# HEALTH MYSELF

**A Directory of UK & Irish Complementary Medicine Experts**

Also available on CD-Rom

Updated daily on **www.healthmyself.com**

**"What has been missing is simple. An easy guide to finding experts by speciality and treatment skills....up until now!!**

HCC Publishing

**The Next Generation Directories**

# HealthMyself

**Publisher:** HCC Publishing Ltd

**Design & Production:** Lucy Hibbert
**Data Researcher:** Lacey Walker
**Production Editor:** Claire Thorpe
**Editorial Programmer:** Matthew Corne
**Marketing Director:** Neil Stokes
**Publishing Director:** Howard C Cox

**ISBN: 1-903897-03-3**




Whilst every effort has been made to ensure the contents of this publication are accurate at the time of publishing, HCC Publishing and those involved in the producing the content of HealthMyself cannot be held responsible for any errors, omissions or changes in the details of this guide or for the consequences of any reliance on the information provided in the same. We have tried to ensure accuracy in this Directory but things do change and we would be grateful if readers would advise us of any inaccuracies they might encounter. Any claims, profiles, characteristic data or descriptions allocated to an entry are not in the editorial control of HCC Publishing, in other words all information has been collected in good faith and with due diligence.

**An entry in HealthMyself does not mean an endorsement or recommendation from HCC Publishing.**


**Further Information:**

**Emails:** information@healthmyself.com
contactus@hccpublishing.co.uk
**Website:** www.healthmyself.com
**Address:** Meaford Power Station, Meaford, Stone, Staffordshire, ST15 0UU.
**Tel:** 0870 7541676
**Fax:** 0870 7541667

HEALTH MYSELF

# CONTENTS

# History

By accessing yet another exciting new “Next Generation Directory” it is pertinent to understand why this publication has been designed in the way it has. Many of the popular “where to find" directories are, to some extent, badly well thought out, because they are limited by the use of difficult to access editorial text and the huge restrictions in the ways of finding salient information. Of course, directories should not become novels but many database publications still transfer what is published on the page, without any noticeable change whatsoever, straight onto the Internet? So the information still remains unsearchable. Most of these publications are rarely updated and so become stale. The majority are published by editorial production personnel who know little about presenting and finding information easily.

Most data suppliers limit searches to simple lines of attack involving broad-brush stroke questions such as finding businesses by location, name and type. The main reasons for these limitations are due to the data delivery of the publication itself, the information layout and even the quality of the data itself. Instead of concentrating on the structure of information, most publishers focus on the limited "word processed" retrieval. This strategy prevents multiple criteria searching. In other words the only way to search for a "business" is by the location or name in the "free text". Nothing more. Very restrictive indeed!

# HCC Publishing Ltd

## Leisure Publications and Information services

The new and exciting "Next Generation Directories" from HCC Publishing comprise an immense listing of relevant addresses, contacts and hugely salient information about specific interest areas such as garden centres, fisheries, golf courses, complementary medicine, night clubs and equestrian services. To the uninitiated these HCC "databases" may be regarded as nothing particularly new, even though on first view the sheer size of the content is obviously more than similar publications. However, once you get to use the HCC products, words such as "astonishing", "amazing" and "incredible" become frequent plaudits.

By using innovative HCC's multi searchable indexing approach, "**for the first time in hard copy format**" it is now possible to access and locate information by what each contact address actually offers to the reader. In other words the way the reader wants to look for a relevant business, address or contact can be achieved by the way they want to find them. Not just by the conventional limited index driven approaches of other, more conventional publications.

HCC offers readers information as to what the contact listing actually does, has to offer and wants to display rather than being pigeonholed in restrictive headings by the editors of those traditional one-dimensional guides! Such guides usually only list by broad cataloguing class, locality and business name.

HCC offers so many more ways to locate the information required. In addition all HCC publications are supplied as hard copy directories such as this one, “lite” and “pro” interactive CD-ROMs together with intuitive membership driven websites.

HCC Next Generation Directories are perfect for the occasional user or the enthusiast making them a 'must have' for the avid devotee and an ideal gift for others. In addition they are even pertinent for the professional, the trade and of course those that sell to the trade.

# HealthMyself Background

In 1982 the next King of Great Britain described "today's un-orthodoxy" as tomorrows convention. Prince Charles was referring to alternative or complementary medicine.

Traditional medical treatments are increasingly taking into account the use of complementary treatments. The main reasons being that:

Alternative practitioners are generally able to offer more time to patients than busy doctors

Patients feel that therapists are more compassionate providing care for the whole patient and not just the indication itself

Patients also seem to like touch as a way of communicating healing

Many of the specialist therapies listed in "Health Myself" now have a place in conventional traditional medicine.

**What has been missing is simple. An easy guide to finding experts by speciality and treatment skills. Welcome to Health Myself.**

The world of medicine is changing empowered by research in areas once disavowed by professionals, to include more ever-widened interest in natural and preventive medicine. More physicians are convincing their patients to use diet and nutritional supplements to treat diseases. Limitations of orthodox (traditional) medicine have clearly realised in the eye of the public. So wishful interest is developed towards alternative medicine.

By definition, alternative medicine is a vast collection of theories and practices, some very ancient, some very recent, some sensible and worthy of study, others seen not so sensible and need more proof to establish their genuine existence and effectiveness.

Such methods are derided in detail in numerous references, along with suggestions for how and when to use them. It is not the purpose of this guide to go into any details of the specific methods or recommendations on their proper use. In here, however, the focus is to create an argument for healthcare professionals, organisations and investors on the feasible possibility of "integrated medicine" that encompasses both orthodox and alternative medicine connected in a well studied plan for both preventive and treatment options.

There is an increasing doubt because of the specificity in orthodox medicine not only because it moved away from nature but also because it just addresses the physical body, or better stated, the physical dimension of the integrated units and systems of our bodies. Mental, emotional and spiritual aspects of health are connected to its physical counterpart yet not serviced correctly through orthodox medicine.

Not only is high-tech medicine expensive, everyone knows, it can also be dangerous. Its methods are potent and invasive and it is frequently harmful. Adverse drug reactions are now so common that most patients will experience one sooner or later. These reactions can be minor and as major as permanent disability or death. The problem is that most pharmaceutical drugs are too strong. They produce very intense effects rapidly. Certainly, in treating emergency conditions such products are useful, but for routine management of common illnesses, the use of such agents is in violation of the famous precept of Hypocrites to Physicians: **First do no harm.**

In the last years of the 20th century, as people became disillusioned with technology, they became restless and uneasy about synthetic chemicals and much more interested in natural products and vitamins. Herbs and natural food has been developed, along with a strong consumer movement opposed to the excess of science and technology. Very slowly and maybe very reluctantly, the medical profession is beginning to respond to demands from consumers for the changes in the way medicine is practised.

Definitely, it would be foolish to seek alternative therapy for conditions that orthodox medicine treats very well, such as bacterial infection, surgical emergencies, immunization and others. The first requirement for taking responsibility in providing health care to a patient is to know when a problem demands immediate intervention by orthodox medicine. Chronic suffering from back pain, arthritis, and the effect of stress are proven to be adequately and successfully handled by other medicine including naturopathy, chiropractic, and homeopathy.

The problem now is to create a system of unbiased thinking towards integration of orthodox medicine with alternative, traditional, natural, holistic, and folk medicines. The American Medical Association has long recognised these forms of medicine, once regarded as quackery, such as hypnotherapy. Such therapies are often safer than invasive procedures, and when they work, are also much less costly. Who knows when they work? The experts? Then experts in different disciplines of alternative medicine are needed to create a panel of therapists, whose goal is to educate modern healthcare providers, physicians, investors, and the public about their strength in providing healing or preventing ailment. Such a panel, by exchange of ideas and expertise, may form an interwoven mesh or fabric that guides us towards an effective, less harmful, less costly health care plan that can be administered to patients to provide both healing, safety, and prevention. Much is to be learned from the venerable healing philosophies and techniques of other cultures, methods that have been handed down over the centuries. While acupuncture has mesmerised the media, herbal medicine is actually so complex and highly regarded in Chinese medicine that students of traditional Chinese medicine must spend at least six years studying it. Herbal medicine is used to restore balance to the system. Acupuncture aims to restore the smooth flow of energy. Ancient Indian philosophers believed that illness develops as a result of internal disharmony and lack of balance with oneself and the environment. This form is the basis of Ayurvedic medicine. It emphasises treatment and prevention. There are some citations in the literature that connect western medicine to Ayurveda.

Homeopathy, where “like cures like”, the "Law of Simulars" cured chronic problems such as allergies, headaches, and arthritis, and it has been recommended as a safer alternative to conventional drugs for pregnant women and for infants and children. In osteopathy, the body is viewed as a whole, interrelated whole, with each system and organ in constant contact. Health is a matter of shifting in balance, and any adverse changes in one part of the body will impair the functioning of other systems or organs.

Self-diagnosis is within the reach of public readers, yet it is unsafe and dangerous. The right person has to be consulted in the proper time. This is only attainable through a proposed health care system that integrates experts in alternative medicine with orthodox medicine in a unified diagnostic panel who decide what, where and how treatment should start. As any project develops, it starts with a simple thought, from which come ideas that formulate a project or plan of action.

# Welcome to HealthMyself

HealthMyself is a unique directory of over 22,000 UK and Irish Complementary Medicine Experts that is available as this hardcopy directory, an Interactive CD-ROM and sophisticated Website.

These experts, together with over 25,000 types of treatment entries, are listed differently to other more conventional directories. Subscribers to HealthMyself can search in many ways to locate the Complementary Medicine Expert or treatment skill of their choice. No other information source compares with HealthMyself.

It is possible to select an expert by location, diseases or problems they treat, therapies, types of expertise and so much more. Only the imagination limits the search opportunities available in HealthMyself.

Designed for every person in the country who is a keen follower of complementary therapy. There is no other guide which allows you to find the therapist of your choice.

The following page shows the number of contacts you can make using HealthMyself.

HEALTH MYSELF

# Treatment Categories and number of entries

| | |
|---|---|
| Absent Healing | 152 |
| Acupressure | 296 |
| Acupuncture | 1259 |
| Alexander Technique | 397 |
| Allergy Testing | 74 |
| Anthroposohical Medicine | 11 |
| Aromatherapy | 1347 |
| Art Therapy | 31 |
| Aura Therapy | 35 |
| Auricular Therapy | 17 |
| Auto Suggestion | 92 |
| Autogenic Training | 44 |
| Aversion Therapy | 49 |
| Ayurvedic Medicine | 26 |
| Baby Massage | 3 |
| Bach Remedies | 494 |
| Bates Method | 16 |
| Beauty Therapy | 22 |
| Bio-energetics | 34 |
| Biofeedback | 51 |
| Biomagnetic Therapy | 4 |
| Biomechanics | 197 |
| Bonesetting | 20 |
| Bowen Therapy | 143 |
| Chinese Herbal Medicine | 53 |
| Chiropody | 616 |
| Chiropractic | 990 |
| Clinical Ecology | 28 |
| Cognitive Therapy | 152 |
| Colonic Hydrotherapy | 8 |
| Colour Therapy | 67 |
| Complementary Therapy | 465 |
| Counselling | 607 |
| Cranial Osteopathy | 250 |
| Cranio-Sacral Therapy | 93 |
| Cryo Surgery | 44 |
| Crystal Healing | 106 |
| Cupping | 98 |
| Cymatics | 1 |
| Dance Movement Therapy | 18 |
| Dietician | 93 |
| Do In | 16 |
| Douching | 2 |
| Dowsing | 68 |

| | |
|---|---|
| Drama Therapy | 13 |
| Electrolipolysis | 10 |
| Electrolysis | 9 |
| Electrotherapy | 155 |
| Encounter Groups | 7 |
| Faith Healing | 54 |
| Family Planning (Natural) | 23 |
| Family Therapy | 58 |
| Feldenkrais Methodology | 10 |
| Feng Shui | 5 |
| Floral Essence Therapy | 51 |
| Flotation Therapy | 8 |
| Gait Analysis | 26 |
| Gem Essence Therapy | 14 |
| Gestalt Therapy | 68 |
| Group Therapy | 70 |
| Hay Diet | 55 |
| Healer | 215 |
| Healing Therapy | 239 |
| Hellerwork | 4 |
| Herbal Medicine | 594 |
| Holistic Healing | 316 |
| Homeopathy | 914 |
| Hopi Ear Candles | 31 |
| Humanistic Psychology | 84 |
| Hypnosis | 1096 |
| Hypnotherapy | 543 |
| Indian Head Massage | 432 |
| Inhalation Therapy | 13 |
| Iridology | 78 |
| Kinesiology | 225 |
| Kirlian Photography | 4 |
| Laser Treatment | 5 |
| Life Style Coaching | 129 |
| Light Therapy | 4 |
| Macrobiotics | 19 |
| Magnetic Therapy | 27 |
| Manipulation | 445 |
| Manual Lymph Drainage | 18 |
| Massage (Therapeutic) | 888 |
| McTimoney Chiropractic | 29 |
| Meditation | 235 |
| Metamorphic Therapy | 45 |
| Miasm Therapy | 22 |
| Micro Manipulation | 31 |
| Moxibustion | 142 |
| Mud Therapy | 4 |
| Music Therapy | 21 |
| Nail Surgery | 166 |
| Naturopathy | 193 |
| Neuro-Linguistic Program | 65 |
| Neurotherapy | 1 |
| Nutritional Therapy | 365 |
| Orgone Therapy | 1 |
| Oriental Diagnosis | 102 |
| Orthomolecular Medicine | 8 |

| | |
|---|---|
| Orthotics | 43 |
| Osteomyology | 4 |
| Osteopathy | 1811 |
| Power Ass. Micro Manipulation | 2 |
| Paranormal Therapies | 20 |
| Pattern Therapies | 5 |
| Physiotherapy | 248 |
| Phytotherapy | 98 |
| Pilates | 54 |
| Podiatry | 203 |
| Polarity Therapy | 35 |
| Postural Integration | 69 |
| Primal Therapy | 5 |
| Psionic Therapy | 3 |
| Psychotherapy | 916 |
| Pyramid Power | 5 |
| Pyscho-Synthesis | 14 |
| Reflexology | 1981 |
| Reichian Therapy | 11 |
| Reiki | 575 |
| Remedial Massage | 79 |
| Rogerian Therapy | 54 |
| Rolfing | 15 |
| Seichem | 43 |
| Sensitivity Training | 8 |
| Shiatsu | 270 |
| Silva Method | 8 |
| Sound Therapy | 19 |
| Spiritual Healing | 208 |
| Sports Massage | 47 |
| Stress Therapy | 440 |
| Swedish Body Massage | 31 |
| T'ai-Chi Ch'uan | 64 |
| Tantra Therapy | 9 |
| Tera-Mai | 19 |
| Thought Field Therapy | 3 |
| Touch Therapy | 66 |
| Transactional Analysis | 39 |
| Tui-na | 5 |
| Ultrasonics | 115 |
| Vibrational Therapy | 33 |
| Visualisation Therapy | 138 |
| Vitamin Therapy | 166 |
| Voice Therapy | 15 |
| X-Ray | 52 |
| Ying & Yang | 45 |
| Yoga | 115 |
| Zen Therapy | 7 |
| Zero Balancing | 14 |

HEALTH MYSELF

# How is the data collected?

Addresses of related businesses are collated from trade publications, magazines and directory services. All are mailed a bespoke questionnaire. Those businesses not completing questionnaires are contacted directly by HCC's team of tele-marketing research personnel.

This directory is a snapshot of a huge dynamic database. It is the largest and most comprehensive UK & Irish Complementary Medical Businesses database ever produced and it is updated and edited daily on the Internet.

It is important to understand however that HCC Publishing cannot guarantee perfection, even though every effort has been made to ensure as much accuracy as possible.

Over 25,000 businesses are contacted twice per year. HealthMyself is a selection of these businesses. There may be errors that you spot, because despite Complementary Medicine being one of the most interesting subjects, it is also one of the hardest and least defined of areas to try and collect current, topical and validated information easily. In our research in building the database, every other magazine, directory and web site examined, exhibited inaccuracies. In many cases there were huge discrepancies, mainly because of the topicality of their reporting.

We need your constructive comments, feedback and support...

# Abbreviations used

Occasionally business names have been shortened in the business headings and use the following abbreviations:

| | |
|---|---|
| Acu | Acupuncture |
| Allgy | Allergy |
| Alt | Alternative |
| Aroma | Aromatherapy |
| Ass | Association |
| Ast | Associates |
| Ave | Avenue |
| Blvd | Boulevard |
| Bty | Beauty |
| Chiro | Chiropractic |
| Chirop | Chiropody |
| Chrtrd | Chartered |
| Cl | Close |
| Clge | College |
| Clnc | Clinic |
| Com | Company |
| Comm | Communities |
| Comp | Complementary |
| Con | Consultancy |
| Consult | Consultant |
| Couns | Counselling |
| Cres | Crescent |
| Ctre | Centre |
| Ctry | Country |
| Dept | Department |
| Ed | Education |
| Fed | Federation |
| Grp | Group |
| Gr | Grove |
| Gt | Great |
| Herb | Herbal |
| Hlth | Health |
| Hol | Holistic |
| Hom | Homeopathic |
| Hosp | Hospital |
| Hse | House |
| Hyp | Hynotherapy |
| Ind | Independent |
| Inj | Injuries |
| Ins | Institute |
| Int | International |
| Mass | Massage |
| Med | Medicine |
| Medi | Medical |
| Mngmt | Management |
| Nat | National |
| Nrth | North |
| Ntrl | Natural |
| Nurs | Nurse |
| Occu | Occupational |
| Org | Organisation |
| Ost | Osteopathic |
| Part | Partnership |
| Phys | Physical |
| Physio | Physiotherapy |
| Pk | Park |
| Pl | Place |
| Pod | Podiatry |
| Pr | Probe |
| Prac | Practice |
| Pract | Practitioner |
| Prde | Parade |
| Prof | Professional |
| Psyc | Psychic |
| Psych | Psychologist |
| Psycho | Psychotherapy |
| Rd | Road |
| Reflex | Reflexology |
| Reg | Registered |
| Sch | School |
| Sgy | Surgery |
| Sprts | Sports |
| Sq | Square |
| St | Street |
| Sv | Service |
| Svs | Services |
| Ther | Therapist |
| Thera | Therapeutic |
| Thrpy | Therapy |
| Trad | Traditional |
| Trce | Terrace |
| Eng | England |
| NIR | Northern Ireland |
| IRE | Ireland |
| Wal | Wales |
| Sco | Scotland |
| UK | United Kingdom |
| GB | Great Britain |

# Glossary - qualifications and professional bodies

| | |
|---|---|
| A.A.C.T | Association of Analytical and Cognitive Therapists |
| AACP | Acupuncture Association of Chartered Physiotherapists |
| AAF | Active Association Foundation |
| AAMT | Association of Advancement of Meridian Therapists |
| AB Phys | Association of British Physiotherapists |
| ABCHyp | Atkinson Ball College of Hypnotherapy |
| Ac.A.C | The Acupuncture Association of the Republic of China |
| ACA | American Chiropractic Association |
| ACH | Academy of Curative Hypnotherapists |
| ACHE | American Council of Hypnotherapist Examiners |
| ADMT UK | Association for Dance Movement Therapy UK |
| AFI | Acupuncture Foundation of Ireland |
| AFT | Association of Family Therapists |
| AGPC | Association of Gold Psychotherapeutic Counsellors |
| AHA | American Hypnosis Association |
| AHPP | The Association of Humanistic Psychology Practitoners |
| AIA | Association of Irish Acupuncturists |
| AIC | Association of International Colleges |
| ALTT | Association of Light Touch Therapists |
| AMFO | Associated Member of the Faculty of Osteopathy |
| AMH | The Association of Master Herbalists |
| AMIH | Association of the Midland Institute of Hypnotherapists |
| AMRSH | Associate Member of the Royal Society of Health |
| AMT | Association of Meridian Therapists |
| ANLP | Association of Neuro Linguistic Programming |
| ANM | Association of Natural Medicine |
| AoA | Association of Aromatherapists |
| AOC | Aromatherapy Organisations Council |
| AoR | Association Of Reflexology |
| APHP | Association of Professional Hypnotherapists and Psychotherapists |
| APNT | Association of Physical and Natural Therapists |
| APS | Association of Professional Sugaring |
| AQCH | Association of Qualified Curative Hypnotherapists |
| ARMT | The Association of Relaxation Massage Therapists |
| ASC | Association of Stress Consultants |
| ASM | Association of Stress Management |
| Ass.Therapeutic Massage | Association of Therapeutic Massage |
| AST | Academy of Sports Therapists |
| ATA | Alexander Technique Association |
| ATC | Aromatherapy Trading Council |
| ATCM UK | Association of Traditional Chinese Medicine UK |
| ATI | Alexander Technique International |
| Azeemi Federation UK | Azeemi Federation UK |
| B.A.Ch.P | The British Association of Chiropody and Podiatry |
| B.A.Th.H | British Association of Therapeutic Hypnotists |
| BA UK | Bowen Association UK |
| BAAC | British Association for Applied Chiropractic |
| BAAT | British Association of Art Therapy |
| BABCP | British Association of Behavioural and Cognative Psychotherapy |
| BABTAC | British Association of Beauty Therapy and Cosmotologists |
| BAcC | British Acupuncture Council |

| | |
|---|---|
| BACP | British Association for Counselling and Psychotherapy |
| BAE | British Association of Electrolysis |
| BAHA | British Alliance of Healing Associations |
| BANT | British Association of Nutritional Therapy |
| BAP | British Association of Psychotherapists |
| BAS | British Autogenic Society |
| BASE | British Academy of Spiritual Enlightenment |
| BASRT | British Association for Sexual and Relationship Therapy |
| BAWAc | British Academy of Western Acupuncture |
| BBA | British Biomagnetic Association |
| BCA | British Chiropractic Association |
| BCC | British Chiropractic Council |
| BCCMA | British Council of Chinese Martial Arts |
| BCHE | British Council of Hypnotist Examiners |
| BCMA | British Complementary Medicine Association |
| BCP | British Confederation of Psychotherapy |
| BCPC | Bath Centre of Psychotherapy And Counselling |
| BDI | Bio Dynamic Institute |
| BEST | British And European Spinal TouchAssociation |
| BFIR | Bach Foundation International Register |
| BFMT | British Federation of Massage Therapist |
| BFRP | Bach Flower Remedy Practitioner |
| BFVEA | British Flower Vibrational Essence Association |
| BHMA | British Herbal Medicine Association |
| BHReg | British Hypnotherapy Register |
| BIAET | British Institute for Allergy and Environmental Therapy |
| BIAT | British Institiute of Allergy Therapists |
| BIH | British Institute of Hypnotherapy |
| BIMM | British Institute of Musculo Skeletal Medicine |
| BIMT | British Institute of Magnetic Therapy |
| BKUSE | Brahma Kumaris University of Spinal Education |
| BMA | British Medical Association |
| BMAS | British Medical Acupuncture Society |
| BNA | British Naturopathic Association |
| BOA | British Osteopathic Association |
| BOrthA | British Orthopaedic Association |
| BOsC | British Osteopathic Council |
| BPA | Bowen Practitioner Association |
| BPS | British Psychological Society |
| BRA | British Reflexology Association |
| BRCP | British Registered Complementary Practitioner |
| BSA | British Shiatsu Association |
| BSCH | British Society of Clinical Hypnosis |
| BSECH | The British Society of Experimental and Clinical Hypnosis |
| BSR | British School of Reflexology |
| BSTF | Brief Strategic Therapy Foundation |
| BSY | British School of Yoga |
| BTAA | Bowen Therapist Association of Australia |
| BTER | Bowen Therapist European Register |
| BVA | British Vetinary Association |
| BWY | British Wheel of Yoga |
| C.P.S.M | Council of Professions Supplementary to Medicine |
| C.Phyto | College of Phytotherapy |
| CAH | Corporation of Advanced Hypnotherapy |
| CAH | The Corporation of Advanced Hypnotherapy |
| CAI | Chiropractic Association of Ireland |
| CC | College of Chiropractors |
| CCEP | Certified Chiropractic Exstramities Practitioner |
| CH | The College of Homeopathy |
| CHA | Corinthian Healing Association |
| CHAss | Complementary Health Association |
| CHO | Confederation of Healing Organisation |
| CIA | Colonic International Association |
| CIBTAC | CIBTAC |
| CMA | Complementary Medical Association |

| | |
|---|---|
| CMIR | Chinese Medical Institute and Register |
| COH | The College of Healing |
| COSCA | COSCA |
| CPM | Council For Professional Medicine |
| CPP | The Centre for Psychoanalytical Psychotherapy |
| CPS | Counselling and Psychotherapy Society |
| CPSM | Council for Professions Supplementary to Medicine |
| CRAH | Central Register of Advanced Hypnotherapy |
| CSM | Confederation of Stress Management |
| CSP | The Chartered Society of Physiotherapy |
| CSTA | The Craniosacral Therapy Association |
| CTA | Colour Therapy Association |
| DACP | Dorset Association of Complementary Practitioners |
| DHA | District Healing Association |
| DOC | Democratic Osteopathic Council |
| DPA | Development Practitioners Association |
| DrEBF | Dr Edward Bach Foundation |
| EABP | European Association For Body Psychotherapists |
| EATA | European Association of Transactional Analysis |
| EChiroU | European Chiropractic Union |
| EHPA | European Herbalists Practitioners Association |
| EMDR | Eye Movement Desensitisation and Reprocessing Association (UK & Ireland) |
| EMPA | Eastern Medicine Practitioners Association |
| EOTA | Essential Oil Trade Association |
| ESIPF | English Societe L'Institute Pierre Franchomme |
| ETSI | European Therapies Studies Institute |
| FAN | Foundation of Applied Nutrition |
| FCPod(s) | Fellow of the College of Podiatrists of the Society of Chiropodists and Podiatrists |
| FFHom | Fellow of the Faculty of Homeopathy |
| FGUK | Feldenkrais Guild UK |
| FHom | Faculty of Homeopathy |
| FHT | Federation of Holistic Therapy |
| FIH | Fellow of the Indian Institute of Homeopaths |
| FNT | Foundation of Natural Therapy |
| FPC | Foundation for Psychotherapy and Counselling |
| FPLR | Federation of Precision Linking Reflexologists |
| FTA | Flotation Tank Association |
| FTAI | Family Therapy Association of Ireland |
| GASW | Group Analysis South West |
| GCBT | Guild of Complementary Beauty Therapists |
| GCC | General Chiropractic Council |
| GCH | Guild of Curative Hypnotherapists |
| GCP | Guild of Complementary Practitioners |
| GCRN | General Council of Registered Naturopaths |
| GCT | Guild of Complementary Therapists |
| GDS | General Dental Surgery |
| GHR | General Hypnotherapy Register |
| GIA | Guild In Aromatherapy |
| GMC | General Medical Council |
| GNC | General Nursing Council |
| GNI | Guild of Naturopathic Iridologists |
| GOsC | General Osteopathic Council |
| GOsS | General Osteopathic Society |
| GPAO | Guild of Practitioners of Alternative Osteopathy |
| GPTI | Gestalt Psychotherapy Training Institute |
| GRO | General Register of Osteopaths |
| GTH | Guild of Therapeutic Hypnotherapists |
| Guild of Reflexologists | Guild of Reflexologists |
| Guild.Prof.Beauty.Th | Guild of Professional Beauty Therapists |
| HA | Hypnotherapy Association |
| HAF | Holistic Aromatherapy Foundation |
| HAR | Holistic Association of Reflexologists |
| HF | Hypnothink Foundation |
| HMA | Homeopathic Medical Association |

| | |
|---|---|
| HPG | Hypnotherapy Guild |
| HRS | Hypnotherapy Research Society |
| HS | Hypnotherapy Society |
| HSEC | Healing Shiatsu Education Centre |
| IAA | International Aromatherapy Association |
| IAC | International Association of Colour |
| IACT | Irish Association of Counselling and Therapy |
| IAH | International Association of Hypno-Analysts |
| IAIM | International Association of Infant Massage |
| IBCA | International Bio Cranial Academy |
| ICA | International Chiropractors Association |
| ICA | International Cranial Association |
| ICAK | International College of Applied Kinesiology |
| ICHP | Institute of Clinical Hypnotherapy and Psychotherapy |
| ICHT | International Council Of Holistic Therapy |
| ICM | Institute of Complementary Medicine |
| ICO | Institute of Classical Osteopaths |
| IET | The Institute of Environmental Therapists |
| IETA | Irish Exercise Teachers Association |
| IFA | International Federation of Aromatherapists |
| IFHB | International Federation of Holistic Beauty Therapists |
| IFR | International Federation of Reflexology |
| IGA | The Institute of Group Analysis |
| IHBC | International Health and Beauty Counselling |
| IHT | Institute of Holistic Therapy |
| IIAA | Irish and International Aromatherapy Association |
| IIBT | International Institute of Beauty Therapists |
| IICH | Irish Institute Of Counselling and Hypnotherapy |
| IIHFT | International Council of Health Fitness and Sports Therapy |
| IIHHT | International Institute of Health Holistic Therapy |
| IIR | International Institute of Reflexology |
| IIST | International Institute of Sports Therapist |
| IMM | The Institute of Massage and Movement |
| Inst.CH.P | The Institute of Chiropodists and Podiatrists |
| Inst.HFR | The Institute of Health Food Retailing |
| Inst.Hom | Institute of Homeopaths |
| InstAET | Institute of Allergy and Environmental Therapists |
| INT | Institute of Natural Therapy |
| Int.Aest | International Aestheticiennes |
| ION | Institute Of Optimum Nutrition |
| IP | Institute of Psychotherapists |
| IPA | International Physiotherapist Association |
| IPCC | Ipswich Psychotherapy & Counselling Centre |
| IPD | Institute of Personal Development |
| IPN | Independent Practitioner Network |
| IPTI | Independent Professional Therapists International |
| IRA | International Reflexology Association |
| IRAFMRH | International Research Association for Functional Medicine and Resonance Homeopathy |
| IRCH | International Register of Consultant Herbalists |
| IRI | Irish Reflexology Institute |
| IROM | The International Register of Oriental Medicine |
| IScB | Institute des Sciences Bio Medicale(French Qualification) |
| ISCP | Irish Society of Chartered Physiotherapists |
| ISH | Irish Society of Homeopaths |
| ISMA | International Stress Management Association |
| ISPA | International Society of Professional Aromatherapists |
| ISRHA | International Self Realisation Healing Association |
| ISRN | Incorporated Society of Registered Naturopaths |
| ISS | Irish Shiatsu Society |
| ISSD | International Society for the Study in Dissociation |
| ISTA | International Shien Therapy Association |
| ITA | Institute for Transactional Analysis |
| ITEC | International Therapy Examination Council |
| ITHMA | Institute of Traditional Herbal Medicine and Aromatherapy |
| KFRP | Kinesiology Federation Registered Practitioner |

| | |
|---|---|
| L.C.C.H | Licentiate of the College of Classical Homeopathy |
| L.I.S.Ch | Licensed School of Chiropody |
| LCH | Licentiate of the College of Homeopathy |
| LCHyp | London College of Hypnotherapy |
| LCIC | London Centre of Indian Champissage |
| LCSP | London Counties Society of Physiologists |
| LLSA | Licentiate of the London School of Aromatherapy |
| MAA | Modern Acupuncture Association |
| MACP | Manipulative Association of Chartered Physiotherapists |
| Maharishi Foundation | Maharishi Foundation |
| MCA | McTimoney Chiropractic Association |
| MedCouns(Ireland) | Medical Council of Ireland |
| MLD(UK) | Manual Lymph Drainage UK |
| MPNLP | Master Practitioner of Neuro Linguistic Programming |
| MSSCh | The School of Surgical Chiropody & Podiatric Medicine |
| MTI | Massage Training Institute |
| NACHP | National Association of Counsellors, Hypnotherapists and Psychotherapists |
| NACM | National Association for Chiropractic Medicine |
| NADA | National Acupuncture Detoxification Association |
| NAHH | National Association of Holistic Hypnotherapists |
| NAHS | National Association of Health Stores |
| Nakamura Foundation | Nakamura Foundation |
| Nat.Back Pain.Ass | National Back Pain Association |
| NCH | National Council for Hypnotherapy |
| NCP | National Council for Psychotherapy |
| NFSH | National Federation of Spiritual Healers |
| NGH(US) | National Guild of Hypnotherapy(US) |
| NHR | National Hypnotherapy Register |
| NIMH | National Institute of Medical Herbalists |
| NKT | Nekadampa Tradition |
| NMA | Northern Massage Association |
| NORA | Natural Oils Research Association |
| NRAH | National Register of Advanced Hypnotherapy |
| NRHP | National Register of Hypnotherapists and Psychotherapists |
| NRSCT | National Register of Smoking Cessation Therapist |
| NSPH | National Society of Professional Hypnotherapists |
| NWCH | The North West College of Honours |
| OCPPP | Organisation of Chartered Physiotherapists Private Practice |
| PA | The Pain Association |
| PAAT | Professional Association of the Alexander Technique |
| PMAS | Professional Massage Association of Scotland |
| PMBCA | Professional Member of the Back Care Association |
| PSI | Psychological Society of Ireland |
| RCBFR | Registered Counsellor in Bach Flower Remedies |
| RCGP | Royal College of General Practitioners |
| RCHM | Register of Chinese Herbal Medicine |
| RCN | Royal College of Nursing |
| RCOG | Royal College of Obstetrics and Gynaecology |
| RCPsych | Royal College of Psychiatrists |
| RCS (Eng) | Royal College of Surgeons |
| RCST | Registered Cranio_Sacral Therapist |
| Reiki Association | Reiki Association |
| Reiki Fed | Reiki Federation |
| RGN | Registered Nurse |
| RMANM | Registered Member of the Association of Natural Medicine |
| RN | Registered Naturopaths |
| RO | Register of Osteomyologists |
| RoN | The Register of Naturopaths |
| RoO | The Register of Osteopaths |
| RPS | Royal Pharmaceutical Society |
| RQA | Registered Qualified Aromatherapist |
| RSA | The Royal Society of Arts |
| RSAss | Reiki and Seichem Association |
| RSM | Royal Society of Medicine |
| RSoH | Royal Society of Homeopaths |

| | |
|---|---|
| RSS | Registered Shiatsu Society |
| RxS | The Reflexologists Society |
| S.C.P | The Society of Chiropodists and Podiatrists |
| S.R.Ch | State Registered Chiropodists |
| SAAc | Society of Auricular Acupuncture |
| SAC | Society Of Applied Cosmeology |
| SBMA | The Scottish Baby Massage Instructors Association |
| SCA | Scottish Chiropractic Association |
| Scottish Chiropodist Assoc | Scottish Chiropodist Association |
| SHA | Sussex Healers Association |
| SHEN | Therapy Specific Human Energy Nexus |
| Shiatsu Society UK | The Shiatsu Society UK |
| SHP | Society of Holistic Practitioners |
| SIR | Scottish Institute of Reflexology |
| SMA | Scottish Massage Association |
| SMAE | S.M.A.E (EAMS) |
| SMN | Spiritual Medical Network |
| SMTO | Scottish Massage Therapist Organisation |
| SNHS | School of Natural Health Sciences |
| Soc.Comp.Therapy | Society of Complementary Therapy |
| Soc.Hom | Society of Homeopaths |
| Soc.SM | Society of Stress Managers |
| SOM | Society of Orthopaedic Medicine |
| SOM | The Society of Orthopaedic Medicine |
| SoP | Society of Physiologists |
| SPCAH | Society for Primary Cause Analysis by Hypnosis |
| SPNT | Society For Promotion of Nutritional Therapy |
| SPTI | Sherwood Psychotherapy Training Institute |
| SRNHV | State Registered Nurse Health Visitor |
| SRP | State Registered Physiotherapist |
| SSCh | School of Surgical Chiropody & Podiatric Medicine |
| SSChA | The Surgical School of Chiropody Association |
| SSM | Society of Sports Massage |
| SSM | The Society for Stress Mangement |
| SSR | Scottish School of Reflexology |
| SST | Society of Sports Therapists |
| Stars Edge International | Star's Edge International |
| STAT | Society for Teachers of the Alexander Technique |
| State.Reg.Psych | State Registered Psychotherapist |
| SVA | Spiritual Venturers Association |
| SYTA | Scottish Yoga Teachers Association |
| TAO | The Association of Osteomyologists |
| TATh | Thermo Auricular Therapy |
| TCUGB | Tai Chi Union of Great Britain |
| TMHA | Tera Mai Healers Association |
| Trager UK | Trager UK |
| TTA | Timeline Therapy Association |
| UKCC | United Kingdom Central Council |
| UKCHO | United Kingdom Confederation Hypnotherapy Organisation |
| UKCP | United Kingdom Council for Psychotherapy |
| UKGH | United Kingdom Guild Hypnotherapy |
| UKGHE | UK Guild of Hypnotist Examiners |
| UKHR | United Kingdon Hypnotherapy Register |
| UKRC | United Kingdom Registered Counsellors |
| Ukreg.Pract.GPs.Hosp | UK Register of Practitioners for GPs and Hospitals |
| UKTCA | United Kingdom Tai-Chi Association |
| WACM | World Association of Chinese Medicine |
| WFH | The World Federation of Healing |
| WIPH | World Institute of Professional Hypnotherapists |
| YTA | Yoga TeachersAssociation |
| ZBA(UK) | The Zero Balancing Association(UK) |

HEALTH MYSELF

# SECTION 1

## A-Z Practitioners

### 1066 SHIATSU

**1066 Shiatsu**, 23 De Cham Rd, St. Leonards-On-Sea, **Sussex (East)**, TN37 6JP, ENG.
(T) 01424 441743
Speciality: Complementary Medicines & Therapy.
● **Owner** Mrs A Cryar
[M] (**Ref:**HM00001)

### 1ST ALTERNATIVE HEALTH CENTRE

**1st Alternative Health Centre**, 172A Field End Rd, Pinner, **London (Greater)**, HA5 1RH, ENG.
(T) 020 8868 0239
Speciality: Alexander Technique, Aromatherapy, Cranial Osteopathy, Cranio-Sacral Therapy, Homeopathy, Manipulation, Massage (Therapeutic), Naturopathy, Osteopathy, Psychotherapy, Shiatsu. ✓
● **Osteopath** Ms J Ovett **Q:** BSc. **M:** GOsC.
● **Osteopath** Ms E Shanahan **Q:** BSc. **M:** GOsC.
● **Osteopath** Peri Phokon **Q:** BSc. **M:** GOsC.
● **Principal/Osteopath/Cranio-Sacral Therapist**
Mr D Harrison **Q:** DO. **M:** GOsC.
[S] Yrs. Est.: 13 (**Ref:**HM00002)

### 1ST CHIROPRACTIC CENTRES

**1st Chiropractic Centres**, 26 Portsmouth Rd, Camberley, **Surrey**, GU15 1JX, ENG.
(T) 01276 681555 (F) 01276 681555
Speciality: Chiropractic.
● **Doctor** Dr Fitzpatrick
[P] [S] [T] (**Ref:**HM00003)

### 1ST CHIROPRACTIC CLINIC

**1st Chiropractic Clinic**, Davis Way, Hurst, Reading, **Berkshire**, RG10 0TR, ENG.
(T) 01189 320555
Speciality: Chiropractic. ✓
● **Owner** Dr R Grey **Q:** BA, BSc, DC. **M:** BCA, GCC.
[P] Yrs. Est.: 1 (**Ref:**HM00004)

### 1ST CHIROPRACTIC UK

**1st Chiropractic UK**, 4b Heathfield Rd, Kings Heath, Birmingham, **Midlands (West)**, B14 7DB, ENG.
(T) 01214 412782
(W) www.firstchiropractic.co.uk
Speciality: Chiropractic. ✓
● **Owner** Mr G Miles **Q:** DC. **M:** SCA.
[P] [S] [T] Yrs. Est.: 2 (**Ref:**HM00005)

### 1ST CHIROPRACTIC UK

**1st Chiropractic UK**, 108 Birmingham Rd, Sutton Coldfield, **Midlands (West)**, B72 1LY, ENG.
(T) 01213 554272 (F) 01216 817258
(W) www.firstchiropractic.co.uk
Speciality: Chiropractic. ✓
● **Owner** Dr D Murray **Q:** DC. **M:** SCA.
[P] Yrs. Est.: 2 (**Ref:**HM00006)

### 1ST CHIROPRACTIC UK

**1st Chiropractic UK**, High Peak Centre, 632 Evesham Rd, Crabbs Cross, Redditch, **Worcestershire**, B97 5LH, ENG.
(T) 01527 404154
(W) www.firstchiropractic.co.uk
Speciality: Chiropractic, Counselling, Sclero Therapy, Forte Skin Peels.
● **Associate** Ms K Thorogood **M:** IIHHT.
● **Associate** Ms C Griffiths
● **Associate** Ms C Harris
● **Partner** Dr T Smythe **Q:** DC.
[P] Yrs. Est.: 1 (**Ref:**HM00007)

### 2 NOW

**2 Now**, 176 Lymington Avenue, London, **London (Greater)**, N22 6JH, ENG.
(T) 020 8881 5147
Speciality: Psychology.
[B] (**Ref:**HM00008)

### 21ST CENTURY HEALTH

**21st Century Health Ltd**, 2 Fitzhardinge St, London, **London (Greater)**, W1H 6EE, ENG.
(T) 020 7935 5440 (F) 020 7487 3710
(W) www.21stcenturyhealth.co.uk
Speciality: Complementary Medicines & Therapy.
● **Director** Mr S Chasan
[C] (**Ref:**HM00009)

### 21ST CENTURY LIVING

**21st Century Living**, Weston Bungalow Cooldrinagh, Leixlip, **County Kildare**, IRE.
(T) 01624 5546
Speciality: Complementary Medicines & Therapy.
[M] (**Ref:**HM00010)

### 3 WAY PHYSIOTHERAPY

**3 Way Physiotherapy**, 11 Headley Rd, Woodley, Reading, **Berkshire**, RG5 4JB, ENG.
(T) 01189 692299 (F) 01189 692299
Speciality: Physiotherapy.
● **Partner** Mrs J Davey
[P] [S] [T] (**Ref:**HM00011)

### 3 WAYS PHYSIOTHERAPY CLINIC

**3 Ways Physiotherapy Clinic**, 1 Pine Drive, St. Ives, Ringwood, **Hampshire**, BH24 2LN, ENG.
(T) 07976 419813
Speciality: Physiotherapy.
● **Owner** Mr P Savage
[P] [S] [T] (**Ref:**HM00012)

### 5 VALLEYS PHYSIOTHERAPY

**Five Valleys Physiotherapy & Sports Injury Clinic**, Brunel Mall, London Rd, Stroud, **Gloucestershire**, GL5 2BP, ENG.
(T) 01453 755948
Speciality: Physiotherapy.
[P] [S] [T] (**Ref:**HM00013)

### 7C'S EXPERIENCE

**7C's Experience**, 5 Cobnor Cl, Crawley, **Sussex (West)**, RH11 8LL, ENG.
(T) 01293 429631
Speciality: Complementary Medicines & Therapy.
● **Owner** Mrs E McGill
[M] (**Ref:**HM00014)

### A & H CHIROPODY SURGERY

**A & H Chiropody Surgery & Sports Clinic**, Unit 6, YMCA Buildings, North Rd, St. Helens, **Merseyside**, WA10 2TZ, ENG.
(T) 01744 23392
Speciality: Chiropodists (Podiatrists).
● **Partner** Ms H Charnock
[S] (**Ref:**HM00015)

### A & H PAIN CLINIC

**A & H Pain Clinic Chinese Acupuncture And Herb Centre**, 9 Concord Way, Dukinfield, **Cheshire**, SK16 4DB, ENG.
(T) 01613 442888 (F) 01613 040006
(E) painclinic@cwcom.net
(W) www.painclinic.cwc.net
Speciality: Acupressure, Acupuncture, Aromatherapy, Manipulation, Reflexology. ✓
● **Practitioner** Mr Lee
(T) 01614 431188
● **Practitioner** Mrs X Lee **Q:** MD. **M:** BAcC.
[O] (**Ref:**HM00016)

### A & L AROMATHERAPY SUPPLIES

**A & L Aromatherapy Supplies**, 42 Bradmore Green, Brookmans Park, Hatfield, **Hertfordshire**, AL9 7QR, ENG.
(T) 01707 656236
(W) www.alas.fsbusiness.co.uk
Speciality: Complementary Medicines & Therapy.
● **Owner** Ms L Garvey
[C] Yrs. Est.: 1 (**Ref:**HM00017)

### A & M KENNEDY

**A & M Kennedy**, Mayfield, Bray Rd, Maidenhead, **Berkshire**, SL6 1UF, ENG.
(T) 01628 624102
Speciality: Complementary Medicines & Therapy.
● **Owner** Anthony Kennedy
[C] [M] (**Ref:**HM00018)

### A 1 ALOE VERA CENTRE

**A 1 Aloe Vera Centre**, 53 Haslemere Gr, Doncaster, **Yorkshire (South)**, DN5 9QA, ENG.
(T) 01302 782317
Speciality: Complementary Medicines & Therapy.
[C] [M] (**Ref:**HM00019)

### A A A HYPNOTHERAPY ADVICE

**A A A Hypnotherapy Advice Helpline**, 281 Sauchiehall St, Glasgow, **Glasgow (City of)**, G2 3HQ, SCO.
(T) 01418 825647
Speciality: Hypnotherapy.
● **Manager** Mr F Kelly
[B] (**Ref:**HM00020)

### A A R H P

**A A R H P**, London Medical Centre, 144 Harley St, London, **London (Greater)**, W1N 1AH, ENG.
(T) 020 7439 1995 (F) 020 7439 3536
Speciality: Hypnotherapy.
● **Owner** Dr T O'Keefe
[B] (**Ref:**HM00021)

### A APOSTLE & MACKAY

**A Apostle & Mackay Clinical Hypnotherapy**, Kenton Bridge Medical Centre, 155-175 Kenton Rd, Harrow, **London (Greater)**, HA3 0YX, ENG.
(T) 020 8424 0056 (F) 020 8424 0056
Speciality: Hypnotherapy.
● **Owner** Mr T Toms
[B] (**Ref:**HM00022)

### A B C HYPNOSIS

**A B C Hypnosis**, 33 Mount Pleasant, Hildenborough, Tonbridge, **Kent**, TN11 9JQ, ENG.
(T) 01474 855568
Speciality: Hypnotherapy.
● **Hypnotherapist**
[B] (**Ref:**HM00023)

### A BARCHAM REFLEXOLOGY

**A Barcham Reflexology**, 214 Moor End Rd, Halifax, **Yorkshire (West)**, HX2 0RU, ENG.
(T) 01422 341687
(E) alihb@aol.com
(W) www.reflextherapyonline.com
Speciality: Reflexology. ✓
● **Reflexologist** Ali Barcham **Q:** MIIR. **M:** IIR.
[T] Yrs. Est.: 20 (**Ref:**HM00024)

### A BODY ORIENTED HUMANISTIC

**A Body Oriented Humanistic Therapist**, 77 Godstow Rd, Wolvercote, Oxford, **Oxfordshire**, OX2 8PE, ENG.
(T) 01865 512430
Speciality: Psychotherapy.
● **Owner** Ms C Birtwhistle
[B] (**Ref:**HM00025)

### A BREATH OF FRESH AIR

**A Breath Of Fresh Air**, 62 Halton Lane, Wendover, Aylesbury, **Buckinghamshire**, HP22 6AZ, ENG.
(T) 07970 305983
Speciality: Aromatherapy.
● **Owner** Mrs C Walton
[M] [O] (**Ref:**HM00026)

### A C H COMPLEMENTARY

**A C H Complementary**, 75 Leigh Rd, Leigh-On-Sea, **Essex**, SS9 1JN, ENG.
(T) 01702 714862 (F) 01702 716969
Speciality: Complementary Medicines & Therapy.
● **Owner** Mrs C Merryfield
[M] (**Ref:**HM00027)

### A C T CLINIC

**A C T Clinic**, 88 Caulfield Rd, Shoeburyness, Southend-On-Sea, **Essex**, SS3 9LW, ENG.
(T) 01702 297265 (F) 01702 297265
Speciality: Acupuncture.
● **Owner** Mr D Jacobs
[O] (**Ref:**HM00028)

### A CHARTERED PHYSIOTHERAPIST

**A Chartered Physiotherapist**, Daresbury Park Physiotherapy Clinic, Daresbury Park Hotel, Daresbury, Warrington, **Cheshire**, WA4 4BB, ENG.
(T) 01925 268424
Speciality: Physiotherapy.
[P] [S] [T] (**Ref:**HM00029)

### A D S THOM

**A D S Thom**, 3 Junction Rd, Kirkwall, **Orkney Isles**, KW15 1LB, SCO.
(T) 01856 873289
Speciality: Biomechanics, Chiropody. ✓

● **Chiropodist** Mr A Thom **Q:** S.R.Ch. **M:** S.C.P.
**M** Yrs. Est.: 33 (**Ref:**HM00030)

## A G C CONSULTANTS
**A G C Consultants Ltd**, 33 Welbeck St, London, **London (Greater)**, W1M 7PG, ENG.
(T) 020 7486 2992 (F) 020 7486 1661
Speciality: Psychology.
● **Director** Mr J Mackay
**B** (**Ref:**HM00031)

## A G C CONSULTANTS
**A G C Consultants Ltd**, Chancery House, 53-64 Chancery Lane, London, **London (Greater)**, WC2A 1QU, ENG.
(T) 020 7831 3406
Speciality: Psychology.
● **Managing Director** Mr S Mackay
**B** (**Ref:**HM00032)

## A G PUSEY & ASSOCIATES
**A G Pusey & Associates**, Awbrook Lodge, Lewes Rd, Haywards Heath, **Sussex (West)**, RH17 7TB, ENG.
(T) 01444 831211 (F) 01444 831211
Speciality: Osteopathy.
● **Owner** Mr G Pusey
**P S T** (**Ref:**HM00033)

## A G PUSEY & ASSOCIATES
**A G Pusey & Associates**, 15 Millwood, Burgess Hill, **Sussex (West)**, RH15 8EB, ENG.
(T) 01444 239333
Speciality: Osteopathy.
● **Manager** Mrs P MacNaughty
**P S T** (**Ref:**HM00034)

## A J F LABORATORIES
**A J F Laboratories**, Orthotics Laboratory, Alveley Industrial Estate, Alveley, Bridgnorth, **Shropshire**, WV15 6HG, ENG.
(T) 01746 780241
Speciality: Chiropractic.
**P S T** (**Ref:**HM00035)

## A JS CHIROPODIST
**A Js Chiropodist**, 1a High St, Bovingdon, Hemel Hempstead, **Hertfordshire**, HP3 0HG, ENG.
(T) 01442 833346
Speciality: Chiropodists (Podiatrists).
● **Owner** Miss A Gurney
**S** (**Ref:**HM00036)

## A K CHINESE HEALTHCARE CENTRE
**A K Chinese Healthcare Centre**, 13 High St, Wealdstone, Harrow, **London (Greater)**, HA3 5BY, ENG.
(T) 020 8863 3686 (F) 020 8863 3686
Speciality: Herbal Medicine.
● **Doctor** Ms Y Han
**M** (**Ref:**HM00037)

## A L J RILEY ASSOCIATES
**A L J Riley Associates**, Surgery House, Halkyn, Holywell, **Flintshire**, CH8 8DL, WAL.
(T) 01352 781138
(E) jose@lifeofrileyclub.co.uk
(W) www.lifeofrileyclub.co.uk
Speciality: Complementary Therapy, Herbal Medicine, Vitamin Therapy, Preventative, Skincare.
● **Owner** Ms J Riley
**H** Yrs. Est.: 7 (**Ref:**HM00038)

## A M M TAYLOR
**A M M Taylor**, Swinford House, Swinford, Witney, **Oxfordshire**, OX8 1BY, ENG.
(T) 01865 881476
Speciality: Physiotherapy.
**P S T** (**Ref:**HM00039)

## A M R THERAPIES
**A M R Therapies**, Elm Villa, 12 Church Rd, Witham, **Essex**, CM8 3LA, ENG.
(T) 01621 891459
Speciality: Aromatherapy, Massage (Therapeutic), Reflexology. ✔
● **Holistic Therapist** Ms F Duddell **Q:** DM. **M:** IFR.
**C** Yrs. Est.: 9 (**Ref:**HM00040)

## A P B ACUPUNCTURE PRACTICE
**A P B Acupuncture Practice**, 2 Lilac Cl, Horsford, Norwich, **Norfolk**, NR10 3EN, ENG.
(T) 01603 898888
Speciality: Acupuncture.
● **Owner** Mr Patrick
**O** (**Ref:**HM00041)

## A P HEALEY CHIROPODY SERVICE
**A P Healey Chiropody Service**, 250 Park Rd, Peterborough, **Cambridgeshire**, PE1 2UR, ENG.
(T) 01733 562920
Speciality: Chiropodists (Podiatrists).
● **Owner** A Healey
**S** (**Ref:**HM00042)

## A P S THERAPY
**A P S Therapy Ltd**, Missing Link House, 3 Eastbury Rd, Northwood, **London (Greater)**, HA6 3AB, ENG.
(T) 01923 836353 (F) 01923 836484
Speciality: Complementary Medicines & Therapy.
● **Manager** Mr M Bradford
**M** (**Ref:**HM00043)

## A Q C H
**Association Of Qualified Curative Hypnotherapists**, 10 Balaclava Rd, Kings Heath, Birmingham, **Midlands (West)**, B14 7SG, ENG.
(T) 01214 411775
(E) info@aqch.org
(W) www.aqch.org
Speciality: Hypnosis, Hypnotherapy, Curative Hypnotherapy, Lesserian Curative Hypnotherapy. ✔
● **Committee Member** Ms H Lesser **Q:** Dip.Hyp.
● **Committee Member** Ms J Hopkins **Q:** C.Hyp.
**B** Yrs. Est.: 15 (**Ref:**HM00044)

## A SIR ROBERTS ALT PLACE
**J A Medicine T A A Sir Roberts AP**, 219 - 221 Old St, Ashton-under-Lyne, **Manchester (Greater)**, OL6 7SR, ENG.
(T) 01613 082518
Speciality: Acupressure, Acupuncture, Aromatherapy, Auto Suggestion, Bach Remedies, Biofeedback, Bonesetting, Chiropractic, Complementary Therapy, Counselling, Cupping, Dowsing, Faith Healing, Healer, Healing Therapy, Herbal Medicine, Holistic Healing, Homeopathy, Hypnosis, Hypnotherapy, Life Style Coaching, Manipulation, Massage (Therapeutic), Meditation, Naturopathy, Osteopathy, Postural Integration, Psychotherapy, Pyramid Power, Reflexology, Shiatsu, Spiritual Healing, Stress Therapy, Touch Therapy, Vibrational Therapy.
● **ALT Medicine Practitioner** Mr J Alternative Medicine
**M** Yrs. Est.: 40 (**Ref:**HM00045)

## A TACTILE BUSINESS
**A Tactile Business**, 30 Rayleigh Rd, Harrogate, **Yorkshire (North)**, HG2 8QR, ENG.
(T) 01423 541171
(E) atactilebusiness@cwcom.net
(W) www.atactilebusiness.co.uk
Speciality: Acupressure, Healer, Indian Head Massage, Reflexology, Acupressure Chair Massage, Body Massage. ✔
● **Sole Trader/Therapist** Mrs G Puckrin **Q:** CIBTAC. **M:** BABTAC.
**C T** Yrs. Est.: 3 (**Ref:**HM00046)

## A TIME FOR YOU
**A Time For You**, 32 Farrant Avenue, Churchdown, Gloucester, **Gloucestershire**, GL3 2BP, ENG.
(T) 01452 536328
Speciality: Electrolysis.
● **Owner** Mrs K Leigh
**T** (**Ref:**HM00047)

## A TOUCH OF HARMONY
**A Touch Of Harmony**, 44 High St, Gnosall, Stafford, **Staffordshire**, ST20 0EX, ENG.
(T) 01785 824262
Speciality: Aromatherapy.
● **Owner** Mrs N Buck
**M O** (**Ref:**HM00048)

## A TOUCH OF HEALTH
**A Touch Of Health**, 363 Curie Avenue, Harwell, Didcot, **Oxfordshire**, OX11 0QQ, ENG.
(T) 01235 821259
Speciality: Complementary Medicines & Therapy.
● **Owner** Mrs A Griffiths
**C M** (**Ref:**HM00049)

## A V CHIROPODY SERVICES
**A V Chiropody Services**, 226 Kingston Rd, Staines, **Surrey**, TW18 1PG, ENG.
(T) 01784 449997
Speciality: Chiropodists (Podiatrists).
● **Owner** Mrs A Varma
**S** (**Ref:**HM00050)

## A WAY WITH THE FAERIES
**A Way With The Faeries**, 6 Arbuthnott Pl, Stonehaven, **Aberdeenshire**, AB39 2JA, SCO.
(T) 01569 766808
Speciality: Aromatherapy, Crystal Healing.
● **Therapist** Mr N Willock
● **Owner** Mrs P Troup
**B C** Yrs. Est.: 3 (**Ref:**HM00051)

## A WELSH COUTTS
**A Welsh Coutts**, 48 Berkeley St, Glasgow, **Glasgow (City of)**, G3 7DS, SCO.
(T) 01412 212972
Speciality: Homeopathy.
● **Practice Manager** Miss T Coutts
**M** (**Ref:**HM00052)

## A1 FOOTCARE
**A1 Footcare**, 97 Kingsgate Avenue, Broadstairs, **Kent**, CT10 3LH, ENG.
(T) 01843 863653
Speciality: Chiropodists (Podiatrists).
● **Partner** Mrs P Corke
**S** (**Ref:**HM00053)

## A2Z COUNSELLING
**A2Z Counselling and Therapy Services**, 139 Lillie Rd, Richmond, London, **London (Greater)**, SW6 7SX, ENG.
(T) 07957 586656or07939314008
Speciality: Spiritual Healing, Thought Field Therapy, Regression Therapy, Transpersonal Psychology, Tantric Teaching.
**H T** (**Ref:**HM00054)

## A6 CHIROPODY PRACTICE
**A6 Chiropody Practice**, In-Step Footcare, 893 Stockport Rd, Manchester, **Manchester (Greater)**, M19 3PG, ENG.
(T) 01612 254300
Speciality: Chiropody, Reflexology. ✔
● **Reflexologist** Ms L Durrands
● **Chiropodist** Mrs J Bailey **Q:** BSc (Hons), M.S.C.P, S.R.Ch. **M:** S.C.P.
● **Chiropodist** Mr Butcher **Q:** M.S.C.P, S.R.Ch. **M:** S.C.P.
**M T** Yrs. Est.: 15 (**Ref:**HM00055)

## A7 ACUPUNCTURE CLINIC
**A7 Acupuncture Clinic**, 259 Harvist Rd, London, **London (Greater)**, NW6 6HH, ENG.
(T) 020 8960 1801
Speciality: Acupuncture.
● **Owner** Ms C Hector
**O** (**Ref:**HM00056)

## AA CHIROPRACTIC CLINIC
**AA Chiropractic Clinic Bramley**, 261 Upper Town St, Leeds, **Yorkshire (West)**, LS17 6PA, ENG.
(T) 01132 370596
Speciality: Chiropractors.
● **Owner** Mr K Pedersen
**P S T** (**Ref:**HM00057)

## AAAAAI HYPNOTISM & TRAINING
**AAAAAI Hypnotism & Training**, Front St, Witton Gilbert, Durham, **County Durham**, DH7 6TQ, ENG.
(T) 01913 710238 (F) 01913 710238
Speciality: Hypnotherapy.
● **Owner** Mr C Turnball
**B** (**Ref:**HM00058)

## AABLE FEET CHIROPODY
**Aable Feet Chiropody**, 55 Kings Rd, Gosport, **Hampshire**, PO12 1PX, ENG.
(T) 023 9225 8363
Speciality: Chiropodists (Podiatrists).
**S** (**Ref:**HM00059)

## AAROMA INTRIGUE
**Aaroma Intrigue**, 17 Herbert St, Dublin, **County Dublin**, IRE.


Key continued: **Yrs.Est:** Years Established **Q:** Qualifications **M:** Professional Membership ✔ Indemnity Insurance Accept Credit Cards

(T) 01286 5738
(E) aaromaintrigue@eircom.net
Speciality: Aromatherapy.
M O (Ref:HM00060)

**AARON ABBA-IMMA CENTRE**

**Aaron Abba-Imma Centre**, Grange Hse, 60 Beaumont Ave, Dublin, **County Dublin**, IRE.
(T) 01298 3352
Speciality: Complementary Medicines & Therapy.
M (Ref:HM00061)

**AARON ABBEY HYPNOTHERAPY**

**Aaron Abbey Hypnotherapy**, 66 Ascot Avenue, Doncaster, **Yorkshire (South)**, DN4 6HE, ENG.
(T) 01302 533349
Speciality: Hypnotherapy.
● **Owner** Mr N Shillitoe
B (Ref:HM00062)

**AARON ACUPUNCTURE & OSTEOPATHY**

**Aaron Acupuncture & Osteopathy Centre**, 7 Malford Gr, London, **London (Greater)**, E18 2DX, ENG.
(T) 020 8989 2635
Speciality: Osteopathy.
P S T (Ref:HM00063)

**AARON ACUPUNCTURE & OSTEOPATHY**

**Aaron Acupuncture & Osteopathy Centre**, 33 Stainforth Rd, London, **London (Greater)**, E17 9RB, ENG.
(T) 020 8520 2464
Speciality: Acupuncture.
● **Principal** Dr Z Malik
O (Ref:HM00064)

**AARON HYPNOTHERAPY SERVICES**

**Aaron Hypnotherapy Services**, 25 Asquith Gardens, Benfleet, **Essex**, SS7 3SZ, ENG.
(T) 01268 771001
Speciality: Hypnotherapy.
B (Ref:HM00065)

**ABABS NIGHT & DAY**

**Ababs Night & Day**, 3-5 Hardwidge St, London, **London (Greater)**, SE1 3SY, ENG.
(T) 020 7378 8377
Speciality: Aromatherapy.
M O (Ref:HM00066)

**ABACADE**

**Abacade**, 3-5 Hardwidge St, London, **London (Greater)**, SE1 3SY, ENG.
(T) 020 7403 6565
Speciality: Complementary Medicines & Therapy.
C M (Ref:HM00067)

**ABACUS THERAPY CENTRE**

**Abacus Therapy Centre**, 195 Main Rd, Romford, **Essex**, RM2 6LT, ENG.
(T) 01708 743544
Speciality: Complementary Medicines & Therapy.
● **Owner** Mr A Bloom
M (Ref:HM00068)

**ABACUS THERAPY CENTRE**

**Abacus Therapy Centre**, 4b East Rd, London, **London (Greater)**, E15 3QR, ENG.
(T) 020 8471 6375
Speciality: Hypnotherapy.
● **Owner** Mr R Bloom
B (Ref:HM00069)

**ABBA, TERRI**

**Terri Abba**, 15 Havenbaulk Avenue, Littleover, Derby, **Derbyshire**, DE23 7BL, ENG.
(T) 01332 518827
Speciality: Reflexology.
S T (Ref:HM00070)

**ABBEY CENTRE**

**Abbey Centre (The)**, 10 Sanderstead Avenue, London, **London (Greater)**, NW2 1SG, ENG.
(T) 020 8452 1533 (F) 020 8452 1533
(E) duri@duri.worldonline.co.uk
Speciality: Counselling, Hypnosis, Hypnotherapy, Physiotherapy, Psychotherapy, Stress Therapy. ✔
● **Owner/Physiotherapist/Hypnotherapist** Dr D Uri Q: Dip.Hyp, Dip.Psych, MIAH, MSc, PhD. M: IAH.
B H Yrs. Est.: 8 (Ref:HM00071)

**ABBEY CHIROPODY CLINIC**

**Abbey Chiropody Clinic**, 14 Bath St, Abingdon, **Oxfordshire**, OX14 3QH, ENG.
(T) 01235 530577
Speciality: Chiropodists (Podiatrists).
● **Owner** Mr P Neighbour
S (Ref:HM00072)

**ABBEY CHIROPODY CLINIC**

**Abbey Chiropody Clinic**, 20 Abbey Court, St Martins Way, Battle, **Sussex (East)**, TN33 0TZ, ENG.
(T) 01424 773295
Speciality: Chiropodists (Podiatrists).
● **Owner** Mrs A Hillman
S (Ref:HM00073)

**ABBEY CHIROPODY SERVICES**

**Abbey Chiropody Services**, The Hearing Aid Centre, 72 Hendford, Yeovil, **Somerset**, BA20 1UY, ENG.
(T) 01935 475926
Speciality: Chiropody. ✔
● **Chiropodist (Podiatrist)**
Mr G Meager Q: MBChA, MSSCh. M: S.C.P.
M Yrs. Est.: 15 (Ref:HM00074)

**ABBEY CHIROPRACTIC CLINIC**

**Abbey Chiropractic Clinic**, 6 Latimer St, Romsey, **Hampshire**, SO51 8DG, ENG.
(T) 01794 518772
Speciality: Chiropractic.
P S T (Ref:HM00075)

**ABBEY CLINIC**

**Abbey Clinic (Bisham)**, National Sports Centre, Bisham, Marlow, **Buckinghamshire**, SL7 1RT, ENG.
(T) 01628 481866 (F) 01628 481866
Speciality: Physiotherapy.
● **Owner** Ms G Morgan
P S T (Ref:HM00076)

**ABBEY CLINIC**

**Abbey Clinic**, 7a Earlsdon St, Earlsdon, Coventry, **Midlands (West)**, CV5 6EP, ENG.
(T) 024 7669 1100
Speciality: Acupressure, Acupuncture, Aromatherapy, Bonesetting, Bowen Therapy, Chiropractic, Counselling, Cranial Osteopathy, Herbal Medicine, Homeopathy, Hypnosis, Indian Head Massage, Manipulation, Massage (Therapeutic), Micro Manipulation, Osteopathy, Phytotherapy, Reflexology, Reiki, Rolfing, Shiatsu, Vitamin Therapy. ✔
● **Osteopath/Nurse** Mr J Stapleton Q: BA, BSc, Hons (OST), RGN. M: GNC, GOsC.
● **Masseuse** Ms M Robinson Q: ITEC.
S Yrs. Est.: 3 (Ref:HM00077)

**ABBEY CLINIC**

**Abbey Clinic (The)**, 6a Albert Rd, Belvedere, **Kent**, DA17 5LJ, ENG.
(T) 01322 436555
Speciality: Complementary Medicines & Therapy.
C M (Ref:HM00078)

**ABBEY CLINIC**

**Abbey Clinic (The)**, First Floor, Lyttleton House, Abbey Rd, Malvern, **Worcestershire**, WR14 3ES, ENG.
(T) 01684 563111
Speciality: Complementary Medicines & Therapy.
● **Manager** Miss K Standon
M (Ref:HM00079)

**ABBEY COMPLEMENTARY**

**Abbey Complementary**, 70 Abbey St, Bangor, **County Down**, BT20 4JB, NIR.
(T) 028 9127 1984
Speciality: Complementary Medicines & Therapy.
● **Owner** Mr B Hazell
M (Ref:HM00080)

**ABBEY FOOT CLINIC**

**Abbey Foot Clinic Ltd**, 71D Rice Lane, Liverpool, **Merseyside**, L9 1AD, ENG.
(T) 01515 250278
Speciality: Chiropodists (Podiatrists).
● **Joint Director** Miss C Latham
S (Ref:HM00081)

**ABBEY FOOT CLINIC**

**Abbey Foot Clinic Ltd**, 99 Wavertree Rd, Liverpool, **Merseyside**, L7 1PG, ENG.
(T) 01512 632056
Speciality: Chiropodists (Podiatrists).
S (Ref:HM00082)

**ABBEY FOOT CLINIC**

**Abbey Foot Clinic**, 7 Lisburn Lane, Liverpool, **Merseyside**, L13 9AE, ENG.
(T) 01512 289837
Speciality: Chiropody, Podiatry. ✔
● **Chiropodist (Podiatrist)**
Miss C Lather Q: DPodM. M: S.C.P.
M Yrs. Est.: 16 (Ref:HM00083)

**ABBEY HILL & ROBSON**

**Abbey Hill & Robson**, 203 Toller Lane, Bradford, **Yorkshire (West)**, BD9 5DS, ENG.
(T) 01274 541732
Speciality: Chiropodists (Podiatrists).
S (Ref:HM00084)

**ABBEY HILL & ROBSON**

**Abbey Hill & Robson**, 4 Westgate, Baildon, Shipley, **Yorkshire (West)**, BD17 5EJ, ENG.
(T) 01274 532953
Speciality: Chiropodists (Podiatrists).
S (Ref:HM00085)

**ABBEY HOUSE HEALTH AND BEAUTY**

**Abbey House Health And Beauty**, 75 Abbey Rd, Cambridge, **Cambridgeshire**, CB5 8HH, ENG.
(T) 01223 525347
Speciality: Complementary Medicines & Therapy.
C M (Ref:HM00086)

**ABBEY HYPNOTHERAPY**

**Abbey Hypnotherapy**, 348 Hoe St, London, **London (Greater)**, E17 9PX, ENG.
(T) 020 8509 1171
Speciality: Hypnotherapy.
B (Ref:HM00087)

**ABBEY VIEW COMP CLINIC**

**Abbey View Complementary Clinic**, Abbey View Medical Centre, Shaftesbury, **Dorset**, SP7 8DH, ENG.
(T) 01747 856719 (F) 01747 856701
(E) david@broo22.freeserve.co.uk
Speciality: Acupuncture, Alexander Technique, Aromatherapy, Chiropody, Counselling, Herbal Medicine, Homeopathy, Hypnotherapy, Nutritional Therapy, Reflexology, Remedial Massage, Shiatsu, Cranial Osteopathy, Allergy Testing, Manual Lymphatic Drainage, Hydrotherapy. ✔
● **Chiropodist (Podiatrist)**
Ms M Knight Q: BSc (Hons), DPodM, S.R.Ch. M: S.C.P.
● **Counsellor** Cinzia Altobelli Q: Dip.Couns, RGN.
● **Medical Herbalist** Dr F James Q: Ch.B, Dip.Phyto, DRCOG, MB, MNIMH. M: NIMH.
● **Manual Lymphatic Drainage**
Ms A Screiber Q: ITEC.
● **Alexander Technique Therapist**
Ms F Robinson Q: ATI, BA, MSTAT. M: STAT.
● **Allergy Tester/Medical Herbalist**
Mr D Broom M: IRCH.
● **Homeopathic Physician**
Dr E Douglas Q: MA, MB, MFHom.
● **Osteoporosis Screener**
Dr G Kempson Q: BSc (Hons), DIC, PhD.
● **Osteopath** Ms D Bendy Q: BSc, Hons (OST).
● **Osteopath** Dr R Gribble Q: BS, MB, MRCP.
● **Massage/Aromatherapist/Reflexologist**
Ms S Millbank Q: ITEC. M: IPTI.
● **Acupuncturist/Physiotherapist**
Mr B Bunn Q: Lic.Ac, SRP. M: CSP.
● **Owner/Acupuncturist** Mrs V Dawson Q: MCSP, SRP. M: BAcC, CSP.
● **Physiotherapist** Ms A Hogan Q: BSc (Hons), MCSP, SRP. M: CSP, SRP.
C Yrs. Est.: 14 (Ref:HM00088)

**ABBEY, AMANDA**

**Amanda Abbey**, 16 Victoria Rd, Clacton-On-Sea,



Key: B Mind-Body Medicine C Complementary Medicine H Self Help Treatment M Medicinal Therapy O Oriental Medicine P Postural Therapy S Manipulative Structural Therapy T Touch Therapy

**Essex**, CO15 6BH, **ENG**.
**(T)** 01255 688069
Speciality: Hypnotherapy.
● **Administrator** Mrs H Robinson
B (**Ref:**HM00089)

## ABBEYMEAD NATURAL HEALTH CTRE

**Abbeymead Natural Health Centre**, 7 Plymouth Rd, Tavistock, **Devon**, PL19 8AU, **ENG**.
**(T)** 01822 614814 **(F)** 01822 610463
**(W)** www.abbey-mead.co.uk
Speciality: Acupuncture, Aromatherapy, Bowen Therapy, Chiropractic, Complementary Therapy, Counselling, Cranial Osteopathy, Drama Therapy, Herbal Medicine, Homeopathy, Hypnotherapy, Indian Head Massage, Iridology, Manipulation, Massage (Therapeutic), Meditation, Naturopathy, Nutritional Therapy, Osteopathy, Psychotherapy, Reflexology, Stress Therapy. ✓
● **Aromatherapist** Ms L Hudson **Q:** Dip.Arom, Dip.Th.Massage. **M:** ANM.
● **Osteopath** Mr P Hartnoll **Q:** DO. **M:** GOsC.
C Yrs. Est.: 10 (**Ref:**HM00090)

## ABBEYWOOD CHIROPODY CLINIC

**Abbeywood Chiropody Clinic**, 108 McLeod Rd, London, **London (Greater)**, SE2 0BS, **ENG**.
**(T)** 020 8310 8923
Speciality: Biomechanics, Chiropody. ✓
● **Chiropodist** Mrs B Patel **Q:** S.R.Ch. **M:** S.R.Ch.
C Yrs. Est.: 10 (**Ref:**HM00091)

## ABBIE HYPNOTHERAPY CENTRE

**Abbie Hypnotherapy Centre**, 20 The Hurst, Moseley, Birmingham, **Midlands (West)**, B13 0DG, **ENG**.
**(T)** 01217 786675 **(F)** 01217 786676
Speciality: Hypnotherapy.
● **Owner** Mrs C Cooke
B (**Ref:**HM00092)

## ABBIE HYPNOTHERAPY CENTRE

**Abbie Hypnotherapy Centre**, 240 Alcester Rd South, Kings Heath, Birmingham, **Midlands (West)**, B14 6DR, **ENG**.
**(T)** 01217 786676 **(F)** 01217 786676
**(W)** www.abbie-hypnotherapy.co.uk
Speciality: Counselling, Hypnosis, Hypnotherapy, Psychotherapy, Stress Therapy. ✓
● **Practice Manager** Carmel Finglass
● **Owner** Mr N Cooke **Q:** Dip.Psych, MNCH. **M:** HS.
B Yrs. Est.: 16 (**Ref:**HM00093)

## ABBOT, JENNY

**Jenny Abbot**, 17 Vicarage Rd, Bletchley, Milton Keynes, **Buckinghamshire**, MK2 2EZ, **ENG**.
**(T)** 01908 371875
Speciality: Physiotherapy.
● **Owner** Ms J Abbot
P S T (**Ref:**HM00094)

## ABBOT, LISA

**Sclare Chiropody Practice**, 119 Eastern Avenue, Redbridge, Ilford, **Essex**, IG4 5AN, **ENG**.
**(T)** 020 8550 9722/5519111
Speciality: Reflexology, Reiki, Shiatsu. ✓
● **Complementary Therapist** Ms L Abbott **Q:** MAR, MIIR. **M:** AoR.
T Yrs. Est.: 5 (**Ref:**HM00095)

## ABBOTT & WILKINSON

**Abbott & Wilkinson**, 57 Talbot St, Southport, **Merseyside**, PR8 1LU, **ENG**.
**(T)** 01704 538245
Speciality: Chiropodists (Podiatrists).
● **Owner** Mr R Wilkinson
S (**Ref:**HM00096)

## ABBOTT HYPNOTHERAPY

**Abbott Hypnotherapy**, 7 Wood View, Newton Abbot, **Devon**, TQ12 1YX, **ENG**.
**(T)** 01626 330930
Speciality: Hypnotherapy.
B (**Ref:**HM00097)

## ABBOTT, LISA

**Rainham Osteopath**, 84 Upminster Rd South, Rainham, **Kent**, RM13 9AA, **ENG**.
**(T)** 01708 551771
Speciality: Reflexology, Reiki, Shiatsu. ✓
● **Owner** Mr J Kirkwood
● **Complementary Therapist** Ms L Abbott **Q:** MAR, MIIR. **M:** AoR.
T Yrs. Est.: 5 (**Ref:**HM00098)

## ABBOTT, LISA

**Sclaire Chiropody Practice**, 535 Rainham Rd South, Dagenham, **Essex**, RM10 7TA, **ENG**.
**(T)** 07966 448234
Speciality: Reflexology, Reiki, Shiatsu.
● **Complementary Therapist** Ms L Abbott **Q:** MAR, MIIR. **M:** AoR.
T Yrs. Est.: 5 (**Ref:**HM00099)

## ABBOTT, LISA

**Lisa Abbott**, 47 Hawthorn Avenue, Rainham, **Kent**, RM13 9AT, **ENG**.
**(T)** 01708 523982
Speciality: Reflexology.
S T (**Ref:**HM00100)

## ABBOTT, LORNA

**Lorna Abbott**, 1 Skippons Cl, Newbury, **Berkshire**, RG14 6SE, **ENG**.
**(T)** 01635 582133
Speciality: Hypnosis.
B (**Ref:**HM00101)

## ABBOTTS OF LEIGH

**Abbotts Of Leigh**, 56 Railway Rd, Leigh, **Manchester (Greater)**, WN7 4AR, **ENG**.
**(T)** 01942 671766
Speciality: Herbalists.
● **Manageress** Mrs J Berry
M (**Ref:**HM00102)

## ABBOTTS ROAD PRACTICE

**Abbotts Road Practice**, Abbotts Rd, Mitcham, **Surrey**, CR4 1JP, **ENG**.
**(T)** 020 8288 9570
Speciality: Psychotherapy.
● **Hypnotherapist** Miss Starrett
B (**Ref:**HM00103)

## ABBYCARE HYPNOTHERAPY

**Abbycare Hypnotherapy**, 49 Holbeck Pk Avenue, Barrow-in-Furness, **Cumbria**, LA13 0RG, **ENG**.
**(T)** 01229 825260
Speciality: Hypnotherapy.
● **Owner** Mr M McGuire
B (**Ref:**HM00104)

## ABDAY-WHITE, R J

**R J Abday-White**, 12 Andover St, Cheltenham, **Gloucestershire**, GL50 2EL, **ENG**.
**(T)** 01242 234027
Speciality: Chiropodists (Podiatrists).
● **Principal** Mr R Abday-White
S (**Ref:**HM00105)

## ABEL HOUSE HYPNOTHERAPY

**Abel House Hypnotherapy**, 24 West Pk Rd, Smethwick, **Midlands (West)**, B67 7JJ, **ENG**.
**(T)** 01216 012526
Speciality: Hypnotherapy.
● **Owner** Mr D Cooper
B (**Ref:**HM00106)

## ABEL, ELAINE

**Elaine Abel**, Emsworth, **Hampshire**, PO10, **ENG**.
**(T)** 01243 376506
Speciality: Bach Remedies.
M (**Ref:**HM00107)

## ABEL, STEFFAN H

**Steffan H Abel**, 22 Oakdale Trce, Chester Le Street, **County Durham**, DH3 3DH, **ENG**.
**(T)** 01913 891866
Speciality: Chiropractic.
P S T (**Ref:**HM00108)

## ABELA, P

**Mrs P Abela**, 93 Castle St, Luton, **Bedfordshire**, LU1 3AJ, **ENG**.
**(T)** 01582 876866
Speciality: Chiropodists (Podiatrists).
S (**Ref:**HM00109)

## ABELIA COUNSELLING

**Abelia Counselling**, 4 Alden Park, Sutton, **County Dublin**, **IRE**.
**(T)** 01832 4576
**(E)** fryder@gofree.indigo.ie
Speciality: Counselling, Hypnosis, Hypnotherapy, Neuro-Linguistic Program. ✓
● **Counsellor/Therapist** Mr F Ryder **Q:** Dip.Couns, Dip.Hyp, NLP. **M:** IICH.
B Yrs. Est.: 2 (**Ref:**HM00110)

## ABELL-FRANCIS, NICKY

**Nicky Abell-Francis**, Laureens Walk, Nevill Rd, Rottingdean, Brighton, **Sussex (East)**, BN2 7HG, **ENG**.
**(T)** 01273 390280
Speciality: Complementary Medicines & Therapy.
● **Owner** Mrs S Troak
M (**Ref:**HM00111)

## ABERCROMBIE, CAROLINE

**Caroline Abercrombie**, 208 Birmingham Rd, Stratford-Upon-Avon, **Warwickshire**, CV37 0AX, **ENG**.
**(T)** 01789 299190
Speciality: Chiropodists (Podiatrists).
● **Owner** Ms Y Kiernan
S (**Ref:**HM00112)

## ABERDEEN CHIROPODY & PODIATRY

**Aberdeen Chiropody & Podiatry Practice**, 9 Victoria St, Aberdeen, **Aberdeenshire**, AB10 1XB, **SCO**.
**(T)** 01224 635806
Speciality: Chiropodists (Podiatrists).
S (**Ref:**HM00113)

## ABERDEEN CHIROPRACTIC CLINIC

**Aberdeen Chiropractic Clinic**, 331 Great Western Rd, Aberdeen, **Aberdeenshire**, AB10 6NW, **SCO**.
**(T)** 01224 585456 **(F)** 01224 572110
Speciality: Chiropractic, Kinesiology. ✓
● **Associate** Dr D Wood
● **Doctor** Mr K Bramberg
P S T Yrs. Est.: 21 (**Ref:**HM00114)

## ABERDEEN HEALING CENTRE

**Aberdeen Healing Centre**, 52 Holburn St, Aberdeen, **Aberdeenshire**, AB10 6BX, **SCO**.
**(T)** 01224 591700
Speciality: Complementary Medicines & Therapy.
● **Chairperson** Ann Moon
C M (**Ref:**HM00115)

## ABERDEEN HYPNOTHERAPY CENTRE

**Aberdeen Hypnotherapy Centre**, 1 Belgrave Trce, Aberdeen, **Aberdeenshire**, AB25 2NR, **SCO**.
**(T)** 01224 658700
Speciality: Hypnotherapy.
● **Owner** Mr M Taylor
B (**Ref:**HM00116)

## ABERDEEN PHYSIOTHERAPY

**Aberdeen Physiotherapy**, 99 Westburn Rd, Aberdeen, **Aberdeenshire**, AB25 2SG, **SCO**.
**(T)** 01224 626266
Speciality: Physiotherapy.
● **Receptionist** Chris Ashbrook
P S T (**Ref:**HM00117)

## ABERDEEN PHYSIOTHERAPY CTRE

**Aberdeen Chartered Physiotherapy Centre**, Arrdeir 25, Craigton Rd, Aberdeen, **Aberdeenshire**, AB15 7US, **SCO**.
**(T)** 01224 316488 **(F)** 01224 208801
Speciality: Physiotherapy.
● **Owner** Mr G Wallace
P S T (**Ref:**HM00118)

## ABERDEEN SPIRITUALIST CENTRE

**Aberdeen Spiritualist Centre & Healing Sanctuary**, 71 Dee St, Aberdeen, **Aberdeenshire**, AB11 6EE, **SCO**.
**(T)** 01224 574916
Speciality: Complementary Medicines & Therapy.
M (**Ref:**HM00119)

## ABERDEEN THERAPY CENTRE

**Aberdeen Therapy Centre**, 232 Holburn St, Aberdeen, **Aberdeenshire**, AB10 6DB, **SCO**.
**(T)** 01224 586958 **(F)** 01224 586958
Speciality: Complementary Medicines & Therapy.
● **Owner** Mr G Duffus


Key continued: **Yrs.Est:** Years Established **Q:** Qualifications **M:** Professional Membership ✓ Indemnity Insurance Accept Credit Cards

M (Ref:HM00120)

**ABERGAVENNY THERAPY CTRE**

**Abergavenny Natural Therapy Centre**, 12 Cross St, Abergavenny, **Monmouthshire**, NP7 5EH, WAL.
(T) 01873 858391
Speciality: Aromatherapy, Hypnotherapy, Reflexology. ✓
● **Manager** Mrs Y Davis Q: Dip.Hyp. M: BHMA.
C Yrs. Est.: 12 (Ref:HM00121)

**ABERGELE CHIROPODY SERVICES**

**Abergele Chiropody Services**, 11A Market St, Abergele, **Conwy**, LL22 7AG, WAL.
(T) 01745 826633
Speciality: Chiropodists (Podiatrists).
S (Ref:HM00122)

**ABERNETHY, HILARY**

**Hilary Abernethy**, 54 London Rd, Blackpool, **Lancashire**, FY3 8DL, ENG.
(T) 01253 391506
Speciality: Aromatherapy, Cognitive Therapy, Complementary Therapy, Group Therapy, Holistic Healing, Life Style Coaching, Massage (Therapeutic), Meditation, Psychotherapy, Reflexology, Sensitivity Training, Stress Therapy. ✓
● **Aromatherapist/Reflexologist**
Ms H Abernethy Q: IIHHT, RGN, RMN. M: IIHHT.
B T Yrs. Est.: 5 (Ref:HM00123)

**ABERTAWE PHYSIOTHERAPY CLINIC**

**Abertawe Physiotherapy & Sports Injury Clinic**, 42 Eaton Cres, Swansea, SA1 4QL, WAL.
(T) 01792 473957
(E) physio@posture.co.uk
Speciality: Acupressure, Acupuncture, Complementary Therapy, Manipulation, Massage (Therapeutic), Meditation, Physiotherapy, Ultrasonics. ✓
● **Practice Principal** Mr D Spowart Q: Grad Dip Phys, MCSP, SRP. M: CSP.
S Yrs. Est.: 10 (Ref:HM00124)

**ABERTILLERY PHYSIOTHERAPY**

**Abertillery Physiotherapy Clinic**, 3 New Houses, Mitre St, Abertillery, **Blaenau Gwent**, NP13 1AE, WAL.
(T) 01495 215655 (F) 01495 215655
(E) anthonyaparker@hotmail.com
Speciality: Acupuncture, Physiotherapy. ✓
● **Physiotherapist** Mr A Parker Q: MCSP, MSc, SRP. M: CSP.
S Yrs. Est.: 10 (Ref:HM00125)

**ABIGAIL'S**

**Abigail's 1st Class Holistic Therapy Clinic**, 196 Shrewsbury Rd, London, **London (Greater)**, E7 8QJ, ENG.
(T) 020 8471 0549
Speciality: Aromatherapy, Reflexology. ✓
● **Aromatherapist/Reflexologist**
Mrs Sawhney Q: Dip.Arom. M: FHT.
C Yrs. Est.: 3 (Ref:HM00126)

**ABILITY FOR YOU**

**Ability For You Ltd**, Unit E14, Marquis Court, Team Valley Trading Estate, Gateshead, **Tyne and Wear**, NE11 0RU, ENG.
(T) 01914 911144 (F) 01914 911824
Speciality: Physiotherapy.
P S T (Ref:HM00127)

**ABINGDON & DIDCOT CLINIC**

**Abingdon & Didcot Chiropractic Clinic**, 6 Broad St, Abingdon, **Oxfordshire**, OX14 3LH, ENG.
(T) 01235 554435
Speciality: Chiropractors.
● **Principal** Dr A Roe
P S T (Ref:HM00128)

**ABNETT, LINDA**

**Linda Abnett**, 42 Oak Farm Gardens, Headcorn, Ashford, **Kent**, TN27 9TZ, ENG.
(T) 01622 891333
Speciality: Chiropodists (Podiatrists).
● **Owner** Mrs L Abnett
S (Ref:HM00129)

**ABNEY, ERIKA R (DR)**

**Dr Erika R Abney**, 5 Elm Trce, Constantine Rd, London, **London (Greater)**, NW3 2LL, ENG.
(T) 020 7267 7070
Speciality: Homeopathy.
● **Practice Manager**
Nicola Bannerman
M (Ref:HM00130)

**ABOUT FACE**

**About Face Electrolysis Beauty & Nail Clinic**, 40 St Enoch Sq, Glasgow, **Glasgow (City of)**, G1 4DH, SCO.
(T) 01412 044060 (F) 01555 840583
(E) info@about-face.co.uk
(W) www.about-face.co.uk
Speciality: Aromatherapy, Electrolysis, Massage (Therapeutic). ✓
● **Owner** Ms H Graham Q: IHBC. M: BABTAC.
S Yrs. Est.: 16 (Ref:HM00131)

**ABRAHAMS & BENNETT**

**Abrahams & Bennett**, Liberty Clinic, 394 Romford Rd, London, **London (Greater)**, E7 8DF, ENG.
(T) 020 8552 6063 (F) 020 8470 6250
Speciality: Osteopathy. ✓
● **Osteopath** Mr L Bennett M: GOsC.
● **Osteopath** Lisa Abrahams M: GOsC.
● **Osteopath** Mr R Wiseman M: GOsC.
● **Osteopath** Mr N Herterich M: GOsC.
S Yrs. Est.: 15 (Ref:HM00132)

**ABRAHAMS & BENNETT**

**Abrahams & Bennett**, The Liberty City Clinic, 3 Ravey St, London, **London (Greater)**, EC2A 4QP, ENG.
(T) 020 7739 8009 (F) 020 7739 0708
Speciality: Osteopathy. ✓
● **Osteopath** Mr P Row M: GOsC.
● **Owner/Osteopath** Mr L Bennett M: GOsC.
● **Osteopath** Mr J Last M: GOsC.
● **Osteopath** Mr K Leeson M: GOsC.
● **Osteopath** Ms L Abrahams M: GOsC.
S Yrs. Est.: 10 (Ref:HM00133)

**ABRAHAMS, LISA**

**Lisa Abrahams**, 434 Romford Rd, London, **London (Greater)**, E7 8DF, ENG.
(T) 020 8552 6063
Speciality: Osteopathy.
● **Owner** L Abraham
P S T (Ref:HM00134)

**ABRAHAMS, SANDRA**

**Sandra Abrahams**, The Terrace, 35 Staplegrove Rd, Taunton, **Somerset**, TA1 1DG, ENG.
(T) 01823 338968
Speciality: Aromatherapy.
● **Owner** Ms J Gotto
M O (Ref:HM00135)

**ABRAMS, CAROLINE**

**Caroline Abrams**, 255 Abingdon Rd, Oxford, **Oxfordshire**, OX1 4TH, ENG.
(T) 01865 245095
Speciality: Osteopathy.
P S T (Ref:HM00136)

**ABSOLUTE AROMAS**

**Absolute Aromas Ltd**, Unit 2, Grove Pk, Mill Lane, Alton, **Hampshire**, GU34 2QG, ENG.
(T) 01420 549991 (F) 01420 540401
Speciality: Aromatherapy.
● **Managing Director** Mr D Tomlinson
M O (Ref:HM00137)

**ABSOLUTE BLISS**

**Absolute Bliss**, 3 Avenue Rd, Swindon, **Wiltshire**, SN1 4BZ, ENG.
(T) 01793 615439
Speciality: Aromatherapy.
● **Owner** Ms L Holmes
M O (Ref:HM00138)

**ABSOLUTE ESSENCE**

**Absolute Essence**, Shaw Cl, Cheshunt, Waltham Cross, **Hertfordshire**, EN8 0HD, ENG.
(T) 01992 626340
Speciality: Complementary Medicines & Therapy.
● **Owner** Ms D Whiteside
M (Ref:HM00139)

**ABSOLUTE MASSAGE & REFLEXOLOGY**

**Absolute Massage & Reflexology Clinic**, 120 Lr Kilmacud Rd, Stillorgan, **County Dublin**, IRE.
(T) 01278 0750
Speciality: Reflexology.
S T (Ref:HM00140)

**ABSOLUTE RELAXING**

**Absolute Relaxing Therapeutic Massage**, Bredgar, Lewisham Park, London, **London (Greater)**, SE13 6QN, ENG.
(T) 020 8690 9690
Speciality: Complementary Medicines & Therapy.
● **Owner** Ms V Mitchell
M (Ref:HM00141)

**ABSOLUTE SOLUTIONS**

**Absolute Solutions**, 11 Daryngton Avenue, Birchington, **Kent**, CT7 9PS, ENG.
(T) 01843 541010 (F) 01843 541010
Speciality: Ayurvedic Medicine, Holistic Healing, Meditation, Stress Therapy, Yoga, Transcendental Meditation. ✓
● **Director/Teacher** Mr C Beckley
B Yrs. Est.: 10 (Ref:HM00142)

**ABSOLUTE THERAPY**

**Absolute Therapy**, 3 Oldcoach Rd, East Kilbride, **Lanarkshire (South)**, G74 4DR, SCO.
(T) 01355 247697
Speciality: Complementary Medicines & Therapy.
● **Manager** Christine Hoey
M (Ref:HM00143)

**ABSOLUTELY YOU**

**Absolutely You**, Longthorne House, 546 Fishponds Rd, Fishponds, Bristol, BS16 3DD, ENG.
(T) 01179 650413
Speciality: Complementary Medicines & Therapy.
● **Joint Manager** Julie
M (Ref:HM00144)

**ABUNDANCE HEALING**

**Abundance Healing**, 8 Orchard Drive, Standon, **Hertfordshire**, SG11 1XD, ENG.
(T) 01920 822954
Speciality: Counselling, Reflexology, Reiki, Occupational Therapy.
S T (Ref:HM00145)

**ACACIA COUNSELLING CENTRE**

**Acacia Counselling Centre**, 16 Ardeevin Dr, Lucan, **County Dublin**, IRE.
(T) 01628 1012
Speciality: Complementary Medicines & Therapy.
M (Ref:HM00146)

**ACADEMY INTERNATIONAL**

**Academy International**, 19 Maypark Malahide Rd, IRE.
(T) 01851 1144
Speciality: Complementary Medicines & Therapy.
M (Ref:HM00147)

**ACADEMY OF HOLISTIC STUDIES**

**Academy of Holistic Studies**, The Professional Centre For Holistic Health, 50 High St, Hastings, **Sussex (East)**, TN34 3EN, ENG.
(T) 01424 465050
Speciality: Reiki. ✓
● **Reiki Master** Ms M Eaton Q: BRCP, MIFA, Reiki Master.
● **Reiki Master** Mrs V Ford
(T) 01424 751441 Q: BRCP, MIFA, Reiki Master.
C Yrs. Est.: 3 (Ref:HM00148)

**ACADEMY PHYSIOTHERAPY CLINIC**

**Academy Physiotherapy & Sports Injury Clinic**, Clifton House Medical Centre, 263 Beverley Rd, Hull, **Humberside (North)**, HU5 2ST, ENG.
(T) 01482 493309
Speciality: Acupuncture, Physiotherapy. ✓
● **Physiotherapist/Owner**
Mr P Johnson Q: DIT, MCSP, SRP. M: CSP, SOM.
S Yrs. Est.: 5 (Ref:HM00149)

**ACARSAID CHIROPODY CLINIC**

**Acarsaid Chiropody Clinic**, 55 Strathmartine



Key: B Mind-Body Medicine C Complementary Medicine H Self Help Treatment M Medicinal Therapy O Oriental Medicine P Postural Therapy S Manipulative Structural Therapy T Touch Therapy

Rd, Dundee, **Angus**, DD3 7RX, SCO.
(T) 01382 833030
Speciality: Chiropody.
● **Owner** Mrs S Wallace
**S** (Ref:HM00150)

## ACCELERATED CHANGE CENTRE
**Accelerated Change Centre**, 30 Victoria Rd, Romford, **Essex**, RM1 2JH, ENG.
(T) 01708 438800
Speciality: Hypnotherapy.
● **Partner** Dr E Neale
**B** (Ref:HM00151)

## ACCELERATED LEARNING
**Accelerated Learning & Therapy Centre**, 565 Cranbrook Rd, Ilford, **Essex**, IG2 6JZ, ENG.
(T) 020 8551 5551 (F) 020 8551 5559
Speciality: Complementary Medicines & Therapy.
● **Principal** Miss M Aligbe
**C** **M** (Ref:HM00152)

## ACCENT ON BEAUTY
**Accent On Beauty**, 39 Mellish Rd, Walsall, **Midlands (West)**, WS4 2DG, ENG.
(T) 01922 644088
Speciality: Electrolysis.
● **Owner** Mrs E Lapsley
**T** (Ref:HM00153)

## ACCOMPLISHED ACUPUNCTURE
**Accomplished Acupuncture By Yasmin Islam**, Flat 8 Masons House, 1-3 Valley Drive, London, **London (Greater)**, NW9 9NG, ENG.
(T) 020 8206 0926
Speciality: Acupuncture.
● **Owner** Yasmin Islam
**O** (Ref:HM00154)

## ACCREDITED HYPNOTHERAPY
**Accredited Hypnotherapy Consultancy**, 109 Navarino Mansions, Dalston Lane, London, **London (Greater)**, E8 1LD, ENG.
(T) 020 7241 2178
Speciality: Hypnotherapy.
● **Owner** Mr P Allan
**B** (Ref:HM00155)

## ACE NUTRITION
**ACE Nutrition**, 2 St Andrews Way, Oxted, **Surrey**, RH8 0TN, ENG.
(T) 01883 723330
(E) tamara@acc-nutrition.co.uk
(W) www.ace-nutrition.co.uk
Speciality: Nutritional Therapy, Reflexology. ✔
● **Owner/Reflexologist/Nutritional Therapist**
Ms T Devane M: BANT, SPNT.
**H** Yrs. Est.: 5 (Ref:HM00157)

## ACHES & PAINS
**Aches & Pains Osteopathic Clinic**, 80 Ruxley Lane, Epsom, **Surrey**, KT19 0HY, ENG.
(T) 020 8393 2050
Speciality: Osteopathy.
**P** **S** **T** (Ref:HM00158)

## ACHIEVE BALANCE
**Achieve Balance**, 25 Parklands Ct, Maynooth, **County Kildare**, IRE.
(T) 01629 1194
Speciality: Psychotherapy.
**B** (Ref:HM00159)

## ACHILLES CENTRE
**Achilles Centre (The)**, 10 Dudley St, Grimsby, **Humberside (South)**, DN31 2AB, ENG.
(T) 01472 250800 (F) 01472 250800
Speciality: Complementary Medicines & Therapy.
● **Owner** Mrs A Cottingham
**M** (Ref:HM00160)

## ACHILLES PHYSIOTHERAPY CLINIC
**Achilles Physiotherapy Clinic (The)**, 7 Tredgold Lane, Napier St, Cambridge, **Cambridgeshire**, CB1 1HN, ENG.
(T) 01223 351933
Speciality: Physiotherapy. ✔
● **Physiotherapist** Mrs J Oliver Q: MCSP, MMACP, SRP. M: CSP, MACP.
**S** Yrs. Est.: 8 (Ref:HM00161)

## ACHILLESPHYSIO
**Achillesphysio**, 3 St Marys Wynd, Hexham, **Northumberland**, NE46 1NQ, ENG.
(T) 01434 609494 (F) 01434 609494
Speciality: Physiotherapy.
● **Manager** Mrs E Strouzer
**P** **S** **T** (Ref:HM00162)

## ACHILLESPHYSIO
**Achillesphysio**, 8 Brentwood Avenue, Newcastle Upon Tyne, **Tyne and Wear**, NE2 3DH, ENG.
(T) 01912 814598 (F) 01912 819947
Speciality: Physiotherapy.
● **Administrator** Ms L Humble
**P** **S** **T** (Ref:HM00163)

## ACKERMAN, FIONA
**Fiona Ackerman**, 3 Crown Rise, Watford, **Hertfordshire**, WD2 6NE, ENG.
(T) 01923 663231
Speciality: Reflexology.
● **Owner** Mrs F Ackerman
**S** **T** (Ref:HM00164)

## ACKERS, R S
**R S Ackers**, 110 Edith Avenue North, Peacehaven, **Sussex (East)**, BN10 8DY, ENG.
(T) 01273 586811
Speciality: Chiropodists (Podiatrists).
**S** (Ref:HM00165)

## ACKLAND, J
**J Ackland**, 75 Leigh Rd, Leigh-On-Sea, **Essex**, SS9 1JN, ENG.
(T) 01702 714862 (F) 01702 716969
Speciality: Psychology.
● **Owner** Mrs C Merryfield
**B** (Ref:HM00166)

## ACKLAND, MAUREEN
**Maureen Ackland**, 31 The Vineries, Burgess Hill, **Sussex (West)**, RH15 0ND, ENG.
(T) 01444 242247
Speciality: Reflexology.
**S** **T** (Ref:HM00167)

## ACNE ECZEMA PSORIASIS CLINIC
**Acne Eczema Psoriasis Lichen Planus Vitiligo Clinic**, 50 Elmcroft Cres, London, **London (Greater)**, NW11 9SY, ENG.
(T) 020 8455 6598
Speciality: Complementary Medicines & Therapy.
**M** (Ref:HM00168)

## ACOMB CHIROPRACTIC CLINIC
**Acomb Chiropractic Clinic**, 60A York Rd, Acomb, York, **Yorkshire (North)**, YO24 4NW, ENG.
(T) 01904 798444
Speciality: Chiropractors.
● **Doctor** Dr H Jacobson
**P** **S** **T** (Ref:HM00169)

## ACORA'S ZODIAC EMPORIUM
**Acora's Zodiac Emporium**, 27 Southside St, Plymouth, **Devon**, PL1 2LD, ENG.
(T) 01752 221711
Speciality: Clairvoyants & Palmists.
**B** (Ref:HM00170)

## ACORN CENTRE
**Acorn Centre For Natural Health**, 57A Railway Approach, East Grinstead, **Sussex (West)**, RH19 1BT, ENG.
(T) 01342 317620
(E) dwilz@cix.co.uk
Speciality: Absent Healing, Acupressure, Aromatherapy, Bach Remedies, Clinical Ecology, Counselling, Dowsing, Healer, Homeopathy, Hypnotherapy, Massage (Therapeutic), Psychotherapy, Reflexology, Shiatsu, Spiritual Healing. ✔
● **Homeopath/Therapist** Mr P Burnett
(T) 020 8776 2536 Q: LCH, MCH, RSHom. M: Soc.Hom.
● **Therapist** Ms P Christie Q: ITEC, MIFA.
● **Healer** Mr D Wilson
**B** **C** Yrs. Est.: 10 (Ref:HM00171)

## ACORN CHIROPODY SERVICES
**Acorn Chiropody Services**, 1 Aubrey Avenue, Cardiff, **Glamorgan (Vale of)**, CF5 1AQ, WAL.
(T) 029 2056 2660
Speciality: Chiropodists (Podiatrists).
**S** (Ref:HM00172)

## ACORN CHIROPODY SURGERY
**Acorn Chiropody Surgery**, 8 Kirkstone Rd North, Liverpool, **Merseyside**, L21 7NS, ENG.
(T) 01519 202112
Speciality: Chiropodists (Podiatrists).
● **Partner** Mrs K Goodison
**S** (Ref:HM00173)

## ACORN CHIROPODY/PODIATRY
**Acorn Chiropody & Sports Podiatry Services**, 87 Holton Rd, Barry, **Glamorgan (Vale of)**, CF63 4HG, WAL.
(T) 01446 745606
Speciality: Chiropodists (Podiatrists).
**S** (Ref:HM00174)

## ACORN CLINIC
**Acorn Clinic**, 17 The Oaks Upr Churchtown Rd, Dublin, **County Dublin**, IRE.
(T) 01296 1551
Speciality: Complementary Medicines & Therapy.
**M** (Ref:HM00175)

## ACORN COUNSELLING
**Acorn Counselling**, Wellington Quay, Drogheda, **County Louth**, IRE.
(T) 04198 44277
Speciality: Complementary Medicines & Therapy.
**M** (Ref:HM00176)

## ACORN HEALTH CLINIC
**Acorn Health Clinic**, 1 Upland Rd, South Croydon, **Surrey**, CR2 6RD, ENG.
(T) 020 8760 0909
Speciality: Acupuncture, Allergy Testing, Homeopathy. ✔
● **Acupuncturist** Mr N Raman Q: PhD.
**C** (Ref:HM00177)

## ACORN HYPNOTHERAPY SERVICES
**Acorn Hypnotherapy Services**, Waterford Cl, Heath Charnock, Chorley, **Lancashire**, PR6 9JQ, ENG.
(T) 01257 480188 (F) 01257 480188
Speciality: Neuro-Linguistic Program, Emotional Freedom Techniques.
● **Owner** Ms C Weston
**B** (Ref:HM00178)

## ACORN PHYSIOTHERAPY CLINIC
**Acorn Physiotherapy Clinic**, Boyces Avenue, Bristol, BS8 4AA, ENG.
(T) 01179 221091
Speciality: Physiotherapy.
● **Owner** Ms S Holmes
**P** **S** **T** (Ref:HM00179)

## ACORN SCHOOL OF REFLEXOLOGY
**Acorn School of Reflexology**, Tetney House, Scarborouh Rd, Driffield, **Humberside (North)**, YO25 5DS, ENG.
(T) 01377 255246
Speciality: Reflexology.
**S** **T** (Ref:HM00180)

## ACORN THERAPY CENTRE
**Acorn Therapy Centre**, The Acorn, 7 Greenlaw Gardens, New Malden, **Surrey**, KT3 6AZ, ENG.
(T) 020 8949 4573
(E) enquiries@acorncentre.fsnet.co.uk
Speciality: Absent Healing, Complementary Therapy, Counselling, Healer, Healing Therapy, Hypnosis, Hypnotherapy, Meditation, Spiritual Healing, Stress Therapy, Visualisation Therapy, Life Coaching. ✔
● **Therapist** Jackie Whitehead Q: Dip.Hyp, MNFSH. M: ASC, NFSH.
**B** Yrs. Est.: 2 (Ref:HM00181)

## ACORN THERAPY CENTRE
**Acorn Therapy Centre**, 40 Creswick Rd, London, **London (Greater)**, W3 9HF, ENG.
(T) 020 8992 4915
Speciality: Hypnosis, Hypnotherapy, Kosmed Therapy. ✔
● **Hypnotherapist** Mr P Carter Q: BHA, CRAH.
**B** Yrs. Est.: 5 (Ref:HM00182)


Key continued: Yrs.Est: Years Established Q: Qualifications M: Professional Membership ✔ Indemnity Insurance Accept Credit Cards

### ACRE HEALTH
**Acre Health**, 1 The Acres, Lower Pilsley, Chesterfield, **Derbyshire**, S45 8DT, **ENG**.
(T) 01246 852565
Speciality: Aromatherapy.
● **Owner** Mr C Hayes
M O (**Ref:**HM00183)

### ACTESON, JENNY
**Jenny Acteson**, 191 High St, Hornchurch, **Essex**, RM11 3XT, **ENG**.
(T) 01708 476677
Speciality: Complementary Medicines & Therapy.
C M (**Ref:**HM00184)

### ACTION ORTHO
**Action Ortho**, 467 Lytham Rd, Blackpool, **Lancashire**, FY4 1JH, **ENG**.
(T) 01253 404907 (F) 01253 403363
Speciality: Osteopathy.
● **Senior Partner** Dr M Lucking
P S T (**Ref:**HM00185)

### ACTIVE BALANCE
**Active Balance**, 50 Clifford Cr, Luton, **Bedfordshire**, LU4 9HR, **ENG**.
(T) 01582 574836
Speciality: Physiotherapy.
P S T (**Ref:**HM00186)

### ACTIVE BALANCE CLINIC
**Active Balance Clinic**, 19 Lowthian Rd, Hartlepool, **Cleveland**, TS24 8BH, **ENG**.
(T) 01429 271961
Speciality: Osteopathy.
● **Owner** Mr P Ainsley
P S T (**Ref:**HM00187)

### ACTIVE BALANCE CLINIC
**Active Balance Clinic**, 29 Alma Rd, Enfield, **London (Greater)**, EN1 4NF, **ENG**.
(T) 07050 262878
Speciality: Osteopathy.
P S T (**Ref:**HM00188)

### ACTIVE BALANCE CLINIC
**Active Balance Clinic**, 43A Seymour St, Lisburn, **County Antrim**, BT27 4SY, **NIR**.
(T) 028 9260 3356
Speciality: Cranial Osteopathy, Dietician, Floral Essence Therapy, Herbal Medicine, Kinesiology, Manipulation, Micro Manipulation, Naturopathy, Osteopathy, Phytotherapy, Stress Therapy, Vitamin Therapy. ✔
● **Owner/Osteopath/Naturopath**
Mr R Dodson **Q:** DO, ND.
S Yrs. Est.: 4 (**Ref:**HM00189)

### ACTIVE BALANCE CLINIC
**Active Balance Clinic**, Collingwood Rd, Uxbridge, **London (Greater)**, UB8 3EJ, **ENG**.
(T) 020 8569 3535
Speciality: Osteopathy.
● **Partner** Mr C Roworth
P S T (**Ref:**HM00190)

### ACTIVE BALANCE CLINIC
**Active Balance Clinic**, 16 Gurteen Pk, Ballyfermot, Dublin, **County Dublin**, **IRE**.
(T) 08827 11215
Speciality: Complementary Medicines & Therapy.
M (**Ref:**HM00191)

### ACTIVE BIRTH CENTRE
**Active Birth Centre**, Dartmouth Park Rd, London, **London (Greater)**, NW5 1SL, **ENG**.
(T) 020 7482 5554
Speciality: Complementary Medicines & Therapy.
● **Managing Director** Mr K Brainin
M (**Ref:**HM00192)

### ACTIVE BIRTH CENTRE
**Active Birth Centre**, 1 Landsdowne Tce, Patricks Hill, Cork, **County Cork**, **IRE**.
(T) 021 4500 509
Speciality: Complementary Medicines & Therapy.
M (**Ref:**HM00193)

### ACTIVE CHIROPRACTIC
**Active Chiropractic**, 69 Milngavie Rd, Bearsden, Glasgow, **Glasgow (City of)**, G61 4SE, **SCO**.
(T) 0141 5637800 (F) 0141 5637900
Speciality: Acupuncture, Chiropractic.
● **Doctor** Mr J Schultz
(T) 01436 674354 **Q:** DC. **M:** SCA.
● **Doctor** Mr G Steiner **Q:** DC. **M:** BCA, SCA.
S Yrs. Est.: 3 (**Ref:**HM00194)

### ACTIVE CHIROPRACTIC
**Active Chiropractic**, 43 West King St, Helensburgh, **Argyll and Bute**, G84 8UL, **SCO**.
(T) 01436 674354
Speciality: Acupuncture, Chiropractic.
● **Doctor** Dr J Schultz **Q:** DC. **M:** SCA.
● **Doctor** Dr G Steiner **Q:** DC. **M:** SCA.
S Yrs. Est.: 3 (**Ref:**HM00195)

### ACTIVE HEALTH CLINIC
**Active Health Clinic**, Fairways Clinic Fairways, Rathfarnham, **County Dublin**, **IRE**.
(T) 01215 7876
Speciality: Acupuncture.
O (**Ref:**HM00196)

### ACTIVE HYPNOSIS
**Active Hypnosis**, 222A Frimley Green Rd, Frimley Green, Camberley, **Surrey**, GU16 6LL, **ENG**.
(T) 01252 838940
Speciality: Hypnotherapy.
● **Director** Mr S Cantwell
B (**Ref:**HM00197)

### ACTIVE LIFE
**Active Life**, 15 Blackfriars St, King's Lynn, **Norfolk**, PE30 1NN, **ENG**.
(T) 01553 772292
Speciality: Physiotherapy.
P S T (**Ref:**HM00198)

### ACTIVE MINDS
**Active Minds**, 16 Carlton House Trce, Halifax, **Yorkshire (West)**, HX1 3LD, **ENG**.
(T) 01422 361248 (F) 01422 361248
(E) activemindselderly@yahoo.co.uk
Speciality: Group Therapy, Stimulation Therapy, Music Therapy, Reality Orientation, Communication skills. ✔
● **Manager** Mr M Fleet
C Yrs. Est.: 6 (**Ref:**HM00199)

### ACTIVE OSTEOPATHS
**Active Osteopaths**, 24 - 26 West Port, Edinburgh, **Edinburgh (City of)**, EH1 2JE, **SCO**.
(T) 01312 211415 (F) 01312 210301
(E) gavin@active-x.co.uk
(W) www.active-x.co.uk
Speciality: Osteopathy. ✔
● **Osteopath** Mr R Dougall **Q:** BSc (Hons). **M:** GOsC.
● **Clinic Director** Mr G Routledge **Q:** DO (Hons). **M:** GOsC.
S Yrs. Est.: 8 (**Ref:**HM00200)

### ACTIVE PHYSICAL THERAPY
**Active Physical Therapy**, 23 Swallow Fields, Liverpool, **Merseyside**, L9 6ED, **ENG**.
(T) 01515 218779
Speciality: Physiotherapy.
● **Owner** Mr P McAuley
P S T (**Ref:**HM00201)

### ACTIVE POWER ELECTRICAL
**Active Power Electrical**, 335B St Johns St, London, **London (Greater)**, EC1V 4LB, **ENG**.
(T) 020 7278 3126
Speciality: Electrolysis.
T (**Ref:**HM00202)

### ACTIVE SPORTS THERAPY
**Active Sports Therapy**, 289 Farnborough Rd, Farnborough, **Hampshire**, GU14 8AU, **ENG**.
(T) 01252 544283 (F) 01252 544283
Speciality: Physiotherapy.
● **Manageress** Mrs J Scard
P S T (**Ref:**HM00203)

### ACTON ACUPUNTURE CLINIC
**Acton Acupuncture Clinic**, The Spinney, Dig Lane, Acton, Nantwich, **Cheshire**, CW5 8PB, **ENG**.
(T) 01270 627704
Speciality: Acupuncture.
● **Owner** Mrs M Wright
O (**Ref:**HM00204)

### ACTON OSTEOPATHS
**Acton Osteopaths**, 15 Brouncker Rd, London, **London (Greater)**, W3 8AE, **ENG**.
(T) 020 8993 1222
Speciality: Osteopathy.
P S T (**Ref:**HM00205)

### ACTON PRACTICE
**Acton Practice**, 146 Old Oak Rd, London, **London (Greater)**, W3 7HE, **ENG**.
(T) 020 8743 5140
Speciality: Osteopathy.
● **Owner** Mr R Fairman
P S T (**Ref:**HM00206)

### ACU ASS OF CHRTRD PHYSIO
**Acupuncture Association Of Chartered Physiotherapists**, Castleton House, Castle St, Mere, Warminster, **Wiltshire**, BA12 6JE, **ENG**.
(T) 01747 861151 (F) 01747 861717
Speciality: Acupuncture.
● **Company Secretary** Mrs V Dawson
O (**Ref:**HM00207)

### ACU ASS OF CHRTRD PHYSIO
**Acupuncture Association Of Chartered Physiotherapists**, Abbey View Medical Centre, Salisbury Rd, Shaftesbury, **Dorset**, SP7 8DH, **ENG**.
(T) 01747 850784
Speciality: Complementary Medicines & Therapy.
● **Owner** Mrs V Dawson
C M (**Ref:**HM00208)

### ACU/HOM/ALLERGY TESTING
**Acupuncture, Homoeopathic & Allergy Testing**, Unit 6 Phibsboro S C, Dublin, **County Dublin**, **IRE**.
(T) 01830 9551 (F) 01830 9551
Speciality: Acupuncture.
O (**Ref:**HM00226)

### ACUCARE
**Acucare**, 93 Fern Drive, Dudley, Cramlington, **Northumberland**, NE23 7AQ, **ENG**.
(T) 01912 500587 (F) 01912 501900
Speciality: Acupuncture, Hypnotherapy, Psychotherapy. ✔
● **Owner** Mr D Rimmer **Q:** MASC, MBHReg.
C Yrs. Est.: 10 (**Ref:**HM00209)

### ACU-DIET CENTRE
**Acu-Diet Centre**, 11 Burnham Avenue, Beaconsfield, **Buckinghamshire**, HP9 2JA, **ENG**.
(T) 01494 676972 (F) 01494 676972
Speciality: Acupuncture.
● **Owner** Dr J Dutta
O (**Ref:**HM00210)

### ACUHEALTH
**AcuHealth**, 8 Lansdown Pl, Cheltenham, **Gloucestershire**, GL50 2HU, **ENG**.
(T) 01242 577533 (F) 01242 257333
Speciality: Acupuncture.
● **Owner** Mrs L Lloyd-Barker
O (**Ref:**HM00211)

### ACUHERB
**Acuherb**, 2 Conway Rd, **Leicestershire**, LE2 1PD, **ENG**.
(T) 01162 218989
Speciality: Herbal Medicine.
M (**Ref:**HM00212)

### ACU-HERB CLINIC
**Acu-Herb Clinic**, 2 Gibson Avenue, Manchester, **Manchester (Greater)**, M18 8TS, **ENG**.
(T) 01613 014601
Speciality: Complementary Medicines & Therapy.
● **Owner** Mrs X Lee
C M (**Ref:**HM00213)

### ACUHERBAL CHINESE MEDICINE
**Acuherbal Chinese Medicine**, 138 Frimley Rd, Camberley, **Surrey**, GU15 2QN, **ENG**.
(T) 01276 469888 (F) 01276 469888
Speciality: Acupressure, Acupuncture, Aromatherapy, Colour Therapy, Herbal Medicine,



Key: B Mind-Body Medicine; C Complementary Medicine; H Self Help Treatment; M Medicinal Therapy; O Oriental Medicine; P Postural Therapy; S Manipulative Structural Therapy; T Touch Therapy

Reflexology. ✔
● **Practitioner** Mrs S Lau **Q:** MBAcC, MRCHM. **M:** BAcC, RCHM.
● **Doctor** Dr Jin
● **Colour Therapist** June McLeod **Q:** ISPA, MAR, NFSH.
O Yrs. Est.: 1 (**Ref:**HM00214)

### ACUHERBS
**Acuherbs**, 6 Aungier St, Dublin, **County Dublin**, IRE.
(T) 01475 0226
Speciality: Acupuncture.
O (**Ref:**HM00215)

### ACUHERBS CHINESE MEDICINE CTRE
**Acuherbs Chinese Medicine Centre**, 469 Bearwood Rd, Smethwick, **Midlands (West)**, B66 4DH, ENG.
(T) 01214 298803
Speciality: Complementary Medicines & Therapy.
● **Manager** Mr Shen
C M (**Ref:**HM00216)

### ACUMEDIC
**Acumedic Ltd**, 101-105 Camden High St, Camden, London, **London (Greater)**, NW1 7JN, ENG.
(T) 020 7388 6704 (F) 020 7387 5766
(E) mfm@acumedic.com
(W) www.acumedic.co.uk
Speciality: Acupressure, Acupuncture, Chinese Herbal Medicine, Oriental Diagnosis, T'ai-Chi Ch'uan.
● **Director** Professor M Mei
O Yrs. Est.: 27 (**Ref:**HM00217)

### ACUMEDIC
**Acumedic Ltd**, 1 Wyle Cop, Forresters Hill, Shrewsbury, **Shropshire**, SY1 1UT, ENG.
(T) 01743 236100 (F) 01743 236100
(E) mfm@acumedic.com
(W) www.acumedic.co.uk
Speciality: Acupressure, Acupuncture, Chinese Herbal Medicine, Oriental Diagnosis, T'ai-Chi Ch'uan.
● **Director** Professor M Mei
O Yrs. Est.: 27 (**Ref:**HM00218)

### ACUMEDIC
**Acumedic**, 2 Talbot Pl, Dublin, **County Dublin**, IRE.
(T) 01856 1230
Speciality: Acupuncture.
O (**Ref:**HM00219)

### ACUMEDIC
**Acumedic Ltd**, St. Johns Chambers, 2 St. Johns St, Manchester, **Manchester (Greater)**, M3 4BD, ENG.
(T) 01618 399283 (F) 01618 399301
(E) mfm@acumedic.com
(W) www.acumedic.com
Speciality: Acupressure, Acupuncture, Chinese Herbal Medicine, Oriental Diagnosis, T'ai-Chi Ch'uan.
● **Director** Man Fong Mai
(T) 020 7388 8381
O Yrs. Est.: 27 (**Ref:**HM00220)

### ACUPOINT - IRJA FOLEY L AC
**Acupoint - Irja Foley L Ac**, 2 Johnsons Pl, Dublin, **County Dublin**, IRE.
(T) 01677 4114
Speciality: Acupuncture.
O (**Ref:**HM00221)

### ACUPOINT CHINESE HERBALIST
**Acupoint Chinese Herbalist Centre**, 42 Goodge St, London, **London (Greater)**, W1P 1FH, ENG.
(T) 020 7436 9735
Speciality: Complementary Medicines & Therapy.
C M (**Ref:**HM00222)

### ACUPOINT MAGNETO CLINIC
**Acupoint Magneto Clinic**, 32 Malmesbury Rd, Birmingham, **Midlands (West)**, B10 0JQ, ENG.
(T) 01217 724253
Speciality: Acupuncture.
● **Owner** Dr S Khan
O (**Ref:**HM00223)

### ACUPOWER
**Acupower**, 24 Balcarres St, Edinburgh, **Edinburgh (City of)**, EH10 5JD, SCO.
(T) 01314 478070
Speciality: Complementary Medicines & Therapy.
M (**Ref:**HM00224)

### ACUPRESSURE
**Acupressure**, 132 St Andrews Rd, Worthing, **Sussex (West)**, BN13 1HH, ENG.
(T) 01903 830563 (F) 01903 526249
Speciality: Acupressure.
● **Owner** Mrs C Armstrong
M (**Ref:**HM00225)

### ACUPRESSURE MASSAGE
**Acupressure Massage - Practitioner Training School**, 82 The Spinney, Beaconsfield, **Buckinghamshire**, HP9 1SA, ENG.
(T) 01494 678221
Speciality: Acupressure, Complementary Therapy.
M (**Ref:**HM00156)

### ACUPUNCTURE
**Acupuncture**, 32 The Mall, Swindon, **Wiltshire**, SN1 4JG, ENG.
(T) 01793 496333 (F) 01793 496333
Speciality: Acupuncture.
● **Owner** Ms S Pready
O (**Ref:**HM00227)

### ACUPUNCTURE
**Dr Wijekoon**, 872 Green Lane, Dagenham, **Essex**, RM8 1BX, ENG.
(T) 020 8599 7151 (F) 020 8983 8784
Speciality: Acupuncture.
● **Acupuncture Practitioner** Dr J Wijekoon **Q:** BS, MB.
O Yrs. Est.: 15 (**Ref:**HM00228)

### ACUPUNCTURE & ALLERGY TESTING
**Acupuncture & Allergy Testing Clinic**, 564 Howth Rd, Raheny, **County Dublin**, IRE.
(T) 01851 0285
Speciality: Acupuncture.
O (**Ref:**HM00229)

### ACUPUNCTURE & BACK PAIN CLINIC
**Acupuncture & Back Pain Clinic**, 2 Greythorn Pk, Glenageary, IRE.
(T) 01280 4821
(E) traynor@iol.ie
Speciality: Acupuncture.
O (**Ref:**HM00230)

### ACUPUNCTURE & CHINESE
**Acupuncture & Chinese**, 2 Fairways, Rathfarnham, **County Dublin**, IRE.
(T) 01494 1534 (F) 01494 5462
(E) traynory@iol.ie
Speciality: Acupuncture.
O (**Ref:**HM00231)

### ACUPUNCTURE & CHINESE MEDICAL
**Acupuncture & Chinese Medical Clinic**, 4 Greythorn Park, Glenageary, Dublin, **County Dublin**, IRE.
(T) 01280 4821 (F) 01494 5462
(E) traynor@iol.ie
Speciality: Acupuncture.
O (**Ref:**HM00239)

### ACUPUNCTURE & HERBAL CLINIC
**Acupuncture & Herbal Clinic**, 871B Finchley Rd, London, **London (Greater)**, NW11 8RR, ENG.
(T) 020 8455 6184
Speciality: Acupuncture. ✔
● **Acupuncturist** Rosalind Beeton **Q:** MBAcC, MRCHM, RCST. **M:** BAcC.
C Yrs. Est.: 15 (**Ref:**HM00240)

### ACUPUNCTURE & HERBAL CLINIC
**Acupuncture & Herbal Clinic**, 1 Upland Rd, South Croydon, **Surrey**, CR2 6RD, ENG.
(T) 020 8688 0188 (F) 020 8688 0188
Speciality: Acupuncture.
● **Manager** Mr K Ramas
O (**Ref:**HM00241)

### ACUPUNCTURE & MASSAGE CLINIC
**Acupuncture & Massage Clinic**, 24 Main St, Blackrock, **County Dublin**, IRE.
(T) 01278 3547
Speciality: Acupuncture.
O (**Ref:**HM00242)

### ACUPUNCTURE & NAT MED CLINIC
**Acupuncture & Natural Medicine Clinic**, 88 Wingrove Rd, Newcastle Upon Tyne, **Tyne and Wear**, NE4 9BY, ENG.
(T) 01912 722424 (F) 01912 722424
Speciality: Acupressure, Acupuncture, Auto Suggestion, Chiropractic, Complementary Therapy, Cupping, Herbal Medicine, Holistic Healing, Manipulation, Massage (Therapeutic), Naturopathy, Nutritional Therapy, Oriental Diagnosis, Osteopathy, Shiatsu, Vitamin Therapy. ✔
● **Owner** Dr C Soong-Shan **Q:** MD. **M:** ATCM UK.
M O S Yrs. Est.: 15 (**Ref:**HM00243)

### ACUPUNCTURE & PAIN CLINIC
**Acupuncture & Pain Clinic**, 12 North Park, Eltham, London, **London (Greater)**, SE9 5AP, ENG.
(T) 020 8850 7099
Speciality: Acupuncture.
O (**Ref:**HM00244)

### ACUPUNCTURE & PHYSIO CLINIC
**Acupuncture & Physiotherapy Clinic**, 132 Bellemoor Rd, Shirley, Southampton, **Hampshire**, SO15 7RA, ENG.
(T) 023 8077 3435 (F) 023 8078 2121
(E) sara@iat.co.uk
(W) www.iat.co.uk
Speciality: Acupressure, Acupuncture, Aromatherapy, Cranial Osteopathy, Cupping, Electrotherapy, Moxibustion, Ultrasonics, Ying & Yang.
● **Principal** Sara Jeevanjee **Q:** Dip.Ac, MCSP, SRP.
O Yrs. Est.: 30 (**Ref:**HM00245)

### ACUPUNCTURE & PHYSIO CLINIC
**Acupuncture & Physiotherapy Clinic (The)**, 19 The Crescent, Truro, **Cornwall**, TR1 3ES, ENG.
(T) 01872 241882
Speciality: Acupuncture.
O (**Ref:**HM00246)

### ACUPUNCTURE & SPORTS INJURY
**Acupuncture & Sports Injury Clinic**, 68 Old Bawn Rd, Dublin, **County Dublin**, IRE.
(T) 01451 3207
Speciality: Acupuncture.
O (**Ref:**HM00247)

### ACUPUNCTURE CENTRE
**Acupuncture Centre**, 17 Tickham Avenue, Stenson Fields, Derby, **Derbyshire**, DE24 3AS, ENG.
(T) 01332 763163
Speciality: Acupuncture.
● **Practitioner** Mr A Qurban
O (**Ref:**HM00249)

### ACUPUNCTURE CENTRE
**Acupuncture Centre**, 46 Mildred Avenue, Watford, **Hertfordshire**, WD1 7DZ, ENG.
(T) 01923 249239 (F) 01923 212005
Speciality: Acupuncture.
● **Owner** Mr M Armstrong
O (**Ref:**HM00250)

### ACUPUNCTURE CENTRE
**Acupuncture Centre**, 6 White Hart Fold, Todmorden, **Yorkshire (West)**, OL14 7BD, ENG.
(T) 01706 813527
Speciality: Acupuncture.
● **Partner** Ms A Rotheram
O (**Ref:**HM00251)

### ACUPUNCTURE CENTRE
**Acupuncture Centre**, 4 St. Aldwyns Rd, Didsbury, Manchester, **Manchester (Greater)**, M20 3JF, ENG.
(T) 01614 457998
Speciality: Acupuncture, Bach Remedies, Cupping, Moxibustion. ✔
● **Owner** Mrs A Bromiley **Q:** Dip.Ac, MBAcC.



Key continued: **Yrs.Est:** Years Established **Q:** Qualifications **M:** Professional Membership ✔ Indemnity Insurance Accept Credit Cards

M: BAcC.
**O** Yrs. Est.: 12 (**Ref:**HM00252)

### ACUPUNCTURE CENTRE
**Acupuncture Centre (The)**, Glynawel, Caio, Llanwrda, **Carmarthenshire**, SA19 8RL, **WAL**.
(T) 01558 650746
Speciality: Acupuncture.
**O** (**Ref:**HM00253)

### ACUPUNCTURE CENTRE
**Acupunture Centre (The)**, 61 Newton Rd, Mumbles, Swansea, SA3 4BL, **WAL**.
(T) 01792 366115 (F) 01558 650746
Speciality: Acupuncture. ✔
● **Acupuncturist** Ms I Cosgrove Q: Lic.Ac, M.Ac. M: BAcC.
● **Acupuncturist** Mr T Davis Q: BSc, Lic.Ac. M: BAcC.
**O** (**Ref:**HM00254)

### ACUPUNCTURE CENTRE
**Acupuncture Centre**, 41 Walton Cres, Oxford, **Oxfordshire**, OX1 2JQ, **ENG**.
(T) 01865 554631
Speciality: Acupuncture.
**O** (**Ref:**HM00255)

### ACUPUNCTURE CLINIC
**Acupuncture Clinic**, Richborough Cottage, Ash Rd, Sandwich, **Kent**, CT13 9JA, **ENG**.
(T) 01304 611963
Speciality: Acupuncture.
**O** (**Ref:**HM00256)

### ACUPUNCTURE CLINIC
**Acupuncture Clinic**, 58 Tower St, Dudley, **Midlands (West)**, DY1 1NG, **ENG**.
(T) 01384 241555
Speciality: Acupuncture.
● **Manager**
**O** (**Ref:**HM00257)

### ACUPUNCTURE CLINIC
**Acupuncture Clinic**, 61 Lakedale Rd, London, **London (Greater)**, SE18 1PR, **ENG**.
(T) 020 8316 6058
Speciality: Acupuncture.
● **Owner** Mr C Moeun
**O** (**Ref:**HM00258)

### ACUPUNCTURE CLINIC
**Acupuncture Clinic**, 79 Mansel St, Swansea, SA1 5TW, **WAL**.
(T) 01792 641784
Speciality: Acupuncture.
● **Partner** Mr J Morris
**O** (**Ref:**HM00259)

### ACUPUNCTURE CLINIC
**Acupuncture Clinic**, Cobble Cottage, 3 Castle Wynd, Richmond, **Yorkshire (North)**, DL10 4JW, **ENG**.
(T) 01748 822944
Speciality: Acupuncture.
**O** (**Ref:**HM00260)

### ACUPUNCTURE CLINIC
**Acupuncture Clinic**, Glen View, New Rd, Porthcawl, Bridgend, CF36 5PL, **WAL**.
(T) 01656 783413
Speciality: Acupuncture.
● **Owner** Mr D Lean
**O** (**Ref:**HM00261)

### ACUPUNCTURE CLINIC
**Acupuncture Clinic**, Kemerton, Tewkesbury, **Gloucestershire**, GL20 7HY, **ENG**.
(T) 01386 725461
Speciality: Acupuncture, Aromatherapy, Moxibustion, Reflexology, Shiatsu. ✔
● **Acupuncturist** Mr T Jennings Q: M.Ac. M: BAcC.
● **Acupuncturist** Ms L Holmes Q: Lic.Ac. M: BAcC.
● **Acupuncturist** Ms M Darby Q: M.Ac.
● **Reflexologist** Ms M Llewellyn
(T) 01684 773957 Q: MAR. M: AoR.
**O** Yrs. Est.: 17 (**Ref:**HM00262)

### ACUPUNCTURE CLINIC
**Acupuncture Clinic**, 608 Woodchurch Rd, Prenton, Birkenhead, **Merseyside**, **ENG**.
(T) 01516 080753
Speciality: Acupuncture, Complementary Therapy, Moxibustion.
● **Doctor** Dr G Nieman Q: MBAWAc. M: BAWAc.
● **Doctor** Dr R Nieman Q: Dr.Ac, MBAWAc, RGN. M: BAWAc.
**O** Yrs. Est.: 42 (**Ref:**HM00263)

### ACUPUNCTURE CLINIC
**Acupuncture Clinic**, The Old School, 10 Kirklington Rd, Southwell, **Nottinghamshire**, NG25 0AY, **ENG**.
(T) 01636 815550
Speciality: Acupuncture. ✔
● **Owner/Acupuncturist**
Mrs A Mowbray Q: BSc, Dip.Ac, MBAcC, RGN. M: BAcC.
**C** Yrs. Est.: 3 (**Ref:**HM00264)

### ACUPUNCTURE CLINIC
**Acupuncture Clinic**, 5 Brouster Hill, East Kilbride, Glasgow, **Glasgow (City of)**, G74 1AQ, **SCO**.
(T) 01355 263999
Speciality: Acupuncture.
● **Owner** Mr R Fraser
**O** (**Ref:**HM00265)

### ACUPUNCTURE CLINIC
**Acupuncture Clinic**, New Copybush, St. Florence, Tenby, **Pembrokeshire**, SA70 8LX, **WAL**.
(T) 01834 871117
Speciality: Acupuncture.
● **Owner** Mr C Ashdown
**O** (**Ref:**HM00266)

### ACUPUNCTURE CLINIC
**Acupuncture Clinic**, 45 Osborne St, Slough, **Berkshire**, SL1 1TT, **ENG**.
(T) 01753 714803
Speciality: Acupuncture.
● **Owner** Mr R Pedley
**O** (**Ref:**HM00267)

### ACUPUNCTURE CLINIC
**Acupuncture Clinic**, 419 Woodborough Rd, Nottingham, **Nottinghamshire**, NG3 5FF, **ENG**.
(T) 01159 623193
Speciality: Acupuncture.
**O** (**Ref:**HM00268)

### ACUPUNCTURE CLINIC
**Acupuncture Clinic**, 46A Northwood End Rd, Haynes, Bedford, **Bedfordshire**, MK45 3HQ, **ENG**.
(T) 01234 381190
Speciality: Acupuncture.
**O** (**Ref:**HM00269)

### ACUPUNCTURE CLINIC
**Acupuncture Clinic**, 319 Osmaston Park Rd, Derby, **Derbyshire**, DE24 8DA, **ENG**.
(T) 01332 384136
Speciality: Acupuncture.
● **Acupuncturist** Mr Lam Q: MBAcC. M: BAcC.
**O** (**Ref:**HM00270)

### ACUPUNCTURE CLINIC
**Acupuncture Clinic**, 26 Astwick Rd, Lincoln, **Lincolnshire**, LN6 7JX, **ENG**.
(T) 01522 682193
Speciality: Acupuncture.
● **Owner** Mr P Scott
**O** (**Ref:**HM00271)

### ACUPUNCTURE CLINIC
**Acupuncture Clinic**, 23A Commercial Rd, Swanage, **Dorset**, BH19 1DF, **ENG**.
(T) 01929 422799
Speciality: Acupuncture.
**O** (**Ref:**HM00272)

### ACUPUNCTURE CLINIC
**Acupuncture Clinic**, 23 Exeter Rd, Kidlington, **Oxfordshire**, OX5 2DY, **ENG**.
(T) 01865 374707
Speciality: Acupuncture.
● **Owner** Dr T Duby
**O** (**Ref:**HM00273)

### ACUPUNCTURE CLINIC
**Acupuncture Clinic**, 19 St Augustines Rd, Canterbury, **Kent**, CT1 1XP, **ENG**.
(T) 01227 786700
Speciality: Acupuncture.
**O** (**Ref:**HM00274)

### ACUPUNCTURE CLINIC
**Acupuncture Clinic**, 12A York Rd, Northampton, **Northamptonshire**, NN1 5QG, **ENG**.
(T) 01604 632129 (F) 01604 632129
Speciality: Acupuncture. ✔
● **Acupuncturist** Mr G Levi Q: LCSP, Lic.Ac, MBAcC. M: BAcC, IROM.
**C** Yrs. Est.: 9 (**Ref:**HM00275)

### ACUPUNCTURE CLINIC
**Acupuncture Clinic (The)**, 241 Torquay Rd, Manor Corner, Preston, Paignton, **Devon**, TQ3 2HW, **ENG**.
(T) 01803 525019
Speciality: Acupressure, Acupuncture, Herbal Medicine, Massage (Therapeutic), Meditation, Oriental Diagnosis, Ying & Yang, Bio-Magnetics, 5 Element Acupuncture, Elecro-Acupuncture, Traditional Chinese Acupuncture. ✔
● **Acupuncturist** Ms K Maidment Q: Lic.Ac. M: BAcC.
**O** Yrs. Est.: 6 (**Ref:**HM00276)

### ACUPUNCTURE CLINIC
**Ninette Sapir**, The Stables, Hammerwood Rd, Ashurst Wood, East Grinstead, **Sussex (West)**, RH19 3RX, **ENG**.
(T) 01342 82374 (F) 01342 82374
Speciality: Acupressure, Acupuncture, Bach Remedies, Cupping, Massage (Therapeutic), Moxibustion. ✔
● **Acupuncturist** Ms N Sapir Q: B.Ac. M: BAcC.
**O** Yrs. Est.: 11 (**Ref:**HM00277)

### ACUPUNCTURE CLINIC
**Acupuncture Clinic (The)**, 326A Woodchurch Rd, Birkenhead, **Merseyside**, CH42 8PQ, **ENG**.
(T) 01516 089168 (F) 01513 439168
Speciality: Acupuncture.
● **Owner** Dr G Niman
**O** (**Ref:**HM00278)

### ACUPUNCTURE CLINIC
**Acupuncture Clinic (The)**, Tao House, Queensway, Leamington Spa, **Warwickshire**, CV31 3LZ, **ENG**.
(T) 01926 831379 (F) 01926 888282
Speciality: Acupuncture, Complementary Therapy, Shiatsu, Holistic Medicine and Chinese Herbs.
● **Therapist** Mr M Reidy M: BAcC.
**O** Yrs. Est.: 22 (**Ref:**HM00279)

### ACUPUNCTURE CLINIC
**Acupuncture Clinic**, 2 Churchview Main St, Lucan, **County Dublin**, **IRE**.
(T) 01621 7057
Speciality: Acupuncture.
**O** (**Ref:**HM00280)

### ACUPUNCTURE CLINIC
**Acupuncture Clinic**, 10 Townhall St, **County Cavan**, **IRE**.
(T) 04943 61414
Speciality: Acupuncture.
**O** (**Ref:**HM00281)

### ACUPUNCTURE CLINIC
**Acupuncture Clinic**, 84 West St, Drogheda, **County Louth**, **IRE**.
(T) 04198 43162
Speciality: Acupuncture.
**O** (**Ref:**HM00282)

### ACUPUNCTURE CLINIC
**Acupuncture Clinic**, 26 Upr John St, **County Kilkenny**, **IRE**.
(T) 05662 196
Speciality: Acupuncture.
**O** (**Ref:**HM00283)

### ACUPUNCTURE CLINIC
**Acupuncture Clinic**, 35 Parnell Ave, Mervue G'way, **IRE**.
(T) 09177 1066
Speciality: Acupuncture.
**O** (**Ref:**HM00284)

### ACUPUNCTURE CLINIC
**Acupuncture Clinic**, Miltown Malbay, **County**

Clare, IRE.
(T) 06570 84494
Speciality: Acupuncture.
O (Ref:HM00285)

## ACUPUNCTURE CLINIC
**Acupuncture Clinic**, 33 Main St, Castleisland, **County Kerry**, IRE.
(T) 06671 42317
Speciality: Acupuncture, Cupping, Herbal Medicine, Moxibustion, Oriental Diagnosis. ✓
● **Acupuncturist** Ms F Maxwell-Smith
Q: Dip.Ac, Lic.Ac. M: AIA.
O Yrs. Est.: 12 (Ref:HM00286)

## ACUPUNCTURE CLINIC
**South Westminster Centre for Health NHS Trust**, 82 Vincent Sq, London, **London (Greater)**, SW1P 2PF, ENG.
(T) 020 8746 5747 (F) 07966 192042
(E) dantapsell@btinternet.com
Speciality: Acupressure, Acupuncture, Bach Remedies, Kinesiology, Meditation, Moxibustion, Reiki, Ying & Yang. ✓
● **Acupuncturist** Mr D Tapsell Q: Lic.Ac.
M: BAcC.
B Yrs. Est.: 6 (Ref:HM00287)

## ACUPUNCTURE CLINIC
**Acupuncture Clinic (The)**, Perth Chiropractic And Osteopathic Centre, The Durn, Isla Rd, Perth, **Perth and Kinross**, SCO.
(T) 01738 442012 (F) 01738 442012
Speciality: Acupressure, Acupuncture. ✓
● **Acupuncturist** Ms M Moore
(T) 01350 728800 Q: Dip.Ac. M: BAcC.
O Yrs. Est.: 3 (Ref:HM00288)

## ACUPUNCTURE CLINIC DUNKELD
**Acupuncture Clinic Dunkeld (The)**, St Ninian's Wynd, Dunkeld, **Perth and Kinross**, PH8 0AT, SCO.
(T) 01350 728800 (F) 01350 728838
Speciality: Acupressure, Acupuncture. ✓
● **Owner/Acupuncturist** Ms M Moore
Q: Dip.Ac. M: BAcC.
O Yrs. Est.: 3 (Ref:HM00289)

## ACUPUNCTURE CLINICS
**Acupuncture Clinics**, Blackrock Acupuncture Clinic, Seafield Ave, Monkstown, **County Cork**, IRE.
(T) 01280 1950
Speciality: Acupuncture.
O (Ref:HM00290)

## ACUPUNCTURE CLINICS
**Acupuncture Clinics**, Greystones Acupuncture Clinic, Cova Trafalgar Tce, Greystones, IRE.
Speciality: Acupuncture.
O (Ref:HM00291)

## ACUPUNCTURE CONSULTANT
**Acupuncture Consultant**, Saat-A-Saat, Burton, Milford Haven, **Pembrokeshire**, SA73 1NT, WAL.
(T) 01646 600531
Speciality: Acupuncture.
● **Owner** Dr T Sheikh
O (Ref:HM00292)

## ACUPUNCTURE ENERGY PRACTICE
**Acupuncture Energy Practice**, 19 Clifton Rd, Harrow, **London (Greater)**, HA3 9NX, ENG.
(T) 020 8204 7887
Speciality: Acupuncture.
● **Owner** Ms Mustafa
O (Ref:HM00293)

## ACUPUNCTURE FOUNDATION
**Acupuncture Foundation**, Celtic Healing Centre, 117 - 119 Renelagh, IRE.
(T) 01491 0689
(E) afi@iol.ie
Speciality: Acupuncture.
O (Ref:HM00294)

## ACUPUNCTURE FOUNDATION
**Acupuncture Foundation**, 274 Sunday Well, Naas, **County Kildare**, IRE.
(T) 04586 6723
(E) afi@iol.ie
Speciality: Acupuncture.
● **Practitioner** Mr K Dowling
O (Ref:HM00295)

## ACUPUNCTURE FOUNDATION
**Acupuncture Foundation**, Kelly Phil Old Bawn Rd, Tallaght, **County Dublin**, IRE.
(T) 01451 3207
(E) afi@iol.ie
Speciality: Acupuncture.
O (Ref:HM00296)

## ACUPUNCTURE FOUNDATION
**Acupuncture Foundation**, 41B St Richmond St, IRE.
(T) 01475 9648
(E) afi@iol.ie
Speciality: Acupuncture.
● **Practitioner** Dr J Li
O (Ref:HM00297)

## ACUPUNCTURE FOUNDATION
**Acupuncture Foundation**, 10 Clonard Pk, Sandyford, **County Dublin**, IRE.
(T) 01295 2209
(E) afi@iol.ie
Speciality: Acupuncture.
O (Ref:HM00298)

## ACUPUNCTURE FOUNDATION
**Acupuncture Foundation**, Main St, Rathcoole, **County Dublin**, IRE.
(T) 01458 9672
(E) afi@iol.ie
Speciality: Acupuncture.
● **Practitioner** Ms N Slattery
O (Ref:HM00299)

## ACUPUNCTURE FOUNDATION
**Acupuncture Foundation**, 17 Kildare St, IRE.
(T) 08685 59074
(E) afi@iol.ie
Speciality: Acupuncture.
● **Acupuncturist** Ms D Walsh
O (Ref:HM00300)

## ACUPUNCTURE FOUNDATION
**Acupuncture Foundation**, 85 Strand St, Skerries, **County Dublin**, IRE.
(T) 01849 4457
(E) afi@iol.ie
Speciality: Acupuncture.
● **Practitioner** Mr G Westby
O (Ref:HM00301)

## ACUPUNCTURE FOUNDATION
**Acupuncture Foundation**, 1st Fl, 18 Upr Georges St, Dun Laoghaire, **County Dublin**, IRE.
(T) 01284 4268
(E) afi@iol.ie
Speciality: Acupuncture.
● **Acupuncturist** Dr H Zhang
O (Ref:HM00302)

## ACUPUNCTURE FOUNDATION
**Acupuncture Foundation**, Mafi Beaumont Pri, Dublin, **County Dublin**, IRE.
(T) 01836 9688
(E) afi@iol.ie
Speciality: Acupuncture.
● **Acupuncturist** Dr L Browne
O (Ref:HM00303)

## ACUPUNCTURE FOUNDATION
**Acupuncture Foundation**, Sutton Co, Dublin, **County Dublin**, IRE.
(T) 01839 4019
(E) afi@iol.ie
Speciality: Acupuncture.
O (Ref:HM00304)

## ACUPUNCTURE FOUNDATION
**Acupuncture Foundation**, 67 Lr Camden St, Dublin, **County Dublin**, IRE.
(T) 08720 75556
(E) afi@iol.ie
Speciality: Acupuncture.
● **Practitioner** Mr S Light
O (Ref:HM00305)

## ACUPUNCTURE FOUNDATION
**Acupuncture Foundation**, 106 Nutgrove Ave, R'farnham, Dublin, **County Dublin**, IRE.
(T) 01493 4736
(E) afi@iol.ie
Speciality: Acupuncture.
● **Practitioner** Ms J McGovern
O (Ref:HM00306)

## ACUPUNCTURE FOUNDATION
**Acupuncture Foundation**, 47 Millview Lawns, Malahide Co, Dublin, **County Dublin**, IRE.
(T) 08684 05493
(E) afi@iol.ie
Speciality: Acupuncture.
● **Practitioner** Mr E O'Donnell
O (Ref:HM00307)

## ACUPUNCTURE FOUNDATION
**Acupuncture Foundation**, 2 Fairways, Rathfarnham, **County Dublin**, IRE.
(T) 01215 7876
(E) afi@iol.ie
Speciality: Acupuncture.
● **Practitioner** Mr J O'Sullivan
O (Ref:HM00308)

## ACUPUNCTURE FOUNDATION
**Acupuncture Foundation**, 3 Leopardstown Gardens, IRE.
(T) 01288 6664
(E) afi@iol.ie
Speciality: Acupuncture.
O (Ref:HM00309)

## ACUPUNCTURE FOUNDATION
**Acupuncture Foundation**, 93A Hillcrest Drive, Lucan Co, Dublin, **County Dublin**, IRE.
(T) 01624 1214
(E) afi@iol.ie
Speciality: Acupuncture.
● **Practitioner** Ms G Lattimore
O (Ref:HM00310)

## ACUPUNCTURE FOUNDATION
**Acupuncture Foundation**, 208 Botanic Ave, Glasnevin, **County Dublin**, IRE.
(T) 01857 4040 (F) 01857 1660
(E) afi@iol.ie
(W) www.acupuncturefoundation.com
Speciality: Acupuncture.
O (Ref:HM00311)

## ACUPUNCTURE HEALTH CLINIC
**Acupuncture Health Clinic**, Warwick House, 87 Warwick Rd, Solihull, **Midlands (West)**, B92 7HP, ENG.
(T) 01217 069621
Speciality: Acupuncture. ✓
● **Acupuncturist** Mr D Bladen Q: Lic.Ac, MBAcC. M: BAcC.
O (Ref:HM00312)

## ACUPUNCTURE HEALTH POINT
**Acupuncture Health Point**, 10 Osborne Ter, Gateshead, **Tyne and Wear**, NE8 1UY, ENG.
(T) 01914 778503
Speciality: Acupuncture.
● **Owner** Mr M Emery
O (Ref:HM00313)

## ACUPUNCTURE HERBAL REMEDIES
**Acupuncture Herbal Remedies & Chinese Medicines**, 70 Thorpe Park Rd, Peterborough, **Cambridgeshire**, PE3 6LJ, ENG.
(T) 01733 555899
Speciality: Acupuncture.
● **Principal** Dr J Whan
O (Ref:HM00314)

## ACUPUNCTURE MOXIBUSTION CLINIC
**Acupuncture Moxibustion Clinic**, 61 Baronswood, Gosforth, Newcastle Upon Tyne, **Tyne and Wear**, NE3 3UB, ENG.
(T) 01912 130307 (F) 01912 130307
Speciality: Acupuncture.
● **Owner** Dr A Zhang
O (Ref:HM00315)

## ACUPUNCTURE PRACTICE
**Acupuncture Practice (The)**, Unit 67, 5 Cannon Drive, London, **London (Greater)**, E14 4AS, ENG.
(T) 020 7277 8350
Speciality: Acupuncture.
● **Owner** Mrs C Fletcher
O (Ref:HM00316)

## ACUPUNCTURE PRIVATE CLINIC
**Acupuncture Private Clinic**, The Health Centre, Railway Rd, Withnell, Chorley,


Key continued: **Yrs.Est:** Years Established **Q:** Qualifications **M:** Professional Membership ✓ Indemnity Insurance Accept Credit Cards

**Lancashire**, PR6 8UA, ENG.
(T) 01254 831877 (F) 01254 832337
(W) www.xsmokers.co.uk
Speciality: Acupuncture, Homeopathy, Psionic Medicine. ✔
● **Acupuncturist** Dr V Mainey M: BMAS.
C Yrs. Est.: 25 (Ref:HM00317)

### ACUPUNCTURE RATHFARNHAM
**Acupuncture Rathfarnham**, 2 Fairways Rathfarnham, IRE.
(T) 01215 7876
Speciality: Acupuncture.
O (Ref:HM00318)

### ACUPUNCTURE SCHOOL
**Acupuncture School Of Five Element & Clinic**, 13 Mandela St, London, **London (Greater)**, NW1 0DU, ENG.
(T) 020 7383 5567 (F) 020 7383 5503
Speciality: Acupuncture.
● **Principal** Mrs L Franglen
O (Ref:HM00319)

### ACUPUNCTURE SERVICES
**Acupuncture Services**, 472 Coventry Rd, Hinckley, **Leicestershire**, LE10 0NH, ENG.
(T) 01455 233995
Speciality: Acupressure, Acupuncture, Massage (Therapeutic), Moxibustion. ✔
● **Acupuncturist** Mr M Cooke Q: Lic.Ac. M: BAcC.
O Yrs. Est.: 15 (Ref:HM00320)

### ACUPUNCTURE SOCIETY
**Acupuncture Society**, 163 Northwood Way, Northwood, **London (Greater)**, HA6 1RA, ENG.
(T) 01923 822972
Speciality: Acupuncture.
● **Sole Director** Paul Mark Robin
O (Ref:HM00321)

### ACUPUNCTURE/ANTI-SMOKING CLNC
**Acupuncture & Anti-Smoking Clinic**, 22 Brookbank Cl, Sunderland, **Tyne and Wear**, SR3 2UE, ENG.
(T) 01915 201125
Speciality: Acupuncture.
● **Owner** Mrs E Fowler
O (Ref:HM00322)

### ACUPUNCTURE/CHINESE HERB SHOP
**Acupuncture & Chinese Herb Shop**, 5 City Arcade, Fore St, Exeter, **Devon**, EX4 3JE, ENG.
(T) 01392 211833
Speciality: Acupuncture.
● **Owner** Mr Y Zude
O (Ref:HM00323)

### ACUPUNCTURE/CHINESE HERBAL
**Acupuncture & Chinese Herbal Medicine Clinic**, 13 Crofton Rd, Orpington, **Kent**, BR6 8AE, ENG.
(T) 01689 603732
Speciality: Acupuncture.
O (Ref:HM00324)

### ACUPUNCTURE/CHINESE HERBAL ASS
**Acupuncture & Chinese Herbal Practitioners Association**, 590 Wokingham Rd, Earley, Reading, **Berkshire**, RG6 7HN, ENG.
(T) 01189 665454 (F) 01189 665454
Speciality: Acupuncture.
● **Chief Executive** Mr B Lee
O (Ref:HM00325)

### ACUPUNCTURE/CHINESE HERBAL MED
**Acupuncture & Chinese Herbal Medicine**, 915 Brighton Rd, Purley, **Surrey**, CR8 2BP, ENG.
(T) 020 8763 1119
Speciality: Acupuncture.
● **Manager** Mr Zhand
O (Ref:HM00326)

### ACUPUNCTURE/CHINESE MEDI ORG
**Acupuncture & Chinese Medicine Organisation**, 2 Johnsons Pl, South King St, Dublin, **County Dublin**, IRE.
(T) 01679 4216
Speciality: Acupuncture.
O (Ref:HM00232)

### ACUPUNCTURE/CHINESE MEDI ORG
**Skerries Healing Centre**, 85 Strand St, Skerries, **County Dublin**, IRE.
(T) 01849 4457
Speciality: Acupuncture.
● **Healer** Mr D Cosgrave
O (Ref:HM00233)

### ACUPUNCTURE/CHINESE MEDI ORG
**Acupuncture & Chinese Medicine Organisation**, 12 Clarinda Park, North Dun Laoighre Co, Dublin, **County Dublin**, IRE.
(T) 01280 1740
Speciality: Acupuncture.
O (Ref:HM00234)

### ACUPUNCTURE/CHINESE MEDI ORG
**Acupuncture & Chinese Medicine Organisation**, Stephanie Davis Walmer Clinic, Millbrook Gr, Dublin, **County Dublin**, IRE.
(T) 01832 7859
Speciality: Acupuncture.
O (Ref:HM00235)

### ACUPUNCTURE/CHINESE MEDI ORG
**Acupuncture & Chinese Medicine Organisation**, Breffin, 32 Church Rd, Dalkey Co, Dublin, **County Dublin**, IRE.
(T) 01280 6419
Speciality: Acupuncture.
O (Ref:HM00236)

### ACUPUNCTURE/CHINESE MEDI ORG
**Acupuncture & Chinese Medicine Organisation**, Old Bawn Clinic, 68 Old Bawn Rd, Dublin, **County Dublin**, IRE.
(T) 01451 3207
Speciality: Acupuncture.
O (Ref:HM00237)

### ACUPUNCTURE/CHINESE MEDI ORG
**Acupuncture & Chinese Medicine Organisation**, Fitzwilliam Chiropractic Centre, Dublin, **County Dublin**, IRE.
(T) 01676 3036
Speciality: Acupuncture.
O (Ref:HM00238)

### ACUPUNCTURE/CHINESE MEDI ORG
**Acupuncture & Chinese Medicine Organisation**, Dingle Acupunture Clinic, Green St, Dingle Co, **County Kerry**, IRE.
(T) 08727 44735
Speciality: Acupuncture.
● **Practitioner** Mr D Hankey
O (Ref:HM00331)

### ACUPUNCTURE/CHINESE MEDI ORG
**Acupuncture & Chinese Medicine Organisation**, Sandhill Rd, Ballybunion Co, **County Kerry**, IRE.
(T) 06827 993
Speciality: Acupuncture.
● **Practitioner** Ms A Lovett
O (Ref:HM00332)

### ACUPUNCTURE/CHINESE MEDI ORG
**Acupuncture & Chinese Medicine Organisation**, The Acupunture Clinic, Turnpike Rd, Ennis, **County Clare**, IRE.
(T) 06568 41280
Speciality: Acupuncture.
● **Practitioner** Ms M McNamara
O (Ref:HM00333)

### ACUPUNCTURE/CHINESE MEDI ORG
**Acupuncture & Chinese Medicine Organisation**, Celine Foxgrove Hse, Rockbarton Bruff Co, **County Limerick**, IRE.
(T) 06138 2151
Speciality: Acupuncture.
● **Practitioner** Casey O'Connor
O (Ref:HM00334)

### ACUPUNCTURE/CHINESE MEDI ORG
**Acupuncture & Chinese Medicine Organisation**, Carbury Clinic, Carbury Hse, Catherine Pl, **County Limerick**, IRE.
(T) 06131 7670
Speciality: Acupuncture.
O (Ref:HM00335)

### ACUPUNCTURE/CHINESE MEDI ORG
**Acupuncture & Chinese Medicine Organisation**, 65 Catherine St, **County Limerick**, IRE.
(T) 06141 9920
Speciality: Acupuncture.
● **Practitioner** Mr J Leboeut
O (Ref:HM00336)

### ACUPUNCTURE/CHINESE MEDI ORG
**Acupunture & Chinese Medicine Organisation**, Crevagh Beg Quin, Ennis, **County Clare**, IRE.
(T) 06568 25801
Speciality: Acupuncture.
● **Practitioner** Mr P Currin
O (Ref:HM00337)

### ACUPUNCTURE/CHIRO CLINIC
**Acupuncture & Chiropractic Clinic**, Parkview, 35 Chesswood Rd, Worthing, **Sussex (West)**, BN11 2AA, ENG.
(T) 01903 230066
Speciality: Acupuncture.
● **Practitioner** Dr Olsen
O (Ref:HM00248)

### ACUPUNCTURE/HERBAL MEDICINE
**Acupuncture & Herbal Medicine Chinese Clinic**, 92 Harley St, London, **London (Greater)**, W1N 1AF, ENG.
(T) 020 7935 6862
Speciality: Acupuncture.
O (Ref:HM00327)

### ACUPUNCTURE/NATURAL THERAPY
**Acupuncture & Natural Therapy Centre**, 13 Pavilion Sq, Scarborough, **Yorkshire (North)**, YO11 2JN, ENG.
(T) 01723 378999
Speciality: Acupuncture.
● **Owner** Mr M Cordell
O (Ref:HM00328)

### ACUPUNCTURE/OSTEO PRACTICE
**Acupuncture & Osteopathic Practice**, 10 Christchurch St West, Frome, **Somerset**, BA11 1EQ, ENG.
(T) 01373 467130
Speciality: Acupuncture.
● **Partner** Ms V Broughton
O (Ref:HM00329)

### ACUPUNCTURE/STRESS THERAPY
**Acupuncture & Stress Therapy Clinic**, 4 Arcade Chambers, 210 Eltham High St, London, **London (Greater)**, SE9 1BG, ENG.
(T) 020 8859 5818 (F) 020 8265 5174
Speciality: Acupuncture.
● **Director** Mr I Chirali
O (Ref:HM00330)

### ACUPUNTURE CENTRE
**Acupunture Centre (The)**, 87 Newton Rd, Mumbles, Swansea, **Glamorgan (Vale of)**, SA3 4BN, WAL.
(T) 01792 366115
Speciality: Acupuncture.
O (Ref:HM00338)

### ACUPUNTURE TAO CLINIC
**Acupunture Tao Clinic**, 2 Gledswood, Hill Brow Rd, Hill Brow, Liss, **Hampshire**, GU33 7PX, ENG.
(T) 01730 892226
Speciality: Acupuncture.
O (Ref:HM00339)

### ACUTECH ACU & ALLERGY CENTRE
**Acutech Acupunture & Allergy Centre (The)**, 47 Colebrook Rd, Shirley, Solihull, **Midlands (West)**, B90 2JZ, ENG.
(T) 01216 934455 (F) 01216 934455
Speciality: Complementary Medicines & Therapy.
● **Owner** Mr R Franks
M (Ref:HM00340)

### ADAIR, JAYNE
**Miss Jayne Adair**, 78 Fencepiece Rd, Ilford, **Essex**, IG6 2JY, ENG.
(T) 020 8501 4647
Speciality: Physiotherapy.
P S T (Ref:HM00341)

### ADAM BUX SPORTS CLINIC
**Adam Bux Sports Injuries Clinic**, Apollo Bldg Dundrum Rd, Dundrum, Dublin, **County Dublin**, IRE.

Key: B Mind-Body Medicine C Complementary Medicine H Self Help Treatment M Medicinal Therapy O Oriental Medicine P Postural Therapy S Manipulative Structural Therapy T Touch Therapy

(T) 01298 8127
**Speciality:** Complementary Medicines & Therapy.
M (Ref:HM00342)

## ADAM, G S

**G S Adam**, 30 Bishop Rd, Bristol, BS7 8LT, ENG.
(T) 01179 426810
**Speciality:** Homeopathy.
● **Owner** Mr G Adam
M (Ref:HM00343)

## ADAM, JAMES

**Adam James**, The Ember Clinic, Canada House, 272 Field End Rd, Ruislip, **London (Greater)**, HA4 9NY, ENG.
(T) 020 8866 4006
**Speciality:** Hypnotherapy.
● **Owner** Mr A James
B (Ref:HM00344)

## ADAMS & YOUNG

**Adams & Young**, 537 Wimborne Rd, Bournemouth, **Dorset**, BH9 2AP, ENG.
(T) 01202 520068
**Speciality:** Chiropodists (Podiatrists).
S (Ref:HM00345)

## ADAMS SMOKERS/SLIMMERS CLINIC

**Adams Smokers & Slimmers Clinic**, 14 Chalbury Cl, Poole, **Dorset**, BH17 8BS, ENG.
(T) 01202 698090
**Speciality:** Hypnotherapy.
● **Owner** Mr J Adams
B (Ref:HM00346)

## ADAMS, C A

**C A Adams**, Taunton Rd Medical Centre, 14-16 Taunton Rd, Bridgwater, **Somerset**, TA6 3LS, ENG.
(T) 01278 423063
**Speciality:** Chiropodists (Podiatrists).
S (Ref:HM00347)

## ADAMS, CHARMAINE

**Charmaine Adams**, Dafen Industrial Park, Dafen, Llanelli, **Carmarthenshire**, SA14 8LX, WAL.
(T) 01554 740509 (F) 01554 740501
**Speciality:** Reflexology.
● **Owner** Mrs C Adams
S T (Ref:HM00348)

## ADAMS, EVE

**Eve Adams**, Lantern Cottage, Stockend, Edge, Stroud, **Gloucestershire**, GL6 6PN, ENG.
(T) 01452 813355
**Speciality:** Psychotherapy.
B (Ref:HM00349)

## ADAMS, HEATHER DAWN

**Heather Dawn Adams**, 49 Post Office Rd, Featherstone, Pontefract, **Yorkshire (West)**, WF7 5EP, ENG.
(T) 01977 599528
**Speciality:** Aromatherapy.
● **Owner** Miss H Adams
M O (Ref:HM00350)

## ADAMS, J R

**J R Adams**, Hunnacott Farm, Bratton Fleming, Barnstaple, **Devon**, EX31 4SG, ENG.
(T) 01598 763216
**Speciality:** Reflexology.
● **Owner** Mrs J Adam
S T (Ref:HM00351)

## ADAMS, JANET

**Janet Adams**, 30 Grange Cres, St. Michaels, Tenterden, **Kent**, TN30 6DZ, ENG.
(T) 01580 762485
**Speciality:** Chiropodists (Podiatrists).
● **Owner** Mrs J Adams
S (Ref:HM00352)

## ADAMS, JENNIFER

**Jennifer Adams**, 5 Thurlow Rd, Torquay, **Devon**, TQ1 3DZ, ENG.
(T) 01803 295652
**Speciality:** Reflexology.
S T (Ref:HM00353)

## ADAMS, JULIA

**Julia Adams**, 12 Providence Way, Waterbeach, Cambridge, **Cambridgeshire**, CB5 9QJ, ENG.
(T) 01223 441733
**Speciality:** Chiropodists (Podiatrists).
● **Owner** Mrs J Adams
S (Ref:HM00354)

## ADAMS, MARGERET REID

**Margeret Reid Adams**, Stockdale Pl, Birmingham, **Midlands (West)**, B15 3XH, ENG.
(T) 01214 550958
**Speciality:** Aromatherapy.
M O (Ref:HM00355)

## ADAMS, MEGAN

**Megan Adams**, Hawthorn Cottage, Church Farm, Church Rd, Dosthill, Tamworth, **Staffordshire**, B77 1LU, ENG.
(T) 01827 281233
**Speciality:** Hypnosis.
● **Owner** Mrs M Adams
B (Ref:HM00356)

## ADAMS, MICHAEL

**Michael Adams**, Eltham Health Centre, 146-148 Eltham Hill, London, **London (Greater)**, SE9 5EA, ENG.
(T) 020 8294 1113
**Speciality:** Osteopathy.
P S T (Ref:HM00357)

## ADAMS, NEIL

**Neil Adams**, 14 Weller Gr, Chelmsford, **Essex**, CM1 4YJ, ENG.
(T) 01245 442485
**Speciality:** Hypnosis.
B (Ref:HM00358)

## ADAMS, PAUL

**Paul Adams**, 67 The Broadway, High St, Chesham, **Buckinghamshire**, HP5 1BX, ENG.
(T) 01494 794606
**Speciality:** Chiropodists (Podiatrists).
● **Owner** Mr P Adams
S (Ref:HM00359)

## ADAMS, PETER

**Peter Adams**, Stroud Natural Health Clinic, Withey's Yard, High St, Stroud, **Gloucestershire**, GL5 1AP, ENG.
(T) 01453 750796
(E) peter@adams9.free-online.co.uk
**Speciality:** Complementary Therapy, Holistic Healing, Homeopathy. ✔
● **Homeopath** Mr P Adams Q: LCH, MA, RSHom. M: Soc.Hom.
M Yrs. Est.: 17 (Ref:HM00360)

## ADAMS, PETER C

**Peter C Adams**, Flat 18 Southlands, Lindisfarne Cl, Portsmouth, **Hampshire**, PO6 2SD, ENG.
(T) 023 9221 9659
**Speciality:** Chiropodists (Podiatrists).
● **Owner** Mr P Adams
S (Ref:HM00361)

## ADAMS, RAYMONDE D

**Raymonde D Adams**, 24 New Rd, Waltham, Grimsby, **Humberside (South)**, DN37 0EN, ENG.
(T) 01472 823589
**Speciality:** Physiotherapy.
● **Owner** Mrs R Adams
P S T (Ref:HM00362)

## ADAMS, S

**Adams Ms S McHs State Registered Chiropodist**, 4 Wellow Cl, Southampton, **Hampshire**, SO16 4PT, ENG.
(T) 023 8049 0194
**Speciality:** Chiropodists (Podiatrists).
S (Ref:HM00363)

## ADAMS, SIOBHAN

**Siobhan Adams**, The Ashcroft Surgery, 2 Ashcroft Drive, Denham, Uxbridge, **London (Greater)**, UB9 5JF, ENG.
(T) 01895 834868
**Speciality:** Acupuncture.
● **Practitioner** S Adams
O (Ref:HM00364)

## ADAMSON, ANGELICA

**Angelica Adamson**, 16 Victoria Rd, Clacton-On-Sea, **Essex**, CO15 6BH, ENG.
(T) 01255 688036
**Speciality:** Clairvoyants & Palmists.
● **Administrator** Mrs H Robinson
B (Ref:HM00365)

## ADASTRAL HEALTH

**Adastral Health Ltd**, The Atrium Court, Apex Plaza, Forbury Rd, Reading, **Berkshire**, RG1 1AX, ENG.
(T) 01189 254209
**Speciality:** Complementary Medicines & Therapy, Occupational Therapy.
M (Ref:HM00366)

## ADATIA, K H (DR)

**Dr K H Adatia**, 221 Cannon Lane, Pinner, **London (Greater)**, HA5 1JA, ENG.
(T) 020 8868 1631
**Speciality:** Physiotherapy.
P S T (Ref:HM00367)

## ADATIA, K H (DR)

**Dr K H Adatia DC, M C S P, S R P, B PHTY**, 163 Ley St, Ilford, **Essex**, IG6 2EL, ENG.
(T) 020 8514 8348
**Speciality:** Physiotherapy.
P S T (Ref:HM00368)

## ADBY, SHEILA

**Ms Sheila Adby**, 6 Wendover Way, Orpington, **Kent**, BR6 0US, ENG.
(T) 01689 818313
**Speciality:** Acupuncture.
● **Owner** Ms S Adby
O (Ref:HM00369)

## ADDENBROOKE, KAREN

**Karen Addenbrooke**, 14 New Cavendish St, London, **London (Greater)**, W1M 7LJ, ENG.
(T) 020 7487 3277 (F) 020 7487 3277
**Speciality:** Physiotherapy.
● **Owner** Mrs K Addenbrook
P S T (Ref:HM00370)

## ADDERBURY CHIROPRACTIC CLINIC

**Adderbury Chiropractic Clinic (The)**, Tythe Barn House, High St, Adderbury, Banbury, **Oxfordshire**, OX17 3LS, ENG.
(T) 01295 811947
**Speciality:** Chiropractors.
P S T (Ref:HM00371)

## ADDINGTON ROAD PRACTICE

**Addington Road Chiropody Practice**, 18 Addington Rd, West Wickham, **Kent**, BR4 9BS, ENG.
(T) 020 8462 6600
**Speciality:** Chiropodists (Podiatrists).
● **Owner** Ms P Murrin
S (Ref:HM00372)

## ADDISON, SYLVIA

**Sylvia Addison**, 6 Bracey Rise, West Bridgford, Nottingham, **Nottinghamshire**, NG2 7AX, ENG.
(T) 01159 235994
**Speciality:** Reflexology.
S T (Ref:HM00373)

## ADDLESTONE THERAPY CENTRE

**Addlestone Therapy Centre**, 164 Station Rd, Addlestone, **Surrey**, KT15 2BD, ENG.
(T) 01932 831616 (F) 01932 831617
**Speciality:** Complementary Medicines & Therapy.
● **Owner** Mr R Bahbra
M (Ref:HM00374)

## ADDRESS THE STRESS

**Address The Stress**, 135 Capstone Rd, Bournemouth, **Dorset**, BH8 8RZ, ENG.
(T) 01202 777893
**Speciality:** Aromatherapy.
M O (Ref:HM00375)

## ADEGOKE, ROTIMI

**Rotimi Adegoke**, 17 Thorney Hedge Rd, London, **London (Greater)**, W4 5SB, ENG.
(T) 020 8987 8581
**Speciality:** Osteopathy.
● **Owner** Mr R Adegoke
P S T (Ref:HM00376)

## ADEGOKE, ROTIMI

**Rotimi Adegoke**, 13A Nolton St, Bridgend, CF31 1BX, WAL.
(T) 01656 645177
**Speciality:** Osteopathy.


Key continued: **Yrs.Est:** Years Established **Q:** Qualifications **M:** Professional Membership ✔ Indemnity Insurance Accept Credit Cards

P S T (Ref:HM00377)

**ADELAIDE CLINIC**

**Adelaide Clinic (The)**, 3 Georgian Passage, Off East St, Blandford Forum, **Dorset**, DT11 8UJ, ENG.
(T) 01258 451345
Speciality: Alexander Technique, Aromatherapy, Chiropody, Counselling, Humanistic Psychology, Massage (Therapeutic), Reflexology, Painless Spinal Touch Therapy, Beauty Treatments, Pedicures and Manicures. ✔
● **Chiropodist** Ms M Newham Q: Inst.CH.P.
● **Teacher of the Alexander Technique** Ms F Robinson Q: ATI, BA, MSTAT. M: ATI, STAT.
● **Therapist** Ms T Randall
S Yrs. Est.: 5 (Ref:HM00378)

**ADELAIDE ROAD CHIROPODY CENTRE**

**Adelaide Road Chiropody Centre**, 15 Adelaide Rd, Leamington Spa, **Warwickshire**, CV31 3PN, ENG.
(T) 01926 450633 (F) 01926 450633
Speciality: Chiropodists (Podiatrists).
● **Owner** Mr T O'Reilly
S (Ref:HM00379)

**ADEN, ROLL**

**Roll Aden**, The Mews, 43-45 Churchgate St, Bury St. Edmunds, **Suffolk**, IP33 1RG, ENG.
(T) 01284 762768 (F) 01284 762768
Speciality: Complementary Medicines & Therapy.
● **Owner** Mrs T Warner
C M (Ref:HM00380)

**ADERCORN PHYSICAL THERAPY**

**Adercorn Physical Therapy Clinic**, Abercorn Business Centre, 101 Abercorn St, Paisley, **Renfrewshire**, PA3 4AT, SCO.
(T) 01415 819009 (F) 01418 489805
Speciality: Physiotherapy.
● **Owner** Mrs E Hirft
P S T (Ref:HM00381)

**ADKIN, JEAN**

**Jean Adkin**, Esher, **Surrey**, KT10, ENG.
(T) 01372 470004
Speciality: Bach Remedies.
M (Ref:HM00382)

**ADLARD, FIONA**

**Fiona Adlard**, 63B Mytton Oak Rd, Shrewsbury, **Shropshire**, SY3 8UQ, ENG.
(T) 01743 248543
Speciality: Osteopathy.
P S T (Ref:HM00383)

**ADLER, DAVID**

**David Adler**, 18 Mivart St, Bristol, BS5 6JF, ENG.
(T) 01179 525424
Speciality: Physiotherapy.
● **Owner** D Adler
P S T (Ref:HM00384)

**ADLINGTON CHIROPODY**

**Adlington Chiropody**, 173 Chorley Rd, Adlington, Chorley, **Lancashire**, PR6 9LP, ENG.
(T) 01257 474050
Speciality: Chiropodists (Podiatrists).
● **Owner** Mr S Dodd
S (Ref:HM00385)

**ADL-TABATABAI, C**

**C Adl-Tabatabai**, 339 Ballards Lane, London, **London (Greater)**, N12 8LJ, ENG.
(T) 020 8445 4397
Speciality: Aromatherapy.
● **Director** Mr E Thankey
M O (Ref:HM00386)

**ADL-TABATABAI, CAROL**

**Carol Adl-Tabatabai**, 33 Meadow Cl, Dollis Valley Way, Barnet, **Hertfordshire**, EN5 2UE, ENG.
(T) 020 8449 9470
Speciality: Reflexology.
● **Owner** Mrs C Adl-Tabatabai
S T (Ref:HM00387)

**ADSHEAD & WESTWOOD**

**Adshead & Westwood**, 9 Quantock Cl, Halesowen, **Midlands (West)**, B63 1HF, ENG.
(T) 01215 506234 (F) 01216 022207
Speciality: Complementary Medicines & Therapy.
● **Partner** Mr R Adshead
C M (Ref:HM00388)

**ADSHEAD, MARK**

**Mark Adshead**, York Lodge, St Peters St, St. Albans, **Hertfordshire**, AL1 3HD, ENG.
(T) 01727 850925 (F) 01727 854330
Speciality: Physiotherapy.
● **Manager** Mrs M Hardman
P S T (Ref:HM00389)

**ADSHEAD, S**

**S Adshead**, Suite 104 The Standish Centre, Cross St, Standish, Wigan, **Lancashire**, WN6 0HQ, ENG.
(T) 01257 427288
Speciality: Chiropodists (Podiatrists).
● **Principal** Mrs S Adshead
S (Ref:HM00390)

**ADULT & CHILD FOOT CLINIC**

**Adult And Child Foot Health Clinic**, 109 Carmarthen Cl, Callands, Warrington, **Cheshire**, WA5 9UT, ENG.
(T) 01925 470925
(E) trevor@ergopod.freeserve.co.uk
Speciality: Chiropody, Complementary Therapy, Nail Surgery, Podiatry, Orthotic Therapy, Bio-Mechanical Assessment. ✔
● **Chiropodist (Podiatrist)** Mrs C Shaw Q: BSc (Hons), S.R.Ch, SRPod. M: S.C.P.
M P S Yrs. Est.: 2 (Ref:HM00391)

**ADUR CLINIC**

**Adur Clinic**, Southlands Hospital, Upper Shoreham Rd, Shoreham-by-Sea, **Sussex (West)**, BN43 6TQ, ENG.
(T) 01273 446018
Speciality: Physiotherapy.
● **Owner** Mr K Sobodu
P S T (Ref:HM00392)

**ADVANCE COUNSELLING SERVICES**

**Advance Counselling & Supervision Services**, 14 Colquitt St, Liverpool, **Merseyside**, L1 4DE, ENG.
(T) 01517 086609
Speciality: Complementary Medicines & Therapy.
● **Director** Ms E Monks
M (Ref:HM00393)

**ADVANCED CHIROPODY SURGERY**

**Advanced Chiropody Surgery**, 2 Acres Lane, Stalybridge, **Manchester (Greater)**, SK15 2JU, ENG.
(T) 01613 382367 (F) 01613 386365
Speciality: Chiropody. ✔ CREDIT
● **Owner** Mr M Smith Q: S.R.Ch.
S Yrs. Est.: 20 (Ref:HM00394)

**ADVANCED CHIROPRACTIC**

**Advanced Chiropractic**, 42 Baggot St, Dublin, **County Dublin**, IRE.
(T) 01677 0554
(E) advancedchiropractic@ireland.com
(W) www.chiropractorireland.com
Speciality: Chiropractors.
P S T (Ref:HM00395)

**ADVANCED CHIROPRACTIC CLINIC**

**Advanced Chiropractic Clinic**, 11 Market St, Galway, **County Galway**, IRE.
(T) 09156 7055
Speciality: Chiropractors.
P S T (Ref:HM00396)

**ADVANCED FOOT THERAPY**

**Advanced Foot Therapy Chiropodist Clinic**, 112 Westbourne Rd, Huddersfield, **Yorkshire (West)**, HD1 4LF, ENG.
(T) 01484 542007
Speciality: Chiropodists (Podiatrists).
● **Owner** Mrs S Ho
S (Ref:HM00397)

**ADVANCED HYP/PSYCHOTHERAPY**

**Advanced Hypnotherapy Psychotherapy Counselling**, 4 Witton Cl, Heacham, King's Lynn, **Norfolk**, PE31 7TD, ENG.
(T) 01485 572547
Speciality: Hypnosis.
● **Owner** Ms S MacKinnon
B (Ref:HM00398)

**ADVANCED HYPNOSIS**

**Advanced Hypnosis**, 95 Kenlor Rd, London, **London (Greater)**, SW17 0DG, ENG.
(T) 020 8682 9325
Speciality: Hypnotherapy.
● **Owner** Mr D Robertson
B (Ref:HM00399)

**ADVANCED HYPNOSIS/HYNOTHERAPY**

**Advanced Hypnosis & Hynotherapy Consultancy**, 10A The Parade, Hengrove Lane, Bristol, BS14 9DB, ENG.
(T) 01179 773402 (F) 01179 773402
Speciality: Hypnotherapy.
● **Owner** Mr A Needham
B (Ref:HM00400)

**ADVANCED HYPNOTHERAPY**

**Advanced Hypnotherapy**, 2 College Rd, Grays, **Essex**, RM17 5PB, ENG.
(T) 01375 385439 (F) 01375 405816
Speciality: Hypnotherapy.
● **Owner** Mrs M Lucas
B (Ref:HM00401)

**ADVANCED HYPNOTHERAPY**

**Advanced Hypnotherapy**, 267 Beoley Rd East, Redditch, **Worcestershire**, B98 8PD, ENG.
(T) 01527 66377
Speciality: Hypnotherapy.
● **Owner** Mr L Cremetti
B (Ref:HM00402)

**ADVANCED PHYSIOTHERAPY CLINIC**

**Advanced Physiotherapy Clinic**, Westernlea Clinic, 131 Denton Rd, Audenshaw, Manchester, **Manchester (Greater)**, M34 5BE, ENG.
(T) 01613 200197 (F) 01613 204409
Speciality: Acupuncture, Chiropody, Electrotherapy, Manipulation, Massage (Therapeutic), Physiotherapy, Reflexology, Ultrasonics, Exercise Therapy, Traction Therapy.
● **Chartered Physiotherapist** Mr C Wych Q: Grad Dip Phys, MCSP, SRP. M: CSP.
S Yrs. Est.: 21 (Ref:HM00403)

**ADVANCED SKIN THERAPY CLINIC**

**Advanced Skin Therapy Clinic**, The Alexandra Hospital, Mill Lane, Cheadle, **Cheshire**, SK8 2PX, ENG.
(T) 01613 749797 (F) 01614 913867
Speciality: Complementary Medicines & Therapy, Hair Removal, Thread Vein Removal.
✔ CREDIT
● **Sister** Sister Evans
● **Consultant/Dermatologist** Dr J Ashworth
● **Manageress** Mrs A Luckett
● **Consultant** Prof M Walker
C (Ref:HM00404)

**ADVANCED THERAPY & TRAINING**

**Advanced Therapy & Training**, 29 Sedgecombe Avenue, Harrow, **London (Greater)**, HA3 0HW, ENG.
(T) 08009 176501 (F) 020 8933 8455
Speciality: Psychotherapy.
● **Partner** Ms N Crawford
B (Ref:HM00405)

**ADVISORY CENTRE**

**Advisory Centre For Stress Management**, The Laurels, 10 Fairview Rd, Headley Down, Bordon, **Hampshire**, GU35 8JP, ENG.
(T) 01428 717413
Speciality: Hypnotherapy.
● **Owner** Mrs W Clarke
B (Ref:HM00406)

**AEQUILIBRIUM**

**AEquilibrium**, 14 Ward Gardens, Harold Wood, Romford, **Essex**, RM3 0WX, ENG.
(T) 01708 349629 (F) 01708 349629
Speciality: Reflexology. ✔
● **Reflexologist** Ms A Cohh Q: MBRA, Reg.Reflex. M: BRA.
S Yrs. Est.: 2 (Ref:HM00407)

**AEQUO ANIMO**

**Aequo Animo**, 8 Russley Cl, Peatmoor, Swindon,

**Wiltshire**, SN5 5AG, **ENG**.
(T) 01793 874578
Speciality: Reflexology.
● **Director** Sue Williams
S T (Ref:HM00408)

## AERON, A

**Mr A Aeron**, Harlequin House, 43 Chester Rd, Ilford, **Essex**, IG3 8PT, **ENG**.
(T) 020 8599 6013
Speciality: Psychotherapy.
B (Ref:HM00409)

## AESTHETIC LASER & COSMETIC

**Aesthetic Laser & Cosmetic Clinic**, Kiltartan Hse, Forster St, **County Galway**, **IRE**.
(T) 09156 7535
Speciality: Complementary Medicines & Therapy.
M (Ref:HM00410)

## AESTHETICA TOTAL SKIN & BODY

**Aesthetica Total Skin And Body Spa**, Aesthetica, 12 Kerse Lane, Falkirk, FK1 1RQ, **SCO**.
(T) 01324 611775
Speciality: Aromatherapy. ✓
● **Owner/Aromatherapist** Ms D Allan Q: ITEC.
C Yrs. Est.: 4 (Ref:HM00411)

## AETHERIUS SOCIETY

**Aetherius Society (The)**, 350 Sheffield Rd, Birdwell, Barnsley, **Yorkshire (South)**, S70 5TU, **ENG**.
(T) 01226 744659
Speciality: Complementary Medicines & Therapy.
● **Manager** Mrs H Moody
C M (Ref:HM00412)

## AFFECTIVE THERAPY

**Affective Therapy**, 89 Shawclough Way, Rochdale, **Lancashire**, OL12 6DR, **ENG**.
(T) 01706 868660
Speciality: Hypnotherapy.
B (Ref:HM00413)

## AFFINITY

**Affinity**, 18E High Rd, London, **London (Greater)**, NW10 2QD, **ENG**.
(T) 020 8459 0253
Speciality: Aromatherapy.
● **Director** Ms H Burnett
M O (Ref:HM00414)

## AGAINST ALLERGY

**Against Allergy**, Po Box 278, Twickenham, **London (Greater)**, TW1 4QQ, **ENG**.
(T) 020 8892 2711
Speciality: Complementary Medicines & Therapy.
M (Ref:HM00415)

## AGASCAR, ROBIN

**Robin Agascar**, 153 Bristol Rd, Quedgeley, Gloucester, **Gloucestershire**, GL2 4PQ, **ENG**.
(T) 01452 728797
Speciality: Hypnosis, Hypnotherapy. ✓
● **Owner/Hypnotherapist** Mr R Gascar Q: Dip.Hyp. M: GHR.
C Yrs. Est.: 9 (Ref:HM00416)

## AGATE, LYNN

**Lynn Agate**, 8 Sandringham Rd, Fareham, **Hampshire**, PO14 3DW, **ENG**.
(T) 01329 313923
Speciality: Chiropodists (Podiatrists).
● **Owner** Mrs L Agate
S (Ref:HM00417)

## AGER, R W

**R W Ager**, Forest Gate Therapies, Hazel Farm Rd, Totton, Southampton, **Hampshire**, SO40 3SJ, **ENG**.
(T) 023 8066 6076
Speciality: Osteopathy.
● **Owner** Mr R Ager
P S T (Ref:HM00418)

## AGINCOURT OSTEOPATHIC CLINIC

**Agincourt Osteopathic Clinic**, 3a Agincourt St, Monmouth, **Monmouthshire**, NP5 3DZ, **WAL**.
(T) 01600 716880
(W) www.ukosteopathy.co.uk
Speciality: Naturopathy, Osteopathy.
P S T (Ref:HM00419)

## AGIUS, ANTHONY J

**Anthony J Agius**, 111 Highbury Park, London, **London (Greater)**, N5 1UB, **ENG**.
(T) 020 7354 3020
Speciality: Osteopathy.
● **Owner** A Agius
P S T (Ref:HM00420)

## AGIUS, ANTHONY JOSEPH

**Anthony Joseph Agius**, 62 Wellington Avenue, London, **London (Greater)**, E4 6RE, **ENG**.
(T) 020 8529 6677
Speciality: Osteopathy.
P S T (Ref:HM00421)

## AGNEW, B K

**B K Agnew**, Daws Wood, Woodhill Lane, Frensham, Farnham, **Surrey**, GU10 3EN, **ENG**.
(T) 01252 792063 (F) 01252 792063
Speciality: Psychotherapy.
● **Owner** Mrs B Agnew
B (Ref:HM00422)

## AGNEW, M D

**M D Agnew**, 215 Kingsway, Dunmurry, Belfast, **County Antrim**, BT17 9SB, **NIR**.
(T) 028 9030 1202
Speciality: Osteopathy.
P S T (Ref:HM00423)

## AHERN, ANNE

**Anne Ahern Hypnotherapy**, 1 Liffey Lawns Clane Co, **County Kildare**, **IRE**.
(T) 04586 8751
Speciality: Hypnotherapy.
B (Ref:HM00424)

## AHMED, NICHOLA

**Nichola Ahmed**, Eastcote, Norfolk Rd, Holmwood, Dorking, **Surrey**, RH5 4LA, **ENG**.
(T) 01306 888191
Speciality: Complementary Medicines & Therapy.
● **Owner** Mrs N Ahmed
M (Ref:HM00425)

## AIDAN WRYNNE HEALING CLINIC

**Aidan Wrynne Healing Clinic**, Satrissaun, Mohill, **County Leitrim**, **IRE**.
(T) 07831 263
Speciality: Healing.
B (Ref:HM00426)

## AIGBURTH MCTIMONEY CLINIC

**Aigburth McTimoney Chiropractic Clinic**, Flat 2, 38 Devonshire Rd, Princess Park, Liverpool, **Merseyside**, L8 3TZ, **ENG**.
(T) 01517 287847
(E) allyn@tenosce.com
(W) www.tenosce.com
Speciality: Bowen Therapy, Chiropractic, Cranio-Sacral Therapy, McTimoney Chiropractic, Ishta Spinal Touch. ✓
● **McTimoney Chiropractor** Ms A Edwards Q: MC. M: ALTT.
S Yrs. Est.: 10 (Ref:HM00427)

## AIHUN, CHARLES

**Charles Aihun**, 330 Kilburn High Rd, London, **London (Greater)**, NW6 2QN, **ENG**.
(T) 020 7624 4477
Speciality: Chiropodists (Podiatrists).
S (Ref:HM00428)

## AINDOW, M J

**M J Aindow**, 16 Welwyn Avenue, Southport, **Merseyside**, PR8 3BE, **ENG**.
(T) 01704 578316
Speciality: Chiropodists (Podiatrists).
S (Ref:HM00429)

## AINGE, S W

**S W Ainge**, Care Of Daniels, 96-112 Uxbridge Rd, London, **London (Greater)**, W13 8RF, **ENG**.
(T) 020 8579 9740
Speciality: Chiropodists (Podiatrists).
S (Ref:HM00430)

## AINSDALE OSTEOPATHIC CLINIC

**Ainsdale Osteopathic Clinic**, Doctors Surgery, 2 Leamington Rd, Southport, **Merseyside**, PR8 3LB, **ENG**.
(T) 01704 572202
Speciality: Osteopathy.
● **Owner** Mr J Bell
P S T (Ref:HM00431)

## AINSDALE PHYSIOTHERAPY

**Ainsdale Physiotherapy**, 722a Liverpool Rd, Southport, **Merseyside**, PR8 2QE, **ENG**.
(T) 01704 576316
Speciality: Physiotherapy.
● **Manager** Mrs Sharpe
P S T (Ref:HM00432)

## AINSLEY, S

**Mrs S Ainsley**, 10 Church St, Kidderminster, **Worcestershire**, DY10 2AD, **ENG**.
(T) 01562 746734
(E) s.ainsley@blueyonder.co.uk
Speciality: Biomechanics, Orthotics. ✓
● **Owner** Mrs S Ainsley Q: SRPod. M: S.C.P.
S Yrs. Est.: 14 (Ref:HM00433)

## AINSWORTH HOMEOPATHIC PHARMACY

**Ainsworth Homeopathic Pharmacy**, 36 New Cavendish St, London, **London (Greater)**, W1M 7LH, **ENG**.
(T) 020 7935 5330 (F) 020 7486 4313
Speciality: Homeopathy.
● **Director** Mr T Pinkus
M (Ref:HM00434)

## AINSWORTH HOMEOPATHIC PHARMACY

**Ainsworths Homeopathic Pharmacy**, 40-44 High St, Caterham, **Surrey**, CR3 5UB, **ENG**.
(T) 01883 340332 (F) 01883 344602
Speciality: Complementary Medicines & Therapy.
● **Manager** Mr J Lee
M (Ref:HM00435)

## AINSWORTH, D & C

**D & C Ainsworth**, 11 Braddyll Trce, Ulverston, **Cumbria**, LA12 0DH, **ENG**.
(T) 01229 587038
Speciality: Chiropodists (Podiatrists).
● **Partner** Mrs C Ainsworth
S (Ref:HM00436)

## AINSWORTH, J

**J Ainsworth**, 535 Chester Rd, Woodford, Stockport, **Cheshire**, SK7 1PR, **ENG**.
(T) 01614 391743
Speciality: Physiotherapy.
P S T (Ref:HM00437)

## AINSWORTH, S R

**S R Ainsworth**, 20 Walter Scott Avenue, Wigan, **Lancashire**, WN1 2RH, **ENG**.
(T) 01942 244612
Speciality: Chiropodists (Podiatrists).
● **Owner** Mr S Ainsworth
S (Ref:HM00438)

## AINTREE OSTEOPATHIC

**Aintree Osteopathic**, 225 Longmoor Lane, Aintree, Liverpool, **Merseyside**, L12 0NF, **ENG**.
(T) 01512 845016 (F) 01512 845016
(E) vthomas@cable.net
Speciality: Acupuncture, Aromatherapy, Chiropody, Complementary Therapy, Cranial Osteopathy, Electrotherapy, Indian Head Massage, Kinesiology, Manipulation, Massage (Therapeutic), Nutritional Therapy, Orthotics, Osteopathy, Reflexology. ✓
● **Osteopath** Mr P Thomas
(T) 01515 467405 Q: DO. M: GOsC.
● **Acupuncturist** Mrs P Sinn Q: Dip.Ac.
● **Osteopath** Mr R Oshea Q: DO. M: GOsC.
● **Osteopath** Mr J Smith Q: DO. M: BOsC.
P S T Yrs. Est.: 12 (Ref:HM00439)

## AION COUNSELLING/PSYCHOTHERAPY

**Aion Counselling & Psychotherapy Services**, Steeple House, Percy St, Coventry, **Midlands (West)**, CV1 3BY, **ENG**.
(T) 024 7622 2828
Speciality: Psychotherapy.
B (Ref:HM00440)

## AIREDALE ALLERGY CENTRE

**Airedale Allergy Centre**, Farfield House, 105 North St, Keighley, **Yorkshire (West)**, BD21 3AA, **ENG**.
(T) 01535 603966 (F) 01535 655456
Speciality: Nutritional Therapy, Skin Prick



Key continued: Yrs.Est: Years Established Q: Qualifications M: Professional Membership ✓ Indemnity Insurance Accept Credit Cards

Testing, Nutritional Status and Neutralisation Technique. ✔
- **Allergy Specialist** Dr E Comns **Q:** LRCP. **M:** RCS (Eng).
- **Joint Director** Elaine Gloria Maberly
- **Principal** Dr D Maberly

**C** Yrs. Est.: 14 (**Ref:**HM00441)

### AIREY, L M
**L M Airey**, Yard 96 Stricklandgate, Kendal, **Cumbria**, LA9 4PU, **ENG**.
**(T)** 01539 735335
Speciality: Aromatherapy.
- **Owner** Mrs L Airey

**M O** (**Ref:**HM00442)

### AIRLIE COMPLEMENTARY CLINIC
**Airlie Complementary Clinic**, 7 Waverley Rd, Nairn, **Highland**, IV12 4RH, **SCO**.
**(T)** 01667 453498
Speciality: Complementary Medicines & Therapy.
- **Manager** Mrs N Salek

**C M** (**Ref:**HM00443)

### AIRMOUNT CHIROPRACTIC CLINIC
**Airmount Chiropractic Clinic**, Rocklands Gracedieu, Waterford, **County Waterford**, **IRE**.
**(T)** 05185 5481
Speciality: Chiropractors.
**P S T** (**Ref:**HM00444)

### AISHA CENTRE
**Aisha Centre**, 66A St Johns Rd, Hedge End, Southampton, **Hampshire**, SO30 4AG, **ENG**.
**(T)** 01489 799766
Speciality: Hypnotherapy.
**B** (**Ref:**HM00445)

### AISHER, CAMILLA
**Camilla Aisher**, Helix Gardens, London, **London (Greater)**, SW2 2JL, **ENG**.
**(T)** 020 8671 4491
Speciality: Aromatherapy.
- **Owner** Ms C Aisher

**M O** (**Ref:**HM00446)

### AISLING CONSULTANTS
**Aisling Consultants**, Marlborough Rd, Donnybrook, **County Dublin**, **IRE**.
**(T)** 01497 6140
**(E)** aishlingi@iol.ie
Speciality: Complementary Medicines & Therapy.
**M** (**Ref:**HM00447)

### AISLING CONSULTANTS
**Aisling Consultants**, Millpark Rd, Enniscorthy, **County Wexford**, **IRE**.
**(T)** 05435 669
**(E)** aishlingi@iol.ie
Speciality: Complementary Medicines & Therapy.
**M** (**Ref:**HM00448)

### AISLING INFORMATION SYSTEMS
**Aisling Information Systems Ltd**, 77A Marlborough Rd, Donnybrook, **County Dublin**, **IRE**.
**(T)** 01497 6140
**(E)** aishlingi@iol.ie
Speciality: Complementary Medicines & Therapy.
**M** (**Ref:**HM00449)

### AITCHISON, JAMES
**James Aitchison**, 10 Upper Craigs, Stirling, FK8 2DG, **SCO**.
**(T)** 01786 474162
Speciality: Chiropodists (Podiatrists).
**S** (**Ref:**HM00450)

### AITCHISON, LYNN
**Lynn Aitchison**, 42 Boundary Park, Seaton, **Devon**, EX12 2UN, **ENG**.
**(T)** 01297 24512
Speciality: Chiropodists (Podiatrists).
**S** (**Ref:**HM00451)

### AITKEN, ANNE
**Anne Aitken**, 11A Saxon Rd, Southport, **Merseyside**, PR8 2AX, **ENG**.
**(T)** 01704 568487
Speciality: Psychotherapy.
- **Owner** Mrs A Aitken

**B** (**Ref:**HM00452)

### AITKEN, LYNNE
**Lynne Aitken**, 41 Armoury Gardens, Shrewsbury, **Shropshire**, SY2 6PL, **ENG**.
**(T)** 01743 365746
Speciality: Osteopathy.
**P S T** (**Ref:**HM00453)

### AITKENHEAD, B P
**B P Aitkenhead**, Fareham Leisure Centre, Park Lane, Fareham, **Hampshire**, PO16 7JU, **ENG**.
**(T)** 023 9251 1076 **(F)** 01329 825396
Speciality: Physiotherapy.
- **Owner** Mr B Aitkinhead

**P S T** (**Ref:**HM00454)

### AJANTA CENTRE
**Ajanta Centre (The)**, 39 Blenkarne Rd, London, **London (Greater)**, SW11 6HZ, **ENG**.
**(T)** 020 7223 7020
Speciality: Psychotherapy.
**B** (**Ref:**HM00455)

### AJMERI
**Ajmeri**, 12 Prince St, Bridlington, **Humberside (North)**, YO15 2NW, **ENG**.
**(T)** 01262 401121
Speciality: Clairvoyants & Palmists.
- **Owner** Mr I Ahmid

**B** (**Ref:**HM00456)

### AJNA
**Ajna-The Teddy Bear & Relaxation Shop**, 45A Thoroughfare, Woodbridge, **Suffolk**, IP12 1AH, **ENG**.
**(T)** 01394 610211
Speciality: Healing Therapy, Reiki. ✔
- **Retailer/Healer/Reiki Master** Mr P Antill **Q:** Reiki Master.

**C** Yrs. Est.: 4 (**Ref:**HM00457)

### AJW CLEMENS OSTEOPATHIC CLINIC
**AJW Clemens Osteopathic Clinic**, 14 Dunmore Rd, Chelmer Village, Chelmsford, **Essex**, CM2 6RY, **ENG**.
**(T)** 01245 468786
Speciality: Osteopathy.
**P S T** (**Ref:**HM00458)

### AJW CLEMENS OSTEOPATHIC CLINIC
**AJW Clemens Osteopathic Clinic**, 80 Greenstead Avenue, Woodford Green, **Essex**, IG8 7ER, **ENG**.
**(T)** 020 8504 1462
Speciality: Osteopathy.
**P S T** (**Ref:**HM00459)

### AJWARD, NONA
**Nona Ajward**, 52 Stoke Newington Church St, London, **London (Greater)**, N16 0NB, **ENG**.
**(T)** 020 7241 5033
Speciality: Aromatherapy.
- **Senior Partner** Mrs J Sheridan

**M O** (**Ref:**HM00460)

### AKERS, D
**D Akers**, 27 Sycamore Rd, Elms Rise, Oxford, **Oxfordshire**, OX2 9EJ, **ENG**.
**(T)** 01865 245926
Speciality: Chiropractors.
- **Owner** Miss D Akers

**P S T** (**Ref:**HM00461)

### AKERS, DENISE
**Denise Akers**, Santé, 40 Buckingham St, Aylesbury, **Buckinghamshire**, HP20 2LH, **ENG**.
**(T)** 01296 482028
**(W)** www.complementary-healthcare.co.uk/info/akers
Speciality: Reflexology.
**S T** (**Ref:**HM00462)

### AKESTER, JANE
**Jane Akester**, Needles View, Kings Saltern Rd, Lymington, **Hampshire**, SO41 3QH, **ENG**.
**(T)** 01590 678344
Speciality: Alexander Technique.
- **Owner** Mrs J Akester

**P S** (**Ref:**HM00463)

### AKHTAR, J
**J Akhtar**, 64 Heidelberg Rd, **Yorkshire (West)**, BD9 5EB, **ENG**.
**(T)** 01274 407984
Speciality: Aromatherapy.
**M O** (**Ref:**HM00464)

### AKIN, K
**K Akin**, 11C Westbourne Rd, Islington, London, **London (Greater)**, N7 8AR, **ENG**.
**(T)** 020 7607 6500
Speciality: Alexander Technique.
- **Owner** Ms K Akin

**P S** (**Ref:**HM00465)

### AKINDELE, KOLA
**Kola Akindele**, 4 Museum Sq, The Crescent, Wisbech, **Cambridgeshire**, PE13 1ES, **ENG**.
**(T)** 01945 583199
Speciality: Chiropractic.
**P S T** (**Ref:**HM00466)

### AKINS CHIROPRACTIC CLINIC
**Akins Chiropractic Clinic**, 1 Parsons Green Lane, London, **London (Greater)**, SW6 4HP, **ENG**.
**(T)** 020 7731 3737
Speciality: Chiropractic.
- **Director** Dr J Akins

**P S T** (**Ref:**HM00467)

### ALADDIN AROMAS
**Aladdin Aromas**, Overwater, Nenthead, Alston, **Cumbria**, CA9 3NT, **ENG**.
**(T)** 01434 382820 **(F)** 01434 382820
Speciality: Aromatherapy.
- **Manager** Mr A Herdman

**M O** (**Ref:**HM00468)

### ALAN BRANNELLY CLNC OF ALT MED
**Alan Brannelly Clinic Of Alternative Medicine**, 33 Shantalla Rd, **County Galway**, **IRE**.
**(T)** 09152 2631
Speciality: Osteopathy.
**P S T** (**Ref:**HM00469)

### ALAN SMITH CHIROPRACTOR
**Alan Smith Chiropractor**, Clarendon House, Judges Trce, East Grinstead, **Sussex (West)**, RH19 3AD, **ENG**.
**(T)** 01342 313396
Speciality: Bonesetting, Chiropractic, Cranial Osteopathy, Electrotherapy, Healer, Manipulation, Reiki. ✔
- **Chiropractor** Mr A Smith **Q:** BSc, DC, MMCA. **M:** GCC.

**S** Yrs. Est.: 8 (**Ref:**HM00470)

### ALARA BEAUTY SALON
**Alara Beauty Salon**, 53 The Village, Ranelagh, **County Dublin**, **IRE**.
**(T)** 01497 0888
Speciality: Complementary Medicines & Therapy.
**M** (**Ref:**HM00471)

### ALASKAN BACH FLOWER REMEDIES
**Alaskan Bach Bush Flower Remedies**, Sharna, 81A West End, Street, **Somerset**, BA16 0LQ, **ENG**.
**(T)** 01458 448448
Speciality: Aromatherapy, Bach Remedies, Massage (Therapeutic), Reflexology. ✔
- **Holistic Therapist** Mr S Hawkins **M:** IPTI.

**B T** Yrs. Est.: 7 (**Ref:**HM00472)

### ALBA CENTRE
**Alba Centre (The)**, 74 Arkleston Rd, Paisley, **Renfrewshire**, PA1 3TR, **SCO**.
**(T)** 01418 897235
**(W)** www.albahealingtherapies.co.uk
Speciality: Anthroposohical Medicine, Aromatherapy, Aura Therapy, Counselling, Meditation, Reflexology, Reiki, Spiritual Healing. ✔
- **Owner** Mrs G Dinning
- **Therapist** Mrs P Reid **Q:** MICHT. **M:** ICHT.

**C** Yrs. Est.: 1 (**Ref:**HM00473)

### ALBAN HEALTH
**Alban Health Ltd**, Cheapside Farmhouse, Sandridgebury Lane, Sandridge, St. Albans, **Hertfordshire**, AL3 6JF, **ENG**.
**(T)** 01727 857714
Speciality: Osteopathy.



Key: **B** Mind-Body Medicine **C** Complementary Medicine **H** Self Help Treatment **M** Medicinal Therapy **O** Oriental Medicine **P** Postural Therapy **S** Manipulative Structural Therapy **T** Touch Therapy

P S T (Ref:HM00474)

## ALBAN THERAPY

**Alban Therapy**, 5 Dickens Cl, St. Albans, **Hertfordshire**, AL3 5PP, ENG.
(T) 01727 851571
Speciality: Hypnotherapy.
● **Sole Director** Mr R Biddle
B (Ref:HM00475)

## ALBANY AROMATHERAPY CLINIC

**Albany Aromatherapy Clinic**, Clifton Ct, Lr Fitzwilliam St, Dublin, **County Dublin**, IRE.
(T) 08726 23266
Speciality: Aromatherapy.
M O (Ref:HM00476)

## ALBANY CLINIC

**Albany Clinic**, 1st Floor Kensington High St, London, **London (Greater)**, W8 4SG, ENG.
(T) 020 7376 1942
Speciality: Osteopathy.
● **Clinic Manager** Mr J Sutton
P S T (Ref:HM00477)

## ALBANY CLINIC

**Albany Clinic**, Fitzwilliam St, Dublin, **County Dublin**, IRE.
(T) 01661 2222
Speciality: Osteopathy.
P S T (Ref:HM00478)

## ALBANY HOUSE

**Albany House Hand Made Cosmetics**, Albany House, 106 Northampton Rd, Market Harborough, **Leicestershire**, LE16 9HF, ENG.
(T) 01858 466737 (F) 01858 466737
(E) joyce.barker@webleicester.co.uk
Speciality: Aromatherapy, Yoga. [Accept Credit Cards]
● **Partner** Ms J De-Borde-Barker Q: QYT.
H Yrs. Est.: 5 (Ref:HM00479)

## ALBERT STREET CLINIC

**Albert Street Chiropractic Clinic**, 45 Albert St, Aberdeen, **Aberdeenshire**, AB25 1XT, SCO.
(T) 01888 569123
Speciality: Chiropractors.
● **Doctor** Mr S Carter
P S T (Ref:HM00480)

## ALBERTBRIDGE ROAD DAY HOSPITAL

**Albertbridge Road Day Hospital**, 225 Albertbridge Rd, Belfast, **County Antrim**, BT5 4PX, NIR.
(T) 028 9045 6007 (F) 028 9045 2638
Speciality: Psychiatry.
● **Manager** Miss M Elliott
B (Ref:HM00481)

## ALBION CHIROPODISTS

**Albion Chiropodists**, 67 Leasowe Rd, Leeds, **Yorkshire (West)**, LS10 2EY, ENG.
(T) 01132 761950
Speciality: Chiropodists (Podiatrists).
● **Owner** Mrs C Lunn
S (Ref:HM00482)

## ALBION CLINIC

**Albion Acupuncture & Chiropractic Clinic**, 1 Albion St, Brighton, **Sussex (East)**, BN2 2NE, ENG.
(T) 01273 628221
Speciality: Acupuncture, Aromatherapy, Chiropractic, Counselling, Cranio-Sacral Therapy, Herbal Medicine, Homeopathy, Massage (Therapeutic), Shiatsu. [✔]
● **Chiropractor** Mr C Garland Q: DC, Dip.Chiro, MMCA. M: BCA.
● **Chiropractor** Ms J Sanders Q: DC. M: BCA.
● **Owner** Ms R Urbanowicz Q: DC. M: BCA.
● **Chiropractor** Mr T Dawson Q: Dip.Chiro. M: BCA.
P Yrs. Est.: 14 (Ref:HM00483)

## ALBION HOMOEOPATHIC CENTRE

**Albion Homoeopathic Centre**, 36 Duke St, Kettering, **Northamptonshire**, NN16 9DY, ENG.
(T) 01536 516220
Speciality: Homeopathy.
● **Owner** Mrs S Walmsley
M (Ref:HM00484)

## ALBROW, B

**B Albrow**, 41 Carlton Mansions, Randolph Avenue, London, **London (Greater)**, W9 1NR, ENG.
(T) 020 7624 0895
Speciality: Complementary Medicines & Therapy.
● **Owner** Mrs B Albrow
M (Ref:HM00485)

## ALBURY, MAVIS

**Mavis Albury**, 14 Windmill Rd, Thame, **Oxfordshire**, OX9 2DR, ENG.
(T) 01844 212562
Speciality: Chiropodists (Podiatrists).
S (Ref:HM00486)

## ALCANTARA, FATIMA

**Fatima Alcantara**, 59 Bedford St, Oxford, **Oxfordshire**, OX4 1SU, ENG.
(T) 01865 249062 (F) 01865 249062
Speciality: Chiropractic.
● **Owner** Mrs F Alcantra
P S T (Ref:HM00487)

## ALCHEMY FOUNDATION

**Alchemy Foundation (The)**, The Birchcliff Centre, Birchcliff Rd, Hebden Bridge, **Yorkshire (West)**, HX7 8DG, ENG.
(T) 01422 844337
Speciality: Complementary Medicines & Therapy.
C M (Ref:HM00488)

## ALCOCK, ANNE

**Anne Alcock**, Sullivan's Quay, **County Cork**, IRE.
(T) 08761 76193
Speciality: Complementary Medicines & Therapy.
M (Ref:HM00489)

## ALCOCK, E C

**E C Alcock**, 85-86 Darlington St, Wolverhampton, **Midlands (West)**, WV1 4EX, ENG.
(T) 01902 425314
Speciality: Biomechanics, Chiropody, Gait Analysis, Nail Surgery. [✔]
● **Podiatrist** Mrs E Alcock Q: BSc (Hons), DPodM. M: S.C.P, S.R.Ch.
C Yrs. Est.: 15 (Ref:HM00490)

## ALDA HOUSE

**Alda House School Of Natural Therapy**, Alda House, Manor House Drive, Coventry, **Midlands (West)**, CV1 2EY, ENG.
(T) 024 7622 2002
Speciality: Complementary Medicines & Therapy.
● **Principal** Linda Stokes
M (Ref:HM00491)

## ALDA HOUSE NATURAL THERAPY

**Alda House Natural Therapy**, Manor House Drive, Coventry, **Midlands (West)**, CV1 2EY, ENG.
(T) 024 7655 3793
(E) jaq@dial.pipex.com
Speciality: Acupressure, Acupuncture, Aromatherapy, Auricular Therapy, Baby Massage, Bach Remedies, Bowen Therapy, Chiropractic, Dowsing, Floral Essence Therapy, Homeopathy, Hopi Ear Candles, Indian Head Massage, Kinesiology, Manipulation, Massage (Therapeutic), Miasm Therapy, Moxibustion, Reflexology, Reiki, Stress Therapy, Parapsychology. [✔]
● **Health Therapist** Ms L Stokes M: GCP, IAIM.
● **Homeopath/Counsellor/Parapsychologist** Ms K Stranks
● **Massage Therapist/Reflexologist** Ms D Hunter Q: IIHHT, ITEC. M: GCP.
● **Natural Health Therapist/Reflexologist** Ms I Frank Q: IIHHT, ITEC. M: GCP.
● **Chiropractor** Mr J Shuttleworth Q: Dip.Chiro. M: BAAC.
● **Acupunturist** Ms S Hopkins Q: Dip.Ac, MBAcC. M: BAcC.
● **Homeopath/Bowen Therapist** Mr M Byng Q: BTAA, BTER. M: BA UK, BTER, HMA.
C Yrs. Est.: 8 (Ref:HM00492)

## ALDAN PHYSIOTHERAPY CLINIC

**Aldan Physiotherapy Clinic**, 2a Pilton St, Barnstaple, **Devon**, EX31 1PE, ENG.
(T) 01271 323737
Speciality: Physiotherapy.
● **Partner** Miss A Longdon
P S T (Ref:HM00493)

## ALDCROFT, R

**Mr R Aldcroft**, Unit 8 Watergate Arc, Watergate St, Whitchurch, **Shropshire**, SY13 1DP, ENG.
(T) 01948 662286
Speciality: Chiropodists (Podiatrists).
S (Ref:HM00494)

## ALDEPHI HOUSE

**Aldephi House**, 20 Queen St, Blackpool, **Lancashire**, FY1 1PD, ENG.
(T) 01253 751155
Speciality: Psychotherapy.
● **Partner** Ms H Liddle
B (Ref:HM00495)

## ALDER, CHRISTINE

**Christine Alder**, Clay House, Clay Lane, Beenham, Reading, **Berkshire**, RG7 5PA, ENG.
(T) 01189 713009
Speciality: Herbal Medicine.
M (Ref:HM00496)

## ALDER, DENNIS

**Dennis Alder**, 36 Fishponds Rd, Hitchin, **Hertfordshire**, SG5 1NR, ENG.
(T) 01462 434655
Speciality: Biomechanics, Chiropody, Cryo Surgery, Nail Surgery, Podiatry. [✔] [Accept Credit Cards]
● **Owner/Podiatrist** Mr A Dennis Q: M.S.C.P, S.R.Ch.
C Yrs. Est.: 22 (Ref:HM00497)

## ALDER, DENNIS

**Dennis Alder**, 21 High St, Baldock, **Hertfordshire**, SG7 6AZ, ENG.
(T) 01462 894386
Speciality: Chiropodists (Podiatrists).
S (Ref:HM00498)

## ALDER, E R

**E R Alder**, 3a Days Lane, Biddenham, Bedford, **Bedfordshire**, MK40 4AD, ENG.
(T) 01234 341800 (F) 01234 356284
Speciality: Physiotherapy.
● **Owner** Mrs E Alder
P S T (Ref:HM00499)

## ALDERBURY CLINIC

**Alderbury Clinic**, 62 Unthank Rd, Norwich, **Norfolk**, NR2 2RN, ENG.
(T) 01603 663186
Speciality: Acupuncture.
● **Owner** Mr J Whines
O (Ref:HM00500)

## ALDERFLEY, YVETTE

**Yvette Alderfley**, 26 Parkside, London, **London (Greater)**, NW2 6RJ, ENG.
(T) 020 8452 6986
Speciality: Chiropodists (Podiatrists).
● **Owner** Mrs Y Aldersley
S (Ref:HM00501)

## ALDERSHOT & FARNHAM CLINIC

**Aldershot & Farnham Chiropody Clinics**, 88a West St, Farnham, **Surrey**, GU9 7EN, ENG.
(T) 01252 716611
Speciality: Chiropodists (Podiatrists).
S (Ref:HM00502)

## ALDOUS, JOSIE

**Josie Aldous**, 6 Leys Lane, Meriden, Coventry, **Midlands (West)**, CV7 7LQ, ENG.
(T) 01676 523014
Speciality: Hopi Ear Candles, Reiki, Seichem, Spiritual Healing. [✔]
● **Owner/Natural Health Therapist** Mrs J Aldhous Q: Cert.Reiki, Cert.Seichem. M: ANM.
C Yrs. Est.: 9 (Ref:HM00503)

## ALDRED, E M

**E M Aldred**, Nottingham Chiropractic Clinic, 3 Hawksworth St, Nottingham, **Nottinghamshire**, NG3 2EG, ENG.
(T) 01159 472131



Key continued: Yrs.Est: Years Established Q: Qualifications M: Professional Membership [✔] Indemnity Insurance [card] Accept Credit Cards

Speciality: Chiropractic.
P S T (Ref:HM00504)

**ALDRED, HELEN**

**Helen Aldred**, 65 Sea Lane, Goring-By-Sea, Worthing, **Sussex (West)**, BN12 4QD, ENG.
(T) 01903 247984
Speciality: Reflexology.
S T (Ref:HM00505)

**ALDRIDGE PHYSIOTHERAPY CLINIC**

**Aldridge Physiotherapy & Sports Injury Clinic**, 48A Paddock Lane, Aldridge, Walsall, **Midlands (West)**, WS9 0BP, ENG.
(T) 01922 451492 (F) 01922 451492
Speciality: Physiotherapy.
● **Owner** Mr S Williams
P S T (Ref:HM00506)

**ALDRIDGE, ANNETTE**

**Annette Aldridge**, 53 Main Rd, East Morton, Keighley, **Yorkshire (West)**, BD20 5TE, ENG.
(T) 01274 564822
Speciality: Hypnotherapy.
B (Ref:HM00507)

**ALDRIDGE, JUDITH**

**Judith Aldridge**, Badham Pharmacy, Sixways, Charlton Kings, Cheltenham, **Gloucestershire**, GL52 6HS, ENG.
(T) 01242 242219
Speciality: Chiropodists (Podiatrists).
S (Ref:HM00508)

**ALDRIDGE, SUSAN**

**Susan Aldridge**, 7 Heather Cl, Ardmore Avenue, Guildford, **Surrey**, GU2 9ZZ, ENG.
(T) 01483 575396
Speciality: Reflexology.
● **Owner** Susan Aldridge
S T (Ref:HM00509)

**ALDRIDGE, VICKI**

**Vicki Aldridge**, Bishops Pk Centre, Lancaster Way, Bishop's Stortford, **Hertfordshire**, CM23 4DA, ENG.
(T) 01279 651859
Speciality: Osteopathy.
● **Owner** Mr D Lindy
P S T (Ref:HM00510)

**ALDRIDGE, VICKI**

**Vicki Aldridge**, 5 Johns Rd, Bishop's Stortford, **Hertfordshire**, CM23 2BS, ENG.
(T) 01279 505292
Speciality: Osteopathy.
● **Owner** Ms V Aldridge
P S T (Ref:HM00511)

**ALDWINCKLE, PAUL**

**Paul Aldwinckle**, 11 Loftsteads, Somersham, Huntingdon, **Cambridgeshire**, PE28 3HX, ENG.
(T) 01487 740497
Speciality: Chiropodists (Podiatrists).
● **Owner** Mr P Aldwinckle
S (Ref:HM00512)

**ALEX TECH TEACHING CENTRE**

**Alexander Technique Teaching Centre (The)**, The Swartmore Centre, 2-7 Woodhouse Sq, Leeds, **Yorkshire (West)**, LS3 1AD, ENG.
(T) 01132 445559
(W) www.alextec.org.uk
Speciality: Alexander Technique. ✔
● **Teacher of the Alexander Technique**
Ms M White Q: MSTAT. M: STAT.
● **Teacher of the Alexander Technique**
Mr G Ragsdale Q: MSTAT. M: STAT.
P Yrs. Est.: 6 (Ref:HM00513)

**ALEXANDER HOUSE PRACTICE**

**Alexander House Chiropody Practice**, 13 Salisbury Rd, Redland, Bristol, BS6 7AL, ENG.
(T) 01179 071113
Speciality: Chiropodists (Podiatrists).
● **Owner** Mrs S Varney
S (Ref:HM00514)

**ALEXANDER STUDIO**

**Alexander Studio (The)**, 16 Balderton St, London, **London (Greater)**, W1Y 1TF, ENG.
(T) 020 7629 1808
Speciality: Alexander Technique.
● **Practitioner** Mrs G Druks-Kok
P S (Ref:HM00515)

**ALEXANDER TEACHERS ASSOCIATION**

**Alexander Teachers Professional Association**, Studio 706-707 The Big Peg, Vyse St, Hockley, Birmingham, **Midlands (West)**, B18 6NF, ENG.
(T) 01212 481133
Speciality: Alexander Technique.
● **Teacher** Mr K Edwards
P S (Ref:HM00516)

**ALEXANDER TECHNIQUE**

**Alexander Technique**, 8 St. Peters Pl, Edinburgh, **Edinburgh (City of)**, EH3 9PJ, SCO.
(T) 01312 299035
Speciality: Alexander Technique. ✔
● **Sole Director/Teacher**
Mr R Harrower Q: ATI. M: ATI, STAT, SYTA.
M Yrs. Est.: 9 (Ref:HM00517)

**ALEXANDER TECHNIQUE**

**Alexander Technique**, 53 Fellside Rd, Whickham, Newcastle Upon Tyne, **Tyne and Wear**, NE16 4JT, ENG.
(T) 01914 887678
Speciality: Alexander Technique.
● **Owner** Mrs K Torkington
P S (Ref:HM00518)

**ALEXANDER TECHNIQUE**

**Alexander Technique**, 56 High St, Ipswich, **Suffolk**, IP1 3QJ, ENG.
(T) 01473 259096
Speciality: Alexander Technique.
P S (Ref:HM00519)

**ALEXANDER TECHNIQUE**

**Alexander Technique**, 69 Willingdon Rd, Eastbourne, **Sussex (East)**, BN21 1TR, ENG.
(T) 01323 739450
Speciality: Alexander Technique.
M (Ref:HM00520)

**ALEXANDER TECHNIQUE**

**Alexander Technique**, 7 Lynedoch St, Glasgow, **Glasgow (City of)**, G3 6EF, SCO.
(T) 01413 530415
Speciality: Alexander Technique.
● **Owner** Mr G McCaffrey
P S (Ref:HM00521)

**ALEXANDER TECHNIQUE**

**Alexander Technique**, Hill St, Coventry, **Midlands (West)**, CV1 4AN, ENG.
(T) 01905 350566
Speciality: Alexander Technique.
● **Owner** Ms M Kirkness
P S (Ref:HM00522)

**ALEXANDER TECHNIQUE**

**Alexander Technique**, 77 Godstow Rd, Wolvercote, Oxford, **Oxfordshire**, OX2 8PE, ENG.
(T) 01865 512430
Speciality: Alexander Technique.
● **Owner** Ms C Birtwhistle
P S (Ref:HM00523)

**ALEXANDER TECHNIQUE**

**Alexander Technique**, Dalton Ellis Hall, Conyngham Rd, Manchester, **Manchester (Greater)**, M14 5RL, ENG.
(T) 01612 489836
Speciality: Alexander Technique.
P S (Ref:HM00524)

**ALEXANDER TECHNIQUE**

**Alexander Technique**, 94 Stowey Rd, Yatton, Bristol, BS49 4EB, ENG.
(T) 01934 876747 (F) 01934 876747
Speciality: Alexander Technique.
● **Manager** Mrs G Ray
P S (Ref:HM00525)

**ALEXANDER TECHNIQUE**

**Alexander Technique**, 98A Baker St, Enfield, **London (Greater)**, EN1 3EZ, ENG.
(T) 020 8342 1404
Speciality: Alexander Technique.
P S (Ref:HM00526)

**ALEXANDER TECHNIQUE**

**Alexander Technique**, Shefford Rd, Clophill, Bedford, **Bedfordshire**, MK45 4BT, ENG.
(T) 01525 861456 (F) 01525 861456
Speciality: Alexander Technique.
● **Owner** Mr R Diss
P S (Ref:HM00527)

**ALEXANDER TECHNIQUE**

**Alexander Technique**, 51 Rose St, Glasgow, **Glasgow (City of)**, G3 6SF, SCO.
(T) 01413 531513
Speciality: Alexander Technique.
P S (Ref:HM00528)

**ALEXANDER TECHNIQUE**

**Alexander Technique**, Holly View Cottage, Mangreen, Swardeston, Norwich, **Norfolk**, NR14 8DD, ENG.
(T) 01508 571370
Speciality: Alexander Technique.
● **Owner** Mr C Goodchild
P S (Ref:HM00529)

**ALEXANDER TECHNIQUE**

**Alexander Technique**, 7 Priory Pl, Wells, **Somerset**, BA5 1SP, ENG.
(T) 01749 670453
Speciality: Alexander Technique.
● **Owner** Mr P Olivieri
P S (Ref:HM00530)

**ALEXANDER TECHNIQUE**

**Alexander Technique**, 103 Woodstock Rd, Broxbourne, **Hertfordshire**, EN10 7PE, ENG.
(T) 01992 421912 (F) 01992 421912
Speciality: Alexander Technique.
● **Owner** Mrs S Burnay
P S (Ref:HM00531)

**ALEXANDER TECHNIQUE**

**Alexander Technique**, 1 Hazel Villa, Valley Rd, Hayfield, High Peak, **Derbyshire**, SK22 2LP, ENG.
(T) 01663 749513
Speciality: Alexander Technique.
● **Owner** Mrs J Osgood
P S (Ref:HM00532)

**ALEXANDER TECHNIQUE**

**Alexander Technique**, 11 Dunollie Rd, London, **London (Greater)**, NW5 2XN, ENG.
(T) 020 7813 2434
Speciality: Alexander Technique.
P S (Ref:HM00533)

**ALEXANDER TECHNIQUE**

**Alexander Technique**, 39 Grosvenor Gardens, Kingston Upon Thames, **Surrey**, KT2 5BE, ENG.
(T) 020 8974 9345 (F) 020 8549 7315
Speciality: Alexander Technique.
● **Owner** Ms J Nutt
P S (Ref:HM00534)

**ALEXANDER TECHNIQUE**

**Alexander Technique**, 13 Moncrieff Trce, Edinburgh, **Edinburgh (City of)**, EH9 1NB, SCO.
(T) 01316 682839
Speciality: Alexander Technique.
● **Manager** Mrs L Wyman
P S (Ref:HM00535)

**ALEXANDER TECHNIQUE**

**Alexander Technique**, 18 Barnpark Rd, Teignmouth, **Devon**, TQ14 8PN, ENG.
(T) 01626 774512
Speciality: Alexander Technique.
● **Owner** Mrs L Lions
C P S (Ref:HM00536)

**ALEXANDER TECHNIQUE**

**Alexander Technique**, 19 Church Wood Avenue, Leeds, **Yorkshire (West)**, LS16 5LF, ENG.
(T) 01132 755687
Speciality: Alexander Technique.
P S (Ref:HM00537)

**ALEXANDER TECHNIQUE**

**Alexander Technique**, 26 Vauxhall Gr, London, **London (Greater)**, SW8 1SY, ENG.
(T) 020 7820 7770
Speciality: Alexander Technique.
P S (Ref:HM00538)

**ALEXANDER TECHNIQUE**

**Alexander Technique**, 26 Woodland Park Rd, Newport, NP19 8LY, WAL.
(T) 01633 223356
Speciality: Alexander Technique.



Key: B Mind-Body Medicine C Complementary Medicine H Self Help Treatment M Medicinal Therapy O Oriental Medicine P Postural Therapy S Manipulative Structural Therapy T Touch Therapy

P S (Ref:HM00539)

**ALEXANDER TECHNIQUE**

**Alexander Technique**, 30 Culliford Rd, Dorchester, **Dorset**, DT1 2AT, ENG.
(T) 01305 257949
Speciality: Alexander Technique.
● **Owner** Ms J Curnow
P S (Ref:HM00540)

**ALEXANDER TECHNIQUE**

**Alexander Technique**, 33 Rathen Rd, Manchester, **Manchester (Greater)**, M20 4QJ, ENG.
(T) 01614 340195
Speciality: Alexander Technique.
P S (Ref:HM00541)

**ALEXANDER TECHNIQUE**

**Alexander Technique**, 35 Montague Rd, Bournemouth, **Dorset**, BH5 2EW, ENG.
(T) 01202 427442
Speciality: Alexander Technique.
P S (Ref:HM00542)

**ALEXANDER TECHNIQUE**

**Alexander Technique**, 23 Westminster Trce, Glasgow, **Glasgow (City of)**, G3 7RU, SCO.
(T) 01414 237578
Speciality: Alexander Technique.
P S (Ref:HM00543)

**ALEXANDER TECHNIQUE**

**Alexander Technique**, 37 Greenway, London, **London (Greater)**, N14 6NR, ENG.
(T) 020 8882 5134
Speciality: Alexander Technique.
● **Owner** Mrs L Feldman
P S (Ref:HM00544)

**ALEXANDER TECHNIQUE**

**Alexander Technique in the City**, 62 Paul St, London, **London (Greater)**, EC2A 4NA, ENG.
(T) 020 7739 0200 (F) 020 8883 5611
(E) enquiries@alextech-city.co.uk
(W) www.alextech-city.co.uk
Speciality: Alexander Technique. ✓
● **Teacher of the Alexander Technique** Fitzmaurice M: STAT.
● **Teacher of the Alexander Technique** Ms M Stone Q: BA (Hons), M.Ed, MSTAT. M: STAT.
● **Teacher of the Alexander Technique** Ms M Hampson M: STAT.
● **Teacher of the Alexander Technique** Ms S Kiefer M: STAT.
P Yrs. Est.: 2 (Ref:HM00545)

**ALEXANDER TECHNIQUE**

**Judy Clover**, 33 Cameron St, Cardiff, **Glamorgan (Vale of)**, CF24 2NW, WAL.
(T) 029 2048 1844
Speciality: Alexander Technique. ✓
● **Therapist** Ms J Clover M: RCPsych, STAT.
P Yrs. Est.: 15 (Ref:HM00546)

**ALEXANDER TECHNIQUE**

**Alexander Technique**, 1 Beattock Rise, Muswell Hill, London, **London (Greater)**, N10 3DS, ENG.
(T) 020 8883 5611 (F) 020 8883 5611
(E) ms@monstone.force9.co.uk
Speciality: Alexander Technique. ✓
● **Teacher of the Alexander Technique** Ms M Stone Q: BA (Hons), M.Ed. M: STAT.
P Yrs. Est.: 15 (Ref:HM00547)

**ALEXANDER TECHNIQUE**

**Alexander Technique**, 19 Eton Rd, Stockton-On-Tees, **Cleveland**, TS18 4DL, ENG.
(T) 01642 644067
(W) www.paat.org.uk
Speciality: Alexander Technique. ✓
● **Teacher of the Alexander Technique** Ms M Marcus M: ATI, PAAT.
B P Yrs. Est.: 20 (Ref:HM00548)

**ALEXANDER TECHNIQUE**

**Alexander Technique**, The Professional Centre Of Holistic Health, 50 High St, Hastings, **Sussex (East)**, TN34 3EN, ENG.
(T) 01424 465050
Speciality: Alexander Technique. ✓
● **Aromatherapist/Reiki Master** Mrs M Eaton
● **Teacher of the Alexander Technique** Ms S Child
(T) 01323 734428 Q: MSTAT. M: STAT.
P Yrs. Est.: 8 (Ref:HM00549)

**ALEXANDER TECHNIQUE**

**Susanne Pearce**, 6 Roeze Cl, Woodhall Spa, **Lincolnshire**, LN10 6PP, ENG.
(T) 01526 354980 (F) 01526 354980
(E) suabsolut@aol.com
Speciality: Alexander Technique, T'ai-Chi Ch'uan. ✓
● **Teacher of the Alexander Technique** Ms S Pearce Q: MSTAT. M: STAT.
P Yrs. Est.: 15 (Ref:HM00550)

**ALEXANDER TECHNIQUE**

**Alexander Technique Cardiff Consultancy**, 20 Princes Avenue, Cardiff, **Glamorgan (Vale of)**, CF24 3SN, WAL.
(T) 029 2048 4171 (F) 029 2048 7617
(W) www.alexandertec.u-net.com
Speciality: Alexander Technique.
● **Therapist** Ms T Miller Q: BSc. M: STAT.
P Yrs. Est.: 18 (Ref:HM00551)

**ALEXANDER TECHNIQUE**

**Alexander Technique**, Optimum Health Clinic, 106 Gordon Rd, Ealing, London, **London (Greater)**, W13 8PJ, ENG.
(T) 020 8998 8873 (F) 020 8998 8873
Speciality: Alexander Technique, Re-education.
● **Therapist** Ms L Godliman Q: MSTAT. M: STAT.
● **Owner** Miss F Sholeh
H Yrs. Est.: 10 (Ref:HM00552)

**ALEXANDER TECHNIQUE**

**Alexander Technique**, 201A Cheriton Rd, Folkestone, **Kent**, CT19 4AT, ENG.
(T) 01303 270389
Speciality: Alexander Technique. ✓
● **Alexander Technique Teacher** Mrs S Lantain M: STAT.
C Yrs. Est.: 15 (Ref:HM00553)

**ALEXANDER TECHNIQUE**

**Alexander Technique**, 34 Orchard Avenue, London, **London (Greater)**, N14 4ND, ENG.
(T) 020 8882 5134
Speciality: Alexander Technique.
P S (Ref:HM00554)

**ALEXANDER TECHNIQUE CENTRE**

**Alexander Technique Centre (The)**, 82 Great Eastern St, London, **London (Greater)**, EC2A 3JL, ENG.
(T) 020 7749 7246
Speciality: Alexander Technique, Bates Method, Neuro-Linguistic Program. ✓
● **Teacher of the Alexander Technique** Mr D Glassman Q: MSTAT.
● **Practitioner** Mr D Howlett
● **Practitioner** Ms D Aubrey
B C H P T
Yrs. Est.: 16 (Ref:HM00555)

**ALEXANDER TECHNIQUE CENTRE**

**F M Alexander Technique**, Dunsinane House, Kilspindie Rd, Dunsinane Estate, Dundee, **Angus**, DD2 3PW, SCO.
(T) 01382 889116
Speciality: Alexander Technique. ✓
● **Alexander Technique Teacher** Mr G Coltart Q: MSTAT. M: STAT.
B Yrs. Est.: 15 (Ref:HM00556)

**ALEXANDER TECHNIQUE CENTRE**

**Alexander Technique Centre Ireland (The)**, Kirkullen Lodge, Tooreeny, Moycullen, **County Galway**, IRE.
(T) 00353 91555800 (F) 00353 91555800
(E) rickbrennan@eircom.net
(W) homepage.eircom.net/~alexandertechnique
Speciality: Alexander Technique.
● **Teacher of the Alexander Technique** Mr R Brennan
P Yrs. Est.: 11 (Ref:HM00557)

**ALEXANDER, A (DR)**

**Dr A Alexander**, 97 Town Lane, Mobberley, Knutsford, **Cheshire**, WA16 7HH, ENG.
(T) 01565 872157
Speciality: Osteopathy.
P S T (Ref:HM00558)

**ALEXANDER, CAROL**

**Carol Alexander**, 7 Peverell Ter, Plymouth, **Devon**, PL3 4JJ, ENG.
(T) 01752 668508
Speciality: Chiropodists (Podiatrists).
● **Owner** Ms C Alexander
S (Ref:HM00559)

**ALEXANDER, EMMA**

**Emma Alexander**, 66 Mellowship Rd, Coventry, **Midlands (West)**, CV5 7BY, ENG.
(T) 024 7646 9913
Speciality: Reflexology.
● **Owner** Ms E Alexander
S T (Ref:HM00560)

**ALEXANDER, F & JAYNE, V**

**Mrs F Alexander & Mrs V Jayne**, 22 Glenside, Billericay, **Essex**, CM11 2LY, ENG.
(T) 01277 656314
Speciality: Physiotherapy.
P S T (Ref:HM00561)

**ALEXANDER, GERRARD**

**Gerrard Alexander**, 91 Sweetloves Lane, Bolton, **Lancashire**, BL1 7EA, ENG.
(T) 01204 306425
Speciality: Herbal Medicine.
M (Ref:HM00562)

**ALEXANDER, JAMES**

**James Alexander**, 77 East High St, Forfar, **Angus**, DD8 2EQ, SCO.
(T) 01307 462434
Speciality: Chiropodists (Podiatrists).
S (Ref:HM00563)

**ALEXANDER, JANE**

**Jane Alexander**, Hillrise, Deanery Rd, Godalming, **Surrey**, GU7 2PG, ENG.
(T) 01483 419195
Speciality: Homeopathy.
M (Ref:HM00564)

**ALEXANDER, KAREN**

**Acupuncturist**, 2 Yew Tree Cottages, Garston Lane, Blagdon, Bristol, BS40 7TF, ENG.
(T) 01761 462022
(E) rdkalex@ukonline.co.uk
Speciality: Acupuncture. ✓
● **Acupuncturist** Ms K Alexander Q: BA, BSc, Lic.Ac, MBAcC. M: BAcC.
O Yrs. Est.: 6 (Ref:HM00565)

**ALEXANDER, LAUREL**

**Laurel Alexander**, 101 Osborne Rd, Brighton, **Sussex (East)**, BN1 6LW, ENG.
(T) 01273 564030
Speciality: Reflexology.
S T (Ref:HM00566)

**ALEXANDER, LINDA**

**Linda Alexander**, 11 Attow Rd, Glasgow, **Glasgow (City of)**, G43 1BZ, SCO.
(T) 01416 321440 (F) 01416 493388
Speciality: Hypnosis.
● **Owner** Mrs L Alexander
B (Ref:HM00567)

**ALEXANDER, M S**

**M S Alexander**, Mid Yorkshire Nuffield Hospital, Outwood Lane, Horsforth, Leeds, **Yorkshire (West)**, LS18 4HP, ENG.
(T) 01132 588756
Speciality: Psychiatry.
B (Ref:HM00568)

**ALEXANDER, MARGARET**

**Margaret Alexander**, 137 Magdalen Rd, Oxford, **Oxfordshire**, OX4 1RJ, ENG.
(T) 01865 396939
Speciality: Homeopathy.
● **Owner** Mr M Franklin
M (Ref:HM00569)

**ALEXANDER, R E**

**R E Alexander**, Milne Field Surgery, 168 Uxbridge Rd, Pinner, **London (Greater)**, HA5 4DR, ENG.
(T) 020 8421 3277
Speciality: Acupuncture.
O (Ref:HM00570)



Key continued: **Yrs.Est:** Years Established **Q:** Qualifications **M:** Professional Membership ✓ Indemnity Insurance Accept Credit Cards

## ALEXANDER, RUPERT
**Rupert Alexander**, 8 Cornfield Cl, Witney, **Oxfordshire**, OX8 5BU, ENG.
(T) 01993 702400
Speciality: Chiropractors.
● **Owner** Mr R Alexander
P S T (Ref:HM00571)

## ALEXANDER, S
**S Alexander**, Dragon House, Edgiock, Astwood Bank, Redditch, **Worcestershire**, B96 6LB, ENG.
(T) 01527 893706
Speciality: Physiotherapy.
● **Owner** Mrs S Alexander
P S T (Ref:HM00572)

## ALEXANDRA FOOT CLINIC
**Alexandra Foot Clinic**, 87 Alexandra Rd, St. Austell, **Cornwall**, PL25 4QW, ENG.
(T) 01726 77577
Speciality: Chiropody.
S (Ref:HM00573)

## ALFONSO & PETERSON
**Alfonso & Peterson**, Coopers Building, Church St, Liverpool, **Merseyside**, L1 3AG, ENG.
(T) 01517 094306
Speciality: Chiropodists (Podiatrists).
● **Partner** Mrs F Alfonso
S (Ref:HM00574)

## ALFORD, B
**B Alford**, Lavender Avenue, London, **London (Greater)**, NW9 8HE, ENG.
(T) 020 8930 0046
Speciality: Reflexology.
● **Owner** Mrs B Alford
S T (Ref:HM00575)

## ALFORD, JO
**Jo Alford**, The Limes, 4 Privett Rd, Waterlooville, **Hampshire**, PO7 5HJ, ENG.
(T) 023 9225 1885
Speciality: Physiotherapy.
● **Owner** J Alford
P S T (Ref:HM00576)

## ALFORD, M A
**Mr M A Alford**, 38-40 Thornton St, Hartlepool, **Cleveland**, TS26 9ET, ENG.
(T) 01429 274082
Speciality: Osteopathy.
● **Owner** Mr M Alford
P S T (Ref:HM00577)

## ALIGNING BODY & SOUL
**Aligning Body & Soul-Judy Burton**, 1 School Bank, Main Rd, Minsterley, Shrewsbury, **Shropshire**, SY5 0BP, ENG.
(T) 01743 791122
Speciality: Homeopathy.
● **Owner** Judy Burton
M (Ref:HM00578)

## ALISON MORTON PHYSIOTHERAPY
**Alison Morton Physiotherapy**, 202 Peverell Park Rd, Plymouth, **Devon**, PL3 4QE, ENG.
(T) 01752 783873 (F) 01752 788143
Speciality: Acupuncture, Physiotherapy. ✔
● **Physiotherapist** Alison Morton Q: MCSP, SRP. M: CSP.
S Yrs. Est.: 7 (Ref:HM00579)

## ALJOE, J
**J Aljoe**, 11 Kingsley Pl, London, **London (Greater)**, N6 5EA, ENG.
(T) 020 8348 2810
Speciality: Chiropodists (Podiatrists).
● **Owner** Ms J Aljoe
S (Ref:HM00580)

## ALL - HEAL ACU & HERB CENTRE
**All - Heal Acupuncture & Herb Centre**, 202 Above Bar St, Southampton, **Hampshire**, SO14 7DW, ENG.
(T) 023 8023 5599 (F) 023 8023 5599
Speciality: Acupressure, Acupuncture, Cupping, Herbal Medicine, Moxibustion.
● **Doctor** Jian Hong Guan Q: MB. M: ATCM UK.
● **Doctor** Daian Zou Q: MB. M: ATCM UK.
● **Doctor** Hua Shang Q: MB. M: ATCM UK, BAcC, RCHM.
C Yrs. Est.: 1 (Ref:HM00581)

## ALL IN THE MIND
**All In The Mind**, 25 Oakbank, Prestwich, Manchester, **Manchester (Greater)**, M25 3AN, ENG.
(T) 01617 739785 (F) 01617 739785
(E) mcook_hypn@hotmail.com
(W) www.allinthemindhypnosis.com
Speciality: Complementary Therapy, Hypnosis, Hypnotherapy, Stress Therapy, Visualisation Therapy. ✔
● **Clinical Hypnotherapist**
Ms M Cook Q: BA (Hons), Dip.Hyp, M.Ed. M: BSCH, HA.
B Yrs. Est.: 4 (Ref:HM00582)

## ALL WELL & GOOD
**All Well & Good**, 89 Ashleigh Rd, London, **London (Greater)**, SW14 8PY, ENG.
(T) 020 8876 6026
Speciality: Aromatherapy, Massage (Therapeutic).
M (Ref:HM00583)

## ALLABOUTPHSYCOTHERAPY.CO.UK
**Allaboutpsychotherapy.Co.UK**, 35 Croftdown Rd, London, **London (Greater)**, NW5 1EL, ENG.
(T) 020 7428 0616
Speciality: Psychotherapy.
● **Principal** Dr M Chatsman
B (Ref:HM00584)

## ALLAN, A
**A Allan**, 16 Victoria Rd, Clacton-On-Sea, **Essex**, CO15 6BH, ENG.
(T) 01255 688036
Speciality: Complementary Medicines & Therapy.
● **Administrator** Mrs H Robinson
M (Ref:HM00585)

## ALLAN, C
**C Allan**, 15 Albert Pl, Stirling, FK8 2RE, SCO.
(T) 01786 475175
Speciality: Chiropodists (Podiatrists).
● **Owner** Mr C Allan
S (Ref:HM00586)

## ALLAN, DIANNE
**Dianne Allan**, Lowside Croft, Nethertown, Egremont, **Cumbria**, CA22 2UH, ENG.
(T) 01946 820483
Speciality: Physiotherapy.
P S T (Ref:HM00587)

## ALLAN, HUGH
**Hugh Allan**, 56 South Hamilton St, Kilmarnock, **Ayrshire (East)**, KA1 2DT, SCO.
(T) 01563 527501
Speciality: Physiotherapy.
P S T (Ref:HM00588)

## ALLAN, PAUL
**Paul Allan**, 52 Stoke Newington Church St, London, **London (Greater)**, N16 0NB, ENG.
(T) 020 7241 5033 (F) 020 7502 1182
Speciality: Hypnotherapy.
● **Senior Partner** Mrs J Sharidan
B (Ref:HM00589)

## ALLAUDDIN, ASIF
**Asif Allauddin**, 9 Bell St, Renfrew, **Renfrewshire**, PA4 8PP, SCO.
(T) 01418 866930
Speciality: Osteopathy.
P S T (Ref:HM00590)

## ALLAUDDIN, ASIF
**Asif Allauddin**, 76A Causeyside St, Paisley, **Renfrewshire**, PA1 1YP, SCO.
(T) 01418 898416
Speciality: Osteopathy.
P S T (Ref:HM00591)

## ALLAWAY, SANDRA
**Sandra Allaway**, 22 Southwick Avenue, Fareham, **Hampshire**, PO16 8JE, ENG.
(T) 023 9238 7340
Speciality: Reflexology.
S T (Ref:HM00592)

## ALLCHORN, MAGGIE
**Maggie Allchorn**, 11 Forest Way, Deanland Wood Park, Golden Cross, **Sussex (East)**, BN27 3SP, ENG.
(T) 01825 872471
Speciality: Reflexology.
S T (Ref:HM00593)

## ALLCOCK, RACHAEL
**Rachael Allcock**, Tan-Y-Ffordd, Bwlch-Y-Ddar, Llangedwyn, Oswestry, **Shropshire**, SY10 9LN, ENG.
(T) 01691 648978
Speciality: Reflexology.
S T (Ref:HM00594)

## ALLDRIDGE, T
**T Alldridge**, 186 Gudge Heath Lane, Fareham, **Hampshire**, PO15 6QB, ENG.
(T) 01329 232213
Speciality: Osteopathy.
● **Owner** Mr T Alldridge
P S T (Ref:HM00595)

## ALLDRIDGE, T D
**T D Alldridge**, 30 College St, Petersfield, **Hampshire**, GU31 4AF, ENG.
(T) 01730 263028 (F) 01730 263028
Speciality: Osteopathy.
● **Owner** Mr T Alldridge
P S T (Ref:HM00596)

## ALLEN ASSOCIATES
**Allen Associates**, 3 Longmeade Gardens, Wilmslow, **Cheshire**, SK9 1DA, ENG.
(T) 07702 714821
Speciality: Hypnotherapy.
B (Ref:HM00597)

## ALLEN HINDE - PHYSIOTHERAPIST
**Allen Hinde - Physiotherapist**, 47 Roberts St, Wellingborough, **Northamptonshire**, NN8 3HY, ENG.
(T) 01933 227663 (F) 01933 227663
(E) ahinde@supanet.com
Speciality: Acupressure, Acupuncture, Electrotherapy, Kinesiology, Manipulation, Massage (Therapeutic), Ultrasonics, Interferential Current Therapy, Exercise Therapy, Postural Re-Education, Spinal(sertebral)Traction, Transcutaneous Electrical Nerve Stimulation, Electro-Acupuncture. ✔
● **Physiotherapist Private Practitioner**
Mr A Hinde Q: BA, Grad Dip Phys, MA, MCSP, SRP. M: CSP.
S Yrs. Est.: 15 (Ref:HM00598)

## ALLEN, BARBARA
**Barbara Allen**, Leamington Rd, Coventry, **Midlands (West)**, CV3 6GF, ENG.
(T) 024 7650 4349
Speciality: Clairvoyants & Palmists.
● **Owner** Mrs B Allen
B (Ref:HM00599)

## ALLEN, BRIAN C
**Brian C Allen**, 15 Gurston Rise, Northampton, **Northamptonshire**, NN3 5HY, ENG.
(T) 01604 406538
Speciality: Hypnosis.
● **Owner** Mr B Allen
B (Ref:HM00600)

## ALLEN, C E
**C E Allen**, Dolgran Isaf, Pencader, **Carmarthenshire**, SA39 9BY, WAL.
(T) 01559 384751
Speciality: Chiropodists (Podiatrists).
● **Owner** Mrs C Allen
S (Ref:HM00601)

## ALLEN, CAROL
**Carol Allen**, 4 Nostell Lane, Ryhill, Wakefield, **Yorkshire (West)**, WF4 2DB, ENG.
(T) 01226 723139
Speciality: Chiropody.
● **Owner** Ms C Allen
S (Ref:HM00602)

## ALLEN, CAROL
**Carol Allen**, 6 Nelson Sq, London, **London (Greater)**, SE1 0PY, ENG.
(T) 020 7207 3370
(W) www.changingtack.com
Speciality: Hypnotherapy, Life Style Coaching. ✔
● **Hypnotherapist** Mr R Allen Q: NLP (Master). M: ANLP.

Key: B Mind-Body Medicine C Complementary Medicine H Self Help Treatment M Medicinal Therapy O Oriental Medicine P Postural Therapy S Manipulative Structural Therapy T Touch Therapy

● **Hypnotherapist** Mrs C Allen M: HA.
C Yrs. Est.: 4 (**Ref:**HM00603)

**ALLEN, CAROL**

**Carol Allen**, 89 The Crescent, Eastleigh, **Hampshire**, SO50 9BQ, **ENG**.
(T) 023 8057 5703
Speciality: Complementary Medicines & Therapy.
C M (**Ref:**HM00604)

**ALLEN, CARRIE**

**Carrie Allen**, Hastings, **Sussex (East)**, TN34, ENG.
(T) 01424 427771
Speciality: Bach Remedies.
M (**Ref:**HM00605)

**ALLEN, CHERYL**

**Cheryl Allen**, Holmbush Rd, St. Austell, **Cornwall**, PL25 3LF, **ENG**.
(T) 01726 69486
Speciality: Psychotherapy.
● **Owner** Ms C Allen
B (**Ref:**HM00606)

**ALLEN, D**

**D Allen**, Diggle, Oldham, **Lancashire**, OL3 5NT, ENG.
(T) 07071 224320
Speciality: Chiropodists (Podiatrists).
● **Owner** Mr D Allen
S (**Ref:**HM00607)

**ALLEN, ELAINE**

**Elaine Allen**, 67 Ivybridge Rd, Coventry, **Midlands (West)**, CV3 5PF, **ENG**.
(T) 024 7641 6753
Speciality: Aromatherapy, Reflexology. ✔
● **Owner/Aromatherapist** Mrs E Allen
Q: Dip.Arom. M: ICHT, IFR.
C Yrs. Est.: 4 (**Ref:**HM00608)

**ALLEN, GEOFFREY**

**Geoffrey Allen**, 7 Brampton Walk, Northampton, **Northamptonshire**, NN3 6EJ, **ENG**.
(T) 01604 495060
Speciality: Hypnosis.
B (**Ref:**HM00609)

**ALLEN, GRAHAM M**

**Graham M Allen**, Dorking Chiropractic Clinic, 316 High St, Dorking, **Surrey**, RH4 1QX, **ENG**.
(T) 01306 887793
Speciality: Chiropractors.
P S T (**Ref:**HM00610)

**ALLEN, J**

**J Allen**, 35 Blagreaves Lane, Littleover, Derby, **Derbyshire**, DE23 7FJ, **ENG**.
(T) 01332 766909
Speciality: Chiropodists (Podiatrists).
S (**Ref:**HM00611)

**ALLEN, J**

**Mr J Allen**, 60 Woodbridge Rd, Guildford, **Surrey**, GU1 4RF, **ENG**.
(T) 01483 571783
Speciality: Physiotherapy.
P S T (**Ref:**HM00612)

**ALLEN, JULIE & LEN**

**Julie & Len Allen**, 10 Fairgreen East, Cockfosters, **Hertfordshire**, EN4 0QR, **ENG**.
(T) 020 8441 2704
Speciality: Cognitive Therapy, Counselling, Homeopathy, Hypnosis, Hypnotherapy, Psychotherapy, Stress Therapy. ✔
● **Therapist** Mr L Allen Q: BSc, MNCH.
● **Therapist** Dr J Allen Q: MHMA, MNCH.
B Yrs. Est.: 28 (**Ref:**HM00613)

**ALLEN, R D**

**R D Allen**, 30 St Peters Way, Chorleywood, Rickmansworth, **Hertfordshire**, WD3 5QE, **ENG**.
(T) 01923 282016
Speciality: Complementary Medicines & Therapy.
C M (**Ref:**HM00614)

**ALLEN, RICHARD**

**Richard Allen**, 41 Armoury Gardens, Shrewsbury, **Shropshire**, SY2 6PL, **ENG**.
(T) 01743 365746
Speciality: Osteopathy.
P S T (**Ref:**HM00615)

**ALLEN, S**

**S Allen**, 109 Shore Rd, Kircubbin, Newtownards, **County Down**, BT22 2RP, **NIR**.
(T) 028 4273 8395
Speciality: Physiotherapy.
P S T (**Ref:**HM00616)

**ALLEN, S**

**S Allen**, 42 Wood Lane, Hucknall, Nottingham, **Nottinghamshire**, NG15 6LR, **ENG**.
(T) 01159 559786
Speciality: Physiotherapy.
● **Owner** Mrs S Allen
P S T (**Ref:**HM00617)

**ALLEN, SANDRA**

**Sandra Allen**, Chapel St, Northwich, **Cheshire**, CW8 1HD, **ENG**.
(T) 01606 781430
Speciality: Complementary Medicines & Therapy.
M (**Ref:**HM00618)

**ALLEN, SUSAN**

**Susan Allen**, 41 Armoury Gardens, Shrewsbury, **Shropshire**, SY2 6PL, **ENG**.
(T) 01743 365746
Speciality: Osteopathy.
P S T (**Ref:**HM00619)

**ALLEN, SUSAN**

**Susan Allen**, P O Box 7, Teddington, **London (Greater)**, TW11 9SZ, **ENG**.
(T) 020 8943 2899
Speciality: Reflexology.
● **Owner** Ms S Allen
S T (**Ref:**HM00620)

**ALLEN, TRICIA**

**Tricia Allen**, 172 Dunstans Rd, London, **London (Greater)**, SE22 0ES, **ENG**.
(T) 020 8693 7701
Speciality: Homeopathy.
● **Owner** Mrs T Allen
M (**Ref:**HM00621)

**ALLEN, W A**

**W A Allen**, 6 The Wayne Way, Leicester, **Leicestershire**, LE5 4PP, **ENG**.
(T) 01162 762306
Speciality: Clairvoyants & Palmists.
B (**Ref:**HM00622)

**ALLEN, WENDY**

**Wendy Allen**, 3 Hocroft Rd, London, **London (Greater)**, NW2 2BN, **ENG**.
(T) 020 7435 9506
Speciality: Osteopathy.
P S T (**Ref:**HM00623)

**ALLEN-DAVIES, GAIL**

**Gail Allen-Davies**, 1st Floor Woburn Court, 8 Guildhall Hill, Norwich, **Norfolk**, NR2 1JG, **ENG**.
(T) 01603 219254
Speciality: Complementary Medicines & Therapy.
● **Partner** Mrs G Allen-Davies
M (**Ref:**HM00624)

**ALLENS**

**Allens & Co**, 67 Gleneagles Way, Fixby, Huddersfield, **Yorkshire (West)**, HD2 2NH, **ENG**.
(T) 01484 519251 (F) 01484 549032
(W) www.allenshealthcare.co.uk
Speciality: Complementary Medicines & Therapy.
● **Therapist** Mr H Dixon
C Yrs. Est.: 30 (**Ref:**HM00625)

**ALLENS**

**Allens & Co**, Fresh Winds, Pentraeth, **Isle of Anglesey**, LL75 8YF, **WAL**.
(T) 01248 450604
Speciality: Complementary Medicines & Therapy.
C M (**Ref:**HM00626)

**ALLERGY & ENVIRONMENTAL MED**

**Allergy & Environmental Medicine**, Complementary Medical Centre, Roynon Way, Cheddar, **Somerset**, BS27 3NZ, **ENG**.
(T) 01934 744574
Speciality: Complementary Medicines & Therapy.
● **Manager** Ms J Harris
M (**Ref:**HM00627)

**ALLERGY CARE**

**Allergy Care**, Flat 17 Gladeside Court, Succombs Hill, Warlingham, **Surrey**, CR6 9JG, ENG.
(T) 01883 626446
Speciality: Complementary Medicines & Therapy.
C M (**Ref:**HM00628)

**ALLERGY CLINIC-EASTBOURNE CLNC**

**Allergy Clinic - Eastbourne Clinic of Natural Medicine**, 69 Meads Rd, Eastbourne, **Sussex (East)**, BN20 7QL, **ENG**.
(T) 01323 734664
Speciality: Homeopathy.
M (**Ref:**HM00629)

**ALLERGY DETECT & NTRL HEALING**

**Allergy Detection & Natural Healing**, 40 Grant Rd, **Hampshire**, PO6 1DX, **ENG**.
(T) 023 9278 9253
Speciality: Complementary Medicines & Therapy.
C M (**Ref:**HM00630)

**ALLERGY SHOP**

**Allergy Shop Ltd (The)**, 15 Beech Hill, Haywards Heath, **Sussex (West)**, RH16 3RY, ENG.
(T) 01444 414290
Speciality: Complementary Medicines & Therapy.
● **Joint Director** Mrs A Lee
C M (**Ref:**HM00631)

**ALLERGY TESTING**

**Allergy Testing**, 1 Leicester Rd, Preston, **Lancashire**, PR1 1PP, **ENG**.
(T) 01772 825529
Speciality: Complementary Medicines & Therapy.
C M (**Ref:**HM00632)

**ALLERGY TESTING**

**Allergy Testing**, Lower Cookham Rd, Maidenhead, **Berkshire**, SL6 8JH, **ENG**.
(T) 01628 412645 (F) 01628 412645
Speciality: Complementary Medicines & Therapy.
● **Owner** Ms B North
C M (**Ref:**HM00633)

**ALLERGY TESTING**

**Allergy Testing**, 2 Livingstone Rd, Gravesend, **Kent**, DA12 5DZ, **ENG**.
(T) 01474 356729 (F) 01474 560326
Speciality: Complementary Medicines & Therapy.
● **Owner** Mr R Baines
M (**Ref:**HM00634)

**ALLERGY TESTING CLINIC**

**Allergy Testing Clinic Ltd**, 564 Howth Rd, Raheny, **County Dublin**, **IRE**.
(T) 01851 0285
Speciality: Complementary Medicines & Therapy.
M (**Ref:**HM00635)

**ALLERGY TESTING SERVICE**

**Allergy Testing Service**, 29 Lyndhurst Avenue, Pinner, **London (Greater)**, HA5 3UZ, **ENG**.
(T) 020 8429 3724
Speciality: Homeopathy.
M (**Ref:**HM00636)

**ALLERGY THERAPY**

**Allergy Therapy & Natural Healing**, 137 Albert Rd, Southsea, Portsmouth, **Hampshire**, PO5 2SQ, **ENG**.
(T) 023 9278 9253
(W) www.arragorn.co.uk
Speciality: Counselling, Healing Therapy, Homeopathy, Indian Head Massage, Reflexology, Reiki, Shiatsu. ✔
● **Owner/Allergy Therapist** Mrs H Humble
C Yrs. Est.: 17 (**Ref:**HM00637)



Key continued: **Yrs.Est:** Years Established **Q:** Qualifications **M:** Professional Membership ✔ Indemnity Insurance Accept Credit Cards

### ALLERTON CLINIC
**Allerton Chiropractic & Acupuncture Clinic**, 2 Queensdale Rd, Liverpool, **Merseyside**, L18 1LT, **ENG**.
**(T)** 01517 335715 **(F)** 01517 335715
**Speciality:** Chiropractic.
● **Owner** Mr L Davies
[P] [S] [T] (**Ref:**HM00638)

### ALLERTON HEALTH CENTRE
**Allerton Health Centre**, 615 Smithdown Rd, Liverpool, **Merseyside**, L15 5AG, **ENG**.
**(T)** 01517 345909
**Speciality:** Acupuncture, Chinese Herbal Medicine, Osteopathy, Remedial Massage. ✔
● **Owner** Mr M McCrink
[O] (**Ref:**HM00639)

### ALLERTON MOBILE PHYSIOTHERAPY
**Allerton Mobile Physiotherapy Service**, 24 Edale Rd, Liverpool, **Merseyside**, L18 5HR, **ENG**.
**(T)** 01517 242780
**Speciality:** Physiotherapy.
● **Partner** Mrs F Cowell
[P] [S] [T] (**Ref:**HM00640)

### ALLERTON MOBILE PHYSIOTHERAPY
**Allerton Mobile Physiotherapy Service**, 89 Elm Hall Drive, Liverpool, **Merseyside**, L18 5HY, **ENG**.
**(T)** 01517 241757
**Speciality:** Physiotherapy.
● **Partner** Mrs J Pope
[P] [S] [T] (**Ref:**HM00641)

### ALLERTON REMEDIAL CLINIC
**Allerton Remedial Clinic**, 4 Greenbank Rd, Liverpool, **Merseyside**, L18 1HN, **ENG**.
**(T)** 01517 337632
**Speciality:** Osteopathy.
● **Owner** Mr M Hammond
[P] [S] [T] (**Ref:**HM00642)

### ALLFREE, J & M (DR)
**Dr J Allfree & Dr M Allfree**, 42 Nottingham Rd, Mansfield, **Nottinghamshire**, NG18 1BL, **ENG**.
**(T)** 01623 641611
**Speciality:** Osteopathy.
[C] [P] [S] [T] (**Ref:**HM00643)

### ALLIANCE OF PSYCHOTHERAPISTS
**Alliance Of Registered Psychotherapists South (The)**, 6 Owen Walk, London, **London (Greater)**, SE20 8BY, **ENG**.
**(T)** 020 8659 8486
**Speciality:** Psychotherapy.
[B] (**Ref:**HM00644)

### ALLIDINA, PARVIZ
**Parviz Allidina**, Fairway Avenue, Borehamwood, **Hertfordshire**, WD6 1PU, **ENG**.
**(T)** 020 8537 1486
**Speciality:** Physiotherapy.
● **Owner** Mr H Allidina
[P] [S] [T] (**Ref:**HM00645)

### ALLIED PHYSIOTHERAPY
**Allied Physiotherapy**, 2 Burlington Cres, Rhyl, **Denbighshire**, LL18 2RA, **WAL**.
**(T)** 01745 339892
**Speciality:** Acupressure, Manipulation, Massage (Therapeutic), Osteopathy. ✔
● **Physiotherapist/Chiropodist**
Mr L Shirt **Q:** MAB Phys, MBChA, SMAE. **M:** AB Phys.
[S] **Yrs. Est.:** 8 (**Ref:**HM00646)

### ALLINSON, IAN
**Ian Allinson**, 188 Tynemouth Rd, North Shields, **Tyne and Wear**, NE30 1EG, **ENG**.
**(T)** 01912 591683
**Speciality:** Chiropodists (Podiatrists).
● **Owner** Mr I Allinson
[S] (**Ref:**HM00647)

### ALLINSON, IAN
**Ian Allinson**, 3 Bedford St, Middlesbrough, **Cleveland**, TS1 2LL, **ENG**.
**(T)** 01642 223442
**Speciality:** Chiropodists (Podiatrists).
● **Owner** Mr I Allinson
[S] (**Ref:**HM00648)

### ALLISON JOY REFLEXOLOGY
**Allison Joy Reflexology**, 22 Carolina House, Dove St, Bristol, BS2 8LJ, **ENG**.
**(T)** 01179 245918
**Speciality:** Reflexology.
[M] (**Ref:**HM00649)

### ALLISON, C (DR)
**Dr C Allison**, Fairfields Clinic, Skippetts Lane West, Basingstoke, **Hampshire**, RG21 3HP, **ENG**.
**(T)** 01256 326980
**Speciality:** Psychotherapy.
[B] (**Ref:**HM00650)

### ALLISON, V C
**V C Allison**, Holly Copse House, Tothill, Burghclere, Newbury, **Berkshire**, RG20 9ED, **ENG**.
**(T)** 01635 278390
**Speciality:** Complementary Medicines & Therapy.
● **Owner** Mrs V Allison
[M] (**Ref:**HM00651)

### ALLMAN, ANNE
**Anne Allman**, 35 Buchanan Avenue, Walsall, **Midlands (West)**, WS4 2ER, **ENG**.
**(T)** 01922 611596
**Speciality:** Hypnotherapy.
● **Owner** Mrs A Allman
[B] (**Ref:**HM00652)

### ALLMAN, JANNINE
**Jannine Allman**, 35 Cornbury Cres, Downhead Park, Milton Keynes, **Buckinghamshire**, MK15 9AR, **ENG**.
**(T)** 01908 606376
**Speciality:** Complementary Medicines & Therapy.
[C] [M] (**Ref:**HM00653)

### ALLMAN, LESLIE
**Leslie Allman**, 32 Grange Lane, Cople, Bedford, **Bedfordshire**, MK44 3TT, **ENG**.
**(T)** 01234 831609 **(F)** 01234 838326
**Speciality:** Psychotherapy.
● **Owner** Miss L Allman
[B] (**Ref:**HM00654)

### ALLONBY, R M
**R M Allonby**, Curlew Cottage, Grasmere, Ambleside, **Cumbria**, LA22 9RQ, **ENG**.
**(T)** 01539 435583
**Speciality:** Physiotherapy.
[P] [S] [T] (**Ref:**HM00655)

### ALLOT, ALISON M
**Alison M Allot**, 43 Ridgebourne Rd, Shrewsbury, **Shropshire**, SY3 9AB, **ENG**.
**(T)** 01743 243273
**Speciality:** Osteopathy.
● **Owner** Mrs A Allot
[P] [S] [T] (**Ref:**HM00656)

### ALLSHORN, S
**S Allshorn**, All Hallows House, Idol Lane, London, **London (Greater)**, EC3R 5DD, **ENG**.
**(T)** 020 7283 8908
**Speciality:** Herbalists.
[M] (**Ref:**HM00657)

### ALLSHORN, SUSAN
**Susan Allshorn**, Hillside, Clay Tye Rd, Upminster, **Essex**, RM14 3PL, **ENG**.
**(T)** 01708 226061
**Speciality:** Herbal Medicine.
● **Owner** Mrs S Allshorn
[M] (**Ref:**HM00658)

### ALLSOP, A
**A Allsop**, 24 Pastureside Ter West, Clayton, Bradford, **Yorkshire (West)**, BD14 6LW, **ENG**.
**(T)** 01274 816098
**Speciality:** Hypnotherapy.
● **Owner** Suzanne Allsop
[B] (**Ref:**HM00659)

### ALLSOP, L M
**L M Allsop**, 8 Clinton Avenue, Luton, **Bedfordshire**, LU2 7LT, **ENG**.
**(T)** 01582 455435
**Speciality:** Physiotherapy.
[P] [S] [T] (**Ref:**HM00660)

### ALLSOP, M A
**M A Allsop**, 5 Southland Park Cres, Wembury, Plymouth, **Devon**, PL9 0HB, **ENG**.
**(T)** 01752 862902
**Speciality:** Chiropodists (Podiatrists).
● **Owner** Mr M Allsop
[S] (**Ref:**HM00661)

### ALLSOPP, EMMA
**Emma Allsopp**, 3 Shute Court, Shute Hill, Bishopsteignton, Teignmouth, **Devon**, TQ14 9QL, **ENG**.
**(T)** 01626 772799
**Speciality:** Reflexology.
[S] [T] (**Ref:**HM00662)

### ALLTREE COMPLEMENTARY THERAPY
**Alltree Complementary Therapy**, Linthorpe Avenue, Wembley, **London (Greater)**, HA0 2HL, **ENG**.
**(T)** 020 8903 7347
**Speciality:** Complementary Medicines & Therapy.
[M] (**Ref:**HM00663)

### ALM, DENISE
**Denise Alm**, South Manse, Abernyte, Perth, **Perth and Kinross**, PH14 9SJ, **SCO**.
**(T)** 01828 686364
**Speciality:** Reflexology.
● **Owner** Ms D Alm
[S] [T] (**Ref:**HM00664)

### ALMOND HOUSE HYPNOTHERAPY
**Almond House Hypnotherapy Centre**, 17 Bell Lane, Orrell, Wigan, **Lancashire**, WN5 0DH, **ENG**.
**(T)** 01942 728605
**Speciality:** Hypnotherapy.
[B] (**Ref:**HM00665)

### ALNWICK CHIROPODY CLINIC
**Alnwick Chiropody Clinic**, Bondgate Without, Alnwick, **Northumberland**, NE66 1PP, **ENG**.
**(T)** 01665 606566
**Speciality:** Chiropodists (Podiatrists).
● **Owner** Miss H Seward
[S] (**Ref:**HM00666)

### ALOE IN ACTION
**Aloe In Action**, 115 Huntingdon Rd, Chatteris, **Cambridgeshire**, PE16 6EF, **ENG**.
**(T)** 01487 773374
**Speciality:** Complementary Medicines & Therapy.
● **Owner** Mrs F Peacock
[C] [M] (**Ref:**HM00667)

### ALOE PRODUCTS
**Aloe Products**, 31 Oak Tree Drive, London, **London (Greater)**, N20 8QJ, **ENG**.
**(T)** 07000 626654 **(F)** 020 8343 7990
**Speciality:** Complementary Medicines & Therapy.
● **Owner** Mr M Barfield
[M] (**Ref:**HM00668)

### ALOE VERA
**Aloe Vera**, 65 Killycowan Rd, Glarryford, Ballymena, **County Antrim**, BT44 9HJ, **NIR**.
**(T)** 028 2568 5521 **(F)** 028 2568 5521
**(E)** tandagraham@onetel.net.uk
**Speciality:** Herbal Medicine.
● **Owner** Mr T Graham
[C] [M] **Yrs. Est.:** 10 (**Ref:**HM00669)

### ALOE VERA ADVICE CENTRE
**Aloe Vera Advice Centre (The)**, 8 Post House Wynd, Wynd, Darlington, **County Durham**, DL3 7LU, **ENG**.
**(T)** 01325 241488
**Speciality:** Complementary Medicines & Therapy.
● **Manager/Owner** Mr D Nattrass
[C] **Yrs. Est.:** 2 (**Ref:**HM00670)

### ALOE VERA ADVISORY SERVICE
**Aloe Vera Advisory Service**, 2 High Beech Farm, Rock Hill, Orpington, **Kent**, BR6 7PJ, **ENG**.
**(T)** 01959 533833 **(F)** 01959 533833
**Speciality:** Complementary Medicines & Therapy.
● **Owner** Miss S Alesbury
[M] (**Ref:**HM00671)

Key: [B] Mind-Body Medicine [C] Complementary Medicine [H] Self Help Treatment [M] Medicinal Therapy [O] Oriental Medicine [P] Postural Therapy [S] Manipulative Structural Therapy [T] Touch Therapy

## ALOE VERA ADVISORY SERVICE

**Aloe Vera Advisory Service**, Wellhill House, Well Hill, Orpington, **Kent**, BR6 7PR, ENG.
(T) 01959 533833
Speciality: Complementary Medicines & Therapy.
C M (Ref:HM00672)

## ALOE VERA CENTRE

**Aloe Vera Centre**, 15 Cabstand, Portishead, Bristol, BS20 7HW, ENG.
(T) 01275 849997 (F) 01275 817762
Speciality: Complementary Medicines & Therapy.
● **Owner** Mrs R Knight
C M (Ref:HM00673)

## ALOE VERA CENTRE

**Aloe Vera Centre (The)**, Casa Del Monte, Hall Cliffe Rd, Horbury, Wakefield, **Yorkshire (West)**, WF4 6BX, ENG.
(T) 01924 261399 (F) 01924 261399
Speciality: Complementary Medicines & Therapy.
● **Owner** Mrs S Firth
C M (Ref:HM00674)

## ALOE VERA DIRECT

**Aloe Vera Direct**, 342 Wellfield St, Warrington, **Cheshire**, WA5 1PX, ENG.
(T) 01925 659425
Speciality: Complementary Medicines & Therapy.
C M (Ref:HM00675)

## ALOE VERA FOREVER LVNG PRDCTS

**Aloe Vera Forever Living Products Centre**, 2 Old Hay Cl, Dore, Sheffield, **Yorkshire (South)**, S17 3GQ, ENG.
(T) 01142 366712
Speciality: Complementary Medicines & Therapy.
C M (Ref:HM00676)

## ALOE VERA INTERNATIONAL

**Aloe Vera International Ltd**, The Coppice, Intakes Lane, Turnditch, Belper, **Derbyshire**, DE56 2LU, ENG.
(T) 01335 372020 (F) 01335 370656
Speciality: Complementary Medicines & Therapy.
● **Director** Mr S Yates
C M (Ref:HM00677)

## ALOE VERA NATURAL HEALTH CTRE

**Aloe Vera Natural Health Centre**, 33 Claremont Rd, Whitley Bay, **Tyne and Wear**, NE26 3TN, ENG.
(T) 01912 970007
Speciality: Complementary Medicines & Therapy.
C M (Ref:HM00678)

## ALOE VERA NATURAL HEALTHCARE

**Aloe Vera Natural Healthcare**, 91 Limbrick Lane, Goring-By-Sea, Worthing, **Sussex (West)**, BN12 6AF, ENG.
(T) 01903 529267
Speciality: Complementary Medicines & Therapy.
C M (Ref:HM00679)

## ALOE VERA PRODUCT CENTRE

**Aloe Vera Product Centre**, Lower Stock Farm East, Bakers Lane, Langford, Bristol, BS40 5HT, ENG.
(T) 01934 862997 (F) 01934 862997
Speciality: Complementary Medicines & Therapy.
● **Owner** Mrs C Baker
M (Ref:HM00680)

## ALOE VERA SPECIALISTS

**Rayvon Enterprises**, Brook House, Water Lane, Kempston, Bedford, **Bedfordshire**, MK42 7BJ, ENG.
(T) 01234 843393 (F) 01234 843017
(E) rayclarke@bigfoot.com
Speciality: Counselling, Herbal Medicine, Vitamin Therapy. ✔ [Credit]
● **Sole Owner** Mr R Clarke
M Yrs. Est.: 22 (Ref:HM00681)

## ALPHA AROMATHERAPY

**Alpha Aromatherapy**, 10 Mill Cl, Haslemere, **Surrey**, GU27 1SA, ENG.
(T) 01428 654421
Speciality: Aromatherapy.
● **Owner** Miss A Benson
M O (Ref:HM00682)

## ALPHA CONSULTANCY

**Alpha Consultancy**, Orchard Cottage, Darby Gardens, Sunbury-On-Thames, **Surrey**, TW16 5JW, ENG.
(T) 01932 789600
Speciality: Hypnotherapy.
● **Owner** Mr H Christensen
B (Ref:HM00683)

## ALPHA HYPNOTHERAPY

**Alpha Hypnotherapy: Hypnosis For Healing**, Garden Flat, 112A Ditchling Rise, Brighton, **Sussex (East)**, BN1 4QR, ENG.
(T) 01273 675435
(E) janeporter@talk21.com
(W) www.uk-therapy.com/alphahypnotherapy
Speciality: Hypnosis, Hypnotherapy, Psychotherapy. ✔
● **Hypnotherapist** Ms J Porter Q: BSc (Hons), Dip.Hyp, Dip.Psych. M: HA.
B Yrs. Est.: 1 (Ref:HM00684)

## ALPHAWAVE

**Alphawave**, 16 Darwen St, Blackburn, **Lancashire**, BB2 2BY, ENG.
(T) 01254 706604
(E) nick@awave.freeserve.co.uk
Speciality: Cognitive Therapy, Hypnotherapy, EMDR - Eye Movement Desensitisation and Reprocessing. ✔
● **Owner** Mr N Crighton Q: BA, C.Hyp, CQSW, DMS. M: BABCP, UKCP.
B Yrs. Est.: 8 (Ref:HM00685)

## ALSING, FABIENNE

**Fabienne Alsing**, 20 Coppice Walk, Shirley, Solihull, **Midlands (West)**, B90 4HY, ENG.
(T) 01564 702186
Speciality: Acupuncture.
● **Partner** Mrs J Spence
O (Ref:HM00686)

## ALSMEER CHIROPODY SERVICE

**Alsmeer Chiropody Service**, 70 Sullington Gardens, Worthing, **Sussex (West)**, BN14 0HS, ENG.
(T) 01903 872831
Speciality: Chiropodists (Podiatrists).
● **Owner** Mr J Weaver
S (Ref:HM00687)

## ALSTON, S R

**S R Alston**, 4 Hazelwood Cl, Basingstoke, **Hampshire**, RG23 8LD, ENG.
(T) 01256 358306 (F) 01256 358306
Speciality: Physiotherapy.
● **Owner** Mr S Alston
P S T (Ref:HM00688)

## ALTERED STATES FLOTATION CTRE

**Altered States Flotation Centre**, 4 Marlborough Rd, Wootton Bassett, Swindon, **Wiltshire**, SN4 7EJ, ENG.
(T) 01793 855414
Speciality: Complementary Medicines & Therapy.
M (Ref:HM00689)

## ALTER-MED

**Alter-Med**, 63 Sandcliffe Rd, Midway, Swadlincote, **Derbyshire**, DE11 7PH, ENG.
(T) 01283 218009
Speciality: Aromatherapy, Massage (Therapeutic), Reflexology, Phrase Reflexology.
● **Therapist** Mrs Brewin
C Yrs. Est.: 10 (Ref:HM00690)

## ALTERNATE THERAPY

**Alternate Therapy**, 17 Swallow Cl, Totton, Southampton, **Hampshire**, SO40 7JA, ENG.
(T) 023 8086 4761
Speciality: Aromatherapy.
M O (Ref:HM00691)

## ALTERNATE WAYS

**Alternate Ways**, 15 Cawardon, Stantonbury, Milton Keynes, **Buckinghamshire**, MK14 6AH, ENG.
(T) 01908 313898
Speciality: Complementary Medicines & Therapy, Body Massage and Colour Puncture (Needle Free Acupunture with Lights). ✔
● **Complementary Practitioner** Mr A Howlings Q: IIHHT, VTCT. M: IIHHT.
● **Complementary Practitioner** Ms M Howlings Q: IIHHT. M: IIHHT.
C Yrs. Est.: 5 (Ref:HM00692)

## ALTERNATIVE ANIMAL CARE

**Alternative Animal Care**, Barley Hill Roscarbery, **County Cork**, IRE.
(T) 08724 94059
(E) alternanimalcare@eircom.net
Speciality: Homeopathy.
M (Ref:HM00693)

## ALTERNATIVE APPROACH

**Alternative Approach**, 154 Leigh Rd, Wimborne, **Dorset**, BH21 2DB, ENG.
(T) 01202 880136
Speciality: Chiropractic, Cranio-Sacral Therapy, Homeopathy. ✔ [Credit]
● **Chiropractor** Dr R Drake Q: BSc, MSc (Chiro).
● **Chiropractor** Dr N Karmazi Q: DC.
P Yrs. Est.: 18 (Ref:HM00694)

## ALTERNATIVE APPROACHES

**Alternative Approaches, Wendy Grace**, 3 Montpelier Avenue, Bexley, **Kent**, DA5 3AP, ENG.
(T) 020 8304 6540
Speciality: Hypnotherapy.
B (Ref:HM00695)

## ALTERNATIVE BACK CARE

**Alternative Back Care**, 5 Wellington Rd, Bilston, **Midlands (West)**, WV14 6AA, ENG.
(T) 01902 408458
Speciality: Osteopathy.
P S T (Ref:HM00696)

## ALTERNATIVE CHOICES

**Alternative Choices**, 28 Beehive Lane, Welwyn Garden City, **Hertfordshire**, AL7 4BQ, ENG.
(T) 01707 320449 (F) 01707 375324
Speciality: Acupuncture, Chinese Herbal Medicine, Crystal Healing, Herbal Medicine, Reiki, Chinese Herbs. ✔ [Credit]
● **Owner/Acupuncturist/Herbalist** Mrs N Todd Q: Lic.Ac, MBAcC. M: BAcC.
B Yrs. Est.: 3 (Ref:HM00697)

## ALTERNATIVE HEALING CENTRE

**Alternative Healing Centre**, 15 Bishopswood, Brackla, Bridgend, CF31 2LT, WAL.
(T) 01656 668427
(E) alternativehealing@hotmail.com
(W) www.alternativehealinguk.com
Speciality: Absent Healing, Auto Suggestion, Aversion Therapy, Colour Therapy, Family Therapy, Group Therapy, Healer, Healing Therapy, Holistic Healing, Hypnosis, Hypnotherapy, Indian Head Massage, Metamorphic Therapy, Psychotherapy, Reiki, Stress Therapy, Visualisation Therapy. ✔
● **Owner/Tutor/Healer** Ms P Broom Q: Dip.Hyp, Reiki Master. M: GTH.
B Yrs. Est.: 10 (Ref:HM00698)

## ALTERNATIVE HEALING CENTRE

**Alternative Healing Centre (The)**, Stonebridge Mill, Kestor Lane, Longridge, Preston, **Lancashire**, PR3 3JX, ENG.
(T) 01772 782782
Speciality: Complementary Medicines & Therapy.
● **Owner** Mrs M Hall
M (Ref:HM00699)

## ALTERNATIVE HEALTH & BEAUTY

**Alternative Health & Beauty**, 15 Bidwell Hill, Houghton Regis, Dunstable, **Bedfordshire**, LU5 5DR, ENG.
(T) 01582 867858 (F) 01582 867858
Speciality: Chiropodists (Podiatrists).
● **Owner** Mrs P Hill
S (Ref:HM00700)



Key continued: Yrs.Est: Years Established Q: Qualifications M: Professional Membership ✔ Indemnity Insurance [Credit] Accept Credit Cards

## ALTERNATIVE HEALTH & BEAUTY

**Alternative Health & Beauty**, 33 Rydal Avenue, Ramsgate, **Kent**, CT11 0PU, ENG.
(T) 01843 850489
Speciality: Beauty Therapy, Trichology.
H T (Ref:HM00701)

## ALTERNATIVE HEALTH CARE

**Alternative Heath Care**, 78 Langley Rd, Chedgrave, Norwich, **Norfolk**, NR14 6HE, ENG.
(T) 01508 520546
(E) alternative-healthcare@ukgateway.net
Speciality: Iridology, Nutritional Therapy, Study of the Eye. ✓
● **Natural Medicine Practitioner** Mrs M Johnson Q: D.Th.D. M: BANT.
C Yrs. Est.: 6 (Ref:HM00702)

## ALTERNATIVE HEALTH CENTRE

**Alternative Health Centre**, 88A Wellingborough Rd, Northampton, **Northamptonshire**, NN1 4DP, ENG.
(T) 01604 629248
Speciality: Aromatherapy.
● **Owner** Mrs K Boyles
M O (Ref:HM00703)

## ALTERNATIVE HEALTH CENTRE

**Alternative Health Centre (Widness)**, 75 Albert Rd, Widnes, **Cheshire**, WA8 6JS, ENG.
(T) 01514 203398
Speciality: Osteopathy.
P S T (Ref:HM00704)

## ALTERNATIVE HEALTH CENTRE

**Alternative Health Centre**, 1369 High Rd, London, **London (Greater)**, N20 9LN, ENG.
(T) 020 8445 2675 (F) 020 8445 4397
Speciality: Complementary Medicines & Therapy.
● **Sales Person** Mrs Thankey
C Yrs. Est.: 11 (Ref:HM00705)

## ALTERNATIVE HEALTH CLINICS

**Alternative Health Clinics**, Bury Complementary Health Centre, 12 Tenterden St, Bury, **Lancashire**, BL9 0EG, ENG.
(T) 01617 631660 (F) 01617 631660
Speciality: Complementary Medicines & Therapy.
C M (Ref:HM00706)

## ALTERNATIVE HEALTH INFORMATION

**Alternative Health Information Bureau**, Orchard Villa, Porters Park Drive, Shenley, Radlett, **Hertfordshire**, WD7 9DS, ENG.
(T) 01923 856222 (F) 01923 587670
Speciality: Complementary Medicines & Therapy.
● **Owner** Mr A Jackson
C M (Ref:HM00707)

## ALTERNATIVE HEALTH STUDIO

**Alternative Health Studio (The)**, 112 Widnes Rd, Widnes, **Cheshire**, WA8 6AX, ENG.
(T) 01514 953202
Speciality: Complementary Medicines & Therapy.
● **Partner** Miss J Chatterton
C M (Ref:HM00708)

## ALTERNATIVE HEALTH THERAPIES

**Alternative Health Therapies**, 42 Skipton Rd, Earby, Barnoldswick, **Lancashire**, BB18 6QB, ENG.
(T) 01282 844713
Speciality: Complementary Medicines & Therapy.
● **Owner** Mrs L Cliffe
M (Ref:HM00709)

## ALTERNATIVE MEDICAL CENTRE

**Alternative Medical Centre**, 34 Westfield St, St. Helens, **Merseyside**, WA10 1QF, ENG.
(T) 01744 451357
Speciality: Osteopathy.
● **Owner** Miss P McDonald
P S T (Ref:HM00710)

## ALTERNATIVE MEDICAL CLINIC

**Alternative Medical Clinic**, Alloa Business Centre, The Whins, Alloa, **Clackmannanshire**, FK10 3SA, SCO.
(T) 01259 723563 (F) 01259 723563
(E) altmed@altmed.ndirect.co.uk
(W) www.altmed.ndirect.co.uk
Speciality: Hypnosis, Magnetic Therapy, Reflexology, Remedial Massage, Passive Manipulation, Energy Release. ✓
● **Doctor** Dr A Campbell Q: D.Mag, DCM.
C Yrs. Est.: 26 (Ref:HM00711)

## ALTERNATIVE MEDICAL CLINIC

**Alternative Medical Clinic (The)**, 87 Upsdell Avenue, London, **London (Greater)**, N13 6JJ, ENG.
(T) 020 8881 6208
Speciality: Complementary Medicines & Therapy.
● **Owner** Mr A Constantis
C M (Ref:HM00712)

## ALTERNATIVE MEDICINE

**Alternative Medicine**, 36 Hollowfields Cl, Redditch, **Worcestershire**, B98 7NR, ENG.
(T) 01527 404012
Speciality: Acupuncture.
● **Owner** Dr N Rao
O (Ref:HM00713)

## ALTERNATIVE MEDICINE

**Alternative Medicine & Physical Rehabilitation**, 61 Waltham Rd, Grimsby, **Humberside (South)**, DN33 2ND, ENG.
(T) 01472 873001
Speciality: Complementary Medicines & Therapy.
● **Owner** Dr M Rao
C M (Ref:HM00714)

## ALTERNATIVE MEDICINE

**Natural Therapy Clinic (The)**, 1 Lindale Rd, Fulwood, Preston, **Lancashire**, PR2 8EQ, ENG.
(T) 01772 774373
Speciality: Acupuncture, Complementary Therapy, Counselling, Dietician, Douching, Electrotherapy, Hay Diet, Holistic Healing, Homeopathy, Hypnotherapy, Manipulation, Naturopathy, Nutritional Therapy, Orthomolecular Medicine, Osteopathy, Psionic Therapy, Reflexology, Ultrasonics, Vitamin Therapy. ✓
● **Therapist** Mr T Ryan Q: DO, MBRA. M: BRA.
● **Alternative Medicine Practitioner** Mr T Ryan Q: DO, MNCH, MNCP, RSHom. M: BRCP, NCP, Soc.Hom.
S Yrs. Est.: 35 (Ref:HM00715)

## ALTERNATIVE MEDICINE

**Alternative Medicine**, 80 Oakly Rd, Redditch, **Worcestershire**, B97 4EE, ENG.
(T) 01527 592172
Speciality: Acupuncture.
O (Ref:HM00716)

## ALTERNATIVE MEDICINE CENTRE

**Acupuncture Alternative Medicine Centre**, 14 Knottingley Rd, Pontefract, **Yorkshire (West)**, WF8 2LG, ENG.
(T) 01977 792738
Speciality: Osteopathy.
● **Owner** Mr T Peake
P S T (Ref:HM00717)

## ALTERNATIVE MEDICINE CENTRE

**Alternative Medicine Centre**, Polstead Rd, Oxford, **Oxfordshire**, OX2 6TN, ENG.
(T) 01865 554326
Speciality: Complementary Medicines & Therapy.
C M (Ref:HM00718)

## ALTERNATIVE MEDICINE CENTRE

**Alternative Medicine Centre**, 6 Cadzow St, Hamilton, **Lanarkshire (South)**, ML3 6DG, SCO.
(T) 01698 428889
Speciality: Complementary Medicines & Therapy.
● **Owner** Ms A Doherty
M (Ref:HM00719)

## ALTERNATIVE MEDICINE CLINIC

**Alternative Medicine Clinic**, 40 William St, **County Limerick**, IRE.
(T) 06141 8383
Speciality: Complementary Medicines & Therapy.
M (Ref:HM00720)

## ALTERNATIVE MEDICINE PRACTICE

**Natural Therapy Clinic (The)**, The Moorings, 7 Gorse Rd, Blackburn, **Lancashire**, BB2 6LY, ENG.
(T) 01254 55526
Speciality: Acupuncture, Complementary Therapy, Counselling, Dietician, Electrotherapy, Hay Diet, Holistic Healing, Homeopathy, Hypnotherapy, Manipulation, Naturopathy, Nutritional Therapy, Orthomolecular Medicine, Osteopathy, Psychotherapy, Reflexology, Ultrasonics, Vitamin Therapy. ✓
● **Alternative Medicine Practitioner** Mr T Ryan Q: DO, MNCH, MNCP, RSHom. M: BRCP, NCP, Soc.Hom.
● **Alternative Medicine Practitioner** Mr T Ryan Q: DO, MBRA. M: BRA.
S Yrs. Est.: 35 (Ref:HM00721)

## ALTERNATIVE MEDICINE PRACTICE

**Alternative Medicine Practice (The)**, 43 Preston New Rd, Blackburn, **Lancashire**, BB2 6AE, ENG.
(T) 01254 689264 (F) 01254 689264
Speciality: Complementary Medicines & Therapy.
● **Practice Manager** Mr M Harrison
C M (Ref:HM00722)

## ALTERNATIVE PRACTICE

**Alternative Practice**, 75 Huntly St, Aberdeen, **Aberdeenshire**, AB10 1TE, SCO.
(T) 01224 620987
Speciality: Aromatherapy, Bach Remedies, Indian Head Massage, Kinesiology, Reflexology, Reiki.
● **Owner/Sports Therapist** Mrs M Whyte
● **Aromatherapist/Reflexologist** Carol Black Q: GSSR, ITEC.
B C Yrs. Est.: 1 (Ref:HM00723)

## ALTERNATIVE REMEDIES

**Alternative Remedies**, 8 Elm Drive, Market Drayton, **Shropshire**, TF9 3HA, ENG.
(T) 01630 657922
Speciality: Complementary Medicines & Therapy.
● **Owner** Mrs P Shufflebotham
M (Ref:HM00724)

## ALTERNATIVE STRESS CENTRE

**Alternative Stress Centre**, 35 Springfield Rd, Glasgow, **Glasgow (City of)**, G40 3EL, SCO.
(T) 01415 504593 (F) 01415 501468
Speciality: Complementary Medicines & Therapy.
● **Manager** Ms L Curran
C M (Ref:HM00725)

## ALTERNATIVE THERAPIES

**Alternative Therapies**, 67 Norfolk St, King's Lynn, **Norfolk**, PE30 1AG, ENG.
(T) 01553 692022
Speciality: Complementary Medicines & Therapy.
● **Owner** Miss T Dix
M (Ref:HM00726)

## ALTERNATIVE THERAPIES

**Alternative Therapies By Tina Dilks**, 18 Exeter Rd, Southsea, **Hampshire**, PO4 9PZ, ENG.
(T) 023 9273 5178
Speciality: Complementary Medicines & Therapy.
C M (Ref:HM00727)

## ALTERNATIVE THERAPIES CENTRE

**Alternative Therapies Centre**, 52-52A Church St, Stoke Newington, London, **London (Greater)**, N16 0NB, ENG.
(T) 020 7249 9671
(W) www.alttherapies.co.uk
Speciality: Acupressure, Acupuncture, Alexander Technique, Aromatherapy, Bach Remedies, Biofeedback, Bowen Therapy, Complementary Therapy, Counselling, Cranial Osteopathy, Crystal Healing, Cupping, Floral Essence Therapy, Healer, Healing Therapy, Herbal Medicine, Holistic Healing, Homeopathy, Humanistic Psychology, Hypnosis, Hypnotherapy,



Key: B Mind-Body Medicine C Complementary Medicine H Self Help Treatment M Medicinal Therapy O Oriental Medicine P Postural Therapy S Manipulative Structural Therapy T Touch Therapy

Indian Head Massage, Manipulation, Massage (Therapeutic), Meditation, Moxibustion, Naturopathy, Nutritional Therapy, Oriental Diagnosis, Osteopathy, Psychotherapy, Pyscho-Synthesis, Reflexology, Reiki, Shiatsu, Stress Therapy, Touch Therapy, Zen Therapy. ✓
● **Teacher of the Alexander Technique** Mr C Neale **Q:** MSTAT.
● **Partner** Mrs J Sheridan
● **Acupuncturist** Ms K Scampton
● **Bowen Therapist** Mrs A Hughes **Q:** MSc.
● **Cranial Therapist** Mr A Wren **Q:** Dip.Psych. **M:** CTA.
**C** Yrs. Est.: 12 (**Ref:**HM00728)

### ALTERNATIVE THERAPIES CENTRE
**Alternative Therapies Centre**, 87 Heanor Rd, Ilkeston, **Derbyshire**, DE7 8DY, ENG.
**(T)** 01159 326152
Speciality: Herbalists.
● **Partner** Mr B Stevenson
**M** (**Ref:**HM00729)

### ALTERNATIVE THERAPIES TRAINING
**Alternative Therapies Training Centre**, 16 Dukes Wood Drive, Gerrards Cross, **Buckinghamshire**, SL9 7LR, ENG.
**(T)** 01753 890202 **(F)** 01753 884069
Speciality: Acupressure, Aromatherapy, Indian Head Massage, Oriental Diagnosis, Reflexology, Reiki, Shiatsu, Macrobotics, Karuna Healing, Anatomy, Physiology. ✓ 💳
● **Owner/Teacher** Mr P Hamouy
**C** Yrs. Est.: 9 (**Ref:**HM00730)

### ALTERNATIVE THERAPY
**Alternative Therapy**, 7 Peartree Avenue, Southampton, **Hampshire**, SO19 7JN, ENG.
**(T)** 023 8043 4273
Speciality: Homeopathy.
● **Owner** Mr F Bradley
**M** (**Ref:**HM00731)

### ALTERNATIVE THERAPY AT WORK
**Alternative Therapy At Work**, 233 Runley Rd, Luton, **Bedfordshire**, LU1 1TY, ENG.
**(T)** 01582 432215
Speciality: Acupressure, Aromatherapy, Complementary Therapy, Indian Head Massage, Massage (Therapeutic), Reflexology, Rolfing, Shiatsu, Stress Therapy, Touch Therapy, Holistic Facial Massage, Work Place Therapy. ✓
● **Principal Therapist** Mr M Bullock
**Q:** Dip.Holistic Therapy, Dip.Indian Head Massage, Dip.Reflex, Dip.StM. **M:** ICHT.
**T** Yrs. Est.: 2 (**Ref:**HM00732)

### ALTERNATIVE THERAPY CENTRE
**Alternative Therapy Centre**, 147 Demesne Rd, Wallington, **Surrey**, SM6 8EW, ENG.
**(T)** 020 8669 9377
Speciality: Homeopathy.
● **Owner** Mr D Soames
**M** (**Ref:**HM00733)

### ALTERNATIVE THERAPY CENTRE
**Alternative Therapy Centre**, 23B New St, Salisbury, **Wiltshire**, SP1 2PH, ENG.
**(T)** 01722 413652 **(F)** 01722 413652
Speciality: Complementary Medicines & Therapy.
● **Owner** Ms J Johnson-Newall
**M** (**Ref:**HM00734)

### ALTERNATIVE THERAPY CENTRE
**Alternative Therapy Centre**, 25 Lower Gungate, Tamworth, **Staffordshire**, B79 7AT, ENG.
**(T)** 01827 68374
**(E)** margaret.mcneill@virgin.net
Speciality: Absent Healing, Acupuncture, Alexander Technique, Aromatherapy, Bach Remedies, Counselling, Crystal Healing, Dowsing, Faith Healing, Healer, Healing Therapy, Herbal Medicine, Holistic Healing, Homeopathy, Hypnosis, Hypnotherapy, Indian Head Massage, Iridology, Life Style Coaching, Massage (Therapeutic), Nutritional Therapy, Osteopathy, Psychotherapy, Reflexology, Spiritual Healing, Stress Therapy, Visualisation Therapy, Vitamin Therapy. ✓
● **Acupuncturist** Ms M McNeill
**(T)** 01675 465726 **Q:** Lic.Ac. **M:** BAcC.
● **Hypnotherapist** Ms M Swinnerton **Q:** Dip.Hyp. **M:** UKGH.
● **Healer/Allergy Tester** Ms S Mercer **Q:** F.Inst.HFR, MNFSH. **M:** Inst.HFR, NFSH.
● **Aromatherapist** Ms B Williscroft **Q:** Dip.Arom. **M:** ISPA.
**M** Yrs. Est.: 18 (**Ref:**HM00735)

### ALTERNATIVELY
**Alternatively**, 74 Grassington Drive, Burnley, **Lancashire**, BB10 2SP, ENG.
**(T)** 01282 424193
Speciality: Reflexology.
● **Owner** Ms C Woskalo
**S** **T** (**Ref:**HM00736)

### ALTERNATIVES
**Alternatives**, 4 Warwick Lane, Warwick St, Worthing, **Sussex (West)**, BN11 3DP, ENG.
**(T)** 01903 211006
Speciality: Complementary Medicines & Therapy.
● **Owner** Ms S Besly
**C** **M** (**Ref:**HM00737)

### ALTERNATIVES
**Alternatives**, 8 Cosdach Avenue, Wallington, **Surrey**, SM6 9RA, ENG.
**(T)** 020 8288 2796
Speciality: Psychotherapy.
**B** (**Ref:**HM00738)

### ALTERNATIVES
**Alternatives**, 102 Park Avenue, Princes Avenue, Hull, **Humberside (North)**, HU5 3ET, ENG.
**(T)** 01482 345482
Speciality: Psychotherapy.
**B** (**Ref:**HM00739)

### ALTERNATIVES
**Alternatives**, Unit 16, Aylesfield Farm Buildings, Froyle Rd, Shalden, Alton, **Hampshire**, GU34 4BY, ENG.
**(T)** 01420 544848
Speciality: Homeopathy.
● **Manager** Mrs E Wills
**M** (**Ref:**HM00740)

### ALTERNATIVES
**Alternatives**, 12 Attingham Drive, Cannock, **Staffordshire**, WS11 2YB, ENG.
**(T)** 01543 270973
Speciality: Aromatherapy, Indian Head Massage, Massage (Therapeutic), Reflexology, Reiki. ✓
● **Alternative Therapist** Ms S Russell **Q:** IIHHT, ITEC. **M:** IHBC, ITEC.
**C** Yrs. Est.: 4 (**Ref:**HM00741)

### ALTERNATIVES
**Alternatives**, 9 Hilton Cl, Belton, Doncaster, **Yorkshire (South)**, DN9 1TJ, ENG.
**(T)** 01427 872907
**(W)** www.complementary-healthcare.co.uk/info/brown
Speciality: Hypnosis, Reflexology, Spiritual Healing.
**B** (**Ref:**HM00742)

### ALTERNATIVES COMP THERAPY CTRE
**Alternatives Ltd**, 118 High St, Northwood, **London (Greater)**, HA6 1BJ, ENG.
**(T)** 01923 828832
**(E)** fiona@alternatives.co.uk
**(W)** www.alternatives.co.uk
Speciality: Acupressure, Acupuncture, Aromatherapy, Bach Remedies, Complementary Therapy, Counselling, Herbal Medicine, Homeopathy, Hypnosis, Hypnotherapy, Massage (Therapeutic), Meditation, Moxibustion, Naturopathy, Nutritional Therapy, Osteopathy, Psychotherapy, Reflexology, Reiki, Shiatsu, Stress Therapy, Vitamin Therapy. ✓ 💳
● **Osteopath/Naturopath** Ms F Roberts **Q:** DO. **M:** GOsC.
● **Owner** Mr P Cook
**T** Yrs. Est.: 8 (**Ref:**HM00743)

### ALTERNATIVES NTRL HLTH CTRE
**Alternatives Natural Health & Fitness Centre**, 121 Eaton Rd, West Derby, Liverpool, **Merseyside**, L12 1LU, ENG.
**(T)** 01512 542424
Speciality: Complementary Medicines & Therapy.
**C** **M** (**Ref:**HM00744)

### ALTIMES, BERYL
**Beryl Altimes**, 136 Hoads Wood Rd, Hastings, **Sussex (East)**, TN34 2BA, ENG.
**(T)** 01424 420134
Speciality: Complementary Medicines & Therapy.
● **Owner** Mrs B Altimes
**C** **M** (**Ref:**HM00745)

### ALTINA, R J
**R J Altina**, 44 Kilburn High Rd, London, **London (Greater)**, NW6 4HJ, ENG.
**(T)** 020 7419 2928
Speciality: Osteopathy.
**P** **S** **T** (**Ref:**HM00746)

### ALTMAN, JEN
**Jen Altman**, Clissold Park Health Centre, 154 Stoke Newington Church St, London, **London (Greater)**, N16 0JU, ENG.
**(T)** 020 7249 2990 **(F)** 020 7249 3977
Speciality: Complementary Medicines & Therapy.
● **Director** Mr D Berg
**M** (**Ref:**HM00747)

### ALTON & JAMES MED HERBAL
**Alton & James Medical Herbalists**, 253 Sharrow Vale Rd, Sheffield, **Yorkshire (South)**, S11 8ZE, ENG.
**(T)** 01142 682468
**(E)** herbalist@cableinet.co.uk
Speciality: Allergy Testing, Bach Remedies, Complementary Therapy, Herbal Medicine, Holistic Healing, Phytotherapy, Allergy Therapy, Hair Analysis for Nutritional Status, Holistic Primary Medical Care. ✓
● **Medical Herbalist** Robyn James **Q:** Dip.Herb.Med. **M:** NIMH.
● **Medical Herbalist** Janet Alton **Q:** Dip.Herb.Med. **M:** NIMH.
**M** Yrs. Est.: 1 (**Ref:**HM00748)

### ALTON, C R
**C R Alton**, 82 Cantley Lane, Doncaster, **Yorkshire (South)**, DN4 6NH, ENG.
**(T)** 01302 537411
Speciality: Chiropractic.
**P** **S** **T** (**Ref:**HM00749)

### ALTONICS
**Altonics**, 119 Holloway Head, Birmingham, **Midlands (West)**, B1 1QP, ENG.
**(T)** 01216 433340 **(F)** 01216 439940
Speciality: Physiotherapy.
● **Owner** Mr A Warren
**P** **S** **T** (**Ref:**HM00750)

### ALTREE, CHRISTOPHER
**Christopher Altree**, 9 The Moorlands, Devizes, **Wiltshire**, SN10 5HF, ENG.
**(T)** 01380 726128 **(F)** 01380 726128
Speciality: Hypnosis.
● **Owner** Mr C Altree
**B** (**Ref:**HM00751)

### ALUNA HOLISTIC THERAPY CENTRE
**Aluna Holistic Therapy Centre**, 26 Lyndhurst Rd, Manchester, **Manchester (Greater)**, M20 6AA, ENG.
**(T)** 01614 453860
Speciality: Complementary Medicines & Therapy.
**C** **M** (**Ref:**HM00752)

### ALVA HOUSE
**Alva House**, Alva Valley Drive, Gravesend, **Kent**, DA12 5UE, ENG.
**(T)** 01474 331120
Speciality: Complementary Medicines & Therapy.
**M** (**Ref:**HM00753)

### ALVAREZ, ANDREA
**Andrea Alvarez**, 22 Lincoln Rd, Reading, **Berkshire**, RG2 0EX, ENG.
**(T)** 01189 871860
Speciality: Reflexology.
**S** **T** (**Ref:**HM00754)



Key continued: **Yrs.Est:** Years Established **Q:** Qualifications **M:** Professional Membership ✓ Indemnity Insurance 💳 Accept Credit Cards

### ALVES-DA SILVA, CARLA
**Carla Alves-Da Silva Hypnotherapy**, 20-26 South St, Raworth Centre, Dorking, **Surrey**, RH4 2HQ, ENG.
(T) 01306 742150
Speciality: Psychotherapy.
B (Ref:HM00755)

### ALVEY, DAVID M
**David M Alvey**, The Old Bakehouse, Bakers Lane, Cuckney, Mansfield, **Nottinghamshire**, NG20 9NE, ENG.
(T) 01623 847104
Speciality: Chiropodists (Podiatrists).
S (Ref:HM00756)

### ALVEY, J W D
**J W D Alvey**, 36 Lumley Rd, Horley, **Surrey**, RH6 7JL, ENG.
(T) 01293 782513
Speciality: Chiropodists (Podiatrists).
S (Ref:HM00757)

### ALYN, PAUL
**Paul Alyn Reflexology**, 27 Solent Drive, Darcy Lever, Bolton, **Lancashire**, BL3 1RN, ENG.
(T) 01204 405253
Speciality: Reflexology.
S T (Ref:HM00758)

### ALYSS, THOMAS
**Thomas Alyss**, The Practice 1 The Plains, Totnes, **Devon**, TQ9 5NJ, ENG.
(T) 01803 862300
Speciality: Psychotherapy.
B (Ref:HM00759)

### AMALA CHIROPODY CENTRE
**Amala Chiropody Centre**, 511 Earlham Rd, Norwich, **Norfolk**, NR4 7HN, ENG.
(T) 01603 499512
(E) amala4us@hotmail.com
Speciality: Biomechanics, Chiropody, Cyro Therapy. ✔
● **Chiropodist** Ms S Spencer Q: F.S.C.P. M: S.C.P.
M Yrs. Est.: 1 (Ref:HM00760)

### AMANN OSTEOPATHIC CLINIC
**Amann Osteopathic Clinic**, 56 St Andrews Avenue, Wembley, **London (Greater)**, HA0 2QD, ENG.
(T) 020 8904 0020
Speciality: Osteopathy.
● **Owner** Mr A Amann
P S T (Ref:HM00761)

### AMATO, CHRISTOPHER
**Mr Christopher Amato**, 205A Garratt Lane, London, **London (Greater)**, SW18 4DS, ENG.
(T) 020 8265 0882
Speciality: Acupuncture.
O (Ref:HM00762)

### AMATSU SPINEWORKS CLINIC
**Amatsu Spineworks Clinic**, 49A High St, Yarm, **Cleveland**, TS15 9BH, ENG.
(T) 01642 785353
Speciality: Physiotherapy.
P S T (Ref:HM00763)

### AMBACARE
**Ambacare**, 374 Dunstable Rd, Luton, **Bedfordshire**, LU4 8JT, ENG.
(T) 01582 591544 (F) 01582 583032
Speciality: Osteopathy.
● **Director** Mrs B Smith
P S T (Ref:HM00764)

### AMBER CONNECTIONS
**Amber Connections**, 208 Birmingham Rd, Stratford-Upon-Avon, **Warwickshire**, CV37 0AX, ENG.
(T) 01789 299190
Speciality: Aromatherapy.
● **Owner** Ms Y Kiernan
M O (Ref:HM00765)

### AMBER LANE
**Amber Lane**, Woodbine Surgery, 40 High St, Chew Magna, Bristol, BS40 8PW, ENG.
(T) 01275 331151
Speciality: Chiropodists (Podiatrists).
● **Owner** Miss A Lane
S (Ref:HM00766)

### AMBER NATURAL THERAPY
**Amber Natural Therapy**, Coate Cottage, London Rd, Binfield, Bracknell, **Berkshire**, RG42 4AA, ENG.
(T) 01344 411175
Speciality: Complementary Medicines & Therapy.
● **Owner** Mrs O Bellia
C M (Ref:HM00767)

### AMBER THERAPEUTIC CLINIC
**Amber Therapeutic Clinic**, 58 Amberwood Rise, New Malden, **Surrey**, KT3 5JG, ENG.
(T) 020 8949 3640
Speciality: Manipulation, Remedial Massage.
● **Owner** Mr N Din
C (Ref:HM00768)

### AMBERGRIS
**Ambergris**, 2 Whitehall St, Halifax, **Yorkshire (West)**, HX3 8NB, ENG.
(T) 01422 204898
Speciality: Aromatherapy.
● **Owner** Mrs A Ambler
M O (Ref:HM00769)

### AMBERLEY HYP & COUNSELLING
**Amberley Hypnotherapy & Counselling**, 19 Knocklyon Dr, Dublin, **County Dublin**, IRE.
(T) 01494 5439
(E) amberley@therapy.net
Speciality: Hypnotherapy.
B (Ref:HM00770)

### AMBERSTONE PHYSIOTHERAPY
**Amberstone Physiotherapy Department**, Carters Corner, Hailsham, **Sussex (East)**, BN27 4HU, ENG.
(T) 01323 849485 (F) 01323 844676
Speciality: Physiotherapy.
● **Manageress** Mrs A Procter
P S T (Ref:HM00771)

### AMBLER, S J
**S J Ambler**, 75 Fakenham Way, Owlsmoor, Sandhurst, **Berkshire**, GU47 0YS, ENG.
(T) 01344 773022
Speciality: Chiropodists (Podiatrists).
● **Owner** Ms S Ambler
S (Ref:HM00772)

### AMBLESIDE CLINIC
**Ambleside Clinic**, 42 Vicars Cross Rd, Vicars Cross, Chester, **Cheshire**, CH3 5NL, ENG.
(T) 01244 344131
Speciality: Acupuncture, Complementary Therapy, Homeopathy, Massage (Therapeutic), Reflexology, Swedish Remedial Massage Therapy. ✔
● **Acupuncturist/Owner** Mr C Reynolds Q: Lic.Ac. M: BAcC.
● **Swedish Remedial Massage Therapist** Ms C Elander-Vickers Q: LCSP. M: SoP.
● **Reflexologist** Ms A Cropper Q: MBSR. M: BSR, HAR.
● **Homeopath** Mrs C Reynolds Q: FFHom, LCH, MCH, RSHom. M: FFHom, LCH.
M Yrs. Est.: 2 (Ref:HM00773)

### AMBROSE, YVONNE D
**Yvonne D Ambrose**, 3 Castle Dene, Maidstone, **Kent**, ME14 2NH, ENG.
(T) 01622 681314
Speciality: Reflexology.
S T (Ref:HM00774)

### AMEE & ASSOCIATES
**Patel Amee & Associates**, East Ham Foot Clinic, 15 Burges Rd, London, **London (Greater)**, E6 2BJ, ENG.
(T) 020 8472 9496
Speciality: Chiropodists (Podiatrists).
S (Ref:HM00775)

### AMELAN, RACHEL
**Rachel Amelan**, Hedgehog Cottage, 19 Briarwood, Wilmslow, **Cheshire**, SK9 2DH, ENG.
(T) 01625 533138
Speciality: Reflexology.
S T (Ref:HM00776)

### AMER, ANDREW R
**Andrew R Amer**, The Old Convent, Beeches Green, Stroud, **Gloucestershire**, GL5 4AD, ENG.
(T) 01453 767363
Speciality: Acupuncture.
● **Owner** Mr A Amer
O (Ref:HM00777)

### AMERICAN HOLISTIC
**American Holistic**, **County Galway**, IRE.
(T) 09152 5941
Speciality: Complementary Medicines & Therapy.
M (Ref:HM00778)

### AMERSHAM CHIROPRACTIC CLINIC
**Amersham Chiropractic Clinic**, 24 The Broadway, Amersham, **Buckinghamshire**, HP7 0HP, ENG.
(T) 01494 434366 (F) 01494 434866
(E) amersham.chiro@virgin.net
Speciality: Acupressure, Acupuncture, Chiropractic, Dietician, Manipulation, Massage (Therapeutic), Orthotics, Phytotherapy, X-Ray. ✔
● **Chiropractor/Director** Dr M Gould Q: BSc, CCEP, DC, MCC, MSc (Chiro). M: BCA, GCC.
S Yrs. Est.: 5 (Ref:HM00779)

### AMERSHAM OSTEOPATHIC CLINIC
**Amersham Osteopathic Clinic**, Caer Sidhe, Chiltern Rd, Amersham, **Buckinghamshire**, HP6 5PH, ENG.
(T) 01494 434651 (F) 01494 431481
(E) frances@laser.uk.com
(W) www.laser.uk.com/aoc
Speciality: Bach Remedies, Cranial Osteopathy, Massage (Therapeutic), Naturopathy, Osteopathy, Reflexology, Reiki. ✔
● **Practice Manager** Frances Smith
● **Osteopath/Naturopath** Ms K Carroll Q: DO, ND. M: GOsC.
● **Osteopath/Reflexologist** Mr R May Q: DO. M: GOsC.
● **Osteopath/Therapist** Mr A Blank Q: BSc, DO. M: GOsC.
S Yrs. Est.: 5 (Ref:HM00780)

### AMESBURY ABBEY CLINIC
**Amesbury Abbey Physiotherapy & Sports Injuries Clinic**, Amesbury, Abbey Church St, Salisbury, **Wiltshire**, SP4 7EX, ENG.
(T) 01980 625245
Speciality: Acupuncture. ✔
● **Physiotherapist/Owner** Christine Thompson Q: MCSP, SRP.
S (Ref:HM00781)

### AMETHYST CENTRE
**Amethyst Centre**, 28 Beechcourt, Killiney, **County Dublin**, IRE.
(T) 01285 0976
Speciality: Complementary Medicines & Therapy.
M (Ref:HM00782)

### AMETHYST HEALING CENTRE
**Amethyst Healing Centre**, 20 Union St, Birstall, Batley, **Yorkshire (West)**, WF17 9ED, ENG.
(T) 01924 446055
(E) vicki@amethystcentrefreeserve.co.uk
Speciality: Colour Therapy, Crystal Healing, Hypnotherapy, Psychotherapy, Reiki, Stress Therapy, Natural Healing. ✔
● **Owner/Hypnotherapist** Ms V White Q: NLP, Reiki Master. M: BAHA, NGH(US).
B Yrs. Est.: 4 (Ref:HM00783)

### AMETHYST HEALING CENTRE
**Amethyst Healing Centre (The)**, Newport House, Commercial St, Llantwit Major, **Glamorgan (Vale of)**, CF61 1RB, WAL.
(T) 01446 790199
Speciality: Aromatherapy, Kinesiology, Reflexology, Bach Flower Remedies, Training in Kinesiology. ✔
● **Owner/Aromatherapist** Miss H Morris Q: IIHHT, ITEC. M: IIR.
C Yrs. Est.: 3 (Ref:HM00784)

### AMIES, SUSAN
**Susan Amies**, Hafod Brynog, Felinfach,

Key: B Mind-Body Medicine · C Complementary Medicine · H Self Help Treatment · M Medicinal Therapy · O Oriental Medicine · P Postural Therapy · S Manipulative Structural Therapy · T Touch Therapy

Lampeter, **Ceredigion**, SA48 8AE, **WAL**.
(T) 01570 470084
Speciality: Chiropody. ✔
● **Owner/Chiropodist** Ms S Amies Q: MBChA, MSSCh. M: B.A.Ch.P.
S Yrs. Est.: 7 (Ref:HM00785)

## AMIN, S
**Miss S Amin**, 174 Kingston Rd, Epsom, **Surrey**, KT19 0SD, **ENG**.
(T) 020 8394 2971
Speciality: Chiropodists (Podiatrists).
S (Ref:HM00786)

## AMIN, S
**S Amin**, 303 Brighton Rd, South Croydon, **Surrey**, CR2 6EQ, **ENG**.
(T) 020 8680 4645
Speciality: Chiropodists (Podiatrists).
S (Ref:HM00787)

## AMIN, S
**S Amin**, Robin Hood Lane Health Centre, Camden Rd, Sutton, **Surrey**, SM1 2SH, **ENG**.
(T) 020 8770 7121
Speciality: Chiropractors.
P S T (Ref:HM00788)

## AMIR, M
**Mr M Amir**, 50B Lower Richmond Rd, London, **London (Greater)**, SW15 1JT, **ENG**.
(T) 020 8870 8686
Speciality: Complementary Medicines & Therapy.
M (Ref:HM00789)

## AMMAROSE HYPNOTHERAPY CLINIC
**Ammarose Hypnotherapy Clinic**, Derryharriff, Castlebar, **County Mayo**, **IRE**.
(T) 09423 654
Speciality: Hypnotherapy.
B (Ref:HM00790)

## AMORA TRADING
**Amora Trading Co Ltd**, Unit 1B Tokenspire Business Park, Hull Rd, Woodmansey, Beverley, **Humberside (North)**, HU17 0TB, **ENG**.
(T) 01482 886158 (F) 01482 887049
Speciality: Complementary Medicines & Therapy.
● **Manager** Mr J Johnston
M (Ref:HM00791)

## AMOS, CLAIRE
**Claire Amos**, Churchside, St Johns Rd, Mardens Hill, Crowborough, **Sussex (East)**, TN6 1XW, **ENG**.
(T) 01892 668852
Speciality: Chiropractors.
● **Owner** Miss C Amos
P S T (Ref:HM00792)

## AMOS, REBECCA
**Rebecca Amos**, Loder Rd, Brighton, **Sussex (East)**, BN1 6PN, **ENG**.
(T) 01273 702177
Speciality: Chiropodists (Podiatrists).
● **Owner** Ms R Amos
S (Ref:HM00793)

## AMPHORA AROMATICS
**Amphora Aromatics**, 36 Cotham Hill, Bristol, BS6 6LA, **ENG**.
(T) 01179 047212 (F) 01179 047212
Speciality: Aromatherapy.
● **Director** Mr P Carroll
M O (Ref:HM00794)

## AMPTHILL & FLITWICK CLINIC
**Ampthill & Flitwick Chartered Physiotherapy Clinic**, 7 Station Sq, Flitwick, Bedford, **Bedfordshire**, MK45 1DP, **ENG**.
(T) 01525 720882 (F) 01525 720884
Speciality: Acupuncture, Physiotherapy.
✔ [credit card]
● **Practice Manager** Mrs A Regan
● **Physiotherapist** Mrs Olney Q: MCSP, SRP.
● **Physiotherapist** Mrs C Ellis Q: MCSP, MMACP, SRP.
S Yrs. Est.: 7 (Ref:HM00795)

## AMYRIS ESSENTIAL OILS
**Amyris Essential Oils**, P O Box 181, Harrogate, **Yorkshire (North)**, HG2 0LX, **ENG**.
(T) 01423 560583
Speciality: Aromatherapy.
● **Partner** Mr J Beavis-Harrison
M O (Ref:HM00796)

## AN TAM HEALING CENTRE
**An Tam Healing Centre**, 1 Marlborough Studios, 12A Finchley Rd, London, **London (Greater)**, NW8 6EG, **ENG**.
(T) 020 7586 6543 (F) 020 7586 6514
Speciality: Complementary Medicines & Therapy.
● **Sole Director** Thi Huy Dinh
C M (Ref:HM00797)

## ANABELLE'S THERAPEUTIC MASSAGE
**Anabelle's Therapeutic Massage**, 200 St Leonards Rd, Windsor, **Berkshire**, SL4 3BP, **ENG**.
(T) 07956 459636
Speciality: Massage (Therapeutic). ✔
● **Owner/Sports Therapist** Mrs A Williams Q: ITEC. M: ITEC.
C Yrs. Est.: 10 (Ref:HM00798)

## ANABELLS
**Anabells**, 1066 Balcombe Rd, Crawley, **Sussex (West)**, RH10 3NL, **ENG**.
(T) 020 8570 7323
Speciality: Aromatherapy.
M O (Ref:HM00799)

## ANALYSIS CENTRE
**Analysis Centre**, 280 Coleshill Rd, Birmingham, **Midlands (West)**, B36 8BG, **ENG**.
(T) 01217 496533
Speciality: Complementary Medicines & Therapy.
C M (Ref:HM00800)

## ANALYSIS UNDER HYPNOSIS
**Analysis Under Hypnosis**, 17 High St, Brymbo, Wrexham, LL11 5BL, **WAL**.
(T) 01978 754447
Speciality: Hypnotherapy.
● **Owner** Mr K Bailey
B (Ref:HM00801)

## ANAM CHARA COUNSELLING
**Anam Chara Counselling Practice**, 77 Glencarraig, Ballinode, **County Sligo**, **IRE**.
(T) 07171 624
Speciality: Art Therapy, Cognitive Therapy, Counselling, Gestalt Therapy, Group Therapy, Humanistic Psychology, Psychotherapy, Rogerian Therapy, Psychodynamic Psychotherapy, Integrative Psychotherapy. ✔
● **Counsellor/Psychotherapist** Ms A O'Connell Q: Dip.Couns, Dip.Psych. M: IACT.
H Yrs. Est.: 5 (Ref:HM00802)

## ANANDA HOMOEOPATHIC CLINIC
**Ananda Homoeopathic Clinic**, Vita Health Food Store, 565 Lea Bridge Rd, Bakers Arms, London, **London (Greater)**, E10 6EN, **ENG**.
(T) 020 8926 7855
Speciality: Homeopathy.
M (Ref:HM00803)

## ANCHORAGE ANALYSIS
**Anchorage Analysis**, 32 Manor Rd, Westcliff-on-Sea, **Essex**, SS0 7SS, **ENG**.
(T) 01702 340077
Speciality: Hypnotherapy.
B (Ref:HM00804)

## ANCIENT HEALING CRYSTALS
**Ancient Healing Crystals**, Unit 9, 43 Old St, Ashton-under-Lyne, **Manchester (Greater)**, OL6 6BB, **ENG**.
(T) 01613 396677
Speciality: Complementary Medicines & Therapy.
● **Owner** Mrs C Wallis
C M (Ref:HM00805)

## ANDERSON & CRAIG CLINIC
**Anderson & Craig Clinic**, 12 Coolafinny Rd, Eglinton, Londonderry, **County Londonderry**, BT47 3PG, **NIR**.
(T) 028 7181 0469 (F) 028 7181 0469
Speciality: Complementary Medicines & Therapy.
● **Owner** Mr G Craig
C M (Ref:HM00806)

## ANDERSON CENTRE
**Anderson Centre (The)**, 1 Dent St, Blyth, **Northumberland**, NE24 3ED, **ENG**.
(T) 01670 360108
Speciality: Complementary Medicines & Therapy.
C M (Ref:HM00807)

## ANDERSON COMPLEMENTARY MED
**Anderson Complementary Medicine Centre**, Priory Stones, Lossenham Lane, Newenden, Cranbrook, **Kent**, TN18 5QQ, **ENG**.
(T) 01797 252458
Speciality: Aromatherapy.
M O (Ref:HM00808)

## ANDERSON DOE PODIATRY CLINIC
**Anderson Doe Poditary Clinic (The)**, 472 Crow Rd, Glasgow, **Glasgow (City of)**, G11 7DR, **SCO**.
(T) 01413 349994 (F) 01413 349994
Speciality: Biomechanics, Chiropody, Nail Surgery, Physiotherapy, Podiatry. ✔
● **Chiropodist (Podiatrist)** Ms G Anderson Q: BSc (Hons), S.R.Ch. M: S.C.P.
● **Chiropodist (Podiatrist)** Ms S Doe Q: BSc (Hons), GSSR, M.S.C.P, S.R.Ch. M: S.C.P.
● **Physiotherapist** Mr C MacBeth Q: SRP. M: CSP.
S (Ref:HM00809)

## ANDERSON, A DUDLEY
**A Dudley Anderson**, Park View, 45 Lemont Rd, Sheffield, **Yorkshire (South)**, S17 4HA, **ENG**.
(T) 01142 368825
(E) andy@synergynet.co.uk
Speciality: Complementary Therapy, Counselling, Hypnosis, Hypnotherapy, Massage (Therapeutic), Psychotherapy, Reiki, Stress Therapy, Touch Therapy, Visualisation Therapy. ✔
● **Owner** Mr D Anderson Q: C.Hyp, CMH. M: UKGHE.
B Yrs. Est.: 18 (Ref:HM00810)

## ANDERSON, A J
**A J Anderson**, 4 Elmstead Rd, Bexhill-on-Sea, **Sussex (East)**, TN40 2HP, **ENG**.
(T) 01424 734027
Speciality: Psychotherapy.
● **Owner** Mr A Anderson
B (Ref:HM00811)

## ANDERSON, A J
**A J Anderson**, The Physiotherapy Clinic, 5 Rachel Pl, Port Glasgow Rd, Kilmacolm, **Inverclyde**, PA13 4ES, **SCO**.
(T) 01505 873078
Speciality: Physiotherapy.
● **Manager** A Anderson
P S T (Ref:HM00812)

## ANDERSON, ANGELA
**Angela Anderson**, 40 Celandine Avenue, Locks Heath, **Hampshire**, SO31 6XA, **ENG**.
(T) 01489 581314
Speciality: Reflexology.
S T (Ref:HM00813)

## ANDERSON, BETTY
**Betty Anderson**, Sylvan Tryst, Bronygarth Rd, Weston Rhyn, Oswestry, **Shropshire**, SY10 7RQ, **ENG**.
(T) 01691 778503
Speciality: Reflexology.
S T (Ref:HM00814)

## ANDERSON, DAVID
**David Anderson**, 14 Mossbank Cr, Motherwell, **Lanarkshire (North)**, ML1 5TE, **SCO**.
(T) 01698 861627
Speciality: Physiotherapy.
● **Owner** Mr D Anderson
P S T (Ref:HM00815)

## ANDERSON, DAVID
**David Anderson**, Bow Cottage, Biddisham, Axbridge, **Somerset**, BS26 2RD, **ENG**.
(T) 01934 750329
Speciality: Chiropody, Nail Surgery. ✔
● **Chiropodist** Mr D Anderson Q: MSSCh.


Key continued: Yrs.Est: Years Established Q: Qualifications M: Professional Membership ✔ Indemnity Insurance [credit card] Accept Credit Cards

M Yrs. Est.: 30 (**Ref:**HM00816)

## ANDERSON, DUNCAN

**Duncan Anderson**, 6-8 West St, Berwick-Upon-Tweed, **Northumberland**, TD15 1AS, SCO.
(T) 01289 306996
Speciality: Chiropodists (Podiatrists).
S (**Ref:**HM00817)

## ANDERSON, G

**G Anderson**, 7 All Saints Rd, Burton-On-Trent, **Staffordshire**, DE14 3LS, ENG.
(T) 01283 533806 (F) 01283 533806
Speciality: Hypnotherapy, Reiki. ✔
● **Hypnotherapist** Mr G Anderson M: IAH, NRAH.
C Yrs. Est.: 6 (**Ref:**HM00818)

## ANDERSON, GILLIAN

**Gillian Anderson**, 6 Thorpeside Cl, Chertsey Lane, Staines, **Surrey**, TW18 3NZ, ENG.
(T) 01784 453738
Speciality: Chiropractors.
P S T (**Ref:**HM00819)

## ANDERSON, GORDON

**Gordon Anderson**, 35 Green Way, Frinton-on-Sea, **Essex**, CO13 9AL, ENG.
(T) 01255 679830
Speciality: Complementary Medicines & Therapy.
● **Owner** Mr G Anderson
M (**Ref:**HM00820)

## ANDERSON, I M

**Mr I M Anderson**, The Health Centre, 7 Denbigh St, Llanrwst, **Conwy**, LL26 0LL, WAL.
(T) 01492 641669
Speciality: Complementary Medicines & Therapy.
M (**Ref:**HM00821)

## ANDERSON, ISOBEL

**Isobel Anderson**, 52 Stoke Newington Church St, London, **London (Greater)**, N16 0NB, ENG.
(T) 020 7249 9671
Speciality: Homeopathy.
● **Senior Partner** Mrs J Sheridan
M (**Ref:**HM00822)

## ANDERSON, J

**J Anderson**, 2 The Bridges, Dalgety Bay, Dunfermline, **Fife**, KY11 9XZ, SCO.
(T) 01383 824578
Speciality: Chiropodists (Podiatrists).
● **Owner** Mrs J Anderson
S (**Ref:**HM00823)

## ANDERSON, J

**J Anderson**, 35 St Leonards Rd, London, **London (Greater)**, SW14 7LY, ENG.
(T) 020 8241 7624
Speciality: Psychotherapy.
B (**Ref:**HM00824)

## ANDERSON, J GAVIN

**J Gavin Anderson**, 37A Aire St, Goole, **Humberside (North)**, DN14 5QW, ENG.
(T) 01405 763519
Speciality: Chiropodists (Podiatrists).
S (**Ref:**HM00825)

## ANDERSON, JANE M

**Jane M Anderson**, 15 Gilbert Rd, Pinner, **London (Greater)**, HA5 1AP, ENG.
(T) 020 8866 1262
Speciality: Homeopathy.
● **Owner** Ms J Anderson
M (**Ref:**HM00826)

## ANDERSON, JUDY

**Judy Anderson**, Hove Manor Clinic, Hove St, Hove, **Sussex (East)**, BN3 2DF, ENG.
(T) 01273 203546
Speciality: Physiotherapy.
P S T (**Ref:**HM00827)

## ANDERSON, K

**K Anderson**, 11 Woodhall Bank, Edinburgh, **Edinburgh (City of)**, EH13 0HL, SCO.
(T) 01314 415652
Speciality: Chiropodists (Podiatrists).
● **Owner** Mrs K Anderson
S (**Ref:**HM00828)

## ANDERSON, KATE

**Kate Anderson**, Liverpool, **Merseyside**, L15, ENG.
(T) 01517 344918
Speciality: Bach Remedies.
M (**Ref:**HM00829)

## ANDERSON, KEITH

**Keith Anderson**, 21 Carnarvon Rd, Bristol, BS6 7DT, ENG.
(T) 01179 247825
Speciality: Bach Remedies, Colour Therapy, Dietician, Dowsing, Paranormal Therapies.
● **Palmistry Consultant**
Mr K Anderson
B Yrs. Est.: 35 (**Ref:**HM00830)

## ANDERSON, LINDA

**Linda Anderson**, Dalswinton, London Rd, Great Chesterford, Saffron Walden, **Essex**, CB10 1NY, ENG.
(T) 01799 531315
Speciality: Reflexology.
● **Owner** Ms L Anderson
S T (**Ref:**HM00831)

## ANDERSON, LOUISE

**Louise Anderson**, The Crescent Consulting Rooms, 30 The Crescent, Salford, **Manchester (Greater)**, M5 4UT, ENG.
(T) 01617 457551
Speciality: Physiotherapy.
● **Managing Director**
Miss L Anderson
P S T (**Ref:**HM00832)

## ANDERSON, LOUISE

**Louise Anderson**, 14 Badger Cl, Feltham, **London (Greater)**, TW13 7HA, ENG.
(T) 020 8751 4541
Speciality: Reflexology.
S T (**Ref:**HM00833)

## ANDERSON, M

**M Anderson - The Chiropractic Clinic**, 34A Fitzroy St, Cambridge, **Cambridgeshire**, CB1 1EW, ENG.
(T) 01223 460467
Speciality: Chiropractic. ✔
● **Chiropractor** Mr M Anderson Q: DC.
P S T Yrs. Est.: 26 (**Ref:**HM00834)

## ANDERSON, MARGOT

**Margot Anderson**, Warnford Court, 29 Throgmorton St, London, **London (Greater)**, EC2N 2AT, ENG.
(T) 020 7256 8019
Speciality: Physiotherapy.
P S T (**Ref:**HM00835)

## ANDERSON, PAUL

**Paul Anderson**, 15 The Rookery, Balsham, Cambridge, **Cambridgeshire**, CB1 6EU, ENG.
(T) 01223 893032
Speciality: Chiropody. ✔
● **Owner/Chiropodist** Mr P Anderson Q: M.S.C.P, SMAE.
M Yrs. Est.: 11 (**Ref:**HM00836)

## ANDERSON, R T

**R T Anderson**, 72 Church St, Portadown, Craigavon, **County Armagh**, BT62 3EU, NIR.
(T) 028 3833 0005
Speciality: Physiotherapy.
● **Owner** Mrs R Anderson
P S T (**Ref:**HM00837)

## ANDERSON, W B

**W B Anderson**, 95 Seagate, Dundee, **Angus**, DD1 2ER, SCO.
(T) 01382 223035
Speciality: Chiropodists (Podiatrists).
S (**Ref:**HM00838)

## ANDERSON-DOBLE, CYNTHIA

**Cynthia Anderson Doble**, 7 College Avenue, Tonbridge, **Kent**, TN9 2NR, ENG.
(T) 01732 361147
Speciality: Chiropodists (Podiatrists).
S (**Ref:**HM00839)

## ANDERTON, NORAH

**Norah Anderton**, 21 Broom Lane, Rotherham, **Yorkshire (South)**, S60 3EL, ENG.
(T) 01709 837046
Speciality: Chiropodists (Podiatrists).
● **Owner** Ms N Anderton
S (**Ref:**HM00840)

## ANDOVER BACK PAIN & PHYSIO

**Andover Back Pain & Physiotherapy Centre**, 12 High St, Andover, **Hampshire**, SP10 1NX, ENG.
(T) 01264 350716
Speciality: Osteopathy.
● **Owner** Mr M Gillott
P S T (**Ref:**HM00841)

## ANDOVER FOOT HEALTH

**Andover Foot Health**, 30 Junction Rd, Andover, **Hampshire**, SP10 3QU, ENG.
(T) 01264 334448
Speciality: Chiropractic.
S (**Ref:**HM00842)

## ANDREA ALLAN CHIROPODIST

**Andrea Allan Chiropodist**, 89-91 Norton Lane, Hammerwich, Burntwood, **Staffordshire**, WS7 0HW, ENG.
(T) 01543 674977
Speciality: Chiropodists (Podiatrists).
S (**Ref:**HM00843)

## ANDREADIS, ANTHONIA

**Anthonia Andreadis**, Claypath Medical Practice, 26 Gilesgate, Durham, **County Durham**, DH1 1QW, ENG.
(T) 01913 832090
Speciality: Acupuncture.
● **Owner** Mrs A Andreadis
O (**Ref:**HM00844)

## ANDREASEN CENTRE

**Andreasen Centre For Holistic Health**, 91-93 Hartington Gr, Cambridge, **Cambridgeshire**, CB1 7UB, ENG.
(T) 01223 892241
Speciality: Complementary Medicines & Therapy.
C M (**Ref:**HM00845)

## ANDREW BATHIE PRACTICE

**Andrew Bathie Practice**, 19 Felbridge Cl, East Grinstead, **Sussex (West)**, RH19 2BN, ENG.
(T) 01342 318043
(E) drandrew@bathie.freeserve.co.uk
(W) www.stress-solutions.net
Speciality: Auto Suggestion, Autogenic Training, Aversion Therapy, Biofeedback, Cognitive Therapy, Complementary Therapy, Counselling, Gestalt Therapy, Humanistic Psychology, Hypnosis, Hypnotherapy, Life Style Coaching, Meditation, Neuro-Linguistic Program, Psychotherapy, Stress Therapy, Visualisation Therapy, Past Life Regression, Gold Psychotherapy Counselling, Solution Focussed Brief Therapy, Parts Therapy, Life Coaching. ✔
● **Stress Management Consultant/Hypnotherapist**
Mr A Bathie Q: Dip.StM, PhD. M: AGPC, BACP, BPS, CPS, ETSI, HA, HRS, HS, NCH, NCP, SSM.
B Yrs. Est.: 12 (**Ref:**HM00846)

## ANDREW JOHNSON HYPNOTHERAPIST

**Andrew Johnson Hypnotherapist**, Room 119, 91 Western Rd, Brighton, **Sussex (East)**, BN1 2NW, ENG.
(T) 01292 286760
Speciality: Hypnotherapy.
B (**Ref:**HM00847)

## ANDREW, CHERYL

**Andrews Cheryl**, 14-16 Bond St, London, **London (Greater)**, W5 5AA, ENG.
(T) 020 8575 5668
Speciality: Complementary Medicines & Therapy.
M (**Ref:**HM00848)

## ANDREWS & DOW

**Andrews & Dow**, 93 Chillingham Rd, Newcastle Upon Tyne, **Tyne and Wear**, NE6 5XL, ENG.
(T) 01912 650295 (F) 01912 650295
Speciality: Chiropodists (Podiatrists).
● **Owner** Mr H Dow
S (**Ref:**HM00849)

Key: B Mind-Body Medicine C Complementary Medicine H Self Help Treatment M Medicinal Therapy O Oriental Medicine P Postural Therapy S Manipulative Structural Therapy T Touch Therapy

**ANDREWS CLINIC**

**Andrews Clinic**, 59 Telford Cres, Leigh, **Manchester (Greater)**, WN7 5LY, ENG.
(T) 01942 678092 (F) 01942 515579
Speciality: Osteopathy.
● **Owner** Mr J Andrews
P S T (Ref:HM00850)

**ANDREWS, ELIZABETH**

**Elizabeth Andrews**, Chapel Cottage, Winkworth Hill, Hascombe Rd, Godalming, **Surrey**, GU8 4AE, ENG.
(T) 01483 208207
Speciality: Chiropractors.
● **Owner** Mrs E Andrews
P S T (Ref:HM00851)

**ANDREWS, HAZEL**

**Hazel Andrews**, 7 Ash Gardens, South Marston, Swindon, **Wiltshire**, SN3 4XX, ENG.
(T) 01793 827507
Speciality: Acupuncture, Cupping, Moxibustion. ✔
● **Acupuncturist** Ms H Andrews Q: Lic.Ac.
M: BAcC.
O Yrs. Est.: 5 (Ref:HM00852)

**ANDREWS, KATHRYN**

**Kathryn Andrews**, 5 Ash Lane, Widnes, **Cheshire**, WA8 8JH, ENG.
(T) 01514 952232
Speciality: Reflexology.
S T (Ref:HM00853)

**ANDREWS, M**

**M Andrews**, Courtyard Physiotherapy Clinic, 28B Bancroft, Hitchin, **Hertfordshire**, SG5 1XA, ENG.
(T) 01462 441205 (F) 01462 441205
Speciality: Physiotherapy.
● **Owner** Mrs M Andrew
P S T (Ref:HM00854)

**ANDREWS, M E**

**Mrs M E Andrews**, The Andrews Physiotherapy Clinic, High St, Horam, Heathfield, **Sussex (East)**, TN21 0EY, ENG.
(T) 01435 812429
Speciality: Physiotherapy.
● **Owner** Mrs M Andrews
P S T (Ref:HM00855)

**ANDREWS, R**

**R Andrews**, 4 Sanders Rd, Brixham, **Devon**, TQ5 8PL, ENG.
(T) 01803 855273
Speciality: Chiropodists (Podiatrists).
● **Owner** Mrs R Andrews
S (Ref:HM00856)

**ANDREWS, S C**

**Simon C Andrews LSCH, RSHom**, 34 Main Rd, Grendon, **Northamptonshire**, NN7 1JW, ENG.
(T) 01933 663849
(E) simonhom@aol
Speciality: Homeopathy. ✔
● **Homeopath** Mr S Andrews M: Soc.Hom.
M Yrs. Est.: 5 (Ref:HM00857)

**ANDREWS, S C W**

**S C W Andrews**, 17 Hagley Rd, Halesowen, **Midlands (West)**, B63 4PU, ENG.
(T) 01215 856143
Speciality: Chiropodists (Podiatrists).
● **Owner** Mr S Andrews
S (Ref:HM00858)

**ANDREWS, SIMON C**

**Simon C Andrews LSCH**, Eastgate Complementary Health Centre, Eastgate House, 19 Humberstone Rd, Leicester, **Leicestershire**, LE5 3GJ, ENG.
(T) 01162 511647
Speciality: Acupressure, Acupuncture, Aromatherapy, Bowen Therapy, Chiropractic, Complementary Therapy, Gestalt Therapy, Homeopathy, Hypnotherapy, Iridology, Kinesiology, Manipulation, Massage (Therapeutic), Reflexology, Reiki, Yoga. ✔
● **Homeopath** Mr S Andrews Q: RSHom.
M: Soc.Hom.
M (Ref:HM00859)

**ANDREWS, SIMON C**

**Simon C Andrews LSCH RSHom**, Physioplus, 28 Harborough Rd, Kingsthorpe, Northampton, **Northamptonshire**, ENG.
(T) 01604 722372
Speciality: Homeopathy. ✔
● **Homeopath** Mr S Andrews Q: RSHom.
M: Soc.Hom.
M (Ref:HM00860)

**ANERLEY NATURAL HEALING CENTRE**

**Anerley Natural Healing Centre**, 34 Wheathill Rd, London, **London (Greater)**, SE20 7XH, ENG.
(T) 020 8778 8635
Speciality: Aromatherapy.
M O (Ref:HM00861)

**ANGALEE'S**

**Angalee's**, 29 Queens Rd, Southend-On-Sea, **Essex**, SS1 1LT, ENG.
(T) 01702 436379
Speciality: Complementary Medicines & Therapy.
● **Owner** Mr R Steele
C M (Ref:HM00862)

**ANGAR, VYAS**

**Vyas Angar**, 28 St Andrews Rd, Watford, **Hertfordshire**, WD1 6AB, ENG.
(T) 020 8428 6475
Speciality: Complementary Medicines & Therapy.
C M (Ref:HM00863)

**ANGEL**

**Angel**, 1 Willow St, London, **London (Greater)**, EC2A 4BH, ENG.
(T) 020 8693 2253
Speciality: Hypnotherapy.
● **Owner** Mr T Morris
B (Ref:HM00864)

**ANGEL AROMATHERAPY CLINIC**

**Angel Aromatherapy Clinic & Beauty Rooms**, Flood St, **County Galway**, IRE.
(T) 09156 8871
(E) angel_aroma@yahoo.com
Speciality: Aromatherapy.
M O (Ref:HM00865)

**ANGEL HEART CENTRE**

**Angel Heart Centre**, 543-547 Ecclesall Rd, Sheffield, **Yorkshire (South)**, S11 8PR, ENG.
(T) 01142 683085
Speciality: Complementary Medicines & Therapy.
C M (Ref:HM00866)

**ANGEL HEART CENTRE**

**Angel Heart Centre**, Cranford Lane, Heston, **London (Greater)**, TW5 9PU, ENG.
(T) 020 8897 7885
(E) barbara.guest@btinternet.com
Speciality: Absent Healing, Group Therapy, Healer, Hypnotherapy, Reiki, Stress Therapy, Workshop-Personal Development, Management & Relaxation Programmes. ✔
● **Owner** Ms B Guest Q: Dip.Adv.Hyp, DSMH, MBA, Reiki Master.
B Yrs. Est.: 2 (Ref:HM00867)

**ANGEL HLTHY LIVING INITIATIVE**

**Angel Healthy Living Initiative (The)**, St Phillips Pl, Off Chapel St, Manchester, **Manchester (Greater)**, M3 2RB, ENG.
(T) 01618 330495 (F) 01618 342532
Speciality: Complementary Medicines & Therapy.
M (Ref:HM00868)

**ANGEL THERAPIES**

**Angel Therapies**, Willow Bank, Hirst Courtney, Selby, **Yorkshire (North)**, YO8 8QT, ENG.
(T) 01757 270585 (F) 01757 270570
Speciality: Aromatherapy.
● **Partner** Mr J Burton
M O (Ref:HM00869)

**ANGEL, LESLEY**

**Lesley Angel**, Wembley Medical Centre, 130 Llanover Rd, Wembley, **London (Greater)**, HA9 7LT, ENG.
(T) 020 8908 1425 (F) 020 8908 1425
Speciality: Reflexology.
S T (Ref:HM00870)

**ANGEL, LESLEY**

**Lesley Angel**, 3 Marlen Court, Napier Rd, Wembley, **London (Greater)**, HA0 4UB, ENG.
(T) 020 8903 0962
Speciality: Reflexology.
S T (Ref:HM00871)

**ANGELA**

**Angela**, 68 Farnhurst Rd, Barnham, Bognor Regis, **Sussex (West)**, PO22 0JW, ENG.
(T) 01243 552627
Speciality: Spiritual Healing, Relaxation Therapy. ✔
● **Owner/Spirtual Healer** Mrs A Wake
M: SHA.
C Yrs. Est.: 13 (Ref:HM00872)

**ANGELA MATTHEWS HOMEOPATH**

**Angela Mathews Homeopath**, 88 Davidgor Rd, Hove, **Sussex (East)**, BN3 1RF, ENG.
(T) 01273 206390
Speciality: Holistic Healing, Homeopathy. ✔
● **Owner/Homeopath** Mrs A Mathews Q: BA.
M: HMA.
C M Yrs. Est.: 2 (Ref:HM00873)

**ANGELA'S NATURAL HEALING**

**Angela's Natural Healing**, Swindon, **Wiltshire**, SN2 2ES, ENG.
(T) 01793 514882
Speciality: Complementary Medicines & Therapy.
M (Ref:HM00874)

**ANGELIS**

**Angelis**, 2 Station Sq, Whitley Bay, **Tyne and Wear**, NE26 2QT, ENG.
(T) 01912 513794
Speciality: Clairvoyants & Palmists.
● **Owner** Mrs M Hepplewhite
B (Ref:HM00875)

**ANGELIS, LUCIA**

**Lucia Angelis**, 69 Endell St, London, **London (Greater)**, WC2H 9AJ, ENG.
(T) 020 7240 6226 (F) 020 7240 6226
Speciality: Complementary Medicines & Therapy.
● **Manager** Mr A James
C M (Ref:HM00876)

**ANGELIS, LUCIA**

**Lucia Angelis**, 8 Turnpin Lane, London, **London (Greater)**, SE10 9JA, ENG.
(T) 020 8858 3353
Speciality: Complementary Medicines & Therapy.
● **Owner** Miss V Grieveson
C M (Ref:HM00877)

**ANGELO, JAN**

**Jan Angelo**, Natural Health Clinic, 98 Cathedral Rd, Cardiff, **Glamorgan (Vale of)**, CF11 9LP, WAL.
(T) 029 2022 2221
Speciality: Complementary Medicines & Therapy.
● **Practice Manager** Mrs L Powell
M (Ref:HM00878)

**ANGELS**

**Angels**, 42 Glenbrook Cr, Nottingham, **Nottinghamshire**, NG8 3GQ, ENG.
(T) 01159 167237
Speciality: Relaxation Technique.
● **Owner** Miss C Carter
H T (Ref:HM00879)

**ANGELS CLAIRVOYANCY**

**Angels Clairvoyancy**, 22 Ormonde Rd, Hythe, **Kent**, CT21 6DN, ENG.
(T) 01303 237567 (F) 01303 268049
Speciality: Clairvoyants & Palmists.
● **Owner** Ms S Aynsley
B (Ref:HM00880)

**ANGLESEY HEALING CENTRE**

**Anglesey Healing Centre**, Tyn Y Lon Farm, Llangoed, Beaumaris, **Isle of Anglesey**, LL58 8NE, WAL.
(T) 01248 490814



Key continued: Yrs.Est: Years Established Q: Qualifications M: Professional Membership ✔ Indemnity Insurance ▬ Accept Credit Cards

Speciality: Complementary Medicines & Therapy.
● **Owner** Mrs V Candlish
M (Ref:HM00881)

### ANGLIA BACK CLINIC
**Anglia Back Clinic**, 56 Broadway, Peterborough, **Cambridgeshire**, PE1 1SU, ENG.
(T) 01733 310978
Speciality: Osteopathy.
P S T (Ref:HM00882)

### ANGLO-AUSTRALIAN SEED
**Anglo-Australian Seed Co**, 2 Applecroft, Park St, St. Albans, **Hertfordshire**, AL2 2AP, ENG.
(T) 01727 768182 (F) 01727 768561
Speciality: Herbal Medicine.
M (Ref:HM00883)

### ANGLO-EUROPEAN COLLEGE
**Anglo-European College Of Chiropractic**, 13-15 Parkwood Rd, Bournemouth, **Dorset**, BH5 2DF, ENG.
(T) 01202 436200 (F) 01202 436312
Speciality: Chiropractic.
● **Principal** Mr K Vall
P S T (Ref:HM00884)

### ANGUS WILLIAMSON CLINIC
**Angus Williamson Therapy Clinic**, 50 Cow Wynd, Falkirk, FK1 1PU, SCO.
(T) 01324 612658
(W) www.taams.co.uk
Speciality: Aromatherapy, Chiropractic, Massage (Therapeutic), Reflexology, Teaches Aromatherapy, Reflexology & Massage to a professional standard. ✓ CREDIT
● **Partner** Mr A Williamson
(T) 01384 612658 Q: Dip.Arom. M: AoR, IPD, IPTI, ISPA, SIR.
C T Yrs. Est.: 20 (Ref:HM00885)

### ANISE-STAR MOBILE AROMATHERAPY
**Anise-Star Mobile Aromatherapy**, 42 Sandringham Way, Bognor Regis, **Sussex (West)**, PO21 2BQ, ENG.
(T) 01243 862274
Speciality: Aromatherapy.
● **Owner** Miss F Bennett
M O (Ref:HM00886)

### ANKERSIDE CLINIC
**Ankerside Clinic**, 3 Bond St, Nuneaton, **Warwickshire**, CV11 4DA, ENG.
(T) 024 7676 6412
Speciality: Physiotherapy.
P S T (Ref:HM00887)

### ANKIN, CHRISTINA
**Christina Ankin**, 18 Brook Way, Anna Valley, Andover, **Hampshire**, SP11 7RY, ENG.
(T) 01264 333174
Speciality: Reflexology.
S T (Ref:HM00888)

### ANN
**Ann**, 19 Leven Walk, Peterlee, **County Durham**, SR8 1HF, ENG.
(T) 01915 863362
Speciality: Clairvoyants & Palmists.
● **Owner** Mrs A Carroll
B (Ref:HM00889)

### ANNA
**Anna**, 22 Willowcroft Drive, Hambleton, Poulton-le-Fylde, **Lancashire**, FY6 9EJ, ENG.
(T) 01253 700081 (F) 01253 700081
Speciality: Clairvoyants & Palmists.
● **Owner** Mrs C Holland
B (Ref:HM00890)

### ANNALA HERBAL CLINIC
**Annala Herbal Clinic**, 44 Mallory House, Teriot St, London, **London (Greater)**, E14 6QF, ENG.
(T) 020 7987 3384
Speciality: Herbalists.
● **Owner** Mrs A Ablorh
M (Ref:HM00891)

### ANNANDALE CLINIC
**Annandale Clinic**, 37 Cobham Rd, Westcliff-on-Sea, **Essex**, SS0 8EG, ENG.
(T) 01702 330656
Speciality: Homeopathy.
● **Manager** Mrs S Hockett
M (Ref:HM00892)

### ANNANDALE PHYSIOTHERAPY CLINIC
**Annandale Physiotherapy Clinic**, 21 Salop Rd, Oswestry, **Shropshire**, SY11 2NR, ENG.
(T) 01691 650986
Speciality: Physiotherapy.
P S T (Ref:HM00893)

### ANNAPURNA NATURAL HEALTHCARE
**Annapurna Natural Healthcare**, 6 Mount Verdon Trce, Wellington Rd, Cork, **County Cork**, IRE.
(T) 08722 55831
(E) annacpurna@eircom.net
Speciality: Acupressure, Aromatherapy, Cranio-Sacral Therapy, Massage (Therapeutic), Reflexology, Reiki, Auricular Therapy. ✓
● **Practitioner** Ms A Cronin Q: BSc, Dip.Arom, Dip.Aur.Th, Dip.Reflex, PgC.Acupr.Mass. M: IFA, IIAA.
T Yrs. Est.: 4 (Ref:HM00894)

### ANNA'S
**Anna's Aromatherapy & Reflexology**, 16 Angler Rd, Salisbury, **Wiltshire**, SP2 9PB, ENG.
(T) 01722 329804
Speciality: Aromatherapy.
M O (Ref:HM00895)

### ANNAS STUDIO PRACTICE
**Annas Studio Practice**, 58 Mar St, Alloa, **Clackmannanshire**, FK10 1HR, SCO.
(T) 01259 216687
Speciality: Complementary Medicines & Therapy.
C M (Ref:HM00896)

### ANNE
**Anne**, 23 Porchester Gardens, London, **London (Greater)**, W2 4DB, ENG.
(T) 020 7727 3861
Speciality: Clairvoyants & Palmists.
B (Ref:HM00897)

### ANNE BERTOLUZZI REFLEXOLOGIST
**Anne Bertoluzzi Reflexologist**, 62 West Hill Rd, St. Leonards-On-Sea, **Sussex (East)**, TN38 0NE, ENG.
(T) 01424 429164
Speciality: Reflexology.
S T (Ref:HM00898)

### ANNE JORDAN CLINIC
**Anne Jordan Clinic**, 171A Wells Rd, Malvern, **Worcestershire**, WR14 4HE, ENG.
(T) 01684 563366 (F) 01684 563366
Speciality: Reflexology.
● **Owner** Mrs A Jordan
M (Ref:HM00899)

### ANNE PENMAN THERAPY
**Anne Penman Therapy Ltd**, 158 Queens Drive, Glasgow, **Glasgow (City of)**, G42 8QN, SCO.
(T) 01414 239923 (F) 01414 236647
(E) anneperman@aol.com
(W) www.annepenmantherapy.co.uk
Speciality: Complementary Therapy, Counselling, Reiki, Smoking cessation using laser, counselling and back up support. Stress and weight control. ✓ CREDIT
● **Laser Therapist** Mrs A Penman
● **Joint Director**
Scott Stuart Penman
C H Yrs. Est.: 9 (Ref:HM00900)

### ANNE RAWLINGS HYPNOTHERAPY
**Anne Rawlings Hypnotherapy**, Barn Court, Washfield, Tiverton, **Devon**, EX16 9QU, ENG.
(T) 01884 256483 (F) 01884 257982
Speciality: Auto Suggestion, Autogenic Training, Aversion Therapy, Cognitive Therapy, Complementary Therapy, Counselling, Family Therapy, Group Therapy, Healer, Healing Therapy, Holistic Healing, Humanistic Psychology, Hypnosis, Hypnotherapy, Life Style Coaching, Meditation, Primal Therapy, Psychotherapy, Pyscho-Synthesis, Rogerian Therapy, Stress Therapy, Transactional Analysis, Visualisation Therapy, Hypno-Analysis. ✓
● **Hypnotherapist** Ms A Rawlings Q: Dip.Hyp, Dip.Psych, MIAH. M: IAH.
B Yrs. Est.: 12 (Ref:HM00901)

### ANNE TOBIN BEAUTY CLINIC
**Anne Tobin Beauty Clinic**, 36 Main St, Castlebar, **County Mayo**, IRE.
(T) 09426 741
Speciality: Complementary Medicines & Therapy.
M (Ref:HM00902)

### ANNE WRIGHT & LARA SEYMOUR
**Anne V V Wright D O & Lara G Seymour B S C (Hons)**, 5 Chichester Avenue, Ruislip, **London (Greater)**, HA4 7EJ, ENG.
(T) 01895 677179
Speciality: Osteopathy.
P S T (Ref:HM00903)

### ANNE, CORCORAN (DR)
**CORCORAN ANNE HHC Dip**, Camden Court Hotel, Dublin, **County Dublin**, IRE.
(T) 01475 9666
Speciality: Complementary Medicines & Therapy.
M (Ref:HM00904)

### ANNE, NINA
**Nina Anne**, 64 Longridge Avenue, Saltdean, Brighton, **Sussex (East)**, BN2 8RB, ENG.
(T) 01273 390190
Speciality: Clairvoyants & Palmists.
● **Owner** Mrs N Anne
B (Ref:HM00905)

### ANNELISE
**Annelise Complementary Therapists**, 42 Washbrook Rd, Rushden, **Northamptonshire**, NN10 9UX, ENG.
(T) 01933 313673
Speciality: Aromatherapy, Auricular Therapy, Complementary Therapy, Group Therapy, Holistic Healing, Hopi Ear Candles, Indian Head Massage, Life Style Coaching, Massage (Therapeutic), Reflexology, Stress Therapy. ✓
● **Aromatherapist** Ms E Dryden Q: ITEC. M: AOC, GCP.
● **Reflexologist** Ms A Mitchell Q: IIHHT, MTI. M: GCP.
C Yrs. Est.: 2 (Ref:HM00906)

### ANNES BEAUTY SALON
**Annes Beauty Salon**, 3 Biddulph Rd, South Croydon, **Surrey**, CR2 6QA, ENG.
(T) 020 8660 6768
Speciality: Aromatherapy.
M O (Ref:HM00907)

### ANNEXE CLINIC
**Annexe Clinic (The)**, 21 Privet Rd, Bournemouth, **Dorset**, BH9 2NS, ENG.
(T) 01202 537067 (F) 01202 536482
Speciality: Chiropractors.
● **Partner** Mr A Sheasby
P S T (Ref:HM00908)

### ANNIES NATURAL HEALTH CENTRE
**Annies Natural Health Centre**, 5 Cherry Trees, Hartley, Longfield, **Kent**, DA3 8DS, ENG.
(T) 01474 707202
Speciality: Complementary Medicines & Therapy.
● **Owner** Mrs A Biggs
C M (Ref:HM00909)

### ANNMARIE
**Annmarie**, Winchester St, Coventry, **Midlands (West)**, CV1 5NU, ENG.
(T) 024 7663 0807
Speciality: Clairvoyants & Palmists.
● **Owner** Ms A Godsmark
B (Ref:HM00910)

### ANN'S MIGRAINE DIETARY PLAN
**Ann's Migraine Dietary Plan**, 58 Laindon Rd, Billericay, **Essex**, CM12 9LD, ENG.
(T) 01277 658080 (F) 01277 631895
Speciality: Acupuncture.
● **Owner** Mrs A Din
O (Ref:HM00911)

### ANSELL, H
**H Ansell**, 64 Appledore Cres, Sidcup, **Kent**, DA14 6RQ, ENG.
(T) 020 8302 8324

Speciality: Chiropodists (Podiatrists).
● **Owner** Mrs H Ansell
**S** (**Ref:**HM00912)

## ANSELL, JOHN

**John Ansell**, 45 Sackville Rd, Hove, **Sussex (East)**, BN3 3WD, ENG.
(T) 01273 736959 (F) 01273 723369
Speciality: Physiotherapy.
● **Owner** Mr J Ansell
**P S T** (**Ref:**HM00913)

## ANSELL, S

**S Ansell**, 17 Badgers Cl, Ivybridge, **Devon**, PL21 9TN, ENG.
(T) 01752 698522
Speciality: Reflexology.
● **Owner** Mrs S Ansell
**S T** (**Ref:**HM00914)

## ANSON CENTRE

**Anson Centre For Complementary Medicine (The)**, Anson House, 183 Horninglow St, Burton-On-Trent, **Staffordshire**, DE14 1NG, ENG.
(T) 01283 516444 (F) 01283 516444
Speciality: Complementary Medicines & Therapy.
● **Manager** Mr G Gargini
**M** (**Ref:**HM00915)

## ANSON, BARRIE

**Barrie Anson**, Rowan House, Mahlerbie Court, Knowle St. Giles, Chard, **Somerset**, TA20 4AZ, ENG.
(T) 01460 63238
(E) barrie.anson@virgin.net
(W) www.barrieanson.50megs.com
Speciality: Absent Healing, Bach Remedies, Biofeedback, Complementary Therapy, Counselling, Faith Healing, Floral Essence Therapy, Healer, Healing Therapy, Herbal Medicine, Holistic Healing, Homeopathy, Hypnosis, Hypnotherapy, Meditation, Nutritional Therapy, Psychotherapy, Spiritual Healing, Stress Therapy, Vitamin Therapy, Food Sensitivity Testing. ✔
● **Practitioner** Mr B Anson
**B** Yrs. Est.: 20 (**Ref:**HM00916)

## ANSTEE, M J

**M J Anstee**, 49 Elm Gr, Woburn Sands, Milton Keynes, **Buckinghamshire**, MK17 8QA, ENG.
(T) 01908 584553 (F) 01908 584553
Speciality: Complementary Medicines & Therapy.
● **Owner** Mrs M Anstee
**C M** (**Ref:**HM00917)

## ANTHONY, JOHN

**John Anthony**, 86 Gordon St, Aberdeen, **Aberdeenshire**, AB11 6EW, SCO.
(T) 01224 580899
Speciality: Psychotherapy.
● **Owner** Mr J Anthony
**B** (**Ref:**HM00918)

## ANTHONY, PETER

**Peter Anthony**, 33 Belsize Lane, London, **London (Greater)**, NW3 5AS, ENG.
(T) 020 7435 6826
Speciality: Complementary Medicines & Therapy, Trichology.
**M** (**Ref:**HM00919)

## ANTHROPOSOPHICAL MEDICAL ASS

**Anthroposophical Medical Association**, Park Attwood Clinic, Trimpley, Bewdley, **Worcestershire**, DY12 1RE, ENG.
(T) 01299 861444
Speciality: Complementary Medicines & Therapy.
● **Doctor** Dr J Dycon
**M** (**Ref:**HM00920)

## ANTI SNORING

**Anti Snoring**, Second Floor, Talbot House, 17 Church St, Rickmansworth, **Hertfordshire**, WD3 1DE, ENG.
(T) 01923 775677
Speciality: Complementary Medicines & Therapy.
● **Office Manager** Mrs S Smith
**M** (**Ref:**HM00921)

## ANTON HOUSE OF AVILON

**Anton House Of Avilon**, 2 Milecastle, Bancroft, Milton Keynes, **Buckinghamshire**, MK13 0QL, ENG.
(T) 01908 312594
Speciality: Clairvoyants & Palmists.
**B** (**Ref:**HM00922)

## ANTRIM CHIROPRACTIC CLINIC

**Antrim Chiropractic Clinic**, 35 Belfast Rd, Antrim, **County Antrim**, BT41 1PB, NIR.
(T) 028 9447 9144 (F) 028 9447 9144
(E) k.l@btinternet.com
Speciality: Acupuncture, Chiropractic, Herbal Medicine. ✔
● **Chiropractor** Dr B McElroy Q: BSc (Hons), MSc (Chiro).
● **Owner** Dr K Loughlin Q: BSc (Chiro), BSc (Hons), DC, RGN. M: BCA, GCC.
**P S T** Yrs. Est.: 5 (**Ref:**HM00923)

## ANTSCHERL, M

**M Antscherl**, 90 Basingstoke Rd, Reading, **Berkshire**, RG2 0EL, ENG.
(T) 01189 871925
Speciality: Physiotherapy.
**P S T** (**Ref:**HM00924)

## AOK INSPIRATIONAL

**AOK Inspirational Hypnotherapy & Counselling**, Inspiration House, Stockton, Southam, **Warwickshire**, CV47 8JU, ENG.
(T) 07000 268537
Speciality: Hypnosis.
● **Managing Director** Ms P Bould
**B** (**Ref:**HM00925)

## AP CHEMIST/HOMOEOPATHIC CTRE

**A P Chemist & Homoeopathic Medical Centre**, 41 High St Colliers Wood, London, **London (Greater)**, SW19 2JE, ENG.
(T) 020 8542 3221 (F) 020 8542 3221
Speciality: Homeopathy.
● **Owner** Mr A Pancholi
**M** (**Ref:**HM00926)

## AP CLINIC OF PHYSICAL MEDICINE

**A P Clinic Of Physical Medicine (Est 1985)**, 337 Muswell Hill Broadway, London, **London (Greater)**, N10 1BX, ENG.
(T) 020 8444 1920
Speciality: Osteopathy.
● **Practitioner** Mr N Patel
**P S T** (**Ref:**HM00927)

## APACHE

**Apache**, Archers Wood Farm, Coppingford Rd, Sawtry, Huntingdon, **Cambridgeshire**, PE28 5XY, ENG.
(T) 01487 832040
(W) www.apache.avieators.net
Speciality: Complementary Medicines & Therapy.
● **Chairman** Ms K Zablotzky
**C** (**Ref:**HM00928)

## APEX HYPNOTHERAPY

**Apex Hypnotherapy**, 16 Wymbush Gdns, Bristol, BS13 0AZ, ENG.
(T) 01179 641048
Speciality: Hypnotherapy.
● **Owner** Mr D Angell
**B** (**Ref:**HM00929)

## APHRODITE'S

**Aphrodite's**, 271 Chesterfield Rd, Sheffield, **Yorkshire (South)**, S8 0RT, ENG.
(T) 01142 812705
Speciality: Complementary Medicines & Therapy.
**C M** (**Ref:**HM00930)

## APL INTERNATIONAL

**APL International Ltd**, 385 High Rd, London, **London (Greater)**, N22 8JA, ENG.
(T) 020 8889 3300 (F) 020 8889 3300
Speciality: Clairvoyants & Palmists.
**B** (**Ref:**HM00931)

## APOTHECARY

**Apothecary**, 103 High St, Syston, Leicester, **Leicestershire**, LE7 1GQ, ENG.
(T) 01162 694590
Speciality: Herbal Medicine.
**M** (**Ref:**HM00932)

## APOTHECARY

**Apothecary (The)**, Brereton Lodge, Goathland, Whitby, **Yorkshire (North)**, YO22 5JR, ENG.
(T) 01947 896038 (F) 01947 896482
Speciality: Herbal Medicine.
● **Manager** Mr J Fernley
**M** (**Ref:**HM00933)

## APOTHECARY 2

**Apothecary 2**, Unit 7 Craven Court, Skipton, **Yorkshire (North)**, BD23 2AP, ENG.
(T) 01756 700295
Speciality: Complementary Medicines & Therapy.
**C M** (**Ref:**HM00934)

## APPEARANCE PLUS

**Appearance Plus**, 129 Browns Lane, Allesley, Coventry, **Midlands (West)**, CV5 9DY, ENG.
(T) 024 7640 4237
Speciality: Electrolysis.
● **Owner** Mrs C Motram
**T** (**Ref:**HM00935)

## APPLE TREE CLINIC

**Apple Tree Clinic (The)**, 91 The Avenue, Kennington, Oxford, **Oxfordshire**, OX1 5PR, ENG.
(T) 01865 735353
Speciality: Acupuncture.
● **Owner** Mrs J White
**O** (**Ref:**HM00936)

## APPLEBEE THERAPY

**Applebee Therapy**, 56 Burnway, Hornchurch, **Essex**, RM11 3SG, ENG.
(T) 01708 472573
Speciality: Hypnotherapy.
● **Owner** Mrs P Steel
**B** (**Ref:**HM00937)

## APPLEBY LEIGH AROMATHERAPIST

**Appleby Leigh Aromatherapist**, 146 Balgores Lane, Romford, **Essex**, RM2 6BP, ENG.
(T) 01708 735195
Speciality: Aromatherapy.
**M O** (**Ref:**HM00938)

## APPLEBY, W

**W Appleby**, 55 Peebles Avenue, St. Helens, **Merseyside**, WA11 9QS, ENG.
(T) 01744 755813
Speciality: Chiropodists (Podiatrists).
● **Owner** Mr W Appleby
**S** (**Ref:**HM00939)

## APPLEDORE CENTRE

**Appledore Centre (The)**, 8 Coronation Avenue, East Tilbury, Tilbury, **Essex**, RM18 8SJ, ENG.
(T) 01375 858657
Speciality: Complementary Medicines & Therapy.
**C M** (**Ref:**HM00940)

## APPLEGARTH

**Applegarth**, 29 Trentside, Keadby, Scunthorpe, **Humberside**, DN17 3EF, ENG.
(T) 01724 782980
Speciality: Complementary Medicines & Therapy.
**C M** (**Ref:**HM00941)

## APPLEGATE AROMATHERAPY

**Applegate Aromatherapy**, 29 Bridle Lane, Norwich, **Norfolk**, NR4 6RU, ENG.
(T) 01603 503966
Speciality: Complementary Medicines & Therapy.
● **Owner** Ms M Ransom
**C M** (**Ref:**HM00942)

## APPLETON, CARRIE

**Carrie Appleton**, Silver Cl, Dukinfield, **Cheshire**, SK16 4XD, ENG.
(T) 01613 083306
Speciality: Chiropodists (Podiatrists).
● **Owner** Mrs C Appleton
**S** (**Ref:**HM00943)

## APPLETREE CHIROPODY

**Appletree Chiropody**, 5 Botany Bay Rd, Southampton, **Hampshire**, SO19 8LT, ENG.
(T) 023 8044 4313



Key continued: **Yrs.Est:** Years Established **Q:** Qualifications **M:** Professional Membership ✔ Indemnity Insurance ▬ Accept Credit Cards

**Speciality:** Chiropodists (Podiatrists).
S (Ref:HM00944)

## APPLETREE COUNSELLING

**Appletree Counselling, Relationships, Bereavement**, 3 Appletree Lane, Spencers Wood, Reading, **Berkshire**, RG7 1EE, ENG.
(T) 01189 884360
**Speciality:** Psychotherapy.
B (Ref:HM00945)

## APPLETREE HEALTHY LIVING CTRE

**Appletree Healthy Living Centre**, 13 Lincoln Rd, Newark, **Nottinghamshire**, NG24 2BU, ENG.
(T) 01636 707156 (F) 01636 707174
**Speciality:** Osteopathy.
● **Owner** Miss A Wilkinson
P S T (Ref:HM00946)

## APPLEYARD, J

**J Appleyard**, 85 Dudwell Lane, Halifax, **Yorkshire (West)**, HX3 0SH, ENG.
(T) 01422 358291
**Speciality:** Physiotherapy.
● **Owner** Mrs J Appleyard
P S T (Ref:HM00947)

## APPLIED PSYCHOLOGY SERVICES

**Applied Psychology Services**, Crewes Pl, Crewes Lane, Warlingham, **Surrey**, CR6 9NS, ENG.
(T) 01883 626185
**Speciality:** Psychology.
B (Ref:HM00948)

## APPS, JENNY

**Jenny Apps**, Tudor Lodge, Hungate Rd, Emneth, Wisbech, **Cambridgeshire**, PE14 8EQ, ENG.
(T) 01945 581671
**Speciality:** Chiropodists (Podiatrists).
S (Ref:HM00949)

## APT LASER THERAPY

**APT Laser Therapy**, Room 22, Victoria Buildings Business Centre, Violet St, Paisley, **Renfrewshire**, PA1 1PA, SCO.
(T) 01415 612007
**Speciality:** Laser Treatment. ✔
● **Partner** Mr M Smith
● **Laser Therapist** Rita McBride
C **Yrs. Est.:** 3 (Ref:HM00950)

## AQCH

**Association Of Qualified Curative Hypnotherapi (The)**, 128 Spring Parklands, Dudley, **Midlands (West)**, DY1 2DN, ENG.
(T) 01384 866481
**Speciality:** Hypnotherapy.
● **Owner** Mr T Lancaster
B (Ref:HM00951)

## AQUA

**Aqua**, 186 Waleton Acres, Carew Rd, Wallington, **Surrey**, SM6 8PY, ENG.
(T) 020 8773 0181
**Speciality:** Clairvoyants & Palmists.
B (Ref:HM00952)

## AQUA OLEUM

**Aqua Oleum**, Unit 3 Lower Wharf, Wallbridge, Stroud, **Gloucestershire**, GL5 3JB, ENG.
(T) 01453 753555 (F) 01453 752179
**Speciality:** Aromatherapy.
● **General Manager** Mr I Wolfenden
M O (Ref:HM00953)

## AQUAMAID

**Aquamaid**, 225-229 Putney Bridge Rd, London, **London (Greater)**, SW15 2WW, ENG.
(T) 020 8874 1130 (F) 020 8871 0066
**Speciality:** Complementary Medicines & Therapy.
● **Managing Director** Mr R Woodward
M (Ref:HM00954)

## AQUARIAN SCHOOL HERTFORDSHIRE

**Aquarian School Hertfordshire**, 67 Haldens, Welwyn Garden City, **Hertfordshire**, AL7 1DH, ENG.
(T) 01707 325976
(W) www.complementary-healthcare.co.uk/info/aquarian
**Speciality:** Reflexology.
S T (Ref:HM00955)

## AQUARIUS AROMATHERAPY

**Aquarius Aromatherapy**, 155 Victoria Rd, Fulwood, Preston, **Lancashire**, PR2 8AJ, ENG.
(T) 01772 468834
**Speciality:** Aromatherapy.
● **Owner** Ms P Saul
M O (Ref:HM00956)

## AQUARIUS ESSENTIAL OILS

**Aquarius Essential Oils**, Suite 26a, Caledonia House, Longford Avenue, Kilwinning, **Ayrshire (North)**, KA13 6EX, SCO.
(T) 01294 558658
**Speciality:** Aromatherapy.
M O (Ref:HM00957)

## AQUARIUS HEALING

**Aquarius Healing**, 13 Belmont Gr, Havant, **Hampshire**, PO9 3PT, ENG.
(T) 023 9264 1358
**Speciality:** Homeopathy.
M (Ref:HM00958)

## AQUARIUS HEALTH CENTRE

**Indira Kotecha**, 213A Passage Rd, Bristol, BS10 7DL, ENG.
(T) 01179 590438
**Speciality:** Acupuncture, Allergy Testing, Aromatherapy, Homeopathy, Nutritional Therapy, Reflexology, Shiatsu, Stress Therapy. ✔
● **Natural/Complementary Medicine Practitioner**
Mrs I Kotecha **Q:** BA, Dip.Ac, Dip.Hom, RMN, SRN.
C **Yrs. Est.:** 20 (Ref:HM00959)

## AQUARONE REMY

**Aquarone Remy**, 11 Pottergate, Norwich, **Norfolk**, NR2 1DS, ENG.
(T) 01603 633115
**Speciality:** Psychotherapy.
B (Ref:HM00960)

## ARAGON, HOLLY

**Holly Aragon**, Park Lane Complementary Health Centre, 70D Park Lane, Chippenham, **Wiltshire**, SN15 1LW, ENG.
(T) 01249 655088
**Speciality:** Acupuncture.
O (Ref:HM00961)

## ARAMINTA

**Araminta**, Marquis House, 2 North St, Winchcombe, Cheltenham, **Gloucestershire**, GL54 5LH, ENG.
(T) 01242 604686
**Speciality:** Clairvoyants & Palmists.
● **Owner** Miss M Blandford
B (Ref:HM00962)

## ARBORETUM/WALSALL CHIROPRACTIC

**Arboretum & Walsall Chiropractic Health Clinic**, 81 Broadway, Walsall, **Midlands (West)**, WS1 3EZ, ENG.
(T) 01922 634959
(W) www.chiro1.net
**Speciality:** Chiropractic, Myofascial Dry Needling.
● **Chiropractor** Dr P Malone
P S T (Ref:HM00963)

## ARBOUR

**Arbour Hypnotherapy Therapeutic Counselling**, 106 London Rd, Liverpool, **Merseyside**, L3 5JY, ENG.
(T) 01512 201554
**Speciality:** Hypnotherapy.
B (Ref:HM00964)

## ARBOURS

**Arbours Chiropody Service**, 21 Paxton Rd, Northampton, **Northamptonshire**, NN3 3RL, ENG.
(T) 01604 410010
(E) jshh20aol.com
**Speciality:** Biomechanics, Chiropody, Nail Surgery, Orthotics. ✔
● **Chiropodist (Podiatrist)**
Mrs J Stiff **Q:** BSc. **M:** S.C.P.
C **Yrs. Est.:** 1 (Ref:HM00965)

## ARBOURS ASSOCIATION

**Arbours Association (The)**, 6 Church Lane, London, **London (Greater)**, N8 7BU, ENG.
(T) 020 8340 7646
**Speciality:** Psychotherapy.
● **Accountant** Mr R Desai
B (Ref:HM00966)

## ARBOURS CRISIS CENTRE

**Arbours Crisis Centre**, 41 Weston Park, London, **London (Greater)**, N8 9SY, ENG.
(T) 020 8340 8125
**Speciality:** Psychotherapy.
B (Ref:HM00967)

## ARC HEALTHCARE

**Arc Healthcare**, 5 Dale Rd, Leigh-On-Sea, **Essex**, SS9 2RQ, ENG.
(T) 01702 476805
(E) arc.healthcare@btinternet.com
**Speciality:** Bach Remedies, Counselling, Homeopathy, Kinesiology, Naturopathy, Nutritional Therapy. ✔
● **Healthcare Practitioner**
Mrs E Gilmore **Q:** C.B.A.K, Dip.Couns, Dip.ION, LCH.
B C **Yrs. Est.:** 4 (Ref:HM00968)

## ARCANIA

**Arcania**, 17 Union Passage, Bath, **Somerset**, BA1 1RE, ENG.
(T) 01225 335233
**Speciality:** Complementary Medicines & Therapy.
● **Owner** Mr R Howard
C M (Ref:HM00969)

## ARCHANGEL MICHAEL SOUL

**Archangel Michael Soul Therapy Centre (The)**, George St, Glastonbury, **Somerset**, BA6 9JH, ENG.
(T) 01458 832482 (F) 01458 832482
**Speciality:** Complementary Medicines & Therapy.
C M (Ref:HM00970)

## ARCHER, ANNE

**Anne Archer**, 9 London Rd, Halstead, Sevenoaks, **Kent**, TN14 7DS, ENG.
(T) 01959 534580
**Speciality:** Acupuncture.
O (Ref:HM00971)

## ARCHER, C A

**C A Archer**, 18 Pentland Cl, Washington, **Tyne and Wear**, NE38 0PG, ENG.
(T) 01914 174962
**Speciality:** Chiropodists (Podiatrists).
S (Ref:HM00972)

## ARCHER, D J B

**D J B Archer**, 8 Ranfurly Avenue, Bangor, **County Down**, BT20 3SN, NIR.
(T) 028 9127 0932 (F) 028 9127 0932
**Speciality:** Physiotherapy.
● **Owner** Mrs D Archer
P S T (Ref:HM00973)

## ARCHER, DEBORAH

**Deborah Archer**, 77 Harston Drive, Enfield, **London (Greater)**, EN3 6GJ, ENG.
(T) 020 8245 1021
**Speciality:** Chiropractic.
P S T (Ref:HM00974)

## ARCHER, J

**J Archer**, 86 Clipstone Rd West, Forest Town, Mansfield, **Nottinghamshire**, NG19 0HL, ENG.
(T) 01623 626564
**Speciality:** Chiropodists (Podiatrists).
● **Owner** Mrs J Archer
S (Ref:HM00975)

## ARCHER, JOANNE

**Joanne Archer**, 5 Willoughby Rd, Kingston Upon Thames, **Surrey**, KT2 6LN, ENG.
(T) 020 8549 5669
**Speciality:** Chiropractors.
● **Owner** Miss J Archer
P S T (Ref:HM00976)

## ARCHER, JULIE

**Julie B Archer Sc(Ost ) DO**, The Burghwood Clinic, 34 Brighton Rd, Banstead, **Surrey**, SM7 1BS, ENG.
(T) 01737 361177
**Speciality:** Osteopathy.

Key: B Mind-Body Medicine · C Complementary Medicine · H Self Help Treatment · M Medicinal Therapy · O Oriental Medicine · P Postural Therapy · S Manipulative Structural Therapy · T Touch Therapy

P S T (Ref:HM00977)

**ARCHER, JULIE**

**Julie Archer**, Beaulieu Cl, Datchet, Slough, **Berkshire**, SL3 9DD, ENG.
(T) 01753 591622
Speciality: Osteopathy.
● **Owner** Mrs J Archer
P S T (Ref:HM00978)

**ARCHER, SARAH**

**Sarah Archer**, Forget-Me-Not Cottage, 12 Denmark Rd, London, **London (Greater)**, SW19 4PG, ENG.
(T) 020 8946 8586
Speciality: Reflexology.
S T (Ref:HM00979)

**ARCHIBALD, LIZ**

**Liz Archibald CHP (NC)**, The Rushes, Sansomes Hill, Milborne Port, Sherborne, **Dorset**, DT9 5AJ, ENG.
(T) 01963 250231
Speciality: Aversion Therapy, Hypnosis, Hypnotherapy, Phytotherapy, Stress Therapy. ✔
● **Hypnotherapist** Ms L Archibald Q: C.Hyp.
H Yrs. Est.: 16 (Ref:HM00980)

**ARCHIBALD, VALERIE**

**Valerie Archibald**, 4 Deepdene Court, London, **London (Greater)**, N21 2NH, ENG.
(T) 020 8360 7405
Speciality: Reflexology.
S T (Ref:HM00981)

**ARCHWAY CLINIC OF HERBAL MED**

**Archway Clinic Of Herbal Medicine (The)**, Highgate Hill, London, **London (Greater)**, N19 5NF, ENG.
(T) 020 7288 3666
Speciality: Herbalists.
● **Manager** Mr M Walia
M (Ref:HM00982)

**ARCHWAY HSE NATURAL HLTH CTRE**

**Archway House Natural Health Centre**, 44 Coventry Rd, Market Harborough, **Leicestershire**, LE16 9BZ, ENG.
(T) 01858 410820 (F) 01858 410820
Speciality: Acupuncture, Aromatherapy, Chiropractic, Reflexology, Reiki, Shiatsu, Zero Balancing, Feng Shui. ✔
● **Reiki Practitioner/Reflexologist**
Ms J Gough
● **Shiatsu Practitioner/Aromatherapist**
Ms M Steadman
● **Owner/Acupuncturist** Mr A Welton
M: BAcC.
C Yrs. Est.: 5 (Ref:HM00983)

**ARCHWAYS-EFFIE GARDNER**

**Archways-Effie Gardner**, 20 Grove Farm Cl, Leeds, **Yorkshire (West)**, LS16 6DB, ENG.
(T) 01132 612658
Speciality: Hypnotherapy.
B (Ref:HM00984)

**ARCIER, MICHELINE**

**Micheline Arcier**, 7 William St, London, **London (Greater)**, SW1X 9HL, ENG.
(T) 020 7235 5282
Speciality: Aromatherapy.
M O (Ref:HM00985)

**ARCOS, LYNNE**

**Lynne Arcos ITEC MAR**, Meyrick House, St Nicholas, Cardiff, **Glamorgan (Vale of)**, CF5 6SG, WAL.
(T) 01446 760631
Speciality: Reflexology.
● **Owner** Ms L Arcos Q: ITEC, MAR.
S T (Ref:HM00986)

**ARCTURUES CLINIC**

**Arcturues Clinic**, 47 Fore St, Totnes, **Devon**, TQ9 5NJ, ENG.
(T) 01803 868282
(E) info@arcturuesclinic.co.uk
Speciality: Acupuncture, Bowen Therapy, Chiropractic, Cranio-Sacral Therapy, Homeopathy, Massage (Therapeutic), Osteopathy, Psychotherapy, Reflexology. ✔
● **Cranio-Sacral Therapist**
Mr L Kaine Q: RCST.
● **Acupuncturist** Dr S Hopwood Q: Ch.B, Lic.Ac, MB, MBAcC.
C Yrs. Est.: 6 (Ref:HM00987)

**ARDAGH ACUPUNCTURE CLINIC**

**Ardagh Acupuncture Clinic**, 25 Ardagh Drive, Blackrock, **County Dublin**, IRE.
(T) 087 2831328
Speciality: Acupuncture, Counselling, Cupping, Moxibustion, Nutritional Therapy, Oriental Diagnosis, Reiki, Ying & Yang. ✔
● **Acupuncturist/Reiki Practitioner**
Mr P Donnelly Q: Dip.Ac, Reiki 1, Reiki 2. M: AFI.
O Yrs. Est.: 3 (Ref:HM00988)

**ARDAGH CLINIC**

**Ardagh Clinic**, 118 Stillorgan Rd, Dublin, **County Dublin**, IRE.
(T) 01260 0115
Speciality: Psychotherapy.
B (Ref:HM00989)

**ARDEN HYPNOTHERAPY**

**Arden Hypnotherapy**, 243 High St, Henley-In-Arden, Solihull, **Warwickshire**, B95 5BG, ENG.
(T) 01564 792144
Speciality: Neuro-Linguistic Program, Personal Development.
● **Owner** Mr J Clarke
C (Ref:HM00990)

**ARDENTE CHIROPODY SERVICE**

**Ardente Chiropody Service**, 4 Fish St, Off Briggate, Leeds, **Yorkshire (West)**, LS1 6DB, ENG.
(T) 01132 457647 (F) 01132 347921
Speciality: Chiropody, Podiatry. ✔
● **Manager** Mr T Irving
● **Chiropodist (Podiatrist)**
Ms S Hamer-Bloom Q: MBChA, MSSCh.
M: B.A.Ch.P.
S Yrs. Est.: 15 (Ref:HM00991)

**ARDERN FOOT & HEALTH CLINIC**

**Ardern Foot & Health Clinic (The)**, 123 St James's St, Brighton, **Sussex (East)**, BN2 1TH, ENG.
(T) 01273 673964
Speciality: Biomechanics, Chiropody, Indian Head Massage, Nutritional Therapy, Podiatry, Reflexology. ✔ CREDIT
● **Therapist** Ms S Ardern Q: MBRA, S.R.Ch.
M: BRA, S.C.P.
M T Yrs. Est.: 10 (Ref:HM00992)

**ARDS CHIROPRACTIC CLINIC**

**Ards Chiropractic Clinic**, 69 Frances St, Newtownards, **County Down**, BT23 7DX, NIR.
(T) 028 9182 6696
Speciality: Acupuncture, Chiropractic. ✔
● **Owner** Dr R Hilary Q: DC, Lic.Ac. M: BCA, GCC.
P Yrs. Est.: 9 (Ref:HM00993)

**ARDUINO, JANE**

**Jane Arduino**, 14 The Pingle, Rugeley, **Staffordshire**, WS15 2UR, ENG.
(T) 01889 585480
Speciality: Clairvoyants & Palmists.
● **Owner** Miss J Arduino
B (Ref:HM00994)

**ARDUNA COUNS & PSYCHOTHPY CTRE**

**Arduna Ltd**, 55 Clontarf Rd, Dublin, **County Dublin**, IRE.
(T) 00 353 18 332733 (F) 01833 1758
Speciality: Cognitive Therapy, Counselling, Family Therapy, Group Therapy, Psychotherapy, Couple Therapy, Child & Adolescent Educational/Psychological Assessment and Therapy.
● **Therapist** Ms B Mackey Q: MB.
● **Therapist** Maeve Daly Q: MB.
M Yrs. Est.: 7 (Ref:HM00995)

**ARGYLL HERBS DIRECT**

**Argyll Herbs Direct**, 9 Chancellors Pound, Redhill, Bristol, BS40 5TZ, ENG.
(T) 01934 863353
Speciality: Complementary Medicines & Therapy.
C M (Ref:HM00996)

**ARIES OSTEOPATHIC HEALTH CLNC**

**Aries Osteopathic Health Clinic**, 14 Woodside Rd, Poole, **Dorset**, BH14 9JJ, ENG.
(T) 01202 743100
Speciality: Osteopathy.
● **Owner** Miss H Annauth
P S T (Ref:HM00997)

**ARIORI, A R**

**A R Ariori**, Hepworth Chambers, Bank Passage, Colchester, **Essex**, CO1 1HZ, ENG.
(T) 01206 578988
Speciality: Chiropodists (Podiatrists).
● **Owner** Mr A Ariori
S (Ref:HM00998)

**ARIORI, A R & B M**

**A R & B M Ariori**, 25 Wellesley Rd, Clacton-On-Sea, **Essex**, CO15 3PW, ENG.
(T) 01255 434364
Speciality: Chiropodists (Podiatrists).
● **Partner** Mr A Ariori
S (Ref:HM00999)

**ARJUNA NATURAL HEALTH CENTRE**

**Arjuna Natural Health Centre Ltd**, 12A Mill Rd, Cambridge, **Cambridgeshire**, CB1 2AB, ENG.
(T) 01223 566122 (F) 01223 303172
Speciality: Acupuncture, Alexander Technique, Aromatherapy, Counselling, Homeopathy, Hypnotherapy, Indian Head Massage, Iridology, Nutritional Therapy, Osteopathy, Reflexology, Reiki, Shiatsu, Herbalism, Massage, Phytobiophysics Flower Formulas, Shen. ✔
● **Nutritional Therapist** Ms J Green
● **Hypnotherapist** Ms T Cheslaw Q: DHP (NC), DipCH.P, UKHR. M: CPS.
● **Homeopath** Ms R Currie Q: Lic.Hom.
● **Pilates Bodywork Therapist**
Michelina Craft Q: MSc.
● **Herbalist/Iridologist/Reflexologist**
Christine Sheila Gray Q: MH.
● **Osteopath** Ms K Binks Q: DO, MSc.
● **Therapeutic Massage**
Nersys Edmonds Q: APNT, BA (Hons), MGCP.
● **Body Psychotherapist/Holistic Massage Therapist**
Ms E Houwen Q: DHP (NC).
● **Shiatsu Therapist** Ms A Woodburn Q: MRSS.
● **Cranio-Sacral Therapist/Biodynamic Massage**
Ms G Edwards Q: BA (Hons), RCST.
● **Counsellor/Psychotherapist**
Ms C Heal Q: BA, Dip.Couns.
● **Acupuncturist** Ms H Barratt Q: Lic.Ac.
M: BAcC.
● **Alexander Technique Therapist**
Pippa Bondy Q: MSTAT.
B Yrs. Est.: 5 (Ref:HM01000)

**ARK CLINIC**

**Ark Clinic**, 59 Mogden Lane, Isleworth, **London (Greater)**, TW7 7LH, ENG.
(T) 020 8891 5435
Speciality: Acupuncture.
O (Ref:HM01001)

**ARK COUNSELLING**

**Ark Counselling**, 122 Churchview Rd, Killiney, **County Dublin**, IRE.
(T) 01284 8766
Speciality: Counselling.
B H (Ref:HM01002)

**ARK HYPNOTHERAPY**

**Ark Hypnotherapy**, 122 Churchview Rd, Killiney, **County Dublin**, IRE.
(T) 01284 8766
Speciality: Hypnotherapy.
B (Ref:HM01003)

**ARK NATURAL HEALING CENTRE**

**Ark Natural Healing Centre (The)**, 17 Quay St, Haverfordwest, **Pembrokeshire**, SA61 1BG, WAL.
(T) 01437 763855
Speciality: Complementary Medicines & Therapy.
C M (Ref:HM01004)

**ARKLEY, BRENDA**

**Brenda Arkley**, 101 Stephens Rd, Tadley,



Key continued: Yrs.Est: Years Established Q: Qualifications M: Professional Membership ✔ Indemnity Insurance CREDIT Accept Credit Cards

**Hampshire**, RG26 3RT, ENG.
(T) 01189 813141
Speciality: Reflexology.
● **Owner** Mrs B Arkley
[S] [T] (Ref:HM01005)

## ARKLOW CHIROPRACTIC CLINIC

**Arklow Chiropractic Clinic**, Inbhearmor Pk, Templerainey, Arklow, **County Wicklow**, IRE.
(T) 07702 91133 (F) 07702 91851
Speciality: Chiropractors.
[P] [S] [T] (Ref:HM01006)

## ARKLOW NATURAL HEALING CENTRE

**Arklow Natural Healing Centre**, 8 St Mary's Rd, Arklow, **County Wicklow**, IRE.
(T) 07702 33933
(E) diane_stauder@hotmail.com
Speciality: Bach Remedies, Floral Essence Therapy, Homeopathy, Indian Head Massage, Macrobiotics, Meditation, Bush Flower Remedies. ✓
● **Homeopath** Ms D Stauder M: ISH.
[M] Yrs. Est.: 3 (Ref:HM01007)

## ARKSEY, LINDA

**Linda Arksey**, The Castle Clinic, 18-20 The Ropewalk, Nottingham, **Nottinghamshire**, NG1 5DT, ENG.
(T) 01159 472263 (F) 01159 556306
Speciality: Aromatherapy.
● **Owner** Mr M Pook
[M] [O] (Ref:HM01008)

## ARMAGH CHIROPRACTIC CLINIC

**Armagh Chiropractic Clinic**, 37A Thomas St, Armagh, **County Armagh**, BT61 7QB, NIR.
(T) 028 3751 1955
Speciality: Chiropractic.
● **Manager** Ms B Mallon
[P] [S] [T] (Ref:HM01009)

## ARMFIELD, L S

**L S Armfield**, Old School, Auchterarder, **Perth and Kinross**, PH3 1JU, SCO.
(T) 01764 664600
Speciality: Osteopathy.
● **Owner** Mr L Armfield
[P] [S] [T] (Ref:HM01010)

## ARMITAGE, D R

**D R Armitage (Sale) Ltd**, 53 Washway Rd, Sale, **Cheshire**, M33 7AB, ENG.
(T) 01619 622968
Speciality: Electrolysis.
● **Director** Mr D Armitage
[T] (Ref:HM01011)

## ARMITAGE, KATHERINE

**Katherine Armitage**, 68 Fallsbrook Rd, London, **London (Greater)**, SW16 6DX, ENG.
(T) 020 8769 9093
Speciality: Complementary Medicines & Therapy.
● **Owner** Ms K Armitage
[M] (Ref:HM01012)

## ARMITAGE, PETER

**Peter Armitage**, 47 Swanage Rd, London, **London (Greater)**, SW18 2DZ, ENG.
(T) 020 8877 9118
Speciality: Osteopathy.
● **Partner** Mrs F Armitage
[P] [S] [T] (Ref:HM01013)

## ARMITAGE, S

**S Armitage**, 149 Lord Lane, Failsworth, Manchester, **Manchester (Greater)**, M35 0QH, ENG.
(T) 01616 834189
Speciality: Osteopathy.
● **Partner** Mr D Armitage
[P] [S] [T] (Ref:HM01014)

## ARMITSTEAD, JOHN

**John Armitstead**, 19 Castle St, High Wycombe, **Buckinghamshire**, HP13 6RU, ENG.
(T) 01494 529763
Speciality: Osteopathy.
[P] [S] [T] (Ref:HM01015)

## ARMSTRONG HEALTH/HERBAL STORE

**Armstrong Health & Herbal Store**, 22 Town Rd, Stoke-On-Trent, **Staffordshire**, ST1 2JQ, ENG.
(T) 01782 215417
Speciality: Herbal Medicine.
● **Manager** Mrs L Dobell
[M] (Ref:HM01016)

## ARMSTRONG, ANNA

**Anna Armstrong**, 22 High St, Overton, **Hampshire**, RG25 3HA, ENG.
(T) 01256 773155
Speciality: Herbal Medicine, Phytotherapy. ✓
● **Medical Herbalist** Ms A Armstrong
(T) 01256 773243 Q: BSc, MNIMH. M: NIMH.
[M] (Ref:HM01017)

## ARMSTRONG, ANNA

**Anna Armstrong**, Narajo Complementary Therapies, 3 Newbury St, Whitchurch, **Hampshire**, RG28 5DW, ENG.
(T) 01256 773155
Speciality: Herbal Medicine, Phytotherapy. ✓
● **Medical Herbalist** Ms A Armstrong Q: BSc, MNIMH. M: NIMH.
[M] (Ref:HM01018)

## ARMSTRONG, CAROLYN

**Carolyn Armstrong**, Old St, Ludlow, **Shropshire**, SY8 1NP, ENG.
(T) 01584 878537
Speciality: Complementary Medicines & Therapy.
[C] [M] (Ref:HM01019)

## ARMSTRONG, DEE

**Dee Armstrong**, 77 Crispin Field, Pitstone, Leighton Buzzard, **Bedfordshire**, LU7 9DX, ENG.
(T) 01296 660161
Speciality: Aromatherapy.
● **Owner** Mrs D Armstrong
[M] [O] (Ref:HM01020)

## ARMSTRONG, ELIZABETH

**Elizabeth Armstrong**, 62 Berkeley Rd, Westbury Park, Bristol, BS6 7PL, ENG.
(T) 01179 742508
Speciality: Chiropractic, McTimoney - Holistic gentle adjustment. ✓
● **Owner/Chiropractor**
Mrs E Armstrong Q: BSc, DC, MMCA.
[P] Yrs. Est.: 8 (Ref:HM01021)

## ARMSTRONG, EVELYN

**Evelyn Armstrong**, 90 Malcolmson House, Tachbrook Estate, Aylesford St, London, **London (Greater)**, SW1V 3RS, ENG.
(T) 020 7630 6582
(W) www.complementary-healthcare.co.uk/info/armstrong
Speciality: Reflexology.
[S] [T] (Ref:HM01022)

## ARMSTRONG, HEATHER

**Heather Armstrong**, 14 The Gardens, Kettering, **Northamptonshire**, NN16 9DU, ENG.
(T) 01536 502722
Speciality: Reflexology.
[S] [T] (Ref:HM01023)

## ARMSTRONG, JOHN

**John Armstrong**, 76 Dukes Avenue, London, **London (Greater)**, W4 2AF, ENG.
(T) 020 8994 0685
Speciality: Osteopathy.
● **Owner** Mr J Armstrong
[P] [S] [T] (Ref:HM01024)

## ARMSTRONG, M G

**M G Armstrong**, 194 Bromley Rd, Beckenham, **Kent**, BR3 6PG, ENG.
(T) 020 8658 9709
Speciality: Physiotherapy.
● **Owner** Mrs M Armstrong
[P] [S] [T] (Ref:HM01025)

## ARMSTRONG, OLWYN

**Olwyn Armstrong**, 96 North Rd, Darlington, **County Durham**, DL1 2EQ, ENG.
(T) 01325 247111
Speciality: Aromatherapy.
● **Owner** Mrs O Armstrong
[M] [O] (Ref:HM01026)

## ARMSTRONG, PAT

**Pat Armstrong**, 481 Queensferry Rd, Edinburgh, **Edinburgh (City of)**, EH4 7ND, SCO.
(T) 01313 365595
Speciality: Chiropodists (Podiatrists).
● **Owner** Mrs P Armstrong
[S] (Ref:HM01027)

## ARMSTRONG, R F

**R F Armstrong**, 218 Ormeau Rd, Belfast, **County Antrim**, BT7 2FY, NIR.
(T) 028 9049 1094
Speciality: Chiropodists (Podiatrists).
[S] (Ref:HM01028)

## ARMSTRONG, SIAN

**Sian Armstrong**, 19 Oaktree Cl, Colden Common, Winchester, **Hampshire**, SO21 1UT, ENG.
(T) 01962 714433
Speciality: Chiropodists (Podiatrists).
[S] (Ref:HM01029)

## ARNAOUT, HUDA

**Huda Arnaout**, 65 Rathbone Rd, Smethwick, **Midlands (West)**, B67 5JF, ENG.
(T) 07970 757878
Speciality: Reflexology.
[S] [T] (Ref:HM01030)

## ARNDALE CHIROPRACTIC

**Arndale Chiropractic**, 28 Ringwood Rd, Poole, **Dorset**, BH14 0RL, ENG.
(T) 01202 661122
Speciality: Chiropractic. ✓
● **Chiropractor** Dr P Moondi Q: DC, PhD.
[P] Yrs. Est.: 15 (Ref:HM01031)

## ARNETT, J I

**J I Arnett**, 25 Princes St, Southend-On-Sea, **Essex**, SS1 1QA, ENG.
(T) 01702 344709
Speciality: Complementary Medicines & Therapy.
● **Owner** Mrs J Arnett
[C] [M] (Ref:HM01032)

## ARNOLD, ANNE

**Anne Arnold**, Fern Brook, 66 Glenhugh Rd, Ahoghill, Ballymena, **County Antrim**, BT42 1JD, NIR.
(T) 028 2587 8448
Speciality: Complementary Medicines & Therapy.
● **Owner** Ms A Arnold
[C] [M] (Ref:HM01033)

## ARNOLD, M S

**M S Arnold**, 10 Cobblestones, Hempstead, Gillingham, **Kent**, ME7 3NT, ENG.
(T) 01634 378459
Speciality: Homeopathy.
● **Owner** Mrs M Arnold
[M] (Ref:HM01034)

## ARNOLD, MARK

**Mark Arnold**, 45 Claremont Rd, Teddington, **London (Greater)**, TW11 8DH, ENG.
(T) 020 8977 4775
Speciality: Complementary Medicines & Therapy.
[C] [M] (Ref:HM01035)

## ARNOLD, PETER & JACKIE

**Peter & Jackie Arnold**, 74 Bedford Rd, Hitchin, **Hertfordshire**, SE5 2UD, ENG.
(T) 01462 450264
(W) www.p-arnold.co.uk
Speciality: Acupuncture, Herbal Medicine, Osteopathy. ✓
● **Chinese Herbalist** Mrs J Arnold Q: MRCHM. M: RCHM.
● **Osteopath/Acupuncturist**
Mr P Arnold Q: BSc, DO, Lic.Ac. M: GOsC.
[S] Yrs. Est.: 18 (Ref:HM01036)

## ARNOLD, SHIRLEY

**Shirley Arnold**, 132 Grenville Rd, Plymouth, **Devon**, PL4 9QA, ENG.
(T) 01752 202265
Speciality: Physiotherapy.
● **Owner** Mrs S Arnold
[P] [S] [T] (Ref:HM01037)

## ARNOLD, SUE

**Sue Arnold**, Willow Cottage, Tallarn Green,

Malpas, **Cheshire**, SY14 7LJ, ENG.
**(T)** 01948 770697
Speciality: Psychotherapy.
● **Owner** Mrs S Arnold
**B** (**Ref:**HM01038)

## ARNOLDS, SHIRLEY

**Shirley Arnolds**, 41 Sherford Rd, Plymouth, **Devon**, PL9 8DA, ENG.
**(T)** 01752 407100
Speciality: Physiotherapy.
● **Owner** Mrs S Arnolds
**P S T** (**Ref:**HM01039)

## ARNOTT, R A B

**R A B Arnott**, 20 Old Harpenden Rd, St. Albans, **Hertfordshire**, AL3 6AX, ENG.
**(T)** 01727 858588
Speciality: Physiotherapy.
● **Owner** Mr R Arnott
**P S T** (**Ref:**HM01040)

## AROMA

**Aroma**, 1a Fields Park Rd, Cardiff, **Glamorgan (Vale of)**, CF11 9JP, WAL.
**(T)** 029 2030 0090
Speciality: Aromatherapy.
● **Owner** Mrs A Taylor
**M O** (**Ref:**HM01041)

## AROMA

**Aroma**, 73B-4 High St, Dunbar, **Lothian (East)**, EH42 1EW, SCO.
**(T)** 01368 865965
Speciality: Aromatherapy, Reiki, Clinical Aromatherapy. ✓
● **Aromatherapist** Miss R Gallegher
Q: Dip.Arom. M: ISPA.
**C** Yrs. Est.: 5 (**Ref:**HM01042)

## AROMA - ZONE

**Aroma - Zone (The)**, 41 Main St, Ballybay, **County Monaghan**, IRE.
**(T)** 04297 41480
Speciality: Aromatherapy, Indian Head Massage, Massage (Therapeutic).
● **Owner/Manager** Ms M Carnew Q: Dip.Arom, Dip.Reflex, ITEC. M: GCP.
**M** Yrs. Est.: 2 (**Ref:**HM01043)

## AROMA BLISS

**Aroma Bliss**, 21 Oakwood Drive, Bingley, **Yorkshire (West)**, BD16 4SJ, ENG.
**(T)** 01274 551332
Speciality: Aromatherapy, Bach Remedies, Reflexology.
**M O** (**Ref:**HM01044)

## AROMA CARE

**Aroma Care**, 30 Market Pl, Uttoxeter, **Staffordshire**, ST14 8HP, ENG.
**(T)** 01889 563561
Speciality: Aromatherapy.
● **Owner** Mrs C Bettany
**M O** (**Ref:**HM01045)

## AROMA ENTERPRISES

**Aroma Enterprises**, 120 Maple Cl, Hayes, **London (Greater)**, UB4 9NH, ENG.
**(T)** 020 8845 7701
Speciality: Aromatherapy.
**M O** (**Ref:**HM01046)

## AROMA HAIR

**Aroma Hair**, 52A Church Rd, Portslade, Brighton, **Sussex (East)**, BN41 1LA, ENG.
**(T)** 01273 414888
Speciality: Aromatherapy, Hypnotherapy, Indian Head Massage, Reflexology, Reiki. ✓
● **Owner/Aromatherapist** Ms T Watson
● **Reflexologist** Mrs J Caulfield M: IIHHT.
**C** Yrs. Est.: 2 (**Ref:**HM01047)

## AROMA HEALTH

**Aroma Health**, 19 Underdown Rd, Herne Bay, **Kent**, CT6 5BP, ENG.
**(T)** 01227 374116
Speciality: Complementary Medicines & Therapy.
**M** (**Ref:**HM01048)

## AROMA HEALTH

**Aroma Health**, Po Box 114, Herne Bay, **Kent**, CT6 5GG, ENG.
**(T)** 01227 370003 **(F)** 01227 370003
Speciality: Complementary Medicines & Therapy.
● **Owner** Mr S Parman-Sibley
**M** (**Ref:**HM01049)

## AROMA HEALTH 2000

**Aroma Health 2000**, 119 Botley Rd, Oxford, **Oxfordshire**, OX2 0HD, ENG.
**(T)** 01865 201441 **(F)** 01865 250231
Speciality: Aromatherapy.
● **Director** Mr A Akhtar
**M O** (**Ref:**HM01050)

## AROMA HEALTH INTERNATIONAL

**Aroma Health International Ltd**, 900 Kingsbury Rd, Erdington, Birmingham, **Midlands (West)**, B24 9PY, ENG.
**(T)** 01216 087200 **(F)** 01216 085260
Speciality: Aromatherapy.
● **Director** Mrs V McLoed
**M O** (**Ref:**HM01051)

## AROMA HEALTH NORTH EAST

**Aroma Health North East**, Unit 8 Leeholme Rd Industrial Estate, Billingham, **Cleveland**, TS23 3TA, ENG.
**(T)** 01642 351299 **(F)** 01642 565378
Speciality: Aromatherapy.
● **Owner** Mr S Morgan
**M O** (**Ref:**HM01052)

## AROMA REMEDY

**Aroma Remedy**, 19 Macpherson St, Hopeman, Elgin, **Moray**, IV30 5TG, SCO.
**(T)** 01343 835857
Speciality: Complementary Medicines & Therapy.
● **Owner** Ms J Oatridge
**M** (**Ref:**HM01053)

## AROMA ROOM

**Aroma Room (The)**, 182B St. Peters St, Lowestoft, **Suffolk**, NR32 2LY, ENG.
**(T)** 01502 565300
Speciality: Aromatherapy.
**M O** (**Ref:**HM01054)

## AROMA ROOM

**Aroma Room (The)**, 6 The Minims, Hatfield, **Hertfordshire**, AL10 0AW, ENG.
**(T)** 01707 894294
Speciality: Aromatherapy, Massage (Therapeutic), Chemical Aromatherapy. ✓
● **Owner** Miss D Myall M: GCP.
**B C T** Yrs. Est.: 2 (**Ref:**HM01055)

## AROMA ROOM

**Aroma Room (The)**, Cedar Farm, Back Lane, Mawdesley, Ormskirk, **Lancashire**, L40 3SY, ENG.
**(T)** 01704 823313
Speciality: Complementary Medicines & Therapy.
● **Owner** Miss N Clift
**M** (**Ref:**HM01056)

## AROMA SANTE

**Aroma Sante**, Brookdale, The Fordrough, Truemans Heath Lane, Shirley, Solihull, **Midlands (West)**, B90 1PP, ENG.
**(T)** 01214 307913
Speciality: Aromatherapy, Indian Head Massage, Reflexology, Reiki. ✓
● **Holistic Therapist** Ms B Thorpe M: BRCP, IFA, RQA.
**M O** Yrs. Est.: 3 (**Ref:**HM01057)

## AROMA SECRETS

**Aroma Secrets**, 50 Hill Rise, Richmond, **Surrey**, TW10 6UB, ENG.
**(T)** 020 8332 2262
Speciality: Aromatherapy.
**M O** (**Ref:**HM01058)

## AROMA SECRETS

**Aroma Secrets**, Bentalls Shopping Centre, Wood St, Kingston Upon Thames, **Surrey**, KT1 1TR, ENG.
**(T)** 020 8546 6742
Speciality: Aromatherapy.
● **Owner** Mrs B Sutton
**M O** (**Ref:**HM01059)

## AROMA SHEET

**Aroma Sheet Ltd**, 1 Holtspur Lane, Wooburn Green, High Wycombe, **Buckinghamshire**, HP10 0AA, ENG.
**(T)** 01628 533066 **(F)** 01628 533066
Speciality: Aromatherapy.
● **Owner** Mr A Aramosheed
**M O** (**Ref:**HM01060)

## AROMA THERAPEUTICS

**Aroma Therapeutics Ltd**, Po Box 3, Bourton-On-The-Water, Cheltenham, **Gloucestershire**, GL54 2YQ, ENG.
**(T)** 01451 822444 **(F)** 01451 822443
Speciality: Aromatherapy.
**M O** (**Ref:**HM01061)

## AROMA THERAPEUTICS

**Aroma Therapeutics Ltd**, Barn Bus Centre, Great Rissington, Cheltenham, **Gloucestershire**, GL54 2LH, ENG.
**(T)** 01451 822444
Speciality: Aromatherapy.
**M O** (**Ref:**HM01062)

## AROMA TRADING

**Aroma Trading Ltd**, Chapel Farm, Hanslope Rd, Hartwell, Northampton, **Northamptonshire**, NN7 2EU, ENG.
**(T)** 01908 511881 **(F)** 01908 511990
Speciality: Aromatherapy.
● **Owner** Mr J Black
**M O** (**Ref:**HM01063)

## AROMA TRANQUILITY

**Aroma Tranquility**, 11 Hillside Gardens, Corfe Mullen, Wimborne, **Dorset**, BH21 3UL, ENG.
**(T)** 01202 692692
Speciality: Aromatherapy, Massage (Therapeutic), Stress Therapy. ✓
● **Owner/Aromatherapist** Mrs J Back Q: ITEC, SRN. M: GCP.
**M O** Yrs. Est.: 2 (**Ref:**HM01064)

## AROMA TREATMENTS

**Aroma Treatments**, 36a Frairs Stile Rd, Richmond, **Surrey**, TW10 6NQ, ENG.
**(T)** 020 8399 0817
Speciality: Complementary Medicines & Therapy.
● **Owner** Joanna Jones
**M** (**Ref:**HM01065)

## AROMA-ACTIVE

**Aroma-Active**, 80A Croydon Rd, Caterham, **Surrey**, CR3 6QD, ENG.
**(T)** 01883 344911
Speciality: Aromatherapy.
**M O** (**Ref:**HM01066)

## AROMACARE

**Aromacare**, 32 Ferguson Avenue, Wirral, **Merseyside**, CH49 1RP, ENG.
**(T)** 01516 060259
Speciality: Aromatherapy.
● **Owner** Mr G Patrick
**M O** (**Ref:**HM01067)

## AROMACARE

**Aromacare**, Stall 33 Neath Market, Green St, Neath, **Glamorgan (Vale of)**, SA11 1DP, WAL.
**(T)** 01639 638031
Speciality: Aromatherapy.
● **Owner** Mrs A Joseph
**M O** (**Ref:**HM01068)

## AROMACARE

**Aromacare**, The Old Rectory, 47 Malvern Rd, Powick, Worcester, **Worcestershire**, WR2 4RP, ENG.
**(T)** 01905 831077
Speciality: Aromatherapy.
● **Owner** Mrs S Hutchinson
**M O** (**Ref:**HM01069)

## AROMACLINIC

**Aromaclinic Ltd**, Camrose Avenue, Edgware, **London (Greater)**, HA8 6EH, ENG.
**(T)** 020 8952 5289
Speciality: Aromatherapy.
● **Director** Mrs J Shichaterry
**M O** (**Ref:**HM01070)



Key continued: **Yrs.Est:** Years Established **Q:** Qualifications **M:** Professional Membership ✓ Indemnity Insurance Accept Credit Cards

**AROMACUSHION**

**Aromacushion Ltd**, Unit B009, Trident Business Centre, 89 Bickersteth Rd, London, **London (Greater)**, SW17 9SH, ENG.
(T) 020 8355 3400 (F) 020 8355 3401
Speciality: Aromatherapy.
● **Manager** Ms C Voilquin
M O (Ref:HM01071)

**AROMACUSHIONS**

**Aromacushions Ltd**, 100 Tollington Way, London, **London (Greater)**, N7 6RY, ENG.
(T) 020 7272 3513 (F) 020 7272 2008
Speciality: Aromatherapy.
● **Manager** Miss N Shockett
M O (Ref:HM01072)

**AROMAFIRE**

**Aromafire**, Chapel Cottage, Whatlington, Battle, **Sussex (East)**, TN33 0NL, ENG.
(T) 01424 870407 (F) 01424 870407
Speciality: Aromatherapy.
● **Owner** Mr F Waghorn
M O (Ref:HM01073)

**AROMAFLEX**

**Aromaflex**, U 17 Mullingar Enterprise Ctr Mullingar, **County Westmeath**, IRE.
(T) 04443 444
Speciality: Aromatherapy.
M O (Ref:HM01074)

**AROMAFLOAT**

**Aromafloat**, 2 Whitebridge Lane, Stone, **Staffordshire**, ST15 8LQ, ENG.
(T) 01785 818879
Speciality: Aromatherapy.
● **Owner** Mr N Tetlow
M O (Ref:HM01075)

**AROMAGLOW**

**Aromaglow**, 12 The Pavilion, Vaughan Rd, Torquay, **Devon**, TQ2 5EQ, ENG.
(T) 01803 292228 (F) 01803 292228
Speciality: Aromatherapy.
● **Area Manager** Mrs C Davies
M O (Ref:HM01076)

**AROMAGLOW**

**Aromaglow**, 68 Fore St, Brixham, **Devon**, TQ5 8EF, ENG.
(T) 01803 859378 (F) 01803 859378
Speciality: Aromatherapy.
● **Owner** Mr D Parkin
M O (Ref:HM01077)

**AROMAHEALTH**

**Aromahealth Natural Therapy Centre**, 19 Oaklands, Bradford, **Yorkshire (West)**, BD10 8RG, ENG.
(T) 01274 619667 (F) 01274 619667
Speciality: Complementary Medicines & Therapy.
● **Owner** Mrs S Kupse
M (Ref:HM01078)

**AROMAKIDS**

**Aromakids**, Barford Cl, Spaxton, Bridgwater, **Somerset**, TA5 1AE, ENG.
(T) 01278 671461 (F) 01278 671715
(E) aromakids@iafrica.com
(W) www.aromakids.com
Speciality: Aromatherapy, Aromatherapy for children. ✔
● **Owner** Mr J Minchin M: ATC.
C Yrs. Est.: 2 (Ref:HM01079)

**AROMANTIC**

**Findhorn Nature Care**, 4 Heathneuk, Findhorn, Forres, **Moray**, IV36 3WN, SCO.
(T) 01309 692000 (F) 01309 691100
(E) info@aromantic.co.uk
(W) www.aromantic.co.uk
Speciality: Aromatherapy, Complementary Therapy, Dietician, Naturopathy.
● **Owner** Mr K Borseth
M O Yrs. Est.: 3 (Ref:HM01080)

**AROMAS OF JOY**

**Aromas Of Joy**, The Shopping Mall, Morton Pk Way, Darlington, **County Durham**, DL1 4PH, ENG.
(T) 01325 387667 (F) 01325 387676
Speciality: Aromatherapy.
● **Owner** Mr D Sidebottom
M O (Ref:HM01081)

**AROMAS OF THE HOMELANDS**

**Aromas Of The Homelands Stress Consultancy**, 47 Gloucester Rd, London, **London (Greater)**, N18 1HW, ENG.
(T) 020 8351 7388
Speciality: Complementary Medicines & Therapy.
C M (Ref:HM01082)

**AROMASPHERE**

**Aromasphere Ltd**, Bowmere House, Birch Heath Rd, Tarporley, **Cheshire**, CW6 9UR, ENG.
(T) 01829 733663 (F) 01829 733854
Speciality: Aromatherapy, Reflexology, Beauty Treatment. ✔
● **Sole Director/Aromatherapist** Mrs A Leach
C Yrs. Est.: 10 (Ref:HM01083)

**AROMATHERAPY**

**Aromatherapy**, 30E Catisfield Lane, Fareham, **Hampshire**, PO15 5NN, ENG.
(T) 01329 844418
Speciality: Aromatherapy.
● **Owner** Miss S Murphy
M O (Ref:HM01084)

**AROMATHERAPY**

**Aromatherapy**, 714 City Rd, Sheffield, **Yorkshire (South)**, S2 1GJ, ENG.
(T) 01142 530340
Speciality: Aromatherapy.
● **Manager** Mr J Williams
M O (Ref:HM01085)

**AROMATHERAPY**

**Aromatherapy Organisations Council**, P O Box 355, Croydon, **Surrey**, CR9 2BN, ENG.
(T) 020 8251 7912
Speciality: Aromatherapy.
● **Owner** Mrs N Ashby
M O (Ref:HM01086)

**AROMATHERAPY & MASSOLOGY CLNC**

**Aromatherapy & Massology Clinic**, First Floor, 14 High St, Carcroft, Doncaster, **Yorkshire (South)**, DN6 8DP, ENG.
(T) 01302 727000
Speciality: Aromatherapy.
M O (Ref:HM01087)

**AROMATHERAPY & REFLEX CENTRE**

**Aromatherapy & Reflexology Centre**, Sanas 2 Landscape Rd, Ch'town, Dublin, **County Dublin**, IRE.
(T) 01295 1808
Speciality: Aromatherapy.
M O (Ref:HM01088)

**AROMATHERAPY & REFLEX CENTRE**

**Aromatherapy & Reflexology Centre**, 49 Rocwood, Leopardstown Rd, Foxrock, Dublin, **County Dublin**, IRE.
(T) 01288 0699
Speciality: Aromatherapy.
M O (Ref:HM01089)

**AROMATHERAPY & REFLEX CTRE**

**Aromatherapy & Reflexology Centre (The)**, 1 Station Approach, Buxton, **Derbyshire**, SK17 6AQ, ENG.
(T) 01298 72260
Speciality: Aromatherapy, Reflexology. ✔
● **Reflexologist** Mrs B Andrew Q: Dip.Reflex. M: FHT.
C Yrs. Est.: 6 (Ref:HM01090)

**AROMATHERAPY & REIKI CLINIC**

**Aromatherapy & Reiki Clinic**, 6 Briarwood Drive, Cardiff, **Glamorgan (Vale of)**, CF23 6SR, WAL.
(T) 029 2075 8965
Speciality: Aromatherapy.
● **Owner** Mrs B Roderick
M O (Ref:HM01091)

**AROMATHERAPY ASSOCIATES**

**Aromatherapy Associates**, 68 Maltings Pl, London, **London (Greater)**, SW6 2BY, ENG.
(T) 020 7371 9878 (F) 020 7371 9894
Speciality: Complementary Medicines & Therapy.
● **Managing Director** Mr G Howard
C M (Ref:HM01092)

**AROMATHERAPY AT PAULINES**

**Aromatherapy At Paulines**, 5 St. Martins Walk, Leicester, **Leicestershire**, LE1 5DG, ENG.
(T) 01162 619331
Speciality: Aromatherapy.
● **Partner** Ms J Hunt
M O (Ref:HM01093)

**AROMATHERAPY BEAUTY CLINIC**

**Aromatherapy Beauty Clinic**, 12 Wicklow St, Dublin2, IRE.
(T) 01677 0512
Speciality: Aromatherapy.
M O (Ref:HM01094)

**AROMATHERAPY BY ANTONIO**

**Aromatherapy Massage By Antonio**, 5 Oxford Avenue, St. Albans, **Hertfordshire**, AL1 5NS, ENG.
(T) 01727 811234 (F) 07970 509193
(W) www.naturistmassage.com
Speciality: Aromatherapy, Massage (Therapeutic), Reflexology. ✔
● **Owner/Aromatherapist** Mr A Casiero Q: RQA. M: IIHHT, RQA.
B Yrs. Est.: 5 (Ref:HM01095)

**AROMATHERAPY BY JOANNA JONES**

**Aromatherapy By Joanna Jones**, 151 Beechwood Avenue, St. Albans, **Hertfordshire**, AL1 4XX, ENG.
(T) 01727 850581
Speciality: Aromatherapy.
M (Ref:HM01096)

**AROMATHERAPY BY R SKILTON**

**Aromatherapy By Rosemary Skilton**, 4 Cricket Lea, Lindford, Bordon, **Hampshire**, GU35 0PY, ENG.
(T) 01420 472669
Speciality: Aromatherapy.
M O (Ref:HM01097)

**AROMATHERAPY BY SARA**

**Aromatherapy By Sara**, 32 Affleck Avenue, Prestolee, Stoneclough, Radcliffe, Manchester, **Manchester (Greater)**, M26 1HN, ENG.
(T) 01204 571802
Speciality: Aromatherapy. ✔
● **Owner/Aromatherapist** Mrs J Jones M: IIHHT.
C Yrs. Est.: 8 (Ref:HM01098)

**AROMATHERAPY BY SHEILA BURWOOD**

**Aromatherapy By Sheila Burwood**, 35 Allbrook Hill, Eastleigh, **Hampshire**, SO50 4NA, ENG.
(T) 023 8061 8556 (F) 023 8061 8556
Speciality: Aromatherapy.
● **Owner** Ms S Burwood
M O (Ref:HM01099)

**AROMATHERAPY CENTRE**

**Aromatherapy Centre**, 176 Chesterfield Rd, Ashford, **Surrey**, TW15 3PU, ENG.
(T) 01784 420943
Speciality: Aromatherapy.
M O (Ref:HM01100)

**AROMATHERAPY CENTRE**

**Aromatherapy Centre (The)**, 117 High St, Crediton, **Devon**, EX17 3LG, ENG.
(T) 01363 772712
Speciality: Aromatherapy.
● **Owner** Ms J Hogan
M O (Ref:HM01101)

**AROMATHERAPY CENTRE**

**Aromatherapy Centre (The)**, Aroma House, 85 Henry Rd, West Bridgford, Nottingham, **Nottinghamshire**, NG2 7ND, ENG.
(T) 01159 815481
Speciality: Aromatherapy.
M O (Ref:HM01102)

**AROMATHERAPY CENTRE**

**Aromatherapy Centre**, Leopardstown Rd, Foxrock, Dublin, **County Dublin**, IRE.
(T) 01289 8699

Key: B Mind-Body Medicine; C Complementary Medicine; H Self Help Treatment; M Medicinal Therapy; O Oriental Medicine; P Postural Therapy; S Manipulative Structural Therapy; T Touch Therapy

Speciality: Aromatherapy.
M O (Ref:HM01103)

### AROMATHERAPY CLINIC

**Aromatherapy Clinic (The)**, 27 Northburn Avenue, Aberdeen, **Aberdeenshire**, AB15 6AH, SCO.
(T) 01224 315124
Speciality: Aromatherapy.
M O (Ref:HM01104)

### AROMATHERAPY CLINIC

**Aromatherapy Clinic (The)**, 227 Pantbach Rd, Rhiwbina, Cardiff, **Glamorgan (Vale of)**, CF14 6AE, WAL.
(T) 029 2052 1206
Speciality: Aromatherapy, Bach Remedies, Reflexology, Reiki, Ayurveda Face/Body Treatment.
● **Therapist** Ms M Collins Q: Dip.Arom, Dip.Reflex, IIHHT. M: IFR, ISPA.
● **Therapist** Ms J Pitten Q: CIDESCO, SRN. M: ISPA.
● **Aromatherapist/Reflexologist** Ms J Newcombe Q: Dip.Arom, Dip.Reflex, IHBC, IIHHT, MIFR. M: IFR, ISPA.
H (Ref:HM01105)

### AROMATHERAPY CLINIC

**Aromatherapy Clinic (The)**, Kings Head Sports, Harts Lane, Bawburgh, Norwich, **Norfolk**, NR9 3LT, ENG.
(T) 01603 744433
Speciality: Aromatherapy.
M O (Ref:HM01106)

### AROMATHERAPY CLINIC

**Aromatherapy Clinic (The)**, 301B New North Rd, Ilford, **Essex**, IG6 3DX, ENG.
(T) 020 8500 2996
Speciality: Aromatherapy, Massage (Therapeutic), Reiki.
● **Aromatherapist** Ms L Barrett Q: ITEC.
M O Yrs. Est.: 3 (Ref:HM01107)

### AROMATHERAPY CLINIC

**Aromatherapy Clinic**, 12 Wicklow St, Dublin, **County Dublin**, IRE.
(T) 01677 0512
Speciality: Aromatherapy.
M O (Ref:HM01108)

### AROMATHERAPY DIRECT

**Aromatherapy Direct**, Antiques & Craft Centre, Kings Walk Arcade, Winchester, **Hampshire**, SO23 8AF, ENG.
(T) 01962 856820
Speciality: Aromatherapy.
● **Owner** Ms K McGregor
M O (Ref:HM01109)

### AROMATHERAPY FOR LADIES

**Aromatherapy For Ladies**, 50 Barrs Court Rd, Barrs Court, Warmley, Bristol, BS30 8DH, ENG.
(T) 01179 677021
Speciality: Aromatherapy, Massage (Therapeutic). ✔
● **Aromatherapy Masseur** Mrs H Justice M: ICHT.
T Yrs. Est.: 2 (Ref:HM01110)

### AROMATHERAPY HEALING CLINIC

**Aromatherapy Healing Clinic**, 9 Cantelowes Rd, London, **London (Greater)**, NW1 9XP, ENG.
(T) 020 7482 1924
Speciality: Complementary Medicines & Therapy.
● **Owner** Miss R Doheny
C M (Ref:HM01111)

### AROMATHERAPY HEALTH & BEAUTY

**Aromatherapy Health & Beauty Clinic**, 21 Eyre Sq, **County Galway**, IRE.
(T) 09156 2597
Speciality: Aromatherapy.
M O (Ref:HM01112)

### AROMATHERAPY HEALTHCARE

**Aromatherapy Healthcare Ltd**, 7 Cookstown Sq, Cookstown Ind E, Dublin, **County Dublin**, IRE.
(T) 01451 0733 (F) 01452 0665
(E) aroma@tinet.ie
Speciality: Aromatherapy.
M O (Ref:HM01113)

### AROMATHERAPY IN PRACTICE

**Aromatherapy In Practice**, 8 Lansdowne Trce, Newcastle Upon Tyne, **Tyne and Wear**, NE3 1HN, ENG.
(T) 01912 131388
Speciality: Aromatherapy, Manual Lymph Drainage. ✔
● **Aromatherapist** Mrs T Magen Q: Dip.Arom. M: IFA, MLD(UK).
C Yrs. Est.: 12 (Ref:HM01114)

### AROMATHERAPY INTERNATIONAL

**Aromatherapy International Ltd**, 5 High St, Waltham On The Wolds, Melton Mowbray, **Leicestershire**, LE14 4AH, ENG.
(T) 01664 464468 (F) 01664 464351
Speciality: Aromatherapy. ✔ [CREDIT]
● **Owner** Mr R Shorthouse
C Yrs. Est.: 8 (Ref:HM01115)

### AROMATHERAPY INTERNATIONAL

**Aromatherapy International Ltd**, Banks House, Baileys Lane, Burton Overy, Leicester, **Leicestershire**, LE8 9DD, ENG.
(T) 01162 590055 (F) 01162 593033
Speciality: Aromatherapy.
● **Managing Director** Mr J Brebner
M O (Ref:HM01116)

### AROMATHERAPY IS FLOWER POWER

**Aromatherapy Is Flower Power**, 19 Hardings, Welwyn Garden City, **Hertfordshire**, AL7 2EQ, ENG.
(T) 01707 336935
Speciality: Aromatherapy.
● **Owner** Mrs H Webberley
M (Ref:HM01117)

### AROMATHERAPY LADIES MASSAGE

**Aromatherapy Ladies Massage**, 2 Lapwing Cl, Stalybridge, **Manchester (Greater)**, SK15 1HP, ENG.
(T) 01613 384983
Speciality: Aromatherapy, Indian Head Massage, Reflexology. ✔
● **Owner/Holistic Therapist** Mrs J Davies Q: IIHHT. M: IIHHT, ISPA.
C T Yrs. Est.: 6 (Ref:HM01118)

### AROMATHERAPY MASSAGE

**Aromatherapy Massage**, 31 Leslie Rd, Barnsley, **Yorkshire (South)**, S70 3JH, ENG.
(T) 01226 296376
Speciality: Aromatherapy.
● **Owner** Ms A Brammer
M O (Ref:HM01119)

### AROMATHERAPY MASSAGE/REFLEX

**Aromatherapy Therapeutic Massage & Reflexology**, 44 Avenue Rd, Leamington Spa, **Warwickshire**, CV31 3PE, ENG.
(T) 01926 428896
Speciality: Aromatherapy, Massage (Therapeutic), Reflexology.
M (Ref:HM01120)

### AROMATHERAPY ORG COUNCIL

**Aromatherapy Organisation Council (A O C)**, Po Box 19834, London, **London (Greater)**, SE25 6WF, ENG.
(T) 020 8251 7912 (F) 020 8251 7942
(W) www.aoc.uk.net
Speciality: Aromatherapy, Complementary Therapy, Massage (Therapeutic).
C Yrs. Est.: 10 (Ref:HM01121)

### AROMATHERAPY PLUS

**Aromatherapy Plus**, Complementary Practice Of Annie Littler, 1 Okehampton St, Exeter, **Devon**, EX4 1DW, ENG.
(T) 01392 203182 (F) 01392 203182
Speciality: Aromatherapy.
● **Owner** Mrs A Littler
M O (Ref:HM01122)

### AROMATHERAPY PLUS OIL SUPPLIER

**Aromatherapy Plus Oil Supplier**, 2 Moorshall Cottages, Kington St. Michael, Chippenham, **Wiltshire**, SN14 6JX, ENG.
(T) 01249 750667
Speciality: Aromatherapy.
M O (Ref:HM01123)

### AROMATHERAPY SHOP

**Aromatherapy Shop (The)**, Flat Lane, Kelsall, Tarporley, **Cheshire**, CW6 0PU, ENG.
(T) 01829 751810
Speciality: Aromatherapy.
● **Owner** Mrs E Jerrard
M (Ref:HM01124)

### AROMATHERAPY STUDIO

**Aromatherapy Studio (The)**, 14 New Lane, Havant, **Hampshire**, PO9 2JJ, ENG.
(T) 023 9249 9466
Speciality: Aromatherapy.
M O (Ref:HM01125)

### AROMATHERAPY THAI MASSAGE

**Aromatherapy Thai Massage**, 27 Old Brompton Rd, London, **London (Greater)**, SW7 3SS, ENG.
(T) 020 7937 0576
Speciality: Aromatherapy.
● **Owner** Ms M Navi
M O (Ref:HM01126)

### AROMATHERAPY TRADE COUNCIL

**Aromatherapy Trade Council (The)**, 3 Latymer Cl, Braybrooke, Market Harborough, **Leicestershire**, LE16 8LN, ENG.
(T) 01858 465731 (F) 01858 465731
Speciality: Aromatherapy.
● **Chairman** Mr G Lythe
M O (Ref:HM01127)

### AROMATHERAPY TRADE COUNCIL

**Aromatherapy Trade Council (The)**, P O Box 387, Ipswich, **Suffolk**, IP2 9AN, ENG.
(T) 01473 603630 (F) 01473 603630
Speciality: Aromatherapy.
M O (Ref:HM01128)

### AROMATHERAPY TREATMENT

**Aromatherapy Treatment**, 15 Bentley Rd, Liverpool, **Merseyside**, L8 0SY, ENG.
(T) 01517 345601
Speciality: Aromatherapy.
● **Owner** Miss V Howell
M (Ref:HM01129)

### AROMATHERAPY WORLD

**Aromatherapy World**, 3 Chequer Lane, Ely, **Cambridgeshire**, CB7 4LN, ENG.
(T) 01353 665499
Speciality: Aromatherapy.
● **Owner** Mrs L Evans
M O (Ref:HM01130)

### AROMATHERAPY/REMEDIAL MASSAGE

**Aromatherapy & Remedial Massage**, Bullimores House, Church Lane, Cranleigh, **Surrey**, GU6 8AR, ENG.
(T) 01483 268221
Speciality: Aromatherapy, Massage (Therapeutic).
M O (Ref:HM01131)

### AROMATHEUTICS

**Aromatheutics**, High St, Irchester, Wellingborough, **Northamptonshire**, NN29 7AB, ENG.
(T) 01933 410055 (F) 01933 410055
Speciality: Aromatherapy.
● **Owner** Mrs C Hammond
M O (Ref:HM01132)

### AROMATIC

**Aromatic**, Unit N Grainger Arcade, Newcastle Upon Tyne, **Tyne and Wear**, NE1 5QE, ENG.
(T) 01912 300392
Speciality: Aromatherapy.
● **Owner** Mr S Douglas
M O (Ref:HM01133)

### AROMATIC

**Aromatic**, 66 Eckington Rd, Coal Aston, Dronfield, **Derbyshire**, S18 3AW, ENG.
(T) 01246 417332
Speciality: Aromatherapy.
● **Owner** Mrs G O'Rourke
M O (Ref:HM01134)

### AROMATICA

**Aromatica**, 49 Cross St, Camborne, **Cornwall**, TR14 8ET, ENG.
(T) 01209 715367



Key continued: **Yrs.Est:** Years Established **Q:** Qualifications **M:** Professional Membership ✔ Indemnity Insurance [CREDIT] Accept Credit Cards

Speciality: Indian Head Massage, Reflexology. ✔
● **Shop Owner** Mrs C Jennings
● **Reflexologist/Masseuse** Ms G Young Q: ITEC. M: GCP, ITEC.
[H] Yrs. Est.: 1 (Ref:HM01135)

### AROMATICA TREATMENT & PRODUCTS
**Aromatica Treatment & Products**, Quay Rd, Lymington, **Hampshire**, SO41 3AX, ENG.
(T) 01590 677889
Speciality: Aromatherapy.
[M] [O] (Ref:HM01136)

### AROMATICA TREATMENT & PRODUCTS
**Aromatica Treatment & Products**, 6 Quay Hill, Lymington, **Hampshire**, SO41 9AR, ENG.
(T) 01590 677889
Speciality: Aromatherapy.
[M] [O] (Ref:HM01137)

### AROMATICS
**Aromatics**, 1a Cresswell Park, London, **London (Greater)**, SE3 9RD, ENG.
(T) 020 8297 1398
Speciality: Aromatherapy.
[M] [O] (Ref:HM01138)

### AROMATICS
**Aromatics**, 42 Harrington Court, Barnsley, **Yorkshire (South)**, S71 5JR, ENG.
(T) 01226 244570
Speciality: Aromatherapy.
[M] [O] (Ref:HM01139)

### AROMATIX
**Aromatix**, 3 The Colonade Piece Hall, Halifax, **Yorkshire (West)**, HX1 1RE, ENG.
(T) 01422 367007 (F) 01422 367007
Speciality: Aromatherapy.
● **Owner** Mrs L Ryder
[M] [O] (Ref:HM01140)

### AROMATIX
**Aromatix**, 5 Hollowgate, Holmfirth, Huddersfield, **Yorkshire (West)**, HD7 1DG, ENG.
(T) 01484 688858 (F) 01484 688858
Speciality: Aromatherapy.
● **Owner** Mrs L Ryder
[M] [O] (Ref:HM01141)

### AROMA-WISE
**Aroma-Wise**, Newhaven, Polbathic, Torpoint, **Cornwall**, PL11 3HA, ENG.
(T) 01503 230991 (F) 01503 230889
Speciality: Aromatherapy.
● **Owner** Mr T Clayton
[M] [O] (Ref:HM01142)

### AROMAZ
**Aromaz**, 47 Fir Gr, Blackpool, **Lancashire**, FY1 6PL, ENG.
(T) 01253 766736
Speciality: Aromatherapy.
● **Owner** Mrs Y Ursell
[M] [O] (Ref:HM01143)

### AROMAZ HOLISTIC CLINIC
**Aromaz Holistic Health & Beauty Clinic**, 22B Albion St, Dunstable, **Bedfordshire**, LU6 1SA, ENG.
(T) 01582 670333
Speciality: Complementary Medicines & Therapy.
● **Owner** Mrs J Curtis
[M] (Ref:HM01144)

### AROMER
**Aromer**, 59 High St, Canvey Island, **Essex**, SS8 7RD, ENG.
(T) 01268 511893
Speciality: Aromatherapy.
[M] [O] (Ref:HM01145)

### ARPINO, MARIA
**Maria Arpino**, 5 Ringmore Cl, Shaldon, Teignmouth, **Devon**, TQ14 0AS, ENG.
(T) 01626 872583
Speciality: Reflexology.
[S] [T] (Ref:HM01146)

### ARRAN YOGA
**Arran Yoga**, 4 Brook St, Tonbridge, **Kent**, TN9 2PJ, ENG.
(T) 01732 353804
Speciality: Complementary Medicines & Therapy.
[C] [M] (Ref:HM01147)

### ARRINDELL, MARK
**Mark Arrindell**, 1-2A Clayhill House, Weyhill, Haslemere, **Surrey**, GU27 1DA, ENG.
(T) 01428 651067
Speciality: Osteopathy.
[P] [S] [T] (Ref:HM01148)

### ARROW BANK CHIROPRACTIC CLINIC
**Arrow Bank Chiropractic Clinic (The)**, 35 Ten Ashes Lane, Rednal, Birmingham, **Midlands (West)**, B45 8PE, ENG.
(T) 01214 477812
Speciality: Chiropractic. ✔
● **Therapist** Dr J Rousseau Q: BSc, DC.
● **Therapist** Mr P Brindley Q: BSc, DC.
[P] [S] Yrs. Est.: 9 (Ref:HM01149)

### ARROWSMITH, BARRIE
**Barrie Arrowsmith**, 64 Standishgate, Wigan, **Lancashire**, WN1 1UP, ENG.
(T) 01942 236239
Speciality: Chiropody.
[S] (Ref:HM01150)

### ARROWSMITH, SUSAN
**Susan Arrowsmith**, 46 Porter Rd, Long Stratton, Norwich, **Norfolk**, NR15 2TY, ENG.
(T) 01508 530926
Speciality: Hypnosis.
● **Owner** Mrs S Arrowsmith
[B] (Ref:HM01151)

### ART DE VIVRE
**Art De Vivre**, 17 Bell St, Romsey, **Hampshire**, SO51 8GY, ENG.
(T) 01794 518131 (F) 01794 518131
Speciality: Aromatherapy.
● **Owner** Mr P Harper
[M] [O] (Ref:HM01152)

### ART OF HEALTH
**Art of Health Ltd**, 280 Balham High Rd, London, **London (Greater)**, SW17 7AL, ENG.
(T) 020 8682 1800 (F) 020 8682 1995
Speciality: Complementary Medicines & Therapy.
● **Manager** Dr F Chao
[C] [M] (Ref:HM01153)

### ART OF REFLEXOLOGY
**Art Of Reflexology (The)**, Parkland Manor, 15 Bodorgan Rd, Bournemouth, **Dorset**, BH2 6NQ, ENG.
(T) 01202 295910
Speciality: Reflexology. ✔
● **Reflexologist/Tutor** Miss T Rich Q: ITEC. M: GCBT.
[T] Yrs. Est.: 6 (Ref:HM01154)

### ART OF WELL-BEING
**Art Of Well-Being Alternative Health Centre**, 38 St. Mildreds Rd, Westgate-on-Sea, **Kent**, CT8 8RF, ENG.
(T) 01843 834843
Speciality: Complementary Medicines & Therapy.
● **Owner** Mr C Brennan
[M] (Ref:HM01155)

### ARTEMIS
**Artemis**, 22 High St, Overton, Basingstoke, **Hampshire**, RG25 3HA, ENG.
(T) 07989 120431 (F) 01256 772194
(E) druicca@aladdinscave.net
Speciality: Hypnosis, Hypnotherapy, Psychotherapy, Stress Therapy. ✔
● **Hypnotherapist** Mr G Armstrong Q: BSc, Dip.Hyp, Dip.Psych, MHA. M: HA.
[B] Yrs. Est.: 1 (Ref:HM01156)

### ARTEMIS AROMATHERAPY
**Artemis Aromatherapy**, 73 Anson Rd, London, **London (Greater)**, N7 0AT, ENG.
(T) 020 7607 2549
Speciality: Aromatherapy.
[M] [O] (Ref:HM01157)

### ARTEMIS HEALING CENTRE
**Artemis Healing Centre**, 9 Newmarket St, Cahirciveen, **County Kerry**, IRE.
(T) 06694 73088
Speciality: Healing.
[B] (Ref:HM01158)

### ARTHEY, ELAINE
**Elaine Arthey**, Ipswich, **Suffolk**, IP7, ENG.
(T) 01473 827636
Speciality: Bach Remedies.
[M] (Ref:HM01159)

### ARTHUR, A R
**A R Arthur**, 15 Ploughmans Cl, London, **London (Greater)**, NW1 0XH, ENG.
(T) 020 7388 6990
Speciality: Psychology.
● **Owner** A Arthur
[B] (Ref:HM01160)

### ARTHUR, ALICIA
**Alicia Arthur**, 142 Henwood Green Rd, Pembury, Tunbridge Wells, **Kent**, TN2 4LR, ENG.
(T) 01892 824387
Speciality: Reflexology.
[S] [T] (Ref:HM01161)

### ARTHUR, J R
**J R Arthur**, 130 Roman Rd, London, **London (Greater)**, E2 0RN, ENG.
(T) 020 8981 7226
Speciality: Chiropodists (Podiatrists).
● **Owner** Mrs M Gore
[S] (Ref:HM01162)

### ARTHUR, JOHN
**John Arthur**, 27 Anchor Lane, Hathern, Loughborough, **Leicestershire**, LE12 5HR, ENG.
(T) 01509 843873
Speciality: Chiropodists (Podiatrists).
[S] (Ref:HM01163)

### ARTHURS WHOLEFOODS
**Arthurs Wholefoods**, 3a Wellington Rd, Dereham, **Norfolk**, NR19 2BP, ENG.
(T) 01362 697750
Speciality: Complementary Medicines & Therapy, Wholefood Shop.
● **Owner** Mr T Park
[M] Yrs. Est.: 15 (Ref:HM01164)

### ARTHURS, BEV
**Bev Arthurs**, 18 Morgan Court, 807 Chester Rd, Erdington, Birmingham, **Midlands (West)**, B24 0BL, ENG.
(T) 01213 738483
Speciality: Reflexology.
[S] [T] (Ref:HM01165)

### ARTHURS, MARY & HUGH
**Arthurs Mary & Hugh**, 22 De Courcy Sq, Glasnevin, **County Dublin**, IRE.
(T) 01830 2187
(E) dubhl@indigo.ie
Speciality: Complementary Medicines & Therapy.
[M] (Ref:HM01166)

### ARTHURWORREY, J
**J Arthurworrey**, 13 Star Post Rd, Camberley, **Surrey**, GU15 4DE, ENG.
(T) 01276 683607
Speciality: Aromatherapy.
● **Owner** Ms J Arthurworry
[M] [O] (Ref:HM01167)

### ARTICHOKE NATURAL HEALTH
**Artichoke Natural Health**, 33 Long St, Wotton-under-Edge, **Gloucestershire**, GL12 7BX, ENG.
(T) 01453 520111 (F) 01453 520196
Speciality: Acupuncture, Alexander Technique, Aromatherapy, Baby Massage, Bowen Therapy, Chiropody, Cranial Osteopathy, Herbal Medicine, Hypnotherapy, Massage (Therapeutic), Osteopathy, Reflexology, Shiatsu, Food Sensitivity Testing. ✔
● **Practice Manager** Mrs K Curan M: AOC.
[B] Yrs. Est.: 1 (Ref:HM01168)

### ARTS PSYCHOLOGY CONSULTANTS
**Arts Psychology Consultants**, 29 Argyll Mansions, Hammersmith Rd, London, **London (Greater)**, W14 8QQ, ENG.
(T) 020 7602 2707 (F) 020 7602 8541
Speciality: Psychology.
● **Director** Mr A Evans



Key: [B] Mind-Body Medicine [C] Complementary Medicine [H] Self Help Treatment [M] Medicinal Therapy [O] Oriental Medicine [P] Postural Therapy [S] Manipulative Structural Therapy [T] Touch Therapy

B (Ref:HM01169)

**ARTURI, S (DR)**

**Dr S Arturi**, Hockerill House, 29 Hockerill St, Bishop's Stortford, **Hertfordshire**, CM23 2DH, ENG.
(T) 01279 466841
Speciality: Acupuncture.
O (Ref:HM01170)

**ARUNDALE, C**

**C Arundale**, 11 Heath Rd, Haywards Heath, **Sussex (West)**, RH16 3AX, ENG.
(T) 01444 450162 (F) 01444 459816
Speciality: Physiotherapy.
● **Practice Manager** Mrs W Langley
P S T (Ref:HM01171)

**ARUNDELL, LINDA**

**Linda Arundell**, 37 Waverley Rd, Bagshot, **Surrey**, GU19 5JL, ENG.
(T) 01276 479898
Speciality: Aromatherapy.
● **Owner** Mrs L Arundell
M O (Ref:HM01172)

**ARYAEENIA, LINDA M**

**Linda M Aryaeenia**, 31 Shenfield Rd, Brentwood, **Essex**, CM15 8AG, ENG.
(T) 01277 212900
Speciality: Osteopathy.
P S T (Ref:HM01173)

**ASARIEL**

**Asariel**, 25 Croxton, Burritt Rd, Kingston Upon Thames, **Surrey**, KT1 3HS, ENG.
(T) 020 8546 2879
Speciality: Clairvoyants & Palmists.
● **Owner** Mrs H Burden
B (Ref:HM01174)

**ASCLEPION**

**Asclepion**, Blackfriars Court, Southside St, The Barbican, Plymouth, **Devon**, PL1 2LA, ENG.
(T) 01752 206018
Speciality: Aromatherapy.
M O (Ref:HM01175)

**ASCLEPION**

**Asclepion**, Unit 23 Angel Gate, 326 City Rd, London, **London (Greater)**, EC1V 2PT, ENG.
(T) 020 7284 0404
Speciality: Psychotherapy.
● **Owner** Mr J Jolliffe
B (Ref:HM01176)

**ASCOT HOMEOPATHIC CLINIC**

**Ascot Homeopathic Clinic**, Little Wood, Kings Rd, Sunninghill, **Surrey**, SL5 0AD, ENG.
(T) 01344 291484
Speciality: Hay Diet, Healer, Homeopathy, Life Style Coaching, Reiki. ✔
● **Homeopath** Ms T Longworth Q: LCH, MCH, RSHom. M: Soc.Hom.
M Yrs. Est.: 8 (Ref:HM01177)

**ASCOT PHYSIOFIRST CENTRE**

**Ascot Physiofirst Centre**, Kingswick House, Kingswick Drive, Ascot, **Berkshire**, SL5 7BH, ENG.
(T) 01344 292213 (F) 01344 872708
Speciality: Alexander Technique, Massage (Therapeutic), Physiotherapy. ✔
● **Physiotherapist** Mrs C Owen Q: MCSP, SRP. M: CSP.
S Yrs. Est.: 20 (Ref:HM01178)

**ASCOTT, TARA**

**Tara Ascott**, The Crossway Clinic, 39 Crossway, Manchester, **Manchester (Greater)**, M20 6TU, ENG.
(T) 01617 282857
Speciality: Osteopathy.
P S T (Ref:HM01179)

**ASH PHYSIOTHERAPY/SPORTS CLNC**

**Ash Physiotherapy & Sports Injury Clinic**, 3 Chequer Lane, Ash, Canterbury, **Kent**, CT3 2ET, ENG.
(T) 01304 813596 (F) 01304 813596
Speciality: Physiotherapy.
● **Owner** Mrs L Cousins
P S T (Ref:HM01180)

**ASH, ANNIE**

**Annie Ash**, 16 Victoria Rd, Clacton-On-Sea, **Essex**, CO15 6BH, ENG.
(T) 01255 423387
Speciality: Psychotherapy.
● **Administrator** Mrs H Robinson
B (Ref:HM01181)

**ASH, GRAHAM M**

**Graham M Ash**, 33 Meadow View Rd, Thornton Heath, **Surrey**, CR7 7HA, ENG.
(T) 020 8689 0913
Speciality: Hypnosis.
● **Owner** Mr G Ash
B (Ref:HM01182)

**ASH, STACEY**

**Stacey Ash**, 118 Dunford Rd, Holmfirth, Huddersfield, **Yorkshire (West)**, HD9 2DT, ENG.
(T) 01484 684245
(W) www.acupunctureyorkshire.co.uk
Speciality: Acupuncture, Chinese Herbal Medicine.
● **Acupuncturist** Ms S Ash M: BAcC.
C Yrs. Est.: 15 (Ref:HM01183)

**ASH, STACEY**

**Stacey Ash**, Middle Cottage, Ben Kaye Row, Holmfirth, Huddersfield, **Yorkshire (West)**, HD7 1EF, ENG.
(T) 01484 684245
Speciality: Acupuncture.
O (Ref:HM01184)

**ASHA MANIPULATIONS**

**Asha Manipulations**, 50 Fore St, Chard, **Somerset**, TA20 1QA, ENG.
(T) 01460 61464
Speciality: Chiropractic.
P S T (Ref:HM01185)

**ASHA, VALERA**

**Valera Asha**, 221 East St, London, **London (Greater)**, SE17 2SS, ENG.
(T) 020 7703 3043 (F) 020 7703 3043
Speciality: Homeopathy.
● **Doctor** Mrs A Valera
M (Ref:HM01186)

**ASHANA**

**Ashana**, 51 Cairngrassie Circle, Portlethen, Aberdeen, **Aberdeenshire**, AB12 4TZ, SCO.
(T) 01224 781747
Speciality: Hypnotherapy.
● **Owner** Ms C Kholer
B (Ref:HM01187)

**ASHBERRY PHYSIOTHERAPY CLINIC**

**Ashberry Physiotherapy & Sports Injury Clinic**, Holtspur Prde, Beaconsfield, **Buckinghamshire**, HP9 1DA, ENG.
(T) 01494 681314
Speciality: Physiotherapy. ✔
● **Physiotherapist** Ms L Harper Q: MCSP, SRP. M: CSP.
● **Physiotherapist** Ms J Thompson Q: MCSP, SRP. M: CSP.
S Yrs. Est.: 2 (Ref:HM01188)

**ASHBOURNE CHIROPRACTIC CLINIC**

**Ashbourne Chiropractic Clinic**, Office 10 Ashbourne Town, Ashbourne, **County Meath**, IRE.
(T) 01835 2736
Speciality: Chiropractors.
P S T (Ref:HM01189)

**ASHBOURNE KNIGHT**

**Ashbourne Knight Ltd**, Unit 15 Westside Industrial Estate, Jackson St, St. Helens, **Merseyside**, WA9 3AT, ENG.
(T) 01744 739716 (F) 01744 754440
Speciality: Aromatherapy.
● **Managing Director** Mr K Mather
M O (Ref:HM01190)

**ASHBOURNE PHYSIOTHERAPY CLINIC**

**Ashbourne Physiotherapy & Sports Injury Clinic**, Constabulary House, 41 Station St, Ashbourne, **Derbyshire**, DE6 1DE, ENG.
(T) 01335 344952 (F) 01335 347475
Speciality: Physiotherapy.
● **Owner** Mrs P Phillips
P S T (Ref:HM01191)

**ASHBROOKE THERAPY**

**Ashbrooke Therapy**, Llwynmelyn, Llandinam, **Powys**, SY17 5AZ, WAL.
(T) 01686 413671
Speciality: Complementary Medicines & Therapy.
C M (Ref:HM01192)

**ASHBURNER, P**

**Mr P Ashburner**, 652 Nottingham Rd, Derby, **Derbyshire**, DE21 6SX, ENG.
(T) 01332 663342
Speciality: Osteopathy.
P S T (Ref:HM01193)

**ASHBY & ASSOCIATES**

**Anthea Ashby & Associates**, The Burntwood Surgery, 27 Shenfield Rd, Brentwood, **Essex**, CM15 8AG, ENG.
(T) 01277 227400 (F) 01277 264938
Speciality: Biomechanics, Chiropody, Cryo Surgery, Nail Surgery, Orthotics, Podiatry. ✔
● **Chiropodist (Podiatrist)** Mrs A Ashby
(T) 01277 222184 Q: MBChA, MSSCh. M: SSCh.
M Yrs. Est.: 12 (Ref:HM01194)

**ASHBY CHIROPODY/PODIATRY CLNC**

**Ashby Chiropody Podiatry Clinic**, 1st Floor, 52 Market St, Ashby-de-la-Zouch, **Leicestershire**, LE65 1AN, ENG.
(T) 01530 564200
Speciality: Chiropodists (Podiatrists).
● **Owner** Mrs F Power
S (Ref:HM01195)

**ASHBY, CAROLINE**

**Caroline Ashby**, 77 Alder Cres, **Dorset**, BH12 4BE, ENG.
(T) 01202 749380
Speciality: Reflexology.
S T (Ref:HM01196)

**ASHBY, F J S**

**F J S Ashby**, Cae Llewelyn, Llansantffraid, **Powys**, SY22 6TE, WAL.
(T) 01691 828111
Speciality: Chiropodists (Podiatrists).
S (Ref:HM01197)

**ASHCROFT CLINIC**

**Ashcroft Clinic**, Ashcroft Clinic, Hudson St, Deddington, Banbury, **Oxfordshire**, OX15 0SW, ENG.
(T) 01869 338854 (F) 01869 338854
(E) iswash@ashcroftclinic.co.uk
(W) www.ashcroftclinic.co.uk
Speciality: Acupuncture, Chiropody, Complementary Therapy, Counselling, Electrotherapy, Herbal Medicine, Manipulation, Massage (Therapeutic), Moxibustion, Nutritional Therapy, Osteopathy, Podiatry, Stress Therapy, Ultrasonics, Vibrational Therapy, Vitamin Therapy, X-Ray.
● **Chiropodist (Podiatrist)** Ms M Mindalia Q: BSc, DPodM, M.S.C.P, S.R.Ch.
● **Radiologist** Dr K Choji Q: MD.
● **Director/Osteopath** Mr I Swash Q: Dip.Ed, DO, FRSH, MSc. M: RoO.
● **Acupuncturist** Ms C Vass Q: BSc (Hons), Lic.Ac, MBAcC. M: BAcC.
S (Ref:HM01198)

**ASHCROFT, D M**

**D M Ashcroft**, La Ends Chiropody Practice, 229 Liverpool Rd, Culcheth, Warrington, **Cheshire**, WA3 5ES, ENG.
(T) 01925 722577
Speciality: Chiropodists (Podiatrists).
S (Ref:HM01199)

**ASHCROFT, E**

**E Ashcroft**, 29 Sutton St, Durham, **County Durham**, DH1 4BW, ENG.
(T) 01913 848590
Speciality: Chiropodists (Podiatrists).
S (Ref:HM01200)

**ASHCROFT, J J**

**J J Ashcroft**, 36 Salusbury Lane, Offley, Hitchin, **Hertfordshire**, SG5 3EG, ENG.



Key continued: Yrs.Est: Years Established Q: Qualifications M: Professional Membership ✔ Indemnity Insurance Accept Credit Cards

(T) 01462 769184 (F) 01462 768666
Speciality: Psychology.
● **Owner** Mrs J Ashcroft
B (Ref:HM01201)

## ASHCROFT, PATSY

**Patsy Ashcroft**, 37 Carr Lane, Willerby, Hull, **Humberside (North)**, HU10 6JP, ENG.
(T) 01482 653706
Speciality: Reflexology.
S T (Ref:HM01202)

## ASHDALE CHIROPODY

**Ashdale Chiropody**, 17 Ashdale, Mount Pleasant, Washington, **Tyne and Wear**, NE38 7BD, ENG.
(T) 01914 173132
Speciality: Chiropodists (Podiatrists).
S (Ref:HM01203)

## ASHDOWN CHIROPRACTIC CLINIC

**Ashdown Chiropractic Clinic**, Royal Oak Cottage, High St, Nutley, Uckfield, **Sussex (East)**, TN22 3NN, ENG.
(T) 01825 713457
Speciality: Chiropractors.
● **Chiropractor** Steven Rudd
P S T (Ref:HM01204)

## ASHDOWN CLINIC

**Ashdown Clinic**, 54 Hatfield Rd, Potters Bar, **Hertfordshire**, EN6 1HT, ENG.
(T) 01707 659978 (F) 01707 659978
(E) ashdownclinic@bigfoot.com
Speciality: Acupuncture, Allergy Testing, Aromatherapy, Biomechanics, Bowen Therapy, Chinese Herbal Medicine, Counselling, Cranial Osteopathy, Dietician, Homeopathy, Hypnotherapy, Indian Head Massage, Manipulation, Massage (Therapeutic), Naturopathy, Nutritional Therapy, Osteopathy, Physiotherapy, Pilates, Reflexology, Reiki, Shiatsu, Vitamin Therapy, X-Ray, Manual Lymphatic Drainage, Low Power Laser.
● **Podiatrist** Ms B Ashdown Q: B.A.Ch.P, DPodM, M.S.C.P, S.R.Ch. M: S.C.P.
S (Ref:HM01205)

## ASHDOWN OSTEOPATHIC CENTRE

**Trevor Strutt T/A - Ashdown Osteopathic Centre**, The Sq, Lewes Rd, Forest Row, **Sussex (East)**, RH18 5ES, ENG.
(T) 01342 822505 (F) 01342 822505
(E) ashdownosteopaths@hotmail.com
(W) www.ashdownosteopathiccentre.co.uk
Speciality: Acupuncture, Autogenic Training, Complementary Therapy, Counselling, Cranial Osteopathy, Homeopathy, Indian Head Massage, Kinesiology, Manipulation, Massage (Therapeutic), Naturopathy, Osteopathy, Pilates, Postural Integration, Psychotherapy, Reiki, Ultrasonics. ✔
● **Osteopath** Ms L Oakenfold
● **Osteopath/Practice Manager** Mr T Strutt Q: DO. M: GOsC.
● **Osteopath** Mr N McCall
● **Osteopath** Mr N Tuckley
S Yrs. Est.: 2 (Ref:HM01206)

## ASHDOWN, LOUISE

**Louise Ashdown**, Bromley, **Kent**, BR2, ENG.
(T) 020 8462 8565
Speciality: Bach Remedies.
M (Ref:HM01207)

## ASHE, SHIRLEY

**Shirley Ashe**, 60 Hawthorn Rd, Clarkston, Glasgow, **Glasgow (City of)**, G76 8EJ, SCO.
(T) 01416 443819
Speciality: Reflexology.
S T (Ref:HM01208)

## ASHELFORD, J L

**J L Ashelford**, 9 The Briary, Wickford, **Essex**, SS12 0HT, ENG.
(T) 01268 769217
Speciality: Chiropodists (Podiatrists).
● **Principal** Mr J Ashelford
S (Ref:HM01209)

## ASHER, PATRICIA

**Patricia Asher**, 18 Butlers Ct Rd, Beaconsfield, **Buckinghamshire**, HP9 1SF, ENG.
(T) 01494 672547
Speciality: Hypnotherapy.
B (Ref:HM01210)

## ASHER, V A

**V A Asher**, Pebbles, 41 Shorefield Way, Milford On Sea, Lymington, **Hampshire**, SO41 0RW, ENG.
(T) 01590 643226
Speciality: Chiropodists (Podiatrists).
● **Owner** Mrs V Asher
S (Ref:HM01211)

## ASHERA THERAPY CENTRE

**Ashera Therapy Centre**, Swansea, SA1 3TX, WAL.
(T) 01792 461413
Speciality: Psychotherapy.
● **Owner** Ms S Hale
B (Ref:HM01212)

## ASHETON, BEVERLEY

**Beverley Asheton**, 3 Hazelwood Drive, St. Albans, **Hertfordshire**, AL4 0UP, ENG.
(T) 01727 843633
Speciality: Alexander Technique.
P S (Ref:HM01213)

## ASHETON, KEVIN

**Kevin Asheton**, 3 Hazelwood Drive, St. Albans, **Hertfordshire**, AL4 0UP, ENG.
(T) 01727 843633
Speciality: Alexander Technique.
P S (Ref:HM01214)

## ASHFORD CHIROPODY CENTRE

**Ashford Chiropody Centre**, 13 North St, Ashford, **Kent**, TN24 8LF, ENG.
(T) 01233 645777
Speciality: Chiropodists (Podiatrists).
● **Partner** Miss K Edwards
S (Ref:HM01215)

## ASHFORD CLINIC

**Ashford Clinic of Complementary Medicine**, Western Avenue, Ashford, **Kent**, TN23 1LY, ENG.
(T) 01233 631530 (F) 01233 637825
Speciality: Homeopathy. ✔
● **Therapist** Ms T Parkington Q: MHMA. M: HMA.
● **Allergy Therapist** Ms S Lane Q: MBPA. M: BPA.
● **Allergy Therapist** Ms R Heddle
C Yrs. Est.: 20 (Ref:HM01216)

## ASHFORD OSTEOPATHIC CLINIC

**Ashford Osteopathic Clinic**, 36 Station Rd, Ashford, **Kent**, TN23 1PH, ENG.
(T) 01233 662929
Speciality: Osteopathy. ✔
● **Osteopath** Ms Z Van-Herbert Q: DO. M: GOsC.
S Yrs. Est.: 8 (Ref:HM01217)

## ASHFORD OSTEOPATHIC CLINIC

**Ashford Osteopathic Clinic**, 23 Feltham Rd, Ashford, **Surrey**, TW15 1DQ, ENG.
(T) 01784 255535 (F) 01784 255536
Speciality: Osteopathy.
● **Owner** Mr P Garnham
P S T (Ref:HM01218)

## ASHFORD, HAYLEY

**Hayley Ashford**, 90 Roydene Cres, **Leicestershire**, LE4 0GP, ENG.
(T) 01162 247794
Speciality: Reflexology.
S T (Ref:HM01219)

## ASHFORD, T

**T Ashford**, 1st Floor Woburn Court, 8 Guildhall Hill, Norwich, **Norfolk**, NR2 1JG, ENG.
(T) 01603 219254
Speciality: Osteopathy.
● **Practice Manager** Mr V Ryan
P S T (Ref:HM01220)

## ASHKEN, JOHN J (DR)

**Dr John J Ashken**, Oriel House, Royston Gr, Pinner, **London (Greater)**, HA5 4HE, ENG.
(T) 020 8428 1253
Speciality: Acupuncture.
● **Owner** Dr J Ashken
O (Ref:HM01221)

## ASHLEIGH PHYSIO & BEAUTY CLNC

**Ashleigh Physiotherapy & Beauty Clinic**, 26 Stoneygate Rd, Leicester, **Leicestershire**, LE2 2AD, ENG.
(T) 01162 707948
Speciality: Physiotherapy.
P S T (Ref:HM01222)

## ASHLEY HEATH CENTRE

**Ashley Heath Aromatherapy & Health Centre**, 39 Gainsborough Rd, Ashley Heath, Ringwood, **Hampshire**, BH24 2HY, ENG.
(T) 01425 476796
Speciality: Physiotherapy.
● **Owner** Mr T Johns
P S T (Ref:HM01223)

## ASHLEY HOUSE

**Ashley House**, Admirals Walk, Hoddesdon, **Hertfordshire**, EN11 8AJ, ENG.
(T) 01992 444323
Speciality: Complementary Medicines & Therapy.
C M (Ref:HM01224)

## ASHLEY, CLIVE

**Clive Ashley**, 1 Mauleverer Rd, London, **London (Greater)**, SW2 5DR, ENG.
(T) 07774 415588
Speciality: Osteopathy.
● **Owner** Mr C Ashley
P S T (Ref:HM01225)

## ASHLEY, PHILLIPA

**Phillipa Ashley**, 6 Berrylands, Liss, **Hampshire**, GU33 7DB, ENG.
(T) 01730 895505
Speciality: Complementary Medicines & Therapy.
C M (Ref:HM01226)

## ASHLIN'S NATURAL HEALTH

**Ashlin's Natural Health**, 181 Hoe St, Walthamstow, London, **London (Greater)**, E17 3AP, ENG.
(T) 020 8520 5268
Speciality: Alexander Technique.
● **Manager** Mr G Croston
P S (Ref:HM01227)

## ASHMOUNT PHYSIOTHERAPY CLINIC

**Ashmount Physiotherapy Clinic**, 5 Nile St, Crewe, **Cheshire**, CW2 7LL, ENG.
(T) 01270 661320
Speciality: Physiotherapy.
● **Owner** Miss S Hurd
P S T (Ref:HM01228)

## ASHROY HYP & COUNSELLING

**Ashroy Hypnotherapy & Counselling**, 22 Rathgar Ave, Dublin, **County Dublin**, IRE.
(T) 01492 1793
Speciality: Hypnotherapy.
B (Ref:HM01229)

## ASHTEAD CHARTERED PHYSIO SV

**D L M Coleman**, 45 Leatherhead Rd, Ashtead, **Surrey**, KT21 2TP, ENG.
(T) 01372 275823 (F) 01372 279009
(E) denise.l.m.coleman@btinternet.com
Speciality: Electrotherapy, Laser Treatment, Manipulation, Massage (Therapeutic), Phytotherapy, Pilates, Ultrasonics.
● **Physiotherapist** Ms D Coleman Q: MCSP, MMACP, MSc. M: CSP.
S Yrs. Est.: 17 (Ref:HM01230)

## ASHTEAD CHIROPRACTIC CLINIC

**Ashtead Chiropractic Clinic**, 6 Rectory Lane, Ashtead, **Surrey**, KT21 2BB, ENG.
(T) 01372 271970
Speciality: Chiropractors.
● **Partner** Dr J De-Graff
P S T (Ref:HM01231)

## ASHTEAD CLINIC

**Ashtead Osteopathy & Natural Health Clinic**, 13 The St, Ashtead, **Surrey**, KT21 2AD, ENG.
(T) 01372 277311
Speciality: Cranial Osteopathy, Homeopathy, Naturopathy, Osteopathy, Reflexology. ✔
● **Osteopath/Naturopath** Ms L Eicke Q: BSc,

DO, ND. M: RN.
● **Practice Manager** Ms J Edwards
**M** (**Ref:**HM01232)

### ASHTON CHIROPRACTIC CENTRE
**Ashton Chiropractic Centre**, 122-124 Mossley Rd, Ashton-under-Lyne, **Manchester (Greater)**, OL6 6ND, ENG.
(T) 01613 083322
Speciality: Chiropractic.
● **Joint Director** Ms A Renkin
**P** **S** **T** (**Ref:**HM01233)

### ASHTON HYPNOTHERAPY CENTRE
**Ashton Hypnotherapy Centre**, 19 Wigan Rd, Ashton-In-Makerfield, Wigan, **Lancashire**, WN4 9AR, ENG.
(T) 01942 720835
Speciality: Hypnotherapy.
● **Manager** Mrs C Spencer
**B** (**Ref:**HM01234)

### ASHTON PRIVATE CLINIC
**Ashton Private Clinic**, 197 Old St, Ashton-under-Lyne, **Manchester (Greater)**, OL6 7SR, ENG.
(T) 01613 309926
Speciality: Osteopathy.
**P** **S** **T** (**Ref:**HM01235)

### ASHTON SCHOOL OF REFLEXOLOGY
**Ashton School Of Reflexology**, 5 Kingwood, Markington, Harrogate, **Yorkshire (North)**, HG3 3NT, ENG.
(T) 01765 677772
Speciality: Reflexology.
**M** (**Ref:**HM01236)

### ASHTON, ANTHONY
**Anthony Ashton**, 26 Castle Mount, Exeter, **Devon**, EX4 4JW, ENG.
(T) 01392 431936
Speciality: Chiropodists (Podiatrists).
● **Owner** Mr A Ashton
**S** (**Ref:**HM01237)

### ASHTON, C M
**Mrs C M Ashton**, 53 Vancouver Rd, Forest Hill, London, **London (Greater)**, SE23 2AH, ENG.
(T) 020 8291 3905
Speciality: Osteopathy.
● **Owner** Mrs C Ashton
**P** **S** **T** (**Ref:**HM01238)

### ASHTON, HAZEL
**Hazel Ashton**, Moelfre Uchaf, Llangynog, Carmarthen, **Carmarthenshire**, SA33 5BS, WAL.
(T) 01267 211566
Speciality: Reflexology.
**S** **T** (**Ref:**HM01239)

### ASHTON, J G
**J G Ashton**, 39 Crossway, Manchester, **Manchester (Greater)**, M20 6TU, ENG.
(T) 01614 451018
Speciality: Hypnosis.
**B** (**Ref:**HM01240)

### ASHTON, JOHN H
**John H Ashton**, 10 Penlee Cl, Edenbridge, **Kent**, TN8 5NA, ENG.
(T) 01732 863612
Speciality: Chiropodists (Podiatrists).
**S** (**Ref:**HM01241)

### ASHTON-GREEN, SUE
**Sue Ashton-Green**, 41 Racecourse Avenue, Shrewsbury, **Shropshire**, SY2 5BS, ENG.
(T) 01743 244150
Speciality: Complementary Medicines & Therapy.
● **Owner** Mrs S Ashbourne-Green
**M** (**Ref:**HM01242)

### ASHTON-GREEN, SUE
**Sue Ashton-Green**, Natural Health Centre, Radbrook Green, Shrewsbury, **Shropshire**, SY3 6DU, ENG.
(T) 01743 248878
Speciality: Chiropodists (Podiatrists).
● **Owner** Ms S Ashton-Green
**S** (**Ref:**HM01243)

### ASHURST WOOD PRACTICE
**Ashurst Wood Osteopathic Practice**, 10 Woods Hill Cl, Ashurst Wood, East Grinstead, **Sussex (West)**, RH19 3RJ, ENG.
(T) 01342 314775
Speciality: Osteopathy.
● **Owner** Mrs M Clarke
**P** **S** **T** (**Ref:**HM01244)

### ASHURST, R F & S A
**R F & S A Ashurst**, 40 Shropshire Brook Rd, Armitage, Rugeley, **Staffordshire**, WS15 4UZ, ENG.
(T) 01543 492894
Speciality: Physiotherapy.
**P** **S** **T** (**Ref:**HM01245)

### ASHWELL, MELBOURN & BALDOCK
**Tim Moynihan**, 84 High St, Ashwell, Baldock, **Hertfordshire**, SG7 5NS, ENG.
(T) 01462 742942
Speciality: Manipulation, Massage (Therapeutic), Osteopathy. ✔
● **Osteopath** Mr T Moynihan Q: DO, ND. M: GOsC.
**S** Yrs. Est.: 10 (**Ref:**HM01246)

### ASHWIN STREET PRACTICE
**Ashwin Street Counselling & Psychotherapy Practice**, The Print House, 18 Ashwin St, London, **London (Greater)**, E8 3DL, ENG.
(T) 020 7254 9202
Speciality: Psychotherapy.
**B** (**Ref:**HM01247)

### ASHWORTH, FREDA
**Freda Ashworth**, Harefield Drive, Heywood, **Manchester (Greater)**, OL10 1RN, ENG.
(T) 01706 368193 (F) 01706 623414
Speciality: Hypnosis.
● **Owner** Mrs F Ashworth
**B** (**Ref:**HM01248)

### ASINYA, MARY
**Mary Asinya**, Nurses Bungalow, High St, Elsenham, Bishop's Stortford, **Hertfordshire**, CM22 6DD, ENG.
(T) 01279 815417
Speciality: Chiropodists (Podiatrists).
**S** (**Ref:**HM01249)

### ASKEW, SUSAN
**Susan Askew**, Clissold Park Health Centre, 154 Stoke Newington Church St, London, **London (Greater)**, N16 0JU, ENG.
(T) 020 7249 2990 (F) 020 7249 3977
Speciality: Psychotherapy.
● **Owner** Mr D Berg
**B** (**Ref:**HM01250)

### ASKEY, LAURIE
**Laurie Askey**, 12 Kingsway, Staines, **Surrey**, TW19 7QE, ENG.
(T) 01784 259820
Speciality: Hypnosis.
● **Owner** Mr L Askey
**B** (**Ref:**HM01251)

### ASKINS, A M
**A M Askins**, Penprom
pren, Llanfihangel-Ar-Arth, Pencader, **Carmarthenshire**, SA39 9JE, WAL.
(T) 01559 395379
Speciality: Chiropodists (Podiatrists).
● **Owner** Mr A Askins
**S** (**Ref:**HM01252)

### ASLING, JULIA
**Julia Asling**, 6 St Mary Magdalene St, Brighton, **Sussex (East)**, BN2 3HU, ENG.
(T) 01273 694958
Speciality: Chiropractors.
● **Owner** Miss J Asling
**P** **S** **T** (**Ref:**HM01253)

### ASMUNS CHIROPRACTIC CLINIC
**Asmuns Chiropractic Clinic**, 28 Asmuns Pl, London, **London (Greater)**, NW11 7XG, ENG.
(T) 020 8458 4135
Speciality: Chiropractic.
**P** **S** **T** (**Ref:**HM01254)

### ASPEN CLINIC
**Aspen Physiotherapy & Sports Injury Clinic**, 620 Wakefield Rd, Huddersfield, **Yorkshire (West)**, HD5 8PZ, ENG.
(T) 01484 452788
Speciality: Acupuncture, Physiotherapy. ✔
● **Physiotherapist/Owner** Ms C Bodsworth Q: Grad Dip Phys, SRP. M: CSP.
**S** Yrs. Est.: 6 (**Ref:**HM01255)

### ASPEN PHYSIOTHERAPY PRACTICE
**Aspen Physiotherapy Practice**, 28 Front St, Prudhoe, **Northumberland**, NE42 5DQ, ENG.
(T) 01661 830980
Speciality: Physiotherapy.
● **Owner** Mr S Robson
**P** **S** **T** (**Ref:**HM01256)

### ASPEY, A
**A Aspey**, 7b Stretford Rd, Urmston, Manchester, **Manchester (Greater)**, M41 9JY, ENG.
(T) 01617 480186
Speciality: Chiropodists (Podiatrists).
**S** (**Ref:**HM01257)

### ASPINALL, JEAN
**Jean Aspinall**, Mingoose Barn, Mount Hawke, Truro, **Cornwall**, TR4 8BU, ENG.
(T) 01872 553013
Speciality: Chiropodists (Podiatrists).
**S** (**Ref:**HM01258)

### ASS FOR GROUP & IND PSYCHO
**Association For Group & Individual Psychotherapy**, 1 Fairbridge Rd, London, **London (Greater)**, N19 3EW, ENG.
(T) 020 7272 7013
Speciality: Psychotherapy.
**B** (**Ref:**HM01259)

### ASS OF CHARTERED PHYSIO
**Association Of Chartered Physiotherapists In Animals**, Moorland House, Salters Lane, Winchester, **Hampshire**, SO22 5JP, ENG.
(T) 01962 844390 (F) 01962 863801
Speciality: Physiotherapy.
**P** **S** **T** (**Ref:**HM01260)

### ASS OF CHIROP/PODIATRISTS
**Association Of Chiropodists & Podiatrists**, 17 Littlemead Rd, Shirley, Solihull, **Midlands (West)**, B90 1DJ, ENG.
(T) 01214 746304 (F) 01214 746304
Speciality: Chiropodists (Podiatrists).
**S** (**Ref:**HM01261)

### ASS OF HUMANISTIC PSYCHOLOGY
**Association Of Humanistic Psychology Practitioners**, Bcm Ahpp, London, **London (Greater)**, WC1N 3XX, ENG.
(T) 08457 660326
(W) www.ahpp.org
Speciality: Psychotherapy.
**B** (**Ref:**HM01262)

### ASS OF IND PSYCHOTHERAPISTS
**Association Of Independent Psychotherapists (The)**, 8 Victoria Mansions, Holloway Rd, London, **London (Greater)**, N7 8LZ, ENG.
(T) 020 7700 1911
Speciality: Psychotherapy.
**B** (**Ref:**HM01263)

### ASS OF NATURAL MEDICINES
**Association Of Natural Medicines Ltd**, 19A Collingwood Rd, Witham, **Essex**, CM8 2DY, ENG.
(T) 01376 502762 (F) 01376 502762
Speciality: Complementary Medicines & Therapy.
● **Chairman** Miss S Handscombe
**C** **M** (**Ref:**HM01264)

### ASS OF WOMEN PSYCHOTHERAPISTS
**Association Of Women Psychotherapists**, 167 Sumatra Rd, London, **London (Greater)**, NW6 1PN, ENG.
(T) 020 8202 0816
Speciality: Psychotherapy.
**B** (**Ref:**HM01265)

### ASS WARRINGTON - REG CHIROP
**Association Of Warrington State Registered Chiropodists**, 152 Bent Lane, Culcheth, Warrington, **Cheshire**, WA3 5ES, ENG.
(T) 01925 754366



Key continued: **Yrs.Est:** Years Established **Q:** Qualifications **M:** Professional Membership ✔ Indemnity Insurance Accept Credit Cards

Speciality: Chiropodists (Podiatrists).
S (Ref:HM01266)

## ASSAD RAISSI

**Assad Raissi**, 22 Hockley Rd, Rayleigh, **Essex**, SS6 8EB, ENG.
(T) 01268 742534
Speciality: Acupuncture.
O (Ref:HM01267)

## ASS-DANCE MOVEMENT THERAPY

**Association For Dance Movement Therapy(UK)**, Quaker Meeting House, Wedmore Vale, Bedminster, Bristol, BS3 5HX, ENG.
(T) 01179 532055
(E) gvery@dmtuk.demon.co.uk
(W) www.dmtuk.demon.co.uk/
Speciality: Dance Movement Therapy.
● **Member of Executive Council**
Ms P Fisher Q: R DMT. M: ADMT UK.
● **Member of Executive Council**
Ms M Ware Q: R DMT. M: ADMT UK.
● **Chair of Association**
Ms J MacDonald Q: R DMT. M: ADMT UK.
C (Ref:HM01268)

## ASSESSMENT SERVICES

**Assessment Services**, P O Box 78, Much Hadham, **Hertfordshire**, SG10 6HA, ENG.
(T) 01279 843052 (F) 01279 843052
Speciality: Psychology.
● **Principal** Mrs J Morris
B (Ref:HM01269)

## ASSOCIATED CHIROPODY SERVICES

**Associated Chiropody Services**, 37 Devon Sq, Newton Abbot, **Devon**, TQ12 2HH, ENG.
(T) 01626 354834
Speciality: Chiropody. ✔
● **Owner/Chiropodist** Mr R Holland Q: FSSCh. M: B.A.Ch.P.
C Yrs. Est.: 23 (Ref:HM01270)

## ASSOCIATED CHIROPRACTIC CLNC

**Associated Chiropractic Clinics**, 126 Clontarf Rd, Clontarf, Dublin, **County Dublin**, IRE.
(T) 01833 4026 (F) 01853 1305
Speciality: Chiropractors.
P S T (Ref:HM01271)

## ASSOCIATED HR SERVICES

**Associated HR Services**, Emmet Hse, Emmet Pl, **County Cork**, IRE.
(T) 021 4278 009 (F) 021 4278 005
(E) ahr@indigo.ie
Speciality: Counselling.
B H (Ref:HM01272)

## ASSOCIATED PHYSIOTHERAPISTS

**Associated Physiotherapists**, Mall Villa, The Mall, Brading, Sandown, **Isle of Wight**, PO36 0BT, ENG.
(T) 01983 402772 (F) 01983 402772
Speciality: Physiotherapy.
● **Owner** Mr P Judge
P S T (Ref:HM01273)

## ASSOCIATED PSYCHOLOGISTS

**Associated Independent Psychologists**, Allington Manor, Allington Lane, Fair Oak, Eastleigh, **Hampshire**, SO50 7DE, ENG.
(T) 023 8069 2621
Speciality: Psychology.
B (Ref:HM01274)

## ASSOCIATES HEAD & SHORT

**Associates Head & Short**, The Bassett Clinic, 5 Port Hill, Hertford, **Hertfordshire**, SG14 1PJ, ENG.
(T) 01992 501659 (F) 01582 766017
Speciality: Chiropodists (Podiatrists).
● **Partner** Mr J Head
S (Ref:HM01275)

## ASSOCIATES HEAD & SHORT

**Associates Head & Short**, 14 Maidenhead St, Hertford, **Hertfordshire**, SG14 1DR, ENG.
(T) 01992 505105 (F) 01582 766017
(W) www.headandshort.co.uk
Speciality: Biomechanics, Chiropody, Cryo Surgery, Gait Analysis, Podiatry, Electrosurgery, Diabetic Assesments and Specialist care, H.I.V foot care and Vascular Assessments. ✔
● **Chiropodist (Podiatrist)**
Mr K Short Q: BSc (Hons), DPodM, M.S.C.P, S.R.Ch. M: S.C.P.
● **Chiropodist (Podiatrist)**
Ms M Charles Q: BSc (Hons), M.S.C.P, S.R.Ch. M: S.C.P.
● **Chiropodist (Podiatrist)**
Mr J Head Q: BSc, M.S.C.P, S.R.Ch. M: S.C.P.
S Yrs. Est.: 3 (Ref:HM01276)

## ASSOCIATES HEAD & SHORT

**Associates Head & Short**, Aberfoyle House, Stapley Rd, St. Albans, **Hertfordshire**, AL3 5EP, ENG.
(T) 01728 56687
(E) mail@headandshort.co.uk
(W) www.headandshort.co.uk
Speciality: Biomechanics, Chiropody, Cryo Surgery, Gait Analysis, Podiatry, Electrosurgery, Diabetic Assessments and Specialist care, H.I.V foot care and Vascular Assessments. ✔
● **Chiropodist (Podiatrist)**
Ms M Charles Q: BSc (Hons), M.S.C.P, S.R.Ch. M: S.C.P.
● **Chiropodist (Podiatrist)**
Mr J Head Q: BSc, M.S.C.P, S.R.Ch. M: S.C.P.
● **Chiropodist (Podiatrist)**
Mr K Short Q: BSc (Hons), DPodM, M.S.C.P, S.R.Ch. M: S.C.P.
S Yrs. Est.: 3 (Ref:HM01277)

## ASSOCIATES HEAD & SHORT

**Associates Head & Short**, Bowers Way Dental Surgery, 29 Bowers Way, Harpenden, **Hertfordshire**, AL5 4EP, ENG.
(T) 01582 467667 (F) 01582 766017
Speciality: Chiropodists (Podiatrists).
● **Partner** Mr J Head
S (Ref:HM01278)

## ASSOCIATES, G B

**G B Associates**, 3 Callows Cross, Brinkworth, Chippenham, **Wiltshire**, SN15 5DY, ENG.
(T) 01666 510661
Speciality: Complementary Medicines & Therapy.
C M (Ref:HM01279)

## ASSOCIATION FOR FAMILY THERAPY

**Association For Family Therapy Ltd (The)**, Woodlands House, 3 Larkstoke Cl, Appleton, Warrington, **Cheshire**, WA4 5AU, ENG.
(T) 01925 264545
Speciality: Psychotherapy.
● **Administrator** Mrs S Kennedy
B (Ref:HM01280)

## ASSOCIATION OF CHILD PSYCHO

**Association Of Child Psychotherapists (The)**, 120 West Heath Rd, London, **London (Greater)**, NW3 7TU, ENG.
(T) 020 8458 1609
Speciality: Psychotherapy.
B (Ref:HM01281)

## ASSOCIATION OF IRISH ACUP

**Association of Irish Acupuncturists**, 1 Raheen Gardens, **County Limerick**, IRE.
(T) 06122 7601
Speciality: Acupuncture.
O (Ref:HM01282)

## ASSOCIATION OF OSTEOMYOLOGY

**Association of Osteomyology (The)**, 80 Greenstead Avenue, Woodford Green, **Essex**, IG8 7ER, ENG.
(T) 020 8504 1462
Speciality: Acupuncture, Aromatherapy, Chiropractic, Cranio-Sacral Therapy, Homeopathy, Kinesiology, Massage (Therapeutic), McTimoney Chiropractic, Naturopathy, Neuro-Linguistic Program, Osteomyology, Osteopathy, Physiotherapy, Remedial Massage, Stress Therapy.
P S T (Ref:HM01283)

## ASSOCIATION OF REFLEXOLOGISTS

**Association Of Reflexologists**, 27 Old Gloucester St, London, **London (Greater)**, WC1N 3XX, ENG.
(T) 08705 673320 (F) 01989 567676
Speciality: Reflexology.
● **Executive Officer** Mr S Duncun
S T (Ref:HM01284)

## ASSOCIATION OF STRESS MANAGERS

**Association Of Stress Managers**, 59 Addiscombe Court Rd, Croydon, **Surrey**, CR0 6TT, ENG.
(T) 020 8656 3310
Speciality: Hypnotherapy.
B (Ref:HM01285)

## ASSOCIATION OF STRESS MNGMT

**Association Of Stress Management**, Mount Farm Clinic, Bitchfield, Grantham, **Lincolnshire**, NG33 4DS, ENG.
(T) 01476 585898
Speciality: Hypnotherapy.
B (Ref:HM01286)

## ASSOCIATION OF STRESS MNGMT

**Association Of Stress Management**, Hoath Hall, Chiddingstone Hoath, Edenbridge, **Kent**, TN8 7DB, ENG.
(T) 01892 870740
Speciality: Hypnotherapy.
● **Principal** Mr J Clarkson
B (Ref:HM01287)

## ASSOCIATION OF STRESS MNGMT

**Association Of Stress Management**, 72 Vicarage Rd, Kings Heath, Birmingham, **Midlands (West)**, B14 7QH, ENG.
(T) 01214 433427
Speciality: Auto Suggestion, Aversion Therapy, Cognitive Therapy, Counselling, Hypnosis, Hypnotherapy, Stress Therapy. ✔
● **Hypnotherapist** Mr D Evans Q: PhD. M: ASM, HA.
H Yrs. Est.: 10 (Ref:HM01288)

## ASSOCIATION OF STRESS MNGMT

**Association Of Stress Management**, 72 Cumbrian Way, Southampton, **Hampshire**, SO16 4AU, ENG.
(T) 023 8078 6848
Speciality: Hypnotherapy.
B (Ref:HM01289)

## ASSOCIATION OF STRESS MNGMT

**Association Of Stress Management**, 6 Hawthorne Avenue, Urmston, Manchester, **Manchester (Greater)**, M41 9NP, ENG.
(T) 01617 180143
Speciality: Hypnotherapy.
B (Ref:HM01290)

## ASSOCIATION OF STRESS MNGMT

**Association Of Stress Management**, 156 Croftside Avenue, Glasgow, **Glasgow (City of)**, G44 5ND, SCO.
(T) 01416 347805 (F) 01416 347805
Speciality: Hypnotherapy.
● **Owner** Dr T Younis
B (Ref:HM01291)

## ASSOCIATION OF STRESS MNGMT

**Association Of Stress Management**, Old Orchard, Grange Lane, Burghwallis, Doncaster, **Yorkshire (South)**, DN6 9JL, ENG.
(T) 01302 700338 (F) 01302 700338
Speciality: Hypnotherapy.
● **Owner** Mrs J Mills
B (Ref:HM01292)

## ASSOCIATION OF STRESS MNGMT

**Anglia Stress Management**, 215 Cambridge Rd, Hitchin, **Hertfordshire**, SG4 0JP, ENG.
(T) 01462 459202 (F) 01462 459202
(E) laurencenicholas@aol.com
Speciality: Counselling, Hypnotherapy, Stress Therapy. ✔
● **Stress Manager** Mr L Nicholas Q: Dip.Hyp, Dip.StM. M: NCH, SSM.
B Yrs. Est.: 11 (Ref:HM01293)

## ASSOCIATION OF STRESS MNGMT

**Association Of Stress Management**, 128 Knights Croft, New Ash Green, Longfield, **Kent**, DA3 8HY, ENG.
(T) 01474 874539
Speciality: Hypnotherapy.
B (Ref:HM01294)

## ASSOCI-SYSTEMATIC KINESIOLOGY

**Association Of Systematic Kinesiology**, 37 Harcourt Green Charlemont St, Dublin, **County**

**Dublin**, IRE.
(T) 08727 19863
(E) kinesiology@ireland.com
(W) www.kinesiology.ie
Speciality: Complementary Medicines & Therapy.
M (Ref:HM01295)

## ASTARRE INT TAROT CONSULTANT

**Astarre International Tarot Consultant**, Telephone Service Only, 44 Gorton St, Blackpool, **Lancashire**, FY1 3HP, ENG.
(T) 01253 620090
Speciality: Clairvoyants & Palmists.
● **Owner** Mrs S Miquel
B (Ref:HM01296)

## ASTBURY, PENNIE

**Pennie Astbury**, 26 Coln Cres, **Wiltshire**, SN25 3NA, ENG.
(T) 01793 703176
Speciality: Reflexology.
S T (Ref:HM01297)

## ASTHMA & ALLERGY CLINIC

**Asthma & Allergy Clinic**, Bishopstown, **County Cork**, IRE.
(T) 021 4343 311
Speciality: Complementary Medicines & Therapy.
M (Ref:HM01298)

## ASTILL-SMITH, A

**A Astill-Smith**, 5 Eastcott Common, Eastcott, Devizes, **Wiltshire**, SN10 4PL, ENG.
(T) 01380 813139
Speciality: Osteopathy.
● **Owner** Mr A Astill-Smith
P S T (Ref:HM01299)

## ASTLEY COMPLEMENTARY CENTRE

**Astley Complementary Therapy Centre**, 8a Higher Green Lane, Astley, Manchester, **Manchester (Greater)**, M29 7HG, ENG.
(T) 01942 870572 (F) 01942 765508
Speciality: Acupuncture, Allergy Testing, Aromatherapy, Bach Remedies, Bowen Therapy, Chinese Herbal Medicine, Cognitive Therapy, Complementary Therapy, Counselling, Cranial Osteopathy, Electrotherapy, Homeopathy, Hypnotherapy, Indian Head Massage, Moxibustion, Oriental Diagnosis, Osteopathy, Psychotherapy, Reflexology, Reiki, Shiatsu, Stress Therapy, Beauty Therapies. ✔
● **Owner** Mr T Hall M: RPS.
● **Centre Co-Ordinator** Mr B Gerami M: IIST.
● **Aromatherapist** Ms J Gerami M: IHT.
● **Homeopathic Practitioner** Ms A Donaldson
B C Yrs. Est.: 2 (Ref:HM01300)

## ASTON CLINIC

**Aston Clinic**, 26 Kingston Rd, New Malden, **Surrey**, KT3 3LS, ENG.
(T) 020 8942 3148 (F) 020 8949 7050
(W) www.astonclinic.co.uk
Speciality: Acupuncture, Alexander Technique, Allergy Testing, Chiropody, Colour Therapy, Herbal Medicine, Hypnotherapy, Kinesiology, Massage (Therapeutic), Osteopathy, Physiotherapy, Reflexology, Anti Smoking Therapy. ✔
● **Osteopath/Herbalist** Mr D Melrose Q: ICAK, MNIMH, UKRC. M: GOsC, UKRC.
M Yrs. Est.: 20 (Ref:HM01301)

## ASTON CLINIC

**Aston Clinic (The)**, 79 Harley St, London, **London (Greater)**, W1N 1DE, ENG.
(T) 020 7487 5926 (F) 020 7487 4608
Speciality: Osteopathy.
● **Owner** Mr D Melrose
P S T (Ref:HM01302)

## ASTRID, KELLY

**Kelly Astrid**, Eldersfield, 4 Church Down Rd, Malvern, **Worcestershire**, WR14 3JX, ENG.
(T) 01684 562123
Speciality: Reflexology.
S T (Ref:HM01303)

## ASTROLOGICAL CONSULTANTS

**Astrological Consultants**, 45 Mickleburgh Hill, Herne Bay, **Kent**, CT6 6DU, ENG.
(T) 01227 741262
Speciality: Clairvoyants & Palmists.
● **Owner** Mr K Gordon
B (Ref:HM01304)

## ASW ALLERGY CONSULTANTS

**ASW Allergy Consultants**, 37 Orchard Rd, Hook, Chessington, **Surrey**, KT9 1AL, ENG.
(T) 020 8397 4978
Speciality: Absent Healing, Complementary Therapy, Dowsing, Healer, Healing Therapy, Herbal Medicine, Holistic Healing, Homeopathy, Kinesiology, Phytotherapy. ✔
● **Senior Consultant** Mr A Wrigglesworth
C M Yrs. Est.: 15 (Ref:HM01305)

## ASWAB

**Aswab**, 41 Arthray Rd, Oxford, **Oxfordshire**, OX2 9AD, ENG.
(T) 01865 248070 (F) 01865 248070
Speciality: Psychotherapy.
● **Partner** Mrs R Harries
B (Ref:HM01306)

## AT HOME WITH HOMEOPATHY

**At Home With Homeopathy**, Westgate, Cowbridge, **Glamorgan (Vale of)**, CF71 7AQ, WAL.
(T) 08007 835917
Speciality: Homeopathy.
● **Owner** Ms C Geary
M (Ref:HM01307)

## ATAR AROMATHERAPY

**Atar Aromatherapy**, 1st Fl 95-97 Nth Main St, **County Wexford**, IRE.
(T) 05321 755
(E) info@atar.ie
(W) www.atar.ie
Speciality: Aromatherapy.
M O (Ref:HM01308)

## ATC

**Aromatherapy Trade Council**, Po Box 387, Ipswich, **Suffolk**, IP2 98N, ENG.
(T) 01473 603630 (F) 01473 603630
(W) www.a-t-c.org.uk
Speciality: Aromatherapy.
H (Ref:HM01309)

## ATHANASIADOU, KATERINA

**Katerina Athanasiadou**, 10 Victoria Rd, Canterbury, **Kent**, CT1 3SG, ENG.
(T) 01227 463432
Speciality: Physiotherapy.
● **Owner** Ms K Athanasiadou
P S T (Ref:HM01310)

## ATHERTON, ANN LOUISE

**Ann Louise Atherton**, The Hertford Chiropractic Clinic, 5 Port Hill, Hertford, **Hertfordshire**, SG14 1PJ, ENG.
(T) 01992 501659
Speciality: Chiropractors.
P S T (Ref:HM01311)

## ATHERTON, H R

**H R Atherton**, 358 Harrogate Rd, Leeds, **Yorkshire (West)**, LS17 6QB, ENG.
(T) 01132 685121 (F) 01132 685121
Speciality: Chiropodists (Podiatrists).
● **Owner** Mr H Atherton
S (Ref:HM01312)

## ATHERTON, NICOLA

**Nicola Atherton**, The Dental Surgery, 273 Stockport Rd, Timperley, Altrincham, **Cheshire**, WA15 7SP, ENG.
(T) 01619 803428
Speciality: Chiropodists (Podiatrists).
S (Ref:HM01313)

## ATHERTON, PAUL

**Paul Atherton**, 51 Parkgate Rd, Chester, **Cheshire**, CH1 4AG, ENG.
(T) 01244 390292
Speciality: Osteopathy.
P S T (Ref:HM01314)

## ATHLONE CHIROPRACTIC CLINIC

**Athlone Chiropractic Clinic**, Unit 4 McCormack Ctr, Dublin Rd, Athlone, **County Westmeath**, IRE.
(T) 09027 6277
Speciality: Chiropractors.
P S T (Ref:HM01315)

## ATKIN, M B

**M B Atkin**, 11 Finlaystone St, Coatbridge, **Lanarkshire (North)**, ML5 1NA, SCO.
(T) 01236 423579
Speciality: Chiropodists (Podiatrists).
● **Owner** Mrs M Atkin
S (Ref:HM01316)

## ATKIN, MORRIS

**Morris Atkin**, Healing Hands House, 1851B Pershore Rd, Kings Norton, Birmingham, **Midlands (West)**, B30 3DJ, ENG.
(T) 01214 861556
Speciality: Complementary Medicines & Therapy.
● **Owner** Mr M Atkin
C M (Ref:HM01317)

## ATKINS, DENISE

**Denise Atkins**, 1 Sutherland Drive, Wombourne, Wolverhampton, **Midlands (West)**, WV5 9BB, ENG.
(T) 01902 892772 (F) 01902 892772
Speciality: Hypnosis.
● **Owner** Mrs D Atkins
B (Ref:HM01318)

## ATKINS, F

**F Atkins**, 170 Pinner Rd, Watford, **Hertfordshire**, WD1 4EW, ENG.
(T) 01923 237406
Speciality: Chiropodists (Podiatrists).
● **Owner** Mrs F Atkins
S (Ref:HM01319)

## ATKINSON NEILSON

**Atkinson Neilson**, The Maple Clinic, 3-5 Horndean Rd, Bracknell, **Berkshire**, RG12 0XQ, ENG.
(T) 01344 862646
Speciality: Osteopathy.
● **Owner** Dr W Baker
P S T (Ref:HM01320)

## ATKINSON, D W

**D W Atkinson**, 417 Woodchurch Rd, Birkenhead, **Merseyside**, CH42 8PF, ENG.
(T) 01516 082835
Speciality: Osteopathy.
● **Owner** Mr D Atkinson
P S T (Ref:HM01321)

## ATKINSON, D W

**D W Atkinson**, First Floor Deysbrook Osteopathic Clinic, 1a Deysbrook Lane, Liverpool, **Merseyside**, L12 8RE, ENG.
(T) 01512 283403
Speciality: Osteopathy.
P S T (Ref:HM01322)

## ATKINSON, MAURICE

**Maurice Atkinson**, 16 Alford Trce, Bradford, **Yorkshire (West)**, BD7 2AU, ENG.
(T) 01274 574562
Speciality: Physiotherapy.
● **Owner** Mr M Atkinson
P S T (Ref:HM01323)

## ATKINSON, N T

**N T Atkinson**, 5 Station Trce, Twyford, Reading, **Berkshire**, RG10 9NE, ENG.
(T) 01189 342187
Speciality: Osteopathy.
● **Owner** Mr N Atkinson
P S T (Ref:HM01324)

## ATKINSON, PEARL

**Pearl Atkinson**, Surgery, 12 Brays Lane, Rochford, **Essex**, SS4 3DW, ENG.
(T) 01702 547311
Speciality: Chiropodists (Podiatrists).
S (Ref:HM01325)

## ATKINSON, R J

**R J Atkinson**, Parkview Clinic, Clough Lane, Oakworth, Keighley, **Yorkshire (West)**, BD22 7HP, ENG.
(T) 01535 646057
Speciality: Physiotherapy.
P S T (Ref:HM01326)



Key continued: **Yrs.Est:** Years Established **Q:** Qualifications **M:** Professional Membership ✔ Indemnity Insurance Accept Credit Cards

**ATKINSON, SOPHIE**

**Sophie Atkinson**, 66 Cranmer Avenue, Northfields, London, **London (Greater)**, W13 9XU, ENG.
(T) 020 8566 2433
Speciality: Reflexology.
S T (Ref:HM01327)

**ATMOSPHERES**

**Atmospheres Indoor Energy Balancing**, Chesterford Gardens, London, **London (Greater)**, NW3 7DE, ENG.
(T) 020 7431 9509
Speciality: Complementary Medicines & Therapy.
M (Ref:HM01328)

**ATTERTON, P**

**P Atterton**, Hapenny Cottage, Chaingate Lane, Winterbourne, Bristol, BS36 1NL, ENG.
(T) 01454 228491
Speciality: Chiropodists (Podiatrists).
S (Ref:HM01329)

**ATTEWELL, D**

**D Attewell**, 12 Market St, Lutterworth, **Leicestershire**, LE17 4EH, ENG.
(T) 01455 558488
Speciality: Chiropodists (Podiatrists).
● **Owner** Mr D Attewell
S (Ref:HM01330)

**ATTEWELL, GAVIN**

**Gavin Attewell**, 133 Wood St, Barnet, **Hertfordshire**, EN5 4BX, ENG.
(T) 020 8441 0231
Speciality: Osteopathy.
● **Owner** Mr M Cole
P S T (Ref:HM01331)

**ATTIA, GINA**

**Gina Attia**, 34 West St, Alresford, **Hampshire**, SO24 9AU, ENG.
(T) 01962 735553
Speciality: Chiropodists (Podiatrists).
● **Owner** Mrs G Attia
S (Ref:HM01332)

**ATTIA, GINA**

**Gina Attia**, 24 High St, Hythe, Southampton, **Hampshire**, SO45 6AH, ENG.
(T) 023 8084 3200
Speciality: Chiropodists (Podiatrists).
● **Owner** Mrs G Attia
S (Ref:HM01333)

**ATTIA, GINA**

**Gina Attia**, 2 Longhouse Green, Winchester, **Hampshire**, SO23 8SH, ENG.
(T) 01962 853528
Speciality: Chiropodists (Podiatrists).
● **Owner** Mrs G Attia
S (Ref:HM01334)

**ATTIC OFFICES**

**Attic Offices**, 96 Town Gate, Wyke, Bradford, **Yorkshire (West)**, BD12 9JB, ENG.
(T) 07702 631115
Speciality: Reflexology.
● **Owner** Mrs H Todd
S T (Ref:HM01335)

**ATTLEE, THOMAS**

**Thomas Attlee**, The Primrose Hill Natural Health Centre, 9 St George's Mews, London, **London (Greater)**, NW1 8XE, ENG.
(T) 020 7586 0148
Speciality: Complementary Medicines & Therapy.
C M (Ref:HM01336)

**ATTLESEY, C**

**C Attlesey**, El Adam, 33 Partridge Cl, Bridlington, **Humberside (North)**, YO15 3LQ, ENG.
(T) 01262 675577
Speciality: Osteopathy.
P S T (Ref:HM01337)

**ATTRIDGE, BRIAN**

**Brian Attridge**, 16 Victoria Gr, Southsea, **Hampshire**, PO5 1NE, ENG.
(T) 023 9286 3266
Speciality: Psychotherapy.
B (Ref:HM01338)

**ATTRIDGE, FAY**

**Fay Attridge**, 38 Lovedean Lane, Waterlooville, **Hampshire**, PO8 8HJ, ENG.
(T) 023 9259 8171
Speciality: Reflexology.
S T (Ref:HM01339)

**ATTWELL, IDA**

**Ida Attwell**, 124 Lower Richmond Rd, London, **London (Greater)**, SW15 1LN, ENG.
(T) 020 8785 9559
Speciality: Hypnotherapy.
● **Owner** Mrs I Attwell
B (Ref:HM01340)

**AUBEELUCK, L**

**L Aubeeluck**, 4 Pipers Avenue, Harpenden, **Hertfordshire**, AL5 1HB, ENG.
(T) 01582 621880
Speciality: Acupuncture.
● **Owner** Mr L Aubeeluck
O (Ref:HM01341)

**AUBREY, C J**

**C J Aubrey**, Room 3 First Floor, Rex Buildings, Alderley Rd, Wilmslow, **Cheshire**, SK9 1HY, ENG.
(T) 01625 530794
Speciality: Physiotherapy.
P S T (Ref:HM01342)

**AUCHTERARDER CHIROPODY**

**Auchterarder Chiropody Practice**, 153 High St, Auchterarder, **Perth and Kinross**, PH3 1AD, SCO.
(T) 01764 661133
Speciality: Biomechanics, Chiropody, Nail Surgery, Orthotics, Podiatry. ✓
● **State Registered Chiropodist**
Mrs C Williamson Q: DPodM, M.S.C.P, S.R.Ch.
C Yrs. Est.: 2 (Ref:HM01343)

**AUCKLAND ACUPUNCTURE CLINIC**

**Auckland Acupuncture Clinic**, Health Centre, Escomb Rd, Bishop Auckland, **County Durham**, DL14 6HT, ENG.
(T) 01325 318760
Speciality: Acupuncture.
● **Doctor** Dr N Pindolia
O (Ref:HM01344)

**AUCOTT, M J**

**M J Aucott**, 65 Jackson Avenue, Mickleover, Derby, **Derbyshire**, DE3 5AS, ENG.
(T) 01332 512240
Speciality: Physiotherapy.
P S T (Ref:HM01345)

**AUDLEY END PHYSIO CLINIC**

**Audley End Physiotherapy Clinic**, The Cottage, London Rd, Wendens Ambo, Saffron Walden, **Essex**, CB11 4JL, ENG.
(T) 01799 542371
Speciality: Physiotherapy.
P S T (Ref:HM01346)

**AUDSLEY, ADRIAN**

**Adrian Audsley**, 160 Hydethorpe Rd, London, **London (Greater)**, SW12 0JD, ENG.
(T) 020 8673 2201
Speciality: Reflexology.
S T (Ref:HM01347)

**AUDSLEY, T**

**T Audsley**, 2 Longlands Rd, Ossett, **Yorkshire (West)**, WF5 0PR, ENG.
(T) 01924 279367
Speciality: Chiropodists (Podiatrists).
● **Owner** Mr T Audsley
S (Ref:HM01348)

**AUGHTON PRIVATE CLINIC**

**Aughton Private Clinic**, 67 Liverpool Rd, Aughton, Ormskirk, **Lancashire**, L39 5AP, ENG.
(T) 01695 424058 (F) 01695 424058
Speciality: Chiropractors.
● **Manager** Mrs S Thumter
P S T (Ref:HM01349)

**AULD & BONN**

**Mrs E R Auld & Mrs J Bonn**, Largs Physiotherapy, 54-56 Gallowgate St, Largs, **Ayrshire (North)**, KA30 8PP, SCO.
(T) 01475 674611
Speciality: Physiotherapy.
P S T (Ref:HM01350)

**AURA**

**Aura**, Unit K17, Green Lanes Shopping Centre, Barnstaple, **Devon**, EX31 1UL, ENG.
(T) 01271 327020
Speciality: Aromatherapy.
● **Partner** Ms S Windsor
M O (Ref:HM01351)

**AURA HYPNOTHERAPY CLINIC**

**Aura Hypnotherapy Clinic**, 53 The Village, Ranelagh, **County Dublin**, IRE.
(T) 01491 0633
(W) www.hypnosiseire.com
Speciality: Hypnotherapy.
B (Ref:HM01352)

**AURA PHOTOGRAPHY**

**Aura Photography**, The Coliseum, 24 Church St, Manchester, **Manchester (Greater)**, M4 1PW, ENG.
(T) 01618 333213
Speciality: Complementary Medicines & Therapy.
● **Partner** Mr K Hurst
M (Ref:HM01353)

**AURA-SOMA**

**Aura-Soma**, South Rd, Tetford, Horncastle, **Lincolnshire**, LN9 6QB, ENG.
(T) 01507 533581 (F) 01507 533412
Speciality: Complementary Medicines & Therapy.
C M (Ref:HM01354)

**AURAVISION**

**Auravision**, 1 Chapel St, St. Ives, **Cornwall**, TR26 2LR, ENG.
(T) 01736 798166
Speciality: Complementary Medicines & Therapy.
● **Owner** Mrs L Quarton-Cats
M (Ref:HM01355)

**AURICULOTHERAPY UK**

**Auriculotherapy UK**, Willowbank, Heol Smyrna, Llangain, Carmarthen, **Carmarthenshire**, SA33 5AD, WAL.
(T) 01267 241376
Speciality: Complementary Medicines & Therapy.
● **Owner** Mr R Harcourt-Riley
C M (Ref:HM01356)

**AUROMA**

**J Clarke**, Friars Oak, Walberton Green, Walberton, Arundel, **Sussex (West)**, BN18 0AT, ENG.
(T) 01243 542528
Speciality: Aromatherapy. ✓
● **Owner/Aromatherapist**
Mrs J Clarke Q: LLSA(Adv). M: IFA.
C Yrs. Est.: 13 (Ref:HM01357)

**AURORA HEALING CENTRE**

**Aurora Healing Centre (The)**, 10 Severn St, Newtown, **Powys**, SY16 2AQ, WAL.
(T) 01686 623344
Speciality: Complementary Medicines & Therapy.
● **Partner** Mrs J Fryer
M (Ref:HM01358)

**AUSSENS, MIEKE**

**Mieke Aussens**, 1 Pyleigh Bungalow, Lydeard St. Lawrence, Taunton, **Somerset**, TA4 3QZ, ENG.
(T) 01984 667370
Speciality: Shiatsu. ✓
● **Healing Shiatsu Practitioner**
Mieke Aussens M: Shiatsu Society UK.
C Yrs. Est.: 7 (Ref:HM01359)

**AUSTEN, HEATHER**

**Heather Austen**, 172 West St, Portchester, Fareham, **Hampshire**, PO16 9XG, ENG.
(T) 023 9242 5422
Speciality: Complementary Medicines & Therapy.
M (Ref:HM01360)

**AUSTEN, S**

**S Austen**, 117 Gledhow Lane, Leeds, **Yorkshire (West)**, LS8 1NJ, ENG.



Key: B Mind-Body Medicine C Complementary Medicine H Self Help Treatment M Medicinal Therapy O Oriental Medicine P Postural Therapy S Manipulative Structural Therapy T Touch Therapy

(T) 01132 667656
Speciality: Hypnosis.
B (Ref:HM01361)

**AUSTERBERRY, HELEN**
**Helen Austerberry - Homeopath**, 47 Woodisarde Rd, Dulwich, London, **London (Greater)**, SE22 8UN, ENG.
(T) 020 7792 2844 (F) 020 7792 2844
Speciality: Homeopathy. ✓
● **Homeopath** Ms H Austerberry Q: BSc, LCH, RSHom. M: Soc.Hom.
B Yrs. Est.: 11 (Ref:HM01362)

**AUSTERBERRY, HELEN**
**Helen Austerberry - Homeopath**, Flat 2, 44 Kensington Gardens Sq, London, **London (Greater)**, W2 4BQ, ENG.
(T) 020 7792 2844 (F) 020 7792 2844
Speciality: Homeopathy. ✓
● **Homeopath** Ms H Austerberry Q: BSc, LCH, RSHom. M: Soc.Hom.
B Yrs. Est.: 11 (Ref:HM01363)

**AUSTIN HEALTH**
**Austin Health**, 2 Bournemouth Arcade, Bournemouth, **Dorset**, BH1 2AF, ENG.
(T) 01202 229007
Speciality: Complementary Medicines & Therapy.
● **Owner** Mrs S Austin
M (Ref:HM01364)

**AUSTIN, DIANA**
**Diana Austin**, 20 The Green, Twickenham, **London (Greater)**, TW2 5AB, ENG.
(T) 020 8977 2947
Speciality: Herbal Medicine.
● **Owner** Ms D Austin
M (Ref:HM01365)

**AUSTIN, H L**
**H L Austin**, 5 Church Lane, Stafford, **Staffordshire**, ST16 2AW, ENG.
(T) 01785 258522
Speciality: Chiropodists (Podiatrists).
S (Ref:HM01366)

**AUSTIN, JENNIFER**
**Jennifer Austin**, Inverness, **Highland**, IV3, SCO.
(T) 01463 861306
Speciality: Bach Remedies.
M (Ref:HM01367)

**AUSTIN, MIRANDA**
**Miranda Austin**, 25 Lower Buckland Rd, Lymington, **Hampshire**, SO41 9DN, ENG.
(T) 01590 678731
Speciality: Complementary Medicines & Therapy.
C M (Ref:HM01368)

**AUSTIN, NEIL**
**Neil Austin**, 140 Harley St, London, **London (Greater)**, W1N 1AH, ENG.
(T) 020 7935 8117
Speciality: Chiropractic.
P S T (Ref:HM01369)

**AUSTIN, P**
**Mrs P Austin**, 58A High St, Pinner, **London (Greater)**, HA5 5PZ, ENG.
(T) 020 8429 0555
Speciality: Chiropodists (Podiatrists).
S (Ref:HM01370)

**AUSTRALIAN BODY CARE UK**
**Australian Body Care UK**, Bodycare House, Sham Farm, Danegate, Eridge Green, Tunbridge Wells, **Kent**, TN3 9JA, ENG.
(T) 01892 750850
(W) www.teatreeoil.com
Speciality: Complementary Medicines & Therapy, Distributes Tea Tree products all over the world.
● **Owner** Mr S Jensen
C Yrs. Est.: 10 (Ref:HM01371)

**AUTOGENIC TRAINING**
**Autogenic Training**, 37 Ramsbury Rd, St. Albans, **Hertfordshire**, AL1 1SN, ENG.
(T) 01727 851574
(E) chris@pinch.co.uk
(W) www.autogenic-therapy.org.uk
Speciality: Autogenic Training. ✓
● **Autogenic Therapist** Mrs C Pinch Q: Dip.AT, SRN. M: BAS, UKCP.
H Yrs. Est.: 15 (Ref:HM01372)

**AUTOGENICS**
**Autogenics**, 2 Combe Lane, Torquay, **Devon**, TQ2 8DY, ENG.
(T) 01803 312098
Speciality: Complementary Medicines & Therapy.
● **Partner** Mr I Collins
C M (Ref:HM01373)

**AVA**
**Ava**, 1 Wentworth Avenue, Whitefield, Manchester, **Manchester (Greater)**, M45 7GQ, ENG.
(T) 01612 806639
Speciality: Aromatherapy.
● **Owner** Ms A Paulden
M O (Ref:HM01374)

**AVA-CLAIRVOYANT**
**Ava-Clairvoyant**, Brownroyd Hill Rd, Bradford, **Yorkshire (West)**, BD6 1RU, ENG.
(T) 01274 521278
Speciality: Clairvoyants & Palmists.
● **Owner** Mr J Goodman
B (Ref:HM01375)

**AVALON CENTRE**
**Avalon Centre For Complementary Medicine Ltd**, 9 Silver St, Glastonbury, **Somerset**, BA6 8BS, ENG.
(T) 01458 830080 (F) 01458 830080
Speciality: Complementary Medicines & Therapy.
● **Principal** Ms B Scott-Alexander
M (Ref:HM01376)

**AVALON CHINESE MEDICINE CLINIC**
**Avalon Chinese Medicine Clinic**, 1 Station Approach, Chiswick, London, **London (Greater)**, W4 3SJ, ENG.
(T) 020 8994 2500 (F) 020 8994 2500
(E) avalonclinic@hotmail.com
(W) www.avalonclinic.co.uk
Speciality: Acupressure, Acupuncture, Cupping, Electrotherapy, Herbal Medicine, Massage (Therapeutic), Moxibustion, Oriental Diagnosis. ✓
● **Doctor** Mr J Galvao-Rogers
O Yrs. Est.: 2 (Ref:HM01377)

**AVALON CLINIC**
**Avalon Clinic Of Traditional Acupuncture**, Croscombe, Wells, **Somerset**, BA5 3RQ, ENG.
(T) 01749 346414
Speciality: Acupuncture.
O (Ref:HM01378)

**AVALON HEALTH & THERAPY CENTRE**
**Avalon Health & Therapy Centre**, 6 St Johns Rd, Clacton-On-Sea, **Essex**, CO15 4BP, ENG.
(T) 01255 436059
Speciality: Complementary Medicines & Therapy.
● **Owner** Mr B Henesy
C M (Ref:HM01379)

**AVALON HEALTH CENTRE**
**Avalon Health Centre**, 39 Park Drive, Rustington, Littlehampton, **Sussex (West)**, BN16 3DY, ENG.
(T) 01903 771504
Speciality: Aromatherapy, Chiropody, Counselling, Herbal Medicine, Homeopathy, Massage (Therapeutic), Nutritional Therapy, Osteopathy, Physiotherapy. ✓
● **Owner** Miss D Stromwall
C Yrs. Est.: 31 (Ref:HM01380)

**AVALON NATURAL HEALTH**
**Avalon Natural Health**, 42 Claremont Avenue, Bournemouth, **Dorset**, BH9 3HA, ENG.
(T) 01202 517598
Speciality: Reflexology.
● **Owner** Mrs J Porter
S T (Ref:HM01381)

**AVALON NATURAL THERAPY CENTRE**
**Avalon Natural Therapy Centre**, 62 High St, Evesham, **Worcestershire**, WR11 4HG, ENG.
(T) 01386 423109
Speciality: Complementary Medicines & Therapy.
● **Owner** Mrs T Morrison
M (Ref:HM01382)

**AVART, GILLIAN**
**Aromatherapy Is At Hand**, 7 South Beech Avenue, Wickford, **Essex**, SS11 8AH, ENG.
(T) 01268 732571
(E) gillianavart@hotmail.com
(W) www.gillianavart.supanet.com
Speciality: Absent Healing, Aromatherapy, Crystal Healing, Dowsing, Faith Healing, Healer, Holistic Healing, Indian Head Massage, Massage (Therapeutic), Paranormal Therapies, Reflexology, Reiki, Spiritual Healing, Sports Injuries, Astrology. ✓
● **Aromatherapist/Tutor** Ms G Avart
B Yrs. Est.: 8 (Ref:HM01383)

**AVATAR**
**Avatar**, 62 Muswell Hill Rd, London, **London (Greater)**, N10 3JR, ENG.
(T) 020 8444 3216
(E) marygellhorn@virgin.net
Speciality: Aromatherapy, Cranio-Sacral Therapy, Massage (Therapeutic), Reflexology. ✓
● **Avatar Master** Ms M Gellhorn Q: ITEC, Licensed Avator Master, MAR. M: AoR, IFA, Stars Edge International.
B Yrs. Est.: 14 (Ref:HM01384)

**AVATARA**
**AvaTara Ltd**, Mill Lane, Uplyme, Lyme Regis, **Dorset**, DT7 3TZ, ENG.
(T) 01297 444772 (F) 01297 445514
Speciality: Complementary Medicines & Therapy.
● **Owner** Mr D Zacks
M (Ref:HM01385)

**AVEBURY HYPNOTHERAPY PRACTICE**
**Avebury Hypnotherapy Practice**, The Old Barn, Beckhampton, Marlborough, **Wiltshire**, SN8 1QJ, ENG.
(T) 01672 539625
Speciality: Cognitive Therapy, Counselling, Hypnosis, Hypnotherapy. ✓
● **Hypnotherapist/Hypno-Analyst** Mr J Brown Q: Dip.Hyp, Dip.Hyp-Anal. M: HA, IAH.
B H Yrs. Est.: 4 (Ref:HM01386)

**AVENA HERBAL PRODUCTS**
**Avena Herbal Products**, 8 Victoria Sq, Skipton, **Yorkshire (North)**, BD23 1JF, ENG.
(T) 01756 701636 (F) 01756 790017
Speciality: Herbal Medicine.
● **Partner** Mr N Spence
M (Ref:HM01387)

**AVENUE CLINIC**
**Avenue Clinic (The)**, 54 The Avenue, Yeovil, **Somerset**, BA21 4BN, ENG.
(T) 01935 422488
Speciality: Acupuncture, Alexander Technique, Aromatherapy, Ayurvedic Medicine, Bach Remedies, Complementary Therapy, Counselling, Cranial Osteopathy, Cupping, Herbal Medicine, Homeopathy, Hypnosis, Hypnotherapy, Indian Head Massage, Massage (Therapeutic), Nutritional Therapy, Osteopathy, Reflexology, Shiatsu, Qi Gong Classes. ✓
● **Manager** Ms J Robinson Q: M.Ac, MBAcC.
● **Manager** Ms G Rhodes Q: M.Ac, MBAcC, SRN.
● **Manager** Mrs L Jenkins Q: M.Ac, MBAcC, SRN.
● **Manager** Mr R Bertschinger Q: BA, Dip.Ac, Dip.Ed, MBAcC. M: BAcC.
B C H M O P S T
(Ref:HM01388)

**AVENUE CLINIC**
**Avenue Clinic**, 76 Bedford Pl, Southampton, **Hampshire**, SO15 2DF, ENG.
(T) 023 8033 0090
(E) robinpauc@excite.co.uk
Speciality: Chiropractic, Manipulation, Sound Therapy, Ultrasonics, Visualisation Therapy, X-Ray. ✓ CREDIT


Key continued: Yrs.Est: Years Established Q: Qualifications M: Professional Membership ✓ Indemnity Insurance CREDIT Accept Credit Cards

● **Chiropractor** Mr R Pauc Q: DC. M: BCA.
S Yrs. Est.: 26 (Ref:HM01389)

## AVENUE PHYSIO & SPORTS CLNC
**Avenue Physiotherapy & Sports Injury Clinic**, 214 Gordon Avenue, Camberley, **Surrey**, GU15 2NT, ENG.
(T) 01276 508408 (F) 01276 516206
Speciality: Physiotherapy. ✔
● **Owner/Physiotherapist** Mr S Evans Q: BSc (Hons), MCSP. M: CSP.
● **Physiotherapist** Ms B MacLead Q: BA, BSc, DPTh, MCSP. M: CSP.
S Yrs. Est.: 1 (Ref:HM01390)

## AVENUE PSYCHOTHERAPY SERVICES
**Avenue Psychotherapy Services Ltd**, 127 City Rd, London, **London (Greater)**, EC1V 1JB, ENG.
(T) 020 7490 3311 (F) 020 7490 3311
(E) 127avenue@compuserve.com
(W) www.avenue-psychotherapy.co.uk
Speciality: Psychotherapy, Individual/Couple Therapy, Training/Consultancy, Employee Assistance Programme. ✔
● **Director/Clinical Therapist** Mr R Neilsen-Cernkovich M: UKCP.
C Yrs. Est.: 5 (Ref:HM01391)

## AVERDUNG, DAN
**Dan Averdung ICNH, BHHSA, MIAH**, "Shalimar", Mullinabro Ferrybank, **County Waterford**, IRE.
(T) 05184 1627
Speciality: Complementary Medicines & Therapy.
M (Ref:HM01392)

## AVERY, MANDA
**Manda Avery**, Gosling Sports Park, Stanborough Rd, Welwyn Garden City, **Hertfordshire**, AL8 7LF, ENG.
(T) 01707 329910
Speciality: Physiotherapy.
P S T (Ref:HM01393)

## AVERY, MARK
**Mark Avery**, 10 Eynsham Rd, Botley, Oxford, **Oxfordshire**, OX2 9BP, ENG.
(T) 01865 865028
Speciality: Homeopathy.
● **Owner** Mr M Avery
M (Ref:HM01394)

## AVERY, N R (DR)
**Dr N R Avery**, 14 Denton Rd, Eastbourne, **Sussex (East)**, BN20 7SU, ENG.
(T) 01323 727474 (F) 01323 729159
Speciality: Acupuncture.
● **Owner** Dr N Avery
O (Ref:HM01395)

## AVERY, PATRICIA
**Patricia Avery**, 9 Stanley Rd, Teddington, **London (Greater)**, TW11 8TP, ENG.
(T) 020 8943 0603
Speciality: Chiropodists (Podiatrists).
S (Ref:HM01396)

## AVES, TREVOR (DR)
**Dr Trevor Aves**, 15 Cawley Rd, Chichester, **Sussex (West)**, PO19 1XT, ENG.
(T) 01243 530623 (F) 01243 782014
Speciality: Psychology.
● **Owner** Dr T Aves
B (Ref:HM01397)

## AVETOOM, CARO
**Caro Avetoom**, 117 Dormers Wells Lane, Southall, **London (Greater)**, UB1 3JA, ENG.
(T) 020 8893 6132
Speciality: Complementary Medicines & Therapy.
● **Owner** Mr C Avetoom
M (Ref:HM01398)

## AVEVA HERBAL
**Aveva Herbal**, 1 Byres Rd, 148 Dumbarton Rd, Glasgow, **Glasgow (City of)**, G11 6XE, SCO.
(T) 01413 340705 (F) 01413 349789
(W) www.aveva.co.uk
Speciality: Herbalists, Herbalist Dispensary on site.
● **Clinic Manager** Ms M Beaton
● **Dispensary Manager** Ms J Robertson
● **Homeopath** Mrs E Tobs-Heirman M: Soc.Hom.
C (Ref:HM01399)

## AVINGTON, GEORGIA
**Georgia Avington**, 80A Nightingale Rd, London, **London (Greater)**, N22 8PP, ENG.
(T) 020 8888 5593
Speciality: Psychology.
● **Owner** Miss L Hesper
B (Ref:HM01400)

## AVIS, JEAN
**Jean Avis**, 1 Britons Lane, Beeston Regis, Sheringham, **Norfolk**, NR26 8SJ, ENG.
(T) 01263 825471
Speciality: Reflexology.
S T (Ref:HM01401)

## AVISION COUNS & PSYCHO SVS
**Avision Counselling & Psychotherapy Services**, 9 Beaufield Gn, Maynooth, **County Kildare**, IRE.
(T) 01628 5353
Speciality: Psychotherapy.
B (Ref:HM01402)

## AVISON, RITA
**Rita Avison**, West Cl, Melmerby, Leyburn, **Yorkshire (North)**, DL8 4TW, ENG.
(T) 01969 640283
Speciality: Chiropodists (Podiatrists).
S (Ref:HM01403)

## AVON COMPLEMENTARY MEDICINE
**Avon Complementary Medicine**, The Old Ship, 548 Bath Rd, Saltford, Bristol, BS31 3JL, ENG.
(T) 01225 874075 (F) 01225 400227
(E) ddowson@appleonline.net
Speciality: Acupuncture, Clinical Ecology, Homeopathy. ✔
● **Practitioner** Dr D Dowson Q: Ch.B, MB.
M Yrs. Est.: 7 (Ref:HM01404)

## AVON COUNSELLING/PSYCHOTHERAPY
**Avon Counselling & Psychotherapy Service**, 11 Orchard St, Bristol, BS1 5EH, ENG.
(T) 01179 304447
Speciality: Psychotherapy.
B (Ref:HM01405)

## AVON HOUSE NATURAL HEALTH CTRE
**Avon House Natural Health Centre**, Avon House, 29 New Broad St, Stratford-Upon-Avon, **Warwickshire**, CV37 6NY, ENG.
(T) 01789 267888
Speciality: Complementary Medicines & Therapy.
● **Owner** Mr K Batchelo
M (Ref:HM01406)

## AVON HYPNOTHERAPY
**Avon Hypnotherapy**, 2 Leamington Cl, Derby, **Derbyshire**, DE23 6HF, ENG.
(T) 01332 769358
Speciality: Hypnotherapy.
● **Owner** Mr B Dawson
B (Ref:HM01407)

## AVONBOURNE CHIROPRACTIC CLINIC
**Avonbourne Chiropractic Clinic**, 31 Salt Lane, Salisbury, **Wiltshire**, SP1 1EG, ENG.
(T) 01722 411998
Speciality: Chiropractic.
● **Partner** Ms H Hooper
P S T (Ref:HM01408)

## AVRIL
**Avril**, 12 Corn Exchange Hall, Manchester, **Manchester (Greater)**, M4 3EY, ENG.
(T) 01614 913081
Speciality: Clairvoyants & Palmists.
B (Ref:HM01409)

## AVSEC, FAY
**Fay Avsec**, 100 Atbara Rd, Teddington, **London (Greater)**, TW11 9PB, ENG.
(T) 020 8977 4075
Speciality: Homeopathy.
M (Ref:HM01410)

## AWAKENING
**Awakening (The)**, 162 Market St, Droylsden, Manchester, **Manchester (Greater)**, M43 7AA, ENG.
(T) 01613 707687
Speciality: Clairvoyants & Palmists.
● **Owner** Miss D Garnet
B (Ref:HM01411)

## AWAKENING HYPNOTHERAPY
**Awakening Hypnotherapy**, 15 Upper Howsell Rd, Malvern, **Worcestershire**, WR14 1TL, ENG.
(T) 01684 892793
Speciality: Hypnotherapy.
B (Ref:HM01412)

## AWARENESS & DEVELOPMENT
**Awareness & Development**, 111 Godfrey House, St Lukes Estate, Bath St, London, **London (Greater)**, EC1V 9ET, ENG.
(T) 020 7253 2022
Speciality: Alexander Technique.
P S (Ref:HM01413)

## AWARENESS CENTRE
**Awareness Centre**, 28 & 29 Walpole St, Weymouth, **Dorset**, DT4 7HJ, ENG.
(T) 01305 766854
Speciality: Complementary Medicines & Therapy.
M (Ref:HM01414)

## AWARENESS CENTRE
**Awareness Centre**, Hanover House, Chard St, Axminster, **Devon**, EX13 5DZ, ENG.
(T) 01297 32331 (F) 01297 631090
(E) awareness@eclipse.co.uk
(W) www.awarenesscentre.co.uk
Speciality: Absent Healing, Acupressure, Acupuncture, Alexander Technique, Aromatherapy, Bowen Therapy, Colour Therapy, Complementary Therapy, Counselling, Cranial Osteopathy, Crystal Healing, Dietician, Dowsing, Faith Healing, Hay Diet, Healer, Healing Therapy, Holistic Healing, Homeopathy, Hypnosis, Hypnotherapy, Indian Head Massage, Macrobiotics, Meditation, Nutritional Therapy, Osteopathy, Psychotherapy, Reiki, Seichem, Shiatsu, Spiritual Healing, T'ai-Chi Ch'uan, Visualisation Therapy, Vitamin Therapy, Yoga. ✔
● **Manager** Mr H Alldritt Q: NFSH.
B C Yrs. Est.: 4 (Ref:HM01415)

## AWDRY, ROBERT
**Robert Awdry**, Orchard Farm, East Orchard, Shaftesbury, **Dorset**, SP7 0LH, ENG.
(T) 01747 811925 (F) 01747 811925
(E) robertawdry@aol.com
(W) www.net-prescriber.co.uk
Speciality: Acupuncture, Bowen Therapy, Homeopathy, Nutritional Therapy. ✔
● **Owner** Mr R Awdry Q: MBRCP. M: ICM.
M Yrs. Est.: 11 (Ref:HM01416)

## AWDRY, ROBERT
**Robert Awdry**, 10 Harley St, London, **London (Greater)**, W1N 1AA, ENG.
(T) 020 7636 6504 (F) 020 7467 8312
Speciality: Homeopathy.
M (Ref:HM01417)

## AXTON, PETER
**Peter Axton**, 93 Penenden, New Ash Green, Longfield, **Kent**, DA3 8LT, ENG.
(T) 01474 871117
Speciality: Chiropractic.
● **Owner** Mr P Axton
P S T (Ref:HM01418)

## AYERS, K
**K Ayers**, 3 Bickham Park Rd, Plymouth, **Devon**, PL3 4QJ, ENG.
(T) 01752 705936
Speciality: Chiropodists (Podiatrists).
S (Ref:HM01419)

## AYERS, WENDY
**Wendy Ayers**, 284 Ecclesall Rd, Sheffield, **Yorkshire (South)**, S11 8PE, ENG.
(T) 01142 664045
Speciality: Reflexology.
● **Owner** Mrs W Ayres
S T (Ref:HM01420)



Key: B Mind-Body Medicine C Complementary Medicine H Self Help Treatment M Medicinal Therapy O Oriental Medicine P Postural Therapy S Manipulative Structural Therapy T Touch Therapy

**AYLARD, P**

**P Aylard**, 2 Clifton Pk, Bristol, BS8 3BS, **ENG**.
**(T)** 01179 737371 **(F)** 01179 730887
Speciality: Psychiatry.
● **Senior Partner** Dr M Sternberg
B (**Ref:**HM01421)

**AYLESBURY CHIROPRACTIC CLINIC**

**Aylesbury Chiropractic Clinic**, Milton House, Gatehouse Rd, Aylesbury, **Buckinghamshire**, HP19 8EA, **ENG**.
**(T)** 01296 489231 **(F)** 01296 394931
Speciality: Chiropractic. ✔
● **Owner** Miss J Benepal **Q:** DC. **M:** CC.
P Yrs. Est.: 14 (**Ref:**HM01422)

**AYLESBURY COMPLEMENTARY HEALTH**

**Aylesbury Complementary Health Ltd**, 16 Walnut Cl, Stoke Mandeville, Aylesbury, **Buckinghamshire**, HP22 5UG, **ENG**.
**(T)** 01296 612930 **(F)** 01296 612930
**(E)** nickyward@supanet.com
Speciality: Absent Healing, Aromatherapy, Complementary Therapy, Counselling, Healing Therapy, Holistic Healing, Hypnosis, Hypnotherapy, Indian Head Massage, Massage (Therapeutic), Neuro-Linguistic Program, Psychotherapy, Reiki, Stress Therapy, Hydrotherm - Massage on a warm water bed, Bodytalk - simple form of Kinesiology and Hatha Yoga. ✔
● **Complementary Therapist** Ms N Ward **Q:** BSc (Hons), CHP, ITEC, NLP. **M:** HA, HS, IPTI, NRHP.
B Yrs. Est.: 6 (**Ref:**HM01423)

**AYLESBURY FOOT HEALTH CENTRE**

**Aylesbury Foot Health Centre**, 21 Buckingham Rd, Aylesbury, **Buckinghamshire**, HP19 9PT, **ENG**.
**(T)** 01296 428065
Speciality: Chiropodists (Podiatrists).
S (**Ref:**HM01424)

**AYLESBURY VALE THERAPY**

**Aylesbury Vale Therapy**, 17 Camborne Avenue, Aylesbury, **Buckinghamshire**, HP21 7UH, **ENG**.
**(T)** 01296 334338
Speciality: Complementary Therapy, Hypnotherapy, Psychotherapy, Stress Therapy, Visualisation Therapy.
● **Hypnotherapist** Mr B Hillyard **Q:** DABCH. **M:** CAH.
B Yrs. Est.: 4 (**Ref:**HM01425)

**AYLESFORD MEDICAL CENTRE**

**Aylesford Medical Centre Osteopath Clinic**, The Aylesford Medical Centre, Admiral Moore Drive, Aylesford, **Kent**, ME20 7SE, **ENG**.
**(T)** 01622 718084
**(E)** philandshurn@yahoo.com
Speciality: Osteopathy. ✔
● **Osteopath** Mr P Austin **Q:** BSc, Hons (OST). **M:** GOsC.
S Yrs. Est.: 1 (**Ref:**HM01426)

**AYLESFORD OSTEOPATHIC PRACTICE**

**Aylesford Osteopathic Practice**, Aylesford Business Centre, 17 High St, Aylesford, **Kent**, ME20 7AX, **ENG**.
**(T)** 01622 710536
Speciality: Osteopathy.
● **Partner** Mr P Martin
P S T (**Ref:**HM01427)

**AYLING, GILL**

**Gill Ayling**, Yarcombe, Willett Way, Orpington, **Kent**, BR5 1QD, **ENG**.
**(T)** 01689 606700
Speciality: Reflexology.
S T (**Ref:**HM01428)

**AYLSHAM OSTEOPATHIC PRACTICE**

**Aylsham Osteopathic Practice**, Burgh House Osteopathic Practice, Burgh Rd, Aylesham, **Kent**, NR11 6AT, **ENG**.
**(T)** 07770 652839
**(E)** yayliffeost@talk21.com
Speciality: Cranial Osteopathy, Manipulation, Naturopathy, Osteopathy, Postural Integration. ✔
● **Osteopath** Ms Y Ayliffe **Q:** DO. **M:** GOsC.
● **Osteopath** Arnaud Geanyt **Q:** DO. **M:** GOsC.
P Yrs. Est.: 3 (**Ref:**HM01429)

**AYRE CENTRE OF HYPNOTHERAPY**

**Ayre Centre Of Hypnotherapy**, 5 Lisvane St, Cardiff, **Glamorgan (Vale of)**, CF24 4LH, **WAL**.
**(T)** 029 2039 7168
**(W)** www.selfdevelopment.ukprofessionals.com
Speciality: Hypnotherapy. ✔
● **Hypnotherapist** Mr D Ayre **Q:** Dip.Hyp (Acc). **M:** NCH.
B Yrs. Est.: 24 (**Ref:**HM01430)

**AYRES, D**

**D Ayres**, 87 Cairnfield Avenue, London, **London (Greater)**, NW2 7PH, **ENG**.
**(T)** 020 8452 2017
Speciality: Chiropodists (Podiatrists).
● **Owner** Mrs D Ayres
S (**Ref:**HM01431)

**AYRES, DAVID**

**David Ayres**, 15 Swanswood Gardens, Westward Ho, Bideford, **Devon**, EX39 1HP, **ENG**.
**(T)** 01237 477913
Speciality: Chiropodists (Podiatrists).
● **Owner** Mr D Ayres
S (**Ref:**HM01432)

**AYRES, ELIZABETH**

**Elizabeth Aryes State Registered Chiropodist**, 65 Newgate St, Morpeth, **Northumberland**, NE61 1AY, **ENG**.
**(T)** 01670 514244
Speciality: Biomechanics, Chiropody, Nail Surgery. ✔
● **Owner/Chiropodist** Miss E Ayres **Q:** DPodM, S.R.Ch. **M:** S.R.Ch.
M Yrs. Est.: 6 (**Ref:**HM01433)

**AYRES, JOHN**

**John Ayres**, South House, Bleathwood, Ludlow, **Shropshire**, SY8 4LT, **ENG**.
**(T)** 01584 811183
**(E)** glassairre@aol.com
Speciality: Aversion Therapy, Cognitive Therapy, Counselling, Family Therapy, Gestalt Therapy, Group Therapy, Humanistic Psychology, Hypnosis, Hypnotherapy, Psychotherapy, Rogerian Therapy, Stress Therapy. ✔
● **Hypnotherapist/Psychotherapist** Mr J Ayres **Q:** MNCH, MNRHP. **M:** NCH.
B Yrs. Est.: 10 (**Ref:**HM01434)

**AYRES, JUDITH**

**Judith Ayres**, 82 Slade Rd, Stokenchurch, High Wycombe, **Buckinghamshire**, HP14 3PX, **ENG**.
**(T)** 01494 482407
Speciality: Reflexology.
S T (**Ref:**HM01435)

**AYRES, KATHLEEN**

**Kathleen Ayres**, Oakwood House, 6 Marshall Avenue, Bognor Regis, **Sussex (West)**, PO21 2TJ, **ENG**.
**(T)** 01243 822263
Speciality: Hypnosis.
● **Owner** Mrs K Ayres
B (**Ref:**HM01436)

**AYRES, M E**

**M E Ayres**, 8 High St, Mill Lane Entrance, Arundel, **Sussex (West)**, BN18 9AB, **ENG**.
**(T)** 01903 882200
Speciality: Chiropodists (Podiatrists).
S (**Ref:**HM01437)

**AYRE-SNOWDEN, MARION**

**Marion Ayre-Snowden**, 4 Arlington Cl, Swindon, **Wiltshire**, SN3 3NB, **ENG**.
**(T)** 01793 524273
Speciality: Chiropodists (Podiatrists).
S (**Ref:**HM01438)

**AYSA SHOES & CHIROPODY**

**Aysa Shoes & Chiropody**, 47 Bell Rd, Hounslow, **London (Greater)**, TW3 3NX, **ENG**.
**(T)** 020 8572 1552 **(F)** 020 8814 1707
Speciality: Chiropodists (Podiatrists).
● **Owner** Mr B Dulloo
S (**Ref:**HM01439)

**AYTON, P E**

**P E Ayton**, 9 Albany Rd, Stockton-On-Tees, **Cleveland**, TS20 2QX, **ENG**.
**(T)** 01642 559690
Speciality: Osteopathy.
● **Owner** Mr P Ayton
P S T (**Ref:**HM01440)

**AYUR VED, MAHARISHI**

**Maharishi Ayur Ved**, 18 Brecknock Rd, Bristol, BS4 2DD, **ENG**.
**(T)** 01179 737651
Speciality: Complementary Medicines & Therapy.
M (**Ref:**HM01441)

**AYURVED HERBELI**

**Ayurved Consultancy Ltd**, 50 Elmcroft Cres, London, **London (Greater)**, NW11 9SY, **ENG**.
**(T)** 020 8455 6598 **(F)** 020 8455 6598
**(E)** elashah@hotmail.com
**(W)** www.ayurved-herbeli.com
Speciality: Ayurvedic Medicine, Herbal Medicine, Yoga. [credit card]
● **Ayur-Veda Expert** Dr E Shah **Q:** BRCP, BS, MB. **M:** ICM.
M O Yrs. Est.: 9 (**Ref:**HM01442)

**AYURVEDIC CO OF GREAT BRITAIN**

**Ayurvedic Co Of Great Britain Ltd**, 81 Wimpole St, London, **London (Greater)**, W1M 7DB, **ENG**.
**(T)** 020 7224 6070 **(F)** 020 7224 6080
Speciality: Complementary Medicines & Therapy.
● **Managing Director** Mr G Warrior
M (**Ref:**HM01443)

**AYURVEDIC HERBAL CLINIC**

**Ayurvedic Herbal Clinic**, 218 Melton Rd, Leicester, **Leicestershire**, LE4 7PG, **ENG**.
**(T)** 01162 663939 **(F)** 01162 663939
**(E)** ayurvedicherbalclinic@aol.com
Speciality: Acupressure, Aromatherapy, Ayurvedic Medicine, Complementary Therapy, Dietician, Herbal Medicine, Indian Head Massage, Life Style Coaching, Massage (Therapeutic), Naturopathy, Nutritional Therapy, Psychotherapy, Reflexology, Stress Therapy, Touch Therapy, Vitamin Therapy, Yoga. ✔
● **Ayur-Veda Consultant** Dr K Patel
B O P Yrs. Est.: 20 (**Ref:**HM01444)

**AYURVEDIC MEDICAL ASSOCIATION**

**Ayurvedic Medical Association**, 1079 Garratt Lane, London, **London (Greater)**, SW17 0LN, **ENG**.
**(T)** 020 8682 3876
Speciality: Complementary Medicines & Therapy.
● **Ayurvedic Doctor** Dr Moorthy
M (**Ref:**HM01445)

**AYURVEDIC TRADING**

**Ayurvedic Trading Co Ltd**, 10 High St, Glastonbury, **Somerset**, BA6 9DU, **ENG**.
**(T)** 01458 833382
Speciality: Complementary Medicines & Therapy.
● **Owner** Ms J Sanders
M (**Ref:**HM01446)

**AZAB, M**

**M Azab**, 88 Intake Lane, Barnsley, **Yorkshire (South)**, S75 2HY, **ENG**.
**(T)** 01226 284271
Speciality: Chiropodists (Podiatrists).
S (**Ref:**HM01447)

**AZRINA**

**Azrina**, 89 Beauvale Rd, Nottingham, **Nottinghamshire**, NG2 2ES, **ENG**.
**(T)** 01159 863692
Speciality: Clairvoyants & Palmists.
● **Owner** Mrs A Serina
B (**Ref:**HM01448)

**B A WILLIAMS CHIROPODY**

**B A Williams Chiropody**, 14-15 Albany Prde, High St, Brentford, **London (Greater)**, TW8 0JW, **ENG**.
**(T)** 020 8560 3834
Speciality: Chiropractors.
P S T (**Ref:**HM01449)

**B A WILLIAMS REFLEXOLOGY**

**B A Williams Reflexology**, 14-15 Albany Prde, High St, Brentford, **London (Greater)**, TW8 0JW,


Key continued: **Yrs.Est:** Years Established **Q:** Qualifications **M:** Professional Membership ✔ Indemnity Insurance [credit card] Accept Credit Cards

ENG.
(T) 020 8560 3834
Speciality: Reflexology.
[S] [T] (Ref:HM01450)

## B M R THERAPY

**B M R Therapy**, 5a Wick Lane, Christchurch, **Dorset**, BH23 1HT, ENG.
(T) 01202 487161 (F) 01202 487161
Speciality: Complementary Medicines & Therapy.
● **Principal** Mrs B Ruskill
[M] (Ref:HM01451)

## B O P

**Broadwater Osteopathic Practice**, 2 Sompting Rd, Worthing, **Sussex (West)**, BN14 9EP, ENG.
(T) 01903 820206 (F) 01903 820206
(E) mike@bostp.freeserve.co.uk
Speciality: Aromatherapy, Electrotherapy, Manipulation, Massage (Therapeutic), Osteopathy, Reflexology, Ultrasonics, Remedial Massage. ✔
● **Remedial Massage Therapist** Ms W Jones Q: LCSP.
● **Remedial Massage Therapist/Reflexologist** Ms S Macpherson Q: LCSP. M: AoR.
● **Osteopath** Ms D Cantrell Q: DO, MD. M: GOsC.
● **Senior Associate** Mr M Morris Q: DO. M: GOsC.
● **Homeopath** Ms D Holmes (T) 01903 208238 Q: DSH.
● **Osteopath** Mr N Mitchell Q: DO. M: GOsC.
● **Osteopath** Mr A Bellamy Q: DO, SRN. M: GOsC.
● **Osteopath** Ms S Bunce Q: BSc, Hons (OST).
● **Aromatherapist/Reflexologist** Ms V Johnson (T) 01903 203360 Q: RQA. M: AOC.
● **Osteopath** Ms H Mayors Q: DO. M: GOsC.
● **Homeopath** Ms P Black (T) 01903 208238 Q: BA, MCH, RSHom.
[P] [S] Yrs. Est.: 24 (Ref:HM01452)

## B P AITKENHEAD PHYSIO SERVICES

**B P Aitkenhead Physiotherapy Services**, 38A St Edwards Rd, Southsea, **Hampshire**, PO5 3DJ, ENG.
(T) 023 9283 7999
Speciality: Physiotherapy.
[P] [S] [T] (Ref:HM01453)

## B SHAW HOLISTIC THERAPIST

**B Shaw Holistic Therapist**, 2a Barley Rd, Thelwall, Warrington, **Cheshire**, WA4 2EZ, ENG.
(T) 01925 604802
Speciality: Complementary Medicines & Therapy.
[C] [M] (Ref:HM01454)

## B WIGRAM HEALING & REFLEXOLOGY

**Bill Wigram Healing And Reflexology**, 1 Moorfield, High West Jesmond, Newcastle Upon Tyne, **Tyne and Wear**, NE2 3NL, ENG.
(T) 01912 845233
(E) bill.wigram@dial.pipex.com
(W) www.the-healer.co.uk
Speciality: Absent Healing, Colour Therapy, Complementary Therapy, Healer, Healing Therapy, Meditation, Reflexology, Spiritual Healing, Visualisation Therapy. ✔
● **Healer/Reflexologist** Mr B Wigram Q: MAR, NFSH. M: AoR, NFSH.
[B] Yrs. Est.: 7 (Ref:HM01455)

## B WILLIAMS CORPORATE PSYCHOL

**Ben Williams Corporate Psychology Ltd**, 2 Randolph Cliff, Edinburgh, **Edinburgh (City of)**, EH3 7TZ, SCO.
(T) 01312 262727 (F) 01312 206333
Speciality: Psychology.
● **Managing Director** Mr B Williams
[B] (Ref:HM01456)

## BA FOR COUNSELLING

**British Association for Counselling**, 1 Regent Pl, Rugby, Rugby, **Warwickshire**, CV21 2BX, ENG.
(T) 01788 550899
Speciality: Complementary Medicines & Therapy.
● **Counsellor** Denise Chaytor
[M] (Ref:HM01457)

## BA FOR COUNSELLING

**British Association For Counselling**, Barbary House, California Lane, Bushey, Watford, **Hertfordshire**, WD2 1EX, ENG.
(T) 020 8950 1006
Speciality: Psychotherapy.
[B] (Ref:HM01458)

## BAARTZ, MARIAN

**Marian Baartz**, Small World, Newdigate Rd, Beare Green, Dorking, **Surrey**, RH5 4QE, ENG.
(T) 01306 711645
Speciality: Reflexology.
[S] [T] (Ref:HM01459)

## BABBACOMBE CHIROPODY CLINIC

**Babbacombe Chiropody Clinic-Evans Hunt**, 86 Babbacombe Rd, Torquay, **Devon**, TQ1 3SW, ENG.
(T) 01803 325657
Speciality: Chiropodists (Podiatrists).
● **Owner** Mrs W Evans
[S] (Ref:HM01460)

## BABBAGE, SARAH

**Sarah Babbage**, 12 Riverside Pk, Severn Beach, Bristol, BS35 4PN, ENG.
(T) 01454 631461
Speciality: Aromatherapy.
● **Owner** Mrs S Babbage
[M] [O] (Ref:HM01461)

## BABBAGE-CLARK, SACHA

**Sacha Babbage-Clark**, Tarring Osteopathic Practice, 105 Tarring Rd, Worthing, **Sussex (West)**, BN11 4HE, ENG.
(T) 01903 235018
Speciality: Osteopathy.
● **Owner** Miss S Babbage-Clark
[P] [S] [T] (Ref:HM01462)

## BABLEE, S

**S Bablee**, 24 Wycherley Cres, New Barnet, Barnet, **Hertfordshire**, EN5 1AR, ENG.
(T) 020 8441 0545
Speciality: Chiropodists (Podiatrists).
● **Owner** Mr S Bablee
[S] (Ref:HM01463)

## BABY HOLISTIC & MASSAGE

**Baby Holistic & Therapeutic Massage**, 7 Greenbank Avenue, Edinburgh, **Edinburgh (City of)**, EH10 5RD, SCO.
(T) 01314 473060
Speciality: Complementary Medicines & Therapy, Massage and movement. ✔
● **Massage Therapist Instructor** Ms L Bendle Q: CBMI. M: SBMA.
[M] Yrs. Est.: 3 (Ref:HM01464)

## BAC, NULA L

**Nula L Bac**, 35 Montague Rd, Bournemouth, **Dorset**, BH5 2EW, ENG.
(T) 01202 427442
Speciality: Psychotherapy.
[B] (Ref:HM01465)

## BACA

**British Acupuncture Association**, 34 Alderney St, London, **London (Greater)**, SW1V 4EU, ENG.
(T) 020 7834 1012
Speciality: Acupuncture.
[O] (Ref:HM01466)

## BACH CENTRE

**Bach Centre**, Mount Vernon, Sotwell, Wallingford, **Oxfordshire**, OX10 0PZ, ENG.
(T) 01491 834678 (F) 01491 825022
Speciality: Complementary Medicines & Therapy.
● **Therapist** Cathy Nicholson
[M] (Ref:HM01467)

## BACH FLOWER REMEDIES

**Bach Flower Remedies**, Baring Rd, London, **London (Greater)**, SE12 0UW, ENG.
(T) 020 8851 6341
Speciality: Complementary Medicines & Therapy.
[M] (Ref:HM01468)

## BACH FLOWER REMEDIES

**Bach Flower Remedies**, 10 The Crescent, New Mills, High Peak, **Derbyshire**, SK22 3DB, ENG.
(T) 01663 742472
Speciality: Bach Remedies, Bach Flower Remedies. ✔
● **Practitioner** Mrs M De-Mierre Q: BFRP.
[C] Yrs. Est.: 18 (Ref:HM01469)

## BACH FLOWER REMEDIES

**Bach Flower Remedies**, 6 Suffolk Way, Abingdon, **Oxfordshire**, OX14 5JX, ENG.
(T) 01235 550444 (F) 01235 523973
Speciality: Complementary Medicines & Therapy.
● **Manager** Mr B Hitchman
[C] [M] (Ref:HM01470)

## BACHE CHIROPODY

**Bache Chiropody**, 9c Mill Lane, Upton, Chester, **Cheshire**, CH2 1BS, ENG.
(T) 01244 381350 (F) 01224 380252
Speciality: Biomechanics, Chiropody, Nail Surgery, Physiotherapy. ✔
● **Chiropodist (Podiatrist)** Mrs H Dodman Q: BSc (Hons), S.R.Ch. M: S.C.P.
● **Chiropodist (Podiatrist)** Ms L Niocon Q: BSc (Hons), S.R.Ch. M: S.C.P.
[M] Yrs. Est.: 11 (Ref:HM01471)

## BACK & HEADACHE CLINIC

**Back & Headache Clinic**, 115 Haddington Rd, Dublin, **County Dublin**, IRE.
(T) 01660 8416
Speciality: Complementary Medicines & Therapy.
[M] (Ref:HM01472)

## BACK & NECK CHIRO CLINIC

**Back & Neck Chiropractic Clinic**, 11 Thornhill Rd, Cardiff, **Glamorgan (Vale of)**, CF14 6PD, WAL.
(T) 029 2075 7444
Speciality: Chiropractors.
● **Partner** Mr R Wieser
[P] [S] [T] (Ref:HM01473)

## BACK & NECK CLINIC

**Back & Neck Clinic**, Nathaniel House, David St, Bridgend Industrial Estate, Bridgend, CF31 3SA, WAL.
(T) 01656 766688
Speciality: Chiropractors.
● **Owner** Mr I Wong
[P] [S] [T] (Ref:HM01474)

## BACK 2 BACK

**Back 2 Back**, 124B Nelson Rd, London, **London (Greater)**, N8 9RN, ENG.
(T) 020 8341 2772
Speciality: Physiotherapy.
[P] [S] [T] (Ref:HM01475)

## BACK 2 FITNESS CHIROPRACTIC

**Back 2 Fitness Chiropractic Clinic**, 5a Churchill Court, 112 The St, Rustington, Littlehampton, **Sussex (West)**, BN16 3DB, ENG.
(T) 01903 775577
Speciality: Chiropractic. ✔
● **Chiropractor** Mr P Curtis Q: DC.
[P] [S] [T] Yrs. Est.: 15 (Ref:HM01476)

## BACK 2 HEALTH

**Back 2 Health Ltd**, 52 Anstey Rd, Alton, **Hampshire**, GU34 2RE, ENG.
(T) 01420 80007
Speciality: Chiropractic.
● **Owner** Mr J Field
[P] [S] [T] (Ref:HM01477)

## BACK 2 HEALTH

**Back 2 Health (T C M C )**, Glenview Park S.C, Tallaght, **County Dublin**, IRE.
(T) 01462 7555 (F) 01462 7444
Speciality: Complementary Medicines & Therapy.
[M] (Ref:HM01478)

## BACK IN BALANCE

**Back In Balance**, 10 Leigh Rd, Wimborne, **Dorset**, BH21 1AF, ENG.
(T) 01202 888812 (F) 01202 888812
Speciality: Chiropractic. ✔



Key: [B] Mind-Body Medicine [C] Complementary Medicine [H] Self Help Treatment [M] Medicinal Therapy [O] Oriental Medicine [P] Postural Therapy [S] Manipulative Structural Therapy [T] Touch Therapy

● **Owner** Dr A Hulkkonen **Q:** DC. **M:** BCA.
● **Associate** Dr M Stephens **Q:** DC. **M:** BCA.
[P] Yrs. Est.: 21 (**Ref:**HM01479)

## BACK IN FORM

**Back In Form**, 54 Parkstone Rd, Poole, **Dorset**, BH15 2PG, ENG.
(T) 01202 649900 (F) 01202 649911
(W) www.backinform.co.uk
Speciality: Chiropractic. [✓]
● **Chiropractor** Mr S Oldale **Q:** BSc, DC, MCC.
[P] Yrs. Est.: 7 (**Ref:**HM01480)

## BACK IN LINE

**Back In Line**, The Old Barn, 79 Beld St, Henley-on-Thames, **Oxfordshire**, RG9 2BD, ENG.
(T) 01491 579712
Speciality: Acupuncture, Chiropractic, Massage (Therapeutic), Pilates. [✓] [CREDIT]
● **Chiropractor** Mrs V Lyke **Q:** DC, Dip.Ac. **M:** GCC.
[P] Yrs. Est.: 1 (**Ref:**HM01481)

## 'BACK IN LINE'

**'Back In Line' Massage & Home Care Service**, The Laurels, 38 Sambourne Rd, Warminster, **Wiltshire**, BA12 8LG, ENG.
(T) 01985 218217
(E) maureen-mike@hibbs-tanner.fsnet.co.uk
Speciality: Aromatherapy, Indian Head Massage, Massage (Therapeutic). [✓]
● **Owner/Masseur** Ms M Hibbs **Q:** IIHHT. **M:** ICHT.
[T] Yrs. Est.: 1 (**Ref:**HM01482)

## BACK IN STEP

**Back In Step**, 43 Booth Rise, Northampton, **Northamptonshire**, NN3 6HP, ENG.
(T) 01604 643948
Speciality: Chiropodists (Podiatrists).
[S] (**Ref:**HM01483)

## BACK IN TOUCH

**Back In Touch**, 19 Appley La North, Appley Bridge, Wigan, **Lancashire**, WN6 9AN, ENG.
(T) 01257 251920
Speciality: Complementary Medicines & Therapy.
[M] (**Ref:**HM01484)

## BACK IN TUNE

**Back in Tune**, 48 Village Rd, London, **London (Greater)**, N3 1TJ, ENG.
(T) 020 8346 5472
Speciality: Alexander Technique.
● **Therapist** Mr G Griffiths
[P] [S] (**Ref:**HM01485)

## BACK ON TRACK

**Back On Track Physiotherapy Ltd**, 204 High St, Cherry Hinton, Cambridge, **Cambridgeshire**, CB1 9HJ, ENG.
(T) 01223 722715 (F) 01223 301422
Speciality: Acupuncture. [✓]
● **Physiotherapist** Ms D Bryson **Q:** MCSP, SRP. **M:** CSP.
● **Physiotherapist** Ms A McGurk **Q:** MCSP, SRP. **M:** CSP.
[S] Yrs. Est.: 3 (**Ref:**HM01486)

## BACK ON TRACK

**Back On Track Physiotherapy Ltd**, 41 Hills Rd, Cambridge, **Cambridgeshire**, CB2 5NT, ENG.
(T) 01223 722715 (F) 01223 301422
Speciality: Acupuncture, Physiotherapy. [✓]
● **Physiotherapist** Ms A McGurk **Q:** MCSP, SRP. **M:** AACP, CSP.
● **Physiotherapist** Ms D Bryson **Q:** MCSP, SRP. **M:** AACP, CSP.
[S] Yrs. Est.: 3 (**Ref:**HM01487)

## BACK ON TRACK

**Back On Track Physiotherapy Ltd**, Hills Rd Sports And Tennis Centre, Purbeck Rd, Cambridge, **Cambridgeshire**, CB2 2PF, ENG.
(T) 01223 722715 (F) 01223 301422
Speciality: Acupuncture, Physiotherapy. [✓]
● **Physiotherapist** Ms D Bryson **Q:** MCSP, SRP. **M:** AACP, CSP.
● **Physiotherapist** Ms A McGurk **Q:** MCSP, SRP. **M:** AACP, CSP.
[S] Yrs. Est.: 3 (**Ref:**HM01488)

## BACK PAIN & COMP MED CENTRE

**Back Pain & Complementary Medicine Centre (The)**, 65 Church St, Leigh, **Manchester (Greater)**, WN7 1AZ, ENG.
(T) 01942 608195
Speciality: Acupuncture.
● **Owner** Dr T Fletcher
[O] (**Ref:**HM01489)

## BACK PAIN & SPORTS CLINIC

**Back Pain & Sports Injuries Clinic**, 17 Broughton Rd, Banbury, **Oxfordshire**, OX16 9QB, ENG.
(T) 01295 265267
Speciality: Osteopathy.
[P] [S] [T] (**Ref:**HM01490)

## BACK PAIN & SPORTS CLINIC

**Back Pain & Sports Injury Clinic**, Mossgiel, Burrell St, Comrie, **Perth and Kinross**, PH6 2JP, SCO.
(T) 01764 670567 (F) 01764 670567
(E) griffiths@mossgiecomrie.freeserve.co.uk
Speciality: Acupressure, Electrotherapy, Holistic Healing, Manipulation, Massage (Therapeutic), Ultrasonics, Manual Lymphatic Drainage, Sports Therapy, Positional Release Therapy. [✓]
● **Physical Therapist** Mr T Griffiths **Q:** LCSP. **M:** LCSP.
[S] Yrs. Est.: 7 (**Ref:**HM01491)

## BACK PAIN & SPORTS INJURIES

**Back Pain & Sports Injuries Clinic**, 3 Hocroft Rd, London, **London (Greater)**, NW2 2BN, ENG.
(T) 024 7638 7449
Speciality: Osteopathy.
[P] [S] [T] (**Ref:**HM01492)

## BACK PAIN & SPORTS INJURY CLNC

**Back Pain & Sports Injury Clinic**, 18 Julians Rd, Stevenage, **Hertfordshire**, SG1 3ET, ENG.
(T) 01438 313540 (F) 01438 317037
Speciality: Physiotherapy.
● **Owner** Mr N Nadri
[P] [S] [T] (**Ref:**HM01493)

## BACK PAIN & SPRTS INJ PRACTICE

**Back Pain & Sports Injuries Practice (The)**, 14 Waverley St, Worcester, **Worcestershire**, WR5 3DH, ENG.
(T) 08003 585853 (F) 01905 764401
Speciality: Complementary Medicines & Therapy.
● **Partner** Mr A Metcalfe
[M] (**Ref:**HM01494)

## BACK PAIN CENTRE

**Back Pain Centre**, Forge Rd, Machynlleth, **Powys**, SY20 8EQ, WAL.
(T) 01654 702959 (F) 01654 702220
Speciality: Chiropractic.
● **Owner** Mr J Riley
[P] [S] [T] (**Ref:**HM01495)

## BACK PAIN CENTRE

**Back Pain Centre**, 67 Clifton Trce, New Rd, Newtown, **Powys**, SY16 1BG, WAL.
(T) 01686 610211
Speciality: Chiropractic.
● **Owner** Ms B Riley
[P] [S] [T] (**Ref:**HM01496)

## BACK PAIN CENTRE

**Back Pain Centre (The)**, 118 Middlesex St, London, **London (Greater)**, E1 7HY, ENG.
(T) 020 7247 8585 (F) 020 7426 0234
(W) www.backpaincentre.co.uk
Speciality: Chiropractic, Osteopathy. [✓] [CREDIT]
● **Chiropractor** Miss C Gallant **Q:** DC. **M:** BCA.
● **Chiropractor** Mr T Chimes **Q:** DC. **M:** BCA.
● **Chiropractor** Mr S Davison **Q:** DC. **M:** BCA.
● **Chiropractor** Mr K Murrey **Q:** DC. **M:** SCA.
[C] [P] Yrs. Est.: 5 (**Ref:**HM01497)

## BACK PAIN CENTRE

**Back Pain Centre (The)**, 2 Cyprus Rd, London, **London (Greater)**, N3 3RY, ENG.
(T) 020 8371 0222 (F) 020 7371 0150
(W) www.backpaincentre.co.uk
Speciality: Chiropractic, Osteopathy. [✓] [CREDIT]
● **Chiropractor** Mr K Murrey **Q:** DC. **M:** SCA.
● **Chiropractor** Mr S Davison **Q:** DC. **M:** BCA.
● **Chiropractor** Mr T Chimes **Q:** DC. **M:** BCA.
● **Chiropractor** Miss C Gallant **Q:** DC. **M:** BCA.
[C] [P] Yrs. Est.: 5 (**Ref:**HM01498)

## BACK PAIN CENTRE

**Back Pain Centre (The)**, 50 Chigwell Rd, South Woodford, London, **London (Greater)**, E18 1LS, ENG.
(T) 020 8989 3330
(W) www.backpaincentre.co.uk
Speciality: Chiropractic. [✓] [CREDIT]
● **Chiropractor** Dr T Chimes **Q:** DC. **M:** BCA.
● **Chiropractor** Mr S Davison **Q:** DC. **M:** BCA.
● **Chiropractor** Miss C Gallant **Q:** DC. **M:** BCA.
● **Chiropractor** Mr K Murrey **Q:** DC. **M:** SCA.
[C] [P] Yrs. Est.: 5 (**Ref:**HM01499)

## BACK PAIN CLINIC

**Back Pain Clinic**, 16 Station Rd, Cheadle Hulme, Cheadle, **Cheshire**, SK8 5AE, ENG.
(T) 08007 9561890
Speciality: Chiropractic. [✓]
● **Chiropractor** Mr J Doherty **Q:** BSc, DC. **M:** BAAC.
[P] Yrs. Est.: 2 (**Ref:**HM01500)

## BACK PAIN CLINIC

**Back Pain Clinic**, 229A High St, Uxbridge, **London (Greater)**, UB8 1LD, ENG.
(T) 01895 273555
Speciality: Chiropractic.
● **Owner** Dr F Ghafoor
[P] [S] [T] (**Ref:**HM01501)

## BACK PAIN CLINIC

**Back Pain Clinic**, 23 Walnut Way, Ruislip, **London (Greater)**, HA4 6ST, ENG.
(T) 020 8842 4420
Speciality: Chiropractic.
[P] [S] [T] (**Ref:**HM01502)

## BACK PAIN CLINIC

**Back Pain Ltd(Trading)**, 92 Harley St, London, **London (Greater)**, W1, ENG.
(T) 07710 901140 (F) 01483 851366
(E) info@body-pain.co.uk
(W) www.back-pain.co.uk
Speciality: Homeopathy, Spinal Rehabilitation(Orthopaedic). [✓]
● **Private Specialist** B. M Luklinski
(T) 020 7487 5482 **Q:** MSc.
[S] Yrs. Est.: 23 (**Ref:**HM01503)

## BACK PAIN CLINIC

**Back Pain Clinic**, Great Heath Farm, Chelmsford Rd, Hatfield Heath, Bishop's Stortford, **Hertfordshire**, CM22 7BQ, ENG.
(T) 01279 730371
Speciality: Complementary Medicines & Therapy.
[C] [M] (**Ref:**HM01504)

## BACK SHOP

**Back Shop (The)**, 140A Longstone St, Lisburn, **County Antrim**, BT28 1TR, NIR.
(T) 028 9266 1435
Speciality: Physiotherapy.
[P] [S] [T] (**Ref:**HM01505)

## BACK TO BACK CHIRO CLINIC

**Back To Back Chiropractic Clinic**, 268 Crawley Green Rd, Luton, **Bedfordshire**, LU2 0SJ, ENG.
(T) 01582 391000
Speciality: Chiropractors.
[P] [S] [T] (**Ref:**HM01506)

## BACK TO BALANCE SHIATSU

**Back To Balance Shiatsu**, 83 Swinley Rd, Wigan, **Lancashire**, WN1 2DJ, ENG.
(T) 01942 204993
Speciality: Complementary Medicines & Therapy.
● **Owner** Mrs V Miles
[M] (**Ref:**HM01507)

## BACK TO HEALTH

**Back To Health Chiropractic Clinic**, 1a Drummond Rd, Croydon, **Surrey**, CR0 1TT, ENG.
(T) 020 8688 8850 (F) 020 8688 8801
(E) adammccarthy@holmail.com
Speciality: Chiropractic, Homeopathy. [✓] [CREDIT]
● **Chiropractor** Dr A McCarthy **Q:** BSc (Chiro),


Key continued: **Yrs.Est:** Years Established **Q:** Qualifications **M:** Professional Membership [✓] Indemnity Insurance [CREDIT] Accept Credit Cards

DC. M: BCA, GCC.
● **Assistant** Ms P Wilson-Laing
● **Assistant** Ms R Clark
● **Chiropractor** Dr A Hyman Q: BSc (Chiro), DC. M: BCA, GCC.
● **Administrator** Ms V Bartholomew
P Yrs. Est.: 2 (**Ref:**HM01508)

## BACK TO HEALTH
**Back To Health**, Omni Pk S.C, Swords Rd, Santry, **County Dublin**, IRE.
(T) 01862 1188
Speciality: Complementary Medicines & Therapy.
M (**Ref:**HM01509)

## BACK TO HEALTH - CHISWICK
**Back To Health Chiropractic Clinics Ltd**, 386A Chiswick High Rd, Cheswick, London, **London (Greater)**, W4 5TQ, **ENG**.
(T) 020 8580 1030 (F) 020 8580 1029
(E) davidaranda@yahoo.com
Speciality: Chiropractic. ✔
● **Chiropractor** Dr D Aranda Q: DC. M: BCA.
P Yrs. Est.: 3 (**Ref:**HM01510)

## BACK TO HEALTH - GUILDFORD
**Back To Health Chiropractic Clinics Ltd**, 5 Jenner Rd, Guildford, **Surrey**, GU1 3PH, **ENG**.
(T) 01483 306538 (F) 01483 306178
(E) giuntinidc@hotmail.com
Speciality: Chiropractic. ✔
● **Administrator** Ms L Perry
● **Chiropractor** Dr G Carlos Q: DC. M: BCA.
P Yrs. Est.: 1 (**Ref:**HM01511)

## BACK TO HEALTH - KINGSTON
**Back To Health Chiropractic Clinics Ltd**, 31 Castle St, Kingston-Upon-Thames, London, **London (Greater)**, KT1 1ST, **ENG**.
(T) 020 8549 5409 (F) 020 8546 9293
Speciality: Chiropractic. ✔
● **Administrator** Ms L Caveth
● **Chiropractor** Dr J Parker Q: DC. M: BCA.
● **Chiropractor** Dr A Grove Q: DC. M: BCA.
P Yrs. Est.: 3 (**Ref:**HM01512)

## BACK TO HEALTH - NORTH FINCHLEY
**Back To Health Chiropractic Clinics Ltd**, 775a High Rd, North Finchley, London, **London (Greater)**, N12 8JY, **ENG**.
(T) 020 8445 4355
Speciality: Chiropractic. ✔
● **Chiropractor** Dr A Cohn Q: DC. M: BCA.
P Yrs. Est.: 1 (**Ref:**HM01513)

## BACK TO HEALTH - RICHMOND
**Back To Health Chiropractic Clinics Ltd**, 21A Sheen Rd, Richmond, **Surrey**, TW9 1AD, **ENG**.
(T) 020 8332 6977 (F) 020 8332 7083
(E) jocelynemiranda@hotmail.com
Speciality: Chiropractic. ✔
● **Chiropractor** Dr M Flanagan Q: DC. M: BCA.
● **Chiropractor** Dr C Briggs Q: DC. M: BCA.
● **Employee** Ms S Whiting Q: DC. M: BCA.
P Yrs. Est.: 2 (**Ref:**HM01514)

## BACK TO HEALTH - SUTTON
**Back To Health Chiropractic Clinics Ltd**, 1 Tudor Court, Brighton Rd, Sutton, **Surrey**, SM2 5AE, **ENG**.
(T) 020 8255 1881 (F) 020 8255 2456
(E) tarachiro@hotmail.com
Speciality: Chiropractic. ✔
● **Chiropractor** Dr S Shiu Q: DC. M: BCA.
● **Chiropractor** Dr T Smith Q: DC. M: BCA.
P Yrs. Est.: 2 (**Ref:**HM01515)

## BACK TO HEALTH - WINDSOR
**Back To Health Chiropractic Clinics Ltd**, 29 Oxford Rd East, Windsor, **Berkshire**, SL4 1EF, **ENG**.
(T) 01753 841980 (F) 01753 841975
Speciality: Chiropractic. ✔
● **Administrator** Ms W Hacault
● **Administrator** Ms C Fletcher
● **Chiropractor** Dr F Hacult Q: DC. M: BCA.
P Yrs. Est.: 1 (**Ref:**HM01516)

## BACK TO HEALTH CHIRO CLINIC
**Back To Health Chiropractic Clinic**, 67 Penrhyn Avenue, London, **London (Greater)**, E17 5BJ, **ENG**.
(T) 020 8523 5621
Speciality: Chiropractors.
● **Owner** Mr G Perry
P S T (**Ref:**HM01517)

## BACK TO HEALTH CHIRO CLINIC
**Back To Health Chiropractic Clinics Ltd**, 2nd Floor, 131 High St, Hounslow, **London (Greater)**, TW3 1QL, **ENG**.
(T) 020 8230 1088 (F) 020 8230 1091
(E) dominganunez@hotmail.com
Speciality: Chiropractic. ✔
● **Chiropractor** Dr A Powell Q: DC. M: BCA.
● **Practice Manager** Ms D Nunez
● **Chiropractor** Dr C Barnhart Q: DC. M: BCA.
P Yrs. Est.: 3 (**Ref:**HM01518)

## BACK TO HEALTH-EALING
**Back To Health Chiropractic Clinics Ltd**, 1st Floor, 9-11 New Broadway, Ealing, London, **London (Greater)**, W5 5AW, **ENG**.
(T) 020 8566 0909 (F) 020 8566 2001
Speciality: Chiropractic. ✔
● **Chiropractor** Dr A Kleinberg Q: DC. M: BCA.
P Yrs. Est.: 4 (**Ref:**HM01519)

## BACK TO NATURE
**Back To Nature**, 9 Thrale Rd, London, **London (Greater)**, SW16 1NS, **ENG**.
(T) 020 8769 9969 (F) 020 8769 9969
Speciality: Complementary Medicines & Therapy.
● **Owner** Miss M Harris
C M (**Ref:**HM01520)

## BACK TO NATURE CLINIC
**Back To Nature Clinic**, 19 Cambuslea Rd, Ayr, **Ayrshire (South)**, KA8 9HT, **SCO**.
(T) 01292 285833
Speciality: Physiotherapy.
● **Owner** Mr C D'Amico
P S T (**Ref:**HM01521)

## BACK TO NORMAL CHIRO CLINIC
**Back To Normal Chiropractic Clinic**, 185 Banbury Rd, Kidlington, **Oxfordshire**, OX5 1AL, **ENG**.
(T) 01865 370777
Speciality: Chiropractic. ✔
● **Chiropractor** Ms D Edens Q: BSc (Chiro), DO. M: GCC.
S Yrs. Est.: 2 (**Ref:**HM01522)

## BACK TO PERFECTION
**Back To Perfection**, 76 Beaconsfield Villas, Brighton, **Sussex (East)**, BN1 6HE, **ENG**.
(T) 01273 555062
Speciality: Chiropractors.
● **Manager** Mr R Mason
P S T (**Ref:**HM01523)

## BACK TO WORK
**Back To Work**, Po Box 67, Basingstoke, **Hampshire**, RG24 8YG, **ENG**.
(T) 01256 351080
Speciality: Physiotherapy.
● **Partner** Mrs L Tagg
P S T (**Ref:**HM01524)

## BACK, R A
**R A Back**, Taunton Rd Medical Centre, 14-16 Taunton Rd, Bridgwater, **Somerset**, TA6 3LS, **ENG**.
(T) 01278 423063
Speciality: Chiropodists (Podiatrists).
S (**Ref:**HM01525)

## BACKCARE & ACUPUNCTURE CLINIC
**Backcare & Acupuncture Clinic**, 2 Bate St, Off Day St, Walsall, **Midlands (West)**, WS2 8EL, **ENG**.
(T) 01922 620047 (F) 01922 611333
(E) helga@thincare.co.uk
(W) www.clusker.co.uk
Speciality: Acupressure, Acupuncture, Chiropody, Complementary Therapy, Cranial Osteopathy, Hypnosis, Hypnotherapy, Life Style Coaching, Manipulation, Massage (Therapeutic), Moxibustion, Neuro-Linguistic Program, Nutritional Therapy, Oriental Diagnosis, Osteopathy, Reflexology, Stress Therapy, Thai Massage. ✔
● **Practice Manager** Ms C Drake Wilkes Q: PhD.
● **Osteopath/Acupuncturist** Mr P Clusker Q: DO, Lic.Ac. M: BAcC, BOrthA, GOsC.
● **Thai Massage Therapist** Ms H Blakemore
● **Reflexologist** Ms T Preece
(T) 01922 713532 Q: IIHHT, RGN. M: ICHT.
O Yrs. Est.: 20 (**Ref:**HM01526)

## BACKCARE CLINIC
**Backcare Clinic**, 2 Station Approach, Worcester Park, **Surrey**, KT4 7NB, **ENG**.
(T) 020 8335 3787 (F) 020 8337 6835
(E) backcareclinic@yahoo.com
(W) www.backpaincentre.com
Speciality: Acupuncture, Osteopathy, Ultrasonics. ✔
● **Osteopath** Ms I Phillips Q: BSc (Hons), DO, Hons (OST). M: GOsC.
S Yrs. Est.: 5 (**Ref:**HM01527)

## BACKS R US
**Backs R Us**, P O Box 100, Plympton, Plymouth, **Devon**, PL7 5YD, **ENG**.
(T) 01752 204060 (F) 01752 202099
Speciality: Osteopathy.
● **Senior Partner** Mrs S Warne
P S T (**Ref:**HM01528)

## BACKS TO BASIC
**Backs To Basic**, 14 Crown St, Brentwood, **Essex**, CM14 4BA, **ENG**.
(T) 01277 224799
Speciality: Osteopathy.
● **Owner** Mr S Wright
P S T (**Ref:**HM01529)

## BACON, D A
**D A Bacon**, 14 Willow Drive, Durrington, Salisbury, **Wiltshire**, SP4 8DE, **ENG**.
(T) 01980 652824
Speciality: Chiropodists (Podiatrists).
S (**Ref:**HM01530)

## BACON, JOELLE
**Joelle Bacon**, 1 Heigh Top Cottages, Blackshawhead, Hebden Bridge, **Yorkshire (West)**, HX7 7JW, **ENG**.
(T) 01422 842975
Speciality: Reflexology.
● **Owner** Mrs J Bacon
S T (**Ref:**HM01531)

## BACUP HOLISTIC THERAPIES
**Bacup Holistic Therapies**, 5 St James St, Bacup, **Lancashire**, OL13 9NJ, **ENG**.
(T) 01706 872217
Speciality: Complementary Medicines & Therapy. ✔
● **Manager** Miss C Dolphin
C Yrs. Est.: 30 (**Ref:**HM01532)

## BADCOCK, ELAINE
**Elaine Badcock**, 68 Millhead Rd, Honiton, **Devon**, EX14 1RD, **ENG**.
(T) 01404 46428
Speciality: Chiropodists (Podiatrists).
● **Owner** Mrs E Badcock
S (**Ref:**HM01533)

## BADDELEY & BANNISTER
**Baddeley & Bannister**, 852a Washwood Heath Rd, Birmingham, **Midlands (West)**, B8 2NL, **ENG**.
(T) 01217 840505
Speciality: Chiropodists (Podiatrists).
● **Partner** Mrs L Bannister
S (**Ref:**HM01534)

## BAGGLEY, HILARY
**Hilary Baggley**, 26 Hawthorne Gr, Burley In Wharfedale, Ilkley, **Yorkshire (West)**, LS29 7RF, **ENG**.
(T) 01943 864307
Speciality: Hypnosis.
B (**Ref:**HM01535)

## BAGGLEY, J M
**J M Baggley**, The Old Vicarage, Somerset Sq, Nailsea, Bristol, BS48 2AQ, **ENG**.
(T) 01275 810910
Speciality: Chiropody, Nail Surgery. ✔

Key: B Mind-Body Medicine C Complementary Medicine H Self Help Treatment M Medicinal Therapy O Oriental Medicine P Postural Therapy S Manipulative Structural Therapy T Touch Therapy

● **Owner/Chiropodist** Mrs J Baggley **Q:** DPodM, S.R.Ch. **M:** S.C.P.
M Yrs. Est.: 32 (**Ref:**HM01536)

### BAGINI, LINDA
**Linda Bagini**, 133 Wood St, Barnet, **Hertfordshire**, EN5 4BX, **ENG**.
(T) 020 8441 0231
Speciality: Hypnotherapy.
● **Owner** Mr M Cole
B (**Ref:**HM01537)

### BAGLEY, ELIZABETH
**Elizabeth Bagley**, 29 Bruce Avenue, Hornchurch, **Essex**, RM12 4JF, **ENG**.
(T) 01708 621119
Speciality: Osteopathy.
● **Owner** Ms E Bagley
P S T (**Ref:**HM01538)

### BAILEY FLOWER ESSENCES
**Bailey Flower Essences Ltd**, 7 Nelson Rd, Ilkley, **Yorkshire (West)**, LS29 8HN, **ENG**.
(T) 01943 432012
Speciality: Complementary Medicines & Therapy.
● **Manager** Ms R Hunter
C (**Ref:**HM01539)

### BAILEY, ALISON
**Alison Bailey**, 21 South Brent Cl, Brent Knoll, Highbridge, **Somerset**, TA9 4BS, **ENG**.
(T) 01278 760189
Speciality: Reflexology.
S T (**Ref:**HM01540)

### BAILEY, ANDREW
**Andrew Bailey**, 8 Nelson Rd, Ilkley, **Yorkshire (West)**, LS29 8HN, **ENG**.
(T) 01943 602177
Speciality: Osteopathy.
P S T (**Ref:**HM01541)

### BAILEY, B M
**B M Bailey**, Crofton, Ryde Rd, Seaview, **Isle of Wight**, PO34 5AD, **ENG**.
(T) 01983 611323
Speciality: Hypnosis, Hypnotherapy. ✔
● **Hypnotherapist** Mrs B Bailey **Q:** BSc (Hons). **M:** IAH, NCH.
C Yrs. Est.: 10 (**Ref:**HM01542)

### BAILEY, BARBARA
**Barbara Bailey**, Whiskers Cottage, Workhouse Lane, Westfield, Hastings, **Sussex (East)**, TN35 4QJ, **ENG**.
(T) 01424 752376
Speciality: Herbalists.
● **Owner** Mrs B Bailey
M (**Ref:**HM01543)

### BAILEY, BARBARA
**Barbara Bailey**, 34A Elms Rd, Burton-On-Trent, **Staffordshire**, DE15 9AQ, **ENG**.
(T) 01283 548696
Speciality: Chiropodists (Podiatrists).
S (**Ref:**HM01544)

### BAILEY, DEREK
**Derek Bailey**, 100 Woodman Rd, Warley, Brentwood, **Essex**, CM14 5AZ, **ENG**.
(T) 01277 234564
Speciality: Chiropractors.
● **Owner** Mr D Bailey
P S T (**Ref:**HM01545)

### BAILEY, E J
**E J Bailey**, 30 Hillmore Gr, London, **London (Greater)**, SE26 5RW, **ENG**.
(T) 020 8244 5874
Speciality: Hypnotherapy.
● **Owner** Mr E Bailey
B (**Ref:**HM01546)

### BAILEY, GILLIAN
**Gillian Bailey**, 1 Hogben Cl, Lyminge, Folkestone, **Kent**, CT18 8ND, **ENG**.
(T) 01303 862093
Speciality: Reflexology.
S T (**Ref:**HM01547)

### BAILEY, GILLIAN
**Gillian Bailey**, Wootton House, Wootton Village, Boars Hill, Oxford, **Oxfordshire**, OX1 5HP, **ENG**.
(T) 01865 730077
Speciality: Reflexology.
S T (**Ref:**HM01548)

### BAILEY, JANE
**Jane Bailey**, Tonetta, 8 St. Georges Cres, Fordingbridge, **Hampshire**, SP6 1ET, **ENG**.
(T) 01425 653433
Speciality: Reflexology.
S T (**Ref:**HM01549)

### BAILEY, JO
**Jo Bailey**, 16 Elenor Drive, Tyldesley, Manchester, **Manchester (Greater)**, M29 7NN, **ENG**.
(T) 01942 893154
Speciality: Reflexology.
● **Owner** Ms J Bailey
S T (**Ref:**HM01550)

### BAILEY, L J
**L J Bailey Registered Osteopaths**, 112 Nightingale Rd, Carshalton, **Surrey**, SM5 2EN, **ENG**.
(T) 020 8669 3818 (F) 020 8669 3818
Speciality: Osteopathy, Sports Massage, Orthotic Prescribing, Acupuncture Pain Control, Remedial Massage. ✔ [credit card]
● **Registered Osteopath** Mr L Bailey **Q:** DO. **M:** GOsC.
● **Remedial/Sports Massage** Ms K Johnson **Q:** DM. **M:** Ass.Therapeutic Massage.
P S T Yrs. Est.: 10 (**Ref:**HM01551)

### BAILEY, LINDA R
**Linda R Bailey**, 63 Silverberry Rd, Worle, Weston-Super-Mare, **Somerset**, BS22 6RY, **ENG**.
(T) 01934 516886 (F) 01934 513268
(E) lindarbailey@aol.com
Speciality: Dowsing, Iridology, Nutritional Therapy.
● **Dietary Therapist** Ms L Bailey **Q:** Dip.DTh.
M Yrs. Est.: 10 (**Ref:**HM01552)

### BAILEY, MATTHEW G
**Matthew G Bailey**, 4 Highbury, Newcastle Upon Tyne, **Tyne and Wear**, NE2 3BX, **ENG**.
(T) 01912 813711
Speciality: Chiropractic.
● **Owner** Dr M Bailey
P S T (**Ref:**HM01553)

### BAILEY, SUE
**Sue Bailey**, 115f Chorlton Rd, Blackheath, London, **London (Greater)**, SE3 8TL, **ENG**.
(T) 020 8293 5997
Speciality: Relaxation Technique.
● **Owner** Sue Bailey
H T (**Ref:**HM01554)

### BAILEY-CONLON, ELIZABETH
**Elizabeth Bailey-Conlon**, Port Erin, **Isle of Man**, IM9, **ENG**.
(T) 01624 825433
Speciality: Bach Remedies.
M (**Ref:**HM01555)

### BAILIE, EILEEN
**Eileen Bailie**, 10 Cairnshill Cres, **County Antrim**, BT8 6RL, **NIR**.
(T) 028 9070 3012
Speciality: Reflexology.
S T (**Ref:**HM01556)

### BAILLIES STUDIO
**Baillies Studio**, R/O 288 Union St, Torquay, **Devon**, TQ2 5QZ, **ENG**.
(T) 01803 212044
Speciality: Aromatherapy.
M O (**Ref:**HM01557)

### BAIN, C
**C Bain**, 10 Angrove Gdns, Sunderland, **Tyne and Wear**, SR4 7TB, **ENG**.
(T) 01915 654321
Speciality: Chiropodists (Podiatrists).
S (**Ref:**HM01558)

### BAIN, J
**J Bain**, Hatchgate Farm, Pennypot Lane, Chobham, Woking, **Surrey**, GU24 8DL, **ENG**.
(T) 01726 856186
Speciality: Homeopathy.
● **Owner** Mrs J Bain
M (**Ref:**HM01559)

### BAIN, J M
**J M Bain**, Focklesbrook Farm, Sandpit Hall Rd, Chobham, Woking, **Surrey**, GU24 8HB, **ENG**.
(T) 01276 856186
Speciality: Homeopathy.
M (**Ref:**HM01560)

### BAIN, S
**S Bain**, Beverley Clinic, 362 Coombe Lane, London, **London (Greater)**, SW20 0RJ, **ENG**.
(T) 020 8241 2515
Speciality: Reflexology.
S T (**Ref:**HM01561)

### BAINBRIDGE, DAVID
**David Bainbridge**, Health Hydro, Milton Rd, Swindon, **Wiltshire**, SN1 5JA, **ENG**.
(T) 01793 465629
Speciality: Alexander Technique.
P S (**Ref:**HM01562)

### BAINBRIDGE, ELLEN
**Ellen Bainbridge**, 1 Capella Gdns, Dibden, Southampton, **Hampshire**, SO45 5UE, **ENG**.
(T) 023 8084 9641
Speciality: Complementary Medicines & Therapy.
● **Owner** Ms E Bainbridge
C M (**Ref:**HM01563)

### BAINES, ALAN
**Alan Baines**, 18 Barton Court, Mansfield, **Nottinghamshire**, NG18 4LT, **ENG**.
(T) 01623 635391
Speciality: Chiropodists (Podiatrists).
● **Owner** A Baines
S (**Ref:**HM01564)

### BAINES, HILARY
**Hilary Baines**, Hillview, Coldstream, **Scottish Borders**, TD12 4ED, **SCO**.
(T) 01890 882895
Speciality: Bach Remedies.
M (**Ref:**HM01565)

### BAINES, JEAN
**Jean Baines**, 36 Phipps Hatch Lane, Enfield, **London (Greater)**, EN2 0HN, **ENG**.
(T) 020 8367 1425 (F) 020 8367 4948
Speciality: Complementary Medicines & Therapy.
● **Owner** Mrs J Baines
C M (**Ref:**HM01566)

### BAINES, PAUL
**Paul Baines**, 30 Colin Drive, London, **London (Greater)**, NW9 6ES, **ENG**.
(T) 020 8200 1630
Speciality: Chiropodists (Podiatrists).
S (**Ref:**HM01567)

### BAINSFORD FOOT CLINIC
**Bainsford Foot Clinic**, 19 Main St, Bainsford, Falkirk, FK2 7PQ, **SCO**.
(T) 01324 622652
Speciality: Chiropodists (Podiatrists).
S (**Ref:**HM01568)

### BAIRD, DAVID
**David Baird**, The Alternative Guide To Health And Healing, Hastings, **Sussex (East)**, TN35 4UB, **ENG**.
(T) 01424 882660
Speciality: Acupressure, Acupuncture, Alexander Technique, Aromatherapy, Bach Remedies, Bowen Therapy, Cranial Osteopathy, Crystal Healing, Hypnosis, Indian Head Massage, Kinesiology, Massage (Therapeutic), McTimoney Chiropractic, Meditation, Naturopathy, Nutritional Therapy, Osteopathy, Physiotherapy, Pilates, Psychotherapy, Reflexology, Reiki, Shiatsu, Yoga.
C (**Ref:**HM01569)

### BAIRD, JANET
**Janet Baird**, London, **London (Greater)**, N19, **ENG**.
(T) 07808 414736
Speciality: Bach Remedies.
M (**Ref:**HM01570)

### BAIRD, MICHAEL
**Michael Baird**, 51 Reddings Rd, Birmingham, **Midlands (West)**, B13 8LW, **ENG**.


Key continued: **Yrs.Est:** Years Established **Q:** Qualifications **M:** Professional Membership ✔ Indemnity Insurance [credit card] Accept Credit Cards

(T) 01214 490971
Speciality: Acupuncture.
**O** (Ref:HM01571)

**BAJJADA, JUNE**

**June Bajjada**, 12 Hampshire Avenue, Newport, NP19 4QA, **WAL**.
(T) 01633 660219
Speciality: Acupressure, Acupuncture, Auto Suggestion, Complementary Therapy, Cupping, Electrotherapy, Meditation, Moxibustion, Reflexology, Stress Therapy. ✓
● **Acupuncturist** Mrs J Bajjada
**O** Yrs. Est.: 2 (Ref:HM01572)

**BAJWA, K S & O'DRISCOLL, P**

**K S Bajwa & Paschal O'Driscoll**, Slough Clinic Of Osteopathy & Sports Injury, 188 Stoke Rd, Slough, **Berkshire**, SL2 5AY, **ENG**.
(T) 01753 528882
Speciality: Osteopathy.
**P S T** (Ref:HM01573)

**BAKER STREET HEALING CTRE**

**Baker Street Natural Healing Centre**, First Floor 4 Baker St, Aberystwyth, **Ceredigion**, SY23 2BJ, **WAL**.
(T) 01970 615232
Speciality: Complementary Medicines & Therapy.
**C M** (Ref:HM01574)

**BAKER, A W**

**A W Baker**, 173 Uxbridge Rd, Rickmansworth, **Hertfordshire**, WD3 2DW, **ENG**.
(T) 01923 772542 (F) 01923 772542
Speciality: Chiropodists (Podiatrists).
● **Owner** Mr A Baker
**S** (Ref:HM01575)

**BAKER, A W J**

**A W J Baker**, Rosewarne Dairy Farm, Rosewarne Downs, Camborne, **Cornwall**, TR14 0BD, **ENG**.
(T) 01209 713023 (F) 01209 713023
Speciality: Complementary Medicines & Therapy.
● **Owner** Mr A Baker
**C M** (Ref:HM01576)

**BAKER, ANN**

**Ann Baker**, 117 Gunners Rd, Shoeburyness, Southend-On-Sea, **Essex**, SS3 9SB, **ENG**.
(T) 01702 296260
Speciality: Chiropodists (Podiatrists).
● **Owner** Mrs A Baker
**S** (Ref:HM01577)

**BAKER, ANNE**

**Anne Baker McTimoney Chiropractor**, The Wellbeing Centre, 11 Musters Rd, Nottingham, **Nottinghamshire**, NG5 3GQ, **ENG**.
(T) 01159 825353
Speciality: Chiropractors.
**P S T** (Ref:HM01578)

**BAKER, BARBARA**

**Barbara Baker**, 12 Mt Eden Model Farm Rd, Cork, **County Cork**, **IRE**.
(T) 021 4345 492
Speciality: Aromatherapy.
**M O** (Ref:HM01579)

**BAKER, C**

**C Baker**, 27 Lower Stone St, Maidstone, **Kent**, ME15 6LH, **ENG**.
(T) 01634 377233
Speciality: Clairvoyants & Palmists.
● **Owner** Miss C Baker
**B** (Ref:HM01580)

**BAKER, CAROLINE**

**Caroline Baker**, The Doctors House Annexe, Victoria Rd, Marlow, **Buckinghamshire**, SL7 1DN, **ENG**.
(T) 01628 477466
Speciality: Osteopathy.
**P S T** (Ref:HM01581)

**BAKER, CAROLINE**

**Caroline Baker**, The Maple Clinic, 3-5 Horndean Rd, Bracknell, **Berkshire**, RG12 0XQ, **ENG**.
(T) 01344 862646
Speciality: Osteopathy.
● **Owner** Mr W Baker
**P S T** (Ref:HM01582)

**BAKER, E**

**E Baker**, 41 Renfrew Avenue, St. Helens, **Merseyside**, WA11 9RW, **ENG**.
(T) 01744 755122
Speciality: Chiropodists (Podiatrists).
**S** (Ref:HM01583)

**BAKER, E**

**E Baker**, 18 Clifton Rd, Worthing, **Sussex (West)**, BN11 4DY, **ENG**.
(T) 01903 236318
Speciality: Chiropodists (Podiatrists).
● **Owner** Mr E Baker
**S** (Ref:HM01584)

**BAKER, IRENE**

**Irene Baker**, Willow Cottage, Nafferton Rd, Wansford, Driffield, **Humberside (North)**, YO25 8NT, **ENG**.
(T) 01377 256835 (F) 01377 256835
Speciality: Osteopathy.
● **Owner** Ms I Baker
**P S T** (Ref:HM01585)

**BAKER, JULIE**

**Julie Baker**, Health Hydro, Milton Rd, Swindon, **Wiltshire**, SN1 5JA, **ENG**.
(T) 01793 465631
Speciality: Aromatherapy.
**M O** (Ref:HM01586)

**BAKER, LINDA**

**Linda Baker**, 25 Kensington St, York, **Yorkshire (North)**, YO23 1JA, **ENG**.
(T) 01904 671460
Speciality: Absent Healing, Aromatherapy, Bates Method, Holistic Healing, Indian Head Massage, Massage (Therapeutic), Reflexology, Reiki, Animal Healing Clinic, Advice centre and complementary therapy centre for animals.
● **Owner** Mrs L Baker Q: Dip.Arom, Dip.Reflex, DM. M: IPTI.
● **Cranial Osteopath for Animal Healing** Rowena Field
(T) 01904 656504
● **Mind Body and Spirit Therapist** Mr M
(T) 01904 622706
**B** Yrs. Est.: 13 (Ref:HM01587)

**BAKER, M A**

**M A Baker**, 3 Maidstone Rd, Gillingham, **Kent**, ME8 0DH, **ENG**.
(T) 01634 387961
Speciality: Chiropodists (Podiatrists).
**S** (Ref:HM01588)

**BAKER, MICHAEL**

**Michael Baker**, 28 Wootton Rd, Abingdon, **Oxfordshire**, OX14 1JD, **ENG**.
(T) 01235 531021
Speciality: Osteopathy.
● **Owner** Mr M Davies
**P S T** (Ref:HM01589)

**BAKER, N**

**N Baker**, 15 Davies Rd, West Bridgford, Nottingham, **Nottinghamshire**, NG2 5JE, **ENG**.
(T) 01159 816840
Speciality: Chiropodists (Podiatrists).
● **Owner** Mrs N Baker
**S** (Ref:HM01590)

**BAKER, P H**

**P H Baker**, 18 Woodfield Rd, Bristol, BS6 6JQ, **ENG**.
(T) 01179 730101
Speciality: Hypnosis.
**B** (Ref:HM01591)

**BAKER, P J**

**P J Baker**, 3 Hallam Rd, Clevedon, **Somerset**, BS21 7SE, **ENG**.
(T) 01275 872181
Speciality: Chiropodists (Podiatrists).
**S** (Ref:HM01592)

**BAKER, P T**

**P T Baker**, 233 Perth Rd, Dundee, **Angus**, DD2 1EJ, **SCO**.
(T) 01382 665717
Speciality: Naturopathy, Osteopathy. ✓
● **Practitioner** Mr P Baker Q: BSc, DO, MSc, ND. M: GOsC.
**C S** Yrs. Est.: 15 (Ref:HM01593)

**BAKER, ROY**

**Roy Baker**, 10 Hazlemere Drive, Gillingham, **Kent**, ME7 2TE, **ENG**.
(T) 01634 572340
Speciality: Hypnosis.
● **Principal** Mr R Baker
**B** (Ref:HM01594)

**BAKER, SANDRA**

**Sandra Baker**, 66 Newstead Avenue, Orpington, **Kent**, BR6 9RN, **ENG**.
(T) 01689 898787
Speciality: Homeopathy.
● **Owner** Miss S Baker
**M** (Ref:HM01595)

**BAKER, SARAH**

**Sarah Baker**, 19 Valley Dene, Newhaven, **Sussex (East)**, BN9 9NF, **ENG**.
(T) 01273 512119
Speciality: Aromatherapy.
● **Owner** Mrs S Baker
**M O** (Ref:HM01596)

**BAKER, V J**

**V J Baker**, 28 Park Rd, Hampton Hill, Hampton, **London (Greater)**, TW12 1HF, **ENG**.
(T) 020 8979 8170
Speciality: Chiropodists (Podiatrists).
**S** (Ref:HM01597)

**BAKHSHI, R S**

**R S Bakhshi**, 49 Lancaster Rd, Southall, **London (Greater)**, UB1 1NP, **ENG**.
(T) 020 8574 8746
Speciality: Homeopathy.
**M** (Ref:HM01598)

**BAKOWSKA, D**

**D Bakowska**, Herne Bay Osteopathic Practice, 21 Park Rd, Herne Bay, **Kent**, CT6 5ST, **ENG**.
(T) 01227 366473
Speciality: Complementary Medicines & Therapy.
● **Owner** Mr A Mathews
**C M** (Ref:HM01599)

**BAKRAN, D M**

**D M Bakran**, 24 Quarry Rd East, Heswall, Wirral, **Merseyside**, CH61 6XD, **ENG**.
(T) 01513 429277
Speciality: Hypnotherapy.
**B** (Ref:HM01600)

**BAKSH, ANITA**

**Anita Baksh**, 30 Howlands, Welwyn Garden City, **Hertfordshire**, AL7 4RE, **ENG**.
(T) 01707 892492
Speciality: Chiropodists (Podiatrists).
● **Owner** Mrs A Baksh
**S** (Ref:HM01601)

**BAL, NORMAN**

**Norman Bal**, Norwood House, West Avenue, Gosforth, Newcastle Upon Tyne, **Tyne and Wear**, NE3 4ES, **ENG**.
(T) 01912 843985
Speciality: Homeopathy.
**M** (Ref:HM01602)

**BALANCE**

**Balance**, 250 King's Rd, London, **London (Greater)**, SW3 5UE, **ENG**.
(T) 020 7565 0333 (F) 020 7565 0334
Speciality: Complementary Medicines & Therapy.
● **Owner** Mrs J Walsh
**M** (Ref:HM01603)

**BALANCE & HARMONY**

**Balance & Harmony**, 663 Stratford Rd, Birmingham, **Midlands (West)**, B11 4DH, **ENG**.
(T) 01217 777144
Speciality: Complementary Medicines & Therapy.
**C M** (Ref:HM01604)

**BALANCE CARE HEALTH**

**Balance Care Health Ltd**, Westleigh, Broomfield, Bridgwater, **Somerset**, TA5 2EH, **ENG**.

(T) 07002 252623 (F) 07000 225262
Speciality: Psychology.
● Managing Director Dr R Sharpe
B (Ref:HM01605)

## BALANCE HOLISTIC HEALTHCARE

**Clare Midgley T/A Balance Holistic Healthcare**, 105 Greathead Cres, Newton Aycliffe, **County Durham**, DL5 5DP, ENG.
(T) 01325 317378
(E) imidgley@yahoo.com
(W) www.balance-holistic-healthcare.co.uk
Speciality: Absent Healing, Bach Remedies, Complementary Therapy, Counselling, Healer, Healing Therapy, Holistic Healing, Reflexology, Reiki. ✔
● Owner/Manager Ms C Midgley Q: IIHHT, ITEC, MGCP. M: DrEBF, GCP.
H Yrs. Est.: 4 (Ref:HM01606)

## BALANCE THERAPY CENTRE

**Balance Therapy Centre**, 45-47 Hill St, Stoke-On-Trent, **Staffordshire**, ST4 1NS, ENG.
(T) 01782 768789 (F) 01782 768789
Speciality: Complementary Medicines & Therapy.
● Owner Ms P Howell
C M (Ref:HM01607)

## BALANCED HEALTH

**Balanced Health**, 46 Snow Hill Lane, Scorton, Preston, **Lancashire**, PR3 1BA, ENG.
(T) 01524 793004
Speciality: Complementary Medicines & Therapy.
● Owner Ms K Chaplin
M (Ref:HM01608)

## BALANCED HEALTH

**Balanced Health (Applied Kinesiology)**, Hardwick Court, Cardiff, **Glamorgan (Vale of)**, CF5 2LB, WAL.
(T) 029 2030 9009 (F) 029 2030 9009
Speciality: Complementary Medicines & Therapy.
● Owner Mrs A Conners
M (Ref:HM01609)

## BALCOMBE, WILLIAM

**William Balcombe**, 9 Kings Rd, St. Leonards-On-Sea, **Sussex (East)**, TN37 6EA, ENG.
(T) 01424 714800
Speciality: Homeopathy.
M (Ref:HM01610)

## BALDACCHINO, PAUL

**Paul Baldacchino**, 8 Cranleigh Avenue, Portsmouth, **Hampshire**, PO1 5LU, ENG.
(T) 023 9229 4037
Speciality: Hypnosis.
B (Ref:HM01611)

## BALDWIN, BERNADETTE

**Bernadette Baldwin**, 7a Bassett Rd, London, **London (Greater)**, W10 6LA, ENG.
(T) 020 8969 1695
Speciality: Reflexology.
S T (Ref:HM01612)

## BALDWIN, G

**G Baldwin & Co**, 171-173 Walworth Rd, London, **London (Greater)**, SE17 1RW, ENG.
(T) 020 7703 5550 (F) 020 7252 6264
Speciality: Complementary Medicines & Therapy.
● Director Mr S Dagnell
C M (Ref:HM01613)

## BALDWIN, G J

**G J Baldwin**, 437 Warrington Rd, Rainhill, Prescot, **Merseyside**, L35 4LL, ENG.
(T) 01514 307694
Speciality: Chiropodists (Podiatrists).
S (Ref:HM01614)

## BALDWIN, JILLIAN

**Jillian Baldwin**, 55 Nineacres Cl, Charlbury, Chipping Norton, **Oxfordshire**, OX7 3RD, ENG.
(T) 01608 810429 (F) 01608 811256
Speciality: Chiropractic.
● Owner Mrs J Baldwin
P S T (Ref:HM01615)

## BALDWIN, M

**M Baldwin**, 18 Hillcrest Avenue, Burnley, **Lancashire**, BB10 4JA, ENG.
(T) 01282 421724
Speciality: Complementary Medicines & Therapy.
C M (Ref:HM01616)

## BALDWIN, MADELEINE

**Madeleine Baldwin**, 1 Sidcup Hill Gardens, Sidcup Hill, Sidcup, **Kent**, DA14 6JP, ENG.
(T) 020 8308 9522
Speciality: Reflexology.
S T (Ref:HM01617)

## BALDWIN, P D

**P D Baldwin**, 164 Juniper, Bracknell, **Berkshire**, RG12 7ZE, ENG.
(T) 01344 428962
Speciality: Chiropodists (Podiatrists).
● Owner Mrs P Baldwin
S (Ref:HM01618)

## BALDWYN ANIMAL PHYSIOTHERAPY

**Baldwyn Animal Physiotherapy**, 24 Seaford Rd, Wokingham, **Berkshire**, RG40 2EL, ENG.
(T) 01189 781380
Speciality: Physiotherapy.
● Owner Ms C Baldwyn
P S T (Ref:HM01619)

## BALFOUR-LAYDEN, ISABEL

**Isabel Balfour-Layden**, Kingfisher Surgery, 26 Elthorne Way, Newport Pagnell, **Buckinghamshire**, MK16 0JR, ENG.
(T) 01908 618265 (F) 01908 217804
Speciality: Chiropodists (Podiatrists).
● Doctor Dr A Paton
S (Ref:HM01620)

## BALGILLO HOMEOPATHIC PRACTICE

**Balgillo Homeopathic Practice**, Albert St, Alyth, Blairgowrie, **Perth and Kinross**, PH11 8AX, SCO.
(T) 01828 633795 (F) 01828 633795
Speciality: Homeopathy.
● Owner Mrs F Finney
M (Ref:HM01621)

## BALGORES SQUARE THERAPY CTRE

**Balgores Square Natural Therapy Centre**, 3 Balgores Sq, Romford, **Essex**, RM2 6AU, ENG.
(T) 01708 723555
Speciality: Osteopathy.
● Practice Manager Ms J Meecham
P S T (Ref:HM01622)

## BALL DELYTH

**Ball Delyth**, 7 Lon Fach, Cardiff, **Glamorgan (Vale of)**, CF14 6DY, WAL.
(T) 029 2062 4004
Speciality: Reflexology.
S T (Ref:HM01623)

## BALL, ADRIAN

**Adrian Ball**, 82 Duchy Drive, Paignton, **Devon**, TQ3 1EX, ENG.
(T) 01803 527373
Speciality: Manipulation, Massage (Therapeutic), Osteopathy. ✔
● Massage/Manipulation Practitioner Mr A Ball Q: DO.
S Yrs. Est.: 24 (Ref:HM01624)

## BALL, GILL

**Gill Ball**, 94 Valley Walk, Croxley Green, Rickmansworth, **Hertfordshire**, WD3 3TG, ENG.
(T) 01923 441663
Speciality: Reflexology.
S T (Ref:HM01625)

## BALL, GREGORY

**Gregory Ball**, 4 Station Rd, Warminster, **Wiltshire**, BA12 9BR, ENG.
(T) 01985 213927
Speciality: Osteopathy.
● Partner Mr J Penny
P S T (Ref:HM01626)

## BALL, J

**Mrs J Ball**, 14 Meadow Way, Reigate, **Surrey**, RH2 8DR, ENG.
(T) 01737 247470
Speciality: Chiropodists (Podiatrists).
● Owner Mrs J Ball
S (Ref:HM01627)

## BALL, JUNE

**June Ball**, 11 Nevill Park, Tunbridge Wells, **Kent**, TN4 8NN, ENG.
(T) 01892 523074 (F) 01892 523074
Speciality: Reflexology.
● Owner Mrs J Ball
S T (Ref:HM01628)

## BALL, LORRAINE

**Lorraine Ball**, 29 Sycamore Rd, Kingsbury, Tamworth, **Staffordshire**, B78 2JD, ENG.
(T) 01827 874085
Speciality: Reflexology.
● Principal Mrs L Ball
S T (Ref:HM01629)

## BALL, S A

**S A Ball**, Trent Bridge, Bridgford Rd, West Bridgford, Nottingham, **Nottinghamshire**, NG2 6AG, ENG.
(T) 01159 821525
Speciality: Physiotherapy.
● Manager Mr S Ball
P S T (Ref:HM01630)

## BALL, SANDRA

**Sandra Ball**, 19 Roedean Cres, London, **London (Greater)**, SW15 5JX, ENG.
(T) 020 8876 0933
Speciality: Reflexology.
S T (Ref:HM01631)

## BALL, VIVIENNE

**Vivienne Ball**, Glen House, Harewood Rd, East Keswick, Leeds, **Yorkshire (West)**, LS17 9HG, ENG.
(T) 01937 572003
Speciality: Physiotherapy.
● Partner Ms V Ball
P S T (Ref:HM01632)

## BALLARD, CATHERINE

**Catherine Ballard**, 36 Chapel Lane, Leeds, **Yorkshire (West)**, LS6 3BW, ENG.
(T) 01132 758395
Speciality: Acupuncture.
O (Ref:HM01633)

## BALLARD, MELISSA

**Melissa Ballard**, Anderson Suite, Chantry & South Park Medical Practice, Sevenoaks, **Kent**, TN13 1ED, ENG.
(T) 01732 364044
Speciality: Complementary Medicines & Therapy.
M (Ref:HM01634)

## BALLY SILLAN FOOT CLINIC

**Bally Sillan Foot Clinic**, 661 Upper Old Park Rd, Belfast, **County Antrim**, BT14 6QY, NIR.
(T) 028 9039 1989
Speciality: Chiropodists (Podiatrists).
S (Ref:HM01635)

## BALLYCLARE CHIROPRACTIC CLINIC

**Ballyclare Chiropractic Clinic**, 53-55 Main St, Ballynure, Ballyclare, **County Antrim**, BT39 9QA, NIR.
(T) 028 9332 4880
Speciality: Chiropractic. ✔
● Owner Dr L Gardener Q: BSc, BSc (Chiro), DC.
P S T Yrs. Est.: 11 (Ref:HM01636)

## BALLYCLARE FOOT CLINIC

**Ballyclare Foot Clinic**, 6 Main St, Ballyclare, **County Antrim**, BT39 9AB, NIR.
(T) 028 9335 4700
Speciality: Chiropodists (Podiatrists).
S (Ref:HM01637)

## BALLYMENA CHIROPRACTIC CLINIC

**Ballymena Chiropractic Clinic**, 1 Henry St, Ballymena, **County Antrim**, BT42 3AA, NIR.
(T) 028 2565 5755 (F) 028 2565 5755
Speciality: Chiropractic.
● Practice Manager Mrs P Donnelly
P S T (Ref:HM01638)

## BALLYMONEY CHIROPRACTIC CLINIC

**Ballymoney Chiropractic Clinic**, 51A Queen St, Ballymoney, **County Antrim**, BT53 6JD, NIR.
(T) 028 2766 6667 (F) 028 2766 6712


Key continued: Yrs.Est: Years Established Q: Qualifications M: Professional Membership ✔ Indemnity Insurance Accept Credit Cards

Speciality: Chiropractic. ✔
● **Owner** Mr T Pronek **Q:** DC.
**P** Yrs. Est.: 5 (**Ref:**HM01639)

### BALMORAL PHYSIOTHERAPY

**Balmoral Physiotherapy**, Balmoral, 19 Bowsden Ter, Newcastle Upon Tyne, **Tyne and Wear**, NE3 1RX, **ENG**.
(T) 01912 840087 (F) 01912 2848180
Speciality: Physiotherapy. ✔
● **Physiotherapist** Ms A Powell **Q:** MCSP, SRP.
● **Physiotherapist** Ms C Evans **Q:** MCSP, SRP.
**S** (**Ref:**HM01640)

### BALOOMBE OSTEOPATHIC & SPORTS

**Tracy Wilkinson**, 1 Haywards Heath Rd, Balcombe, Haywards Heath, **Sussex (West)**, RH17 6NG, **ENG**.
(T) 01444 811092 (F) 01444 811092
Speciality: Osteopathy, Dry Needles Technique. ✔
● **Owner/Osteopath** Mrs T Wilkinson **Q:** BSc. **M:** GOsC.
**S** Yrs. Est.: 10 (**Ref:**HM01641)

### BAMBER, KAREN

**Karen Bamber**, 2 Clarence St, Leyland, Preston, **Lancashire**, PR5 2WX, **ENG**.
(T) 01772 452432
Speciality: Chiropodists (Podiatrists).
● **Owner** Miss K Bamber
**S** (**Ref:**HM01642)

### BAMBROUGH, J

**J Bambrough**, 33 Glebe Villas, Hove, **Sussex (East)**, BN3 5SL, **ENG**.
(T) 01273 416557
Speciality: Chiropodists (Podiatrists).
● **Owner** Mr J Bambrough
**S** (**Ref:**HM01643)

### BAMFORD, G X

**G X Bamford**, 5 South View Rd, Southampton, **Hampshire**, SO15 5JD, **ENG**.
(T) 023 8077 2955
Speciality: Chiropodists (Podiatrists).
**S** (**Ref:**HM01644)

### BANBURY CHIROPRACTIC CLINIC

**Banbury Chiropractic Clinic**, 37 The Green, South Bar, Banbury, **Oxfordshire**, OX16 9AE, **ENG**.
(T) 01295 253434 (F) 01295 251869
Speciality: Chiropractic.
● **Owner** Dr K Sissins
**P S T** (**Ref:**HM01645)

### BANBURY, A E

**A E Banbury**, 3 Manley Trce, Station Rd, Liskeard, **Cornwall**, PL14 4DW, **ENG**.
(T) 01579 342273
Speciality: Osteopathy. ✔
● **Owner** Mr A Banbury **Q:** DO. **M:** GOsC.
**S** Yrs. Est.: 40 (**Ref:**HM01646)

### BANBURY, KAREN

**Karen Banbury**, 11 St James Place East, Plymouth, **Devon**, PL1 3AS, **ENG**.
(T) 01752 670479
Speciality: Chiropodists (Podiatrists).
● **Owner** Miss K Banbury
**S** (**Ref:**HM01647)

### BANBURY, KATE

**Kate Banbury**, 14 Galloway Rd, London, **London (Greater)**, W12 0PJ, **ENG**.
(T) 020 8740 0639
Speciality: Reflexology.
● **Owner** Ms K Banbury
**S T** (**Ref:**HM01648)

### BANCHORY CHIROPODY PRACTICE

**Banchory Chiropody Practice**, Bridge St, Banchory, **Aberdeenshire**, AB31 5SX, **SCO**.
(T) 01330 825333
Speciality: Chiropody. ✔
● **Chiropodist** Mrs P Rumbles **Q:** BSc, S.R.Ch. **M:** S.C.P.
**M** Yrs. Est.: 7 (**Ref:**HM01649)

### BAND, GILLIAN

**Gillian Band Therapies**, 13 Sheepgate Drive, Tottington, Bury, **Lancashire**, BL8 3JZ, **ENG**.
(T) 01204 887732
Speciality: Complementary Medicines & Therapy.
**M** (**Ref:**HM01650)

### BAND, NEIL M

**Neil M Band**, Bellwood Park, Perth, **Perth and Kinross**, PH2 7AJ, **SCO**.
(T) 01738 626909
Speciality: Osteopathy.
● **Owner** Mr N Band
**P S T** (**Ref:**HM01651)

### BANDON ACUPUNCTURE CLINIC

**Bandon Acupuncture Clinic**, Lavanoise Laurel Walk, Bandon, **County Cork**, **IRE**.
(T) 023 4418 6
Speciality: Acupuncture.
**O** (**Ref:**HM01652)

### BANDON CHIROPRACTIC CLINIC

**Bandon Chiropractic Clinic**, Millbrook Clinic, Bandon, **County Cork**, **IRE**.
(T) 023 4363 8
Speciality: Chiropractic, Manipulation, Massage (Therapeutic), Ultrasonics, Dry Needling. ✔
● **Chiropractor** Mr C Wood **Q:** BSc (Chiro), DC. **M:** CAI.
**S** Yrs. Est.: 4 (**Ref:**HM01653)

### BANDON THERAPY ROOMS

**Bandon Therapy Rooms**, Marion Hse, Oliver Plunkett St, Bandon, **County Cork**, **IRE**.
(T) 08681 90648
Speciality: Complementary Medicines & Therapy.
**M** (**Ref:**HM01654)

### BANE, M

**M Bane**, High Rd, Saddlebow, King's Lynn, **Norfolk**, PE34 3AW, **ENG**.
(T) 01553 617853
Speciality: Chiropodists (Podiatrists).
● **Owner** Mrs M Bane
**S** (**Ref:**HM01655)

### BANERJEE, R K

**R K Banerjee**, 64 Branksome Avenue, Barnsley, **Yorkshire (South)**, S70 6HX, **ENG**.
(T) 01226 241911
Speciality: Chiropodists (Podiatrists).
**S** (**Ref:**HM01656)

### BANFIELD, KATIE

**Katie Banfield Osteopathy/Naturopathy**, The Belmore Centre, Lower Rd, Stoke Mandeville, **Buckinghamshire**, HP21 9DR, **ENG**. (F) 0870 1313965
(E) katie.banfield@btinternet.com
Speciality: Aromatherapy, Cranial Osteopathy, Manipulation, Massage (Therapeutic), Naturopathy, Nutritional Therapy, Osteopathy, Vitamin Therapy, Visceral Osteopathy. ✔
● **Osteopath/Naturopath** Ms K Banfield
(T) 01296 612361 **Q:** BSc (Hons), ND. **M:** BNA, GOsC.
**S** Yrs. Est.: 8 (**Ref:**HM01657)

### BANFIELD, KEITH

**Keith Banfield**, Marleyfields, Leighton Buzzard, **Bedfordshire**, LU7 8WL, **ENG**.
(T) 01525 371375
Speciality: Hypnosis.
**B** (**Ref:**HM01658)

### BANGOR CHIROPRACTIC CLINIC

**Bangor Chiropractic Clinic**, 186 Rathgael Rd, Bangor, **County Down**, BT19 1RT, **NIR**.
(T) 028 9127 5556 (F) 028 9127 5323
Speciality: Chiropractic, Sports Science. ✔
● **Specialist of Sports Science** Dr N Quodling **Q:** BSc.
● **Owner** Dr K Prideman
**P** Yrs. Est.: 20 (**Ref:**HM01659)

### BANGOR OSTEOPATHIC CLINIC

**Bangor Osteopathic Clinic**, 118A High St, Bangor, **County Down**, BT20 5BB, **NIR**.
(T) 028 9147 1712
Speciality: Naturopathy, Osteopathy. ✔
● **Osteopath** Mr N Perkes **Q:** BSc, Hons (OST), ND. **M:** GOsC.
**S** Yrs. Est.: 2 (**Ref:**HM01660)

### BANI, SUSAN

**Susan Bani**, 66 Washington Gr, Doncaster, **Yorkshire (South)**, DN5 9RL, **ENG**.
(T) 01302 875878
Speciality: Reflexology.
● **Owner** Mrs S Bani
**S T** (**Ref:**HM01661)

### BANI, SUSAN

**Susan Bani**, 67 High St, Bentley, Doncaster, **Yorkshire (South)**, DN5 0AA, **ENG**.
(T) 01302 820160
Speciality: Reflexology.
**S T** (**Ref:**HM01662)

### BANKS, ALASTAIR

**Alastair Banks**, Aldrens Lane, Lancaster, **Lancashire**, LA1 2DU, **ENG**.
(T) 01524 69864 (F) 01524 848155
Speciality: Complementary Medicines & Therapy.
● **Owner** A Banks
**M** (**Ref:**HM01663)

### BANKS, DENISE

**Denise Banks**, 54 The Meadows, Ingrave, Brentwood, **Essex**, CM13 3RW, **ENG**.
(T) 01277 810376
Speciality: Aromatherapy.
● **Owner** Mrs D Banks
**M O** (**Ref:**HM01664)

### BANKS, LINDA

**Linda Banks**, Birmington House, 73 Station Rd, Brimington, Chesterfield, **Derbyshire**, S43 1LJ, **ENG**.
(T) 01246 235947 (F) 01246 235947
Speciality: Indian Head Massage, Reflexology, Reiki. ✔
● **Owner/Reflexologist** Mrs L Banks **Q:** IIHHT, MICHT. **M:** FHT.
**H** Yrs. Est.: 2 (**Ref:**HM01665)

### BANKS, M H (DR)

**Dr M H Banks**, Queens Buildings, 55 Queen St, Sheffield, **Yorkshire (South)**, S1 2DX, **ENG**.
(T) 01142 769970 (F) 01142 769965
Speciality: Psychology.
● **Owner** Dr M Banks
**B** (**Ref:**HM01666)

### BANKS, RON

**Ron Banks**, 149 Clifford Bridge Rd, Binley, Coventry, **Midlands (West)**, CV3 2DX, **ENG**.
(T) 024 7645 5856
Speciality: Chiropodists (Podiatrists).
**S** (**Ref:**HM01667)

### BANKS, RONALD

**Ronald Banks**, Littlebrook House, The Brownings, Box, Corsham, **Wiltshire**, SN13 8HP, **ENG**.
(T) 01225 742898 (F) 01225 742898
Speciality: Psychotherapy.
● **Owner** Mr R Banks
**B** (**Ref:**HM01668)

### BANN, P

**P Bann**, 31 Sycamore Drive, Radcliffe, Manchester, **Manchester (Greater)**, M26 4SA, **ENG**.
(T) 01617 233858
Speciality: Chiropodists (Podiatrists).
● **Owner** Ms P Bann
**S** (**Ref:**HM01669)

### BANNATYNES HEALTH CLUB

**Bannatynes Health Club**, 43 Queen St, Edinburgh, **Edinburgh (City of)**, EH2 3NH, **SCO**.
(T) 01312 258384
Speciality: Physiotherapy.
**P S T** (**Ref:**HM01670)

### BANNERMAN CHIROPODY CLINIC

**Bannerman Chiropody Clinic**, 69 Plymouth Rd, Scunthorpe, **Humberside**, DN17 1SS, **ENG**.
(T) 01724 854807
Speciality: Chiropodists (Podiatrists).
**S** (**Ref:**HM01671)

### BANNISTER, M

**M Bannister**, 36 Eslington Trce, Newcastle Upon Tyne, **Tyne and Wear**, NE2 4RN, **ENG**.

Key: **B** Mind-Body Medicine **C** Complementary Medicine **H** Self Help Treatment **M** Medicinal Therapy **O** Oriental Medicine **P** Postural Therapy **S** Manipulative Structural Therapy **T** Touch Therapy

(T) 01912 812204
Speciality: Osteopathy.
● Owner Mr M Bannister
P S T (Ref:HM01672)

## BANNISTER, PETER
**Peter Bannister**, 31 Shenfield Rd, Brentwood, **Essex**, CM15 8AG, ENG.
(T) 01277 210664
Speciality: Complementary Medicines & Therapy.
● Partner Mrs L Lemmon
M (Ref:HM01673)

## BANNISTER, PETER J
**Peter J Bannister**, 568 Longbridge Rd, Dagenham, **Essex**, RM8 2AR, ENG.
(T) 020 8590 6467
Speciality: Complementary Medicines & Therapy, Trichology.
M (Ref:HM01674)

## BANNON, C
**C Bannon**, 54 Keyhaven Rd, Milford On Sea, Lymington, **Hampshire**, SO41 0QY, ENG.
(T) 01590 645129
Speciality: Chiropodists (Podiatrists).
● Owner Mrs C Bannon
S (Ref:HM01675)

## BANNON, P
**P Bannon**, 30 Ladeside Court, Kilbirnie, **Ayrshire (North)**, KA25 6HE, SCO.
(T) 01505 683853
Speciality: Physiotherapy.
● Owner Mr P Bannon
P S T (Ref:HM01676)

## BANSAL, SATPAL
**Satpal Bansal**, 13 Kingsley Rd, Hounslow, **London (Greater)**, TW3 1PA, ENG.
(T) 020 8577 9731
Speciality: Osteopathy.
● Owner Mr S Bansal
P S T (Ref:HM01677)

## BANTICK, ANGELA
**Angela Bantick**, 32 Canbury Park Rd, Kingston Upon Thames, **Surrey**, KT2 6JX, ENG.
(T) 020 8946 2331
Speciality: Chiropodists (Podiatrists).
S (Ref:HM01678)

## BARAN, G
**G Baran**, 57 Coleridge Rd, London, **London (Greater)**, N8 8EH, ENG.
(T) 020 8340 1307
Speciality: Homeopathy.
M (Ref:HM01679)

## BARBARA
**Barbara**, Nautilus House, 17 Erskine Rd, South Shields, **Tyne and Wear**, NE33 2TQ, ENG.
(T) 01914 567227
Speciality: Complementary Medicines & Therapy.
● Owner Ms B Whale
C M (Ref:HM01680)

## BARBER, C J
**C J Barber**, 28 Alice Driver Rd, Grundisburgh, Woodbridge, **Suffolk**, IP13 6XH, ENG.
(T) 01473 738432 (F) 01473 738432
Speciality: Physiotherapy.
● Owner Mrs C Barber
P S T (Ref:HM01682)

## BARBER, FIONA M
**Fiona M Barber**, 73 Leadside Rd, Aberdeen, **Aberdeenshire**, AB25 1RX, SCO.
(T) 01224 643661 (F) 01224 643661
Speciality: Chiropodists (Podiatrists).
● Owner Miss F Barber
S (Ref:HM01683)

## BARBER, JOANNE
**Joanne Barber**, 24 Ladbroke Rd, Epsom, **Surrey**, KT18 5BG, ENG.
(T) 01372 749691
Speciality: Osteopathy.
● Owner Miss J Barber
P S T (Ref:HM01684)

## BARBER, JULIE
**Julie Barber**, 24 Springfield Avenue, Muswell Hill, London, **London (Greater)**, N10 3SU, ENG.
(T) 020 8883 5950 (F) 020 8883 5950
Speciality: Alexander Technique.
● Owner Ms J Barber
P S (Ref:HM01685)

## BARBER, M J
**M J Barber**, 17 Pulborough Rd, London, **London (Greater)**, SW18 5UN, ENG.
(T) 020 8877 9474
Speciality: Physiotherapy.
P S T (Ref:HM01686)

## BARBER, MAVIS
**Mavis Barber**, 129 Falconwood Rd, Croydon, **Surrey**, CR0 9BF, ENG.
(T) 01689 843297
Speciality: Chiropodists (Podiatrists).
S (Ref:HM01687)

## BARBER, NICHOLAS J
**Nicholas J Barber**, The Folly, 18 Hadham Rd, Bishop's Stortford, **Hertfordshire**, CM23 2QR, ENG.
(T) 01279 655052
Speciality: Osteopathy.
P S T (Ref:HM01688)

## BARBER, SMITH & ASSOCIATES
**Mrs B Barber, Miss V Smith & Associates**, Roundwood, 110 Dodworth Rd, Barnsley, **Yorkshire (South)**, S70 6HL, ENG.
(T) 01226 282560
Speciality: Physiotherapy.
P S T (Ref:HM01689)

## BARBER, TOM
**Tom Barber**, 96 Frinton Rd, Kirby Cross, Frinton-on-Sea, **Essex**, CO13 0HJ, ENG.
(T) 08000 283071 (F) 01255 679829
Speciality: Hypnotherapy.
● Owner Mr T Barber
B (Ref:HM01690)

## BARBER, TOM
**Tom Barber**, 110 Thorpe Rd, Kirby Cross, Frinton-on-Sea, **Essex**, CO13 0ND, ENG.
(T) 01255 679829
Speciality: Hypnosis.
B (Ref:HM01691)

## BARBERY, GAERY
**Gaery Barbery**, 14 Holyoake Rd, Headington, Oxford, **Oxfordshire**, OX3 8AE, ENG.
(T) 01865 761802
Speciality: Chiropractors.
P S T (Ref:HM01692)

## BARBICAN CENTRE
**Barbican Centre**, Bupa Wellness, 3 White Lyon Court, London, **London (Greater)**, EC2Y 8EA, ENG.
(T) 020 7588 3146 (F) 020 7628 1831
Speciality: Biomechanics, Chiropody, Cryo Surgery, Gait Analysis, Nail Surgery, Podiatry. ✔
● Chiropodist Ms F Cooper Q: F.S.C.P, FCPod(s). M: FCPod(s), S.C.P.
C Yrs. Est.: 10 (Ref:HM01693)

## BARBICAN PODIATRY PRACTICE
**Barbican Podiatry Practice**, 1 Wallside, Wood St, Barbican, London, **London (Greater)**, EC2Y 8BH, ENG.
(T) 020 7588 8803 (F) 020 7588 8803
Speciality: Biomechanics, Gait Analysis, Podiatric Surgery. ✔ 💳
● Podiatrist/Podiatric Surgeon Mr R David Q: DPodM, FCPod(s), S.R.Ch, SRN.
S Yrs. Est.: 16 (Ref:HM01694)

## BARCLAY, JAMES
**James Barclay Alexander Technique**, 4 Grove Court, Egham, **Surrey**, TW20 9PZ, ENG.
(T) 01784 472855
Speciality: Alexander Technique.
P S (Ref:HM01695)

## BARCROFT, J M
**J M Barcroft**, 629 Uttoxeter Rd, Stoke-On-Trent, **Staffordshire**, ST3 5PZ, ENG.
(T) 01782 313769
Speciality: Biomechanics, Chiropody, Nail Surgery, Podiatry, Physical Therapy, Medical Massage. ✔
● Chiropodist (Podiatrist) Mrs J Barcroft Q: M.S.C.P. M: S.C.P, S.R.Ch.
● Physical Therapist Ms J Snape Q: BSc (Hons).
C Yrs. Est.: 33 (Ref:HM01696)

## BARDEN, JOANNE
**Joanne Barden**, 23 Winchester Avenue, Upminster, **Essex**, RM14 3LP, ENG.
(T) 01708 227693
Speciality: Complementary Medicines & Therapy.
● Owner Mrs J Barden
C M (Ref:HM01697)

## BARDSLEY PHYSIOTHERAPY CLINIC
**Bardsley Physiotherapy Clinic**, 360 Wells Rd, Bristol, BS4 2QL, ENG.
(T) 01179 774159
Speciality: Physiotherapy.
● Partner Mrs C Bardsley
P S T (Ref:HM01698)

## BAREFIELD, SHIRLEY
**Shirley Barefield**, 18 Mill Rd, Caversham, Reading, **Berkshire**, RG4 8DP, ENG.
(T) 01189 481209
Speciality: Reflexology.
S T (Ref:HM01699)

## BARGOED CHIROPODY CLINIC
**Bargoed Chiropody Clinic**, 6 Gwerthonor Pl, Gilfach, Bargoed, **Caerphilly**, CF81 8JQ, WAL.
(T) 01443 838040
Speciality: Chiropodists (Podiatrists).
● Owner Mr M Crowley
S (Ref:HM01700)

## BARHAM, PENNY
**Penny Barham**, 32 The Sq, Brill, Aylesbury, **Buckinghamshire**, HP18 9RP, ENG.
(T) 01844 238558
Speciality: Physiotherapy.
● Owner Mrs P Barham
P S T (Ref:HM01701)

## BARKER & BENNELL
**Mrs A R Barker & Mrs J L Bennell**, Rear Of 37 Upper Wickham Lane, Welling, **Kent**, DA16 3AB, ENG.
(T) 020 8298 0202
Speciality: Chiropodists (Podiatrists).
● Partner Mrs A Barker
S (Ref:HM01702)

## BARKER, A D
**A D Barker**, 12 Arfryn Trce, Tylorstown, Ferndale, **Rhondda Cynon Taff**, CF43 3DR, WAL.
(T) 01443 733510 (F) 01443 733510
Speciality: Homeopathy.
● Owner Mrs A Barker
M (Ref:HM01703)

## BARKER, C
**C Barker**, 8a Arundel St, Brighton, **Sussex (East)**, BN2 5TG, ENG.
(T) 01273 699933
Speciality: Hypnosis.
B (Ref:HM01704)

## BARKER, DENNIS
**Dennis Barker**, 12 MacAuley House, Woodlea Rd, London, **London (Greater)**, N16 0TR, ENG.
(T) 07973 439813
Speciality: Complementary Medicines & Therapy.
● Owner Mr D Barker
C M (Ref:HM01705)

## BARKER, GREG
**Greg Barker**, The Reve Pavilion Natural Health Clinic, 2a Guildford Park Rd, Guildford, **Surrey**, GU2 7ND, ENG.
(T) 01483 579500
Speciality: Osteopathy.
P S T (Ref:HM01706)

## BARKER, JACQUI
**Jacqui Barker**, 77 Stoughton Avenue, Sutton, **Surrey**, SM3 8PH, ENG.
(T) 020 8641 7947
Speciality: Hypnotherapy.
B (Ref:HM01707)



Key continued: Yrs.Est: Years Established Q: Qualifications M: Professional Membership ✔ Indemnity Insurance 💳 Accept Credit Cards

### BARKER, JEAN

**Jean Barker**, 29 Fewston Cr, Harrogate, **Yorkshire (North)**, HG1 2BP, ENG.
(T) 01423 503203
Speciality: Chiropodists (Podiatrists).
● **Owner** Mrs J Barker
S (Ref:HM01708)

### BARKER, JILL

**Jill Barker**, 108 Verney Rd, London, **London (Greater)**, SE16 3DB, ENG.
(T) 020 7252 0148
Speciality: Reflexology.
● **Owner** Ms J Barker
S T (Ref:HM01709)

### BARKER, JOHN

**John Barker Osteopath**, 51 Numa Ct Justin Cl, Brentford, **London (Greater)**, TW8 8QG, ENG.
(T) 020 8568 9342
Speciality: Osteopathy.
● **Owner** Dr J Barker
P S T (Ref:HM01710)

### BARKER, KAY E

**Kay E Barker**, Southport Osteopathic Practice, 55 Princes St, Southport, **Merseyside**, PR8 1HA, ENG.
(T) 01704 500905
Speciality: Osteopathy.
P S T (Ref:HM01711)

### BARKER, LINDA

**Linda Barker**, 149 Sandhurst Rd, London, **London (Greater)**, N9 8BB, ENG.
(T) 020 8804 1547
Speciality: Clairvoyants & Palmists.
● **Owner** Ms L Barker
B (Ref:HM01712)

### BARKHAM, KATHRYN

**Kathryn Barkham**, 43 Swallow Rise, Knaphill, Woking, **Surrey**, GU21 2LH, ENG.
(T) 01483 476302
Speciality: Chiropodists (Podiatrists).
S (Ref:HM01713)

### BARKHILL OSTEOPATHIC CLINIC

**Barkhill Osteopathic Clinic (The)**, 263 Highfield Rd, Idle, Bradford, **Yorkshire (West)**, BD10 8QY, ENG.
(T) 01274 618488
Speciality: Osteopathy.
● **Manager** Mr R Hold
P S T (Ref:HM01714)

### BARKING PHYSICAL THERAPY CTRE

**Barking Physical Therapy Centre**, 90B Longbridge Rd, Barking, **Essex**, IG11 8SF, ENG.
(T) 020 8507 8169
Speciality: Acupuncture, Massage (Therapeutic), Psychotherapy. ✔
● **Physiotherapist** Mr A Apsey Q: Grad Dip Phys.
● **Physiotherapist** Mr R Alasi Q: MCSP, SRP. M: CSP.
S Yrs. Est.: 7 (Ref:HM01715)

### BARKWORTH & ASSOCIATES

**John Barkworth & Associates**, 12 College Rd, Eastbourne, **Sussex (East)**, BN21 4HZ, ENG.
(T) 01323 638606 (F) 01323 722726
Speciality: Osteopathy.
P S T (Ref:HM01716)

### BARLEY, ANDREW

**Andrew Barley**, 18 Atwood Rd, Manchester, **Manchester (Greater)**, M20 6TD, ENG.
(T) 01614 462470
Speciality: Psychotherapy.
B (Ref:HM01717)

### BARLING, J

**J Barling**, 9 Long St, Middleton, Manchester, **Manchester (Greater)**, M24 6TE, ENG.
(T) 01616 535092
Speciality: Chiropodists (Podiatrists).
S (Ref:HM01718)

### BARLOW, A

**A Barlow**, 18 Underhill Rd, London, **London (Greater)**, SE22 0AH, ENG.
(T) 020 8693 2849
Speciality: Alexander Technique.
● **Owner** Mrs A Barlow
P S (Ref:HM01719)

### BARLOW, CHRISTINA

**Christina Barlow**, 109 Swindon Rd, Wroughton, Swindon, **Wiltshire**, SN4 9AD, ENG.
(T) 01793 812422
Speciality: Chiropodists (Podiatrists).
● **Owner** Ms C Barlow
S (Ref:HM01720)

### BARLOW, GAIL

**Gail Barlow**, 12 The Green, Richmond, **Yorkshire (North)**, DL10 4RG, ENG.
(T) 01748 850553 (F) 01748 850553
Speciality: Alexander Technique.
P S (Ref:HM01721)

### BARLOW, J A

**J A Barlow**, Lead Hall Farm, Saxton, Tadcaster, **Yorkshire (North)**, LS24 9QL, ENG.
(T) 01937 557565
Speciality: Osteopathy.
● **Owner** Mr J Barlow
P S T (Ref:HM01722)

### BARLOW, MADELEINE

**Madeleine Barlow**, 28 Chewton Way, Walkford, Christchurch, **Dorset**, BH23 5LS, ENG.
(T) 01425 272490
Speciality: Chiropodists (Podiatrists).
S (Ref:HM01723)

### BARLOW, V

**V Barlow**, 4 Garstang Rd East, Poulton-le-Fylde, **Lancashire**, FY6 7EH, ENG.
(T) 01253 885439
Speciality: Physiotherapy.
P S T (Ref:HM01724)

### BARLOWS

**Barlows**, 27 Standish St, Burnley, **Lancashire**, BB11 1AP, ENG.
(T) 01282 423374
Speciality: Herbal Medicine.
M (Ref:HM01725)

### BARN HOUSE PHYSIO CLINIC

**Barn House Physiotherapy Clinic**, Main Rd, Tallington, Stamford, **Lincolnshire**, PE9 4RP, ENG.
(T) 01780 740242 (F) 01780 740586
Speciality: Psychotherapy. ✔
● **Practice Manager** Mrs M Goodall
● **Physiotherapist** Ms Knox Q: MCSP, MMACP, SRP. M: CSP.
S Yrs. Est.: 5 (Ref:HM01726)

### BARNACLE, MARIAN

**Marian Barnacle**, Aquarius, 33 Park St, Bristol, BS1 5JG, ENG.
(T) 01179 251140
Speciality: Chiropodists (Podiatrists).
● **Owner** Ms M Barnacle
S (Ref:HM01727)

### BARNACLE, MARION

**Marion Barnacle**, Westbourne House, Shuttern, Taunton, **Somerset**, TA1 4ES, ENG.
(T) 01823 322516
Speciality: Chiropodists (Podiatrists).
● **Owner** Miss M Barnacle
S (Ref:HM01728)

### BARNARD, JUDY

**Judy Barnard**, 77 Rosemary Lane, Blackwater, Camberley, **Surrey**, GU17 0LT, ENG.
(T) 01276 32647 (F) 01276 32647
Speciality: Aromatherapy.
● **Owner** Mrs J Barnard
M O (Ref:HM01729)

### BARNARD, S P

**S P Barnard**, 4 Nelson Rd, Southsea, **Hampshire**, PO5 2AR, ENG.
(T) 023 9282 4153
Speciality: Physiotherapy.
P S T (Ref:HM01730)

### BARNARD, SIMON

**Simon Barnard**, Todd House Surgery, Market Pl, Easingwold, York, **Yorkshire (North)**, YO61 3AD, ENG.
(T) 01347 822946
Speciality: Osteopathy.
P S T (Ref:HM01731)

### BARNARD, SIMON

**Simon Barnard**, Natural Therapy Centre, 7 Westgate Rd, Guisborough, **Cleveland**, TS14 6EA, ENG.
(T) 01287 633591
Speciality: Complementary Therapy, Cranial Osteopathy, Holistic Healing, Manipulation, Massage (Therapeutic), Osteopathy, Postural Integration.
● **Owner** Mr S Barnard
S (Ref:HM01732)

### BARNARD, SUSAN

**Susan Barnard**, Lavender House, Pett Level Rd, Pett Level, Hastings, **Sussex (East)**, TN35 4EH, ENG.
(T) 01424 813183
Speciality: Aromatherapy.
● **Owner** Mrs S Barnard
M O (Ref:HM01733)

### BARNARD-HADLEY, JEAN

**Jean Barnard-Hadley**, Hackney Osteopathic Practice, The Print House, 18 Ashwin St, London, **London (Greater)**, E8 3DL, ENG.
(T) 020 7254 6425
Speciality: Osteopathy.
P S T (Ref:HM01734)

### BARNARD-HADLEY, JEAN

**Jean Barnard-Hadley**, St Peters Centre, Reardon St, Wapping, London, **London (Greater)**, E1W 2QH, ENG.
(T) 020 7702 9286
Speciality: Osteopathy.
● **Owner** Ms J Barnard-Hadley
P S T (Ref:HM01735)

### BARNATT, A J

**A J Barnatt**, 6 Hillfoot Drive, Pudsey, **Yorkshire (West)**, LS28 7QL, ENG.
(T) 01132 563179
Speciality: Chiropodists (Podiatrists).
● **Owner** Mr A Barnatt
S (Ref:HM01736)

### BARNATT, D J

**D J Barnatt**, 122 Salisbury Rd, Andover, **Hampshire**, SP10 2LJ, ENG.
(T) 01264 337103
Speciality: Chiropodists (Podiatrists).
● **Owner** Mr D Barnatt
S (Ref:HM01737)

### BARNES & ASSOCIATES

**Francesca Barnes & Associates**, 112 Barnsole Rd, Gillingham, **Kent**, ME7 4DY, ENG.
(T) 01634 281388
Speciality: Osteopathy.
P S T (Ref:HM01738)

### BARNES & WILLCOCK

**Barnes & Willcock**, 16 Chorley Old Rd, Bolton, **Lancashire**, BL1 3AA, ENG.
(T) 01204 393020
Speciality: Chiropodists (Podiatrists).
S (Ref:HM01739)

### BARNES CHIROPRACTIC HEALTHCARE

**Barnes Chiropractic Healthcare**, Claridge House, 29 Barnes High St, Barnes, London, **London (Greater)**, SW13 9LW, ENG.
(T) 020 8282 1661 (F) 020 8282 1660
Speciality: Chiropractic, Manipulation, Massage (Therapeutic), X-Ray, Applied Kinesiology, Cranial Therapy. ✔
● **Chiropractor** Mr J Keel Q: BSc, DC. M: BCA.
● **Chiropractor** Hemi Patel Q: DC, MSc. M: BCA.
S Yrs. Est.: 1 (Ref:HM01740)

### BARNES HOMOEOPATHY CENTRE

**Barnes Homoeopathy Centre**, Ambassador House, 37 Church Rd, London, **London (Greater)**, SW13 9HQ, ENG.
(T) 020 8748 4244
Speciality: Homeopathy.
M (Ref:HM01741)

### BARNES SPORTS CLINIC

**Barnes Sports Clinic**, 50 Box Rd, Bath, **Somerset**, BA1 7QH, ENG.

Key: B Mind-Body Medicine C Complementary Medicine H Self Help Treatment M Medicinal Therapy O Oriental Medicine P Postural Therapy S Manipulative Structural Therapy T Touch Therapy

(T) 01225 859047
Speciality: Physiotherapy.
● **Principal** Mr S Barnes
P S T (Ref:HM01742)

## BARNES, A K R
**A K R Barnes**, 49 Oatlands Drive, Weybridge, **Surrey**, KT13 9LU, ENG.
(T) 01932 225288
Speciality: Osteopathy. ✔
● **Osteopath** Mr A Barnes Q: DO, MSc. M: GOsC.
S Yrs. Est.: 22 (Ref:HM01743)

## BARNES, CHARMAINE
**Charmaine Barnes**, 19 Victoria St, Carrickfergus, **County Antrim**, BT38 8AQ, NIR.
(T) 028 9336 0049
Speciality: Chiropodists (Podiatrists).
S (Ref:HM01744)

## BARNES, J
**J Barnes**, 8 Royster Cl, Poole, **Dorset**, BH17 9LQ, ENG.
(T) 01202 602044
Speciality: Chiropodists (Podiatrists).
● **Owner** Mrs J Barnes
S (Ref:HM01745)

## BARNES, J
**J Barnes**, Link House, Oakway, Amersham, **Buckinghamshire**, HP6 5PQ, ENG.
(T) 01494 725034
Speciality: Chiropodists (Podiatrists).
● **Owner** Mrs J Barnes
S (Ref:HM01746)

## BARNES, JACQUI
**Jacqui Barnes**, 1 South View, Littlethorpe, Ripon, **Yorkshire (North)**, HG4 3LL, ENG.
(T) 01765 605390
Speciality: Aromatherapy.
● **Owner** Mrs J Barnes
M O (Ref:HM01747)

## BARNES, JEREMY
**Jeremy Barnes**, 139 Wolverhampton Rd, Burgess Bridge, Codsall, Wolverhampton, **Midlands (West)**, WV8 1PD, ENG.
(T) 01902 844030 (F) 01902 845177
Speciality: Physiotherapy.
● **Partner** Mr J Barnes
P S T (Ref:HM01748)

## BARNES, JONATHAN P
**Jonathan P Barnes**, Salisbury Neck & Back Pain Clinic, 57 Milford St, Salisbury, **Wiltshire**, SP1 2BP, ENG.
(T) 01722 414214
Speciality: Osteopathy.
P S T (Ref:HM01749)

## BARNES, M
**M Barnes**, The Lilacs, The St, Steeple, Southminster, **Essex**, CM0 7LF, ENG.
(T) 01621 774218
Speciality: Psychotherapy.
● **Owner** Mr M Barnes
B (Ref:HM01750)

## BARNES, MICHAEL W
**Michael W Barnes**, 149 Lee Gate, Bolton, **Lancashire**, BL2 4BQ, ENG.
(T) 01204 597587
Speciality: Physiotherapy.
P S T (Ref:HM01751)

## BARNES, RICHARD
**Richard Barnes**, 25 Burns St, Northampton, **Northamptonshire**, NN1 3QE, ENG.
(T) 01604 231735
Speciality: Herbal Medicine.
M (Ref:HM01752)

## BARNES, S C
**S C Barnes**, 26 Highfield Grange Avenue, Wigan, **Lancashire**, WN3 6TA, ENG.
(T) 01942 239593
Speciality: Hypnosis.
B (Ref:HM01753)

## BARNES, SHEENA
**Sheena Barnes**, 478 Bushey Mill Lane, Bushey, Watford, **Hertfordshire**, WD2 2AS, ENG.
(T) 01923 220426
Speciality: Aromatherapy.
● **Owner** Mrs S Barnes
M O (Ref:HM01754)

## BARNES, T V
**T V Barnes**, 19 Glebe Way, Frinton-on-Sea, **Essex**, CO13 9HR, ENG.
(T) 01255 672966
Speciality: Physiotherapy.
● **Principal** Mr T Barnes
P S T (Ref:HM01755)

## BARNES, VINCENT
**Vincent Barnes**, 88 Bramerton Rd, Beckenham, **Kent**, BR3 3PD, ENG.
(T) 020 8650 5001
Speciality: Osteopathy.
● **Owner** Mr V Barnes
P S T (Ref:HM01756)

## BARNET CHIROPODY SURGERY
**Barnet Chiropody Surgery**, 178 East Barnet Rd, Barnet, **Hertfordshire**, EN4 8RD, ENG.
(T) 020 8440 5518
Speciality: Biomechanics, Chiropody, Cryo Surgery. ✔
● **Chiropodist** Ms T Dawes M: Inst.CH.P.
● **Chiropodist** Ms G Neville Q: M.S.C.P., S.R.Ch.
M Yrs. Est.: 30 (Ref:HM01757)

## BARNETT, ANNE
**Anne Barnett**, 3 Hounster Drive, Millbrook, Torpoint, **Cornwall**, PL10 1BZ, ENG.
(T) 01752 822589 (F) 01752 822589
Speciality: Complementary Medicines & Therapy.
M (Ref:HM01758)

## BARNETT, RUTH
**Ruth Barnett**, 73 Fortune Green Rd, London, **London (Greater)**, NW6 1DR, ENG.
(T) 020 7431 0837
Speciality: Psychotherapy.
B (Ref:HM01759)

## BARNETT, SAMANTHA
**Samantha Barnett**, Flat 10 Block A, Dufferin St, London, **London (Greater)**, EC1Y 8PA, ENG.
(T) 07939 141451
Speciality: Reflexology.
S T (Ref:HM01760)

## BARNETT, SUE
**Sue Barnett**, Chigwell, **Essex**, IG7, ENG.
(T) 020 8504 1897
Speciality: Bach Remedies.
M (Ref:HM01761)

## BARNFIELD, HILARY
**Hilary Barnfield**, 20A Lyefield Rd East, Charlton Kings, Cheltenham, **Gloucestershire**, GL53 8AY, ENG.
(T) 07946 401829
Speciality: Reflexology.
S T (Ref:HM01762)

## BARNNETT, ANN
**Ann Barnnett**, 1 Heskyn View, Tideford, Saltash, **Cornwall**, PL12 5JP, ENG.
(T) 01752 851398
Speciality: Bowen Therapy. ✔
● **Bowen Therapist** Ms A Barnnett Q: BTER, MAR. M: BTER.
C Yrs. Est.: 2 (Ref:HM01763)

## BARNS, MICHAEL
**Michael Barns**, 7 Kingsbridge Rd, Poole, **Dorset**, BH14 8TL, ENG.
(T) 01202 737600 (F) 01202 734581
Speciality: Psychotherapy.
● **Owner** Mr M Barns
B (Ref:HM01764)

## BARNSDALE, K
**K Barnsdale**, 42 Nethermoor Rd, New Tupton, Chesterfield, **Derbyshire**, S42 6EL, ENG.
(T) 01246 864520
Speciality: Chiropodists (Podiatrists).
● **Owner** Mr J Barnsdale
S (Ref:HM01765)

## BARNSLEY CHIROPRACTIC CENTRE
**Barnsley Chiropractic Centre**, 45 High St, Dodworth, Barnsley, **Yorkshire (South)**, S75 3RF, ENG.
(T) 01226 208106 (F) 01226 208106
Speciality: Chiropractors.
● **Doctor** Dr L Bystrom
P S T (Ref:HM01766)

## BARNSLEY, C
**C Barnsley**, 61 Westbury Hill, Bristol, BS9 3AD, ENG.
(T) 01179 624337
Speciality: Chiropodists (Podiatrists).
● **Owner** Mr C Barnsley
S (Ref:HM01767)

## BARNSTAPLE HYPNOTHERAPY
**Barnstaple Hypnotherapy & Psychotherapy Centre**, Peregrins, Fort Hill, Barnstaple, **Devon**, EX32 8BS, ENG.
(T) 01271 346613
Speciality: Hypnotherapy.
● **Owner** Mrs M Wolfe-Emery
B (Ref:HM01768)

## BARNSTEAD VILLAGE CLINIC
**Barnstead Village Clinic**, 146 High St, Banstead, **Surrey**, SM7 2NZ, ENG.
(T) 01737 373684
(E) morgan@globelnet.co.uk
Speciality: Acupuncture, Chinese Herbal Medicine, Chiropody, Homeopathy, Osteopathy. ✔
● **Chiropodist** Mr Morgan Q: S.R.Ch.
● **Osteopath** Mr C Pinches Q: DO.
O Yrs. Est.: 8 (Ref:HM01769)

## BARNT GREEN
**Barnt Green**, 81A Hewell Rd, Barnt Green, Birmingham, **Midlands (West)**, B45 8NL, ENG.
(T) 01214 453949
Speciality: Physiotherapy.
● **Owner** Ms K Hamflett
P S T (Ref:HM01770)

## BARNT GREEN ACUPUNCTURE CLINIC
**Barnt Green Acupuncture Clinic**, 111 Hewell Rd, Barnt Green, Birmingham, **Midlands (West)**, B45 8NW, ENG.
(T) 01214 453118
Speciality: Acupuncture.
O (Ref:HM01771)

## BARON, COLIN M (DR)
**Dr Colin M Baron**, 3 Fir Rd, Doune, **Stirling**, FK16 6HU, SCO.
(T) 01786 841517
Speciality: Hypnotherapy.
● **Owner** Dr C Barron
B (Ref:HM01772)

## BARON, MARTA
**Marta Baron**, 2 Sinclair Gardens, London, **London (Greater)**, W14 0AT, ENG.
(T) 020 7602 4933
Speciality: Alexander Technique.
● **Owner** Ms M Baron
P S (Ref:HM01773)

## BARR, ISABEL
**Isabel Barr**, 11 Coleridge Avenue, Bothwell, Glasgow, **Glasgow (City of)**, G71 8TH, SCO.
(T) 01698 853857 (F) 01698 853857
Speciality: Chiropodists (Podiatrists).
● **Owner** Mrs I Barr
S (Ref:HM01774)

## BARRA LANE
**Barra Lane**, 2 Fairways, Rathfarnham, **County Dublin**, IRE.
(T) 08723 09808
Speciality: Osteopathy.
P S T (Ref:HM01775)

## BARRACLOUGH, HELEN
**Helen Barraclough**, 160 Leeds Rd, Wakefield, **Yorkshire (West)**, WF1 2QA, ENG.
(T) 01924 365119
Speciality: Chiropodists (Podiatrists).
● **Owner** Mrs H Barraclough
S (Ref:HM01776)

## BARRAS, L
**L Barras (Mobile)**, West Auckland Rd, Darlington, **County Durham**, DL3 9EJ, ENG.
(T) 01325 361311 (F) 01325 361311
Speciality: Chiropodists (Podiatrists).


Key continued: Yrs.Est: Years Established Q: Qualifications M: Professional Membership ✔ Indemnity Insurance Accept Credit Cards

● **Owner** Mr L Barras
S (Ref:HM01777)

## BARRASS, K I

**K I Barrass**, 76 Castle Rd, Scarborough, **Yorkshire (North)**, YO11 1XE, ENG.
(T) 01723 377187
(E) keith@castlerdfreeserve.co.uk
Speciality: Chiropody, Nail Surgery, Orthotics, Podiatry. ✓
● **Chiropodist (Podiatrist)**
Mr K Barrass Q: BA (Hons), DPodM, M.S.C.P, S.R.Ch.
C Yrs. Est.: 15 (Ref:HM01778)

## BARRATT, JAN

**Jan Barratt**, 274 Shobnall St, Burton-On-Trent, **Staffordshire**, DE14 2HR, ENG.
(T) 01283 562694
Speciality: Complementary Medicines & Therapy.
C M (Ref:HM01779)

## BARRATT'S HOMEOPATHY

**J Barratt**, 95 Albert St, Rugby, **Warwickshire**, CV21 2SW, ENG.
(T) 01788 562843 (F) 01788 575795
(E) james@homeopath.co.uk
(W) www.homoeopath.co.uk
Speciality: Complementary Therapy, Counselling, Herbal Medicine, Holistic Healing, Homeopathy, Iridology, Naturopathy, Phytotherapy, Vitamin Therapy. ✓
● **Homeopath** Mr J Barratt Q: BIH, Dip.Hom, MHMA. M: HMA.
M Yrs. Est.: 21 (Ref:HM01780)

## BARRELL, L A

**L A Barrell**, 30 Station Rd, Wokingham, **Berkshire**, RG40 2AE, ENG.
(T) 01189 783453
Speciality: Chiropodists (Podiatrists).
● **Owner** Mrs L Barrell
S (Ref:HM01781)

## BARRELL, PETER

**Peter Barrell**, 17 Mellstock Rd, Aylesbury, **Buckinghamshire**, HP21 7NU, ENG.
(T) 01296 422953
Speciality: Chiropodists (Podiatrists).
● **Owner** Mr B Barrell
S (Ref:HM01782)

## BARRETT & LIPTROTT

**Barrett & Liptrott**, 21 Rossall Rd, Thornton, **Lancashire**, FY5 1DX, ENG.
(T) 01253 826413
Speciality: Chiropody, Nail Surgery. ✓
● **Chiropodist** Ms B Barrett Q: BSc, S.R.Ch. M: S.C.P.
● **Chiropodist** Ms C Liptrott Q: BSc, S.R.Ch. M: S.C.P.
M Yrs. Est.: 20 (Ref:HM01783)

## BARRETT BOWEN TREATMENT

**S Barrett Bowen Treatment**, 2 Crown Lane, Littleport, Ely, **Cambridgeshire**, CB6 1PP, ENG.
(T) 01353 863218
Speciality: Complementary Medicines & Therapy.
M (Ref:HM01784)

## BARRETT, C

**C Barrett**, 2 Wimborne Cl, Sawbridgeworth, **Hertfordshire**, CM21 0EA, ENG.
(T) 01279 724789
Speciality: Chiropodists (Podiatrists).
S (Ref:HM01785)

## BARRETT, C J & M

**C J & M Barrett**, 26 Cheriton Gardens, Folkestone, **Kent**, CT20 2AS, ENG.
(T) 01303 850077 (F) 01303 226225
Speciality: Chiropodists (Podiatrists).
● **Owner** Mr T Drion
S (Ref:HM01786)

## BARRETT, CARMEL

**Carmel Barrett**, 101 Carlton Vale, London, **London (Greater)**, NW6 5HG, ENG.
(T) 020 7372 8103
Speciality: Reflexology.
S T (Ref:HM01787)

## BARRETT, CAROL-ANN

**Carol-Ann Barrett**, Lavandula, 9 Willow Cl, Bishop's Stortford, **Hertfordshire**, CM23 2RY, ENG.
(T) 01279 656737
Speciality: Reflexology.
S T (Ref:HM01788)

## BARRETT, CAROLYN

**Carolyn Barrett**, West Lane, Sutton-In-Craven, Keighley, **Yorkshire (West)**, BD20 7NT, ENG.
(T) 01535 630126
Speciality: Complementary Medicines & Therapy.
M (Ref:HM01789)

## BARRETT, J

**J Barrett**, 96 Weston Park Rd, Plymouth, **Devon**, PL3 4NP, ENG.
(T) 01752 205969
Speciality: Chiropody. ✓
● **Owner/Chiropodist** Mrs J Barrett Q: MBChA, MSSCh. M: B.A.Ch.P, SSCh.
C Yrs. Est.: 3 (Ref:HM01790)

## BARRETT, JACQUELINE

**Jacqueline Barrett**, Little Potters, Middle St, Nazeing, Waltham Abbey, **Essex**, EN9 2LQ, ENG.
(T) 01992 892110
Speciality: Reflexology.
S T (Ref:HM01791)

## BARRETT, LINDA

**Linda Barrett**, 7 Lauderdale, Farnborough, **Hampshire**, GU14 0RR, ENG.
(T) 01252 662983
Speciality: Complementary Medicines & Therapy.
● **Owner** Mrs L Barrett
M (Ref:HM01792)

## BARRETT, P M

**P M Barrett**, The Firs, Uxbridge Rd, Hillingdon Village, Uxbridge, **London (Greater)**, UB10 0LF, ENG.
(T) 01895 232185
Speciality: Chiropodists (Podiatrists).
S (Ref:HM01793)

## BARRETT, ROS

**Ros Barrett**, 29 Eglise Rd, Warlingham, **Surrey**, CR6 9SE, ENG.
(T) 01883 625584
Speciality: Aromatherapy.
M O (Ref:HM01794)

## BARRETT, ROSEMARY

**Rosemary Barrett**, 18 Francis Rd, Broadstairs, **Kent**, CT10 3NG, ENG.
(T) 01843 868906
Speciality: Reflexology.
S T (Ref:HM01795)

## BARRETT, SHEILA

**Barrett Sheila MISCP MCSPMSOM Lic Ac**, 9 New Cork Rd, Midleton, **County Cork**, IRE.
(T) 021 4633 455
Speciality: Complementary Medicines & Therapy.
M (Ref:HM01796)

## BARRETT-BOYCE, PATRICK

**Patrick Barrett-Boyce**, 47 Coombe Rd, Croydon, **Surrey**, CR0 1BQ, ENG.
(T) 020 8688 0345 (F) 020 8688 0345
Speciality: Osteopathy.
● **Owner** Mr P Barrett-Boyce
P S T (Ref:HM01797)

## BARRIE, ALEXANDER

**Alexander Barrie**, 200 Vaughan Rd, Harrow, **London (Greater)**, HA1 4EB, ENG.
(T) 020 8423 5659 (F) 020 8423 5659
(E) alexander.barrie@talk21.com
(W) www.alexanderbase.fsnet.co.uk
Speciality: Complementary Therapy, Counselling, Cranial Osteopathy, Cranio-Sacral Therapy, Cupping, Do-In, Faith Healing, Healer, Manipulation, Meditation, Moxibustion, Oriental Diagnosis, Postural Integration, Shiatsu, Stress Therapy, Yoga, Mr Barrie is the founder of The Alexander Barrie System of Pelvic Correction TM. This deals successfully with back-pain. Also known as the Pelvic Correction System. The Alexander Barrie System Of Pelvic Correction. ✓
● **Consultant** Mr A Barrie Q: QTHY, RCST, Reg.Shiatsu Therapist. M: BWY, CSTA, Shiatsu Society UK.
C S Yrs. Est.: 15 (Ref:HM01798)

## BARRIE, S C

**S C Barrie**, 33 Warren Rd, Wickersley, Rotherham, **Yorkshire (South)**, S66 2HE, ENG.
(T) 01709 547990
Speciality: Chiropodists (Podiatrists).
● **Owner** Mr S Barrie
S (Ref:HM01799)

## BARRINGTON-WARD, H B

**H B Barrington-Ward**, Dolphin House, The Hill, Burford, **Oxfordshire**, OX18 4RE, ENG.
(T) 01993 823604
Speciality: Acupuncture.
● **Owner** Mrs H Barrington-Ward
O (Ref:HM01800)

## BARRON CHIROPRACTIC CLINICS

**Barron Chiropractic Clinics**, 29 Hersham Rd, Walton-On-Thames, **Surrey**, KT12 1LF, ENG.
(T) 01932 227360 (F) 01932 254395
Speciality: Chiropractic.
● **Principal** Mr S Barron
P S T (Ref:HM01801)

## BARRON, ANGELA L

**Angela L Barron**, Dental Practice (Kerruish), 15a High St, Normanby, Middlesbrough, **Cleveland**, TS6 0NQ, ENG.
(T) 01642 466460
Speciality: Chiropodists (Podiatrists).
S (Ref:HM01802)

## BARRON, DEIRDRE

**Deirdre Barron**, Alyth, **Perth and Kinross**, PH11, SCO.
(T) 01828 632325
Speciality: Reflexology.
S T (Ref:HM01803)

## BARROW, J

**Mrs J Barrow**, 76 Parkfield Avenue, Harrow, **London (Greater)**, HA2 6NP, ENG.
(T) 020 8428 8170 (F) 020 8428 8170
Speciality: Chiropodists (Podiatrists).
● **Owner** Mrs J Barrow
S (Ref:HM01804)

## BARROW, P W

**P W Barrow**, Clifton Rd Chiropody & Podiatry Practice, 71-73 Clifton Rd, Rugby, **Warwickshire**, CV21 3QG, ENG.
(T) 01788 572798
Speciality: Chiropodists (Podiatrists).
● **Owner** Mr P Barrow
S (Ref:HM01805)

## BARROWCLIFFE, GRAHAM (DR)

**Dr Graham Barrowcliffe**, 11 Holmesfield Rd, Dronfield, Woodhouse, Dronfield, **Derbyshire**, S18 8WS, ENG.
(T) 01142 890798
(E) graham@lifestyledoctor.fq.co.uk
(W) www.lifestyledoctor.co.uk
Speciality: Acupuncture, Autogenic Training, Cognitive Therapy, Electrolipolysis, Hypnosis, Hypnotherapy, Life Style Coaching, Manipulation, Manual Lymph Drainage, Psychotherapy, Stress Therapy, Visualisation Therapy, Medical and Natural Product Treatments of Overweight and Skin Aging, Prevention of Osteoporosis. ✓
● **Doctor** Dr G Barrowcliffe Q: Ch.B, LRCP, MB.
B H M S Yrs. Est.: 40 (Ref:HM01806)

## BARROWCLOUGH, LISA

**Lisa Barrowclough**, Canada House, 1 Carrick Way, New Milton, **Hampshire**, BH25 6UD, ENG.
(T) 01425 622233 (F) 01425 639099
Speciality: Physiotherapy.
● **Owner** Ms L Barrowclough
P S T (Ref:HM01807)

## BARROWFORD CLINIC

**Barrowford Clinic**, 5-6 Cromwell Ter, Barrowford, Nelson, **Lancashire**, BB9 8PT, ENG.
(T) 01282 618881 (F) 01282 618881
Speciality: Physiotherapy.
● **Owner** Mr E Salmon

Key: B Mind-Body Medicine, C Complementary Medicine, H Self Help Treatment, M Medicinal Therapy, O Oriental Medicine, P Postural Therapy, S Manipulative Structural Therapy, T Touch Therapy

P S T (Ref:HM01808)

## BARRY OSTEOPATHIC CLINIC

**Barry Osteopathic Clinic**, 68 High St, Barry, **Glamorgan (Vale of)**, CS62 7DU, WAL.
(T) 01446 775080
Speciality: Osteopathy. ✓
● **Osteopath** Mr P Pearce Q: DO. M: GOsC.
S Yrs. Est.: 2 (Ref:HM01809)

## BARRY WEST ASSOCIATES

**Barry West Associates**, 21 Nixon Cl, Dewsbury, **Yorkshire (West)**, WF12 0JA, ENG.
(T) 01924 468110
Speciality: Hypnotherapy.
B (Ref:HM01810)

## BARRY, D J

**D J Barry**, 32 Eveswell St, Newport, NP19 8EP, WAL.
(T) 01633 270868
Speciality: Hypnosis.
● **Owner** Mr D Barry
B (Ref:HM01811)

## BARRY, JOHN

**John Barry**, First Floor, 107 Arthur Rd, London, **London (Greater)**, SW19 7DR, ENG.
(T) 020 8946 5730
Speciality: Hypnotherapy.
B (Ref:HM01812)

## BARRYMORE, MIKE

**Mike Barrymore**, 4 Handel Walk, Colchester, **Essex**, CO4 3YX, ENG.
(T) 01206 862211
Speciality: Clairvoyants & Palmists.
● **Owner** Mr M Barrymore
B (Ref:HM01813)

## BARSELL, R H

**R H Barsell**, 119 Cockett Rd, Cockett, Swansea, SA2 0FG, WAL.
(T) 01792 582372
Speciality: Physiotherapy.
● **Owner** Mr R Barsell
P S T (Ref:HM01814)

## BARSKY, S

**S Barsky**, 15 East St, Weymouth, **Dorset**, DT4 8BW, ENG.
(T) 01305 789949
Speciality: Chiropodists (Podiatrists).
S (Ref:HM01815)

## BARSKY, S & HAWKINS, R W

**S Barsky & R W Hawkins**, 63 High West St, Dorchester, **Dorset**, DT1 1UY, ENG.
(T) 01305 265850 (F) 01305 265850
Speciality: Chiropodists (Podiatrists).
● **Owner** Mr P Wallis
S (Ref:HM01816)

## BARSTOW & CLAY

**Barstow & Clay**, City Sq, Leeds, **Yorkshire (West)**, LS1 1PL, ENG.
(T) 01132 452610
Speciality: Chiropodists (Podiatrists).
● **Partner** Mr K Barstow
S (Ref:HM01817)

## BARTHOLOMEW WAY CLINIC

**Mr H M Jenkins T/A The Bartholomew Way Clinic**, 13A Bartholomew Way, Horsham, **Sussex (West)**, RH12 5JL, ENG.
(T) 01403 276272 (F) 01403 254604
(E) podman100@aol.com
Speciality: Chiropody, Gait Analysis, Kinesiology, Manipulation, Massage (Therapeutic), Orthotics, Osteopathy, Physiotherapy, Podiatry, X-Ray, Video Gait Analysis, Pressure Plate Analysis and Prescription Footwear. ✓ 💳
● **Chiropodist (Podiatrist)**
Mr M Jenkins Q: D.S.Ch. M: Inst.CH.P.
● **Sports Massage Therapist**
Ms H Chishome Q: FSMT. M: SSM.
● **Osteopath** Ms A Brown Q: BSc, Reg.Osteopath.
● **Physiotherapist** Mr C Greenfield Q: BSc (Hons), MCSP, MSc, SRP. M: CSP, SRP.
S (Ref:HM01818)

## BARTHROPP, VICTORIA

**Victoria Barthropp**, 12 Buckingham Rd, Kingston-upon-Thames, London, **London (Greater)**, KT1 3BH, ENG.
(T) 020 8546 7894
Speciality: Reflexology.
S T (Ref:HM01819)

## BARTIG, ANDREA

**Andrea Bartig**, 24 Morritt Avenue, Leeds, **Yorkshire (West)**, LS15 7EP, ENG.
(T) 01132 930345
Speciality: Homeopathy.
M (Ref:HM01820)

## BARTLETT, CLAIRE

**Claire Bartlett**, Camberley Natural Therapy Centre, 9 Tekels Park, Camberley, **Surrey**, GU15 2LE, ENG.
(T) 01276 23300
Speciality: Hypnotherapy.
B (Ref:HM01821)

## BARTLETT, GODFREY

**Godfrey Bartlett**, 13 Mayfield Gdns, Brentwood, **Essex**, CM14 4UJ, ENG.
(T) 01277 223894
Speciality: Acupuncture.
● **Owner** Mr G Bartlett
O (Ref:HM01822)

## BARTLETT, LOUIS

**Louis Bartlett**, 100 High St, Crediton, **Devon**, EX17 3LF, ENG.
(T) 01363 774175
Speciality: Osteopathy.
P S T (Ref:HM01823)

## BARTLETT, M J

**M J Bartlett**, 22 Westmount Rd, London, **London (Greater)**, SE9 1JD, ENG.
(T) 020 8850 4316
Speciality: Physiotherapy.
P S T (Ref:HM01824)

## BARTLETT, PETER

**Peter Bartlett**, Hale Clinic, 7 Park Cresent, London, **London (Greater)**, W1N 3HE, ENG.
(T) 020 7631 0156
Speciality: Osteopathy.
P S T (Ref:HM01825)

## BARTLETT, PHILIPPA

**Philippa Bartlett**, 86 Highbury Park, London, **London (Greater)**, N5 2XE, ENG.
(T) 020 7359 2609
Speciality: Acupuncture.
O (Ref:HM01826)

## BARTLETT, S G A

**S G A Bartlett**, 88 Vale Rd, Ash Vale, Aldershot, **Hampshire**, GU12 5HS, ENG.
(T) 01252 312412 (F) 01252 312412
Speciality: Hypnosis.
● **Owner** Dr S Bartlett
B (Ref:HM01827)

## BARTON HARTSHORN MANOR

**Barton Hartshorn Manor**, Manor House, Barton Hartshorn, Buckingham, **Buckinghamshire**, MK18 4JU, ENG.
(T) 01280 848943 (F) 01892 667525
Speciality: Complementary Medicines & Therapy.
● **Manager** Ms S Petszaft
C M (Ref:HM01828)

## BARTON, C

**C Barton**, 3 Babworth Rd, Retford, **Nottinghamshire**, DN22 7BP, ENG.
(T) 01777 703458
Speciality: Chiropodists (Podiatrists).
● **Owner** Mrs C Barton
S (Ref:HM01829)

## BARTON, CHRISTINE

**Christine Barton**, 66 Victoria Rd, Polegate, **Sussex (East)**, BN26 6BY, ENG.
(T) 01323 487193
Speciality: Chiropodists (Podiatrists).
● **Owner** Mr T Barton
S (Ref:HM01830)

## BARTON, MARGOT

**Margot Barton**, The Studio, Gilhurst, The Street, Warninglid, Haywards Heath, **Sussex (West)**, RH17 5SZ, ENG.
(T) 01444 461486
Speciality: Homeopathy.
M (Ref:HM01831)

## BARTON, VIRGINIA

**Virginia Barton**, 4 Queen St, Bideford, **Devon**, EX39 2JG, ENG.
(T) 01237 474076
Speciality: Chiropodists (Podiatrists).
S (Ref:HM01832)

## BARTOSZEWICZ, PATRICIA

**Patricia Bartoszewicz**, 131 Constance Rd, Twickenham, **London (Greater)**, TW2 7HX, ENG.
(T) 020 8894 7875
Speciality: Aromatherapy.
● **Owner** Mrs P Bartoszewi
M O (Ref:HM01833)

## BARTSTRA, R

**R Bartstra**, Gin Mill, Garrigill, Alston, **Cumbria**, CA9 3DH, ENG.
(T) 01434 382222
Speciality: Physiotherapy.
P S T (Ref:HM01834)

## BARTSTRA, RINSKE

**Rinske Bartstra**, Bridge End, Hexham, **Northumberland**, NE46 4JH, ENG.
(T) 01434 600088
Speciality: Osteopathy.
● **Manager** Ms R Bartstra
P S T (Ref:HM01835)

## BARTUP, ALISON

**Alison Bartup**, 16 Ridgmont Rd, Bramhall, Stockport, **Cheshire**, SK7 1JY, ENG.
(T) 01614 408970
Speciality: Physiotherapy.
● **Owner** Mrs A Bartup
P S T (Ref:HM01836)

## BARUCH, LEONARD A

**Leonard A Baruch**, 19 Pettits Lane, Romford, **Essex**, RM1 4HL, ENG.
(T) 01708 763488
Speciality: Chiropodists (Podiatrists).
S (Ref:HM01837)

## BARWICK & LEVEN SPORTS CLINIC

**Barwick & Leven Sports & Injury Clinic**, Healaugh Park, Thirsk Park, Yarm, **Cleveland**, TS15 9XN, ENG.
(T) 01642 785578
Speciality: Physiotherapy.
● **Principal** Mr M Nile
P S T (Ref:HM01838)

## BARWICK, M E

**M E Barwick**, 2 Liddell Trce, Gateshead, **Tyne and Wear**, NE8 1YN, ENG.
(T) 01914 901234
Speciality: Chiropodists (Podiatrists).
● **Owner** Mrs M Barwick
S (Ref:HM01839)

## BASCOMBE, K E

**K E Bascombe**, 28 Regina Rd, London, **London (Greater)**, W13 9EF, ENG.
(T) 020 8579 5232
Speciality: Osteopathy.
P S T (Ref:HM01840)

## BASE

**Base (The)**, 34 South Molton St, London, **London (Greater)**, W1Y 2BP, ENG.
(T) 020 7355 4300
Speciality: Complementary Medicines & Therapy.
● **Partner** Mrs V Robinson
M (Ref:HM01841)

## BASFORD CHIROPRACTIC CLINIC

**Basford Chiropractic Clinic**, 513 Etruria Rd, Stoke-On-Trent, **Staffordshire**, ST4 6HT, ENG.
(T) 01782 627133 (F) 01782 627133
Speciality: Chiropractic. ✓
● **Chiropractor** Dr V Stanley Q: BSc (Chiro), DC. M: GCC.
P Yrs. Est.: 8 (Ref:HM01842)

## BASHALL, L (DR)

**Dr L Bashall**, 130-132 Gloucester Rd, Bishopston, Bristol, BS7 8NL, ENG.
(T) 01179 245842



Key continued: Yrs.Est: Years Established Q: Qualifications M: Professional Membership ✓ Indemnity Insurance 💳 Accept Credit Cards

Speciality: Chiropractors.
● **Doctor** Mr J Jensen
P S T (Ref:HM01843)

### BASHFORD, JANET

**Janet Bashford**, 13 High St, Emberton, Olney, **Buckinghamshire**, MK46 5JB, ENG.
(T) 01234 711241
Speciality: Hypnosis.
● **Owner** Mrs J Bashford
B (Ref:HM01844)

### BASHFUL ALLEY CENTRE

**Bashful Alley Centre**, Bashful Alley, Lancaster, **Lancashire**, LA1 1LF, ENG.
(T) 01524 844299
Speciality: Alexander Technique.
● **Owner** Mr J Woodward
P S (Ref:HM01845)

### BASILDON CHIROPRACTIC CLINIC

**Basildon Chiropractic Clinic**, 1 Vange Riverview Centre, Vange, Basildon, **Essex**, SS16 4NE, ENG.
(T) 01268 557313 (F) 01268 583835
Speciality: Chiropractors.
● **Owner** Mr G Webber
P S T (Ref:HM01846)

### BASINGSTOKE CHIROPRACTIC

**Basingstoke Chiropractic Clinic (The)**, 18 Cliddesden Rd, Basingstoke, **Hampshire**, RG21 3DU, ENG.
(T) 01256 328128
Speciality: Chiropractors.
● **Partner** Mrs A Williams
P S T (Ref:HM01847)

### BASINGSTOKE FOOT CLINIC

**Basingstoke Foot Clinic**, 23A London St, Basingstoke, **Hampshire**, RG21 7PG, ENG.
(T) 01256 355555
Speciality: Chiropodists (Podiatrists).
● **Owner** Mr M Chatee
S (Ref:HM01848)

### BASS, CATHERINE

**Catherine Bass**, Thorncliffe, Ballure Rd, Ramsey, **Isle of Man**, IM8 1NE, ENG.
(T) 01624 813885
Speciality: Chiropractors.
● **Owner** Miss C Bass
P S T (Ref:HM01849)

### BASS, MIKE

**Mike Bass**, 141 Rayleigh Drive, Wideopen, Newcastle Upon Tyne, **Tyne and Wear**, NE13 6AL, ENG.
(T) 01912 367291
(E) mike/bass@lineone.net
Speciality: Reflexology. ✔
● **Owner/Reflexologist** Mr M Bass Q: MIFR.
C Yrs. Est.: 5 (Ref:HM01850)

### BASSETT & ASSOCIATES

**Bassett M L D C & Associates**, The Hertford Chiropractic Clinic, 5 Port Hill, Hertford, **Hertfordshire**, SG14 1PJ, ENG.
(T) 01992 501659
Speciality: Chiropractors.
P S T (Ref:HM01851)

### BASSETT & ASSOCIATES

**Bassett M L D C & Associates**, Watford Chiropractic Centre, 27 Eastbury Rd, Watford, **Hertfordshire**, WD1 4PU, ENG.
(T) 01923 225578
Speciality: Chiropractic.
● **Owner** Mrs M Bassett
P S T (Ref:HM01852)

### BASSETT CLINIC

**M L Bassett DC & Associates**, Aberfoyle House, Stapley Rd, St. Albans, **Hertfordshire**, AL3 5EP, ENG.
(T) 01727 856687
(E) bassettclinic@cellnetuk.com
Speciality: Acupuncture, Aromatherapy, Chiropractic, Counselling, Homeopathy, Hypnotherapy, Indian Head Massage, Manipulation, Massage (Therapeutic), Reflexology, X-Ray, The above therapies can also be found at The Bassett Clinic including Chinese Herbs and Integrative Massage Therapy. ✔
● **Chiropractor** Mr S Bassett Q: BSc (Hons), MSc (Chiro). M: BCA, GCC.
● **Chiropractor** Mr M Bassett Q: CCEP, DC, FCC. M: BCA, GCC.
M (Ref:HM01853)

### BASSETT PHYSIOTHERAPY CLINIC

**Bassett Physiotherapy Clinic (The)**, 23 Bassett Crescent West, Southampton, **Hampshire**, SO16 7EB, ENG.
(T) 023 8079 1001
Speciality: Physiotherapy.
P S T (Ref:HM01854)

### BASSETT, LESLEY

**Lesley Bassett**, 37 Homefield Rd, Warlingham, **Surrey**, CR6 9HU, ENG.
(T) 01883 625044
Speciality: Reflexology.
S T (Ref:HM01855)

### BASSETT, MIKE

**Mike Bassett**, Aberfoyle House, Stapley Rd, St. Albans, **Hertfordshire**, AL3 5EP, ENG.
(T) 01727 856687
Speciality: Chiropractors.
● **Manager** Mrs S Bassett
P S T (Ref:HM01856)

### BASSETT, N S

**N S Bassett**, 74 Canute Rd, Hastings, **Sussex (East)**, TN35 5HT, ENG.
(T) 01424 433991
Speciality: Acupuncture, Alexander Technique, Cranial Osteopathy, Homeopathy, Osteopathy, Shiatsu.
● **Osteopath** Mr M Green Q: DO. M: GOsC, RoO.
● **Osteopath** Miss S Birks Q: DO. M: GOsC, RoO.
● **Osteopath** Miss S White Q: DO. M: GOsC, RoO.
● **Osteopath** Mr N Bassett Q: DO, MRO. M: GOsC, RoO.
S Yrs. Est.: 16 (Ref:HM01857)

### BASSETTS CHIROPRACTIC CLINIC

**Bassetts Chiropractic Clinic (The)**, 305 Winchester Rd, Southampton, **Hampshire**, SO16 6TX, ENG.
(T) 023 8078 3321
Speciality: Chiropractic.
● **Owner** Dr C Webb
P S T (Ref:HM01858)

### BASSEY, DAWN

**Dawn Bassey**, The Body Shop, 194 Portobello Rd, London, **London (Greater)**, W11 1LA, ENG.
(T) 020 7243 8211
Speciality: Complementary Medicines & Therapy.
C M (Ref:HM01859)

### BASSEY, DAWN

**Dawn Bassey**, 34-36A Warwick Way, London, **London (Greater)**, SW1V 1RY, ENG.
(T) 020 7834 0861
Speciality: Complementary Medicines & Therapy.
● **Owner** Mr M Cozzi
M (Ref:HM01860)

### BASSIL, L

**L Bassil**, 83 Penyston Rd, Maidenhead, **Berkshire**, SL6 6ED, ENG.
(T) 01628 624981
Speciality: Clairvoyants & Palmists.
● **Owner** Mrs L Bassil
B (Ref:HM01861)

### BASTON, MYRA V

**Myra V Baston**, 15A Dene St, Dorking, **Surrey**, RH4 2DB, ENG.
(T) 01306 889680
Speciality: Physiotherapy.
● **Owner** Miss M Baston
P S T (Ref:HM01862)

### BATCHELOR, C

**C Batchelor**, 46 Westville Rd, Thames Ditton, **Surrey**, KT7 0UJ, ENG.
(T) 020 8398 1053 (F) 020 8398 5990
Speciality: Counselling, Psychotherapy. ✔
● **Owner** Carol Batchelor Q: MSc. M: BACP, BPS, UKCP.
M Yrs. Est.: 14 (Ref:HM01863)

### BATCHELOR, R V

**R V Batchelor**, 93 St. Leonards Rd, Hove, **Sussex (East)**, BN3 4QQ, ENG.
(T) 01273 413155
Speciality: Chiropodists (Podiatrists).
● **Owner** Mr R Batcholor
S (Ref:HM01864)

### BATE, ALAN

**Alan Bate**, 9 Abbey Hill Rd, Allestree, Derby, **Derbyshire**, DE22 2PT, ENG.
(T) 01332 541057
Speciality: Hypnotherapy.
● **Owner** Mr A Bate
B (Ref:HM01865)

### BATE, AMANDA

**Amanda Bate**, 122 Tibbs Hill Rd, Abbots Langley, **Hertfordshire**, WD5 0LL, ENG.
(T) 01923 443240
Speciality: Homeopathy.
● **Owner** Ms A Bate
M (Ref:HM01866)

### BATE, CAROLE

**Carole Bate**, 39 Oxford Drive, Halewood, Liverpool, **Merseyside**, L26 0TN, ENG.
(T) 01514 877491
Speciality: Electrolysis.
T (Ref:HM01867)

### BATE, J M

**J M Bate**, 166 Knowlton Rd, Poole, **Dorset**, BH17 9ED, ENG.
(T) 01202 659638
Speciality: Chiropodists (Podiatrists).
● **Owner** Mrs J Bate
S (Ref:HM01868)

### BATE, ROBIN

**Robin Bate**, 69 Portobello High St, Edinburgh, **Edinburgh (City of)**, EH15 1BQ, SCO.
(T) 01316 699476
Speciality: Homeopathy.
M (Ref:HM01869)

### BATEMAN, JANE

**Jane Bateman**, 11 Rydes Hill Cres, Guildford, **Surrey**, GU2 9UH, ENG.
(T) 01483 232217
Speciality: Hypnosis.
B (Ref:HM01870)

### BATEMAN, P W

**P W Bateman**, 4 Market Strand, Redruth, **Cornwall**, TR15 2AS, ENG.
(T) 01209 314131
Speciality: Chiropodists (Podiatrists).
● **Owner** Mr P Bateman
S (Ref:HM01871)

### BATEMAN, P W

**P W Bateman**, 92 Daniels Lane, St. Austell, **Cornwall**, PL25 3HT, ENG.
(T) 01726 76699
Speciality: Chiropodists (Podiatrists).
● **Owner** Mr P Bateman
S (Ref:HM01872)

### BATEMAN, R A (DR)

**Dr R A Bateman**, 67 Mersea Rd, Colchester, **Essex**, CO2 7QR, ENG.
(T) 01206 549809 (F) 01206 549852
Speciality: Chiropractors.
● **Principal** Dr I Garrod
P S T (Ref:HM01873)

### BATEMAN, STEPHEN W

**Stephen W Bateman**, Devonport House, Skye Gardens, Tibshelf, Alfreton, **Derbyshire**, DE55 5PL, ENG.
(T) 01773 872991
Speciality: Complementary Medicines & Therapy.
C M (Ref:HM01874)

### BATES ASS FOR VISION ED

**Bates Association For Vision Education (The)**, P O Box 25, Shoreham-by-Sea, **Sussex (West)**, BN43 6ZF, ENG.
(T) 01273 422090 (F) 01273 279983
Speciality: Complementary Medicines & Therapy.

Key: B Mind-Body Medicine C Complementary Medicine H Self Help Treatment M Medicinal Therapy O Oriental Medicine P Postural Therapy S Manipulative Structural Therapy T Touch Therapy

● **Company Secretary** Mr P Manson
C M (**Ref:**HM01875)

## BATES METHOD

**Bates Method**, 128 Merton Rd, London, **London (Greater)**, SW18 5SP, ENG.
(T) 020 8874 7337
Speciality: Complementary Medicines & Therapy.
● **Teacher** Mr A Attenborough
M (**Ref:**HM01876)

## BATES METHOD VISION EDUCATION

**Bates Method Vision Education**, Claverley, North Rd, Glossop, **Derbyshire**, SK13 7AX, ENG.
(T) 01457 853268
Speciality: Complementary Medicines & Therapy.
● **Owner** Ms S Davenport
M (**Ref:**HM01877)

## BATES VISION EDUCATION

**Bates Vision Education**, 24 Abbotsford Gr, West Timperley, Altrincham, **Cheshire**, WA14 5AZ, ENG.
(T) 01619 693888
(E) stewart.wilson@photoshot.com
Speciality: Bates Method. ✔
● **Vision Teacher** Mr S Wilson Q: BSc.
H Yrs. Est.: 3 (**Ref:**HM01878)

## BATES, DAVID J

**David J Bates**, 333 Field End Rd, Ruislip, **London (Greater)**, HA4 9NS, ENG.
(T) 020 8866 7897
Speciality: Chiropodists (Podiatrists).
S (**Ref:**HM01879)

## BATES, DILYS

**Dilys Bates**, Witheys Yard, High St, Stroud, **Gloucestershire**, GL5 1AP, ENG.
(T) 01453 750796
Speciality: Complementary Medicines & Therapy.
M (**Ref:**HM01880)

## BATES, EDWARD (DR)

**Dr Edward Bates D C**, Dungarvan Co, **County Waterford**, IRE.
(T) 025 2765 3
Speciality: Chiropractors.
P S T (**Ref:**HM01881)

## BATES, K

**K Bates**, Chelsea Lane, Inverurie, **Aberdeenshire**, AB51 3QQ, SCO.
(T) 01467 624888 (F) 01467 624888
Speciality: Complementary Medicines & Therapy.
● **Partner** Mrs C Craigmile
M (**Ref:**HM01882)

## BATES, K A C

**K A C Bates**, 34 Elm Grove South, Barnham, Bognor Regis, **Sussex (West)**, PO22 0EL, ENG.
(T) 01243 552899
Speciality: Chiropodists (Podiatrists).
● **Owner** Mrs K Bates
S (**Ref:**HM01883)

## BATES, MARGARET

**Margaret Bates**, 26 Lime Grove Avenue, Beeston, Nottingham, **Nottinghamshire**, NG9 4AR, ENG.
(T) 01159 255568
Speciality: Complementary Medicines & Therapy.
C M (**Ref:**HM01884)

## BATES, SANDIE

**Sandie Bates**, 2 Fox Lane, Brackley, **Northamptonshire**, NN13 6BG, ENG.
(T) 01280 709997
Speciality: Chiropractors.
● **Owner** Mrs S Bates
P S T (**Ref:**HM01885)

## BATES, SUE

**Sue Bates**, Oakington Therapy Centre, 12 High St, Oakington, Cambridge, **Cambridgeshire**, CB4 5AG, ENG.
(T) 01223 237459 (F) 01223 237459
Speciality: Aromatherapy.
● **Director** Mr R Giddings
M O (**Ref:**HM01886)

## BATES, SUSAN

**Susan Bates**, 'Catkins', 12 Manor Garth, Pakenham, Bury St. Edmunds, **Suffolk**, IP31 2LB, ENG.
(T) 01359 232582
Speciality: Reflexology.
S T (**Ref:**HM01887)

## BATES, SUSAN M

**Susan M Bates**, 5 Hawke Rd, Kewstoke, Weston-Super-Mare, **Somerset**, BS22 9LB, ENG.
(T) 01934 522133
Speciality: Physiotherapy.
● **Owner** Miss S Bates
P S T (**Ref:**HM01888)

## BATEY, PATRICIA

**Patricia Batey**, 10 Porchester Rd, Bingham, Nottingham, **Nottinghamshire**, NG13 8ES, ENG.
(T) 01949 875117
Speciality: Chiropodists (Podiatrists).
S (**Ref:**HM01889)

## BATH ALEXANDER TECHNIQUE

**Bath Alexander Technique Practice**, 6 Hatfield Buildings, Widcombe Hill, Bath, **Somerset**, BA1 6AF, ENG.
(T) 01225 331136
Speciality: Alexander Technique. ✔
● **Teacher of the Alexander Technique** Ms F Rietchel M: STAT.
P S Yrs. Est.: 16 (**Ref:**HM01890)

## BATH BACK CLINIC

**Bath Back Clinic**, 7-9 Comfortable Pl, Upper Bristol Rd, Bath, **Somerset**, ENG.
(T) 01225 461463
Speciality: Acupuncture, Chiropractic, Nutritional Therapy, Yoga.
O (**Ref:**HM01891)

## BATH CHIROPODY CLINIC

**Bath Chiropody Clinic**, 1 Bladud Buildings, Bath, **Somerset**, BA1 5LS, ENG.
(T) 01225 422222
Speciality: Chiropodists (Podiatrists).
● **Owner** Mrs J Wildgoose
S (**Ref:**HM01892)

## BATH NATURAL MEDICAL CENTRE

**Bath Natural Medical Centre**, 7 Laura Pl, Bath, **Somerset**, BA2 4BJ, ENG.
(T) 01225 442119
Speciality: Acupuncture, Chiropractic, Homeopathy, Indian Head Massage, Nutritional Therapy, Psychotherapy, Shiatsu, Bio-Dynamics. ✔
● **Therapist** Mr E Mansell
● **Therapist** Ms L Irvine
● **Therapist** Mr D Green
● **Therapist** Mr C Smith
● **Therapist** Ms R Davies
● **Therapist** Ms R Brown
C Yrs. Est.: 21 (**Ref:**HM01893)

## BATH PRACTICE

**Bath Practice**, 26 Monmouth St, Bath, **Somerset**, BA1 2AP, ENG.
(T) 01225 331136
Speciality: Osteopathy.
● **Therapist** Ms F Rietchel
P S (**Ref:**HM01894)

## BATH ROAD MASSAGE

**Bath Road Massage**, 387 Bath Rd, Arnos Vale, Bristol, BS4 3EU, ENG.
(T) 01179 720310
Speciality: Aromatherapy.
M O (**Ref:**HM01895)

## BATH RUGBY CLINIC

**Bath Rugby Clinic (The)**, 11 Argyle St, Bath, **Somerset**, BA2 4BQ, ENG.
(T) 01225 425444
Speciality: Physiotherapy.
P S T (**Ref:**HM01896)

## BATH STREET CHIROPODIST

**Bath Street Chiropodist**, 162 Bath St, Ilkeston, **Derbyshire**, DE7 8FH, ENG.
(T) 01159 320032
Speciality: Chiropodists (Podiatrists).
● **Owner** Mr W Hall
S (**Ref:**HM01897)

## BATH STREET THERAPY CENTRE

**Bath Street Therapy Centre**, 204 Bath St, Glasgow, **Glasgow (City of)**, G2 4HL, SCO.
(T) 01415 721134
Speciality: Complementary Medicines & Therapy.
● **Owner** Mrs M Sommerville
C M (**Ref:**HM01898)

## BATH, ANN

**Ann Bath**, 319 Burringham Rd, Scunthorpe, **Humberside**, DN17 2BJ, ENG.
(T) 01724 859340 (F) 01724 859340
Speciality: Aromatherapy. ✔
● **Owner** Mrs A Bath Q: Dip.Arom, TIDHA. M: RQA.
C Yrs. Est.: 10 (**Ref:**HM01899)

## BATHPOOL CHIROPRACTIC CLINIC

**Bath Chiropractic Clinic**, 152 Bridgwater Rd, Bathpool, Taunton, **Somerset**, TA2 8BJ, ENG.
(T) 01823 412489
Speciality: Aromatherapy, Chiropractic, Complementary Therapy, Indian Head Massage, Massage (Therapeutic), Reflexology, Stress Therapy, Lymphatic Drainage. ✔ CREDIT
● **Chiropractor** Mrs A Archibald Q: Dip.Chiro. M: BCA, GCC.
● **Chiropractor** Ms J Deans Q: BSc (Chiro). M: BCA.
● **Complementary Therapist** Viv Giles
(T) 01278 784159 Q: AOC, ITEC, MGCP. M: GCP.
● **Chiropractor** Mr D Westlake Q: BSc. M: BCA, GCC.
S Yrs. Est.: 60 (**Ref:**HM01900)

## BATLEY, KAREN

**Karen Batley**, 28 Woodhall Drive, Leeds, **Yorkshire (West)**, LS5 3LG, ENG.
(T) 01132 588791
Speciality: Hypnosis.
B (**Ref:**HM01901)

## BATSON, BARBARA

**Barbara Batson**, 67 Buckingham St, Aylesbury, **Buckinghamshire**, HP20 2NF, ENG.
(T) 01296 337788
Speciality: Bach Remedies.
● **Owner** Mrs B Batson
C (**Ref:**HM01902)

## BATSTONE, I

**I Batstone**, 14 Juniper Cl, Chineham, Basingstoke, **Hampshire**, RG24 8XH, ENG.
(T) 01256 324540
Speciality: Chiropodists (Podiatrists).
● **Owner** Mrs I Batstone
S (**Ref:**HM01903)

## BATT, M

**M Batt**, Frid Farm, Bethersden, Ashford, **Kent**, TN26 3DX, ENG.
(T) 01233 820274
Speciality: Chiropodists (Podiatrists).
S (**Ref:**HM01904)

## BATTEN, C

**C Batten**, 86 Longbrook St, Exeter, **Devon**, EX4 6AP, ENG.
(T) 01392 434074
Speciality: Osteopathy.
P S T (**Ref:**HM01905)

## BATTEN, CHRISTOPHER

**Christopher Batten**, 28 Lancaster Pk, Richmond, **Surrey**, TW10 6AB, ENG.
(T) 020 8940 5080
Speciality: Alexander Technique.
P S (**Ref:**HM01906)

## BATTEN, P R

**P R Batten**, 25 Farncombe Hill, Godalming, **Surrey**, GU7 2AU, ENG.
(T) 01483 421251
Speciality: Chiropodists (Podiatrists).
S (**Ref:**HM01907)

## BATTERSBY, TANIA

**Tania Battersby**, East London Homoeopathic Group Practice, 18 Martello St, London, **London**



Key continued: **Yrs.Est:** Years Established **Q:** Qualifications **M:** Professional Membership ✔ Indemnity Insurance CREDIT Accept Credit Cards

**(Greater)**, E8 3PE, ENG.
**(T)** 020 7241 2171
Speciality: Aromatherapy.
**M O** (**Ref:**HM01908)

### BATTERSEA & CLAPHAM PHYSIO

**Battersea & Clapham Junction Physiotherapy Clinic**, The Metropolitan Club, Sheepcote Lane, London, **London (Greater)**, SW11 2NL, ENG.
**(T)** 020 7924 3890
Speciality: Physiotherapy.
**P S T** (**Ref:**HM01909)

### BATTERSEA BACK CLINIC

**Battersea Back Clinic**, 4 Ransomes Dock, Parkgate Rd, London, **London (Greater)**, SW11 4NP, ENG.
**(T)** 020 7223 7223
Speciality: Chiropractic.
**P S T** (**Ref:**HM01910)

### BATTERSEA SCALP & HAIR CLINIC

**Battersea Scalp & Hair Clinic**, 108 St John's Hill, London, **London (Greater)**, SW11 1SY, ENG.
**(T)** 020 7924 2195
Speciality: Complementary Medicines & Therapy, Trichology.
**M** (**Ref:**HM01911)

### BATTERSHALL, J E

**J E Battershall**, 8 Berwick Rd, Rainham, **Kent**, RM13 9QU, ENG.
**(T)** 01708 558050
Speciality: Reflexology.
**S T** (**Ref:**HM01912)

### BATTLE, J M

**J M Battle**, 179 Greenhill Avenue, Sheffield, **Yorkshire (South)**, S8 7TJ, ENG.
**(T)** 01142 745364
Speciality: Chiropodists (Podiatrists).
**S** (**Ref:**HM01913)

### BATTLEY, STEVEN

**Steven Battley**, 36 Whitemore Rd, Guildford, **Surrey**, GU1 1QT, ENG.
**(T)** 01483 827387
Speciality: Complementary Medicines & Therapy.
**M** (**Ref:**HM01914)

### BATTY, JILL

**Jill Batty**, 163 Northchurch Rd, London, **London (Greater)**, N1 3NT, ENG.
**(T)** 020 7359 7644
Speciality: Complementary Medicines & Therapy.
● **Owner** Mrs J Batty
**C M** (**Ref:**HM01915)

### BATTY, PETER

**Peter Batty**, 39 Gloster Drive, Bognor Regis, **Sussex (West)**, PO21 3JL, ENG.
**(T)** 01243 264851
Speciality: Complementary Medicines & Therapy.
**C M** (**Ref:**HM01916)

### BAWDRIP CHIROPRACTIC CLINIC

**Bawdrip Chiropractic Clinic**, Goldmead Cottage, Bradney Lane, Bawdrip, Bridgwater, **Somerset**, TA7 8PQ, ENG.
**(T)** 01278 445564
Speciality: Chiropractic.
● **Owner** Ms H Parsons
**P S T** (**Ref:**HM01917)

### BAWTRY PHYSIOTHERAPY PRACTICE

**Bawtry Physiotherapy Practice**, 20B Station Rd, Bawtry, Doncaster, **Yorkshire (South)**, DN10 6PT, ENG.
**(T)** 01302 711799
Speciality: Physiotherapy. ✔
● **Physiotherapist** Mr R Johnson **Q:** MCSP, SRP.
**S** Yrs. Est.: 6 (**Ref:**HM01918)

### BAXTER CLINIC

**Baxter Clinic**, 2 Bushwood, London, **London (Greater)**, E11 3AY, ENG.
**(T)** 020 8989 2292
Speciality: Physiotherapy.
**P S T** (**Ref:**HM01919)

### BAXTER WILD, IAN

**Ian Baxter Wild**, 117 Drake St, Rochdale, **Lancashire**, OL16 1PZ, ENG.
**(T)** 01706 358515
Speciality: Chiropodists (Podiatrists).
**S** (**Ref:**HM01920)

### BAXTER, A

**A Baxter**, 4-10 Pellon Lane, Halifax, **Yorkshire (West)**, HX1 5SP, ENG.
**(T)** 01422 350179
Speciality: Hypnotherapy.
● **Owner** Mr A Baxter
**B** (**Ref:**HM01921)

### BAXTER, BEVERLEY J

**Beverley J Baxter**, 22 Stowting Rd, Orpington, **Kent**, BR6 9SJ, ENG.
**(T)** 01689 851889
Speciality: Reflexology.
**S T** (**Ref:**HM01922)

### BAXTER, C

**C Baxter**, 14 Meynell Rise, Ashbourne, **Derbyshire**, DE6 1RU, ENG.
**(T)** 01335 345562
Speciality: Chiropodists (Podiatrists).
● **Owner** Mrs C Baxter
**S** (**Ref:**HM01923)

### BAXTER, E

**E Baxter**, Gammons Farm, Gammons Farm Lane, Newchurch, Romney Marsh, **Kent**, TN29 0ED, ENG.
**(T)** 01303 872207
Speciality: Physiotherapy.
● **Owner** Mrs E Baxter
**P S T** (**Ref:**HM01924)

### BAXTER, E

**E Baxter**, Oak Hall Surgery, 41-43 High St, New Romney, **Kent**, TN28 8BW, ENG.
**(T)** 01797 367363
Speciality: Physiotherapy.
● **Owner** Ms E Baxter
**P S T** (**Ref:**HM01925)

### BAXTER, F J

**F J Baxter**, 41 London Rd, Edinburgh, **Edinburgh (City of)**, EH7 5SW, SCO.
**(T)** 01316 614196
Speciality: Chiropodists (Podiatrists).
● **Owner** Mr F Baxter
**S** (**Ref:**HM01926)

### BAXTER, GILLIAN

**Gillian Baxter**, White Friars House, 14 White Friars, Chester, **Cheshire**, CH1 1NZ, ENG.
**(T)** 01244 322275
Speciality: Chiropody. ✔
● **Chiropodist** Mrs G Baxter
**M** Yrs. Est.: 16 (**Ref:**HM01927)

### BAXTER, HELEN

**Helen Baxter**, 175 Padgate Lane, Warrington, **Cheshire**, WA1 3SW, ENG.
**(T)** 01925 244666
Speciality: Physiotherapy.
**P S T** (**Ref:**HM01928)

### BAXTER, LISA

**Lisa Baxter**, 14 Falkirk Cl, Hornchurch, **Essex**, RM11 3QJ, ENG.
**(T)** 01708 476446 **(F)** 01708 476446
Speciality: Aromatherapy, Indian Head Massage, Massage (Therapeutic), Reflexology, Baby Massage. ✔
● **Owner/Complementary Therapist**
Miss L Baxter **Q:** IIHHT.
**C** Yrs. Est.: 4 (**Ref:**HM01929)

### BAXTER, PAUL

**Paul Baxter**, 337-339 Norwich Rd, Ipswich, **Suffolk**, IP1 4BN, ENG.
**(T)** 01473 464300
Speciality: Complementary Medicines & Therapy.
**M** (**Ref:**HM01930)

### BAXTER, ROSEMARIE

**Rosemarie Baxter**, 50 Crown Woods Way, London, **London (Greater)**, SE9 2NN, ENG.
**(T)** 020 8850 2284
Speciality: Reflexology.
● **Owner** Mrs R Baxter
**S T** (**Ref:**HM01931)

### BAXTER, S M

**S M Baxter**, 20a The Quomp, Ringwood, **Hampshire**, BH24 1NS, ENG.
**(T)** 01425 480053
Speciality: Hypnosis.
**B** (**Ref:**HM01932)

### BAXTER, STEPHEN

**Stephen Baxter**, The Raworth Centre, 20-26 South St, Dorking, **Surrey**, RH4 2HQ, ENG.
**(T)** 020 8878 7896
Speciality: Alexander Technique. ✔
● **Teacher of the Alexander Technique**
Mr S Baxter **Q:** BSc, MSTAT. **M:** STAT.
**P S** Yrs. Est.: 8 (**Ref:**HM01933)

### BAXTER, STEPHEN

**Stephen Baxter**, 4 Cleveland Rd, Barnes, London, **London (Greater)**, SW13 0AB, ENG.
**(T)** 020 8878 7896
Speciality: Alexander Technique. ✔
● **Teacher of the Alexander Technique**
Mr S Baxter **Q:** BSc, MSTAT. **M:** STAT.
**P S** Yrs. Est.: 8 (**Ref:**HM01934)

### BAY HOUSE AROMATICS

**Bay House Aromatics**, 88 St Georges Rd, Brighton, **Sussex (East)**, BN2 1EE, ENG.
**(T)** 01273 601109 **(F)** 01273 601174
Speciality: Complementary Medicines & Therapy.
● **Manageress** Miss S Vinicombe
**M** (**Ref:**HM01935)

### BAY HOUSE AROMATICS

**Bay House Aromatics**, 9 Church Lane, Seaford, **Sussex (East)**, BN25 1HJ, ENG.
**(T)** 01323 892809 **(F)** 01323 873339
Speciality: Aromatherapy.
● **Owner** Mr M Fears
**M O** (**Ref:**HM01936)

### BAY TRADITIONAL REMEDY

**Bay Traditional Remedy**, 51 North Clive St, Cardiff, **Glamorgan (Vale of)**, CF11 6NQ, WAL.
**(T)** 029 2033 3395
Speciality: Complementary Medicines & Therapy.
● **Owner** Mr T Ahmed
**C M** (**Ref:**HM01937)

### BAYLEY SCHOOL OF REFLEXOLOGY

**Bayley School of Reflexology (The)**, Monks Orchard, Whitbourne, Worcester, **Worcestershire**, WR6 5RB, ENG.
**(T)** 01886 821207
Speciality: Reflexology.
● **Director** Miss N Hall
**S T** (**Ref:**HM01938)

### BAYLEY, EVA

**Eva Bayley**, 125 Addison Rd, Guildford, **Surrey**, GU1 3QE, ENG.
**(T)** 01483 531552
Speciality: Psychotherapy.
● **Owner** Ms E Bayley
**B** (**Ref:**HM01939)

### BAYLISS, CATHERINE

**Catherine Bayliss**, 130 Gilders Rd, Chessington, **Surrey**, KT9 2EA, ENG.
**(T)** 020 8397 3146
Speciality: Hypnosis.
**B** (**Ref:**HM01940)

### BAYLISS, IRENE

**Irene Bayliss**, 1a The Gdns, Langford, Lechlade, **Gloucestershire**, GL7 3LW, ENG.
**(T)** 01367 860496
Speciality: Chiropractors.
● **Owner** Mrs I Bayliss
**P S T** (**Ref:**HM01941)

### BAYLISS, JOHN

**Mr John Bayliss**, Bayliss Osteopathic Clinic, 3 Moor Lane, Chessington, **Surrey**, KT9 1BJ, ENG.
**(T)** 020 8397 3802
Speciality: Osteopathy.
**P S T** (**Ref:**HM01942)

### BAYNES, COLETTE

**Colette Baynes**, Athenry Rd, Loughrea, Galway,

Key: **B** Mind-Body Medicine **C** Complementary Medicine **H** Self Help Treatment **M** Medicinal Therapy **O** Oriental Medicine **P** Postural Therapy **S** Manipulative Structural Therapy **T** Touch Therapy

**County Galway**, IRE.
(T) 09184 1837
Speciality: Complementary Medicines & Therapy.
M (Ref:HM01943)

## BAYSIDE HOLISTIC CENTRE

**Bayside Holistic Centre**, 13D Bayside S C, Dublin, **County Dublin**, IRE.
(T) 01839 4019
Speciality: Complementary Medicines & Therapy.
M (Ref:HM01944)

## BAZALGETTE, R A

**R A Bazalgette**, 1 Springfield Cres, Poole, **Dorset**, BH14 0LL, ENG.
(T) 01202 744090
Speciality: Osteopathy.
● **Owner** Mr R Bazalgette
P S T (Ref:HM01945)

## BAZELEY, J

**J Bazeley**, 170 Clay Lane, Coventry, **Midlands (West)**, CV2 4LT, ENG.
(T) 024 7644 1028
Speciality: Chiropodists (Podiatrists).
S (Ref:HM01946)

## BCMA

**British Complementary Medicine Association**, The Hoths Centre, 249 Fosse Rd South, Leicester, **Leicestershire**, LE3 1AE, ENG.
(T) 01162 825511 (F) 01162 825611
Speciality: Complementary Medicines & Therapy.
● **Secretary** Mr J Hopson
C M (Ref:HM01947)

## BEACH, CARYL

**Caryl Beach**, 71 Tempsford, Welwyn Garden City, **Hertfordshire**, AL7 2PA, ENG.
(T) 01707 324322
Speciality: Complementary Medicines & Therapy.
C M (Ref:HM01948)

## BEACH, P J

**P J Beach**, Top Floor Flat, 99 South Hill Park, London, **London (Greater)**, NW3 2SP, ENG.
(T) 020 7794 1140
Speciality: Osteopathy.
● **Owner** Mr P Beach
P S T (Ref:HM01949)

## BEACHAM, SONJA

**Sonja Beacham**, Carlton Rd, Manchester, **Manchester (Greater)**, M16 8BQ, ENG.
(T) 01612 268489 (F) 01612 268489
Speciality: Psychotherapy.
● **Owner** Miss S Beacham
B (Ref:HM01950)

## BEACHER, D R

**D R Beacher**, 90 Junction Rd, Andover, **Hampshire**, SP10 3JB, ENG.
(T) 01264 355566
Speciality: Chiropodists (Podiatrists).
S (Ref:HM01951)

## BEACON CENTRE

**Beacon Centre (The)**, Cutteridge Farm, Whitestone, Exeter, **Devon**, EX4 2HE, ENG.
(T) 01392 811203
Speciality: Complementary Medicines & Therapy.
C M (Ref:HM01952)

## BEACONLINK

**Beaconlink**, Beaconsfield House, 135 Park Avenue, Princes Avenue, Hull, **Humberside (North)**, HU5 3EX, ENG.
(T) 01482 449823 (F) 01482 449823
Speciality: Psychology.
● **Owner** Ms M Drummond
B (Ref:HM01953)

## BEACONSFIELD CHIRO CLINIC

**Beaconsfield Chiropractic Clinic at Lanes**, 80 Gregories Rd, Beaconsfield, **Buckinghamshire**, HP9 1HL, ENG.
(T) 01494 681881
Speciality: Acupuncture, Chiropody, Chiropractic. ✔ [credit card]
● **Chiropractor** Dr J Napier Q: DC. M: GCC.
P Yrs. Est.: 23 (Ref:HM01954)

## BEACONTREE HYPNOTHERAPY

**Beacontree Hypnotherapy**, 134 Temple Avenue, Dagenham, **Essex**, RM8 1NB, ENG.
(T) 020 8592 3506
Speciality: Hypnosis.
● **Owner** Mr T Didcott
B (Ref:HM01955)

## BEADLE HOUSE CLINIC

**Beadle House Clinic**, London Rd, Sevenoaks, **Kent**, TN13 2JD, ENG.
(T) 01732 741641 (F) 01732 455919
Speciality: Physiotherapy.
● **Manager** Mr D Jones
P S T (Ref:HM01956)

## BEADLE, TRUDY

**Trudy Beadle**, 5 Hazel Gr, Bishop Auckland, **County Durham**, DL14 7RF, ENG.
(T) 01388 450258
Speciality: Complementary Medicines & Therapy.
● **Owner** Mrs T Beadle
C M (Ref:HM01957)

## BEAGLEY, D R

**D R Beagley**, 16 Prices Avenue, Margate, **Kent**, CT9 2NT, ENG.
(T) 01843 227251
Speciality: Physiotherapy.
P S T (Ref:HM01958)

## BEAL, J P

**J P Beal**, 14 Walpole Rd, Twickenham, **London (Greater)**, TW2 5SN, ENG.
(T) 020 8898 3734
Speciality: Chiropodists (Podiatrists).
● **Owner** Mr J Beal
S (Ref:HM01959)

## BEAN, GARY

**Gary Bean**, 83 Kingston Rd, Teddington, **London (Greater)**, TW11 9JX, ENG.
(T) 020 8977 3612
Speciality: Hypnosis.
B (Ref:HM01960)

## BEARA CIRCLE

**Beara Circle Ltd**, Beara Circle, Castletownbere, **County Cork**, IRE.
(T) 027 7074 4 (F) 027 7074 5
Speciality: Complementary Medicines & Therapy.
M (Ref:HM01961)

## BEARD, A

**A Beard**, 27 Malpas Rd, Newport, NP20 5PB, WAL.
(T) 01633 855180
Speciality: Chiropodists (Podiatrists).
● **Owner** Mrs A Beard
S (Ref:HM01962)

## BEARD, ANN CHRISTINE

**Ann Christine Beard**, 10 Castlemaine Drive, Cheltenham, **Gloucestershire**, GL51 0UA, ENG.
(T) 01242 577774
Speciality: Chiropodists (Podiatrists).
● **Partner** Mr D Beard
S (Ref:HM01963)

## BEARD, HELEN

**Helen Beard**, 21 Langdale, White Court, Black Notley, Braintree, **Essex**, CM7 8XA, ENG.
(T) 01376 331143
(W) www.complementary-healthcare.co.uk/info/hbeard
Speciality: Reflexology, Shiatsu.
S T (Ref:HM01964)

## BEARD, JANE

**Jane Beard**, 78 Stansted Rd, Bishop's Stortford, **Hertfordshire**, CM23 2DZ, ENG.
(T) 01279 655268
Speciality: Reflexology.
● **Owner** Mrs J Beard
S T (Ref:HM01965)

## BEARD, ROSE

**Rose Beard**, 2 Greencroft Cottage, Farley Common, Westerham, **Kent**, TN16 1UB, ENG.
(T) 01959 562938
Speciality: Hypnosis.
● **Owner** Mrs R Roberts
B (Ref:HM01966)

## BEARDMORE, CHRIS

**Chris Beardmore**, 96 Newdigate Rd, Bedworth, **Warwickshire**, CV12 8EF, ENG.
(T) 024 7631 5817
Speciality: Hypnosis.
B (Ref:HM01967)

## BEARE, M E

**M E Beare**, 35 Pennance Rd, Falmouth, **Cornwall**, TR11 4ED, ENG.
(T) 01326 313064
(E) mbeare@supanet.com
Speciality: Chiropody, Nail Surgery, Podiatry. ✔
● **Chiropodist** Mrs M Beare Q: M.S.C.P. M: S.C.P.
M Yrs. Est.: 25 (Ref:HM01968)

## BEARLEY, CAROL

**Carol Bearley**, 53 Horne St, Bury, **Lancashire**, BL9 9BW, ENG.
(T) 01617 612293
Speciality: Reflexology. ✔
● **Reflexologist** Ms C Bearley Q: IIHHT. M: BRCP.
T Yrs. Est.: 2 (Ref:HM01969)

## BEARMAN, PATRICIA

**Patricia Bearman**, Lindisfarne, Ulgham, Morpeth, **Northumberland**, NE61 3AR, ENG.
(T) 01670 790261
Speciality: Hypnosis.
● **Owner** Mrs P Bearman
B (Ref:HM01970)

## BEARSDEN CHIROPRACTIC CLINIC

**Bearsden Chiropractic Clinic**, 152 Drymen Rd, Bearsden, Glasgow, **Glasgow (City of)**, G61 3RE, SCO.
(T) 01415 700090
Speciality: Chiropractic.
● **Doctor** Dr M Stopa M: BCA, GCC.
S Yrs. Est.: 4 (Ref:HM01971)

## BEARSTED CHIROPODY & PODIATRY

**Bearsted Chiropody & Podiatry Centre**, 126 Ashford Rd, Bearsted, Maidstone, **Kent**, ME14 4LX, ENG.
(T) 01622 630393
Speciality: Chiropodists (Podiatrists).
● **Owner** Mr S Gray
S (Ref:HM01972)

## BEASLEY, CAROL

**Carol Beasley**, 41 Welbeck Avenue, Hinckley, **Leicestershire**, LE10 2JH, ENG.
(T) 01455 635376
Speciality: Hypnosis.
● **Owner** Mrs C Beasley
B (Ref:HM01973)

## BEASLEY, D

**D Beasley**, 45 Wellington Rd, Mablethorpe, **Lincolnshire**, LN12 1HT, ENG.
(T) 01507 477730 (F) 01507 477730
Speciality: Chiropodists (Podiatrists).
● **Owner** Mr D Beasley
S (Ref:HM01974)

## BEASLEY, URSULA E

**Ursula E Beasley**, 4 Buckingham Rd, Hampton, **London (Greater)**, TW12 3JA, ENG.
(T) 020 8979 5956
Speciality: Chiropodists (Podiatrists).
● **Owner** Mrs E Beasley
S (Ref:HM01975)

## BEATRICE ST CHIROPODY CLINIC

**Beatrice Street Chiropody Clinic**, 94 Beatrice St, Swindon, **Wiltshire**, SN2 1BE, ENG.
(T) 01793 420556
Speciality: Chiropodists (Podiatrists).
S (Ref:HM01976)

## BEATTIE, J

**J Beattie**, 2 The Green, Manston, Ramsgate, **Kent**, CT12 5AZ, ENG.
(T) 01843 823422
Speciality: Chiropodists (Podiatrists).
● **Owner** Mrs J Beattie



Key continued: Yrs.Est: Years Established Q: Qualifications M: Professional Membership ✔ Indemnity Insurance [credit card] Accept Credit Cards

**S** (Ref:HM01977)

## BEATTIE, JOHN

**John Beattie**, Wayside Cottage, Thurlands Drove, Upwell, Wisbech, **Cambridgeshire**, PE14 9AP, ENG.
(T) 01945 773954
Speciality: Clairvoyants & Palmists.
● **Owner** Mr J Beattie
**B** (Ref:HM01978)

## BEATTIE, R G

**R G Beattie**, Castle Clinic, St Marys St, Bridgnorth, **Shropshire**, WV16 4DW, ENG.
(T) 01746 763735
Speciality: Nail Surgery. ✓
● **Chiropodist (Podiatrist)** Mr R Beattie Q: M.S.C.P, S.R.Ch. M: S.R.Ch.
**C** Yrs. Est.: 10 (Ref:HM01979)

## BEATTIE, R G

**R G Beattie**, 796 High St, Kingswinford, **Midlands (West)**, DY6 8AA, ENG.
(T) 01384 288077
Speciality: Chiropodists (Podiatrists).
● **Owner** Mr R Beattie
**S** (Ref:HM01980)

## BEATTIE, ROBERT

**Robert Beattie**, 68 Monifieth Rd, Broughty Ferry, Dundee, **Angus**, DD5 2RX, SCO.
(T) 01382 776620
Speciality: Chiropodists (Podiatrists).
**S** (Ref:HM01981)

## BEATTY, CAROLINE

**Caroline Beatty**, 1 Dorsley Cottages, Harberton, Totnes, **Devon**, TQ9 6DL, ENG.
(T) 01803 862706
Speciality: Herbal Medicine.
● **Owner** Mrs C Beatty
**M** (Ref:HM01982)

## BEAUCHAMP BAGENAL

**Beauchamp Bagenal**, 15 Springfields, Welwyn Garden City, **Hertfordshire**, AL8 6XS, ENG.
(T) 01707 331391
Speciality: Alexander Technique, Complementary Therapy, Life Style Coaching, Stress Therapy, Voice Therapy. ✓
● **Owner** Mrs B Bagenal M: STAT.
**P** Yrs. Est.: 12 (Ref:HM01983)

## BEAUCHAMP COLCLOUGH

**Beauchamp Colclough**, 90 Harley St, London, **London (Greater)**, W1N 1AF, ENG.
(T) 020 7486 0274
Speciality: Psychology.
**B** (Ref:HM01984)

## BEAUCHAMP FOOT & BODY CARE

**Beauchamp Foot & Body Care**, 41 Beauchamp Pl, London, **London (Greater)**, SW3 1NX, ENG.
(T) 020 7225 0794
Speciality: Chiropodists (Podiatrists).
● **Manager** Mrs M Callagher
**S** (Ref:HM01985)

## BEAUMONT COLLEGE OF NAT MED

**Beaumont College of Natural Medicine**, Premier House, 23 Hinton Rd, Bournemouth, **Dorset**, BH1 2EF, ENG.
(T) 01202 708887
Speciality: Aromatherapy, Indian Head Massage, Massage (Therapeutic), Reflexology, Sports Massage.
● **Principal** Mrs D Brown
**C** (Ref:HM01986)

## BEAUMONT, ANNA

**Anna Beaumont**, 22 Church Rd, Ascot, **Berkshire**, SL5 9EX, ENG.
(T) 01344 620132
Speciality: Homeopathy.
● **Owner** Miss A Beaumont
**M** (Ref:HM01987)

## BEAUMONT, JOHN M

**John M Beaumont**, 11 Pinchbeck Rd, Spalding, **Lincolnshire**, PE11 1QD, ENG.
(T) 01775 767007
Speciality: Chiropodists (Podiatrists).
● **Owner** Mr J Beaumont
**S** (Ref:HM01988)

## BEAUMONT, ROWENA

**Rowena Beaumont**, 10 High St, Glastonbury, **Somerset**, BA6 9DU, ENG.
(T) 01458 834236
Speciality: Complementary Medicines & Therapy.
● **Director** Ms J Sanders
**M** (Ref:HM01989)

## BEAUMONT, SUSAN LAW

**Susan Law Beaumont**, Roundwood, 110 Dodworth Rd, Barnsley, **Yorkshire (South)**, S70 6HL, ENG.
(T) 01226 282560
Speciality: Acupuncture.
**O** (Ref:HM01990)

## BEAUTE PLUS

**Beaute Plus**, 36 Williamsons Pl, Dundalk, **County Louth**, IRE.
(T) 04293 52783
Speciality: Complementary Medicines & Therapy.
**M** (Ref:HM01991)

## BEAUTIFORM COLLEGE

**Beautiform College**, 10 Balaclava Rd, Kings Heath, Birmingham, **Midlands (West)**, B14 7SG, ENG.
(T) 01214 445435
(E) hypnosis@lesserion.co.uk
Speciality: Electrotherapy, Massage (Therapeutic), Relaxation and Beauty. ✓
● **Teacher/Therapist** Ms F Lesser Q: IRMT, ITEC. M: Guild.Prof.Beauty.Th.
**C** **T** Yrs. Est.: 11 (Ref:HM01992)

## BEAUTY & AROMATHERAPY

**Beauty & Aromatherapy With Katherine**, 23 Regent Trce, Harrogate, **Yorkshire (North)**, HG1 4BL, ENG.
(T) 01423 525772
Speciality: Aromatherapy.
● **Owner** Miss K Welsh
**M** **O** (Ref:HM01993)

## BEAUTY & ELECTROLYSIS CLINIC

**Beauty & Electrolysis Clinic**, 18A Church St, Oswestry, **Shropshire**, SY11 2SP, ENG.
(T) 01691 656929
Speciality: Electrolysis.
**T** (Ref:HM01994)

## BEAUTY BOX THE BEAUTY SALON

**Beauty Box The Beauty Salon**, Waltham Abbey Swimming Pool, Roundhills, Waltham Abbey, **Essex**, EN9 1UP, ENG.
(T) 01992 700925
Speciality: Electrolysis.
**T** (Ref:HM01995)

## BEAUTY CLINIC

**Beauty Clinic (The)**, 104A King St, Cottingham, **Humberside (North)**, HU16 5QE, ENG.
(T) 01482 875329
Speciality: Electrolysis.
● **Owner** Mrs J McKee
**T** (Ref:HM01996)

## BEAUTY CLINIC

**Beauty Clinic (The)**, 9 Hove Manor Prde, Hove St, Hove, **Sussex (East)**, BN3 2DF, ENG.
(T) 01273 778871
Speciality: Chiropodists (Podiatrists).
● **Owner** Mrs S Armes
**S** (Ref:HM01997)

## BEAUTY IN HARMONY

**Beauty In Harmony**, The Harmony Centre, 14A Anyards Rd, Cobham, **Surrey**, KT11 2JZ, ENG.
(T) 01932 864309
Speciality: Complementary Medicines & Therapy.
● **Owner** Mrs M Langley
**C** **M** (Ref:HM01998)

## BEAUTY IS YOURS

**Beauty Is Yours**, 121 Mill Way, Bushey, **Herefordshire**, WD23 2AE, ENG.
(T) 01923 237730
(E) sue@beautyisyours.org.uk
(W) www.beautyisyours.org.uk
Speciality: Aromatherapy, Bowen Therapy, Complementary Therapy, Crystal Healing, Indian Head Massage, Massage (Therapeutic), Nutritional Therapy, Reiki, Touch Therapy. ✓ CREDIT
● **Beauty Therapist** Ms S Bryan Q: BABTAC, CIDESCO. M: BABTAC.
**T** Yrs. Est.: 21 (Ref:HM01999)

## BEAUTY NOW

**Beauty Now**, 18 Canberra Rd, Bexleyheath, **Kent**, DA7 5SG, ENG.
(T) 020 8310 7436
Speciality: Electrolysis.
● **Owner** Miss S Robinson
**T** (Ref:HM02000)

## BEAUTY REGAIN

**Beauty Regain**, 33 Grand Prde, **County Cork**, IRE.
(T) 021 4277 181 (F) 021 4277 181
Speciality: Complementary Medicines & Therapy.
**M** (Ref:HM02001)

## BEAUTY ROOM

**Beauty Room (The)**, 253 Lodge Lane, Grays, **Essex**, RM17 5PX, ENG.
(T) 01375 381692
Speciality: Electrolysis.
● **Owner** Mrs S Richardson
**T** (Ref:HM02002)

## BEAUTY SPA

**Beauty Spa (The)**, 23 Racca Green, Knottingley, **Yorkshire (West)**, WF11 8AT, ENG.
(T) 01977 671190
Speciality: Reflexology.
● **Owner** Miss L Lee
**S** **T** (Ref:HM02003)

## BEAUTY SPOT

**Beauty Spot (The)**, Market Gate, Salop Rd, Oswestry, **Shropshire**, SY11 2NR, ENG.
(T) 01691 657707
Speciality: Complementary Medicines & Therapy.
● **Owner** Ms F Mullings
**C** **M** (Ref:HM02004)

## BEAUTY SPOT

**Beauty Spot (The)**, 11A Reva Syke Rd, Clayton, Bradford, **Yorkshire (West)**, BD14 6RA, ENG.
(T) 01274 880779
Speciality: Electrolysis.
**T** (Ref:HM02005)

## BEAUTY THERAPY CENTRE

**Beauty Therapy Centre (The)**, 77 School Lane, Manchester, **Manchester (Greater)**, M20 6WN, ENG.
(T) 01614 454445
Speciality: Complementary Medicines & Therapy, Body Massage and Waxing. ✓ CREDIT
● **Therapist** Mrs V Zarabbi M: GCT.
**C** Yrs. Est.: 3 (Ref:HM02006)

## BEAUTY WITH COMFORT

**Beauty With Comfort**, 54 Petteril, Washington, **Tyne and Wear**, NE38 9EQ, ENG.
(T) 01914 194750
Speciality: Aromatherapy.
**M** **O** (Ref:HM02007)

## BEAVEN STRESS CLINIC

**Beaven Stress Clinic**, Woodlands, Chew Hill, Chew Magna, Bristol, BS40 8SA, ENG.
(T) 01275 333795 (F) 01275 333745
Speciality: Physiotherapy.
● **Owner** Mrs D Beaven
**P** **S** **T** (Ref:HM02008)

## BEAVER, STEPHEN

**Stephen Beaver**, 23 North Rd, London, **London (Greater)**, SW19 1AQ, ENG.
(T) 020 8543 3673
Speciality: Osteopathy.
● **Owner** Mr S Beaver
**P** **S** **T** (Ref:HM02009)

## BEAVIS, ANN

**Ann Beavis**, 5 Sussex Cl, Chalfont St. Giles, **Buckinghamshire**, HP8 4PP, ENG.
(T) 01494 872359
Speciality: Physiotherapy.

Key: **B** Mind-Body Medicine **C** Complementary Medicine **H** Self Help Treatment **M** Medicinal Therapy **O** Oriental Medicine **P** Postural Therapy **S** Manipulative Structural Therapy **T** Touch Therapy

● **Owner** Mrs A Beavis
P S T (**Ref:**HM02010)

## BEAZLEIGH, SALLY

**Sally Beazleigh**, Ely Complementary Health Centre, 29a St Marys St, Ely, **Cambridgeshire**, CB7 4HF, ENG.
(T) 01353 664476
Speciality: Osteopathy.
● **Owner** Mr A Spence
P S T (**Ref:**HM02011)

## BEBER, SHEILA E

**Sheila E Beber**, 94 Station Lane, Hornchurch, **Essex**, RM12 6LX, ENG.
(T) 01708 451702
Speciality: Chiropodists (Podiatrists).
● **Owner** Mrs S Beber
S (**Ref:**HM02012)

## BECCLES ACUPUNCTURE CLINIC

**Beccles Acupuncture Clinic**, 42 Station Rd, Beccles, **Suffolk**, NR34 9QJ, ENG.
(T) 01502 715708
Speciality: Acupuncture.
O (**Ref:**HM02013)

## BECCLES PSYCHO & COUNS CTRE

**Beccles Psychotherapy & Counselling Centre**, 23A New Market, Beccles, **Suffolk**, NR34 9HD, ENG.
(T) 01502 710960
Speciality: Psychotherapy.
● **Director** Mr M Wood-Bevan
B (**Ref:**HM02014)

## BECERRA, P

**P Becerra**, London House, Bell St, Sawbridgeworth, **Hertfordshire**, CM21 9AR, ENG.
(T) 01279 600825
Speciality: Hypnosis.
B (**Ref:**HM02015)

## BECK, JAMES

**James Beck**, 1 Moor Drive, Moor Rd, Leeds, **Yorkshire (West)**, LS6 4BY, ENG.
(T) 01132 786606
Speciality: Osteopathy.
P S T (**Ref:**HM02016)

## BECKENHAM & BROMLEY

**Beckenham and Bromley Chiropratic Clinic**, 18 Oaklands Rd, Bromley, **Kent**, BR1 3SL, ENG.
(T) 020 8460 5800
Speciality: Chiropractic. ✔
● **Chiropractor** Dr S Kenneally **Q:** BSc (Chiro), DC.
● **Chiropractor** Dr J Lucas **Q:** BSc (Chiro), DC.
● **Owner** Dr C Metcalfe **Q:** BCA, DC.
P S T Yrs. Est.: 20 (**Ref:**HM02017)

## BECKENHAM ACUPUNCTURE CLINIC

**Beckenham Acupuncture Clinic**, 65 Stone Park Avenue, Beckenham, **Kent**, BR3 3LU, ENG.
(T) 020 8658 3484
Speciality: Acupuncture.
● **Owner** Mr B Pancham
O (**Ref:**HM02018)

## BECKENHAM CHINESE MED CTRE

**Beckenham Chinese Medicine Centre**, 140 High St, Beckenham, **Kent**, BR3 1EA, ENG.
(T) 020 8663 3823
Speciality: Acupuncture, Herbal Medicine. ✔
● **Owner** Mr B Zhu **Q:** MB, MSc. **M:** BAcC.
C Yrs. Est.: 2 (**Ref:**HM02019)

## BECKENHAM PHYSIOTHERAPY CLINIC

**Beckenham Physiotherapy Clinic**, 20 Bushey Way, Beckenham, **Kent**, BR3 6TB, ENG.
(T) 020 8650 0438
Speciality: Physiotherapy.
P S T (**Ref:**HM02020)

## BECKER, AMELY

**Amely Becker**, 15a Langdon Park Rd, London, **London (Greater)**, N6 5PS, ENG.
(T) 020 8348 6253
(E) amely@globalnet.co.uk
Speciality: Counselling, Gestalt Therapy, Group Therapy, Humanistic Psychology, Meditation, Psychotherapy.
● **Spiritual Counsellor/Gestalt Psychotherapist** Amely Becker **M:** AHPP, UKCP.
M (**Ref:**HM02021)

## BECKER, JACKI

**Jacki Becker RS Hom**, The Homeopathy Centre, Totnes, **Devon**, TQ9 5PG, ENG.
(T) 01803 840614
Speciality: Homeopathy.
M (**Ref:**HM02022)

## BECKETT, DALE (DR)

**Dr Dale Beckett**, 18 Ockendon Rd, London, **London (Greater)**, N1 3NP, ENG.
(T) 020 7704 9999 (F) 020 7354 5170
Speciality: Hypnosis.
● **Principal** Dr D Beckett
B (**Ref:**HM02023)

## BECKETT, L J

**L J Beckett**, 2 Guildford Rd, Bagshot, **Surrey**, GU19 5JH, ENG.
(T) 01276 472040
Speciality: Physiotherapy.
P S T (**Ref:**HM02024)

## BECKETT, MAURICE

**Maurice Beckett**, 4 Finnick Glen, Alloway, Ayr, **Ayrshire (South)**, KA7 4RF, SCO.
(T) 01292 445174
Speciality: Hypnosis.
B (**Ref:**HM02025)

## BECKETT, MICHAEL D

**Michael D Beckett**, 23 Poole Rd, Bournemouth, **Dorset**, BH4 9DF, ENG.
(T) 01202 764161
Speciality: Osteopathy.
P S T (**Ref:**HM02026)

## BECKETT, V C

**V C Beckett**, 5 Highlands Park, Halifax, **Yorkshire (West)**, HX2 9UL, ENG.
(T) 01422 244874
Speciality: Chiropodists (Podiatrists).
● **Owner** Mr V Beckett
S (**Ref:**HM02027)

## BECKETT-GEORGE, D

**D Beckett-George**, 33 Welholme Avenue, Grimsby, **Humberside (South)**, DN32 0DZ, ENG.
(T) 01472 342329
Speciality: Acupuncture.
O (**Ref:**HM02028)

## BECKWITH, JONATHAN

**Jonathan Beckwith**, 32A Northampton Rd, Wellingborough, **Northamptonshire**, NN8 3HG, ENG.
(T) 01933 228568
Speciality: Reflexology.
S T (**Ref:**HM02029)

## BECONTREE NHS THERAPY

**Becontree NHS Therapy Service**, 508 Beacontree Avenue, Dagenham, **Essex**, RM8 3HR, ENG.
(T) 020 8984 1234 (F) 020 8593 7318
Speciality: Psychotherapy.
● **Manager** Mr I Brown
B (**Ref:**HM02030)

## BEDDEN, TONY

**Tony Bedden**, Andelain, Drift Rd, Whitehill, Bordon, **Hampshire**, GU35 9DZ, ENG.
(T) 01420 474651
Speciality: Complementary Medicines & Therapy.
● **Owner** Mr T Bedden
C M (**Ref:**HM02031)

## BEDFORD ACUPUNCTURE CLINIC

**Bedford Acupuncture Clinic**, 27 Colchester Way, Bedford, **Bedfordshire**, MK41 8BG, ENG.
(T) 01234 261932
Speciality: Acupuncture. ✔
● **Owner** Mr O Ali **Q:** RMANM. **M:** RMANM.
O Yrs. Est.: 19 (**Ref:**HM02032)

## BEDFORD CHIROPRACTIC SURGERY

**Bedford Chiropractic Surgery**, 20 De Parys Avenue, Bedford, **Bedfordshire**, MK40 2TW, ENG.
(T) 01234 353937
Speciality: Chiropractic. ✔
● **Owner** Dr C Wain **Q:** DC. **M:** GCC.
P Yrs. Est.: 23 (**Ref:**HM02033)

## BEDFORD HOUSE CLINIC

**Bedford House Clinic**, Bedford House, Havelock Pl, Stoke-On-Trent, **Staffordshire**, ST1 4PR, ENG.
(T) 01782 425010 (F) 01782 425006
Speciality: Chiropodists (Podiatrists).
S (**Ref:**HM02034)

## BEDFORD PHYSIOTHERAPY CENTRE

**Bedford Physiotherapy Centre**, 31 Chiltern Avenue, Bedford, **Bedfordshire**, MK41 9EQ, ENG.
(T) 01234 266222 (F) 01234 266222
(W) www.betterpatientcare.co.uk
Speciality: Acupuncture, Physiotherapy. ✔
● **Physiotherapist** Ms J Johnson **Q:** MCSP, SRP. **M:** CSP.
● **Partner** Mrs R Kier **Q:** MCSP, SRP. **M:** CSP.
S Yrs. Est.: 8 (**Ref:**HM02035)

## BEDFORD PHYSIOTHERAPY CLINIC

**Bedford Physiotherapy Clinic**, Hassett House, Hassett St, Bedford, **Bedfordshire**, MK40 1HA, ENG.
(T) 01234 271090 (F) 01234 271090
Speciality: Physiotherapy.
● **Owner** Mrs S Tucker
P S T (**Ref:**HM02036)

## BEDFORD PSYCHOTHERAPY PRACTICE

**Bedford Psycotherapy Practice**, Flat 4 Priory Trce, Roise St, Bedford, **Bedfordshire**, MK40 1JE, ENG.
(T) 01234 267903
Speciality: Psychotherapy.
● **Partner** Mr A Dutton
B (**Ref:**HM02037)

## BEDFORD, H & B

**H & B Bedford**, 114 Osborne Rd, Farnborough, **Hampshire**, GU14 6AS, ENG.
(T) 01252 523808
Speciality: Chiropodists (Podiatrists).
● **Partner** Mr H Bedford
S (**Ref:**HM02038)

## BEDFORD, JANET

**Janet Bedford**, 8 Dewhurst Rd, Cheshunt, Waltham Cross, **Hertfordshire**, EN8 9PE, ENG.
(T) 01992 622575
Speciality: Reflexology.
S T (**Ref:**HM02039)

## BEDFORD, PAULINE

**Pauline Bedford**, The Anchorage, Harwich Rd, Beaumont, Clacton-On-Sea, **Essex**, CO16 0AS, ENG.
(T) 01255 861417
Speciality: Herbalists.
● **Owner** Mrs P Bedford
M (**Ref:**HM02040)

## BEDFORD, SUSAN

**Susan Bedford**, The Burns Practice, 4 Albion Pl, Doncaster, **Yorkshire (South)**, DN1 2EG, ENG.
(T) 01302 329311
Speciality: Homeopathy.
● **Owner** Ms S Bedford
M (**Ref:**HM02041)

## BEDFORD, TOM

**Tom Bedford**, 34 Cowley Rd, Oxford, **Oxfordshire**, OX4 1HZ, ENG.
(T) 01865 200678
Speciality: Osteopathy.
● **Professor** Mr T Bedford
P S T (**Ref:**HM02042)

## BEDI, N P S (DR)

**Dr N P S Bedi**, 139 Humberston Avenue, Humberston, Grimsby, **Humberside (South)**, DN36 4ST, ENG.
(T) 01472 210444 (F) 01472 313412
Speciality: Acupuncture.
● **Owner** Dr N Bedi
O (**Ref:**HM02043)

## BEDINGFELD, ANN

**Ann Bedingfeld**, 48A Carminia Rd, Balham,



Key continued: **Yrs.Est:** Years Established **Q:** Qualifications **M:** Professional Membership ✔ Indemnity Insurance Accept Credit Cards

London, **London (Greater)**, SW17 8AH, ENG.
**(T)** 020 8675 5744
Speciality: Reflexology.
● **Owner** Ms A Bedingfeld
**S T** (**Ref:**HM02044)

## BEE NATURAL PRODUCTS

**Bee Natural Products**, 26 Beacon Rd, Broadstairs, **Kent**, CT10 3DF, ENG.
**(T)** 01843 871050 **(F)** 01843 871050
Speciality: Complementary Medicines & Therapy.
● **Owner** Mr N Girolami
**P** (**Ref:**HM02045)

## BEECH HOUSE CLINIC

**Vinewood Healthcare**, Station Rd, Ilminster, **Somerset**, TA19 9BE, ENG.
**(T)** 01460 54888
Speciality: Acupuncture, Chinese Herbal Medicine, Chiropractic, Osteopathy. ✔
● **Chiropractor** Dr J Vine **Q:** DC. **M:** BCA.
● **Therapist** Mrs M Harris
● **Osteopath** Dr P Hands **M:** BACP.
**C** Yrs. Est.: 25 (**Ref:**HM02046)

## BEECH, MICHAEL

**Michael Beech**, West Midland House, Gipsy Lane, Willenhall, **Midlands (West)**, WV13 2HA, ENG.
**(T)** 01902 482440
Speciality: Chiropodists (Podiatrists).
● **Owner** Mr M Beech
**S** (**Ref:**HM02047)

## BEECH, STEVEN

**Steven Beech**, 13 Marnhull Rd, Poole, **Dorset**, BH15 2EX, ENG.
**(T)** 01202 686429
Speciality: Alexander Technique.
● **Owner** Mr S Beech
**P S** (**Ref:**HM02048)

## BEECHES PHYSICAL THERAPY

**Beeches Physical Therapy Clinic (The)**, 35 Beeches Avenue, Carshalton, **Surrey**, SM5 3LJ, ENG.
**(T)** 020 8773 8760
Speciality: Complementary Medicines & Therapy.
**C M** (**Ref:**HM02049)

## BEECHGROVE CLINIC

**Beechgrove Clinic**, 60 Midstocket Rd, Aberdeen, **Aberdeenshire**, AB15 5JB, SCO.
**(T)** 01224 635644
Speciality: Autogenic Training, Biofeedback, Biomechanics, Cranial Osteopathy, Electrotherapy, Manipulation, Massage (Therapeutic), Osteopathy, Postural Integration, Ultrasonics, Yoga. ✔
● **Osteopath** Dr P Wilson **Q:** BSc, DO, PhD. **M:** GOsC.
● **Physiotherapist** Ms L Newcombe **Q:** MCSP, SRP. **M:** CSP.
**S** Yrs. Est.: 8 (**Ref:**HM02050)

## BEECHWOOD CENTRE

**Beechwood Centre (The)**, The Cottage, Forrabury, Boscastle, **Cornwall**, PL35 0DJ, ENG.
**(T)** 01840 250776
Speciality: Hypnotherapy.
● **Owner** Mr N Beechwood
**B** (**Ref:**HM02051)

## BEECHWOOD CHIROPODY

**Beechwood Chiropody**, 8a Beechwood Centre, Church St, Woodlesford, Leeds, **Yorkshire (West)**, LS26 8RE, ENG.
**(T)** 01132 826431
Speciality: Chiropodists (Podiatrists).
● **Owner** Mr D Buchanan
**S** (**Ref:**HM02052)

## BEENEY, CHERYL

**Cheryl Beeney**, 87 Bodmin Rd, Chelmsford, **Essex**, CM1 6LN, ENG.
**(T)** 01245 351561
Speciality: Reflexology.
● **Owner** Mrs C Beeney
**S T** (**Ref:**HM02053)

## BEER, L & M

**L & M Beer**, Tenby House, Keycol Hill, Newington, Sittingbourne, **Kent**, ME9 7LG, ENG.
**(T)** 01795 844499 **(F)** 01795 843460
Speciality: Aromatherapy.
● **Partner** Mrs L Beer
**M O** (**Ref:**HM02054)

## BEER, SUSAN

**Susan Beer**, 8b Beresford Rd, St. Albans, **Hertfordshire**, AL1 5NP, ENG.
**(T)** 01727 842300
Speciality: Chiropodists (Podiatrists).
● **Owner** Mrs S Beer
**S** (**Ref:**HM02055)

## BEES CRYSTAL SHOP

**Bees Crystal Shop**, 64 Victoria Rd, Horley, **Surrey**, RH6 7PZ, ENG.
**(T)** 01293 772526
Speciality: Complementary Medicines & Therapy.
● **Owner** Mrs B Blackburn
**C M** (**Ref:**HM02056)

## BEESLEY, RODERICK

**Roderick Beesley**, 56 St Barnabas Rd, Cambridge, **Cambridgeshire**, CB1 2DE, ENG.
**(T)** 01223 350543
Speciality: Alexander Technique.
**P S** (**Ref:**HM02057)

## BEESTON CHIROPRACTIC CLINIC

**Beeston Chiropractic Clinic**, 191 Queens Rd, Beeston, Nottingham, **Nottinghamshire**, NG9 2BZ, ENG.
**(T)** 01159 225085
Speciality: Chiropractic.
● **Owner** Dr A Newton
**P S T** (**Ref:**HM02058)

## BEESTON NATURAL THERAPY CENTRE

**Beeston Natural Therapy Centre**, 1 Marlborough Rd, Beeston, Nottingham, **Nottinghamshire**, NG9 2HG, ENG.
**(T)** 01159 431204
Speciality: Osteopathy.
● **Owner** Mr R Hepple
**P S T** (**Ref:**HM02059)

## BEESTON PHYSIO & SPORTS CLNC

**Beeston Physiotherapy & Sports Injury Clinic**, 12 Chilwell Rd, Beeston, Nottingham, **Nottinghamshire**, NG9 1EJ, ENG.
**(T)** 01159 431230 **(F)** 01159 431230
Speciality: Physiotherapy. ✔
● **Physiotherapist** Mr S McVeigh **Q:** MCSP, SRP. **M:** CSP.
● **Manager** Mr I Tomlinson
**S** (**Ref:**HM02060)

## BEESTON, J

**John Beeston**, 759 Rochdale Rd, Royton, Oldham, **Lancashire**, OL2 5UW, ENG.
**(T)** 01616 248424
Speciality: Electrotherapy, Herbal Medicine, Manipulation, Massage (Therapeutic), Ultrasonics. ✔
● **Physiotherapist** Mr J Beeston **Q:** Grad Dip Phys, MCSP, SRP. **M:** CSP.
**S** Yrs. Est.: 50 (**Ref:**HM02061)

## BEGBIE, GARY

**Gary Begbie**, 9 Athelstan Rd, Hastings, **Sussex (East)**, TN35 5JB, ENG.
**(T)** 01424 719674
Speciality: Chiropodists (Podiatrists).
**S** (**Ref:**HM02062)

## BEGINNERS YOGA VIDEO

**Beginners Yoga Video**, 10 Cunningham Avenue, Wrexham, LL13 8SY, WAL.
**(T)** 01978 353127
Speciality: Relaxation Technique.
● **Owner** Mr J Patel
**H T** (**Ref:**HM02063)

## BEHAN, J C

**J C Behan**, 9 Green St, Sandbach, **Cheshire**, CW11 1GX, ENG.
**(T)** 01270 763770
Speciality: Chiropodists (Podiatrists).
● **Partner** Mrs M Behan
**S** (**Ref:**HM02064)

## BEHAVIORAL PSYCHOTHERAPY SVS

**Behavioral Psychotherapy Services Ltd**, 92 Tuam Rd, London, **London (Greater)**, SE18 2QU, ENG.
**(T)** 020 8473 5937
Speciality: Psychotherapy.
**B** (**Ref:**HM02065)

## BEHAVIOUR TRANSFORMATION

**Behaviour Transformation Ltd**, Flat 22, Bridge Wharf, 156 Caledonian Rd, London, **London (Greater)**, N1 9UU, ENG.
**(T)** 020 7278 6006 **(F)** 020 7278 0255
Speciality: Psychology.
● **Owner** Mr M Wellin
**B** (**Ref:**HM02066)

## BEHESHT

**Behesht**, 3 St Andrews Rd South, Lytham St. Annes, **Lancashire**, FY8 1SX, ENG.
**(T)** 01253 723030
Speciality: Aromatherapy.
● **Partner** Miss J McLaren
**M O** (**Ref:**HM02067)

## BEHIND THE VEIL

**Behind The Veil**, 1239-1241 Cathcart Rd, Mount Florida, Glasgow, **Glasgow (City of)**, G42 9HA, SCO.
**(T)** 01416 332444
Speciality: Absent Healing, Aromatherapy, Aura Therapy, Crystal Healing, Dowsing, Healer, Healing Therapy, Holistic Healing, Indian Head Massage, Massage (Therapeutic), Reiki, Spiritual Healing. ✔
● **Spiritual Healer** Ms E Hooper
**(T)** 01414 400608
● **Holistic Therapist** Frances Marriot
● **Clinical Aromatherapist** Ms V Bell
● **Reiki Healer** Ms P McGuire **Q:** Reiki 1, Reiki 2.
**B** (**Ref:**HM02068)

## BEIGHTON, J W

**J W Beighton/V R Beighton**, 10 Cobden St, Cross Keys, Newport, NP11 7PF, WAL.
**(T)** 01495 272167 **(F)** 01495 272167
Speciality: Acupuncture, Complementary Therapy, Homeopathy, Reflexology. ✔
● **Reflexologist** Victoria Beighton **Q:** Dip.Reflex. **M:** BRCP.
● **Homeopath/Acupuncturist** Joseph Beighton **Q:** MMAA, RSHom. **M:** MAA, Soc.Hom.
**C M** Yrs. Est.: 15 (**Ref:**HM02069)

## BEIGHTON, JOSEPH

**Joseph Beighton**, 9 Church St, Bridgwater, **Somerset**, TA6 5AT, ENG.
**(T)** 01278 457730
Speciality: Homeopathy.
● **Principal** Mr S Woods
**M** (**Ref:**HM02070)

## BEIJING ACUPUNCTURE CLINIC

**Beijing Acupuncture Clinic**, 105 London Rd, Morden, **Surrey**, SM4 5HP, ENG.
**(T)** 020 8288 9038
Speciality: Acupuncture.
**O** (**Ref:**HM02071)

## BEISLY, N L (DR)

**Dr N L Beisly**, 14a Chapel St, Newport, **Isle of Wight**, PO30 1PY, ENG.
**(T)** 01983 529646
Speciality: Osteopathy.
● **Owner** Dr N Beisly **Q:** BS, LRCP, MB.
**P S T** (**Ref:**HM02072)

## BEITGHTON, JO

**Jo Beitghton**, Natural Health Clinic, 98 Cathedral Rd, Cardiff, **Glamorgan (Vale of)**, CF11 9LP, WAL.
**(T)** 029 2022 2221
Speciality: Homeopathy.
● **Practice Manager** Mrs L Powell
**M** (**Ref:**HM02073)

## BEITH, W R

**W R Beith**, 31 Moorway, Poulton-le-Fylde, **Lancashire**, FY6 7EX, ENG.
**(T)** 01253 885222
Speciality: Physiotherapy.
**P S T** (**Ref:**HM02074)

Key: **B** Mind-Body Medicine **C** Complementary Medicine **H** Self Help Treatment **M** Medicinal Therapy **O** Oriental Medicine **P** Postural Therapy **S** Manipulative Structural Therapy **T** Touch Therapy

**BEJING TONG REN TANG**

**Bejing Tong Ren Tang (UK) Ltd**, Shaftesbury Avenue, London, **London (Greater)**, W1V 7DJ, ENG.
(T) 020 7287 2308 (F) 020 7287 0068
Speciality: Herbal Medicine.
● **Professor** Mr L Lou
M (Ref:HM02075)

**BELDER, TAMARA**

**Tamara Belder**, Scott St Complementary Therapy Centre, 58 Scott St, Barrow-in-Furness, **Cumbria**, LA14 1QE, ENG.
(T) 01229 826700
Speciality: Complementary Medicines & Therapy.
M (Ref:HM02076)

**BELFAST CHIROPRACTIC CLINIC**

**Belfast Chiropractic Clinic (The)**, 228 Ormeau Rd, Belfast, **County Antrim**, BT7 2FZ, NIR.
(T) 028 9064 1111
Speciality: Chiropractic.
● **Owner** Mr R Mackie
P S T (Ref:HM02077)

**BELGRAVE**

**Belgrave**, 3 Charleston Rd, Rathmines, **County Dublin**, IRE.
(T) 01497 5666
Speciality: Complementary Medicines & Therapy.
M (Ref:HM02078)

**BELGRAVE ACUPUNCTURE CLINIC**

**Belgrave Acupuncture Clinic**, The Basement, 17 Belgrave Sq, Monkstown, **County Dublin**, IRE.
(T) 01284 5400
Speciality: Acupuncture.
O (Ref:HM02079)

**BELL CLINIC**

**Bell Clinic**, 69 Downscroft Gardens, Hedge End, **Hampshire**, SO30 4RS, ENG.
(T) 01489 789189
Speciality: Acupuncture.
O (Ref:HM02080)

**BELL, C M**

**C M Bell**, 4 Granville Sq, Scarborough, **Yorkshire (North)**, YO11 2QZ, ENG.
(T) 01723 375487
Speciality: Physiotherapy.
● **Owner** Mr C Bell
P S T (Ref:HM02081)

**BELL, DERYN**

**Deryn Bell**, Arden House, 15 Harrington Villas, Brighton, **Sussex (East)**, BN1 6RG, ENG.
(T) 01273 507412 (F) 01273 507412
Speciality: Osteopathy.
● **Owner** Ms D Bell
P S T (Ref:HM02082)

**BELL, DOUGLAS W**

**Douglas W Bell**, 2 Wheatfield Rd, Ayr, **Ayrshire (South)**, KA7 2XB, SCO.
(T) 01292 280494 (F) 01292 287142
Speciality: Complementary Medicines & Therapy.
● **Owner** Mr W Bell
C M (Ref:HM02083)

**BELL, LIZ**

**Liz Bell**, 38B Argyle Rd, London, **London (Greater)**, W13 8AA, ENG.
(T) 020 8998 0381
Speciality: Reflexology.
S T (Ref:HM02084)

**BELL, MARTYN**

**Martyn Bell**, 15 Marshworth, Tinkers Bridge, Milton Keynes, **Buckinghamshire**, MK6 3DA, ENG.
(T) 01908 609575
Speciality: Chiropodists (Podiatrists).
● **Owner** Mr M Bell
S (Ref:HM02085)

**BELL, MAUREEN**

**Maureen Bell**, North St, Armadale, Bathgate, **Lothian (West)**, EH48 3QB, SCO.
(T) 01506 633713
Speciality: Chiropodists (Podiatrists).
S (Ref:HM02086)

**BELL, MIDGE**

**Midge Bell**, 36 Rodney St, Rochdale, **Lancashire**, OL11 3DF, ENG.
(T) 01706 341207
Speciality: Chiropodists (Podiatrists).
● **Owner** Mrs M Bell
S (Ref:HM02087)

**BELL, PATRICIA**

**Patricia Bell**, 274 Highfield Rd, Hall Green, Birmingham, **Midlands (West)**, B28 0DP, ENG.
(T) 01217 772676
Speciality: Hypnosis.
B (Ref:HM02088)

**BELL, PHILIP (DR)**

**Dr Philip Bell**, Blackberry Orthopaedic Clinic, Blackberry Court, Walnut Tree, Milton Keynes, **Buckinghamshire**, MK7 7PB, ENG.
(T) 01908 604666
Speciality: Osteopathy.
P S T (Ref:HM02089)

**BELL, T A**

**T A Bell**, Cowley Gore, Cowley Lane, Holmesfield, Dronfield, **Derbyshire**, S18 7SD, ENG.
(T) 01142 890187
Speciality: Physiotherapy.
P S T (Ref:HM02090)

**BELL, W DOUGLAS**

**W Douglas Bell**, 11 Stonefield Pk, Ayr, **Ayrshire (South)**, KA7 4HS, SCO.
(T) 01292 440730
(W) www.nutriherb.co.uk
Speciality: Chiropody, Magnetic Therapy, Reflexology, Cymatic Therapy. ✔ [credit card]
● **Practitioner** Dr W Bell M: IIR.
C Yrs. Est.: 17 (**Ref:**HM02091)

**BELL, Y**

**Y Bell**, 49 Aspley Hill, Woburn Sands, Milton Keynes, **Buckinghamshire**, MK17 8NW, ENG.
(T) 01908 282992
Speciality: Reflexology.
● **Owner** Mr Y Bell
S T (Ref:HM02092)

**BELLAMY PARTNERSHIP**

**Bellamy Partnership**, 210 Upper Shoreham Rd, Shoreham-by-Sea, **Sussex (West)**, BN43 6BG, ENG.
(T) 01273 464900 (F) 01273 454176
(E) abellamy@mistral.co.uk
Speciality: Acupuncture, Osteopathy. ✔
● **Osteopath** Mr A Bellamy Q: DO, SRN. M: GOsC.
S Yrs. Est.: 11 (**Ref:**HM02093)

**BELLAMY, ANTHO A P**

**Antho A P Bellamy**, 32 Mill Lane, Shoreham-by-Sea, **Sussex (West)**, BN43 5AG, ENG.
(T) 01273 464900
Speciality: Osteopathy.
P S T (Ref:HM02094)

**BELLAMY, ELIZABETH**

**Elizabeth Bellamy**, 11 Bennetts Hill, Dunton Bassett, Lutterworth, **Leicestershire**, LE17 5JJ, ENG.
(T) 01455 209314
Speciality: Reflexology.
S T (Ref:HM02095)

**BELLAMY, K J**

**K J Bellamy**, 30 Hatfield Rd, Margate, **Kent**, CT9 5AT, ENG.
(T) 01843 223607
Speciality: Osteopathy.
● **Owner** Mr K Bellamy
P S T (Ref:HM02096)

**BELLAMY, R D**

**R D Bellamy**, 69 Douglas Cres, Houghton Regis, Dunstable, **Bedfordshire**, LU5 5AS, ENG.
(T) 01582 661199
(E) robert.bellamy@virgin.net
Speciality: Osteopathy. ✔
● **Osteopath** Mr R Bellamy Q: BSc, Hons (OST). M: GOsC.
S Yrs. Est.: 4 (**Ref:**HM02097)

**BELLAMY, YVONNE**

**Yvonne Bellamy**, 18 School Rd, Laughton, Sheffield, **Yorkshire (South)**, S25 1YP, ENG.
(T) 01909 567816
Speciality: Chiropodists (Podiatrists).
S (Ref:HM02098)

**BELLE, M**

**M Belle**, 44A Green Lane, Sale, **Cheshire**, M33 5PP, ENG.
(T) 01613 745817
Speciality: Complementary Medicines & Therapy.
● **Owner** Miss M Knowles
M (Ref:HM02099)

**BELLEW, CHRIS**

**Chris Bellew**, 276 Coalway Rd, Wolverhampton, **Midlands (West)**, WV3 7NP, ENG.
(T) 01902 333166
Speciality: Chiropodists (Podiatrists).
● **Owner** Mr C Bellew
S (Ref:HM02100)

**BELLINGER, A**

**A Bellinger**, Cornwall Buildings, 45 Newhall St, Birmingham, **Midlands (West)**, B3 3QR, ENG.
(T) 01212 369016
Speciality: Chiropodists (Podiatrists).
● **Partner** Miss A Bellinger
S (Ref:HM02101)

**BELLINGHAM, JANE**

**Jane Bellingham**, 72 Abington Avenue, Northampton, **Northamptonshire**, NN1 4PA, ENG.
(T) 01604 624638
Speciality: Osteopathy.
● **Owner** Mrs J Bellingham
P S T (Ref:HM02102)

**BELLISSIMA**

**Bellissima**, 34 St Marks Rd, Bush Hill Park, Enfield, **London (Greater)**, EN1 1BE, ENG.
(T) 020 8367 4510
(W) www.complementary-healthcare.co.uk/info/bellissima
Speciality: Reflexology.
S T (Ref:HM02103)

**BELLMAN, ERICA**

**Erica Bellman**, 9 Wyndham Avenue, High Wycombe, **Buckinghamshire**, HP13 5EP, ENG.
(T) 01494 474926
Speciality: Homeopathy.
● **Owner** Ms E Bellman
M (Ref:HM02104)

**BELLO, L A**

**L A Bello**, 1a Forest Rd, Loughton, **Essex**, IG10 1DR, ENG.
(T) 020 8502 2625
Speciality: Osteopathy.
P S T (Ref:HM02105)

**BELLO, L A**

**L A Bello**, 40 Stronsa Rd, Shepherds Bush, London, **London (Greater)**, W12 9LB, ENG.
(T) 020 8743 5976
Speciality: Osteopathy.
P S T (Ref:HM02106)

**BELLRINGER INTERNATIONAL**

**Bellringer International**, 13 Dowding Way, Bowerhill, Melksham, **Wiltshire**, SN12 6SG, ENG.
(T) 01225 709138
Speciality: Complementary Medicines & Therapy.
C M (Ref:HM02107)

**BELMONT PHYSIOTHERAPY PRACTICE**

**Belmont Physiotherapy Practice**, 572 Kenton Lane, Harrow, **London (Greater)**, HA3 7LJ, ENG.
(T) 020 8863 8503
Speciality: Acupuncture, Physiotherapy. ✔
● **Physiotherapist** Mr P Rao Q: MCSP, SRP. M: CSP.
S Yrs. Est.: 4 (**Ref:**HM02108)

**BELMONTE, P**

**P Belmonte**, Flat 6 The Old School, Frome, **Somerset**, BA11 1EU, ENG.
(T) 01373 464968



Key continued: Yrs.Est: Years Established Q: Qualifications M: Professional Membership ✔ Indemnity Insurance [credit card] Accept Credit Cards

Speciality: Complementary Medicines & Therapy.
M (Ref:HM02109)

## BELPER BACKPAIN CLINIC

**Belper Backpain Clinic**, 5a North Mill Office Suites, Bridge Foot, Belper, **Derbyshire**, DE56 1YD, ENG.
(T) 01773 822523
Speciality: Absent Healing, Crystal Healing, Electrotherapy, Iridology, Kinesiology, Manipulation, Massage (Therapeutic), Reiki, Remedial Massage, Ultrasonics, Neural Massage, Mobilisation. ✓
● **Owner** Mr M Thacker M: LCSP.
C S (Ref:HM02110)

## BELPER HOMEOPATHY

**Belper Homeopathy**, 18 Brookside, Belper, **Derbyshire**, DE56 1UR, ENG.
(T) 01773 828032
(E) lorraine@belpham.screaming.net
Speciality: Homeopathy. ✓
● **Homeopath** Ms L Hart Q: RSHom. M: Soc.Hom.
C Yrs. Est.: 12 (Ref:HM02111)

## BELPER NATURAL HEALTH CENTRE

**Belper Natural Health Centre**, 12 Chapel St, Belper, **Derbyshire**, DE56 1AR, ENG.
(T) 01773 820220
Speciality: Acupuncture, Aromatherapy, Counselling, Cranial Osteopathy, Faith Healing, Healer, Herbal Medicine, Homeopathy, Indian Head Massage, Kinesiology, Manipulation, Massage (Therapeutic), Moxibustion, Naturopathy, Nutritional Therapy, Oriental Diagnosis, Osteopathy, Reflexology, Reiki, Spiritual Healing, Stress Therapy, Vitamin Therapy. ✓
● **Homeopath** Mr T Grinney Q: RSHom. M: NWCH.
● **Clinic Manager/Osteopath** Mr I Rumbold Q: DO.
● **Homeopath** Fiona Winstanley Q: Dip.Hom.
● **Acupuncturist** Dr X Lu Q: BSc, MB, MD.
● **Medical Herbalist** Mrs J Paulson Q: MNIMH.
● **Acupuncturist** Mr N Lintott Q: BA, Lic.Ac, MBAcC.
● **Osteopath** Rachel Shaw Q: BSc (Hons).
● **Reflexologist/Reiki Healer** Shelia Heywood Q: MAR.
H O S Yrs. Est.: 8 (Ref:HM02112)

## BELPER PHYSIOTHERAPY CLINIC

**Belper Physiotherapy Clinic**, 57 Bridge St, Belper, **Derbyshire**, DE56 1AY, ENG.
(T) 01773 829623
Speciality: Physiotherapy.
● **Owner** Ms S Walker
P S T (Ref:HM02113)

## BELSHAW, KAREN

**Karen Belshaw B Sc Hons**, 53B Raglan Rd, Ballsbridge, **County Dublin**, IRE.
(T) 01668 7934
Speciality: Complementary Medicines & Therapy.
M (Ref:HM02114)

## BELSIZE HOUSE

**Belsize House**, Bradford St, Walsall, **Midlands (West)**, WS1 1PN, ENG.
(T) 01922 649779
Speciality: Chiropodists (Podiatrists).
S (Ref:HM02115)

## BELTAIN CENTRE

**Beltain Centre Of Natural Therapies**, Courtyard, 1 Colliton Walk, Dorchester, **Dorset**, DT1 1TZ, ENG.
(T) 01305 267069
Speciality: Absent Healing, Counselling, Faith Healing, Healer, Healing Therapy, Meditation, Reiki. ✓
● **Reiki Master** Ms P Garland Q: Reiki Master.
H Yrs. Est.: 7 (Ref:HM02116)

## BELTAIN CENTRE

**R M Sleet & S Gale T/A Beltain Consultancy**, The Courtyard, 1 Colliton Walk, Dorchester, **Dorset**, DT1 1TZ, ENG.
(T) 01305 267069
Speciality: Complementary Therapy, Counselling, Healing Therapy, Holistic Healing, Hypnosis, Hypnotherapy, Meditation, Psychotherapy, Stress Therapy, Visualisation Therapy, Hypno-Analytical/Investigative Techniques. ✓
● **Partner/Hypnotherapist** Ms S Gale M: INT.
● **Co-ordinator/Tutor** Mr R Sleet Q: BA (Hons). M: INT.
B H O Yrs. Est.: 10 (Ref:HM02117)

## BELVAIN, E

**E Belvain**, 30 Waterloo St, Hove, **Sussex (East)**, BN3 1AN, ENG.
(T) 01273 777740
(W) www.lichfieldhouse.freeserve.co.uk
Speciality: Acupressure, Aromatherapy, Massage (Therapeutic), Reflexology, Shiatsu. ✓
● **Aromatherapist** Ms E Belvain M: ISPA.
C (Ref:HM02118)

## BELVEDERE PHYSIO CLINIC

**Belvedere Physiotherapy Clinic (The)**, 40 Belvedere Rd, Coventry, **Midlands (West)**, CV5 6PG, ENG.
(T) 024 7667 2725
Speciality: Physiotherapy.
● **Owner** Mrs L Pateman
P S T (Ref:HM02119)

## BENATAR, WENDY

**Wendy Benatar**, 12 Woodhouse Eaves, Northwood, **London (Greater)**, HA6 3NF, ENG.
(T) 01923 824032
Speciality: Acupuncture.
● **Owner** Mrs W Benatar
O (Ref:HM02120)

## BENCH, PAUL

**Paul Bench**, Shrewsbury, **Shropshire**, SY2, ENG.
(T) 01743 233164
Speciality: Bach Remedies.
M (Ref:HM02121)

## BENDER, J

**J Bender**, 153 Elgin Cres, London, **London (Greater)**, W11 2JH, ENG.
(T) 020 7229 5796
Speciality: Chiropodists (Podiatrists).
S (Ref:HM02122)

## BENDER, S

**S Bender**, 153 Elgin Cres, London, **London (Greater)**, W11 2JH, ENG.
(T) 020 7792 1922
Speciality: Aromatherapy.
● **Owner** Mrs S Bender
M O (Ref:HM02123)

## BENDLE CALDER

**Bendle Calder**, 183 Whitham Rd, Sheffield, **Yorkshire (South)**, S10 2SN, ENG.
(T) 01142 665902 (F) 01142 665902
Speciality: Herbalists.
● **Owner** Dr M Hayes-Allen
M (Ref:HM02124)

## BENEDICTA

**Benedicta**, Blake House Craft Centre, Blake End, Braintree, **Essex**, CM7 8SH, ENG.
(T) 01376 550940 (F) 01376 550940
(E) aroma21@aol.com
(W) www.benedicta.co.uk
Speciality: Aromatherapy, Bach Remedies, Complementary Therapy, Counselling, Holistic Healing, Indian Head Massage, Massage (Therapeutic), Metamorphic Therapy, Reflexology, Reiki, Stress Therapy. ✓
● **Owner** Ms A Nubbert Q: IIHHT. M: BABTAC, FHT, ITEC.
B Yrs. Est.: 1 (Ref:HM02125)

## BENEDICT-SMITH, M

**M Benedict-Smith**, 91 Compstall Rd, Romiley, Stockport, **Cheshire**, SK6 4HT, ENG.
(T) 01614 942437
Speciality: Chiropodists (Podiatrists).
● **Owner** Miss M Benedict-Smith
S (Ref:HM02126)

## BENEFEET

**Benefeet**, 21 Stafford Rd, Wallington, **Surrey**, SM6 9AN, ENG.
(T) 020 8773 3696
Speciality: Chiropodists (Podiatrists).
● **Owner** Miss M Nolan
S (Ref:HM02127)

## BENES, G B

**G B Benes**, Bank House Clinic, 5 High St, Milford On Sea, Lymington, **Hampshire**, SO41 0QF, ENG.
(T) 01590 642749
Speciality: Chiropractic.
● **Owner** Dr G Benes
P S T (Ref:HM02128)

## BENFIELD, R E

**R E Benfield**, 1 St. Nicholas Cl, Newport, **Isle of Wight**, PO30 1NA, ENG.
(T) 01983 525063
Speciality: Chiropodists (Podiatrists).
● **Owner** Mr R Benfield
S (Ref:HM02129)

## BENFLEET PHYSIOTHERAPY

**Benfleet Physiotherapy**, 28 High Rd, Benfleet, **Essex**, SS7 5LH, ENG.
(T) 01268 751181 (F) 01268 751181
Speciality: Physiotherapy.
● **Owner** Mr N Kempton
P S T (Ref:HM02130)

## BENFLEET THERAPIES

**Benfleet Therapies**, 224 London Rd, Benfleet, **Essex**, SS7 5SJ, ENG.
(T) 01268 757098
Speciality: Chiropodists (Podiatrists).
● **Owner** Mrs C Bland
S (Ref:HM02131)

## BENHAM, CHARLES

**Charles Benham**, 193 London Rd, High Wycombe, **Buckinghamshire**, HP11 1BT, ENG.
(T) 01494 437409
Speciality: Complementary Medicines & Therapy.
C M (Ref:HM02132)

## BENJAMIN, K

**K Benjamin**, 108 Lady Margaret Rd, London, **London (Greater)**, N19 5EX, ENG.
(T) 020 7607 4415
Speciality: Alexander Technique.
● **Owner** Ms K Benjamin
P S (Ref:HM02133)

## BENJAMIN, MAUREEN

**Maureen Benjamin**, Cambrook House, 17 Eastcourt Rd, Temple Cloud, Bristol, BS39 5BU, ENG.
(T) 01761 452862
Speciality: Complementary Medicines & Therapy.
● **Owner** Ms M Benjamin
M (Ref:HM02134)

## BENNER, LAWRENCE M

**Lawrence M Benner**, Pontardulais Health Clinic, Dulais Rd, Pontarddulais, Swansea, **Glamorgan (Vale of)**, SA4 1RH, WAL.
(T) 01792 881488
Speciality: Chiropractic.
● **Administrator** Ms H Jones
P S T (Ref:HM02135)

## BENNETT, A

**A Bennett**, 7 Kiver Rd, London, **London (Greater)**, N19 4PE, ENG.
(T) 020 7272 6695
Speciality: Osteopathy.
P S T (Ref:HM02136)

## BENNETT, B

**B Bennett**, 2 Comer Rd, Cheddar, **Somerset**, BS27 3AS, ENG.
(T) 01934 743164
Speciality: Chiropodists (Podiatrists).
S (Ref:HM02137)

## BENNETT, CHARLES R

**Charles R Bennett**, Sandwood, 15 Church Lane, Sarratt, Rickmansworth, **Hertfordshire**, WD3 6HN, ENG.
(T) 01923 262491
Speciality: Osteopathy.
● **Principal** Mr C Bennett
P S T (Ref:HM02138)



Key: B Mind-Body Medicine C Complementary Medicine H Self Help Treatment M Medicinal Therapy O Oriental Medicine P Postural Therapy S Manipulative Structural Therapy T Touch Therapy

### BENNETT, ELIZABETH

**Elizabeth Bennett**, 26 The Glade, Fetcham, Leatherhead, **Surrey**, KT22 9TH, ENG.
(T) 01372 458316
Speciality: Reflexology.
S T (Ref:HM02139)

### BENNETT, GINETTE

**Ginette Bennett**, 77 Wood St, Castleford, **Yorkshire (West)**, WF10 1LN, ENG.
(T) 01977 513642
Speciality: Osteopathy.
P S T (Ref:HM02140)

### BENNETT, J C

**J C Bennett**, 7 Snatts Hill, Oxted, **Surrey**, RH8 0BL, ENG.
(T) 01883 712268
Speciality: Hypnosis.
● **Owner** Mr J Bennett
B (Ref:HM02141)

### BENNETT, J P

**J P Bennett**, 59 St Dunstans St, Canterbury, **Kent**, CT2 8BS, ENG.
(T) 01227 780033
Speciality: Hypnosis.
B (Ref:HM02142)

### BENNETT, J P

**J P Bennett, FHS, FHRS**, 13 St Johns Lane, Canterbury, **Kent**, CT1 2QG, ENG.
(T) 01227 780033
(E) jb@scorpian.net
Speciality: Auto Suggestion, Cognitive Therapy, Group Therapy, Hypnotherapy, Past Life Therapy.
✔
● **Hypnotherapist** Mr J Bennett Q: FHA. M: HRS.
B Yrs. Est.: 15 (Ref:HM02143)

### BENNETT, JANET

**Janet Bennett**, 18 Sundorne Avenue, Shrewsbury, **Shropshire**, SY1 4JN, ENG.
(T) 01743 367048
Speciality: Reflexology.
S T (Ref:HM02144)

### BENNETT, JAYNE

**Jayne Bennett**, 1 Hill Cres, Finstock, Chipping Norton, **Oxfordshire**, OX7 3BT, ENG.
(T) 01993 868062
Speciality: Complementary Medicines & Therapy.
C M (Ref:HM02145)

### BENNETT, JOHN B

**John B Bennett**, 42 Dickinson Court, Wakefield, **Yorkshire (West)**, WF1 3PU, ENG.
(T) 01924 201950
Speciality: Hypnosis.
B (Ref:HM02146)

### BENNETT, LIAM

**Liam Bennett**, 98 High St, **County Kilkenny**, IRE.
(T) 05623 373
Speciality: Reflexology.
S T (Ref:HM02147)

### BENNETT, LOIS

**Lois Bennett**, The Studio, Astwood Bank, Redditch, **Worcestershire**, B96 6HF, ENG.
(T) 01527 893624
Speciality: Complementary Medicines & Therapy.
● **Owner** Mrs L Bennett
M (Ref:HM02148)

### BENNETT, M A

**M A Bennett**, 39 Royston Rd, Urmston, Manchester, **Manchester (Greater)**, M41 0GQ, ENG.
(T) 01617 482280
Speciality: Physiotherapy.
P S T (Ref:HM02149)

### BENNETT, MARGARET

**Margaret Bennett**, 43 Woodhouse Lane, Bishop Auckland, **County Durham**, DL14 6JX, ENG.
(T) 01388 607592
Speciality: Reflexology.
S T (Ref:HM02150)

### BENNETT, MAUREEN E

**Maureen E Bennett**, 39 Dib Lane, Leeds, **Yorkshire (West)**, LS8 3DF, ENG.
(T) 01132 652889
Speciality: Physiotherapy.
P S T (Ref:HM02151)

### BENNETT, MO

**Mo Bennett**, 36 Mellalieu St, Middleton, Manchester, **Manchester (Greater)**, M24 5DN, ENG.
(T) 01616 431306
Speciality: Psychotherapy.
● **Owner** Ms M Bennett
B (Ref:HM02152)

### BENNETT, ROGER

**Roger Bennett**, 49 West St, Tavistock, **Devon**, PL19 8JZ, ENG.
(T) 01822 614471
Speciality: Psychotherapy.
B (Ref:HM02153)

### BENNETT, ROSEMARY

**Rosemary Bennett**, 538 Allerton Rd, Allerton, Liverpool, **Merseyside**, L18 9UZ, ENG.
(T) 01514 941082 (F) 01514 941082
Speciality: Reflexology.
● **Owner** Ms R Bennett
S T (Ref:HM02154)

### BENNETT, ROSS

**Ross Bennett**, Kwanti, Jermyns Lane, Ampfield, Romsey, **Hampshire**, SO51 0QA, ENG.
(T) 01794 368012
Speciality: Psychotherapy.
● **Owner** Ms R Bennett
B (Ref:HM02155)

### BENNETT, ROSS

**Ross Bennett**, Portsmouth Natural Health Centre, 20 Landport Trce, Portsmouth, **Hampshire**, PO1 2RG, ENG.
(T) 023 9283 0558
Speciality: Complementary Medicines & Therapy.
C M (Ref:HM02156)

### BENNETT, RUSSELL

**Russell Bennett**, Guildford Chiropractic Centre, 1 Abbotswood, Guildford, **Surrey**, GU1 1AG, ENG.
(T) 01483 562830
Speciality: Chiropractors.
P S T (Ref:HM02157)

### BENNETT, S M

**S M Bennett**, 22 Breinton Rd, Hereford, **Herefordshire**, HR4 0JX, ENG.
(T) 01432 268099
Speciality: Chiropodists (Podiatrists).
● **Owner** Mrs S Bennett
S (Ref:HM02158)

### BENNETT, SHEILA

**Sheila Bennett**, 21 Hill View, Uffington, Faringdon, **Oxfordshire**, SN7 7RZ, ENG.
(T) 01367 820700
Speciality: Reflexology.
S T (Ref:HM02159)

### BENNETT, W P

**W P Bennett**, 112 Primley Park, Paignton, **Devon**, TQ3 3JX, ENG.
(T) 01803 526133
Speciality: Herbal Medicine.
M (Ref:HM02160)

### BENNETTO, CHRIS

**Chris Bennetto**, Pendene Complementary Medical Centre, Beechwood Hou, 7 Summe, Wolverhampton, **Midlands (West)**, WV1 4PR, ENG.
(T) 01902 426486 (F) 01902 717920
Speciality: Complementary Medicines & Therapy.
● **Owner** Mr C Benetto
C M (Ref:HM02161)

### BENNISON, A J

**A J Bennison**, 30 Tor O Moor Rd, Woodhall Spa, **Lincolnshire**, LN10 6TD, ENG.
(T) 01526 353467
Speciality: Chiropodists (Podiatrists).
● **Owner** Mr A Bennison
S (Ref:HM02162)

### BENNISON, DIANE

**Diane Bennison**, Hemner Hill House, South Harting, Petersfield, **Hampshire**, GU31 5PH, ENG.
(T) 01730 825868
Speciality: Hypnosis.
B (Ref:HM02163)

### BENRENE HEALTH INTERNATIONAL

**Benrene Health International**, 122 Northwood Avenue, Hornchurch, **Essex**, RM12 4PX, ENG.
(T) 01708 443999
Speciality: Complementary Medicines & Therapy.
● **Owner** Mrs L Button
C M (Ref:HM02164)

### BENRENE HEALTH INTERNATIONAL

**Benrene Health International**, 34 Ravenswood Cl, Romford, **Essex**, RM5 2UD, ENG.
(T) 01708 768793
Speciality: Herbal Medicine.
● **Owner** Mrs M Forshaw
M (Ref:HM02165)

### BENSON, BRIDGET

**Bridget Benson**, 8 Regent Pl, Sowerby Bridge, **Yorkshire (West)**, HX6 2HG, ENG.
(T) 01422 834006 (F) 01422 834006
Speciality: Clairvoyants & Palmists.
● **Owner** Mrs B Benson
B (Ref:HM02166)

### BENSON, HAZEL

**Hazel Benson**, 31 Kingsfield Rd, Dane End, Ware, **Hertfordshire**, SG12 0LY, ENG.
(T) 01920 438416
Speciality: Reflexology.
S T (Ref:HM02167)

### BENSON, HUGH

**Hugh Benson**, 82 Norwich St, Cambridge, **Cambridgeshire**, CB2 1NE, ENG.
(T) 01223 316503
Speciality: Holistic Healing, Homeopathy. ✔
● **Homeopath** Mr H Benson Q: BA. M: LCH.
C Yrs. Est.: 15 (Ref:HM02168)

### BENSON, KAREN

**Karen Benson**, Crouch Hall Rd Surgery, 48 Crouch Hall Rd, London, **London (Greater)**, N8 8HJ, ENG.
(T) 020 8340 7736 (F) 020 8340 3384
Speciality: Acupuncture.
● **Practice Manager**
Mrs M Maciesczek
O (Ref:HM02169)

### BENSON, MICHAEL

**Michael Benson**, 8 Augusta Rd, Ramsgate, **Kent**, CT11 8JP, ENG.
(T) 01843 590630
Speciality: Aromatherapy.
M O (Ref:HM02170)

### BENSTED, LUCINDA

**Lucinda Bensted**, Memorial Medical Centre, Bell Rd, Sittingbourne, **Kent**, ME10 4XX, ENG.
(T) 01795 477764
Speciality: Osteopathy.
P S T (Ref:HM02171)

### BENTLEY AND ASSOCIATES

**Alison Bentley and Associates**, 5a Bacup Rd, Rawtenstall, **Lancashire**, BB4 7NG, ENG.
(T) 01706 227428
(E) bentleyal@aol.com
Speciality: Acupuncture, Chiropody, Cognitive Therapy, Counselling, Electrotherapy, Family Therapy, Manipulation, Massage (Therapeutic), Physiotherapy, Podiatry, Stress Therapy, Youth Counselling, Drug Abuse Counselling, Bio-Mechanical Assessments. ✔ [credit card]
● **Counsellor** Ms J Morrison Q: Dip.Couns.
● **Counsellor/Supervisor**
Ms L Woodings Q: Dip.Couns, RMN, SRN.
● **Physiotherapist** Mr I Liversedge Q: MCSP, SRP. M: CSP.
● **Chiropodist (Podiatrist)**
Ms A Bentley Q: DPodM, S.R.Ch. M: S.C.P.
C Yrs. Est.: 17 (Ref:HM02172)



Key continued: Yrs.Est: Years Established Q: Qualifications M: Professional Membership ✔ Indemnity Insurance [credit card] Accept Credit Cards

**BENTLEY, J H**

**J H Bentley**, 11 Crag Hill Avenue, Leeds, **Yorkshire (West)**, LS16 7LU, ENG.
(T) 01132 672798
Speciality: Massage (Therapeutic), Reiki. ✓
● **Massage and Reiki Master**
Mrs J Bentley M: NMA.
T Yrs. Est.: 9 (Ref:HM02173)

**BENTLEY, JANE**

**Jane Bentley**, Eden Vale House, 32 Victoria Avenue, Bristol, BS5 9NG, ENG.
(T) 01179 542255
Speciality: Chiropodists (Podiatrists).
● **Owner** Mrs J Bentley
S (Ref:HM02174)

**BENTLEY, JOHN**

**John Bentley**, The Barn Clinic, Crinow, Narberth, **Pembrokeshire**, SA67 8UB, WAL.
(T) 01834 861488
Speciality: Chiropractic.
P S T (Ref:HM02175)

**BENTLEY, M J**

**M J Bentley**, 666 Hollins Rd, Oldham, **Lancashire**, OL8 4JZ, ENG.
(T) 01616 886191 (F) 01616 886191
Speciality: Chiropractic.
● **Owner** Mr M Bentley
P S T (Ref:HM02176)

**BENTON, LINDSEY**

**Lindsey Benton**, 45 Clarence Rd, Chesterfield, **Derbyshire**, S40 1LQ, ENG.
(T) 01246 550330 (F) 01246 550330
Speciality: Complementary Medicines & Therapy.
● **Owner** Mrs L Benton
M (Ref:HM02177)

**BENWELL, NATALIE**

**Natalie Benwell**, 62 Tithe Rd, Plymouth, **Devon**, PL7 4QQ, ENG.
(T) 01752 343833
Speciality: Reflexology.
● **Owner** Mrs N Benwell
S T (Ref:HM02178)

**BERESFORD, G S**

**G S Beresford**, 1 Collets Court, Lansdown, Bourton-On-The-Water, Cheltenham, **Gloucestershire**, GL54 2AR, ENG.
(T) 01451 810086
Speciality: Osteopathy.
P S T (Ref:HM02179)

**BERESFORD, G S**

**G S Beresford**, 14 Clarence Sq, Cheltenham, **Gloucestershire**, GL50 4JN, ENG.
(T) 01242 516048
Speciality: Osteopathy.
● **Partner** Mr G Beresford
P S T (Ref:HM02180)

**BERESFORD, GUY S**

**Guy S Beresford**, 12 Windsor Rd, Evesham, **Worcestershire**, WR11 4QE, ENG.
(T) 01386 41219
Speciality: Osteopathy.
● **Owner** Mr G Beresford
P S T (Ref:HM02181)

**BERESFORD, KATE**

**Mrs Kate Beresford**, The Hand Clinic, Dedworth Rd, Windsor, **Berkshire**, SL4 4LH, ENG.
(T) 01753 831333 (F) 01753 832109
Speciality: Physiotherapy.
● **Manager** Ms K Beresford Q: MCSP, SRP.
P S T (Ref:HM02182)

**BERESFORD, KATHLEEN**

**Kathleen Beresford**, 23 Swan St, Congleton, **Cheshire**, CW12 4BN, ENG.
(T) 01260 290106
Speciality: Alexander Technique, Bach Remedies, Colour Therapy, Homeopathy, Nutritional Therapy, Reflexology. ✓
● **Owner/Reflexologist**
Miss K Beresford Q: MAR. M: AoR.
T Yrs. Est.: 11 (Ref:HM02183)

**BERETTA, P**

**P Beretta**, 68 Grove Rd, Blaby, Leicester, **Leicestershire**, LE8 4DG, ENG.
(T) 01162 771324
Speciality: Chiropodists (Podiatrists).
S (Ref:HM02184)

**BERG, DAVID**

**David Berg**, 154 Stoke Newington Church St, London, **London (Greater)**, N16 0JU, ENG.
(T) 020 7249 2990
Speciality: Acupuncture.
O (Ref:HM02185)

**BERG, DAVID**

**David Berg**, 18 Gloucester Rd, Teignmouth, **Devon**, TQ14 9HN, ENG.
(T) 01626 777626
Speciality: Acupuncture.
● **Owner** Mr D Berg
O (Ref:HM02186)

**BERG, STELLA**

**Stella Berg**, Clissold Park Health Centre, 154 Stoke Newington Church St, London, **London (Greater)**, N16 0JU, ENG.
(T) 020 7249 2990 (F) 020 7249 3977
Speciality: Homeopathy.
● **Director** Mr D Berg
M (Ref:HM02187)

**BERG, WENDY**

**Wendy Berg**, Clissold Park Health Centre, 154 Stoke Newington Church St, London, **London (Greater)**, N16 0JU, ENG.
(T) 020 7249 2990 (F) 020 7249 3977
Speciality: Complementary Medicines & Therapy.
● **Director** Mr D Berg
M (Ref:HM02188)

**BERGIN, ALICE**

**Alice Bergin**, 4 Lynwood Avenue, Lowton, Warrington, **Cheshire**, WA3 1HJ, ENG.
(T) 01942 673494
Speciality: Complementary Medicines & Therapy.
C M (Ref:HM02189)

**BERGMANN, MARIA (DR)**

**Nuffield Hospital**, Park House, Nuffield Hospital, Kingswood Rd, Tunbridge Wells, **Kent**, TN2 4UL, ENG.
(T) 01892 552940 (F) 01892 552904
Speciality: Herbal Medicine, Phytotherapy.
● **Medical Herbalist** Dr M Bergmann Q: MD, MNIMH. M: NIMH.
C (Ref:HM02190)

**BERKE, JOSEPH**

**Joseph Berke**, 5 Shepherds Cl, London, **London (Greater)**, N6 5AG, ENG.
(T) 020 8348 4492
Speciality: Psychotherapy.
● **Doctor** Dr J Berke
B (Ref:HM02191)

**BERKHAMSTED CHIRO CLINIC**

**Berkhamsted Chiropractic Clinic**, 69 High St, Berkhamsted, **Hertfordshire**, HP4 2DE, ENG.
(T) 01442 863800
Speciality: Chiropractors.
P S T (Ref:HM02192)

**BERKHAMSTED PHYSIO CLINIC**

**Berkhamsted Physiotherapy Clinic**, Victory Rd, Berkhamsted, **Hertfordshire**, HP4 1DL, ENG.
(T) 01442 874458 (F) 01442 878387
Speciality: Physiotherapy. ✓
● **Physiotherapist** Ms K Moule Q: MCSP, SRP. M: CSP.
S (Ref:HM02193)

**BERKLEYS HEALTH STUDIO**

**Berkleys Health Studio**, 33 Portswood Rd, Southampton, **Hampshire**, SO17 2ET, ENG.
(T) 023 8032 2625
Speciality: Aromatherapy.
M O (Ref:HM02194)

**BERKSHIRE CHIROPRACTIC**

**Berkshire Chiropractic**, 1 Grove Cottage, Billingbear, Binfield, Bracknell, **Berkshire**, RG42 5PR, ENG.
(T) 01344 482851
(E) e.roberts@tinyonline.co.uk
Speciality: Acupressure, Aromatherapy, Chiropractic, Complementary Therapy, Dietician, Healing Therapy, Manipulation, Massage (Therapeutic), Naturopathy, Ultrasonics, Physical Therapy, Animal Chiropractic Treatment, Cranio-Sacral Manipulation, McTimoney-Chorley Chiropractic Technique. ✓
● **Chiropractor** Dr E Roberts Q: BSc, DC. M: BAAC, GCC.
P S Yrs. Est.: 5 (Ref:HM02195)

**BERNARD, ELAINE**

**Elaine Bernard**, 5 North St, Leigh-On-Sea, **Essex**, SS9 1QE, ENG.
(T) 01702 712192
Speciality: Alexander Technique.
● **Owner** Miss E Bernard
P S (Ref:HM02196)

**BERNARD-SMITH, H (DR)**

**Dr H Bernard-Smith**, Lleifior, Malltraeth, Bodorgan, **Isle of Anglesey**, LL62 5AF, WAL.
(T) 01407 840688
Speciality: Hypnosis.
● **Owner** Dr H Bernard-Smith
B (Ref:HM02197)

**BERNE INSTITUTE**

**Berne Institute (The)**, Berne House, 29 Derby Rd, Kegworth, Derby, **Derbyshire**, DE74 2EN, ENG.
(T) 01509 673649
Speciality: Psychotherapy.
B (Ref:HM02198)

**BERNER, ERICH**

**Erich Berner**, 6 Ashley Court, 51-53 Somerset Rd, New Barnet, Barnet, **Hertfordshire**, EN5 1RQ, ENG.
(T) 07833 125087
Speciality: Reflexology.
S T (Ref:HM02199)

**BERNEY, SUSAN**

**Susan Berney**, 64 Bethel St, Norwich, **Norfolk**, NR2 1NR, ENG.
(T) 01603 666546
Speciality: Aromatherapy.
M O (Ref:HM02200)

**BERNICE**

**Bernice**, 15 Dumbarton Cl, Stockport, **Cheshire**, SK5 7EG, ENG.
(T) 01614 297741
Speciality: Clairvoyants & Palmists.
● **Owner** Miss B Rostron
B (Ref:HM02201)

**BERNSTEIN, R**

**R Bernstein**, The Lodge, Holly Trce, West Hill, London, **London (Greater)**, N6 6LX, ENG.
(T) 020 8348 7467
Speciality: Complementary Medicines & Therapy.
● **Owner** Mr R Bernstein
M (Ref:HM02202)

**BERNSTEIN, S**

**S Bernstein**, 83 Abbotswood Gardens, Ilford, **Essex**, IG5 0BH, ENG.
(T) 020 8550 5542
Speciality: Hypnosis.
● **Owner** Mr S Bernstein
B (Ref:HM02203)

**BERNSTEIN, SAMUEL**

**Samuel Bernstein**, The Penthouse, Flat 42, Manor Court Lodge, 175 High Rd, South Woodford, London, **London (Greater)**, E18 2PD, ENG.
(T) 020 8504 6622 (F) 020 8504 6622
Speciality: Complementary Therapy, Counselling, Healing Therapy, Hypnotherapy, Psychotherapy, Stress Therapy, Visualisation Therapy. ✓
● **Therapist/Counsellor**
Mr S Bernstein M: BRCP, HS.
B Yrs. Est.: 14 (Ref:HM02204)

**BERRIE, INGE**

**Inge Berrie**, 73 Connaught Rd, Sutton, **Surrey**, SM1 3PJ, ENG.
(T) 020 8644 6481
Speciality: Reflexology.



Key: B Mind-Body Medicine C Complementary Medicine H Self Help Treatment M Medicinal Therapy O Oriental Medicine P Postural Therapy S Manipulative Structural Therapy T Touch Therapy

S T (Ref:HM02205)

## BERRILL, P
**P Berrill**, 60 Leyland Rd, Southport, **Merseyside**, PR9 9JA, ENG.
(T) 01704 534725 (F) 01704 501062
Speciality: Hypnotherapy.
● **Owner** Mr P Berrill
B (Ref:HM02206)

## BERRY, A R
**A R Berry**, Butterleigh, Cullompton, **Devon**, EX15 1PQ, ENG.
(T) 01884 855678
Speciality: Complementary Medicines & Therapy.
● **Owner** Mrs R Berry
M (Ref:HM02207)

## BERRY, ELIZABETH
**Elizabeth Berry**, 46 Hardinge Rd, Ashford, **Kent**, TN24 8HA, ENG.
(T) 01233 643018
Speciality: Reflexology.
S T (Ref:HM02208)

## BERRY, K L
**K L Berry**, 23 Irwell Rd, Warrington, **Cheshire**, WA4 6BA, ENG.
(T) 01925 658371
Speciality: Chiropodists (Podiatrists).
● **Owner** Mrs K Berry
S (Ref:HM02209)

## BERRY, LISA
**Lisa Berry**, 42 Newbridge Rd, Bath, **Somerset**, BA1 3JZ, ENG.
(T) 01225 338141
Speciality: Chiropodists (Podiatrists).
● **Owner** Ms L Berry
S (Ref:HM02210)

## BERRY, M E
**M E Berry**, 2 Mornington Villas, Bradford, **Yorkshire (West)**, BD8 7HB, ENG.
(T) 01274 546665
Speciality: Chiropodists (Podiatrists).
S (Ref:HM02211)

## BERRY, M E
**M E Berry**, 1a Exchange Buildings, Main St, Cross Hills, Keighley, **Yorkshire (West)**, BD20 8TH, ENG.
(T) 01535 636247
Speciality: Chiropodists (Podiatrists).
S (Ref:HM02212)

## BERRY, RUTH
**Ruth Berry**, 14 High Gr, Whitehaven, **Cumbria**, CA28 6TA, ENG.
(T) 01946 694478
Speciality: Complementary Medicines & Therapy.
C M (Ref:HM02213)

## BERTH-JONES, D
**D Berth-Jones**, Aldwyn House, Meifod, **Powys**, SY22 6BY, WAL.
(T) 01938 500570 (F) 01938 500570
Speciality: Hypnotherapy.
● **Owner** Mr D Berth-Jones
B (Ref:HM02214)

## BERTRAM-SMITH, MICHAEL R
**Michael R Bertram-Smith**, Conifers, 22 Netley Dell, Letchworth, **Hertfordshire**, SG6 2TF, ENG.
(T) 01462 672385
Speciality: Chiropodists (Podiatrists).
● **Owner** Mr M Bertram-Smith
S (Ref:HM02215)

## BERWICK FOOT CLINIC
**Berwick Foot Clinic**, 8 Sandgate, Berwick-Upon-Tweed, **Northumberland**, TD15 1EP, SCO.
(T) 01289 331218
Speciality: Chiropodists (Podiatrists).
S (Ref:HM02216)

## BERWICK PHYSIOTHERAPY CENTRE
**Berwick Physiotherapy Centre**, 1 The Chandlery, Quayside, Berwick-Upon-Tweed, **Northumberland**, TD15 1HE, SCO.
(T) 01289 303070
Speciality: Physiotherapy.
● **Partner** Miss A Grant
P S T (Ref:HM02217)

## BERWICK, E
**E Berwick**, 30 Jupiter Rd, Ipswich, **Suffolk**, IP4 4NT, ENG.
(T) 01473 278355
Speciality: Chiropodists (Podiatrists).
● **Owner** Miss E Berwick
S (Ref:HM02218)

## BERWICK, MARK
**Mark Berwick**, 79 Aldsworth Avenue, Goring-By-Sea, Worthing, **Sussex (West)**, BN12 4XG, ENG.
(T) 01903 243894
Speciality: Complementary Medicines & Therapy.
● **Owner** Mr M Berwick
C M (Ref:HM02219)

## BERWITZ, ANDREW
**Andrew Berwitz**, 1 Burnthouse Cottage, Bucklow Hill Lane, Mere, Knutsford, **Cheshire**, WA16 6LD, ENG.
(T) 01565 830700 (F) 01565 830700
Speciality: Homeopathy.
● **Owner** Mr A Berwitz
M (Ref:HM02220)

## BEST FOOT FORWARD
**Caroline Nolder Of Best Foot Forward**, The Wharf, Couch Lane, Devizes, **Wiltshire**, SN10 1EB, ENG.
(T) 01380 729103
Speciality: Chiropodists (Podiatrists).
S (Ref:HM02221)

## BEST OF HEALTH THERAPY CENTRE
**Best Of Health Therapy Centre**, 127 High St, Wootton Bassett, Swindon, **Wiltshire**, SN4 7AY, ENG.
(T) 01793 855266
Speciality: Complementary Medicines & Therapy.
● **Partner** Mrs A Edwards
C M (Ref:HM02222)

## BEST, BONITA
**Bonita Best**, Sharella, Main Rd, Appleford, Abingdon, **Oxfordshire**, OX14 4PD, ENG.
(T) 01235 847005 (F) 01235 848101
Speciality: Chiropodists (Podiatrists).
● **Owner** Mrs B Best
S (Ref:HM02223)

## BEST, JOHN G E
**G E Best-John**, 77 Blyth Rd, Hayes, **London (Greater)**, UB3 1DB, ENG.
(T) 020 8848 1425
Speciality: Osteopathy. ✔
● **Owner/Osteopath** Mrs G Best-John Q: DO. M: BOA.
S Yrs. Est.: 17 (Ref:HM02224)

## BEST, S
**S Best**, The Halifax Clinic Of Natural Medicine, 22 Clare Rd, Halifax, **Yorkshire (West)**, HX1 2HX, ENG.
(T) 01422 340919
Speciality: Complementary Medicines & Therapy.
M (Ref:HM02225)

## BEST, SALLY
**Sally Best**, Tara, Rawdon Hall Drive, Rawdon, Leeds, **Yorkshire (West)**, LS19 6HD, ENG.
(T) 01132 503011
Speciality: Physiotherapy.
● **Owner** Mrs S Best
P S T (Ref:HM02226)

## BESTEL & ASSOCIATES
**Heather Bestel & Associates**, 248 Hale Rd, Hale Village, Liverpool, **Merseyside**, L24 5RD, ENG.
(T) 01514 254541
Speciality: Psychotherapy.
B (Ref:HM02227)

## BESWICK, MARGARET
**Margaret Beswick**, Riverbank House, Riverbank Rd, Wirral, **Merseyside**, CH60 4SQ, ENG.
(T) 01513 422591 (F) 01513 343912
Speciality: Physiotherapy.
● **Owner** Mrs M Beswick
P S T (Ref:HM02228)

## BETA HEALTH CLINIC
**Beta Health Clinic**, 67 Marlowes, Hemel Hempstead, **Hertfordshire**, HP1 1LE, ENG.
(T) 01442 249080
Speciality: Acupuncture, Chiropody, Homeopathy, Hypnotherapy, Massage (Therapeutic), Osteopathy, Physiotherapy, Shiatsu. ✔
● **Owner/Osteopath** Mr G Pritchard Q: DO. M: BOA, GOsC.
● **Chiropodist** J Govan Q: MBChA, MSSCh.
● **Acupuncturist** Mr M Stilliton Q: Dip.Ac, Dip.CHM.
O (Ref:HM02229)

## BETHESDA
**Bethesda**, Mall Hse, Tuam, **County Galway**, IRE.
(T) 09328 300
Speciality: Complementary Medicines & Therapy.
M (Ref:HM02230)

## BETSER, J
**J Betser**, Codicote Osteopathy & Sports Injury Clinic, 101 High St, Codicote, Hitchin, **Hertfordshire**, SG4 8XE, ENG.
(T) 01438 820234
Speciality: Osteopathy.
● **Owner** Mr J Betser
P S T (Ref:HM02231)

## BETSER, J
**J Betser**, The Surgery, 1 Leighton Rd, Leighton Buzzard, **Bedfordshire**, LU7 7LB, ENG.
(T) 01525 211444
Speciality: Osteopathy.
● **Owner** Mr J Betser
P S T (Ref:HM02232)

## BETTER HEALTH
**Better Health**, 6 Shaftesbury Avenue, South Harrow, Harrow, **London (Greater)**, HA2 0PH, ENG.
(T) 020 8248 8441
Speciality: Reflexology.
● **Owner** Miss B Williams
S T (Ref:HM02233)

## BETTER HEALTH CLINIC
**Better Health Clinic**, 4a Hunter St, Chester, **Cheshire**, CH1 2AR, ENG.
(T) 01244 322822 (F) 01244 344533
Speciality: Complementary Medicines & Therapy.
● **Managing Director** Dr R Jones
C M (Ref:HM02234)

## BETTER HEALTH REFLEXOLOGY
**Better Health Reflexology**, 11 Rectory Lane, Guisborough, **Cleveland**, TS14 7DJ, ENG.
(T) 01287 630113
Speciality: Complementary Medicines & Therapy.
● **Manager** Mrs L Forest
C M (Ref:HM02235)

## BETTER UNDERSTANDINGS
**Better Understandings**, Mill House, 12 Millway, Halebarns, Altrincham, **Cheshire**, WA15 0AE, ENG.
(T) 01619 806292 (F) 01619 806292
Speciality: Complementary Medicines & Therapy.
● **Owner** Ms L Thompson
M (Ref:HM02236)

## BETTERIDGE, SHIRLEY
**Shirley Betteridge**, 47 Alexandra Rd, Southampton, **Hampshire**, SO15 5DH, ENG.
(T) 023 8063 2154
Speciality: Hypnosis.
● **Owner** Mrs S Betteridge
B (Ref:HM02237)

## BETTERWORLD
**Betterworld**, 75 Springholm Drive, Airdrie, **Lanarkshire (North)**, ML6 6NF, SCO.
(T) 01236 607894 (F) 01236 607894
Speciality: Complementary Medicines & Therapy.



Key continued: Yrs.Est: Years Established Q: Qualifications M: Professional Membership ✔ Indemnity Insurance Accept Credit Cards

● **Owner** Mr I Marsh
C M (Ref:HM02238)

## BETTS, DAVID
**David Betts**, 9 Cuthbert Cl, North Wootton, King's Lynn, **Norfolk**, PE30 3XG, ENG.
(T) 01553 675633
Speciality: Physiotherapy.
P S T (Ref:HM02239)

## BEVAN, K J
**Mrs K J Bevan**, Rayleigh Physiotherapy Sports & Spinal Clinic, 41 High Rd, Rayleigh, **Essex**, SS6 7SA, ENG.
(T) 01268 771868
Speciality: Physiotherapy.
● **Owner** Mrs K Bevan
P S T (Ref:HM02240)

## BEVAN, L
**L Bevan**, Hurst Lane Surgery, Chapel Lane, Milford, Godalming, **Surrey**, GU8 5JG, ENG.
(T) 01483 424505
Speciality: Physiotherapy.
P S T (Ref:HM02241)

## BEVAN, RUSS
**Russ Bevan**, 1a Lovells Hill, Hanham, Bristol, BS15 3AN, ENG.
(T) 01179 672367
(E) russ@kscotland.net
Speciality: Biofeedback, Hypnosis, Hypnotherapy, Stress Therapy, Curative Hypnotherapy. ✔
● **Curative Hypnotherapist** Mr R Bevan Q: C.Hyp.
B Yrs. Est.: 13 (Ref:HM02242)

## BEVERLEY CHIROPRACTIC CLINIC
**Beverley Chiropractic Clinic**, 24 Railway St, Beverley, **Humberside (North)**, HU17 0DX, ENG.
(T) 01482 870934 (F) 01482 872076
Speciality: Chiropractic. ✔
● **Chiropractor** Dr P Allison Q: BSc, DC, MCC. M: BCA.
S Yrs. Est.: 11 (Ref:HM02243)

## BEVERLEY CLINIC
**Beverley Clinic Ltd**, 362 Coombe Lane, West Wimbledon, London, **London (Greater)**, SW20 0RJ, ENG.
(T) 020 8241 2515
Speciality: Acupuncture, Chiropody, Chiropractic, Counselling, Homeopathy, Hypnotherapy. ✔
● **Chiropodist (Podiatrist)** Mr B White Q: DPodM, M.S.C.P, S.R.Ch.
● **Chiropodist (Podiatrist)** Ms C Harris Q: BSc, DPodM, M.S.C.P, S.R.Ch.
● **Dental Surgeon** A Du Toit Q: BDS.
● **Chiropractor/Clinic Director** A F Kerrigan Q: BA, BCA, BSc (Chiro), DC. M: BCA, GCC.
● **Acupuncturist** Mr M Barry Q: Lic.Ac, MBAcC. M: BAcC.
● **Homeopath** Mr G Martin Q: LCPH.
● **Chiropractor** Ms S Nielsen Q: BCA, BSc (Chiro), DC. M: BCA.
● **Counsellor** Mrs S Harris Q: RGN.
S Yrs. Est.: 8 (Ref:HM02244)

## BEVERLEY, SHEILA
**Sheila Beverley**, 4 The Beeches, Great Habton, Malton, **Yorkshire (North)**, YO17 6RS, ENG.
(T) 01653 669055
Speciality: Reflexology.
S T (Ref:HM02245)

## BEVERLEYS
**Beverleys**, 54-56 Queen St, Market Rasen, **Lincolnshire**, LN8 3EN, ENG.
(T) 01673 849106 (F) 01673 849106
(W) www.bevs.co.uk
Speciality: Acupressure, Aromatherapy, Colour Therapy, Hypnotherapy, Indian Head Massage, Reflexology, Yoga, Magnet Therapy and Sports Injuries. ✔
● **Complementary Therapist** Miss B Farrow Q: Dip.Arom, Dip.Hyp, Dip.Indian Head Massage, Dip.Reflex. M: ASC.
C Yrs. Est.: 4 (Ref:HM02246)

## BEVINGTON, ANN
**Ann Bevington**, 5 West St, Earls Barton, Northampton, **Northamptonshire**, NN6 0EW, ENG.
(T) 01604 811040
Speciality: Reflexology.
S T (Ref:HM02247)

## BEVIS, J P
**J P Bevis**, 3 Cawley Rd, Chichester, **Sussex (West)**, PO19 1UZ, ENG.
(T) 01243 789444
Speciality: Osteopathy.
● **Owner** Mr J Bevis
P S T (Ref:HM02248)

## BEVIS, STUART
**Stuart Bevis**, 34 Cotman Rd, Clacton-On-Sea, **Essex**, CO16 8YB, ENG.
(T) 01255 431390
Speciality: Physiotherapy.
● **Partner** Mr S Bevis
P S T (Ref:HM02249)

## BEWDLEY CHIROPRACTOR CLINIC
**Bewdley Chiropractor Clinic**, The Old Snuff Mill Warehouse, Park Lane, Bewdley, **Worcestershire**, DY12 2EL, ENG.
(T) 01299 404699
Speciality: Chiropractic.
● **Manager** Mr N Fullerton
P S T (Ref:HM02250)

## BE-WELL CLINIC
**Be-Well Clinic**, Hughendon, London Rd, Crays Hill, Billericay, **Essex**, CM11 2UY, ENG.
(T) 01268 272757 (F) 01268 272757
(W) www.bewell-clinic.co.uk
Speciality: Bio-energetics, Homeopathy, Iridology, Trager. ✔
● **Homeopathic Practitioner** Ms K Meader Q: MBRI, RSHom. M: Soc.Hom.
M Yrs. Est.: 15 (Ref:HM02251)

## BEWLEY, COLIN A
**Colin A Bewley**, Derby Cathedral, St. Michaels House, Queen St, Derby, **Derbyshire**, DE1 3DT, ENG.
(T) 01332 346178
Speciality: Chiropodists (Podiatrists).
● **Owner** Mr C Bewley
S (Ref:HM02252)

## BEWLEY-JONES, ELIZABETH
**Elizabeth Bewley-Jones**, 6 Washabrook Way, Kingsbridge, **Devon**, TQ7 1RJ, ENG.
(T) 01548 857130
Speciality: Physiotherapy.
P S T (Ref:HM02253)

## BEXHILL CHIROPODY CENTRE
**Bexhill Chiropody Centre**, 16 Windsor Rd, Bexhill-on-Sea, **Sussex (East)**, TN39 3PB, ENG.
(T) 01424 730822
Speciality: Chiropodists (Podiatrists).
● **Owner** Mr C Miles
S (Ref:HM02254)

## BEXHILL CHIROPRACTIC
**Bexhill Chiropractic**, 21a Ocklynge Cl, Bexhill-on-Sea, **Sussex (East)**, TN39 4PF, ENG.
(T) 01424 842098 (F) 01424 842098
(E) pdupker@hotmail.com
Speciality: Acupressure, Aromatherapy, Bach Remedies, Chiropractic, Complementary Therapy, Manipulation, Massage (Therapeutic), Reflexology, Stress Therapy. ✔
● **Owner** Mr P Dupker Q: Dip.Chiro. M: B.A.Ch.P.
● **Therapist** Ms A Dupker Q: Dip.Arom, Dip.Reflex, Dip.Th.Massage, RGN. M: AoR, FHT, LCSP.
S Yrs. Est.: 6 (Ref:HM02255)

## BEXHILL CHIROPRACTIC CLINIC
**Bexhill Chiropractic Clinic**, Endwell Chambers, 8 Endwell Rd, Bexhill-on-Sea, **Sussex (East)**, TN40 1EA, ENG.
(T) 01424 214215
Speciality: Chiropractors.
● **Partner** Mr H Hilton
P S T (Ref:HM02256)

## BEXHILL OSTEOPATHIC PRACTICE
**Bexhill Osteopathic Practice**, 16 Endwell Rd, Bexhill-on-Sea, **Sussex (East)**, TN40 1EA, ENG.
(T) 01424 734734
Speciality: Acupuncture, Alexander Technique, Cranial Osteopathy, Homeopathy, Osteopathy, Shiatsu. ✔
● **Osteopath** Ms S White Q: BSc, Hons (OST). M: GOsC.
● **Osteopath** Ms S Birks Q: BSc, Hons (OST). M: GOsC.
● **Osteopath** Mr M Green Q: BSc, Hons (OST). M: GOsC.
● **Osteopath** Mr N Bassett Q: DO. M: GOsC.
S Yrs. Est.: 8 (Ref:HM02257)

## BEXLEY HEATH SURGERY
**Bexley Heath Surgery**, 16-18 Lion Rd, Bexleyheath, **Kent**, DA6 8NR, ENG.
(T) 020 8304 0019
Speciality: Chiropodists (Podiatrists).
● **Owner** Mrs F Povey
S (Ref:HM02258)

## BEXLEY OSTEOPATHIC CLINIC
**Bexley Osteopathic Clinic**, 16A Bexley High St, Bexley, **Kent**, DA5 1AD, ENG.
(T) 01322 529326
Speciality: Aromatherapy, Cranial Osteopathy, Osteopathy. ✔
● **Joint Director** Ms A Western
● **Osteopath** Mr G Western M: GOsC.
S Yrs. Est.: 14 (Ref:HM02259)

## BEXLEYHEATH CHIRO CLINIC
**Bexleyheath Chiropractic Clinic**, 18 Avenue Rd, Bexleyheath, **Kent**, DA7 4ER, ENG.
(T) 020 8301 5859
Speciality: Chiropractors.
● **Owner** Mr C Krumins
P S T (Ref:HM02260)

## BEXLEYHEATH CHIROPRACTIC
**Bexleyheath Chiropractic Clinic**, 306 Broadway, Bexleyheath, **Kent**, DA6 8AA, ENG.
(T) 020 8301 5859
Speciality: Chiropractic.
P S T (Ref:HM02261)

## BEXLEYHEATH NATURAL HEALTH
**Bexleyheath Natural Health Clinic**, 284 Broadway, Bexleyheath, **Kent**, DA6 8AJ, ENG.
(T) 020 8303 6288 (F) 020 8303 6288
Speciality: Acupuncture, Bowen Therapy, Chiropody, Homeopathy, Hypnotherapy, Osteopathy, Reflexology.
● **Hypnotherapist** Mr P Cousins
C Yrs. Est.: 16 (Ref:HM02262)

## BEYNON, E
**E Beynon**, 4 Slape Moor Cottages, Croford, Wiveliscombe, Taunton, **Somerset**, TA4 2TR, ENG.
(T) 01984 623642
Speciality: Physiotherapy.
● **Owner** Miss E Beynon
P S T (Ref:HM02263)

## BEYNON, MARTIN
**Martin Beynon**, 253 Gower Rd, Sketty, Swansea, SA2 9JL, WAL.
(T) 01792 201040
Speciality: Osteopathy.
● **Owner** Mr M Beynon
P S T (Ref:HM02264)

## BFMP
**British Federation Of Massage Practitioners**, 78 Meadow St, Preston, **Lancashire**, PR1 1TS, ENG.
(T) 01772 881063 (F) 01772 881063
(E) jolanta@jolanta.co.uk
(W) www.jolanta.co.uk
Speciality: Acupuncture, Aromatherapy, Bach Remedies, Complementary Therapy, Electrotherapy, Holistic Healing, Homeopathy, Indian Head Massage, Massage (Therapeutic), Osteopathy, Reflexology, Reiki, Stress Therapy, Ultrasonics. ✔
● **Therapist** Ms J Basnyet Q: BA (Hons), BSc, ITEC, MAR, MIFA. M: AoR, IFA.
C S Yrs. Est.: 5 (Ref:HM02265)



Key: B Mind-Body Medicine C Complementary Medicine H Self Help Treatment M Medicinal Therapy O Oriental Medicine P Postural Therapy S Manipulative Structural Therapy T Touch Therapy

## BHAGAT, PRITI

**Priti Bhagat**, The Surgery, 297 Greenford Rd, Greenford, **London (Greater)**, UB6 8RE, ENG.
(T) 020 8575 0174
Speciality: Aromatherapy.
M O (Ref:HM02266)

## BHAGWAT-BROWN, GINA

**Gina Bhagwat-Brown**, Care Of Lifestyle, 110 High St, Newport Pagnell, **Buckinghamshire**, MK16 8EH, ENG.
(T) 01908 614642
Speciality: Chiropodists (Podiatrists).
S (Ref:HM02267)

## BHATTI, HUSSAIN (DR)

**Dr Hussain Bhatti Homoeopath**, Kiltartan Hse, Forster St, **County Galway**, IRE.
(T) 09156 8804
Speciality: Homeopathy.
M (Ref:HM02268)

## BHMA

**British Herbal Medicine Association**, Sun House, Church St, Stroud, **Gloucestershire**, GL5 1JL, ENG.
(T) 01453 751389
Speciality: Herbal Medicine.
M (Ref:HM02269)

## BHMA

**British Herbal Medicine Association Ltd**, 1 Wickham Rd, Bournemouth, **Dorset**, BH7 6JX, ENG.
(T) 01202 433691 (F) 01202 417079
Speciality: Complementary Medicines & Therapy.
● **Chairman** Mr H Mitchell
C M (Ref:HM02270)

## BHOGAL, V R K

**V R K Bhogal**, 61 Wilson St, Derby, **Derbyshire**, DE1 1PL, ENG.
(T) 01332 344631
Speciality: Chiropodists (Podiatrists).
● **Owner** Mrs V Bhogal
S (Ref:HM02271)

## BIANCARDI, J

**J Biancardi**, 9 Stratford Gr, Newcastle Upon Tyne, **Tyne and Wear**, NE6 5AT, ENG.
(T) 01912 659664
Speciality: Psychotherapy.
B (Ref:HM02272)

## BIANCO, MOIRA

**Moira Bianco**, 27 Cherry Tree Rise, Walkern, Stevenage, **Hertfordshire**, SG2 7JL, ENG.
(T) 01438 861895
Speciality: Electrolysis.
● **Owner** Ms M Bianco
T (Ref:HM02273)

## BI-AURA THERAPY

**Bi-Aura Therapy Foundation**, De Light House, Corlurgan, Bailieborough, **County Cavan**, IRE.
(T) 04296 66779
(E) bio@iol.ie
(W) www.bi-aura.com
Speciality: Aura Therapy, Bio-energetics.
● **Bi-Aura Head Consultant** Mr M D'alton M: CMA.
T Yrs. Est.: 10 (Ref:HM02274)

## BIBBY, JANET

**Janet Bibby**, Brookland Farm, Brighouse, **Yorkshire (West)**, HD6 2RB, ENG.
(T) 01484 720084
Speciality: Clairvoyants & Palmists.
B (Ref:HM02275)

## BIBBY, KEITH

**Keith Bibby**, 49 Klea Avenue, London, **London (Greater)**, SW4 9HG, ENG.
(T) 020 8673 6311
Speciality: Hypnosis.
● **Owner** Mr K Bibby
B (Ref:HM02276)

## BICESTER CHIROPRACTIC CLINIC

**Bicester Chiropractic Clinic**, 21 Causeway, Bicester, **Oxfordshire**, OX6 7AN, ENG.
(T) 01869 321166 (F) 01869 321166
Speciality: Chiropractic.
● **Owner** Mr S Hudson
P S T (Ref:HM02277)

## BICESTER CHIROPRACTIC CLINIC

**Bicester Chiropractic Clinic**, The Old Post Office, Cherry St, Stratton Audley, Bicester, **Oxfordshire**, OX6 9BA, ENG.
(T) 01869 277111 (F) 01869 277111
Speciality: Chiropractic.
● **Owner** Mr S Hudson
P S T (Ref:HM02278)

## BIDBOROUGH CHIROPRACTIC CLINIC

**Bidborough Chiropractic Clinic**, Cockleberry Cottage, Penshurst Rd, Bidborough, Tunbridge Wells, **Kent**, TN3 0LW, ENG.
(T) 01892 870587
Speciality: Chiropractic.
● **Manager** Mrs L Summarsell
P S T (Ref:HM02279)

## BIDDER, N

**N Bidder**, 10 Fox Green, Great Bradley, Newmarket, **Suffolk**, CB8 9NR, ENG.
(T) 01420 409176
Speciality: Acupuncture.
● **Owner** Ms N Bidder
O (Ref:HM02280)

## BIDDLECOMBE, D L

**D L Biddlecombe**, 13 Barfield, Ryde, **Isle of Wight**, PO33 2JP, ENG.
(T) 01983 562855
Speciality: Chiropodists (Podiatrists).
● **Owner** Miss D Biddlecombe
S (Ref:HM02281)

## BIDDLESTONE, ANN R

**Ann R Biddlestone**, 24 Knighton Park, Sea Rd, Barton On Sea, New Milton, **Hampshire**, BH25 7PG, ENG.
(T) 01425 612747
Speciality: Chiropodists (Podiatrists).
● **Owner** Mrs A Biddlestone
S (Ref:HM02282)

## BIDEFORD CHIROPRACTIC CLINIC

**Jean Tallantire**, 127 Bay View Rd, Northam, Bideford, **Devon**, EX39 1BJ, ENG.
(T) 01237 472222
Speciality: Chiropractic, Naturopathy. ✔
● **Chiropractor** Ms J Tallantire Q: BSc (Chiro), ND. M: BCA, CC.
S Yrs. Est.: 7 (Ref:HM02283)

## BIDMEAD, MARGARET

**Margaret Bidmead**, Hadleigh, **Essex**, SS7, ENG.
(T) 01702 510231
Speciality: Bach Remedies.
M (Ref:HM02284)

## BIDWELL, KAREN

**Karen Bidwell**, 136 Water Lane, Totton, **Hampshire**, SO40 3GS, ENG.
(T) 023 8086 4358
Speciality: Reflexology.
S T (Ref:HM02285)

## BIDWELL, L H

**L H Bidwell**, Poplar Cottage, Poplar Lane, Bransgore, Christchurch, **Dorset**, BH23 8JE, ENG.
(T) 01425 672683
Speciality: Complementary Medicines & Therapy.
● **Owner** Mrs L Bidwell
C M (Ref:HM02286)

## BIEZANEK, A C

**A C Biezanek**, Cluney, Manor Rd, Wallasey, **Merseyside**, CH45 7RG, ENG.
(T) 01516 304000
Speciality: Homeopathy.
● **Owner** Dr A Biezanek
M (Ref:HM02287)

## BIGDEN, ROGER

**Roger Bigden**, 75 Boutport St, Barnstaple, **Devon**, EX31 1SR, ENG.
(T) 01271 327330
Speciality: Homeopathy.
M (Ref:HM02288)

## BIGG, V

**V Bigg**, 2 Kenwood Rd, Sheffield, **Yorkshire (South)**, S7 1NP, ENG.
(T) 01142 552048
Speciality: Osteopathy.
● **Owner** Mr D Wainwright
P S T (Ref:HM02289)

## BIGG, VANESSA

**Vanessa Bigg**, 24 High St, Dronfield, **Derbyshire**, S18 1PY, ENG.
(T) 01246 411067
Speciality: Osteopathy.
P S T (Ref:HM02290)

## BIGGIN, ALISON

**Alison Biggin**, 61 Northampton Rd, Market Harborough, **Leicestershire**, LE16 9HD, ENG.
(T) 01858 465503
Speciality: Osteopathy.
● **Owner** A Biggin
P S T (Ref:HM02291)

## BIGGINS, NICHOLAS

**Nicholas Biggins**, 97 London Rd, Sawbridgeworth, **Hertfordshire**, CM21 9JJ, ENG.
(T) 01279 724140
Speciality: Homeopathy.
● **Owner** Mr N Biggins
M (Ref:HM02292)

## BIGGS, MARGARET

**Mrs Margaret Biggs**, 42 Erskine Rd, Sutton, **Surrey**, SM1 3BQ, ENG.
(T) 020 8644 2132
Speciality: Homeopathy.
M (Ref:HM02293)

## BIGGS, SYLVIA

**Sylvia Biggs**, Juniper, Marlow Rd, Marlow, **Buckinghamshire**, SL7 3DE, ENG.
(T) 01628 484719
Speciality: Bowen Therapy. ✔
● **Therapist** Sylvia Biggs
(T) 01628 788770 Q: BTER. M: BTER.
C Yrs. Est.: 3 (Ref:HM02294)

## BIGWOOD, SIMON

**Simon Bigwood**, 43 The Ridgeway, Sutton, **Surrey**, SM2 5JX, ENG.
(T) 020 8643 2599
Speciality: Acupuncture.
● **Owner/Acupuncturist** Mr S Bigwood
C (Ref:HM02295)

## BILBE, MARIANNE

**Marianne Bilbe**, 150 Thorne Rd, Doncaster, **Yorkshire (South)**, DN2 5AE, ENG.
(T) 01302 349886
Speciality: Reflexology.
S T (Ref:HM02296)

## BILES, TINA

**Tina Biles**, Cherry Trees, 36 Milverton Rd, Winchester, **Hampshire**, SO22 5AU, ENG.
(T) 01962 620094
Speciality: Reflexology.
● **Owner** Mrs T Biles
S T (Ref:HM02297)

## BILL TAYLOR PHYSIOTHERAPY

**Bill Taylor Physiotherapy**, 50 Learmonth Gr, Edinburgh, **Edinburgh (City of)**, EH4 1BN, SCO.
(T) 01313 328837
Speciality: Physiotherapy.
● **Partner** Miss J Hazel
P S T (Ref:HM02298)

## BILLERICAY PHYSIO & SPORTS

**Billericay Physiotherapy & Sports Injury Clinic**, 60 Prince Edward Rd, Billericay, **Essex**, CM11 2HB, ENG.
(T) 01277 653143
Speciality: Physiotherapy.
● **Owner** Mr K Howells
P S T (Ref:HM02299)

## BILLINGHAM, K

**K Billingham**, 17 Norfolk Pl, Penrith, **Cumbria**, CA11 9BE, ENG.
(T) 01768 865763
Speciality: Chiropodists (Podiatrists).
● **Owner** Mrs K Billingham
S (Ref:HM02300)



Key continued: Yrs.Est: Years Established Q: Qualifications M: Professional Membership ✔ Indemnity Insurance Accept Credit Cards

## BILLINGHAM, S
**Mrs S J Billingham**, 9 Bowstoke Rd, Great Barr, Birmingham, **Midlands (West)**, B43 5EB, ENG.
(T) 01213 575348
Speciality: Chiropody, Reflexology. ✔
● **Reflexologist** Mrs S Billingham Q: ITEC. M: Inst.CH.P.
T Yrs. Est.: 8 (Ref:HM02301)

## BILLINGHAMS
**Billinghams**, 148A Margam Rd, Port Talbot, **Neath Port Talbot**, SA13 2BW, WAL.
(T) 01639 775353
Speciality: Aromatherapy.
M O (Ref:HM02302)

## BILLINGHURST, D M
**D M Billinghurst**, Glen Helen, Exeter Cross, Liverton, Newton Abbot, **Devon**, TQ12 6EY, ENG.
(T) 01626 821760
Speciality: Clairvoyants & Palmists.
B (Ref:HM02303)

## BILLINGS, A
**A Billings**, 2 Crown Lane, Littleport, Ely, **Cambridgeshire**, CB6 1PP, ENG.
(T) 01353 863218
Speciality: Psychotherapy.
● **Clinical Director** Mr B Beber
B (Ref:HM02304)

## BILLINGSHURST OSTEO PRACTICE
**Billingshurst Osteopathic Practice**, 74 High St, Billingshurst, **Sussex (West)**, RH14 9QS, ENG.
(T) 01403 786081
Speciality: Osteopathy.
● **Owner** Mr J Meadows
P S T (Ref:HM02305)

## BILLINGTON, JANE
**Mrs Jane Billington**, 36C London Rd, Alderley Edge, **Cheshire**, SK9 7DZ, ENG.
(T) 01625 586229
Speciality: Aromatherapy.
M O (Ref:HM02306)

## BILLINGTON, JANE
**Jane Billington**, Tower Hill Cottage, Tower Hill, Rainow, Macclesfield, **Cheshire**, SK10 5TX, ENG.
(T) 01625 614466
Speciality: Acupuncture.
O (Ref:HM02307)

## BILLINGTON, JILL M
**Jill M Billington**, 487 Garstang Rd, Broughton, Preston, **Lancashire**, PR3 5JA, ENG.
(T) 01772 861224
Speciality: Physiotherapy.
● **Owner** Mrs J Billington
P S T (Ref:HM02308)

## BILLINGTON, P J
**P J Billington**, Chaddesley Cottage, Chestnut Avenue, Chichester, **Sussex (West)**, PO19 4QD, ENG.
(T) 01243 781610
Speciality: Osteopathy.
● **Owner** Miss P Billington
P S T (Ref:HM02309)

## BILLINGTON, PEGGY
**Peggy Billington**, 36 Hale Pit Rd, Bookham, Leatherhead, **Surrey**, KT23 4BS, ENG.
(T) 01372 459099 (F) 01372 459099
Speciality: Osteopathy.
● **Owner** Miss P Billington
P S T (Ref:HM02310)

## BIMPSON, PETER
**Peter Bimpson**, 67 Halsall Rd, Southport, **Merseyside**, PR8 3DB, ENG.
(T) 01704 566479
Speciality: Massage (Therapeutic), Reflexology. ✔
● **Physical Therapist** Mr P Bimpson Q: ITEC.
C T Yrs. Est.: 15 (Ref:HM02311)

## BINE, NICHOLAS
**Nicholas Bine**, 39 Crossway, Manchester, **Manchester (Greater)**, M20 6TU, ENG.
(T) 01614 451018
Speciality: Osteopathy.
P S T (Ref:HM02312)

## BINGHAM, JULIA
**Julia Bingham**, Elmsall Kennels, Doncaster Rd, North Elmsall, Pontefract, **Yorkshire (West)**, WF9 2DY, ENG.
(T) 01977 640321
Speciality: Reflexology.
S T (Ref:HM02313)

## BINGHAM, JULIE
**Julie Bingham**, 4 Limmer Cl, Barkham, Wokingham, **Berkshire**, RG41 4DF, ENG.
(T) 01189 785784
Speciality: Kinesiology.
M (Ref:HM02314)

## BINGLEY HOMOEOPATHIC PRACTICE
**Bingley Homoeopathic Practice**, 2a Bradley St, Bingley, **Yorkshire (West)**, BD16 4DU, ENG.
(T) 01274 781360
Speciality: Acupuncture, Aromatherapy, Counselling, Holistic Healing, Homeopathy, Hypnotherapy, Massage (Therapeutic), Osteopathy, Reflexology, Reiki. ✔
● **Hypnotherapist** Ms D Chippendale
● **Acupuncturist** Mr A Watkinson Q: Dip.Ac. M: BAcC.
● **Practitioner** Ms P Gregory
● **Reflexologist** Ms C Bedell Q: IIHHT.
● **Practitioner** Ms H Rawling Q: ITEC.
● **Owner** Mr A Robinson M: BRCP.
● **Practitioner** Ms M Potterton Q: BA, MA.
● **Osteopath** Ms S Austin Q: BSc, Hons (OST).
● **Therapist** Ms G Parker Q: BA. M: BACP.
● **Owner** Mrs M Robinson M: BRCP.
C Yrs. Est.: 10 (Ref:HM02315)

## BINMORE & ASSOCIATE
**B J Binmore & Associate**, 41 High St, Chard, **Somerset**, TA20 1QL, ENG.
(T) 01460 61411
Speciality: Chiropodists (Podiatrists).
S (Ref:HM02316)

## BINMORE, B J
**B J Binmore**, Clover Cl, Shute, Axminster, **Devon**, EX13 7QJ, ENG.
(T) 01297 552706
Speciality: Chiropodists (Podiatrists).
S (Ref:HM02317)

## BINMORE, F
**F Binmore**, 34 Berry Drive, Paignton, **Devon**, TQ3 3QW, ENG.
(T) 01803 521562
Speciality: Kinesiology. ✔
● **Health Kinesiologist**
Mr F Binmore Q: KFRP. M: KFRP.
● **Health Kinesiologist**
Mrs B Binmore Q: KFRP. M: KFRP.
C Yrs. Est.: 10 (Ref:HM02318)

## BINNIE, D
**Mrs D Binnie**, West Point, 4 Reigate Hill Cl, Reigate, **Surrey**, RH2 9PG, ENG.
(T) 01737 247459
Speciality: Physiotherapy.
P S T (Ref:HM02319)

## BIO ENERGY HEALING
**Bio Energy Healing**, Balbriggan Co, Dublin, **County Dublin**, IRE.
(T) 01841 5647
Speciality: Complementary Medicines & Therapy.
M (Ref:HM02320)

## BIO ENERGY HEALING
**Bio Energy Healing**, Blackrock Co, Dublin, **County Dublin**, IRE.
(T) 01288 9919
Speciality: Complementary Medicines & Therapy.
M (Ref:HM02321)

## BIO ENERGY HEALING
**Bio Energy Healing**, Drimnagh, Dublin, **County Dublin**, IRE.
(T) 01455 6904
Speciality: Complementary Medicines & Therapy.
M (Ref:HM02322)

## BIO ENERGY HEALING
**Bio Energy Healing**, Finglas & Wicklow St, IRE.
(T) 08729 66468
Speciality: Complementary Medicines & Therapy.
M (Ref:HM02323)

## BIO ENERGY HEALING
**Bio Energy Healing**, Rathmines, **County Dublin**, IRE.
(T) 08722 06382
Speciality: Complementary Medicines & Therapy.
M (Ref:HM02324)

## BIO ENERGY HEALING
**Bio Energy Healing**, Rush Co, Dublin, **County Dublin**, IRE.
(T) 01843 7448
Speciality: Complementary Medicines & Therapy.
M (Ref:HM02325)

## BIO ENERGY HEALING
**Bio Energy Healing**, Bailieboro Co, **County Cavan**, IRE.
(T) 04296 66779
(W) www.bioenergyhealing.co.uk
Speciality: Complementary Medicines & Therapy.
M (Ref:HM02326)

## BIO ENERGY THERAPY
**Bio Energy Therapy**, 4 Abbeyfield Killester, Dublin, **County Dublin**, IRE.
(T) 01831 0544
Speciality: Complementary Medicines & Therapy.
M (Ref:HM02327)

## BIO HEALTH
**Bio Health Ltd**, Culpeper Cl, Medway City Estate, Rochester, **Kent**, ME2 4HU, ENG.
(T) 01634 290115 (F) 01634 290761
Speciality: Complementary Medicines & Therapy.
● **Marketing Director**
June Olive Crisp
M (Ref:HM02328)

## BIO SYNERGY
**Bio Synergy Ltd**, 55 Paddington St, London, **London (Greater)**, W1M 3RQ, ENG.
(T) 020 7935 5291 (F) 020 7487 2581
Speciality: Complementary Medicines & Therapy.
● **Marketing Manager** Mr R ONeil
M (Ref:HM02329)

## BIO UNIT
**Bio Unit**, 25 St Johns Cres, Canton, Cardiff, **Glamorgan (Vale of)**, CF5 1NX, WAL.
(T) 029 2022 5066 (F) 029 2022 5066
Speciality: Aromatherapy.
● **Partner** Mrs M Angove
M O (Ref:HM02330)

## BIODYNAMIC BODY THERAPY
**Biodynamic Body Therapy**, Rivendell Hse, 76 Bayside Blvd, Bayside, Dublin, **County Dublin**, IRE.
(T) 01839 4862
Speciality: Complementary Medicines & Therapy.
M (Ref:HM02331)

## BIODYNAMICS
**Biodynamics**, 41 Upper Halliford Rd, Shepperton, **Surrey**, TW17 8RX, ENG.
(T) 01932 886754
Speciality: Herbal Medicine, Naturopathy, Nutritional Therapy, Vitamin Therapy.
● **Nutritional Therapist** Mr MacDuff
M Yrs. Est.: 1 (Ref:HM02332)

## BIOENERGETIC MEDICINE CLINIC
**Bioenergetic Medicine Clinic**, Carlow, Kilkenny, **County Kilkenny**, IRE.
(T) 05033 5358
Speciality: Complementary Medicines & Therapy.
M (Ref:HM02333)



Key: B Mind-Body Medicine; C Complementary Medicine; H Self Help Treatment; M Medicinal Therapy; O Oriental Medicine; P Postural Therapy; S Manipulative Structural Therapy; T Touch Therapy

## BIOENERGY PARTNERSHIP

**Bioenergy Partnership**, 27 Welcombe Gr, Solihull, **Midlands (West)**, B91 1PD, ENG.
**(T)** 01217 051979
Speciality: Holistic Healing, Yoga, Nutritional Therapy. ✔
● **Manager** Ms A Garland **Q:** Dip.AP.
● **Therapist** Mr J Kelsey **Q:** PhD.
**C** Yrs. Est.: 6 (**Ref:**HM02334)

## BIO-ENERGY THERAPY

**Bio-Energy Therapy**, 33 West Avenue, Donnington, Telford, **Shropshire**, TF2 8BL, ENG.
**(T)** 01952 677163
Speciality: Complementary Medicines & Therapy.
● **Owner** Mrs L Girling
**C** **M** (**Ref:**HM02335)

## BIOFEEDBACK

**Biofeedback**, 18 Farm Cl, Bracknell, **Berkshire**, RG42 1SD, ENG.
**(T)** 01344 640749
Speciality: Complementary Medicines & Therapy.
● **Owner** Dr V Adams
**C** **M** (**Ref:**HM02336)

## BIOFLOW

**Bioflow**, 25 Park House, 39 Park Pl, Cheltenham, **Gloucestershire**, GL50 2RF, ENG.
**(T)** 01242 224107 **(F)** 01242 224107
Speciality: Complementary Medicines & Therapy.
● **Owner** Mr M Baker
**C** **M** (**Ref:**HM02337)

## BIOFLOW

**Bioflow**, Pannier Market, Back Quay, Truro, **Cornwall**, TR1 2LL, ENG.
**(T)** 01872 264222
Speciality: Complementary Medicines & Therapy.
● **Owner** Mrs L Hearn
**C** **M** (**Ref:**HM02338)

## BIOFLOW MAGNOTHERAPY

**Bioflow Magnotherapy**, Potters Farm, Bethersden, Ashford, **Kent**, TN26 3JX, ENG.
**(T)** 01233 820341
Speciality: Complementary Medicines & Therapy.
**C** **M** (**Ref:**HM02339)

## BIOMAG

**BIOMAG**, Bagenalstown, **County Carlow**, IRE.
**(T)** 05032 2422 **(F)** 05032 2433
Speciality: Complementary Medicines & Therapy.
**M** (**Ref:**HM02340)

## BIOMED INTERNATIONAL

**Biomed International**, 55 Queens Rd, East Grinstead, **Sussex (West)**, RH19 1BG, ENG.
**(T)** 01342 322854 **(F)** 01342 324574
Speciality: Complementary Medicines & Therapy.
● **Owner** Mr M Allen
**C** **M** (**Ref:**HM02341)

## BIOPHYSICAL TREATMENT SERVICE

**Biophysical Treatment Service**, 134 Darras Rd, Ponteland, Newcastle Upon Tyne, **Tyne and Wear**, NE20 9PG, ENG.
**(T)** 01661 822050
Speciality: Acupuncture.
**O** (**Ref:**HM02342)

## BIORADIANT HEALTH

**Bioradiant Health**, 3 Blair St, Edinburgh, **Edinburgh (City of)**, EH1 1QR, SCO.
**(T)** 01312 253099
Speciality: Acupuncture, Aromatherapy, Massage (Therapeutic), Mineral & Nutritional Therapy. Onsite massage practitioner for the work place - needle free acupuncture, Chair Massage. Instant Management Therapy. ✔
● **Owner** Mrs L Bennett **Q:** Lic.Ac.
**C** Yrs. Est.: 7 (**Ref:**HM02343)

## BIOS NATURE CLINIC

**Bios Nature Clinic**, 36 Darwen St, Blackburn, **Lancashire**, BB2 2BH, ENG.
**(T)** 01254 676071
**(E)** bionature@aol.com
Speciality: Biofeedback, Clinical Ecology, Herbal Medicine, Homeopathy, Naturopathy, Gerson Therapy. ✔ CREDIT
● **Manager** Ms K Adele
● **Practitioner** Mr D Adele **Q:** MSc.
**B** Yrs. Est.: 17 (**Ref:**HM02344)

## BIOTECH HEALTH & NUTRITION

**Biotech Health & Nutrition Centre**, 48 East St, Andover, **Hampshire**, SP10 1ES, ENG.
**(T)** 01264 323287 **(F)** 01264 323297
Speciality: Complementary Medicines & Therapy.
● **Manager** Mr J Grew
**C** **M** (**Ref:**HM02345)

## BIOTECHNIQUE

**Biotechnique**, 24 Darenth Rise, Chatham, **Kent**, ME5 8QU, ENG.
**(T)** 01634 865020 **(F)** 01634 865020
Speciality: Complementary Medicines & Therapy.
● **Partner** Mr P Fairchild
**C** **M** (**Ref:**HM02346)

## BIOTHERAPY

**Biotherapy**, 116 Weston Park Rd, Plymouth, **Devon**, PL3 4NR, ENG.
**(T)** 01752 674367
Speciality: Homeopathy.
● **Owner** Dr A O'Connel
**M** (**Ref:**HM02347)

## BIOTHERAPY

**Biotherapy Ltd**, 20 Kieth Avenue, Basildon, **Essex**, SS11 7BE, ENG.
**(T)** 01268 453120
Speciality: Complementary Medicines & Therapy.
● **Manager** Mr Clarry
**M** (**Ref:**HM02348)

## BIRCH STREET CLINIC

**Birch Street Clinic For Physiotherapy (The)**, 3 South Vennel, Lanark, **Lanarkshire (South)**, ML11 7JT, SCO.
**(T)** 01555 665703
Speciality: Physiotherapy.
● **Owner** Miss L Seath
**P** **S** **T** (**Ref:**HM02349)

## BIRCH, DIANA

**Diana Birch**, Caradon, Pluckley, Ashford, **Kent**, TN27 0SL, ENG.
**(T)** 01233 840353
Speciality: Reflexology.
● **Owner** Ms D Birch
**S** **T** (**Ref:**HM02350)

## BIRCH, GILLIAN

**Gillian Birch**, 236 Marshmont Way, New Oscott, Birmingham, **Midlands (West)**, B23 5YN, ENG.
**(T)** 01213 508558
Speciality: Reflexology.
**S** **T** (**Ref:**HM02351)

## BIRCH, MARGARET

**Margaret Birch**, 22 Dennis Park Cr, London, **London (Greater)**, SW20 8QH, ENG.
**(T)** 020 8542 0754
Speciality: Aromatherapy, Massage (Therapeutic), Reflexology.
● **Owner** Mrs M Birch
**M** **O** (**Ref:**HM02352)

## BIRCH, R F

**R F Birch**, 1 Paignton Avenue, Portsmouth, **Hampshire**, PO3 6LL, ENG.
**(T)** 023 9266 7038
Speciality: Chiropodists (Podiatrists).
● **Owner** Mr R Birch
**S** (**Ref:**HM02353)

## BIRCH, ROBIN

**Robin Birch**, 44 Fletcher Rd, Oxford, **Oxfordshire**, OX4 2UF, ENG.
**(T)** 01865 395498
Speciality: Hypnotherapy.
● **Owner** Mr R Birch
**B** (**Ref:**HM02354)

## BIRCH, SONIA Y

**Sonia Y Birch**, 74 Ashley Lane, Killamarsh, Sheffield, **Yorkshire (South)**, S21 1AB, ENG.
**(T)** 01142 511521
Speciality: Hypnosis.
**B** (**Ref:**HM02355)

## BIRCHALL, ANNE V

**Anne V Birchall**, 15 Sandy Lane, Orrell, Wigan, **Lancashire**, WN5 7AY, ENG.
**(T)** 01942 519224
Speciality: Chiropodists (Podiatrists).
● **Owner** Mrs A Birchall
**S** (**Ref:**HM02356)

## BIRD, C

**C Bird**, The Aromatherapy Clinic, Kings Head Sports, Harts Lane, Bawburgh, Norwich, **Norfolk**, NR9 3LT, ENG.
**(T)** 01603 744433
Speciality: Aromatherapy.
**M** **O** (**Ref:**HM02357)

## BIRD, CAROLINE

**Caroline Bird**, 49 Winterley Lane, Walsall, **Midlands (West)**, WS4 1LP, ENG.
**(T)** 01922 632990
Speciality: Reflexology.
**S** **T** (**Ref:**HM02358)

## BIRD, D

**D Bird**, 40 Victor Gdns, Hockley, **Essex**, SS5 4DS, ENG.
**(T)** 01702 200921
Speciality: Complementary Medicines & Therapy.
● **Owner** Mr D Bird
**C** **M** (**Ref:**HM02359)

## BIRD, DAPHNE

**Daphne Bird**, 37 Palmers Avenue, Grays, **Essex**, RM17 5TX, ENG.
**(T)** 01375 372865
Speciality: Osteopathy.
● **Owner** Mrs D Bird
**P** **S** **T** (**Ref:**HM02360)

## BIRD, DEBBY

**Debby Bird**, 69 Lloyds Head, Jackfield, Telford, **Shropshire**, TF8 7LZ, ENG.
**(T)** 01952 883927
Speciality: Chiropodists (Podiatrists).
● **Owner** Mr A Bird
**S** (**Ref:**HM02361)

## BIRD, ELAINE

**Elaine Bird**, 17 Gibson Rd, High Wycombe, **Buckinghamshire**, HP12 4QW, ENG.
**(T)** 01494 526573
Speciality: Chiropodists (Podiatrists).
**S** (**Ref:**HM02362)

## BIRD, G F

**G F Bird**, 289A Prince Avenue, Westcliff-on-Sea, **Essex**, SS0 0JP, ENG.
**(T)** 01702 432432
Speciality: Hypnotherapy.
**B** (**Ref:**HM02363)

## BIRD, IAN M

**Ian M Bird**, 17 Kynaston Cl, Harrow, **London (Greater)**, HA3 6TQ, ENG.
**(T)** 020 8954 4394
Speciality: Osteopathy.
● **Owner** Mr I Bird
**P** **S** **T** (**Ref:**HM02364)

## BIRD, J

**J Bird**, 24 Church Rd, Hove, **Sussex (East)**, BN3 2FN, ENG.
**(T)** 01273 329453
Speciality: Chiropodists (Podiatrists).
● **Owner** Mr J Bird
**S** (**Ref:**HM02365)

## BIRD, J K

**J K Bird**, 94 Weston Drive, Stanmore, **London (Greater)**, HA7 2EN, ENG.
**(T)** 020 8907 3997 **(F)** 020 8909 2861
Speciality: Osteopathy.
● **Owner** Mr J Bird
**P** **S** **T** (**Ref:**HM02366)



Key continued: **Yrs.Est:** Years Established **Q:** Qualifications **M:** Professional Membership ✔ Indemnity Insurance CREDIT Accept Credit Cards

### BIRD, JANE
**Jane Bird**, 22 Bella Vista Rd, Brixham, **Devon**, TQ5 8BQ, ENG.
(T) 01803 853528
Speciality: Hypnosis.
● **Owner** Mrs J Bird
B (Ref:HM02367)

### BIRD, LYNN
**Mrs Lynn Bird**, 9 Caithness Cl, Oakley, Basingstoke, **Hampshire**, RG23 7NG, ENG.
(T) 01256 780202
Speciality: Acupuncture.
O (Ref:HM02368)

### BIRD, MICHELLE
**Michelle Bird**, 22 Llandaff Rd, Cardiff, **Glamorgan (Vale of)**, CF11 9NJ, WAL.
(T) 029 2037 7656
Speciality: Chiropodists (Podiatrists).
S (Ref:HM02369)

### BIRD, NEIL
**Neil Bird**, 49 Etterby St, Carlisle, **Cumbria**, CA3 9JD, ENG.
(T) 01228 546588 (F) 01228 546588
Speciality: Osteopathy.
● **Partner** Miss S McGregor
P S T (Ref:HM02370)

### BIRD, SUZANNE
**Suzanne Bird**, 22 Fleetwood Way, Thame, **Oxfordshire**, OX9 3DE, ENG.
(T) 01844 216878 (F) 01844 216927
Speciality: Chiropractic.
● **Owner** Mrs S Bird
P S T (Ref:HM02371)

### BIRKBECK, C A
**C A Birkbeck**, 172 Maidstone Rd, Borough Green, Sevenoaks, **Kent**, TN15 8JD, ENG.
(T) 01732 883271
Speciality: Chiropodists (Podiatrists).
● **Owner** Mrs C Birkbeck
S (Ref:HM02372)

### BIRKDALE CHIROPRACTIC CLINIC
**Birkdale Chiropractic Clinic**, 37 Westbourne Rd, Southport, **Merseyside**, PR8 2HY, ENG.
(T) 01704 569695 (F) 01704 569695
Speciality: Chiropractic.
● **Principal** Mr J Fulwood
P S T (Ref:HM02373)

### BIRKDALE PAEDI & NEURO CLNC
**Birkdale Paediatric & Adult Neuro Clinic**, 34 Birkdale Rd, London, **London (Greater)**, W5 1JZ, ENG.
(T) 020 8998 9403
Speciality: Physiotherapy.
P S T (Ref:HM02374)

### BIRKENHEAD CHIROPODY CENTRE
**Birkenhead Chiropody Centre**, 108 Claughton Rd, Birkenhead, **Merseyside**, CH41 6ES, ENG.
(T) 01516 475917
Speciality: Chiropodists (Podiatrists).
● **Owner** Mr P Davies
S (Ref:HM02375)

### BIRKENHEAD CHIROPRACTIC CLNC
**Birkenhead Chiropractic Clinic**, 33 Hamilton Sq, Birkenhead, **Merseyside**, CH41 6AZ, ENG.
(T) 01516 477989 (F) 01516 476261
Speciality: Chiropractic.
● **Principal** Miss M Mouss
P S T (Ref:HM02376)

### BIRKIN, H
**H Birkin**, 76 Moorland Rd, Stoke-On-Trent, **Staffordshire**, ST6 1DY, ENG.
(T) 01782 813166
Speciality: Chiropodists (Podiatrists).
● **Owner** Mrs H Birkin
S (Ref:HM02377)

### BIRKS, W KEITH
**W Keith Birks**, 10 The Crescent, Middlesbrough, **Cleveland**, TS5 6SQ, ENG.
(T) 01642 850018
Speciality: Osteopathy.
● **Owner** Mr W Birks
P S T (Ref:HM02378)

### BIRLESON, G
**G Birleson**, 43 Castle St, Trowbridge, **Wiltshire**, BA14 8AY, ENG.
(T) 01225 763898
Speciality: Chiropodists (Podiatrists).
S (Ref:HM02379)

### BIRLEY, PAUL
**Paul Birley**, 15 Lee Rd, Hollywood, Birmingham, **Midlands (West)**, B47 5NY, ENG.
(T) 01564 822967
Speciality: Hypnotherapy.
B (Ref:HM02380)

### BIRMINGHAM & DISTRICT
**Birmingham & District Osteopathic Clinic**, Vaughan McDermott House, 955 Stratford Rd, Hall Green, Birmingham, **Midlands (West)**, B28 8EE, ENG.
(T) 01217 775757
Speciality: Osteopathy.
P S T (Ref:HM02381)

### BIRMINGHAM ACU/CHIRO CLNC
**Chiromed**, 26 Wake Green Rd, Birmingham, **Midlands (West)**, B13 9PA, ENG.
(T) 01214 493578
Speciality: Acupuncture, Chiropractic, Counselling, Massage (Therapeutic). ✔
● **Associate** John William Duncombe Q: DC. M: MCA.
● **Associate** Ms B Husband Q: DC. M: MCA.
● **Associate** Ms L Wilkes Q: DC, RGN. M: MCA.
● **Owner** Mr K Grant Q: BA (Hons), DC. M: CC, MCA.
P Yrs. Est.: 13 (Ref:HM02382)

### BIRMINGHAM CHINESE MEDICINE
**Birmingham Centre For Chinese Medicine**, 245 Alcester Rd South, Birmingham, **Midlands (West)**, B14 6DT, ENG.
(T) 01214 412757
Speciality: Complementary Medicines & Therapy.
● **Owner** Mr N Lampert
C M (Ref:HM02383)

### BIRMINGHAM CTRE-ARTS THERAPIES
**Birmingham Centre For Arts Therapies**, Friends Institute, 220 Moseley Rd, Birmingham, **Midlands (West)**, B12 0DG, ENG.
(T) 01214 404455 (F) 01214 404455
Speciality: Complementary Medicines & Therapy.
● **Manager** Ms A Fenwick
C M (Ref:HM02384)

### BIRMINGHAM DIATHERMY
**Birmingham Diathermy Specialists**, 21 Albert Rd, Harborne, Birmingham, **Midlands (West)**, B17 0AP, ENG.
(T) 01214 271721
Speciality: Electrolysis.
● **Owner** Ms J Banks
T (Ref:HM02385)

### BIRMINGHAM HYPNOTHERAPY
**Birmingham Hypnotherapy**, 44 Lea House, Woodview Drive, Birmingham, **Midlands (West)**, B15 2HE, ENG.
(T) 01214 405228
Speciality: Aromatherapy, Colour Therapy, Complementary Therapy, Counselling, Crystal Healing, Healing Therapy, Hypnosis, Indian Head Massage, Life Style Coaching, Neuro-Linguistic Program, Spiritual Healing, Stress Therapy, Chakra and Aura Healing, Personal Development, Regression Therapy.
● **Owner** Mr D Green
C (Ref:HM02386)

### BIRMINGHAM MOBILE CHIRO CTRE
**Birmingham Mobile Chiropody Centre**, 16 Weoley Hill, Birmingham, **Midlands (West)**, B29 4AD, ENG.
(T) 01214 721524 (F) 01214 721524
Speciality: Chiropodists (Podiatrists).
● **Owner** Mr M Blom-Hamm
S (Ref:HM02387)

### BIRMINGHAM PHYSIO CLINIC
**Birmingham Physiotherapy Clinic**, 1376 Coventry Rd, Yardley, Birmingham, **Midlands (West)**, B25 8AE, ENG.
(T) 01217 074393
Speciality: Acupuncture, Manipulation, Psychotherapy. ✔
● **Physiotherapist** Mr C Rushton Q: SRP.
S Yrs. Est.: 10 (Ref:HM02388)

### BIRMINGHAM SCHOOL OF PODIATRY
**Birmingham School Of Podiatry**, Sherlock St, Birmingham, **Midlands (West)**, B5 7DB, ENG.
(T) 01214 464532
Speciality: Chiropodists (Podiatrists).
S (Ref:HM02389)

### BIRMINGHAM TRAD ACU CENTRE
**Birmingham Traditional Acupuncture Centre**, 131A Alcester Rd, Birmingham, **Midlands (West)**, B13 8JP, ENG.
(T) 01214 499500
Speciality: Acupuncture, Zero Balancing. ✔
● **Therapist** Ms R Ansell Davis M: BAcC.
● **Therapist** Mrs H Timmermans M: BAcC.
● **Therapist** Ms L Fox M: BAcC.
S (Ref:HM02390)

### BIRMINGHAM WOMENS COUNS
**Birmingham Womens Counselling & Therapy Centre (The)**, The Lodge, Queensbridge Rd, Birmingham, **Midlands (West)**, B13 8QB, ENG.
(T) 01214 422241
Speciality: Psychotherapy.
B (Ref:HM02391)

### BIRMINGHAM, LINDA
**Linda Birmingham**, 172A Field End Rd, Pinner, **London (Greater)**, HA5 1RH, ENG.
(T) 020 8868 0239
Speciality: Alexander Technique.
● **Owner** Miss L Birmingham
P S (Ref:HM02392)

### BIRMINGHAM, MURROUGH (DR)
**Dr Murrough**, Inverarie Ramelton Rd, Ballyrai, Letterkenny, **County Donegal**, IRE.
(T) 07424 559
Speciality: Complementary Medicines & Therapy.
M (Ref:HM02393)

### BIRNIE, KATHLEEN
**Kathleen Birnie**, Natural Way, 5 Harvey Pl, Banff, **Aberdeenshire**, AB45 1EJ, SCO.
(T) 01261 812312
Speciality: Reflexology.
S T (Ref:HM02394)

### BIROFLOW INDEPENDENT DIST
**Biroflow Independent Distributor**, 1 Virginia Cl, Lofthouse, Wakefield, **Yorkshire (West)**, WF3 3TB, ENG.
(T) 01924 820536
Speciality: Complementary Medicines & Therapy.
● **Manager** Mrs S Mitchell-Gears
M (Ref:HM02395)

### BIRRAN, VERONICA
**Veronica Birran**, Chandlers, Town Hill, Hebden, Skipton, **Yorkshire (North)**, BD23 5D, ENG.
(T) 01733 286176
Speciality: Acupuncture.
● **Owner** Ms V Birran
O (Ref:HM02396)

### BIRRELL, M
**M Birrell**, Allerton, Hall Lane, Upper Farringdon, Alton, **Hampshire**, GU34 3EA, ENG.
(T) 01420 587352
Speciality: Hypnosis.
● **Owner** Ms M Birrell
B (Ref:HM02397)

### BIRT, JANET
**Janet Birt**, 3 Church Meadow, Boverton, Llantwit Major, **Glamorgan (Vale of)**, CF61 2AT, WAL.
(T) 01446 792073
Speciality: Chiropodists (Podiatrists).
● **Owner** Ms J Birt
S (Ref:HM02398)

### BIRTHWORKS
**Birthworks**, 14-15 Fiddlebridge Ind Centre, Hatfield, **Hertfordshire**, AL10 0DE, ENG.

(T) 01707 880333 (F) 01707 880333
(E) birthworks@ic24.net
(W) www.birthworks.co.uk
Speciality: Metamorphic Therapy. ✔ CREDIT
● **Therapist** Mr J O'Grady
● **Partner** Debbie Summers
● **Therapist** Mrs C Sadler
**H** Yrs. Est.: 12 (**Ref:**HM02399)

## BIRTWELL, ANDREW

**Holycombe Complementary Health Centre**, Whichford, Shipston on Stour, **Warwickshire**, CV36 5PH, ENG.
(T) 01608 684500 (F) 01608 684501
(E) birtwell@globalnet.co.uk
Speciality: Counselling, Family Therapy, Gestalt Therapy, Group Therapy, Psychotherapy, Rogerian Therapy, Stress Therapy. ✔
● **Head of Practice** Mr A Birtwell
(T) 01608 684239 M: GPTI.
**B** Yrs. Est.: 4 (**Ref:**HM02400)

## BISBY, TIFFANY

**Tiffany Bisby**, Offshoot Clinic, Cavendish St, Keighley, **Yorkshire (West)**, BD21 3RG, ENG.
(T) 01274 542114
Speciality: Homeopathy.
● **Owner** Ms T Bisby
**M** (**Ref:**HM02401)

## BISDÉE, EMMA

**Emma Bisdée**, 2 Brocklebank Rd, London, **London (Greater)**, SW18 3AU, ENG.
(T) 020 8870 1565
(W) www.complementary-healthcare.co.uk/info/headtotoe
Speciality: Reflexology.
**S T** (**Ref:**HM02402)

## BISH, M A & J

**M A & J Bish**, Tanglewood, Mill Lane, Bardsey, Leeds, **Yorkshire (West)**, LS17 9AN, ENG.
(T) 01937 572957
Speciality: Physiotherapy.
● **Partner** Mrs J Bish
**P S T** (**Ref:**HM02403)

## BISHOP AUCKLAND CHIROPODY

**Bishop Auckland Chiropody Training School**, Watling Rd, Bishop Auckland, **County Durham**, DL14 6RP, ENG.
(T) 01388 605161
Speciality: Chiropodists (Podiatrists).
**S** (**Ref:**HM02404)

## BISHOP, HEATHER

**Heather Bishop**, 6 Tregarne Trce, St. Austell, **Cornwall**, PL25 4BE, ENG.
(T) 01726 72345 (F) 01726 68957
Speciality: Physiotherapy.
● **Owner** Miss S Bishop
**P S T** (**Ref:**HM02405)

## BISHOP, N

**N Bishop**, 73 Hackthorn Rd, Sheffield, **Yorkshire (South)**, S8 8TB, ENG.
(T) 01142 490115
Speciality: Reflexology.
● **Owner** Ms N Bishop
**S T** (**Ref:**HM02406)

## BISHOP, PATRICIA

**Patricia Bishop**, 26 Greenways, Flitwick, Bedford, **Bedfordshire**, MK45 1DA, ENG.
(T) 01525 712204
Speciality: Osteopathy.
● **Owner** Mrs P Bishop
**P S T** (**Ref:**HM02407)

## BISHOP, RONALD C

**Ronald C Bishop**, British Acupuncture Association, 34 Alderney St, London, **London (Greater)**, SW1V 4EU, ENG.
(T) 020 7834 1012
Speciality: Osteopathy.
**P S T** (**Ref:**HM02408)

## BISHOP, S

**Mrs S Bishop**, Broadleas Lodge, Hartmoor Rd, Devizes, **Wiltshire**, SN10 5HQ, ENG.
(T) 01380 721765
Speciality: Acupuncture.
● **Owner** Mrs S Bishop
**O** (**Ref:**HM02409)

## BISHOP, S J

**S J Bishop**, Sunnybank, Login, Whitland, **Carmarthenshire**, SA34 0XB, WAL.
(T) 01994 419725
Speciality: Chiropractic.
**P S T** (**Ref:**HM02410)

## BISHOP, SARAH

**Sarah Bishop**, 3 Dixwell Cl, Rainham, Gillingham, **Kent**, ME8 9TB, ENG.
(T) 01634 230388
Speciality: Aromatherapy, Bowen Therapy, Massage (Therapeutic), Hopi Ear Candles. ✔
● **Complementary Therapist**
Sarah Bishop Q: BTER, ITEC, TATQ. M: GCP, ITEC.
**C** Yrs. Est.: 4 (**Ref:**HM02411)

## BISHOP-COMPTON, JENNY

**Jenny Bishop-Compton**, 44 Lakenheath, London, **London (Greater)**, N14 4RP, ENG.
(T) 020 8886 7093
Speciality: Hypnosis.
**B** (**Ref:**HM02412)

## BISHOPS CLEEVE PHYSIO & SPORTS

**Bishops Cleeve Physiotherapy & Sports Injuries**, 4 Pecked Lane, Bishops Cleeve, Cheltenham, **Gloucestershire**, GL52 4JE, ENG.
(T) 01242 677655 (F) 01242 677755
Speciality: Physiotherapy. ✔
● **Physiotherapist** Mr D Snape Q: MCSP, SRP. M: CSP.
**S** Yrs. Est.: 1 (**Ref:**HM02413)

## BISHOPS LODGE

**Bishops Lodge**, Oakley Green Rd, Oakley Green, Windsor, **Berkshire**, SL4 5UL, ENG.
(T) 01753 869433
Speciality: Physiotherapy.
**P S T** (**Ref:**HM02414)

## BISHOPS STORTFORD CHIRO CLINIC

**Bishops Stortford Chiropractic Clinic**, Hockerhill House, 29 Hockerill St, Bishop's Stortford, **Hertfordshire**, CM23 2DH, ENG.
(T) 01279 466841
Speciality: Chiropractic.
**P S T** (**Ref:**HM02415)

## BISHOP'S STORTFORD HOMEOPATHIC

**Bishop's Stortford Homeopathic Clinic**, 9 Nelson Rd, Bishop's Stortford, **Hertfordshire**, CM23 3LH, ENG.
(T) 01279 658138
(E) margit.w@talk21.com
Speciality: Allergy Testing, Bach Remedies, Dowsing, Homeopathy, Kinesiology, Naturopathy, Australian Bush Flower Remedies. ✔
● **Homeopath**
Mrs M Wendelberger-James Q: MA (Hons), RSHom. M: Soc.Hom.
**M** Yrs. Est.: 7 (**Ref:**HM02416)

## BITS & BOBS

**Bits & Bobs**, 3 Fore St, Liskeard, **Cornwall**, PL14 3JA, ENG.
(T) 01579 348750
Speciality: Complementary Medicines & Therapy.
● **Owner** Mrs W Pritchard
**M** (**Ref:**HM02417)

## BIZONY, STELLA

**Stella Bizony**, Wild Hay Cottage, Buttsfield Lane, Laughton, Lewes, **Sussex (East)**, BN8 6BJ, ENG.
(T) 01825 841001
Speciality: Clairvoyants & Palmists.
**B** (**Ref:**HM02418)

## BJARNASON, MARGARET

**Margaret Bjarnason**, 20 Marlborough Rd, Oxford, **Oxfordshire**, OX1 4LP, ENG.
(T) 01865 201965
Speciality: Aromatherapy.
**M O** (**Ref:**HM02419)

## BJORK, CARINA

**Carina Bjork**, Complementary Health Centre, 29a St Marys St, Ely, **Cambridgeshire**, CB7 4HF, ENG.
(T) 01353 664476
Speciality: Homeopathy.
● **Owner** Mr A Specne
**M** (**Ref:**HM02420)

## BLACK, CATHY

**Cathy Black**, 150 Oakleigh Park Drive, Leigh-On-Sea, **Essex**, SS9 1RU, ENG.
(T) 07967 208442
Speciality: Reflexology.
**S T** (**Ref:**HM02421)

## BLACK, G

**G Black**, Bembury House, Bembury Lane, Thornford, Sherborne, **Dorset**, DT9 6QF, ENG.
(T) 01935 873320 (F) 01935 872308
Speciality: Acupuncture.
● **Owner** Mrs G Black
**O** (**Ref:**HM02422)

## BLACK, G

**G Black**, 22 West Avenue, Worthing, **Sussex (West)**, BN11 5LU, ENG.
(T) 01903 240796
Speciality: Physiotherapy.
● **Owner** Miss G Black
**P S T** (**Ref:**HM02423)

## BLACK, JIM

**Jim Black**, 42 Torridon Avenue, Glasgow, **Glasgow (City of)**, G41 5NS, SCO.
(T) 01414 274973
Speciality: Biomechanics, Chiropody, Nail Surgery, Podiatry. ✔ CREDIT
● **Owner/Chiropodist** Mr J Black Q: DPodM, M.S.C.P, S.R.Ch.
**M** Yrs. Est.: 36 (**Ref:**HM02424)

## BLACK, PAULINE

**Pauline Black**, Broadwater Osteopathic Practice, 2 Sompting Rd, Worthing, **Sussex (West)**, BN14 9EP, ENG.
(T) 01903 208238 (F) 01903 203360
(E) paulineblack@cwctv.net
Speciality: Homeopathy, Accredited Journey Therapist. ✔
● **Homeopath** Ms P Black Q: BA, MCH, RSHom. M: Soc.Hom.
**B** Yrs. Est.: 10 (**Ref:**HM02425)

## BLACK, R N

**R N Black**, Cassidy Rd Medical Centre, 651A Fulham Rd, London, **London (Greater)**, SW6 5PX, ENG.
(T) 020 7731 2511 (F) 020 7371 7857
Speciality: Chiropodists (Podiatrists).
● **Manager** Mr L McNulty
**S** (**Ref:**HM02426)

## BLACK, R N

**R N Black**, 162A Balham High Rd, Balham, London, **London (Greater)**, SW12 9BW, ENG.
(T) 020 8673 6789
Speciality: Chiropodists (Podiatrists).
**S** (**Ref:**HM02427)

## BLACK, SAUL

**Saul Black**, 5a Skinner St, Whitby, **Yorkshire (North)**, YO21 3AH, ENG.
(T) 01947 825137
(E) annette@naturalorigins.co.uk
Speciality: Biomechanics, Chiropody, Nail Surgery. ✔
● **Chiropodist (Podiatrist)**
Mr S Black
**C** Yrs. Est.: 2 (**Ref:**HM02428)

## BLACKBERRY HILL HOSPITAL

**Blackberry Hill Hospital Natural Therapy Centre**, Manor Rd, Fishponds, Bristol, BS16 2EW, ENG.
(T) 01179 656061 (F) 01179 656061
Speciality: Acupuncture.
● **Manager** Mrs M Neery
**O** (**Ref:**HM02429)

## BLACKBERRY ORTHO & SPRTS CLNC

**Blackberry Orthopaedic & Sports Clinic**, Blackberry Court, Walnut Tree, Milton Keynes, **Buckinghamshire**, MK7 7PB, ENG.
(T) 01908 604666
Speciality: Osteopathy.
**P S T** (**Ref:**HM02430)

## BLACKBOROW, R A

**R A Blackborow**, 10 St Peters Avenue, Weston-Super-Mare, **Somerset**, BS23 2JU, ENG.



Key continued: **Yrs.Est:** Years Established **Q:** Qualifications **M:** Professional Membership ✔ Indemnity Insurance CREDIT Accept Credit Cards

(T) 01934 632580
Speciality: Chiropodists (Podiatrists).
● **Owner** Mr R Blackborow
S (Ref:HM02431)

## BLACKBOURN, STEPHEN
**Stephen Blackbourn**, 9 Clevely Way, Nottingham, **Nottinghamshire**, NG11 8AY, ENG.
(T) 01159 749939
Speciality: Chiropodists (Podiatrists).
S (Ref:HM02432)

## BLACKBURN PHYSIOTHERAPY CLINIC
**Blackburn Physiotherapy Clinic**, Royal Infirmary Hospital, Infirmary Rd, Blackburn, **Lancashire**, BB2 3LR, ENG.
(T) 01254 294172
Speciality: Physiotherapy.
● **Manageress** Mrs R Nuttall
P S T (Ref:HM02433)

## BLACKBURN, JENNIFER M
**Jennifer M Blackburn**, Kennedy Rd, Bracebridge Heath, Lincoln, **Lincolnshire**, LN4 2LG, ENG.
(T) 01522 529651
Speciality: Chiropodists (Podiatrists).
S (Ref:HM02434)

## BLACKBURN, MARK
**Mark Blackburn**, 6 Dalesman Drive, Oldham, **Lancashire**, OL1 4PU, ENG.
(T) 01706 299805
Speciality: Chiropodists (Podiatrists).
S (Ref:HM02435)

## BLACKBURN, OLIVE
**Olive Blackburn**, Broadstone Centre Of Complementary Medicine, 11 Dunyeats Rd, Broadstone, **Dorset**, BH18 8AA, ENG.
(T) 01202 692493
Speciality: Hypnotherapy.
B (Ref:HM02436)

## BLACKBURN, ROBERT W
**Mr Robert W Blackburn**, The Osteopathic Clinic, 92b Widemarsh St, Hereford, **Herefordshire**, HR4 9HG, ENG.
(T) 01432 273234
Speciality: Osteopathy.
● **Principal** Mr R Blackburn
P S T (Ref:HM02437)

## BLACKBURN, SUSAN
**Susan Blackburn**, The Owlers, Burlees Lane, Hebden Bridge, **Yorkshire (West)**, HX7 8PS, ENG.
(T) 01422 843156
Speciality: Chiropodists (Podiatrists).
● **Owner** Mrs S Blackburn
S (Ref:HM02438)

## BLACKBURN, V
**V Blackburn**, Eastry Clinic, Lower St, Eastry, Sandwich, **Kent**, CT13 0HX, ENG.
(T) 01304 611751
Speciality: Herbalists.
● **Owner** Ms V Blackburn
M (Ref:HM02439)

## BLACKDEN, J M
**J M Blackden**, St Michaels Cottage, Kings Rd, St. Albans, **Hertfordshire**, AL3 4TG, ENG.
(T) 01727 867569
Speciality: Hypnosis.
● **Owner** Mrs J Blackden
B (Ref:HM02440)

## BLACKER, JOHN
**John Blacker**, 25 Harrington Villas, Brighton, **Sussex (East)**, BN1 6RG, ENG.
(T) 01273 540670
Speciality: Counselling, Hypnosis, Hypnotherapy. ✓
● **Owner** Mr J Blacker Q: CRAH.
B Yrs. Est.: 7 (Ref:HM02441)

## BLACKFEN HYPNOTHERAPY
**Blackfen Hypnotherapy**, 267 Days Lane, Sidcup, **Kent**, DA15 8JX, ENG.
(T) 020 8302 3289 (F) 020 8302 3289
(E) t.g.a.smith@lineone.co.uk
Speciality: Cognitive Therapy, Counselling, Gestalt Therapy, Hypnosis, Hypnotherapy, Psychotherapy, Rogerian Therapy, Stress Therapy.
● **Hypnotherapist** Mr T Smith Q: Dip.Hyp, Dip.Psych, NLP.
H Yrs. Est.: 20 (Ref:HM02442)

## BLACKHALL CHIROP & PODIATRY
**Blackhall Chiropody & Podiatry Clinic**, 5 Marischal Pl, Edinburgh, **Edinburgh (City of)**, EH4 3NE, SCO.
(T) 01313 323255
Speciality: Chiropodists (Podiatrists).
● **Owner** Mrs J Johnson
S (Ref:HM02443)

## BLACKHALL PARK CENTRE
**Blackhall Park Natural Therapy Centre**, 32 Hunterhill Rd, Paisley, **Renfrewshire**, PA2 6ST, SCO.
(T) 01418 877930 (F) 01418 877930
Speciality: Allergy Testing, Bowen Therapy, Kinesiology, Massage (Therapeutic), Reflexology, Reiki, On-Site Massge.
● **Therapist** Mr S Reid
● **Owner** Miss F Gass
C Yrs. Est.: 9 (Ref:HM02444)

## BLACKHALL PHYSIOTHERAPY CLINIC
**Blackhall Physiotherapy Clinic**, 1 House O'Hill Gardens, Edinburgh, **Edinburgh (City of)**, EH4 2AR, SCO.
(T) 01313 432000
Speciality: Psychotherapy. ✓
● **Physiotherapist**
Mr G Paterson Brown Q: MCSP, SRP.
S Yrs. Est.: 14 (Ref:HM02445)

## BLACKHEATH & BROCKLEY
**Blackheath & Brockley Counselling & Psychotherapy**, 153 Pepys Rd, London, **London (Greater)**, SE14 5SG, ENG.
(T) 020 7635 5809
Speciality: Psychotherapy.
● **Owner** Ms L Seear
B (Ref:HM02446)

## BLACKHEATH CENTRE
**Blackheath Alexander Technique Centre**, 184-186 Westcombe Hill, London, **London (Greater)**, SE3 7DR, ENG.
(T) 020 8854 5080
Speciality: Alexander Technique.
● **Owner** Miss B McAuliffe
P S (Ref:HM02447)

## BLACKHEATH CHIROPRACTIC CLINIC
**Blackheath Chiropractic Clinic**, 7 Southvale Rd, London, **London (Greater)**, SE3 0TP, ENG.
(T) 020 8852 5369
Speciality: Chiropractic.
P S T (Ref:HM02448)

## BLACKHEATH COMP HEALTH CTRE
**Blackheath Complementary Health Centre**, 184-186 Westcombe Hill, London, **London (Greater)**, SE3 7DH, ENG.
(T) 020 8293 5380
Speciality: Complementary Medicines & Therapy.
● **Manager** Ms S Pritchard
M (Ref:HM02449)

## BLACKHEATH COMP THERAPIES CTRE
**Blackheath Complementary Therapies Centre**, 42 Blacklands Rd, London, **London (Greater)**, SE6 3AF, ENG.
(T) 020 8697 7861 (F) 020 8697 7861
Speciality: Acupuncture. ✓
● **Manager** Mr K Hammond
● **Therapist** Dr M Hammond Q: MD(AM).
C Yrs. Est.: 10 (Ref:HM02450)

## BLACKHEATH OSTEO & ACU CLINIC
**Blackheath Osteopathy & Acupuncture Clinic**, 19 Tranquil Vale, London, **London (Greater)**, SE3 0BU, ENG.
(T) 020 8852 1706
Speciality: Osteopathy.
P S T (Ref:HM02451)

## BLACKHILL HEALTH CARE
**Blackhill Health Care**, 209 Pitshanger Lane, London, **London (Greater)**, W5 1RQ, ENG.
(T) 020 8566 7539 (F) 020 8998 2791
Speciality: Psychology.
● **Owner** Mr P Karataos
B (Ref:HM02452)

## BLACKLAW-JONES, R
**R Blacklaw-Jones**, 15 North St, Haverfordwest, **Pembrokeshire**, SA61 2JE, WAL.
(T) 01437 769713 (F) 01437 769713
Speciality: Osteopathy.
● **Owner** Mr R Blacklaw-Jones
P S T (Ref:HM02453)

## BLACKLAW-JONES, RICHARD
**Richard Blacklaw-Jones**, 78 Mansel St, Swansea, SA1 5TW, WAL.
(T) 01792 654751
Speciality: Osteopathy.
P S T (Ref:HM02454)

## BLACKLEDGE, VIVIAN
**Vivian Blackledge**, 1st Floor Woburn Court, 8 Guildhall Hill, Norwich, **Norfolk**, NR2 1JG, ENG.
(T) 01603 219254
Speciality: Reflexology.
● **Partner** Mrs V Blackledge
S T (Ref:HM02455)

## BLACKLER, G G
**G G Blackler**, Sea Call, Cliff Rd, Wembury, Plymouth, **Devon**, PL9 0HW, ENG.
(T) 01752 862069
Speciality: Aromatherapy.
● **Owner** Mr G Blackler
M O (Ref:HM02456)

## BLACKMAN, G P
**G P Blackman**, 199 Burnt Oak Broadway, Edgware, **London (Greater)**, HA8 5EG, ENG.
(T) 020 8952 4405
Speciality: Chiropodists (Podiatrists).
S (Ref:HM02457)

## BLACKPOOL CHIROPRACTIC CLINIC
**Blackpool Chiropractic Clinic**, 2a Alfred St, Blackpool, **Lancashire**, FY1 4LH, ENG.
(T) 01253 291000
Speciality: Chiropractic.
● **Owner** Mr A Lambeth
P S T (Ref:HM02458)

## BLACKPOOL OSTEOPATHY CLINIC
**Blackpool Osteopathy Clinic**, 47 Springfield Rd, Blackpool, **Lancashire**, FY1 1PZ, ENG.
(T) 01253 625578
Speciality: Osteopathy.
P S T (Ref:HM02459)

## BLACKROCK
**Blackrock Counselling & Psychotherapy**, 47 Carysford Downs, Blackrock, **County Dublin**, IRE.
(T) 01288 6773
Speciality: Psychotherapy.
B (Ref:HM02460)

## BLACKROCK ACUPUNCTURE
**Blackrock Acupuncture & Reflexology Clinic**, 6 Clontarf Est, Skehard Rd, Blackrock, Cork, **County Cork**, IRE.
(T) 021 4358 777
Speciality: Acupuncture.
O (Ref:HM02461)

## BLACKROCK OSTEOPATHS
**Blackrock Osteopaths**, 28 Lakelands Ave, Kilmacud Rd, U, Blackrock, **County Dublin**, IRE.
(T) 01288 6514
Speciality: Osteopathy.
P S T (Ref:HM02462)

## BLACKSTONE PHYSIO & SPORTS
**Blackstone Physiotherapy & Sports Injury Clinic**, 101 Main St, Moira, Craigavon, **County Armagh**, BT67 0LH, NIR.
(T) 028 9261 1211
Speciality: Physiotherapy.
● **Owner** Mrs K McArthy
P S T (Ref:HM02463)

## BLACKSTONE, VICTORIA (DR)
**Dr Victoria Blackstone**, 14 Ellington Rd, London, **London (Greater)**, N10 3DG, ENG.
(T) 020 8883 4242 (F) 020 8883 0983
Speciality: Homeopathy.
● **Owner** Dr V Blackstone
M (Ref:HM02464)

Key: B Mind-Body Medicine C Complementary Medicine H Self Help Treatment M Medicinal Therapy O Oriental Medicine P Postural Therapy S Manipulative Structural Therapy T Touch Therapy

**BLACKWELL, HEATHER**

**Heather Blackwell**, 13 Gressingham Walk, Lancaster, **Lancashire**, LA1 4RD, ENG.
(T) 01524 36532
Speciality: Chiropodists (Podiatrists).
● **Owner** Mrs H Blackwell
S (Ref:HM02465)

**BLACKWELL, Z**

**Z Blackwell**, 74 Albemarle Rd, York, **Yorkshire (North)**, YO23 1HB, ENG.
(T) 01904 651547
Speciality: Chiropodists (Podiatrists).
● **Owner** Mrs Z Blackwell
S (Ref:HM02466)

**BLACKWOOD, JANE**

**Jane Blackwood**, 9 Bradley Drive, Sittingbourne, **Kent**, ME10 1RB, ENG.
(T) 01795 426692
Speciality: Reflexology.
S T (Ref:HM02467)

**BLACKWOOD, R H W**

**R H W Blackwood**, 7 Whitecrook St, Clydebank, **Argyll and Bute**, G81 1QN, SCO.
(T) 01419 525215
Speciality: Chiropodists (Podiatrists).
S (Ref:HM02468)

**BLADEN, DAVE**

**Dave Bladen**, 25 Lower Gungate, Tamworth, **Staffordshire**, B79 7AT, ENG.
(T) 01827 68374
Speciality: Acupuncture.
O (Ref:HM02469)

**BLADES, S**

**S Blades**, 3 Hillside Cottages, South Brent, **Devon**, TQ10 9BA, ENG.
(T) 01364 73440
Speciality: Acupuncture.
O (Ref:HM02470)

**BLAGG, NIGEL**

**Nigel Blagg**, 39 Staplegrove Rd, Taunton, **Somerset**, TA1 1DG, ENG.
(T) 01823 336204 (F) 01823 332201
Speciality: Psychology.
● **Owner** Dr N Blagg
B (Ref:HM02471)

**BLAIR, GRAHAM**

**Graham Blair**, 325 Tettenhall Rd, Wolverhampton, **Midlands (West)**, WV6 0JZ, ENG.
(T) 01902 565965
Speciality: Hypnotherapy.
● **Owner** Mr G Blair
B (Ref:HM02472)

**BLAIR, GRAHAM**

**Graham Blair**, Bus Development Centre, 21 Temple St, **Midlands (West)**, WV2 4AN, ENG.
(T) 01902 773076
Speciality: Hypnosis.
B (Ref:HM02473)

**BLAIR, R C**

**R C Blair**, 18 Cushendall Rd, Ballymena, **County Antrim**, BT43 6HE, NIR.
(T) 028 2565 2624
Speciality: Physiotherapy.
P S T (Ref:HM02474)

**BLAIR, RICHARD**

**Richard Blair**, 23 Forbes Rd, Edinburgh, **Edinburgh (City of)**, EH10 4EG, SCO.
(T) 01312 298200
(E) blair @shiatsuscot.co.uk
(W) www.shiatsuscot.co.uk
Speciality: Shiatsu. ✔
● **Principal/Shiatsu therapist**
Mr R Blair Q: MRSS.
O Yrs. Est.: 10 (Ref:HM02475)

**BLAKE, A**

**Miss A Blake**, Bank Court, Manor Rd, Verwood, **Dorset**, BH31 6DW, ENG.
(T) 01202 827609
Speciality: Chiropodists (Podiatrists).
S (Ref:HM02476)

**BLAKE, ADRIAN**

**Adrian Blake**, 42 East St, Bromley, **Kent**, BR1 1QX, ENG.
(T) 020 8300 5465
Speciality: Hypnotherapy.
● **Owner** A Blake
B (Ref:HM02477)

**BLAKE, D**

**D Blake**, Harequin House, 43 Chester Rd, Ilford, **Essex**, IG3 8PT, ENG.
(T) 020 8599 6013
Speciality: Complementary Medicines & Therapy.
C M (Ref:HM02478)

**BLAKE, D H**

**D H Blake**, 1 St Augustines Court, 269 Hagley Rd, Birmingham, **Midlands (West)**, B16 9JU, ENG.
(T) 01214 559087
Speciality: Acupuncture, Osteopathy, Injection Treatments. ✔
● **Osteopath** Dr D Blake Q: BS. M: BOA, GOsC.
C Yrs. Est.: 40 (Ref:HM02479)

**BLAKE, JANET**

**Janet Blake**, 74 Dymchurch Rd, St. Marys Bay, Romney Marsh, **Kent**, TN29 0RN, ENG.
(T) 01303 875424
Speciality: Reflexology.
● **Owner** Ms J Blake
S T (Ref:HM02480)

**BLAKE, JANET**

**Janet Blake**, New Romney, **Kent**, TN29, ENG.
(T) 01303 875424
Speciality: Bach Remedies.
M (Ref:HM02481)

**BLAKE, SHEILA**

**Sheila Blake**, 22 Alford Rd, Erith, **Kent**, DA8 1PP, ENG.
(T) 020 8852 3108
Speciality: Reflexology.
S T (Ref:HM02482)

**BLAKE, SHEILA**

**Sheila Blake**, 94 Snowsfields, London, **London (Greater)**, SE1 3SS, ENG.
(T) 020 7403 2571
Speciality: Aromatherapy.
● **Owner** Mr K Harris
M O (Ref:HM02483)

**BLAKELEY, K**

**K Blakeley**, 30 Kinnoull Causeway, Perth, **Perth and Kinross**, PH2 8HQ, SCO.
(T) 01738 622864
Speciality: Osteopathy.
P S T (Ref:HM02484)

**BLAKEMAN, S M**

**S M Blakeman**, 44 Copperfield Rd, Rochester, **Kent**, ME1 2JE, ENG.
(T) 01634 814402
Speciality: Acupuncture.
● **Owner** Ms S Blakeman
O (Ref:HM02485)

**BLAKLEY, PAMELA**

**Pamela Blakley**, 47 Chaplains Avenue, Waterlooville, **Hampshire**, PO8 8QH, ENG.
(T) 023 9225 8934
Speciality: Reflexology.
S T (Ref:HM02486)

**BLAKOE**

**Blakoe Ltd**, 225-229 Putney Bridge Rd, London, **London (Greater)**, SW15 2PP, ENG.
(T) 020 8874 1130 (F) 020 8871 0066
Speciality: Complementary Medicines & Therapy.
● **Managing Director** Mr R Woodward
M (Ref:HM02487)

**BLAMPIED ST HILL**

**Blampied St Hill**, 42 London Rd, Guildford, **Surrey**, GU1 2AF, ENG.
(T) 01483 532452
Speciality: Chiropodists (Podiatrists).
S (Ref:HM02488)

**BLAMPIED ST HILL**

**Blampied St Hill**, 16 Terrace Rd, Walton-On-Thames, **Surrey**, KT12 2SB, ENG.
(T) 01932 226749
Speciality: Chiropodists (Podiatrists).
● **Principal** Mrs D Blanpied
S (Ref:HM02489)

**BLANCH, KATE**

**Kate Blanch**, The Surgery, Queens Sq, Attleborough, **Norfolk**, NR17 2AF, ENG.
(T) 01953 453166
Speciality: Osteopathy.
P S T (Ref:HM02490)

**BLANCHE, M**

**M Blanche**, 155 Southbank Rd, Southport, **Merseyside**, PR8 6LZ, ENG.
(T) 01704 233038 (F) 01704 506496
Speciality: Aromatherapy.
● **Owner** Ms M Blanche
M O (Ref:HM02491)

**BLANCK, E H**

**E H Blanck**, 25 Claremont Rd, Dudley, **Midlands (West)**, DY3 1HW, ENG.
(T) 01902 663646
Speciality: Chiropodists (Podiatrists).
S (Ref:HM02492)

**BLAND, AMANDA**

**Amanda Bland**, 100 High St, Crediton, **Devon**, EX17 3LF, ENG.
(T) 01363 774175
Speciality: Aromatherapy.
M O (Ref:HM02493)

**BLAND, C R**

**Mrs C R Bland**, 35 Pittfields, Basildon, **Essex**, SS16 6RD, ENG.
(T) 01268 416603
Speciality: Chiropodists (Podiatrists).
S (Ref:HM02494)

**BLAND, L**

**L Bland**, 3 Spital Trce, Gainsborough, **Lincolnshire**, DN21 2HD, ENG.
(T) 01427 614420
Speciality: Chiropodists (Podiatrists).
S (Ref:HM02495)

**BLANDFORD OSTEOPATHY PRACTICE**

**Blandford Osteopathy Practice**, Berlin Court, Salisbury St, Blandford Forum, **Dorset**, DT11 7AU, ENG.
(T) 01258 480885
Speciality: Osteopathy.
● **Owner** Miss A Burrows
P S T (Ref:HM02496)

**BLANE, LAURA**

**Laura Blane**, 433 Green Lanes, London, **London (Greater)**, N4 1HA, ENG.
(T) 020 8347 6154
Speciality: Chiropodists (Podiatrists).
S (Ref:HM02497)

**BLANE, LAURA J**

**Laura J Blane**, Health Care Centre, 44A High St, Hoddesdon, **Hertfordshire**, EN11 8DA, ENG.
(T) 01992 443462
Speciality: Chiropodists (Podiatrists).
S (Ref:HM02498)

**BLANK, CHRISTOPHER**

**Christopher Blank**, 37 Myott Avenue, Newcastle, **Staffordshire**, ST5 2EP, ENG.
(T) 01782 629105
Speciality: Chiropody. ✔
● **Chiropodist** Mr C Blank Q: M.S.C.P, S.R.Ch.
C Yrs. Est.: 8 (Ref:HM02499)

**BLANK, JUNE**

**June Blank**, 34 Daylesford Rd, Cheadle, **Cheshire**, SK8 1LF, ENG.
(T) 01614 282085
Speciality: Chiropodists (Podiatrists).
● **Owner** Mrs J Blank
S (Ref:HM02500)

**BLARNEY ACU & REFLEXOLOGY CTRE**

**Blarney Acupuncture & Reflexology Centre**, 2 Sunset Pl, Killeens, Cork, **County Cork**, IRE.
(T) 021 4381 280



Key continued: Yrs.Est: Years Established Q: Qualifications M: Professional Membership ✔ Indemnity Insurance Accept Credit Cards

Speciality: Acupuncture.
O (Ref:HM02501)

**BLAZEY, PHILLIPA**

**Phillipa Blazey**, 6 Danetree Cl, Epsom, **Surrey**, KT19 9SU, **ENG**.
(T) 020 8394 2965
Speciality: Homeopathy.
● **Owner** Mrs P Blazey
M (Ref:HM02502)

**BLEBY, J**

**J Bleby**, 74 Colebourne Rd, Birmingham, **Midlands (West)**, B13 0EY, **ENG**.
(T) 01217 776047
Speciality: Reflexology.
● **Owner** Ms J Bleby
S T (Ref:HM02503)

**BLENHEIM BACK PAIN CENTRE**

**Blenheim Back Pain & Natural Therapy Centre**, Dresden House, 51 High St, Evesham, **Worcestershire**, WR11 4DA, **ENG**.
(T) 01386 422330
Speciality: Complementary Medicines & Therapy.
● **Owner** Ms S Henderson
M (Ref:HM02504)

**BLENHEIM CHIROPODY PRACTICE**

**Blenheim Chiropody Practice**, 3 New Rd, Donaghadee, **County Down**, BT21 0DR, **NIR**.
(T) 028 9188 3177
Speciality: Chiropodists (Podiatrists).
● **Owner** Mr W Nickell
S (Ref:HM02505)

**BLENKINSOP, KAREN**

**Karen Blenkinsop**, 37 Landseer Avenue, Warrington, **Cheshire**, WA4 6DH, **ENG**.
(T) 01925 630895
Speciality: Reflexology.
● **Owner** Mrs K Blenkinsop
S T (Ref:HM02506)

**BLISS**

**Bliss**, 333 Portobello Rd, London, **London (Greater)**, W10 5SA, **ENG**.
(T) 01707 661501
Speciality: Healing Therapy, Hypnosis, Massage (Therapeutic), Psychotherapy, Stress Therapy.
C (Ref:HM02507)

**BLISS REMEDIES**

**Bliss Clinic**, Second Floor, 53 High St, Burford, **Oxfordshire**, OX18 4QA, **ENG**.
(T) 01993 824595
(E) bliss.remedies@virgin.net
Speciality: Complementary Medicines & Therapy. ✔
● **Therapist** Ms P Quirke
● **Therapist** Ms S Hawkins
● **Chiropodist** Ms K Nicholas Q: M.S.C.P, S.R.Ch.
● **Homeopath** Ms A Bryant
● **Owner** Miss S Bliss
C (Ref:HM02508)

**BLITHE SPIRIT**

**Blithe Spirit**, 83 St Dunstans St, Canterbury, **Kent**, CT2 8AD, **ENG**.
(T) 01227 455444
Speciality: Aromatherapy.
● **Partner** Mr M Shilling
M O (Ref:HM02509)

**BLOCH, PETER**

**Peter Bloch**, 4 Chapel Lane, Wilmslow, **Cheshire**, SK9 5HX, **ENG**.
(T) 01625 548233
Speciality: Alexander Technique. ✔
● **Owner** Mr P Bloch M: STAT.
P Yrs. Est.: 14 (Ref:HM02510)

**BLOCK, GEORGINA**

**Georgina Block**, 12 Lewis Rd, Kettering, **Northamptonshire**, NN15 6HE, **ENG**.
(T) 01536 392433
Speciality: Hypnosis.
B (Ref:HM02511)

**BLOGG, G**

**G Blogg**, Cl Farm, Walkerith Rd, Morton, Gainsborough, **Lincolnshire**, DN21 3DB, **ENG**.
(T) 01427 617171
Speciality: Complementary Medicines & Therapy.
● **Owner** Mr G Blogg
M (Ref:HM02512)

**BLOMFIELD, VAL**

**Val Blomfield**, 12 Woodlands Park Rd, London, **London (Greater)**, SE10 9XD, **ENG**.
(T) 020 8853 0772
Speciality: Psychotherapy.
● **Owner** Ms V Blomfield
B (Ref:HM02513)

**BLOOM, MARTINE**

**Martine Bloom**, 13 Northgate St, Bath, **Somerset**, BA1 5AS, **ENG**.
(T) 01225 480504
Speciality: Reflexology.
● **Owner** Mrs M Bloom
S T (Ref:HM02514)

**BLOOMFIELD, MICHAEL**

**Michael Bloomfield**, 126 Brookhill St, Stapleford, Nottingham, **Nottinghamshire**, NG9 7GG, **ENG**.
(T) 01159 390772
Speciality: Osteopathy.
P S T (Ref:HM02515)

**BLOOMSBURY ALEXANDER CENTRE**

**Bloomsbury Alexander Centre**, Bristol House, 80A Southampton Row, London, **London (Greater)**, WC1B 4BB, **ENG**.
(T) 020 7404 5348
(W) www.alexander.com
Speciality: Alexander Technique, Bates Method, Bowen Therapy, Holistic Healing, Homeopathy, Humanistic Psychology, Massage (Therapeutic), Postural Integration, Psychotherapy, Reflexology, Cranial Sacral. Remedial, Holistic & Bio Dynamic Massage. Lymphatic Drainage. ✔
● **Teacher of the Alexander Technique** Mr J Fuller M: STAT.
● **Teacher of the Alexander Technique** Mr H Goodlisse M: STAT.
● **Teacher of the Alexander Technique** Mrs E Higginson M: STAT.
● **Teacher of the Alexander Technique** Ms M Ashford M: STAT.
● **Teacher of the Alexander Technique** Ms J Bari M: STAT.
● **Teacher of the Alexander Technique** Mr R Bernstein M: STAT.
● **Teacher of the Alexander Technique** Ms I Weskin M: STAT.
● **Teacher of the Alexander Technique** Ms Y Inada M: STAT.
● **Teacher of the Alexander Technique** Mr A Bignell M: STAT.
● **Teacher of the Alexander Technique** Mr G Higginson M: STAT.
● **Teacher of the Alexander Technique** Ms M Galai M: STAT.
● **Teacher of the Alexander Technique** Ms M Cole M: STAT.
● **Teacher of the Alexander Technique** Mr S Cooper M: STAT.
● **Teacher of the Alexander Technique** Ms B Forstrom M: STAT.
● **Teacher of the Alexander Technique** Ms M Garcia M: STAT.
● **Teacher of the Alexander Technique** Miss S Manford M: STAT.
● **Teacher of the Alexander Technique** Mr P Palon M: STAT.
H Yrs. Est.: 13 (Ref:HM02516)

**BLOOMSBURY CLINIC**

**Bloomsbury Clinic**, 16 Brownlow Mews, London, **London (Greater)**, WC1N 2LD, **ENG**.
(T) 020 7405 9689
Speciality: Osteopathy.
● **Owner** Mrs B Muhleisen
P S T (Ref:HM02517)

**BLOOMSBURY THERAPY CENTRE**

**Bloomsbury Therapy Centre**, 80A Southampton Row, London, **London (Greater)**, WC1B 4BB, **ENG**.
(T) 020 7831 7924
(W) www.alexander.com
Speciality: Alexander Technique, Bates Method, Bowen Therapy, Cranio-Sacral Therapy, Remedial, Holistic, Bio Dynamic Massage, Lymphatic Drainage. ✔
● **Teacher of the Alexander Technique** Ms S Bernstein M: STAT.
● **Teacher of the Alexander Technique** Mr G Higginson M: STAT.
● **Teacher of the Alexander Technique** Ms E Higginson M: STAT.
● **Teacher of the Alexander Technique** Mr S Cooper M: STAT.
● **Teacher of the Alexander Technique** Mr P Palon M: STAT.
● **Teacher of the Alexander Technique** Ms M Cole M: STAT.
● **Teacher of the Alexander Technique** Mr H Goodlisse M: STAT.
● **Teacher of the Alexander Technique** Mr J Fuller M: STAT.
● **Teacher of the Alexander Technique** Mr M Garcia M: STAT.
● **Teacher of the Alexander Technique** Ms B Forsstrom M: STAT.
● **Teacher of the Alexander Technique** Ms M Galai M: STAT.
● **Teacher of the Alexander Technique** Mr A Bignall M: STAT.
● **Teacher of the Alexander Technique** Mr R Bernstein M: STAT.
● **Teacher of the Alexander Technique** Ms I Weskin M: STAT.
● **Teacher of the Alexander Technique** Ms Y Inada M: STAT.
● **Teacher of the Alexander Technique** Ms M Ashford M: STAT.
● **Teacher of the Alexander Technique** Ms J Bari
C H Yrs. Est.: 13 (Ref:HM02518)

**BLOOR, HILARY**

**Hilary Bloor**, 834 Fishponds Rd, Fishponds, Bristol, BS16 3XA, **ENG**.
(T) 01179 491290
Speciality: Chiropodists (Podiatrists).
S (Ref:HM02519)

**BLORE, ANNE**

**Anne Blore**, 9 Dewlands Way, Verwood, **Dorset**, BH31 6JN, **ENG**.
(T) 01202 820628
Speciality: Reflexology.
S T (Ref:HM02520)

**BLOSSOM AROMATHERAPY CENTRE**

**Blossom Aromatherapy Centre**, Blossom House, Alma Rd, Folkestone, **Kent**, CT20 3LU, **ENG**.
(T) 01303 274800
Speciality: Aromatherapy. ✔
● **Partner** Mrs S Bushell M: ISPA.
● **Therapist** Ms A Roberts M: ISPA.
C Yrs. Est.: 6 (Ref:HM02521)

**BLOWES, K L**

**Mrs K L Blowes**, 39 Brighton Rd, Surbiton, **Surrey**, KT6 5LR, **ENG**.
(T) 07956 482370
Speciality: Chiropodists (Podiatrists).
S (Ref:HM02522)

**BLOXHAM, R J**

**R J Bloxham**, 231 Clarendon Park Rd, Leicester, **Leicestershire**, LE2 3AN, **ENG**.
(T) 01162 707145
Speciality: Chiropodists (Podiatrists).
● **Senior Partner** Mr S Parton
S (Ref:HM02523)

**BLOXSOM, R J**

**R J Bloxsom**, 28 Bridge St, Loughborough, **Leicestershire**, LE11 1NH, **ENG**.
(T) 01509 211909
Speciality: Chiropodists (Podiatrists).
● **Owner** Mr R Bloxsom
S (Ref:HM02524)

**BLUE CRYSTAL RELAXATION MUSIC**

**Blue Crystal Relaxation Music Ltd**, Yew Tree Farm, Stone St, Stanford, Ashford, **Kent**, TN25 6DH, **ENG**.
(T) 01303 814880 (F) 01303 814884
Speciality: Complementary Medicines &



Key: B Mind-Body Medicine C Complementary Medicine H Self Help Treatment M Medicinal Therapy O Oriental Medicine P Postural Therapy S Manipulative Structural Therapy T Touch Therapy

Therapy.
● **Owner** Mr G Milner
C M (**Ref:**HM02525)

**BLUE HAZE**

**Blue Haze**, 91 Tennyson Rd, Stafford, **Staffordshire**, ST17 9SS, ENG.
(T) 01785 212752
Speciality: Complementary Medicines & Therapy.
● **Owner** Mrs P Wareham
C M (**Ref:**HM02526)

**BLUE PERSON**

**Blue Person Ltd (The)**, P.O.Box 523, Rochford, **Essex**, SS4 1SX, ENG.
(T) 01702 543523
Speciality: Meditation, Trantric Teaching.
M (**Ref:**HM02527)

**BLUE ROOM**

**Blue Room - Bennetsbridge Healing Centre (The)**, Chapel St, Bennettsbridge, **County Kilkenny**, IRE.
(T) 05627 004
Speciality: Absent Healing, Art Therapy, Bach Remedies, Bio-energetics, Complementary Therapy, Counselling, Dance Movement Therapy, Faith Healing, Floral Essence Therapy, Group Therapy, Healer, Holistic Healing, Humanistic Psychology, Kinesiology, Massage (Therapeutic), Meditation, Music Therapy, Nutritional Therapy, Paranormal Therapies, Phytotherapy, Psychotherapy, Reichian Therapy, Reiki, Sensitivity Training, Sound Therapy, Spiritual Healing, Stress Therapy, Tantra Therapy, Touch Therapy, Visualisation Therapy, Vitamin Therapy, Voice Therapy, Yoga, Breath Awareness Work, Dream Analysis. ✔
● **Therapist** Ms E Mountain
(T) 05623 573 Q: BA.
● **Therapist** Caoimbhe Purcell Q: BA.
● **Complementary Health Practitioner** Ms J Ashton Q: BA, ITEC.
B Yrs. Est.: 2 (**Ref:**HM02528)

**BLUFF, ANN**

**Ann Bluff**, 621A Greenland Rd, Sheffield, **Yorkshire (South)**, S9 5HH, ENG.
(T) 01142 436081
Speciality: Chiropody. ✔
● **Chiropodist** Ms A Bluff Q: MBChA.
M: B.A.Ch.P.
C Yrs. Est.: 12 (**Ref:**HM02529)

**BLUNDELL, ALISON**

**Alison Blundell**, The Studio, North Bridge Rd, Berkhamsted, **Hertfordshire**, HP4 1EH, ENG.
(T) 01442 874410
Speciality: Chiropodists (Podiatrists).
● **Owner** A Blundell
S (**Ref:**HM02530)

**BLUNDELL, STEPHEN**

**Stephen Blundell**, 4 London Rd, Grays, **Essex**, RM17 5XY, ENG.
(T) 01375 380912
Speciality: Chiropodists (Podiatrists).
● **Owner** Mr S Blundell
S (**Ref:**HM02531)

**BLUNDELL, WAYNE**

**Wayne Blundell**, The Studio, North Bridge Rd, Berkhamsted, **Hertfordshire**, HP4 1EH, ENG.
(T) 01442 874410
Speciality: Chiropodists (Podiatrists).
● **Owner** Mrs A Blundell
S (**Ref:**HM02532)

**BLUNSDON ABBEY PHYSIOTHERAPY**

**Blunsdon Abbey Physiotherapy**, Elstree Way, Swindon, **Wiltshire**, SN2 3YX, ENG.
(T) 01793 701333 (F) 01793 701444
Speciality: Acupuncture, Aromatherapy, Physiotherapy, Podiatry. ✔ [credit card]
● **Physiotherapist** Mr A Tobin
● **Manager** Mr B Reed
S (**Ref:**HM02533)

**BLUNT, W W**

**W W Blunt**, 41 Branthwaite Brow, Kendal, **Cumbria**, LA9 4TP, ENG.
(T) 01539 720965
Speciality: Complementary Medicines & Therapy, Trichology.
M (**Ref:**HM02534)

**BLUSH**

**Blush**, 36 Byng Rd, Tunbridge Wells, **Kent**, TN4 8EJ, ENG.
(T) 01892 531500
Speciality: Electrolysis.
T (**Ref:**HM02535)

**BLYTH CHIROPRACTIC CLINIC**

**Blyth Chiropractic Clinic**, Sideways Cottage, High St, Blyth, Worksop, **Nottinghamshire**, S81 8EW, ENG.
(T) 01909 591866
Speciality: Chiropractors.
● **Office Manager** Mrs M Slaney
P S T (**Ref:**HM02536)

**BLYTH, DANIEL**

**Daniel Blyth**, 16 Clarence Sq, Cheltenham, **Gloucestershire**, GL50 4JN, ENG.
(T) 01242 241933
Speciality: Acupuncture.
O (**Ref:**HM02537)

**BLYTH, DON**

**Don Blyth**, 1 Hylton Surgery, Seafield Lane, Sidmouth, **Devon**, EX10 8HF, ENG.
(T) 01395 577473 (F) 01395 577473
Speciality: Osteopathy.
● **Partner** Mrs A Jackson
P S T (**Ref:**HM02538)

**BLYTH, JOSEPHINE**

**Josephine Blyth**, 186 Red Lion Rd, Surbiton, **Surrey**, KT6 7QZ, ENG.
(T) 020 8391 5244 (F) 020 8391 5652
Speciality: Hypnosis.
● **Owner** Mrs J Blyth
B (**Ref:**HM02539)

**BLYTH, SALLY**

**Sally Blyth**, 1 Hylton Surgery, Seafield Lane, Sidmouth, **Devon**, EX10 8HF, ENG.
(T) 01395 577473 (F) 01395 577473
Speciality: Osteopathy.
● **Partner** Mrs A Jackson
P S T (**Ref:**HM02540)

**BLYTH, SIMON**

**Simon Blyth**, 28 Farmers Way, Cox Green, Maidenhead, **Berkshire**, SL6 3PL, ENG.
(T) 01628 823289
Speciality: Acupuncture.
O (**Ref:**HM02541)

**BOA**

**British Osteopathic Association**, Langham House East, 29-37 Mill St, Luton, **Bedfordshire**, LU1 2NA, ENG.
(T) 01582 488455 (F) 01582 481533
Speciality: Osteopathy.
● **Chief Executive** Mr M Murray
P S T (**Ref:**HM02542)

**BOADEN, PAM**

**Pam Boaden**, 59 Beechwood Avenue, Orpington, **Kent**, BR6 7EZ, ENG.
(T) 01689 861814
Speciality: Hypnotherapy.
● **Owner** Mrs P Boaden
B (**Ref:**HM02543)

**BOALER, DAVID M**

**David M Boaler**, 11 Hayfield Avenue, Boston Spa, Wetherby, **Yorkshire (West)**, LS23 6EG, ENG.
(T) 01937 842396
Speciality: Chiropodists (Podiatrists).
● **Owner** Mr D Boaler
S (**Ref:**HM02544)

**BOARDMAN, C J**

**C J Boardman**, Summertown Clinic, 362 Banbury Rd, Oxford, **Oxfordshire**, OX2 7PP, ENG.
(T) 01865 513239
Speciality: Acupuncture.
● **Owner** Mr C Boardman
O (**Ref:**HM02545)

**BOARDMAN, SARA**

**Sara Boardman**, 43A Argyle St, St. Andrews, **Fife**, KY16 9BX, SCO.
(T) 01334 479003
Speciality: Chiropodists (Podiatrists).
S (**Ref:**HM02546)

**BOBY, KEITH**

**Keith Boby**, 44 Thorncliffe Rd, Oxford, **Oxfordshire**, OX2 7BB, ENG.
(T) 01865 516517
Speciality: Psychotherapy.
B (**Ref:**HM02547)

**BOCOCK, RICHARD**

**Richard Bocock**, 67a St Peter's St, Islington, London, **London (Greater)**, N1 8JR, ENG.
(T) 020 7226 8705
(E) richjb@lineone.net
(W) www.rbocock.healingonline.co.uk
Speciality: Homeopathy, Career counselling. ✔
● **Owner** Mr R Bocock Q: DSH, RSHom.
M: Soc.Hom.
M Yrs. Est.: 5 (**Ref:**HM02548)

**BODDAM-WHETHAM, C**

**C Boddam-Whetham**, Greystone, Rockness Hill, Nailsworth, Stroud, **Gloucestershire**, GL6 0JT, ENG.
(T) 01453 834834
Speciality: Physiotherapy.
● **Owner** Mrs C Boddam-Whetham
P S T (**Ref:**HM02549)

**BODELL, TERRI**

**Terri Bodell**, Park Avenue, Potters Bar, **Hertfordshire**, EN6 5EN, ENG.
(T) 01707 855338
Speciality: Hypnosis.
B (**Ref:**HM02550)

**BODY & BEAUTY STUDIO**

**Body & Beauty Studio (The)**, 86 Maybury Rd, Woking, **Surrey**, GU21 5JH, ENG.
(T) 01483 773113
Speciality: Electrolysis.
● **Owner** Ms N Scannella
T (**Ref:**HM02551)

**BODY & BREATH WORK**

**Body & Breath Work**, 464 Merton Rd, London, **London (Greater)**, SW18 5AE, ENG.
(T) 020 8874 1635
Speciality: Complementary Medicines & Therapy.
● **Owner** Mrs E McNabe
M (**Ref:**HM02552)

**BODY & MIND THERAPY CENTRE**

**Body & Mind Therapy Centre**, 1 Kenworthy St, Stalybridge, **Manchester (Greater)**, SK15 2DX, ENG.
(T) 01613 049272 (F) 01613 049272
Speciality: Complementary Medicines & Therapy.
● **Employee** Mrs H Bourguignon
C M (**Ref:**HM02553)

**BODY & SOLE**

**Body & Sole**, 3 Manor Croft, Burton-On-Trent, **Staffordshire**, DE14 1HJ, ENG.
(T) 01283 515656
Speciality: Reflexology.
● **Owner** Ms C Keegan
S T (**Ref:**HM02554)

**BODY & SOLE**

**Body & Sole**, Glebe Farm, Main Rd, Haltham, Horncastle, **Lincolnshire**, LN9 6JE, ENG.
(T) 01507 522210
Speciality: Complementary Medicines & Therapy.
● **Owner** Mr J Garner
C M (**Ref:**HM02555)

**BODY & SOLE**

**Body & Sole Complementary & Beauty Therapies**, 93 Bradford Rd, Shipley, **Yorkshire (West)**, BD18 3BX, ENG.
(T) 01274 598294
Speciality: Complementary Medicines & Therapy.
● **Owner** Mrs L Danson
M (**Ref:**HM02556)



Key continued: **Yrs.Est:** Years Established **Q:** Qualifications **M:** Professional Membership ✔ Indemnity Insurance [credit card] Accept Credit Cards

**BODY & SOLE CENTRE**

**Body & Sole Centre**, 8 Ely Pl, Sea Rd, Galway, **County Galway**, IRE.
(T) 09158 9363 (F) 09158 9369
Speciality: Complementary Medicines & Therapy.
M (Ref:HM02557)

**BODY & SOLE HEALTH & SPORTS**

**Body & Sole Health & Sports Clinic**, 2a Shore St, Donaghadee, **County Down**, BT21 0DG, NIR.
(T) 028 9188 4800
Speciality: Complementary Medicines & Therapy.
● **Manageress**
Ms L Hammel-Fitzpatrick
C M (Ref:HM02558)

**BODY & SOLE REFLEXOLOGY**

**Body& Sole Reflexology**, 118 Sydney Rd, Hornsey, London, **London (Greater)**, N8 0EX, ENG.
(T) 020 8340 6188
Speciality: Reflexology.
S T (Ref:HM02559)

**BODY & SOLE REFLEXOLOGY**

**Body& Sole Reflexology**, 118 Sydney Rd, Hornsey, London, **London (Greater)**, N8 0EX, ENG.
(T) 020 8340 6188
Speciality: Reflexology, Sunflower Method.
S T (Ref:HM02560)

**BODY & SOUL**

**Body & Soul Complementary Healthcare Ltd**, 76 High St, Sunninghill, Ascot, **Berkshire**, SL5 9NN, ENG.
(T) 01344 872754 (F) 01344 873803
(E) geoff@bodyandsoulhydrotherapy.co.uk
(W) www.bodyandsoul-hydrotherapy.co.uk
Speciality: Complementary Therapy, Healing Therapy, Herbal Medicine, Massage (Therapeutic). ✔
● **Managing Director** Mr G Olden
H Yrs. Est.: 12 (Ref:HM02561)

**BODY & SOUL**

**Body & Soul**, 10 Water St, Bakewell, **Derbyshire**, DE45 1EW, ENG.
(T) 01629 814495
Speciality: Aromatherapy.
M O (Ref:HM02562)

**BODY & SOUL**

**Body & Soul**, 127 High St, Wootton Bassett, Swindon, **Wiltshire**, SN4 7AY, ENG.
(T) 01793 849111
Speciality: Aromatherapy.
● **Owner** Mrs V Oral
M O (Ref:HM02563)

**BODY & SOUL**

**Body & Soul**, 42 Kilwinning Rd, Irvine, **Ayrshire (North)**, KA12 8RY, SCO.
(T) 01294 275018
Speciality: Aromatherapy.
● **Owner** Mrs M Lindsay
M O (Ref:HM02564)

**BODY & SOUL**

**Body & Soul (MK)**, 21 Stainton Drive, Heelands, Milton Keynes, **Buckinghamshire**, MK13 7QW, ENG.
(T) 01908 313383
Speciality: Aromatherapy, Reflexology. ✔
● **Aromatherapist** Miss F Harries Q: Dip.Arom. M: FHT.
C Yrs. Est.: 1 (Ref:HM02565)

**BODY & SOUL**

**Body & Soul (Norwich) Ltd**, 22 Bridewell Alley, Norwich, **Norfolk**, NR2 1AQ, ENG.
(T) 01603 660030
Speciality: Aromatherapy.
● **Joint Director**
Kathleen Susan Soanes
M O (Ref:HM02566)

**BODY & SOUL BEAUTY CLINIC**

**Body & Soul Beauty Clinic**, New St, **County Kilkenny**, IRE.
(T) 05663 517
(E) bodysoul@eircom.net
Speciality: Complementary Medicines & Therapy.
M (Ref:HM02567)

**BODY & SOUL NAT HLTH AND BTY**

**Body & Soul Natural Health And Beauty Studio**, 38 East St, Newquay, **Cornwall**, TR7 1BH, ENG.
(T) 01637 877394
Speciality: Complementary Medicines & Therapy.
● **Owner** Mrs S Crossman
M (Ref:HM02568)

**BODY BALANCE**

**Body Balance**, 153 Oldchurch Rd, Romford, **Essex**, RM7 0BD, ENG.
(T) 01708 762288 (F) 01708 501150
Speciality: Acupuncture, Psychotherapy.
● **Partner** Mr J Chaffey
P S T (Ref:HM02569)

**BODY BALANCE**

**Body Balance**, King St, Hartlepool, **Cleveland**, TS25 1PH, ENG.
(T) 01429 268847 (F) 01429 268276
Speciality: Massage (Therapeutic), Sport Injuries and Tension. ✔
● **Owner** Mr S Hunter Q: IIST.
C S T Yrs. Est.: 2 (Ref:HM02570)

**BODY BALANCE HEALTH SOLUTIONS**

**Body Balance Health Solutions**, 153 Oldchurch Rd, Romford, **Essex**, RM7 0BD, ENG.
(T) 01708 702200
Speciality: Acupuncture, Biomechanics, Chiropody, Homeopathy, Osteopathy. ✔
● **Osteopath** Mr J Chaffey Q: BSc (Chiro), DO.
B Yrs. Est.: 13 (Ref:HM02571)

**BODY BALANCE HOLISTIC THERAPY**

**Body Balance Holistic Therapy**, 1 Home Farm Cottages, Blagdon Estate, Seaton Burn, Newcastle Upon Tyne, **Tyne and Wear**, NE13 6DB, ENG.
(T) 01670 789922
Speciality: Aromatherapy, Sonar Light and Advanced Sound Wave Energy. ✔
● **Alternative Practitioner**
Ms B Kelly M: FHT.
C Yrs. Est.: 3 (Ref:HM02572)

**BODY BALANCE THERAPIES**

**Body Balance Therapies**, 39 Riversdale Rd, Halton, Runcorn, **Cheshire**, WA7 2AP, ENG.
(T) 01928 564444
Speciality: Complementary Medicines & Therapy.
M (Ref:HM02573)

**BODY BALANCE THERAPY**

**Body Balance Therapy**, 25 Eyre Sq, **County Galway**, IRE.
(T) 09156 4244
Speciality: Complementary Medicines & Therapy.
M (Ref:HM02574)

**BODY BASIC**

**Body Basic**, 20 Brookside Cl, Waterlooville, **Hampshire**, PO7 6ET, ENG.
(T) 023 9226 6599
Speciality: Aromatherapy.
M O (Ref:HM02575)

**BODY BEAUTIFUL**

**Mrs L Scowen**, Threeways, Beech Rd, Scratby, Great Yarmouth, **Norfolk**, NR29 3PG, ENG.
(T) 01493 732247
(E) linda@body-beautiful.co.uk
(W) www.bodybeautiful.co.uk
Speciality: Aromatherapy, Massage (Therapeutic), Reflexology, Reiki. ✔
● **Complementary Therapist**
Ms L Scowen M: AOC, IFA.
B Yrs. Est.: 2 (Ref:HM02576)

**BODY BEAUTIFUL**

**Body Beautiful**, 53 Orchard Rd, Gravesend, **Kent**, DA11 8HU, ENG.
(T) 01474 362818
Speciality: Aromatherapy.
M O (Ref:HM02577)

**BODY BENEFITS**

**Body Benefits**, 5b The Mews, Watts Lane, Eastbourne, **Sussex (East)**, BN21 1NP, ENG.
(T) 01323 647280
Speciality: Complementary Medicines & Therapy.
C M (Ref:HM02578)

**BODY CALM**

**Body Calm Therapeutic Massage For Women**, Kingsway, Woking, **Surrey**, GU21 1NS, ENG.
(T) 01483 765300
Speciality: Aromatherapy.
● **Owner** Mrs L Thomas
M O (Ref:HM02579)

**BODY CLINIC**

**Body Clinic**, Petworth Court, Felpham Rd, Bognor Regis, **Sussex (West)**, PO22 7PQ, ENG.
(T) 01243 868688
Speciality: Complementary Medicines & Therapy.
C M (Ref:HM02580)

**BODY CONTROL PILATES OXFORD**

**Body Control Pilates Oxford**, Bagley Wood Lodge, Bagley Wood Rd, Kennington, **Oxfordshire**, OX1 5LY, ENG.
(T) 01865 730429
Speciality: Pilates.
M (Ref:HM02581)

**BODY CONTROL PILATES STUDIO**

**Body Control Pilates Studio**, Enterprise Point, Melbourne St, Brighton, **Sussex (East)**, BN2 3LH, ENG.
(T) 01273 276323
Speciality: Complementary Medicines & Therapy.
● **Owner** Mrs H Fisher
M (Ref:HM02582)

**BODY CONTROL STUDIOS**

**Body Control Studios**, London Studio Centre, 42-50 York Way, London, **London (Greater)**, N1 9AB, ENG.
(T) 020 7837 8511
Speciality: Pilates.
M (Ref:HM02583)

**BODY ELEGANCE**

**Body Elegance**, 30 Weston Way Weston Pk, Lucan, **County Dublin**, IRE.
(T) 01628 3502
(E) annoreilly1@eircom.net
Speciality: Complementary Medicines & Therapy.
M (Ref:HM02584)

**BODY ESSENCE**

**Body Essence by Julie Haigh**, 5 Bankfield Trce, Armitage Bridge, Huddersfield, **Yorkshire (West)**, HD1 7PE, ENG.
(T) 01484 316353
Speciality: Aromatherapy, Indian Head Massage, Massage (Therapeutic), Reflexology. ✔
● **Aromatherapist/Reflexologist**
Julie Haigh Q: ITEC. M: GCP.
C Yrs. Est.: 5 (Ref:HM02585)

**BODY ESSENCES**

**Blakemere Craft Centre**, Unit 16 Chester Rd, Sandiway, Northwich, **Cheshire**, CW8 2EB, ENG.
(T) 01606 888842
Speciality: Aromatherapy, Beauty Therapy. ✔
● **Therapist** Mrs J Flanagan Q: IIHHT. M: IIHHT.
● **Partner** Mrs D Farrow Q: IIHHT. M: ICHT.
C Yrs. Est.: 2 (Ref:HM02586)

**BODY ESSENTIALS**

**Body Essentials**, 153 Lavernock Rd, Penarth, **Glamorgan (Vale of)**, CF64 3RN, WAL.
(T) 029 2070 2910
Speciality: Aromatherapy. ✔
● **Aromatherapist** Mrs W Jones M: IHBC.
C Yrs. Est.: 7 (Ref:HM02587)

**BODY FACTOR**

**Body Factor**, 99 Fordwater Rd, Chertsey, **Surrey**, KT16 8HH, ENG.

Key: B Mind-Body Medicine C Complementary Medicine H Self Help Treatment M Medicinal Therapy O Oriental Medicine P Postural Therapy S Manipulative Structural Therapy T Touch Therapy

(T) 01932 574930 (F) 01932 574920
Speciality: Physiotherapy.
● **Partner** Mr T Williams
P S T (Ref:HM02588)

## BODY FOCUS

**Body Focus**, Lucerne, Whitford, Axminster, **Devon**, EX13 7PG, ENG.
(T) 01297 21134
Speciality: Aromatherapy.
● **Owner** Miss S Davey
M O (Ref:HM02589)

## BODY GARAGE

**Body Garage (The)**, 3rd Floor, 46 Kingsway, London, **London (Greater)**, WC2B 6EN, ENG.
(T) 020 7242 2709
Speciality: Physiotherapy.
P S T (Ref:HM02590)

## BODY GOLD /CLOVERWOOD

**Body Gold /Cloverwood Aromatherapy**, Wotton Rd, Kings North Business Park, Ashford, **Kent**, TN23 6LN, ENG.
Speciality: Aromatherapy.
M O (Ref:HM02591)

## BODY HARMONY

**Body Harmony**, 3 Farmhill Rd, Roebuck Shopping Mall, Dublin, **County Dublin**, IRE.
(T) 01298 2312
Speciality: Complementary Medicines & Therapy.
M (Ref:HM02592)

## BODY LANGUAGE

**Body Language**, Ullswater Rd, Congleton, **Cheshire**, CW12 4JE, ENG.
(T) 01260 273386
Speciality: Aromatherapy.
● **Owner** Ms A Jackson
S T (Ref:HM02593)

## BODY MAINTENANCE STUDIO

**Body Maintenance Studio**, 7 Langley St, London, **London (Greater)**, WC2H 9JA, ENG.
(T) 020 7379 6043
Speciality: Complementary Medicines & Therapy.
● **Owner** Ms L Ackland
C M (Ref:HM02594)

## BODY MATTERS

**Body Matters**, 47 Pendre, Cardigan, **Carmarthenshire**, SA43 1JS, WAL.
(T) 01239 614581
Speciality: Complementary Medicines & Therapy.
● **Owner** Miss W Ceridwen
C M (Ref:HM02595)

## BODY MATTERS

**Body Matters**, Malt Mill House, 159 Low St, Collingham, Newark, **Nottinghamshire**, NG23 7NL, ENG.
(T) 01636 893412
Speciality: Complementary Medicines & Therapy.
● **Partner** Mrs D Palfreeman
M (Ref:HM02596)

## BODY MATTERS

**Body Matters**, 31 Park Rd, Burgess Hill, **Sussex (West)**, RH15 8EU, ENG.
(T) 01444 871369 (F) 01444 230523
Speciality: Complementary Medicines & Therapy.
● **Owner** Mrs K Soper
C M (Ref:HM02597)

## BODY MECHANICS THERAPY CLINIC

**Body Mechanics Therapy Clinic**, 22 Baldock St, Ware, **Hertfordshire**, SG12 9DZ, ENG.
(T) 01920 485265
(E) body.mechanics@btinternet.com
Speciality: Bowen Therapy, Psychotherapy, Reflexology. ✔
● **Manager** Mr P Collins
● **Psychotherapist** Mrs O Collins M: BCMA.
C Yrs. Est.: 9 (Ref:HM02598)

## BODY MECHANICS THERAPY CLINIC

**Body Mechanics Therapy Clinic**, The Lodge, Marlesford, Woodbridge, **Suffolk**, IP13 0AT, ENG.
(T) 01728 747925
(E) body.mechanics@btconnect.com
Speciality: Bowen Therapy, Psychotherapy, Reflexology. ✔
● **Psychotherapist** Mrs O Collins Q: ALTT. M: BCMA.
● **Manager** Mr P Collins
C Yrs. Est.: 9 (Ref:HM02599)

## BODY MIND & SOLE

**Body Mind & Sole**, 176-178 Pensby Rd, Heswall, Wirral, **Merseyside**, CH60 7RJ, ENG.
(T) 07041 580140
Speciality: Complementary Medicines & Therapy.
● **Owner** Mrs N Titley
M (Ref:HM02600)

## BODY MIND & SOLE

**Body Mind & Sole**, 1st Floor, 13 Bridge St, Lampeter, **Carmarthenshire**, SA48 7HG, WAL.
(T) 01570 421412
Speciality: Complementary Medicines & Therapy.
● **Partner** Mr M Clarke
M (Ref:HM02601)

## BODY MIND & SPIRIT ACUPUNCTURE

**Body Mind & Spirit Acupuncture**, 111 Hermon Hill, South Woodford, London, **London (Greater)**, E18 1QE, ENG.
(T) 020 8989 6322
Speciality: Complementary Medicines & Therapy.
M (Ref:HM02602)

## BODY 'N' SOLE

**Body 'n' Sole**, 12a Park Rd, Holbeach, Spalding, **Lincolnshire**, PE12 7EE, ENG.
(T) 01406 490479
Speciality: Aromatherapy.
M O (Ref:HM02603)

## BODY PERFECTION

**Body Perfection**, 117- St. Peters Cl, Moreton-On-Lugg, Hereford, **Herefordshire**, HR4 8DW, ENG.
(T) 01432 761124
Speciality: Naturopathy, Nutritional Therapy, Vitamin Therapy, Sports Therapy/Personal Fitness Training.
M (Ref:HM02604)

## BODY PRACTICE

**Body Practice (The)**, 7 Church St, Market Harborough, **Leicestershire**, LE16 7AA, ENG.
(T) 01858 466160
Speciality: Osteopathy.
● **Owner** Mr R Montgomery
P S T (Ref:HM02605)

## BODY SCENT

**Body Scent**, 4 Portland St, Southampton, **Hampshire**, SO14 7EB, ENG.
(T) 023 8063 3040
Speciality: Aromatherapy.
M O (Ref:HM02606)

## BODY STRESS RELEASE

**Body Stress Release**, The Pheasantry, Vicarage Hill, Westerham, **Kent**, TN16 1AY, ENG.
(T) 01959 565926
Speciality: Complementary Medicines & Therapy.
C M (Ref:HM02607)

## BODY SUITE

**Body Suite (The)**, 4 Ashwood Gr, Morley, Leeds, **Yorkshire (West)**, LS27 7AQ, ENG.
(T) 01132 524806
Speciality: Aromatherapy.
● **Owner** Ms K Bollard
M O (Ref:HM02608)

## BODY THERAPY

**Body Therapy**, 116 Ledburn, Skelmersdale, **Lancashire**, WN8 6TX, ENG.
(T) 01695 51461
Speciality: Complementary Medicines & Therapy.
● **Owner** Ms L McKenna
M (Ref:HM02609)

## BODY WORK

**Body Work**, 49 New Exeter St, Chudleigh, Newton Abbot, **Devon**, TQ13 0DA, ENG.
(T) 01626 852575
Speciality: Complementary Medicines & Therapy.
● **Owner** Mr M Colquhoun
C M (Ref:HM02610)

## BODY WORK CENTRE

**Body Work Centre (The)**, 19 St Marys Chare, Hexham, **Northumberland**, NE46 1NQ, ENG.
(T) 01434 601577
Speciality: Complementary Medicines & Therapy.
C M (Ref:HM02611)

## BODY WORKSHOP

**Body Workshop**, 3 Hall Park Centre, Forest Drive, Lytham St. Annes, **Lancashire**, FY8 4QF, ENG.
(T) 01253 795100
Speciality: Aromatherapy.
M O (Ref:HM02612)

## BODYBASIC UK

**Bodybasic UK Ltd**, 68 High St, Cosham, Portsmouth, **Hampshire**, PO6 3AJ, ENG.
(T) 023 9237 7099 (F) 023 9237 7775
Speciality: Aromatherapy.
● **Owner** Mr M Eaves
M O (Ref:HM02613)

## BODYCARE CLINIC

**Bodycare Clinic (The)**, 59 Heron Way, Horsham, **Sussex (West)**, RH13 6DW, ENG.
(T) 01403 242624 (F) 01403 242624
Speciality: Osteopathy.
● **Owner** Mr S Palmer
P S T (Ref:HM02614)

## BODYCARE INJURY CLINIC

**Bodycare Injury Clinic**, 1a Clarendon St, Londonderry, **County Londonderry**, BT48 7EP, NIR.
(T) 028 7126 0324 (F) 028 7126 0324
Speciality: Physiotherapy.
● **Owner** Mr M Kerr
P S T (Ref:HM02615)

## BODYCENTRE

**Bodycentre**, 3 Cross Rd, Feltham, **London (Greater)**, TW13 6QP, ENG.
(T) 020 8707 2026 (F) 020 8707 2021
Speciality: Osteopathy.
● **Owner** Mr N Birdi
P S T (Ref:HM02616)

## BODYCHECK

**Bodycheck**, 1 Church Farm, Ashley, Market Drayton, **Shropshire**, TF9 4QT, ENG.
(T) 01630 673525
Speciality: Complementary Medicines & Therapy.
● **Partner** Mrs S Pollock
C M (Ref:HM02617)

## BODY-FOOT REFLEX

**Body-Foot Reflex**, 67A De Lacy St, Ashton-On-Ribble, Preston, **Lancashire**, PR2 2DD, ENG.
(T) 01772 563349
Speciality: Reflexology.
● **Owner** Ms V Corner
S T (Ref:HM02618)

## BODYGUIDE ALTERNATE

**Bodyguide Alternate & Holistic Therapies**, 115D South Rd, Haywards Heath, **Sussex (West)**, RH16 4LR, ENG.
(T) 01444 474543
Speciality: Aromatherapy, Reflexology, Reiki. ✔
● **Owner** Mrs P Esmond M: IIHHT.
C Yrs. Est.: 2 (Ref:HM02619)

## BODYHARMONICS CENTRE

**Bodyharmonics Centre**, 54 Fleckers Drive, Cheltenham, **Gloucestershire**, GL51 5BD, ENG.
(T) 01242 582168
Speciality: Acupuncture.
O (Ref:HM02620)

## BODY-INTEGRATION CO UK

**Body-Integration Co UK**, Dolphin House, Woodgreen, Witney, **Oxfordshire**, OX8 6DH,



Key continued: Yrs.Est: Years Established Q: Qualifications M: Professional Membership ✔ Indemnity Insurance ▬ Accept Credit Cards

ENG.
(T) 01993 700370
Speciality: Physiotherapy.
● Owner Mrs W Hills
P S T (Ref:HM02621)

## BODYLIFE CENTRE

**Derek Osborn**, Bayliffe's House, 60 Spout Lane, Benthall, Broseley, **Shropshire**, TF12 5QZ, ENG.
(T) 08454 589280or01952883135
(E) derekosborn@cwcom.net
Speciality: Autogenic Training, Indian Head Massage, Life Style Coaching, Massage (Therapeutic), Meditation, Yoga, Yoga Massage, Bodylife - Combining Yoga, Massage & Other Techniques. ✔
● **Owner/Yoga Teacher/ Masseur**
Mr D Osborn
(T) 08454 589280
C Yrs. Est.: 20 (Ref:HM02622)

## BODYLINE HEALTH

**Bodyline Health**, Burwash Manor Barns, New Rd, Barton, Cambridge, **Cambridgeshire**, CB3 7AY, ENG.
(T) 01223 264443
Speciality: Reflexology.
● **Owner** Mr T Smart
S T (Ref:HM02623)

## BODYMATTERS

**Bodymatters**, 217 Bath Rd, Cheltenham, **Gloucestershire**, GL53 7NA, ENG.
(T) 01242 257030
Speciality: Chiropodists (Podiatrists).
S (Ref:HM02624)

## BODYMIND

**Bodymind**, 4 Little Thurbans Cl, Farnham, **Surrey**, GU9 8SG, ENG.
(T) 01252 717868
Speciality: Complementary Medicines & Therapy.
● **Owner** Mrs J Maach
M (Ref:HM02625)

## BODYMIND

**Bodymind**, Po Box 14, Robertsbridge, **Sussex (East)**, TN32 5ZA, ENG.
(T) 01580 882252
Speciality: Hypnotherapy.
● **Owner** Mrs J Price
B (Ref:HM02626)

## BODY-MIND HYPNOTHERAPY

**Body-Mind Hypnotherapy**, 208 Banstead Rd, Banstead, **Surrey**, SM7 1QG, ENG.
(T) 020 8786 7314
Speciality: Hypnotherapy.
B (Ref:HM02627)

## BODYMIND THERAPY

**Bodymind Therapy**, 9a Ennis Rd, London, **London (Greater)**, N4 3HD, ENG.
(T) 020 7263 1667 (F) 020 7263 1667
Speciality: Complementary Medicines & Therapy.
● **Owner** Mr S Heale
M (Ref:HM02628)

## BODYNEEDS

**Bodyneeds**, 10 Thistle Trce, Leven, **Fife**, KY8 4QR, SCO.
(T) 01592 611108
Speciality: Aromatherapy, Indian Head Massage, Massage (Therapeutic), Reflexology, Sports Massage, Swedish Body Massage.
✔ CREDIT
● **Reflexologist** Mr J Kerr Q: Dip.Rem.Massage, Dip.Swedish Massage, MBRA. M: BRA, SMA.
● **Aromatherapist** Mrs S Kerr Q: LLSA, MIFA. M: IFA.
C T Yrs. Est.: 7 (Ref:HM02629)

## BODYNEEDS

**Bodyneeds**, 9 Unicorn Way, Glenrothes, **Fife**, KY7 5NU, SCO.
(T) 01592 611108
Speciality: Aromatherapy.
M O (Ref:HM02630)

## BODYSCENTS

**Bodyscents**, 58 Turnberry Wynd, Irvine, **Ayrshire (North)**, KA11 4DP, SCO.
(T) 01294 279110
Speciality: Aromatherapy. ✔
● **Owner** Mrs E Bryden
C Yrs. Est.: 5 (Ref:HM02631)

## BODYSPACE

**Bodyspace**, The Open Centre, 188 Old St, London, **London (Greater)**, EC1V 9FR, ENG.
(T) 020 7272 6672
Speciality: Bio-energetics, Counselling, Group Therapy, Humanistic Psychology, Psychotherapy, Pulsing. ✔
● **Psychotherapist/Bodywork Practitioner**
Mr G Gladstone Q: IPSS, ITEC, MAHPP. M: GCP.
B Yrs. Est.: 17 (Ref:HM02632)

## BODYTECH

**Bodytech**, 82 Wilson Rd, Stoke-On-Trent, **Staffordshire**, ST4 4QQ, ENG.
(T) 01782 646421
Speciality: Complementary Medicines & Therapy.
● **Owner** Ms J Mountford
C M (Ref:HM02633)

## BODYTONE

**BodyTone**, 38 Stockport Rd, Marple, Stockport, **Cheshire**, SK, ENG.
(T) 01614 279484
Speciality: Aromatherapy, Bowen Therapy, Hopi Ear Candles, Indian Head Massage, Reflexology, Reiki.
M O (Ref:HM02634)

## BODYTUNE

**Bodytune**, 20 Abbey Cl, Ampthill, Bedford, **Bedfordshire**, MK45 2SH, ENG.
(T) 01525 404339
Speciality: Physiotherapy.
● **Owner** Mr R Edwards
P S T (Ref:HM02635)

## BODYWATCH

**Bodywatch Limited**, Unit 20C, Terryland House, Terryland Retail Park, Headford Road, Galway, **County Galway**, IRE.
(T) 08682 34337 (F) 09156 5812
(W) www.bodywatch.ie
Speciality: Complementary Therapy, Counselling, Pilates, Psychotherapy. ✔
● **Sports Psychologist** Ms N Flynn Q: BA, M.Med.Sc, MBA. M: IETA.
B Yrs. Est.: 4 (Ref:HM02636)

## BODYWISE

**Bodywise**, 119 Roman Rd, Bethnal Green, London, **London (Greater)**, E2 0QN, ENG.
(T) 020 8981 6938
Speciality: Herbal Medicine, Massage (Therapeutic). ✔
● **Medical Herbalist**
Alexandra Knowles Q: BSc (Hons). M: NIMH.
M Yrs. Est.: 2 (Ref:HM02637)

## BODYWISE

**Bodywise**, 16-20 Turner St, Manchester, **Manchester (Greater)**, M4 1DZ, ENG.
(T) 01618 332528
Speciality: Complementary Medicines & Therapy.
● **Secretary** Ms C Howitt
C M (Ref:HM02638)

## BODYWORK HEALTH CLUB & CLINIC

**Bodywork Health Club & Clinic**, The Lodge, Browney Lane, Browney, Durham, **County Durham**, DH7 8HU, ENG.
(T) 01913 789209
Speciality: Homeopathy, Reflexology, Reiki. ✔
● **Owner** Mr B Petre M: BRCP.
C Yrs. Est.: 5 (Ref:HM02639)

## BODYWORKERS

**Bodyworkers**, Suite 211 Coppergate House, 16 Brune St, London, **London (Greater)**, E1 7NJ, ENG.
(T) 020 7721 7833
Speciality: Physiotherapy.
P S T (Ref:HM02640)

## BODYWORKS

**Bodyworks**, 10 Market St, Ellon, **Aberdeenshire**, AB41 9JD, SCO.
(T) 01358 723175
Speciality: Complementary Medicines & Therapy.
● **Owner** Mr J Walls
M (Ref:HM02641)

## BODYWORKS

**Bodyworks**, Doctors Surgery, 81 Kingston Hill, Kingston Upon Thames, **Surrey**, KT2 7PX, ENG.
(T) 020 8974 8742 (F) 020 8547 0075
Speciality: Physiotherapy.
● **Partner** Mrs N Burrows
P S T (Ref:HM02642)

## BODYWORKS COMPLETE

**Bodyworks Complete**, 29 Chapel St, Dunfermline, **Fife**, KY12 7AW, SCO.
(T) 01383 741151
Speciality: Physiotherapy.
● **Owner** Mr B McNeill
P S T (Ref:HM02643)

## BODYWORLD

**Bodyworld**, 20 Market Pl, Chorley, **Lancashire**, PR7 1DA, ENG.
(T) 01257 262833 (F) 01257 411315
Speciality: Aromatherapy.
● **Owner** Mrs M Gardener
M O (Ref:HM02644)

## BOES, AGNES M

**Agnes M Boes**, 28 Withleigh Rd, Bristol, BS4 2LQ, ENG.
(T) 01179 073381 (F) 01179 073380
Speciality: Complementary Medicines & Therapy.
● **Owner** Ms A Boes
M (Ref:HM02645)

## BOGART, R S

**R S Bogart**, Bankfield House, Bankfield St, Bacup, **Lancashire**, OL13 8LW, ENG.
(T) 01706 875911
Speciality: Psychology.
B (Ref:HM02646)

## BOHACZ, KIM

**Kim Bohacz**, 92 Newington Rd, Ramsgate, **Kent**, CT12 6EJ, ENG.
(T) 01843 589934
Speciality: Reflexology.
● **Owner** Mrs K Bokacz
S T (Ref:HM02647)

## BOHNET, CAROLE

**Carole Bohnet**, Honer Farm, South Mundham, Chichester, **Sussex (West)**, PO20 6LZ, ENG.
(T) 01243 261747 (F) 01243 262472
(E) carole@bohnet.co.uk
Speciality: Aromatherapy, Colour Therapy, Complementary Therapy, Healing Therapy, Holistic Healing, Indian Head Massage, Massage (Therapeutic), Reflexology, Reiki, Remedial Massage. ✔
● **Owner** Ms C Bohnet Q: IIHHT, MAR, Reiki 1, Reiki 2. M: AoR.
B Yrs. Est.: 3 (Ref:HM02648)

## BOITEUX, FRANK

**Frank Boiteux**, 32 Loudoun Rd, Newmilns, **Ayrshire (East)**, KA16 9HF, SCO.
(T) 01560 324242
Speciality: Hypnosis.
● **Owner** Mr F Boiteux
B (Ref:HM02649)

## BOLD, PHILIP

**Philip Bold**, Therapy Room, Ashford Health Stores, 10 Station Rd, Ashford, **Surrey**, TW15 2UP, ENG.
(T) 01784 244975
Speciality: Homeopathy.
● **Owner** Mr P Bold
M (Ref:HM02650)

## BOLDICK, K J

**K J Boldick**, 157 South St, Andover, **Hampshire**, SP10 2BS, ENG.
(T) 01264 356254
Speciality: Complementary Medicines & Therapy.
C M (Ref:HM02651)



Key: B Mind-Body Medicine C Complementary Medicine H Self Help Treatment M Medicinal Therapy O Oriental Medicine P Postural Therapy S Manipulative Structural Therapy T Touch Therapy

## BOLDICK, KATHLEEN
**Kathleen Boldick**, 54 East St, Andover, **Hampshire**, SP10 1ES, ENG.
(T) 01264 365910
Speciality: Cranio-Sacral Therapy, Reflexology. ✔
● **Owner/Reflexologist**
Mrs K Boldick Q: LCSP, RCST. M: ITEC.
C Yrs. Est.: 1 (Ref:HM02652)

## BOLDMERE HYPNOTHERAPY
**Boldmere Hypnotherapy**, 6 Wyvern Rd, Sutton Coldfield, **Midlands (West)**, B74 2PT, ENG.
(T) 01213 548037
(E) rosterryuk@yahoo.com
Speciality: Auto Suggestion, Aversion Therapy, Biofeedback, Counselling, Hypnosis, Hypnotherapy, Life Style Coaching, Stress Therapy. ✔
● **Owner** Ms R Terry Q: BSc, MNCH. M: NCH.
B Yrs. Est.: 18 (Ref:HM02653)

## BOLGER, MAEVE
**Bolger Maeve B A , M Sc Couns**, 71 The Palms, Clonskeagh, **County Dublin**, IRE.
(T) 01283 3129
Speciality: Complementary Medicines & Therapy.
M (Ref:HM02654)

## BOLTON CHINESE MEDICAL CENTRE
**Bolton Chinese Medical Centre**, 76 Bradford St, Bolton, **Lancashire**, BL2 1JR, ENG.
(T) 01204 399116 (F) 01204 399116
Speciality: Complementary Medicines & Therapy.
● **Doctor** Dr X Her
C M (Ref:HM02655)

## BOLTON CHIROPRATIC CLINIC
**Bolton Chiropratic Clinic**, The Newlands Centre, Chorley New Rd, Bolton, **Lancashire**, BL1 5BP, ENG.
(T) 01204 848887 (F) 01204 847073
Speciality: Chiropractic. ✔
● **Chiropractor** Dr D Darwent Q: BSc, DC. M: GCC.
P Yrs. Est.: 9 (Ref:HM02656)

## BOLTON CLINIC OF ACUPUNCTURE
**Bolton Clinic Of Acupuncture**, 557 Chorley Old Rd, Bolton, **Lancashire**, BL1 6AE, ENG.
(T) 01204 841060
Speciality: Acupuncture, Hypnotherapy, Osteopathy.
● **Owner** Mrs G Sumner Q: LCSP, Lic.Ac, MB.
● **Practitioner** Ms D Wrathal Q: LCSP.
● **Therapist** Mr M Smith Q: BA (Hons), MNRHP, PGCE.
● **Osteopath** Ms D Stackwood Q: DO. M: GOsC.
B H P (Ref:HM02657)

## BOLTON PHYSIOTHERAPY CLINIC
**Bolton Physiotherapy Clinic**, Stocks House, Chorley Old Rd, Horwich, Bolton, **Lancashire**, BL6 6BQ, ENG.
(T) 01204 691144 (F) 01204 691144
Speciality: Acupuncture, Physiotherapy. ✔
● **Physiotherapist** Mr G Pearson Q: BSc, MCSP.
S Yrs. Est.: 50 (Ref:HM02658)

## BOLTON THERAPY CENTRE
**Bolton Therapy Centre**, 13 Chorley Old Rd, Bolton, **Lancashire**, BL1 3AD, ENG.
(T) 01204 386170 (F) 01204 386170
(E) langridge@supanet.com
(W) www.boltontherapycentre.co.uk
Speciality: Acupuncture, Alexander Technique, Aromatherapy, Complementary Therapy, Counselling, Electrotherapy, Homeopathy, Hypnotherapy, Manipulation, Massage (Therapeutic), Micro Manipulation, Moxibustion, Postural Integration, Reflexology, Reiki, Stress Therapy, Ultrasonics. ✔
● **Counsellor/Supervisor**
Ms J Langridge
(T) 01204 700926 Q: BEd (Hons), Cert.Couns, Cert.Couns.Groupwork, Cert.Ed, Dip.Adv.Couns, Dip.Hyp, Dip.Psych, RGN. M: BACP, NRHP.
● **Homeopath** Ms C Searson
(T) 01254 676156 Q: BSc, DSH, RSHom. M: Soc.Hom.
● **Clinical Reflexologist**
Ms G Magdour Q: Dip.Reflex. M: AoR.
● **Aromatherapist/Reiki Master**
Ms P Barlow Q: ICHT, IIHHT. M: ICHT.
● **Principal** Ms K Wilcock Q: Chart.Acup, Chartered Physio. M: BAcC, CSP.
● **Teacher of the Alexander Technique**
Mr C Tully
(T) 01619 479184 Q: BA, MSTAT. M: STAT.
B S Yrs. Est.: 10 (Ref:HM02659)

## BOLTON, D A
**D A Bolton**, 65 Cleveland Rd, London, **London (Greater)**, E18 2AE, ENG.
(T) 020 8989 2949
Speciality: Chiropodists (Podiatrists).
● **Owner** Mr D Bolton
S (Ref:HM02660)

## BOLTON, HAZEL
**Hazel Bolton**, 37 Ormskirk Rd, Preston, **Lancashire**, PR1 2QP, ENG.
(T) 01772 821942
Speciality: Electrolysis.
T (Ref:HM02661)

## BOLTON, STEVEN
**Steven Bolton**, Nature Cure Clinic, 15 Oldbury Pl, London, **London (Greater)**, W1M 3AL, ENG.
(T) 020 7402 6339
Speciality: Hypnosis.
● **Owner** Mr S Bolton
B (Ref:HM02662)

## BOLTON, TOM
**Tom Bolton**, 161A Manor Rd, Wallasey, **Merseyside**, CH44 0EN, ENG.
(T) 01516 386706
(W) www.freezone.co.uk/tranquilife
Speciality: Aromatherapy, Holistic Healing, Hypnotherapy, Massage (Therapeutic), Nutritional Therapy, Psychotherapy, Meridian Energy Therapy, Freeway Technique, Regression Therapy, Emotional Freedom Technique, Couples Therapy. ✔
● **Hypnotherapist/Holistic Practitioner**
Mr T Bolton Q: Dip.Arom, Dip.Holistic Healing, Dip.Hyp, Dip.Massage, Dip.Nut.Th, Dip.Psych. M: DHA, WFH.
B Yrs. Est.: 10 (Ref:HM02663)

## BOLTON, VANESSA
**Vanessa Bolton - Reflexology**, The Standish Therapy Centre, 28 High St, Standish, Wigan, **Lancashire**, WN6 0HL, ENG.
(T) 01257 472661
Speciality: Acupressure, Chiropody, Physiotherapy, Psychotherapy, Reflexology, Stress Therapy. ✔
● **Reflexologist** Mrs V Bolton
(T) 01257 473018 Q: ART(Reg), Cert.Ed, ITEC. M: RxS.
T Yrs. Est.: 5 (Ref:HM02664)

## BOLTON, VANESSA
**Vanessa Bolton**, 7 Broadlands, Shevington, Wigan, **Lancashire**, WN6 8DH, ENG.
(T) 01257 473018
Speciality: Reflexology.
S T (Ref:HM02665)

## BOMAR AROMA OILS & SUPPLIES
**Bomar Aromatherapy Oils & Supplies**, Sea Rd, Kilcoole, **County Wicklow**, IRE.
(T) 01287 5110 (F) 01287 6717
Speciality: Aromatherapy.
M O (Ref:HM02666)

## BON-ACCORD CHIROPODY
**Bon-Accord Chiropody**, 60 Bon Accord St, Aberdeen, **Aberdeenshire**, AB11 6EL, SCO.
(T) 01224 783552
Speciality: Chiropody. ✔
● **Chiropodist** Mrs S Duncan Q: MBChA, MSSCh.
M Yrs. Est.: 2 (Ref:HM02667)

## BOND, D
**D Bond**, 66 Bulford Rd, Durrington, Salisbury, **Wiltshire**, SP4 8DJ, ENG.
(T) 01980 652524
Speciality: Chiropodists (Podiatrists).
● **Owner** Mr D Bond
S (Ref:HM02668)

## BOND, DIANORA
**Chartered Physiotherapist**, Burgage Manor Cottage, Southwell, **Nottinghamshire**, NG25 0EP, ENG.
(T) 01636 814878 (F) 01636 816844
Speciality: Alexander Technique, Electrotherapy, Manipulation, Massage (Therapeutic), Osteopathy, Reflexology, Ultrasonics. ✔
● **Physiotherapist** Ms D Bond Q: MCSP, SRP. M: CSP.
S Yrs. Est.: 20 (Ref:HM02669)

## BOND, J
**J Bond**, 55A Andover Way, Aldershot, **Hampshire**, GU11 3RJ, ENG.
(T) 01252 324555
Speciality: Alexander Technique.
● **Owner** Miss J Bond
P S (Ref:HM02670)

## BOND, LESLEY
**Lesley Bond**, Liberty Clinic, 394 Romford Rd, London, **London (Greater)**, E7 8DF, ENG.
(T) 020 8555 8869
Speciality: Psychotherapy.
● **Owner** Mrs L Bond
B (Ref:HM02671)

## BOND, LYNNE
**Lynne Bond**, 213 Leach Lane, Sutton Leach, St. Helens, **Merseyside**, WA9 4PH, ENG.
(T) 01744 818444
Speciality: Reflexology.
● **Owner** Mrs L Bond
S T (Ref:HM02672)

## BONDY, PIPPA
**Pippa Bondy**, 59 St Johns Rd, Stansted, **Essex**, CM24 8JS, ENG.
(T) 01279 813886
Speciality: Alexander Technique.
● **Owner** Ms P Bondy
P S (Ref:HM02673)

## BONE, ELIZABETH
**Elizabeth Bone**, Addington Palace Country Club, Gravel Hill, Croydon, **Surrey**, CR0 5BB, ENG.
(T) 020 8688 0737
Speciality: Acupuncture.
O (Ref:HM02674)

## BONE, LEMAYAH
**Lemayah Bone**, 26 Lansdown, Stroud, **Gloucestershire**, GL5 1BG, ENG.
(T) 01453 752141 (F) 01453 752141
Speciality: Complementary Medicines & Therapy.
● **Owner** Ms L Bone
M (Ref:HM02675)

## BONESETTER AND MANIPULATOR
**Adrian Green**, 1 Danum Rd, Bennetthorpe, Doncaster, **Yorkshire (South)**, DN4 5HE, ENG.
(T) 01302 366371
Speciality: Manipulation, Osteopathy. ✔ [credit card]
● **Bonesetter/Manipulator**
Mr A Green
S Yrs. Est.: 40 (Ref:HM02676)

## BONFIELD, D M
**D M Bonfield**, 88 Laburnum Rd, Fareham, **Hampshire**, PO16 0SW, ENG.
(T) 01329 220753
Speciality: Chiropodists (Podiatrists).
S (Ref:HM02677)

## BONIFACE, SANDRA
**Sandra Boniface**, 37 Strathcona Gardens, Knaphill, Woking, **Surrey**, GU21 2AY, ENG.
(T) 01483 473094
Speciality: Chiropractors.
● **Owner** Mrs S Boniface
P S T (Ref:HM02678)

## BONIFACE, SANDRA
**Sandra Boniface**, 2 Barley Mow Cl, Knaphill, Woking, **Surrey**, GU21 2JA, ENG.
(T) 01483 473094
Speciality: Chiropractic.
P S T (Ref:HM02679)



Key continued: Yrs.Est: Years Established Q: Qualifications M: Professional Membership ✔ Indemnity Insurance [credit card] Accept Credit Cards

## BONIFACE, SANDY J

**Sandy J Boniface**, Cranleigh Chiropractic Clinic, Ruffold Lodge, Guildford Rd, Cranleigh, **Surrey**, GU6 8LT, ENG.
(T) 01483 274002
Speciality: Chiropractors.
P S T (Ref:HM02680)

## BONN, JANET

**Janet Bonn**, 1 Miller Avenue, Fairlie, Largs, **Ayrshire (North)**, KA29 0EJ, SCO.
(T) 01475 568382
Speciality: Physiotherapy.
● **Owner** Mrs J Bonn
P S T (Ref:HM02681)

## BONNEBAIGT, ANDRE

**Andre Bonnebaigt**, 17 Spruce Gr, Rode Heath, Stoke-On-Trent, **Staffordshire**, ST7 3SQ, ENG.
(T) 01270 876672
Speciality: Hypnotherapy, Phytotherapy, I B S Therapy. ✔
● **Owner/Hypnotherapist**
Mr A Bonnebaigt Q: Dip.Psych. M: HA, UKCP.
C Yrs. Est.: 3 (Ref:HM02682)

## BONNER, DAVID

**David Bonner**, 88 Heath Rd, Twickenham, **London (Greater)**, TW1 4BW, ENG.
(T) 020 8892 2356
Speciality: Hypnotherapy.
● **Principal** Mr D Bonner
B (Ref:HM02683)

## BONNER, DAVID

**David Bonner**, 26 Compton Cres, London, **London (Greater)**, W4 3JA, ENG.
(T) 020 8994 5520 (F) 020 8994 5520
Speciality: Hypnosis.
● **Principal** Mr D Bonner
B (Ref:HM02684)

## BONNYRIGG CHIROPODY CENTRE

**Bonnyrigg Chiropody Centre**, 33 High St, Bonnyrigg, **Lothian (Mid)**, EH19 2DA, SCO.
(T) 01316 634802
Speciality: Chiropodists (Podiatrists).
S (Ref:HM02685)

## BONTEIN, SARA

**Sara Bontein**, Myrtle Cottage, Milltown, Muddiford, Barnstaple, **Devon**, EX31 4HG, ENG.
(T) 01271 850355
Speciality: Reflexology.
S T (Ref:HM02686)

## BONTHRON, SARAH

**Sarah Bonthron**, 39 Berne Rd, Thornton Heath, **Surrey**, CR7 7BJ, ENG.
(T) 020 8240 1760
Speciality: Reflexology.
S T (Ref:HM02687)

## BOOBIER, A

**A Boobier**, 40 Retreat Rd, Topsham, Exeter, **Devon**, EX3 0LF, ENG.
(T) 01392 874934
Speciality: Chiropodists (Podiatrists).
S (Ref:HM02688)

## BOODAN, D

**D Boodan**, 86 Longbrook St, Exeter, **Devon**, EX4 6AP, ENG.
(T) 01392 434074
Speciality: Homeopathy.
M (Ref:HM02689)

## BOON, G M

**G M Boon**, 394 Ecclesall Rd, Sheffield, **Yorkshire (South)**, S11 8PJ, ENG.
(T) 01142 669255
Speciality: Biomechanics, Chiropody, Nail Surgery, Podiatry. ✔
● **Owner** Mr G Boon Q: S.R.Ch. M: S.C.P.
H Yrs. Est.: 18 (Ref:HM02690)

## BOON, JEAN

**Jean Boon**, 15 Hunters Chase, Caversham, Reading, **Berkshire**, RG4 7XE, ENG.
(T) 01189 483866
Speciality: Homeopathy.
M (Ref:HM02691)

## BOORER, ALISON

**Alison Boorer**, Plaistow Lane, Bromley, **Kent**, BR1 3TP, ENG.
(T) 020 8466 6645
Speciality: Physiotherapy.
● **Owner** A Boorer
P S T (Ref:HM02692)

## BOORMAN, CATHERINE

**Catherine Boorman**, Bardan Cottage, High Rd, Guyhirn, Wisbech, **Cambridgeshire**, PE13 4EQ, ENG.
(T) 01945 450711
Speciality: Reflexology.
● **Owner** Mrs C Boorden
S T (Ref:HM02693)

## BOORMAN, JUNE

**June Boorman**, 28 South View Rise, Loxley, Sheffield, **Yorkshire (South)**, S6 6SZ, ENG.
(T) 01142 340452
Speciality: Hypnosis.
B (Ref:HM02694)

## BOOTH, CLARE

**Clare Booth**, Aberfoyle House, Stapley Rd, St. Albans, **Hertfordshire**, AL3 5EP, ENG.
(T) 01727 856687
Speciality: Hypnotherapy.
● **Manager** Mrs S Bassett
B (Ref:HM02695)

## BOOTH, CORINNE

**Corinne Booth**, 2 Wensleydale Drive, Camberley, **Surrey**, GU15 1SP, ENG.
(T) 01276 677207
Speciality: Reflexology.
S T (Ref:HM02696)

## BOOTH, HILARY

**Hilary Booth**, 74 Worsted Green, Redhill, **Surrey**, RH1 3PW, ENG.
(T) 01737 642193
Speciality: Chiropodists (Podiatrists).
S (Ref:HM02697)

## BOOTH, I G P

**I G P Booth**, 219 Rochdale Rd, Middleton, Manchester, **Manchester (Greater)**, M24 2QJ, ENG.
(T) 01616 437561
Speciality: Chiropodists (Podiatrists).
S (Ref:HM02698)

## BOOTH, JACQUELINE

**Jacqueline Booth**, 56 Paget Avenue, Birstall, **Leicestershire**, LE4 4HX, ENG.
(T) 01162 671921
Speciality: Reflexology.
S T (Ref:HM02699)

## BOOTH, JAMES

**James Booth**, 52 Bonnington Sq, London, **London (Greater)**, SW8 1TQ, ENG.
(T) 020 7735 1875
Speciality: Acupuncture.
O (Ref:HM02700)

## BOOTH, JANICE

**Janice Booth**, 131 Goddard Avenue, Swindon, **Wiltshire**, SN1 4HX, ENG.
(T) 01793 641107
Speciality: Acupuncture.
● **Owner** Mrs J Booth
O (Ref:HM02701)

## BOOTH, JANICE

**Janice Booth**, Health Hydro, Milton Rd, Swindon, **Wiltshire**, SN1 5JA, ENG.
(T) 01793 465631
Speciality: Acupuncture.
O (Ref:HM02702)

## BOOTH, JUDY

**Judy Booth**, 3 Prince Arthur Rd, London, **London (Greater)**, NW3 6AX, ENG.
(T) 020 7794 7484
Speciality: Aromatherapy, Reflexology, Remedial Massage.
M O (Ref:HM02703)

## BOOTH, KATHERYN

**Katheryn Booth**, 12 Bronte Drive, Oakworth, Keighley, **Yorkshire (West)**, BD22 7LX, ENG.
(T) 01535 604682
Speciality: Reflexology.
● **Owner** Mrs K Booth
S T (Ref:HM02704)

## BOOTH, LYNNE

**Lynne Booth**, 9 Glenavon Park, Bristol, BS9 1RS, ENG.
(T) 01179 626746
Speciality: Reflexology.
S T (Ref:HM02705)

## BOOTH, MARK

**Mark Booth**, 99 Wolverton Rd, Newport Pagnell, **Buckinghamshire**, MK16 8HX, ENG.
(T) 01908 615045 (F) 01908 615045
Speciality: Osteopathy.
● **Principal** Mr M Booth
P S T (Ref:HM02706)

## BOOTH, N

**N Booth**, 4 Waterden Rd, Guildford, **Surrey**, GU1 2AW, ENG.
(T) 01483 503240 (F) 01483 531177
Speciality: Homeopathy.
● **Practice Manager** Mrs C Don
M (Ref:HM02707)

## BOOTH, PHILLIP

**Phillip Booth**, 6 Clare Rd, Cotham, Bristol, BS6 5TB, ENG.
(T) 01179 870142
Speciality: Psychotherapy.
● **Owner** Mr P Booth
B (Ref:HM02708)

## BOOTH, ROBERT

**Robert Booth**, Hillside, Hopton, Nesscliffe, Shrewsbury, **Shropshire**, SY4 1DG, ENG.
(T) 01743 741544
Speciality: Acupuncture, Physiotherapy. ✔
● **Practice Manager** Mrs D Booth
● **Owner/Physiotherapist** Mr R Booth Q: MCSP, SRP. M: CSP.
S Yrs. Est.: 9 (Ref:HM02709)

## BOOTH, ROBERT

**Robert Booth**, Lilleshall National Sports Centre, Lilleshall, Newport, **Shropshire**, TF10 9AT, ENG.
(T) 01952 605828 (F) 01952 820924
Speciality: Physiotherapy.
● **Owner** Mr R Booth
P S T (Ref:HM02710)

## BOOTS HEALTHCARE SERVICES

**Boots Chiropody & Footcare**, Unit 7, Broughton Shopping Pk, Near Chester, Broughton, **Flintshire**, CH4 0DP, WAL.
(T) 01244 539254
(E) toby@toby76freeserve.com
Speciality: Biomechanics, Chiropody, Podiatry.
✔ CREDIT
● **Senior Chiropodist** Mr T Edwards Q: SRPod. M: S.C.P.
● **Chiropodist** Helen Crawford Q: SRPod. M: S.C.P.
S Yrs. Est.: 2 (Ref:HM02711)

## BOOTY, STEPHEN

**Stephen Booty**, 327 Farnborough Rd, Farnborough, **Hampshire**, GU14 8AY, ENG.
(T) 01252 510284 (F) 01252 510284
Speciality: Chiropractic.
● **Owner** Mr S Booty
P S T (Ref:HM02712)

## BOR, ROBERT (DR)

**Dr Robert Bor**, City University, Northampton Sq, London, **London (Greater)**, EC1V 0HB, ENG.
(T) 020 7477 8523
Speciality: Psychology.
B (Ref:HM02713)

## BORDERS HEALTH BOARD

**Borders Health Board**, 42 Bridgend, Duns, **Scottish Borders**, TD11 3EX, SCO.
(T) 01361 882162 (F) 01361 882167
Speciality: Psychiatry.
● **Manager** Dr B Lowe
B (Ref:HM02714)

## BORDISS, DEBORAH

**Deborah Bordiss**, 2 St. Albans Rd, Kingston Upon Thames, **Surrey**, KT2 5HQ, ENG.

Key: B Mind-Body Medicine C Complementary Medicine H Self Help Treatment M Medicinal Therapy O Oriental Medicine P Postural Therapy S Manipulative Structural Therapy T Touch Therapy

(T) 020 8541 3207
Speciality: Reflexology.
S T (Ref:HM02715)

## BORE ST POD & CHIROP PRACTICE

**Bore St Podiatry & Chiropody Practice**, 24-26 Bore St, Lichfield, **Staffordshire**, WS13 6LL, ENG.
(T) 01543 250093
(E) vg2@btinternet.com
Speciality: Biomechanics, Chiropody, Nail Surgery, Orthotics, Bone surgery, Dentistry.
● **Chiropodist** Mr P Thompson Q: DPodM. M: S.C.P.
B Yrs. Est.: 15 (Ref:HM02716)

## BOREHAMWOOD CHIRO CLINIC

**Claudio Merkier**, Wellswood House, Fairway Avenue, Borehamwood, **Hertfordshire**, WD6 1PU, ENG.
(T) 020 8953 4515 (F) 020 8953 4372
Speciality: Chiropractic, Manipulation, Massage (Therapeutic), Spinal Rehabilitation Exercises. ✔
● **Chiropractor** Ms C Merkier Q: BSc, DC, MCC. M: BCA, CC.
S Yrs. Est.: 2 (Ref:HM02717)

## BORKETT, RALPH

**Ralph Borkett**, Forest Hill Leisure Centre, Dartmouth Rd, London, **London (Greater)**, SE23 3XU, ENG.
(T) 020 8690 7418
Speciality: Complementary Medicines & Therapy.
● **Owner** Mr R Borkett
M (Ref:HM02718)

## BOROUGHBRIDGE

**Boroughbridge Chiropody & Beauty**, 4 Fishergate, Boroughbridge, York, **Yorkshire (North)**, YO51 9AL, ENG.
(T) 01423 325375
Speciality: Chiropodists (Podiatrists).
● **Owner** Mrs A Little
S (Ref:HM02719)

## BORRELLI, SCOTT E (DR)

**Dr Scott E Borrelli**, 55 Ossington Buildings, London, **London (Greater)**, W1M 3HZ, ENG.
(T) 020 7224 4402 (F) 020 7224 4402
Speciality: Psychology.
● **Owner** Dr S Borrelli
B (Ref:HM02720)

## BORTH, H

**H Borth**, Rainbows, Thurleston Lodge Cottages, Thurleston Lane, Ipswich, **Suffolk**, IP1 6TF, ENG.
(T) 01473 226650
Speciality: Reflexology.
● **Partner** Ms W Seal
S T (Ref:HM02721)

## BORTHWICK, C M

**C M Borthwick**, 15 Longlands Drive, Heybrook Bay, Plymouth, **Devon**, PL9 0BL, ENG.
(T) 01752 862909
Speciality: Chiropodists (Podiatrists).
S (Ref:HM02722)

## BOSCOMBE MANOR MEDICAL CENTRE

**Boscombe Manor Medical Centre**, 40 Florence Rd, Bournemouth, **Dorset**, BH5 1HQ, ENG.
(T) 01202 251075 (F) 01202 303014
Speciality: Reflexology.
● **Manager** Mrs L Cluer
S T (Ref:HM02723)

## BOSSERT, ELAINE HARRISON

**Elaine Harrison Bossert**, 30 Sidney Rd, Walton-On-Thames, **Surrey**, KT12 2LZ, ENG.
(T) 01932 254597
Speciality: Reflexology.
S T (Ref:HM02724)

## BOSTON CHIROPODY CLINIC

**Boston Chiropody Clinic**, C/O Bella Karen, 12 Boston Prde, Boston Rd, London, **London (Greater)**, W7 2DG, ENG.
(T) 020 8567 7126
Speciality: Biomechanics, Chiropody, Manipulation, Podiatry. ✔
● **Chiropodist (Podiatrist)** Mr B Forde Q: BSc, DPodM, M.S.C.P., S.R.Ch. M: S.C.P.
C Yrs. Est.: 3 (Ref:HM02725)

## BOSTON CHIROPRACTIC CLINIC

**Boston Chiropractic Clinic**, 11 Main Ridge West, Boston, **Lincolnshire**, PE21 6QQ, ENG.
(T) 01205 311115 (F) 01205 311128
Speciality: Chiropractic. ✔
● **Partner** Dr C Ball Q: DC. M: GCC, SCA.
● **Owner** Ms K Royle
P S T Yrs. Est.: 4 (Ref:HM02726)

## BOSTON, SANDY

**Sandy Boston**, 22 Eltham Park Gardens, London, **London (Greater)**, SE9 1AW, ENG.
(T) 020 8265 9494
Speciality: Reflexology.
● **Owner** Mrs S Boston
S T (Ref:HM02727)

## BOSTWICK, A

**A Bostwick**, 230 Sladepool Farm Rd, Birmingham, **Midlands (West)**, B14 5EE, ENG.
(T) 01216 042163
Speciality: Chiropodists (Podiatrists).
S (Ref:HM02728)

## BOSTWICK, B

**B Bostwick**, 57 Christ Church Rd, Doncaster, **Yorkshire (South)**, DN1 2QS, ENG.
(T) 01302 840315
Speciality: Electrolysis.
● **Owner** Mrs B Bostwick
T (Ref:HM02729)

## BOSWELL, EVA

**Eva Boswell**, 34 Kent Rd, Margate, **Kent**, CT9 3SN, ENG.
(T) 01843 295960
Speciality: Chiropodists (Podiatrists).
● **Owner** Mrs E Boswell
S (Ref:HM02730)

## BOTANIC CHIROPODY

**Botanic Chiropody Practitioners**, 19 Middleflat, Auchtermuchty, Cupar, **Fife**, KY14 7DG, SCO.
(T) 01337 828003
Speciality: Chiropodists (Podiatrists).
● **Owner** Mrs M Adam
S (Ref:HM02731)

## BOTHA, M E

**M E Botha**, 70 Bradbourne Rd, Sevenoaks, **Kent**, TN13 3QA, ENG.
(T) 01732 455903
Speciality: Psychotherapy.
B (Ref:HM02732)

## BOTHWELL PHYSIOTHERAPY

**Bothwell Physiotherapy**, 28 Hamilton Rd, Bothwell, Glasgow, **Glasgow (City of)**, G71 8NA, SCO.
(T) 01698 854474 (F) 01698 854631
Speciality: Physiotherapy. ✔ [credit card]
● **Physiotherapist** Ms J Constable Q: MCSP. M: SRP.
● **Physiotherapist** Mrs J Wells Q: MCSP.
S Yrs. Est.: 18 (Ref:HM02733)

## BOTHWICK, JOHN

**John Bothwick I T E C**, 31 Southsea Trce, Southsea, **Hampshire**, PO5 3AU, ENG.
(T) 023 9275 4689
Speciality: Massage (Therapeutic). ✔
● **Therapist** Mr J Bothwick Q: ITEC. M: ITEC.
C Yrs. Est.: 11 (Ref:HM02734)

## BOTT, JENNY

**Jenny Bott**, Kew House, 23 Anchor Rd, Calne, **Wiltshire**, SN11 8DY, ENG.
(T) 01249 813021
Speciality: Physiotherapy.
P S T (Ref:HM02735)

## BOTTERILL, V C

**V C Botterill**, 21 Rib Vale, Hertford, **Hertfordshire**, SG14 3LE, ENG.
(T) 01992 500922
Speciality: Complementary Medicines & Therapy.
C M (Ref:HM02736)

## BOTTING, MELANIE

**Melanie Botting**, 15 Monceux Rd, Eastbourne, **Sussex (East)**, BN21 1RD, ENG.
(T) 01323 639917
Speciality: Chiropodists (Podiatrists).
● **Owner** Mrs M Botting
S (Ref:HM02737)

## BOULANGER, S

**S Boulanger**, 28 Hallowell Rd, Northwood, **London (Greater)**, HA6 1DN, ENG.
(T) 01923 827833
Speciality: Osteopathy.
P S T (Ref:HM02738)

## BOULEVARD PHARMACY

**V G Evans Ltd**, 23 Waterloo St, Weston-Super-Mare, **Somerset**, BS23 1LF, ENG.
(T) 01934 628845
Speciality: Acupressure, Acupuncture, Aromatherapy, Bach Remedies, Chinese Herbal Medicine, Chiropody, Complementary Therapy, Counselling, Dietician, Herbal Medicine, Homeopathy, Hypnosis, Hypnotherapy, Indian Head Massage, Massage (Therapeutic), Meditation, Physiotherapy, Phytotherapy, Psychotherapy, Reflexology, Reiki, Shiatsu, Spiritual Healing, Stress Therapy, Yoga. ✔ [credit card]
● **Pharmacist** Ms V Evans Q: BSc (Hons), Cert.Ed.
M (Ref:HM02739)

## BOULTER, NIGEL

**Nigel Boulter**, Carlton Clinic, 147 Balcombe Rd, Horley, **Surrey**, RH6 9BX, ENG.
(T) 01293 784200
Speciality: Hypnotherapy.
B (Ref:HM02740)

## BOULTON, A

**A Boulton**, 47 Campion Trce, Leamington Spa, **Warwickshire**, CV32 4SU, ENG.
(T) 01926 335932 (F) 01926 339574
Speciality: Osteopathy.
● **Osteopath** Jane O'Conner
P S T (Ref:HM02741)

## BOULTON, ERIC C

**Eric C Boulton**, 63 Holmes Chapel Rd, Congleton, **Cheshire**, CW12 4NU, ENG.
(T) 01260 273913
Speciality: Hypnosis.
● **Owner** Mr E Boulton
B (Ref:HM02742)

## BOULTON, FRANCES

**Frances Boulton**, 6 Brownrigg Rd, Ashford, **Surrey**, TW15 2TL, ENG.
(T) 01784 244419
Speciality: Reflexology.
S T (Ref:HM02743)

## BOUND, A J

**A J Bound**, 28 Dunraven Trce, Treorchy, **Rhondda Cynon Taff**, CF42 6EL, WAL.
(T) 01443 772214
Speciality: Chiropodists (Podiatrists).
● **Owner** Mrs A Bound
S (Ref:HM02744)

## BOUNDY, C

**C Boundy**, 5 Retreat Rd, Topsham, Exeter, **Devon**, EX3 0LF, ENG.
(T) 01392 874349
Speciality: Chiropodists (Podiatrists).
● **Owner** Mrs C Boundy
S (Ref:HM02745)

## BOUNDY, ELIZABETH

**Elizabeth Boundy**, Hillside, Shawford, Winchester, **Hampshire**, SO21 2AA, ENG.
(T) 01962 712324
Speciality: Physiotherapy.
P S T (Ref:HM02746)

## BOURGARD, FRANCOISE

**Francoise Bourgard**, 18 Shelley Cl, Greenford, **London (Greater)**, UB6 8RT, ENG.
(T) 020 8813 0731
Speciality: Aromatherapy.
● **Owner** Miss F Bourgard
M O (Ref:HM02747)



Key continued: Yrs.Est: Years Established Q: Qualifications M: Professional Membership ✔ Indemnity Insurance [credit card] Accept Credit Cards

## BOURGUIGNON, PASCAL
**Pascal Bourguignon**, 1 Kenworthy St, Stalybridge, **Manchester (Greater)**, SK15 2DX, ENG.
(T) 01613 383080
Speciality: Hypnosis.
● **Owner** Mr P Bourguignon
B (Ref:HM02748)

## BOURKE, JOHN (DR)
**Dr John Bourke**, Liscarroll, Mallow, **County Cork**, IRE.
(T) 022 4834 0
Speciality: Acupuncture.
O (Ref:HM02749)

## BOURKE, SEAN M
**Sean M Bourke**, 54 Vernon Ave, Clontarf, **County Dublin**, IRE.
(T) 01833 6648
Speciality: Psychotherapy.
B (Ref:HM02750)

## BOURN, M
**M Bourne**, Beverley Clinic, 362 Coombe Lane, London, **London (Greater)**, SW20 0RJ, ENG.
(T) 020 8241 2515
Speciality: Complementary Medicines & Therapy.
M (Ref:HM02751)

## BOURNE CONSULTANCY
**Bourne Consultancy (The)**, 25 Bilberry Drive, Marchwood, Southampton, **Hampshire**, SO40 4YR, ENG.
(T) 023 8087 0228
Speciality: Hypnosis.
● **Owner** Miss J Bourne
B (Ref:HM02752)

## BOURNE HEALTH
**Bourne Health**, Bourne House, Horsell Park, Woking, **Surrey**, GU21 4LY, ENG.
(T) 01483 722122
Speciality: Aromatherapy, Homeopathy, Massage (Therapeutic), Reiki, Remedial Massage. ✔
● **Homeopath** Ms Y Stone Q: RSHom.
● **Therapist** Ms T Laws Q: ITEC, TIDHA. M: IPTI, ITEC.
C Yrs. Est.: 4 (Ref:HM02753)

## BOURNE, DAVID
**David Bourne**, 39 Melton Rd, West Bridgford, Nottingham, **Nottinghamshire**, NG2 7NE, ENG.
(T) 01159 810001
Speciality: Chiropractic.
● **Owner** Mr D Bourne
P S T (Ref:HM02754)

## BOURNE, JOHN
**John Bourne**, 40 Edburton Avenue, Brighton, **Sussex (East)**, BN1 6EJ, ENG.
(T) 01273 552832
Speciality: Indian Head Massage, Massage (Therapeutic), Reflexology.
S T (Ref:HM02755)

## BOURNE, LIZ
**Liz Bourne**, 2 Myrtle Cottages, Flint Hill, Dorking, **Surrey**, RH4 2LJ, ENG.
(T) 01306 884966
Speciality: Aromatherapy.
● **Owner** Mrs L Bourne
M O (Ref:HM02756)

## BOURNE, STACEY
**Stacey Bourne**, 588 Eastern Avenue, Ilford, **Essex**, IG2 6PQ, ENG.
(T) 020 8554 6166
Speciality: Osteopathy.
P S T (Ref:HM02757)

## BOURNE, VIV
**Viv Bourne**, 41 Church Rd, Poole, **Dorset**, BH14 0NN, ENG.
(T) 01202 749514 (F) 01202 718906
Speciality: Physiotherapy.
● **Partner** Mrs C Swinhoe
P S T (Ref:HM02758)

## BOURNEMOUTH & POOLE PRACTICE
**Bournemouth & Poole Homeopathic Practice**, 14 Woodside Rd, Poole, **Dorset**, BH14 9JJ, ENG.
(T) 01202 739730
Speciality: Homeopathy.
M (Ref:HM02759)

## BOURNEMOUTH CHIRO & NTRL HLTH
**Bournemouth Chiropractic & Natural Health Clinic**, 36 Iddesleigh Rd, Bournemouth, **Dorset**, BH3 7NQ, ENG.
(T) 01202 513838
Speciality: Chiropractic.
● **Owner** Ms R Clarke
P S T (Ref:HM02760)

## BOURNEMOUTH CTRE FOR COMP MED
**Bournemouth Centre for Complementary Medicine**, 51A Christchurch Rd, Bournemouth, **Dorset**, BH1 3PA, ENG.
(T) 01202 295128
Speciality: Acupuncture, Aromatherapy, Homeopathy, Hypnosis, Indian Head Massage, Massage (Therapeutic), Osteopathy, Reflexology, Reiki, Swedish Body Massage. ✔
● **Owner** Mrs J Hussey
● **Osteopath** Mr S Hussey Q: BSc, DO. M: GOsC.
● **Acupuncturist** Mr G Hussey Q: Dip.Ac, MBAcC.
P T (Ref:HM02761)

## BOURNEMOUTH PHYSIO CLINIC
**Bournemouth Physiotherapy Clinic**, 1626 Wimborne Rd, Bournemouth, **Dorset**, BH11 9AH, ENG.
(T) 01202 576731 (F) 01202 576731
Speciality: Physiotherapy. ✔
● **Physiotherapist** Mr J Chick Q: MCSP, SRP. M: CSP.
S Yrs. Est.: 20 (Ref:HM02762)

## BOURNEMOUTH THERAPY CLINIC
**Bournemouth Therapy Clinic**, 1120 Christchurch Rd, Bournemouth, **Dorset**, BH7 6DT, ENG.
(T) 01202 434361
Speciality: Complementary Medicines & Therapy.
C M (Ref:HM02763)

## BOUSFIELD, A M
**A M Bousfield**, 13 Burtons Rd, Hampton Hill, Hampton, **London (Greater)**, TW12 1DB, ENG.
(T) 020 8977 9922
Speciality: Chiropodists (Podiatrists).
S (Ref:HM02764)

## BOVEY, MARK
**Mark Bovey**, 28 Wootton Rd, Abingdon, **Oxfordshire**, OX14 1JD, ENG.
(T) 01235 531021
Speciality: Osteopathy.
● **Owner** Mr M Davies
P S T (Ref:HM02765)

## BOW HOUSE PHYSIO PRACTICE
**Bow House Physiotherapy Practice**, Bow House, Bow St, Langport, **Somerset**, TA10 9PQ, ENG.
(T) 01458 253388
Speciality: Physiotherapy.
P S T (Ref:HM02766)

## BOWBURN PHYSICAL THERAPY CLNC
**Bowburn Physical Therapy Clinic**, 4 Durham Rd, Bowburn, Durham, **County Durham**, DH6 5AT, ENG.
(T) 01913 773553
Speciality: Complementary Medicines & Therapy.
C M (Ref:HM02767)

## BOWCOCK, HELEN
**Helen Bowcock**, 22 Clare Rd, Halifax, **Yorkshire (West)**, HX1 2HX, ENG.
(T) 01422 340919
Speciality: Homeopathy.
M (Ref:HM02768)

## BOWDEN, ANN
**Ann Bowden**, 1 Wainwright, Peterborough, **Cambridgeshire**, PE4 5AG, ENG.
(T) 01733 579375
Speciality: Chiropodists (Podiatrists).
S (Ref:HM02769)

## BOWDEN, KAREN
**Karen Bowden**, 21 St Marys Rd, Sileby, Loughborough, **Leicestershire**, LE12 7TL, ENG.
(T) 01509 814550
Speciality: Reflexology.
● **Owner** Mrs K Bowden
S T (Ref:HM02770)

## BOWEN CLINIC
**Bowen Clinic (The)**, 122 The Grove, Moordown, Bournemouth, **Dorset**, BH9 2UA, ENG.
(T) 01202 518152
(E) russell.jenkins@tesco.net
Speciality: Acupressure, Bowen Therapy, Electrotherapy, Healer, Massage (Therapeutic), Reiki, Spiritual Healing. ✔
● **Bowen Therapist** Mr R Jenkins Q: MBEC.
T Yrs. Est.: 6 (Ref:HM02771)

## BOWEN TECHNIQUE
**Bowen Technique (The)**, P O Box 57, Batley, **Yorkshire (West)**, WF17 8YX, ENG.
(T) 01924 402205 (F) 01924 402205
Speciality: Complementary Medicines & Therapy.
● **Owner** Mr Y Patch
M (Ref:HM02772)

## BOWEN TECHNIQUE
**Bowen Technique (The)**, 24 Westmead Cres, Trowbridge, **Wiltshire**, BA14 0LY, ENG.
(T) 01225 752246
Speciality: Complementary Medicines & Therapy.
C M (Ref:HM02773)

## BOWEN TECHNIQUE EURO REG
**Bowen Technique European Register (The)**, Bow House, Bow St, Langport, **Somerset**, TA10 9PQ, ENG.
(T) 01458 252599
Speciality: Complementary Medicines & Therapy.
● **Bowen Therapist/Administrator** Mr I Roberts M: BTER.
C (Ref:HM02774)

## BOWEN TECHNIQUE STUDIO
**Bowen Technique Studio (The)**, Wentworth Park, Hexham, **Northumberland**, NE46 3PD, ENG.
(T) 01434 609500 (F) 01434 652357
Speciality: Bowen Therapy. ✔
● **Bowen Therapist** Mr J Wilson Q: BTER. M: BTER.
● **Secretary** Ms J Lambert
M Yrs. Est.: 6 (Ref:HM02775)

## BOWEN THERAPY
**Bowen Therapy**, 10 High St, Banstead, **Surrey**, SM7 2LJ, ENG.
(T) 01737 371007
Speciality: Complementary Medicines & Therapy.
● **Owner** Ms E Thompson
C M (Ref:HM02776)

## BOWEN THERAPY
**Bowen Therapy**, 1 Park Cottages, Westerham Rd, Keston, London, **London (Greater)**, BR2 6HG, ENG.
(T) 01689 858818
Speciality: Complementary Medicines & Therapy.
● **Owner** Mrs M Wilson
M (Ref:HM02777)

## BOWEN THERAPY
**Bowen Therapy**, 62 Springpark Drive, Beckenham, **Kent**, BR3 6QD, ENG.
(T) 020 8650 3095
Speciality: Complementary Medicines & Therapy.
C M (Ref:HM02778)

## BOWEN, CHRISTINE
**Christine Bowen**, Stone Hayne, Stone St, Stanford, Ashford, **Kent**, TN25 6DN, ENG.
(T) 01303 814671
Speciality: Reflexology.
S T (Ref:HM02779)



Key: B Mind-Body Medicine, C Complementary Medicine, H Self Help Treatment, M Medicinal Therapy, O Oriental Medicine, P Postural Therapy, S Manipulative Structural Therapy, T Touch Therapy

### BOWEN, KAREN
**Karen Bowen**, 13 Laurel Gr, Hoole, Chester, **Cheshire**, CH2 3HU, ENG.
(T) 01244 320378
Speciality: Reflexology.
S T (Ref:HM02780)

### BOWEN, LINDA
**Linda Bowen**, 15 Redvers St, Newport, NP19 0FR, WAL.
(T) 01633 882235
Speciality: Chiropodists (Podiatrists).
● **Owner** Mr L Bowen
S (Ref:HM02781)

### BOWEN, MARGARET
**Margaret Bowen**, 18 Twycross Gr, Hodgehill, Birmingham, **Midlands (West)**, B36 8LB, ENG.
(T) 01217 831882
Speciality: Reflexology.
S T (Ref:HM02782)

### BOWEN, SARAH
**Sarah Bowen**, 52 Stoke Newington Church St, London, **London (Greater)**, N16 0NB, ENG.
(T) 020 7249 9671
Speciality: Chiropodists (Podiatrists).
S (Ref:HM02783)

### BOWEN, SARAH
**Sarah Bowen**, 81 Offord Rd, London, **London (Greater)**, N1 1PG, ENG.
(T) 020 7607 4458
Speciality: Chiropodists (Podiatrists).
S (Ref:HM02784)

### BOWER MOUNT CLINIC
**Bower Mount Clinic**, 62 Bower Mount Rd, Maidstone, **Kent**, ME16 8AT, ENG.
(T) 01622 674656
Speciality: Osteopathy.
● **Therapist** Miss M Perrichon
P S T (Ref:HM02785)

### BOWER, BRENDA (DR)
**Dr Brenda Bower B Sc D C**, Omni Park S.C, Swords Rd, Santry, **County Dublin**, IRE.
(T) 01862 1188
Speciality: Chiropractors.
P S T (Ref:HM02786)

### BOWER, JOAN
**Joan Bower**, Romney House, Romney Rd, Willesborough, Ashford, **Kent**, TN24 0RW, ENG.
(T) 01233 643095
Speciality: Chiropodists (Podiatrists).
● **Owner** Mrs J Bower
S (Ref:HM02787)

### BOWER, PHILIPPA
**Philippa Bower**, 17 South View, East Preston, Littlehampton, **Sussex (West)**, BN16 1PX, ENG.
(T) 01903 773969
Speciality: Chiropodists (Podiatrists).
S (Ref:HM02788)

### BOWER, V
**Mrs V Bower**, 23 Sutton Park Rd, Seaford, **Sussex (East)**, BN25 1RH, ENG.
(T) 01323 892002
Speciality: Chiropodists (Podiatrists).
S (Ref:HM02789)

### BOWIE, R
**R Bowie**, 6a The Villas, Stoke-On-Trent, **Staffordshire**, ST4 5AQ, ENG.
(T) 01782 846915
Speciality: Alexander Technique.
P S (Ref:HM02790)

### BOWIE, S
**S Bowie**, 23 Green Farm Rd, Bagshot, **Surrey**, GU19 5LB, ENG.
(T) 01276 475677
Speciality: Chiropodists (Podiatrists).
S (Ref:HM02791)

### BOWKETT, LYN
**Lyn Bowkett**, 24 Stow Park Avenue, Newport, NP20 4FL, WAL.
(T) 01633 661088
Speciality: Kinesiology, Massage (Therapeutic), Reflexology, Reiki, Golden Rai Work and Past Life Therapy. ✔
● **Owner** Ms L Bowkett Q: BA, DIBAK, Dip.Reflex, NLP, Reiki Master.
C Yrs. Est.: 7 (Ref:HM02792)

### BOWKETT, STEPHEN
**Stephen Bowkett**, 88A Northampton Rd, Market Harborough, **Leicestershire**, LE16 9HF, ENG.
(T) 01858 433244
Speciality: Hypnosis.
B (Ref:HM02793)

### BOWLER, ANNIE
**Annie Bowler**, Ash Cottage, Bentley, Farnham, **Surrey**, GU10 5NF, ENG.
(T) 01420 520003
Speciality: Reflexology.
S T (Ref:HM02794)

### BOWLES, D
**D Bowles**, 8 High St, Mill Lane Entrance, Arundel, **Sussex (West)**, BN18 9AB, ENG.
(T) 01903 882200
Speciality: Osteopathy.
P S T (Ref:HM02795)

### BOWLES, JANICE
**Janice Bowles**, 69 Southern Rd, Thame, **Oxfordshire**, OX9 2ED, ENG.
(T) 01844 212511
Speciality: Hypnosis.
B (Ref:HM02796)

### BOWLES, LESLEY-ANN
**Lesley-Ann Bowles**, 3 Strathnairn St, London, **London (Greater)**, SE1 5BN, ENG.
(T) 020 7394 6403
Speciality: Reflexology.
S T (Ref:HM02797)

### BOWLING, ANDREW
**Andrew Bowling**, 28 Morrison Rd, Folkestone, **Kent**, CT20 1PQ, ENG.
(T) 01303 257938
Speciality: Reflexology.
S T (Ref:HM02798)

### BOWMAN, D
**D Bowman**, 11 Sandelwood Avenue, Coleraine, **County Londonderry**, BT52 1JW, NIR.
(T) 028 7035 5242
Speciality: Chiropodists (Podiatrists).
● **Owner** Mr D Bowman
S (Ref:HM02799)

### BOWMAN, D
**D Bowman**, 33 Church Rd, Holywood, **County Down**, BT18 9BU, NIR.
(T) 028 9042 3991
Speciality: Complementary Medicines & Therapy.
C M (Ref:HM02800)

### BOWMER, S
**S Bowmer**, 14 Dale View Rd, Lower Pilsley, Chesterfield, **Derbyshire**, S45 8DR, ENG.
(T) 01246 851004
Speciality: Reflexology.
● **Owner** Mr S Bowmer
S T (Ref:HM02801)

### BOWN, LYNNE
**Lynne Bown**, 51 Syddall St, Hyde, **Cheshire**, SK14 1JH, ENG.
(T) 01613 688910
Speciality: Aromatherapy.
● **Owner** Mrs L Bown
M O (Ref:HM02802)

### BOWNESS, B
**B Bowness**, Rose Bank, East Rd, Egremont, **Cumbria**, CA22 2ED, ENG.
(T) 01946 823582
Speciality: Chiropodists (Podiatrists).
● **Owner** Mr B Bowness
S (Ref:HM02803)

### BOWOOD HEALTH & BEAUTY CENTRE
**Bowood Health & Beauty Centre**, 3 Wellington Rd, Bournemouth, **Dorset**, BH8 8JQ, ENG.
(T) 01202 554137
Speciality: Aromatherapy. ✔
● **Aromatherapist** Mr C Button M: IFA, LCSP.
C Yrs. Est.: 2 (Ref:HM02804)

### BOWRY, HEATHER
**Heather Bowry**, 33 Mayfair Avenue, Worcester Park, **Surrey**, KT4 7SH, ENG.
(T) 020 8337 2408
Speciality: Reflexology.
S T (Ref:HM02805)

### BOWYER, E
**E Bowyer**, Brackenbury Natural Health Clinic, 30 Brackenbury Rd, London, **London (Greater)**, W6 0BA, ENG.
(T) 020 8741 9264
Speciality: Homeopathy.
M (Ref:HM02806)

### BOWYER, MARGARET
**Margaret Bowyer**, 19 Willow Court, St Peters Park Rd, Broadstairs, **Kent**, CT10 2BQ, ENG.
(T) 01843 863284
Speciality: Osteopathy.
● **Owner** Mrs M Bowyer
P S T (Ref:HM02807)

### BOWYER, MO
**Mo Bowyer**, Flat 8, Regatta Point, 38 Kew Bridge Rd, Brentford, **London (Greater)**, TW8 0EB, ENG.
(T) 020 8580 5576
Speciality: Reflexology.
S T (Ref:HM02808)

### BOWYER, SARAH
**Sarah Bowyer**, The Old Police House, Lower Binton, Binton, Stratford-Upon-Avon, **Warwickshire**, CV37 9TE, ENG.
(T) 01789 751122
Speciality: Chiropodists (Podiatrists).
S (Ref:HM02809)

### BOXALL, KERRY
**Kerry Boxall**, The Folly, 18 Hadham Rd, Bishop's Stortford, **Hertfordshire**, CM23 2QR, ENG.
(T) 01279 507066
Speciality: Physiotherapy.
P S T (Ref:HM02810)

### BOXALL, R J
**R J Boxall**, 64 Edward St, Southborough, Tunbridge Wells, **Kent**, TN4 0EY, ENG.
(T) 01892 525409
Speciality: Chiropodists (Podiatrists).
S (Ref:HM02811)

### BOXALL, RICHARD
**Richard Boxall**, Gainborough, Station Rd, Tenterden, **Kent**, TN30 6HN, ENG.
(T) 01580 762351
Speciality: Chiropodists (Podiatrists).
● **Owner** Mr R Boxall
S (Ref:HM02812)

### BOXER, IRVING S
**Irving S Boxer**, 51 Chartley Avenue, Stanmore, **London (Greater)**, HA7 3RB, ENG.
(T) 020 8954 2254
Speciality: Osteopathy.
P S T (Ref:HM02813)

### BOYCE, MICHAEL
**Michael Boyce**, 55 Weatherby, Dunstable, **Bedfordshire**, LU6 1TP, ENG.
(T) 01582 665348
Speciality: Kinesiology. ✔
● **Owner/Kinesiologist** Mr M Boyce Q: KFRP. M: KFRP.
C T Yrs. Est.: 15 (Ref:HM02814)

### BOYCE, NIGEL
**Nigel Boyce**, 56 Railway Rd, Coleraine, **County Londonderry**, BT52 1PF, NIR.
(T) 028 7035 2412
Speciality: Chiropodists (Podiatrists).
● **Owner** Mr N Boyce
S (Ref:HM02815)

### BOYD HYPNOTHERAPY
**Garth Boyd**, 8 Park Rd, Halifax, **Yorkshire (West)**, HX1 2TS, ENG.
(T) 01422 361226
(E) garth@boyd.fsnet.co.uk
(W) www.hypnotherapist.org.uk
Speciality: Auto Suggestion, Aversion Therapy, Cognitive Therapy, Humanistic Psychology, Hypnosis, Hypnotherapy, Psychotherapy.


Key continued: Yrs.Est: Years Established Q: Qualifications M: Professional Membership ✔ Indemnity Insurance Accept Credit Cards

● **Owner** Mr G Boyd **Q:** BSc. **M:** NCH.
**B** Yrs. Est.: 16 (**Ref:**HM02816)

**BOYD, A**

**A Boyd**, 3 Castle Wynd North, Edinburgh, **Edinburgh (City of)**, EH1 2NQ, **SCO**.
(T) 01312 256537
Speciality: Psychotherapy.
● **Owner** Mr A Boyd
**B** (**Ref:**HM02817)

**BOYD, JOHN**

**John Boyd**, 5 Inkerman Trce, Whitehaven, **Cumbria**, CA28 7TY, **ENG**.
(T) 01946 692597
Speciality: Acupuncture.
**O** (**Ref:**HM02818)

**BOYD, LESLEY**

**Lesley Boyd**, Unit 6 Riverside Business Park, Gosport St, Lymington, **Hampshire**, SO41 9BB, **ENG**.
(T) 01590 688788
Speciality: Physiotherapy.
**P** **S** **T** (**Ref:**HM02819)

**BOYD, M C**

**M C Boyd**, First Floor Room, 9 Rex Buildings, Alderley Rd, Wilmslow, **Cheshire**, SK9 1HY, **ENG**.
(T) 01625 522750
Speciality: Chiropodists (Podiatrists).
**S** (**Ref:**HM02820)

**BOYD-JONES, KERVIN (DR)**

**Dr Kervin Boyd-Jones**, 4 Hallam Rd, Godalming, **Surrey**, GU7 3HW, **ENG**.
(T) 01483 429183
Speciality: Osteopathy.
**P** **S** **T** (**Ref:**HM02821)

**BOYES, LESLEY**

**Lesley Boyes**, The Old Convent, Beeches Green, Stroud, **Gloucestershire**, GL5 4AD, **ENG**.
(T) 01453 751140
Speciality: Osteopathy.
● **Director** Ms L Boyes
**P** **S** **T** (**Ref:**HM02822)

**BOYLAN, SEAN**

**Boylan Sean**, Edenmore, Dunboyne, **County Meath**, **IRE**.
(T) 01825 5250 (F) 01825 5751
Speciality: Herbalists.
**M** (**Ref:**HM02823)

**BOYLE, A**

**A Boyle**, 32 Station Rd, Ainsdale, Southport, **Merseyside**, PR8 3HS, **ENG**.
(T) 01704 578040
Speciality: Chiropodists (Podiatrists).
● **Partner** Mrs J Collins
**S** (**Ref:**HM02824)

**BOYLE, A M**

**A M Boyle**, 6 Liverpool Rd North, Liverpool, **Merseyside**, L31 2PN, **ENG**.
(T) 01515 203322
Speciality: Chiropodists (Podiatrists).
● **Owner** Mr M Boyle
**S** (**Ref:**HM02825)

**BOYLE, ANDREW**

**Andrew Boyle - State Registered Chiropodist**, 3 Duke St, Formby, Liverpool, **Merseyside**, L37 4AL, **ENG**.
(T) 01704 833301
(E) a.boyle@btinternet.co.uk
Speciality: Acupressure, Acupuncture, Aromatherapy, Biomechanics, Chiropody, Complementary Therapy, Electrotherapy, Indian Head Massage, Manipulation, Massage (Therapeutic), Moxibustion, Nail Surgery, Orthotics, Pilates, Podiatry, Reflexology, Reiki, Ultrasonics. ✔
● **Complementary Therapist**
Ms M Kristiansen
(T) 01704 876645 **Q:** IIHHT, LCSP. **M:** LCSP.
● **Physiotherapist** Ms J Lovelady
(T) 01704 386447 **Q:** MCSP, MSc, SRP. **M:** CSP.
● **Chiropodist (Podiatrist)**
Mr A Boyle **Q:** DPodM, M.S.C.P, S.R.Ch. **M:** S.C.P.
**P** Yrs. Est.: 9 (**Ref:**HM02826)

**BOYLE, JACK (DR)**

**Dr Jack Boyle**, 38 Fernleigh Rd, Glasgow, **Glasgow (City of)**, G43 2UB, **SCO**.
(T) 01416 370659
Speciality: Psychology.
**B** (**Ref:**HM02827)

**BOYLE, MARY**

**Mary Boyle**, 51 Plymouth Rd, Penarth, **Glamorgan (Vale of)**, CF64 3DD, **WAL**.
(T) 029 2070 0220
Speciality: Acupuncture.
● **Owner** Ms M Boyle
**O** (**Ref:**HM02828)

**BOYLE, MICHAEL**

**Michael Boyle**, 14 Cassel Avenue, Poole, **Dorset**, BH13 6JD, **ENG**.
(T) 01202 757522 (F) 01202 757522
Speciality: Psychotherapy.
● **Owner** Mr M Boyle
**B** (**Ref:**HM02829)

**BRABANT HOUSE CLINIC**

**Brabant House Clinic**, Brabant House, Portsmouth Rd, Thames Ditton, **Surrey**, KT7 0EY, **ENG**.
(T) 020 8398 7592 (F) 020 8873 3792
Speciality: Acupressure, Acupuncture, Alexander Technique, Aromatherapy, Bach Remedies, Chiropody, Chiropractic, Cognitive Therapy, Counselling, Cranial Osteopathy, Crystal Healing, Dowsing, Hay Diet, Healer, Herbal Medicine, Homeopathy, Hypnosis, Hypnotherapy, Indian Head Massage, Kinesiology, Life Style Coaching, Manipulation, Massage (Therapeutic), Meditation, Moxibustion, Naturopathy, Osteopathy, Psychotherapy, Reflexology, Reiki, Shiatsu, Spiritual Healing, Ultrasonics, Colonic Irrigation, Trichology, Osteoporosis Screening.
● **Osteopath** Mr M Metliss **Q:** Reg.Osteopath. **M:** GOsC.
● **Osteopath** Mr P Ladrowski **Q:** Reg.Osteopath. **M:** GOsC.
● **Osteopath** Mr J Morton Bell **Q:** Reg.Osteopath. **M:** GOsC.
● **Osteopath** Mr M Burt **Q:** Reg.Osteopath. **M:** GOsC.
**S** Yrs. Est.: 33 (**Ref:**HM02830)

**BRABNER, JANNINE**

**Jannine Brabner**, 1 Marwood Cl, Burnham-on-Sea, **Somerset**, TA8 2ED, **ENG**.
(T) 01278 780749
Speciality: Clairvoyants & Palmists.
**B** (**Ref:**HM02831)

**BRACEWELL, J**

**Mrs J Bracewell**, Milton Villas, 125 Wendover Rd, Aylesbury, **Buckinghamshire**, HP21 9LW, **ENG**.
(T) 01296 486925
Speciality: Chiropodists (Podiatrists).
**S** (**Ref:**HM02832)

**BRACEWELL, P J**

**P J Bracewell**, 43 Cwmrhydyceirw Rd, Cwmrhydyceirw, Swansea, SA6 6LJ, **WAL**.
(T) 01792 700723
Speciality: Homeopathy.
**M** (**Ref:**HM02833)

**BRACEY, RON**

**Ron Bracey**, St. Martins, Lavant, Chichester, **Sussex (West)**, PO18 0BG, **ENG**.
(T) 01243 774473
Speciality: Psychology.
● **Owner** Mr R Bracey
**B** (**Ref:**HM02834)

**BRACHER, C J**

**C J Bracher**, 144 North High St, Musselburgh, **Lothian (Mid)**, EH21 6AS, **SCO**.
(T) 01316 652330
Speciality: Chiropodists (Podiatrists).
**S** (**Ref:**HM02835)

**BRACHER, C J**

**C J Bracher**, 2 Croft St, Dalkeith, **Lothian (Mid)**, EH22 3BA, **SCO**.
(T) 01316 633414
Speciality: Chiropodists (Podiatrists).
**S** (**Ref:**HM02836)

**BRACKENBURY NTRL HEALTH CLNC**

**Brackenbury Natural Health Clinic**, 30 Brackenbury Rd, Hammersmith, London, **London (Greater)**, W6 0BA, **ENG**.
(T) 020 8741 9264
(W) www.brackenburyclinic.co.uk
Speciality: Acupuncture, Alexander Technique, Allergy Testing, Aromatherapy, Chiropody, Counselling, Homeopathy, Indian Head Massage, Massage (Therapeutic), Naturopathy, Osteopathy, Podiatry, Psychotherapy, Reflexology, Reiki, Shiatsu, Dietary Therapy, Lymphatic Drainage Technique, Australian Flower Essences, Colon Hydrotherapy. ✔
● **Shiatsu Practitioner** Mr O Ron
● **Teacher of the Alexander Technique**
Mr J Fuller **M:** STAT.
● **Osteopath/Herbal Medicine**
Mr C Leonard **Q:** Dip.Ac, Dip.CHM.
● **Reflexologist/Indian Head Massage**
Ms M Weber **Q:** MAR.
● **Colon Hydrotherapist/Dietary Therapist**
Ms A Easton
● **Counsellor/Physiotherapist**
Ms C Pocapaglia
● **Osteopath** Ms B Pickwoad **Q:** DO.
● **Hypnotherapist** Ms S Thomas
● **Psychotherapist** Ms R Hooper **Q:** BA (Hons) Psychol.
● **Therapist** Ms S Psyllas
● **Chinese Medicine Practitioner**
Dr K Song
● **Reflexologist/Therapeutic Massage**
Ms J Shaw **Q:** BA, ITEC, MA, MAR.
● **Colon Hydrotherapist/Dietary Therapist**
Ms J Barnes **M:** SPNT.
● **Homeopath** Ms I Spencer **Q:** LCH.
● **Homeopath** Ms R Chisholm
● **Colon Hydrotherapist/Dietary Therapist**
Ms D Gannon
● **Chiropodist** Ms P Sagara
● **Counselling** Mr B Mankowitz
● **Therapeutic Massage** Ms S Thomas **Q:** ITEC.
● **Homeopath** Mr J Buchanan **Q:** BA (Hons).
● **Homeopath** Mr E Bowyer **Q:** BA (Hons), RSHom.
● **Acupuncturist/Chinese Herbal Medicine**
Mr A Cowley **M:** BAcC.
● **Osteopath** Ms K Eastwood **Q:** BSc (Hons).
● **Owner** Mr M Semper
● **Therapeutic Massage**
Ms E Sturgess-Lief **M:** MTI.
● **Therapeutic Massage** Mr J Guyer
● **Aromatherapy/Sports Massage**
Ms B Knox **Q:** BA (Hons), ITEC, NLP. **M:** IPTI.
**C** Yrs. Est.: 18 (**Ref:**HM02837)

**BRACKNELL CHIROPRACTIC CLINIC**

**Bracknell Chiropractic Clinic**, 2 Albert Rd, Bracknell, **Berkshire**, RG42 2AE, **ENG**.
(T) 01344 302992
(W) www.bracknellclinic.co.uk
Speciality: Chiropractic, Phytotherapy. ✔
● **Owner** Dr M Pokath **Q:** BSc, DC.
● **Tenant** Mr A Larsen
● **Tenant** Ms C Hillitsoe
● **Chiropractor** Dr J Anderson **Q:** BSc (Hons), MSc (Chiro). **M:** BCA.
**P** Yrs. Est.: 2 (**Ref:**HM02838)

**BRACKNELL PHYSIOTHERAPY CLINIC**

**Bracknell Physiotherapy Clinic**, 49 Avebury, Little Foxes, Bracknell, **Berkshire**, RG12 8SQ, **ENG**.
(T) 01344 481894
Speciality: Physiotherapy.
**P** **S** **T** (**Ref:**HM02839)

**BRADBURY, C J**

**C J Bradbury**, 15 Newhall St, Cannock, **Staffordshire**, WS11 1AB, **ENG**.
(T) 01543 503430
Speciality: Chiropodists (Podiatrists).
● **Owner** Mr C Bradbury
**S** (**Ref:**HM02840)

**BRADBURY, SHARON**

**Sharon Bradbury**, The Keele Centre, Three Mile Lane, Keele, Newcastle, **Staffordshire**, ST5 5AR, **ENG**.
(T) 01782 612500 (F) 01782 612600

Speciality: Osteopathy.
● **Owner** Ms S Bradbury
P S T (**Ref:**HM02841)

## BRADBURY, SHARON

**Sharon Bradbury**, 104 King St, Newcastle, **Staffordshire**, ST5 1JJ, ENG.
(T) 01782 610500
Speciality: Osteopathy. ✔
● **Osteopath** Ms S Bradbury Q: BSc (Hons), DO. M: GOsC.
S Yrs. Est.: 13 (**Ref:**HM02842)

## BRADBURY, TANYA

**Tanya Bradbury**, 8a Dell Cl, Harpenden, **Hertfordshire**, AL5 4HP, ENG.
(T) 01582 767433
Speciality: Aromatherapy.
M O (**Ref:**HM02843)

## BRADBURY, VALMA

**Valma Bradbury**, Chepstow, 44 Purfield Drive, Wargrave, Reading, **Berkshire**, RG10 8AR, ENG.
(T) 01189 406268
Speciality: Reflexology.
S T (**Ref:**HM02844)

## BRADEN, WENDY

**Wendy Braden**, 2 Grange Rd, Weymouth, **Dorset**, DT4 7PH, ENG.
(T) 01305 777765
Speciality: Aromatherapy.
● **Owner** Mrs W Bradan
M O (**Ref:**HM02845)

## BRADFORD CHIROPODY & BIO CLNC

**Bradford Chiropody & Biomechanics Clinic**, 2b Green End, Clayton, Bradford, **Yorkshire (West)**, BD14 6BB, ENG.
(T) 01274 880169 (F) 01274 816764
Speciality: Biomechanics, Chiropody, Orthotics, Phytotherapy. ✔
● **Physiotherapist** Ms S Scott Q: SRP.
● **Chiropodist** Mr R Churchill-Kenningham Q: S.R.Ch. M: S.C.P.
M Yrs. Est.: 7 (**Ref:**HM02846)

## BRADFORD CHIROPRACTIC CLINIC

**Bradford Chiropractic Clinic**, 3 Mount Pleasant, Oakfield Gr, Bradford, **Yorkshire (West)**, BD9 4QA, ENG.
(T) 01274 545510
Speciality: Chiropractic.
P S T (**Ref:**HM02847)

## BRADFORD CLINIC OF ALT MED

**Bradford Clinic Of Alternative Medicine**, 24 Victoria Rd, Shipley, **Yorkshire (West)**, BD18 3JR, ENG.
(T) 01274 532661
(W) www.alternative-health-therapies.co.uk
Speciality: Acupuncture, Aromatherapy, Autogenic Training, Chinese Herbal Medicine, Counselling, Cranio-Sacral Therapy, Herbal Medicine, Homeopathy, Massage (Therapeutic), Neuro-Linguistic Program, Reflexology, Spiritual Healing, Spiritual Healing, Health Kinesiology and Shamballa Reiki. ✔
● **Autogenic Training** Mr M Clifford Q: Cert.Ed, NFSH.
● **Medical Herbalist** Miss M Kearney Q: BVSc, MNIMH, MRCVS.
● **Reflexologist** Valerie Banks Q: BSR.
● **Aromatherapist/Sports Massage** Patti Gregory Q: ITEC.
● **Homeopath** Mr D Fairfax Q: RMN, RSHom, SRN.
● **Cranio-Sacral Therapist** Mr N Edwards Q: RCST, RMN.
● **Homeopath** Ms L Harrison Q: Dip.Hom, RGN, RM.
● **Homeopath** Ms D Bennett Q: Dip.Hom. M: Soc.Hom.
● **Acupuncturist/Chinese Herbalist** Mr C Widdup Q: Dip.Ac, Dip.Chinese Studies, MSc. M: BAcC.
● **Homeopath** Ms C Deheera Q: Dip.Adv.Hom, RSHom.
● **Time Line Therapist** Mr J Ellis Q: C.Hyp, Cert T.L.T.
C Yrs. Est.: 12 (**Ref:**HM02848)

## BRADFORD HOUSE CHIRO CLINIC

**Bradford House Chiropractic Clinic**, St Clements House, Tanner St, Winchester, **Hampshire**, SO23 8AD, ENG.
(T) 01962 861188 (F) 01962 856010
(E) max.atkinson@dial.pipex.com
(W) www.communitychiropracticclinics.com
Speciality: Acupuncture, Chiropractic, Complementary Therapy, Cranio-Sacral Therapy, Manipulation, Massage (Therapeutic), Postural Integration, Ultrasonics, X-Ray, Interferential Therapy, TENS, Sacro-Occipital Technique, Posture Analysis, Ergonomic Analysis. ✔
● **Chiropractor** Ms M Heming Q: MSc (Chiro).
● **Chiropractor** Dr M Atkinson Q: BSc, DC. M: BCA, GCC.
P S Yrs. Est.: 12 (**Ref:**HM02849)

## BRADFORD ON AVON CHIRO CLINIC

**Bradford On Avon Chiropractic Clinic**, 18 Woolley St, Bradford-on-Avon, **Wiltshire**, BA15 1AE, ENG.
(T) 01225 862140
Speciality: Chiropractors.
● **Owner** Mr P Dickson
P S T (**Ref:**HM02850)

## BRADFORD ON AVON OSTEO CENTRE

**Bradford On Avon Osteopathy Centre**, 15A Church St, Bradford-on-Avon, **Wiltshire**, BA15 1LN, ENG.
(T) 01225 868282
Speciality: Osteopathy.
● **Owner** Mr C Sullivan
P S T (**Ref:**HM02851)

## BRADFORD PSYCHOTHERAPY & COUNS

**Bradford Psychotherapy & Counselling Service**, 505A Otley Rd, Bradford, **Yorkshire (West)**, BD2 4QL, ENG.
(T) 01274 641152
Speciality: Psychotherapy.
B (**Ref:**HM02852)

## BRADFORD, ANN

**Ann Bradford**, 62 Paul St, London, **London (Greater)**, EC2A 4NA, ENG.
(T) 020 7251 4429 (F) 020 7613 4737
Speciality: Complementary Medicines & Therapy.
M (**Ref:**HM02853)

## BRADFORD, S H

**S H Bradford**, Parkway, North Prde, Horsham, **Sussex (West)**, RH12 2BH, ENG.
(T) 01403 217557 (F) 01403 218401
Speciality: Chiropractors.
P S T (**Ref:**HM02854)

## BRADFORD, SONIA

**Sonia Bradford**, 36 Jonathans, Coffee Hall, Milton Keynes, **Buckinghamshire**, MK6 5DF, ENG.
(T) 01908 670307
Speciality: Aromatherapy.
● **Owner** Mrs S Bradford
M O (**Ref:**HM02855)

## BRADLEY & ASSOCIATES

**John Bradley & Associates**, 411 Whalley Rd, Clayton Le Moors, Accrington, **Lancashire**, BB5 5QZ, ENG.
(T) 01254 381545
Speciality: Osteopathy.
● **Owner** Mr J Bradley
P S T (**Ref:**HM02856)

## BRADLEY & ASSOCIATES

**John Bradley & Associates**, 5 Station Sq, Lytham St. Annes, **Lancashire**, FY8 5PA, ENG.
(T) 01253 795406
Speciality: Osteopathy.
● **Owner** Mr J Bradley
P S T (**Ref:**HM02857)

## BRADLEY ASSOCIATES

**Bradley Associates**, 92 Edenfield Rd, Rochdale, **Lancashire**, OL11 5AE, ENG.
(T) 01706 522922 (F) 01706 522922
Speciality: Physiotherapy.
● **Partner** Ms T Bradley
P S T (**Ref:**HM02858)

## BRADLEY, ALAN

**Alan Bradley**, 3 Yarm Rd, Stockton-On-Tees, **Cleveland**, TS18 3NJ, ENG.
(T) 01642 862333 (F) 01642 862444
Speciality: Psychology.
● **Owner** Dr A Bradley
B (**Ref:**HM02859)

## BRADLEY, ANDREW

**Andrew Bradley**, 7 Blake Cl, Blacon, Chester, **Cheshire**, CH1 5XL, ENG.
(T) 01244 380921
Speciality: Chiropodists (Podiatrists).
● **Owner** Mr A Bradley
S (**Ref:**HM02860)

## BRADLEY, AUDREY (DR)

**Dr Audrey Bradley MB BCH BAO**, Wrightville Douglas Rd, Cork, **County Cork**, IRE.
(T) 021 4314 044
Speciality: Complementary Medicines & Therapy.
M (**Ref:**HM02861)

## BRADLEY, DAVID & JEAN

**David & Jean Bradley**, 7 Colin St, Wigan, **Lancashire**, WN1 1XY, ENG.
(T) 01942 491449
Speciality: Physiotherapy.
P S T (**Ref:**HM02862)

## BRADLEY, DAWN

**Dawn Bradley**, 70 Spruce Drive, Lightwater, **Surrey**, GU18 5YX, ENG.
(T) 01276 453314
Speciality: Complementary Medicines & Therapy.
● **Owner** Mrs D Anderson
M (**Ref:**HM02863)

## BRADLEY, F

**F Bradley**, 3a High St, Congleton, **Cheshire**, CW12 1BN, ENG.
(T) 01260 298190
Speciality: Hypnosis.
● **Owner** Mr F Bradley
B (**Ref:**HM02864)

## BRADLEY, HAZEL

**Miss Hazel Bradley**, 27A Valentines Rd, Ilford, **Essex**, IG1 4RZ, ENG.
(T) 020 8518 1977
Speciality: Osteopathy.
P S T (**Ref:**HM02865)

## BRADLEY, J H

**J H Bradley**, 31 Shore Rd, Belfast, **County Antrim**, BT15 3PG, NIR.
(T) 028 9077 4514
Speciality: Chiropodists (Podiatrists).
S (**Ref:**HM02866)

## BRADLEY, JOANNAH

**Joannah Bradley**, 403A Lynmouth Avenue, Morden, **Surrey**, SM4 4RZ, ENG.
(T) 020 8330 3721
Speciality: Reflexology.
S T (**Ref:**HM02867)

## BRADLEY, JUDITH A

**Judith A Bradley**, 10 Wendron Way, Bradford, **Yorkshire (West)**, BD10 8TW, ENG.
(T) 01274 615304
Speciality: Chiropodists (Podiatrists).
S (**Ref:**HM02868)

## BRADLEY, M A

**M A Bradley**, Cogges Hill Surgery, Cogges Hill Rd, Witney, **Oxfordshire**, OX8 6FP, ENG.
(T) 01993 779775
Speciality: Chiropodists (Podiatrists).
● **Partner** Mrs M Bradley
S (**Ref:**HM02869)

## BRADLEY, MICHELLE

**Michelle Bradley**, 16 Cherry Fields, **Yorkshire (West)**, BD2 1LB, ENG.
(T) 01274 728770
Speciality: Reflexology.
S T (**Ref:**HM02870)

## BRADLEY, R M

**R M Bradley**, 28 Rathmore, Cookstown, **County Tyrone**, BT80 8JD, NIR.



Key continued: **Yrs.Est:** Years Established **Q:** Qualifications **M:** Professional Membership ✔ Indemnity Insurance Accept Credit Cards

(T) 028 8676 4344
Speciality: Chiropody, Podiatry. ✓
● **Owner/Chiropodist** Mrs R Bradley Q: DPodM, M.S.C.P, S.R.Ch.
[M] (Ref:HM02871)

**BRADLEY, S**

**S Bradley**, 1 Ferrybridge Rd, Knottingley, **Yorkshire (West)**, WF11 8JF, ENG.
(T) 01977 672513
Speciality: Chiropodists (Podiatrists).
[S] (Ref:HM02872)

**BRADLEY, SUSIE**

**Susie Bradley**, 96 South Gipsy Rd, Welling, **Kent**, DA16 1JD, ENG.
(T) 020 8304 2000
Speciality: Aromatherapy.
[M] [O] (Ref:HM02873)

**BRADSHAW COMP MEDICINE**

**Bradshaw Complementary Medicine**, 5 Beechlawns, Mullingar, **County Westmeath**, IRE.
(T) 04445 053
(W) www.midnet.ie
Speciality: Complementary Medicines & Therapy.
[M] (Ref:HM02874)

**BRADSHAW, C**

**Mrs C Bradshaw**, Middle Row, Chipping Norton, **Oxfordshire**, OX7 5NH, ENG.
(T) 01608 645608
Speciality: Physiotherapy.
[P] [S] [T] (Ref:HM02875)

**BRADSHAW, DIANNE**

**Dianne Bradshaw**, 2 Hawthorn Walk, Wilmslow, **Cheshire**, SK9 5BS, ENG.
(T) 01625 527063
Speciality: Chiropractors.
[P] [S] [T] (Ref:HM02876)

**BRADSHAW, J**

**J Bradshaw**, Langside, South Rd, Puckeridge, Ware, **Hertfordshire**, SG11 1TH, ENG.
(T) 01920 822555 (F) 01920 822555
Speciality: Hypnotherapy.
● **Owner** Mrs J Bradshaw
[B] (Ref:HM02877)

**BRADSHAW, P J**

**Polly J Bradshaw**, 9 Merchant St, Derby, **Derbyshire**, DE22 3AN, ENG.
(T) 01332 295071
Speciality: Auto Suggestion, Bio-energetics, Cognitive Therapy, Counselling, Gestalt Therapy, Hypnosis, Hypnotherapy, Meditation, Psychotherapy, Pyscho-Synthesis, Rogerian Therapy, Silva Method, Transactional Analysis. ✓
● **Psychotherapist** Polly J Bradshaw
Q: Cert.CounsSkills, Dip.Clin.Hyp, Dip.Couns.
M: BACP, NCH, NCP.
[H] Yrs. Est.: 10 (Ref:HM02878)

**BRADSHAW, S R**

**S R Bradshaw**, 8 Longcroft Lane, Welwyn Garden City, **Hertfordshire**, AL8 6EA, ENG.
(T) 01707 321318
Speciality: Chiropodists (Podiatrists).
● **Owner** Mr S Bradshaw
[S] (Ref:HM02879)

**BRADWAY COMP THERAPY CENTRE**

**Bradway Complementary Therapy Centre**, 298 Twentywell Lane, Sheffield, **Yorkshire (South)**, S17 4QH, ENG.
(T) 01142 360675
Speciality: Chiropody, Massage (Therapeutic), Reflexology.
[C] (Ref:HM02880)

**BRADY, J**

**J Brady**, 77 Rotherham Rd, Coventry, **Midlands (West)**, CV6 4FF, ENG.
(T) 024 7668 0118
Speciality: Chiropodists (Podiatrists).
[S] (Ref:HM02881)

**BRADY, KATIE**

**Katie Brady**, 19 The Hundred, Romsey, **Hampshire**, SO51 8GD, ENG.
(T) 01794 523653 (F) 01794 523653
Speciality: Chiropodists (Podiatrists).
● **Owner** Miss K Brady
[S] (Ref:HM02882)

**BRADY, MAUREEN**

**Maureen Brady**, Church Cottage, Orsett Rd, Horndon-On-The-Hill, Stanford-Le-Hope, **Essex**, SS17 8NS, ENG.
(T) 01375 360700
Speciality: Chiropodists (Podiatrists).
[S] (Ref:HM02883)

**BRAEMAR HOMEOPATHIC CENTRE**

**Braemar Homeopathic Centre**, 14 Woodlands Rd, Sale, **Cheshire**, M33 2DW, ENG.
(T) 01619 733116
Speciality: Homeopathy.
● **Partner** Miss A Manogue
[M] (Ref:HM02884)

**BRAGG, SHARON**

**Sharon Bragg**, 4 Bridge St, Mansfield, **Nottinghamshire**, NG18 1AL, ENG.
(T) 01623 627038
Speciality: Chiropodists (Podiatrists).
● **Owner** Mrs S Bragg
[S] (Ref:HM02885)

**BRAHMA KUMARIS INNER SPACE**

**Brahma Kumaris Inner Space Wembley**, 528 High Rd, Wembley, **London (Greater)**, HA9 7BS, ENG.
(T) 020 8903 1911 (F) 020 8902 4530
(W) www.bkwsu.org.uk
Speciality: Meditation, Spiritual Meditation.
● **Teacher** Mr A Bhai M: BKUSE.
[C] (Ref:HM02886)

**BRAHMA KUMARIS MEDITATION CTRE**

**Brahma Kumaris Meditation Centre**, 24 Oakbrook Rd, Sheffield, **Yorkshire (South)**, S11 7EA, ENG.
(T) 01142 306781 (F) 01142 306781
Speciality: Complementary Medicines & Therapy.
● **Manager** Miss G Valentine
[C] [M] (Ref:HM02887)

**BRAHMA KUMARIS MEDITATION CTRE**

**Brahma Kumaris Meditation Centre**, 241 Otley Rd, Leeds, **Yorkshire (West)**, LS16 5LQ, ENG.
(T) 01132 757727
Speciality: Complementary Medicines & Therapy.
[C] [M] (Ref:HM02888)

**BRAHMA KUMARIS RAJA YOGA CTRE**

**Brahma Kumaris Raja Yoga Centre**, 82 Leman St, Derby, **Derbyshire**, DE22 3UX, ENG.
(T) 01332 202419
Speciality: Yoga.
● **Director** Miss D Ypung
[M] (Ref:HM02889)

**BRAHMA KUMARIS WORLD**

**Brahma Kumaris World Spiritual University**, 17 Shrigley Gardens, Newcastle Upon Tyne, **Tyne and Wear**, NE3 3AY, ENG.
(T) 01912 847681
(W) www.bkwsu.org.uk
Speciality: Meditation, Positive Thinking.
● **Teacher** Mrs S Hammond
● **Teacher** Ms W White
[C] [H] Yrs. Est.: 18 (Ref:HM02890)

**BRAHMA KUMARIS WORLD**

**Brahma Kumaris World Spiritual University**, Raja Yoga Meditation Centre, 90 Trent Blvd, West Bridgford, Nottingham, **Nottinghamshire**, NG2 5BL, ENG.
(T) 01159 817331
(W) www.bkwsu.org.uk
Speciality: Meditation, Yoga.
● **Co-ordinator** Mrs Nehra
[B] [C] Yrs. Est.: 16 (Ref:HM02891)

**BRAHMA KUMARIS WORLD**

**Brahma Kumaris World Spitirual University**, Nuneham Park, Nuneham Courtenay, Oxford, **Oxfordshire**, OX44 9PG, ENG.
(T) 01865 343551
Speciality: Complementary Medicines & Therapy.
[C] [M] (Ref:HM02892)

**BRAHMBHATT, H B**

**H B Brahmbhatt**, 309 Kenton Rd, Harrow, **London (Greater)**, HA3 0HT, ENG.
(T) 020 8907 9983
Speciality: Acupuncture.
● **Owner** Dr H Brahmbhatt
[O] (Ref:HM02893)

**BRAIME, MARTINA**

**Martina Braime**, 42 Riviera Gardens, Leeds, **Yorkshire (West)**, LS7 3DW, ENG.
(T) 01132 758741
Speciality: Aromatherapy.
[M] [O] (Ref:HM02894)

**BRAINTREE CHIROPRACTIC CENTRE**

**Braintree Chiropractic Centre**, 26 Manor St, Braintree, **Essex**, CM7 3HP, ENG.
(T) 01376 327474
Speciality: Chiropractic.
● **Employee** Mrs J Craig
[P] [S] [T] (Ref:HM02895)

**BRAITHWAITE FOOT CLINIC**

**Braithwaite Foot Clinic**, 83 Milton St, Maidstone, **Kent**, ME16 8LD, ENG.
(T) 01622 721173 (F) 01622 729619
Speciality: Chiropodists (Podiatrists).
● **Owner** Ms C Bateson
[S] (Ref:HM02896)

**BRAKE, C L**

**C L Brake**, 19 Penybryn Trce, Penybryn, Hengoed, **Caerphilly**, CF82 7GF, WAL.
(T) 01443 813420
Speciality: Physiotherapy.
[P] [S] [T] (Ref:HM02897)

**BRAMHALL CHIROPRACTIC CLINIC**

**Dr E Heinonen**, 3 Syddal Rd, Bramhall, **Manchester (Greater)**, SK7 1AB, ENG.
(T) 01614 390439 (F) 01565 755837
(E) info@health-select.com
Speciality: Chiropractic, Manipulation, Massage (Therapeutic), X-Ray. ✓
● **Chiropractor** Ms K Haslam Q: BSc, DC. M: BCA, GCC.
● **Chiropractor** Dr E Heinonen Q: BSc, DC. M: BCA, GCC.
[S] Yrs. Est.: 10 (Ref:HM02898)

**BRAMHALL PARK PHYSIO CLINIC**

**Bramhall Park Physiotherapy Clinic**, 235 Bramhall Lane South, Bramhall, Stockport, **Cheshire**, SK7 3EP, ENG.
(T) 01614 395330 (F) 01614 407671
Speciality: Physiotherapy. ✓
● **Physiotherapist/Owner**
Ms E Bradbury Q: MCSP, SRP. M: CSP.
[S] Yrs. Est.: 10 (Ref:HM02899)

**BRAMIN CLINIC**

**Bramin Clinic**, 8 Beechroyd Trce, Bingley, **Yorkshire (West)**, BD16 1EJ, ENG.
(T) 01274 568122 (F) 01274 551677
Speciality: Chiropractic, Homeopathy, Osteopathy Scanning. ✓
● **Neuro Spinal Specialist**
Mr R Taiwo
[P] Yrs. Est.: 30 (Ref:HM02900)

**BRAMLEY COMP THERAPY CLINIC**

**Bramley Complementary Therapy Clinic**, Raynville Rd, Bramley, Leeds, **Yorkshire (West)**, LS13 2PZ, ENG.
(T) 01132 741034
(E) lifecoach@synergynet.co.uk
(W) www.onlinecoaching.co.uk
Speciality: Absent Healing, Acupressure, Acupuncture, Aromatherapy, Auto Suggestion, Ayurvedic Medicine, Bach Remedies, Chiropody, Cognitive Therapy, Complementary Therapy, Counselling, Crystal Healing, Cupping, Dietician, Dowsing, Electrotherapy, Faith Healing, Floral Essence Therapy, Gem Essence Therapy, Gestalt Therapy, Group Therapy, Hay Diet, Healer, Healing Therapy, Herbal Medicine, Holistic Healing, Homeopathy, Hypnosis, Hypnotherapy, Indian Head Massage, Iridology, Life Style Coaching, Macrobiotics, Manipulation, Massage

Key: [B] Mind-Body Medicine [C] Complementary Medicine [H] Self Help Treatment [M] Medicinal Therapy [O] Oriental Medicine [P] Postural Therapy [S] Manipulative Structural Therapy [T] Touch Therapy

(Therapeutic), Metamorphic Therapy, Micro Manipulation, Moxibustion, Naturopathy, Nutritional Therapy, Vega Allergy Testing, Sports Therapy, Weight Control, Chinese Herbalism, Remedial Massage. ✔
● **Hypnotherapist** Mr D Vickers M: BIH.
● **Owner/Physiotherapist** Mrs A Warren M: APNT.
● **Acupuncturist** Dr L Wang Q: MD. M: BAcC, BRCP.
● **Herbalist/Naturopath/Ayurvedic** Ms B Gosling Q: MH, ND. M: NIMH, RoN.
B C Yrs. Est.: 5 (Ref:HM02901)

## BRAMLEY HALL CLINIC
**Bramley Hall Clinic**, Bramley Hall, Bramley Hall Rd, Sheffield, **Yorkshire (South)**, S13 8TX, ENG.
(T) 01142 694909 (F) 01142 694909
(E) beckwith@bramleyhallfreeserve.co.uk
Speciality: Acupuncture, Bach Remedies, Complementary Therapy, Cranial Osteopathy, Dietician, Hay Diet, Herbal Medicine, Kinesiology, Manipulation, Massage (Therapeutic), Naturopathy, Osteopathy, Vitamin Therapy. ✔
● **Owner/Osteopath/Naturopath** Mr K Beckwith Q: DCR(R), DO, ND, RN. M: GCRN, GOsC.
S Yrs. Est.: 2 (Ref:HM02902)

## BRAMLEY NATURAL HEALTH STUDIO
**Bramley Natural Health Studio**, 10 High St, Bramley, Guildford, **Surrey**, GU5 0HF, ENG.
(T) 01483 890377
Speciality: Complementary Medicines & Therapy.
● **Owner** Miss S Aldrige
C M (Ref:HM02903)

## BRAMLEY, S
**S Bramley**, 106 Keswick Rd, Blackpool, **Lancashire**, FY1 5PA, ENG.
(T) 01253 293123
Speciality: Physiotherapy.
● **Owner** Mrs S Bramley
P S T (Ref:HM02904)

## BRAMMELL, A L
**A L Brammell**, 38a Queens Rd, Sketty, Swansea, SA2 0SB, WAL.
(T) 01792 205837
Speciality: Physiotherapy.
● **Owner** Mr A Brammall
P S T (Ref:HM02905)

## BRAMPTON CHIROPRACTIC CLINIC
**Brampton Chiropractic Clinic**, 84 High St, Brampton, Huntingdon, **Cambridgeshire**, PE28 4TH, ENG.
(T) 01480 436435
Speciality: Chiropractic. ✔
● **Chiropractor** Dr N Broe M: BCA.
S (Ref:HM02906)

## BRAMPTON SCIEN FOOD ALLERGY
**Brampton Scientific Services Food Allergy Clinic**, Head Office, 19 Manor Farm Cl, Barton-Le-Clay, Bedford, **Bedfordshire**, MK45 4TB, ENG.
(T) 01582 883014 (F) 01582 883014
Speciality: Complementary Medicines & Therapy.
● **Owner** Mrs L McEwan
C M (Ref:HM02907)

## BRAMPTON TREES CLINIC
**Brampton Trees Clinic**, Hanover St, Newcastle, **Staffordshire**, ST5 1AU, ENG.
(T) 01782 714937 (F) 01782 717334
Speciality: Physiotherapy. ✔
● **Physiotherapist** Ms C Montgomery Q: MCSP, SRP. M: CSP.
● **Physiotherapist** Ms G French Q: MCSP, SRP. M: CSP.
● **Physiotherapist/Owner** Mrs G Wade Q: MCSP, SRP. M: CSP.
S Yrs. Est.: 20 (Ref:HM02908)

## BRANCH, SUE
**Sue Branch**, Timberline, Plaisters Lane, Sutton Poyntz, Weymouth, **Dorset**, DT3 6LQ, ENG.
(T) 01305 834583
Speciality: Acupuncture.
O (Ref:HM02909)

## BRAND, R
**R Brand**, 10 Gaynes Park Rd, Upminster, **Essex**, RM14 2HJ, ENG.
(T) 01708 220754
Speciality: Chiropodists (Podiatrists).
● **Owner** Mr R Brand
S (Ref:HM02910)

## BRANDLER, H
**H Brandler**, 134 Hutton Rd, Shenfield, Brentwood, **Essex**, CM15 8NQ, ENG.
(T) 01277 211804
Speciality: Physiotherapy.
● **Owner** Mr H Brandler
P S T (Ref:HM02911)

## BRANDON, DAVE
**Dave Brandon**, Forest View, Gaunts Common, Wimborne, **Dorset**, BH21 4JP, ENG.
(T) 01258 841422 (F) 01258 841422
Speciality: Bach Remedies, Holistic Healing, Homeopathy, Nutritional Therapy, Electronic Gem Therapy. ✔
● **Owner** Mr D Brandon Q: BIH.
C Yrs. Est.: 20 (Ref:HM02912)

## BRANDON, LEON
**Leon Brandon**, 158 North St, Romford, **Essex**, RM1 1DR, ENG.
(T) 01708 747519
Speciality: Chiropodists (Podiatrists).
● **Owner** Mr L Brandon
S (Ref:HM02913)

## BRANDON, NICHOLAS
**Nicholas Brandon**, 44 Lansdowne Cres, London, **London (Greater)**, W11 2NN, ENG.
(T) 020 7792 1347
(E) n.brandon@virgin.net
Speciality: Alexander Technique, Aromatherapy, Yoga.
● **Teacher of the Alexander Technique** Mr N Brandon M: STAT.
H P Yrs. Est.: 5 (Ref:HM02914)

## BRANDWOOD-CORMACK, HAYLEY
**Hayley Brandwood-Cormack**, Flat 8 'Trocadero', 14 High St, Swanage, **Dorset**, BH19 2NT, ENG.
(T) 01929 421610
Speciality: Reflexology.
S T (Ref:HM02915)

## BRANKIN, K
**K Brankin**, Above 38 King St, Hoyland, Barnsley, **Yorkshire (South)**, S74 9JT, ENG.
(T) 01226 743727
Speciality: Chiropodists (Podiatrists).
● **Partner** Mr M Brankin
S (Ref:HM02916)

## BRANKIN, M & K
**M & K Brankin**, 1a Booth St, Above 38 King St, Hoyland, Barnsley, **Yorkshire (South)**, S74 9JT, ENG.
(T) 01226 743727
(E) user@brankin.softnet.co.uk
Speciality: Biomechanics, Chiropody, Nail Surgery. ✔ CREDIT
● **Chiropodist** Mrs K Brankin Q: S.R.Ch.
● **Chiropodist** Mr M Brankin Q: S.R.Ch.
C Yrs. Est.: 15 (Ref:HM02917)

## BRANKLIN, M & K
**M & K Branklin**, 42 Huddersfield Rd, Barnsley, **Yorkshire (South)**, S75 1DW, ENG.
(T) 01226 284571
(E) user@brankin.softnet.co.uk
Speciality: Biomechanics, Chiropody, Nail Surgery. ✔ CREDIT
● **Chiropodist** Mrs K Branklin Q: S.R.Ch.
● **Chiropodist** Mr M Branklin Q: S.R.Ch.
S Yrs. Est.: 15 (Ref:HM02918)

## BRANNELLY, ALAN
**Brannelly Alan**, 1 McDara Rd, Shantalla, **County Galway**, IRE.
(T) 09152 2631
Speciality: Osteopathy.
P S T (Ref:HM02919)

## BRANSON, H J L
**H J L Branson**, Green Lane, Stamford, **Lincolnshire**, PE9 1HE, ENG.
(T) 01780 763670
Speciality: Osteopathy.
P S T (Ref:HM02920)

## BRAS, I
**Miss I Bras**, 28 St. Clements Way, Bishopdown, Salisbury, **Wiltshire**, SP1 3FF, ENG.
(T) 01722 416006
Speciality: Osteopathy.
● **Owner** Mr G Gobell
P S T (Ref:HM02921)

## BRATERMAN, ELEANOR
**Eleanor Braterman**, 36E Portland Rise, London, **London (Greater)**, N4 2PP, ENG.
(T) 020 8802 9206
Speciality: Hypnosis.
● **Owner** Ms E Braterman
B (Ref:HM02922)

## BRATHERTON, W J
**W J Bratherton**, 34 Rustat Rd, Cambridge, **Cambridgeshire**, CB1 3QT, ENG.
(T) 01223 240491
Speciality: Psychotherapy.
● **Owner** Mrs W Bratherton
B (Ref:HM02923)

## BRATLEY-ATKINS, MARY
**Mary Bratley-Atkins**, 2 Lismore Rd, Highworth, Swindon, **Wiltshire**, SN6 7HU, ENG.
(T) 01793 763440
Speciality: Aromatherapy.
● **Owner** Mrs M Bratley-Atkins
M O (Ref:HM02924)

## BRAY HOLISTIC HEALTH CLINIC
**Bray Holistic Health Clinic**, U4 79 Castle St, Bray, **County Wicklow**, IRE.
(T) 01286 6611
Speciality: Complementary Medicines & Therapy.
M (Ref:HM02925)

## BRAY, CAROLINE
**Caroline Bray**, 20 Goddards Cl, Cranbrook, **Kent**, TN17 3LJ, ENG.
(T) 01580 713554 (F) 01580 713554
Speciality: Reflexology.
● **Owner** Ms C Bray
S T (Ref:HM02926)

## BRAY, CAROLINE
**Caroline Bray**, 26 The Avenue, Claygate, Esher, **Surrey**, KT10 0RY, ENG.
(T) 01372 810133 (F) 01372 810133
Speciality: Physiotherapy.
● **Owner** Mrs C Bray
P S T (Ref:HM02927)

## BRAY, D N
**D N Bray**, 25 Sutherland Avenue, Leeds, **Yorkshire (West)**, LS8 1BY, ENG.
(T) 01132 664260
Speciality: Manipulation. ✔
● **Therapist/Consultant** D. N Bray Q: DC. M: BCA, ISMA.
S Yrs. Est.: 23 (Ref:HM02928)

## BRAY, J M
**J M Bray**, 7 Osborn Rd, Farnham, **Surrey**, GU9 9QT, ENG.
(T) 01252 714228
Speciality: Chiropodists (Podiatrists).
S (Ref:HM02929)

## BRAY, STEPHEN
**Stephen Bray**, 2 Albert Pl, Blandford Forum, **Dorset**, DT11 7JA, ENG.
(T) 01258 458889 (F) 08453 336343
Speciality: Psychotherapy.
● **Owner** Mr S Bray
B (Ref:HM02930)

## BRAYFIELD, A IMRIE
**A Imrie Brayfield**, 7 Rope Walk, Garstang, Preston, **Lancashire**, PR3 1NS, ENG.
(T) 01995 602512
Speciality: Physiotherapy.
● **Owner** A Imrie Brayfield
P S T (Ref:HM02931)

## BRAYFIELD, GLYN C
**Glyn C Brayfield**, 7 Rope Walk, Garstang,



Key continued: Yrs.Est: Years Established Q: Qualifications M: Professional Membership ✔ Indemnity Insurance CREDIT Accept Credit Cards

Preston, **Lancashire**, PR3 1NS, ENG.
(T) 01995 600222
Speciality: Physiotherapy.
P S T (Ref:HM02932)

## BRAYNE, PAULINE

**Pauline Brayne**, Blake House, Orchard Mead, Nailsworth, Stroud, **Gloucestershire**, GL6 0RE, ENG.
(T) 01453 833908
Speciality: Chiropodists (Podiatrists).
● **Owner** Mrs P Brayne
S (Ref:HM02933)

## BRAZENALL, A R

**A R Brazenall**, 143 Balmuildy Rd, Bishopbriggs, Glasgow, **Glasgow (City of)**, G64 3ER, SCO.
(T) 01417 723629
Speciality: Manipulation, Osteomyology, Osteopathy, Physiotherapy.
P S T (Ref:HM02934)

## BREADING, MARGARET

**Margaret Breading**, 1 Broadway, Exeter, **Devon**, EX2 9LT, ENG.
(T) 01392 25505
Speciality: Reflexology.
S T (Ref:HM02935)

## BREADON, ROBBIE & HAAG, JUDY

**Robbie Breadon & Judy Haag**, Grove Cottage, Southam Rd, Napton, Southam, **Warwickshire**, CV47 8NG, ENG.
(T) 01926 810491
Speciality: Acupuncture.
● **Partner** Mr R Breadon
O (Ref:HM02936)

## BREARE, SARAH

**Sarah Breare**, 44 Westerham Rd, Sevenoaks, **Kent**, TN13 2PZ, ENG.
(T) 01732 450979
Speciality: Osteopathy.
● **Owner** Mrs J Mew
P S T (Ref:HM02937)

## BREARE, SARAH

**Sarah Breare**, 47 Lawrence Hill Rd, Dartford, **Kent**, DA1 3AG, ENG.
(T) 01322 220928
Speciality: Osteopathy.
P S T (Ref:HM02938)

## BREARLEY, JILL

**Jill Brearley**, 34 Woodhall Croft, Stanningley, Pudsey, **Yorkshire (West)**, LS28 7TU, ENG.
(T) 01132 394041
Speciality: Reflexology.
● **Owner** Ms J Brearley
S T (Ref:HM02939)

## BREARLEY, SYLVIA

**Sylvia Brearley School Of Therapy (The)**, 105 Otley Rd, Harrogate, **Yorkshire (North)**, HG2 0AG, ENG.
(T) 01423 505707 (F) 01425 505707
Speciality: Complementary Medicines & Therapy.
● **Owner** Ms S Brearley
C M (Ref:HM02940)

## BREATHWORK & BODYWORK

**Breathwork & Bodywork**, Flat 1, Stalbridge Flats, Lumley St, London, **London (Greater)**, W1Y 1TA, ENG.
(T) 020 7355 4796
Speciality: Complementary Medicines & Therapy.
● **Owner** Ms M Breathwork
M (Ref:HM02941)

## BREATNACH, MARY

**Mary Breatnach**, 2 Kenley Rd, Model Farm Rd, Cork, **County Cork**, IRE.
(T) 021 4541 179
Speciality: Acupuncture.
O (Ref:HM02942)

## BRECKLAND PROMOTIONS

**Breckland Promotions Ltd**, Po Box 103, Thetford, **Norfolk**, IP24 2RD, ENG.
(T) 01842 820635
Speciality: Complementary Medicines & Therapy.
● **Owner** Mr B Trainor
C M (Ref:HM02943)

## BRECON CLINIC

**Brecon Clinic Of Acupuncture And Chinese Herbal Medicine**, Oak House, 12 The Bulwark, Brecon, **Powys**, LD3 7AD, WAL.
(T) 01874 623577
Speciality: Acupressure, Acupuncture, Aromatherapy, Complementary Therapy, Healer, Herbal Medicine, Massage (Therapeutic), Moxibustion, Oriental Diagnosis, Reiki. ✔
● **Acupuncturist/Herbalist**
Mr D Smith Q: Lic.Ac, MSc. M: BAcC.
● **Acupuncturist/Aromatherapist**
Ms D Smith Q: IIHHT, Lic.Ac, MA, MSc, Reiki Master. M: BAcC.
O Yrs. Est.: 11 (Ref:HM02944)

## BRECON COMPLEMENTARY MED CTRE

**Brecon Complementary Medicine Centre**, Ty Henry Vaughan, Bridge St, Brecon, **Powys**, LD3 8AH, WAL.
(T) 01874 610420
(E) catriona@btclick.com
Speciality: Acupuncture, Allergy Testing, Aromatherapy, Bowen Therapy, Chiropody, Counselling, Hypnotherapy, Massage (Therapeutic), Reflexology, Reiki, Seichem, Holistic Therapy, Equine Bowen Therapy and Flower Remedy. ✔
● **Acupuncturist** Ms J Flinning Q: Lic.Ac. M: BAcC.
● **Reflexologist/Allergy Therapist**
Mrs J Abbott
(T) 01874 665495 Q: ITEC, MRxS. M: ITEC, RxS.
● **Therapist** Ms C Mirylees
(T) 01497 821646 Q: Dip.CHM, Dip.SPA. M: IPTI.
● **Osteopath** Mr D Rodway Q: DO. M: GOsC.
● **Hypnotherapist/Chiropodist**
Ms S Peace
(T) 01591 620339 Q: MSSCh. M: B.A.Ch.P, NRHP, UKCP.
● **Homeopath** Ms M Wainwright
(T) 01550 720615
● **Medical Herbalist** Ms S Owen
(T) 01982 553398 M: NIMH.
C Yrs. Est.: 3 (Ref:HM02945)

## BREDON HOUSE SPORTS & PHYSIO

**Bredon House Sports & Physiotherapy Clinic**, 321 Tettenhall Rd, Wolverhampton, **Midlands (West)**, WV6 0JZ, ENG.
(T) 01902 756334 (F) 01902 754823
Speciality: Physiotherapy.
P S T (Ref:HM02946)

## BREE, JOHN

**Reiki Healing**, 2 Hillsbrook Drive, Perrystown, **County Dublin**, IRE.
(T) 01456 2232
(W) www.how.to/reiki
Speciality: Absent Healing, Counselling, Healing Therapy, Hypnotherapy, Reiki, Stress Therapy.
● **Healer** Mr J Bree Q: Reiki Master.
B T Yrs. Est.: 10 (Ref:HM02947)

## BREE, SEAN

**Sean Bree**, 20 Argyle Avenue, Aylesbury, **Buckinghamshire**, HP19 9JZ, ENG.
(T) 01296 432459
Speciality: Physiotherapy.
● **Owner** Mr S Bree
P S T (Ref:HM02948)

## BREEDON, GARY

**Gary Breedon**, 149 Hurst Rd, Smethwick, **Midlands (West)**, B67 6LZ, ENG.
(T) 01214 343847 (F) 01214 343847
Speciality: Chiropodists (Podiatrists).
● **Owner** Mr G Breedon
S (Ref:HM02949)

## BREEN, BRENDAN

**Brendan Breen**, 32 Collins Ave, Killester, Dublin, **County Dublin**, IRE.
(T) 01831 5919
Speciality: Relaxation Technique.
H T (Ref:HM02950)

## BREEZE, T

**T Breeze**, 1 Pennington Rd, Chalfont St. Peter, Gerrards Cross, **Buckinghamshire**, SL9 9PH, ENG.
(T) 01753 889247 (F) 01753 889247
Speciality: Chiropractic, Spinal Manipulation. ✔
● **Chiropractor** Mr T Breeze Q: Dip.MC. M: GCC.
S Yrs. Est.: 5 (Ref:HM02951)

## BREINBURG, DERYCK

**Deryck Breinburg**, Rochford Rd Clinic, 32 Rochford Rd, Chelmsford, **Essex**, CM2 0EF, ENG.
(T) 01245 283626
Speciality: Osteopathy.
P S T (Ref:HM02952)

## BRENCHLEY, NICOLA

**Nicola Brenchley**, Lewes Physiotherapy Clinic, St Andrews Lane, Lewes, **Sussex (East)**, BN7 1UW, ENG.
(T) 01273 480033
Speciality: Physiotherapy.
● **Owner** Mrs N Brenchley
P S T (Ref:HM02953)

## BRENDA'S BEAUTY SALON

**Brenda's Beauty Salon**, The Gables S.C, Dunshaughlin, **County Meath**, IRE.
(T) 01825 9909
Speciality: Complementary Medicines & Therapy.
M (Ref:HM02954)

## BRENNAN, CAROL

**Carol Brennan Counselling Dip Psychotherapy MIAHM**, Rathfarnham, **County Dublin**, IRE.
(T) 01490 9690
Speciality: Psychotherapy.
B (Ref:HM02955)

## BRENNAN, J

**J Brennan**, 8 Ennerdale Trce, Low Westwood, Newcastle Upon Tyne, **Tyne and Wear**, NE17 7PN, ENG.
(T) 01207 561863
Speciality: Alexander Technique.
P S (Ref:HM02956)

## BRENNAN, JULIA

**Julia Brennan**, 12 Hemlington Rd, Stainton, Middlesbrough, **Cleveland**, TS8 9AJ, ENG.
(T) 01642 592845
Speciality: Physiotherapy.
P S T (Ref:HM02957)

## BRENNAN, M A

**M A Brennan**, 29 Upton Rd, Wirral, **Merseyside**, CH46 0PE, ENG.
(T) 01516 788833
(E) markbrennanchiropody@tinyworld.co.uk
Speciality: Biomechanics, Chiropody, Cryo Surgery, Nail Surgery, Orthotics, Podiatry. ✔
● **Chiropodist (Podiatrist)** Mrs J Q: DPodM, S.R.Ch. M: S.C.P.
● **Chiropodist (Podiatrist)**
Mr M Brennan Q: DPodM, S.R.Ch. M: S.C.P.
S Yrs. Est.: 13 (Ref:HM02958)

## BRENNAN, STANLEY

**Stanley Brennan**, 7 Montague Rd, London, **London (Greater)**, N8 9PJ, ENG.
(T) 020 8340 9690
(E) stan.brennan@virgin.net
Speciality: Psychotherapy. ✔
● **Psychotherapist** Mr S Brennan Q: BA, UKCP (Reg).
B Yrs. Est.: 10 (Ref:HM02959)

## BRENNAN-JESSON, L

**L Brennan-Jesson**, Ashdown Osteopathic Centre, The Sq, Lewes Rd, Forest Row, **Sussex (East)**, RH18 5ES, ENG.
(T) 01342 822505 (F) 01342 822505
Speciality: Osteopathy.
● **Owner** Mr T Strutt
P S T (Ref:HM02960)

## BRENT CENTRE

**Brent Centre Of Natural Therapy**, Pippins, Brent St, Brent Knoll, Highbridge, **Somerset**, TA9



Key: B Mind-Body Medicine C Complementary Medicine H Self Help Treatment M Medicinal Therapy O Oriental Medicine P Postural Therapy S Manipulative Structural Therapy T Touch Therapy

4DX, ENG.
(T) 01278 760813
Speciality: Complementary Medicines & Therapy.
● Partner Mrs S Allen
M (Ref:HM02961)

## BRENT, GILL
**Gill Brent**, 8 Harthill Lane, Gildersome, Morley, Leeds, **Yorkshire (West)**, LS27 7BP, ENG.
(T) 01132 525848
Speciality: Physiotherapy.
P S T (Ref:HM02962)

## BRENTWOOD CHIROPODY SURGERY
**Brentwood Chiropody Surgery**, 14 Crown St, Brentwood, **Essex**, CM14 4BA, ENG.
(T) 01277 203010
Speciality: Biomechanics, Chiropody, Nail Surgery, Orthotics, Podiatry. ✓
● Chiropodist (Podiatrist)
Ms K Williams Q: BSc (Hons), MBChA, MSSCh, S.R.Ch.
● Chiropodist (Podiatrist)
Ms J Williams Q: BSc (Hons), MBChA. M: SMAE.
M Yrs. Est.: 10 (Ref:HM02963)

## BRENTWOOD CHIROPRACTIC CLINIC
**Brentwood Chiropractic Clinic (The)**, 54 Doddinghurst Rd, Brentwood, **Essex**, CM15 9EH, ENG.
(T) 01277 222221
Speciality: Chiropractic.
● Owner Mr B Carter
P S T (Ref:HM02964)

## BRENTWOOD HYPNO/PSYCHOTHERAPY
**Brentwood Hypnotherapy & Psychotherapy**, 205 Brentwood Rd, Herongate, Brentwood, **Essex**, CM13 3PH, ENG.
(T) 01277 812221
Speciality: Hypnosis.
B (Ref:HM02965)

## BRENTWOOD HYPNOTHERAPY
**Brentwood Hypnotherapy**, 3 Hatch Rd, Pilgrims Hatch, Brentwood, **Essex**, CM15 9PU, ENG.
(T) 01277 375750
Speciality: Hypnotherapy.
● Owner Mrs S Cotgrove
B (Ref:HM02966)

## BRESLIN, CATHY
**Breslin Cathy**, 149 Rathgar Rd, Dublin, **County Dublin**, IRE.
(T) 01491 2157
(E) catymb@eircom.net
Speciality: Complementary Medicines & Therapy.
M (Ref:HM02967)

## BRESSEY OSTEOPATHIC CLINIC
**Bressey Osteopathic Clinic (The)**, 30 Bressey Gr, London, **London (Greater)**, E18 2HU, ENG.
(T) 020 8532 9889 (F) 020 8989 9164
Speciality: Osteopathy.
● Owner Mr S Neil-Asher
P S T (Ref:HM02968)

## BRETFORDTON CLINIC
**Bretfordton Academy**, Bretforton Hall, Vale Of Evesham, Bretforton, Evesham, **Worcestershire**, WR11 5JH, ENG.
(T) 01386 830537 (F) 01356 830918
Speciality: Acupressure, Acupuncture, Aromatherapy, Bach Remedies, Bio-energetics, Chiropractic, Colour Therapy, Complementary Therapy, Cranial Osteopathy, Cymatics, Electrotherapy, Healer, Healing Therapy, Herbal Medicine, Holistic Healing, Homeopathy, Kinesiology, Manipulation, Massage (Therapeutic), Music Therapy, Naturopathy, Osteopathy, Psychotherapy, Reflexology, Sound Therapy, Vibrational Therapy. ✓
● Director Dr P Manners
M S T Yrs. Est.: 30 (Ref:HM02969)

## BRETHERTON, S M
**S M Bretherton**, 11 Church End, Biddenham, Bedford, **Bedfordshire**, MK40 4AR, ENG.
(T) 01234 355390
Speciality: Chiropodists (Podiatrists).
S (Ref:HM02970)

## BRETHERTON-CROWE, LINDA
**Linda Bretherton-Crowe**, Warrington, **Cheshire**, WA4, ENG.
(T) 01925 232466
Speciality: Bach Remedies.
M (Ref:HM02971)

## BRETT, HALLIDAY
**Brett Halliday**, Corner Of Church & Henry St, Tullamore, **County Offaly**, IRE.
(T) 08624 570
Speciality: Complementary Medicines & Therapy.
M (Ref:HM02972)

## BRETT, T
**T Brett**, Laburnum Cottage, Cumwhinton, Carlisle, **Cumbria**, CA4 8DL, ENG.
(T) 01604 645533
Speciality: Osteopathy.
● Owner Mr T Brett
P S T (Ref:HM02973)

## BREUKEL, CORINA
**Corina Breukel**, 29a Head St, Halstead, **Essex**, CO9 2AU, ENG.
(T) 01787 476010 (F) 01787 476010
Speciality: Osteopathy.
● Owner Ms C Breukel
P S T (Ref:HM02974)

## BREW, LESLEY
**Lesley Brew**, Meridian Acupuncture & Chinese Herbal Medicine, London, **London (Greater)**, WC2E 8BE, ENG.
(T) 020 7836 4007
Speciality: Acupuncture.
O (Ref:HM02975)

## BREW, LESLEY
**Lesley Brew**, Bexleyheath Natural Health Clinic, 284 Broadway, Bexleyheath, **Kent**, DA6 8AJ, ENG.
(T) 020 8303 6288 (F) 020 8303 6288
Speciality: Acupuncture.
● Owner Mr P Cousins
O (Ref:HM02976)

## BREW, LESLIE
**Ms Leslie Brew**, Shooters Hill Practice, Flat 2 145 Eglinton Hill, London, **London (Greater)**, SE18 3DU, ENG.
(T) 020 8854 8787
Speciality: Acupuncture.
O (Ref:HM02977)

## BREWOOD NATURAL THERAPY CENTRE
**Brewood Natural Therapy Centre**, 5 Market Pl, Brewood, Stafford, **Staffordshire**, ST19 9BS, ENG.
(T) 01902 851294
Speciality: Complementary Medicines & Therapy.
C M (Ref:HM02978)

## BREWSTER, CARL A
**Carl A Brewster**, 29 Tollington Rd, London, **London (Greater)**, N7 6PB, ENG.
(T) 020 7607 3666
Speciality: Chiropodists (Podiatrists).
● Owner Mr C Brewster
S (Ref:HM02979)

## BREWSTER, DAVID J
**David J Brewster Ph D**, 4 Park Court, Hill View Rd, Woking, **Surrey**, GU22 7NW, ENG.
(T) 01483 767911
Speciality: Auto Suggestion, Cognitive Therapy, Counselling, Hypnosis, Hypnotherapy, Psychotherapy, Rogerian Therapy, Stress Therapy, Visualisation Therapy. ✓
● Hypnotherapist Mr D Brewster Q: Dip.Couns. M: CPS, HS, NCH.
B Yrs. Est.: 18 (Ref:HM02980)

## BREWSTER, J B
**J B Brewster**, Farfield House, 105 North St, Keighley, **Yorkshire (West)**, BD21 3AA, ENG.
(T) 01535 606881
Speciality: Osteopathy.
P S T (Ref:HM02981)

## BREWSTER, JOHN J
**John J Brewster**, Farfield House, 105 North St, Keighley, **Yorkshire (West)**, BD21 3AA, ENG.
(T) 01535 690055
Speciality: Osteopathy.
P S T (Ref:HM02982)

## BRIAN, MCCARTHY (DR)
**Dr Brian McCarthy B Sc D C**, North Mall, Westport, **County Mayo**, IRE.
(T) 09828 545
Speciality: Chiropractors.
P S T (Ref:HM02983)

## BRIAR
**Briar**, 2 Briar Walk, Tonbridge, **Kent**, TN10 3NR, ENG.
(T) 01732 352821 (F) 01732 773624
Speciality: Hypnosis.
● Owner Ms Z Balch
B (Ref:HM02984)

## BRIARS
**Briars (The)**, Bull St, Gornal Wood, Dudley, **Midlands (West)**, DY3 2NQ, ENG.
(T) 01384 236924
Speciality: Chiropodists (Podiatrists).
S (Ref:HM02985)

## BRIARS CLINIC
**Briars Clinic (The)**, Gardener St, Herstmonceux, Hailsham, **Sussex (East)**, BN27 4LB, ENG.
(T) 01323 832426
Speciality: Herbal Medicine.
M (Ref:HM02986)

## BRICK LANE NATURAL HEALTH CTRE
**Brick Lane Natural Health Centre**, 216 Brick Lane, London, **London (Greater)**, E1 6SA, ENG.
(T) 020 7729 7710
Speciality: Alexander Technique.
● Therapist Mr A Shields
P S (Ref:HM02987)

## BRIDGE CENTRE
**Bridge Centre for Natural Health**, 185 Ladybank Rd, Mickleover, Derby, **Derbyshire**, DE3 5QL, ENG.
(T) 01332 521270
Speciality: Alexander Technique.
● Therapist Ms Y White
C P S (Ref:HM02988)

## BRIDGE COUNSELLING CENTRE
**Bridge Counselling Centre (The)**, Beechfield, Waldens Rd, Horsell, Woking, **Surrey**, GU21 4RH, ENG.
(T) 01483 755953
Speciality: Psychotherapy.
B (Ref:HM02989)

## BRIDGE HOUSE CLINIC
**Bridge House Clinic**, Fairway House, 73 Village Rd, Higher Bebington, Wirral, **Merseyside**, L63 8PS, ENG.
(T) 01519 200738
Speciality: Alexander Technique.
● Therapist Mrs B King
P S (Ref:HM02990)

## BRIDGE OF ALLAN THERAPY CENTRE
**Bridge Of Allan Therapy Centre**, 37 Murray Pl, Stirling, FK8 1DQ, SCO.
(T) 01786 834616
Speciality: Complementary Medicines & Therapy.
M (Ref:HM02991)

## BRIDGE OF ALLAN THERAPY CENTRE
**Bridge Of Allan Therapy Centre**, Tigh-Beag, Stirling St, Blackford, Auchterarder, **Perth and Kinross**, PH4 1QG, SCO.
(T) 01764 682508
Speciality: Hypnosis.
● Owner Ms M Daley
B (Ref:HM02992)

## BRIDGE OF WEIR CHIRO CLINIC
**Bridge Of Weir Chiropractic Clinic**, 10 Castle Ter, Bridge Of Weir, **Renfrewshire**, PA11 3EF, SCO.
(T) 01505 615777 (F) 01505 615888
Speciality: Chiropractors.
P S T (Ref:HM02993)

## BRIDGE PSYCHOTHERAPY
**Bridge Psychotherapy**, 30 Borough High St,



Key continued: Yrs.Est: Years Established Q: Qualifications M: Professional Membership ✓ Indemnity Insurance Accept Credit Cards

London, **London (Greater)**, SE1 1XU, ENG.
(T) 020 7407 7879 (F) 020 7407 7880
Speciality: Psychotherapy.
● **Director** Mrs D McConnell
**B** (Ref:HM02994)

**BRIDGE ST CLINIC**

**Bridge St Clinic (The)**, 6 Bridge St, Gainsborough, **Lincolnshire**, DN21 2AE, ENG.
(T) 01427 677101
Speciality: Acupuncture.
**O** (Ref:HM02995)

**BRIDGE ST CTRE FOR COMP MED**

**Bridge Street Centre For Complementary Medicine (The)**, 12 Bridge St, Bradford-on-Avon, **Wiltshire**, BA15 1BY, ENG.
(T) 01225 867346
Speciality: Complementary Medicines & Therapy.
● **Owner** Mr Z Bozic
**C M** (Ref:HM02996)

**BRIDGE STREET CHIROPODY**

**Bridge Street Chiropody Surgery**, 9 Bridge St, Darwen, **Lancashire**, BB3 2AA, ENG.
(T) 01254 772882
Speciality: Chiropodists (Podiatrists).
● **Owner** Mrs J Forshaw
**S** (Ref:HM02997)

**BRIDGE TO HEALTH**

**Bridge To Health (The)**, 696-702 Chigwell Rd, Woodford Green, **Essex**, IG8 8AL, ENG.
(T) 020 8502 9200
Speciality: Complementary Medicines & Therapy.
● **Owner** Mr M Hartzel
**C M** (Ref:HM02998)

**BRIDGE VIEW CHIROPODY CLINIC**

**Bridge View Chiropody Clinic**, Guildford Rd, Bagshot, **Surrey**, GU19 5JH, ENG.
(T) 01276 472245
Speciality: Chiropodists (Podiatrists).
**S** (Ref:HM02999)

**BRIDGE WAY CLINIC**

**Bridge Way Clinic**, 113 High St, Whitton, Twickenham, **London (Greater)**, TW2 7LD, ENG.
(T) 020 8894 3186
Speciality: Chiropodists (Podiatrists).
● **Owner** Mr G Woods
**S** (Ref:HM03000)

**BRIDGE, DANIEL**

**Daniel Bridge**, 21B Park Cres, Brighton, **Sussex (East)**, BN2 3HA, ENG.
(T) 01273 702413
Speciality: Complementary Medicines & Therapy.
● **Owner** Mr D Bridge
**C M** (Ref:HM03001)

**BRIDGEMAN CENTRE**

**Bridgeman Centre**, 18 Bridgeman Ter, Wigan, **Lancashire**, WN1 1TD, ENG.
(T) 01942 321235
Speciality: Physiotherapy.
**P S T** (Ref:HM03002)

**BRIDGEND**

**Bridgend Physiotherapy Dept**, Princess Of Wales Hospital, Bridgend, CF31 1RQ, WAL.
(T) 01656 645134
Speciality: Physiotherapy.
● **Manager** Mrs J Convery
**P S T** (Ref:HM03003)

**BRIDGER, ADAM**

**Adam Bridger**, 7 York Pl, Wetherby, **Yorkshire (West)**, LS22 6NZ, ENG.
(T) 01937 584775
Speciality: Osteopathy.
● **Owner** A Bridger
**P S T** (Ref:HM03004)

**BRIDGER, ADAM**

**Bridger Adam**, 1 Moor Drive, Moor Rd, Leeds, **Yorkshire (West)**, LS6 4BY, ENG.
(T) 01132 786606
Speciality: Osteopathy.
**P S T** (Ref:HM03005)

**BRIDGER, MARY**

**Mary Bridger**, 7 York Pl, Wetherby, **Yorkshire (West)**, LS22 6NZ, ENG.
(T) 01937 584775
Speciality: Osteopathy.
**P S T** (Ref:HM03006)

**BRIDGES, GLYNIS**

**Glynis Bridges**, 7 Springfield Rd, Tunbridge Wells, **Kent**, TN4 0RD, ENG.
(T) 01892 527880
Speciality: Electrolysis.
**T** (Ref:HM03007)

**BRIDGET HEALING CENTRE**

**Bridget Healing Centre**, The Courtyard, 2-4 High St, Glastonbury, **Somerset**, BA6 9DU, ENG.
(T) 01458 833317
Speciality: Aromatherapy, Indian Head Massage, Reflexology, Reiki, Shiatsu, Alignment Therapy, Clairvoyant, Tarot Readings, Healing with Sound, Higher Profection Reading, Holistic Massage, Hypno-Regression, Rune Reading. ✓
● **Therapist** Ms Y Fields Q: ITEC, VTCT.
● **Therapist** Mr S Benfield Q: Dip.Shiatsu.
● **Therapist** Kestrel Gerrard Q: ITEC, NFSH.
● **Natural Clairvoyant** Ms J Taylor
● **Owner/Holistic Therapist**
Mano Warren Q: BA, Dip.Arom, Dip.Massage, Dip.Orient.Med, ITEC. M: COH, IPTI, ITEC.
● **Therapist** Ms M Chipper Q: BSc, MIFA. M: IFA.
**C** Yrs. Est.: 8 (Ref:HM03008)

**BRIDGET READER ALTERNATIVE**

**Bridget Reader (Alternative Approaches)**, 3 Montpelier Ave, Bexley, **Kent**, DA5 3AP, ENG.
(T) 020 8304 6540
Speciality: Complementary Medicines & Therapy.
**C M** (Ref:HM03009)

**BRIDGETON PSYCHOLOGICAL SVS**

**Bridgeton Psychological Services**, Springfield Primary School, 106 Allan St, Glasgow, **Glasgow (City of)**, G40 4TD, SCO.
(T) 01415 561141 (F) 01415 562981
Speciality: Psychology.
● **Manageress** Miss S Dolan
**B** (Ref:HM03010)

**BRIDGETT, A**

**Mr A Bridgett**, The Old Church, Shelton New Rd, Stoke-On-Trent, **Staffordshire**, ST5 1EH, ENG.
(T) 01782 260062
Speciality: Acupressure, Complementary Therapy, Manipulation, Massage (Therapeutic), Phytotherapy, Stress Therapy. ✓
● **Physiotherapist** Mr A Bridgett Q: MAB Phys, SMAE. M: BPA, SMAE.
**M** Yrs. Est.: 36 (Ref:HM03011)

**BRIDGEVIEW PHYSIO & SPORTS**

**Bridgeview Physiotherapy & Sports Clinic**, 2 Guildford Rd, Bagshot, **Surrey**, GU19 5JH, ENG.
(T) 01276 472040
Speciality: Physiotherapy.
**P S T** (Ref:HM03012)

**BRIDGMONT, NICHOLAS**

**Nicholas Bridgmont**, 25 Howard House, 161 Cleveland St, London, **London (Greater)**, W1P 5PF, ENG.
(T) 020 7388 4142
Speciality: Reflexology.
**S T** (Ref:HM03013)

**BRIDGNORTH CHIROPRACTIC CLINIC**

**Bridgnorth Chiropractic Clinic**, Lasyard House, Underhill St, Bridgnorth, **Shropshire**, WV16 4BB, ENG.
(T) 01746 769073
Speciality: Chiropractic.
● **Owner** Mr J Oliver
**P S T** (Ref:HM03014)

**BRIDGWATER HEALING CENTRE**

**Bridgwater Healing Centre**, 11 Dorset Rd, Bridgwater, **Somerset**, TA6 5PP, ENG.
(T) 01278 424475
Speciality: Complementary Medicines & Therapy.
● **Partner** Mr E Bray
**C M** (Ref:HM03015)

**BRIDGWATER, K A**

**K A Bridgwater**, 14 Marsden St, Westhoughton, Bolton, **Lancashire**, BL5 3AQ, ENG.
(T) 01942 810318
(E) kbridgewater'homeopathy'sch.org
Speciality: Homeopathy. ✓
● **Owner** Mrs K Bridgewater Q: LCH, RSHom.
**C** Yrs. Est.: 9 (Ref:HM03016)

**BRIDGWATER, K A**

**K A Bridgwater**, 10 Bankfield, Westhoughton, Bolton, **Lancashire**, BL5 2QG, ENG.
(T) 01942 818480
Speciality: Homeopathy.
**M** (Ref:HM03017)

**BRIDLINGTON CHIROPODY SURGERY**

**Bridlington Chiropody Surgery**, 6 Prospect Arcade, Prospect St, Bridlington, **Humberside (North)**, YO15 2AL, ENG.
(T) 01262 674116 (F) 01262 674116
Speciality: Biomechanics, Chiropody, Massage (Therapeutic), Podiatry, Orthotics, Orthopaedic Shoefitting. ✓
● **Chiropodist (Podiatrist)**
Mr D Butler Q: MBChA, MSSCh. M: B.A.Ch.P.
**M** Yrs. Est.: 5 (Ref:HM03018)

**BRIDPORT COMP MEDICINE CTRE**

**David Howlett**, Bridport Clinic Of Complementary Medicines, 32 South St, Bridport, **Dorset**, DT6 3JP, ENG.
(T) 01308 427777 (F) 01308 427777
Speciality: Alexander Technique, Counselling, Homeopathy, Massage (Therapeutic), Nutritional Therapy, Osteopathy, Reflexology, Shiatsu. ✓
● **Chiropodist** Moria Lucas Q: DPodM.
● **Teacher of the Alexander Technique**
Mr D Howlett Q: BA, MSTAT.
● **Practice Manager** Mrs S Marsh
**C** Yrs. Est.: 1 (Ref:HM03019)

**BRIEF COUNS & PSYCHOTHERAPY SV**

**Brief Counselling & Psychotherapy Service**, 12 New St, Kenilworth, **Warwickshire**, CV8 2EZ, ENG.
(T) 01926 851065 (F) 01926 851165
(E) bob@brief-psychotherapy.co.uk
(W) www.brief-psychotherapy.co.uk
Speciality: Cognitive Therapy, Counselling, Humanistic Psychology, Psychotherapy, Rogerian Therapy, Stress Therapy, Psychodynamic Therapy. ✓
● **Independent Psychotherapist**
Mr R Tummey Q: Dip.Psych, MSc, RMN.
**H** Yrs. Est.: 2 (Ref:HM03020)

**BRIERLEY, ANTHONY**

**Anthony Brierley**, Green Haven, Nolton Rd, Simpson Cross, Haverfordwest, **Pembrokeshire**, SA62 6ES, WAL.
(T) 01437 710756
Speciality: Reflexology.
**S T** (Ref:HM03021)

**BRIERLEY, D**

**D Brierley**, Maracaibo, Frome Rd, Radstock, Bath, **Somerset**, BA3 3JZ, ENG.
(T) 01761 436346
Speciality: Chiropodists (Podiatrists).
● **Owner** Mr M Brierley
**S** (Ref:HM03022)

**BRIERLEY, M**

**M Brierley**, 16 Jensen Rd, Bracebridge Heath, Lincoln, **Lincolnshire**, LN4 2QU, ENG.
(T) 01522 529883
Speciality: Chiropodists (Podiatrists).
● **Owner** Mrs M Brierley
**S** (Ref:HM03023)

**BRIERLEY, MATTHEW**

**Matthew Brierley**, 58 Church St, Falmouth, **Cornwall**, TR11 3DS, ENG.
(T) 01326 312466
Speciality: Osteopathy.
● **Owner** Mr M Brierley
**P S T** (Ref:HM03024)

**BRIERLEY, V A**

**V A Brierley**, 19 St Augustines Rd, Canterbury, **Kent**, CT1 1XP, ENG.



Key: **B** Mind-Body Medicine **C** Complementary Medicine **H** Self Help Treatment **M** Medicinal Therapy **O** Oriental Medicine **P** Postural Therapy **S** Manipulative Structural Therapy **T** Touch Therapy

(T) 01227 768884
Speciality: Chiropractors.
● **Owner** Dr F Collingwood
**P S T** (**Ref:**HM03025)

## BRIGDEN, JENNIFER

**Jennifer Brigden**, 13A North St, Havant, **Hampshire**, PO9 1PW, ENG.
(T) 023 9247 1757
Speciality: Alexander Technique.
**P S** (**Ref:**HM03026)

## BRIGDEN, JENNIFER

**Jennifer Brigden**, 30 Stirling Rd, Chichester, **Sussex (West)**, PO19 2ES, ENG.
(T) 01243 787507
Speciality: Alexander Technique.
● **Owner** Mr T York
**P S** (**Ref:**HM03027)

## BRIGG CHIROPRACTIC CLINIC

**Brigg Chiropractic Clinic**, Bridge St, Brigg, **Humberside**, DN20 8NF, ENG.
(T) 01652 650032 (F) 01652 650300
Speciality: Chiropractic. ✔
● **Owner** Dr J Ashley Q: DC. M: GCC.
**P** Yrs. Est.: 15 (**Ref:**HM03028)

## BRIGG PHYSIOTHERAPY

**Brigg Physiotherapy**, Health Pl, Wrawby Rd, Brigg, **Humberside**, DN20 8DW, ENG.
(T) 01652 652281
Speciality: Physiotherapy.
**P S T** (**Ref:**HM03029)

## BRIGG SKIN SURGERY

**Brigg Skin Surgery**, Albert St, Brigg, **Humberside**, DN20 8HU, ENG.
(T) 01652 653021 (F) 01652 653021
Speciality: Electrolysis, Skin surgery. [Credit]
● **Owner** Miss K Dae Q: ASB, MGBT.
**T** (**Ref:**HM03030)

## BRIGGS, AGNES

**Agnes Briggs**, 5 Thorn Rd, Bearsden, Glasgow, **Glasgow (City of)**, G61 4PP, SCO.
(T) 01419 427185
Speciality: Chiropodists (Podiatrists).
● **Owner** Mrs A Briggs
**S** (**Ref:**HM03031)

## BRIGGS, J

**J Briggs**, 1 Ghyll Mount, Yeadon, Leeds, **Yorkshire (West)**, LS19 7GA, ENG.
(T) 01132 509669
Speciality: Homeopathy.
**M** (**Ref:**HM03032)

## BRIGGS, JENNI

**Jenni Briggs**, Stillpoint, Broad St Pl, Bath, **Somerset**, BA1 5LH, ENG.
(T) 01225 460106
Speciality: Osteopathy.
**P S T** (**Ref:**HM03033)

## BRIGGS, JO

**Jo Briggs**, St Rumbold, Gawcott Rd, Buckingham, **Buckinghamshire**, MK18 1TL, ENG.
(T) 01280 815789
Speciality: Chiropodists (Podiatrists).
● **Owner** Mrs J Briggs
**S** (**Ref:**HM03034)

## BRIGGS, JOHN C

**John C Briggs**, 81 Earnsdale Avenue, Darwen, **Lancashire**, BB3 1JR, ENG.
(T) 01254 761640 (F) 01254 600119
Speciality: Hypnosis.
● **Owner** Mr J Briggs
**B** (**Ref:**HM03035)

## BRIGGS, MARGARETE

**Margarete Briggs**, 11 Home Cl, Harlow, **Essex**, CM20 3PD, ENG.
(T) 01279 423093
Speciality: Psychotherapy.
● **Owner** Mrs M Briggs
**B** (**Ref:**HM03036)

## BRIGGS-WILSON, A

**Relaxation Company (The)**, 78 The Thatchers, Bishop's Stortford, **Hertfordshire**, CM23 4FN, ENG.
(T) 07885 809327
(E) mwandajw@aol.com
Speciality: Absent Healing, Aromatherapy, Complementary Therapy, Healing Therapy, Holistic Healing, Indian Head Massage, Massage (Therapeutic), Reflexology, Reiki, Reiki Attainments (Teaching Reiki for self treatments). ✔
● **Alternative Therapist/Reiki Master** Ms A Briggs-Wilson Q: Cert.Arom, Cert.IHM, Cert.Massage, Cert.Reflex, IHBC, IIHHT, Reiki 1, Reiki 2, Reiki 3. M: AoR, ICHT.
**T** Yrs. Est.: 4 (**Ref:**HM03037)

## BRIGHT, JENNY

**Jenny Bright**, 48 Dovecote Rd, Eastwood, Nottingham, **Nottinghamshire**, NG16 3EZ, ENG.
(T) 01773 719490
Speciality: Clairvoyants & Palmists.
● **Owner** Mrs J Bright
**B** (**Ref:**HM03038)

## BRIGHTER FUTURE

**Brighter Future**, 71 Wareham Rd, Corfe Mullen, Wimborne, **Dorset**, BH21 3JX, ENG.
(T) 01202 659883
(E) andy.tomlinson@virgin.net
(W) www.brighterfuture.org.uk
Speciality: Cognitive Therapy, Holistic Healing, Hypnosis, Hypnotherapy, Psychotherapy, Spiritual Healing, Past Life Regression Therapy. ✔
● **Past Life Therapist** Mr A Tomlinson Q: BSc, DipTHP. M: UKCP.
**B** Yrs. Est.: 5 (**Ref:**HM03039)

## BRIGHTER FUTURE

**Brighter Future**, 11 Liberty Way, Dragoon Way, Christchurch, **Dorset**, BH23 2TZ, ENG.
(T) 01202 659883
(E) andy.tomlinson@virgin.net
Speciality: Cognitive Therapy, Holistic Healing, Hypnosis, Hypnotherapy, Psychotherapy, Spiritual Healing, Past Life Regression Therapy. ✔
● **Past Life Therapist** Mr A Tomlinson Q: BSc, DipTHP. M: UKCP.
**B** Yrs. Est.: 5 (**Ref:**HM03040)

## BRIGHTON & HOVE SPORTS CLINIC

**Brighton & Hove Sports Injury Clinic**, 62 Palmeira Avenue, Hove, **Sussex (East)**, BN3 3GF, ENG.
(T) 01273 329557 (F) 01273 329557
Speciality: Physiotherapy. ✔ [Credit]
● **Physiotherapist/Owner** Mr M Grant Q: MCSP, SRP. M: CSP.
**S** (**Ref:**HM03041)

## BRIGHTON ACUPUNCTURE CLINIC

**Brighton Acupuncture Clinic**, 22 Spring St, Brighton, **Sussex (East)**, BN1 3EF, ENG.
(T) 01273 326896
Speciality: Acupuncture. ✔
● **Acupuncturist** Ms S Downey Q: B.Ac. M: BAcC.
● **Acupuncturist** Ms S Truce Q: B.Ac. M: BAcC.
**O** Yrs. Est.: 11 (**Ref:**HM03042)

## BRIGHTON ALEXANDER TRAINING

**Brighton Alexander Training Centre**, 57A Beaconsfield Villas, Brighton, **Sussex (East)**, BN1 6HB, ENG.
(T) 01273 501612 (F) 08702 840307
Speciality: Alexander Technique. ✔
● **Teacher of the Alexander Technique** Mr J Nicholls Q: MA, MSTAT.
**T** Yrs. Est.: 10 (**Ref:**HM03043)

## BRIGHTON CHIROPRACTIC CLINIC

**Brighton Chiropractic Clinic**, 34 Palmeira Sq, Hove, **Sussex (East)**, BN3 2JP, ENG.
(T) 01273 733469
Speciality: Chiropractic, Massage (Therapeutic). ✔ [Credit]
● **Partner** Dr J Lyndon M: BCA, SCA.
● **Massage Therapist** Miss S Knee Q: LCSP.
● **Owner** Dr P Harris Q: DC. M: BCA, SCA.
● **Partner** Dr C Robilliard Q: BSc (Chiro), DC. M: BCA, SCA.
**P** Yrs. Est.: 30 (**Ref:**HM03044)

## BRIGHTON HEALTH & RACQUET CLUB

**Lewes Sports Injuries & Physiotherapy Clinic**, Village Way, Falmer, **Sussex (East)**, BN2 1BL, ENG.
(T) 01273 667826
Speciality: Physiotherapy. ✔
● **Sole Director** Nigel John Baker
● **Physiotherapist** Penny Lucy Q: BSc, MCSP, MSc, SRP.
**S** Yrs. Est.: 5 (**Ref:**HM03045)

## BRIGHTON NATURAL CLINIC

**Brighton Natural Clinic**, 94 St James's St, Brighton, **Sussex (East)**, BN2 1TP, ENG.
(T) 01273 672952
Speciality: Complementary Medicines & Therapy.
**M** (**Ref:**HM03046)

## BRIGHTON NATURAL HEALTH CENTRE

**Brighton Natural Health Centre**, 27 Regent St, Brighton, **Sussex (East)**, BN1 2LR, ENG.
(T) 01273 605226
Speciality: Alexander Technique.
● **Therapist** Mr C Element
**P S** (**Ref:**HM03047)

## BRIGHTON PHYSIOTHERAPY CLINIC

**Brighton Physiotherapy Clinic**, 56A Marine Prde, Brighton, **Sussex (East)**, BN2 1PN, ENG.
(T) 01273 621248 (F) 01273 621248
Speciality: Acupuncture, Aromatherapy, Physiotherapy. ✔ [Credit]
● **Physiotherapist/Owner** Mrs S Baxter Q: MCSP, SRP. M: CSP.
● **Physiotherapist** Ms D McGuinness Q: MCSP, SRP. M: CSP.
**S** Yrs. Est.: 20 (**Ref:**HM03048)

## BRIGHTWELL, TONY

**Tony Brightwell**, 4 Lombardy Rd, Sudbury, **Suffolk**, CO10 1LQ, ENG.
(T) 01787 376957
Speciality: Chiropodists (Podiatrists).
● **Owner** Mr T Brightwell
**S** (**Ref:**HM03049)

## BRIGNALL, PENELOPE

**Penelope Brignall**, Ashridge, Hurtis Hill, Crowborough, **Sussex (East)**, TN6 3BL, ENG.
(T) 01892 653892
Speciality: Chiropractic.
● **Owner** Mrs P Brignall
**P S T** (**Ref:**HM03050)

## BRILL, PAULINE

**Pauline Brill**, 28 Avondale Rd, Chesterfield, **Derbyshire**, S40 4TF, ENG.
(T) 01246 220956
Speciality: Reflexology.
**S T** (**Ref:**HM03051)

## BRIMELOW, KEITH

**Keith Brimelow**, Flat 2 Highland Apartments, Breadalbane St, Oban, **Argyll and Bute**, PA34 5PA, SCO.
(T) 01631 565226
Speciality: Osteopathy.
**P S T** (**Ref:**HM03052)

## BRIND, KEVIN

**Kevin Brind**, 266 Baldwins Lane, Croxley Green, Rickmansworth, **Hertfordshire**, WD3 3LG, ENG.
(T) 01923 240524 (F) 01923 240524
Speciality: Acupuncture, Physiotherapy. ✔
● **Owner/Physiotherapist** Mr K Brind Q: BSc (Hons), MCSP, SRP. M: CSP.
**S** Yrs. Est.: 3 (**Ref:**HM03053)

## BRIND, S

**S Brind**, 7 Rockhampton Rd, South Croydon, **Surrey**, CR2 7AQ, ENG.
(T) 020 8688 8496
Speciality: Chiropodists (Podiatrists).
● **Partner** Mrs S Brind
**S** (**Ref:**HM03054)

## BRINDLEY, ELAINE

**Elaine Brindley**, The Old Farm House, Main St, Brandesburton, Driffield, **Humberside (North)**, YO25 8RL, ENG.
(T) 01964 543774
Speciality: Psychotherapy.
**B** (**Ref:**HM03055)

## BRINSON, L

**L Brinson**, Physiotherapy Sports Injury Clinic, Brook Way, Bradley Stoke, Bristol, BS32 9DS,



Key continued: Yrs.Est: Years Established Q: Qualifications M: Professional Membership ✔ Indemnity Insurance [Credit] Accept Credit Cards

ENG.
(T) 01454 616026
Speciality: Physiotherapy.
P S T (Ref:HM03056)

**BRINTON, MEG**

**Meg Brinton**, High Wycombe, **Buckinghamshire**, HP15, ENG.
(T) 01494 711644
Speciality: Homeopathy.
M (Ref:HM03057)

**BRISCOE, WARREN**

**Warren Briscoe**, 5 Granada Rd, Southsea, **Hampshire**, PO4 0RD, ENG.
(T) 023 9286 2529
Speciality: Hypnosis.
● **Owner** Mr J Warren
B (Ref:HM03058)

**BRISFETT, E T**

**E T Brisfett**, 57 Camberwell Church St, London, **London (Greater)**, SE5 8TR, ENG.
(T) 020 7708 3036
Speciality: Chiropodists (Podiatrists).
S (Ref:HM03059)

**BRISTOL ALOE CENTRE**

**Bristol Aloe Centre (The)**, 7 Etloe Rd, Bristol, BS6 7PG, ENG.
(T) 01179 735007
Speciality: Complementary Medicines & Therapy.
C M (Ref:HM03060)

**BRISTOL BUDDHIST CENTRE**

**Bristol Buddhist Centre**, 162 Gloucester Rd, Bishopstone, Bristol, BS7 8NT, ENG.
(T) 01179 249991
Speciality: Complementary Medicines & Therapy.
M (Ref:HM03061)

**BRISTOL HAIR & SCALP CENTRE**

**Bristol Hair & Scalp Centre**, 111 Old Church Rd, Clevedon, **Somerset**, BS21 7XP, ENG.
(T) 01275 877120
Speciality: Complementary Medicines & Therapy, Trichology.
M (Ref:HM03062)

**BRISTOL HYPNOTHERAPY CLINIC**

**Bristol Hypnotherapy Clinic**, The Old Bank Buildings, 263 Southmead Rd, Westbury-On-Trym, Bristol, BS10 5EL, ENG.
(T) 01179 686886
(W) www.hypnotherapy-clinic.co.uk
Speciality: Cognitive Therapy, Hypnosis, Hypnotherapy, Psychotherapy. ✔
● **Owner/Clinical Hypnotherapist/Psychotherapist** Mr D Kato Q: Dip.Hyp, Dip.Psych. M: GHR, IAH, UKCC.
B Yrs. Est.: 6 (Ref:HM03063)

**BRISTOL NATURAL HEALTH SERVICE**

**Bristol Natural Health Service**, 310 Gloucester Rd, Horfield, Bristol, BS7 8TJ, ENG.
(T) 01179 444448
(E) richardgibbons@beeb.net
Speciality: Acupuncture, Alexander Technique, Aromatherapy, Chiropractic, Counselling, Herbal Medicine, Homeopathy, Hypnosis, Hypnotherapy, Massage (Therapeutic), Moxibustion, Naturopathy, Reflexology, Reiki, Shiatsu. ✔
● **Partner/Acupuncturist** Mr R Gibbons
(T) 01179 739541 Q: Lic.Ac. M: BAcC.
● **Partner/Acupuncturist** Ms A Lane-Willan
(T) 01275 873793 Q: Lic.Ac. M: BAcC.
B C Yrs. Est.: 6 (Ref:HM03064)

**BRISTOL SCHOOL**

**Bristol School Of Aromatherapy & Reflexology**, 14 Orchard St, Bristol, BS1 5EH, ENG.
(T) 01179 055007 (F) 01179 055001
Speciality: Aromatherapy.
● **Director** Mrs K Ward
M O (Ref:HM03065)

**BRISTOL SCHOOL OF SHIATSU**

**Bristol School Of Shiatsu**, 18 Lilymead Avenue, Bristol, BS4 2BX, ENG.
(T) 01179 772809
Speciality: Shiatsu.
M (Ref:HM03066)

**BRISTOW, M P**

**M P Bristow**, Unicorn House, Market Pl, Coleford, **Gloucestershire**, GL16 8AA, ENG.
(T) 01594 837296
Speciality: Chiropodists (Podiatrists).
● **Owner** Mr M Bristow
S (Ref:HM03067)

**BRITCHIRO CLINIC**

**Dr P Westergaard**, 13 West St, Horsham, **Sussex (West)**, RH12 1PB, ENG.
(T) 01403 275000
(W) www.britchiro.com
Speciality: Chiropractic. ✔
● **Chiropractor** Dr P Westergaard Q: BSc, DC, MSc (Hons). M: BCA.
P Yrs. Est.: 1 (Ref:HM03068)

**BRITISH ACUPUNCTURE COUNCIL**

**British Acupuncture Council**, Suite D Park House, 206-208 Latimer Rd, London, **London (Greater)**, W10 6UB, ENG.
(T) 020 8964 0222 (F) 020 8964 0333
Speciality: Acupuncture.
O (Ref:HM03069)

**BRITISH AIRWAYS TRAVEL CLINICS**

**British Airways Travel Clinics**, East St, Tonbridge, **Kent**, TN9 1LA, ENG.
(T) 01732 772815
Speciality: Complementary Medicines & Therapy.
C M (Ref:HM03070)

**BRITISH ASS FOR DRAMA THRPY**

**British Associations For Drama Therapists (The)**, 41 Broomhouse Lane, London, **London (Greater)**, SW6 3DP, ENG.
(T) 020 7731 0160 (F) 020 7731 0160
Speciality: Complementary Medicines & Therapy.
C M (Ref:HM03071)

**BRITISH ASS OF CLAIRVOYANT**

**British Association Of Clairvoyant Consultants (The)**, 20 Albion St, Broadstairs, **Kent**, CT10 1LU, ENG.
(T) 01843 863322 (F) 01843 863346
Speciality: Clairvoyants & Palmists.
● **Owner** Mrs C Rhodes
B (Ref:HM03072)

**BRITISH ASS OF GROUP PSYCHO**

**British Association Of Group Psychotherapists**, 48 Godolphin Rd, London, **London (Greater)**, W12 8JF, ENG.
(T) 020 8743 4743 (F) 020 8749 2373
Speciality: Psychotherapy.
● **Chairman** Mr D Glyn
B (Ref:HM03073)

**BRITISH ASS OF PSYCHO**

**British Association Of Psychotherapists**, 37 Mapesbury Rd, London, **London (Greater)**, N16 STQ, ENG.
(T) 020 8452 9823 (F) 020 8452 5182
Speciality: Psychotherapy.
B (Ref:HM03074)

**BRITISH ASS-PSYCHOPHARMACOLOGY**

**British Association For Psychopharmacology**, 6 Regent Ter, Cambridge, **Cambridgeshire**, CB2 1AA, ENG.
(T) 01223 358395
Speciality: Psychiatry.
B (Ref:HM03075)

**BRITISH AUTOGENIC SOCIETY**

**British Autogenic Society**, Royal London Homeopathic Hospital, Great Ormond St, London, **London (Greater)**, WC1N 3HR, ENG.
(T) 020 7713 6336
(E) autosoc@lineone.net
(W) www.autogenic-therapy.org.uk
Speciality: Autogenic Training, Group Therapy, Humanistic Psychology, Psychotherapy, Stress Therapy. ✔
● **Administrator**
H Yrs. Est.: 17 (Ref:HM03076)

**BRITISH CHIROPODY & POD ASS**

**British Chiropody & Podiatry Association**, Kilmoyley South Ardfert, Tralee, **County Kerry**, IRE.
(T) 08728 88131
(E) greenwood.podiatrics@oceanfree.net
Speciality: Chiropodists (Podiatrists).
S (Ref:HM03077)

**BRITISH CHIROPRACTIC ASS**

**British Chiropractic Association (The)**, Blagrave House, 17 Blagrave St, Reading, **Berkshire**, RG1 1QB, ENG.
(T) 01189 505950
Speciality: Chiropractors.
● **Chiropractor** Sue Wakefield
P S T (Ref:HM03078)

**BRITISH COLLEGE-NATURO & OSTEO**

**British College Of Naturopathy & Osteopathy**, Lief House, 3 Sumpter Cl, 120-122 Finchley Rd, London, **London (Greater)**, NW3 5HR, ENG.
(T) 020 7435 7830
Speciality: Osteopathy.
P S T (Ref:HM03079)

**BRITISH CONFEDERATION-PSYCHO**

**British Confederation Of Psychotherapists**, 37 Mapesbury Rd, London, **London (Greater)**, NW2 4HJ, ENG.
(T) 020 8830 5173 (F) 020 8452 3684
Speciality: Psychotherapy.
B (Ref:HM03080)

**BRITISH HOLISTIC MEDICAL ASS**

**British Holistic Medical Association**, Rowland Thomas House, Royal Shrewsbury Hospital South, Shrewsbury, **Shropshire**, SY3 8XF, ENG.
(T) 01743 261155
Speciality: Complementary Medicines & Therapy.
M (Ref:HM03081)

**BRITISH HOM DENTAL ASS**

**British Homeopathic Dental Association**, 2b Franklin Rd, Watford, **Hertfordshire**, WD1 1QD, ENG.
(T) 01923 233336
Speciality: Homeopathy.
M (Ref:HM03082)

**BRITISH HYPNOTHERAPY ASS**

**British Hypnotherapy Association National Register**, 14 Crown St, Chorley, **Lancashire**, PR7 1DX, ENG.
(T) 01257 262124
Speciality: Hypnosis.
● **Secretary** Mr J Dove
B (Ref:HM03083)

**BRITISH HYPNOTHERAPY ASS**

**British Hypnotherapy Association**, 67 Upper Berkeley St, Portman Sq, London, **London (Greater)**, W1H 7QX, ENG.
(T) 020 7723 4443
Speciality: Hypnotherapy, Psychotherapy, Hypno- Analysis and Pyscho-Analysis. All are qualified Psychotherapists. All are required to continue to have high standards of competence and ethics in their work. ✔
● **Manager** Ms A Wookey
B Yrs. Est.: 43 (Ref:HM03084)

**BRITISH INSTITUTE-HYPNOTHERAPY**

**British Institute Of Hypnotherapy**, 12 Heycroft Rd, Eastwood, Leigh-On-Sea, **Essex**, SS9 5SW, ENG.
(T) 01702 524484
(E) bih@globalnet.co.uk
Speciality: Auto Suggestion, Autogenic Training, Cognitive Therapy, Hypnosis, Hypnotherapy, Psychotherapy, Stress Therapy, Visualisation Therapy. ✔
● **Owner** P C Lawrence Q: BSc, BSCMEH. M: BIH.
B Yrs. Est.: 20 (Ref:HM03085)

**BRITISH MED ACUPUNCTURE SOC**

**British Medical Acupuncture Society**, 12 Marbury House, Higher Whitley, Warrington, **Cheshire**, WA4 4QW, ENG.



Key: B Mind-Body Medicine; C Complementary Medicine; H Self Help Treatment; M Medicinal Therapy; O Oriental Medicine; P Postural Therapy; S Manipulative Structural Therapy; T Touch Therapy

(T) 01925 730727 (F) 01925 730492
Speciality: Acupuncture.
● **Acupuncturist** Ms V Edgerley
O (Ref:HM03086)

## BRITISH MED ACUPUNCTURE SOC
**British Medical Acupuncture Society Ltd**, 60 Great Ormond St, London, **London (Greater)**, WC1N 3HR, ENG.
(T) 020 7278 1615 (F) 020 7278 1615
Speciality: Complementary Medicines & Therapy.
● **Chief Executive** Mr J Price
M (Ref:HM03087)

## BRITISH PSYCHO ANALYTICAL SOC
**British Psycho Analytical Society**, 63 New Cavendish St, London, **London (Greater)**, W1M 7RD, ENG.
(T) 020 7580 4952 (F) 020 7323 5312
Speciality: Psychoanalysis.
B (Ref:HM03088)

## BRITISH REG-COMP PRACTITIONERS
**British Register Of Complementary Practitioners**, 15 Tavern Quay, Sweden Gate, Off Plough Way, London, **London (Greater)**, SE16 7QZ, ENG.
(T) 020 7237 5165
Speciality: Complementary Medicines & Therapy.
M (Ref:HM03089)

## BRITISH SCHOOL OF HOMOEOPATHY
**British School Of Homoeopathy**, Parkham Lane, Brixham, **Devon**, TQ5 9JR, ENG.
(T) 01803 855646
Speciality: Homeopathy.
M (Ref:HM03090)

## BRITISH SCHOOL OF REFLEXOLOGY
**British School Of Reflexology (The)**, Holistic Healing Centre, 92 Sheering Rd, Harlow, **Essex**, CM17 0JW, ENG.
(T) 01279 429060 (F) 01279 445234
Speciality: Reflexology.
● **Manager** Mr D King
M (Ref:HM03091)

## BRITISH SCHOOL OF SHIATSU DO
**British School Of Shiatsu Do (London)**, 97-99 Seven Sisters Rd, London, **London (Greater)**, N7 7QP, ENG.
(T) 020 7281 1412
Speciality: Complementary Medicines & Therapy.
● **Owner** Mrs H Tutah
C M (Ref:HM03092)

## BRITISH SCHOOL OF SHIATSU-DO
**British School Of Shiatsu-Do**, 33 The Parade, Roath, Cardiff, **Glamorgan (Vale of)**, CF24 3AD, WAL.
(T) 029 2022 5230
Speciality: Shiatsu.
● **Owner** Mr D Jones
M (Ref:HM03093)

## BRITISH SOC OF CLINICAL HYPNO
**British Society Of Clinical Hypnotherapists**, 2 The Tarns, Gatley, Cheadle, **Cheshire**, SK8 4RU, ENG.
(T) 01614 288202
Speciality: Hypnosis.
B (Ref:HM03094)

## BRITISH SOC OF MED/DENT HYP
**British Society Of Medical & Dental Hypnosis**, 17 Keppel View Rd, Rotherham, **Yorkshire (South)**, S61 2AR, ENG.
(T) 07000 560309 (F) 01709 554558
Speciality: Hypnosis.
● **Company Secretary** Mrs R Jackson
B (Ref:HM03095)

## BRITISH SOC OF MED/DENT HYP
**British Society Of Medical & Dental Hypnosis**, P O Box 1007, Glasgow, **Glasgow (City of)**, G31 2LE, SCO.
(T) 01415 561606 (F) 01415 519104
Speciality: Hypnosis.
● **Administrator** Mrs R Summers
B (Ref:HM03096)

## BRITISH SOC OF MED/DENT HYP
**British Society Of Medical & Dental Hypnosis (The)**, 23 Broadfields Heights, Broadfields Avenue, Edgware, **London (Greater)**, HA8 8PF, ENG.
(T) 020 8905 4342 (F) 020 8958 8069
Speciality: Hypnosis.
B (Ref:HM03097)

## BRITISH SOCIETY-CLINICAL HYP
**British Society Of Clinical Hypnotherapists**, 229a Sussex Gardens, London, **London (Greater)**, W2 2RL, ENG.
(T) 020 7499 2813
Speciality: Hypnosis.
B (Ref:HM03098)

## BRITISH WHEEL OF YOGA
**British Wheel Of Yoga**, 25 Jermyn St, Sleaford, **Lincolnshire**, NG34 7RU, ENG.
(T) 01529 303233 (F) 01529 303233
Speciality: Relaxation Technique.
● **Yoga Teacher** Denny Gibson
H T (Ref:HM03099)

## BRITISH WHEEL OF YOGA
**British Wheel Of Yoga**, 1 Hamilton Pl, Boston Rd, Sleaford, **Lincolnshire**, NG34 7ES, ENG.
(T) 01529 306851
Speciality: Relaxation Technique.
H T (Ref:HM03100)

## BRITTAIN, HAL
**Hal Brittain**, 63 Windsor Rd, Southport, **Merseyside**, PR9 9BX, ENG.
(T) 01704 501271 (F) 01704 501271
Speciality: Osteopathy.
● **Owner** Mr H Brittain
O (Ref:HM03101)

## BRITTAIN-DODD, RUTH
**Ruth Brittain-Dodd**, Cae Newydd, Pentre, Cilcain, Mold, **Flintshire**, CH7 5PF, WAL.
(T) 01352 740153
Speciality: Chiropractic.
● **Owner** Mrs R Brittain-Dodd
P S T (Ref:HM03102)

## BRITTON, JADE
**Jade Britton**, New Cross Natural Therapy Centre, 394 New Cross Rd, London, **London (Greater)**, SE14 6TY, ENG.
(T) 020 8469 0858
Speciality: Herbalists.
M (Ref:HM03103)

## BRITTON, JAN
**Jan Britton**, 34 Parc-Y-Coed, Creigiau, Cardiff, **Glamorgan (Vale of)**, CF15 9LX, WAL.
(T) 029 2089 1084
Speciality: Reflexology.
S T (Ref:HM03104)

## BRIXHAM HEALING HANDS CENTRE
**Brixham Healing Hands Centre**, 1st Floor, 6 Fore St, Brixham, **Devon**, TQ5 8DS, ENG.
(T) 01803 850288
(E) annette@hcb.freeserve.co.uk
Speciality: Spiritual Healing, Clairvoyant.
● **Spiritualist** Mrs A Powell
C Yrs. Est.: 5 (Ref:HM03105)

## BRIXTON TAI CHI
**Kate Taylor T/A Brixton Tai Chi**, 82 Sudbourne Rd, Brixton, London, **London (Greater)**, SW2 5AH, ENG.
(T) 020 7652 1231
(E) instructors@brixtontaichi.com
(W) www.brixtontaichi.com
Speciality: T'ai-Chi Ch'uan, Chi Kung, Ba Gua, Push Hands. ✔
● **Senior Instructor** Ms K Taylor
● **Instructor** Mr R Senior
C P Yrs. Est.: 4 (Ref:HM03106)

## BROAD STREET PRACTICE
**Broad Street Practice (The)**, 20-21 Broad St, Stamford, **Lincolnshire**, PE9 1PG, ENG.
(T) 01780 480889
Speciality: Osteopathy.
● **Partner** Ms L Lipman
P S T (Ref:HM03107)

## BROAD, H M
**H M Broad**, 4 Besbury Park, Minchinhampton, Stroud, **Gloucestershire**, GL6 9EN, ENG.
(T) 01453 885526
Speciality: Chiropodists (Podiatrists).
S (Ref:HM03108)

## BROADBENT, ELAINE
**Elaine Broadbent**, 4 Barley Hill Rd, Garforth, Leeds, **Yorkshire (West)**, LS25 1DY, ENG.
(T) 01132 320060
Speciality: Chiropodists (Podiatrists).
● **Owner** Mrs E Broadbent
S (Ref:HM03109)

## BROADBENT, KARL
**Karl Broadbent**, 185 Bennetthorpe, Doncaster, **Yorkshire (South)**, DN2 6AH, ENG.
(T) 01302 342531 (F) 01302 342531
Speciality: Physiotherapy.
P S T (Ref:HM03110)

## BROADBENT, S
**S Broadbent**, 18-20 East St, Littlehampton, **Sussex (West)**, BN17 6AW, ENG.
(T) 01903 731111
Speciality: Osteopathy.
P S T (Ref:HM03111)

## BROADBENT, SUSAN
**Susan Broadbent**, 59 Sea Rd, East Preston, Littlehampton, **Sussex (West)**, BN16 1JN, ENG.
(T) 01903 783459 (F) 01903 783459
Speciality: Osteopathy.
● **Senior Partner** Dr T Davies
P S T (Ref:HM03112)

## BROADGATE CHIROPRACTIC CLINIC
**Broadgate Chiropractic Clinic**, 65 London Wall, London, **London (Greater)**, EC2M 5TU, ENG.
(T) 020 7638 4330
Speciality: Chiropractic.
P S T (Ref:HM03113)

## BROADHEAD, J N & M
**J N & M Broadhead**, 60 Gladstone St, Scarborough, **Yorkshire (North)**, YO12 7BN, ENG.
(T) 01723 500686
Speciality: Biomechanics, Chiropody, Gait Analysis, Podiatry, Cyro-Surgery. ✔
● **Chiropodist** J N Broadhead Q: MBChA, MSSCh. M: B.A.Ch.P.
● **Podiatrist** Mrs M Broadhead Q: DPodM, FSSCh, MBChA. M: B.A.Ch.P.
C Yrs. Est.: 8 (Ref:HM03114)

## BROADHEAD, MARILYN
**Marilyn Broadhead**, 53 Yeovil Rd, Owlsmoor, Sandhurst, **Berkshire**, GU47 0TD, ENG.
(T) 01276 34701
Speciality: Chiropodists (Podiatrists).
● **Owner** Mrs M Broadhead
S (Ref:HM03115)

## BROADLEY, RICHARD
**Richard Broadley**, 1 Villa Court, 16 Villa Rd, Nottingham, **Nottinghamshire**, NG3 4GG, ENG.
(T) 01159 693106
Speciality: Counselling, Psychotherapy. ✔
● **Psychotherapist** Mr R Broadley Q: Dip.Couns. M: BACP.
B Yrs. Est.: 16 (Ref:HM03116)

## BROADSTONE CENTRE COMP MED
**Broadstone Centre Complementary Medicine**, 11 Dunyeats Rd, Poole, **Dorset**, BH18 8AA, ENG.
(T) 01202 692493
(W) www.compmedicine-dorset.co.uk
Speciality: Shiatsu. ✔
● **Complementary Therapist** Ms J Curnow Q: Dip.Shiatsu, MRSS. M: Shiatsu Society UK.
C Yrs. Est.: 12 (Ref:HM03117)

## BROADSTONE CENTRE OF COMP MED
**Broadstone Centre of Complementary Medicine**, 11 Dunyeats Rd, Broadstone, **Dorset**, BH18 8AA, ENG.
(T) 01202 692493 (F) 01202 658515
(W) www.compmedicine-dorset.co.uk



Key continued: Yrs.Est: Years Established Q: Qualifications M: Professional Membership ✔ Indemnity Insurance Accept Credit Cards

Speciality: Acupressure, Acupuncture, Alexander Technique, Allergy Testing, Aromatherapy, Chinese Herbal Medicine, Chiropody, Counselling, Cranial Osteopathy, Herbal Medicine, Homeopathy, Hypnotherapy, Indian Head Massage, Manual Lymph Drainage, Massage (Therapeutic), Nutritional Therapy, Podiatry, Psychotherapy, Reflexology, Remedial Massage, Shiatsu, Stress Therapy, Hydrotherapy, Swimming Therapy, Cranial Osteopathy, Orthopaedic Physician, and Private Midwife. ✔
- **Orthopaedic Physician** Dr D Murgatroyd
- **Aromatherapist/Reflexologist** Ms J Vestey Q: ITEC. M: IPTI.
- **Counsellor** Ms J Sheridan Q: Dip.Couns.
- **Cranial Osteopath** Ms D Whitchello Q: BSc, DO, MIFR. M: IFR.
- **Allergy Testing/Medical Herbalism Therapist** Mr D Broom
- **Osteopath/Clinic Director** Mr D Allen Q: BSc (Hons), DO.
- **Osteoporosis Screener** Dr G Kempson Q: BSc (Hons), DIC, PhD.
- **Practitioner** Dr M Mackay-James Q: MA.
- **Chiropodist (Podiatrist)** Ms S Clarke Q: DPodM, M.S.C.P, S.R.Ch. M: S.C.P.
- **Shiatsu Practitioner** Ms J Pridmore Q: MRSS.
- **Homeopath** Ms R Rees Q: BA, MHMA. M: HMA.
- **Alexander Technique Therapist** Ms J Curnow Q: BA, MSTAT. M: STAT.
- **Allergy Testing/Medical Herbalism Therapist** Ms L Harrold Q: ITEC. M: IPTI.
- **Acupuncturist/Chinese Herbal Medicine** Mr G Wadlow Q: B.Ac, BA, MBAcC. M: BAcC.
- **Acupuncturist/Chinese Herbal Medicine** Ms F Mason Q: Lic.Ac, MBAcC. M: BAcC.
- **Teacher of The Therapy of Swimming** Mr A Spiroc-Tica
- **Chiropodist (Podiatrist)** Ms J Moore Q: DPodM, M.S.C.P, S.R.Ch. M: S.C.P.
- **Osteopath** Mr G Saxby Q: BSc (Hons), DO.
- **Private Midwife** Ms M Algate
- **Hypnotherapist** Ms O Blackburn Q: MIAH. M: IAH.

C P Yrs. Est.: 8 (**Ref:**HM03118)

## BROADVIEW NATURAL HEALTH CTRE

**Broadview Natural Health Centre**, Greytree Rd, Ross-on-Wye, **Herefordshire**, HR9 7DQ, ENG.
(T) 01594 823041 (F) 01594 825823
(W) www.integrativehealthcare.co.uk
Speciality: Acupuncture, Aromatherapy, Counselling, Massage (Therapeutic), Psychotherapy, Shiatsu, Holistic Medicine. ✔
- **Holistic Doctor/Acupuncturist/Psychotherapist** Dr R James Q: BSc, Dip.Med.Ac, Lic.Ac. M: BAcC, BMAS, GMC.
- **Owner** Mr D Smythe

C (**Ref:**HM03119)

## BROADVIEW NATURAL HEALTH CTRE

**Broadview Natural Health Centre**, 46 Broad St, Ross-on-Wye, **Herefordshire**, HR9 7DY, ENG.
(T) 01989 564513
Speciality: Acupuncture.
O (**Ref:**HM03120)

## BROADWATER, ANNE

**Anne Broadwater**, Dairy Farm Cottage, Dumbwomans Lane, Udimore, Rye, **Sussex (East)**, TN31 6AD, ENG.
(T) 01797 223707
Speciality: Chiropodists (Podiatrists).
- **Owner** Miss A Broadwater

S (**Ref:**HM03121)

## BROADWAY CHIROPRACTIC CLINIC

**Broadway Chiropractic Clinic**, 67 Broadway, Peterborough, **Cambridgeshire**, PE1 1SY, ENG.
(T) 01733 562638
Speciality: Chiropractic.
P S T (**Ref:**HM03122)

## BROADWAY CHIROPRACTIC CLINIC

**Broadway Chiropractic Clinic**, 199 Burnt Oak Broadway, Edgware, **London (Greater)**, HA8 5EG, ENG.
(T) 020 8950 4245
Speciality: Chiropractors.
- **Owner** Mr S Amelkin

P S T (**Ref:**HM03123)

## BROADWAY HOUSE

**Broadway House**, 35 High St, Topsham, Exeter, **Devon**, EX3 0ED, ENG.
(T) 01392 877241
Speciality: Chiropodists (Podiatrists).
S (**Ref:**HM03124)

## BROADWAY NAT THERAPY CLINIC

**Broadway Natural Therapy Clinic**, 52 The Broadway, London, **London (Greater)**, W5 5JN, ENG.
(T) 020 8579 4323
Speciality: Complementary Medicines & Therapy.
- **Owner** Chris Eedy

M (**Ref:**HM03125)

## BROCK, ROBERT

**Robert Brock**, 125 Weydon Hill Rd, Farnham, **Surrey**, GU9 8NZ, ENG.
(T) 01252 728252 (F) 01252 728252
Speciality: Chiropractic.
- **Owner** Mr R Brock

P S T (**Ref:**HM03126)

## BROCK, S

**S Brock**, 4 Paddock Fields, Basingstoke, **Hampshire**, RG21 4AR, ENG.
(T) 01256 354688 (F) 01256 462293
Speciality: Psychotherapy.
- **Owner** Mrs S Brock

B (**Ref:**HM03127)

## BROCK, SUSAN

**Susan Brock**, 34 Mason St, Wolverhampton, **Midlands (West)**, WV2 3AG, ENG.
(T) 01902 659887
Speciality: Complementary Medicines & Therapy.
- **Owner** Mrs S Brock

C M (**Ref:**HM03128)

## BROCKBANK, BRETT

**Brett Brockbank**, 180 Copthorne Rd, Shrewsbury, **Shropshire**, SY3 8LP, ENG.
(T) 01743 247759
Speciality: Osteopathy.
- **Owner** Mr B Brockbank

P S T (**Ref:**HM03129)

## BROCKBANK, N

**N Brockbank**, 1 Gospond Rd, Barnham, Bognor Regis, **Sussex (West)**, PO22 0EU, ENG.
(T) 01243 552662
Speciality: Alexander Technique.
- **Owner** Mr N Brockbank

P S (**Ref:**HM03130)

## BROCKWELL, BADGER

**Badger Brockwell**, 60 Cross Rd, Watford, **Hertfordshire**, WD1 4DQ, ENG.
(T) 01923 229060
Speciality: Psychotherapy.
- **Owner** Mr B Brockwell

B (**Ref:**HM03131)

## BRODIE, JACQUELINE

**Jacqueline Brodie**, Nairn, **Highland**, IV12, SCO.
(T) 01667 404254
Speciality: Bach Remedies.
M (**Ref:**HM03132)

## BRODIE, JEAN M

**Jean M Brodie**, The Pharmacy, High St, Newnham, **Gloucestershire**, GL14 1AA, ENG.
(T) 01594 516276
Speciality: Homeopathy.
M (**Ref:**HM03133)

## BRODIE, JOANNE

**Joanne Brodie**, 58 Branston St, Birmingham, **Midlands (West)**, B18 6BP, ENG.
(T) 01212 368122
Speciality: Complementary Medicines & Therapy.
- **Owner** Mrs J Brodie

M (**Ref:**HM03134)

## BRODY, S M

**S M Brody**, 21 Church Rd, Eccles, Manchester, **Manchester (Greater)**, M30 0DL, ENG.
(T) 01617 891028
Speciality: Chiropodists (Podiatrists).
S (**Ref:**HM03135)

## BROE, NEIL

**Neil Broe**, Spinney Cl, Warmington, Peterborough, **Cambridgeshire**, PE8 6TF, ENG.
(T) 01832 280601
Speciality: Chiropractic.
P S T (**Ref:**HM03136)

## BROEKHOFF, MARIA

**Maria Broekhoff**, 16 School Lane, Pinner, **London (Greater)**, HA5 5NF, ENG.
(T) 020 8866 1488
Speciality: Reflexology.
S T (**Ref:**HM03137)

## BROMBLEY, E

**E Brombley**, Wood Pk, Sageston, Tenby, **Pembrokeshire**, SA70 8SQ, WAL.
(T) 01646 651048
Speciality: Reflexology.
S T (**Ref:**HM03138)

## BROME & SCHIMMER

**Brome & Schimmer Ltd**, 25 Abbey Enterprise Centre, Premier Way, Romsey, **Hampshire**, SO51 9AQ, ENG.
(T) 01794 518222
Speciality: Complementary Medicines & Therapy.
C M (**Ref:**HM03139)

## BROMILEY, A P

**A P Bromiley**, 563 Kingsway, Manchester, **Manchester (Greater)**, M19 1RA, ENG.
(T) 01614 324998
Speciality: Acupuncture.
O (**Ref:**HM03140)

## BROMILEY, MARY

**Mary Bromiley**, Downs House, Baydon, Marlborough, **Wiltshire**, SN8 2JS, ENG.
(T) 01488 71055
Speciality: Physiotherapy.
P S T (**Ref:**HM03141)

## BROMLEY CHIROPODY CENTRE

**Bromley Chiropody Centre (The)**, 1a West Way, Petts Wood, Orpington, **Kent**, BR5 1LN, ENG.
(T) 020 8466 7575
Speciality: Biomechanics, Chiropody, Nail Surgery. ✔
- **Chiropodist** Mr J O'Brian Q: MSSCh. M: B.A.Ch.P.

M Yrs. Est.: 2 (**Ref:**HM03142)

## BROMLEY CHIROPRACTIC CLINIC

**Bromley Chiropractic Clinic**, 55 Tweedy Rd, Bromley, **Kent**, BR1 3NH, ENG.
(T) 020 8313 1577 (F) 020 8290 0768
Speciality: Acupuncture, Chinese Herbal Medicine, Chiropractic, Kinesiology, Osteopathy. ✔
- **Associate** Dr J Bryant
- **Chiropractor** Dr K Elad Q: BSc, DC. M: BCA.
- **Associate** Dr A Boness Q: B.Ed, BSc, Hons (OST).
- **Owner** Dr T Simon Q: MBAcC, MRCHM. M: RCHM.

P Yrs. Est.: 11 (**Ref:**HM03143)

## BROMLEY CROSS THERAPY CLINIC

**Bromley Cross Therapy Clinic**, 12 Hough Lane, Bromley Cross, Bolton, **Lancashire**, BL7 9DA, ENG.
(T) 01204 592020
Speciality: Complementary Medicines & Therapy.
C M (**Ref:**HM03144)

## BROMLEY OSTEOPATHIC CLINIC

**Bromley Osteopathic Clinic**, 46 London Lane, Bromley, **Kent**, BR1 4HE, ENG.
(T) 020 8460 0694
Speciality: Acupuncture, Osteopathy. ✔



Key: B Mind-Body Medicine C Complementary Medicine H Self Help Treatment M Medicinal Therapy O Oriental Medicine P Postural Therapy S Manipulative Structural Therapy T Touch Therapy

● **Osteopath** Mrs D Callaghan **Q:** BSc.
**M:** GOsC.
**S** Yrs. Est.: 36 (**Ref:**HM03145)

## BROMLEY STRESS MANAGEMENT CTRE

**Bromley Stress Management Centre**, 2 East St, Bromley, **Kent**, BR1 1QU, ENG.
(T) 020 8402 5421
Speciality: Complementary Medicines & Therapy.
**M** (**Ref:**HM03146)

## BROMLEY STRESS MANAGEMENT CTRE

**Bromley Stress Management Centre**, 42A East St, Bromley, **Kent**, BR1 1QW, ENG.
(T) 020 8402 5421
Speciality: Hypnotherapy.
**B** (**Ref:**HM03147)

## BROMLEY, DAVID

**David Bromley**, 38 Dereham Court, Leamington Spa, **Warwickshire**, CV32 5UN, ENG.
(T) 01926 314352
Speciality: Hypnosis.
● **Owner** Mr D Bromley
**B** (**Ref:**HM03148)

## BROMLEY, RIA

**Ria Bromley**, 3 Old Inn Rd, Portlethen, Aberdeen, **Aberdeenshire**, AB12 3RT, SCO.
(T) 01224 782464
Speciality: Aromatherapy.
● **Owner** Mrs R Bromley
**M** **O** (**Ref:**HM03149)

## BROMPTON ELECTROLYSIS

**Brompton Electrolysis**, 305 Brompton Rd, London, **London (Greater)**, SW3 2DY, ENG.
(T) 020 7823 9713
Speciality: Electrolysis.
● **Owner** Mrs B Skrkrwska-Posnic
**T** (**Ref:**HM03150)

## BROMSGROVE CHIROPRACTIC CLINIC

**Bromsgrove Chiropractic Clinic**, 21 New Rd, Bromsgrove, **Worcestershire**, B60 2JQ, ENG.
(T) 01527 831467 (F) 01527 831467
Speciality: Chiropractic. ✔
● **Owner** Mr T Beardsley **Q:** BSc (Hons), DC.
**M:** BCA.
**P** Yrs. Est.: 7 (**Ref:**HM03151)

## BRONKS, IAN G

**Ian G Bronks**, 27 Friargate, Derby, **Derbyshire**, DE1 1NL, ENG.
(T) 01332 344329
Speciality: Psychiatry.
**B** (**Ref:**HM03152)

## BRONZE DRAGON HOLISTIC CENTRE

**Bronze Dragon Holistic Centre**, 18 Emerald St, York, **Yorkshire (North)**, YO31 8LQ, ENG.
(T) 01904 636216
Speciality: Complementary Medicines & Therapy.
● **Owner** Ms S Bellini
**M** (**Ref:**HM03153)

## BROOK GREEN CHIRO CLINIC

**Brook Green Chiropractic Clinic**, 232 Blythe Rd, London, **London (Greater)**, W14 0HJ, ENG.
(T) 020 7602 1007
Speciality: Chiropractors.
● **Dentist** Mr A Gardey
**P** **S** **T** (**Ref:**HM03154)

## BROOK GREEN OSTEOPATHY

**Brook Green Osteopathy**, 121 Shepherds Bush Rd, Brook Green, Hammersmith, London, **London (Greater)**, W6 7LP, ENG.
(T) 020 7610 5459
Speciality: Osteopathy. ✔
● **Osteopath** Miss A Havard **Q:** BSc, Hons (OST).
**M:** GOsC.
**S** Yrs. Est.: 1 (**Ref:**HM03155)

## BROOK HYP & COUNS PRACTICE

**Brook Hypnotherapy & Counselling Practice (The)**, Premier House, 112 Station Rd, Edgware, **London (Greater)**, HA8 7BJ, ENG.
(T) 020 8952 1395
Speciality: Hypnotherapy.
**B** (**Ref:**HM03156)

## BROOK NATURAL HEALTH CENTRE

**Brook Natural Health Centre**, 338 Long Rd, Canvey Island, **Essex**, SS8 0JU, ENG.
(T) 01268 515101
Speciality: Complementary Medicines & Therapy.
● **Owner** Mrs E Veal
**C** **M** (**Ref:**HM03157)

## BROOK, ELIZABETH

**Elizabeth Brook**, 6 Gorse Bank Rd, Halebarns, Altrincham, **Cheshire**, WA15 0AL, ENG.
(T) 01619 807795
Speciality: Physiotherapy.
● **Owner** Mrs E Brook
**P** **S** **T** (**Ref:**HM03158)

## BROOK, SHEILA

**Sheila Brook**, 1 Lewins Court, Mount St, Battle, **Sussex (East)**, TN33 0EP, ENG.
(T) 01424 775839
Speciality: Aromatherapy.
**M** **O** (**Ref:**HM03159)

## BROOKE, JUDITH

**Judith Brooke**, 10 The Crescent, Moggerhanger, Bedford, **Bedfordshire**, MK44 3RE, ENG.
(T) 01767 640124
Speciality: Bach Remedies.
● **Owner** Ms J Brooke
**C** (**Ref:**HM03160)

## BROOKES, CLIVE

**Clive Brookes**, 173 Dunbabin Rd, Liverpool, **Merseyside**, L16 7QQ, ENG.
(T) 01517 223070
Speciality: Chiropodists (Podiatrists).
● **Owner** Mr C Brookes
**S** (**Ref:**HM03161)

## BROOKES, J R

**J R Brookes**, 24 Widley Rd, Cosham, Portsmouth, **Hampshire**, PO6 2DT, ENG.
(T) 023 9237 1467
Speciality: Chiropodists (Podiatrists).
● **Owner** Mrs J Brookes
**S** (**Ref:**HM03162)

## BROOKES, MICHAEL

**Michael Brookes**, 3 Hanging Lees, Newhay, Rochdale, **Lancashire**, OL16 3SG, ENG.
(T) 01706 846040 (F) 01706 846040
Speciality: Acupressure, Complementary Therapy, Dietician, Naturopathy, Nutritional Therapy. ✔
● **Allergy/Nutritional Therapist**
Mr M Brookes **Q:** BIAT. **M:** BIAT.
**T** Yrs. Est.: 3 (**Ref:**HM03163)

## BROOKES, N

**N Brookes**, Einor Homoeopathic Scientific Clinic, 128 Roseneath Rd, Urmston, Manchester, **Manchester (Greater)**, M41 5AZ, ENG.
(T) 01617 484308
Speciality: Homeopathy.
**M** (**Ref:**HM03164)

## BROOKES, N ( DR)

**Dr N Brookes**, 6 Church Rd, Urmston, Manchester, **Manchester (Greater)**, M41 9BU, ENG.
(T) 01617 553993
Speciality: Homeopathy.
**M** (**Ref:**HM03165)

## BROOKES, S

**S Brookes**, 91 Hurstbourne Rd, London, **London (Greater)**, SE23 2AQ, ENG.
(T) 020 8699 8308
Speciality: Chiropodists (Podiatrists).
● **Owner** Mrs S Brookes
**S** (**Ref:**HM03166)

## BROOKFIELD PHYSIOTHERAPY

**Brookfield Physiotherapy**, Ardmanning Ave, Tocher, Cork, **County Cork**, IRE.
(T) 021 4962 268 (F) 021 4312 488
Speciality: Reiki. ✔
● **Physiotherapist/Reiki Master**
Ms T Collins **Q:** Reiki Master. **M:** ISCP.
**B** Yrs. Est.: 8 (**Ref:**HM03167)

## BROOKHOUSE, S

**S Brookhouse**, Flat 2, 25 Edge Lane, Manchester, **Manchester (Greater)**, M21 9JH, ENG.
(T) 01618 811677 (F) 01618 820376
Speciality: Psychotherapy.
● **Owner** Dr S Brookhouse
**B** (**Ref:**HM03168)

## BROOKMAN, U H

**U H Brookman**, 54 The Avenue, Yeovil, **Somerset**, BA21 4BN, ENG.
(T) 01935 422488
Speciality: Complementary Medicines & Therapy.
**M** (**Ref:**HM03169)

## BROOKMANS OSTEOPATHY CLINIC

**Brookmans Osteopathy Clinic**, 83-85 Bradmore Green, Brookmans Park, Hatfield, **Hertfordshire**, AL9 7QT, ENG.
(T) 01707 664321
Speciality: Osteopathy.
**P** **S** **T** (**Ref:**HM03170)

## BROOKS, A P

**A P Brooks**, 9 North St Prde, Sudbury, **Suffolk**, CO10 1GL, ENG.
(T) 01787 372164
Speciality: Chiropodists (Podiatrists).
● **Owner** Mr A Brooks
**S** (**Ref:**HM03171)

## BROOKS, ANN

**Ann Brooks**, 2-4 Castle House, Long St, Sherborne, **Dorset**, DT9 3BU, ENG.
(T) 01935 816372
Speciality: Chiropodists (Podiatrists).
**S** (**Ref:**HM03172)

## BROOKS, BERNARD

**Bernard Brooks**, 56 Bouchers Mead, Chelmsford, **Essex**, CM1 6PJ, ENG.
(T) 01245 450075
Speciality: Psychotherapy.
**B** (**Ref:**HM03173)

## BROOKS, CAROLE

**Carole Brooks**, 5 Hampshire Cl, Basingstoke, **Hampshire**, RG22 5JT, ENG.
(T) 01256 356763
Speciality: Reflexology.
**S** **T** (**Ref:**HM03174)

## BROOKS, CATHY

**Cathy Brooks - Homeopath**, 34 Chislehurst Avenue, London, **London (Greater)**, N12 0HU, ENG.
(T) 020 8346 9385
(E) cc69w@homeopath.fsnet.co.uk
Speciality: Homeopathy, Reiki, Anti/Post-Natal Doula. ✔
● **Homeopath** Mrs C Brooks **Q:** LCH, RSHom.
**M:** Soc.Hom.
**M** Yrs. Est.: 5 (**Ref:**HM03175)

## BROOKS, HELEN

**Helen Brooks**, 21 Colchester Rd, White Colne, Colchester, **Essex**, CO6 2PW, ENG.
(T) 01787 223476
Speciality: Chiropodists (Podiatrists).
● **Owner** Ms H Brooks
**S** (**Ref:**HM03176)

## BROOKS, JANE

**Psychotherapist/Counsellor**, 41 Church Rd, Hayes, **London (Greater)**, UB3 2LB, ENG.
(T) 020 8573 7140
Speciality: Aversion Therapy, Cognitive Therapy, Counselling, Faith Healing, Family Therapy, Gestalt Therapy, Hay Diet, Healer, Humanistic Psychology, Meditation, Psychotherapy, Rogerian Therapy, Spiritual Healing, Stress Therapy.
● **Owner** Mrs J Brooks **Q:** Dip.Couns.
**H** Yrs. Est.: 12 (**Ref:**HM03177)

## BROOKS, KENNETH

**Kenneth Brooks**, The Osteopathic Clinic, 25 The Tything, Worcester, **Worcestershire**, WR1 1JL, ENG.
(T) 01905 22264
Speciality: Osteopathy.
● **Owner** Mr K Brooks
**P** **S** **T** (**Ref:**HM03178)


Key continued: **Yrs.Est:** Years Established **Q:** Qualifications **M:** Professional Membership ✔ Indemnity Insurance ▭ Accept Credit Cards

**BROOKS, M**

**M Brooks**, 41 Upper Abbey Rd, Brighton, **Sussex (East)**, BN2 2AD, ENG.
(T) 01273 699620
Speciality: Osteopathy.
P S T (Ref:HM03179)

**BROOKS, MAGGIE**

**Maggie Brooks**, 24 Ellon Rd, Bridge Of Don, Aberdeen, **Aberdeenshire**, AB23 8BX, SCO.
(T) 01224 822956 (F) 01224 822960
Speciality: Osteopathy.
● **Director** Mrs M Brooks
P S T (Ref:HM03180)

**BROOKS, S J**

**S J Brooks**, 71 Rochdale Rd, Shaw, Oldham, **Lancashire**, OL2 7JT, ENG.
(T) 01706 848774
Speciality: Chiropodists (Podiatrists).
S (Ref:HM03181)

**BROOKS, V L J**

**V L J Brooks**, Walnut Cottage, 10 Bonegate Rd, Brighouse, **Yorkshire (West)**, HD6 1SP, ENG.
(T) 01484 712378
Speciality: Hypnosis.
● **Owner** Mr V Brooks
B (Ref:HM03182)

**BROOKS, WENDY J**

**Wendy J Brooks**, 82 Crawthorne Rd, Peterborough, **Cambridgeshire**, PE1 4AE, ENG.
(T) 01733 352802
Speciality: Chiropodists (Podiatrists).
S (Ref:HM03183)

**BROOKSIDE PHYSIO PRACTICE**

**Brookside Physiotherapy Practice**, 47 Wonastow Rd, Monmouth, **Monmouthshire**, NP25 5DG, WAL.
(T) 01600 716335
(E) price@brooksidephysio.fsnet.co.uk
Speciality: Acupressure, Acupuncture, Complementary Therapy, Electrotherapy, Manipulation, Massage (Therapeutic), Moxibustion, Physiotherapy, Ultrasonics, Electro Acupuncture. ✓
● **Physiotherapist** Mr C Cook Q: MCSP, SRP. M: AACP, CSP, OCPPP.
● **Physiotherapist** Mr D Price Q: MCSP, SRP.
S Yrs. Est.: 20 (Ref:HM03184)

**BROOKSIDE PHYSIOTHERAPY SVS**

**Brookside Physiotherapy Services**, Broadway, Totland Bay, **Isle of Wight**, PO39 0BW, ENG.
(T) 01983 755799 (F) 01983 752407
Speciality: Physiotherapy.
● **Owner** Mrs B Pinkard
P S T (Ref:HM03185)

**BROOM, DAVID**

**David Broom**, Abbey View Complementary Clinic, Abbey View Medical Centre, Shaftesbury, **Dorset**, SP7 8DH, ENG.
(T) 01747 856719 (F) 01747 856701
Speciality: Herbalists.
M (Ref:HM03186)

**BROOME, ALISON**

**Alison Broome**, 8 Park St, Kendal, **Cumbria**, LA9 5QP, ENG.
(T) 01539 740423
Speciality: Reflexology.
S T (Ref:HM03187)

**BROOME, RAYMOND T**

**Dr Raymond T Broome**, North Hinksey Lane, Oxford, **Oxfordshire**, OX2 0JW, ENG.
(T) 01865 204246
Speciality: Chiropractors.
P S T (Ref:HM03188)

**BROOMFIELD HYPNOTHERAPY CENTRE**

**Broomfield Hypnotherapy Centre**, 15 Broomfield Avenue, London, **London (Greater)**, N13 4JJ, ENG.
(T) 020 8882 6425
Speciality: Hypnotherapy.
B (Ref:HM03189)

**BROOMFIELD, HELEN**

**Helen Broomfield**, 14 Borden Avenue, Enfield, **London (Greater)**, EN1 2BZ, ENG.
(T) 020 8366 6122
Speciality: Chiropodists (Podiatrists).
S (Ref:HM03190)

**BROOMHEAD, S J**

**S J Broomhead**, 28 Crofts Bank Rd, Urmston, Manchester, **Manchester (Greater)**, M41 0UH, ENG.
(T) 01612 832822
Speciality: Chiropodists (Podiatrists).
S (Ref:HM03191)

**BROOMHILL CHIROPRACTIC CLINIC**

**Broomhill Chiropractic Clinic**, 172 Whitham Rd, Sheffield, **Yorkshire (South)**, S10 2SR, ENG.
(T) 01142 666076 (F) 01142 666084
Speciality: Chiropractic.
● **Partner** Mrs L Carruthers
P S T (Ref:HM03192)

**BROOMHILL MEDICAL CENTRE**

**Broomhill Medical Centre**, 183 Whitham Rd, Sheffield, **Yorkshire (South)**, S10 2SN, ENG.
(T) 01142 665902 (F) 01142 665902
Speciality: Aromatherapy. ✓
● **Aromatherapist** Ms A Cousins Q: Cert.Arom.
● **Doctor** Dr M Hayes-Allen
C Yrs. Est.: 10 (Ref:HM03193)

**BROPHY, MARTHA**

**Martha Brophy**, 'Carlovia', St. Vincents Rd, Torquay, **Devon**, TQ1 4EH, ENG.
(T) 01803 380334
Speciality: Reflexology.
S T (Ref:HM03194)

**BROS, GODFREY**

**Godfrey Bros**, 29 Wormgate, Boston, **Lincolnshire**, PE21 6NR, ENG.
(T) 01205 367457
Speciality: Herbal Medicine.
● **Partner** Mr C Godfrey
M (Ref:HM03195)

**BROSNAN, J V**

**J V Brosnan**, 2 Wootten Drive, Iffley, Oxford, **Oxfordshire**, OX4 4DS, ENG.
(T) 01865 716771
Speciality: Psychotherapy.
● **Owner** Ms J Brosnan
B (Ref:HM03196)

**BROTHERTON & STEVENSON**

**Brotherton & Stevenson**, Norwood House, West Avenue, Gosforth, Newcastle Upon Tyne, **Tyne and Wear**, NE3 4ES, ENG.
(T) 01912 843985
Speciality: Chiropodists (Podiatrists).
S (Ref:HM03197)

**BROTHERTON, MARY**

**Mary Brotherton**, 30 Albany Rd, Stratford-Upon-Avon, **Warwickshire**, CV37 6PG, ENG.
(T) 01789 292052
Speciality: Physiotherapy.
P S T (Ref:HM03198)

**BROUGHAM CHIROPODY CLINIC**

**Brougham Chiropody Clinic**, 3 Drumdryan St, Edinburgh, **Edinburgh (City of)**, EH3 9JZ, SCO.
(T) 01312 296283
Speciality: Chiropodists (Podiatrists).
S (Ref:HM03199)

**BROUGHAM, PENNY (DR)**

**Dr Penny Brougham**, 5 Alvia Gdns, Sutton, **Surrey**, SM1 4RU, ENG.
(T) 020 8642 4022
Speciality: Acupuncture.
O (Ref:HM03200)

**BROUGHTON, C**

**C Broughton**, 6 Doris Court, Beeston, Nottingham, **Nottinghamshire**, NG9 6GS, ENG.
(T) 01159 731301
Speciality: Reflexology.
S T (Ref:HM03201)

**BROUGHTON, G G**

**G G Broughton**, 417 Mansfield Rd, Nottingham, **Nottinghamshire**, NG5 2DP, ENG.
(T) 01159 605068
Speciality: Osteopathy.
P S T (Ref:HM03202)

**BROUGHTY FERRY HEALTH CENTRE**

**Broughty Ferry Health Centre**, Brown St, Broughty Ferry, Dundee, **Angus**, DD5 1EP, SCO.
(T) 01382 737107
Speciality: Chiropodists (Podiatrists).
● **Manager** Mr B Christie
S (Ref:HM03203)

**BROUWER JOOP**

**Brouwer Joop**, 43 Cavendish Rd, St. Albans, **Hertfordshire**, AL1 5EF, ENG.
(T) 01727 836478
Speciality: Acupuncture.
O (Ref:HM03204)

**BROWN & ASSOCIATES**

**Brown S L & Associates**, Wentwood House, Stockton Avenue, Fleet, **Hampshire**, GU13 8NP, ENG.
(T) 01252 616511
Speciality: Chiropractic.
● **Owner** Dr S Brown
P S T (Ref:HM03205)

**BROWN & PARTNERS OSTEO**

**Denis Brown & Partners Osteopaths**, 23 Cumberland St, Macclesfield, **Cheshire**, SK10 1DD, ENG.
(T) 01625 434202
Speciality: Osteopathy.
P S T (Ref:HM03206)

**BROWN & ROBINSON**

**Denis Brown & Caroline Robinson**, Parsonage Chambers, The Parsonage, Manchester, **Manchester (Greater)**, M3 2BQ, ENG.
(T) 01618 344076
Speciality: Osteopathy.
P S T (Ref:HM03207)

**BROWN, A D**

**A D Brown**, 6 Barns Rd, Ferndown, **Dorset**, BH22 8AG, ENG.
(T) 01202 897870
Speciality: Chiropody. ✓
● **Chiropodist** Mr A Brown Q: MSSCh.
M Yrs. Est.: 10 (Ref:HM03208)

**BROWN, A M**

**A M Brown**, 73 Westgate, Guiseley, Leeds, **Yorkshire (West)**, LS20 8HH, ENG.
(T) 01943 872281
Speciality: Physiotherapy.
● **Owner** Mrs A Brown
P S T (Ref:HM03209)

**BROWN, ALISON R**

**Alison R Brown**, 1 Ernald Avenue, London, **London (Greater)**, E6 3AL, ENG.
(T) 020 8470 8678 (F) 020 8470 8678
Speciality: Cranial Osteopathy, Osteopathy. ✓
● **Osteopath** Mrs A Brown Q: DO. M: GOsC.
● **Osteopath** Mr B Davies Q: BSc (Hons). M: GOsC.
● **Osteopath** Ms K Hall Q: BSc (Hons), RGN. M: GOsC.
S Yrs. Est.: 16 (Ref:HM03210)

**BROWN, AMANDA**

**Amanda Brown**, 2 Orchard View, Manor Rd, Gussage St. Michael, Wimborne, **Dorset**, BH21 5HY, ENG.
(T) 01258 840995
Speciality: Aromatherapy.
● **Owner** Mr M Brown
M O (Ref:HM03211)

**BROWN, ANGELA**

**Angela Brown**, 18 Mayfield Avenue, Gr, Wantage, **Oxfordshire**, OX12 7LZ, ENG.
(T) 01235 765936
Speciality: Hypnosis.
● **Owner** Mrs A Brown
B (Ref:HM03212)

**BROWN, ANN**

**Ann Brown**, 85A Oakley Lane, Oakley, Basingstoke, **Hampshire**, RG23 7JT, ENG.
(T) 01256 781641
Speciality: Reflexology.
S T (Ref:HM03213)



Key: B Mind-Body Medicine C Complementary Medicine H Self Help Treatment M Medicinal Therapy O Oriental Medicine P Postural Therapy S Manipulative Structural Therapy T Touch Therapy

## BROWN, ANNE

**Anne Brown**, 22 Merthyr Dyfan Rd, Barry, **Glamorgan (Vale of)**, CF62 9TG, WAL.
**(T)** 01446 737722
Speciality: Acupuncture, Electrotherapy, Massage (Therapeutic), Phytotherapy. ✔
● **Physiotherapist** Mrs A Brown **Q:** MCSP, SRP. **M:** AACP, CSP, SRP.
S Yrs. Est.: 11 (**Ref:**HM03214)

## BROWN, AVRIL

**Avril Brown**, 113 University St, Belfast, **County Antrim**, BT7 1HP, NIR.
**(T)** 028 9031 2942
**(E)** avril.brown@dnet.co.uk
Speciality: Psychotherapy, Psychosexual Therapy. ✔
● **Psychosexual Therapist**
Ms A Brown **Q:** CertCC(Relate), Dip.PST, Dip.Psych. **M:** BASRT, UKCP.
C Yrs. Est.: 9 (**Ref:**HM03215)

## BROWN, B T

**B T Brown**, St Davids Health Centre, Richmond Rd, Exeter, **Devon**, EX4 4JA, ENG.
**(T)** 01392 275079
Speciality: Chiropodists (Podiatrists).
S (**Ref:**HM03216)

## BROWN, CLAIRE

**Claire Brown**, 29A Salts Rd, West Walton, Wisbech, **Cambridgeshire**, PE14 7EJ, ENG.
**(T)** 01945 585684
Speciality: Chiropodists (Podiatrists).
● **Owner** Mrs C Brown
S (**Ref:**HM03217)

## BROWN, DEBRA

**Debra Brown**, Chiropody Surgery Crackenedge Lane, Dewsbury, **Yorkshire (West)**, WF13 1QD, ENG.
**(T)** 01924 459163
Speciality: Chiropodists (Podiatrists).
S (**Ref:**HM03218)

## BROWN, F H

**F H Brown**, 5 School Lane, South Croxton, Leicester, **Leicestershire**, LE7 3RT, ENG.
**(T)** 01664 840508
Speciality: Osteopathy.
● **Owner** Mr F Brown
P S T (**Ref:**HM03219)

## BROWN, F K

**F K Brown**, Cringle Farm, Grendon Rd, Wollaston, Wellingborough, **Northamptonshire**, NN29 7PT, ENG.
**(T)** 01933 664221
Speciality: Electrolysis.
T (**Ref:**HM03220)

## BROWN, F R

**F R Brown**, 10 North Lane, Headingley, Leeds, **Yorkshire (West)**, LS6 3HE, ENG.
**(T)** 01132 784269
Speciality: Chiropodists (Podiatrists).
● **Owner** Mr F Brown
S (**Ref:**HM03221)

## BROWN, GEORGINA

**Georgina Brown**, Marisfield Pl, Selsey, Chichester, **Sussex (West)**, PO20 0PD, ENG.
**(T)** 01243 607031
Speciality: Chiropodists (Podiatrists).
● **Owner** Mrs G Brown
S (**Ref:**HM03222)

## BROWN, HELEN

**Helen Brown**, Dial Cottage, Handley Lane, Handley, Clay Cross, Chesterfield, **Derbyshire**, S45 9AT, ENG.
**(T)** 01246 862783 **(F)** 01246 862783
Speciality: Reflexology.
● **Owner** Mrs H Brown
S T (**Ref:**HM03223)

## BROWN, HELEN

**Helen Brown**, 29 Romilly Rd, Cardiff, **Glamorgan (Vale of)**, CF5 1FJ, WAL.
**(T)** 029 2034 1793
Speciality: Reflexology.
S T (**Ref:**HM03224)

## BROWN, IAN

**Ian Brown**, 4 Drumjoan Trce, Ochiltree, Cumnock, **Ayrshire (East)**, KA18 2RS, SCO.
**(T)** 01292 591936
Speciality: Complementary Medicines & Therapy.
C M (**Ref:**HM03225)

## BROWN, IAN

**Ian Brown (Assoc)**, 13 The Birches, Hurworth, Darlington, **County Durham**, DL2 2BD, ENG.
**(T)** 01325 721357
Speciality: Physiotherapy.
● **Owner** Mr I Brown
P S T (**Ref:**HM03226)

## BROWN, ISLA M

**Isla M Brown**, 5 Station Rd, Galston, **Ayrshire (East)**, KA4 8HS, SCO.
**(T)** 01563 822244
Speciality: Osteopathy.
● **Owner** Miss I Brown
P S T (**Ref:**HM03227)

## BROWN, J

**J Brown**, 18 Lansdowne Rd, London, **London (Greater)**, W11 3LL, ENG.
**(T)** 020 7727 7222
Speciality: Alexander Technique.
● **Employee** Mr J Brown
P S (**Ref:**HM03228)

## BROWN, J E

**J E Brown**, 14 Malyons Rd, Swanley, **Kent**, BR8 7RE, ENG.
**(T)** 01322 669141
Speciality: Physiotherapy.
● **Owner** Mr J Brown
P S T (**Ref:**HM03229)

## BROWN, JAMES

**James Brown**, 6 William St, Kilmarnock, **Ayrshire (East)**, KA3 1EE, SCO.
**(T)** 01563 529987
Speciality: Chiropodists (Podiatrists).
S (**Ref:**HM03230)

## BROWN, JULIET

**Juliet Brown**, 9 Patwell St, Bruton, **Somerset**, BA10 0EQ, ENG.
**(T)** 01749 812422
Speciality: Psychotherapy.
● **Owner** Ms J Brown
B (**Ref:**HM03231)

## BROWN, K J

**K J Brown**, 22 Russell St, Eccles, Manchester, **Manchester (Greater)**, M30 0NU, ENG.
**(T)** 01617 894825
Speciality: Chiropodists (Podiatrists).
● **Owner** Mr K Brown
S (**Ref:**HM03232)

## BROWN, KAREN

**Karen Brown**, 104 Tangier Rd, Richmond, **Surrey**, TW10 5DN, ENG.
**(T)** 020 8878 9827
Speciality: Aromatherapy.
M O (**Ref:**HM03233)

## BROWN, L

**L Brown**, Somersbury, 6 Stoneyfields, Farnham, **Surrey**, GU9 8DX, ENG.
**(T)** 01252 713491
Speciality: Chiropodists (Podiatrists).
● **Owner** Mrs L Brown
S (**Ref:**HM03234)

## BROWN, L R

**L R Brown**, Sarah Key Physiotherapy Centre, 30 Weymouth St, London, **London (Greater)**, W1N 3FA, ENG.
**(T)** 020 7636 3433
Speciality: Physiotherapy.
P S T (**Ref:**HM03235)

## BROWN, LAWRIE

**Lawrie Brown**, 150 Mottram Rd, Stalybridge, **Manchester (Greater)**, SK15 2RF, ENG.
**(T)** 01613 382434
Speciality: Physiotherapy.
P S T (**Ref:**HM03236)

## BROWN, LOUISE

**Louise Brown**, 3 North Rd, Torpoint, **Cornwall**, PL11 2DH, ENG.
**(T)** 01752 813358
Speciality: Chiropodists (Podiatrists).
● **Owner** Mrs L Brown
S (**Ref:**HM03237)

## BROWN, LYNN

**Lynn Brown**, 10 Nunroyd Avenue, **Yorkshire (West)**, LS17 6PN, ENG.
**(T)** 01132 680559
Speciality: Reflexology.
S T (**Ref:**HM03238)

## BROWN, N W J

**N W J Brown**, 38 Abbey Gardens, Canterbury, **Kent**, CT2 7EU, ENG.
**(T)** 01227 452497
Speciality: Chiropodists (Podiatrists).
S (**Ref:**HM03239)

## BROWN, NILI

**Nili Brown**, 20A Central Avenue, West Bridgeford, West Bridgford, Nottingham, **Nottinghamshire**, NG2 5GR, ENG.
**(T)** 01159 143311
Speciality: Acupuncture.
O (**Ref:**HM03240)

## BROWN, OLWEN

**Olwen Brown**, Millfield Cottage, Wesley St, Ossett, **Yorkshire (West)**, WF5 8HD, ENG.
**(T)** 01924 271876
Speciality: Complementary Medicines & Therapy.
● **Owner** Mrs O Brown
C M (**Ref:**HM03241)

## BROWN, P A

**P A Brown**, St Davids Health Centre, Richmond Rd, Exeter, **Devon**, EX4 4JA, ENG.
**(T)** 01392 275079
Speciality: Chiropractors.
P S T (**Ref:**HM03242)

## BROWN, PAT

**Pat Brown**, 19 Fearnville View, Leeds, **Yorkshire (West)**, LS8 3DJ, ENG.
**(T)** 01132 738842
**(E)** patbrown19fv@hotmail.com
Speciality: Alexander Technique. ✔
● **Teacher of the Alexander Technique**
Pat Brown **Q:** BEd (Hons), MSTAT. **M:** STAT.
P Yrs. Est.: 7 (**Ref:**HM03243)

## BROWN, R

**R Brown**, 1 Preston Cl, Chepstow, **Monmouthshire**, NP16 5TB, WAL.
**(T)** 01291 622523
Speciality: Chiropodists (Podiatrists).
● **Owner** Mrs R Brown
S (**Ref:**HM03244)

## BROWN, RAY

**Ray Brown**, Po Box 5836, Lutterworth, **Leicestershire**, LE17 4WL, ENG.
**(T)** 01455 559880 **(F)** 01455 559880
Speciality: Complementary Medicines & Therapy, Spiritual Healer. ✔
● **Owner/Spiritual Healer**
Mr R Brown **M:** CHA.
C Yrs. Est.: 15 (**Ref:**HM03245)

## BROWN, RITA

**Rita Brown**, 7 Kilby Cl, Wellingborough, **Northamptonshire**, NN8 2BG, ENG.
**(T)** 01933 382568
Speciality: Reflexology.
S T (**Ref:**HM03246)

## BROWN, S M

**S M Brown**, Farleigh Mortimer, Farleigh Wallop, Basingstoke, **Hampshire**, RG25 2HY, ENG.
**(T)** 01256 336853 **(F)** 01256 818064
Speciality: Chiropodists (Podiatrists).
● **Owner** Mr S Brown
S (**Ref:**HM03247)

## BROWN, SARAH

**Sarah Brown**, 9 Thorndale Mews, Bristol, BS8 2HX, ENG.
**(T)** 01179 737757
Speciality: Reflexology.


Key continued: **Yrs.Est:** Years Established **Q:** Qualifications **M:** Professional Membership ✔ Indemnity Insurance Accept Credit Cards

S T (Ref:HM03248)

**BROWN, T**

**T Brown**, 1 St Margarets Drive, Chesterfield, **Derbyshire**, S40 4SY, ENG.
(T) 01246 232511
Speciality: Physiotherapy.
P S T (Ref:HM03249)

**BROWN, TOM**

**Tom Brown**, 13 Willmore End, London, **London (Greater)**, SW19 3DE, ENG.
(T) 020 8544 1278 (F) 020 8287 1639
Speciality: Complementary Medicines & Therapy.
● **Owner** Mr T Brown
C M (Ref:HM03250)

**BROWN, V C**

**V C Brown**, 38 Russell Trce, Leamington Spa, **Warwickshire**, CV31 1HE, ENG.
(T) 01926 422388
Speciality: Acupuncture.
O (Ref:HM03251)

**BROWN, VAL**

**Val Brown**, 43 Shepshed Rd, Hathern, Loughborough, **Leicestershire**, LE12 5LL, ENG.
(T) 01509 843103
Speciality: Reflexology.
S T (Ref:HM03252)

**BROWN, VICTORIA**

**Victoria Brown**, 22 Pearl St, Cardiff, **Glamorgan (Vale of)**, CF24 1HD, WAL.
(T) 029 2021 8831
Speciality: Reflexology.
S T (Ref:HM03253)

**BROWNBILL-LOWE, GAIL**

**Gail Brownbill-Lowe**, 21 Siskin Chase, Cullompton, **Devon**, EX15 1UD, ENG.
(T) 01884 35011
Speciality: Aromatherapy.
M O (Ref:HM03254)

**BROWNE, ANNE**

**Anne Browne**, 34 Duporth Rd, St. Austell, **Cornwall**, PL25 3NU, ENG.
(T) 01726 71475
Speciality: Reflexology.
S T (Ref:HM03255)

**BROWNE, MICHELE**

**Michele Browne MIRI MNHII MIIAA**, Ballintemple, Cork, **County Cork**, IRE.
(T) 021 4294 499
Speciality: Complementary Medicines & Therapy.
M (Ref:HM03256)

**BROWNHILL, D G**

**Hypno-Analyst**, 27 Laburnum Rd, Stowheath, Wolverhampton, **Midlands (West)**, WV1 2TD, ENG.
(T) 01902 839239 (F) 01902 839239
Speciality: Auto Suggestion, Hypnotherapy, Psychotherapy. ✔
● **Hypnotherapist/Psychotherapist** Mr D Brownhill Q: Dip.Hyp, Dip.Psych. M: IAH.
B Yrs. Est.: 3 (Ref:HM03257)

**BROWNING, JOY**

**Joy Browning**, The Oxford Physiotherapy Service, 162 Banbury Rd, Oxford, **Oxfordshire**, OX2 7BT, ENG.
(T) 01865 311686
Speciality: Physiotherapy.
P S T (Ref:HM03258)

**BROWNING, JOY K**

**Joy K Browning**, University Running Ground, Iffley Rd, Oxford, **Oxfordshire**, OX4 1EQ, ENG.
(T) 01865 243590
Speciality: Physiotherapy.
P S T (Ref:HM03259)

**BROWNING, KAREN**

**Karen Browning**, Wani, Highfield Rd, Whiteshill, Stroud, **Gloucestershire**, GL6 6AJ, ENG.
(T) 01453 765088
Speciality: Reflexology.
S T (Ref:HM03260)

**BRUCE, A**

**A Bruce**, 29 High St, Harlow, **Essex**, CM17 0DN, ENG.
(T) 01279 438444
Speciality: Chiropodists (Podiatrists).
● **Partner** Mr N Bruce
S (Ref:HM03261)

**BRUCE, A R**

**A R Bruce**, 57 Gratton Rd, Cheltenham, **Gloucestershire**, GL50 2BZ, ENG.
(T) 01242 227437
Speciality: Physiotherapy.
● **Owner** Ms A Bruce
P S T (Ref:HM03262)

**BRUCE, ADAM**

**Adam Bruce**, 50 Arnold St, Nantwich, **Cheshire**, CW5 5QB, ENG.
(T) 01270 625066
Speciality: Physiotherapy.
● **Owner** Mr A Bruce
P S T (Ref:HM03263)

**BRUCE, ANN**

**Ann Bruce**, 25 Shepherds Hill, Bracknell, **Berkshire**, RG12 2LS, ENG.
(T) 01344 421481
(E) ann@hypnotics.org.uk
(W) www.hypnotics.org.uk
Speciality: Hypnosis, Hypnotherapy. ✔
● **Hypnotherapist** Ms A Bruce M: NCH.
B Yrs. Est.: 13 (Ref:HM03264)

**BRUCE, BOB**

**Bob Bruce**, 15 Kings Park, Scotland Gate, Choppington, **Northumberland**, NE62 5SD, ENG.
(T) 01670 829580
Speciality: Reflexology.
S T (Ref:HM03265)

**BRUCE, CLAIRE**

**Claire Bruce**, 2 Costly St, Ivybridge, **Devon**, PL21 0DB, ENG.
(T) 01752 691499
Speciality: Chiropodists (Podiatrists).
● **Owner** Mrs C Bruce
S (Ref:HM03266)

**BRUCE, F N**

**F N Bruce**, 29 High St, Harlow, **Essex**, CM17 0DN, ENG.
(T) 01279 438444
Speciality: Osteopathy.
● **Partner** Mr N Bruce
P S T (Ref:HM03267)

**BRUCE, JAN**

**Jan Bruce**, 10 Arundel Rd, Eastbourne, **Sussex (East)**, BN21 2EL, ENG.
(T) 01323 735536
Speciality: Physiotherapy.
● **Owner** Miss J Bruce
P S T (Ref:HM03268)

**BRUCE, K**

**K Bruce**, 27 Berners St, Ipswich, **Suffolk**, IP1 3LN, ENG.
(T) 01473 253870
Speciality: Chiropodists (Podiatrists).
S (Ref:HM03269)

**BRUCE, KATHRYN**

**Kathryn Bruce**, Dean Mead Cottage, David St, Meopham, Gravesend, **Kent**, DA13 0BT, ENG.
(T) 01474 815467
Speciality: Homeopathy.
M (Ref:HM03270)

**BRUCE, KATIE**

**Katie Bruce**, 48 Saxon Way, Melton, Woodbridge, **Suffolk**, IP12 1PJ, ENG.
(T) 01394 383784
Speciality: Chiropodists (Podiatrists).
● **Owner** Mrs K Bruce
S (Ref:HM03271)

**BRUCE, NEIL**

**Neil Bruce**, 36 Sun St, Waltham Abbey, **Essex**, EN9 1EJ, ENG.
(T) 01992 713033
Speciality: Osteopathy.
● **Owner** Mr N Bruce
P S T (Ref:HM03272)

**BRUCE, P L**

**P L Bruce**, 49 Earlsdon Avenue, Middlesbrough, **Cleveland**, TS5 8SZ, ENG.
(T) 01642 815129
Speciality: Physiotherapy.
● **Owner** Miss P Bruce
P S T (Ref:HM03273)

**BRUCKNER, R J**

**R J Bruckner**, 203 Golders Green Rd, London, **London (Greater)**, NW11 9BY, ENG.
(T) 020 8458 1523 (F) 020 8458 1523
Speciality: Chiropodists (Podiatrists).
● **Owner** Mr R Bruckner
S (Ref:HM03274)

**BRUEN, MARY**

**Mary Bruen**, 44 Leinster St, Phibsboro, Dublin, **County Dublin**, IRE.
(T) 01830 4285
Speciality: Complementary Medicines & Therapy.
M (Ref:HM03275)

**BRUGGEMEYER'S**

**Bruggemeyer's**, 99 Herne Hill, London, **London (Greater)**, SE24 9LY, ENG.
(T) 020 7274 6182
Speciality: Osteopathy.
● **Owner** Mr W Bruggemeyer
P S T (Ref:HM03276)

**BRUMMITT, V A**

**V A Brummitt**, 32 Panfield Lane, Braintree, **Essex**, CM7 2TH, ENG.
(T) 01376 343891
Speciality: Chiropodists (Podiatrists).
● **Owner** Mrs V Brummitt
S (Ref:HM03277)

**BRUNGER, ANDREW**

**Andrew Brunger**, 153 Pizien Well Rd, Wateringbury, Maidstone, **Kent**, ME18 5HX, ENG.
(T) 01622 813030
Speciality: Chiropodists (Podiatrists).
S (Ref:HM03278)

**BRUNSKILL, DAVID**

**David Brunskill**, 23A Wood St, Wootton Bassett, Swindon, **Wiltshire**, SN4 7BD, ENG.
(T) 01793 848093
Speciality: Osteopathy.
● **Owner** Mr D Brunskill
P S T (Ref:HM03279)

**BRUNSWICK PHYSIO**

**Brunswick Physio**, 5 Brunswick Rd, Norwich, **Norfolk**, NR2 2HA, ENG.
(T) 01603 612149 (F) 01603 624497
Speciality: Physiotherapy. ✔
● **Physiotherapist** Ms F Sutton Q: BSc (Hons), MCSP, SRP. M: CSP.
● **Physiotherapist** Mrs G Deddis Q: BSc (Hons), MCSP, SRP. M: CSP.
S Yrs. Est.: 23 (Ref:HM03280)

**BRUNT, LINDA**

**Linda Brunt**, Hentervene, Crackington Haven, Bude, **Cornwall**, EX23 0LF, ENG.
(T) 01840 230106
Speciality: Reflexology.
S T (Ref:HM03281)

**BRUNTON, A**

**A Brunton**, 110 Cleaver St, Burnley, **Lancashire**, BB10 3DN, ENG.
(T) 01282 430666
Speciality: Osteopathy.
● **Owner** Mr A Brunton
P S T (Ref:HM03282)

**BRUNTON, DEIRDRE**

**Deirdre Brunton**, 34 Hanover Trce, Brighton, **Sussex (East)**, BN2 2SN, ENG.
(T) 01273 689810
Speciality: Acupuncture.
O (Ref:HM03283)

**BRUNTSFIELD CTRE-HYPNOTHERAPY**

**Bruntsfield Centre For Hypnotherapy (The)**, 16 Granville Trce, Edinburgh, **Edinburgh (City of)**, EH10 4PQ, SCO.
(T) 01312 297823



Key: B Mind-Body Medicine C Complementary Medicine H Self Help Treatment M Medicinal Therapy O Oriental Medicine P Postural Therapy S Manipulative Structural Therapy T Touch Therapy

Speciality: Hypnosis.
**B** (Ref:HM03284)

### BRYAN, SUE

**Sue Bryan**, 121 Mill Way, Bushey, **Herefordshire**, WD23 2AE, ENG.
(T) 01923 237730
Speciality: Complementary Medicines & Therapy.
● **Bowen Therapist** Sue Bryan
**M** (Ref:HM03285)

### BRYANT, C

**C Bryant**, 5 Glenrosa Rd, Tilehurst, Reading, **Berkshire**, RG30 6AN, ENG.
(T) 01189 424773
Speciality: Electrolysis.
● **Owner** Mrs C Bryant
**T** (Ref:HM03286)

### BRYANT, I E

**I E Bryant**, 6 Wentworth Way, South Croydon, **Surrey**, CR2 9EU, ENG.
(T) 020 8657 1435
Speciality: Physiotherapy.
**P S T** (Ref:HM03287)

### BRYANT, JACQUELINE

**Jacqueline Bryant**, 26 Chyngton Cl, Eastbourne, **Sussex (East)**, BN23 8HQ, ENG.
(T) 01323 764657
Speciality: Reflexology.
**S T** (Ref:HM03288)

### BRYANT, M L

**M L Bryant**, 49 Weston Rd, Rochester, **Kent**, ME2 3HB, ENG.
(T) 01634 297340
Speciality: Chiropodists (Podiatrists).
**S** (Ref:HM03289)

### BRYCE, EDWARD

**Mr Edward Bryce**, Fife Natural Therapies, Albany Osteopathic Clinic, Albany St, Dunfermline, **Fife**, KY12 0QZ, SCO.
(T) 01383 732195 (F) 01383 726649
Speciality: Osteopathy.
● **Partner** Mr E Bryce
**P S T** (Ref:HM03290)

### BRYDEN & KEER

**Bryden & Keer**, 5 Elm Trce, Constantine Rd, London, **London (Greater)**, NW3 2LL, ENG.
(T) 020 7267 4222
Speciality: Physiotherapy.
● **Owner** Ms A Power
**P S T** (Ref:HM03291)

### BRYSON & ASSOCIATES

**Anne Bryson & Associates**, 30 Claremont Rd, Wivenhoe, Colchester, **Essex**, CO7 9NU, ENG.
(T) 08000 263549
Speciality: Hypnosis.
● **Owner** Ms A Bryson
**B** (Ref:HM03292)

### BRZOZOWSKI-MAN, ISABELLA

**Isabella Brzozowski-Man**, 27 Craven Rd, Newbury, **Berkshire**, RG14 5NG, ENG.
(T) 01635 31679
Speciality: Acupuncture.
**O** (Ref:HM03293)

### BST FOUNDATION

**BST Foundation**, 34 Arthur Rd, New Malden, **Surrey**, KT3 6LX, ENG.
(T) 020 8241 0353 (F) 020 8942 6307
(W) www.bstfoundation.co.uk
Speciality: Hypnosis, Hypnotherapy. ✓
● **Hypnotherapist** Mr G Emerson Q: Dip.BST, Dip.Hyp. M: BSTF.
**B** Yrs. Est.: 10 (Ref:HM03294)

### BST FOUNDATION

**BST Foundation**, 10 Harley St, London, **London (Greater)**, W1, ENG.
(T) 020 8241 0353 (F) 020 8942 6307
(W) www.bstfoundation.co.uk
Speciality: Hypnosis, Hypnotherapy, Clinical Hypnosis, Brief Therapy. ✓
● **Hypnotherapist** Mr G Emerson
(T) 020 8942 6307 Q: Dip.BST, Dip.Hyp. M: BSTF.
**B** Yrs. Est.: 10 (Ref:HM03295)

### BTAC

**Blossomfields Traditional Acupuncture Clinic**, 306 Blossomfield Rd, Solihull, **Midlands (West)**, B91 1TH, ENG.
(T) 01217 044909
Speciality: Absent Healing, Acupressure, Acupuncture, Aura Therapy, Cupping, Electrotherapy, Faith Healing, Healer, Healing Therapy, Holistic Healing, Life Style Coaching, Meditation, Moxibustion, Naturopathy, Nutritional Therapy, Oriental Diagnosis, Polarity Therapy, Reflexology, Shiatsu, Spiritual Healing, T'ai-Chi Ch'uan, Visualisation Therapy, Ying & Yang. ✓
● **Director** Ms J Morgan Q: Dip.Jap.Ac, Dip.TCHM, Lic.Ac. M: BAcC.
**O** Yrs. Est.: 11 (Ref:HM03296)

### BUBBLES

**Bubbles**, 22 Blandford Sq, Newcastle Upon Tyne, **Tyne and Wear**, NE1 4HZ, ENG.
(T) 01912 220982
Speciality: Aromatherapy.
**M O** (Ref:HM03297)

### BUCHAN, DAVID (DR)

**Dr David Buchan**, The Health Hydro, Milton Rd, Swindon, **Wiltshire**, SN1 5JA, ENG.
(T) 01793 693787
Speciality: Hypnosis.
**B** (Ref:HM03298)

### BUCHAN, L

**L Buchan**, 32 Chaplet Avenue, Glasgow, **Glasgow (City of)**, G13 3LX, SCO.
(T) 01419 597193
Speciality: Hypnotherapy.
**B** (Ref:HM03299)

### BUCHANAN, ANGELA

**Physiotherapy Practice**, 353 Upper Richmond Rd, Putney, London, **London (Greater)**, SW15 5QJ, ENG.
(T) 020 8876 6543
Speciality: Electrotherapy, Kinesiology, Manipulation, Phytotherapy, Ultrasonics, Mobilisation.
● **Physiotherapist** Ms A Buchanan Q: MCSP. M: CSP, SRP.
**P S T** Yrs. Est.: 11 (Ref:HM03300)

### BUCHANAN, ELIZABETH

**Elizabeth Buchanan**, 110 Harley St, London, **London (Greater)**, W1N 1AF, ENG.
(T) 020 7224 4588 (F) 020 7224 4588
Speciality: Physiotherapy.
**P S T** (Ref:HM03301)

### BUCHANAN, JO

**Jo Buchanan**, 14 Bradmore Park Rd, London, **London (Greater)**, W6 0DS, ENG.
(T) 020 8748 1079
Speciality: Homeopathy.
● **Owner** Ms J Buchanan
**M** (Ref:HM03302)

### BUCHANAN, LEONORA

**Leonora Buchanan**, 80 Forrest St, Airdrie, **Lanarkshire (North)**, ML6 7AG, SCO.
(T) 01236 768060 (F) 01236 768060
Speciality: Chiropodists (Podiatrists).
● **Owner** Mrs L Buchanan
**S** (Ref:HM03303)

### BUCHHOLZ, D

**D Buchholz**, 376 Grays Inn Rd, London, **London (Greater)**, WC1X 8BB, ENG.
(T) 020 7837 5530
Speciality: Chiropodists (Podiatrists).
**S** (Ref:HM03304)

### BUCK, IAN

**Ian Buck**, 70 Mountbatten Cl, Yate, Bristol, BS37 5TE, ENG.
(T) 01454 880502
Speciality: Chiropodists (Podiatrists).
● **Owner** Mr I Buck
**S** (Ref:HM03305)

### BUCK, PETER

**Peter Buck**, Outwood, 34A Westover Rd, Fleet, **Hampshire**, GU13 9DB, ENG.
(T) 01252 614380
Speciality: Chiropody. ✓
● **Chiropodist** Mr P Buck Q: MBChA, MSSCh. M: B.A.Ch.P.
**M** Yrs. Est.: 1 (Ref:HM03306)

### BUCK, SUE

**Sue Buck**, 26 Hermitage Rd, Roche, St. Austell, **Cornwall**, PL26 8QD, ENG.
(T) 01726 891301
Speciality: Reflexology.
● **Owner** Ms S Buck
**S T** (Ref:HM03307)

### BUCKBERRY, TINA

**Tina Buckberry**, The Maples, 75 Walsby Drive, Kemsley, Sittingbourne, **Kent**, ME10 2TT, ENG.
(T) 01795 427378
Speciality: Reflexology.
**S T** (Ref:HM03308)

### BUCKHURST HILL HEALTH PRACTICE

**Buckhurst Hill Good Health Practice**, 161 Queens Rd, Buckhurst Hill, **Essex**, IG9 5AZ, ENG.
(T) 020 8505 8353
Speciality: Homeopathy.
● **Owner** Mr R Woodleigh
**M** (Ref:HM03309)

### BUCKINGHAM CHIROPRACTIC CLINIC

**Buckingham Chiropractic Clinic (The)**, 12 Brackley Rd, Buckingham, **Buckinghamshire**, MK18 1JD, ENG.
(T) 01280 816623 (F) 01280 824648
Speciality: Chiropractic, Cranio-Sacral Therapy. ✓
● **Chiropractor** Ms F Dondell Q: AMC, DC. M: MCA.
● **Owner** Ms K Jarman Q: AMC, DC. M: MCA.
● **Chiropractor** Mr A Redrup Q: AMC, DC. M: MCA.
**P** Yrs. Est.: 13 (Ref:HM03310)

### BUCKINGHAM CLINIC

**Buckingham Clinic**, 24 Buckingham Trce, Glasgow, **Glasgow (City of)**, G12 8ED, SCO.
(T) 01413 394340 (F) 01413 397704
Speciality: Osteopathy.
● **Partner** Mrs C Sneddon
**P S T** (Ref:HM03311)

### BUCKINGHAM, MARK

**Mark Buckingham**, St Georges House, 56 Billing Rd, Northampton, **Northamptonshire**, NN1 5DB, ENG.
(T) 01604 601641 (F) 01604 601641
Speciality: Physiotherapy.
● **Partner** Mr P Whitty
**P S T** (Ref:HM03312)

### BUCKLAND, CAROLINE

**Caroline Buckland**, 26 Tournay Rd, London, **London (Greater)**, SW6 7UF, ENG.
(T) 020 7381 3523
Speciality: Reflexology.
**S T** (Ref:HM03313)

### BUCKLE, SHARON ELIZABETH

**Sharon Elizabeth Buckle**, 24 Bostock House, Scoe Cl, Hounslow, **London (Greater)**, TW5 0UW, ENG.
(T) 020 8569 6914
Speciality: Complementary Medicines & Therapy.
**C M** (Ref:HM03314)

### BUCKLE, WENDY-ANNE

**Wendy-Anne Buckle**, The Therapy Room, 181 Tachbrook Rd, Leamington Spa, **Warwickshire**, CV31 3EN, ENG.
(T) 01926 430264
Speciality: Aromatherapy, Massage (Therapeutic), Reflexology.
**S T** (Ref:HM03315)

### BUCKLEY, A S

**Buckley A S**, Cres Chambers, 6-8 Clifton Cresent, Birkenhead, **Merseyside**, CH41 2QD, ENG.
(T) 01516 477498
Speciality: Chiropodists (Podiatrists).
**S** (Ref:HM03316)

### BUCKLEY, B

**B Buckley**, 110 North Rd, Glossop, **Derbyshire**, SK13 7AX, ENG.


Key continued: Yrs.Est: Years Established Q: Qualifications M: Professional Membership ✓ Indemnity Insurance Accept Credit Cards

(T) 01457 863247
Speciality: Chiropodists (Podiatrists).
● **Owner** Mrs B Buckley
S (Ref:HM03317)

## BUCKLEY, BILLIE
**Mrs Billie Buckley**, 6 Trevor Pl, London, **London (Greater)**, SW7 1LA, ENG.
(T) 020 7581 3987
(E) bbsi@bigfoot.com
Speciality: Cognitive Therapy, Counselling, Family Therapy, Psychotherapy, Stress Therapy. ✓
● **Psychotherapist** Mrs B Buckley M: FPC.
H Yrs. Est.: 10 (Ref:HM03318)

## BUCKLEY, JUDY
**Judy Buckley**, 21 Private Rd, Enfield, **London (Greater)**, EN1 2EH, ENG.
(T) 020 8367 3392
Speciality: Psychotherapy.
● **Owner** Ms J Buckley
B (Ref:HM03319)

## BUCKLEY, MAUREEN
**Maureen Buckley**, Rosebank, 15 St Johns Cres, Huddersfield, **Yorkshire (West)**, HD1 5DY, ENG.
(T) 01484 421178 (F) 01484 421178
Speciality: Hypnosis.
● **Owner** Miss M Buckley
B (Ref:HM03320)

## BUCKMAN, C M
**C M Buckman**, 76 Haddo House, Haddo St, London, **London (Greater)**, SE10 9SF, ENG.
(T) 020 8293 1114
Speciality: Homeopathy.
M (Ref:HM03321)

## BUDD, CHRISTINE
**Christine Budd**, 84B Highbury Park, London, **London (Greater)**, N5 2XE, ENG.
(T) 020 7359 5777
Speciality: Osteopathy.
P S T (Ref:HM03322)

## BUDD, M L
**M L Budd**, 29 Ferncroft Rd, Bournemouth, **Dorset**, BH10 6BY, ENG.
(T) 01202 578640
Speciality: Osteopathy.
P S T (Ref:HM03323)

## BUDD, M L
**M L Budd**, The New Surgery, Brookley Rd Car Park, Brockenhurst, **Hampshire**, SO42 7RR, ENG.
(T) 01590 623311
Speciality: Osteopathy.
● **Owner** Mrs M Budd
P S T (Ref:HM03324)

## BUDD, RICHARD
**Richard Budd**, The Flat Above, East Court Nursing, Home, 156-160 Havant Road, Drayton, **Hampshire**, PO6 2JQ, ENG.
(T) 023 9221 5843
Speciality: Reflexology.
S T (Ref:HM03325)

## BUDD, S
**S Budd**, 43 Luxborough Towers, Luxborough St, London, **London (Greater)**, W1M 3LL, ENG.
(T) 020 7486 5095
Speciality: Reflexology.
● **Owner** Mrs S Budd
S T (Ref:HM03326)

## BUDDEN, ANDREW M
**Andrew M Budden**, 57 Lansdowne Hill, London, **London (Greater)**, SE27 0LS, ENG.
(T) 020 8670 9019
Speciality: Osteopathy.
P S T (Ref:HM03327)

## BUDDEN, CLARE
**Clare Budden**, 10 Brendon Rd, London, **London (Greater)**, SE9 3RP, ENG.
(T) 020 8313 2813
Speciality: Reflexology.
S T (Ref:HM03328)

## BUDDEN, O
**Mrs O Budden**, 111 Milford Rd, Lymington, **Hampshire**, SO41 8DN, ENG.
(T) 01590 671492
Speciality: Physiotherapy.
● **Owner** Mrs O Budden
P S T (Ref:HM03329)

## BUDDHIST SOCIETY
**Buddhist Society**, 58 Eccleston Sq, London, **London (Greater)**, SW1V 1PH, ENG.
(T) 020 7834 5858
Speciality: Complementary Medicines & Therapy.
● **General Secretary** R Maddox
M (Ref:HM03330)

## BUDZYNSKI, LESLIE A
**Leslie A Budzynski**, Enfield Chiropractic Clinic, 94 Ridge Avenue, London, **London (Greater)**, N21 2AU, ENG.
(T) 020 8360 0204
Speciality: Chiropractic.
P S T (Ref:HM03331)

## BUENO, JULIA
**Julia Bueno**, 74 Oxford Gardens, London, **London (Greater)**, W10 5UW, ENG.
(T) 07956 476808
Speciality: Reflexology.
● **Owner** Ms J Bueno
S T (Ref:HM03332)

## BUGLASS, I G
**I G Buglass**, 44 Halifax Rd, Todmorden, **Yorkshire (West)**, OL14 5QJ, ENG.
(T) 01706 818118
Speciality: Complementary Medicines & Therapy.
C M (Ref:HM03333)

## BUILDERS, MEJ
**Mej Builders**, 26 Dean Lane, Merstham, Redhill, **Surrey**, RH1 3AH, ENG.
(T) 01737 555850
Speciality: Complementary Medicines & Therapy.
C M (Ref:HM03334)

## BUILDING FUTURES
**Building Futures**, 32 Cantwell Rd, London, **London (Greater)**, SE18 3LW, ENG.
(T) 020 8854 0606
Speciality: Psychotherapy.
B (Ref:HM03335)

## BULINSKI, JAN
**Jan Bulinski**, 6 Acomb Rd, York, **Yorkshire (North)**, YO24 4EW, ENG.
(T) 01904 793758
Speciality: Chiropodists (Podiatrists).
S (Ref:HM03336)

## BULL, C S
**C S Bull**, 99 High Rd West, Felixstowe, **Suffolk**, IP11 9AB, ENG.
(T) 01394 277689
Speciality: Osteopathy.
● **Owner** Mr C Bull
P S T (Ref:HM03337)

## BULL, J
**J Bull**, 45 Priests Avenue, Romford, **Essex**, RM1 4RJ, ENG.
(T) 01708 742555
Speciality: Chiropodists (Podiatrists).
S (Ref:HM03338)

## BULL, MARGARET
**Margaret Bull**, 25 The Poplars, Horsham, **Sussex (West)**, RH13 5RH, ENG.
(T) 01403 254123
Speciality: Reflexology.
S T (Ref:HM03339)

## BULL, MARTIN
**Martin Bull**, 22 Cow Lane, Rampton, Cambridge, **Cambridgeshire**, CB4 8QG, ENG.
(T) 01954 250791
Speciality: Hypnotherapy.
B (Ref:HM03340)

## BULL, OWEN MORGAN
**Owen Morgan Bull**, 70 Woodbridge Rd East, Ipswich, **Suffolk**, IP4 5PH, ENG.
(T) 01473 716340 (F) 01473 716340
Speciality: Hypnosis.
● **Owner** Mr O Bull
B (Ref:HM03341)

## BULLEN-SPICER ASSOCIATES
**Bullen-Spicer Associates**, 76 Hallam Rd, Mapperley, Nottingham, **Nottinghamshire**, HG3 6HR, ENG.
(T) 01159 504336
Speciality: Counselling, Encounter Groups, Family Therapy, Gestalt Therapy, Group Therapy, Humanistic Psychology, Life Style Coaching, Meditation, Psychotherapy, Stress Therapy, Visualisation Therapy. ✓
● **Psychotherapist/Manager**
Mr R Spicer Q: Dip.Psych. M: AHPP, SPTI, UKCP.
B Yrs. Est.: 13 (Ref:HM03342)

## BULLER, JEMIMA
**Jemima Buller**, 41 Highfield Green, Epping, **Essex**, CM16 5HD, ENG.
(T) 01992 578105
Speciality: Psychotherapy.
B (Ref:HM03343)

## BULLOCK, JULIE
**Julie Bullock**, 20 Colinwood Cl, Walsall, **Midlands (West)**, WS6 6JF, ENG.
(T) 01922 416713
Speciality: Chiropody. ✓
● **Owner/Chiropodist** Ms J Bullock Q: MBChA, MSSCh.
C Yrs. Est.: 5 (Ref:HM03344)

## BULLOCK, WILLIAM
**William Bullock**, 32 Regent Drive, Skipton, **Yorkshire (North)**, BD23 1AY, ENG.
(T) 01756 790186
Speciality: Reflexology.
S T (Ref:HM03345)

## BULOS, K C
**K C Bulos**, 56 Lakeside Drive, Bromley, **Kent**, BR2 8QJ, ENG.
(T) 01689 854823
Speciality: Chiropodists (Podiatrists).
● **Owner** Mr K Bulos
S (Ref:HM03346)

## BUMBLE - BEE'S PHYSIO
**Barbara Hummel MCSP**, Lentach Cottage, Dulnain Bridge, Grantown-on-Spey, **Highland**, PH26 3NE, SCO.
(T) 01479 851293
Speciality: Electrotherapy, Indian Head Massage, Manipulation, Massage (Therapeutic), Metamorphic Therapy, Physiotherapy, Reflexology, Self help exercise programmes. ✓
● **Holistic Physiotherapist**
Barbara Hummell Q: SRP. M: CSP, OCPPP.
S Yrs. Est.: 5 (Ref:HM03347)

## BUMFREY, CAROL
**Carol Bumfrey**, 41 High St, Westoning, Bedford, **Bedfordshire**, MK45 5JQ, ENG.
(T) 01525 755020
Speciality: Reflexology.
S T (Ref:HM03348)

## BUNCE THERAPEUTIC MASSAGE
**Bunce Therapeutic Massage**, 2 Chantry Cl, Windsor, **Berkshire**, SL4 5EP, ENG.
(T) 01753 852162
Speciality: Complementary Medicines & Therapy.
● **Owner** Mrs L Bunce
C M (Ref:HM03349)

## BUNCE, J
**J Bunce**, Southdown Physiotherapy Clinic, 11 Stafford Rd, Seaford, **Sussex (East)**, BN25 1UE, ENG.
(T) 01323 894354
Speciality: Physiotherapy.
● **Partner** Mrs S Bunce
P S T (Ref:HM03350)

## BUNCE, S
**S Bunce**, Southdown Physiotherapy Clinic, 11 Stafford Rd, Seaford, **Sussex (East)**, BN25 1UE, ENG.
(T) 01323 894354
Speciality: Physiotherapy.
● **Partner** Mrs S Bunce
P S T (Ref:HM03351)



Key: B Mind-Body Medicine C Complementary Medicine H Self Help Treatment M Medicinal Therapy O Oriental Medicine P Postural Therapy S Manipulative Structural Therapy T Touch Therapy

## BUNGAY, SHERILYN
**Sherilyn Bungay Do**, 104 Grattons Drive, Crawley, **Sussex (West)**, RH10 3DD, ENG.
(T) 01293 888600
Speciality: Osteopathy.
P S T (Ref:HM03352)

## BUNN, ANDREW
**Andrew Bunn**, 30 Winnington Lane, Northwich, **Cheshire**, CW8 4DE, ENG.
(T) 01606 79668
Speciality: Chiropodists (Podiatrists).
● **Owner** Mr A Bunn
S (Ref:HM03353)

## BUNTON, LYNN
**Miss Lynn Bunton**, Delabere Health & Racketts Club, Southam, Cheltenham, **Gloucestershire**, GL52 3NJ, ENG.
(T) 01242 673329
Speciality: Massage (Therapeutic), Reflexology, On-Site Massage, Vertical Reflexology Treatment. ✔
● **Owner/Complementary Therapist** Miss L Bunton Q: ITEC. M: GCP, ITEC.
B C P T Yrs. Est.: 6 (Ref:HM03354)

## BUPA DUNEDIN HOSPITAL
**BUPA Dunedin Hospital**, 16 Bath Rd, Reading, **Berkshire**, RG1 6NB, ENG.
(T) 01189 553413
Speciality: Physiotherapy.
P S T (Ref:HM03355)

## BUPA HOSPITAL
**BUPA Hospital (Norwich)**, Old Watton Rd, Norwich, **Norfolk**, NR4 7TD, ENG.
(T) 01603 456181
Speciality: Physiotherapy.
● **General Manager** Mrs L Nerney
P S T (Ref:HM03356)

## BUPA HOSPITAL ELLAND
**BUPA Hospital Elland**, Elland Lane, Elland, **Yorkshire (West)**, HX5 9EB, ENG.
(T) 01422 375577
Speciality: Physiotherapy.
P S T (Ref:HM03357)

## BUPA MURRAYFIELD HOSPITAL
**Bupa Murrayfield Hospital**, 122 Corstorphine Rd, Edinburgh, **Edinburgh (City of)**, EH12 6UD, SCO.
(T) 01313 162526
Speciality: Physiotherapy.
P S T (Ref:HM03358)

## BUQI COLLEGE U K
**Buqi College U K**, Care Of Kailash, 7 Newcourt St, London, **London (Greater)**, NW8 7AA, ENG.
(T) 020 8771 7237
Speciality: Complementary Medicines & Therapy.
● **Manager** Ms S Bracke
M (Ref:HM03359)

## BURCH, E
**E Burch**, Steart Farm, Marhamchurch, Bude, **Cornwall**, EX23 0HF, ENG.
(T) 01288 361513
Speciality: Complementary Medicines & Therapy.
● **Owner** Mrs E Burch
M (Ref:HM03360)

## BURCH, NIGEL
**Nigel Burch**, 1a Laurier Rd, London, **London (Greater)**, NW5 1SD, ENG.
(T) 020 7267 2785
Speciality: Psychotherapy.
B (Ref:HM03361)

## BURCHELL & ASSOCIATES
**Burchell M B & Associates**, 210 Fulham Palace Rd, Hammersmith, London, **London (Greater)**, W6 9NT, ENG.
(T) 020 7385 0554 (F) 020 7386 0935
Speciality: Chiropodists (Podiatrists).
● **Practice Manager** Mr R Burchell
S (Ref:HM03362)

## BURCHELL & ASSOCIATES
**Burchell M B & Associates**, 99 Moore Pk Rd, Fulham, London, **London (Greater)**, SW6 2DA, ENG.
(T) 020 7736 4715 (F) 020 7736 4715
Speciality: Chiropodists (Podiatrists).
● **Owner** Mr M Burchell
S (Ref:HM03363)

## BURCHELL & ASSOCIATES
**M B Burchell & Associates**, 30 Farley Rd, South Croydon, **Surrey**, CR2 8DA, ENG.
(T) 020 8657 1648 (F) 020 8651 4199
Speciality: Chiropodists (Podiatrists).
● **Owner** Mr R Birchell
S (Ref:HM03364)

## BURCHELL, DIANE SUE
**Diane Sue Burchell**, 12 Smithy Cl, Holybourne, Alton, **Hampshire**, GU34 4EE, ENG.
(T) 01420 549267
Speciality: Reflexology.
S T (Ref:HM03365)

## BURCHFIELD PHYSIO PRACTICE
**Burchfield Physiotherapy Practice**, 66 Lymington Bottom Rd, Medstead, Alton, **Hampshire**, GU34 5EP, ENG.
(T) 01420 563200
Speciality: Physiotherapy.
P S T (Ref:HM03366)

## BURDEN, C
**C Burden**, 2 Newport Trce, Millbrook, Torpoint, **Cornwall**, PL10 1BS, ENG.
(T) 01752 823024 (F) 01752 823024
Speciality: Chiropodists (Podiatrists).
● **Owner** Mrs C Burden
S (Ref:HM03367)

## BURDEN, GILLIAN
**Gillian Burden**, Pummy's Cottage, Sutton, Witney, **Oxfordshire**, OX8 1RY, ENG.
(T) 01865 884443
Speciality: Reflexology.
S T (Ref:HM03368)

## BURDEN, PHILIPPA
**Philippa Burden**, 33 Northgate, Canterbury, **Kent**, CT1 1BL, ENG.
(T) 01227 451317
Speciality: Complementary Medicines & Therapy.
C M (Ref:HM03369)

## BURDEN, RICHARD
**Richard Burden**, Swansea Clinic Of Natural Medicine, 20 Walter Rd, Swansea, SA1 5NQ, WAL.
(T) 01792 654751
Speciality: Naturopathy, Osteopathy, Colonic Hydrotherapy. ✔
● **Owner/Naturopath/Osteopath** Mr R Burden Q: DO, ND. M: RoN.
S Yrs. Est.: 13 (Ref:HM03370)

## BUREN, VAN
**Van Buren**, 181 Everton Drive, Stanmore, **London (Greater)**, HA7 1EB, ENG.
(T) 020 8204 5951
Speciality: Hypnotherapy. ✔
● **Owner** Mr L Buren Q: MIAH.
C Yrs. Est.: 4 (Ref:HM03371)

## BURFORD, DOMINIQUE
**Dominique Burford**, 48 Sunley Gardens, Greenford, **London (Greater)**, UB6 7PE, ENG.
(T) 020 8810 5366
Speciality: Reflexology.
S T (Ref:HM03372)

## BURGE, ROBERT A
**Robert A Burge**, Hawzelwood House, 197 Frindsbury Rd, Rochester, **Kent**, ME2 4JN, ENG.
(T) 01634 710051
Speciality: Osteopathy.
P S T (Ref:HM03373)

## BURGER, SALLY
**Sally Burger**, 40 Durham Rd, London, **London (Greater)**, N2 9DT, ENG.
(T) 020 8444 1160
Speciality: Alexander Technique.
● **Owner** Mrs S Burger
P S (Ref:HM03374)

## BURGESS ROAD NAT THERAPY CTRE
**Burgess Road Natural Therapy Centre**, 7 Burges Rd, London, **London (Greater)**, E6 2BJ, ENG.
(T) 020 8548 9020
Speciality: Complementary Medicines & Therapy.
C M (Ref:HM03375)

## BURGESS, DAVINA
**Davina Burgess**, 141 Burnham Tower, Fellows Rd, London, **London (Greater)**, NW3 3JN, ENG.
(T) 020 7209 3870
Speciality: Reflexology.
S T (Ref:HM03376)

## BURGESS, KAREN
**Karen Burgess**, 131 Denton Rd, Audenshaw, Manchester, **Manchester (Greater)**, M34 5BE, ENG.
(T) 01613 200917
(E) physiotherapy@breathmail.net
(W) www.physiotherapy.uk.net
Speciality: Chiropody, Physiotherapy. ✔
● **Physiotherapist** Mr C Wych
(T) 01613 204409 Q: Grad Dip Phys, MCSP, SRP. M: CSP.
● **Owner/Chiropodist** Ms K Burgess Q: S.R.Ch. M: S.R.Ch.
S Yrs. Est.: 22 (Ref:HM03377)

## BURGESS, KAY
**Kay Burgess**, 34 Norris Cl, Chiseldon, Swindon, **Wiltshire**, SN4 0LR, ENG.
(T) 01793 740790
Speciality: Chiropodists (Podiatrists).
● **Owner** Mrs K Burgess
S (Ref:HM03378)

## BURGESS, MARGARET
**Margaret Burgess**, 3 Shelford Rd, Southsea, **Hampshire**, PO4 8NT, ENG.
(T) 023 9273 0909
Speciality: Chiropodists (Podiatrists).
S (Ref:HM03379)

## BURGESS, P
**P Burgess**, Victoria Court, Victoria St, Grimsby, **Humberside (South)**, DN31 1PT, ENG.
(T) 01472 242771
Speciality: Osteopathy.
● **Owner** Mr P Burgess
P S T (Ref:HM03380)

## BURGESS, PAUL
**Paul Burgess**, 21 Berryhill, Cannock, **Staffordshire**, WS12 5UJ, ENG.
(T) 01543 423965
Speciality: Chiropodists (Podiatrists).
● **Owner** Mr P Burgess
S (Ref:HM03381)

## BURGESS, SANDY
**Sandy Burgess**, 533 Waterside, Chesham, **Buckinghamshire**, HP5 1QG, ENG.
(T) 01494 772898
Speciality: Chiropodists (Podiatrists).
● **Owner** Mrs S Burgess
S (Ref:HM03382)

## BURGIS, TESSA
**Tessa Burgis**, 4 North Rd, Hythe, **Kent**, CT21 5UH, ENG.
(T) 01303 268736
Speciality: Reflexology.
S T (Ref:HM03383)

## BURKE, ANDREW
**Andrew Burke**, 90 Whalley Rd, Manchester, **Manchester (Greater)**, M16 8AZ, ENG.
(T) 01612 265417
Speciality: Hypnotherapy.
● **Owner** Mr A Burke
B (Ref:HM03384)

## BURKE, E
**E Burke**, Little Greenfields Farm, Jack Haye Lane, Light Oaks, Stoke-On-Trent, **Staffordshire**, ST2 7NG, ENG.
(T) 01782 304909 (F) 01782 305463
Speciality: Acupuncture, Auto Suggestion, Counselling, Dietician, Hypnosis, Hypnotherapy, Psychotherapy, Stress Therapy, Visualisation Therapy.
● **Hypnotherapist** Mr E Burke M: NCP.
B Yrs. Est.: 25 (Ref:HM03385)


Key continued: Yrs.Est: Years Established Q: Qualifications M: Professional Membership ✔ Indemnity Insurance Accept Credit Cards

### BURKE, EIMEAR
**Eimear Burke**, 8 Havelock Sq, Sandymount, **IRE**.
(T) 01667 7902
Speciality: Psychology.
● **Psychologist** Eimar Burke **Q:** BA, MSc, Reg.Psychol.
**B** (**Ref:**HM03386)

### BURKE, EMER
**Emer Burke Councelling Psycologist MSc Reg Pfycol Afpff**, 8 Havelock Sq, Dublin, **County Dublin**, IRE.
(T) 01667 7902
Speciality: Psychology.
**B** (**Ref:**HM03387)

### BURKE, JAYNE
**Jayne Burke**, 62 Great Rd, Winchcombe, Cheltenham, **Gloucestershire**, GL54 5JT, **ENG**.
(T) 01242 604312
Speciality: Aromatherapy, Crystal Healing, Holistic Healing, Metamorphic Therapy, Reflexology, Spiritual Healing, Laughter and Happiness Therapy, Deep Tissue Massage. ✔
● **Reflexologist** Ms J Burke **M:** LCIC, MTI, RxS, SVA.
**C T** Yrs. Est.: 3 (**Ref:**HM03388)

### BURKE, PAUL E
**Paul E Burke**, 15 Station Rd, Woodhouse, Sheffield, **Yorkshire (South)**, S13 7QH, **ENG**.
(T) 01142 697601
Speciality: Chiropodists (Podiatrists).
● **Owner** Mr P Burke
**S** (**Ref:**HM03389)

### BURKE, SHARON
**Sharon Burke (Mobile)**, 51 Carnation Way, Aylesbury, **Buckinghamshire**, HP21 8TX, **ENG**.
(T) 01296 415717
Speciality: Complementary Medicines & Therapy.
● **Owner** Mrs S Burke
**C M** (**Ref:**HM03390)

### BURLINSON, RENEE
**Renee Burlinson**, 12 Engine St, Chadderton, Oldham, **Lancashire**, OL9 7JG, **ENG**.
(T) 01613 450255
Speciality: Hypnosis.
**B** (**Ref:**HM03391)

### BURN, I
**I Burn**, 3 High Ridge, Bedlington, **Northumberland**, NE22 6EF, **ENG**.
(T) 01670 823445
Speciality: Osteopathy.
● **Owner** Mr I Burn
**P S T** (**Ref:**HM03392)

### BURN, LOIC (DR)
**Dr Loic Burn**, Hermitage House, Church Trce, Richmond, **Surrey**, TW10 6SE, **ENG**.
(T) 020 8940 0164
Speciality: Acupuncture.
**O** (**Ref:**HM03393)

### BURNE, JANET
**Janet Burne**, 38 Widgeon Cl, Gosport, **Hampshire**, PO12 4JG, **ENG**.
(T) 023 9234 5951
Speciality: Reflexology.
**S T** (**Ref:**HM03394)

### BURNELL, SUE
**Sue Burnell**, Horthorne Cottage, The Downs, Bromyard, Hereford, **Herefordshire**, HR7 4NX, **ENG**.
(T) 01885 482834
Speciality: Bach Remedies.
**M** (**Ref:**HM03395)

### BURNES, DAVID T
**David T Burnes**, 373 Wellington Rd North, Stockport, **Cheshire**, SK4 5AQ, **ENG**.
(T) 01614 323792
Speciality: Hypnosis.
● **Owner** Mr D Burnes
**B** (**Ref:**HM03396)

### BURNETT, A
**A Burnett**, 5 Thunderton Pl, Elgin, **Moray**, IV30 1BH, **SCO**.
(T) 01343 549177
Speciality: Chiropodists (Podiatrists).
**S** (**Ref:**HM03397)

### BURNETT, AILEEN
**Aileen Burnett**, 40 High St, Fochabers, **Moray**, IV32 7DU, **SCO**.
(T) 01343 820467
Speciality: Chiropodists (Podiatrists).
● **Owner** Mrs A Burnett
**S** (**Ref:**HM03398)

### BURNETT, BOB
**Bob Burnett**, 44 Preston Rd, Southport, **Merseyside**, PR9 9EE, **ENG**.
(T) 01704 549308
Speciality: Physiotherapy.
● **Owner** Mr B Burnett
**P S T** (**Ref:**HM03399)

### BURNETT, JAMES P
**James P Burnett**, 394 Rayners Lane, Pinner, **London (Greater)**, HA5 5DX, **ENG**.
(T) 020 8429 1808
Speciality: Chiropodists (Podiatrists).
**S** (**Ref:**HM03400)

### BURNETT, KIM
**Mrs Kim Burnett**, The Natural Health Centre, 33 Pound St, Newbury, **Berkshire**, RG14 6AE, **ENG**.
(T) 01635 580200
Speciality: Osteopathy.
**P S T** (**Ref:**HM03401)

### BURNETT, KIM
**Kim Burnett**, Beech Cottage, Aldbourne, Marlborough, **Wiltshire**, SN8 2EJ, **ENG**.
(T) 01672 541198 (F) 01672 541203
Speciality: Osteopathy.
● **Owner** Mrs K Burnett
**P S T** (**Ref:**HM03402)

### BURNETT, PAUL
**Paul Burnett**, Natural Therapies, 9 North Rd, West Wickham, **Kent**, BR4 0JS, **ENG**.
(T) 020 8776 2536
Speciality: Homeopathy.
● **Owner** Mr P Burnett
**M** (**Ref:**HM03403)

### BURNHAM CHIROPRACTIC CLINIC
**Helen Tweedale**, 1 Lincoln Hatch Lane, Burnham, Slough, **Berkshire**, SL1 7HA, **ENG**.
(T) 01628 669117
Speciality: Chiropractic. ✔
● **Chiropractor** Mr P Chambers **Q:** DC.
● **Chiropractor** Mr M Storr **Q:** DC.
**P** Yrs. Est.: 6 (**Ref:**HM03404)

### BURNHAM PHYSIOTHERAPY CLINIC
**Burnham Physiotherapy Clinic**, 50 High St, Burnham-on-Crouch, **Essex**, CM0 8AA, **ENG**.
(T) 01621 782194
Speciality: Physiotherapy. ✔
● **Physiotherapist** Ms B Houlding **Q:** Grad Dip Phys, MCSP, SRP. **M:** CSP.
● **Physiotherapist** Ms M Bell **Q:** MCSP, SRP. **M:** CSP.
**P S T** Yrs. Est.: 15 (**Ref:**HM03405)

### BURNHAM, EMMA-JANE
**Emma-Jane Burnham**, 73 Harrow Drive, Hornchurch, **Essex**, RM11 1NT, **ENG**.
(T) 01708 473070
Speciality: Reflexology.
**S T** (**Ref:**HM03406)

### BURNING DESIRE
**Burning Desire Ltd**, 251 Farm Hill, Exeter, **Devon**, EX4 2NW, **ENG**.
(T) 01392 411717
Speciality: Aromatherapy.
● **Managing Director** Mr S Jordan
**M O** (**Ref:**HM03407)

### BURNLEY CLINIC OF OSTEOPATHY
**Burnley Clinic Of Osteopathy**, 257 Rossendale Rd, Burnley, **Lancashire**, BB11 5BZ, **ENG**.
(T) 01282 831811
Speciality: Osteopathy.
● **Owner** Mr V Seal
**P S T** (**Ref:**HM03408)

### BURNS VOYLE PARTNERSHIP
**Burns Voyle Partnership**, 80 Dew St, Haverfordwest, **Pembrokeshire**, SA61 1NR, **WAL**.
(T) 01437 762899
Speciality: Physiotherapy.
● **Partner** Mrs J Voyle
**P S T** (**Ref:**HM03409)

### BURNS, ALAN STEWART
**Alan Stewart Burns**, 65 Main St, Kilwinning, **Ayrshire (North)**, KA13 6AN, **SCO**.
(T) 01294 552230
Speciality: Chiropody, Nail Surgery. ✔
● **Chiropodist** Mr G Burns **Q:** M.S.C.P. **M:** S.C.P.
● **Chiropodist** Mr A Burns **Q:** L.V.Ch.C. **M:** S.C.P.
**M** Yrs. Est.: 14 (**Ref:**HM03410)

### BURNS, ALEX
**Alex Burns**, Flat 26, 119 Haverstock Hill, London, **London (Greater)**, NW3 4RS, **ENG**.
(T) 020 7586 7076
Speciality: Psychotherapy.
● **Owner** Alex Burns
**B** (**Ref:**HM03411)

### BURNS, E M
**E M Burns**, Downs View, Westcott Rd, Dorking, **Surrey**, RH4 3DP, **ENG**.
(T) 01306 889077
Speciality: Chiropodists (Podiatrists).
● **Owner** Mrs E Burns
**S** (**Ref:**HM03412)

### BURNS, J G
**J G Burns**, Hebrides, Station Rd, Rustington, Littlehampton, **Sussex (West)**, BN16 3BH, **ENG**.
(T) 01903 859500 (F) 01903 859500
Speciality: Chiropodists (Podiatrists).
● **Owner** Mrs L Burns
**S** (**Ref:**HM03413)

### BURNS, JOLANDA
**Jolanda Burns**, 56 The Highway, Stanmore, **London (Greater)**, HA7 3PN, **ENG**.
(T) 020 8954 3619 (F) 020 8954 3619
Speciality: Homeopathy.
● **Owner** Mr P Burns
**M** (**Ref:**HM03414)

### BURNS, JON
**Jon Burns**, 197 Wolverhampton Rd West, Wolverhampton, **Midlands (West)**, WV6 0RW, **ENG**.
(T) 01902 746789
Speciality: Clairvoyants & Palmists.
**B** (**Ref:**HM03415)

### BURNS, K P
**K P Burns**, York Chiropractic Clinic, 312 Stockton Lane, **Yorkshire (North)**, YO3 0JW, **ENG**.
(T) 01904 430300
Speciality: Chiropractic.
**P S T** (**Ref:**HM03416)

### BURNS, L C
**L C Burns**, Hebrides, Station Rd, Rustington, Littlehampton, **Sussex (West)**, BN16 3BH, **ENG**.
(T) 01903 859500 (F) 01903 859500
Speciality: Physiotherapy. ✔
● **Owner** Mrs L Burns **Q:** MCSP, SRP.
**S** Yrs. Est.: 10 (**Ref:**HM03417)

### BURNS, M J
**M J Burns**, 16A Lower Sloane St, London, **London (Greater)**, SW1W 8BJ, **ENG**.
(T) 020 7823 4941
Speciality: Chiropodists (Podiatrists).
● **Owner** Mr M Burns
**S** (**Ref:**HM03418)

### BURNS, MICHAEL & ASSOCIATES
**Michael Burns & Associates**, 82-86 Sheen Rd, Richmond, **Surrey**, TW9 1UF, **ENG**.
(T) 020 8948 8439
Speciality: Chiropodists (Podiatrists).
● **Senior Partner** Mr M Burns
**S** (**Ref:**HM03419)

### BURNS, RICHARD
**Richard Burns**, 2 Piper Cl, Loughborough, **Leicestershire**, LE11 3LG, **ENG**.
(T) 01509 269929
Speciality: Chiropodists (Podiatrists).
● **Owner** Mr R Burns

Key: **B** Mind-Body Medicine **C** Complementary Medicine **H** Self Help Treatment **M** Medicinal Therapy **O** Oriental Medicine **P** Postural Therapy **S** Manipulative Structural Therapy **T** Touch Therapy

S (Ref:HM03420)

**BURRIDGE, C**
**C Burridge**, Laurel Farm, Station Rd, Pulham St. Mary, Diss, **Norfolk**, IP21 4QS, ENG.
(T) 01379 676221
Speciality: Reflexology.
S T (Ref:HM03421)

**BURROWS, A**
**A Burrows**, 37 Bellevue Cres, Bristol, BS8 4TF, ENG.
(T) 01179 872989
Speciality: Alexander Technique.
● **Owner** A Burrows
P S (Ref:HM03422)

**BURROWS, BARBARA**
**Barbara Burrows**, 39 Is-Y-Llan, Llanddarog, Carmarthen, **Carmarthenshire**, SA32 8NX, WAL.
(T) 01267 275653
Speciality: Complementary Medicines & Therapy.
● **Owner** Mrs B Burrows
C M (Ref:HM03423)

**BURROWS, MARY**
**Mary Burrows**, Lynchens Cottage, High St, Bembridge, **Isle of Wight**, PO35 5SF, ENG.
(T) 01983 873917
Speciality: Chiropody. ✔
● **Owner/Chiropodist** Mrs M Burrows Q: MBChA.
C Yrs. Est.: 14 (Ref:HM03424)

**BURSCOUGH PHYSIOTHERAPY**
**Burscough Physiotherapy**, 51 Liverpool Rd South, Burscough, Ormskirk, **Lancashire**, L40 7SU, ENG.
(T) 01704 896107 (F) 01704 896107
Speciality: Manipulation, Pattern Therapies, Neuro-Rehabilitation.
● **Owner** Ms A Wade Q: MCSP, SRP. M: CSP.
S Yrs. Est.: 12 (Ref:HM03425)

**BURT, JANE**
**Jane Burt**, 4 Friars Walk, Exeter, **Devon**, EX2 4AY, ENG.
(T) 01392 434922
Speciality: Chiropodists (Podiatrists).
S (Ref:HM03426)

**BURT, JOHN**
**John Burt**, 49B Peach St, Wokingham, **Berkshire**, RG40 1XP, ENG.
(T) 01189 770800
Speciality: Hypnosis.
B (Ref:HM03427)

**BURT, P**
**P Burt**, 40 Grange Rd, Felixstowe, **Suffolk**, IP11 2JR, ENG.
(T) 01394 285450
Speciality: Chiropodists (Podiatrists).
● **Owner** Mr P Burt
S (Ref:HM03428)

**BURT, S**
**S Burt**, Carefree Cottage, Furzebrook Rd, Wareham, **Dorset**, BH20 5AR, ENG.
(T) 01929 551701
(E) sarahbur@natmed.fsnet.co.uk
Speciality: Bach Remedies, Complementary Therapy, Counselling, Floral Essence Therapy, Herbal Medicine, Holistic Healing, Homeopathy, Iridology, Life Style Coaching, Naturopathy, Nutritional Therapy, Vitamin Therapy. ✔
● **Naturopath** Ms S Burt Q: Dip.Hom, Dip.Nutrition, ND. M: GCRN.
M Yrs. Est.: 2 (Ref:HM03429)

**BURT, VALERIE**
**Valerie Burt**, 44 Bent Lane, Leyland, Preston, **Lancashire**, PR5 2HQ, ENG.
(T) 01772 497135
Speciality: Reflexology.
● **Owner** Mrs V Burt
S T (Ref:HM03430)

**BURTON & KERR**
**Burton & Kerr**, 107 St Marys Rd, Faversham, **Kent**, ME13 8EG, ENG.
(T) 01795 591232
Speciality: Chiropodists (Podiatrists).
● **Partner** Mrs B Burton
S (Ref:HM03431)

**BURTON CHIROPRACTIC CLINIC**
**Burton Chiropractic Clinic**, 41 New St, Burton-On-Trent, **Staffordshire**, DE14 3QW, ENG.
(T) 01283 539090 (F) 01283 539191
Speciality: Chiropractic.
● **Owner** Mr P Hicks
P S T (Ref:HM03432)

**BURTON, F J**
**F J Burton**, Pinks Cottage, London Rd, Fairford, **Gloucestershire**, GL7 4AR, ENG.
(T) 01285 711246 (F) 01285 711246
Speciality: Psychology.
● **Owner** Mrs F Burton
B (Ref:HM03433)

**BURTON, GAYLE**
**Gayle Burton**, 20 Craigrigg Cottages, Westfield, Bathgate, **Lothian (West)**, EH48 3DH, SCO.
(T) 01501 733721
Speciality: Complementary Medicines & Therapy.
M (Ref:HM03434)

**BURTON, GEOFFREY**
**Geoffrey Burton**, 13 Station Rd, Thames Ditton, **Surrey**, KT7 0NU, ENG.
(T) 020 8224 9554 (F) 020 8224 9554
Speciality: Hypnosis.
● **Owner** Mr G Burton
B (Ref:HM03435)

**BURTON, J S**
**J S Burton**, Aston Heath House, Sheppenhall Gr, Aston, Nantwich, **Cheshire**, CW5 8DF, ENG.
(T) 01270 780638
Speciality: Biomechanics, Chiropody, Nail Surgery, Orthotics. ✔
● **Chiropodist** Ms J Burton Q: BSc, MBChA, MSSCh. M: B.A.Ch.P.
M Yrs. Est.: 12 (Ref:HM03436)

**BURTON, JENIFER**
**Jenifer Burton**, Pershore, Worcester, **Worcestershire**, WR10, ENG.
(T) 01386 553440
Speciality: Bach Remedies.
M (Ref:HM03437)

**BURTON, JOAN**
**Joan Burton**, Physio & Hyrdrotherpay Clinic, Southgate, Ripon, **Yorkshire (North)**, HG4 1PG, ENG.
(T) 01765 604700
Speciality: Physiotherapy.
● **Owner** Mrs J Burton
P S T (Ref:HM03438)

**BURTON, KIM**
**Kim Burton**, 36 Newboundmill Lane, Pleasley, Mansfield, **Nottinghamshire**, NG19 7PT, ENG.
(T) 01623 810587
Speciality: Chiropodists (Podiatrists).
S (Ref:HM03439)

**BURTON, LESLEY**
**Lesley Burton**, 10 Gledhow Park Cres, Leeds, **Yorkshire (West)**, LS7 4JY, ENG.
(T) 01132 629718
Speciality: Homeopathy.
● **Owner** Mrs L Burton
M (Ref:HM03440)

**BURTON, M**
**Miss M Burton**, 212 Oldham Rd, Ashton-under-Lyne, **Manchester (Greater)**, OL7 9AW, ENG.
(T) 01613 397732
Speciality: Chiropodists (Podiatrists).
S (Ref:HM03441)

**BURTON, M**
**M Burton**, 5 Westfield Rd, Dumfries, **Dumfries and Galloway**, DG1 4AA, SCO.
(T) 01387 266285
Speciality: Chiropodists (Podiatrists).
S (Ref:HM03442)

**BURTON, MAUREEN**
**Maureen Burton**, 37 Norborough Rd, Doncaster, **Yorkshire (South)**, DN2 4AT, ENG.
(T) 01302 349450
Speciality: Psychotherapy.
● **Owner** Mrs M Burton
B (Ref:HM03443)

**BURTON, MERILYNN**
**Merilynn Burton**, 24 East Court, Goldington Green, Bedford, **Bedfordshire**, MK41 0AH, ENG.
(T) 01234 271345
Speciality: Aromatherapy, Chiropody, Massage (Therapeutic), Podiatry, Foot Massage. ✔
● **Chiropodist** Ms M Burton Q: MBChA, MSSCh, RN. M: B.A.Ch.P, SSCh.
S Yrs. Est.: 4 (Ref:HM03444)

**BURTON, S J**
**S J Burton**, Flat 71 Lawrence Moorings, Sheering Mill Lane, Sawbridgeworth, **Hertfordshire**, CM21 9PE, ENG.
(T) 01279 725382
Speciality: Complementary Medicines & Therapy.
C M (Ref:HM03445)

**BURTON, VICKI**
**Vicki Burton**, Kennox House, Kilwinning Rd, Stewarton, Kilmarnock, **Ayrshire (East)**, KA3 3EF, SCO.
(T) 01294 850285
Speciality: Reflexology.
● **Owner** Ms V Burton
S T (Ref:HM03446)

**BURTON, VICKY**
**Vicky Burton**, Erkinholm, Drove Rd, Langholm, **Dumfries and Galloway**, DG13 0JW, SCO.
(T) 01387 381770 (F) 01387 381770
Speciality: Reflexology, Reiki. ✔
● **Reflexologist** Ms V Burton Q: GSSR. M: SIR.
M Yrs. Est.: 5 (Ref:HM03447)

**BURVILL, J A**
**Mr & Mrs J A Burvill**, 32 Chapel St, Billericay, **Essex**, CM12 9LU, ENG.
(T) 01277 659110
Speciality: Chiropodists (Podiatrists).
● **Owner** Mr N Burvill
S (Ref:HM03448)

**BURY NATURAL HEALTH CENTRE**
**Bury Natural Health Centre**, The Barn, Bury St Edmunds Golf Club, Tut Hill, Fornham All Saints, Bury St. Edmunds, **Suffolk**, IP28 6LG, ENG.
(T) 01284 760020
Speciality: Complementary Medicines & Therapy.
● **Therapist** Mrs A Baeppler
M (Ref:HM03449)

**BURY PHYSIO & SPORTS CLINIC**
**Bury Physiotherapy & Sports Clinic (The)**, 75 Guildhall St, Bury St. Edmunds, **Suffolk**, IP33 1QD, ENG.
(T) 01284 703794 (F) 01284 765170
Speciality: Physiotherapy.
● **Chief Executive** Mrs N Hunter
P S T (Ref:HM03450)

**BURY PRACTICE**
**Bury Practice For Counselling & Psychotherapy (The)**, 64 Southgate St, Bury St. Edmunds, **Suffolk**, IP33 2BJ, ENG.
(T) 01284 705772
Speciality: Psychotherapy.
B (Ref:HM03451)

**BURY ST EDMUNDS PHYSIO CLINIC**
**Bury St Edmunds Physiotherapy Clinic**, Maynewater Lane, Bury St. Edmunds, **Suffolk**, IP33 2AB, ENG.
(T) 01284 748200 (F) 01284 748201
Speciality: Physiotherapy.
● **General Manager** Mr A Hunter
P S T (Ref:HM03452)

**BURY, CHRIS**
**Chris Bury**, 100 High St, Crediton, **Devon**, EX17 3LF, ENG.
(T) 01363 774175
Speciality: Osteopathy.
P S T (Ref:HM03453)

**BURY, CHRIS**
**Chris Bury**, Argyle House, New Buildings Lane,


Key continued: Yrs.Est: Years Established Q: Qualifications M: Professional Membership ✔ Indemnity Insurance Accept Credit Cards

Gandy St, Exeter, **Devon**, EX4 3LS, ENG.
(T) 01392 213899
Speciality: Osteopathy.
P S T (Ref:HM03454)

**BURY, D R**
**D R Bury**, 47 Mayfield Rd, London, **London (Greater)**, N8 9LL, ENG.
(T) 020 8348 9181
Speciality: Psychotherapy.
B (Ref:HM03455)

**BURYHILL PHYSIOTHERAPY**
**Buryhill Physiotherapy**, 33 Bancroft, Hitchin, **Hertfordshire**, SG5 1LA, ENG.
(T) 01462 438853
(W) www.buryhillphysio.co.uk
Speciality: Acupuncture, Manipulation, Physiotherapy.
● **Physiotherapist** Mr A Cockhill Q: MCSP, SRP.
S Yrs. Est.: 3 (Ref:HM03456)

**BUSH & MEADOWS**
**Bush & Meadows**, 60 East St Chambers, Taunton, **Somerset**, TA1 3LX, ENG.
(T) 01823 278996
Speciality: Chiropodists (Podiatrists).
S (Ref:HM03457)

**BUSH HILL PK SPIRITUAL HEALING**
**Bush Hill Park Spiritual Healing Centre**, 1a Ladbroke Rd, Enfield, **London (Greater)**, EN1 1HY, ENG.
(T) 020 8367 1166
Speciality: Complementary Medicines & Therapy.
● **Owner** Mr D Brooks
C M (Ref:HM03458)

**BUSH HOUSE OSTEO PRACTICE**
**Bush House Osteopathic Practice**, Bush House, Upper Redbrook, Monmouth, **Monmouthshire**, NP25 4LU, WAL.
(T) 01600 772166 (F) 01600 772251
Speciality: Osteopathy.
● **Partner** Ms C Kramer
P S T (Ref:HM03459)

**BUSH, ANTONY J**
**Antony J Bush**, Croft End, Neston Rd, Willaston, Neston, **Cheshire**, CH64 2TG, ENG.
(T) 01513 276757
Speciality: Osteopathy.
● **Owner** Mr A Bush
P S T (Ref:HM03460)

**BUSH, RON**
**Ron Bush**, 7 Willow Avenue, Broadstairs, **Kent**, CT10 2LP, ENG.
(T) 01843 869948
Speciality: Reflexology.
S T (Ref:HM03461)

**BUSHEY HEATH PHYSIO CLINIC**
**Bushey Heath Physiotherapy Clinic**, Belle Vue Lane, Bushey Heath, Watford, **Hertfordshire**, WD2 3TL, ENG.
(T) 020 8950 4644 (F) 020 8421 8662
Speciality: Physiotherapy.
● **Owner** Mrs S Letheren
P S T (Ref:HM03462)

**BUSHEY HYPNOTHERAPY CENTRE**
**Bushey Hypnotherapy Centre**, 46 Belmont Rd, Bushey, Watford, **Hertfordshire**, WD2 2JP, ENG.
(T) 01923 223739
Speciality: Hypnosis.
● **Principal** Mr I McIntosh
B (Ref:HM03463)

**BUSHEY PRACTICE**
**Bushey Practice**, County End, Magpie Hall Rd, Bushey Heath, Watford, **Hertfordshire**, WD2 1NY, ENG.
(T) 020 8950 9992 (F) 020 8905 4463
Speciality: Osteopathy.
● **Owner** Mrs S King
P S T (Ref:HM03464)

**BUSINESS PSYCHOLOGY**
**Business Psychology**, 2 Jocelyn Pl, Dundalk, **County Louth**, IRE.
(T) 04293 51800
Speciality: Psychology.
B (Ref:HM03465)

**BUSINESS PSYCHOLOGY WALES**
**Business Psychology Wales Ltd**, 16 Cowbridge Rd, Pontyclun, **Rhondda Cynon Taff**, CF72 9ED, WAL.
(T) 01443 230555 (F) 01443 230666
Speciality: Psychology.
● **Managing Director** Mrs K Collier
B (Ref:HM03466)

**BUSINESS PSYCHOL-WEST ASS**
**Business Psychologists-West Associates**, 11 Berkeley St, London, **London (Greater)**, W1X 6BU, ENG.
(T) 020 7355 5051
Speciality: Psychology.
B (Ref:HM03467)

**BUSOLINI, DON**
**Don Busolini**, 45 Valley Rd, Welwyn Garden City, **Hertfordshire**, AL8 7DH, ENG.
(T) 01707 330557
Speciality: Hypnosis.
● **Owner** Mr D Busolini
B (Ref:HM03468)

**BUSSUNT, M**
**M Bussunt**, 2 St Pauls Rd, Shipley, **Yorkshire (West)**, BD18 3EP, ENG.
(T) 01274 530580
Speciality: Hypnosis.
B (Ref:HM03469)

**BUSWELL, PRISILLA J**
**Prisilla J Buswell**, 33 Carlton Green, Redhill, **Surrey**, RH1 2DB, ENG.
(T) 01737 762282
Speciality: Osteopathy.
P S T (Ref:HM03470)

**BUSWELL, RONA**
**Mrs Rona Buswell**, Beech Cottage, Beech Lane, Spofforth, Harrogate, **Yorkshire (North)**, HG3 1AN, ENG.
(T) 01937 590297
Speciality: Healer, Reflexology, Remedial Massage.
● **Complementary Therapist** Mrs R Buswell Q: MBPA. M: BRA, COH.
C Yrs. Est.: 12 (Ref:HM03471)

**BUSY BODIES**
**Busy Bodies**, 33 Market Hall, Aldridge, Walsall, **Midlands (West)**, WS9 8QS, ENG.
(T) 01922 456772
Speciality: Aromatherapy.
● **Owner** Mrs P Luff
M O (Ref:HM03472)

**BUTCHER, GERARD**
**Gerard Butcher**, 69 Lr Baggot St, Dublin, **County Dublin**, IRE.
(T) 01662 5148
Speciality: Psychology.
B (Ref:HM03473)

**BUTCHER, P O**
**P O Butcher**, 49 Amherst Rd, Bexhill-on-Sea, **Sussex (East)**, TN40 1QN, ENG.
(T) 01424 224164
Speciality: Physiotherapy.
● **Owner** Mr P Butcher
P S T (Ref:HM03474)

**BUTCHER, PETER**
**Peter Butcher**, Centr For Whole Health, 12 Victoria Pl, Bristol, BS3 3BP, ENG.
(T) 01179 231138
Speciality: Acupuncture.
O (Ref:HM03475)

**BUTCHER, PETER**
**Peter Butcher**, Newport Clinic Of Holistic Health, 36 Godfrey Rd, Newport, NP20 4PE, WAL.
(T) 01633 843333
Speciality: Complementary Medicines & Therapy.
● **Owner** Mr J Francis
M (Ref:HM03476)

**BUTEYKO**
**Buteyko**, Feargal Tobin Terenure, Dublin, **County Dublin**, IRE.
(T) 01465 0030
(W) www.buteykoireland.com
Speciality: Complementary Medicines & Therapy.
M (Ref:HM03477)

**BUTEYKO**
**Buteyko**, 6 Barons Court, Sanquhar, **Dumfries and Galloway**, DG4 6EB, SCO.
(T) 01659 50628
Speciality: Complementary Medicines & Therapy, Butkeyko.
M (Ref:HM03478)

**BUTEYKO BREATHING CENTRE**
**Buteyko Breathing Centre**, 70 Winchester Rd, Blaby, Leicester, **Leicestershire**, LE8 4HJ, ENG.
(T) 01162 772051 (F) 01162 778311
Speciality: Complementary Medicines & Therapy.
● **Owner** Mr D Brooks
C M (Ref:HM03479)

**BUTEYKO BREATHING CLINIC**
**Buteyko Breathing Clinic**, Willow Cottage, Brook Lane, Doddinghurst, Brentwood, **Essex**, CM15 0RT, ENG.
(T) 01277 823973
Speciality: Complementary Medicines & Therapy.
● **Partner** Mr A Brinderly
M (Ref:HM03480)

**BUTHE, PETER**
**Peter Buthe**, Natural Health Clinic, 98 Cathedral Rd, Cardiff, **Glamorgan (Vale of)**, CF11 9LP, WAL.
(T) 029 2022 2221
Speciality: Complementary Medicines & Therapy.
● **Practice Manager** Mrs L Powell
M (Ref:HM03481)

**BUTLER & ASSOCIATES**
**Gareth C Butler & Associates**, 83 Old Woking Rd, West Byfleet, **Surrey**, KT14 6JA, ENG.
(T) 01932 345287
Speciality: Osteopathy.
P S T (Ref:HM03482)

**BUTLER, A**
**A Butler**, 17 John St, Helensburgh, **Argyll and Bute**, G84 8BA, SCO.
(T) 01436 672230
Speciality: Chiropodists (Podiatrists).
● **Owner** Miss A Butler
S (Ref:HM03483)

**BUTLER, CHERYL**
**Cheryl Butler**, 7 Solway Avenue, Patcham, Brighton, **Sussex (East)**, BN1 8UJ, ENG.
(T) 01273 708307
Speciality: Reflexology.
S T (Ref:HM03484)

**BUTLER, D A**
**D A Butler**, 6 Prospect Arc, Off Prospect St, Bridlington, **Humberside (North)**, YO15 2RR, ENG.
(T) 01262 674116
Speciality: Chiropractic.
P S T (Ref:HM03485)

**BUTLER, ELVERA**
**Elvera Butler M A DIP HYP M Prac**, 77 Haddington Rd, Dublin, **County Dublin**, IRE.
(T) 01660 1578
Speciality: Complementary Medicines & Therapy.
M (Ref:HM03486)

**BUTLER, J H C**
**J H C Butler**, High Standings, Rye Rd, Sandhurst, Cranbrook, **Kent**, TN18 5PJ, ENG.
(T) 01580 850666
Speciality: Physiotherapy.
● **Owner** Mrs J Butler
P S T (Ref:HM03487)

**BUTLER, KAREN**
**Karen Butler**, Beaver Lodge, St Michaels Cl, Stourport-on-Severn, **Worcestershire**, DY13 8EQ, ENG.
(T) 01299 879052
Speciality: Chiropodists (Podiatrists).



Key: B Mind-Body Medicine; C Complementary Medicine; H Self Help Treatment; M Medicinal Therapy; O Oriental Medicine; P Postural Therapy; S Manipulative Structural Therapy; T Touch Therapy

● **Professor** Mrs K Butler
S (**Ref:**HM03488)

## BUTLER, LAWRENCE

**Lawrence Butler**, 97 College Rd, Epsom, **Surrey**, KT17 4HY, ENG.
(T) 01372 726080
Speciality: Osteopathy.
● **Senior Partner** Mr B Hounsfield
P S T (**Ref:**HM03489)

## BUTLER, M

**M Butler**, 31 Burnaby Rd, Coventry, **Midlands (West)**, CV6 4BE, ENG.
(T) 024 7663 7197
Speciality: Clairvoyants & Palmists.
● **Owner** Miss M Butler
B (**Ref:**HM03490)

## BUTLER, RAYMOND

**Raymond Butler**, 32 Ormerod Avenue, St. Leonards-On-Sea, **Sussex (East)**, TN38 9LN, ENG.
(T) 01424 852431
Speciality: Chiropodists (Podiatrists).
S (**Ref:**HM03491)

## BUTLER, SUZANNE

**Suzanne Butler**, 23 Church View, Walkhampton, Yelverton, **Devon**, PL20 6JS, ENG.
(T) 01822 854439
Speciality: Chiropodists (Podiatrists).
● **Owner** Mrs S Butler
S (**Ref:**HM03492)

## BUTSON, JUDITH

**Judith Butson**, 26 Castle View, Colyton, **Devon**, EX13 6DN, ENG.
(T) 01297 552985
Speciality: Reflexology.
S T (**Ref:**HM03493)

## BUTT, M

**M Butt**, 69 West Green Rd, London, **London (Greater)**, N15 5DA, ENG.
(T) 020 8800 8414
Speciality: Chiropodists (Podiatrists).
S (**Ref:**HM03494)

## BUTTERBUR & SAGE

**Butterbur & Sage Ltd**, 7 Tessa Rd, Reading, **Berkshire**, RG1 8HH, ENG.
(T) 01189 505100 (F) 01189 576300
Speciality: Aromatherapy.
● **Managing Director** Mr S Sandhu
M O (**Ref:**HM03495)

## BUTTERFIELD, ROBIN

**Robin Butterfield**, 95 Western Rd, Tring, **Hertfordshire**, HP23 4BN, ENG.
(T) 01442 890111 (F) 01442 890734
(W) www.healingmassage.co.uk
Speciality: Complementary Therapy, Cranial Osteopathy, Dowsing, Healing Therapy, Holistic Healing, Indian Head Massage, Kinesiology, Manipulation, Manual Lymph Drainage, Massage (Therapeutic), Naturopathy, Osteomyology, Osteopathy, Psychotherapy, Stress Therapy, Tantra Therapy. ✔
● **Owner** Mr R Butterfield Q: APNT, DO, MAO, ND, RN. M: DOC.
S Yrs. Est.: 15 (**Ref:**HM03496)

## BUTTERFIELD, SUSAN A

**Susan A Butterfield**, Squirrel Lane, High Wycombe, **Buckinghamshire**, HP12 4RS, ENG.
(T) 01494 451124
Speciality: Chiropodists (Podiatrists).
S (**Ref:**HM03497)

## BUTTERFILL, M T

**M T Butterfill**, 14 Winter Drive, Hawkinge, Folkestone, **Kent**, CT18 7QX, ENG.
(T) 01303 892732
Speciality: Reflexology.
S T (**Ref:**HM03498)

## BUTTERWORTH, MARK

**Mark Butterworth**, 14 Holyoake Rd, Headington, Oxford, **Oxfordshire**, OX3 8AE, ENG.
(T) 01865 761802
Speciality: Chiropractors.
P S T (**Ref:**HM03499)

## BUTTREY, BEATRICE M

**Beatrice M Buttrey**, 99 High St, Hoddesdon, **Hertfordshire**, EN11 8TN, ENG.
(T) 01992 463958
Speciality: Chiropodists (Podiatrists).
S (**Ref:**HM03500)

## BUTTRUMS MILL

**Buttrums Mill**, Burkitt Rd, Woodbridge, **Suffolk**, IP12 4JH, ENG.
(T) 01394 388863
Speciality: Complementary Medicines & Therapy.
C M (**Ref:**HM03501)

## BUXTED OSTEOPATHIC PRACTICE

**Buxted Osteopathic Practice**, Chesworth House, Pound Green, Buxted, Uckfield, **Sussex (East)**, TN22 4JW, ENG.
(T) 01825 733766
Speciality: Osteopathy.
P S T (**Ref:**HM03502)

## BUXTON, ANNE

**Anne Buxton**, 69 Meadow Gate Avenue, Sothall, Sheffield, **Yorkshire (South)**, S20 2PG, ENG.
(T) 01142 510449
Speciality: Reflexology.
S T (**Ref:**HM03503)

## BUXTON, JOHN

**John Buxton**, 46 Bramhall Lane, Stockport, **Cheshire**, SK2 6HZ, ENG.
(T) 01614 296639
Speciality: Chiropodists (Podiatrists).
● **Owner** Mr J Buxton
S (**Ref:**HM03504)

## BUXTON, PETER

**Peter Buxton**, 44A Gladstone St, Sunderland, **Tyne and Wear**, SR6 0HZ, ENG.
(T) 01915 673230
Speciality: Osteopathy.
P S T (**Ref:**HM03505)

## B-WELL HYPNOTHERAPY CLINIC

**B-Well Hypnotherapy Clinic**, 63 Tynhall Avenue, Kingswood, Tallaght, Dublin, **County Dublin**, IRE.
(T) 01451 5166
(E) bwellclinic@yahoo.co.uk
(W) www.hypnosiseire.com
Speciality: Absent Healing, Acupressure, Aura Therapy, Auto Suggestion, Bio-energetics, Hypnosis, Hypnotherapy, Meditation, Psychotherapy, Reflexology, Reiki, Seichem, Spiritual Healing, Tera-Mai.
● **Hypnotherapist** Mr D O'Neill Q: Dip.Hyp, Dip.Psych, MIAH. M: ICHP.
● **Hypnotherapist** Mrs L O'Neill M: ICHP.
H Yrs. Est.: 6 (**Ref:**HM03506)

## BWT PHYSIOTHERAPY CENTRE

**BWT Physiotherapy Centre**, 2 Clarendon Rd, Bournemouth, **Dorset**, BH4 8AH, ENG.
(T) 01202 768638 (F) 01202 751038
Speciality: Physiotherapy.
P S T (**Ref:**HM03507)

## BWT PODIATRY

**BWT Physiotherapists**, 41 Church Rd, Parkstone, Poole, **Dorset**, BH14 0NN, ENG.
(T) 01202 739059
Speciality: Biomechanics, Gait Analysis, Nail Surgery, Podiatry.
● **Podiatrist** Mrs J Hadlow Q: DPodM, M.S.C.P, S.R.Ch, SRPod. M: CPM.
M Yrs. Est.: 10 (**Ref:**HM03508)

## BYATT, J M

**Mrs J M Byatt**, 13 South View Cl, Bexley, **Kent**, DA5 1EG, ENG.
(T) 01322 527073
Speciality: Chiropodists (Podiatrists).
S (**Ref:**HM03509)

## BYERS, PAULINE

**Pauline Byers**, Clavendine, The Chase, Foxearth, Sudbury, **Suffolk**, CO10 7LD, ENG.
(T) 01787 377111
Speciality: Reflexology.
S T (**Ref:**HM03510)

## BYFLEET, ROSEMARY

**Rosemary Byfleet**, North House, St. Marys St, Brecon, **Powys**, LD3 7AA, WAL.
(T) 01874 625506
Speciality: Chiropody.
● **Owner** Mrs R Byfleet
S (**Ref:**HM03511)

## BYNG, MELANIE

**Melanie Byng**, 2a Eliot Park, London, **London (Greater)**, SE13 7EG, ENG.
(T) 020 8318 1150
Speciality: Alexander Technique.
● **Owner** Mrs M Byng
P S (**Ref:**HM03512)

## BYRNE ASSUMPTA

**Byrne Assumpta**, The Banks Manor Kilbride, **County Wicklow**, IRE.
(T) 01458 2407
Speciality: Complementary Medicines & Therapy.
M (**Ref:**HM03513)

## BYRNE, ALISON

**Alison Byrne**, 33 Tumulus Way, Colchester, **Essex**, CO2 9SD, ENG.
(T) 01206 520017
Speciality: Reflexology.
S T (**Ref:**HM03514)

## BYRNE, ANGELA

**Angela Byrne**, 83 Amberwood Rise, New Malden, **Surrey**, KT3 5JQ, ENG.
(T) 020 8949 4787
Speciality: Reflexology.
S T (**Ref:**HM03515)

## BYRNE, JUDY

**Judy Byrne**, 96 Wellmeadow Rd, London, **London (Greater)**, SE6 1HW, ENG.
(T) 020 8697 3227
Speciality: Cognitive Therapy, Counselling, Hypnosis, Hypnotherapy, Psychotherapy, EMDR-Eye Movement Desensitisation and Reprocessing. ✔
● **Psychotherapist** Mrs J Byrne Q: Adv.Dip.PHTA, BA (Hons), Dip.BHR. M: HS, NCH, NCP.
B Yrs. Est.: 10 (**Ref:**HM03516)

## BYRNE, M

**M Byrne**, 160 Woodwarde Rd, London, **London (Greater)**, SE22 8UR, ENG.
(T) 020 8693 6867
Speciality: Homeopathy.
M (**Ref:**HM03517)

## BYRNE, MARTIN

**Martin Byrne**, James St, Claremorris, **County Mayo**, IRE.
(T) 09462 333
Speciality: Complementary Medicines & Therapy.
M (**Ref:**HM03518)

## BYRNE, STEVE

**Steve Byrne**, Bishopswood, Portarlington, **County Laois**, IRE.
(T) 05024 07961
Speciality: Complementary Medicines & Therapy.
M (**Ref:**HM03519)

## BYWATER, FAYE

**Faye Bywater**, Nancy Doyle Clinic, 27 New Rd, Bromsgrove, **Worcestershire**, B60 2JL, ENG.
(T) 01527 578001
Speciality: Chiropodists (Podiatrists).
S (**Ref:**HM03520)

## C CARTLEDGE REFLEXOLOGY

**Christine Cartledge Reflexology**, 16 Gale, Todmorden Rd, Littleborough, **Manchester (Greater)**, OL15 9ER, ENG.
(T) 01706 373603
(E) reflexology@christinecartledge.co.uk
Speciality: Indian Head Massage, Reflexology. ✔
● **Reflexologist** Ms C Cartledge Q: ART(Reg), MAR. M: AoR.
T Yrs. Est.: 4 (**Ref:**HM03521)



Key continued: **Yrs.Est:** Years Established **Q:** Qualifications **M:** Professional Membership ✔ Indemnity Insurance Accept Credit Cards

## C D THERAPIES
**C D Therapies**, 5 Bethel Avenue, Failsworth, Manchester, **Manchester (Greater)**, M35 0AG, ENG.
(T) 01616 886824
Speciality: Complementary Medicines & Therapy.
C M (Ref:HM03522)

## C F C M
**Centre for Complementary Medicine**, Orchard Paddock, Bugbrooke, Northampton, **Northamptonshire**, NN7 3QR, ENG.
(T) 01604 832256 (F) 01604 832256
Speciality: Acupressure, Acupuncture, Herbal Medicine, Homeopathy, Hypnosis, Hypnotherapy, Manipulation, Moxibustion, Ying & Yang, Orthopaedic Medicine. ✓
● **Practitioner** Dr D Paine Q: Ch.B, Dip.Ac, MB, MFHom, MRCGP. M: BMAS, FHom.
M Yrs. Est.: 5 (Ref:HM03523)

## C H M SWANPOEL
**C H M Swanpoel**, Valley View, Diddies Rd, Stratton, Bude, **Cornwall**, EX23 9DW, ENG.
(T) 01288 352146 (F) 01288 352146
Speciality: Acupuncture.
● **Owner** Mr C Swanpoel
O (Ref:HM03524)

## C I M TEST PUBLISHERS
**C I M Test Publishers**, 23 Dunkeld Rd, Sheffield, **Yorkshire (South)**, S11 9HN, ENG.
(T) 01142 363811
Speciality: Psychology.
B (Ref:HM03525)

## C PHILIP & J FOSTER & A MULA
**Courtney Philip & Jennifer Foster & Ania Mula & Ho**, 15 West St, Carshalton, **Surrey**, SM5 2PT, ENG.
(T) 020 8647 5105
Speciality: Osteopathy.
P S T (Ref:HM03526)

## C R PHYSIOTHERAPY
**C R Physiotherapy**, Allan Park, Stirling, FK8 2QD, SCO.
(T) 01224 890433
Speciality: Physiotherapy.
P S T (Ref:HM03527)

## C TAYLOR BEAUTY THERAPY
**Christine Taylor Beauty Therapy**, 67 Westwater Way, Didcot, **Oxfordshire**, OX11 7RZ, ENG.
(T) 01235 814755
Speciality: Electrolysis.
T (Ref:HM03528)

## CABOURNE CHIROPODY
**Cabourne Chiropody**, Cabourne Av Health Care Complex, Nettleham Rd, Lincoln, **Lincolnshire**, LN2 2JP, ENG.
(T) 01522 530645
Speciality: Chiropodists (Podiatrists).
S (Ref:HM03529)

## CADDEN, D C
**D C Cadden**, Pentre Cottage, Long Compton, Haughton, Stafford, **Staffordshire**, ST18 9JT, ENG.
(T) 01785 824016
Speciality: Hypnosis.
B (Ref:HM03530)

## CADDY, G
**G Caddy**, 63 Tower Hill Rd, Brown Lees, Stoke-On-Trent, **Staffordshire**, ST8 6PA, ENG.
(T) 01782 515541
Speciality: Chiropodists (Podiatrists).
● **Owner** Mrs G Caddy
S (Ref:HM03531)

## CADE, ANNA
**Anna Cade**, 6 Kingston Rd, Oxford, **Oxfordshire**, OX2 6EF, ENG.
(T) 01865 311900
Speciality: Hypnotherapy.
B (Ref:HM03532)

## CADENHEAD, SHEENA
**Sheena Cadenhead**, 66 Berkeley St, Glasgow, **Glasgow (City of)**, G3 7DS, SCO.
(T) 01412 267779 (F) 01412 217838
Speciality: Physiotherapy.
● **Owner** Mrs S Cadenhead
P S T (Ref:HM03533)

## CADGE, A E H
**A E H Cadge**, 76 Arden Rd, Acocks Green, Birmingham, **Midlands (West)**, B27 6AQ, ENG.
(T) 01217 063364
Speciality: Chiropodists (Podiatrists).
● **Owner** Mrs A Cadge
S (Ref:HM03534)

## CADMAN, STEPHEN
**Stephen Cadman**, 52 Rockford Cl, Redditch, **Worcestershire**, B98 7SZ, ENG.
(T) 01527 402521
Speciality: Chiropodists (Podiatrists).
● **Owner** Mr S Cadman
S (Ref:HM03535)

## CADWALLADER, PENNY
**Penny Cadwallader**, 113 High Rd, Loughton, **Essex**, IG10 4HZ, ENG.
(T) 020 8502 1984
Speciality: Osteopathy.
P S T (Ref:HM03536)

## CAHILL, T
**Mrs T Cahill**, 105 Garth Rd, Morden, **Surrey**, SM4 4LF, ENG.
(T) 020 8330 7407
Speciality: Chiropodists (Podiatrists).
S (Ref:HM03537)

## CAIN, SHEILA
**Sheila Cain**, Culver Croft, Margaretting Rd, Writtle, Chelmsford, **Essex**, CM1 3PJ, ENG.
(T) 01245 420957 (F) 01245 420957
(E) scain@callnetuk.com
Speciality: Bach Remedies, Complementary Therapy, Holistic Healing, Indian Head Massage, Reflexology, Bodytalk. ✓
● **Reflexologist** Ms S Cain Q: Dip.Indian Head Massage, Dip.Reflex, PGD.Reflex. M: BSR, GCP.
B C Yrs. Est.: 9 (Ref:HM03538)

## CAIN, SUSAN
**Susan Cain**, 30 Glenridding Drive, Barrow-in-Furness, **Cumbria**, LA14 4PE, ENG.
(T) 01229 831762
Speciality: Reflexology.
S T (Ref:HM03539)

## CAINES, J A
**Mrs J A Caines**, The Old Manse, Scarr, Lydeard St. Lawrence, Taunton, **Somerset**, TA4 3RH, ENG.
(T) 01984 667416
Speciality: Chiropodists (Podiatrists).
S (Ref:HM03540)

## CAIRD, DOUGLAS
**Douglas Caird**, 9 Dean Park Mews, Edinburgh, **Edinburgh (City of)**, EH4 1EE, SCO.
(T) 01316 247173
Speciality: Reflexology.
● **Owner** Mr D Caird
S T (Ref:HM03541)

## CAIRDEAS REMEDIAL
**Cairdeas Remedial And On Site Services Ltd**, Unit 6, Abbeymount Techbase, 2 Easter Rd, Edinburgh, **Edinburgh (City of)**, EH7 5AN, SCO.
(T) 01314 783478 (F) 01314 783444
Speciality: Complementary Medicines & Therapy.
● **Managing Director** Mr D Holmes
C M (Ref:HM03542)

## CAIRNS, GUY
**Guy Cairns**, 26A Fareham Enterprise Centre, Newgate Lane, Fareham, **Hampshire**, PO14 1TH, ENG.
(T) 01329 515111
Speciality: Physiotherapy.
P S T (Ref:HM03543)

## CALCUTT, GILLIAN
**Gillian Calcutt**, 49 Wykeham Pk, Thame, **Oxfordshire**, OX9 3JU, ENG.
(T) 01844 212261
Speciality: Reflexology.
● **Owner** Mrs G Calcutt
S T (Ref:HM03544)

## CALDERBANK, W
**W Calderbank**, 121 London Rd, Preston, **Lancashire**, PR1 4BA, ENG.
(T) 01772 556405
Speciality: Chiropodists (Podiatrists).
● **Owner** Mr W Calderbank
S (Ref:HM03545)

## CALDICOT CHIROPRACTOR CENTRE
**Caldicot Chiropractor Centre**, Newport Rd, Caldicot, **Monmouthshire**, NP26 4HX, WAL.
(T) 01291 425553 (F) 01291 425553
Speciality: Chiropractors.
● **Owner** Dr B Bacon
P S T (Ref:HM03546)

## CALLAGHAN, DENISE
**Denise Callaghan**, 46 High Beeches, Orpington, **Kent**, BR6 6EF, ENG.
(T) 01689 858068
Speciality: Osteopathy.
P S T (Ref:HM03547)

## CALLAGHAN, M M
**M M Callaghan**, Star Yard, Horsemarket, Barnard Castle, **County Durham**, DL12 8LY, ENG.
(T) 01833 637651
Speciality: Chiropody. ✓
● **Chiropodist** Mrs M Callaghan Q: S.R.Ch. M: S.C.P.
M Yrs. Est.: 20 (Ref:HM03548)

## CALLAGHAN, R M & J
**R M & J Callaghan**, 596 Warwick Rd, Solihull, **Midlands (West)**, B91 1AD, ENG.
(T) 01217 051431 (F) 01217 051431
Speciality: Biomechanics, Chiropody, Podiatry.
✓ CREDIT
● **Chiropodist** Mr R Callaghan Q: DPodM, M.S.C.P, S.R.Ch.
● **Chiropodist** Mr J Callaghan Q: DPodM. M: S.R.Ch.
M Yrs. Est.: 10 (Ref:HM03549)

## CALLAN, KAY
**Kay Callan**, 12 Distillery Lane, Dundalk, **County Louth**, IRE.
(T) 04293 31908
Speciality: Complementary Medicines & Therapy.
M (Ref:HM03550)

## CALLANAN NOIRIN HEALER
**Callanan Noirin Healer**, Dublin Naas & Bray Co, **County Wicklow**, IRE.
(T) 01276 0766
Speciality: Healing.
B (Ref:HM03551)

## CALLANAN, NOIRIN
**Noirin Callanan**, 15 Ledwidge Cres, Bray, **County Wicklow**, IRE.
(T) 01276 0766
Speciality: Complementary Medicines & Therapy.
M (Ref:HM03552)

## CALLAWAY, PETER
**Peter Callaway**, 36 Midway, Sutton, **Surrey**, SM3 9EL, ENG.
(T) 020 8641 0179
Speciality: Hypnosis, Emotional Freedom Techniques.
● **Owner** Mr P Callaway
B (Ref:HM03553)

## CALLIE INT CLAIRVOYANT
**Callie International Clairvoyant**, Starley Rd, Coventry, **Midlands (West)**, CV1 3JU, ENG.
(T) 024 7622 5121
Speciality: Clairvoyants & Palmists.
B (Ref:HM03554)

## CALLIS THERAPY FOUNDATION
**Callis Therapy Foundation**, 18 Oxford St, Wellingborough, **Northamptonshire**, NN8 4HY, ENG.
(T) 01933 224454 (F) 01933 224699
Speciality: Alexander Technique, Allergy Testing, Aromatherapy, Bach Remedies, Beauty Therapy, Counselling, Cranio-Sacral Therapy, Crystal Healing, Homeopathy, Hypnotherapy, Kinesiology, Metamorphic Therapy, Nutritional



Key: B Mind-Body Medicine; C Complementary Medicine; H Self Help Treatment; M Medicinal Therapy; O Oriental Medicine; P Postural Therapy; S Manipulative Structural Therapy; T Touch Therapy

Therapy, Reflexology, Remedial Massage, Shiatsu, Physical / Manipulative Therapy, Neuro Muscular Transmission. ✔
● **Allergy Testing** Margaret Oakley
● **Reflexologist** Margaret Patterson **Q:** MAR, MIIR, RCST.
● **Physical/Manipulative Therapy** Jo Brewis
● **Nutritional Therapy** Barbara Swift **Q:** Dip.Nutrition.
● **Metamorphic Technique Practitioner** Nicia Voss **Q:** MA.
● **Hypnotherapist** Laura Lindell
● **Homeopath** Marianne Ryan **Q:** ITEC, LCH.
● **Crystal Therapist** Keith Jayne
● **Crystal Therapist** Judith Jayne **Q:** IIHHT.
● **Aromatherapist** Frankie Boyes
● **Counselling** Charles Callis **Q:** Dip.Couns. **M:** MCA.
● **Allergy Tester** Shusha Walmsley **Q:** MAR, RSHom. **M:** BIAET.
● **Teacher of the Alexander Technique** Elaine Nicolas **M:** STAT.
● **Aromatherapist** Heena Bhojani **Q:** IIHHT. **M:** AoR.
● **Aromatherapist** Linda Callis
● **Aromatherapist** Ms D Richardson
● **Aromatherapist** Jane Ward **Q:** IIHHT.
● **Counselling** Davina Williams **Q:** Dip.Couns.
**C** Yrs. Est.: 2 (**Ref:**HM03555)

## CALLIS, CHARLES

**Charles Callis**, Wellingborough, **Northamptonshire**, NN8, ENG.
**(T)** 01933 224454
Speciality: Bach Remedies.
**M** (**Ref:**HM03556)

## CALM WATERS

**Calm Waters**, 2 Park Cl, Cosby, Leicester, **Leicestershire**, LE9 1RP, ENG.
**(T)** 01162 864454
Speciality: Reiki, Sports Massage, 16 types of massage. Specialist in massage techniques. Swedish, Turkish, Relaxation and Remedial.
● **Holistic Therapist** Mr Hutchins **Q:** IIHHT, IIST.
**C** Yrs. Est.: 5 (**Ref:**HM03557)

## CALMARINE

**Calmarine**, 2-3 Conduit St, London, **London (Greater)**, W1R 9TG, ENG.
**(T)** 020 7499 6565
Speciality: Relaxation Technique.
● **Director** Mr B Leeson
**H T** (**Ref:**HM03558)

## CALMING EFFECTS

**Calming Effects**, 9 Grove End, Rectory Gr, Leigh-On-Sea, **Essex**, SS9 2HB, ENG.
**(T)** 01702 713470
Speciality: Aromatherapy.
● **Partner** Mrs K Page
**M O** (**Ref:**HM03559)

## CALVER, AMANDA

**Amanda Calver**, 1 Clayfield Mews, Newcomen Rd, Tunbridge Wells, **Kent**, TN4 9PA, ENG.
**(T)** 01892 545443
Speciality: Aromatherapy.
**M O** (**Ref:**HM03560)

## CALVERLEY ACUPUNCTURE CLINIC

**Calverley Acupuncture Clinic**, 1 Portman St, Calverley, Pudsey, **Yorkshire (West)**, LS28 5PG, ENG.
**(T)** 01132 563262
Speciality: Acupressure, Acupuncture, Complementary Therapy, Cupping, Electrotherapy, Massage (Therapeutic), Moxibustion. ✔
● **Acupuncturist** Ms C Haige **Q:** BSc (Hons), Dip.Ac. **M:** BAcC.
**O** Yrs. Est.: 3 (**Ref:**HM03561)

## CALVERT, D R

**D R Calvert**, 1d Old Torquay Rd, Paignton, **Devon**, TQ3 2QY, ENG.
**(T)** 01803 526912
Speciality: Chiropodists (Podiatrists).
● **Owner** Mr D Calvert
**S** (**Ref:**HM03562)

## CALVERT, G A

**G A Calvert**, 15 Dean Way, Storrington, Pulborough, **Sussex (West)**, RH20 4QN, ENG.
**(T)** 01903 744587
Speciality: Chiropodists (Podiatrists).
● **Owner** Mr G Calvert
**S** (**Ref:**HM03563)

## CALVERT, S M

**S M Calvert**, 66 Pingle Rd, Sheffield, **Yorkshire (South)**, S7 2LL, ENG.
**(T)** 01142 368559 **(F)** 01142 960525
Speciality: Reflexology.
● **Owner** Mrs S Calvert
**S T** (**Ref:**HM03564)

## CAMBERLEY CHIROPRACTIC CLINIC

**Camberley Chiropractic Clinic**, 62 Frimley Rd, Camberley, **Surrey**, GU15 3EG, ENG.
**(T)** 01276 21637
Speciality: Chiropractic.
● **Owner** Dr C Walker
**P S T** (**Ref:**HM03565)

## CAMBERLEY NATURAL THERAPY CTRE

**Camberley Natural Therapy Centre**, 9 Tekels Park, Camberley, **Surrey**, GU15 2LE, ENG.
**(T)** 01276 23300
**(E)** cntc@zyworld.com
**(W)** www.kalicinska.freeserve.co.uk
Speciality: Acupuncture, Aromatherapy, Colour Therapy, Healing Therapy, Massage (Therapeutic), Meditation, Reflexology. ✔
● **Acupuncturist** Rachel Maguire **Q:** B.Ac, MBAcC.
● **Acupuncturist** Mr M Barry **Q:** B.Ac, MBAcC.
● **Owner/Acupuncturist** Sue Kalicinska **Q:** B.Ac, BSc, LCSP, MBAcC, MIAC, MSc. **M:** BAcC.
● **Aromatherapist/Reflexologist** Mr D Cole **Q:** ITEC, RAWDip.
**O** Yrs. Est.: 10 (**Ref:**HM03566)

## CAMBERLEY OSTEOPATHIC CLINIC

**Camberley Osteopathic Clinic**, 272 Gordon Avenue, Camberley, **Surrey**, GU15 2NU, ENG.
**(T)** 01276 20411 **(F)** 01276 20411
Speciality: Osteopathy.
● **Owner** Mr S Green
**P S T** (**Ref:**HM03567)

## CAMBERLEY PHYSIO & SPORTS CLNC

**Camberley Physiotherapy & Sports Injury Clinic**, 37 Upper Gordon Rd, Camberley, **Surrey**, GU15 2HJ, ENG.
**(T)** 01276 65552
Speciality: Physiotherapy.
● **Owner** Miss M Kosse
**P S T** (**Ref:**HM03568)

## CAMBORNE COMP HEALTH CENTRE

**Camborne Complementary Health Centre**, 21A Basset Rd, Camborne, **Cornwall**, TR14 8SH, ENG.
**(T)** 01209 711504
Speciality: Complementary Medicines & Therapy.
● **Owner** Mr M Rowland
**C M** (**Ref:**HM03569)

## CAMBRAY, ANDREW

**Andrew Cambray**, 35 Calcott Pk, Yateley, **Hampshire**, GU46 6JJ, ENG.
**(T)** 01252 890622 **(F)** 01252 890622
Speciality: Acupuncture.
● **Owner** Mr A Cambray
**M** (**Ref:**HM03570)

## CAMBRIDGE BIODYNAMIC PRACTICE

**Cambridge Biodynamic Practice**, New Sq, Cambridge, **Cambridgeshire**, CB1 1EZ, ENG.
**(T)** 01223 740289
Speciality: Complementary Medicines & Therapy.
● **Partner** Mrs J Harcourt
**M** (**Ref:**HM03571)

## CAMBRIDGE CHIROPRACTIC CENTRE

**Cambridge Chiropractic Centre**, 19 Hamilton Rd, Cambridge, **Cambridgeshire**, CB4 1BP, ENG.
**(T)** 01223 312020 **(F)** 01223 515250
Speciality: Chiropractic, Homeopathy.
● **Chiropractor** Dr J Blake
● **Chiropractor** Dr G Stevens **Q:** DC.
● **Practitioner** Dr B Taylor **Q:** MRCGP, MSc (Chiro). **M:** BMAS, FHom.
● **Chiropractor** Dr A Edwards **Q:** BSc (Chiro), DC. **M:** CC.
● **Principal** Dr P Millbank **Q:** DC. **M:** BCA.
**P** Yrs. Est.: 25 (**Ref:**HM03572)

## CAMBRIDGE COMP HEALTH PRACTICE

**Cambridge Complementary Health Practice**, 34 Rustat Rd, Cambridge, **Cambridgeshire**, CB1 3QT, ENG.
**(T)** 01223 244980
Speciality: Complementary Medicines & Therapy.
● **Partner** Mr R Savage
**C M** (**Ref:**HM03573)

## CAMBRIDGE MEDICAL HERBALIST

**Cambridge Medical Herbalist**, 19 Swaynes Lane, Comberton, Cambridge, **Cambridgeshire**, CB3 7EF, ENG.
**(T)** 01223 264159 **(F)** 01223 262081
Speciality: Herbal Medicine.
● **Owner** Mrs A Davies
**M** (**Ref:**HM03574)

## CAMBRIDGE NUTRITIONAL SCIENCES

**Cambridge Nutritional Sciences Ltd**, Eden Research Park, Henry Crabb Rd, Littleport, **Cambridgeshire**, CB6 1SE, ENG.
**(T)** 01353 862220
Speciality: Complementary Medicines & Therapy.
**M** (**Ref:**HM03575)

## CAMBRIDGE PHYSIOTHERAPY CLINIC

**Cambridge Physiotherapy Clinic**, 36 Sedley Taylor Rd, Cambridge, **Cambridgeshire**, CB2 2PN, ENG.
**(T)** 01223 211606
Speciality: Physiotherapy.
● **Partner** Miss S Inman
**P S T** (**Ref:**HM03576)

## CAMBRIDGE PSYCHOTHERAPY

**Cambridge Psychotherapy Practice**, 26 Newnham Rd, Cambridge, **Cambridgeshire**, CB3 9EY, ENG.
**(T)** 01223 369894
Speciality: Psychotherapy.
**B** (**Ref:**HM03577)

## CAMBRIDGE TRAD ACUPUNC CENTRE

**Cambridge Traditional Acupuncture Centre**, 5 Tredgold Lane, Napier St, Cambridge, **Cambridgeshire**, CB1 1HN, ENG.
**(T)** 01223 323473
Speciality: Acupuncture, Zero Balancing. ✔
● **Manager/Acupuncturist** Mr A Hext **Q:** Cert.ZB, M.Ac, MBAcC. **M:** BAcC.
● **Acupuncturist** Francious Hawkridge **Q:** Cert.ZB, Lic.Ac, MBAcC. **M:** BAcC.
● **Acupuncturist** Ms J Tart **Q:** Lic.Ac, MBAcC. **M:** BAcC.
**O** Yrs. Est.: 18 (**Ref:**HM03578)

## CAMDEN PSYCHOTHERAPY UNIT

**Camden Psychotherapy Unit**, Instrument House, 207-215 King's Cross Rd, London, **London (Greater)**, WC1X 9DB, ENG.
**(T)** 020 7837 5628
Speciality: Psychotherapy.
**B** (**Ref:**HM03579)

## CAMELON CHIROPODY CENTRE

**Camelon Chiropody Centre**, 32 Glasgow Rd, Camelon, Falkirk, FK1 4HJ, SCO.
**(T)** 01324 877877
Speciality: Chiropodists (Podiatrists).
**S** (**Ref:**HM03580)

## CAMERON CLINIC

**Cameron Clinic**, 25 Albany St, Edinburgh, **Edinburgh (City of)**, EH1 3QN, SCO.
**(T)** 01315 581875
Speciality: Physiotherapy.
**P S T** (**Ref:**HM03581)

## CAMERON, ALISON

**Alison Cameron**, 41 Houndiscombe Rd, Plymouth, **Devon**, PL4 6EX, ENG.
**(T)** 01752 223518
Speciality: Osteopathy.
● **Owner** Ms A Cameron

P S T (Ref:HM03582)

## CAMERON, ANNE

**Anne Cameron**, 47 Woodside Avenue, Flackwell Heath, High Wycombe, **Buckinghamshire**, HP10 9LG, ENG.
(T) 01628 522198
Speciality: Reflexology.
S T (Ref:HM03583)

## CAMERON, IAN L

**Ian L Cameron**, 26 Monmouth St, Bath, **Somerset**, BA1 2AP, ENG.
(T) 01225 427835 (F) 01225 333866
Speciality: Osteopathy.
● **Owner** Mr I Cameron
P S T (Ref:HM03584)

## CAMERON, LOUISE E

**Louise E Cameron**, Woodsend Medical Centre, School Pl, Corby, **Northamptonshire**, NN18 0QP, ENG.
(T) 01536 268589
Speciality: Osteopathy.
● **Owner** Mrs L Prestage
P S T (Ref:HM03585)

## CAMERON, SARAH

**Sarah Cameron**, 21 High St, Redbourn, St. Albans, **Hertfordshire**, AL3 7LE, ENG.
(T) 01582 794441 (F) 01582 794441
Speciality: Physiotherapy.
● **Owner** Mr G Cameron
P S T (Ref:HM03586)

## CAMERON, W M

**W M Cameron**, 33D Glasgow Rd, Wishaw, **Lanarkshire (North)**, ML2 7PG, SCO.
(T) 01698 357131
Speciality: Physiotherapy.
P S T (Ref:HM03587)

## CAMERON, WILLIAM

**William Cameron**, Pendeen, Haughgate St, Leven, **Fife**, KY8 4SF, SCO.
(T) 01333 423927
Speciality: Biomechanics, Chiropody, Nail Surgery, Podiatry. ✔
● **Chiropodist (Podiatrist)**
Mrs R Cameron Q: DPodM, S.R.Ch. M: S.C.P.
● **Chiropodist (Podiatrist)**
Mr W Cameron Q: DPodM, S.R.Ch. M: S.C.P.
M Yrs. Est.: 31 (Ref:HM03588)

## CAMERON-KIRBY, E

**E Cameron-Kirby**, 3 Edmund Rd, Oxford, **Oxfordshire**, OX4 3EH, ENG.
(T) 01865 770067
Speciality: Acupuncture.
● **Owner** Ms E Cameron
O (Ref:HM03589)

## CAMILLA HEY HOLISTIC PRACTICE

**Camilla Hey Holistic & Remedial Massage Practice**, 2 Lockhart Pl, St. Andrews, **Fife**, KY16 9XB, SCO.
(T) 01334 477505
Speciality: Remedial Massage.
C (Ref:HM03590)

## CAMPBELL & ASSOCIATES

**F D Campbell & Associates**, 10 Westow St, London, **London (Greater)**, SE19 3AH, ENG.
(T) 020 8771 9050
Speciality: Osteopathy.
P S T (Ref:HM03591)

## CAMPBELL & ASSOCIATES

**F D Campbell & Associates**, 242 Lower Addiscombe Rd, Croydon, **Surrey**, CR0 7AB, ENG.
(T) 020 8656 9573
Speciality: Osteopathy.
P S T (Ref:HM03592)

## CAMPBELL ALLERGY TESTING

**Campbell Allergy Testing**, Canford Heath Group Practice, 9 Mitchell Rd, Poole, **Dorset**, BH17 8UE, ENG.
(T) 01258 450127
Speciality: Complementary Medicines & Therapy.
C M (Ref:HM03593)

## CAMPBELL, ANNE

**Campbell Anne LIC AC**, 12 Rye River Gdns Duncarrig, Leixlip, **County Kildare**, IRE.
(T) 01624 6255
Speciality: Acupuncture.
O (Ref:HM03594)

## CAMPBELL, CAROLINE

**Caroline Campbell**, Jacksons Cl, 209 Royal Mile, Edinburgh, **Edinburgh (City of)**, EH1 1PZ, SCO.
(T) 01312 258092
Speciality: Hypnotherapy.
B (Ref:HM03595)

## CAMPBELL, EDITHA

**Editha Campbell**, 40 Archers Rd, Eastleigh, **Hampshire**, SO50 9AY, ENG.
(T) 023 8032 0641
Speciality: Complementary Medicines & Therapy.
C M (Ref:HM03596)

## CAMPBELL, ELSPETH

**Elspeth Campbell**, 7 Prince Consort Cottages, Alexandra Rd, Windsor, **Berkshire**, SL4 1JA, ENG.
(T) 01753 857051
Speciality: Art Therapy, Complementary Therapy, Counselling, Healing Therapy, Holistic Healing, Hypnosis, Hypnotherapy, Meditation, Neuro-Linguistic Program, Psychotherapy, Spiritual Healing, Stress Therapy, Visualisation Therapy, Ying & Yang, Ericksonian Hypnotherapy, Metaphor Therapy - Past Life Therapy, Qi Gong - Huagong Self Healing. ✔
● **Psychotherapist/Hypnotherapist**
Ms E Campbell Q: BSc, EH.P, MBHReg, MNCP, NLP. M: GHR, NCH, NCP.
B Yrs. Est.: 14 (Ref:HM03597)

## CAMPBELL, FIONA

**Fiona Campbell**, 14 Russell St, Armagh, **County Armagh**, BT61 7SD, NIR.
(T) 07751 131056
Speciality: Chiropody. ✔
● **Chiropodist** Mrs F Campbell Q: C.P.S.M, S.R.Ch. M: S.C.P.
S Yrs. Est.: 4 (Ref:HM03598)

## CAMPBELL, HELEN

**Helen Campbell**, Southpark House, 28 Station Rd, Armadale, Bathgate, **Lothian (West)**, EH48 3LH, SCO.
(T) 01501 730935
Speciality: Homeopathy.
● **Owner** Ms H Campbell
M (Ref:HM03599)

## CAMPBELL, HELEN

**Helen Campbell C Hyp**, 13 Ecklington, Eldene, Swindon, **Wiltshire**, SN3 3TJ, ENG.
(T) 01793 528262
Speciality: Hypnosis.
B (Ref:HM03600)

## CAMPBELL, JOHN D

**John D Campbell**, 31 Main St, Stewarton, Kilmarnock, **Ayrshire (East)**, KA3 5BS, SCO.
(T) 01560 482490
Speciality: Chiropodists (Podiatrists).
● **Owner** Mr J Campbell
S (Ref:HM03601)

## CAMPBELL, KRYSTYNA

**Krystyna Campbell**, 11 Westerdale Cl, Keyingham, Hull, **Humberside (North)**, HU12 9TT, ENG.
(T) 01964 622973
Speciality: Reflexology.
S T (Ref:HM03602)

## CAMPBELL, LISA

**Lisa Campbell**, 518A Bury Rd, Rochdale, **Lancashire**, OL11 4DQ, ENG.
(T) 01706 861186
Speciality: Chiropodists (Podiatrists).
● **Owner** Ms L Campbell
S (Ref:HM03603)

## CAMPBELL, LOUISE

**Louise Campbell**, 26 Highmoor, Amersham, **Buckinghamshire**, HP7 9BU, ENG.
(T) 01494 722622
Speciality: Aromatherapy, Beauty Therapy, Reflexology. ✔
● **Owner/Reflexologist**
Mrs L Campbell Q: IHBC. M: IHBC.
C Yrs. Est.: 20 (Ref:HM03604)

## CAMPBELL, NIKKI

**Nikki Campbell**, 4 Barnards Hill, Marlow, **Buckinghamshire**, SL7 2NZ, ENG.
(T) 01628 482967
(E) nikki.cst@zoom.co.uk
Speciality: Cranio-Sacral Therapy, Dance Movement Therapy, Reflexology. ✔
● **Therapist** Ms N Campbell Q: BA (Hons). M: IPTI.
B C Yrs. Est.: 5 (Ref:HM03605)

## CAMPBELL, ROSEMARY

**Rosemary Campbell**, 20A Walnut Ct, Dublin, **County Dublin**, IRE.
(T) 01836 8201
Speciality: Complementary Medicines & Therapy.
M (Ref:HM03606)

## CAMPBELL, RUTH

**Ruth Campbell**, 216 Stapleford Lane, Beeston, Nottingham, **Nottinghamshire**, NG9 6GB, ENG.
(T) 01159 724079
Speciality: Osteopathy.
● **Owner** Ms R Campbell
P S T (Ref:HM03607)

## CAMPBELL, SEAN

**Sean Campbell**, Flat 2, 18 Smoke Lane, Reigate, **Surrey**, RH2 7HJ, ENG.
(T) 01737 240108
Speciality: Acupuncture.
● **Owner** Mr S Campbell
O (Ref:HM03608)

## CAMPBELL, SEAN D

**Sean D Campbell**, Wellbrook Clinic, 21 Stafford Rd, Wallington, **Surrey**, SM6 9AN, ENG.
(T) 020 8401 0011
Speciality: Acupuncture.
O (Ref:HM03609)

## CAMPBELL-BEATTIE, JOHN

**John Campbell-Beattie**, 64A Underlane, Plymstock, Plymouth, **Devon**, PL9 9JZ, ENG.
(T) 01752 484265
Speciality: Hypnotherapy.
● **Owner** Mr J Campbell-Beattie
B (Ref:HM03610)

## CAMPBELL-COATES, EVEANN

**Eveann Campbell-Coates**, 60 Freebrough Rd, Moorsholm, Saltburn-by-the-Sea, **Cleveland**, TS12 3JB, ENG.
(T) 01287 660441
Speciality: Complementary Medicines & Therapy.
● **Owner** Ms E Campbell-Coates
C M (Ref:HM03611)

## CAMPBELL-PARKER, PATRICIA

**Patricia Campbell-Parker**, Kingston-upon-Thames, London, **London (Greater)**, KT2, ENG.
(T) 020 8549 2721
Speciality: Bach Remedies.
M (Ref:HM03612)

## CAMPHILL MEDICAL PRACTICE

**Camphill Medical Practice**, St John, Murtle Estate, Bieldside, Aberdeen, **Aberdeenshire**, AB15 9EP, SCO.
(T) 01224 868935 (F) 01224 868971
Speciality: Complementary Medicines & Therapy.
● **Partner** Dr S Geider
M (Ref:HM03613)

## CAMPION & ASSOCIATES

**R Campion & Associates**, 15 South St, Yeovil, **Somerset**, BA20 1QG, ENG.
(T) 01935 476855
Speciality: Osteopathy.
● **Owner** Mr R Campion
P S T (Ref:HM03614)

## CAMPION, RICHARD

**Richard Campion**, Norvale, Combe Batch,



Key: B Mind-Body Medicine C Complementary Medicine H Self Help Treatment M Medicinal Therapy O Oriental Medicine P Postural Therapy S Manipulative Structural Therapy T Touch Therapy

Wedmore, **Somerset**, BS28 4DX, ENG.
(T) 01934 712489
Speciality: Osteopathy.
● **Owner** Mr R Campion
P S T (**Ref:**HM03615)

### CAMPLING, J

**J Campling**, Harrogate Holistic Health Centre, 43-45 Tower St, Harrogate, **Yorkshire (North)**, HG1 1HS, ENG.
(T) 01423 887203
Speciality: Complementary Medicines & Therapy.
● **Owner** Mrs J Kampling
M (**Ref:**HM03616)

### CANALE-PAROLA, AUDREY

**Audrey Canale-Parola**, 15 Longrood Rd, Rugby, **Warwickshire**, CV22 7RG, ENG.
(T) 01788 817961
Speciality: Acupuncture.
O (**Ref:**HM03617)

### CANALS, FRANCESC XAVIER

**Francesc Xavier Canals**, 27 Elm Gr, London, **London (Greater)**, NW2 3AE, ENG.
(T) 020 8450 6869
Speciality: Reflexology.
● **Owner** Mr F Canals
S T (**Ref:**HM03618)

### CANAVAN, JOHN (DR)

**Dr John Canavan**, 11 Cashel Pk, Castlebar, **County Mayo**, IRE.
(T) 09438 055
Speciality: Complementary Medicines & Therapy.
M (**Ref:**HM03619)

### CANAVAN, JOHN (DR)

**Dr John Canavan**, Castlebar Mayo, **County Mayo**, IRE.
(T) 09428 918
Speciality: Complementary Medicines & Therapy.
M (**Ref:**HM03620)

### CANCER INFORMATION & SUPPORT

**Cancer Information & Support**, 7 Groveherst Rd, Dartford, **Kent**, DA1 5JD, ENG.
(T) 01322 270597
Speciality: Complementary Medicines & Therapy.
● **Owner** Mrs S Batchelor
C M (**Ref:**HM03621)

### CANDICE READING

**Candice Reading**, Greenhill House, 90-93 Cowcross St, London, **London (Greater)**, EC1M 6BH, ENG.
(T) 020 7628 2585
Speciality: Osteopathy.
P S T (**Ref:**HM03622)

### CANDLEWELL CLINIC

**Candlewell Clinic**, Well Cottage, Cadmore End Common, High Wycombe, **Buckinghamshire**, HP14 3PT, ENG.
(T) 01494 883970
Speciality: Cranial Osteopathy, Healer, Naturopathy, Osteopathy.
● **Cranial Osteopath** Ms L Evans **Q:** BSc, Hons (OST).
● **Cranial Osteopath** Ms S Clark **Q:** DO, MRO.
● **Cranial Osteopath** Ms P Vaill - Carter **Q:** BSc, Hons (OST), MRO.
● **Cranial Osteopath** Ms A O'Connor **Q:** BA (Hons), BSc (Hons), DO.
T Yrs. Est.: 3 (**Ref:**HM03623)

### CANDY, TIM

**Mr Tim Candy**, Combe House, Combe Lane, Wedmore, **Somerset**, BS28 4DZ, ENG.
(T) 01934 713496
Speciality: Chiropractors, Animal Chiropractic. ✔
● **Owner** Mrs J Candy **Q:** DC(OCC).
P S T Yrs. Est.: 7 (**Ref:**HM03624)

### CANE, FENELLA

**Fenella Cane**, Little Acres, 5 Alders Rd, Reigate, **Surrey**, RH2 0EA, ENG.
(T) 01737 247125
Speciality: Physiotherapy.
P S T (**Ref:**HM03625)

### CANE, PAT

**Pat Cane**, 14 The Greenway, The Wells, Epsom, **Surrey**, KT18 7HZ, ENG.
(T) 01372 727403
Speciality: Indian Head Massage, Reflexology.
S T (**Ref:**HM03626)

### CANFOR, HAZEL

**Hazel Canfor**, Physiotherapy Clinic, 79 New Market Rd, Norwich, **Norfolk**, NR2 2HW, ENG.
(T) 01603 625959
Speciality: Physiotherapy.
P S T (**Ref:**HM03627)

### CANN, D

**D Cann**, Pontygwaith Farm, Pontygwaith, Treharris, **Glamorgan (Vale of)**, CF46 5PD, WAL.
(T) 01443 411137
Speciality: Physiotherapy.
P S T (**Ref:**HM03628)

### CANNEY, E

**E Canney**, 10 Eldon Rd, Reading, **Berkshire**, RG1 4DH, ENG.
(T) 01189 502002
Speciality: Physiotherapy.
P S T (**Ref:**HM03629)

### CANNEY, J

**J Canney**, 16 Blackdown Rd, Worthing, **Sussex (West)**, BN13 2EZ, ENG.
(T) 01903 261881
Speciality: Chiropodists (Podiatrists).
S (**Ref:**HM03630)

### CANNING, D M

**D M Canning**, 4 Orchard Lane, Amersham, **Buckinghamshire**, HP6 5AB, ENG.
(T) 01494 721803 (F) 01494 726228
Speciality: Chiropodists (Podiatrists).
● **Owner** Mrs D Canning
S (**Ref:**HM03631)

### CANNING, LINDA

**Linda Canning**, 25 Austins Mead, Bovingdon, Hemel Hempstead, **Hertfordshire**, HP3 0JX, ENG.
(T) 01442 834049
Speciality: Reflexology.
S T (**Ref:**HM03632)

### CANNING, LORRAINE

**Lorraine Canning**, 22 Priest Avenue, Wokingham, **Berkshire**, RG40 2LX, ENG.
(T) 01189 786145
Speciality: Reflexology.
S T (**Ref:**HM03633)

### CANNING, PATRICIA

**Patricia Canning**, 265 Green Lanes, London, **London (Greater)**, N13 4XE, ENG.
(T) 020 8886 9977
Speciality: Physiotherapy.
● **Owner** Mr S Thurgood
P S T (**Ref:**HM03634)

### CANNON, VALERIE

**Valerie Cannon**, 7 Garden Cl, Royston, **Hertfordshire**, SG8 7HX, ENG.
(T) 01763 243538
Speciality: Reflexology, Reiki. ✔
● **Owner/Reflexologist** Mrs V Cannon **Q:** MAR. **M:** AoR, BRA.
C Yrs. Est.: 16 (**Ref:**HM03635)

### CANO, D

**D Cano**, Winding Way, Bittams Lane, Chertsey, **Surrey**, KT16 9RF, ENG.
(T) 01932 873169
Speciality: Complementary Medicines & Therapy.
C M (**Ref:**HM03636)

### CANONBURY CLINIC OF OSTEOPATHY

**Canonbury Clinic Of Osteopathy**, 265 Upper St, London, **London (Greater)**, N1 2UQ, ENG.
(T) 020 7226 0011 (F) 020 7226 0011
Speciality: Osteopathy.
● **Partner** Mrs H Eshref
P S T (**Ref:**HM03637)

### CANONBURY PRODUCTS

**Canonbury Products Ltd**, Unit 7 Boundary Rd, Buckingham Rd Industrial Es, Buckingham Road Industrial Est, Brackley, **Northamptonshire**, NN13 7ES, ENG.
(T) 01280 706661 (F) 01280 706671
Speciality: Chiropodists (Podiatrists).
● **Owner** Mr H Bakker
S (**Ref:**HM03638)

### CANONS HEALTH CLUB

**Canons Health Club**, Cousin Lane, London, **London (Greater)**, EC4R 3TE, ENG.
(T) 020 7283 9797
Speciality: Alexander Technique.
● **Therapist** Ms J Messenger
P S (**Ref:**HM03639)

### CANTASSIUM

**Cantassium**, 225-229 Putney Bridge Rd, London, **London (Greater)**, SW15 2AY, ENG.
(T) 020 8874 1130 (F) 020 8871 0066
Speciality: Complementary Medicines & Therapy.
● **Managing Director** Mr R Woodward
C M (**Ref:**HM03640)

### CANTERBURY OSTEOPATHIC CLINIC

**Canterbury Osteopathic Clinic**, 11 Best Lane, Canterbury, **Kent**, CT1 2JB, ENG.
(T) 01227 454848
(E) hms@cantost.com
(W) www.cantost.com
Speciality: Absent Healing, Auricular Therapy, Bio-energetics, Biofeedback, Colour Therapy, Complementary Therapy, Counselling, Cranial Osteopathy, Cranio-Sacral Therapy, Dietician, Dowsing, Family Planning (Natural), Hay Diet, Healing Therapy, Hypnosis, Manipulation, Massage (Therapeutic), Naturopathy, Nutritional Therapy, Osteopathy, Vitamin Therapy, Osteomyology, Blood Group Nutrition, Thermo-(Ear Candle Therapy). ✔ CREDIT
● **Osteomyologist** Angela Coslett-Derby **Q:** DO, MAO. **M:** RO, TATh.
● **Owner** Mr T Greenfield **Q:** DO, ND, RCST. **M:** GCRN, RCST, RN.
H Yrs. Est.: 5 (**Ref:**HM03641)

### CANTERBURY SCHOOL

**Canterbury School Of Natural Therapies**, Frogham Farm, Frogham, Dover, **Kent**, CT15 7JF, ENG.
(T) 01304 849080
Speciality: Complementary Medicines & Therapy.
● **Principal** Mr M Yates
M (**Ref:**HM03642)

### CANTERLA, MARGARET

**Mrs M Canterla**, 4 Cuthbert Rd, Brighton, **Sussex (East)**, BN2 2EN, ENG.
(T) 01273 692550
Speciality: Holistic Healing, Homeopathy. ✔
● **Homeopath** Mrs M Canterla **Q:** Dip.Hom. **M:** Soc.Hom.
C Yrs. Est.: 16 (**Ref:**HM03643)

### CANTILLON, REGINA (DR)

**Dr Regina Cantillon**, Ivy Tce, Princess St, Tralee, **County Kerry**, IRE.
(T) 06671 23876
Speciality: Chiropractors.
P S T (**Ref:**HM03644)

### CANTO, HILARY

**Hilary Canto**, Dormston, Worcester, **Worcestershire**, WR7, ENG.
(T) 01386 793879
Speciality: Bach Remedies.
M (**Ref:**HM03645)

### CANTWELL, JOHN

**John Cantwell**, Pembroke Hse, Pembroke St, **County Cork**, IRE.
(T) 021 4346 211
(E) hypnosiscork@eircom.net
(W) homepage.eircom.net/~hpynosiscork
Speciality: Complementary Medicines & Therapy.
M (**Ref:**HM03646)



Key continued: **Yrs.Est:** Years Established **Q:** Qualifications **M:** Professional Membership ✔ Indemnity Insurance CREDIT Accept Credit Cards

## CAPEL PHYSIOTHERAPY CLINIC
**Capel Physiotherapy Clinic**, 12 Little Tufts, Capel St. Mary, Ipswich, **Suffolk**, IP9 2UD, ENG.
(T) 01473 311866
Speciality: Physiotherapy.
● **Manager** Mrs J Fenton
P S T (Ref:HM03647)

## CAPEL, TERRY
**Terry Capel**, White Oaks Paynesfield Rd, Tatsfield, Westerham, **Kent**, TN16 2BQ, ENG.
(T) 01959 577360
Speciality: Acupuncture.
● **Owner** Mr T Capel
O (Ref:HM03648)

## CAPEWELL, L
**L Capewell**, 3 St Leonards St, Stamford, **Lincolnshire**, PE9 2HU, ENG.
(T) 01780 482038
Speciality: Chiropodists (Podiatrists).
● **Partner** Mr R Capewell
S (Ref:HM03649)

## CAPLAN, JOHN S
**John S Caplan**, 3b Lutton Pl, Edinburgh, **Edinburgh (City of)**, EH8 9PD, SCO.
(T) 01316 676760
Speciality: Chiropodists (Podiatrists).
● **Owner** Mr J Caplan
S (Ref:HM03650)

## CAPLE, J
**Mrs J Caple**, Litfield Ho Medical Centre, 1 Litfield Pl, Bristol, BS8 3LS, ENG.
(T) 01179 733387
Speciality: Physiotherapy.
P S T (Ref:HM03651)

## CAPOT, ARLENE
**Arlene Capot**, Radisson Sas St, Helens Hotel Stillorgan Rd, IRE.
(T) 01218 8198
Speciality: Complementary Medicines & Therapy.
M (Ref:HM03652)

## CAPOT, ARLENE
**Arlene Capot B A Hons Lic T C M**, 9 Radisson Sas Hotel, Stillorgan, **County Dublin**, IRE.
(T) 01218 8198
Speciality: Complementary Medicines & Therapy.
M (Ref:HM03653)

## CARA
**Cara**, 61A Watergate Row, Chester, **Cheshire**, CH1 2LE, ENG.
(T) 01244 316310
Speciality: Clairvoyants & Palmists.
● **Owner** Mrs S Gable-Clee
B (Ref:HM03654)

## CARACCIOS NATURAL THERAPY CTRE
**Caraccios Natural Therapy Centre**, 83 St Dunstans St, Canterbury, **Kent**, CT2 8AD, ENG.
(T) 01227 455411
Speciality: Complementary Medicines & Therapy.
C M (Ref:HM03655)

## CARADON CHIROPRACTIC CLINIC
**Caradon Chiropractic Clinic**, Parade House, The Parade, Liskeard, **Cornwall**, PL14 6AH, ENG.
(T) 01579 344292
Speciality: Chiropractic. ✔
● **Owner/Chiropractor** Mr W Horsley **Q:** BSc (Chiro). **M:** SCA.
P Yrs. Est.: 5 (Ref:HM03656)

## CARBERY PRACTICE
**Carbery Practice**, 73 Carbery Avenue, Bournemouth, **Dorset**, BH6 3LW, ENG.
(T) 01202 420637 (F) 01202 420637
Speciality: Aromatherapy, Bach Remedies, Hypnotherapy, Indian Head Massage, Manipulation, Massage (Therapeutic), Naturopathy, Osteopathy, Psychotherapy, Stress Therapy, X-Ray. ✔
● **Osteopath/Naturopath** Mr F Hill **Q:** DO, ND. **M:** GOsC.
S Yrs. Est.: 20 (Ref:HM03657)

## CARBONEL-DEERE, M
**M Carbonel-Deere**, 82 Highgate Rd, Whitstable, **Kent**, CT5 3HP, ENG.
(T) 01227 276874
Speciality: Chiropodists (Podiatrists).
● **Owner** Mrs M Carbonel-Deere
S (Ref:HM03658)

## CARBONNEL, JOEL
**Joel Carbonnel**, 4a Berrymede Rd, London, **London (Greater)**, W4 5JF, ENG.
(T) 020 8747 8583 (F) 020 8994 8520
Speciality: Alexander Technique.
● **Owner** Mr J Carbonnel
P S (Ref:HM03659)

## CARD, J P
**J P Card**, 2 St Johns Rd, Sandown, **Isle of Wight**, PO36 8ER, ENG.
(T) 01983 402771
Speciality: Chiropodists (Podiatrists).
● **Owner** Miss J Card
S (Ref:HM03660)

## CARD, K
**K Card**, Red Tiles, Pear Tree Lane, Shorne, Gravesend, **Kent**, DA12 3JX, ENG.
(T) 01474 822644
Speciality: Chiropodists (Podiatrists).
● **Owner** Mr K Card
S (Ref:HM03661)

## CARDEN COMPLEMENTARY CENTRE
**Carden Complementary Centre**, 14 Carden Pl, Aberdeen, **Aberdeenshire**, AB10 1UR, SCO.
(T) 01224 634737
Speciality: Complementary Medicines & Therapy.
C M (Ref:HM03662)

## CARDEW & ASSOCIATES
**E Cardew & Associates**, 141 Burngreave Rd, Sheffield, **Yorkshire (South)**, S3 9DL, ENG.
(T) 01142 730319 (F) 01142 813028
Speciality: Physiotherapy.
● **Practice Manager** Mr G Cardew
P S T (Ref:HM03663)

## CARDFF/CWMBRN/PONTYPL CHIROP
**Cardiff & Cwmbran & Pontypool Chiropody**, 111 The Highway, New Inn, Pontypool, **Monmouthshire**, NP4 0PJ, WAL.
(T) 01495 750851
Speciality: Chiropodists (Podiatrists).
S (Ref:HM03664)

## CARDIFF & CWMBRAN CHIROPODY
**Cardiff & Cwmbran Chiropody**, 371 Caerphilly Rd, Cardiff, **Glamorgan (Vale of)**, CF14 4SH, WAL.
(T) 029 2061 3434
Speciality: Chiropodists (Podiatrists).
● **Owner** Mrs S Fleming
S (Ref:HM03665)

## CARDIFF CHIROPRACTIC CLINIC
**Gareth Lloyd & Associates**, 154 Pen-Y-Lan Rd, Cardiff, **Glamorgan (Vale of)**, CF23 5RE, WAL.
(T) 029 2048 8733
Speciality: Chiropractic. ✔
● **Chiropractor** Dr S Gareth-Lloyd **Q:** BSc, DC. **M:** BCA.
P Yrs. Est.: 22 (Ref:HM03666)

## CARDIFF CLINIC OF TRICHOLOGY
**Cardiff Clinic Of Trichology**, First Floor 2 High St Arcade, Chambers, Cardiff, **Glamorgan (Vale of)**, CF1 2BE, WAL.
(T) 029 2034 1824
Speciality: Complementary Medicines & Therapy, Trichology.
M (Ref:HM03667)

## CARDIFF CONSULTANCY
**Cardiff Consultancy for the Alexander Technique**, 20 Princes Ave, Roath, Cardiff, **Glamorgan (Vale of)**, CF2 3XN, WAL.
(T) 029 2048 5521
Speciality: Alexander Technique.
P S (Ref:HM03668)

## CARDIFF ELECTRO & BTY CLNC
**Cardiff Electrolysis & Beauty Clinic**, 1st Floor, 2 High St Arcade Chambers, Cardiff, **Glamorgan (Vale of)**, CF10 1BE, WAL.
(T) 029 2034 1824
Speciality: Electrolysis.
● **Managing Director** Ms S Tantrum
T (Ref:HM03669)

## CARDIFF HEALTH PRACTICE
**Cardiff Health Practice**, 39 Tydfil Pl, Cardiff, **Glamorgan (Vale of)**, CF23 5HP, WAL.
(T) 029 2048 4555
Speciality: Chiropractic. ✔
● **Chiropractor** Dr C Taylor **Q:** DC. **M:** GCC.
P S T Yrs. Est.: 8 (Ref:HM03670)

## CARDIFF HOMEOPATHIC CLINIC
**Cardiff Homeopathic Clinic**, 30 Riversdale, Llandaff, Cardiff, **Glamorgan (Vale of)**, CF5 2QL, WAL.
(T) 029 2057 8820
Speciality: Holistic Healing, Homeopathy. ✔
● **Owner** Mr P Collins **Q:** MSc.
C Yrs. Est.: 17 (Ref:HM03671)

## CARDINAL, PAUL
**Paul Cardinal**, 26 Longfield Rd, Bristol, BS7 9AG, ENG.
(T) 01179 836349
Speciality: Physiotherapy.
P S T (Ref:HM03672)

## CARDWELL, MARTIN
**Martin Cardwell**, 18 Grasmere Rd, Bromley, **Kent**, BR1 4BA, ENG.
(T) 020 8460 1173 (F) 020 8460 1173
(E) martincardwell@compuserve.com
(W) www.fengshuiexperience.org.uk
Speciality: Absent Healing, Complementary Therapy, Crystal Healing, Dowsing, Faith Healing, Healer, Healing Therapy, Herbal Medicine, Indian Head Massage, Massage (Therapeutic), Meditation, Reiki, Seichem, Spiritual Healing, Stress Therapy, Karuna Reiki. ✔
● **Healer/Teacher** Mr M Cardwell **Q:** NFSH, Reiki Master. **M:** NFSH, Reiki Association, Reiki Fed.
T Yrs. Est.: 8 (Ref:HM03673)

## CARDY BEAVER PHYSIO CENTRE
**Cardy Beaver Physiotherapy Centre**, Reading Rd, Pangbourne, Reading, **Berkshire**, RG8 7LR, ENG.
(T) 01189 844217
Speciality: Physiotherapy.
● **Accountant** Mr G Coia
P S T (Ref:HM03674)

## CARE FOR YOUR HEALTH
**Care For Your Health**, Gillygate, York, **Yorkshire (North)**, YO31 7EQ, ENG.
(T) 01759 318616 (F) 01759 318616
Speciality: Reflexology.
● **Owner** Ms C Cunningham
S T (Ref:HM03675)

## CARE THROUGH HYPNOSIS
**Care Through Hypnosis**, Sunbury Court Island, Sunbury-On-Thames, **Surrey**, TW16 5PP, ENG.
(T) 01932 781903
Speciality: Hypnotherapy.
B (Ref:HM03676)

## CAREER SEARCH
**Career Search**, 15 Stancomb Avenue, Trowbridge, **Wiltshire**, BA14 7HS, ENG.
(T) 01225 775900 (F) 01225 355802
Speciality: Psychology.
● **Owner** Mr P Wilkins
B (Ref:HM03677)

## CARE-TECH AROMATHERAPY
**Care-Tech Aromatherapy**, 5 Merchant St, Aberdare, **Glamorgan (Vale of)**, CF44 7EF, WAL.
(T) 01685 881750 (F) 01685 876315
Speciality: Aromatherapy.
● **Owner** Mr J Davies
M O (Ref:HM03678)

## CAREY BOYCE CENTRE-KINESIOLOGY
**Carey Boyce Centre For Kinesiology**, 19A Gloucester St, Faringdon, **Oxfordshire**, SN7 7JA, ENG.
(T) 01367 241641
Speciality: Complementary Medicines & Therapy.

Key: B Mind-Body Medicine · C Complementary Medicine · H Self Help Treatment · M Medicinal Therapy · O Oriental Medicine · P Postural Therapy · S Manipulative Structural Therapy · T Touch Therapy

C M (Ref:HM03679)

### CAREY-MORGAN, SIMON

**Simon Carey-Morgan**, Ingledale, 1 Tanhouse Rd, Oxted, **Surrey**, RH8 9PE, ENG.
(T) 01883 717277
Speciality: Acupuncture.
O (Ref:HM03680)

### CARGILL, APRIL

**April Cargill**, 16 Coniston Avenue, Upminster, **Essex**, RM14 2NS, ENG.
(T) 01708 229676
Speciality: Chiropodists (Podiatrists).
S (Ref:HM03681)

### CARING CLINIC

**Caring Clinic (The)**, 35 Barkers Rd, Sheffield, **Yorkshire (South)**, S7 1SD, ENG.
(T) 01142 551345
(E) pham@thecaringclinic.co.uk
(W) www.thecaringclinic.co.uk
Speciality: Aromatherapy, Bach Remedies, Colour Therapy, Counselling, Crystal Healing, Healer, Healing Therapy, Hypnotherapy, Indian Head Massage, Meditation, Metamorphic Therapy, Nutritional Therapy, Reflexology, Stress Therapy, Visualisation Therapy, Vitamin Therapy. ✔ CREDIT
● **Healer/Counsellor** Ms P Hampton Q: Dip.Ed, ITEC, NFSH. M: IPTI, NFSH.
● **Clinical Nutritionist** Mr B Hampton Q: Dip.ION. M: BANT.
M Yrs. Est.: 16 (Ref:HM03682)

### CARING HANDS

**Caring Hands**, 9 Kelsborrow Way, Kelsall, Tarporley, **Cheshire**, CW6 0NL, ENG.
(T) 01829 752268
Speciality: Aromatherapy, Reflexology, Remedial Massage.
● **Owner** Mrs S Owen
M (Ref:HM03683)

### CARING HANDS

**Caring Hands**, Little Lane, Kimberley, Nottingham, **Nottinghamshire**, NG16 2PE, ENG.
(T) 01159 385491
Speciality: Homeopathy.
● **Owner** Miss J Hand
M (Ref:HM03684)

### CARING HANDS CLINIC

**Caring Hands Clinic Of Alternative Therapy (The)**, 45 Rhosddu Rd, Wrexham, LL11 2NS, WAL.
(T) 01978 361921
Speciality: Complementary Medicines & Therapy.
M (Ref:HM03685)

### CARING HYPNOTHERAPY CENTRE

**Caring Hypnotherapy Centre**, 297 Alcester Rd South, Birmingham, **Midlands (West)**, B14 6EB, ENG.
(T) 01214 415914 (F) 01216 282442
Speciality: Hypnosis.
● **Secretary** Mrs W Ryan
B (Ref:HM03686)

### CARISBROOKE HEALTH CENTRE

**Carisbrooke Health Centre**, 22 High St, Carisbrooke, Newport, **Isle of Wight**, ENG.
(T) 01983 520211 (F) 01983 825902
(E) footstepsuk@netscapeonline.co.uk
Speciality: Alexander Technique, Bach Remedies, Biomechanics, Chiropody, Nail Surgery, Podiatry. ✔
● **Manager** Ms S Parry Q: MSTAT.
● **Chiropodist** Mr G Knapper Q: M.S.C.P, S.R.Ch.
B H P Yrs. Est.: 15 (Ref:HM03687)

### CARITAS NATURAL HEALTH CLINIC

**Caritas Natural Health Clinic**, 24A Chilwell Rd, Beeston, Nottingham, **Nottinghamshire**, NG9 1EJ, ENG.
(T) 01159 871581
Speciality: Massage (Therapeutic), Osteopathy, Sports Massage. ✔
● **Sports Therapist** Ms S McKinnon Q: VTCT. M: FHT.
S (Ref:HM03688)

### CARLE, J

**J Carle**, 20 Turner Cl, Kemsley, Sittingbourne, **Kent**, ME10 2UE, ENG.
(T) 01795 425029
Speciality: Chiropractic.
● **Owner** Mrs J Carle
P S T (Ref:HM03689)

### CARLEY, R J

**R J Carley**, Maidstone Physiotherapy Clinic, 116A London Rd, Maidstone, **Kent**, ME16 0DJ, ENG.
(T) 01622 691251
Speciality: Physiotherapy.
P S T (Ref:HM03690)

### CARLING, ANNA

**Anna Carling**, Health Hydro, Milton Rd, Swindon, **Wiltshire**, SN1 5JA, ENG.
(T) 01793 465631
Speciality: Aromatherapy.
M O (Ref:HM03691)

### CARLISLE PHYSIO & SPORTS CLNC

**Carlisle Physiotherapy & Sports Injury Clinic**, Chapel Court, 40-44 Cecil St, Carlisle, **Cumbria**, CA1 1NT, ENG.
(T) 01228 592979
Speciality: Physiotherapy.
P S T (Ref:HM03692)

### CARLISLE, L

**L Carlisle**, Churchill Medical Centre, 1 Churchill Trce, London, **London (Greater)**, E4 8DA, ENG.
(T) 020 8524 1505
Speciality: Homeopathy.
M (Ref:HM03693)

### CARLISLE, L

**L Carlisle**, Goldings Hill Clinic, 1 Lower Rd, Loughton, **Essex**, IG10 2RS, ENG.
(T) 020 8508 7514
Speciality: Homeopathy.
M (Ref:HM03694)

### CARLISLE, L

**L Carlisle**, Magnolia Cottage, Silver Birch Avenue, North Weald, Epping, **Essex**, CM16 6LB, ENG.
(T) 01992 579333 (F) 01992 613859
Speciality: Homeopathy.
● **Owner** Ms L Carlisle
M (Ref:HM03695)

### CARLISLE, L

**L Carlisle**, 4 Laburnum Rd, Coopersale, Epping, **Essex**, CM16 7RA, ENG.
(T) 01992 613859
Speciality: Homeopathy.
M (Ref:HM03696)

### CARLOW HYPNOTHERAPY CLINIC

**Carlow Hypnotherapy Clinic**, The Paddock Mountain, View House, **County Carlow**, IRE.
(T) 05033 3288
Speciality: Hypnotherapy.
B (Ref:HM03697)

### CARLSEN, CHRISTINA

**Christina Carlsen**, 10A Corfton Rd, London, **London (Greater)**, W5 2HS, ENG.
(T) 020 8998 1388
Speciality: Physiotherapy.
P S T (Ref:HM03698)

### CARLSON, PATRICIA

**Patricia Carlson**, 20 Westcliffe Way, South Shields, **Tyne and Wear**, NE34 9HF, ENG.
(T) 01914 893274
Speciality: Reflexology.
S T (Ref:HM03699)

### CARLTON CLINIC

**Carlton Clinic**, Carlton Clinic, 147-9 Balcombe Rd, Horley, **Surrey**, RH6 9BX, ENG.
(T) 01293 784200 (F) 01293 452222
(E) carlton clinic.co
Speciality: Acupressure, Acupuncture, Alexander Technique, Aromatherapy, Bach Remedies, Bonesetting, Bowen Therapy, Chiropody, Chiropractic, Complementary Therapy, Counselling, Cranial Osteopathy, Cupping, Dietician, Electrolipolysis, Electrotherapy, Faith Healing, Floral Essence Therapy, Hay Diet, Healer, Healing Therapy, Herbal Medicine, Holistic Healing, Homeopathy, Humanistic Psychology, Hypnosis, Hypnotherapy, Indian Head Massage, Inhalation Therapy, Kinesiology, Life Style Coaching, Manipulation, Massage (Therapeutic), Micro Manipulation, Moxibustion, Naturopathy, Nutritional Therapy, Oriental Diagnosis, Osteopathy, Podiatrics via Podiatric Surgeon. ✔ CREDIT
● **Medial Chinese Medicine/Acupuncturist** Dr D Pezeshkifar M: GMC.
● **Naturopath/Visceral/Obstetric Osteopath** Beate Gunther Q: Reg.Osteopath, RN. M: BOrthA, GOsC.
● **Naturopath/Osteopath** Mr C Bates Q: Reg.Osteopath. M: BOrthA, GOsC.
● **Osteopath/Naturopath** Jon Cove Q: Reg.Osteopath. M: BOrthA, GOsC.
S Yrs. Est.: 17 (Ref:HM03700)

### CARLTON SPORTS & PHYSIO CLINIC

**Carlton Sports & Physiotherapy Clinic**, 35 High St, Sandridge, St. Albans, **Hertfordshire**, AL4 9DD, ENG.
(T) 01727 855111
Speciality: Physiotherapy.
P S T (Ref:HM03701)

### CARLYLE EON

**Carlyle Eon**, Lambert House, Bramham, Wetherby, **Yorkshire (West)**, LS23 6QG, ENG.
(T) 01937 843109
Speciality: Homeopathy.
M (Ref:HM03702)

### CARMA HEALING SANCTUARY

**Carma Healing Sanctuary**, 15 The Uplands, Gerrards Cross, **Buckinghamshire**, SL9 7JQ, ENG.
(T) 07071 780229
Speciality: Colour Therapy, Crystal Healing, Past Life Therapy, Acupuncture Colour. ✔
● **Holistic Therapist** Mrs Y Ferrell
B C Yrs. Est.: 25 (Ref:HM03703)

### CARMAN, CAROL

**Carol Carman**, Highgate House, Wednesday Market, Beverley, **Humberside (North)**, HU17 0DG, ENG.
(T) 01482 871029
Speciality: Hypnosis, Neuro-Linguistic Program, Psychotherapy.
B (Ref:HM03704)

### CARMARTHEN

**Carmarthen**, 17 Spilman St, Carmarthen, **Carmarthenshire**, SA31 1JY, WAL.
(T) 01267 231097
Speciality: Chiropodists (Podiatrists).
● **Owner** Ms A Byrne
S (Ref:HM03705)

### CARMEL, BRADLEY

**Bradley Carmel TCM Lic Ac (China)**, 138 Philipsburgh Ave, Fairview, **County Dublin**, IRE.
(T) 01837 0543
Speciality: Complementary Medicines & Therapy.
M (Ref:HM03706)

### CARMEN NATURAL THERAPIES

**Carmen Natural Therapies**, 1 Orion, Bracknell, **Berkshire**, RG12 7YX, ENG.
(T) 01344 425301
Speciality: Aromatherapy.
M O (Ref:HM03707)

### CARMICHAEL CLINIC

**Carmichael Clinic Of Physiotherapy And Acupuncture**, Regent House, Bexton Lane, Knutsford, **Cheshire**, WA16 9AB, ENG.
(T) 01565 750035
Speciality: Acupuncture, Cupping, Electrotherapy, Manipulation, Massage (Therapeutic), Physiotherapy, Ultrasonics.
● **Physiotherapist/Acupuncturist** Ms J Middleton
● **Physiotherapist** Mrs C Davies
● **Physiotherapist** Ms G Crawford
S Yrs. Est.: 10 (Ref:HM03708)

### CARMICHAEL, GORDON

**Gordon Carmichael**, 14 Cayman Cl, Basingstoke, **Hampshire**, RG24 9AG, ENG.
(T) 01256 364141
Speciality: Massage (Therapeutic), Sports


Key continued: Yrs.Est: Years Established Q: Qualifications M: Professional Membership ✔ Indemnity Insurance CREDIT Accept Credit Cards

Massage, Stress Therapy. ✓
● **Massage Therapist**
Mr G Carmichael **Q:** ITEC. **M:** ITEC.
**C** Yrs. Est.: 10 (**Ref:**HM03709)

## CARMICHAEL, KAREN
**Karen Carmichael**, 3 Thirlmere Avenue, Prenton, **Merseyside**, CH43 9SQ, ENG.
(T) 01516 782710
Speciality: Reflexology.
**S T** (**Ref:**HM03710)

## CARMICHAEL, R
**R Carmichael**, 6 The Hollow, Child Okeford, Blandford Forum, **Dorset**, DT11 8EX, ENG.
(T) 01258 860169
Speciality: Complementary Medicines & Therapy.
● **Owner** Miss R Carmichael
**C M** (**Ref:**HM03711)

## CARNEAL COTTAGE
**Carneal Cottage**, Main St, Hickling, Melton Mowbray, **Leicestershire**, LE14 3AH, ENG.
(T) 01664 822234
Speciality: Physiotherapy.
**P S T** (**Ref:**HM03712)

## CARNELIAN HEALTH PARTNERSHIP
**Carnelian Health Partnership (The)**, The Grange, 35 Wedmans Lane, Rotherwick, Hook, **Hampshire**, RG27 9BN, ENG.
(T) 01256 769400 (F) 01256 769400
Speciality: Complementary Medicines & Therapy.
● **Partner** Mrs S Enoch
**M** (**Ref:**HM03713)

## CARNELIAN NTRL TREATMENT CTRE
**Carnelian Natural Treatment Centre**, 63 Olive Avenue, Leigh-on-Sea, **Essex**, SS9 3PU, ENG.
(T) 01702 558009
Speciality: Bach Remedies, Indian Head Massage, Reflexology, Reiki.
**S T** (**Ref:**HM03714)

## CAROL
**Carol**, 2 Arthur Green Avenue, Kirkby-In-Ashfield, Nottingham, **Nottinghamshire**, NG17 9FY, ENG.
(T) 01623 750212
Speciality: Clairvoyants & Palmists.
● **Owner** Mrs C Morley
**B** (**Ref:**HM03715)

## CAROLAN, PAUL
**Paul Carolan**, 13 Moatfield Pk, St Brendans, Dublin, **County Dublin**, IRE.
(T) 01867 0343
Speciality: Complementary Medicines & Therapy.
**M** (**Ref:**HM03717)

## CAROLE'S MOBILE THERAPIST
**Carole's Mobile Therapist**, 16 Brankholm Lane, Rosyth, Dunfermline, **Fife**, KY11 2AJ, SCO.
(T) 01383 419364
Speciality: Massage (Therapeutic), Reiki. ✓
● **Owner/Therapist** Mrs C Stryker
**C S T** Yrs. Est.: 3 (**Ref:**HM03718)

## CAROLINE, BOBBY
**Bobby Caroline**, 205A Ashmore Rd, Queens Park, London, **London (Greater)**, W9 3DB, ENG.
(T) 020 8960 2325
Speciality: Complementary Medicines & Therapy.
**C M** (**Ref:**HM03719)

## CAROL'S TWILIGHT ZONE
**Carol's Twilight Zone**, 29A Ripon Mall, Station Lane, Hornchurch, **Essex**, RM12 6JL, ENG.
(T) 07956 673832
Speciality: Clairvoyants & Palmists.
● **Owner** Mrs C West
**B** (**Ref:**HM03720)

## CAROLYN'S BEAUTY
**Carolyn's Beauty**, 10 Heron Cl, Mountsorrel, Loughborough, **Leicestershire**, LE12 7FH, ENG.
(T) 01162 374613
Speciality: Aromatherapy.
● **Owner** Ms C Saddington
**M O** (**Ref:**HM03721)

## CAROLYN'S BEAUTY SALON
**Carolyn's Beauty Salon**, 21 Sea Rd, **County Galway**, IRE.
(T) 09158 7738
Speciality: Beauty Therapy.
**H T** (**Ref:**HM03722)

## CARPANI, HANS
**Hans Carpani**, 102 Chosen Drive, Churchdown, Gloucester, **Gloucestershire**, GL3 2QU, ENG.
(T) 01452 714511 (F) 01452 541369
Speciality: Osteopathy.
● **Partner** Mr C Hayden
**P S T** (**Ref:**HM03723)

## CARPANINI, REGINALD & PENELOPE
**Reginald W Carpanini & Penelope M Carpanini**, 2 Blake Rd, Croydon, **Surrey**, CR0 6UH, ENG.
(T) 020 8688 5210
Speciality: Osteopathy.
● **Partner** Mr R Carpanini
**M** (**Ref:**HM03724)

## CARPENDALE, O
**O Carpendale**, 22 Queens Gardens, London, **London (Greater)**, W5 1SF, ENG.
(T) 020 8997 0423
Speciality: Chiropodists (Podiatrists).
● **Owner** Mrs O Carpendale
**S** (**Ref:**HM03725)

## CARPENTER
**Carpenter**, 53 Tidings Hill, Halstead, **Essex**, CO9 1BL, ENG.
(T) 01787 479922
Speciality: Chiropodists (Podiatrists).
**S** (**Ref:**HM03726)

## CARPENTER, DAVID
**David Carpenter**, 136 Lichfield Rd, Walsall Wood, Walsall, **Midlands (West)**, WS9 9PD, ENG.
(T) 01543 820092 (F) 01543 820387
(W) www.helpishere.co.uk
Speciality: Counselling, Hypnosis, Hypnotherapy, Neuro-Linguistic Program, Psychotherapy, Stress Therapy, Visualisation Therapy. ✓
● **Hypnotherapist/Psychotherapist**
Mr D Carpenter **Q:** CQSW, MNCH, UKCP (Reg). **M:** BACP, HS, NCH, UKCP.
**B C** Yrs. Est.: 11 (**Ref:**HM03727)

## CARPENTER, ELAINE
**Elaine Carpenter**, 3 Groton St, Groton, Sudbury, **Suffolk**, CO10 5EE, ENG.
(T) 01787 210601
Speciality: Hypnosis.
● **Owner** Mrs E Carpenter
**B** (**Ref:**HM03728)

## CARPENTER, FIONA
**Fiona Carpenter**, Clobells Cottage, Clobells, South Brent, **Devon**, TQ10 9JW, ENG.
(T) 01364 72344
Speciality: Complementary Medicines & Therapy.
**C M** (**Ref:**HM03729)

## CARPENTER, G W
**G W Carpenter**, 14 Record Rd, Emsworth, **Hampshire**, PO10 7NS, ENG.
(T) 01243 374855
Speciality: Acupuncture.
● **Owner** Miss G Carpenter
**O** (**Ref:**HM03730)

## CARPENTER, HEATHER
**Heather Carpenter McTimoney**, Little Ridge, 14 Whittlebury Rd, Silverstone, Towcester, **Northamptonshire**, NN12 8UD, ENG.
(T) 01327 857468 (F) 01327 858166
Speciality: Chiropractic.
● **Owner** Mrs H Carpenter
**P S T** (**Ref:**HM03731)

## CARPENTER, M P
**M P Carpenter**, 7 Stirling Cl, Windsor, **Berkshire**, SL4 4PW, ENG.
(T) 01753 861868
Speciality: Chiropodists (Podiatrists).
● **Owner** Mrs M Carpenter
**S** (**Ref:**HM03732)

## CARPENTER, P M
**P M Carpenter**, Higher Tregadra, Cury Cross Lanes, Helston, **Cornwall**, TR12 7BB, ENG.
(T) 01326 240225
Speciality: Chiropodists (Podiatrists).
● **Owner** Mrs P Carpenter
**S** (**Ref:**HM03733)

## CARPENTER, PAUL
**Paul Carpenter**, 8 Clarence Pl, Morice Town, Plymouth, **Devon**, PL2 1SF, ENG.
(T) 01752 219092
Speciality: Chiropody, Reflexology. ✓
● **Owner/Surgical Chiropodist/Reflexologist**
Mr P Carpenter **Q:** MAR, MBChA, MSSCh.
**C** Yrs. Est.: 6 (**Ref:**HM03734)

## CARR, CATHERINE
**Catherine Carr**, 1 De Lacy St, Clitheroe, **Lancashire**, BB7 2EE, ENG.
(T) 01200 427735
Speciality: Alexander Technique.
● **Owner** Mrs C Carr
**P S** (**Ref:**HM03735)

## CARR, CHRISTINE
**Christine Carr**, 11 Dale View, Ilkley, **Yorkshire (West)**, LS29 9BP, ENG.
(T) 01943 603145
Speciality: Complementary Medicines & Therapy.
**C M** (**Ref:**HM03736)

## CARR, J M
**J M Carr**, 96 Queens Rd, Buckhurst Hill, **Essex**, IG9 5BS, ENG.
(T) 020 8504 1341
Speciality: Chiropodists (Podiatrists).
● **Partner** Mr R Carr
**S** (**Ref:**HM03737)

## CARR, PAUL
**Paul Carr**, 5 Church St, Ewell, Epsom, **Surrey**, KT17 2AU, ENG.
(T) 020 8393 3441
Speciality: Osteopathy.
**P S T** (**Ref:**HM03738)

## CARR, R
**R Carr**, The Newcastle Clinic, 52 Mitchell Avenue, Newcastle Upon Tyne, **Tyne and Wear**, NE2 3LA, ENG.
(T) 01912 810193
Speciality: Osteopathy.
**P S T** (**Ref:**HM03739)

## CARR, R
**R Carr**, 19 Carlton St, Blyth, **Northumberland**, NE24 2DB, ENG.
(T) 01670 363334
Speciality: Acupuncture.
**O** (**Ref:**HM03740)

## CARR, R N D
**R N D Carr**, 12 Garden Drive, Penrhyn Bay, Llandudno, **Conwy**, LL30 3LL, WAL.
(T) 01492 544445
Speciality: Osteopathy.
**P S T** (**Ref:**HM03741)

## CARRICK CLINIC
**Carrick Clinic**, 33 Ayr Rd, Prestwick, **Ayrshire (South)**, KA9 1SY, SCO.
(T) 01292 478888
(E) ipgill@globalnet.co.uk
Speciality: Acupressure, Acupuncture, Alexander Technique, Aromatherapy, Complementary Therapy, Dietician, Electrotherapy, Herbal Medicine, Homeopathy, Iridology, Kinesiology, Manipulation, Massage (Therapeutic), Naturopathy, Osteopathy, Reflexology, Ultrasonics, Vitamin Therapy, Magnetic Field Therapy, Impact Therapy, Celloid Mineral Therapy. ✓
● **Remedial Therapist/Naturopath**
Pat Leith **Q:** AMRSH. **M:** AMRSH, Nat.Back Pain.Ass.
● **Osteopath/Naturopath** Mr P Gill **Q:** DO, FLCSP. **M:** LCSP.
**S** Yrs. Est.: 10 (**Ref:**HM03742)



Key: **B** Mind-Body Medicine **C** Complementary Medicine **H** Self Help Treatment **M** Medicinal Therapy **O** Oriental Medicine **P** Postural Therapy **S** Manipulative Structural Therapy **T** Touch Therapy

**CARRICK STREET PHYSIO & SPORT**

**Carrick Street Physiotherapy & Sport Injury Clinic**, 45C Carrick St, Glasgow, **Glasgow (City of)**, G2 8PJ, SCO.
(T) 01412 422800 (F) 01412 211525
Speciality: Physiotherapy, Sports Therapy. ✔
● **Administrator** Mrs J McLeod
● **Owner/Physiotherapist** Mr G Smith
Q: Cert.Ed, Grad Dip Phys, MCSP, SRP.
● **Sports Therapist** Mr J Mc Creadie
● **Therapist** Mr C Jackson Q: BSc (Hons), MSST.
S (Ref:HM03743)

**CARRICK-SMITH, L**

**L Carrick-Smith & Associates Chartered Psychologists**, Highfields House, Sheffield Rd, Clowne, Chesterfield, **Derbyshire**, S43 4AP, ENG.
(T) 01246 810669
Speciality: Counselling, Humanistic Psychology, Psychotherapy, Rogerian Therapy. ✔
● **Practice Principal**
Mr L Carrick-Smith Q: BA, MSc. M: BPS.
B Yrs. Est.: 12 (Ref:HM03744)

**CARRIE, CLARE**

**Clare Carrie**, 40 Free School Lane, Halifax, **Yorkshire (West)**, HX1 2PW, ENG.
(T) 01422 367641
Speciality: Acupuncture.
● **Owner** Mrs C Clare
O (Ref:HM03745)

**CARRINGTON, A J & C D**

**Mr A J Carrington & Mrs C D Carrington**, Carrington Physiotherapy, 14 Myddleton Park, London, **London (Greater)**, N20 0HX, ENG.
(T) 020 8445 2660
Speciality: Physiotherapy.
P S T (Ref:HM03746)

**CARRINGTON, DAVID**

**David Carrington**, 47 Woodlands Ave, Sidcup, **Kent**, DA15 8HB, ENG.
(T) 020 8309 0042
Speciality: Chiropodists (Podiatrists).
S (Ref:HM03747)

**CARRINGTON, DORA**

**Dora Carrington**, Whassett House, Whassett, Milnthorpe, **Cumbria**, LA7 7DN, ENG.
(T) 01539 563488
Speciality: Reflexology.
S T (Ref:HM03748)

**CARRINGTON, MARTIN**

**Martin Carrington**, 13 Pantbach Rd, Cardiff, **Glamorgan (Vale of)**, CF14 1TU, WAL.
(T) 029 2062 1764
Speciality: Chiropodists (Podiatrists).
S (Ref:HM03749)

**CARRINGTON, W H M**

**W H M Carrington**, 18 Lansdowne Rd, London, **London (Greater)**, W11 3LL, ENG.
(T) 020 7727 7222
Speciality: Alexander Technique.
P S (Ref:HM03750)

**CARRINGTON'S CONSULTANCY GROUP**

**Carrington's Consultancy Group**, Britannia House, High St, Cowbridge, **Glamorgan (Vale of)**, CF71 7YT, WAL.
(T) 01446 771302 (F) 01446 771302
Speciality: Complementary Medicines & Therapy.
● **Owner** Mrs S Carrington
C M (Ref:HM03751)

**CARR-JONES, MICHAEL**

**Michael Carr-Jones**, E F T, 17 Church Rd, Poole, **Dorset**, BH14 8UF, ENG.
(T) 01202 739369 (F) 01202 715008
Speciality: Hypnosis.
● **Director** Mr M Carr-Jones
B (Ref:HM03752)

**CARROLL, ALISON**

**Alison Carroll**, 36 High St, Market Harborough, **Leicestershire**, LE16 7NL, ENG.
(T) 01858 410982
Speciality: Chiropodists (Podiatrists).
S (Ref:HM03753)

**CARROLL, D**

**D Carroll**, 12 Bath Rd, Slough, **Berkshire**, SL1 3SA, ENG.
(T) 01753 520544 (F) 01753 536060
Speciality: Hypnosis.
● **Owner** Mr I Carling
B (Ref:HM03754)

**CARROLL, P**

**P Carroll**, 1 Philip Lane, London, **London (Greater)**, N15 4JA, ENG.
(T) 020 8809 3426
Speciality: Osteopathy.
● **Owner** Mr P Carroll
P S T (Ref:HM03755)

**CARROLL, P**

**P Carroll**, Park Rd Pools, Park Rd, London, **London (Greater)**, N8 8JN, ENG.
(T) 020 8809 3426
Speciality: Osteopathy.
● **Owner** Mr P Carroll
P S T (Ref:HM03756)

**CARROLL, S F**

**S F Carroll**, Hoath Cottage, Chiddingstone Hoath, Edenbridge, **Kent**, TN8 7DB, ENG.
(T) 01342 850426
Speciality: Chiropodists (Podiatrists).
● **Owner** Mrs S Carroll
S (Ref:HM03757)

**CARROLL, VINCENT (DR)**

**Dr Vincent Carroll**, Fairfield Hse, Newbridge Ave, Dublin, **County Dublin**, IRE.
(T) 01660 1487
Speciality: Complementary Medicines & Therapy.
M (Ref:HM03758)

**CARROLL-PHELAN, BERNICE (DR)**

**Dr Bernice Carroll-Phelan PHD**, Main St, Carrigaline, **County Cork**, IRE.
(T) 021 4832 249
Speciality: Complementary Medicines & Therapy.
M (Ref:HM03759)

**CARROTT, EMMA**

**Emma Carrott**, 30 Deerleap Way, New Milton, **Hampshire**, BH25 5EU, ENG.
(T) 01425 617840
Speciality: Chiropodists (Podiatrists).
● **Owner** Mrs E Carrott
S (Ref:HM03760)

**CARRS LANE CHURCH CENTRE**

**Carrs Lane Church Centre**, Carrs Lane, Birmingham, **Midlands (West)**, B4 7SX, ENG.
(T) 01216 436667
Speciality: Alexander Technique.
P S (Ref:HM03761)

**CARRS, ALLEN**

**Allen Carrs**, 48 Eastfield, Edinburgh, **Edinburgh (City of)**, EH15 2PN, SCO.
(T) 01316 606688
(W) www.allencarr.com
Speciality: Psychotherapy.
● **Therapist** Mr D McCuff
H Yrs. Est.: 5 (Ref:HM03762)

**CARRUTHERS, D**

**D Carruthers**, Portsmouth Natural Health Centre, 20 Landport Trce, Portsmouth, **Hampshire**, PO1 2RG, ENG.
(T) 023 9283 0558
Speciality: Complementary Medicines & Therapy.
M (Ref:HM03763)

**CARRUTHERS, G (DR)**

**Dr G Carruthers**, Chesterfield Clinic, Holywell Annexe, Holywell St, Chesterfield, **Derbyshire**, S41 7SH, ENG.
(T) 01246 200311 (F) 01246 200311
Speciality: Chiropractors.
● **Practice Manager** Mrs J Cole
P S T (Ref:HM03764)

**CARRUTHERS, P**

**P Carruthers**, 16 The Hawthornes, Broad Oak, Rye, **Sussex (East)**, TN31 6EN, ENG.
(T) 01424 882666
Speciality: Chiropodists (Podiatrists).
● **Owner** Mr P Carruthers
S (Ref:HM03765)

**CARRUTHERS, P**

**P Carruthers**, Iden Green Rd, Iden Green, Cranbrook, **Kent**, TN17 4HA, ENG.
(T) 01580 240668
Speciality: Chiropodists (Podiatrists).
S (Ref:HM03766)

**CARSON, BRONWYN**

**Bronwyn Carson**, Exeter, **Devon**, EX4, ENG.
(T) 01392 494716
Speciality: Osteopathy.
P S T (Ref:HM03767)

**CARSON, C**

**C Carson**, Dolphin House, St Peter St, Winchester, **Hampshire**, SO23 8BW, ENG.
(T) 01962 829735 (F) 01962 866116
Speciality: Psychiatry.
B (Ref:HM03768)

**CARSON, D**

**D Carson**, 11 Old Market Way, Moreton-in-Marsh, **Gloucestershire**, GL56 0AJ, ENG.
(T) 01608 652066
Speciality: Chiropodists (Podiatrists).
● **Owner** Dr D Carson
S (Ref:HM03769)

**CARSON, KAREN**

**La Carson**, 1 The Willows, Oriel Avenue, Gorleston, Great Yarmouth, **Norfolk**, NR31 7JJ, ENG.
(T) 01493 669661 (F) 01493 669661
(E) nick@carson20.freeserve.co.uk
Speciality: Chiropody. ✔
● **Surgical Chiropodist**
Mrs K Carson Q: MSSCh. M: B.A.Ch.P, SMAE.
● **Owner** Mr N Carsons
C Yrs. Est.: 2 (Ref:HM03770)

**CARSON, NICHOLAS**

**Nicholas Carson**, The Surgery, 10 Glebelands Rd, Tiverton, **Devon**, EX16 4EB, ENG.
(T) 01884 258736
Speciality: Osteopathy.
P S T (Ref:HM03771)

**CARSON, STEPHEN**

**Stephen Carson**, 45 Michleham Down, London, **London (Greater)**, N12 7JJ, ENG.
(T) 020 8445 8529
Speciality: Complementary Medicines & Therapy, Trichology.
M (Ref:HM03772)

**CARSTAIRS, K (DR)**

**Dr K Carstairs**, 7 Mayfield Rd, Bromley, **Kent**, BR1 2HB, ENG.
(T) 020 8325 1697 (F) 020 8325 1697
Speciality: Psychology.
● **Doctor** Dr K Carstairs
B (Ref:HM03773)

**CARTER, AMANDA**

**Amanda Carter**, 14 Douglas Avenue, Hythe, **Kent**, CT21 5JT, ENG.
(T) 01303 261459
Speciality: Reflexology.
S T (Ref:HM03774)

**CARTER, F J**

**F J Carter**, 45 Lime Tree Avenue, Retford, **Nottinghamshire**, DN22 7BB, ENG.
(T) 01777 703120
Speciality: Psychology.
B (Ref:HM03775)

**CARTER, G G**

**G G Carter**, 16 The Brittox, Devizes, **Wiltshire**, SN10 1AJ, ENG.
(T) 01380 728394
Speciality: Chiropodists (Podiatrists).
S (Ref:HM03776)

**CARTER, G R**

**G R Carter**, 13 Rolleston Drive, Wallasey, **Merseyside**, CH45 6XE, ENG.
(T) 01516 386026
Speciality: Chiropodists (Podiatrists).
● **Owner** Mr G Carter
S (Ref:HM03777)



Key continued: Yrs.Est: Years Established Q: Qualifications M: Professional Membership ✔ Indemnity Insurance Accept Credit Cards

**CARTER, G R**

**G R Carter**, 23 Westbourne Rd, Wirral, **Merseyside**, CH48 4DG, ENG.
(T) 01516 386026 (F) 01515 386026
Speciality: Biomechanics, Chiropody, Cryo Surgery, Nail Surgery, Orthotics, Podiatry. ✓
● **Chiropodist (Podiatrist)**
Mr G Carter Q: DPodM, S.R.Ch. M: S.C.P.
M Yrs. Est.: 25 (Ref:HM03778)

**CARTER, GERALD R**

**Gerald R Carter**, Apartment 2, Bramley Arms, 1 Bramley Rd, London, **London (Greater)**, W10 6SZ, ENG.
(T) 020 7792 3953
Speciality: Osteopathy.
P S T (Ref:HM03779)

**CARTER, J P**

**J P Carter**, 30 Burns Drive, Hemel Hempstead, **Hertfordshire**, HP2 7NR, ENG.
(T) 01442 261416
Speciality: Homeopathy.
● **Owner** Mrs J Carter
M (Ref:HM03780)

**CARTER, LINDA**

**Linda Carter**, 27 Warbleton Rd, Chineham, Basingstoke, **Hampshire**, RG24 8RF, ENG.
(T) 01256 478800
Speciality: Reflexology.
● **Owner** Ms L Carter
S T (Ref:HM03781)

**CARTER, LINDA P**

**Linda P Carter**, 58 Sidlaws Rd, Farnborough, **Hampshire**, GU14 9JN, ENG.
(T) 01252 548961
Speciality: Chiropodists (Podiatrists).
S (Ref:HM03782)

**CARTER, NICK**

**Nick Carter**, 24 Ellon Rd, Bridge Of Don, Aberdeen, **Aberdeenshire**, AB23 8BX, SCO.
(T) 01224 822956 (F) 01224 822960
Speciality: Osteopathy.
● **Director** Mrs M Brooks
P S T (Ref:HM03783)

**CARTER, S**

**S Carter**, The Wesley Lane Clinic, 6 Wesley Lane, Bicester, **Oxfordshire**, OX6 7JU, ENG.
(T) 01869 248538
Speciality: Chiropodists (Podiatrists).
S (Ref:HM03784)

**CARTER, SHEILA**

**Sheila Carter**, The Old Brewery House, Bath Rd, Shaw, Melksham, **Wiltshire**, SN12 8EG, ENG.
(T) 01225 700905 (F) 01225 700894
Speciality: Chiropodists (Podiatrists).
● **Partner** Mrs S Carter
S (Ref:HM03785)

**CARTER, SUSAN**

**Susan Carter**, 6 Quisters, Lyppard Hanford, Worcester, **Worcestershire**, WR4 0UT, ENG.
(T) 01905 617402
Speciality: Reflexology.
S T (Ref:HM03786)

**CARTER, T**

**T Carter**, The Wesley Lane Clinic, 6 Wesley Lane, Bicester, **Oxfordshire**, OX6 7JU, ENG.
(T) 01869 248538
Speciality: Chiropodists (Podiatrists).
S (Ref:HM03787)

**CARTER, TERRI**

**Terri Carter**, London Rd, Ramsgate, **Kent**, CT11 0DR, ENG.
(T) 01843 594744
Speciality: Chiropodists (Podiatrists).
● **Owner** Mrs T Carter
S (Ref:HM03788)

**CARTER, YVONNE**

**Yvonne Carter**, Drayton Crossroads Farmhouse, Newton Rd, Drayton Parslow, Milton Keynes, **Buckinghamshire**, MK17 0LB, ENG.
(T) 01908 373581 (F) 01908 373581
Speciality: Reflexology.
● **Owner** Mrs Y Carter
S T (Ref:HM03789)

**CARTER-REES, A G**

**A G Carter-Rees**, 42 Itchen Avenue, Eastleigh, **Hampshire**, SO50 8JZ, ENG.
(T) 023 8060 0344
Speciality: Physiotherapy.
● **Owner** A Carter-Rees
P S T (Ref:HM03790)

**CARTER-WEBER, LEE**

**Lee Carter-Weber**, 24 Coronation Avenue, Braintree, **Essex**, CM7 1EZ, ENG.
(T) 01376 554861
Speciality: Reflexology.
● **Owner** Ms L Carter-Weber
S T (Ref:HM03791)

**CARTEY, SARAH**

**Sarah Cartey**, 37 Walnut Avenue, Chichester, **Sussex (West)**, PO19 3EF, ENG.
Speciality: Reflexology.
S T (Ref:HM03792)

**CARTHY, MARY**

**Carthy Mary**, Keeragh View Ballygow Bannon, **County Wexford**, IRE.
(T) 05156 1400
Speciality: Healing.
B (Ref:HM03793)

**CARTLAND, ANN**

**Ann Cartland**, 63 Hills Rd, Steyning, **Sussex (West)**, BN44 3QG, ENG.
(T) 01903 814533 (F) 01903 814533
Speciality: Chiropody, Podiatry. ✓
● **Chiropodist (Podiatrist)**
Mrs A Cartland Q: MSSCh. M: SMAE.
M Yrs. Est.: 20 (Ref:HM03794)

**CARTLIDGE, S**

**S Cartlidge**, 39 Tydfil Pl, Cardiff, **Glamorgan (Vale of)**, CF23 5HP, WAL.
(T) 029 2048 4555
Speciality: Chiropractors.
P S T (Ref:HM03795)

**CARTLIDGE, S**

**S Cartlidge**, All Hallows House, Idol Lane, London, **London (Greater)**, EC3R 5DD, ENG.
(T) 020 7283 8908
Speciality: Chiropractors.
P S T (Ref:HM03796)

**CARTS, K P**

**K P Carts**, The Village Works, London Rd, East Hoathly, Lewes, **Sussex (East)**, BN8 6QA, ENG.
(T) 01825 841012 (F) 01825 841166
Speciality: Complementary Medicines & Therapy.
● **Owner** Mrs A Cousins
C M (Ref:HM03797)

**CARTWRIGHT, CECILIA**

**Cecilia Cartwright**, 105 Snape Hill Rd, Darfield, Barnsley, **Yorkshire (South)**, S73 9LR, ENG.
(T) 01226 752719 (F) 01226 752719
Speciality: Clairvoyants & Palmists.
● **Owner** Mrs C Cartwright
B (Ref:HM03798)

**CARTWRIGHT-ADAMS, NATALIE**

**Natalie Cartwright-Adams**, 4 Hartsbourne Rd, Bushey, Watford, **Hertfordshire**, WD2 1JH, ENG.
(T) 020 8950 7810
Speciality: Osteopathy.
P S T (Ref:HM03799)

**CARTWRIGHT-RAY, JOY**

**Joy Cartwright-Ray**, 18 Summer Lane, Minworth, Sutton Coldfield, **Midlands (West)**, B76 9AU, ENG.
(T) 01213 514505
Speciality: Hypnosis.
B (Ref:HM03800)

**CARVALHO, CAROL**

**Carol Carvalho**, 7 Cockshoot Cl, Stonesfield, Witney, **Oxfordshire**, OX8 8ED, ENG.
(T) 01993 898860
Speciality: Homeopathy.
M (Ref:HM03801)

**CARVELL, B R**

**B R Carvell**, 24 Coalpit Fields Rd, Bedworth, **Warwickshire**, CV12 9HW, ENG.
(T) 024 7664 0650
Speciality: Chiropodists (Podiatrists).
S (Ref:HM03802)

**CARVER-HARDY, LOUISE**

**Louise Carver-Hardy**, 3 Manor Cottages, Mary La South, Great Bromley, Colchester, **Essex**, CO7 7UD, ENG.
(T) 01206 250538
Speciality: Chiropodists (Podiatrists).
● **Owner** Mrs L Carver-Hardy
S (Ref:HM03803)

**CARYL, M D**

**M D Caryl**, 66 Friar St, Droitwich, **Worcestershire**, WR9 8EF, ENG.
(T) 01905 771405
Speciality: Chiropody. ✓
● **Chiropodist** Mrs M Caryl Q: L.I.S.Ch. M: L.I.S.Ch.
C Yrs. Est.: 32 (Ref:HM03804)

**CASA DELL' AROMA**

**Casa Dell' Aroma**, 71 St. Winifreds Av West, Harrogate, **Yorkshire (North)**, HG2 8LS, ENG.
(T) 01423 884830
Speciality: Aromatherapy.
M O (Ref:HM03805)

**CASE MANAGEMENT SERVICES**

**Case Management Services Ltd**, 17A Main St, Balerno, **Edinburgh (City of)**, EH14 7EQ, SCO.
(T) 01314 515265 (F) 01314 495158
Speciality: Psychology.
B (Ref:HM03806)

**CASE, BRENDA**

**Brenda Case**, 1 The Cl, Halton, Aylesbury, **Buckinghamshire**, HP22 5NJ, ENG.
(T) 01296 622716
Speciality: Osteopathy.
● **Owner** Ms B Case
P S T (Ref:HM03807)

**CASEMENT THERAPY CENTRE**

**Casement Therapy Centre**, Casement St, Ballina, **County Mayo**, IRE.
(T) 09672 900
Speciality: Complementary Medicines & Therapy.
M (Ref:HM03808)

**CASEY, MAXINE**

**Maxine Casey**, 33 Church Rd, Urmston, Manchester, **Manchester (Greater)**, M41 9FH, ENG.
(T) 01617 477295
Speciality: Chiropodists (Podiatrists).
S (Ref:HM03809)

**CASEY-KENNEDY, MARGARET**

**Margaret Casey-Kennedy**, 2 Farmside Green, Wolverhampton, **Midlands (West)**, WV9 5QW, ENG.
(T) 01902 784157
Speciality: Chiropodists (Podiatrists).
● **Owner** Mrs M Casey-Kenn
S (Ref:HM03810)

**CASH, G G**

**G G Cash Chiropodist**, 36 Foxes Croft, Barnham, Bognor Regis, **Sussex (West)**, PO22 0JT, ENG.
(T) 01243 554045
(E) gordon.cash@virigin.net
Speciality: Chiropody. ✓
● **Chiropodist** Mr C Cash Q: MBChA.
C Yrs. Est.: 176 (Ref:HM03811)

**CASKEY, ANYA**

**Anya Caskey**, 80 Nightingale Rd, Rickmansworth, **Hertfordshire**, WD3 2BT, ENG.
(T) 01923 897514
Speciality: Physiotherapy.
● **Owner** Mrs A Caskey
P S T (Ref:HM03812)

**CASSANDRA**

**Cassandra**, 1 Elizabeth Rd, Basingstoke, **Hampshire**, RG22 6AX, ENG.
(T) 01256 417731
Speciality: Clairvoyants & Palmists.
● **Owner** Ms C Watmore

Key: B Mind-Body Medicine; C Complementary Medicine; H Self Help Treatment; M Medicinal Therapy; O Oriental Medicine; P Postural Therapy; S Manipulative Structural Therapy; T Touch Therapy

B (Ref:HM03813)

## CASSELL, JOHN

**John Cassell**, 34 Northover Rd, Portsmouth, **Hampshire**, PO3 6NT, ENG.
(T) 023 9266 4720
Speciality: Cranio-Sacral Therapy. ✓
● **Owner** Mr J Cassell Q: RCST.
C Yrs. Est.: 8 (Ref:HM03814)

## CASSIDY MEDICAL CENTRE

**Cassidy Medical Centre**, 651A Fulham Rd, Fulham, London, **London (Greater)**, SW6 5PX, ENG.
(T) 020 7731 2511
Speciality: Manipulation, Massage (Therapeutic), Osteopathy. ✓
● **Osteopath** Mr T Stafford Q: DO. M: GOsC.
S Yrs. Est.: 6 (Ref:HM03815)

## CASSIDY, D J

**D J Cassidy**, Suite 2 28 The Spain, Petersfield, **Hampshire**, GU32 3LA, ENG.
(T) 01730 267645
Speciality: Physiotherapy.
P S T (Ref:HM03816)

## CASSIDY, LINDA

**Linda Cassidy**, 48 Elizabeth Avenue, Stockport, **Cheshire**, SK1 3QA, ENG.
(T) 01614 779270
Speciality: Electrolysis.
T (Ref:HM03817)

## CASSIDY, M

**M Cassidy**, 137 Almond Rd, Gorleston, Great Yarmouth, **Norfolk**, NR31 8EN, ENG.
(T) 01493 440860
Speciality: Physiotherapy.
P S T (Ref:HM03818)

## CASSIDY, SUSAN

**Susan Cassidy B S St CQSW, M S Sc Psy**, Liffey Bdge Hse, 1 Main St, Lucan, **County Dublin**, IRE.
(T) 01628 3431
Speciality: Complementary Medicines & Therapy.
M (Ref:HM03819)

## CASSIDY, TRISH

**Trish Cassidy**, 4 Sandringham Avenue, West Bridgford, Nottingham, **Nottinghamshire**, NG2 7QS, ENG.
(T) 01159 815530
Speciality: Aromatherapy, Reflexology.
M O (Ref:HM03820)

## CASSIN SCOTT ASSOCIATES

**Cassin Scott Associates Ltd**, Bishops Walk House, 19-23 High St, Pinner, **London (Greater)**, HA5 5PJ, ENG.
(T) 020 8866 5735 (F) 020 8866 6927
Speciality: Psychology.
● **Sole Director** Ms S Scott
B (Ref:HM03821)

## CAST, BRIAN

**Brian Cast**, High St, Beckenham, **Kent**, BR3 1AH, ENG.
(T) 020 8658 0795
Speciality: Chiropodists (Podiatrists).
S (Ref:HM03822)

## CASTELL, JENNIE

**Jennie Castell**, 8a Napier Rd, Edinburgh, **Edinburgh (City of)**, EH10 5BD, SCO.
(T) 01314 475364
Speciality: Homeopathy.
● **Owner** Mrs J Castell
M (Ref:HM03823)

## CASTELL, JENNIE

**Jennie Castell**, Bridgend, Yarrow Trce, Selkirk, **Scottish Borders**, TD7 5AS, SCO.
(T) 01314 475364
Speciality: Homeopathy.
M (Ref:HM03824)

## CASTELL, PHILIPPA

**Philippa Castell**, 25 Hillside Cres, Uplands, Swansea, SA2 0RD, WAL.
(T) 01792 473415
Speciality: Alexander Technique.
● **Owner** Ms P Castell
P S (Ref:HM03825)

## CASTERBRIDGE CHIROPRACTIC

**Casterbridge Chiropractic Clinic (The)**, 7 Icen Way, Dorchester, **Dorset**, DT1 1EW, ENG.
(T) 01305 263048 (F) 01305 251375
Speciality: Chiropractors.
● **Owner** Mr L Plunkett
P S T (Ref:HM03826)

## CASTLE CENTRE

**Castle Centre (The)**, 14a Broughton St Lane, Edinburgh, **Edinburgh (City of)**, EH1 3LY, SCO.
(T) 01315 566641
Speciality: Alexander Technique.
● **Teacher** Mr J Snell
P S (Ref:HM03827)

## CASTLE CHIROPODY CLINIC

**Castle Chiropody Clinic**, 14 The Plain, Thornbury, Bristol, BS35 2BD, ENG.
(T) 01454 416772
Speciality: Biomechanics, Chiropody, Nail Surgery, Orthotics. ✓
● **Partner/Chiropodist** Mrs A Down Q: BSc, M.S.C.P, S.R.Ch. M: S.C.P.
M Yrs. Est.: 16 (Ref:HM03828)

## CASTLE CHIROPRACTIC CLINIC

**ME & TH Stone T/A Castle Chiropractic Clinic**, 26 Castle St, Barnstaple, **Devon**, EX31 1DR, ENG.
(T) 01271 327444 (F) 01271 329166
Speciality: Chiropractic, Manipulation, Vitamin Therapy, X-Ray. ✓ [credit card]
● **Chiropractor** Dr M Stone Q: BA, DC. M: BCA.
S Yrs. Est.: 8 (Ref:HM03829)

## CASTLE CLINIC

**Castle Clinic (The)**, Castle Clinic, 5 Castle Hill Rd, Dover, **Kent**, CT16 1QG, ENG.
(T) 01304 202352 (F) 01304 216366
Speciality: Acupuncture, Aromatherapy, Counselling, Hypnosis, Hypnotherapy, Massage (Therapeutic), Osteopathy, Psychotherapy. ✓
● **Osteopath** Mr J Morgan Q: DO, MSc.
● **Nutritional Therapist** Ms V Carter M: ION.
● **Chiropodist (Podiatrist)** Ms K Toone-Jackson Q: M.S.C.P, S.R.Ch. M: S.C.P.
● **Aromatherapist/Reflexologist** Ms F Hollis Q: IIHHT, IIST, MIFA. M: IFA.
● **Sports Massage Therapist/Personal Trainer** Ms K Bradford Q: IIST.
● **Osteopath** Ms P Morgan Q: DO.
● **Hypnotherapist** Ms A Rozard
● **Homeopath** Mr K Smith Q: LCPH, MHMA. M: HMA.
● **Acupuncturist** Ms L Wilson Q: BA, BSc, MBAcC.
B T Yrs. Est.: 12 (Ref:HM03830)

## CASTLE CLINIC

**Castle Clinic (The)**, 23 St Marys St, Bridgnorth, **Shropshire**, WV16 4DW, ENG.
(T) 01746 768886
Speciality: Homeopathy.
● **Owner** Mr L Marlow
M (Ref:HM03831)

## CASTLE CLINIC

**Castle Clinic (The)**, 18-20 The Ropewalk, Nottingham, **Nottinghamshire**, NG1 5DT, ENG.
(T) 01159 472263 (F) 01159 556306
Speciality: Complementary Medicines & Therapy.
● **Owner** Mr M Pook
M (Ref:HM03832)

## CASTLE HILL CLINIC

**Castle Hill Chiropody Clinic**, 1c Tilehurst Rd, Reading, **Berkshire**, RG1 7TW, ENG.
(T) 01189 586766 (F) 01189 509244
Speciality: Acupuncture, Chiropody, Cryo Surgery, Homeopathy, Hypnotherapy, Indian Head Massage, Nutritional Therapy. [credit card]
● **Nutritional Therapist** Luis Alberto Nafig Q: Dip.Nutrition. M: BCMA.
● **Hypnotist** Mr P Haynes
● **Acupuncturist** Dr R Sharma
● **Masseur/Homeopath** Ms M Ralph
C (Ref:HM03833)

## CASTLE POINT PHYSIO CLINIC

**Castle Point Physiotherapy Clinic**, 4 Park Chase, Benfleet, **Essex**, SS7 2BZ, ENG.
(T) 01702 551177 (F) 01702 551177
Speciality: Physiotherapy.
● **Practice Manager** Mrs J Taylorson
P S T (Ref:HM03834)

## CASTLE ROAD OSTEO PRACTICE

**Castle Road Osteopathic Practice**, 64A Castle Rd, London, **London (Greater)**, NW1 8SN, ENG.
(T) 020 7267 8847 (F) 020 7916 9200
Speciality: Osteopathy.
P S T (Ref:HM03835)

## CASTLE STREET CHIRO CLINIC

**Castle Street Chiropractic Clinic**, 43 Castle St, Trowbridge, **Wiltshire**, BA14 8AS, ENG.
(T) 01225 766662
Speciality: Chiropractic.
● **Owner** Mr W Rhodes Q: DC, NACM.
H Yrs. Est.: 10 (Ref:HM03836)

## CASTLE STREET CLINIC

**Castle Street Clinic**, 19 Castle St, High Wycombe, **Buckinghamshire**, HP13 6RU, ENG.
(T) 01494 530004
(E) robert@pettingell.fsnet.co.uk
Speciality: Acupuncture, Alexander Technique, Aromatherapy, Cranial Osteopathy, Homeopathy, Hypnosis, Hypnotherapy, Kinesiology, Manipulation, Nutritional Therapy, Osteopathy, Pilates, Psychotherapy, Reflexology. ✓
● **Acupuncturist** Ms M Marsland Q: Lic.Ac. M: BAcC.
● **Osteopath** Ms A Wright Q: DO. M: GOsC.
● **Osteopath** Mr P Middle Q: BSc. M: GOsC.
● **Osteopath** Mr R Pettingell Q: DO. M: GOsC.
● **Osteopath** Ms L Seymour Q: DO. M: GOsC.
C S Yrs. Est.: 15 (Ref:HM03837)

## CASTLE STREET CLINIC

**Castle Street Clinic**, 36-37 Castle St, Guildford, **Surrey**, GU1 3UQ, ENG.
(T) 01483 300400
Speciality: Complementary Medicines & Therapy.
M (Ref:HM03838)

## CASTLE STREET CLINIC

**Castle Street Clinic (The)**, 43 Castle St, Trowbridge, **Wiltshire**, BA14 8AY, ENG.
(T) 01225 763898
Speciality: Chiropractic.
S (Ref:HM03839)

## CASTLE SURGERY

**Vinewood Healthcare**, 9 Church St, Bridgwater, **Somerset**, TA6 5AT, ENG.
(T) 01278 457730
Speciality: Acupuncture, Aromatherapy, Chiropractic, Counselling, Homeopathy, Osteopathy, Reflexology. ✓
● **Osteopath/Acupuncturist** Mr S Woods Q: DO.
● **Homeopath/Associate** Mr J Reighton Q: DACH, L.C.C.H.
● **Chiropractor** Dr C France Q: BSc (Chiro).
● **Chiropractor** Dr A Stewart Q: DC. M: BCA.
P S T Yrs. Est.: 25 (Ref:HM03840)

## CASTLE TAROT

**Castle Tarot**, The Old Post Office, Davis Way, Hurst, Reading, **Berkshire**, RG10 0TR, ENG.
(T) 01189 320607
Speciality: Clairvoyants & Palmists.
● **Owner** Mrs L Lajer
B (Ref:HM03841)

## CASTLE VALE CHIROPODY SERVICE

**Castle Vale Chiropody Service**, Clifford Coombes Centre, 70 Tangmere Drive, Birmingham, **Midlands (West)**, B35 7QX, ENG.
(T) 01217 475181
Speciality: Chiropodists (Podiatrists).
S (Ref:HM03842)

## CASTLEBAR HEALTHCARE CLINIC

**Castlebar Healthcare Clinic**, Linenhall St, Castlebar, **County Mayo**, IRE.
(T) 09425 655



Key continued: Yrs.Est: Years Established Q: Qualifications M: Professional Membership ✓ Indemnity Insurance [credit card] Accept Credit Cards

Speciality: Complementary Medicines & Therapy.
M (Ref:HM03843)

## CASTLEBRIDGE CHIRO & REFLEX
**Castlebridge Chiropody & Reflexology**, 13A Bridgetown, Totnes, **Devon**, TQ9 5AB, ENG.
(T) 01803 865345 (F) 01803 211616
(W) www.castlebridge-chiropody.co.uk
Speciality: Chiropody, Reflexology. ✔
● **Owner** Mr P Grantham Q: MICHT, MSSCh. M: AMRSH, B.A.Ch.P.
M Yrs. Est.: 10 (Ref:HM03844)

## CASTLEBRIDGE CHIRO & REFLEX
**Castlebridge Chiropody & Reflexology**, Suite 26, Castle Circus House, Union St, Torquay, **Devon**, TQ2 5QG, ENG.
(T) 01803 211616
Speciality: Chiropodists (Podiatrists).
S (Ref:HM03845)

## CASTLEFIELDS SURGERY
**Castlefields Surgery**, Castleway, Castlefields, Stafford, **Staffordshire**, ST16 1BS, ENG.
(T) 01785 248298
Speciality: Osteopathy. ✔
● **Osteopath** Mr D Cooper Q: DO. M: GOsC.
● **Osteopath** Mr K Chew Q: BSc, Hons (OST). M: GOsC.
● **Osteopath** Ian Whyte Q: DO. M: GOsC.
S Yrs. Est.: 23 (Ref:HM03846)

## CASTLEGATE OSTEO PRACTICE
**Castlegate Osteopathic Practice (The)**, 70 Castlegate, Grantham, **Lincolnshire**, NG31 6SH, ENG.
(T) 01476 590845
Speciality: Osteopathy. ✔
● **Osteopath** Mr R Montgomery Q: BSc, Hons (OST). M: GOsC.
● **Osteopath** Ms R Shaw Q: BSc, Hons (OST). M: GOsC.
● **Practice Manager** Mrs W Drew
● **Osteopath** Mr M Buffree Q: DO, M.Med.Sc. M: GOsC.
P S Yrs. Est.: 11 (Ref:HM03847)

## CASTLEKNOCK PHYSIOTHERAPY
**Castleknock Physiotherapy & Acupuncture Clinic**, 1 Auburn Gn, Castleknock, Dublin, **County Dublin**, IRE.
(T) 01820 1668
Speciality: Acupuncture.
O (Ref:HM03848)

## CASTLETON, DAVID
**David Castleton**, Wellbrook Clinic, 21 Stafford Rd, Wallington, **Surrey**, SM6 9AN, ENG.
(T) 020 8401 0011
Speciality: Psychotherapy.
B (Ref:HM03849)

## CASTLETON, S
**S Castleton**, 18 Park Rd North, Middlesbrough, **Cleveland**, TS1 3LF, ENG.
(T) 01642 217557 (F) 01642 231806
Speciality: Osteopathy.
● **Owner** Mr S Castleton
P S T (Ref:HM03850)

## CASWELL, KERI
**Keri Caswell**, Lavender Cottage, 11 The Brook, Old Alresford, Alresford, **Hampshire**, SO24 9DQ, ENG.
(T) 01962 734189
Speciality: Reflexology.
S T (Ref:HM03851)

## CATCHPOLE, J
**J Catchpole**, 30 Princethorpe Rd, Kesgrave, Ipswich, **Suffolk**, IP5 2NY, ENG.
(T) 01473 271171 (F) 01473 271171
Speciality: Chiropodists (Podiatrists).
● **Partner** Mr J Catchpole
S (Ref:HM03852)

## CATERHAM CHIROPRACTIC CLINIC
**Caterham Chiropractic Clinic**, 9a Station Avenue, Caterham, **Surrey**, CR3 6LB, ENG.
(T) 01883 344354
Speciality: Chiropractic. ✔
● **Owner** Dr S Norton Q: DC. M: BCA, GCC.
P Yrs. Est.: 15 (Ref:HM03853)

## CATERHAM OSTEOPATHIC PRACTICE
**Caterham Osteopathic Practice**, 70 High St, Caterham, **Surrey**, CR3 5UD, ENG.
(T) 01883 344301
Speciality: Osteopathy.
● **Employee** Mr G Reilly
P S T (Ref:HM03854)

## CATERHAM VALLEY CHIROPRACTIC
**Caterham Valley Chiropractic Clinic (The)**, Eothen House, Eothen Cl, Caterham, **Surrey**, CR3 6JU, ENG.
(T) 01883 331221 (F) 01883 331221
Speciality: Chiropractors.
● **Director** Mr C Hamp
P S T (Ref:HM03855)

## CATHAY CHINESE HERBS
**Cathay Chinese Herbs & Health**, 28 Blackheath Village, London, **London (Greater)**, SE3 9SY, ENG.
(T) 020 8852 6118
Speciality: Herbalists.
M (Ref:HM03856)

## CATHCART, ALISON
**Alison Cathcart**, 64 Wellington Rd, Enfield, **London (Greater)**, EN1 2PH, ENG.
(T) 020 8360 9416
Speciality: Physiotherapy.
P S T (Ref:HM03857)

## CATHRINA'S CLINIC
**Cathrina's Clinic**, 1a Lower Catherine St, Newry, **County Down**, BT35 6DE, **NIR**.
(T) 028 3026 6293
Speciality: Chiropodists (Podiatrists).
● **Owner** Mrs C Love
S (Ref:HM03858)

## CATON, PETER
**Peter Caton**, 46 Wanstead Lane, Ilford, **Essex**, IG1 3SD, ENG.
(T) 020 8554 9063
Speciality: Auto Suggestion, Autogenic Training, Biofeedback, Cognitive Therapy, Counselling, Dietician, Family Therapy, Herbal Medicine, Hypnosis, Meditation, Nutritional Therapy, Psychotherapy, Stress Therapy, Visualisation Therapy, Vitamin Therapy, Voice Therapy. ✔
● **Hypnotherapist** Mr P Caton Q: Dip.Hyp, Dip.Psych. M: HS, NCH.
H Yrs. Est.: 20 (Ref:HM03859)

## CATTERALL, KEVIN
**Kevin Catterall**, Aldrens Lane, Lancaster, **Lancashire**, LA1 2DU, ENG.
(T) 01524 69864 (F) 01524 848155
Speciality: Chiropodists (Podiatrists).
S (Ref:HM03860)

## CATTO & ASSOCIATES
**A G Catto & Associates**, 370A Upper Richmond Rd West, London, **London (Greater)**, SW14 7JU, ENG.
(T) 020 8876 5063
Speciality: Chiropodists (Podiatrists).
S (Ref:HM03861)

## CAULKIN, CHRISTOPHER
**Christopher Caulkin**, 58-60 King Edward St, Hull, **Humberside (North)**, HU1 3SQ, ENG.
(T) 01482 589516
Speciality: Chiropodists (Podiatrists).
● **Owner** Mr C Caulkin
S (Ref:HM03862)

## CAVANAGH, CHERYL
**Cheryl Cavanagh**, 8 Beech Drive, Bridgwater, **Somerset**, TA6 4DU, ENG.
(T) 01278 458866
Speciality: Reflexology.
S T (Ref:HM03863)

## CAVERSHAM CHIROPRACTIC CLINC
**Caversham Chiropractic Clinic**, 85 Kidmore Rd, Caversham, Reading, **Berkshire**, RG4 7NQ, ENG.
(T) 01189 471115
Speciality: Chiropractic. ✔
● **Chiropractor** Dr R Pim Q: DC. M: BCA, GCC.
P S T Yrs. Est.: 17 (Ref:HM03864)

## CAVERSHAM COUN & PSYCHOTHERAPY
**Caversham Counselling & Psychotherapy**, 38A Priest Hill, Caversham, Reading, **Berkshire**, RG4 7RY, ENG.
(T) 01189 473686
Speciality: Psychotherapy.
● **Administrator** Ms L Banks
B (Ref:HM03865)

## CAVERSHAM FOOT CLINIC
**Caversham Foot Clinic**, 25 Prospect St, Caversham, Reading, **Berkshire**, RG4 8JB, ENG.
(T) 01189 482999
Speciality: Absent Healing, Aromatherapy, Chiropody, Complementary Therapy, Counselling, Crystal Healing, Faith Healing, Healer, Healing Therapy, Holistic Healing, Homeopathy, Indian Head Massage, Life Style Coaching, Meditation, Nutritional Therapy, Psychotherapy, Reflexology, Reiki, Seichem, Stress Therapy, Tera-Mai, Visualisation Therapy. ✔
● **Therapist** Ms M Ralph
● **Owner** Mrs E Burt
(T) 01189 482999or01189478996 Q: Reiki Master. M: S.C.P.
● **Senior Reflexologist** Mr A Campbell
S (Ref:HM03866)

## CAVIL, A J
**A J Cavil**, 9a Gelliwastad Rd, Pontypridd, **Rhondda Cynon Taff**, CF37 2BW, **WAL**.
(T) 01443 485302
Speciality: Osteopathy.
● **Owner** Mrs A Cavil
P S T (Ref:HM03867)

## CAWDRON, TESSA
**Tessa Cawdron**, Castleton House, Castle St, Mere, Warminster, **Wiltshire**, BA12 6JE, ENG.
(T) 01747 860161
Speciality: Alexander Technique.
P S (Ref:HM03868)

## CAWLEY, LOUISE
**Louise Cawley**, 28 Wedderburn Rd, Malvern, **Worcestershire**, WR14 2DG, ENG.
(T) 01242 863739
Speciality: Reflexology.
S T (Ref:HM03869)

## CAWLEY, MICHAEL
**Michael Cawley Ac (China)**, Centrepoint Main St, Cabinteely, Dublin, **County Dublin**, IRE.
(T) 01285 2831
Speciality: Complementary Medicines & Therapy.
M (Ref:HM03870)

## CAWLEY, TONY
**Anthony Cawley**, 44 Wellesley Rd, Liverpool, **Merseyside**, L8 3SU, ENG.
(T) 01517 271485
Speciality: Cognitive Therapy, Counselling, Humanistic Psychology, Hypnosis, Hypnotherapy, Meditation, Psychotherapy, Rogerian Therapy, Stress Therapy, Visualisation Therapy. ✔
● **Hypno-Psychotherapist** Mr T Cawley Q: DHP (NC). M: NRHP, UKCP.
B Yrs. Est.: 14 (Ref:HM03871)

## CAYNE, J COUN & PSYCHOTHERAPY
**Cayne Julia Counselling & Psychotherapy**, Vindomis Cl, Holybourne, Alton, **Hampshire**, GU34 4HL, ENG.
(T) 01420 85539
Speciality: Psychotherapy.
B (Ref:HM03872)

## CECIL, MARGO
**Margo Cecil**, 27 Garden Cl, Shoreham-by-Sea, **Sussex (West)**, BN43 6BR, ENG.
(T) 01273 452747
Speciality: Clairvoyants & Palmists.
B (Ref:HM03873)

## CEDAR LODGE
**Cedar Lodge**, 53 Stoneham Lane, Southampton, **Hampshire**, SO16 2NZ, ENG.
(T) 023 8034 9185
Speciality: Aromatherapy.
● **Owner** Mrs T Gradidge
M O (Ref:HM03874)



Key: B Mind-Body Medicine C Complementary Medicine H Self Help Treatment M Medicinal Therapy O Oriental Medicine P Postural Therapy S Manipulative Structural Therapy T Touch Therapy

## CEDAR LODGE
**Cedar Lodge**, 100 Cedar Rd, **Hampshire**, SO14 6TH, ENG.
(T) 023 8034 9185
Speciality: Aromatherapy.
M O (Ref:HM03875)

## CEDARBANK CENTRE PSYCHOL SVS
**Cedarbank Centre Psychological Services**, Ladywell East, Livingston, **Lothian (West)**, EH54 6DR, SCO.
(T) 01506 775800
Speciality: Psychology.
B (Ref:HM03876)

## CEDARFIELD
**Cedarfield**, 30 Waterloo St, Weston-Super-Mare, **Somerset**, BS23 1LN, ENG.
(T) 01278 794331
Speciality: Complementary Medicines & Therapy.
● **Owner** Mrs J Quinlan
C M (Ref:HM03877)

## CEDARS OSTEOPATH CLINIC
**Cedars Osteopath Clinic**, 197 Headstone Lane, Harrow, **London (Greater)**, HA2 6ND, ENG.
(T) 020 8428 2629 (F) 020 8428 2629
Speciality: Osteopathy.
● **Owner** Mr H Davdani
P S T (Ref:HM03878)

## CEDARWOOD CLINIC
**Cedarwood Clinic (The)**, 4 Girton Gdns, Croydon, **Surrey**, CR0 8PX, ENG.
(T) 020 8654 4461
Speciality: Reflexology.
S T (Ref:HM03879)

## CELBRIDGE PHYSIOTHERAPY
**Celbridge Physiotherapy & Acupuncture Clinic**, Main St, Celbridge, **County Kildare**, IRE.
(T) 01627 5628
Speciality: Acupuncture.
O (Ref:HM03880)

## CELEBRITY CENTRE LONDON
**Celebrity Centre London**, 27 Westbourne Gr, London, **London (Greater)**, W2 4UA, ENG.
(T) 020 7229 1065
Speciality: Complementary Medicines & Therapy.
M (Ref:HM03881)

## CELESTIAL DESIGNS AROMATHERAPY
**Celestial Designs Aromatherapy**, 4 Tan Y Gyrt Hall, Nantglyn, Denbigh, **Denbighshire**, LL16 5PD, WAL.
(T) 01745 550411
(W) www.aroma-shop.co.uk
Speciality: Aromatherapy.
● **Partner** Mrs J Whittaker
● **Partner** Mr D Whittaker
C Yrs. Est.: 9 (Ref:HM03882)

## CELTIC AROMATICS
**Celtic Aromatics**, 156 Greenbank Rd, Edinburgh, **Edinburgh (City of)**, EH10 5RN, SCO.
(T) 01314 474129 (F) 01314 479833
Speciality: Aromatherapy.
● **Owner** Mrs Y Jevons
M O (Ref:HM03883)

## CELTIC GRAINBAGS
**Celtic Grainbags**, Unit 13, Visicks Works, Perranarworthal, Truro, **Cornwall**, TR3 7NR, ENG.
(T) 01872 870706
Speciality: Complementary Medicines & Therapy.
● **Partner** Mr M Meppley
M (Ref:HM03884)

## CELTIC HEALTH CENTRE
**Celtic Health Centre**, 117-119, Ranelagh, **County Dublin**, IRE.
(T) 01491 0689
(E) celtichealth@clubi.ie
Speciality: Complementary Medicines & Therapy.
M (Ref:HM03885)

## CELTIC HEALTH CLINIC
**Celtic Health Clinic**, 117 Ranelagh Rd, Dublin, **County Dublin**, IRE.
(T) 01491 0689
Speciality: Complementary Medicines & Therapy.
M (Ref:HM03886)

## CENTRAL CHARTERED PHYSIO
**Central Chartered Physiotherapist**, Kedleston House, Aspen Drive, Spondon, Derby, **Derbyshire**, DE21 7SS, ENG.
(T) 01332 281411
Speciality: Physiotherapy.
P S T (Ref:HM03887)

## CENTRAL CHIROPODY CLINIC
**Central Chiropody Clinic**, 49 Bull St, West Bromwich Ringway, West Bromwich, **Midlands (West)**, B70 6EU, ENG.
(T) 01216 016677
Speciality: Chiropody. ✔
● **Owner** Mr G Uppal Q: S.R.Ch.
T Yrs. Est.: 2 (Ref:HM03888)

## CENTRAL CHIROPODY CLINIC
**Central Chiropody Clinic**, 21 Orchard St, Swansea, SA1 5AG, WAL.
(T) 01792 646000
Speciality: Chiropodists (Podiatrists).
S (Ref:HM03889)

## CENTRAL CHIROPRACTIC CLINIC
**Central Chiropractic Clinic**, 96 London Rd, Southend-On-Sea, **Essex**, SS1 1PG, ENG.
(T) 01702 342329
Speciality: Chiropractic.
● **Partner** Mr L Graham
P S T (Ref:HM03890)

## CENTRAL CHIROPRACTIC CLINIC
**Central Chiropractic Clinic**, North Hinksey Lane, Oxford, **Oxfordshire**, OX2 0JW, ENG.
(T) 01865 204246
Speciality: Chiropractic.
P S T (Ref:HM03891)

## CENTRAL HEALTH CLINIC
**Central Health Clinic**, Mulberry St, Sheffield, **Yorkshire (South)**, S1 2PJ, ENG.
(T) 01142 716798
Speciality: Chiropodists (Podiatrists).
S (Ref:HM03892)

## CENTRAL HYPNOTHERAPY UNIT
**Central Hypnotherapy Unit**, 7a Chepstow Villas, London, **London (Greater)**, W11 3EE, ENG.
(T) 020 7229 4726
Speciality: Hypnosis.
B (Ref:HM03893)

## CENTRAL LONDON PHYSIO CLINIC
**Central London Physiotherapy Clinic**, 106 Harley St, London, **London (Greater)**, W1N 1AF, ENG.
(T) 020 7486 5238
Speciality: Physiotherapy.
● **Partner** Ms R Keer
P S T (Ref:HM03894)

## CENTRAL LONDON SCHOOL-REFLEX
**Central London School Of Reflexology**, 15 King St, London, **London (Greater)**, WC2E 8HN, ENG.
(T) 020 7240 1438
Speciality: Complementary Medicines & Therapy.
C M (Ref:HM03895)

## CENTRAL PHYSIOTHERAPY SERVICES
**Central Physiotherapy Services**, 12 Cedar Rd, Redditch, **Worcestershire**, B97 6HN, ENG.
(T) 01527 585090
Speciality: Physiotherapy.
P S T (Ref:HM03896)

## CENTRE
**Centre (The)**, The Old Police Station, 18 Prospect Rd, Hythe, **Kent**, CT21 5NH, ENG.
(T) 01303 270389 (F) 01303 230800
Speciality: Acupuncture, Allergy Testing, Aromatherapy, Counselling, Homeopathy, Hypnotherapy, Meditation, Nutritional Therapy, Osteopathy, Reflexology, Reiki, Spiritual Healing, Chinese Herbs and Sports Therapy. ✔
● **Therapist** Ms J Plummer Q: Reiki Master.
C Yrs. Est.: 1 (Ref:HM03897)

## CENTRE ASSOCIATION OF PSYCHO
**Centre Association Of Psychotherapists**, 145 Chapel Lane, Longton, Preston, **Lancashire**, PR4 5NA, ENG.
(T) 01772 617663 (F) 01772 617663
Speciality: Psychotherapy.
● **Office Manager** Miss S Washington
B (Ref:HM03898)

## CENTRE FOR COMP HEALTHCARE
**Centre For Complementary Healthcare Ltd**, Unit 3 Old Sarum House, The Plocks, Blandford Forum, **Dorset**, DT11 7AA, ENG.
(T) 01258 458120
Speciality: Complementary Medicines & Therapy.
● **Administrator** Alyson Joann Black
M (Ref:HM03899)

## CENTRE FOR COMP MEDICINE
**Centre For Complementary Medicine (The)**, 18 Church St, Adlington, Chorley, **Lancashire**, PR7 4EX, ENG.
(T) 01257 481456
Speciality: Homeopathy.
● **Manager** Mrs K Maidment
M (Ref:HM03900)

## CENTRE FOR COMP MEDICINE
**Centre For Complementary Medicine (The)**, 20 Lavant St, Petersfield, **Hampshire**, GU32 3EW, ENG.
(T) 01730 231655
Speciality: Homeopathy. ✔
● **Homeopath** Mr R Cook Q: BSc, MCH, RSHom. M: Soc.Hom.
C M Yrs. Est.: 10 (Ref:HM03901)

## CENTRE FOR COMP THERAPIES
**Centre For Complementary Therapies**, Maslin House, Kinmylies Way, Inverness, **Highland**, IV3 8TP, SCO.
(T) 01463 713614
Speciality: Chiropodists (Podiatrists).
● **Director** Mr L McKerrow
S (Ref:HM03902)

## CENTRE FOR CREATIVE CHANGE
**Centre For Creative Change**, 14 Upr Clanbrassil St, Dublin, **County Dublin**, IRE.
(T) 01453 8356
Speciality: Complementary Medicines & Therapy.
M (Ref:HM03903)

## CENTRE FOR HEALTH AND HEALING
**Centre for Health and Healing**, Christ Church, 27 Blackfriars Rd, London, **London (Greater)**, SE1 8NY, ENG.
(T) 020 7928 6378
Speciality: Alexander Technique.
● **Therapist** Mr M Gothill
P S (Ref:HM03904)

## CENTRE FOR HEALTH HEALING
**Centre For Health Healing & Self Development**, Croft Bank, Malvern, **Worcestershire**, WR14 4DU, ENG.
(T) 01684 573868 (F) 01684 892047
Speciality: Complementary Medicines & Therapy.
● **Director** Mr A Neate
C M (Ref:HM03905)

## CENTRE FOR HOLISTIC HEALTH
**Centre For Holistic Health**, 70 Douglas St, **County Cork**, IRE.
(T) 021 4321 857
(W) www.corkfloats.com
Speciality: Complementary Medicines & Therapy.
M (Ref:HM03906)

## CENTRE FOR HOLISTIC THERAPIES
**Centre For Holistic Therapies**, Blackwell Building, Brook St, Neston, **Cheshire**, CH64 9XJ, ENG.
(T) 01513 366222
Speciality: Complementary Medicines & Therapy.
● **Partner** Mrs J Hayes



Key continued: Yrs.Est: Years Established Q: Qualifications M: Professional Membership ✔ Indemnity Insurance Accept Credit Cards

**M** (**Ref:**HM03907)

## CENTRE FOR HYPNOSIS

**Centre For Hypnosis**, Care Of Good Life Natural Health Clinic, 1 Waterloo Rd, Epsom, **Surrey**, KT19 8AY, ENG.
(T) 01372 742095
Speciality: Hypnotherapy.
● **Owner** Mrs J Panchaud
**B** (**Ref:**HM03908)

## CENTRE FOR HYPNOSIS

**Centre For Hypnosis**, Woodland House, Cripplegate Lane, Southwater, Horsham, **Sussex (West)**, RH13 7HN, ENG.
(T) 01403 738472
Speciality: Hypnotherapy.
● **Owner** Mrs J Panchaud
**B** (**Ref:**HM03909)

## CENTRE FOR NATURAL HEALING

**Centre For Natural Healing (The)**, 268 Penn Rd, Wolverhampton, **Midlands (West)**, WV4 4AD, ENG.
(T) 01902 339877 (F) 01902 620668
Speciality: Complementary Medicines & Therapy.
● **Owner** Mrs L Porter
**C** **M** (**Ref:**HM03910)

## CENTRE FOR NATURAL HEALTH

**Centre For Natural Health**, Ainderby Hall, Ainderby Steeple, Northallerton, **Yorkshire (North)**, DL7 9QJ, ENG.
(T) 01609 770953
Speciality: Complementary Medicines & Therapy.
● **Manager** Mrs A Barnett
**C** **M** (**Ref:**HM03911)

## CENTRE FOR NATURAL HEALTH

**Centre For Natural Health (The)**, 2 Marshall Pl, Perth, **Perth and Kinross**, PH2 8AH, SCO.
(T) 01738 630353 (F) 01738 442275
Speciality: Complementary Medicines & Therapy.
● **Owner** Mr J Page
**C** **M** (**Ref:**HM03912)

## CENTRE FOR NATURAL THERAPIES

**Centre For Natural Therapies (The)**, 31 Acfold Rd, Birmingham, **Midlands (West)**, B20 1HD, ENG.
(T) 01213 570701
Speciality: Aromatherapy, Bowen Therapy, Chiropody, Homeopathy, Hypnotherapy, Reflexology, Reiki. ✔
● **Owner** Miss A Bell Q: B.V.M.S, LCPH, MRCVS.
**B** **C** Yrs. Est.: 6 (**Ref:**HM03913)

## CENTRE FOR POSITIVE HEALTH

**Centre For Positive Health (The)**, 11 Whitchurch Rd, Wellington, Telford, **Shropshire**, TF1 3DS, ENG.
(T) 01952 242596
Speciality: Aromatherapy.
**M** **O** (**Ref:**HM03914)

## CENTRE FOR RATIONAL EMOTIVE

**Centre For Rational Emotive**, Behaviour & Therapy Centre, 156 Westcombe Hill, London, **London (Greater)**, SE3 7DH, ENG.
(T) 020 8293 1441
Speciality: Psychology.
**B** (**Ref:**HM03915)

## CENTRE FOR SELF HEALING ART

**Centre For Self Healing Art**, 2 Dilston Rd, Durham, **County Durham**, DH1 5ND, ENG.
(T) 01738 449443
Speciality: Complementary Medicines & Therapy.
● **Manager** Mrs T Shower
**M** (**Ref:**HM03916)

## CENTRE FOR SHIATSU

**Centre For Shiatsu (The)**, 37 Oxford Pl, 7 Oxford Rd, Manchester, **Manchester (Greater)**, M1 6EY, ENG.
(T) 01612 743280
Speciality: Shiatsu.
● **Partner** Mr R Graham
**M** (**Ref:**HM03917)

## CENTRE FOR STRESS MANAGEMENT

**Centre For Stress Management**, 156 Westcombe Hill, London, **London (Greater)**, SE3 7DH, ENG.
(T) 020 8293 4114
Speciality: Psychotherapy.
**B** (**Ref:**HM03918)

## CENTRE FOR STRESS RELEASE

**Centre For Stress Release (The)**, 5 Charles Way South, Limekilns, Dunfermline, **Fife**, KY11 3JW, SCO.
(T) 01383 872086 (F) 01383 872086
Speciality: Complementary Medicines & Therapy.
**C** **M** (**Ref:**HM03919)

## CENTRE FOR TRANSFORMATION

**Dr Lindsay Nash**, 47 Goring Rd, London, **London (Greater)**, N11 2BT, ENG.
(T) 020 8888 1252
(E) tranformation@vithami-freeserve.co.uk
Speciality: Bates Method, Family Planning (Natural), Homeopathy, Nutritional Therapy, Reiki, Vitamin Therapy, Preparation for death, Spiritual insight work. ✔
● **Practitioner** Dr L Nash Q: LCH, M.Med.Sc, MCH, PhD, RSHom. M: Soc.Hom.
**M** Yrs. Est.: 16 (**Ref:**HM03920)

## CENTRE FOR TRANSFORMATION

**Dr Lindsay Nash**, 15 Second Avenue Off Sherwood Rise, Nottingham, **Nottinghamshire**, NG7 6JJ, ENG.
(T) 01159 692190
(E) transformation@vithami.freeserve.co.uk
Speciality: Bates Method, Family Planning (Natural), Homeopathy, Nutritional Therapy, Reiki, Vitamin Therapy, Preparation for death, Spritiual insight work, Teaches Reiki rather than practices Reiki. ✔
● **Practitioner** Dr L Nash Q: LCH, M.Med.Sc, MCH, PhD, RSHom. M: Soc.Hom.
**M** Yrs. Est.: 16 (**Ref:**HM03921)

## CENTRE FOR WELL BEING

**Centre For Well Being**, 16 Skinner St, Caernarfon, **Gwynedd**, LL55 1RB, WAL.
(T) 01286 671789
Speciality: Aromatherapy, Relaxation. ✔
● **Owner/Aromatherapist** Mr P Cooper
M: IPTI.
**C** Yrs. Est.: 2 (**Ref:**HM03922)

## CENTRE FOR WELLBEING

**Centre for WellBeing**, Mallow Rd, **County Cork**, IRE.
(T) 021 4307 012
Speciality: Complementary Medicines & Therapy.
**M** (**Ref:**HM03923)

## CENTRE OF HOLISTIC HEALING

**Centre Of Holistic Healing**, O'Connor Sq, Tullamore, **County Offaly**, IRE.
(T) 05064 1308
Speciality: Healing.
**B** (**Ref:**HM03924)

## CENTRE OF NATURAL MEDICINE

**Centre Of Natural Medicine**, Above The Gallery, Long St, Newport, **Pembrokeshire**, SA42 0TL, WAL.
(T) 01239 820050
Speciality: Complementary Medicines & Therapy.
**C** **M** (**Ref:**HM03925)

## CENTRE OF TRADITIONAL HEALING

**Centre Of Traditional Healing**, 53 West St, Fishguard, **Pembrokeshire**, SA65 9NG, WAL.
(T) 01348 874384
Speciality: Acupuncture, Alexander Technique, Chiropractic, Homeopathy, McTimoney Chiropractic, Reflexology, Shiatsu, Holistic Massage, Herbalist. ✔ CREDIT
● **Herbalist** Ms C Jabroo
● **McTimoney Chiropractor**
Mr N Dowsett Q: DC, MMCA. M: MCA.
● **Owner** Ms P Gillespie Q: VTCT.
● **Reflexologist** Ms J Griffiths Q: MBRA.
M: BRA.
● **Acupuncturist** Niki Oates Q: MA, MBAcC.
M: BAcC.
● **Homeopath** Ms H Gillam Q: BSc, DSH.
● **Shiatsu Practitioner**
Ms C Kedward M: HSEC.
● **Holistic Massage** Ina Thompson Q: ITEC.
● **Teacher of the Alexander Technique**
Mr A Lambert Q: MSTAT.
● **Shaitsu Practitioner** Ms A Jones
**C** Yrs. Est.: 11 (**Ref:**HM03926)

## CENTREPOINT CLINIC

**Centrepoint Clinic**, 86 Worsley Rd, Newport, **Isle of Wight**, PO30 5JD, ENG.
(T) 01983 525577
Speciality: Complementary Medicines & Therapy.
● **Owner** Mrs V Lane
**C** **M** (**Ref:**HM03927)

## CEPHAS CONSULTANCY

**Cephas Consultancy**, 367 Prescot Rd, Old Swan, Liverpool, **Merseyside**, L13 3BS, ENG.
(T) 01515 122600
Speciality: Complementary Medicines & Therapy.
**C** **M** (**Ref:**HM03928)

## CERAMIC WATERFALLS

**Ceramic Waterfalls**, The Studio, Twitham Court Farm, Staple Rd, Wingham, Canterbury, **Kent**, CT3 1LP, ENG.
(T) 01227 722324
Speciality: Complementary Medicines & Therapy.
**C** **M** (**Ref:**HM03929)

## CEROSIMO, JOSEPH

**Joseph Cerosimo**, Flintoff Way, Preston, **Lancashire**, PR1 5AF, ENG.
(T) 01772 655533
Speciality: Chiropractic.
● **Owner** Ms N Walker
**P** **S** **T** (**Ref:**HM03930)

## CEROSIMO, JOSEPH

**Joseph Cerosimo**, Wood Croft Cl, Penwortham, Preston, **Lancashire**, PR1 9BX, ENG.
(T) 01772 746492
Speciality: Chiropractic.
**P** **S** **T** (**Ref:**HM03931)

## CHACKETT, LINDA

**Linda Chackett**, Wolverhampton Rd, Wedges Mills, Cannock, **Staffordshire**, WS11 1SX, ENG.
(T) 01922 416190
Speciality: Aromatherapy.
**M** **O** (**Ref:**HM03932)

## CHADHA, PRADEEP K (DR)

**Dr Pradeep K Chadha**, Apartment 5, Verdemont, Blanchardstown, Dublin, **County Dublin**, IRE.
(T) 01824 2666 (F) 01824 2666
(E) chadhap@indigo.ie
(W) www.druglesspsychiatrist.com
Speciality: Cognitive Therapy, Counselling, Hypnosis, Hypnotherapy, Meditation, Psychotherapy. ✔ CREDIT
● **Psychotherapist** Dr P Chadha Q: BS, DCP, Dip.Psychol.Med, FAAETS, FHRS, MB. M: IACT.
**B** Yrs. Est.: 5 (**Ref:**HM03933)

## CHADWICK, ANTHONY

**Anthony Chadwick**, 3 Oakampton House, Great Barton, Bury St. Edmunds, **Suffolk**, IP31 2RF, ENG.
(T) 01284 787110
Speciality: Reiki.
● **Owner** Mr A Chadwick M: Reiki Fed.
**T** (**Ref:**HM03934)

## CHADWICK, ATOSHA

**Atosha Chadwick**, 17 Kelvon Cl, Glenfield, **Leicestershire**, LE3 8AT, ENG.
(T) 01162 874558
Speciality: Reflexology.
**S** **T** (**Ref:**HM03935)

## CHADWICK, BRIAN L

**Brian L Chadwick**, 9 Oak Tree Cres, Stalybridge, **Manchester (Greater)**, SK15 2HQ, ENG.
(T) 01613 384389
Speciality: Homeopathy.
● **Owner** Mr B Chadwick



Key: **B** Mind-Body Medicine **C** Complementary Medicine **H** Self Help Treatment **M** Medicinal Therapy **O** Oriental Medicine **P** Postural Therapy **S** Manipulative Structural Therapy **T** Touch Therapy

M (Ref:HM03936)

## CHADWICK, CAROL
**Carol Chadwick**, 26 Hawthorn Lane, Wilmslow, **Cheshire**, SK9 5DD, ENG.
(T) 01625 529718
Speciality: Physiotherapy.
● **Owner** Mrs C Chadwick
P S T (Ref:HM03937)

## CHADWICK, JAMES L
**James L Chadwick**, Mews House, Hassall Rd, Alsager, Stoke-On-Trent, **Staffordshire**, ST7 2SL, ENG.
(T) 01270 878140
Speciality: Osteopathy.
P S T (Ref:HM03938)

## CHADWICK, PAUL R
**Paul R Chadwick**, 27 Rodney St, Liverpool, **Merseyside**, L1 9EH, ENG.
(T) 01517 097335
Speciality: Physiotherapy.
P S T (Ref:HM03939)

## CHAFER, D W
**D W Chafer**, 46 Church Rd, Plymstock, Plymouth, **Devon**, PL9 9BA, ENG.
(T) 01752 401864
Speciality: Chiropodists (Podiatrists).
S (Ref:HM03940)

## CHAIR MASSAGE
**Chair Massage**, 75 Morley Gr, Harlow, **Essex**, CM20 1ED, ENG.
(T) 01279 424203
Speciality: Aromatherapy.
● **Owner** Mrs A Searle
M O (Ref:HM03941)

## CHAKRA ROSE
**Chakra Rose Alternative and Complementary Therapy Clinic**, 4a Fairfield Rd, Braintree, **Essex**, CM7 3HF, ENG.
(T) 01376 347689
(E) chrissie@chakrarose-clinic.co.uk
(W) www.chakrarose-clinic.co.uk
Speciality: Aromatherapy, Bach Remedies, Cognitive Therapy, Complementary Therapy, Group Therapy, Hay Diet, Humanistic Psychology, Hypnosis, Hypnotherapy, Massage (Therapeutic), Nutritional Therapy, Psychotherapy, Reflexology, Stress Therapy, Visualisation Therapy, Aromatherapy Skin Preparations, Aroma Sauna Therapy, Aroma Diffusion Therapy, Chakra Balancing, Detoxification, Intolerance Testing, Magnet Therapy and Skincare Prescriptions. ✔
● **Owner** Ms C Lord Q: BHA, BSc, Cert.Ed, Dip.APMASS, Dip.Arom, Dip.SACH.Hyp, DipHCE, MBHReg, MGCP, MRCN.
● **Therapist** Ms J Brown Q: IIHHT. M: AoR, ICHT.
B C Yrs. Est.: 2 (Ref:HM03942)

## CHAKRAVERTY, R C (DR)
**Dr R C Chakraverty**, 27 Belle Vue Gardens, Shrewsbury, **Shropshire**, SY3 7JQ, ENG.
(T) 01743 244000
Speciality: Osteopathy.
● **Owner** Dr R Chakraverty
P S T (Ref:HM03943)

## CHAKRAVERTY, R C (DR)
**Dr R C Chakraverty**, Hodnet Medical Centre, Drayton Rd, Hodnet, Market Drayton, **Shropshire**, TF9 3NF, ENG.
(T) 01630 685230
Speciality: Osteopathy.
● **Owner** Dr R Chakraverty
P S T (Ref:HM03944)

## CHALICE CRYSTALS
**Chalice Crystals**, 3 Bosham Walk, Bosham Lane, Bosham, Chichester, **Sussex (West)**, PO18 8HX, ENG.
(T) 01243 574564
Speciality: Complementary Medicines & Therapy.
C M (Ref:HM03945)

## CHALINDER-MORGAN, H
**H Chalinder-Morgan**, 33 Mary St, Porthcawl, Bridgend, CF36 3YN, WAL.
(T) 01656 782362 (F) 01656 782362
Speciality: Physiotherapy.
● **Owner** Mrs H Chalander-Morgan
P S T (Ref:HM03946)

## CHALKLEY, E & S
**E & S Chalkley**, 42 Harvesters Way, Weavering, Maidstone, **Kent**, ME14 5SJ, ENG.
(T) 01622 730735
Speciality: Chiropodists (Podiatrists).
● **Partner** Mr S Chalkley
S (Ref:HM03947)

## CHALKLIN, J
**J Chalklin**, 18 Trinity Cl, West Mersea, Colchester, **Essex**, CO5 8RW, ENG.
(T) 01206 385339
Speciality: Electrolysis.
● **Owner** Mrs J Chalklin
T (Ref:HM03948)

## CHALLENER HYPNOTHERAPY
**Challener Hypnotherapy**, 43 Challener Rd, High Wycombe, **Buckinghamshire**, HP12 4PW, ENG.
(T) 01494 441195
Speciality: Hypnosis.
B (Ref:HM03949)

## CHALLIS, R T
**R T Challis**, 85-91 Derby Rd, Sandiacre, Nottingham, **Nottinghamshire**, NG10 5HZ, ENG.
(T) 01159 606116
Speciality: Hypnosis.
B (Ref:HM03950)

## CHALMERS, D G
**Douglas Grant Chalmers**, Sunny Hill Clinic, Rhostrehwfa, Llangefni, **Isle of Anglesey**, LL77 7YU, WAL.
(T) 01248 724184
Speciality: Acupressure, Bonesetting, Electrotherapy, Kinesiology, Manipulation, Massage (Therapeutic), Ultrasonics. ✔
● **Physiotherapist** Mr D Chalmers Q: LCSP. M: LCSP.
S Yrs. Est.: 15 (Ref:HM03951)

## CHALMERS, RICHARD
**Richard Chalmers**, 10A Chequer St, St. Albans, **Hertfordshire**, AL1 3XZ, ENG.
(T) 01727 845246 (F) 01727 833667
Speciality: Hypnosis.
● **Owner** Mr R Chalmers
B (Ref:HM03952)

## CHALMERS, RICHARD
**Richard Chalmers**, 73 Loom Lane, Radlett, **Hertfordshire**, WD7 8NX, ENG.
(T) 01923 853055
Speciality: Hypnosis.
B (Ref:HM03953)

## CHALTON, SANDRA
**Sandra Chalton**, 100 High St, Crediton, **Devon**, EX17 3LF, ENG.
(T) 01363 774175
Speciality: Herbal Medicine.
M (Ref:HM03954)

## CHAMBERLAIN CONSULTANTS
**Chamberlain Consultants**, 13A Chamberlain Rd, Edinburgh, **Edinburgh (City of)**, EH10 4DJ, SCO.
(T) 01314 528083
Speciality: Psychology.
B (Ref:HM03955)

## CHAMBERLAIN, A G
**A G Chamberlain**, 2 Town Hall Rd, Havant, **Hampshire**, PO9 1AN, ENG.
(T) 023 9248 3316
Speciality: Chiropodists (Podiatrists).
● **Owner** Mr A Chamberlain
S (Ref:HM03956)

## CHAMBERS, AINE
**Aine Chambers**, 6 Grove Lea, Hatfield, **Hertfordshire**, AL10 8LA, ENG.
(T) 01707 272842
Speciality: Psychotherapy.
● **Psychotherapist** A Chambers
B (Ref:HM03957)

## CHAMBERS, HANNAH
**Hannah Chambers**, Coedcae, Rock House Rd, Llandrindod Wells, **Powys**, LD1 6AF, WAL.
(T) 01597 823672
Speciality: Reflexology.
S T (Ref:HM03958)

## CHAMBERS, I M
**I M Chambers**, 3 High St, Nairn, **Highland**, IV12 4AG, SCO.
(T) 01667 453494
Speciality: Chiropodists (Podiatrists).
S (Ref:HM03959)

## CHAMBERS, MICHAEL R C
**Michael R C Chambers**, The Doctors House, Victoria Rd, Marlow, **Buckinghamshire**, SL7 1DS, ENG.
(T) 01628 477377
Speciality: Chiropodists (Podiatrists).
S (Ref:HM03960)

## CHAMELEON OILS
**Chameleon Oils**, 10 Hewett Cl, Taunton, **Somerset**, TA1 4YQ, ENG.
(T) 01823 282413 (F) 01823 282413
(E) chameleon-oils@freezone.co.uk
(W) www.chameleon-oils.co.uk
Speciality: Aromatherapy, Reflexology. ✔
● **Partner** Mrs J Watson Q: ITEC. M: IPTI.
● **Partner** Mr J Watson
H Yrs. Est.: 8 (Ref:HM03961)

## CHAMPANERIA
**Champaneria**, 245 Manningham Lane, Bradford, **Yorkshire (West)**, BD8 7ER, ENG.
(T) 01274 783811 (F) 01274 522980
Speciality: Acupuncture.
● **Owner** Mr S Champaneria
O (Ref:HM03962)

## CHAMPANERIA, S K
**S K Champaneria**, 2 Mornington Villas, Bradford, **Yorkshire (West)**, BD8 7HB, ENG.
(T) 01274 607002 (F) 01274 783811
(E) champaneria@aol.com
(W) www.bioresonance.uk.com
Speciality: Acupressure, Acupuncture, Bach Remedies, Bio-energetics, Biofeedback, Complementary Therapy, Cupping, Floral Essence Therapy, Herbal Medicine, Holistic Healing, Indian Head Massage, Massage (Therapeutic), Naturopathy, Nutritional Therapy, Oriental Diagnosis, Orthomolecular Medicine, Phytotherapy, Stress Therapy, Vibrational Therapy, Bio-Resonance Therapy (BICOM).
● **Senior Practitioner** Ms S Champaneria Q: BSc, Dip.Ac, Dip.CHM, PhD. M: BAcC.
M Yrs. Est.: 8 (Ref:HM03963)

## CHAMPION, ALISON
**Alison Champion**, White Gates Lodge, Coach Rd, Acrise, Folkestone, **Kent**, CT18 8JU, ENG.
(T) 01303 892303
Speciality: Reflexology.
S T (Ref:HM03964)

## CHAMPS
**Champs**, Sterling House, 21 Winchester Rd, Basingstoke, **Hampshire**, RG21 8UE, ENG.
(T) 01256 843434 (F) 01256 352242
Speciality: Hypnosis.
● **Partner** Mrs M Atuahene
B (Ref:HM03965)

## CHAN ACUPUNCTURE
**Dr Keith F K Chan Acupuncture & Private Clinic**, 19 Long Lane, Halesowen, **Midlands (West)**, B62 9LL, ENG.
(T) 01215 592044
Speciality: Acupuncture.
O (Ref:HM03966)

## CHAN, C
**C Chan**, British Acupuncture Association, 34 Alderney St, London, **London (Greater)**, SW1V 4EU, ENG.
(T) 020 7834 1012
Speciality: Acupuncture.
O (Ref:HM03967)

## CHAN, K P
**K P Chan**, 4 Sandown Drive, Halebarns, Altrincham, **Cheshire**, WA15 0BA, ENG.
(T) 01619 806756


Key continued: Yrs.Est: Years Established Q: Qualifications M: Professional Membership ✔ Indemnity Insurance Accept Credit Cards

Speciality: Acupuncture.
**O** (Ref:HM03968)

## CHANCE, G D

**G D Chance**, 41 High St, Lymington, **Hampshire**, SO41 9AF, ENG.
(T) 01590 676770
Speciality: Chiropodists (Podiatrists).
**S** (Ref:HM03969)

## CHANCE, G D

**G D Chance**, 11 Salisbury Rd, Totton, Southampton, **Hampshire**, SO40 3HW, ENG.
(T) 023 8086 3127
Speciality: Chiropodists (Podiatrists).
● **Owner** Mr G Chance
**S** (Ref:HM03970)

## CHANCE, SUE

**Sue Chance**, 8 Hanover Court, Riverside, Guildford, **Surrey**, GU1 1LD, ENG.
(T) 01483 453400
Speciality: Psychology.
● **Owner** Mr G Chance
**B** (Ref:HM03971)

## CHANCERY LANE PHYSIOTHERAPY

**Chancery Lane Physiotherapy**, Chancery House, 53-64 Chancery Lane, London, **London (Greater)**, WC2A 1QU, ENG.
(T) 020 7404 6343 (F) 020 7404 6343
Speciality: Physiotherapy.
● **Owner** Mr S Shepard
**P S T** (Ref:HM03972)

## CHANDLER, ANN

**Ann Chandler**, The Grange, 62 Spixworth Rd, Norwich, **Norfolk**, NR6 7NF, ENG.
(T) 01603 402010 (F) 01603 482611
Speciality: Acupuncture, Physiotherapy. ✔
● **Physiotherapist** Mrs A Chandler Q: MCSP, SRP. M: AACP.
**S** Yrs. Est.: 5 (Ref:HM03973)

## CHANDLER, J

**Miss J Chandler**, 10 Dersingham Rd, London, **London (Greater)**, NW2 1SL, ENG.
(T) 020 8450 0448
Speciality: Chiropodists (Podiatrists).
● **Owner** Miss J Chandler
**S** (Ref:HM03974)

## CHANDLER, LENA

**Lena Chandler**, 67 Barnfield Rd, Harpenden, **Hertfordshire**, AL5 5TH, ENG.
(T) 01582 620143
(W) www.complementary-healthcare.co.uk/info/chandler
Speciality: Aromatherapy, Reflexology.
**S T** (Ref:HM03975)

## CHANDLER, M D

**M D Chandler**, 9 Basil Gardens, Croydon, **Surrey**, CR0 8XD, ENG.
(T) 020 8656 9209
Speciality: Psychotherapy.
**B** (Ref:HM03976)

## CHANDLER, PAT

**Pat Chandler**, Fairfields Clinic, Skippetts Lane West, Basingstoke, **Hampshire**, RG21 3HP, ENG.
(T) 01256 326980
Speciality: Aromatherapy.
**M O** (Ref:HM03977)

## CHANDLER, PETER E

**Peter E Chandler**, Bay Rd, Bracknell, **Berkshire**, RG12 2NR, ENG.
(T) 01344 300404
Speciality: Osteopathy.
**P S T** (Ref:HM03978)

## CHANDLER, ROBERT & ELIZABETH

**Robert & Elizabeth Chandler**, 42 Milson Rd, London, **London (Greater)**, W14 0LD, ENG.
(T) 020 7603 3862
Speciality: Alexander Technique.
**P S** (Ref:HM03979)

## CHANDLERS FORD CHIRO CLINIC

**Chandlers Ford Chiropody Clinic**, 26 The Precinct, Winchester Rd, Chandler's Ford, Eastleigh, **Hampshire**, SO53 2GA, ENG.
(T) 023 8026 2614
Speciality: Chiropodists (Podiatrists).
● **Owner** Ms M Atterbury
**S** (Ref:HM03980)

## CHANDLERS FORD PHYSIO

**Chandlers Ford Physiotherapy & Sports Injury Clinic**, 110 Winchester Rd, Chandler's Ford, Eastleigh, **Hampshire**, SO53 2GJ, ENG.
(T) 023 8027 3777
Speciality: Physiotherapy.
**P S T** (Ref:HM03981)

## CHANDRA PDS

**Chandra - Personal Development Services**, Richardsons Farm, Crowhurst Lane, West Kingsdown, **Kent**, TN15 6JE, ENG.
(T) 01474 853576 (F) 07020 970476
(E) gaura@cwcom.net
(W) www.chandra-pds.freeserve.co.uk
Speciality: Acupressure, Acupuncture, Kinesiology, Reflexology, Stress Therapy, Emotional Freedom Technique (EFT), Meridian Therapy. ✔
● **Workshop Facilitator** Gaura Dasi
● **Therapist/Workshop Facilitator** Mrs A Sivyer
**H** Yrs. Est.: 2 (Ref:HM03982)

## CHANEY, JOHN

**John Chaney**, 10 High St, Glastonbury, **Somerset**, BA6 9DU, ENG.
(T) 01458 834236
Speciality: Complementary Medicines & Therapy.
● **Director** Ms J Sanders
**M** (Ref:HM03983)

## CHANGE OF LIFE

**Herbalife**, 2 Hill Farm Cl, High Halstow, Rochester, **Kent**, ME3 8SS, ENG.
(T) 01634 251181
Speciality: Nutritional Therapy.
● **Healer** Ms R Martin
(T) 01634 719947
● **Hypnotherapist** Mr R Cole
(T) 01474 874539 Q: BEd (Hons), FIHP. M: ASM.
● **Reiki Healer** Ms Y Lesley
(T) 01634 845005 Q: Reiki Master. M: CHA.
● **Therapist** Ms E Castleden
(T) 01634 683491
**B** Yrs. Est.: 22 (Ref:HM03984)

## CHANGES

**Changes**, Rear Of The Market House, 29 Cantelupe Rd, East Grinstead, **Sussex (West)**, RH19 3BH, ENG.
(T) 01342 311215
Speciality: Aromatherapy, Bach Remedies, Floral Essence Therapy, Gem Essence Therapy, Hay Diet, Healer, Homeopathy, Iridology, Kinesiology, Reflexology, Spiritual Healing, Vitamin Therapy. ✔
● **Homeopath** Ms D Jones Q: LCPH, MCPH.
● **Homeopath** Ms S Benmassoud Q: BABTAC, CIDESCO, LCPH. M: BABTAC.
**B** Yrs. Est.: 7 (Ref:HM03985)

## CHANGES HYPNOTHERAPY

**Changes Hypnotherapy/Counselling Clinic**, Plunkett Chambers Business Cnt 21 Oliver Plunkett, Cork, **County Cork**, IRE.
(T) 021 4271 020
Speciality: Hypnotherapy.
**B** (Ref:HM03986)

## CHANNEL VIEW COMP HEALTH

**Channel View Complementary Health Clinic**, Channel View Surgery, 3 Courtenay Pl, Teignmouth, **Devon**, TQ14 8AY, ENG.
(T) 01626 774656
Speciality: Complementary Medicines & Therapy.
**C M** (Ref:HM03987)

## CHANNING, N & A M

**N & A M Channing**, 195 High St, Honiton, **Devon**, EX14 1LQ, ENG.
(T) 01404 43032
Speciality: Chiropodists (Podiatrists).
● **Partner** Mrs A Channing
**S** (Ref:HM03988)

## CHANNON, CHRISTINA

**Christina Channon**, The Smile Centre, Nottingham, **Nottinghamshire**, NG2 2JY, ENG.
(T) 01159 259813
Speciality: Psychotherapy.
● **Owner** Ms C Channon
**B** (Ref:HM03989)

## CHANNON, P M

**P M Channon**, 49 Francis Avenue, Southsea, **Hampshire**, PO4 0HL, ENG.
(T) 023 9273 1062
Speciality: Chiropodists (Podiatrists).
**S** (Ref:HM03990)

## CHAO, FENG (DR)

**Dr Feng Chao**, 30 Wimbledon Hill Rd, London, **London (Greater)**, SW19 7PA, ENG.
(T) 020 8879 0555
Speciality: Acupuncture.
● **Manager** Dr F Chao
**O** (Ref:HM03991)

## CHAPEL COURT CENTRE

**Chapel Court Centre (The)**, 74 Hospital St, Nantwich, **Cheshire**, CW5 5RP, ENG.
(T) 01270 611702 (F) 01270 611702
Speciality: Psychotherapy.
● **Owner** Mr D Rogers
**B** (Ref:HM03992)

## CHAPEL HOUSE CLINIC

**Chapel House Clinic**, Chapel House Clinic, Boars Head, Crowborough, **Sussex (East)**, TN6 3HD, ENG.
(T) 01892 610096
Speciality: Osteopathy.
● **Owner** Mr R Anderson
**P S T** (Ref:HM03993)

## CHAPELL, D (DR)

**Dr D Chapell**, 69A Brent St, London, **London (Greater)**, NW4 2EA, ENG.
(T) 020 8203 7372
Speciality: Homeopathy.
● **Owner** Dr D Chappell
**M** (Ref:HM03994)

## CHAPLIN-SMITH, S J

**Mrs S J Chaplin-Smith**, Harriers, Hunters Way, Chichester, **Sussex (West)**, PO19 4RB, ENG.
(T) 01243 527827
Speciality: Physiotherapy.
**P S T** (Ref:HM03995)

## CHAPMAN, A

**A Chapman**, 1 Holt Cl, Church Lane, Leeds, **Yorkshire (West)**, LS16 8DJ, ENG.
(T) 01132 673497
Speciality: Chiropodists (Podiatrists).
**S** (Ref:HM03996)

## CHAPMAN, A G

**A G Chapman**, Flat 4, Evelyn Mansions, Carlisle Pl, London, **London (Greater)**, SW1P 1NH, ENG.
(T) 020 7630 0304
Speciality: Osteopathy.
● **Owner** Mr A Chapman
**P S T** (Ref:HM03997)

## CHAPMAN, ALAN

**Alan Chapman**, 29 Ernest Rd, Hornchurch, **Essex**, RM11 3JG, ENG.
(T) 01708 455650
Speciality: Osteopathy.
● **Owner** Mr A Chapman
**P S T** (Ref:HM03998)

## CHAPMAN, ANNA

**Anna Chapman**, 195B Ware Rd, Hertford, **Hertfordshire**, SG13 7EQ, ENG.
(T) 01992 503399
Speciality: Osteopathy.
● **Owner** Ms A Chapman
**P S T** (Ref:HM03999)

## CHAPMAN, E

**E Chapman**, 31 Nelson Rd, Ilkley, **Yorkshire (West)**, LS29 8HN, ENG.
(T) 01943 817879
Speciality: Acupuncture.
**O** (Ref:HM04000)

Key: **B** Mind-Body Medicine **C** Complementary Medicine **H** Self Help Treatment **M** Medicinal Therapy **O** Oriental Medicine **P** Postural Therapy **S** Manipulative Structural Therapy **T** Touch Therapy

### CHAPMAN, GILLIAN
**Gillian Chapman**, 2 Asher Drive, Ascot, **Berkshire**, SL5 8LJ, ENG.
(T) 01344 883219 (F) 01344 883219
Speciality: Chiropodists (Podiatrists).
● **Owner** Mrs G Chapman
S (Ref:HM04001)

### CHAPMAN, J
**J Chapman**, 99 Barrow Rd, London, **London (Greater)**, SW16 5PB, ENG.
(T) 020 8677 8254
Speciality: Reflexology.
● **Senior Partner** Mrs J Chapman
S T (Ref:HM04002)

### CHAPMAN, J D
**J D Chapman**, 11 Bridge St, Winchester, **Hampshire**, SO23 0HL, ENG.
(T) 01962 853260
Speciality: Osteopathy.
● **Manager** Mr D Chapman
P S T (Ref:HM04003)

### CHAPMAN, JANE
**Jane Chapman**, 28 Parkland Avenue, Upminster, **Essex**, RM14 2EX, ENG.
(T) 01708 223230
Speciality: Chiropodists (Podiatrists).
● **Owner** Mrs J Chapman
S (Ref:HM04004)

### CHAPMAN, M J
**M J Chapman**, 58 Colwyn Rd, Bramhall, Stockport, **Cheshire**, SK7 2JQ, ENG.
(T) 01614 396601
Speciality: Chiropodists (Podiatrists).
● **Owner** Mrs M Chapman
S (Ref:HM04005)

### CHAPMAN, MARILYN
**Marilyn Chapman**, Shoreham-by-Sea, **Sussex (West)**, BN43, ENG.
(T) 01273 464740
Speciality: Bach Remedies.
M (Ref:HM04006)

### CHAPMAN, PETE
**Pete Chapman**, 396 High St, Lincoln, **Lincolnshire**, LN5 7SS, ENG.
(T) 01522 887887
Speciality: Relaxation Technique.
● **Owner** Mr P Chapman
H T (Ref:HM04007)

### CHAPMAN, ROBERT
**Robert Chapman**, 396 High St, Lincoln, **Lincolnshire**, LN5 7SS, ENG.
(T) 01522 887887
Speciality: Reflexology.
● **Owner** Mr R Chapman
S T (Ref:HM04008)

### CHAPMAN, RUPERT
**Rupert Chapman**, 34-36A Warwick Way, Victoria, London, **London (Greater)**, SW1V 1RY, ENG.
(T) 020 7834 0861
Speciality: Osteopathy.
● **Osteopath** Mr R Chapman Q: DO (Hons). M: GOsC.
H P S Yrs. Est.: 12 (Ref:HM04009)

### CHAPMAN, SHEILA
**Chapman Sheila**, 137 Dorchester Rd, Worcester Park, **Surrey**, KT4 8PA, ENG.
(T) 020 8715 1145
Speciality: Reflexology.
● **Owner** Mrs C Felten
S T (Ref:HM04010)

### CHAPMAN, STEPHEN
**Stephen Chapman**, 20 Vale Rd, Northfleet, Gravesend, **Kent**, DA11 8BZ, ENG.
(T) 01474 536500
Speciality: Chiropodists (Podiatrists).
● **Owner** Mr S Chapman
S (Ref:HM04011)

### CHAPPELL, D
**D Chappell**, 16A High St, Sandy, **Bedfordshire**, SG19 1AQ, ENG.
(T) 01767 691960
Speciality: Homeopathy.
M (Ref:HM04012)

### CHAPPELL, D S
**D S Chappell**, 21 Grove Rd, Ilkley, **Yorkshire (West)**, LS29 9PD, ENG.
(T) 01943 607231
Speciality: Physiotherapy.
P S T (Ref:HM04013)

### CHAPPELL, J
**J Chappell**, 94 Peaks Lane, New Waltham, Grimsby, **Humberside (South)**, DN36 4LY, ENG.
(T) 01472 812644
Speciality: Chiropodists (Podiatrists).
● **Owner** Mr J Chappell
S (Ref:HM04014)

### CHAPPELL, L
**L Chappell**, 86A Liverpool Rd South, Liverpool, **Merseyside**, L31 7AG, ENG.
(T) 01515 263780
Speciality: Chiropodists (Podiatrists).
S (Ref:HM04015)

### CHAPPLE, MAUREEN
**Maureen Chapple**, 49 Greenwich High Rd, London, **London (Greater)**, SE10 8JL, ENG.
(T) 020 8691 4401
Speciality: Homeopathy.
M (Ref:HM04016)

### CHARD ELECTROLYSIS CENTRE
**Chard Electrolysis Centre**, 43 Holyrood St, Chard, **Somerset**, TA20 2DN, ENG.
(T) 01460 63700
Speciality: Electrolysis.
T (Ref:HM04017)

### CHARLBURY NAT HEALTH CLINIC
**Charlbury Natural Health Clinic**, 5 Spendlove Centre, Enstone Rd, Charlbury, Chipping Norton, **Oxfordshire**, OX7 3PQ, ENG.
(T) 01608 810019
Speciality: Complementary Medicines & Therapy.
● **Manager** Mrs R Jodka-Narkiewicz
M (Ref:HM04018)

### CHARLES BARR HYPNOTHERAPIST
**Charles Barr Hypnotherapist**, 17 London Rd, Potters Bar, **Hertfordshire**, EN6 1UP, ENG.
(T) 01707 652939
Speciality: Hypnotherapy.
● **Owner** Mr M Powell
B (Ref:HM04019)

### CHARLES CLINIC
**Charles Clinic (The)**, 3 Cotham Rd, Bristol, BS6 6DG, ENG.
(T) 01179 745084
Speciality: Cranial Osteopathy, Osteopathy.
✔
● **Osteopath** Ms K Burns Q: DO, MA. M: GOsC.
● **Osteopath** Mrs C Steel Q: DO, RGN. M: GOsC.
● **Osteopath** Mr N Hainsford Q: BSc, Hons (OST). M: GOsC.
● **Osteopath** Mr G Cleghorn Q: DO, DSH, M.App.Sc. M: GOsC.
S (Ref:HM04020)

### CHARLES STREET CHIROPODY
**Charles Street Chiropody**, 5 Charles St, Wrexham, LL13 8BT, WAL.
(T) 01978 313190
Speciality: Chiropodists (Podiatrists).
● **Owner** Ms V Turner
S (Ref:HM04021)

### CHARLES, J H
**J H Charles**, 61 Little Common Rd, Bexhill-on-Sea, **Sussex (East)**, TN39 4HU, ENG.
(T) 01424 731138
Speciality: Chiropodists (Podiatrists).
● **Owner** Mr J Charles
S (Ref:HM04022)

### CHARLES, JANICE
**Janice Charles**, 18 Beechcroft Rd, Laverstock, Salisbury, **Wiltshire**, SP1 1PF, ENG.
(T) 01722 326766
Speciality: Reflexology.
S T (Ref:HM04023)

### CHARLES, L
**L Charles**, 21 St Catherine St, Carmarthen, **Carmarthenshire**, SA31 1RE, WAL.
(T) 01267 222095
Speciality: Aromatherapy.
M O (Ref:HM04024)

### CHARLES, L M (DR)
**Dr L M Charles**, 26 Swan Walk, Shepperton, **Surrey**, TW17 8LY, ENG.
(T) 01932 222182
Speciality: Hypnotherapy.
● **Doctor** Dr M Charles
B (Ref:HM04025)

### CHARLES, SARAH
**Sarah Charles**, 35 West St, Trowbridge, **Wiltshire**, BA14 0AH, ENG.
(T) 01225 353633
Speciality: Aromatherapy.
M O (Ref:HM04026)

### CHARLES-DAVIS, S
**S Charles-Davis**, The Practice, The Old Sawmills, Hawkerland Rd, Colaton Raleigh, Sidmouth, **Devon**, EX10 0HP, ENG.
(T) 01395 568824
Speciality: Osteopathy.
● **Owner** Mr S Charles-Davis
P S T (Ref:HM04027)

### CHARLESWORTH, L M
**L M Charlesworth**, 16 Loweswater Drive, Loughborough, **Leicestershire**, LE11 3RS, ENG.
(T) 01509 231529
Speciality: Hypnosis.
B (Ref:HM04028)

### CHARLESWORTH, M
**M Charlesworth**, 23 Arncliffe Drive, Barnsley, **Yorkshire (South)**, S70 6QX, ENG.
(T) 01226 293781
Speciality: Chiropodists (Podiatrists).
● **Owner** Mrs M Charlesworth
S (Ref:HM04029)

### CHARLESWORTH, MARIAN
**Marian Charlesworth**, 42 Canal St, Thurmaston, **Leicestershire**, LE4 8AA, ENG.
(T) 01162 692892
Speciality: Reflexology.
S T (Ref:HM04030)

### CHARLETT, DEBORAH
**Deborah Charlett**, 9 Bentley Court, 15 Winn Rd, **Hampshire**, SO17 1EX, ENG.
(T) 023 8057 1548
Speciality: Reflexology.
S T (Ref:HM04031)

### CHARLEY, EMMA
**Charley Emma**, Care Of In-Sight Opticians, 4 Leegate, London, **London (Greater)**, SE12 8SS, ENG.
(T) 020 8463 0281
Speciality: Chiropodists (Podiatrists).
S (Ref:HM04032)

### CHARLTON CLINIC
**Charlton Clinic**, 1 Merville, Carlton Colville, Lowestoft, **Suffolk**, NR33 8UF, ENG.
(T) 01502 584470 (F) 01502 560721
(E) errolawilliams@aol.com
Speciality: Aromatherapy, Electrotherapy, Nutritional Therapy, Pilates, Reflexology, Ultrasonics, Cryotherapy when required, Mechanical Massage, Various Massage Tecniques such as STR - Soft Tissue Release, NMT - Neuro Muscular Tecnique, MET - Muscular Energy Tecniques, CTM- Connective Tissue Manipulation. Also remedial exercises. ✔
● **Owner/Physical/Sports Therapist** Mr E Williams Q: ICHT, IIHHT, MIFA. M: BRCP, FHT, IFA.
S Yrs. Est.: 1 (Ref:HM04033)

### CHARLTON, P
**P Charlton**, 36 Windermere Avenue, Ilkeston, **Derbyshire**, DE7 4FQ, ENG.
(T) 01159 325139
Speciality: Chiropodists (Podiatrists).
● **Owner** Mr P Charlton
S (Ref:HM04034)


Key continued: Yrs.Est: Years Established Q: Qualifications M: Professional Membership ✔ Indemnity Insurance Accept Credit Cards

## CHARLTON, STEPHANIE
**Stephanie Charlton**, 19 College Rd, Cheltenham, **Gloucestershire**, GL53 7HY, ENG.
(T) 01242 231962
Speciality: Acupuncture.
● **Owner** Ms S Charlton
O (Ref:HM04035)

## CHARMINSTER CHIRO CLINIC
**Charminster Chiropractic Clinic**, 2 Milton Rd, Bournemouth, **Dorset**, BH8 8LN, ENG.
(T) 01202 296756
Speciality: Chiropractic. ✔
● **Owner** Dr M Kiri Q: DC. M: BCA.
P Yrs. Est.: 12 (Ref:HM04036)

## CHARMWOOD CHIROPRACTIC CLINIC
**Charmwood Chiropractic Clinic**, 53 Tiverton Rd, Loughborough, **Leicestershire**, LE11 2RU, ENG.
(T) 01509 267673
Speciality: Chiropractic.
● **Owner** Mr A Watt
P S T (Ref:HM04037)

## CHARNWOOD PHYSIOTHERAPY
**Charnwood Physiotherapy**, 37 Main St, Woodhouse Eaves, Loughborough, **Leicestershire**, LE12 8RY, ENG.
(T) 01509 891115
Speciality: Physiotherapy.
● **Owner** Mr A Clements
P S T (Ref:HM04038)

## CHART LANE CLINIC
**Chart Lane Clinic**, 36A Chart Lane, Reigate, **Surrey**, RH2 7DZ, ENG.
(T) 01737 243601
Speciality: Bach Remedies, Counselling, Homeopathy. ✔
● **Homeopath** Mr K Smeaton Q: MCH, RSHom. M: Soc.Hom.
M Yrs. Est.: 13 (Ref:HM04039)

## CHARTER MEDICAL CENTRE
**Charter Medical Centre**, 88 Davigdor Rd, Hove, **Sussex (East)**, ENG.
(T) 01273 306616
Speciality: Alexander Technique.
● **Practitioner** Ms K McKeown
P S (Ref:HM04040)

## CHARTERED PHYSIO & SPORTS
**Chartered Physiotherapy & Sports Injury Clinic**, 654 Blackburn Rd, Bolton, **Lancashire**, BL1 7AJ, ENG.
(T) 01204 596086
Speciality: Acupuncture, Manipulation, Physiotherapy. ✔
● **Owner/Physiotherapist** Mr A Butt Q: MCSP, SRP.
S Yrs. Est.: 12 (Ref:HM04041)

## CHARTERED PHYSIOTHERAPIST
**Chartered Physiotherapist**, 23 Wellpond Cl, Sharnbrook, Bedford, **Bedfordshire**, MK44 1PL, ENG.
(T) 01234 781777
(E) claudia@voncaronfreeserve.co.uk
Speciality: Chiropractic, Electrotherapy, Kinesiology, Manipulation, Massage (Therapeutic), Osteopathy, Physiotherapy, Postural Integration, Stress Therapy, Ultrasonics, Sports Therapy. ✔
● **Physiotherapist** Mrs C Von-Caron Q: MCSP, SRP. M: CSP, OCPPP.
S Yrs. Est.: 10 (Ref:HM04042)

## CHARTERED PHYSIOTHERAPISTS
**Chartered Physiotherapists**, Elizabeth Cottage, Upper Highway, Kings Langley, **Hertfordshire**, WD4 8PP, ENG.
(T) 01923 261220
Speciality: Physiotherapy.
P S T (Ref:HM04043)

## CHARTERED PHYSIOTHERAPY
**Chartered Physiotherapy**, 13 Ulsterville Avenue, Belfast, **County Antrim**, BT9 7AS, NIR.
(T) 028 9066 4224
Speciality: Physiotherapy.
● **Owner** Mrs J Wilson
P S T (Ref:HM04044)

## CHARTERED PHYSIOTHERAPY
**Chartered Physiotherapy Ltd**, Croesnewydd Hall, Wrexham Technology Centre, Wrexham, LL13 7TB, WAL.
(T) 01978 312407
Speciality: Physiotherapy.
● **Owner** Mrs J Miles
P S T (Ref:HM04045)

## CHARTERED PHYSIOTHERAPY CLINIC
**Hodgson & Hardman Ltd T/A Chartered Physiotherapy Clinic**, 31-33 Booth St, Ashton-under-Lyne, **Manchester (Greater)**, OL6 7LB, ENG.
(T) 01613 303142 (F) 01613 303142
Speciality: Acupuncture, Chiropractic, Electrotherapy, Manipulation, Massage (Therapeutic), Moxibustion, Osteopathy, Physiotherapy, Ultrasonics. ✔
● **Physiotherapist/Partner**
Mr S Hardman Q: MCSP, SRP. M: CSP.
● **Physiotherapist/Partner**
Mr N Hodgson Q: MCSP, SRP. M: CSP.
C Yrs. Est.: 29 (Ref:HM04046)

## CHARTERED PSYCHOLOGISTS
**Chartered Psychologists**, 9 Kedleston Gardens, Derby, **Derbyshire**, DE1 1RE, ENG.
(T) 01332 383590 (F) 01332 383590
Speciality: Psychology.
● **Owner** Mr R Wojciechowski
B (Ref:HM04047)

## CHARTERHOUSE PHYSIOTHERAPY
**Charterhouse Physiotherapy**, 31 Queen Anne St, London, **London (Greater)**, W1M 9FB, ENG.
(T) 020 7323 4263
Speciality: Physiotherapy. ✔
● **Owner/Physiotherapist**
Mrs C Rugman Q: MCSP, SRP. M: CSP.
S Yrs. Est.: 10 (Ref:HM04048)

## CHARTERHOUSE PHYSIOTHERAPY
**Charterhouse Physiotherapy**, 35 Cloth Fair, London, **London (Greater)**, EC1A 7JQ, ENG.
(T) 020 7606 2435 (F) 020 7606 2351
Speciality: Acupuncture, Physiotherapy. ✔
● **Owner/Physiotherapist**
Ms C Rugman Q: MCSP, SRP. M: CSP.
S Yrs. Est.: 10 (Ref:HM04049)

## CHARTERS PHYSIO & SPORTS
**Charters Physiotherapy & Sports Injury Clinic**, 198 Church Rd, Hove, **Sussex (East)**, BN3 2DJ, ENG.
(T) 01273 735283 (F) 01273 747788
Speciality: Physiotherapy. ✔
● **Partner/Physiotherapist**
Mrs L Burroughs Q: Grad Dip Phys, MCSP, ONC, SRP. M: CSP.
● **Partner/Physiotherapist**
Ms N Saunders Q: Grad Dip Phys, MCSP, SRP. M: CSP.
S Yrs. Est.: 13 (Ref:HM04050)

## CHARTERS, EUNICE
**Eunice Charters**, 3a Cambridge Rd, Colchester, **Essex**, CO3 3NS, ENG.
(T) 01206 542842
Speciality: Complementary Medicines & Therapy.
● **Owner** Mrs E Charters
M (Ref:HM04051)

## CHARTIER, SUSAN
**Susan Chartier**, Ashley, White Horse Lane, Otham, Maidstone, **Kent**, ME15 8RQ, ENG.
(T) 01622 861333
Speciality: Reflexology.
S T (Ref:HM04052)

## CHARVET, BARBARA
**Barbara Charvet**, Wern Derys, Michaelchurch Escley, Hereford, **Herefordshire**, HR2 0JZ, ENG.
(T) 01981 510659
Speciality: Reflexology.
S T (Ref:HM04053)

## CHASE CHIROPODY SERVICES
**Chase Chiropody Services**, Meriden House, 10 Mill St, Cannock, **Staffordshire**, WS11 3DL, ENG.
(T) 01543 577566
Speciality: Chiropodists (Podiatrists).
S (Ref:HM04054)

## CHASE HEALTH FOODS
**Chase Health Foods**, 4 Mill St, Stafford, **Staffordshire**, ST16 2AJ, ENG.
(T) 01785 608181 (F) 01785 608181
(E) julie@brynholmes.freeserve.co.uk
Speciality: Aromatherapy, Homeopathy, Indian Head Massage, Reflexology, Sekham Healing. ✔
● **Reflexologist/Aromatherapist**
Ms J Lancs Q: MBRA. M: BRA, BRCP.
C T Yrs. Est.: 2 (Ref:HM04055)

## CHASE HOPKINS, MARY
**Mary Chase Hopkins**, 7 Park Cr, London, **London (Greater)**, W1N 3HE, ENG.
(T) 020 7631 0604
Speciality: Complementary Medicines & Therapy.
M (Ref:HM04056)

## CHASE HYPNOTHERAPY
**Chase Hypnotherapy**, 327 The Chase, Benfleet, **Essex**, SS7 3DN, ENG.
(T) 01702 551513
Speciality: Hypnosis.
B (Ref:HM04057)

## CHASE NATURAL HEALTH CENTRE
**Chase Natural Health Centre (The)**, 33 The Chase, Edgware, **London (Greater)**, HA8 5DW, ENG.
(T) 020 8621 3068
Speciality: Complementary Medicines & Therapy.
C M (Ref:HM04058)

## CHASE NATURAL THERAPY CENTRE
**Chase Natural Therapy Centre**, 385 Pye Green Rd, Cannock, **Staffordshire**, WS11 2RW, ENG.
(T) 01543 500765 (F) 01543 500765
Speciality: Acupuncture, Aromatherapy, Bowen Therapy, Homeopathy, Hypnotherapy, Indian Head Massage, Massage (Therapeutic), Reflexology, Reiki, Swedish Body Massage, Sports Therapy, Light Therapy, Diet & Nutritional, Medical Dowsing. ✔
● **Owner/Holistic Therapist**
Mrs J Eagles M: ICHT, IHBC, IIHHT, ITEC.
C Yrs. Est.: 4 (Ref:HM04059)

## CHASE PARK PRACTICE
**Chase Park Practice**, 119 Elvington, King's Lynn, **Norfolk**, PE30 4TB, ENG.
(T) 01553 776915
Speciality: Counselling, Gestalt Therapy, Psychotherapy, Rogerian Therapy. ✔
● **Counsellor** Ms J Stone Q: Dip.Adv.Couns. M: IPCC.
● **Psychotherapist** Mr R Brown Q: Dip.Psych. M: SPTI.
B Yrs. Est.: 3 (Ref:HM04060)

## CHASE, PETER
**Peter Chase**, 1 Ettrick Rd, Chichester, **Sussex (West)**, PO19 2EU, ENG.
(T) 01243 785885
Speciality: Chiropody. ✔
● **Owner/Chiropodist** Mr P Chase Q: MBChA, MSSCh. M: B.A.Ch.P, MSSCh.
C Yrs. Est.: 12 (Ref:HM04061)

## CHATFIELD, KATE
**Kate Chatfield**, 23 Bannister Cl, Higher Walton, Preston, **Lancashire**, PR5 4DD, ENG.
(T) 01772 339800
Speciality: Homeopathy.
M (Ref:HM04062)

## CHATSWORTH CLINIC
**Chatsworth Clinic**, 4 Chatsworth Rd, London, **London (Greater)**, NW2 4BN, ENG.
(T) 020 8451 4754 (F) 07092 056094
(E) ssi5@aol.com
Speciality: Acupressure, Acupuncture, Aromatherapy, Bach Remedies, Complementary Therapy, Counselling, Cranial Osteopathy, Floral Essence Therapy, Healing Therapy, Holistic Healing, Homeopathy, Indian Head Massage, Manipulation, Massage (Therapeutic), Meditation,

Key: B Mind-Body Medicine C Complementary Medicine H Self Help Treatment M Medicinal Therapy O Oriental Medicine P Postural Therapy S Manipulative Structural Therapy T Touch Therapy

Moxibustion, Nutritional Therapy, Oriental Diagnosis, Osteopathy, Postural Integration, Psychotherapy, Reiki, Rolfing, Shiatsu, Vitamin Therapy, Radionics, Sexual and Relationship Psychotherapy, Alchemical Healing Process, Astrology, Astrological Counselling and Psychological Astrology. ✔
- **Therapist** Ms M Reinhart
- **Therapist** Ms B Perse
- **Therapist** Mr S Frank
- **Therapist** Ms N Leech
- **Therapist** Ms G Drewe
- **Therapist** Ms S McGee
- **Therapist** Ms F Canais
- **Therapist** Ms S Wharton
- **Therapist** Mr D Kellett
- **Therapist** Ms D Cohen
- **Therapist** Mr S Trotter
- **Therapist** Dr M Houston
- **Therapist** Mr J Buhler
- **Therapist** Mr S Silver

**B C** Yrs. Est.: 15 (**Ref:**HM04063)

## CHAUDHRY, M D
**M D Chaudhry**, 46 Greywell Rd, Havant, **Hampshire**, PO9 5AL, ENG.
(T) 023 9247 1781
Speciality: Homeopathy.
**M** (**Ref:**HM04064)

## CHAUHAN, D K
**D K Chauhan**, 52 Waverley Rd, St. Albans, **Hertfordshire**, AL3 5PE, ENG.
(T) 01727 851448 (F) 01727 851448
Speciality: Complementary Medicines & Therapy, Homeopathic medicine, herbal medicine and Aromatherapy oils. [credit card]
- **Pharmacist** Mr D Chauhan

**C** Yrs. Est.: 10 (**Ref:**HM04065)

## CHAVDA, ANJNA
**Anjna Chavda**, 24 Meadow View, Birmingham, **Midlands (West)**, B13 0AP ENG.
(T) 01217 773174
Speciality: Reflexology.
**S T** (**Ref:**HM04066)

## CHAWDHARY, B S
**B S Chawdhary**, 19 Broadway Rd, Bishopston, Bristol, BS7 8ES, ENG.
(T) 01179 422182
Speciality: Psychotherapy.
- **Owner** Mr B Chawdhary

**B** (**Ref:**HM04067)

## CHAWTONS
**Chawtons**, 48 High St, Market Harborough, **Leicestershire**, LE16 7AF, ENG.
(T) 01858 410886
Speciality: Aromatherapy.
- **Partner** Mr P Crotty

**M O** (**Ref:**HM04068)

## CHAWTONS
**Chawtons**, 77 St. Giles St, Northampton, **Northamptonshire**, NN1 1JF, ENG.
(T) 01604 626527
Speciality: Aromatherapy.
- **Partner** Mr P Crotty

**M O** (**Ref:**HM04069)

## CHEADLE HULME NATURAL HEALTH
**Cheadle Hulme Natural Health Care Centre**, 16 Station Rd, Cheadle Hulme, Stockport, **Cheshire**, SK8 5AE, ENG.
(T) 01614 854009
Speciality: Aromatherapy, Chiropractic, Counselling, Homeopathy, Hypnotherapy, Massage (Therapeutic), Meditation, Nutritional Therapy, Reflexology, Reiki, Stress Therapy, Past Life Therapy. ✔
- **Manager** Mrs B Jones

**C** Yrs. Est.: 13 (**Ref:**HM04070)

## CHEADLE SPORTS INJURIES CLINIC
**Cheadle Sports Injuries Clinic**, 11 Park Gates Drive, Cheadle Hulme, Cheadle, **Cheshire**, SK8 7DD, ENG.
(T) 01614 851437
Speciality: Physiotherapy.
**P S T** (**Ref:**HM04071)

## CHEAH, R F S
**R F S Cheah**, 463 Falls Rd, Belfast, **County Antrim**, BT12 6DD, NIR.
(T) 028 9024 3593 (F) 028 9033 0499
Speciality: Acupuncture.
- **Owner** Dr R Cheah

**O** (**Ref:**HM04072)

## CHEANEY, JOANNA C
**Joanna C Cheaney**, 57 Woodford Rd, Bramhall, Stockport, **Cheshire**, SK7 1JR, ENG.
(T) 01614 400298
Speciality: Osteopathy.
- **Owner** Ms J Cheaney

**P S T** (**Ref:**HM04073)

## CHECCHIA, TERESSA
**Teressa Checchia**, Ely Complmentary Health Centre, 29a St Marys St, Ely, **Cambridgeshire**, CB7 4HF, ENG.
(T) 01353 664476
Speciality: Osteopathy.
- **Owner** Mr A Spence

**P S T** (**Ref:**HM04074)

## CHEDDAR COMP MEDICINE CTRE
**Cheddar Complementary Medicine Centre**, Complementary Medical Centre, Roynon Way, Cheddar, **Somerset**, BS27 3NZ, ENG.
(T) 01934 744574
Speciality: Acupuncture, Alexander Technique, Aromatherapy, Chiropody, Counselling, Healing Therapy, Herbal Medicine, Homeopathy, Hypnotherapy, Massage (Therapeutic), Naturopathy, Osteopathy, Physiotherapy, Psychotherapy, Reiki. ✔
- **Manager** Mrs J Harris
- **Acupuncturist** Jackie Tuckey Q: BA, Lic.Ac, MBAcC.
- **Osteopath/Naturopath** Mr J Muscaty Q: BSc (Hons), DO, MIIR, ND, RN.
- **Psychotherapist/Counselling** Amanda Haskayne Q: BSc (Hons), MA. M: NRHP, UKCP.
- **Physiotherapy** Kathy Gardner Q: MCSP, SRP.
- **Herbal Medicine (Phytotherapy)** Mr D Keogh M: NIMH.
- **Acupuncturist** Ms R Vilensky Q: BSc, Lic.Ac, MBAcC.
- **Teacher of the Alexander Technique** Mr A Phillips Q: MSTAT.
- **Classical Homeopath** Mr R Napper Q: RSHom.
- **Massage/Aromatherapist/Counsellor** Shan Ford Q: BA (Hons), ITEC.
- **Environmental Medicine/Homeopath** Dr D Dowson Q: Dip.Med.Ac, MB.
- **Chiropodist** Mr P Small Q: Inst.CH.P.

**C** Yrs. Est.: 12 (**Ref:**HM04075)

## CHEDGEY, PAUL
**Paul Chedgey**, 3 Hurst Rd, Eastbourne, **Sussex (East)**, BN21 2PJ, ENG.
(T) 01323 411900
Speciality: Herbal Medicine.
- **Owner** Ms A Rambaut

**M** (**Ref:**HM04076)

## CHEE KUNG HEALTH CENTRE
**Chee Kung Health Centre**, 47 Coronation Rd, Southville, Bristol, BS3 1AR, ENG.
(T) 01179 660122
Speciality: Acupuncture.
**C O** (**Ref:**HM04077)

## CHEE SOO HOLISTIC CLINIC
**Chee Soo Holistic Clinic**, Unit 9, Blaenau Gwent Workshops, Pond Rd, Nantyglo, Ebbw Vale, **Blaenau Gwent**, NP23 4BL, WAL.
(T) 01495 315315
Speciality: Complementary Medicines & Therapy.
- **Owner** Mr P Murphey

**M** (**Ref:**HM04078)

## CHEEK 2 CHEEK BEAUTY SALON
**Cheek 2 Cheek Beauty Salon**, 108 Drumcondra Rd, Upr Drumcondra, Dublin, **County Dublin**, IRE.
(T) 01837 5437
Speciality: Complementary Medicines & Therapy.
**M** (**Ref:**HM04079)

## CHEEK, SUSAN
**Susan Cheek**, 7 The Barn, Mount Rd, Wheathampstead, St. Albans, **Hertfordshire**, AL4 8BX, ENG.
(T) 01582 831687 (F) 01582 831695
Speciality: Alexander Technique.
**P S** (**Ref:**HM04080)

## CHEEMA, M
**M Cheema**, 111 Wolverhampton Rd South, Birmingham, **Midlands (West)**, B32 2AX, ENG.
(T) 01214 266924
Speciality: Chiropodists (Podiatrists).
- **Owner** Mr M Cheema

**S** (**Ref:**HM04081)

## CHEER, MARIE
**Marie Cheer**, 39 Fletchers Lane, Willenhall, **Midlands (West)**, WV13 2QW, ENG.
(T) 01902 416290
Speciality: Acupressure, Aromatherapy, Herbal Medicine, Indian Head Massage, Reflexology.
- **Owner** Ms M Cheer

**C** Yrs. Est.: 1 (**Ref:**HM04082)

## CHEETHAM, D
**D Cheetham**, Park House Physiotherapy Clinic, Park Rd, Tydd St. Giles, Wisbech, **Cambridgeshire**, PE13 5NH, ENG.
(T) 01945 870515 (F) 01945 870515
Speciality: Physiotherapy.
- **Owner** Mrs D Cheetham

**P S T** (**Ref:**HM04083)

## CHEFLAND, GERTI
**Gerti Chetland**, 48 Redlands Rd, Reading, **Berkshire**, RG1 5HR, ENG.
(T) 01189 866635 (F) 01189 874461
(W) www.rosedaleclinic.co.uk
Speciality: Reflexology.
- **Reflexologist** Ms G Chetland Q: BRCP. M: ICM.

**T** Yrs. Est.: 2 (**Ref:**HM04084)

## CHELMSFORD CHIROPRACTIC CLINIC
**Chelmsford Chiropractic Clinic**, 5 First Avenue, Chelmsford, **Essex**, CM1 1RX, ENG.
(T) 01245 353078
Speciality: Chiropractic.
**P S T** (**Ref:**HM04085)

## CHELMSLEY WOOD FOOT CLINIC
**Chelmsley Wood Foot Care Clinic**, 2-8 Greenwood Way, Birmingham, **Midlands (West)**, B37 5TL, ENG.
(T) 01217 703040
Speciality: Aromatherapy, Chiropody, Indian Head Massage, Reflexology, Reiki. ✔
- **Owner/Chiropodist** Mr V Martin

**M T** Yrs. Est.: 2 (**Ref:**HM04086)

## CHELSEA AROMATHERAPISTS
**Chelsea Aromatherapists (The)**, 147 Beaufort St, London, **London (Greater)**, SW3 6BS, ENG.
(T) 020 7352 0556
Speciality: Aromatherapy.
**M O** (**Ref:**HM04087)

## CHELSEA COMPLEMENTARY CLINIC
**Chelsea Complementary Clinic**, 174 Ifield Rd, London, **London (Greater)**, SW10 9AF, ENG.
(T) 020 7373 8575
Speciality: Complementary Medicines & Therapy.
**M** (**Ref:**HM04088)

## CHELSEA HOUSE CLINIC
**Chelsea House Clinic**, 215 North Deeside Rd, Peterculter, **Aberdeenshire**, AB14 0UJ, SCO.
(T) 01224 733303 (F) 01224 733303
Speciality: Complementary Medicines & Therapy.
- **Owner** Ms C Craigmile

**M** (**Ref:**HM04089)

## CHELSEA HOUSE CLINIC
**Chelsea House Clinic**, Chelsea Lane, Inverurie, **Aberdeenshire**, AB51 3QQ, SCO.
(T) 01467 624888 (F) 01467 624888
Speciality: Acupuncture, Aromatherapy, Chiropody, Homeopathy, Podiatry, Reflexology, Reiki. ✔
- **Chiropodist** Mrs C Craigmile



Key continued: **Yrs.Est:** Years Established **Q:** Qualifications **M:** Professional Membership ✔ Indemnity Insurance [credit card] Accept Credit Cards

M O Yrs. Est.: 10 (**Ref:**HM04090)

### CHELSEA PRACTICE

**Chelsea Practice (The)**, 186 Fulham Rd, London, **London (Greater)**, SW10 9PN, **ENG**.
**(T)** 020 7352 9385
Speciality: Osteopathy.
P S T (**Ref:**HM04091)

### CHELSTON CHIROPODY PRACTICE

**Chelston Chiropody Practice**, 42 Walnut Rd, Torquay, **Devon**, TQ2 6HS, **ENG**.
**(T)** 01803 690420
**(E)** taycaul@aol.com
Speciality: Chiropody. ✔
- **Chiropodist** Ms K Banbury **Q:** MBChA, MSSCh. **M:** B.A.Ch.P, MSSCh.
- **Chiropodist** Ms J Taylor **Q:** Inst.CH.P. **M:** Inst.CH.P.
- **Reflexologist** Ms B Pierce **Q:** ITEC, MAR. **M:** AoR.

C Yrs. Est.: 6 (**Ref:**HM04092)

### CHELTENHAM CLINIC & TRAD ACU

**Cheltenham Clinic & Traditional Acupuncture**, 16 Clarence Sq, Cheltenham, **Gloucestershire**, GL50 4JN, **ENG**.
**(T)** 01242 241933
**(E)** mike.eatough@virgin.net
Speciality: Acupuncture, Bach Remedies, Chiropractic, Cranial Osteopathy, Herbal Medicine, Metamorphic Therapy, Reflexology, T'ai-Chi Ch'uan. ✔
- **Owner/Therapist** Mr M Eatough **Q:** B.Ac, Lic.Ac. **M:** BAcC.

O Yrs. Est.: 22 (**Ref:**HM04093)

### CHELTENHAM HOLISTIC HLTH CTRE

**Cheltenham Holistic Health Centre**, Cheltenham Holistic Centre, 66 Suffolk Rd, Cheltenham, **Gloucestershire**, GL50 2ED, **ENG**.
**(T)** 01242 584140
Speciality: Acupuncture, Alexander Technique, Allergy Testing, Aromatherapy, Chiropractic, Cranio-Sacral Therapy, Homeopathy, Hypnotherapy, Indian Head Massage, Kinesiology, Massage (Therapeutic), Meditation, Nutritional Therapy, Osteopathy, Psychotherapy, Reflexology, Remedial Massage, Shiatsu, Spiritual Healing, Yoga, Chinese Herbalism, Emotional Therapy, NLP, Optimum Nutrition Consultancy, Viniyoga. ✔
- **NLP Practitioner/Hypnotherapist** Mr S Tromans **Q:** BA (Hons).
- **Optimum Nutritionist** Ms S Whitman **Q:** Lic.ION, MA (Hons).
- **Shiatsu Therapist** Ms H Tucker
- **Massage/Aromatherapist** Ms L Buckland **Q:** BABTAC, CIBTAC, MIFA.
- **Hypnotherapist** Mr J Ramsey **Q:** Dip.Hyp, NACHP.
- **Osteopath/Cranial Osteopath** Karl J A Turner **Q:** BSc, Hons (OST).
- **Homeopath** Ms C Keef **Q:** BA, MCH, RSHom.
- **Reflexologist** Ms S Tromans **Q:** ART(Reg), MAR.
- **Massage/Aromatherapist/Emotional Therapist** Ms J Rochfort **Q:** MIFA.
- **Alexander Technique/Cranio-Sacral Therapist** Mr J Underhill **Q:** BSc, RCST. **M:** ATI.
- **Indian Head Massage/Yoga** Ms M Harris **Q:** Cert.Champ, SRN.
- **Acupuncturist** Mr E Goodchild **Q:** BA, Lic.Ac, MBAcC. **M:** BAcC.
- **Psychotherapist/Counselling/Hynotherapist** Ms A Cooper **Q:** BA (Hons), DHC, MSc.
- **Allergy Testing** Ms C Hoare **Q:** RNT. **M:** InstAET, SPNT.
- **Acupuncturist/Chinese Herbalist** Ms L Upton **Q:** B.Ac, Cert.Ac, MBAcC, MRCHM. **M:** BAcC, RCHM.
- **Acupuncturist** Ms A Collings-Wells **Q:** Lic.Ac, MBAcC. **M:** BAcC.

C Yrs. Est.: 18 (**Ref:**HM04094)

### CHELTENHAM HOMEOPATHIC CLINIC

**Cheltenham Homeopathic Clinic**, Waverley, Western Rd, Cheltenham, **Gloucestershire**, GL50 3RN, **ENG**.
**(T)** 01242 520704
Speciality: Homeopathy.
- **Owner** Mr R Nichols

M (**Ref:**HM04095)

### CHELTENHAM HYPNOTHERAPY

**Nicholas Norman**, 9 Ryeworth Rd, Charlton Kings, Cheltenham, **Gloucestershire**, GL52 6LG, **ENG**.
**(T)** 01242 252316
**(E)** hypnotherapy@cheltenham1999.freeserve.co.uk
Speciality: Auto Suggestion, Aversion Therapy, Hypnosis, Hypnotherapy, Psychotherapy, Psycho Analysis, Systematic Desensitisation. ✔
- **Owner** Mr N Norman **Q:** Dip.Hyp, Dip.Psych, MIAH, MNCH. **M:** IAH, NCH.

B Yrs. Est.: 6 (**Ref:**HM04096)

### CHELTENHAM PHYSIO/SPRTS CLNC

**Cheltenham Physiotherapy & Sports Injuries Clinic**, 27A St Georges Rd, Cheltenham, **Gloucestershire**, GL50 3DT, **ENG**.
**(T)** 01242 239078
Speciality: Acupuncture, Physiotherapy, Hydrotherapy. ✔
- **Physiotherapist** Ms S Copp **Q:** SRP. **M:** CSP.
- **Physiotherapist** Ms A Knight **Q:** SRP. **M:** CSP.
- **Physiotherapist** Ms F Hines **Q:** SRP. **M:** CSP.
- **Physiotherapist** Ms S Hine **Q:** SRP. **M:** CSP.
- **Physiotherapist** Jossette Farrugia **Q:** SRP. **M:** CSP.
- **Owner** Mrs J Griffin
- **Physiotherapist** Ms I Loughton **Q:** SRP. **M:** CSP.
- **Physiotherapist** Ms L Chesterton **Q:** SRP. **M:** CSP.
- **Physiotherapist** Ms G Rache **Q:** SRP. **M:** CSP.
- **Physiotherapist** Ms C Mayers **Q:** SRP. **M:** CSP.
- **Physiotherapist** Ms S McKenzie **Q:** SRP. **M:** CSP.

S Yrs. Est.: 30 (**Ref:**HM04097)

### CHEMIN, CHRISTIAN

**Christian Chemin**, Penswell, Rattery, **Devon**, TQ10 9LF, **ENG**.
**(T)** 01364 642790
Speciality: Cranial Osteopathy, Osteopathy. ✔
- **Osteopath** Mr C Chemin **Q:** BSc, DO, SRN. **M:** GOsC.

B Yrs. Est.: 15 (**Ref:**HM04098)

### CHEN, AC C

**Ac C Chen**, 29 Gordon Rd, Haywards Heath, **Sussex (West)**, RH16 1EL, **ENG**.
**(T)** 01444 451152
Speciality: Acupuncture.
O (**Ref:**HM04099)

### CHEN, LO KUEI

**Lo Kuei Chen**, Top Maisonette, 10 Glazbury Rd, Barons Court, London, **London (Greater)**, W14 9AS, **ENG**.
**(T)** 020 7602 0770
Speciality: Acupuncture.
O (**Ref:**HM04100)

### CHEN, LU

**Lu Chen**, 35 Park Rd, Coventry, **Midlands (West)**, CV1 2LE, **ENG**.
**(T)** 024 7667 5302
Speciality: Acupuncture.
- **Owner** Dr L Chen

O (**Ref:**HM04101)

### CHENERY, P N

**P N Chenery**, Town Park Farm, Oakham Rd, Brooke, Oakham, **Leicestershire**, LE15 8DG, **ENG**.
**(T)** 01572 757440 **(F)** 01572 770808
Speciality: Complementary Medicines & Therapy.
- **Owner** Mr P Chenery

M (**Ref:**HM04102)

### CHENG, MIGGI

**Miggi Cheng**, Flat B, 36 Upper Grosvenor Rd, Tunbridge Wells, **Kent**, TN1 2EP, **ENG**.
**(T)** 01892 541256
Speciality: Reflexology.
S T (**Ref:**HM04103)

### CHENUBE, ROY

**Chenube Roy Advanced Hypnotherapist**, 22C Woodchurch Rd, West Hampstead, London, **London (Greater)**, NW6 3PN, **ENG**.
**(T)** 020 8566 3885
Speciality: Hypnosis.
B (**Ref:**HM04105)

### CHENUBE, ROY ADV HYP

**Roy Chenube Advanced Hypnotherapist**, 24 Lancaster Gdns, London, **London (Greater)**, W13 9JY, **ENG**.
**(T)** 020 8566 3885
Speciality: Hypnotherapy.
- **Owner** Mrs G Roy

B (**Ref:**HM04104)

### CHERINGTON PRACTICE

**Cherington Practice (The)**, 1 Cherington Rd, Bristol, BS10 5BH, **ENG**.
**(T)** 01179 625195 **(F)** 01179 625209
Speciality: Physiotherapy, Mr Patterson is a Specialist Orthopedic Physiotherapist. ✔
- **Physiotherapist** Mr R Patterson **Q:** MCSP, SRP. **M:** CSP.

S Yrs. Est.: 1 (**Ref:**HM04106)

### CHERRY GRANGE

**Cherry Grange Ltd**, 32 Peatling Rd, Countesthorpe, Leicester, **Leicestershire**, LE8 5RD, **ENG**.
**(T)** 01162 773007 **(F)** 01162 773330
Speciality: Herbal Medicine.
- **Managing Director** Mrs J Brown

M (**Ref:**HM04107)

### CHERRY PLUS

**Cherry Plus Ltd**, 6a Furlong Rd, Bourne End, **Buckinghamshire**, SL8 5DG, **ENG**.
**(T)** 01628 850666 **(F)** 01628 850670
Speciality: Electrolysis.
- **Director** Ms C Edwards

T (**Ref:**HM04108)

### CHERRY TREE CTRE FOR NTRL MED

**Cherry Tree Centre For Natural Medicine (The)**, 12 Baker St, Aberystwyth, **Ceredigion**, SY23 2BJ, **WAL**.
**(T)** 01970 610030
Speciality: Acupuncture. ✔
- **Acupuncturist** Ms S Morgan **Q:** B.Ac, Dip.Ac. **M:** BAcC.

C Yrs. Est.: 18 (**Ref:**HM04109)

### CHERRY, CHRIS

**Chris Cherry**, Clissold Park Health Centre, 154 Stoke Newington Church St, London, **London (Greater)**, N16 0JU, **ENG**.
**(T)** 020 7249 2990 **(F)** 020 7249 3977
Speciality: Psychotherapy.
- **Owner** Mr D Berg

B (**Ref:**HM04110)

### CHERTSEY OSTEOPATHIC CLINIC

**Chertsey Osteopathic Clinic**, 21A London St, Chertsey, **Surrey**, KT16 9AU, **ENG**.
**(T)** 01932 563081
Speciality: Osteopathy.
P S T (**Ref:**HM04111)

### CHESHAM HOSPITAL

**Chesham Hospital**, Physiotherapy Department, Hospital Hill, Waterside, Chesham, **Buckinghamshire**, HP5 1PJ, **ENG**.
**(T)** 01494 784484
Speciality: Physiotherapy.
P S T (**Ref:**HM04112)

### CHESHIRE FOOT-HEALTH CENTRE

**Cheshire Foot-Health Centre (The)**, 174 London Rd, Northwich, **Cheshire**, CW9 8AA, **ENG**.
**(T)** 01606 49641
Speciality: Chiropodists (Podiatrists).
S (**Ref:**HM04113)

### CHESHIRE FOUNDATION

**Cheshire Foundation Homes For The Physically Disabled**, The Marian Centre, Old Highway, Colwyn Bay, **Conwy**, LL28 5YA, **WAL**.
**(T)** 01492 535153 **(F)** 01492 535782
Speciality: Physiotherapy.

Key: B Mind-Body Medicine; C Complementary Medicine; H Self Help Treatment; M Medicinal Therapy; O Oriental Medicine; P Postural Therapy; S Manipulative Structural Therapy; T Touch Therapy

● **Manageress**
Mrs K Fortescue-Joseph
**P S T** (**Ref:**HM04114)

## CHESHIRE HEALTH CLINIC
**Cheshire Health Clinic**, 84 Congleton Rd, Sandbach, **Cheshire**, CW11 1HG, ENG.
(T) 01270 763926
Speciality: Acupuncture, Alexander Technique, Aromatherapy, Bowen Therapy, Counselling, Homeopathy, Hypnotherapy, Nail Surgery, Osteopathy, Psychotherapy. ✔
● **Aromatherapist** Ms A Holmes Q: IHBC, IIHHT. M: IHBC.
● **Chiropodist (Podiatrist)**
Ms K Richards Q: S.R.Ch.
● **Teacher of the Alexander Technique**
Binni King
● **Hypnotherapist/Psychotherapist**
Andre' Bonnebaigt Q: BA (Hons), MHA, UKCP (Reg).
● **Homeopath** Ms M Hargreaves
● **Remedial/Reflexologist**
Ms S Beardsmore M: AoR.
● **Acupuncturist/Bowen Therapist**
Ms J Keating Q: Lic.Ac, MBAcC, MBAWAc.
● **Chiropodist (Podiatrist)**
Ms J Burrows Q: BSc (Hons), S.R.Ch.
● **Osteopath** Mr P Owen Q: DO. M: GOsC.
● **Osteopath** Miss L Curphey Q: BSc (Hons). M: GOsC.
● **Owner/Osteopath** Ms L Potter Q: BSc. M: GOsC.
● **Counselling Psychologist**
Mr S McNab Q: BA.
**S** Yrs. Est.: 10 (**Ref:**HM04115)

## CHESHIRE, A R E
**A R E Cheshire**, 9 Portman Cres, Bournemouth, **Dorset**, BH5 2ER, ENG.
(T) 01202 427901
Speciality: Chiropodists (Podiatrists).
● **Owner** Mr A Cheshire
**S** (**Ref:**HM04116)

## CHESHUNT CHIROPRACTIC CLINIC
**Cheshunt Chiropractic Clinic**, 1 Russells Ride, Cheshunt, Waltham Cross, **Hertfordshire**, EN8 8TS, ENG.
(T) 01992 627717
Speciality: Chiropractic.
● **Sole Director** Kevin Joel Leizer
**P S T** (**Ref:**HM04117)

## CHESHUNT OSTEOPATHIC CLINIC
**Cheshunt Osteopathic Clinic**, 86 Windmill Lane, Cheshunt, Waltham Cross, **Hertfordshire**, EN8 9AD, ENG.
(T) 01992 635667
Speciality: Osteopathy.
**P S T** (**Ref:**HM04118)

## CHESNEY, SIMON
**Simon Chesney**, The Lantern House, 7 Clifton Rd, Amersham, **Buckinghamshire**, HP6 5PU, ENG.
(T) 01494 725431 (F) 01494 728196
Speciality: Osteopathy.
● **Owner** Mr S Chesney
**P S T** (**Ref:**HM04119)

## CHESSELL, KAREN
**Karen Chessell**, 329 Upland Rd, London, **London (Greater)**, SE22 0DL, ENG.
(T) 020 8299 2890
Speciality: Psychotherapy.
**B** (**Ref:**HM04120)

## CHESSER, HELEN
**Helen Chesser**, The Battersea Practice, 40 Webbs Rd, London, **London (Greater)**, SW11 6SF, ENG.
(T) 020 7228 2141
Speciality: Physiotherapy.
● **Partner** Mrs H Chesser
**P S T** (**Ref:**HM04121)

## CHESSER, HELEN
**Helen Chesser**, The Chelsea Practice, 186 Fulham Rd, London, **London (Greater)**, SW10 9PN, ENG.
(T) 020 7351 9918
Speciality: Physiotherapy.
● **Partner** Mrs H Chesser
**P S T** (**Ref:**HM04122)

## CHESSINGTON OSTEOPATHIC CLINIC
**Chessington Osteopathic Clinic**, 25 Oakcroft Villas, Chessington, **Surrey**, KT9 1RJ, ENG.
(T) 020 8255 9389
Speciality: Osteopathy.
● **Owner** Mr D Chandler
**P S T** (**Ref:**HM04123)

## CHESTER & HALTON COM
**Chester & Halton Community NHS Trust**, Victoria House, Holloway, Runcorn, **Cheshire**, WA7 4TH, ENG.
(T) 01928 593623
Speciality: Chiropodists (Podiatrists).
**S** (**Ref:**HM04124)

## CHESTER ALEXANDER TECH ST
**Chester Alexander Technique Studio**, 27 Gladstone Rd, Chester, **Cheshire**, CH1 4BZ, ENG.
(T) 01244 377955
Speciality: Alexander Technique. ✔
● **Teacher of the Alexander Technique**
Mrs J Pinder-Emery Q: GRSM, MSTAT, PGCE. M: STAT.
**H T** Yrs. Est.: 14 (**Ref:**HM04125)

## CHESTER CHIROPODY
**Chester Chiropody**, Rosecliffe, Rowton Lane, Rowton, Chester, **Cheshire**, CH3 6AT, ENG.
(T) 01244 336981
Speciality: Biomechanics, Chiropody. ✔
● **Chiropodist** Mr D Richards
(T) 01244 314875 Q: BA, MBChA, MSSCh. M: S.C.P, SMAE.
● **Chiropodist** Ms J Ellison Q: MBChA, MSSCh. M: S.C.P, SMAE.
**M** Yrs. Est.: 12 (**Ref:**HM04126)

## CHESTER CHIROPRACTIC CLINIC
**Chester Chiropractic Clinic**, 9a Canadian Avenue, Hoole, Chester, **Cheshire**, CH2 3HG, ENG.
(T) 01244 343236
Speciality: Chiropractic. ✔
● **Chiropractor** Ms M Broughton Q: DC. M: BCA, GCC.
● **Chiropractor** Mr P Gordon Q: BA, DC. M: BCA, GCC.
● **Owner** Dr L Cooper Q: DC. M: BCA, GCC.
● **Chiropractor** Mr H Gardener Q: DC. M: BCA, GCC.
**P** Yrs. Est.: 14 (**Ref:**HM04127)

## CHESTER CLINIC
**Chester Clinic For Complementary Medicine (The)**, 68 Heath Rd, Upton, Chester, **Cheshire**, CH2 1HX, ENG.
(T) 01244 390411 (F) 01244 398585
(E) 100677-2300@compuserve.com
(W) www.chesterclinic.com
Speciality: Acupressure, Acupuncture, Aromatherapy, Bowen Therapy, Chinese Herbal Medicine, Clinical Ecology, Counselling, Cupping, Herbal Medicine, Homeopathy, Hypnotherapy, Indian Head Massage, Kinesiology, Manipulation, Massage (Therapeutic), Moxibustion, Nutritional Therapy, Oriental Diagnosis, Psychotherapy, Reflexology, Reiki, Shiatsu, Vitamin Therapy. ✔
● **Acupuncturist** Ms M Buck Q: Dip.Ac, MSc. M: BAcC.
● **Acupuncturist/Physiotherapist**
Ms T Hunter Q: Dip.Ac, MSc. M: BAcC.
● **Homeopath** Mr A Kirk Q: RSHom.
● **Clinic Director** Mr C Buck Q: B.Ac, BSc (Hons), MSc. M: BAcC, RCHM.
**O** Yrs. Est.: 22 (**Ref:**HM04128)

## CHESTER HEALTH
**Chester Health & Beauty Studios**, Eccleston Wellness Centre, Hill Rd, Eccleston, Chester, **Cheshire**, CH4 9HQ, ENG.
(T) 01244 680214/7
Speciality: Aromatherapy, Complementary Therapy, Healing Therapy, Holistic Healing, Indian Head Massage, Massage (Therapeutic), Nutritional Therapy, Reflexology, Reiki, Touch Therapy, Vitamin Therapy, Laser Hair Removal. ✔
● **Owner** Ms J Stananought Q: ITEC, Reiki 2.
● **Owner** Mr J Bills
**T** Yrs. Est.: 2 (**Ref:**HM04129)

## CHESTER HEALTH & BEAUTY STUDIO
**Chester Health & Beauty Studio**, Unit 57C Chester Enterprise Centre, Hoole Bridge, Chester, **Cheshire**, CH2 3NE, ENG.
(T) 01244 344668
Speciality: Aromatherapy, Complementary Therapy, Healing Therapy, Holistic Healing, Indian Head Massage, Massage (Therapeutic), Nutritional Therapy, Reflexology, Reiki, Touch Therapy, Vitamin Therapy, Laser Hair Removal. ✔
● **Therapist** Mr J Bills
● **Owner** Ms J Stananought Q: ITEC, Reiki 2.
**T** Yrs. Est.: 12 (**Ref:**HM04130)

## CHESTER HOMEOPATHIC CLINIC
**Chester Homeopathic Clinic**, 230 Hoole Lane, Chester, **Cheshire**, CH2 3EF, ENG.
(T) 01244 313885 (F) 01829 261310
Speciality: Homeopathy, Miasm Therapy. ✔
● **Homeopathic Practitioner**
Ms E Yeardsley Q: RSHom. M: NWCH, Soc.Hom.
● **Homeopathic Practitioner**
Mrs M Denholm-Thomson Q: Lic.Hom. M: NWCH, Soc.Hom.
**B** Yrs. Est.: 6 (**Ref:**HM04131)

## CHESTER LE STREET HEALTH CTRE
**Chester Le Street Health Centre**, Chiropody, Newcastle Rd, Chester Le Street, **County Durham**, DH3 3UR, ENG.
(T) 01913 333861
Speciality: Chiropodists (Podiatrists).
**S** (**Ref:**HM04132)

## CHESTER PODIATRY GROUP
**Chester Podiatry Group**, 34 Meadows Lane, Chester, **Cheshire**, CH4 7BH, ENG.
(T) 01244 677799
Speciality: Chiropodists (Podiatrists).
● **Owner** Mr J Schooling
**S** (**Ref:**HM04133)

## CHESTER THERAPY CENTRE
**Chester Therapy Centre**, 20 Walpole St, Chester, **Cheshire**, CH1 4HG, ENG.
(T) 01244 390121 (F) 01244 390374
(E) c+c@chestertherapycentre.com
Speciality: Cognitive Therapy, Psychotherapy, Psychology. ✔
● **Consultant/Psychologist**
Ms J McIntee Q: BA (Hons), MSc. M: BPS, UKCP.
**B** Yrs. Est.: 13 (**Ref:**HM04134)

## CHESTER, A
**A Chester**, 7 Church St, Market Harborough, **Leicestershire**, LE16 7AA, ENG.
(T) 01858 431929
Speciality: Herbal Medicine.
● **Manager** A Chester
**M** (**Ref:**HM04135)

## CHESTER, MARTIN
**Martin Chester**, 21 Oxford Rd, Colchester, **Essex**, CO3 3HT, ENG.
(T) 01206 572642
Speciality: Complementary Medicines & Therapy.
**C M** (**Ref:**HM04136)

## CHESTERFIELD CHIROP & PODIATRY
**Chesterfield Chiropody & Podiatry Clinic**, William St North, Old Whittington, Chesterfield, **Derbyshire**, S41 9DT, ENG.
(T) 01246 451208
Speciality: Chiropodists (Podiatrists).
● **Owner** Mrs M Hall
**S** (**Ref:**HM04137)

## CHESTERGATE CLINIC
**Chestergate Clinic**, Suit 4, Ford House, Chestergate, Macclesfield, **Cheshire**, SK11 6DG, ENG.
(T) 01625 502840 (F) 01625 502906
Speciality: Complementary Medicines & Therapy.
● **Partner** Miss A Trinder
**C M** (**Ref:**HM04138)

## CHESTERMAN, ANNE-MARIE
**Anne-Marie Chesterman**, 13 Darling Rd, London, **London (Greater)**, SE4 1YQ, ENG.
(T) 020 8692 7274
Speciality: Hypnotherapy.


Key continued: Yrs.Est: Years Established Q: Qualifications M: Professional Membership ✔ Indemnity Insurance Accept Credit Cards

B (Ref:HM04139)

### CHETSINGH, R

**R Chetsingh**, 339 Ballards Lane, London, **London (Greater)**, N12 8LJ, ENG.
(T) 020 8445 4397
Speciality: Reflexology.
● **Director** Mr E Thankey
S T (Ref:HM04140)

### CHEUNG, DANIEL

**Daniel Cheung**, 7 Lancaster Rd, London, **London (Greater)**, SE25 4BJ, ENG.
(T) 020 8771 2070 (F) 020 8653 4976
Speciality: Chiropractors.
● **Owner** Mr D Cheung
P S T (Ref:HM04141)

### CHEUNG, JAMES T (DR)

**Dr James T Cheung**, 8 Frensham Rd, Crowthorne, **Berkshire**, RG45 6QH, ENG.
(T) 01344 774777
Speciality: Acupuncture, Herbal Medicine.
● **Acupuncturist** Dr J Cheung
O Yrs. Est.: 4 (Ref:HM04142)

### CHEUNG, LILY

**Lily Cheung**, 15 Porchester Gardens, London, **London (Greater)**, W2 4DB, ENG.
(T) 020 7727 6778
Speciality: Acupuncture.
● **Owner** Dr L Cheung
O (Ref:HM04143)

### CHEVALLIER, ANDREW

**Andrew Chevallier**, Clissold Park Health Centre, 154 Stoke Newington Church St, London, **London (Greater)**, N16 0JU, ENG.
(T) 020 7249 2990 (F) 020 7249 3977
Speciality: Herbalists.
● **Director** Mr D Berg
M (Ref:HM04144)

### CHEVINGTON CHIROPRACTIC CLINIC

**Chevington Chiropractic Clinic**, Chevington Farm, Waterhouse Lane, Bletchingley, Redhill, **Surrey**, RH1 4LU, ENG.
(T) 01883 743355
Speciality: Chiropractic.
P S T (Ref:HM04145)

### CHEW, J KENDALL

**J Kendall Chew**, The Weaver House Clinic, 19A Pillory St, Nantwich, **Cheshire**, CW5 5BZ, ENG.
(T) 01270 629933
Speciality: Osteopathy.
P S T (Ref:HM04146)

### CHEYLESMORE PHYSIO CLINIC

**Cheylesmore Physiotherapy Clinic**, 60 The Park Paling, Coventry, **Midlands (West)**, CV3 5LJ, ENG.
(T) 024 7650 3599
(E) petersargent@physiofirst.org.uk
Speciality: Electrotherapy, Phytotherapy, Ultrasonics. ✔
● **Physiotherapist** Mr P Sargent Q: BA, Grad Dip Phys, MCSP, SRP. M: CSP.
P S T Yrs. Est.: 25 (Ref:HM04147)

### CHI CLINIC

**Chi Clinic (The)**, 98 Church Hill Rd, Sutton, **Surrey**, SM3 8LJ, ENG.
(T) 020 8641 3756 (F) 020 8641 1540
(W) www.chi-do.com
Speciality: Acupressure, Crystal Healing, Massage (Therapeutic), Reflexology, Shiatsu, Chi Kung (Qi Gong) Massage, Teaches Martial Arts. ✔
● **Therapist** Ms V Ahern Q: ITEC. M: ICM.
● **Therapist** Mr T Hardiman Q: BRCP. M: BRCP, ICM.
B C O T Yrs. Est.: 2 (Ref:HM04148)

### CHI CTRE FOR TRAD CHINESE MED

**CHI Centre For Traditional Chinese Medicine**, 10 Greycoat Pl, London, **London (Greater)**, SW1P 1SB, ENG.
(T) 020 7222 1888 (F) 020 7799 2388
Speciality: Complementary Medicines & Therapy.
C M (Ref:HM04149)

### CHI HEALTH CENTRES

**Chi Health Centres**, 1 Lower Grosvenor Pl, London, **London (Greater)**, SW1W 0EJ, ENG.
(T) 020 7233 5566 (F) 020 7931 8181
Speciality: Complementary Medicines & Therapy.
● **Owner** Ms R Delman
M (Ref:HM04150)

### CHIA, G R

**G R Chia**, 81 Wilkinson St, Sheffield, **Yorkshire (South)**, S10 2GJ, ENG.
(T) 01142 761997
Speciality: Physiotherapy.
P S T (Ref:HM04151)

### CHIANALINO, M L

**M L Chianalino**, Highfield, Main Rd, Kingsley, Bordon, **Hampshire**, GU35 9LZ, ENG.
(T) 01420 489463
Speciality: Chiropodists (Podiatrists).
● **Owner** Ms M Chianalino
S (Ref:HM04152)

### CHICHESTER ACUPUNCTURE CLINIC

**Chichester Acupuncture Clinic**, 4 Marsh Barns, Runcton, Chichester, **Sussex (West)**, PO20 6LG, ENG.
(T) 01243 778159
Speciality: Acupuncture.
O (Ref:HM04153)

### CHICHESTER CHIROPRACTORS

**Chichester Chiropractors**, 119 The Hornet, Chichester, **Sussex (West)**, PO19 4JP, ENG.
(T) 01243 774336
Speciality: Chiropractic.
P S T (Ref:HM04154)

### CHICHESTER HOMOEOPATHIC MED

**Chichester Homoeopathic Medical Practice**, 107 Westgate, Chichester, **Sussex (West)**, PO19 3HB, ENG.
(T) 01243 773292
Speciality: Homeopathy.
M (Ref:HM04155)

### CHICHESTER NATURAL HEALTH CTRE

**Chichester Natural Health Centre**, 5 City Business Centre, Basin Rd, Chichester, **Sussex (West)**, PO19 2DU, ENG.
(T) 01243 786946
Speciality: Homeopathy. ✔
● **Homeopath** Mr R Cook Q: BSc, MCH, RSHom. M: Soc.Hom.
M Yrs. Est.: 10 (Ref:HM04156)

### CHICHESTER PHYSIO & SPORTS

**Chichester Physiotherapy & Sports Injury Clinic**, Harriers, Hunters Way, Chichester, **Sussex (West)**, PO19 4RB, ENG.
(T) 01243 527827
Speciality: Physiotherapy.
P S T (Ref:HM04157)

### CHICK, MARY

**Mary Chick**, Minehead, **Somerset**, TA24, ENG.
(T) 01643 707503
Speciality: Bach Remedies.
M (Ref:HM04158)

### CHICK, TREVOR J

**Trevor J Chick**, 7 Hillcrest Avenue, Aberdare, **Glamorgan (Vale of)**, CF44 6YH, WAL.
(T) 01685 876881
Speciality: Chiropodists (Podiatrists).
● **Owner** Mr T Chick
S (Ref:HM04159)

### CHIDWICK, SAMUEL

**Samuel Chidwick**, 17 River St, River, Dover, **Kent**, CT17 0RB, ENG.
(T) 01304 825117
(W) www.complementary-healthcare.co.uk/info/chidwick
Speciality: Healing Therapy, Reflexology.
S T (Ref:HM04160)

### CHIEN ACUPUNCTURE CLINIC

**Chien Acupuncture Clinic (The)**, 51 South Park, Lincoln, **Lincolnshire**, LN5 8ER, ENG.
(T) 01522 520918
(E) tony.brewer@btclick.com
Speciality: Acupuncture, Homeopathy, Massage (Therapeutic), Physiotherapy. ✔
● **Massage Therapist** Ms K Ward
● **Acupuncturist** Ms J Tonde Q: MBAcC. M: BAcC.
● **Acupuncturist/Owner** Mr T Brewer Q: MBAcC, MCSP. M: BAcC.
● **Homeopath** Ms J Tree Q: Dip.Hom, MA. M: Soc.Hom.
C O Yrs. Est.: 11 (Ref:HM04161)

### CHIGWELL HOLISTIC CLINIC

**Chigwell Holistic Health Clinic**, 93 Grange Cres, Chigwell, **Essex**, IG7 5JD, ENG.
(T) 020 8500 9558
Speciality: Complementary Medicines & Therapy.
M (Ref:HM04162)

### CHI-KIN, PO

**Mr Po Chi-Kin**, 35 The Vineyard, Richmond, **Surrey**, TW10 6PP, ENG.
(T) 020 8948 0404
Speciality: Acupuncture.
O (Ref:HM04163)

### CHILD & ADOLESCENT PSYCH DEPT

**Child & Adolescent Psychiatry Department**, Abbey Hulton Clinic, Leek Rd, Stoke-On-Trent, **Staffordshire**, ST2 8BP, ENG.
(T) 01782 538148 (F) 01782 538151
Speciality: Psychiatry.
● **Manager** Mrs G Owen
B (Ref:HM04164)

### CHILD & ADOLESCENT PSYCHIATRY

**Child & Adolescent Psychiatry Service**, Stoney Stanton Rd, Coventry, **Midlands (West)**, CV1 4FH, ENG.
(T) 024 7622 4055
Speciality: Psychiatry.
B (Ref:HM04165)

### CHILD & FAMILY SERVICES

**Child & Family Services**, Care Of Newtown Hospital, Newtown Rd, Worcester, **Worcestershire**, WR5 1JG, ENG.
(T) 01905 760446 (F) 01905 760314
Speciality: Psychiatry.
● **Chief Executive** Mrs J Coupe
B (Ref:HM04166)

### CHILD PSYCHOLOGY SERVICE

**Child Psychology Service**, 12 Grange Rd, West Bromwich, **Midlands (West)**, B70 8PD, ENG.
(T) 01215 537411 (F) 01215 801522
Speciality: Psychology.
B (Ref:HM04167)

### CHILD, HILARY

**Hilary Child**, 10 Station Prde, Harrogate, **Yorkshire (North)**, HG1 1UE, ENG.
(T) 01423 521272
Speciality: Chiropodists (Podiatrists).
● **Owner** Mrs H Child
S (Ref:HM04168)

### CHILD, SARAH

**Sarah Child**, Eastbourne Clinic Of Natural Medicine, 69 Meads Rd, Eastbourne, **Sussex (East)**, BN20 7QL, ENG.
(T) 01323 734664 (F) 01323 734664
Speciality: Alexander Technique.
● **Employee** Mr H Boys
P S (Ref:HM04169)

### CHILDS, HAZEL

**Hazel Childs**, 30 Commercial St, Cornsay Colliery, Durham, **County Durham**, DH7 9BW, ENG.
(T) 01913 732836
Speciality: Chiropodists (Podiatrists).
● **Owner** Mrs H Childs
S (Ref:HM04170)

### CHILMAN CLINIC

**Chilman Clinic**, 42 Highland Rd, Norwich, **Norfolk**, NR2 3NN, ENG.
(T) 01603 455982 (F) 01603 455982
Speciality: Physiotherapy.
● **Owner** Mrs S Chamberlin
P S T (Ref:HM04171)

### CHILTERN AROMATHERAPY

**Chiltern Aromatherapy**, Langley House, Tudor

Key: B Mind-Body Medicine; C Complementary Medicine; H Self Help Treatment; M Medicinal Therapy; O Oriental Medicine; P Postural Therapy; S Manipulative Structural Therapy; T Touch Therapy

Rd, Hazlemere, High Wycombe, **Buckinghamshire**, HP15 7PD, ENG.
(T) 01494 816651
Speciality: Aromatherapy.
● **Aromatherapist** Mr C Vassie Q: ISPA.
C (Ref:HM04172)

**CHILTERN CHIROPODY SERVICE**

**Chiltern Chiropody Service**, Podiatry Administration Amersham Hospital Whielden, Amersham, **Buckinghamshire**, HP7 0JD, ENG.
(T) 01494 734800 (F) 01494 734815
Speciality: Chiropractic.
● **Manager** Mrs V Aldred
S (Ref:HM04173)

**CHILTERN CHIROPRACTIC CLINIC**

**Chiltern Chiropractic Clinic (The)**, 4 Gold Hill West, Chalfont St. Peter, Gerrards Cross, **Buckinghamshire**, SL9 9JR, ENG.
(T) 01753 886643
Speciality: Chiropractors.
P S T (Ref:HM04174)

**CHILTERN COTTAGE CLINIC**

**Carol I Scicluna**, Chiltern Cottage, 6 Wood Lane, Fleet, **Hampshire**, GU51 3DX, ENG.
(T) 01252 624001
Speciality: Homeopathy. ✔
● **Homeopath** Ms C Scicluna M: Soc.Hom.
M Yrs. Est.: 4 (Ref:HM04175)

**CHILTERN NATURAL THERAPY**

**Chiltern Natural Therapy**, 191 Boundary Rd, Wooburn Green, High Wycombe, **Buckinghamshire**, HP10 0DL, ENG.
(T) 01628 819130
Speciality: Hypnosis.
B (Ref:HM04176)

**CHILTERN OSTEOPATHIC PRACTICE**

**Chiltern Osteopathic Practice (The)**, 7 Brays Meadow, Hyde Heath, Amersham, **Buckinghamshire**, HP6 5RY, ENG.
(T) 01494 783962
Speciality: Osteopathy.
P S T (Ref:HM04177)

**CHILTERNS COMPLEMENTARY CARE**

**Chilterns Complementary Care**, High St, Klane End, Marlow, High Wycombe, **Buckinghamshire**, HP14 3ER, ENG.
(T) 01494 883946
Speciality: Complementary Medicines & Therapy.
C M (Ref:HM04178)

**CHIMES AROMATHERAPY**

**Chimes Aromatherapy Clinic/School Of Natural Therapies**, Chimes Cottage, 321 Poole Rd, Branksome, **Dorset**, BH12 1AD, ENG.
(T) 01202 762180
Speciality: Aromatherapy.
M O (Ref:HM04179)

**CHIMES THERAPY CENTRE**

**Chimes Therapy Centre**, 21 Parkstone Rd, Poole, **Dorset**, BH15 2NN, ENG.
(T) 01202 661966
Speciality: Aromatherapy.
● **Partner** Mrs M Harding
M O (Ref:HM04180)

**CHIMES, MAXINE**

**Maxine Chimes**, Brabant House, Portsmouth Rd, Thames Ditton, **Surrey**, KT7 0EY, ENG.
(T) 020 8398 7592
Speciality: Chiropractors.
P S T (Ref:HM04181)

**CHINESE & COMPLEMENTARY**

**Chinese & Complementary**, 80 Upper Lisburn Rd, Finaghy, Belfast, **County Antrim**, BT10 0AD, NIR.
(T) 028 9060 0600 (F) 028 9040 3582
Speciality: Complementary Medicines & Therapy.
● **Owner** Mrs S Eastwood
C M (Ref:HM04182)

**CHINESE & MEDICINE CENTRE**

**Chinese & Medicine Centre**, 176 High St, Hornchurch, **Essex**, RM12 6QP, ENG.
(T) 01708 454888

Speciality: Complementary Medicines & Therapy.
● **Manager** Mrs S Ylu
C M (Ref:HM04183)

**CHINESE ACUPUNCTURE CLINIC**

**Chinese Acupuncture Clinic**, 22 Mark St, Cardiff, **Glamorgan (Vale of)**, CF11 6LL, WAL.
(T) 029 2038 3777 (F) 029 2038 3654
Speciality: Acupuncture.
● **Owner** Mr L Ng
O (Ref:HM04184)

**CHINESE ACUPUNCTURE CLINIC**

**Chinese Acupuncture Clinic**, 42 Glen Eyre Drive, Southampton, **Hampshire**, SO16 3NR, ENG.
(T) 023 8076 9003 (F) 023 8076 9003
Speciality: Acupuncture.
● **Partner** Mrs Q Zhang
O (Ref:HM04185)

**CHINESE ACUPUNCTURE CLINIC**

**Chinese Acupuncture Clinic**, 12 Wooddale Gro, Ballycullen, IRE.
(T) 01493 8141
Speciality: Acupuncture.
O (Ref:HM04186)

**CHINESE ACUPUNCTURE CLINIC**

**Chinese Acupuncture Clinic**, 62 Dame St, Dublin, **County Dublin**, IRE.
(T) 01677 3591
Speciality: Acupuncture.
O (Ref:HM04187)

**CHINESE CLINIC**

**Chinese Clinic (The)**, 3 Station Prde, Burlington Lane, London, **London (Greater)**, W4 3HD, ENG.
(T) 020 8995 1355 (F) 020 8941 7791
Speciality: Herbal Medicine.
● **Doctor** Dr G Xu
M (Ref:HM04188)

**CHINESE HEALTH CARE CENTRE**

**Chinese Health Care Centre**, 85 Chamberlayne Rd, London, **London (Greater)**, NW10 3NU, ENG.
(T) 020 8964 2421 (F) 020 8964 9447
Speciality: Complementary Medicines & Therapy.
● **Manager** Mr N Georgio
C M (Ref:HM04189)

**CHINESE HEALTH CENTRE**

**Chinese Health Centre**, 359 New Cross Rd, London, **London (Greater)**, SE14 6AT, ENG.
(T) 020 8694 7987
Speciality: Complementary Medicines & Therapy.
● **Partner** Ms A Liu
C M (Ref:HM04190)

**CHINESE HEALTH CENTRE**

**Chinese Health Centre (The)**, 4 Tudor St, Cardiff, **Glamorgan (Vale of)**, CF11 6AF, WAL.
(T) 029 2034 3733 (F) 029 2034 3733
Speciality: Complementary Medicines & Therapy.
● **Owner** Mr P Lam
M (Ref:HM04191)

**CHINESE HERB HOUSE**

**Chinese Herb House**, 3 Upper George St, Luton, **Bedfordshire**, LU1 2QX, ENG.
(T) 01582 481889 (F) 01582 481889
Speciality: Complementary Medicines & Therapy.
● **Owner** Mr W Wu
C M (Ref:HM04192)

**CHINESE HERB MEDICINE CENTRE**

**Chinese Herb Medicine Centre**, 1 Lower Richmond Rd, London, **London (Greater)**, SW15 1EJ, ENG.
(T) 020 8780 1112
Speciality: Complementary Medicines & Therapy.
● **Owner** Mr S Li
C M (Ref:HM04193)

**CHINESE HERBAL & ACU CENTRE**

**Chinese Herbal & Acupuncture Centre**, 16 Nicholas St, Manchester, **Manchester (Greater)**, M1 4EJ, ENG.
(T) 01612 280131
Speciality: Acupuncture.
O (Ref:HM04194)

**CHINESE HERBAL & MEDICAL CTRE**

**Chinese Herbal & Medical Centre**, 203 Moulsham St, Chelmsford, **Essex**, CM2 0LG, ENG.
(T) 01245 281808
Speciality: Complementary Medicines & Therapy.
● **Owner** Mr P Wong
C M (Ref:HM04195)

**CHINESE HERBAL HEALING CENTRE**

**Chinese Herbal Healing Centre**, 1st Floor 260 Upper Tooting Rd, London, **London (Greater)**, SW17 0DN, ENG.
(T) 020 8767 6870
Speciality: Herbal Medicine.
● **Director** Mrs L Cooper
M (Ref:HM04196)

**CHINESE HERBAL MED & ACU**

**Chinese Herbal Medicine & Acupuncture**, 114 Heath St, London, **London (Greater)**, NW3 1DR, ENG.
(T) 020 7431 3510
Speciality: Herbal Medicine.
M (Ref:HM04199)

**CHINESE HERBAL MED & ACU CTRE**

**Chinese Herbal Medicine & Acupuncture Centre**, 42 Bath St, Leamington Spa, **Warwickshire**, CV31 3AE, ENG.
(T) 01926 833368 (F) 01926 833368
Speciality: Complementary Medicines & Therapy.
● **Owner** Dr Y Tian
M (Ref:HM04197)

**CHINESE HERBAL MED & ACU CTRE**

**Chinese Herbal Medicines & Acupuncture Centre**, 34 Belgrave Gate, Leicester, **Leicestershire**, LE1 3GP, ENG.
(T) 01162 538828
Speciality: Complementary Medicines & Therapy.
● **Owner** Dr Y Liu
M (Ref:HM04198)

**CHINESE HERBAL MED & HLTH CARE**

**Chinese Herbal Medicine & Health Care**, 5 St. Botolphs Rd, Sevenoaks, **Kent**, TN13 3AJ, ENG.
(T) 01732 458810
Speciality: Chinese Herbal Medicine, Chinese Acupuncture. ✔
● **Acupuncturist** Mrs Y Yin M: BAcC.
O Yrs. Est.: 10 (Ref:HM04200)

**CHINESE HERBAL MED & HLTH CARE**

**Chinese Herbal Medicine & Healthcare**, 31 Smallbrook Queensway, Birmingham, **Midlands (West)**, B5 4HQ, ENG.
(T) 01216 438909
Speciality: Herbal Medicine.
● **Owner** Mrs S Jin
M (Ref:HM04201)

**CHINESE HERBAL MED & HLTH CARE**

**Chinese Herbal Medicine & Healthcare Ltd**, 6 High St, Tonbridge, **Kent**, TN9 1EJ, ENG.
(T) 01732 771611
Speciality: Herbal Medicine.
● **Owner** Dr D Gao
M (Ref:HM04202)

**CHINESE HERBAL MED & HLTH CARE**

**Chinese Herbal Medicine & Healthcare Ltd**, 193 Rushey Green, London, **London (Greater)**, SE6 4BD, ENG.
(T) 020 8695 9898
Speciality: Complementary Medicines & Therapy.
● **Sole Director** Duo Gao
C M (Ref:HM04203)

**CHINESE HERBAL MED & HLTH CARE**

**Chinese Herbal Medicine & Healthcare Ltd**, 1a Cheam Rd, Sutton, **Surrey**, SM1 1SN, ENG.
(T) 020 8814 2654 (F) 020 8643 1555
Speciality: Herbal Medicine.



Key continued: **Yrs.Est:** Years Established **Q:** Qualifications **M:** Professional Membership ✔ Indemnity Insurance Accept Credit Cards

● **Director** Dr Y Shen
**M** (**Ref:**HM04204)

**CHINESE HERBAL MED ACU CTRE**

**Chinese Herbal Medicine Acupuncture Centre**, 186 High St, Orpington, **Kent**, BR6 0JW, ENG.
(T) 01689 829664
(W) www.chinese-herbal.co.uk
Speciality: Acupuncture, Chinese Herbal Medicine.
● **Acupuncturist** Mrs R Wei **Q:** Cert.Ac, Dip.Ac.
**C O** Yrs. Est.: 2 (**Ref:**HM04205)

**CHINESE HERBAL MEDICAL CENTRE**

**Chinese Herbal Medical Centre**, 6 Adams House, Harlow, **Essex**, CM20 1BD, ENG.
(T) 01279 438585
Speciality: Complementary Medicines & Therapy.
● **Owner** Mr J Wu
**M** (**Ref:**HM04206)

**CHINESE HERBAL MEDICAL CENTRE**

**Chinese Herbal Medical Centre**, 161 Hamlet Ct Rd, Westcliff-on-Sea, **Essex**, SS0 7EL, ENG.
(T) 01702 213889
Speciality: Acupuncture.
● **Manager** Mr P Wong
**O** (**Ref:**HM04207)

**CHINESE HERBAL MEDICAL CENTRE**

**Chinese Herbal Medical Centre**, 43 George St, Hastings, **Sussex (East)**, TN34 3EA, ENG.
(T) 01424 466100
Speciality: Complementary Medicines & Therapy.
**C M** (**Ref:**HM04208)

**CHINESE HERBAL MEDICINE**

**Chinese Herbal Medicine**, The Therapy Centre, 92B Broad St, Canterbury, **Kent**, CT1 2LU, ENG.
(T) 01227 452202
Speciality: Herbalists.
**M** (**Ref:**HM04209)

**CHINESE HERBAL MEDICINE**

**Chinese Herbal Medicine**, 45 Station Rd, London, **London (Greater)**, E4 7BJ, ENG.
(T) 020 8559 3480
Speciality: Herbal Medicine.
**M** (**Ref:**HM04210)

**CHINESE HERBAL MEDICINE**

**Chinese Herbal Medicine**, 243 Chingford Mount Rd, London, **London (Greater)**, E4 8LP, ENG.
(T) 020 8524 1819 (F) 020 8523 3464
Speciality: Herbalists.
● **Owner** Mr H Qi
**M** (**Ref:**HM04211)

**CHINESE HERBAL MEDICINE**

**Chinese Herbal Medicine**, 25 West Gate, Harlow, **Essex**, CM20 1JR, ENG.
(T) 01279 413888 (F) 01279 413888
Speciality: Complementary Medicines & Therapy.
**M** (**Ref:**HM04212)

**CHINESE HERBAL MEDICINE CENTRE**

**Chinese Herbal Medicine Centre**, 34 Knights Hill, London, **London (Greater)**, SE27 0HY, ENG.
(T) 020 8670 7477
Speciality: Herbal Medicine.
**M** (**Ref:**HM04213)

**CHINESE HERBAL MEDICINE CENTRE**

**Chinese Herbal Medicine Centre**, 1-2 Cornmarket, High Wycombe, **Buckinghamshire**, HP11 2BW, ENG.
(T) 01494 512818
Speciality: Complementary Medicines & Therapy.
● **Manager** Mr D Yu
**M** (**Ref:**HM04214)

**CHINESE HERBAL REMEDY CENTRE**

**Chinese Herbal Remedy Centre**, 305 Bethnal Green Rd, London, **London (Greater)**, E2 6AH, ENG.
(T) 020 7729 5100
Speciality: Herbalists.
● **Doctor** Dr Y Huang
**M** (**Ref:**HM04215)

**CHINESE HERBAL WAY**

**Chinese Herbal Way**, 81 High St, Kings Heath, Birmingham, **Midlands (West)**, B14 7BH, ENG.
(T) 01214 448866
Speciality: Herbalists.
● **Owner** Ms C Cai
**M** (**Ref:**HM04216)

**CHINESE HERBALIST**

**Chinese Herbalist**, 288 Derby Rd, Nottingham, **Nottinghamshire**, NG7 1PZ, ENG.
(T) 01159 859096 (F) 01159 859096
Speciality: Herbal Medicine.
● **Owner** Mr K Situ
**M** (**Ref:**HM04217)

**CHINESE HERBS**

**Chinese Herbs**, 4 Nursery Prde, Marsh Rd, Luton, **Bedfordshire**, LU3 2QP, ENG.
(T) 01582 707766
Speciality: Herbalists.
**M** (**Ref:**HM04218)

**CHINESE HERBS & MEDICINE**

**Chinese Herbs & Medicine**, 26 St Loyes St, Bedford, **Bedfordshire**, MK40 1EP, ENG.
(T) 01234 307744 (F) 01582 650389
Speciality: Complementary Medicines & Therapy.
**C M** (**Ref:**HM04219)

**CHINESE MED & ACUPUNCTURE CTRE**

**Chinese Medicine & Acupuncture Centre**, 122 St. James's St, Brighton, **Sussex (East)**, BN2 1TH, ENG.
(T) 01273 699852
Speciality: Acupuncture.
**O** (**Ref:**HM04220)

**CHINESE MED & HEALTHCARE CTRE**

**Chinese Medicine & Healthcare Centre**, 24 Bernard St, Edinburgh, **Edinburgh (City of)**, EH6 6PP, SCO.
(T) 01315 547888 (F) 01315 547888
Speciality: Complementary Medicines & Therapy.
● **Practice Manager** Mrs J Foster
**M** (**Ref:**HM04221)

**CHINESE MEDI CTRE OF LONDON**

**Chinese Medical Centre Of London (The)**, 90 Kingsley Rd, Hounslow, **London (Greater)**, TW3 1QA, ENG.
(T) 020 8570 9998 (F) 020 8423 7887
Speciality: Complementary Medicines & Therapy.
● **Owner** Mrs V Zhu
**C M** (**Ref:**HM04222)

**CHINESE MEDICAL & SKIN CENTRE**

**Chinese Medical & Skin Centre**, 17 Padgate Lane, Warrington, **Cheshire**, WA1 3RS, ENG.
(T) 01925 571333 (F) 01925 571333
Speciality: Acupuncture.
● **Principal** Dr X Her
**O** (**Ref:**HM04223)

**CHINESE MEDICAL & SKIN CENTRE**

**Chinese Medical & Skin Centre (The)**, 75a Cross St, Sale, **Cheshire**, M33 7HF, ENG.
(T) 01619 053666 (F) 01619 053999
Speciality: Complementary Medicines & Therapy.
● **Owner** Dr G Bai
**M** (**Ref:**HM04224)

**CHINESE MEDICAL & SKIN CENTRE**

**Chinese Medical & Skin Centre (The)**, 103 Walshway Rd, Sale, Sale, **Cheshire**, M33 7TY, ENG.
(T) 01619 053666
Speciality: Complementary Medicines & Therapy.
**C M** (**Ref:**HM04225)

**CHINESE MEDICAL CENTRE**

**Chinese Medical Centre**, 112 Alder Rd, Poole, **Dorset**, BH12 4AB, ENG.
(T) 01202 748459 (F) 01202 730670
Speciality: Acupuncture.
● **Practice Manager** Mr L Haung
**O** (**Ref:**HM04226)

**CHINESE MEDICAL CENTRE**

**Chinese Medical Centre**, 33 High St, Maidstone, **Kent**, ME14 1JF, ENG.
(T) 01622 664606
Speciality: Complementary Medicines & Therapy.
● **Owner** Dr P Luo
**M** (**Ref:**HM04227)

**CHINESE MEDICAL CENTRE**

**Chinese Medical Centre**, 217 Stainbeck Rd, Leeds, **Yorkshire (West)**, LS7 2LR, ENG.
(T) 01132 888877 (F) 01132 681229
Speciality: Acupressure, Acupuncture, Chinese Herbal Medicine, Herbal Medicine.
● **Owner** Mr Y Xiu
**C** (**Ref:**HM04228)

**CHINESE MEDICAL CENTRE**

**Chinese Medical Centre**, 2 St John St, Manchester, **Manchester (Greater)**, M3 4DA, ENG.
(T) 01618 399283
Speciality: Complementary Medicines & Therapy.
● **Manager** Mrs W Zhang
**C M** (**Ref:**HM04229)

**CHINESE MEDICAL CENTRE**

**Chinese Medical Centre**, 166 High St, Watford, **Hertfordshire**, WD1 2EG, ENG.
(T) 01923 244635
Speciality: Acupuncture.
● **Director** Ms L Ji
**O** (**Ref:**HM04230)

**CHINESE MEDICAL CENTRE**

**Chinese Medical Centre**, 150 Station Rd, London, **London (Greater)**, N3 2SG, ENG.
(T) 020 8343 4393
Speciality: Acupuncture.
**O** (**Ref:**HM04231)

**CHINESE MEDICAL CENTRE**

**Chinese Medical Centre**, 31 Princesshay, Exeter, **Devon**, EX1 1NG, ENG.
(T) 01392 438683 (F) 01392 438683
Speciality: Complementary Medicines & Therapy.
● **Owner** Mr P Wren
**M** (**Ref:**HM04232)

**CHINESE MEDICAL CENTRE**

**Chinese Medical Centre**, 1 The Strand, Castlerock, Coleraine, **County Londonderry**, BT51 4RA, NIR.
(T) 028 7032 8090 (F) 028 7032 9383
Speciality: Complementary Medicines & Therapy.
● **Principal** Mr I Fu
**C M** (**Ref:**HM04233)

**CHINESE MEDICAL CENTRE**

**Chinese Medical Centre**, 1 Marlborough Court, London, **London (Greater)**, W1V 1PJ, ENG.
(T) 020 7437 5147
Speciality: Complementary Medicines & Therapy.
**C M** (**Ref:**HM04234)

**CHINESE MEDICAL CENTRE**

**Chinese Medical Centre**, 45 Eastlake St, Plymouth, **Devon**, PL1 1BU, ENG.
(T) 01752 600009
Speciality: Complementary Medicines & Therapy.
● **Owner** Mr P Ren
**M** (**Ref:**HM04235)

**CHINESE MEDICAL CENTRE**

**Chinese Medical Centre**, 160B Drake St, Rochdale, **Lancashire**, OL16 1QD, ENG.
(T) 01706 346688
Speciality: Acupuncture.
● **Owner** Mr D Xiu
**O** (**Ref:**HM04236)

**CHINESE MEDICAL CENTRE**

**Chinese Medical Centre**, 8 Upper Brook St, Ipswich, **Suffolk**, IP4 1EE, ENG.
(T) 01473 225700
Speciality: Complementary Medicines &

Key: **B** Mind-Body Medicine **C** Complementary Medicine **H** Self Help Treatment **M** Medicinal Therapy **O** Oriental Medicine **P** Postural Therapy **S** Manipulative Structural Therapy **T** Touch Therapy

Therapy.
● **Owner** Mr P Wren
C M (**Ref:**HM04237)

**CHINESE MEDICAL CENTRE**
**Acumedic Ltd**, Manvers Chambers, Manvers St, Bath, **Somerset**, BA1 1PE, ENG.
(T) 01225 483393 (F) 01225 422037
(E) mfm@acumedic.com
Speciality: Acupressure, Acupuncture, Chinese Herbal Medicine, Oriental Diagnosis, T'ai-Chi Ch'uan.
● **Director** Professor M Mei
(T) 020 7388 8381
● **Consultant Professor** Dr Chen M: ATCM UK, CMIR.
● **Doctor** Dr Zhou Q: MB. M: BAcC, CMIR.
O Yrs. Est.: 27 (**Ref:**HM04238)

**CHINESE MEDICAL CENTRE**
**Chinese Medical Centre**, 208 Poulton Rd, Wallasey, **Merseyside**, CH44 4DA, ENG.
(T) 01516 380016 (F) 01516 380016
Speciality: Complementary Medicines & Therapy.
M (**Ref:**HM04239)

**CHINESE MEDICAL CENTRE**
**Chinese Medical Centre**, 52 Chiltern St, London, **London (Greater)**, W1M 1PP, ENG.
(T) 020 7224 7225
Speciality: Complementary Medicines & Therapy.
C M (**Ref:**HM04240)

**CHINESE MEDICAL CENTRE**
**Chinese Medical Centre Ltd**, 401 Lisburn Rd, Belfast, **County Antrim**, BT9 7EW, NIR.
(T) 028 9066 6212 (F) 028 9066 6801
Speciality: Complementary Medicines & Therapy.
● **Manager** Mr A Sherwani
C M (**Ref:**HM04241)

**CHINESE MEDICAL CENTRE**
**Chinese Medical Centre**, 47 Upr Georges St, Dun Laoghaire, **County Dublin**, IRE.
(T) 01280 0268 (F) 01280 9160
Speciality: Complementary Medicines & Therapy.
M (**Ref:**HM04242)

**CHINESE MEDICAL CENTRE-HERBFIT**
**Chinese Medical Centre-Herbfit**, 35 Hythe St, Dartford, **Kent**, DA1 1BE, ENG.
(T) 01322 290570 (F) 01322 290570
Speciality: Complementary Medicines & Therapy.
● **Owner** Dr K Wuan
C M (**Ref:**HM04243)

**CHINESE MEDICAL CLINIC**
**Chinese Medical Clinic**, 33 Peterson Rd, Wakefield, **Yorkshire (West)**, WF1 4DU, ENG.
(T) 01924 298238
Speciality: Acupuncture.
● **Chief Executive** Mr A Barlow
O (**Ref:**HM04244)

**CHINESE MEDICAL CTRE OF LONDON**
**Chinese Medical Centre of London**, 337 Kilburn High Rd, London, **London (Greater)**, NW6 7QB, ENG.
(T) 020 7372 2184
Speciality: Acupuncture, Cupping, Herbal Medicine, Moxibustion. ✔
● **Doctor** Dr W Wang M: ATCM UK.
● **Doctor** Dr V Yu M: BRCP, RCHM.
O Yrs. Est.: 8 (**Ref:**HM04245)

**CHINESE MEDICINE**
**Chinese Medicine**, Ballinamona Slieverue, **County Waterford**, IRE.
(T) 05185 1530
Speciality: Acupuncture.
O (**Ref:**HM04246)

**CHINESE MEDICINE & ACU CENTRE**
**Chinese Medicine & Acupuncture Centre**, 3 Castleknock Rd, IRE.
(T) 01820 9181
Speciality: Acupuncture.
O (**Ref:**HM04247)

**CHINESE MEDICINE & ACU CENTRE**
**Chinese Medicine & Acupuncture Centre**, 196 Rathmines Rd, Upr, Dublin, **County Dublin**, IRE.
(T) 01496 1533
Speciality: Acupuncture.
O (**Ref:**HM04248)

**CHINESE MEDICINE & ACUPUNCTURE**
**Chinese Medicine & Acupuncture**, 225 Broadway, Bexleyheath, **Kent**, DA6 7AJ, ENG.
(T) 020 8304 0203
Speciality: Complementary Medicines & Therapy.
C M (**Ref:**HM04249)

**CHINESE MEDICINE CENTRE**
**Chinese Medicine Centre**, 36 Westbourne Gr, London, **London (Greater)**, W2 5SH, ENG.
(T) 020 7792 8626
Speciality: Complementary Medicines & Therapy.
● **Owner** Mrs B Bian
C M (**Ref:**HM04250)

**CHINESE MEDICINE CENTRE**
**Chinese Medicine Centre**, 64 Fife Rd, Kingston Upon Thames, **Surrey**, KT1 1SP, ENG.
(T) 020 8546 3886
Speciality: Complementary Medicines & Therapy.
● **Owner** Mr S Li
C M (**Ref:**HM04251)

**CHINESE MEDICINE CENTRE**
**Chinese Medicine Centre**, 61 Watling Avenue, Edgware, **London (Greater)**, HA8 0LD, ENG.
(T) 020 8952 4583
Speciality: Complementary Medicines & Therapy.
● **Owner** Miss T Zsu
M (**Ref:**HM04252)

**CHINESE MEDICINE CENTRE**
**Chinese Medicine Centre**, 537 Great Western Rd, Glasgow, **Glasgow (City of)**, G12 8HN, SCO.
(T) 01413 342122 (F) 01413 343828
Speciality: Complementary Medicines & Therapy.
● **Manager** Mr A Lam
C M (**Ref:**HM04253)

**CHINESE MEDICINE CENTRE**
**Chinese Medicine Centre**, 311 Wimborne Rd, Bournemouth, **Dorset**, BH9 2AB, ENG.
(T) 01202 859988 (F) 01202 859988
Speciality: Acupuncture, Herbal Medicine. ✔
● **Owner** Mrs A Zong Q: Dip.Ac.
● **Practitioner** Dr Kang
O Yrs. Est.: 2 (**Ref:**HM04254)

**CHINESE MEDICINE CENTRE**
**Chinese Medicine Centre**, 3 West Ter, Folkestone, **Kent**, CT20 1RR, ENG.
(T) 01303 243870
Speciality: Complementary Medicines & Therapy.
● **Director** Mr W Hu
M (**Ref:**HM04255)

**CHINESE MEDICINE CENTRE**
**Chinese Medicine Centre**, 375 Nechells Pk Rd, Birmingham, **Midlands (West)**, B7 5NT, ENG.
(T) 01213 289642
Speciality: Acupuncture.
● **Owner** Mr T Long
O (**Ref:**HM04256)

**CHINESE MEDICINE CENTRE**
**Chinese Medicine Centre (The)**, 44 Pillory St, Nantwich, **Cheshire**, CW5 5BG, ENG.
(T) 01270 629222
(W) www.acupuncture.fsnet.co.uk
Speciality: Acupressure, Acupuncture, Chinese Herbal Medicine. ✔
● **Acupuncturist** Mrs J Hu Q: BSc, MBAcC, MRCHM. M: RCHM.
O Yrs. Est.: 4 (**Ref:**HM04257)

**CHINESE MEDICINE CLINIC**
**Chinese Medicine Clinic**, 696 Christchurch Rd, Bournemouth, **Dorset**, BH7 6BY, ENG.
(T) 01202 390399
Speciality: Acupuncture, Chinese Herbal Medicine. ✔
● **Chinese Medicine Practitioner** Mrs S Szhang Q: MD, PhD. M: ATCM UK.
C Yrs. Est.: 4 (**Ref:**HM04258)

**CHINESE MEDICINE CLINIC**
**Chinese Medicine Clinic**, 79 Kings Rd, Chelmsford, **Essex**, CM1 2BB, ENG.
(T) 01245 257085
Speciality: Acupuncture.
● **Owner** Mr H Trinh
O (**Ref:**HM04259)

**CHINESE MEDICINE RENJI CLINIC**
**Chinese Medicine Renji Clinic**, 314 Bradford Rd, Huddersfield, **Yorkshire (West)**, HD1 6LQ, ENG.
(T) 01484 480222
Speciality: Complementary Medicines & Therapy.
● **Owner** Mr G Whitehead
C M (**Ref:**HM04260)

**CHINESE MEDICINE TECH DEVPT**
**Chinese Medicine Technology Development Corporatio**, 369 Eastern Avenue, Ilford, **Essex**, IG2 6NE, ENG.
(T) 020 8550 3888
Speciality: Complementary Medicines & Therapy.
C M (**Ref:**HM04261)

**CHINESE MEDICINE TECH DEVPT**
**Chinese Medicine Technology Development Ltd**, West Gate, Harlow, **Essex**, CM20 1JR, ENG.
(T) 01279 412888
Speciality: Complementary Medicines & Therapy.
● **Manager** Mr H Yu
M (**Ref:**HM04262)

**CHINESE MEDICINE TECH DEVPT**
**Chinese Medicine Technology Development Ltd**, 45 Station Rd, London, **London (Greater)**, E4 7BJ, ENG.
(T) 020 8559 3481 (F) 020 8559 3480
Speciality: Herbal Medicine.
● **Managing Director** Wei Guang Hu
M (**Ref:**HM04263)

**CHINESE MEDICINE TRADITIONAL**
**Chinese Medicine Traditional**, 52 Stoke Newington Church St, London, **London (Greater)**, N16 0NB, ENG.
(T) 020 7249 9671
Speciality: Complementary Medicines & Therapy.
● **Senior Partner** Mrs J Sheridan
M (**Ref:**HM04264)

**CHINESE NAT HEALTHY LIVING**
**Chinese National Healthy Living Centre**, 29-30 Soho Sq, London, **London (Greater)**, W1V 5DH, ENG.
(T) 020 7534 6546 (F) 020 7534 6545
Speciality: Complementary Medicines & Therapy.
● **Manager** Mrs A Kan
C M (**Ref:**HM04265)

**CHINESE NATURAL HEALTH CARE**
**Chinese Natural Health Care**, Tas North London Chinese Herbal Centre, 104 Seven Sisters Rd, London, **London (Greater)**, N7 6AE, ENG.
(T) 020 7607 3143
Speciality: Complementary Medicines & Therapy.
● **Owner** Dr C Que
M (**Ref:**HM04266)

**CHINESE NATURAL HERBAL CENTRE**
**Chinese Natural Herbal Centre**, 93 Turnpike Lane, London, **London (Greater)**, N8 0DY, ENG.
(T) 020 8348 0568 (F) 020 8886 5170
Speciality: Herbal Medicine.
● **Owner** Mrs R Liang
M (**Ref:**HM04267)

**CHINESE NATURAL HERBAL CENTRE**
**Chinese Natural Herbal Centre**, 80 Aungier St, Dublin, **County Dublin**, IRE.
(T) 01475 6974


Key continued: Yrs.Est: Years Established Q: Qualifications M: Professional Membership ✔ Indemnity Insurance Accept Credit Cards

Speciality: Herbalists.
M (Ref:HM04268)

## CHINESE SHOP

**Chinese Shop (The)**, 150 Sandy Hill Rd, Woolwich, London, **London (Greater)**, SE18 7BA, ENG.
(T) 020 8855 0771 (F) 020 8856 9063
Speciality: Acupressure, Acupuncture, Herbal Medicine, Oriental Diagnosis, T'ai-Chi Ch'uan. ✔
● **Owner** Ms D Homan
● **Doctor** Mr H Wang Q: MD. M: ATCM UK.
C O Yrs. Est.: 15 (Ref:HM04269)

## CHINESE THERAPY CLINIC

**Chinese Therapy Clinic**, Yoredale House, Kangel Cl, Ripon, **Yorkshire (North)**, HG4 1DE, ENG.
(T) 01765 607010
Speciality: Acupuncture, Shiatsu, T'ai-Chi Ch'uan.
● **Owner** Mr A Clarke
M (Ref:HM04270)

## CHINESE THERAPY CLINIC

**Chinese Therapy Clinic**, 8a Low Skellgate, Ripon, **Yorkshire (North)**, HG4 1BE, ENG.
(T) 01765 607010
Speciality: Complementary Medicines & Therapy.
C M (Ref:HM04271)

## CHINESE TRAD HEALTH CENTRE

**Chinese Traditional Health Centre**, 3 Southgate, Urmston, Manchester, **Manchester (Greater)**, M41 9FS, ENG.
(T) 01617 473233
Speciality: Complementary Medicines & Therapy.
● **Manageress** Mrs Y Liu
C M (Ref:HM04272)

## CHINESE TRAD HEALTH CENTRE

**Chinese Traditional Health Centre**, 60 Russell Rd (Off Lancaster Rd), Salford, **Manchester (Greater)**, M6 8NR, ENG.
(T) 01617 362163 (F) 01617 362163
Speciality: Complementary Medicines & Therapy.
● **Manager** Mr S Mo
M (Ref:HM04273)

## CHINGFORD FOOT CLINIC

**Chingford Foot Clinic**, 66 Station Rd, London, **London (Greater)**, E4 7BA, ENG.
(T) 020 8529 1298
Speciality: Chiropodists (Podiatrists).
S (Ref:HM04274)

## CHINN, HEDLEY

**Hedley Chinn**, Blackberry Orthopaedic Clinic, Blackberry Court, Walnut Tree, Milton Keynes, **Buckinghamshire**, MK7 7PB, ENG.
(T) 01908 604666
Speciality: Osteopathy.
P S T (Ref:HM04275)

## CHIOTIS, ANNE

**Anne Chiotis**, 15 Regent St, Bilston, **Midlands (West)**, WV14 6AP, ENG.
(T) 01902 409164
Speciality: Herbalists.
M (Ref:HM04276)

## CHIPPENDALE, M

**M Chippendale**, 366 Croydon Rd, Beckenham, **Kent**, BR3 4EX, ENG.
(T) 020 8663 3878 (F) 020 8663 3878
Speciality: Chiropractors.
● **Doctor** Dr M Chippendale
P S T (Ref:HM04277)

## CHIPPER, MARY

**Mary Chipper**, 27 Hill Head, Glastonbury, **Somerset**, BA6 8AW, ENG.
(T) 01458 833317
Speciality: Aromatherapy, Indian Head Massage, Manual Lymph Drainage, Massage (Therapeutic), Stress Therapy. ✔
● **Owner/Aromatherapist**
Mrs M Chipper Q: BSc. M: IFA.
B T Yrs. Est.: 8 (Ref:HM04278)

## CHIPPERFIELD, CAMILLA J

**Camilla J Chipperfield**, 4 The Glade, Ashley Heath, Ringwood, **Hampshire**, BH24 2HR, ENG.
(T) 01425 473797
Speciality: Chiropodists (Podiatrists).
● **Owner** Miss C Chipperfield
S (Ref:HM04279)

## CHIRO & OCCU ADVISORY SV

**Chiropractic & Occupational Health Advisory Servic**, The Hale Clinic, 7 Park Cresent, London, **London (Greater)**, W1N 3HE, ENG.
(T) 020 7631 0156
Speciality: Chiropractors.
P S T (Ref:HM04280)

## CHIRO CENTRE

**Chiro Centre**, Terenure, Dublin, **County Dublin**, IRE.
(T) 01465 0030
(W) www.buteykoireland.com
Speciality: Chiropractors.
P S T (Ref:HM04281)

## CHIRO HEALTH CARE CLINIC

**Chiropractic Health Care Clinic**, 23 Montgomerie Cres, Saltcoats, **Ayrshire (North)**, KA21 5BT, SCO.
(T) 01294 462882
Speciality: Aromatherapy, Chiropractic, Nutritional Therapy. ✔
● **Associate** Miss L Cooper
● **Owner** Dr B Gilmore Q: DC. M: GCC.
P Yrs. Est.: 27 (Ref:HM04282)

## CHIRO MED

**Birmingham Acupuncture & Chiropractic Centre**, 26 Wake Green Rd, Birmingham, **Midlands (West)**, B13 9PA, ENG.
(T) 01214 499515
Speciality: Acupressure, Acupuncture, Aromatherapy, Chiropractic, Cognitive Therapy, Complementary Therapy, Counselling, Cupping, Family Therapy, Gestalt Therapy, Healing Therapy, Holistic Healing, Hypnotherapy, Manipulation, Massage (Therapeutic), Phytotherapy, Stress Therapy, Remedial Massage, Personal Training, Quit Smoking Groups/Japenese Techniques. (Acupuncture Needline). ✔
● **Associate Practitioner**
Lynn Wilkes Q: DC, RGN. M: MCA.
● **Senior Practitioner**
Barbara Husband Q: DC. M: MCA.
● **Senior Practitioner** Mr K Grant Q: BSc (Hons), DC.
● **Senior Acupuncturist** Mr M Scully Q: Lic.Ac. M: BAcC.
S Yrs. Est.: 3 (Ref:HM04283)

## CHIRO SPORTS INJURY CLINIC

**Chiropractic Sports Injury Clinic**, 9 Newman St, Burton Latimer, Kettering, **Northamptonshire**, NN15 5SH, ENG.
(T) 01536 724221
Speciality: Chiropractic.
● **Doctor** Dr M Ganga
P S T (Ref:HM04284)

## CHIROCARE

**Chirocare**, 9 Park Lane, Harefield, Uxbridge, **London (Greater)**, UB9 6BJ, ENG.
(T) 01895 822775
Speciality: Chiropodists (Podiatrists).
S (Ref:HM04285)

## CHIRON

**Chiron**, 370-372 Sharrow Vale Rd, Sheffield, **Yorkshire (South)**, S11 8ZP, ENG.
(T) 01142 664751 (F) 01142 665513
Speciality: Complementary Medicines & Therapy.
● **Owner** Ms J Binns
C M (Ref:HM04286)

## CHIRON CENTRE

**Chiron Centre For Body Psychotherapy**, 90 Harvist Rd, London, **London (Greater)**, NW6 6HL, ENG.
Speciality: Physiotherapy, Body Psychotherapy, Bio-Dynamics. ✔
● **Managing Director** Mr Eidon
(T) 020 8997 5219 Q: Dip.Psych, MA. M: AHPP, EABP, UKCP.
● **Managing Director** Mr Lude Q: Dip.Psych, MA. M: AHPP, EABP, UKCP.
B Yrs. Est.: 18 (Ref:HM04287)

## CHIRON CTRE-BODY PSYCHOTHERAPY

**Chiron Centre For Body Psychotherapy**, 26 Eaton Rise, London, **London (Greater)**, W5 2ER, ENG.
(T) 020 8997 5219 (F) 020 8997 5219
Speciality: Psychotherapy, Body Psychotherapy, Bio-Dynamic Massage. ✔
● **Managing Director** Mr Eidon Q: Dip.Psych, MA. M: AHPP, EABP, UKCP.
● **Managing Director** Mr J Lude Q: Dip.Psych, MA. M: AHPP, EABP, UKCP.
B (Ref:HM04288)

## CHIRONIC ENERGY HEALING CENTRE

**Chironic Energy Healing Centre**, Oxford House, Derbyshire St, London, **London (Greater)**, E2 6HG, ENG.
(T) 020 7739 0100
Speciality: Complementary Medicines & Therapy.
● **Owner** Mr G Leury
M (Ref:HM04289)

## CHIROPODIST

**Miss Heather Todd**, 86 Main St, Larne, **County Antrim**, BT40 1RE, NIR.
(T) 028 2827 3998
Speciality: Biomechanics, Chiropody. ✔
● **Chiropodist** Miss H Todd Q: M.S.C.P.
C Yrs. Est.: 9 (Ref:HM04290)

## CHIROPODIST

**Chiropodist**, 1 Bank Loke, Market Pl, North Walsham, **Norfolk**, NR28 9BP, ENG.
(T) 01692 403355
Speciality: Chiropody, Nail Surgery. ✔
● **Chiropodist** Ms E Bown
S Yrs. Est.: 26 (Ref:HM04291)

## CHIROPODIST

**Chiropodist (The)**, 27 Micklegate, York, **Yorkshire (North)**, YO1 6JH, ENG.
(T) 01904 541293
Speciality: Chiropody. ✔
● **Chiropodist** Mrs J Perry Q: Inst.CH.P. M: Inst.CH.P.
S (Ref:HM04292)

## CHIROPODIST

**Chiropodist (The)**, 724 Pollokshaws Rd, Glasgow, **Glasgow (City of)**, G41 2AD, SCO.
(T) 01414 233231
Speciality: Chiropodists (Podiatrists).
● **Owner** Miss N Melly
S (Ref:HM04293)

## CHIROPODIST & REMEDIAL MASSAGE

**Chiropodist & Remedial Massage**, 106 Denton St, Carlisle, **Cumbria**, CA2 5HB, ENG.
(T) 01228 515457
Speciality: Chiropodists (Podiatrists).
S (Ref:HM04294)

## CHIROPODIST SURGERY

**Chiropodist Services**, 67 Warwick Rd, Stockport, **Cheshire**, SK4 2NL, ENG.
(T) 01617 18371
Speciality: Chiropody, Complementary Therapy, Massage (Therapeutic), Orthotics, Biogun Treatment. ✔
● **Owner** Ms G Thomason M: Inst.CH.P.
● **Chiropodist** Ms D Reeves M: Inst.CH.P.
C M Yrs. Est.: 2 (Ref:HM04295)

## CHIROPODIST/PODIATRIST

**Chiropodist/ Podiatrist**, Heightlea, Old Falmouth Rd, Truro, **Cornwall**, TR1 2HN, ENG.
(T) 01872 260278
Speciality: Biomechanics, Chiropody, Podiatry. ✔
● **Chiropodist (Podiatrist)**
Mrs L Edwards Q: S.R.Ch. M: S.R.Ch.
C (Ref:HM04296)

## CHIROPODISTS

**Chiropodists**, 66 Norwich Rd, Dereham, **Norfolk**, NR20 3AR, ENG.
(T) 01362 696204
Speciality: Chiropody. ✔
● **Chiropodist** Sue Ringer Q: MBChA, MSSCh.

Key: B Mind-Body Medicine, C Complementary Medicine, H Self Help Treatment, M Medicinal Therapy, O Oriental Medicine, P Postural Therapy, S Manipulative Structural Therapy, T Touch Therapy

C Yrs. Est.: 10 (Ref:HM04297)

### CHIROPODISTS SURGERY

**Mrs A C Hibbert**, 4 Chester Rd West, Queensferry, Deeside, **Flintshire**, CH5 1SA, WAL.
(T) 01244 815198
Speciality: Chiropody, Podiatry. ✔
● **Chiropodist (Podiatrist)**
Mrs A Hibbert Q: DPodM, M.S.C.P, S.R.Ch.
M: S.C.P.
H Yrs. Est.: 21 (Ref:HM04298)

### CHIROPODY

**Chiropody**, 15 High St, Mansfield Woodhouse, Mansfield, **Nottinghamshire**, NG19 8NP, ENG.
(T) 01623 648322
Speciality: Chiropractors.
P S T (Ref:HM04299)

### CHIROPODY

**Chiropody**, 6 Meadowbank, Watford, **Hertfordshire**, WD1 4NP, ENG.
(T) 01923 245822
Speciality: Chiropodists (Podiatrists).
● **Owner** Mrs J Feldman
S (Ref:HM04300)

### CHIROPODY

**Chiropody**, 6 Victoria Rd, Poole, **Dorset**, BH12 3BB, ENG.
(T) 01202 734466
Speciality: Chiropody.
● **Owner** Mrs S Smith
S (Ref:HM04301)

### CHIROPODY & AROMATHERAPY

**Chiropody & Aromatherapy Practice**, 11a Grange Pl, Kilmarnock, **Ayrshire (East)**, KA1 2AB, SCO.
(T) 01563 525207
Speciality: Chiropodists (Podiatrists).
● **Partner** Mrs I Young
S (Ref:HM04302)

### CHIROPODY & PHYSIOTHERAPY

**Margaret Street**, 3 George St, Glossop, **Derbyshire**, SK13 8AY, ENG.
(T) 01457 865063
Speciality: Reflexology. ✔
● **Podiatrist/Reflexologist**
Ms M Street Q: DPodM, M.S.C.P, MAR, S.R.Ch.
M: AoR.
T Yrs. Est.: 12 (Ref:HM04303)

### CHIROPODY & PODIATRY CLINIC

**Chiropody & Podiatry Clinic**, 13 Bromley Common, Bromley, **Kent**, BR2 9LS, ENG.
(T) 020 8290 0052
Speciality: Chiropodists (Podiatrists).
S (Ref:HM04304)

### CHIROPODY & REFLEX PRACTICE

**Chiropody & Reflexology Practice**, 22 Downing Cr, Stamford, **Lincolnshire**, PE9 1JD, ENG.
(T) 01780 481788
Speciality: Reflexology.
● **Partner** Mrs J Watson
S T (Ref:HM04305)

### CHIROPODY ADMINISTRATION

**Chiropody Administration (The)**, Stockwell Gate, Mansfield, **Nottinghamshire**, NG18 5QJ, ENG.
(T) 01623 785208
Speciality: Chiropodists (Podiatrists).
● **Manageress** Ms S Knott
S (Ref:HM04306)

### CHIROPODY AT FERNDALE CLINIC

**Chiropody At Ferndale Clinic**, Oakland Ter, Ferndale, **Rhondda Cynon Taff**, CF43 4UD, WAL.
(T) 01443 730533
Speciality: Chiropodists (Podiatrists).
S (Ref:HM04307)

### CHIROPODY AT MUNRO'S

**Chiropody At Munro's**, 693 Great Western Rd, Glasgow, **Glasgow (City of)**, G12 8RA, SCO.
(T) 01413 373115
Speciality: Chiropodists (Podiatrists).
S (Ref:HM04308)

### CHIROPODY CARE

**Chiropody Care**, St. Gilgen, Homer, Much Wenlock, **Shropshire**, TF13 6NE, ENG.
(T) 01952 727647
Speciality: Chiropodists (Podiatrists).
S (Ref:HM04309)

### CHIROPODY CARE CENTRE

**Chiropody Care Centre**, 11 Barstow Sq, Wakefield, **Yorkshire (West)**, WF1 2SF, ENG.
(T) 01924 201213
Speciality: Chiropodists (Podiatrists).
● **Owner** Mrs L Meek
S (Ref:HM04310)

### CHIROPODY CENTRE

**Chiropody Centre (Whitton) (The)**, Minal Pharmacy, 11 High St, Whitton, Twickenham, **London (Greater)**, TW2 7LA, ENG.
(T) 020 8894 4260
Speciality: Chiropody.
● **Owner** Mrs J Crane
S (Ref:HM04311)

### CHIROPODY CENTRE

**Chiropody Centres**, 5 India Pl, Edinburgh, **Edinburgh (City of)**, EH3 6EH, SCO.
(T) 01312 609200
Speciality: Chiropodists (Podiatrists).
S (Ref:HM04312)

### CHIROPODY CENTRE

**Chiropody Centres**, The Glebe, Kirkliston, **Edinburgh (City of)**, EH29 9AS, SCO.
(T) 01313 333383
Speciality: Chiropodists (Podiatrists).
S (Ref:HM04313)

### CHIROPODY CLINIC

**Chiropody Clinic**, 63A Cinque Ports St, Rye, **Sussex (East)**, TN31 7AN, ENG.
(T) 01797 224472
Speciality: Chiropodists (Podiatrists).
● **Partner** Mrs K Luff
S (Ref:HM04314)

### CHIROPODY CLINIC

**Chiropody Clinic**, 748 Upper Newtownards Rd, Dundonald, Belfast, **County Antrim**, BT16 1RJ, NIR.
(T) 028 9048 4686
Speciality: Chiropodists (Podiatrists).
● **Owner** Ms G Marks
S (Ref:HM04315)

### CHIROPODY CLINIC

**Chiropody Clinic**, Hill Pk House, Hill Pk, Launceston, **Cornwall**, PL15 9EP, ENG.
(T) 01566 772662
Speciality: Chiropodists (Podiatrists).
● **Owner** Mr B Pink
S (Ref:HM04316)

### CHIROPODY CLINIC

**Chiropody Clinic**, High St, Paisley, **Renfrewshire**, PA1 2AZ, SCO.
(T) 01418 894745
Speciality: Chiropodists (Podiatrists).
S (Ref:HM04317)

### CHIROPODY CLINIC

**Chiropody Clinic**, Bingley Health Centre, 23 Myrtle Pl, Bingley, **Yorkshire (West)**, BD16 2TL, ENG.
(T) 01274 569131
Speciality: Chiropodists (Podiatrists).
S (Ref:HM04318)

### CHIROPODY CLINIC

**Chiropody Clinic**, 45 Charlotte Rd, Stirchley, Birmingham, **Midlands (West)**, B30 2BT, ENG.
(T) 01214 513393
Speciality: Chiropodists (Podiatrists).
S (Ref:HM04319)

### CHIROPODY CLINIC

**Chiropody Clinic**, Central Health Clinic, Avon Approach, Salisbury, **Wiltshire**, SP1 3SL, ENG.
(T) 01722 422257
Speciality: Chiropodists (Podiatrists).
S (Ref:HM04320)

### CHIROPODY CLINIC

**Chiropody Clinic**, 31 St Johns St, Devizes, **Wiltshire**, SN10 1BN, ENG.
(T) 01380 721177
Speciality: Chiropodists (Podiatrists).
● **Partner** Mrs L Grant
S (Ref:HM04321)

### CHIROPODY CLINIC

**Chiropody Clinic**, 2 Sawyers Cl, Wraxall, Bristol, BS48 1LY, ENG.
(T) 01275 857316
Speciality: Chiropodists (Podiatrists).
S (Ref:HM04322)

### CHIROPODY CLINIC

**Chiropody Clinic**, 19 Westfield Rd, Eastbourne, **Sussex (East)**, BN21 2QT, ENG.
(T) 01323 733506
Speciality: Chiropodists (Podiatrists).
S (Ref:HM04323)

### CHIROPODY CLINIC

**Chiropody Clinic (The)**, 55 Station Rd, Hetton-Le-Hole, Houghton le Spring, **Tyne and Wear**, DH5 0AT, ENG.
(T) 01915 260070
Speciality: Biomechanics, Chiropody, Nail Surgery, Orthotics, Podiatry, Reflexology. ✔
● **Reflexologist** Ms P Hudspeth M: FHT, ICHT, IIHHT.
● **Chiropodist (Podiatrist)**
Mrs P Middleditch Q: DPodM, S.R.Ch. M: S.C.P.
S (Ref:HM04324)

### CHIROPODY CLINIC

**Chiropody Clinic (The)**, 24 Rose St, London, **London (Greater)**, WC2E 9EA, ENG.
(T) 020 7836 1050
Speciality: Chiropodists (Podiatrists).
S (Ref:HM04325)

### CHIROPODY CLINIC

**Chiropody Clinic (The)**, Vicarage Lane, Ashford, **Kent**, TN23 1NJ, ENG.
(T) 01233 204102 (F) 01233 204115
Speciality: Chiropodists (Podiatrists).
S (Ref:HM04326)

### CHIROPODY CLINIC

**Chiropody Clinic (The)**, 29 Fleet St, London, **London (Greater)**, EC4Y 1AA, ENG.
(T) 020 7353 5678 (F) 020 7353 5500
Speciality: Chiropodists (Podiatrists).
● **Owner** Miss N Martinelli
S (Ref:HM04327)

### CHIROPODY CLINIC LODDON

**Chiropody Clinic Loddon NHS Trust**, Bramblys Drive, Basingstoke, **Hampshire**, RG21 8UW, ENG.
(T) 01256 356630 (F) 01256 357986
Speciality: Chiropodists (Podiatrists).
S (Ref:HM04328)

### CHIROPODY CLINIC OFFICE

**Chiropody Clinic Office & Appliance Centre (The)**, Sanderson Hospital, Salters Rd, Newcastle Upon Tyne, **Tyne and Wear**, NE3 4EL, ENG.
(T) 01912 847224
Speciality: Chiropodists (Podiatrists).
S (Ref:HM04329)

### CHIROPODY CORNER

**Chiropody Corner**, 26 Monkswood Cl, Callands, Warrington, **Cheshire**, WA5 5SE, ENG.
(T) 01925 470584
Speciality: Chiropody. ✔
● **Chiropodist** Mr N Corner Q: Inst.CH.P.
M: Inst.CH.P.
C Yrs. Est.: 2 (Ref:HM04330)

### CHIROPODY DEPARTMENT

**Chiropody Department**, Prince Philip House, St Matthews Health & Community Centre, Leicester, **Leicestershire**, LE1 2NZ, ENG.
(T) 01162 244664
Speciality: Chiropodists (Podiatrists).
S (Ref:HM04331)

### CHIROPODY NHS

**Chiropody NHS**, Kings Park Community Hospital, Gloucester Rd, Bournemouth, **Dorset**, BH7 6JE, ENG.
(T) 01202 303757
Speciality: Chiropodists (Podiatrists).


Key continued: Yrs.Est: Years Established Q: Qualifications M: Professional Membership ✔ Indemnity Insurance Accept Credit Cards

● **General Manager** Mr J Assey
**S** (**Ref:**HM04332)

**CHIROPODY PRACTICE**

**Chiropody Practice (The)**, 38 Oxford St, Whitstable, **Kent**, CT5 1DG, **ENG**.
(T) 01227 262483
Speciality: Chiropodists (Podiatrists).
**S** (**Ref:**HM04333)

**CHIROPODY PRACTICE**

**Chiropody Practice (The)**, 6 Sandford St, Lichfield, **Staffordshire**, WS13 6QA, **ENG**.
(T) 01543 256306
Speciality: Chiropodists (Podiatrists).
**S** (**Ref:**HM04334)

**CHIROPODY PRACTICE**

**Chiropody Practice (The)**, 1 Clarendon Rd, Borehamwood, **Hertfordshire**, WD6 1BD, **ENG**.
(T) 020 8953 9052
Speciality: Chiropodists (Podiatrists).
**S** (**Ref:**HM04335)

**CHIROPODY SERVICE**

**Chiropody Service**, 41 Upper Rock Gdns, Brighton, **Sussex (East)**, BN2 1QF, **ENG**.
(T) 01273 690546
Speciality: Chiropodists (Podiatrists).
● **Owner** Mrs C McLeod
**S** (**Ref:**HM04336)

**CHIROPODY SERVICES**

**Chiropody Services**, Durrington Health Centre, Durrington Lane, Worthing, **Sussex (West)**, BN13 2RX, **ENG**.
(T) 01903 843860
Speciality: Chiropodists (Podiatrists).
**S** (**Ref:**HM04337)

**CHIROPODY SERVICES**

**Chiropody Services**, Sovereign Centre, Christchurch Rd, Bournemouth, **Dorset**, BH1 4SX, **ENG**.
(T) 01202 390951
Speciality: Chiropody. ✔
● **Chiropodist (Podiatrist)**
Miss M Farrant **Q:** S.R.Ch. **M:** S.C.P.
**M** Yrs. Est.: 3 (**Ref:**HM04338)

**CHIROPODY SERVICES**

**Chiropody Services**, 7 Coombe Lane, Tenterden, **Kent**, TN30 6HN, **ENG**.
(T) 01580 762040
Speciality: Chiropodists (Podiatrists).
**S** (**Ref:**HM04339)

**CHIROPODY SERVICES**

**Chiropody Services**, Central Clinic, Stoke Abbott Rd, Worthing, **Sussex (West)**, BN11 1HE, **ENG**.
(T) 01903 843503
Speciality: Chiropodists (Podiatrists).
**S** (**Ref:**HM04340)

**CHIROPODY SERVICES**

**Chiropody Services (The)**, 28 St Mary St, Cardiff, **Glamorgan (Vale of)**, CF10 1AT, **WAL**.
(T) 029 2066 6617
Speciality: Chiropodists (Podiatrists).
● **Owner** Mr V Kerry
**S** (**Ref:**HM04341)

**CHIROPODY SURGERY**

**Chiropody Surgery**, 203 Crookes Valley Rd, Sheffield, **Yorkshire (South)**, S10 1BA, **ENG**.
(T) 01142 664101
Speciality: Chiropody, Cryo Surgery, Gait Analysis, Nail Surgery. ✔
● **Chiropodist** Mr R Sallay **Q:** Inst.CH.P.
**S** Yrs. Est.: 22 (**Ref:**HM04342)

**CHIROPODY SURGERY**

**Chiropody Surgery**, 7 Barmouth Rd, London, **London (Greater)**, SW18 2DT, **ENG**.
(T) 020 8870 0184
Speciality: Chiropodists (Podiatrists).
● **Owner** Mr M Patel
**S** (**Ref:**HM04343)

**CHIROPODY SURGERY**

**Chiropody Surgery**, 1 Parkhouse Rd, Minehead, **Somerset**, TA24 8AB, **ENG**.
(T) 01643 702122
Speciality: Biomechanics, Chiropody, Nail Surgery. ✔
● **Chiropodist** Mr M Cavell **Q:** BSc (Hons), DPodM, M.S.C.P, S.R.Ch. **M:** C.P.S.M.
**S** Yrs. Est.: 20 (**Ref:**HM04344)

**CHIROPODY SURGERY**

**Chiropody Surgery (The)**, Pigmeadow Lane, The Parade, Liskeard, **Cornwall**, PL14 6AF, **ENG**.
(T) 01579 344090
Speciality: Chiropodists (Podiatrists).
● **Owner** Mrs T Teasdale
**S** (**Ref:**HM04345)

**CHIROPODY SURGERY**

**Chiropody Surgery (The)**, 7a High St, Emsworth, **Hampshire**, PO10 7AQ, **ENG**.
(T) 01243 375603
Speciality: Chiropodists (Podiatrists).
● **Owner** Ms J Crayton
**S** (**Ref:**HM04346)

**CHIROPODY SURGERY**

**Chiropody Surgery (The)**, 47 Villa Rd, Birmingham, **Midlands (West)**, B19 1BH, **ENG**.
(T) 01215 236916
Speciality: Chiropodists (Podiatrists).
● **Owner** Mr J White
**S** (**Ref:**HM04347)

**CHIROPRACTIC & CRANIAL CENTRE**

**Chiropractic & Cranial Centre**, 60 Testwood Cres, Totton, Southampton, **Hampshire**, SO40 3NH, **ENG**.
(T) 023 8066 7205
Speciality: Chiropractic.
**P S T** (**Ref:**HM04348)

**CHIROPRACTIC & HERBAL CENTRE**

**Chiropractic & Herbal Treatment Centre**, 38 Upper Grosvenor Rd, Tunbridge Wells, **Kent**, TN1 2ET, **ENG**.
(T) 01892 536732
Speciality: Chiropractic.
**P S T** (**Ref:**HM04349)

**CHIROPRACTIC AND MYOFACIAL**

**Chiropractic and Myofacial Pain Clinic**, 61 Shearwater Drive, The Willows, Torquay, **Devon**, TQ2 7TL, **ENG**.
(T) 01803 615605
Speciality: Acupressure, Acupuncture, Chiropractic, Complementary Therapy, Manipulation, Physiotherapy, Myofascial Dry Needling.
**P S T** (**Ref:**HM04350)

**CHIROPRACTIC ASS OF IRELAND**

**Kilworth Chiropractic Clinic**, Kilworth Chiropractic Clinic, Kilworth, **County Cork**, IRE.
(T) 025 2743 6
Speciality: Chiropractors.
**P S T** (**Ref:**HM04351)

**CHIROPRACTIC ASS OF IRELAND**

**Chiropractic Association Of Ireland**, Ennis Chiropractic Clinic, IRE.
(T) 06568 24600
Speciality: Chiropractors.
**P S T** (**Ref:**HM04352)

**CHIROPRACTIC ASS OF IRELAND**

**Chiropractic Association Of Ireland**, Ed Sordillo, IRE.
(T) 06141 6082
Speciality: Chiropractors.
**P S T** (**Ref:**HM04353)

**CHIROPRACTIC ASS OF IRELAND**

**Tralee Chiropractic Cllinic**, St Brendans Rd, Upper Rock St, Tralee, **County Kerry**, IRE.
(T) 06671 23876
Speciality: Chiropractors.
**P S T** (**Ref:**HM04354)

**CHIROPRACTIC ASS OF IRELAND**

**Chiropractic Association Of Ireland**, Dungarvan Alternative Health Clinic, IRE.
(T) 025 2765 3
Speciality: Chiropractors.
**P S T** (**Ref:**HM04355)

**CHIROPRACTIC ASS OF IRELAND**

**Chiropractic Association Of Ireland**, Mullingar, **County Westmeath**, IRE.
(T) 04448 374
Speciality: Chiropractors.
● **Chiropractor** Rory Murphy
**P S T** (**Ref:**HM04356)

**CHIROPRACTIC ASS OF IRELAND**

**Chiropractic Association Of Ireland**, Dean St, **County Kilkenny**, IRE.
(T) 05651 959
Speciality: Chiropractors.
● **Doctor** Mary Sheedy
**P S T** (**Ref:**HM04357)

**CHIROPRACTIC ASS OF IRELAND**

**Chiropractic Association Of Ireland**, Rory Hayes D.C., Thurles, **County Tipperary**, IRE.
(T) 05042 2250
Speciality: Chiropractors.
**P S T** (**Ref:**HM04358)

**CHIROPRACTIC ASS OF IRELAND**

**Chiropractic Association Of Ireland**, Noel Ryan D.C. Gracedieu, **County Waterford**, IRE.
(T) 05185 5481
Speciality: Chiropractors.
**P S T** (**Ref:**HM04359)

**CHIROPRACTIC ASS OF IRELAND**

**Chiropractic Association Of Ireland**, Unit 9 Penrose Wharf, Penrose, **County Cork**, IRE.
(T) 021 4551 747
Speciality: Chiropractors.
● **Chiropractor** Dr J Cosgrave
**P S T** (**Ref:**HM04360)

**CHIROPRACTIC ASS OF IRELAND**

**Chiropractic Association Of Ireland**, Market Hse, Kilworth, IRE.
(T) 025 2743 6
Speciality: Chiropractors.
● **Chiropractor** Dr E Bates
**P S T** (**Ref:**HM04361)

**CHIROPRACTIC ASS OF IRELAND**

**Chiropractic Association Of Ireland**, Bellevue Surgery, Mallow, **County Cork**, IRE.
(T) 022 2147 8
Speciality: Chiropractors.
● **Chiropractor** Dr M Blumenthal
**P S T** (**Ref:**HM04362)

**CHIROPRACTIC ASS OF IRELAND**

**Chiropractic Association Of Ireland**, Millbrook Clinic, Bandon, **County Cork**, IRE.
(T) 023 4363 8
Speciality: Chiropractors.
**P S T** (**Ref:**HM04363)

**CHIROPRACTIC ASS OF IRELAND**

**Chiropractic Association Of Ireland**, C/O Cork Chiropractic Clinic, 2a Harley Court, **County Cork**, IRE.
(T) 021 4342 933 (F) 021 2726 6
Speciality: Chiropractors.
**P S T** (**Ref:**HM04364)

**CHIROPRACTIC ASS OF IRELAND**

**Chiropractic Association Of Ireland (CAI)**, Rehins, Foxford, **County Mayo**, IRE.
(T) 09670 664
Speciality: Chiropractors.
**P S T** (**Ref:**HM04365)

**CHIROPRACTIC ASS OF IRELAND**

**Chiropractic Association Of Ireland (CAI)**, Ballinasloe, **County Galway**, IRE.
(T) 09054 5326
Speciality: Chiropractors.
**P S T** (**Ref:**HM04366)

**CHIROPRACTIC ASS OF IRELAND**

**Chiropractic Association Of Ireland (CAI)**, Ballincar, **County Sligo**, IRE.
(T) 07147 049
Speciality: Chiropractors.
**P S T** (**Ref:**HM04367)

**CHIROPRACTIC ASS OF IRELAND**

**Chiropractic Association Of Ireland (CAI)**, Killybegs Rd, **County Donegal**, IRE.
(T) 07323 838
Speciality: Chiropractors.
**P S T** (**Ref:**HM04368)

**CHIROPRACTIC ASS OF IRELAND**

**Chiropractic Association Of Ireland (CAI)**,

Key: **B** Mind-Body Medicine **C** Complementary Medicine **H** Self Help Treatment **M** Medicinal Therapy **O** Oriental Medicine **P** Postural Therapy **S** Manipulative Structural Therapy **T** Touch Therapy

Castlebar, **County Mayo**, IRE.
(T) 09426 516
Speciality: Chiropractors.
P S T (Ref:HM04369)

### CHIROPRACTIC ASS OF IRELAND
**Chiropractic Association Of Ireland (CAI)**, Letterkenny Co, **County Donegal**, IRE.
(T) 08723 93535
Speciality: Chiropractors.
P S T (Ref:HM04370)

### CHIROPRACTIC ASS OF IRELAND
**Chiropractic Association Of Ireland (CAI)**, Pearse Rd, **County Sligo**, IRE.
(T) 07160 001
Speciality: Chiropractors.
P S T (Ref:HM04371)

### CHIROPRACTIC ASS OF IRELAND
**Chiropractic Association Of Ireland (CAI)**, Williamstown Co, **County Galway**, IRE.
(T) 09074 3235
Speciality: Chiropractors.
P S T (Ref:HM04372)

### CHIROPRACTIC ASS OF IRELAND
**Chiropractic Association Of Ireland (CAI)**, Tuam Rd, **County Galway**, IRE.
(T) 09175 5205
Speciality: Chiropractors.
P S T (Ref:HM04373)

### CHIROPRACTIC ASS OF IRELAND
**Chiropractic Association Of Ireland (CAI)**, Riverstown, **County Sligo**, IRE.
(T) 07167 686
Speciality: Chiropractors.
P S T (Ref:HM04374)

### CHIROPRACTIC ASS OF IRELAND
**Chiropratic Association Of Ireland**, C/O Dr Jesse Lawrence Limerick Moyrhee Phares Rd, Nth Limerick, **County Limerick**, IRE.
(T) 06132 7716
Speciality: Chiropractors.
P S T (Ref:HM04375)

### CHIROPRACTIC ASSOCIATES
**Chiropractic Associates**, 1/L.H.P.C., Forest Drive, Lytham St. Annes, **Lancashire**, FY8 4QF, ENG.
(T) 01253 739052
Speciality: Acupuncture.
O (Ref:HM04376)

### CHIROPRACTIC ASSOCIATES
**Chiropractic Associates**, 133 Chorley Rd, Walton-Le-Dale, Preston, **Lancashire**, PR5 4JR, ENG.
(T) 01772 696611 (F) 01772 629691
Speciality: Chiropractic.
● **Director** Mr J Shurr
P S T (Ref:HM04377)

### CHIROPRACTIC ASSOCIATES
**Chiropractic Associates**, 16-26 Darwen St, Blackburn, **Lancashire**, BB2 2BY, ENG.
(T) 01254 261706
Speciality: Chiropractic.
● **Director** Dr J Shurr
P S T (Ref:HM04378)

### CHIROPRACTIC CARE
**Chiropractic Care**, 193 High St, Honiton, **Devon**, EX14 1LQ, ENG.
(T) 01297 35844 (F) 01297 35844
Speciality: Chiropractors.
● **Owner** Mr R Stenning
P S T (Ref:HM04379)

### CHIROPRACTIC CENTRE
**Chiropractic Centre**, Borough High St, London, **London (Greater)**, SE1 4HT, ENG.
(T) 020 7378 9494
Speciality: Chiropractors.
P S T (Ref:HM04380)

### CHIROPRACTIC CENTRE
**Chiropractic Centre**, 5 North St, Oadby, Leicester, **Leicestershire**, LE2 5AH, ENG.
(T) 01162 712255
(E) npainter@stayfree.co.uk
Speciality: Chiropractic. ✔
● **Principal** Mr N Painter Q: DC. M: BCA.
S Yrs. Est.: 10 (Ref:HM04381)

### CHIROPRACTIC CENTRE
**Chiropractic Centre (The)**, 1st-2nd-3rd Floor, 9a George St, Croydon, **Surrey**, CR0 1LA, ENG.
(T) 020 8680 4777 (F) 028 0649 8188
Speciality: Chiropractic. ✔ CREDIT
● **Clinical Director** Dr C Merkier Q: DC. M: BCA.
● **Chiropractor** Dr H Madsen Q: DC. M: BCA.
P Yrs. Est.: 10 (Ref:HM04382)

### CHIROPRACTIC CLINIC
**Chiropractic Clinic**, 16 Keyberry Park, Newton Abbot, **Devon**, TQ12 1BZ, ENG.
(T) 01626 366840 (F) 01626 353334
Speciality: Chiropractors.
● **Senior Partner** Mr F Verwey
P S T (Ref:HM04383)

### CHIROPRACTIC CLINIC
**Chiropractic Clinic**, 84 Tettenhall Rd, Wolverhampton, **Midlands (West)**, WV1 4TF, ENG.
(T) 01902 772446
Speciality: Chiropractic.
● **Senior Partner** Dr H Kulyna
P S T (Ref:HM04384)

### CHIROPRACTIC CLINIC
**Chiropractic Clinic**, 79 Gales Drive, Crawley, **Sussex (West)**, RH10 1QA, ENG.
(T) 01293 535381 (F) 01293 535382
Speciality: Chiropractic.
● **Doctor** Dr D Hales
P S T (Ref:HM04385)

### CHIROPRACTIC CLINIC
**Chiropractic Clinic**, Corbin Avenue, Ferndown, **Dorset**, BH22 8AZ, ENG.
(T) 01202 897989
Speciality: Chiropractors.
P S T (Ref:HM04386)

### CHIROPRACTIC CLINIC
**Chiropractic Clinic**, 313 High Rd, Romford, **Essex**, RM6 6AX, ENG.
(T) 020 8252 1010 (F) 020 8252 1010
Speciality: Chiropractic.
● **Doctor** Dr S Alonzolmedo
P S T (Ref:HM04387)

### CHIROPRACTIC CLINIC
**Chiropractic Clinic**, 131 Edgbaston Rd, Birmingham, **Midlands (West)**, B12 9QA, ENG.
(T) 01214 497766 (F) 01214 424357
Speciality: Chiropractic. ✔ CREDIT
● **Chiropractor** Dr J Rousseau Q: DC.
● **Chiropractor** Dr H Hold Q: DC.
P Yrs. Est.: 30 (Ref:HM04388)

### CHIROPRACTIC CLINIC
**Chiropractic Clinic**, 106 Wellingborough Rd, Northampton, **Northamptonshire**, NN1 4DR, ENG.
(T) 01604 786107
Speciality: Chiropractic.
● **Owner** Dr M Ganger
P S T (Ref:HM04389)

### CHIROPRACTIC CLINIC
**Chiropractic Clinic**, 101 Watcombe Rd, Bournemouth, **Dorset**, BH6 5LP, ENG.
(T) 01202 427632
Speciality: Chiropractic.
P S T (Ref:HM04390)

### CHIROPRACTIC CLINIC
**Chiropractic Clinic**, 14 Percy St, Rotherham, **Yorkshire (South)**, S65 1ED, ENG.
(T) 01709 837738
Speciality: Chiropractic.
P S T (Ref:HM04391)

### CHIROPRACTIC CLINIC
**Chiropractic Clinic Ltd**, 19 St Augustines Rd, Canterbury, **Kent**, CT1 1XP, ENG.
(T) 01227 768884
Speciality: Chiropractic.
● **Owner** Dr F Collingwood
P S T (Ref:HM04392)

### CHIROPRACTIC CLINIC
**Chiropractic Clinic (The)**, 141 Golders Green Rd, London, **London (Greater)**, NW11 8HG, ENG.
(T) 020 8458 3311 (F) 020 8201 8578
Speciality: Acupuncture, Chiropractic, Health and Beauty Clinic. ✔ CREDIT
● **Owner** Dr J Napier Q: DC. M: GCC.
P Yrs. Est.: 20 (Ref:HM04393)

### CHIROPRACTIC CLINIC
**Chiropractic Clinic (The)**, 71 Westborough, Scarborough, **Yorkshire (North)**, YO11 1YS, ENG.
(T) 01723 507207
Speciality: Chiropractic.
P S T (Ref:HM04394)

### CHIROPRACTIC CONSULTANT SVS
**Chiropractic Consultant Services**, 146 Sundon Park Rd, Luton, **Bedfordshire**, LU3 3AH, ENG.
(T) 01582 579687 (F) 01582 493512
Speciality: Chiropractors.
● **Principal** Mr G Heale
P S T (Ref:HM04395)

### CHIROPRACTIC CONSULTANT SVS
**Chiropractic Consultant Services**, Hitchin Chiropractic Clinic, 133 Cambridge Rd, Hitchin, **Hertfordshire**, SG4 0JH, ENG.
(T) 01462 420077 (F) 01462 420033
Speciality: Chiropractic.
● **Partner** Mr G Heale
P S T (Ref:HM04396)

### CHIROPRACTIC CONSULTANT SVS
**Chiropractic Consultant Services**, 5 Hockliffe St, Leighton Buzzard, **Bedfordshire**, LU7 8HE, ENG.
(T) 01525 853002 (F) 01525 370320
Speciality: Chiropractic.
● **Employee** Mr M Horrelll
P S T (Ref:HM04397)

### CHIROPRACTIC FIRST
**Chiropractic First**, Unit 1 Church Hill, Navan, **County Meath**, IRE.
(T) 07767 1066
Speciality: Chiropractors.
P S T (Ref:HM04398)

### CHIROPRACTIC HEALTH CENTRE
**Chiropractic Health Centre**, 13 Leeds Rd, Harrogate, **Yorkshire (North)**, HG2 8AW, ENG.
(T) 01423 701777
Speciality: Chiropractors.
● **Partner** Dr D Cheung
P S T (Ref:HM04399)

### CHIROPRACTIC HEALTHCARE CLINIC
**Chiropractic Healthcare Clinic**, 48A Barton Hill Rd, Torquay, **Devon**, TQ2 8JD, ENG.
(T) 01803 329799
Speciality: Chiropractic.
P S T (Ref:HM04400)

### CHIROPRACTIC PATIENTS ASS
**Chiropractic Patients Association**, 8 Centre One, Lysander Way, Old Sarum, Salisbury, **Wiltshire**, SP4 6BU, ENG.
(T) 01722 415027 (F) 01722 415028
Speciality: Chiropractic.
● **Chairman** Mr A Atkinson
P S T (Ref:HM04401)

### CHIROPRACTIC PLUS
**Chiropractic Plus**, 11-15 The Old High St, Folkestone, **Kent**, CT20 1RL, ENG.
(T) 01303 249249 (F) 01843 599366
Speciality: Chiropractic, Iridology, Nutritional Therapy, Reiki. ✔
● **Chiropractor** Dr A Plenty Q: DC, F.I.A.M.A. M: BRCP, CC.
C Yrs. Est.: 2 (Ref:HM04402)

### CHIROPRACTIC TREATMENT CENTRE
**Chiropractic Treatment Centre**, 20 St Swithuns Rd South, Bournemouth, **Dorset**, BH1 3RQ, ENG.
(T) 01202 551010 (F) 01202 554433
Speciality: Chiropractic. ✔
● **Chiropractor** Dr A Zahedi Q: DC. M: BCA.
P Yrs. Est.: 30 (Ref:HM04403)

### CHIROPRACTIC WELLNESS CENTRE
**Chiropractic Wellness Centre**, 73 Hucclecote


Key continued: Yrs.Est: Years Established Q: Qualifications M: Professional Membership ✔ Indemnity Insurance CREDIT Accept Credit Cards

Rd, Gloucester, **Gloucestershire**, GL3 3TW, ENG.
**(T)** 01452 372222 **(F)** 01452 372222
Speciality: Chiropractors.
● **Practice Manager** Mrs L Collin
P S T (**Ref:**HM04404)

## CHIROPRACTICE

**Chiropractice**, 2 Redburn Sq, Holywood, **County Down**, BT18 9HZ, NIR.
**(T)** 028 9042 1511 **(F)** 028 9042 6282
Speciality: Chiropody, Chiropractic, Massage (Therapeutic), Podiatry. ✓
● **Chiropodist** Miss A McClean **Q:** BSc (Hons), M.S.C.P, S.R.Ch. **M:** S.C.P, S.R.Ch.
● **Therapeutic/Remedial Massage Therapist** Mr J Earls **Q:** BA (Hons), MIRI.
● **Chiropractor** Dr S Kaushal **Q:** BSc (Chiro), DC. **M:** CC.
P Yrs. Est.: 3 (**Ref:**HM04405)

## CHIROPRACTORS MCTIMONEY

**Chiropractors McTimoney**, 32A Sun St, Hitchin, **Hertfordshire**, SG5 1AH, ENG.
**(T)** 01462 433777
Speciality: Chiropractic.
● **Owner** Mr R Tant
P S T (**Ref:**HM04406)

## CHIROPRACTORS OF WARWICK ROAD

**Chiropractors Of Warwick Road (The)**, 451 Warwick Rd, Solihull, **Midlands (West)**, B91 1AL, ENG.
**(T)** 01217 051876 **(F)** 01216 817258
Speciality: Chiropractic. ✓
● **Chiropractor** Dr T Smythe **Q:** B.App.Sc, BSc (Chiro).
● **Chiropractor** Dr A O'Neill **Q:** BSc (Chiro), DC.
● **Chiropractor** Dr C Sawyer **Q:** BSc (Chiro), DC.
P Yrs. Est.: 2 (**Ref:**HM04407)

## CHIROPRATIC & HOM HEALTH CTRE

**Chiropratic & Homeopathic Health Centre**, 6 North Brink, Wisbech, **Cambridgeshire**, PE13 1JR, ENG.
**(T)** 01945 588330 **(F)** 01945 476065
Speciality: Acupressure, Acupuncture, Aromatherapy, Chiropractic, Massage (Therapeutic), Nutritional Therapy, Stress Therapy, Laser Therapy. ✓
● **Chiropractor** Dr Stuart
● **Reflexologist** Nicky Smith **Q:** IIHHT. **M:** IIHHT.
● **Chiropractor** Dr Kola **Q:** DC.
● **Manageress** Ms V Akinderle
C (**Ref:**HM04408)

## CHISLEHURST CHIROPODY PRACTICE

**Chislehurst Chiropody Practice**, 54B Green Lane, Chislehurst, **Kent**, BR7 6AQ, ENG.
**(T)** 020 8295 1066 **(F)** 020 8295 1066
Speciality: Chiropodists (Podiatrists).
● **Partner** Mr J McNeil
S (**Ref:**HM04409)

## CHISLEHURST NATURAL HEALTH

**Chislehurst Natural Health Centre**, 40 High St, Chislehurst, **Kent**, BR7 5AQ, ENG.
**(T)** 020 8467 1910
Speciality: Acupuncture, Aromatherapy, Chiropody, Hypnotherapy, Osteopathy, Reflexology, Shiatsu. ✓
● **Therapist** Leong-Sen Liu
**(T)** 01689 898920 **Q:** ITEC, MRSS.
● **Osteopath** Mrs R Godec **Q:** DC.
● **Owner** Mrs M Birkbeck
**(T)** 01732 450049 **Q:** ITEC.
● **Therapist** Ms G Allsop
**(T)** 01812 950893 **Q:** B.Ac, MBAcC.
● **Chiropodist** Mr A Saunders **Q:** BSc (Chiro), DPodM, M.S.C.P.
C Yrs. Est.: 8 (**Ref:**HM04410)

## CHISTLEHURST NATURAL HLTH CTRE

**Chistlehurst Natural Health Centre**, Chislehurst Natural Health Centre, 40 High St, Chislehurst, **Kent**, BR7 5AQ, ENG.
**(T)** 020 8467 1910
Speciality: Acupuncture, Aromatherapy, Chiropody, Holistic Healing, Homeopathy, Hypnotherapy, Indian Head Massage, Massage (Therapeutic), Osteopathy, Reflexology, Shiatsu.
✓
● **Owner** Ms R Godeck
P Yrs. Est.: 7 (**Ref:**HM04411)

## CHISWICK CHIROPRACTIC CLINIC

**Chiswick Chiropractic Clinic (The)**, 103 Duke Rd, London, **London (Greater)**, W4 2BX, ENG.
**(T)** 08003 283260
Speciality: Acupuncture, Chiropractic, Manipulation. ✓
● **Chiropractor** Mr J Sykes **Q:** DC. **M:** BCA.
P S T Yrs. Est.: 3 (**Ref:**HM04412)

## CHISWICK CHIROPRACTIC CLINIC

**Chiswick Chiropractic Clinic**, 3 Pleydell Av, Stamford Book, London, **London (Greater)**, W4 2NW, ENG.
**(T)** 020 8741 3556
Speciality: Chiropractic.
P S T (**Ref:**HM04413)

## CHISWICK HYPNOTHERAPY CENTRE

**Chiswick Hypnotherapy Centre**, 83 Airedale Avenue, London, **London (Greater)**, W4 2NN, ENG.
**(T)** 020 8994 9992
Speciality: Hypnosis.
B (**Ref:**HM04414)

## CHIU, ANGELA

**Angela Chiu**, Harbour Lodge, Haven Rd, Poole, **Dorset**, BH13 7LZ, ENG.
**(T)** 01202 701108
Speciality: Aromatherapy.
M O (**Ref:**HM04415)

## CHIVERS, JAMES

**James Chivers**, 19 Stoddart Avenue, Southampton, **Hampshire**, SO19 4ED, ENG.
**(T)** 023 8068 5592
Speciality: Clairvoyants & Palmists.
● **Owner** Mr J Chivers
B (**Ref:**HM04416)

## CHIVERS, JEAN

**Jean Chivers S R Ch D Pod M**, 7 Godfrey Rd, Newport, NP20 4NX, WAL.
**(T)** 01633 258560
Speciality: Chiropractors.
P S T (**Ref:**HM04417)

## CHIVERS, JEAN

**Jean Chivers**, 27 Malpas Rd, Newport, NP20 5PB, WAL.
**(T)** 01633 821909
Speciality: Chiropodists (Podiatrists).
● **Owner** Ms J Chivers
S (**Ref:**HM04418)

## CHLOE'S HERBS

**Chloe's Herbs**, Clugston Mill, Spittal Croft, Kirkcowan, Newton Stewart, **Dumfries and Galloway**, DG8 0DA, SCO.
**(T)** 01671 830390
**(E)** chloesherbs@netscapeonline.co.uk
**(W)** www.wigtown.co.uk
Speciality: Bach Remedies, Herbal Medicine, Iridology, Naturopathy, Nutritional Therapy. ✓
● **Herbalist/Natural Healer** Ms C Bruce **Q:** CT, Ir, MH. **M:** AMH, EHPA.
M (**Ref:**HM04419)

## CHOHAN, SUKHI

**Mrs Sukhi Chohan**, 4 Princess Park Avenue, Hayes, **London (Greater)**, UB3 1LD, ENG.
**(T)** 020 8581 3842
Speciality: Psychotherapy.
M (**Ref:**HM04420)

## CHOICE AROMAS

**Choice Aromas**, 345 Bradford Rd, Cleckheaton, **Yorkshire (West)**, BD19 3UQ, ENG.
**(T)** 01274 876621
Speciality: Aromatherapy, Counselling, Indian Head Massage, Massage (Therapeutic), Reiki. ✓
● **Aromatherapist** Mrs J Frearson **M:** ISPA.
B Yrs. Est.: 14 (**Ref:**HM04421)

## CHOICE NATURAL HEALTH CENTRE

**Choice Natural Health Centre**, Holistic Health Centre, 3 Highgate, Kendal, **Cumbria**, LA9 4DA, ENG.
**(T)** 01539 734132
Speciality: Complementary Medicines & Therapy.
● **Employee** Mr A Rubenstien
C M (**Ref:**HM04422)

## CHOICES HYPNOTHERAPY

**Choices Hypnotherapy**, Plunkett Chambers, 21-23 Oliver Plunkett St, **County Cork**, IRE.
**(T)** 021 4271 020
Speciality: Hypnotherapy.
B (**Ref:**HM04423)

## CHOLSEY CHIROPODY SURGERY

**Cholsey Chiropody Surgery**, 2b Honey Lane, Cholsey, Wallingford, **Oxfordshire**, OX10 9NP, ENG.
**(T)** 01491 652574
Speciality: Chiropodists (Podiatrists).
S (**Ref:**HM04424)

## CHOPPEN, M

**M Choppen**, The Old Vicarage, Ogden Lane, Brighouse, **Yorkshire (West)**, HD6 3HF, ENG.
**(T)** 01484 720841
Speciality: Chiropodists (Podiatrists).
● **Owner** Mrs M Choppen
S (**Ref:**HM04425)

## CHOPRA, S

**Mrs S Chopra**, 39 Leys Avenue, Letchworth, **Hertfordshire**, SG6 3EE, ENG.
**(T)** 01462 682526 **(F)** 01462 682526
Speciality: Biomechanics, Chiropody, Cryo Surgery, Gait Analysis. ✓
● **Chiropodist** Mrs S Chopra **Q:** DPodM, M.S.C.P, S.R.Ch. **M:** S.C.P, S.R.Ch.
C Yrs. Est.: 10 (**Ref:**HM04426)

## CHOPRA, S

**S Chopra**, Health First Group, King George Surgery, 135 High St, Stevenage, **Hertfordshire**, SG1 3HT, ENG.
**(T)** 01438 218222
Speciality: Biomechanics, Chiropody, Cryo Surgery, Gait Analysis, Nail Surgery, Orthotics. ✓
● **Owner/Chiropodist** Mrs S Chopra **Q:** DPodM, M.S.C.P, S.R.Ch. **M:** S.C.P, S.R.Ch.
C Yrs. Est.: 6 (**Ref:**HM04427)

## CHORLEY & DISTRICT CLINIC

**Chorley & District Clinic Of Manipulative Therapy**, 16 Victoria St, Chorley, **Lancashire**, PR7 2TX, ENG.
**(T)** 01257 266977
Speciality: Osteopathy.
● **Owner** Mr C Curtis
P S T (**Ref:**HM04428)

## CHORLEY CHIROPODY PRACTICE

**Chorley Chiropody Practice**, 69 Union St, Chorley, **Lancashire**, PR7 1AB, ENG.
**(T)** 01257 231776
Speciality: Chiropodists (Podiatrists).
● **Owner** Mr I Sager
S (**Ref:**HM04429)

## CHORLTON STRESS MANAGEMENT

**Costa Lambrias**, The Bungalow, 550b Wilbraham Rd, Manchester, **Manchester (Greater)**, M21 9LB, ENG.
**(T)** 01618 604797 **(F)** 01618 816843
**(E)** costa@soulconcern.co.uk
**(W)** www.soulconcern.force9.co.uk
Speciality: Healer, Hypnotherapy, Paranormal Therapies, Psychotherapy, Reiki, Stress Therapy, Visualisation Therapy, Past Life Healing, Emotional Freedom Techniques, Regression Therapy, Soul Retrieval Therapy. ✓
● **Owner/Principal Consultant** Mr C Lambrias **Q:** Dip.Hyp, FIHP, MABCH, MCAH. **M:** ACH, HA, NHR.
H Yrs. Est.: 10 (**Ref:**HM04430)

## CHOUDHRY, MAUREEN

**Maureen Choudhry**, 88 Sewardstone Gardens, London, **London (Greater)**, E4 7QE, ENG.
**(T)** 020 8524 8329
Speciality: Reflexology.
S T (**Ref:**HM04431)

## CHOY, STEPHEN

**Stephen Choy**, 88A Northchurch Rd, London,

Key: B Mind-Body Medicine, C Complementary Medicine, H Self Help Treatment, M Medicinal Therapy, O Oriental Medicine, P Postural Therapy, S Manipulative Structural Therapy, T Touch Therapy

**London (Greater)**, N1 3NY, ENG.
(T) 020 7354 2314
Speciality: Osteopathy.
P S T (Ref:HM04432)

## CHRIS MOSLIN HYPNOTHERAPIST

**Linrick Home Mades**, 48 Trenchard Cres, Nabbotts Farm Estate, North Springfield, Chelmsford, **Essex**, CM1 6FG, ENG.
(T) 01245 465007
(E) ccmoslin@freenetnane.co.uk
Speciality: Holistic Healing, Hypnosis, Hypnotherapy, Psychotherapy, Stress Therapy, Age Regression Therapy, Past Life Regression Therapy. ✔
● **Therapist** Mr C Moslin Q: BSc (Hons). M: RCST.
B Yrs. Est.: 19 (Ref:HM04433)

## CHRIS SMITH HYPNOTHERAPY

**Chris Smith Hypnotherapy**, 81 Aldermans Drive, Peterborough, **Cambridgeshire**, PE3 6AX, ENG.
(T) 01733 313204
Speciality: Hypnosis.
B (Ref:HM04434)

## CHRISTCHURCH CHIROPRACTIC CTRE

**Christchurch Chiropractic Centre**, 1 Twynham Avenue, Christchurch, **Dorset**, BH23 1QU, ENG.
(T) 01202 483281 (F) 01202 418317
(E) g.meal@btinternet.com
(W) www.xchiro.co.uk
Speciality: Bach Remedies, Chiropractic, Manipulation, Reflexology, X-Ray. ✔ CREDIT
● **Reflexologist** Ms S Meal Q: Dip.Reflex, MAR. M: AoR.
● **Partner/Chiropractor** Mr G Meal Q: DC. M: BCA.
● **Chiropractor** Mr T Webb Q: BSc. M: SCA.
S Yrs. Est.: 24 (Ref:HM04435)

## CHRISTCHURCH PHYSIO PRACTICE

**Christchurch Physiotherapy Practice**, 1 Purewell Cross Rd, Christchurch, **Dorset**, BH23 3AF, ENG.
(T) 01202 477335
Speciality: Acupuncture, Electrotherapy, Manipulation, Massage (Therapeutic), Physiotherapy. ✔
● **Physiotherapist** Ms A Booth Q: MCSP, SRP. M: CSP.
● **Physiotherapist** Ms A Duncan Q: MCSP, SRP. M: CSP.
● **Physiotherapist** Ms S Hillier Q: MCSP, SRP. M: CSP.
S Yrs. Est.: 1 (Ref:HM04436)

## CHRISTIAN SCIENCE PRACTITIONER

**Christian Science Practitioner**, 26 Albany Cres, Claygate, Esher, **Surrey**, KT10 0PF, ENG.
(T) 01372 800551
Speciality: Complementary Medicines & Therapy.
● **Owner** Mr F Clark-Brown
C M (Ref:HM04437)

## CHRISTIE, ADRIAN

**Adrian Christie**, 37 Coates Gardens, Edinburgh, **Edinburgh (City of)**, EH12 5LF, SCO.
(T) 01313 372483
Speciality: Counselling, Hypnosis, Hypnotherapy, Psychotherapy. ✔
● **Hypnotherapist** Mr A Christie M: HA, NCH.
B Yrs. Est.: 16 (Ref:HM04438)

## CHRISTIE, ANITA

**Anita Christie M N I M H**, 14 Munster Rd, Teddington, **London (Greater)**, TW11 9LL, ENG.
(T) 020 8977 8468 (F) 020 8977 8468
Speciality: Herbalists.
● **Owner** Ms A Christie
M (Ref:HM04439)

## CHRISTIE, ELIZABETH

**Elizabeth Christie**, 37 Millbrook St, Cheltenham, **Gloucestershire**, GL50 3RR, ENG.
(T) 01242 222015
Speciality: Acupuncture.
● **Owner** Miss E Christie
O (Ref:HM04440)

## CHRISTIE, S A

**Christie S A**, 98 Penton Rd, Staines, **Surrey**, TW18 2LJ, ENG.
(T) 01784 462768
Speciality: Chiropodists (Podiatrists).
S (Ref:HM04441)

## CHRISTIENSEN, MARK

**Mark Christiensen**, Back To Health, 2 Charles St, Petersfield, **Hampshire**, GU32 3EH, ENG.
(T) 01730 267423
Speciality: Chiropractors.
P S T (Ref:HM04442)

## CHRISTINA, HALLAM

**Hallam Christina**, Aberfoyle House, Stapley Rd, St. Albans, **Hertfordshire**, AL3 5EP, ENG.
(T) 01727 856687
Speciality: Homeopathy.
M (Ref:HM04443)

## CHRISTINE

**Christine**, Annworth Cottage, Chapel St, Kirk Merrington, Spennymoor, **County Durham**, DL16 7JA, ENG.
(T) 01388 815535 (F) 01388 815535
Speciality: Clairvoyants & Palmists.
● **Owner** Ms C Kean
B (Ref:HM04444)

## CHRISTINE & LINDA

**Christine & Linda**, Liongate Clinic, 8 Chilston Rd, Tunbridge Wells, **Kent**, TN4 9LT, ENG.
(T) 01892 543535
Speciality: Chiropodists (Podiatrists).
S (Ref:HM04445)

## CHRISTINE CHINNERY COMP THER

**Christine Chinnery Complementary Therapist**, 18 Willow House, Hackfield, Ashford, **Kent**, TN2 34X, ENG.
(T) 01233 633835
Speciality: Aromatherapy, Complementary Therapy, Massage (Therapeutic), Reflexology. ✔
● **Therapist** Ms C Chinnery Q: MBRA. M: CIBTAC, IIHHT.
C Yrs. Est.: 1 (Ref:HM04446)

## CHRISTINE KEY HYPNOTHERAPIST

**Christine Key Hypnotherapist**, 7 Giles Travers Cl, Egham, **Surrey**, TW20 8UQ, ENG.
(T) 01932 560725 (F) 01932 560725
(E) chriskey1@aol.com
Speciality: Counselling, Hypnosis, Hypnotherapy, Neuro-Linguistic Program, Psychotherapy. ✔
● **Owner/Hypnotherapist/Psychotherapist** Ms C Key Q: MNCH. M: NCP.
B Yrs. Est.: 11 (Ref:HM04447)

## CHRISTINES MASSAGE THERAPY

**Christines Massage Therapy**, 94B Sidwell St, Exeter, **Devon**, EX4 6PH, ENG.
(T) 01392 499160
Speciality: Complementary Medicines & Therapy.
M (Ref:HM04448)

## CHRISTOFI, KATERINA

**Katerina Christofi Hypnotherapy & Psychotherapy**, 16 Newpark Avenue, London, **London (Greater)**, N13 5NB, ENG.
(T) 020 8245 8529
Speciality: Hypnotherapy.
B (Ref:HM04449)

## CHRISTOPHER J FANTHOME HYP

**Christopher J Fanthome Hypnotherapist**, Wellbrook Clinic, 21 Stafford Rd, Wallington, **Surrey**, SM6 9AN, ENG.
(T) 020 8401 0011
Speciality: Hypnotherapy.
B (Ref:HM04450)

## CHRISTOPHER, CLARE

**Clare Christopher**, 24 Catherine St, Salisbury, **Wiltshire**, SP1 2DA, ENG.
(T) 01722 411766
Speciality: Homeopathy.
M (Ref:HM04451)

## CHRISTOPHER, DEBORAH

**Deborah Christopher**, Orgeris Villa, Les Rouvets, Vale, **Guernsey**, GY6 8NH, ENG.
(T) 01481 56592
Speciality: Reflexology.
S T (Ref:HM04452)

## CHRISTOPHER, JERRY

**Jerry Christopher**, Good Robins, Atherfield, Ventnor, **Isle of Wight**, PO38 2LQ, ENG.
(T) 01983 551380
Speciality: Homeopathy.
● **Partner** Mrs J Christopher
M (Ref:HM04453)

## CHRISTOPHER, T

**T Christopher**, 8 Newland St, Gloucester, **Gloucestershire**, GL1 3PA, ENG.
(T) 01452 502721
Speciality: Chiropodists (Podiatrists).
S (Ref:HM04454)

## CHRISTOU, Z

**Z Christou**, 106 Gallants Farm Rd, East Barnet, Barnet, **Hertfordshire**, EN4 8EP, ENG.
(T) 020 8368 2870
Speciality: Hypnosis.
● **Owner** Mrs Z Christou
B (Ref:HM04455)

## CHRISTY, KERRIE

**Kerrie Christy**, Roseview Newton, Elgin, **Moray**, IV30 8XW, SCO.
(T) 01343 541512
Speciality: Complementary Medicines & Therapy.
M (Ref:HM04456)

## CHROMASOUND

**Chromasound**, Park Stables, Upton Lane, Upton, Northampton, **Northamptonshire**, NN5 4UX, ENG.
(T) 01604 581382 (F) 01604 581382
Speciality: Psychology.
● **Owner** Mrs B Fothergill
B (Ref:HM04457)

## CHRYSALIS

**Chrysalis**, Crystal House, New Bedford Rd, Luton, **Bedfordshire**, LU1 1HS, ENG.
(T) 01582 414949
Speciality: Hypnosis.
● **Director** Ms M Franklin
B (Ref:HM04458)

## CHRYSALIS NATURAL HEALING CTRE

**Chrysalis Natural Healing Centre**, 85B Headstone Rd, Harrow, **London (Greater)**, HA1 1PG, ENG.
(T) 020 8861 3077
Speciality: Complementary Medicines & Therapy.
M (Ref:HM04459)

## CHUMBLEY, COLIN

**Colin Chumbley**, 36 Kidmore Rd, Caversham, Reading, **Berkshire**, RG4 7LU, ENG.
(T) 01189 470762
Speciality: Chiropodists (Podiatrists).
S (Ref:HM04460)

## CHUMBLEY, SYLVIA

**Sylvia Chumbley**, 36 Kidmore Rd, Caversham, Reading, **Berkshire**, RG4 7LU, ENG.
(T) 01189 470762
Speciality: Chiropodists (Podiatrists).
S (Ref:HM04461)

## CHURCH HOUSE PRACTICE

**Church House Practice**, Church House, Church Yard, South Molton, **Devon**, EX36 3BW, ENG.
(T) 01769 573142
Speciality: Aromatherapy.
● **Owner** Mrs L Roulstone
M O (Ref:HM04462)

## CHURCH LAWFORD CHIRO CLINIC

**Church Lawford Chiropractic Clinic**, 1a Kings Newnham Rd, Church Lawford, Rugby, **Warwickshire**, CV23 9EP, ENG.
(T) 024 7654 5865
(E) ggibbon@globalnet
Speciality: Acupressure, Bach Remedies, Chiropractic, Cranial Osteopathy, Electrotherapy, Holistic Healing, Manipulation, Massage (Therapeutic), Postural Integration, Reiki. ✔



Key continued: Yrs.Est: Years Established Q: Qualifications M: Professional Membership ✔ Indemnity Insurance CREDIT Accept Credit Cards

● **Chiropractor** Mr G Gibbon **Q:** C of C, DC.
M: GCC, MCA.
**S** Yrs. Est.: 8 (**Ref:**HM04463)

### CHURCH OF SCIENTOLOGY
**Church Of Scientology Celebrity Centre London**, 27 Westbourne Gr, London, **London (Greater)**, W2 4UA, ENG.
(T) 020 7229 1065
Speciality: Complementary Medicines & Therapy.
**C** **M** (**Ref:**HM04464)

### CHURCH ROAD PHYSIOTHERAPY
**Church Road Physiotherapy**, Hanwell Health Centre, 20 Church Rd, London, **London (Greater)**, W7 1DR, ENG.
(T) 020 8840 0144
Speciality: Physiotherapy.
● **Owner** Mr P Rao
**P** **S** **T** (**Ref:**HM04465)

### CHURCH, CAROL & STEVEN
**Carol & Steven Church**, 3 The Grove, Coulsdon, **London (Greater)**, CR5 2BH, ENG.
(T) 020 8660 0425
Speciality: Herbal Medicine.
● **Partner** Mrs C Church
**M** (**Ref:**HM04466)

### CHURCH, PAULINE
**Pauline Church**, Redthorne House, Mill St, Eynsham, Witney, **Oxfordshire**, OX8 1JU, ENG.
(T) 01865 880641
Speciality: Chiropractic.
**P** **S** **T** (**Ref:**HM04467)

### CHURCHDOWN CHIROPODY CLINIC
**Churchdown Chiropody Clinic**, 56 Albemarle Rd, Churchdown, Gloucester, **Gloucestershire**, GL3 2HE, ENG.
(T) 01452 712114
Speciality: Chiropodists (Podiatrists).
**S** (**Ref:**HM04468)

### CHURCHER, L A
**L A Churcher**, Trappe House, Ewyas Harold, Hereford, **Herefordshire**, HR2 0HU, ENG.
(T) 01981 240007
Speciality: Hypnosis.
**B** (**Ref:**HM04469)

### CHURCHES OSTEOPATHIC PRACTICE
**Churches Osteopathic Practice**, 12 Market Sq, Horsham, **Sussex (West)**, RH12 1EU, ENG.
(T) 01403 252228
Speciality: Osteopathy.
● **Senior Partner** Mr K Beckwith
**P** **S** **T** (**Ref:**HM04470)

### CHURCHILL, MARION
**Marion Churchill**, Blade Mill, Yarde, Williton, Taunton, **Somerset**, TA4 4HW, ENG.
(T) 08003 285215
Speciality: Chiropractors.
● **Owner** Mrs M Churchill
**P** **S** **T** (**Ref:**HM04471)

### CHURCHILL, MARION
**Marion Churchill**, 28 Angel Cres, Bridgwater, **Somerset**, TA6 3EW, ENG.
(T) 01278 433077
Speciality: Chiropractic.
● **Owner** Mrs L Lord
**P** **S** **T** (**Ref:**HM04472)

### CHURCHILL, VANESSA
**Vanessa Churchill**, Doctors Hill, Sherfield English, Romsey, **Hampshire**, SO51 6JX, ENG.
(T) 01794 340914
Speciality: Complementary Medicines & Therapy.
**C** **M** (**Ref:**HM04473)

### CHURCHLEY, RUBY
**Ruby Churchley**, 29 Brock St, Bath, **Somerset**, BA1 2LN, ENG.
(T) 01225 424601
Speciality: Hypnosis.
● **Dentist** Mr R Talbot
**B** (**Ref:**HM04474)

### CHURCHMAN & ASS REG OST
**Beryl Churchman DO & Associates Registered Osteopaths**, 71 Boom Hill Rd, Ipswich, **Suffolk**, IP1 4EH, ENG.
(T) 01473 410708
(E) beryl.churchman@havenhealth.co.uk
Speciality: Cranial Osteopathy, Manipulation, Osteopathy. ✔
● **Registered Osteopath**
Ms B Churchman **Q:** DO. M: GOsC.
● **Registered Osteopath**
Ms S Chapman **Q:** Hons (OST). M: GOsC.
**S** Yrs. Est.: 10 (**Ref:**HM04475)

### CHURCHMAN, B
**B Churchman**, 37 Springfield Avenue, Felixstowe, **Suffolk**, IP11 9JZ, ENG.
(T) 01394 277501
Speciality: Osteopathy.
**P** **S** **T** (**Ref:**HM04476)

### CHURCHMAN, B E
**B E Churchman**, 15 Grundisburgh Rd, Woodbridge, **Suffolk**, IP12 4HH, ENG.
(T) 01394 386540 (F) 01394 386540
Speciality: Osteopathy.
● **Owner** Ms J Wright
**P** **S** **T** (**Ref:**HM04477)

### CHURCHMAN, BERYL
**Beryl Churchman DO & Associates Registered Osteopaths**, Haven Health, Grange Farm Avenue, Felixstowe, **Suffolk**, IP11 2FB, ENG.
(T) 01394 670107 (F) 01394 282872
(E) beryl.churchman@havenhealth.co.uk
Speciality: Cranial Osteopathy, Manipulation, Osteopathy. ✔
● **Osteopath** Ms S Chapman **Q:** BSc, Hons (OST). M: GOsC.
● **Osteopath** Ms B Churchman **Q:** DO. M: GOsC.
**S** Yrs. Est.: 10 (**Ref:**HM04478)

### CHURTON, JAMES E
**James E Churton**, 19 Market St, Hindley, Wigan, **Lancashire**, WN2 3AE, ENG.
(T) 01942 254163
Speciality: Chiropodists (Podiatrists).
**S** (**Ref:**HM04479)

### CHUTER-KIRK, SAMANTHA
**Samantha Chuter-Kirk**, 32 Hill Top Drive, Harrogate, **Yorkshire (North)**, HG1 3BU, ENG.
(T) 01423 538647
Speciality: Chiropodists (Podiatrists).
● **Owner** Mrs S Chuter
**S** (**Ref:**HM04480)

### CIRCUS HOUSE
**Circus House**, The Circus, Bath, **Somerset**, BA1 2EX, ENG.
(T) 01225 421328
Speciality: Physiotherapy.
**P** **S** **T** (**Ref:**HM04481)

### CIRENCESTER NATURAL THERAPIES
**Cirencester Natural Therapies**, 14 Dollar St, Cirencester, Gloucester, **Gloucestershire**, GL7 2AJ, ENG.
(T) 01285 656393
Speciality: Alexander Technique.
**P** **S** (**Ref:**HM04482)

### CITISPORT
**Citisport**, The Chalk Pit, College Rd, Epsom, **Surrey**, KT17 4JA, ENG.
(T) 01372 743166 (F) 01372 743538
Speciality: Acupuncture, Dietician, Electrotherapy, Herbal Medicine, Life Style Coaching, Manipulation, Massage (Therapeutic), Naturopathy, Nutritional Therapy, Physiotherapy, Podiatry, Sports Massage, Personal Fitness Training. ✔
● **Senior Physiotherapist**
Sharon Bolton **Q:** MCSP, SRP. M: AACP, CSP.
● **Physiotherapist** Libby Garry **Q:** MCSP, SRP. M: CSP.
● **Nutritionist** Deborah Bant **Q:** Dip.ION. M: BANT.
● **Consultant in Orthopaedic Medicine**
Dr J Reynolds M: GMC.
**S** Yrs. Est.: 16 (**Ref:**HM04483)

### CITRUS NATURAL THERAPY CLINIC
**Citrus Natural Therapy Clinic**, 14 New St, Cahirciveen, **County Kerry**, IRE.
(T) 06694 73377
Speciality: Complementary Medicines & Therapy.
**M** (**Ref:**HM04484)

### CITY & COUNTY CHIROPRACTIC
**City & County Chiropractic**, 55 West Cross Avenue, West Cross, Swansea, SA3 5TX, WAL.
(T) 01792 405500
Speciality: Chiropractors.
● **Owner** Mr C Beckett
**P** **S** **T** (**Ref:**HM04485)

### CITY BEACH
**City Beach**, 381 North Deeside Rd, Cults, Aberdeen, **Aberdeenshire**, AB15 9SX, SCO.
(T) 01224 869882 (F) 01224 869909
Speciality: Aromatherapy, Electrolysis, Laser hair removal and Non Surgical face lift. ✔
● **Owner** Miss J Barrow
● **Manageress** Mrs D Henderson **Q:** HND.
**C** Yrs. Est.: 10 (**Ref:**HM04486)

### CITY CENTRE CHIRO CLINIC
**City Centre Chiropractic Clinic**, 9 Marsh St, Bristol, BS1 4AA, ENG.
(T) 01179 220551
Speciality: Chiropractors.
● **Owner** Mr A Sanni
**P** **S** **T** (**Ref:**HM04487)

### CITY CENTRE CHIRO CLINIC
**City Centre Chiropractic Clinic**, 39 Charles St, Cardiff, **Glamorgan (Vale of)**, CF10 2GB, WAL.
(T) 029 2066 4964
Speciality: Chiropractic. ✔
● **Owner** Dr A Sanni **Q:** DC. M: NACM.
**P** Yrs. Est.: 7 (**Ref:**HM04488)

### CITY CENTRE THERAPISTS
**City Centre Therapists**, 24 Barry St, Bradford, **Yorkshire (West)**, BD1 2AW, ENG.
(T) 01274 780277
Speciality: Complementary Medicines & Therapy.
● **Director** Mrs C Dawson
**M** (**Ref:**HM04489)

### CITY CHIROPRACTIC CENTRE
**City Chiropractic Centre**, Bankside House, 107-112 Leadenhall St, London, **London (Greater)**, EC3A 4AA, ENG.
(T) 020 7378 9494
Speciality: Chiropractors.
**P** **S** **T** (**Ref:**HM04490)

### CITY CHIROPRACTIC CENTRE
**City Chiropractic Centre**, Second Floor 88 Cannon St, London, **London (Greater)**, EC4N 6HT, ENG.
(T) 020 7929 4556
Speciality: Chiropractic.
● **Owner** Mr N Foley
**P** **S** **T** (**Ref:**HM04491)

### CITY CHIROPRACTIC CLINIC
**Christine L Kusiar**, 40 Epworth St, Stoke-On-Trent, **Staffordshire**, ST4 1NR, ENG.
(T) 01782 848184 (F) 01782 746555
Speciality: Acupuncture, Chiropractic, Nutritional Therapy. ✔
● **Chiropractor** Dr C Kusiar **Q:** DC. M: BCA, GCC.
● **Therapist** Ms S Jackson M: BANT.
● **Acupuncturist** Mr I Markham **Q:** BA, Lic.Ac.
**P** Yrs. Est.: 4 (**Ref:**HM04492)

### CITY CHIROPRACTIC CLINIC
**City Chiropractic Clinic**, 111 Hagley Rd, Birmingham, **Midlands (West)**, B16 8LB, ENG.
(T) 01214 525040
Speciality: Chiropractors.
● **Owner** Dr A Allard
**P** **S** **T** (**Ref:**HM04493)

### CITY CHIROPRACTIC CLINIC
**City Chiropractic Clinic**, Armour House, Brunswick Sq, Southampton, **Hampshire**, SO14 3AR, ENG.
(T) 023 8023 4477
Speciality: Chiropractic.
**P** **S** **T** (**Ref:**HM04494)

Key: **B** Mind-Body Medicine **C** Complementary Medicine **H** Self Help Treatment **M** Medicinal Therapy **O** Oriental Medicine **P** Postural Therapy **S** Manipulative Structural Therapy **T** Touch Therapy

## CITY FOOT HEALTH
**City Foot Health**, 5 London Wall Buildings, London, **London (Greater)**, EC2M 5NS, ENG.
(T) 020 7628 3359
Speciality: Chiropodists (Podiatrists).
S (Ref:HM04495)

## CITY HEALTH CENTRE
**City Health Centre**, The Gestalt Centre, 62 Paul St, London, **London (Greater)**, EC2A 4NA, ENG.
(T) 020 7729 8525
(E) compmed@cityhealthcentre.co.uk
(W) www.cityhealthcentre.nildram.co.uk
Speciality: Complementary Therapy, Cranial Osteopathy, Herbal Medicine, Homeopathy, Manipulation, Moxibustion, Oriental Diagnosis, Osteopathy, Ying & Yang. ✔
● **Acupuncturist/Herbalist** Yizhen Jia Q: MBAcC, MRCHM.
● **Osteopath/Cranial Osteopath** Ms H Makin M: GOsC.
● **Herbalist** Ms E Farrant Q: MRCHM.
● **Osteopath/Cranial Osteopath** Ms J Vetterlein M: GOsC.
● **Homeopath** Ms J Redmond Q: LCPH. M: HMA.
● **Acupuncturist** Ms A Bradford Q: MBAcC.
● **Homeopath** Ms H Fairclough Q: RSHom.
C Yrs. Est.: 20 (Ref:HM04496)

## CITY OSTEOPATHIC CLINIC
**City Osteopathic Clinic**, 30 Carlton Cresent, Southampton, **Hampshire**, SO15 2EW, ENG.
(T) 023 8023 4080
Speciality: Osteopathy.
● **Director** Mr J Rouse
P S T (Ref:HM04497)

## CITY OSTEOPATHS
**City Osteopaths**, 100 Wellington St, Leeds, **Yorkshire (West)**, LS1 4LT, ENG.
(T) 01132 373033 (F) 01132 422433
Speciality: Osteopathy.
● **Owner** Mr R Kingston
P S T (Ref:HM04498)

## CITY PHYSIO
**City Physio**, The Sporting Club, 49 Oldham St, Manchester, **Manchester (Greater)**, M1 1JR, ENG.
(T) 01618 346050 (F) 01618 346023
Speciality: Physiotherapy.
● **Owner** Mr J Spencer
P S T (Ref:HM04499)

## CITY PHYSIOTHERAPY CENTRE
**City Physiotherapy Centre**, 61 Granada Rd, Southsea, **Hampshire**, PO4 0RQ, ENG.
(T) 023 9283 2921 (F) 023 9283 2921
Speciality: Physiotherapy.
● **Owner** Mr D Dentry
P S T (Ref:HM04500)

## CLACTON CHIROPRACTIC CLINIC
**Clacton Chiropractic Clinic**, 124 Wellesley Rd, Clacton-On-Sea, **Essex**, CO15 3PT, ENG.
(T) 01255 422337
Speciality: Chiropractic. ✔
● **Chiropractor** Dr I Nothling Q: DC, M.S.C.P. M: ICA.
P Yrs. Est.: 2 (Ref:HM04501)

## CLACTON REFLEX & THERAPY CTRE
**Clacton Reflexology & Natural Therapy Centre**, Suite 22 Empire Court, 169 Old Rd, Clacton-On-Sea, **Essex**, CO15 3AU, ENG.
(T) 01255 434399
Speciality: Reflexology.
C (Ref:HM04502)

## CLAGUE, LAURA
**Laura Clague**, 33 Glenluce Rd, London, **London (Greater)**, SE3 7SD, ENG.
(T) 020 8305 1759
Speciality: Psychotherapy.
● **Owner** Ms L Clague
B (Ref:HM04503)

## CLAIR, EILEEN
**Eileen Clair**, Carnacalla, Kilrush, **County Clare**, IRE.
(T) 06590 52239
Speciality: Complementary Medicines & Therapy.
M (Ref:HM04504)

## CLAIRBAUX CLINIC
**Clairbaux Clinic**, 35 Craignabo Rd, Peterhead, **Aberdeenshire**, AB42 2YE, SCO.
(T) 01779 472006 (F) 01779 472006
Speciality: Acupuncture, Nutritional Therapy, Physiotherapy. ✔
● **Acupuncturist** Mrs I Spence Q: MBAcC, MCSP.
C S (Ref:HM04505)

## CLAIRBAUX CLINIC
**Clairbaux Clinic**, Clairbaux House, South Lee, **Aberdeenshire**, AB41 6AU, SCO.
Speciality: Acupuncture, Nutritional Therapy, Physiotherapy.
● **Therapist** Mrs I Spence Q: Cert.ION, MBAcC, MCSP. M: BAcC.
C (Ref:HM04506)

## CLAIRE CHOUDHURY HERBAL PRAC
**Claire Choudhury Herbal Practice**, 280 Balham High Rd, London, **London (Greater)**, SW17 7AJ, ENG.
(T) 020 8675 6023
Speciality: Herbal Medicine. ✔
● **Owner/Medical Herbalist** Ms C Choudhury Q: BA (Hons), Dip.Herb.Med. M: NIMH.
M Yrs. Est.: 1 (Ref:HM04507)

## CLAIRE FRETWELL'S ALLERGY CLNC
**Claire Fretwell's Allergy Clinic**, 7 Berry Lane, Longridge, Preston, **Lancashire**, PR3 3JA, ENG.
(T) 01772 784777
Speciality: Complementary Medicines & Therapy.
C M (Ref:HM04508)

## CLAIRE FRETWELL'S ALLERGY CLNC
**Claire Fretwell's Allergy Clinic**, School House, High St, Brant Broughton, Lincoln, **Lincolnshire**, LN5 0SL, ENG.
(T) 01400 273277 (F) 01400 273277
Speciality: Complementary Medicines & Therapy.
● **Owner** Ms C Fretwell
C M (Ref:HM04509)

## CLAIRE LOUISE
**Claire Louise**, 3 Knowle Cl, Stannington, Sheffield, **Yorkshire (South)**, S6 6BJ, ENG.
(T) 01142 340333
Speciality: Chiropody, Foot and Leg Massage. ✔
● **Chiropodist (Podiatrist)** Miss C Smith M: B.A.Ch.P.
C Yrs. Est.: 3 (Ref:HM04510)

## CLAIRE LOUISE
**Claire Louise**, 4 Norris Rd, Sheffield, **Yorkshire (South)**, S6 4QS, ENG.
(T) 01142 852522
Speciality: Chiropodists (Podiatrists).
● **Owner** Ms C Louise
S (Ref:HM04511)

## CLAIRE'S THERAPEUTIC SPA CTRE
**Claire's Therapeutic Spa & Beauty Centre**, 8 Lower Market St, Ennis, **County Clare**, IRE.
(T) 06568 23814
Speciality: Complementary Medicines & Therapy.
M (Ref:HM04512)

## CLAIRVOYANT
**Clairvoyant**, 14 Cranley Rd, Westcliff-on-Sea, **Essex**, SS0 8AL, ENG.
(T) 01702 342717
Speciality: Clairvoyants & Palmists.
● **Owner** Mr K Wade
B (Ref:HM04513)

## CLAIRVOYANT - MEDIUM - HEALER
**Clairvoyant - Medium - Healer**, Wood Dale, 23 Mons Avenue, Bognor Regis, **Sussex (West)**, PO21 5JN, ENG.
(T) 01243 823083
Speciality: Absent Healing, Counselling, Healer, Healing Therapy, Spiritual Healing, Clairvoyant.
● **Owner** Mr K Harvey
C Yrs. Est.: 20 (Ref:HM04514)

## CLAIRVOYANT & MEDIUM
**Clairvoyant & Medium**, 56 Sefton Rd, Dosthill, Tamworth, **Staffordshire**, B77 1PN, ENG.
(T) 01827 251681
Speciality: Clairvoyants & Palmists.
B (Ref:HM04515)

## CLAIRVOYANT & TAROT
**Clairvoyant & Tarot**, 1 St Marys Rd, London, **London (Greater)**, SE25 6UT, ENG.
(T) 020 8771 4043
Speciality: Clairvoyants & Palmists.
B (Ref:HM04516)

## CLAIRVOYANT PREDICTIONS
**Clairvoyant Predictions**, Creswicke House, 9 Small St, Bristol, BS1 1DB, ENG.
(T) 01179 077781
Speciality: Clairvoyants & Palmists.
B (Ref:HM04517)

## CLAIRVOYANT SERVICES
**Clairvoyant Services**, 17 Danes Court, Great Cornard, Sudbury, **Suffolk**, CO10 0JW, ENG.
(T) 01787 881653
Speciality: Counselling, Spiritual Healing.
● **Owner** Mrs F Rhodes
B Yrs. Est.: 10 (Ref:HM04518)

## CLAIRVOYANT TAROT READER
**Clairvoyant Tarot Reader Palmist & Runes**, 15 Corby Cl, Englefield Green, Egham, **Surrey**, TW20 0TX, ENG.
(T) 01784 431884
Speciality: Clairvoyants & Palmists.
● **Owner** Ms L Skeels
B (Ref:HM04519)

## CLAIRVOYANT VERONICA
**Clairvoyant Veronica**, London, **London (Greater)**, SW11 4LE, ENG.
(T) 020 7738 8095
Speciality: Clairvoyants & Palmists.
● **Owner** Ms V Adam
B (Ref:HM04520)

## CLAIRVOYANT, ANDREW
**Andrew Clairvoyant**, 2 Sunnyhurst Avenue, Blackpool, **Lancashire**, FY4 2HP, ENG.
(T) 01253 349833
Speciality: Clairvoyants & Palmists.
● **Owner** Mr A Poulton
B (Ref:HM04521)

## CLAIRVOYANTS & REIKI
**Clairvoyants & Reiki**, 2 Brickmakers Lane, Hemel Hempstead, **Hertfordshire**, HP3 8NY, ENG.
(T) 01442 243134
Speciality: Clairvoyants & Palmists.
B (Ref:HM04522)

## CLAIVOYANTS SHOP
**Claivoyants Shop (The)**, 18 St Mary's St, Edinburgh, **Edinburgh (City of)**, EH1 1SU, SCO.
(T) 01315 583446
Speciality: Clairvoyants & Palmists.
B (Ref:HM04523)

## CLANE ACUPUNCTURE
**Clane Acupuncture**, Betaghstown Clane Co, **County Kildare**, IRE.
(T) 04586 1892
Speciality: Acupuncture.
O (Ref:HM04524)

## CLANE COUNSELLING/HYPNOTHERAPY
**Clane Counselling & Hypnotherapy**, 1 Liffey Lawns Clane, **County Kildare**, IRE.
(T) 04586 8751
Speciality: Hypnotherapy.
B (Ref:HM04525)

## CLANRICARDE CLINIC
**Clanricarde Clinic**, 28 Grendon Gardens, Wembley Park, **Middlesex**, HA9 9NE, ENG.
(T) 020 8904 5801
(E) tomurray@virgin.net
Speciality: Biomechanics, Bowen Therapy, Chiropody, Cranial Osteopathy, Cryo Surgery, Electrotherapy, Manipulation, Massage (Therapeutic), Osteopathy, Orthotics. ✔
● **Osteopath/Bowen Therapist**


Key continued: Yrs.Est: Years Established Q: Qualifications M: Professional Membership ✔ Indemnity Insurance Accept Credit Cards

Dr T Murray Q: BTER, DO, PhD. M: BTER, GOsC.
**S** Yrs. Est.: 11 (**Ref:**HM04526)

### CLAPHAM COMMON CLINIC
**Clapham Common Clinic**, 151-153 Clapham High St, London, **London (Greater)**, SW4 7SS, ENG.
(T) 020 7627 8890
Speciality: Complementary Medicines & Therapy.
● **Owner** Mr M Knight
**M** (**Ref:**HM04527)

### CLAPHAM PHYSIOTHERAPY
**Clapham Physiotherapy**, 38 North St, London, **London (Greater)**, SW4 0HD, ENG.
(T) 020 7627 0291
Speciality: Physiotherapy.
**P** **S** **T** (**Ref:**HM04528)

### CLAPHAM, EUGENIE
**Eugenie Clapham**, Cheltenham, **Gloucestershire**, GL52, ENG.
(T) 01242 620731
Speciality: Bach Remedies.
**M** (**Ref:**HM04529)

### CLAPHAM, J W
**J W Clapham Ltd**, 16 George St, Leeds, **Yorkshire (West)**, LS2 7HY, ENG.
(T) 01132 453145
Speciality: Herbal Medicine.
● **Manageress** Mrs L Clark
**M** (**Ref:**HM04530)

### CLAPP, T
**T Clapp**, 10 Willow Rd, Enfield, **London (Greater)**, EN1 3NE, ENG.
(T) 020 8366 7338
Speciality: Psychotherapy.
● **Owner** Mr T Clapp
**B** (**Ref:**HM04531)

### CLARE JAMES HEALTH FOODS
**Clare James**, 13A Hempstead Rd, Kings Langley, **Hertfordshire**, WD4 8BJ, ENG.
(T) 01923 263195
Speciality: Anthroposohical Medicine, Aromatherapy, Bach Remedies, Hay Diet, Herbal Medicine, Homeopathy, Vitamin Therapy.
✔ CREDIT
● **Owner** Ms B Johnstone Q: BSc.
**H** Yrs. Est.: 17 (**Ref:**HM04532)

### CLARE, A E
**A E Clare**, The Croft, Bourne Rd, Langtoft, Peterborough, **Cambridgeshire**, PE6 9NJ, ENG.
(T) 01778 343573
Speciality: Physiotherapy.
● **Owner** Mrs A Clare
**P** **S** **T** (**Ref:**HM04533)

### CLARE, MONICA G
**Monica G Clare**, Mallard Cottage, High St, Thornham, Hunstanton, **Norfolk**, PE36 6LY, ENG.
(T) 01485 512473
Speciality: Chiropodists (Podiatrists).
● **Owner** Mrs M Clare
**S** (**Ref:**HM04534)

### CLARE, S M
**S M Clare**, Flat 1 Highcliffe, 32 Albemarle Rd, Beckenham, **Kent**, BR3 5HJ, ENG.
(T) 020 8778 8156
Speciality: Hypnosis.
● **Owner** Ms S Clare
**B** (**Ref:**HM04535)

### CLAREMONT
**Claremont**, 4 Claremont Rd, Blackpool, **Lancashire**, FY1 2QF, ENG.
(T) 01253 626733
Speciality: Hypnotherapy.
● **Owner** Mrs J Ikin
**B** (**Ref:**HM04536)

### CLAREMONT FOOTCARE SURGERY
**Claremont Footcare Surgery**, 19a Claremont Cres, Whitley Bay, **Tyne and Wear**, NE26 3HL, ENG.
(T) 01912 910140
Speciality: Chiropody.
● **Owner** Mr N Lewis
**S** (**Ref:**HM04537)

### CLAREMONT HOMEOPATHIC CLINIC
**Claremont Homeopathic Clinic**, 11b North Claremont St, Glasgow, **Glasgow (City of)**, G3 7NR, **SCO**.
(T) 01413 310393
Speciality: Homeopathy.
● **Owner** Dr R Malcolm
**M** (**Ref:**HM04538)

### CLARENDON CHIROPRACTIC CLINIC
**Clarendon Chiropractic Clinic**, 5 Clarendon St, Londonderry, **County Londonderry**, BT48 7EP, NIR.
(T) 028 7137 3822 (F) 028 7137 2487
Speciality: Chiropractic. ✔ CREDIT
● **Chiropractor** Dr R Vackery Q: BA, BSc (Chiro), DC. M: BAS, SCA.
● **Owner** Dr M McHenney Q: DC, MSc (Chiro). M: BCA.
**P** Yrs. Est.: 4 (**Ref:**HM04539)

### CLARENDON CLINIC
**Clarendon Clinic**, 115 Chorley Rd, Swinton, Manchester, **Manchester (Greater)**, M27 4AA, ENG.
(T) 01617 935990
(E) ipgill@globalnet.co.uk
(W) www.ipgill.com
Speciality: Acupressure, Acupuncture, Aromatherapy, Electrotherapy, Iridology, Kinesiology, Manipulation, Massage (Therapeutic), Naturopathy, Osteopathy, Reflexology, Ultrasonics, Vitamin Therapy, Magnetic Field Therapy, Celloid Mineral Therapy, Impact Therapy. ✔
● **Osteopath** Mr P Gill Q: DO, FLCSP. M: LCSP.
● **Manipulative Therapist** Mr S Evans Q: LCSP. M: LCSP.
**S** Yrs. Est.: 23 (**Ref:**HM04540)

### CLARENDON DENTAL PRACTICE
**Clarendon Dental Practice**, 1 Borough Arcade, Off Market St, Hyde, **Cheshire**, SK14 2AA, ENG.
(T) 01613 681224
Speciality: Chiropodists (Podiatrists).
**S** (**Ref:**HM04541)

### CLARE'S BEAUTY CLINIC
**Clare's Beauty Clinic**, 48 Goring Rd, Goring-By-Sea, Worthing, **Sussex (West)**, BN12 4AD, ENG.
(T) 01903 241114
Speciality: Aromatherapy.
● **Owner** Ms C Robrts
**M** **O** (**Ref:**HM04542)

### CLARIDGE HOUSE HEALING CENTRE
**Claridge House Healing Centre**, Dormans Rd, Dormansland, Lingfield, **Surrey**, RH7 6QH, ENG.
(T) 01342 832150 (F) 01342 836730
Speciality: Complementary Medicines & Therapy.
● **Manager** Mrs C Lynsey
**M** (**Ref:**HM04543)

### CLARIDGE, B M
**B M Claridge**, 86 Argyll Avenue, Luton, **Bedfordshire**, LU3 1EH, ENG.
(T) 01582 736513
Speciality: Physiotherapy.
● **Owner** Mrs B Claridge
**P** **S** **T** (**Ref:**HM04544)

### CLARIDGE, PATRICIA
**Patricia Claridge**, 20 Newgate Cl, St. Albans, **Hertfordshire**, AL4 9JE, ENG.
(T) 01727 847149
Speciality: Reflexology.
**S** **T** (**Ref:**HM04545)

### CLARK & ASSOCIATES
**A P Clark & Associates**, 147 St. James St, Burnley, **Lancashire**, BB11 1PD, ENG.
(T) 01282 457716
Speciality: Chiropodists (Podiatrists).
● **Owner** Mr A Clark
**S** (**Ref:**HM04546)

### CLARK & ASSOCIATES
**A P Clark & Associates**, 45 Church St, Padiham, Burnley, **Lancashire**, BB12 8HF, ENG.
(T) 01282 775716
Speciality: Chiropodists (Podiatrists).
● **Owner** Mr A Clark
**S** (**Ref:**HM04547)

### CLARK, A L
**A L Clark**, 14 The Drive, Fareham, **Hampshire**, PO16 7NL, ENG.
(T) 01329 235919 (F) 023 9246 8642
Speciality: Chiropodists (Podiatrists).
● **Owner** Mr A Clark
**S** (**Ref:**HM04548)

### CLARK, A L
**A L Clark**, 78 Elm Gr, Hayling Island, **Hampshire**, PO11 9EH, ENG.
(T) 023 9246 8642
Speciality: Chiropodists (Podiatrists).
● **Owner** Mr A Clark
**S** (**Ref:**HM04549)

### CLARK, ALAN
**Alan Clark**, 13 Bridus Mead, Blewbury, Didcot, **Oxfordshire**, OX11 9PJ, ENG.
(T) 01235 851168
Speciality: Hypnotherapy.
● **Owner** A Clark
**B** (**Ref:**HM04550)

### CLARK, ANGELA
**Angela Clark**, 20A Station Rd, Birchington, **Kent**, CT7 9DQ, ENG.
(T) 01843 848292
Speciality: Chiropodists (Podiatrists).
● **Partner** Mrs G Connelly
**S** (**Ref:**HM04551)

### CLARK, BARRY J
**Barry J Clark**, 5 Salisbury Cl, Bishop's Stortford, **Hertfordshire**, CM23 3NS, ENG.
(T) 01279 657177
Speciality: Chiropodists (Podiatrists).
● **Owner** Mr B Clark
**S** (**Ref:**HM04552)

### CLARK, BRIAN
**Brian Clark**, 27 Hyland Way, Hornchurch, **Essex**, RM11 1DN, ENG.
(T) 01708 474186
Speciality: Chiropodists (Podiatrists).
● **Owner** Mr B Clark
**S** (**Ref:**HM04553)

### CLARK, C Z
**C Z Clark**, 53 Calton Avenue, London, **London (Greater)**, SE21 7DF, ENG.
(T) 020 8693 3204
Speciality: Physiotherapy.
● **Owner** Mrs C Clark
**P** **S** **T** (**Ref:**HM04554)

### CLARK, D
**D Clark**, Newburn, Grangewood, Wexham, Slough, **Berkshire**, SL3 6LP, ENG.
(T) 01753 552725
Speciality: Chiropodists (Podiatrists).
● **Owner** Mrs D Clark
**S** (**Ref:**HM04555)

### CLARK, GEOFFREY
**Geoffrey Clark**, 19 Muswell Hill Rd, London, **London (Greater)**, N10 3JB, ENG.
(T) 020 8883 2130
Speciality: Osteopathy.
**P** **S** **T** (**Ref:**HM04556)

### CLARK, GERALD
**Gerald Clark**, Flat 2, 2 Belsize Rd, Worthing, **Sussex (West)**, BN11 4RG, ENG.
(T) 01903 213906
Speciality: Osteopathy.
● **Owner** Mr G Clark
**P** **S** **T** (**Ref:**HM04557)

### CLARK, HAZEL
**Hazel Clark**, 17 Park Avenue, Darley Dale, Matlock, **Derbyshire**, DE4 2FX, ENG.
(T) 01629 734102
Speciality: Aromatherapy.
● **Owner** Ms H Clark
**M** **O** (**Ref:**HM04558)

### CLARK, J
**J Clark**, 7 St. Peters Avenue, Caversham, Reading, **Berkshire**, RG4 7DD, ENG.
(T) 01189 476317 (F) 01189 462804
Speciality: Acupuncture.

Key: **B** Mind-Body Medicine **C** Complementary Medicine **H** Self Help Treatment **M** Medicinal Therapy **O** Oriental Medicine **P** Postural Therapy **S** Manipulative Structural Therapy **T** Touch Therapy

● **Owner** Ms J Clark
**O** (**Ref:**HM04559)

**CLARK, J**

**J Clark**, 25 Woburn Cl, Caversham, Reading, **Berkshire**, RG4 7HB, ENG.
(T) 01189 476317
Speciality: Acupuncture.
**O** (**Ref:**HM04560)

**CLARK, JOYCE**

**Joyce Clark**, Brooklyn, Gadbrook Rd, Betchworth, **Surrey**, RH3 7AN, ENG.
(T) 01306 611320
Speciality: Aromatherapy, Reflexology.
**S T** (**Ref:**HM04561)

**CLARK, KATHRYN**

**Kathryn Clark**, 445 Springvale Rd, Sheffield, **Yorkshire (South)**, S10 1LQ, ENG.
(T) 01142 678419
Speciality: Aromatherapy.
**M O** (**Ref:**HM04562)

**CLARK, L A**

**L A Clark**, 31 Bridge St, Thorne, Doncaster, **Yorkshire (South)**, DN8 5NR, ENG.
(T) 01405 813112
Speciality: Chiropodists (Podiatrists).
**S** (**Ref:**HM04563)

**CLARK, LEE**

**Lee Clark**, 17 Branksome Gr, Stockton-On-Tees, **Cleveland**, TS18 5DD, ENG.
(T) 01642 351515
Speciality: Physiotherapy.
● **Owner** Mr L Clark
**P S T** (**Ref:**HM04564)

**CLARK, LUCY**

**Lucy Clark**, 177 King St, Castle Douglas, **Dumfries and Galloway**, DG7 1DZ, SCO.
(T) 01556 504104 (F) 01556 504552
Speciality: Acupuncture.
● **Partner** Mr G Carlo
**O** (**Ref:**HM04565)

**CLARK, LYN**

**Lyn Clark**, Ashley Hill, Bristol, BS7 9BE, ENG.
(T) 01179 445542 (F) 01179 445542
Speciality: Counselling, Homeopathy. ✔
● **Homeopath** Mrs L Clark **Q:** B.Ac, Dip.Couns, RSHom. **M:** L.C.C.H.
**C** Yrs. Est.: 16 (**Ref:**HM04566)

**CLARK, LYNDA**

**Lynda Clark**, 8 School Lane, St. Ives, Ringwood, **Hampshire**, BH24 2PF, ENG.
(T) 01425 470882
Speciality: Chiropractors.
● **Employee** Miss L Clark
**P S T** (**Ref:**HM04567)

**CLARK, LYNN**

**Mrs Lynn Clark**, 55B Seamoor Rd, Bournemouth, **Dorset**, BH4 9AE, ENG.
(T) 01202 764179
Speciality: Chiropody, Nail Surgery, Orthotics. ✔
● **Owner/Chiropodist** Mrs L Clark **Q:** BSc, M.S.C.P.
**M** Yrs. Est.: 3 (**Ref:**HM04568)

**CLARK, M**

**M Clark**, Centre For Study Of Complementary Medicine, 51 Bedford Pl, Southampton, **Hampshire**, SO15 2DT, ENG.
(T) 023 8033 4752 (F) 023 8023 1835
Speciality: Complementary Medicines & Therapy.
● **Practice Manager** Mrs J Tuson
**M** (**Ref:**HM04569)

**CLARK, M D C**

**M D C Clark**, 60 St Pancras Rd, Lewes, **Sussex (East)**, BN7 1JG, ENG.
(T) 01273 473945
Speciality: Osteopathy.
**P S T** (**Ref:**HM04570)

**CLARK, MADELEINE**

**Madeleine Clark**, 6 Lakewood Rd, Ashurst, Southampton, **Hampshire**, SO40 7DJ, ENG.
(T) 023 8029 2680
Speciality: Hypnosis.

● **Owner** Ms M Clark
**B** (**Ref:**HM04571)

**CLARK, MALCOLM**

**Malcolm Clark**, 74 High St, Battle, **Sussex (East)**, TN33 0AG, ENG.
(T) 01424 772075
Speciality: Osteopathy.
● **Owner** Mr M Clark
**P S T** (**Ref:**HM04572)

**CLARK, MICHELLE**

**Michelle Clark**, 58 Marlins Turn, Hemel Hempstead, **Hertfordshire**, HP1 3LL, ENG.
(T) 01442 397667
Speciality: Reflexology.
**S T** (**Ref:**HM04573)

**CLARK, PETER**

**Peter Clark**, 318 Newton Rd, Rushden, **Northamptonshire**, NN10 0SY, ENG.
(T) 01933 317320
Speciality: Hypnosis.
● **Owner** Mr P Clark
**B** (**Ref:**HM04574)

**CLARK, R (DR)**

**Dr R Clark**, 130-132 Gloucester Rd, Bishopston, Bristol, BS7 8NL, ENG.
(T) 01179 245842
Speciality: Chiropractors.
● **Doctor** Mr J Jensen
**P S T** (**Ref:**HM04575)

**CLARK, S J**

**S J Clark**, High St, Buckden, St Neots, Huntingdon, **Cambridgeshire**, PE18 9TA, ENG.
(T) 01480 810667 (F) 01480 810667
Speciality: Hypnosis.
● **Owner** Mr S Clark
**B** (**Ref:**HM04576)

**CLARK, S L**

**S L Clark**, 2 Parliament St, Harrogate, **Yorkshire (North)**, HG1 2QZ, ENG.
(T) 01423 569158
Speciality: Chiropodists (Podiatrists).
**S** (**Ref:**HM04577)

**CLARK, SIMON**

**Simon Clark**, 18 Twyford Avenue, Acton, London, **London (Greater)**, W3 9QA, ENG.
(T) 07956 323898 (F) 020 8966 2461
Speciality: Reflexology.
● **Owner** Mr S Clark
**S T** (**Ref:**HM04578)

**CLARK, STEPHEN**

**Stephen Clark**, 70A Stanstead Rd, Hoddesdon, **Hertfordshire**, EN11 0RL, ENG.
(T) 01992 471794
Speciality: Physiotherapy.
**P S T** (**Ref:**HM04579)

**CLARK, STEPHEN**

**Stephen Clark**, 71 Nursery Rd, Hoddesdon, **Hertfordshire**, EN11 9LD, ENG.
(T) 01992 443393
Speciality: Physiotherapy.
● **Owner** Mr S Clark
**P S T** (**Ref:**HM04580)

**CLARKE GAIL & RAWLINSON MIKE**

**Gail Clarke & Mike Rawlinson**, 42 St James St, South Petherton, **Somerset**, TA13 5BN, ENG.
(T) 01460 242549
(E) mikeandgail@supanet.com
Speciality: Alexander Technique, Cranio-Sacral Therapy. ✔
● **Teacher of the Alexander Technique** Mr M Rawlinson **Q:** MSTAT. **M:** STAT.
● **Teacher/Cranio-Sacral Therapist** Ms G Clarke **Q:** MSTAT, RCST. **M:** CSTA, STAT.
**P** Yrs. Est.: 10 (**Ref:**HM04581)

**CLARKE, ANNE MARI**

**Anne Mari Clarke**, 61 Granville Rd, Oxted, **Surrey**, RH8 0BY, ENG.
(T) 01883 382280 (F) 01883 382280
Speciality: Complementary Medicines & Therapy.
● **Owner** Mrs A Clarke
**C M** (**Ref:**HM04582)

**CLARKE, C**

**C Clarke**, 192 Baslow Rd, Sheffield, **Yorkshire (South)**, S17 4DS, ENG.
(T) 01142 364101
Speciality: Chiropodists (Podiatrists).
● **Owner** Mrs C Clarke
**S** (**Ref:**HM04583)

**CLARKE, CHRIS**

**Chris Clarke**, 13 Clandon Drive, Eastleigh, **Hampshire**, SO50 4QQ, ENG.
(T) 023 8061 9059
Speciality: Aromatherapy.
● **Owner** Mr C Clarke
**M O** (**Ref:**HM04584)

**CLARKE, DAVID**

**David Clarke**, 2a Bridge House, Walton Lea Rd, Higher Walton, Warrington, **Cheshire**, WA4 6SN, ENG.
(T) 01925 266343
Speciality: Complementary Medicines & Therapy.
● **Owner** Mr D Clarke
**M** (**Ref:**HM04585)

**CLARKE, DON**

**Don Clarke**, 3 Dale Villas, Horsforth, Leeds, **Yorkshire (West)**, LS18 4JN, ENG.
(T) 01132 959752
Speciality: Acupuncture. ✔
● **Owner/Acupuncturist** Mr D Clarke **Q:** Dip.Ac, MBAcC, MSc.
**O** (**Ref:**HM04586)

**CLARKE, H G**

**H G Clarke**, 25 Allanson Rd, Manchester, **Manchester (Greater)**, M22 4HN, ENG.
(T) 01619 988288
Speciality: Chiropodists (Podiatrists).
**S** (**Ref:**HM04587)

**CLARKE, IRENE**

**Irene Clarke**, 38 Twatling Rd, Barnt Green, Birmingham, **Midlands (West)**, B45 8HU, ENG.
(T) 01214 452149
Speciality: Electrolysis.
● **Owner** Mrs I Clarke
**T** (**Ref:**HM04588)

**CLARKE, J**

**J Clarke**, Corner Farm Barns, Main St, South Scarle, Newark, **Nottinghamshire**, NG23 7JH, ENG.
(T) 01636 893062 (F) 01636 893062
Speciality: Chiropractic.
● **Owner** Mrs J Clarke
**P S T** (**Ref:**HM04589)

**CLARKE, J A**

**J A Clarke**, Highcliffe Private Clinic, 248 Lymington Rd, Highcliffe, Christchurch, **Dorset**, BH23 5ET, ENG.
(T) 01425 277505 (F) 01425 271086
Speciality: Physiotherapy.
● **Practice Manager** Mrs P Jones
**P S T** (**Ref:**HM04590)

**CLARKE, LORRAINE**

**Lorraine Clarke**, 17 Harwood Park, Carrickfergus, **County Antrim**, BT38 7LZ, NIR.
(T) 028 9336 7304
Speciality: Reflexology.
**S T** (**Ref:**HM04591)

**CLARKE, M D**

**M D Clarke**, 2 Bowles St, Bootle, **Merseyside**, L20 4QF, ENG.
(T) 01519 226902
Speciality: Chiropodists (Podiatrists).
**S** (**Ref:**HM04592)

**CLARKE, M R**

**Michael Raymond Clarice BSc Ost Hons**, 39C Mersea Rd, Colchester, **Essex**, CO2 7QS, ENG.
(T) 01206 549325
Speciality: Cranial Osteopathy, Manipulation, Massage (Therapeutic), Osteopathy. ✔
● **Osteopath** Ms K Perkins **Q:** BSc, Hons (OST). **M:** GOsC.
● **Osteopath** Mr M Clarke **Q:** BSc, Hons (OST). **M:** GOsC.


Key continued: **Yrs.Est:** Years Established **Q:** Qualifications **M:** Professional Membership ✔ Indemnity Insurance Accept Credit Cards

**S** Yrs. Est.: 4 (**Ref:**HM04593)

### CLARKE, MARGARET
**Margaret Clarke B A ,M A ,Reg Psychol ,Ps S I**, 23 Lr Albert Rd, Sandycove, **County Dublin**, IRE.
(T) 01280 8989
Speciality: Psychology.
**B** (**Ref:**HM04594)

### CLARKE, MO
**Mo Clarke**, Windhill Cottage, Windhill, Bishop's Stortford, **Hertfordshire**, CM23 2NJ, ENG.
(T) 01279 659292
Speciality: Complementary Medicines & Therapy.
● **Owner** Mrs M Clarke
**C M** (**Ref:**HM04595)

### CLARKE, NICK
**Nick Clarke**, 102 Geary Rd, Dollis Hill, London, **London (Greater)**, NW10 1HR, ENG.
(T) 020 8450 8688
Speciality: Acupuncture.
● **Owner** Mr J Dela-Cruz
**O** (**Ref:**HM04596)

### CLARKE, P P
**P P Clarke**, Tanelorn, Strete, Dartmouth, **Devon**, TQ6 0RH, ENG.
(T) 01803 770638
Speciality: Chiropodists (Podiatrists).
**S** (**Ref:**HM04597)

### CLARKE, PAUL G
**Paul G Clarke**, 82 Grange Rd, West Kirby, Wirral, **Merseyside**, CH48 4EQ, ENG.
(T) 01516 252953 (F) 01516 253953
Speciality: Physiotherapy.
● **Owner** Mr P Clarke
**P S T** (**Ref:**HM04598)

### CLARKE, R J
**R J Clarke**, Glebe House, 7 Glebe Rd, Leicester, **Leicestershire**, LE2 2LD, ENG.
(T) 01162 704244
Speciality: Chiropodists (Podiatrists).
**S** (**Ref:**HM04599)

### CLARKE, RACHEL
**Rachel Clarke**, 50 Bill Todd Way, Taverham, Norwich, **Norfolk**, NR8 6GF, ENG.
(T) 01603 867900
Speciality: Reflexology.
**S T** (**Ref:**HM04600)

### CLARKE, ROSALEEN
**Rosaleen Clarke**, 41 Parkwood Avenue, Wivenhoe, Colchester, **Essex**, CO7 9AW, ENG.
(T) 01206 823742
Speciality: Reflexology.
**S T** (**Ref:**HM04601)

### CLARKE, ROSEMARY
**Rosemary Clarke**, 11 Crawford Cl, Leamington Spa, **Warwickshire**, CV32 7HA, ENG.
(T) 01926 421928
Speciality: Psychotherapy.
**B** (**Ref:**HM04602)

### CLARKE, SAM
**Sam Clarke**, 56 Alum Chine Rd, Bournemouth, **Dorset**, BH4 8DZ, ENG.
(T) 01202 769976
Speciality: Chiropodists (Podiatrists).
**S** (**Ref:**HM04603)

### CLARKE, STEVEN
**Steven Clarke**, 75 Winchester Rd, Tilgate, Crawley, **Sussex (West)**, RH10 5HL, ENG.
(T) 01293 408214
Speciality: Auto Suggestion, Aversion Therapy, Complementary Therapy, Counselling, Holistic Healing, Hypnosis, Hypnotherapy, Psychotherapy, Stress Therapy.
● **Psychoanalyst/Hypnotherapist** Mr S Clarke Q: Dip.Hyp, Dip.Psych.
**B** Yrs. Est.: 6 (**Ref:**HM04604)

### CLARKE, SUSAN AMANDA
**Susan Amanda Clarke**, 140 Chew Valley Rd, Greenfield, Oldham, **Lancashire**, OL3 7DD, ENG.
(T) 01457 878764
Speciality: Aromatherapy.
● **Owner** Mrs S Clarke
**M O** (**Ref:**HM04605)

### CLASSIC CLINIC
**Classic Clinic**, 104 Worcester St, Brynmawr, Ebbw Vale, **Blaenau Gwent**, NP23 4EY, WAL.
(T) 01495 313870
Speciality: Acupuncture, Aromatherapy, Chiropody, Nutritional Therapy, Sports Massage. ✓
● **Owner** Mrs J Jones
● **Aromatherapist** Mrs Parry
**C** Yrs. Est.: 3 (**Ref:**HM04606)

### CLASSIC THERAPIES
**Classic Therapies**, The Studio, Pinner Rd, Northwood, **London (Greater)**, HA6 1BT, ENG.
(T) 01923 826892
Speciality: Complementary Medicines & Therapy.
**C M** (**Ref:**HM04607)

### CLASSICAL OSTEOPATH
**Classical Osteopath**, 1 Grove Cottage, Orange Hill, Binfield, Bracknell, **Berkshire**, RG42 5PR, ENG.
(T) 01344 482851
Speciality: Osteopathy.
**P S T** (**Ref:**HM04608)

### CLASSICAL OSTEOPATH
**Classical Osteopath**, The Life Story Centre, 17 Eldon Sq, Reading, **Berkshire**, RG1 4DP, ENG.
(T) 01189 580806
Speciality: Osteopathy.
**P S T** (**Ref:**HM04609)

### CLASSICAL OSTEOPATH
**Classical Osteopath**, Professionails, 3a Coulgate St, Brockley, London, **London (Greater)**, SE4 2RW, ENG.
(T) 020 8691 1051
Speciality: Absent Healing, Acupressure, Complementary Therapy, Cranial Osteopathy, Faith Healing, Healer, Healing Therapy, Manipulation, Massage (Therapeutic), Micro Manipulation, Osteopathy, Reflexology, Reiki, Seichem, Tera-Mai. ✓
● **Osteopath** Mr N Fennel Q: DO, ITEC, MICO. M: GOsC, ICO.
**S** Yrs. Est.: 9 (**Ref:**HM04610)

### CLASSICAL OSTEOPATH
**Classical Osteopath**, 32 Gaywood Hall Drive, King's Lynn, **Norfolk**, PE30 4ED, ENG.
Speciality: Absent Healing, Acupressure, Aromatherapy, Complementary Therapy, Cranial Osteopathy, Faith Healing, Healer, Healing Therapy, Manipulation, Massage (Therapeutic), Micro Manipulation, Osteopathy, Reflexology, Reiki, Seichem, Tera-Mai, Bioflow Magnectic wrist device to improve exchange of nutrients from blood to cells and stabilise blood PH. Usually enhances energy levels, reduces tiredness and pain - usually helps a person recover much more quickly after very tiring activities. ✓
● **Osteopath** Mr N Fennel Q: DO, ITEC, MICO. M: GOsC, ICO.
**S** Yrs. Est.: 2 (**Ref:**HM04611)

### CLAUDY CHIROPRACTIC CLINIC
**Claudy Chiropractic Clinic**, 520-522 Glenshane Rd, Claudy, Londonderry, **County Londonderry**, BT47 4BT, NIR.
(T) 028 7133 8748 (F) 028 7133 7116
Speciality: Chiropractic. ✓
● **Chiropractor** Dr K Prideman Q: DC.
**P** Yrs. Est.: 20 (**Ref:**HM04612)

### CLAXTON, VICKI
**Vicki Claxton**, Campscott, Assher Rd, Walton-On-Thames, **Surrey**, KT12 4RA, ENG.
(T) 01932 225221
Speciality: Reflexology.
**S T** (**Ref:**HM04613)

### CLAY, ANITA (DR)
**Dr Anita Clay**, The Herbal Clinic, 23 Southernhay West, Exeter, **Devon**, EX1 1PR, ENG.
(T) 01392 253222
Speciality: Herbalists.
● **Owner** Dr A Clay
**M** (**Ref:**HM04614)

### CLAY, M
**M Clay**, 74 Elers Rd, London, **London (Greater)**, W13 9QD, ENG.
(T) 020 8567 3537
Speciality: Physiotherapy.
● **Owner** Miss M Clay
**P S T** (**Ref:**HM04615)

### CLAY, P A
**P A Clay**, 126 St Cross Rd, Winchester, **Hampshire**, SO23 9RJ, ENG.
(T) 01962 877122 (F) 01962 841872
Speciality: Acupuncture.
● **Owner** Mr P Clay
**O** (**Ref:**HM04616)

### CLAYDON, JOHN
**John Claydon**, 60 Woodside Rd, Tunbridge Wells, **Kent**, TN4 8PZ, ENG.
(T) 01892 512337 (F) 01892 512337
Speciality: Complementary Medicines & Therapy.
● **Owner** Mr J Claydon
**C M** (**Ref:**HM04617)

### CLAYDON, L
**L Claydon**, 24A Orchard Rd, Melbourn, Royston, **Hertfordshire**, SG8 6HH, ENG.
(T) 01763 263260
Speciality: Chiropodists (Podiatrists).
**S** (**Ref:**HM04618)

### CLAYPATH MEDICAL PRACTICE
**Claypath Medical Practice**, 26 Gilesgate, Durham, **County Durham**, DH1 1QW, ENG.
(T) 01913 332830
Speciality: Acupuncture.
**O** (**Ref:**HM04619)

### CLAYSON, V
**V Clayson**, The Castle Clinic, 18-20 The Ropewalk, Nottingham, **Nottinghamshire**, NG1 5DT, ENG.
(T) 01159 472263 (F) 01159 556306
Speciality: Acupuncture.
● **Owner** Mr M Pook
**O** (**Ref:**HM04620)

### CLAYTON, DEBBIE
**Debbie Clayton**, 27 Ash Cl, Elswick, Preston, **Lancashire**, PR4 3YG, ENG.
(T) 01995 671074
Speciality: Reflexology.
● **Owner** Mrs D Clayton
**S T** (**Ref:**HM04621)

### CLAYTON, DEBRA
**Debra Clayton**, 40 Exeter Gardens, Ilford, **Essex**, IG1 3LB, ENG.
(T) 020 8554 5745
Speciality: Reflexology.
**S T** (**Ref:**HM04622)

### CLAYTON, E A
**E A Clayton**, Great North Way, London, **London (Greater)**, NW4 1PS, ENG.
(T) 020 8959 0823
Speciality: Osteopathy.
● **Owner** Mrs E Clayton
**P S T** (**Ref:**HM04623)

### CLAYTON, EMMA
**Emma Clayton**, 208 Birmingham Rd, Stratford-Upon-Avon, **Warwickshire**, CV37 0AX, ENG.
(T) 01789 299190
Speciality: Chiropodists (Podiatrists).
● **Owner** Mrs E Clayton
**S** (**Ref:**HM04624)

### CLAYTON, HELEN
**Helen Clayton**, Derrymullen, Ballinasloe, **County Galway**, IRE.
(T) 09054 2311
Speciality: Chiropractors.
**P S T** (**Ref:**HM04625)

### CLAYTON, P A
**P A Clayton**, 9 Anchorsholme Lane East, Thornton, **Lancashire**, FY5 3QH, ENG.
(T) 01253 855499
Speciality: Chiropodists (Podiatrists).
**S** (**Ref:**HM04626)

Key: **B** Mind-Body Medicine **C** Complementary Medicine **H** Self Help Treatment **M** Medicinal Therapy **O** Oriental Medicine **P** Postural Therapy **S** Manipulative Structural Therapy **T** Touch Therapy

### CLAYTON, SUSAN
**Susan Clayton**, 8 Henry Drive, Leigh-On-Sea, **Essex**, SS9 3QQ, ENG.
(T) 01702 474048
Speciality: Reflexology.
S T (Ref:HM04627)

### CLAYTON-ROBB, WAYNE
**Wayne Clayton-Robb**, 82 Mildred Avenue, Watford, **Hertfordshire**, WD1 7DX, ENG.
(T) 01923 350380
Speciality: Hypnosis.
B (Ref:HM04628)

### CLAYTON'S
**Clayton's**, 94A Bank St, Mexborough, **Yorkshire (South)**, S64 9LG, ENG.
(T) 01709 583816 (F) 01977 706619
Speciality: Herbalists.
● **Manageress** Mrs G Thornhill
M (Ref:HM04629)

### CLEAR, SEAN
**Sean Clear**, Rosedale Clinic, 48 Redlands Rd, Reading, **Berkshire**, RG1 5HR, ENG.
(T) 01189 860879
Speciality: Acupuncture.
● **Owner** Mr S Clear
O (Ref:HM04630)

### CLEASSON, HAZEL
**Hazel Cleasson**, North Cottage, Fairlands Rd, Guildford, **Surrey**, GU3 3JB, ENG.
(T) 01483 234404
Speciality: Aromatherapy.
● **Owner** Miss H Cleasson
M O (Ref:HM04631)

### CLEERE, SEAN
**Sean Cleere**, 48 Redlands Rd, Reading, **Berkshire**, RG1 5HR, ENG.
(T) 01189 866635 (F) 01189 874461
Speciality: Acupuncture.
● **Director** Mr J Boardman
O (Ref:HM04632)

### CLEGG, D P
**D P Clegg**, 41 Laburnum Gr, Portsmouth, **Hampshire**, PO2 0HQ, ENG.
(T) 023 9266 2715
Speciality: Hypnotherapy.
● **Owner** Mr D Clegg
B (Ref:HM04633)

### CLEGG, D P
**D P Clegg**, 23 Strand Hill, Dawlish, **Devon**, EX7 9JJ, ENG.
(T) 01626 867210
Speciality: Hypnotherapy.
● **Owner** Mr D Clegg
B (Ref:HM04634)

### CLEGG, N A
**N A Clegg**, 22 New Rd, Mytholmroyd, Hebden Bridge, **Yorkshire (West)**, HX7 5DZ, ENG.
(T) 01422 885455
Speciality: Chiropodists (Podiatrists).
S (Ref:HM04635)

### CLEGHORN, ANNE
**Anne Cleghorn**, 24 Western Avenue, Barton On Sea, New Milton, **Hampshire**, BH25 7PZ, ENG.
(T) 01425 620105
Speciality: Chiropodists (Podiatrists).
● **Owner** Mrs A Cleghorn
S (Ref:HM04636)

### CLEGHORN, BURNES & HOWNSFIELD
**Cleghorn Burnes & Hownsfield**, 3 Cotham Rd, Bristol, BS6 6DG, ENG.
(T) 01179 735999
Speciality: Osteopathy.
P S T (Ref:HM04637)

### CLEIN, LEWIS (DR)
**Dr Lewis Clein**, 80 Harley St, London, **London (Greater)**, W1N 1AE, ENG.
(T) 020 7935 4647
Speciality: Psychiatry.
● **Practice Manager** Dr L Clein
B (Ref:HM04638)

### CLELLAND, J
**J Clelland**, Trinity Medical Centre, Thornhill St, Wakefield, **Yorkshire (West)**, WF1 1PG, ENG.
(T) 01977 732665
Speciality: Acupuncture.
● **Owner** Mrs J Clelland
O (Ref:HM04639)

### CLEMENCY
**Clemency**, 5 The Shambles, Sevenoaks, **Kent**, TN13 1XH, ENG.
(T) 01732 450049
Speciality: Complementary Medicines & Therapy.
C M (Ref:HM04640)

### CLEMENT, RITA
**Rita Clement**, 13 Newlands Rd, Barwell, Leicester, **Leicestershire**, LE9 8AN, ENG.
(T) 01455 445161
Speciality: Reflexology.
● **Owner** Mrs R Clement
S T (Ref:HM04641)

### CLEMENTS, CHRISTINE
**Christine Clements BSc(Hons)Ost**, 45 Gordon Rd, Aldershot, **Hampshire**, GU11 1ND, ENG.
(T) 01252 322419
Speciality: Aromatherapy, Bach Remedies, Cranial Osteopathy, Manipulation, Massage (Therapeutic), Osteopathy. ✔
● **Osteopath** Miss C Clements Q: BSc, DO, Hons (OST). M: GOsC.
S Yrs. Est.: 3 (Ref:HM04642)

### CLEMENTS, CHRISTINE
**Christine Clements**, Foxglove, Foxhills Lodge, Stonehill Rd, Ottershaw, Chertsey, **Surrey**, KT16 0EL, ENG.
(T) 01932 875077
Speciality: Osteopathy.
● **Owner** Miss C Clements
P S T (Ref:HM04643)

### CLEMENTS, J
**J Clements**, 68A The Avenue, Worcester Park, **Surrey**, KT4 7HJ, ENG.
(T) 020 8335 3202
Speciality: Nutritional Therapy, Reflexology, Baby Massage. ✔
● **Natural Therapist** Ms J Clements Q: ITEC. M: APNT, ITEC.
C Yrs. Est.: 14 (Ref:HM04644)

### CLEMENTS, MICHAEL
**Michael Clements**, 175 Bexley Rd, London, **London (Greater)**, SE9 2PP, ENG.
(T) 020 8850 0035
Speciality: Acupuncture.
O (Ref:HM04645)

### CLEMIT, MIKE
**Mike Clemit**, 23 Pullan Avenue, Eccleshill, Bradford, **Yorkshire (West)**, BD2 3RS, ENG.
(T) 01274 641918
Speciality: Hypnosis.
● **Owner** Mr M Clemit
B (Ref:HM04646)

### CLEMO, ANNE
**Anne Clemo**, 53 Bonnington Gr, Exeter, **Devon**, EX1 2QY, ENG.
(T) 01392 274072
Speciality: Reflexology.
S T (Ref:HM04647)

### CLEOPATRA
**Cleopatra**, First Floor, 140 Eastgate, Louth, **Lincolnshire**, LN11 9AA, ENG.
(T) 01507 607387
Speciality: Reflexology.
● **Owner** Mrs H Sherif
S T (Ref:HM04648)

### CLERE PHYSIOTHERAPY
**Clere Physiotherapy**, Greenacre Leisure, Greenham Rd, Greenham, Thatcham, **Berkshire**, RG19 8XF, ENG.
(T) 01635 528887
Speciality: Physiotherapy.
P S T (Ref:HM04649)

### CLEREY, J D
**J D Clerey**, 3 Burton House, Kents Bank Rd, Grange-over-Sands, **Cumbria**, LA11 7EY, ENG.
(T) 01539 532135
Speciality: Chiropodists (Podiatrists).
S (Ref:HM04650)

### CLERKIN, G
**G Clerkin**, 10 Walker St, Paisley, **Renfrewshire**, PA1 2EF, SCO.
(T) 01418 899438
Speciality: Chiropodists (Podiatrists).
S (Ref:HM04651)

### CLEVELAND CHIROPODY/SPORTS INJ
**Cleveland Chiropody & Sports Injuries**, 8 Westgate Rd, Guisborough, **Cleveland**, TS14 6EA, ENG.
(T) 01287 633799
Speciality: Chiropodists (Podiatrists).
● **Owner** Mrs E Roger
S (Ref:HM04652)

### CLEVELAND HOMEOPATHIC CLINIC
**Cleveland Homeopathic Clinic**, 72A Parliament Rd, Middlesbrough, **Cleveland**, TS1 4JS, ENG.
(T) 01642 244337
Speciality: Homeopathy.
M (Ref:HM04653)

### CLEVELAND NAT HEALTH CLINIC
**Cleveland Natural Health Clinic**, 73 Queen St, Redcar, **Cleveland**, TS10 1BG, ENG.
(T) 01642 489682
Speciality: Osteopathy.
P S T (Ref:HM04654)

### CLEVERLEY, ALUN
**Alun Cleverley**, 8 Market Sq, South Petherton, **Somerset**, TA13 5BT, ENG.
(T) 01460 242474
Speciality: Chiropodists (Podiatrists).
S (Ref:HM04655)

### CLEVERLEY, PAULINE
**Pauline Cleverley**, 5 Sherbrooke Cl, Calverton, Nottingham, **Nottinghamshire**, NG14 6LN, ENG.
(T) 01159 654733
Speciality: Chiropodists (Podiatrists).
S (Ref:HM04656)

### CLEVERLY, BARBARA
**Barbara Cleverly**, 5 The Moorings, Hindhead, **Surrey**, GU26 6SD, ENG.
(T) 01428 604310
Speciality: Reflexology.
S T (Ref:HM04657)

### CLEVERLY, MARAGRET
**Maragret Cleverly**, 22 Chatburn Rd, Chorlton, Manchester, **Manchester (Greater)**, M21 0XW, ENG.
(T) 07989 471934
Speciality: Aromatherapy, Hypnosis, Reflexology.
S T (Ref:HM04658)

### CLEZY, G M
**Mrs G M Clezy**, 28 Arcot Park, Sidmouth, **Devon**, EX10 9HS, ENG.
(T) 01395 512100
Speciality: Psychotherapy.
● **Owner** Mrs G Clezy
B (Ref:HM04659)

### CLGE OF CLINICAL REFLEX/HOL MASS
**College Of Clinical Reflexology & Holistic Massage (The)**, 15 Hartfield Cl, Tonbridge, **Kent**, TN10 4JP, ENG.
(T) 01732 350629
Speciality: Complementary Medicines & Therapy.
C M (Ref:HM04660)

### CLIFF, R
**Mrs R Cliff**, The Stables, 10 The Green, Quenington, Cirencester, **Gloucestershire**, GL7 5BS, ENG.
(T) 01285 750760
Speciality: Chiropractic.
● **Owner** Mrs R Cliff
P S T (Ref:HM04661)

### CLIFFORD, CORNELIUS
**Clifford Cornelius**, Liverpool Hypnotherapy, 45a Rodney St, Liverpool, **Merseyside**, L1 9ER, ENG.
(T) 01517 343313


Key continued: Yrs.Est: Years Established Q: Qualifications M: Professional Membership ✔ Indemnity Insurance Accept Credit Cards

Speciality: Hypnotherapy.
● **Hypnotherapist** Mr C Clifford
B (Ref:HM04662)

### CLIFFORD, S H
**Mrs S H Clifford**, Shendao 1A Melrose Rd, Pinner, **London (Greater)**, HA5 5RA, ENG.
(T) 020 8933 1676
Speciality: Physiotherapy.
P S T (Ref:HM04663)

### CLIFT, HELEN
**Helen Clift**, 7 St Stephens Walk, Ashford, **Kent**, TN23 5AD, ENG.
(T) 01233 334717
Speciality: Clairvoyants & Palmists.
● **Owner** Ms H Clift
B (Ref:HM04664)

### CLIFTON ACUPUNCTURE CLINIC
**Clifton Acupuncture Clinic**, 13 Clifton Vale, Bristol, BS8 4PT, ENG.
(T) 01179 260474
Speciality: Acupuncture.
O (Ref:HM04665)

### CLIFTON CHIROPRACTIC CLINIC
**Hugh C Hurst TA Clifton Chiropractic Clinic**, 123 Pembroke Rd, Clifton, Bristol, BS8 3EU, ENG.
(T) 01179 744217 (F) 01179 238045
(E) cliftonchiropractic@freeserve.co.uk
Speciality: Acupressure, Acupuncture, Chinese Herbal Medicine, Chiropractic, Macrobiotics, Manipulation, Massage (Therapeutic), Moxibustion, Oriental Diagnosis, Pilates, Vitamin Therapy, X-Ray, Back and Neck Rehabilitation. ✔
● **Chiropractor** Ms C Clothier Q: DC, MCC, MSc. M: BCA, GCC.
● **Chiropractor** Mr D Ingrams Q: BSc, DC, MCC. M: BCA, GCC.
● **Acupuncturist/Chinese Herbalist** Mr N Johnson Q: Dip.CHM, Lic.Ac, MBAcC. M: BAcC, RCHM.
● **Chiropractor** Dr H Hurst Q: DC, FCC. M: BCA, GCC.
P S Yrs. Est.: 13 (Ref:HM04666)

### CLIFTON COMPLEMENTARY MED CTRE
**Clifton Complementary Medicine Centre**, 56 Royal York Cres, Bristol, BS8 4JP, ENG.
(T) 01179 734594
Speciality: Chiropodists (Podiatrists).
● **Partner** Mr E Jones
S (Ref:HM04667)

### CLIFTON COURT COMP HEALTH CTRE
**Clifton Court Complementary Health Centre**, 48 High St, Newport Pagnell, **Buckinghamshire**, MK16 8AQ, ENG.
(T) 01908 611004 (F) 01908 611004
Speciality: Complementary Medicines & Therapy.
C M (Ref:HM04668)

### CLIFTON OSTEOPATHIC PRACTICE
**Clifton Osteopathic Practice**, 131 Clifton Rd, Rugby, **Warwickshire**, CV21 3QJ, ENG.
(T) 01788 579595
(E) mail@wholebodiesfsnet.co.uk
Speciality: Complementary Therapy, Cranial Osteopathy, Cupping, Family Planning (Natural), Herbal Medicine, Holistic Healing, Homeopathy, Life Style Coaching, Manipulation, Massage (Therapeutic), Naturopathy, Nutritional Therapy, Osteopathy, Myofascial Dry Needling. ✔
● **Osteopath/Naturopath** Ms A Donley Q: BSc, DO, Hons (OST), ND, RN. M: GCRN, GOsC.
● **Osteopath/Naturopath** Mr S Harris Q: DO, ND, RN. M: GCRN, GOsC.
S Yrs. Est.: 1 (Ref:HM04669)

### CLIFTON PRACTICE
**Clifton Practice (The)**, 88 Princess Victoria St, Bristol, BS8 4DB, ENG.
(T) 01179 733260
Speciality: Acupuncture, Alexander Technique, Aromatherapy, Chiropractic, Homeopathy, Hypnosis, Indian Head Massage, Kinesiology, Massage (Therapeutic), Osteopathy, Reflexology, Reiki, Shiatsu. ✔
● **Owner** Mr D Newton Q: AccHyp, Dip.Hyp, Dip.Psych, MNCH. M: HS.
C Yrs. Est.: 9 (Ref:HM04670)

### CLIFTON, C
**C Clifton**, 20 Taylor Rd, Lydd On Sea, Romney Marsh, **Kent**, TN29 9PA, ENG.
(T) 01797 366689
Speciality: Chiropodists (Podiatrists).
● **Owner** Ms C Clifton
S (Ref:HM04671)

### CLIFTON, NIGEL
**Nigel Clifton**, 65 Townley Rd, Bexleyheath, **Kent**, DA6 7HZ, ENG.
(T) 020 8303 6698
Speciality: Hypnosis.
B (Ref:HM04672)

### CLIFTON, SARAH
**Sarah Clifton**, 1 Wodehouse St, Norwich, **Norfolk**, NR3 4TY, ENG.
(T) 01603 631391
Speciality: Reflexology.
● **Owner** Ms S Clifton
S T (Ref:HM04673)

### CLIFTON, SARAH
**Sarah Clifton**, 64 Bethel St, Norwich, **Norfolk**, NR2 1NR, ENG.
(T) 01603 666546 (F) 01603 666759
Speciality: Reflexology.
● **Owner** Ms S Clifton
S T (Ref:HM04674)

### CLINCH, ADELE
**Adele Clinch**, 216 South Coast Rd, Peacehaven, **Sussex (East)**, BN10 8JR, ENG.
(T) 01273 582999
Speciality: Chiropody, Podiatry. ✔
● **Receptionist/Partner** Mr S Gibbs
● **Owner** Miss A Clinch M: B.A.Ch.P.
M Yrs. Est.: 9 (Ref:HM04675)

### CLINIC
**Clinic (The)**, 163 Felixstowe Rd, Ipswich, **Suffolk**, IP3 8EB, ENG.
(T) 01473 272742
Speciality: Chiropodists (Podiatrists).
● **Owner** Mrs M Smith
S (Ref:HM04676)

### CLINIC
**Clinic (The)**, 71 Park St, London, **London (Greater)**, W1Y 3HB, ENG.
(T) 020 7629 3763
Speciality: Physiotherapy.
P S T (Ref:HM04677)

### CLINIC 2000
**Clinic 2000**, 1st Floor 106 Bradshawgate, Leigh, **Manchester (Greater)**, WN7 4NP, ENG.
(T) 01942 269920
Speciality: Electrolysis.
T (Ref:HM04678)

### CLINIC AT CHARING CROSS
**Clinic At Charing Cross (The)**, 257 Renfrew St, Glasgow, **Glasgow (City of)**, G3 6TT, SCO.
(T) 01413 321928
Speciality: Acupuncture, Hypnosis, Hypnotherapy. ✔
● **Owner** Mr V Van Middell Q: BSCH. M: BSCH.
B Yrs. Est.: 40 (Ref:HM04679)

### CLINIC FOR COUNSELLING
**Clinic For Counselling**, 10 Harley St, London, **London (Greater)**, W1N 1AA, ENG.
Speciality: Counselling, Family Therapy. ✔
● **Counsellor** S. I Nejad
(T) 020 8202 1836 Q: BA (Hons), MA, NVQ L4. M: BACP.
C Yrs. Est.: 5 (Ref:HM04680)

### CLINIC FOR COUNSELLING
**Clinic For Counselling**, 18-24 High St, Edgware, **London (Greater)**, HA8 7RP, ENG.
(T) 020 8202 1836
Speciality: Counselling, Family Therapy, Psychotherapy. ✔
● **Counsellor** S. I Nejad Q: BA (Hons), MA, NVQ L4. M: BACP.
C Yrs. Est.: 5 (Ref:HM04681)

### CLINIC FOR PHYSICAL MEDICINE
**Clinic For Physical Medicine & Sports Injuries**, 1 Kilminster Court, Cheltenham Rd East, Gloucester, **Gloucestershire**, GL3 1AN, ENG.
(T) 01452 714013
Speciality: Osteopathy.
● **Owner** Mr R Rolleston
P S T (Ref:HM04682)

### CLINIC OF ACUPUNCTURE
**Clinic Of Acupuncture**, Hill House, Petworth Rd, Haslemere, **Surrey**, GU27 3AX, ENG.
(T) 01428 654380 (F) 01428 656005
Speciality: Acupuncture.
● **Owner** Mr H Hill
O (Ref:HM04683)

### CLINIC OF ACUPUNCTURE
**Clinic Of Acupuncture**, 18 North Park Rd, Bramhall, Stockport, **Cheshire**, SK7 3JR, ENG.
(T) 01614 398605
Speciality: Acupressure, Acupuncture, Moxibustion, Oriental Diagnosis, Ying & Yang. ✔
● **Acupuncturist** Mr R Powell Q: BA (Hons), Lic.Ac. M: BAcC.
O Yrs. Est.: 18 (Ref:HM04684)

### CLINIC OF CHINESE MED & ACU
**Clinic Of Chinese Medicine & Acupuncture (The)**, 46 Grove Rd, Eastbourne, **Sussex (East)**, BN21 4TY, ENG.
(T) 01323 727238
Speciality: Acupuncture, Herbal Medicine. ✔
● **Chinese Doctor** Dr Ben
● **Owner** Mr G Yu
O (Ref:HM04685)

### CLINIC OF CHINESE MEDICINE
**Clinic Of Chinese Medicine**, 107 Walter Rd, Swansea, SA1 5QQ, WAL.
(T) 01792 474488 (F) 01792 281041
Speciality: Acupuncture.
● **Owner** Dr L Zhu
O (Ref:HM04686)

### CLINIC OF CHINESE MEDICINE
**Clinic of Chinese Medicine**, Clinic Of Traditional Chinese Medicine, 10 New North Rd, Exeter, **Devon**, EX4 4HF, ENG.
(T) 01392 217422
Speciality: Acupuncture, Herbal Medicine. ✔
● **Acupunturist** Mr S King Q: MBAcC.
● **Herbal Assistant** Susie Brown
● **Acupuncturist** Ms J Dallas Q: MBAcC.
O Yrs. Est.: 5 (Ref:HM04687)

### CLINIC OF CHINESE MEDICINE
**Clinic Of Chinese Medicine**, 888 Christchurch Rd, **Dorset**, BH7 6DJ, ENG.
(T) 01202 417080
Speciality: Complementary Medicines & Therapy.
C M (Ref:HM04688)

### CLINIC OF COMP MEDICINE
**Clinic of Complementary Medicine**, 54 The Avenue, Yeovil, **Somerset**, BA21 4BN, ENG.
(T) 01935 422488
(E) homeopath@bigfoot.com
Speciality: Homeopathy, Osteopathy, Oxygen Therapy. ✔
● **Osteopath/Homeopath** Mr A Bickley Q: LCSP, MHMA, Reg.Osteopath, RSHom. M: Soc.Hom.
M Yrs. Est.: 21 (Ref:HM04689)

### CLINIC OF HERBAL MEDICINE
**Clinic Of Herbal Medicine**, 174 Otley Rd, Leeds, **Yorkshire (West)**, LS16 5LG, ENG.
(T) 01132 745319
Speciality: Herbal Medicine.
● **Practice Manager** Mrs M Knowles
M (Ref:HM04690)

### CLINIC OF HERBAL MEDICINE
**Clinic Of Herbal Medicine**, 354 Mansfield Rd, Nottingham, **Nottinghamshire**, NG5 2EF, ENG.
(T) 01159 147153
Speciality: Herbalists.
● **Owner** Mrs M Elliottsmith
M (Ref:HM04691)

### CLINIC OF HERBAL MEDICINE
**Clinic Of Herbal Medicine**, 101 Newlands Rd, Birmingham, **Midlands (West)**, B30 2SA, ENG.
(T) 01214 583781

Key: B Mind-Body Medicine, C Complementary Medicine, H Self Help Treatment, M Medicinal Therapy, O Oriental Medicine, P Postural Therapy, S Manipulative Structural Therapy, T Touch Therapy

Speciality: Herbal Medicine.
● **Owner** Mrs L Klovrza
M (Ref:HM04692)

### CLINIC OF HOLISTIC HEALTH
**Newport Clinic of Holistic Health**, 4 Llanthewy Rd, Newport, NP20 4JR, **WAL**.
(T) 01633 843333
(W) www.newportclinic.co.uk
Speciality: Acupuncture, Allergy Testing, Aromatherapy, Chiropody, Counselling, Herbal Medicine, Holistic Healing, Homeopathy, Hypnotherapy, Massage (Therapeutic), Osteopathy, Psychotherapy, Reflexology, Shiatsu, Stop Smoking Clinic. ✔
● **Therapist** Mr B Rowlands Q: BSc, DHP (NC), MNRHP, NLP.
● **Therapist** Mr J Plowman Q: MNRHP, PhD.
● **Therapist** Mr R Napper Q: RSHom.
● **Shiatsu Therapist** Mr A Penman Q: MRSS.
● **Aromatherapist** Mr R Lougher Q: IIHHT.
M: ISPA.
● **Owner/Therapist** Mr G Adam Q: RSHom.
● **Counsellor** Ms C Hoad
C Yrs. Est.: 12 (Ref:HM04693)

### CLINIC OF HOLISTIC MEDICINE
**Clinic of Holistic Medicine**, Basement 50 Merrion Sq, East, Dublin, **County Dublin**, IRE.
(T) 01676 4640
Speciality: Complementary Medicines & Therapy.
M (Ref:HM04694)

### CLINIC OF HOLISTIC MEDICINE
**Clinic of Holistic Medicine**, 34 Abbeygate St, Upr, **County Galway**, IRE.
(T) 09156 7416
Speciality: Complementary Medicines & Therapy.
M (Ref:HM04695)

### CLINIC OF HYP & STRESS MNGMT
**Clinic Of Hypnosis & Stress Management**, Natural Health & Healing Centre, 175 Outland Rd, Plymouth, **Devon**, PL6 5QT, ENG.
(T) 01752 788321
Speciality: Hypnosis, Stress Therapy.
B (Ref:HM04696)

### CLINIC OF HYPNOTHERAPY
**Clinic Of Hypnotherapy**, Kings Toye Common Lane, Kings Langley, **Hertfordshire**, WD4 8BL, ENG.
(T) 01923 265802
Speciality: Hypnosis.
B (Ref:HM04697)

### CLINIC OF NATURAL HEALTH
**Clinic Of Natural Health**, Church Grange Health Centre, Bramblys Drive, Basingstoke, **Hampshire**, RG21 8QN, ENG.
(T) 01256 475728 (F) 01256 475728
Speciality: Complementary Medicines & Therapy.
● **Owner** Dr P Godwin
C M (Ref:HM04698)

### CLINIC OF NATURAL MEDICINE
**Clinic Of Natural Medicine**, 7 Church St, Crewkerne, **Somerset**, TA18 7HR, ENG.
(T) 01460 77990
Speciality: Complementary Medicines & Therapy.
C M (Ref:HM04699)

### CLINIC OF NATURAL MEDICINE
**Clinic Of Natural Medicine**, 652 Nottingham Rd, Derby, **Derbyshire**, DE21 6SX, ENG.
(T) 01332 663342
Speciality: Physiotherapy.
P S T (Ref:HM04700)

### CLINIC OF NATURAL MEDICINE
**Clinic Of Natural Medicine**, 362 Banbury Rd, Oxford, **Oxfordshire**, OX2 7PT, ENG.
(T) 01865 512392
Speciality: Herbal Medicine.
M (Ref:HM04701)

### CLINIC OF NATURAL MEDICINE
**Clinic Of Natural Medicine**, 19 Fore St, Bovey Tracey, Newton Abbot, **Devon**, TQ13 9AD, ENG.
(T) 01626 835068
Speciality: Complementary Medicines & Therapy.
C M (Ref:HM04702)

### CLINIC OF NATURAL MEDICINE
**Clinic of Natural Medicine**, 90 Foster St, Lincoln, **Lincolnshire**, LN5 7QF, ENG.
(T) 01522 526292 (F) 01522 526292
Speciality: Acupuncture, Bach Remedies, Cranial Osteopathy, Electrotherapy, Kinesiology, Manipulation, Osteopathy, Vibrational Therapy, Cranial Osteopathy, Bioresonance. ✔
● **Osteopath** Mr S Allen Q: DO, DPO. M: GOsC.
● **Osteopath** Mr J Booth Q: DO. M: GOsC.
● **Osteopath** Mr V Henighan
P S T Yrs. Est.: 9 (Ref:HM04703)

### CLINIC OF NATURAL MEDICINE
**Clinic Of Natural Medicine (The)**, 126 Whiteladies Rd, Cliffton, Bristol, BS8 2RP, ENG.
(T) 01179 466035 (F) 01179 466034
Speciality: Aromatherapy, Massage (Therapeutic), Reflexology. ✔
● **Reflexologist** Mrs C File
T Yrs. Est.: 6 (Ref:HM04704)

### CLINIC OF NATURAL MEDICINE
**Clinic of Natural Medicine**, 570 Howth Rd, Raheny, **County Dublin**, IRE.
(T) 01832 7399
Speciality: Complementary Medicines & Therapy.
M (Ref:HM04705)

### CLINIC OF NATURAL THERAPIES
**Clinic Of Natural Therapies (The)**, 187 Ember Lane, East Molesey, **Surrey**, KT8 0BU, ENG.
(T) 020 8398 6943 (F) 020 8398 9396
Speciality: Complementary Medicines & Therapy.
● **Owner** Mr M Faure-Alderson
M (Ref:HM04706)

### CLINIC OF PHYSICAL MEDICINE
**Clinic Of Physical Medicine**, Plough Farm Barn, Pyecombe St, Pyecombe, Brighton, **Sussex (East)**, BN45 7EE, ENG.
(T) 01273 857856
Speciality: Osteopathy.
P S T (Ref:HM04707)

### CLINIC OF REFLEXOLOGY
**Clinic Of Reflexology**, Main Rd, Radcliffe-On-Trent, Nottingham, **Nottinghamshire**, NG12 2GD, ENG.
(T) 01159 333181
Speciality: Reflexology.
● **Owner** Mrs B Bilkhu
S T (Ref:HM04708)

### CLINIC OF TRAD CHINESE MED
**Clinic Of Traditional Chinese Medicine (The)**, 20 Ramsden Rd, London, **London (Greater)**, N11 3JE, ENG.
(T) 020 8361 5522
Speciality: Acupuncture.
O (Ref:HM04709)

### CLINIC OFF THE SQUARE
**Clinic Off The Square**, 33 Ribblesdale Pl, Preston, **Lancashire**, PR1 3NA, ENG.
(T) 01772 511335
Speciality: Complementary Medicines & Therapy.
● **Partner** Mr D Ellis
M (Ref:HM04710)

### CLINICAL AROMATHERAPY
**Clinical Aromatherapy**, The Pines, Alloa, **Clackmannanshire**, FK10 2DQ, SCO.
(T) 01259 218057
Speciality: Aromatherapy.
● **Owner** Mrs J Booth
M O (Ref:HM04711)

### CLINICAL CENTRE OF CHINESE MED
**Clinical Centre Of Chinese Medicine (The)**, 98 The Drive, Hove, **Sussex (East)**, BN3 6GP, ENG.
(T) 01273 776499
Speciality: Acupuncture, Chinese Herbal Medicine, Cranial Osteopathy, Cranio-Sacral Therapy, Herbal Medicine, Osteopathy, Shiatsu.
C (Ref:HM04712)

### CLINICAL HYPNOTHERAPY
**Clinical Hypnotherapy**, 74 The Avenue, Lowestoft, **Suffolk**, NR33 7LN, ENG.
(T) 01502 588055
Speciality: Hypnosis.
● **Owner** Mr T Bailey
B (Ref:HM04713)

### CLINICAL HYPNO-THERAPY
**Clinical Hypno-Therapy**, 16 Piershill Trce, Edinburgh, **Edinburgh (City of)**, EH8 7EU, SCO.
(T) 01316 611475
Speciality: Hypnotherapy.
B (Ref:HM04714)

### CLINICAL PSYCHOLOGY SERVICE
**Clinical Psychology Service**, 1 Rawstorn Rd, Colchester, **Essex**, CO3 3JE, ENG.
(T) 01206 564992 (F) 01206 564992
Speciality: Psychology.
B (Ref:HM04715)

### CLINICAL REFLEXOLOGY
**Clinical Reflexology**, 30 Bolton Rd, Farnworth, Bolton, **Lancashire**, BL4 7JW, ENG.
(T) 01204 438760
Speciality: Reflexology.
● **Owner** Mrs C Knowles
S T (Ref:HM04716)

### CLINIC-COMP & ALT THERAPY
**Clinic For Complementary & Alternative Therapy**, 37 St Peter St, Tiverton, **Devon**, EX16 6NW, ENG.
(T) 01884 255990
Speciality: Complementary Medicines & Therapy.
● **Manager** Ms R Lacey
M (Ref:HM04717)

### CLINIQUE DE SANTE
**Clinique De Sante**, 12a Marion Cr, Orpington, **Kent**, BR5 2DD, ENG.
(T) 01689 878433
Speciality: Complementary Medicines & Therapy.
● **Partner** Ms A Pateman
M (Ref:HM04718)

### CLINTON HOUSE CHIROPODY
**Clinton House Chiropody Surgery**, 23A Oliver St, Northampton, **Northamptonshire**, NN2 7JH, ENG.
(T) 01604 719484
(E) michael/scs@hotmail.co
Speciality: Biomechanics, Chiropody. ✔
● **Chiropodist (Podiatrist)**
Ms S McConaughy Q: BSc (Hons), M.S.C.P., S.R.Ch. M: S.C.P., S.R.Ch.
C Yrs. Est.: 2 (Ref:HM04719)

### CLINTON, D H
**D H Clinton**, 16 Hampson Way, Bearsted, Maidstone, **Kent**, ME14 4AP, ENG.
(T) 01622 736557
Speciality: Physiotherapy.
P S T (Ref:HM04720)

### CLIPSHAM, VANESSA
**Vanessa Clipsham**, 18 Devoke Cl, Huntingdon, **Cambridgeshire**, PE29 6XE, ENG.
(T) 01480 435718
Speciality: Reflexology.
S T (Ref:HM04721)

### CLISBY, JANE
**Jane Clisby**, Haydon Drove, Haydon, Wells, **Somerset**, BA5 3EH, ENG.
(T) 01749 672648
Speciality: Reflexology. ✔
● **Reflexologist** Ms J Clisby Q: ITEC. M: BRCP.
T Yrs. Est.: 3 (Ref:HM04722)

### CLISSOLD PK NATURAL HLTH CTRE
**Clissold Park Natural Health Centre**, 154 Church St, Stoke Newington, London, **London (Greater)**, N16 0JU, ENG.
(T) 020 7249 2990
Speciality: Alexander Technique.
● **Therapist** Ms J Wise
P S (Ref:HM04723)

### CLISSOLD PK NATURAL HLTH CTRE
**Clissold Park Natural Health Centre**,


Key continued: Yrs.Est: Years Established Q: Qualifications M: Professional Membership ✔ Indemnity Insurance Accept Credit Cards

Clissold Park Health Centre, 154 Stoke Newington Church St, London, **London (Greater)**, N16 0JU, ENG.
(T) 020 7249 2990 (F) 020 7249 3977
Speciality: Psychotherapy.
● **Director** Mr D Berg
M (Ref:HM04724)

**CLITHEROE PHYSIOTHERAPY CENTRE**

**Clitheroe Physiotherapy Centre**, New Market St, Clitheroe, **Lancashire**, BB7 2JW, ENG.
(T) 01200 423805
Speciality: Physiotherapy.
● **Manager** Mrs A Ashdown
P S T (Ref:HM04725)

**CLNC OF ACU & CHINESE HERB MED**

**Clinic of Acupuncture & Chinese Herbal Medicine**, 1 Brook Cottages, Ivinghoe Aston, Leighton Buzzard, **Bedfordshire**, HP4 2DG, ENG.
(T) 01525 221125 (F) 01525 229666
(E) melvynepstein@onetel.net.uk
(W) www.acupuncture-online.co.uk
Speciality: Acupuncture, Complementary Therapy, Cupping, Herbal Medicine, Holistic Healing, Magnetic Therapy, Moxibustion, Oriental Diagnosis. ✔
● **Acupuncturist/Chinese Herbalist** Mr M Epstein Q: BSc, Dip.Ac, Dip.CHM. M: BAcC, RCHM.
O Yrs. Est.: 6 (Ref:HM04726)

**CLNC OF ACU & CHINESE HRBL MED**

**Clinic of Acupuncture & Chinese Herbal Medicine**, 109 High St, Berkhamsted, **Hertfordshire**, ENG.
(T) 01442 863430 (F) 01525 229666
(E) melvynepstein@onetel.net.uk
(W) www.acupuncture-online.co.uk
Speciality: Acupuncture, Complementary Therapy, Cupping, Herbal Medicine, Holistic Healing, Magnetic Therapy, Moxibustion, Oriental Diagnosis. ✔
● **Acupuncturist/Chinese Herbalist** Mr M Epstein Q: BSc, Dip.Ac, Dip.CHM. M: BAcC, BBA, RCHM.
O Yrs. Est.: 6 (Ref:HM04727)

**CLOCKHOUSE CLINIC**

**Clockhouse Clinic**, Cobblestone Walk, 74 High St, Steyning, **Sussex (West)**, BN44 3RD, ENG.
(T) 01903 816483 (F) 01903 816483
Speciality: Alexander Technique.
● **Partner** Mr M Bourne
M (Ref:HM04728)

**CLOISTERS**

**Cloisters (The)**, Lower Leam St, Leamington Spa, **Warwickshire**, CV31 1DJ, ENG.
(T) 01926 316420 (F) 01926 886053
Speciality: Physiotherapy.
P S T (Ref:HM04729)

**CLONDALKIN ACUPUNCTURE**

**Clondalkin Acupuncture & Herbal Clinic**, Desmond Hse, Boot Rd, IRE.
(T) 01464 0050 (F) 01464 0496
Speciality: Acupuncture.
O (Ref:HM04730)

**CLONDALKIN ACUPUNCTURE CLINIC**

**Clondalkin Acupuncture Clinic**, Desmond Hse, Boot Rd, Dublin, **County Dublin**, IRE.
(T) 01464 0050 (F) 01464 0496
Speciality: Acupuncture.
O (Ref:HM04731)

**CLONTARF HOLISTIC CENTRE**

**Clontarf Holistic Centre**, 57 Lawrence Rd, Clontarf, **County Dublin**, IRE.
(T) 01853 1296
Speciality: Aromatherapy.
M O (Ref:HM04732)

**CLOUD 10**

**Cloud 10**, 2 Danbury Rd, Shirley, Solihull, **Midlands (West)**, B90 2BU, ENG.
(T) 01217 449581
Speciality: Complementary Medicines & Therapy.
● **Owner** Mrs J Swingler
C M (Ref:HM04733)

**CLOUGH, G J**

**G J Clough**, 106 Manchester Rd, Warrington, **Cheshire**, WA1 3AN, ENG.
(T) 01925 570461
Speciality: Chiropodists (Podiatrists).
● **Owner** Mr G Clough
S (Ref:HM04734)

**CLOUGHS - CHRTRD PHYSIO CLINIC**

**Cloughs The Chartered Physiotherapy Clinic**, 51 High St, Lees, Oldham, **Lancashire**, OL4 3BN, ENG.
(T) 01616 245858
Speciality: Aromatherapy, Physiotherapy. ✔
● **Physiotherapist** Ms D Clough Q: MCSP, SRP.
S (Ref:HM04735)

**CLOVELLY NATURAL THERAPY CTRE**

**Clovelly Natural Therapy Centre**, 12 Argyll Rd, Gloucester, **Gloucestershire**, GL2 0QR, ENG.
(T) 01452 503910
Speciality: Complementary Medicines & Therapy.
● **Owner** Mrs D Bates
M (Ref:HM04736)

**CLOVER HOUSE**

**Clover House**, 98-100 Cloverlea Rd, Oldland Common, Bristol, BS30 8TX, ENG.
(T) 01179 079466
Speciality: Aromatherapy, Nutritional Therapy.
M O (Ref:HM04737)

**CLOVERWOOD**

**Cloverwood Ltd**, Unit 8 St Johns Court, Foster Rd, Ashford Business Park, Sevington, Ashford, **Kent**, TN24 0SJ, ENG.
(T) 01233 628018 (F) 01233 500551
Speciality: Aromatherapy.
● **Owner** Mrs C Hollis
M O (Ref:HM04738)

**CLOWES, JOANNE**

**Joanne Clowes**, 21 Marl Pit Lane, Denstone, Uttoxeter, **Staffordshire**, ST14 5HH, ENG.
(T) 01889 591393
Speciality: Reflexology.
● **Owner** Mrs J Clowes
S T (Ref:HM04739)

**CLOWES, M**

**M Clowes**, 111 Highgate Lane, Lepton, Huddersfield, **Yorkshire (West)**, HD8 0HQ, ENG.
(T) 01484 303003
Speciality: Complementary Medicines & Therapy.
● **Owner** Mr M Clowes
C M (Ref:HM04740)

**CLUB INDIGO**

**Club Indigo**, Avondale Rd, Cwmbran, **Torfaen**, NP44 1TX, WAL.
(T) 01633 877822
Speciality: Physiotherapy. ✔
● **Physiotherapist** Ms A Walter Q: BSc, MCSP, MSc, SRP. M: CSP.
S (Ref:HM04741)

**CLUDERAY, DAVID**

**David Cluderay**, 2a Church Rd, Armley, Leeds, **Yorkshire (West)**, LS12 1TZ, ENG.
(T) 01132 798080
Speciality: Chiropodists (Podiatrists).
● **Owner** Mr D Cluderay
S (Ref:HM04742)

**CLUSKER, P**

**P Clusker**, 44 High St, Sutton Coldfield, **Midlands (West)**, B72 1UJ, ENG.
(T) 01213 544629
Speciality: Acupuncture.
O (Ref:HM04743)

**CLUSKEY, LYNN M**

**Lynn M Cluskey**, 102 Park Lane, Poynton, Stockport, **Cheshire**, SK12 1RQ, ENG.
(T) 01625 874578
Speciality: Chiropodists (Podiatrists).
● **Owner** Miss L Cluskey
S (Ref:HM04744)

**CLUTTERBUCK, B**

**B Clutterbuck**, Ashwood, Rushy Lake, Saunders Foot, Pembroke, **Pembrokeshire**, SA69 9NY, WAL.
(T) 01834 813736
Speciality: Reflexology.
● **Owner** Bernice Clutterbuck
S T (Ref:HM04745)

**CLYDE HOUSE CHIRO CLINIC**

**Clyde House Chiropractic Clinic**, 16 Princes St South, Exeter, **Devon**, EX2 9AW, ENG.
(T) 01392 217418
Speciality: Chiropractic.
P S T (Ref:HM04746)

**CMG ASS NEURO PHYSIOTHERAPY**

**CMG Associates Neurological Physiotherapy**, 2 Moorlands, Ripponden Rd, Denshaw, Oldham, **Lancashire**, OL3 5UN, ENG.
(T) 01457 810079
Speciality: Physiotherapy.
P S T (Ref:HM04747)

**COACH HOUSE**

**Coach House (The)**, 21A Oxford Rd, Colchester, **Essex**, CO3 3HT, ENG.
(T) 01206 571246
Speciality: Complementary Medicines & Therapy.
C M (Ref:HM04748)

**COACH HOUSE CLINIC**

**Coach House Clinic (The)**, The Coach House Clinic, 155 High St, Tenterden, **Kent**, TN30 6JS, ENG.
(T) 01580 763481 (F) 01580 763481
Speciality: Osteopathy.
● **Owner** Mr J Stevens
P S T (Ref:HM04749)

**COACHING FOR SUCCESS**

**Coaching For Success Ltd**, Sheldon House, 3 Plomer Hill, High Wycombe, **Buckinghamshire**, HP13 5JQ, ENG.
(T) 01494 473504 (F) 01494 473504
(W) www.coachingforsuccess.co.uk
Speciality: Auto Suggestion, Cognitive Therapy, Dietician, Hypnosis, Hypnotherapy, Life Style Coaching, Psychotherapy, Stress Therapy, Visualisation Therapy, Vitamin Therapy. ✔
● **Life Coach** Mr M Duckett Q: BA (Hons) Psychol, CSCT, Dip.CT, Dip.EH, NLP. M: ANLP, BIH, BPS, ISSD.
H Yrs. Est.: 4 (Ref:HM04750)

**COAKLEY, NOIRIN**

**Noirin Coakley**, Highgate, London, **London (Greater)**, N6, ENG.
(T) 020 8348 1185
Speciality: Bach Remedies.
M (Ref:HM04751)

**COAST CLINIC**

**Coast Clinic (The)**, Whites Lane, Fawley, Southampton, **Hampshire**, SO45 1DG, ENG.
(T) 023 8089 8990 (F) 023 8089 8990
Speciality: Aromatherapy, Counselling, Reiki, Sports Massage. ✔
● **Owner/Therapist** Mr J D'albert Q: Dip.Clin.Sp.Th, ITEC, Reg.KP, Reiki Master. M: AAF, GCP.
● **Counsellor** Mrs F D'albert
C Yrs. Est.: 4 (Ref:HM04752)

**COAST CLINIC**

**Coast Clinic (The)**, 2 South St, Hythe, Southampton, **Hampshire**, SO45 6EB, ENG.
(T) 023 8020 7776
Speciality: Complementary Medicines & Therapy.
● **Owner** Mr J Dalbert
M (Ref:HM04753)

**COATES, ALAN**

**Alan Coates**, Duchy Rd, Heathpark Industrial Estate, Honiton, **Devon**, EX14 1YD, ENG.
(T) 01404 45333
Speciality: Chiropodists (Podiatrists).
● **Owner** Mr A Coates
S (Ref:HM04754)

**COATES, ELIZABETH**

**Elizabeth Coates**, Dale End, Longsleddale, Kendal, **Cumbria**, LA8 9BA, ENG.
(T) 01539 823213

Key: B Mind-Body Medicine, C Complementary Medicine, H Self Help Treatment, M Medicinal Therapy, O Oriental Medicine, P Postural Therapy, S Manipulative Structural Therapy, T Touch Therapy

**Speciality:** Reflexology.
S T (Ref:HM04755)

## COATES, MARY

**Mary Coates**, 17 Springfields Cl, Colden Common, Winchester, **Hampshire**, SO21 1SU, ENG.
(T) 01962 712417
**Speciality:** Hypnosis.
B (Ref:HM04756)

## COATES, SUSAN E

**Susan E Coates**, 137 Chessfield Park, Amersham, **Buckinghamshire**, HP6 6RU, ENG.
(T) 01494 764249
**Speciality:** Chiropodists (Podiatrists).
S (Ref:HM04757)

## COBB, ADRIAN

**Adrian Cobb**, Pagham Rd, Bognor Regis, **Sussex (West)**, PO21 3QD, ENG.
(T) 01243 268787 (F) 01243 267391
**Speciality:** Chiropractic.
● **Owner** Dr A Cobb
P S T (Ref:HM04758)

## COBB, JOANNA

**Joanna Cobb**, 63 Summerland Avenue, Minehead, **Somerset**, TA24 5BW, ENG.
(T) 01643 702363
**Speciality:** Osteopathy.
● **Owner** Mr A Patten
P S T (Ref:HM04759)

## COBB, JOANNA

**Joanna Cobb**, Burrow Farm, Timberscombe, Minehead, **Somerset**, TA24 7UD, ENG.
(T) 01643 841361
**Speciality:** Osteopathy.
● **Owner** Ms J Cobb
P S T (Ref:HM04760)

## COBBE, DEREK G

**Cobbe Derek G**, Earl St, **County Longford**, IRE.
(T) 04345 912 (F) 04341 039
**Speciality:** Complementary Medicines & Therapy.
M (Ref:HM04761)

## COBHAM COMPLEMENTARY THERAPIES

**Cobham Complementary Therapies**, Tiltmead, 8 Woodend Park, Cobham, **Surrey**, KT11 3BX, ENG.
(T) 01932 862276
**Speciality:** Aromatherapy.
● **Owner** Ms L Brodie
M O (Ref:HM04762)

## COBURN CTRE FOR NATURAL HEALTH

**Coburn Centre For Natural Health (The)**, School Lane, Ashurst Wood, East Grinstead, **Sussex (West)**, RH19 3QW, ENG.
(T) 01342 823650
**Speciality:** Herbal Medicine.
● **Owner** Mrs D Coburn
M (Ref:HM04763)

## COCHRANE, NIALL

**Niall Cochrane**, 42 Dromore St, Ballynahinch, **County Down**, BT24 8AG, NIR.
(T) 028 9756 1540
**Speciality:** Chiropody, Nail Surgery. ✓
● **Chiropodist** Mr N Cochrane Q: S.R.Ch. M: S.C.P.
M **Yrs. Est.:** 15 (Ref:HM04764)

## COCKCROFT, SIMON

**Simon Cockcroft**, 112 Weeland Rd, Knottingley, **Yorkshire (West)**, WF11 8BG, ENG.
(T) 01977 671791
**Speciality:** Chiropodists (Podiatrists).
S (Ref:HM04765)

## COCKELL, J

**J Cockell**, 2 Woodburcote, Wood Burcote, Towcester, **Northamptonshire**, NN12 6JR, ENG.
(T) 01327 350842
**Speciality:** Chiropodists (Podiatrists).
● **Owner** Mr S Cockell
S (Ref:HM04766)

## COCKELL, VALERIE

**Valerie Cockell**, 41 Penerley Rd, London, **London (Greater)**, SE6 2LH, ENG.
(T) 020 8480 9905
**Speciality:** Homeopathy.
● **Owner** Ms V Cockell
M (Ref:HM04767)

## COCKELL, VALERIE

**Valerie Cockell**, 185a Torridon Rd, London, **London (Greater)**, SE6 1RG, ENG.
(T) 020 8480 9905
**Speciality:** Homeopathy.
● **Owner** Ms L Griffin
M (Ref:HM04768)

## COCKERELL, IAN

**Ian Cockerell**, 87 Blenheim Rd, Deal, **Kent**, CT14 7DE, ENG.
(T) 01304 371558
**Speciality:** Chiropodists (Podiatrists).
● **Owner** Mr I Cockrell
S (Ref:HM04769)

## COCKHILL, PETER

**Peter Cockhill**, Stillpoint, Broad St Pl, Bath, **Somerset**, BA1 5LH, ENG.
(T) 01225 460106
**Speciality:** Osteopathy.
P S T (Ref:HM04770)

## COCKINGS-MASON, FIONA

**Fiona Cockings-Mason**, Blackberry Orthopaedic Clinic, Blackberry Court, Walnut Tree, Milton Keynes, **Buckinghamshire**, MK7 7PB, ENG.
(T) 01908 604666
**Speciality:** Osteopathy.
P S T (Ref:HM04771)

## COCKINGTON FRAGRANCES

**Cockington Fragrances**, Cockington Court, Cockington Village, Torquay, **Devon**, TQ2 6XA, ENG.
(T) 01803 607007 (F) 01803 312634
**Speciality:** Aromatherapy.
● **Owner** Mrs M Barnard
M O (Ref:HM04772)

## COCKMAN, MICHAEL

**Michael Cockman**, 105 Havelock Rd, Brighton, **Sussex (East)**, BN1 6GL, ENG.
(T) 01273 565212
**Speciality:** Physiotherapy.
● **Senior Partner** Mrs S Foulds
P S T (Ref:HM04773)

## COCKSEDGE, JOHN M

**John M Cocksedge**, The Surgery, Pwllyberllan, Llanrhystud, **Ceredigion**, SY23 5ED, WAL.
(T) 01974 272026
(E) john@feetfirst.freeserve.co.uk
**Speciality:** Biomechanics, Chiropody. ✓
● **Chiropodist** Mr J Cocksledge Q: MBChA, MSSCh.
C **Yrs. Est.:** 5 (Ref:HM04774)

## COCOON REIKI CENTRE

**Cocoon Reiki Centre**, 21 Woodside, Howth, **County Dublin**, IRE.
(T) 01832 1255
**Speciality:** Complementary Medicines & Therapy.
M (Ref:HM04775)

## CO-CO'S

**Co-Co's**, 140 Melton Rd, Leicester, **Leicestershire**, LE4 5EE, ENG.
(T) 01162 666485
**Speciality:** Aromatherapy.
● **Owner** Ms B Kaur
M O (Ref:HM04776)

## COCQUEREL, DENISE

**Denise Cocquerel**, 7 Gravel Walk, Faringdon, **Oxfordshire**, SN7 7JN, ENG.
(T) 01367 242106
**Speciality:** Chiropodists (Podiatrists).
● **Owner** Miss D Cocquerel
S (Ref:HM04777)

## CODSALL COMP THERAPIES

**Codsall Complementary Therapies**, Development House, Station Rd, Codsall, Wolverhampton, **Midlands (West)**, WV8 1BX, ENG.
(T) 01902 840040
(E) suemoore@ucf.net
(W) www.dph.co.uk
**Speciality:** Aromatherapy, Beauty Therapy, Bowen Therapy, Chiropody, Indian Head Massage, Reichian Therapy, Reiki, Visualisation Therapy, Weight Management Clinic and Sunbed Centre. ✓
● **Therapist** Ms S Mortiner Q: BPS, BSc (Hons), PGD.Eat.Dis.
● **Therapist** Ms P Baddoms Q: BPS, BSc (Hons), PGD.Eat.Dis.
● **Reflexologist** Mrs S Moor M: BSY.
C **Yrs. Est.:** 2 (Ref:HM04778)

## COE HELEN ALTERNATIVE MEDICINE

**Coe Helen Alternative Medicine**, 52 Craddockstown Way, Naas, **County Kildare**, IRE.
(T) 04589 5958
**Speciality:** Complementary Medicines & Therapy.
M (Ref:HM04779)

## COE, J NICHOLAS

**Mr J Nicholas Coe**, 9 Russell Avenue, St. Albans, **Hertfordshire**, AL3 5ES, ENG.
(T) 01727 832359
**Speciality:** Osteopathy.
P S T (Ref:HM04780)

## COE, J NICHOLAS

**Mr J Nicholas Coe**, 15 Oster St, St. Albans, **Hertfordshire**, AL3 5JN, ENG.
(T) 01727 832359
**Speciality:** Osteopathy.
P S T (Ref:HM04781)

## COFFEY, AIDAN

**Aidan Coffey**, 13A North St, Havant, **Hampshire**, PO9 1PW, ENG.
(T) 023 9247 1757
**Speciality:** Hypnotherapy.
● **Owner** A Coffey
B (Ref:HM04782)

## COFFEY, EILEEN

**Eileen Coffey**, 100 Station Prde, Harrogate, **Yorkshire (North)**, HG1 1HQ, ENG.
(T) 01423 561566 (F) 01423 567379
**Speciality:** Osteopathy.
● **Owner** Mr T Cree
P S T (Ref:HM04783)

## COFFEY, RICHARD

**Richard Coffey**, 14 Moat Rd, East Grinstead, **Sussex (West)**, RH19 3JY, ENG.
(T) 01342 323314
**Speciality:** Physiotherapy.
● **Owner** Mr R Coffey
P S T (Ref:HM04784)

## COGGAN, ABBY

**Abby Coggan**, Flat 1, 5 Clarendon Villas, Hove, **Sussex (East)**, BN3 3RD, ENG.
(T) 01273 380568
**Speciality:** Complementary Medicines & Therapy.
● **Owner** Ms A Coggan
M (Ref:HM04785)

## COGGAN, ABBY

**Abby Coggan**, Flat 2, 33 Westbourne Villas, Hove, **Sussex (East)**, BN3 4GF, ENG.
(T) 01273 380568
**Speciality:** Complementary Medicines & Therapy.
C M (Ref:HM04786)

## COGGER, N

**N Cogger**, 52 London Rd, Newington, Sittingbourne, **Kent**, ME9 7NR, ENG.
(T) 01795 842373
**Speciality:** Chiropodists (Podiatrists).
S (Ref:HM04787)

## COGHLAN, HELENA

**Helena Coghlan**, 41 Lr Baggot St, Dublin, **County Dublin**, IRE.
(T) 01660 9490
**Speciality:** Complementary Medicines & Therapy.
M (Ref:HM04788)

## COHEN, D (DR)

**Dr D Cohen**, 8 Ashbourne Gr, Salford, **Manchester (Greater)**, M7 4DD, ENG.


Key continued: **Yrs.Est:** Years Established **Q:** Qualifications **M:** Professional Membership ✓ Indemnity Insurance Accept Credit Cards

(T) 01617 924477 (F) 01617 924477
Speciality: Homeopathy. ✔
● **Homeopathic Doctor** Dr D Cohen Q: MFHom. M: FHom, GMC.
M Yrs. Est.: 5 (Ref:HM04789)

**COHEN, DAVID**

**David Cohen**, 31 The Crescent, Spalding, **Lincolnshire**, PE11 1AF, ENG.
(T) 01775 766966
Speciality: Osteopathy.
P S T (Ref:HM04790)

**COHEN, DAVID**

**David Cohen**, 99 Eastgate, Deeping St. James, Peterborough, **Cambridgeshire**, PE6 8HH, ENG.
(T) 01778 347858 (F) 01778 347858
Speciality: Osteopathy.
● **Owner** Mr D Cohen
P S T (Ref:HM04791)

**COHEN, JANE**

**Jane Cohen**, 1 Kings Avenue, London, **London (Greater)**, N10 1PA, ENG.
(T) 020 8883 4273
Speciality: Physiotherapy.
● **Owner** Miss J Cohen
P S T (Ref:HM04792)

**COHEN, MICHAEL**

**Michael Cohen**, 12 Fairford Court, Grange Rd, Sutton, **Surrey**, SM2 6RY, ENG.
(T) 020 8643 4925
(E) info2coheen@aol.com
Speciality: Auto Suggestion, Autogenic Training, Cognitive Therapy, Counselling, Hypnosis, Hypnotherapy, Life Style Coaching, Psychotherapy, Stress Therapy, Visualisation Therapy. ✔
● **Psychotherapist/Hypnotherapist** Mr M Cohen Q: Dip.Couns, Dip.Hyp. M: BRCP, NCH.
B Yrs. Est.: 15 (Ref:HM04793)

**COHEN, P N**

**P N Cohen**, 54 Manor Drive, London, **London (Greater)**, N20 0DU, ENG.
(T) 020 8368 0600
Speciality: Chiropractic.
● **Owner** Dr P Cohen
P S T (Ref:HM04794)

**COHN, HANS H**

**Hans H Cohn**, 128 Walm Lane, London, **London (Greater)**, NW2 4RT, ENG.
(T) 020 8452 8336
Speciality: Physiotherapy.
● **Partner** Mrs H Cohn
P S T (Ref:HM04795)

**COIA, GRACE**

**Grace Coia**, 10 Carment Drive, Glasgow, **Glasgow (City of)**, G41 3PP, SCO.
(T) 01416 326663
Speciality: Hypnosis.
B (Ref:HM04796)

**COISCEIM NATURAL THERAPY CTRE**

**Coisceim Natural Therapy Centre**, Church St, Tralee, **County Kerry**, IRE.
(T) 06671 81855
Speciality: Complementary Medicines & Therapy.
M (Ref:HM04797)

**COKAYNE, FRANK**

**Frank Cokayne DHP MIACH MAPATH**, 101 Dorothy Av North, Peacehaven, **Sussex (East)**, BN10 8DP, ENG.
(T) 01273 580617
Speciality: Hypnotherapy.
● **Owner** Mr F Cokayne
B (Ref:HM04798)

**COKAYNE, FRANK**

**Frank Cokayne**, 156 Arundel Rd, Peacehaven, **Sussex (East)**, BN10 8HH, ENG.
(T) 07976 420929
Speciality: Hypnosis.
B (Ref:HM04799)

**COKER, EILEEN**

**Eileen Coker**, 18 Norfolk Cl, Laindon West, Basildon, **Essex**, SS15 6QR, ENG.
(T) 01268 418686 (F) 01268 418686
(E) eileen_coker@hotmail.com
(W) www.eileencoker.co.uk
Speciality: Aromatherapy, Complementary Therapy, Indian Head Massage, Massage (Therapeutic), Reflexology, Swedish Body Massage, Facial Treatments. ✔
● **Holistic Therapist** Ms E Coker Q: IIHHT, ITEC, MIFA. M: GCP, IFA, IIHHT, ITEC.
T Yrs. Est.: 2 (Ref:HM04800)

**COKER, M**

**M Coker**, 2 Arundel Way, Newquay, **Cornwall**, TR7 3BB, ENG.
(T) 01637 872085
Speciality: Physiotherapy.
P S T (Ref:HM04801)

**COKER, MARCIA**

**Marcia Coker**, 10 Graham Rd, London, **London (Greater)**, E8 1BZ, ENG.
(T) 07768 263221
Speciality: Reflexology.
S T (Ref:HM04802)

**COLBECK, R M E**

**R M E Colbeck**, 35 Highbury Rd, Hitchin, **Hertfordshire**, SG4 9SA, ENG.
(T) 01462 436092
Speciality: Chiropodists (Podiatrists).
● **Owner** Mrs R Colbeck
S (Ref:HM04803)

**COLBERT, BRIAN**

**Colbert Brian**, 84 Sundrive Rd, Kimmage, **County Dublin**, IRE.
(T) 01492 1447
Speciality: Life Style Coaching, Neuro-Linguistic Program.
B (Ref:HM04804)

**COLBOURNE, C H**

**C H Colbourne**, 53 Railway Rd, Leigh, **Manchester (Greater)**, WN7 4AE, ENG.
(T) 01942 672930
Speciality: Chiropodists (Podiatrists).
S (Ref:HM04805)

**COLCHESTER CHIROPRACTIC CENTRE**

**Colchester Chiropractic Centre**, 67 Mersea Rd, Colchester, **Essex**, CO2 7QR, ENG.
(T) 01206 549809 (F) 01206 549852
Speciality: Chiropractic.
● **Principal** Dr I Garrod
P S T (Ref:HM04806)

**COLCHESTER OSTEOPATHIC CENTRE**

**Colchester Osteopathic Centre**, 27 Oaks Drive, Colchester, **Essex**, CO3 3QZ, ENG.
(T) 01206 769935 (F) 01206 575644
Speciality: Osteopathy.
● **Owner** Mr G Sharpe
P S T (Ref:HM04807)

**COLCLOUGH, CAROL**

**Carol Colclough**, The Nook, Thames St, Wallingford, **Oxfordshire**, OX10 0BH, ENG.
(T) 01491 839906
Speciality: Hypnosis.
B (Ref:HM04808)

**COLDHAM, M**

**M Coldham**, 6a Sloane Sq, London, **London (Greater)**, SW1W 8EE, ENG.
(T) 020 7730 8437
Speciality: Physiotherapy.
P S T (Ref:HM04809)

**COLDWELL, VERONICA**

**Veronica Coldwell**, 12 Lanner Walk, Eaglestone, Milton Keynes, **Buckinghamshire**, MK6 5BT, ENG.
(T) 01525 403435
Speciality: Absent Healing, Acupressure, Aromatherapy, Crystal Healing, Healer, Healing Therapy, Holistic Healing, Homeopathy, Hypnosis, Hypnotherapy, Indian Head Massage, Massage (Therapeutic), Paranormal Therapies, Reflexology, Reiki, Stress Therapy.
● **Owner** Ms V Coldwell
B H T Yrs. Est.: 10 (Ref:HM04810)

**COLDWELL, VERONICA**

**Veronica Coldwell**, 3 The Paddock, Lidlington, Bedford, **Bedfordshire**, MK43 0RW, ENG.
(T) 01525 403435
Speciality: Complementary Medicines & Therapy.
C M (Ref:HM04811)

**COLE, B**

**B Cole**, 4 Offham Trce, Lewes, **Sussex (East)**, BN7 2QP, ENG.
(T) 01273 473113
Speciality: Psychotherapy.
B (Ref:HM04812)

**COLE, C F**

**C F Cole**, 7-9 Hawley Sq, Margate, **Kent**, CT9 1PF, ENG.
(T) 01843 292056 (F) 01843 299347
Speciality: Homeopathy.
M (Ref:HM04813)

**COLE, EVA**

**Eva Cole**, Letchworth, **Hertfordshire**, SG6, ENG.
(T) 01462 677722
Speciality: Bach Remedies.
M (Ref:HM04814)

**COLE, HARVEY M**

**Harvey M Cole**, 64 High St, Porthmadog, **Gwynedd**, LL49 9LW, WAL.
(T) 01766 514680
Speciality: Osteopathy.
● **Senior Partner** Mrs S Foskett
P S T (Ref:HM04815)

**COLE, JEAN**

**Jean Cole**, 22 Broomfield Rd, Sevenoaks, **Kent**, TN13 3EL, ENG.
(T) 01732 458289
Speciality: Homeopathy.
● **Owner** Mrs J Cole
M (Ref:HM04816)

**COLE, JEAN**

**Jean Cole**, 48 Newlands Park, London, **London (Greater)**, SE26 5NE, ENG.
(T) 020 8659 5001
Speciality: Homeopathy.
M (Ref:HM04817)

**COLE, JULIETTE**

**Juliette Cole**, Geoffrey Lloyd Foulkes Clinic, York Rd, Ilford, **Essex**, IG1 3AD, ENG.
(T) 020 8478 0443
Speciality: Osteopathy.
P S T (Ref:HM04818)

**COLE, S**

**S Cole**, Aldrens Lane, Lancaster, **Lancashire**, LA1 2DU, ENG.
(T) 01524 69864 (F) 01524 848155
Speciality: Hypnotherapy.
B (Ref:HM04819)

**COLEBROOK, G**

**G Colebrook**, 3 Chichester Drive, Lowestoft, **Suffolk**, NR33 8PX, ENG.
(T) 01502 12966
Speciality: Chiropodists (Podiatrists). ✔
● **Chiropodist** Mrs G Colebrook Q: MBChA, MBRA. M: B.A.Ch.P, BRA.
C Yrs. Est.: 18 (Ref:HM04820)

**COLEBROOKE, DAVID**

**David Colebrooke**, 50 Maylings Farm Rd, Fareham, **Hampshire**, PO16 7QS, ENG.
(T) 01329 288639 (F) 01329 288639
Speciality: Osteopathy.
● **Owner** Mr D Colebrooke
O (Ref:HM04821)

**COLEBROOKE, LINDA**

**Linda Colebrooke**, 15 Hartlands Rd, Fareham, **Hampshire**, PO16 0NJ, ENG.
(T) 01329 286203
Speciality: Osteopathy.
● **Owner** Mrs L Colebrooke
P S T (Ref:HM04822)

**COLEBY CENTRE**

**Coleby Centre (The)**, 91 Station Rd, Sidcup, **Kent**, DA15 7DP, ENG.
(T) 020 8300 4044
Speciality: Relaxation Technique.
● **Manager** Jill Coleby

Key: B Mind-Body Medicine, C Complementary Medicine, H Self Help Treatment, M Medicinal Therapy, O Oriental Medicine, P Postural Therapy, S Manipulative Structural Therapy, T Touch Therapy

**H** **T** (**Ref:**HM04823)

## COLEMAN, B

**B Coleman**, Unity Hall Chiropody Centre, 20 St Thomas Sq, Newport, **Isle of Wight**, PO30 1SG, ENG.
(T) 01983 523001
Speciality: Chiropodists (Podiatrists).
**S** (**Ref:**HM04824)

## COLEMAN, D T H

**D T H Coleman**, 10 Cambridge Rd, Hastings, **Sussex (East)**, TN34 1DJ, ENG.
(T) 01424 426908
Speciality: Chiropodists (Podiatrists).
● **Partner** Mr R Coleman
**S** (**Ref:**HM04825)

## COLEMAN, G P

**G P Coleman**, 13 Glen Eyre Drive, Southampton, **Hampshire**, SO16 3NQ, ENG.
(T) 023 8076 0149
Speciality: Osteopathy.
● **Owner** Mr G Coleman
**P** **S** **T** (**Ref:**HM04826)

## COLEMAN, JOHN

**John Coleman**, 159 Coleshill Rd, Birmingham, **Midlands (West)**, B36 8DY, ENG.
(T) 01217 832914
Speciality: Osteopathy.
● **Owner** Mr J Coleman
**P** **S** **T** (**Ref:**HM04827)

## COLEMAN, M C

**M C Coleman**, 10 Cambridge Rd, Hastings, **Sussex (East)**, TN34 1DJ, ENG.
(T) 01424 426908
Speciality: Chiropodists (Podiatrists).
● **Partner** Mr R Coleman
**S** (**Ref:**HM04828)

## COLEMAN, R

**R Coleman**, 10 Cambridge Rd, Hastings, **Sussex (East)**, TN34 1DJ, ENG.
(T) 01424 426908
Speciality: Chiropodists (Podiatrists).
● **Partner** Mr R Coleman
**S** (**Ref:**HM04829)

## COLERAINE CHIROPRACTIC CENTRE

**Coleraine Chiropractic Centre**, 10 Lodge Rd, Coleraine, **County Londonderry**, BT52 1NB, NIR.
(T) 028 7032 8157 (F) 028 7032 8157
Speciality: Chiropractic.
**P** **S** **T** (**Ref:**HM04830)

## COLERIDGE, JUDY

**Judy Coleridge**, 10 Dorset St, Shrewsbury, **Shropshire**, SY1 2JB, ENG.
(T) 01743 364157
Speciality: Counselling, Massage (Therapeutic), Psychotherapy, Reflexology, Stress Therapy, Touch Therapy. ✔
● **Therapist of Therapeutic Massage/Counselling**
Ms J Coleridge Q: Dip.Adv.Couns, Dip.Th.Massage. M: SHP.
**C** **T** Yrs. Est.: 10 (**Ref:**HM04831)

## COLES CHIROPODY

**Coles Chiropody**, 37 Conway Avenue, Thornton, **Lancashire**, FY5 3JQ, ENG.
(T) 01253 863439 (F) 01253 863439
Speciality: Chiropodists (Podiatrists).
● **Owner** Mr R Coles
**S** (**Ref:**HM04832)

## COLES, BARBARA

**Barbara Coles**, St. Neots, **Cambridgeshire**, PE19, ENG.
(T) 01480 352485
Speciality: Bach Remedies.
**M** (**Ref:**HM04833)

## COLES, G B

**G B Coles**, 80 Bedford Rd, Rushden, **Northamptonshire**, NN10 0NB, ENG.
(T) 01933 358448
Speciality: Chiropodists (Podiatrists).
**S** (**Ref:**HM04834)

## COLES, L

**L Coles**, 31 Ridgeway Rd, Risinghurst, Oxford, **Oxfordshire**, OX3 8DT, ENG.
(T) 01865 769650
Speciality: Complementary Medicines & Therapy.
**C** **M** (**Ref:**HM04835)

## COLES, RONNIE

**Ronnie Coles**, 2 St Georges Avenue, Thornton, **Lancashire**, FY5 3NH, ENG.
(T) 01253 852845
Speciality: Chiropody, Nail Surgery. ✔
● **Owner/Chiropodist** Mr R Coles Q: SSChA. M: SSChA.
**M** Yrs. Est.: 2 (**Ref:**HM04836)

## COLESHILL, AMANDA Y

**Amanda Y Coleshill**, 50 Havelock St, Wellingborough, **Northamptonshire**, NN8 4PZ, ENG.
(T) 01933 278391
Speciality: Osteopathy.
● **Owner** Mrs A Coleshill
**P** **S** **T** (**Ref:**HM04837)

## COLETTE

**Colette**, 90 Quarry St, Hamilton, **Lanarkshire (South)**, ML3 7AX, SCO.
(T) 01698 891900
Speciality: Clairvoyants & Palmists.
● **Owner** Mrs C Halket
**B** (**Ref:**HM04838)

## COLETTE, CUNNINGHAM

**Colette Cunningham ADHP MICHP**, 358 Griffith Ave, Drumcondra, **County Dublin**, IRE.
(T) 01837 4742
(W) www.hypnosiseire.com
Speciality: Complementary Medicines & Therapy.
**M** (**Ref:**HM04839)

## COLEY, LESLEY

**Lesley Coley**, Aston Clinic, 26 Kingston Rd, New Malden, **Surrey**, KT3 3LS, ENG.
(T) 020 8942 3148 (F) 020 8949 7050
Speciality: Chiropodists (Podiatrists).
**S** (**Ref:**HM04840)

## COLHOUN, P S

**P S Colhoun**, 22 Bath St, Rugby, **Warwickshire**, CV21 3JF, ENG.
(T) 01788 562843
Speciality: Chiropodists (Podiatrists).
**S** (**Ref:**HM04841)

## COLHOUN, PETER

**Peter Colhoun - Mobile Chiropody**, 3 Victoria Rd, Chester, **Cheshire**, CH4 8ST, ENG.
(T) 07880 702475
(E) pcolhoun@hotmail.com
(W) www.proudfeet.com
Speciality: Chiropody, Herbal Medicine, Homeopathy, Foot Care Advice, Orthodox & Alternative Therapies prescribed in Podiatry.
✔ CREDIT
● **Chiropodist (Podiatrist)**
Mr P Colhoun
(T) 01244 681219 Q: MBChA, MSSCh. M: B.A.Ch.P.
**S** Yrs. Est.: 5 (**Ref:**HM04842)

## COLLEDGE, SUSAN

**Susan Colledge**, 128 Great Tattenhams, Epsom, **Surrey**, KT18 5SE, ENG.
(T) 01737 355281
Speciality: Chiropodists (Podiatrists).
● **Owner** Mrs S Colledge
**S** (**Ref:**HM04843)

## COLLEGE MASSAGE

**College Massage (The)**, 176 Lakedale Rd, London, **London (Greater)**, SE18 1PU, ENG.
(T) 020 8317 9042
Speciality: Complementary Medicines & Therapy.
**C** **M** (**Ref:**HM04844)

## COLLEGE OF AYURVEDA

**College of Ayurveda (UK) (The)**, 20 Annes Gr, Great Linford, **Buckinghamshire**, MK14 5DR, ENG.
(T) 01908 664518
Speciality: Ayurvedic Medicine, Complementary Therapy.
**M** (**Ref:**HM04845)

## COLLEGE OF HEALING

**College Of Healing (The)**, Runnings Park, Croft Bank, Malvern, **Worcestershire**, WR14 4DU, ENG.
(T) 01684 566450
Speciality: Complementary Therapy, Healing Therapy.
**C** (**Ref:**HM04846)

## COLLEGE OF HOLISTIC MEDICINE

**College Of Holistic Medicine**, 4 Craigpark, Glasgow, **Glasgow (City of)**, G31 2NA, SCO.
(T) 01415 544017
Speciality: Complementary Medicines & Therapy.
**M** (**Ref:**HM04847)

## COLLEGE OF INTEG CHINESE MED

**College Of Integrated Chinese Medicine**, Castle St, Reading, **Berkshire**, RG1 7SB, ENG.
(T) 01189 508889 (F) 01189 508890
Speciality: Complementary Medicines & Therapy.
**C** **M** (**Ref:**HM04848)

## COLLEGE OF INTEGRATIVE

**College of Integrative**, Woodquay, **County Galway**, IRE.
(T) 09156 1676
Speciality: Acupuncture.
**O** (**Ref:**HM04849)

## COLLEGE OF MEDICAL

**College Of Medical**, 50 Merrion Sq, East, Dublin, **County Dublin**, IRE.
(T) 01676 4640
Speciality: Complementary Medicines & Therapy.
**M** (**Ref:**HM04850)

## COLLEGE OF NATURAL NUTRITION

**College Of Natural Nutrition (The)**, 1 Halthaies, Bradninch, Exeter, **Devon**, EX5 4LQ, ENG.
(T) 01392 881091 (F) 01392 882368
(E) cnn@globalnet.co.uk
(W) www.natnut.co.uk
Speciality: Complementary Therapy, Dietician, Holistic Healing, Naturopathy, Nutritional Therapy.
✔ CREDIT
● **Principal** Mr B Wren Q: Dip.N.Nut. M: ICA, ICM.
**B** **C** Yrs. Est.: 9 (**Ref:**HM04851)

## COLLEGE OF OSTEOPATHS

**College Of Osteopaths Training Clinic (The)**, 13 Furzehill Rd, Borehamwood, **Hertfordshire**, WD6 2DG, ENG.
(T) 020 8953 7552 (F) 020 8953 0320
Speciality: Osteopathy.
**P** **S** **T** (**Ref:**HM04852)

## COLLEGE OF PHYTOTHERAPY

**College Of Phytotherapy**, Bucksteep Manor, Bodle St, Hailsham, **Sussex (East)**, BN27 4RJ, ENG.
(T) 01323 834800 (F) 01323 834801
Speciality: Phytotherapy.
● **Chief Executive Officer**
Mr G Jeffs
**M** (**Ref:**HM04853)

## COLLEGE-PRACTICAL HOMEOPATHY

**College Of Practical Homeopathy**, 60 Ballards Lane, London, **London (Greater)**, N3 2BY, ENG.
(T) 020 8346 7800 (F) 020 8343 3376
Speciality: Homeopathy.
**M** (**Ref:**HM04854)

## COLLEGE-PRACTICAL HOMEOPATHY

**College Of Practical Homeopathy**, 760 High Rd, London, **London (Greater)**, N12 9QH, ENG.
(T) 07000 777654 (F) 020 8445 3784
(W) www.learnhomeopathy.co.uk
Speciality: Homeopathy. ✔
● **Teacher** Mr R Davidson Q: MHMA.
**C** Yrs. Est.: 15 (**Ref:**HM04855)

## COLLIER & HARVEY

**Jennie Collier & Jenny Harvey**, 8 Clay Hill, Enfield, **London (Greater)**, EN2 9AA, ENG.


Key continued: **Yrs.Est:** Years Established **Q:** Qualifications **M:** Professional Membership ✔ Indemnity Insurance CREDIT Accept Credit Cards

HEALTH MYSELF

# Website

Contact Details

Categories

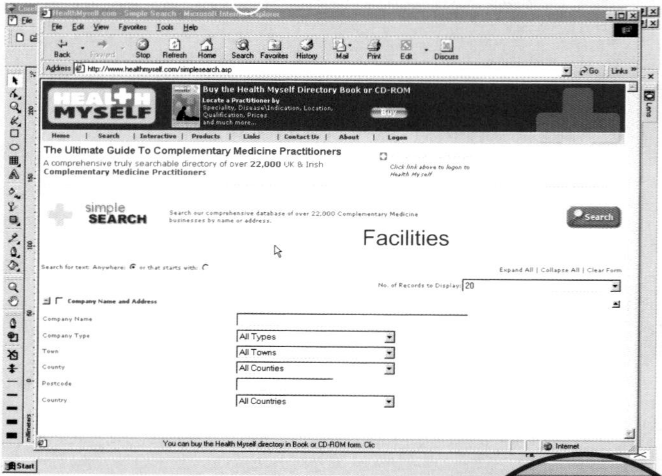


# Even more ways to search...

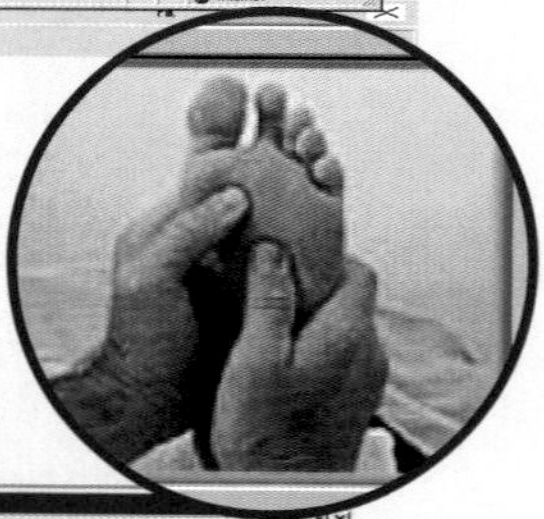

Photos

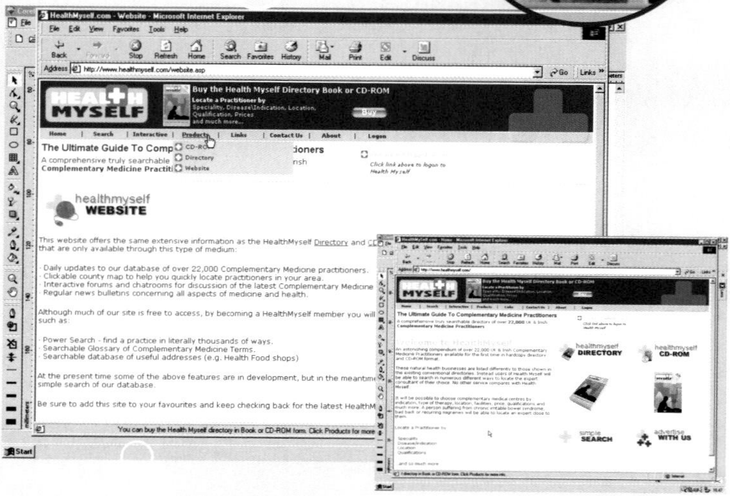


www.healthmyself.com

(T) 020 8366 0470
Speciality: Reflexology.
S T (Ref:HM04856)

## COLLIER, A
**A Collier**, 114 Winter Hay Lane, Horwich, Bolton, **Lancashire**, BL6 7PJ, ENG.
(T) 01204 669557
Speciality: Chiropodists (Podiatrists).
● **Owner** Miss A Collier
S (Ref:HM04857)

## COLLIER, A M
**A M Collier**, 17 Droke Lane, East Dean, Chichester, **Sussex (West)**, PO18 0JH, ENG.
(T) 01243 811473
Speciality: Reflexology.
● **Owner** Mrs A Collier
S T (Ref:HM04858)

## COLLIER, ELAINE M
**Elaine M Collier**, 8 Lawrence Avenue, Simonstone, Burnley, **Lancashire**, BB12 7HX, ENG.
(T) 01282 771837
Speciality: Aromatherapy.
● **Owner** Ms E Collier
M O (Ref:HM04859)

## COLLIGAN, H
**H Colligan**, 60 Front St, Blaydon-on-Tyne, **Tyne and Wear**, NE21 6AE, ENG.
(T) 01914 140802
Speciality: Chiropodists (Podiatrists).
S (Ref:HM04860)

## COLLING, K A
**K A Colling**, 84 Severn Pl, Plymouth, **Devon**, PL3 6JJ, ENG.
(T) 01752 220123
Speciality: Complementary Medicines & Therapy.
C M (Ref:HM04861)

## COLLINGE, IAN
**Ian Collinge**, 9 Langley Park, London, **London (Greater)**, NW7 2AA, ENG.
(T) 020 8959 3388 (F) 020 8959 3388
Speciality: Osteopathy.
● **Owner** Mr I Collinge
P S T (Ref:HM04862)

## COLLINGE, J C
**Mrs J C Collinge**, 55 Bury And Bolton Rd, Radcliffe, Manchester, **Manchester (Greater)**, M26 4LF, ENG.
(T) 01617 648982 (F) 01617 648982
(E) jan.collinge@zen.co.uk
Speciality: Phytotherapy, Ultrasonics. ✔
● **Proprietor** Mrs J Collinge
H M (Ref:HM04863)

## COLLINGS, S
**S Collings**, 3 Old Row Court, Rose St, Wokingham, **Berkshire**, RG40 1XZ, ENG.
(T) 01189 894525
Speciality: Osteopathy.
● **Owner** Mr S Collings
P S T (Ref:HM04864)

## COLLINGS-WELLS, ANNA
**Anna Collings-Wells**, Witheys Yard, High St, Stroud, **Gloucestershire**, GL5 1AP, ENG.
(T) 01453 750796
Speciality: Acupuncture.
O (Ref:HM04865)

## COLLINGWOOD, F J G
**F J G Collingwood**, 19 St Augustines Rd, Canterbury, **Kent**, CT1 1XP, ENG.
(T) 01227 768884
Speciality: Chiropractors.
● **Owner** Dr F Collingwood
P S T (Ref:HM04866)

## COLLINS & ASSOCIATES
**Brian Collins & Associates**, 63 Garrett St, Nuneaton, **Warwickshire**, CV11 4PP, ENG.
(T) 024 7638 7449 (F) 024 7638 7449
Speciality: Osteopathy.
P S T (Ref:HM04867)

## COLLINS, CLARE
**Clare Collins**, 16B Chandos Rd, Bristol, BS6 6PE, ENG.
(T) 01179 739418
Speciality: Chiropodists (Podiatrists).
S (Ref:HM04868)

## COLLINS, D
**D Collins**, 12 Hillcrest Gardens, Burton Joyce, Nottingham, **Nottinghamshire**, NG14 5DE, ENG.
(T) 01159 313853
Speciality: Complementary Medicines & Therapy.
● **Owner** Mrs D Collins
C M (Ref:HM04869)

## COLLINS, J
**J Collins**, 32 Station Rd, Ainsdale, Southport, **Merseyside**, PR8 3HS, ENG.
(T) 01704 578040
Speciality: Chiropodists (Podiatrists).
● **Partner** Mrs J Collins
S (Ref:HM04870)

## COLLINS, JOHN
**John Collins**, 4 Sudbury Rd, Bures, **Suffolk**, CO8 5JW, ENG.
(T) 01787 227142
Speciality: Massage (Therapeutic), Metamorphic Therapy, Reiki, Remedial Massage.
H T (Ref:HM04871)

## COLLINS, M
**M Collins**, Sandy Lane South, Wallington, **Surrey**, SM6 9NR, ENG.
(T) 020 8395 0126 (F) 020 8395 0126
Speciality: Psychology.
B (Ref:HM04872)

## COLLINS, M (DR)
**Dr M Collins**, Harley St, London, **London (Greater)**, W1N 1AA, ENG.
(T) 020 7467 8426
Speciality: Psychology.
● **Principal** Dr M Collins
B (Ref:HM04873)

## COLLINS, MARY
**Mary Collins**, 62-64 Milner Rd, Wirral, **Merseyside**, CH60 5RZ, ENG.
(T) 01513 429665
Speciality: Chiropodists (Podiatrists).
● **Owner** Mrs M Collins
S (Ref:HM04874)

## COLLINS, MARY
**Mary Collins ICNHS (Dip) IIAA**, 104 Oliver Plunkett St, **County Cork**, IRE.
(T) 021 4274 130
Speciality: Complementary Medicines & Therapy.
M (Ref:HM04875)

## COLLINS, MICHAEL
**Michael Collins**, 52 Monastery Gate Ave, Dublin, **County Dublin**, IRE.
(T) 01459 1990
Speciality: Complementary Medicines & Therapy.
M (Ref:HM04876)

## COLLINS, N T
**N T Collins**, 14 Burslem Cl, Walsall, **Midlands (West)**, WS3 3YD, ENG.
(T) 01922 406780
Speciality: Chiropractors.
P S T (Ref:HM04877)

## COLLINS, N T
**N T Collins**, Whittingham Rd, Nottingham, **Nottinghamshire**, NG3 6BL, ENG.
(T) 01159 621548
Speciality: Physiotherapy.
P S T (Ref:HM04878)

## COLLINS, STUART
**Stuart Collins**, 22 Lock Rd, Marlow, **Buckinghamshire**, SL7 1QW, ENG.
(T) 01628 472952
Speciality: Osteopathy.
● **Owner** Mr S Collins
P S T (Ref:HM04879)

## COLLINS, V
**V Collins**, Mowbray Rd, London, **London (Greater)**, NW6 7QS, ENG.
(T) 020 8451 1256 (F) 020 8451 1256
Speciality: Hypnosis.
● **Owner** Ms V Collins
B (Ref:HM04880)

## COLLINS, VERNON
**Vernon Collins**, Raintree, 129 North Rd, Stoke Gifford, Bristol, BS34 8PE, ENG.
(T) 01179 311261
Speciality: Chiropodists (Podiatrists).
● **Owner** Mr V Collins
S (Ref:HM04881)

## COLLINSON, J
**J Collinson**, 35 Cheviot Avenue, Oldham, **Lancashire**, OL8 4HD, ENG.
(T) 01616 203580 (F) 01616 335309
Speciality: Complementary Medicines & Therapy.
● **Owner** Mr J Collinson
C M (Ref:HM04882)

## COLLINSON, J
**J Collinson**, 72 High St, Lees, Oldham, **Lancashire**, OL4 5AA, ENG.
(T) 01616 335309
Speciality: Acupuncture.
O (Ref:HM04883)

## COLLINWOOD, LOUIS
**Louis Collinwood**, 10 Sandbourne Rd, Bournemouth, **Dorset**, BH4 8JH, ENG.
(T) 01202 768508
Speciality: Chiropractic. ✔
● **Owner/Chiropractor**
Dr L Collinwood Q: DC. M: BCA.
P Yrs. Est.: 18 (Ref:HM04884)

## COLLISON, PETER
**Peter Collison**, 174 Kingston Rd, Epsom, **Surrey**, KT19 0SD, ENG.
(T) 020 8394 2971
Speciality: Chiropodists (Podiatrists).
S (Ref:HM04885)

## COLLISON, SUSAN
**Susan Collison**, 143 Parkside Drive, Watford, **Hertfordshire**, WD1 3BA, ENG.
(T) 01923 220993
Speciality: Electrolysis.
● **Owner** Mrs S Collison
T (Ref:HM04886)

## COLLITON WALK PSYCHO SVS
**Colliton Walk Psychotherapy Services**, 1 Colliton Walk, Dorchester, **Dorset**, DT1 1TZ, ENG.
(T) 01305 259212 (F) 01308 898146
Speciality: Psychotherapy.
● **Manager** Ms M Lister
B (Ref:HM04887)

## COLOMBI, F
**F Colombi**, Whimple Wood Cottage, Whimple, Exeter, **Devon**, EX5 2QR, ENG.
(T) 01404 822893
Speciality: Alexander Technique.
P S (Ref:HM04888)

## COLOMBI, FELICITY
**Felicity Colombi**, 122 Alexandria Rd, Sidmouth, **Devon**, EX10 9HG, ENG.
(T) 01395 519101
Speciality: Alexander Technique.
● **Owner** Mrs F Colombi
P S (Ref:HM04889)

## COLONIC IRRIGATION
**Colonic Irrigation**, 15 Chelmsford Village Model Farm Rd, Cork, **County Cork**, IRE.
(T) 021 4872 337
Speciality: Complementary Medicines & Therapy.
M (Ref:HM04890)

## COLONIC IRRIGATION SERVICES
**Colonic Irrigation Services**, 75 Gloucester Rd, London, **London (Greater)**, SW7 4SS, ENG.
(T) 020 7373 7833
Speciality: Complementary Medicines & Therapy.
● **Owner** Mrs J Vervialle
C M (Ref:HM04891)

## COLOUR THERAPY ASSOCIATION
**Colour Therapy Association**, Po Box 16756, London, **London (Greater)**, SW20 8TE, ENG.
(T) 020 8540 3540



Key: B Mind-Body Medicine C Complementary Medicine H Self Help Treatment M Medicinal Therapy O Oriental Medicine P Postural Therapy S Manipulative Structural Therapy T Touch Therapy

Speciality: Complementary Medicines & Therapy.
M (Ref:HM04892)

### COLTMAN, J B

**J B Coltman**, 302 Hipswell Highway, Coventry, **Midlands (West)**, CV2 5FS, **ENG**.
(T) 024 7645 3218
Speciality: Chiropodists (Podiatrists).
S (Ref:HM04893)

### COLUMN OF LIGHT HEALING CENTRE

**Column Of Light Healing Centre**, The Yews, 7 Victoria Rd, Tamworth, **Staffordshire**, B79 7HS, ENG.
(T) 01827 58257 (F) 01827 58257
Speciality: Complementary Medicines & Therapy.
● **Partner** Mrs V Ives
C M (Ref:HM04894)

### COLVILE, RICHARD

**Herbalife Independent Distributor**, Green Acre, Hatchet Green, Hale, Fordingbridge, **Hampshire**, SP6 2NB, **ENG**.
(T) 01725 513452 (F) 01725 511057
(E) dietwell@net
Speciality: Counselling, Herbal Medicine, Nutritional Therapy, Herbal-Skin.
● **Director** Ms D Colvile
● **Managing Director** Mr R Colvile
C Yrs. Est.: 20 (Ref:HM04895)

### COLVIN, P C (DR)

**Dr P C Colvin**, Woodside Osteopathic Clinic, 47A Bancroft, Hitchin, **Hertfordshire**, SG5 1LA, ENG.
(T) 01462 452929
Speciality: Osteopathy.
● **Senior Partner** Mr A El-Sayed
P S T (Ref:HM04896)

### COMER OSTEOPATHIC CLINIC

**Cromer Osteopathic Clinic**, 26 West St, Cromer, **Norfolk**, NR27 9DS, **ENG**.
(T) 01263 514610
Speciality: Manipulation, Naturopathy, Osteopathy. ✓
● **Osteopath** Mr M Warner Q: DO, ND.
P Yrs. Est.: 13 (Ref:HM04897)

### COMERTON, LIZ

**Liz Comerton**, **County Antrim**, BT7, **NIR**.
(T) 028 9064 3630
Speciality: Bach Remedies.
M (Ref:HM04898)

### COMFORT, EMMA

**Emma Comfort**, Crantock, Shelburne Rd, Calne, **Wiltshire**, SN11 8EW, **ENG**.
(T) 01249 811024
Speciality: Aromatherapy.
● **Owner** Ms E Comfort
M O (Ref:HM04899)

### COMFORT, STEVEN V

**Steven V Comfort**, 27 Clanwilliam Rd, Deal, **Kent**, CT14 7BX, **ENG**.
(T) 01304 375658
Speciality: Osteopathy.
● **Owner** Mr S Comfort
P S T (Ref:HM04900)

### COMING UP FOR AIR

**Coming Up For Air**, 8a Market Sq, Witney, **Oxfordshire**, OX8 7BB, **ENG**.
(T) 01993 776787 (F) 01993 779499
Speciality: Relaxation Technique.
● **Owner** Mr U Jariseh
H T (Ref:HM04901)

### COMMANDER, J

**J Commander M Inst Ch P**, 3 Meadow Hill, Purley, **Surrey**, CR8 3HL, **ENG**.
(T) 020 8763 0899
Speciality: Chiropodists (Podiatrists).
● **Owner** Mrs J Commander
S (Ref:HM04902)

### COMMON SCENTS

**Common Scents**, 11 St Annes Rd, Faversham, **Kent**, ME13 8RH, **ENG**.
(T) 01795 536920 (F) 01795 536920
Speciality: Aromatherapy.
● **Owner** Mr C Callaghan
M O (Ref:HM04903)

### COMMONSCENTS

**CommonScents**, 102-103 Queensgate Market Hall, Princess Alexandra Walk, Huddersfield, **Yorkshire (West)**, HD1 2UJ, **ENG**.
(T) 01484 530507
Speciality: Aromatherapy.
● **Owner** Mrs Y Bedford
M O (Ref:HM04904)

### COMMUNICATE

**Communicate**, 7 Grammar School Rd, Warrington, **Cheshire**, WA4 1JN, **ENG**.
(T) 01925 635662
Speciality: Hypnosis.
B (Ref:HM04905)

### COMMUNITY CHIROPRACTIC CLINIC

**Community Chiropractic Clinic**, Bank Court, Manor Rd, Verwood, **Dorset**, BH31 6DW, **ENG**.
(T) 01202 827609 (F) 01202 829413
Speciality: Chiropractic. ✓
● **Chiropractor** Mr J Sharp Q: BSc (Hons), DC, MSc (Chiro).
● **Chiropractor** Miss M Heming Q: BSc (Hons), MSc (Chiro).
P Yrs. Est.: 10 (Ref:HM04906)

### COMMUNITY HEALTH CARE TRUST

**Community Health Care Trust**, Chiropody Dept, Folkestone Health Centre, Dover Rd, Folkestone, **Kent**, CT20 1PG, **ENG**.
(T) 01303 228880 (F) 01303 228888
Speciality: Chiropodists (Podiatrists).
S (Ref:HM04907)

### COMMUNITY PSYCHIATRIC NURSING

**Community Psychiatric Nursing**, Poplar Rd Clinic, 58-64 Poplar Rd, Kings Heath, Birmingham, **Midlands (West)**, B14 7AG, **ENG**.
(T) 01214 411637 (F) 01214 444501
Speciality: Psychiatry.
● **Manager** Mr H Mattis
B (Ref:HM04908)

### COMMUNITY PSYCHIATRIC TEAM

**Community Psychiatric Team**, Blomfield House, Looms Lane, Bury St. Edmunds, **Suffolk**, IP33 1HE, **ENG**.
(T) 01284 775250 (F) 01284 775259
Speciality: Psychiatry.
● **Manager** Mr M Mansfield
B (Ref:HM04909)

### COMMUNITY PSYCHIATRIST NURSING

**Community Psychiatrist Nursing**, Shankhill Health Centre, 135 Shankill Prde, Belfast, **County Antrim**, BT13 1SD, **NIR**.
(T) 028 9024 7181
Speciality: Psychiatry.
B (Ref:HM04910)

### COMP HEALTH & TREATMENT CLNC

**Complementary Health & Treatment Clinic**, 86A Stranmillis Rd, Belfast, **County Antrim**, BT9 5AD, **NIR**.
(T) 028 9080 9888
Speciality: Complementary Medicines & Therapy.
● **Teacher** Mr D White
M (Ref:HM04911)

### COMP HEALTH INITIATIVE

**Complementary Health Initiative**, Tall Trees, Trencrom Lane, Carbis Bay, St. Ives, **Cornwall**, TR26 2TA, **ENG**.
(T) 01736 797711
(E) chi@feenetname.co.uk
Speciality: Absent Healing, Acupuncture, Aromatherapy, Bach Remedies, Chiropractic, Complementary Therapy, Counselling, Crystal Healing, Dowsing, Family Planning (Natural), Family Therapy, Healer, Herbal Medicine, Holistic Healing, Homeopathy, Humanistic Psychology, Hypnotherapy, Indian Head Massage, Kinesiology, Life Style Coaching, Massage (Therapeutic), Meditation, Metamorphic Therapy, Nutritional Therapy, Polarity Therapy, Psychotherapy, Reflexology, Reiki, Shiatsu, Spiritual Healing. ✓
● **Chairperson-C.H.I** Mrs L Lane Q: Reiki Master. M: NFSH.
B Yrs. Est.: 1 (Ref:HM04912)

### COMP MEDI ASS

**Complementary Medical Association**, The Meridian, 142A Greenwich High Rd, London, **London (Greater)**, SE10 8NN, **ENG**.
(T) 01344 360720 (F) 020 8305 9571
Speciality: Acupressure, Acupuncture, Alexander Technique, Aromatherapy, Ayurvedic Medicine, Bach Remedies, Bowen Therapy, Chinese Herbal Medicine, Chiropractic, Complementary Therapy, Cranial Osteopathy, Cranio-Sacral Therapy, Crystal Healing, Feng Shui, Herbal Medicine, Holistic Healing, Hypnosis, Indian Head Massage, Iridology, Kinesiology, Light Therapy, Magnetic Therapy, Massage (Therapeutic), Meditation, Naturopathy, Neuro-Linguistic Program, Nutritional Therapy, Physiotherapy, Phytotherapy, Psychotherapy, Reflexology, Reiki, Remedial Massage, Shiatsu, Spiritual Healing, Stress Therapy, T'ai-Chi Ch'uan, Tui-na, Vitamin Therapy, Yoga, Ba Gua, Butkeyko, Chakra and Aura Healing, Chi Kung, Personal Development, Radionics, The Alexander Barrie System Of Pelvic Correction, Trichology.
C (Ref:HM04913)

### COMP THERAPIES INFORMATION SVS

**Complementary Therapies Information Service**, 21 Richmond Avenue, Handforth, Wilmslow, **Cheshire**, SK9 3JD, **ENG**.
(T) 01625 522613 (F) 01625 522613
Speciality: Complementary Medicines & Therapy.
● **Owner** Mrs C Hardisty
M (Ref:HM04914)

### COMP THERAPY & TRAINING CENTRE

**Complementary Therapy & Training Centre**, 41 Terminus Rd, Eastbourne, **Sussex (East)**, BN21 3QL, **ENG**.
(T) 01323 430025 (F) 01323 648452
(E) andrew@acupuncture-uk.net
(W) www.acupuncture-uk.net
Speciality: Acupressure, Acupuncture, Bowen Therapy, Chiropractic, Counselling, Holistic Healing, Homeopathy, Hypnotherapy, Indian Head Massage, Phytotherapy, Reflexology, Reiki, Shiatsu, Metamorphic Technique, Neuro-Linguistic Programming, Painless Spinal Touch. ✓
● **Therapist** Ms L Dean Q: ITEC. M: GCP.
● **Owner** Mr T Josling
● **Owner** Mrs S Josling Q: RSHom.
● **Therapist** Mr P Burley Q: BTER.
● **Acupuncturist** Mr A Parfitt Q: Lic.Ac, MBAcC. M: BAcC.
C O Yrs. Est.: 8 (Ref:HM04915)

### COMPLEMENTARY CARE

**Complementary Care**, 3 Riverdale Rd, Bexley, **Kent**, DA5 1RD, **ENG**.
(T) 01322 524079 (F) 01322 524079
Speciality: Reflexology.
● **Owner** Mrs S Botwright
S T (Ref:HM04916)

### COMPLEMENTARY CARE CLINIC

**Complementary Care Clinic**, 8 Elwes St, Brigg, **Humberside**, DN20 8LB, **ENG**.
(T) 01652 659300
Speciality: Complementary Medicines & Therapy.
● **Owner** Mr M Barton
M (Ref:HM04917)

### COMPLEMENTARY CLINIC

**Complementary Clinic (The)**, 4 Dragon Rd, Harrogate, **Yorkshire (North)**, HG1 5DF, **ENG**.
(T) 01423 504445
Speciality: Complementary Medicines & Therapy.
● **Owner** Mrs N Gill
C M (Ref:HM04918)

### COMPLEMENTARY HEALING CENTRE

**Complementary Healing Centre**, 4b Heathfield Rd, Kings Heath, Birmingham, **Midlands (West)**, B14 7DB, **ENG**.
(T) 01214 433154 (F) 01214 433154
Speciality: Crystal Healing, Hopi Ear Candles, Indian Head Massage, Massage (Therapeutic), Reflexology, Spiritual Healing, Therapeutic Massage, Clarvoyance, Tarot Card Reading, Hopi



Key continued: **Yrs.Est:** Years Established **Q:** Qualifications **M:** Professional Membership ✓ Indemnity Insurance Accept Credit Cards

Ear Candle Treatment.
● **Owner** Mrs P Mawby
B C Yrs. Est.: 4 (Ref:HM04919)

## COMPLEMENTARY HEALING CENTRE
**Complementary Healing Centre**, 91 Terenure Rd, Nth Dublin 6W, IRE.
(T) 01492 9077
Speciality: Complementary Medicines & Therapy.
C M (Ref:HM04920)

## COMPLEMENTARY HEALTH
**Aylesbury Complementary Health Ltd**, Whitchurch Doctors Surgery, Oving Rd, Whitchurch, **Buckinghamshire**, ENG.
(T) 01296 612930 (F) 01296 612930
(E) nickyward@jasmineholistic.freeserve.co.uk
Speciality: Absent Healing, Aromatherapy, Complementary Therapy, Counselling, Healing Therapy, Holistic Healing, Hypnosis, Hypnotherapy, Indian Head Massage, Massage (Therapeutic), Neuro-Linguistic Program, Psychotherapy, Reiki, Stress Therapy, Hydrotherm, Body Talk. ✔
● **Therapist** Ms N Ward Q: BSc (Hons), ITEC, NLP. M: HA, IPTI, NRHP.
B Yrs. Est.: 2 (Ref:HM04921)

## COMPLEMENTARY HEALTH CENTRE
**Complementary Health Centre**, 9 Combie St, Oban, **Argyll and Bute**, PA34 4HN, SCO.
(T) 01631 567054
Speciality: Aromatherapy, Chiropody, Herbal Medicine, Hypnosis, Hypnotherapy, Massage (Therapeutic), Osteopathy. ✔
● **Chiropodist** Mr N Jones Q: BSc, MBChA, MSSCh. M: SMAE.
● **Aromatherapist** Ms J Todd
● **Remedial Massage Therapist** Ms G Rogers
● **Osteopath** Mrs I Grey M: GOsC.
● **Hypnotherapist** Mr D Canning
● **Remedial Massage Therapist** Ms S Waltham
● **Medical Herbalist** Mr B Cleve Q: BSc.
C Yrs. Est.: 8 (Ref:HM04922)

## COMPLEMENTARY HEALTH CENTRE
**Complementary Health Centre (The)**, Castle Park Rd, Wendover, Aylesbury, **Buckinghamshire**, HP22 6AE, ENG.
(T) 01296 622611 (F) 01296 423488
(E) reflexology@lineone.net
Speciality: Aromatherapy, Bach Remedies, Complementary Therapy, Dietician, Hypnosis, Kinesiology, Massage (Therapeutic), Reflexology, Reiki, Stress Therapy, Hydrotherm, NLP, Body Talk. ✔
● **Complementary Therapist** Ms N Ward Q: BSc (Hons), CHP, CSCT, ITEC, NLP (Master). M: HA, HS, IPTI, ISSD, NRHP.
● **Complementary Therapist** Ms C Watson - Bartlam Q: BFASK, Dip.App.Kin, Dip.ION, MAR. M: AoR.
B C Yrs. Est.: 2 (Ref:HM04923)

## COMPLEMENTARY HEALTH CENTRE
**Complementary Health Centre (The)**, 2a Broad St, Long Eaton, Nottingham, **Nottinghamshire**, NG10 1JH, ENG.
(T) 01158 499449
Speciality: Complementary Medicines & Therapy.
M (Ref:HM04924)

## COMPLEMENTARY HEALTH CENTRE
**Complementary Health Centre (The)**, 35 North Rd, Lerwick, **Shetland Islands**, ZE1 0NT, SCO.
(T) 01595 695225
Speciality: Complementary Medicines & Therapy.
M (Ref:HM04925)

## COMPLEMENTARY HEALTH CLINIC
**Complementary Health Clinic**, Downham Market, **Norfolk**, PE38 9JU, ENG.
(T) 01366 383840 (F) 01366 383840
Speciality: Acupuncture, Aromatherapy, Cranial Osteopathy, Hypnotherapy, Massage (Therapeutic), Osteopathy, Reflexology. ✔
● **Chiropodist** Mrs K Bays Q: MBChA, MSSCh. M: B.A.Ch.P.
● **Homeopath** Mr J Foulkes Q: MCPH.
● **Acupuncturist** Ms K Stewart Q: Dip.Ac, MBAcC.
● **Osteopath** Dr N Watson Q: Ch.B, MB, MLCOM, MRO. M: GOsC.
S Yrs. Est.: 10 (Ref:HM04926)

## COMPLEMENTARY HEALTH CLINIC
**Complementary Health Clinic**, 24 West Park St, Chatteris, **Cambridgeshire**, PE16 6AL, ENG.
(T) 01354 694050 (F) 01354 694050
Speciality: Acupuncture, Aromatherapy, Cranial Osteopathy, Hypnotherapy, Massage (Therapeutic), Osteopathy, Reflexology. ✔
● **Osteopath** Dr N Watson M: GOsC.
● **Chiropodist** Mrs K Bays Q: MBChA, MSSCh.
S Yrs. Est.: 10 (Ref:HM04927)

## COMPLEMENTARY HEALTH PART
**Complementary Health Partnership**, 5-6 Sydney Trce, The Green, Claygate, Esher, **Surrey**, KT10 0JJ, ENG.
(T) 01372 464659
Speciality: Complementary Medicines & Therapy.
● **Partner** Mr P Sullivan
C M (Ref:HM04928)

## COMPLEMENTARY HEALTH SERVICES
**Complementary Health Services**, 219 Stamford Rd, Lees, Oldham, **Lancashire**, OL4 3NJ, ENG.
(T) 01616 781824
Speciality: Chiropractic, Homeopathy, Manipulation, Massage (Therapeutic). ✔
● **Chiropractor** Ms L Mills Q: BA, DC. M: GCC.
S Yrs. Est.: 10 (Ref:HM04929)

## COMPLEMENTARY HEALTH STUDIO
**Complementary Healthcare Studio**, 11 St Alphonsus Villas, Dundalk, **County Louth**, IRE.
(T) 04293 39779
Speciality: Complementary Medicines & Therapy.
M (Ref:HM04930)

## COMPLEMENTARY HEALTH SUITE
**Complementary Health Suite (The)**, 5 Victoria Embankment, Nottingham, **Nottinghamshire**, NG2 2JY, ENG.
(T) 01159 864745
Speciality: Acupuncture.
O (Ref:HM04931)

## COMPLEMENTARY HEALTHCARE
**Complementary Healthcare**, 15 Bedford St, Carrhall, Barrowford, Nelson, **Lancashire**, BB9 6DA, ENG.
(T) 01282 611505
Speciality: Complementary Medicines & Therapy.
● **Owner** Mr A Abbott
C M (Ref:HM04932)

## COMPLEMENTARY MEDICAL CENTRE
**Complementary Medical Centre**, 1 Cranmore Park, Belfast, **County Antrim**, BT9 6JF, NIR.
(T) 028 9066 2942
Speciality: Homeopathy.
M (Ref:HM04933)

## COMPLEMENTARY MEDICINE CENTRE
**Complementary Medicine Centre**, Manor House Surgery, Manor St, Glossop, **Derbyshire**, SK13 8PS, ENG.
(T) 01457 860860
Speciality: Alexander Technique.
● **Therapist** Mr P Grundy-White
P S (Ref:HM04934)

## COMPLEMENTARY MEDICINE CENTRE
**Complementary Medicine Centre**, 24 St Stephens Rd, Norwich, **Norfolk**, NR1 3QU, ENG.
(T) 01603 614914
Speciality: Complementary Medicines & Therapy.
C M (Ref:HM04935)

## COMPLEMENTARY MEDICINE CENTRE
**Complementary Medicine Centre**, 4 Market St, Musselburgh, **Lothian (Mid)**, EH21 6PT, SCO.
(T) 01316 651441 (F) 01316 651441
Speciality: Homeopathy.
● **Owner** Mrs S Eeles
M (Ref:HM04936)

## COMPLEMENTARY MEDICINE CENTRE
**Complementary Medicine Centre**, 20 Coppice Walk, Shirley, Solihull, **Midlands (West)**, B90 4HY, ENG.
(T) 01564 702186
Speciality: Acupuncture, Aromatherapy, Auto Suggestion, Aversion Therapy, Healer, Herbal Medicine, Homeopathy.
● **Partner** Mrs J Spence
C (Ref:HM04937)

## COMPLEMENTARY MEDICINE CLINIC
**Complementary Medicine Clinic**, 21 Shirlea View, Battle, **Sussex (East)**, TN33 0UU, ENG.
(T) 01424 775332
Speciality: Complementary Medicines & Therapy.
● **Owner** Mrs A Horton
C M (Ref:HM04938)

## COMPLEMENTARY MEDICINE SERVICE
**Complementary Medicine Service**, Mitcheldean Surgery, Mitcheldean, **Gloucestershire**, GL17 0AU, ENG.
(T) 01594 544566
Speciality: Osteopathy.
P S T (Ref:HM04939)

## COMPLEMENTARY THERAPIES
**Complementary Therapies In Loose**, 18 Copper Tree Court, Maidstone, **Kent**, ME15 9RW, ENG.
(T) 01622 747125
Speciality: Aromatherapy.
M O (Ref:HM04940)

## COMPLEMENTARY THERAPIES
**Complementary Therapies**, 43 Overton Lane, Hammerwich, **Staffordshire**, WS7 0LQ, ENG.
(T) 01543 672108
Speciality: Hopi Ear Candles, Indian Head Massage, Reflexology.
S T (Ref:HM04941)

## COMPLEMENTARY THERAPIES CON
**Complementary Therapies Consultancy**, 12 Rudyard Gr, Sale, **Cheshire**, M33 4RR, ENG.
(T) 01619 735248
Speciality: Complementary Medicines & Therapy.
● **Owner** Mr P Morris
C M (Ref:HM04952)

## COMPLEMENTARY THERAPY
**Complementary Therapy**, Newbridge Surgery, 129 Newbridge Hill, Bath, **Somerset**, BA1 3PT, ENG.
(T) 01225 475508
(E) ddawson@appleanline.net
Speciality: Acupuncture, Clinical Ecology, Homeopathy. ✔
● **Homeopath** Dr D Dawson Q: Ch.B, MB.
C M Yrs. Est.: 7 (Ref:HM04942)

## COMPLEMENTARY THERAPY CENTRE
**Complementary Therapy Centre**, Warstone Tower, 1 Bromford Drive, Birmingham, **Midlands (West)**, B36 8TU, ENG.
(T) 01216 858858
Speciality: Complementary Medicines & Therapy, Spineologist. ✔
● **Owner/Spineologist** Mr M Glenn Q: DSc, IIHFT. M: IIHFT.
C Yrs. Est.: 4 (Ref:HM04943)

## COMPLEMENTARY THERAPY CENTRE
**Complementary Therapy Centre**, 43 Preston New Rd, Blackburn, **Lancashire**, BB2 6AE, ENG.
(T) 01254 698558
Speciality: Hypnosis.
● **Owner** Mr P Jackson
B (Ref:HM04944)

## COMPLEMENTARY THERAPY CENTRE
**Complementary Therapy Centre**, 33 Peterson Rd, Wakefield, **Yorkshire (West)**, WF1 4DU, ENG.
(T) 01924 298238
Speciality: Complementary Medicines & Therapy.



Key: B Mind-Body Medicine C Complementary Medicine H Self Help Treatment M Medicinal Therapy O Oriental Medicine P Postural Therapy S Manipulative Structural Therapy T Touch Therapy

● **Chief Executive** Mr A Barlow
C M (Ref:HM04945)

## COMPLEMENTARY THERAPY CENTRE
**Complementary Therapy Centre**, 115 Victoria Rd, Maplethorpe, Lincoln, **Lincolnshire**, LN12 2AL, ENG.
(T) 01507 478183
(E) therapies@kirp.demon.co.uk
Speciality: Absent Healing, Acupressure, Bowen Therapy, Complementary Therapy, Hypnosis, Hypnotherapy, Indian Head Massage, Meditation, Music Therapy, Reiki, Seichem, Stress Therapy, Tera-Mai. ✓
● **Bowen Therapist** Mr G Kirkup Q: BTER. M: ALTT, BTER, UKGHE.
● **Therapist** Ms S Kirkup Q: BTER. M: ALTT, BTER, UKGHE.
B Yrs. Est.: 3 (Ref:HM04946)

## COMPLEMENTARY THERAPY CENTRE
**Complementary Therapy Centre**, 113 High St, Coleshill, Birmingham, **Midlands (West)**, ENG.
(T) 01675 466166
Speciality: Osteopathy, Sports Massage, Spineologist. ✓
● **Spineologist** Mr M Glenn Q: IIHFT. M: IIHFT.
C Yrs. Est.: 4 (Ref:HM04947)

## COMPLEMENTARY THERAPY CLINIC
**Complementary Therapy Clinic**, 141 Balby Rd, Doncaster, **Yorkshire (South)**, DN4 0RG, ENG.
(T) 01302 859109
Speciality: Complementary Medicines & Therapy.
● **Owner** Mrs J Lockwood
C M (Ref:HM04948)

## COMPLEMENTARY THERAPY CLINIC
**Complementary Therapy Clinic**, 179 Commercial St, Kirkcaldy, **Fife**, KY1 2NS, SCO.
(T) 01592 641014
Speciality: Absent Healing, Aromatherapy, Bowen Therapy, Cognitive Therapy, Complementary Therapy, Counselling, Electrotherapy, Group Therapy, Psychotherapy, Reiki, Stress Therapy, T'ai-Chi Ch'uan, Touch Therapy, Transactional Analysis, Vitamin Therapy, Electro Point Stimulation, Back Swing Therapy. ✓
● **Complementary Therapist** Mr R Ross M: BTER, IPTI.
● **Hearing Aid Dispenser** Ms C Deplacido Q: MSc. M: BAAT, BSA.
● **Counsellor** Mr G Davidson Q: Dip.Couns. M: BACP.
T Yrs. Est.: 3 (Ref:HM04949)

## COMPLEMENTARY TOUCH
**Complementary Touch**, Court Lane, Newent, **Gloucestershire**, GL18 1AR, ENG.
(T) 01531 822772
(E) marie@netscapeonline.co.uk
Speciality: Acupuncture, Chiropractic, Counselling, Holistic Healing, Homeopathy, McTimoney Chiropractic, Reflexology. ✓
● **Counsellor** Mrs J David Q: B.Ac, UKRC. M: BACP.
C Yrs. Est.: 3 (Ref:HM04950)

## COMPLEMENTARY TREATMENT CENTRE
**Complementary Treatment Centre (The)**, 48 Durham Avenue, Plymouth, **Devon**, PL4 8SP, ENG.
(T) 01752 229481 (F) 01752 229538
Speciality: Aromatherapy.
● **Owner** Mrs S Privett
M O (Ref:HM04951)

## COMPLEMENTS
**Complements**, 6 Market Sq, Stafford, **Staffordshire**, ST16 2JN, ENG.
(T) 01785 258647
Speciality: Complementary Medicines & Therapy.
● **Owner** Mrs F Scott
C M (Ref:HM04953)

## COMPLEMENTS HOLISTIC THERAPIES
**Complements Holistic Therapies**, 11 Watson Trce, Irvine, **Ayrshire (North)**, KA12 0JA, SCO.
(T) 01294 273010
Speciality: Hypnotherapy.
B (Ref:HM04954)

## COMPLETE ANGEL HEALING CENTRE
**Complete Angel Healing Centre**, 30 Glenbrook Walk, Fareham, **Hampshire**, PO14 3AH, ENG.
(T) 01329 311229
Speciality: Aromatherapy, Indian Head Massage, Reflexology, Reiki, Metaphysical Teaching and Personal Life Coaching. ✓
● **Receptionist** Ms R Horswell Q: IIHHT. M: FHT.
C Yrs. Est.: 8 (Ref:HM04955)

## COMPLETE CARE CLINICAL AROMA
**Complete Care Clinical Aromatherapy**, 72 Birmingham Rd, Bromsgrove, **Worcestershire**, B61 0DD, ENG.
(T) 01527 878267
Speciality: Aromatherapy.
M O (Ref:HM04956)

## COMPLETE CHIROPRACTIC
**Complete Chiropractic**, Suite 2, 88 Broomfield Rd, Chelmsford, **Essex**, CM1 1SS, ENG.
(T) 01245 358742 (F) 01245 345657
Speciality: Chiropractic. ✓
● **Chiropractor** Dr T Kelly Q: DC. M: GCC.
● **Owner** Dr K Murray Q: BSc, DC. M: GCC.
P Yrs. Est.: 2 (Ref:HM04957)

## COMPLETE HEALTH CARE
**Complete Health Care Ltd**, 160 City Rd, London, **London (Greater)**, EC1V 2NP, ENG.
(T) 020 7336 0466 (F) 020 7336 8073
(W) www.completehealthcare.co.uk
Speciality: Acupressure, Acupuncture, Alexander Technique, Aromatherapy, Bach Remedies, Biofeedback, Chinese Herbal Medicine, Complementary Therapy, Counselling, Cranial Osteopathy, Healer, Healing Therapy, Holistic Healing, Homeopathy, Hypnotherapy, Manipulation, Manual Lymph Drainage, Massage (Therapeutic), Metamorphic Therapy, Nutritional Therapy, Osteopathy, Pilates, Psychotherapy, Reflexology, Reiki, Shiatsu, Sports Massage, Stress Therapy, Swedish Body Massage, Personal Training, Detox Programs, Beauty Treatments, Life Style Coaching, Past Life Therapy. ✓ [credit cards]
● **Director** How Griffiths Q: MBAcC. M: BAcC.
● **Aromatherapist** Ms C Stiling Q: ITEC.
● **Osteopath** Alex Milledge
● **Chinese Medicine Practitioner** Ms S Horrocks M: BAcC.
C Yrs. Est.: 5 (Ref:HM04958)

## COMPLEXIONS BEAUTY THERAPY
**Complexions Beauty Therapy**, High St, Newton Poppleford, Sidmouth, **Devon**, EX10 0DW, ENG.
(T) 01395 567894
Speciality: Complementary Medicines & Therapy.
● **Owner** Mrs A Earp
M (Ref:HM04959)

## COMPLIMENTARY HEALTH CLINIC
**Complimentary Health Clinic**, Newtown, Bantry, **County Cork**, IRE.
(T) 027 5202 0
Speciality: Complementary Medicines & Therapy.
M (Ref:HM04960)

## COMPTON HOMOEOPATHY CENTRE
**Compton Homoeopathy Centre (The)**, The Cloisters, Down Lane, Compton, Guildford, **Surrey**, GU3 1DQ, ENG.
(T) 01483 811060
Speciality: Homeopathy.
M (Ref:HM04961)

## COMP-U-CLIC
**Comp-U-Clic**, 268 Penn Rd, Wolverhampton, **Midlands (West)**, WV4 4AD, ENG.
(T) 01902 654488
Speciality: Complementary Medicines & Therapy.
M (Ref:HM04962)

## CONBA, THOMAS J
**Thomas J Conba**, 20 Drumcree Ct Kildare Town, **County Kildare**, IRE.
(T) 04552 2292
Speciality: Complementary Medicines & Therapy.
M (Ref:HM04963)

## CONBOYE, M CLARE
**M Clare Conboye**, Ryde House Clinic, 15 Morrab Rd, Penzance, **Cornwall**, TR18 4EZ, ENG.
(T) 01736 364603
Speciality: Osteopathy.
● **Owner** Ms M Conboye
P S T (Ref:HM04964)

## CONCANNON, DEIRDRE
**Deirdre Concannon**, 86 Fishers Lane, Wirral, **Merseyside**, CH61 5XG, ENG.
(T) 01516 487236
Speciality: Bach Remedies, Chiropractic, Herbal Medicine. ✓
● **Owner** Mrs D Concannon Q: BSc, DC.
P Yrs. Est.: 9 (Ref:HM04965)

## CONCANNON, MAUREEN (DR)
**Dr Maureen Concannon**, 96 St Stephens Gn, Dublin, **County Dublin**, IRE.
(T) 01475 1710
Speciality: Counselling.
B H (Ref:HM04966)

## CONCANNON, MAUREEN (DR)
**Dr Maureen Concannon Reg Psychol**, 96 St Stephens Gn, IRE.
(T) 01475 1710
Speciality: Psychotherapy.
B (Ref:HM04967)

## CONCANON, A
**A Concanon**, Lynchmere End, Linchmere Ridge, Haslemere, **Surrey**, GU27 3PS, ENG.
(T) 01428 651181
Speciality: Chiropodists (Podiatrists).
S (Ref:HM04968)

## CONCANON, ANNABELL
**Annabell Concanon**, 14 Marten Rd, London, **London (Greater)**, E17 4NN, ENG.
(T) 020 8531 7714
Speciality: Chiropodists (Podiatrists).
S (Ref:HM04969)

## CONCEPTS PHYSIO & NUTRITION
**Concepts Physiotherapy & Nutrition Clinic**, 9 Charleston Rd, Motcombe, Eastbourne, **Sussex (East)**, BN21 1SE, ENG.
(T) 01323 410084 (F) 01323 410084
(E) kevinicollins@yahoo.com
(W) www.i-concepts.co.uk
Speciality: Absent Healing, Acupressure, Acupuncture, Alexander Technique, Anthroposohical Medicine, Aromatherapy, Art Therapy, Complementary Therapy, Counselling, Electrolipolysis, Electrotherapy, Hay Diet, Homeopathy, Kinesiology, Life Style Coaching, Manipulation, Massage (Therapeutic), Naturopathy, Nutritional Therapy, Physiotherapy, Polarity Therapy, Reflexology, Reiki, Seichem, Stress Therapy, Touch Therapy, Ultrasonics, Vitamin Therapy, Post natal rehabilitation, weight loss, obstetric tens hire. ✓
● **Partner** Mrs L Wynn Q: Dip.Nut.Th, Grad Dip Phys. M: CMA, CSP.
H Yrs. Est.: 5 (Ref:HM04970)

## CONCORDA HEALTH-SPORTS THERAPY
**Concorda Natural Health & Sports Therapy**, 32 York Rd, Marlow, **Buckinghamshire**, SL7 2QB, ENG.
(T) 01628 472420
Speciality: Complementary Medicines & Therapy.
● **Owner** Ms P Douglas-Barton
C M (Ref:HM04971)

## CONDUIT, E
**E Conduit**, 68 Worcester St, Stourbridge, **Midlands (West)**, DY8 1AY, ENG.
(T) 01384 390044
Speciality: Psychology.
B (Ref:HM04972)

## CONFEDERATION OF HEALING ORG
**Confederation Of Healing Organisations**, 113 High St, Berkhamsted, **Hertfordshire**, HP4 2DJ, ENG.


Key continued: Yrs.Est: Years Established Q: Qualifications M: Professional Membership ✓ Indemnity Insurance [card] Accept Credit Cards

(T) 01442 870667
Speciality: Complementary Medicines & Therapy.
● **Chairman** Mr J Repard
**M** (Ref:HM04973)

## CONFIDENTIAL COUNSELLING

**Confidential Counselling**, 10 Corbawn Ct, Shankill, **County Dublin**, IRE.
(T) 01282 1817
Speciality: Counselling.
**B** **H** (Ref:HM04974)

## CONFIDENTIAL COUNSELLING SVS

**Confidential Counselling Services**, 51 Grove Way, Esher, **Surrey**, KT10 8HQ, ENG.
(T) 020 8398 5013
Speciality: Counselling, Trains trauma therapy, Trauma counsellor of natural disasters. ✔
● **Owner/Trauma Counsellor**
Judy Aitkens Q: DipCH.P, MAHPP, UKRC.
M: AHPP, UKRC.
**S** Yrs. Est.: 10 (Ref:HM04975)

## CONFIDENTIAL COUNSELLING SVS

**Confidential Counselling Services**, 9 Summerville Pk, Rathmines, **County Dublin**, IRE.
(T) 08682 37230
Speciality: Counselling.
**B** **H** (Ref:HM04976)

## CONGLETON COUNSELLING PRACTICE

**Congleton Counselling Practice**, 16 Kestrel Cl, Congleton, **Cheshire**, CW12 3FA, ENG.
(T) 01260 279924
(E) counselling@bbharrison.freeserve.co.uk
(W) www.congletoncounsellingpractice.co.uk
Speciality: Cognitive Therapy, Counselling, Life Style Coaching, Psychotherapy, Rogerian Therapy, Stress Therapy.
● **Counsellor/Psychotherapist**
Ms B Harrison Q: Cert.Couns, Cert.Couns.Groupwork, Dip.Couns. M: BACP.
**C** (Ref:HM04977)

## CONGLETON HOMEOPATHIC PRACTICE

**Congleton Homeopathic Practice**, 3 High St, Congleton, **Cheshire**, CW12 1BN, ENG.
(T) 01260 273804
Speciality: Homeopathy.
**M** (Ref:HM04978)

## CONISBROUGH CENTRE

**Conisbrough Centre For Natural Healing (The)**, 74 Elm Green Lane, Conisbrough, Doncaster, **Yorkshire (South)**, DN12 3HS, ENG.
(T) 01709 858697
Speciality: Complementary Medicines & Therapy.
● **Owner** Mrs K Burnage
**M** (Ref:HM04979)

## CONISTON PHYSIOTHERAPY CLINIC

**Seraphia**, 42 Coniston Rd, Kings Langley, **Hertfordshire**, WD4 8BU, ENG.
(T) 07956 569115 (F) 01923 269947
(E) rstevens@seraphia.co.uk
(W) www.seraphia.co.uk
Speciality: Acupuncture, Aura Therapy, Chiropractic, Complementary Therapy, Cranial Osteopathy, Crystal Healing, Electrotherapy, Holistic Healing, Life Style Coaching, Manipulation, Osteopathy, Spiritual Healing, Stress Therapy, Ultrasonics, Vitamin Therapy.
✔
● **Practice Principal** Mr R Stevens Q: FCO, MCSP, SRP. M: CSP.
**S** Yrs. Est.: 10 (Ref:HM04980)

## CONLAN, HEATHER

**Heather Conlan**, 20 St. Petersburgh Pl, London, **London (Greater)**, W2 4LB, ENG.
(T) 07798 844301
Speciality: Reflexology.
● **Owner** Mrs H Conlan
**S** **T** (Ref:HM04981)

## CONLIFFE, LOUISE

**Louise Cunliffe L C Hom**, Manor Cottage, 10 Cedar St, Braunston-In-Rutland, Oakham, **Leicestershire**, LE15 8QS, ENG.
(T) 01572 770220
Speciality: Aromatherapy, Complementary Therapy, Homeopathy, Massage (Therapeutic), Miasm Therapy, Reflexology. ✔
● **Owner** Ms L Cunliffe M: LCH.
**M** Yrs. Est.: 9 (Ref:HM04982)

## CONLIN, TOM

**Tom Conlin**, Eltham Health Clinic, 93 Eltham Hill, London, **London (Greater)**, SE9 5EA, ENG.
(T) 020 8294 1113
Speciality: Chiropodists (Podiatrists).
**S** (Ref:HM04983)

## CONN, RONALD & SHALINI

**Ronald & Shalini Conn**, 15 Broomfield Avenue, London, **London (Greater)**, N13 4JT, ENG.
(T) 020 8882 6425
Speciality: Hypnosis.
**B** (Ref:HM04984)

## CONNAUGHT PRACTICE

**Connaught Practice (The)**, 1a Connaught Rd, London, **London (Greater)**, E11 4AB, ENG.
(T) 020 8539 9830
Speciality: Hypnosis.
● **Owner** Mr S Harold
**B** (Ref:HM04985)

## CONNAUGHT SQUARE HYPNOTHERAPY

**Thames Lectures Ltd**, 15 Connaught Sq, London, **London (Greater)**, W2 2HG, ENG.
(T) 020 8946 0320 (F) 020 8262 1237
(E) ursulajames@mindbody.org.uk
(W) www.stopsmokingatonce.co.uk
Speciality: Hypnotherapy, Life Style Coaching.
✔
● **Owner** Ursula James Q: BSCH. M: BSCH.
**B** Yrs. Est.: 7 (Ref:HM04986)

## CONNAWOOD AROMATHERAPY CENTRE

**Connawood Aromatherapy Centre**, 5 Connawood Lawn Old Connaught, Bray, **County Wicklow**, IRE.
(T) 01272 0013
Speciality: Aromatherapy.
**M** **O** (Ref:HM04987)

## CONNECT ASSOCIATES

**Connect Assocs**, Lonsdale Hse, Avoca Ave, Blackrock, **County Dublin**, IRE.
(T) 01288 4155
Speciality: Counselling.
**B** **H** (Ref:HM04988)

## CONNECT PHYSICAL HEALTH CTRE

**Connect Physical Health Centres Ltd**, Head Office, 2 Ivy Rd, Gosforth, Newcastle Upon Tyne, **Tyne and Wear**, NE3 1DB, ENG.
(T) 01912 135116 (F) 01912 135117
Speciality: Acupuncture, Aromatherapy, Biofeedback, Chiropody, Complementary Therapy, Dietician, Electrotherapy, Homeopathy, Indian Head Massage, Manipulation, Massage (Therapeutic), Nutritional Therapy, Physiotherapy, Pilates, Podiatry, Postural Integration, Reflexology.
✔
**S** Yrs. Est.: 10 (Ref:HM04989)

## CONNECT THERAPEUTIC COMMUNITY

**Connect Therapeutic Community Ltd**, 19 Park Rd, Moseley, Birmingham, **Midlands (West)**, B13 8AB, ENG.
(T) 01214 492204 (F) 01214 496124
Speciality: Psychotherapy.
● **Partner** Ms J Robinson
**B** (Ref:HM04990)

## CONNELLY, CHRISTINA

**Christina Connelly**, Ranelagh, **County Dublin**, IRE.
(T) 08726 75602
Speciality: Complementary Medicines & Therapy.
**M** (Ref:HM04991)

## CONNELLY, G M

**G M Connelly**, 20A Station Rd, Birchington, **Kent**, CT7 9DQ, ENG.
(T) 01843 848292
Speciality: Chiropodists (Podiatrists).
● **Partner** Mrs G Connelly
**S** (Ref:HM04992)

## CONNER, CAROL

**Carol Conner**, 27 Plane Tree Way, Woodstock, **Oxfordshire**, OX20 1PE, ENG.
(T) 01993 811120
Speciality: Chiropractic.
**P** **S** **T** (Ref:HM04993)

## CONNER, MATTHEW

**Chiropractic Association Of Ireland Dr Matthew Conner B Sc (CHIRO)D C**, Skibbereen Chiropractic Clinic, 49b Townshend St, Skibbereen, IRE.
(T) 028 2312 9
Speciality: Chiropractors.
**P** **S** **T** (Ref:HM04994)

## CONNER, MATTHEW (DR)

**Dr Matthew Conner D C**, The Sq, Bantry Co, **County Cork**, IRE.
(T) 027 5279 0
Speciality: Chiropractors.
**P** **S** **T** (Ref:HM04995)

## CONNERY, PAUL

**Paul Connery**, 41 Eastern Avenue, Reading, **Berkshire**, RG1 5RX, ENG.
(T) 01189 267438
Speciality: Chiropractors.
● **Senior Partner** Mr S Carpenter
**P** **S** **T** (Ref:HM04996)

## CONNEXIONS

**Connexions**, 64 Manor Drive, London, **London (Greater)**, N20 0DU, ENG.
(T) 020 8361 3740 (F) 020 8368 7878
Speciality: Psychotherapy.
● **Owner** Mrs G Simmons
**B** (Ref:HM04997)

## CONNOLLY COUNSELLING

**Connolly Counselling**, 38 Neville Rd, Bognor Regis, **Sussex (West)**, PO22 8BJ, ENG.
(T) 01243 827411
Speciality: Psychotherapy.
● **Owner** Mrs L Connolly
**B** (Ref:HM04998)

## CONNOLLY, JOHN (DR)

**Dr John A Connolly PH D**, 24 Dornden Pk, Booterstown, Dublin, **County Dublin**, IRE.
(T) 01269 7830
Speciality: Complementary Medicines & Therapy.
**M** (Ref:HM04999)

## CONNOLLY, MARTINA

**Martina Connolly**, Berkana Lisnalurg, **County Sligo**, IRE.
(T) 07171 734
Speciality: Aromatherapy.
**M** **O** (Ref:HM05000)

## CONNOLLY, MICHAEL

**Michael Connolly**, 27 Johns Hill, **County Waterford**, IRE.
(T) 08761 13232
Speciality: Complementary Medicines & Therapy.
**M** (Ref:HM05001)

## CONNOLLY, SANDRA

**Sandra Connolly**, 26 Edward Rd, Great Sankey, Warrington, **Cheshire**, WA5 3LT, ENG.
(T) 01925 487873
Speciality: Reflexology.
**S** **T** (Ref:HM05002)

## CONNOR, JEANETTE

**Jeanette Connor**, 30 Delmer, Enfield, **County Meath**, IRE.
(T) 08682 07530
Speciality: Complementary Medicines & Therapy.
**M** (Ref:HM05003)

## CONNOR, L K J

**L K J Connor**, 2 Sewardstone Rd, Waltham Abbey, **Essex**, EN9 1NA, ENG.
(T) 01992 715804
Speciality: Physiotherapy.
**P** **S** **T** (Ref:HM05004)

## CONRAD, H

**H Conrad**, Heathfield, Market St, Ruthin, **Denbighshire**, LL15 1BE, WAL.
(T) 01824 705574
Speciality: Chiropodists (Podiatrists).

Key: **B** Mind-Body Medicine **C** Complementary Medicine **H** Self Help Treatment **M** Medicinal Therapy **O** Oriental Medicine **P** Postural Therapy **S** Manipulative Structural Therapy **T** Touch Therapy

● **Owner** Miss H Conrad
S (**Ref:**HM05005)

**CONRAN, JAN**

**Jan Conran**, 63 Chalk Farm Rd, Stokenchurch, High Wycombe, **Buckinghamshire**, HP14 3TB, ENG.
(T) 01494 483034
Speciality: Reflexology.
S T (**Ref:**HM05006)

**CONROY, CHRISTINE**

**Osteopathic Practice**, Canolfan Harmdden Bro Ddyfi, Machynlleth, **Powys**, SY20 9TQ, WAL.
(T) 01654 703076 (F) 01654 703013
Speciality: Absent Healing, Cranial Osteopathy, Healer, Osteopathy.
● **Osteopath** Ms C Conroy Q: DO (Hons), MSc. M: GOsC.
C (**Ref:**HM05007)

**CONROY, GILLIAN**

**Gillian Conroy**, 32 Churchfield Rd, Liverpool, **Merseyside**, L25 3SF, ENG.
(T) 01514 879564
Speciality: Reflexology.
S T (**Ref:**HM05008)

**CONSETT PHYSIOTHERAPY**

**Consett Physiotherapy**, 43A Albert Rd, Consett, **County Durham**, DH8 5QU, ENG.
(T) 01207 582222
Speciality: Physiotherapy.
P S T (**Ref:**HM05009)

**CONSTABLE, JOY**

**Joy Constable**, Ty Cum, Pandy, Glyn Ceiriog, Llangollen, **Denbighshire**, LL20 7PD, WAL.
(T) 01691 718698
Speciality: Reflexology.
S T (**Ref:**HM05010)

**CONSTABLE, R N**

**R N Constable**, Green Gables, Willow Gr, Fair Oak, Eastleigh, **Hampshire**, SO50 7BJ, ENG.
(T) 023 8069 2421
Speciality: Chiropodists (Podiatrists).
S (**Ref:**HM05011)

**CONSTANTINE, J C**

**J C Constantine DO**, 5 Walnut Lane, Hartford, Northwich, **Cheshire**, CW8 1QN, ENG.
(T) 01606 74746 (F) 01606 74746
(E) john@jcdo.co.uk
Speciality: Cranial Osteopathy, Osteopathy. ✓
● **Osteopath** Mr J Constantine Q: DO. M: GOsC.
S Yrs. Est.: 34 (**Ref:**HM05012)

**CONSTANTINE, V**

**V Constantine**, 41 Durdham Park, Bristol, BS6 6XE, ENG.
(T) 01179 466626
Speciality: Reflexology.
● **Owner** Mrs V Constantine
S T (**Ref:**HM05013)

**CONSULTANT CLINICAL PSYCH**

**Consultant Clinical Psychologist**, 121 Harley St, London, **London (Greater)**, W1N 1DH, ENG.
(T) 020 7224 0639
Speciality: Psychotherapy.
B (**Ref:**HM05014)

**CONSULTANT CLINICAL PSYCH**

**Consultant Clinical Psychologist**, 90 Grove End Gdns, London, **London (Greater)**, NW8 9LP, ENG.
(T) 020 7286 3126 (F) 020 7286 2126
Speciality: Psychology.
● **Owner** Dr V Mouratoglou
B (**Ref:**HM05015)

**CONSULTANT HYP ANALYST**

**Consultant Hypnotherapist Analyst**, 21A Forrester Park Drive, Edinburgh, **Edinburgh (City of)**, EH12 9AT, SCO.
(T) 01313 349784
Speciality: Hypnosis.
B (**Ref:**HM05016)

**CONSULTANT, NUTRITION**

**Nutrition Consultant**, 25A Broad St, Blaenavn, Pontypool, **Monmouthshire**, NP4 9NE, WAL.
(T) 01495 790170
Speciality: Complementary Medicines & Therapy.
C M (**Ref:**HM05017)

**CONTENT, A J**

**A J Content**, 33 Church Rd, London, **London (Greater)**, SW13 9HQ, ENG.
(T) 020 8748 3229
Speciality: Alexander Technique.
● **Owner** Mrs A Content
P S (**Ref:**HM05018)

**CONTINENTAL CRAFTS**

**Continental Crafts**, 40 Bolton St, Dublin, **County Dublin**, IRE.
(T) 01872 6915
Speciality: Complementary Medicines & Therapy.
M (**Ref:**HM05019)

**CONTINENTAL SKIN CLINIC**

**Continental Skin Clinic**, 6a Nelson St, Swansea, SA1 3QE, WAL.
(T) 01792 648874
Speciality: Holistic Healing, Skin conditions. ✓
● **Owner** Mrs E Lewis
C Yrs. Est.: 17 (**Ref:**HM05020)

**CONTOUR DESIGNS**

**Contour Designs**, Melbourne Hall, Church Sq, Melbourne, Derby, **Derbyshire**, DE73 1EN, ENG.
(T) 01332 865222
Speciality: Hypnosis, Hypnotherapy. ✓
● **Therapist** Mr J Conway
(T) 020 7433 1757 Q: MNCH.
B Yrs. Est.: 6 (**Ref:**HM05021)

**CONTOUR THERAPY SCHOOL**

**Contour Therapy School**, The Old Sawmill, Church Sq, Melbourne, Derby, **Derbyshire**, DE73 1EN, ENG.
(T) 01242 539000
Speciality: Complementary Medicines & Therapy.
M (**Ref:**HM05022)

**CONVERGENCE CENTRE**

**Convergence Centre (The)**, 44-45 Queen St, Exeter, **Devon**, EX4 3SR, ENG.
(T) 01392 434441
Speciality: Complementary Medicines & Therapy.
C M (**Ref:**HM05023)

**CONWAY, C**

**C Conway**, Crossbank House, 116 Highgate, Kendal, **Cumbria**, LA9 4HE, ENG.
(T) 01539 741447
Speciality: Osteopathy.
P S T (**Ref:**HM05024)

**CONWAY, CLIFFORD**

**Clifford Conway**, Kirkby Lonsdale Natural Health Clinic, 1 Jingling Court, Kirkby Lonsdale, Carnforth, **Lancashire**, LA6 2FD, ENG.
(T) 01524 272998
Speciality: Osteopathy.
P S T (**Ref:**HM05025)

**CONWAY, J**

**J Conway**, Crossbank House, 116 Highgate, Kendal, **Cumbria**, LA9 4HE, ENG.
(T) 01539 741447
Speciality: Reflexology.
S T (**Ref:**HM05026)

**CONWAY, JANET**

**Janet Conway**, Kirkby Lonsdale Natural Health Clinic, 1 Jingling Court, Kirkby Lonsdale, Carnforth, **Lancashire**, LA6 2FD, ENG.
(T) 01524 272998
Speciality: Acupuncture.
O (**Ref:**HM05027)

**CONWAY, JONATHAN**

**Jonathan Conway**, 25 Maresfield Gardens, London, **London (Greater)**, NW3 5SD, ENG.
(T) 020 7433 1757 (F) 020 7433 1758
Speciality: Hypnosis, Hypnotherapy. ✓
● **Ericksonian Hypnotherapist/NLP Practitioner**
Mr J Conway M: ACH, ANLP, NCH, NRAH.
B Yrs. Est.: 6 (**Ref:**HM05028)

**CONWAY, JONATHON**

**Jonathon Conway**, The Ability Centre, 29 Crawford St, London, **London (Greater)**, W1H 1PL, ENG.
(T) 020 7723 5676
Speciality: Hypnosis, Hypnotherapy. ✓
● **Ericksonian Hypnotherapist/NLP Practitioner**
Jonathon Kent Q: Dip.EH, Dip.Psych, NLP. M: ACH, MPNLP, NCH, NRAH.
B Yrs. Est.: 6 (**Ref:**HM05029)

**CONWAY, PENELOPE L**

**Penelope L Conway**, 14 Eversley Park Rd, London, **London (Greater)**, N21 1JU, ENG.
(T) 020 8882 0026
Speciality: Osteopathy.
P S T (**Ref:**HM05030)

**CONWAY, RONALD**

**Ronald Conway**, 3 Peacock Way, Histon, Cambridge, **Cambridgeshire**, CB4 9XZ, ENG.
(T) 01223 576440
Speciality: Hypnosis.
● **Owner** Mr R Conway
B (**Ref:**HM05031)

**CONWAY, SUSAN**

**Susan Conway**, 154a Church Rd, Hove, **Sussex (East)**, BN3 2DL, ENG.
(T) 01273 739482
Speciality: Hypnosis.
B (**Ref:**HM05032)

**CONWAY, V A (DR)**

**Dr V A Conway**, 22 Sandyford Pl, Glasgow, **Glasgow (City of)**, G3 7NG, SCO.
(T) 01416 395318 (F) 01416 395318
Speciality: Homeopathy.
● **Doctor** Dr V Conway
M (**Ref:**HM05033)

**CONWAY, VALERIE (DR)**

**Dr Valerie Conway**, 87 Barrington Drive, Glasgow, **Glasgow (City of)**, G4 9ES, SCO.
(T) 01413 390894
Speciality: Homeopathy. ✓
● **Homeopathic Physician**
Dr V Conway Q: Ch.B, MB, MFHom. M: GMC.
M Yrs. Est.: 21 (**Ref:**HM05034)

**CONWAY, VALERIE A (DR)**

**Dr Valerie A Conway**, Health And Stress Clinic, 407 Clarkston Rd, Glasgow, **Glasgow (City of)**, G44 3LL, SCO.
(T) 01416 333338
Speciality: Homeopathy. ✓
● **Homeopath** Dr V Conway Q: Ch.B, MB, MFHom. M: FHom, GMC.
M Yrs. Est.: 12 (**Ref:**HM05035)

**CONYERD, D**

**D Conyerd**, 90 Compton Rd West, Wolverhampton, **Midlands (West)**, WV3 9DZ, ENG.
(T) 01902 424103
Speciality: Physiotherapy.
● **Owner** Mr D Conyerd
P S T (**Ref:**HM05036)

**CONYERS, MIKE**

**Mike Conyers**, 247 Rayleigh Rd, Hutton, Brentwood, **Essex**, CM13 1PJ, ENG.
(T) 01277 232585
Speciality: Physiotherapy.
P S T (**Ref:**HM05037)

**COOK, ALISON**

**Alison Cook**, 18 Kingsholm Sq, Gloucester, **Gloucestershire**, GL1 2QJ, ENG.
(T) 01452 500042
Speciality: Psychotherapy.
● **Owner** Mrs A Cook
B (**Ref:**HM05038)

**COOK, ANN**

**Ann Cook**, 8 Upper Guildown Rd, Guildford, **Surrey**, GU2 4EZ, ENG.
(T) 01483 504508
Speciality: Osteopathy.
P S T (**Ref:**HM05039)

**COOK, AUBREY**

**Aubrey Cook**, 7 Withipoll St, Ipswich, **Suffolk**,


Key continued: **Yrs.Est:** Years Established **Q:** Qualifications **M:** Professional Membership ✓ Indemnity Insurance Accept Credit Cards

IP4 2BZ, ENG.
(T) 01473 221108
Speciality: Reflexology.
● **Owner** Mr A Cook
S T (Ref:HM05040)

**COOK, COLIN**

**Colin Cook Chartered Physiotherapist**, 3 Park Rd, Lower Weston, Bath, **Somerset**, BA1 3EE, ENG.
(T) 01225 445963
Speciality: Acupressure, Acupuncture, Complementary Therapy, Electrotherapy, Manipulation, Massage (Therapeutic). ✔
● **Chartered Physiotherapist**
Mr C Cook Q: MCSP, SRP. M: AACP, CSP, OCPPP.
S Yrs. Est.: 20 (Ref:HM05041)

**COOK, ELAINE**

**Elaine Cook**, The Dyke Rd Natural Health Clinic, 274 Dyke Rd, Brighton, **Sussex (East)**, BN1 5AE, ENG.
(T) 01273 561844
Speciality: Acupuncture, Moxibustion. ✔
● **Acupuncturist** Ms E Cook
(T) 01273 701276 Q: Dip.Ac. M: BAcC.
O Yrs. Est.: 9 (Ref:HM05042)

**COOK, GARETH**

**Gareth Cook**, 47 High St, Bangor, **Gwynedd**, LL57 1NR, WAL.
(T) 01248 354984
Speciality: Chiropodists (Podiatrists).
● **Owner** Mr G Cook
S (Ref:HM05043)

**COOK, I M**

**I M Cook**, 16 Scotlands Rd, Coalville, **Leicestershire**, LE67 3RD, ENG.
(T) 01530 835978
Speciality: Chiropodists (Podiatrists).
● **Owner** Mrs I Cook
S (Ref:HM05044)

**COOK, J C H**

**J C H Cook**, Redland House Clinic, 118 Redland Rd, Bristol, BS6 6QT, ENG.
(T) 01179 247502
Speciality: Chiropractors.
P S T (Ref:HM05045)

**COOK, J E**

**J E Cook**, Rolle Rd, Budleigh Salterton, **Devon**, EX9 6JZ, ENG.
(T) 01395 442437
Speciality: Chiropodists (Podiatrists).
● **Owner** Mrs J Cook
S (Ref:HM05046)

**COOK, JACKIE**

**Jackie Cook**, 6 Ryland Cl, Tetbury, **Gloucestershire**, GL8 8TF, ENG.
(T) 01666 504253
Speciality: Reflexology.
S T (Ref:HM05047)

**COOK, JOE**

**Joe Cook Hypnotherapy**, 2 Keats Avenue, Braintree, **Essex**, CM7 1HB, ENG.
(T) 01376 325042
Speciality: Biofeedback, Counselling, Hypnosis, Hypnotherapy, Psychotherapy, Stress Therapy, Visualisation Therapy, Solution Focus Therapy. ✔
● **Owner/Hypnotherapist/Analyist**
Mr J Cook Q: Doctorship.Hyp.Psychol. M: BIH.
H Yrs. Est.: 15 (Ref:HM05048)

**COOK, JULIE**

**Julie Cook**, 44 Manly Dixon Drive, Enfield, **London (Greater)**, EN3 6BQ, ENG.
(T) 01992 652506
Speciality: Reflexology.
S T (Ref:HM05049)

**COOK, LORNA**

**Lorna Cook**, 44 Chevallier St, Ipswich, **Suffolk**, IP1 2PB, ENG.
(T) 01473 214316
Speciality: Hypnosis.
● **Owner** Ms L Cook
B (Ref:HM05050)

**COOK, M V**

**M V Cook**, 66 Sullivan Walk, Hebburn, **Tyne and Wear**, NE31 1YN, ENG.
(T) 01914 896406
Speciality: Chiropodists (Podiatrists).
S (Ref:HM05051)

**COOK, RICHARD**

**Richard Cook**, 5 City Business Centre, Basin Rd, Chichester, **Sussex (West)**, PO19 2DU, ENG.
(T) 01243 786946
Speciality: Homeopathy.
M (Ref:HM05052)

**COOK, RICHARD**

**Richard Cook**, 1st Floor, 20 Lavant St, Petersfield, **Hampshire**, GU32 3EW, ENG.
(T) 01730 231655
Speciality: Homeopathy.
● **Manager** Ms G Silverthorn
M (Ref:HM05053)

**COOK, RICHARD**

**Richard Cook**, 25 Osborne Rd, Southsea, **Hampshire**, PO5 3LR, ENG.
(T) 023 9287 4748
Speciality: Homeopathy.
M (Ref:HM05054)

**COOK, S C HUDSON**

**S C Hudson Cook**, 78 East Avenue, Bournemouth, **Dorset**, BH3 7DB, ENG.
(T) 01202 769100
Speciality: Chiropractors.
P S T (Ref:HM05055)

**COOK, S H W**

**S H W Cook**, 133 Walton Rd, Frinton-on-Sea, **Essex**, CO13 0AD, ENG.
(T) 01255 851428
Speciality: Chiropodists (Podiatrists).
● **Owner** Mr S Cook
S (Ref:HM05056)

**COOK, SUE**

**Sue Cook**, Namaste Clinic, Fullbridge Quay, Maldon, **Essex**, CM9 4LE, ENG.
(T) 01621 841863
Speciality: Homeopathy.
● **Owner** Mrs S Cook
M (Ref:HM05057)

**COOK, TOM**

**Tom Cook**, 4 Devon Pl, Bridgetown, Totnes, **Devon**, TQ9 5AE, ENG.
(T) 01803 863015
Speciality: Alexander Technique.
● **Owner** Mr T Cook
P S (Ref:HM05058)

**COOKE, A D**

**A D Cooke**, 199 Burnt Oak Broadway, Edgware, **London (Greater)**, HA8 0AS, ENG.
(T) 020 8952 4597
Speciality: Hypnotherapy.
● **Owner** Mrs A Cooke
B (Ref:HM05059)

**COOKE, ANNIE**

**Annie Cooke**, 37 Old Exeter Rd, Tavistock, **Devon**, PL19 0JE, ENG.
(T) 01822 613286
Speciality: Reflexology.
S T (Ref:HM05060)

**COOKE, BRENDA**

**Brenda Cooke**, Nottingham Natural Health Centre, 354 Mansfield Rd, Nottingham, **Nottinghamshire**, NG5 2EF, ENG.
(T) 01159 608855
Speciality: Herbalists.
M (Ref:HM05061)

**COOKE, C**

**C Cooke**, 23 Sutton Pk Rd, Seaford, **Sussex (East)**, BN25 1RH, ENG.
(T) 01323 892002
Speciality: Chiropodists (Podiatrists).
● **Owner** Mrs C Cooke
S (Ref:HM05062)

**COOKE, C Y**

**Mrs C Y Cooke**, The Atman Clinic, 108 St. Johns Rd, Tunbridge Wells, **Kent**, TN4 9PH, ENG.
(T) 01892 544783
Speciality: Chiropodists (Podiatrists).
S (Ref:HM05063)

**COOKE, D M**

**D M Cooke**, 121 Wallasey Rd, Wallasey, **Merseyside**, CH44 2AB, ENG.
(T) 01516 382114
Speciality: Reflexology.
● **Owner** Mrs D Cooke
S T (Ref:HM05064)

**COOKE, DIANE**

**Diane Cooke**, Clissold Park Health Centre, 154 Stoke Newington Church St, London, **London (Greater)**, N16 0JU, ENG.
(T) 020 7249 2990 (F) 020 7249 3977
Speciality: Aromatherapy.
● **Owner** Mr D Berg
M O (Ref:HM05065)

**COOKE, E M**

**E M Cooke**, 48 West Lane, Ripon, **Yorkshire (North)**, HG4 2NP, ENG.
(T) 01765 605512
Speciality: Chiropodists (Podiatrists).
S (Ref:HM05066)

**COOKE, R M**

**R M Cooke**, 7 Southam Rd, Banbury, **Oxfordshire**, OX16 2ED, ENG.
(T) 01295 263978
Speciality: Chiropodists (Podiatrists).
S (Ref:HM05067)

**COOKHAM CHIROPRACTIC CLINIC**

**Cookham Chiropractic Clinic**, Yew Lodge, Maidenhead Rd, Cookham, Maidenhead, **Berkshire**, SL6 9DA, ENG.
(T) 01628 532163
(E) anngalpin@yewlodge.clara.uk
Speciality: Chiropractic, Cranial Osteopathy, Cranio-Sacral Therapy, Feldenkrais Methodology, Herbal Medicine, Holistic Healing, Kinesiology, Manipulation, Massage (Therapeutic), McTimoney Chiropractic, Meditation, Nutritional Therapy, Physiotherapy, Remedial Massage, Spiritual Healing, Stress Therapy, Visualisation Therapy, Yoga, Physical Therapy. ✔
● **Chiropractor** Mrs A Galphin Q: DC, LCSP, MMCA. M: LCSP, MCA.
● **Practitioner** Mr P Deguara Q: DC, MMCA. M: MCA.
● **Practitioner** Mr D Bostock Q: DC, MMCA. M: MCA.
P Yrs. Est.: 10 (Ref:HM05068)

**COOKSLEY, L J**

**L J Cooksley**, 103 Chesterfield Rd, Goring-By-Sea, Worthing, **Sussex (West)**, BN12 6BY, ENG.
(T) 01903 249660
Speciality: Homeopathy.
M (Ref:HM05069)

**COOKSON, LORRAINE**

**Lorraine Cookson**, Glen House, Harewood Rd, East Keswick, Leeds, **Yorkshire (West)**, LS17 9HG, ENG.
(T) 01937 572003
Speciality: Physiotherapy.
● **Partner** Ms V Ball
P S T (Ref:HM05070)

**COOKSON, N**

**N Cookson**, Norland, Main St, Baycliff, Ulverston, **Cumbria**, LA12 9RN, ENG.
(T) 01229 869234
Speciality: Chiropodists (Podiatrists).
S (Ref:HM05071)

**COOKSTOWN CHIROPRACTIC CLINIC**

**Cookstown Chiropractic Clinic**, 37 Molesworth St, Cookstown, **County Tyrone**, BT80 8NX, NIR.
(T) 028 8676 6454 (F) 028 8676 6454
Speciality: Chiropractic.
● **Owner** Dr A Hufnagl
P S T (Ref:HM05072)

**COOKSTOWN HERBAL CLINIC**

**Cookstown Herbal Clinic (The)**, 4 Fairhill Rd, Cookstown, **County Tyrone**, BT80 8AG, NIR.
(T) 028 8676 1661
Speciality: Herbal Medicine. ✔



Key: B Mind-Body Medicine C Complementary Medicine H Self Help Treatment M Medicinal Therapy O Oriental Medicine P Postural Therapy S Manipulative Structural Therapy T Touch Therapy

● **Medical Herbalist** Mr Elliott M: NIMH.
C Yrs. Est.: 10 (Ref:HM05073)

## COOKSTOWN PHYSIO & SPORTS

**Cookstown Physiotherapy & Sports Injury Clinic**, 28 Fairhill Rd, Cookstown, **County Tyrone**, BT80 8AG, **NIR**.
(T) 028 8676 1996
Speciality: Physiotherapy.
● **Owner** Mr D McCollum
P S T (Ref:HM05074)

## COOMBES, ALISON

**Alison Coombes**, 9 The Holt, Bishops Cleeve, Cheltenham, **Gloucestershire**, GL52 8NQ, ENG.
(T) 01242 678121
Speciality: Reflexology.
S T (Ref:HM05075)

## COOMBES, JOY

**Joy Coombes**, 109 Upper Brighton Rd, Worthing, **Sussex (West)**, BN14 9HX, ENG.
(T) 01903 209643
Speciality: Hypnosis.
● **Owner** Mrs J Coombes
B (Ref:HM05076)

## COOMBS

**Mr & Mrs Coombs**, 28 Belmont Rd, Bushey, Watford, **Hertfordshire**, WD2 2JP, ENG.
(T) 01923 233739
Speciality: Chiropodists (Podiatrists).
● **Owner** Mr R Coombs
S (Ref:HM05077)

## COOMBS & COOMBS

**Coombs & Coombs**, The Ilford Chiropody Practice, 91 Clements Rd, Ilford, **Essex**, IG1 1BE, ENG.
(T) 020 8478 0758
Speciality: Chiropodists (Podiatrists).
● **Partner** Mr R Coombs
S (Ref:HM05078)

## COOMBS, ANNIE S

**Annie S Coombs**, 69A High St, Chislehurst, **Kent**, BR7 5AG, ENG.
(T) 020 8295 0893
Speciality: Psychotherapy.
B (Ref:HM05079)

## COOMBS, NICOLA

**Nicola Coombs**, 36 Wilman Way, Salisbury, **Wiltshire**, SP2 8QS, ENG.
(T) 01722 330666
Speciality: Chiropodists (Podiatrists).
● **Owner** Ms N Coombs
S (Ref:HM05080)

## COONEY-SMITH, P M

**P M Cooney-Smith**, 39 Crossway, Manchester, **Manchester (Greater)**, M20 6TU, ENG.
(T) 01614 451018
Speciality: Chiropodists (Podiatrists).
S (Ref:HM05081)

## COOP, JOE

**Joe Coop**, 111 Nuns Moor Rd, Newcastle Upon Tyne, **Tyne and Wear**, NE4 9BA, ENG.
(T) 01912 734628
Speciality: Hypnosis, Hypnotherapy. ✓
● **Owner/Hypnotherapist** Mr J Coop Q: BA.
B Yrs. Est.: 22 (Ref:HM05082)

## COOPER CLINIC

**Cooper Clinic (The)**, 72 Updown Hill, Windlesham, **Surrey**, GU20 6DT, ENG.
(T) 01276 476200 (F) 01276 453270
Speciality: Complementary Medicines & Therapy.
● **Owner** Mr G Cooper
C M (Ref:HM05083)

## COOPER TOM & PATERSON STUART

**Tom Cooper & Stuart Paterson**, 7 Endymion Rd, London, **London (Greater)**, N4 1EE, ENG.
(T) 020 8342 9594
Speciality: Psychotherapy.
B (Ref:HM05084)

## COOPER, A

**A Cooper**, Castle Lodge, Wye St, Ross-on-Wye, **Herefordshire**, HR9 7BS, ENG.
(T) 01989 562154
Speciality: Psychotherapy.
● **Owner** Miss A Cooper
B (Ref:HM05085)

## COOPER, A

**A Cooper**, 8 Kings Head Mews, Chipping Norton, **Oxfordshire**, OX7 5LR, ENG.
(T) 01608 642018 (F) 01608 645411
Speciality: Physiotherapy.
● **Owner** Mrs A Cooper
P S T (Ref:HM05086)

## COOPER, A

**A Cooper**, 36 Church St, Dorking, **Surrey**, RH4 1DJ, ENG.
(T) 01306 882336
Speciality: Alexander Technique.
P S (Ref:HM05087)

## COOPER, A R

**A R Cooper**, 4 Market St, Newmarket, **Suffolk**, CB8 8EE, ENG.
(T) 01638 662840
Speciality: Chiropody, Nail Surgery. ✓
● **Chiropodist** Mr A Cooper Q: BSc, S.R.Ch. M: S.C.P.
M Yrs. Est.: 20 (Ref:HM05088)

## COOPER, ANGELA

**Angela Cooper**, Cheltenham Holistic Health Centre, 66 Suffolk Rd, Cheltenham, **Gloucestershire**, GL50 2ED, ENG.
(T) 01242 584140 (F) 01242 256567
(E) angela@psmail.net
(W) www.chch.co.uk
Speciality: Counselling, Hypnotherapy, Psychotherapy. ✓
● **Psychotherapist Counsellor/Hypnotherapist** Ms A Cooper
(T) 01989 562154 Q: BA (Hons), Dip.Couns, Dip.Hyp, MSc. M: BACP.
B Yrs. Est.: 12 (Ref:HM05089)

## COOPER, ANN

**Ann Cooper**, 4 Aston Farm Cottages, Cherington, Tetbury, **Gloucestershire**, GL8 8SW, ENG.
(T) 01285 841440
(W) www.moorglade.co.uk
Speciality: Reflexology. ✓ CREDIT
● **Reflexologist** Mrs A Cooper Q: MAR.
T Yrs. Est.: 2 (Ref:HM05090)

## COOPER, ANTHONY

**Anthony Cooper**, 14 Park Rd, Bridport, **Dorset**, DT6 5DA, ENG.
(T) 01308 421854
Speciality: Chiropodists (Podiatrists).
● **Owner** Mr A Cooper
S (Ref:HM05091)

## COOPER, BARBARA

**Barbara Cooper**, 12 Station Rd, Chapeltown, Sheffield, **Yorkshire (South)**, S35 2XH, ENG.
(T) 01142 450971
Speciality: Chiropodists (Podiatrists).
● **Owner** Mr A Cooper
S (Ref:HM05092)

## COOPER, BARRINGTON (DR)

**Dr Barrington Cooper**, 10 Devonshire Pl, London, **London (Greater)**, W1N 1PB, ENG.
(T) 020 7935 9335 (F) 020 7935 1093
Speciality: Psychotherapy.
● **Owner** Dr B Cooper
B (Ref:HM05093)

## COOPER, C J C

**C J C Cooper**, 11 Arden St, Edinburgh, **Edinburgh (City of)**, EH9 1BR, SCO.
(T) 01312 294859
Speciality: Alexander Technique.
● **Owner** Ms C Cooper
P S (Ref:HM05094)

## COOPER, D V

**D V Cooper**, 2 Greenside, Shirley, Solihull, **Midlands (West)**, B90 4HH, ENG.
(T) 01564 702135
Speciality: Chiropodists (Podiatrists).
S (Ref:HM05095)

## COOPER, D W

**D W Cooper**, 12 Aurania Avenue, Norwich, **Norfolk**, NR1 2RD, ENG.
(T) 01603 625409
Speciality: Osteopathy.
● **Owner** Mr D Cooper
P S T (Ref:HM05096)

## COOPER, DAVID

**David Cooper**, 320 Liverpool Rd, Newcastle, **Staffordshire**, ST5 9DY, ENG.
(T) 01782 633483
Speciality: Osteopathy.
● **Partner** Mr D Cooper
P S T (Ref:HM05097)

## COOPER, DAVID

**David Cooper**, 19 Lichfield St, Stone, **Staffordshire**, ST15 8NA, ENG.
(T) 01785 816481
Speciality: Osteopathy.
P S T (Ref:HM05098)

## COOPER, DIANA

**Diana Cooper**, 12 Frobisher Gardens, Guildford, **Surrey**, GU1 2NT, ENG.
(T) 01483 566961
Speciality: Complementary Medicines & Therapy.
C M (Ref:HM05099)

## COOPER, EMILY

**Emily Cooper**, 2 Colwick Crossing, Nottingham, **Nottinghamshire**, NG2 4BD, ENG.
(T) 01159 240806
Speciality: Hypnotherapy.
● **Owner** Miss E Cooper
B (Ref:HM05100)

## COOPER, FELICITY

**Felicity Cooper**, The Old Surgery, High St, Much Hadham, **Hertfordshire**, SG10 6DA, ENG.
(T) 01279 842567
Speciality: Chiropody, Cryo Surgery, Gait Analysis, Nail Surgery, Podiatry. ✓ CREDIT
● **Chiropodist** Ms F Cooper Q: F.S.C.P, FCPod(s). M: FCPod(s), S.C.P.
C Yrs. Est.: 20 (Ref:HM05101)

## COOPER, FELICITY

**Felicity Cooper**, 7-8 Wych Elm House, Hamstel Rd, Harlow, **Essex**, CM20 1QP, ENG.
(T) 01279 410136
Speciality: Chiropodists (Podiatrists).
S (Ref:HM05102)

## COOPER, FELICITY

**Felicity Cooper**, 3 North View Cottages, Ware Rd, Widford, Ware, **Hertfordshire**, SG12 8RF, ENG.
(T) 01279 842969
Speciality: Chiropodists (Podiatrists).
S (Ref:HM05103)

## COOPER, FELICITY

**Felicity Cooper**, 42 Market St, Old Harlow, **Essex**, CM17 0AQ, ENG.
(T) 01279 626219
Speciality: Biomechanics, Chiropody, Cryo Surgery, Gait Analysis, Nail Surgery, Podiatry. ✓ CREDIT
● **Chiropodist** Ms F Cooper Q: F.S.C.P, FCPod(s). M: FCPod(s), S.C.P.
C Yrs. Est.: 10 (Ref:HM05104)

## COOPER, G R

**G R Cooper**, Barrows Ford, Markington, Harrogate, **Yorkshire (North)**, HG3 3PQ, ENG.
(T) 01765 677483 (F) 01765 677483
Speciality: Chiropodists (Podiatrists).
● **Owner** Mr G Cooper
S (Ref:HM05105)

## COOPER, GEOFFREY M

**Geoffrey M Cooper**, 2 Sutton Cl, Mickle Trafford, Chester, **Cheshire**, CH2 4QP, ENG.
(T) 01244 300217
Speciality: Reflexology.
S T (Ref:HM05106)

## COOPER, H J

**H J Cooper**, St Michaels, 134 Windsor Rd, Torquay, **Devon**, TQ1 1SR, ENG.
(T) 01803 296728 (F) 01803 215820
Speciality: Osteopathy.
● **Owner** Mr H Cooper
P S T (Ref:HM05107)



Key continued: **Yrs.Est:** Years Established **Q:** Qualifications **M:** Professional Membership ✓ Indemnity Insurance CREDIT Accept Credit Cards

### COOPER, HEATHER
**Heather Cooper**, 69 The St, Fetcham, Leatherhead, **Surrey**, KT22 9RB, ENG.
(T) 01372 376548
Speciality: Complementary Medicines & Therapy.
M (Ref:HM05108)

### COOPER, J
**Mrs J Cooper**, 22 Wembley Avenue, Lancing, **Sussex (West)**, BN15 9JZ, ENG.
(T) 01903 762064
Speciality: Complementary Medicines & Therapy.
M (Ref:HM05109)

### COOPER, J A
**J A Cooper**, Farnham House, Harewood Avenue, London, **London (Greater)**, NW1 6NT, ENG.
(T) 020 7402 7587
Speciality: Complementary Medicines & Therapy.
● **Owner** Mr J Cooper
C M (Ref:HM05110)

### COOPER, JACQUELINE
**Jacqueline Cooper**, 28 Victoria Rd, Swindon, **Wiltshire**, SN1 3AW, ENG.
(T) 01793 435494
Speciality: Chiropodists (Podiatrists).
● **Owner** Ms J Cooper
S (Ref:HM05111)

### COOPER, JAMES
**James Cooper**, 3 Finch Rd, Doncaster, **Yorkshire (South)**, DN4 9AL, ENG.
(T) 01302 859142
Speciality: Chiropodists (Podiatrists).
S (Ref:HM05112)

### COOPER, JEFFREY C
**Jeffrey C Cooper**, 31 Straight Rd, Boxted, Colchester, **Essex**, CO4 5HN, ENG.
(T) 01206 272757
Speciality: Osteopathy.
P S T (Ref:HM05113)

### COOPER, JOHN M
**John M Cooper**, 13 Selden Rd, Worthing, **Sussex (West)**, BN11 2LL, ENG.
(T) 01903 234214
Speciality: Chiropodists (Podiatrists).
● **Owner** Mr J Cooper
S (Ref:HM05114)

### COOPER, KAY
**Kay Cooper**, Evergreens, Main St, Beeford, Driffield, **Humberside (North)**, YO25 8AZ, ENG.
(T) 01262 488879
Speciality: Complementary Medicines & Therapy.
● **Owner** Mrs K Cooper
C M (Ref:HM05115)

### COOPER, LAURA
**Laura Cooper**, 130-131 High St, Uxbridge, **London (Greater)**, UB8 1JX, ENG.
(T) 01895 234017
Speciality: Chiropractic.
● **Owner** Ms L Cooper
P S T (Ref:HM05116)

### COOPER, LESLEY
**Lesley Cooper**, 7 Ottervale Rd, Budleigh Salterton, **Devon**, EX9 6JE, ENG.
(T) 01395 443677
Speciality: Alexander Technique.
● **Owner** Mrs L Cooper
P S (Ref:HM05117)

### COOPER, LESLEY
**Lesley Cooper**, 'Sidside', Packhorse Cl, Sidfird, Sidmouth, **Devon**, EX10 9RR, ENG.
(T) 01395 57922
Speciality: Alexander Technique.
P S (Ref:HM05118)

### COOPER, M L
**Mrs M L Cooper**, Redholme, The Ridge, Little Baddow, Chelmsford, **Essex**, CM3 4RT, ENG.
(T) 01245 224436
Speciality: Physiotherapy.
P S T (Ref:HM05119)

### COOPER, MARGARET
**Margaret Cooper**, 8 Broad Leys, Princes Risborough, **Buckinghamshire**, HP27 9JT, ENG.
(T) 01844 344580
Speciality: Chiropodists (Podiatrists).
● **Owner** Mrs M Cooper
S (Ref:HM05120)

### COOPER, P G
**P G Cooper**, Jameston Court, Jameston, Tenby, **Pembrokeshire**, SA70 8QD, WAL.
(T) 01834 871616
Speciality: Physiotherapy.
● **Owner** Mr P Cooper
P S T (Ref:HM05121)

### COOPER, P W
**P W Cooper**, 34 Prince Andrews Rd, Norwich, **Norfolk**, NR6 6XG, ENG.
(T) 01603 411101
Speciality: Osteopathy.
● **Owner** Mr P Cooper
P S T (Ref:HM05122)

### COOPER, PETER
**Peter Cooper**, Rosegarth Clinic Of Natural Medicine, 56 Sutton Rd, Mansfield, **Nottinghamshire**, NG18 5EU, ENG.
(T) 01623 658224
Speciality: Homeopathy.
M (Ref:HM05123)

### COOPER, R P
**R P Cooper**, 11 Victoria Rd, Salford, **Manchester (Greater)**, M6 8FZ, ENG.
(T) 01617 895917
Speciality: Chiropodists (Podiatrists).
● **Owner** Mr R Cooper
S (Ref:HM05124)

### COOPER, S
**S Cooper**, Farfield House, 105 North St, Keighley, **Yorkshire (West)**, BD21 3AA, ENG.
(T) 01535 606881
Speciality: Osteopathy.
P S T (Ref:HM05125)

### COOPER, SAFFRON
**Saffron Cooper**, 43 Bradford Rd, Shipley, **Yorkshire (West)**, BD18 3DJ, ENG.
(T) 01274 582367
Speciality: Homeopathy. ✓
● **Homeopath** Ms S Cooper Q: RSHom. M: Soc.Hom.
C Yrs. Est.: 13 (Ref:HM05126)

### COOPER, SARAH E J
**Sarah E J Cooper**, 35 Chesswood Rd, Worthing, **Sussex (West)**, BN11 2AA, ENG.
(T) 01903 230066
Speciality: Acupuncture.
O (Ref:HM05127)

### COOPER, STEPHEN
**Stephen Cooper**, 10 York Rd, Headington, Oxford, **Oxfordshire**, OX3 8NW, ENG.
(T) 01865 765511
(E) s.c@btinternet.com
(W) www.hatso.com
Speciality: Alexander Technique. ✓
● **Teacher** Mr S Cooper Q: MSTAT. M: STAT.
H Yrs. Est.: 20 (Ref:HM05128)

### COOPER, STEPHEN
**Stephen Cooper**, 137 Magdalen Rd, Oxford, **Oxfordshire**, OX4 1RJ, ENG.
(T) 01865 396939
Speciality: Alexander Technique.
● **Owner** Mr M Franklin
P S (Ref:HM05129)

### COOPER, STUART
**Stuart Cooper**, Farfield House, 105 North St, Keighley, **Yorkshire (West)**, BD21 3AA, ENG.
(T) 01535 690055
Speciality: Osteopathy.
P S T (Ref:HM05130)

### COOPER, VAUGHAN
**Vaughan Cooper**, 15 St Johns St, Long Eaton, Nottingham, **Nottinghamshire**, NG10 1BW, ENG.
(T) 01159 461699
Speciality: Osteopathy.
P S T (Ref:HM05131)

### COOTE, JACKIE
**Jackie Coote**, 27 Britannia Rd, London, **London (Greater)**, SW6 2HJ, ENG.
(T) 020 7731 1061
Speciality: Alexander Technique.
● **Owner** Ms J Coote
P S (Ref:HM05132)

### COPCUTT
**Copcutt**, 129 Ditton Walk, Cambridge, **Cambridgeshire**, CB5 8QD, ENG.
(T) 01223 740326
Speciality: Complementary Medicines & Therapy.
● **Principal** Miss M Winstanley
C M (Ref:HM05133)

### COPE, ANNE
**Anne Cope DO ND MRN**, 22 Majorfield Rd, Topsham, Exeter, **Devon**, EX3 0ES, ENG.
(T) 01392 875004
Speciality: Acupressure, Bach Remedies, Cranial Osteopathy, Hay Diet, Herbal Medicine, Manipulation, Massage (Therapeutic), Naturopathy, Nutritional Therapy, Osteopathy, Postural Integration, Reflexology. ✓
● **Naturopath** Ms A Cope Q: DO, ND. M: RoN.
S Yrs. Est.: 9 (Ref:HM05134)

### COPE, ANNE
**Anne Cope**, Moss Pharmacy, 70 High St, Honiton, **Devon**, EX14 1PD, ENG.
(T) 01392 875004
Speciality: Osteopathy.
● **Owner** Mrs A Cope
P S T (Ref:HM05135)

### COPE, C G
**C G Cope**, 70 Lullington Rd, Overseal, Swadlincote, **Derbyshire**, DE12 6NG, ENG.
(T) 01283 762596
Speciality: Chiropodists (Podiatrists).
● **Owner** Mr C Cope
S (Ref:HM05136)

### COPE, KAY
**Kay Cope**, 15 Rievaulx Cl, Knaresborough, **Yorkshire (North)**, HG5 8NG, ENG.
(T) 01423 869856
Speciality: Chiropodists (Podiatrists).
S (Ref:HM05137)

### COPE, PAUL
**Paul Cope**, 6 Marlborough House, Langton Cl, Lincoln, **Lincolnshire**, LN2 2HJ, ENG.
(T) 01522 541314
Speciality: Hypnosis.
B (Ref:HM05138)

### COPELAND, ELAINE
**Elaine Copeland**, 7 Ingrams Cl, Hersham, **Surrey**, KT12 5JH, ENG.
(T) 07973 846934
Speciality: Bach Remedies, Kinesiology.
M (Ref:HM05139)

### COPELAND, KATIE
**Katie Copeland**, 76 Lower Bridge St, Chester, **Cheshire**, CH1 1RU, ENG.
(T) 01244 311880
Speciality: Physiotherapy.
P S T (Ref:HM05140)

### COPELAND, LIZ
**Liz Copeland**, 36 Welcomes Rd, Purley, **Surrey**, CR8 4HG, ENG.
(T) 020 8668 3502
Speciality: Herbal Medicine.
M (Ref:HM05141)

### COPELAND, M E
**M E Copeland**, Lakeside Physiotherapy Clinic, Festival Way, Stoke-On-Trent, **Staffordshire**, ST1 5PU, ENG.
(T) 01782 205707 (F) 01782 260771
Speciality: Physiotherapy.
● **Owner** Mr M Copeland
P S T (Ref:HM05142)

### COPLAND-GRIFFITHS, M C
**M C Copland-Griffiths**, Wingfield Chiropractic Clinic, Trowle House, Wingfield, Trowbridge, **Wiltshire**, BA14 9LE, ENG.

(T) 01225 752199 (F) 01225 769842
Speciality: Chiropractic.
● **Owner** Mr M Copland-Griffiths
P S T (Ref:HM05143)

### COPLEY, F

**F Copley**, 14 Toronto Pl, Leeds, **Yorkshire (West)**, LS7 4LJ, ENG.
(T) 01132 623668
Speciality: Hypnosis.
● **Owner** Mrs F Copley
B (Ref:HM05144)

### COPNOR OSTEOPATHICS

**Copnor Osteopathics**, 305 Copnor Rd, Portsmouth, **Hampshire**, PO3 5EG, ENG.
(T) 023 9267 8582
Speciality: Osteopathy.
● **Owner** Mr A Taylor
P S T (Ref:HM05145)

### COPPEN, J

**J Coppen**, Constitutional Buildings, High St, East Grinstead, **Sussex (West)**, RH19 3AW, ENG.
(T) 01342 323463
Speciality: Chiropodists (Podiatrists).
● **Owner** Mrs M Lawrence
S (Ref:HM05146)

### COPPERTHWAITE, ERIC

**Eric Copperthwaite**, 20 Harts Leap Rd, Sandhurst, **Berkshire**, GU47 8EW, ENG.
(T) 01344 774318
Speciality: Hypnosis, Hypnotherapy, Psychotherapy, Electro-Crystal Therapy. ✔
● **Psychotherapist/Hypnotherapist** Mr E Copperthwaite M: NCH, NCP.
B Yrs. Est.: 40 (Ref:HM05147)

### COPPING, A G

**A G Copping**, 147 Gilbert Rd, Cambridge, **Cambridgeshire**, CB4 3PA, ENG.
(T) 01223 314408
Speciality: Physiotherapy.
● **Owner** Mrs A Copping
P S T (Ref:HM05148)

### COPPING, P

**P Copping**, 14 The St, Melton, Woodbridge, **Suffolk**, IP12 1PW, ENG.
(T) 01394 383495
Speciality: Chiropodists (Podiatrists).
S (Ref:HM05149)

### COPY CENTRE

**Copy Centre (The)**, 44 Osborne Rd, Willesborough, Ashford, **Kent**, TN24 0EF, ENG.
(T) 01233 660767
Speciality: Aromatherapy.
M O (Ref:HM05150)

### CORAL CALCIUM

**Coral Calcium**, Trafalgar House, Grenville Pl, London, **London (Greater)**, NW7 3SA, ENG.
(T) 020 8201 0300 (F) 020 8906 1700
Speciality: Complementary Medicines & Therapy.
● **Owner** Mr P Steyne
C M (Ref:HM05151)

### CORBETT, D

**D Corbett**, The Wellbeing Centre, 11 Musters Rd, West Bridgford, Nottingham, **Nottinghamshire**, NG2 7PP, ENG.
(T) 01159 825353
Speciality: Aromatherapy.
M O (Ref:HM05152)

### CORBETT, DIANE

**Diane Corbett**, 12 Berkeley Avenue, Nottingham, **Nottinghamshire**, NG3 5BU, ENG.
(T) 01159 602702
Speciality: Aromatherapy.
● **Owner** Ms D Corbett
M O (Ref:HM05153)

### CORBIN, CLARE A

**Clare A Corbin**, Robin Hood Health Centre, 1 Camden Rd, Sutton, **Surrey**, SM1 2SH, ENG.
(T) 020 8770 7119
Speciality: Chiropodists (Podiatrists).
● **Owner** Mrs C Corbin
S (Ref:HM05154)

### CORBIN, L

**L Corbin**, 25 Lower Church St, Chepstow, **Monmouthshire**, NP16 5HJ, WAL.
(T) 01291 623538
Speciality: Chiropodists (Podiatrists).
S (Ref:HM05155)

### CORBY, MICHAEL

**Michael Corby**, 14 Woodland Rd, Darlington, **County Durham**, DL3 7PL, ENG.
(T) 01913 712147
Speciality: Hypnosis.
● **Owner** Mr M Corby
B (Ref:HM05156)

### CORBY, VERONICA

**Veronica Corby**, 11 Bristowe Drive, Orsett, Grays, **Essex**, RM16 3DB, ENG.
(T) 01375 892472
Speciality: Reflexology.
S T (Ref:HM05157)

### CORBYN, SANJEE

**Sanjee Corbyn**, 16b Abbey Rd, South Croydon, **Surrey**, CR2 8NG, ENG.
(T) 020 8657 8434
Speciality: Herbal Medicine.
M (Ref:HM05158)

### CORCORAN, ANNE

**Anne Corcoran HHC DIP**, 2 Derrynane Gdns Sandymount, Dublin, **County Dublin**, IRE.
(T) 08729 96316
Speciality: Complementary Medicines & Therapy.
M (Ref:HM05159)

### CORDEL, MICHAEL

**Michael Cordel**, Gibson And Moretta, 63 Falsgrave Rd, Scarborough, **Yorkshire (North)**, YO12 6EA, ENG.
(T) 01723 366455
Speciality: Acupressure, Acupuncture, Cupping, Massage (Therapeutic), Moxibustion. ✔
● **Acupuncturist** Mr M Cordel Q: Lic.Ac. M: BAcC.
O Yrs. Est.: 7 (Ref:HM05160)

### CORELLO, LOUISE

**Louise Corello**, School House, School Lane, Sheet, Petersfield, **Hampshire**, GU32 2AS, ENG.
(T) 01730 268301
Speciality: Acupuncture, Zero Balancing. ✔
● **Acupuncturist** Ms L Corello Q: BA, MBAcC. M: BAcC.
O Yrs. Est.: 9 (Ref:HM05161)

### CORIN, E

**Mrs E Corin**, 59 Huddleston Rd, London, **London (Greater)**, N7 0AD, ENG.
(T) 020 7609 6697
Speciality: Alexander Technique.
P S (Ref:HM05162)

### CORK CHIROPRACTIC CLINIC

**Cork Chiropractic Clinic**, 2a Harley Ct, Whiteoaks Wilton, **County Cork**, IRE.
(T) 021 4342 933
Speciality: Chiropractors.
P S T (Ref:HM05163)

### CORK HYPNOTHERAPY CLINIC

**Cork Hypnotherapy Clinic**, Therapy Hse, 6 Tuckey St, **County Cork**, IRE.
(T) 021 4273 575
Speciality: Hypnotherapy.
B (Ref:HM05164)

### CORK SCHOOL OF SHIATSU

**Cork School of Shiatsu**, 61 Westcourt Heights, Ballincollig, **County Cork**, IRE.
(T) 021 4872 324
Speciality: Complementary Medicines & Therapy.
M (Ref:HM05165)

### CORK, STEPHEN

**Stephen Cork**, 4 Old Pk Cottages, Slaugham Lane, Warninglid, Haywards Heath, **Sussex (West)**, RH17 5TJ, ENG.
(T) 01444 461451
Speciality: Hypnosis.
B (Ref:HM05166)

### CORKE, A J

**A J & S Corke**, Dove Leys, Homer, Much Wenlock, **Shropshire**, TF13 6NF, ENG.
(T) 01952 728166 (F) 01952 728166
(E) tonysand/acorke@aol.com
Speciality: Auto Suggestion, Autogenic Training, Biofeedback, Counselling, Hypnosis, Hypnotherapy, Stress Therapy. ✔
● **Hypnotherapist** Mr T Corke Q: Dip.Hyp, Dip.Psych, LCSP, NACHP. M: LCSP, NACHP.
B Yrs. Est.: 23 (Ref:HM05167)

### CORKE, AMI

**Ami Corke**, 'Les Bouchons', 10 Freeman Rd, Didcot, **Oxfordshire**, OX11 7DE, ENG.
(T) 01235 212004
Speciality: Reflexology.
S T (Ref:HM05168)

### CORKE, TONY

**Tony Corke**, 18 Waldemar Avenue, London, **London (Greater)**, W13 9PY, ENG.
(T) 020 8567 3271
Speciality: Hypnotherapy.
● **Owner** Mr T Corke
B (Ref:HM05169)

### CORKER, E

**E Corker**, 55 The Avenue, Stoke-On-Trent, **Staffordshire**, ST4 6BT, ENG.
(T) 01782 662655
Speciality: Psychotherapy.
● **Owner** Miss E Corker
B (Ref:HM05170)

### CORLET, LOUISE

**Louise Corlet**, 29 Attleborough Rd, Nuneaton, **Warwickshire**, CV11 4HZ, ENG.
(T) 024 7638 3138
Speciality: Chiropractic.
P S T (Ref:HM05171)

### CORLET, LOUISE

**Louise Corlet**, 380 Walsgrave Rd, Coventry, **Midlands (West)**, CV2 4AF, ENG.
(T) 024 7645 2357 (F) 024 7645 9924
Speciality: Chiropractors.
● **Owner** Mr R Hatfield
P S T (Ref:HM05172)

### CORLETT, D A (DR )

**Dr D A Corlett**, 21 Yates Lane, Huddersfield, **Yorkshire (West)**, HD3 4NW, ENG.
(T) 01484 461440
Speciality: Chiropractic.
P S T (Ref:HM05173)

### CORLEY, H V

**H V Corley**, Pucketty Farm, Faringdon, **Oxfordshire**, SN7 8JP, ENG.
(T) 01367 240181
Speciality: Chiropractors.
P S T (Ref:HM05174)

### CORLEY, SHIAN

**Shian Corley**, The Whole Works, Jacksons Cl, 209 The Royal Mile, Edinburgh, **Edinburgh (City of)**, EH1 1PZ, SCO.
(T) 01312 258092
Speciality: Complementary Medicines & Therapy.
C M (Ref:HM05175)

### CORMACK, SUSAN

**Susan Cormack**, 13 Sheriffs Park, Linlithgow, **Lothian (West)**, EH49 7SR, SCO.
(T) 01506 847418
Speciality: Reflexology.
S T (Ref:HM05176)

### CORNCROFT

**Corncroft (UK) Ltd**, 10 Winsford Rd, Sheffield, **Yorkshire (South)**, S6 1HT, ENG.
(T) 01142 344443 (F) 07070 600106
Speciality: Complementary Medicines & Therapy.
● **Managing Director** Mr B Wheatcroft
C M (Ref:HM05177)

### CORNELL, LESLEY

**Lesley Cornell**, Phoenix House, Overdale, Ashtead, **Surrey**, KT21 1PW, ENG.
(T) 01372 274442



Key continued: Yrs.Est: Years Established Q: Qualifications M: Professional Membership ✔ Indemnity Insurance Accept Credit Cards

Speciality: Chiropodists (Podiatrists).
S (Ref:HM05178)

## CORNER SURGERY

**Corner Surgery (The)**, Waunbant Rd, Kenfig Hill, Bridgend, CF33 6DE, **WAL**.
(T) 01656 742674 (F) 01656 742674
Speciality: Chiropodists (Podiatrists).
● **Owner** Mr C Williams
S (Ref:HM05179)

## CORNER, CAROLYN

**Carolyn Corner**, 12 Southend Avenue, Darlington, **County Durham**, DL3 7HL, **ENG**.
(T) 01325 286225
Speciality: Physiotherapy.
● **Owner** Mrs C Corner
P S T (Ref:HM05180)

## CORNER, GLENYS

**Glenys Corner**, 4 Westminster Avenue, Sandiacre, Nottingham, **Nottinghamshire**, NG10 5AT, **ENG**.
(T) 01159 395796
Speciality: Chiropodists (Podiatrists).
● **Owner** Miss G Corner
S (Ref:HM05181)

## CORNERSTONES PRACTICE

**Cornerstones Practice (The)**, 108 Crewe Rd, Alsager, Stoke-On-Trent, **Staffordshire**, ST7 2JA, **ENG**.
(T) 01782 380034
Speciality: Counselling, Homeopathy, Psychotherapy, Reiki. ✓
● **Homeopath** Mrs J Marshall Q: RSHom. M: Soc.Hom.
● **Practice Manager** Mrs C Dickens
(T) 01270 883097
C Yrs. Est.: 2 (Ref:HM05182)

## CORNERWEIGHS

**Cornerweighs**, Elm Lodge, Caudle St, Henfield, **Sussex (West)**, BN5 9DQ, **ENG**.
(T) 01273 492794 (F) 01273 492794
(E) cornerweighs@netscapeonline.co.uk
Speciality: Anthroposohical Medicine, Aromatherapy, Bach Remedies, Naturopathy, Phytotherapy, Vitamin Therapy.
● **Owner** Mrs S Marchbanks
H Yrs. Est.: 4 (Ref:HM05183)

## CORNISH, B A

**B A Cornish**, Heaton Consulting Rooms, Heaton Medical Centre, 2 Lucy St, Bolton, **Lancashire**, BL1 5PU, **ENG**.
(T) 01204 848686
Speciality: Chiropodists (Podiatrists).
● **Owner** Mrs B Cornish
S (Ref:HM05184)

## CORNWALL CHIROPRACTIC SERVICES

**Cornwall Chiropractic Services**, Unit 2 Bridge House, St Clement St, Truro, **Cornwall**, TR1 1ER, **ENG**.
(T) 01872 262988 (F) 01872 262988
Speciality: Chiropractors.
● **Manager** Dr P Stick
P S T (Ref:HM05185)

## CORNWELL, K J

**K J Cornwell**, 175 Burnley Rd, Rossendale, **Lancashire**, BB4 8HY, **ENG**.
(T) 01706 210772
Speciality: Chiropodists (Podiatrists).
S (Ref:HM05186)

## CORNWELL, S

**S Cornwell**, 20 Chichester Way, Burgess Hill, **Sussex (West)**, RH15 0RH, **ENG**.
(T) 01444 232828
Speciality: Reflexology.
● **Owner** Mrs S Cornwell
S T (Ref:HM05187)

## CORNWELL, SUE

**Sue Cornwell**, Fenkirk, Green Rd, Wivelsfield Green, Haywards Heath, **Sussex (West)**, RH17 7QL, **ENG**.
(T) 01444 471353
Speciality: Reflexology.
S T (Ref:HM05188)

## CORONELLI, DANIELLA

**Daniella Coronelli**, Centre For Whole Health, 12 Victoria Pl, Bristol, BS3 3BP, **ENG**.
(T) 01179 231138
Speciality: Complementary Medicines & Therapy.
M (Ref:HM05189)

## CORPORATE COUNSELLING IRELAND

**Corporate Counselling Ireland**, 15 Straffan Rd, Maynooth, **County Kildare**, **IRE**.
(T) 01 628 9939 (F) 01 628 9598
Speciality: Counselling.
B H (Ref:HM05190)

## CORPORATE STRESS MANAGEMENT

**Corporate Stress Management**, 27 Tooley St, London, **London (Greater)**, SE1 2PR, **ENG**.
(T) 020 7700 5930
Speciality: Psychotherapy.
B (Ref:HM05191)

## CORRIE REIKI HEALING

**Francis and Susie Corrie**, 25 Flatford Pl, Kidlington, **Oxfordshire**, OX5 1TQ, **ENG**.
(T) 01865 379670
(E) franciscorrie@uahoo.com
Speciality: Reiki. ✓
● **Healer** Mr F Corrie Q: Reiki Master.
● **Healer** Ms S Corrie Q: Reiki Master.
T Yrs. Est.: 1 (Ref:HM05192)

## CORRIE, D F

**D F Corrie**, 48 St. Baldreds Rd, North Berwick, **Lothian (East)**, EH39 4PU, **SCO**.
(T) 01620 892453
Speciality: Chiropodists (Podiatrists).
● **Owner** Mrs D Corrie
S (Ref:HM05193)

## CORRIGAN, A J

**A J Corrigan**, The Sudbury Chiropractic, The Old Bakery, King St, Sudbury, **Suffolk**, CO10 6EB, **ENG**.
(T) 01787 377300
Speciality: Chiropractic.
P S T (Ref:HM05194)

## CORRIGAN, PETER

**Peter Corrigan**, 29 Grasmere Rd, Chestfield, Whitstable, **Kent**, CT5 3LY, **ENG**.
(T) 01227 792359
Speciality: Hypnosis, Hypnotherapy, Neuro-Linguistic Program, Reflexology. ✓
● **Owner/Hypnotherapist**
Mr P Corrigan Q: BHA, Reg.Hyp, Reg.Reflex, RGN. M: NCH.
B Yrs. Est.: 8 (Ref:HM05195)

## CORRY, MICHAEL M (DR)

**Dr Michael M Corry**, 2 Eden Pk, Sandycove, **County Dublin**, **IRE**.
(T) 01280 0084
Speciality: Complementary Medicines & Therapy.
M (Ref:HM05196)

## CORTEEN, PAOLA

**Paola Corteen**, 10A Eversley Park Rd, London, **London (Greater)**, N21 1JU, **ENG**.
(T) 020 8882 7898
Speciality: Alexander Technique.
● **Owner** Mrs P Corteen
P S (Ref:HM05197)

## CORTHINE, S

**S Corthine**, 139 Grove Lane, London, **London (Greater)**, SE5 8BG, **ENG**.
(T) 020 7274 2621
Speciality: Chiropodists (Podiatrists).
S (Ref:HM05198)

## CORTON, JOHN

**John Corton**, 36 Melton Rd, Sprotbrough, Doncaster, **Yorkshire (South)**, DN5 7NJ, **ENG**.
(T) 01302 784092
Speciality: Acupuncture.
O (Ref:HM05199)

## COSGROVE, CORRINNE

**Corrinne Cosgrove**, 42 Thornleigh Rd, Huddersfield, **Yorkshire (West)**, HD4 5PY, **ENG**.
(T) 01484 321872
Speciality: Complementary Medicines & Therapy.
● **Owner** Mrs C Cosgrove
C M (Ref:HM05200)

## COSGROVES PHYSIO-FIT CENTRE

**Cosgroves Physio-Fit Centre**, Station Approach, Atherton, Manchester, **Manchester (Greater)**, M46 9LJ, **ENG**.
(T) 01942 883407
Speciality: Acupressure, Acupuncture, Dietician, Electrotherapy, Manipulation, Massage (Therapeutic), Ultrasonics, Yoga. ✓
● **Owner/Senior Physiotherapist**
Mr S Cosgrove Q: Grad Dip Phys, MCSP, SRP. M: CSP, OCPPP.
● **Physiotherapist** Mr S Hooten Q: BSc, MCSP, SRP. M: CSP.
● **Physiotherapist** Mr G Morris Q: BSc, MCSP, SRP. M: CSP.
P S T Yrs. Est.: 18 (Ref:HM05201)

## COSHAM OSTEOPATHIC CLINIC

**Cosham Osteopathic Clinic**, 13 Spur Rd, Cosham, Portsmouth, **Hampshire**, PO6 3DY, **ENG**.
(T) 023 9220 0000
Speciality: Osteopathy.
P S T (Ref:HM05202)

## COSMIC CONNECTIONS

**Cosmic Connections**, 20 Essex Avenue, Sudbury, **Suffolk**, CO10 1YZ, **ENG**.
(T) 01379 240243
Speciality: Vibrational Therapy, Personal Development.
M (Ref:HM05203)

## COSMIC FLOW

**Cosmic Flow**, Studio 12 St Georges Studios, 93-97 St Georges Rd, Glasgow, **Glasgow (City of)**, G3 6JA, **SCO**.
(T) 01415 721127 (F) 01415 721128
Speciality: Clairvoyants & Palmists.
● **Owner** Mr D Cameron
B (Ref:HM05204)

## COSMOS HERBS

**Cosmos Herbs**, 329 Chiswick High Rd, London, **London (Greater)**, W4 4HS, **ENG**.
(T) 020 8995 7239
Speciality: Herbal Medicine.
M (Ref:HM05205)

## COSSINS, M

**M Cossins**, 26 Moorland Rd, Yate, Bristol, BS37 4BX, **ENG**.
(T) 01454 310361
Speciality: Chiropodists (Podiatrists).
● **Owner** Mr M Cossins
S (Ref:HM05206)

## COSTAR, MARK

**Mark Costar**, 1 Dene House, Cockshaw, Hexham, **Northumberland**, NE46 3EB, **ENG**.
(T) 01434 322651
Speciality: Aromatherapy.
● **Owner** Mr M Costar
M O (Ref:HM05207)

## COSTELLO, JILL

**Jill Costello MIRI MAR ITEC**, 37 St Kevins Sq, Bray, **County Wicklow**, **IRE**.
(T) 01286 6629
Speciality: Complementary Medicines & Therapy.
M (Ref:HM05208)

## COSTIGAN, LUCY

**Lucy Costigan (MIAH)**, 14 Thomas St, **County Wexford**, **IRE**.
(T) 05322 923
Speciality: Complementary Medicines & Therapy.
M (Ref:HM05209)

## COSTIN, A E

**A E Costin**, Tower Rd, Orpington, **Kent**, BR6 0SG, **ENG**.
(T) 01689 833817
Speciality: Osteopathy.
● **Owner** Mr A Costin
P S T (Ref:HM05210)



Key: B Mind-Body Medicine C Complementary Medicine H Self Help Treatment M Medicinal Therapy O Oriental Medicine P Postural Therapy S Manipulative Structural Therapy T Touch Therapy

**COSTIN, KAREN**

**Karen Costin**, 3 Craiglands, Dalkey, **County Dublin**, IRE.
(T) 01285 0874
Speciality: Complementary Medicines & Therapy.
M (Ref:HM05211)

**COTEBROOK NATURAL HEALTH CTRE**

**Cotebrook Natural Health Centre**, Tarporley Rd, Cotebrook, Tarporley, **Cheshire**, CW6 9DY, ENG.
(T) 01829 760999
Speciality: Complementary Medicines & Therapy.
● **Director** Ms S Shepherd
C M (Ref:HM05212)

**COTSWOLD CHIROPODY**

**Cotswold Chiropody**, 121 Parkland, Wotton-under-Edge, **Gloucestershire**, GL12 7NR, ENG.
(T) 01453 521737
Speciality: Chiropodists (Podiatrists).
S (Ref:HM05213)

**COTSWOLD COMP THERAPY CTRE**

**Cotswold Complementary Therapy Centre (The)**, 17 Castle St, Banbury, **Oxfordshire**, OX16 5NU, ENG.
(T) 01295 266807 (F) 01295 266807
Speciality: Complementary Medicines & Therapy.
● **Owner** Mrs C Horner
M (Ref:HM05214)

**COTSWOLD PHYSIOTHERAPY CENTRE**

**Cotswold Physiotherapy Centre**, 105-107 Bath Rd, Cheltenham, **Gloucestershire**, GL53 7LE, ENG.
(T) 01242 228019 (F) 01242 230193
(E) physio@cotswold105.freeserve.co.uk
(W) www.cotswoldphysiotherapy.co.uk
Speciality: Acupuncture, Electrotherapy, Massage (Therapeutic), Physiotherapy, Pilates, Sports Massage, Hydrotherapy. ✔ CREDIT
● **Physiotherapist** Ms G Brown Q: MCSP, SRP. M: CSP.
● **Physiotherapist** Ms A Hackett Q: MCSP, SRP. M: CSP.
● **Physiotherapist** Ms R Heaton Q: MCSP, SRP. M: CSP.
● **Physiotherapist** Ms J Kent Q: MCSP, SRP. M: CSP.
● **Practice Manager** Mrs I Goldby
S Yrs. Est.: 12 (Ref:HM05215)

**COTSWOLD PODIATRY & CHIROPODY**

**Cotswold Podiatry & Chiropody**, 36A Griffiths Avenue, Cheltenham, **Gloucestershire**, GL51 7BL, ENG.
(T) 01242 514103
Speciality: Chiropodists (Podiatrists).
S (Ref:HM05216)

**COTTAGE CHIROPRACTIC CLINIC**

**Cottage Chiropractic Clinic**, Cherry Tree Lodge, High St, Cranworth, Thetford, **Norfolk**, IP25 7TA, ENG.
(T) 01362 820875
Speciality: Chiropractic. ✔
● **Chiropractor** Dr P Cooper Q: DC. M: BCA.
P Yrs. Est.: 1 (Ref:HM05217)

**COTTAGE CLINIC**

**Cottage Clinic**, 1 Higher Hill Lane, Cullompton, **Devon**, ENG.
(T) 01884 33669
Speciality: Complementary Medicines & Therapy.
● **Manager** Christina Huffer
M (Ref:HM05218)

**COTTAGE CLINIC**

**Cottage Clinic (The)**, Milton Cottage, Vicarage St, Painswick, Stroud, **Gloucestershire**, GL6 6XS, ENG.
(T) 01452 812344
Speciality: Physiotherapy.
P S T (Ref:HM05219)

**COTTAGE CLINIC**

**Self Heal School For Herbalists & Natural Healers (The)**, The Cabins, Station Rd, Pulham Market, **Norfolk**, IP21 4XF, ENG.
(T) 01379 608082 (F) 01379 608201
(E) selfheal@aol.com
(W) www.herbshandshealing.co.uk
Speciality: Herbal Medicine. ✔ CREDIT
● **Master Herbalist** Ms J Davies Q: PhD. M: AMH.
H M Yrs. Est.: 20 (Ref:HM05220)

**COTTAGE CLINIC**

**Cottage Clinic**, 63A Windmill Rd, Headington, Oxford, **Oxfordshire**, OX3 7BP, ENG.
(T) 01865 742215 (F) 01865 432691
Speciality: Absent Healing, Moxibustion, Reflexology, Reiki, Shiatsu, Tera-Mai, Tai Massage. ✔
● **Practitioner** Ms K Melbye Q: MRSS, Reiki 2. M: Shiatsu Society UK.
C Yrs. Est.: 5 (Ref:HM05221)

**COTTAGE NTRL HEALTH CLINIC**

**Cottage Natural Health Clinic (The)**, 2 Bridge Farm Cottages, Station Rd, Pulham Market, Diss, **Norfolk**, IP21 4TF, ENG.
(T) 01379 608007
Speciality: Complementary Medicines & Therapy, Herbalist, Natural Healers. ✔ CREDIT
● **Herbalist** Ms J Davies M: AMH, BHMA, EHPA.
● **Director** Mr Nityanada
C Yrs. Est.: 15 (Ref:HM05222)

**COTTAM, MARILYN**

**Marilyn Cottam**, 41 Windsor Drive, Leek, **Staffordshire**, ST13 6NP, ENG.
(T) 01538 385672
Speciality: Reflexology.
● **Owner** Mrs M Cottam
S T (Ref:HM05223)

**COTTAM, O N**

**Mrs O N Cottam**, 23A West Bank Avenue, Lytham St. Annes, **Lancashire**, FY8 5RB, ENG.
(T) 01253 733262
Speciality: Chiropody. ✔
● **Owner/Chiropodist** Mrs O Cottam Q: M.S.C.P.
M Yrs. Est.: 40 (Ref:HM05224)

**COTTERIDGE CHIROPRACTIC CLINIC**

**Cotteridge Chiropractic Clinic**, 8-10 Watford Rd, Birmingham, **Midlands (West)**, B30 1JA, ENG.
(T) 01214 513838
Speciality: Chiropractic.
● **Owner** Mr P Cooper
P S T (Ref:HM05225)

**COTTERILL, F**

**F Cotterill**, Chiropody Department, Garrison Clinic, Millport, **Ayrshire (North)**, KA28 0BY, SCO.
(T) 01475 530448
Speciality: Chiropodists (Podiatrists).
S (Ref:HM05226)

**COTTERILL, JENNY**

**Jenny Cotterill**, 'Bylands', Maidstone Rd, Charing, Ashford, **Kent**, TN27 0JS, ENG.
(T) 01233 712528
Speciality: Reflexology.
S T (Ref:HM05227)

**COTTON, A**

**A Cotton**, New Cross Natural Therapy Centre, 394 New Cross Rd, London, **London (Greater)**, SE14 6TY, ENG.
(T) 020 8469 0858
Speciality: Osteopathy.
● **Osteopath** A Cotton
P S T (Ref:HM05228)

**COTTON, PAULA**

**Paula Cotton**, Durants Rd, Enfield, **London (Greater)**, EN3 7AN, ENG.
(T) 020 8804 6995
Speciality: Aromatherapy.
● **Owner** Miss P Cotton
M O (Ref:HM05229)

**COTTRELL, SANDRA**

**Sandra Cottrell**, 3 Stanhope Cl, Durham, **County Durham**, DH1 5SR, ENG.
(T) 01913 849734
Speciality: Complementary Medicines & Therapy.
C M (Ref:HM05230)

**COUGHLAN & COUGHLAN**

**Coughlan & Coughlan**, 4 Ashwood, Locks Heath, Southampton, **Hampshire**, SO31 6RH, ENG.
(T) 01489 589804
Speciality: Chiropodists (Podiatrists).
● **Partner** Mr M Coughlan
S (Ref:HM05231)

**COUGHLAN, EILEEN**

**Eileen Coughlan**, 24 Shawley Way, Epsom, **Surrey**, KT18 5PB, ENG.
(T) 01737 357705
Speciality: Complementary Medicines & Therapy.
● **Owner** Mrs E Coughlan
C M (Ref:HM05232)

**COUGHLAN, SHEILA & THOMAS**

**Sheila & Thomas Coughlan**, 1 Summerstown Gro, Wilton, Cork, **County Cork**, IRE.
(T) 021 4341 300
Speciality: Complementary Medicines & Therapy.
M (Ref:HM05233)

**COUGHLIN, V IAN**

**V Ian Coughlin**, 135 Old Hale Way, Hitchin, **Hertfordshire**, SG5 1XT, ENG.
(T) 01462 457551
Speciality: Herbal Medicine.
● **Owner** Mr V Coughlin
M (Ref:HM05234)

**COULING, J**

**J Couling**, 41 Main Rd, Hextable, Swanley, **Kent**, BR8 7RA, ENG.
(T) 01322 665166
Speciality: Osteopathy.
P S T (Ref:HM05235)

**COULL, JUDY**

**Judy Coull**, 157 Waterworks Rd, Norwich, **Norfolk**, NR2 4DF, ENG.
(T) 01603 667713
Speciality: Homeopathy.
M (Ref:HM05236)

**COULSON, D W H**

**D W H Coulson**, 63 Roberts Yard, Beeston, Nottingham, **Nottinghamshire**, NG9 2LJ, ENG.
(T) 01159 253887
Speciality: Chiropodists (Podiatrists).
● **Owner** Mr D Coulson
S (Ref:HM05237)

**COULSON, GERALD**

**Gerald Coulson**, Glebe House, Front St, Chedzoy, Bridgwater, **Somerset**, TA7 8RB, ENG.
(T) 01278 423754
Speciality: Homeopathy.
● **Owner** Mr G Coulson
M (Ref:HM05238)

**COULSTOCK, JUDY**

**Judy Coulstock**, 47 Atterbury Avenue, Leighton Buzzard, **Bedfordshire**, LU7 8LE, ENG.
(T) 01525 374842
Speciality: Reflexology, Reiki. ✔
● **Owner/Reiki Master** Ms J Coulstock Q: Reiki Master.
C T Yrs. Est.: 7 (Ref:HM05239)

**COULTER, M**

**M Coulter**, 3 Ogwen Avenue, Kinmel Bay, Rhyl, **Denbighshire**, LL18 5ER, WAL.
(T) 01745 361018
Speciality: Clairvoyants & Palmists.
● **Owner** Mrs M Coulter
B (Ref:HM05240)

**COULTER, T H L**

**T H L Coulter**, 16 Cromwell Rd, Southsea, **Hampshire**, PO4 9PN, ENG.
(T) 023 9273 7474
Speciality: Chiropodists (Podiatrists).
S (Ref:HM05241)

**COUNCIL FOR COMP ALT MEDICINE**

**Council For Complementary & Alternative Medicine**, Suite D Park House, 206-208 Latimer Rd, London, **London (Greater)**, W10 6SZ, ENG.



Key continued: Yrs.Est: Years Established Q: Qualifications M: Professional Membership ✔ Indemnity Insurance CREDIT Accept Credit Cards

(T) 020 8968 3862
Speciality: Complementary Medicines & Therapy.
M (Ref:HM05242)

## COUNCIL FOR COMP/ALT MEDICINE

**Council For Complementary & Alternative Medicine**, Suite D., Park House, 206-208 Latimer Rd, London, **London (Greater)**, W10 6RE, ENG.
(T) 020 8968 3862
Speciality: Complementary Medicines & Therapy.
C M (Ref:HM05243)

## COUNS & HYPNOTHERAPY PRACTICE

**Counselling & Hypnotherapy Practice (The)**, 4 Crown Rise, Watford, **Hertfordshire**, WD2 6NE, ENG.
(T) 01923 440031
Speciality: Hypnosis.
B (Ref:HM05244)

## COUNSELLING & HYPNOTHERAPY SV

**Counselling & Hypnotherapy Service (West Wiltshire**, 45 Avenue Rd, Trowbridge, **Wiltshire**, BA14 0AQ, ENG.
(T) 01225 754585
Speciality: Hypnotherapy.
● **Owner** Ms I De-Souza
B (Ref:HM05245)

## COUNSELLING & PSYCHOTHERAPY

**Counselling & Psychotherapy Associates**, Flat 4, 9 Welbeck St, Marylebone, London, **London (Greater)**, W1G 7PB, ENG.
(T) 020 7486 8914 (F) 020 7935 6687
(E) london.uk@bigfoot.com
(W) www.counselling.org
Speciality: Counselling, Family Therapy, Group Therapy, Humanistic Psychology, Physiotherapy, Psychotherapy. ✔
● **Psychiatrist** Dr M Best Q: FRCP. M: RCPsych.
● **Psychotherapist** Mr I Brown Q: BA, BACP, PGCE, UKCP (Reg). M: BACP, UKCP.
● **Psychotherapist** Mr T Wader Q: BA (Hons) Psychol, UKCP (Reg). M: BAP, UKCP.
B Yrs. Est.: 9 (Ref:HM05246)

## COUNSELLING & PSYCHOTHERAPY

**Counselling & Psychotherapy Network**, 2 Provost Rd, London, **London (Greater)**, NW3 4ST, ENG.
(T) 020 7722 7573
Speciality: Psychotherapy.
B (Ref:HM05247)

## COUNSELLING AT ST PETER'S HSE

**Counselling at St Peter's House**, 4 Exchange St, **Midlands (West)**, WV1 1TS, ENG.
(T) 01902 773375
Speciality: Psychotherapy.
B (Ref:HM05248)

## COUNSELLING CENTRE

**Counselling Centre (The)**, 66 Colinton Rd, Edinburgh, **Edinburgh (City of)**, EH14 1AT, SCO.
(T) 01314 440100
Speciality: Hypnosis.
● **Owner** Mr G Dickson
B (Ref:HM05249)

## COUNSELLING CENTRE

**Counselling Centre**, 7 Fr Mathew St, **County Cork**, IRE.
(T) 021 4274 951
Speciality: Counselling.
B H (Ref:HM05250)

## COUNSELLING CLINIC

**Counselling Clinic Of Psychotherapy & Hypnotherapy (The)**, The Lodge, 1 Oakford Cl, Banks, Southport, **Merseyside**, PR9 8BP, ENG.
(T) 01704 214713
Speciality: Psychotherapy.
B (Ref:HM05251)

## COUNSELLING SERVICE

**Counselling Service**, 1017 Harrow Rd, Sudbury Hill, London, **London (Greater)**, HA0 2SJ, ENG.
(T) 020 8904 8239
(E) samandar9@aol.com
Speciality: Counselling, Family Therapy, Stress Therapy, Life Style Assessment, Relaxation, Visualisation.
● **Owner** S Samari
C Yrs. Est.: 5 (Ref:HM05252)

## COUNSULTING ROOMS

**Counsulting Rooms (The)**, 28 College St, Burnham-on-Sea, **Somerset**, TA8 1AT, ENG.
(T) 01278 784490
(E) theconsulting.rooms@virgin.net
Speciality: Auto Suggestion, Autogenic Training, Aversion Therapy, Biofeedback, Cognitive Therapy, Complementary Therapy, Counselling, Group Therapy, Hypnosis, Hypnotherapy, Life Style Coaching, Stress Therapy, Transactional Analysis, Visualisation Therapy. ✔
● **Hypnotherapist/Stress Management Practitioner**
Mrs S McIntyre Q: Cert.Couns, Cert.Couns.Groupwork, Dip.Adv.Hyp, Dip.Hyp. M: NCH.
B Yrs. Est.: 11 (Ref:HM05253)

## COUNTRY CLINIC

**Country Clinic (The)**, 60A Bloomfield Avenue, Belfast, **County Antrim**, BT5 5AD, NIR.
(T) 028 9045 1438 (F) 028 9045 1438
Speciality: Complementary Medicines & Therapy.
● **Owner** Dr J Li
M (Ref:HM05254)

## COUNTRY GARDEN HOLISTICS

**Country Garden Holistics**, Welford Grange Farm, Naseby Rd, Welford, Northampton, **Northamptonshire**, NN6 6HZ, ENG.
(T) 01858 575834
Speciality: Complementary Medicines & Therapy.
C M (Ref:HM05255)

## COUNTRY PRACTICE

**Country Practice (The)**, Unit 2, 63 Thorpe St, Thorpe Hesley, Rotherham, **Yorkshire (South)**, S61 2RP, ENG.
(T) 01142 455990 (F) 01142 455990
Speciality: Aromatherapy, Complementary Therapy, Inhalation Therapy, Massage (Therapeutic), Nail Surgery, Stress Therapy, Aromatic Herbal Medicine (internal use of aromatic waters). ✔
● **Podiatrist/Aromatherapist**
Ms D Wilson Q: BSc, ISPA, MA. M: ISPA, S.C.P.
B Yrs. Est.: 3 (Ref:HM05256)

## COUNTRYSIDE HYPNOTHERAPIST

**Countryside Hypnotherapist**, Toseland Rd, Graveley, Huntingdon, **Cambridgeshire**, PE18 9PS, ENG.
(T) 08005 21449
Speciality: Hypnotherapy.
● **Owner** Mr M Thody
B (Ref:HM05257)

## COUNTY BEAUTY CLINIC

**County Beauty Clinic Ltd**, 251 Seymour Gr, Manchester, **Manchester (Greater)**, M16 0DS, ENG.
(T) 01618 815306
Speciality: Electrolysis.
● **Owner** Mrs E Derbyshire
T (Ref:HM05258)

## COUNTY HEALTH

**County Health**, 15 High St, Holt, **Norfolk**, NR25 6BB, ENG.
(T) 01263 713974
Speciality: Homeopathy. ✔
● **Homeopath** Jo Reay Q: BSc (Hons), LCH. M: HMA.
M (Ref:HM05259)

## COUNTY PSYCHOLOGY SERVICE

**County Psychology Service**, County Offices, Newland, Lincoln, **Lincolnshire**, LN1 1YQ, ENG.
(T) 01522 553341 (F) 01522 553224
Speciality: Psychology.
● **Manager** Mr D Dickenson
B (Ref:HM05260)

## COUPAR, A M

**A M Coupar**, The Clock Tower, Llanerch Park, St. Asaph, **Denbighshire**, LL17 0BD, WAL.
(T) 01745 730571
Speciality: Psychology.
B (Ref:HM05261)

## COUPLAND, J E

**J E Coupland**, 38 Eastgate St, Stafford, **Staffordshire**, ST16 2LZ, ENG.
(T) 01785 255810
Speciality: Chiropodists (Podiatrists).
S (Ref:HM05262)

## COURAGE, VANESSA

**Vanessa Courage**, **Hampshire**, SO32, ENG.
(T) 01489 891996
Speciality: Bach Remedies.
M (Ref:HM05263)

## COURT, C A

**C A Court**, 7 The Paddocks, Thornbury, Bristol, BS35 2HP, ENG.
(T) 01454 419255
Speciality: Chiropodists (Podiatrists).
● **Owner** Mrs C Court
S (Ref:HM05264)

## COURT, SUSAN

**Susan Court**, 9 Greenwood Cl, Petts Wood, Orpington, **Kent**, BR5 1QG, ENG.
(T) 01689 822830
Speciality: Chiropractic, Manipulation, Massage (Therapeutic), Hopi Ear Candles. ✔
● **McTimoney Chiropractor**
Ms S Court Q: Dip.Chiro. M: MCA.
● **Remedial Masseuse** Ms C Campbell
(T) 01892 680451 Q: Dip.NIM. M: LCSP.
S Yrs. Est.: 10 (Ref:HM05265)

## COURT, SUSAN

**Susan Court**, 2 Lodge Rd, Tonbridge, **Kent**, TN9 1JA, ENG.
(T) 01732 366543
Speciality: Chiropractic, Manipulation, Massage (Therapeutic), Hopi Ear Candles. ✔
● **Remedial Masseuse** Ms C Campbell
(T) 01892 680451 Q: Dip.NIM. M: LCSP.
● **McTimoney Chiropractor**
Ms S Court Q: Dip.Chiro. M: MCA.
S Yrs. Est.: 10 (Ref:HM05266)

## COURTLAND

**Courtland**, 24 Forge Rd, Port Talbot, **Neath Port Talbot**, SA13 1NU, WAL.
(T) 01639 882088
Speciality: Chiropodists (Podiatrists).
● **Owner** Mr L Price
S (Ref:HM05267)

## COURTNEY, JOHN

**John Courtney**, Ashford Clinic Of Complementary Medicine, Western Avenue, Ashford, **Kent**, TN23 1LY, ENG.
(T) 01233 631530
Speciality: Hypnotherapy.
B (Ref:HM05268)

## COURTYARD CLINIC

**Courtyard Clinic (The)**, 7a The Courtyard, Market Sq, Westerham, **Kent**, TN16 1AZ, ENG.
(T) 01959 561242
Speciality: Complementary Medicines & Therapy.
● **Owner** Miss M Hunn
C M (Ref:HM05269)

## COURTYARD STOURBRIDGE CENTRE

**Courtyard Stourbridge Complementary Health Cen (The)**, 50A High St, Wollaston, Stourbridge, **Midlands (West)**, DY8 4NL, ENG.
(T) 01384 825678
Speciality: Complementary Medicines & Therapy.
C M (Ref:HM05270)

## COUSANS, W E

**W E Cousans**, 34 Station Rd West, Canterbury, **Kent**, CT2 8AN, ENG.
(T) 01227 463369
Speciality: Chiropodists (Podiatrists).
● **Owner** Mr W Cousans
S (Ref:HM05271)

## COUSENS, BRENDA

**Brenda Cousens**, 75 Leigh Rd, Leigh-On-Sea, **Essex**, SS9 1JN, ENG.
(T) 01702 714862 (F) 01702 716969

Speciality: Aromatherapy.
● **Owner** Mrs C Merryfield
M O (Ref:HM05272)

### COUSINS, MARILYN

**Marilyn Cousins**, Bexleyheath Natural Health Clinic, 284 Broadway, Bexleyheath, **Kent**, DA6 8AJ, ENG.
(T) 020 8303 6288 (F) 020 8303 6288
Speciality: Hypnotherapy.
● **Owner** Mr P Cousins
B (Ref:HM05273)

### COUSINS, MATHEW

**Mathew Cousins**, The Radlett Practice, 107 Watling St, Radlett, **Hertfordshire**, WD7 7NG, ENG.
(T) 01923 855884
Speciality: Osteopathy.
P S T (Ref:HM05274)

### COUSINS, MATHEW

**Mathew Cousins**, Treatment Centre, Portmill Lane, Hitchin, **Hertfordshire**, SG4 9TH, ENG.
(T) 01462 713031
Speciality: Osteopathy.
P S T (Ref:HM05275)

### COUSSENS, C A

**C A Coussens**, 44 Coronation Gardens, Hurst Green, Etchingham, **Sussex (East)**, TN19 7PH, ENG.
(T) 01580 860519
Speciality: Osteopathy.
● **Owner** Mrs C Coussens
P S T (Ref:HM05276)

### COUTTS & SONS

**J Coutts & Sons**, 2 Cross Lane, North Frodingham, Driffield, **Humberside (North)**, YO25 8JY, ENG.
(T) 01262 488414
Speciality: Electrolysis.
T (Ref:HM05277)

### COUTTS, L

**L Coutts**, Chelsea Lane, Inverurie, **Aberdeenshire**, AB51 3QQ, SCO.
(T) 01467 624888 (F) 01467 624888
Speciality: Complementary Medicines & Therapy.
● **Partner** Mrs C Craigmile
M (Ref:HM05278)

### COUZENS, D R

**D R Couzens**, 12 Coley Avenue, Reading, **Berkshire**, RG1 6LQ, ENG.
(T) 01189 572102
Speciality: Chiropodists (Podiatrists).
S (Ref:HM05279)

### COVENT HOUSE NTRL HEALTH CTRE

**Covent House Natural Health Centre**, 27a Maengwyn St, Machynlleth, **Powys**, SY20 8UP, WAL.
(T) 01654 703289
Speciality: Acupuncture, Alexander Technique, Chiropody, Counselling, Cranio-Sacral Therapy, Homeopathy, Massage (Therapeutic), Pyscho-Synthesis, Reflexology, Shiatsu. ✔
● **Reflexologist** Ms S Fisher Q: MAR. M: AoR.
● **Homeopath** Ms V Reed Q: BA, DSH, RSHom. M: Soc.Hom.
B Yrs. Est.: 5 (Ref:HM05280)

### COVENTON, DOROTHY

**Dorothy Coventon**, Dolphins, 2 Trelawney Cl, Maenporth, Falmouth, **Cornwall**, TR11 5HS, ENG.
(T) 01326 250751
Speciality: Reflexology.
S T (Ref:HM05281)

### COVENTRY CTRE OF OSTEO & ACU

**Coventry Centre Of Osteopathy & Acupuncture**, 8 Dugdale Rd, Coventry, **Midlands (West)**, CV6 1PB, ENG.
(T) 024 7659 0478
Speciality: Osteopathy.
P S T (Ref:HM05282)

### COVERDALE, ANNE

**Anne Coverdale**, 38 Eastfield Rd, Westbury-On-Trym, Bristol, BS9 4AD, ENG.
(T) 01179 079516
Speciality: Reflexology.
● **Partner** Ms A Coverdale
S T (Ref:HM05283)

### COVERLEY PHYSIOTHERAPY CLINIC

**Coverley Physiotherapy Clinic (The)**, 2 Sett Cl, Off Market St, New Mills, High Peak, **Derbyshire**, SK22 4AQ, ENG.
(T) 01663 744552
Speciality: Manipulation, Physiotherapy. ✔
● **Physiotherapist** Ms S Coverley Q: MCSP, SRP. M: CSP.
S Yrs. Est.: 10 (Ref:HM05284)

### COVIELLO, LINDA

**Linda Coviello**, 14 Jersey Rd, London, **London (Greater)**, W7 2JF, ENG.
(T) 020 8566 4478
Speciality: Acupuncture.
O (Ref:HM05285)

### COWAN, KAREN

**Karen Cowan**, 39 - 41 High St, Holywood, **County Down**, BT18 9AB, NIR.
(T) 028 9080 5090 (F) 028 9080 5090
Speciality: Complementary Medicines & Therapy.
● **Owner** Miss K Cowan
C M (Ref:HM05286)

### COWARD, JANICE

**Janice Coward**, 282 St. Johns Rd, Hemel Hempstead, **Hertfordshire**, HP1 1QG, ENG.
(T) 01442 863683
Speciality: Reflexology.
● **Owner** Mrs J Coward
S T (Ref:HM05287)

### COWBRIDGE & VALE CLINIC

**Cowbridge & Vale Homeopathic Clinic**, 33 Westgate, Cowbridge, **Glamorgan (Vale of)**, CF71 7AQ, WAL.
(T) 01446 772489
Speciality: Homeopathy.
● **Owner** Ms C Geary
M (Ref:HM05288)

### COWBRIDGE CHIRO/SPINAL REHAB

**Cowbridge Chiropractic & Spinal Rehabilitation Clinic**, 87 Eastgate, Cowbridge, **Glamorgan (Vale of)**, CF71 7AA, WAL.
(T) 01446 771114 (F) 01446 771114
Speciality: Acupuncture, Chiropractic, Homeopathy. ✔
● **Chiropractor** Dr M Barber Q: DC, FCC. M: BCA, GCC.
● **Chiropractor** Dr A Kier Q: DC, FCC. M: BCA, GCC.
● **Homeopath** Dr H Barber Q: MCPH. M: HMA.
● **Chiropractor** Dr D Byfield Q: DC. M: BCA, GCC.
P Yrs. Est.: 24 (Ref:HM05289)

### COWBRIDGE OSTEOPATH CLINIC

**Cowbridge Osteopath Clinic**, 23 High St, Cowbridge, **Glamorgan (Vale of)**, CF71 7AE, WAL.
(T) 01446 775080
Speciality: Manipulation, Massage (Therapeutic), Osteopathy. ✔
● **Osteopath** Mr P Pearce Q: DO. M: GOsC.
S Yrs. Est.: 5 (Ref:HM05290)

### COWBRIDGE PRACTICE

**Cowbridge Practice**, Mill Cottage, Monknash, Cowbridge, **Glamorgan (Vale of)**, CF71 7QQ, WAL.
(T) 01656 890700
Speciality: Homeopathy.
● **Owner** Mrs V Thompson
M (Ref:HM05291)

### COWELL, D E (DR)

**Dr D E Cowell**, 62 Priory Green, Highworth, Swindon, **Wiltshire**, SN6 7NU, ENG.
(T) 01793 763267
Speciality: Psychology.
B (Ref:HM05292)

### COWELL, IAN

**Ian Cowell**, 8a Brook Prde, High Rd, Chigwell, **Essex**, IG7 6PB, ENG.
(T) 020 8501 1449
Speciality: Physiotherapy.
P S T (Ref:HM05293)

### COWELL, SARAH

**Sarah Cowell**, 24 Catherine St, Salisbury, **Wiltshire**, SP1 2DA, ENG.
(T) 01722 411766
Speciality: Homeopathy.
M (Ref:HM05294)

### COWEN, E

**Mrs E Cowen**, 46 Upper St James's St, Brighton, **Sussex (East)**, BN2 1JN, ENG.
(T) 01273 673033
Speciality: Chiropodists (Podiatrists).
S (Ref:HM05295)

### COWIESON, MARY

**Mary Cowieson**, Lattice Cottage, Crawley Ridge, Camberley, **Surrey**, GU15 2AN, ENG.
(T) 01276 23072
Speciality: Reflexology.
S T (Ref:HM05296)

### COWLINGS FOOT CLINIC

**Cowlings Foot Clinic**, 38 Broad St, Syston, Leicester, **Leicestershire**, LE7 1GH, ENG.
(T) 01162 608834
Speciality: Chiropodists (Podiatrists).
S (Ref:HM05297)

### COWPER, F M

**F M Cowper**, The Accord Clinic, Church House, 20 Hightown, Middlewich, **Cheshire**, CW10 9AN, ENG.
(T) 01606 836214
Speciality: Chiropodists (Podiatrists).
● **Owner** Mrs F Cowper
S (Ref:HM05298)

### COX ASSOCIATES

**Cox Associates**, Riverdale House, 89 Graham Rd, Sheffield, **Yorkshire (South)**, S10 3GP, ENG.
(T) 01142 295050 (F) 01142 295151
Speciality: Psychology.
● **Owner** Mr M Cox
B (Ref:HM05299)

### COX, ANGELA

**Angela Cox**, 28 Springfield Rd, Bexleyheath, **Kent**, DA7 6DX, ENG.
(T) 01322 523783
Speciality: Reflexology.
S T (Ref:HM05300)

### COX, B L

**B L Cox**, 13 The Graylands, Coventry, **Midlands (West)**, CV3 6EW, ENG.
(T) 024 7641 2528
Speciality: Physiotherapy.
P S T (Ref:HM05301)

### COX, BARBARA

**Barbara Cox**, 20A Central Avenue, West Bridgeford, West Bridgford, Nottingham, **Nottinghamshire**, NG2 5GR, ENG.
(T) 01159 143311
Speciality: Reflexology.
S T (Ref:HM05302)

### COX, CHRISTINE

**Christine Cox**, 28 Fern Rd, St. Leonards-On-Sea, **Sussex (East)**, TN38 0UH, ENG.
(T) 01424 424797
Speciality: Hypnotherapy.
● **Owner** Mrs C Cox
B (Ref:HM05303)

### COX, H J E (DR)

**Dr H J E Cox**, Sozo Clinic, 14 Ayleswater, Aylesbury, **Buckinghamshire**, HP19 0FB, ENG.
(T) 01296 399317
Speciality: Complementary Medicines & Therapy.
M (Ref:HM05304)

### COX, IAN

**Ian Cox**, Surgery, 38-40 Sea Rd, Bexhill-on-Sea, **Sussex (East)**, TN40 1ED, ENG.
(T) 01424 216488
Speciality: Chiropodists (Podiatrists).
● **Owner** Mr I Cox
S (Ref:HM05305)


Key continued: Yrs.Est: Years Established Q: Qualifications M: Professional Membership ✔ Indemnity Insurance Accept Credit Cards

### COX, J G

**J G Cox**, 2a Railway Trce, Grantham, **Lincolnshire**, NG31 6NB, ENG.
(T) 01476 562483
Speciality: Chiropodists (Podiatrists).
S (Ref:HM05306)

### COX, JULIET

**Juliet Cox**, Croydon Buddhist Centre, 96-98 High St, Croydon, **Surrey**, CR0 1, ENG.
(T) 020 8688 8624
(E) juliet@brighton16.freeserve
Speciality: Alexander Technique, Voice Therapy. ✓
● **Therapist** Ms J Cox Q: BA. M: STAT.
P Yrs. Est.: 4 (Ref:HM05307)

### COX, JULIET

**Juliet Cox**, Evolution Arts And Natural Health Centre, 2 Sillwood Trce, Brighton, **Sussex (East)**, BN1 2LR, ENG.
(T) 01273 729803
(E) juliet@brighton16.freeserve.co.uk
Speciality: Alexander Technique, Voice Therapy. ✓
● **Teacher of the Alexander Technique/Voice Worker**
Ms J Cox
(T) 01273 387862 Q: BA. M: STAT.
C Yrs. Est.: 5 (Ref:HM05308)

### COX, K

**K Cox**, 65 Marshall Rd, Gillingham, **Kent**, ME8 0AN, ENG.
(T) 01634 232341
Speciality: Osteopathy.
P S T (Ref:HM05309)

### COX, KATHERINE

**Katherine Cox**, The Elms Medical Centre, Hoo, Rochester, **Kent**, ME3 9AE, ENG.
(T) 01634 250142 (F) 01634 255029
Speciality: Osteopathy.
● **Practice Manager** Mrs H Rayner
P S T (Ref:HM05310)

### COX, LESLEY

**Lesley Cox**, 82 Dewlands Rd, Verwood, **Dorset**, BH31 6PN, ENG.
(T) 01202 824885
Speciality: Reflexology.
S T (Ref:HM05311)

### COX, LINDY

**Lindy Cox**, Sundial House, Bernards Cl, Great Missenden, **Buckinghamshire**, HP16 0BU, ENG.
(T) 01494 864705
Speciality: Acupuncture.
● **Owner** Mrs L Cox
O (Ref:HM05312)

### COX, M M

**M M Cox**, Chiropractic Health Care Clinic, 23 Montgomerie Cresent, Saltcoats, **Ayrshire (North)**, KA21 5BT, SCO.
(T) 01294 462882
Speciality: Chiropractors.
P S T (Ref:HM05313)

### COX, MADDI

**Maddi Cox**, 42 Watling St, St. Albans, **Hertfordshire**, AL1 2QB, ENG.
(T) 01727 854904
Speciality: Reflexology.
S T (Ref:HM05314)

### COX, MARTIN

**Martin Cox**, 54 York Rd, Montpelier, Bristol, BS6 5QF, ENG.
(T) 01179 541755
Speciality: Alexander Technique.
● **Owner** Mr M Cox
P S (Ref:HM05315)

### COX, MIRANDA

**Miranda Cox**, 3 St. Helens, Heywood Rd, Bideford, **Devon**, EX39 3PQ, ENG.
(T) 01237 473252 (F) 01237 473252
(E) miranda.cox@care4free.com
Speciality: Cognitive Therapy, Counselling, Gestalt Therapy, Group Therapy, Humanistic Psychology, Inhalation Therapy, Meditation, Psychotherapy, Rogerian Therapy, Stress Therapy, Transactional Analysis. ✓
● **Psychotherapist/Counsellor**
Ms M Cox Q: BA (Hons), Dip.Psych. M: UKCP.
B Yrs. Est.: 10 (Ref:HM05316)

### COX, PETER R

**Peter R Cox**, 2 Stratford Rd, Shirley, Solihull, **Midlands (West)**, B90 3LT, ENG.
(T) 01217 451968
Speciality: Physiotherapy.
P S T (Ref:HM05317)

### COX, R W

**R W Cox**, 55 Fair St, Broadstairs, **Kent**, CT10 2JL, ENG.
(T) 01843 867302
Speciality: Chiropodists (Podiatrists).
S (Ref:HM05318)

### COX, RITA

**Rita Cox**, 153 Berengrave Lane, Rainham, Gillingham, **Kent**, ME8 7UJ, ENG.
(T) 01634 232640
Speciality: Reflexology.
● **Owner** Mrs R Cox
S T (Ref:HM05319)

### COX, S

**S Cox**, 15 Ridgeway Rd, Headington, Oxford, **Oxfordshire**, OX3 8DS, ENG.
(T) 01865 762376
Speciality: Acupuncture.
● **Owner** Mrs S Cox
O (Ref:HM05320)

### COX, SUSAN

**Susan Cox**, Brabant House, Portsmouth Rd, Thames Ditton, **Surrey**, KT7 0EY, ENG.
(T) 020 8398 7592
Speciality: Acupuncture.
O (Ref:HM05321)

### COX, T

**T Cox**, 35-37 High St, Wheathampstead, St. Albans, **Hertfordshire**, AL4 8BB, ENG.
(T) 01582 834004
Speciality: Osteopathy.
● **Owner** Mr T Cox
P S T (Ref:HM05322)

### COXAN, PATRICIA

**Patricia Coxan**, 50 Learmonth Gr, Edinburgh, **Edinburgh (City of)**, EH4 1BN, SCO.
(T) 01313 328837
Speciality: Complementary Medicines & Therapy.
● **Partner** Miss J Hazel
C M (Ref:HM05323)

### COXELL REMEDIAL CLINIC

**Coxell Remedial Clinic (The)**, 15 Clifton Avenue, Peterborough, **Cambridgeshire**, PE3 6AY, ENG.
(T) 01733 343815
Speciality: Electrotherapy, Manipulation, Massage (Therapeutic), Micro Manipulation, Specific Reflex Techniques of the late Mr S.G Coxell. ✓
● **Manipulative Therapist**
Mr M Dodsworth Q: LCSP. M: LCSP.
S Yrs. Est.: 20 (Ref:HM05324)

### COXHEAD, ANN

**Ann Coxhead**, 106 High St, Rottingdean, Brighton, **Sussex (East)**, BN2 7HF, ENG.
(T) 01273 305350
Speciality: Osteopathy.
P S T (Ref:HM05325)

### COXON CLINIC

**Coxon Clinic (The)**, Care Of In Trim, 81 Knight St, Pinchbeck, Spalding, **Lincolnshire**, PE11 3RA, ENG.
(T) 01775 710734
(E) roycoxon@globalnet.co.uk
Speciality: Allergy Testing, Bach Remedies, Osteopathy, Reiki, Electro Acupuncture. ✓
● **Owner** Mr R Coxon Q: LCSP. M: BIAET, LCSP.
C Yrs. Est.: 16 (Ref:HM05326)

### COXON, THOMAS

**Thomas Coxon**, 26 Mere Rd, Wigston, **Leicestershire**, LE18 3RJ, ENG.
(T) 01162 886068
Speciality: Complementary Medicines & Therapy.
C M (Ref:HM05327)

### COYLE, DAVID

**David Coyle**, The Spindles, 227 Brow Foot Gate Lane, Halifax, **Yorkshire (West)**, HX2 7LS, ENG.
(T) 01422 346459
Speciality: Chiropodists (Podiatrists).
● **Owner** Mr D Coyle
S (Ref:HM05328)

### COYNE, ANTHONY

**Anthony Coyne**, Trim Rd, Athboy, **County Meath**, IRE.
(T) 04630 383
(E) coynea@indigo.ie
(W) www.animalherbcompany.com
Speciality: Complementary Medicines & Therapy.
M (Ref:HM05329)

### COYNE, MARTINA

**Martina Coyne**, 11 Main St, Lucan, **County Dublin**, IRE.
(T) 01628 3467
Speciality: Healing.
B (Ref:HM05330)

### COYNE, MAUREEN ELLEN

**Maureen Ellen Coyne**, 18 Old Oak Cl, Leeds, **Yorkshire (West)**, LS16 5HD, ENG.
(T) 01132 780602
Speciality: Clairvoyants & Palmists.
● **Owner** Mrs M Clairvoyant
B (Ref:HM05331)

### COYSTEN & ASSOCIATES

**Tim Coysten & Associates**, L.A. Fitness, Market Sq, Tunbridge Wells, **Kent**, TN1 2SW, ENG.
(T) 01892 513444
Speciality: Cranial Osteopathy, Manipulation, Massage (Therapeutic), Osteopathy, Postural Integration. ✓
● **Osteopath** Mrs J Coysten Q: BSc, Hons (OST). M: GOsC.
● **Osteopath** Mr T Coysten Q: DO. M: GOsC.
S Yrs. Est.: 8 (Ref:HM05332)

### COYSTEN, T

**T Coysten**, Denewood, 74 Woodlands Avenue, Rustington, Littlehampton, **Sussex (West)**, BN16 3EY, ENG.
(T) 01903 773074
Speciality: Osteopathy.
● **Owner** Mr B Walsh
P S T (Ref:HM05333)

### COZANS, EDDIE

**Eddie Cozans**, 7 Cragside House, Anglesey Rd, Sunderland, **Tyne and Wear**, SR3 3ED, ENG.
(T) 01915 281990
Speciality: Clairvoyants & Palmists.
● **Owner** Mr E Cozans
B (Ref:HM05334)

### COZENS, DAVID R

**David R Cozens**, 27 Queensway, Caversham, Reading, **Berkshire**, RG4 6SQ, ENG.
(T) 01189 470411
Speciality: Chiropodists (Podiatrists).
S (Ref:HM05335)

### CRABTREE, JANET

**Janet Crabtree**, 6 Vine Ter East, Bradford, **Yorkshire (West)**, BD8 0LF, ENG.
(T) 01274 493248
Speciality: Reflexology.
● **Owner** Ms J Crabtree
S T (Ref:HM05336)

### CRABTREE, JENNY R

**Jenny R Crabtree**, 4 Raven Cl, Bradwell, Great Yarmouth, **Norfolk**, NR31 8JX, ENG.
(T) 01493 667585
Speciality: Chiropodists (Podiatrists).
● **Partner** Mr P Crabtree
S (Ref:HM05337)

### CRABTREE, P W

**P W Crabtree**, 6b Smallgate, Beccles, **Suffolk**, NR34 9AD, ENG.
(T) 01502 716418

Key: B Mind-Body Medicine, C Complementary Medicine, H Self Help Treatment, M Medicinal Therapy, O Oriental Medicine, P Postural Therapy, S Manipulative Structural Therapy, T Touch Therapy

Speciality: Chiropodists (Podiatrists).
● **Owner** Mr P Crabtree
S (Ref:HM05338)

## CRABTREE, P W

**P W Crabtree**, 4 Raven Cl, Bradwell, Great Yarmouth, **Norfolk**, NR31 8JX, ENG.
(T) 01493 667585
Speciality: Chiropodists (Podiatrists).
● **Partner** Mr P Crabtree
S (Ref:HM05339)

## CRACKNELL, ANGELA

**Angela Cracknell**, 20 Eastville Rd, Swindon, **Wiltshire**, SN2 3BA, ENG.
(T) 01793 613334
Speciality: Chiropodists (Podiatrists).
S (Ref:HM05340)

## CRACKNELL, ANNE

**Anne Cracknell**, 45C Leeming St, Mansfield, **Nottinghamshire**, NG18 1NB, ENG.
(T) 01623 635084
Speciality: Physiotherapy.
P S T (Ref:HM05341)

## CRACKNELL, F J

**F J Cracknell**, 1 Woodland Gardens, Isleworth, **London (Greater)**, TW7 6LN, ENG.
(T) 020 8568 4184
Speciality: Physiotherapy.
● **Owner** Mr F Cracknell
P S T (Ref:HM05342)

## CRACKNELL, JANICE

**Janice Cracknell**, Sidcup, Rochester, **Kent**, DA15, ENG.
(T) 01634 723205
Speciality: Bach Remedies.
M (Ref:HM05343)

## CRAFT, DEREK A

**Derek A Craft**, 17 Marine Drive West, Bognor Regis, **Sussex (West)**, PO21 2QA, ENG.
(T) 01243 829514
Speciality: Chiropodists (Podiatrists).
S (Ref:HM05344)

## CRAIB, MARGARET

**Margaret Craib**, Ashridge Farm, Ringshall, Berkhamsted, **Hertfordshire**, HP4 1ND, ENG.
(T) 01442 842729
Speciality: Chiropractic.
P S T (Ref:HM05345)

## CRAIG GREGG & RUSSELL

**Craig Gregg & Russell Ltd**, Crossway, Manchester, **Manchester (Greater)**, M20 6TU, ENG.
(T) 01614 450916
Speciality: Psychology.
B (Ref:HM05346)

## CRAIG, C J

**C J Craig**, 21C Market Sq, Antrim, **County Antrim**, BT41 4AW, NIR.
(T) 028 9446 2423
Speciality: Chiropodists (Podiatrists).
● **Owner** Mr C Craig
S (Ref:HM05347)

## CRAIG, DIANE

**Diane Craig**, 267a High St, Chasetown, Burntwood, **Staffordshire**, WS7 8XJ, ENG.
(T) 01543 676612
Speciality: Physiotherapy.
P S T (Ref:HM05348)

## CRAIG, J

**J Craig**, Windermere Business Centre, Oldfield Court, Windermere, **Cumbria**, LA23 2HJ, ENG.
(T) 01539 447888
Speciality: Acupuncture.
● **Owner** Mrs J Craig
O (Ref:HM05349)

## CRAIG, MARIANNE

**Marianne Craig**, 57 Stanford Rd, Brighton, **Sussex (East)**, BN1 5PR, ENG.
(T) 01273 563518
Speciality: Hypnotherapy.
● **Owner** Ms M Craig
B (Ref:HM05350)

## CRAIG, MARY

**Mary Craig**, Amherst, Montrose Trce, Bridge Of Weir, **Renfrewshire**, PA11 3DH, SCO.
(T) 01505 614675 (F) 01505 614675
Speciality: Physiotherapy.
● **Owner** Mrs M Craig
P S T (Ref:HM05351)

## CRAIG, MAUREEN

**Maureen Craig**, 3 Brookland Avenue, Crewe, **Cheshire**, CW2 8EJ, ENG.
(T) 01270 567983
Speciality: Chiropodists (Podiatrists).
● **Owner** Ms M Craig
S (Ref:HM05352)

## CRAIG, PETER

**Peter Craig**, 63 Barton Drive, Barton On Sea, New Milton, **Hampshire**, BH25 7JH, ENG.
(T) 01425 615094
Speciality: Chiropody. ✔
● **Owner/Chiropodist** Mr P Craig Q: M.S.C.P, S.R.Ch.
M Yrs. Est.: 45 (Ref:HM05353)

## CRAIG, THOMAS M

**Thomas M Craig**, 86 Hamilton Avenue, Glasgow, **Glasgow (City of)**, G41 4HD, SCO.
(T) 01414 270756
Speciality: Physiotherapy.
● **Owner** Mr T Craig
P S T (Ref:HM05354)

## CRAIGAVON CHIROPRACTIC CLINIC

**Craigavon Chiropractic Clinic**, 25 High St, Lurgan, Craigavon, **County Armagh**, BT66 8AH, NIR.
(T) 028 3834 9495 (F) 028 3834 9495
(E) kl@btinternet.com
Speciality: Chiropractic. ✔
● **Owner** Dr K Loughlin
(T) 07775 70070 Q: BSc (Chiro), BSc (Hons), DC, RGN. M: BCA, GCC.
● **Chiropractor** Dr B McElroy Q: BSc (Chiro), MSc (Chiro).
P Yrs. Est.: 5 (Ref:HM05355)

## CRAIGLEITH CHIROPRACTIC CLINIC

**Craigleith Chiropractic Clinic**, 128 Queensferry Rd, Edinburgh, **Edinburgh (City of)**, EH4 2BG, SCO.
(T) 01313 320063
Speciality: Chiropractors.
P S T (Ref:HM05356)

## CRAIG-WOOD, SAMANTHA

**Samantha Craig-Wood**, Cranleigh Osteopathic Practice, High St, Cranleigh, **Surrey**, GU6 8AS, ENG.
(T) 01483 268628 (F) 01306 731264
Speciality: Osteopathy.
● **Owner** Miss S Craig-Wood
P S T (Ref:HM05357)

## CRAM, ALEXANDER

**Alexander Cram**, 168 Cumbernauld Rd, Muirhead, Chryston, Glasgow, **Glasgow (City of)**, G69 9NB, SCO.
(T) 01417 791132
Speciality: Osteopathy.
● **Owner** Alexander Cram
P S T (Ref:HM05358)

## CRAM, D

**D Cram**, 3 Old Coach Rd, East Kilbride, Glasgow, **Glasgow (City of)**, G74 4DR, SCO.
(T) 01355 225995
Speciality: Osteopathy.
P S T (Ref:HM05359)

## CRAM, DENNIS

**Dennis Cram**, 87 Barrington Drive, Glasgow, **Glasgow (City of)**, G4 9ES, SCO.
(T) 01413 394164
Speciality: Osteopathy.
P S T (Ref:HM05360)

## CRAM, F

**Mr F Cram**, Maypole Oak, Maypole, Monmouth, **Monmouthshire**, NP25 5QH, WAL.
(T) 01600 713527
Speciality: Cranio-Sacral Therapy, Phytotherapy.
C (Ref:HM05361)

## CRAM, JULIANA

**Juliana Cram**, 834 Fishponds Rd, Fishponds, Bristol, BS16 3XA, ENG.
(T) 01179 491290
Speciality: Osteopathy.
P S T (Ref:HM05362)

## CRAM, KATHY

**Mrs Kathy Cram**, Monmouth Natural Health Centre, Monnow St, Monmouth, **Monmouthshire**, NP25 3EQ, WAL.
(T) 01600 772622
Speciality: Chiropractic, Cranio-Sacral Therapy.
P S T (Ref:HM05363)

## CRAM, NORMUND

**Normund Cram**, 8a Montgomerie Trce, Ayr, **Ayrshire (South)**, KA7 1JL, SCO.
(T) 01292 265075
Speciality: Osteopathy.
P S T (Ref:HM05364)

## CRAMLINGTON CHIRO CLINIC

**Cramlington Chiropractic Clinic**, Ground Floor, 3 West Farm Court, Cramlington, **Northumberland**, NE23 1AX, ENG.
(T) 01670 737788 (F) 01670 738850
Speciality: Chiropractors.
● **Owner** Mrs A Ramsey
P S T (Ref:HM05365)

## CRAN, LORAINE

**Loraine Cran**, 6 Princess Rd, Stonehaven, **Aberdeenshire**, AB39 2DR, SCO.
(T) 01569 762973
Speciality: Reflexology.
S T (Ref:HM05366)

## CRANE SCHOOL OF REFLEXOLOGY

**Crane School Of Reflexology**, 135 Collins Meadow, Harlow, **Essex**, CM19 4EJ, ENG.
(T) 01279 421682
Speciality: Reflexology.
M (Ref:HM05367)

## CRANE, B

**B Crane**, 33 Hickling Way, Harpenden, **Hertfordshire**, AL5 4RP, ENG.
(T) 01582 713909
Speciality: Homeopathy.
● **Owner** Mrs B Crane
M (Ref:HM05368)

## CRANE, B

**B Crane**, 58 Tennyson Rd, Harpenden, **Hertfordshire**, AL5 4BB, ENG.
(T) 01582 713909
Speciality: Homeopathy.
● **Owner** Mr B Crane
M (Ref:HM05369)

## CRANE, DAVID S

**David S Crane**, 27 Brougham St, Gosport, **Hampshire**, PO12 3JF, ENG.
(T) 023 9251 0839
Speciality: Chiropodists (Podiatrists).
● **Owner** Mr D Crane
S (Ref:HM05370)

## CRANE-GRIFFIN, DIANE

**Diane Crane-Griffin**, 40 Wynn Rd, Wolverhampton, **Midlands (West)**, WV4 4AL, ENG.
(T) 01902 340807
Speciality: Clairvoyants & Palmists.
● **Owner** Mrs D Crane-Griffin
B (Ref:HM05371)

## CRANFOLD PHYSIOTHERAPY CENTRE

**Cranfold Physiotherapy Centre**, Lea Cottage, The St, Ewhurst, Cranleigh, **Surrey**, GU6 7QD, ENG.
(T) 01483 267747 (F) 01483 267077
Speciality: Physiotherapy.
● **Owner** Ms W Harrison
P S T (Ref:HM05372)

## CRANHAM HOLISTIC THERAPY

**Cranham Holistic Therapy**, PO Box 6870, Upper Bentley, Redditch, **Worcestershire**, B97 5ST, ENG.
(T) 01527 459869
Speciality: Complementary Medicines &


Key continued: Yrs.Est: Years Established Q: Qualifications M: Professional Membership ✔ Indemnity Insurance ▬ Accept Credit Cards

Therapy.
**M** (**Ref:**HM05373)

### CRANHAM, NIGEL

**Nigel Cranham**, 38 Eastfield Rd, Westbury-On-Trym, Bristol, BS9 4AD, ENG.
(T) 01179 079516
Speciality: Healing Therapy, Reflexology.
● **Partner** Mr N Cranham
**M** (**Ref:**HM05374)

### CRANHAMS

**Cranhams**, 12 Marine Court, St. Leonards-On-Sea, **Sussex (East)**, TN38 0DX, ENG.
(T) 01424 441520
Speciality: Aromatherapy.
**M** **O** (**Ref:**HM05375)

### CRANIOSACRAL SOCIETY

**Craniosacral Society (The)**, 2 Marshal Pl, Perth, **Perth and Kinross**, PH2 8AH, SCO.
(T) 01738 444404
Speciality: Complementary Medicines & Therapy.
● **Therapist** John Page
**M** (**Ref:**HM05376)

### CRANIOSACRAL THERAPY

**Craniosacral Therapy**, 11 Grange Farm Rd, Ash, Aldershot, **Hampshire**, GU12 6SJ, ENG.
(T) 01252 333738
(E) trish.spence@ntlworld.com
Speciality: Cranio-Sacral Therapy, Floral Essence Therapy, Massage (Therapeutic). ✔
● **Therapist** Mrs P Spence Q: ITEC. M: ICA, IPTI.
● **Director** Mr D Spence
**B** **T** Yrs. Est.: 3 (**Ref:**HM05377)

### CRANIOSACRAL THERAPY

**Craniosacral Therapy**, 33 Ilminster Gdns, London, **London (Greater)**, SW11 1PJ, ENG.
(T) 020 7978 4519
Speciality: Complementary Medicines & Therapy.
● **Owner** Ms M Deaechevarria
**M** (**Ref:**HM05378)

### CRANIOSACRAL THERAPY

**CranioSacral Therapy**, 33 Laurel Drive, Bradwell, Great Yarmouth, **Norfolk**, NR31 8PB, ENG.
(T) 01493 442215
Speciality: Complementary Medicines & Therapy.
**M** (**Ref:**HM05379)

### CRANIOSACRAL THERAPY ED TRUST

**Craniosacral Therapy Educational Trust**, 10 Normington Cl, Leigham Court Rd, London, **London (Greater)**, SW16 2QS, ENG.
(T) 07000 785778
Speciality: Complementary Therapy, Cranio-Sacral Therapy.
**M** (**Ref:**HM05380)

### CRANLEIGH CHIROPRACTIC CLINIC

**Cranleigh Chiropractic Clinic**, Ruffold Lodge, Guildford Rd, Cranleigh, **Surrey**, GU6 8LT, ENG.
(T) 01483 274002
Speciality: Acupressure, Aromatherapy, Chiropractic, Homeopathy, Massage (Therapeutic), Reflexology, Reiki, Ultrasonics, X-Ray. ✔
● **Chiropractor** Ms P Edwards - Moss Q: DC. M: BCA, CC, GCC.
**S** Yrs. Est.: 21 (**Ref:**HM05381)

### CRANSHAW, D V

**D V Cranshaw**, 9 Gosditch St, Cirencester, **Gloucestershire**, GL7 2AG, ENG.
(T) 01285 653624
Speciality: Chiropodists (Podiatrists).
**S** (**Ref:**HM05382)

### CRASKE, DAVID

**David Craske**, 19 Houlton Court, Bagshot, **Surrey**, GU19 5QQ, ENG.
(T) 01276 479530
Speciality: Complementary Medicines & Therapy.
● **Owner** Mr D Craske
**M** (**Ref:**HM05383)

### CRAVEN CLINIC

**Craven Clinic Of Homeopathy & Complementary Therapy**, Mount Pleasant, High St, Skipton, **Yorkshire (North)**, BD23 1JT, ENG.
(T) 01756 796690
(W) www.cravenclinic.co.uk
Speciality: Acupressure, Acupuncture, Alexander Technique, Allergy Testing, Aromatherapy, Bach Remedies, Chiropractic, Complementary Therapy, Counselling, Cranial Osteopathy, Healer, Healing Therapy, Holistic Healing, Homeopathy, Hypnotherapy, Indian Head Massage, Manipulation, Massage (Therapeutic), Meditation, Metamorphic Therapy, Moxibustion, Osteopathy, Psychotherapy, Reflexology, Reiki, Sensitivity Training, Shiatsu, Spiritual Healing, Stress Therapy, T'ai-Chi Ch'uan, Touch Therapy. ✔
● **Homeopath** Ms S Asquith Q: Dip.Hom, RSHom. M: Soc.Hom.
● **Acupuncturist** Ms H Coles Q: BSc, Dip.Ac, Dip.Arom, Dip.H.E, MBAcC, RGN. M: BAcC.
● **Aromatherapist** Ms K Ward Q: IIHHT. M: IIHHT.
● **Shiatsu Practitioner** Ms H Blandin Q: Dip.BSA, MRSS, MSc. M: Shiatsu Society UK.
**B** Yrs. Est.: 8 (**Ref:**HM05384)

### CRAVEN CLINIC

**Craven Clinic (The)**, 54 Cambridge Gr, London, **London (Greater)**, W6 0LA, ENG.
(T) 020 8563 8133
(W) www.thecravenclinic.co.uk
Speciality: Acupuncture, Allergy Testing, Aromatherapy, Counselling, Homeopathy, Hypnotherapy, Iridology, Naturopathy, Osteopathy, Reflexology, Reiki, Zero Balancing, Bowen Technique, Energy Healing, Holistic Massage, Sports Injuries Massage.
● **Owner** Ms H Craven
**C** (**Ref:**HM05385)

### CRAVEN STREET CHIROPODY CLINIC

**Craven Street Chiropody Clinic**, 1 Craven St, Droylsden, Manchester, **Manchester (Greater)**, M43 7UD, ENG.
(T) 01613 011112
Speciality: Chiropodists (Podiatrists).
● **Manager** Mr J Hanson
**S** (**Ref:**HM05386)

### CRAVEN, CLAIRE

**Claire Craven**, 20 West Drive, Sutton, **Surrey**, SM2 7NA, ENG.
(T) 020 8643 9184
Speciality: Osteopathy.
**P** **S** **T** (**Ref:**HM05387)

### CRAVEN, INGA

**Inga Craven**, 25 Hamstead Marshall, Hamstead Marshall, Newbury, **Berkshire**, RG20 0HR, ENG.
(T) 01488 658744
Speciality: Complementary Medicines & Therapy.
● **Owner** Mrs I Craven
**M** (**Ref:**HM05388)

### CRAWFORD, ANDREW

**Andrew Crawford**, Woodley Physio & Sports Injury Clinic, 1 Springbank Rd, Woodley, Stockport, **Cheshire**, SK6 1NY, ENG.
(T) 01614 067788 (F) 01614 946078
Speciality: Physiotherapy.
● **Owner** Mrs P Crawford
**P** **S** **T** (**Ref:**HM05389)

### CRAWFORD, D C

**D C Crawford**, 24 Penn St, Horwich, Bolton, **Lancashire**, BL6 5NR, ENG.
(T) 07976 208723
Speciality: Psychology.
**B** (**Ref:**HM05390)

### CRAWFORD, J

**J Crawford**, 34 High St, Inverness, **Highland**, IV1 1JQ, SCO.
(T) 01463 715563
Speciality: Chiropodists (Podiatrists).
**S** (**Ref:**HM05391)

### CRAWFORD, J G

**J G Crawford**, 44 Sunnyside St, Belfast, **County Antrim**, BT7 3EX, NIR.
(T) 028 9064 0026
Speciality: Chiropody, Nail Surgery. ✔
● **Practice Manager** Mrs E Crawford
● **Owner/Chiropodist** Mr J Crawford Q: M.S.C.P, S.R.Ch. M: S.C.P.
**M** Yrs. Est.: 26 (**Ref:**HM05392)

### CRAWFORD, S

**S Crawford**, 7 Woodhead Drive, Hale, Altrincham, **Cheshire**, WA15 9LG, ENG.
(T) 01619 806592
Speciality: Chiropodists (Podiatrists).
**S** (**Ref:**HM05393)

### CRAWLEY CHIROPRACTIC CLINIC

**Crawley Chiropractic Clinic**, 204 Gossops Drive, Crawley, **Sussex (West)**, RH11 8LJ, ENG.
(T) 01293 614127 (F) 01293 614127
Speciality: Chiropractic.
**P** **S** **T** (**Ref:**HM05394)

### CRAWLEY, K

**K Crawley**, 35 Kessingland Avenue, Stevenage, **Hertfordshire**, SG1 2JR, ENG.
(T) 01438 354777
Speciality: Chiropodists (Podiatrists).
● **Owner** Mrs K Crawley
**S** (**Ref:**HM05395)

### CREATIVE CHANGES

**Creative Changes**, 24 Daisy Rd, Birmingham, **Midlands (West)**, B16 9DZ, ENG.
(T) 01214 521131
Speciality: Hypnosis.
● **Owner** Mr J Middleton
**B** (**Ref:**HM05396)

### CREATIVE HEALTH CENTRE

**Creative Health Centre**, 39A Regent St, Leamington Spa, **Warwickshire**, CV32 5EE, ENG.
(T) 01926 316500
Speciality: Aromatherapy, Bach Remedies, Chiropractic, Colonic Hydrotherapy, Cranio-Sacral Therapy, Herbal Medicine, Massage (Therapeutic), McTimoney Chiropractic, Meditation, Psychotherapy, Shiatsu, Yoga.
**C** (**Ref:**HM05397)

### CREATIVE HEALTH CENTRE

**Creative Health Centre (The)**, 52 Hagley Rd, Stourbridge, **Midlands (West)**, DY8 1QD, ENG.
(T) 01384 379141
(W) www.creativehealth.co.uk
Speciality: Acupuncture, Alexander Technique, Aromatherapy, Counselling, Homeopathy, Hopi Ear Candles, Hypnotherapy, Indian Head Massage, Kinesiology, Massage (Therapeutic), Reflexology, Reiki, Shiatsu, Sports Massage, Swedish Body Massage, Tui Na Massage and Spinal Touch. ✔
● **Therapist** Ms L Richards Cooper Q: ITEC.
● **Homeopath** Mr A Bateman Q: LCPH.
● **Therapist** Ms S Aitken
● **Teacher of the Alexander Technique** Ms C Pillath M: STAT.
● **Manager** Mr W Cooper
● **Therapist** Mr T Concannon Q: B.Ac, Lic.Ac, MBAcC.
● **Therapist** Ms L Ireland Q: Dip.Couns.
● **Hypnotherapist** Ms J Whitehouse Q: BA (Hons), BSCH.
● **Teacher** Ms M Telling Q: ITEC.
**C** Yrs. Est.: 12 (**Ref:**HM05398)

### CREATIVE INSIGHTS

**Jacqueline Stevens**, 83 Delaware Mansions, Delaware Rd, Maida Vale, London, **London (Greater)**, W9 2LJ, ENG.
(T) 020 7286 8911
(E) j_stevens@skybiz.com
Speciality: Auto Suggestion, Aversion Therapy, Cognitive Therapy, Counselling, Faith Healing, Hypnosis, Hypnotherapy, Indian Head Massage, Life Style Coaching, Neuro-Linguistic Program, Psychotherapy, Silva Method, Spiritual Healing, Stress Therapy, Visualisation Therapy, Pain Control Therapy, Storytelling. ✔
● **Hypnotherapist/Practitioner** Ms J Stevens M: BIH, LCIC, NCH, UKCHO.

Key: **B** Mind-Body Medicine **C** Complementary Medicine **H** Self Help Treatment **M** Medicinal Therapy **O** Oriental Medicine **P** Postural Therapy **S** Manipulative Structural Therapy **T** Touch Therapy

C Yrs. Est.: 5 (Ref:HM05399)

## CREATIVE LIFE INTERNATIONAL

**Creative Life International**, 68 Clarence St, Cheltenham, **Gloucestershire**, GL50 3LE, ENG.
(T) 01242 702262 (F) 01242 702263
Speciality: Clairvoyants & Palmists.
● **Accountant** Mr M Cott
B (Ref:HM05400)

## CREATIVE THERAPIES

**Creative Therapies**, 7 Water Row, Glasgow, **Glasgow (City of)**, G51 3UW, SCO.
(T) 01414 456000
Speciality: Complementary Medicines & Therapy.
C M (Ref:HM05401)

## CREATIVITY

**Creativity**, 10 Meeting House Lane, Brighton, **Sussex (East)**, BN1 1HB, ENG.
(T) 01273 325497
Speciality: Aromatherapy.
● **Owner** Ms E Nugent
M O (Ref:HM05402)

## CREATON, SUE

**Mrs Sue Creaton**, 1 New St, Paignton, **Devon**, TQ3 3HL, ENG.
(T) 01803 557635
Speciality: Chiropodists (Podiatrists).
S (Ref:HM05403)

## CRECY MASSAGE STUDIO

**Crecy Massage Studio**, 91 Sidwell St, Exeter, **Devon**, EX4 6PH, ENG.
(T) 01392 439942
Speciality: Massage (Therapeutic).
● **Owner** Mrs A Walton
M (Ref:HM05404)

## CREDITON CHIROPRACTIC CLINIC

**Crediton Chiropractic Clinic (The)**, 16 St Lawrence Green, Crediton, **Devon**, EX17 2BD, ENG.
(T) 01363 776156
Speciality: Chiropractic.
● **Partner** Mr C Voysey
P S T (Ref:HM05405)

## CREDO THERAPIES FIRST

**Credo Therapies First**, The Meadows, 342 Grange Rd, Gillingham, **Kent**, ME7 2UB, ENG.
(T) 01634 326302 (F) 01634 326302
Speciality: Physiotherapy.
● **Owner** Mr T Claybrook
P S T (Ref:HM05406)

## CREE PHYSIOTHERAPY CLINIC

**Cree Physiotherapy Clinic (The)**, 101 Cheviot View, Ponteland, Newcastle Upon Tyne, **Tyne and Wear**, NE20 9BH, ENG.
(T) 01661 823319 (F) 01661 823319
Speciality: Physiotherapy.
● **Owner** Mr G Cree
P S T (Ref:HM05407)

## CREE, L

**L Cree**, 9 Poplar Way, Ayr, **Ayrshire (South)**, KA7 3PQ, SCO.
(T) 01292 290557
Speciality: Chiropodists (Podiatrists).
● **Owner** Mrs L Cree
S (Ref:HM05408)

## CREE, TOM

**Tom Cree**, 100 Station Prde, Harrogate, **Yorkshire (North)**, HG1 1HQ, ENG.
(T) 01423 561566 (F) 01423 567379
Speciality: Osteopathy.
● **Owner** Mr T Cree
P S T (Ref:HM05409)

## CREED, GLENN

**Glenn Creed**, Watchbell House, 8 Lugley St, Newport, **Isle of Wight**, PO30 5HD, ENG.
(T) 01983 522477
Speciality: Chiropractors.
● **Owner** Mr G Creed
P S T (Ref:HM05410)

## CREEK, N

**N Creek**, 26 Gibbs Leaze, Hilperton, Trowbridge, **Wiltshire**, BA14 7QN, ENG.
(T) 01225 767220 (F) 01225 767220
Speciality: Alexander Technique.
● **Owner** Mrs N Creek
P S (Ref:HM05411)

## CREGAGH CHIROPRACTIC CLINIC

**Cregagh Chiropractic Clinic**, 162 Upper Knockbreda Rd, Belfast, **County Antrim**, BT6 9QF, NIR.
(T) 028 9040 2266 (F) 028 9079 4724
Speciality: Chiropractic. ✔
● **Employee** Dr S Sorensen Q: B.App.Sc, BSc, DC. M: SCA.
P Yrs. Est.: 11 (Ref:HM05412)

## CREIGHTMORE, R & D

**Richard & Diane Creightmore**, Beech View, Crowborough Rd, Nutley, Uckfield, **Sussex (East)**, TN22 3HY, ENG.
(T) 01825 713215
Speciality: Acupuncture.
O (Ref:HM05413)

## CREMONA, R J

**Mr R J Cremona**, 81 High St, Horsell, Woking, **Surrey**, GU21 4UA, ENG.
(T) 01483 730615
Speciality: Chiropractors.
P S T (Ref:HM05414)

## CREMONA, ROB

**Rob Cremona**, Thorncombe, Church Rd, Windlesham, **Surrey**, GU20 6BT, ENG.
(T) 01276 473371
Speciality: Chiropodists (Podiatrists).
S (Ref:HM05415)

## CRENOL, J P

**J P Crenol**, 56 Highbridge Rd, Burnham-on-Sea, **Somerset**, TA8 1LN, ENG.
(T) 01278 785915
Speciality: Chiropodists (Podiatrists).
S (Ref:HM05416)

## CRESCENT CLINIC

**Crescent Clinic**, 32 Burton Manor Rd, Stafford, **Staffordshire**, ST17 9QJ, ENG.
(T) 01785 242061
Speciality: Acupuncture, Allergy Testing, Aromatherapy, Herbal Medicine, Homeopathy, Kinesiology, Manipulation, Psychotherapy, Reflexology, Remedial Massage, T'ai-Chi Ch'uan, Acu Therapy. ✔
● **Reflexologist** Mr B Dunkan Q: MAR, MBRA.
● **Practice Manager** Mrs Bents-Martin
● **Acupuncturist** Mr I Markem M: GMC.
● **Kinesiologist** Kim Lichfield M: ICAK.
● **Owner/Physiotherapist** Ms K Bents Q: MCSP, MISBM, ONC, SRP. M: CSP.
C Yrs. Est.: 15 (Ref:HM05417)

## CRESCENT CLINIC FOR COMP MED

**Crescent Clinic For Complementary Medicine (The)**, 32 Burton Manor Rd, Stafford, **Staffordshire**, ST17 9QJ, ENG.
(T) 01785 242061 (F) 01785 220240
Speciality: Acupuncture, Allergy Testing, Aromatherapy, Herbal Medicine, Homeopathy, Kinesiology, Manipulation, Physiotherapy, Reflexology, Remedial Massage, T'ai-Chi Ch'uan, Acutherapy. ✔
● **Owner/Physiotherapist** Mrs K Bents Q: MCSP, MISBM, ONC, SRP. M: CSP.
C Yrs. Est.: 14 (Ref:HM05418)

## CRESCENT MOON

**Crescent Moon**, Po Box 287, Sheffield, **Yorkshire (South)**, S9 2RW, ENG.
(T) 01494 883688 (F) 01494 881033
Speciality: Complementary Medicines & Therapy.
● **Office Manager** Mr M Donovan
M (Ref:HM05419)

## CRESCENT OSTEOPATHIC CENTRE

**Crescent Osteopathic Centre (The)**, 1 The Crescent, Maidenhead, **Berkshire**, SL6 6AA, ENG.
(T) 01628 620897
Speciality: Osteopathy.
P S T (Ref:HM05420)

## CRESCENT THERAPIES

**Crescent Therapies**, 19 The Crescent, Taunton, **Somerset**, TA1 4EB, ENG.
(T) 01823 339000
Speciality: Complementary Medicines & Therapy.
● **Owner** Mrs L Brown
C M (Ref:HM05421)

## CRESENT CLINIC

**Cresent Clinic Of Complementary Medicine (The)**, 37 Vernon Trce, Brighton, **Sussex (East)**, BN1 3JH, ENG.
(T) 01273 202221 (F) 01273 202221
Speciality: Aromatherapy, Bach Remedies, Bowen Therapy, Chiropractic, Counselling, Herbal Medicine, Holistic Healing, Homeopathy, Hypnotherapy, Kinesiology, Manipulation, Massage (Therapeutic), Naturopathy, Nutritional Therapy, Osteopathy, Physiotherapy, Reflexology, Ultrasonics, Neuro Linguistic Counselling. ✔
● **Homeopath** Mr S Deeks Q: LCH.
● **Clinical Osteopath/Hypnotherapist** Mr B Cull
(T) 01273 580370 Q: Dip.Clin.Hyp, DO. M: GOsC.
● **Physiotherapist** Ms M Penny
(T) 01273 723279 Q: MCSP, SRP. M: CSP.
● **Owner** Marek Urban Awicz
C H M P S
Yrs. Est.: 10 (Ref:HM05422)

## CRESSWELL, C

**C Cresswell**, 3 Phillips Cr, Needham Market, Ipswich, **Suffolk**, IP6 8TF, ENG.
(T) 01449 722104
Speciality: Chiropodists (Podiatrists).
● **Owner** Mrs C Cresswell
S (Ref:HM05423)

## CRESSWELL, JAN

**Jan Cresswell**, 14 Bryan Rd, Blackpool, **Lancashire**, FY3 9BE, ENG.
(T) 01253 301727
Speciality: Aromatherapy.
M O (Ref:HM05424)

## CRESSWELL, R

**R Cresswell**, The Garden Clinic, 43 Clifton Rd, London, **London (Greater)**, SE25 6PX, ENG.
(T) 020 8653 8750
Speciality: Reflexology.
● **Owner** Mrs R Cresswell
S T (Ref:HM05425)

## CREST HYPNOTHERAPY

**Crest Hypnotherapy**, 18 Radcliffe New Rd, Whitefield, Manchester, **Manchester (Greater)**, M45 7GY, ENG.
(T) 01617 965126
Speciality: Hypnosis.
● **Owner** Mrs D Higgins
B (Ref:HM05426)

## CREW, D

**Mrs D Crew**, Park House, 12 Old Portsmouth Rd, Camberley, **Surrey**, GU15 1JJ, ENG.
(T) 01276 66280
Speciality: Reflexology.
● **Owner** Mr D Crew
S T (Ref:HM05427)

## CREW, DAVID A

**David A Crew**, Park House, 12 Old Portsmouth Rd, Camberley, **Surrey**, GU15 1JJ, ENG.
(T) 01276 66280
Speciality: Chiropodists (Podiatrists).
● **Owner** Mr D Crew
S (Ref:HM05428)

## CREW, R

**R Crew**, 4 Hawthorne Trce, Aberdare, **Glamorgan (Vale of)**, CF44 7HE, WAL.
(T) 01685 881819
Speciality: Complementary Medicines & Therapy.
● **Owner** Mrs R Crew
C M (Ref:HM05429)

## CREWE & NANT PHYSIO CLINIC

**Crewe & Nantwich Physiotherapy Clinic**, Mary St, Crewe, **Cheshire**, CW1 4AJ, ENG.
(T) 01270 588244 (F) 01270 505055
Speciality: Acupuncture, Physiotherapy. ✔
● **Physiotherapist** Mr R Carter Q: MCSP, SRP.


Key continued: Yrs.Est: Years Established Q: Qualifications M: Professional Membership ✔ Indemnity Insurance Accept Credit Cards

M: CSP.
● **Physiotherapist** Mr A Leach **Q:** BSc (Chiro), MCSP, SRP. **M:** CSP.
● **Manager** Ms C Kirby
S (**Ref:**HM05431)

## CREWE & NANT PHYSIO CLINIC

**Crewe & Nantwich Physiotherapy Clinic**, The Bungalow, 499 Crewe Rd, Wistaston, Crewe, **Cheshire**, CW2 6QP, ENG.
(T) 01270 652260
Speciality: Physiotherapy.
P S T (**Ref:**HM05432)

## CREWE & NANTWICH HOLISTIC

**Crewe & Nantwich Holistic Clinic**, Sandringham Drive, Crewe, **Cheshire**, CW2 8JF, ENG.
(T) 01270 665403
Speciality: Acupuncture.
● **Owner** Mrs V Hayes
O (**Ref:**HM05430)

## CREWE, G

**G Crewe**, 9 Barkers Rd, Sheffield, **Yorkshire (South)**, S7 1SD, ENG.
(T) 01142 508882
Speciality: Alexander Technique.
P S (**Ref:**HM05433)

## CREWE, GRAHAM

**Graham Crewe**, The Wellbeing Centre, 11 Musters Rd, Nottingham, **Nottinghamshire**, NG5 3GQ, ENG.
(T) 01159 825353
Speciality: Alexander Technique.
P S (**Ref:**HM05434)

## CREWE, N V

**N V Crewe**, Hawthorne Cottage, Wootton Green, Wootton, Bedford, **Bedfordshire**, MK43 9EE, ENG.
(T) 01234 768483
Speciality: Physiotherapy.
P S T (**Ref:**HM05435)

## CREWKERNE CHIROPRACTIC CLINIC

**Crewkerne Chiropractic Clinic**, Market Sq, Crewkerne, **Somerset**, TA18 7LE, ENG.
(T) 01460 78400 (F) 01460 78400
Speciality: Chiropractors.
● **Manager** Mrs R Cartwright
P S T (**Ref:**HM05436)

## CRIBB, PAULINE

**Pauline Cribb**, Thanet Cottage, 1 Dickens Lane, Tilsworth, Leighton Buzzard, **Bedfordshire**, LU7 9PX, ENG.
(T) 01525 210348
Speciality: Aromatherapy.
M O (**Ref:**HM05437)

## CRICK, PAUL

**Paul Crick L C S P (Assoc)**, 37 Station Avenue, Filey, **Yorkshire (North)**, YO14 9AE, ENG.
(T) 01723 512337
Speciality: Massage (Therapeutic).
M (**Ref:**HM05438)

## CRICKLADE ROAD PRACTICE

**Cricklade Road Osteopathy Clinic**, 530 Cricklade Rd, Swindon, **Wiltshire**, SN2 7AQ, ENG.
(T) 01793 722913 (F) 01793 722913
(E) osteopath@scharneck.com
Speciality: Acupuncture, Allergy Testing, Aromatherapy, Dietician, Homeopathy, Manipulation, Massage (Therapeutic), Osteopathy. ✔
● **Aromatherapist/Sports Massage Therapist**
Ms L Hardiman **Q:** ONC, RGN. **M:** RCN.
● **Osteopath** Ms S Spencer Chapman **Q:** DO. M: GOsC.
● **Homeopath** Ms J Janeway **Q:** BA, CQSW, LSH.
● **Owner** Mrs F Scharneck **Q:** DO. **M:** GOsC.
M O P S Yrs. Est.: 14 (**Ref:**HM05439)

## CRICKMERE, S D

**S D Crickmere**, Crofton House, 31 The Avenue, Newmarket, **Suffolk**, CB8 9AY, ENG.
(T) 01638 663906
Speciality: Chiropodists (Podiatrists).
● **Owner** Mrs S Crickmere
S (**Ref:**HM05440)

## CRIGHTON, TINA

**Tina Crighton**, 9 Elm Rd, Worthing, **Sussex (West)**, BN11 1PG, ENG.
(T) 01903 204893
Speciality: Complementary Medicines & Therapy.
● **Owner** Ms T Crighton
C M (**Ref:**HM05441)

## CRILL, J

**J Crill**, 29 Geraldine Rd, London, **London (Greater)**, SW18 2NR, ENG.
(T) 020 8874 9601
Speciality: Physiotherapy.
● **Owner** Miss J Crill
P S T (**Ref:**HM05442)

## CRIMMINS, JOHN

**John Crimmins**, 103 Beaumont Ave, Dublin, **County Dublin**, IRE.
(T) 01296 4218
(E) ati@indigo.ie
Speciality: Counselling.
B H (**Ref:**HM05443)

## CRIPPS, C

**C Cripps**, 18 Valleyway Rd, Nailsea, Bristol, BS48 1HQ, ENG.
(T) 01275 857048
Speciality: Chiropodists (Podiatrists).
● **Owner** Mr C Cripps
S (**Ref:**HM05444)

## CRISP, D M

**D M Crisp**, 19 Stour St, Sudbury, **Suffolk**, CO10 2AX, ENG.
(T) 01787 372294
Speciality: Chiropodists (Podiatrists).
● **Owner** Mrs D Crisp
S (**Ref:**HM05445)

## CRISTA GALLI OSTEOPATHS

**Crista Galli Osteopaths**, 52 Porchester Rd, Bayswater, London, **London (Greater)**, W2 6ET, ENG.
(T) 020 7221 3557 (F) 020 7221 3557
(E) cristagalli@mail.com
Speciality: Cranial Osteopathy, Osteopathy. ✔
● **Osteopath** Ms N Constaninou **Q:** DO. M: GOsC.
● **Osteopath** Mr J Gilbey **Q:** DO. **M:** GOsC.
● **Osteopath** Ms H Makin **Q:** DO. **M:** GOsC.
● **Osteopath** Mr A Heller **Q:** DO. **M:** GOsC.
● **Osteopath** Mr C Contandinou **Q:** DO. M: GOsC.
S Yrs. Est.: 10 (**Ref:**HM05446)

## CRITERION PARTNERSHIP

**Criterion Partnership**, Churchward Court, 15 Western Rd, Lewes, **Sussex (East)**, BN7 1RL, ENG.
(T) 01273 480583 (F) 01273 487271
Speciality: Psychology.
● **Principal** Mr R Hunter
B (**Ref:**HM05447)

## CRITTELL, SANDRA

**Sandra Crittell**, School House, Millers Lane, Outwood, Redhill, **Surrey**, RH1 5PY, ENG.
(T) 01342 843661
Speciality: Psychotherapy.
● **Owner** Mrs S Crittell
B (**Ref:**HM05448)

## CROCKETT, NEVILLE

**Neville Crockett**, Birches Cl, The Cricket Green, Mitcham, **Surrey**, CR4 4LA, ENG.
(T) 020 8640 6548
Speciality: Chiropodists (Podiatrists).
● **Owner** Mr N Crockett
S (**Ref:**HM05449)

## CROCKETT, P

**P Crockett**, All Hallows House, Idol Lane, London, **London (Greater)**, EC3R 5DD, ENG.
(T) 020 7283 8908
Speciality: Homeopathy.
M (**Ref:**HM05450)

## CROFT CLINIC

**Croft Clinic**, 3 Wards End, Halifax, **Yorkshire (West)**, HX1 1DD, ENG.
(T) 01422 346269
Speciality: Osteopathy.
P S T (**Ref:**HM05451)

## CROFT HOUSE CLINIC

**Joanna Waterworth Registered Osteopath**, 1 Crosby Rd, Northallerton, **Yorkshire (North)**, DL6 1AA, ENG.
(T) 01609 783600 (F) 01609 783600
Speciality: Acupuncture, Cranial Osteopathy, Herbal Medicine, Homeopathy, Osteopathy, Reflexology. ✔
● **Osteopath** Ms J Waterworth **Q:** BSc. M: GOsC.
● **Osteopath** Ms Hibbard **Q:** BSc, Hons (OST). M: GOsC.
● **Osteopath** Mr Bentley **Q:** BSc, Hons (OST). M: GOsC.
S Yrs. Est.: 3 (**Ref:**HM05452)

## CROFT, ANGELA

**Angela Croft**, Murray's Chemist, Queens Way, Halesowen, **Midlands (West)**, ENG.
(T) 01384 412854
Speciality: Reflexology, Stress Therapy, Reflexology has an overall re-balancing quality, good for keeping you in good health aswell as treating disorders. ✔
● **Reflexologist** Ms A Croft **Q:** MBRA. **M:** BRA.
T Yrs. Est.: 7 (**Ref:**HM05453)

## CROFT, DAVID

**David Croft**, 22 Aubrey Cl, Chelmsford, **Essex**, CM1 4EJ, ENG.
(T) 01245 440502
Speciality: Chiropodists (Podiatrists).
S (**Ref:**HM05454)

## CROFT, JOANNA

**Joanna Croft**, Steeple Bumpstead, **Essex**, CB9, ENG.
(T) 01440 730742
Speciality: Bach Remedies.
M (**Ref:**HM05455)

## CROFT, LESLEY

**Lesley Croft**, Gloucester Park Swimming Pool, Broadmayne, Basildon, **Essex**, SS14 2EB, ENG.
(T) 01268 767727
Speciality: Aromatherapy.
● **Owner** Mrs L Croft
M O (**Ref:**HM05456)

## CROFTON HOUSE OSTEO CLINIC

**Crofton House Osteopathic Clinic**, Wych Hill, Woking, **Surrey**, GU22 0ES, ENG.
(T) 01483 770529 (F) 01483 770529
Speciality: Osteopathy.
● **Principal** Mr I Lawler
P S T (**Ref:**HM05457)

## CROFTS, TREVOR

**Trevor Crofts**, 1 Basingbourne Cl, Fleet, **Hampshire**, GU13 9TF, ENG.
(T) 01252 617552
Speciality: Physiotherapy.
P S T (**Ref:**HM05458)

## CROIX, E C DE SAINTE

**E C De Sainte Croix**, 40 Gervis Rd, Bournemouth, **Dorset**, BH1 3DH, ENG.
(T) 01202 292199
Speciality: Chiropodists (Podiatrists).
● **Owner** Mrs E Destcroix
S (**Ref:**HM05459)

## CROIX, LINDA LA

**Linda La Croix**, 203 Yorkland Avenue, Welling, **Kent**, DA16 2LH, ENG.
(T) 020 8301 0332
Speciality: Aromatherapy. ✔
● **Owner/Aromatherapist**
Ms L Lacroix **Q:** ITEC. **M:** GCP.
C Yrs. Est.: 1 (**Ref:**HM05460)

## CROMER PHYSIOTHERAPY

**Cromer Physiotherapy**, 19A Cliff Avenue, Cromer, **Norfolk**, NR27 0AN, ENG.
(T) 01263 515201
Speciality: Physiotherapy.
P S T (**Ref:**HM05461)



Key: B Mind-Body Medicine C Complementary Medicine H Self Help Treatment M Medicinal Therapy O Oriental Medicine P Postural Therapy S Manipulative Structural Therapy T Touch Therapy

**CROMPTON, CHRISTINE**

**Christine Crompton**, 25 Westhaven Cres, Aughton, Ormskirk, **Lancashire**, L39 5BN, ENG.
(T) 01695 421557
Speciality: Chiropodists (Podiatrists).
● **Owner** Mrs C Crompton
S (Ref:HM05462)

**CROMWELL CHIROPRACTIC CLINIC**

**Cromwell Chiropractic Clinic**, Marston House, Cromwell Park, Banbury Rd, Chipping Norton, **Oxfordshire**, OX7 5SR, ENG.
(T) 01608 643704 (F) 01608 643704
Speciality: Chiropractic.
● **Owner** Mrs S James-Hudson
P S T (Ref:HM05463)

**CRONIN, CLAIRE E**

**Claire E Cronin**, 5 Grosvenor Court, Mayfare, Croxley Green, Rickmansworth, **Hertfordshire**, WD3 3DH, ENG.
(T) 01923 230724
Speciality: Chiropodists (Podiatrists).
● **Owner** Mrs C Cronin
S (Ref:HM05464)

**CRONIN, DECLAN**

**Declan Cronin D Psych A D H P MI**, 2 Grange Erin Mews Douglas, Cork, **County Cork**, IRE.
(T) 021 4892 510
Speciality: Complementary Medicines & Therapy.
M (Ref:HM05465)

**CROOK LOG CHIROPODY SURGERY**

**Crook Log Chiropody Surgery**, 4 Clarence Rd, Bexleyheath, **Kent**, DA6 8ER, ENG.
(T) 020 8304 5936
Speciality: Chiropodists (Podiatrists).
S (Ref:HM05466)

**CROOK LOG PHYSIO & SPORTS**

**Crook Log Physiotherapy & Sports Injury Clinic**, Splashworld, Crook Log, Bexleyheath, **Kent**, DA6 8EQ, ENG.
(T) 020 8303 5781
Speciality: Physiotherapy.
P S T (Ref:HM05467)

**CROOK, ALAN**

**Alan Crook**, Wingletang, Southview Rd, Crowborough, **Sussex (East)**, TN6 1HG, ENG.
(T) 01892 655217
Speciality: Homeopathy.
● **Owner** Mr A Crook
M (Ref:HM05468)

**CROOK, D E**

**D E Crook**, 95 The Fairway, Bognor Regis, **Sussex (West)**, PO21 4EW, ENG.
(T) 01243 262126
Speciality: Physiotherapy.
P S T (Ref:HM05469)

**CROOK, G C**

**G C Crook**, 13 Gorse Rd, Blackburn, **Lancashire**, BB2 6LY, ENG.
(T) 01254 661194
Speciality: Psychotherapy.
B (Ref:HM05470)

**CROOK, J L**

**J L Crook**, 8 Green Finch Drive, Moulton, Northampton, **Northamptonshire**, NN3 7HX, ENG.
(T) 01604 492312
Speciality: Chiropodists (Podiatrists).
● **Owner** Mrs J Crook
S (Ref:HM05471)

**CROOKES ACUPUNCTURE CENTRE**

**Crookes Acupuncture Centre**, 8 Cobden View Rd, Sheffield, **Yorkshire (South)**, S10 1HQ, ENG.
(T) 01142 661499
Speciality: Acupuncture.
O (Ref:HM05472)

**CROPPER, AGNES**

**Agnes Cropper**, 25 West Drive, Neston, **Cheshire**, CH64 0SA, ENG.
(T) 01513 361123
Speciality: Reflexology. ✔
● **Reflexologist** Mrs A Cropper
S T Yrs. Est.: 4 (Ref:HM05473)

**CROPPER, JAN**

**Jan Cropper**, 33 Bath Rd, Felixstowe, **Suffolk**, IP11 7JN, ENG.
(T) 01394 671450
Speciality: Reflexology.
● **Owner** Mrs J Cropper
S T (Ref:HM05474)

**CROPPER, LINDA**

**Linda Cropper**, 24 The Firs, Chester Rd, Whitchurch, **Shropshire**, SY13 1NL, ENG.
(T) 01948 664075
Speciality: Hypnotherapy.
● **Owner** Mrs L Cropper
B (Ref:HM05475)

**CROSBY PHYSIOTHERAPY**

**Crosby Physiotherapy**, 90 College Rd, Liverpool, **Merseyside**, L23 0RP, ENG.
(T) 01519 244784 (F) 01512 263034
Speciality: Physiotherapy.
● **Owner** Mrs S Jones
P S T (Ref:HM05476)

**CROSS CLINIC**

**Cross Clinic (The)**, 20 The Cross, Lymm, **Cheshire**, WA13 0HU, ENG.
(T) 01925 757513 (F) 01625 614466
Speciality: Complementary Medicines & Therapy.
● **Manager** Mrs J Bilington
M (Ref:HM05477)

**CROSS HANDS CHIRO CLINIC**

**Cross Hands Chiropractic Clinic**, Northwick Rd, Alveston, Bristol, BS35 3JE, ENG.
(T) 01454 633622
Speciality: Chiropractic, Kinesiology. ✔
● **Practice Manager** Mrs H Miller
● **Clinic Manager** Dr C De Groot Q: DC.
P Yrs. Est.: 10 (Ref:HM05478)

**CROSS HANDS CHIRO CLINIC**

**Cross Purposes Physiotherapy Clinic**, 1 Penhaligon Court, Guithavon St, Witham, **Essex**, CM8 1BQ, ENG.
(T) 01376 514675
Speciality: Physiotherapy. ✔
● **Physiotherapist** Ms G Gillespie Q: MCSP, SRP.
● **Manager** Ms M Anderson
P S Yrs. Est.: 30 (Ref:HM05479)

**CROSS, ANDREW**

**Andrew Cross**, 22 Clare Rd, Halifax, **Yorkshire (West)**, HX1 2HX, ENG.
(T) 01422 340919
Speciality: Osteopathy.
P S T (Ref:HM05480)

**CROSS, ANDREW**

**Andrew Cross**, Osteopathic Clinic, 216 Marton Rd, Middlesbrough, **Cleveland**, TS4 2ET, ENG.
(T) 01642 253515
Speciality: Osteopathy.
P S T (Ref:HM05481)

**CROSS, ANN-LOUISE**

**Ann-Louise Cross**, The Hollyhocks, 30 Fleet End Rd, Warsash, Southampton, **Hampshire**, SO31 9JG, ENG.
(T) 01489 589892
Speciality: Chiropodists (Podiatrists).
● **Owner** Miss A Cross
S (Ref:HM05482)

**CROSS, D J**

**D J Cross**, The Vineyard, Berkeley St, Cheltenham, **Gloucestershire**, GL52 2SX, ENG.
(T) 01242 228368
Speciality: Chiropodists (Podiatrists).
● **Owner** Mr S Davies
S (Ref:HM05483)

**CROSS, J D**

**J D Cross**, 11 Handleys Lane, Wickham Bishops, Witham, **Essex**, CM8 3NJ, ENG.
(T) 01621 893235
Speciality: Chiropodists (Podiatrists).
● **Owner** Ms J Cross
S (Ref:HM05484)

**CROSS, PHILIPPA**

**Philippa Cross**, Criss Cross Cottage, 6 Coxhill Lane, Potterne, Devizes, **Wiltshire**, SN10 5PH, ENG.
(T) 01380 728522 (F) 01380 728522
Speciality: Alexander Technique.
● **Owner** Mrs P Cross
P S (Ref:HM05485)

**CROSS, R**

**R Cross**, 2 Godstone Rd, Oxted, **Surrey**, RH8 9JT, ENG.
(T) 01883 714036
Speciality: Acupuncture.
O (Ref:HM05486)

**CROSSFIELD CLINIC-OSTEOPATHY**

**Crossfield Clinic Of Osteopathy**, 6a Crossfield Rd, London, **London (Greater)**, NW3 4NS, ENG.
(T) 020 7586 2868 (F) 020 7813 5215
Speciality: Osteopathy.
● **Director** Mrs N Soonasra
P S T (Ref:HM05487)

**CROSSLEY CLINIC**

**Crossley Clinic (The)**, Broadwater Way, Eastbourne, **Sussex (East)**, BN22 9PZ, ENG.
(T) 01323 511222 (F) 01323 648066
Speciality: Osteopathy.
● **Owner** Mr S Crossley
P S T (Ref:HM05488)

**CROSSLEY, C**

**C Crossley**, 114A Stricklandgate, Kendal, **Cumbria**, LA9 4PU, ENG.
(T) 01539 720236
Speciality: Complementary Medicines & Therapy.
C M (Ref:HM05489)

**CROSSLEY-JONES, SYLVIA**

**Miss Sylvia Crossley-Jones**, 26 Hallastone Rd, Helsby, Frodsham, **Cheshire**, WA6 0PR, ENG.
(T) 01928 723115
Speciality: Psychotherapy.
B (Ref:HM05490)

**CROSSWAY CLINIC**

**Crossway Clinic (The)**, 39 Crossway, Didsbury, Manchester, **Manchester (Greater)**, M20 6TZ, ENG.
(T) 01614 451018 (F) 01614 489494
(E) ost@vine.freeserve.co.uk
(W) www.crosswayclinic.co.uk
Speciality: Acupuncture, Alexander Technique, Aromatherapy, Counselling, Cranial Osteopathy, Hypnotherapy, Iridology, Manipulation, Massage (Therapeutic), Osteopathy, Reflexology, Stress Therapy. ✔
● **Osteopath** Mr N Vine Q: BSc. M: GOsC.
S Yrs. Est.: 12 (Ref:HM05491)

**CROSTON, GRAHAM**

**Graham Croston**, 20 Stanley Buildings, Stanley Passage, London, **London (Greater)**, NW1 2TD, ENG.
(T) 020 7837 8457
Speciality: Alexander Technique.
● **Owner** Mr G Croston
P S (Ref:HM05492)

**CROUCH END NATIONAL HLTH CTRE**

**Crouch End National Health Centre**, 24 Hermiston Avenue, Hornsey, London, **London (Greater)**, N8 8NL, ENG.
(T) 020 8340 6832
Speciality: Complementary Medicines & Therapy.
● **Therapist** Ms C Havard
M (Ref:HM05493)

**CROUCH, JANET**

**Janet Crouch**, 31 Pearce Pl, Lamberhurst, Tunbridge Wells, **Kent**, TN3 8EJ, ENG.
(T) 01892 890454
Speciality: Reflexology.
S T (Ref:HM05494)

**CROUCH, ROBERTA**

**Roberta Crouch**, The Muirs Natural Health Centre, The Muirs Business Centre, Kinross, **Perth and Kinross**, KY13 8AU, SCO.
(T) 01577 864455
Speciality: Complementary Medicines & Therapy.



Key continued: Yrs.Est: Years Established Q: Qualifications M: Professional Membership ✔ Indemnity Insurance Accept Credit Cards

M (Ref:HM05495)

## CROUTEAR, SARAH

**Sarah Croutear**, 19 Westwood Cl, Cowes, **Isle of Wight**, PO31 7NS, ENG.
(T) 01983 299964
Speciality: Reflexology.
● **Owner** Ms S Croutear
S T (Ref:HM05496)

## CROWBERRY CHIROPODY

**Crowberry Chiropody**, Manor Rd, Hayling Island, **Hampshire**, PO11 0QH, ENG.
(T) 023 9246 8468
Speciality: Chiropodists (Podiatrists).
S (Ref:HM05497)

## CROWBOROUGH CHIRO/COMP HLTH

**Crowborough Chiropractic & Complementary Health Centre**, The Broadway, Crowborough, **Sussex (East)**, TN6 1DE, ENG.
(T) 01892 610022
Speciality: Acupuncture, Chiropractic, Complementary Therapy, Counselling, Dietician, Healing Therapy, Homeopathy, Manipulation, Massage (Therapeutic), Meditation, Nutritional Therapy, Reflexology, Reiki, T'ai-Chi Ch'uan, Visualisation Therapy. ✓
● **Chiropractor** Ms C Amos
(T) 01892 668852 Q: DC, RGN. M: GCC.
● **Chiropractor** Ms P Brignall
(T) 01892 653892 Q: DC, S.E.N. M: GCC.
S Yrs. Est.: 10 (Ref:HM05498)

## CROWBOROUGH COMP THERAPISTS

**Crowborough Complementary Therapists**, 2 Beaver Cl, Crowborough, **Sussex (East)**, TN6 2NZ, ENG.
(T) 01892 660246
Speciality: Aromatherapy, Bowen Therapy, Counselling, Homeopathy, Indian Head Massage, Kinesiology, Massage (Therapeutic), Reflexology, Reiki, Themo-Auricular Therapy. ✓
● **Manager/Reflexologist**
Mrs T Smithers Q: MAR. M: AoR.
● **Counsellor** Leilan Mitchell
● **Homeopath** Sheila Royal Q: LCH, RGN.
● **Touch Therapist (Bowen)**
Ms J McDougal Q: BTER.
C Yrs. Est.: 2 (Ref:HM05499)

## CROWDEN-NAYLOR ASSOCIATES

**Crowden-Naylor Associates Ltd**, 112 St Marys Rd, Market Harborough, **Leicestershire**, LE16 7DX, ENG.
(T) 01858 468469
Speciality: Complementary Medicines & Therapy.
● **Sales Manager**
Ms S Crowden-Naylor
M (Ref:HM05500)

## CROWDER, C H J

**C H J Crowder**, Osteopathic Surgery, 2 Highlands Gardens, Ilford, **Essex**, IG1 3LD, ENG.
(T) 020 8554 3849
Speciality: Osteopathy.
● **Owner** Mr C Crowder
P S T (Ref:HM05501)

## CROWDER, E M

**E M Crowder**, 3 Walkers Lane, Killamarsh, Sheffield, **Yorkshire (South)**, S21 1ER, ENG.
(T) 01142 483764
Speciality: Chiropodists (Podiatrists).
● **Owner** Mrs E Crowder
S (Ref:HM05502)

## CROWDER, SUZANNE

**Suzanne Crowder**, Ely Complementary Health Centre, 29a St Marys St, Ely, **Cambridgeshire**, CB7 4HF, ENG.
(T) 01353 664476
Speciality: Reflexology.
● **Owner** Mr A Spence
S T (Ref:HM05503)

## CROWE, A

**A Crowe Holistic Aromatherapy Massage & Reflexology**, 3 Riverside, Clayton West, Huddersfield, **Yorkshire (West)**, HD8 9QN, ENG.
(T) 01484 863696
Speciality: Aromatherapy, Massage (Therapeutic), Reflexology.
M (Ref:HM05504)

## CROWEST, E

**E Crowest**, 98 Denmark St, Diss, **Norfolk**, IP22 4LF, ENG.
(T) 01379 644535
Speciality: Chiropodists (Podiatrists).
● **Owner** Mrs E Crowest
S (Ref:HM05505)

## CROWLEY, HEATHER

**Heather Crowley**, Court Field, De Burgh Park, Banstead, **Surrey**, SM7 2PP, ENG.
(T) 01737 358742
Speciality: Reflexology.
S T (Ref:HM05506)

## CROWN CHIROPRACTIC CLINIC

**Crown Chiropractic Clinic**, 14 Crown St, Brentwood, **Essex**, CM14 4BA, ENG.
(T) 01277 212277
Speciality: Chiropractic.
● **Owner** Dr C Cockerton Q: DC. M: BCA.
P S T Yrs. Est.: 10 (Ref:HM05507)

## CROWN CHIROPRACTIC CLINIC

**Crown Chiropractic Clinic**, 40 Rayne Rd, Braintree, **Essex**, CM7 2QP, ENG.
(T) 01376 340399 (F) 01376 340399
Speciality: Chiropractic. ✓
● **Owner** Mrs C Cockerton Q: BSc, DC, MBAcC. M: GCC.
P Yrs. Est.: 4 (Ref:HM05508)

## CROWN TREATMENT CENTRE

**Crown Treatment Centre**, 2 Crown Lane, Littleport, Ely, **Cambridgeshire**, CB1 5PA, ENG.
(T) 01353 863218
Speciality: Complementary Medicines & Therapy.
● **Therapist** Ms E Tarmy
M (Ref:HM05509)

## CROWNGATE PHYSIOTHERAPY CLINIC

**Crowngate Physiotherapy Clinic**, 48 Friary Walk, Worcester, **Worcestershire**, WR1 3LE, ENG.
(T) 01905 27922
Speciality: Physiotherapy.
P S T (Ref:HM05510)

## CROWNHILL CHIROPODY PRACTICE

**Crownhill Chiropody Practice (The)**, 10 Morshead Rd, Plymouth, **Devon**, PL6 5AJ, ENG.
(T) 01752 790490
Speciality: Chiropodists (Podiatrists).
● **Owner** Mr W Robins
S (Ref:HM05511)

## CROWTHER, GEORGE

**George Crowther**, Little Hill, Colley Manor Drive, Reigate, **Surrey**, RH2 9JS, ENG.
(T) 01737 243286
Speciality: Psychology.
B (Ref:HM05512)

## CROWTHORNE CHIROPODIST CLINIC

**Crowthorne Chiropodist Clinic (The)**, Suite 8, Talbot House, High St, Crowthorne, **Berkshire**, RG45 7AQ, ENG.
(T) 01344 777105 (F) 01344 427364
Speciality: Chiropodists (Podiatrists).
● **Employee** Mr P Hayward
S (Ref:HM05513)

## CROYDON BUDDHIST CENTRE

**Croydon Buddhist Centre**, 96-98 High St, Croydon, **Surrey**, CR0 1, ENG.
(T) 020 8688 8624
Speciality: Alexander Technique.
● **Teacher of the Alexander Technique**
Ms J Cox
P S (Ref:HM05514)

## CROYDON HEALING CENTRE

**Croydon Healing Centre**, Friends Meeting House, Park Lane, Croydon, **Surrey**, CR2 7DX, ENG.
(T) 020 8688 1751 (F) 020 8688 1751
(E) croydon.healing.centre@ukgateway.net
Speciality: Absent Healing, Complementary Therapy, Faith Healing, Healer, Healing Therapy, Spiritual Healing. ✓
● **Secretary/Healer** Tonie Lambie Q: MNFSH. M: NFSH.
B Yrs. Est.: 17 (Ref:HM05515)

## CROYDON HYPNOTHERAPY

**Croydon Hypnotherapy & Primary Cause Analysis Centre**, 13 Beechwood Rd, Sanderstead, South Croydon, **Surrey**, CR2 0AE, ENG.
(T) 020 8657 3624 (F) 020 8657 3624
(E) hamish@pitceathly.freeserve.co.uk
Speciality: Counselling, Hypnosis, Hypnotherapy, Hypno Analysis. ✓
● **President of SPCAH**
Mr H Pitceathly Q: Dip.PCAH, FHA, FHRS, FSPCAH, MCPS. M: CPS, HRS, HS, SPCAH.
B Yrs. Est.: 21 (Ref:HM05516)

## CROYDON PRACTICE-PSYCHOTHERAPY

**Croydon Practice & Centre For Psychotherapy (The)**, 23 Addiscombe Court Rd, Croydon, **Surrey**, CR0 6TT, ENG.
(T) 020 8656 3075
Speciality: Psychotherapy.
● **Owner** Ms M Rabe
B (Ref:HM05517)

## CRUICKSHANK-ROBB, S

**S Cruickshank-Robb**, Hove St, Hove, **Sussex (East)**, BN3 2TR, ENG.
(T) 01273 203546
Speciality: Physiotherapy.
P S T (Ref:HM05518)

## CRUICKSHANKS, P

**P Cruickshanks**, 6 Warrener St, Sale, **Cheshire**, M33 3GE, ENG.
(T) 01619 735596
Speciality: Hypnosis.
● **Owner** Mrs P Cruickshanks
B (Ref:HM05519)

## CRUISE, M & M

**M & M Cruise**, 25 Portland Rd, Kilmarnock, **Ayrshire (East)**, KA1 2BT, SCO.
(T) 01563 525112
Speciality: Biomechanics, Chiropody, Cryo Surgery, Nail Surgery. ✓
● **Chiropodist** Mr M Cruise Q: M.S.C.P, S.R.Ch.
M Yrs. Est.: 32 (Ref:HM05520)

## CRUISE, M & M

**M & M Cruise**, The Consulting Rooms, 12 Barns St, Ayr, **Ayrshire (South)**, KA7 1XA, SCO.
(T) 01292 260024
Speciality: Chiropodists (Podiatrists).
● **Manageress** Mrs A Smith
S (Ref:HM05521)

## CRUISE, M & M

**M & M Cruise**, 24 Wellington Sq, Ayr, **Ayrshire (South)**, KA7 1EZ, SCO.
(T) 01563 525112
Speciality: Biomechanics, Chiropody, Nail Surgery, Cyro-Surgery. ✓
● **Chiropodist** Mr M Cruise Q: S.R.Ch. M: S.C.P.
M Yrs. Est.: 32 (Ref:HM05522)

## CRUTCHINGTON, JEAN

**Jean Crutchington**, 47 Carlton Rd, Redhill, **Surrey**, RH1 2BY, ENG.
(T) 01737 768900
Speciality: Chiropodists (Podiatrists).
S (Ref:HM05523)

## CRYSTAL & REIKI

**Crystal & Reiki**, 62 West Bradford Rd, Waddington, Clitheroe, **Lancashire**, BB7 3JD, ENG.
(T) 01200 426061 (F) 01200 444776
(W) www.iacht.co.uk
Speciality: Crystal Healing, Reiki. ✓
● **Therapist** Susan Baron Q: BA (Hons).
B Yrs. Est.: 15 (Ref:HM05524)

## CRYSTAL AROMATICS

**Crystal Aromatics**, 48 Roe St, Macclesfield, **Cheshire**, SK11 6XD, ENG.
(T) 01625 511551
Speciality: Aromatherapy.
M O (Ref:HM05525)



Key: B Mind-Body Medicine C Complementary Medicine H Self Help Treatment M Medicinal Therapy O Oriental Medicine P Postural Therapy S Manipulative Structural Therapy T Touch Therapy

## CRYSTAL BALL

**Crystal Ball (The)**, 44 Station Rd, Ossett, **Yorkshire (West)**, WF5 8AY, ENG.
(T) 01924 274944
Speciality: Clairvoyants & Palmists.
● **Owner** Ms L Davies
B (**Ref:**HM05526)

## CRYSTAL CLEAR

**Crystal Clear**, Unit 67, B S S House, Cheney Manor Industrial Estate, Swindon, **Wiltshire**, SN2 2PJ, ENG.
(T) 01793 520770
Speciality: Aromatherapy.
● **Owner** Mrs K Tombling
M O (**Ref:**HM05527)

## CRYSTAL CLEAR PRACTICE

**Crystal Clear Practice**, 851 Chester Rd, Erdington, Birmingham, **Midlands (West)**, B24 0BT, ENG.
(T) 01213 826444 (F) 01213 826444
Speciality: Aromatherapy, Reiki. ✓
● **Reiki Master/Holistic Therapist** Mrs J Ashworth **Q:** C&GFAETC, Dip.ITHMA, ITHMA, Louise Hay Trainer, RQA.
C Yrs. Est.: 4 (**Ref:**HM05528)

## CRYSTAL CLEAR PSYCHIC READINGS

**Crystal Clear Psychic Readings**, 3 Stubbington Avenue, Portsmouth, **Hampshire**, PO2 0HP, ENG.
(T) 023 9267 2392 (F) 023 9267 2392
Speciality: Clairvoyants & Palmists.
● **Owner** Mrs P Phipps
B (**Ref:**HM05529)

## CRYSTAL GARDEN

**Crystal Garden (The)**, 270 London Rd, Croydon, **London (Greater)**, CR0 2TH, ENG.
(T) 020 8667 1944
(E) crystalgarden@spiralspider.demon.co.uk
(W) www.spiralspider.demon.co.uk
Speciality: Complementary Medicines & Therapy.
● **Owner** Ms K Langley
C Yrs. Est.: 1 (**Ref:**HM05530)

## CRYSTAL HARMONY

**Crystal Harmony**, 8 Alexandra Pk, Kirkintilloch, Glasgow, **Glasgow (City of)**, G66 5BH, SCO.
(T) 01417 752584 (F) 01417 752584
Speciality: Complementary Medicines & Therapy.
● **Owner** Mrs A Gillchrist
M (**Ref:**HM05531)

## CRYSTAL SANCTUARY

**Crystal Sanctuary (The)**, 164 North High St, Musselburgh, **Lothian (Mid)**, EH21 6AR, SCO.
(T) 01316 650878
(E) cs@thesanctuary.org.uk
Speciality: Aromatherapy, Holistic Healing, Homeopathy, Massage (Therapeutic), Reflexology, Reiki, Clinical Aromatherapy. ✓
● **Reiki Teacher** Ms E Walker **Q:** Reiki Master. **M:** IPTI.
● **Owner** Mr A Haines
C Yrs. Est.: 4 (**Ref:**HM05532)

## CRYSTAL THERAPY

**Crystal Therapy**, 52 The Broadway, London, **London (Greater)**, W5 5JN, ENG.
(T) 020 8866 6435
Speciality: Complementary Medicines & Therapy.
M (**Ref:**HM05533)

## CT & IM LEITH

**CT Leith & IM Leith**, 16 Melton Hill, Woodbridge, **Suffolk**, IP12 1AY, ENG.
(T) 01394 380701
(E) i.leith@cwcom.net
Speciality: Acupuncture, Bach Remedies, Homeopathy, Magnetic Therapy, Manipulation, Nutritional Therapy, Reiki, X-Ray, Electro-Acupuncture. ✓
● **Homeopath** Mrs C Leith **Q:** RMANM. **M:** ANM.
● **Orthopedic Physician/Medical Acupuncturist** Mr I Leith **Q:** BS, Dip.Med.Ac, MB. **M:** BIMM, BMAS.
S Yrs. Est.: 12 (**Ref:**HM05534)

## CTIC

**CTIC**, 83 Baldwin Rd, Birmingham, **Midlands (West)**, B30 3LD, ENG.
(T) 01214 333606
Speciality: Aromatherapy, Hypnotherapy, Indian Head Massage, Nutritional Therapy, Reflexology, Remedial Massage, Holistic Therapy, NLP. ✓
● **Director** Mr D Harpe **Q:** IIHHT, NLP. **M:** FHT.
M Yrs. Est.: 1 (**Ref:**HM05535)

## CTRE - INTEGRAL PSYCHOANALYSIS

**Centre Of Integral Psychoanalysis**, 6a Colville Rd, London, **London (Greater)**, W11 2BP, ENG.
(T) 020 7727 4404
Speciality: Psychotherapy.
B (**Ref:**HM05536)

## CTRE FOR ADVANCED REFLEXOLOGY

**Centre For Advanced Reflexology**, 204 Mauldeth Rd, Manchester, **Manchester (Greater)**, M19 1AJ, ENG.
(T) 01614 431582 (F) 01612 862336
Speciality: Reflexology.
● **Owner** Mr C O'Hara
S T (**Ref:**HM05537)

## CTRE FOR COMPLEMENTARY HEALTH

**Centre For Complementary Health**, 6 Cambridge Rd, Godmanchester, Huntingdon, **Cambridgeshire**, PE29 2BW, ENG.
(T) 01480 455221 (F) 01480 411588
Speciality: Complementary Medicines & Therapy.
● **Practice Manager** Mrs H Lawrence
M (**Ref:**HM05538)

## CTRE FOR COUNS/PSYCHO ED

**Centre For Counselling & Psychotherapy Education**, 2 Warwick Cres, London, **London (Greater)**, W2 6NE, ENG.
(T) 020 7266 3006 (F) 020 7266 3691
Speciality: Psychotherapy.
B (**Ref:**HM05539)

## CTRE FOR CRANIO-SACRAL THERAPY

**Centre for Cranio-Sacral Therapy**, 9 St Georges Mews, London, **London (Greater)**, NW1 8XE, ENG.
(T) 020 7483 0120 (F) 020 7586 9550
(E) info@ccst.co.uk
(W) www.ccst.co.uk
Speciality: Acupuncture, Alexander Technique, Aromatherapy, Bowen Therapy, Chiropractic, Counselling, Cranial Osteopathy, Cranio-Sacral Therapy, Herbal Medicine, Homeopathy, Hypnosis, Hypnotherapy, Manipulation, Massage (Therapeutic), Metamorphic Therapy, Osteopathy, Phytotherapy, Psychotherapy, Reflexology, Reiki, Shiatsu. ✓
● **Homeopath** Ms J Parkin **Q:** RSHom.
● **Cranio-Sacral Therapist** Mr T Attlee **Q:** DO, RCST. **M:** CSTA.
● **Massage Therapist** Ms M Berrisford
● **Osteopath** Mr D Picknett **Q:** BSc. **M:** GOsC.
B Yrs. Est.: 10 (**Ref:**HM05540)

## CTRE FOR HEALTH/PASTORAL CARE

**Centre for Health and Pastoral Care**, Holyrood House, 10 Sowerby Rd, Sowerby, Thirsk, **Yorkshire (North)**, YO7 1HX, ENG.
(T) 01845 522580
Speciality: Psychology.
● **Therapist** Mr S Baxter
B (**Ref:**HM05541)

## CTRE FOR KINESIOLOGY

**Centre For Kinesiology & Phytobiophysics (The)**, 321 Nore Rd, Portishead, Bristol, BS20 8EN, ENG.
(T) 01275 846683 (F) 01275 846683
(W) www.mesk.org
Speciality: Bach Remedies, Clinical Ecology, Complementary Therapy, Holistic Healing, Kinesiology, Nutritional Therapy, Reiki, Seichem, Vibrational Therapy, Phytobiophysics. ✓
● **Therapist** Ms M King
● **Therapist** Ms P Noakes **Q:** BA (Hons), RCT.
B Yrs. Est.: 10 (**Ref:**HM05542)

## CTRE FOR THE STUDY OF COMP MED

**Boots Health And Beauty Ltd**, 51 Bedford Pl, Southampton, **Hampshire**, SO15 2DT, ENG.
(T) 023 8033 4752 (F) 023 8023 1835
(E) enquiries@complemed.co.uk
(W) www.complemed.co.uk
Speciality: Acupuncture, Alexander Technique, Autogenic Training, Bach Remedies, Clinical Ecology, Complementary Therapy, Counselling, Dietician, Herbal Medicine, Homeopathy, Hypnosis, Macrobiotics, Meditation, Nutritional Therapy. ✓
● **Consultant** Ms J Worden **Q:** MRCGP. **M:** FHom.
● **Consultant** Mr M Clark **Q:** BSc, Ch.B, Dip.Med.Ac, MB. **M:** FHom.
● **Consultant** Mr D Marshall **Q:** MRCGP. **M:** FHom.
● **Consultant** Mr N Avery **Q:** BS, MB. **M:** FHom.
● **Consultant** Mr G Lewith **Q:** Dip.Med.Ac, FRCP, MA.
M Yrs. Est.: 20 (**Ref:**HM05543)

## CTRE FOR THE STUDY OF COMP MED

**Boots Health And Beauty Ltd**, 14 Harley House, Brunswick Pl, London, **London (Greater)**, NW1 4PR, ENG.
(T) 020 7935 7848 (F) 020 7224 4159
(E) enquiries@complemed.co.uk
(W) www.complemed.co.uk
Speciality: Acupuncture, Alexander Technique, Autogenic Training, Bach Remedies, Clinical Ecology, Complementary Therapy, Counselling, Dietician, Herbal Medicine, Homeopathy, Hypnosis, Macrobiotics, Meditation, Nutritional Therapy. ✓
● **Consultant** Mr M Clarke **Q:** BSc, Dip.Med.Ac. **M:** FHom.
● **Consultant** Mr D Marshall **Q:** MRCGP. **M:** FHom.
● **Consultant** Mr G Lewith **Q:** MRCGP. **M:** FHom.
● **Consultant** Ms J Worden **Q:** MRCGP. **M:** FHom.
● **Consultant** Mr N Avery **Q:** BS, MB.
M Yrs. Est.: 20 (**Ref:**HM05544)

## CTRE-ATTACH BASED PSYCHOAN

**Centre For Attachment Based Psychoanalytic Psychotherapy**, 356 Holloway Rd, London, **London (Greater)**, N7 6PA, ENG.
(T) 020 7794 4306
Speciality: Psychoanalysis.
B (**Ref:**HM05545)

## CTRE-CLASSICAL HOMEOPATHY

**Centre For Classical Homeopathy**, Chaucer Building, 57 Grainger St, Newcastle Upon Tyne, **Tyne and Wear**, NE1 5LE, ENG.
(T) 01912 324700
Speciality: Homeopathy.
● **Owner** Mr F Hannon
M (**Ref:**HM05546)

## CTRE-COMPLEMENTARY THERAPY

**Centre For Complementary Therapy**, 130 New St, Andover, **Hampshire**, SP10 1DR, ENG.
(T) 01264 335333
Speciality: Aromatherapy, Chiropractic, Cranio-Sacral Therapy, Homeopathy, Hypnosis, Indian Head Massage, Massage (Therapeutic), McTimoney Chiropractic, Naturopathy, Physiotherapy, Reflexology, Reiki, Yoga, Radionics.
C (**Ref:**HM05547)

## CTRE-PSYCHOANALY PSYCHOTHERAPY

**Centre For Psychoanalytical Psychotherapy**, 538 Finchley Rd, London, **London (Greater)**, NW11 8DD, ENG.
(T) 020 8922 8551
Speciality: Psychotherapy.
B (**Ref:**HM05548)

## CTRE-REFLEX & AROMATHERAPY

**Centre Of Reflexology & Aromatherapy**, 160 Westminster Rd, Handsworth, Birmingham, **Midlands (West)**, B20 3NA, ENG.
(T) 01213 565588
Speciality: Aromatherapy, Bach Remedies, Healer, Hopi Ear Candles, Indian Head Massage, Reflexology, Reiki. ✓
● **Owner/Therapist** Mrs S Gohil **Q:** MAR, S.E.N.



Key continued: **Yrs.Est:** Years Established **Q:** Qualifications **M:** Professional Membership ✓ Indemnity Insurance Accept Credit Cards

M: AoR.
C T Yrs. Est.: 12 (Ref:HM05549)

### CUDDEFORD, C
**C Cuddeford**, 62 High St, Hadleigh, Ipswich, **Suffolk**, IP7 5EF, ENG.
(T) 01473 828585
Speciality: Osteopathy.
P S T (Ref:HM05550)

### CUDDEFORD, C
**C Cuddeford**, Station Rd, Sudbury, **Suffolk**, CO10 2SU, ENG.
(T) 01787 375656
Speciality: Osteopathy.
P S T (Ref:HM05551)

### CUDLIPP, G
**G Cudlipp**, 40 Summerdown Rd, Eastbourne, **Sussex (East)**, BN20 8DR, ENG.
(T) 01323 733539
Speciality: Osteopathy.
● **Owner** Mr G Cudlipp
P S T (Ref:HM05552)

### CUERDEN, I
**I Cuerden**, 50 Plungington Rd, Preston, **Lancashire**, PR1 7RB, ENG.
(T) 01772 556520
Speciality: Chiropodists (Podiatrists).
● **Partner** Mr I Cuerdon
S (Ref:HM05553)

### CULCHETH REMEDIAL CLINIC
**Culcheth Remedial Therapy Clinic**, 17 Sundial House, Common Lane, Culcheth, Warrington, **Cheshire**, WA3 4EH, ENG.
(T) 01925 767979
Speciality: Hypnosis.
B (Ref:HM05554)

### CULL, BEN
**Ben Cull**, 37 Vernon Trce, Brighton, **Sussex (East)**, BN1 3JH, ENG.
(T) 01273 202221
Speciality: Osteopathy.
P S T (Ref:HM05555)

### CULL, BEN
**Ben Cull D O**, 227A South Coast Rd, Peacehaven, **Sussex (East)**, BN10 8LB, ENG.
(T) 01273 580370
Speciality: Hypnosis, Osteopathy. ✔
● **Osteopath** Mr B Cull Q: DO.
S Yrs. Est.: 12 (Ref:HM05556)

### CULL, KAREN
**Karen Cull**, 12A Church St, London, **London (Greater)**, NW8 8EP, ENG.
(T) 020 7402 2936
Speciality: Hypnosis.
B (Ref:HM05557)

### CULLEN, D
**D Cullen**, 6 West Drive, Mickleover, Derby, **Derbyshire**, DE3 5EX, ENG.
(T) 01332 511656
Speciality: Chiropodists (Podiatrists).
● **Owner** Mr D Cullen
S (Ref:HM05558)

### CULLEN, FRANCESCA
**Francesca Cullen**, Bates St, Sheffield, **Yorkshire (South)**, S10 1NQ, ENG.
(T) 01142 682088
Speciality: Reflexology.
● **Owner** Mrs F Cullen
S T (Ref:HM05559)

### CULLEN, KEVIN
**Kevin Cullen**, Swale Chiropractic Clinic, 167A London Rd, Sittingbourne, **Kent**, ME10 1PA, ENG.
(T) 01795 520707 (F) 01795 520799
Speciality: Chiropractic.
● **Owner** Mr K Cullen
P S T (Ref:HM05560)

### CULLEN, MARGARET
**Margaret Cullen**, 64 Elm Gr, Brighton, **Sussex (East)**, BN2 3DD, ENG.
(T) 01273 683623
Speciality: Clairvoyants & Palmists, Palmistry. ✔
● **Owner/Palmist** Mrs M Cullen
B Yrs. Est.: 51 (Ref:HM05561)

### CULLEN, T C
**T C Cullen**, 7 Oriel Bank, Scarborough, **Yorkshire (North)**, YO11 2SZ, ENG.
(T) 01723 371248
Speciality: Osteopathy.
● **Owner** Mr T Cullen
P S T (Ref:HM05562)

### CULLENS, IONA
**Iona Cullens**, Alva, **Clackmannanshire**, FK12, SCO.
(T) 01259 760243
Speciality: Aromatherapy.
M O (Ref:HM05563)

### CULLETON, L
**L Culleton**, 29 High St, Harlow, **Essex**, CM17 0DN, ENG.
(T) 01279 438444
Speciality: Acupuncture.
● **Partner** Mr N Bruce
O (Ref:HM05564)

### CULLINANE/GARDINER
**Cullinane/Gardiner**, Sports Injuries Clinic 36 Gled, Dublin, **County Dublin**, IRE.
(T) 01260 0090
Speciality: Complementary Medicines & Therapy.
M (Ref:HM05565)

### CULLING, ADRIAN
**Adrian Culling**, 56 Alum Chine Rd, Bournemouth, **Dorset**, BH4 8DZ, ENG.
(T) 01202 769976
Speciality: Osteopathy.
P S T (Ref:HM05566)

### CULLING, CHARMAINE
**Charmaine Culling**, 56 Alum Chine Rd, Bournemouth, **Dorset**, BH4 8DZ, ENG.
(T) 01202 769976
Speciality: Osteopathy.
P S T (Ref:HM05567)

### CULLOMPTON CHIROPRACTIC CLINIC
**Cullompton Chiropractic Clinic**, 11A Exeter Rd, Cullompton, **Devon**, EX15 1DX, ENG.
(T) 01884 38134
Speciality: Chiropractic.
● **Owner** Ms C Elgom
P S T (Ref:HM05568)

### CULPEPER
**Culpeper Ltd**, 43 County Arcade, Leeds, **Yorkshire (West)**, LS1 6BH, ENG.
(T) 01132 471870 (F) 01132 471870
Speciality: Herbalists.
● **Manager** Ms K Chaplin
M (Ref:HM05569)

### CULPEPER
**Culpeper Ltd**, Unit 2 Upper Mall, Royal Priors Shopping Centre, Leamington Spa, **Warwickshire**, CV32 4XT, ENG.
(T) 01926 450067
Speciality: Herbal Medicine.
● **Branch Manager** Ms L Ashbourne
M (Ref:HM05570)

### CULPEPER
**Culpeper Ltd**, Unit 2 Orchard Sq, Sheffield, **Yorkshire (South)**, S1 2FB, ENG.
(T) 01142 769788
Speciality: Herbal Medicine.
M (Ref:HM05571)

### CULPEPER
**Culpeper Ltd**, Hadstock Rd, Linton, Cambridge, **Cambridgeshire**, CB1 6NJ, ENG.
(T) 01223 891196 (F) 01223 893104
Speciality: Herbalists.
● **Director** Mrs E Harrison
M (Ref:HM05572)

### CULPEPER
**Culpeper Ltd**, 8 The Market, The Piazza, London, **London (Greater)**, WC2E 8RB, ENG.
(T) 020 7379 6698 (F) 020 7379 6698
Speciality: Herbal Medicine.
● **Manageress** Mrs E James
M (Ref:HM05573)

### CULPEPER
**Culpeper Ltd**, 7 New Inn Hall St, Oxford, **Oxfordshire**, OX1 2DH, ENG.
(T) 01865 249754
Speciality: Herbal Medicine.
● **Manager** Ms M Jones
M (Ref:HM05574)

### CULPEPER
**Culpeper Ltd**, 43 Low Petergate, York, **Yorkshire (North)**, YO1 7HT, ENG.
(T) 01904 651654
Speciality: Herbal Medicine.
● **Manager** Miss H Bligh
M (Ref:HM05575)

### CULPEPER
**Culpeper Ltd**, 34 The Pavilions, High St, Birmingham, **Midlands (West)**, B4 7SL, ENG.
(T) 01216 430100 (F) 01216 430100
Speciality: Herbal Medicine.
● **Manageress** Miss S Dale
M (Ref:HM05576)

### CULPEPER
**Culpeper Ltd**, 28 Milsom St, Bath, **Somerset**, BA1 1DG, ENG.
(T) 01225 425875 (F) 01225 425875
Speciality: Herbal Medicine.
● **Manager** Mrs K Curle
M (Ref:HM05577)

### CULPEPER
**Culpeper Ltd**, 1 Post Office Rd, Bournemouth, **Dorset**, BH1 1BB, ENG.
(T) 01202 557107
Speciality: Herbal Medicine.
M (Ref:HM05578)

### CULPEPER
**Culpeper Ltd**, 5 White Lion St, Norwich, **Norfolk**, NR2 1QA, ENG.
(T) 01603 619153 (F) 01603 619153
Speciality: Herbal Medicine.
● **Manager** Miss E Davison
M (Ref:HM05579)

### CULPEPER
**Culpeper Ltd**, 1 Cavern Walk, 8 Mathew St, Liverpool, **Merseyside**, L2 6RE, ENG.
(T) 01512 365780 (F) 01512 365780
Speciality: Herbal Medicine.
● **Manager** Miss H Peers
M (Ref:HM05580)

### CULPEPER
**Culpeper Ltd**, 25 The Maltings, Salisbury, **Wiltshire**, SP1 1BD, ENG.
(T) 01722 326159 (F) 01722 326159
Speciality: Herbal Medicine.
● **Manager** Ms M Giscos
M (Ref:HM05581)

### CULPEPER
**Culpeper Ltd**, 10 Swan Lane, Guildford, **Surrey**, GU1 4EQ, ENG.
(T) 01483 560008
Speciality: Herbal Medicine.
● **Chairman** Ian Mitchell Thomas
M (Ref:HM05582)

### CULPEPER
**Culpeper Ltd**, 11 Marlowe Arcade, Canterbury, **Kent**, CT1 2TJ, ENG.
(T) 01227 451121
Speciality: Herbal Medicine.
● **Assistant Manager** Miss J Burns
M (Ref:HM05583)

### CULPEPER
**Culpeper Ltd**, 12D Meeting House Lane, Brighton, **Sussex (East)**, BN1 1HB, ENG.
(T) 01273 327939 (F) 01273 327939
Speciality: Herbal Medicine.
● **Manager** Miss L McMorrin
M (Ref:HM05584)

### CULPEPER
**Culpeper Ltd**, 17 Pittville St, Cheltenham, **Gloucestershire**, GL52 2LN, ENG.
(T) 01242 571784 (F) 01242 571784
Speciality: Herbal Medicine.
● **Area Manager** Ms V Bolton
M (Ref:HM05585)



Key: B Mind-Body Medicine C Complementary Medicine H Self Help Treatment M Medicinal Therapy O Oriental Medicine P Postural Therapy S Manipulative Structural Therapy T Touch Therapy

**CULPEPER**

**Culpeper Ltd**, 21 Bruton St, London, **London (Greater)**, W1X 7DA, ENG.
(T) 020 7629 4559 (F) 020 7629 4559
Speciality: Herbal Medicine.
● **Manager** Ms A Clark
M (Ref:HM05586)

**CULPEPER**

**Culpeper Ltd**, 24 Bridge St, Chester, **Cheshire**, CH1 1NQ, ENG.
(T) 01244 317774
Speciality: Herbal Medicine.
M (Ref:HM05587)

**CULPEPER**

**Culpeper Ltd**, 25 Lion Yard, Cambridge, **Cambridgeshire**, CB2 3NA, ENG.
(T) 01223 367370
Speciality: Herbal Medicine.
M (Ref:HM05588)

**CULPIN, J I**

**J I Culpin**, 1 Evington Parks Rd, Leicester, **Leicestershire**, LE2 1PS, ENG.
(T) 01162 730371
Speciality: Chiropodists (Podiatrists).
S (Ref:HM05589)

**CULPIN, SANDRA**

**Sandra Culpin**, 27 Castle Drive, South Cave, Brough, **Humberside (North)**, HU15 2ES, ENG.
(T) 01430 424602
Speciality: Reflexology.
S T (Ref:HM05590)

**CULSHAW, S**

**S Culshaw**, 6 Fowler Rd, Blacon, Chester, **Cheshire**, CH1 5PT, ENG.
(T) 01244 375777
Speciality: Aromatherapy.
M O (Ref:HM05591)

**CULTRON SERVICES**

**Cultron Services**, 32 Hilliard Drive, Bradwell, Milton Keynes, **Buckinghamshire**, MK13 9EG, ENG.
(T) 01908 317943 (F) 01908 317943
Speciality: Complementary Medicines & Therapy.
● **Owner** Mr T Cullip
C M (Ref:HM05592)

**CULVER, COLETTE**

**Colette Culver R G N A D H P**, Pembroke Hse, Pembroke St, **County Cork**, IRE.
(T) 08660 82627
Speciality: Hypnotherapy.
B (Ref:HM05593)

**CULVERHOUSE, DAVID**

**David Culverhouse**, 75A High St, Dunmow, **Essex**, CM6 1AE, ENG.
(T) 01371 872332
Speciality: Chiropodists (Podiatrists).
● **Owner** Mr D Culverhouse
S (Ref:HM05594)

**CUMBERLEDGE, P J**

**P J Cumberledge**, 1 Park Rd, Consett, **County Durham**, DH8 5EA, ENG.
(T) 01207 504478
Speciality: Chiropodists (Podiatrists).
● **Partner** Mrs E Cumberledge
S (Ref:HM05595)

**CUMBERLEDGE, PAUL JAMES**

**Paul James Cumberledge**, 66-68 Station Rd, Stanley, **County Durham**, DH9 0JP, ENG.
(T) 01207 232329
Speciality: Chiropodists (Podiatrists).
S (Ref:HM05596)

**CUMBERLIDGE, CAROL**

**Carol Cumberlidge**, 10 Kinnibrugh Drive, Dormansland, Lingfield, **Surrey**, RH7 6QF, ENG.
(T) 01342 832631
Speciality: Reflexology.
S T (Ref:HM05597)

**CUMBRIA PHYSIO & SPORTS CLINIC**

**Cumbria Physiotherapy & Sports Injuries Clinic**, 1 Castlegate, Cockermouth, **Cumbria**, CA13 9EU, ENG.
(T) 01900 825314 (F) 01900 823363
(W) www.cumbriaphysiotherapy.co.uk
Speciality: Physiotherapy. ✔
● **Physiotherapist** Mrs N Fraser Q: MCSP, SRP.
C (Ref:HM05598)

**CUMMING, BETTE**

**Bette Cumming**, 26 Mons Avenue, Billericay, **Essex**, CM11 2HG, ENG.
(T) 01277 653939
Speciality: Complementary Medicines & Therapy.
● **Owner** Bette Cummings
M (Ref:HM05599)

**CUMMING, DENISE**

**Denise Cumming**, 37 Inglethorpe St, London, **London (Greater)**, SW6 6NS, ENG.
(T) 020 7381 6879
Speciality: Reflexology.
S T (Ref:HM05600)

**CUMMING, JANE**

**Mrs Jane Cumming**, 6 Willand Rd, Braunton, **Devon**, EX33 1AX, ENG.
(T) 01271 817058
Speciality: Physiotherapy.
● **Owner** Mrs J Cumming
P S T (Ref:HM05601)

**CUMMING, JOHN**

**John Cumming**, 36A Prince Of Wales Drive, London, **London (Greater)**, SW11 4SF, ENG.
(T) 020 7924 2955
Speciality: Homeopathy.
● **Owner** Mr J Cumming
M (Ref:HM05602)

**CUMMING, JOHN D**

**John D Cumming**, 44 Falkland Park Rd, Ayr, **Ayrshire (South)**, KA8 8LL, SCO.
(T) 01292 285060
Speciality: Chiropodists (Podiatrists).
● **Owner** Mr J Cummings
S (Ref:HM05603)

**CUMMING, LESLEY**

**Lesley Cumming**, Unit 6 Riverside Business Park, Gosport St, Lymington, **Hampshire**, SO41 9BB, ENG.
(T) 01590 688788
Speciality: Physiotherapy.
P S T (Ref:HM05604)

**CUMMING, LLOYD**

**Lloyd Cumming**, 468 Trelawney Avenue, Slough, **Berkshire**, SL3 7TS, ENG.
(T) 01753 580640
Speciality: Chiropodists (Podiatrists).
S (Ref:HM05605)

**CUMMING, NIGEL A**

**Nigel A Cumming**, 44E Station Rd, Sheringham, **Norfolk**, NR26 8RG, ENG.
(T) 01263 823733
Speciality: Chiropodists (Podiatrists).
● **Owner** Mr N Cummings
S (Ref:HM05606)

**CUMMING, S W**

**S W Cumming**, 20 Park Pl, Stirling, FK7 9JR, SCO.
(T) 01786 463184
Speciality: Physiotherapy.
● **Owner** Mrs S Cumming
P S T (Ref:HM05607)

**CUMMINGS, ALEX M L**

**Alex M L Cummings**, 16 Orchard St, Paisley, **Renfrewshire**, PA1 1UZ, SCO.
(T) 01418 896929
Speciality: Chiropodists (Podiatrists).
● **Chief Executive** Mr A Cummings
S (Ref:HM05608)

**CUMMINGS, ALISON**

**Alison Cummings**, 39 Roman Rd, Weymouth, **Dorset**, DT3 5JH, ENG.
(T) 01305 773824
Speciality: Reflexology.
● **Owner** Ms A Cummings
S T (Ref:HM05609)

**CUMMINGS, ELIZABETH**

**Elizabeth Cummings Holistic Reflexology**, Freegrove, Red St, Southfleet, Gravesend, **Kent**, DA13 9QL, ENG.
(T) 01474 833422
Speciality: Reflexology.
M (Ref:HM05610)

**CUMMINGS, J S**

**J S Cummings**, 98 Cambridge St, Wolverton, Milton Keynes, **Buckinghamshire**, MK12 5AH, ENG.
(T) 01908 313357
Speciality: Chiropodists (Podiatrists).
● **Owner** Mr J Cummings
S (Ref:HM05611)

**CUMMINGS, M**

**M Cummings**, 110 Lower Richmond Rd, London, **London (Greater)**, SW15 1LN, ENG.
(T) 020 8788 1991
Speciality: Osteopathy.
P S T (Ref:HM05612)

**CUMMINGS, MAUREEN**

**Maureen Cummings**, 44E Station Rd, Sheringham, **Norfolk**, NR26 8RG, ENG.
(T) 01263 823733
Speciality: Electrolysis.
● **Owner** Mr N Cummings
T (Ref:HM05613)

**CUMMINS, DECLAN**

**Declan Cummins**, 1 Hyde Lane, Frogmore, St. Albans, **Hertfordshire**, AL2 2LE, ENG.
(T) 01727 873015
Speciality: Chiropodists (Podiatrists).
S (Ref:HM05614)

**CUMMINS, LYNN**

**Lynn Cummins**, Greenlea, 20 Millbank, Cupar, **Fife**, KY15 5DP, SCO.
(T) 01334 653367
Speciality: Reflexology.
S T (Ref:HM05615)

**CUMMINS, R**

**R Cummins**, 9 Beeches Avenue, Carshalton, **Surrey**, SM5 3LB, ENG.
(T) 020 8773 4508
Speciality: Reflexology.
S T (Ref:HM05616)

**CUMMINS, ROZ**

**Roz Cummins**, 57 Nonsuch Walk, Sutton, **Surrey**, SM2 7LG, ENG.
(T) 020 8393 2707
Speciality: Bach Remedies, Nutritional Therapy, Reflexology, Reiki, Spiritual Healing. ✔
● **Owner/Nutritionist** Mrs R Cummins
M: BANT.
C Yrs. Est.: 10 (Ref:HM05617)

**CUNLIFFE PHARMACY**

**Cunliffe Pharmacy**, 12 Southbourne Gr, Bournemouth, **Dorset**, BH6 3QZ, ENG.
(T) 01202 428181
Speciality: Complementary Medicines & Therapy.
C M (Ref:HM05618)

**CUNLIFFE, H B**

**H B Cunliffe**, York House, 15 York St, Heywood, **Manchester (Greater)**, OL10 4NN, ENG.
(T) 01706 623178
Speciality: Chiropodists (Podiatrists).
● **Owner** Mrs H Cunliffe
S (Ref:HM05619)

**CUNLIFFE, IAN**

**Ian Cunliffe**, 32 Evans St, Prescot, **Merseyside**, L34 6HU, ENG.
(T) 01514 931618
Speciality: Hypnotherapy.
● **Owner** Mr I Cunliffe
B (Ref:HM05620)

**CUNNIFFE, J M & J CHIROPODISTS**

**J M Cunniffe & J Chiropodists**, 1 Hollins Park Prde, Leeds, **Yorkshire (West)**, LS8 3AS, ENG.
(T) 01132 359760
Speciality: Chiropodists (Podiatrists).
S (Ref:HM05621)

**CUNNING, I**

**I Cunning**, 12 Hopetoun St, Bathgate, **Lothian (West)**, EH48 4EU, SCO.



Key continued: Yrs.Est: Years Established Q: Qualifications M: Professional Membership ✔ Indemnity Insurance Accept Credit Cards

(T) 01506 633458
Speciality: Chiropodists (Podiatrists).
● **Owner** Mr J Cunning
S (Ref:HM05622)

## CUNNINGHAM, CAROL
**Cunningham Carol**, The Rectory Donadea, **County Kildare**, IRE.
(T) 04586 9204
Speciality: Psychotherapy.
B (Ref:HM05623)

## CUNNINGHAM, DAVID L
**David L Cunningham**, The Hale Clinic, 7 Park Cresent, London, **London (Greater)**, W1N 3HE, ENG.
(T) 020 7631 0604 (F) 020 7323 1693
Speciality: Complementary Medicines & Therapy.
● **Owner** Mr D Cunningham
C M (Ref:HM05624)

## CUNNINGHAM, H P
**H P Cunningham**, 45 Thomas St, Armagh, **County Armagh**, BT61 7QB, NIR.
(T) 028 3752 2818
Speciality: Chiropodists (Podiatrists).
S (Ref:HM05625)

## CUNNINGHAM, MARJORIE
**Marjorie Cunningham**, The Wellbeing Centre, 11 Musters Rd, Nottingham, **Nottinghamshire**, NG5 3GQ, ENG.
(T) 01159 825353
Speciality: Homeopathy.
M (Ref:HM05626)

## CUNNINGTON, A
**A Cunnington**, 34 Hyde Park Rd, Halifax, **Yorkshire (West)**, HX1 3LH, ENG.
(T) 01422 320225
Speciality: Osteopathy.
P S T (Ref:HM05627)

## CURATIVE HYPNOTHERAPY CENTRE
**Curative Hypnotherapy Centre**, 58 Watchetts Drive, Camberley, **Surrey**, GU15 2PQ, ENG.
(T) 01276 28118
Speciality: Hypnosis.
● **Owner** Mr M Emery
B (Ref:HM05628)

## CURRAN, M J
**M J Curran**, 1 Queen St, Rushden, **Northamptonshire**, NN10 0AA, ENG.
(T) 01933 410419
Speciality: Chiropodists (Podiatrists).
S (Ref:HM05629)

## CURRAN, MAUREEN
**Maureen Curran**, 11 Osprey Drive, Londonderry, **County Londonderry**, BT47 2LE, NIR.
(T) 028 7134 6500
Speciality: Aromatherapy, Beauty Therapy, Electrolysis, Massage (Therapeutic), Reflexology, Reiki, Stress Therapy. ✔
● **Owner/Electrolysist** Ms M Curran
Q: Dip.Arom, Dip.Electrol. M: BAE, RQA.
T Yrs. Est.: 19 (Ref:HM05630)

## CURRIE, A M
**A M Currie**, 44 The Murray Sq, East Kilbride, Glasgow, **Glasgow (City of)**, G75 0BH, SCO.
(T) 01355 222561
Speciality: Chiropodists (Podiatrists).
● **Owner** Mr A Currie
S (Ref:HM05631)

## CURRIEHILL CLINIC
**Curriehill Clinic**, Nether Currie Clinic, 23 Thomson Cr, Currie, **Edinburgh (City of)**, EH14 5JR, SCO.
(T) 01314 495118
Speciality: Physiotherapy.
P S T (Ref:HM05632)

## CURRY, AINE
**Aine Curry**, 26 Oldmeldrum Rd, Newmachar, Aberdeen, **Aberdeenshire**, AB21 0UE, SCO.
(T) 01651 863197
Speciality: Chiropodists (Podiatrists).
● **Owner** Ms A Curry
S (Ref:HM05633)

## CURTIN, D
**D Curtin**, Doctors Surgery, 28 Beaumont St, Oxford, **Oxfordshire**, OX1 2NP, ENG.
(T) 01865 512673
Speciality: Homeopathy.
● **Principal** Dr D Curtin
M (Ref:HM05634)

## CURTIS, AIDEEN
**Aideen Curtis**, 16 Approach Rd, Bethnal Green, London, **London (Greater)**, E2 9LY, ENG.
(T) 020 8981 0091
Speciality: Complementary Medicines & Therapy.
● **Owner** Ms A Curtis
M (Ref:HM05635)

## CURTIS, MORAG
**Morag Curtis**, 177 King St, Castle Douglas, **Dumfries and Galloway**, DG7 1DZ, SCO.
(T) 01556 504104 (F) 01556 504552
Speciality: Reflexology.
● **Partner** Mr G Carlo
S T (Ref:HM05636)

## CURTIS, P A
**P A Curtis**, 25 Alexandra Rd, Watford, **Hertfordshire**, WD1 3QX, ENG.
(T) 01923 255632 (F) 01923 211172
Speciality: Chiropodists (Podiatrists).
● **Owner** Mr P Curtis
S (Ref:HM05637)

## CURTIS, PETER
**Peter Curtis**, Harlequin House, 43 Chester Rd, Ilford, **Essex**, IG3 8PT, ENG.
(T) 020 8599 6013
Speciality: Psychotherapy.
B (Ref:HM05638)

## CURZON, A
**A Curzon**, 94 High St, Epping, **Essex**, CM16 4AE, ENG.
(T) 01992 572624
Speciality: Chiropodists (Podiatrists).
S (Ref:HM05639)

## CUSS, JEAN
**Jean Cuss**, 30 Trumlands Rd, Torquay, **Devon**, TQ1 4RN, ENG.
(T) 01803 325413
Speciality: Acupuncture.
● **Owner** Mrs J Cuss
O (Ref:HM05640)

## CUSWORTH, BRIAN
**Brian Cusworth**, 9 Northridge Way, Hemel Hempstead, **Hertfordshire**, HP1 2AE, ENG.
(T) 01442 255610
Speciality: Osteopathy.
P S T (Ref:HM05641)

## CUSWORTH, L E
**L E Cusworth**, 24 Barnsley Rd, Wombwell, Barnsley, **Yorkshire (South)**, S73 8DD, ENG.
(T) 01226 210444 (F) 01226 750390
Speciality: Reflexology.
● **Owner** Ms L Cusworth
S T (Ref:HM05642)

## CUTCLIFFE, PETER G
**Peter G Cutcliffe**, 39 Woodlands Rd, Headington, Oxford, **Oxfordshire**, OX3 7RU, ENG.
(T) 01865 765805
Speciality: Chiropodists (Podiatrists).
S (Ref:HM05643)

## CUTLER, AMANDA
**Amanda Cutler**, 32 Foxholes, Rudgwick, **Sussex (West)**, RH12 3DX, ENG.
(T) 01403 823437
Speciality: Aromatherapy, Massage (Therapeutic).
M O (Ref:HM05644)

## CUTLER, JENNY
**Jenny Cutler**, 17 Battery End, Newbury, **Berkshire**, RG14 6NX, ENG.
(T) 01635 43430
Speciality: Hypnosis.
B (Ref:HM05645)

## CUTLER, PAULINE
**Pauline Cutler**, 7 Plum Lane, London, **London (Greater)**, SE18 3AF, ENG.
(T) 020 8854 1606 (F) 020 8854 1606
Speciality: Homeopathy.
● **Owner** Ms P Cutler
M (Ref:HM05646)

## CUTTING, MELANIE
**Melanie Cutting**, 1a Trinity Avenue, Westcliff-on-Sea, **Essex**, SS0 7PU, ENG.
(T) 01702 430430
Speciality: Chiropractors.
P S T (Ref:HM05647)

## CUTTING, VALERIE
**Valerie Cutting**, 10 Inverness Cl, Cambridge, **Cambridgeshire**, CB4 1RB, ENG.
(T) 01223 360080
Speciality: Reflexology. ✔
● **Owner/Reflexologist**
Mrs V Cutting Q: BSR.
T Yrs. Est.: 8 (Ref:HM05648)

## CWMBRAN PHYSIOTHERAPY CENTRE
**Cwmbran Physiotherapy Centre**, 223 Llantarnam Rd, Llantarnam, Cwmbran, **Torfaen**, NP44 3BG, WAL.
(T) 01633 865465
Speciality: Physiotherapy.
P S T (Ref:HM05649)

## CWYNAR, B (DR)
**Dr B Cwynar**, 101 Vernon Cres, Ravenshead, Nottingham, **Nottinghamshire**, NG15 9BP, ENG.
(T) 01623 796905
Speciality: Hypnotherapy.
B (Ref:HM05650)

## CYGNET HOSPITAL EALING
**Cygnet Hospital Ealing**, 22 Corfton Rd, London, **London (Greater)**, W5 2HT, ENG.
(T) 020 8991 6699 (F) 020 8991 0440
Speciality: Psychiatry.
● **Director** Mr J Hoar
B (Ref:HM05651)

## CYNTHIA MOORES REFLEXOLOGY
**Cynthia Moores Reflexology**, 28 Wychbury Rd, Wolverhampton, **Midlands (West)**, WV3 8DN, ENG.
(T) 01902 650817
Speciality: Reflexology.
S T (Ref:HM05652)

## CZERKAWSKI, MARK
**Mark Czerkawski**, 106 Charter Avenue, Ilford, **Essex**, IG2 7AD, ENG.
(T) 020 8252 2881
Speciality: Chiropodists (Podiatrists).
S (Ref:HM05653)

## CZERNEK, J
**J Czernek**, 334 Upper Richmond Rd West, London, **London (Greater)**, SW14 7JR, ENG.
(T) 020 8878 2731
Speciality: Osteopathy.
● **Owner** Mr J Czernek
P S T (Ref:HM05654)

## D A F CLINIC
**David Antony Fairclough**, 17 Inglewood Rd, Rainford, St. Helens, **Merseyside**, WA11 7QL, ENG.
(T) 07050 396611 (F) 07050 005180
(E) david@fairclough5@virgin.net
Speciality: Counselling, Holistic Healing, Massage (Therapeutic), Moxibustion, Nutritional Therapy, Reflexology, Stress Therapy, Visualisation Therapy, Holistic Chiropody using animal free and non animal tested products, Vegetarian and Vegan Nutritional Therapy and Vegetarian and Vegan Sports Nutrition. ✔
● **Partner** Mr D Fairclough
(T) 01744 454495 Q: Dip.Nut.Th, Dip.Nutrition, G.C.S.Ch, TCCAR. M: B.A.Ch.P, SPNT.
M Yrs. Est.: 6 (Ref:HM05655)

## D 'ARCY, LARRAINE
**Larraine D 'Arcy**, Tall Pines, Harestone Drive, Caterham, **Surrey**, CR3 6HX, ENG.
(T) 01883 331165
Speciality: Hypnosis.
B (Ref:HM05656)

### D GELDARD PHYSIOTHERAPIST

**Mr D Geldard Physiotherapist**, 50B Scarisbrick New Rd, Southport, **Merseyside**, PR8 6PF, ENG.
(T) 01704 532880
Speciality: Physiotherapy.
P S T (Ref:HM05657)

### D HEALY IND FINANCIAL ADV

**David Healy E L A Independant Financial Advisor**, 5 Springmead, Braintree, **Essex**, CM7 2LT, ENG.
(T) 01376 329182 (F) 01376 342130
Speciality: Chiropodists (Podiatrists).
● **Owner** Mr D Healy
S (Ref:HM05658)

### D SEXTON HYPNOTHERAPY NLP

**Denis Sexton Hypnotherapy NLP**, Barrettstown, Newbridge, **County Kildare**, IRE.
(T) 04543 3291
Speciality: Hypnotherapy.
B (Ref:HM05659)

### D T R CLINIC

**D T R Clinic**, 220 Cathays Trce, Cardiff, **Glamorgan (Vale of)**, CF24 4JA, WAL.
(T) 029 2038 2811
Speciality: Physiotherapy.
P S T (Ref:HM05660)

### D VAN-BENTUM CHIROPODIST

**D Van-Bentum Chiropodist**, 118 Radcliffe New Rd, Whitefield, Manchester, **Manchester (Greater)**, M45 7WQ, ENG.
(T) 01617 246220
Speciality: Chiropodists (Podiatrists).
S (Ref:HM05661)

### D, CAIN

**Cain D**, 171 Sandown Rd, Deal, **Kent**, CT14 6NX, ENG.
(T) 01304 364879
Speciality: Chiropractors.
P S T (Ref:HM05662)

### DA COSTA, SALLY

**Sally D A Costa**, 37 Gloucester Rd, London, **London (Greater)**, W5 4JA, ENG.
(T) 020 8567 3529
Speciality: Alexander Technique.
P S (Ref:HM05663)

### DA RIN, MANUELA

**Manuela Da Rin**, 40 Church Lane, Oxted, **Surrey**, RH8 9LB, ENG.
(T) 01883 715127
Speciality: Osteopathy.
P S T (Ref:HM05664)

### DA SILVA, CAROLE

**Carole Da Silva**, Shepherd Maze, Copper Beech Way, Leighton Buzzard, **Bedfordshire**, LU7 8BD, ENG.
(T) 01525 377277
Speciality: Alexander Technique. ✓
● **Teacher of the Alexander Technique**
Mrs C Da Silva Q: MSTAT. M: STAT.
P Yrs. Est.: 7 (Ref:HM05665)

### DAB HANDS MASSAGE

**Dab Hands**, 23 Wallfield Cres, Aberdeen, **Aberdeenshire**, AB25 2LD, SCO.
(T) 01224 643734 (F) 01224 643734
Speciality: Massage (Therapeutic).
● **Massage Therapist** Mr D Shepherd
Q: Dip.Swedish Massage, MA.
C S Yrs. Est.: 5 (Ref:HM05666)

### DACRELANDS CLINIC

**Dacrelands Clinic**, Aldrens Lane, Lancaster, **Lancashire**, LA1 2DU, ENG.
(T) 01524 69864 (F) 01524 848155
Speciality: Acupuncture, Aromatherapy, Bowen Therapy, Chinese Herbal Medicine, Chiropody, Cranial Osteopathy, Cranio-Sacral Therapy, Healing Therapy, Herbal Medicine, Hypnosis, Osteopathy, Podiatry, Psychotherapy, Reflexology, Remedial Massage, Shiatsu, Spiritual Healing, Butkeyko, Sports Therapy/Personal Fitness Training.
C (Ref:HM05667)

### DADSON, D G

**D G Dadson**, 113 St James Rd, Tunbridge Wells, **Kent**, TN1 2HG, ENG.
(T) 01892 523220
Speciality: Chiropodists (Podiatrists).
● **Owner** Mr D Dadson
S (Ref:HM05668)

### DADSON, D G

**D G Dadson**, Rear Of 313a Broadway, Bexleyheath, **Kent**, DA6 8DT, ENG.
(T) 020 8301 5589
Speciality: Chiropodists (Podiatrists).
● **Owner** Mr D Dadson
S (Ref:HM05669)

### DADSWELL, CLAIRE

**Claire Dadswell Homeopathic Consultant**, 1 The Oast, Crouchs Farm, East Hoathly, **Sussex (East)**, BN8 6QX, ENG.
(T) 01825 880046
(E) calire.dadswell@tesco.net
Speciality: Biofeedback, Homeopathy, Electro-Acupuncture, Homotoxicology, Bio Functional Diagnosis. ✓
● **Homeopathic Consultant**
Miss C Dadswell Q: BEd (Hons), Dip.Hom, E.A.V.
M Yrs. Est.: 3 (Ref:HM05670)

### DAGNALL, J C

**J C Dagnall**, 300 Bramhall Lane South, Bramhall, Stockport, **Cheshire**, SK7 3DJ, ENG.
(T) 01614 391138
Speciality: Chiropodists (Podiatrists).
● **Owner** Mr J Dagnall
S (Ref:HM05671)

### DAHL, JESPER

**Jesper Dahl**, The Ashford Rd Chiropractic Clinic, 24 Ashford Rd, Maidstone, **Kent**, ME14 5BH, ENG.
(T) 01622 661883
Speciality: Chiropractors.
P S T (Ref:HM05672)

### DAHMS, A

**A Dahms**, The Hearing Aid Centre, 8b South Prde, Weston-Super-Mare, **Somerset**, BS23 1JN, ENG.
(T) 01934 623201
Speciality: Chiropodists (Podiatrists).
● **Owner** A Dahms
S (Ref:HM05673)

### DAINES, MARY

**Mary Daines**, 9 Skye Cl, Norwich, **Norfolk**, NR5 9DL, ENG.
(T) 01603 746721
Speciality: Chiropodists (Podiatrists).
S (Ref:HM05674)

### DAINTREE, FREDERICA JEAN

**Frederica Jean Daintree**, 7 Burlington Court, Burlington Rd, Altrincham, **Cheshire**, WA14 1JT, ENG.
(T) 01619 289777
Speciality: Psychotherapy.
● **Owner** Mrs F Daintree
B (Ref:HM05675)

### DAIRY PSYCHOTHERAPY

**Dairy Psychotherapy**, 3 Scarcroft Rd, York, **Yorkshire (North)**, YO23 1ND, ENG.
(T) 01904 639367
Speciality: Psychotherapy.
● **Owner** Mrs C Andrade
B (Ref:HM05676)

### DAKIN, C M

**C M Dakin**, 30 Exeter Rd, Ellesmere Port, **Merseyside**, CH65 8AW, ENG.
(T) 01513 563822 (F) 01513 563822
Speciality: Physiotherapy.
● **Owner** Mrs C Dakin
P S T (Ref:HM05677)

### DALAL, X R

**Mr X R Dalal**, White House, The Bishops Avenue, London, **London (Greater)**, N2 0BN, ENG.
(T) 020 8201 9092
Speciality: Osteopathy.
● **Owner** Mr X Dalal
P S T (Ref:HM05678)

### DALCROFT COUNSELLING SERVICES

**Dalcroft Counselling Services**, 7 Sands Lane, Elloughton, Brough, **Humberside (North)**, HU15 1JH, ENG.
(T) 01482 667354
Speciality: Psychotherapy.
B (Ref:HM05679)

### DALE, JANET

**Janet Dale**, 24 Seaton Pl, Stourbridge, **Midlands (West)**, DY8 5BY, ENG.
(T) 01384 277287
Speciality: Complementary Medicines & Therapy.
● **Owner** Ms J Dale
C M (Ref:HM05680)

### DALE, K

**K Dale**, 11 Heath Rd, Haywards Heath, **Sussex (West)**, RH16 3AX, ENG.
(T) 01444 450162 (F) 01444 459816
Speciality: Physiotherapy.
● **Practice Manager** Mrs W Langley
P S T (Ref:HM05681)

### DALE, LYNNE

**Lynne Dale**, 6 Tidnock Avenue, Congleton, **Cheshire**, CW12 2HW, ENG.
(T) 01260 299697
Speciality: Reflexology.
● **Owner** Mrs L Dale
S T (Ref:HM05682)

### DALE, M J

**M J Dale**, 16 Cleveland Avenue, Wigan, **Lancashire**, WN3 6DT, ENG.
(T) 01942 217310
Speciality: Chiropodists (Podiatrists).
● **Owner** Mrs M Dale
S (Ref:HM05683)

### DALE, ROGER

**Roger Dale**, 187 Addington Rd, South Croydon, **Surrey**, CR2 8LN, ENG.
(T) 020 8651 5551
Speciality: Reflexology.
S T (Ref:HM05684)

### DALE, SUZANNE

**Suzanne Dale**, 248 Oxford Rd, Newcastle, **Staffordshire**, ST5 0QB, ENG.
(T) 01782 634614
Speciality: Hypnosis.
● **Owner** Ms S Dale
B (Ref:HM05685)

### DALE, TILLY

**Tilly Dale**, 111 Clifton St, Swindon, **Wiltshire**, SN1 3QA, ENG.
(T) 01793 642832
Speciality: Acupuncture.
● **Owner** Mrs T Dale
O (Ref:HM05686)

### DALEMILL ESSENTIAL OILS

**Dalemill Essential Oils Ltd**, Holmes Mill, Holmes St, Rochdale, **Lancashire**, OL12 6AQ, ENG.
(T) 01706 342234 (F) 01706 344511
Speciality: Complementary Medicines & Therapy.
● **Sales Director** Mr R Hall
C M (Ref:HM05687)

### DALE-ROBERTS, PAULETTE

**Paulette Dale-Roberts**, Green Pastures, North St, Punnetts Town, Heathfield, **Sussex (East)**, TN21 9DT, ENG.
(T) 01435 830564
Speciality: Reflexology.
S T (Ref:HM05688)

### DALKEITH, MICHAEL

**Michael Dalkeith**, Compton House, 87 High St, Hampton, **London (Greater)**, TW12 2SX, ENG.
(T) 020 8979 3119
Speciality: Osteopathy.
P S T (Ref:HM05689)

### DALLAS, JENNIE

**Jennie Dallas**, 100 High St, Crediton, **Devon**, EX17 3LF, ENG.
(T) 01363 774175
Speciality: Acupuncture.



Key continued: Yrs.Est: Years Established Q: Qualifications M: Professional Membership ✓ Indemnity Insurance Accept Credit Cards

O (**Ref:**HM05690)

### DALLAS, PETER

**Peter Dallas**, Greenfields Farmhouse, Crawley Rd, Horsham, **Sussex (West)**, RH12 4HF, ENG.
(T) 01403 248482 (F) 020 7404 0670
(E) pete@dallasdesign.co.uk
Speciality: Acupressure, Shiatsu, T'ai-Chi Ch'uan. ✓
● **Shiatsu Practitioner** Mr P Dallas
T Yrs. Est.: 4 (**Ref:**HM05691)

### D'ALMEIDA, KAREN

**Karen D'almeida**, 1 Stevens Cl, Snodland, **Kent**, ME6 5DU, ENG.
(T) 01634 243613
Speciality: Reflexology.
● **Owner** Ms K D'almeida
S T (**Ref:**HM05692)

### DALMUIR CLINIC

**Dalmuir Clinic**, 235 Dumbarton Rd, Clydebank, **Argyll and Bute**, G81 6AA, SCO.
(T) 01419 412095
Speciality: Chiropodists (Podiatrists).
S (**Ref:**HM05693)

### DALRYMPLE, S D (DR)

**Dr S D Dalrymple**, 30 The Drive, Hove, **Sussex (East)**, BN3 3JD, ENG.
(T) 01273 778123 (F) 01273 776266
Speciality: Psychiatry.
● **Practice Manager** Mrs M Ward
B (**Ref:**HM05694)

### DALTON CHIROPODY CENTRE

**Dalton Chiropody Centre (The)**, 28 Sangley Rd, London, **London (Greater)**, SE6 2JL, ENG.
(T) 020 8697 2072
Speciality: Chiropodists (Podiatrists).
● **Manager** Ms I Taylor
S (**Ref:**HM05695)

### DALTON, CARRIE

**Carrie Dalton**, 1 Ard Auling St, Lukes, Cork, **County Cork**, IRE.
(T) 021 4502 480
Speciality: Complementary Medicines & Therapy.
M (**Ref:**HM05696)

### DALTON, EMMA

**Emma Dalton**, Drift Cottage, The Drift, Henley, Ipswich, **Suffolk**, IP6 0RS, ENG.
(T) 01473 831273
Speciality: Reflexology.
S T (**Ref:**HM05697)

### DALTON, HELEN

**Helen Dalton LCPH**, 37 Hawkesfield Rd, Forest Hill, London, **London (Greater)**, SE23 2TN, ENG.
(T) 020 8291 7353
Speciality: Bach Remedies, Floral Essence Therapy, Homeopathy. ✓
● **Homeopath** Ms H Dalton **Q:** LCPH.
M Yrs. Est.: 2 (**Ref:**HM05698)

### DALY, CHARLES

**Charles Daly**, Medical Centre Clonalour, Tralee, **County Kerry**, IRE.
(T) 06671 21792
(E) chmdaly@eircom.net
Speciality: Complementary Medicines & Therapy.
M (**Ref:**HM05699)

### DALY, JEAN N

**Jean N Daly**, Roseville Barnakyle Patrickswell, Limerick, **County Limerick**, IRE.
(T) 06135 5171
Speciality: Psychotherapy.
B (**Ref:**HM05700)

### DALY, JENNIFER (DR)

**Dr Jennifer Daly**, Natural Medicine Clinic 2 Nova Ct, Carrigaline, **County Cork**, IRE.
(T) 021 4372 787
Speciality: Complementary Medicines & Therapy.
M (**Ref:**HM05701)

### DALY, ROWENA

**Rowena Daly**, Dagenham, **Essex**, RM9, ENG.
(T) 020 8517 6762
Speciality: Bach Remedies.
M (**Ref:**HM05702)

### DAMAN, WENDY

**Wendy Daman (Freeman-Pope)**, 3 Richmond Park Avenue, Bournemouth, **Dorset**, BH8 9DL, ENG.
(T) 01202 536741
Speciality: Acupuncture.
O (**Ref:**HM05703)

### DAMIAN P JOHNS

**Damian P Johns**, 15 Wednesday Market, Beverley, **Humberside (North)**, HU17 0DH, ENG.
(T) 01482 868448
Speciality: Biomechanics, Chiropody, Cryo Surgery, Nail Surgery, Orthotics, Podiatry.
✓
● **Chiropodist (Podiatrist)**
Mr D Johns **Q:** DPodM, S.R.Ch.
M Yrs. Est.: 11 (**Ref:**HM05704)

### DANBURY CLINIC

**Danbury Clinic**, 9 Maldon Rd, Danbury, **Essex**, CM3 4QH, ENG.
(T) 01245 222804
Speciality: Osteopathy.
● **Manager** Gordon Service
P S T (**Ref:**HM05705)

### DANBY, CAROL

**Carol Danby**, Hazel Dene, Sandy Lane, Stockton On The Forest, York, **Yorkshire (North)**, YO32 9UT, ENG.
(T) 01904 400382
Speciality: Reflexology.
S T (**Ref:**HM05706)

### DANBY, J

**J Danby**, Remedy Centre For Health, 166 Tulketh Rd, Ashton-On-Ribble, Preston, **Lancashire**, PR2 1ER, ENG.
(T) 01772 733007
Speciality: Osteopathy.
● **Owner** Mrs J Danby
P S T (**Ref:**HM05707)

### DANCE MOVEMENT THERAPY

**Dance Movement Therapy(Association)**, The Art Therapies Department, Springfield Hospital, 61 Glenburnie Rd, London, **London (Greater)**, SW17 7DJ, ENG.
(T) 020 8672 9911
Speciality: Complementary Medicines & Therapy.
● **Head of Department** Alison Barnes
M (**Ref:**HM05708)

### DANCE VOICE THERAPY CENTRE

**Dance Voice Plc And Registered Charity**, Quaker House, Wedmore Vale, Bedminster, Bristol, BS8 5HX, ENG.
(T) 01179 532055 (F) 01179 532055
(E) dance.voice@cablenet.co.uk
(W) www.dancevoice.org.uk
Speciality: Dance Movement Therapy. ✓
● **Therapist** Ms P Fisher
● **Therapist** Pat Morgan
● **Director/Therapist** Ms M Ware
● **Therapist** Ms B Feldtkeller
B Yrs. Est.: 11 (**Ref:**HM05709)

### DANCE, M G

**M G Dance**, 68 Glasgow Rd, Edinburgh, **Edinburgh (City of)**, EH12 8LN, SCO.
(T) 01313 341966
Speciality: Chiropodists (Podiatrists).
S (**Ref:**HM05710)

### DANCES WITH UNICORNS

**Dances With Unicorns**, 47 Greenmarket, Newcastle Upon Tyne, **Tyne and Wear**, NE1 7YB, ENG.
(T) 01912 211200
Speciality: Clairvoyants & Palmists.
B (**Ref:**HM05711)

### DAND, A

**A Dand**, 58 Park Prde, Whitley Bay, **Tyne and Wear**, NE26 1DX, ENG.
(T) 01912 524834 (F) 01912 524834
Speciality: Complementary Medicines & Therapy.
● **Owner** Mr A Dand
C M (**Ref:**HM05712)

### DANDO, PAUL

**Paul Dando**, St Andrews Rd, Droitwich, **Worcestershire**, WR9 8DN, ENG.
(T) 01905 794793
Speciality: Physiotherapy.
P S T (**Ref:**HM05713)

### DANDO, PAUL

**Paul Dando**, Watson Reef & Dando/Physiotherapy & Sports Injury, Halesowen, **Midlands (West)**, B63 4QQ, ENG.
(T) 01215 505778
Speciality: Physiotherapy.
● **Partner** Mr P Dando
P S T (**Ref:**HM05714)

### DANDO, PAUL

**Paul Dando**, Physiotherapy & Sports Injury Clinic, 3 Franchise St, Kidderminster, **Worcestershire**, DY11 6RE, ENG.
(T) 01562 67129
Speciality: Physiotherapy.
● **Senior Partner** Mrs R Watson
P S T (**Ref:**HM05715)

### DANESH, MOJDEH

**Ms Mojdeh Danesh**, Viakuntha, Private Rd, Rodborough Common, Stroud, **Gloucestershire**, GL5 5BT, ENG.
(T) 01453 872334 (F) 01453 872334
Speciality: Acupuncture.
● **Owner** Ms M Danesh
O (**Ref:**HM05716)

### DANESTRETE CENTRE

**Danestrete Centre**, Child Development Centre, Southgate, Stevenage, **Hertfordshire**, SG1 1HB, ENG.
(T) 01438 781457
Speciality: Physiotherapy.
P S T (**Ref:**HM05717)

### DANFORD, P H

**P H Danford**, 157A Kew Rd, Richmond, **Surrey**, TW9 2PN, ENG.
(T) 020 8948 2744
Speciality: Chiropractic.
P S T (**Ref:**HM05718)

### DANIEL, EILEEN

**Eileen Daniel B Sc (Hons) Ost**, 11 Oliver Plunkett St, Bandon, Cork, **County Cork**, IRE.
(T) 023 4225 3
Speciality: Osteopathy.
P S T (**Ref:**HM05719)

### DANIEL, L G

**L G Daniel**, Keepers Lodge, Trebursye, Launceston, **Cornwall**, PL15 7ES, ENG.
(T) 01566 776451
Speciality: Hypnosis.
● **Owner** Mr L Daniel
B (**Ref:**HM05720)

### DANIEL-BAYLE, M

**M Daniel-Bayle**, The Barn, Bury St Edmunds Golf Club, Tut Hill, Fornham All Saints, Bury St. Edmunds, **Suffolk**, IP28 6LG, ENG.
(T) 01284 760020
Speciality: Aromatherapy.
M O (**Ref:**HM05721)

### DANIELLS, JONATHAN

**Jonathan Daniells**, Chelsfield Osteopathic Practice, Neals Ho Church Rd, Chelsfield, Orpington, **Kent**, BR6 7RE, ENG.
(T) 01689 877500
Speciality: Osteopathy.
P S T (**Ref:**HM05722)

### DANIELS, FRANK

**Frank Daniels**, 103 Hands Rd, Heanor, **Derbyshire**, DE75 7HB, ENG.
(T) 01773 532195
Speciality: Hypnosis.
● **Owner** Mr F Daniels
B (**Ref:**HM05723)

### DANIELS, FRANK

**Frank Daniels**, The Wellbeing Centre, 11 Musters Rd, West Bridgford, Nottingham, **Nottinghamshire**, NG2 7PP, ENG.

(T) 01159 825353
Speciality: Hypnotherapy.
B (Ref:HM05724)

**DANIELS, INGRID**

**Ingrid Daniels**, 1 Upland Rd, South Croydon, **Surrey**, CR2 6RD, ENG.
(T) 020 8681 8665
Speciality: Homeopathy.
M (Ref:HM05725)

**DANIELS, INGRID**

**Ingrid Daniels**, 15 Talbot Rd, Carshalton, **Surrey**, SM5 3BP, ENG.
(T) 020 8395 6550
Speciality: Homeopathy.
● **Owner** Ms I Daniels
M (Ref:HM05726)

**DANIELS, PENNY**

**Penny Daniels**, 9 Newton Cl, Ledbury, **Herefordshire**, HR8 2XG, ENG.
(T) 01531 634448
Speciality: Hypnosis.
B (Ref:HM05727)

**DANKS, K W**

**K W Danks**, 37 Wignals Gate, Holbeach, Spalding, **Lincolnshire**, PE12 7HL, ENG.
(T) 01406 426667
Speciality: Chiropodists (Podiatrists).
● **Owner** Mr K Danks
S (Ref:HM05728)

**DANNE, IVAN**

**Ivan Danne**, 3 Dowry Pl, Bristol, BS8 4QL, ENG.
(T) 01179 298384
Speciality: Chiropractors.
● **Owner** Ms A Archibald
P S T (Ref:HM05729)

**DANS CHINESE MEDICINE CLINIC**

**Dans Chinese Medicine Clinic**, 884 Dunstable Rd, Luton, **Bedfordshire**, LU4 0HH, ENG.
(T) 01582 495040 (F) 01582 822958
Speciality: Acupuncture.
● **Owner** Dr L Dan
O (Ref:HM05730)

**DAO CLINIC OF CHINESE MEDICINE**

**Dao Clinic Of Chinese Medicine**, 30 Beaumont St, Oxford, **Oxfordshire**, OX1 2NY, ENG.
(T) 01865 311871
Speciality: Acupuncture.
● **Owner** Dr G Shia
O (Ref:HM05731)

**DAOUST, YVETTE**

**Yvette Daoust**, 82 Beverley Gardens, Wembley, **London (Greater)**, HA9 9RA, ENG.
(T) 020 8908 2604
Speciality: Alexander Technique.
● **Owner** Mrs Y Daoust
P S (Ref:HM05732)

**DAPAYNE, IMEL**

**Imel Dapayne**, 116 Broughton Rd, Crewe, **Cheshire**, CW1 4NS, ENG.
(T) 01270 581991
Speciality: Reflexology.
● **Owner** Ms I Depayne
S T (Ref:HM05733)

**DARBY HOUSE HEALING & LEARNING**

**Darby House Healing & Learning Centre**, Southey St, Nottingham, **Nottinghamshire**, NG7 4BQ, ENG.
(T) 01159 704977
Speciality: Complementary Medicines & Therapy.
C M (Ref:HM05734)

**DARBY, ANN**

**Ann Darby**, P O Box 5566, Derby, **Derbyshire**, DE1 9EY, ENG.
(T) 01332 273658 (F) 01332 273658
Speciality: Reiki. ✔
● **Owner** Mrs A Darby Q: Reiki Master.
C Yrs. Est.: 4 (Ref:HM05735)

**D'ARCY, LARRAINE**

**Larraine D'arcy**, 31 Hilltop Rd, Whyteleafe, **Surrey**, CR3 0DF, ENG.
(T) 01883 331165 (F) 01883 343474
Speciality: Hypnotherapy.
● **Owner** Ms L D'arcy
B (Ref:HM05736)

**D'ARCY, M**

**M D'arcy**, St Judes, Tring Rd, Edlesborough, Dunstable, **Bedfordshire**, LU6 2EQ, ENG.
(T) 01525 220127
Speciality: Physiotherapy.
● **Owner** Mrs M D'arcy
P S T (Ref:HM05737)

**D'ARCY, PATRICK**

**Patrick D'Arcy D O M G O Phys**, 5a Castle St, Bray, **County Wicklow**, IRE.
(T) 01286 7025
Speciality: Osteopathy.
P S T (Ref:HM05738)

**DARE TO CARE**

**Dare To Care**, 112 Mill St, Liverpool, **Merseyside**, L8 5UB, ENG.
(T) 01517 099528 (F) 01517 092139
Speciality: Aromatherapy, Indian Head Massage, Reflexology, Reiki, Shiatsu, Yoga, Herbal Remedies, Tai Chi. ✔
● **Director/Acupuncturist**
Miss C Darby-Darton
● **Company Secretary**
Ruben Dolowitch
O Yrs. Est.: 9 (Ref:HM05739)

**DARGIE ANDERSON, G**

**G Dargie Anderson**, 2 The Fourways, The Weir, Broad Hinton, Swindon, **Wiltshire**, SN4 9NE, ENG.
(T) 01793 731676
Speciality: Hypnotherapy.
B (Ref:HM05740)

**DARINA, JOYCE**

**Joyce Darina**, Ard Ri Hse, Lr Abbeygate St, Galway, **County Galway**, IRE.
(T) 09156 3329
Speciality: Acupuncture.
O (Ref:HM05741)

**DARLING, ANNE**

**Anne Darling**, 99 Lammermuir Cres, Dunbar, **Lothian (East)**, EH42 1EZ, SCO.
(T) 01368 862079
Speciality: Clairvoyants & Palmists.
B (Ref:HM05742)

**DARLINGTON CHIROPRACTIC CLINIC**

**Darlington Chiropractic Clinic**, 1 Bondgate, Darlington, **County Durham**, DL3 7JA, ENG.
(T) 01325 485200
Speciality: Chiropractic.
P S T (Ref:HM05743)

**DARLINGTON CTRE OF ORIENTL MED**

**Darlington Centre Of Oriental Medicine (The)**, 65 Duke St, Darlington, **County Durham**, DL3 7SD, ENG.
(T) 01325 467287
Speciality: Complementary Medicines & Therapy.
● **Partner** Mr K Thomas
M (Ref:HM05744)

**DARLINGTON F C SPORTS CLINIC**

**Darlington F C Sports Clinic**, Feethams Ground, South Ter, Darlington, **County Durham**, DL1 5JB, ENG.
(T) 01325 369155
Speciality: Physiotherapy.
P S T (Ref:HM05745)

**DARLINGTON HOMEOPATHIC CLINIC**

**Darlington Homeopathic Health Clinic**, 9 Hilda St, Darlington, **County Durham**, DL1 1SY, ENG.
(T) 01325 467544
Speciality: Homeopathy.
● **Owner** Mr R Laver
M (Ref:HM05746)

**DARLINGTON STREET PRACTICE**

**Darlington Street Practice**, Premier House, Darlington St, Wolverhampton, **Midlands (West)**, WV1 4ND, ENG.
(T) 01902 717172 (F) 01902 717174
Speciality: Hypnotherapy.
● **Owner** Mr P Wesson
B (Ref:HM05747)

**DARNELL, PATRICIA**

**Patricia Darnell**, 58 St Stephens Gardens, London, **London (Greater)**, W2 5NJ, ENG.
(T) 07956 165137
Speciality: Homeopathy.
M (Ref:HM05748)

**DARNLEY HOUSE**

**Darnley House**, 23 Darnley Gardens, Glasgow, **Glasgow (City of)**, G41 4NQ, SCO.
(T) 01414 236881
Speciality: Hypnosis.
B (Ref:HM05749)

**DARRALL, BETH**

**Beth Darrall**, Cheltenham, **Gloucestershire**, GL50, ENG.
(T) 01242 251465
Speciality: Bach Remedies.
M (Ref:HM05750)

**DARTFORD NATURAL HEALTH CENTRE**

**Dartford Natural Health Centre**, 37A Lowfield St, Dartford, **Kent**, DA1 1HP, ENG.
(T) 01322 284898
Speciality: Osteopathy.
P S T (Ref:HM05751)

**DARWEN PHYSIOTHERAPY CLINIC**

**Darwen Physiotherapy Clinic**, Victoria St, Darwen, **Lancashire**, BB3 3HB, ENG.
(T) 01254 703151
Speciality: Physiotherapy.
● **Senior Partner** Mrs L Mills
P S T (Ref:HM05752)

**DARWIN, EDWARD**

**Edward Darwin**, 2 Priors Gate House, The Precincts, Rochester, **Kent**, ME1 1SR, ENG.
(T) 01634 407955
Speciality: Hypnosis.
● **Owner** Mr E Darwin
B (Ref:HM05753)

**DASHWOOD, ANJA**

**Anja Dashwood**, 14 Neals Yard, London, **London (Greater)**, WC2H 9DP, ENG.
(T) 020 7497 0321
Speciality: Complementary Medicines & Therapy.
C M (Ref:HM05754)

**DATE, M S**

**M S Date**, Sheldon House, Sheldwich, Faversham, **Kent**, ME13 0LU, ENG.
(T) 01795 532418 (F) 01795 532418
Speciality: Osteopathy.
● **Owner** Mr M Date
P S T (Ref:HM05755)

**DATE, SUSAN**

**Susan Date Natural & Holistic Therapies**, 3 Eastley Cl, Falfield, **Gloucestershire**, GL12 8BZ, ENG.
(T) 01454 261775
Speciality: Holistic Healing, Hopi Ear Candles, Life Style Coaching, Nutritional Therapy, Reflexology, Reiki.
S T (Ref:HM05756)

**DATHAN, PENNY**

**Penny Dathan**, Aylesbury Rd, Wendover, Aylesbury, **Buckinghamshire**, HP22 6LD, ENG.
(T) 01296 696999
Speciality: Osteopathy.
P S T (Ref:HM05757)

**DAULTRY, CLIFF**

**Cliff Daultry**, 66 Thackeray Rd, London, **London (Greater)**, E6 3BW, ENG.
(T) 07958 357671
Speciality: Reflexology.
● **Owner** Mr C Daultry
S T (Ref:HM05758)

**DAUNCEY, CLARE M**

**Clare M Dauncey**, 7 Carlton Rd South, Weymouth, **Dorset**, DT4 7PL, ENG.
(T) 01305 782582
Speciality: Physiotherapy.
P S T (Ref:HM05759)



Key continued: Yrs.Est: Years Established Q: Qualifications M: Professional Membership ✔ Indemnity Insurance Accept Credit Cards

**DAVALA, CHRISTOPHER**
**Christopher Davala**, 12 Clarinda Pk, Nth, Dun Laoghaire, **County Dublin**, IRE.
(T) 01280 1740
Speciality: Acupuncture.
O (Ref:HM05760)

**DAVALA, CHRISTOPHER**
**Davala Christopher Lic TCM MIATCM**, 12 Clarinda Pk, Nth, Dun Laoghaire, **County Dublin**, IRE.
(T) 01280 1740
Speciality: Acupuncture.
O (Ref:HM05761)

**DAVE WILLIAMSON COUNS PSYCH**
**Dave Williamson Counselling Psychologist**, St. Stephens Cottage, East Harting, Petersfield, **Hampshire**, GU31 5NE, ENG.
(T) 01730 825250
Speciality: Psychology.
B (Ref:HM05762)

**DAVEENA ASSOCIATES**
**Daveena Associates**, 9 High Lane, Chorlton, Manchester, **Manchester (Greater)**, M21 9DJ, ENG.
(T) 01617 183089
Speciality: Counselling. ✓
● **Owner** Ms D McGarthy
H Yrs. Est.: 2 (Ref:HM05763)

**DAVEIGAS, DOUGLAS**
**Douglas Daveigas**, 87 Tolcarne Drive, Pinner, **London (Greater)**, HA5 2DJ, ENG.
(T) 020 8429 0098
Speciality: Hypnosis.
● **Owner** Mr D Daveigas
B (Ref:HM05764)

**DAVENPORT, ANNETTE**
**Annette Davenport**, Natural Medicine Centre, 86 Queens Rd, Nuneaton, **Warwickshire**, CV11 5LE, ENG.
(T) 024 7634 1122
Speciality: Homeopathy.
M (Ref:HM05765)

**DAVENPORT-FRY, ELIZABETH**
**Elizabeth Davenport-Fry**, Liongate Clinic, 8 Chilston Rd, Tunbridge Wells, **Kent**, TN4 9LT, ENG.
(T) 01892 543535
Speciality: Osteopathy.
P S T (Ref:HM05766)

**DAVENTRY NATUREWORKS**
**Daventry Natureworks**, 40 High St, Daventry, **Northamptonshire**, NN11 4HU, ENG.
(T) 01327 311507
Speciality: Acupuncture.
O (Ref:HM05767)

**DAVENTRY NATUREWORKS**
**Daventry Natureworks**, 7 Bishops Court, Daventry, **Northamptonshire**, NN11 4NP, ENG.
(T) 01327 300852
Speciality: Acupuncture, Allergy Testing, Aromatherapy, Bowen Therapy, Chiropractic, Homeopathy, Hypnotherapy, Nutritional Therapy, Osteopathy, Reflexology, Zero Balancing, Bowen Technique, Cranial Osteopathy. ✓
● **Owner/Senior Osteopath** Jane Bellingham Q: DO. M: GOsC.
● **Practice Manager** Carol Howe
● **Acupuncturist** Mrs R Price Q: Adv.Lic.Ac, Cert.Ac, MBAcC. M: BAcC.
O (Ref:HM05768)

**DAVEY, JOAN**
**Joan Davey**, 2 Bridge Rd, Torquay, **Devon**, TQ2 5AX, ENG.
(T) 01803 297975
Speciality: Chiropodists (Podiatrists).
● **Owner** Mrs J Davey
S (Ref:HM05769)

**DAVEY, SARAH**
**Sarah Davey**, 10 Sundew Rd, Hemel Hempstead, **Hertfordshire**, HP1 2DQ, ENG.
(T) 01442 250712
Speciality: Alexander Technique.
P S (Ref:HM05770)

**DAVID**
**David**, 71 Lumsden Avenue, Southampton, **Hampshire**, SO15 5EJ, ENG.
(T) 023 8077 5039
Speciality: Clairvoyants & Palmists.
● **Owner** Mr M Cross
B (Ref:HM05771)

**DAVID ALLAN CLINIC**
**David Allan Clinic**, 19 Cammo Cres, Edinburgh, **Edinburgh (City of)**, EH4 8DZ, SCO.
(T) 01313 392038
Speciality: Osteopathy.
● **Owner** Mr D Allan
P S T (Ref:HM05772)

**DAVID CECIL SURGICAL CHIROPODY**
**David Cecil Surgical Chiropodist & Podiatrist**, 44 Whalebone Gr, Romford, **Essex**, RM6 6BT, ENG.
(T) 020 8597 6403
Speciality: Chiropodists (Podiatrists).
S (Ref:HM05773)

**DAVID HERBERT REFLEXOLOGY**
**David Herbert Reflexology**, 16 Fontmell Cl, Bernards Heath, St. Albans, **Hertfordshire**, AL3 5HU, ENG.
(T) 01727 764081
(E) david_herbert@ntlworld.com
Speciality: Healing Therapy, Holistic Healing, Indian Head Massage, Reflexology. ✓
● **Reflexologist** Mr D Herbert Q: MBSR. M: BCMA, HAR.
C Yrs. Est.: 4 (Ref:HM05774)

**DAVID HOPE PERSONAL DEV**
**David Hope Personal Development**, 41 Weston Lane, Bedworth, Bulkington, **Warwickshire**, CV12 9RS, ENG.
(T) 08007 9561318
Speciality: Psychotherapy, Personal Development.
B (Ref:HM05775)

**DAVID LIST**
**David List**, 20 Grassmere Way, Waterlooville, **Hampshire**, PO7 8RU, ENG.
(T) 023 9224 1475
Speciality: Chiropodists (Podiatrists).
● **Owner** Mr D List
S (Ref:HM05776)

**DAVID ROBERTS PHYSIO CLINIC**
**David Roberts Physiotherapy Clinic**, 474 Broadeay, Chadderton, Oldham, **Lancashire**, OL9 9NS, ENG.
(T) 01616 810822
Speciality: Physiotherapy.
P S T (Ref:HM05777)

**DAVID ROBERTS PHYSIO CLINIC**
**David Roberts Physiotherapy Clinic**, 49-51 Mount Rd, Middleton, Manchester, **Manchester (Greater)**, M24 1DY, ENG.
(T) 01616 535853
Speciality: Physiotherapy.
P S T (Ref:HM05778)

**DAVID THERAPY CLINIC**
**David Therapy Clinic (The)**, 15 Beaconsfield St, Long Eaton, Nottingham, **Nottinghamshire**, NG10 1AY, ENG.
(T) 01159 727711
Speciality: Complementary Medicines & Therapy.
● **Owner** Ms S Mackenzie
M (Ref:HM05779)

**DAVID TIDSALL REIKI PRAC**
**David Tidsall Reiki Practitioner**, 50 Anglesey Avenue, Farnborough, **Hampshire**, GU14 8SQ, ENG.
(T) 01252 544844
Speciality: Reiki.
M (Ref:HM05780)

**DAVID WEISS HOMEOPATHY**
**David Weiss Homeopathy**, 71 Cambridge Cres, Teddington, **London (Greater)**, TW11 8DX, ENG.
(T) 020 8943 9573
(E) dweiss@cwcom.net
Speciality: Acupuncture, Homeopathy, Moxibustion. ✓
● **Homeopath** Mr D Weiss Q: LCH, RSHom. M: Soc.Hom.
M O Yrs. Est.: 4 (Ref:HM05781)

**DAVID, B**
**B David**, 19 Sandilands, Sevenoaks, **Kent**, TN13 2SP, ENG.
(T) 01732 456536
Speciality: Aromatherapy.
M O (Ref:HM05782)

**DAVID, HOLMS, & COFFEY**
**David Davies John Holms & Eileen Coffey**, 2 Bachelor Lane, Horsforth, Leeds, **Yorkshire (West)**, LS18 5NA, ENG.
(T) 01132 589687
Speciality: Osteopathy.
O (Ref:HM05783)

**DAVIDGE, AMANDA**
**Amanda Davidge**, 4 Sheppards, Harlow, **Essex**, CM19 5PL, ENG.
(T) 07775 834967
Speciality: Reflexology.
S T (Ref:HM05784)

**DAVIDSON, ANGELA**
**Angela Davidson**, 2 Gleneagles Avenue, Glenrothes, **Fife**, KY6 2QA, SCO.
(T) 01592 570318
Speciality: Chiropody, Podiatry, Reflexology, Reiki. ✓
● **Owner/Chiropodist/Reflexologist** Ms A Davidson Q: DPodM, M.S.C.P.
M T Yrs. Est.: 6 (Ref:HM05785)

**DAVIDSON, H L**
**H L Davidson**, 521 Foxhall Rd, Ipswich, **Suffolk**, IP3 8LW, ENG.
(T) 01473 723552
Speciality: Herbal Medicine.
O (Ref:HM05786)

**DAVIDSON, MICHAEL S**
**Michael S Davidson**, Gilletts Farm House, Woodville, Stour Provost, Gillingham, **Dorset**, SP8 5LX, ENG.
(T) 01747 838553
Speciality: Chiropractic.
● **Owner** Mr M Davidson
P S T (Ref:HM05787)

**DAVIDSON, MORAG**
**Morag Davidson**, Dunreggan, Moniaive, Thornhill, **Dumfries and Galloway**, DG3 4HH, SCO.
(T) 01848 200200
Speciality: Chiropody. ✓
● **Chiropodist** Ms M Davidson Q: DPodM. M: B.A.Ch.P.
M Yrs. Est.: 5 (Ref:HM05788)

**DAVIDSON, NIKKI**
**Nikki Davidson**, 2 Newnham Grounds Cottages, Newnham, Daventry, **Northamptonshire**, NN11 3EP, ENG.
(T) 01327 705206
Speciality: Reflexology.
S T (Ref:HM05789)

**DAVIDSON, SUSAN**
**Susan Davidson**, Aspasia, 19 Turbary Avenue, Worcester, **Worcestershire**, WR4 0PS, ENG.
(T) 01905 724821
Speciality: Reflexology.
S T (Ref:HM05790)

**DAVIES & ASSOCIATES**
**Martin K Davies & Associates**, 59 Valley Rd, Wistaston, Crewe, **Cheshire**, CW2 8JZ, ENG.
(T) 01270 661593
Speciality: Bonesetting, Complementary Therapy, Cranial Osteopathy, Life Style Coaching, Manipulation, Massage (Therapeutic), Naturopathy, Osteopathy, Rolfing. ✓
● **Osteopath** Mr M Davies Q: DO. M: GOsC.
● **Osteopath** Mr P Nye Q: BSc. M: GOsC.
● **Osteopath** Ms L Spiby Q: DO. M: GOsC.
● **Osteopath** Mr S Hale Q: DO. M: GOsC.
S Yrs. Est.: 15 (Ref:HM05791)

**DAVIES PODIATRY**
**Davies Podiatry**, 73 High St, Droitwich,



Key: B Mind-Body Medicine C Complementary Medicine H Self Help Treatment M Medicinal Therapy O Oriental Medicine P Postural Therapy S Manipulative Structural Therapy T Touch Therapy

Worcestershire, WR9 8EP, ENG.
(T) 01905 798806
Speciality: Biomechanics, Chiropody, Nail Surgery, Podiatry, Cryo Therapy. ✓
● Chiropodist (Podiatrist) Mr S Davies Q: DPodM, S.R.Ch.
C Yrs. Est.: 1 (Ref:HM05792)

**DAVIES, (DR)**

**Dr Davies**, 48 Trinity St, Salisbury, **Wiltshire**, SP1 2BD, ENG.
(T) 01722 411884
Speciality: Acupuncture.
O (Ref:HM05793)

**DAVIES, ANDREW**

**Andrew Davies**, 2b Church St, Kirkham, Preston, **Lancashire**, PR4 2SE, ENG.
(T) 01772 671925
Speciality: Chiropody.
● Owner Mr A Davies
S (Ref:HM05794)

**DAVIES, ANGELA**

**Angela Davies**, 5 Sandy Bank Rd, Gravesend, **Kent**, DA12 1JR, ENG.
(T) 01474 329335
Speciality: Reflexology.
S T (Ref:HM05795)

**DAVIES, ANITA**

**Anita Davies**, 21 Lushington Rd, Eastbourne, **Sussex (East)**, BN21 4LG, ENG.
(T) 01323 410441
Speciality: Homeopathy.
M (Ref:HM05796)

**DAVIES, ANNE**

**Anne Davies**, 5 Beaufort Gardens, Kittle, Swansea, SA3 3LE, WAL.
(T) 01792 233419
Speciality: Physiotherapy.
P S T (Ref:HM05797)

**DAVIES, ANTHONY J**

**Anthony J Davies**, Ottershaw Dental Practice, 2 Brox Rd, Ottershaw, Chertsey, **Surrey**, KT16 0HL, ENG.
(T) 01932 875000
Speciality: Chiropodists (Podiatrists).
S (Ref:HM05798)

**DAVIES, B D**

**B D Davies**, 5 Cumberland Avenue, Basingstoke, **Hampshire**, RG22 4BG, ENG.
(T) 01256 321556
Speciality: Acupuncture.
● Partner Ms B Davies
O (Ref:HM05799)

**DAVIES, BARBARA**

**Barbara Davies**, The Lammas, Churchtown, Belton, Doncaster, **Yorkshire (South)**, DN9 1PB, ENG.
(T) 01427 873443
Speciality: Reflexology.
S T (Ref:HM05800)

**DAVIES, BERYL**

**Beryl Davies**, 103 Grove Rd, Kings Heath, Birmingham, **Midlands (West)**, B14 6SX, ENG.
(T) 01216 242383
Speciality: Aromatherapy.
● Owner Mrs B Davies
M O (Ref:HM05801)

**DAVIES, C G**

**C G Davies**, 5 Clarence Rd, Wotton-under-Edge, **Gloucestershire**, GL12 7EX, ENG.
(T) 01453 843535
Speciality: Osteopathy.
P S T (Ref:HM05802)

**DAVIES, C M**

**C M Davies**, 1 Ship St, Frodsham, **Cheshire**, WA6 7NW, ENG.
(T) 01928 735323
Speciality: Chiropodists (Podiatrists).
S (Ref:HM05803)

**DAVIES, CYNTHIA**

**Cynthia Davies**, 48 Swithland Lane, Rothley, Leicester, **Leicestershire**, LE7 7SE, ENG.
(T) 01162 302162
Speciality: Acupuncture.
● Owner Mrs C Davies
O (Ref:HM05804)

**DAVIES, D B**

**D B Davies**, 29 Brancker Rd, Plymouth, **Devon**, PL2 3DW, ENG.
(T) 01752 564789
Speciality: Chiropodists (Podiatrists).
● Owner Mr D Davies
S (Ref:HM05805)

**DAVIES, DAVID**

**David Davies**, 100 Station Prde, Harrogate, **Yorkshire (North)**, HG1 1HQ, ENG.
(T) 01423 561566 (F) 01423 567379
Speciality: Osteopathy.
● Owner Mr T Cree
P S T (Ref:HM05806)

**DAVIES, DEBRA**

**Debra Davies**, 11 Attfield Walk, Eastbourne, **Sussex (East)**, BN22 9JP, ENG.
(T) 01323 511261
Speciality: Chiropodists (Podiatrists).
S (Ref:HM05807)

**DAVIES, E**

**E Davies**, Tygwennol, Nantmel, Llandrindod Wells, **Powys**, LD1 6EH, WAL.
(T) 01597 824305
Speciality: Osteopathy.
P S T (Ref:HM05808)

**DAVIES, E R**

**E R Davies**, 57 Basterfield House, Golden Lane Estate, London, **London (Greater)**, EC1Y 0TR, ENG.
(T) 020 7490 2310
Speciality: Hypnosis.
● Owner Mr E Davies
B (Ref:HM05809)

**DAVIES, FIONA**

**Fiona Davies**, 29 Blackmead, Riverhead, Sevenoaks, **Kent**, TN13 2QU, ENG.
(T) 01732 453985
Speciality: Reflexology.
S T (Ref:HM05810)

**DAVIES, G W**

**G W Davies**, 64 Needingworth Rd, St. Ives, **Cambridgeshire**, PE27 5JT, ENG.
(T) 01480 466390
Speciality: Chiropodists (Podiatrists).
S (Ref:HM05811)

**DAVIES, H A**

**H A Davies**, 34 Westfield St, St. Helens, **Merseyside**, WA10 1QF, ENG.
(T) 01744 29119
Speciality: Herbal Medicine.
● Owner Ms H Davies
M (Ref:HM05812)

**DAVIES, H A**

**H A Davies**, 32 Grosvenor Rd, Prescot, **Merseyside**, L34 6HZ, ENG.
(T) 01514 306483
Speciality: Herbal Medicine.
M (Ref:HM05813)

**DAVIES, J C**

**J C Davies**, 86 Fair Rd, Bradford, **Yorkshire (West)**, BD6 1QL, ENG.
(T) 01274 678894
Speciality: Chiropodists (Podiatrists).
S (Ref:HM05814)

**DAVIES, J G**

**J G Davies**, 203 The Homend, Ledbury, **Herefordshire**, HR8 1BS, ENG.
(T) 01531 634492
Speciality: Physiotherapy.
P S T (Ref:HM05815)

**DAVIES, JACKIE**

**Jackie Davies**, First Floor, 10 Nelson St, Swansea, SA1 3QE, WAL.
(T) 01792 457770
Speciality: Chiropodists (Podiatrists).
● Owner Mrs J Davies
S (Ref:HM05816)

**DAVIES, JACQUELINE**

**Jacqueline Davies**, 41 Tower Cl, Bassingbourn, Royston, **Hertfordshire**, SG8 5JX, ENG.
(T) 01763 244629
Speciality: Reflexology.
S T (Ref:HM05817)

**DAVIES, JOAN**

**Joan Davies**, Rosehill Cottage, The Village, Gorsedd, Holywell, **Flintshire**, CH8 8QZ, WAL.
(T) 01352 710108 (F) 01352 712533
Speciality: Physiotherapy.
● Owner Mrs J Davies
P S T (Ref:HM05818)

**DAVIES, JOHNATHON**

**Johnathon Davies**, 13 Duchess Drive, Blackpool, **Lancashire**, FY2 9PQ, ENG.
(T) 01253 353461
Speciality: Chiropody, Nail Surgery. ✓
● Owner/Chiropodist Mr J Davies Q: DPodM. M: B.A.Ch.P.
M Yrs. Est.: 2 (Ref:HM05819)

**DAVIES, JUDITH**

**Judith Davies**, 26 Davies Rd, West Bridgford, Nottingham, **Nottinghamshire**, NG2 5JD, ENG.
(T) 01159 815190
Speciality: Complementary Medicines & Therapy.
● Owner Miss J Davies
M (Ref:HM05820)

**DAVIES, JULIA**

**Julia Davies**, The Terrace, 35 Staplegrove Rd, Taunton, **Somerset**, TA1 1DG, ENG.
(T) 01823 338968
Speciality: Aromatherapy.
● Owner Ms J Gotto
M O (Ref:HM05821)

**DAVIES, L**

**L Davies**, Oxford Natural Health Centre, 3 Church Cowley Rd, Oxford, **Oxfordshire**, OX4 3JR, ENG.
(T) 01865 715615
Speciality: Chiropractors.
● Owner Mrs L Davies
P S T (Ref:HM05822)

**DAVIES, L**

**L Davies**, 99 Singleton Rd, Salford, **Manchester (Greater)**, M7 4LX, ENG.
(T) 01617 950883
Speciality: Hypnosis.
● Owner Dr L Davies
B (Ref:HM05823)

**DAVIES, LARRY**

**Larry Davies**, 15 Rhydypenau Rd, Cardiff, **Glamorgan (Vale of)**, CF23 6PX, WAL.
(T) 029 2075 6470
Speciality: Chiropodists (Podiatrists).
S (Ref:HM05824)

**DAVIES, LORNA**

**Lorna Davies**, 33 Oak Lane, Barston, Solihull, **Midlands (West)**, B92 0JR, ENG.
(T) 01675 442003
Speciality: Chiropodists (Podiatrists).
● Owner Mrs L Davies
S (Ref:HM05825)

**DAVIES, LOUISE**

**Louise Davies**, 2b Heol Y Deri, Cardiff, **Glamorgan (Vale of)**, CF14 6HF, WAL.
(T) 029 2061 4728
Speciality: Complementary Medicines & Therapy.
● Owner Mrs L Davies
C M (Ref:HM05826)

**DAVIES, M D**

**M D Davies**, 35 Faulder Avenue, Carterton, **Oxfordshire**, OX18 3LP, ENG.
(T) 01993 843922
Speciality: Chiropodists (Podiatrists).
● Owner Mr M Davies
S (Ref:HM05827)

**DAVIES, M K**

**M K Davies**, 55A Beam St, Nantwich, **Cheshire**, CW5 5NF, ENG.
(T) 01270 610288
Speciality: Osteopathy.
P S T (Ref:HM05828)



Key continued: Yrs.Est: Years Established Q: Qualifications M: Professional Membership ✓ Indemnity Insurance Accept Credit Cards

## DAVIES, MARTIN K
**Martin K Davies**, 102 Crewe Rd, Alsager, Stoke-On-Trent, **Staffordshire**, ST7 2JA, ENG.
(T) 01270 883242
Speciality: Osteopathy.
● **Manager** Mrs J Sutton
P S T (Ref:HM05829)

## DAVIES, MERYL
**Meryl Davies**, Nethercott Clinic, 6 Station Approach Rd, Tadworth, **Surrey**, KT20 5AF, ENG.
(T) 01737 813600
Speciality: Chiropodists (Podiatrists).
● **Owner** Mrs M Davies
S (Ref:HM05830)

## DAVIES, MICHAEL
**Michael Davies - Physiotherapy Surgery**, The Cottage, Back Of 61 Littlefield Lane, Grimsby, **Humberside (South)**, DN34 4NU, ENG.
(T) 01472 251420
(E) mike@pamtherapist.fq.co.uk
Speciality: Physiotherapy, Power Assisted Micro Manipulation. ✔
● **PAM Therapist/Physiotherapist**
Mr M Davies Q: MAB Phys.
S Yrs. Est.: 14 (Ref:HM05831)

## DAVIES, N G
**N G Davies**, 1 Bryn Lane, The Bryn, Pontllanfraith, Blackwood, **Caerphilly**, NP12 2PG, WAL.
(T) 01495 225655
Speciality: Osteopathy.
P S T (Ref:HM05832)

## DAVIES, NOEL
**Noel Davies**, 13 Union St, Greenock, **Inverclyde**, PA16 8JL, SCO.
(T) 01475 721752
Speciality: Physiotherapy.
P S T (Ref:HM05833)

## DAVIES, P J
**P J Davies**, 2 The Crescent, Canterbury, **Kent**, CT2 7AG, ENG.
(T) 01227 454200 (F) 01227 763151
Speciality: Physiotherapy.
● **Owner** Mrs P Davies
P S T (Ref:HM05834)

## DAVIES, PETER
**Peter Davies**, 125 Willowbrae Rd, Edinburgh, **Edinburgh (City of)**, EH8 7HN, SCO.
(T) 01316 612804
Speciality: Physiotherapy.
● **Owner** Mr P Davies
P S T (Ref:HM05835)

## DAVIES, PETER
**Peter Davies**, Kinesiology Muscle Balancing, Thorncombe, Church Rd, Windlesham, **Surrey**, GU20 6BT, ENG.
(T) 01276 473371
Speciality: Complementary Medicines & Therapy.
M (Ref:HM05836)

## DAVIES, ROBERT
**Robert Davies**, 28 Gorse Drive, Smallfield, Horley, **Surrey**, RH6 9GJ, ENG.
(T) 01342 842330
Speciality: Reflexology.
S T (Ref:HM05837)

## DAVIES, S M
**S M Davies**, 15 Thirsk Rd, Northallerton, **Yorkshire (North)**, DL6 1PE, ENG.
(T) 01609 772517
Speciality: Complementary Medicines & Therapy.
● **Owner** Mrs L Davies
C M (Ref:HM05838)

## DAVIES, S W
**S W Davies**, The Vineyard, Berkeley St, Cheltenham, **Gloucestershire**, GL52 2SX, ENG.
(T) 01242 574311
Speciality: Osteopathy.
● **Owner** Mr S Davies
P S T (Ref:HM05839)

## DAVIES, SALLY
**Sally Davies**, Dairy Court, Wales, Queen Camel, Yeovil, **Somerset**, BA22 7PA, ENG.
(T) 01935 850003
Speciality: Aromatherapy, Reflexology. ✔
● **Owner/Aromatherapist/Reflexologist**
Mrs S Davies Q: Dip.Arom, Dip.Reflex. M: AoR, ITEC.
C Yrs. Est.: 3 (Ref:HM05840)

## DAVIES, TERESA
**Teresa Davies**, 34 Hoole Rd, Chester, **Cheshire**, CH2 3NJ, ENG.
(T) 01244 342040
Speciality: Chiropodists (Podiatrists).
● **Owner** Mrs T Davies
S (Ref:HM05841)

## DAVIES, TRACY A
**Tracy A Davies**, Radiant Health Clinic, Albion Chambers, 1 High St, Leighton Buzzard, **Bedfordshire**, LU7 7DN, ENG.
(T) 01525 372311
Speciality: Osteopathy.
P S T (Ref:HM05842)

## DAVIES, V E
**Mrs V E Davies**, 1 Rutland Avenue, Wolverhampton, **Midlands (West)**, WV4 4JB, ENG.
(T) 01902 332847
Speciality: Chiropodists (Podiatrists).
S (Ref:HM05843)

## DAVIES, VIVIEN
**Vivien Davies**, Combe Cottage, Sandford Orcas, Sherborne, **Dorset**, DT9 4RP, ENG.
(T) 01963 220749
Speciality: Reflexology.
S T (Ref:HM05844)

## DAVINSKY, MARZO
**Marzo Davinsky Ltd**, Unit A Fox Pitt, Shingle Barn Lane, West Farleigh, Maidstone, **Kent**, ME15 0PN, ENG.
(T) 01622 820733 (F) 01622 820744
Speciality: Aromatherapy.
● **Director** Mr D Marsh
M O (Ref:HM05845)

## DAVIS A STARKEY REM THERAP
**Davis A Starkey Remedial Therapist**, 98 Ashmore Lake Rd, Willenhall, **Midlands (West)**, WV12 4LN, ENG.
(T) 01902 608328 (F) 01902 410590
Speciality: Complementary Medicines & Therapy, Remedial Therapy. ✔
● **Remedial Therapist** Mr D Starkey Q: ITEC, LCSP, MBRA. M: PMBCA.
C Yrs. Est.: 11 (Ref:HM05846)

## DAVIS, ANDREW & VICTORIA
**Andrew & Victoria Davis Ltd**, Brookfields, Westridge, Highclere, Newbury, **Berkshire**, RG20 9RX, ENG.
(T) 01635 253973
Speciality: Physiotherapy.
● **Sole Director**
Andrew Anthony Davis
P S T (Ref:HM05847)

## DAVIS, ANN
**Ann Davis**, 49 Westville Oval, Harrogate, **Yorkshire (North)**, HG1 3JN, ENG.
(T) 01423 507219
Speciality: Complementary Medicines & Therapy.
● **Owner** Mrs A Davis
C M (Ref:HM05848)

## DAVIS, BEVERLEY
**Beverley Davis**, 51 Llwydarth Rd, Maesteg, Bridgend, CF34 9EY, WAL.
(T) 01656 736514
Speciality: Chiropodists (Podiatrists).
● **Owner** Ms B Davis
S (Ref:HM05849)

## DAVIS, GEOFFREY
**Geoffrey Davis**, 17 Broomhills, Welwyn Garden City, **Hertfordshire**, AL7 1RG, ENG.
(T) 01707 332636
Speciality: Chiropodists (Podiatrists).
● **Owner** Mr G Davis
S (Ref:HM05850)

## DAVIS, IRIS
**Iris Davis**, 282 Station Rd, Aylesford, **Kent**, ME20 7JH, ENG.
(T) 01622 710484
Speciality: Chiropodists (Podiatrists).
S (Ref:HM05851)

## DAVIS, J H
**J H Davis**, 10 Monmouth Rd, Abergavenny, **Monmouthshire**, NP7 5HH, WAL.
(T) 01873 854712
Speciality: Physiotherapy.
P S T (Ref:HM05852)

## DAVIS, JAMES E
**James E Davis**, 67 Rosslyn Rd, Vicars Cross, Chester, **Cheshire**, CH3 5HR, ENG.
(T) 01244 316047
Speciality: Chiropodists (Podiatrists).
● **Owner** Mr J Davis
S (Ref:HM05853)

## DAVIS, JULIA
**Julia Davis**, 2 Beechcroft Rd, Tooting Bec, London, **London (Greater)**, SW17 7BY, ENG.
(T) 020 8672 0455
(E) juliad@mcmail.com
Speciality: Acupuncture. ✔
● **Acupuncturist** Miss J Davis Q: Lic.Ac. M: BAcC.
O Yrs. Est.: 7 (Ref:HM05854)

## DAVIS, LOUISE
**Louise Davis**, 3 Beswick Gardens, Bracknell, **Berkshire**, RG12 2QL, ENG.
(T) 01344 489374
Speciality: Complementary Medicines & Therapy.
C M (Ref:HM05855)

## DAVIS, MELANIE
**Melanie Davis**, 32 Stocks Lane, Kelvedon Hatch, Brentwood, **Essex**, CM15 0BN, ENG.
(T) 01277 374573
Speciality: Hypnosis.
B (Ref:HM05856)

## DAVIS, MICHAEL
**Michael Davis**, St Marys House, 55-56 Cheap St, Newbury, **Berkshire**, RG14 5DH, ENG.
(T) 01635 30252
Speciality: Osteopathy.
P S T (Ref:HM05857)

## DAVIS, P R
**P R Davis**, 8 Ivy Cl, Sunbury-On-Thames, **Surrey**, TW16 5JX, ENG.
(T) 01932 785815
Speciality: Physiotherapy.
● **Owner** Mrs P Davis
P S T (Ref:HM05858)

## DAVIS, R J (DR)
**Dr R J Davis**, 36 Greenhill St, Stratford-Upon-Avon, **Warwickshire**, CV37 6LE, ENG.
(T) 01789 415123
Speciality: Chiropodists (Podiatrists).
● **Owner** Mr R Davis
S (Ref:HM05859)

## DAVIS, ROSE
**Rose Davis**, 13 Eden Avenue, Rainford, St. Helens, **Merseyside**, WA11 8HT, ENG.
(T) 01744 885781
Speciality: Homeopathy.
● **Owner** Mrs R Davis
M (Ref:HM05860)

## DAVIS, S
**S Davis**, 34 Sycamore Gr, Braintree, **Essex**, CM7 2LT, ENG.
(T) 01376 344989
Speciality: Hypnosis.
B (Ref:HM05861)

## DAVIS, TIM
**Tim Davis**, 8 Laytons Lane, Sunbury-On-Thames, **Surrey**, TW16 6LR, ENG.
(T) 01932 765946
Speciality: Hypnosis.
● **Owner** Mr T Davis
B (Ref:HM05862)

Key: B Mind-Body Medicine C Complementary Medicine H Self Help Treatment M Medicinal Therapy O Oriental Medicine P Postural Therapy S Manipulative Structural Therapy T Touch Therapy

**DAVIS-JONES, ANN**

**Ann Davis-Jones**, North View, Sherburn Hill, Durham, **County Durham**, DH6 1PN, ENG.
(T) 01913 720966
Speciality: Hypnotherapy.
● **Owner** Ms A Davis-Jones
B (Ref:HM05863)

**DAVISON, DAVID J**

**David J Davison**, 64 King George Rd, Shoreham-by-Sea, **Sussex (West)**, BN43 6YL, ENG.
(T) 01273 870779
Speciality: Chiropodists (Podiatrists).
● **Owner** Mr D Davison
S (Ref:HM05864)

**DAVISON, FIONA**

**Fiona Davison**, 85 Leadside Rd, Aberdeen, **Aberdeenshire**, AB25 1RX, SCO.
(T) 01224 635999
Speciality: Osteopathy. ✓
● **Osteopath** Ms F Davison M: GOsC.
S Yrs. Est.: 9 (Ref:HM05865)

**DAVIS-PARRY, CLARISSA J B**

**Mrs Clarissa J B Davis-Parry**, 56 Gravel Hill Trce, Hemel Hempstead, **Hertfordshire**, HP1 1RJ, ENG.
(T) 01442 217092
Speciality: Osteopathy.
P S T (Ref:HM05866)

**DAVY, TERRY**

**Terry Davy**, 15 Leas Rd, Warlingham, **Surrey**, CR6 9LN, ENG.
(T) 01883 625866
Speciality: Chiropodists (Podiatrists).
● **Owner** Mr T Davy
S (Ref:HM05867)

**DAVYS, MICHAEL**

**Michael Davys**, 14 Henniker Mews, Callow St, Chelsea, London, **London (Greater)**, SW3 6BL, ENG.
(T) 020 7352 4679
Speciality: Psychiatry.
● **Owner** Dr M Davys
B (Ref:HM05868)

**DAWBER, PAULINE**

**Pauline Dawber**, 255 Hinton Way, Great Shelford, Cambridge, **Cambridgeshire**, CB2 5AN, ENG.
(T) 01223 842075
Speciality: Homeopathy.
● **Owner** Miss P Dawber
M (Ref:HM05869)

**DAWE, PATRICIA**

**Patricia Dawe Holistic Therapist**, 27 Bells Lane, Fareham, **Hampshire**, PO14 2BA, ENG.
(T) 01329 667795
Speciality: Complementary Medicines & Therapy.
C M (Ref:HM05870)

**DAWE, S**

**S Dawe**, Overne, Exeter Rd, Teignmouth, **Devon**, TQ14 8PB, ENG.
(T) 01626 779292
Speciality: Chiropodists (Podiatrists).
S (Ref:HM05871)

**DAWED, HELEN**

**Helen Dawed**, 2 Rye River Pk, Dun Carraig, Leixlip, **County Kildare**, IRE.
(T) 01624 4604
Speciality: Complementary Medicines & Therapy.
M (Ref:HM05872)

**DAWES, LESLEY**

**Lesley Dawes**, 7 Lower Park Drive, Telford, **Shropshire**, TF1 3PY, ENG.
(T) 01952 256444
Speciality: Reflexology.
● **Owner** Ms L Dawes
S T (Ref:HM05873)

**DAWES, T**

**T Dawes**, 178 East Barnet Rd, Barnet, **Hertfordshire**, EN4 8QS, ENG.
(T) 020 8440 5518
Speciality: Chiropodists (Podiatrists).
S (Ref:HM05874)

**DAWINDER, JOHAL**

**Johal Dawinder**, 19 Honeybourne Way, Willenhall, **Midlands (West)**, WV13 1HN, ENG.
(T) 01902 637815
Speciality: Chiropodists (Podiatrists).
S (Ref:HM05875)

**DAWKINS, S**

**S Dawkins**, Dolphin House, St Peter St, Winchester, **Hampshire**, SO23 8BW, ENG.
(T) 01962 829735 (F) 01962 866116
Speciality: Psychiatry.
B (Ref:HM05876)

**DAWKINS, SUSAN**

**Susan Dawkins**, 57 Milford St, Salisbury, **Wiltshire**, SP1 2BP, ENG.
(T) 01722 414114
Speciality: Chiropodists (Podiatrists).
● **Owner** Miss S Dawkins
S (Ref:HM05877)

**DAWN AWAKENING MUSIC**

**Dawn Awakening Music Ltd**, Foxhole, Dartington, Totnes, **Devon**, TQ9 6EB, ENG.
(T) 01803 864866 (F) 01803 864881
Speciality: Complementary Medicines & Therapy.
● **Senior Partner** Mr P Lewis
C M (Ref:HM05878)

**DAWNS**

**Dawns**, 2 Silver St, Bridgwater, **Somerset**, TA6 3EG, ENG.
(T) 01278 450588
Speciality: Complementary Medicines & Therapy.
● **Owner** Mrs D Saunders
C M (Ref:HM05879)

**DAWSON, DAVID (DR)**

**Dr David Dawson**, 126 Harley St, London, **London (Greater)**, W1N 1AH, ENG.
(T) 020 7935 2030
Speciality: Clinical Ecology, Homeopathy. ✓
● **Homeopath** Dr D Dawson Q: Ch.B, MB.
M Yrs. Est.: 7 (Ref:HM05880)

**DAWSON, GILLIAN**

**Gillian Dawson**, 137 Dorchester Rd, Worcester Park, **Surrey**, KT4 8PA, ENG.
(T) 020 8715 1145
Speciality: Chiropodists (Podiatrists).
● **Owner** Mrs C Felten
S (Ref:HM05881)

**DAWSON, J P**

**J P Dawson**, 67 London Rd, Alderley Edge, **Cheshire**, SK9 7DY, ENG.
(T) 01625 584667
Speciality: Chiropodists (Podiatrists).
● **Owner** Mr J Dawson
S (Ref:HM05882)

**DAWSON, JEAN**

**Jean Dawson**, Mayfield, 40 Church Rd, Leyland, Preston, **Lancashire**, PR5 2AA, ENG.
(T) 01772 432971
Speciality: Chiropodists (Podiatrists).
S (Ref:HM05883)

**DAWSON, KAREN**

**Karen Dawson**, 63 Dyffryn Rd, Alltwen, Pontardawe, **Neath Port Talbot**, SA8 3BY, WAL.
(T) 01792 830793
Speciality: Reflexology.
S T (Ref:HM05884)

**DAWSON, TONY**

**Tony Dawson**, 18 High St, Cuckfield, Haywards Heath, **Sussex (West)**, RH17 5JU, ENG.
(T) 01444 440857
Speciality: Chiropractors.
● **Owner** Mr T Dawson
P S T (Ref:HM05885)

**DAWSON, VIVIENNE**

**Vivienne Dawson**, 107C Grosvenor Avenue, Carshalton, **Surrey**, SM5 3EN, ENG.
(T) 020 8286 0612
Speciality: Acupuncture.
● **Owner** Mrs V Dawson
O (Ref:HM05886)

**DAY, A C**

**A C Day**, 91 Ferndale, Waterlooville, **Hampshire**, PO7 7PQ, ENG.
(T) 023 9225 1658
Speciality: Chiropodists (Podiatrists).
● **Owner** Mrs A Day
S (Ref:HM05887)

**DAY, BRIAN J**

**Brian J Day**, 75 Maxse Rd, Bristol, BS4 2JQ, ENG.
(T) 01179 771648 (F) 01179 771648
Speciality: Complementary Medicines & Therapy.
● **Owner** Mr B Day
C M (Ref:HM05888)

**DAY, BRIDGET**

**Bridget Day**, 12 Norman Court, Chatsworth Rd, Chichester, **Sussex (West)**, PO19 2XU, ENG.
(T) 01243 532190
Speciality: Alexander Technique.
P S (Ref:HM05889)

**DAY, JOSEPHINE (DR)**

**Dr Josephine Day**, 2 Berenger Tower, Worlds End Estate, London, **London (Greater)**, SW10 0EF, ENG.
(T) 020 7351 2220
Speciality: Clairvoyants & Palmists.
● **Owner** Dr J Day
B (Ref:HM05890)

**DAY, JULIE**

**Julie Day**, Cassidy Rd Medical Centre, 651A Fulham Rd, London, **London (Greater)**, SW6 5PX, ENG.
(T) 020 7731 2511 (F) 020 7371 7857
Speciality: Chiropodists (Podiatrists).
● **Manager** Mr L Senior
S (Ref:HM05891)

**DAY, JULIE C**

**Julie C Day**, 273 Fulham Rd, London, **London (Greater)**, SW10 9PZ, ENG.
(T) 020 7351 4889
Speciality: Chiropodists (Podiatrists).
● **Owner** Ms J Day
S (Ref:HM05892)

**DAY, MELINA**

**Melina Day**, 53 East Hill, London, **London (Greater)**, SW18 2QE, ENG.
(T) 020 8874 1636 (F) 020 8874 1636
Speciality: Osteopathy.
● **Owner** Ms M Day
P S T (Ref:HM05893)

**DAY, PHILIP**

**Philip Day**, 8 Victoria Rd, Peterhead, **Aberdeenshire**, AB42 1UB, SCO.
(T) 01779 478263
Speciality: Chiropodists (Podiatrists).
S (Ref:HM05894)

**DAY, R M**

**R M Day**, 28 Danywern Drive, Winnersh, Wokingham, **Berkshire**, RG41 5NR, ENG.
(T) 01189 794964
Speciality: Osteopathy.
● **Owner** Mrs R Day
P S T (Ref:HM05895)

**DAY, RUKMANI G**

**Rukmani G Day**, Chestnut Osteopathic Practice, High St, Culworth, Banbury, **Oxfordshire**, OX17 2BD, ENG.
(T) 01295 768488
Speciality: Osteopathy.
● **Owner** Mrs R Day
P S T (Ref:HM05896)

**DAY, SYLVIA**

**Sylvia Day**, Holly Pl, Lower Rd, Cookham, Maidenhead, **Berkshire**, SL6 9EJ, ENG.
(T) 01628 527291
Speciality: Reflexology.
S T (Ref:HM05897)

**DAYDREAMS**

**Daydreams**, 2 Denmark Rd, Northampton, **Northamptonshire**, NN1 5QR, ENG.
(T) 01604 602891



Key continued: **Yrs.Est:** Years Established **Q:** Qualifications **M:** Professional Membership ✓ Indemnity Insurance ▬ Accept Credit Cards

Speciality: Complementary Medicines & Therapy.
C M (Ref:HM05898)

## DAYTON-LEWIS, R

**R Dayton-Lewis**, 63 London Rd, Horsham, **Sussex (West)**, RH12 1AN, ENG.
(T) 01403 252092
Speciality: Chiropodists (Podiatrists).
S (Ref:HM05899)

## D'CRUZE, INGRID

**Ingrid D'Cruze**, 9 Dronfield Rd, Manchester, **Manchester (Greater)**, M22 4AW, ENG.
(T) 01619 983302
Speciality: Complementary Medicines & Therapy.
C M (Ref:HM05900)

## DE A'ECHEVARRIA, MARY-CLARE

**Mary-Clare De A'echevarria**, 100 Ferndale Rd, London, **London (Greater)**, E11 3DN, ENG.
(T) 020 8558 1331
Speciality: Psychotherapy.
● **Owner** Ms M Deechevarria
B (Ref:HM05901)

## DE ALMEDIA, ALTAIR

**Altair De Almedia**, The Malvern Natural Health Centre, 15 Abbey Rd, Malvern, **Worcestershire**, WR14 3ES, ENG.
(T) 01684 562528
Speciality: Acupuncture.
O (Ref:HM05902)

## DE BOER, GILLIAN

**Gillian De Boer**, The Leeds Centre Of Homoeopathy, 148 Harrogate Rd, Leeds, **Yorkshire (West)**, LS7 4NZ, ENG.
(T) 01132 783547
Speciality: Homeopathy.
● **Owner** Dr G De-Boer
M (Ref:HM05903)

## DE BURGH, JULIE

**Julie De Burgh**, 12 Sutherland Avenue, West Ealing, London, **London (Greater)**, W13 8LE, ENG.
(T) 020 8997 7966
(E) juliedeburgh@hotmail.com
Speciality: Hypnosis, Hypnotherapy, Psychotherapy, Vortex Healing, Past life/Between Lives Regressions. ✔
● **Hypnotherapist/Psychotherapist** Mrs J De-Burgh **Q:** CQSW, DipTHP, NLP (Master). **M:** HS.
B Yrs. Est.: 21 (Ref:HM05904)

## DE FERE, SUSANNA

**Susanna De Fere**, 142A Gloucester Pl, London, **London (Greater)**, NW1 6DT, ENG.
(T) 020 7723 4137 (F) 020 7723 9203
Speciality: Hypnosis.
● **Owner** Mrs S De-Fere
B (Ref:HM05905)

## DE GROOT, CHRISTINE

**Christine De Groot**, The Well Spring Clinic, 90-92 Islington High St, London, **London (Greater)**, N1 8EG, ENG.
(T) 020 7704 1777
Speciality: Homeopathy.
M (Ref:HM05906)

## DE GROOT, CHRISTINE

**Christine De Groot**, 44 Madeira Rd, London, **London (Greater)**, SW16 2DE, ENG.
(T) 020 8677 6212
Speciality: Homeopathy.
M (Ref:HM05907)

## DE JODE, S

**S De Jode**, 10 Eldon Rd, Reading, **Berkshire**, RG1 4DH, ENG.
(T) 01189 502002
Speciality: Alexander Technique.
P S (Ref:HM05908)

## DE LA HOYDE, HUGH

**Hugh De La Hoyde Registered Osteopath**, 8 Enterprise Centre, King Edward St, Grimsby, **Humberside (South)**, DN31 3JH, ENG.
(T) 01472 320611
Speciality: Osteopathy.
P S T (Ref:HM05909)

## DE LA HOYDE, JUDY

**Judy De La Hoyde**, 2 Seymour Cottages, Vanderbreen St, Bisley, Stroud, **Gloucestershire**, GL6 7BW, ENG.
(T) 01452 770737
Speciality: Complementary Medicines & Therapy.
M (Ref:HM05910)

## DE LIMA, RENUKA

**Renuka De Lima**, 29 Woodlands Avenue, Worcester Park, **Surrey**, KT4 7AL, ENG.
(T) 020 8330 7675
Speciality: Osteopathy.
P S T (Ref:HM05911)

## DE LOURDES DE SOUSA, MARIA

**Maria de Lourdes de Sousa**, 78 Woodford Court, Shepherds Bush Green, London, **London (Greater)**, W12 8QZ, ENG.
(T) 020 8740 4105
Speciality: Reflexology.
S T (Ref:HM05912)

## DE LOWE, V

**V De Lowe**, 576 Warrington Rd, Wigan, **Lancashire**, WN3 6QQ, ENG.
(T) 01942 236897
Speciality: Osteopathy.
● **Owner** Mrs V De Lowe
P S T (Ref:HM05913)

## DE MENTHON, FRANCOIS

**Mr Francois De Menthon**, 41 Hills Rd, Cambridge, **Cambridgeshire**, CB2 1NT, ENG.
(T) 01223 315541
Speciality: Acupuncture.
O (Ref:HM05914)

## DE MIERRE, MAVIS

**Mavis De Mierre**, High Peak, **Derbyshire**, SK22, ENG.
(T) 01663 742472
Speciality: Bach Remedies.
M (Ref:HM05915)

## DE PRINCE, THESSALONIA

**Thessalonia De Prince**, 23 Woodmere, Luton, **Bedfordshire**, LU3 4DL, ENG.
(T) 01582 571777
Speciality: Hypnosis.
● **Owner** Mrs V Patel
B (Ref:HM05916)

## DE REYHER, ISABELLE

**Isabelle De Reyher**, 64A Castle Rd, London, **London (Greater)**, NW1 8SN, ENG.
(T) 020 7267 8847 (F) 020 7916 9200
Speciality: Osteopathy.
P S T (Ref:HM05917)

## DE SALENGRE & SPENCER

**De Salengre & Spencer**, 8 Church Walk, Bideford, **Devon**, EX39 2BP, ENG.
(T) 01237 471110
Speciality: Osteopathy.
P S T (Ref:HM05918)

## DE SILVA, M

**M De Silva**, 6 Elton, Woughton Park, Milton Keynes, **Buckinghamshire**, MK6 3BJ, ENG.
(T) 01908 604704
Speciality: Acupuncture.
O (Ref:HM05919)

## DE TUTE, MARY

**Mary De Tute**, Rosemary Mount, Broom Hill, Flimwell, Wadhurst, **Sussex (East)**, TN5 7NJ, ENG.
(T) 01580 879386
Speciality: Reflexology.
S T (Ref:HM05920)

## DE VERE, G R & R J

**G R & R J De Vere**, 7 South Hawksworth St, Ilkley, **Yorkshire (West)**, LS29 9DX, ENG.
(T) 01943 608345 (F) 01943 608345
Speciality: Chiropodists (Podiatrists).
● **Partner** Mr G De-Vere
S (Ref:HM05921)

## DE VERE, SUSAN

**Susan De Vere**, 42 Seymours, Harlow, **Essex**, CM19 5NG, ENG.
(T) 01279 423102
Speciality: Clairvoyants & Palmists.
● **Owner** Ms S De-Vere
B (Ref:HM05922)

## DE VRIES, JAN

**Jan De Vries**, Auchenkyle, Southwood Rd, Troon, **Ayrshire (South)**, KA10 7EL, SCO.
(T) 01292 311414 (F) 01292 317372
Speciality: Complementary Medicines & Therapy.
● **Owner** Mr J De-Vries
C M (Ref:HM05923)

## DE WOLFF, MAARTJE

**Maartje De Wolff**, Flat 3, 39 Holdenhurst Avenue, London, **London (Greater)**, N12 0JA, ENG.
(T) 020 8343 4805
Speciality: Alexander Technique.
P S (Ref:HM05924)

## DEACH, I

**I Deach**, Dental Surgery, 1 Great Cheetham St West, Salford, **Manchester (Greater)**, M7 2JB, ENG.
(T) 01617 926695
Speciality: Chiropodists (Podiatrists).
● **Owner** Mr I Deach
S (Ref:HM05925)

## DEACH, I

**I Deach**, Greyland Medical Centre, 468 Bury Old Rd, Prestwich, Manchester, **Manchester (Greater)**, M25 1NL, ENG.
(T) 01617 989818 (F) 01617 739219
Speciality: Chiropodists (Podiatrists).
● **Partner** Dr B Rosenberg
S (Ref:HM05926)

## DEACKES, C

**C Deackes**, 9 Beeches Avenue, Carshalton, **Surrey**, SM5 3LB, ENG.
(T) 020 8773 4508
Speciality: Chiropodists (Podiatrists).
S (Ref:HM05927)

## DEACON, ALISON

**Alison Deacon**, 8 Packington Cl, Off Angus Cl, Shaw, Swindon, **Wiltshire**, SN5 9PB, ENG.
(T) 01793 887809
Speciality: Reflexology.
S T (Ref:HM05928)

## DEACON, ALISON

**Alison Deacon**, 41 Arran Rd, Birmingham, **Midlands (West)**, B34 6DD, ENG.
(T) 01217 477411
Speciality: Reflexology.
S T (Ref:HM05929)

## DEACON, MAX

**Max Deacon**, 107 Westgate, Chichester, **Sussex (West)**, PO19 3HB, ENG.
(T) 01243 773292
Speciality: Homeopathy.
● **Administrator** Mrs M Stenning
M (Ref:HM05930)

## DEACON, MAX (DR)

**Dr Max Deacon**, 63 Rowan Rd, London, **London (Greater)**, W6 7DT, ENG.
(T) 020 7602 1006
Speciality: Homeopathy.
● **Owner** Dr M Deacon
M (Ref:HM05931)

## DEADMAN, P J

**P J Deadman**, 11 Main St, West Leake, Loughborough, **Leicestershire**, LE12 5RF, ENG.
(T) 01509 856548
Speciality: Complementary Medicines & Therapy, Clairvoyant.
● **Clairvoyant** Mr P Deadman
C Yrs. Est.: 15 (Ref:HM05932)

## DEAKIN, T

**T Deakin**, 39 Warren Way, Folkestone, **Kent**, CT19 6DT, ENG.
(T) 01303 850761
Speciality: Psychotherapy.
● **Owner** Mr T Deakin
B (Ref:HM05933)



Key: B Mind-Body Medicine C Complementary Medicine H Self Help Treatment M Medicinal Therapy O Oriental Medicine P Postural Therapy S Manipulative Structural Therapy T Touch Therapy

**DEAL CHIROPRACTIC CLINIC**

**Deal Chiropractic Clinic**, 19 Sandown Rd, Deal, **Kent**, CT14 6PG, ENG.
(T) 01304 381831
Speciality: Chiropractic.
● **Owner** Mr D Hipkiss
P S T (Ref:HM05934)

**DEAL PHYSIOTHERAPY CLINIC**

**Deal Physiotherapy Clinic**, 87 Blenheim Rd, Deal, **Kent**, CT14 7DE, ENG.
(T) 01304 373229
Speciality: Physiotherapy.
● **Owner** Mr S Roper
P S T (Ref:HM05935)

**DEAN RUSSELL & BRYDGES ROBERT**

**Dean Russell & Brydges Robert**, 1 Dorset Rd, Windsor, **Berkshire**, SL4 3BA, ENG.
(T) 01753 833244
Speciality: Chiropody, Chiropractic, Massage (Therapeutic), Pilates, Reflexology. ✔
● **Chiropractor** Ms T Mellstrom Q: DC.
● **Owner** Mr R Dean
● **Chiropractor** Mr F Caristo Q: DC.
P S T Yrs. Est.: 1 (Ref:HM05936)

**DEAN, BRIAN**

**Brian Dean**, 240 Chester Rd, Helsby, Frodsham, **Cheshire**, WA6 0PW, ENG.
(T) 01928 724173
Speciality: Hypnotherapy.
B (Ref:HM05937)

**DEAN, JAN**

**Jan Dean**, 11 Clarke Cl, Whitwick, Coalville, **Leicestershire**, LE67 5FG, ENG.
(T) 01530 839900
Speciality: Hypnosis.
B (Ref:HM05938)

**DEAN, JOSIE**

**Josie Dean**, 151 Glen Rd, Oadby, **Leicestershire**, LE2 4RH, ENG.
(T) 07720 746025
Speciality: Reflexology.
S T (Ref:HM05939)

**DEAN, KATHY**

**Kathy Dean**, 3 North View, Thorpe Willoughby, Selby, **Yorkshire (North)**, YO8 9PQ, ENG.
(T) 01757 704131
Speciality: Clairvoyants & Palmists.
● **Owner** Ms K Dean
B (Ref:HM05940)

**DEAN, L**

**L Dean**, 3 Toothill Cl, Ashton-In-Makerfield, Wigan, **Lancashire**, WN4 8BJ, ENG.
(T) 01942 271425
Speciality: Acupuncture.
● **Employee** Mr R Dean
O (Ref:HM05941)

**DEAN, MARTIN**

**Martin Dean**, 44 Sevenoaks Cres, Bramcote, Nottingham, **Nottinghamshire**, NG9 3FP, ENG.
(T) 01159 251184
(E) martin@seventhmoon.co.uk
(W) www.seventhmoon.co.uk
Speciality: Absent Healing, Acupuncture, Aura Therapy, Aversion Therapy, Bach Remedies, Complementary Therapy, Crystal Healing, Cupping, Dowsing, Faith Healing, Healer, Healing Therapy, Holistic Healing, Indian Head Massage, Massage (Therapeutic), Moxibustion, Oriental Diagnosis, Reflexology, Reiki, Seichem, Stress Therapy, Tera-Mai. ✔
● **Acupuncturist/Healer** Mr M Dean Q: MBAcC. M: BAcC.
B Yrs. Est.: 6 (Ref:HM05942)

**DEAN, S**

**S Dean**, 31 Toronto Rd, Exeter, **Devon**, EX4 6LE, ENG.
(T) 01392 218968
Speciality: Homeopathy.
● **Owner** Miss S Dean
M (Ref:HM05943)

**DEANE, MICHAEL**

**Michael Deane**, 64 Northern Rd, Portsmouth, **Hampshire**, PO6 3DP, ENG.
(T) 023 9238 0653
Speciality: Chiropodists (Podiatrists).
S (Ref:HM05944)

**DEANS, GRACE**

**Grace Deans**, 46 Chestnut Gr, Larkhall, **Lanarkshire (South)**, ML9 2AF, SCO.
(T) 01698 885987
Speciality: Physiotherapy.
● **Owner** Mrs G Deans
P S T (Ref:HM05945)

**DEAR, DIANA**

**Diana Dear**, 15 Aycliffe Cl, Bromley, **Kent**, BR1 2LX, ENG.
(T) 020 8467 8699
Speciality: Physiotherapy.
P S T (Ref:HM05946)

**DEARLING, FIONA**

**Fiona Dearling**, 69 Addison Rd, Kings Heath, Birmingham, **Midlands (West)**, B14 7EN, ENG.
(T) 01214 411160
Speciality: Reflexology.
S T (Ref:HM05947)

**DEARSLEY, GILL**

**Gill Dearsley**, 9 Beeches Avenue, Carshalton, **Surrey**, SM5 3LB, ENG.
(T) 020 8773 4508
Speciality: Aromatherapy.
M O (Ref:HM05948)

**DEAS, VALERIE JOHNSTON**

**Valerie Johnston Deas**, 28 Princes Rd, Cheltenham, **Gloucestershire**, GL50 2UR, ENG.
(T) 01242 224283
Speciality: Aromatherapy.
● **Owner** Mrs V Deas
M O (Ref:HM05949)

**DE-BANKE, MARGARET**

**Margaret De-Banke**, 17 Thorburn Rd, Northampton, **Northamptonshire**, NN3 3DA, ENG.
(T) 01604 788988
Speciality: Hypnosis.
● **Owner** Mrs M De-Banke
B (Ref:HM05950)

**DEBRA DARKE CHIROPODY CLINIC**

**Debra Darke Chiropody Clinic**, 250 Fulwell Rd, Sunderland, **Tyne and Wear**, SR6 9EU, ENG.
(T) 01915 493696 (F) 01915 493696
Speciality: Chiropodists (Podiatrists).
● **Owner** Mrs D Darke
S (Ref:HM05951)

**DECHOW, DELAINE**

**Delaine Dechow**, 41 Church Rd, Poole, **Dorset**, BH14 0NN, ENG.
(T) 01202 749514
Speciality: Physiotherapy.
P S T (Ref:HM05952)

**DECKER ASSOCIATES**

**Decker Associates**, 2 Montague Rd, Berkhamsted, **Hertfordshire**, HP4 3DS, ENG.
(T) 01442 876997 (F) 01442 876997
Speciality: Psychology.
● **Partner** Ms A Decker
B (Ref:HM05953)

**DECLERCQ, LAURENCE**

**Laurence Declercq**, 15 Bridewell St, Devizes, **Wiltshire**, SN10 1NQ, ENG.
(T) 01380 728453
Speciality: Osteopathy.
P S T (Ref:HM05954)

**DEDMAN, PAUL**

**Paul Dedman**, 2 Clifton Pk, Bristol, BS8 3BS, ENG.
(T) 01179 737371 (F) 01179 730887
Speciality: Psychiatry.
● **Senior Partner** Dr M Sternberg
B (Ref:HM05955)

**DEEKS, STUART**

**Stuart Deeks**, 30 Norton Trce, Newhaven, **Sussex (East)**, BN9 0BT, ENG.
(T) 01273 513107
Speciality: Homeopathy. ✔
● **Owner/Homeopath** Mr S Deeks Q: LCH.
C Yrs. Est.: 11 (Ref:HM05956)

**DEEP RELAXING MASSAGE**

**Deep Relaxing Massage**, Flat 4, 92 Madeley Rd, London, **London (Greater)**, W5 2LX, ENG.
(T) 020 8248 6056
Speciality: Complementary Medicines & Therapy.
● **Owner** Mrs J Cox
C M (Ref:HM05957)

**DEERING, C**

**C Deering**, 18 Cold Harbour Lane, Bushey, Watford, **Hertfordshire**, WD2 3NS, ENG.
(T) 020 8950 5151
Speciality: Psychotherapy.
B (Ref:HM05958)

**DEERING, CHRISTINE**

**BCP Registered Psychotherapist**, 92 Kentsford Rd, Grange-over-Sands, **Cumbria**, LA11 7BB, ENG.
(T) 01539 535035 (F) 01539 535035
Speciality: Psychotherapy. ✔
● **Psychotherapist** Ms C Deering Q: BSc. M: BCP.
C Yrs. Est.: 12 (Ref:HM05959)

**DEEVIEW AROMATHERAPY**

**Deeview Aromatherapy**, 35 Deeview Rd South, Cults, Aberdeen, **Aberdeenshire**, AB15 9NA, SCO.
(T) 01224 868553
Speciality: Aromatherapy, Massage (Therapeutic), Music Therapy. ✔
● **Aromatherapist** Mrs A Low Q: MRCA, RGN. M: Int.Aest.
T Yrs. Est.: 12 (Ref:HM05960)

**DEGANWY OSTEOPATHIC CLINIC**

**Deganwy Osteopathic Clinic**, Station Rd, Deganwy, **Conwy**, LL31 9EX, WAL.
(T) 01492 573500
Speciality: Osteopathy.
● **Owner** Miss T Harcourt
P S T (Ref:HM05961)

**DEJODE, SONIA**

**Sonia Dejode**, South Lodge Manor Farm, Manor Rd, Shurlock Row, Reading, **Berkshire**, RG10 0PX, ENG.
(T) 01189 343771
Speciality: Alexander Technique, Counselling, Postural Integration. ✔
● **Owner** Mrs S Dejode Q: BACP, MSTAT. M: STAT.
P Yrs. Est.: 6 (Ref:HM05962)

**DEL MAR, ANTONIA**

**Antonia Del Mar**, Appalachian Spring, Coplands Corner, Dartington, Totnes, **Devon**, TQ9 6DJ, ENG.
(T) 01803 862484
(E) tonidartington@hotmail.com
Speciality: Alexander Technique. ✔
● **Teacher** Mr A Del Mar Q: MSTAT. M: STAT.
C Yrs. Est.: 24 (Ref:HM05963)

**DELAP & SIMPSON**

**Dan Delap & Peter Simpson**, 80 Royal Hill, London, **London (Greater)**, SE10 8RT, ENG.
(T) 020 8692 2831
Speciality: Osteopathy.
P S T (Ref:HM05964)

**DELFOSSE, PATRICIA**

**Ms Patricia Delfosse**, 133 Pomona St, Sheffield, **Yorkshire (South)**, S11 8JN, ENG.
(T) 01142 670540 (F) 01142 670540
Speciality: Acupuncture.
● **Owner** Ms P Delfosse
O (Ref:HM05965)

**DELICATE ESSENCE CLINIC**

**Delicate Essence Clinic (The)**, 22 Grays Hill, Bangor, **County Down**, BT20 3BB, NIR.
(T) 028 9147 3123
Speciality: Aromatherapy.
M O (Ref:HM05966)

**DELOOZE, ANNE**

**Anne Delooze**, Beauty & Holistic Clinic, Lymm, **Cheshire**, WA13 0JX, ENG.
(T) 01925 757493
Speciality: Complementary Medicines & Therapy.



Key continued: Yrs.Est: Years Established Q: Qualifications M: Professional Membership ✔ Indemnity Insurance Accept Credit Cards

● **Owner** Miss A Delooze
C M (Ref:HM05967)

### DELROY, SANDRA (DR)

**Dr Sandra Delroy**, 52 Howcroft Cres, Finchley, London, **London (Greater)**, N3 1PB, ENG.
(T) 020 8346 4010
(E) psychologist@drsandradelroy.com
(W) www.drsandradelroy.com
Speciality: Counselling, Family Therapy, Group Therapy, Psychotherapy, Couples Therapy, Individual Therapy, One off Psychological Consultations.
● **Psychologist/Consultant**
Dr S Delroy Q: BS, MA. M: BPS.
B Yrs. Est.: 17 (Ref:HM05968)

### DELTA MEDI CLINIC

**Delta Medi Clinic**, The Woodstock Club, Broadoak Rd, Sittingbourne, **Kent**, ME9 8AQ, ENG.
(T) 01795 420705 (F) 01795 420705
(E) sue@delta65.freeserve.co.uk
Speciality: Acupuncture, Aromatherapy, Electrotherapy, Manipulation, Massage (Therapeutic), Traction and Personal Training.
● **Owner** Ms S Daisy M: CSP, OCPPP.
M (Ref:HM05969)

### DELTER REFLEXOLOGY

**Delter Reflexology**, 61 Wishings Rd, Brixham, **Devon**, TQ5 9PB, ENG.
(T) 01803 859304
Speciality: Reflexology.
● **Owner** Mr T Salisbury
S T (Ref:HM05970)

### DELVE, PHILIP

**Philip Delve**, Tudor House, 49 Wolborough St, Newton Abbot, **Devon**, TQ12 1JQ, ENG.
(T) 01626 335567
Speciality: Osteopathy.
P S T (Ref:HM05971)

### DEMETER, GLENNA

**Glenna Demeter**, The Myrtles, 19 Knoll Rd, Bexley, **Kent**, DA5 1AY, ENG.
(T) 01322 559171 (F) 01322 526310
Speciality: Clairvoyants & Palmists.
● **Owner** Mrs G Demeter
B (Ref:HM05972)

### DEMETRIUS, B

**B Demetrius**, Flat 3, 31 West St, Buckingham, **Buckinghamshire**, MK18 1HE, ENG.
(T) 07970 920240
Speciality: Psychotherapy.
● **Owner** Mr B Demetrius
B (Ref:HM05973)

### DEMOOR, MANON

**Manon DeMoor**, 151 Prestbury Rd, Macclesfield, **Cheshire**, SK10 3DF, ENG.
(T) 01625 501784 (F) 01625 433854
Speciality: Aromatherapy.
● **Owner** Mrs M Demoor
M O (Ref:HM05974)

### DENEHOLM THERAPY

**Deneholm Therapy**, 26 Kirkintilloch Rd, Kirkintilloch, Glasgow, **Glasgow (City of)**, G66 4RL, SCO.
(T) 01417 777233
Speciality: Hypnosis.
● **Owner** Mrs J Tumilty
B (Ref:HM05975)

### DENENY, MARY

**Mary Deneny**, 5 The Elms Froster Street, **County Galway**, IRE.
(T) 08726 24023
Speciality: Psychotherapy.
B (Ref:HM05976)

### DENGATE, L J

**L J Dengate**, 42 Bengal Rd, Bournemouth, **Dorset**, BH9 2NF, ENG.
(T) 01202 517814
Speciality: Complementary Medicines & Therapy.
● **Owner** Mrs A Dengate
C M (Ref:HM05977)

### DENGLER, REGINA

**Regina Dengler**, 16 Luther Cl, Nottingham, **Nottinghamshire**, NG3 3PD, ENG.
(T) 01159 584113
Speciality: Aromatherapy.
M O (Ref:HM05978)

### DENHAM, A M

**A M Denham**, 66 Victoria Gardens, Horsforth, Leeds, **Yorkshire (West)**, LS18 4PH, ENG.
(T) 01132 583194
Speciality: Herbal Medicine.
● **Manager** Mr A Denham
M (Ref:HM05979)

### DENIM, M F

**M F Denim**, 166 Leavesden Rd, Watford, **Hertfordshire**, WD2 5EG, ENG.
(T) 01923 233600
Speciality: Chiropodists (Podiatrists).
S (Ref:HM05980)

### DENIM, M F

**M F Denim**, 405C Neasden Lane North, London, **London (Greater)**, NW10 0BD, ENG.
(T) 07973 175403
Speciality: Chiropodists (Podiatrists).
● **Owner** Mr M Denim
S (Ref:HM05981)

### DENIM, M F

**M F Denim**, 738A Holloway Rd, London, **London (Greater)**, N19 3JF, ENG.
(T) 020 8205 0179
Speciality: Chiropodists (Podiatrists).
S (Ref:HM05982)

### DENISE PALMIST & INT CLAIR

**Denise Palmist & International Clairvoyant**, 175B Lord St, Walsall, **Midlands (West)**, WS1 4DU, ENG.
(T) 01922 612269 (F) 01922 612269
Speciality: Clairvoyants & Palmists.
● **Owner** Miss D Bakewell
B (Ref:HM05983)

### DENLEY, KAREN L

**Karen L Denley**, 32 Lake Hill, Sandown, **Isle of Wight**, PO36 9HE, ENG.
(T) 01983 405615
Speciality: Chiropodists (Podiatrists).
● **Owner** Mrs K Denley
S (Ref:HM05984)

### DENNEY, ANDREA

**Andrea Denney**, Anden Farm, Grimeford Lane, Anderton, Chorley, **Lancashire**, PR6 9HL, ENG.
(T) 01257 482264
Speciality: Herbal Medicine.
M (Ref:HM05985)

### DENNING, JOHN V

**John V Denning**, Cardigan Cottage, Pell Green, Wadhurst, **Sussex (East)**, TN5 6EE, ENG.
(T) 01892 783429
Speciality: Acupuncture.
O (Ref:HM05986)

### DENNING, MICHAEL

**Michael Denning**, 29 Princess St, Crewe, **Cheshire**, CW1 3TU, ENG.
(T) 01270 213857
Speciality: Psychotherapy.
● **Owner** Mr M Denning
B (Ref:HM05987)

### DENNIS & ASSOCIATES

**Dr Owen Dennis & Ass**, 126 Terenure Rd, Nth 6W, IRE.
(T) 01490 5287
Speciality: Chiropractors.
P S T (Ref:HM05988)

### DENNIS & ASSOCIATES

**Dr Owen Dennis & Assoc**, Trafalgar Rd, Greystones, **County Wicklow**, IRE.
(T) 01287 5944
Speciality: Chiropractors.
P S T (Ref:HM05989)

### DENNIS MICHAEL PRACTICE

**Dennis G Michael**, 6 Pavilion Mews, Finchley, London, **London (Greater)**, N3 3QD, ENG.
(T) 020 8343 3423 (F) 020 8343 4456
Speciality: Acupuncture, Biomagnetic Therapy, Complementary Therapy, Cranial Osteopathy, Dietician, Manipulation, Massage (Therapeutic), Moxibustion, Naturopathy, Nutritional Therapy, Osteopathy, Vitamin Therapy.
● **Owner** Mr D Michael Q: BSc, Dip.Ac, DO, ND. M: GCRN, GOsC.
S Yrs. Est.: 20 (Ref:HM05990)

### DENNIS, CLIVE (DR)

**Dr Clive Dennis**, New Rd, Naas Co, **County Kildare**, IRE.
(T) 04587 6355
Speciality: Chiropractors.
P S T (Ref:HM05991)

### DENNIS, CLIVE (DR)

**Dr Clive Dennis**, 58 Main St, , Swords, Co, Dublin, **County Dublin**, IRE.
(T) 01840 3305
Speciality: Chiropractors.
P S T (Ref:HM05992)

### DENNIS, CLIVE (DR)

**Dr Clive Dennis**, 56 Main St, Swords, **County Dublin**, IRE.
(T) 01840 3305
Speciality: Chiropractors.
P S T (Ref:HM05993)

### DENNIS, CLIVE (DR)

**Dr Clive Dennis**, Sallins Rd, Naas, **County Kildare**, IRE.
(T) 04587 6355
Speciality: Chiropractors.
P S T (Ref:HM05994)

### DENNIS, L

**L Dennis**, 3 Leicester Cres, Atherstone, **Warwickshire**, CV9 3BH, ENG.
(T) 01827 717781
Speciality: Chiropodists (Podiatrists).
S (Ref:HM05995)

### DENNISON, IAN

**Ian Dennison**, 38 Tankerville Rd, London, **London (Greater)**, SW16 5LP, ENG.
(T) 020 8764 4958
Speciality: Remedial Massage.
● **Remedial Massage** Mr I Dennison Q: LCSP. M: LCSP.
C Yrs. Est.: 6 (Ref:HM05996)

### DENNISONS CONSULTANCY

**Dennisons Consultancy**, The Oast House, Wyck Lane, East Worldham, Alton, **Hampshire**, GU34 3AW, ENG.
(T) 01420 544290
Speciality: Psychology.
B (Ref:HM05997)

### DENTON, A

**A Denton**, Holly Ridge, Barlow Rd, Barlow, Blaydon-on-Tyne, **Tyne and Wear**, NE21 6JT, ENG.
(T) 01207 542301
Speciality: Kinesiology, Reflexology.
● **Reflexologist** Mrs A Denton M: BSR.
C Yrs. Est.: 8 (Ref:HM05998)

### DENTON, B

**B Denton**, 2 Seacroft Rd, Broadstairs, **Kent**, CT10 1TL, ENG.
(T) 01843 861877
Speciality: Osteopathy.
● **Owner** Mr B Denton
P S T (Ref:HM05999)

### DENTON, D

**D Denton**, Wayside Cottage, Great Hatfield, Hull, **Humberside (North)**, HU11 4UR, ENG.
(T) 01964 534567 (F) 01964 535568
Speciality: Physiotherapy.
● **Senior Partner** Mrs D Denton
P S T (Ref:HM06000)

### DENTON, KATHRYN

**Kathryn Denton**, Barnsley Medical Consulting Rooms, 13 Churchfield Court, Barnsley, **Yorkshire (South)**, S70 2BP, ENG.
(T) 01226 390032
Speciality: Physiotherapy.
● **Owner** Ms K Denton
P S T (Ref:HM06001)



Key: B Mind-Body Medicine C Complementary Medicine H Self Help Treatment M Medicinal Therapy O Oriental Medicine P Postural Therapy S Manipulative Structural Therapy T Touch Therapy

**DEOL, SUE**
**Sue Deol**, The Sherborne Clinic, 2 Sir Thomas Whites Rd, Coventry, **Midlands (West)**, CV5 8DQ, ENG.
(T) 024 7667 0147
Speciality: Complementary Medicines & Therapy.
M (Ref:HM06002)

**DEORA, MARC**
**Marc Deora**, The Barn, Bury St Edmunds Golf Club, Tut Hill, Fornham All Saints, Bury St. Edmunds, **Suffolk**, IP28 6LG, ENG.
(T) 01284 760020
Speciality: Complementary Medicines & Therapy.
C M (Ref:HM06003)

**DEPARTMENT OF COMP MEDICINE**
**Department Of Complementary Medicine**, University Of Exeter/S P M H S, 25 Victoria Pk Rd, Exeter, **Devon**, EX2 4NT, ENG.
(T) 01392 424989 (F) 01392 424989
Speciality: Complementary Medicines & Therapy.
● **Director** Mr E Ernst
C M (Ref:HM06004)

**DEPARTMENT OF FOOT HEALTH**
**Department Of Foot Health**, Princess Royal Health Centre, Greenhead Rd, Huddersfield, **Yorkshire (West)**, HD1 4EW, ENG.
(T) 01484 482308
Speciality: Chiropodists (Podiatrists).
● **Manager** Ms H Chauhan
S (Ref:HM06005)

**DEPARTMENT OF PSYCHOTHERAPY**
**Department Of Psychotherapy**, 1 St. Annes Rd, Lincoln, **Lincolnshire**, LN2 5RA, ENG.
(T) 01522 512000 (F) 01522 532445
Speciality: Psychotherapy.
● **Principal** Dr G Fisk
B (Ref:HM06006)

**DEPART-PSYCHOLOGICAL THERAPY**
**Department Of Psychological Therapy**, Herbert Hospital, Alumhurst Rd, Bournemouth, **Dorset**, BH4 8EP, ENG.
(T) 01202 766422 (F) 01202 757192
Speciality: Psychology.
B (Ref:HM06007)

**DEPENDABILITY**
**Dependability**, Research House, Fraser Rd, Greenford, **London (Greater)**, UB6 7AQ, ENG.
(T) 020 8998 3707
Speciality: Complementary Medicines & Therapy, Occupational Therapy.
M (Ref:HM06008)

**DEPILLE**
**Depille**, 42 Salisbury Rd, Reading, **Berkshire**, RG30 1BJ, ENG.
(T) 01189 589241
Speciality: Electrolysis.
T (Ref:HM06009)

**DEPTFORD PSYCHOTHERAPY CENTRE**
**Deptford Psychotherapy Centre Ltd**, 311a New Cross Rd, London, **London (Greater)**, SE14 6AS, ENG.
(T) 020 8691 9771
Speciality: Psychotherapy.
B (Ref:HM06010)

**DERBY ACUPUNCTURE CENTRE**
**Derby Acupuncture Centre**, 2nd Floor, 10 Iron Gate, Derby, **Derbyshire**, DE1 3FJ, ENG.
(T) 01332 344117
Speciality: Acupuncture.
● **Owner** Ms A Pottinger
O (Ref:HM06011)

**DERBY GESTALT CENTRE**
**Derby Gestalt Centre (The)**, 10 Hampden Gr, Beeston, Nottingham, **Nottinghamshire**, NG9 1FG, ENG.
(T) 01159 259083
Speciality: Psychotherapy.
B (Ref:HM06012)

**DERBY HOMEOPATHIC PRACTICE**
**Derby Homeopathic Practice (The)**, 38 Oregon Way, Chaddesden, Derby, **Derbyshire**, DE21 6UL, ENG.
(T) 01332 662004
Speciality: Homeopathy.
● **Owner** Mr D McAllister
M (Ref:HM06013)

**DERBYSHIRE SPORTS INJURIES**
**Derbyshire Sports Injuries Clinic (The)**, Riverside Rd, Pride Park, Derby, **Derbyshire**, DE24 8HY, ENG.
(T) 01332 369713
Speciality: Acupuncture, Physiotherapy. ✔
● **Physiotherapist** Ms L Wood Q: MCSP, SRP. M: CSP.
● **Physiotherapist** Ms L Henry Q: MCSP, SRP. M: CSP.
● **Physiotherapist** Ms K Buckley Q: MCSP, SRP.
● **Practice Manager** Mr D Lendon
● **Partner/Physiotherapist** Ms A Brentnall Q: MCSP, SRP. M: CSP.
● **Partner/Physiotherapist** Ms P Lendon Q: MCSP, SRP. M: CSP.
S Yrs. Est.: 15 (Ref:HM06014)

**DERBYSHIRE, GILL**
**Gill Derbyshire**, 2 Dartmoor Drive, Huntingdon, **Cambridgeshire**, PE18 8XT, ENG.
(T) 01480 412631 (F) 01480 412140
Speciality: Reflexology.
● **Owner** Mrs G Derbyshire
S T (Ref:HM06015)

**DEREK MOSS THERAPEUTIC MASSAGE**
**Derek Moss Therapeutic Massage**, 73B Egmont Rd, Sutton, **Surrey**, SM2 5JS, ENG.
(T) 020 8643 4092
Speciality: Complementary Medicines & Therapy.
C M (Ref:HM06016)

**DERMALUX**
**Dermalux Ltd**, 99 Windmill St, Gravesend, **Kent**, DA12 1LE, ENG.
(T) 01474 357479
Speciality: Complementary Medicines & Therapy.
● **Partner** Mr B Blizard
M (Ref:HM06017)

**DERRYN THERAPEUTIC**
**Derryn Therapeutic**, 472 Edenfield Rd, Rochdale, **Lancashire**, OL12 7QL, ENG.
(T) 01706 631909
Speciality: Physiotherapy.
P S T (Ref:HM06018)

**DERWEN ELECTROLYSIS CLINIC**
**Derwen Electrolysis Clinic**, 18 Dunraven Pl, Bridgend, CF31 1JD, WAL.
(T) 01656 654474
Speciality: Electrolysis.
T (Ref:HM06019)

**DERWENT CENTRE**
**Derwent Centre**, 20A Derwent St, Sunderland, **Tyne and Wear**, SR1 3NU, ENG.
(T) 01915 101322
Speciality: Acupuncture, Aromatherapy, Aura Therapy, Counselling, Crystal Healing, Healing Therapy, Indian Head Massage, Spiritual Healing, Chakra Balancing, Chakra Cleansing, Aura Healing and Cleansing, Aura Health Readings and Past Life Readings.
● **Healer/Clairvoyant** Mr K Thompson
T Yrs. Est.: 10 (Ref:HM06020)

**DESIDERIO, SONIA**
**Sonia Desiderio**, 248 Ashmore Rd, London, **London (Greater)**, W9 3DD, ENG.
(T) 020 8969 8966
Speciality: Complementary Medicines & Therapy.
C M (Ref:HM06021)

**DESIGNING CHANGE**
**Designing Change**, 20 Duchy Avenue, Bradford, **Yorkshire (West)**, BD9 5NE, ENG.
(T) 01274 824320
Speciality: Counselling, Hypnosis, Hypnotherapy, Neuro-Linguistic Program, Psychotherapy. ✔
● **Owner/NLP Therapist** Mr I Bracegirdle Q: BA, Cert.Ed, M.Hyp, NLP. M: ANLP.
C Yrs. Est.: 4 (Ref:HM06022)

**DE-SILVA & WHITTINGHAM**
**J De-Silva & B Whittingham**, Plymouth Chiropractic Clinic, 152 Mannamead Rd, Plymouth, **Devon**, PL3 5QL, ENG.
(T) 01752 770131 (F) 01752 255148
Speciality: Chiropractic.
● **Partner** Mr B Whittingham
P S T (Ref:HM06023)

**DE-STRESS**
**De-Stress**, 2 Abbotsford Rd, Clydebank, **Argyll and Bute**, G81 1PA, SCO.
(T) 01419 514321
Speciality: Complementary Medicines & Therapy.
C M (Ref:HM06024)

**DEVA OSTEOPATHIC CLINIC**
**Deva Osteopathic Clinic**, 31 Seller St, Chester, **Cheshire**, CH1 3NA, ENG.
(T) 01244 403449 (F) 01244 394214
Speciality: Osteopathy.
● **Owner** Mrs F Franco
P S T (Ref:HM06025)

**DEVAUDEN, D**
**Mrs D Devauden**, Victoria Dairies, 2 Wonastow Rd, Monmouth, **Monmouthshire**, NP25 5AH, WAL.
(T) 01600 713111
Speciality: Chiropodists (Podiatrists).
● **Owner** Mrs D Devauden
S (Ref:HM06026)

**DEVELOPING**
**Developing Co (The)**, 9 Southwood Lawn Rd, London, **London (Greater)**, N6 5SD, ENG.
(T) 020 8348 1300
Speciality: Psychotherapy.
B (Ref:HM06027)

**DEVELOPMENTAL HEALTH CONSULT**
**Developmental Health Consultancy**, 110 Bryn Rd, Brynmill, Swansea, SA2 0AT, WAL.
(T) 01558 823147
Speciality: Relaxation Technique.
● **Owner** Miss K Billings
H T (Ref:HM06028)

**DEVENISH MUTTON, SUSAN**
**Susan Devenish Mutton**, 2 Raphael Cl, Plymouth, **Devon**, PL9 8HB, ENG.
(T) 01752 404716
Speciality: Complementary Medicines & Therapy, Trichology.
M (Ref:HM06029)

**DEVEREAUX M A CHIROPODIST**
**Devereaux M A Chiropodist**, 376A Walsall Rd, Great Wyrley, Walsall, **Midlands (West)**, WS6 6DN, ENG.
(T) 01922 419947
Speciality: Chiropodists (Podiatrists).
S (Ref:HM06030)

**DEVERILL, PAMELA**
**Pamela Deverill**, 3 Dilly Lane, Barton On Sea, New Milton, **Hampshire**, BH25 7DQ, ENG.
(T) 01425 614661
Speciality: Chiropodists (Podiatrists).
● **Owner** Ms P Deverill
S (Ref:HM06031)

**DEVERY, D**
**D Devery**, 1 Queensway, Wotton-under-Edge, **Gloucestershire**, GL12 7HA, ENG.
(T) 01453 843535
Speciality: Osteopathy.
P S T (Ref:HM06032)

**DEVEY, BRENDA**
**Brenda Devey**, Maghull Physiotherapy Clinic, 160 Liverpool Rd North, Liverpool, **Merseyside**, L31 2HP, ENG.
(T) 01515 318941
Speciality: Physiotherapy.
P S T (Ref:HM06033)

**DEVI, JOSEPHA**
**Josepha Devi**, 22 Prentis Rd, London, **London (Greater)**, SW16 6QD, ENG.
(T) 020 8696 7228


Key continued: Yrs.Est: Years Established Q: Qualifications M: Professional Membership ✔ Indemnity Insurance Accept Credit Cards

Speciality: Reflexology.
S T (Ref:HM06034)

## DEVINE, C

**C Devine**, 47 Church Lees, Great Linford, Milton Keynes, **Buckinghamshire**, MK14 5ED, ENG.
(T) 01908 676455
Speciality: Clairvoyants & Palmists.
● **Owner** Mrs C Devine
B (Ref:HM06035)

## DEVINE, MARY

**Mary Devine**, Upstairs Downstairs Hair Salon, 230 St. Albans Rd, Watford, **Hertfordshire**, WD2 4AU, ENG.
(T) 01923 251625
Speciality: Chiropody. ✓
● **Chiropodist** Ms M Devine Q: Inst.CH.P. M: Inst.CH.P.
M Yrs. Est.: 3 (Ref:HM06036)

## DEVIZES ACUPUNCTURE PRACTICE

**Devizes Acupuncture Practice (The)**, 9a Monday Market St, Devizes, **Wiltshire**, SN10 1DN, ENG.
(T) 01380 730042
Speciality: Acupuncture.
● **Partner** Ms S Bishop
O (Ref:HM06037)

## DEVLIN, JULIE

**Julie Devlin**, 24A Chilwell Rd, Beeston, Nottingham, **Nottinghamshire**, NG9 1EJ, ENG.
(T) 01159 258345
Speciality: Acupuncture.
● **Owner** Mrs J Devlin
O (Ref:HM06038)

## DEVLIN, JULIE

**Julie Devlin**, 83 Nottingham Rd, Keyworth, Nottingham, **Nottinghamshire**, NG12 5GS, ENG.
(T) 01159 893572
Speciality: Acupuncture.
O (Ref:HM06039)

## DEVLIN, MARGARET

**Margaret Devlin**, Rodmill Clinic, 9 Fennells Cl, Eastbourne, **Sussex (East)**, BN21 2RJ, ENG.
(T) 01323 731213
Speciality: Chiropodists (Podiatrists).
● **Owner** Miss M Devlin
S (Ref:HM06040)

## DEVON PARADE CLINIC

**Devon Parade Clinic And Northampton Sports Injury Clinic (The)**, 322 Wellingborough Rd, Northampton, **Northamptonshire**, NN1 4EP, ENG.
(T) 01604 622999 (F) 01604 604249
(E) office@paradeclinic.co.uk
Speciality: Acupressure, Acupuncture, Aromatherapy, Biomechanics, Chiropractic, Cognitive Therapy, Complementary Therapy, Counselling, Cranial Osteopathy, Cryo Surgery, Electrotherapy, Gait Analysis, Homeopathy, Humanistic Psychology, Indian Head Massage, Manipulation, Massage (Therapeutic), Nail Surgery, Osteopathy, Physiotherapy, Postural Integration, Psychotherapy, Reflexology, Sports Massage, Stress Therapy, X-Ray, Ying & Yang, Clinical and Sports Psychology. Sports Injuries, Asian Bridal Service and Henna Body Art. ✓
● **Chiropodist (Podiatrist)** Mr A Costain Q: DPodM, M.S.C.P, S.R.Ch. M: S.C.P.
● **Osteopath** Mr C Becquhereah Q: BSc (Hons).
● **Physiotherapist** Mr G Singh Q: BSc (Hons), MCSP, SRP.
● **Acupuncturist** Miss H Patel Q: BA (Hons), MBAcC.
P Yrs. Est.: 25 (Ref:HM06041)

## DEVON SCHOOL OF SHIATSU

**Devon School Of Shiatsu (The)**, The Coach House, Buvhyette Farm, Littlehempston, Totnes, **Devon**, TQ9 6ND, ENG.
(T) 01803 762593
Speciality: Complementary Medicines & Therapy.
● **Director** Mr O Cowmeadow
C M (Ref:HM06042)

## DEVONSHIRE HEALTH & RAQUET

**Devonshire Health And Raquet Club**, Plymbridge Lane, Plymouth, **Devon**, PL6, ENG.
(T) 01752 796333
Speciality: Physiotherapy. ✓
● **Physiotherapist** Mr N Baker Q: BSc, MCSP, MSc, SRP. M: CSP.
S (Ref:HM06043)

## DEVONSHIRE SURGERY

**Vinewood Healthcare**, Devonshire Surgery, 75 Sunnyside Rd, Weston-Super-Mare, **Somerset**, BS23 3QB, ENG.
(T) 01934 618480
Speciality: Chiropractic. ✓
● **Owner/Chiropractor** Dr J Vine Q: DC. M: BCA.
● **Chiropractor** Dr C Francis Q: DC. M: BCA.
P Yrs. Est.: 25 (Ref:HM06044)

## DEWANE, JENNY

**Jenny Dewane**, 6 Raymond Court, Raymond Rd, London, **London (Greater)**, SW19 4AR, ENG.
(T) 020 8946 4659
Speciality: Hypnosis.
B (Ref:HM06045)

## DEWBERRY, MAY

**May Dewberry MAR**, Crogen, Lodgevale Park, Chirk, **Denbighshire**, LL15 5BJ, WAL.
(T) 01691 777509
Speciality: Reflexology.
S T (Ref:HM06046)

## DEWDNEY, JOSEPHINE

**Josephine Dewdney**, 6 Windermere Cl, Rugby, **Warwickshire**, CV21 1NA, ENG.
(T) 01788 332800
Speciality: Reflexology.
S T (Ref:HM06047)

## DEWERT, ERWIN

**Erwin DeWert**, 6 The Cl, Lathbury, Newport Pagnell, **Buckinghamshire**, MK16 8JZ, ENG.
(T) 01908 611314
Speciality: Chiropodists (Podiatrists).
● **Owner** Mr E Dewert
S (Ref:HM06048)

## DEWHURST, PATRICA A

**Patrica A Dewhurst**, 4 Birkdale Pl, Little Ees Lane, Sale, **Cheshire**, M33 5BR, ENG.
(T) 01619 620433
Speciality: Allergy Testing, Herbal Medicine. ✓
● **Owner/Allergy Tester/Medical Herbalist** Miss P Dewhurst Q: BSc (Hons), Dip.Herb.Med, PGCE, RGN. M: UKCC.
M Yrs. Est.: 4 (Ref:HM06049)

## DEXTER, NICOLA

**Nicola Dexter**, 10 Mount Gr, Edgware, **London (Greater)**, HA8 9SX, ENG.
(T) 020 8201 0406
Speciality: Hypnosis.
B (Ref:HM06050)

## DEZELU, B J M

**B J M Dezelu**, 36 Southerndown Avenue, Mayals, Swansea, SA3 5EL, WAL.
(T) 01792 405099
Speciality: Chiropodists (Podiatrists).
● **Owner** Mr B Dezelu
S (Ref:HM06051)

## DHANA, P N

**P N Dhana**, 17A Western Rd, Hagley, Stourbridge, **Midlands (West)**, DY9 0LA, ENG.
(T) 01562 886777 (F) 01562 886777
Speciality: Chiropodists (Podiatrists).
● **Owner** Mrs P Dhana
S (Ref:HM06052)

## DHANA, P N

**P N Dhana**, 45 Hagley Rd, Stourbridge, **Midlands (West)**, DY8 1QR, ENG.
(T) 01384 394708
Speciality: Biomechanics, Chiropody, Podiatry. ✓
● **Chiropodist (Podiatrist)** Mrs P Dhana Q: DPodM, S.R.Ch. M: S.C.P.
M Yrs. Est.: 31 (Ref:HM06053)

## DHANABALAN, K

**K Dhanabalan**, 9 Elgar Cl, Benfleet, **Essex**, SS7 4BZ, ENG.
(T) 01268 751881
Speciality: Acupuncture.
● **Owner** Mr K Dhanabalan
O (Ref:HM06054)

## DHANJI, FARRA

**Farra Dhanji**, Bodywise, 119 Roman Rd, London, **London (Greater)**, E2 0QN, ENG.
(T) 020 8981 6938
Speciality: Osteopathy.
P S T (Ref:HM06055)

## DHILLON, K

**K Dhillon**, 20 St Thomas Sq, Newport, **Isle of Wight**, PO30 1SG, ENG.
(T) 01983 523001
Speciality: Chiropodists (Podiatrists).
S (Ref:HM06056)

## DIACK, A

**A Diack**, Physiotherapy Department, Garrison Clinic, Millport, **Ayrshire (North)**, KA28 0HB, SCO.
(T) 01475 530448
Speciality: Physiotherapy.
● **Physiotherapist** A Diack
P S T (Ref:HM06057)

## DIAL-A-MEDIUM

**Dial-A-Medium Ltd**, 353 Smithdown Rd, Liverpool, **Merseyside**, L15 3JJ, ENG.
(T) 01517 350888 (F) 01517 350777
Speciality: Clairvoyants & Palmists.
● **Manager** Mrs C Eyton
B (Ref:HM06058)

## DIAMOND HOLISTIC CENTRE

**Diamond Holistic Centre**, 27 Craven Rd, Newbury, **Berkshire**, RG14 5NG, ENG.
(T) 01635 31679
Speciality: Complementary Medicines & Therapy.
M (Ref:HM06059)

## DIANA'S JOY

**Diana's Joy**, 1 Mercers Row, Saffron Walden, **Essex**, CB10 1HD, ENG.
(T) 01799 520302 (F) 01799 520302
Speciality: Complementary Medicines & Therapy.
● **Owner** Mrs D Fisher
C M (Ref:HM06060)

## DIANETICS INFORMATION CENTRE

**Dianetics Information Centre (The)**, 68 Tottenham Court Rd, London, **London (Greater)**, W1P 0BB, ENG.
(T) 020 7580 3601
Speciality: Complementary Medicines & Therapy.
C M (Ref:HM06061)

## DIARMUID, LAVELLE

**Lavelle Diarmuid BA Dip**, Canavan Hse, Nuns Island, Galway, **County Galway**, IRE.
(T) 09156 9770
Speciality: Complementary Medicines & Therapy.
M (Ref:HM06062)

## DIAS, E

**E Dias**, 53 Wolveleigh Trce, Newcastle Upon Tyne, **Tyne and Wear**, NE3 1UP, ENG.
(T) 01912 844156
Speciality: Physiotherapy.
P S T (Ref:HM06063)

## DIATHERMY CLINIC

**Diathermy (Skin) Clinic**, 22 Queens Drive, Ossett, **Yorkshire (West)**, WF5 0ND, ENG.
(T) 01924 273819 (F) 01924 280022
Speciality: Electrolysis. ✓
● **Owner/Electrologist/Diathermist** Mrs J Turner Q: BABTAC, CIBTAC.
C Yrs. Est.: 18 (Ref:HM06064)

## DICE, JOHN

**John Dice**, 9 Hall Cl, Godalming, **Surrey**, GU7 3PW, ENG.
(T) 01483 424933
Speciality: Acupuncture.



Key: B Mind-Body Medicine C Complementary Medicine H Self Help Treatment M Medicinal Therapy O Oriental Medicine P Postural Therapy S Manipulative Structural Therapy T Touch Therapy

O (Ref:HM06065)

**DICK, K**

**K Dick**, 3 Castle Walk, Lower St, Stansted, **Essex**, CM24 8LY, ENG.
(T) 01279 647337
Speciality: Chiropodists (Podiatrists).
● **Owner** Mrs K Dick
S (Ref:HM06066)

**DICKASON, J T**

**J T Dickason**, 80 Panfield Lane, Braintree, **Essex**, CM7 2TL, ENG.
(T) 01376 322528
Speciality: Osteopathy. ✓
● **Osteopath** Mr Dickason Q: BA, DO. M: GOsC.
S Yrs. Est.: 20 (Ref:HM06067)

**DICKENSON, A G**

**A G Dickenson**, Warwick House, 4 Stanley Pl, Chester, **Cheshire**, CH1 2LU, ENG.
(T) 01244 318963
Speciality: Acupuncture.
● **Owner** A G Dickenson
O (Ref:HM06068)

**DICKENSON, R**

**R Dickenson**, 16 North Prde, Leeds, **Yorkshire (West)**, LS16 5AY, ENG.
(T) 01132 374449
Speciality: Complementary Medicines & Therapy.
C M (Ref:HM06069)

**DICKER, W**

**W Dicker**, 63 Durley Avenue, Waterlooville, **Hampshire**, PO8 8UZ, ENG.
(T) 023 9226 2811
Speciality: Chiropodists (Podiatrists).
● **Owner** Mrs W Dicker
S (Ref:HM06070)

**DICKINS CHIROPRACTIC CLINIC**

**Dickins Chiropractic Clinic**, Meadow Cl, Bridge, Canterbury, **Kent**, CT4 5AT, ENG.
(T) 01227 830287 (F) 01227 830287
Speciality: Chiropractors.
● **Owner** Dr G Dickins
P S T (Ref:HM06071)

**DICKINS, BEVERLEY**

**Beverley Dickins**, 20 Unthank Rd, Norwich, **Norfolk**, NR2 2RA, ENG.
(T) 01603 621008
Speciality: Acupuncture.
O (Ref:HM06072)

**DICKINSON, A**

**A Dickinson**, 20 Peveril Avenue, Scunthorpe, **Humberside**, DN17 1BE, ENG.
(T) 01724 848622
Speciality: Complementary Medicines & Therapy.
● **Owner** Mr A Dickinson
C M (Ref:HM06073)

**DICKINSON, ANN**

**Ann Dickinson**, The Courtyard, Cavendish Farm, Cavendish Bridge, Shardlow, Derby, **Derbyshire**, DE72 2HL, ENG.
(T) 01332 792808
Speciality: Osteopathy.
P S T (Ref:HM06074)

**DICKINSON, E H**

**E H Dickinson**, 18 The Avenue, Old Windsor, Windsor, **Berkshire**, SL4 2RS, ENG.
(T) 01753 863855
Speciality: Chiropodists (Podiatrists).
S (Ref:HM06075)

**DICKINSON, ELIZABETH A**

**Elizabeth A Dickinson**, 6 Lathom Hall Avenue, Springhead, Oldham, **Lancashire**, OL4 4RG, ENG.
(T) 01616 336708
Speciality: Chiropodists (Podiatrists).
● **Owner** Ms E Dickinson
S (Ref:HM06076)

**DICKINSON, KATE**

**Kate Dickinson**, 208 White Lane, Sheffield, **Yorkshire (South)**, S12 3GL, ENG.
(T) 01142 531633
Speciality: Chiropodists (Podiatrists).
S (Ref:HM06077)

**DICKINSON, LYNNE**

**Lynne Dickinson**, 12 Hurstbrook Cl, Glossop, **Derbyshire**, SK13 8PL, ENG.
(T) 01457 856618
Speciality: Chiropodists (Podiatrists).
● **Owner** Mrs L Dickinson
S (Ref:HM06078)

**DICKINSON, R**

**R Dickinson**, 24 Stanmore Avenue, Blackpool, **Lancashire**, FY4 3LU, ENG.
(T) 01253 696672
Speciality: Chiropodists (Podiatrists).
S (Ref:HM06079)

**DICKMAN, ANNIE**

**Annie Dickman**, 28 Forde Avenue, Bromley, **Kent**, BR1 3EX, ENG.
(T) 020 8460 4275 (F) 020 8460 6100
(E) adic333@aol.com
Speciality: Aromatherapy, Massage (Therapeutic), Reflexology, Yoga. ✓
● **Reflexologist** Mrs A Dickman Q: ITEC, MSBR. M: BSR.
T Yrs. Est.: 6 (Ref:HM06080)

**DICKMAN, KAREN**

**Karen Dickman**, Pickering Lodge, Moss Lane, Timperley, Altrincham, **Cheshire**, WA15 6LE, ENG.
(T) 01619 802947
Speciality: Reflexology.
S T (Ref:HM06081)

**DICKS, ALISON**

**Alison Dicks**, 2 Chale Cl, Gosport, **Hampshire**, PO13 0PD, ENG.
(T) 01329 317398
Speciality: Aromatherapy.
● **Owner** Ms A Dicks
M O (Ref:HM06082)

**DICKS, DEBORAH**

**Deborah Dicks**, Bank House Clinic, 5 High St, Milford On Sea, Lymington, **Hampshire**, SO41 0QF, ENG.
(T) 01590 642749
Speciality: Chiropodists (Podiatrists).
● **Owner** Dr G Benes
S (Ref:HM06083)

**DICKSON, JANE**

**Jane Dickson**, 104 Pennsylvania Rd, Exeter, **Devon**, EX4 6DQ, ENG.
(T) 01392 279761
Speciality: Osteopathy.
P S T (Ref:HM06084)

**DICKSON, JOHN J**

**John J Dickson**, 11 Ashgrove, Musselburgh, **Lothian (Mid)**, EH21 7LS, SCO.
(T) 01316 652040
Speciality: Physiotherapy.
P S T (Ref:HM06085)

**DICKSON, STUART**

**Stuart Dickson**, 15 Victoria Gdns, Neath, **Glamorgan (Vale of)**, SA11 3AY, WAL.
(T) 01639 645559 (F) 01639 630886
Speciality: Physiotherapy.
● **Owner** Mr S Dickson
P S T (Ref:HM06086)

**DIDCOCK, ELLEN**

**Ellen Didcock**, 20 Braidwood Rd, London, **London (Greater)**, SE6 1QX, ENG.
(T) 020 8244 0740
Speciality: Reflexology.
S T (Ref:HM06087)

**DIDDERIENS, BETSY**

**Betsy Didderiens Lic Ac M A I A**, Guangming Townshend St, Skibbereen, **County Cork**, IRE.
(T) 028 2261 6
Speciality: Acupuncture.
O (Ref:HM06088)

**DIDHAM, JUDI**

**Judi Didham**, 55 Gordon Rd, Cowes, **Isle of Wight**, PO31 7SL, ENG.
(T) 01983 294203
Speciality: Reflexology.
S T (Ref:HM06089)

**DIDSBURY CHIROPRACTIC CLINIC**

**Dr Stephen K Roberts**, Calderbank Medical Chambers, 87 Palantine Rd, West Didsbury, Manchester, **Manchester (Greater)**, M20 3JQ, ENG.
(T) 01614 462009 (F) 01614 457468
Speciality: Chiropractic, Manipulation, Massage (Therapeutic), X-Ray. ✓
● **Chiropractor** Mr S Roberts Q: BSc, DC. M: BCA.
S Yrs. Est.: 6 (Ref:HM06090)

**DIEBSCHLAG, FRANCESCA**

**Francesca Diebschlag**, 2 West View Gardens, East Grinstead, **Sussex (West)**, RH19 4EH, ENG.
(T) 01342 313973
Speciality: Acupuncture, Herbal Medicine, Psychotherapy.
● **Owner** Mrs F Diebschlag
M (Ref:HM06091)

**DIEGAN, M**

**M Diegan**, Paultons Sq Practice, 5 Paultons Sq, London, **London (Greater)**, SW3 5AP, ENG.
(T) 020 7352 5172
Speciality: Physiotherapy.
P S T (Ref:HM06092)

**DIEHL, D**

**D Diehl**, 280 Balham High Rd, London, **London (Greater)**, SW17 7AL, ENG.
(T) 020 8682 3662
Speciality: Chiropractic.
P S T (Ref:HM06093)

**DIEHL, DOUGLAS (DR)**

**Dr Douglas Diehl**, 16 Balderton St, London, **London (Greater)**, W1Y 1TF, ENG.
(T) 020 7409 0327
Speciality: Chiropractors.
● **Owner** Mr D Diehl
P S T (Ref:HM06094)

**DIET CENTRE**

**Diet Centre (The)**, 23A Oxton Rd, Birkenhead, **Merseyside**, CH41 2QQ, ENG.
(T) 01516 700082
Speciality: Complementary Medicines & Therapy.
● **Owner** Dr V Bolton
C M (Ref:HM06095)

**DIGBY, DAVID**

**David Digby**, Broad St Pl, Bath, **Somerset**, BA1 5LH, ENG.
(T) 01225 471174
Speciality: Alexander Technique.
● **Owner** Mr D Digby
P S (Ref:HM06096)

**DIGGENS, SUE**

**Sue Diggens**, Newbury, **Berkshire**, RG19, ENG.
(T) 01635 864556
Speciality: Aromatherapy.
M O (Ref:HM06097)

**DIGNAM, P**

**P Dignam**, Wakefield Rd, Fitzwilliam, Pontefract, **Yorkshire (West)**, WF9 5AN, ENG.
(T) 01977 618198
Speciality: Hypnosis.
B (Ref:HM06098)

**DILIS, CLARE (DR)**

**Dr Clare Dilis**, 11 William St, West, **County Galway**, IRE.
(T) 09158 3260
(E) clareherbs@eircom.net
(W) www.clareherbs.com
Speciality: Complementary Medicines & Therapy.
M (Ref:HM06099)

**DILLON, MICHAEL**

**Michael Dillon**, 34 Ash Cresent, Higham, Rochester, **Kent**, ME3 7BA, ENG.
(T) 01474 823611
Speciality: Auto Suggestion, Autogenic Training, Cognitive Therapy, Complementary Therapy, Counselling, Group Therapy, Hypnosis, Hypnotherapy, Psychotherapy, Stress Therapy, Visualisation Therapy. ✓
● **Hypnotherapist** Dr M Dillon Q: Dip.Hyp.



Key continued: Yrs.Est: Years Established Q: Qualifications M: Professional Membership ✓ Indemnity Insurance Accept Credit Cards

FHRS, MHA, MNCH, PhD. M: HA, Soc.SM, SSM.
**H** Yrs. Est.: 11 (**Ref:**HM06100)

### DI-LUZIO, HARRIET
**Harriet Di-Luzio**, 48 Burlington Lane, London, **London (Greater)**, W4 2RR, ENG.
(T) 020 8995 9959
Speciality: Reflexology.
**S** **T** (**Ref:**HM06101)

### DI-MARI REFLEXOLOGY CLINIC
**Di-Mari Reflexology Clinic (The)**, 19A Station Rd, Westcliff-on-Sea, **Essex**, SS0 7RA, ENG.
(T) 01702 391393
Speciality: Complementary Medicines & Therapy.
**M** (**Ref:**HM06102)

### DIMASCIO, CAROLINE
**Caroline Dimascio**, 17 Adderly Gate, Emersons Green, Bristol, BS16 7DR, ENG.
(T) 01179 574498
Speciality: Reflexology.
**S** **T** (**Ref:**HM06103)

### DIMASCIO, CHRISTINE
**Christine Dimascio**, 2 Mornington Villas, Bradford, **Yorkshire (West)**, BD8 7HB, ENG.
(T) 01274 574570
Speciality: Physiotherapy.
● **Owner** Mrs C Dimascio
**P** **S** **T** (**Ref:**HM06104)

### DIMENT, GORDON L
**Gordon L Diment**, Colrosa, 203 Tonbridge Rd, Wateringbury, Maidstone, **Kent**, ME18 5NY, ENG.
(T) 01622 813032
Speciality: Cognitive Therapy, Counselling, Hypnosis, Hypnotherapy, Psychotherapy, Rogerian Therapy, Stress Therapy. ✔
● **Hypnotherapist/Psychotherapist**
Mr G Diment Q: BA (Hons) Psychol, DHP (NC), Dip.CPC. M: BCMA, HS, NCH, NCP, NRHP.
**B** Yrs. Est.: 10 (**Ref:**HM06105)

### DIMITRI-COOPER, CHRISSIE
**Chrissie Dimitri-Cooper**, Vinings Natural Health Centre, Church Rd, Haywards Heath, **Sussex (West)**, RH16 3UF, ENG.
(T) 01273 834478 (F) 01273 831094
Speciality: Reflexology.
● **Owner** Mrs C Cooper
**S** **T** (**Ref:**HM06106)

### DIMMOCK, K
**K Dimmock**, 7 Whitburn Trce, Sunderland, **Tyne and Wear**, SR6 8JB, ENG.
(T) 01915 487945
Speciality: Chiropodists (Podiatrists).
**S** (**Ref:**HM06107)

### DIMPNA CENTRE
**Dimpna Centre**, 83 Princes Rd, Teddington, **London (Greater)**, TW11 0RZ, ENG.
(T) 020 8977 3587 (F) 020 8977 3587
Speciality: Psychotherapy.
● **Director** Mr F Franklin
**B** (**Ref:**HM06108)

### DING, LEE
**Lee Ding**, 249 Kenilworth Rd, Basingstoke, **Hampshire**, RG23 8JP, ENG.
(T) 01256 841276
Speciality: Acupuncture.
**O** (**Ref:**HM06109)

### DINGWALL HEALTH CENTRE
**Dingwall Health Centre**, Ferry Rd, Dingwall, **Highland**, IV15 9QT, SCO.
(T) 01349 863047
Speciality: Chiropodists (Podiatrists).
**S** (**Ref:**HM06110)

### DINGWALL, J T
**J T Dingwall**, 121 Barkers Butts Lane, Coventry, **Midlands (West)**, CV6 1EB, ENG.
(T) 024 7659 2359
Speciality: Chiropodists (Podiatrists).
**S** (**Ref:**HM06111)

### DINNAGE, DAWN
**Dawn Dinnage**, 28 The Ashway, Brixworth, Northampton, **Northamptonshire**, NN6 9TZ, ENG.
(T) 01604 882427
Speciality: Reflexology.
**S** **T** (**Ref:**HM06112)

### DINNAGE, GERARD
**Gerard Dinnage**, 49 Eastcourt Rd, Burbage, Marlborough, **Wiltshire**, SN8 3AJ, ENG.
(T) 01672 811091
Speciality: Hypnosis.
● **Owner** Mr G Dinnage
**B** (**Ref:**HM06113)

### DIRECT HEALING
**Direct Healing**, 223 Great Chalfield, Melksham, **Wiltshire**, SN12 8NL, ENG.
(T) 01225 782459
Speciality: Reiki.
**M** (**Ref:**HM06114)

### DIRLIK-MERCY
**Dirlik-Mercy**, 25 Stour Rd, Christchurch, **Dorset**, BH23 1PS, ENG.
(T) 01202 484164
Speciality: Homeopathy.
● **Owner** Ms M Dirlik-Mercy
**M** (**Ref:**HM06115)

### DISLEY PHYSIO SERVICES
**Disley Physio Services**, 3 Redhouse Lane, Disley, Stockport, **Cheshire**, SK12 2EW, ENG.
(T) 01663 762254 (F) 01663 762254
Speciality: Physiotherapy.
● **Owner** Mrs M Storah
**P** **S** **T** (**Ref:**HM06116)

### DISPENSERY
**Dispensery (The)**, 7 London St, Londonderry, **County Londonderry**, BT48 6RQ, NIR.
(T) 028 7127 1500
Speciality: Acupuncture, Bach Remedies, Counselling, Dietician, Herbal Medicine, Homeopathy, Indian Head Massage, Kinesiology, Life Style Coaching, Massage (Therapeutic), Moxibustion, Reflexology, Reiki, Shiatsu, Sports Massage, Yoga, Injury Treatment. ✔
● **Sports Massage** Glynis Hughes Q: BA (Hons), Cert.Sports Massage. M: IIST.
● **Homeopath** Ms M Bradley M: ISH.
● **Acupuncturist** Mr J O'Mahony Q: Lic.Ac. M: AIA.
● **Owner/Medical Herbalist**
Mr D Foley Q: MNIMH, MRCHM. M: NIMH.
**C** Yrs. Est.: 2 (**Ref:**HM06117)

### DISS CHIROPODY CLINIC
**Diss Chiropody Clinic**, 1 Roydon Rd, Diss, **Norfolk**, IP22 4LN, ENG.
(T) 01379 640370 (F) 01379 650020
Speciality: Chiropodists (Podiatrists).
● **Owner** Mrs C Leroy
**S** (**Ref:**HM06118)

### DISS CHIROPRACTIC CLINIC
**Diss Chiropractic Clinic**, 1 Roydon Rd, Diss, **Norfolk**, IP22 4LN, ENG.
(T) 01379 650020
Speciality: Chiropractors.
**P** **S** **T** (**Ref:**HM06119)

### DISS NATURAL HEALTH CARE CTRE
**Diss Natural Health Care Centre**, 28 Victoria Rd, Diss, **Norfolk**, IP22 4HP, ENG.
(T) 01379 640740 (F) 01379 640740
Speciality: Complementary Medicines & Therapy.
**M** (**Ref:**HM06120)

### DISS NATURAL HEALTH CLINIC
**Diss Natural Health Clinic**, Pegusos House, 16/17 Chapel St, Diss, **Norfolk**, IP22 3AN, ENG.
(T) 01379 644407
Speciality: Acupuncture, Bach Remedies, Cognitive Therapy, Complementary Therapy, Cranial Osteopathy, Dietician, Healer, Herbal Medicine, Homeopathy, Hypnotherapy, Iridology, Manipulation, Massage (Therapeutic), Nutritional Therapy, Osteopathy, Reflexology, Reiki, Stress Therapy, Vitamin Therapy. ✔
● **Owner** Mr W Allchin
**P** **S** **T** Yrs. Est.: 3 (**Ref:**HM06121)

### DISS, KATHRYN
**Kathryn Diss**, Clophill Fruit Farm, Shefford Rd, Clophill, Bedford, **Bedfordshire**, MK45 4BT, ENG.
(T) 01525 862278
Speciality: Alexander Technique. ✔
● **Owner** Mrs K Diss Q: MSTAT.
**P** Yrs. Est.: 8 (**Ref:**HM06122)

### DISTANT HEALING
**Distant Healing For Humans and Animals**, B M Box 2894, London, **London (Greater)**, WC1N 3XX, ENG.
(T) 020 7690 5821
Speciality: Absent Healing, Crystal Healing, Faith Healing, Healer, Healing Therapy, Reiki, Spiritual Healing, Stress Therapy, Angelic Energies. ✔
● **Healer** Mr B Sohon Q: BSc, NFSH, Reiki Master. M: NFSH.
**C** **H** Yrs. Est.: 12 (**Ref:**HM06123)

### DISTANT HEALING
**Distant Healing**, 15 Parkhouse, 314-322 Severn Sisters Rd, London, **London (Greater)**, N42 LR, ENG.
(T) 020 7690 5821
Speciality: Complementary Medicines & Therapy.
● **Owner** Mr B Sohon
**M** (**Ref:**HM06124)

### DIXON & ASSOCIATES
**Peter Dixon & Associates**, 207 London Rd East, Batheaston, Bath, **Somerset**, BA1 7NB, ENG.
(T) 01225 852371
Speciality: Chiropractic.
**P** **S** **T** (**Ref:**HM06125)

### DIXON, CLAIRE
**Claire Dixon**, 19 Old Palace Rd, Guildford, **Surrey**, GU2 7TU, ENG.
(T) 01483 535768
Speciality: Reflexology.
**S** **T** (**Ref:**HM06126)

### DIXON, GAYLE
**Gayle Dixon**, East Barnwell Health Centre, Ditton Lane, Cambridge, **Cambridgeshire**, CB5 8SP, ENG.
(T) 01223 277919
Speciality: Osteopathy.
**P** **S** **T** (**Ref:**HM06127)

### DIXON, HANNAH
**Hannah Dixon**, 26 Emmott Drive, Rawdon, Leeds, **Yorkshire (West)**, LS19 6RF, ENG.
(T) 01132 507539
Speciality: Reflexology.
● **Owner** Ms H Dixon
**S** **T** (**Ref:**HM06128)

### DIXON, HEATHER
**Heather Dixon**, Esplanade, Scarborough, **Yorkshire (North)**, YO11 2AG, ENG.
(T) 01723 372232
Speciality: Chiropodists (Podiatrists).
● **Owner** Mrs A Kenny
**S** (**Ref:**HM06129)

### DIXON, LYNNE
**Lynne Dixon**, 52 Old Elvet, Durham, **County Durham**, DH1 3HN, ENG.
(T) 01913 830677
Speciality: Physiotherapy.
**P** **S** **T** (**Ref:**HM06130)

### DIXON, M L
**M L Dixon**, 8 Central Drive, Morecambe, **Lancashire**, LA4 5JU, ENG.
(T) 01524 417233
Speciality: Chiropodists (Podiatrists).
**S** (**Ref:**HM06131)

### DIXON, MARY
**Mary Dixon**, 61 Manor Rd, Worthing, **Sussex (West)**, BN11 4SE, ENG.
(T) 01903 237853
Speciality: Complementary Medicines & Therapy.
● **Owner** Mrs M Dixon
**C** **M** (**Ref:**HM06132)

### DIXON, RUTH
**Ruth Dixon**, 48 Diban Avenue, Hornchurch, **Essex**, RM12 4YF, ENG.
(T) 01708 703653

Key: **B** Mind-Body Medicine **C** Complementary Medicine **H** Self Help Treatment **M** Medicinal Therapy **O** Oriental Medicine **P** Postural Therapy **S** Manipulative Structural Therapy **T** Touch Therapy

Speciality: Reflexology.
S T (Ref:HM06133)

## DLP HYPNOTHERAPY CENTRE

**DLP Hypnotherapy Centre**, 14 Stanfield Rd, Winton, Bournemouth, **Dorset**, BH9 2NW, ENG.
(T) 01202 546145 (F) 01202 546145
(E) david_1_preston@hotmail.com
(W) www.david_preston.co.uk
Speciality: Auto Suggestion, Aversion Therapy, Counselling, Hypnosis, Hypnotherapy, Visualisation Therapy. ✓
● **Owner** Mr D Lawrence-Preston Q: BSc, Dip.Hyp, Dip.Psych, MHA, MSc. M: HA.
B Yrs. Est.: 8 (Ref:HM06134)

## DMH

**DMH**, 31 Musgrove Rd, London, **London (Greater)**, SE14 5PP, ENG.
(T) 020 7639 5792
Speciality: Complementary Medicines & Therapy.
● **Owner** Mr D Haynes
M (Ref:HM06135)

## DOBBINS, ALISON

**Alison Dobbins**, 40A Brean Down Avenue, Bristol, BS9 4JF, ENG.
(T) 01179 622992
Speciality: Reflexology.
S T (Ref:HM06136)

## DOBELL, R

**R Dobell**, 132 Engaine Drive, Shenley Church End, Milton Keynes, **Buckinghamshire**, MK5 6DH, ENG.
(T) 01908 504744
Speciality: Chiropodists (Podiatrists).
● **Owner** Ms R Dobell
S (Ref:HM06137)

## DOBIE, CLARE

**Clare Dobie**, 8 Riverside, Churnet View Rd, Oakamoor, Stoke-On-Trent, **Staffordshire**, ST10 3AE, ENG.
(T) 01538 702956
Speciality: Acupuncture.
● **Owner** Ms C Dobie
O (Ref:HM06138)

## DOBSON, SUE

**Sue Dobson**, 89 Telford Cres, Woodley, Reading, **Berkshire**, RG5 4QT, ENG.
(T) 01189 695457
Speciality: Electrolysis.
● **Owner** Mrs S Dobson
T (Ref:HM06139)

## DOCKLANDS CHIROPODY CENTRE

**Docklands Chiropody Centre**, Docklands Dental Centre, 27 Skylines Village, Limeharbour, London, **London (Greater)**, E14 9XZ, ENG.
(T) 020 7538 9990 (F) 020 7538 9996
Speciality: Osteopathy.
● **Owner** Mrs S Sharma
S (Ref:HM06140)

## DOCKLANDS DENTAL/COMP HLTH

**Docklands Dental and Complementary Health Centre**, Docklands Dental Centre, 27 Skylines Village, Limeharbour, London, **London (Greater)**, E14 9XZ, ENG.
(T) 020 7538 9990 (F) 020 7538 9996
(W) www.dockdent.co.uk
Speciality: Chiropody, Osteopathy, Dentist and Hygienist. ✓ CREDIT
● **Dentist** Dr C Tarazi Q: BDS.
● **Owner/Dentist** Mrs S Sharma Q: BDS.
● **Dentist** Dr S Waddington Q: BSc (Hons).
● **Dentist** Dr S Soo Q: BDS, MSc.
● **Osteopath** Joanne Larner Q: BA (Hons), DO. M: GOsC.
● **Chiropodist** Csaba Barody Q: DPodM, MBRCP, S.R.Ch.
P S T Yrs. Est.: 8 (Ref:HM06141)

## DOCKLANDS HOMEOPATHY CENTRE

**Docklands Homeopathy Centre**, Docklands Dental Centre/27 Skylines Village, Limeharbour, London, **London (Greater)**, E14 9XZ, ENG.
(T) 020 7538 9990 (F) 020 7538 9996
Speciality: Homeopathy.
● **Owner** Mrs S Sharma
M (Ref:HM06142)

## DOCKLANDS OSTEOPATHIC CLINIC

**Docklands Osteopathic Clinic**, Tiller Rd, London, **London (Greater)**, E14 8PX, ENG.
(T) 020 7345 0051
Speciality: Osteopathy.
P S T (Ref:HM06143)

## DOCTOR BENSONS HEALTH PRACTICE

**Doctor Bensons Health Practice**, 12 St Georges Rd, London, **London (Greater)**, NW11 0LR, ENG.
(T) 020 8905 5509 (F) 020 8455 1955
Speciality: Complementary Medicines & Therapy.
● **Owner** Dr H Benson
C M (Ref:HM06144)

## DODDS, L

**L Dodds**, Bradley Stoke Surgery, Brook Way, Bradley Stoke, Bristol, BS32 9DS, ENG.
(T) 01454 618525
Speciality: Physiotherapy.
P S T (Ref:HM06145)

## DODDS, S C

**S C Dodds**, 52 Chalkwell Park Drive, Leigh-On-Sea, **Essex**, SS9 1NJ, ENG.
(T) 01702 478093
Speciality: Chiropodists (Podiatrists).
S (Ref:HM06146)

## DODGSON, PHILIP (DR)

**Dr Philip Dodgson**, 30 The Drive, Hove, **Sussex (East)**, BN3 3JD, ENG.
(T) 01273 778123 (F) 01273 776266
Speciality: Psychology.
● **Practice Manager** Mrs M Ward
B (Ref:HM06147)

## DODSON, E S P

**E S P Dodson**, 21 Cowlersley Lane, Huddersfield, **Yorkshire (West)**, HD4 5TY, ENG.
(T) 01484 641982
Speciality: Osteopathy.
● **Owner** Mr E Dodson
P S T (Ref:HM06148)

## DOEY, ROSEMARY

**Rosemary Doey**, 27 Craven Rd, Newbury, **Berkshire**, RG14 5NG, ENG.
(T) 01635 31679
Speciality: Osteopathy.
P S T (Ref:HM06149)

## DOGGETT, C

**C Doggett**, 6 Cliff Avenue, Gorleston, Great Yarmouth, **Norfolk**, NR31 6EQ, ENG.
(T) 01493 669619
Speciality: Complementary Medicines & Therapy.
● **Owner** Mrs C Doggett
M (Ref:HM06150)

## DOHERTY, ALISON J

**Alison J Doherty**, 37 Woodhouse Rd, London, **London (Greater)**, N12 9ET, ENG.
(T) 020 8371 9971
Speciality: Reflexology.
S T (Ref:HM06151)

## DOHERTY, ANN

**Ann Doherty**, 11A Earls Avenue, Folkestone, **Kent**, CT20 2HW, ENG.
(T) 01303 243727
Speciality: Physiotherapy.
P S T (Ref:HM06152)

## DOHERTY, COLIN

**Colin Doherty**, 29 Strandview Rd, Ballycastle, **County Antrim**, BT54 6AJ, NIR.
(T) 028 2076 2843
Speciality: Reflexology.
S T (Ref:HM06153)

## DOHERTY, P C

**P C Doherty**, Dolphin House, St Peter St, Winchester, **Hampshire**, SO23 8BW, ENG.
(T) 01962 829735 (F) 01962 866116
Speciality: Psychiatry.
B (Ref:HM06154)

## DOIDGE, FRAN

**Fran Doidge**, 12 Pixiefields, Cradley, Malvern, **Worcestershire**, WR13 5ND, ENG.
(T) 01886 880100
Speciality: Aromatherapy.
● **Owner** Ms F Doidge
M O (Ref:HM06155)

## DOIG, B

**B Doig**, 1 Brittany Mews, Brittany Rd, St. Leonards-On-Sea, **Sussex (East)**, TN38 0YU, ENG.
(T) 01424 440257
Speciality: Homeopathy.
● **Owner** Mrs B Doig
M (Ref:HM06156)

## DOIG, M

**M Doig**, Balbirnie Rd, Glenrothes, **Fife**, KY7 5ED, SCO.
(T) 01592 611125
Speciality: Physiotherapy.
● **Owner** Miss M Doig
P S T (Ref:HM06157)

## DOIG, PAUL

**Mr Paul Doig - Homeopath**, 7 Sycamore Dene, Chesham, **Buckinghamshire**, HP5 3JT, ENG.
(T) 01494 775458
Speciality: Homeopathy. ✓
● **Homeopath** Mr P Doig Q: Dip.Chom. M: Inst.Hom.
M Yrs. Est.: 2 (Ref:HM06158)

## DOLAN, JAMES A (DR)

**Dolan Dr James A**, 191 Howth Rd, Killester, IRE.
(T) 01833 5962
Speciality: Osteopathy.
P S T (Ref:HM06159)

## DOLEMAN, P

**P Doleman**, 123 Scotforth Rd, Lancaster, **Lancashire**, LA1 4JN, ENG.
(T) 01524 33146
Speciality: Chiropractors.
● **Owner** Mr P Doleman
P S T (Ref:HM06160)

## DOLPHIN & THE UNICORN

**Dolphin & The Unicorn**, U15B Innisfallen Mall, Killarney, **County Kerry**, IRE.
(T) 06436 933
Speciality: Complementary Medicines & Therapy.
M (Ref:HM06161)

## DOLPHIN CONNECTION

**Dolphin Connection (The)**, 6 Laing St, Kirkwall, **Orkney Isles**, KW15 1NW, SCO.
(T) 01856 874746
Speciality: Complementary Medicines & Therapy.
● **Owner** Miss M Kidd
M (Ref:HM06162)

## DOLPHIN HOUSE CLINIC

**Dolphin House Clinic**, 14 New Rd, Brighton, **Sussex (East)**, BN1 1UF, ENG.
(T) 01273 324790
Speciality: Complementary Medicines & Therapy.
● **Practice Manager** Ms S Irvine
C M (Ref:HM06163)

## DOLPHIN STAR

**Dolphin Star**, 20 Gregory Avenue, Lenton, Nottingham, **Nottinghamshire**, NG7 2EQ, ENG.
(T) 01159 412123
Speciality: Clairvoyants & Palmists.
● **Owner** Mr J Weeks
B (Ref:HM06164)

## DOLPHIN STUDIOS

**Dolphin Studios**, 27a Penny St, Old Portsmouth, Portsmouth, **Hampshire**, PO1 2NH, ENG.
(T) 023 9286 3561
(W) www.cisweb.co.uk/dolphinstudios
Speciality: Absent Healing, Complementary Therapy, Counselling, Hypnosis, Hypnotherapy, Meditation, Oriental Diagnosis, Psychotherapy, Reiki, Shiatsu, Spiritual Healing, Visualisation Therapy, Past Life Regression Therapy. ✓
● **Hypnotherapist/Shiatsu Practitioner** Mrs M Banbury Q: BA, ESS.TM.Dip, MNRHP. M: NRHP.
B Yrs. Est.: 12 (Ref:HM06165)



Key continued: Yrs.Est: Years Established Q: Qualifications M: Professional Membership ✓ Indemnity Insurance CREDIT Accept Credit Cards

**DON, ANITA**

**Anita Don**, 29 Swain Court, Lumbertubs, Northampton, **Northamptonshire**, NN3 8HT, ENG.
(T) 01604 412851
(W) www.anitadon.co.uk
Speciality: Aromatherapy, Indian Head Massage, Reflexology, Remedial Massage, Swedish Body Massage.
S T (Ref:HM06166)

**DON, ANNETTE**

**Annette Don**, 4 Milford House, 7 Queen Anne St, London, **London (Greater)**, W1M 9FD, ENG.
(T) 020 7637 0202
Speciality: Osteopathy.
P S T (Ref:HM06167)

**DONALD, B**

**B Donald**, 35 Longfield Drive, Rodley, Leeds, **Yorkshire (West)**, LS13 1JX, ENG.
(T) 01132 564464
Speciality: Chiropodists (Podiatrists).
● **Owner** Mr B Donald
S (Ref:HM06168)

**DONALDSON, J F**

**J F Donaldson**, Park Rd Medical Centre, 1a Park Rd, Wallington, **Surrey**, SM6 8AA, ENG.
(T) 020 8647 7336
Speciality: Homeopathy.
M (Ref:HM06169)

**DONCASTER CHIROPRACTIC CLINIC**

**Doncaster Chiropractic Clinic**, 26 High Rd, Balby, Doncaster, **Yorkshire (South)**, DN4 0PL, ENG.
(T) 01302 811322
Speciality: Chiropractic.
P S T (Ref:HM06170)

**DONCASTER PHYSIO & SPORTS**

**Doncaster Physiotherapy & Sports Injury Clinic**, Thorne Rd, Doncaster, **Yorkshire (South)**, DN2 5LT, ENG.
(T) 01302 553210
Speciality: Physiotherapy.
P S T (Ref:HM06171)

**DONEGAN, P T**

**P T Donegan**, 593 Woodchurch Rd, Prenton, **Merseyside**, CH43 3AL, ENG.
(T) 01516 083431
Speciality: Chiropodists (Podiatrists).
● **Owner** Mr P Donegan
S (Ref:HM06172)

**DONLEY, ALISON**

**Alison Donley**, 63 Garrett St, Nuneaton, **Warwickshire**, CV11 4PP, ENG.
(T) 024 7638 7449
Speciality: Osteopathy.
P S T (Ref:HM06173)

**DONNA-MARIA FRAHER**

**Donna-Maria Fraher**, 15 Farm Drive, Alvaston, Derby, **Derbyshire**, DE24 0HB, ENG.
(T) 01332 757424
Speciality: Psychotherapy.
● **Owner** Miss D Faher
B (Ref:HM06174)

**DONNAMARIE**

**Donnamarie**, 112 Cooksey Lane, Birmingham, **Midlands (West)**, B44 9QS, ENG.
(T) 01216 088672
Speciality: Hypnosis.
● **Owner** Miss D Leonard
B (Ref:HM06175)

**DONNA'S AROMATHERAPY & GIFTS**

**Donna's Aromatherapy & Gifts**, 41 North Bridge St, Bathgate, **Lothian (West)**, EH48 4PL, SCO.
(T) 01506 653233
Speciality: Aromatherapy.
● **Owner** Mrs D Henley
M O (Ref:HM06176)

**DONNELL, N**

**N Donnell**, 1 West St, Mexborough, **Yorkshire (South)**, S64 9HZ, ENG.
(T) 01709 583041
Speciality: Chiropodists (Podiatrists).
S (Ref:HM06177)

**DONNELLY, D**

**D Donnelly**, 117 Tweed Cres, Dundee, **Angus**, DD2 4DJ, SCO.
(T) 01382 643742
Speciality: Chiropodists (Podiatrists).
● **Owner** Mr D Donnelly
S (Ref:HM06178)

**DONNELLY, LUCY**

**Lucy Donnelly**, The Surgery, 919 Abbeydale Rd, Sheffield, **Yorkshire (South)**, S7 2BJ, ENG.
(T) 01142 507557
Speciality: Chiropodists (Podiatrists).
● **Owner** Miss L Donnelly
S (Ref:HM06179)

**DONNELLY, MARGARET**

**Margaret Donnelly**, 5 Black Bull Lane, Fulwood, Preston, **Lancashire**, PR2 3PT, ENG.
(T) 01772 718604
Speciality: Chiropodists (Podiatrists).
● **Owner** Mrs M Donnelly
S (Ref:HM06180)

**DONNELLY, PAUL**

**Paul Donnelly**, Active Healthcare Clinic, 388 Ecclesall Rd, Sheffield, **Yorkshire (South)**, S11 8PJ, ENG.
(T) 01142 671901 (F) 01142 671901
Speciality: Osteopathy.
● **Owner** Mr P Donnelly
P S T (Ref:HM06181)

**DONNYBROOK MEDICAL CENTRE**

**Donnybrook Medical Centre**, 6 Main St, Donnybrook, **County Dublin**, IRE.
(T) 01283 8792
Speciality: Complementary Medicines & Therapy.
M (Ref:HM06182)

**DONOVAN, BRENDA**

**Brenda Donovan**, 128 West St, Carshalton, **Surrey**, SM5 2NR, ENG.
(T) 020 8773 3771
Speciality: Reflexology.
● **Owner** Mrs B Donovan
S T (Ref:HM06183)

**DONOVAN, DAVID M**

**David M Donovan**, 22 Foresters Cl, Rags Lane, Cheshunt, Waltham Cross, **Hertfordshire**, EN7 6TF, ENG.
(T) 01992 628592 (F) 01992 628592
Speciality: Chiropodists (Podiatrists).
● **Owner** Mr D Donovan
S (Ref:HM06184)

**DONOVAN, J A**

**J A Donovan**, 30 Lacey Cres, Poole, **Dorset**, BH15 3NZ, ENG.
(T) 01202 741718
Speciality: Chiropodists (Podiatrists).
● **Owner** Mrs J Donovan
S (Ref:HM06185)

**DOODY, ANDREW**

**Andrew Doody**, 43 Fairway, Fleetwood, **Lancashire**, FY7 8QZ, ENG.
(T) 01253 874462
Speciality: Osteopathy.
● **Owner** Mr A Doody
P S T (Ref:HM06186)

**DOODY, COLLEEN**

**Colleen Doody**, 43 Fairway, Fleetwood, **Lancashire**, FY7 8QZ, ENG.
(T) 01253 874462
Speciality: Physiotherapy.
P S T (Ref:HM06187)

**DOOLAN, M F**

**M F Doolan**, 6 Wentworth Cl, Hatfield Peverel, Chelmsford, **Essex**, CM3 2JS, ENG.
(T) 01245 381963
Speciality: Chiropodists (Podiatrists).
● **Owner** Mr M Doolan
S (Ref:HM06188)

**DOOLAN, MARTIN**

**Doolan Martin M A**, 15 Marble Crest, **County Kilkenny**, IRE.
(T) 05661 619
Speciality: Complementary Medicines & Therapy.
M (Ref:HM06189)

**DOOLEY, ELIZABETH**

**Elizabeth Dooley**, 27 Hadrian Avenue, Southwick, Brighton, **Sussex (East)**, BN42 4LJ, ENG.
(T) 01273 597143 (F) 01273 597143
Speciality: Chiropodists (Podiatrists).
● **Owner** Mrs E Dooley
S (Ref:HM06190)

**DOONAN & MCSHANE**

**Doonan & McShane**, 11 Grange Cres, Sunderland, **Tyne and Wear**, SR2 7BN, ENG.
(T) 01915 670775
Speciality: Chiropodists (Podiatrists).
S (Ref:HM06191)

**DOONAN, A**

**A Doonan**, 29 Sutton St, Durham, **County Durham**, DH1 4BW, ENG.
(T) 01913 848590
Speciality: Chiropodists (Podiatrists).
● **Owner** A Doonan
S (Ref:HM06192)

**DOORWAY TO HEALTH**

**Doorway to Health**, 24 Blackrock Park, Mallow, **County Cork**, IRE.
(T) 022 4328 6
Speciality: Complementary Medicines & Therapy.
● **Owner** Mrs C O'Callaghan Q: RGN, RM.
M (Ref:HM06193)

**DORAN, LESLEY**

**Lesley Doran**, Priory Deep, Culver Hill, Amberley, Stroud, **Gloucestershire**, GL5 5AS, ENG.
(T) 01453 872958
Speciality: Reflexology.
S T (Ref:HM06194)

**DORCHESTER HOUSE OSTEOPATHY**

**Dorchester House Osteopathy Clinic**, 137 Dorchester Rd, Worcester Park, **Surrey**, KT4 8PA, ENG.
(T) 020 8715 1145
Speciality: Aromatherapy, Chiropody, Osteopathy. ✔
● **Aromatherapist** Mrs J Reilly
● **Owner/Osteopath** Mrs C Felten M: GOsC.
C Yrs. Est.: 5 (Ref:HM06195)

**DORE PHYSIOTHERAPY PRACTICE**

**Dore Physiotherapy Practise**, 56A Dore Rd, Sheffield, **Yorkshire (South)**, S17 3NB, ENG.
(T) 01142 621255
Speciality: Electrotherapy, Manipulation, Massage (Therapeutic). ✔
● **Physiotherapist** Mrs E Hague Q: BSc (Hons). M: CSP.
S Yrs. Est.: 8 (Ref:HM06196)

**DOREY, JANE**

**Jane Dorey**, Holmes Pl, Upper Richmond Rd, Putney, London, **London (Greater)**, SW15 2SS, ENG.
(T) 07641 105453
Speciality: Physiotherapy.
P S T (Ref:HM06197)

**DOREY, STELLA**

**Stella Dorey**, 266 Watling St, Dartford, **Kent**, DA2 6EW, ENG.
(T) 01322 225230
Speciality: Reflexology.
S T (Ref:HM06198)

**DORKING CHIROPRACTIC**

**Dorking Chiropractic**, 316 High St, Dorking, **Surrey**, RH4 1QX, ENG.
(T) 01306 887793
Speciality: Chiropractic.
P S T (Ref:HM06199)

**DORKING, PAUL**

**Dorking Paul**, 19 Tolworth Pk Rd, Surbiton, **Surrey**, KT6 7RN, ENG.
(T) 020 8390 6189
(E) paul dorkin@email.com
Speciality: Hypnosis, Hypnotherapy,



Key: B Mind-Body Medicine C Complementary Medicine H Self Help Treatment M Medicinal Therapy O Oriental Medicine P Postural Therapy S Manipulative Structural Therapy T Touch Therapy

Phytotherapy. ✔
● **Hypnotherapist/Psychotherapist** Mr P Dorking M: CRAH.
B Yrs. Est.: 9 (**Ref:**HM06200)

**DORMAN, KARL**

**Karl Dorman**, 375 High St, Lincoln, **Lincolnshire**, LN5 7RY, ENG.
(T) 01522 567630
Speciality: Chiropractic. ✔
● **Chiropractor** Mr K Dorman Q: BSc, M.Ed, MMCA. M: CC, MCA.
C Yrs. Est.: 10 (**Ref:**HM06201)

**DORMAN, KARL**

**Karl Dorman**, 37 Newcastle St, Tuxford, Newark, **Nottinghamshire**, NG22 0LN, ENG.
(T) 01777 871255
Speciality: Chiropractic.
P S T (**Ref:**HM06202)

**DORON, LORRAINE**

**Lorraine Doron**, 56 The Glades, East Grinstead, **Sussex (West)**, RH19 3XW, ENG.
(T) 01342 314117
Speciality: Reflexology.
● **Owner** Mrs L Doron
S T (**Ref:**HM06203)

**DORRICOTT, C J**

**C J Dorricott**, Claws Reach, Crablands, Selsey, Chichester, **Sussex (West)**, PO20 9AY, ENG.
(T) 01243 603442 (F) 01245 603442
Speciality: Physiotherapy.
● **Owner** Mrs C Dorricott
P S T (**Ref:**HM06204)

**DORSET RACQUETS & HEALTH CLUB**

**Dorset Racquets and Health Club**, Cabot Lane, Poole, **Dorset**, BH17 7BX, ENG.
(T) 01202 642630
(W) www.esporta.co.uk
Speciality: Alexander Technique, Indian Head Massage, Reflexology, Reiki. ✔ [credit card]
● **Therapist** Mr F Willets Q: MSTAT, PhD.
● **Indian Head Massage** Julie Bennett
● **Reflexologist** Samatha Whild
B Yrs. Est.: 4 (**Ref:**HM06205)

**DORWEST HERBS**

**Dorwest Herbs**, Shipton Rd, Shipton Gorge, Bridport, **Dorset**, DT6 4LP, ENG.
(T) 01308 897272 (F) 01308 897929
Speciality: Bowen Therapy, Herbal Medicine.
C (**Ref:**HM06206)

**DOUGAN**

**Mrs Dougan**, 53 Albany Rd, Walton-On-Thames, **Surrey**, KT12 5QG, ENG.
(T) 01932 244133
Speciality: Chiropodists (Podiatrists).
S (**Ref:**HM06207)

**DOUGAN, PAT**

**Pat Dougan**, Brabant House, Portsmouth Rd, Thames Ditton, **Surrey**, KT7 0EY, ENG.
(T) 020 8398 7592
Speciality: Chiropractors.
P S T (**Ref:**HM06208)

**DOUGLAS BEAUTY CLINIC**

**Douglas Beauty Clinic**, Irish Nationwide Hse, Douglas Village, **County Cork**, IRE.
(T) 021 4891 044
Speciality: Beauty Therapy.
H T (**Ref:**HM06209)

**DOUGLAS, A H**

**A H Douglas**, 534 Queens Promenade, Thornton, **Lancashire**, FY5 1PQ, ENG.
(T) 01253 824459
Speciality: Chiropodists (Podiatrists).
● **Owner** A Douglas
S (**Ref:**HM06210)

**DOUGLAS, ANGELA**

**Angela Douglas**, 5a Westgate, Otley, **Yorkshire (West)**, LS21 3AT, ENG.
(T) 01943 468443
Speciality: Psychotherapy.
B (**Ref:**HM06211)

**DOUGLAS, ANNE S**

**Anne S Douglas**, North Kaim, Lochwinnoch, **Renfrewshire**, PA12 4LD, SCO.
(T) 01505 843351 (F) 01505 843351
Speciality: Physiotherapy, Reiki. ✔
● **Owner** Ms A Douglas M: CSP.
S (**Ref:**HM06212)

**DOUGLAS, CAROLINE**

**Caroline Douglas**, 20 Parkside Avenue, Chorley, **Lancashire**, PR7 1JY, ENG.
(T) 01257 263173
Speciality: Chiropody. ✔
● **Owner/Chiropodist** Miss C Douglas Q: MBChA, MSSCh. M: SSCh.
C Yrs. Est.: 14 (**Ref:**HM06213)

**DOUGLAS, ELAINE**

**Elaine Douglas**, 36 Parma Cresent, London, **London (Greater)**, SW11 1LT, ENG.
(T) 020 7223 7022
Speciality: Electrolysis.
T (**Ref:**HM06214)

**DOUGLAS, ERICA**

**Erica Douglas**, Abbey View Complementary Clinic, Abbey View Medical Centre, Shaftesbury, **Dorset**, SP7 8DH, ENG.
(T) 01747 856719 (F) 01747 856701
Speciality: Homeopathy.
M (**Ref:**HM06215)

**DOUGLAS, G**

**G Douglas**, 3 Eversley Way, Folkestone, **Kent**, CT20 3QP, ENG.
(T) 01303 259019
Speciality: Chiropodists (Podiatrists).
● **Owner** Mrs G Douglas
S (**Ref:**HM06216)

**DOUGLAS, JACK**

**Jack Douglas**, 33 Glasgow Rd, Wishaw, **Lanarkshire (North)**, ML2 7PG, SCO.
(T) 01698 360400
Speciality: Chiropodists (Podiatrists).
● **Owner** Mr D Jack
S (**Ref:**HM06217)

**DOUGLAS, O A**

**O A Douglas**, 181 New Line, Bradford, **Yorkshire (West)**, BD10 0BN, ENG.
(T) 01274 613369
Speciality: Hypnotherapy.
● **Owner** Mrs O Douglas
B (**Ref:**HM06218)

**DOUGLAS, S**

**S Douglas**, 31 Desborough Rd, Eastleigh, **Hampshire**, SO50 5NY, ENG.
(T) 023 8061 6006
Speciality: Chiropodists (Podiatrists).
● **Owner** Mrs S Douglas
S (**Ref:**HM06219)

**DOUGLAS, W**

**W Douglas**, 23 Trent Lane, Burton Joyce, Nottingham, **Nottinghamshire**, NG14 5EY, ENG.
(T) 01159 312553
Speciality: Chiropractic.
P S T (**Ref:**HM06220)

**DOUGLAS-MORT, D J & R F**

**D J & R F Douglas-Mort**, Fawnsmoor Farm, Lyme Rd, Axminster, **Devon**, EX13 5SW, ENG.
(T) 01297 32221
Speciality: Osteopathy.
P S T (**Ref:**HM06221)

**DOUGLAS-MORT, D J & R F**

**D J & R F Douglas-Mort**, First Floor, 143 High St, Honiton, **Devon**, EX14 1LJ, ENG.
(T) 01404 41678 (F) 01404 41678
Speciality: Osteopathy.
● **Partner** Mr D Douglas-Mort
P S T (**Ref:**HM06222)

**DOUGLAS-RILEY, PENELOPE**

**Penelope Douglas-Riley**, Smallack House, Smallack Drive, Plymouth, **Devon**, PL6 5EB, ENG.
(T) 01752 773148
Speciality: Reflexology.
S T (**Ref:**HM06223)

**DOVE CENTRE**

**Dove Centre**, 2 Potto St, Shotton Colliery, Durham, **County Durham**, DH6 2LA, ENG.
(T) 01915 263503
Speciality: Chiropodists (Podiatrists).
● **Owner** Mrs L Bramfitt
S (**Ref:**HM06224)

**DOVE COURT CENTRE**

**Dove Court Centre**, Haxby Shopping Centre, The Village, Haxby, York, **Yorkshire (North)**, YO3 3HU, ENG.
(T) 01904 750199
Speciality: Acupressure, Acupuncture, Swedish Body Massage. ✔
● **Acupuncturist** Sarah Dixon Q: Dip.Ac. M: BAcC.
C Yrs. Est.: 3 (**Ref:**HM06225)

**DOVE, COLIN**

**Colin Dove**, 70 Eastern Rd, Romford, **Essex**, RM1 3QA, ENG.
(T) 01708 762441 (F) 01708 739719
Speciality: Osteopathy.
● **Owner** Mr C Dove
P S T (**Ref:**HM06226)

**DOVE, JOHN**

**John Dove**, 262 Spendmore Lane, Coppull, Chorley, **Lancashire**, PR7 5DE, ENG.
(T) 01257 792993 (F) 01257 792993
Speciality: Hypnosis.
● **Owner** Mr J Dove
B (**Ref:**HM06227)

**DOVE, JULIE**

**Julie Dove**, 25 Idmiston Rd, London, **London (Greater)**, E15 1RP, ENG.
(T) 020 8555 4117
Speciality: Hypnosis.
B (**Ref:**HM06228)

**DOVE, L**

**L Dove**, 18 Spring Gr, Harrogate, **Yorkshire (North)**, HG1 2HS, ENG.
(T) 01423 563103
Speciality: Hypnosis.
B (**Ref:**HM06229)

**DOVES THERAPY CENTRE**

**Doves Therapy Centre**, 2 Merrifield Rd, Lowestoft, **Suffolk**, NR33 7HB, ENG.
(T) 01502 501189
Speciality: Complementary Medicines & Therapy.
C M (**Ref:**HM06230)

**DOVESTONES HEALING CENTRE**

**Dovestones Healing & Awareness Centre**, 8-10 Thorne Rd, Doncaster, **Yorkshire (South)**, DN1 2HS, ENG.
(T) 01302 811142 (F) 01302 811145
Speciality: Complementary Medicines & Therapy.
● **Owner** Mr R Bennett
C M (**Ref:**HM06231)

**DOWDALL, ROBERT**

**Robert Dowdall Alternative Medicine**, 12 Birchview Cl, Kilnamanagh, Tallaght, **County Dublin**, IRE.
(T) 01451 0212
Speciality: Complementary Medicines & Therapy.
M (**Ref:**HM06232)

**DOWDALL, TONY**

**Tony Dowdall**, 40 Moss House Rd, Blackpool, **Lancashire**, FY4 5JE, ENG.
(T) 01253 697858
Speciality: Homeopathy.
● **Owner** Mr T Dowdall
M (**Ref:**HM06233)

**DOWDELL, FIONA K**

**Fiona K Dowdell**, Moat Farm, Nearton End, Swanbourne, Milton Keynes, **Buckinghamshire**, MK17 0SL, ENG.
(T) 01296 720695 (F) 01296 720695
Speciality: Chiropractic, McTimoney Chiropractic. ✔
● **Owner** Miss F Dowdell Q: AMC, DC, MMCA. M: MCA.
P Yrs. Est.: 5 (**Ref:**HM06234)

**DOWDING, C J**

**C J Dowding**, 105 Langham Rd, Raunds, Wellingborough, **Northamptonshire**, NN9 6LB,



Key continued: **Yrs.Est:** Years Established **Q:** Qualifications **M:** Professional Membership ✔ Indemnity Insurance [credit card] Accept Credit Cards

ENG.
(T) 01933 625070
Speciality: Aromatherapy.
● **Owner** Mrs C Dowding
M O (**Ref:**HM06235)

### DOWER EQUINE RADIONIC THER

**Dower Equine Radionic Therapist**, Swinbrook Cottage, Swinbrook, Burford, **Oxfordshire**, OX18 4DY, ENG.
(T) 01993 822267 (F) 01993 823782
Speciality: Complementary Medicines & Therapy.
● **Owner** Mrs A Dower
C M (**Ref:**HM06236)

### DOWIE, SUSANNA

**Susanna Dowie**, 66 The Avenue, London, **London (Greater)**, N10 2QL, ENG.
(T) 020 8444 4956
Speciality: Acupuncture.
O (**Ref:**HM06237)

### DOWLE, C M

**C M Dowle**, Missenden Rd, Great Kingshill, High Wycombe, **Buckinghamshire**, HP15 6DN, ENG.
(T) 01494 713020
Speciality: Physiotherapy.
P S T (**Ref:**HM06238)

### DOWLING, E

**E Dowling**, 37 Globe Pond Rd, London, **London (Greater)**, SE16 6NR, ENG.
(T) 020 7237 4166
Speciality: Hypnosis.
● **Owner** Ms E Dowling
B (**Ref:**HM06239)

### DOWLING, R

**R Dowling**, Cressland Farm, Cranbrook Rd, Frittenden, Cranbrook, **Kent**, TN17 2BL, ENG.
(T) 01580 715155
Speciality: Osteopathy.
● **Owner** Mrs V Clarke
P S T (**Ref:**HM06240)

### DOWLING, SHEILA

**Sheila Dowling**, First Floor, Royal Bank Of Scotland Chambers, 2 Longworth Rd, Horwich, Bolton, **Lancashire**, BL6 7BA, ENG.
(T) 01204 693500
Speciality: Electrolysis.
T (**Ref:**HM06241)

### DOWN TO EARTH HOLISTIC HEALTH

**Down To Earth Holistic Health**, 209 Tangier Rd, Portsmouth, **Hampshire**, PO3 6PQ, ENG.
(T) 023 9279 3720 (F) 023 9279 3720
Speciality: Complementary Medicines & Therapy.
● **Owner** Mrs P Courtney-Dickens
C M (**Ref:**HM06242)

### DOWNEND COUNS & PSYCHOTHERAPY

**Downend Counselling & Psychotherapy Service**, 23 Glenside Cl, Bristol, BS16 2QY, ENG.
(T) 01179 567646
Speciality: Psychotherapy.
● **Owner** Mrs B Radburn
B (**Ref:**HM06243)

### DOWNES, JOHN

**John Downes**, Ashtree Court, Mill Lane, Skegness, **Lincolnshire**, PE25 1HW, ENG.
(T) 01754 766527
Speciality: Clairvoyants & Palmists.
● **Owner** Mr J Downes
B (**Ref:**HM06244)

### DOWNES, STEVEN C

**Steven C Downes**, 14 Woodspring Avenue, Weston-Super-Mare, **Somerset**, BS22 9RP, ENG.
(T) 01934 419600
Speciality: Chiropodists (Podiatrists).
● **Owner** Mr S Downes
S (**Ref:**HM06245)

### DOWNES, W P

**W P Downes**, Lower Brocks, Dunsford, Exeter, **Devon**, EX6 7AB, ENG.
(T) 01647 252767
Speciality: Osteopathy.
● **Owner** Mr W Downes
P S T (**Ref:**HM06246)

### DOWNEY, D R

**D R Downey**, Lulworth House, Monk St, Abergavenny, **Monmouthshire**, NP7 5NP, WAL.
(T) 01873 853235
Speciality: Chiropodists (Podiatrists).
S (**Ref:**HM06247)

### DOWNEY, FRANCES

**Frances Downey**, 53 Giles Rd, Lichfield, **Staffordshire**, WS13 7JY, ENG.
(T) 01543 416361
Speciality: Reflexology.
S T (**Ref:**HM06248)

### DOWNEY, JOHN (DR)

**Dr John Downey**, Health Clinic Pearse Sq, Carrick-On-Suir, **County Tipperary**, IRE.
(T) 05164 0542
Speciality: Acupuncture.
O (**Ref:**HM06249)

### DOWNEY, P A

**P A Downey**, 12 Highgrove, West Denton, Newcastle Upon Tyne, **Tyne and Wear**, NE5 1RT, ENG.
(T) 01912 677985
Speciality: Chiropodists (Podiatrists).
● **Owner** Mr P Downey
S (**Ref:**HM06250)

### DOWNIE, F W

**F W Downie**, 8 Edgeley Rd, Stockport, **Cheshire**, SK3 9NB, ENG.
(T) 01614 805951
Speciality: Chiropodists (Podiatrists).
● **Owner** Mr F Downie
S (**Ref:**HM06251)

### DOWNS HOUSE EQUINE

**Downs House Equine**, Combeleigh Farm, Wheddon Cross, Minehead, **Somerset**, TA24 7AT, ENG.
(T) 01643 841354 (F) 01643 841171
Speciality: Physiotherapy.
● **Senior Partner** Mrs M Bamiley
P S T (**Ref:**HM06252)

### DOWNS, GEORGE

**George Downs**, 240 Middle Drive, Ponteland, Newcastle Upon Tyne, **Tyne and Wear**, NE20 9LU, ENG.
(T) 01661 825109
Speciality: Chiropodists (Podiatrists).
S (**Ref:**HM06253)

### DOWNS, TINA

**Tina Downs**, 47 Waveney Rd, Hunstanton, **Norfolk**, PE36 5DG, ENG.
(T) 01485 534947
Speciality: Aromatherapy.
M O (**Ref:**HM06254)

### DOWRY CHIROPRACTIC CLINIC

**Dowry Chiropractic Clinic (The)**, 3 Dowry Pl, Bristol, BS8 4QL, ENG.
(T) 01179 298384
(E) alisonarchibald@totalise.co.uk
Speciality: Chiropractic, Manipulation, Massage (Therapeutic). ✔ CREDIT
● **Chiropractor** Ms J Deans Q: BCA, BSc, DC. M: BCA.
● **Massage Therapist** Mr J Mearns Q: BA, MA, MTI. M: MTI.
● **Owner/Chiropractor**
Ms A Archibald Q: BCA, DC, GCC (Reg). M: BCA, GCC.
P S Yrs. Est.: 15 (**Ref:**HM06255)

### DOWSING FOR HEALTH

**Dowsing For Health**, Shinehill Lane, South Littleton, Evesham, **Worcestershire**, WR11 5TR, ENG.
(T) 01386 833899
Speciality: Complementary Medicines & Therapy.
C M (**Ref:**HM06256)

### DOYLE, AUDREY

**Audrey Doyle**, 64 Fore St, Hertford, **Hertfordshire**, SG14 1BT, ENG.
(T) 01992 582965
(E) janeconyer@hotmail.com
Speciality: Biomechanics, Chiropody, Cryo Surgery, Indian Head Massage, Nail Surgery, Physiotherapy, Reflexology. ✔
● **Reflexologist/Indian Head Massage Therapist**
Jane Conyers Q: VTCT. M: FHT.
● **Chiropodist (Podiatrist)**
Ms A Doyle
C Yrs. Est.: 3 (**Ref:**HM06257)

### DOYLE, CAITRIONA

**Caitriona Doyle**, Main St, Kiltimagh, **County Mayo**, IRE.
(T) 09482 010
Speciality: Complementary Medicines & Therapy.
M (**Ref:**HM06258)

### DOYLE, D R

**D R Doyle**, 44 Silverwood Walk, Halifax, **Yorkshire (West)**, HX2 0QR, ENG.
(T) 01422 258946
Speciality: Chiropodists (Podiatrists).
● **Owner** Mrs D Doyle
S (**Ref:**HM06259)

### DOYLE, J

**J Doyle**, 6 Rommany Court, Gipsy Rd, London, **London (Greater)**, SE27 9QX, ENG.
(T) 020 8761 5514
Speciality: Osteopathy.
P S T (**Ref:**HM06260)

### DOYLE, JAMES

**James Doyle D O M B E O A**, 17 Windsor Tce, Portobello, Dublin, **County Dublin**, IRE.
(T) 01473 0828
Speciality: Osteopathy.
P S T (**Ref:**HM06261)

### DOYLE, JOHN

**John Doyle**, 95 Nethercraigs Rd, Paisley, **Renfrewshire**, PA2 8SG, SCO.
(T) 01418 846954
Speciality: Chiropodists (Podiatrists).
● **Owner** Mr J Doyle
S (**Ref:**HM06262)

### DOYLE, JOSEPHINE

**Josephine Doyle MRSI/ITEC**, 22 Ormond Ct, Clonmel, **County Tipperary**, IRE.
(T) 05280 029
Speciality: Complementary Medicines & Therapy.
M (**Ref:**HM06263)

### DOYLE, JULIA

**Julia Doyle**, 12 Terence Avenue, Norwich, **Norfolk**, NR7 8EH, ENG.
(T) 01603 403453
Speciality: Reflexology.
S T (**Ref:**HM06264)

### DOYLE, KATH

**Kath Doyle**, 23D High St, Puckeridge, Ware, **Hertfordshire**, SG11 1RN, ENG.
(T) 01920 822957
Speciality: Reflexology.
S T (**Ref:**HM06265)

### DOYLE, RAY (DR)

**Dr Ray Doyle**, 33 Woodquay, **County Galway**, IRE.
(T) 09156 2165
Speciality: Complementary Medicines & Therapy.
M (**Ref:**HM06266)

### DOYLE, TERRY

**Terry Doyle**, Natural Therapy Centre, 7 Westgate Rd, Guisborough, **Cleveland**, TS14 6EA, ENG.
(T) 01287 633591
Speciality: Acupuncture.
O (**Ref:**HM06267)

### DOYLES

**Doyles**, 5 Jarratt St, Hull, **Humberside (North)**, HU1 3HB, ENG.
(T) 01482 581776
Speciality: Aromatherapy.
M O (**Ref:**HM06268)

### DR & HERBS

**Dr & Herbs**, 134 Market Way, Manchester, **Manchester (Greater)**, M4 2EA, ENG.
(T) 01618 317688 (F) 01618 317688

Key: B Mind-Body Medicine C Complementary Medicine H Self Help Treatment M Medicinal Therapy O Oriental Medicine P Postural Therapy S Manipulative Structural Therapy T Touch Therapy

Speciality: Complementary Medicines & Therapy.
● **Doctor** Dr J Sun
M (Ref:HM06269)

## DR & HERBS
**Dr & Herbs**, Unit 16 The Royals, High St, Southend-On-Sea, **Essex**, SS1 1DQ, ENG.
(T) 01702 469888
Speciality: Complementary Medicines & Therapy.
● **Manager** Miss J Pang
C M (Ref:HM06270)

## DR EDWARD BACH FOUNDATION
**Dr Edward Bach Foundation Ltd (The)**, The Bach Centre, Mount Vernon, Bakers Lane, Sotwell, Wallingford, **Oxfordshire**, OX10 0PZ, ENG.
(T) 01491 833712
(E) info@bachcentre.com
(W) www.bachcentre.com
Speciality: Homeopathy.
● **Director** Ms J Howard
C (Ref:HM06271)

## DR K P BURNS & ASS
**Dr K P Burns & Associates**, 378 Ecclesall Rd, Sheffield, **Yorkshire (South)**, S11 8PJ, ENG.
(T) 01142 670010
Speciality: Chiropractic.
P S T (Ref:HM06272)

## DR LI
**Dr Li**, Kent Clinic, 104 Walton Rd, East Molesey, **Surrey**, KT8 0DL, ENG.
(T) 020 8224 0200
Speciality: Complementary Medicines & Therapy.
C M (Ref:HM06273)

## DR LIP ONG CRANIOSACRAL
**Dr Lip Ong Craniosacral Therapy Shiatsu**, The Lane Medical Centre, Plough Lane, Stoke Poges, Slough, **Berkshire**, SL2 4JW, ENG.
(T) 01753 662244
Speciality: Acupuncture, Cranio-Sacral Therapy, Shiatsu.
O (Ref:HM06274)

## DR NIELSON'S HEALTH CLINIC
**Dr Nielson's Health Clinic**, Unit 1 Supervalu Shopping Cent Firhouse, Dublin, **County Dublin**, IRE.
(T) 01462 5322
Speciality: Complementary Medicines & Therapy.
M (Ref:HM06275)

## DR SANDRA RICHER CHIRO SPEC
**Dr Sandra Richer Chiropractic Specialist**, 73 Penshurst Gdns, Edgware, **London (Greater)**, HA8 9TT, ENG.
(T) 020 8343 1234
Speciality: Chiropractors.
P S T (Ref:HM06276)

## DRAGE, MARJORIE
**Marjorie Drage**, 20A King St, Desborough, Kettering, **Northamptonshire**, NN14 2RD, ENG.
(T) 01536 482523
Speciality: Chiropodists (Podiatrists).
● **Owner** Mrs M Drage
S (Ref:HM06277)

## DRAGE, RONALD A
**Ronald A Drage**, 32 Henlow Rise, Shrewsbury, **Shropshire**, SY3 6BL, ENG.
(T) 01743 354517
Speciality: Chiropodists (Podiatrists).
● **Owner** Mr R Drage
S (Ref:HM06278)

## DRAGE, STEPHEN
**Stephen Drage**, 1 Kingsway, Par, **Cornwall**, PL24 2AY, ENG.
(T) 01726 812209
(E) stephen@eurobell.co.uk
Speciality: Herbal Medicine, Hypnosis, Hypnotherapy, Vitamin Therapy. ✓
● **Hypnotherapist** Mr S Drage **Q:** PGD.Hyp. **M:** BSCH.
B Yrs. Est.: 2 (Ref:HM06279)

## DRAGONSWAY ACUPUNCTURE CLINIC
**Dragonsway Acupuncture Clinic**, 9 Roseberry St, Nottingham, **Nottinghamshire**, NG6 0DF, ENG.
(T) 01159 708197
Speciality: Acupuncture.
O (Ref:HM06280)

## DRAKE, S G
**S G Drake**, 5a Fridays Cross Mews, Christchurch Rd, Ringwood, **Hampshire**, BH24 1DG, ENG.
(T) 01425 477466
Speciality: Chiropodists (Podiatrists).
S (Ref:HM06281)

## DRAKEFIELD HOMEOPATHIC CENTRE
**Drakefield Homeopathic Centre**, 239 Balham High Rd, London, **London (Greater)**, SW17 7BE, ENG.
(T) 020 8672 5253
Speciality: Homeopathy.
● **Manageress** Mrs A Marriot
M (Ref:HM06282)

## DRAKES, M
**M Drakes**, 178 East Barnet Rd, Barnet, **Hertfordshire**, EN4 8RD, ENG.
(T) 020 8449 7754 (F) 020 8449 0174
Speciality: Complementary Medicines & Therapy.
● **Principal** Mr L Hartman
M (Ref:HM06283)

## DRANSFIELD, D M
**D M Dransfield**, 51 Rae St, Dumfries, **Dumfries and Galloway**, DG1 1JD, SCO.
(T) 01387 262225
Speciality: Chiropodists (Podiatrists).
S (Ref:HM06284)

## DRANSFIELD, GILL
**Gill Dransfield**, Penvith Farmhouse, St. Martin, Looe, **Cornwall**, PL13 1NZ, ENG.
(T) 01503 240425
Speciality: Homeopathy.
M (Ref:HM06285)

## DRANSFIELD, L J
**L J Dransfield**, 38A Tilehouse Green Lane, Knowle, Solihull, **Midlands (West)**, B93 9EY, ENG.
(T) 01564 777698
Speciality: Physiotherapy.
● **Owner** Mrs L Dransfield
P S T (Ref:HM06286)

## DRAPER, DEREK
**Derek Draper**, Hender Heath, 8 Tensing Rd, Christchurch, **Dorset**, BH23 3AX, ENG.
(T) 01202 486544
Speciality: Magnetic Therapy.
M (Ref:HM06287)

## DRAPER, J
**J Draper**, 8 Pembroke Court, Lillington Avenue, Leamington Spa, **Warwickshire**, CV32 5TT, ENG.
(T) 01926 315201
Speciality: Clairvoyants & Palmists.
B (Ref:HM06288)

## DRAPER, J M
**J M Draper**, 59 Park Lane, Macclesfield, **Cheshire**, SK11 6TX, ENG.
(T) 01625 422759
Speciality: Chiropodists (Podiatrists).
S (Ref:HM06289)

## DRAPER, MARK R
**Mark R Draper**, 107 Westgate, Chichester, **Sussex (West)**, PO19 3HB, ENG.
(T) 01243 782890
Speciality: Homeopathy.
● **Administrator** Mrs M Stenning
M (Ref:HM06290)

## DRAPER, RHOADA
**Rhoada Draper B A (Psych),Dip C H**, 118 Stillorgan Rd, Dublin, **County Dublin**, IRE.
(T) 01260 0118
Speciality: Psychotherapy.
B (Ref:HM06291)

## DRASPA, J
**J Draspa**, White Friars House, 14 White Friars, Chester, **Cheshire**, CH1 1NZ, ENG.
(T) 01244 322275
Speciality: Physiotherapy.
P S T (Ref:HM06292)

## DRAYSON, SAMANTHA
**Samantha Drayson**, Chilton Centre, Chilton Gardens, Ash, Canterbury, **Kent**, CT3 2HA, ENG.
(T) 01304 615442
Speciality: Reflexology.
● **Owner** Miss S Drayson
S T (Ref:HM06293)

## DRAYTON GREEN CHIRO CLINIC
**Drayton Green Chiropractic Clinic**, 6 Drayton Green Rd, London, **London (Greater)**, W13 8RY, ENG.
(T) 020 8566 3757
Speciality: Chiropractors.
● **Owner** Dr J Jeronimus
P S T (Ref:HM06294)

## DREAM AIR
**Dream Air**, Business & Technology Centre, Radway Green, Crewe, **Cheshire**, CW2 5PR, ENG.
(T) 01270 883234 (F) 01270 883234
Speciality: Aromatherapy.
● **Owner** Miss M Williams
M O (Ref:HM06295)

## DREAM LINE
**Practical Results Unit**, 49 Romulus Court, Justin Cl, Brentford, London, **London (Greater)**, TW8 8QW, ENG.
(T) 020 8758 2050
Speciality: Acupressure, Art Therapy, Cognitive Therapy, Complementary Therapy, Counselling, Gestalt Therapy, Humanistic Psychology, Psychotherapy, Silva Method, Stress Therapy.
● **Consultant** Ms P Turner
C Yrs. Est.: 20 (Ref:HM06296)

## DREAM RESEARCH CENTRE
**Dream Research Centre**, 8 Willow Rd, London, **London (Greater)**, NW3 1TJ, ENG.
(T) 020 7794 8717
Speciality: Psychology.
● **Owner** Mr S Mayerson
B (Ref:HM06297)

## DREAMCATCHER
**Dreamcatcher (The)**, 60 Bridge St, Pinner, **London (Greater)**, HA5 3JF, ENG.
(T) 020 8426 1400 (F) 020 8426 1400
Speciality: Reiki. ✓
● **Reiki Teacher/Practitioner** Ms C Warren **Q:** Reiki Master. **M:** GCP.
C Yrs. Est.: 1 (Ref:HM06298)

## DREAMLAND BIO-ENERGY
**Dreamland Bio-Energy & Healing Centre**, Dreamland Farm Kilmihill, Kilmallock, **County Limerick**, IRE.
(T) 06398 518
Speciality: Complementary Medicines & Therapy.
M (Ref:HM06299)

## DREAMS
**Dreams**, Flat 1, 5 Meadow Rd, Beeston, Nottingham, **Nottinghamshire**, NG9 1JN, ENG.
(T) 01159 222066
Speciality: Relaxation Technique.
● **Owner** Miss N Perry
H T (Ref:HM06300)

## DREHER-BROGAN, S K (DR)
**Dr S K Dreher-Brogan**, 75 George St, Croydon, **Surrey**, CR0 1LD, ENG.
(T) 020 8656 6000
Speciality: Homeopathy.
● **Owner** Dr S Dreher-Brogan
M (Ref:HM06301)

## DREIFUSS, L & S
**L & S Dreifuss**, 136 Tuckton Rd, Bournemouth, **Dorset**, BH6 3JX, ENG.
(T) 01202 427658
Speciality: Chiropodists (Podiatrists).
● **Partner** Mrs S Dreifuss
S (Ref:HM06302)

## DREW
**Drew**, 258 High St, Glasgow, **Glasgow (City of)**,



Key continued: **Yrs.Est:** Years Established **Q:** Qualifications **M:** Professional Membership ✓ Indemnity Insurance Accept Credit Cards

G4 0QT, **SCO**.
**(T)** 01415 531990
**Speciality:** Clairvoyants & Palmists.
● **Owner** Miss S Cooper
**B** (**Ref:**HM06303)

## DREW, ADA

**Ada Drew**, 107 Whitecotes Lane, Chesterfield, **Derbyshire**, S40 3HJ, **ENG**.
**(T)** 01246 220839
**Speciality:** Hypnotherapy.
● **Owner** Mrs A Drew
**B** (**Ref:**HM06304)

## DREW, DAVID

**C S Management**, Blue Cloud Lodge, Church Walks, Llandudno, **Conwy**, LL30 2HG, **WAL**.
**(T)** 01492 875560 **(F)** 01492 875560
**(E)** drewpsychic1@aol.com
**Speciality:** Absent Healing, Aromatherapy, Complementary Therapy, Counselling, Faith Healing, Healer, Healing Therapy, Holistic Healing, Massage (Therapeutic), Meditation, Paranormal Therapies, Spiritual Healing, Stress Therapy.
● **Spiritual Medium** Mr D Drew M: BASE.
**T** Yrs. Est.: 30 (**Ref:**HM06305)

## DREW, JOCELYN

**Jocelyn Drew**, 12 Windsor Rd, Evesham, **Worcestershire**, WR11 4QE, **ENG**.
**(T)** 01386 41219
**Speciality:** Osteopathy.
● **Owner** Mr G Beresford
**P** **S** **T** (**Ref:**HM06306)

## DREW, MALCOLM

**Malcolm Drew**, Pertwood, The Green, East Knoyle, Salisbury, **Wiltshire**, SP3 6BN, **ENG**.
**(T)** 01747 830617
**Speciality:** Complementary Medicines & Therapy.
● **Owner** Mr M Drew
**C** **M** (**Ref:**HM06307)

## DREWITT, ALAN J

**Alan J Drewitt**, Garfield House, 9 Bank St, Castleford, **Yorkshire (West)**, WF10 1JD, **ENG**.
**(T)** 01977 676695
**Speciality:** Physiotherapy.
● **Owner** A Drewitt
**P** **S** **T** (**Ref:**HM06308)

## DREWITT, JENNIFER

**Jennifer Drewitt**, Taunton, **Somerset**, TA1, **ENG**.
**(T)** 01823 272227
**Speciality:** Bach Remedies.
**M** (**Ref:**HM06309)

## DREWITT, N R

**N R Drewitt**, 511 Woodborough Rd, Nottingham, **Nottinghamshire**, NG3 5FR, **ENG**.
**(T)** 01159 626304
**Speciality:** Chiropodists (Podiatrists).
● **Practice Manager** Mr N Drewitt
**S** (**Ref:**HM06310)

## DRION & ASSOCIATES

**T L Drion & Associates**, 26 Cheriton Gardens, Folkestone, **Kent**, CT20 2AS, **ENG**.
**(T)** 01303 850077 **(F)** 01303 226225
**Speciality:** Osteopathy.
● **Owner** Mr T Drion
**P** **S** **T** (**Ref:**HM06311)

## DRION, FRANCOISE

**Francoise Drion**, Fairgreen Holistic Clinic, Naas, **County Kildare**, **IRE**.
**(T)** 04589 8243
**Speciality:** Complementary Medicines & Therapy.
**M** (**Ref:**HM06312)

## DRISCOLL & ASSOCIATES

**Lyne Driscoll & Associates**, 5 Mabeys Walk, High Wych, Sawbridgeworth, **Hertfordshire**, CM21 0HN, **ENG**.
**(T)** 01279 722323
**Speciality:** Hypnosis.
**B** (**Ref:**HM06313)

## DRIVE OSTEO AND SPORTS CLINIC

**Drive Osteopathic and Sports Injury Clinic (The)**, 72 The Drive, Hove, **Sussex (East)**, BN3 3PE, **ENG**.
**(T)** 01273 203820
**Speciality:** Aromatherapy, Counselling, Cranial Osteopathy, Homeopathy, Manipulation, Massage (Therapeutic), Osteopathy, Sports Medicine - Rehabilitation. ✔
● **Osteopath** Mr M Pendry **Q:** BSc (Hons). M: GOsC.
● **Osteopath** Mr J Buck **Q:** DO. M: GOsC.
● **Osteopath** Ms E Ross **Q:** DO. M: GOsC.
● **Orthopaedic Physician** Dr U Jannoun M: GMC.
**S** Yrs. Est.: 16 (**Ref:**HM06314)

## DRIVER, D

**D Driver**, 6 Bourne Cres, Inchinnan, Renfrew, **Renfrewshire**, PA4 9PP, **SCO**.
**(T)** 01418 120327
**Speciality:** Complementary Medicines & Therapy.
● **Owner** Mrs D Driver
**C** **M** (**Ref:**HM06315)

## DRIVER, M

**M Driver**, Holmleigh, Doncaster Rd, Mexborough, **Yorkshire (South)**, S64 0JD, **ENG**.
**(T)** 01709 587247
**Speciality:** Chiropodists (Podiatrists).
● **Owner** Mr M Driver
**S** (**Ref:**HM06316)

## DROITWICH CHIROPRACTIC CLINIC

**Droitwich Chiropractic Clinic**, 1 Corbett Avenue, Droitwich, **Worcestershire**, WR9 7BD, **ENG**.
**(T)** 01905 797939 **(F)** 01905 797939
**Speciality:** Chiropractors.
**P** **S** **T** (**Ref:**HM06317)

## DROITWICH KNEE CLINIC

**Droitwich Knee Clinic**, St. Andrews Rd, Droitwich, **Worcestershire**, WR9 8YX, **ENG**.
**(T)** 01905 794858 **(F)** 01905 795916
**Speciality:** Physiotherapy.
**P** **S** **T** (**Ref:**HM06318)

## DRONFIELD NAT HEALTH CLINIC

**Dronfield Natural Health Clinic**, 24 High St, Dronfield, **Derbyshire**, S18 1PY, **ENG**.
**(T)** 01246 411067
**Speciality:** Acupressure, Acupuncture, Aromatherapy, Complementary Therapy, Counselling, Homeopathy, Hypnotherapy, Indian Head Massage, Manipulation, Massage (Therapeutic), Miasm Therapy, Nutritional Therapy, Osteopathy, Psychotherapy, Reflexology, Reiki, Shiatsu, Vitamin Therapy, Yoga. ✔
● **Reiki Healer** Ms F Flynn
● **Hypnotherapist** Ms J Boorman **Q:** B.Ac. M: BAS.
● **Owner** Ms J Cosgrove **Q:** Lic.Hom, MFTCom. M: Soc.Hom.
● **Medical Herbalist** Ms J Meakin **Q:** MNIMH. M: NIMH.
● **Chiropodist** Ms R Kay
● **Sports Massage** Christine Hensey **Q:** ICHT, IIHHT, MCHSF.
● **Osteopath** Vanessa Ellis **Q:** BSc.
● **Physiotherapy** Angela Hill **Q:** BSc (Hons), MCSP, SRP.
● **Shiatsu Masseur/Acupuncturist** Mr P Kay **Q:** Dip.Aur.Th, Lic.Ac.
● **Reflexology** Wendy Myers **Q:** IIST, MAR.
● **Counselling** Ellen Gelsthorpe **Q:** BACP, UKRC.
● **Aromatherapist** Ms Y Fenn
**B** **C** Yrs. Est.: 3 (**Ref:**HM06319)

## DRONFIELD PHYSIOTHERAPY CLINIC

**Dronfield Physiotherapy Clinic**, 264A Chesterfield Rd, Dronfield, **Derbyshire**, S18 1XJ, **ENG**.
**(T)** 01246 290683 **(F)** 01246 292252
**Speciality:** Physiotherapy. ✔
● **Owner/Physiotherapist** Miss C Miller **Q:** MCSP, SRP.
**S** (**Ref:**HM06320)

## DROP-IN CENTRE

**Drop-In Centre (The)**, 39 Wellcome Avenue, Dartford, **Kent**, DA1 5JL, **ENG**.
**(T)** 01322 278404
**Speciality:** Complementary Medicines & Therapy.
● **Owner** Mrs P Abbott
**C** **M** (**Ref:**HM06321)

## D'ROSE, NICKY

**Nicky D'Rose**, 52 Stoke Newington Church St, London, **London (Greater)**, N16 0NB, **ENG**.
**(T)** 020 7249 9671
**Speciality:** Complementary Medicines & Therapy.
● **Senior Partner** Mrs J Sheridan
**M** (**Ref:**HM06322)

## DRUCE, Y L

**Y L Druce**, Market House Surgery, 18B Bampton St, Tiverton, **Devon**, EX16 6AA, **ENG**.
**(T)** 01884 258570
**Speciality:** Chiropodists (Podiatrists).
**S** (**Ref:**HM06323)

## DRUMCHAPEL PSYCHOLOGICAL SVS

**Drumchapel Psychological Services**, Summerhill Primary School, 5 Saddell Rd, Glasgow, **Glasgow (City of)**, G15 7JS, **SCO**.
**(T)** 01419 448513
**Speciality:** Psychology.
**B** (**Ref:**HM06324)

## DRUMMOND, HEATHER

**Heather Drummond**, Keys Counselling & Psychotherapy, 131A Alcester Rd, Birmingham, **Midlands (West)**, B13 8JP, **ENG**.
**(T)** 01214 431580
**Speciality:** Aromatherapy.
● **Doctor** Mr D King
**M** **O** (**Ref:**HM06325)

## DRUMMOND, IAN

**Ian Drummond**, Flat 1, 31 South Bridge, Edinburgh, **Edinburgh (City of)**, EH1 1LL, **SCO**.
**(T)** 01315 581092
**Speciality:** Hypnosis, Hypnotherapy. ✔
● **Hypnotherapist** Mr I Drummond
**B** Yrs. Est.: 6 (**Ref:**HM06326)

## DRUMMOND, JOANNE

**Joanne Drummond**, 1st Floor Flat, 41 St. Pauls Avenue, London, **London (Greater)**, NW2 5SY, **ENG**.
**(T)** 07976 806152
**Speciality:** Reflexology.
**S** **T** (**Ref:**HM06327)

## DRUMMOND, TARA W

**Tara W Drummond**, 37 Frederick St, Edinburgh, **Edinburgh (City of)**, EH2 1EP, **SCO**.
**(T)** 01312 204077
**Speciality:** Osteopathy.
● **Owner** Miss T Drummond
**P** **S** **T** (**Ref:**HM06328)

## DRURY, ANNE

**Anne Drury**, 29 Ferndale Rd, Lichfield, **Staffordshire**, WS13 7DJ, **ENG**.
**(T)** 01543 257926
**Speciality:** Psychotherapy.
● **Owner** Mrs A Drury
**B** (**Ref:**HM06329)

## DRURY, GILLIAN

**Gillian Drury**, 1 Northgate Cl, Rottingdean, Brighton, **Sussex (East)**, BN2 7DZ, **ENG**.
**(T)** 01273 309177
**Speciality:** Hypnosis.
● **Owner** Mrs G Drury
**B** (**Ref:**HM06330)

## DRURY, WENDY

**Wendy Drury MBRA**, 61 Chester Rd, Akroydon, Halifax, **Yorkshire (West)**, HX3 6LS, **ENG**.
**(T)** 01422 367834 **(F)** 01422 367834
**(E)** ben@drury.com
**Speciality:** Reflexology. ✔
● **Reflexologist** Ms W Drury **Q:** MBRA. M: BRA.
**T** Yrs. Est.: 5 (**Ref:**HM06331)

## DRYDEN, B A

**B A Dryden**, 44 Beauharrow Rd, St. Leonards-On-Sea, **Sussex (East)**, TN37 7BL, **ENG**.
**(T)** 01424 853164
**Speciality:** Hypnosis, Hypnotherapy, Psychotherapy. ✔
● **Owner/Hypnotherapist/Psychotherapist** Mr B Dryden **Q:** MNRHP. M: NRHP.
**S** Yrs. Est.: 9 (**Ref:**HM06332)

Key: **B** Mind-Body Medicine **C** Complementary Medicine **H** Self Help Treatment **M** Medicinal Therapy **O** Oriental Medicine **P** Postural Therapy **S** Manipulative Structural Therapy **T** Touch Therapy

**DRYDEN, PHILIP**

**Philip Dryden**, 10 Dalhousie Rd, Broughty Ferry, Dundee, **Angus**, DD5 2SQ, **SCO**.
(T) 01382 778067
Speciality: Chiropody, Nail Surgery. ✓
● **Owner/Chiropodist** Mr P Dryden Q: M.S.C.P, MBChA.
M Yrs. Est.: 13 (**Ref:**HM06333)

**DRYER, DIANA**

**Diana Dryer**, 20 Twyford Gardens, Bishop's Stortford, **Hertfordshire**, CM23 3EH, ENG.
(T) 01279 833549
Speciality: Reflexology.
S T (**Ref:**HM06334)

**DRYSDALE, IAN**

**Ian Drysdale**, 36 Pepys Cl, Uxbridge, **London (Greater)**, UB10 8NY, ENG.
(T) 01895 633870
Speciality: Osteopathy.
P S T (**Ref:**HM06335)

**D'SOUZA, MARGARET**

**Margaret D'Souza**, 11 Glenbank Rd, Kirkintilloch, Glasgow, **Glasgow (City of)**, G66 5AG, SCO.
(T) 01417 761008
Speciality: Reflexology.
S T (**Ref:**HM06336)

**D'SOUZA, R J**

**R J D'Souza**, Physiofirst Centre, 19 The Crescent, Truro, **Cornwall**, TR1 3ES, ENG.
(T) 01872 241882
Speciality: Physiotherapy.
P S T (**Ref:**HM06337)

**D'SOUZA, S A**

**S A D'Souza**, 35 Scholars Rd, London, **London (Greater)**, SW12 0PF, ENG.
(T) 020 8673 3366
Speciality: Osteopathy.
P S T (**Ref:**HM06338)

**DTR THERAPEUTICS**

**DTR Therapeutics**, Empress Business Centre, Chester Rd, Manchester, **Manchester (Greater)**, M16 9EA, ENG.
(T) 01618 776887
Speciality: Physiotherapy.
P S T (**Ref:**HM06339)

**DUBLIN CENTRE FOR CHINESE MED**

**Dublin Centre For Chinese Medicine**, 65 Kenilworth Sq, Dublin, **County Dublin**, IRE.
(T) 01497 8958
(E) tcm@iol.ie
Speciality: Complementary Medicines & Therapy.
M (**Ref:**HM06340)

**DUBLIN COUNS & THERAPY CTRE**

**Dublin Counselling & Therapy Centre**, 41 Gardiner St, Upr, Dublin, **County Dublin**, IRE.
(T) 01878 8236
Speciality: Counselling.
B H (**Ref:**HM06341)

**DUBLIN COUNSELLING**

**Dublin Counselling &**, 41 Gardiner St, Upr, IRE.
(T) 01878 8236
Speciality: Counselling.
B H (**Ref:**HM06342)

**DUBLIN HYPNOTHERAPY CLINIC**

**Dublin Hypnotherapy Clinic**, 91 Terence Rd, North, 6W, IRE.
(T) 01490 1391
(W) www.hypnosiseire.com
Speciality: Hypnotherapy.
B (**Ref:**HM06343)

**DUCAS, KENNETH**

**Kenneth Ducas**, Devereux House, 69 Albert Rd, Farnborough, **Hampshire**, GU14 6SL, ENG.
(T) 01252 512967
Speciality: Chiropodists (Podiatrists).
S (**Ref:**HM06344)

**DUCHY CHIROPRACTIC CLINIC**

**Duchy Chiropractic Clinic (The)**, 2 Mount Folly, Bodmin, **Cornwall**, PL31 2DB, ENG.
(T) 01208 78777
Speciality: Chiropractic.
● **Owner** Dr K Tomes-Nicholson
P S T (**Ref:**HM06345)

**DUCIE, SONIA**

**Sonia Ducie**, 30 Bloemfontein Avenue, London, **London (Greater)**, W12 7BL, ENG.
Speciality: Reflexology.
S T (**Ref:**HM06346)

**DUCKWORTH, JEAN**

**Jean Duckworth - Homeopath**, Ashgreen House, Somerset Avenue, Blackburn, **Lancashire**, BB1 9JD, ENG.
(T) 01254 249970 (F) 01254 249970
(E) jean@homeopath.fsnet.co.uk
Speciality: Homeopathy. ✓
● **Homeopath** Mrs J Duckworth Q: MNWCH, RSHom. M: Soc.Hom.
M Yrs. Est.: 5 (**Ref:**HM06347)

**DUCKWORTH, JEAN**

**Jean Duckworth**, 11 Acrefield, Blackburn, **Lancashire**, BB2 7BJ, ENG.
(T) 01254 667849
Speciality: Homeopathy.
M (**Ref:**HM06348)

**DUCKWORTH, NIGEL**

**Nigel Duckworth**, 2 Nelsons Walk, Tenby, **Pembrokeshire**, SA70 7JD, WAL.
(T) 01834 844088
Speciality: Chiropodists (Podiatrists).
S (**Ref:**HM06349)

**DUCKWORTH, ROGER**

**Roger Duckworth**, 15 Rectory Rd, Wokingham, **Berkshire**, RG40 1DJ, ENG.
(T) 01189 786149
Speciality: Physiotherapy.
● **Owner** Mr R Duckworth
P S T (**Ref:**HM06350)

**DUCKWORTH, ROSEMARY**

**Rosemary Duckworth**, The Guilder Centre, 16A-18 Guilder Lane, Laverstock, Salisbury, **Wiltshire**, SP1 1QE, ENG.
(T) 01722 421404
Speciality: Physiotherapy.
P S T (**Ref:**HM06351)

**DUCROTOY, M**

**M Ducrotoy**, Market St, Deal, **Kent**, CT14 6HS, ENG.
(T) 01304 360916
Speciality: Chiropodists (Podiatrists).
● **Owner** Mr M Ducrotoy
S (**Ref:**HM06352)

**DUDGEON, DELIA**

**Delia Dudgeon**, 30 The Front, Potten End, Berkhamsted, **Hertfordshire**, HP4 2QR, ENG.
(T) 01442 874187 (F) 01442 874187
(E) deliadudge@supanet.com
Speciality: Alexander Technique, Bach Remedies, Counselling, Metamorphic Therapy, Reflexology, Reiki, Focusing Therapy. ✓
● **Therapist** Ms J Shuffrey
(T) 01442 244854
● **Owner** Ms D Dudgeon M: BACP, BRA.
C Yrs. Est.: 13 (**Ref:**HM06353)

**DUDLEY PHYSIOTHERAPY CLINIC**

**Dudley Physiotherapy Clinic**, 1a Parsons St, Dudley, **Midlands (West)**, DY1 1JJ, ENG.
(T) 01384 233306 (F) 01384 250042
Speciality: Acupuncture, Physiotherapy. ✓
● **Practice manager** Mrs Andersen
● **Owner/Physiotherapist** Mr T Andersen Q: MCSP, SRP.
S Yrs. Est.: 20 (**Ref:**HM06354)

**DUDLEY, J A**

**J A Dudley**, 40 Blackmore, Letchworth, **Hertfordshire**, SG6 2SZ, ENG.
(T) 01462 672794
Speciality: Chiropodists (Podiatrists).
S (**Ref:**HM06355)

**DUDMAN, E J**

**E J Dudman**, 47b Woodlands Rd, Lytham St. Annes, **Lancashire**, FY8 1DA, ENG.
(T) 01253 734100
Speciality: Chiropodists (Podiatrists).
● **Owner** Mr E Dudman
S (**Ref:**HM06356)

**DUELL, C**

**C Duell**, 11 Harland Pl, Stockton-On-Tees, **Cleveland**, TS20 1AL, ENG.
(T) 01642 531033
Speciality: Chiropodists (Podiatrists).
S (**Ref:**HM06357)

**DUFF, G**

**G Duff**, 138 Harley St, London, **London (Greater)**, W1N 1AH, ENG.
(T) 020 7935 9438 (F) 020 7935 9438
Speciality: Physiotherapy.
● **Owner** Mrs G Duff
P S T (**Ref:**HM06358)

**DUFF, M H**

**M H Duff**, 71 Lismore Rd, Downpatrick, **County Down**, BT30 7EY, NIR.
(T) 028 4484 1125
Speciality: Physiotherapy.
P S T (**Ref:**HM06359)

**DUFFIELD**

**Duffield**, 24 Love Lane, Pontefract, **Yorkshire (West)**, WF8 4AN, ENG.
(T) 01977 780500 (F) 01977 780500
Speciality: Reflexology. ✓
● **Reflexologist** Ms J Duffield M: AoR.
T (**Ref:**HM06360)

**DUFFIELD, G**

**G Duffield**, 110 Beckett Rd, Doncaster, **Yorkshire (South)**, DN2 4AX, ENG.
(T) 01302 361383
Speciality: Aromatherapy.
● **Owner** Mrs G Duffield
M O (**Ref:**HM06361)

**DUFFIN, INGRID**

**Ingrid Duffin**, Haven Cottage, Cliff Rd, Fareham, **Hampshire**, PO14 3JT, ENG.
(T) 01329 667825
Speciality: Physiotherapy.
● **Owner** Mrs I Duffin
P S T (**Ref:**HM06362)

**DUFFY, CATHERINE**

**Catherine Duffy**, Health Hydro, Milton Rd, Swindon, **Wiltshire**, SN1 5JA, ENG.
(T) 01793 465631
Speciality: Aromatherapy.
M O (**Ref:**HM06363)

**DUFFY, MELANIE**

**Melanie Duffy**, 1 Clayfield Mews, Newcomen Rd, Tunbridge Wells, **Kent**, TN4 9PA, ENG.
(T) 01892 545443
Speciality: Psychotherapy.
B (**Ref:**HM06364)

**DUFFY, MELANIE**

**Melanie Duffy**, Harvest Bank, Lenham Heath Rd, Sandway, Maidstone, **Kent**, ME17 2NB, ENG.
(T) 01622 850921
Speciality: Psychotherapy.
● **Owner** Dr M Duffy
B (**Ref:**HM06365)

**DUFFY, MICHELLE**

**Michelle Duffy**, 11 Cumberland St, Portsmouth, **Hampshire**, PO1 3JL, ENG.
(T) 023 9287 2772
Speciality: Hypnosis.
● **Owner** Ms M Duffy
B (**Ref:**HM06366)

**DUFFY, P W**

**P W Duffy**, 44 Derby Lane, Liverpool, **Merseyside**, L13 3DL, ENG.
(T) 01512 283615
Speciality: Chiropodists (Podiatrists).
● **Owner** Mr P Duffy
S (**Ref:**HM06367)

**DUGGAN, JOY**

**Joy Duggan**, Natural Path Health Centre, 3 Holyrood St, Chard, **Somerset**, TA20 2AH, ENG.
(T) 01460 62953 (F) 01460 63809
Speciality: Hypnosis.
● **Owner** Mr M Newbound
B (**Ref:**HM06368)


Key continued: **Yrs.Est:** Years Established **Q:** Qualifications **M:** Professional Membership ✓ Indemnity Insurance Accept Credit Cards

**DUGGAN, JOY M**

**Joy M Duggan**, 15 Silver St, Ilminster, **Somerset**, TA19 0DH, **ENG**.
(T) 01460 61922
Speciality: Hypnosis.
B (Ref:HM06369)

**DUGGAN, NORA**

**Nora Duggan**, 20 Merllyn Avenue, Deeside, **Flintshire**, CH5 4TB, **WAL**.
(T) 01244 818641
Speciality: Reflexology.
S T (Ref:HM06370)

**DUHY, CHRISTINE**

**Christine Duhy**, 8 London Rd, Markfield, **Leicestershire**, LE67 9UR, **ENG**.
(T) 01530 242681 (F) 01530 242681
Speciality: Complementary Medicines & Therapy.
● **Owner** Mrs C Duhy
C M (Ref:HM06371)

**DUIGNAN, KAREN**

**Karen Duignan**, 5 Golf Course Rd, Livingston, **Lothian (West)**, EH54 8QF, **SCO**.
(T) 01506 438056
Speciality: Hypnosis, Hypnotherapy, Neuro-Linguistic Program. ✔
● **Hypnotherapist** Mrs K Duignan Q: C.Hyp, Cert.Ed, CMH, NLP. M: UKGHE.
B Yrs. Est.: 15 (Ref:HM06372)

**DUKE STREET CHIROPODY**

**Duke Street Chiropody**, 65 Duke St, Darlington, **County Durham**, DL3 7SD, **ENG**.
(T) 01325 356900
Speciality: Chiropodists (Podiatrists).
● **Owner** Mr C Auton
S (Ref:HM06373)

**DUKES, MARTIN**

**Martin Dukes**, St. Georges Chambers, 2 St. Georges Avenue, Thornton, **Lancashire**, FY5 3NH, **ENG**.
(T) 01253 851167
Speciality: Hypnosis.
B (Ref:HM06374)

**DULCAMARA**

**Dulcamara**, Seskin, Windgap, **County Kilkenny**, **IRE**.
(T) 00353 51648356
Speciality: Anthroposohical Medicine, Herbal Medicine, Homeopathy.
● **Herbalist** Ms C Maxwell Q: Dip.Phyto.
M Yrs. Est.: 19 (Ref:HM06375)

**DULDZIN BUDHIST CENTRE**

**Duldzin Budhist Centre**, 25 Aigburth Drive, Liverpool, **Merseyside**, L17 4JH, **ENG**.
(T) 01517 268900
Speciality: Relaxation Technique.
H T (Ref:HM06376)

**DULEWICZ & AST**

**Fletcher Dulewicz & Associates**, 89 Rodenhurst Rd, London, **London (Greater)**, SW4 8AF, **ENG**.
(T) 020 8674 1940 (F) 020 8674 1940
Speciality: Psychology.
● **Partner** Mr C Fletcher
B (Ref:HM06377)

**DULIEU, FIONA**

**Fiona Dulieu**, 10 Greenstead, Sawbridgeworth, **Hertfordshire**, CM21 9NY, **ENG**.
(T) 01279 722064
Speciality: Chiropodists (Podiatrists).
● **Owner** Mrs F Dulieu
S (Ref:HM06378)

**DULLER, R V**

**R V Duller**, 3 Honeysuckle Rd, Widmer End, High Wycombe, **Buckinghamshire**, HP15 6BW, **ENG**.
(T) 01494 713227
Speciality: Chiropodists (Podiatrists).
● **Owner** Mr R Duller
S (Ref:HM06379)

**DULWICH AROMATHERAPY & AST**

**Dulwich Aromatherapy & Associates**, Dulwich Medical Centre, 163-169 Crystal Palace Rd, London, **London (Greater)**, SE22 9EP, **ENG**.
(T) 020 8693 3330
Speciality: Aromatherapy.
M O (Ref:HM06380)

**DULWICH CHIROPODY SURGERY**

**Dulwich Chiropody Surgery**, 6 Woodwarde Rd, London, **London (Greater)**, SE22 8UJ, **ENG**.
(T) 020 8693 6000
Speciality: Chiropodists (Podiatrists).
● **Owner** Mrs D Small
S (Ref:HM06381)

**DULWICH CHIROPRACTIC CLINIC**

**Dulwich Chiropractic Clinic**, Dulwich Medical Centre, 163-169 Crystal Palace Rd, London, **London (Greater)**, SE22 9EP, **ENG**.
(T) 020 8693 1115
Speciality: Chiropractic.
P S T (Ref:HM06382)

**DULWICH PHYSIOTHERAPY**

**Dulwich Physiotherapy**, 163-169 Crystal Palace Rd, London, **London (Greater)**, SE22 9EP, **ENG**.
(T) 020 8693 9930
Speciality: Physiotherapy. ✔
● **Owner/Physiotherapist**
Sarah Parsons Q: MCSP, SRP.
S Yrs. Est.: 11 (Ref:HM06383)

**DUMASIA, HELGA**

**Helga Dumasia**, Church Rd, Windlesham, **Surrey**, GU20 6BT, **ENG**.
(T) 01276 473371
Speciality: Complementary Medicines & Therapy.
M (Ref:HM06384)

**DUMFIRES NATURAL HEALTH CLINIC**

**Dumfires Natural Health Clinic**, 62 Academy St, Dumfries, **Dumfries and Galloway**, DG1 1BZ, **SCO**.
(T) 01387 247844
Speciality: Complementary Medicines & Therapy.
C M (Ref:HM06385)

**DUMFRIES HOLISTIC HEALTH CTRE**

**Dumfries Holistic Health Centre**, 98 Loreburn St, Dumfries, **Dumfries and Galloway**, DG1 1HW, **SCO**.
(T) 01387 267617
Speciality: Acupressure, Acupuncture, Alexander Technique, Aromatherapy, Colour Therapy, Counselling, Crystal Healing, Dietician, Homeopathy, Massage (Therapeutic), Osteopathy, Psychotherapy, Reflexology, Remedial Massage, Spiritual Healing, Aromatherapy Massage. ✔
● **Osteopath** Ms E Wilson Q: DO. M: GOsC.
C Yrs. Est.: 8 (Ref:HM06386)

**DUMFRIES NATURAL HEALTH CENTRE**

**Dumfries Natural Health Centre**, 47 Castle St, Dumfries, **Dumfries and Galloway**, DG1 1DU, **SCO**.
(T) 01387 256644
Speciality: Hypnosis.
B (Ref:HM06387)

**DUN LAOGHAIRE CHIROPRACTIC**

**Dun Laoghaire Chiropractic Clinic**, 12 Clarinda Pk, Nth, Dun Laoghaire, **County Dublin**, **IRE**.
(T) 01280 0488
Speciality: Chiropractors.
P S T (Ref:HM06388)

**DUN LAOIRE HEALING ROOM**

**Dun Laoire Healing Room**, 3 Carriglea Gardens, Kill Avenue, Dun Laoghaire, **County Dublin**, **IRE**.
(T) 01280 0692
Speciality: Spiritual Healing. ✔
● **Spiritual Healer** Ms C Martin Q: BA, Dip.H.E. M: NFSH.
M Yrs. Est.: 3 (Ref:HM06389)

**DUNBAR CHIROPODY CLINIC**

**Dunbar Chiropody Clinic**, 2 High St, Dunbar, **Lothian (East)**, EH42 1EL, **SCO**.
(T) 01368 863269
Speciality: Chiropodists (Podiatrists).
● **Owner** Ms H Anderson
S (Ref:HM06390)

**DUNBAR PHYSIOTHERAPY**

**Dunbar Physiotherapy**, 2 High St, Dunbar, **Lothian (East)**, EH42 1EL, **SCO**.
(T) 01368 864989
Speciality: Osteopathy.
● **Owner** Mr T McNullwn
P S T (Ref:HM06391)

**DUNBAR, MAURICE**

**Maurice Dunbar**, 17 Cannon St, Birmingham, **Midlands (West)**, B2 5EN, **ENG**.
(T) 01216 430314
Speciality: Clairvoyants & Palmists.
● **Owner** Mr M Dunbar
B (Ref:HM06392)

**DUNBAR, NEIL**

**Neil Dunbar**, 26 Farm Lane, Purley, **Surrey**, CR8 3PU, **ENG**.
(T) 020 8660 8712
Speciality: Physiotherapy.
● **Owner** Mr N Dunbar
P S T (Ref:HM06393)

**DUNCAN, E**

**E Duncan**, Farnbarn House, Main St, Tallentire, Cockermouth, **Cumbria**, CA13 0PS, **ENG**.
(T) 01900 827377
Speciality: Osteopathy.
P S T (Ref:HM06394)

**DUNCAN, M**

**M Duncan**, 13 Fairford Rd, Maidenhead, **Berkshire**, SL6 7AL, **ENG**.
(T) 01628 622920
Speciality: Chiropodists (Podiatrists).
● **Owner** Mrs M Duncan
S (Ref:HM06395)

**DUNCAN, SIMON**

**Simon Duncan**, 2a High St, Bromborough, Wirral, **Merseyside**, CH62 7HA, **ENG**.
(T) 01513 530028 (F) 01513 439123
Speciality: Reflexology.
● **Owner** Mr S Duncan
S T (Ref:HM06396)

**DUNCANSON, S**

**S Duncanson**, 59 Spixworth Rd, Norwich, **Norfolk**, NR6 7NQ, **ENG**.
(T) 01603 405333
Speciality: Alexander Technique.
P S (Ref:HM06397)

**DUNCOMBE CLNC OF PHYSICAL MED**

**Duncombe Clinic Of Physical Medicine**, 5 Rochester Rd, Coventry, **Midlands (West)**, CV5 6AB, **ENG**.
(T) 024 7667 7447
Speciality: Osteopathy.
● **Owner** Mr S Duncombe
M (Ref:HM06398)

**DUNCOMBE, MARTIN**

**Martin Duncombe**, 17 Dorset Avenue, Chelmsford, **Essex**, CM2 9TZ, **ENG**.
(T) 01245 267296
Speciality: Homeopathy.
● **Owner** Mr M Duncombe
M (Ref:HM06399)

**DUNDEE, ROKPA**

**Rokpa Dundee**, 51 Reform St, Dundee, **Angus**, DD1 1SL, **SCO**.
(T) 01382 872020 (F) 01382 872010
Speciality: Complementary Medicines & Therapy.
● **Director** Mr K Jiga
M (Ref:HM06400)

**DUNDRUM GESTALT CENTRE**

**Dundrum Gestalt Centre**, Park House Eglington Tce, Off K, Dublin, **County Dublin**, **IRE**.
(T) 01296 2015
Speciality: Complementary Medicines & Therapy.
M (Ref:HM06401)

**DUNEDIN CHIROPODY CLINIC**

**Dunedin Chiropody Clinic**, 40 Westgate, Patrington, Hull, **Humberside (North)**, HU12 0NB, **ENG**.
(T) 01964 630377
Speciality: Chiropodists (Podiatrists).



Key: B Mind-Body Medicine C Complementary Medicine H Self Help Treatment M Medicinal Therapy O Oriental Medicine P Postural Therapy S Manipulative Structural Therapy T Touch Therapy

● **Owner** Ms E Swain
S (Ref:HM06402)

**DUNFORD, BRYAN**

**Bryan Dunford**, Clifton Lodge, 1 Long Acre East, Bingham, Nottingham, **Nottinghamshire**, NG13 8BY, ENG.
(T) 01949 839069
Speciality: Chiropodists (Podiatrists).
S (Ref:HM06403)

**DUNFORD, LIZ**

**Liz Dunford**, Midland Rd, Leeds, **Yorkshire (West)**, LS6 1BQ, ENG.
(T) 01132 751084
Speciality: Homeopathy.
M (Ref:HM06404)

**DUNGANNON CHIROPRACTIC CLINIC**

**Dungannon Chiropractic Clinic**, 7 Ranfurly Rd, Dungannon, **County Tyrone**, BT71 6ED, NIR.
(T) 028 8775 3663 (F) 028 8775 3805
Speciality: Chiropractic. ✓ CREDIT
● **Owner** Dr J Braund Q: BSc, DC.
P Yrs. Est.: 1 (Ref:HM06405)

**DUNGARVAN ALTERNATIVE HEALTH**

**Dungarvan Alternative Health Clinic**, Main St, Dungarvan, **County Waterford**, IRE.
(T) 05844 299
Speciality: Complementary Medicines & Therapy.
M (Ref:HM06406)

**DUNKLEY, KITTY**

**Kitty Dunkley**, 24 Catherine St, Salisbury, **Wiltshire**, SP1 2DA, ENG.
(T) 01747 871576
Speciality: Aromatherapy.
● **General Manager** Ms S Cowell
M O (Ref:HM06407)

**DUNLEA, TONY**

**Tony Dunlea**, Healing Palms Clinic Kenilworth, Youghal, **County Cork**, IRE.
(T) 024 9199 1
Speciality: Complementary Medicines & Therapy.
M (Ref:HM06408)

**DUNLOP, JAMES R W**

**James R W Dunlop**, 100 Warwick Rd, Carlisle, **Cumbria**, CA1 1JU, ENG.
(T) 01228 520412
Speciality: Osteopathy.
P S T (Ref:HM06409)

**DUNLOP, JAMES R W**

**James R W Dunlop**, 2 Lovers Walk, Dumfries, **Dumfries and Galloway**, DG1 1LP, SCO.
(T) 01387 254249
Speciality: Osteopathy.
● **Owner** Mr J Dunlop
P S T (Ref:HM06410)

**DUNLOP, JEAN**

**Jean Dunlop**, The Oxford Physiotherapy Service, 162 Banbury Rd, Oxford, **Oxfordshire**, OX2 7BT, ENG.
(T) 01865 311686
Speciality: Physiotherapy.
P S T (Ref:HM06411)

**DUNLOP, JOAN**

**Joan Dunlop**, 10 Balliol Cl, Bognor Regis, **Sussex (West)**, PO21 5QE, ENG.
(T) 01243 863720
Speciality: Psychotherapy.
B (Ref:HM06412)

**DUNLOP, MARION**

**Marion Dunlop**, Brackley Clinic, Hartley House, 29 Market Pl, Brackley, **Northamptonshire**, NN13 7AB, ENG.
(T) 01280 707083
Speciality: Hypnosis.
● **Owner** Mrs M Dunlop
B (Ref:HM06413)

**DUNMOW PHYSIOTHERAPY SERVICE**

**Dunmow Physiotherapy Service**, Town Farm, High St, Stebbing, Dunmow, **Essex**, CM6 3SG, ENG.
(T) 01371 874333
Speciality: Physiotherapy.

● **Owner** Ms T Holton
P S T (Ref:HM06414)

**DUNN, HELEN**

**Helen Dunn**, Rear Of Whitehill Post Office, Whitehill Rd, Crowborough, **Sussex (East)**, TN6 1JS, ENG.
(T) 01892 665291
Speciality: Osteopathy.
P S T (Ref:HM06415)

**DUNN, LLOYD**

**Lloyd Dunn**, 17 Brackenfield Drive, Giltbrook, Nottingham, **Nottinghamshire**, NG16 2US, ENG.
(T) 01159 386017
Speciality: Chiropodists (Podiatrists).
S (Ref:HM06416)

**DUNNE, ALISON**

**Alison Dunne**, Hazelwood Drive, St. Albans, **Hertfordshire**, AL4 0UP, ENG.
(T) 01727 832603
Speciality: Reflexology.
S T (Ref:HM06417)

**DUNNE, CAROL**

**Carol Dunne**, 33 Highfield Lane, Tyttenhanger, St. Albans, **Hertfordshire**, AL4 0RH, ENG.
(T) 01727 867160
Speciality: Psychotherapy.
● **Owner** Ms C Dunne
B (Ref:HM06418)

**DUNNE, CONOR W**

**Conor W Dunne**, 13 Eagle Rd, Wembley, **London (Greater)**, HA0 4SQ, ENG.
(T) 020 8902 1725
Speciality: Chiropodists (Podiatrists).
● **Owner** Mr C Dunne
S (Ref:HM06419)

**DUNNE, SALLY**

**Sally Dunne**, 9 Eden Rd, Dun Laoighre, Dublin, **County Dublin**, IRE.
(T) 01284 2003
Speciality: Complementary Medicines & Therapy.
M (Ref:HM06420)

**DUNNE, TERESA**

**Teresa Dunne**, The Old Surgery, Warden Court, St Davids St, Presteigne, **Powys**, LD8 2BP, WAL.
(T) 01544 267532
Speciality: Osteopathy.
P S T (Ref:HM06421)

**DUNNE, TRISH**

**Trish Dunne**, 24 Manor Gro, Tralee, **County Kerry**, IRE.
(T) 06671 28335
Speciality: Complementary Medicines & Therapy.
M (Ref:HM06422)

**DUNNET, GILLIAN**

**Gillian Dunnet**, 8 Pye Cl, Caterham, **Surrey**, CR3 5FQ, ENG.
(T) 01883 348631
Speciality: Reflexology.
S T (Ref:HM06423)

**DUNNETT, PAM**

**Pam Dunnett**, 337-339 Norwich Rd, Ipswich, **Suffolk**, IP1 4BN, ENG.
(T) 01473 464300
Speciality: Chiropodists (Podiatrists).
S (Ref:HM06424)

**DUNNING, CAROL**

**Carol Dunning**, 38 Orford Green, Warrington, **Cheshire**, WA2 8PH, ENG.
(T) 01925 635564
Speciality: Clairvoyants & Palmists.
B (Ref:HM06425)

**DUNNINGS & ASSOCIATES**

**D N & J E Dunnings & Associates**, 91 Hassell St, Newcastle, **Staffordshire**, ST5 1AX, ENG.
(T) 01782 661199 (F) 01782 662260
Speciality: Chiropodists (Podiatrists).
● **Practice Manager** Mrs D Plant
S (Ref:HM06426)

**DUNSTER, M**

**M Dunster**, 396 High St, Lincoln, **Lincolnshire**, LN5 7SS, ENG.
(T) 01522 887887
Speciality: Complementary Medicines & Therapy.
● **Owner** Ms M Dunster
M (Ref:HM06427)

**DUNTON CTRE-COUN/PSYCHOTHERAPY**

**Dunton Centre For Counselling & Psychotherapy**, 13 Church St, Dunton, Biggleswade, **Bedfordshire**, SG18 8RR, ENG.
(T) 01767 601259
Speciality: Counselling, Family Therapy, Gestalt Therapy, Humanistic Psychology, Primal Therapy, Psychotherapy, Stress Therapy. ✓ CREDIT
● **Counsellor** Ms M Fosbrook
(T) 01767 262229 Q: Adv.Dip.Psyco.Couns. M: BACP.
● **Counsellor** Ms K Lee
(T) 01767 313839 Q: Cert.Couns, Cert.Couns.Groupwork, Cert.Sup.Sk, CQSW. M: BACP.
● **Counsellor** Ms M Brindle Q: PGD.Couns. M: BACP.
● **Psychotherapist** Ms B Morgan
(T) 01462 733267 Q: Dip.GesTh. M: UKCP.
● **Counsellor** Ms S Murray
(T) 01462 894190 Q: BA (Hons), Cert.Astrol, Dip.Couns.
● **Therapist** Ms S Aldred
(T) 01462 480336 Q: BA (Hons), Dip.Superv, PgDip.Couns.Psych. M: UKCP.
B Yrs. Est.: 5 (Ref:HM06428)

**DUPKER, PAUL**

**Paul Dupker**, 118 Royal Prde, Eastbourne, **Sussex (East)**, BN21 3QL, ENG.
(T) 01323 430025 (F) 01323 648452
Speciality: Chiropractors.
● **Partner** Mrs S Josling
P S T (Ref:HM06429)

**DURBAN, PAMELA**

**Pamela Durban**, 24 Chiltern Cl, Warmley, Bristol, BS30 8UJ, ENG.
(T) 01179 677674
Speciality: Hypnosis.
● **Owner** Mrs P Durban
B (Ref:HM06430)

**DURCAN MARIE KINESIOLOGIST**

**Marie Durcan Kinesiologist**, 3 Miscaun View, **County Sligo**, IRE.
(T) 07161 467
Speciality: Complementary Medicines & Therapy.
M (Ref:HM06431)

**DURCAN, CAROLE**

**Carole Durcan**, Wanstead Village Health Centre, 24 High St, London, **London (Greater)**, E11 2AQ, ENG.
(T) 020 8530 2126
Speciality: Physiotherapy.
P S T (Ref:HM06432)

**DURNDELL, CLAIRE**

**Claire Durndell**, 17 Brill Rd, Oakley, Aylesbury, **Buckinghamshire**, HP18 9QH, ENG.
(T) 01844 237497
Speciality: Complementary Medicines & Therapy.
● **Owner** Mrs C Durndell
C M (Ref:HM06433)

**DURRANS, P J**

**P J Durrans**, 8 Beechwood Drive, Royton, Oldham, **Lancashire**, OL2 5XR, ENG.
(T) 01616 523977
Speciality: Chiropodists (Podiatrists).
● **Owner** Mrs P Durrans
S (Ref:HM06434)

**DURRANT, D**

**D Durrant**, Friars Clinic, Friars St, Sudbury, **Suffolk**, CO10 2AG, ENG.
(T) 01787 374964 (F) 01787 374964
Speciality: Physiotherapy.
● **Partner** Mrs D Durrant
P S T (Ref:HM06435)

**DURRANT, M**

**M Durrant**, 58 Stratford Rd, Shirley, Solihull,



Key continued: Yrs.Est: Years Established Q: Qualifications M: Professional Membership ✓ Indemnity Insurance CREDIT Accept Credit Cards

**Midlands (West)**, B90 3LP, ENG.
(T) 01217 441012
Speciality: Chiropodists (Podiatrists).
● **Owner** Mr M Durrant
S (Ref:HM06436)

## DURRANT, NICOLA
**Nicola Durrant**, 1 Lowfield Rd, Slinfold, Horsham, **Sussex (West)**, RH13 7SG, ENG.
(T) 01403 791275
Speciality: Reflexology.
S T (Ref:HM06437)

## DUSKYS TREATMENTS
**Duskys Treatments**, St Kilda's Rd, Harrow, **London (Greater)**, HA1 1QA, ENG.
(T) 020 8424 0693
Speciality: Complementary Medicines & Therapy.
M (Ref:HM06438)

## DUTT, G C (DR)
**Dr G C Dutt**, Bethnal Green Health Centre, 60 Florida St, London, **London (Greater)**, E2 6LL, ENG.
(T) 020 7739 4837
Speciality: Homeopathy.
M (Ref:HM06439)

## DUTTON, N S
**N S Dutton**, 11 Malpas Drive, Timperley, Altrincham, **Cheshire**, WA14 5BH, ENG.
(T) 01619 622642 (F) 01619 622642
Speciality: Chiropodists (Podiatrists).
● **Owner** Mr N Dutton
S (Ref:HM06440)

## DUVALL, V
**V Duvall**, Spinners Court, 53 West End, Witney, **Oxfordshire**, OX8 6NJ, ENG.
(T) 01993 704099 (F) 01993 704099
Speciality: Chiropractors.
● **Owner** Mrs V Duvall
P S T (Ref:HM06441)

## DUXBURY, HELEN
**Helen Duxbury**, 202 Preston New Rd, Blackburn, **Lancashire**, BB2 6PN, ENG.
(T) 01254 52143
Speciality: Complementary Medicines & Therapy.
M (Ref:HM06442)

## DWYER, F A M
**F A M Dwyer Sc Consl Psych**, 9 Albany Rd, Ranelagh, **County Dublin**, IRE.
(T) 01497 3425
Speciality: Complementary Medicines & Therapy.
M (Ref:HM06443)

## DYER & ASSOCIATES
**C D Dyer & Associates**, 25 St Georges Rd, Worthing, **Sussex (West)**, BN11 2DS, ENG.
(T) 01903 200748 (F) 01903 238612
Speciality: Acupuncture, Aromatherapy, Counselling, Homeopathy, Hypnotherapy, Osteopathy, Sports Massage. ✔
● **Osteopath** Mr P Skates Q: BSc (Hons). M: BOA, GOsC.
● **Osteopath** Ms A Brown Q: BSc. M: BOA, GOsC.
● **Aromatherapist/Reflexologist/Masseur** Lynne Halsey Q: IIHHT, IIST.
● **Practitioner** Sue Finlayson Q: BA (Hons).
● **Acupuncturist** Ms P Macklin-Creasy Q: Lic.Ac, MBAcC.
● **Hypnotherapist** Mr R Muir Q: Dip.Hyp. M: NRAH.
● **Osteopath** Mr C Dyer Q: DO. M: BOA, GOsC.
● **Homeopath** Mr G Beattle Q: LCH.
S Yrs. Est.: 14 (Ref:HM06444)

## DYER, A
**A Dyer**, 17 London Rd, Hailsham, **Sussex (East)**, BN27 1DE, ENG.
(T) 01323 840519
Speciality: Chiropodists (Podiatrists).
S (Ref:HM06445)

## DYER, DAVID
**David Dyer**, 256 Halfway St, Sidcup, **Kent**, DA15 8DT, ENG.
(T) 020 8294 2704 (F) 020 8294 2704
Speciality: Osteopathy.
● **Owner** Mr D Dyer
P S T (Ref:HM06446)

## DYER, ERIC W
**Eric W Dyer**, 17 London Rd, Hailsham, **Sussex (East)**, BN27 1DE, ENG.
(T) 01323 840519
Speciality: Chiropodists (Podiatrists).
S (Ref:HM06447)

## DYER, JOHN
**John Dyer**, Mainway, Lancaster, **Lancashire**, LA1 2AY, ENG.
(T) 01524 847809
Speciality: Chiropodists (Podiatrists).
● **Manager** Mrs M Mason
S (Ref:HM06448)

## DYER, RICHARD J
**Richard J Dyer**, 113 Osborne Rd, Newcastle Upon Tyne, **Tyne and Wear**, NE2 2TA, ENG.
(T) 01912 811497
Speciality: Osteopathy.
● **Owner** Mr R Dyer
P S T (Ref:HM06449)

## DYKE ROAD NATURAL HEALTH
**Dyke Road Natural Health**, 274 Dyke Rd, Brighton, **Sussex (East)**, BN1 5AE, ENG.
(T) 01273 561844
Speciality: Acupuncture, Alexander Technique, Aromatherapy, Drama Therapy, Homeopathy, Massage (Therapeutic), Nutritional Therapy, Osteopathy, Reflexology, Shiatsu, Bio-Energy Healing, Sports Therapeutic Massage. ✔
● **Homeopath** Mr C Taylor
● **Acupuncturist** Mr S Guthrie Q: B.Ac, MBAcC.
● **Baby Massage** Ms S Cranfield
● **Osteopath** Jasveer Bansel
● **Osteopath** Mr S Murray Q: DO.
● **Bio Energy Healing** Chris Gohl
● **Homeopath** Sohani Gonzalez Q: BA, MCH, RSHom.
● **Nutritionist** Ms S Perry Q: BSc, Dip.ION, Hons (OST).
● **Aromatherapist/Reflexologist** Ms J Balkam
● **Osteopath** Ms B Burnett Q: DO.
● **Osteopath** Mr J Hutson
● **Drama Therapist** Ms D Harrison
● **Alexander Technique Therapist** Ms G Schepokat Q: MSTAT.
● **Acupuncturist** Ms E Cook
● **Massage** Ms M Peck Q: ITEC, RSA.
● **Shiatsu Therapist** Zeb Glover Q: MRSS.
● **Teacher (Viniyoga)** Ms L Gillam
● **Teacher (Viniyoga)** Mr A Payne
● **Teacher (Chi Gung)** Mr B Cooper
● **Teacher (Yoga)** Ms L Warrington
● **Osteopath** Aaras Patel
● **Aromatherapist** Ms I Alexander
● **Psychotherapist** Ms R Field
M Yrs. Est.: 10 (Ref:HM06450)

## DYKINS, PAUL
**Paul Dykins**, 34A Chester St, Wrexham, LL13 8AH, **WAL**.
(T) 01978 310197 (F) 01978 310197
Speciality: Osteopathy.
● **Owner** Mr P Dykins
P S T (Ref:HM06451)

## DYMOND-HAMMILL, C
**C Dymond-Hammill**, 40 Parkside, Horsforth, Leeds, **Yorkshire (West)**, LS18 4DJ, ENG.
(T) 01132 588398
Speciality: Chiropodists (Podiatrists).
● **Owner** Mrs C Dymond-Hamill
S (Ref:HM06452)

## DYMOTT, ANGIE C K
**Angie C K Dymott**, 56 Janet St, Cardiff, **Glamorgan (Vale of)**, CF24 2BE, WAL.
(T) 029 2049 0673
Speciality: Reflexology.
S T (Ref:HM06453)

## DYNAMIC DEV STRESS MNGMT
**Dynamic Developement Stress Management**, Middleton Rd, Morden, **Surrey**, SM4 6RR, ENG.
(T) 020 8640 5865
Speciality: Clairvoyants & Palmists.
● **Owner** Miss M Campbell
B (Ref:HM06454)

## DYNAMIC HEALTH
**Dynamic Health (UK) Ltd**, St Andrews Ho High St, Epsom, **Surrey**, KT19 8AJ, ENG.
(T) 01372 724333 (F) 01372 724999
Speciality: Complementary Medicines & Therapy.
M (Ref:HM06455)

## DYNAMICS INTER SKILLS TRAINING
**Dynamics Interpersonal Skills Training**, 4 Wynnefield Rd, Rathmines, **County Dublin**, IRE.
(T) 01497 3498
(E) fmacliam@iol.ie
Speciality: Complementary Medicines & Therapy.
M (Ref:HM06456)

## DYSLEXIA ADVISORY BUREAU
**Dyslexia Advisory Bureau**, Pine View Lodge, Latchwood Lane, Lower Bourne, Farnham, **Surrey**, GU10 3HB, ENG.
(T) 01252 793067
Speciality: Psychology.
B (Ref:HM06457)

## DYSON, ELIZABETH
**Elizabeth Dyson**, 1 Yorke St, Burnley, **Lancashire**, BB11 1HD, ENG.
(T) 01282 431711
Speciality: Electrolysis.
T (Ref:HM06458)

## DYSON, F T & S J
**F T & S J Dyson**, Percy House, Percy Ter, Alnwick, **Northumberland**, NE66 1AF, ENG.
(T) 01665 602523
Speciality: Physiotherapy.
● **Owner** Mrs S Dyson
P S T (Ref:HM06459)

## DYSON, PETER
**Peter Dyson**, 97 Riversdale Rd, London, **London (Greater)**, N5 2SU, ENG.
(T) 020 7704 6544
Speciality: Psychotherapy.
● **Owner** Mr P Dyson
B (Ref:HM06460)

## DYSON, R
**Mr R Dyson**, Newlands Park Natural Health Centre, 48 Newlands Park, London, **London (Greater)**, SE26 5NE, ENG.
(T) 020 8659 5001
Speciality: Homeopathy.
M (Ref:HM06461)

## DYSON, S M
**S M Dyson**, 40 Jenny Lane, Woodford, Stockport, **Cheshire**, SK7 1PE, ENG.
(T) 01614 395565
Speciality: Physiotherapy.
P S T (Ref:HM06462)

## DYSON, VICTORIA
**Victoria Dyson**, 9 Blackburn Rd, Turton, Bolton, **Lancashire**, BL7 0BA, ENG.
(T) 08001 950675
Speciality: Chiropodists (Podiatrists).
● **Owner** Miss V Dyson
S (Ref:HM06463)

## E & E CAINE-WILMOT
**E & E Caine-Wilmot**, 62 Petworth Rd, Haslemere, **Surrey**, GU27 3AU, ENG.
(T) 01428 643912 (F) 01428 643912
Speciality: Psychotherapy.
● **Owner** Mr E Wimot
B (Ref:HM06464)

## E A O C
**Essex Acupuncture & Osteopathic Centre**, 250 Eastwood Rd, Rayleigh, **Essex**, SS6 7LS, ENG.
(T) 01268 772212
(E) osteoac@lineone.net
Speciality: Acupressure, Acupuncture, Bowen Therapy, Cupping, Manipulation, Massage (Therapeutic), Moxibustion, Oriental Diagnosis, Osteopathy, Postural Integration, Ying & Yang. ✔

Key: B Mind-Body Medicine; C Complementary Medicine; H Self Help Treatment; M Medicinal Therapy; O Oriental Medicine; P Postural Therapy; S Manipulative Structural Therapy; T Touch Therapy

● **Owner** Mr B Wood **Q:** DO, Lic.Ac, MBAcC, MGOsC. **M:** BAcC, GOsC.
**M** Yrs. Est.: 35 (**Ref:**HM06465)

## E A V

**E A V Ltd**, Hoar Cross Hall, Hoar Cross, Burton-On-Trent, **Staffordshire**, DE13 8QS, ENG.
(T) 01283 575040 (F) 01283 575030
Speciality: Complementary Medicines & Therapy.
● **Chief Executive Officer**
Simon Julian Freethy
**M** (**Ref:**HM06466)

## E B H

**E B H**, 526 Babbacombe Rd, Torquay, **Devon**, TQ1 1HH, ENG.
(T) 01803 201316 (F) 01803 201316
Speciality: Complementary Medicines & Therapy.
● **Owner** Mr E Hill
**M** (**Ref:**HM06467)

## E G H P

**Edinburgh Group Of Hypno-Psychotherapy (The)**, 4 St Peters Buildings, Edinburgh, **Edinburgh (City of)**, EH3 9PG, SCO.
(T) 01312 289777
(E) peter@eghp.co
Speciality: Cognitive Therapy, Counselling, Hypnosis, Hypnotherapy, Psychotherapy, Visualisation Therapy. ✔
● **Owner/Physiotherapist/Counsellor**
Mr P Pateluch **Q:** DHP (NC), MNRHP. **M:** ETSI, NRHP.
**B** Yrs. Est.: 5 (**Ref:**HM06468)

## E K CURATIVE CENTRE

**E K Curative Centre**, 103a Union St, Oldham, **Lancashire**, OL1 1QH, ENG.
(T) 01616 202165 (F) 01616 202165
Speciality: Hypnotherapy.
● **Owner** Mr E King
**B** (**Ref:**HM06469)

## E LOM COMPLEXIONS COM LTD

**Eve Lom Complexions Com Ltd**, 2 Spanish Pl, London, **London (Greater)**, W1M 5AN, ENG.
(T) 020 7935 9988 (F) 020 7224 0515
Speciality: Complementary Medicines & Therapy.
● **Owner** Mrs E Lom
**C** **M** (**Ref:**HM06470)

## E M D I

**E M D I Ltd**, Felaw Maltings, Felaw St, Ipswich, **Suffolk**, IP2 8SJ, ENG.
(T) 01473 407333 (F) 01473 407334
Speciality: Magnetic Therapy.
● **Managing Director** Mr J Campbell
**M** (**Ref:**HM06471)

## E M D TRADING

**E M D Trading**, Unit 2-3 Mamhilad Trading Estate, Pontypool, **Monmouthshire**, NP4 0HZ, WAL.
(T) 01495 762800
Speciality: Aromatherapy.
**M** **O** (**Ref:**HM06472)

## E M S

**E M S**, Tenerife, Broadlayings, Woolton Hill, Newbury, **Berkshire**, RG20 9TT, ENG.
(T) 01635 254828 (F) 01635 254828
Speciality: Complementary Medicines & Therapy.
● **Owner** Mr P Doyle
**M** (**Ref:**HM06473)

## E ROWBOTTOM STATE REG CHIROP

**E Rowbottom State Registered Chiropodist**, 336-338 Hollinwood Avenue, Manchester, **Manchester (Greater)**, M40 0JB, ENG.
(T) 01616 817526
Speciality: Chiropodists (Podiatrists).
**S** (**Ref:**HM06474)

## E RU CHU

**E Ru Chu**, 38A Stanhope Rd, London, **London (Greater)**, N6 5NG, ENG.
(T) 020 8341 0224
Speciality: Acupuncture.
● **Owner** Mrs E Chu
**O** (**Ref:**HM06475)

## E S PHYSICAL-THERAPY

**E S Physical-Therapy**, 22 Harley St, London, **London (Greater)**, W1N 1AP, ENG.
(T) 020 7636 3830 (F) 020 7636 3830
Speciality: Physiotherapy.
● **Director** Mrs E Sharp
**P** **S** **T** (**Ref:**HM06476)

## E T C CONSULT

**E T C Consult**, 17 Leeson Pk, Dublin, **County Dublin**, IRE.
(T) 01497 2067 (F) 01497 2518
(E) alphacol@iol.ie
Speciality: Psychology.
**B** (**Ref:**HM06477)

## E TULLY HOMEOPATHIC PRACT

**E Tully Homeopathic Practitioner**, Avalon Clinic, 270 Manchester Rd, Warrington, **Cheshire**, WA1 3RB, ENG.
(T) 01925 635670
Speciality: Complementary Medicines & Therapy.
● **Owner** Ms E Tulley
**C** **M** (**Ref:**HM06478)

## E.LONDON COMPLEMENTARY HEALTH

**East London Complementary Health**, 18 Martello St, London, **London (Greater)**, E8 3PE, ENG.
(T) 020 7923 4444 (F) 020 7923 4420
Speciality: Aromatherapy, Complementary Therapy, Cranial Osteopathy, Homeopathy, Indian Head Massage, Osteopathy, Reflexology. ✔
● **Homeopath** Jo Millican **Q:** LCPH. **M:** HMA.
● **Aromatherapist** Tania Battersby **Q:** MRQA. **M:** RQA.
● **Reflexologist** Emma Burton
● **Osteopath** Michael Snee **Q:** BSc, DO. **M:** GOsC.
**B** **P** **S** **T** Yrs. Est.: 4 (**Ref:**HM06479)

## EAGLE'S WING

**Eagle's Wing Centre For Contemporary Shamanism**, 58 Westbere Rd, London, **London (Greater)**, NW2 3RU, ENG.
(T) 020 7435 8174
Speciality: Psychology.
**B** (**Ref:**HM06480)

## EAGLES, EILEEN

**Eileen Eagles**, Garrington, Rolfe Lane, New Romney, **Kent**, TN28 8JJ, ENG.
(T) 01797 363500
Speciality: Electrolysis.
● **Owner** Mrs E Eagles
**T** (**Ref:**HM06481)

## EAKIN, LINDA

**Linda Eakin**, 21 Bendooragh Rd, Ballymoney, **County Antrim**, BT53 7NF, NIR.
(T) 028 2766 5549
Speciality: Reflexology.
**S** **T** (**Ref:**HM06482)

## EALING ACUP/CHINESE HERBAL MED

**Ealing Acupuncture & Chinese Herbal Medicines**, 62A Pitshanger Lane, London, **London (Greater)**, W5 1QX, ENG.
(T) 020 8810 8287
Speciality: Acupuncture.
● **Owner** Mr P Stavrides
**O** (**Ref:**HM06483)

## EALING BOWEN CLINIC

**Ealing Bowen Clinic**, 21 Bond St, Ealing, West London, Ealing, W5 5AP, ENG.
(T) 07802 762089or02085793386
Speciality: Massage (Therapeutic), Physiotherapy, Remedial Massage, Stress Therapy, Personal Development.
**C** (**Ref:**HM06484)

## EALING CHIROPODY CENTRE

**Ealing Chiropody Centre**, 35 Culmington Rd, London, **London (Greater)**, W13 9NJ, ENG.
(T) 020 8579 6969
Speciality: Chiropodists (Podiatrists).
**S** (**Ref:**HM06485)

## EALING CHIROPRACTIC CLINIC

**Ealing Chiropractic Clinic**, 23 Haven Green, London, **London (Greater)**, W5 2UP, ENG.
(T) 020 8566 8868
Speciality: Chiropractic.
● **Owner** Dr C Pittam
**P** **S** **T** (**Ref:**HM06486)

## EALING CLINIC

**Ealing Clinic (The)**, 3 Fielding Trce, Uxbridge Rd, London, **London (Greater)**, W5 3HQ, ENG.
(T) 020 8992 0321
Speciality: Chiropodists (Podiatrists).
**S** (**Ref:**HM06487)

## EALING COUNS & THERAPY CTRE

**Reliberate**, 6a The Park, London, **London (Greater)**, W5 5NE, ENG.
(T) 020 8579 8110
Speciality: Colour Therapy, Complementary Therapy, Counselling, Family Therapy, Holistic Healing, Iridology, Psychotherapy. ✔
● **Iridologist** Mr J Mahabir **Q:** BSc, Dip.Couns, Dip.Med.Irid, Dip.Psych. **M:** BACP, GNI.
**B** Yrs. Est.: 10 (**Ref:**HM06488)

## EALING PHYSIOTHERAPY

**Ealing Physiotherapy**, 228 South Ealing Rd, London, **London (Greater)**, W5 4RP, ENG.
(T) 020 8847 1887
Speciality: Physiotherapy.
● **Owner** Ms C Carlson
**P** **S** **T** (**Ref:**HM06489)

## EAMES, MARGARET (DR)

**Dr Margaret Eames**, Middleton, Church St, Combe Martin, Ilfracombe, **Devon**, EX34 0LQ, ENG.
(T) 01271 882427
Speciality: Homeopathy.
● **Owner** Dr M Eames
**M** (**Ref:**HM06490)

## EAMES, MAX E

**Max E Eames**, Brixton, London, **London (Greater)**, SW9 7JU, ENG.
(T) 020 7978 9214
Speciality: Hypnotherapy.
**B** (**Ref:**HM06491)

## EARDLEY, D & J

**D & J Eardley Chiropodist**, Room 1, First Floor, Half Moon Chambers, 10 Bigg Market, Newcastle Upon Tyne, **Tyne and Wear**, NE1 1UW, ENG.
(T) 01912 325896
(E) podiatrists@cwcom.net
Speciality: Aromatherapy, Chiropody, Reflexology. ✔
● **Chiropodist (Podiatrist)**
Mr D Eardley **Q:** Dip.Reflex, S.R.Ch.
● **Therapist** Ms J Emmonds **Q:** Dip.Arom, Dip.Body Massage, IIHHT.
**T** Yrs. Est.: 10 (**Ref:**HM06492)

## EARDLEY, S

**S Eardley**, 43 Silverdale Park, Silverton, Exeter, **Devon**, EX5 4JF, ENG.
(T) 01392 861361
Speciality: Chiropodists (Podiatrists).
● **Owner** Mrs S Eardley
**S** (**Ref:**HM06493)

## EAREY, C A

**C A Earey**, 122 Sough Rd, South Normanton, Alfreton, **Derbyshire**, DE55 2LE, ENG.
(T) 01773 819911
Speciality: Chiropodists (Podiatrists).
● **Senior Partner** Mr C Earey
**S** (**Ref:**HM06494)

## EAREY, C A

**C A Earey**, Serenity, Warren Lane, Woolpit, Bury St. Edmunds, **Suffolk**, IP30 9RT, ENG.
(T) 01359 244133
Speciality: Chiropractic.
**P** **S** **T** (**Ref:**HM06495)

## EARL, A

**A Earl**, 20 Surrey Rd, Cliftonville, Margate, **Kent**, CT9 2LA, ENG.
(T) 01843 227063
Speciality: Hypnotherapy, Psychotherapy.
✔
● **Hypnotherapist** Mrs A Earl **Q:** DHP (NC). **M:** IAH.
**C** Yrs. Est.: 3 (**Ref:**HM06496)



Key continued: **Yrs.Est:** Years Established **Q:** Qualifications **M:** Professional Membership ✔ Indemnity Insurance Accept Credit Cards

## EARLS, JAMES

**James Earls**, 62 Greenore St, Belfast, **County Antrim**, BT18 0DG, **NIR**.
(T) 028 9059 0594
(E) jearls@eim.dnet.co.uk
Speciality: Aromatherapy, Massage (Therapeutic), Reflexology. ✔
● **Therapist** Mr J Earls Q: BA. M: ISPA.
C S Yrs. Est.: 9 (Ref:HM06497)

## EARLSWOOD PHYSIOTHERAPY CLINIC

**Earlswood Physiotherapy Clinic**, Baytree, Bayfield, Chepstow, **Monmouthshire**, NP16 6AD, **WAL**.
(T) 01291 623894
Speciality: Physiotherapy.
P S T (Ref:HM06498)

## EARLY, KAY

**Kay Early**, 11 The Crescent, Hest Bank, Lancaster, **Lancashire**, LA2 6DP, **ENG**.
(T) 01524 823966
Speciality: Aromatherapy.
● **Owner** Mrs K Early
M O (Ref:HM06499)

## EARNSHAW, E (DR)

**Dr E Earnshaw**, 8 Littlemill Pl, Rankinston, Ayr, **Ayrshire (South)**, KA6 7HB, **SCO**.
(T) 01292 590102
Speciality: Complementary Medicines & Therapy.
C M (Ref:HM06500)

## EARNSHAW, P

**P Earnshaw**, The Bungalow, Airedale Drive, Castleford, **Yorkshire (West)**, WF10 2QA, **ENG**.
(T) 01977 553619
Speciality: Chiropodists (Podiatrists).
● **Owner** Mr P Earnshaw
S (Ref:HM06501)

## EARTH GARDEN

**Earth Garden**, 2 Fairview Prde, Mawney Rd, Romford, **Essex**, RM7 7HH, **ENG**.
(T) 01708 722633 (F) 01708 722633
Speciality: Aromatherapy.
● **Owner** Ms V Worwood
M O (Ref:HM06502)

## EARTHWORKING HEALING CENTRE

**Earthworking Healing Centre**, The Brae, Auchterhouse, Dundee, **Angus**, DD3 0QU, **SCO**.
(T) 01382 320233
Speciality: Complementary Medicines & Therapy.
C M (Ref:HM06503)

## EASBY, DAVID N

**David N Easby**, 86 Liverpool Rd, Reading, **Berkshire**, RG1 3PQ, **ENG**.
(T) 01189 265706
Speciality: Psychotherapy.
● **Owner** Mr D Easby
B (Ref:HM06504)

## EASE

**Ease**, 6 Atlantic Dr, Lisdoonvarna, **County Clare**, **IRE**.
(T) 06570 74431
Speciality: Complementary Medicines & Therapy.
M (Ref:HM06505)

## EASE MANAGEMENT CENTRE

**Ease Management Centre**, 7 Newport St, Old Town, Swindon, **Wiltshire**, SN1 3DX, **ENG**.
(T) 01793 433422 (F) 01793 435544
(W) www.easemanagement.co.uk
Speciality: Biofeedback, Cognitive Therapy, Counselling, Family Therapy, Humanistic Psychology, Life Style Coaching, Psychotherapy, Rogerian Therapy, Stress Therapy, Transactional Analysis, CBT (Cognitive Behavioral Therapy) Relational Therapy, Clinical Supervision. ✔
● **Principal/Psychologist**
Mr A MacGregor Q: MA, MISMA, PGD.Couns, UKCP (Reg). M: BABCP, BACP, BPS, ISMA, UKCP.
B Yrs. Est.: 30 (Ref:HM06506)

## EASEN & GAMAGE

**Easen & Gamage**, 31 Little London, Chichester, **Sussex (West)**, PO19 1PL, **ENG**.
(T) 01243 783904
Speciality: Chiropodists (Podiatrists).
S (Ref:HM06507)

## EASON, GUY

**Guy Eason**, Oakdale Farm House, Weare St, Ockley, Dorking, **Surrey**, RH5 5NN, **ENG**.
(T) 01306 627598
Speciality: Hypnosis.
● **Owner** Mr G Eason
B (Ref:HM06508)

## EAST BOURNE CLINIC

**East Bourne Clinic of Natural Medicine**, Eastbourne Clinic Of Natural Medicine, 69 Meads Rd, Eastbourne, **Sussex (East)**, BN20 7QL, **ENG**.
(T) 01323 734664 (F) 01323 734664
Speciality: Acupuncture, Alexander Technique, Allergy Testing, Aromatherapy, Chiropody, Chiropractic, Counselling, Cranio-Sacral Therapy, Herbal Medicine, Homeopathy, Iridology, Kinesiology, Nutritional Therapy, Reflexology, Remedial Massage. ✔
● **Acupuncturist** Ms K Germann Q: Lic.Ac, MBAcC.
● **Aromatherapist** Lucilla Kader Q: ITEC.
● **Medical Herbalist** Anna Piper Q: MH.
● **Chiropodist (Podiatrist)**
Charmain Hewett Q: BSc (Hons), M.S.C.P, S.R.Ch.
● **Chinese Acupuncture** Mr J Gavin Q: BSc, Dip.CHM, Lic.Ac. M: RCHM.
● **Homeopath** Mr R Ravenhill Q: BA, LCH, MHMA.
● **Chiropractor** Mr G Becvar Q: BSc (Chiro), DC.
● **Phytotherapy** Mr H Boys
● **Hypnotherapist** Mr J Hirst Q: DHP (NC), MA. M: NRHP.
C Yrs. Est.: 5 (Ref:HM06509)

## EAST BRIDGEFORD PHYSIO NEEDS

**East Bridgeford Physio Needs**, 1 Main St, East Bridgeford, Nottingham, **Nottinghamshire**, NG13 8PA, **ENG**.
(T) 01949 21354 (F) 01949 21354
Speciality: Physiotherapy. ✔
● **Physiotherapist** Ms H Cooke Q: MCSP, SRP. M: CSP.
● **Owner** Mr I Tomlinson
S (Ref:HM06510)

## EAST CORK PHYSIOTHERAPY

**East Cork Physiotherapy & Acupuncture Clinic**, 9 New Cork Rd, Midleton, **County Cork**, **IRE**.
(T) 021 4633 455 (F) 021 4663 3910
(E) barrettseng@circom.net
Speciality: Acupressure, Acupuncture, Biofeedback, Complementary Therapy, Cupping, Electrotherapy, Manipulation, Massage (Therapeutic), Moxibustion, Oriental Diagnosis, Stress Therapy, Touch Therapy, Ultrasonics, Vibrational Therapy, Vitamin Therapy. ✔
● **Chartered Physiotherapist**
Mr D Angland Q: MCSP. M: ISCP.
● **Physiotherapist** Shelia Barrett Q: Lic.Ac, MCSP. M: ISCP, SOM.
● **Chartered Physiotherapist**
Anne Browne
O S Yrs. Est.: 4 (Ref:HM06511)

## EAST DEVON CONSULTANCY

**East Devon Consultancy**, Whitwell, Colyton, **Devon**, EX24 6HS, **ENG**.
(T) 01297 553803 (F) 01297 552911
(E) 100755.66@compuserve.com
Speciality: Hay Diet, Kinesiology, Naturopathy, Nutritional Therapy, Electro Crystal Therapy, Electro Magnetic Radiation Surveying. ✔
● **Allergy Therapist** Mr M Williams
C H Yrs. Est.: 17 (Ref:HM06512)

## EAST FIFE SPORTS INJURY CLINIC

**East Fife Sports Injury Clinic**, Care Of St Andrews University, St Leonards Rd, St. Andrews, **Fife**, KY16 9DY, **SCO**.
(T) 01334 462180
Speciality: Physiotherapy.
● **Secretary** Mrs J Finlay
P S T (Ref:HM06513)

## EAST GRINSTAED OSTEOPATHS

**East Grinstaed Osteopaths**, Nunney, Snow Hill, Crawley Down, Crawley, **Sussex (West)**, RH10 3EG, **ENG**.
(T) 01342 712764
Speciality: Osteopathy.
● **Owner** Miss K Pelling
P S T (Ref:HM06514)

## EAST KILBRIDE SPORTS CLINIC

**East Kilbride Sports Injury Clinic**, 3 Old Coach Rd, East Kilbride, Glasgow, **Glasgow (City of)**, G74 4DR, **SCO**.
(T) 01355 225955
Speciality: Physiotherapy.
● **Owner** Mr G Crawford
P S T (Ref:HM06515)

## EAST LONDON ALEXANDER CENTRE

**East London Alexander Centre**, Bodywise, 119 Roman Rd, London, **London (Greater)**, E2 0QN, **ENG**.
(T) 020 8981 6938
Speciality: Alexander Technique.
● **Teacher of the Alexander Technique**
Ms S Rughani
P S (Ref:HM06516)

## EAST LONDON HOM GROUP PRACTICE

**East London Homeopathic Group Practice (The)**, Martello House, 18 Martello St, London, **London (Greater)**, E8 3PE, **ENG**.
(T) 020 7923 4444
Speciality: Homeopathy.
M (Ref:HM06517)

## EAST LOTHIAN PHYSIO CENTRE

**East Lothian Physiotherapy Centre**, 14 Church St, Haddington, **Lothian (East)**, EH41 3EX, **SCO**.
(T) 01620 825380 (F) 01620 825380
(E) elpcphysio@aol.com
Speciality: Acupuncture, Electrotherapy, Manipulation, Massage (Therapeutic), Physiotherapy, Stress Therapy, Ultrasonics. ✔
● **Physiotherapist** Ms G Mitchell Q: MCSP, OCPPP, SRP. M: CSP.
● **Physiotherapist** Ms J Kerr Q: BSc, MCSP, OCPPP, SRP. M: CSP.
S Yrs. Est.: 4 (Ref:HM06518)

## EAST MEETS WEST

**East Meets West**, Meadowview House, 191 Queens Rd, Norwich, **Norfolk**, NR1 3PP, **ENG**.
(T) 01603 768208
Speciality: Herbal Medicine.
● **Owner** Mrs G Hunter
M (Ref:HM06519)

## EAST MIDLANDS NUFFIELD HOSP

**East Midlands Nuffield Hospital**, Rykneld Rd, Littleover, Derby, **Derbyshire**, DE23 7SN, **ENG**.
(T) 01332 521169
Speciality: Physiotherapy.
● **Manager** Mrs M Treece
P S T (Ref:HM06520)

## EAST MIDLANDS PHYSIO CLINIC

**East Midlands Physiotherapy Clinic**, 107 Ashby Rd, Loughborough, **Leicestershire**, LE11 3AB, **ENG**.
(T) 01509 215614 (F) 01509 238505
Speciality: Physiotherapy.
P S T (Ref:HM06521)

## EAST OF EDEN

**East Of Eden**, 41A High St, Halstead, **Essex**, CO9 2AA, **ENG**.
(T) 01787 479879 (F) 01440 785060
Speciality: Complementary Medicines & Therapy.
● **Partner** Mrs K Wardle
M (Ref:HM06522)

## EAST PECKHAM OSTEO PRACTICE

**East Peckham Osteopathic Practice**, 23 Old Rd, East Peckham, Tonbridge, **Kent**, TN12 5AR, **ENG**.
(T) 01622 873481
Speciality: Osteopathy.
P S T (Ref:HM06523)

## EAST RIDING COLLEGE

**East Riding College of Reflexology**, 97 Finkle St, Cottingham, **Humberside (North)**, HU16 4AU, **ENG**.

Key: B Mind-Body Medicine C Complementary Medicine H Self Help Treatment M Medicinal Therapy O Oriental Medicine P Postural Therapy S Manipulative Structural Therapy T Touch Therapy

(T) 01482 840022
Speciality: Aromatherapy, Herbal Medicine, Reflexology, Reiki.
M O (Ref:HM06524)

### EAST STREET CENTRE
**East Street Centre**, 17 South St, Bromley, **Kent**, BR1 1RH, ENG.
(T) 020 8466 7760 (F) 020 8466 7760
Speciality: Complementary Medicines & Therapy.
● **Practice Manager** Mrs A Stephen
C M (Ref:HM06525)

### EAST SURREY HOSPITAL PHYSIO
**East Surrey Hospital Private Physiotherapy Clinic**, Canada Avenue, Redhill, **Surrey**, RH1 5RH, ENG.
(T) 01737 782805
Speciality: Physiotherapy.
● **Partner** Mr C Mallows
P S T (Ref:HM06526)

### EAST WEST HERB SHOP
**Pure Health Ltd**, 3 Neal's Yard, Covent Garden, London, **London (Greater)**, WC2H 9DP, ENG.
(T) 020 7379 1312 (F) 020 7379 4414
(W) www.eastwestherbshop.co.uk
Speciality: Acupuncture, Herbal Medicine, Oriental Diagnosis, Shiatsu. ✓ CREDIT
● **Manager** Mr M Powell Q: Dip.Ac, Dip.CHM. M: RCHM.
O Yrs. Est.: 10 (Ref:HM06527)

### EAST WEST HERBS
**East West Herbs**, Langston Priory, Station Rd, Kingham, Chipping Norton, **Oxfordshire**, OX7 6UP, ENG.
(T) 01608 658862 (F) 01608 658816
Speciality: Herbal Medicine.
M (Ref:HM06528)

### EAST WEST THERAPIES
**Vivienne Drummond**, 71 Greenham Rd, London, **London (Greater)**, N10 1LN, ENG.
(T) 020 8444 1789 (F) 020 844 1789
(E) vdrummond@eastwest71.freeserve.co.uk
(W) www.eastwesthealth.co.uk
Speciality: Absent Healing, Acupressure, Bach Remedies, Complementary Therapy, Do-In, Dowsing, Healer, Healing Therapy, Holistic Healing, Indian Head Massage, Manipulation, Massage (Therapeutic), Meditation, Reflexology, Reiki, Seichem, Stress Therapy, Touch Therapy, Tui-na, Australian Bush Flower Remedies, Vertical Reflex Therapy. ✓
● **Complementary Health Therapist** Ms V Drummond Q: ITEC, MIFR, MTI. M: IFR, MTI.
T Yrs. Est.: 4 (Ref:HM06529)

### EAST, MARY
**Mary East**, 42 High St, Ashford, **Kent**, TN24 8TE, ENG.
(T) 01233 660882
Speciality: Homeopathy.
M (Ref:HM06530)

### EAST, MARY EDGINTON
**Mary Edginton East**, Toad Hall, The Old Brickyard, Rye, **Sussex (East)**, TN31 7EE, ENG.
(T) 01797 224871
Speciality: Homeopathy. ✓
● **Homeopath** Mrs M Edginton East Q: LCPH. M: HMA.
M Yrs. Est.: 8 (Ref:HM06531)

### EAST, R J
**R J East**, 15 Windsor St, Bletchley, Milton Keynes, **Buckinghamshire**, MK2 2LN, ENG.
(T) 01908 372265
Speciality: Chiropodists (Podiatrists).
● **Partner** Mr R East
S (Ref:HM06532)

### EAST, R J
**R J East**, Masonic House Surgery, 26 High St, Buckingham, **Buckinghamshire**, MK18 1NU, ENG.
(T) 01280 813821
Speciality: Chiropodists (Podiatrists).
S (Ref:HM06533)

### EASTBOURNE CHIROPODY CARE
**Eastbourne Chiropody Care**, 1st Floor 2 Terminus Rd, Eastbourne, **Sussex (East)**, BN21 3LP, ENG.
(T) 01323 728722
Speciality: Chiropodists (Podiatrists).
● **Owner** Mrs H Cutler
S (Ref:HM06534)

### EASTBOURNE CHIROPRACTIC CLINIC
**Kelly D Hilton**, Eastbourne Chiropratic Clinic, 5 Old Orchard Rd, Eastbourne, **Sussex (East)**, BN21 1DB, ENG.
(T) 01323 733361
Speciality: Chiropractic. ✓
● **Chiropractor** Mr H Kelly
● **Chiropractor** Mr D Taylor Q: DC, PhD.
P Yrs. Est.: 8 (Ref:HM06535)

### EASTCOTE NFSH HEALING CENTRE
**Eastcote NFSH Healing Centre**, Cavendish Pavilion, Field End Rd, Pinner, **London (Greater)**, HA5 1PP, ENG.
(T) 020 8868 7831
Speciality: Complementary Medicines & Therapy.
● **Treasurer** Mrs J Jolley
C M (Ref:HM06536)

### EASTERHOUSE PSYCHOLOGICAL SVS
**Easterhouse Psychological Services**, St Leonard's Secondary School, 62 Lochend Rd, Glasgow, **Glasgow (City of)**, G34 0EH, SCO.
(T) 01417 730940
Speciality: Psychology.
B (Ref:HM06537)

### EASTERN CLINIC
**Eastern Clinic**, 1079 Garratt Lane, London, **London (Greater)**, SW17 0LN, ENG.
(T) 020 8682 3876
Speciality: Acupuncture.
● **Therapist** Ms A Larkum
O (Ref:HM06538)

### EASTERN SCENTS
**Eastern Scents Ltd**, Unit 23 Fisherrow Industrial Estate, Newhailes Rd, Musselburgh, **Lothian (Mid)**, EH21 6RU, SCO.
(T) 01316 536160
Speciality: Aromatherapy.
M O (Ref:HM06539)

### EASTERN THERAPIES
**Eastern Therapies**, 73 Mossdale Court, Teesdale, Luton, **Bedfordshire**, LU4 9JL, ENG.
(T) 01582 593363
Speciality: Complementary Medicines & Therapy.
● **Owner** Mr P Pabari
C M (Ref:HM06540)

### EASTGATE HYPNOTHERAPY CENTRE
**Eastgate Hypnotherapy Centre**, Eastgate, Louth Rd, Wragby, Market Rasen, **Lincolnshire**, LN8 5PH, ENG.
(T) 01673 858418
Speciality: Hypnotherapy. ✓ CREDIT
● **Hypnotherapist** Ms L Bowser Q: C.Hyp, Dip.Hyp, MSTT. M: NCH.
M Yrs. Est.: 1 (Ref:HM06541)

### EASTHAM, D
**D Eastham**, 13 Walters Way, London, **London (Greater)**, SE23 3LH, ENG.
(T) 020 8291 3554
Speciality: Homeopathy.
● **Owner** Miss D Eastham
M (Ref:HM06542)

### EASTLEIGH CHIROPRACTIC CENTRE
**Eastleigh Chiropractic Centre**, 52 Leigh Rd, Eastleigh, **Hampshire**, SO50 9DT, ENG.
(T) 023 8061 6069 (F) 023 8061 6069
Speciality: Chiropractic.
● **Owner** Dr G King
P S T (Ref:HM06543)

### EASTLEIGH OSTEOPATHIC CLINIC
**Eastleigh Osteopathic Clinic**, 169 Leigh Rd, Eastleigh, **Hampshire**, SO50 9DW, ENG.
(T) 023 8061 2166
(W) www.eastleighosteopaths.co.uk
Speciality: Acupuncture, Aromatherapy, Chiropractic, Cranial Osteopathy, Moxibustion, Naturopathy, Osteopathy, Reiki. ✓ CREDIT
● **Osteopath/Naturopath/Acupuncturist** Mr R Cartwright Q: DO, Lic.Ac, ND. M: GCRN, GOsC.
● **Osteopath** Mr P Hull Q: BSc, Hons (OST). M: GOsC.
● **Chiropractor/Acupuncturist** Ms A Murphy Q: DC, Lic.Ac. M: BCA.
● **Osteopath/Naturopath** Mr J Rouse Q: DO, ND. M: GCRN, GOsC.
S Yrs. Est.: 20 (Ref:HM06544)

### EASTON CHINESE MEDICAL CLINIC
**Easton Chinese Medical Clinic**, 16 Fulham High St, London, **London (Greater)**, SW6 3LQ, ENG.
(T) 020 7731 7888
Speciality: Complementary Medicines & Therapy.
C M (Ref:HM06545)

### EASTON, BRIAN
**Brian Easton**, 52-52A Stoke Newington Church St, London, **London (Greater)**, N16 0NB, ENG.
(T) 020 7241 5033 (F) 020 7502 1182
Speciality: Complementary Medicines & Therapy.
● **Senior Partner** Mrs J Sharidan
M (Ref:HM06546)

### EASTON, JOSEPHINE
**Josephine Easton**, 12 Brook Court, Horton, Northampton, **Northamptonshire**, NN7 2BL, ENG.
(T) 01604 870026
Speciality: Reflexology.
S T (Ref:HM06547)

### EASTON, MERRETT
**Merrett Easton**, 16 Helena Rd, Southsea, **Hampshire**, PO4 9RH, ENG.
(T) 023 9283 1457
Speciality: Psychology.
B (Ref:HM06548)

### EASTWEST CLINIC
**Eastwest Clinic**, 91 Claypath, Durham, **County Durham**, DH1 1RG, ENG.
(T) 01913 868894
Speciality: Acupuncture.
O (Ref:HM06549)

### EASTWOOD, KAREN
**Karen Eastwood**, 78 Main Rd, Biggin Hill, Westerham, **Kent**, TN16 3DT, ENG.
(T) 01959 573456
Speciality: Chiropodists (Podiatrists).
S (Ref:HM06550)

### EASTY, JANE C
**Jane C Easty**, 9 Coton Lane, Birmingham, **Midlands (West)**, B23 6TP, ENG.
(T) 01213 502018
Speciality: Osteopathy.
P S T (Ref:HM06551)

### EASTY, JAYNE
**Jayne Easty**, 59 Albert Rd, Tamworth, **Staffordshire**, B79 7JN, ENG.
(T) 01827 65568
Speciality: Osteopathy.
● **Owner** Ms J Easty
P S T (Ref:HM06552)

### EASY WAY TO STOP SMOKING
**Allen Carrs Easy Way To Stop Smoking**, 1c Amity Gr, Raynes Park, London, **London (Greater)**, SW20 0LQ, ENG.
(T) 020 8944 7761
Speciality: Hypnotherapy.
B (Ref:HM06553)

### EASY WAY TO STOP SMOKING
**Allen Carr's Easy Way To Stop Smoking**, Unit 13 The Coach House, 2 Upper York St, Bristol, BS2 8QN, ENG.
(T) 01179 081106
Speciality: Hypnotherapy.
B (Ref:HM06554)

### EASY WAY TO STOP SMOKING
**Easy Way To Stop Smoking (The)**,


Key continued: Yrs.Est: Years Established Q: Qualifications M: Professional Membership ✓ Indemnity Insurance CREDIT Accept Credit Cards

Christchurch Business Centre, Grange Rd, Christchurch, **Dorset**, BH23 4JD, **ENG**.
(T) 01425 272757
Speciality: Hypnosis.
● **Owner** Mrs A Emery
**B** (**Ref:**HM06555)

### EASY WAY TO STOP SMOKING

**Allen Carr's Easy Way To Stop Smoking**, 123 Coolamber Pk, Dublin, **County Dublin**, **IRE**.
(T) 01493 9313 (F) 01493 9313
(E) seansw@iol.ie
Speciality: Counselling.
**B** **H** (**Ref:**HM06556)

### EASY WAY YORKSHIRE

**Allen Carr's Easy Way To Stop Smoking**, 185 Burtonstone Lane, York, **Yorkshire (North)**, YO30 6DG, **ENG**.
(T) 01904 656703 (F) 01904 340159
(E) diana@fsbdial.co.uk
(W) www.dianaevans.co.uk
Speciality: Cognitive Therapy, Psychotherapy.
● **Owner** Ms D Evans
**C** Yrs. Est.: 5 (**Ref:**HM06557)

### EATOCK, J A

**J A Eatock**, 25 Silver St, Kidderminster, **Worcestershire**, DY10 2EQ, **ENG**.
(T) 01562 822117
Speciality: Physiotherapy.
● **Owner** Mr J Eatock
**P** **S** **T** (**Ref:**HM06558)

### EATOCK, SARAH

**Sarah Eatock**, 3 Redcar Court, Downend, Bristol, BS16 6RW, **ENG**.
(T) 01179 879082
Speciality: Chiropodists (Podiatrists).
● **Owner** Ms S Eatock
**S** (**Ref:**HM06559)

### EATON, A M

**A M Eaton**, 30 Devon Drive, Ruddington, Nottingham, **Nottinghamshire**, NG11 6GA, **ENG**.
(T) 01159 213682
Speciality: Chiropodists (Podiatrists).
**S** (**Ref:**HM06560)

### EATON, JOHN

**John Eaton**, 158 London Rd, Newbury, **Berkshire**, RG14 2AX, **ENG**.
(T) 01635 44444 (F) 01635 569289
Speciality: Hypnosis.
● **Owner** Mr J Eaton
**B** (**Ref:**HM06561)

### EATON, MARGARET

**Margaret Eaton**, Lister House, 71 Ruabon Rd, **Wrexham**, LL13 7PL, **WAL**.
(T) 01978 263487
Speciality: Reflexology.
**S** **T** (**Ref:**HM06562)

### EATON, MARION

**Mrs Marion Eaton**, The Professional Centre For Holistic Health, 50 High St, Old Town, Hastings, **Sussex (East)**, TN34 3EN, **ENG**.
(T) 01424 465050
(W) www.professionalcentre.co.uk
Speciality: Aromatherapy, Auricular Therapy, Hopi Ear Candles, Reiki. ✓
● **Aromatherapist/Reiki Master**
Mrs M Eaton **Q:** BRCP, MIFA, Reiki Master. **M:** IFA.
**M** Yrs. Est.: 3 (**Ref:**HM06563)

### EATON, MAX

**Max Eaton**, 3 Dunstan Steads Farm Cottages, Embleton, Alnwick, **Northumberland**, NE66 3DT, **ENG**.
(T) 01665 576166
Speciality: Reflexology.
**S** **T** (**Ref:**HM06564)

### EATON, T C

**T C Eaton**, 20 Abbey Lane, Sheffield, **Yorkshire (South)**, S8 0BL, **ENG**.
(T) 01142 745700
Speciality: Biomechanics, Chiropody, Nail Surgery, Podiatry. ✓
● **Chiropodist (Podiatrist)**
Mr T Eaton **Q:** BSc, M.S.C.P. **M:** S.C.P.
**M** Yrs. Est.: 6 (**Ref:**HM06565)

### EAU DE VIE

**Eau De Vie**, 34 Cowley Rd, Oxford, **Oxfordshire**, OX4 1HZ, **ENG**.
(T) 01865 200678
Speciality: Complementary Medicines & Therapy.
● **Owner** Mr J Pontey
**M** (**Ref:**HM06566)

### EAVES, ALLAN

**Allan Eaves**, 14-16 Wigan Rd, Ashton-In-Makerfield, Wigan, **Lancashire**, WN4 9BJ, **ENG**.
(T) 01942 727668
Speciality: Chiropodists (Podiatrists).
● **Owner** Mr A Eaves
**S** (**Ref:**HM06567)

### EAVES, HELEN

**Helen Eaves**, Flat 4, 37 Merton Rd, London, **London (Greater)**, SW18 5SU, **ENG**.
(T) 020 8874 8082
Speciality: Aromatherapy.
**M** **O** (**Ref:**HM06568)

### EBONY MASSAGE

**Ebony Massage**, 39A Faversham Rd, London, **London (Greater)**, SE6 4XE, **ENG**.
(T) 020 8690 8413
Speciality: Complementary Medicines & Therapy.
● **Owner** Miss F Simmons
**C** **M** (**Ref:**HM06569)

### EBRAHIM, D W

**D W Ebrahim**, 75 Kenilworth Rd, Coventry, **Midlands (West)**, CV4 7AF, **ENG**.
(T) 024 7641 8667
Speciality: Psychotherapy.
**B** (**Ref:**HM06570)

### EBRAHIMI, SOROUSH

**Soroush Ebrahimi**, 23 Cornwallis Drive, South Woodham Ferrers, Chelmsford, **Essex**, CM3 5YE, **ENG**.
(T) 01245 325460
Speciality: Homeopathy.
● **Owner** Mr E Soroush
**M** (**Ref:**HM06571)

### ECCLES CHIROPODY SERVICES

**Eccles Chiropody Services**, 250 East Prescot Rd, Knotty Ash, Liverpool, **Merseyside**, L14 5NG, **ENG**.
(T) 01512 287848
Speciality: Chiropody, Podiatry.
● **Chiropodist (Podiatrist)**
Mrs D Eccles **Q:** Inst.CH.P., LCH, S.R.Ch. **M:** Inst.CH.P.
● **Chiropodist (Podiatrist)**
Mr H Eccles **Q:** Inst.CH.P., M.S.C.P., S.R.Ch. **M:** Inst.CH.P., S.C.P.
**S** Yrs. Est.: 54 (**Ref:**HM06572)

### ECCLES, H R

**H R Eccles**, 31 Court Hey Drive, Liverpool, **Merseyside**, L16 2NB, **ENG**.
(T) 01514 895201
Speciality: Chiropodists (Podiatrists).
**S** (**Ref:**HM06573)

### ECCLESHALL ACUPUNCTURE CLINIC

**Eccleshall Acupuncture Clinic**, 54 High St, Eccleshall, Stafford, **Staffordshire**, ST21 6BZ, **ENG**.
(T) 01785 851461
Speciality: Aromatherapy.
**M** **O** (**Ref:**HM06574)

### ECCLESTON, MERVYN E

**Mervyn E Eccleston**, 57 Waveney Rd, Ballymena, **County Antrim**, BT43 5BB, **NIR**.
(T) 028 2564 4207
Speciality: Chiropodists (Podiatrists).
● **Owner** Mr M Eccleston
**S** (**Ref:**HM06575)

### ECHO ESSENTIAL OILS

**Echo Essential Oils**, 44 Chestnut Drive, Congleton, **Cheshire**, CW12 4UB, **ENG**.
(T) 01260 277680
Speciality: Complementary Medicines & Therapy.
**C** **M** (**Ref:**HM06576)

### ECHOS CENTRE

**Echos Centre (The)**, 51B High St, Wombwell, Barnsley, **Yorkshire (South)**, S73 8HS, **ENG**.
(T) 01226 270800
Speciality: Complementary Medicines & Therapy.
● **Owner** Mrs D Wadsworth
**C** **M** (**Ref:**HM06577)

### ECKERSLEY, PETER D

**Peter D Eckersley**, 320 Lapwing Lane, Manchester, **Manchester (Greater)**, M20 6UW, **ENG**.
(T) 01614 457989
Speciality: Physiotherapy.
● **Owner** Mr P Eckersley
**P** **S** **T** (**Ref:**HM06578)

### ECLIPSE

**Eclipse**, 52 Weatherhill Rd, Smallfield, Horley, **Surrey**, RH6 9JQ, **ENG**.
(T) 01342 843570
Speciality: Relaxation Technique.
● **Owner** Mrs C Brown
**H** **T** (**Ref:**HM06579)

### ECOFLOW

**Ecoflow Ltd**, 21 Brunel Rd, Saltash, **Cornwall**, PL12 6LF, **ENG**.
(T) 01752 841661 (F) 01752 841044
Speciality: Complementary Medicines & Therapy.
● **Sales Manager** Mr N Broderick
**C** **M** (**Ref:**HM06580)

### ECOGENIX BODYCARE

**Ecogenix Bodycare Ltd**, The Laurels, 9 Brethergate, Westwoodside, Doncaster, **Yorkshire (South)**, DN9 2AU, **ENG**.
(T) 01427 754110
Speciality: Aromatherapy.
**M** **O** (**Ref:**HM06581)

### ECOLIBRIUM

**Ecolibrium**, The Eco Centre, Windmill Way, Hebburn, **Tyne and Wear**, NE31 1SR, **ENG**.
(T) 01914 835700
Speciality: Complementary Medicines & Therapy.
● **Partner** Mr G Butterworth
**C** **M** (**Ref:**HM06582)

### ECONS, A (DR)

**Dr A Econs**, 29 Hersham Rd, Walton-On-Thames, **Surrey**, KT12 1LF, **ENG**.
(T) 01932 252425
Speciality: Nutritional Therapy.
**M** (**Ref:**HM06583)

### ECZEMA THERAPY

**Eczema Therapy**, Tintagel House, Western Rd, Cheltenham, **Gloucestershire**, GL50 3RN, **ENG**.
(T) 01242 221708
Speciality: Complementary Medicines & Therapy.
**M** (**Ref:**HM06584)

### EDDIE, DAVID

**David Eddie**, 95 Park Lane, Poynton, **Cheshire**, SK12 1RB, **ENG**.
(T) 01625 879113
Speciality: Naturopathy, Osteopathy. ✓
● **Owner/Naturotherapist** Mr D Eddie **Q:** RN.
**C** Yrs. Est.: 16 (**Ref:**HM06585)

### EDDIE, DAVID

**David Eddie**, 95 Park Lane, Poynton, Stockport, **Cheshire**, SK12 1RB, **ENG**.
(T) 01625 879113
Speciality: Osteopathy.
**P** **S** **T** (**Ref:**HM06586)

### EDDLESTON, SUE

**Sue Eddleston**, 2 Dale Bank, Harrogate, **Yorkshire (North)**, HG1 2LP, **ENG**.
(T) 01423 508666
Speciality: Reflexology.
**C** **S** **T** (**Ref:**HM06587)

### EDELMAN, JACQUELINE

**Jacqueline Edelman**, 21 Woodhouse Rd, London, **London (Greater)**, N12 9EN, **ENG**.
(T) 020 8343 9942
Speciality: Chiropodists (Podiatrists).

S (Ref:HM06588)

**EDELMAN, JACQUELINE**

**Jacqueline Edelman**, 41 Pine Gr, London, **London (Greater)**, N20 8LA, ENG.
(T) 020 8445 1947
Speciality: Chiropodists (Podiatrists).
● **Owner** Mrs J Edelman
S (Ref:HM06589)

**EDEN DREAM**

**Eden Dream**, 281 Hale End Rd, Woodford Green, **Essex**, IG8 9LU, ENG.
(T) 020 8531 0089
Speciality: Complementary Medicines & Therapy.
● **Owner** Mrs M Bright
M (Ref:HM06590)

**EDEN PHYSIO & SPORTS**

**Eden Physiotherapy & Sports Injuries Clinic**, 7 Southend Trce, Penrith, **Cumbria**, CA11 8JQ, ENG.
(T) 01768 891122
Speciality: Physiotherapy.
P S T (Ref:HM06591)

**EDEN, FRANCES**

**Frances Eden**, 57 Hilary Cres, Rayleigh, **Essex**, SS6 8NB, ENG.
(T) 01268 776850
Speciality: Chiropodists (Podiatrists).
S (Ref:HM06592)

**EDEN, PATRICIA**

**Patricia Eden**, 39 Ingleton Avenue, Welling, **Kent**, DA16 2JY, ENG.
(T) 020 8301 3659
Speciality: Reflexology.
S T (Ref:HM06593)

**EDEN, SHARON**

**Sharon Eden**, 128 Meads Lane, Ilford, **Essex**, IG3 8PE, ENG.
(T) 020 8590 3850
Speciality: Psychotherapy.
● **Owner** Ms S Eden
B (Ref:HM06594)

**EDENS ESSENTIALS**

**Edens Essentials**, 167 St Peters Rs, Bradley Stoke, Bristol, BS32 9DD, ENG.
(T) 01179 832418
Speciality: Complementary Medicines & Therapy.
M (Ref:HM06595)

**EDGAR, A**

**A Edgar**, 18 Western Way, Gosport, **Hampshire**, PO12 2NG, ENG.
(T) 023 9258 2277 (F) 023 9258 2277
Speciality: Chiropody. ✔
● **Chiropodist** Mr A Edgar Q: MSSCh.
C Yrs. Est.: 12 (Ref:HM06596)

**EDGBASTON ACUPUNCTURE CLINIC**

**Edgbaston Acupuncture Clinic**, 6 Chad Rd, Birmingham, **Midlands (West)**, B15 3EN, ENG.
(T) 01214 547779
Speciality: Acupuncture.
O (Ref:HM06597)

**EDGBASTON HEALTH CLINIC**

**Edgbaston Health Clinic**, 24 Somerset Rd, Edgbaston, Birmingham, **Midlands (West)**, B15 2QD, ENG.
(T) 01214 561435 (F) 01214 543909
Speciality: Physiotherapy.
● **Practice Manager** Mr B Maddox
P S T (Ref:HM06598)

**EDGELL, MARJORY**

**Marjory Edgell**, 23 Crescent Gr, London, **London (Greater)**, SW4 7AF, ENG.
(T) 020 7622 4755
Speciality: Counselling, Hypnosis, Hypnotherapy, Psychotherapy, Stress Therapy, Visualisation Therapy.
● **Therapist** Ms M Edgell Q: DHP (NC), MNRHP, SRN, UKCP (Reg).
B Yrs. Est.: 15 (Ref:HM06599)

**EDGERTON, NICK**

**Nick Edgerton**, 13 Camden Row, London, **London (Greater)**, SE3 0QA, ENG.
(T) 020 8297 8600
Speciality: Psychology.
B (Ref:HM06600)

**EDGWARE CHIROPRACTIC CLINIC**

**Edgware Chiropractic Clinic**, 174 Deans Lane, Edgware, **London (Greater)**, HA8 9NT, ENG.
(T) 020 8906 3323
Speciality: Chiropractic.
P S T (Ref:HM06601)

**EDGWARE CLINIC**

**Edgware Clinic (The)**, 4 Whitchurch Lane, Edgware, **London (Greater)**, HA8 6JZ, ENG.
(T) 020 8951 5833
Speciality: Chiropodists (Podiatrists).
● **Owner** Mr D Davies
S (Ref:HM06602)

**EDGWARE MEDICAL ACUPUNCTURE**

**Edgware Medical Acupuncture**, 63 The Drive, Edgware, **London (Greater)**, HA8 8PS, ENG.
(T) 020 8958 5113
Speciality: Acupuncture.
O (Ref:HM06603)

**EDGWARE NATURAL HEALTH CENTRE**

**Edgware Centre For Natural Health**, 128 High St, Edgware, **London (Greater)**, HA8 7EL, ENG.
(T) 020 8951 3475/89529566 (F) 020 8952 4120
Speciality: Absent Healing, Acupressure, Acupuncture, Alexander Technique, Counselling, Homeopathy, Hypnotherapy, Indian Head Massage, Nutritional Therapy, Osteopathy, Reflexology, Reiki, Stress Therapy, Visualisation Therapy, Vitamin Therapy. ✔ 💳
● **Owner** Dr G Visick
● **Therapist** Ms L Siddall Q: Dip.Indian Head Massage, Dip.StM, S.E.N. M: CSM.
B Yrs. Est.: 20 (Ref:HM06604)

**EDGWARE PRACTICE**

**Edgware Practice**, 194A Station Rd, Edgware, **London (Greater)**, HA8 7AT, ENG.
(T) 020 8905 4427
Speciality: Osteopathy.
● **Employee** Mr D Powers
P S T (Ref:HM06605)

**EDINBURGH ALEXANDER CENTRE**

**Edinburgh Alexander Centre**, The South Side Centre, 86 Causewayside, Edinburgh, **Edinburgh (City of)**, EH9 1PY, SCO.
(T) 01316 675251
(E) richard@casebow.net
(W) www.alexandertech.org.uk
Speciality: Alexander Technique. ✔
● **Teacher of the Alexander Technique** Mr R Casebow Q: MSTAT. M: STAT.
P Yrs. Est.: 6 (Ref:HM06606)

**EDINBURGH CLINIC**

**Edinburgh Clinic (The)**, 24 & 26 West Port, Edinburgh, **Edinburgh (City of)**, EH1 2JE, SCO.
(T) 01316 575704
Speciality: Alexander Technique.
● **Teacher** Mrs A Longden
● **Teacher** Mr B Longden
P S (Ref:HM06607)

**EDINBURGH COLLEGE-HOMEOPATHY**

**Edinburgh College Of Classical Homeopathy**, 21 Abercromby Pl, Edinburgh, **Edinburgh (City of)**, EH3 6QE, SCO.
(T) 01315 589988
Speciality: Complementary Medicines & Therapy.
M (Ref:HM06608)

**EDINBURGH COLLEGE-HOMEOPATHY**

**Edinburgh College Of Classical Homeopathy**, 39A York Pl, Edinburgh, **Edinburgh (City of)**, EH1 3HP, SCO.
(T) 01315 583118
Speciality: Homeopathy.
M (Ref:HM06609)

**EDINBURGH EAST PSYCHOLOGIC SV**

**Edinburgh East Psychological Service**, 7 Merchiston Park, Edinburgh, **Edinburgh (City of)**, EH10 4PR, SCO.
(T) 01312 294223 (F) 01312 294223
Speciality: Psychology.
B (Ref:HM06610)

**EDINBURGH FLOATARIUM**

**Edinburgh Floatarium Ltd (The)**, 29 North West Circus Pl, Stockbridge, Edinburgh, **Edinburgh (City of)**, EH3 6TP, SCO.
(T) 01312 253350 (F) 01312 253351
(E) edinburgh.floatarium@scotland.com
(W) www.edinburghfloatarium.co.uk
Speciality: Alexander Technique, Aromatherapy, Beauty Therapy, Chiropody, Complementary Therapy, Crystal Healing, Flotation Therapy, Massage (Therapeutic), Reflexology, Reiki, Shiatsu, Skin Care Therapy. ✔ 💳
● **Owner** Mrs D Brown
C Yrs. Est.: 10 (Ref:HM06611)

**EDINBURGH HEALTH CARE**

**Edinburgh Health Care N H S Trust**, Dept Of Chiropody & Podiatric Medicine, 26 Ardmillan Trce, Edinburgh, **Edinburgh (City of)**, EH11 2JL, SCO.
(T) 01315 377470 (F) 01315 377471
Speciality: Chiropodists (Podiatrists).
● **Manager** Mrs L Hamilton
S (Ref:HM06612)

**EDINBURGH HOMEOPATHIC CENTRE**

**Edinburgh Homeopathic Centre**, 4b Randolph Pl, Edinburgh, **Edinburgh (City of)**, EH3 7TQ, SCO.
(T) 01312 251875 (F) 01314 760309
(W) www.homeopathy.sco.fm
Speciality: Acupuncture, Herbal Medicine, Homeopathy. ✔
● **Homeopath/Owner** Mr Clogstoun-Willmott Q: RSHom.
C (Ref:HM06613)

**EDINBURGH OSTEOPATHIC CLINIC**

**Edinburgh Osteopathic Clinic**, 27 Mountcastle Drive North, Edinburgh, **Edinburgh (City of)**, EH8 7SL, SCO.
(T) 01316 697960
Speciality: Osteopathy.
● **Owner** Mr D Iannarelli
P S T (Ref:HM06614)

**EDINBURGH OSTEOPATHIC SURGERY**

**Edinburgh Osteopathic Surgery**, Edinburgh Osteopathic Surgery, 187 Dalkeith Rd, Edinburgh, **Edinburgh (City of)**, EH16 5DS, SCO.
(T) 01316 671234
(E) paul@osteos.co.uk
Speciality: Acupuncture, Cranial Osteopathy, Manipulation, Osteopathy. ✔
● **Osteopath** Mr P Barratt Q: DO. M: GOsC.
S Yrs. Est.: 21 (Ref:HM06615)

**EDINBURGH PHYSIOTHERAPY CENTRE**

**Edinburgh Physiotherapy Centre (The)**, 36 Henderson Row, Edinburgh, **Edinburgh (City of)**, EH3 5DN, SCO.
(T) 01315 561116 (F) 01315 566620
Speciality: Acupuncture, Beauty Therapy, Chiropractic, Massage (Therapeutic). ✔ 💳
● **Owner/Physiotherapist** Kirsten Mord Q: MCSP, SRP. M: CSP.
S Yrs. Est.: 9 (Ref:HM06616)

**EDINBURGH WEST PSYCHOLOGIC SV**

**Edinburgh West Psychological Service**, Easter Drylaw Drive, Edinburgh, **Edinburgh (City of)**, EH4 2RY, SCO.
(T) 01313 436181
Speciality: Psychology.
B (Ref:HM06617)

**EDMETT, C**

**C Edmett**, 12 Quantock Rd, Weston-Super-Mare, **Somerset**, BS23 4DT, ENG.
(T) 01934 624728
Speciality: Chiropodists (Podiatrists).
S (Ref:HM06618)

**EDMONDS, ANN**

**Ann Edmonds**, 36 Cowslip Cres, Thatcham, **Berkshire**, RG18 4BZ, ENG.
(T) 01635 865612
Speciality: Reflexology.
S T (Ref:HM06619)



Key continued: Yrs.Est: Years Established Q: Qualifications M: Professional Membership ✔ Indemnity Insurance 💳 Accept Credit Cards

### EDMONDS, PHILIP
**Philip Edmonds**, 30 Kents Rd, Haywards Heath, **Sussex (West)**, RH16 4HQ, ENG.
(T) 01444 457851 (F) 01444 457851
Speciality: Homeopathy.
● **Owner** Mr P Edmonds
**M** (**Ref:**HM06620)

### EDMONDS, SANDRA
**Sandra Edmonds**, 53 High St, South Kyme, Lincoln, **Lincolnshire**, LN4 4AE, ENG.
(T) 01526 860943
Speciality: Electrolysis.
**T** (**Ref:**HM06621)

### EDMONDS, SCOTT J
**Scott J Edmonds**, 65 Durley Avenue, Waterlooville, **Hampshire**, PO8 8UZ, ENG.
(T) 023 9225 1718
Speciality: Chiropodists (Podiatrists).
**S** (**Ref:**HM06622)

### EDMONDSON, MICHAEL
**Michael Edmondson**, 18 Mansel Cl, Poole, **Dorset**, BH12 5HS, ENG.
(T) 01202 512394
Speciality: Acupuncture.
**O** (**Ref:**HM06623)

### EDMUNDSON & WHITE-COOPER
**Edmundson & White-Cooper**, 18 Wilmington Cl, Newcastle Upon Tyne, **Tyne and Wear**, NE3 2SF, ENG.
(T) 01912 865053 (F) 01912 865053
Speciality: Homeopathy.
● **Partner** Mrs E Edmundson
**M** (**Ref:**HM06624)

### EDNEY, C S
**C S Edney**, 5 Foxcote, Finchampstead, Wokingham, **Berkshire**, RG40 3PG, ENG.
(T) 01189 735340
(W) www.holistic-haven.com
Speciality: Indian Head Massage, Massage (Therapeutic), Shiatsu, Tantsui - face Reading. ✔
● **Owner** Mrs C Edney **Q:** MRSS.
**C** Yrs. Est.: 12 (**Ref:**HM06625)

### EDUCATION PSYCHOLOGY SERVICE
**Education Psychology Service**, Maitland House, 17 Spa Rd, Gloucester, **Gloucestershire**, GL1 1UY, ENG.
(T) 01452 426961 (F) 01452 426971
Speciality: Psychology.
**B** (**Ref:**HM06626)

### EDUCATIONAL & PSYCHOL SVS
**Educational & Psychological Services**, 42 St Christophers Rd, Porthcawl, Bridgend, CF36 5RY, WAL.
(T) 01656 773730 (F) 01656 773730
Speciality: Psychology.
● **Owner** Dr C Tyre
**B** (**Ref:**HM06627)

### EDUCATIONAL COUNSELLING
**Educational Counselling**, 91 West End Lane, Esher, **Surrey**, KT10 8LF, ENG.
(T) 01372 469030
Speciality: Psychology.
● **Owner** Mrs R Thornton
**B** (**Ref:**HM06628)

### EDUCATIONAL CTRE FOR COMP MED
**Educational Centre For Complementary Medicine Ltd**, Spring Waters, Lower New Rd, Cheddar, **Somerset**, BS27 3DY, ENG.
(T) 01934 743154
Speciality: Complementary Medicines & Therapy.
**M** (**Ref:**HM06629)

### EDUCATIONAL PSYCHOLOGY
**Educational Psychology**, School House, Buckingham Rd, Bletchley, Milton Keynes, **Buckinghamshire**, MK3 5HP, ENG.
(T) 01908 367333
Speciality: Psychology.
● **Manager** Mr J Spicer
**B** (**Ref:**HM06630)

### EDUCATIONAL PSYCHOLOGY ASS
**Educational Psychology Associates**, 17 Warren Way, Wirral, **Merseyside**, CH60 9HU, ENG.
(T) 01513 425055 (F) 01513 425055
Speciality: Psychology.
● **Owner** Mr B Bourne
**B** (**Ref:**HM06631)

### EDUCATIONAL PSYCHOLOGY SERVICE
**Educational Psychology Service**, Westwood St, Manchester, **Manchester (Greater)**, M14 4PH, ENG.
(T) 01612 265404 (F) 01612 262821
Speciality: Psychology.
**B** (**Ref:**HM06632)

### EDUCATIONAL PSYCHOLOGY SERVICE
**Educational Psychology Service**, 9 North Avenue, Coventry, **Midlands (West)**, CV2 4DH, ENG.
(T) 024 7645 9718 (F) 01205 445211
Speciality: Psychology.
● **Manager** Ms L Hinnigan
**B** (**Ref:**HM06633)

### EDUCATIONAL PSYCHOLOGY SERVICE
**Educational Psychology Service**, Battledown Centre, Harp Hill, Charlton Kings, Cheltenham, **Gloucestershire**, GL52 6PZ, ENG.
(T) 01242 525448 (F) 01242 228321
Speciality: Psychology.
● **Area Manager** Ms K Linston
**B** (**Ref:**HM06634)

### EDUCATIONAL PSYCHOLOGY SERVICE
**Educational Psychology Service**, Education Support Services, Queensferry Campus, Queensferry, Deeside, **Flintshire**, CH5 1SE, WAL.
(T) 01244 822818 (F) 01244 812234
Speciality: Psychology.
● **Principal** Mr I Spence
**B** (**Ref:**HM06635)

### EDUCATIONAL PSYCHOLOGY SERVICE
**Educational Psychology Service**, Health Centre, Stroud, **Gloucestershire**, GL5 4BH, ENG.
(T) 01453 751090
Speciality: Psychology.
**B** (**Ref:**HM06636)

### EDUCATIONAL TAPES
**Educational Tapes Ltd**, P O Box 4, Hemel Hempstead, **Hertfordshire**, HP3 8BT, ENG.
(T) 01442 268484
Speciality: Complementary Medicines & Therapy.
**M** (**Ref:**HM06637)

### EDULJEE, STELLA
**Stella Eduljee**, 12 Fruitlands, Eynsham, Witney, **Oxfordshire**, OX8 1RB, ENG.
(T) 01865 880446
Speciality: Aromatherapy, Holistic Massage. ✔
● **Owner/Reflexologist** Ms S Eduljee **Q:** ITEC, RM. **M:** AOC, GCP.
**C** Yrs. Est.: 3 (**Ref:**HM06638)

### EDWARDS HEALTH CLINIC
**Edwards Health Clinic**, 59 Blakes Lane, New Malden, **Surrey**, KT3 6NS, ENG.
(T) 020 8949 4572
(E) eileen@eileenedwards.co.uk
(W) www.edwardsdhp.freeserve.co.uk
Speciality: Auto Suggestion, Complementary Therapy, Counselling, Humanistic Psychology, Hypnosis, Hypnotherapy, Life Style Coaching, Psychotherapy, Rogerian Therapy, Silva Method, Transactional Analysis, Visualisation Therapy. ✔
● **Hypnotherapist/Psychotherapist** Mrs E Edwards **Q:** Dip.Hyp, Dip.Psych, MNRHP. **M:** NRHP.
**B** **C** Yrs. Est.: 22 (**Ref:**HM06639)

### EDWARDS, A D
**A D Edwards**, 4 Abbey Court, High St, Newport, **Shropshire**, TF10 7BW, ENG.
(T) 01952 813219
Speciality: Acupuncture.
● **Owner** A Edwards
**O** (**Ref:**HM06640)

### EDWARDS, ALLYN
**Allyn Edwards**, The Ishta Centre, 26 Kings Avenue, Stone, **Staffordshire**, ST15 8HD, ENG.
(T) 01785 616010 (F) 01785 616010
(E) allyn@ishta.co.uk
(W) www.ishta.co.uk
Speciality: Complementary Medicines & Therapy, Ishta Spinal Touch. ✔
● **Spinal Touch Therapist** Allyn Edwards **M:** ALTT.
**P** Yrs. Est.: 5 (**Ref:**HM06641)

### EDWARDS, ANNE
**Anne Edwards**, 17 Kent Cl, Rogerstone, Newport, NP10 0BE, WAL.
(T) 01633 894768
Speciality: Reflexology.
● **Owner** Mrs A Edwards
**S** **T** (**Ref:**HM06642)

### EDWARDS, BEN
**Ben Edwards**, 9 Kings Rd, St. Leonards-On-Sea, **Sussex (East)**, TN37 6EA, ENG.
(T) 01424 714800
Speciality: Herbalists.
**M** (**Ref:**HM06643)

### EDWARDS, BRIAN
**Brian Edwards**, Flat 31, Lindsay Manor, 47 Lindsay Rd, Poole, **Dorset**, BH13 6BE, ENG.
(T) 01202 767956
Speciality: Clairvoyants & Palmists.
● **Owner** Mr B Edwards
**B** (**Ref:**HM06644)

### EDWARDS, CHERYL
**Cheryl Edwards**, 25 Woodbines Avenue, Kingston Upon Thames, **Surrey**, KT1 2AX, ENG.
(T) 020 8547 1259
Speciality: Homeopathy.
● **Owner** Mrs C Edwards
**M** (**Ref:**HM06645)

### EDWARDS, CHRISTINA
**Christina Edwards**, 30 Albany Rd, Stratford-Upon-Avon, **Warwickshire**, CV37 6PG, ENG.
(T) 01789 292052
Speciality: Acupuncture.
**O** (**Ref:**HM06646)

### EDWARDS, CHRISTINA
**Christina Edwards**, Riverside, 14 Common Rd, Evesham, **Worcestershire**, WR11 4PU, ENG.
(T) 01386 47617
Speciality: Acupuncture.
● **Owner** Mrs C Edwards
**O** (**Ref:**HM06647)

### EDWARDS, D E
**D E Edwards**, 29 Arthur St, Penrith, **Cumbria**, CA11 7TX, ENG.
(T) 01768 862169
Speciality: Counselling, Psychotherapy.
● **Psychologist** Mrs D Edwards **Q:** BA, L.D.P.
**B** Yrs. Est.: 8 (**Ref:**HM06648)

### EDWARDS, E M
**Mrs E M Edwards**, 8 Mellor Brook Drive, Platt Bridge, Wigan, **Lancashire**, WN2 5HL, ENG.
(T) 01942 861337
Speciality: Chiropractors.
● **Owner** Mrs E Edwards
**P** **S** **T** (**Ref:**HM06649)

### EDWARDS, EMMA
**Emma Edwards**, Chesham Open Air Pool, Moor Rd, Amersham, **Buckinghamshire**, HP5, ENG.
(T) 01494 764136 (F) 01494 764136
(E) emma@rjedwards.f9.co.uk
Speciality: Aromatherapy, Indian Head Massage, Reflexology, Reiki. ✔
● **Reflexologist** Ms E Edwards **Q:** ITEC. **M:** LCSP.
**T** Yrs. Est.: 5 (**Ref:**HM06650)

### EDWARDS, G E
**G E Edwards**, Care Of Moss Chemist, 801-803 Southchurch Rd, Southend-On-Sea, **Essex**, SS1 2PP, ENG.
(T) 01702 466585
Speciality: Chiropody. ✔
● **Chiropodist** Mr G Edwards **Q:** MBChA.
**C** Yrs. Est.: 15 (**Ref:**HM06651)

### EDWARDS, G E
**G E Edwards**, Unit 2, Kingsleigh House, 17 High St, Rayleigh, **Essex**, SS6 7ET, ENG.

(T) 01268 772228 (F) 01268 772228
Speciality: Chiropody. ✓
● **Chiropodist** Mr G Edwards Q: MBChA. M: B.A.Ch.P.
C Yrs. Est.: 16 (**Ref:**HM06652)

## EDWARDS, G J

**G J Edwards**, 11 Walmesley Avenue, Rishton, Blackburn, **Lancashire**, BB1 4HQ, ENG.
(T) 01254 883466
Speciality: Chiropodists (Podiatrists).
S (**Ref:**HM06653)

## EDWARDS, G J

**G J Edwards**, Lee Carter Health Studio, Lee Carter Leisure, Off Lowergate, Clitheroe, **Lancashire**, BB7 1AD, ENG.
(T) 01200 424475
Speciality: Chiropodists (Podiatrists).
● **Owner** Mr G Edwards
S (**Ref:**HM06654)

## EDWARDS, HARRY

**Harry Edwards Spiritual Healing Sanctuary (The)**, Burrows Lea, Hook Lane, Shere, Guildford, **Surrey**, GU5 9QG, ENG.
(T) 01483 202054
Speciality: Complementary Medicines & Therapy.
C M (**Ref:**HM06655)

## EDWARDS, IRENE & PETER

**Irene & Peter Edwards**, 55 Beverley Rd, Leamington Spa, **Warwickshire**, CV32 6PW, ENG.
(T) 01926 334212 (F) 01926 833466
Speciality: Hypnosis, Hypnotherapy, Magna Therapy. ✓ (Credit Cards)
● **Hypnotherapist** Mrs I Edwards Q: LCIP. M: CPS, HA.
● **Partner** Mr P Edwards Q: LCIP. M: CPS, HA.
B Yrs. Est.: 9 (**Ref:**HM06656)

## EDWARDS, J B

**J B Edwards**, 18 Orchard Avenue, Cannock, **Staffordshire**, WS11 1JD, ENG.
(T) 01543 462889
Speciality: Complementary Medicines & Therapy.
● **Owner** Mr J Edwards
C M (**Ref:**HM06657)

## EDWARDS, J E

**J E Edwards**, 13 St Andrews St, Droitwich, **Worcestershire**, WR9 8DY, ENG.
(T) 01905 772458
Speciality: Osteopathy.
P S T (**Ref:**HM06658)

## EDWARDS, JOHN

**John Edwards**, 7 Allison Gardens, Purley On Thames, Reading, **Berkshire**, RG8 8DF, ENG.
(T) 01189 422955
Speciality: Auto Suggestion, Autogenic Training, Biofeedback, Cognitive Therapy, Counselling, Hypnosis, Hypnotherapy, Meditation, Psychotherapy, Stress Therapy, Transactional Analysis, Visualisation Therapy. ✓
● **Psychotherapist** Mr J Edwards
H Yrs. Est.: 29 (**Ref:**HM06659)

## EDWARDS, JOHN

**John Edwards**, 37 Rosslyn Hill, London, **London (Greater)**, NW3 5UJ, ENG.
(T) 020 7431 3016
Speciality: Psychotherapy.
B (**Ref:**HM06660)

## EDWARDS, JOHN

**John Edwards**, 627 Dumbarton Rd, Glasgow, **Glasgow (City of)**, G11 6HY, SCO.
(T) 01413 573527 (F) 01413 573527
Speciality: Complementary Medicines & Therapy.
● **Owner** Mr J Edwards
C M (**Ref:**HM06661)

## EDWARDS, KAREEN

**Kareen Edwards**, 39 Desswood Pl, Aberdeen, **Aberdeenshire**, AB25 2EE, SCO.
(T) 01224 642947
Speciality: Psychotherapy.
● **Owner** Mrs K Edwards
B (**Ref:**HM06662)

## EDWARDS, MATTHEW

**Matthew Edwards**, Westbourne House, Westbourne Trce, Shuttern, Taunton, **Somerset**, TA1 4ES, ENG.
(T) 01823 332871
Speciality: Osteopathy.
P S T (**Ref:**HM06663)

## EDWARDS, MICHAEL

**Michael Edwards**, 14 Finnamore Wood Camp, Frieth Rd, Marlow, **Buckinghamshire**, SL7 2HU, ENG.
Speciality: Reflexology.
S T (**Ref:**HM06664)

## EDWARDS, P A

**P A Edwards**, 12 Asquith Cl, Biddulph, Stoke-On-Trent, **Staffordshire**, ST8 7LN, ENG.
(T) 01782 514242
Speciality: Chiropodists (Podiatrists).
● **Owner** Mr P Edwards
S (**Ref:**HM06665)

## EDWARDS, P A

**P A Edwards**, 2 Hyde Court, Market Pl, Leek, **Staffordshire**, ST13 5HH, ENG.
(T) 01538 399727
Speciality: Chiropodists (Podiatrists).
● **Owner** Mr P Edwards
S (**Ref:**HM06666)

## EDWARDS, R

**R Edwards**, 41 Downs Pk, Herne Bay, **Kent**, CT6 6BZ, ENG.
(T) 01227 740542
Speciality: Chiropractic.
● **Owner** Mr R Edwards
P S T (**Ref:**HM06667)

## EDWARDS, R

**R Edwards**, 47 Thanet Rd, Ramsgate, **Kent**, CT11 8EQ, ENG.
(T) 01843 590281
Speciality: Chiropractic. ✓
● **Chiropractor** Dr Tattersfield Q: DC. M: GCC.
● **Chiropractor** Dr Edwards Q: DC. M: GCC.
P Yrs. Est.: 15 (**Ref:**HM06668)

## EDWARDS, R L

**R L Edwards**, 66A Pembroke Rd, Clifton, Bristol, BS8 3DX, ENG.
(T) 01179 736989
Speciality: Acupuncture.
O (**Ref:**HM06669)

## EDWARDS, R, HERNE BAY

**R Edwards The Herne Bay Chiropractic**, 26 Cheriton Pl, Folkestone, **Kent**, CT20 2AZ, ENG.
(T) 01303 226933
Speciality: Chiropractic. ✓
● **Chiropractor** Mr R Edwards Q: DC. M: GCC.
P Yrs. Est.: 15 (**Ref:**HM06670)

## EDWARDS, SIMON

**Simon Edwards**, 35 Barnsite Gardens, Rustington, Littlehampton, **Sussex (West)**, BN16 3QG, ENG.
(T) 01903 859525
Speciality: Chiropractic.
P S T (**Ref:**HM06671)

## EDWARDS, SIMON

**Simon Edwards**, 15 Station Rd, Quainton, Aylesbury, **Buckinghamshire**, HP22 4BW, ENG.
(T) 01296 651259
Speciality: Hypnotherapy.
● **Owner** Mr S Edwards
B (**Ref:**HM06672)

## EDWARDS, T W

**T W Edwards**, 28 Wilford Lane, West Bridgford, Nottingham, **Nottinghamshire**, NG2 7QX, ENG.
(T) 01159 696085
Speciality: Osteopathy.
● **Owner** Mr T Edwards
P S T (**Ref:**HM06673)

## EDWARDS, TINA

**Tina Edwards**, 9 Groesfaen Trce, Deri, Bargoed, **Caerphilly**, CF81 9GH, WAL.
(T) 01443 836106
Speciality: Reflexology.
● **Owner** Miss T Edwards
S T (**Ref:**HM06674)

## EDWARDS, ZENA

**Zena Edwards**, 44 Grange Rd, South Croydon, **Surrey**, CR2 0NA, ENG.
(T) 020 8645 9761
Speciality: Reflexology.
S T (**Ref:**HM06675)

## EDWARDS-FOWLER, A

**A Edwards-Fowler**, 106 Harley St, London, **London (Greater)**, W1N 1AF, ENG.
(T) 020 7486 5238
Speciality: Physiotherapy.
● **Owner** A Edwards-Fowler
P S T (**Ref:**HM06676)

## EDWARDS-FOWLER, A

**A Edwards-Fowler**, Central London Physiotherapy Clinic, 150 Lambeth Rd, London, **London (Greater)**, SE1 7DF, ENG.
(T) 020 7928 9216 (F) 020 7401 8980
Speciality: Physiotherapy.
● **Partner** Mrs A Edwards-Fowler
P S T (**Ref:**HM06677)

## EDWINSTOWE PHYSIO CLINIC

**Edwinstowe Physiotherapy Clinic (The)**, 110 Fourth Avenue, Edwinstowe, Mansfield, **Nottinghamshire**, NG21 9NT, ENG.
(T) 01623 822374
Speciality: Physiotherapy.
● **Owner** Mr J Brown
P S T (**Ref:**HM06678)

## EELES, MEGAN

**Megan Eeles**, 31A Great George St, Above Rumpoles, Leeds, **Yorkshire (West)**, LS1 3BB, ENG.
(T) 01132 343366
Speciality: Complementary Medicines & Therapy.
M (**Ref:**HM06679)

## EFFLEURAGE

**Effleurage**, 10 Winchelsea Drive, Chelmsford, **Essex**, CM2 9TL, ENG.
(T) 01245 353629
Speciality: Aromatherapy.
M O (**Ref:**HM06680)

## EGAN, F

**F Egan**, 7 Surrey Gardens, Birchington, **Kent**, CT7 9SA, ENG.
(T) 01843 846012
Speciality: Chiropodists (Podiatrists).
S (**Ref:**HM06681)

## EGAN, P K

**P K Egan**, 27A High St, Aberdare, **Glamorgan (Vale of)**, CF44 7AA, WAL.
(T) 01685 872772
Speciality: Chiropodists (Podiatrists).
● **Owner** Mr P Egan
S (**Ref:**HM06682)

## EGERTON, S

**S Egerton**, First Floor Flat, Albion Rd, Fordingbridge, **Hampshire**, SP6 1EL, ENG.
(T) 01425 652789
Speciality: Chiropodists (Podiatrists).
S (**Ref:**HM06683)

## EGGINTON, KATHRYN

**Kathryn Egginton**, 2 Farm Cl, Chedgrave, Norwich, **Norfolk**, NR14 6HQ, ENG.
(T) 01508 520521
Speciality: Chiropodists (Podiatrists).
S (**Ref:**HM06684)

## EGHAM HYPNOTHERAPY

**Egham Hypnotherapy**, 47 Hummer Rd, Egham, **Surrey**, TW20 9BS, ENG.
(T) 01784 431929
Speciality: Complementary Medicines & Therapy.
● **Owner** Mrs B Traynor
M (**Ref:**HM06685)

## EGLINTON, DOMINIC

**Dominic Eglinton**, Osteopathic Clinic, 34 Millway, London, **London (Greater)**, NW7 3RA, ENG.
(T) 020 8959 1123 (F) 020 8201 1038
Speciality: Osteopathy.
● **Owner** Mr D Eglinton



Key continued: Yrs.Est: Years Established Q: Qualifications M: Professional Membership ✓ Indemnity Insurance (Credit Cards) Accept Credit Cards

P S T (Ref:HM06686)

## EGNER, JULIE

**Julie Egner**, 24 Spring Rd, Brightlingsea, Colchester, **Essex**, CO7 0PJ, ENG.
(T) 01206 303892
Speciality: Reflexology.
S T (Ref:HM06687)

## EIGENWELT, AMIDA

**Amida Eigenwelt**, 53 Grosvenor Pl, Newcastle Upon Tyne, **Tyne and Wear**, NE2 2RD, ENG.
(T) 01912 815592
Speciality: Psychotherapy.
● **Owner** Mr D Brazier
B (Ref:HM06688)

## EIGHAN, PENELOPE

**Cloud Nine Complementary Health Care**, At Cloud Nine, Unit 3 Eight Bells Arcade, Bartholomew St, Newbury, **Berkshire**, RG14 5DY, ENG.
(T) 01635 581701
Speciality: Acupressure, Aromatherapy, Complementary Therapy, Counselling, Cranio-Sacral Therapy, Cupping, Healing Therapy, Indian Head Massage, Massage (Therapeutic), Oriental Diagnosis, Reflexology, Shiatsu. ✔
● **Complementary Health Therapist** Coralie Bromley Q: IIHHT. M: FHT.
● **Owner/Complementary Health Therapist** Mrs P Eighan Q: ITEC. M: IPTI.
● **Counsellor/Craniosacral Therapist** Jo Cullen
(T) 01635 44854 Q: Dip.Couns. M: CSTA.
B (Ref:HM06689)

## EIGHT WINDS ACUPUNCTURE

**Eight Winds Acupuncture & Shiatsu Clinic**, 21 Cedar Chase, Rectory Rd, Maidenhead, **Berkshire**, SL6 4JY, ENG.
(T) 01628 621683
Speciality: Acupuncture, Shiatsu. ✔
● **Acupuncturist** Mr S Cook Q: Dip.Ac.
O Yrs. Est.: 20 (Ref:HM06690)

## EILEEN TAYLOR CHIROPODIST

**Eileen Taylor Chiropodist**, 34 Armthorpe Drive, Little Sutton, Ellesmere Port, **Merseyside**, CH66 4NW, ENG.
(T) 01513 396828
Speciality: Chiropodists (Podiatrists).
S (Ref:HM06691)

## EINSIEDEL, H

**H Einsiedel**, 63 Wood Vale, London, **London (Greater)**, SE23 3DT, ENG.
(T) 020 8299 6311
Speciality: Homeopathy.
● **Owner** Mrs H Einsiedel
M (Ref:HM06692)

## EISENHAUER, G

**G Eisenhauer**, 80 Ashburnham Rd, London, **London (Greater)**, NW10 5SE, ENG.
(T) 020 8968 4568
Speciality: Psychotherapy.
● **Partner** Mrs S Nelson
B (Ref:HM06693)

## EKE, L

**L Eke**, 114 The St, Brundall, Norwich, **Norfolk**, NR13 5LP, ENG.
(T) 01603 713555
Speciality: Chiropodists (Podiatrists).
● **Owner** Mrs L Eke
S (Ref:HM06694)

## EKF PHYSIOTHERAPY SERVICES

**EKF Physiotherapy Services**, 31 Hayling Rise, High Salvington, Worthing, **Sussex (West)**, BN13 3AL, ENG.
(T) 01903 264817
Speciality: Physiotherapy.
● **Owner** Miss E French
P S T (Ref:HM06695)

## EKSTS, ANNE

**Anne Eksts**, 9 Bryanstone Avenue, Guildford, **Surrey**, GU2 9UN, ENG.
(T) 01483 573164
Speciality: Reflexology.
S T (Ref:HM06696)

## ELAINE ATKINS ASSOCIATES

**Elaine Atkins Associates**, 154 High Rd, Woodford Green, **Essex**, IG8 9EF, ENG.
(T) 020 8504 0478
Speciality: Physiotherapy.
P S T (Ref:HM06697)

## ELAINE MCCARTHY REFLEXOLOGIST

**Elaine McCarthy Reflexologist**, 9 Harcourt, Bradwell, Milton Keynes, **Buckinghamshire**, MK13 9EN, ENG.
(T) 01908 322043
Speciality: Reflexology. ✔
● **Owner/Reflexologist** Mrs E McCarthy Q: MAR. M: AoR.
T Yrs. Est.: 9 (Ref:HM06698)

## ELBAHJA, MOHAMMED

**Mohammed Elbahja**, 94 Snowsfields, London, **London (Greater)**, SE1 3SS, ENG.
(T) 020 7403 2571
Speciality: Hypnotherapy.
● **Owner** Mr K Harris
B (Ref:HM06699)

## ELBAHJA, MOHAMMED

**Mohammed Elbahja**, Flat 8, Stopher House, 90 Webber St, London, **London (Greater)**, SE1 0RE, ENG.
(T) 020 7401 2088
Speciality: Hypnosis.
● **Owner** Mr M Elbahja
B (Ref:HM06700)

## ELCOCK, B J

**B J Elcock**, 134 Wyndham Court, Commercial Rd, Southampton, **Hampshire**, SO15 1GU, ENG.
(T) 023 8022 0488
Speciality: Chiropodists (Podiatrists).
S (Ref:HM06701)

## ELDEN, GAYE

**Gaye Elden**, 121 Main Rd, Danbury, Chelmsford, **Essex**, CM3 4DL, ENG.
(T) 01245 224503
Speciality: Chiropodists (Podiatrists).
● **Owner** Mrs G Elden
S (Ref:HM06702)

## ELDER, SUSANNA

**Susanna Elder**, 2 The Knowe, Troon, **Ayrshire (South)**, KA10 6UZ, SCO.
(T) 01292 314095
Speciality: Chiropodists (Podiatrists).
● **Owner** Mrs S Elder
S (Ref:HM06703)

## ELDERGILL, D J

**D J Eldergill**, 297 High St, Worle, Weston-Super-Mare, **Somerset**, BS22 6JW, ENG.
(T) 01934 511516
Speciality: Chiropodists (Podiatrists).
● **Owner** Mr D Eldergill
S (Ref:HM06704)

## ELDON HEALTH CLINIC

**Eldon Health Clinic (The)**, The Eldon Health Clinic, 12 Torquay Rd, Newton Abbot, **Devon**, TQ12 1AH, ENG.
(T) 01626 205400 (F) 01626 205402
(E) eldon@eclipse.co.uk
Speciality: Acupressure, Acupuncture, Aromatherapy, Biofeedback, Clinical Ecology, Cognitive Therapy, Counselling, Electrotherapy, Homeopathy, Hypnotherapy, Iridology, Manipulation, Massage (Therapeutic), Moxibustion, Naturopathy, Nutritional Therapy, Orthomolecular Medicine, Osteopathy, Physiotherapy, Pilates, Reflexology, Shiatsu, Vitamin Therapy, X-Ray, Laser Therapy, Occupational Medicine, Musculo Skeletal Medicine.
● **Counsellor** Ms I Ash Q: BABTAC.
● **Shiatsu Therapist** Ms S Heygate
● **Osteopath/Naturopath** Mr M Ash Q: BSc (Hons), DO, ND.
● **Homeopath** Ms E Ludgrove Q: Dip.Hom.
● **Nutritionist** Leonie Ash Q: BSR.
● **Physiotherapist/Laser Therapist** Ms L MacDonald Q: MCSP, SRP.
● **Masseuse/Reflexologist/Aromatherapist** Ms J Britton Q: NLP.
● **Doctor/Osteopath/Acupuncturist** Mr P Baker Q: MB.
● **Masseuse/Reflexologist** Ms K Ruth Q: Dip.Reflex, ITEC.
● **Psychologist** Dr B Cripps Q: BEd (Hons), PhD.
S (Ref:HM06705)

## ELDON, MARTIN

**Martin Eldon**, Broomfield Cottage, The Heath, Hatfield Heath, Bishop's Stortford, **Hertfordshire**, CM22 7DZ, ENG.
(T) 01279 731649
Speciality: Hypnosis.
● **Owner** Mr M Eldon
B (Ref:HM06706)

## ELDRAS, T P

**T P Eldras**, Elm Tree House, 13 Netherhall Gardens, London, **London (Greater)**, NW3 5RN, ENG.
(T) 020 7431 6920
Speciality: Hypnotherapy.
● **Chief Executive** Mr T Eldras
B (Ref:HM06707)

## ELDRETT, RACHAEL

**Rachael Eldrett**, 38 Maple Avenue, Heybridge, Maldon, **Essex**, CM9 4BP, ENG.
(T) 01621 857239
Speciality: Reflexology.
S T (Ref:HM06708)

## ELDRIDGE, NICOLA

**Nicola Eldridge**, Falkner House, Falkners Cl, Ancells Farm, Fleet, **Hampshire**, GU13 8XF, ENG.
(T) 01252 614818
Speciality: Chiropractic.
● **Owner** Mrs V Amerongen
P S T (Ref:HM06709)

## ELECTROLYSIS & BEAUTY CLINIC

**Electrolysis & Beauty Clinic**, 50 The Grove, Gravesend, **Kent**, DA12 1DP, ENG.
(T) 01474 535062
Speciality: Electrolysis.
● **Partner** Mrs S Swales
T (Ref:HM06710)

## ELECTROLYSIS & BEAUTY CLINIC

**Electrolysis & Beauty Clinic (The)**, 21 St Georges Rd, Cheltenham, **Gloucestershire**, GL50 3DT, ENG.
(T) 01242 224723
Speciality: Electrolysis.
● **Owner** Mrs N Bhumgara
T (Ref:HM06711)

## ELECTROLYSIS & BEAUTY CLINIC

**Electrolysis & Beauty Clinic (The)**, 466A Hoe St, London, **London (Greater)**, E17 9AH, ENG.
(T) 020 8556 6518
Speciality: Electrolysis.
● **Owner** Ms S Wilson
T (Ref:HM06712)

## ELECTROLYSIS & BEAUTY CLINIC

**Electrolysis & Beauty Clinic (The)**, The Annexe, The Old Vicarage, 31St Dunstans St, Canterbury, **Kent**, CT2 8BZ, ENG.
(T) 01227 762364
Speciality: Electrolysis.
● **Owner** Mrs C Finnis
T (Ref:HM06713)

## ELECTROLYSIS 2000

**Electrolysis 2000**, 19A London Rd, Southampton, **Hampshire**, SO15 2AE, ENG.
(T) 023 8063 0425
Speciality: Electrolysis.
T (Ref:HM06714)

## ELECTROLYSIS CENTRE

**Electrolysis Centre**, 6 Romney Pl, Maidstone, **Kent**, ME15 6LE, ENG.
(T) 01622 758635
Speciality: Electrolysis.
T (Ref:HM06715)

## ELECTROLYSIS CLINIC

**Electrolysis Clinic**, 15 Rowallen Prde, Green Lane, Dagenham, **Essex**, RM8 1XU, ENG.
(T) 020 8597 1514 (F) 020 8597 7168
Speciality: Electrolysis, Hair removal, Skin Care, Body Care. ✔



Key: B Mind-Body Medicine C Complementary Medicine H Self Help Treatment M Medicinal Therapy O Oriental Medicine P Postural Therapy S Manipulative Structural Therapy T Touch Therapy

● **Consultant** Mr I Sheikh
[C] Yrs. Est.: 3 (**Ref:**HM06716)

## ELECTROLYSIS CLINIC

**Electrolysis Clinic**, 38 Queen St, Magherafelt, **County Londonderry**, BT45 6AB, NIR.
(T) 028 7963 3988
Speciality: Electrolysis.
[T] (Ref:HM06717)

## ELECTROLYSIS CLINIC

**Electrolysis Clinic**, 72 Brook Lane, Walsall Wood, Walsall, **Midlands (West)**, WS9 9NA, ENG.
(T) 01543 373507
Speciality: Electrolysis. ✔
● **Principal** Mr A Fisher Q: DRE, FIE.
[T] Yrs. Est.: 31 (**Ref:**HM06718)

## ELECTROLYSIS CLINIC

**Electrolysis Clinic**, Pemchurch Chambers, 30-32 Cradock St, Swansea, SA1 3EP, WAL.
(T) 01792 643049
Speciality: Electrolysis.
[T] (Ref:HM06719)

## ELECTROLYSIS CLINIC

**Electrolysis Clinic (The)**, 14 Cloth Hall St, Huddersfield, **Yorkshire (West)**, HD1 2EG, ENG.
(T) 01484 514553
Speciality: Electrolysis.
● **Owner** Ms S Ali
[T] (Ref:HM06720)

## ELECTROMAGNETIC PRODUCTS

**Medcross Ltd**, Ker Menez, Lower Race, Pontypool, **Monmouthshire**, NP4 5UH, WAL.
(T) 01495 752122 (F) 08707 060168
(W) www.mag-lab.com
Speciality: Complementary Medicines & Therapy, Magnet Therapy.
● **Director** Mr R Coghill Q: C.Biol, MA. M: BIMT.
● **Director** Ms T Coghill
[B] [H] [P] Yrs. Est.: 20 (**Ref:**HM06721)

## ELEMENT, JOANNE

**Joanne Element**, 3 Oak Vale, Grampound, Truro, **Cornwall**, TR2 4QY, ENG.
(T) 01726 882220
Speciality: Hypnotherapy.
● **Owner** Miss J Element
[B] (Ref:HM06722)

## ELEMENT, SUE

**Sue Element**, 116 Victoria Rd, Farnborough, **Hampshire**, GU14 7PN, ENG.
(T) 01252 524301
Speciality: Reflexology.
[S] [T] (Ref:HM06723)

## ELEMENTAL

**Elemental**, 46A Main St, Davidsons Mains, Edinburgh, **Edinburgh (City of)**, EH4 5AA, SCO.
(T) 01313 128019 (F) 01313 128019
Speciality: Complementary Medicines & Therapy.
● **Owner** Ms D Phillips
[C] [M] (Ref:HM06724)

## ELEMENTS OF HEALTH

**Elements of Health**, Bethal St, Norwich, **Norfolk**, NR2 1NR, ENG.
(T) 01603 666546 (F) 01603 666546
(W) www.elementsofhealth.co.uk
Speciality: Acupuncture, Aromatherapy, Counselling, Herbal Medicine, Homeopathy, Hypnosis, Hypnotherapy, Indian Head Massage, Massage (Therapeutic), Nutritional Therapy, Postural Integration, Reflexology, Reiki, Shiatsu, Stress Therapy, Trager Therapy. ✔
● **Chiropractor** Mr B Moore
● **Aromatherapist** Ms L Gardenchild
● **Tai Chi/Chi Kung Teacher** Bo Ou Mander
● **Nutritional Consultancy/Iridology** Ms R Biggins Q: Dip.Iridol.
● **Reflexologist/Yoga** Ms S Clifton Q: MBRA.
● **Image Consultant** Ms B Bowler
● **Homeopathy/Foresight Fertility Programmer** Ms S Suanders Q: RSHom.
● **Hypnotherapist** Ms L Jeckells
● **Reflexologist/Indian Head Massage Therapist** Ms S Leich Q: BA.
● **NLP Practitioner/Hypnotherapist** Mr R Maczka
● **Back Manipulation** Ms S Seely Q: DO, LCSP.
● **Acupuncturist/Mind Body Therapy** Balbir Bhogal Q: Dip.Ac, LCSP.
● **Shiatsu Practitioner** Ms S Ward Q: MRSS.
● **Beauty Therapist** Ms J Skipper
● **Acupuncturist/Chinese Herbal Medicine** Mr N Malak Q: M.Ac, MBAcC, MRCHM. M: BAcC.
● **Massage** Ms E Read
● **Osteomyologist using P.A.M** Mr N Aldous
[C] Yrs. Est.: 3 (**Ref:**HM06725)

## ELEMIS

**Elemis Ltd**, Harrow Weald Lodge, 92 Uxbridge Rd, Harrow, **London (Greater)**, HA3 6BZ, ENG.
(T) 020 8909 5000
Speciality: Aromatherapy.
● **Managing Director** Mr S Harrison
[M] [O] (Ref:HM06726)

## ELF CRAFT

**Elf Craft**, 14 Coronation Drive, Felixstowe, **Suffolk**, IP11 2NU, ENG.
(T) 01394 670080
Speciality: Complementary Medicines & Therapy.
● **Owner** Ms K Orchard
[C] [M] (Ref:HM06727)

## ELFICK, J

**J Elfick**, 21 Longfield, Hemel Hempstead, **Hertfordshire**, HP3 8HN, ENG.
(T) 01442 251473
Speciality: Hypnotherapy.
● **Owner** Mr J Elfick
[B] (Ref:HM06728)

## ELGIN CHIROPRACTIC CLINIC

**Karen Robertson**, 1 South St, Elgin, **Moray**, IV30 1JZ, SCO.
(T) 01343 552721
Speciality: Chiropractic, Carpal Tunnel. ✔
● **Owner/Chiropractor** Mrs K Robertson Q: DC. M: BCA.
● **Associate/Chiropractor** Mr M Marino Q: DC.
[P] Yrs. Est.: 20 (**Ref:**HM06729)

## ELHALHULI, OTHMAN

**Othman Elhalhuli**, Adlington Medical Centre, 22-24 Babylon Lane, Anderton, Chorley, **Lancashire**, PR6 9NW, ENG.
(T) 01257 482076
Speciality: Acupuncture.
[O] (Ref:HM06730)

## ELIAS, GEORGE

**George Elias**, Clerkenwells, 11 Portpool Lane (Off Leather Lane), London, **London (Greater)**, EC1N 7UJ, ENG.
(T) 020 7833 1283
Speciality: Chiropodists (Podiatrists).
[S] (Ref:HM06731)

## ELIAS, IAN

**Ian Elias**, 8 Tibberton Rd, Malvern, **Worcestershire**, WR14 3AN, ENG.
(T) 01684 575379
Speciality: Osteopathy.
[P] [S] [T] (Ref:HM06732)

## ELIAS, IAN R

**Ian R Elias**, 242 Cathedral Rd, Cardiff, **Glamorgan (Vale of)**, CF11 9JG, WAL.
(T) 029 2023 5220
Speciality: Osteopathy.
[P] [S] [T] (Ref:HM06733)

## ELITA HEALING DIVISION

**Elita Healing Division**, 28 Camelford St, Brighton, **Sussex (East)**, BN2 1TQ, ENG.
(T) 01273 686330
Speciality: Complementary Medicines & Therapy.
[M] (Ref:HM06734)

## ELIXAROME

**Elixarome**, Hop Pocket Lane, Paddock Wood, Tonbridge, **Kent**, TN12 6DQ, ENG.
(T) 01892 833334 (F) 01892 833335
Speciality: Aromatherapy.
● **Managing Director** Mr A Phillips
[M] [O] (Ref:HM06735)

## ELIZABETH ANNE

**Elizabeth Anne**, High Spirits Lodge, 89 Edwin Rd, Rainham, **Kent**, ME8 0AE, ENG.
(T) 01634 233426 (F) 01634 233426
(E) elizabethannehyp@aol.com
(W) www.elizabethanne.co.uk
Speciality: Hypnosis, Hypnotherapy, Colonic Irrigation. ✔
● **Hypnotherapist/Colonic Therapist** Mrs E Batcheler Q: C.Hyp, Dip.Hyp, Dip.Psych. M: CIA, HA.
[H] Yrs. Est.: 18 (**Ref:**HM06736)

## ELIZABETH BECK CHIROPODY

**Elizabeth Beck Chiropody**, Unit 4 Doncaster Rd, Rotherham, **Yorkshire (South)**, S65 3SR, ENG.
(T) 01709 854772
Speciality: Chiropodists (Podiatrists).
[S] (Ref:HM06737)

## ELIZABETH BLAYLOCK REIKI PRACT

**Elizabeth Blaylock Reiki Practitioner**, 9 The Grange, Newton Aycliffe, **County Durham**, DL5 4SZ, ENG.
(T) 01325 315586 (F) 01325 315586
Speciality: Aromatherapy.
● **Owner** Mrs E Blaylock
[M] (Ref:HM06738)

## ELIZABETH HELEN BEAUTY THER

**Elizabeth Helen Beauty Therapist**, 8 Dedmere Rise, Marlow, **Buckinghamshire**, SL7 1PH, ENG.
(T) 01628 473917
Speciality: Aromatherapy.
● **Owner** Ms H Smith
[M] [O] (Ref:HM06739)

## ELIZABETH, KENT

**Elizabeth Kent MISCP**, 2 Dara Ct, Naas, **County Kildare**, IRE.
(T) 04586 6075
Speciality: Psychotherapy.
[B] (Ref:HM06740)

## ELIZABETH, WENDY

**Wendy Elizabeth**, Clarence Cottage, York Rd, Totland Bay, **Isle of Wight**, PO39 0HB, ENG.
(T) 01983 754538
Speciality: Clairvoyants & Palmists.
● **Owner** Mrs W Wittingham
[B] (Ref:HM06741)

## ELKAN, MIRIAM

**Miriam Elkan**, 853 Finchley Rd, London, **London (Greater)**, NW11 8LX, ENG.
(T) 020 8455 5646
Speciality: Osteopathy.
[P] [S] [T] (Ref:HM06742)

## ELKINS, P A (DR)

**Dr P A Elkins**, The Botley Clinic, 7a High St, Botley, Southampton, **Hampshire**, SO30 2EA, ENG.
(T) 01489 787170
Speciality: Chiropractic.
[P] [S] [T] (Ref:HM06743)

## ELLALLAM, AISHA

**Aisha Ellallam**, Emberly, Harvest Hill, East Grinstead, **Sussex (West)**, RH19 4BU, ENG.
(T) 01342 324717
Speciality: Complementary Medicines & Therapy.
● **Owner** Mrs A Elallam
[C] [M] (Ref:HM06744)

## ELLAM, VALERIE

**Valerie Ellam**, 69 Southend, Garsington, Oxford, **Oxfordshire**, OX44 9DJ, ENG.
(T) 01865 361495
Speciality: Reflexology.
[S] [T] (Ref:HM06745)

## ELLAN, JAN

**Jan Ellan**, 21 West Cliffe Gr, Harrogate, **Yorkshire (North)**, HG2 0PS, ENG.



Key continued: **Yrs.Est:** Years Established **Q:** Qualifications **M:** Professional Membership ✔ Indemnity Insurance Accept Credit Cards

(T) 01423 506246
Speciality: Alexander Technique.
● **Owner** Mrs J Ellan
P S (Ref:HM06746)

## ELLE BEAUTY SALON

**Elle Beauty Salon**, Village Ct Strand Rd, Portmarnock, **County Dublin**, IRE.
(T) 01846 2754
Speciality: Complementary Medicines & Therapy.
M (Ref:HM06747)

## ELLIOT-SMITH, A

**A Elliot-Smith**, Springfield, Larkins Lane, Headington, Oxford, **Oxfordshire**, OX3 9DW, ENG.
(T) 01865 742894
Speciality: Chiropodists (Podiatrists).
● **Owner** A Elliot-Smith
S (Ref:HM06748)

## ELLIOTT CHIROPRACTIC CLINIC

**Elliott Chiropractic Clinic**, 12 Moss Side Rd, Glasgow, **Glasgow (City of)**, G41 3TL, SCO.
(T) 01416 496333
Speciality: Chiropractic.
P S T (Ref:HM06749)

## ELLIOTT, A T

**A T Elliott**, 31 Woodside St, Cinderford, **Gloucestershire**, GL14 2NL, ENG.
(T) 01594 826979
Speciality: Physiotherapy.
● **Owner** A T Elliott
P S T (Ref:HM06750)

## ELLIOTT, BRIAN

**Brian Elliott**, 143 Markfield, Court Wood Lane, Croydon, **Surrey**, CR0 9HQ, ENG.
(T) 020 8657 4632
Speciality: Chiropodists (Podiatrists).
S (Ref:HM06751)

## ELLIOTT, DAVID W

**David W Elliott**, 8 Vernon St, Derby, **Derbyshire**, DE1 1FR, ENG.
(T) 07971 016866 (F) 07977 436866
Speciality: Chiropodists (Podiatrists).
● **Owner** Mr D Elliott
S (Ref:HM06752)

## ELLIOTT, J E

**J E Elliott**, 54 Derwent Cl, Rugby, **Warwickshire**, CV21 1JX, ENG.
(T) 01788 567890
Speciality: Chiropodists (Podiatrists).
S (Ref:HM06753)

## ELLIOTT, JUDITH

**Judith Elliott**, 6 Whiteway Head, Knaresborough, **Yorkshire (North)**, HG5 8LE, ENG.
(T) 01423 864369
Speciality: Alexander Technique.
P S (Ref:HM06754)

## ELLIOTT, KATHI

**Kathi Elliott**, Beals Cottage, Beals Lane, Tilehurst, Reading, **Berkshire**, RG31 5UD, ENG.
(T) 01189 421500
Speciality: Electrolysis.
● **Owner** Mrs K Elliott
T (Ref:HM06755)

## ELLIOTT, KATHRYN L

**Kathryn L Elliott**, 3 Park Lane, Knaresborough, **Yorkshire (North)**, HG5 0DQ, ENG.
(T) 01423 868388
Speciality: Osteopathy.
● **Owner** Miss K Elliott
P S T (Ref:HM06756)

## ELLIOTT, MAUREEN

**Maureen Elliott**, Stanbridge Cl, Ifield, Crawley, **Sussex (West)**, RH11 0TP, ENG.
(T) 01293 534956
Speciality: Chiropodists (Podiatrists).
S (Ref:HM06757)

## ELLIOTT, N S & ROYFFE, G B

**N S Elliott & G B Royffe**, 69 Crouch St, Colchester, **Essex**, CO3 3EY, ENG.
(T) 01206 572659
Speciality: Chiropodists (Podiatrists).
● **Partner** Mr G Royffe
S (Ref:HM06758)

## ELLIOTT, TIMOTHY

**Timothy Elliott**, Chy-Cocha, Greenbottom, Chacewater, Truro, **Cornwall**, TR4 8QJ, ENG.
(T) 01872 561099
Speciality: Chiropodists (Podiatrists).
S (Ref:HM06759)

## ELLIS & ASSOCIATES

**David Ellis & Associates**, 2 Lee Rd, Snodland, **Kent**, ME6 5NN, ENG.
(T) 01634 241901
Speciality: Psychology.
● **Owner** Mr D Ellis
B (Ref:HM06760)

## ELLIS, A C

**A C Ellis**, 105 King St, Knutsford, **Cheshire**, WA16 6EQ, ENG.
(T) 01565 632010
Speciality: Chiropodists (Podiatrists).
S (Ref:HM06761)

## ELLIS, CHRISTOPHER

**Christopher Ellis**, Hill Brow, 18 Upper Old Pk Lane, Farnham, **Surrey**, GU9 0AT, ENG.
(T) 01252 714480
Speciality: Homeopathy.
● **Owner** Mr C Ellis
M (Ref:HM06762)

## ELLIS, DAVID

**David Ellis**, 18 Warwick St, Rugby, **Warwickshire**, CV21 3DH, ENG.
(T) 01788 544076
Speciality: Hypnosis.
B (Ref:HM06763)

## ELLIS, DAVID S

**David S Ellis**, 19 Leafields, Northampton, **Northamptonshire**, NN3 9UY, ENG.
(T) 01604 407152
Speciality: Hypnosis.
● **Owner** Mr D Ellis
B (Ref:HM06764)

## ELLIS, E A

**E A Ellis**, 105 King St, Knutsford, **Cheshire**, WA16 6EQ, ENG.
(T) 01565 632010
Speciality: Chiropodists (Podiatrists).
S (Ref:HM06765)

## ELLIS, ELIZABETH

**Elizabeth Ellis**, 39 Lamb Hall Rd, Huddersfield, **Yorkshire (West)**, HD3 3TJ, ENG.
(T) 01484 648544
Speciality: Chiropodists (Podiatrists).
S (Ref:HM06766)

## ELLIS, G R

**Mrs G R Ellis**, 2 Ashfield Rd, Birstall, Batley, **Yorkshire (West)**, WF17 0EF, ENG.
(T) 01924 477347
Speciality: Chiropodists (Podiatrists).
S (Ref:HM06767)

## ELLIS, H

**H Ellis**, 15 Gaywood Rd, King's Lynn, **Norfolk**, PE30 1QT, ENG.
(T) 01553 775730
Speciality: Chiropodists (Podiatrists).
● **Owner** Mrs H Ellis
S (Ref:HM06768)

## ELLIS, J

**J Ellis**, 12 Bridport Rd, Verwood, **Dorset**, BH31 6UP, ENG.
(T) 01202 821026
Speciality: Complementary Medicines & Therapy.
● **Owner** Ms G Ellis
M (Ref:HM06769)

## ELLIS, JUNE

**June Ellis**, 19 Redford Loan, Edinburgh, **Edinburgh (City of)**, EH13 0AY, SCO.
(T) 01314 411029
Speciality: Physiotherapy.
● **Owner** Mrs J Ellis
P S T (Ref:HM06770)

## ELLIS, M J H

**M J H Ellis**, 169 Dalkeith Rd, Edinburgh, **Edinburgh (City of)**, EH16 5BY, SCO.
(T) 01316 672676
Speciality: Chiropodists (Podiatrists).
● **Owner** Mrs M Ellis
S (Ref:HM06771)

## ELLIS, STEPHEN

**Stephen Ellis MBAcC**, The Common, Mulbarton, Norwich, **Norfolk**, NR14 8AE, ENG.
(T) 01508 570122
Speciality: Acupuncture. ✔
● **Acupuncturist** Mr S Ellis Q: Lic.Ac, MBAcC. M: BAcC.
● **Manager** Mrs K Lindholme
C Yrs. Est.: 6 (Ref:HM06772)

## ELLIS, SUE

**Sue Ellis**, Tossels House, Fore St, Chulmleigh, **Devon**, EX18 7BR, ENG.
(T) 01769 580970
(E) sue.ellis@btinternet.com
Speciality: Acupressure, Chiropractic, Complementary Therapy, Holistic Healing, Manipulation, Massage (Therapeutic), Spine, Joint and Muscle Therapy. ✔
● **Therapist** Ms S Ellis Q: DC, MAO.
S Yrs. Est.: 8 (Ref:HM06773)

## ELLISON, ANNE

**Anne Ellison**, 15 Station Rd, South Brent, **Devon**, TQ10 9BE, ENG.
(T) 01364 73149
Speciality: Osteopathy.
● **Owner** Mrs A Ellison
P S T (Ref:HM06774)

## ELLISON, ANNE

**Anne Ellison**, 30 Victoria Rd, Dartmouth, **Devon**, TQ6 9SA, ENG.
(T) 01803 835196
Speciality: Osteopathy.
● **Owner** Mrs A Ellison
P S T (Ref:HM06775)

## ELLISON, JENNY

**Jenny Ellison**, Cherwood House, Buckingham Rd, Bicester, **Oxfordshire**, OX6 9RA, ENG.
(T) 01869 240376
Speciality: Physiotherapy.
● **Owner** Mrs J Ellison
P S T (Ref:HM06776)

## ELLISON, TIM

**Surgical Chiropodist**, 25 Shearwater Lane, Crooksbarn, Stockton-On-Tees, **Cleveland**, TS20 1SH, ENG.
(T) 01642 551586
Speciality: Chiropodists (Podiatrists). ✔
● **Surgical Chiropodist** Mr T Ellison Q: MBChA, MSSCh. M: B.A.Ch.P, MSSCh.
S Yrs. Est.: 13 (Ref:HM06777)

## ELLISON-PERRIN

**Ellison-Perrin**, 45 Chew Vale, Greenfield, Oldham, **Lancashire**, OL3 7EQ, ENG.
(T) 01457 874758
Speciality: Clairvoyants & Palmists.
● **Owner** Ms N Ellison-Perrin
B (Ref:HM06778)

## ELLSON, S E

**S E Ellson**, 33 Windsor Rd, Swindon, **Wiltshire**, SN3 1JP, ENG.
(T) 01793 535722
Speciality: Chiropodists (Podiatrists).
S (Ref:HM06779)

## ELLWOOD, CAROLINE

**Caroline Ellwood**, 17 Claremont Sq, Islington, London, **London (Greater)**, N1 9LY, ENG.
(T) 020 7837 3451
Speciality: Cranial Osteopathy, Homeopathy, Naturopathy, Osteopathy. ✔
● **Homeopath/Osteopath/Naturopath** Ms C Ellwood Q: DO, ND, RGN, RN. M: RO, RoN.
S Yrs. Est.: 11 (Ref:HM06780)

## ELMER CHIROPODY & PODIATRY SVS

**Elmer Chiropody & Podiatry Services**, 6 Elmer Avenue, Southend-On-Sea, **Essex**, SS1 1NB, ENG.
(T) 01702 343666
Speciality: Biomechanics, Chiropody, Nail

Surgery, Podiatry. ✓
● **Chiropodist (Podiatrist)**
Miss L Hepworth **Q:** BSc (Hons), DPodM, M.S.C.P, S.R.Ch. **M:** S.C.P, S.R.Ch.
● **Chiropodist (Podiatrist)**
Mrs C Oxley **Q:** BSc, DPodM, M.S.C.P, S.R.Ch. **M:** S.C.P, S.R.Ch.
● **Chiropodist (Podiatrist)**
Mrs J Gillies **Q:** DPodM, M.S.C.P, S.R.Ch. **M:** S.C.P, S.R.Ch.
C Yrs. Est.: 30 (**Ref:**HM06781)

## ELMIDORO, JANE
**Jane Elmidoro**, Coombe Barn, Coombe Lane, Naphill, High Wycombe, **Buckinghamshire**, HP14 4QR, ENG.
(T) 01494 565821
Speciality: Reflexology.
S T (**Ref:**HM06782)

## ELMSLEIGH PARK CHIRO CLINIC
**Elmsleigh Park Chiropractic Clinic**, 4 Elmsleigh Pk, Paignton, **Devon**, TQ4 5AT, ENG.
(T) 01803 559916
Speciality: Chiropractic.
P S T (**Ref:**HM06783)

## ELPHINSTONE, D C R
**D C R Elphinstone**, 53A High St, Burnham-on-Crouch, **Essex**, CM0 8AG, ENG.
(T) 01621 784755
Speciality: Chiropodists (Podiatrists).
● **Owner** Mr D Elphinstone
S (**Ref:**HM06784)

## ELSON, M
**M Elson**, 64 Rokesly Avenue, London, **London (Greater)**, N8 8NH, ENG.
(T) 020 8340 4340
Speciality: Psychotherapy.
● **Owner** Ms M Elson
B (**Ref:**HM06785)

## ELSON, MONICA
**Monica Elson**, 44 St Peters Way, Mickle Trafford, Chester, **Cheshire**, CH2 4EJ, ENG.
(T) 01244 300679
Speciality: Psychotherapy.
● **Owner** Mrs M Elson
B (**Ref:**HM06786)

## ELSWORTH, K
**K Elsworth**, Horsmonden Clinic, Enterprise House, The Heath, Brenchley Rd, Horsmonden, Tonbridge, **Kent**, TN12 8JE, ENG.
(T) 01892 724377
Speciality: Physiotherapy.
● **Owner** Mrs K Elsworth
P S T (**Ref:**HM06787)

## ELTHAM HEALTH CLINIC
**Eltham Health Clinic**, 93 Eltham Hill, London, **London (Greater)**, SE9 5SU, ENG.
(T) 020 8294 1113
Speciality: Osteopathy.
P S T (**Ref:**HM06788)

## ELTHAM HYPNOTHERAPY ANALYSIS
**Peter Williams**, 4 Glenesk Rd, London, **London (Greater)**, SE9 1AG, ENG.
(T) 020 8850 3096
Speciality: Auto Suggestion, Aversion Therapy, Cognitive Therapy, Counselling, Family Therapy, Humanistic Psychology, Hypnosis, Hypnotherapy, Psychotherapy, Stress Therapy, Transactional Analysis. ✓
● **Hypnotherapist** Mr P Williams **Q:** Dip.Psych, MNCH.
H Yrs. Est.: 14 (**Ref:**HM06789)

## ELTON, KATHRYN
**Kathryn Elton**, 7 Pitton Cl, Wigston, **Leicestershire**, LE18 2RP, ENG.
(T) 01162 208177
Speciality: Reflexology.
S T (**Ref:**HM06790)

## ELVIN, CHRISTINA
**Christina Elvin PhD**, 12 Kimble Cl, Northampton, **Northamptonshire**, NN4 0RF, ENG.
(T) 01604 768343 (F) 01604 706609
Speciality: Hypnosis.
● **Owner** Dr C Elvin
B (**Ref:**HM06791)

## ELWELL, R S
**R S Elwell**, Lamberts Barn, Cropredy, Banbury, **Oxfordshire**, OX17 1QA, ENG.
(T) 01295 750758
Speciality: Chiropractic, Cranio-Sacral Therapy, McTimoney Chiropractic.
● **Owner** Dr R Elwell
P S T (**Ref:**HM06792)

## ELWELL, T M
**T M Elwell**, Lamberts Barn, Cropredy, Banbury, **Oxfordshire**, OX17 1QA, ENG.
(T) 01295 750758
Speciality: Chiropractors.
P S T (**Ref:**HM06793)

## ELWIN, E J
**E J Elwin**, 4 Portesham Hill, Portesham, Weymouth, **Dorset**, DT3 4EU, ENG.
(T) 01305 871358 (F) 01305 871358
Speciality: Chiropodists (Podiatrists).
● **Owner** Mr E Elwin
S (**Ref:**HM06794)

## ELY COMPLEMENTARY HEALTH CTRE
**Ely Complementary Health Centre**, 29A St Marys St, Ely, **Cambridgeshire**, CB7 4HF, ENG.
(T) 01353 664476
Speciality: Complementary Medicines & Therapy.
● **Owner** Mr A Spence
M (**Ref:**HM06795)

## ELYSE, GALE
**Gale Elyse**, Westwinds, Lyth Bank, Shrewsbury, **Shropshire**, SY3 0BE, ENG.
(T) 01743 873142
Speciality: Homeopathy.
● **Owner** Mrs E Gale
M (**Ref:**HM06796)

## ELYSIUM
**Elysium**, 2 Wallfield Pl, Aberdeen, **Aberdeenshire**, AB25 2JN, SCO.
(T) 01224 624226
Speciality: Complementary Medicines & Therapy.
● **Owner** Ms L Sibbett
M (**Ref:**HM06797)

## EMANUEL, G J
**G J Emanuel**, The Reddings, Beaulieu Avenue, Fareham, **Hampshire**, PO16 9SY, ENG.
(T) 01329 281829
Speciality: Chiropodists (Podiatrists).
● **Owner** Mr G Emanuel
S (**Ref:**HM06798)

## EMER, PURCELL
**Purcell Emer**, The Lodge Marlfield Hse, Clonmel, **County Tipperary**, IRE.
(T) 05222 297
Speciality: Complementary Medicines & Therapy.
M (**Ref:**HM06799)

## EMERGENCY LIFE SUPPORT
**Emergency Life Support Training Ltd**, 108 London Rd, Neath, **Glamorgan (Vale of)**, SA11 1HL, WAL.
(T) 01639 760102
Speciality: Chiropodists (Podiatrists).
S (**Ref:**HM06800)

## EMERSON, MICHAEL
**Michael Emerson**, 44 Manchester Old Rd, Bury, **Lancashire**, BL9 0TR, ENG.
(T) 01617 052207
Speciality: Physiotherapy.
P S T (**Ref:**HM06801)

## EMERY HOUSE CLINIC
**Emery House Clinic (The)**, 1 Emery Lane, Chippenham, **Wiltshire**, SN15 3JP, ENG.
(T) 01249 447147 (F) 01249 447661
Speciality: Chiropractic.
● **Director** Mr J Cotton-Griffiths
P S T (**Ref:**HM06802)

## EMERY, CHRISTINE
**Christine Emery**, 12 Broadlands Avenue, Hockley, **Essex**, SS5 5EW, ENG.
(T) 01702 202398
Speciality: Aromatherapy.
● **Owner** Mrs C Emery
M O (**Ref:**HM06803)

## EMERY, FREDA
**Freda Emery B A ,M (PSYCH ) SC**, 40B Popes Qy, **County Cork**, IRE.
(T) 021 4508 854
Speciality: Complementary Medicines & Therapy.
M (**Ref:**HM06804)

## EMINATIONS ACUPUNCTURE CLINIC
**Eminations Acupuncture Clinic**, 193 Three Bridges Rd, Three Bridges, Crawley, **Sussex (West)**, RH10 1LG, ENG.
(T) 01293 550079
Speciality: Acupressure, Acupuncture, Bach Remedies, Cupping, Massage (Therapeutic), Moxibustion, Oriental Diagnosis, Spiritual Healing. ✓
● **Senior Acupuncturist**
Mr T Burrows **Q:** Lic.Ac. **M:** BAcC.
O Yrs. Est.: 3 (**Ref:**HM06805)

## EMM, PHILIP & BERYL
**Philip & Beryl Emm**, 160 Manchester Rd, Handforth, Wilmslow, **Cheshire**, SK9 3DJ, ENG.
(T) 01625 528919
Speciality: Physiotherapy.
P S T (**Ref:**HM06806)

## EMMETT, S
**S Emmett**, Westwood, Main Rd, Ryton, **Tyne and Wear**, NE40 3AJ, ENG.
(T) 01914 132349 (F) 01914 132349
Speciality: Chiropodists (Podiatrists).
● **Owner** Mrs S Emmett
S (**Ref:**HM06807)

## EMPTAGE, MARGARET
**Margaret Emptage**, Braeside, Strachan, Banchory, **Aberdeenshire**, AB31 6NN, SCO.
(T) 01330 824708
Speciality: Hypnosis.
● **Owner** Mrs M Emptage
B (**Ref:**HM06808)

## EMS CHIROPODY
**EMS Chiropody**, 587 Southleigh Rd, Emsworth, **Hampshire**, PO10 7TE, ENG.
(T) 01243 372834
Speciality: Chiropodists (Podiatrists).
● **Owner** Mrs W Salmon
S (**Ref:**HM06809)

## ENCHANTMENT
**Enchantment**, 1a Crescent Rd, Birchington, **Kent**, CT7 9DP, ENG.
(T) 01843 848600
Speciality: Complementary Medicines & Therapy.
● **Owner** Mrs K Arnold
C M (**Ref:**HM06810)

## ENCOMPASS THERAPIES
**Encompass Therapies**, P O Box 5244, Pilgrims Hatch, Brentwood, **Essex**, CM15 9PF, ENG.
(T) 01277 202054
Speciality: Complementary Medicines & Therapy.
● **Owner** Mr D Randall
C M (**Ref:**HM06811)

## ENDER, BECKETT
**Beckett Ender**, 3 Tavistock Rd, Newcastle Upon Tyne, **Tyne and Wear**, NE2 3HY, ENG.
(T) 01912 818500
Speciality: Psychotherapy.
B (**Ref:**HM06812)

## ENDORPHIN RELEASE CLINICS
**Endorphin Release Clinics Ltd**, 24 Errigal Rd, Dublin, **County Dublin**, IRE.
(T) 01455 8266
Speciality: Complementary Medicines & Therapy.
M (**Ref:**HM06813)

## ENERGY CENTRE
**Energy Centre (The)**, 44 Bliss Way, Cambridge, **Cambridgeshire**, CB1 9YE, ENG.
(T) 01223 525106
Speciality: Complementary Medicines &

Therapy.
● **Owner** Ms N Lloyd-Butting
C M (**Ref:**HM06814)

### ENERGY EXCHANGE
**Energy Exchange**, Royal Albert Walk, Albert Rd, Southsea, **Hampshire**, PO4 0JX, **ENG**.
**(T)** 023 9236 6968
**Speciality:** Complementary Medicines & Therapy.
C M (**Ref:**HM06815)

### ENERGY EXCHANGE HOLISTIC CTRE
**Energy Exchange Holistic Centre (The)**, Unit G Royal Albert Walk, 196 Albert Rd, Southsea, **Hampshire**, PO4 0JT, **ENG**.
**(T)** 023 9236 6968
**Speciality:** Absent Healing, Aromatherapy, Aura Therapy, Colour Therapy, Healer, Holistic Healing, Hypnotherapy, Indian Head Massage, Massage (Therapeutic), Meditation, Reflexology, Reiki, Shiatsu, Tarot Counselling. Astrological training, Reiki training. ✓
● **Therapist** Yvonne Young **Q:** IIHHT. **M:** FHT.
● **Therapist** Audery De-Ste-Croix **Q:** IIHHT.
M **Yrs. Est.:** 3 (**Ref:**HM06816)

### ENFIELD CHIROPRACTIC CLINIC
**Enfield Chiropractic Clinic**, 94 Ridge Avenue, London, **London (Greater)**, N21 2AU, **ENG**.
**(T)** 020 8360 0406
**Speciality:** Chiropractors.
P S T (**Ref:**HM06817)

### ENFIELD CLINIC OF HERBAL MED
**Enfield Clinic of Herbal Medicine**, 93 St. Marks Rd, Enfield, **London (Greater)**, EN1 1BJ, **ENG**.
**(T)** 020 8482 1112 **(F)** 020 8482 1112
**(E)** hurleyherb@yahoo.co.uk
**Speciality:** Herbal Medicine, Phytotherapy. ✓
● **Medical Herbalist** Ms Hurley **Q:** BSc (Hons). **M:** NIMH.
M **Yrs. Est.:** 6 (**Ref:**HM06818)

### ENFIELD HYP & COUNSELLING
**Enfield Hypnotherapy & Counselling**, 35 Ladysmith Rd, Enfield, **London (Greater)**, EN1 3AJ, **ENG**.
**(T)** 020 8367 0712 **(F)** 020 8367 0712
**(E)** dennisshadbolt1@popntlworld.com
**Speciality:** Counselling, Hypnosis, Hypnotherapy.
● **Owner/Hypnotherapist/Counsellor** Mr D Shadbolt
B **Yrs. Est.:** 7 (**Ref:**HM06819)

### ENFIELD, CLAUDIA
**Claudia Enfield**, Prestwood Osteopathic & Natural Health Centre, 118 High St, Prestwood, Great Missenden, **Buckinghamshire**, HP16 9HD, **ENG**.
**(T)** 01494 445478 **(F)** 01494 445478
**Speciality:** Aromatherapy, Bowen Therapy, Indian Head Massage, Manual Lymph Drainage. ✓
● **Complementary Therapist** Ms C Enfield **Q:** BTER, MAR. **M:** BTER, MLD(UK), RQA.
C **Yrs. Est.:** 3 (**Ref:**HM06820)

### ENFIELD, CLAUDIA
**Claudia Enfield**, 62 Coningsby Rd, High Wycombe, **Buckinghamshire**, HP13 5NZ, **ENG**.
**(T)** 01494 445478
**Speciality:** Complementary Medicines & Therapy.
C M (**Ref:**HM06821)

### ENGBERG, ANNELI
**Anneli Engberg**, 22 Fromefield, Frome, **Somerset**, BA11 2HE, **ENG**.
**(T)** 01373 467719
**Speciality:** Acupuncture.
● **Owner** Ms A Enberg
O (**Ref:**HM06822)

### ENGELKAMP, JOANNA
**Joanna Engelkamp**, 4 Baker St, Aberystwyth, **Ceredigion**, SY23 2BJ, **WAL**.
**(T)** 01970 832638
**Speciality:** Alexander Technique.
P S (**Ref:**HM06823)

### ENGELKAMP, JOANNA
**Joanna Engelkamp**, Alderbaran, Bontgoch, Talybont, **Ceredigion**, SY24 5DP, **WAL**.
**(T)** 01970 832638
**Speciality:** Alexander Technique.
P S (**Ref:**HM06824)

### ENGELKAMP, JOANNA
**Joanna Engelkamp**, Covent House, Heol Maengwyn St, Machynlleth, **Powys**, SY20 8EB, **WAL**.
**(T)** 01970 832638
**Speciality:** Alexander Technique.
P S (**Ref:**HM06825)

### ENGEL-WARSHAW
**Engel-Warshaw**, 35 Pages Lane, London, **London (Greater)**, N10 1PU, **ENG**.
**(T)** 020 8444 6033
**Speciality:** Acupuncture.
O (**Ref:**HM06826)

### ENGLAND, ANITA
**Anita England**, 'Wayside', Strete, Dartmouth, **Devon**, TQ6 0RQ, **ENG**.
**(T)** 01803 770947
**Speciality:** Reflexology.
S T (**Ref:**HM06827)

### ENGLAND, PAMELA
**Pamela England**, 6 St. Margarets Rd, Oxford, **Oxfordshire**, OX2 6RU, **ENG**.
**(T)** 01865 510054
**Speciality:** Reflexology.
S T (**Ref:**HM06828)

### ENGLAND, SUSAN
**Susan England**, Hampton Corner, Warwick Rd, Stratford-Upon-Avon, **Warwickshire**, CV37 0NZ, **ENG**.
**(T)** 01789 414520 **(F)** 01789 414520
**Speciality:** Physiotherapy.
● **Owner** Mrs S England
P S T (**Ref:**HM06829)

### ENGLISH, AILEEN
**Aileen English**, 33 Dartmouth Rd, London, **London (Greater)**, NW2 4ET, **ENG**.
**(T)** 020 8452 2221
**Speciality:** Hypnotherapy.
● **Owner** Ms A English
B (**Ref:**HM06830)

### ENGLISH, D A
**D A English**, The Coach House, Caenshill Rd, Weybridge, **Surrey**, KT13 0SN, **ENG**.
**(T)** 01932 820208
**Speciality:** Osteopathy.
P S T (**Ref:**HM06831)

### ENGLISH, J
**J English**, Chesterfield Hospital, 3 Clifton Hill, Bristol, BS8 1BP, **ENG**.
**(T)** 01179 730391
**Speciality:** Physiotherapy.
P S T (**Ref:**HM06832)

### ENGLISH, JEREMY A
**Jeremy A English**, 798 St. Albans Rd, Bushey, Watford, **Hertfordshire**, WD2 2JP, **ENG**.
**(T)** 020 8845 7881
**Speciality:** Alexander Technique.
P S (**Ref:**HM06833)

### ENGLISH, JOHN M (DR)
**Dr John M English**, 87 Greencroft St, Salisbury, **Wiltshire**, SP1 1JF, **ENG**.
**(T)** 01722 410416
**(E)** john_english@bigfoot.com
**Speciality:** Acupuncture, Autogenic Training, Bach Remedies, Clinical Ecology, Complementary Therapy, Hay Diet, Holistic Healing, Homeopathy, Humanistic Psychology, Kinesiology, Visualisation Therapy. ✓
● **Doctor** Dr J English **Q:** Ch.B, Dip.Med.Ac, FFHom, MB. **M:** BAS, BMAS, FHom.
B C (**Ref:**HM06834)

### ENHANCED SUCCESS PERFORMANCE
**Enhanced Success Performance Ltd**, 152 Blackamoor Lane, Maidenhead, **Berkshire**, SL6 8RN, **ENG**.
**(T)** 01628 418424
**Speciality:** Psychotherapy.
B (**Ref:**HM06835)

### ENJOY SPORT
**Enjoy Sport, Sports Therapy Clinic**, 2 Ash Cl, Allestree, Derby, **Derbyshire**, DE22 2JF, **ENG**.
**(T)** 01332 556293
**Speciality:** Aromatherapy, Electrotherapy, Manipulation, Massage (Therapeutic), Osteopathy. ✓
● **Osteopath** Ms J Potts **Q:** DO. **M:** BOA, GOsC.
● **Manipulative Therapist** Mr R Tipper **Q:** BSc. **M:** BOA.
S **Yrs. Est.:** 12 (**Ref:**HM06836)

### ENLIGHTENMENT
**Enlightenment**, 20 Albion St, Broadstairs, **Kent**, CT10 1LU, **ENG**.
**(T)** 01843 601700 **(F)** 01843 863346
**Speciality:** Clairvoyants & Palmists.
● **Owner** Mrs C Rhodes
B (**Ref:**HM06837)

### ENNESS, SALLY
**Sally Enness**, Park Field, Grovehurst Lane, Horsmonden, Tonbridge, **Kent**, TN12 8BG, **ENG**.
**(T)** 01892 723402 **(F)** 01892 723402
**Speciality:** Clairvoyants & Palmists.
● **Owner** Mrs S Enness
B (**Ref:**HM06838)

### ENNEVER, M
**M Ennever**, 49 Parkland Avenue, Upminster, **Essex**, RM14 2EX, **ENG**.
**(T)** 01708 220854
**Speciality:** Electrolysis.
T (**Ref:**HM06839)

### ENNIS ACUPUNCTURE CLINIC
**Ennis Acupuncture Clinic**, 10 Francis St, Ennis, **County Clare**, **IRE**.
**(T)** 06568 43940
**Speciality:** Acupuncture.
O (**Ref:**HM06840)

### ENNIS, CHRIS
**Chris Ennis**, 255-259 London Rd, Greenhithe, **Kent**, DA9 9DA, **ENG**.
**(T)** 01322 387271
**Speciality:** Complementary Medicines & Therapy.
● **Owner** Mr C Ennis
C M (**Ref:**HM06841)

### ENNISKEANE NATURAL THRPY CTRE
**Enniskeane Natural Therapy Centre**, 13 North Main St, Bandon, **County Cork**, **IRE**.
**(T)** 08783 01053
**Speciality:** Complementary Medicines & Therapy.
M (**Ref:**HM06842)

### ENNISKEANE NATURAL THRPY CTRE
**Enniskeane Natural Therapy Centre**, Enniskeane Co, **County Cork**, **IRE**.
**(T)** 023 4796 1
**Speciality:** Complementary Medicines & Therapy.
M (**Ref:**HM06843)

### ENNISKILLEN CHIRO CLINIC
**Enniskillen Chiropractic Clinic**, 22 New St, Enniskillen, **County Fermanagh**, BT74 6AH, **NIR**.
**(T)** 028 6632 5774 **(F)** 028 6632 9158
**(E)** j-pedersen@freeuk.com
**Speciality:** Chiropractic. ✓
● **Chiropractor** Dr J Pedersen **Q:** DC. **M:** BCA.
S **Yrs. Est.:** 11 (**Ref:**HM06844)

### ENOCK-SHORE, ANGELA
**Offstress Ltd**, 9 Clarence Rd, Hersham, Walton-On-Thames, **Surrey**, KT12 5JU, **ENG**.
**(T)** 01932 883239 **(F)** 01932 880033
**(W)** www.offstress.com
**Speciality:** Hypnosis, Hypnotherapy, Kinesiology, Life Style Coaching, Stress Therapy, Visualisation Therapy. ✓
● **Stress Manager/Life Skills Coach** Ms A Enock-Shore **Q:** Dip.Hyp. **M:** ANLP, HA.
H **Yrs. Est.:** 5 (**Ref:**HM06845)

### ENRIGHT, VALERIE
**Valerie Enright**, 1a Capadocia St, Southend-On-Sea, **Essex**, SS1 3AQ, **ENG**.

(T) 01702 589311
Speciality: Reflexology.
● Owner Mrs V Enright
S T (Ref:HM06846)

**ENTERPRISE**

**Enterprise Psychological Consultancy**, Bolton Enterprise Centre, Washington St, Bolton, **Lancashire**, BL3 5EY, ENG.
(T) 01204 524262
Speciality: Psychology.
B (Ref:HM06847)

**ENTERPRISE Q**

**Enterprise Q Ltd**, 17 Rivington Court, Hardwick Grange, Woolston, Warrington, **Cheshire**, WA1 4RT, ENG.
(T) 01925 820033 (F) 01925 820044
Speciality: Complementary Medicines & Therapy.
● Manager Mrs J Miller
M (Ref:HM06848)

**ENTHEOS HOLISTIC REFLEXOLOGY**

**Entheos Holistic Reflexology**, 10 Farndon Cl, Sale, **Cheshire**, M33 2QR, ENG.
(T) 01619 624454
Speciality: Complementary Medicines & Therapy.
C M (Ref:HM06849)

**ENZYME PROCESS**

**Enzyme Process**, 4 Broadgate House, Westlode St, Spalding, **Lincolnshire**, PE11 2AF, ENG.
(T) 01775 761927 (F) 01775 761104
Speciality: Complementary Medicines & Therapy.
● Managing Director Mr R Girdlestone
C M (Ref:HM06850)

**EPHRAIM, NONA**

**Nona Ephraim**, Plas Paradwys, Paradwys, Bodorgan, **Isle of Anglesey**, LL62 5PE, WAL.
(T) 01407 40706
Speciality: Psychotherapy. ✔
● Psychotherapist Ms N Ephraim M: BACP.
C Yrs. Est.: 17 (Ref:HM06851)

**EPILATION SUITE**

**Epilation Suite**, 3 Dunlop St, Strathaven, **Lanarkshire (South)**, ML10 6LA, SCO.
(T) 01357 523633
Speciality: Electrolysis.
● Owner Mrs D Hunter
T (Ref:HM06852)

**EPONA HOMEOPATHIC**

**Epona Homeopathic**, 19 High St, Newmarket, **Suffolk**, CB8 8LX, ENG.
(T) 01638 508432
Speciality: Homeopathy.
● Principal Miss S Jundors
M (Ref:HM06853)

**EPPING OSTEOPATHY AND SPORTS**

**Epping Osteopathy and Sports Injuries Clinic**, 19 Church Hill, Epping, **Essex**, CM16 4RA, ENG.
(T) 01992 577606
Speciality: Osteopathy. ✔
● Osteopath Mr K Roberts Q: BSc. M: GOsC.
S Yrs. Est.: 13 (Ref:HM06854)

**EPPING PHYSIOTHERAPY PRACTICE**

**Epping Physiotherapy Practice (The)**, 267 High St, Epping, **Essex**, CM16 4BP, ENG.
(T) 01992 561112
Speciality: Acupuncture, Physiotherapy. ✔
● Owner/Acupuncturist Mr A Cornelius M: AACP.
O (Ref:HM06855)

**EPSOM & EWELL ACUPUNCTURE**

**Epsom & Ewell Acupuncture Clinic**, 39 West St, Ewell, Epsom, **Surrey**, KT17 1XD, ENG.
(T) 020 8393 0434
Speciality: Acupuncture.
O (Ref:HM06856)

**EPSOM CHIROPRACTIC CLINIC**

**Epsom Chiropractic Clinic**, 5 Alexandra Rd, Epsom, **Surrey**, KT17 4BH, ENG.
(T) 01372 741151
Speciality: Chiropractic. ✔ 
● Owner Dr S Norton Q: DC. M: BCA, GCC.
P Yrs. Est.: 20 (Ref:HM06857)

**EPSOM HEALTH CARE NHS TRUST**

**Epsom Health Care NHS Trust**, Horton Lane, Epsom, **Surrey**, KT19 8AT, ENG.
(T) 01372 720327 (F) 01372 720327
Speciality: Chiropodists (Podiatrists).
● Manageress Miss V Graham
S (Ref:HM06858)

**EPSTEIN, IAN**

**Ian Epstein ADHP MICHP Psy Masc**, 116 Barton Rd, East, Dundrum, **County Dublin**, IRE.
(T) 01296 0611
(W) www.hypnosiseire.com
Speciality: Hypnotherapy.
B (Ref:HM06859)

**EPSTEIN, IAN**

**Ian Epstein Counselling Hypnotherapy**, 116 Barton Rd, Dundrum, **County Dublin**, IRE.
(T) 01296 0611
(E) ianepstein@eircom.net
Speciality: Hypnotherapy.
B (Ref:HM06860)

**EPSTEIN, WENDY**

**Wendy Epstein**, Claypath Medical Practice, 26 Gilesgate, Durham, **County Durham**, DH1 1QW, ENG.
(T) 01913 832090
Speciality: Acupuncture.
● Owner Mrs A Andreadis
O (Ref:HM06861)

**EPWORTH, STEVEN**

**Steven Epworth**, 910 Woodborough Rd, Nottingham, **Nottinghamshire**, NG3 5QR, ENG.
(T) 01159 856560
Speciality: Chiropodists (Podiatrists).
S (Ref:HM06862)

**EQUA-LIBRA**

**Equa-Libra**, 2 Peninne Cl, Upperthong, Holmfirth, **Yorkshire (West)**, HD9 3EY, ENG.
(T) 01484 680095
Speciality: Aromatherapy, Complementary Therapy, Indian Head Massage, Massage (Therapeutic), Reflexology. ✔
● Therapist Ms J Longbottom Q: IIHHT.
B (Ref:HM06863)

**EQUANIMITY**

**Equanimity**, 10-11 Milroy Walk, London, **London (Greater)**, SE1 9LW, ENG.
(T) 020 7384 3150
Speciality: Complementary Medicines & Therapy.
C M (Ref:HM06864)

**EQUANIMITY NATURAL THERAPY**

**Equanimity Natural Therapy Practice**, 31 Inman Rd, London, **London (Greater)**, SW18 3BB, ENG.
(T) 020 8870 1268
Speciality: Complementary Medicines & Therapy.
C M (Ref:HM06865)

**EQUILIBRIUM**

**Equilibrium**, Dark Lane North, Steeple Ashton, Trowbridge, **Wiltshire**, BA14 6EY, ENG.
(T) 01380 870041
Speciality: Aromatherapy.
● Owner Mr G Leake
M O (Ref:HM06866)

**EQUILIBRIUM**

**Equilibrium**, The Happy House Surgery, Durham Rd, Sunderland, **Tyne and Wear**, SR3 2PY, ENG.
(T) 01915 214550 (F) 01915 214550
Speciality: Nutritional Therapy. ✔
● Clinical Nutritionist Ms S Crossley Q: Dip.ION. M: BANT.
M Yrs. Est.: 5 (Ref:HM06867)

**EQUILIBRIUM**

**Equilibrium**, 65a Piccadilly, Stoke-On-Trent, **Staffordshire**, ST1 1HR, ENG.
(T) 01782 855763 (F) 01782 855763
Speciality: Complementary Medicines & Therapy.
● Owner Mr P Cooke
M (Ref:HM06868)

**EQUILIBRIUM**

**Equilibrium - Complementary Therapies and Alternative Medicine**, 40 Station Rd, Penge, London, **London (Greater)**, SE20 7BJ, ENG.
(T) 020 8778 0888
(W) www.equilibrium.co.uk
Speciality: Aromatherapy, Ayurvedic Medicine, Complementary Therapy, Counselling, Cranio-Sacral Therapy, Holistic Healing, Homeopathy, Hypnotherapy, Indian Head Massage, Massage (Therapeutic), McTimoney Chiropractic, Naturopathy, Reflexology, Reiki, Shiatsu. ✔
● Massage Therapist Marney Lawson
(T) 01322 860878 Q: ITEC.
B C Yrs. Est.: 3 (Ref:HM06869)

**EQUILIBRIUM**

**Equilibrium**, 150 Chiswick High Rd, London, **London (Greater)**, W4 1PR, ENG.
(T) 020 8742 7701 (F) 020 8742 7710
Speciality: Complementary Medicines & Therapy.
● Principal Mr M Rutherford
M (Ref:HM06870)

**EQUILIBRIUM CENTRE**

**Equilibrium Centre For Stress Transformation**, Little Abshot Rd, Fareham, **Hampshire**, PO14 4LN, ENG.
(T) 01489 572451 (F) 01489 572451
Speciality: Complementary Medicines & Therapy.
C M (Ref:HM06871)

**EQUILIBRIUM CLINIC**

**Equilibrium Clinic (The)**, Staddon Lea, Nut Bush Lane, Torquay, **Devon**, TQ2 6SG, ENG.
(T) 01803 690433
Speciality: Complementary Medicines & Therapy.
● Owner Miss T Charalambos
C M (Ref:HM06872)

**EQUILIBRIUM COUNS/THRPY CTRE**

**Equilibrium Counselling & Therapy Centre**, 88 Pulborough Rd, London, **London (Greater)**, SW18 5UJ, ENG.
(T) 020 8870 8761
Speciality: Acupuncture, Counselling, Cranial Osteopathy, Gestalt Therapy, Homeopathy, Humanistic Psychology, Hypnosis, Hypnotherapy, Massage (Therapeutic), Naturopathy, Osteopathy, Psychotherapy. ✔
● Manager Ms V Mathews Q: Dip.Couns, Dip.Supervision. M: BACP.
B S Yrs. Est.: 16 (Ref:HM06873)

**EQUILIBRIUM FLOATATION CENTRE**

**Equilibrium Floatation Natural Therapy Centre**, 22 Lark Lane, Liverpool, **Merseyside**, L17 8US, ENG.
(T) 01517 277295
Speciality: Complementary Medicines & Therapy.
● Owner Mr J Durrant
C M (Ref:HM06874)

**EQUILIBRIUM HOLISTIC CLINIC**

**Equilibrium Holistic Therapy Clinic**, 18 Craft Village, Shipquay St, Londonderry, **County Londonderry**, BT48 6AR, NIR.
(T) 028 7137 2798
Speciality: Aromatherapy, Bach Remedies, Massage (Therapeutic), Meditation, Reflexology, Reiki, T'ai-Chi Ch'uan, Yoga, Bioforce, Herbal Remedies. ✔ 
● Therapist Ms M Walker Q: Dip.Arom, Dip.Reiki.
● Therapist Ms B Hackett Q: ITEC. M: ITEC.
B C Yrs. Est.: 3 (Ref:HM06875)

**EQUILIBRIUM OSTEOPATHIC**

**Equilibrium Osteopathic And Naturopathic Clinic**, 8 Tanners Dean, Leatherhead, **Surrey**, KT22 8RU, ENG.
(T) 01372 374530 (F) 01372 374530
(E) matt-w-osteo@usa.net
(W) www.wallden.co.uk
Speciality: Complementary Therapy, Cranial Osteopathy, Holistic Healing, Life Style Coaching,



Key continued: Yrs.Est: Years Established Q: Qualifications M: Professional Membership ✔ Indemnity Insurance Accept Credit Cards

Manipulation, Massage (Therapeutic), Naturopathy, Nutritional Therapy, Osteopathy, Postural Integration, Vitamin Therapy, High Performance Exercise Kinesiologist, Rehabilitation Specialist. ✓
● **Therapist** Mr M Wallden Q: MSc. M: GOsC.
S Yrs. Est.: 3 (**Ref:**HM06876)

### EQUILIBRUIM HOLISTIC HEALTH
**Equilibruim Holistic Health & Therapy Centre**, 15 Boston Rd, Kirton, Boston, **Lincolnshire**, PE20 1DT, ENG.
(T) 01205 723101
Speciality: Aromatherapy.
● **Owner** Ms J McGuire
M O (**Ref:**HM06877)

### EQUINOX ORGANICS
**Equinox Organics Ltd**, 29 Low Farm Pl, Moulton Park Industrial Estate, Northampton, **Northamptonshire**, NN3 6HY, ENG.
(T) 01604 671718
Speciality: Aromatherapy.
● **Sole Director**
Christopher Michael Buckmaster
M O (**Ref:**HM06878)

### ERABADDA, ERIC
**Eric Erabadda**, 54 Purbrock Avenue, Watford, **Hertfordshire**, WD2 6AD, ENG.
(T) 01923 662573
Speciality: Physiotherapy.
P S T (**Ref:**HM06879)

### ERDINGTHON NATURAL HEALTH CLNC
**Mr Stephen W-Ling**, 9 Coton Lane, Birmingham, **Midlands (West)**, B23 6TP, ENG.
(T) 01213 502018
Speciality: Acupuncture, Aromatherapy, Homeopathy, Indian Head Massage, Osteopathy, Reflexology, Reiki. ✓
● **Associate** Mrs B Stotczynka Q: DO.
● **Owner** Mr S W-Ling Q: DO.
● **Associate** Dr A Zhou
(T) 01213 5020118 M: BACP.
● **Associate** Miss A Clamp Q: IIHHT. M: FHT.
● **Associate** Mr A Flower Q: RSHom.
C Yrs. Est.: 29 (**Ref:**HM06880)

### ERDOS CHINESE MEDICAL CENTRE
**Erdos Chinese Medical Centre**, 7 Ickenham Rd, Ruislip, **London (Greater)**, HA4 7BT, ENG.
(T) 01895 622288
Speciality: Complementary Medicines & Therapy.
● **Owner** Dr Y Yang
C M (**Ref:**HM06881)

### EREVNA
**Erevna**, 26 The Hill, Church Hill, Caterham, **Surrey**, CR3 6SD, ENG.
(T) 08000 749645
Speciality: Aromatherapy, Bach Remedies, Herbal Medicine, Natural Skin Care.
C (**Ref:**HM06882)

### ERICA, GUSTAVSSON
**Erica Gustavsson**, 33 Strathmore Rd, Teddington, **London (Greater)**, TW11 8UJ, ENG.
(T) 020 8977 2503
Speciality: Homeopathy.
M (**Ref:**HM06883)

### ERLICK, STEVEN
**Steven Erlick**, 106 Spinney Lane, Aspley Guise, Milton Keynes, **Buckinghamshire**, MK17 8JL, ENG.
(T) 01908 281412 (F) 01908 585771
Speciality: Homeopathy.
M (**Ref:**HM06884)

### ERSKINE, SUE
**Sue Erskine**, Hayling Gr, Redcar, **Cleveland**, TS10 2NW, ENG.
(T) 01642 470152
Speciality: Complementary Medicines & Therapy.
● **Employee** Mrs S Erskine
M (**Ref:**HM06885)

### ESCOBAR-FRANCO, A
**A Escobar-Franco**, 19 Lynn Rd, Ely, **Cambridgeshire**, CB6 1AA, ENG.
(T) 01353 662618
Speciality: Chiropodists (Podiatrists).
● **Owner** Mr A Escobar-Franco
S (**Ref:**HM06886)

### ESCREET, PENNY
**Penny Escreet**, 7 Hall Orchards Avenue, Wetherby, **Yorkshire (West)**, LS22 6SN, ENG.
(T) 01937 587317
Speciality: Physiotherapy.
P S T (**Ref:**HM06887)

### ESSENCE OF BEAUTY
**Essence of Beauty**, U6 Riverview, Ballinasloe, **County Galway**, IRE.
(T) 09054 5070
Speciality: Beauty Therapy.
H T (**Ref:**HM06888)

### ESSENCE OF ELOAH
**Essence of Eloah**, Po Box 8354, Birmingham, **Midlands (West)**, B20 2ST, ENG.
(T) 01216 817260
Speciality: Complementary Medicines & Therapy.
M (**Ref:**HM06889)

### ESSENCE OF HEALTH
**Essence Of Health**, 6 Garden St, Ayr, **Ayrshire (South)**, KA8 0BB, SCO.
(T) 01292 268472 (F) 01292 268472
Speciality: Alexander Technique, Aromatherapy, Bach Remedies, Beauty Therapy, Chiropody, Herbal Medicine, Holistic Healing, Homeopathy, Massage (Therapeutic), Reflexology, Reiki, Seichem, Shiatsu, Spiritual Healing. ✓
● **Owner** Mr I Louden
C Yrs. Est.: 1 (**Ref:**HM06890)

### ESSENCE OF HEALTH THERAPIES
**Essence Of Health Natural Therapies Clinic**, 75 Park Drive, Sprotbrough, Doncaster, **Yorkshire (South)**, DN5 7LP, ENG.
(T) 01302 859249
Speciality: Complementary Medicines & Therapy.
C M (**Ref:**HM06891)

### ESSENCE OF LIFE
**Essence Of Life**, Kenyon Court, 2 Suite 5, Wellington St, Widnes, **Cheshire**, WA8 0QH, ENG.
(T) 01514 205588
Speciality: Complementary Medicines & Therapy.
● **Owner** Ms M Herron
M (**Ref:**HM06892)

### ESSENCE OF NATURE
**Essence Of Nature**, 366 London Rd, Westcliff-on-Sea, **Essex**, SS0 7HZ, ENG.
(T) 01702 432444 (F) 01702 437431
Speciality: Aromatherapy.
● **Director** Mrs G Sullivan
M O (**Ref:**HM06893)

### ESSENCES OF AROMA/NTRL THRPY
**Essences Of Aromatherapy & Natural Therapies**, 49 Barfield, Sutton At Hone, Dartford, **Kent**, DA4 9EJ, ENG.
(T) 01322 863791
Speciality: Aromatherapy.
● **Owner** Mrs L Sparkes
M O (**Ref:**HM06894)

### ESSENTIA
**Essentia**, 101 Granby St, Leicester, **Leicestershire**, LE1 6FD, ENG.
(T) 01162 992018
Speciality: Aromatherapy.
● **Owner** Miss N Wright
M O (**Ref:**HM06895)

### ESSENTIAL AROMATICS
**Essential Aromatics**, 3 College Court, Gloucester, **Gloucestershire**, GL1 2NJ, ENG.
(T) 01452 332219
Speciality: Aromatherapy.
M O (**Ref:**HM06896)

### ESSENTIAL BEAUTY
**Essential Beauty (Mobile)**, 26 Burra Gardens, Bishopbriggs, Glasgow, **Glasgow (City of)**, G64 1UP, SCO.
(T) 01415 631902
Speciality: Aromatherapy, Massage (Therapeutic), Reflexology.
S T (**Ref:**HM06897)

### ESSENTIAL BEING AROMATHERAPY
**Essential Being Aromatherapy Centre**, 5 Ivegate, Yeadon, Leeds, **Yorkshire (West)**, LS19 7RE, ENG.
(T) 01132 504711
Speciality: Complementary Medicines & Therapy.
● **Partner** Mrs S Stott
M (**Ref:**HM06898)

### ESSENTIAL BODYWORKS COMPANY
**Mark Darryl Williams**, 3 Gladstone Buildings, Bridge Rd, Ebley, Stroud, **Gloucestershire**, GL5 4TR, ENG.
(T) 01453 751377
Speciality: Complementary Therapy, Indian Head Massage, Massage (Therapeutic), Sports Massage, Touch Therapy, Injuries, ISHTA Spinal Touch, Hopi Ear Candles. ✓
● **Therapist** Mr M Williams Q: ITEC. M: GCP.
P Yrs. Est.: 1 (**Ref:**HM06899)

### ESSENTIAL CARE TRAINING
**Essential Care Training**, 8 George St, Croydon, **Surrey**, CR0 1PA, ENG.
(T) 020 8680 7761
Speciality: Complementary Medicines & Therapy.
● **Owner** Mrs J West
C M (**Ref:**HM06900)

### ESSENTIAL ELEMENTS
**Essential Elements**, 134 Bath Rd, Thatcham, **Berkshire**, RG18 3HH, ENG.
(T) 01635 873323
Speciality: Complementary Medicines & Therapy.
● **Owner** Mr S Pace
C M (**Ref:**HM06901)

### ESSENTIAL ENERGIES
**Essential Energies**, 3 Abbeyfields Cl, **London**, NW10 7EF, ENG.
(T) 020 8961 7509 (F) 020 8961 7509
Speciality: Complementary Medicines & Therapy.
● **Director** Ms N Zaman
M (**Ref:**HM06902)

### ESSENTIAL ENERGIES
**Essential Energies**, 1 Leicester Mews, East Finchley, London, **London (Greater)**, N2 9EJ, ENG.
(T) 020 8961 7509
Speciality: Complementary Medicines & Therapy.
C M (**Ref:**HM06903)

### ESSENTIAL ESSENCE
**Essential Essence**, 4 Seaville Drive, Eastbourne, **Sussex (East)**, BN23 6LH, ENG.
(T) 01323 749494
Speciality: Complementary Medicines & Therapy.
● **Owner** Miss S Scarlett
M (**Ref:**HM06904)

### ESSENTIAL GAEL
**Essential Gael (The)**, Bus Station, Margaret St, Inverness, **Highland**, IV1 1LT, SCO.
(T) 01463 237812
Speciality: Aromatherapy.
● **Owner** Mr W Frazer
M O (**Ref:**HM06905)

### ESSENTIAL HARMONY
**Essential Harmony Ltd**, The Barn, Bullock Fayre, Harleston, **Norfolk**, IP20 9AX, ENG.
(T) 01379 855444
Speciality: Complementary Medicines & Therapy.
● **Partner** Mr S Walpole
M (**Ref:**HM06906)

### ESSENTIAL HARMONY
**L Hurley**, 142 Cross Hill, Ecclesfield, Sheffield, **Yorkshire (South)**, S35 9WU, ENG.
(T) 01142 578007
(E) lesley@essentialharmony.co.uk
(W) www.essentialharmony.fsnet.co.uk

Key: B Mind-Body Medicine · C Complementary Medicine · H Self Help Treatment · M Medicinal Therapy · O Oriental Medicine · P Postural Therapy · S Manipulative Structural Therapy · T Touch Therapy

Speciality: Absent Healing, Aromatherapy, Indian Head Massage, Reiki, Swedish Body Massage. ✔
● **Aromatherapist** Ms L Hurley Q: Dip.Indian Head Massage, NVQ L3, Reiki 2. M: FHT.
T Yrs. Est.: 1 (Ref:HM06907)

## ESSENTIAL HARMONY CLINIC

**Essential Harmony Natural Health Clinic**, 96 High St, Billingshurst, **Sussex (West)**, RH14 9QS, ENG.
(T) 01403 786661
Speciality: Complementary Medicines & Therapy.
C M (Ref:HM06908)

## ESSENTIAL HEALTH

**Essential Health**, 4 The Crescent, Solihull, **Midlands (West)**, B91 1JP, ENG.
(T) 01217 056036 (F) 01217 111267
Speciality: Aromatherapy, Auricular Therapy, Reflexology, Reiki, Stress Therapy. ✔
● **Aromatherapist** Mrs J Smillie Q: Dip.Arom, Dip.Reflex. M: ISPA.
B H Yrs. Est.: 2 (Ref:HM06909)

## ESSENTIAL HEALTH

**Essential Health**, 355 Wakefield Rd, Denby Dale, Huddersfield, **Yorkshire (West)**, HD8 8RP, ENG.
(T) 01484 866546
Speciality: Complementary Medicines & Therapy.
● **Owner** Mrs S Fillingham
C M (Ref:HM06910)

## ESSENTIAL HEALTH

**Essential Health**, 17 Osprey Cl, Whittington, Lichfield, **Staffordshire**, WS14 9HT, ENG.
(T) 01543 433520
(E) sally.shoesmith@virgin.net
Speciality: Aromatherapy, Auricular Therapy, Reflexology, Reiki, Nutrition Advisor, Thermo-(Hopi Ear Candles). ✔
● **Owner/Therapist** Ms S Shoesmith Q: MIFA. M: AoR, IFA.
C Yrs. Est.: 3 (Ref:HM06911)

## ESSENTIAL HEALTH MANAGEMENT

**Essential Health Management**, Lower Rd, Orpington, **Kent**, BR5 4AL, ENG.
(T) 020 8264 1003
Speciality: Complementary Medicines & Therapy.
C M (Ref:HM06912)

## ESSENTIAL OIL WORKS

**Essential Oil Works (The)**, 77 Wilmslow Rd, Handforth, Wilmslow, **Cheshire**, SK9 3EN, ENG.
(T) 01625 536651
Speciality: Aromatherapy.
● **Owner** Miss C Hackney
M O (Ref:HM06913)

## ESSENTIAL OILS DIRECT

**Essential Oils Direct**, P O Box 161, Royton, Oldham, **Lancashire**, OL2 6FA, ENG.
(T) 01616 333952 (F) 01616 529693
Speciality: Aromatherapy.
● **Owner** Mr D Freer
M O (Ref:HM06914)

## ESSENTIAL SELECTION

**Essential Selection (The)**, 17 Free Lane, Leicester, **Leicestershire**, LE1 1JX, ENG.
(T) 01162 536162 (F) 01162 626666
Speciality: Aromatherapy.
● **Owner** Mr J Vandyke
M O (Ref:HM06915)

## ESSENTIAL THERAPEUTIC

**Essential Therapeutic**, 25 Buckley Rd, London, **London (Greater)**, NW6 7LY, ENG.
(T) 020 7624 1022 (F) 020 7624 1022
Speciality: Aromatherapy.
● **Managing Director**
Mrs M Roques-O'neill
M O (Ref:HM06916)

## ESSENTIAL THERAPEUTIC MASSAGE

**Essential Therapeutic & Relaxation Massage**, 1 Cambridge Trce, Otley, **Yorkshire (West)**, LS21 1JS, ENG.
(T) 01943 461971 (F) 01943 461971
Speciality: Complementary Medicines & Therapy.
● **Owner** Mrs E Stewart
C M (Ref:HM06917)

## ESSENTIAL THERAPY

**Essential Therapy**, 15 Long Ridge Lane, Nether Poppleton, York, **Yorkshire (North)**, YO26 6LX, ENG.
(T) 01904 794129
Speciality: Aromatherapy.
M O (Ref:HM06918)

## ESSENTIAL TOUCH

**Essential Touch**, 6 Gable Trce, Wheatley Hill, Durham, **County Durham**, DH6 3JT, ENG.
(T) 01429 820606
Speciality: Aromatherapy.
M O (Ref:HM06919)

## ESSENTIAL TRANCE

**Essential Trance Co**, 28A Brondesbury Villas, London, **London (Greater)**, NW6 6AA, ENG.
(T) 020 8357 2523
Speciality: Hypnotherapy.
● **Owner** Mr J Livingstone
B (Ref:HM06920)

## ESSENTIALLY GREEN

**Essentially Green**, Roseville, First Avenue, Hook End, Brentwood, **Essex**, CM15 0HL, ENG.
(T) 01277 824525
Speciality: Aromatherapy.
● **Owner** Mrs K Green
M O (Ref:HM06921)

## ESSENTIALLY NATURAL

**Essentially Natural**, 1-5 Cank St, **Leicestershire**, LE1 5GX, ENG.
(T) 01162 510101
Speciality: Complementary Medicines & Therapy.
C M (Ref:HM06922)

## ESSENTIALLY OILS

**Essentially Oils Ltd**, 8-10 Mount Farm, Junction Rd, Churchill, Chipping Norton, **Oxfordshire**, OX7 6NP, ENG.
(T) 01608 659544 (F) 01608 659566
Speciality: Aromatherapy.
● **Accountant** Mr J Clemence
M O (Ref:HM06923)

## ESSENTIALLY YOU

**Essentially You**, Mizpah, Cornmill Lane, Tutbury, Burton-On-Trent, **Staffordshire**, DE13 9HA, ENG.
(T) 01283 814696
Speciality: Aromatherapy.
● **Owner** Miss E Cockayne
M O (Ref:HM06924)

## ESSENTIALLY YOURS

**Essentially Yours**, 10 Nether Hall Rd, Doncaster, **Yorkshire (South)**, DN1 2PW, ENG.
(T) 01302 349925
Speciality: Aromatherapy.
● **Owner** Miss M King
M O (Ref:HM06925)

## ESSENTIALLY YOURS

**Essentially Yours**, Brinkworth House, Brinkworth, Chippenham, **Wiltshire**, SN15 5DF, ENG.
(T) 01666 510229 (F) 01666 510886
Speciality: Aromatherapy.
● **Owner** Mrs K Osbourne
M O (Ref:HM06926)

## ESSENTIALLY YOURS

**Essentially Yours**, New Lane, Penwortham, Preston, **Lancashire**, PR1 9JE, ENG.
(T) 01772 464060
Speciality: Complementary Medicines & Therapy.
● **Owner** Mr G Maddox
C M (Ref:HM06927)

## ESSENTIALS

**Essentials**, 12 Bridge Rd, East Molesey, **Surrey**, KT8 9HA, ENG.
(T) 020 8783 0371
Speciality: Aromatherapy.
● **Owner** Mrs R White
M O (Ref:HM06928)

## ESSENTIALS

**Essentials**, Harrogate Rd, Huby, Leeds, **Yorkshire (West)**, LS17 0EF, ENG.
(T) 01423 734293
Speciality: Complementary Medicines & Therapy.
C M (Ref:HM06929)

## ESSENTIALS

**Essentials**, 117 Burges Rd, London, **London (Greater)**, E6 2BL, ENG.
(T) 020 8597 4100
Speciality: Complementary Medicines & Therapy.
● **Owner** Mr S Ahluwalia
C M (Ref:HM06930)

## ESSER, ROB J

**Rob J Esser**, 47 Castle St, Canterbury, **Kent**, CT1 2PY, ENG.
(T) 01227 454404
Speciality: Acupuncture.
O (Ref:HM06931)

## ESSERY, PATRICIA

**Patricia Essery**, Northampton, **Northamptonshire**, NN2, ENG.
(T) 01604 718118
Speciality: Bach Remedies.
M (Ref:HM06932)

## ESSERY, TRICIA

**Tricia Essery**, 18 Harborough Rd, Northampton, **Northamptonshire**, NN2 7AZ, ENG.
(T) 01604 718118
Speciality: Bach Remedies, Crystal Healing, Holistic Healing. ✔
● **Holistic Therapist** Ms T Essery Q: MFHT. M: FHT.
C Yrs. Est.: 7 (Ref:HM06933)

## ESSEX COUNS/PSYCHOTHERAPY SV

**Essex Counselling & Psychotherapy Service**, 6 Brentwood Pl, Brentwood, **Essex**, CM15 9DN, ENG.
(T) 01277 212070
Speciality: Psychotherapy.
B (Ref:HM06934)

## ESSEX FENG SHUI

**Essex Feng Shui Co**, St. Andrews, Station Rd, Cold Norton, Chelmsford, **Essex**, CM3 6HX, ENG.
(T) 01621 829720
Speciality: Feng Shui.
● **Owner** Ms A Arthur
M (Ref:HM06935)

## ESSEX NATURAL HEALTH CENTRE

**Essex Natural Health Centre**, 7 King Edwards Rd, South Woodham Ferrers, Chelmsford, **Essex**, CM3 5PQ, ENG.
(T) 01245 325037 (F) 01245 324533
Speciality: Complementary Medicines & Therapy.
● **Senior Partner**
Mrs A Purillard-Medam
M (Ref:HM06936)

## ESSEX OSTEOPATHIC CLINICS

**Essex Osteopathic Clinics**, 70 Guernsey Gardens, Wickford, **Essex**, SS11 7BB, ENG.
(T) 07711 521233
Speciality: Osteopathy.
P S T (Ref:HM06937)

## ESSEX PHYSIO & SPORTS INJ CTRE

**Essex Physiotherapy & Sports Injury Centre (The)**, 7 King Edwards Rd, South Woodham Ferrers, Chelmsford, **Essex**, CM3 5PQ, ENG.
(T) 01245 325037 (F) 01245 324533
(E) angela@essexphysio.fsnet.co.uk
Speciality: Acupuncture, Aromatherapy, Indian Head Massage, Physiotherapy, Reiki. ✔
● **Owner/Physiotherapist**
Mrs A Purillard-Medam Q: Dip.Phys, Grad.Dip.Man.Phys, MCSP, SRP.
S (Ref:HM06938)

## ESSINGTON CHIROPRACTIC CLINIC

**Essington Chiropractic Clinic**, 132 Birmingham Rd, Lichfield, **Staffordshire**, WS14 9BW, ENG.
(T) 01543 256844


Key continued: Yrs.Est: Years Established Q: Qualifications M: Professional Membership ✔ Indemnity Insurance Accept Credit Cards

Speciality: Chiropractors.
● **Manager** Mrs M Leason
P S T (Ref:HM06939)

## ESTEEM COUNSELLING & THERAPY
**Esteem Councelling & Therapy**, Monkstown, **County Cork**, IRE.
(T) 01280 6772
Speciality: Counselling.
B H (Ref:HM06940)

## ETHERINGTON, B
**B Etherington**, 16 North Prde, Bradford, **Yorkshire (West)**, BD1 3HT, ENG.
(T) 01274 721280
Speciality: Electrolysis.
T (Ref:HM06941)

## EURASIA DEVELOPMENT
**Eurasia Development Ltd**, 61 Alfred St, Weston-Super-Mare, **Somerset**, BS23 1PP, ENG.
(T) 01934 420202 (F) 01934 420202
Speciality: Complementary Medicines & Therapy.
● **Doctor** Dr X Thun
M (Ref:HM06942)

## EURO THERAPY PRACTICE
**Euro Therapy Practice (The)**, 78 Low Rd, Worlaby, Brigg, **Humberside**, DN20 0ND, ENG.
(T) 01652 618077 (F) 01652 618077
Speciality: Hypnosis.
● **Partner** Mr P Scott
B (Ref:HM06943)

## EUROPEAN AYUR-VEDA
**European Ayur-Veda Ltd**, 11 Daryngton Avenue, Birchington, **Kent**, CT7 9PS, ENG.
(T) 01843 841010
(W) www.europeanayurveda.com
Speciality: Aromatherapy, Ayurvedic Medicine, Indian Head Massage, Life Style Coaching, Meditation, Stress Therapy, Yoga. ✔
● **Director/Chairman** Mr C Beckley
● **Ayur-Veda Therapist**
Danny Cavanagh
● **Ayur-Veda Therapist** Ms C Willis
B Yrs. Est.: 5 (Ref:HM06944)

## EUROPEAN COLLEGE
**European College Of Traditional Chinese Medicine**, 6 Aungiers St, Dublin, **County Dublin**, IRE.
(T) 01475 2551
Speciality: Complementary Medicines & Therapy.
M (Ref:HM06945)

## EUROPEAN COLLEGE-BOWEN STUDIES
**European College Of Bowen Studies**, 38 Portway, Frome, **Somerset**, BA11 1QU, ENG.
(T) 01373 461873 (F) 01373 461873
(E) julian@thebowentechnique.com
(W) www.healthk.co.uk
Speciality: Bowen Therapy, Complementary Therapy. ✔
● **Director/Principal Instructor**
Mr J Baker Q: BTER. M: ALTT, BCMA, BTER.
T Yrs. Est.: 6 (Ref:HM06946)

## EUROPEAN JOURNAL
**European Journal Of Oriental Medicine**, 63 Jeddo Rd, London, **London (Greater)**, W12 9HQ, ENG.
(T) 020 8749 1300 (F) 020 8749 1301
Speciality: Complementary Medicines & Therapy.
● **Manager** Mrs C Daglish
C M (Ref:HM06947)

## EUROPEAN SCHOOL OF OSTEOPATHY
**European School Of Osteopathy**, Styles Lane, Boxley, Maidstone, **Kent**, ME14 3DZ, ENG.
(T) 01622 671558
Speciality: Osteopathy.
● **Principal** Mr R Molimari
P S T (Ref:HM06948)

## EUROPEAN SCHOOL OF OSTEOPATHY
**European School Of Osteopathy Clinic**, 104 Tonbridge Rd, Maidstone, **Kent**, ME16 8SL, ENG.
(T) 01622 685989
Speciality: Osteopathy.
P S T (Ref:HM06949)

## EUROPEAN SHIATSU SCHOOL
**European Shiatsu School**, High Bank, Lockeridge, Marlborough, **Wiltshire**, SN8 4EQ, ENG.
(T) 01672 861362
Speciality: Complementary Medicines & Therapy.
● **Director** Mr C Jarmy
M (Ref:HM06950)

## EUSTACE-GREAVES, M
**M Eustace-Greaves**, 17 Abbeydale Rd, Birmingham, **Midlands (West)**, B31 3TL, ENG.
(T) 01216 045082
Speciality: Electrolysis.
● **Owner** Ms M Eustace-Greaves
T (Ref:HM06951)

## EVA
**Eva**, 28 Newton Drive, Birstall, Leicester, **Leicestershire**, LE4 4GW, ENG.
(T) 01162 207134
Speciality: Clairvoyants & Palmists.
● **Owner** Mrs M Stubbs
B (Ref:HM06952)

## EVANS
**Mrs Sara J Evans**, 102 Beaufort Rd, Church Crookham, Fleet, **Hampshire**, GU13 0AY, ENG.
(T) 01252 815341
Speciality: Chiropody, Cryo Surgery. ✔
● **Chiropodist (Podiatrist)**
Mrs S Evans Q: MSSCh. M: B.A.Ch.P.
M Yrs. Est.: 9 (Ref:HM06953)

## EVANS, A
**Mrs A Evans**, 22 Harborough Avenue, Sidcup, **Kent**, DA15 8HP, ENG.
(T) 020 8302 2261
Speciality: Chiropodists (Podiatrists).
S (Ref:HM06954)

## EVANS, A R
**A R Evans**, 70 Devonshire Rd, Bristol, BS6 7NL, ENG.
(T) 01179 241727
Speciality: Acupuncture.
● **Owner** A R Evans
O (Ref:HM06955)

## EVANS, ANDY
**Andy Evans**, 51 Elmhurst Avenue, Northampton, **Northamptonshire**, NN3 2LD, ENG.
(T) 01604 404760
Speciality: Chiropodists (Podiatrists).
● **Owner** Mr A Evans
S (Ref:HM06956)

## EVANS, ANNE
**Anne Evans**, Natural Path Health Centre, 3 Holyrood St, Chard, **Somerset**, TA20 2AH, ENG.
(T) 01460 62953 (F) 01460 63809
Speciality: Chiropodists (Podiatrists).
● **Owner** Mr M Newbound
S (Ref:HM06957)

## EVANS, BRUCE (DR)
**Dr Bruce Evans**, 50 Church St, Shildon, **County Durham**, DL4 1DY, ENG.
(T) 01388 777113
Speciality: Manipulation, Micro Manipulation, Osteopathy. ✔
● **Musculo Skeletal Physician**
Dr B Evans Q: Ch.B, MB, MLCOM. M: GMC.
S Yrs. Est.: 16 (Ref:HM06958)

## EVANS, C
**C Evans**, 178 East Barnet Rd, Barnet, **Hertfordshire**, EN4 8RD, ENG.
(T) 020 8449 7754 (F) 020 8449 0174
Speciality: Osteopathy.
● **Principal** Mr L Hartman
P S T (Ref:HM06959)

## EVANS, C
**C Evans**, 272 Gordon Avenue, Camberley, **Surrey**, GU15 2NU, ENG.
(T) 01276 20411 (F) 01276 20411
Speciality: Osteopathy.
● **Owner** Mr S Green
P S T (Ref:HM06960)

## EVANS, CAROL
**Carol Evans**, Physiotherapy & Sports Injury Clinic, 14 Old Hall Rd, Gatley, Cheadle, **Cheshire**, SK8 4BE, ENG.
(T) 01614 284222
Speciality: Physiotherapy.
P S T (Ref:HM06961)

## EVANS, CHRISTINE
**Christine Evans**, 14 Merryfield Rd, Petersfield, **Hampshire**, GU31 4BS, ENG.
(T) 01730 264689
Speciality: Chiropodists (Podiatrists).
S (Ref:HM06962)

## EVANS, CHRISTINE
**Christine Evans**, 32 Cowbridge Rd, Pontyclun, **Rhondda Cynon Taff**, CF72 9EE, WAL.
(T) 01443 225471
Speciality: Physiotherapy.
● **Owner** Mrs C Evans
P S T (Ref:HM06963)

## EVANS, CHRISTINE
**Mrs Christine Evans**, 6 Fabyc House, Cumberland Rd, Richmond, **Surrey**, TW9 3HH, ENG.
(T) 020 8940 1597
Speciality: Alexander Technique.
P S (Ref:HM06964)

## EVANS, D A
**D A Evans**, 16 Berkeley Rd, Bournemouth, **Dorset**, BH3 7JL, ENG.
(T) 01202 514343
Speciality: Chiropodists (Podiatrists).
● **Owner** Mr D Evans
S (Ref:HM06965)

## EVANS, D G
**D G Evans**, North Rd, Ambleside, **Cumbria**, LA22 9DT, ENG.
(T) 01539 431766
Speciality: Homeopathy.
● **Partner** Mr D Evans
M (Ref:HM06966)

## EVANS, DAVID
**David Evans Hypnotherapy**, 33-37 Grosvenor St, Office 8 Denham House, Stalybridge, **Manchester (Greater)**, SK15 2JP, ENG.
(T) 01613 038282
Speciality: Auto Suggestion, Counselling, Healer, Healing Therapy, Hypnosis, Hypnotherapy, Psychotherapy, Reiki, Stress Therapy, Visualisation Therapy, Hypno Healing. ✔
● **Hypnotherapist** Mr D Evans Q: Dip.Hyp, Dip.Psych, MABCH. M: CAH.
B Yrs. Est.: 10 (Ref:HM06967)

## EVANS, DI
**Di Evans**, 12 Brooke Avenue, Chester, **Cheshire**, CH2 1HQ, ENG.
(T) 01244 378601
Speciality: Bowen Therapy, Reflexology, Reiki. ✔
● **Reflexologist** Mrs D Evans Q: BTER, MRxS.
T Yrs. Est.: 4 (Ref:HM06968)

## EVANS, ELIZABETH
**Elizabeth Evans**, 72 Tangley Park Rd, Hampton, **London (Greater)**, TW12 3LX, ENG.
(T) 020 8979 9120
Speciality: Reflexology.
S T (Ref:HM06969)

## EVANS, F S
**F S Evans**, 3 George St, Swansea, SA1 4HH, WAL.
(T) 01792 643613
Speciality: Chiropodists (Podiatrists).
S (Ref:HM06970)

## EVANS, G
**G Evans**, 23 St. Mary St, Winchester, **Hampshire**, SO22 4AQ, ENG.
(T) 01962 866680 (F) 01962 870833
Speciality: Physiotherapy.
● **Owner** Mr G Evans
P S T (Ref:HM06971)

## EVANS, GARFIELD
**Garfield Evans**, 2 Dunraven Pl, Bridgend, CF31 1JD, WAL.
(T) 01656 650641
Speciality: Chiropodists (Podiatrists).

● **Owner** Mr G Evans
S (Ref:HM06972)

**EVANS, GAYLE**

**Gayle Evans**, Pen Y Banc, School Lane, Llanfairtalhaiarn, Abergele, **Conwy**, LL22 8RT, WAL.
(T) 01745 720448
Speciality: Chiropodists (Podiatrists).
S (Ref:HM06973)

**EVANS, H**

**H Evans**, 10 Eldon Rd, Reading, **Berkshire**, RG1 4DH, ENG.
(T) 01189 502002
Speciality: Physiotherapy.
P S T (Ref:HM06974)

**EVANS, HELEN**

**Helen Evans**, 301 High St, Berkhamsted, **Hertfordshire**, HP4 1AJ, ENG.
(T) 01442 875139
Speciality: Chiropody. ✔
● **Chiropodist** Ms H Evans Q: M.S.C.P, S.R.Ch.
M Yrs. Est.: 15 (Ref:HM06975)

**EVANS, HELEN**

**Helen Evans**, The Elms, 24 Hall Place Gardens, St. Albans, **Hertfordshire**, AL1 3SF, ENG.
(T) 01727 865057 (F) 01727 847937
Speciality: Chiropody, Nail Surgery. ✔
● **Chiropodist** Ms H Evans Q: M.S.C.P, S.R.Ch. M: S.C.P.
M Yrs. Est.: 15 (Ref:HM06976)

**EVANS, HELEN**

**Helen Evans**, 23 Maesyderi, Pentre-Cwrt, Llandysul, **Carmarthenshire**, SA44 5DJ, WAL.
(T) 01559 363784
Speciality: Reflexology.
S T (Ref:HM06977)

**EVANS, JENNY**

**Jenny Evans**, Ditchling, Newton Purcell, Buckingham, **Buckinghamshire**, MK18 4BA, ENG.
(T) 01280 848622
Speciality: Reflexology.
● **Owner** Mrs J Evans
S T (Ref:HM06978)

**EVANS, JOANNE**

**Joanne Evans**, 30 Elizabeth Rd, Kington, **Herefordshire**, HR5 3DB, ENG.
(T) 01544 230788
Speciality: Reflexology.
S T (Ref:HM06979)

**EVANS, JUDITH**

**Judith Evans**, 166 Raeburn Avenue, Surbiton, **Surrey**, KT5 9ED, ENG.
(T) 020 8390 2258
Speciality: Aromatherapy.
M O (Ref:HM06980)

**EVANS, LINDA**

**Linda Evans**, 7 Newstead Way, Bedford, **Bedfordshire**, MK41 8RH, ENG.
(T) 01234 347031
Speciality: Electrolysis.
T (Ref:HM06981)

**EVANS, M I**

**M I Evans**, Scotland House, 11 Scotland St, Ellesmere, **Shropshire**, SY12 0DG, ENG.
(T) 01691 622970
Speciality: Chiropodists (Podiatrists).
● **Owner** Miss M Evans
S (Ref:HM06982)

**EVANS, MARGARET**

**Margaret Evans**, 27 Grange Rd, Colwyn Bay, **Conwy**, LL29 7RL, WAL.
(T) 01492 531087
Speciality: Reflexology.
● **Principal** Miss M Evans
S T (Ref:HM06983)

**EVANS, MARI**

**Mari Evans**, 156 Pencisely Rd, Cardiff, **Glamorgan (Vale of)**, CF5 1DP, WAL.
(T) 029 2021 4552
Speciality: Osteopathy.
P S T (Ref:HM06984)

**EVANS, MARI**

**Mari Evans**, 242 Cathedral Rd, Cardiff, **Glamorgan (Vale of)**, CF11 9JG, WAL.
(T) 029 2023 5220
Speciality: Osteopathy.
P S T (Ref:HM06985)

**EVANS, PAT**

**Pat Evans**, 17 Haws Hill, Carnforth, **Lancashire**, LA5 9DD, ENG.
(T) 01524 736755
Speciality: Complementary Medicines & Therapy.
C M (Ref:HM06986)

**EVANS, PHILIP**

**Philip Evans**, 11 Earls Avenue, Folkestone, **Kent**, CT20 2HW, ENG.
(T) 01303 226656
Speciality: Herbal Medicine.
M (Ref:HM06987)

**EVANS, REBECCA MARY**

**Rebecca Mary Evans**, 185b Tuckton Rd, Bournemouth, **Dorset**, BH6 3LA, ENG.
(T) 01202 417656
Speciality: Osteopathy. ✔
● **Osteopath** Ms R Evans Q: BSc. M: GOsC.
S Yrs. Est.: 8 (Ref:HM06988)

**EVANS, RICHARD**

**Richard Evans**, 40 Post Office Rd, Alrewas, Burton-On-Trent, **Staffordshire**, DE13 7BS, ENG.
(T) 01283 790403
Speciality: Reflexology, Reiki. ✔
● **Reflexologist** Mr R Evans Q: MAR. M: AoR.
T Yrs. Est.: 7 (Ref:HM06989)

**EVANS, STEVE**

**Steve Evans**, 127 London Rd, Neath, **Glamorgan (Vale of)**, SA11 1HF, WAL.
(T) 01639 636666
Speciality: Physiotherapy. ✔
● **Manipulative Therapist** Mr S Evans M: FHT.
S (Ref:HM06990)

**EVANS, SUE**

**Sue Evans**, 24A Sunderland Trce, London, **London (Greater)**, W2 5PA, ENG.
(T) 020 7221 8101 (F) 020 7221 8101
Speciality: Reflexology.
● **Owner** Ms S Evans
S T (Ref:HM06991)

**EVANS, SUSAN**

**Susan Evans**, 59 Valley Rd, Crewe, **Cheshire**, CW2 8JZ, ENG.
(T) 01270 652273
Speciality: Acupuncture.
● **Owner** Mrs S Evans
O (Ref:HM06992)

**EVANS, WENDY**

**Wendy Evans**, Old Forge, Woodhouse Rd, Quorn, Loughborough, **Leicestershire**, LE12 8AL, ENG.
(T) 01509 416647
Speciality: Complementary Medicines & Therapy.
● **Bowen Therapist** Wendy Evans
M (Ref:HM06993)

**EVANS-FOSTER, YVETTE**

**Yvette Evans-Foster**, 131 Plimsoll Rd, London, **London (Greater)**, N4 2ED, ENG.
(T) 020 7359 5365 (F) 020 7226 6616
Speciality: Acupuncture.
● **Owner** Ms Y Evans-Foster
O (Ref:HM06994)

**EVE GRAYWOLF LUNG PSYC CONS**

**Eve Graywolf Lung Psychic Consultant**, Flat 1, 218 Yardley Wood Rd, Moseley, Birmingham, **Midlands (West)**, B13 9JQ, ENG.
(T) 01212 462672
Speciality: Clairvoyants & Palmists, Shamamism. ✔
● **Owner** Miss E Graywolf Lung
B Yrs. Est.: 15 (Ref:HM06995)

**EVEGATE CLINIC**

**Evegate Clinic**, The Old Barn, Station Rd, Smeeth, Ashford, **Kent**, TN25 6SX, ENG.
(T) 01303 813712
Speciality: Acupuncture, Chiropractic, Homeopathy, Hypnotherapy, Osteopathy, Reflexology, Reiki, Shiatsu. ✔
● **Joint Owner** Mr K Pugh
● **Joint Owner** T Tutt
● **Acupuncturist/Osteopath** Ms Kiener M: BAcC.
C Yrs. Est.: 14 (Ref:HM06996)

**EVENKEEL**

**Evenkeel**, 11 Eagle St, Ipswich, **Suffolk**, IP4 1JA, ENG.
(T) 01473 253322
Speciality: Flotation Therapy, Healing Therapy, Holistic Healing, Indian Head Massage, Massage (Therapeutic), Stress Therapy.
● **Therapist** Ms C Keeling
● **Masseur** Miss P Whyte
● **Masseur** Mr A Dosher
M Yrs. Est.: 2 (Ref:HM06997)

**EVENNETT, P J**

**P J Evennett**, Exeter Physio & Sports Clinic, 11-15 Dixs Field, Exeter, **Devon**, EX1 1QA, ENG.
(T) 01392 211066
Speciality: Physiotherapy.
P S T (Ref:HM06998)

**EVERETT HEALTH CARE**

**Everett Health Care**, Poundshill House, Pounds Hill, Crediton, **Devon**, EX17 1AA, ENG.
(T) 01363 772029
Speciality: Complementary Medicines & Therapy.
C M (Ref:HM06999)

**EVERETT, G W**

**G W Everett**, Serpentine Rd, Cleckheaton, **Yorkshire (West)**, BD19 3HU, ENG.
(T) 01274 871350
Speciality: Chiropodists (Podiatrists).
S (Ref:HM07000)

**EVERETT, J**

**J Everett**, 51 Chestnut Drive, Sale, **Cheshire**, M33 4HN, ENG.
(T) 01619 761404 (F) 01619 761404
Speciality: Homeopathy.
● **Owner** Mr J Everett
M (Ref:HM07001)

**EVERETT, PAUL**

**Paul Everett**, Flat 5, 9 Cavendish Pl, **Dorset**, BH1 1RQ, ENG.
(T) 01202 297566
Speciality: Reflexology.
S T (Ref:HM07002)

**EVERETT, PETER**

**Peter Everett D O,M R O**, Burnham Medical Centre, Love Lane, Burnham-on-Sea, **Somerset**, TA8 1EY, ENG.
(T) 01278 793223
Speciality: Osteopathy.
● **Owner** Mr P Everett Q: MRO.
P S T (Ref:HM07003)

**EVERETT, U**

**U Everett**, 78 Station Rd, Hayling Island, **Hampshire**, PO11 0EL, ENG.
(T) 023 9246 8512
Speciality: Physiotherapy.
P S T (Ref:HM07004)

**EVERGREEN CLNC OF NATURAL MED**

**Evergreen Clinic of Natural Medicine**, 79 Evergreen Rd, **County Cork**, IRE.
(T) 021 4966 209
Speciality: Complementary Medicines & Therapy.
M (Ref:HM07005)

**EVERITT, ELAINE**

**Elaine Everitt**, Unit 3, Stockwell Lodge Medical Village, Rosedale Way, Cheshunt, Waltham Cross, **Hertfordshire**, EN7 6QQ, ENG.
(T) 01992 637677
Speciality: Osteopathy.
● **Owner** Mrs E Everitt
P S T (Ref:HM07006)

**EVERITT, ELAINE M**

**Elaine M Everitt**, The Well House, Robins Nest Hill, Little Berkhamsted, Hertford, **Hertfordshire**,


Key continued: Yrs.Est: Years Established Q: Qualifications M: Professional Membership ✔ Indemnity Insurance Accept Credit Cards

SG13 8LS, **ENG**.
(T) 01707 873057
Speciality: Osteopathy.
● **Owner** Ms E Everitt
P S T (**Ref:**HM07007)

### EVERSFIELD HOSPITAL

**Eversfield Hospital**, 111-117 West Hill Rd, St. Leonards-On-Sea, **Sussex (East)**, TN38 0NG, **ENG**.
(T) 01424 710104 (F) 01424 433870
Speciality: Physiotherapy.
P S T (**Ref:**HM07008)

### EVESHAM NATURAL HEALTH CENTRE

**Evesham Natural Health Centre**, 98 High St, Evesham, **Worcestershire**, WR11 4EU, **ENG**.
(T) 01386 421821
(E) info@eveshamnaturalhealth.co.uk
(W) www.eveshamnaturalhealth.co.uk
Speciality: Acupuncture, Alexander Technique, Aromatherapy, Cranial Osteopathy, Hypnotherapy, Manipulation, Osteopathy, Psychotherapy, Reflexology, Reiki, Yoga. ✔
● **Osteopath** Mr R Sutton Q: DO. M: GOsC.
● **Osteopath** Ms R Quickenden Q: DO. M: GOsC.
● **Hypnotherapist/Psychotherapist** Ms D Murray Q: MCAH. M: ABCHyp.
● **Aromatherapist/Reflexologist** Ms S O'Carroll Q: ITEC. M: GCP.
● **Teacher of the Alexander Technique** Mr T Foxton Q: BSc, MSTAT. M: STAT.
● **Acupuncturist** Mr J Hayllar Q: Lic.Ac. M: BAcC.
● **Yoga Teacher/Reiki Practitioner** Ms J Harrison Q: BWY.Dip. M: BWY.
S Yrs. Est.: 7 (**Ref:**HM07009)

### EVETTS-SECKER, JOSEPHINE

**Josephine Evetts-Secker**, 16 York Pl, Scarborough, **Yorkshire (North)**, YO11 2NP, **ENG**.
(T) 01723 354949
Speciality: Psychotherapy.
B (**Ref:**HM07010)

### EVINGTON THERAPY CENTRE

**Evington Therapy Centre**, 4 The Common, Evington, Leicester, **Leicestershire**, LE5 6EA, **ENG**.
(T) 01162 737324
Speciality: Hypnotherapy.
B (**Ref:**HM07011)

### EVISON, ALEX

**Alex Evison - Stress Management and Hypnotherapy**, 20 Meal Market, Hexham, **Northumberland**, NE46 1NF, **ENG**.
(T) 01434 601330 (F) 01434 605220
(E) alexevison@aol.com
Speciality: Counselling, Hypnosis, Hypnotherapy, Stress Therapy, Visualisation Therapy. ✔
● **Stress Manager** Mr A Evison Q: Dip.Hyp, FSSM. M: SSM.
H Yrs. Est.: 8 (**Ref:**HM07012)

### EVOLUTION

**Evolution**, 117 Fore St, Exeter, **Devon**, EX4 3JQ, **ENG**.
(T) 01392 410759
Speciality: Complementary Medicines & Therapy.
C M (**Ref:**HM07013)

### EVOLUTION HEALTH

**Evolution Health**, 45 Oxford St, Whitstable, **Kent**, CT5 1DB, **ENG**.
(T) 01227 273821 (F) 01227 771360
(W) www.evolutionhealth.co.uk
Speciality: Aromatherapy, Chiropractic, Counselling, Herbal Medicine, Massage (Therapeutic), Nutritional Therapy, Reflexology, Chiropractic Craniopathy. ✔ CREDIT
● **Chiropractor** Tanya Scott Q: DC, MSc. M: BCA, GCC.
● **Chiropractor** Mrs A Wreford Q: Cert.Cranio, DC. M: BCA, GCC.
P S T Yrs. Est.: 18 (**Ref:**HM07014)

### EWELL CHIROPRACTIC CENTRE

**Ewell Chiropractic Centre**, 9a Cheam Rd, Epsom, **Surrey**, KT17 1SP, **ENG**.
(T) 020 8393 8834 (F) 020 8393 8834
Speciality: Chiropractic.
● **Owner** Dr P Delport
P S T (**Ref:**HM07015)

### EWINGS, D V

**D V Ewings**, 76 Fish Dam Lane, Barnsley, **Yorkshire (South)**, S71 2PY, **ENG**.
(T) 01226 299563
Speciality: Chiropodists (Podiatrists).
S (**Ref:**HM07016)

### EWINS, DAVID

**David Ewins**, The London Lane Clinic, 37-39 London Lane, Bromley, **Kent**, BR1 4HX, **ENG**.
(T) 020 8466 0246
Speciality: Hypnotherapy.
B (**Ref:**HM07017)

### EXCALIBUR

**Excalibur**, 16 Croham Rd, South Croydon, **Surrey**, CR2 7BA, **ENG**.
(T) 020 8649 8622
Speciality: Complementary Medicines & Therapy.
C M (**Ref:**HM07018)

### EXCLUSIVE HYPNOTHERAPY

**Robin W Thorburn**, 10 Biggar Rd, Edinburgh, **Edinburgh (City of)**, EH10 7BQ, **SCO**.
(T) 01314 452485
(E) rwt@exclusivehypnotherapy.co.uk
(W) www.exclusivehypnotherapy.co.uk
Speciality: Auto Suggestion, Aversion Therapy, Cognitive Therapy, Hypnosis, Hypnotherapy, Psychotherapy, Rogerian Therapy. ✔
● **Owner** Mr R Thorburn Q: DHP (NC), MNRHP. M: NRHP.
B Yrs. Est.: 9 (**Ref:**HM07019)

### EXECUTIVE ROOMS

**Executive Rooms**, 115 Uttoxeter Rd, Stoke-On-Trent, **Staffordshire**, ST3 1PF, **ENG**.
(T) 01782 333433
Speciality: Complementary Medicines & Therapy.
● **Owner** Ms C Jackson
C M (**Ref:**HM07020)

### EXECUTIVE SUITE

**Executive Suite (The)**, 152 Sheffield Rd, Barnsley, **Yorkshire (South)**, S70 1JH, **ENG**.
(T) 01226 248500
Speciality: Aromatherapy.
M O (**Ref:**HM07021)

### EXETER CHIROPRACTIC CLINIC

**Exeter Chiropractic Clinic**, 323 Pinhoe Rd, Exeter, **Devon**, EX4 8AD, **ENG**.
(T) 01392 467438
Speciality: Chiropractors.
● **Owner** Mr G Jackson
P S T (**Ref:**HM07022)

### EXETER SKIN CARE CENTRE

**Exeter Skin Care Centre**, Market St, Exeter, **Devon**, EX1 1BW, **ENG**.
(T) 01392 218600
Speciality: Electrolysis.
T (**Ref:**HM07023)

### EXETER, SHARON

**Sharon Exeter**, 84 Roestock Lane, Colney Heath, St. Albans, **Hertfordshire**, AL4 0QQ, **ENG**.
(T) 07976 219083
Speciality: Reflexology.
S T (**Ref:**HM07024)

### EXMOUTH CHIROPODY

**Exmouth Chiropody**, 51 Imperial Rd, Exmouth, **Devon**, EX8 1DQ, **ENG**.
(T) 01395 274188
Speciality: Chiropodists (Podiatrists).
● **Owner** Mr D Wilkes
S (**Ref:**HM07025)

### EXQUISITE BEAUTY SALON

**Exquisite Beauty Salon**, 42A-44 Avery Hill Rd, London, **London (Greater)**, SE9 2BJ, **ENG**.
(T) 020 8859 5766
Speciality: Electrolysis.
T (**Ref:**HM07026)

### EYLES, C

**C Eyles**, 5 Radway Rd, Southampton, **Hampshire**, SO15 7PT, **ENG**.
(T) 023 8077 3500
Speciality: Homeopathy.
● **Owner** Mrs C Eyles
M (**Ref:**HM07027)

### EYRE, E M

**Miss E M Eyre**, 468 Narborough Rd, Leicester, **Leicestershire**, LE3 2FT, **ENG**.
(T) 01162 892026
Speciality: Chiropodists (Podiatrists).
● **Owner** Miss E Eyre
S (**Ref:**HM07028)

### EYRE, JACQUELINE

**Jacqueline Eyre**, 3 Hartford Avenue, Wilmslow, **Cheshire**, SK9 6LP, **ENG**.
(T) 01625 522840
Speciality: Reflexology.
S T (**Ref:**HM07029)

### EYRES, BELINDA

**Belinda Eyres**, Woodbine Surgery, 40 High St, Chew Magna, Bristol, BS40 8PW, **ENG**.
(T) 01275 333587
Speciality: Osteopathy.
P S T (**Ref:**HM07030)

### EYRES, M R

**M R Eyres**, 2 Dellors Cl, Barnet, **Hertfordshire**, EN5 2SU, **ENG**.
(T) 020 8449 3746 (F) 020 8449 3746
Speciality: Osteopathy.
● **Owner** Mr M Eyres
P S T (**Ref:**HM07031)

### EZRA REMEDIAL AROMATHERAPY

**Ezra Remedial Aromatherapy Massage**, 73 Birchwood Cres, Birmingham, **Midlands (West)**, B12 8BW, **ENG**.
(T) 01212 464546
Speciality: Complementary Medicines & Therapy.
M (**Ref:**HM07032)

### F GHAFOOR (DR)

**Dr F Ghafoor**, 229A High St, Uxbridge, **London (Greater)**, UB8 1LD, **ENG**.
(T) 01895 273555
Speciality: Chiropractors.
● **Owner** Dr F Ghafoor
P S T (**Ref:**HM07033)

### F VON - MEHREN

**F Von - Mehren**, Castle Way, Park Avenue, Ventnor, **Isle of Wight**, PO38 1LE, **ENG**.
(T) 01983 854586
Speciality: Chiropody, Nail Surgery. ✔
● **Chiropodist** Miss F Von-Mehren Q: MBChA, MSSCh. M: B.A.Ch.P, SSCh.
C (**Ref:**HM07034)

### FACE & FIGURE

**Face & Figure**, 64 Claughton St, St. Helens, **Merseyside**, WA10 1SN, **ENG**.
(T) 01744 739797
Speciality: Electrolysis.
T (**Ref:**HM07035)

### FACE AND BODY OPTIONS

**Face And Body Options**, 69 New Park St, Shrewsbury, **Shropshire**, SY1 2LE, **ENG**.
(T) 01743 243386
Speciality: Complementary Medicines & Therapy.
● **Owner** Mrs J Millington
M (**Ref:**HM07036)

### FACE UP FOR BEAUTY

**Face Up For Beauty**, 48 Babington Lane, Derby, **Derbyshire**, DE1 1SX, **ENG**.
(T) 01332 368195
Speciality: Electrolysis.
T (**Ref:**HM07037)

### FACIAL REJUVINATION AYURVEDIC

**Facial Rejuvination Ayurvedic Face Lift**, 141-151 Drummond St, London, **London (Greater)**, NW1 2PB, **ENG**.
(T) 020 7388 9795 (F) 020 8348 6976
Speciality: Complementary Medicines & Therapy.

● **Owner** Mrs S Patel
[M] (**Ref:**HM07038)

**FACULTY OF CHIROPODY**

**Faculty Of Chiropody Ltd**, King St Remedial Clinic, 69 King St, Dukinfield, **Cheshire**, SK16 4NQ, ENG.
(T) 01613 308220
Speciality: Chiropodists (Podiatrists).
[S] (**Ref:**HM07039)

**FACULTY OF HOMEOPATHY**

**Faculty of Homeopathy**, 15 Clerkenwell Cl, London, **London (Greater)**, ENG.
(T) 020 7566 7810
(W) www.trusthomeopathy.org
Speciality: Homeopathy, Promote & Teaches Homeopathy.
● **Administrator**
[H] (**Ref:**HM07040)

**FACULTY OF HOMEOPATHY**

**Faculty Of Homeopathy**, Cotham Hill, Bristol, BS6 6JU, ENG.
(T) 01179 466087
Speciality: Homeopathy.
[M] (**Ref:**HM07041)

**FAGAN, B W**

**B W Fagan Chartered Physiotherapist**, Bridge House Medical Centre, 11 Ladybridge Rd, Cheadle Hulme, Cheadle, **Cheshire**, SK8 5LL, ENG.
(T) 01614 855700 (F) 01614 884465
Speciality: Acupuncture, Manipulation, Massage (Therapeutic), Physiotherapy, Ultrasonics, Sports Injury Therapy. ✓
● **Physiotherapist** Mr B Fagan Q: Grad Dip Phys, MCSP, SRP. M: CSP, OCPPP.
[S] Yrs. Est.: 25 (**Ref:**HM07042)

**FAGAN, FRANCES M**

**Frances M Fagan**, The Imperial Physiotherapy Clinic, 33 Imperial Avenue, Leicester, **Leicestershire**, LE3 1AH, ENG.
(T) 01162 630119
Speciality: Physiotherapy.
● **Owner** Mrs F Fagan
[P] [S] [T] (**Ref:**HM07043)

**FAGAN, RUTH**

**Ruth Fagan**, 67 Lower Camden St, Dublin, **County Dublin**, IRE.
(T) 08723 70020
Speciality: Counselling.
[B] [H] (**Ref:**HM07044)

**FAGAN, RUTH**

**Ruth Fagan**, 67 Camden St, Lr, IRE.
(T) 01478 5022
Speciality: Counselling.
[B] [H] (**Ref:**HM07045)

**FAGAN, STEVE**

**Steve Fagan**, 1 Gildenburgh Avenue, Peterborough, **Cambridgeshire**, PE1 4RF, ENG.
(T) 01733 559063
Speciality: Chiropodists (Podiatrists).
● **Owner** Mr S Fagan
[S] (**Ref:**HM07046)

**FAGG, A P**

**A P Fagg**, 1 Somerset Trce, Bristol, BS3 4LL, ENG.
(T) 01179 661008 (F) 01179 661008
Speciality: Complementary Medicines & Therapy.
● **Owner** Mr A Fagg
[C] [M] (**Ref:**HM07047)

**FAIR, ANNETTE**

**Miss Annette Fair**, Kelmscott Leisure Centre, Markhouse Rd, Walthamstow, London, **London (Greater)**, E17, ENG.
(T) 020 8509 1910
Speciality: Osteopathy, Structural Therapy. ✓
● **Osteopath** Miss A Fair Q: BSc, Hons (OST). M: GOsC.
[S] (**Ref:**HM07048)

**FAIRBAIM, SARAH**

**Sarah Fairbaim**, 11 Hillerstone Avenue, Barnes, Richmond, **Surrey**, SW13 0EG, ENG.
(T) 020 8878 4101
Speciality: Complementary Medicines & Therapy.
● **Bowen Therapist** Sarah Fairbaim
[M] (**Ref:**HM07049)

**FAIRBAIRN, KAREN**

**Karen Fairbairn**, 26 Ashcroft Avenue, Lennoxtown, Glasgow, **Glasgow (City of)**, G66 7EN, SCO.
(T) 01360 311054
Speciality: Reflexology.
[S] [T] (**Ref:**HM07050)

**FAIRBOURNE CLINIC**

**Fairbourne Clinic (The)**, 17 Wendan Rd, Newbury, **Berkshire**, RG14 7AG, ENG.
(T) 01635 44200 (F) 01635 40033
(E) wendy@fairbourneclinic.co.uk
(W) www.fairbourneclinic.co.uk
Speciality: Acupuncture, Bach Remedies, Complementary Therapy, Counselling, Cranial Osteopathy, Holistic Healing, Homeopathy, Hypnotherapy, Indian Head Massage, Massage (Therapeutic), Osteopathy, Podiatry, Psychotherapy, Reflexology, Reiki, Manual Lymphatic Drainage, Bio-Resonance Allergy Testing. ✓
● **Homeopath** Ms E Lilwall Q: LCH. M: LCH.
● **Osteopath** Mr T Dennis Q: DO. M: GOsC.
● **Chiropodist** Ms A May Q: FSSCh, MBChA.
● **Osteopath** Ms J Butler Q: DO. M: GOsC.
[M] Yrs. Est.: 12 (**Ref:**HM07051)

**FAIRCHILD, HAZEL**

**Hazel Fairchild**, Flat 4, 45 Ditchling Rise, Brighton, **Sussex (East)**, ENG.
(T) 01273 270925 (F) 01273 270925
Speciality: Counselling, Gestalt Therapy, Group Therapy, Stress Therapy, Visualisation Therapy, Person Centered/Humanistic Counselling, Transpersonal. ✓
● **Counsellor** Ms H Fairchild Q: BSc, Dip.Adv.Couns, PGCE. M: BACP.
[B] Yrs. Est.: 3 (**Ref:**HM07052)

**FAIRCLOUGH, LOUISE**

**Louise Fairclough**, 17 Woolgreaves Avenue, Wakefield, **Yorkshire (West)**, WF2 6DX, ENG.
(T) 01924 256023
Speciality: Reflexology.
[S] [T] (**Ref:**HM07053)

**FAIRCROSS COMP MEDICAL CLINIC**

**Faircross Complementary Medical Clinic (The)**, 60 Upney Lane, Barking, **Essex**, IG11 9LP, ENG.
(T) 020 8594 3667 (F) 020 8594 5594
Speciality: Homeopathy.
● **Senior Partner** Mrs S Bourne
[M] (**Ref:**HM07054)

**FAIRDOWN CENTRE**

**Fairdown Centre (The)**, 173 Alresford Rd, Winchester, **Hampshire**, SO23 0JZ, ENG.
(T) 01962 865999
Speciality: Hypnosis.
● **Director** Mr D Mansfield
[B] (**Ref:**HM07055)

**FAIRFAX PRIVATE THERAPY**

**Fairfax Private Therapy**, 76 Marsh Lane, Birmingham, **Midlands (West)**, B23 6PJ, ENG.
(T) 01213 821862
Speciality: Aromatherapy, Hypnotherapy. ✓
● **Owner** Mr A Stanley Q: ITEC, MIPTI. M: IPTI, ITEC.
[C] Yrs. Est.: 10 (**Ref:**HM07056)

**FAIRFAX, A B (DR)**

**Dr A B Fairfax**, 12 Langley Rd, Trowbridge, **Wiltshire**, BA14 0LL, ENG.
(T) 01225 751486
Speciality: Acupuncture.
● **Principal** Dr A Fairfax
[O] (**Ref:**HM07057)

**FAIRFIELD, MARGARET**

**Margaret Fairfield**, 68B Leicester Rd, Loughborough, **Leicestershire**, LE11 2AG, ENG.
(T) 01509 234522
Speciality: Hypnotherapy.
[B] (**Ref:**HM07058)

**FAIRFIELDS LANE WEST**

**Fairfields Clinic Of Complementary Medicine**, Skippetts Lane West, Basingstoke, **Hampshire**, RG21 3HP, ENG.
(T) 01256 326980 (F) 01256 326980
Speciality: Acupressure, Acupuncture, Alexander Technique, Allergy Testing, Aromatherapy, Bach Remedies, Bowen Therapy, Cognitive Therapy, Complementary Therapy, Counselling, Family Therapy, Healing Therapy, Hellerwork, Herbal Medicine, Homeopathy, Hypnotherapy, Indian Head Massage, Kirlian Photography, Massage (Therapeutic), Nutritional Therapy, Osteopathy, Psychotherapy, Reflexology, Reiki, Shiatsu, Spiritual Healing, Stress Therapy, Yoga. ✓
● **Acupuncturist** Mr R Piercy Q: Lic.Ac, MBAcC.
● **Director** Mr C Allison Q: Dip.Psych.
● **Medical Herbalist** Ishret Mirza Q: BSc (Hons), MNIMH.
● **Nutritionist** Delcia Willmott
[C] Yrs. Est.: 10 (**Ref:**HM07059)

**FAIRGREEN HOLISTIC CLINIC**

**Fairgreen Holistic Clinic**, Fairgreen, Naas, **County Kildare**, IRE.
(T) 04589 8243
Speciality: Complementary Medicines & Therapy.
[M] (**Ref:**HM07060)

**FAIRHEAD, RICHARD**

**Richard Fairhead**, 132 Sunrise Avenue, Chelmsford, **Essex**, CM1 4JR, ENG.
(T) 01245 269082
Speciality: Complementary Medicines & Therapy.
[C] [M] (**Ref:**HM07061)

**FAIRMAN, ROBIN**

**Robin Fairman**, Acton Practice, 146 Old Oak Rd, London, **London (Greater)**, W3 7HE, ENG.
(T) 020 8743 5140
Speciality: Osteopathy.
[P] [S] [T] (**Ref:**HM07062)

**FAIRNINGTON, A & B**

**A & B Fairnington**, 1 Tenter Hill, Wooler, **Northumberland**, NE71 6DB, ENG.
(T) 01668 281721
Speciality: Chiropodists (Podiatrists).
[S] (**Ref:**HM07063)

**FAIRNINGTON, A & B**

**A & B Fairnington**, 6 Bridge St, Kelso, **Scottish Borders**, TD5 7JD, SCO.
(T) 01668 281721
Speciality: Chiropodists (Podiatrists).
● **Partner** Mr A Fairnington
[S] (**Ref:**HM07064)

**FAIRVIEW NAT THERAPY CLINIC**

**Fairview Natural Therapy Clinic**, Wintles Hill, Westbury-on-Severn, **Gloucestershire**, GL14 1QB, ENG.
(T) 01452 760360
Speciality: Complementary Medicines & Therapy.
[C] [M] (**Ref:**HM07065)

**FAIRVIEW THERAPY CENTRE**

**Fairview Therapy Centre**, 10 Fairview Strand Fairview, Dublin, **County Dublin**, IRE.
(T) 01856 1289
Speciality: Acupressure, Acupuncture, Aromatherapy, Bio-energetics, Counselling, Family Therapy, Gestalt Therapy, Homeopathy, Humanistic Psychology, Indian Head Massage, Life Style Coaching, Massage (Therapeutic), Moxibustion, Psychotherapy, Reflexology, Reiki, Rogerian Therapy, Shiatsu. ✓
● **Psychotherapist** Ms K OConnor Q: Dip.Psych. M: IACT.
● **Holistic Massage Therapist** Ms N Farrell Q: Dip.Hol.Mass. M: ITEC.
● **Acupuncturist** Ms A OConnor Q: RGN, S.C.M.
● **Reflexologist/Aromatherapist** Ms A Heery Q: Dip.Arom, Dip.Reflex. M: IRI.
[T] Yrs. Est.: 2 (**Ref:**HM07066)

**FAIRWAY PHYSIOTHERAPY CLINIC**

**Fairway Physiotherapy Clinic**, 28 Western Gales Way, Normanton, **Yorkshire (West)**, WF6



Key continued: Yrs.Est: Years Established Q: Qualifications M: Professional Membership ✓ Indemnity Insurance Accept Credit Cards

1UA, ENG.
(T) 01924 898901
Speciality: Physiotherapy.
P S T (Ref:HM07067)

**FAIRWEATHER, S & E**

**Stephen & Elaine Fairweather**, 98 Willow Cres, Market Harborough, **Leicestershire**, LE16 9DT, ENG.
(T) 01858 431323
Speciality: Counselling, Hypnotherapy, Massage (Therapeutic), Remedial Massage. ✔
● **Massage Therapist**
Mr S Fairweather Q: IIST, ITEC. M: ITEC.
● **Counsellor/Hypnotherapist**
Mrs E Fairweather Q: CertCC(Relate), DHP (NC), MNRHP. M: NRHP.
M Yrs. Est.: 10 (Ref:HM07068)

**FAITH, GORDON**

**Gordon Faith**, 1 Wavel Mews, London, **London (Greater)**, NW6 3AB, ENG.
(T) 020 7328 0446
Speciality: Hypnosis.
B (Ref:HM07069)

**FAITH, JAVAD**

**Javad Faith**, 36 Brent St, London, **London (Greater)**, NW4 2ET, ENG.
(T) 020 8201 5429
Speciality: Osteopathy.
● **Owner** Mr J Faith
P S T (Ref:HM07070)

**FALCON YARD CHIROPODY**

**Falcon Yard Chiropody**, 12 Falcon Yard, Low Pavement, Chesterfield, **Derbyshire**, S40 1PF, ENG.
(T) 01246 203195
Speciality: Chiropodists (Podiatrists).
S (Ref:HM07071)

**FALCONER, N**

**N Falconer**, 357 King St, Broughty Ferry, Dundee, **Angus**, DD5 2HA, SCO.
(T) 01382 774200
Speciality: Osteopathy.
P S T (Ref:HM07072)

**FALCONER, PATRICIA**

**Patricia Falconer**, Newlands, Hilders Lane, Edenbridge, **Kent**, TN8 6LD, ENG.
(T) 01732 865949
Speciality: Aromatherapy. ✔
● **Owner/Aromatherapist**
Mrs P Falconer Q: AOC.
C Yrs. Est.: 5 (Ref:HM07073)

**FALKIRK CHIROPRACTIC CLINIC**

**Falkirk Chiropractic Clinic**, 97 Grahams Rd, Falkirk, FK2 7DD, SCO.
(T) 01324 610000
Speciality: Chiropractic. ✔
● **Owner** Dr M Dalziel Q: DC. M: GCC.
P Yrs. Est.: 6 (Ref:HM07074)

**FALKNER-HEYLINGS, J**

**J Falkner-Heylings**, 12 Beeches Rd, Birmingham, **Midlands (West)**, B42 2HF, ENG.
(T) 01213 573562
Speciality: Chiropodists (Podiatrists).
S (Ref:HM07075)

**FALKOUS, R J**

**R J Falkous**, 6 Lavender Gardens, Gateshead, **Tyne and Wear**, NE9 5TB, ENG.
(T) 01914 876863
Speciality: Chiropodists (Podiatrists).
● **Owner** Mr R Faulkous
S (Ref:HM07076)

**FALLOWS, R D**

**RD Fallows BSc (physio) MCSP SRP**, The Clinic, 4 Tyrone House Church St, Wellington, Telford, **Shropshire**, TF1 1DR, ENG.
(T) 01952 260983
Speciality: Complementary Medicines & Therapy.
● **Owner** Mr R Fallows
C M (Ref:HM07077)

**FALLSHAW, ELIZABETH**

**Elizabeth Fallshaw**, 2 Douglas Avenue, Hythe, **Kent**, CT21 5JT, ENG.
(T) 01303 266535
Speciality: Reflexology.
S T (Ref:HM07078)

**FALMOUTH CHIROPRACTIC CLINIC**

**Falmouth Chiropractic Clinic**, Waterside House, Falmouth Rd, Penryn, **Cornwall**, TR10 8BE, ENG.
(T) 01326 375900 (F) 01326 375905
Speciality: Chiropractic.
P S T (Ref:HM07079)

**FALMOUTH HOMEOPATHIC PRACTICE**

**Falmouth Homeopathic Practice**, Admiralty House, Bank Pl, Falmouth, **Cornwall**, TR11 4AT, ENG.
(T) 01326 241284
Speciality: Homeopathy.
M (Ref:HM07080)

**FAMILY CHIRO & ALT MED CTRE**

**Posthouse Family Chiropractic & Alternative Medical Centre**, 15B High St, Alton, **Hampshire**, GU34 1AW, ENG.
(T) 01420 80050 (F) 01420 80070
(E) siruis639@hotmail.com
(W) www.family-chiropractic.co.uk
Speciality: Acupressure, Acupuncture, Alexander Technique, Aromatherapy, Ayurvedic Medicine, Bach Remedies, Chiropractic, Colour Therapy, Complementary Therapy, Cranial Osteopathy, Healer, Herbal Medicine, Homeopathy, Hypnosis, Hypnotherapy, Indian Head Massage, Kinesiology, Manipulation, Massage (Therapeutic), Meditation, Nutritional Therapy, Polarity Therapy, Postural Integration, Reflexology, Reiki, Seichem, Silva Method, Stress Therapy, Tera-Mai, Vitamin Therapy, X-Ray, Blood Group Diet Program and Sports Therapy. ✔ CREDIT
● **Therapist** Mr A Anderson Q: Dip.Arom, IIST, ITEC.
● **Chiropractor** Ms S Glen Q: DC. M: BCA.
● **Owner/Therapist** Dr H Rower Q: BSc, DC. M: BCA.
● **Chiropractor** Mr D Edwards
● **Therapist** Ms Y Sinclare M: ALTT.
● **Neuro Linguistic Programmer/Hypnotherapist**
Mr B Taylor
● **Acupuncturist** Ms E Bone
S Yrs. Est.: 1 (Ref:HM07081)

**FAMILY CHIRO CLINIC BALLYMENA**

**Family Chiropractic Clinic of Ballymena**, 19 Cullybackey Rd, Ballymena, **County Antrim**, BT43 5DF, NIR.
(T) 028 2563 0778
Speciality: Chiropractic.
● **Chiropractor** Dr C Stant Q: BSc, DC. M: GCC.
H Yrs. Est.: 4 (Ref:HM07082)

**FAMILY CHIRO WELLNESS CENTRE**

**Family Chiropractic Wellness Centre**, 234A Chillingham Rd, Heaton, Newcastle Upon Tyne, **Tyne and Wear**, NE6 5LP, ENG.
(T) 01912 094511
Speciality: Chiropractic. ✔
● **Owner** Mr R Millo Q: DC. M: SCA.
S Yrs. Est.: 1 (Ref:HM07083)

**FAMILY CHIROPRACTIC CENTRE**

**Family Chiropractic Centre**, 159 Kings Rd, Kingston Upon Thames, **Surrey**, KT2 5GG, ENG.
(T) 020 8286 2606
Speciality: Chiropractic.
P S T (Ref:HM07084)

**FAMILY CHIROPRACTIC CLINIC**

**Family Chiropractic Clinic**, 16-18 Glen Rd, Cumber, **County Down**, BT23 5EL, NIR.
(T) 028 9187 0770 (F) 028 2563 2951
(W) www.in8intelligence.co.uk
Speciality: Chiropractic.
● **Owner/Chiropractor** Dr C Stange Q: BSc, DC. M: GCC.
H Yrs. Est.: 4 (Ref:HM07085)

**FAMILY CLINIC**

**Family Clinic (The)**, 47 Central Drive, Romiley, Stockport, **Cheshire**, SK6 4PH, ENG.
(T) 01614 305980
Speciality: Homeopathy.
● **Owner** Mrs G Moore
M (Ref:HM07086)

**FAMILY FIRST**

**Family First**, 41 Terminus Rd, Eastbourne, **Sussex (East)**, BN21 3QL, ENG.
(T) 01323 734505
(E) paul@successuk.co.uk
(W) www.successuk.co.uk
Speciality: Bowen Therapy, Cognitive Therapy, Counselling, Holistic Healing, Hypnotherapy, Life Style Coaching, Neuro-Linguistic Program, Nutritional Therapy, Psychotherapy, Reiki. ✔
● **Owner** Mr P Burley Q: NLP. M: ALTT, ANLP, BTAA, BTER.
B Yrs. Est.: 3 (Ref:HM07087)

**FAMILY FOOT CARE SERVICES**

**Family Foot Care Services**, Guild House, 30-32 Worple Rd, London, **London (Greater)**, SW19 4EF, ENG.
(T) 020 8946 1038
Speciality: Chiropodists (Podiatrists).
● **Owner** Mrs L Papanicola
S (Ref:HM07088)

**FAMILY INSTITUTE**

**Family Institute**, Church St, Ballaghaderreen, **County Roscommon**, IRE.
(T) 09076 1000
Speciality: Psychotherapy.
B (Ref:HM07089)

**FAMILY NATURAL HEALTH CENTRE**

**Family Natural Health Centre (The)**, 106 Lordship Lane, London, **London (Greater)**, SE22 8HF, ENG.
(T) 020 8693 5515
Speciality: Complementary Medicines & Therapy.
● **Manager** Mrs T Brittaen
C M (Ref:HM07090)

**FAMILY PLANNING CLINIC**

**Family Planning Clinic**, Smithfield St, Amesbury, Salisbury, **Wiltshire**, SP4 7AL, ENG.
(T) 01980 625313
Speciality: Chiropodists (Podiatrists).
S (Ref:HM07091)

**FAMILY SCALP & HAIR CLINIC**

**Family Scalp & Hair Clinic (The)**, Claughton Medical Centre, 161 Park Rd North, Birkenhead, **Merseyside**, CH41 0DD, ENG.
(T) 01516 521688
Speciality: Complementary Medicines & Therapy, Trichology.
M (Ref:HM07092)

**FANE, AMANDA**

**Amanda Fane**, 77 De Vigier Avenue, Saffron Walden, **Essex**, CB10 2AY, ENG.
(T) 01799 523091
Speciality: Reflexology.
S T (Ref:HM07093)

**FANNING, DOUGLAS**

**Douglas Fanning**, Suite 5, 44 High St, Daventry, **Northamptonshire**, NN11 4HU, ENG.
(T) 01327 310018
Speciality: Chiropodists (Podiatrists).
S (Ref:HM07094)

**FANNING, M W**

**M W Fanning**, 1 Hutton Avenue, Houston, Johnstone, **Renfrewshire**, PA6 7JS, SCO.
(T) 01505 614897 (F) 01505 614897
Speciality: Herbal Medicine.
● **Medical Herbalist** Mrs M Fanning
C Yrs. Est.: 10 (Ref:HM07095)

**FANTHOM, J K**

**Mrs J K Fanthom**, 43 Starkie Drive, Oldbury, **Midlands (West)**, B68 9NX, ENG.
(T) 01215 521809
Speciality: Chiropodists (Podiatrists).
S (Ref:HM07096)

**FANTOM, L**

**L Fantom**, Castle Clinic, 5 Castle Hill Rd, Dover, **Kent**, CT16 1QG, ENG.
(T) 01304 202352 (F) 01304 216366
Speciality: Osteopathy.
● **Practice Manager** Ms J Lehane



Key: B Mind-Body Medicine C Complementary Medicine H Self Help Treatment M Medicinal Therapy O Oriental Medicine P Postural Therapy S Manipulative Structural Therapy T Touch Therapy

P S T (Ref:HM07097)

## FANYA, M M

**M M Fanya**, Coney Berry, Coneyhurst Lane, Ewhurst, Cranleigh, **Surrey**, GU6 7PL, ENG.
(T) 01483 277252
Speciality: Physiotherapy.
P S T (Ref:HM07098)

## FAR EASTERN MASSAGE

**Far Eastern Massage**, 8 St Stephens Cres, London, **London (Greater)**, W2 5QT, ENG.
(T) 020 7243 0577
Speciality: Aromatherapy.
● **Owner** Miss S Yeoh
M O (Ref:HM07099)

## FARAGO CLINIC

**Farago Clinic**, 47 Alma Rd, Windsor, **Berkshire**, SL4 3HH, ENG.
(T) 01753 861082 (F) 01753 869447
Speciality: Hypnosis.
● **Owner** Mr R Farago
B (Ref:HM07100)

## FARBER, AARON

**Aaron Farber**, Little Bees, Whitemans Green, Cuckfield, Haywards Heath, **Sussex (West)**, RH17 5DB, ENG.
(T) 01444 452220
Speciality: Chiropractic.
● **Owner** Mr A Farber
P S T (Ref:HM07101)

## FAREHAM CHIROPRACTIC CENTRE

**Fareham Chiropractic Centre**, Croad Court, 6a High St, Fareham, **Hampshire**, PO16 7AN, ENG.
(T) 01329 828822
Speciality: Chiropractic.
P S T (Ref:HM07102)

## FAREHAM PHYSIOTHERAPHY SVS

**Fareham Physiotheraphy Services**, Frosthole Cl, Fareham, **Hampshire**, PO15 6DE, ENG.
(T) 01329 232263 (F) 01329 284049
Speciality: Physiotherapy.
P S T (Ref:HM07103)

## FARIS, MUTAIRI

**Mutairi Faris**, 3 Charleston Rd, Rathmines, **County Dublin**, IRE.
(T) 01497 5666
Speciality: Psychology.
B (Ref:HM07104)

## FARLEIGH, CLARE E

**Clare E Farleigh**, St Mary's Practice, Lower Olland St, Bungay, **Suffolk**, NR35 1BY, ENG.
(T) 01986 892846
Speciality: Osteopathy.
P S T (Ref:HM07105)

## FARMACIA F2

**Farmacia F2**, 42 Shorts Gdns, London, **London (Greater)**, WC2H 9AB, ENG.
(T) 020 7836 3179
Speciality: Complementary Medicines & Therapy.
● **Branch Manager** Mr I Ahmed
C M (Ref:HM07106)

## FARMACIA URBAN HEALING

**Farmacia Urban Healing**, 169 Drury Lane, Covent Garden, London, **London (Greater)**, WC2B 5QA, ENG.
(T) 020 7404 8808
Speciality: Acupuncture, Aromatherapy, Cranio-Sacral Therapy, Herbal Medicine, Hypnosis, Indian Head Massage, Massage (Therapeutic), Naturopathy, Neuro-Linguistic Program, Nutritional Therapy, Osteopathy, Reflexology, Shiatsu, Swedish Body Massage.
P S T (Ref:HM07107)

## FARMER, BARBARA

**Barbara J Farmer - Physiotherapist**, 65A Bidston Rd, Oxton, Prenton, **Merseyside**, CH43 6TR, ENG.
(T) 01516 521002
(E) bjfarmer@btclick.com
Speciality: Electrotherapy, Phytotherapy, Stress Therapy, Ultrasonics. ✔
● **Physiotherapist** Mrs B Farmer Q: MCSP, SRP.
M: CSP.
M P S Yrs. Est.: 10 (Ref:HM01681)

## FARMER, F F

**F F Farmer**, 19 Alma Rd, Cardiff, **Glamorgan (Vale of)**, CF23 5BD, WAL.
(T) 029 2049 5762
Speciality: Acupuncture.
● **Owner** Ms F Farmer
O (Ref:HM07108)

## FARMER, RON

**Ron Farmer**, Three Gables, Woolsery, Bideford, **Devon**, EX39 5PZ, ENG.
(T) 01237 431698
Speciality: Hypnosis.
B (Ref:HM07109)

## FARMER, VAL

**Val Farmer**, Ashover, **Derbyshire**, S45, ENG.
(T) 01246 590995
Speciality: Bach Remedies.
M (Ref:HM07110)

## FARNBOROUGH CHIRO CLINIC

**Farnborough Chiropractic Clinic**, 101A Mytchett Rd, Mytchett, Camberley, **Surrey**, GU16 6ES, ENG.
(T) 01252 404240 (F) 01252 404239
(E) farnborough.chiropratic@virgin.net
Speciality: Chiropractic. ✔
● **Chiropractor** Mr R Scott Q: BSc (Chiro).
M: BCA, GCC.
S Yrs. Est.: 5 (Ref:HM07111)

## FARNHAM CHIROPRACTIC CLINIC

**Farnham Chiropractic Clinic**, 1 South Avenue, Heath End, Farnham, **Surrey**, GU9 0QY, ENG.
(T) 01252 710549
Speciality: Chiropractic.
P S T (Ref:HM07112)

## FARNHILL, SANDRA M

**Sandra M Farnhill**, Seedhill Chambers, 38A Church St, Littleborough, **Manchester (Greater)**, OL15 9AA, ENG.
(T) 01706 377620
Speciality: Chiropodists (Podiatrists).
S (Ref:HM07113)

## FAROOQ AHMED, KHAN

**Khan Farooq Ahmed**, 121 Liverpool Rd, Upton, Chester, **Cheshire**, CH2 1BB, ENG.
(T) 01244 375277
Speciality: Osteopathy.
P S T (Ref:HM07114)

## FAROOQ AHMED, KHAN

**Khan Farooq Ahmed**, 4th Floor, City Buildings, 21-23 Old Hall St, Liverpool, **Merseyside**, L3 9BS, ENG.
(T) 01512 369722 (F) 01244 375277
Speciality: Osteopathy.
● **Principal** Mr F Khan
P S T (Ref:HM07115)

## FARQUHAR, KATE

**Kate Farquhar**, 169 Peckham Rye, London, **London (Greater)**, SE15 3HZ, ENG.
(T) 020 7277 6890
Speciality: Psychotherapy.
B (Ref:HM07116)

## FARRAND, ELAINE

**Elaine Farrand**, 15 Toseland Way, Lower Earley, Reading, **Berkshire**, RG6 7YA, ENG.
(T) 01189 662335
Speciality: Chiropodists (Podiatrists).
S (Ref:HM07117)

## FARRANT, A

**A Farrant**, Mangreen Hall, Swardeston, Norwich, **Norfolk**, NR14 8DD, ENG.
(T) 01508 578899
Speciality: Acupuncture.
● **Owner** A Farrant
O (Ref:HM07118)

## FARRANT, A F

**A F Farrant**, 1st Floor Woburn Court, 8 Guildhall Hill, Norwich, **Norfolk**, NR2 1JG, ENG.
(T) 01603 219254
Speciality: Acupuncture.
● **Practice Manager** Mrs V Ryan
O (Ref:HM07119)

## FARRANT, A F

**A F Farrant**, Washlane Barn, Shotesham St. Mary, Norwich, **Norfolk**, NR15 1XX, ENG.
(T) 01508 550214
Speciality: Acupuncture.
● **Owner** Ms A Farrant
O (Ref:HM07120)

## FARRANT, EMMA

**Emma Farrant**, 62 Paul St, London, **London (Greater)**, EC2A 4NA, ENG.
(T) 020 7251 4429 (F) 020 7613 4737
Speciality: Complementary Medicines & Therapy.
M (Ref:HM07121)

## FARRANT, F L

**F L Farrant**, Cynlas, Rhostryfan, Caernarfon, **Gwynedd**, LL54 7NL, WAL.
(T) 01286 831433
Speciality: Homeopathy.
● **Owner** Mrs F Farrant
M (Ref:HM07122)

## FARRANT, K E

**K E Farrant**, 11 Beach Rd, West Mersea, Colchester, **Essex**, CO5 8AA, ENG.
(T) 01206 385362
Speciality: Osteopathy.
P S T (Ref:HM07123)

## FARRAR, JOHN

**John Farrar**, Health Hydro, Milton Rd, Swindon, **Wiltshire**, SN1 5JA, ENG.
(T) 01793 465631
Speciality: Complementary Medicines & Therapy.
M (Ref:HM07124)

## FARRAR, JOHN A

**John A Farrar**, 22 Greywethers Avenue, Swindon, **Wiltshire**, SN3 1QF, ENG.
(T) 01793 520544
Speciality: Complementary Medicines & Therapy.
● **Owner** Mr J Farrar
C M (Ref:HM07125)

## FARRAR, SHARON

**Sharon Farrar**, 9 Swinecarr Avenue, Yeadon, Leeds, **Yorkshire (West)**, LS19 7PF, ENG.
(T) 01132 509978
Speciality: Chiropodists (Podiatrists).
● **Owner** Ms S Farrar
S (Ref:HM07126)

## FARRELL, BARBARA

**Barbara Farrell**, 19 Tudor Grange, Lisburn, **County Antrim**, BT28 3PJ, NIR.
(T) 028 9260 1613
Speciality: Reflexology.
S T (Ref:HM07127)

## FARRELL, CARMEL

**Carmel Farrell D O , M R O**, Friary Ct Friary St, **County Kilkenny**, IRE.
(T) 05665 221
Speciality: Complementary Medicines & Therapy.
M (Ref:HM07128)

## FARRELL, DEREK P

**Derek P Farrell**, Charter House, 11-13 Downham Rd South, Wirral, **Merseyside**, CH60 5RG, ENG.
(T) 01513 429601
Speciality: Psychotherapy.
● **Owner** Mr D Farrell
B (Ref:HM07129)

## FARRER, PAMELA PALMER

**Pamela Palmer Farrer**, 29 Mount Park Cres, London, **London (Greater)**, W5 2RN, ENG.
(T) 020 8991 1313 (F) 020 8991 1313
Speciality: Hypnotherapy.
● **Owner** Mrs P Palmer-Farrer
B (Ref:HM07130)

## FARRER, R H

**R H Farrer**, 43 Half Moon Cr, Oadby, Leicester, **Leicestershire**, LE2 4HD, ENG.
(T) 01162 712520
Speciality: Acupuncture.
● **Owner** Mr R Farrer



Key continued: Yrs.Est: Years Established Q: Qualifications M: Professional Membership ✔ Indemnity Insurance Accept Credit Cards

O (Ref:HM07131)

## FARRER-BROWN HISTOPATHOLOGY

**Farrer-Brown Histopathology Ltd**, Bewlay House, 32 Jamestown Rd, London, **London (Greater)**, NW1 7BY, ENG.
(T) 020 7333 0585 (F) 020 7333 0586
Speciality: Complementary Medicines & Therapy.
● **Manager** Dr J Firth
C M (Ref:HM07132)

## FARRIER, M

**M Farrier**, 31 Kiln Rd, Fareham, **Hampshire**, PO16 7UQ, ENG.
(T) 01329 287690 (F) 01329 826488
Speciality: Hypnosis.
● **Owner** Mr M Farrier
B (Ref:HM07133)

## FARRINGTON, C

**C Farrington**, 17 Park Cres, Cardiff, **Glamorgan (Vale of)**, CF14 7AQ, WAL.
(T) 029 2061 0730
Speciality: Reflexology.
● **Owner** Mrs C Farrinton
S T (Ref:HM07134)

## FARROW, VICKI

**Vicki Farrow**, 4 Port Lane, Colchester, **Essex**, CO1 2JF, ENG.
(T) 01206 525155
(E) vicki.farrow@ntlworld.com
Speciality: Aromatherapy, Complementary Therapy, Crystal Healing, Healing Therapy, Indian Head Massage, Reflexology, Reiki. ✔
● **Aromatherapist/Reflexologist**
Ms V Farrow M: ICHT.
B Yrs. Est.: 2 (Ref:HM07135)

## FARTHING, ANN

**Ann Farthing**, The Basement, 2 Northumberland Pl, North Shields, **Tyne and Wear**, NE30 1QP, ENG.
(T) 01912 962159
Speciality: Osteopathy.
P S T (Ref:HM07136)

## FARUKI, SHIRLEY

**Shirley Faruki**, 38 Pulteney Rd, London, **London (Greater)**, E18 1PS, ENG.
(T) 020 8989 6734
Speciality: Hypnosis.
● **Owner** Mrs S Faruki
B (Ref:HM07137)

## FARVIS, KEITH

**Keith Farvis**, 1 Jackson's Cl, 209 High St, Edinburgh, **Edinburgh (City of)**, EH1 1PZ, SCO.
(T) 01314 478292
Speciality: Complementary Medicines & Therapy.
C M (Ref:HM07138)

## FARWELL, S E

**S E Farwell**, 40 Grafton Rd, London, **London (Greater)**, W3 6PB, ENG.
(T) 020 8993 1994 (F) 020 8992 1945
Speciality: Osteopathy.
● **Owner** Miss S Farwell
P S T (Ref:HM07139)

## FARYNA, WARREN G

**Warren G Faryna**, 48A Barton Hill Rd, Torquay, **Devon**, TQ2 8JD, ENG.
(T) 01803 329799
Speciality: Chiropractors.
P S T (Ref:HM07140)

## FAULKNER, CINDY

**Cindy Faulkner BA MRSS**, 35 Finchams Cl, Linton, Cambridge, **Cambridgeshire**, CB1 6ND, ENG.
(T) 01223 890832
(E) pwhite@i12.com
Speciality: Acupressure, Acupuncture, Massage (Therapeutic), Shiatsu. ✔
● **Acupuncturist** Mr P White Q: BA, MBAcC. M: BAcC.
● **Shiatsu Practitioner**
Ms C Faulkner Q: BA, MRSS. M: Shiatsu Society UK.
O Yrs. Est.: 1 (Ref:HM07141)

## FAULKNER, JAMES

**James Faulkner**, 37 Glenmore Rd, Carterton, **Oxfordshire**, OX18 1TU, ENG.
(T) 01993 846717
Speciality: Hypnosis.
B (Ref:HM07142)

## FAULKNER, M

**M Faulkner**, 39 Tydfil Pl, Cardiff, **Glamorgan (Vale of)**, CF23 5HP, WAL.
(T) 029 2048 4555
Speciality: Chiropractors.
P S T (Ref:HM07143)

## FAULKNER, MICHELLE

**Michelle Faulkner**, 2 Acres Lane, Stalybridge, **Manchester (Greater)**, SK15 2JU, ENG.
(T) 01613 387690
Speciality: Chiropodists (Podiatrists).
● **Owner** Mr M Smith
S (Ref:HM07144)

## FAULKNER, SUSAN

**Susan Faulkner**, 31 Hathaway Rd, Coventry, **Midlands (West)**, CV4 9HW, ENG.
(T) 024 7647 3727
Speciality: Chiropractic.
● **Owner** Mrs S Faulkner
P S T (Ref:HM07145)

## FAVERSHAM CLINIC

**Faversham Clinic Of Classical Homoeopathy**, 42 Ospringe Rd, Faversham, **Kent**, ME13 7LJ, ENG.
(T) 01795 535143
Speciality: Homeopathy.
M (Ref:HM07146)

## FAWKES, CAROL

**Carol Fawkes**, 301 Daventry Rd, Coventry, **Midlands (West)**, CV3 5HJ, ENG.
(T) 024 7650 5997
Speciality: Osteopathy.
● **Owner** Miss C Fawkes
P S T (Ref:HM07147)

## FAWKES, R E

**R E Fawkes**, 1 Crowther Cl, Staplehurst, Tonbridge, **Kent**, TN12 0NQ, ENG.
(T) 01580 892097
Speciality: Chiropodists (Podiatrists).
● **Owner** Mr R Fawkes
S (Ref:HM07148)

## FAWKES, R H

**R H Fawkes**, 51 Stamford Avenue, Coventry, **Midlands (West)**, CV3 5BW, ENG.
(T) 024 7641 4451
Speciality: Chiropodists (Podiatrists).
● **Owner** Mr R Fawkes
S (Ref:HM07149)

## FAY, ESTHER

**Esther Fay**, 81 Glenfield Avenue, **Hampshire**, SO18 4ET, ENG.
(T) 023 8055 3936
Speciality: Reflexology.
S T (Ref:HM07150)

## FAY, GLENDA

**Glenda Fay**, 24 Scotter Rd, Eastleigh, **Hampshire**, SO50 6AJ, ENG.
(T) 023 8061 3802
Speciality: Clairvoyants & Palmists.
● **Owner** Mrs G Kimber
B (Ref:HM07151)

## FAY, JOHN (DR)

**Dr John Fay**, 126 Cloncaf Rd, Dublin, **County Dublin**, IRE.
(T) 01853 2011
Speciality: Chiropractors.
P S T (Ref:HM07152)

## FAY, PAULINE

**Pauline Fay**, 174A London Rd, Worcester, **Worcestershire**, WR5 2EJ, ENG.
(T) 01905 354555 (F) 01905 354555
Speciality: Physiotherapy.
● **Practice Manager** Mrs M Dring
P S T (Ref:HM07153)

## FEARGAL, TOBIN

**Tobin Feargal**, 3 The Cova 163 Whitehall Rd, Dublin, **County Dublin**, IRE.
(T) 01465 0030
(W) www.buteykoireland.com
Speciality: Chiropractors.
P S T (Ref:HM07154)

## FEATHER, A J

**A J Feather**, 17 Mayhurst Cres, Woking, **Surrey**, GU22 8DG, ENG.
(T) 01483 772101
Speciality: Cranio-Sacral Therapy, Osteopathy. ✔
● **Owner** A Feather
C Yrs. Est.: 21 (Ref:HM07155)

## FEATHERSTONE (DR)

**Dr Featherstone**, Health Works, 5 Bank Lane, Forres, **Moray**, IV36 1NU, SCO.
(T) 01309 690943
Speciality: Complementary Medicines & Therapy.
C M (Ref:HM07156)

## FEATHERSTONE, ROSIE

**Rosie Featherstone**, 52 Mount St, Shrewsbury, **Shropshire**, SY3 8QH, ENG.
(T) 01743 232636
Speciality: Homeopathy.
● **Owner** Ms R Featherston
M (Ref:HM07157)

## FEATHERSTONE, ROSIE

**Rosie Featherstone**, The Cottage Hospital Care Centre, Edgmond, Newport, **Shropshire**, TF10 8JN, ENG.
(T) 01743 232636
Speciality: Homeopathy.
● **Owner** Ms R Featherstone
M (Ref:HM07158)

## FEATHERSTONE-GRIFFIN, B

**B Featherstone-Griffin**, 102 Grosvenor Avenue, Carshalton, **Surrey**, SM5 3EP, ENG.
(T) 020 8647 1860
Speciality: Chiropodists (Podiatrists).
● **Owner** Mrs B Featherstone-Griffin
S (Ref:HM07159)

## FEATURES OF HOVE

**Features Of Hove**, 58A New Church Rd, Hove, **Sussex (East)**, BN3 4FL, ENG.
(T) 01273 726575
Speciality: Chiropodists (Podiatrists).
● **Partner** Miss J Haydon
S (Ref:HM07160)

## FED OF HOLISTIC THERAPISTS

**Federation Of Holistic Therapists**, Eastleigh House, Market St, Eastleigh, **Hampshire**, SO50 9FD, ENG.
(T) 023 8048 8900 (F) 023 8048 8970
(W) www.fht.org.uk
Speciality: Complementary Medicines & Therapy.
● **Chief Executive Officer**
Wallace Samuel Sharps
● **Manager** Mrs J Palmer
C (Ref:HM07161)

## FEDER, A P

**A P Feder**, 163 Wincheap, Canterbury, **Kent**, CT1 3SE, ENG.
(T) 01227 457105
Speciality: Chiropodists (Podiatrists).
● **Owner** Mrs A Feder
S (Ref:HM07162)

## FEEHAN, SEAMAS

**Feehan Seamas**, Corrinview, Fermoy, **County Cork**, IRE.
(T) 025 3291 0
Speciality: Complementary Medicines & Therapy.
M (Ref:HM07163)

## FEEL GOOD AROMATHERAPY

**Feel Good Aromatherapy**, Feel Good House, 1 Hartley Gardens, Sunderland, **Tyne and Wear**, SR5 1PY, ENG.
(T) 01915 498626 (F) 01915 498626
Speciality: Aromatherapy, Complementary Therapy, Counselling, Dietician, Healer, Herbal Medicine, Life Style Coaching, Naturopathy, Psychotherapy, Vitamin Therapy. ✔



Key: B Mind-Body Medicine C Complementary Medicine H Self Help Treatment M Medicinal Therapy O Oriental Medicine P Postural Therapy S Manipulative Structural Therapy T Touch Therapy

● **Therapist** Ms S Morton
**B** (Ref:HM07164)

## FEEL GOOD FACTOR

**Feel Good Factor (The)**, 93 Blaby Rd, Wigston, **Leicestershire**, LE18 4PB, ENG.
(T) 01162 778373
Speciality: Complementary Medicines & Therapy.
**C M** (Ref:HM07165)

## FEEL GOOD FACTORY

**Feel Good Factory**, 252 Lavender Hill, London, **London (Greater)**, SW11 1LJ, ENG.
(T) 020 7350 1600 (F) 020 7924 1600
Speciality: Complementary Medicines & Therapy.
● **Director** Mr R Hewitt
**C M** (Ref:HM07166)

## FEET FIRST

**Feet First**, 10 Bramley Pl, Crayford, **Kent**, DA1 4NB, ENG.
(T) 01322 400902
Speciality: Reflexology. ✔
● **Reflexologist** Miss L Cope Q: MBRA. M: BRA.
**C** (Ref:HM07167)

## FEET FIRST

**Feet First**, 80 Austhorpe Rd, Leeds, **Yorkshire (West)**, LS15 8DZ, ENG.
(T) 01132 266677
Speciality: Chiropodists (Podiatrists).
**S** (Ref:HM07168)

## FEET FIRST

**Feet First**, Derby Chambers, 6 The Rock, Bury, **Lancashire**, BL9 0NT, ENG.
(T) 01617 972040
Speciality: Chiropodists (Podiatrists).
● **Owner** Miss N McEntyre
**S** (Ref:HM07169)

## FEET FIRST

**Feet First**, Care Of Mahogany Hair & Beauty, Cockleton Lane, Cowes, **Isle of Wight**, PO31 8QE, ENG.
(T) 01983 282520
Speciality: Reflexology.
● **Owner** Mrs C Hurley
**S T** (Ref:HM07170)

## FEET FIRST

**Feet First**, 10 Station Rd, Poole, **Dorset**, BH14 8UB, ENG.
(T) 01202 736749
Speciality: Chiropody. ✔ [credit card]
● **Owner** Ms K Harris Q: S.R.Ch. M: S.C.P.
**M** Yrs. Est.: 11 (Ref:HM07171)

## FEET FIRST

**Feet First**, 94 Cutenhoe Rd, Luton, **Bedfordshire**, LU1 3NF, ENG.
(T) 01582 526724 (F) 01582 391515
Speciality: Reflexology.
● **Owner** Mrs Z Rankin
**S T** (Ref:HM07172)

## FEET FIRST

**Feet First**, 70 Market St, Edenfield, Ramsbottom, Bury, **Lancashire**, BL0 0JL, ENG.
(T) 01706 823637
Speciality: Reflexology.
**S T** (Ref:HM07173)

## FEET FIRST

**Feet First**, 5 Pump St, Londonderry, **County Londonderry**, BT48 6JG, NIR.
(T) 028 7128 4010
Speciality: Biomechanics, Chiropody, Nail Surgery, Podiatry. ✔
● **Chiropodist** Ms L Whiley Q: BSc, S.R.Ch. M: S.C.P.
**M** Yrs. Est.: 3 (Ref:HM07174)

## FEET FIRST

**Feet First**, 33 Causewayside, Edinburgh, **Edinburgh (City of)**, EH9 1QF, SCO.
(T) 01316 629686
Speciality: Chiropodists (Podiatrists).
**S** (Ref:HM07175)

## FEET FIRST

**Feet First**, 17 Barracks Rd, Newcastle, **Staffordshire**, ST5 1LF, ENG.
(T) 01782 712111
Speciality: Biomechanics, Chiropody, Nail Surgery, Podiatry. ✔
● **Chiropodist (Podiatrist)**
Mr P Reece Q: BSc (Hons). M: S.C.P, S.R.Ch.
**C** Yrs. Est.: 3 (Ref:HM07176)

## FEET FIRST

**Feet First**, 16 Queens Rd, Southend-On-Sea, **Essex**, SS1 1LU, ENG.
(T) 01702 390855
Speciality: Chiropodists (Podiatrists).
**S** (Ref:HM07177)

## FEET FIRST

**Feet First**, Brook Farm Cottage, Old Moss Lane, Tarvin, Chester, **Cheshire**, CH3 8HN, ENG.
(T) 01829 741653
Speciality: Reflexology.
● **Owner** Miss H Atkins
**S T** (Ref:HM07178)

## FEET FIRST

**Feet First**, 44 Aylesbury Rd, Thame, **Oxfordshire**, OX9 3AW, ENG.
(T) 01844 261023
(E) lou@feet-first.org
(W) www.feet-first.org
Speciality: Chiropody, Reflexology. ✔
● **Chiropodist/Reflexologist**
Ms L Hallewell Q: MAR, MBChA, MSSCh. M: AoR, B.A.Ch.P.
**T** Yrs. Est.: 5 (Ref:HM07179)

## FEET FIRST

**Feet First**, 49 Devoran Lane, Devoran, Truro, **Cornwall**, TR3 6PD, ENG.
(T) 01872 864906
Speciality: Naturopathy, Reflexology.
● **Owner** Ms M Francis Q: ITEC, MAR, NAT. M: AoR.
**T** (Ref:HM07180)

## FEET FIRST CHIROPODY

**Feet First Chiropody**, 1 Shelley Lane, Kirkburton, Huddersfield, **Yorkshire (West)**, HD8 0SJ, ENG.
(T) 01484 607615
Speciality: Chiropodists (Podiatrists).
**S** (Ref:HM07181)

## FEET FIRST CHIROPODY CLINIC

**Feet First Chiropody Clinic**, 161 Hook Rd, Surbiton, **Surrey**, KT6 5AR, ENG.
(T) 020 8397 6311
Speciality: Chiropodists (Podiatrists).
● **Owner** Mrs C Samson
**S** (Ref:HM07182)

## FEET FIRST MOBILE CHIROPODY SV

**Feet First Mobile Chiropody Service**, Beechcroft Hunts Lane, Stockton Heath, Warrington, **Cheshire**, WA4 2DT, ENG.
(T) 01925 602181
Speciality: Chiropody. ✔
● **Owner** Mr M Holmes M: Inst.CH.P.
**P** Yrs. Est.: 6 (Ref:HM07183)

## FEET FOR LIFE

**Feet For Life**, 12 Bishopstoke Rd, Eastleigh, **Hampshire**, SO50 6AE, ENG. .
(T) 023 8065 0676
Speciality: Chiropodists (Podiatrists).
● **Partner** Miss E Scott
**S** (Ref:HM07184)

## FEET ON THE HILL

**Feet On The Hill**, 3 High St, Hampton Hill, Hampton, **London (Greater)**, TW12 1NP, ENG.
(T) 020 8941 9616
Speciality: Chiropodists (Podiatrists).
**S** (Ref:HM07185)

## FEET TREAT

**Feet Treat**, Park Cottage, Warren Rd, Wash Common, Newbury, **Berkshire**, RG14 6NH, ENG.
(T) 01635 31597
(E) janecullimore@feettreatfsbusiness.co.uk
Speciality: Floral Essence Therapy, Indian Head Massage, Reflexology. ✔
● **Reflexologist** Ms J Cullimore
**T** Yrs. Est.: 2 (Ref:HM07186)

## FEILDER, JEREMY P

**Mr Jeremy P Feilder**, East Finchley Osteopathic Practice, 168 High Rd, London, **London (Greater)**, N2 9AS, ENG.
(T) 020 8365 2841
Speciality: Osteopathy.
**P S T** (Ref:HM07187)

## FEIST, ANNE

**Anne Feist**, Thorne Oast Clinic, Ninfield Rd, Bexhill-on-Sea, **Sussex (East)**, TN39 5JP, ENG.
(T) 01424 892272
Speciality: Homeopathy.
● **Owner** Mrs A Feist
**M** (Ref:HM07188)

## FELCE, S E

**S E Felce**, 161 Box End Rd, Moorend, Bromham, Bedford, **Bedfordshire**, MK43 8LU, ENG.
(T) 01234 853056
Speciality: Chiropodists (Podiatrists).
**S** (Ref:HM07189)

## FELDENKRAIS CENTRE

**Feldenkrais Centre(London) (The)**, 10 Fernside Court, London, **London (Greater)**, NW4 1JT, ENG.
(T) 020 8346 0258 (F) 020 8346 0258
Speciality: Feldenkrais Methodology. ✔
● **Practitioner** Dr Pfeffer Q: PhD. M: FGUK.
**C T** Yrs. Est.: 5 (Ref:HM07190)

## FELDENKRAIS GUILD UK

**Feldenkrais Guild UK**, P.O. Box 370, London, **London (Greater)**, NW11 7EA, ENG.
(T) 020 8458 9200
Speciality: Complementary Medicines & Therapy.
**C M** (Ref:HM07191)

## FELDENKRAIS METHOD

**Feldenkrais Method**, 112 Kidbrooke Pk Rd, London, **London (Greater)**, SE3 0DX, ENG.
(T) 020 8856 3850
Speciality: Complementary Medicines & Therapy.
● **Owner** Ms J Atkins
**M** (Ref:HM07192)

## FELDMAN, L H

**L H Feldman**, 23 Merrivale Avenue, Ilford, **Essex**, IG4 5PQ, ENG.
(T) 020 8550 5675 (F) 020 8550 5675
Speciality: Homeopathy.
● **Owner** Mr L Feldman
**M** (Ref:HM07193)

## FELDMAN, L H

**L H Feldman**, 399 Stradbroke Gr, Ilford, **Essex**, IG5 0DE, ENG.
(T) 020 8550 5675
Speciality: Homeopathy.
**M** (Ref:HM07194)

## FELDMAN, LARAINE

**Laraine Feldman**, 37 Greenway, London, **London (Greater)**, N14 6NR, ENG.
(T) 020 8882 5134
Speciality: Alexander Technique.
● **Owner** L Feldman
**P S** (Ref:HM07195)

## FELDMANN, MARGARET

**Margaret Feldmann**, 274 Knightsfield, Welwyn Garden City, **Hertfordshire**, AL8 7RB, ENG.
(T) 01707 372829
Speciality: Electrolysis.
● **Owner** Mrs M Feldmann
**T** (Ref:HM07196)

## FELFELLI, FARA

**Fara Felfelli**, 588 Eastern Avenue, Ilford, **Essex**, IG2 6PQ, ENG.
(T) 020 8554 6166
Speciality: Osteopathy.
**P S T** (Ref:HM07197)

## FELIX, S Z

**S Z Felix**, 20 Ashleigh Rd, Barnstaple, **Devon**, EX32 8JY, ENG.
(T) 01271 329897
Speciality: Chiropodists (Podiatrists).
● **Owner** Mrs S Felix
**S** (Ref:HM07198)



Key continued: Yrs.Est: Years Established Q: Qualifications M: Professional Membership ✔ Indemnity Insurance [credit card] Accept Credit Cards

## FELIX, S Z
**S Z Felix**, Boutport Chiropody Clinic, Loverings Court, 27 Boutport St, Barnstaple, **Devon**, EX31 1RP, ENG.
(T) 01271 323392
Speciality: Chiropodists (Podiatrists).
S (Ref:HM07199)

## FELIXSTOWE CHIROPRACTIC CLINIC
**Felixstowe Chiropractic Clinic**, 1 Kiligarth Court, Wolsey Gdns, Felixstowe, **Suffolk**, IP11 7NU, ENG.
(T) 01394 672014 (F) 01473 463344
Speciality: Chiropractic.
● **Owner** Mr J Wilhelm
P S T (Ref:HM07200)

## FELIXSTOWE COUNS & PYSCHO CTRE
**Felixstowe Counselling & Pyschotherapy Centre (The)**, Walton House, 218 High St, Felixstowe, **Suffolk**, IP11 9DS, ENG.
(T) 01394 385915
Speciality: Psychotherapy.
● **Director** Mr M Rivers
B (Ref:HM07201)

## FELIXSTOWE HEALING SANCTUARY
**Felixstowe Healing Sanctuary**, 16 Manwick Rd, Felixstowe, **Suffolk**, IP11 2DQ, ENG.
(T) 01394 286671
Speciality: Complementary Medicines & Therapy.
C M (Ref:HM07202)

## FELIXSTOWE PHYSIO PRACTICE
**Felixstowe Physiotherapy Practice**, Walton House, 218 High St, Felixstowe, **Suffolk**, IP11 9DS, ENG.
(T) 01394 282002 (F) 01394 286105
Speciality: Physiotherapy, Hydrotherapy. ✔
● **Physiotherapist** J Morgan Q: MCSP, SRP. M: CSP.
● **Owner/Physiotherapist** Ms K Wickens Q: MCSP, MMACP, SRP. M: CSP.
● **Physiotherapist** S Di Ponio Q: MCSP, SRP. M: CSP.
● **Physiotherapist** Mrs M Stephens Q: MCSP, SRP. M: CSP.
● **Physiotherapist** Mr M Rapkin Q: MCSP, SRP. M: CSP.
● **Practice Manager** Mrs C Gabriel
S Yrs. Est.: 14 (Ref:HM07203)

## FELL, HELEN
**Helen Fell**, 64 Lynwood Avenue, Plymouth, **Devon**, PL7 4SF, ENG.
(T) 01752 335314
Speciality: Reflexology.
S T (Ref:HM07204)

## FELLOWS, DOROTHY
**Dorothy Fellows**, 91 Highdown Drive, Wick, Littlehampton, **Sussex (West)**, BN17 6HT, ENG.
(T) 01903 721429
Speciality: Complementary Medicines & Therapy.
C M (Ref:HM07205)

## FELPHAM NATURAL HEALTH CLINIC
**Felpham Natural Health Clinic**, Ventura, 12 Roundle Sq Rd, Bognor Regis, **Sussex (West)**, PO22 8JX, ENG.
(T) 01243 583963
Speciality: Allergy Testing, Bach Remedies, Complementary Therapy, Healer, Healing Therapy, Indian Head Massage, Manipulation, Massage (Therapeutic), Reflexology, Spiritual Healing, Stress Therapy, Pelvic Alignmment, Vitamin and mineral Deficiency, Massage during pregnancy. ✔
● **Complementary Health Therapist** Mr S Leftwich Q: ITEC. M: BCMA, IFR, IPTI.
● **Complementary Health Therapist** Mrs C Leftwich Q: ITEC. M: BCMA, IFR.
S Yrs. Est.: 8 (Ref:HM07206)

## FELSTEAD, PETER
**Peter Felstead**, 12 Trefusis Rd, Falmouth, **Cornwall**, TR11 4QQ, ENG.
(T) 01326 319152
Speciality: Reflexology.
S T (Ref:HM07207)

## FELTHAM, N
**Mrs N Feltham**, Westfield, 13 Hill Rd, Carshalton, **Surrey**, SM5 3RA, ENG.
(T) 020 8669 4309
Speciality: Physiotherapy.
P S T (Ref:HM07208)

## FEMME BEAUTY CLINIC
**Femme Beauty Clinic**, 52 Market St, Ashby-de-la-Zouch, **Leicestershire**, LE65 1AN, ENG.
(T) 01530 413678
Speciality: Electrolysis.
● **Owner** Mrs L Reading
T (Ref:HM07209)

## FENG SHUI
**Feng Shui**, Unit 38, The Guildhall, Derby, **Derbyshire**, DE1 2DB, ENG.
(T) 01332 360000 (F) 01332 360000
Speciality: Feng Shui.
● **Owner** Miss T Brooks
M (Ref:HM07210)

## FENG SHUI
**Feng Shui (Authentic)**, **County Cork**, IRE.
(T) 021 4897 229
(E) email:fengshuimasterint@email.net
Speciality: Complementary Medicines & Therapy.
M (Ref:HM07211)

## FENG SHUI
**Feng Shui**, Parchey Cottage, Chedzoy, Bridgwater, **Somerset**, TA7 8RW, ENG.
(T) 01278 433523
Speciality: Complementary Medicines & Therapy.
C M (Ref:HM07212)

## FENG SHUI ACADEMY
**Feng Shui Academy (The)**, Eastgate House, Ann St, Leicester, **Leicestershire**, LE1 1SR, ENG.
(T) 01162 244991 (F) 01162 244992
Speciality: Feng Shui.
● **Manager** Miss K McKgouh
M (Ref:HM07213)

## FENG, W W
**W W Feng**, First Floor Suite 1, Norden House, 41 Stowell St, Newcastle Upon Tyne, **Tyne and Wear**, NE1 4YB, ENG.
(T) 01912 210090
Speciality: Acupuncture.
O (Ref:HM07214)

## FENN, AILEEN
**Aileen Fenn**, 4 Mount View, Northwood, **London (Greater)**, HA6 3NZ, ENG.
(T) 01923 827756
Speciality: Osteopathy.
P S T (Ref:HM07215)

## FENN, JASON
**Jason Fenn**, 25 Stour Avenue, Felixstowe, **Suffolk**, IP11 2NR, ENG.
(T) 01394 277162
Speciality: Reflexology.
S T (Ref:HM07216)

## FENN, SHEILA
**Sheila Fenn**, 50 Hillside Cres, Enfield, **London (Greater)**, EN2 0HR, ENG.
(T) 020 8363 7226
Speciality: Chiropodists (Podiatrists).
● **Owner** Mrs S Fenn
S (Ref:HM07217)

## FENNELL, JOHN
**John Fennell**, Ballykett, **County Clare**, IRE.
(T) 06590 51230
Speciality: Acupuncture.
O (Ref:HM07218)

## FENSTANTON PHYSIOTHERAPY
**Fenstanton Physiotherapy**, Montagu House, The Gables, Hilton Rd, Fenstanton, Huntingdon, **Cambridgeshire**, PE18 9LJ, ENG.
(T) 01480 460049
Speciality: Physiotherapy.
P S T (Ref:HM07219)

## FENTON, D
**D Fenton**, 22 Lough Rd, Lisburn, **County Antrim**, BT27 6TS, NIR.
(T) 028 9263 9083
Speciality: Chiropodists (Podiatrists).
● **Owner** Mr D Fenton
S (Ref:HM07220)

## FENTON, J M
**J M Fenton**, 328 Harrogate Rd, Leeds, **Yorkshire (West)**, LS17 6PE, ENG.
(T) 01132 685992
Speciality: Osteopathy.
P S T (Ref:HM07221)

## FENTON, MICHELLE
**Michelle Fenton**, 48 Waldeck Rd, Dartford, **Kent**, DA1 1UA, ENG.
(T) 01322 280559
Speciality: Complementary Medicines & Therapy.
C M (Ref:HM07222)

## FENTON, P
**P Fenton**, 328 Harrogate Rd, Leeds, **Yorkshire (West)**, LS17 6PE, ENG.
(T) 01132 685992
Speciality: Osteopathy.
P S T (Ref:HM07223)

## FENWICK, J
**J Fenwick**, 3 Chislehurst Rd, Richmond, **Surrey**, TW10 6PW, ENG.
(T) 020 8940 7222 (F) 020 8940 7222
Speciality: Alexander Technique.
● **Owner** Mrs J Fenwick
P S (Ref:HM07224)

## FERDA
**Ferda Ltd**, 54 Clifford Lane, Glasgow, **Glasgow (City of)**, G51 1NR, SCO.
(T) 01414 277003
Speciality: Clairvoyants & Palmists.
B (Ref:HM07225)

## FERGIE-WOODS, D (DR)
**Dr D Fergie-Woods**, 9 Trinity Rd, Hurstpierpoint, Hassocks, **Sussex (West)**, BN6 9UY, ENG.
(T) 01273 832546
Speciality: Homeopathy.
● **Owner** Dr D Fergie-Woods
M (Ref:HM07226)

## FERGUSON, A J
**A J Ferguson**, 8 Shambles, York, **Yorkshire (North)**, YO1 7LZ, ENG.
(T) 01904 629128
Speciality: Chiropodists (Podiatrists).
S (Ref:HM07227)

## FERGUSON, AGNES
**Agnes Ferguson**, 16 Druid Drive, Kilwinning, **Ayrshire (North)**, KA13 7AZ, SCO.
(T) 01294 553554
Speciality: Reflexology.
● **Owner** Mrs A Ferguson
S T (Ref:HM07228)

## FERGUSON, D
**D Ferguson**, Doctors Surgery, 28 Beaumont St, Oxford, **Oxfordshire**, OX1 2NP, ENG.
(T) 01865 512673
Speciality: Homeopathy.
● **Principal** Dr D Curtin
M (Ref:HM07229)

## FERGUSON, PHIL
**Phil Ferguson**, 32 Great Hales St, Market Drayton, **Shropshire**, TF9 1JN, ENG.
(T) 01630 658274
Speciality: Complementary Medicines & Therapy.
● **Owner** Mr P Ferguson
C M (Ref:HM07230)

## FERGUSON, SUSAN
**Susan Ferguson**, 2 St. Benets Court, Tenterden, **Kent**, TN30 6QS, ENG.
(T) 01580 765546
Speciality: Reflexology.
S T (Ref:HM07231)

## FERGUSON, WILMA
**Wilma Ferguson**, 24a Udney Park Rd, Teddington, **London (Greater)**, TW11 9BG, ENG.
(T) 020 8977 3246
(E) wilma@penandpills.co.uk
Speciality: Homeopathy. ✔

Key: B Mind-Body Medicine C Complementary Medicine H Self Help Treatment M Medicinal Therapy O Oriental Medicine P Postural Therapy S Manipulative Structural Therapy T Touch Therapy

● **Homeopath** Mrs W Ferguson **Q:** BRCP, MHA. **M:** BRCP.
**M** Yrs. Est.: 10 (**Ref:**HM07232)

## FERINGA, MARLIES

**Alternative Health Practice**, 200 Windsor Rd, Maidenhead, **Berkshire**, SL6 2DW, ENG.
(T) 01628 671209
(E) feringa@onetel.net.uk
Speciality: Acupuncture, Bach Remedies, Complementary Therapy, Hay Diet, Iridology, Massage (Therapeutic), Naturopathy, Nutritional Therapy, Stress Therapy, Vitamin Therapy, Herbal Medicine (as part of Nutritional Therapy).
● **Therapist** Ms M Feringa
**M** Yrs. Est.: 9 (**Ref:**HM07233)

## FERMOY NTRL HLTH & CHIRO CTRE

**Fermoy Natural Health & Chiropody Centre**, 2 Abbey St, Fermoy, **County Cork**, IRE.
(T) 025 3296 6
Speciality: Chiropodists (Podiatrists).
**S** (**Ref:**HM07234)

## FERN & CUTTER

**Fern & Cutter**, Thursday Cottage, Kilnbridge Cl, East Farleigh, Maidstone, **Kent**, ME15 0LW, ENG.
(T) 01622 728488
Speciality: Aromatherapy.
● **Owner** Mrs V Ramsey
**M O** (**Ref:**HM07235)

## FERNANDEZ, M

**M Fernandez**, 103 Silkstream Rd, Edgware, **London (Greater)**, HA8 0DE, ENG.
(T) 020 8906 2843
Speciality: Reflexology.
● **Owner** Mrs M Fernandez
**S T** (**Ref:**HM07236)

## FERNANDO, OLIVER

**Oliver Fernando**, 67 Church Rd, Bexleyheath, **Kent**, DA7 4DL, ENG.
(T) 020 8301 1589
Speciality: Physiotherapy.
● **Owner** Mr K Fernando
**P S T** (**Ref:**HM07237)

## FERNDOWN ACUPUNCTURE CLINIC

**Ferndown Acupuncture Clinic**, Corbin Avenue, Ferndown, **Dorset**, BH22 8AZ, ENG.
(T) 01202 861527
Speciality: Acupuncture.
**O** (**Ref:**HM07238)

## FERNDOWN CHIROPRACTIC CLINIC

**Ferndown Chiropractic Clinic**, 331 New Rd, Ferndown, **Dorset**, BH22 8EJ, ENG.
(T) 01202 893445 (F) 01590 624257
Speciality: Chiropractic. ✓
● **Associate** Dr V Wyle **Q:** DC, MSc. **M:** BCA.
● **Associate** Dr R Wilkinson **Q:** BSc, DC. **M:** BCA.
● **Chiropractor** Dr D Daivs **Q:** BSc, DC. **M:** BCA.
● **Owner** Dr K Vall **Q:** DC, FCC. **M:** BCA.
**P** Yrs. Est.: 20 (**Ref:**HM07239)

## FERNDOWN PHYSIOTHERAPY CLINIC

**Ferndown Physiotherapy Clinic**, 331 New Rd, Ferndown, **Dorset**, BH22 8EJ, ENG.
(T) 01202 897100
Speciality: Physiotherapy.
**P S T** (**Ref:**HM07240)

## FERNLEY, B

**B Fernley**, 30 Lumn Rd, Hyde, **Cheshire**, SK14 2RR, ENG.
(T) 01613 683144
Speciality: Chiropodists (Podiatrists).
**S** (**Ref:**HM07241)

## FERNS, J

**J Ferns**, 644 Whitworth Rd, Rochdale, **Lancashire**, OL12 0TB, ENG.
(T) 01706 658175
Speciality: Osteopathy.
**P S T** (**Ref:**HM07242)

## FERRELLY, HELEN

**Helen Ferrelly**, Brabant House, Portsmouth Rd, Thames Ditton, **Surrey**, KT7 0EY, ENG.
(T) 020 8398 7592
Speciality: Hypnotherapy.
**B** (**Ref:**HM07243)

## FERRIER, K

**K Ferrier**, The Surgery, 1 Manor Rd, Rugby, **Warwickshire**, CV21 5SX, ENG.
(T) 01788 550542
Speciality: Reflexology.
● **Owner** Mrs K Ferrier
**S T** (**Ref:**HM07244)

## FERRIS, JANET

**Janet Ferris**, 124 Grenfell Avenue, Hornchurch, **Essex**, RM12 4DS, ENG.
(T) 01708 438748
Speciality: Hypnosis.
● **Owner** Miss J Ferris
**B** (**Ref:**HM07245)

## FERRUCCI, LORETTA

**Loretta Ferrucci**, Chiltern Chiropractic Clinic, 12 High St, Bovingdon, Hemel Hempstead, **Hertfordshire**, HP3 0HG, ENG.
(T) 01442 832008 (F) 01442 832008
Speciality: Homeopathy.
● **Owner** Ms L Ferrucci
**M** (**Ref:**HM07246)

## FERTILITY ENTHERAPY GROUP

**Fertility Enhancement Therapy Group (The)**, 7 Wimpole St, London, **London (Greater)**, W1M 7AB, ENG.
(T) 01507 607336
Speciality: Complementary Medicines & Therapy.
**M** (**Ref:**HM07247)

## FEU, DU

**D Du Feu**, Sedgecroft, Hawkchurch, Axminster, **Devon**, EX13 5XB, ENG.
(T) 01297 678267
Speciality: Physiotherapy.
● **Owner** Mrs D Du-Deu
**P S T** (**Ref:**HM07248)

## FEVAR, R

**R Fevar**, 26 Whiteclosegate, Carlisle, **Cumbria**, CA3 0JD, ENG.
(T) 01228 531691
Speciality: Homeopathy.
● **Owner** Dr R Fevar
**M** (**Ref:**HM07249)

## FEWELL, FRANCES

**Frances Fewell**, 80 Beeleigh Link, Chelmsford, **Essex**, CM2 6RG, ENG.
(T) 01245 495656
Speciality: Complementary Medicines & Therapy.
● **Owner** Mrs F Fewell
**C M** (**Ref:**HM07250)

## FEWSTER, DAMON

**Damon Fewster**, 67 Buckingham St, Aylesbury, **Buckinghamshire**, HP20 2NF, ENG.
(T) 01296 337788
Speciality: Acupuncture.
**O** (**Ref:**HM07251)

## FEWSTER, DAVE

**Dave Fewster**, 123 Peregrine Rd, Sunbury-On-Thames, **Surrey**, TW16 6JH, ENG.
(T) 01932 782950
Speciality: Complementary Medicines & Therapy.
● **Owner** Mr D Fewster
**C M** (**Ref:**HM07252)

## FEWSTER, HELEN

**Helen Fewster**, 2 Plumtree Cottages, High St, Prestwood, Great Missenden, **Buckinghamshire**, HP16 9ER, ENG.
(T) 01494 865997
Speciality: Acupuncture.
**O** (**Ref:**HM07253)

## FEWSTER, HELEN

**Helen Fewster**, 36 Kings Lane, South Heath, Great Missenden, **Buckinghamshire**, HP16 0QY, ENG.
(T) 01494 862713 (F) 01494 862713
Speciality: Acupuncture.
● **Owner** Mrs H Fewster
**O** (**Ref:**HM07254)

## FEWTRELL, SALLY

**Sally Fewtrell**, 748 College Rd, Birmingham, **Midlands (West)**, B44 0AJ, ENG.
(T) 01213 503518
Speciality: Chiropody.
● **Owner** Miss S Fewtrell
**S** (**Ref:**HM07255)

## FFYNNONWEN NATURAL THRPY CTRE

**British Institute for Allergy and Environmental Therapy (The)**, Ffynnonwen, Llangwyryfon, Aberystwyth, **Ceredigion**, SY23 4EY, WAL.
(T) 01974 241376
(W) www.allergy.org.uk
Speciality: Allergy Testing, Bach Remedies, Bowen Therapy, Counselling, Herbal Medicine, Homeopathy, Hypnotherapy, Kinesiology, Manipulation, Massage (Therapeutic), Phytotherapy, Reflexology, Reichian Therapy.
✓ CREDIT
● **Complementary Therapist** Mrs C Morice **Q:** ITEC, RGN.
● **Complementary Therapist** Mrs S Harrison **Q:** RGN.
● **Principal** Mr D Harrsion **Q:** BA (Hons) Psychol, BSc. **M:** BPS, RPS.
**M** Yrs. Est.: 20 (**Ref:**HM07256)

## FIDLER, MAL

**Mal Fidler**, Woodshaw Studios, 17 Mizzy Rd, Rochdale, **Lancashire**, OL12 6HW, ENG.
(T) 01706 653561
Speciality: Aromatherapy.
**M O** (**Ref:**HM07257)

## FIELD END COMP HEALTH CLINIC

**Field End Complementary Health Clinic**, 716A Field End Rd, Ruislip, **London (Greater)**, HA4 0QP, ENG.
(T) 020 8422 4163
Speciality: Osteopathy.
**P S T** (**Ref:**HM07258)

## FIELD VIEW SURGERY

**R W Wood D S Ch M A I C**, Field View Surgery, 135 Wistaston Green Rd, Wistaston, Crewe, **Cheshire**, CW2 8RA, ENG.
(T) 01270 668851 (F) 01270 668851
Speciality: Biomechanics, Chiropody, Chiropractic, Orthotics, Reflexology. ✓
● **Surgical Chiropodist** Mr R Wood **Q:** Dip.S.L.S. **M:** AIC.
**P** Yrs. Est.: 12 (**Ref:**HM07259)

## FIELD, JONATHAN

**Jonathan Field**, Back To Health, 2 Charles St, Petersfield, **Hampshire**, GU32 3EH, ENG.
(T) 01730 267423
Speciality: Chiropractic.
**P S T** (**Ref:**HM07260)

## FIELD, JULIA

**Julia Field**, 69 Oakwood Court, London, **London (Greater)**, W14 8JF, ENG.
(T) 020 7602 8941
Speciality: Reflexology.
**S T** (**Ref:**HM07261)

## FIELD, KATIE

**Katie Field**, 52 Spur Rd, Orpington, **Kent**, BR6 0QL, ENG.
(T) 01689 828459
Speciality: Reflexology.
**S T** (**Ref:**HM07262)

## FIELD, MERIEL

**Meriel Field**, 128 Shaftesbury Avenue, Swindon, **Wiltshire**, SN3 2AF, ENG.
(T) 01793 611980
Speciality: Reflexology.
● **Owner** Ms M Field
**S T** (**Ref:**HM07263)

## FIELD, P M

**P M Field**, 266 Shenley Rd, Borehamwood, **Hertfordshire**, WD6 1TJ, ENG.
(T) 020 8953 9627
Speciality: Osteopathy.
**P S T** (**Ref:**HM07264)

## FIELD, PAUL

**Mr Paul Field**, 101 Longmore Ave, Barnet,



Key continued: **Yrs.Est:** Years Established **Q:** Qualifications **M:** Professional Membership ✓ Indemnity Insurance CREDIT Accept Credit Cards

**Hertfordshire**, EN4 8UN, ENG.
(T) 020 8441 8726
Speciality: Osteopathy.
P S T (Ref:HM07265)

## FIELD, RICHARD

**Richard Field**, 2 Kenwood Rd, Sheffield, **Yorkshire (South)**, S7 1NP, ENG.
(T) 01142 552048
Speciality: Osteopathy.
● **Owner** Mr D Wainwright
P S T (Ref:HM07266)

## FIELD, ROWENA

**Rowena Field**, 151 Huntington Rd, York, **Yorkshire (North)**, YO31 9BP, ENG.
(T) 01904 656504
Speciality: Homeopathy.
M (Ref:HM07267)

## FIELD, ZOFIA

**Zofia Field**, 44 The Mall, London, **London (Greater)**, W5 3TJ, ENG.
(T) 020 8840 7374
Speciality: Electrolysis.
● **Owner** Mrs Z Field
T (Ref:HM07268)

## FIELD-COULING, KIM

**Kim Field-Couling**, 12 Thornhill Gardens, Barking, **Essex**, IG11 9TX, ENG.
(T) 020 8594 8874
Speciality: Reflexology.
S T (Ref:HM07269)

## FIELDER, R

**R Fielder**, Alberta House, Kings Park Drive, Bournemouth, **Dorset**, BH7 7AG, ENG.
(T) 01202 396282
Speciality: Psychotherapy.
B (Ref:HM07270)

## FIELDING, ANNA

**Anna Fielding**, 21 Wroxham Rd, Woodley, Reading, **Berkshire**, RG5 3AY, ENG.
(T) 01189 699932
(W) www.complementary-healthcare.co.uk/info/fielding
Speciality: Aromatherapy, Nutritional Therapy, Reflexology, Remedial Massage.
M O (Ref:HM07271)

## FIELDING, DEBORAH

**Deborah Fielding**, The Bower Mount Clinic, 62 Bower Mount Rd, Maidstone, **Kent**, ME16 8AT, ENG.
(T) 01622 674656
Speciality: Acupuncture.
O (Ref:HM07272)

## FIELDING, HELEN

**Helen Fielding**, 126 Whiteladies Rd, Bristol, BS8 2RP, ENG.
(T) 01179 098113
Speciality: Acupuncture.
● **Owner** Ms H Fielding
O (Ref:HM07273)

## FIELDING, J

**J Fielding**, 22 Airedale Avenue, London, **London (Greater)**, W4 2NW, ENG.
(T) 020 8995 6322
Speciality: Physiotherapy.
P S T (Ref:HM07274)

## FIELDING, S H

**S H Fielding**, 45 Springfield Rd, Leicester, **Leicestershire**, LE2 3BB, ENG.
(T) 01162 219691
Speciality: Acupuncture.
● **Owner** Mr S Fielding
O (Ref:HM07275)

## FIELDS OF FRAGRANCE

**Fields Of Fragrance Ltd**, Westwood, High St, Maresfield, Uckfield, **Sussex (East)**, TN22 2EH, ENG.
(T) 01825 766996 (F) 01825 766996
Speciality: Aromatherapy.
● **Joint Director**
Patricia Ann Kennedy
M O (Ref:HM07276)

## FIELDS, SHIRLEY

**Shirley Fields**, 9 Lower Loughborough, Tiverton, **Devon**, EX16 5AD, ENG.
(T) 01884 257797
Speciality: Reflexology.
● **Owner** Mrs S Field
S T (Ref:HM07277)

## FIELDSEND, SARAH

**Sarah Fieldsend**, 20 Downsell Rd, Redditch, **Worcestershire**, B97 5RT, ENG.
(T) 01527 403204
Speciality: Reflexology.
S T (Ref:HM07278)

## FIERMAN B, & KOHNSTAMM B

**Bolt Fierman & Barbara Kohnstamm**, 5 Tivloi Tce, East, Dun Laoghaire, **County Dublin**, IRE.
(T) 01280 3789
Speciality: Complementary Medicines & Therapy.
M (Ref:HM07279)

## FIFE CHIRO & SPORTS INJURY

**Fife Chiropody & Sports Injury Clinic**, 3 Huntsman Court, Glenrothes, **Fife**, KY7 6SX, SCO.
(T) 01592 744499
Speciality: Chiropodists (Podiatrists).
S (Ref:HM07280)

## FIFTH ELEMENT

**Fifth Element**, 1 Darren Pk, Pontypridd, **Rhondda Cynon Taff**, CF37 2AN, WAL.
(T) 01443 480333
Speciality: Aromatherapy.
● **Owner** Miss N Pribay
M O (Ref:HM07281)

## FIGHT

**Stratford Orthopaedic Clinic**, 6 Mansell St, Stratford-Upon-Avon, **Warwickshire**, CV37 6NR, ENG.
(T) 01789 414289 (F) 01789 299003
(E) sales@hairremoval.co.uk
(W) www.hairremoval.co.uk
Speciality: Acupressure, Bio-energetics, Bonesetting, Chiropody, Complementary Therapy, Manipulation, Massage (Therapeutic), Micro Manipulation, Osteopathy, Podiatry, Rolfing, Shiatsu, Vitamin Therapy, Cosmetic Dermatherapy, Permanent Hair Removal. ✔
● **Orthopaedic Physician**
Dr H Kitchen Q: Ch.B, DO, MB. M: GMC.
● **Osteopath** Mr J Kitchen Q: DO. M: GOsC.
S Yrs. Est.: 12 (Ref:HM07282)

## FIGURA, CATHERINE MARIA

**Catherine Maria Figura**, 11 Highfield Avenue, Brighouse, **Yorkshire (West)**, HD6 4EB, ENG.
(T) 01484 720545
Speciality: Aromatherapy. ✔
● **Owner/Aromatherapist** Ms C Figura Q: ITEC. M: GCP.
C Yrs. Est.: 5 (Ref:HM07283)

## FIGURE WISE THERAPY CLINIC

**Figure Wise Therapy Clinic**, 4 North St, New Romney, **Kent**, TN28 8DW, ENG.
(T) 01797 362798
Speciality: Physiotherapy.
P S T (Ref:HM07284)

## FIGUREFIRM HOLISTIC CENTRE

**Figurefirm Holistic Centre**, 9 Midfield Prde, Mayplace Rd East, Bexleyheath, **Kent**, DA7 6ND, ENG.
(T) 01322 550855
Speciality: Complementary Medicines & Therapy.
C M (Ref:HM07285)

## FIGURESHAPERS

**Figureshapers**, 59 Maywood Ave, Raheny, **County Dublin**, IRE.
(T) 01832 8256
Speciality: Complementary Medicines & Therapy.
M (Ref:HM07286)

## FILBY, P

**P Filby**, 55 The Hordens, Barns Green, Horsham, **Sussex (West)**, RH13 7PH, ENG.
(T) 01403 731125 (F) 01403 791153
Speciality: Physiotherapy.
● **Manager** Mrs P Filby
P S T (Ref:HM07287)

## FILE, CHRISTINE

**Christine File**, 125 Mina Rd, Bristol, BS2 9YF, ENG.
(T) 01179 350852
Speciality: Aromatherapy, Massage (Therapeutic), Reflexology. ✔
● **Reflexologist** Mrs C File
T Yrs. Est.: 6 (Ref:HM07288)

## FILEY THERAPIST

**Filey Therapist**, 37 Station Avenue, **Yorkshire (North)**, YO14 9AE, ENG.
(T) 01723 512337
Speciality: Massage (Therapeutic).
M (Ref:HM07289)

## FILIPOVIC, S

**S Filipovic**, 5 King Edwards Avenue, Gloucester, **Gloucestershire**, GL1 5DA, ENG.
(T) 01452 526807
Speciality: Hypnosis.
● **Owner** Mr S Filipovic
B (Ref:HM07290)

## FILLAUDEAU, SARAH-JAYNE

**Sarah-Jayne Fillaudeau**, Cat & Lion, Tarporley Rd, Stretton, Warrington, **Cheshire**, WA4 4NB, ENG.
(T) 01925 730451
Speciality: Reflexology.
S T (Ref:HM07291)

## FILLERY, PAUL L

**Paul L Fillery**, 6 Baring Cres, Exeter, **Devon**, EX1 1TL, ENG.
(T) 01392 410549
Speciality: Osteopathy.
P S T (Ref:HM07292)

## FILLINGHAM, MAGGIE

**Maggie Fillingham**, Cirencester, **Gloucestershire**, GL7, ENG.
(T) 01285 655254
Speciality: Aromatherapy.
M O (Ref:HM07293)

## FILSON, SUSAN

**Susan Filson**, The Physical Therapy Clinic, 1 Victoria Rd, Hale, Altrincham, **Cheshire**, WA15 9AF, ENG.
(T) 01619 415922 (F) 01619 255402
Speciality: Physiotherapy.
● **Owner** Ms S Filson
P S T (Ref:HM07294)

## FINAGHY CHIROPRACTIC CLINIC

**Finaghy Chiropractic Clinic**, 122E Upper Lisburn Rd, Finaghy, Belfast, **County Antrim**, BT10 0BD, NIR.
(T) 028 9060 4294 (F) 028 9030 0671
Speciality: Chiropractic. ✔
● **Chiropractor** Dr R Cathcart Q: DC.
P Yrs. Est.: 14 (Ref:HM07295)

## FINCH, ALTHEA

**Althea Finch**, 30 Wimbledon Hill Rd, London, **London (Greater)**, SW19 7PA, ENG.
(T) 020 8540 8789
Speciality: Complementary Medicines & Therapy.
● **Owner** Miss A Finch
C M (Ref:HM07296)

## FINCH, ANNE

**Anne Finch**, 14 Russell St, Gloucester, **Gloucestershire**, GL1 1NE, ENG.
(T) 01452 307767
Speciality: Homeopathy.
M (Ref:HM07297)

## FINCH, ANNE

**Anne Finch**, 1st Floor The Old Post Office, Bank Cres, Ledbury, **Herefordshire**, HR8 1AA, ENG.
(T) 01531 634220
Speciality: Homeopathy.
M (Ref:HM07298)

## FINCH, CHRIS

**Chris Finch**, 11 Plinston Avenue, Warrington, **Cheshire**, WA4 1QU, ENG.
(T) 01925 243676
Speciality: Physiotherapy.
● **Owner** Mr C Finch
P S T (Ref:HM07299)



Key: B Mind-Body Medicine C Complementary Medicine H Self Help Treatment M Medicinal Therapy O Oriental Medicine P Postural Therapy S Manipulative Structural Therapy T Touch Therapy

**FINCH, CHRISTOPHER**

**Christopher Finch**, 15 Manchester Rd, Warrington, **Cheshire**, WA1 3AB, **ENG**.
(T) 01925 243676
Speciality: Complementary Medicines & Therapy.
● **Owner** Christopher Finch
[M] (**Ref:**HM07300)

**FINCH, MARGARET**

**Margaret Finch**, The Laboratory, The Avenue, Muswell Hill, London, **London (Greater)**, N10 2QE, **ENG**.
(T) 020 8482 3000
Speciality: Reflexology.
● **Owner** Mrs M Finch
[S] [T] (**Ref:**HM07301)

**FINCH, WENDY**

**Wendy Finch**, 74 Queens Drive, Nantwich, **Cheshire**, CW5 5JH, **ENG**.
(T) 01270 624303
Speciality: Physiotherapy, Bates Vision Education, Remedial Massage. ✔
● **Owner** Mrs W Finch Q: LCSP M: CSP
[P] [S] [T] Yrs. Est.: 6 (**Ref:**HM07302)

**FINCHAM, JOHNNY**

**Johnny Fincham**, 39 Union St, Norwich, **Norfolk**, NR2 2SL, **ENG**.
(T) 01603 666646
Speciality: Clairvoyants & Palmists.
● **Owner** Mr J Fincham
[B] (**Ref:**HM07303)

**FINCHLEY ALTERNATIVE MED CTRE**

**Finchley Alternative Medical Centre**, 253 Ballards Lane, London, **London (Greater)**, N3 1NG, **ENG**.
(T) 020 8445 2631 (F) 020 8446 6880
Speciality: Complementary Medicines & Therapy.
● **Owner** Dr H Shivadikar
[C] [M] (**Ref:**HM07304)

**FINCHLEY HYPNOTHERAPY PRACTICE**

**Finchley Hypnotherapy Practice**, 808a High Rd, London, **London (Greater)**, N12 9QU, **ENG**.
(T) 020 8446 8088
Speciality: Hypnotherapy.
● **Owner** Mr G Philips
[B] (**Ref:**HM07305)

**FIND YOUR RAINBOW**

**Find Your Rainbow**, 62 Shipstone Rd, Norwich, **Norfolk**, NR3 1JY, **ENG**.
(T) 01603 764473
Speciality: Clairvoyants & Palmists.
● **Owner** Miss A Bright
[B] (**Ref:**HM07306)

**FINDHORN FLOWER ESSENCES**

**Findhorn Flower Essences**, 'Wellspring', 31 The Park, Findhorn Bay, Forres, **Moray**, IV36 3TZ, **SCO**.
(T) 01309 690129 (F) 01309 691300
(E) info@findhornessences.com
(W) www.findhornessences.com
Speciality: Bach Remedies, Homeopathy. [CREDIT]
● **Homeopath** Ms M Leigh
● **Sales Director** Mr D Steel
[C] Yrs. Est.: 8 (**Ref:**HM07307)

**FINDLAY, MARIE-ANNE**

**Marie-Anne Findlay**, 3 Belle Vue Walk, West Parley, Ferndown, **Dorset**, BH22 8QB, **ENG**.
(T) 01202 894084
Speciality: Homeopathy.
● **Owner** Ms M Findlay
[M] (**Ref:**HM07308)

**FINDLOW, GLENDA**

**Glenda Findlow**, 10 Clifford Rd, Poynton, Stockport, **Cheshire**, SK12 1HY, **ENG**.
(T) 01625 873779
Speciality: Hypnotherapy.
[B] (**Ref:**HM07309)

**FINE FRAGRANCES**

**Fine Fragrances**, 171-177 High St, West Bromwich, **Midlands (West)**, B70 7HS, **ENG**.
(T) 01215 803432 (F) 01215 207176
Speciality: Aromatherapy.
● **Owner** Mrs H Priest
[M] [O] (**Ref:**HM07310)

**FINESSE**

**Finesse**, Maple Croft, Bay View Rd, Looe, **Cornwall**, PL13 1JN, **ENG**.
(T) 01503 265211
Speciality: Electrolysis.
[T] (**Ref:**HM07311)

**FINIMORE-SHERMAN & ASS**

**D M Finimore-Sherman & Associates**, 3 Elmcroft Avenue, London, **London (Greater)**, NW11 0RS, **ENG**.
(T) 020 8458 1763 (F) 020 8458 1763
Speciality: Chiropodists (Podiatrists).
● **Owner** Mrs D Finimore-Sherman
[S] (**Ref:**HM07312)

**FINISHING TOUCHES**

**Finishing Touches**, 1st Floor, 15 Upper Baggot St, Dublin, **County Dublin**, **IRE**.
(T) 01660 0221
(E) lipstick@iol.ie
Speciality: Aromatherapy, Healer, Massage (Therapeutic), Nutritional Therapy, Spiritual Healing, Stress Therapy, Touch Therapy. ✔ [CREDIT]
● **Owner** Mr M Weymes Q: ITEC. M: ITEC.
[T] Yrs. Est.: 8 (**Ref:**HM07313)

**FINKE, MARTYN**

**Martyn Finke**, The Therapy Clinic, 11D Market Pl, Long Buckby, Northampton, **Northamptonshire**, NN6 7RR, **ENG**.
(T) 01327 844646
Speciality: Reflexology.
[S] [T] (**Ref:**HM07314)

**FINKE, WENDY**

**Wendy Finke**, The Therapy Clinic, 11D Market Pl, Long Buckby, Northampton, **Northamptonshire**, NN6 7RR, **ENG**.
(T) 01327 844646
Speciality: Reflexology.
[S] [T] (**Ref:**HM07315)

**FINLAY, BRUCE**

**Bruce Finlay**, 322 Banbury Rd, Oxford, **Oxfordshire**, OX2 7ED, **ENG**.
(T) 01865 511072
Speciality: Chiropodists (Podiatrists).
● **Owner** Mr B Finlay
[S] (**Ref:**HM07316)

**FINLAY, TAMARA**

**Tamara Finlay**, 18 Sleights Drive, Wisbech, **Cambridgeshire**, PE14 7BT, **ENG**.
(T) 01945 461082
Speciality: Reflexology.
● **Owner** Mrs T Finlay
[S] [T] (**Ref:**HM07317)

**FINLAYTER, LENNOX**

**Lennox Finlayter**, 22 Watford Way, London, **London (Greater)**, NW4 3AD, **ENG**.
(T) 020 8202 3235
Speciality: Osteopathy.
● **Owner** Mr L Finlayter
[P] [S] [T] (**Ref:**HM07318)

**FINLEY CHIROPRACTIC CENTRE**

**Chiropractic Association Of Ireland (Finley Chiropractic Centre)**, Newtownpark Ave, Blackrock, **County Dublin**, **IRE**.
(T) 01288 2801
Speciality: Chiropractors.
[P] [S] [T] (**Ref:**HM07319)

**FINLEY CHIROPRACTIC CENTRE**

**Finley Chiropractic Centre**, Newtown Park Ave, Blackrock, **County Dublin**, **IRE**.
(T) 01288 2801
Speciality: Chiropractors.
[P] [S] [T] (**Ref:**HM07320)

**FINLEY-MCKENNA, LINDA (DR)**

**Dr Linda Finley-McKenna**, Dublin Rd, ,, Maynooth, **County Kildare**, **IRE**.
(T) 01628 5962
Speciality: Complementary Medicines & Therapy.
[M] (**Ref:**HM07321)

**FINN, G T & S E**

**G T & S E Finn**, 16 First Avenue, Catherington, Waterlooville, **Hampshire**, PO8 0JR, **ENG**.
(T) 023 9259 4243
Speciality: Homeopathy.
● **Owner** Mr E Finn
[M] (**Ref:**HM07322)

**FINN, JANE**

**Jane Finn**, 4 Hornbeam Avenue, Upminster, **Essex**, RM14 2NH, **ENG**.
(T) 01708 225319
Speciality: Reflexology.
[S] [T] (**Ref:**HM07323)

**FINN, PATRICK (DR)**

**Dr Patrick Finn M B ,M R O**, U M Northside S.C, Coolock, Dublin, **County Dublin**, **IRE**.
(T) 01848 3179
Speciality: Complementary Medicines & Therapy.
[M] (**Ref:**HM07324)

**FINNERTY, ML (DR)**

**Dr Ml Finnerty**, 17 Ashe St, Tralee, **County Kerry**, **IRE**.
(T) 06671 27699
Speciality: Osteopathy.
[P] [S] [T] (**Ref:**HM07325)

**FINNIS, ELIZABETH**

**Elizabeth Finnis**, 8 Well Cross, Edith Weston, Oakham, **Rutland**, LE15 8HG, **ENG**.
(T) 01780 720069
Speciality: Reflexology.
[S] [T] (**Ref:**HM07326)

**FIONA BROOKES & MORNA ELLIOTT**

**Fiona Brookes & Morna Elliott**, Whitebeam Drive, Hornbeam Rd, Reigate, **Surrey**, RH2 7LS, **ENG**.
(T) 01737 221030
Speciality: Chiropodists (Podiatrists).
[S] (**Ref:**HM07327)

**FIONA BROOKES & MORNA ELLIOTT**

**Fiona Brookes & Morna Elliott**, Somers House, Linkfield Corner, Redhill, **Surrey**, RH1 6AA, **ENG**.
(T) 01737 762990
Speciality: Osteopathy.
● **Owner** Mr M Piraino
[P] [S] [T] (**Ref:**HM07328)

**FIONA OTTEWELL CHRTRD PHYSIO**

**Fiona Ottewell Chartered Physiotherapist**, Woodside House Farm, Witton Park, Bishop Auckland, **County Durham**, DL14 0DU, **ENG**.
(T) 01388 607160
(E) ottewell@aol.com
Speciality: Acupuncture, Electrotherapy, Manipulation, Massage (Therapeutic), Pilates.
● **Physiotherapist** Mrs F Ottewell Q: MCSP. M: CSP.
[S] Yrs. Est.: 10 (**Ref:**HM07329)

**FIRBANK, KENNETH A**

**Kenneth A Firbank**, 35a Welbeck Rd, Doncaster, **Yorkshire (South)**, DN4 5EY, **ENG**.
(T) 01302 327195
Speciality: Chiropodists (Podiatrists).
[S] (**Ref:**HM07330)

**FIRESTONE, ELLIS**

**Ellis Firestone**, 26 Dixon Avenue, Glasgow, **Glasgow (City of)**, G42 8EE, **SCO**.
(T) 01414 236976
Speciality: Chiropodists (Podiatrists).
[S] (**Ref:**HM07331)

**FIRMAN, BARBARA**

**Barbara Firman**, 54 Burkes Rd, Beaconsfield, **Buckinghamshire**, HP9 1EE, **ENG**.
(T) 01494 671802
Speciality: Absent Healing, Beauty Therapy, Do-In, Dowsing, Healing Therapy, Hopi Ear Candles, Indian Head Massage, Massage (Therapeutic), Reflexology, Reiki, T'ai-Chi Ch'uan, Vertical Reflexology, Endometriosis, Lymphatic Drainage Massage and Earache. ✔
● **Reflexologist/Reiki Healer/Beauty Therapist**
Ms B Firman Q: ITEC, MAR, Reiki 2. M: AoR, BRA, FHT.
[T] Yrs. Est.: 20 (**Ref:**HM07332)



Key continued: Yrs.Est: Years Established Q: Qualifications M: Professional Membership ✔ Indemnity Insurance [CREDIT] Accept Credit Cards

### FIRST ACUPUNCTURE CLINIC
**First Acupuncture Clinic**, 3 Central Prde, Station Rd, Harrow, **London (Greater)**, HA1 2TW, ENG.
(T) 020 8863 1699
Speciality: Acupuncture.
O (Ref:HM07333)

### FIRST CHIROPRACTIC CLINIC
**First Chiropractic Clinic**, 72 Stanley Gr, Penwortham, Preston, **Lancashire**, PR1 0JJ, ENG.
(T) 01772 465394
Speciality: Chiropractors.
● **Owner** Dr J Cerosimo
P S T (Ref:HM07334)

### FIRST CLASS
**First Class**, 614 Bristol Rd, Selly Oak, Birmingham, **Midlands (West)**, B29 6AE, ENG.
(T) 01214 723668
Speciality: Aromatherapy.
M O (Ref:HM07335)

### FIRST CLASS FOOT CARE
**First Class Foot Care**, 92 High St, Lincoln, **Lincolnshire**, LN5 7QW, ENG.
(T) 01522 888823
Speciality: Chiropodists (Podiatrists).
● **Owner** Mr M Soons
S (Ref:HM07336)

### FIRST HAND PHYSIO PRACTICE
**First Hand Physiotherapy Practice**, Exeter Arena, Summer Lane, Exeter, **Devon**, EX4 8NN, ENG.
(T) 01392 460546
Speciality: Physiotherapy.
● **Owner** Mr T Edbrooke
P S T (Ref:HM07337)

### FIRST PATH HYPNOTHERAPY
**First Path Hypnotherapy & NLP**, Wanstead Village, Dental Health Centre, 24 High St, **London**, E11 2AQ, ENG.
(T) 020 8926 1297
(E) firstpath@btinternet.com
(W) www.firstpath.btinternet.co.uk
Speciality: Hypnotherapy. ✔
● **Owner** Ms N Zaman Q: NLP. M: NCH.
B Yrs. Est.: 3 (Ref:HM07338)

### FIRST PATH HYPNOTHERAPY
**First Path Hypnotherapy**, 28 New Wanstead, Wanstead, London, **London (Greater)**, E11 2SN, ENG.
(T) 020 8989 5806
Speciality: Hypnosis.
B (Ref:HM07339)

### FIRST STEP FOOTCARE
**First Step Footcare**, Unit 24 2-4 Heigham St, Norwich, **Norfolk**, NR2 4TE, ENG.
(T) 01603 767855
Speciality: Biomechanics, Chiropody, Nail Surgery. ✔
● **Owner/Chiropodist** Miss G Hewitt Q: S.R.Ch. M: S.C.P.
C Yrs. Est.: 10 (Ref:HM07340)

### FIRTH, J
**J Firth**, 110 Dodworth Rd, Barnsley, **Yorkshire (South)**, S70 6HL, ENG.
(T) 01226 282560
Speciality: Reflexology.
● **Owner** Mrs J Firth
S T (Ref:HM07341)

### FIRTH, JOHN
**John Firth**, 12 Church Lane, Arley, Coventry, **Midlands (West)**, CV7 8FW, ENG.
(T) 01676 541586
Speciality: Homeopathy.
● **Owner** Mr J Firth
M (Ref:HM07342)

### FIRTH, SUE
**Sue Firth**, Flat 2, 51 West Cliffe Ter, Harrogate, **Yorkshire (North)**, HG2 0PU, ENG.
(T) 01423 507856
Speciality: Alexander Technique.
● **Owner** Ms S Firth
P S (Ref:HM07343)

### FISH, ALINA
**Alina Fish**, 30 West Gr Rd, Exeter, **Devon**, EX2 4LU, ENG.
(T) 01392 211323
Speciality: Homeopathy.
● **Owner** A Fish
M (Ref:HM07344)

### FISH, BARBARA A
**Barbara A Fish**, 97 Billy Lows Lane, Potters Bar, **Hertfordshire**, EN6 1UY, ENG.
(T) 01707 653364
Speciality: Chiropodists (Podiatrists).
● **Owner** Mrs B Fish
S (Ref:HM07345)

### FISH, DAVID
**David Fish**, 32 Mount Pleasant Rd, London, **London (Greater)**, NW10 3EL, ENG.
(T) 020 8459 4595
Speciality: Osteopathy.
P S T (Ref:HM07346)

### FISHER, ANDREW
**Andrew Fisher**, 9 Fourth Avenue, Clipstone Village, Mansfield, **Nottinghamshire**, NG21 9DQ, ENG.
(T) 01623 625250
Speciality: Chiropodists (Podiatrists).
● **Owner** Mr A Fisher
S (Ref:HM07347)

### FISHER, C
**C Fisher**, 90 Barton Rd, Lancaster, **Lancashire**, LA1 4EL, ENG.
(T) 01524 64706
Speciality: Physiotherapy.
P S T (Ref:HM07348)

### FISHER, CHRISTINE A
**Christine A Fisher**, 114 Elm Lane, Sheffield, **Yorkshire (South)**, S5 7TW, ENG.
(T) 01142 400734
Speciality: Chiropody, Nail Surgery. ✔
● **Chiropodist** Ms C Fisher Q: DPodM, M.S.C.P. M: S.C.P.
S Yrs. Est.: 17 (Ref:HM07349)

### FISHER, CLAIRE
**Claire Fisher**, 54 Isaacson Drive, Wavendon Gate, **Buckinghamshire**, MK7 7RU, ENG.
(T) 01908 586173
Speciality: Reflexology.
S T (Ref:HM07350)

### FISHER, DEIRDRE
**Deirdre Fisher (Mobile)**, 21 Bridgeway East, Windmill Hill, Runcorn, **Cheshire**, WA7 6LD, ENG.
(T) 01928 717968
Speciality: Reflexology.
● **Owner** Mrs D Fisher
S T (Ref:HM07351)

### FISHER, E
**E Fisher**, 602 Yarm Rd, Eaglescliffe, Stockton-On-Tees, **Cleveland**, TS16 0DF, ENG.
(T) 01642 780204
Speciality: Physiotherapy.
● **Owner** Mr E Fisher
P S T (Ref:HM07352)

### FISHER, HEATHER
**Heather Fisher**, 5 Drake Cl, Bracknell, **Berkshire**, RG12 7JP, ENG.
(T) 01344 429781
Speciality: Chiropodists (Podiatrists).
S (Ref:HM07353)

### FISHER, J W
**J W Fisher**, 8 Bailleul Gr, Hawick, **Scottish Borders**, TD9 9PP, SCO.
(T) 01450 377584
Speciality: Chiropodists (Podiatrists).
S (Ref:HM07354)

### FISHER, JACK E
**Jack E Fisher**, South View, Burnt St, Wells-next-the-Sea, **Norfolk**, NR23 1HN, ENG.
(T) 01328 711025
(E) jackfisher@hotmail.com
Speciality: Electrotherapy, Hypnosis, Hypnotherapy, Manipulation, Massage (Therapeutic), Osteopathy. ✔
● **Owner** Mr J Fisher Q: DO, MAO. M: LCSP.
S Yrs. Est.: 20 (Ref:HM07355)

### FISHER, MIKE
**Mike Fisher**, Clissold Park Health Centre, 154 Stoke Newington Church St, London, **London (Greater)**, N16 0JU, ENG.
(T) 020 7249 2990 (F) 020 7249 3977
Speciality: Psychotherapy.
● **Owner** Mr D Berg
B (Ref:HM07356)

### FISHER, NIGEL
**Nigel Fisher**, Westfield Dental Practice, 1 Westfield Rd, Woking, **Surrey**, GU22 9LZ, ENG.
(T) 01483 725600
Speciality: Chiropractors.
P S T (Ref:HM07357)

### FISHER, PAUL
**Paul Fisher**, 14 Cleeve Hill Gardens, Waterthorpe, Sheffield, **Yorkshire (South)**, S20 7NP, ENG.
(T) 01142 480441
Speciality: Chiropodists (Podiatrists).
S (Ref:HM07358)

### FISHER, SUSAN
**Susan Fisher**, Bronant, Penegoes, Machynlleth, **Powys**, SY20 8UN, WAL.
(T) 01654 702051
Speciality: Reflexology.
S T (Ref:HM07359)

### FIT FEET
**Fit Feet Ltd**, 176 The Parade, Sutton Coldfield, **Midlands (West)**, B72 1PA, ENG.
(T) 01213 211162
Speciality: Chiropodists (Podiatrists).
● **Partner** Miss J Laden
S (Ref:HM07360)

### FIT FEET CHIROPODY
**Fit Feet Chiropody**, Monmouth House, Drake Rd, Lee-On-The-Solent, **Hampshire**, PO13 9NS, ENG.
(T) 023 9255 1823
Speciality: Chiropody, Reflexology. ✔
● **Chiropodist/Reflexologist** Mrs S Medley Q: MBChA. M: B.A.Ch.P.
C Yrs. Est.: 12 (Ref:HM07361)

### FITENI, SUZANNE
**Suzanne Fiteni**, 50 Chigwell Rd, London, **London (Greater)**, E18 1LS, ENG.
(T) 020 8514 3479
Speciality: Homeopathy.
● **Owner** Ms S Fiteni
M (Ref:HM07362)

### FITNESS FIRST
**Fitness First**, 234-244 Stockwell Rd, London, **London (Greater)**, SW9 9SP, ENG.
(T) 020 7733 2267
Speciality: Physiotherapy.
● **Owner** Mr C Barber
P S T (Ref:HM07363)

### FITZGERALD HYP-PSYCHOTHERAPY
**Fitzgerald Hypno-Psychotherapy**, 1 Chelmsford Rd, Ranelagh, **County Dublin**, IRE.
(T) 01295 7991 (F) 01294 3125
Speciality: Holistic Healing, Hypnosis, Hypnotherapy, Meditation, Psychotherapy, Rogerian Therapy, Stress Therapy. ✔
● **Hypnotherapist/Psychotherapist** Ms P Fitzgerald Q: Dip.Hyp, Dip.Psych, MA. M: CRAH.
H Yrs. Est.: 4 (Ref:HM07364)

### FITZGERALD, D
**D Fitzgerald**, 2 Grainger Rd, Isleworth, **London (Greater)**, TW7 6PQ, ENG.
(T) 020 8847 0138
Speciality: Alexander Technique.
● **Owner** Ms D Fitzgerald
P S (Ref:HM07365)

### FITZGERALD, M F
**M F Fitzgerald**, 297A Hertford Rd, London, **London (Greater)**, N9 7ET, ENG.
(T) 020 8804 2651
Speciality: Chiropodists (Podiatrists).
● **Owner** Miss M Fitzgerald



Key: B Mind-Body Medicine; C Complementary Medicine; H Self Help Treatment; M Medicinal Therapy; O Oriental Medicine; P Postural Therapy; S Manipulative Structural Therapy; T Touch Therapy

S (Ref:HM07366)

## FITZGERALD, ROSEMARY

**Rosemary Fitzgerald**, 123 High St, Newmarket, **Suffolk**, CB8 9AE, **ENG**.
(T) 01638 669641
Speciality: Acupuncture.
O (Ref:HM07367)

## FITZ-HENRY, THOMAS J

**Thomas J Fitz-Henry**, 20A Brockdish Avenue, Barking, **Essex**, IG11 9DS, **ENG**.
(T) 020 8594 6395
Speciality: Osteopathy.
P S T (Ref:HM07368)

## FITZHERBERT, TINA

**Tina Fitzherbert**, 52 Hillcrest Gardens, Esher, **Surrey**, KT10 0BX, **ENG**.
(T) 020 8390 8481
Speciality: Reflexology.
● **Owner** Mrs T Fitzherbert
S T (Ref:HM07369)

## FITZMAURICE, KIERON

**Kieron Fitzmaurice**, Flat 13 Moccatta House, Brady St, London, **London (Greater)**, E1 5DL, **ENG**.
(T) 020 7375 1962
Speciality: Alexander Technique.
● **Owner** Mr K Fitzmaurice
P S (Ref:HM07370)

## FITZPATRICK, BRENDAN (DR)

**Dr Brendan Fitzpatrick M R C P I**, 115 Morehampton Rd, Dublin, **County Dublin**, **IRE**.
(T) 01269 7768
Speciality: Complementary Medicines & Therapy.
M (Ref:HM07371)

## FITZPATRICK, BRENDAN (DR)

**Dr Brendan Fitzpatrick MRCPI, UK Med Ac Soc**, 115 Morehampton Rd, **IRE**.
(T) 01269 7768
Speciality: Complementary Medicines & Therapy.
M (Ref:HM07372)

## FITZPATRICK, G

**G Fitzpatrick**, 22 Osborne Avenue, Newcastle Upon Tyne, **Tyne and Wear**, NE2 1JQ, **ENG**.
(T) 01912 813379
Speciality: Physiotherapy.
● **Owner** Mrs A Moodie
P S T (Ref:HM07373)

## FITZPATRICK, J H

**J H Fitzpatrick**, 1447 Dumbarton Rd, Glasgow, **Glasgow (City of)**, G14 9DP, **SCO**.
(T) 01419 598401
Speciality: Chiropody, Cryo Surgery, Nail Surgery, Podiatry. ✔
● **Chiropodist (Podiatrist)**
Mr J Fitzpatrick Q: DPodM, S.R.Ch. M: S.C.P.
M Yrs. Est.: 27 (Ref:HM07374)

## FITZPATRICK, ROISIN

**Roisin Fitzpatrick**, 1 Queens Ct Queens Pk, Monkstown, **County Dublin**, **IRE**.
(T) 01284 3502
Speciality: Homeopathy.
M (Ref:HM07375)

## FITZPATRICK, TRISH

**Trish Fitzpatrick**, 5 Redland Avenue, Carlton, Nottingham, **Nottinghamshire**, NG4 3EW, **ENG**.
(T) 01159 530786
Speciality: Homeopathy.
● **Owner** Mrs T Fitzpatrick
M (Ref:HM07376)

## FITZPATRICK, TRISH

**Trish Fitzpatrick**, 11 Station Avenue, Gedling, Nottingham, **Nottinghamshire**, NG4 3GZ, **ENG**.
(T) 01159 530786
Speciality: Homeopathy.
M (Ref:HM07377)

## FITZROY PARTNERSHIP

**Fitzroy Partnership (The)**, 49 Rooley Avenue, Bradford, **Yorkshire (West)**, BD6 1BT, **ENG**.
(T) 01274 734652
Speciality: Complementary Medicines & Therapy.
● **Owner** Mr J Stead
C M (Ref:HM07378)

## FITZWILLIAM ACUPUNCTURE

**Fitzwilliam Acupuncture & Allergy Clinic**, 68 Fitzwilliam Sq, Dublin, **County Dublin**, **IRE**.
(T) 01661 6082
Speciality: Acupuncture.
O (Ref:HM07379)

## FITZWILLIAM CHIROPRACTOR

**Fitzwilliam Chiropractor Clinic**, 9 Herbert St, Dublin, **County Dublin**, **IRE**.
(T) 01661 5809
Speciality: Chiropractors.
P S T (Ref:HM07380)

## FIVE WAYS OSTEOPATHIC SURGERY

**Five Ways Osteopathic Surgery (The)**, 74 Macclesfield Rd, Hazel Gr, Stockport, **Cheshire**, SK7 6DT, **ENG**.
(T) 01625 876682
Speciality: Osteopathy. ✔
● **Osteopath** Mr J Gaskill Q: BSc (Hons). M: GOsC.
● **Owner/Osteopath** Mr M Davies Q: DO. M: GOsC.
● **Osteopath** Mr P Nye Q: BSc (Hons). M: GOsC.
● **Osteopath** Mr M Morris Q: BSc (Hons). M: GOsC.
S Yrs. Est.: 16 (Ref:HM07381)

## FIVEWAYS OSTEOPATHIC PRACTICE

**Fiveways Osteopathic Practice**, 308 Ditchling Rd, Brighton, **Sussex (East)**, BN1 6JG, **ENG**.
(T) 01273 566172
(E) nicmit@supanet.com
Speciality: Manipulation, Massage (Therapeutic), Osteopathy, Postural Integration. ✔
● **Osteopath** Mr N Mitchell Q: DO. M: GOsC.
S Yrs. Est.: 5 (Ref:HM07382)

## FIXBY OSTEOPATHIC PRACTICE

**Fixby Osteopathic Practice (The)**, 1 Gleneagles Way, Huddersfield, **Yorkshire (West)**, HD2 2NH, **ENG**.
(T) 01484 454845
Speciality: Osteopathy.
● **Owner** Ms N Gallagher
P S T (Ref:HM07383)

## FIZZIOSTUFF UK

**Fizziostuff UK Ltd**, Swan Mews, Parsons Green Lane, London, **London (Greater)**, SW6 4QT, **ENG**.
(T) 020 7371 7686
Speciality: Physiotherapy.
● **Sole Director** Mr H Turner
P S T (Ref:HM07384)

## FLACK, G

**G Flack**, 205 Robin Hood Lane, Walderslade, Chatham, **Kent**, ME5 9NJ, **ENG**.
(T) 01634 861513
Speciality: Chiropodists (Podiatrists).
S (Ref:HM07385)

## FLACK, G

**G Flack**, Longley Rd, Rochester, **Kent**, ME1 2TH, **ENG**.
(T) 01634 880633
Speciality: Chiropodists (Podiatrists).
● **Owner** Mrs G Flack
S (Ref:HM07386)

## FLAME HYPNOTHERAPY

**Flame Hypnotherapy**, 10 Bees Corner, Wainfleet, Skegness, **Lincolnshire**, PE24 4PB, **ENG**.
(T) 01754 881065
Speciality: Hypnosis.
● **Owner** Mr K Watson
B (Ref:HM07387)

## FLANAGAN, D

**D Flanagan**, 28 Park Lane, Hayes, **London (Greater)**, UB4 8AB, **ENG**.
(T) 020 8573 6413
Speciality: Homeopathy.
M (Ref:HM07388)

## FLANAGAN, DENIS

**Denis Flanagan**, Cherrymount Natural Healing Clinic, Drumcoo, Enniskillen, **County Fermanagh**, BT74 4FY, **NIR**.
(T) 028 6632 2622
Speciality: Physiotherapy.
● **Owner** Mr D Flanagan
P S T (Ref:HM07389)

## FLANAGAN, PATRICK

**Patrick Flanagan Dip Ch , M I I C H**, 176 Castlelawn Heights, **County Galway**, **IRE**.
(T) 09176 0313
Speciality: Complementary Medicines & Therapy.
M (Ref:HM07390)

## FLANDERS, H

**H Flanders**, 99 School Green Rd, Freshwater, **Isle of Wight**, PO40 9AX, **ENG**.
(T) 01983 755557
Speciality: Chiropody. ✔
● **Owner/Chiropodist** Mr H Flanders Q: MBChA, MSSCh.
C Yrs. Est.: 3 (Ref:HM07391)

## FLANIGAN, JANICE

**Janice Flanigan**, 3 School Rd, Crossnacreevy, Belfast, **County Antrim**, BT5 7UA, **NIR**.
(T) 028 9044 8829
Speciality: Reflexology.
S T (Ref:HM07392)

## FLANNERY, ANNE

**Anne Flannery**, 83 Main St, Winchburgh, Broxburn, **Lothian (West)**, EH52 6RA, **SCO**.
(T) 01506 890864
Speciality: Chiropodists (Podiatrists).
● **Owner** Miss A Flannery
S (Ref:HM07393)

## FLANNERY, BARNEY

**Barney Flannery**, 1a Mary St, Drogheda, **County Louth**, **IRE**.
(T) 04198 30741
Speciality: Complementary Medicines & Therapy.
M (Ref:HM07394)

## FLANNERY, ELIZABETH

**Elizabeth Flannery ADHP MICHP**, BlanchaRoadstown, **IRE**.
(T) 01820 1602
(W) www.hypnosiseire.com
Speciality: Hypnotherapy.
B (Ref:HM07395)

## FLANNERY, GERALDINE

**Geraldine Flannery**, 2 Bellair Dr, Tuam, **County Galway**, **IRE**.
(T) 09325 180
Speciality: Acupuncture.
O (Ref:HM07396)

## FLATT, JUNE

**June Flatt**, 10 McKenzie Way, Kiveton Park, Sheffield, **Yorkshire (South)**, S26 6QN, **ENG**.
(T) 01909 774989
Speciality: Chiropodists (Podiatrists).
● **Owner** Mrs J Flatt
S (Ref:HM07397)

## FLAVELL, MARGARET

**Margaret Flavell**, Dorchester, **Dorset**, DT2, **ENG**.
(T) 01300 320689
Speciality: Healer.
B (Ref:HM07398)

## FLEET & DISTRICT HYP CENTRE

**Fleet & District Hypnotherapy Centre (The)**, 8 Kiln Workshops, Pilcot Rd, Crookham Village, Fleet, **Hampshire**, GU13 0SL, **ENG**.
(T) 01252 815682
(E) smale@hypnofleet.demon.co.uk
(W) www.hypnofleet.demon.co.uk
Speciality: Hypnosis, Stress Therapy, Vibrational Therapy. ✔
● **Practitioner** Mr J Smale Q: BA (Hons), DHP (NC). M: HS, IAH, NCH.
B Yrs. Est.: 5 (Ref:HM07399)

## FLEET N F S H HEALING CENTRE

**Fleet N F S H Healing Centre**, 3 Goldcrest Cl,

Yateley, **Hampshire**, GU46 6PA, ENG.
(T) 01252 683914
Speciality: Complementary Medicines & Therapy.
C M (Ref:HM07400)

## FLEET PHYSIOTHERAPY

**Fleet Physiotherapy**, Church Rd, Fleet, **Hampshire**, GU13 8LB, ENG.
(T) 01483 782736 (F) 01483 782798
Speciality: Physiotherapy.
● **Manager** Mr D Smith
P S T (Ref:HM07401)

## FLEET, BARBARA

**Barbara Fleet**, 7 Christian Court, Milton Keynes, **Buckinghamshire**, MK15 9LH, ENG.
(T) 01908 691545
Speciality: Acupressure, Aromatherapy, Massage (Therapeutic), Uses Legend Aromatic Essential Oils. ✔
● **Owner** Barbara Fleet
C Yrs. Est.: 4 (Ref:HM07402)

## FLEETWOOD, REBECCA

**Rebecca Fleetwood**, 416b High St, Lincoln, **Lincolnshire**, LN5 8HX, ENG.
(T) 01522 530268
Speciality: Aromatherapy.
● **Owner** Miss R Fleetwood
M O (Ref:HM07403)

## FLEMING, A (DR)

**A Fleming ITECH TCOL MHA ANP NLC**, Ratoath Est, IRE.
(T) 01868 0707
Speciality: Aromatherapy.
M O (Ref:HM07404)

## FLEMING, J

**J Fleming**, 5 Alexandra Trce, Truro, **Cornwall**, TR1 3HN, ENG.
(T) 01872 264205
Speciality: Hypnotherapy.
B (Ref:HM07405)

## FLEMING, M K

**M K Fleming**, 22 Swallow Way, Wokingham, **Berkshire**, RG41 3TQ, ENG.
(T) 01189 794365
Speciality: Chiropodists (Podiatrists).
S (Ref:HM07406)

## FLEMING, P

**P Fleming**, Newholme Therapy Centre, Littlewick Rd, Knaphill, Woking, **Surrey**, GU21 2JU, ENG.
(T) 01483 480883
Speciality: Psychotherapy.
● **Owner** Mr P Fleming
B (Ref:HM07407)

## FLEMING, R D

**R D Fleming**, 5 Alexandra Trce, Truro, **Cornwall**, TR1 3HN, ENG.
(T) 01872 264205
Speciality: Hypnosis.
B (Ref:HM07408)

## FLETCHER, B C

**B C Fletcher**, 130A High St, Newport, **Shropshire**, TF10 7BH, ENG.
(T) 01952 813008
Speciality: Homeopathy.
M (Ref:HM07409)

## FLETCHER, CLARE

**Clare Fletcher**, 164 Erlanger Rd, London, **London (Greater)**, SE14 5TJ, ENG.
(T) 020 7277 8356
Speciality: Acupuncture. ✔
● **Acupuncturist** Ms C Fletcher Q: Lic.Ac. M: BAcC.
O (Ref:HM07410)

## FLETCHER, J

**J Fletcher**, 20 Jays Mead, Wotton-under-Edge, **Gloucestershire**, GL12 7JF, ENG.
(T) 01453 844363
Speciality: Reflexology.
● **Owner** Mrs J Fletcher
S T (Ref:HM07411)

## FLETCHER, J E

**J E Fletcher**, 74 King St, Farnworth, Bolton, **Lancashire**, BL4 7AP, ENG.
(T) 01204 575566
Speciality: Osteopathy.
P S T (Ref:HM07412)

## FLETCHER, KATIE

**Katie Fletcher**, 22 Rowand Avenue, Giffnock, Glasgow, **Glasgow (City of)**, G46 7PE, SCO.
(T) 01416 210661
Speciality: Osteopathy.
● **Owner** Ms K Fletcher
P S T (Ref:HM07413)

## FLETCHER, R C

**R C Fletcher**, 49 Old Church Rd, Clevedon, **Somerset**, BS21 6NP, ENG.
(T) 01275 876109
Speciality: Chiropodists (Podiatrists).
● **Owner** Mr R Fletcher
S (Ref:HM07414)

## FLETCHER, S & V M

**S & V M Fletcher**, 18 Imperial Rd, Matlock, **Derbyshire**, DE4 3NL, ENG.
(T) 01629 57066
Speciality: Chiropodists (Podiatrists).
S (Ref:HM07415)

## FLETCHER, VICTOR JOHN

**Victor John Fletcher**, Market Chambers, Rowley Regis, **Midlands (West)**, B65 0HP, ENG.
(T) 01215 599921
Speciality: Chiropody. ✔
● **Chiropodist** Mr V Fletcher Q: FCPod(s).
M Yrs. Est.: 15 (Ref:HM07416)

## FLEUR

**Fleur**, Pembroke Rd, London, **London (Greater)**, N10 2JE, ENG.
(T) 020 8444 7424 (F) 020 8444 0704
Speciality: Aromatherapy.
● **Managing Director** Mrs S Baker
M O (Ref:HM07417)

## FLEUROMA

**Fleuroma Aromatherapy & Reflexology**, 1 Wistoria Court, Blackthorn Avenue, Colchester, **Essex**, CO4 3QH, ENG.
(T) 01206 864629
(E) fleuroma@btinternet.com
Speciality: Aromatherapy, Complementary Therapy, Cupping, Holistic Healing, Indian Head Massage, Manipulation, Massage (Therapeutic), Reflexology, Swedish Body Massage, Deep Muscle Relaxation Techniques,. ✔
● **Owner/Therapist** Mrs S Gray Q: BSY.Arom, BSY.Reflex. M: BHMA.
C T Yrs. Est.: 1 (Ref:HM07418)

## FLEURY, DENISE

**Denise Fleury**, Oaklea, Maldon Rd, Stanway, Colchester, **Essex**, CO3 5SJ, ENG.
(T) 01206 331982
Speciality: Reflexology.
S T (Ref:HM07419)

## FLEXIBLE HOUR

**Tai Chi and Health**, 82 Ashville Rd, Leyton Stone, London, **London (Greater)**, E11 4DU, ENG.
(T) 020 8558 9676
(E) tony@taichiandhealth.com
(W) www.taichiandhealth.com
Speciality: Acupressure, Cupping, Massage (Therapeutic), Shiatsu, T'ai-Chi Ch'uan, Push Hands. ✔
● **Therapist** Mr T Rusli Q: MIIR, MRSS, TCUGB. M: RSS, Shiatsu Society UK, TCUGB.
C O Yrs. Est.: 16 (Ref:HM07420)

## FLIGHT, J

**J Flight**, Carmel, Hardwick Cl, Rayleigh, **Essex**, SS6 7QP, ENG.
(T) 01268 776789
Speciality: Chiropodists (Podiatrists).
● **Owner** Miss J Flight
S (Ref:HM07421)

## FLINNING, J

**J Flinning**, 25 The Struet, Brecon, **Powys**, LD3 7LW, WAL.
(T) 01874 610387
Speciality: Acupuncture.
O (Ref:HM07422)

## FLINT, J

**J Flint**, 4 Occupation Lane, Kirkby-In-Ashfield, Nottingham, **Nottinghamshire**, NG17 8FD, ENG.
(T) 01623 751972
Speciality: Chiropodists (Podiatrists).
S (Ref:HM07423)

## FLOAT WORKS

**Float Works (The)**, Winchester Wharf, Clink St, London, **London (Greater)**, SE1 9DG, ENG.
(T) 020 7357 0111
(W) www.floatworks.com
Speciality: Acupuncture, Indian Head Massage, Reiki, Shiatsu, T'ai-Chi Ch'uan, Astanga, Iyengar-Yoga. ✔
● **Joint Director** Peter Marsh
● **Joint Director** Timothy John Strudwick
● **Acupuncturist** Ms J Hobbs Q: BSc (Hons). M: BAcC.
● **Practitioner** Ms M Luckhurst M: RSS.
M Yrs. Est.: 8 (Ref:HM07424)

## FLOATATION RETREAT

**Floatation Retreat**, 14 Eastern Promenade, Point Clear Bay, Clacton-On-Sea, **Essex**, CO16 8LG, ENG.
(T) 01255 820631 (F) 01255 820631
Speciality: Relaxation Technique.
● **Owner** Mr P Bailie
H T (Ref:HM07425)

## FLOATATION TANK CENTRE

**Floatation Tank Centre**, 24 Lr Baggot St, IRE.
(T) 01662 7556
(W) www.harvestmoon.ie
Speciality: Complementary Medicines & Therapy.
M (Ref:HM07426)

## FLOATER, R

**R Floater**, 5 West Kensington Mansions, Beaumont Cresent, London, **London (Greater)**, W14 9PE, ENG.
(T) 020 7385 4091 (F) 020 7385 4091
Speciality: Psychotherapy.
● **Owner** Mr R Horrocks
B (Ref:HM07427)

## FLOOD, RICHARD

**Richard Flood**, 11 Tuscan Court, Pakenham Cl, Cambridge, **Cambridgeshire**, CB4 1PN, ENG.
(T) 01223 368935
Speciality: Aromatherapy.
M O (Ref:HM07428)

## FLOOKBURGH CLINIC

**Flookburgh Clinic**, 5 Market St, Flookburgh, Grange-over-Sands, **Cumbria**, LA11 7JU, ENG.
(T) 01539 559062
Speciality: Physiotherapy.
● **Owner** Mr P Fitchett
P S T (Ref:HM07429)

## FLORASSENTIALS

**Florassentials**, 10 Emerson Drive, Hornchurch, **Essex**, RM11 1XH, ENG.
(T) 01708 475419
Speciality: Aromatherapy.
● **Owner** Ms T Bates
M O (Ref:HM07430)

## FLORENCE SHARPE CHIROPODIST

**Florence Sharpe Chiropodist**, 77 Belmont Rd, Belfast, **County Antrim**, BT4 2AA, NIR.
(T) 028 9065 1771
Speciality: Biomechanics, Chiropody, Nail Surgery, Podiatry. ✔
● **Chiropodist (Podiatrist)** Mrs F Sharpe Q: DPodM, M.S.C.P, S.R.Ch. M: S.C.P.
● **Chiropodist (Podiatrist)** Ms G Withers Q: DPodM, S.R.Ch. M: S.C.P.
M Yrs. Est.: 10 (Ref:HM07431)

## FLOTATION TANK

**Flotation Tank**, 239 Liverpool Rd, Islington, London, **London (Greater)**, N1 1LX, ENG.
(T) 020 7607 5096
Speciality: Complementary Medicines & Therapy.
C M (Ref:HM07432)

Key: B Mind-Body Medicine, C Complementary Medicine, H Self Help Treatment, M Medicinal Therapy, O Oriental Medicine, P Postural Therapy, S Manipulative Structural Therapy, T Touch Therapy

**FLOURA, H S**
**H S Floura**, 1a Moore Avenue, Bradford, **Yorkshire (West)**, BD6 3HH, ENG.
(T) 01274 600659
Speciality: Osteopathy.
● **Owner** Mr H Floura
P S T (Ref:HM07433)

**FLOWERDEW, M**
**M Flowerdew**, Lower Olland St, Bungay, **Suffolk**, NR35 1BY, ENG.
(T) 01986 892846
Speciality: Acupuncture.
O (Ref:HM07434)

**FLOWERDEW, M**
**M Flowerdew**, 14 Thoroughfare, Halesworth, **Suffolk**, IP19 8AH, ENG.
(T) 01986 872899
Speciality: Acupuncture.
O (Ref:HM07435)

**FLOWERS AROMATICS**
**Flowers Aromatics**, 606 Leeds Rd, Dewsbury, **Yorkshire (West)**, WF12 7QG, ENG.
(T) 01924 430344
Speciality: Aromatherapy.
M O (Ref:HM07436)

**FLOWERS, H M**
**H M Flowers**, 41 St Albans Rd, Northampton, **Northamptonshire**, NN3 2RH, ENG.
(T) 01604 401180
Speciality: Chiropodists (Podiatrists).
● **Owner** Mrs H Flowers
S (Ref:HM07437)

**FLOYD, MICHELLE**
**Homoeopath**, 56 Osborne Rd, Brighton, **Sussex (East)**, BN1 6LQ, ENG.
(T) 01273 563727
Speciality: Complementary Therapy, Homeopathy, Meditation. ✔
● **Owner** Ms M Floyd
M Yrs. Est.: 7 (Ref:HM07438)

**FLYNN, FRANCESCA**
**Francesca Flynn**, 24 High St, Dronfield, **Derbyshire**, S18 1PY, ENG.
(T) 01246 411067
Speciality: Complementary Medicines & Therapy.
M (Ref:HM07439)

**FLYNN, FRANCESCA**
**Francesca Flynn**, 62 Bower Rd, Sheffield, **Yorkshire (South)**, S10 1ER, ENG.
(T) 01142 686247
Speciality: Reflexology.
S T (Ref:HM07440)

**FLYNN, GERARD**
**Gerard Flynn D O M R O**, 3 Merrion Ct Ailesbury Rd, Ballsbridge, **County Dublin**, IRE.
(T) 01269 5525
Speciality: Osteopathy.
P S T (Ref:HM07441)

**FLYNN, GILLIAN**
**Gillian Flynn**, 9 Moor Cl, Finchampstead, Wokingham, **Berkshire**, RG40 4EZ, ENG.
(T) 01189 328350 (F) 01189 328350
Speciality: Reflexology.
S T (Ref:HM07442)

**FLYNN, GIRON DE**
**GIRON de FLYNN MCH BA ADHP**, Balrothery, Balbriggan, **County Dublin**, IRE.
(T) 01841 6272
(W) www.hypnosiseire.com
Speciality: Complementary Medicines & Therapy.
M (Ref:HM07443)

**FLYNN, JANE C**
**Jane C Flynn**, Ascot Complementary Health Centre, 57 High St, Ascot, **Berkshire**, SL5 7HP, ENG.
(T) 01344 620174 (F) 01344 623378
Speciality: Acupuncture.
● **Owner** Mrs J Flynn
O (Ref:HM07444)

**FLYNN, JOHN K**
**John K Flynn**, 264 Bath St, Glasgow, **Glasgow (City of)**, G2 4JP, SCO.
(T) 01413 321390
Speciality: Chiropodists (Podiatrists).
S (Ref:HM07445)

**FLYNN, K**
**K Flynn**, The Surgery, Canada Rd, Cromer, **Norfolk**, NR27 9AH, ENG.
(T) 01263 511911 (F) 01263 515577
Speciality: Chiropodists (Podiatrists).
● **Owner** Mr K Flynn
S (Ref:HM07446)

**FLYNN, LISA**
**Lisa Flynn**, 11A Litchdon St, Barnstaple, **Devon**, EX32 8ND, ENG.
(T) 01271 376456
Speciality: Osteopathy.
● **Owner** Miss L Flynn
P S T (Ref:HM07447)

**FLYNN, T G**
**T G Flynn**, 1a Tait St, Carlisle, **Cumbria**, CA1 1RU, ENG.
(T) 01228 528084
Speciality: Chiropodists (Podiatrists).
● **Owner** Mr T Flynn
S (Ref:HM07448)

**FOCUS 4 HEALTH**
**Focus 4 Health**, 235 Cowley Rd, Oxford, **Oxfordshire**, OX1 4XG, ENG.
(T) 01865 790235
Speciality: Complementary Medicines & Therapy.
● **Owner** Miss N Plested
C M (Ref:HM07449)

**FOCUS COUNSELLING AND THERAPY**
**Focus Counselling And Therapy**, West End Hse, West St, Drogheda, **County Louth**, IRE.
(T) 04198 44322
Speciality: Counselling.
B H (Ref:HM07450)

**FOGDEN, O**
**O Fogden**, 27 Springfield Rd, Aughton, Ormskirk, **Lancashire**, L39 6ST, ENG.
(T) 01695 422697
Speciality: Physiotherapy.
● **Owner** Mr O Fogden
P S T (Ref:HM07451)

**FOGG, HELEN**
**Helen Fogg**, 1 Penrith Rd, Basingstoke, **Hampshire**, RG21 8XN, ENG.
(T) 01256 325946
Speciality: Holistic Healing, Hypnosis, Kinesiology, Reiki.
● **Owner** Ms H Fogg
C (Ref:HM07452)

**FOGGETT, GLENDA**
**Glenda Foggett**, 19 St Anselms Rd, Worthing, **Sussex (West)**, BN14 7EW, ENG.
(T) 01903 217577
Speciality: Reflexology.
● **Owner** Mrs G Foggett
S T (Ref:HM07453)

**FOGGIE, MARGARET**
**Margaret Foggie**, 468 Perth Rd, Dundee, **Angus**, DD2 1NG, SCO.
(T) 01382 669691 (F) 01382 21275
Speciality: Chiropody, Indian Head Massage. ✔
● **Owner/Chiropodist** Mrs M Foggie Q: MBChA, MSSCh.
T Yrs. Est.: 2 (Ref:HM07454)

**FOGGIN, SYLVIA**
**Sylvia Foggin**, 15 Glamis Avenue, Newcastle Upon Tyne, **Tyne and Wear**, NE3 5SY, ENG.
(T) 01912 363446
Speciality: Reflexology.
S T (Ref:HM07455)

**FOLEY, EILISH**
**Eilish Foley**, Ballynoran, Charleville, **County Cork**, IRE.
(T) 06381 228
Speciality: Complementary Medicines & Therapy.
M (Ref:HM07456)

**FOLEY, G B & ASSOCIATES**
**G B Foley & Associates**, Sandal Health Centre, Asdale Rd, Wakefield, **Yorkshire (West)**, WF2 7JE, ENG.
(T) 01924 256009
Speciality: Chiropodists (Podiatrists).
● **Owner** Mr G Foley
S (Ref:HM07457)

**FOLEY, TRISHA**
**Trisha Foley**, 3 Park View Victoria Rd, Cork, **County Cork**, IRE.
(T) 021 4975 529
Speciality: Complementary Medicines & Therapy.
M (Ref:HM07458)

**FOLKER, N**
**N Folker**, Norwich Chiropractic Clinic, 109 Newmarket Rd, Norwich, **Norfolk**, NR2 2HT, ENG.
(T) 01603 250980
Speciality: Chiropractic.
P S T (Ref:HM07459)

**FOLKESTONE PHYSIO CENTRE**
**Folkestone Physiotherapy Centre**, Folkestone Sports Centre, 18 Radnor Park Avenue, Folkestone, **Kent**, CT19 5HX, ENG.
(T) 01303 850595
Speciality: Physiotherapy.
P S T (Ref:HM07460)

**FONTANA, YVONNE**
**Yvonne Fontana**, Flat 3, Parkham Court, Shortlands Rd, Bromley, **Kent**, BR2 0JF, ENG.
(T) 020 8460 0577
Speciality: Reflexology.
● **Partner** Mr J Fontana
S T (Ref:HM07461)

**FONTWELL PHYSIOTHERAPY CLINIC**
**Fontwell Physiotherapy Clinic**, Newlands, Arundel Rd, Fontwell, Arundel, **Sussex (West)**, BN18 0SD, ENG.
(T) 01243 544806 (F) 01243 544806
Speciality: Physiotherapy.
● **Partner** Mrs K Shrimpton
P S T (Ref:HM07462)

**FOORD, AUDREY**
**Audrey Foord**, 11 Nevill Park, Tunbridge Wells, **Kent**, TN4 8NN, ENG.
(T) 01892 523074
Speciality: Chiropody, Indian Head Massage, Physiotherapy, Reflexology.
● **Partner** Mrs A Foord
C (Ref:HM07463)

**FOOT & ANKLE CLINIC**
**Foot & Ankle Clinic**, 14 Russell St, Armagh, **County Armagh**, BT61 9AA, NIR.
(T) 028 3752 8882
Speciality: Chiropodists (Podiatrists).
● **Owner** Miss F Campbell
S (Ref:HM07464)

**FOOT & BACK CLINIC**
**Foot & Back Clinic (The)**, 53 Carlton Rd, Boston, **Lincolnshire**, PE21 8PA, ENG.
(T) 01205 357011
Speciality: Chiropodists (Podiatrists).
S (Ref:HM07465)

**FOOT CARE CENTRE**
**Foot Care Centre (The)**, 30 Elm Pk Gdns, South Croydon, **Surrey**, CR2 8RU, ENG.
(T) 020 8651 4202
Speciality: Chiropody. ✔ 💳
● **Owner/Chiropodist** Mr K Harris Q: M.S.C.P. M: S.R.Ch.
P S T Yrs. Est.: 15 (Ref:HM07466)

**FOOT CARE CLINIC**
**Foot Care Clinic (The)**, 87 New Sq, Chesterfield, **Derbyshire**, S40 1AH, ENG.
(T) 01246 207774
Speciality: Chiropodists (Podiatrists).
● **Owner** Miss K Harrison
S (Ref:HM07467)

**FOOT CARE NORTHERN IRELAND**
**Foot Care Northern Ireland**, 22 Carwood Park,



Key continued: **Yrs.Est:** Years Established **Q:** Qualifications **M:** Professional Membership ✔ Indemnity Insurance 💳 Accept Credit Cards

Newtownabbey, **County Antrim**, BT36 5JU, NIR.
**(T)** 028 9084 1103
Speciality: Chiropodists (Podiatrists).
● **Owner** Mr D Hallowell
S (**Ref:**HM07468)

## FOOT CENTRE
**Foot Centre (The)**, 1st Floor, Eothen House, Eothen Cl, Caterham, **Surrey**, CR3 6JU, ENG.
**(T)** 01883 348544
Speciality: Chiropodists (Podiatrists).
● **Owner** Mrs A Bullen
S (**Ref:**HM07469)

## FOOT CLINIC
**Foot Clinic**, 89 High St Wimbledon, London, **London (Greater)**, SW19 5EG, ENG.
**(T)** 020 8879 1345
Speciality: Chiropodists (Podiatrists).
S (**Ref:**HM07470)

## FOOT CLINIC
**Foot Clinic (The)**, 4 Newstead Rd, Wakefield, **Yorkshire (West)**, WF1 2DA, ENG.
**(T)** 01924 364581
Speciality: Chiropodists (Podiatrists).
S (**Ref:**HM07471)

## FOOT CLINIC
**Foot Clinic (The)**, 191 Old Rd West, Gravesend, **Kent**, DA11 0LU, ENG.
**(T)** 01474 535373 **(F)** 07010 700564
Speciality: Chiropodists (Podiatrists).
● **Owner** Mr A Randhawa
S (**Ref:**HM07472)

## FOOT CLINIC
**Foot Clinic (The)**, Canterbury House, 85 Newhall St, Birmingham, **Midlands (West)**, B3 1LH, ENG.
**(T)** 01212 361983
Speciality: Chiropodists (Podiatrists).
S (**Ref:**HM07473)

## FOOT CLINIC & THERAPY ROOM
**Foot Clinic & Therapy Room (The)**, 300A Torquay Rd, Paignton, **Devon**, TQ3 2ER, ENG.
**(T)** 01803 525533
Speciality: Acupuncture, Chiropody, Indian Head Massage, Massage (Therapeutic), Podiatry. ✓
● **Reflexologist** Ms T Hooks Q: Dip.Reflex. M: AoR.
● **Masseur** Mr D Hall Q: ITEC. M: ITEC.
● **Acupuncturist** Pat Price Q: Cert.Soc.Serv, Lic.Ac, MBAcC. M: BAcC.
● **Chiropodist** Mr S Acres Q: BSc (Hons), M.S.C.P, S.R.Ch. M: S.C.P.
S Yrs. Est.: 4 (**Ref:**HM07474)

## FOOT FIRST
**Foot First**, North West London Medical Centre, 56 Maida Vale, London, **London (Greater)**, W9 1PP, ENG.
**(T)** 020 7287 5531
Speciality: Chiropodists (Podiatrists).
S (**Ref:**HM07475)

## FOOT FLEX
**Foot Flex**, 10 Raby Cl, Tividale, Oldbury, **Midlands (West)**, B69 1US, ENG.
**(T)** 01384 241678
Speciality: Reflexology.
S T (**Ref:**HM07476)

## FOOT GALLERY
**Foot Gallery (The)**, 4 Station Rd, Biddulph, Stoke-On-Trent, **Staffordshire**, ST8 6BJ, ENG.
**(T)** 01782 522449 **(F)** 01782 832872
Speciality: Chiropodists (Podiatrists).
● **Owner** Mr C Bradley
S (**Ref:**HM07477)

## FOOT HEALTH CENTRE
**Foot Health Centre**, 178 Brighton Rd, Coulsdon, **London (Greater)**, CR5 2NF, ENG.
**(T)** 020 8660 0349
Speciality: Chiropodists (Podiatrists).
● **Manager** Miss A Barton
S (**Ref:**HM07478)

## FOOT HEALTH CENTRE
**Foot Health Centre (The)**, Therapies Dept, East Surrey Hospital, Canada Avenue, Redhill, **Surrey**, RH1 5RH, ENG.
**(T)** 01737 782922
Speciality: Chiropodists (Podiatrists).
S (**Ref:**HM07479)

## FOOT HEALTH CLINIC
**Foot Health Clinic**, Woodhatch Centre, Whitebeam Drive, Reigate, **Surrey**, RH2 7LS, ENG.
**(T)** 01737 242442 **(F)** 01737 823851
Speciality: Chiropodists (Podiatrists).
● **Partner** Ms M Elliott
S (**Ref:**HM07480)

## FOOT HEALTH CLINIC
**Foot Health Clinic**, 27 Market Pl, Pontefract, **Yorkshire (West)**, WF8 1AG, ENG.
**(T)** 01977 792985
Speciality: Chiropodists (Podiatrists).
● **Owner** Mr S Bradley
S (**Ref:**HM07481)

## FOOT HEALTH CLINIC
**Foot Health Clinic (The)**, 69 High St, Saffron Walden, **Essex**, CB10 1AA, ENG.
**(T)** 01799 521496
Speciality: Biomechanics, Podiatry, Foot Surgery. ✓
● **Chiropodist** Ms P Brooks Q: M.S.C.P, S.R.Ch. M: S.C.P.
● **Podiatrist** Mr G Howell Q: DPodM, FCPod(s), M.S.C.P, S.R.Ch. M: S.C.P.
P Yrs. Est.: 20 (**Ref:**HM07482)

## FOOT HEALTH CLINIC
**Foot Health Clinic (The)**, 1 Crompton St, Bury, **Lancashire**, BL9 0AD, ENG.
**(T)** 01617 644479
Speciality: Chiropody.
S (**Ref:**HM07483)

## FOOT MECHANIX
**Foot Mechanix**, 22 Station Approach, West Byfleet, **Surrey**, KT14 6NF, ENG.
**(T)** 01932 353568
Speciality: Chiropodists (Podiatrists).
● **Owner** Mrs K Knightly
S (**Ref:**HM07484)

## FOOT SHOP
**Foot Shop**, Savoy Centre, Sauchiehall St, Glasgow, **Glasgow (City of)**, G2 3ER, SCO.
**(T)** 01413 322860
Speciality: Chiropodists (Podiatrists).
● **Owner** Mrs J Hutchinson
S (**Ref:**HM07485)

## FOOT SHOP
**Foot Shop (The)**, 18 Whitefield Rd, New Milton, **Hampshire**, BH25 6DF, ENG.
**(T)** 01425 638474
Speciality: Chiropody. ✓
M Yrs. Est.: 20 (**Ref:**HM07486)

## FOOT SOUL & BODYWORKS
**Foot Soul & Bodyworks**, 44 Lyndhurst Rd, Heath Hayes, Cannock, **Staffordshire**, WS12 5HD, ENG.
**(T)** 01543 274221
Speciality: Acupressure, Aromatherapy, Bach Remedies, Complementary Therapy, Dowsing, Healer, Holistic Healing, Indian Head Massage, Meditation, Metamorphic Therapy, Nutritional Therapy, Reflexology, Reiki, Touch Therapy. ✓
● **Natural Health Practitioner** Ms G Ferriday Q: BFRP, IIHHT, ITEC, MAR. M: AoR.
T Yrs. Est.: 8 (**Ref:**HM07487)

## FOOT STUDIO
**Foot Studio (The)**, The Spinney House, Old Down Hill, Severn Beach, Bristol, BS35 4PA, ENG.
**(T)** 01454 618342
Speciality: Chiropodists (Podiatrists).
S (**Ref:**HM07488)

## FOOT TREATMENT SURGERY
**Foot Treatment Surgery**, 330B Soho Rd, Birmingham, **Midlands (West)**, B21 9NA, ENG.
**(T)** 01212 405445
Speciality: Chiropodists (Podiatrists).
● **Owner** Mr S Miah
S (**Ref:**HM07489)

## FOOT WISE CHIROPODY
**Foot Wise Chiropody**, 144 Boldmere Rd, Sutton Coldfield, **Midlands (West)**, B73 5UD, ENG.
**(T)** 01213 557242
Speciality: Chiropodists (Podiatrists).
● **Owner** Mrs S Bharakhada
S (**Ref:**HM07490)

## FOOTCARE
**Footcare**, Nant Llys, Penisa, Dyserth, Rhyl, **Denbighshire**, LL18 6BW, WAL.
**(T)** 01745 571740
Speciality: Chiropodists (Podiatrists).
● **Owner** Mrs G Carr
S (**Ref:**HM07491)

## FOOTCARE
**Footcare**, 2 Gurneys Mews, Gurneys Lane, Camborne, **Cornwall**, TR14 8JR, ENG.
**(T)** 01209 612888 **(F)** 01736 40030
**(E)** jmattchir@aol.com
Speciality: Chiropody, Podiatry. ✓
● **Owner/Chiropodist** Mr J Matthews
**(T)** 01209 6612888 Q: D.B.Ch, D.S.Ch. M: B.A.Ch.P.
C Yrs. Est.: 15 (**Ref:**HM07492)

## FOOTCARE CENTRE
**Footcare Centre**, 9-11 Turnpike House, Market St, Leigh, **Manchester (Greater)**, WN7 1DT, ENG.
**(T)** 01942 262212
Speciality: Chiropody.
● **Owner** Mr P Corbett
S (**Ref:**HM07493)

## FOOTCARE CENTRE
**Footcare Centre (The)**, 9 Woodcock Hill, Harrow, **London (Greater)**, HA3 0XP, ENG.
**(T)** 020 8907 9901
Speciality: Chiropodists (Podiatrists).
S (**Ref:**HM07494)

## FOOTCARE CENTRE
**Footcare Centre (The)**, 94 Snowsfields, London, **London (Greater)**, SE1 3SS, ENG.
**(T)** 020 7403 2571
Speciality: Reflexology.
● **Owner** Mr K Harris
S T (**Ref:**HM07495)

## FOOTCARE CLINIC
**Footcare Clinic**, 149 Bradford Rd, Stanningley, Pudsey, **Yorkshire (West)**, LS28 6AT, ENG.
**(T)** 01132 552111
Speciality: Chiropodists (Podiatrists).
● **Owner** Mr M Hector
S (**Ref:**HM07496)

## FOOTCARE NI
**Footcare NI**, Unit 1 Mallusk Park, Mallusk Rd, Newtownabbey, **County Antrim**, BT36 4FS, NIR.
**(T)** 028 9034 2088
Speciality: Chiropodists (Podiatrists).
● **Owner** Mr D Holliwell
S (**Ref:**HM07497)

## FOOTCARE SERVICE
**Footcare Service**, 9 The Village, London, **London (Greater)**, SE7 8UG, ENG.
**(T)** 020 8265 5223
Speciality: Chiropodists (Podiatrists).
S (**Ref:**HM07498)

## FOOT-EASE CHIROPODIST
**Foot-Ease Chiropodist**, 7 Kirk Rd, Manchester, **Manchester (Greater)**, M19 2RH, ENG.
**(T)** 01612 920487
Speciality: Chiropodists (Podiatrists).
● **Owner** Mrs J Mollard
S (**Ref:**HM07499)

## FOOTEC MEDICAL
**Footec Medical**, 3 Cherry Tree Drive, Brixton, Plymouth, **Devon**, PL8 2DD, ENG.
**(T)** 01752 880218 **(F)** 01752 880218
**(E)** footec@footcare1freeserve.co.uk
**(W)** www.footec.co.uk
Speciality: Biomechanics, Chiropody, Cryo Surgery, Gait Analysis, Nail Surgery, Podiatry. ✓
● **Chiropodist (Podiatrist)** Mr M Couchman Q: BSc, Inst.CH.P, S.R.Ch. M: Inst.CH.P.



Key: B Mind-Body Medicine C Complementary Medicine H Self Help Treatment M Medicinal Therapy O Oriental Medicine P Postural Therapy S Manipulative Structural Therapy T Touch Therapy

C H Yrs. Est.: 18 (Ref:HM07500)

### FOOTEZE
**Footeze**, 14 Woodland Rd, Darlington, **County Durham**, DL3 7PL, ENG.
(T) 01325 363433
Speciality: Reflexology.
S T (Ref:HM07501)

### FOOTHOLD REFLEXOLOGY
**Foothold Reflexology**, 9 Church Lane, Killamarsh, Sheffield, **Yorkshire (South)**, S21 1AS, ENG.
(T) 01142 475060 (F) 01142 510130
Speciality: Reflexology.
● **Owner** Mr C Weston
S T (Ref:HM07502)

### FOOTLOOSE CHIROPODY CLINIC
**Footloose Chiropody Clinic**, 17 Fulham High St, London, **London (Greater)**, SW6 3JH, ENG.
(T) 020 7610 9161 (F) 020 7736 6114
Speciality: Chiropody.
S (Ref:HM07503)

### FOOTMARK, G & P
**G & P Footmark**, 38 Thurloe Pl, London, **London (Greater)**, SW7 2HP, ENG.
(T) 020 7838 0838
Speciality: Chiropractic.
P S T (Ref:HM07504)

### FOOTMATTERS PODIATRY CLINIC
**Footmatters Podiatry Clinic**, 7-8 The Triangle, Cobden Avenue, Southampton, **Hampshire**, SO18 1FZ, ENG.
(T) 023 8055 5372 (F) 023 8055 5334
Speciality: Chiropodists (Podiatrists).
● **Owner** Mrs S O'Donnell
S (Ref:HM07505)

### FOOTPAD
**Footpad**, 4 Paddington St, London, **London (Greater)**, W1M 3LA, ENG.
(T) 020 7487 3998
Speciality: Chiropody.
S (Ref:HM07506)

### FOOTPRINTS
**Footprints**, 24 Front St, Sherburn, Durham, **County Durham**, DH6 1HB, ENG.
(T) 01913 722736
Speciality: Biomechanics, Chiropody, Nail Surgery, Podiatry. ✔
● **Chiropodist** Joanne Woods Q: BSc (Hons), M.S.C.P, S.R.Ch.
● **Owner/Chiropodist** Mr D Nicholls Q: BSc (Hons), M.S.C.P, S.R.Ch.
M Yrs. Est.: 1 (Ref:HM07507)

### FOOTSTEP CHIROPODY
**Footstep Chiropody**, Red Oaks, Ipplepen, Newton Abbot, **Devon**, TQ12 5UA, ENG.
(T) 01803 872054
Speciality: Chiropodists (Podiatrists).
● **Owner** Mrs A Cutts
S (Ref:HM07508)

### FOOTSTEP CHIROPODY
**Footstep Chiropody**, 67 Fore St, Bovey Tracey, Newton Abbot, **Devon**, TQ13 9AB, ENG.
(T) 01626 836837
Speciality: Chiropodists (Podiatrists).
● **Owner** Mrs A Cutts
S (Ref:HM07509)

### FOOTSTEPS
**Footsteps**, 4 Clarence Rd, Shanklin, **Isle of Wight**, PO37 7BH, ENG.
(T) 01983 868288 (F) 01983 868279
(E) footstepsuk@netscapeonline.co.uk
(W) members.netscapeonline.co.uk/footstepsuk
Speciality: Biomechanics, Chiropody, Nail Surgery, Podiatry. ✔
● **Podiatrist** Mr G Knapper Q: M.S.C.P, S.R.Ch. M: S.C.P.
M Yrs. Est.: 4 (Ref:HM07510)

### FOOTSTEPS
**Footsteps**, 14A South St, Braunton, **Devon**, EX33 2AA, ENG.
(T) 01271 814257
Speciality: Chiropodists (Podiatrists).
● **Owner** Mrs L Troot
S (Ref:HM07511)

### FOOTSTEPS
**Footsteps**, 12 Malvern Gardens, Loughton, **Essex**, IG10 3AD, ENG.
(T) 020 8508 6282
Speciality: Reflexology.
● **Owner** Ms S Johns
S T (Ref:HM07512)

### FOOTSTEPS THERAPY CENTRE
**Footsteps Therapy Centre**, 113A High St, Ryde, **Isle of Wight**, PO33 2SU, ENG.
(T) 01983 868288 (F) 01983 868279
(E) footstepsuk@netscapeonline.co.uk
(W) members.netscapeonline.co.uk/footstepsuk/
Speciality: Biomechanics, Chiropody, Nail Surgery.
● **Podiatrist** Mr G Knapper Q: M.S.C.P, S.R.Ch. M: S.C.P, S.R.Ch.
M Yrs. Est.: 4 (Ref:HM07513)

### FOOTSURE
**Footsure**, 4 Viaduct Rd, Clarkston, Glasgow, **Glasgow (City of)**, G76 8BW, SCO.
(T) 01416 443752
Speciality: Chiropody.
● **Chiropodist** Mrs A Kermack Q: L.V.Ch.C. M: Scottish Chiropodist Assoc.
S Yrs. Est.: 14 (Ref:HM07514)

### FOOTWORKS
**Footworks**, 15 Low Mill, Greta Side, Keswick, **Cumbria**, CA12 5LL, ENG.
(T) 01768 774744 (F) 01768 775654
Speciality: Biomechanics, Chiropody, Nail Surgery, Podiatry. ✔ [credit card]
● **Chiropodist (Podiatrist)** Ms V Stewart Q: BSc (Hons), DPodM, S.R.Ch. M: S.C.P.
M Yrs. Est.: 6 (Ref:HM07515)

### FOOTWORKS
**Footworks**, 8a Wilkinson Walk, Market Drayton, **Shropshire**, TF9 1PW, ENG.
(T) 01630 653533 (F) 01630 653533
Speciality: Chiropodists (Podiatrists).
● **Owner** Mr R Aldcroft
S (Ref:HM07516)

### FOOTWORKS
**Footworks (Louise Hussey)**, 12 Hawkeshead Rd, Burtonwood, Warrington, **Cheshire**, WA5 4PW, ENG.
(T) 01925 222183
Speciality: Chiropodists (Podiatrists).
● **Owner** Mrs L Hussey
S (Ref:HM07517)

### FORBES, D LOCKHART
**D Lockhart Forbes**, 7 Lomond Pl, Balmullo, St. Andrews, **Fife**, KY16 0DL, SCO.
(T) 01334 870510
Speciality: Chiropodists (Podiatrists).
S (Ref:HM07518)

### FORCE CENTRE
**Force Centre For Alternative Healing (The)**, Dovecot Cottage, Kirkby Fleetham Hall, Kirkby Fleetham, Northallerton, **Yorkshire (North)**, DL7 0SU, ENG.
(T) 01609 748133 (F) 01609 748133
Speciality: Complementary Medicines & Therapy.
● **Director** Mr D Austen
M (Ref:HM07519)

### FORCE, GAYLE
**Gayle Force**, Eastholme, Boldventure Rd, Boscoppa, St. Austell, **Cornwall**, PL25 3EA, ENG.
(T) 01726 70786
Speciality: Absent Healing, Colour Therapy, Counselling, Crystal Healing, Dowsing, Faith Healing, Meditation, Paranormal Therapies, Sound Therapy, Visualisation Therapy, Voice Therapy, Clairvoyance, Clairaudio, Phychometry.
● **Healer** Mrs G Force M: BAHA.
B Yrs. Est.: 5 (Ref:HM07520)

### FORD OSTEOPATHIC CLINIC
**Ford Osteopathic Clinic Ltd (The)**, Briarbank, 27 Croxton Rd, Thetford, **Norfolk**, IP24 1AF, ENG.
(T) 01842 750650
(E) andrew.hamilton3@btinternet.co.uk
Speciality: Osteopathy, Reiki. ✔
● **Osteopath** Ms H Edwards Q: BSc (Hons), DO. M: GOsC.
● **Reiki Therapist** Ms R Hamilton
(T) 01842 751213 Q: Reiki 2.
● **Osteopath** Philippe Gely Q: BSc (Hons), DO. M: GOsC.
● **Osteopath** Mr A Hamilton Q: DO. M: GOsC.
S Yrs. Est.: 10 (Ref:HM07521)

### FORD, A (DR)
**Dr A Ford**, 82 Lowlands Rd, Harrow, **London (Greater)**, HA1 3AN, ENG.
(T) 020 8864 6768
Speciality: Chiropractors.
P S T (Ref:HM07522)

### FORD, AUDREY
**Audrey Ford**, The New Medical Centre, 264 Brentwood Rd, Romford, **Essex**, RM2 5SU, ENG.
(T) 07956 161410
Speciality: Chiropractic.
P S T (Ref:HM07523)

### FORD, G
**G Ford**, 18-20 East St, Littlehampton, **Sussex (West)**, BN17 6AL, ENG.
(T) 01903 731111
Speciality: Osteopathy.
P S T (Ref:HM07524)

### FORD, MARGARET
**Margaret Ford**, 12 Gray Park, Perth Rd, Cowdenbeath, **Fife**, KY4 9EZ, SCO.
(T) 01383 513611
Speciality: Reflexology.
S T (Ref:HM07525)

### FORD, MARIA
**Maria Ford**, 22 Farnham Rd, Birmingham, **Midlands (West)**, B21 8EG, ENG.
(T) 01215 236176
Speciality: Floral Essence Therapy, Homeopathy, Reiki. ✔
● **Homeopath** Ms M Ford Q: LCPH. M: HMA.
C Yrs. Est.: 6 (Ref:HM07526)

### FORD, PETER A
**Peter A Ford**, 316 High St, Dorking, **Surrey**, RH4 1QX, ENG.
(T) 01306 887793
Speciality: Chiropractors.
P S T (Ref:HM07527)

### FORD, SUSAN
**Susan Ford**, 304 Knightsfield, Welwyn Garden City, **Hertfordshire**, AL8 7NQ, ENG.
(T) 01707 332535
Speciality: Chiropodists (Podiatrists).
● **Owner** Mrs S Ford
S (Ref:HM07528)

### FORD, SUSAN
**Susan Ford**, 89 New North Rd, Huddersfield, **Yorkshire (West)**, HD1 5ND, ENG.
(T) 01484 548134
Speciality: Physiotherapy.
● **Owner** Mr P Leary
P S T (Ref:HM07529)

### FORD, ZARA & ASSOCIATES
**Zara Ford & Associates**, Walnut Gr, Slade Rd, Portishead, Bristol, BS20 6BB, ENG.
(T) 01275 818303
Speciality: Osteopathy.
● **Owner** Mrs Z Ford
P S T (Ref:HM07530)

### FORDE, M
**M Forde BA, Dip App Psych HDipEd, Reg Psychol, MIAHM**, 316 Howth Rd, Dublin, **County Dublin**, IRE.
(T) 01833 9902
Speciality: Psychology.
B (Ref:HM07531)

### FORDE, MARGARET
**Margaret Forde Dip APP PSYCH**, 316 Howth Rd, Dublin, **County Dublin**, IRE.
(T) 01833 9902
Speciality: Psychotherapy.
B (Ref:HM07532)

### FORDE, MARGARET
**Margaret Forde Reg Psychol**, 316 Howth Rd,


Key continued: Yrs.Est: Years Established Q: Qualifications M: Professional Membership ✔ Indemnity Insurance [credit card] Accept Credit Cards

IRE.
(T) 01833 9902
Speciality: Psychology.
B (Ref:HM07533)

## FORDHAM, ANNICK S

**Annick S Fordham**, Dental Practice, 136 Reading Rd, Henley-on-Thames, **Oxfordshire**, RG9 1DN, ENG.
(T) 01491 412027
Speciality: Osteopathy.
● **Owner** Ms A Fordham
P S T (Ref:HM07534)

## FORDHAM, BOB

**Bob Fordham**, Newcastle Homoeopathic Clinic, 87 Holly Avenue, Jesmond, Newcastle Upon Tyne, **Tyne and Wear**, NE2 2QB, ENG.
(T) 01912 817539
Speciality: Homeopathy.
M (Ref:HM07535)

## FORDHAM, S

**S Fordham**, 7 Hurst Way, Pyrford, Woking, **Surrey**, GU22 8PH, ENG.
(T) 01932 347857 (F) 01932 351043
Speciality: Electrolysis.
● **Owner** Mrs S Fordham
T (Ref:HM07536)

## FORDHAM, SHARON

**Sharon Fordham**, College Rd, Isleworth, **London (Greater)**, TW7 5DW, ENG.
(T) 020 8560 7641
Speciality: Hypnosis.
● **Owner** Mrs S Fordham
B (Ref:HM07537)

## FORD-HAMMOND, BARBARA

**Barbara Ford-Hammond**, 2 Barnfield Cottages, Newton Valence, Alton, **Hampshire**, GU34 3RH, ENG.
(T) 01420 588619
Speciality: Hypnosis.
B (Ref:HM07538)

## FORE STREET CHIROPODY

**Fore Street Chiropody**, 50 Fore St, St. Marychurch, Torquay, **Devon**, TQ1 4LX, ENG.
(T) 01803 329369
Speciality: Chiropodists (Podiatrists).
● **Owner** Mrs P Haddican
S (Ref:HM07539)

## FORE STREET CTRE OF COMP MED

**Fore Street Centre Of Complementary Medicine (The)**, 322 Fore St, London, **London (Greater)**, N9 0PN, ENG.
(T) 020 8803 8102
Speciality: Complementary Medicines & Therapy.
● **Partner** Ms J Mithell
C M (Ref:HM07540)

## FOREMAN, R

**R Foreman**, 91 Brierton Lane, Hartlepool, **Cleveland**, TS25 5DW, ENG.
(T) 01429 267527
Speciality: Hypnosis.
● **Owner** Mr R Foreman
B (Ref:HM07541)

## FORENSIC PSYCHOLOGY AGENCY

**Forensic Psychology Agency (The)**, P O Box 150, Wakefield, **Yorkshire (West)**, WF1 3YX, ENG.
(T) 01924 377997
Speciality: Psychology.
B (Ref:HM07542)

## FORERO-CASAS, SANDYRA

**Sandyra Forero-Casas**, 49B Danby St, London, **London (Greater)**, SE15 4BS, ENG.
(T) 020 8265 6562
Speciality: Hypnosis.
● **Owner** Ms S Forero-Casas
B (Ref:HM07543)

## FOREST CHIROPODY

**Forest Chiropody**, 1 The Parade, Southampton Rd, Cadnam, Southampton, **Hampshire**, SO40 2NG, ENG.
(T) 023 8081 4903
Speciality: Chiropodists (Podiatrists).
S (Ref:HM07544)

## FOREST COMPLEMENTARY CLINIC

**Forest Complementary Clinic**, 843 Forest Rd, London, **London (Greater)**, E17 4AT, ENG.
(T) 020 8531 7188
Speciality: Osteopathy.
P S T (Ref:HM07545)

## FOREST COMPLEMENTARY CLINIC

**Forest Complementary Clinic**, 86a The Broadway, Leigh-On-Sea, **Essex**, SS9 1AE, ENG.
(T) 01702 715203
Speciality: Osteopathy.
P S T (Ref:HM07546)

## FOREST GATE PHYSIOTHERAPY

**Forest Gate Physiotherapy**, 4 Forest Gate, Blackpool, **Lancashire**, FY3 9AW, ENG.
(T) 01253 398742 (F) 01253 304306
Speciality: Physiotherapy.
● **Owner** Mr C Cornah
P S T (Ref:HM07547)

## FOREST LODGE PSYCHOTHERAPY

**Forest Lodge Psychotherapy**, Forest Lodge, Cascob, Presteigne, **Powys**, LD8 2NT, WAL.
(T) 01547 560232
Speciality: Hypnosis.
● **Owner** Mr J Pugh
B (Ref:HM07548)

## FOREST ROW HOMEOPATHY

**Forest Row Homeopathy**, The Community Centre, Hartfield Rd, Forest Row, **Sussex (East)**, RH18 5DZ, ENG.
(T) 01342 826930
Speciality: Homeopathy.
M (Ref:HM07549)

## FOREST ROW OSTEOPATHIC CLINIC

**Forest Row Osteopathic Clinic**, First Floor, 13a Hartfield Rd, Forest Row, **Sussex (East)**, RH18 5DN, ENG.
(T) 01342 823722
Speciality: Osteopathy.
● **Partner** Mr G Ganson
P S T (Ref:HM07550)

## FOREST-HYPNOPSYCHOTHERAPY

**Forest Agency Hypnopsychotherapy**, 10 Eastwood Cl, London, **London (Greater)**, E18 1BX, ENG.
(T) 020 8502 4674 (F) 020 8508 6032
Speciality: Hypnosis, Psychotherapy.
● **Managing Director** Ms S Grant
B (Ref:HM07551)

## FORESTRIDGE HLTH & DRUG STORE

**Forestridge Health & Drug Store**, 50 High St, Tarvin, Chester, **Cheshire**, CH3 8EE, ENG.
(T) 01829 741874
Speciality: Complementary Medicines & Therapy.
C M (Ref:HM07552)

## FOREVER LIVING PRODUCTS

**Forever Living Products**, York House, 12 Drury Lane, Wakefield, **Yorkshire (West)**, WF1 2TE, ENG.
(T) 01924 372931 (F) 01924 381796
Speciality: Complementary Medicines & Therapy.
● **Manager** Mr K James
M (Ref:HM07553)

## FOREVER LIVING PRODUCTS

**Forever Living Products**, Little Hesteyri, Coxbury Lane, St. Briavels, Lydney, **Gloucestershire**, GL15 6QJ, ENG.
(T) 01594 810500 (F) 01594 810200
Speciality: Complementary Medicines & Therapy.
● **Owner** Mr R White
C M (Ref:HM07554)

## FOREVER LIVING PRODUCTS

**Forever Living Products**, Fintragh House, Sherfield Green, Sherfield-On-Loddon, Hook, **Hampshire**, RG27 0DE, ENG.
(T) 01256 883488
Speciality: Counselling, Permanent Hair Removal, Relationship Problems, Depression and Assertiveness Training. ✔
● **Manager** Mrs C Nightingale **Q:** C.Hyp, CMH, SRN. **M:** FHT, IHBC.
C Yrs. Est.: 11 (Ref:HM07555)

## FOREVER LIVING PRODUCTS

**Forever Living Products (UK) Ltd**, Foxholes, Bay Horse, Lancaster, **Lancashire**, LA2 9DB, ENG.
(T) 01524 792697
Speciality: Complementary Medicines & Therapy.
M (Ref:HM07556)

## FORLAND, ELAINA

**Elaina Forland**, 10 Hanyards Lane, Cuffley, Potters Bar, **Hertfordshire**, EN6 4AT, ENG.
(T) 01707 872308
Speciality: Hypnosis.
B (Ref:HM07557)

## FORMAN, LESLEY J

**Lesley J Forman**, 149 Ravenswood Rd, Arnold, Nottingham, **Nottinghamshire**, NG5 7GB, ENG.
(T) 01159 269107
Speciality: Aromatherapy.
M O (Ref:HM07558)

## FORMBY PHYSIOTHERAPY

**Formby Physiotherapy**, 95 Larkhill Lane, Formby, Liverpool, **Merseyside**, L37 1LU, ENG.
(T) 01704 874866 (F) 01704 874866
Speciality: Physiotherapy.
● **Owner** Mrs J Hughes
P S T (Ref:HM07559)

## FORMOSA CENTRE

**Formosa Centre**, 26 Wigmore St, London, **London (Greater)**, W1H 9DF, ENG.
(T) 020 7224 2884 (F) 020 7224 0869
Speciality: Complementary Medicines & Therapy.
● **Owner** Miss H Tang
C M (Ref:HM07560)

## FORMOSA HOUSE HOMEO CLINIC

**Formosa House Homeopathic Clinic**, 143 Alexandra Rd, Farnborough, **Hampshire**, GU14 6RR, ENG.
(T) 01252 658117 (F) 01252 658117
Speciality: Homeopathy.
● **Owner** Mrs J Malyon
M (Ref:HM07561)

## FORREST, E

**E Forrest**, 86 Babbacombe Rd, Torquay, **Devon**, TQ1 3SW, ENG.
(T) 01803 325657
Speciality: Chiropodists (Podiatrists).
● **Owner** Mrs W Evans
S (Ref:HM07562)

## FORREST, E A

**E A Forrest**, 12 Wellis Gardens, Margate, **Kent**, CT9 5RG, ENG.
(T) 01843 292992
Speciality: Chiropodists (Podiatrists).
S (Ref:HM07563)

## FORREST, LISA M

**Lisa M Forrest**, 80 Lichfield Rd, Sutton Coldfield, **Midlands (West)**, B74 2SY, ENG.
(T) 01213 548923 (F) 01213 544258
Speciality: Chiropodists (Podiatrists).
● **Owner** Mrs L Forrest
S (Ref:HM07564)

## FORREST, SAMANTHA

**Samantha Forrest**, 3 Frederick Pl, Wokingham, **Berkshire**, RG41 2YB, ENG.
(T) 01189 774113
Speciality: Reflexology, Reiki.
S T (Ref:HM07565)

## FORRESTER, CATHY

**Mrs Cathy Forrester**, 22 Auchavan Gardens, Glenrothes, **Fife**, KY7 4TU, SCO.
(T) 01592 631227
Speciality: Reflexology.
● **Owner** Mrs C Forrester
S T (Ref:HM07566)

## FORSHAW, ROBYN S

**Robyn S Forshaw**, Anscombe Rd, Worthing, **Sussex (West)**, BN11 5EN, ENG.
(T) 01903 506129

Key: B Mind-Body Medicine · C Complementary Medicine · H Self Help Treatment · M Medicinal Therapy · O Oriental Medicine · P Postural Therapy · S Manipulative Structural Therapy · T Touch Therapy

Speciality: Reflexology.
● **Owner** Ms R Forshaw
S T (Ref:HM07567)

## FORSHAW, VERONICA

**Veronica Forshaw**, 3 Otter Drive, Pickering, **Yorkshire (North)**, YO18 8TQ, ENG.
(T) 01751 473557
Speciality: Aromatherapy.
● **Owner** Mrs V Forshaw
M O (Ref:HM07568)

## FORSTER, FIONA

**Fiona Forster**, 35 Elworth St, Sandbach, **Cheshire**, CW11 1HA, ENG.
(T) 01270 760440
Speciality: Complementary Medicines & Therapy.
● **Owner** Fiona Forster
M (Ref:HM07569)

## FORSTER, LINDA

**Linda Forster**, Rowan Cottage, Hartford Bridge, Bedlington, **Northumberland**, NE22 6AN, ENG.
(W) www.therapycentre.net
Speciality: Nutritional Therapy, Speech Therapist. ✔
● **Nutritional Therapist** Mrs L Forster Q: ECNT, RNT.
C (Ref:HM07570)

## FORSTER, M

**M Forster**, 27 Ashby Rd, Watford, **Hertfordshire**, WD2 5HS, ENG.
(T) 01923 462346
Speciality: Reflexology.
● **Owner** Ms M Forster
S T (Ref:HM07571)

## FORSTER, M M

**M M Forster**, 4 Chatfields, Crawley, **Sussex (West)**, RH11 8PZ, ENG.
(T) 01293 544131
Speciality: Chiropodists (Podiatrists).
● **Owner** Mrs M Forster
S (Ref:HM07572)

## FORSYTH, CHARLES (DR)

**Dr Charles Forsyth**, 17 Nottingham Rd, South Croydon, **Surrey**, CR2 6AR, ENG.
(T) 01737 226338
Speciality: Homeopathy.
● **Owner** Dr C Forsyth
M (Ref:HM07573)

## FORSYTH, CHARLES (DR)

**Dr Charles Forsyth**, North Cottage, Dovers Green Rd, Reigate, **Surrey**, RH2 8BU, ENG.
(T) 01737 226338
Speciality: Homeopathy.
M (Ref:HM07574)

## FORSYTH, ELNA

**Elna Forsyth**, 43 Kingsdown Avenue, London, **London (Greater)**, W13 9PS, ENG.
(T) 020 7731 8197
Speciality: Reflexology.
S T (Ref:HM07575)

## FORSYTH, J M

**J M Forsyth**, George House, Long Buckby Wharf, Long Buckby, Northampton, **Northamptonshire**, NN6 7PP, ENG.
(T) 01327 844977 (F) 01327 842762
Speciality: Chiropodists (Podiatrists).
● **Owner** Mr J Forsyth
S (Ref:HM07576)

## FORSYTH, JILLIAN

**Jillian Forsyth**, 479 Wellingborough Rd, Northampton, **Northamptonshire**, NN3 3HN, ENG.
(T) 01604 714821
Speciality: Osteopathy.
P S T (Ref:HM07577)

## FORSYTH, JUSTIN

**Justin Forsyth**, 31B Market Pl, Ripley, **Derbyshire**, DE5 3HA, ENG.
(T) 01773 741777
Speciality: Chiropodists (Podiatrists).
● **Owner** Mr J Forsythe
S (Ref:HM07578)

## FORTEY, C J

**George Lane Podiatry**, 56 George Lane, Lichfield, **Staffordshire**, WS13 6DX, ENG.
(T) 01543 262639
Speciality: Podiatry, Biomechanical Assessments. ✔
● **Podiatric Specialist** Ms C Fortey Q: BSc (Hons), M.S.C.P, S.R.Ch. M: S.C.P.
P Yrs. Est.: 6 (Ref:HM07579)

## FORTEY, KEVIN

**Kevin Fortey**, 117 Wellington Hill West, Bristol, BS9 4QX, ENG.
(T) 01179 851495 (F) 01179 042935
Speciality: Clairvoyants & Palmists.
● **Owner** Mr K Fortey-Jones
B (Ref:HM07580)

## FORTON, LINDA

**Linda Forton**, Rose View, Field Head Lane, Halifax, **Yorkshire (West)**, HX2 9UL, ENG.
(T) 01422 244953
Speciality: Reflexology.
S T (Ref:HM07581)

## FORTUNES

**Fortunes**, 8a Union Rd, Ryde, **Isle of Wight**, PO33 2ER, ENG.
(T) 01983 812246
Speciality: Clairvoyants & Palmists.
● **Owner** Mrs R Mowbray
B (Ref:HM07582)

## FORUM FOR INDEPENDENT PSYCHO

**Forum For Independent Psychotherapists**, 167 Sumatra Rd, London, **London (Greater)**, NW6 1PN, ENG.
(T) 020 7431 8638
Speciality: Psychotherapy.
● **Employee** Mrs G Ghiaci
B (Ref:HM07583)

## FOSKETT, SARAH J

**Sarah J Foskett**, 64 High St, Porthmadog, **Gwynedd**, LL49 9LW, WAL.
(T) 01766 514680
Speciality: Osteopathy.
● **Partner** Ms S Foskett
P S T (Ref:HM07584)

## FOSSEY, LYNETTE

**Lynette Fossey**, 58 Privett Rd, Gosport, **Hampshire**, PO12 3SX, ENG.
(T) 023 9252 1118
Speciality: Aromatherapy, Massage (Therapeutic), Reflexology. ✔
● **Reflexologist** Ms L Fossey M: ICHT.
C Yrs. Est.: 4 (Ref:HM07585)

## FOSTER CLINIC

**Foster Clinic**, 148 Bells Rd, Gorleston, Great Yarmouth, **Norfolk**, NR31 6AG, ENG.
(T) 01493 604690 (F) 01493 604690
Speciality: Complementary Medicines & Therapy.
● **Owner** Mr S Foster
C M (Ref:HM07586)

## FOSTER, C

**C Foster**, 10 Ashley Rd, Salisbury, **Wiltshire**, SP2 7BZ, ENG.
(T) 01722 328675
Speciality: Chiropodists (Podiatrists).
S (Ref:HM07587)

## FOSTER, CHRIS

**Chris Foster**, Cygnus House, Black Swan Walk, Leominster, **Herefordshire**, HR6 8HU, ENG.
(T) 01568 614486
Speciality: Chiropodists (Podiatrists).
● **Owner** Mr C Foster
S (Ref:HM07588)

## FOSTER, E H

**E H Foster**, 152 Intake Lane, Barnsley, **Yorkshire (South)**, S75 2HU, ENG.
(T) 01226 284939 (F) 01226 284939
Speciality: Physiotherapy.
● **Owner** Mr E Foster
P S T (Ref:HM07589)

## FOSTER, G S

**G S Foster**, 7 Victoria Rd East, Hebburn, **Tyne and Wear**, NE31 1XG, ENG.
(T) 01914 285000
Speciality: Chiropodists (Podiatrists).
● **Owner** Mr G Foster
S (Ref:HM07590)

## FOSTER, J

**J Foster**, The Cottage, Speltham Hill, Hambledon, Waterlooville, **Hampshire**, PO7 4RU, ENG.
(T) 023 9263 2306
Speciality: Physiotherapy.
P S T (Ref:HM07591)

## FOSTER, J D

**J D Foster**, 428 Soundwell Rd, Bristol, BS15 1JU, ENG.
(T) 01179 615437
Speciality: Chiropodists (Podiatrists).
● **Owner** Mr J Foster
S (Ref:HM07592)

## FOSTER, JAMES M ASSOCIATES

**James M Foster Associates**, 158 Gudge Heath Lane, Fareham, **Hampshire**, PO15 6PS, ENG.
(T) 01329 280009
Speciality: Biomechanics, Chiropody, Cryo Surgery, Gait Analysis.
● **Owner/Chiropodist** Mr J Foster Q: Inst.CH.P.
C Yrs. Est.: 3 (Ref:HM07593)

## FOSTER, JENNIE

**Jennie Foster**, 100 High St, Crediton, **Devon**, EX17 3LF, ENG.
(T) 01363 774175
Speciality: Complementary Medicines & Therapy.
M (Ref:HM07594)

## FOSTER, JOY

**Joy Foster**, Flat 2, 23-24 Richmond Trce, Clifton, Bristol, BS8 1AA, ENG.
(T) 01179 239627
Speciality: Hypnosis.
● **Owner** Mrs J Foster
B (Ref:HM07595)

## FOSTER, M

**M Foster**, 5 Ferndown Gardens, Wolverhampton, **Midlands (West)**, WV11 3TE, ENG.
(T) 01902 368658
Speciality: Chiropodists (Podiatrists).
S (Ref:HM07596)

## FOSTER, MARGARET

**Margaret Foster**, Devizes, **Wiltshire**, SN10, ENG.
(T) 01380 828138
Speciality: Bach Remedies.
M (Ref:HM07597)

## FOSTER, P R

**P R Foster**, The Cottage, Speltham Hill, Hambledon, Waterlooville, **Hampshire**, PO7 4RU, ENG.
(T) 023 9263 2306
Speciality: Physiotherapy.
P S T (Ref:HM07598)

## FOSTER, ROSALYN

**Rosalyn Foster**, 6 Brooklands Trce, Green St, Sunbury-On-Thames, **Surrey**, TW16 6RW, ENG.
(T) 01932 789779
Speciality: Osteopathy.
P S T (Ref:HM07599)

## FOSTER, S

**S Foster**, 339 Ballards Lane, London, **London (Greater)**, N12 8LJ, ENG.
(T) 020 8445 4397
Speciality: Reflexology.
● **Director** Mr E Thankey
S T (Ref:HM07600)

## FOSTER, SHERRIE

**Sherrie Foster**, 3 Sunset View, Barnet, **Hertfordshire**, EN5 4LB, ENG.
(T) 020 8449 3993
Speciality: Complementary Medicines & Therapy.
M (Ref:HM07601)

## FOSTER, SUE

**Sue Foster**, 60 Waterloo Rd, Waterloo, Liverpool, **Merseyside**, L22 1RF, ENG.
(T) 01514 749356



Key continued: **Yrs.Est:** Years Established **Q:** Qualifications **M:** Professional Membership ✔ Indemnity Insurance Accept Credit Cards

Speciality: Chiropodists (Podiatrists).
● **Owner** Mrs S Foster
S (Ref:HM07602)

### FOSTER, W

**W Foster**, Aldrens Lane, Lancaster, **Lancashire**, LA1 2DU, ENG.
(T) 01524 69864 (F) 01524 848155
Speciality: Aromatherapy.
M O (Ref:HM07603)

### FOTHERBY, J

**Mrs J Fotherby**, 17 Maythorn Gardens, Wolverhampton, **Midlands (West)**, WV6 8NP, ENG.
(T) 01902 755953
Speciality: Physiotherapy.
P S T (Ref:HM07604)

### FOTHERBY, ROZ

**Roz Fotherby**, 11 Crompton Rd, Lowestoft, **Suffolk**, NR33 9NG, ENG.
(T) 01502 514168
Speciality: Hypnosis.
● **Owner** Mrs R Fotherby
B (Ref:HM07605)

### FOTHERGILL, MICHAEL

**Michael Fothergill**, 42 Twyford Cl, Cramlington, **Northumberland**, NE23 1PH, ENG.
(T) 01670 716622
Speciality: Reflexology.
S T (Ref:HM07606)

### FOULDS, PHILLIP

**Phillip Foulds**, 5 Cumberland Avenue, Basingstoke, **Hampshire**, RG22 4BG, ENG.
(T) 01256 321556
Speciality: Chiropodists (Podiatrists).
● **Partner** Ms B Davies
S (Ref:HM07607)

### FOULGER, SONIA

**Sonia Foulger Chiropody**, Care Of Stewarts Pharmacy, 120 St Peters St, Lowestoft, **Suffolk**, NR32 1UD, ENG.
(T) 01502 538082
Speciality: Chiropodists (Podiatrists).
S (Ref:HM07608)

### FOULKES, GEOFFREY LLOYD

**Geoffrey Lloyd Foulkes Clinic Of Complementary Medicine (The)**, 27 York Rd, Ilford, **Essex**, IG1 3AD, ENG.
(T) 020 8478 0443
(W) www.geoffreylloydfouklescompmed.co.uk
Speciality: Acupuncture, Aromatherapy, Bach Remedies, Complementary Therapy, Cranial Osteopathy, Cupping, Dietician, Electrotherapy, Hay Diet, Herbal Medicine, Holistic Healing, Homeopathy, Kinesiology, Manipulation, Massage (Therapeutic), Meditation, Moxibustion, Naturopathy, Nutritional Therapy, Oriental Diagnosis, Osteopathy, Reiki, Stress Therapy, Ultrasonics, Vitamin Therapy, X-Ray, Ying & Yang. ✔
● **Homeopath** Mr A Bajpai Q: BSc, LCPH, MA, MHMA, PGCE. M: HMA.
● **Practice Manager** Mrs G Foulkes
● **Osteopath/Acupuncturist** Mr D Shukla Q: DO, MBAcC. M: BAcC, GOsC.
● **Osteopath/Acupuncturist** Mr C Papapetrou Q: BSc, MBAcC. M: BAcC, GOsC.
● **Practitioner of Traditional Chinese Medicine** Ms D Matal Q: MBAcC. M: BAcC, RCHM.
S Yrs. Est.: 37 (Ref:HM07609)

### FOULKES, L

**L Foulkes**, 18 Water St, Newcastle, **Staffordshire**, ST5 1HN, ENG.
(T) 01782 615184
Speciality: Homeopathy.
M (Ref:HM07610)

### FOUNDATION FOR HOLISTIC CONSC

**Foundation For Holistic Consciousness**, 201 Selhurst Rd, London, **London (Greater)**, SE25 6LB, ENG.
(T) 020 8410 4846 (F) 020 8251 7942
Speciality: Complementary Medicines & Therapy.
● **Partner** Mr D Ashby
M (Ref:HM07611)

### FOUNDATION FOR INT SPIR

**Foundation For International Spiritual Unfoldment**, 58 Marlborough Rd, London, **London (Greater)**, E4 9AL, ENG.
(T) 020 8523 3133 (F) 020 8523 2028
Speciality: Complementary Medicines & Therapy.
● **Managing Director** Mr R Ward
C M (Ref:HM07612)

### FOUNDATION HEALTH

**Foundation Health**, 21 George Trce, St. Monans, **Fife**, KY10 2AY, SCO.
(T) 01333 730506
Speciality: Cranio-Sacral Therapy, Kinesiology, Massage (Therapeutic), Nutritional Therapy, Vitamin Therapy.
M (Ref:HM07613)

### FOUNDATION NATURAL THRPY CTRE

**Foundation Natural Therapy Centre**, 17-21 High St, Ruddington, Nottingham, **Nottinghamshire**, NG11 6DT, ENG.
(T) 01159 405565
Speciality: Complementary Medicines & Therapy.
C M (Ref:HM07614)

### FOUNDATION, ANGELGATE

**Angelgate Foundation for Complementary Therapies**, 6 Combermere Rd, St. Leonards-On-Sea, **Sussex (East)**, TN38 0RR, ENG.
(T) 01424 430001 (F) 01424 430001
(E) ga@angelgate.co.uk
Speciality: Absent Healing, Aromatherapy, Bach Remedies, Complementary Therapy, Healing Therapy, Holistic Healing, Indian Head Massage, Life Style Coaching, Massage (Therapeutic), Metamorphic Therapy, Nutritional Therapy, Reflexology, Reiki, Spiritual Healing, Touch Therapy. ✔
● **Therapist** Ms G Ayres Q: BSc (Hons), MA. M: ITEC.
B Yrs. Est.: 10 (Ref:HM07615)

### FOUNDATIONS PSYCHOTHERAPY

**Foundations Psychotherapy**, 37a Killigrew St, Falmouth, **Cornwall**, TR11 3PW, ENG.
(T) 01326 314999
Speciality: Psychotherapy.
● **Owner** Mr A Hanks
B (Ref:HM07616)

### FOUNTAIN OF HEALTH

**Fountain Of Health**, 35 Sutton Park Rd, Seaford, **Sussex (East)**, BN25 1HH, ENG.
(T) 01323 896192
Speciality: Complementary Medicines & Therapy.
C M (Ref:HM07617)

### FOUR ALL SEASONS

**Four All Seasons**, 8 West St, Marlow, **Buckinghamshire**, SL7 2NB, ENG.
(T) 01628 477594
Speciality: Complementary Medicines & Therapy.
● **Owner** Mrs L Nicholls
M (Ref:HM07618)

### FOUR OAKS

**Four Oaks**, 54a Mere Green Rd, Sutton Coldfield, **Midlands (West)**, B75 5BT, ENG.
(T) 01213 233281 (F) 01213 233281
Speciality: Physiotherapy.
● **Partner** Mr A Holdon
P S T (Ref:HM07619)

### FOUR WINDS HEALING CENTRE

**Four Winds Healing Centre (The)**, St Teilos House, Merthyr Dyfan Lane, Barry, **Glamorgan (Vale of)**, CF62 9TL, WAL.
(T) 01446 420155
Speciality: Complementary Medicines & Therapy.
● **Owner** Mr K Jones
M (Ref:HM07620)

### FOURNIER, C

**C Fournier**, St Boswells Chiropractic Clinic, 16 Jenny Moores Rd, St. Boswells, Melrose, **Scottish Borders**, TD6 0AL, SCO.
(T) 01835 823645 (F) 01835 823930
Speciality: Chiropractors.
● **Partner** Dr C How
P S T (Ref:HM07621)

### FOURTH MOUNTAIN HOM AND ACU

**Fourth Mountain Homeopathy And Acupuncture**, Coolnagee, Forth Mountain, Wexford, **County Wexford**, IRE.
(T) 05347 671
Speciality: Acupuncture, Homeopathy, Also a practising GP, which is separate from the Acupuncture and Homeopathy practice, with a special interest in women's health.
● **General Practitioner** Dr C Thornley Q: BS, Dip.Med.Ac, MB, MRCGP, PC.Hom. M: BMAS, FHom, MedCouns(Ireland), RCGP.
M Yrs. Est.: 5 (Ref:HM07622)

### FOWDEN, M G

**M G Fowden**, 14 St Annes Cl, St. George, Bristol, BS5 8DQ, ENG.
(T) 01179 542223
Speciality: Aromatherapy.
● **Owner** Mr M Fowden
M O (Ref:HM07623)

### FOWKES, S R

**Mrs S R Fowkes**, 113A Uxbridge Rd, Harrow, **London (Greater)**, HA3 6DN, ENG.
(T) 020 8954 2555
Speciality: Hypnotherapy.
B (Ref:HM07624)

### FOWKES, SUSIE

**Mrs Susie Fowkes**, The Garth, 8 Lodge Rd, Writtle, Chelmsford, **Essex**, CM1 3HB, ENG.
(T) 01245 420504
Speciality: Physiotherapy.
P S T (Ref:HM07625)

### FOWLER, B R & V A

**B R & V A Fowler**, 114 Upper Tooting Rd, London, **London (Greater)**, SW17 7EN, ENG.
(T) 020 8672 8670
Speciality: Chiropodists (Podiatrists).
● **Partner** Mrs V Fowler
S (Ref:HM07626)

### FOWLER, B R & V A

**B R & V A Fowler**, Alstonefields, Tandridge Rd, Warlingham, **Surrey**, CR6 9LS, ENG.
(T) 01883 624788
Speciality: Chiropodists (Podiatrists).
● **Owner** Mr B Fowler
S (Ref:HM07627)

### FOWLER, CHRISTINE

**Christine Fowler**, 2 The Cloisters, Newcastle Upon Tyne, **Tyne and Wear**, NE7 7LS, ENG.
(T) 01912 847615 (F) 01912 847615
Speciality: Bowen Therapy, Kinesiology, Reiki. ✔
● **Holistic Therapist** Mrs C Fowler Q: BA (Hons), CQSW. M: BTER, KFRP.
B C T Yrs. Est.: 20 (Ref:HM07628)

### FOWLER, J A

**J A Fowler**, Portland House, Priest Bridge, Tritlington, Morpeth, **Northumberland**, NE61 3DT, ENG.
(T) 01670 787391
Speciality: Homeopathy.
M (Ref:HM07629)

### FOWNES, SUZANNE

**Suzanne Fownes**, 52 Dovercourt Rd, London, **London (Greater)**, SE22 8ST, ENG.
(T) 020 8693 4007
Speciality: Alexander Technique.
P S (Ref:HM07630)

### FOX, ANTONY D (DR)

**Dr Antony D Fox**, 54 Barton Court Avenue, Barton-On-Sea, New Milton, **Hampshire**, BH25 7HG, ENG.
(T) 01425 618801 (F) 01425 618337
Speciality: Bach Remedies, Homeopathy, Nutritional Therapy, Vitamin Therapy, Allergy diagnosis and treatments. ✔
● **Principal** Dr A Fox Q: MRCGP.
M Yrs. Est.: 20 (Ref:HM07631)



Key: B Mind-Body Medicine, C Complementary Medicine, H Self Help Treatment, M Medicinal Therapy, O Oriental Medicine, P Postural Therapy, S Manipulative Structural Therapy, T Touch Therapy

## FOX, DIANA
**Diana Fox**, Egham Sports Centre, Vicarage Rd, Egham, **Surrey**, TW20 8NL, ENG.
(T) 01784 437695
Speciality: Reflexology.
S T (Ref:HM07632)

## FOX, E
**E Fox**, 48 Redlands Rd, Reading, **Berkshire**, RG1 5HR, ENG.
(T) 01189 866635 (F) 01189 874461
Speciality: Aromatherapy.
● **Director** Mr J Boardman
M O (Ref:HM07633)

## FOX, E
**E Fox**, 23 Quarry Hill Rd, Tonbridge, **Kent**, TN9 2RN, ENG.
(T) 01732 355634
Speciality: Osteopathy.
P S T (Ref:HM07634)

## FOX, G A
**G A Fox**, High St South, Dunstable, **Bedfordshire**, LU6 3RZ, ENG.
(T) 01582 605346
Speciality: Psychotherapy.
● **Owner** Mr G Fox
B (Ref:HM07635)

## FOX, GLYNIS
**Glynis Fox**, 52 Stoke Newington Church St, London, **London (Greater)**, N16 0NB, ENG.
(T) 020 7241 5033
Speciality: Osteopathy.
P S T (Ref:HM07636)

## FOX, GLYNIS
**Glynis Fox**, 23 Eyre Pl, Edinburgh, **Edinburgh (City of)**, EH3 5EX, SCO.
(T) 01315 572211
Speciality: Osteopathy.
P S T (Ref:HM07637)

## FOX, J
**J Fox**, 16 Tower Hill, Witney, **Oxfordshire**, OX8 5ER, ENG.
(T) 01993 708583
Speciality: Hypnotherapy.
● **Owner** Mr J Fox
B (Ref:HM07638)

## FOX, J P
**J P Fox**, 47 Bournehall Avenue, Bushey, Watford, **Hertfordshire**, WD2 3AU, ENG.
(T) 020 8950 0727
Speciality: Osteopathy.
P S T (Ref:HM07639)

## FOX, JACKY
**Jacky Fox**, 4 South Rd, Hailsham, **Sussex (East)**, BN27 3JQ, ENG.
(T) 01323 843079
Speciality: Reiki.
M (Ref:HM07640)

## FOX, SOPHIE LANE
**Sophie Lane Fox**, 32 Ouseley Rd, London, **London (Greater)**, SW12 8EF, ENG.
(T) 020 8767 7768
Speciality: Reflexology.
S T (Ref:HM07641)

## FOX, Z
**Z Fox**, 8 Smore Slade Hills, Oadby, Leicester, **Leicestershire**, LE2 4UX, ENG.
(T) 01162 713954
Speciality: Chiropodists (Podiatrists).
S (Ref:HM07642)

## FOX-DAVIES, DAWN
**Dawn Fox-Davies**, 17 Hayfield Rd, Chapel-En-Le-Frith, High Peak, **Derbyshire**, SK23 0JF, ENG.
(T) 01298 814031
Speciality: Hypnosis.
● **Owner** Mrs D Fox-Davies
B (Ref:HM07643)

## FOXWELL, CORALIE
**Coralie Foxwell**, Tarka Clinic, Paiges Lane, Barnstaple, **Devon**, EX31 1EF, ENG.
(T) 01271 345546 (F) 01271 327808
Speciality: Osteopathy.
P S T (Ref:HM07644)

## FOXWELL, CORALIE
**Coralie Foxwell**, 5 South St, Torrington, **Devon**, EX38 8HE, ENG.
(T) 01805 622591
Speciality: Osteopathy.
P S T (Ref:HM07645)

## FOYLE HYPNOTHERAPY CENTRE
**Hypnotherapy Centre (The)**, 2 Brentwood Park, Foyle Springs, Derry City, Londonderry, **County Londonderry**, BT48 0NS, NIR.
(T) 028 7126 1767
(E) richardglen@therapist.net
(W) www.richardglenn.com
Speciality: Acupressure, Acupuncture, Auto Suggestion, Aversion Therapy, Cognitive Therapy, Colour Therapy, Complementary Therapy, Counselling, Electrotherapy, Healer, Healing Therapy, Holistic Healing, Hypnosis, Hypnotherapy, Psychotherapy, Stress Therapy, Visualisation Therapy, Ying & Yang. ✔ CREDIT
● **Hypnotherapist/Psychotherapist**
Mr R Glen Q: Dip.Hyp. M: HA, ICHP.
B Yrs. Est.: 21 (Ref:HM07646)

## FOZZARD, JOANNA M
**Joanna M Fozzard**, 11 Elmes Arcade, 50 High St, Stevenage, **Hertfordshire**, SG1 3EF, ENG.
(T) 01438 318722
Speciality: Osteopathy.
● **Owner** Ms J Fozzard
P S T (Ref:HM07647)

## FOZZARD, JOANNA M
**Joanna M Fozzard**, 1 Norfolk Rd, Buntingford, **Hertfordshire**, SG9 9AN, ENG.
(T) 01763 272365
Speciality: Osteopathy.
● **Owner** Mrs J Fozzard
P S T (Ref:HM07648)

## FRAGRANT HAVEN
**Fragrant Haven**, First Flr 36 William St, Listowel, **County Kerry**, IRE.
(T) 06822 970
Speciality: Beauty Therapy.
H T (Ref:HM07649)

## FRAGRANT MOODS
**Fragrant Moods**, 106 Mirren Drive, Clydebank, **Argyll and Bute**, G81 6LD, SCO.
(T) 01389 380551
Speciality: Aromatherapy.
● **Owner** Ms C Thomson
M O (Ref:HM07650)

## FRAGRANT RETREAT
**Fragrant Retreat (The)**, The Bell Hotel, Market Pl, Driffield, **Humberside (North)**, YO25 6AN, ENG.
(T) 01377 252700
Speciality: Aromatherapy.
● **Owner** Mrs V Fallowfield
M O (Ref:HM07651)

## FRAGRANT ROOM
**Fragrant Room**, Unit 12C Hatton Country World, Hatton, Warwick, **Warwickshire**, CV35 8XA, ENG.
(T) 01926 843506
Speciality: Aromatherapy.
● **Owner** Mrs J Watts
M O (Ref:HM07652)

## FRAGRANT ROOM
**Fragrant Room**, 37 Coventry St, Southam, Leamington Spa, **Warwickshire**, CV33 0EP, ENG.
(T) 01926 811933
Speciality: Aromatherapy.
M O (Ref:HM07653)

## FRAMAR NATURAL HEALTH CLINIC
**Framar Health**, 595 Lisburn Rd, Belfast, **County Antrim**, BT9 7GS, NIR.
(T) 028 9068 1018/5 (F) 028 9066 2891
(E) pearl@framarhealth.com
(W) www.framarhealth.com
Speciality: Acupressure, Acupuncture, Aromatherapy, Bach Remedies, Complementary Therapy, Counselling, Herbal Medicine, Homeopathy, Indian Head Massage, Iridology, Kinesiology, Manipulation, Massage (Therapeutic), Naturopathy, Nutritional Therapy, Osteopathy, Phytotherapy, Reflexology, Reiki, Vitamin Therapy. ✔ CREDIT
● **Owner** Mr J De Vries
● **Owner** Mr F MacOnaghie
● **Therapist** Stella Couglan
● **Therapist** Pearl MacOnaghie
M Yrs. Est.: 20 (Ref:HM07654)

## FRAMLINGHAM PHYSIO PRACTICE
**Framlingham Physiotherapy Practice**, 31B Market Hill, Framlingham, Woodbridge, **Suffolk**, IP13 9AS, ENG.
(T) 07770 923873
Speciality: Physiotherapy.
● **Owner** Mrs L Patrick
P S T (Ref:HM07655)

## FRANCE, C A
**C A France**, 62 Beresford Drive, Southport, **Merseyside**, PR9 7LQ, ENG.
(T) 01704 227423
Speciality: Hypnosis.
● **Owner** Mr C France
B (Ref:HM07656)

## FRANCE, C J
**C J France**, 5b Three Tuns Lane, Liverpool, **Merseyside**, L37 4AG, ENG.
(T) 01704 879221
Speciality: Chiropodists (Podiatrists).
● **Owner** Mr C France
S (Ref:HM07657)

## FRANCES
**Frances**, 3 Lockton Cl, South Reddish, Stockport, **Cheshire**, SK5 7SU, ENG.
(T) 01614 297495
Speciality: Clairvoyants & Palmists.
B (Ref:HM07658)

## FRANCES ST CLAIR
**Frances St Clair**, 151 Cambridge St, Pimlico, London, **London (Greater)**, SW1V 4JZ, ENG.
(T) 020 7630 1505
Speciality: Aromatherapy.
M O (Ref:HM07659)

## FRANCES, JOAN
**Joan Frances New Vision Complementary Therapy**, 7 Comely Bank, Hamilton, **Lanarkshire (South)**, ML3 9TR, SCO.
(T) 01698 331008
Speciality: Complementary Medicines & Therapy.
C M (Ref:HM07660)

## FRANCES, LEE
**Lee Frances Lic ,Ac**, Abbey Hse, Medical Ctr Abbey Rd, Navan, **County Meath**, IRE.
(T) 04622 126
Speciality: Acupuncture.
O (Ref:HM07661)

## FRANCES, ROBBIE
**Robbie Frances**, 23 Ivydene, Knaphill, Woking, **Surrey**, GU21 2TA, ENG.
(T) 01483 480808
Speciality: Chiropodists (Podiatrists).
● **Owner** Mrs F Robbie
S (Ref:HM07662)

## FRANCESCA
**Francesca**, 24 Vernon Cl, Cheadle Hulme, Cheadle, **Cheshire**, SK8 6AN, ENG.
(T) 01614 851158
Speciality: Electrolysis.
● **Owner** Ms F Herman
T (Ref:HM07663)

## FRANCE-SHELTON FOOT HLTH CTRE
**France-Shelton Foot Health Centre**, 1st Floor 390 Birmingham Rd, Sutton Coldfield, **Midlands (West)**, B72 1YJ, ENG.
(T) 01213 843244
Speciality: Chiropodists (Podiatrists).
S (Ref:HM07664)

## FRANCES-WHITAKER, J A
**J A Frances-Whitaker**, Melbourne House, 36 Chamberlain St, Wells, **Somerset**, BA5 2PJ, ENG.
(T) 01749 676201
Speciality: Chiropody. ✔
● **Practice Manager**
Mrs K Frances- Whitaker



Key continued: Yrs.Est: Years Established Q: Qualifications M: Professional Membership ✔ Indemnity Insurance CREDIT Accept Credit Cards

● **Chiropodist (Podiatrist)**
Mr J Frances-Whitaker Q: BSc, DPodM, S.R.Ch. M: S.C.P.
● **Chiropodist (Podiatrist)**
Mr K Walker Q: DPodM. M: S.C.P.
M Yrs. Est.: 18 (Ref:HM07665)

**FRANCIS J H WILSON CHIRO**
**Francis J H Wilson Chiropractor**, Woodbridge Hill Surgery, 1 Deerbarn Rd, Guildford, **Surrey**, GU2 6AT, ENG.
(T) 01483 454422
Speciality: Chiropractic.
P S T (Ref:HM07666)

**FRANCIS, A**
**A Francis**, 43 Front St, Cleadon, Sunderland, **Tyne and Wear**, SR6 7PG, ENG.
(T) 01915 367224
Speciality: Osteopathy.
● **Owner** A Francis
P S T (Ref:HM07667)

**FRANCIS, BARRY**
**Mr Barry Francis**, 10 Harley St, London, **London (Greater)**, W1N 1AA, ENG.
(T) 020 7467 8356 (F) 020 7467 8312
Speciality: Chiropodists (Podiatrists).
● **Owner** Mr B Francis
S (Ref:HM07668)

**FRANCIS, D**
**D Francis**, 348 Waterloo Rd, Manchester, **Manchester (Greater)**, M8 9AB, ENG.
(T) 01617 404314
Speciality: Chiropodists (Podiatrists).
S (Ref:HM07669)

**FRANCIS, D**
**D Francis**, The Chiropodist Centre, 334 Moston Lane, Manchester, **Manchester (Greater)**, M40 9JS, ENG.
(T) 01616 880377
Speciality: Chiropodists (Podiatrists).
● **Owner** Mr D Francis
S (Ref:HM07670)

**FRANCIS, HELEN**
**Helen Francis**, The Bryn, Bryn Lane, Newtown, **Powys**, SY16 3LZ, WAL.
(T) 01686 626948
Speciality: Reflexology.
S T (Ref:HM07671)

**FRANCIS, JAKKI**
**Jakki Francis**, 109 Hillmorton Rd, Rugby, **Warwickshire**, CV22 5AT, ENG.
(T) 01788 337203
Speciality: Reflexology.
S T (Ref:HM07672)

**FRANCIS, JOHN**
**John Francis**, Newport Clinic Of Holistic Health, Westgate Chambers, Commercial St, Newport, NP9, WAL.
(T) 01633 843333
Speciality: Complementary Medicines & Therapy.
● **Owner** Mr J Francis
M (Ref:HM07673)

**FRANCIS, MARILYN**
**Marilyn Francis**, 45 Silver Birch Avenue, Stotfold, Hitchin, **Hertfordshire**, SG5 4AS, ENG.
(T) 01462 730773
Speciality: Chiropodists (Podiatrists).
S (Ref:HM07674)

**FRANCIS, PATRICIA**
**Patricia Francis**, 35 Barrow Hill Rd, Bristol, BS11 9QY, ENG.
(T) 01179 827486
Speciality: Aromatherapy, Massage (Therapeutic). ✔
● **Owner** Mrs P Francis Q: Dip.Arom.
T Yrs. Est.: 10 (Ref:HM07675)

**FRANCIS, SUE**
**Sue Francis**, Prescot House, Bridge St, Kineton, Warwick, **Warwickshire**, CV35 0JR, ENG.
(T) 01926 642900
Speciality: Homeopathy.
● **Owner** Mrs S Francis
M (Ref:HM07676)

**FRANCIS-JONES, T**
**T Francis-Jones**, 10 High St, Orpington, **Kent**, BR6 0JG, ENG.
(T) 01689 873130
Speciality: Chiropractors.
● **Owner** Dr M Chippendale
P S T (Ref:HM07677)

**FRANCIS-JONES, T**
**T Francis-Jones**, 366 Croydon Rd, Beckenham, **Kent**, BR3 4EX, ENG.
(T) 020 8663 3878 (F) 020 8663 3878
Speciality: Chiropractors.
● **Doctor** Dr M Chippendale
P S T (Ref:HM07678)

**FRANCIS-JONES, TREVOR (DR)**
**Dr Trevor Francis-Jones Chiropractor**, 50 High St, Orpington, **Kent**, BR6 0JQ, ENG.
(T) 01689 890894
Speciality: Chiropractic. ✔
● **Assistant Chiropractor**
Miss L Clending
● **Chiropractor** Dr T Francis-Jones
P S Yrs. Est.: 4 (Ref:HM07679)

**FRANCOISE, JORDAN**
**Jordan Francoise**, 46 Khyber Rd, London, **London (Greater)**, SW11 2PZ, ENG.
(T) 020 7223 6343
Speciality: Reflexology.
S T (Ref:HM07680)

**FRANELLI**
**Franelli**, 70 Castle Avenue, Rochester, **Kent**, ME1 2DY, ENG.
(T) 01634 819889
Speciality: Complementary Medicines & Therapy.
● **Owner** Mr F Marinelli
M (Ref:HM07681)

**FRANEY, JAMES R**
**James R Franey**, 308 Washway Rd, Sale, **Cheshire**, M33 4RU, ENG.
(T) 07885 422516 (F) 01619 738877
Speciality: Chiropodists (Podiatrists).
● **Owner** Mr J Franey
S (Ref:HM07682)

**FRANK RYDER HYPNOTHERAPY**
**Frank Ryder Hypnotherapy**, 4 Alden Pk, Sutton, **County Dublin**, IRE.
(T) 01832 4576
Speciality: Hypnotherapy.
B (Ref:HM07683)

**FRANK, KRIS**
**Kris Frank**, 100 High St, Crediton, **Devon**, EX17 3LF, ENG.
(T) 01363 774175
Speciality: Homeopathy.
M (Ref:HM07684)

**FRANKCOM, DAVID J**
**David J Frankcom**, Glenthorne, 4 West Rd, Guildford, **Surrey**, GU1 2AT, ENG.
(T) 01483 576438
Speciality: Osteopathy.
● **Owner** Mr D Francom
P S T (Ref:HM07685)

**FRANKEISS, PETER**
**Peter Frankeiss**, Bank St, Bishops Waltham, Southampton, **Hampshire**, SO32 1AN, ENG.
(T) 01489 891880
Speciality: Osteopathy.
● **Partner** Mr P Frankeiss
P S T (Ref:HM07686)

**FRANKLAND, JULIE D**
**Julie D Frankland**, 5 Longfield Avenue, Pudsey, **Yorkshire (West)**, LS28 7DB, ENG.
(T) 01132 575805
Speciality: Chiropodists (Podiatrists).
S (Ref:HM07687)

**FRANKLIN CHIROPODY**
**Franklin Chiropody**, 185 Caerleon Rd, Newport, NP18 1QA, WAL.
(T) 08000 743050
Speciality: Chiropodists (Podiatrists).
● **Owner** Mr M Franklin
S (Ref:HM07688)

**FRANKLYN CHIROPODY**
**Franklyn Chiropody**, 123 Bute St, Cardiff, **Glamorgan (Vale of)**, CF10 5AE, WAL.
(T) 029 2048 5674
Speciality: Chiropodists (Podiatrists).
S (Ref:HM07689)

**FRANKS, PAUL**
**Paul Franks**, 378 Ecclesall Rd, Sheffield, **Yorkshire (South)**, S11 8PJ, ENG.
(T) 01142 680236
Speciality: Acupuncture.
O (Ref:HM07690)

**FRASER HOUSE CHIROPRACTIC**
**Fraser House Chiropractic Clinic (The)**, The Mount, Salters Lane, Tamworth, **Staffordshire**, B79 8BH, ENG.
(T) 01827 310910
Speciality: Chiropractic.
● **Owner** Dr D Eldridge
P S T (Ref:HM07691)

**FRASER, ANNE**
**Anne Fraser**, 3 Lakeside Avenue, Long Eaton, Nottingham, **Nottinghamshire**, NG10 3GJ, ENG.
(T) 01159 727416
Speciality: Chiropodists (Podiatrists).
● **Owner** Mrs A Fraser
S (Ref:HM07692)

**FRASER, DINGWALL & ASSOCIATES**
**Gillian Fraser Ian Dingwall & Associate**, 1 Donaldson Pl, Kirkintilloch, Glasgow, **Glasgow (City of)**, G66 1XA, SCO.
(T) 01417 761581
Speciality: Chiropractic.
P S T (Ref:HM07693)

**FRASER, ELIZABETH**
**Elizabeth Fraser**, 33 Nasmyth St, London, **London (Greater)**, W6 0HA, ENG.
(T) 020 8748 0177
Speciality: Reflexology.
S T (Ref:HM07694)

**FRASER, EMMA L**
**Emma L Fraser**, 17 Wharfedale Pl, Harrogate, **Yorkshire (North)**, HG2 0AY, ENG.
(T) 01423 509580
Speciality: Reflexology.
● **Owner** Miss E Fraser
S T (Ref:HM07695)

**FRASER, GORDON**
**Gordon Fraser**, 84 High St, North Berwick, **Lothian (East)**, EH39 4HF, SCO.
(T) 01620 892353 (F) 01620 892353
Speciality: Aromatherapy, Holistic Healing, Homeopathy, Hypnotherapy, Iridology, Reiki, Shiatsu, Needle free Acupuncture (laser).
✔ CREDIT
● **Owner/Complementary Therapist**
Mr G Fraser Q: IHT. M: IHT.
C Yrs. Est.: 20 (Ref:HM07696)

**FRASER, GORDON**
**Gordon Fraser**, 4 Church Rd, North Berwick, **Lothian (East)**, EH39 4AD, SCO.
(T) 01620 892353
Speciality: Complementary Medicines & Therapy.
C M (Ref:HM07697)

**FRASER, HUGH ROSS**
**Hugh Ross Fraser**, 51 Holmewood Gardens, London, **London (Greater)**, SW2 3NB, ENG.
(T) 020 8674 2235
Speciality: Psychotherapy.
B (Ref:HM07698)

**FRASER, SANDY**
**Sandy Fraser**, 108 High St, Montrose, **Angus**, DD10 8JE, SCO.
(T) 01674 675355
Speciality: Complementary Medicines & Therapy.
● **Owner** Mr S Fraser
M (Ref:HM07699)

**FRASER, SANDY**
**Sandy Fraser**, 22 Provost Mitchell Rd, Montrose, **Angus**, DD10 9DH, SCO.
(T) 01674 675355

Key: B Mind-Body Medicine C Complementary Medicine H Self Help Treatment M Medicinal Therapy O Oriental Medicine P Postural Therapy S Manipulative Structural Therapy T Touch Therapy

Speciality: Osteopathy.
P S T (Ref:HM07700)

## FRAWLEY MICHAEL BIO THERAP

**Michael Frawley Biodynamic Therapist & Counsellor**, 2 Ballybane Rd, **County Galway**, IRE.
(T) 09175 5998
Speciality: Complementary Medicines & Therapy.
M (Ref:HM07701)

## FRAZER, C C

**C C Frazer**, Dental Surgery, 78 Harborne Rd, Birmingham, **Midlands (West)**, B15 3HN, ENG.
(T) 01214 542413 (F) 01214 542413
Speciality: Chiropodists (Podiatrists).
● **Owner** Mr C Frazer
S (Ref:HM07702)

## FRAZER, P

**P Frazer**, 44 Angelton Green, Pen-Y-Fai, Bridgend, CF31 4LQ, WAL.
(T) 01656 724775
Speciality: Reflexology.
● **Owner** Mr P Frazer
S T (Ref:HM07703)

## FREASHFIELDS

**Freashfields**, P.O. Box 12, Aldeburgh, **Suffolk**, IP15 5JB, ENG.
(T) 01728 454299
Speciality: Complementary Medicines & Therapy.
C M (Ref:HM07704)

## FREDA, ROSE

**Rose Freda**, Craneswater House, 2 Craneswater Gate, Southsea, **Hampshire**, PO4 0NZ, ENG.
(T) 023 9275 6087
Speciality: Aromatherapy.
● **Owner** Mrs F Woolsgrove
M O (Ref:HM07705)

## FREE, HUGH

**Hugh Free**, 25 Mill Lane, Saffron Walden, **Essex**, CB10 2AS, ENG.
(T) 01799 527190
Speciality: Reflexology.
S T (Ref:HM07706)

## FREED CLINIC

**Freed Clinic (The)**, 351A Whitehorse Rd, Croydon, **Surrey**, CR0 2HS, ENG.
(T) 020 8665 5042 (F) 020 8689 2537
Speciality: Acupuncture.
● **Director** Mr P Curson
M (Ref:HM07707)

## FREEDMAN & ASSOCIATES

**M H Freedman & Associates**, 66B Station Rd, London, **London (Greater)**, E4 7BA, ENG.
(T) 020 8524 3916
Speciality: Chiropodists (Podiatrists).
● **Owner** Mr M Freedman
S (Ref:HM07708)

## FREEDMAN, AUSTIN

**Austin Freedman**, 5 Uplands Rd, East Barnet, Barnet, **Hertfordshire**, EN4 8NY, ENG.
(T) 020 8361 6028
Speciality: Hypnotherapy.
● **Owner** Mr A Freedman
B (Ref:HM07709)

## FREEDMAN, L

**L Freedman**, 48 Stanhope Avenue, London, **London (Greater)**, N3 3NA, ENG.
(T) 020 8346 2636 (F) 020 8346 2636
Speciality: Chiropodists (Podiatrists).
● **Owner** Mr L Freedman
S (Ref:HM07710)

## FREEDMAN, M

**M Freedman**, Lakeside Avenue, Ilford, **Essex**, IG4 5PJ, ENG.
(T) 020 8550 5193
Speciality: Chiropodists (Podiatrists).
● **Owner** Mrs M Freedman
S (Ref:HM07711)

## FREEDMAN, M

**M Freedman**, 48 Stanhope Avenue, London, **London (Greater)**, N3 3NA, ENG.
(T) 020 8346 2636 (F) 020 8346 2636
Speciality: Relaxation Technique.
● **Owner** Mr L Freedman
H T (Ref:HM07712)

## FREEDMAN, SIMON

**Simon Freedman**, Soho Osteopathic Health Clinic, 6 Denmark St, London, **London (Greater)**, WC2H 8LP, ENG.
(T) 020 7379 5531
Speciality: Osteopathy.
P S T (Ref:HM07713)

## FREEDOM HOLISTIC CENTRE

**Freedom Holistic Centre**, Church Mews Church La, Midleton, **County Cork**, IRE.
(T) 021 4633 421
Speciality: Complementary Medicines & Therapy.
M (Ref:HM07714)

## FREEDOM WITHIN

**Freedom Within**, 4 Wynn Avenue, Rhos-ddu, **Wrexham**, LL11 2EP, WAL.
(T) 01978 291390
Speciality: Aromatherapy, Massage (Therapeutic), Psychotherapy.
C (Ref:HM07715)

## FREEGARD, CHANTAL

**Chantal Freegard**, 15 Highgate Cl, London, **London (Greater)**, N6 4SD, ENG.
(T) 020 8341 2521
Speciality: Reflexology.
S T (Ref:HM07716)

## FREEGROVE CENTRE

**Freegrove Centre**, 26 Freegrove Rd, London, **London (Greater)**, N7 9RQ, ENG.
(T) 020 7609 1597 (F) 020 7609 4837
Speciality: Psychotherapy.
● **Director** Dr R Young
B (Ref:HM07717)

## FREEMAN DUCKMANTON & MASON

**Freeman Duckmanton & Mason**, 98 High St, Ware, **Hertfordshire**, SG12 9AP, ENG.
(T) 01920 462705
Speciality: Chiropodists (Podiatrists).
S (Ref:HM07718)

## FREEMAN, ANN

**Ann Freeman**, 4 St Matthews Rd, Bristol, BS6 5TS, ENG.
(T) 01179 246681
Speciality: Allergy Testing, Herbal Medicine, Spiritual Healing, Western Herbalism. ✔
● **Medical Herbalist** Ms A Freeman Q: MNIMH. M: NIMH.
M Yrs. Est.: 12 (Ref:HM07719)

## FREEMAN, BELINDA

**Belinda Freeman**, 1 Clanricard Gardens, Tunbridge Wells, **Kent**, TN1 1PE, ENG.
(T) 01892 861040
Speciality: Reflexology.
S T (Ref:HM07720)

## FREEMAN, FRANCES

**Frances Freeman**, 7 Hamilton Rd, St. Albans, **Hertfordshire**, AL1 4PZ, ENG.
(T) 01727 842443
Speciality: Homeopathy. ✔
● **Homeopath** Ms F Freeman Q: MHMA.
C Yrs. Est.: 9 (Ref:HM07721)

## FREEMAN-ATWOOD, R

**R Freeman-Atwood**, All Hallows House, Idol Lane, London, **London (Greater)**, EC3R 5DD, ENG.
(T) 020 7283 8908
Speciality: Aromatherapy.
M O (Ref:HM07722)

## FREENEY, JOSEPHINE (DR)

**Dr Josephine Freeney**, 5 Lakelands Dr Kilmacud, Stillorgan, **County Dublin**, IRE.
(T) 01288 8174
Speciality: Complementary Medicines & Therapy.
M (Ref:HM07723)

## FREESPIRIT

**Freespirit**, 40 Easton St, Easton, Isle Of Portland, **Dorset**, DT5 1BT, ENG.
(T) 01305 822296 (F) 01305 822296
Speciality: Colour Therapy, Complementary Therapy, Counselling, Healing Therapy, Meditation, Stress Therapy, Thermotherapy, Spectro-chrome.
● **Owner** Mr P Stewart-Staniforth M: IAC.
B (Ref:HM07724)

## FREESTONE, EILEEN

**Eileen Freestone**, 25E Woodruff Avenue, Conniburrow, Milton Keynes, **Buckinghamshire**, MK14 7AA, ENG.
(T) 01908 661455
Speciality: Reflexology.
● **Owner** Ms E Freestone
S T (Ref:HM07725)

## FREESTON-SMITH, M P

**M P Freeston-Smith**, 102 Saltergate, Chesterfield, **Derbyshire**, S40 1NE, ENG.
(T) 01246 235639
Speciality: Complementary Medicines & Therapy.
C M (Ref:HM07726)

## FREILICH, ELINOR

**Elinor Freilich**, 19 Hercules St, London, **London (Greater)**, N7 6AT, ENG.
(T) 020 7281 9140
Speciality: Acupuncture.
O (Ref:HM07727)

## FRENCH, ANNE

**Anne French**, Natural Health Centre, 86 The Green, Kings Norton, Birmingham, **Midlands (West)**, B38 8RS, ENG.
(T) 01214 585069
Speciality: Hypnosis.
B (Ref:HM07728)

## FRENCH, BELINDA

**Belinda French**, 15 Bruton Way, London, **London (Greater)**, W13 0BY, ENG.
(T) 020 8357 1196
Speciality: Electrolysis.
● **Owner** Ms B French
T (Ref:HM07729)

## FRENCH, DAVID

**David French**, 35 Manor Rd, Stilton, Peterborough, **Cambridgeshire**, PE7 3XA, ENG.
(T) 01733 242408
Speciality: Hypnotherapy.
B (Ref:HM07730)

## FRENCH, EILEEN (DR)

**Dr Eileen French**, The Leather Market, Weston St, London, **London (Greater)**, SE1 4XE, ENG.
(T) 020 7357 0357
Speciality: Psychotherapy.
B (Ref:HM07731)

## FRENCH, JULIE

**Julie French**, Pumphouse, High St, Henfield, **Sussex (West)**, BN5 9DA, ENG.
(T) 01273 493822
Speciality: Osteopathy.
● **Owner** Mrs L Mayers
P S T (Ref:HM07732)

## FRENCH, K J

**K J French**, Tudor Cottage, Lenacre St, Eastwell, Ashford, **Kent**, TN26 1JD, ENG.
(T) 01233 631101
Speciality: Alexander Technique.
P S (Ref:HM07733)

## FRENCH, M

**M French**, 104 Upper Brighton Rd, Worthing, **Sussex (West)**, BN14 9HR, ENG.
(T) 01903 234144
Speciality: Electrolysis.
● **Owner** Mrs M French
T (Ref:HM07734)

## FRENCH, N

**N French**, The Complementary Health Centre, Westover Trading Estate, Langport, **Somerset**, TA10 9RB, ENG.
(T) 01458 252041 (F) 01458 253072
Speciality: Homeopathy.
● **Owner** Mrs N French
M (Ref:HM07735)

## FRESH HORIZONS

**Fresh Horizons**, 50 Ditton Ct Rd, Westcliff-on-



Key continued: **Yrs.Est:** Years Established **Q:** Qualifications **M:** Professional Membership ✔ Indemnity Insurance Accept Credit Cards

Sea, **Essex**, SS0 7HF, ENG.
(T) 01702 304931
Speciality: Complementary Medicines & Therapy.
● **Employee** Mrs L Cummins
C M (Ref:HM07736)

## FRESHFIELDS OF ALDEBURGH

**Freshfields of Aldeburgh**, 152 High St, Aldebugh, Ipswich, **Suffolk**, IP15 5AX, ENG.
(T) 01728 454299
Speciality: Acupuncture, Aromatherapy, Chiropody, Complementary Therapy, Homeopathy, Indian Head Massage, Nutritional Therapy, Osteopathy, Podiatry, Reflexology, Shiatsu, Vitamin Therapy, Health and Beauty. ✓
● **Owner** Dr E Kerrigan Q: CMA.
● **Osteopath** Ms S Kimber
(T) 01502 740427 Q: BSc (Hons).
● **Homeopath** Ms N Coulson
(T) 01728 830152
● **Podiatrist** Ms P Burrell-Saward
(T) 01394 450315or01728832998 Q: MBChA, MSSCh. M: B.A.Ch.P.
● **Shiatsu Teacher** Ms C Paola
(T) 01728 452775 Q: MRSS. M: RSS.
● **Complementary Therapist** Ms S Balls
(T) 01394 460903 Q: AOC, ITEC. M: GCP.
● **Complementary Therapist** Ms E Mayhew
(T) 01728 832998or01728832861 Q: IIHHT, MIFA. M: IFA, IIHHT.
C (Ref:HM07737)

## FRESHLEA PRIVATE CLINICS

**Freshlea Private Clinics**, 6 Kew Rd, Liverpool, **Merseyside**, L37 2HB, ENG.
(T) 01704 873213
Speciality: Osteopathy, Remedial Massage. ✓
● **Osteopath** Mr Howard Q: DO. M: GOsC.
● **Partner** Mrs Howard
S (Ref:HM07738)

## FRESHWATER, WILLIAM T

**William T Freshwater**, 12 Middle Rd, London, **London (Greater)**, E13 0DQ, ENG.
(T) 020 8552 8209
Speciality: Psychotherapy.
● **Principal** Mr W Freshwater
B (Ref:HM07739)

## FRESHWINDS CHARITABLE TRUST

**Freshwinds Charitable Trust**, 13 Gravelly Hill North, Birmingham, **Midlands (West)**, B23 6BT, ENG.
(T) 01214 568100 (F) 01214 568119
(E) freshwinds@btinternet.com
(W) www.freshwinds.org.uk
Speciality: Acupuncture, Alexander Technique, Aromatherapy, Chiropractic, Counselling, Healer, Healing Therapy, Homeopathy, Hypnosis, Hypnotherapy, Indian Head Massage, Meditation, Moxibustion, Osteopathy, Psychotherapy, Reflexology, Reiki, Shiatsu, Sound Therapy, Spiritual Healing, T'ai-Chi Ch'uan, Yoga, Tui Na and Magna Therapy. ✓
● **Director** Mr M Al-Rahim
● **Centre Manager** Dr P Shah
● **Teacher** Dr R Lee Q: Dip.Arom.
C Yrs. Est.: 10 (Ref:HM07740)

## FREUND, S M

**S M Freund**, Norton Lodge, 83 The Park, Cheltenham, **Gloucestershire**, GL50 2RP, ENG.
(T) 01242 224894
Speciality: Chiropodists (Podiatrists).
● **Owner** Mrs S Freund
S (Ref:HM07741)

## FREY, YVES

**Yves Frey**, 17 Nottingham St, London, **London (Greater)**, W1M 3RD, ENG.
(T) 020 7935 9354
Speciality: Complementary Medicines & Therapy.
● **Owner** Mr Y Frey
C M (Ref:HM07742)

## FRIAR, CARL

**Carl Friar**, 49 Deben Avenue, Martlesham Heath, Ipswich, **Suffolk**, IP5 3QP, ENG.
(T) 01473 630499
Speciality: Reflexology.
S T (Ref:HM07743)

## FRIARS HEALING/SPIRITUAL CTRE

**Friars Healing & Spiritual Centre**, 10 St. Peters St, Canterbury, **Kent**, CT1 2AT, ENG.
(T) 01227 477171
Speciality: Complementary Medicines & Therapy.
M (Ref:HM07744)

## FRIDAY, SARA

**Sara Friday**, 49-51 South St, Dorking, **Surrey**, RH4 2JX, ENG.
(T) 01306 880488
Speciality: Physiotherapy.
P S T (Ref:HM07745)

## FRIEDRICH STAEBLER

**Friedrich Staebler**, 3a Ladbroke Rd, London, **London (Greater)**, W11 3PA, ENG.
(T) 020 7221 2479
Speciality: Acupuncture.
O (Ref:HM07746)

## FRIEND, JONATHAN

**Jonathan Friend**, 29 Highcliffe Gardens, Ilford, **Essex**, IG4 5HP, ENG.
(T) 020 8550 0982
Speciality: Osteopathy.
● **Owner** Mr J Friend
P S T (Ref:HM07747)

## FRIENDLY FROG

**Friendly Frog**, 9 West Quay, Bridgwater, **Somerset**, TA6 3HL, ENG.
(T) 01278 452544
Speciality: Aromatherapy.
● **Owner** Mrs C Huck
M O (Ref:HM07748)

## FRIGHT, ANGELA M

**Angela M Fright**, 2 Park Farm, Stoneham Lane, Eastleigh, **Hampshire**, SO50 9HS, ENG.
(T) 023 8061 2960
Speciality: Complementary Medicines & Therapy.
C M (Ref:HM07749)

## FRINTON PHYSIOTHERAPY CLINIC

**Frinton Physiotherapy Clinic**, 78 Rochford Way, Walton On The Naze, **Essex**, CO14 8SP, ENG.
(T) 01255 671563 (F) 01255 671563
Speciality: Physiotherapy.
● **Owner** Mrs J Iveson
P S T (Ref:HM07750)

## FRISBY, JOHN

**John Frisby**, 155 Glenfields, Whittlesey, Peterborough, **Cambridgeshire**, PE7 1HY, ENG.
(T) 01733 204954 (F) 01733 204954
Speciality: Hypnotherapy.
● **Partner** Mr J Frisby
B (Ref:HM07751)

## FRISBY, S

**S Frisby**, Ashdown Osteopathic Centre, The Sq, Lewes Rd, Forest Row, **Sussex (East)**, RH18 5ES, ENG.
(T) 01342 822505 (F) 01342 822505
Speciality: Osteopathy.
● **Owner** Mr T Strutt
P S T (Ref:HM07752)

## FRIS-LAWRENCE, J

**J Fris-Lawrence**, 252 Cheriton Rd, Folkestone, **Kent**, CT19 4DN, ENG.
(T) 01303 278188
Speciality: Homeopathy.
● **Owner** Mr P Smith
M (Ref:HM07753)

## FROBISHER, LYNDA

**Lynda Frobisher**, 7 Delamere Cres, Harrogate, **Yorkshire (North)**, HG2 7HG, ENG.
(T) 01423 543523
Speciality: Reflexology.
S T (Ref:HM07754)

## FROME PHYSIO & SPORTS CLINIC

**Frome Physiotherapy & Sports Injury Clinic**, 14 Bath Rd, Frome, **Somerset**, BA11 2HH, ENG.
(T) 01373 452604 (F) 01373 452604
Speciality: Physiotherapy.
● **Principal** Mrs P Laarberg
P S T (Ref:HM07755)

## FROME VALLEY PHYSIO CLINIC

**Frome Valley Physiotherapy Clinic**, 35 Crescent Rd, Bristol, BS16 2TW, ENG.
(T) 01179 563103
Speciality: Physiotherapy.
● **Owner** Ms V Paver
P S T (Ref:HM07756)

## FRONTIA

**Frontia Complementary Health Care Centre**, 4 Bath Rd, Worcester, **Worcestershire**, WR5 3EJ, ENG.
(T) 01905 763481
(E) fiona@frontia.co.uk
(W) www.frontia.co.uk
Speciality: Acupuncture, Alexander Technique, Aromatherapy, Bach Remedies, Chiropractic, Complementary Therapy, Counselling, Cranial Osteopathy, Crystal Healing, Healer, Homeopathy, Hypnotherapy, Indian Head Massage, Kinesiology, Massage (Therapeutic), Nutritional Therapy, Psychotherapy, Reflexology, Reiki, Spiritual Healing, Stress Therapy, Visualisation Therapy. ✓
● **Aromatherapist** Ms R Davies Q: ITEC, MTI. M: IPTI, MTI.
● **Reflexologist** Mrs F Clarke Q: RGN, TCCAR. M: AoR.
C Yrs. Est.: 5 (Ref:HM07757)

## FROST, ANDREA

**Andrea Frost**, 58 Hartington St, Barrow-in-Furness, **Cumbria**, LA14 5SR, ENG.
(T) 01229 832855 (F) 01229 832855
Speciality: Physiotherapy.
● **Partner** Mrs A Frost
P S T (Ref:HM07758)

## FROST, CAROLINE

**Caroline Frost**, 8 Tilmans Mead, Farningham, Dartford, **Kent**, DA4 0BY, ENG.
(T) 01322 862508
Speciality: Acupuncture.
● **Owner** Ms C Frost
O (Ref:HM07759)

## FROST, CHARLES

**Charles Frost**, 5 Searles View, Horsham, **Sussex (West)**, RH12 4FG, ENG.
(T) 01403 264665
Speciality: Allergy Testing, Auto Suggestion, Aversion Therapy, Cognitive Therapy, Counselling, Humanistic Psychology, Hypnosis, Hypnotherapy, Rogerian Therapy, Stress Therapy, Visualisation Therapy. ✓
● **Hypnotherapist/Counsellor** Mr C Frost Q: Dip.Hyp, Dip.Psych, MNCH, NACHP. M: GHR, NACHP, NCH, NCP.
B Yrs. Est.: 22 (Ref:HM07760)

## FROST, JANICE

**Janice Frost**, 193 Manor Rd, Benfleet, **Essex**, SS7 4JD, ENG.
(T) 01268 793159
Speciality: Reflexology. ✓
● **Reflexologist** Ms J Frost Q: IIHHT. M: FHT, ICHT.
C Yrs. Est.: 4 (Ref:HM07761)

## FROST, JEREMY

**Jeremy Frost**, 301b New North Rd, Ilford, **Essex**, IG6 3DX, ENG.
(T) 020 8270 7829
Speciality: Osteopathy.
● **Owner** Mr J Frost
P S T (Ref:HM07762)

## FROST, JEREMY

**Jeremy Frost**, 75 Risbygate St, Bury St. Edmunds, **Suffolk**, IP33 3AQ, ENG.
(T) 01284 769153
Speciality: Osteopathy.
P S T (Ref:HM07763)

## FROST, LESLEY

**Lesley Frost**, 2 White Hart Lane, Shaftesbury, **Dorset**, SP7 8HH, ENG.
(T) 01747 853375
Speciality: Reflexology.



Key: B Mind-Body Medicine C Complementary Medicine H Self Help Treatment M Medicinal Therapy O Oriental Medicine P Postural Therapy S Manipulative Structural Therapy T Touch Therapy

S T (Ref:HM07764)

## FROST, M J

**M J Frost**, 126 Norwood Rd, London, **London (Greater)**, SE24 9AY, ENG.
(T) 020 8669 0388
Speciality: Chiropodists (Podiatrists).
S (Ref:HM07765)

## FROST, P

**P Frost**, Bushey Country Club, Bushey House, High St, Bushey, Watford, **Hertfordshire**, WD2 1BJ, ENG.
(T) 020 8421 8384 (F) 020 8421 8355
Speciality: Chiropodists (Podiatrists).
● **Owner** Miss P Frost
S (Ref:HM07766)

## FROST, PATRICIA

**Patricia Frost**, Durham, **County Durham**, DH1 5YT, ENG.
(T) 01913 865175
Speciality: Homeopathy.
M (Ref:HM07767)

## FROST, RICHARD L

**Richard L Frost**, 28 Court Yard, London, **London (Greater)**, SE9 5QA, ENG.
(T) 020 8850 7623
Speciality: Chiropodists (Podiatrists).
● **Owner** Miss L McGucken
S (Ref:HM07768)

## FROST, SAMANTHIA

**Samanthia Frost**, Friar Lane, Nottingham, **Nottinghamshire**, NG1 6DQ, ENG.
(T) 01159 523324
Speciality: Clairvoyants & Palmists.
B (Ref:HM07769)

## FROSTICK, DAVID

**David Frostick**, 31 King St, Stanford-Le-Hope, **Essex**, SS17 0HJ, ENG.
(T) 01375 360626
Speciality: Homeopathy.
M (Ref:HM07770)

## FRY, HOWARD

**Howard Fry**, 18 Acorn Cl, Enfield, **London (Greater)**, EN2 8LX, ENG.
(T) 020 8372 7809
Speciality: Chiropodists (Podiatrists).
S (Ref:HM07771)

## FRY, HOWARD

**Howard Fry**, All Hallows House, Idol Lane, London, **London (Greater)**, EC3R 5DD, ENG.
(T) 020 7283 8908
Speciality: Chiropody, Nail Surgery. ✔
● **Chiropodist** Mr H Fry Q: DPodM, M.S.C.P.
M Yrs. Est.: 5 (Ref:HM07772)

## FRY, MARGARET

**Margaret Fry**, 544 Green Lane, Ilford, **Essex**, IG3 9LL, ENG.
(T) 020 8599 2444
Speciality: Complementary Medicines & Therapy.
● **Partner** Ms T Couzens
M (Ref:HM07773)

## FRYER-DOUGLAS, PATRICIA

**Patricia Fryer-Douglas**, 52 Stoke Newington Church St, London, **London (Greater)**, N16 0NB, ENG.
(T) 020 7249 9671
Speciality: Hypnotherapy.
● **Senior Partner** Mrs J Sheridan
B (Ref:HM07774)

## FRYMORGEN, A

**A Frymorgen**, 182 Algernon Rd, London, **London (Greater)**, SE13 7AN, ENG.
(T) 020 8690 2608
Speciality: Homeopathy.
● **Owner** Mrs A Frymorgan
M (Ref:HM07775)

## FUCHSIA AROMATHERAPY

**Fuchsia Aromatherapy**, 10 Cornmarket St, **County Cork**, IRE.
(T) 021 4279 106
Speciality: Aromatherapy.
M O (Ref:HM07776)

## FUDGE, H

**H Fudge - Osteopath**, Market House Surgery, 18b Bampton St, Tiverton, **Devon**, EX16 6AA, ENG.
(T) 01884 258570
Speciality: Complementary Therapy, Counselling, Kinesiology, Manipulation, Massage (Therapeutic), Osteopathy. ✔
● **Counsellor** Mrs R Fudge Q: Dip.Couns. M: BACP.
● **Osteopath** Mr H Fudge Q: DO. M: BOA, GOsC.
S Yrs. Est.: 10 (Ref:HM07777)

## FUDGE, JOHN

**John Fudge**, The Brownswood Practice, 24 Wilberforce Rd, London, **London (Greater)**, N4 2SW, ENG.
(T) 020 7226 1193
Speciality: Osteopathy.
P S T (Ref:HM07778)

## FUDGE, Z

**Z Fudge**, 42 Moss Lane, Pinner, **London (Greater)**, HA5 3AX, ENG.
(T) 020 8866 1778
Speciality: Electrolysis.
● **Owner** Mrs Z Fudge
T (Ref:HM07779)

## FULBRIDGE REFLEXOLOGY

**Fulbridge Reflexology**, 554 Fulbridge Rd, Peterborough, **Cambridgeshire**, PE4 6SB, ENG.
(T) 01733 320989
Speciality: Reflexology.
S T (Ref:HM07780)

## FULHAM CLINIC

**Fulham Clinic Ltd (The)**, 4 Fulham Park Studios, Rear Of 895/921 Fulham Rd, London, **London (Greater)**, SW6 5HU, ENG.
(T) 01717 315329 (F) 020 7731 5329
Speciality: Acupressure, Acupuncture, Aromatherapy, Bach Remedies, Chiropractic, Complementary Therapy, Counselling, Cranial Osteopathy, Herbal Medicine, Holistic Healing, Homeopathy, Hypnotherapy, Indian Head Massage, Massage (Therapeutic), Osteopathy, Reflexology, Shiatsu, Lymphatic Drainage Technique, Vertical Reflex Therapy.
● **Shiatsu Practitioner** Mr S Pucelle
● **Reflexologist** Ms C Pegg Q: MAR.
● **Deep Tissue Massage Therapist** Mr A Mercuri
● **Cranio-Sacral Therapist** Ms M Molloy Q: Dip.Reflex, ITEC.
● **Aromatherapist** Ms S Anderson Q: ITEC.
● **Acupuncturist** Ms J Hall Q: BA (Hons), Lic.Ac, MBAcC.
● **Osteopath** Ms D Ryan Q: BSc.
● **Homeopath** Ms P Nalty Q: LCPH.
● **Therapist** Ms S Woodford
● **Acupuncturist/Chinese Herbalist** Ms S Subner Q: BSc (Hons), Dip.Ac, MRCHM.
● **Acupuncturist** Miss A Rolt Q: Lic.Ac, MBAcC.
● **Chiropractor** Krister Harm Q: BSc, DC.
M Yrs. Est.: 2 (Ref:HM07781)

## FULHAM MEDICAL CENTRE

**Fulham Medical Centre (The)**, 446 Fulham Rd, London, **London (Greater)**, SW6 1BG, ENG.
(T) 020 7385 6001
Speciality: Osteopathy.
P S T (Ref:HM07782)

## FULHAM OSTEOPATHIC PRACTICE

**Fulham Osteopathic Practice**, 53 Finlay St, London, **London (Greater)**, SW6 6HF, ENG.
(T) 020 7384 1851
(W) www.fop.co.uk
Speciality: Cranial Osteopathy, Osteopathy, Physiotherapy.
P S T (Ref:HM07783)

## FULHAM PALACE

**Fulham Palace Chiropractic & Health**, 381 Lillie Rd, Corner Of Fulham Place Rd, London, **London (Greater)**, SW6 7PJ, ENG.
(T) 020 7386 9993
Speciality: Chiropractic.
P S T (Ref:HM07784)

## FULHAM PHYSIOTHERAPY

**Fulham Physiotherapy**, Swan Mews, London, **London (Greater)**, SW6 4QT, ENG.
(T) 020 7371 7666 (F) 020 7371 7686
Speciality: Physiotherapy.
● **Owner** Mr M Bender
P S T (Ref:HM07785)

## FULL SPECTRUM THERAPY CENTRE

**Full Spectrum Therapy Centre**, 218 New Rd, West Parley, Ferndown, **Dorset**, BH22 8EN, ENG.
(T) 01202 594494
Speciality: Hypnotherapy, Electro Crystal Therapy, PIP~Scanning, Ozone/Oxygen Therapy. ✔
● **Therapist** Mrs L Brady
● **Hypnotherapist** Mr Brady
C Yrs. Est.: 4 (Ref:HM07786)

## FULL, D M

**D M Full**, Keepers Cottage, Walton, Presteigne, **Powys**, LD8 2RE, WAL.
(T) 01544 350388
Speciality: Chiropodists (Podiatrists).
● **Owner** Mr D Full
S (Ref:HM07787)

## FULLALOVE, D

**D Fullalove**, 172 Springfield Rd, Plymouth, **Devon**, PL9 8PT, ENG.
(T) 01752 492450
Speciality: Reflexology.
S T (Ref:HM07788)

## FULLER, HILARY

**Hilary Fuller**, 10 Castlegate, Prestbury, Macclesfield, **Cheshire**, SK10 4AZ, ENG.
(T) 01625 827619
Speciality: Reflexology.
S T (Ref:HM07789)

## FULLER, MICHAEL A

**Michael A Fuller**, 105 Kings Rd, Haslemere, **Surrey**, GU27 2QG, ENG.
(T) 01428 642434
Speciality: Osteopathy.
● **Owner** Mr M Fuller
P S T (Ref:HM07790)

## FULLERTON, DERMOT M

**Dermot M Fullerton**, Cooleen St, Orans Rd, Buncrana, **County Donegal**, IRE.
(T) 07761 191 (F) 07762 487
Speciality: Homeopathy.
M (Ref:HM07791)

## FULLERTON, N P

**Ludlow Chiropractic Clinic**, Holcombe House, Gravel Hill, Ludlow, **Shropshire**, SY8 1QU, ENG.
(T) 01584 874200
(E) npfullerton@netmatters.co.uk
Speciality: Chiropractic, Kinesiology, Manipulation, Massage (Therapeutic), Nutritional Therapy. ✔
● **Doctor** Dr N Fullerton Q: DC. M: BCA, GCC.
S Yrs. Est.: 20 (Ref:HM07792)

## FULLING, JACK

**Jack Fulling**, 3 Ashville Cl, Harrogate, **Yorkshire (North)**, HG2 9LZ, ENG.
(T) 01423 879722
Speciality: Physiotherapy.
● **Partner** Mrs P Fulling
P S T (Ref:HM07793)

## FULLWOOD, D

**D Fullwood**, 32 Upper High St, Wednesbury, **Midlands (West)**, WS10 7HJ, ENG.
(T) 01215 560891
Speciality: Chiropodists (Podiatrists).
● **Owner** Mr D Fullwood
S (Ref:HM07794)

## FULTON, A J

**A J Fulton**, 1 Willow Cl, Canvey Island, **Essex**, SS8 9HQ, ENG.
(T) 01268 474319
Speciality: Biomechanics, Chiropody, Nail Surgery, Podiatry. ✔
● **Chiropodist (Podiatrist)** Mr A Fulton
C Yrs. Est.: 30 (Ref:HM07795)



Key continued: **Yrs.Est:** Years Established **Q:** Qualifications **M:** Professional Membership ✔ Indemnity Insurance Accept Credit Cards

## FULTON, A J

**A J Fulton**, Body Balance, 11A Billet Lane, Hornchurch, **Essex**, RM11 1TS, ENG.
(T) 01708 621194 (F) 01708 501150
Speciality: Biomechanics, Chiropody, Nail Surgery, Podiatry. ✔
● **Owner/Chiropodist** A J Fulton Q: SRPod.
C Yrs. Est.: 12 (Ref:HM07796)

## FUN, MAE

**Mae Fun**, 2 Cliff Way, Frinton-on-Sea, **Essex**, CO13 9NL, ENG.
(T) 01255 675256
Speciality: Acupuncture.
O (Ref:HM07797)

## FUNCTIONAL HEALTH CARE

**Functional Health Care**, 11 Newham Grange Avenue, Stockton-On-Tees, **Cleveland**, TS19 0SB, ENG.
(T) 01642 675341
Speciality: Complementary Medicines & Therapy.
M (Ref:HM07798)

## FURLONG, CATHIE

**Cathie Furlong**, 8 South Common, Redbourn, St. Albans, **Hertfordshire**, AL3 7LU, ENG.
(T) 01582 793076
Speciality: Complementary Medicines & Therapy.
● **Owner** Mr M Furlong
C M (Ref:HM07799)

## FURNACE GREEN CHIRO CTRE

**Furnace Green Chiropractic Centre**, 50 The Glades, Furnace Green, Crawley, **Sussex (West)**, RH10 6JN, ENG.
(T) 01293 612793
Speciality: Chiropractic, Complementary Therapy, Manipulation, Massage (Therapeutic), Vitamin Therapy, Mineral and Diet Therapist.
● **Chiropractor** Mr J Lafitte Q: DC, MCC. M: CC, GCC.
S Yrs. Est.: 5 (Ref:HM07800)

## FURSDON, S V

**S V Fursdon**, 201 Holdenhurst Rd, Bournemouth, **Dorset**, BH8 8DE, ENG.
(T) 01202 557283
Speciality: Chiropodists (Podiatrists).
● **Owner** Mr N Welsh
S (Ref:HM07801)

## FURSEY, STEPHEN

**Stephen Fursey**, 126 High St, Lymington, **Hampshire**, SO41 9AQ, ENG.
(T) 01590 679560
Speciality: Herbal Medicine.
● **Senior Partner** Dr P Hardy
M (Ref:HM07802)

## FURZE CORNER NATURAL THERAPIES

**Furze Corner Natural Therapies**, Tatsfield Approach Rd, Tatsfield, Westerham, **Kent**, TN16 2JT, ENG.
(T) 01959 577240
Speciality: Complementary Medicines & Therapy.
● **Owner** Mr G Litchfield
C M (Ref:HM07803)

## FURZER, LINDA

**Linda Furzer**, The Terrace, 35 Staplegrove Rd, Taunton, **Somerset**, TA1 1DG, ENG.
(T) 01823 338968
Speciality: Homeopathy.
● **Owner** Ms J Gotto
M (Ref:HM07804)

## FYFE, M J

**M J Fyfe**, 48 Alexandra St, Southend-On-Sea, **Essex**, SS1 1BJ, ENG.
(T) 01702 393737
Speciality: Chiropodists (Podiatrists).
● **Owner** Mr M Fyfe
S (Ref:HM07805)

## FYSON, MELANIE

**Melanie Fyson Homeopath**, 73 Five Mile Drive, Oxford, **Oxfordshire**, OX2 8HW, ENG.
(T) 01865 429336
(E) melanie.fyson@ntlworld.com
(W) www.fyson.freeserve.co.uk
Speciality: Homeopathy. ✔
● **Homeopath** Mrs M Fyson Q: Dip.Hom. M: Soc.Hom.
M Yrs. Est.: 2 (Ref:HM07806)

## G & G FOOD SUPPLIES

**G & G Vitamin**, Vitatility House, 2-3 Imberhorne Way, East Grinstead, **Sussex (West)**, RH19 1RL, ENG.
(T) 01342 312811 (F) 01342 315938
(W) www.gandgvitamins.com
Speciality: Herbal Medicine, Vitamin Therapy.
● **Promotions/Marketing Manager** Mr M Wood
H Yrs. Est.: 36 (Ref:HM07807)

## G H B CHIROPODY SERVICES

**G H B Chiropody Services**, Oap Hut, Wishaw Rd, Wishaw, **Lanarkshire (North)**, ML2 8ES, SCO.
(T) 01698 357186
Speciality: Chiropodists (Podiatrists).
● **Owner** Mr G Bicknell
S (Ref:HM07808)

## G H M VICKERS

**G H M Vickers**, 12 Byron Pl, Bristol, BS8 1JT, ENG.
(T) 01179 264881
Speciality: Chiropodists (Podiatrists).
S (Ref:HM07809)

## G HAMER NUTRITION

**G Hamer Nutrition**, All Hallows House, Idol Lane, London, **London (Greater)**, EC3R 5DD, ENG.
(T) 020 7283 8908
Speciality: Complementary Medicines & Therapy.
M (Ref:HM07810)

## G J D ELECTRICAL SERVICES

**G J D Electrical Services**, 75 Dovedale Cres, Belper, **Derbyshire**, DE56 1HJ, ENG.
(T) 01773 821198
Speciality: Electrolysis.
T (Ref:HM07811)

## G NORTHWOOD PSYCHOTHERAPY

**Graham Northwood Psychotherapy & Clinical Hypnosis**, 8 Mount Rd, Chessington, **Surrey**, KT9 1JG, ENG.
(T) 020 8397 5441 (F) 020 8241 4719
Speciality: Hypnosis.
● **Owner** Mr G Northwood
B (Ref:HM07812)

## G P F CONSULTANCY

**G P F Consultancy**, 41 Maple Rd, Bristol, BS7 8RE, ENG.
(T) 01179 421600
Speciality: Reflexology.
S T (Ref:HM07813)

## G P S

**G P S**, Animals Only, Tatham Rd, Ruabon, Wrexham, LL14 6RF, WAL.
(T) 01978 824361 (F) 01978 824361
Speciality: Herbalists.
● **Owner** Mrs R Williams
M (Ref:HM07814)

## G T CONSULTANCY

**G T Consultancy**, 56 Biddulph Mansions, Elgin Avenue, Maida Vale, London, **London (Greater)**, W9 1HT, ENG.
(T) 020 7286 0887
(E) gtconsult@gtconsult.co.uk
(W) www.gtconsult.co.uk
Speciality: Counselling, Healing Therapy, Hypnosis, Hypnotherapy, Psychotherapy, Stress Therapy. ✔
● **Hypno-Psychotherapist** Mr G Thomas Q: BSc (Hons), Dip.Psych, MA. M: BPS, CRAH, HA, NCH.
B Yrs. Est.: 5 (Ref:HM07815)

## GABB, ELIZABETH DESMOND

**Elizabeth Desmond Gabb**, 28 Mansell Rd, London, **London (Greater)**, W3 7QH, ENG.
(T) 020 8749 0528
Speciality: Electrolysis.
T (Ref:HM07816)

## GABLECROFT-NATURAL THERAPY

**Gablecroft College Of Natural Therapy**, Church St, Whittington, Oswestry, **Shropshire**, SY11 4DT, ENG.
(T) 01691 659631
Speciality: Complementary Medicines & Therapy.
C M (Ref:HM07817)

## GABLES CLINIC NHS

**Gables Clinic NHS**, Chiropodists, 402 Marton Rd, Middlesbrough, **Cleveland**, TS4 2PB, ENG.
(T) 01642 245090
Speciality: Chiropodists (Podiatrists).
S (Ref:HM07818)

## GABLES NATURAL HEALTH CLINIC

**Gables Natural Health Clinic**, 108 High St, Uckfield, **Sussex (East)**, TN22 1PX, ENG.
(T) 01825 766529
Speciality: Complementary Medicines & Therapy.
● **Practice Manager** Ms V Hunot
M (Ref:HM07819)

## GABRIEL PROGRAMME

**Gabriel Programme (The)**, 104 Dartmouth Park Hill, London, **London (Greater)**, N19 5HU, ENG.
(T) 020 7609 1586
Speciality: Psychotherapy.
● **Owner** Mr M Gabriel
B (Ref:HM07820)

## GABRIEL, CLARE

**Clare Gabriel**, Treeway House, 134 Forest Rd, Narborough, Leicester, **Leicestershire**, LE9 5ET, ENG.
(T) 01162 849890
Speciality: Clairvoyants & Palmists.
B (Ref:HM07821)

## GADD, A

**A Gadd**, 8 High St, Arundel, **Sussex (West)**, BN18 9AB, ENG.
(T) 01903 882200
Speciality: Osteopathy.
● **Owner** A Gadd
P S T (Ref:HM07822)

## GADD, K

**K Gadd**, 1 Larke Rise, Southend-On-Sea, **Essex**, SS2 6GQ, ENG.
(T) 01702 434515
Speciality: Chiropodists (Podiatrists).
● **Owner** Mrs K Gadd
S (Ref:HM07823)

## GADHER, SATYEN P

**Satyen P Gadher**, 26 Monmouth St, Bath, **Somerset**, BA1 2AP, ENG.
(T) 01225 427835
Speciality: Osteopathy.
P S T (Ref:HM07824)

## GADSBEY, GORDON

**Gordon Gadsbey**, 47 Milton Cres, Leicester, **Leicestershire**, LE4 0PA, ENG.
(T) 01162 352204
Speciality: Acupuncture.
● **Owner** Mr G Gadsby
O (Ref:HM07825)

## GAELEN

**Gaelen**, Stud Cottage, Bishops Down, Sherborne, **Dorset**, DT9 5PN, ENG.
(T) 07071 676869
Speciality: Clairvoyants & Palmists.
B (Ref:HM07826)

## GAFFNEY, ALMA

**A Gaffney**, 94 High St, Mold, **Flintshire**, CH7 1BH, WAL.
(T) 01352 700095
Speciality: Biomechanics, Chiropody, Cryo Surgery, Nail Surgery, Orthotics, Podiatry. ✔
● **Chiropodist (Podiatrist)** Mrs A Gaffney Q: DPodM, S.R.Ch.
M Yrs. Est.: 36 (Ref:HM07827)

## GAGNON THERAPIES

**Gagnon Therapies**, 67 Wigmore St, London, **London (Greater)**, W1H 9LG, ENG.
(T) 020 7224 2332 (F) 020 7224 5995
Speciality: Complementary Medicines &



Key: B Mind-Body Medicine C Complementary Medicine H Self Help Treatment M Medicinal Therapy O Oriental Medicine P Postural Therapy S Manipulative Structural Therapy T Touch Therapy

Therapy.
● **Manageress** Miss B Gagoyle
M (Ref:HM07828)

## GAIA CENTRE FOR HEALTHY LIVING
**GAIA Centre For Healthy Living**, 27-29 High St, Droitwich, **Worcestershire**, WR9 8EJ, ENG.
(T) 01905 795404
Speciality: Complementary Medicines & Therapy.
C M (Ref:HM07829)

## GAIA HEALTH
**Gaia Health**, 127 Park Gr, Barnsley, **Yorkshire (South)**, S70 1QG, ENG.
(T) 01226 286690 (F) 01226 282904
Speciality: Aromatherapy.
● **Owner** Mrs S Dawson
M O (Ref:HM07830)

## GAIER, HARALD C
**Harald C Gaier**, The Hale Clinic, 7 Park Cresent, London, **London (Greater)**, W1N 3HE, ENG.
(T) 020 7631 0156
Speciality: Osteopathy.
C P S T (Ref:HM07831)

## GAINBOROUGH CHIROPODY CLINIC
**Gainborough Chiropody Clinic**, Gainborough, Station Rd, Tenterden, **Kent**, TN30 6HN, ENG.
(T) 01580 762351
Speciality: Chiropodists (Podiatrists).
● **Owner** Mr R Boxall
S (Ref:HM07832)

## GAINES, GWEN
**Gwen Gaines**, 4 Hawke Cl, Norton, Doncaster, **Yorkshire (South)**, DN6 9PG, ENG.
(T) 01302 709119
Speciality: Physiotherapy.
● **Owner** Mrs G Gaines
P S T (Ref:HM07833)

## GAITERO-ARROYO, CRISTINA
**Cristina Gaitero-Arroyo**, 117 Chambers Lane, London, **London (Greater)**, NW10 2RP, ENG.
(T) 020 8459 3783
Speciality: Reflexology.
S T (Ref:HM07834)

## GAJAHARSINGH, GERRY
**Gerry Gajaharsingh**, 96 Harley St, London, **London (Greater)**, W1N 1AF, ENG.
(T) 020 7487 4204 (F) 020 7487 4274
Speciality: Osteopathy.
● **Owner** Mr G Gajadharsingh
P S T (Ref:HM07835)

## GALE CENTRE
**Gale Centre**, Stable Cottage, Whitakers Way, Loughton, **Essex**, IG10 1SQ, ENG.
(T) 020 8508 9344
Speciality: Psychotherapy.
● **Owner** Derek Gale
B (Ref:HM07836)

## GALE, M H
**M H Gale**, 71 Queensland Avenue, Coventry, **Midlands (West)**, CV5 8FF, ENG.
(T) 024 7671 2569
Speciality: Chiropodists (Podiatrists).
● **Owner** Mr N Gale
S (Ref:HM07837)

## GALGUT, CORDELIA
**Cordelia Galgut**, 52 Stoke Newington Church St, London, **London (Greater)**, N16 0NB, ENG.
(T) 020 7249 9671
Speciality: Psychotherapy.
● **Senior Partner** Mrs J Sheridan
B (Ref:HM07838)

## GALLACHER, J
**J Gallacher**, 2 Wessex Rd, Poole, **Dorset**, BH14 8BG, ENG.
(T) 01202 721904
Speciality: Hypnotherapy.
● **Owner** Mr J Gallacher
B (Ref:HM07839)

## GALLAGHER, ARTHUR
**Arthur Gallagher**, 1a Wynsome St, Southwick, Trowbridge, **Wiltshire**, BA14 9RB, ENG.
(T) 01225 755736
Speciality: Chiropodists (Podiatrists).
● **Owner** Mr A Gallagher
S (Ref:HM07840)

## GALLEN, ANNE
**Anne Gallen**, Luton, **Bedfordshire**, LU21, ENG.
(T) 01582 487100
Speciality: Bach Remedies.
M (Ref:HM07841)

## GALLEY, D G
**D G Galley**, 127 Marsh Lane, Belper, **Derbyshire**, DE56 1GU, ENG.
(T) 01773 820942
Speciality: Chiropractic.
P S T (Ref:HM07842)

## GALLEY, D G
**D G Galley**, 65 Heage Rd, Ripley, **Derbyshire**, DE5 3GE, ENG.
(T) 01773 743293
Speciality: Chiropractic.
P S T (Ref:HM07843)

## GALLIENNE-SMITH, HELEN
**Helen Gallienne-Smith**, 114 Robin Hood Lane, Helsby, Frodsham, **Cheshire**, WA6 9NL, ENG.
(T) 01928 722344
Speciality: Chiropodists (Podiatrists).
● **Owner** Mrs H Gallienne-Smith
S (Ref:HM07844)

## GALLIVAN, NOEL M (DR)
**Dr Noel M Gallivan**, 5 Lr Hatch St, Dublin, **County Dublin**, IRE.
(T) 01676 0311
Speciality: Complementary Medicines & Therapy.
M (Ref:HM07845)

## GALLOWAY, BEVERLEY
**Beverley Galloway**, 113 Probert Rd, Wolverhampton, **Midlands (West)**, WV10 6UB, ENG.
(T) 01902 782594
Speciality: Reflexology.
M (Ref:HM07846)

## GALLOWAY, CHRISTOPHER
**Christopher Galloway**, Forest Edge Clinic, Salisbury Rd, Totton, Southampton, **Hampshire**, SO40 3NH, ENG.
(T) 023 8066 7205
Speciality: Osteopathy.
P S T (Ref:HM07847)

## GALLOWAY, N
**N Galloway**, Brundholme House, Threlkeld, Keswick, **Cumbria**, CA12 4TB, ENG.
(T) 01768 779674
Speciality: Complementary Medicines & Therapy.
● **Owner** Mr N Galloway
M (Ref:HM07848)

## GALLOWAY, NEIL
**Neil Galloway**, North Friarage, Friargate, Penrith, **Cumbria**, CA11 7XR, ENG.
(T) 01768 892567
Speciality: Complementary Medicines & Therapy.
C M (Ref:HM07849)

## GALLOWAY, TRUDY J
**Trudy J Galloway**, 49-51 Mill St, Montrose, **Angus**, DD10 8NE, SCO.
(T) 01674 675042
Speciality: Chiropodists (Podiatrists).
● **Owner** Miss T Galloway
S (Ref:HM07850)

## GALSTON CLINIC
**Galston Clinic**, 7 Henrietta St, Galston, **Ayrshire (East)**, KA4 8HN, SCO.
(T) 01563 822709
Speciality: Chiropodists (Podiatrists).
● **Owner** Mr K Brown
S (Ref:HM07851)

## GALVIN, LILIAN
**Lilian Galvin**, 10 Doyle Gardens, Kensal Rise, London, **London (Greater)**, NW10 3DA, ENG.
(T) 020 8969 5115
Speciality: Osteopathy.
P S T (Ref:HM07852)

## GALWAY BACKCARE & HEALTH
**Galway Backcare & Health Clinic**, Pollnaclough, Moycullen, **County Galway**, IRE.
(T) 09155 5025
Speciality: Complementary Medicines & Therapy.
M (Ref:HM07853)

## GALWAY CHIROPRACTIC CLINIC
**Galway Chiropractic Clinic (The)**, Estel Galway, **County Galway**, IRE.
(T) 09175 5205
Speciality: Chiropractors.
● **Chiropractor** Dr L Martensson
● **Chiropractor** Dr J Fay
P S T (Ref:HM07854)

## GALWAY HYPNOTHERAPY CLINIC
**Galway Hypnotherapy Clinic**, 10 Montpellier Trce, The Crescent, **County Galway**, IRE.
(T) 09158 2561
(E) hypnowest@eircom.net
Speciality: Hypnotherapy.
B (Ref:HM07855)

## GALWAY PSYCHOLOGICAL SERVICES
**Galway Psychological Services**, 40 Tudor Lawns Newcastle, **County Galway**, IRE.
(T) 09152 8808
Speciality: Psychology.
B (Ref:HM07856)

## GAMBLE, ADRIAN P
**Adrian P Gamble**, 69 Prettygate Rd, Colchester, **Essex**, CO3 4ED, ENG.
(T) 01206 543621
Speciality: Chiropodists (Podiatrists).
● **Owner** Mr A Gamble
S (Ref:HM07857)

## GAMBLE-CLEE, SARA
**Sara Gamble-Clee**, 61A Watergate Row, Chester, **Cheshire**, CH1 2LE, ENG.
(T) 01244 316310
Speciality: Hypnosis.
● **Owner** Mrs S Gamble-Clee
B (Ref:HM07858)

## GAMP, C
**C Gamp**, 28 Richmond Rd, Gillingham, **Kent**, ME7 1LN, ENG.
(T) 07071 221418
Speciality: Chiropodists (Podiatrists).
● **Owner** Mr C Gamp
S (Ref:HM07859)

## GANDHI, MEERA
**Meera Gandhi**, 35 Lamorna Gr, Stanmore, **London (Greater)**, HA7 1PH, ENG.
(T) 020 8951 3828
Speciality: Clairvoyants & Palmists.
B (Ref:HM07860)

## GANDY, R S
**R S Gandy**, 5 Avenue Mansions, Sisters Avenue, London, **London (Greater)**, SW11 5SL, ENG.
(T) 020 7223 4269
Speciality: Psychology.
● **Owner** Mr R Gandy
B (Ref:HM07861)

## GANF, JENNIFER
**Jennifer Ganf**, 11 Columbine Rd, Basingstoke, **Hampshire**, RG22 5RN, ENG.
(T) 01256 359384
Speciality: Complementary Medicines & Therapy.
● **Owner** Ms J Ganf
C M (Ref:HM07862)

## GANNON, P
**P Gannon**, 32 Bader Walk, Northfleet, Gravesend, **Kent**, DA11 8PU, ENG.
(T) 01474 356574
Speciality: Chiropodists (Podiatrists).
S (Ref:HM07863)

## GAPPER, MILES
**Miles Gapper**, 110 Bishopdown Rd, Salisbury, **Wiltshire**, SP1 3ED, ENG.
(T) 01722 504940
Speciality: Hypnosis.
● **Owner** Mr M Gapper
B (Ref:HM07864)



Key continued: Yrs.Est: Years Established Q: Qualifications M: Professional Membership Indemnity Insurance Accept Credit Cards

**GARD, GRAHAM**

**Graham Gard**, 2 Clement St, Ware, **Hertfordshire**, SG12 7AG, ENG.
(T) 01920 465345
Speciality: Osteopathy.
P S T (Ref:HM07865)

**GARDEN CLINIC**

**Garden Clinic**, 43 Clifton Rd, London, **London (Greater)**, SE25 6PX, ENG.
(T) 020 8405 3274
Speciality: Alexander Technique.
● **Therapist** Ms F Horsfield
P S (Ref:HM07866)

**GARDEN LANE PHYSIO SERVICE**

**Garden Lane Physiotherapy Service**, 19 Garden Lane, Chester, **Cheshire**, CH1 4EN, ENG.
(T) 01244 346677 (F) 01244 310094
Speciality: Physiotherapy.
● **Practice Manager** Mrs R Mallett
P S T (Ref:HM07867)

**GARDENER, B**

**B Gardener**, 4 Kendall Rd, Beckenham, **Kent**, BR3 4PZ, ENG.
(T) 020 8659 9998
Speciality: Osteopathy.
● **Owner** Mr B Gardener
P S T (Ref:HM07868)

**GARDENER, DAPHNE**

**Daphne Gardener**, Banstead Village Clinic, 146 High St, Banstead, **Surrey**, SM7 2NZ, ENG.
(T) 01737 359632/373684
Speciality: Reflexology.
S T (Ref:HM07869)

**GARDENER, STEFANJA**

**Stefanja Gardener**, Springfield, S Gorsey Lane, Wythall, Birmingham, **Midlands (West)**, B47 6JH, ENG.
(T) 01564 823001
Speciality: Reflexology.
S T (Ref:HM07870)

**GARDINER, C C**

**C C Gardiner**, 4 Brackenhill Cl, Nunthorpe, Middlesbrough, **Cleveland**, TS7 0LX, ENG.
(T) 01642 324698
Speciality: Reflexology.
● **Owner** Mr C Gardiner
S T (Ref:HM07871)

**GARDINER, F**

**Fiona Gardiner**, 6 Stafford St, Edinburgh, **Edinburgh (City of)**, EH3 7AU, SCO.
(T) 01312 264611
Speciality: Aromatherapy, Indian Head Massage, Reflexology. ✔
● **Reflexologist** Miss F Gardiner Q: GSSR. M: ISPA, SIR.
C Yrs. Est.: 4 (Ref:HM07872)

**GARDINER, JOHN MICHAEL**

**John Michael Gardiner**, 277 Buxton Rd, Macclesfield, **Cheshire**, SK11 7ET, ENG.
(T) 01625 611183
Speciality: Osteopathy.
P S T (Ref:HM07873)

**GARDINER, NICKY**

**Nicky Gardiner**, Chypons, Nancledra, Penzance, **Cornwall**, TR20 8NA, ENG.
(T) 01736 740131 (F) 01736 740131
Speciality: Aromatherapy.
● **Owner** Miss N Gardiner
M O (Ref:HM07874)

**GARDINER, S D**

**S D Gardiner**, Rhode Lane, Bridgwater, **Somerset**, TA6 6HU, ENG.
(T) 07889 035560
Speciality: Hypnotherapy.
● **Owner** Mrs S Gardiner
B (Ref:HM07875)

**GARDINER, SAM**

**Sam Gardiner**, 20 Capstan Drive, Littlehampton, **Sussex (West)**, BN17 6RW, ENG.
(T) 07889 035560
(E) sammysixtynine@aol.com
Speciality: Counselling, Hypnosis, Hypnotherapy. ✔
● **Hypnotherapist** Sam Gardiner Q: DipCH.P. M: BSCH.
B Yrs. Est.: 3 (Ref:HM07876)

**GARDNER, E**

**E Gardner**, Littledoone, London Rd, Bracknell, **Berkshire**, RG12 2UL, ENG.
(T) 01344 483838
Speciality: Aromatherapy.
M O (Ref:HM07877)

**GARDNER, J**

**J Gardner**, 50 Postmill Cl, Croydon, **Surrey**, CR0 5DY, ENG.
(T) 020 8656 9090
Speciality: Psychotherapy.
B (Ref:HM07878)

**GARDNER, J**

**J Gardner**, 83 Lawsons Rd, Thornton, **Lancashire**, FY5 4PP, ENG.
(T) 01253 866696
Speciality: Chiropodists (Podiatrists).
● **Owner** Mrs K Gardner
S (Ref:HM07879)

**GARDNER, K**

**K Gardner**, 83 Lawsons Rd, Thornton, **Lancashire**, FY5 4PP, ENG.
(T) 01253 866696
Speciality: Clairvoyants & Palmists.
● **Owner** Mrs K Gardner
B (Ref:HM07880)

**GARDNER, KATHLEEN A**

**Kathleen A Gardner**, 50 Foreland Rd, Cardiff, **Glamorgan (Vale of)**, CF14 7AS, WAL.
(T) 029 2062 1124
Speciality: Physiotherapy.
P S T (Ref:HM07881)

**GARDNER, MARIE**

**Marie Gardner**, 22 St Georges Avenue, Hornchurch, **Essex**, RM11 3PD, ENG.
(T) 01708 475421
Speciality: Reflexology.
● **Owner** Ms M Gardner
S T (Ref:HM07882)

**GARDNER, MARION**

**Marion Gardner**, Glen Torr, Portling, Dalbeattie, **Dumfries and Galloway**, DG5 4PZ, SCO.
(T) 01556 630251
Speciality: Homeopathy.
M (Ref:HM07883)

**GARDNER, PETER (DR)**

**Dr Peter Gardner**, Harpers Batch, Felton Lane, Winford, Bristol, BS40 8AF, ENG.
(T) 01275 472598 (F) 01275 474467
Speciality: Psychology.
B (Ref:HM07884)

**GARDNER, PHILIP**

**Philip Gardner**, 60 Mainstone Avenue, Plymouth, **Devon**, PL4 9NB, ENG.
(T) 01752 250322
Speciality: Chiropodists (Podiatrists).
S (Ref:HM07885)

**GARDNER, S**

**S Gardner**, 6 Grange Rd, St. Leonards, Ringwood, **Hampshire**, BH24 2QE, ENG.
(T) 01202 892334 (F) 01202 892334
Speciality: Chiropodists (Podiatrists).
● **Owner** Mrs S Gardner
S (Ref:HM07886)

**GARFORTH CHIROPODY SURGERY**

**Garforth Chiropody Surgery**, The Surgery, 11 Wakefield Rd, Garforth, Leeds, **Yorkshire (West)**, LS25 1AN, ENG.
(T) 01132 864428
Speciality: Chiropodists (Podiatrists).
S (Ref:HM07887)

**GARIOCH, J**

**J Garioch**, 492 George St, Aberdeen, **Aberdeenshire**, AB25 3XH, SCO.
(T) 01224 636703
Speciality: Chiropodists (Podiatrists).
S (Ref:HM07888)

**GARLAND, C**

**C Garland**, 36 Poplar Rd, Warmley, Bristol, BS30 5JU, ENG.
(T) 01179 498359
Speciality: Aromatherapy, Reflexology. ✔
● **Reflexologist/Aromatherapist** Mrs C Garland Q: ITEC.
C Yrs. Est.: 7 (Ref:HM07889)

**GARLAND, GLENN D**

**Glenn D Garland**, Fordingbridge Chiropractic Clinic, 71 High St, Fordingbridge, **Hampshire**, SP6 1AS, ENG.
(T) 01425 652951
Speciality: Chiropractic.
P S T (Ref:HM07890)

**GARLICK, STUART**

**Stuart Garlick**, 21 Queen Elizabeth 11 Sq, South Woodham Ferrers, Chelmsford, **Essex**, CM3 5TD, ENG.
(T) 01245 322114
Speciality: Osteopathy.
● **Owner** Mr S Garlick
P S T (Ref:HM07891)

**GARNER, ANGELA**

**Angela Garner Electrolysis**, 20 Ridge Lane, Watford, **Hertfordshire**, WD1 3TA, ENG.
(T) 01923 248181
Speciality: Electrolysis.
● **Owner** Mrs A Garner
T (Ref:HM07892)

**GARNER, J**

**J Garner**, 21 Lamington Rd, Glasgow, **Glasgow (City of)**, G52 2SE, SCO.
(T) 01418 821032
Speciality: Chiropodists (Podiatrists).
S (Ref:HM07893)

**GARNER, MARGARET**

**Margaret Garner**, 40 Studley Rd, Harrogate, **Yorkshire (North)**, HG1 5JU, ENG.
(T) 01423 521765
Speciality: Hypnosis.
● **Owner** Dr M Garner
B (Ref:HM07894)

**GARNER, SOPHIE**

**Sophie Garner**, 7 Monmouth Rd, Watford, **Hertfordshire**, WD1 1QW, ENG.
(T) 01923 220756
Speciality: Complementary Medicines & Therapy.
● **Owner** Ms S Garner
C M (Ref:HM07895)

**GARNETHILL CENTRE**

**Garnethill Centre Ltd**, 28 Rose St, Glasgow, **Glasgow (City of)**, G3 6RE, SCO.
(T) 01413 330730 (F) 01413 330737
Speciality: Psychotherapy.
B (Ref:HM07896)

**GARNETT, JANE**

**Jane Garnett**, Steel St, Askam-in-Furness, **Cumbria**, LA16 7BP, ENG.
(T) 01229 467700
Speciality: Aromatherapy, Hypnotherapy, Reflexology. ✔
● **Owner Health Therapist** Ms J Garnett Q: BA (Hons), MIAH.
C Yrs. Est.: 7 (Ref:HM07897)

**GARNETT, R J S**

**R J S Garnett**, 55 Ploughmans Lea, East Goscote, Leicester, **Leicestershire**, LE7 3ZR, ENG.
(T) 01162 640717
Speciality: Chiropodists (Podiatrists).
● **Owner** Mrs R Garnett
S (Ref:HM07898)

**GARRARD, J**

**J Garrard**, 15 Downland Avenue, Southwick, Brighton, **Sussex (East)**, BN42 4RF, ENG.
(T) 01273 871102
Speciality: Chiropodists (Podiatrists).
S (Ref:HM07899)

**GARRATT, J R**

**J R Garratt**, 22 Station Rd, Woburn Sands, Milton Keynes, **Buckinghamshire**, MK17 8RW, ENG.
(T) 01908 583158

Key: B Mind-Body Medicine C Complementary Medicine H Self Help Treatment M Medicinal Therapy O Oriental Medicine P Postural Therapy S Manipulative Structural Therapy T Touch Therapy

Speciality: Osteopathy.
P S T (Ref:HM07900)

**GARRATT, L J**
**L J Garratt**, 56 Union Rd, Abergavenny, **Monmouthshire**, NP7 7RH, WAL.
(T) 01873 856818
Speciality: Osteopathy.
P S T (Ref:HM07901)

**GARRETTLEY, U**
**U Garrettley**, 26 Ellacombe Church Rd, Torquay, **Devon**, TQ1 1LG, ENG.
(T) 01803 297781
Speciality: Reflexology. ✔
● **Owner/Reflexologist**
Mrs U Garrattley Q: MAR. M: AoR.
C Yrs. Est.: 5 (Ref:HM07902)

**GARRETT-SIMPSON, E A**
**E A Garrett-Simpson**, 23 Silvester Rd, Waterlooville, **Hampshire**, PO8 8TJ, ENG.
(T) 023 9225 8026
Speciality: Complementary Medicines & Therapy.
C M (Ref:HM07903)

**GARRINGTON, N**
**N Garrington**, 3 Sutherland Avenue, Fort William, **Highland**, PH33 6JS, SCO.
(T) 01397 703833
Speciality: Physiotherapy.
P S T (Ref:HM07904)

**GARRISON-TODD, WENDY**
**Wendy Garrison-Todd**, 45 Clarence Rd, Chesterfield, **Derbyshire**, S40 1LQ, ENG.
(T) 01246 235970
Speciality: Reflexology, Reiki. ✔
● **Reflexologist/Reiki Master Practitioner**
Mrs W Garrison - Todd M: AoR.
B C Yrs. Est.: 13 (Ref:HM07905)

**GARRISON-TODD, WENDY**
**Wendy Garrison-Todd**, 71 Park Rd, Chesterfield, **Derbyshire**, S40 2LP, ENG.
(T) 01246 235970
Speciality: Complementary Medicines & Therapy.
● **Owner** Mrs W Garrison-Todd
C M (Ref:HM07906)

**GARROD, I T (DR)**
**Dr I T Garrod**, 67 Mersea Rd, Colchester, **Essex**, CO2 7QR, ENG.
(T) 01206 549809 (F) 01206 549852
Speciality: Chiropractors.
● **Principal** Dr I Garrod
P S T (Ref:HM07907)

**GARRONE, J B**
**J B Garrone**, 366 Croydon Rd, Beckenham, **Kent**, BR3 4EX, ENG.
(T) 020 8663 3878 (F) 020 8663 3878
Speciality: Chiropractors.
● **Doctor** Dr M Chippendale
P S T (Ref:HM07908)

**GARSIDE, CATHERINE**
**Catherine Garside**, Devereux House, 69 Albert Rd, Farnborough, **Hampshire**, GU14 6SL, ENG.
(T) 01252 512967
Speciality: Osteopathy.
P S T (Ref:HM07909)

**GARSIDE, D**
**D Garside**, 16 Weymouth Rd, Ashton-under-Lyne, **Manchester (Greater)**, OL6 9EP, ENG.
(T) 01613 397626
Speciality: Chiropodists (Podiatrists).
● **Owner** Mr D Garside
S (Ref:HM07910)

**GARSON, J E**
**Mrs J E Garson**, Greenways, Glaziers Lane, Normandy, Guildford, **Surrey**, GU3 2DQ, ENG.
(T) 01483 811287
Speciality: Physiotherapy.
P S T (Ref:HM07911)

**GARSTANG, LINDA**
**Linda Garstang**, 225 Coppull Moor Lane, Coppull, Chorley, **Lancashire**, PR7 5JA, ENG.
(T) 01257 792388
Speciality: Reflexology.
S T (Ref:HM07912)

**GARTLAND, LINDA**
**Linda Gartland**, 23 Finsen Rd, London, **London (Greater)**, SE5 9AX, ENG.
(T) 020 7733 7183
Speciality: Homeopathy.
M (Ref:HM07913)

**GARVEY-WILLIAMS, RICHARD**
**Richard Garvey-Williams**, Abingdon Park Osteopathy Clinic, 479 Wellingborough Rd, Northampton, **Northamptonshire**, NN3 3HN, ENG.
(T) 01604 714821
Speciality: Cranial Osteopathy, Homeopathy, Manipulation, Naturopathy, Osteopathy. ✔
● **Osteopath** Mr R Garvey-Williams Q: DO. M: GOsC.
S Yrs. Est.: 12 (Ref:HM07914)

**GARVEY-WILLIAMS, RICHARD**
**Richard Garvey-Williams**, Abington Park Homeopathy Clinic, 479 Wellingborough Rd, Northampton, **Northamptonshire**, NN3 3HN, ENG.
(T) 01604 791222
Speciality: Cranial Osteopathy, Homeopathy, Manipulation, Naturopathy, Osteopathy. ✔
● **Homeopath** Mr R Garvey-Williams Q: LCPH. M: HMA.
B Yrs. Est.: 2 (Ref:HM07915)

**GARWOOD, CATHERINE**
**Catherine Garwood**, The Chiropody Podiatry Clinic, Myton Rd, Ingleby Barwick, Stockton-On-Tees, **Cleveland**, TS17 0WA, ENG.
(T) 01642 760333
Speciality: Chiropodists (Podiatrists).
S (Ref:HM07916)

**GASCOIGNE, DOROTHY**
**Dorothy Gascoigne**, 6 Bramfield Drive, Newcastle, **Staffordshire**, ST5 0ST, ENG.
(T) 01782 715605
Speciality: Aromatherapy, Reflexology. ✔
● **Complementary Therapist**
Mrs D Gascoigne Q: Dip.Arom.
C Yrs. Est.: 11 (Ref:HM07917)

**GASCOIGNE, S (DR)**
**Dr S Gascoigne Clinic of Chinese Medicine**, O'Rahilly St, Clonakilty, **County Cork**, IRE.
(T) 023 3332 3
Speciality: Complementary Medicines & Therapy.
M (Ref:HM07918)

**GASCOYNE, L**
**L Gascoyne**, 13 Church St, Haddington, **Lothian (East)**, EH41 3EX, SCO.
(T) 01620 825570
Speciality: Chiropodists (Podiatrists).
S (Ref:HM07919)

**GASCOYNE, P**
**P Gascoyne**, 1 Top Corner, Market St, Penkridge, Stafford, **Staffordshire**, ST19 5DH, ENG.
(T) 01785 716607
Speciality: Chiropody, Nail Surgery, Phytotherapy. ✔
● **Chiropodist** Mr P Gascoyne Q: Inst.CH.P. M: Inst.CH.P.
C Yrs. Est.: 4 (Ref:HM07920)

**GASKELL, CATHERINE**
**Catherine Gaskell**, 100 Station Prde, Harrogate, **Yorkshire (North)**, HG1 1HQ, ENG.
(T) 01423 561566 (F) 01423 567379
Speciality: Osteopathy.
● **Owner** Mr T Cree
P S T (Ref:HM07921)

**GASKIN, CAROLINE**
**Caroline Gaskin**, Flat 59, St. John's Pk Mansions, Pemberton Gardens, London, **London (Greater)**, N19 5RT, ENG.
(T) 020 7263 0767
Speciality: Homeopathy.
● **Owner** Ms C Gaskin
M (Ref:HM07922)

**GASKIN, T**
**T Gaskin**, 88 Quantock Rd, Bristol, BS3 4PE, ENG.
(T) 01179 141456 (F) 01179 141457
Speciality: Homeopathy.
● **Owner** Mr T Gaskin
M (Ref:HM07923)

**GATEAUD, S**
**S Gateaud**, 70-72 Grange Rd, West Kirby, Wirral, **Merseyside**, CH48 4EG, ENG.
(T) 01516 250030 (F) 01516 250030
(E) doctorjane@firstcallnutrition.co.uk
Speciality: Aromatherapy, Counselling, Cranial Osteopathy, Homeopathy, Nutritional Therapy, Osteopathy, Reflexology, Reiki, Cranial Oseopathy. ✔
● **Homeopath** Ms K Shay-Stephenson
(T) 05156 251395 Q: BSc, LCH, MSc.
● **Chiropodist** Ms L Elliott
(T) 01516 709656
● **Nutritionist** Dr J Jones
(T) 01516 255510 Q: PhD.
● **Counsellor** Ms J Beckham
(T) 05156 480853
● **Shiastu Practitioner** Mr M Day
(T) 01516 251116
● **Owner** Mr S Gateaud
● **Reflexologist** Ms M Skinner Q: MIFR.
C Yrs. Est.: 4 (Ref:HM07924)

**GATEHOUSE THERAPY CENTRE**
**Hazel Redsell Gatehouse Therapy Centre**, Gatehouse Therapy Centre, Staplecorss Rd, Northiam, Rye, **Sussex (East)**, TN31 6JN, ENG.
(T) 01580 831756 (F) 01580 830964
(E) hazel@redsulltherapyfreeserve.co.uk
Speciality: Counselling, Group Therapy, Psychotherapy. ✔
● **Owner** Mrs H Redsell Q: SRAaT. M: BAAT.
B Yrs. Est.: 2 (Ref:HM07925)

**GATES & ASSOCIATES**
**T S Gates & Associates**, Doneechka, Mill Straight, Southwater, Horsham, **Sussex (West)**, RH13 7EY, ENG.
(T) 01403 734321 (F) 01403 732689
Speciality: Osteopathy.
● **Principal** Miss T Gates
P S T (Ref:HM07926)

**GATESHEAD COMPLEMENTARY HEALTH**
**David Postlewaite**, 219 Coatsworth Rd, Gateshead, **Tyne and Wear**, NE8 1SR, ENG.
(T) 01914 205460
Speciality: Acupuncture, Aromatherapy, Counselling, Hypnosis, Hypnotherapy, Massage (Therapeutic), Reflexology. ✔
● **Owner** Mr D Postlewaite Q: BSc. M: BACP, BPS.
● **Aromatherapist/Beauty Therapist**
Sue Graham Q: BTEC, HND. M: BPS.
B Yrs. Est.: 9 (Ref:HM07927)

**GATEWAYS CENTRE**
**Gateways Centre**, Tzaneen, Blackhorse Rd, Woking, **Surrey**, GU22 0RE, ENG.
(T) 01482 232030
Speciality: Psychotherapy. ✔
● **Psychotherapist** Ms K Pearman Q: MSc. M: BACP, UKCP, UKRC.
B Yrs. Est.: 25 (Ref:HM07928)

**GAUNT, DAVID**
**David Gaunt**, Traditional Acupuncture Clinic, 55 Hill St, Totterdown, Bristol, BS3 4TS, ENG.
(T) 01179 774853
Speciality: Acupuncture.
● **Owner** Mr D Gaunt
O (Ref:HM07929)

**GAUNT, DAVID**
**David Gaunt**, Blackberry Hill Hospital, Manor Rd, Fishponds, Bristol, BS16 2EW, ENG.
(T) 01179 656061
Speciality: Acupuncture.
O (Ref:HM07930)

**GAUNT, GAYNOR**
**Gaynor Gaunt**, 16 Ashcombe Gdns, Edgware, **London (Greater)**, HA8 8HS, ENG.
(T) 020 8958 9121
Speciality: Chiropodists (Podiatrists).
● **Owner** Mrs G Gaunt
S (Ref:HM07931)


Key continued: Yrs.Est: Years Established Q: Qualifications M: Professional Membership ✔ Indemnity Insurance Accept Credit Cards

**GAUNT, THERESA**

**Theresa Gaunt**, Spring Dale, South Milton, Kingsbridge, **Devon**, TQ7 3JQ, ENG.
(T) 01548 560603 (F) 01548 560603
Speciality: Physiotherapy.
● **Owner** Mrs T Gaunt
P S T (**Ref:**HM07932)

**GAUNTLETT, E J**

**E J Gauntlett**, 74 Broad St, Chipping Sodbury, Bristol, BS37 6AG, ENG.
(T) 01454 319083
Speciality: Chiropodists (Podiatrists).
● **Owner** Mrs E Gauntlett
S (**Ref:**HM07933)

**GAUVAIN, TONY**

**Tony Guavain**, Rumbeams Farm Cottage, Ewhurst Green, Cranleigh, **Surrey**, GU6 7RR, ENG.
(T) 01483 267027
(E) aygee@talk21.com
Speciality: Cognitive Therapy, Counselling, Hypnosis, Hypnotherapy, Life Style Coaching, Neuro-Linguistic Program, Phytotherapy, Stress Therapy, Visualisation Therapy, Vitamin Therapy, Emotional Freedom Technique, Relaxation Therapy, Self Hypnosis. ✔
● **Owner/Consultant** Mr T Gauvain Q: NRHP (Assoc). M: NRHP.
H Yrs. Est.: 2 (**Ref:**HM07934)

**GAVAN, JUDITH**

**Judith Gavan**, Falmouth, **Cornwall**, TR11, ENG.
(T) 01326 314115
Speciality: Reflexology.
S T (**Ref:**HM07935)

**GAVICAN, CHRIS**

**Chris Gavican**, Cloonart Ruskey, **County Leitrim**, IRE.
(T) 07838 063
(E) cgavican@iol.ie
Speciality: Complementary Medicines & Therapy.
M (**Ref:**HM07936)

**GAVIN, H T H**

**H T H Gavin**, 28 Cairndow Court, Glasgow, **Glasgow (City of)**, G44 3BU, SCO.
(T) 01416 331929
Speciality: Chiropodists (Podiatrists).
● **Owner** Mr H Gavin
S (**Ref:**HM07937)

**GAW, MARY**

**Mary Gaw**, 43 Buckingham Avenue, London, **London (Greater)**, N20 9DG, ENG.
(T) 020 8445 2459
Speciality: Chiropodists (Podiatrists).
● **Owner** Mrs M Gaw
S (**Ref:**HM07938)

**GAWEN & ASSOCIATES**

**Gawen Rachel & Associates**, Tawstock Medical Centre, 7 High St, Chard, **Somerset**, TA20 1QF, ENG.
(T) 01460 67763
Speciality: Osteopathy.
P S T (**Ref:**HM07939)

**GAWLINSKA, CATHERINE**

**Catherine Gawlinska**, 7-8 Wych Elm House, Hamstel Rd, Harlow, **Essex**, CM20 1EP, ENG.
(T) 01279 410136
Speciality: Osteopathy.
P S T (**Ref:**HM07940)

**GAWNE, HEATHER**

**Heather Gawne**, 22 Liverpool Rd North, Burscough, Ormskirk, **Lancashire**, L40 5TP, ENG.
(T) 01704 892904
Speciality: Chiropodists (Podiatrists).
● **Owner** Mrs H Gawne
S (**Ref:**HM07941)

**GAY, E A**

**Miss E A Gay**, 8 Mountfield Rd, Tunbridge Wells, **Kent**, TN1 1SG, ENG.
(T) 01892 536022
Speciality: Chiropodists (Podiatrists).
● **Owner** Miss E Gay
S (**Ref:**HM07942)

**GAYER, PETER**

**Peter Gayer**, 26 Lake Pl, Wirral, **Merseyside**, CH47 2DW, ENG.
(T) 01516 322874
Speciality: Complementary Medicines & Therapy.
● **Owner** Mr P Gayer
M (**Ref:**HM07943)

**GAYLOR, A A**

**A A Gaylor**, New Park, Axminster, **Devon**, EX13 5UQ, ENG.
(T) 01297 33287
Speciality: Chiropodists (Podiatrists).
● **Owner** Miss A Gaylor
S (**Ref:**HM07944)

**GAYNOR BULLER CLINIC**

**Gaynor Buller Clinic (The)**, 1227 Warwick Rd, Acocks Green, Birmingham, **Midlands (West)**, B27 6PX, ENG.
(T) 01217 076776
Speciality: Acupuncture.
● **Owner** Mrs G Buller
O (**Ref:**HM07945)

**GAYNOR, JOHN**

**John Gaynor**, 44 Pyle Rd, Bishopston, Swansea, SA3 3HJ, WAL.
(T) 01792 391212
Speciality: Chiropodists (Podiatrists).
● **Owner** Mrs G John
S (**Ref:**HM07946)

**GAZE, JENNY**

**Jenny Gaze**, 111 Horns Rd, Stroud, **Gloucestershire**, GL5 1EE, ENG.
(T) 01453 757399 (F) 01453 757399
Speciality: Herbalists.
● **Owner** Ms J Gaze
M (**Ref:**HM07947)

**GAZELEY, HELEN**

**Helen Gazeley**, 43 Chaffers Mead, Ashtead, **Surrey**, KT21 1NA, ENG.
(T) 01372 276360
Speciality: Reflexology.
● **Owner** Miss H Gazeley
S T (**Ref:**HM07948)

**GEALL, SUSAN**

**Susan Geall**, Solitude, Vines Cross, Heathfield, **Sussex (East)**, TN21 9HH, ENG.
(T) 01435 813120
Speciality: Herbal Medicine.
● **Owner** Mrs S Geall
M (**Ref:**HM07949)

**GEARING, JOHN**

**John Gearing**, 14 Harefield Rd, Bognor Regis, **Sussex (West)**, PO22 6EE, ENG.
(T) 01243 586689
Speciality: Chiropodists (Podiatrists).
● **Owner** Mr J Gearing
S (**Ref:**HM07950)

**GEARY, A G**

**A G Geary**, 20 West End St, Norwich, **Norfolk**, NR2 4JJ, ENG.
(T) 01603 452739
Speciality: Biomechanics, Chiropody, Orthotics. ✔
● **Chiropodist** Mr A Geary Q: MBChA. M: B.A.Ch.P.
C Yrs. Est.: 18 (**Ref:**HM07951)

**GEBAL, ANNE**

**Anne Gebal**, 8 Burnhouse Drive, Dechmont, Broxburn, **Lothian (West)**, EH52 6NA, SCO.
(T) 01506 811118
Speciality: Chiropodists (Podiatrists).
S (**Ref:**HM07952)

**GEBALA, K**

**K Gebala**, Woodlands, 64 Laurel Avenue, Bideford, **Devon**, EX39 3AZ, ENG.
(T) 01237 479474
Speciality: Reflexology.
S T (**Ref:**HM07953)

**GEBBIE, JAMES**

**James Gebbie**, 5 Drumsheugh Gardens, Edinburgh, **Edinburgh (City of)**, EH3 7QJ, SCO.
(T) 01312 255710
Speciality: Physiotherapy.
P S T (**Ref:**HM07954)

**GEDDES, PIPPA**

**Pippa Geddes**, 3 Poplar Rise, Wappenham, Towcester, **Northamptonshire**, NN12 8RR, ENG.
(T) 01327 860861 (F) 01327 860861
(E) pippageddes@lineone.net
Speciality: Reflexology. ✔
● **Reflexologist** Mrs P Geddes Q: MAR.
C Yrs. Est.: 3 (**Ref:**HM07955)

**GEE**

**Mrs Gee**, Stoney Rd, Coventry, **Midlands (West)**, CV3 6HY, ENG.
(T) 024 7650 3831
Speciality: Clairvoyants & Palmists.
B (**Ref:**HM07956)

**GEE, D**

**D Gee**, 1st Floor, 43 Garstang Rd, Preston, **Lancashire**, PR1 1LA, ENG.
(T) 01772 562300
Speciality: Chiropody. ✔
● **Chiropodist** Miss D Gee Q: Inst.CH.P.
C Yrs. Est.: 4 (**Ref:**HM07957)

**GEE, L**

**L Gee**, 24 Manners Rd, Southsea, **Hampshire**, PO4 0BB, ENG.
(T) 023 9273 0972 (F) 023 9273 0972
(W) www.southseafsschoolnet.co.uk
Speciality: Complementary Medicines & Therapy, Deep Tissue Massage. ✔
● **Owner/Masseur** Mr L Gee Q: A.I.P.T.I, ITEC.
C Yrs. Est.: 10 (**Ref:**HM07958)

**GEE, PHILL**

**Phill Gee**, 39a Stansfield Rd, Brixton, London, **London (Greater)**, SW9 9RY, ENG.
(T) 020 7326 1675
(E) phill.jazz@virgin.net
Speciality: Clairvoyants & Palmists, Tarot Readings, Numerology and Dream Interpretations.
● **Tarot/Numerologist** Mr P Gee
B Yrs. Est.: 8 (**Ref:**HM07959)

**GEE, SUSAN**

**Susan Gee**, 153 Church End, Cambridge, **Cambridgeshire**, CB1 3LF, ENG.
(T) 01223 515479
Speciality: Complementary Medicines & Therapy.
● **Owner** Miss S Gee
C M (**Ref:**HM07960)

**GEEN, SHERYLE**

**Sheryle Geen**, 95B Leighton Rd, London, **London (Greater)**, NW5 2QJ, ENG.
(T) 020 7482 4537 (F) 020 7482 4450
Speciality: Psychotherapy.
● **Owner** Ms S Geen
B (**Ref:**HM07961)

**GEERE, HELEN**

**Helen Geere**, 38A Main St, Woodhouse Eaves, Loughborough, **Leicestershire**, LE12 8RZ, ENG.
(T) 01509 891353
Speciality: Chiropodists (Podiatrists).
● **Owner** Mrs H Geere
S (**Ref:**HM07962)

**GEESON, D**

**D Geeson**, 27 Berners St, Ipswich, **Suffolk**, IP1 3LN, ENG.
(T) 01473 253870
Speciality: Chiropodists (Podiatrists).
S (**Ref:**HM07963)

**GEESON, MARK**

**Mark Geeson**, 12 Marsden Avenue, Queniborough, Leicester, **Leicestershire**, LE7 3FL, ENG.
(T) 01162 606790
Speciality: Physiotherapy.
● **Owner** Mr M Geeson
P S T (**Ref:**HM07964)

**GEGG, SARAH**

**Sarah Gegg**, 62 Market Pl, Henley-on-Thames, **Oxfordshire**, RG9 2AG, ENG.
(T) 01491 574179
Speciality: Chiropodists (Podiatrists).
S (**Ref:**HM07965)



Key: B Mind-Body Medicine C Complementary Medicine H Self Help Treatment M Medicinal Therapy O Oriental Medicine P Postural Therapy S Manipulative Structural Therapy T Touch Therapy

### GEGGUS, PAM
**Pam Geggus**, 116 Southmoor Rd, Oxford, **Oxfordshire**, OX2 6RB, ENG.
(T) 01865 554005
Speciality: Acupuncture.
● **Owner** Mrs P Geggus
O (**Ref:**HM07966)

### GEIGES, STEPHANIE
**Stephanie Geiges**, Flat 1, 144 London Rd, Brighton, **Sussex (East)**, BN1 4JH, ENG.
(T) 01273 694436 (F) 01273 694436
Speciality: Alexander Technique. ✔
● **Owner** Ms S Gregis Q: BA (Hons). M: STAT.
P S Yrs. Est.: 5 (**Ref:**HM07967)

### GELSON, C J
**C J Gelson**, 1st Floor Hogarth House, Princes St, Corbridge, **Northumberland**, NE45 5AE, ENG.
(T) 01434 632427
Speciality: Osteopathy.
P S T (**Ref:**HM07968)

### GEMS
**Gems**, Botley Rd, Hemel Hempstead, **Hertfordshire**, HP2 7JL, ENG.
(T) 01442 401591
Speciality: Crystal Healing, Reiki. ✔
● **Reiki Master** Mrs Delph Q: Reiki Master.
C Yrs. Est.: 3 (**Ref:**HM07969)

### GENERAL HYPNOTHERAPY REGISTER
**General Hypnotherapy Register (The)**, P O Box 204, Sway, Lymington, **Hampshire**, SO41 6WP, ENG.
(T) 01590 683770 (F) 01590 683770
Speciality: Hypnosis.
B (**Ref:**HM07970)

### GENGE, DAVID
**David Genge**, 30 Howard Avenue, Slough, **Berkshire**, SL2 1LE, ENG.
(T) 01753 528500 (F) 01753 528500
Speciality: Hypnosis.
● **Owner** Mr D Genge
B (**Ref:**HM07971)

### GENT, B
**B Gent**, Larklands Clinic, Andriesse, Lower Stanton Rd, Ilkeston, **Derbyshire**, DE7 4BJ, ENG.
(T) 01159 440239
Speciality: Complementary Medicines & Therapy.
C M (**Ref:**HM07972)

### GENT, WENDY
**Wendy Gent**, Cumbers Cottage, Farmbridge End, Good Easter, Chelmsford, **Essex**, CM1 4RY, ENG.
(T) 01245 231344
(W) www.ray-gent.co.uk
Speciality: Massage (Therapeutic), Reiki, Remedial Massage, Remedial Medical Massage. ✔
● **Therapist** Mr R Gent Q: BA (Hons), Cert.Ed, Dip.Th.Massage. M: SHP.
● **Therapist** Mrs W Gent Q: ITEC. M: IFA.
C Yrs. Est.: 5 (**Ref:**HM07973)

### GENTLE CARE CLINIC
**Gentle Care Clinic**, 4 Banbury Lane, Byfield, Daventry, **Northamptonshire**, NN11 6UX, ENG.
(T) 01327 261747
Speciality: Complementary Medicines & Therapy.
● **Owner** Mrs M Lowe
C M (**Ref:**HM07974)

### GENTLE COLON IRRIGATION
**Gentle Colon Irrigation**, 26 Mulberry Way, London, **London (Greater)**, E18 1ED, ENG.
(T) 020 8530 8804
Speciality: Complementary Medicines & Therapy.
C M (**Ref:**HM07975)

### GENTLE COLON IRRIGATION
**Gentle Colon Irrigation**, 140 Harley St, London, **London (Greater)**, W1N 1AH, ENG.
(T) 020 7486 4227
Speciality: Complementary Medicines & Therapy.
● **Principal** Mr B Loverchic
C M (**Ref:**HM07976)

### GENTLE FEET
**Gentle Feet**, 4 Jenningsbury Court, Hertford Heath, Hertford, **Hertfordshire**, SG13 7NS, ENG.
(T) 01992 50058 (F) 01992 500558
(E) janeconyers@hotmail.com
Speciality: Indian Head Massage, Reflexology. ✔
● **Reflexologist/Indian Head Massage Therapist**
Jane Conyers Q: VTCT. M: FHT.
C Yrs. Est.: 1 (**Ref:**HM07977)

### GENTLE HEALTH & BEAUTY
**Gentle Health & Beauty**, 9 Station Rd, Ossett, **Yorkshire (West)**, WF5 8AB, ENG.
(T) 01924 283521
Speciality: Complementary Medicines & Therapy.
● **Owner** Mrs L North
C M (**Ref:**HM07978)

### GENTLE TOUCH
**Gentle Touch**, Davenport House, Carr Lane, Alderley Edge, **Cheshire**, SK9 7SL, ENG.
(T) 01625 585586 (F) 01625 586795
Speciality: Complementary Medicines & Therapy, Clinical Nutritionist. ✔
● **Owner** Mrs D Birchinall Q: Dip.ION. M: BANT.
C Yrs. Est.: 6 (**Ref:**HM07979)

### GENTLE WAYS
**Gentle Ways**, West Tomachoin, Abriachan, Inverness, **Highland**, IV3 8LB, SCO.
(T) 01463 861306
(E) jennie.austin@btinternet.com
(W) www.www.jennieaustin.co.uk
Speciality: Absent Healing, Aromatherapy, Bach Remedies, Complementary Therapy, Healer, Healing Therapy, Meditation, Reflexology, Reiki, Life Skills Coaching, Energy Healing - Animals. ✔
● **Teacher/Health Practitioner**
Ms J Austin M: BFRP, BRCP, RxS.
B Yrs. Est.: 15 (**Ref:**HM07980)

### GENTLEMANS CLUB
**Gentlemans Club (The)**, 94 Union St, Plymouth, **Devon**, PL1 3EZ, ENG.
(T) 01752 263860
Speciality: Complementary Medicines & Therapy.
● **Manageress** Mrs C Hocking
C M (**Ref:**HM07981)

### GENTRY, V
**V Gentry**, 30 Hinton Avenue, Cambridge, **Cambridgeshire**, CB1 7AS, ENG.
(T) 01223 212821
Speciality: Psychotherapy.
● **Owner** Mrs V Gentry
B (**Ref:**HM07982)

### GENTRY'S NATURAL MEDICINE
**Gentry's Natural Medicine**, 4 Marcia Cl, Eastbourne, **Sussex (East)**, BN20 9DG, ENG.
(T) 01323 505529 (F) 01323 505529
Speciality: Complementary Medicines & Therapy.
● **Owner** Miss G Gentry
C M (**Ref:**HM07983)

### GEOFF & JAYNE PLUMMER
**Geoff & Jayne Plummer**, 134 Bricknell Avenue, Hull, **Humberside (North)**, HU5 4QQ, ENG.
(T) 01482 342685 (F) 01482 342685
Speciality: Physiotherapy.
● **Partner** Mr G Plummer
P S T (**Ref:**HM07984)

### GEOFF PICK PSYCHOTHERAPY
**Geoff Pick Psychotherapy**, 78 Aylward Rd, London, **London (Greater)**, SW20 9AF, ENG.
(T) 020 8408 2975
Speciality: Psychotherapy.
B (**Ref:**HM07985)

### GEOFF THIEL, COUNS & PSYCHO
**Geoff Thiel, Counsellor & Psychotherapist**, 17 Browning Rd, Harpenden, **Hertfordshire**, AL5 4TS, ENG.
(T) 01582 764579
Speciality: Counselling, Psychotherapy. ✔
● **Counsellor/Psychotherapist**
Mr G Thiel Q: BA, Dip.Psych. M: BACP, UKCP.
B Yrs. Est.: 10 (**Ref:**HM07986)

### GEORGE
**Mrs J M George**, 35 Spratt Hall Rd, Wanstead, London, **London (Greater)**, E11 2RQ, ENG.
(T) 020 8989 6573
(E) wanstead35@55net.co.uk
Speciality: Biomechanics, Chiropody, Nail Surgery.
● **Chiropodist** Mrs J George
(T) 020 8989 573 Q: M.S.C.P. M: S.C.P.
S Yrs. Est.: 20 (**Ref:**HM07987)

### GEORGE A BOWDLER CHIROPODIST
**George A Bowdler Chiropodist**, 4 Clyde Rd, St. Leonards-On-Sea, **Sussex (East)**, TN38 0QE, ENG.
(T) 01424 427728
Speciality: Chiropody.
S (**Ref:**HM07988)

### GEORGE, CHRISTOPHER
**Christopher George**, 7 Keelton Cl, Bicton Heath, Shrewsbury, **Shropshire**, SY3 5PS, ENG.
(T) 01743 364243
Speciality: Acupuncture.
● **Owner** Mr C George
O (**Ref:**HM07989)

### GEORGE, DIANA
**Diana George**, Holly Lodge, Belle Vue Lane, Guilden Sutton, Chester, **Cheshire**, CH3 7EJ, ENG.
(T) 01244 301487
Speciality: Reflexology.
S T (**Ref:**HM07990)

### GEORGE, ROSALIND
**Rosalind George**, Imperial College, Princes Gdns, London, **London (Greater)**, SW7 1LU, ENG.
(T) 020 7603 8600
Speciality: Homeopathy.
M (**Ref:**HM07991)

### GEORGINA'S
**Georgina's**, 27 Bentley Rd, Doncaster, **Yorkshire (South)**, DN5 9SD, ENG.
(T) 01302 789332
Speciality: Clairvoyants & Palmists.
B (**Ref:**HM07992)

### GEORGIOU, C A
**C A Georgiou**, 43 Epps Rd, Sittingbourne, **Kent**, ME10 1JD, ENG.
(T) 01795 428817
Speciality: Osteopathy.
P S T (**Ref:**HM07993)

### GERAGHTY, B
**B Geraghty**, 77 Kenilworth Avenue, London, **London (Greater)**, SW19 7LP, ENG.
(T) 020 8946 4950
Speciality: Homeopathy.
● **Owner** Mr B Geraghty
M (**Ref:**HM07994)

### GERALD, KENNY
**Kenny Gerald**, 40 Ballymun Rd, Dublin, **County Dublin**, IRE.
(T) 01836 0669
Speciality: Complementary Medicines & Therapy.
M (**Ref:**HM07995)

### GERBER, E
**E Gerber**, 123 Rye St, Bishop's Stortford, **Hertfordshire**, CM23 2HD, ENG.
(T) 01279 506216
Speciality: Chiropodists (Podiatrists).
S (**Ref:**HM07996)

### GERETY, PATRICIA
**Patricia Gerety**, 9 Hillcrest Templeogue Dublin 6W, IRE.
(T) 01464 0050
Speciality: Acupuncture.
O (**Ref:**HM07997)

### GERMAIN, SUE
**Sue Germain**, 12 Wigmore Rd, Tadley, **Hampshire**, RG26 4HH, ENG.
(T) 01189 814742
Speciality: Chiropodists (Podiatrists).


Key continued: Yrs.Est: Years Established Q: Qualifications M: Professional Membership ✔ Indemnity Insurance Accept Credit Cards

S (Ref:HM07998)

## GERMAN, PATRICIA

**Patricia German**, 41 Nightingale Rd, Hampton, **London (Greater)**, TW12 3HX, ENG.
(T) 020 8979 5385
Speciality: Herbal Medicine.
● **Owner** Mrs P German
M (Ref:HM07999)

## GERMANN, KIRSTEN

**Kirsten Germann**, 8 Chilston Rd, Tunbridge Wells, **Kent**, TN4 9LT, ENG.
(T) 01892 546551
Speciality: Acupuncture.
O (Ref:HM08000)

## GERRARD, BARBARA

**Barbara Gerrard**, Barron Surgery, Crosshill Bus Centre, Main St, Crosshill, Lochgelly, **Fife**, KY5 8BJ, SCO.
(T) 01592 861180
Speciality: Complementary Medicines & Therapy.
C M (Ref:HM08001)

## GERRARD, K

**K Gerrard**, 2-4 High St, Glastonbury, **Somerset**, BA6 9DU, ENG.
(T) 01458 833317
Speciality: Complementary Medicines & Therapy.
M (Ref:HM08002)

## GERRARD, RITA

**Rita Gerrard**, 16 Pine Valley Dr, Dublin, **County Dublin**, IRE.
(T) 01493 9024
Speciality: Complementary Medicines & Therapy.
M (Ref:HM08003)

## GERRARDS CROSS SPORTS & BACK

**Gerrards Cross Sports Injury & Back Pain Clinic**, Silvana, Camp Rd, Gerrards Cross, **Buckinghamshire**, SL9 7PB, ENG.
(T) 01753 883044
Speciality: Acupressure, Acupuncture, Electrotherapy, Manipulation, Massage (Therapeutic), Postural Integration, Ultrasonics, Muscle stimulation for weak pelvic floor muscles causing incontinence. ✔
● **Physiotherapist** Mrs E Sykes Q: MCSP, SRP. M: CSP, SRP.
S Yrs. Est.: 10 (Ref:HM08004)

## GESTALT CENTRE

**Gestalt Centre (The)**, First Floor, 62 Paul St, London, **London (Greater)**, EC2A 4NA, ENG.
(T) 020 7613 4480 (F) 020 7613 4737
(E) gestaltcentre@dialpipex.com
Speciality: Counselling, Gestalt Therapy, Group Therapy, Phytotherapy. ✔
● **Centre Co-Ordinator** Jacqueline Wearn Q: BACP. M: UKCP.
H Yrs. Est.: 20 (Ref:HM08005)

## GESTALT CONSORTIUM

**Gestalt Consortium**, Psychotherapy Centre, The Garden Flat, 33 Croftdown Rd, London, **London (Greater)**, NW5 1EN, ENG.
(T) 020 7284 1701
Speciality: Psychotherapy.
B (Ref:HM08006)

## GESTALT PSYCHOTHERAPY

**Gestalt Psychotherapy**, 18 Empire Rd, Sheffield, **Yorkshire (South)**, S7 1GL, ENG.
(T) 01142 550645
Speciality: Psychotherapy.
● **Owner** Ms J Caw
B (Ref:HM08007)

## GESTALT SOUTHWEST

**Gestalt Southwest**, The Pavilion, Winford Manor, Winford, Bristol, BS40 8DW, ENG.
(T) 01275 474470 (F) 01275 474470
Speciality: Complementary Medicines & Therapy.
M (Ref:HM08008)

## GESTALT STUDIO

**Gestalt Studio (The)**, 33 Croftdown Rd, London, **London (Greater)**, NW5 1EL, ENG.
(T) 020 7485 2316
Speciality: Psychotherapy.
● **Partner** Ms V Marsden
B (Ref:HM08009)

## GETHIN, CHRISTOPHER

**Christopher Gethin**, Higher Pudsham, Ashburton, Newton Abbot, **Devon**, TQ13 7HW, ENG.
(T) 01364 652207
Speciality: Homeopathy.
M (Ref:HM08010)

## GHAFOOR, F (DR)

**Dr F Ghafoor**, 23 Walnut Way, Ruislip, **London (Greater)**, HA4 6TA, ENG.
(T) 020 8842 4420
Speciality: Chiropractors.
P S T (Ref:HM08011)

## GHAMY, M R

**M R Ghamy**, 1 Shamrock Rd, Bristol, BS5 6RL, ENG.
(T) 01179 518548 (F) 01179 518548
Speciality: Acupuncture.
● **Owner** Mr M Ghamy
O (Ref:HM08012)

## GHELICH, S BATMAN (DR)

**Dr S Batman Ghelich**, 1st Floor Equity House, 6-7 Duke St, Cardiff, **Glamorgan (Vale of)**, CF10 1AY, WAL.
(T) 029 2022 2915
Speciality: Physiotherapy.
● **Doctor** Dr S Batmanghelich
P S T (Ref:HM08013)

## GHEORGHIU, E (DR)

**Dr E Gheorghiu**, 2 Boyn Valley Rd, Maidenhead, **Berkshire**, SL6 4ED, ENG.
(T) 01628 672005
Speciality: Homeopathy.
● **Owner** Mr H Lye
M (Ref:HM08014)

## GHOSH, A

**A Ghosh**, Consulting Rooms, 31 Rodney St, Liverpool, **Merseyside**, L1 9EH, ENG.
(T) 01517 098522
Speciality: Homeopathy.
● **Professor** Mr J Verbov
M (Ref:HM08015)

## GHOURI HOMEOPATHIC CLINIC

**Ghouri Homeopathic Clinic**, 510 Coventry Rd, Small Heath, Birmingham, **Midlands (West)**, B10 0UN, ENG.
(T) 01217 727089 (F) 01217 727089
Speciality: Homeopathy.
● **Managing Director** Mr A Ghouri
M (Ref:HM08016)

## GIANFAGNA, CARMELA

**Carmela Gianfagna**, 7a Perth Rd, Beckenham, **Kent**, BR3 6PP, ENG.
(T) 020 8249 1282
Speciality: Acupuncture.
● **Owner** Ms C Gianfagna
O (Ref:HM08017)

## GIANFAGNU, CARMELA

**Carmela Gianfagnu**, 185A Torridon Rd, London, **London (Greater)**, SE6 1RG, ENG.
(T) 020 8480 9905
Speciality: Acupuncture.
● **Owner** Ms L Griffin
O (Ref:HM08018)

## GIARDINO

**Giardino**, Unit 2 Sutton Hall Farm, Sutton Maddock, Shifnal, **Shropshire**, TF11 9NQ, ENG.
(T) 01952 730304 (F) 01952 730616
Speciality: Aromatherapy.
● **Director** Mr P Moseley
M O (Ref:HM08019)

## GIBANI, CAROL

**Carol Gibani**, Garregwen, Llanfairpwllgwyngyll, **Isle of Anglesey**, LL61 5YR, WAL.
(T) 01248 713973 (F) 01248 713973
Speciality: Physiotherapy.
● **Owner** Mrs C Gibani
P S T (Ref:HM08020)

## GIBBENS, JOAN

**Joan Gibbens**, 21 Mendip Avenue, Eastbourne, **Sussex (East)**, BN23 8ER, ENG.
(T) 01323 768571
Speciality: Hypnosis.
B (Ref:HM08021)

## GIBBINS, JONATHAN

**Jonathan Gibbins**, The McTimoney Chiropractic Clinic, 17 Alexandra Rd, Malvern, **Worcestershire**, WR14 1HA, ENG.
(T) 01684 567480
Speciality: Chiropractic. ✔
● **Chiropractor** Mr J Gibbins Q: AMC, DC, MMCA. M: MCA.
S Yrs. Est.: 15 (Ref:HM08022)

## GIBBON, MALCOLM

**Malcolm Gibbon**, 80 Hart St, Southport, **Merseyside**, PR8 6BN, ENG.
(T) 01704 538359
Speciality: Hypnosis.
B (Ref:HM08023)

## GIBBONS, ELAINE

**Elaine Gibbons**, Preston Park Clinic, 207-209 Ditchling Rd, Brighton, **Sussex (East)**, BN1 6JB, ENG.
(T) 01273 504488
Speciality: Acupuncture.
● **Owner** Mrs E Gibbons
O (Ref:HM08024)

## GIBBONS, J

**J Gibbons**, 66 Malmains Way, Beckenham, **Kent**, BR3 6SF, ENG.
(T) 020 8658 6718 (F) 020 8658 7436
Speciality: Reflexology.
● **Owner** Mrs J Gibbons
S T (Ref:HM08025)

## GIBBONS, J A

**J A Gibbons**, Physiotherapy Clinic, 1 High St, Houghton Regis, Dunstable, **Bedfordshire**, LU5 5BE, ENG.
(T) 01582 867831
Speciality: Physiotherapy.
P S T (Ref:HM08026)

## GIBBONS, JUNE

**June Gibbons**, 2 Kenwood Rd, Sheffield, **Yorkshire (South)**, S7 1NP, ENG.
(T) 01142 552048
Speciality: Homeopathy.
● **Owner** Mr D Wainwright
M (Ref:HM08027)

## GIBBONS, RICHARD

**Richard Gibbons**, 8 Gloucester Row, Bristol, BS8 4AW, ENG.
(T) 01179 739541
Speciality: Acupuncture.
O (Ref:HM08028)

## GIBBS, ALEXANDER

**Alexander Gibbs D O M R O**, C/O 10 Winton Ave, Rathgar, **County Dublin**, IRE.
(T) 01269 5281
Speciality: Osteopathy.
P S T (Ref:HM08029)

## GIBBS, LOUIS

**Louis Gibbs**, 24 New Rd, Shoreham-by-Sea, **Sussex (West)**, BN43 6RA, ENG.
(T) 01273 463334
Speciality: Hypnosis.
● **Owner** Mr L Gibbs
B (Ref:HM08030)

## GIBBS, NICOLA

**Nicola Gibbs**, 13 Manor Rd, Lymm, **Cheshire**, WA13 0AY, ENG.
(T) 01925 759367
Speciality: Reflexology.
S T (Ref:HM08031)

## GIBBS, T

**T Gibbs**, The New Therapy Care Centre, Gundry Lane, Bridport, **Dorset**, DT6 3RL, ENG.
(T) 01308 422544
Speciality: Complementary Medicines & Therapy.
● **Owner** Mr T Gibbs
C M (Ref:HM08032)



Key: B Mind-Body Medicine; C Complementary Medicine; H Self Help Treatment; M Medicinal Therapy; O Oriental Medicine; P Postural Therapy; S Manipulative Structural Therapy; T Touch Therapy

**GIBSON LYNDA & MURRAY ANNE**

**Miss Lynda Gibson & Miss Anne Murray**, 6 Woolton St, Liverpool, **Merseyside**, L25 5JA, ENG.
(T) 01514 287141
Speciality: Physiotherapy.
● **Partner** Miss L Gibson
P S T (Ref:HM08033)

**GIBSON, A E**

**A E Gibson**, 45 Bryansford Rd, Newcastle, **County Down**, BT33 0DW, NIR.
(T) 028 4372 4627
Speciality: Osteopathy.
● **Owner** Ms A Gibson
P S T (Ref:HM08034)

**GIBSON, A E**

**A E Gibson**, 41 Finaghy Rd South, Belfast, **County Antrim**, BT10 0BW, NIR.
(T) 028 9061 7510
Speciality: Osteopathy.
● **Owner** Ms A Gibson
P S T (Ref:HM08035)

**GIBSON, ANDREW**

**Andrew Gibson**, 170 Roebank St, Glasgow, **Glasgow (City of)**, G31 3EB, SCO.
(T) 01415 510583
Speciality: Chiropodists (Podiatrists).
S (Ref:HM08036)

**GIBSON, E M**

**E M Gibson**, Hylands, The Downs, Stebbing, Dunmow, **Essex**, CM6 3RA, ENG.
(T) 01371 856434
Speciality: Chiropodists (Podiatrists).
● **Owner** Mrs E Gibson
S (Ref:HM08037)

**GIBSON, J B**

**J B Gibson**, 3 Wakefield Avenue, Morecambe, **Lancashire**, LA4 6DY, ENG.
(T) 01524 420429
Speciality: Chiropodists (Podiatrists).
● **Owner** Mr J Gibson
S (Ref:HM08038)

**GIBSON, J S**

**Gibson J S FRCSI**, St Davids Castle, Naas, **County Kildare**, IRE.
(T) 04589 7389
Speciality: Complementary Medicines & Therapy.
M (Ref:HM08039)

**GIBSON, JAN**

**Jan Gibson**, 3 Dawson Avenue, St Pauls Cray, Orpington, **Kent**, BR5 3AY, ENG.
(T) 01689 873262 (F) 01689 873262
Speciality: Absent Healing, Aura Therapy, Auto Suggestion, Aversion Therapy, Bach Remedies, Cognitive Therapy, Colour Therapy, Complementary Therapy, Counselling, Faith Healing, Family Therapy, Group Therapy, Healer, Healing Therapy, Holistic Healing, Humanistic Psychology, Hypnosis, Hypnotherapy, Indian Head Massage, Life Style Coaching, Meditation, Psychotherapy, Spiritual Healing, Stress Therapy, Transactional Analysis, Visualisation Therapy. ✔
● **Therapist** Ms J Gibson Q: MABCH, MCAH, NFSH. M: CAH.
H Yrs. Est.: 10 (Ref:HM08040)

**GIBSON, LINDA**

**Linda Gibson**, 74 Starring Way, Halifax Rd, Littleborough, **Manchester (Greater)**, OL15 8NT, ENG.
(T) 01706 372540
Speciality: Chiropractic.
P S T (Ref:HM08041)

**GIBSON, MALCOLM**

**Malcolm Gibson**, 37 High Town Rd, Maidenhead, **Berkshire**, SL6 1PA, ENG.
(T) 01628 788420
Speciality: Acupuncture.
● **Owner** Mrs C Sanders
O (Ref:HM08042)

**GIBSON, NEIL**

**Neil Gibson**, 23 Templesheen Rd, Bognor Regis, **Sussex (West)**, PO22 6JB, ENG.
(T) 01243 584866
Speciality: Hypnosis.
● **Owner** Mr N Gibson
B (Ref:HM08043)

**GIBSON, R G**

**R G Gibson**, 354 Albert Drive, Glasgow, **Glasgow (City of)**, G41 5PJ, SCO.
(T) 01414 271505 (F) 01414 271505
Speciality: Homeopathy.
● **Owner** Dr R Gibson
M (Ref:HM08044)

**GIBSON, RONALD J**

**Chiropodist and Reflexologist**, 27 East Princes St, Helensburgh, **Argyll and Bute**, CT84 7DE, SCO.
(T) 01436 676882
Speciality: Chiropody, Podiatry, Reflexology. ✔
● **Owner** Mr R Gibson Q: GSSR, M.Ch.A. M: SSR.
T Yrs. Est.: 12 (Ref:HM08045)

**GIBSON, STEPHEN J**

**J Stephen Gibson**, Brook House, 544 Blackpool Rd, Ashton-On-Ribble, Preston, **Lancashire**, PR2 1HY, ENG.
(T) 01772 728798
Speciality: Hypnosis.
B (Ref:HM08046)

**GIBSON, VERONICA**

**Veronica Gibson**, 76 Paisley Rd, **Dorset**, BH6 5ED, ENG.
(T) 01202 250067
Speciality: Reflexology.
S T (Ref:HM08047)

**GIBSON-FORTY, J**

**J Gibson-Forty**, Chase Rd, Ross-on-Wye, **Herefordshire**, HR9 5JQ, ENG.
(T) 01989 767673
Speciality: Osteopathy.
● **Owner** Mr J Gibson-Forty
P S T (Ref:HM08048)

**GIBSON-FORTY, JOHN**

**John Gibson-Forty**, 3 Strensham Hill, Birmingham, **Midlands (West)**, B13 8AG, ENG.
(T) 01214 492323
Speciality: Osteopathy.
● **Principal** Mr J Gibson-Forty
P S T (Ref:HM08049)

**GIDDINGS, JANE**

**Jane Giddings**, 4 Chilwood Cl, Iron Acton, Bristol, BS37 9US, ENG.
(T) 01454 228393
Speciality: Reflexology.
S T (Ref:HM08050)

**GIDDINGS, R**

**R Giddings**, 15 Tuesday Market Pl, King's Lynn, **Norfolk**, PE30 1JN, ENG.
(T) 01553 760044
Speciality: Osteopathy.
● **Practice Manager** Mrs C Zimmer
P S T (Ref:HM08051)

**GIDDINGS, STARMER-JONES, BEAZL**

**Roger Giddings, Richard Starmer-Jones & Sally Beazl**, Oakington Therapy Centre, 12 High St, Oakington, Cambridge, **Cambridgeshire**, CB4 5AG, ENG.
(T) 01223 237459 (F) 01223 237459
Speciality: Osteopathy.
● **Director** Mr R Giddings
P S T (Ref:HM08052)

**GIL, JOHN**

**John Gil**, Top Flat, 3 South Rd, Redland, Bristol, BS6 6QP, ENG.
(T) 01179 428867 (F) 01179 428867
Speciality: Alexander Technique.
● **Owner** Mr J Gil
P S (Ref:HM08053)

**GILBERDYKE SPORTS & INJURY**

**Gilberdyke Sports & Recent Injury Clinic**, Clementhorpe Rd, Gilberdyke, Brough, **Humberside (North)**, HU15 2UB, ENG.
(T) 01430 441411
Speciality: Phytotherapy. ✔
● **Psychotherapist** Mr J Ratcliffe Q: MCSP, SRP. M: CSP.
S Yrs. Est.: 3 (Ref:HM08054)

**GILBERT RD OSTEOPATHIC**

**Gilbert Rd Osteopathic Clinic**, 46 Gilbert Rd, Cambridge, **Cambridgeshire**, CB4 3PE, ENG.
(T) 01223 563704
(E) graham.house@ntlworld.com
Speciality: Manipulation, Osteopathy. ✔
● **Physical Therapist** Mr G House Q: BSc, DO, MSc.
● **Osteopath** Ms C Doherty Q: BA (Hons), CQSW, DO, SRN. M: BOA.
S Yrs. Est.: 1 (Ref:HM08055)

**GILBERT, CATHERINE**

**Catherine Gilbert**, 50 Church St, Ruddington, Nottingham, **Nottinghamshire**, NG11 6HD, ENG.
(T) 01159 211163
Speciality: Clairvoyants & Palmists.
● **Owner** Ms C Gilbert
B (Ref:HM08056)

**GILBERT, CHARLES**

**Charles Gilbert**, 107 Uxbridge Rd, Harrow, **London (Greater)**, HA3 6DN, ENG.
(T) 020 8954 0404 (F) 020 8954 0404
Speciality: Chiropodists (Podiatrists).
● **Owner** Mr C Gilbert
S (Ref:HM08057)

**GILBERT, CHARLES N**

**Charles N Gilbert**, 215-217 Edgware Rd, London, **London (Greater)**, W2 1ES, ENG.
(T) 020 7723 5424
Speciality: Chiropodists (Podiatrists).
S (Ref:HM08058)

**GILBERT, EDWARD J**

**Edward J Gilbert**, 10 The Plain, Thornbury, Bristol, BS35 2AG, ENG.
(T) 01454 281243
Speciality: Osteopathy.
● **Owner** Mr E Gilbert
P S T (Ref:HM08059)

**GILBEY, BRIGETTE**

**Brigette Gilbey**, 52 Porchester Rd, London, **London (Greater)**, W2 6ET, ENG.
(T) 020 7221 3557
Speciality: Osteopathy.
● **Owner** Ms B Gilbey
P S T (Ref:HM08060)

**GILBEY, J**

**J Gilbey**, 28 Hallowell Rd, Northwood, **London (Greater)**, HA6 1DN, ENG.
(T) 01923 827833
Speciality: Osteopathy.
P S T (Ref:HM08061)

**GILCHRIST, A**

**A Gilchrist**, 37 Lisburn Rd, Belfast, **County Antrim**, BT9 7AA, NIR.
(T) 028 9033 3303
Speciality: Hypnotherapy.
B (Ref:HM08062)

**GILCHRIST, A**

**A Gilchrist**, 243 Great Clowes St, Salford, **Manchester (Greater)**, M7 2DZ, ENG.
(T) 01617 926565
Speciality: Homeopathy.
● **Owner** Mr A Gilchrist
M (Ref:HM08063)

**GILCHRIST, F**

**F Gilchrist**, 24 Derwent Drive, Hayes, **London (Greater)**, UB4 8DR, ENG.
(T) 020 8561 4703
Speciality: Chiropodists (Podiatrists).
● **Owner** Mrs F Gilchrist
S (Ref:HM08064)

**GILCHRIST, P**

**P Gilchrist**, Ashburnham Cottage, Ashburnham Drive, Walters Ash, High Wycombe, **Buckinghamshire**, HP14 4UD, ENG.
(T) 01494 562704
Speciality: Psychology.
B (Ref:HM08065)

**GILCREST, P**

**P Gilcrest**, 259 Park West, London, **London**

**(Greater)**, W2 2QZ, ENG.
(T) 020 7402 7532
Speciality: Psychiatry.
● **Partner** Mr R Shuttleworth
**B** (**Ref:**HM08066)

## GILES, CHRISTOPHER

**Christopher Giles**, 44 Bassett Rd, Headington, Oxford, **Oxfordshire**, OX3 9PE, ENG.
(T) 01865 751272
Speciality: Reflexology.
**S** **T** (**Ref:**HM08067)

## GILES, KAY

**Kay Giles**, 17 Middle Avenue, Loughborough, **Leicestershire**, LE11 5HZ, ENG.
(T) 01509 552779
Speciality: Chiropodists (Podiatrists).
● **Owner** Mrs K Giles
**S** (**Ref:**HM08068)

## GILES, KAY

**Kay Giles**, 52 Leslie Rd, London, **London (Greater)**, E11 4HG, ENG.
(T) 020 8556 3934
Speciality: Reflexology.
**S** **T** (**Ref:**HM08069)

## GILES, ROSEMARY

**Rosemary Giles**, Frimley, **Surrey**, GU16, ENG.
(T) 01276 501953
Speciality: Reflexology.
**S** **T** (**Ref:**HM08070)

## GILES-TODHUNTER THERAPY CLINIC

**Giles-Todhunter Therapy Clinic**, 75A Liverpool Rd, Penwortham, Preston, **Lancashire**, PR1 9XD, ENG.
(T) 01772 751404
Speciality: Complementary Medicines & Therapy.
● **Owner** Mrs S Giles
**M** (**Ref:**HM08071)

## GILHEAD, M A

**M A Gilhead**, 44 Princes Avenue, London, **London (Greater)**, N3 2DB, ENG.
(T) 020 8346 4923
Speciality: Physiotherapy.
● **Owner** Mrs M Gilhead
**P** **S** **T** (**Ref:**HM08072)

## GILKERSON, PATRICIA

**Patricia Gilkerson**, 21 Chrystel Cl, Tipton St. John, Sidmouth, **Devon**, EX10 0AY, ENG.
(T) 01404 814398
Speciality: Reflexology.
**S** **T** (**Ref:**HM08073)

## GILL JULIE

**Gill Julie**, Kingston Rise, New Haw, Addlestone, **Surrey**, KT15 3EY, ENG.
(T) 01932 352223
Speciality: Aromatherapy.
**M** **O** (**Ref:**HM08074)

## GILL, A

**A Gill**, 10 Eldon Rd, Reading, **Berkshire**, RG1 4DH, ENG.
(T) 01189 502002
Speciality: Psychology.
**B** (**Ref:**HM08075)

## GILL, G M

**G M Gill**, 48A Belvoir Rd, Coalville, **Leicestershire**, LE67 3PP, ENG.
(T) 01530 833533
Speciality: Physiotherapy.
**P** **S** **T** (**Ref:**HM08076)

## GILL, JUNE

**June Gill**, 28 Andrew St, Mossley, Ashton-under-Lyne, **Manchester (Greater)**, OL5 0DN, ENG.
(T) 01457 834961
Speciality: Alexander Technique.
**P** **S** (**Ref:**HM08077)

## GILL, SARAH

**Sarah Gill**, Trehayle, Whitecross, Wadebridge, **Cornwall**, PL27 7JD, ENG.
(T) 01208 813068
Speciality: Reflexology.
● **Owner** Mrs S Gill
**S** **T** (**Ref:**HM08078)

## GILL, SHEILA

**Sheila Gill**, Macclesfield, **Cheshire**, SK11, ENG.
(T) 01625 860455
Speciality: Bach Remedies.
**M** (**Ref:**HM08079)

## GILL, SHIRLEY

**Shirley Gill**, 37 Jones Green, Livingston, **Lothian (West)**, EH54 8QB, SCO.
(T) 01506 490730
Speciality: Reflexology. ✔
● **Reflexologist** Ms S Gill Q: GSSR, RMN. M: SIR.
**C** Yrs. Est.: 2 (**Ref:**HM08080)

## GILL, Y

**Y Gill**, 2 Beauly Cl, Ramsbottom, Bury, **Lancashire**, BL0 9WB, ENG.
(T) 01204 880469
Speciality: Chiropodists (Podiatrists).
● **Owner** Mrs Y Gill
**S** (**Ref:**HM08081)

## GILLARD, J

**Mr J Gillard**, 17 Shell Cl, Plymouth, **Devon**, PL6 8NU, ENG.
(T) 01752 786971
Speciality: Homeopathy.
● **Owner** Mr J Gillard
**M** (**Ref:**HM08082)

## GILLATT, A C

**A C Gillatt**, 39 Woodgate, Loughborough, **Leicestershire**, LE11 2TZ, ENG.
(T) 01509 263533
Speciality: Chiropodists (Podiatrists).
● **Owner** A C Gillatt
**S** (**Ref:**HM08083)

## GILLBRIDE, S A

**Mr S A Gillbride**, 3 Baswich Lane, Stafford, **Staffordshire**, ST17 0BH, ENG.
(T) 01785 247106
Speciality: Physiotherapy.
**P** **S** **T** (**Ref:**HM08084)

## GILLENDER, P L

**P L Gillender**, 61 St Andrews Drive, Skegness, **Lincolnshire**, PE25 1DJ, ENG.
(T) 01754 763884
Speciality: Physiotherapy.
● **Owner** Mr P Gillender
**P** **S** **T** (**Ref:**HM08085)

## GILLESPIE, B

**B Gillespie**, 43 Beechwood Gr, Horbury, Wakefield, **Yorkshire (West)**, WF4 5JG, ENG.
(T) 01924 274260
Speciality: Aromatherapy.
● **Owner** Mrs B Gillespie
**M** **O** (**Ref:**HM08086)

## GILLETT, E

**E Gillett**, Natural Health Clinic, 98 Cathedral Rd, Cardiff, **Glamorgan (Vale of)**, CF11 9LP, WAL.
(T) 029 2022 2221
Speciality: Chiropractors.
**P** **S** **T** (**Ref:**HM08087)

## GILLETT, LIZ

**Mrs Liz Gillett**, 5 Roman Mount, Leeds, **Yorkshire (West)**, LS8 2DP, ENG.
(T) 01132 664651
Speciality: Nutritional Therapy, Reflexology, Magnet Therapy. ✔
● **Owner/Reflexologist**
Mrs L Gillett Q: PGD.Reflex. M: BSR.
**T** Yrs. Est.: 13 (**Ref:**HM08088)

## GILLETT, PHILIP

**Philip Gillett**, 94 Northview Drive, Westcliff-on-Sea, **Essex**, SS0 9NF, ENG.
(T) 01702 332936
Speciality: Herbal Medicine.
● **Owner** Mr P Gillett
**M** (**Ref:**HM08089)

## GILLEY, EUNICE

**Eunice Gilley**, 3 Elmwood Avenue, Newton Mearns, Glasgow, **Glasgow (City of)**, G77 6EH, SCO.
(T) 01416 398748
Speciality: Physiotherapy.
**P** **S** **T** (**Ref:**HM08090)

## GILLHAM, ALISON

**Alison Gillham**, 181 Cuckfield Rd, Hurstpierpoint, Hassocks, **Sussex (West)**, BN6 9RT, ENG.
(T) 01273 832502
Speciality: Physiotherapy.
**P** **S** **T** (**Ref:**HM08091)

## GILLIARD, J H

**Mr J H Gilliard**, 86 Barbourne Rd, Worcester, **Worcestershire**, WR1 1SE, ENG.
(T) 01905 24027
Speciality: Physiotherapy.
● **Physiotherapist** Mr J Gilliard Q: MCSP, SRP.
**P** **S** **T** (**Ref:**HM08092)

## GILLIBRAND, M

**M Gillibrand**, 16 Broad Robin, Gillingham, **Dorset**, SP8 4PJ, ENG.
(T) 01747 824541
Speciality: Chiropodists (Podiatrists).
● **Partner** Mr R Gillibrand
**S** (**Ref:**HM08093)

## GILLIGAN, TONI

**Toni Gilligan**, 22 Cottage, Tilesford, Pershore, **Worcestershire**, WR10 2LA, ENG.
(T) 01386 561528
Speciality: Psychology.
**B** (**Ref:**HM08094)

## GILLING, LINDA

**Linda Gilling - Reflexology**, Barringtons Beauty Salon, Elstree Moat House Hotel, Borehamwood, **Hertfordshire**, WD6 5PU, ENG.
(T) 020 8953 9375
(E) abbie.g@cwctv.net
Speciality: Complementary Therapy, Indian Head Massage, Reflexology. ✔
● **Owner/Reflexologist**
Mrs L Gilling M: BRA.
**B** Yrs. Est.: 10 (**Ref:**HM08095)

## GILLINGHAM CHIROPRACTIC CLINIC

**Gillingham Chiropractic Clinic**, Gillingham Chiropractic Clinic, 2 Station Rd, Gillingham, **Dorset**, SP8 4PY, ENG.
(T) 01747 825583 (F) 01747 825583
Speciality: Chiropractic.
● **Owner** Mr C Richardson
**P** **S** **T** (**Ref:**HM08096)

## GILLINGHAM CLINIC OF COMP MED

**Gillingham Clinic of Complementary Medicine**, 50 Watling St, Gillingham, **Kent**, ME7 2YN, ENG.
(T) 01634 576292 (F) 01634 854087
Speciality: Acupressure, Acupuncture, Complementary Therapy, Dietician, Holistic Healing, Homeopathy, Naturopathy, Osteopathy, Reflexology, Stress Therapy. ✔ CREDIT
● **Acupuncturist** Linda Wilson Q: Reg.Acu.
● **Homeopath** Sandra Baker Q: RSHom.
● **Stress Counsellor/Hypnotherapist**
Linda Coutts
● **Therapist** Mr D Leigh Q: DO, ND. M: GOsC.
**S** Yrs. Est.: 20 (**Ref:**HM08097)

## GILLINGHAM, GLENNA

**Glenna Gillingham**, The Park Clinic, 22 Park Rd, Bath, **Somerset**, BA1 3EE, ENG.
(T) 01225 333021
Speciality: Acupuncture.
**O** (**Ref:**HM08098)

## GILLINGS, SONIA

**Sonia Gillings**, 161 Queens Rd, Buckhurst Hill, **Essex**, IG9 5AZ, ENG.
(T) 020 8505 8353
Speciality: Hypnotherapy.
● **Owner** Mr R Woodleigh
**B** (**Ref:**HM08099)

## GILLMAN, C M

**C M Gillman**, 2 Fryatts Way, Bexhill-on-Sea, **Sussex (East)**, TN39 4LW, ENG.
(T) 01424 224996
Speciality: Physiotherapy.
● **Owner** Miss C Gillmann
**P** **S** **T** (**Ref:**HM08100)

## GILLMAN, G J

**G J Gillman**, 40 Rosslyn Rd, Heald Green,

Key: **B** Mind-Body Medicine **C** Complementary Medicine **H** Self Help Treatment **M** Medicinal Therapy **O** Oriental Medicine **P** Postural Therapy **S** Manipulative Structural Therapy **T** Touch Therapy

Cheadle, **Cheshire**, SK8 3DJ, ENG.
(T) 01614 361543
Speciality: Chiropodists (Podiatrists).
● **Owner** Mr G Gillman
S (Ref:HM08101)

## GILLON, RACHEL

**Rachel Gillon**, 6 Glencairn Rd, Langbank, Port Glasgow, **Renfrewshire**, PA14 6XL, SCO.
(T) 01475 540632
Speciality: Reflexology.
S T (Ref:HM08102)

## GILLY-CRUYSMANS, FABIENNE

**Fabienne Gilly-Cruysmans**, 79A Deodar Rd, London, **London (Greater)**, SW15 2NU, ENG.
(T) 020 8874 1472
Speciality: Reflexology.
S T (Ref:HM08103)

## GILMORE, E M J

**E M J Gilmore**, Gilmore, Somerton Rd, North Aston, Bicester, **Oxfordshire**, OX6 4HX, ENG.
(T) 01869 347480 (F) 01869 347480
Speciality: Chiropractic.
● **Owner** Mr R Gilmore
P S T (Ref:HM08104)

## GILMORE, J J (DR)

**Dr J J Gilmore**, 12 Clarinda Pk, Nth, Dun Laoghaire, **County Dublin**, IRE.
(T) 01280 0488
Speciality: Chiropractors.
P S T (Ref:HM08105)

## GILMORE, V M

**V M Gilmore**, 20 Hendred St, Oxford, **Oxfordshire**, OX4 2ED, ENG.
(T) 01865 778684
Speciality: Psychotherapy.
● **Owner** Ms V Gilmore
B (Ref:HM08106)

## GILMOUR, PIPER & ASSOCIATES

**A Gilmour M Piper & Assoicates**, 10 Fonnereau Rd, Ipswich, **Suffolk**, IP1 3JP, ENG.
(T) 01473 217592 (F) 01473 286646
Speciality: Osteopathy.
● **Partner** Mr A Gilmour
P S T (Ref:HM08107)

## GINA

**Gina**, 17a Saville Row, Newcastle Upon Tyne, **Tyne and Wear**, NE1 8JE, ENG.
(T) 01912 324832
Speciality: Clairvoyants & Palmists.
B (Ref:HM08108)

## GINAS AROMATHERAPY

**Ginas Aromatherapy**, 44 Duchess Way, Bristol, BS16 1ET, ENG.
(T) 01179 659500
Speciality: Aromatherapy.
● **Owner** Miss G Chandler
M O (Ref:HM08109)

## GINN, ALAN

**Alan Ginn**, 76 Tollgate, Bretton, Peterborough, **Cambridgeshire**, PE3 9XB, ENG.
(T) 01733 267301
Speciality: Hypnotherapy.
● **Owner** Mr A Ginn
B (Ref:HM08110)

## GINSBERG, ANNE

**Anne Ginsberg: Spiritual Teacher**, 61 Conisborough, Freehold Estate, Rochdale, **Lancashire**, OL11 4JS, ENG.
(T) 01706 343519
(E) anneginsberg@ask.co.uk
(W) www.homestead.com/AnneGinsberg/homesteadindexPAGE1
Speciality: Absent Healing, Aura Therapy, Colour Therapy, Healer, Healing Therapy, Holistic Healing, Life Style Coaching, Meditation, Paranormal Therapies, Spiritual Healing, Visualisation Therapy.
● **Spiritual Teacher/Healer** Mrs A Ginsberg
B Yrs. Est.: 4 (Ref:HM08111)

## GINSENG

**Ginseng Co (The)**, The Granary, Railway Hill, Barham, Canterbury, **Kent**, CT4 6LA, ENG.
(T) 01227 832475
Speciality: Herbal Medicine.
M (Ref:HM08112)

## GIRLING, SUSAN

**Susan Girling**, Unit 6 Riverside Business Park, Gosport St, Lymington, **Hampshire**, SO41 9BB, ENG.
(T) 01590 688788
Speciality: Physiotherapy.
P S T (Ref:HM08113)

## GIRON, DANIEL

**Daniel Giron (Irl) Ltd**, 62 Clontarf Rd, Clontarf, Dublin, **County Dublin**, IRE.
(T) 01833 6687
Speciality: Complementary Medicines & Therapy.
M (Ref:HM08114)

## GIVEN, CLIVE

**Clive Given**, 11 Fountain Hill, Antrim, **County Antrim**, BT41 1LZ, NIR.
(T) 028 9446 7862
Speciality: Indian Head Massage, Reflexology, Reiki. ✔
● **Reflexologist** Mr C Given
(T) 028 9446 1964 Q: Adv.Cert.Ch.Reflex, BA (Hons), Cert.Ed, Cert.Reiki, Dip.Indian Head Massage, Dip.Reflex, IIHHT.
C Yrs. Est.: 1 (Ref:HM08115)

## GLADSTONE, A R

**A R Gladstone**, 199 Old St, London, **London (Greater)**, EC1V 9NP, ENG.
(T) 020 7253 2586
Speciality: Chiropodists (Podiatrists).
● **Owner** Mr A Gladstone
S (Ref:HM08116)

## GLADWIN, DENIS

**Denis Gladwin**, 28 Hatchcroft Gardens, Elmstead Market, Colchester, **Essex**, CO7 7AJ, ENG.
(T) 01206 823383
Speciality: Reflexology.
S T (Ref:HM08117)

## GLADWIN, G L

**G L Gladwin**, 19 Castle St, High Wycombe, **Buckinghamshire**, HP13 6RU, ENG.
(T) 01494 530004
Speciality: Hypnotherapy.
B (Ref:HM08118)

## GLADWIN, JOHN F C

**John F C Gladwin**, 18 Springvalley Trce, Edinburgh, **Edinburgh (City of)**, EH10 4PY, SCO.
(T) 01314 472404
Speciality: Physiotherapy.
● **Owner** Mr J Gladwin
P S T (Ref:HM08119)

## GLAISTER, BRIAN (DR)

**Dr Brian Glaister**, 135 Foxley Lane, Purley, Croydon, **Surrey**, CR8 3HR, ENG.
(T) 020 8660 7465
Speciality: Cognitive Therapy, Counselling, Psychotherapy. ✔
● **Psychologist** Dr B Glaister Q: PhD.
H Yrs. Est.: 20 (Ref:HM08120)

## GLAISTER, J E

**J E Glaister**, 37 Bank St, Carlisle, **Cumbria**, CA3 8HJ, ENG.
(T) 01228 523761
Speciality: Chiropodists (Podiatrists).
● **Owner** Mrs J Glaister
S (Ref:HM08121)

## GLAMORGAN HEALTH & RACQUET

**Glamorgan Health And Racquet Club**, Llandarcy, Neath, **Glamorgan (Vale of)**, SA10 6GZ, WAL.
(T) 01792 324300
Speciality: Physiotherapy. ✔
● **Physiotherapist** Cabella Wigley Q: BSc, MCSP, MSc, SRP. M: CSP.
S (Ref:HM08122)

## GLASBY, H R

**H R Glasby**, 1 Broad St, Bungay, **Suffolk**, NR35 1EE, ENG.
(T) 01986 892426
Speciality: Chiropodists (Podiatrists).
● **Owner** Mr H Glasby
S (Ref:HM08123)

## GLASGOW CHIROPRACTIC CLINIC

**Glasgow Chiropractic Clinic**, 994 Crow Rd, Glasgow, **Glasgow (City of)**, G13 1JN, SCO.
(T) 01414 340370 (F) 01414 340470
Speciality: Chiropractic.
● **Owner** Dr H Cameron
P S T (Ref:HM08124)

## GLASGOW, KY

**Ky Glasgow**, 82 Gordon St, Glasgow, **Glasgow (City of)**, G1 3RS, SCO.
(T) 01412 483188 (F) 01414 272400
Speciality: Complementary Medicines & Therapy.
● **Owner** Mrs D Bell
M (Ref:HM08125)

## GLASSBOROW, G W

**G W Glassborow**, Red Tiles, Portsmouth Rd, Milford, Godalming, **Surrey**, GU8 5HW, ENG.
(T) 01483 416893
Speciality: Hypnosis.
● **Owner** Mr G Glassborow
B (Ref:HM08126)

## GLASSER, E C

**E C Glasser**, 1 Lonsdale Avenue, Giffnock, Glasgow, **Glasgow (City of)**, G46 6HG, SCO.
(T) 01416 380717 (F) 01416 380159
Speciality: Physiotherapy.
● **Owner** Mrs E Glasser
P S T (Ref:HM08127)

## GLASSMAN, DAVID

**David Glassman**, 26 Cleveland Gardens, London, **London (Greater)**, NW2 1DY, ENG.
(T) 020 8455 1317
Speciality: Alexander Technique, Bates Method, Neuro-Linguistic Program, Neuro-Linguistic Programming. ✔
● **Owner/Teacher** Mr D Glassman Q: B.A.V.E. M: STAT.
B C H P T
(Ref:HM08128)

## GLASSMAN, RUTH

**Ruth Glassman**, Hendon Natural Health Centre, 12 Golders Rise, London, **London (Greater)**, NW4 2HR, ENG.
(T) 020 8202 9747 (F) 020 8202 3890
Speciality: Reflexology.
● **Owner** Ms K McCarroll
S T (Ref:HM08129)

## GLASSPOOL, PATRICIA

**Patricia Glasspool**, 12 Hocombe Drive, Chandler's Ford, Eastleigh, **Hampshire**, SO53 5QE, ENG.
(T) 023 8025 5678
Speciality: Hypnosis.
● **Owner** Mrs P Glasspool
B (Ref:HM08130)

## GLASTONBURY CHIROPRACTIC

**Glastonbury Chiropractic Clinic (The)**, 14 Northload St, Glastonbury, **Somerset**, BA6 9JJ, ENG.
(T) 01458 833779
Speciality: Aromatherapy, Chiropractic, Counselling, Kinesiology, Manipulation, Nutritional Therapy, Reflexology, Reiki. ✔
● **Chiropractor** Ms J Gill Q: DC, RGN. M: MCA.
● **Chiropractor** Mr C Smith Q: DC. M: MCA.
● **Owner** Mrs A Tynan Q: DC. M: MCA.
P Yrs. Est.: 2 (Ref:HM08131)

## GLASTONBURY EAST WEST CENTRE

**Glastonbury East West Centre**, 10 High St, Glastonbury, **Somerset**, BA6 9DU, ENG.
(T) 01458 834236
(W) www.eastwestcentre.com
Speciality: Acupuncture, Aromatherapy, Counselling, Floral Essence Therapy, Herbal Medicine, Iridology, Kinesiology, Massage (Therapeutic), Nutritional Therapy, Osteopathy, Psychotherapy, Shiatsu, Stress Therapy, Yoga, Chinese, Western & Ayurvedic herbal medicine, Radionics psychotherapy core process. ✔



Key continued: Yrs.Est: Years Established Q: Qualifications M: Professional Membership ✔ Indemnity Insurance Accept Credit Cards

● **Medical Herbalist** Mr A Johnson **Q:** D.Th.D, MH.
● **Psychotherapist** Ms J Sanders **Q:** Dip.Psych. **M:** UKCP.
**C** Yrs. Est.: 15 (**Ref:**HM08132)

**GLASTONBURY HEALING CENTRE**

**N F S H Glastonbury Healing Centre**, 8 Market Pl, Glastonbury, **Somerset**, BA6 9HW, ENG.
**(T)** 01458 832549
Speciality: Complementary Medicines & Therapy.
● **Manager** Mrs M Payne
**C M** (**Ref:**HM08133)

**GLATT, M M (DR)**

**Dr M M Glatt**, 16 Southbourne Cres, London, **London (Greater)**, NW4 2JY, ENG.
**(T)** 020 8346 4810
Speciality: Psychotherapy.
**B** (**Ref:**HM08134)

**GLEADALL, A D**

**A D Gleadall**, Birkdale Clinic, Clifton Lane, Rotherham, **Yorkshire (South)**, S65 2AJ, ENG.
**(T)** 01709 540723 **(F)** 01709 828372
Speciality: Physiotherapy.
● **Owner** A Gleadall
**P S T** (**Ref:**HM08135)

**GLEAVE, V W**

**V W Gleave**, Bury Knowle Health Centre, 207 London Rd, Headington, Oxford, **Oxfordshire**, OX3 9JA, ENG.
**(T)** 01865 742815
Speciality: Physiotherapy.
**P S T** (**Ref:**HM08136)

**GLEAVE, VAL**

**Val Gleave**, The Helix Centre, Woodbrook House, 27 Bridge St, Loughborough, **Leicestershire**, LE11 1NH, ENG.
**(T)** 01509 230200
Speciality: Acupuncture.
**O** (**Ref:**HM08137)

**GLEDHILL, MAUREEN (DR)**

**Dr Maureen Gledhill**, 528 Finchley Rd, London, **London (Greater)**, NW11 8DD, ENG.
**(T)** 020 8731 8642 **(F)** 020 8455 7211
Speciality: Psychotherapy.
● **Owner** Mrs M Gledhill
**B** (**Ref:**HM08138)

**GLEDHILL, RACHEL**

**Rachel Gledhill**, 30 Dudwell Lane, Halifax, **Yorkshire (West)**, HX3 0SD, ENG.
**(T)** 01422 366143 **(F)** 01422 366143
Speciality: Physiotherapy.
● **Owner** Mrs R Gledhill
**P S T** (**Ref:**HM08139)

**GLEESON, CATHERINE**

**Catherine Gleeson BA HDip DipPsy DHPM MIAHM**, Prospect Ave, Clontarf, **County Dublin**, IRE.
**(T)** 01833 4025
Speciality: Complementary Medicines & Therapy.
**M** (**Ref:**HM08140)

**GLEESON, KAREN**

**Karen Gleeson**, 12 The Nook, Chilwell, Beeston, Nottingham, **Nottinghamshire**, NG9 5AB, ENG.
**(T)** 01159 228341
Speciality: Hypnosis.
● **Owner** Mrs K Gleeson
**B** (**Ref:**HM08141)

**GLEESON, ROISIN B (DR)**

**Roisin B Gleeson Physio MISCP Lic Ac**, Swords Physiotherapy & Acupuncture Clinic 59 Main, Swords, IRE.
**(T)** 01840 7907
Speciality: Complementary Medicines & Therapy.
**M** (**Ref:**HM08142)

**GLEICH, M T**

**M T Gleich**, Fir Way House, Fir Way, Grayshott, Hindhead, **Surrey**, GU26 6JQ, ENG.
**(T)** 01428 712262
Speciality: Osteopathy.
● **Owner** Mr M Gleich
**P S T** (**Ref:**HM08143)

**GLEICH, M T**

**M T Gleich**, 29 Salisbury Rd, Southsea, **Hampshire**, PO4 9QY, ENG.
**(T)** 023 9273 4422
Speciality: Osteopathy.
**P S T** (**Ref:**HM08144)

**GLENCAIRE CLINIC**

**Glencaire Clinic of Complementary Medicine**, Suite 1 Glencairn, South St, Sherborne, **Dorset**, DT9 3NQ, ENG.
**(T)** 01935 817442 **(F)** 01935 817706
Speciality: Osteopathy. ✔
● **Osteopath** Mr A Gibbs **Q:** DO. **M:** GOsC.
● **Osteopath** Dr Hegerty **Q:** BSc, DO, PhD. **M:** GOsC.
**C** Yrs. Est.: 20 (**Ref:**HM08145)

**GLENCAIRN HOUSE**

**Glencairn House**, South St, Sherborne, **Dorset**, DT9 3NQ, ENG.
**(T)** 01935 814943 **(F)** 01935 814943
Speciality: Physiotherapy.
● **Practice Manager** Mrs S England
**P S T** (**Ref:**HM08146)

**GLENCOURT REFLEXOLOGY**

**Glencourt Reflexology**, Domewood, Copthorne, Crawley, **Sussex (West)**, RH10 3HD, ENG.
**(T)** 01342 713061 **(F)** 01342 716219
Speciality: Reflexology.
● **Owner** Mrs B Garton
**S T** (**Ref:**HM08147)

**GLENDINNING, CATHERINE**

**Catherine Glendinning**, 20 Prestonville Court, 134 Dyke Rd, Brighton, **Sussex (East)**, BN1 3UG, ENG.
**(T)** 01273 884303
Speciality: Reflexology.
**S T** (**Ref:**HM08148)

**GLENDON, NOEL**

**Noel Glendon**, 2 North St, Chester, **Cheshire**, CH3 5DS, ENG.
**(T)** 01244 340337
Speciality: Psychotherapy.
● **Owner** Mr N Glendon
**B** (**Ref:**HM08149)

**GLENFIELD PRACTICE**

**Glenfield Practice**, 123 Station Rd, Glenfield, Leicester, **Leicestershire**, LE3 8GS, ENG.
**(T)** 01162 241358 **(F)** 01162 241358
Speciality: Acupuncture, Cranial Osteopathy, Hypnosis, Manipulation, Osteopathy. ✔
● **Osteopath** Graham Spowage **Q:** Reg.Osteopath.
● **Acupuncturist** Ms J Smith **Q:** Dip.TCM.
**O S** Yrs. Est.: 20 (**Ref:**HM08150)

**GLENGORMLEY CHIRO CLINIC**

**Glengormley Chiropractic Clinic**, 57 Ballyclare Rd, Newtownabbey, **County Antrim**, BT36 5HQ, NIR.
**(T)** 028 9084 8938 **(F)** 028 9084 8938
Speciality: Chiropractic. ✔
● **Chiropractor** Dr P Davis **Q:** DC.
**P** Yrs. Est.: 5 (**Ref:**HM08151)

**GLENGORMLEY FOOT CARE**

**Glengormley Foot Care**, 4a Portland Avenue, Newtownabbey, **County Antrim**, BT36 5EY, NIR.
**(T)** 028 9083 3568
Speciality: Chiropodists (Podiatrists).
● **Partner** Mr D Hallowell
**S** (**Ref:**HM08152)

**GLENNON, PATRICK & BERNIE**

**Glennon Patrick & Bernie**, The Beeches Kilconnell, Ballinasloe, **County Galway**, IRE.
**(T)** 09058 6800
Speciality: Complementary Medicines & Therapy.
**M** (**Ref:**HM08153)

**GLENTHORNE**

**Glenthorne**, 44 Glenthorne Rd, London, **London (Greater)**, N11 3HJ, ENG.
**(T)** 020 8368 3883
Speciality: Chiropractors.
● **Owner** Mr C Merkier
**P S T** (**Ref:**HM08154)

**GLOBAL CHIROPRACTIC CENTRE**

**Global Chiropractic Centre**, 143 Ormeau Rd, Belfast, **County Antrim**, BT7 1SL, NIR.
**(T)** 028 9031 0538
Speciality: Chiropractors.
● **Doctor** Dr P Fraser
**P S T** (**Ref:**HM08155)

**GLOBAL HEALTH SERVICES**

**Global Health Services**, 7 Meadow Cl, Trench, Telford, **Shropshire**, TF2 6PA, ENG.
**(T)** 01952 414038
Speciality: Complementary Medicines & Therapy.
● **Owner** Mr P Fernley
**C M** (**Ref:**HM08156)

**GLOBAL HEALTHCARE**

**Global Healthcare**, 17 Elgin St, Belfast, **County Antrim**, BT7 3AG, NIR.
**(T)** 028 9020 2880 **(F)** 028 9020 3647
Speciality: Complementary Medicines & Therapy.
● **Owner** Mr G Martin
**C M** (**Ref:**HM08157)

**GLORIA JEANS FASC FOR LAVENDER**

**Gloria Jeans Fascination For Lavender**, 6 Bow Wharf, Grove Rd, Bow, London, **London (Greater)**, E3 5AX, ENG.
**(T)** 020 8980 2331
Speciality: Aromatherapy.
**M O** (**Ref:**HM08158)

**GLOUCESTER CHIROPRACTIC CLINIC**

**Gloucester Chiropractic Clinic**, 31 St Michaels Sq, Gloucester, **Gloucestershire**, GL1 1HX, ENG.
**(T)** 01452 304386
Speciality: Chiropractors.
**P S T** (**Ref:**HM08159)

**GLOUCESTER NAT THERAPIES**

**Gloucester Natural Therapies Clinic**, 11A Kingsholm Rd, Gloucester, **Gloucestershire**, GL1 3AY, ENG.
**(T)** 01452 505550 **(F)** 01452 505550
Speciality: Acupuncture.
● **Owner** Mr D Smythe
**M** (**Ref:**HM08160)

**GLOUCESTER ROAD PRACTITIONER**

**Gloucester Road Practitioner (The)**, 79a Gloucester Rd, Bishopston, Bristol, BS7 8AS, ENG.
**(T)** 01179 420226
Speciality: Complementary Medicines & Therapy.
● **Partner** Ms A Hartley
**C M** (**Ref:**HM08161)

**GLOVER, ELEANOR L**

**Eleanor L Glover**, 70A Ashby Rd, Loughborough, **Leicestershire**, LE11 3AE, ENG.
**(T)** 01509 235653
Speciality: Osteopathy.
**P S T** (**Ref:**HM08162)

**GLOVER, ELEANOR L**

**Eleanor L Glover**, Corner House, 11 Imperial Rd, Beeston, Nottingham, **Nottinghamshire**, NG9 1ET, ENG.
**(T)** 01159 431433
Speciality: Osteopathy.
**P S T** (**Ref:**HM08163)

**GLOVER, J**

**J Glover**, 30 Bishop Rd, Bristol, BS7 8LT, ENG.
**(T)** 01179 426810
Speciality: Acupuncture.
**O** (**Ref:**HM08164)

**GLOVER, JEAN**

**Jean Glover**, 5 Forge End, Amersham, **Buckinghamshire**, HP7 0JP, ENG.
**(T)** 01494 726515
Speciality: Chiropodists (Podiatrists).
● **Owner** Mrs J Glover
**S** (**Ref:**HM08165)

**GLOVER, PATRICIA**

**Patricia Glover**, 31 Rowsley Rd, Lytham St.

Key: **B** Mind-Body Medicine **C** Complementary Medicine **H** Self Help Treatment **M** Medicinal Therapy **O** Oriental Medicine **P** Postural Therapy **S** Manipulative Structural Therapy **T** Touch Therapy

Annes, **Lancashire**, FY8 2NT, ENG.
(T) 01253 780242
Speciality: Chiropodists (Podiatrists).
S (Ref:HM08166)

## GLOVER, ROBERT

**Robert Glover**, 17 Lady Matildas Drive, Skegness, **Lincolnshire**, PE25 1ES, ENG.
(T) 01754 764316
Speciality: Chiropodists (Podiatrists).
● **Owner** Mr R Glover
S (Ref:HM08167)

## GLYNN, CLAIR

**Clair Glynn**, Crown Inn House, The St, Hinderclay, Diss, **Norfolk**, IP22 1HX, ENG.
(T) 01379 890175
Speciality: Reflexology.
S T (Ref:HM08168)

## GLYNN, ELIZABETH

**Elizabeth Glynn**, 7 Parslow Court, Aylesbury, **Buckinghamshire**, HP21 9HJ, ENG.
(T) 01296 425398
Speciality: Reflexology.
S T (Ref:HM08169)

## GOACHER, J

**J Goacher**, 10 High St, Banstead, **Surrey**, SM7 2LJ, ENG.
(T) 01372 721282
Speciality: Homeopathy.
● **Owner** Mrs J Goacher
M (Ref:HM08170)

## GOBELL, C G

**C G Gobell**, 71B High St, Lymington, **Hampshire**, SO41 9AL, ENG.
(T) 01590 670706
Speciality: Osteopathy.
P S T (Ref:HM08171)

## GOBIN, JOHN

**John Gobin**, 12 Deansgate Lane, Liverpool, **Merseyside**, L37 3LG, ENG.
(T) 01704 872283
Speciality: Chiropodists (Podiatrists).
S (Ref:HM08172)

## GOBLE, L M

**L M Goble**, 18 Fisher St, Carlisle, **Cumbria**, CA3 8RH, ENG.
(T) 01228 522185
Speciality: Chiropodists (Podiatrists).
● **Owner** Ms L Goble
S (Ref:HM08173)

## GODAGAMA, S

**S Godagama**, 16 Cannon Hill Clinic, London, **London (Greater)**, N14 7HD, ENG.
(T) 020 8882 2131
Speciality: Acupuncture.
O (Ref:HM08174)

## GODAGAMA, S (DR)

**Dr S Godagama**, 322A St Albans Rd, Watford, **Hertfordshire**, WD2 5PQ, ENG.
(T) 01923 246010 (F) 01923 246010
Speciality: Acupuncture.
● **Owner** Dr S Dodagama
O (Ref:HM08175)

## GODAGAMA, SHANTA (DR)

**Dr Shanta Godagama**, 66 London Rd, Hemel Hempstead, **Hertfordshire**, HP3 9SD, ENG.
(T) 01442 266880
Speciality: Acupuncture.
● **Owner** Dr S Godagama
O (Ref:HM08176)

## GODAGAMA, SHANTHA

**Shantha Godagama**, 17 Bromham Mill, Giffard Park, Milton Keynes, **Buckinghamshire**, MK14 5QP, ENG.
(T) 01908 617089 (F) 01908 617102
Speciality: Acupuncture.
● **Director** Mr S Godagama
O (Ref:HM08177)

## GODALMING CHIROPRACTIC CLINIC

**Godalming Chiropractic Clinic**, Meadowcroft, Bridge Rd, Godalming, **Surrey**, GU7 3DT, ENG.
(T) 01483 419538
Speciality: Chiropractic.
P S T (Ref:HM08178)

## GODDARD, E A

**E A Goddard**, 1 Church Rd, North Waltham, Basingstoke, **Hampshire**, RG25 2BG, ENG.
(T) 01256 397548
Speciality: Chiropodists (Podiatrists).
S (Ref:HM08179)

## GODDARD, TERRI

**Terri Goddard MRSS**, Greenwood By The Lake, Station Rd, Wraysbury, Staines, **Surrey**, TW19, ENG.
(T) 01784 482186
Speciality: Acupressure, Complementary Therapy, Do-In, Healing Therapy, Holistic Healing, Oriental Diagnosis, Shiatsu, Ying & Yang, Ki Development. ✓
● **Shiatsu/Jin Shin Acupressure Practitioner**
Ms T Goddard Q: MHTN, MRSS. M: Shiatsu Society UK.
O Yrs. Est.: 10 (Ref:HM08180)

## GODDEN, PATRICIA

**Patricia Godden**, The Willows, Ashlake Copse Rd, Ryde, **Isle of Wight**, PO33 4EY, ENG.
(T) 01983 884952
Speciality: Reflexology.
S T (Ref:HM08181)

## GODDENOUGH, J

**J Goddenough**, 5 Mallory Lane, Stamford, **Lincolnshire**, PE9 2FW, ENG.
(T) 01780 480645
Speciality: Chiropractic.
● **Doctor** Dr J Goddenough
P S T (Ref:HM08182)

## GODFREY, BRIAN

**Brian Godfrey**, 19 Downleaze, Portishead, Bristol, BS20 8BJ, ENG.
(T) 01275 848608
Speciality: Hypnosis.
● **Owner** Mr B Godfrey
B (Ref:HM08183)

## GODFREY, BRIAN

**Brian Godfrey C Hyp**, 25 Sweethill Lane, Southwell, Isle of Portland, **Dorset**, DT5 2DT, ENG.
(T) 01305 820038
Speciality: Healer, Hypnotherapy. ✓
● **Owner** Mr B Godfrey Q: C.Hyp, MCAH, NFSH.
● **Healer** Ms A Godfrey Q: NFSH.
B H T Yrs. Est.: 13 (Ref:HM08184)

## GODLEY, C

**C Godley**, 178 East Barnet Rd, Barnet, **Hertfordshire**, EN4 8RD, ENG.
(T) 020 8449 7754 (F) 020 8449 0174
Speciality: Acupuncture.
● **Principal** Mr L Hartman
O (Ref:HM08185)

## GODLEY, C

**C Godley**, 339 Ballards Lane, London, **London (Greater)**, N12 8LJ, ENG.
(T) 020 8445 4397
Speciality: Acupuncture.
● **Director** Mr E Thankey
O (Ref:HM08186)

## GODLEY, CATHERINE

**Catherine Godley**, 102 Geary Rd, London, **London (Greater)**, NW10 1HR, ENG.
(T) 020 8450 8688
Speciality: Acupuncture.
O (Ref:HM08187)

## GODLIMAN, BEN

**Ben Godliman**, Feng Shui, 52 Stoke Newington Church St, London, **London (Greater)**, N16 0NB, ENG.
(T) 020 7249 9671
Speciality: Complementary Medicines & Therapy.
M (Ref:HM08188)

## GODLIMAN, LINDA

**Linda Godliman**, 6 Ingram Way, Greenford, **London (Greater)**, UB6 8QG, ENG.
(T) 020 8578 3120
Speciality: Alexander Technique.
P S (Ref:HM08189)

## GODLIMAN, LINDA

**Linda Godliman**, Chiswick Health Centre, Fishers Lane, London, **London (Greater)**, W4 1RX, ENG.
(T) 020 8578 3120
Speciality: Alexander Technique.
● **Owner** Mrs L Godliman
P S (Ref:HM08190)

## GODSWELL NATURAL THRPY CTRE

**Godswell Natural Therapy Centre (The)**, Godswell Lodge, Church St, Bloxham, Banbury, **Oxfordshire**, OX15 4ES, ENG.
(T) 01295 720347
Speciality: Acupuncture, Alexander Technique, Aromatherapy, Art Therapy, Bach Remedies, Chiropody, Chiropractic, Cranio-Sacral Therapy, Herbal Medicine, Hypnosis, Massage (Therapeutic), McTimoney Chiropractic, Neuro-Linguistic Program, Nutritional Therapy, Physiotherapy, Psychotherapy, Reflexology, Reiki, Shiatsu, Vitamin Therapy, Yoga, Hypericum.
C (Ref:HM08191)

## GODWIN, E

**E Godwin**, 31 St. Johns St, Devizes, **Wiltshire**, SN10 1BN, ENG.
(T) 01380 721177
Speciality: Chiropodists (Podiatrists).
● **Partner** Mrs L Grant
S (Ref:HM08192)

## GODWIN, PAUL & JENNY

**Paul & Jenny Godwin**, Church Grange Health Centre, Bramblys Drive, Basingstoke, **Hampshire**, RG21 8QN, ENG.
(T) 01256 329021 (F) 01256 817466
Speciality: Chiropractic.
● **Practice Manager** Mrs L Newton
P S T (Ref:HM08193)

## GODWIN, ROME

**Rome Godwin**, 11 Argyll Mansions, Bishop Kings Rd, London, **London (Greater)**, W14 8QQ, ENG.
(T) 020 7603 2250
(E) godwinj@aol.com
Speciality: Alexander Technique. ✓
● **Teacher of the Alexander Technique**
Ms R Godwin Q: MSTAT. M: STAT.
P Yrs. Est.: 10 (Ref:HM08194)

## GOGIA, D R (DR)

**Dr D R Gogia**, 11 St John St, Manchester, **Manchester (Greater)**, M3 4DW, ENG.
(T) 01618 343090
Speciality: Osteopathy. ✓
● **Osteopath** Dr D Gogia
S Yrs. Est.: 30 (Ref:HM08195)

## GOGIA, D R (DR)

**Dr D R Gogia**, 4 Brent Rd, Brentford, **London (Greater)**, TW8 8BP, ENG.
(T) 020 8568 9683 (F) 020 8568 9683
Speciality: Osteopathy.
● **Doctor** Mr D Gogia
P S T (Ref:HM08196)

## GOHIL, SUMAN

**Suman Gohil**, 25 Lower Gungate, Tamworth, **Staffordshire**, B79 7AT, ENG.
(T) 01827 68374
Speciality: Complementary Medicines & Therapy.
M (Ref:HM08197)

## GOJ, STEPHANIE

**Stephanie Goj**, Clissold Park Health Centre, 154 Stoke Newington Church St, London, **London (Greater)**, N16 0JU, ENG.
(T) 020 7249 2990 (F) 020 7249 3977
Speciality: Complementary Medicines & Therapy.
● **Owner** Mr D Berg
M (Ref:HM08198)

## GOKANI, M

**M Gokani**, 32 Church Rd, Northolt, **London (Greater)**, UB5 5AB, ENG.
(T) 020 8841 1585 (F) 020 8841 1585
Speciality: Chiropodists (Podiatrists).
● **Owner** Mr M Gokani
S (Ref:HM08199)



Key continued: Yrs.Est: Years Established Q: Qualifications M: Professional Membership ✓ Indemnity Insurance Accept Credit Cards

## GOLD PURE ESSENTIAL OILS

**Gold Pure Essential Oils**, Highfields House, Rempstone Rd, Belton, Loughborough, **Leicestershire**, LE12 9XA, ENG.
(T) 01509 600433 (F) 01509 600433
Speciality: Aromatherapy.
● **Managing Director** Ms G Mathias
M O (Ref:HM08200)

## GOLD, HELENA S

**Helena S Gold**, 67 Knox Green, Binfield, Bracknell, **Berkshire**, RG42 4NZ, ENG.
(T) 01344 459371
Speciality: Chiropodists (Podiatrists).
● **Owner** Mrs H Gold
S (Ref:HM08201)

## GOLD, LULU

**Lulu Gold**, Ravenscroft Medical Centre, 166-168 Golders Green Rd, London, **London (Greater)**, NW11 8BB, ENG.
(T) 020 8209 0922
Speciality: Physiotherapy.
P S T (Ref:HM08202)

## GOLD, P

**P Gold**, Hillside, Blairlogie, Stirling, FK9 5PX, SCO.
(T) 01259 769909 (F) 01259 769909
Speciality: Homeopathy.
● **Owner** Mrs P Gold
M (Ref:HM08203)

## GOLD, STEPHEN

**Stephen Gold**, 18 Park Lane, Newmarket, **Suffolk**, CB8 8AX, ENG.
(T) 01638 667282 (F) 01638 667282
Speciality: Osteopathy.
● **Owner** Mr S Gold
P S T (Ref:HM08204)

## GOLDEN ARROW LEISURE

**Golden Arrow Leisure Ltd**, Irnham Grange, Irnham Rd, Corby Glen, Grantham, **Lincolnshire**, NG33 4NE, ENG.
(T) 01476 550218
Speciality: Aromatherapy.
M O (Ref:HM08205)

## GOLDEN HANDS

**Golden Hands**, 25 Branchalmuir Cres, Newmains, Wishaw, **Lanarkshire (North)**, ML2 9DY, SCO.
(T) 01698 381779
Speciality: Physiotherapy.
● **Owner** Mr G Shaw
P S T (Ref:HM08206)

## GOLDEN PALMS

**Golden Palms**, 96 Station St, Wednesbury, **Midlands (West)**, WS10 8BL, ENG.
(T) 01215 267091
Speciality: Acupressure, Aromatherapy, Bowen Therapy, Holistic Healing, Indian Head Massage, Manipulation, Massage (Therapeutic). ✔
● **Holistic Therapist** Ms N Webb **Q:** IHBC, IIHHT, IIST. **M:** IIBT.
B Yrs. Est.: 5 (Ref:HM08207)

## GOLDEN ROSE

**Golden Rose**, 101C Coldharbour Rd, Bristol, BS6 7SD, ENG.
(T) 01179 420425
Speciality: Complementary Medicines & Therapy.
C M (Ref:HM08208)

## GOLDEN SAFFRON

**Golden Saffron**, Hartington Rd, Toxteth, Liverpool, **Merseyside**, L8 0SH, ENG.
(T) 01512 815233
Speciality: Biomagnetic Therapy, Zero Balancing.
● **Owner** Miss P Loyd
M (Ref:HM08209)

## GOLDEN SQUARE

**Golden Square**, 4 Warwick Pl, Worthing, **Sussex (West)**, BN11 3EU, ENG.
(T) 01903 228044
Speciality: Chiropodists (Podiatrists).
● **Manager** Ms S Gough
S (Ref:HM08210)

## GOLDEN SQUARE

**Golden Square**, Golden Sq, Whaphams, High St, Henfield, **Sussex (West)**, BN5 9DP, ENG.
(T) 01273 493467
Speciality: Chiropodists (Podiatrists).
● **Manager** Ms S Gough
S (Ref:HM08211)

## GOLDEN, JEREMY

**Jeremy Golden**, 5 Elm Trce, Constantine Rd, London, **London (Greater)**, NW3 2LL, ENG.
(T) 020 7267 4222
Speciality: Complementary Medicines & Therapy.
● **Owner** Mr J Golden
M (Ref:HM08212)

## GOLDENBERG, ILANA

**Ilana Goldenberg**, 106 Whitchurch Gardens, Edgware, **London (Greater)**, HA8 6PB, ENG.
(T) 020 8952 2197
Speciality: Osteopathy.
● **Owner** Mrs H Hubbers
P S T (Ref:HM08213)

## GOLDENHEAD HYPNOSIS

**Goldenhead Hypnosis**, 1 Willow Gr, Elton, Chester, **Cheshire**, CH2 4PA, ENG.
(T) 01928 725300
Speciality: Hypnotherapy.
● **Sole Director** Mr C Newton
B (Ref:HM08214)

## GOLDIE, BRENDA

**Brenda Goldie**, Clifton Physiotherapy Clinic, 111 Pembroke Rd, Clifton, Bristol, BS8 3EU, ENG.
(T) 01179 706390
Speciality: Physiotherapy.
P S T (Ref:HM08215)

## GOLDIE, L (DR)

**Dr L Goldie**, 111 Harley St, London, **London (Greater)**, W1N 1DG, ENG.
(T) 020 7935 0977 (F) 020 7935 0728
Speciality: Psychotherapy.
● **Owner** Dr L Goldie
B (Ref:HM08216)

## GOLDIE, RICHARD

**Richard Goldie**, 3 Links View Avenue, Poole, **Dorset**, BH14 9QT, ENG.
(T) 01202 707577
Speciality: Physiotherapy.
● **Owner** Mr R Goldie
P S T (Ref:HM08217)

## GOLDIE, S

**S Goldie**, 133 Wood St, Barnet, **Hertfordshire**, EN5 4BX, ENG.
(T) 020 8449 7656
Speciality: Reflexology.
S T (Ref:HM08218)

## GOLDIE, SUSIE

**Susie Goldie**, 28 Queensborough Court, North Circular Rd, London, **London (Greater)**, N3 3JP, ENG.
(T) 020 8343 1957
Speciality: Reflexology.
S T (Ref:HM08219)

## GOLDIN PAUL CLINIC

**Goldin Paul Clinic**, Knapton Ct York Rd, Dun Laoghaire, **County Dublin**, IRE.
(T) 01280 2797 (F) 01284 4284
Speciality: Hypnotherapy.
B (Ref:HM08220)

## GOLDING, KATE

**Kate Golding**, 21 Bexhill Rd, London, **London (Greater)**, SE4 1RZ, ENG.
(T) 020 8314 5613
Speciality: Homeopathy.
● **Owner** Mrs K Golding
M (Ref:HM08221)

## GOLDING, PAULINE

**Pauline Golding**, 32 The Rowans, Chalfont St. Peter, Gerrards Cross, **Buckinghamshire**, SL9 8SE, ENG.
(T) 01753 883062 (F) 01753 883062
Speciality: Hypnosis.
● **Owner** Mrs P Golding
B (Ref:HM08222)

## GOLDINGHAM, ROMEY

**Romey Goldingham**, Wildings Farm, Beales Lane, Northiam, Rye, **Sussex (East)**, TN31 6LW, ENG.
(T) 01797 253497
Speciality: Reflexology.
S T (Ref:HM08223)

## GOLDMAN, ALAN J

**Alan J Goldman**, 92A Brent St, London, **London (Greater)**, NW4 2ES, ENG.
(T) 020 8202 6008
Speciality: Chiropodists (Podiatrists).
● **Owner** Mr A Goldman
S (Ref:HM08224)

## GOLDMAN, ELLEN

**Ellen Goldman**, 200 King Lane, Moortown, **Yorkshire (West)**, LS17 6AA, ENG.
(T) 01132 160844
Speciality: Hypnosis, Psychotherapy.
B (Ref:HM08225)

## GOLDMAN, T

**T Goldman**, 9 Shirehall Park, London, **London (Greater)**, NW4 2QJ, ENG.
(T) 020 8202 2564
Speciality: Chiropodists (Podiatrists).
S (Ref:HM08226)

## GOLDSMITH, ANNE

**Anne Goldsmith**, 67 Toms Lane, Kings Langley, **Hertfordshire**, WD4 8NJ, ENG.
(T) 01923 265015
Speciality: Reflexology.
● **Owner** Mrs A Goldsmith
S T (Ref:HM08227)

## GOLDSMITH, D

**D Goldsmith**, St Georges Physiotherapy, 22 Carisbrooke High St, Newport, **Isle of Wight**, PO30 1NR, ENG.
(T) 01983 521078
Speciality: Physiotherapy.
P S T (Ref:HM08228)

## GOLDSTONE CLINIC

**Cornelia S Nicholas**, The Goldstone Clinic, 35 Goldstone Villas, Hove, **Sussex (East)**, BN3 3RT, ENG.
(T) 01273 206868
Speciality: Chiropractic, Hypnotherapy. ✔
● **Chiropractor** Ms C Hall **Q:** BA (Hons), BSc (Hons), MSc (Chiro).
● **Chiropractor** Ms C Nicolas **Q:** BCA, DC, MCC, RCST.
● **Chiropractor**
Mr R Brayley Hodgetts **Q:** BA (Hons), Dip.Hyp, ITEC, MRSS.
P Yrs. Est.: 18 (Ref:HM08229)

## GOLDSTONE CLINIC

**Goldstone Clinic (The)**, The Goldstone Clinic, 35 Goldstone Villas, Hove, **Sussex (East)**, BN3 3RT, ENG.
(T) 01273 206868
Speciality: Chiropractic, Massage (Therapeutic), Shiatsu. ✔
● **Chiropractor** Mrs C Nicholas **Q:** DC. **M:** BCA, CC, GCC, RCST.
C T Yrs. Est.: 15 (Ref:HM08230)

## GOLTEN, ROGER

**Roger Golten Hellerwork Practice**, 36 Langley Hill, Kings Langley, **Hertfordshire**, WD4 9HE, ENG.
(T) 01923 400521
Speciality: Hellerwork.
M (Ref:HM08231)

## GOMAN, J

**J Goman**, Nottingham Natural Health Centre, 354 Mansfield Rd, Nottingham, **Nottinghamshire**, NG5 2EF, ENG.
(T) 01159 608855
Speciality: Chiropractors.
P S T (Ref:HM08232)

## GOMAN, JOHN

**John Goman**, 24 Kirk Lane, Ruddington, Nottingham, **Nottinghamshire**, NG11 6NN, ENG.
(T) 01159 405005
Speciality: Chiropractic.

Key: B Mind-Body Medicine C Complementary Medicine H Self Help Treatment M Medicinal Therapy O Oriental Medicine P Postural Therapy S Manipulative Structural Therapy T Touch Therapy

● **Owner** Mr J Goman
P S T (Ref:HM08233)

**GONSTEAD CLINICS UK**

**Gonstead Clinics UK**, 22 Harley St, London, **London (Greater)**, W1N 1AP, ENG.
(T) 020 7637 2920
Speciality: Chiropractors.
P S T (Ref:HM08234)

**GONZALEZ, M A**

**M A Gonzalez**, 6 The Hollows, Wilton, Salisbury, **Wiltshire**, SP2 0JD, ENG.
(T) 01722 744551
Speciality: Reflexology.
S T (Ref:HM08235)

**GONZALEZ, PHYLLIS**

**Phyllis Gonzalez**, Natural Path Health Centre, 3 Holyrood St, Chard, **Somerset**, TA20 2AH, ENG.
(T) 01460 62953 (F) 01460 63809
Speciality: Complementary Medicines & Therapy.
● **Owner** Mr M Newbound
M (Ref:HM08236)

**GONZALEZ, SOHANI**

**Sohani Gonzalez**, 14 Cuthbert Rd, Brighton, **Sussex (East)**, BN2 2EN, ENG.
(T) 01273 689194 (F) 01273 689194
(E) sohani@sohanifsnet.co
Speciality: Holistic Healing, Homeopathy, Naturopathy, Nutritional Therapy. ✔
● **Owner/Homeopath** Mrs S Gonzalez Q: BA, MCH, RSHom. M: Soc.Hom.
B Yrs. Est.: 18 (Ref:HM08237)

**GOOCH, GILL**

**Gill Gooch**, 117 Nunnery Lane, York, **Yorkshire (North)**, YO23 1AH, ENG.
(T) 01904 671191
Speciality: Chiropodists (Podiatrists).
● **Owner** Miss G Gooch
S (Ref:HM08238)

**GOOCH, K W**

**K W Gooch**, Linken Health Natural Therapy Centre, 22 Pallister Rd, Clacton-On-Sea, **Essex**, CO15 1PG, ENG.
(T) 01255 221651
Speciality: Chiropodists (Podiatrists).
● **Owner** Ms L Robinson
S (Ref:HM08239)

**GOOCH, S**

**S Gooch**, 54 Queens Rd, Littlestone, New Romney, **Kent**, TN28 8LY, ENG.
(T) 01797 363875
Speciality: Chiropodists (Podiatrists).
S (Ref:HM08240)

**GOOD HEALTHKEEPING**

**Good Healthkeeping Ltd**, Unit 4, Thames St, Louth, **Lincolnshire**, LN11 7AD, ENG.
(T) 01507 601655 (F) 01507 606655
(E) amanosambodhi@yahoo.com
(W) www.good-healthkeeping.co.uk
Speciality: Anthroposohical Medicine, Bach Remedies, Chiropody, Clinical Ecology, Colour Therapy, Counselling, Crystal Healing, Dietician, Dowsing, Family Planning (Natural), Floral Essence Therapy, Gem Essence Therapy, Hay Diet, Herbal Medicine, Holistic Healing, Homeopathy, Hypnosis, Life Style Coaching, Miasm Therapy, Naturopathy, Nutritional Therapy, Orthomolecular Medicine, Psionic Therapy, Reflexology, Reiki, Rogerian Therapy, Sound Therapy, Vitamin Therapy, Yoga, Non Standard Immunisation Schedules, Non Specific Desensitisation, EDTA Chelation Therapy. ✔ 
● **Health Advisor** Mr R Heighton
(T) 01507 450013 Q: Reiki 3.
● **Health Advisor** Ms P Wilson
(T) 01507 606353 Q: BA, Dip.Couns, Reiki 3, RGN, RM.
● **Health Advisor**
Aline MacInnes-Hurd
(T) 01507 480626 Q: Dip.Couns. M: BACP.
● **Director** Dr P Mansfield Q: MA, MB. M: GMC.
C H Yrs. Est.: 15 (Ref:HM08241)

**GOOD, JEAN**

**Jean Good**, Plush Cloverhill, Cavan, **County Cavan**, IRE.
(T) 04943 38429
Speciality: Aromatherapy.
M O (Ref:HM08242)

**GOODALL, DAVID**

**David Goodall**, 24 Orkney Rd, Portsmouth, **Hampshire**, PO6 3UE, ENG.
(T) 023 9237 1055
Speciality: Chiropodists (Podiatrists).
● **Owner** Mr D Goodall
S (Ref:HM08243)

**GOODALL, L G**

**L G Goodall**, 83 Snape Hill Lane, Dronfield, **Derbyshire**, S18 2GN, ENG.
(T) 01246 412162
Speciality: Chiropodists (Podiatrists).
● **Owner** Mr L Goodall
S (Ref:HM08244)

**GOODALL, PAULINE**

**Pauline Goodall**, 6 Baring Cres, Exeter, **Devon**, EX1 1TL, ENG.
(T) 01392 495405
Speciality: Osteopathy.
● **Owner** Mrs P Goodall
P S T (Ref:HM08245)

**GOODBODYS NATURAL BEAUTY**

**Goodbodys Natural Beauty**, U26 Shopping Ctre, **County Monaghan**, IRE.
(T) 04772 161
Speciality: Beauty Therapy.
H T (Ref:HM08246)

**GOODCHILD & ORR ASSOCIATES**

**Goodchild & Orr Associates**, 2 Trine Court Waldegrave Park, Twickenham, **London (Greater)**, TW1 4TH, ENG.
(T) 020 8891 3267
Speciality: Hypnosis.
B (Ref:HM08247)

**GOODCHILD, GARY J**

**Gary J Goodchild**, 24 The Hawthorns, Marlow Rd, Bishops Waltham, Southampton, **Hampshire**, SO32 1JX, ENG.
(T) 01489 896496
Speciality: Chiropodists (Podiatrists).
● **Owner** Mr G Goodchild
S (Ref:HM08248)

**GOODCHILD, ROGER**

**Roger Goodchild**, 14 Taunton Rd, Bridgwater, **Somerset**, TA6 3LS, ENG.
(T) 01278 444067 (F) 01278 444067
Speciality: Physiotherapy.
● **Owner** Mr R Goodchild
P S T (Ref:HM08249)

**GOODCHILD, ROGER**

**Roger Goodchild**, Ryefields, Cliff Rd, North Petherton, Bridgwater, **Somerset**, TA6 6NY, ENG.
(T) 01278 663098
Speciality: Physiotherapy.
● **Owner** Mr R Goodchild
P S T (Ref:HM08250)

**GOODCHILD, ROGER A**

**Roger A Goodchild**, 10 Brigham Gardens, Biggleswade, **Bedfordshire**, SG18 0LW, ENG.
(T) 01767 220466
Speciality: Osteopathy.
● **Owner** Mr R Goodchild
P S T (Ref:HM08251)

**GOODE, CAROLINE**

**Caroline Goode**, 31 Heol Esgyn, Cardiff, **Glamorgan (Vale of)**, CF23 6JT, WAL.
(T) 029 2076 2141
Speciality: Chiropodists (Podiatrists).
S (Ref:HM08252)

**GOODFELLOW, DONNA**

**Donna Goodfellow**, 82 Godolphin Rd, London, **London (Greater)**, W12 8JW, ENG.
(T) 020 8743 9616
Speciality: Aromatherapy.
● **Owner** Ms D Goodfellow
M O (Ref:HM08253)

**GOODFELLOW, NORMAN S**

**Norman S Goodfellow**, 50 Windermere Rd, Cheltenham, **Gloucestershire**, GL51 5PH, ENG.
(T) 01242 583881
Speciality: Chiropodists (Podiatrists).
S (Ref:HM08254)

**GOODING, NIGEL (DR)**

**Dr Nigel Gooding**, 21 Alma Rd, Reigate, **Surrey**, RH2 0DH, ENG.
(T) 01737 246388
Speciality: Complementary Medicines & Therapy.
M (Ref:HM08255)

**GOODLIFE NATURAL HEALTH CENTRE**

**Goodlife Natural Health Centre**, 207 High St, Sutton, **Surrey**, SM2 5DL, ENG.
(T) 020 8643 0251
Speciality: Osteopathy, Ultrasonics. ✔
● **Osteopath** Ms K Nunn Q: DO. M: GOsC.
S Yrs. Est.: 16 (Ref:HM08256)

**GOODLIFE, JOHN**

**John Goodlife**, 124 Bramcote Lane, Nottingham, **Nottinghamshire**, NG8 2QG, ENG.
(T) 01159 283268
Speciality: Chiropodists (Podiatrists).
● **Owner** Mr J Goodliffe
S (Ref:HM08257)

**GOODMAN, HENRY**

**Henry Goodman**, 1 Simmonds Rise, Hemel Hempstead, **Hertfordshire**, HP3 9EA, ENG.
(T) 01442 257503
(E) h.goodman1@tinyworld.co.uk
Speciality: Cognitive Therapy, Hypnosis, Hypnotherapy, Psychotherapy, Stress Therapy.
● **Owner** Mr H Goodman Q: DipCH.P M: BSCH, NCH.
B Yrs. Est.: 13 (Ref:HM08258)

**GOODMAN, JEAN**

**Jean Goodman**, St. Neots, **Cambridgeshire**, PE19, ENG.
(T) 01480 391303
Speciality: Bach Remedies.
M (Ref:HM08259)

**GOODMAN, JOSEPH & LINDA**

**Joseph & Linda Goodman**, 11 Alderton Cres, London, **London (Greater)**, NW4 3XU, ENG.
(T) 020 8202 6242 (F) 020 8202 6686
Speciality: Osteopathy.
● **Owner** Mr J Goodman
P S T (Ref:HM08260)

**GOODMAN, K (DR)**

**Dr K Goodman**, Brunswick St, Manchester, **Manchester (Greater)**, M13 9ST, ENG.
(T) 01612 732446 (F) 01612 732446
Speciality: Homeopathy.
● **Owner** Dr G Burns
M (Ref:HM08261)

**GOODMAN, LESLEY**

**Lesley Goodman**, Health Hydro, Milton Rd, Swindon, **Wiltshire**, SN1 5JA, ENG.
(T) 01793 465631
Speciality: Chiropractors.
P S T (Ref:HM08262)

**GOODMAN, STEVEN**

**Steven Goodman**, Health Hydro, Milton Rd, Swindon, **Wiltshire**, SN1 5JA, ENG.
(T) 01793 465629
Speciality: Chiropractors.
P S T (Ref:HM08263)

**GOODMAN, WENDY**

**Wendy Goodman**, 86 Cambridge St, St. Neots, **Cambridgeshire**, PE19 1PJ, ENG.
(T) 01480 394715
Speciality: Acupuncture.
O (Ref:HM08264)

**GOODSON, KAREN**

**Karen Goodson**, Tan House, Mill Lane, Longhope, **Gloucestershire**, GL17 0AA, ENG.
(T) 01452 830030
Speciality: Hypnosis, Psychotherapy.
B (Ref:HM08265)

**GOODWILLIE, GILL**

**Gill Goodwillie**, 15 North Hermitage, Shrewsbury, **Shropshire**, SY3 7JW, ENG.
(T) 01743 249194
Speciality: Psychotherapy.



Key continued: **Yrs.Est:** Years Established **Q:** Qualifications **M:** Professional Membership ✔ Indemnity Insurance ▬ Accept Credit Cards

B (Ref:HM08266)

## GOODWIN, HELEN

**Helen Goodwin**, 199 Addington Rd, South Croydon, **Surrey**, CR2 8LN, ENG.
(T) 020 8406 7050
Speciality: Complementary Medicines & Therapy.
M (Ref:HM08267)

## GOODWIN, JO

**Jo Goodwin**, 2 Kenwood Rd, Sheffield, **Yorkshire (South)**, S7 1NP, ENG.
(T) 01142 552048
Speciality: Complementary Medicines & Therapy.
● **Owner** Mr D Wainwright
M (Ref:HM08268)

## GOODWIN, S P

**S P Goodwin**, 13 Edge Lane, Stretford, Manchester, **Manchester (Greater)**, M32 8HN, ENG.
(T) 01618 658126
Speciality: Chiropodists (Podiatrists).
S (Ref:HM08269)

## GOODWIN, SALLY

**Sally Goodwin**, Clermont Rd, Brighton, **Sussex (East)**, BN1, ENG.
(T) 07887 553598
Speciality: Life Style Coaching.
M (Ref:HM08270)

## GOODWIN, SIMON P

**Simon P Goodwin**, 82 Wilmslow Rd, Handforth, Wilmslow, **Cheshire**, SK9 3EW, ENG.
(T) 01625 520382
Speciality: Chiropodists (Podiatrists).
● **Owner** Mr S Goodwin
S (Ref:HM08271)

## GOODWIN, SUSAN

**Susan Goodwin**, Hebdenbridge Centre For Natural Medicine, 33 West End, Hebden Bridge, **Yorkshire (West)**, HX7 8UQ, ENG.
(T) 01422 843517
Speciality: Herbal Medicine.
M (Ref:HM08272)

## GOODYEAR, MARGARET

**Margaret Goodyear**, 1st Floor Woburn Court, 8 Guildhall Hill, Norwich, **Norfolk**, NR2 1JG, ENG.
(T) 01603 219254
Speciality: Homeopathy.
● **Partner** Mrs M Goodyear
M (Ref:HM08273)

## GOOSTREY NATURAL THERAPY CTRE

**Goostrey Natural Therapy Centre**, 174 Main Rd, Goostrey, Crewe, **Cheshire**, CW4 8PA, ENG.
(T) 01477 549040
Speciality: Complementary Medicines & Therapy.
● **Owner** Mrs V Young
C M (Ref:HM08274)

## GOPAUL, V

**V Gopaul**, 40 Church Lane, Oxted, **Surrey**, RH8 9LB, ENG.
(T) 01883 715127
Speciality: Osteopathy.
P S T (Ref:HM08275)

## GORANIA, V D (DR)

**Dr V D Gorania**, 11 Grove Rd, Houghton Regis, Dunstable, **Bedfordshire**, LU5 5PD, ENG.
(T) 01582 861321 (F) 01582 861321
Speciality: Homeopathy.
● **Owner** Dr V Gorania
M (Ref:HM08276)

## GORDON, CHARLES

**Charles Gordon**, 3 Rothbury Trce, Newcastle Upon Tyne, **Tyne and Wear**, NE6 5XH, ENG.
(T) 01912 655358
Speciality: Physiotherapy.
P S T (Ref:HM08277)

## GORDON, JOSEPH

**Joseph Gordon**, Kirklee House, Manor Walk, Fulbourn, Cambridge, **Cambridgeshire**, CB1 5BN, ENG.
(T) 01223 881872
Speciality: Reflexology.
S T (Ref:HM08278)

## GORDON, KAREN

**Karen Gordon**, 95 Ascot Rd, Stafford, **Staffordshire**, ST17 0AQ, ENG.
(T) 01785 259615
Speciality: Reflexology.
● **Owner** Ms K Gordon
S T (Ref:HM08279)

## GORDON, MARIA

**Maria Gordon**, 15 Upton Cl, Ipswich, **Suffolk**, IP4 2QQ, ENG.
(T) 01473 225319
Speciality: Chiropodists (Podiatrists).
● **Owner** Mrs M Gordon
S (Ref:HM08280)

## GORDON, REBECCA

**Rebecca Gordon**, Field Way, St. Leonards-On-Sea, **Sussex (East)**, TN38 8DU, ENG.
(T) 01424 442108
Speciality: Chiropodists (Podiatrists).
● **Owner** Mrs R Gordon
S (Ref:HM08281)

## GORDON, SARAH

**Sarah Gordon**, 78 Richmond Rd, Thornton Heath, **Surrey**, CR7 7QD, ENG.
(T) 020 8665 7704
Speciality: Aromatherapy. ✔
● **Owner/Aromatherapist**
Mrs S Gordon Q: Dip.Hol.Arom. M: IFA.
C Yrs. Est.: 2 (Ref:HM08282)

## GORDON, STEPHEN

**Stephen Gordon**, School House, Market Pl, Kenninghall, Norwich, **Norfolk**, NR16 2AH, ENG.
(T) 01953 887521
Speciality: Homeopathy.
M (Ref:HM08283)

## GORDON, STEVEN

**Steven Gordon**, W E I Clinic, 57A Garland St, Bury St. Edmunds, **Suffolk**, IP33 1EZ, ENG.
(T) 01284 704228
Speciality: Complementary Medicines & Therapy.
M (Ref:HM08284)

## GORDON, TIM (DR)

**Dr Tim Gordon**, 9 Hammersmith Trce, London, **London (Greater)**, W6 9TS, ENG.
(T) 020 8748 9673
Speciality: Acupuncture.
O (Ref:HM08285)

## GORE, JONATHAN & ASSOCIATES

**Jonathan Gore & Associates**, 2 New Church Rd, Hove, **Sussex (East)**, BN3 4FH, ENG.
(T) 01273 770377
Speciality: Osteopathy.
● **Owner** Mr J Gore
P S T (Ref:HM08286)

## GOREY HOLISTIC THERAPIES CTRE

**Gorey Holistic Therapies Centre**, Hillcrest Fort Rd, Gorey, **County Wexford**, IRE.
(T) 05522 849
Speciality: Complementary Medicines & Therapy.
M (Ref:HM08287)

## GORING & STREATLEY OSTEOPATHIC

**Goring & Streatley Osteopathic Clinic**, The Old Golf House, Rectory Rd, Streatley, Reading, **Berkshire**, RG8 9QA, ENG.
(T) 01491 873874 (F) 01491 875587
Speciality: Osteopathy.
● **Owner** Mrs S Swan
P S T (Ref:HM08288)

## GORING PHYSIOTHERAPY & SPORTS

**Goring Physiotherapy & Sports Injury Clinic**, 177 Goring Rd, Goring-By-Sea, Worthing, **Sussex (West)**, BN12 4PA, ENG.
(T) 01903 242261
Speciality: Physiotherapy.
P S T (Ref:HM08289)

## GORING-THOMAS, DIANE

**Diane Goring-Thomas**, Hildenborough, Tonbridge, **Kent**, TN11, ENG.
(T) 01732 838734
Speciality: Aromatherapy, Massage (Therapeutic), Reflexology.
S T (Ref:HM08290)

## GORMAN, J

**J Gorman**, Beta Health Clinic, 67 Marlowes, Hemel Hempstead, **Hertfordshire**, HP1 1LE, ENG.
(T) 01442 249080
Speciality: Chiropodists (Podiatrists).
● **Owner** Mr G Pritchard
S (Ref:HM08291)

## GORMAN, J

**J Gorman**, 110 High St, Tring, **Hertfordshire**, HP23 4AF, ENG.
(T) 01442 822990
Speciality: Chiropodists (Podiatrists).
● **Owner** Mr M Thornton
S (Ref:HM08292)

## GORMAN, JOHN

**John Gorman**, Oaklands, New Mill Lane, Eversley, Hook, **Hampshire**, RG27 0RA, ENG.
(T) 01189 732365 (F) 01189 730250
Speciality: Chiropractic.
● **Partner** Mrs Y Gorman
P S T (Ref:HM08293)

## GORMAN, PETER

**Peter Gorman**, 46 Three Shires Oak Rd, Smethwick, **Midlands (West)**, B67 5BS, ENG.
(T) 01214 291100
Speciality: Chiropodists (Podiatrists).
S (Ref:HM08294)

## GORMLEY, A

**A Gormley**, 60 Glen Rd, Comber, Newtownards, **County Down**, BT23 5QW, NIR.
(T) 028 9187 3136
Speciality: Physiotherapy.
● **Owner** Mrs A Gormley
P S T (Ref:HM08295)

## GORNEY, C

**C Gorney**, 26 Westwood Rd, Sheffield, **Yorkshire (South)**, S11 7EY, ENG.
(T) 01142 295792
(W) www.carry-gorney.co.uk
Speciality: Psychotherapy, Systemic Psychotherapy, Short term solution focused. ✔
● **Owner** Mrs C Gorney Q: BA (Hons), PGD.S.T. M: UKCP.
B Yrs. Est.: 10 (Ref:HM08296)

## GORSE HILL CHIROPODY PRACTICE

**Gorse Hill Chiropody Practice**, Gorse Hill Medical Centre, 879 Chester Rd, Stretford, Manchester, **Manchester (Greater)**, M32 0RN, ENG.
(T) 01618 818101
Speciality: Chiropodists (Podiatrists).
● **Owner** Miss F Shafi
S (Ref:HM08297)

## GOSCHEN, MORIORA

**Moriora Goschen**, The Hale Clinic, 7 Park Cr, London, **London (Greater)**, W1N 3HE, ENG.
(T) 020 7631 0604
Speciality: Complementary Medicines & Therapy.
● **Owner** Ms M Goschen
M (Ref:HM08298)

## GOSHENS THERAPIES

**Goshens Therapies**, 18-20 Tennyson Avenue, Bury, **Lancashire**, BL9 9RF, ENG.
(T) 01617 634954
Speciality: Complementary Medicines & Therapy.
● **Owner** Mrs M Entwithle
C M (Ref:HM08299)

## GOSLING, IMOGEN

**Imogen Gosling**, 36 Yorick Rd, West Mersea, Colchester, **Essex**, CO5 8HU, ENG.
(T) 01206 383436
Speciality: Homeopathy.
● **Owner** Ms I Gosling
M (Ref:HM08300)

## GOSNAY, SHIRLEY ANNE

**Shirley Anne Gosnay**, 3 Holme Way, Ossett, **Yorkshire (West)**, WF5 8DT, ENG.
(T) 01924 264149

Speciality: Complementary Medicines & Therapy.
● Owner Mrs S Gosnay
C M (Ref:HM08301)

## GOSS, LEN

**Len Goss**, 12A St Marys Cl, Epsom, **Surrey**, KT17 2BA, ENG.
(T) 020 8393 6423 (F) 020 8393 6423
Speciality: Clairvoyants & Palmists.
● Owner Mr L Goss
B (Ref:HM08302)

## GOSS, TOM

**Tom Goss**, Rose Cottage, Pound Lane, Stanton St. John, Oxford, **Oxfordshire**, OX33 1HF, ENG.
(T) 01865 351765
Speciality: Psychotherapy.
● Owner Mr T Goss
B (Ref:HM08303)

## GOSSET & HALES

**E Nicholas Gosset & Diane Hales**, 37 High St, Uckfield, **Sussex (East)**, TN22 5DL, ENG.
(T) 01825 763355
Speciality: Osteopathy.
P S T (Ref:HM08304)

## GOSSET, N E

**N E Gosset**, Tile Barn, Lewes Rd, Forest Row, **Sussex (East)**, RH18 5AN, ENG.
(T) 01342 825244
Speciality: Osteopathy.
P S T (Ref:HM08305)

## GOSSIT, N

**N Gossit**, Ferndale, Fox Hill, Haywards Heath, **Sussex (West)**, RH16 4RF, ENG.
(T) 01444 473202 (F) 01444 417652
Speciality: Osteopathy.
● Owner Mr N Gossit
P S T (Ref:HM08306)

## GOSWELL HOUSE CLINIC

**Goswell House Clinic**, 2 Goswell Rd, Street, **Somerset**, BA16 0JG, ENG.
(T) 01458 840071 (F) 01458 840075
Speciality: Osteopathy.
● Owner Mr M Szewiel
P S T (Ref:HM08307)

## GOTHAM VILLAGE PHSYO CLINIC

**Gotham Village Physotherapy Clinic**, 4 Naylor Avenue, Gotham, Nottingham, **Nottinghamshire**, NG11 0HS, ENG.
(T) 01159 830261 (F) 01159 830261
Speciality: Physiotherapy. ✔
● **Physiotherapist** Mrs G Weightman Q: Cert.Ed, Grad Dip Phys, MCSP, SRP.
S Yrs. Est.: 11 (Ref:HM08308)

## GOTHAM, SUE

**Sue Gotham**, Matthews House, 85 Epsom Rd, Guildford, **Surrey**, GU1 3PA, ENG.
(T) 01483 575876
Speciality: Physiotherapy.
P S T (Ref:HM08309)

## GOTHIC

**Gothic**, Market Hall, The Mall, Hyde, **Cheshire**, SK14 2QT, ENG.
(T) 01613 677939
Speciality: Clairvoyants & Palmists.
B (Ref:HM08310)

## GOUDIE, A V

**A V Goudie (M C S P S R P)**, 38 Mill View, Waltham, Grimsby, **Humberside (South)**, DN37 0HQ, ENG.
(T) 01472 822573
Speciality: Physiotherapy.
● Owner Mrs A Goudie
P S T (Ref:HM08311)

## GOUGH, B

**B Gough**, 116 Dartmouth Rd, London, **London (Greater)**, NW2 4HB, ENG.
(T) 020 8452 7517
Speciality: Osteopathy.
P S T (Ref:HM08312)

## GOUGH, B

**B Gough**, Sutherland House, 1a Ashbourne Avenue, London, **London (Greater)**, NW11 0DP, ENG.
(T) 020 8458 7869
Speciality: Osteopathy.
P S T (Ref:HM08313)

## GOUGH, E & P T

**E & P T Gough**, 71 Marsh Rd, Luton, **Bedfordshire**, LU3 2QF, ENG.
(T) 01582 574432
(E) eric@ergo/uk.demon.com
Speciality: Chiropody. ✔
● **Chiropodist** Mr E Gough Q: DPodM, S.R.Ch. M: S.R.Ch.
M Yrs. Est.: 35 (Ref:HM08314)

## GOUGH, J

**J Gough**, 81 Hedgerley Lane, Beaconsfield, **Buckinghamshire**, HP9 2JS, ENG.
(T) 01494 672448
Speciality: Chiropodists (Podiatrists).
● Owner Mrs J Gough
S (Ref:HM08315)

## GOUGH, LOUISE

**Louise Gough**, Penzance Chiropractic Clinic, 7 Chyandour Sq, Penzance, **Cornwall**, TR18 3LW, ENG.
(T) 01736 364912
Speciality: Chiropractic.
P S T (Ref:HM08316)

## GOULD, JENNY

**Jenny Gould**, 7 Mapperley Cl, New Wanstead, London, **London (Greater)**, E11 2SF, ENG.
(T) 020 8518 8732
Speciality: Reflexology.
S T (Ref:HM08317)

## GOULDEN, KATHLEEN

**Kathleen Goulden**, 31 Monastery Rd, Paignton, **Devon**, TQ3 3BU, ENG.
(T) 01803 559971
Speciality: Reflexology.
S T (Ref:HM08318)

## GOURLAY, B

**B Gourlay**, 2 Pendley Bridge Cottages, Tring Station, Tring, **Hertfordshire**, HP23 5QU, ENG.
(T) 01442 822206
Speciality: Psychotherapy.
B (Ref:HM08319)

## GOURLAY, LINDA

**Linda Gourlay**, 28 Cedar Drive, Milton Of Campsie, Glasgow, **Glasgow (City of)**, G66 8AY, SCO.
(T) 01360 310828
Speciality: Complementary Medicines & Therapy.
● Owner Mrs L Gourlay
C M (Ref:HM08320)

## GOURLAY, STEPHEN

**Stephen Gourlay**, 261 Kilmarnock Rd, Glasgow, **Glasgow (City of)**, G41 3JF, SCO.
(T) 01416 323283
Speciality: Chiropodists (Podiatrists).
S (Ref:HM08321)

## GOVAN PSYCHOLOGICAL SERVICES

**Govan Psychological Services**, 102 Copland Rd, Glasgow, **Glasgow (City of)**, G51 2RR, SCO.
(T) 01414 451628
Speciality: Psychology.
B (Ref:HM08322)

## GOVE, J J

**J J Gove**, 56 Normandy St, Alton, **Hampshire**, GU34 1DE, ENG.
(T) 01420 87756
Speciality: Osteopathy.
● Owner Miss J Gove
P S T (Ref:HM08323)

## GOWER, CATHERINE

**Catherine Gower**, Flat 9 Nevile Court, Nevile Rd, Salford, **Manchester (Greater)**, M7 3BS, ENG.
(T) 01617 926966
Speciality: Reflexology.
● Owner Miss C Gower
S T (Ref:HM08324)

## GOWER, MONICA

**Monica Gower**, 109 Brompton Drive, Brierley Hill, **Midlands (West)**, DY5 3NZ, ENG.
(T) 01384 897693
Speciality: Homeopathy.
● Owner Ms M Gower
M (Ref:HM08325)

## GOWING, JOSIE

**Josie Gowing**, 8 Lincoln Rd, Harrow, **London (Greater)**, HA2 7RN, ENG.
(T) 020 8866 8034
Speciality: Reflexology.
S T (Ref:HM08326)

## GOWING, KAY

**Kay Gowing**, Holmdale Cottage, South St, Litlington, Royston, **Hertfordshire**, SG8 0QR, ENG.
(T) 01763 852572
Speciality: Aromatherapy.
M O (Ref:HM08327)

## GOWING, LYNN

**Lynn Gowing**, Jessamines, Station Rd, Woodmancote, Cheltenham, **Gloucestershire**, GL52 9HN, ENG.
(T) 01242 672439
Speciality: Reflexology.
S T (Ref:HM08328)

## GOWLDING, P & N

**P & N Gowlding**, 1 Hartington St, Barrow-in-Furness, **Cumbria**, LA14 5SL, ENG.
(T) 01229 812002
Speciality: Chiropodists (Podiatrists).
● Owner Mr P Gowlding
S (Ref:HM08329)

## GRACE & ASSOCIATES

**Kathryn Grace & Associates**, Unit 30, Sundial House Common Lane, Culcheth, Warrington, **Cheshire**, WA4 2RS, ENG.
(T) 01925 762404
Speciality: Biomechanics, Chiropody, Podiatry. ✔
● **Chiropodist (Podiatrist)** Kathryn Grace Q: S.R.Ch.
M Yrs. Est.: 16 (Ref:HM08331)

## GRACE, MARIE

**Marie Grace**, 76 Pool Farm Rd, Birmingham, **Midlands (West)**, B27 7HD, ENG.
(T) 01217 077264
Speciality: Clairvoyants & Palmists.
B (Ref:HM08332)

## GRACE, NIGEL

**Nigel Grace**, 24A - Trinity Church Gate, Wakefield, **Yorkshire (West)**, WF1 1TX, ENG.
(T) 01924 373353
Speciality: Indian Head Massage, Massage (Therapeutic).
M (Ref:HM08333)

## GRACE, R C E

**R C E Grace**, Redland House Clinic, 118 Redland Rd, Bristol, BS6 6QT, ENG.
(T) 01179 247502
Speciality: Chiropractors.
P S T (Ref:HM08334)

## GRACELINGS NATURAL HEALTH

**Gracelings Natural Health and Beauty Clinic**, 70 Godfreys Gardens, Bow, Crediton, **Devon**, EX17 6HT, ENG.
(T) 01363 82768
Speciality: Aromatherapy, Healing Therapy, Indian Head Massage, Magnetic Therapy, Massage (Therapeutic), Nutritional Therapy, Reflexology, Remedial Massage, Stress Therapy, Swedish Body Massage.
H T (Ref:HM08335)

## GRAHAM & KERSTIN ELLIOTT

**Graham & Kerstin Elliott**, 27 Marshals Drive, St. Albans, **Hertfordshire**, AL1 4RQ, ENG.
(T) 01727 760067
(E) gje@ntlworld.com
Speciality: Alexander Technique, Kinesiology, Re-Education Process. ✔
● Owner Mrs K Elliott M: ATI, STAT.
● Owner Mr G Elliott M: ATI, STAT.
P Yrs. Est.: 7 (Ref:HM08336)

## GRAHAM COOMBE - MCTIMONEY

**Graham Coombe - McTimoney Chiropractor**, 170 Burton Rd, West Didsbury,



Key continued: Yrs.Est: Years Established Q: Qualifications M: Professional Membership ✔ Indemnity Insurance Accept Credit Cards

Manchester, **Manchester (Greater)**, M20 8LH, ENG.
(T) 01614 342723
Speciality: McTimoney Chiropractic, Reiki. ✔
● **McTimoney Chiropractor**
Mr G Coombe Q: Dip.Chiro, RGN. M: GCC.
S Yrs. Est.: 10 (Ref:HM08337)

**GRAHAM COOMBE - MCTIMONEY**
**Graham Coombe - McTimoney Chiropractor**, 221-223 London Rd, Hazel Gr, Stockport, **Cheshire**, SK7 4HS, ENG.
(T) 01614 833314
Speciality: Chiropractic, Reiki. ✔
● **McTimoney Chiropractor**
Mr G Coombe Q: Dip.Chiro, RGN. M: GCC.
S Yrs. Est.: 10 (Ref:HM08338)

**GRAHAM PRIVATE CLINIC**
**Graham Private Clinic M I A H**, Limerick Appointments, IRE.
(T) 08687 76307
(E) tvgraham@gofree.indigo.ie
Speciality: Complementary Medicines & Therapy.
M (Ref:HM08339)

**GRAHAM SPOWAGE OSTEOPATHIC SVS**
**Graham Spowage Osteopathic Services**, 19 St Johns Rd, Stoneygate, Leicester, **Leicestershire**, LE2 2BL, ENG.
(T) 01162 705348
Speciality: Osteopathy. ✔
● **Osteopath** Mr G Spowage Q: BSc, Hons (OST). M: GOsC.
S Yrs. Est.: 5 (Ref:HM08340)

**GRAHAM, CHRISTINE**
**Christine Graham**, 13 Furness Rd, Urmston, Manchester, **Manchester (Greater)**, M41 0UQ, ENG.
(T) 01617 487569
Speciality: Chiropodists (Podiatrists).
● **Owner** Mrs C Graham
S (Ref:HM08341)

**GRAHAM, CHRISTINE**
**Christine Graham**, 373 Bolton Rd, Salford, **Manchester (Greater)**, M6 7NJ, ENG.
(T) 01617 360768
Speciality: Chiropodists (Podiatrists).
S (Ref:HM08342)

**GRAHAM, D (DR)**
**Dr D Graham Psy ,BSc ,PhD ,MIAH**, Psychotherapy/Hypnotherapy Nlp Clinic Main St, Tramore, **County Waterford**, IRE.
(T) 05138 6651
(E) tvgraham@gofree.indigo.ie
Speciality: Complementary Medicines & Therapy.
M (Ref:HM08343)

**GRAHAM, G S**
**G S Graham**, 7 Fellside Rd, Whickham, Newcastle Upon Tyne, **Tyne and Wear**, NE16 4AL, ENG.
(T) 01914 881870
Speciality: Psychotherapy.
● **Owner** Mr G Graham
B (Ref:HM08344)

**GRAHAM, GEOFF**
**Geoff Graham**, 32 Higher Drive, Dawlish, **Devon**, EX7 0AS, ENG.
(T) 01626 864774
Speciality: Hypnosis.
● **Owner** Mr G Graham
B (Ref:HM08345)

**GRAHAM, GILLIAN**
**Gillian Graham**, Primrose Gardens, London, **London (Greater)**, NW3 4TP, ENG.
(T) 020 7586 4456
Speciality: Clairvoyants & Palmists.
● **Owner** Ms G Graham
B (Ref:HM08346)

**GRAHAM, HILARY E**
**Hilary E Graham**, 25 George Rd, West Bridgford, Nottingham, **Nottinghamshire**, NG2 7PT, ENG.
(T) 01159 455290
Speciality: Hypnosis, Psychotherapy.
B (Ref:HM08347)

**GRAHAM, HILARY E**
**Hilary E Graham Hypnotherapist**, 100 Derby Rd, Long Eaton, Nottingham, **Nottinghamshire**, NG10 4LS, ENG.
(T) 01159 726151
Speciality: Hypnosis.
B (Ref:HM09762)

**GRAHAM, J**
**J Graham**, 10 Francis Drive, Chatham, **Kent**, ME5 9LG, ENG.
(T) 01634 681138
Speciality: Osteopathy.
P S T (Ref:HM08348)

**GRAHAM, JANE**
**Jane Graham**, 39 Claddens Quadrant, Glasgow, **Glasgow (City of)**, G22 6LR, SCO.
(T) 01413 367639
Speciality: Reflexology.
S T (Ref:HM08349)

**GRAHAM, JEAN**
**Jean Graham**, Colas Tonne, Collaton, Malborough, Kingsbridge, **Devon**, TQ7 3DJ, ENG.
(T) 01548 561553
Speciality: Physiotherapy.
● **Owner** Mrs J Graham
P S T (Ref:HM08350)

**GRAHAM, KATIE**
**Katie Graham**, 108 London Rd, Neath, **Glamorgan (Vale of)**, SA11 1HL, WAL.
(T) 01639 633292
Speciality: Osteopathy.
P S T (Ref:HM08351)

**GRAHAM, LINDA**
**Linda Graham**, 187 Upper Shoreham Rd, Shoreham-by-Sea, **Sussex (West)**, BN43 6TA, ENG.
(T) 01273 705776
Speciality: Chiropodists (Podiatrists).
S (Ref:HM08352)

**GRAHAM, N**
**N Graham**, Clifton House, 2 Clifton Rd, **Dorset**, BH6 3PA, ENG.
(T) 01202 770007
Speciality: Osteopathy.
P S T (Ref:HM08353)

**GRAHAM, NIGEL**
**Nigel Graham**, The Cottage, 2b Ravensdale Avenue, London, **London (Greater)**, N12 9HS, ENG.
(T) 020 8445 3344
Speciality: Osteopathy.
P S T (Ref:HM08354)

**GRAHAM, NIGEL**
**Nigel Graham**, 199 Burnt Oak Broadway, Edgware, **London (Greater)**, HA8 5EG, ENG.
(T) 020 8952 4405 (F) 020 8445 3344
Speciality: Osteopathy.
P S T (Ref:HM08355)

**GRAHAM, P D**
**P D Graham**, 11 Park Rd, Sutton, **Surrey**, SM3 8QB, ENG.
(T) 020 8643 2086
Speciality: Chiropodists (Podiatrists).
S (Ref:HM08356)

**GRAHAM, P D & M E**
**P D & M E Graham**, 53C North St, Carshalton, **Surrey**, SM5 2HG, ENG.
(T) 020 8669 6485
Speciality: Chiropodists (Podiatrists).
S (Ref:HM08357)

**GRAHAM, PATRICIA**
**Patricia Graham**, 36 Abbotsford Avenue, Birmingham, **Midlands (West)**, B43 6HD, ENG.
(T) 01213 582423
Speciality: Hypnosis.
B (Ref:HM08358)

**GRAHAM, R B**
**R B Graham**, 6 Orchards, Witham, **Essex**, CM8 1DW, ENG.
(T) 01376 511202
Speciality: Chiropodists (Podiatrists).
S (Ref:HM08359)

**GRAHAM, S E**
**S E Graham**, The Bridgeman Centre, 18 Bridgeman Trce, Wigan, **Lancashire**, WN1 1TD, ENG.
(T) 01942 321235
Speciality: Physiotherapy.
P S T (Ref:HM08360)

**GRAHAM, THERESA**
**Theresa Graham BA(Hons) CMIC**, Graham Clinic, Tramore, **County Waterford**, IRE.
(T) 05138 6651
(E) tvgraham@gofree.indigo.ie
Speciality: Complementary Medicines & Therapy.
M (Ref:HM08361)

**GRAHAM, V**
**V Graham**, 61 Meredith Rd, Clacton-On-Sea, **Essex**, CO15 3AG, ENG.
(T) 01255 254595
Speciality: Chiropodists (Podiatrists).
● **Owner** Mr V Graham
S (Ref:HM08362)

**GRAHAM, W A**
**W A Graham**, 10 Ingrebourne Rd, Rainham, **Kent**, RM13 9AL, ENG.
(T) 01708 508641
Speciality: Hypnosis.
● **Owner** Mr W Graham
B (Ref:HM08363)

**GRAHAM-ROWE, CHRISTOPHER P**
**Christopher P Graham-Rowe**, The Chiropodists Surgery, Seemore Shopping Centre, Ossett, **Yorkshire (West)**, WF5 9BN, ENG.
(T) 01924 274003
Speciality: Chiropodists (Podiatrists).
● **Owner** Mr C Graham-Rowe
S (Ref:HM08364)

**GRAINEY**
**Grainey**, Main St, Scariff, **County Clare**, IRE.
(T) 06192 1265
Speciality: Complementary Medicines & Therapy.
M (Ref:HM08365)

**GRAINGER, RACHEL**
**Rachel Grainger**, Grimsby Rd, Caistor, Market Rasen, **Lincolnshire**, LN7 6QY, ENG.
(T) 01472 852053
Speciality: Reflexology.
S T (Ref:HM08366)

**GRAINNE, MULLANY**
**Grainne Mullany**, 12 St. Marys, Victoria Rd, Weybridge, **Surrey**, KT13 9QG, ENG.
(T) 01932 842215
Speciality: Reflexology.
S T (Ref:HM08367)

**GRAMPIAN HOMEOPATHIC PRACTICE**
**Grampian Homeopathic Practice**, 381 Union St, Aberdeen, **Aberdeenshire**, AB11 6BX, SCO.
(T) 01224 590780
Speciality: Complementary Medicines & Therapy.
● **Owner** Ms V Sutherland
M (Ref:HM08368)

**GRANGE CLINIC**
**Grange Clinic**, 39 The Grange, Newbridge, **County Kildare**, IRE.
(T) 04543 1266
Speciality: Complementary Medicines & Therapy.
M (Ref:HM08369)

**GRANGE CONSULTING ROOMS**
**Grange Consulting Rooms (The)**, 92 Whitcliffe Rd, Cleckheaton, **Yorkshire (West)**, BD19 3DR, ENG.
(T) 01274 878600 (F) 01274 869898
Speciality: Psychiatry.
● **Doctor** Dr P Wood
B (Ref:HM08370)

**GRANGE HYPNOTHERAPY**
**Grange Hypnotherapy**, 68 Grange Cres, Chigwell, **Essex**, IG7 5JF, ENG.
(T) 020 8501 4877
Speciality: Hypnosis.



Key: B Mind-Body Medicine C Complementary Medicine H Self Help Treatment M Medicinal Therapy O Oriental Medicine P Postural Therapy S Manipulative Structural Therapy T Touch Therapy

● **Owner** Mrs R Stanley
B (Ref:HM08371)

## GRANGE, DIANA
**Diana Grange**, 19 Elm Gr, Allestree, **Derbyshire**, DE22 2HB, ENG.
(T) 01332 551403
Speciality: Reflexology.
S T (Ref:HM08372)

## GRANGER, J B
**Mr J B Granger**, 26 Thunder Lane, Norwich, **Norfolk**, NR7 0PX, ENG.
(T) 01603 431074
Speciality: Physiotherapy.
P S T (Ref:HM08373)

## GRANNY M'S AROMATHERAPY PRODS
**Granny M's Aromatherapy Products**, Three Corners, Scarcewater Vean, St. Clement, Truro, **Cornwall**, TR1 1TA, ENG.
(T) 01872 242157 (F) 01872 242157
Speciality: Aromatherapy.
● **Owner** Mrs M Whatley
M O (Ref:HM08374)

## GRANT SMITH ASSOCIATES
**Grant Smith Associates**, 52 Clifton Drive, Lytham St. Annes, **Lancashire**, FY8 1AT, ENG.
(T) 01253 735578 (F) 01253 795504
Speciality: Physiotherapy.
● **Owner** Mr M Smith
P S T (Ref:HM08375)

## GRANT SMITH ASSOCIATES
**Grant Smith Associates**, 25 Westby St, Lytham St. Annes, **Lancashire**, FY8 5JF, ENG.
(T) 01253 735728
Speciality: Physiotherapy.
P S T (Ref:HM08376)

## GRANT, C B T (DR)
**Dr C B T Grant**, Chowles, East St, Rusper, Horsham, **Sussex (West)**, RH12 4RH, ENG.
(T) 01293 871425
Speciality: Acupuncture.
● **Owner** Dr C Grant
O (Ref:HM08377)

## GRANT, CARL
**Carl Grant**, 36 Renwick Rd, Blyth, **Northumberland**, NE24 2RG, ENG.
(T) 01670 352053
Speciality: Chiropodists (Podiatrists).
S (Ref:HM08378)

## GRANT, CARL
**Carl Grant**, Fawcett House, Fawcetts Yard, Morpeth, **Northumberland**, NE61 1BG, ENG.
(T) 01670 513205
Speciality: Chiropodists (Podiatrists).
S (Ref:HM08379)

## GRANT, JANE
**Jane Grant**, 12 Nassington Rd, London, **London (Greater)**, NW3 2UD, ENG.
(T) 020 7794 8603
Speciality: Reflexology.
S T (Ref:HM08380)

## GRANT, K
**K Grant**, 16 Cullard Rd, Inverness, **Highland**, IV2 4DL, SCO.
(T) 01463 225391
Speciality: Chiropodists (Podiatrists).
● **Owner** Mrs K Grant
S (Ref:HM08381)

## GRANT, K
**K Grant**, 28 Orchard Rd, Ebley, Stroud, **Gloucestershire**, GL5 4UA, ENG.
(T) 01453 823061 (F) 01453 823061
Speciality: Hypnosis.
● **Owner** Mrs K Grant
B (Ref:HM08382)

## GRANT, L
**L Grant**, 31 St Johns St, Devizes, **Wiltshire**, SN10 1BN, ENG.
(T) 01380 721177
Speciality: Chiropodists (Podiatrists).
● **Partner** Mrs L Grant
S (Ref:HM08383)

## GRANT, L
**L Grant**, 86 Longbrook St, Exeter, **Devon**, EX4 6AP, ENG.
(T) 01392 434074
Speciality: Alexander Technique.
P S (Ref:HM08384)

## GRANT, LESLIE & DAWN
**Leslie & Dawn Grant**, The Tower, 36 Braehead, Bo'ness, **Falkirk**, EH51 9DW, SCO.
(T) 01506 826286
Speciality: Biomechanics, Chiropody, Cryo Surgery, Nail Surgery, Podiatry. ✔
● **Chiropodist (Podiatrist)**
Dawn Grant Q: DPodM, M.S.C.P, S.R.Ch.
● **Chiropodist (Podiatrist)**
Mr L Grant Q: DPodM, M.S.C.P, S.R.Ch.
M Yrs. Est.: 20 (Ref:HM08385)

## GRANT, LESLIE AND DAWN
**Leslie And Dawn Grant**, 14 Kerse Lane, Falkirk, FK1 1RQ, SCO.
(T) 01324 621809
Speciality: Biomechanics, Chiropody, Nail Surgery, Podiatry, Cyro-Surgery. ✔
● **Chiropodist (Podiatrist)**
Leslie Grant Q: DPodM, S.R.Ch. M: S.C.P.
● **Chiropodist (Podiatrist)**
Mrs D Grant Q: DPodM, S.R.Ch. M: S.C.P.
C Yrs. Est.: 20 (Ref:HM08386)

## GRANT, MARION
**Marion Grant**, Country Curls, Main St, Polmont, Falkirk, FK2 0PX, SCO.
(T) 01324 711410
Speciality: Chiropodists (Podiatrists).
● **Owner** Mrs M Grant
S (Ref:HM08387)

## GRANT, MARY
**Mary Grant Lifespring**, 111 Cliftonville Rd, Belfast Bt14 6Jq, IRE.
(T) 04890 748236
Speciality: Complementary Medicines & Therapy.
M (Ref:HM08388)

## GRANT, SUE
**Sue Grant**, 10 Eastwood Cl, London, **London (Greater)**, E18 1BX, ENG.
(T) 020 8502 4674 (F) 020 8508 6032
Speciality: Psychotherapy.
● **Owner** Mrs S Grant
B (Ref:HM08389)

## GRANT, SUSAN
**Susan Grant**, 3 Wychbury Rd, Birmingham, **Midlands (West)**, B32 4DH, ENG.
(T) 01214 757590
Speciality: Reflexology.
S T (Ref:HM08390)

## GRANT, SYLVIA
**Sylvia Grant**, 74 Hillside Gardens, Edgware, **London (Greater)**, HA8 8HD, ENG.
(T) 020 8958 7522
Speciality: Hypnosis.
● **Owner** Mrs S Grant
B (Ref:HM08391)

## GRANTHAM CHIROPODY PRACTICE
**Grantham Chiropody Practice**, 24 St Catherines Rd, Grantham, **Lincolnshire**, NG31 6TT, ENG.
(T) 01476 590029
Speciality: Chiropodists (Podiatrists).
S (Ref:HM08392)

## GRANTHAM CHIROPRACTIC CLINIC
**Grantham Chiropractic Clinic Ltd**, 2-6 North Prde, Grantham, **Lincolnshire**, NG31 8AN, ENG.
(T) 01476 400100 (F) 01476 400101
Speciality: Chiropractic.
● **Owner** Mr S King
P S T (Ref:HM08393)

## GRANTHAM PHYSIO PRACTICE
**Grantham Physiotherapy Practice**, 10 St Catherines Rd, Grantham, **Lincolnshire**, NG31 6TS, ENG.
(T) 01476 593778
(E) beverleymyers@yahoo.co.uk
Speciality: Physiotherapy. ✔
● **Chartered Physiotherapist**
Ms B Myers Q: MCSP, SRP. M: SRP.
S Yrs. Est.: 10 (Ref:HM08394)

## GRANTHAM, P M
**P M Grantham**, 13A Bridgetown, Totnes, **Devon**, TQ9 5AB, ENG.
(T) 01803 865345
Speciality: Chiropodists (Podiatrists).
S (Ref:HM08395)

## GRANVILLE, MARION
**Marion Granville**, Davina House, Fordwych Rd, London, **London (Greater)**, NW2 3TN, ENG.
(T) 020 8452 0308
Speciality: Psychotherapy.
● **Owner** Mrs M Granville
B (Ref:HM08396)

## GRANVILLE, MICHELLE
**Michelle Granville**, 155 High St, Tenterden, **Kent**, TN30 6JS, ENG.
(T) 01580 763481 (F) 01580 763481
Speciality: Reflexology.
● **Owner** Mr J Stevens
S T (Ref:HM08397)

## GRAPEVINE
**Grapevine (The)**, 49 Victoria St, Rothesay, **Argyll and Bute**, PA20 0AP, SCO.
(T) 01700 504414 (F) 01700 504414
Speciality: Crystal Healing, Reiki, Spiritual Healing. ✔
● **Crystal Healer** Ms S McKay
T Yrs. Est.: 7 (Ref:HM08398)

## GRAPEVINE HEALTH
**Grapevine Health**, 18 Gisborne Rd, Sheffield, **Yorkshire (South)**, S11 7HA, ENG.
(T) 01142 683217
(E) nicola@grapevinehealth.co.uk
(W) www.grapevinehealth.co.uk
Speciality: Nutritional Therapy, Reflexology. ✔
● **Therapist** Ms N Gilbert Q: BA (Hons), Dip.Nutrition, Inst.CH.P, MAR. M: AoR, Inst.CH.P.
C Yrs. Est.: 7 (Ref:HM08399)

## GRATION, CHARLIE
**Charlie Gration**, Heathville, Highleadon, Newent, **Gloucestershire**, GL18 1HH, ENG.
(T) 01452 790213
Speciality: Chiropodists (Podiatrists).
● **Owner** Mr C Gration
S (Ref:HM08400)

## GRAVELL, NICOLA
**Nicola Gravell**, The Middle House, 6 Upper Edgeborough Rd, Guildford, **Surrey**, GU1 2BG, ENG.
(T) 01483 571962
Speciality: Hypnosis, Hypnotherapy.
● **Hypnotherapist/Psychotherapist**
Ms N Gravell Q: BA (Hons), Dip.Hyp, Dip.Psych. M: NCH, NRHP.
H Yrs. Est.: 19 (Ref:HM08401)

## GRAVELLS, M
**M Gravells**, 19 Main St, Heslington, York, **Yorkshire (North)**, YO10 5EA, ENG.
(T) 01904 431244
Speciality: Homeopathy.
M (Ref:HM08402)

## GRAVES, CELIA
**Celia Graves**, 18 Oakfield, Lodsworth, Petworth, **Sussex (West)**, GU28 9BL, ENG.
(T) 01798 861903 (F) 01798 861820
Speciality: Acupuncture.
● **Owner** Mr C Graves
O (Ref:HM08403)

## GRAVESEND HOMOEOPATHY CLINIC
**Gravesend Homoeopathy Clinic**, 20 Pine Avenue, Gravesend, **Kent**, DA12 1QZ, ENG.
(T) 01474 355204
(E) homeopath@consultant.com
Speciality: Homeopathy.
● **Homeopath**
Giovanna Farrugia-Forrester Q: BA (Hons), LCH. M: Soc.Hom.
M Yrs. Est.: 6 (Ref:HM08404)


Key continued: Yrs.Est: Years Established Q: Qualifications M: Professional Membership ✔ Indemnity Insurance Accept Credit Cards

## GRAVILLE, CHRIS
**Chris Graville**, 2 Ferrymead Court, The Meadway, Shoreham-by-Sea, **Sussex (West)**, BN43 5RN, ENG.
(T) 01273 440599
Speciality: Aromatherapy. ✔
● **Aromatherapist** C Graville Q: Dip.Arom. M: IHBC, ITEC.
C Yrs. Est.: 25 (Ref:HM08405)

## GRAVINA, A (DR)
**Dr A Gravina MB BCH**, 6 Block B Harley Ct White Oaks Wilton, **County Cork**, IRE.
(T) 021 4546 087
Speciality: Complementary Medicines & Therapy.
M (Ref:HM08406)

## GRAVITT CLINIC
**Gravitt Clinic (The)**, Physiotherapy Centre, 7 Boughton Prde, Loose Rd, Maidstone, **Kent**, ME15 9QD, ENG.
(T) 01622 743439
Speciality: Physiotherapy.
P S T (Ref:HM08407)

## GRAY, ALAN
**Alan Gray**, 133 Staincliffe Rd, Dewsbury, **Yorkshire (West)**, WF13 4EF, ENG.
(T) 01924 468142
Speciality: Hypnotherapy.
● **Owner** Mr A Gray
B (Ref:HM08408)

## GRAY, BARBARA
**Barbara Gray**, 254 Smedley St, Matlock, **Derbyshire**, DE4 3LH, ENG.
(T) 01629 584419
Speciality: Complementary Medicines & Therapy.
● **Owner** Ms B Gray
C M (Ref:HM08409)

## GRAY, CHRISTINE
**Christine Gray**, 2 Ravens Court, Neath, **Glamorgan (Vale of)**, SA11 3SX, WAL.
(T) 01639 632525
Speciality: Chiropodists (Podiatrists).
● **Owner** Mrs C Gray
S (Ref:HM08410)

## GRAY, F
**F Gray**, 1 Garden Trce, Lothersdale, Keighley, **Yorkshire (West)**, BD20 8ER, ENG.
(T) 01535 630675
Speciality: Chiropodists (Podiatrists).
S (Ref:HM08411)

## GRAY, FRANCESCA
**Francesca Gray**, Clissold Park Health Centre, 154 Stoke Newington Church Stre, London, **London (Greater)**, N16 0JU, ENG.
(T) 020 7249 2990 (F) 020 7249 3977
Speciality: Homeopathy.
● **Owner** Mr D Berg
M (Ref:HM08412)

## GRAY, J F
**J F Gray**, Kuchana, 11 St Martins Lane, Marshfield, Chippenham, **Wiltshire**, SN14 8LZ, ENG.
(T) 01225 891115
Speciality: Homeopathy.
M (Ref:HM08413)

## GRAY, MARGARET
**Margaret Gray**, Bournside Court, Bournside Rd, Cheltenham, **Gloucestershire**, GL51 5AH, ENG.
(T) 01242 254207
Speciality: Reflexology.
S T (Ref:HM08414)

## GRAY, NORMAN R
**Norman R Gray**, 1 Abbey Trce, Tewkesbury, **Gloucestershire**, GL20 5SP, ENG.
(T) 01684 298053 (F) 01684 298053
Speciality: Reflexology.
● **Owner** Mr N Gray
S T (Ref:HM08415)

## GRAY, P A
**P A Gray**, The Surgery, 3 Anson Cl, South Woodham Ferrers, Chelmsford, **Essex**, CM3 5YJ, ENG.
(T) 01245 323767
Speciality: Chiropodists (Podiatrists).
S (Ref:HM08416)

## GRAY, P A
**P A Gray**, Shencot, Alexander Lane, Hutton, Brentwood, **Essex**, CM13 1AG, ENG.
(T) 01277 263122
(W) www.pgray.co.uk
Speciality: Biomechanics, Chiropody, Nail Surgery, Orthotics. ✔
● **Chiropodist** Mr P Gray Q: M.S.C.P, S.R.Ch. M: S.C.P.
M Yrs. Est.: 18 (Ref:HM08417)

## GRAY, S
**S Gray**, 1 Wistoria Court, Westbourne, **Essex**, CO4 3QH, ENG.
(T) 07718 946161
Speciality: Complementary Medicines & Therapy.
● **Owner** Samantha Gray
M (Ref:HM08418)

## GRAY, SHEILA
**Sheila Gray**, Yew Tree Cottage, Methlick, Ellon, **Aberdeenshire**, AB41 7DU, SCO.
(T) 01651 806471
Speciality: Bowen Therapy, Reflexology, Reiki, Personal Coaching. ✔
● **Therapist** Ms S Gray Q: BTER, GSSR, MA. M: BTER, SIR.
T Yrs. Est.: 10 (Ref:HM08419)

## GRAY, W R
**W R Gray**, Southgate Lodge, Middle Handley, Sheffield, **Yorkshire (South)**, S21 5RN, ENG.
(T) 01246 435450
Speciality: Psychotherapy.
B (Ref:HM08420)

## GRAY, WENDY
**Wendy Gray**, 25 Lower Gungate, Tamworth, **Staffordshire**, B79 7AT, ENG.
(T) 01827 68374
Speciality: Aromatherapy.
M O (Ref:HM08421)

## GRAYBURN-HALE, DAVID
**David Grayburn Hale**, 69 Chichester Avenue, Dudley, **Midlands (West)**, DY2 9JL, ENG.
(T) 01384 235009 (F) 01384 235009
Speciality: Hypnosis.
● **Owner** Mr D Hale
B (Ref:HM08422)

## GRAYLING, N P
**N P Grayling**, 13 Grenada Cl, Bexhill-on-Sea, **Sussex (East)**, TN39 3TN, ENG.
(T) 01424 842456
Speciality: Chiropodists (Podiatrists).
● **Owner** Mrs N Grayling
S (Ref:HM08423)

## GRAYS CHIROPRACTIC CLINIC
**Grays Chiropractic Clinic**, 6 London Rd, Grays, **Essex**, RM17 5XY, ENG.
(T) 01375 391999
Speciality: Chiropractic.
P S T (Ref:HM08424)

## GRAYSHOTT ELECTRO-ACUPUNCTURE
**Grayshott Electro-Acupuncture**, Woodlands, 87 Wheelwrights Lane, Grayshott, Hindhead, **Surrey**, GU26 6EB, ENG.
(T) 01428 606158
Speciality: Acupuncture.
● **Owner** Mr A Chandler
O (Ref:HM08425)

## GRAYSON, C M & R J
**C M & R J Grayson**, 38 Deepdale Rd, Rotherham, **Yorkshire (South)**, S61 2NT, ENG.
(T) 01709 556186
Speciality: Chiropodists (Podiatrists).
S (Ref:HM08426)

## GRAYSON, NEIL W
**Neil W Grayson**, 1 Burbo Way, Wallasey, **Merseyside**, CH45 3NP, ENG.
(T) 01516 391936
Speciality: Herbalists.
M (Ref:HM08427)

## GRAYSTON, SUE
**Mrs Sue Grayston**, 32 Galsworthy Rd, Tilbury, **Essex**, RM18 8JS, ENG.
(T) 01375 846964
Speciality: Chiropodists (Podiatrists).
● **Owner** Mrs S Graystone
S (Ref:HM08428)

## GREAR, M D
**M D Grear**, 36 Lumley Rd, Horley, **Surrey**, RH6 7JL, ENG.
(T) 01293 782513
Speciality: Chiropodists (Podiatrists).
S (Ref:HM08429)

## GREAT BARR OSTEO PRACTICE
**Great Barr Osteopathic Practice**, 7a Newton Rd, Great Barr, Birmingham, **Midlands (West)**, B43 6AA, ENG.
(T) 01213 579078
Speciality: Osteopathy. ✔
● **Osteopath** Mamta Narayan Q: DO. M: GOsC.
S Yrs. Est.: 3 (Ref:HM08430)

## GREAT SANKEY PHYSIOTHERAPY
**Great Sankey Physiotherapy**, Great Sankey Leisure Centre, Barrow Hall Lane, Great Sankey, Warrington, **Cheshire**, WA5 3AA, ENG.
(T) 01925 729981
Speciality: Physiotherapy.
● **Owner** Mrs J Barnfield
P S T (Ref:HM08431)

## GREAVES HERBALIST
**Greaves Herbalist**, 167 Alfreton Rd, Nottingham, **Nottinghamshire**, NG7 3JR, ENG.
(T) 01159 106606
Speciality: Herbal Medicine.
● **Owner** Mr R Fincham
M (Ref:HM08432)

## GREAVES, N
**N Greaves**, 155 Alfreton Rd, Nottingham, **Nottinghamshire**, NG7 3JR, ENG.
(T) 01159 786173
Speciality: Herbalists.
● **Owner** Mr N Greaves
M (Ref:HM08433)

## GREEN BATT PHYSIOTHERAPY
**Green Batt Physiotherapy & Sports Injuries Clinic**, 22 Green Batt, Alnwick, **Northumberland**, NE66 1TS, ENG.
(T) 01665 602427 (F) 01665 602427
(E) gandjfeltham@onetel.net.uk
Speciality: Bach Remedies, Electrotherapy, Manipulation, Massage (Therapeutic), Ultrasonics. ✔
● **Owner** Mr G Feltham Q: MCSP, SRP. M: CSP.
S Yrs. Est.: 15 (Ref:HM08434)

## GREEN FARM CLINIC
**Green Farm Clinic**, Green Farm, The St, Pettistree, Woodbridge, **Suffolk**, IP13 0HU, ENG.
(T) 01728 747511
Speciality: Manipulation, Physiotherapy, Hydrotherapy. ✔
● **Physiotherapist** Ms J Whinney M: CSP.
● **Owner** Dr P Hayward Q: BS, MB. M: GMC.
P S (Ref:HM08435)

## GREEN LODGE CENTRE
**Green Lodge Centre For Intergrated Natural Med (The)**, Russells Rd, Halstead, **Essex**, CO9 1SN, ENG.
(T) 01787 475195
Speciality: Complementary Medicines & Therapy.
C M (Ref:HM08436)

## GREEN MAN (THE)
**Green Man (The)**, 1 Meadway, Woolavington, Bridgwater, **Somerset**, TA7 8HA, ENG.
(T) 01278 685085
Speciality: Clairvoyants & Palmists.
● **Owner** Mr R Cooper
B (Ref:HM08437)

## GREEN MEDIC
**Green Medic**, 47 Blackstock Rd, London, **London (Greater)**, N4 2JF, ENG.
(T) 020 7359 8836 (F) 020 7359 8836
Speciality: Complementary Medicines &

Key: B Mind-Body Medicine; C Complementary Medicine; H Self Help Treatment; M Medicinal Therapy; O Oriental Medicine; P Postural Therapy; S Manipulative Structural Therapy; T Touch Therapy

Therapy.
● **Manager** Mr J Cao
M (**Ref:**HM08438)

### GREEN PARK CLASSICAL OSTEOPATH

**Green Park Classical Osteopath**, Room 116, 11 Berkeley St, London, **London (Greater)**, W1X 6BU, ENG.
(T) 020 7355 5018 (F) 020 7355 5050
Speciality: Osteopathy.
● **Owner** Mr J Donald
P S T (**Ref:**HM08439)

### GREEN PHARMACY COMP MED

**Green Pharmacy Complementary Medicine**, 128 London Rd North, Lowestoft, **Suffolk**, NR32 1HB, ENG.
(T) 01502 587654
Speciality: Complementary Medicines & Therapy.
C M (**Ref:**HM08440)

### GREEN ROAD HEALING CENTRE

**Green Road Healing Centre**, Green Rd, The Curragh, **County Kildare**, IRE.
(T) 04544 2323 (F) 04544 2323
(E) greenrd@eircom.net
Speciality: Aromatherapy, Bach Remedies, Complementary Therapy, Holistic Healing, Indian Head Massage, Massage (Therapeutic), Reflexology, Touch Therapy. ✔
● **Therapist** Maura Barry Q: ITEC.
T Yrs. Est.: 3 (**Ref:**HM08441)

### GREEN ROOMS

**Green Rooms (The)**, 22 Mountfield Rd, Eastbourne, **Sussex (East)**, BN22 9BS, ENG.
(T) 01323 520813
Speciality: Complementary Medicines & Therapy.
C M (**Ref:**HM08442)

### GREEN VALLEY THERAPY CENTRE

**Green Valley Therapy Centre**, 135 Stratford Rd, Shirley, Solihull, **Midlands (West)**, B90 3AY, ENG.
(T) 01217 443600
Speciality: Acupuncture, Allergy Testing, Aromatherapy, Bowen Therapy, Counselling, Holistic Healing, Homeopathy, Hypnotherapy, Indian Head Massage, Kinesiology, Massage (Therapeutic), Nutritional Therapy, Energy Field Therapy, Personal Training, Wellness Screening. ✔
● **Aromatherapist** Ms J Mason
● **Homeopath** Mr B Taylor Q: BSc (Hons), LCPH, MCPH, MHMA. M: HMA.
● **Kinesiology** Mr S Kempson
● **Hypnotherapist** Meryl Mulat
● **Nutritionist** Mr J Kelsy Q: Dip.Nutrition, PhD.
● **Energy Field Therapy** Anita Tailer
● **Manager** Mr A Ryder
● **Bowen Technique** Sandria Marks
● **Personal Trainer** Grant Allen
● **Owner/Aromatherapist** Mrs D Ryder Q: Dip.APMASS, Dip.Arom, DM, MICHT. M: ICHT.
C Yrs. Est.: 1 (**Ref:**HM08443)

### GREEN YARDS NATURAL HEALTH

**Green Yards Natural Health Clinic**, 12 Allerton Rd, Wallasey, **Merseyside**, CH45 6UW, ENG.
(T) 01516 301870
Speciality: Acupuncture.
O (**Ref:**HM08444)

### GREEN, A J

**A J Green**, Greenacres, Forthvean Rd, Porthtowan, Truro, **Cornwall**, TR4 8AY, ENG.
(T) 01209 890170 (F) 01209 890170
Speciality: Chiropodists (Podiatrists).
● **Owner** Mrs A Green
S (**Ref:**HM08445)

### GREEN, A L

**A L Green**, The Mount, Salters Lane, Tamworth, **Staffordshire**, B79 8BH, ENG.
(T) 01827 310910
Speciality: Chiropractors.
● **Owner** Dr D Eldridge
P S T (**Ref:**HM08446)

### GREEN, ANN

**Ann Green**, 15 Millway Drive, Bishops Tachbrook, Leamington Spa, **Warwickshire**, CV33 9SE, ENG.
(T) 01926 424199
Speciality: Chiropodists (Podiatrists).
● **Owner** Mrs A Green
S (**Ref:**HM08447)

### GREEN, B

**B Green**, 14 Eastcote Lane, Harrow, **London (Greater)**, HA2 8BP, ENG.
(T) 020 8422 1411
Speciality: Chiropodists (Podiatrists).
S (**Ref:**HM08448)

### GREEN, BRIAN

**Brian Green**, 85 Nixons Lane, Blakehall, Skelmersdale, **Lancashire**, WN8 9BE, ENG.
(T) 01695 721245
Speciality: Chiropodists (Podiatrists).
● **Owner** Mr B Green
S (**Ref:**HM08449)

### GREEN, C M

**C M Green**, 105A High St, Fraserburgh, **Aberdeenshire**, AB43 9EX, SCO.
(T) 01346 518062
Speciality: Chiropodists (Podiatrists).
S (**Ref:**HM08450)

### GREEN, C M

**C M Green**, 187 Princes St, Dundee, **Angus**, DD4 6DQ, SCO.
(T) 01382 452222
Speciality: Chiropodists (Podiatrists).
S (**Ref:**HM08451)

### GREEN, DANA

**Dana Green**, 7 Holly Rd, Northampton, **Northamptonshire**, NN1 4QL, ENG.
(T) 01604 231088
Speciality: Chiropractors.
P S T (**Ref:**HM08452)

### GREEN, DAVID

**David Green**, 12 High St South, Dunstable, **Bedfordshire**, LU6 3HA, ENG.
(T) 01582 727453
Speciality: Chiropodists (Podiatrists).
● **Owner** Mr D Green
S (**Ref:**HM08453)

### GREEN, ELIZABETH

**Elizabeth Green**, 32 Old Crossing Rd, Margate, **Kent**, CT9 5JH, ENG.
(T) 01843 231949
Speciality: Reflexology.
S T (**Ref:**HM08454)

### GREEN, GEOFFREY C

**Geoffrey C Green**, Braeside, Station Rd, Steyning, **Sussex (West)**, BN44 3YL, ENG.
(T) 01903 812458
Speciality: Osteopathy.
P S T (**Ref:**HM08455)

### GREEN, GILLIAN

**Gillian Green**, The Watermill, Mill Lane, Heyington, Lincoln, **Lincolnshire**, LN4 1RQ, ENG.
(T) 01522 793564 (F) 01522 794941
Speciality: Reflexology.
● **Owner** Mrs G Green
S T (**Ref:**HM08456)

### GREEN, J

**J Green**, 19 Isis Avenue, Bicester, **Oxfordshire**, OX6 8GR, ENG.
(T) 01869 244120
Speciality: Chiropodists (Podiatrists).
● **Employee** Mrs J Green
S (**Ref:**HM08457)

### GREEN, J

**J Green**, 5 Copperfields, Tarporley, **Cheshire**, CW6 0UP, ENG.
(T) 01829 732629
Speciality: Physiotherapy.
P S T (**Ref:**HM08458)

### GREEN, J

**J Green**, 12 Park Hill, Bury Old Rd, Prestwich, Manchester, **Manchester (Greater)**, M25 0FX, ENG.
(T) 01617 958101
Speciality: Chiropodists (Podiatrists).
● **Owner** Mrs J Green
S (**Ref:**HM08459)

### GREEN, J A

**J A Green**, 7 Oundle Rd, Chesterton, Peterborough, **Cambridgeshire**, PE7 3UA, ENG.
(T) 01733 233213
Speciality: Chiropodists (Podiatrists).
S (**Ref:**HM08460)

### GREEN, JENNY

**Jenny Green**, 28 Wilbury Rd, Hove, **Sussex (East)**, BN3 3JP, ENG.
(T) 01273 733830
Speciality: Hypnosis.
B (**Ref:**HM08461)

### GREEN, JESSICA

**Jessica Green**, 102 Rowheath Rd, Birmingham, **Midlands (West)**, B30 2EX, ENG.
(T) 01214 511018
Speciality: Electrolysis.
● **Owner** Mrs J Green
T (**Ref:**HM08462)

### GREEN, JULIA

**Julia Green**, 286 Ashley Down Rd, Bristol, BS7 9BQ, ENG.
(T) 01179 248133
Speciality: Herbal Medicine.
M (**Ref:**HM08463)

### GREEN, JULIA

**Julia Green**, 40 Lansdown Rd, Redland, Bristol, BS6 6NS, ENG.
(T) 01179 731520
Speciality: Alexander Technique.
● **Partner** Mr C Tully
P S (**Ref:**HM08464)

### GREEN, JULIA A

**Julia A Green**, 1 Oak Farm Cottages, Hog Lane, Ashley Green, Chesham, **Buckinghamshire**, HP5 3PS, ENG.
(T) 01442 870733
Speciality: Osteopathy.
P S T (**Ref:**HM08465)

### GREEN, K B

**K B Green**, The Laurels, 39 Rickmansworth Rd, Watford, **Hertfordshire**, WD1 7HS, ENG.
(T) 01923 221303
Speciality: Osteopathy.
● **Owner** Mr M Tunmore
P S T (**Ref:**HM08466)

### GREEN, M

**M Green**, 7-9 Hawley Sq, Margate, **Kent**, CT9 1PF, ENG.
(T) 01843 292056 (F) 01843 299347
Speciality: Osteopathy.
P S T (**Ref:**HM08467)

### GREEN, MEG

**Meg Green**, 90 George St, Basingstoke, **Hampshire**, RG21 7RW, ENG.
(T) 01256 410126
Speciality: Hypnotherapy.
● **Owner** Ms M Green
B (**Ref:**HM08468)

### GREEN, NANCY

**Nancy Green**, 20 Hartington Rd, Manchester, **Manchester (Greater)**, M21 8UY, ENG.
(T) 01618 810733
Speciality: Homeopathy.
M (**Ref:**HM08469)

### GREEN, PAULINE

**Pauline Green**, 16 Ridgeway, Barrowford, Nelson, **Lancashire**, BB9 8QP, ENG.
(T) 01282 611263 (F) 01282 611262
Speciality: Clairvoyants & Palmists.
● **Owner** Mrs P Green
B (**Ref:**HM08470)

### GREEN, PAULINE

**Pauline Green**, 164 Rochfords Gardens, Slough, **Berkshire**, SL2 5XL, ENG.
(T) 01753 537267
Speciality: Complementary Medicines & Therapy.



Key continued: **Yrs.Est:** Years Established **Q:** Qualifications **M:** Professional Membership ✔ Indemnity Insurance [card] Accept Credit Cards

C M (Ref:HM08471)

## GREEN, PETER J
**Peter J Green**, 70 High St, Pershore, **Worcestershire**, WR10 1DU, ENG.
(T) 01386 555365
Speciality: Osteopathy.
P S T (Ref:HM08472)

## GREEN, S
**S Green**, 272 Gordon Avenue, Camberley, **Surrey**, GU15 2NU, ENG.
(T) 01276 20411 (F) 01276 20411
Speciality: Osteopathy.
● **Owner** Mr S Green
P S T (Ref:HM08473)

## GREEN, S P
**S P Green**, 21 Lees Rd, Nottingham, **Nottinghamshire**, NG3 6HB, ENG.
(T) 01159 530282
Speciality: Chiropodists (Podiatrists).
S (Ref:HM08474)

## GREEN, STEVE
**Steve Green**, 2 Plumtree Cottages, High St, Prestwood, Great Missenden, **Buckinghamshire**, HP16 9ER, ENG.
(T) 01494 865997
Speciality: Chiropodists (Podiatrists).
S (Ref:HM08475)

## GREEN, T
**T Green**, 29 High St, Stalbridge, Sturminster Newton, **Dorset**, DT10 2LH, ENG.
(T) 01963 363127
Speciality: Aromatherapy.
● **Owner** Miss T Green
M O (Ref:HM08476)

## GREEN, TRACEY
**Tracey Green**, 45B Clavering Avenue, London, **London (Greater)**, SW13 8DX, ENG.
(T) 020 8408 2765
Speciality: Reflexology.
S T (Ref:HM08477)

## GREEN, VICTORIA
**Victoria Green**, 137 Magdalen Rd, Oxford, **Oxfordshire**, OX4 1RJ, ENG.
(T) 01865 396939
Speciality: Reflexology.
● **Owner** Mr M Franklin
S T (Ref:HM08478)

## GREEN, W
**W Green**, 10 Eldon Rd, Reading, **Berkshire**, RG1 4DH, ENG.
(T) 01189 502002
Speciality: Physiotherapy.
P S T (Ref:HM08479)

## GREENCADES
**Greencades**, 5 Watermill Way, London, **London (Greater)**, SW19 2RD, ENG.
(T) 020 8543 0519 (F) 020 8543 3553
Speciality: Aromatherapy.
● **Manager** Mrs J Waddon
M O (Ref:HM08480)

## GREENCROFT THERAPY CLINIC
**Greencroft Therapy Clinic**, Carey Hill Rd, Stoney Stanton, Leicester, **Leicestershire**, LE9 4LA, ENG.
(T) 01455 271533
Speciality: Complementary Medicines & Therapy.
C M (Ref:HM08481)

## GREENE, STEFANI
**Stefani Greene**, 281 Sauchiehall St, Glasgow, **Glasgow (City of)**, G2 3HQ, SCO.
(T) 01413 531633
Speciality: Aromatherapy.
M O (Ref:HM08482)

## GREENFIELD AVE CONSULTING ROOM
**Greenfield Avenue Consulting Room**, 19 Greenfield Avenue, Stourbridge, **Midlands (West)**, DY8 1SX, ENG.
(T) 01384 394033
Speciality: Physiotherapy.
P S T (Ref:HM08483)

## GREENFIELD, BRIAN
**Brian Greenfield**, 88 Swan Lane, Sellindge, Ashford, **Isle of Wight**, PO33 2TU, ENG.
(T) 01303 813549
(E) braingreenfield@btinternet.com
Speciality: Acupressure, Aromatherapy, Auricular Therapy, Colour Therapy, Complementary Therapy, Healer, Healing Therapy, Holistic Healing, Indian Head Massage, Massage (Therapeutic), Meditation, Spiritual Healing, Stress Therapy, Creative Visualisation, Relaxation, Thermo - (Ear Candles). ✓
● **Owner/Stress Management Counsultant** Mr B Greenfield Q: Cert.Ed, ITEC, MIAC, NFSH. M: IAC, NFSH.
B Yrs. Est.: 3 (Ref:HM08484)

## GREENFIELD, J
**J Greenfield**, 30 Ruskin Avenue, Rogerstone, Newport, NP10 0AA, WAL.
(T) 01633 893467
Speciality: Reflexology.
S T (Ref:HM08485)

## GREENFIELD, KAREN
**Karen Greenfield**, 24 Norbury Drive, Lancing, **Sussex (West)**, BN15 0QN, ENG.
(T) 01903 751535
Speciality: Reflexology. ✓
● **Reflexologist** Ms K Greenfield
T Yrs. Est.: 2 (Ref:HM08486)

## GREENFIELD, T A
**T A Greenfield**, First Floor, 157 Ashley Rd, Hale, Altrincham, **Cheshire**, WA14 2UW, ENG.
(T) 01619 290361
Speciality: Psychology.
● **Principal** Dr T Greenfield
B (Ref:HM08487)

## GREENFORD, S P
**S P Greenford**, 11 Park Cres, Abingdon, **Oxfordshire**, OX14 1DF, ENG.
(T) 01235 521724
Speciality: Chiropodists (Podiatrists).
● **Owner** Ms S Greenford
S (Ref:HM08488)

## GREENHALGH, A J T
**A J T Greenhalgh**, 58A King St, Blackburn, **Lancashire**, BB2 2DT, ENG.
(T) 01254 682268
Speciality: Chiropody, Nail Surgery, Podiatry. ✓
● **Owner/Chiropodist**
Mr A Greenhalgh Q: DPodM, S.R.Ch. M: S.C.P.
M Yrs. Est.: 11 (Ref:HM08489)

## GREENHALGH, KEITH
**Keith Greenhalgh**, 69 Marine Drive, Rhos On Sea, Colwyn Bay, **Conwy**, LL28 4HT, WAL.
(T) 01492 547525
Speciality: Osteopathy.
P S T (Ref:HM08490)

## GREENHALGH, P
**P Greenhalgh**, 110 Conway Rd, Colwyn Bay, **Conwy**, LL29 7LL, WAL.
(T) 01492 531542
Speciality: Osteopathy.
● **Partner** Mrs A Greenhalgh
P S T (Ref:HM08491)

## GREENHALGH, S
**S Greenhalgh**, 115 Blackburn Rd, Darwen, **Lancashire**, BB3 1ET, ENG.
(T) 01254 773203
Speciality: Chiropodists (Podiatrists).
S (Ref:HM08492)

## GREENMOUNT HYPNOTHERAPY CENTRE
**Greenmount Hypnotherapy Centre**, 5 Kimble Cl, Greenmount, Bury, **Lancashire**, BL8 4QQ, ENG.
(T) 01204 884826
Speciality: Hypnosis.
● **Owner** Mr M Barlow
B (Ref:HM08493)

## GREENS HEALTH FOODS
**Greens Health Foods**, 175 High St, Lincoln, **Lincolnshire**, LN5 7AF, ENG.
(T) 01522 524874 (F) 01522 523533
Speciality: Aromatherapy, Bach Remedies, Herbal Medicine, Homeopathy, Vitamin Therapy. CREDIT
● **Owner** Mr W Heath M: BHMA, Inst.HFR, NAHS.
H M Yrs. Est.: 91 (Ref:HM08494)

## GREENWAY CONSULTANCY
**Greenway Consultancy**, 15 Greenway St, Llanelli, **Carmarthenshire**, SA15 3BS, WAL.
(T) 01554 771667 (F) 01554 771667
(E) gbt@geoffreysmail.com
(W) www.greenwayconsultancy.com
Speciality: Absent Healing, Aromatherapy, Auto Suggestion, Cognitive Therapy, Complementary Therapy, Counselling, Healer, Holistic Healing, Homeopathy, Hypnosis, Hypnotherapy, Massage (Therapeutic), Meditation, Psychotherapy, Spiritual Healing, Stress Therapy, Touch Therapy, Voice Therapy. ✓
● **Psychotherapist/Therapist**
Mr G Bowen-Thomas Q: MHA. M: BRCP, HA.
B H M T Yrs. Est.: 12 (Ref:HM08495)

## GREENWAY, ROSEMARY J
**Rosemary J Greenway**, 52 Broad St, Lyme Regis, **Dorset**, DT7 3QF, ENG.
(T) 01297 442423
Speciality: Chiropodists (Podiatrists).
S (Ref:HM08496)

## GREENWAYS NATURAL HEALTH CTRE
**Greenways Natural Health Centre**, 180 Baslow Rd, Sheffield, **Yorkshire (South)**, S17 4DS, ENG.
(T) 01142 360890 (F) 01142 362142
Speciality: Complementary Medicines & Therapy.
● **Owner** Mrs P Lyon
C M (Ref:HM08497)

## GREENWELL, DAVID
**David Greenwell**, 25 London Rd, Cheltenham, **Gloucestershire**, GL52 6EY, ENG.
(T) 01242 221000 (F) 01242 242075
(E) greenwell@compuserve.com
(W) www.dghypnotherapy.co.uk
Speciality: Complementary Therapy, Counselling, Hypnotherapy, Psychotherapy, Stress Therapy, Brief Therapy, Solution Focusing. ✓ CREDIT
● **Hypnotherapist/Stress Counsellor**
Mr D Greenwell Q: Dip.Hyp. M: NCH, NCP.
B Yrs. Est.: 9 (Ref:HM08498)

## GREENWICH HOMEOPATHY CENTRE
**Greenwich Homeopathy Centre**, 137 Greenwich South St, London, **London (Greater)**, SE10 8NX, ENG.
(T) 020 8691 1533
Speciality: Homeopathy.
M (Ref:HM08499)

## GREENWICH NATURAL HEALTH CTRE
**Greenwich Natural Health Centre**, Neptune House, 70 Royal Hill, Greenwich, London, **London (Greater)**, SE10 8RF, ENG.
(T) 020 8869 15408
(E) contact@ur2.net
(W) www.greenwichnaturalhealth.co.uk
Speciality: Acupuncture, Alexander Technique, Allergy Testing, Aromatherapy, Bach Remedies, Chinese Herbal Medicine, Chiropody, Complementary Therapy, Counselling, Cranial Osteopathy, Cranio-Sacral Therapy, Herbal Medicine, Homeopathy, Hypnotherapy, Indian Head Massage, Massage (Therapeutic), Osteopathy, Psychotherapy, Pyscho-Synthesis, Reflexology, Reiki, Shiatsu, Stress Therapy. ✓
● **Osteopath** Ms C Williams Q: DO. M: GOsC.
● **Osteopath** Ms C Plumridge Q: DO. M: GOsC.
● **Osteopath** Mr D Kean Q: DO. M: GOsC.
● **Homeopath** Ms L Razzell Q: RSHom. M: Soc.Hom.
B S Yrs. Est.: 7 (Ref:HM08500)

## GREENWOLD'S THERAPY CENTRE
**Greenwold's Therapy Centre**, The Old Post Office, Main Rd, West Keal, Spilsby, **Lincolnshire**, PE23 4BE, ENG.
(T) 01790 754444
Speciality: Physiotherapy.
● **Owner** Mr G Codd



Key: B Mind-Body Medicine C Complementary Medicine H Self Help Treatment M Medicinal Therapy O Oriental Medicine P Postural Therapy S Manipulative Structural Therapy T Touch Therapy

P S T (Ref:HM08501)

**GREENWOOD, A**
**A Greenwood**, Victoria House Physiotherapy Clinic, 102 George St, Ryde, **Isle of Wight**, PO33 2JE, ENG.
(T) 01983 812576
Speciality: Physiotherapy.
● **Owner** A Greenwood
P S T (Ref:HM08502)

**GREENWOOD, A J**
**A J Greenwood**, Woodlands, 103 High St, Bembridge, **Isle of Wight**, PO35 5SF, ENG.
(T) 01983 875177
Speciality: Physiotherapy.
● **Owner** A J Greenwood
P S T (Ref:HM08503)

**GREENWOOD, CLARE**
**Clare Greenwood**, 103 Lavernock Point, Fort Rd, Lavernock, Penarth, **Glamorgan (Vale of)**, CF64 5XQ, WAL.
(T) 029 2070 6881
Speciality: Reflexology.
S T (Ref:HM08504)

**GREENWOOD, ELAINE**
**Elaine Greenwood**, Cirencester, **Gloucestershire**, GL7, ENG.
(T) 01285 654067
Speciality: Bach Remedies.
M (Ref:HM08505)

**GREENWOOD, J**
**J Greenwood**, 5 Grand Cres, Rottingdean, Brighton, **Sussex (East)**, BN2 7GL, ENG.
(T) 01273 305649
Speciality: Physiotherapy.
● **Owner** Mrs J Greenwood
P S T (Ref:HM08506)

**GREENWOOD, JULIA**
**Julia Greenwood**, 43A Watnall Rd, Hucknall, Nottingham, **Nottinghamshire**, NG15 7JQ, ENG.
(T) 01159 680391
Speciality: Biomechanics, Chiropody. ✔
● **Owner/Chiropodist**
Mrs J Greenwood Q: DPodM, M.S.C.P, S.R.Ch.
M Yrs. Est.: 10 (Ref:HM08507)

**GREENWOOD, LINDA**
**Linda Greenwood**, Vineyard House, Knowle Syke St, Wardle, Rochdale, **Lancashire**, OL12 9PG, ENG.
(T) 01706 377073
Speciality: Acupuncture.
● **Owner** Mrs L Greenwood
O (Ref:HM08508)

**GREENWOOD, SUSAN L**
**Susan L Greenwood**, 7 Townsend Rd, Harpenden, **Hertfordshire**, AL5 4BQ, ENG.
(T) 01582 713880
Speciality: Chiropodists (Podiatrists).
● **Owner** Mrs S Greenwood
S (Ref:HM08509)

**GREER, M**
**M Greer**, 88 Comiston Drive, Edinburgh, **Edinburgh (City of)**, EH10 5QT, SCO.
(T) 01314 472685
Speciality: Alexander Technique.
● **Owner** Mrs M Greer
P S (Ref:HM08510)

**GREER, RITA**
**Rita Greer**, 23 Woodhall Rd, Calverley, Pudsey, **Yorkshire (West)**, LS28 5NL, ENG.
(T) 01132 564409
Speciality: Hypnosis.
● **Owner** Mrs R Greer
B (Ref:HM08511)

**GREETHAM PHYSIOTHERAPY**
**Greetham Physiotherapy & Specialist Knee Clinic (The)**, 37 Main St, Greetham, Oakham, **Leicestershire**, LE15 7NJ, ENG.
(T) 01572 813394
Speciality: Physiotherapy.
P S T (Ref:HM08512)

**GREETHAM, ALISTAIR**
**Alistair Greetham**, Blackberry Orthopaedic Clinic, Blackberry Court, Walnut Tree, Milton Keynes, **Buckinghamshire**, MK7 7PB, ENG.
(T) 01908 604666
Speciality: Physiotherapy.
P S T (Ref:HM08513)

**GREEVES, JANET**
**Janet Greeves**, Newport Clinic Of Holistic Health, 36 Godfrey Rd, Newport, NP20 4PE, WAL.
(T) 01633 843333
Speciality: Complementary Medicines & Therapy.
● **Owner** Mr J Francis
M (Ref:HM08514)

**GREG KELLOWAY IND ECO FL DIST**
**Greg Kelloway Independent ECO Flow Distributor**, 27 Hollybrook Park, Bordon, **Hampshire**, GU35 0DL, ENG.
(T) 01420 479383
Speciality: Complementary Medicines & Therapy.
M (Ref:HM08515)

**GREGORIADIS, SUE**
**Sue Gregoriadis**, 32 Gade Cl, Rickmansworth Rd, Watford, **Hertfordshire**, WD18 7JH, ENG.
(T) 01923 226009
Speciality: Reflexology.
S T (Ref:HM08516)

**GREGORY, BRIAN**
**Brian Gregory**, 2 Eastfield Cl, Beverley, **Humberside (North)**, HU17 9PW, ENG.
(T) 01482 861707
Speciality: Hypnosis.
B (Ref:HM08517)

**GREGORY, F**
**F Gregory**, 27 Chequers Rd, Basingstoke, **Hampshire**, RG21 7PT, ENG.
(T) 01256 352241
Speciality: Complementary Medicines & Therapy.
M (Ref:HM08518)

**GREGORY, K M**
**K M Gregory**, 11 Blenheim Rd, Wroughton, Swindon, **Wiltshire**, SN4 9HL, ENG.
(T) 01793 815120
Speciality: Chiropodists (Podiatrists).
S (Ref:HM08519)

**GREGORY, T R**
**T R Gregory**, 22 Heald Cl, Littleborough, **Manchester (Greater)**, OL15 0DL, ENG.
(T) 01706 378988
Speciality: Chiropodists (Podiatrists).
● **Owner** Mr T Gregory
S (Ref:HM08520)

**GREGSON, D**
**D Gregson**, 5 Richmond Court, Leyland, Preston, **Lancashire**, PR5 3YH, ENG.
(T) 01772 435416
Speciality: Chiropodists (Podiatrists).
● **Owner** Mr D Gregson
S (Ref:HM08521)

**GREGSON, MICHAEL**
**Michael Gregson**, 2 Albert Rd, Fulwood, Preston, **Lancashire**, PR2 8PJ, ENG.
(T) 01772 712048
Speciality: Complementary Medicines & Therapy.
● **Owner** Mr M Gregson
C M (Ref:HM08522)

**GREGSON, NEIL R**
**Neil R Gregson**, 3 Coulsdon Rd, Coulsdon, **London (Greater)**, CR5 2LG, ENG.
(T) 020 8660 0304
Speciality: Osteopathy.
● **Owner** Mr N Gregson
P S T (Ref:HM08523)

**GREIDINGER, CLIVE**
**Clive Greidinger**, 3 Delamere Gardens, Mill Hill, London, **London (Greater)**, NW7 3EA, ENG.
(T) 020 8906 8504
Speciality: Healing Therapy, Hypnosis, Hypnotherapy. ✔
● **Owner** Mr C Greidinger Q: Dip.Hyp, MIAH. M: IAH.
B Yrs. Est.: 6 (Ref:HM08524)

**GREIG, A D**
**A D Greig**, 47 Station Rd, Horrabridge, Yelverton, **Devon**, PL20 7ST, ENG.
(T) 01822 852018
Speciality: Chiropractic.
● **Owner** Mr A Greig
P S T (Ref:HM08525)

**GREIG, ANDREW**
**Andrew Greig**, 48A Barton Hill Rd, Torquay, **Devon**, TQ2 8JD, ENG.
(T) 01803 329799
Speciality: Chiropractors.
P S T (Ref:HM08526)

**GREIG, E**
**Elizabeth Greig - Natural Health Consultancy**, The Linwood, 1 Northbourne Drive, Nuneaton, **Warwickshire**, CV11 4GA, ENG.
(T) 024 7635 2329
Speciality: Aromatherapy, Bach Remedies, Cognitive Therapy, Hay Diet, Hypnotherapy, Neuro-Linguistic Program, Nutritional Therapy, Reflexology, Stress Therapy, Visualisation Therapy. ✔
● **Hypnotherapist** Ms E Greig Q: Dip.BHR. M: BIH, GHR.
B Yrs. Est.: 11 (Ref:HM08527)

**GREIG, ELIZABETH**
**Elizabeth Greig**, 76 Quinton Rd, Cheylesmore, Coventry, **Midlands (West)**, CV3 5FD, ENG.
(T) 024 7650 6463
Speciality: Aromatherapy.
M O (Ref:HM08528)

**GREIG, LISA**
**Lisa Greig**, 27 Eastbury Rd, Watford, **Hertfordshire**, WD1 4PU, ENG.
(T) 01923 225578
Speciality: Chiropractors.
● **Owner** Mrs M Bassett
P S T (Ref:HM08529)

**GREIG, LISA**
**Lisa Greig**, Aberfoyle House, Stapley Rd, St. Albans, **Hertfordshire**, AL3 5EP, ENG.
(T) 01727 856687
Speciality: Chiropractors.
● **Manager** Mrs S Bassett
P S T (Ref:HM08530)

**GREIG, LISA**
**Lisa Greig**, The Hertford Chiropractic Clinic, 5 Port Hill, Hertford, **Hertfordshire**, SG14 1PJ, ENG.
(T) 01992 501659
Speciality: Chiropractors.
P S T (Ref:HM08531)

**GREIG, LISA A**
**Lisa A Greig**, Chitern Chiropractic Clinic, 12 High St, Bovingdon, Hemel Hempstead, **Hertfordshire**, HP3 0HG, ENG.
(T) 01442 832008 (F) 01442 832008
Speciality: Chiropractic.
● **Owner** Dr L Greig
P S T (Ref:HM08532)

**GREIG, MARIANNE**
**Marianne Greig**, 58 Privett Rd, Gosport, **Hampshire**, PO12 3SX, ENG.
(T) 023 9252 1795
Speciality: Chiropodists (Podiatrists).
S (Ref:HM08533)

**GREKIN CHIROPRACTIC CLINIC**
**Grekin Chiropractic Clinic**, Myre Rd, Forfar, **Angus**, DD8 1AZ, SCO.
(T) 01307 462208
Speciality: Chiropractic.
● **Owner** Dr M Cashley
P S T (Ref:HM08534)

**GRENHAM, HELENA**
**Helena Grenham**, 43 Castleknock Ave, Dublin, **County Dublin**, IRE.
(T) 01822 1778
Speciality: Complementary Medicines & Therapy.
M (Ref:HM08535)

**GRENOSIDE PHYSIOTHERAPY**
**Grenoside Physiotherapy & Sports Injury**




Key continued: Yrs.Est: Years Established Q: Qualifications M: Professional Membership ✔ Indemnity Insurance Accept Credit Cards

**Clinic**, Norfolk House, 40 Norfolk Hill, Grenoside, Sheffield, **Yorkshire (South)**, S35 8QB, ENG.
(T) 01142 400677
Speciality: Physiotherapy. ✔
● **Physiotherapist** Mr D Doherty **Q:** MCSP, SRP.
**S** (**Ref:**HM08536)

**GRESHAM, CLARE**

**Clare Gresham**, 18 Peterborough Cl, Grantham, **Lincolnshire**, NG31 8SH, ENG.
(T) 01476 575710
Speciality: Reflexology.
**S** **T** (**Ref:**HM08537)

**GREVIS, MICHAEL**

**Michael Grevis**, 46 Cottenham Rd, Histon, Cambridge, **Cambridgeshire**, CB4 9ES, ENG.
(T) 01223 563403
Speciality: Hypnotherapy.
● **Owner** Mr M Grevis
**B** (**Ref:**HM08538)

**GREWCOCK, N**

**N Grewcock**, The Cottage, Station Rd, Hinckley, **Leicestershire**, LE10 1AP, ENG.
(T) 01455 634320
Speciality: Electrolysis.
● **Owner** Mrs N Grewcock
**T** (**Ref:**HM08539)

**GREY, CHRISTOPHER**

**Christopher Grey**, Herne House, Heath Rd, Petersfield, **Hampshire**, GU31 4EJ, ENG.
(T) 01730 233802
Speciality: Osteopathy.
● **Manager** Mr C Grey
**P** **S** **T** (**Ref:**HM08540)

**GREYSTONE CHARTERED PHYSIO**

**Greystone Chartered Physiotherapy Clinic**, 1 Rinkway Business Park, Rink Drive, Swadlincote, **Derbyshire**, DE11 8JL, ENG.
(T) 01283 224669
Speciality: Physiotherapy.
● **Owner** Mrs B Holloway
**P** **S** **T** (**Ref:**HM08541)

**GREYSTONES ALTERNATIVE MED**

**Greystones Alternative Medicine**, 48 Oakpark Demesne, Tralee, **County Kerry**, IRE.
(T) 06671 80344
Speciality: Complementary Medicines & Therapy.
**M** (**Ref:**HM08542)

**GREYSTONES CHIROPRACTIC CLINIC**

**Greystones Chiropractic Clinic**, The Cova, Trafalgar Rd, Greystones, **County Wicklow**, IRE.
(T) 01287 5944
Speciality: Chiropractors.
**P** **S** **T** (**Ref:**HM08543)

**GRGIC, IGOR**

**Igor Grgic**, 14 Holyoake Rd, Headington, Oxford, **Oxfordshire**, OX3 8AE, ENG.
(T) 01865 761802
Speciality: Chiropractors.
**P** **S** **T** (**Ref:**HM08544)

**GRICE, ANNIE**

**Annie Grice**, 44 Gunthorpe Rd, Marlow, **Buckinghamshire**, SL7 1UH, ENG.
(T) 01628 483045
Speciality: Aromatherapy.
**M** **O** (**Ref:**HM08545)

**GRIER, A R**

**A R Grier**, 11 Woodside Rd, Poole, **Dorset**, BH14 9JH, ENG.
(T) 01202 742365 (F) 01202 742365
Speciality: Chiropodists (Podiatrists).
● **Owner** Mr A Grier
**S** (**Ref:**HM08546)

**GRIER, PHILIPPA**

**Philippa Grier**, Avalon, 141 Victoria Gr, Bridport, **Dorset**, DT6 3AG, ENG.
(T) 01308 423952
Speciality: Reflexology.
**S** **T** (**Ref:**HM08547)

**GRIEVE, J M**

**J M Grieve**, Thorn Farm, Fowlis Wester, Crieff, **Perth and Kinross**, PH7 3NL, SCO.
(T) 01764 683382
Speciality: Physiotherapy.
● **Owner** Mrs J Grieve
**P** **S** **T** (**Ref:**HM08548)

**GRIFFIN ROY HYPNOTHERAPIST**

**Griffin Roy Hypnotherapist**, 67 Camden St, Dublin, **County Dublin**, IRE.
(T) 01478 7927
Speciality: Hypnotherapy.
**B** (**Ref:**HM08549)

**GRIFFIN, A D**

**A D Griffin**, Pinfield, Lady Gate, Diseworth, Derby, **Derbyshire**, DE74 2QF, ENG.
(T) 01332 850349
Speciality: Chiropodists (Podiatrists).
**S** (**Ref:**HM08550)

**GRIFFIN, A H**

**A H Griffin**, 80A Bow Court, Church St, Inverness, **Highland**, IV1 1HB, SCO.
(T) 01463 715377
Speciality: Chiropodists (Podiatrists).
● **Owner** Mr A Griffin
**S** (**Ref:**HM08551)

**GRIFFIN, CORRINNE**

**Corrinne Griffin**, Springfield Rd, Oundle, Peterborough, **Cambridgeshire**, PE8 4LU, ENG.
(T) 01832 272883
Speciality: Aromatherapy.
● **Owner** Mrs C Griffin
**M** **O** (**Ref:**HM08552)

**GRIFFIN, ED**

**Ed Griffin**, 396 High St, Lincoln, **Lincolnshire**, LN5 7SS, ENG.
(T) 01522 887887
Speciality: Hypnotherapy.
● **Owner** Mr E Griffin
**B** (**Ref:**HM08553)

**GRIFFIN, SANDRA**

**Sandra Griffin**, 25 Craigweil Cres, Stockton-On-Tees, **Cleveland**, TS19 0DU, ENG.
(T) 01642 650773
Speciality: Chiropodists (Podiatrists).
**S** (**Ref:**HM08554)

**GRIFFIN, TRICIA**

**Tricia Griffin - Homeopath**, 2 Wellington Trce, Whitby, **Yorkshire (North)**, YO21 3HF, ENG.
(T) 01947 821747
Speciality: Homeopathy. ✔
● **Homeopath** Ms T Griffin **Q:** BSc (Hons), RSHom. M: Soc.Hom.
**M** Yrs. Est.: 15 (**Ref:**HM08555)

**GRIFFITH, ALISON**

**Alison Griffith**, Fairfields Clinic, Skippetts Lane West, Basingstoke, **Hampshire**, RG21 3HP, ENG.
(T) 01256 326980
Speciality: Hypnotherapy.
**B** (**Ref:**HM08556)

**GRIFFITH, C J**

**C J Griffith**, The Manse Health Centre, 54 East St, Andover, **Hampshire**, SP10 1ES, ENG.
(T) 01264 359780
Speciality: Chiropodists (Podiatrists).
● **Owner** Mr C Griffiths
**S** (**Ref:**HM08557)

**GRIFFITH, G D**

**Miss G D Griffith**, Belmont Surgery, 11 Belmont Cresent, Maidenhead, **Berkshire**, SL6 6LS, ENG.
(T) 01628 639480
Speciality: Chiropodists (Podiatrists).
**S** (**Ref:**HM08558)

**GRIFFITHS & ASSOCIATES**

**Lindy Griffiths & Associates**, 20 Westgate, Chichester, **Sussex (West)**, PO19 3EU, ENG.
(T) 01243 783040 (F) 01243 528337
Speciality: Physiotherapy.
● **Owner** Miss L Griffiths
**P** **S** **T** (**Ref:**HM08559)

**GRIFFITHS, C**

**C Griffiths**, 12 Alder Avenue, Widnes, **Cheshire**, WA8 6QG, ENG.
(T) 01514 232651
Speciality: Chiropodists (Podiatrists).
**S** (**Ref:**HM08560)

**GRIFFITHS, C**

**C Griffiths**, The Lynwood Physiotherapy Clinic, 18 Lynwood Drive, Worcester Park, **Surrey**, KT4 7AB, ENG.
(T) 020 8337 8970
Speciality: Physiotherapy.
**P** **S** **T** (**Ref:**HM08561)

**GRIFFITHS, C J**

**C J Griffiths**, 69A Brent St, Hendon, London, **London (Greater)**, NW4 2EA, ENG.
(T) 020 8203 6652
Speciality: Chiropodists (Podiatrists).
**S** (**Ref:**HM08562)

**GRIFFITHS, CAROL**

**Carol Griffiths**, 12 Lancaster Gardens, Kingston Upon Thames, **Surrey**, KT2 5NL, ENG.
(T) 020 8549 0511 (F) 020 8549 0511
Speciality: Physiotherapy.
● **Owner** Mrs C Griffiths
**P** **S** **T** (**Ref:**HM08563)

**GRIFFITHS, DOROTHY**

**Dorothy Griffiths**, 166 Tulketh Rd, Ashton-On-Ribble, Preston, **Lancashire**, PR2 1ER, ENG.
(T) 01772 761166
Speciality: Osteopathy.
● **Owner** Mrs D Griffiths
**P** **S** **T** (**Ref:**HM08564)

**GRIFFITHS, IAN**

**Ian Griffiths**, 49 Park St, Bridgend, CF31 4AX, WAL.
(T) 01656 646446
Speciality: Osteopathy.
**P** **S** **T** (**Ref:**HM08565)

**GRIFFITHS, IAN**

**Ian Griffiths**, Llanelli Osteopathic Clinic, 29 West End, Llanelli, **Carmarthenshire**, SA15 4EN, WAL.
(T) 01554 755772
Speciality: Osteopathy.
**P** **S** **T** (**Ref:**HM08566)

**GRIFFITHS, J**

**J Griffiths**, Clackhams Lane, Crowborough, **Sussex (East)**, TN6 3RN, ENG.
(T) 01892 655468 (F) 01892 655468
(E) jan-griffiths@lineone.net
Speciality: Cranio-Sacral Therapy, Massage (Therapeutic), Remedial Massage. ✔
● **Physical Therapist**
Mr J Wedlake Griffiths **Q:** LCSP. M: LCSP.
● **Cranio-Sacral Therapist**
Mrs J Griffiths
**C** Yrs. Est.: 14 (**Ref:**HM08567)

**GRIFFITHS, J A**

**J A Griffiths**, Physiotherapy Clinic, 13 Alexandra Rd, Gloucester, **Gloucestershire**, GL1 3DR, ENG.
(T) 01452 506512
Speciality: Physiotherapy.
**P** **S** **T** (**Ref:**HM08568)

**GRIFFITHS, JAMES (DR)**

**Dr James Griffiths**, Blackberry Orthopaedic Clinic, Blackberry Court, Walnut Tree, Milton Keynes, **Buckinghamshire**, MK7 7PB, ENG.
(T) 01908 604666
Speciality: Osteopathy.
**P** **S** **T** (**Ref:**HM08569)

**GRIFFITHS, JOANNE**

**Joanne Griffiths**, Park House, The St, High Roding, Dunmow, **Essex**, CM6 1NW, ENG.
(T) 01371 873934
Speciality: Homeopathy.
● **Owner** Mrs J Griffiths
**M** (**Ref:**HM08570)

**GRIFFITHS, JOHN E**

**John E Griffiths**, Stanley Mews, Stanley St, Macclesfield, **Cheshire**, SK11 6AU, ENG.
(T) 01625 432152
Speciality: Physiotherapy.
**P** **S** **T** (**Ref:**HM08571)

**GRIFFITHS, R J**

**R J Griffiths**, 15 Westlake Cl, Torpoint, **Cornwall**, PL11 2BZ, ENG.
(T) 08081 000639

Speciality: Chiropodists (Podiatrists).
● Owner Mr R Griffiths
S (Ref:HM08572)

**GRIFFITHS, SAIDA K**

**Saida K Griffiths**, 1 Petercroft Lane, Dunnington, York, **Yorkshire (North)**, YO1 5NA, ENG.
(T) 01904 481048
Speciality: Psychotherapy.
B (Ref:HM08573)

**GRIFFITH-WARD, JANE**

**Jane Griffith-Ward M R S**, 56 Richmond Rd, Staines, **Surrey**, TW18 2AB, ENG.
(T) 01784 450042
Speciality: Osteopathy.
P S T (Ref:HM08574)

**GRIGGS, LESLEY**

**Lesley Griggs**, 3 Somers Rd, Reigate, **Surrey**, RH2 9DU, ENG.
(T) 01737 224488
Speciality: Osteopathy.
● Owner Mrs L Griggs
P S T (Ref:HM08575)

**GRIMES, JUNE**

**June Grimes**, 6 Seaburn Cl, Sunderland, **Tyne and Wear**, SR6 8BU, ENG.
(T) 01915 294131
Speciality: Reflexology.
S T (Ref:HM08576)

**GRIMES-SAMUEL, EDNA A**

**Edna A Grimes-Samuel**, 109 Masons Hill, Bromley, **Kent**, BR2 9HT, ENG.
(T) 020 8460 2798
Speciality: Chiropodists (Podiatrists).
● Owner Mrs E Grimes-Samuel
S (Ref:HM08577)

**GRIMMINGER, C**

**C Grimminger**, Essex House Medical Centre, Fore St, Chard, **Somerset**, TA20 1QA, ENG.
(T) 01460 65046
Speciality: Chiropodists (Podiatrists).
S (Ref:HM08578)

**GRIMMINGER, C**

**C Grimminger**, 7 High St, Chard, **Somerset**, TA20 1QF, ENG.
(T) 01460 67763
Speciality: Chiropodists (Podiatrists).
S (Ref:HM08579)

**GRIMMINGER, J**

**J Grimminger**, Essex House Medical Centre, Fore St, Chard, **Somerset**, TA20 1QA, ENG.
(T) 01460 65046
Speciality: Chiropodists (Podiatrists).
S (Ref:HM08580)

**GRIMMINGER, J**

**J Grimminger**, 7 High St, Chard, **Somerset**, TA20 1QF, ENG.
(T) 01460 67763
Speciality: Chiropodists (Podiatrists).
S (Ref:HM08581)

**GRIMSBY CHIROPRACTIC CLINIC**

**Grimsby Chiropractic Clinic**, 5 Hainton Avenue, Grimsby, **Humberside (South)**, DN32 9AS, ENG.
(T) 01472 344904
Speciality: Chiropractic.
P S T (Ref:HM08582)

**GRIMSEY, ALAN R**

**Alan R Grimsey**, 6 Mulberry Cl, Mildenhall, Bury St. Edmunds, **Suffolk**, IP28 7LL, ENG.
(T) 01638 715581
Speciality: Hypnotherapy.
● Owner Mr A Grimsey
B (Ref:HM08583)

**GRIMSHAW, R**

**R Grimshaw**, 98 Balfour Rd, Brighton, **Sussex (East)**, BN1 6ND, ENG.
(T) 01273 552111
Speciality: Physiotherapy.
P S T (Ref:HM08584)

**GRIMWADE, J C**

**J C Grimwade**, 30 Plassey St, Penarth, **Glamorgan (Vale of)**, CF64 1EJ, WAL.
(T) 029 2071 1399
Speciality: Physiotherapy.
● Owner Mr J Grimwade
P S T (Ref:HM08585)

**GRIMWADE, S**

**Mrs S Grimwade**, 27 Butleigh Avenue, Llandaff, Cardiff, **Glamorgan (Vale of)**, WAL.
(T) 029 2056 5378
(E) samantha@sgrimwade.freeserve.co.uk
Speciality: Cranial Osteopathy, Manipulation, Massage (Therapeutic), Osteopathy. ✔
● Osteopath Mrs S Grimwade Q: DO. M: BOA.
S Yrs. Est.: 10 (Ref:HM08586)

**GRIMWADE, S**

**S Grimwade**, 148 Pencisely Rd, Cardiff, **Glamorgan (Vale of)**, CF5 1DR, WAL.
(T) 029 2056 5378
Speciality: Osteopathy.
P S T (Ref:HM08587)

**GRINDLEY, E M**

**E M Grindley**, The Findhorn Foundation, Findhorn, Forres, **Moray**, IV36 3TZ, SCO.
(T) 01309 690217
Speciality: Complementary Medicines & Therapy.
C M (Ref:HM08588)

**GRISHKOV, AMANDA**

**Amanda Grishkov**, Gables, Drapers Corner, Greensted, Ongar, **Essex**, CM5 9LS, ENG.
(T) 01277 366353
Speciality: Chiropodists (Podiatrists).
● Owner Mrs A Grishkov
S (Ref:HM08589)

**GROCHOLSKI, SABINE**

**Sabine Grocholski**, 6 Talbot Rd, Twickenham, **London (Greater)**, TW2 6SJ, ENG.
(T) 020 8898 1952
Speciality: Homeopathy.
M (Ref:HM08590)

**GROFSKI, JANE**

**Jane Grofski**, 15A Vaughan Avenue, London, **London (Greater)**, W6 0XS, ENG.
(T) 020 8748 0377
Speciality: Reflexology.
S T (Ref:HM08591)

**GROGAN, DIANA E**

**Diana E Grogan**, St Davids House, 8 Strawberry Bank, Blackburn, **Lancashire**, BB2 6AA, ENG.
(T) 01254 263728
(E) diana.grogan@tinyworld.co.uk
Speciality: Acupuncture, Bach Remedies, Chiropody, Counselling, Cupping, Homeopathy, Hypnotherapy, Manipulation, Massage (Therapeutic), Moxibustion. ✔
● Counselling Psychologist
Ms L Abbott
(T) 01254 673461 Q: BPS, BSc (Hons), Dip.Couns. M: BACP, BPS.
● Acupuncturist/Manipulative Therapist
Ms D Grogan Q: Dip.MSc, G.C.S.Ch, Lic.Ac, MBAcC, MSc. M: Ass.Therapeutic Massage, BAcC.
● Hypnotherapist Ms V Brown
(T) 01254 265987 Q: BA (Hons) Psychol, NRHP (Assoc). M: NRHP.
O Yrs. Est.: 12 (Ref:HM08592)

**GROMADZKA, B**

**B Gromadzka**, 2 Devonshire Pl, London, **London (Greater)**, W1N 1PA, ENG.
(T) 020 7935 8139
Speciality: Psychology.
B (Ref:HM08593)

**GROOM, C**

**C Groom**, Queens Rd, Harrogate, **Yorkshire (North)**, HG2 0HF, ENG.
(T) 01423 567136
Speciality: Aromatherapy.
M O (Ref:HM08594)

**GROSS, A**

**A Gross**, Ravenscroft Medical Centre, 166-168 Golders Green Rd, London, **London (Greater)**, NW11 8BB, ENG.
(T) 020 8209 0922
Speciality: Osteopathy.
● Osteopath A Gross
P S T (Ref:HM08595)

**GROSVENOR PHYSIOTHERAPY CLINIC**

**Grosvenor Physiotherapy Clinic**, Grosvenor House, Hambledon Rd, Denmead, Waterlooville, **Hampshire**, PO7 6NU, ENG.
(T) 023 9223 3288
Speciality: Physiotherapy.
P S T (Ref:HM08596)

**GROSVENOR PHYSIOTHERAPY CLINIC**

**Grosvenor Physiotherapy Clinic**, 154A High St, Newmarket, **Suffolk**, CB8 9AQ, ENG.
(T) 01638 667606
Speciality: Physiotherapy. ✔
● Physiotherapist/Owner
Ms F Morton Q: MCSP, SRP.
● Physiotherapist Rosemary Pratten Q: MCSP, SRP.
S Yrs. Est.: 20 (Ref:HM08597)

**GROSVENOR REFLEXOLOGY**

**Grosvenor Reflexology**, 11 Grosvenor Pl, Bath, **Somerset**, BA1 6AX, ENG.
(T) 01225 311290
Speciality: Reflexology.
● Owner Mrs E Bridgen
S T (Ref:HM08598)

**GROUNDS, L**

**L Grounds**, 19 Longmeadow Drive, Ickleford, Hitchin, **Hertfordshire**, SG5 3TJ, ENG.
(T) 01462 625083
(E) lynn.grounds@ntlworld.com
Speciality: Reflexology. ✔
● Reflexologist Mrs L Grounds Q: MAR.
C Yrs. Est.: 10 (Ref:HM08599)

**GROUNDS, L**

**L Grounds**, 11 Harding Avenue, Wirral, **Merseyside**, CH63 3HL, ENG.
(T) 01513 347328
Speciality: Chiropody. ✔
● Chiropodist Lesley Tanner Q: DPodM, M.S.C.P, S.R.Ch.
M Yrs. Est.: 23 (Ref:HM08600)

**GROUNDS, S J**

**S J Grounds**, 11 Battishill St, London, **London (Greater)**, N1 1TE, ENG.
(T) 020 7359 8762
Speciality: Physiotherapy.
P S T (Ref:HM08601)

**GROUP & INTERPERSONAL TRAINING**

**Group & Interpersonal Training**, 48 The Pines Howth Road, Dublin, **County Dublin**, IRE.
(T) 01832 8016
Speciality: Complementary Medicines & Therapy.
M (Ref:HM08602)

**GROUP ANALYSIS-ROSENDALE**

**Group Analysis-Rosendale**, 43 Rosendale Rd, London, **London (Greater)**, SE21 8DY, ENG.
(T) 020 8670 5023
Speciality: Psychotherapy.
B (Ref:HM08603)

**GROUP ANALYTIC NETWORK WEST**

**Group Analytic Network West**, 12 Sydenham Rd, Cotham, Bristol, BS6 5SH, ENG.
(T) 01179 441005
Speciality: Psychotherapy.
B (Ref:HM08604)

**GROUP ANALYTIC PRACTICE**

**Group Analytic Practice (The)**, 88 Montagu Mansions, London, **London (Greater)**, W1H 1LF, ENG.
(T) 020 7935 3103 (F) 020 7935 1397
(E) members@gapractice.org.uk
Speciality: Counselling, Group Therapy, Psychotherapy. ✔
● Practice Manager Mrs J Ansall
B Yrs. Est.: 40 (Ref:HM08605)

**GROUP ANALYTIC PRACTICE**

**Group Analytic Practice**, Global Hse, 29 Abbey St, Lr, Dublin, **County Dublin**, IRE.
(T) 01878 6486 (F) 01878 6451
(E) gap@clubi.ie
Speciality: Complementary Medicines &



Key continued: Yrs.Est: Years Established Q: Qualifications M: Professional Membership ✔ Indemnity Insurance Accept Credit Cards

Therapy.
M (Ref:HM08606)

## GROVE CHIROPODY PRACTICE

**Grove Chiropody Practice**, 43 Harmer St, Gravesend, **Kent**, DA12 2AP, ENG.
(T) 01474 533393
Speciality: Chiropodists (Podiatrists).
S (Ref:HM08607)

## GROVE COMP HEALTH CENTRE

**Grove Complementary Health Centre (The)**, 182-184 Kensington Church St, London, **London (Greater)**, W8 4DP, ENG.
(T) 020 7221 2266 (F) 020 7243 2112
Speciality: Complementary Medicines & Therapy.
● **Owner** Miss V Young
M (Ref:HM08608)

## GROVE NATURAL THERAPY CENTRE

**Grove Natural Therapy Centre (The)**, 22 Grosvenor Rd, Southampton, **Hampshire**, SO17 1RT, ENG.
(T) 023 8058 2245
Speciality: Acupuncture, Alexander Technique, Aromatherapy, Bach Remedies, Chinese Herbal Medicine, Chiropractic, Colonic Hydrotherapy, Cranio-Sacral Therapy, Healing Therapy, Homeopathy, Indian Head Massage, Manipulation, Massage (Therapeutic), McTimoney Chiropractic, Meditation, Metamorphic Therapy, Naturopathy, Nutritional Therapy, Osteopathy, Psychotherapy, Reflexology, Reiki, Shiatsu, Spiritual Healing, Stress Therapy, Vitamin Therapy, Yoga.
C (Ref:HM08609)

## GROVE NATURAL THERAPY CLINIC

**Grove Natural Therapy Clinic (The)**, 7a High St Mews, 28 High St, Leighton Buzzard, **Bedfordshire**, LU7 7EA, ENG.
(T) 01525 851588
(W) www.grovetherapycentre.co.uk
Speciality: Allergy Testing, Aromatherapy, Chiropractic, Colonic Hydrotherapy, Counselling, Cranial Osteopathy, Homeopathy, Massage (Therapeutic), McTimoney Chiropractic, Naturopathy, Nutritional Therapy, Osteopathy, Psychotherapy, Reflexology, Reiki, Shiatsu, Yoga, Learning Difficulties and Behavioral Problems.
✔
● **Chiropractor** Ms C Williams Q: DC, MMCA. M: GCC.
● **Owner** Ms B Deacon Q: DC, MMCA. M: CC, GCC.
● **Chiropractor** Mr J Brickell Q: DC, MMCA. M: GCC.
P Yrs. Est.: 10 (Ref:HM08610)

## GROVE, D

**D Grove**, 14 Market Pl, Olney, **Buckinghamshire**, MK46 4BA, ENG.
(T) 01234 713104
Speciality: Chiropodists (Podiatrists).
S (Ref:HM08611)

## GROVE, M

**M Grove**, Ananda House, Franks Hollow Rd, Bidborough, Tunbridge Wells, **Kent**, TN3 0UD, ENG.
(T) 01892 514288
Speciality: Homeopathy.
M (Ref:HM08612)

## GROVE, NICHOLAS

**Nicholas Grove**, 6 Lionel Avenue, Wendover, Aylesbury, **Buckinghamshire**, HP22 6LL, ENG.
(T) 01296 622363
Speciality: Physiotherapy.
● **Owner** Mr N Grove
P S T (Ref:HM08613)

## GROVES, FRAN

**Fran Groves**, The Mill House, Pencelli, Brecon, **Powys**, LD3 7LX, WAL.
(T) 01874 610420 (F) 01874 665436
(E) frangroves@aol.com
Speciality: Bowen Therapy, Equine Bowen Therapy. ✔
● **Bowen Therapist** Ms F Groves Q: Cert.ECBS.
C Yrs. Est.: 1 (Ref:HM08614)

## GROVES, MURIEL

**Muriel Groves**, Sutton Coldfield, **Midlands (West)**, B74, ENG.
(T) 01213 534486
Speciality: Bach Remedies.
M (Ref:HM08615)

## GROVES, P A

**P A Groves**, Highcliffe Private Clinic, 248 Lymington Rd, Highcliffe, Christchurch, **Dorset**, BH23 5ET, ENG.
(T) 01425 277505 (F) 01425 271086
Speciality: Chiropodists (Podiatrists).
● **Practice Manager** Mrs P Jones
S (Ref:HM08616)

## GROVES, VALERIE

**Valerie Groves**, 130 Wendover Rd, Staines, **Surrey**, TW18 3DQ, ENG.
(T) 01784 453367
Speciality: Chiropodists (Podiatrists).
S (Ref:HM08617)

## GROWNEY, SHAUN

**Shaun Growney**, 15 Sangora Rd, London, **London (Greater)**, SW11 1RL, ENG.
(T) 020 7924 7327
Speciality: Psychotherapy.
● **Owner** Mr S Growney
B (Ref:HM08618)

## GRUMBALL, J D

**J D Grumball**, 51 Frimley Avenue, Hornchurch, **Essex**, RM11 3PX, ENG.
(T) 01708 474961
Speciality: Osteopathy.
● **Owner** Mr J Grumball
P S T (Ref:HM08619)

## GRUNDBERG, SIBYL

**Sibyl Grundberg**, 52 Warham Rd, London, **London (Greater)**, N4 1AT, ENG.
(T) 020 8341 2904
Speciality: Osteopathy.
P S T (Ref:HM08620)

## GT YARMOUTH PHYSICAL THERAPY

**Great Yarmouth Physical Therapy**, 70 Salisbury Rd, Great Yarmouth, **Norfolk**, NR30 4LA, ENG.
(T) 01493 330252
(E) gypt@supanet.com
Speciality: Electrotherapy, Manipulation, Massage (Therapeutic). ✔
● **Manipulative Therapist** Mr G Smith Q: LCSP. M: CSP.
S Yrs. Est.: 7 (Ref:HM08330)

## GUBBAY, R

**R Gubbay**, Berkhamsted Chiropractic Clinic, 69 High St, Berkhamsted, **Hertfordshire**, HP4 2DE, ENG.
(T) 01442 863800
Speciality: Chiropractors.
P S T (Ref:HM08621)

## GUERRINI, HEATHER

**Heather Guerrini**, 30 Redesdale St, London, **London (Greater)**, SW3 4BJ, ENG.
(T) 020 7352 0245
Speciality: Reflexology.
S T (Ref:HM08622)

## GUEST, GRAHAM

**Graham Guest**, 162 Sylvan Rd, London, **London (Greater)**, SE19 2SA, ENG.
(T) 020 8653 1694
Speciality: Healing Therapy, Personal Development.
M (Ref:HM08623)

## GUEST, J F

**J F Guest**, 13 Harrison Gr, Sandycroft, Deeside, **Flintshire**, CH5 2PH, WAL.
(T) 01244 532413
Speciality: Complementary Medicines & Therapy.
● **Owner** Mr J Guest
C M (Ref:HM08624)

## GUIDING LIGHTS

**Guiding Lights**, 5 Cannon St, Chesterfield, **Derbyshire**, S40 1SH, ENG.
(T) 01246 563188
Speciality: Aromatherapy.
● **Partner** Mrs D Barnett
M O (Ref:HM08625)

## GUILD OF COMP PRACTITIONERS

**Guild Of Complementary Practitioners (The)**, Liddell House, 6 Liddell Cl, Finchampstead, Wokingham, **Berkshire**, RG40 4NS, ENG.
(T) 01189 735757 (F) 01189 735767
Speciality: Complementary Medicines & Therapy.
● **Secretary** Mr J Beeney
C M (Ref:HM08626)

## GUILD OF PRACTITIONERS

**Guild Of Practitioners Of Alternative Osteopathy (The)**, 221 Old St, Ashton-under-Lyne, **Manchester (Greater)**, OL6 7SR, ENG.
(T) 01613 435908
Speciality: Bonesetting, Chiropractic, Complementary Therapy, Cupping, Stress Therapy, Touch Therapy, Vibrational Therapy.
● **Secretary** Ms E Mackay M: GPAO.
S Yrs. Est.: 1 (Ref:HM08627)

## GUILD OF PSYCHOTHERAPISTS

**Guild Of Psychotherapists (The)**, 47 Nelson Sq, London, **London (Greater)**, SE1 0QA, ENG.
(T) 020 8540 4454
Speciality: Psychotherapy.
B (Ref:HM08628)

## GUILD, M D (DR)

**Dr M D Guild**, 16 Cairns Pl, Muckhart, Dollar, **Clackmannanshire**, FK14 7LH, SCO.
(T) 01259 781435
Speciality: Homeopathy.
● **Principal** Dr M Guild
M (Ref:HM08629)

## GUILDER CENTRE

**Guilder Centre**, Guilder Lane, Salisbury, **Wiltshire**, ENG.
(T) 01794 340664
Speciality: Alexander Technique.
● **Therapist** Ms P Lyon
P S (Ref:HM08630)

## GUILDFORD CTRE-PSYCHOTHERAPY

**Guildford Centre For Psychotherapy**, P O Box 63, Guildford, **Surrey**, GU1 2SU, ENG.
(T) 01483 560607
Speciality: Hypnotherapy.
B (Ref:HM08631)

## GUILDFORD PHYSIO & SPORTS

**Guildford Physiotherapy & Sports Clinic**, Matthews House, 85 Epsom Rd, Guildford, **Surrey**, GU1 3PA, ENG.
(T) 01483 575876 (F) 01483 302691
Speciality: Physiotherapy. ✔
● **Physiotherapist** Mr D Wood Q: MCSP. M: CSP.
C Yrs. Est.: 50 (Ref:HM08632)

## GUILDFORD, DILYS

**Dilys Guildford**, Woodside, Hallsands, Kingsbridge, **Devon**, TQ7 2EY, ENG.
(T) 01803 770977 (F) 01803 770977
Speciality: Clairvoyants & Palmists.
● **Owner** Ms D Guildford
B (Ref:HM08633)

## GUILDHALL SCHOOL

**Guildhall School of Music and Drama**, Silk St, Barbican, London, **London (Greater)**, EC2Y 8DT, ENG.
(T) 020 7628 2571
Speciality: Alexander Technique.
● **Practitioner** Miss N Ben-Or
P S (Ref:HM08634)

## GUILD-NATUROPATHIC IRIDOLOGY

**Guild Of Naturopathic Iridology**, 94 Grosvenor Rd, London, **London (Greater)**, SW1V 3LF, ENG.
(T) 020 7821 0255 (F) 020 7821 0255
Speciality: Iridology.
● **Chairman** Mr P Bradbury
M (Ref:HM08635)

## GUISELEY CHIROPODY CENTRE

**Guiseley Chiropody Centre**, 40 Victoria Rd,



Key: B Mind-Body Medicine; C Complementary Medicine; H Self Help Treatment; M Medicinal Therapy; O Oriental Medicine; P Postural Therapy; S Manipulative Structural Therapy; T Touch Therapy

Guiseley, Leeds, **Yorkshire (West)**, LS20 8DG, ENG.
(T) 01943 872716
Speciality: Chiropodists (Podiatrists).
S (Ref:HM08636)

**GULATI, R K (DR)**
**Dr R K Gulati**, Viran Medical Centre, 291 Hesketh Lane, Tarleton, Preston, **Lancashire**, PR4 6RJ, ENG.
(T) 01772 812207
Speciality: Acupuncture.
O (Ref:HM08637)

**GULLIFORD, A W R**
**A W R Gulliford**, 22 Swan Lane, Wickford, **Essex**, SS11 7DD, ENG.
(T) 01268 732398
Speciality: Chiropodists (Podiatrists).
● **Owner** Mr A Gulliford
S (Ref:HM08638)

**GUNDRY, N**
**N Gundry**, All Hallows House, Idol Lane, London, **London (Greater)**, EC3R 5DD, ENG.
(T) 020 7283 8908
Speciality: Psychotherapy.
B (Ref:HM08639)

**GUNGADIN, G**
**G Gungadin**, 198 Elmsleigh Drive, Leigh-On-Sea, **Essex**, SS9 4JQ, ENG.
(T) 01702 711532
Speciality: Chiropodists (Podiatrists).
● **Owner** Mr G Gungadin
S (Ref:HM08640)

**GUNN, HARRY**
**Harry Gunn**, 18 Gloucester Walk, London, **London (Greater)**, W8 4HZ, ENG.
(T) 020 7937 6194
Speciality: Osteopathy.
P S T (Ref:HM08641)

**GUNN, JASON**
**Jason Gunn**, 17 Lesley Cl, Bexley, **Kent**, DA5 1LR, ENG.
(T) 01322 527292
Speciality: Cranial Osteopathy, Homeopathy, Osteopathy. ✓
● **Osteopath** Mr J Gunn Q: BSc. M: GOsC.
S Yrs. Est.: 5 (Ref:HM08642)

**GUNNING, R**
**R Gunning**, 5 Knocklofty Park, Belfast, **County Antrim**, BT4 3NA, NIR.
(T) 028 9047 1627
Speciality: Physiotherapy.
● **Owner** Mrs R Gunning
P S T (Ref:HM08643)

**GUNNING, ROSALIND**
**Rosalind Gunning**, 2a Mill Lane, Broomfield, Chelmsford, **Essex**, CM1 7BQ, ENG.
(T) 01245 441277
Speciality: Physiotherapy.
P S T (Ref:HM08644)

**GUNNS, C M**
**C M Gunns**, 98 Old Rectory Rd, Portsmouth, **Hampshire**, PO6 1AJ, ENG.
(T) 023 9237 3019
Speciality: Chiropodists (Podiatrists).
S (Ref:HM08645)

**GUNTER, MARIGOLD**
**Marigold Gunter**, 1 Farrer Rd, London, **London (Greater)**, N8 8LD, ENG.
(T) 020 8340 8887
Speciality: Reflexology.
S T (Ref:HM08646)

**GUO, B**
**B Guo**, 67 Jesmond Park West, Newcastle Upon Tyne, **Tyne and Wear**, NE7 7BX, ENG.
(T) 01912 120773
Speciality: Acupuncture.
O (Ref:HM08647)

**GUO, J (DR)**
**Dr J Guo**, 1 Collin St, Nottingham, **Nottinghamshire**, NG1 7EQ, ENG.
(T) 01159 502070 (F) 01159 237678
Speciality: Complementary Medicines & Therapy.
● **Doctor** Dr J Guo
M (Ref:HM08648)

**GUPTA, P**
**P Gupta**, 48 Altys Lane, Ormskirk, **Lancashire**, L39 4RQ, ENG.
(T) 01695 572175
Speciality: Acupuncture.
● **Doctor** Dr P Gupta
O (Ref:HM08649)

**GUPTA, S**
**S Gupta**, Valentine, St Georges Rd, Bromley, **Kent**, BR1 2AX, ENG.
(T) 020 8467 6142 (F) 020 8467 6142
Speciality: Osteopathy.
● **Owner** Mr S Gupta
P S T (Ref:HM08650)

**GURNET, CATHERINE**
**Catherine Gurnet**, 24 Willow Rd, London, **London (Greater)**, NW3 1TL, ENG.
(T) 020 7433 1237
Speciality: Reflexology.
S T (Ref:HM08651)

**GURNEY, CHRISTINE**
**Christine Gurney**, 1 Betts Folly, Warninglid Lane, Warninglid, Haywards Heath, **Sussex (West)**, RH17 5TQ, ENG.
(T) 01444 461553
Speciality: Reflexology.
S T (Ref:HM08652)

**GURNEY, JACQUELINE**
**Jacqueline Gurney**, 39 London Rd, Woolmer Green, Knebworth, **Hertfordshire**, SG3 6JE, ENG.
(T) 01438 813050
Speciality: Chiropodists (Podiatrists).
● **Owner** Ms J Green
S (Ref:HM08653)

**GURNEY, SHARON**
**Sharon Gurney**, 28 Glenhurst Rd, Southend-On-Sea, **Essex**, SS2 5DS, ENG.
(T) 01702 462381
Speciality: Reflexology.
S T (Ref:HM08654)

**GURPAL SINGH AROMA/REFLEX**
**Mr Gurpal Singh Aromatherapist & Reflexologist**, 171 Bushbury Rd, Wolverhampton, **Midlands (West)**, WV10 0LZ, ENG.
(T) 01902 729076
Speciality: Aromatherapy, Reflexology, Reiki. ✓
● **Owner/Therapist** Mr G Singh Q: ITEC. M: IPTI.
C Yrs. Est.: 8 (Ref:HM08655)

**GURR, J**
**J Gurr**, 8 Inverary Cl, Kenilworth, **Warwickshire**, CV8 2NZ, ENG.
(T) 01926 512171
Speciality: Chiropodists (Podiatrists).
S (Ref:HM08656)

**GURRY, N J**
**N J Gurry**, 118 The Grove, Christchurch, **Dorset**, BH23 2HE, ENG.
(T) 01202 482986
Speciality: Chiropodists (Podiatrists).
● **Owner** Mrs N Gurry
S (Ref:HM08657)

**GUTH & ASSOCIATES**
**Moira A Guth & Associates**, Birbeck Natural Health Clinic, 45 Birkbeck Rd, Sidcup, **Kent**, DA14 4DB, ENG.
(T) 020 8302 2624
Speciality: Osteopathy.
P S T (Ref:HM08658)

**GUTTERIDGE, A C (DR)**
**Dr A C Gutteridge**, Garthside, Storrs Park, Bowness-On-Windermere, Windermere, **Cumbria**, LA23 3JP, ENG.
(T) 01539 442964
Speciality: Osteopathy.
● **Owner** Dr A Gutteridge
P S T (Ref:HM08659)

**GUTTERIDGE, DAVID**
**David Gutteridge**, 202 Preston New Rd, Blackburn, **Lancashire**, BB2 6PN, ENG.
(T) 01254 52143
Speciality: Osteopathy.
P S T (Ref:HM08660)

**GUTTERIDGE, L**
**L Gutteridge**, 10 Holden Way, Upminster, **Essex**, RM14 1BP, ENG.
(T) 01708 227786
Speciality: Osteopathy.
P S T (Ref:HM08661)

**GUY, R A**
**R A Guy**, 18 Manor Rd, Aylesbury, **Buckinghamshire**, HP20 1JD, ENG.
(T) 01296 424043
Speciality: Chiropodists (Podiatrists).
S (Ref:HM08662)

**GUYLL, S**
**S Guyll**, 1 Gretton Rd, Winchcombe, Cheltenham, **Gloucestershire**, GL54 5EE, ENG.
(T) 01242 602672
Speciality: Chiropodists (Podiatrists).
S (Ref:HM08663)

**GUYS & ST THOMAS HOSP TRUST**
**Guys & St Thomas Hospital Trust Private Physiotherapist**, Lambeth Palace Rd, London, **London (Greater)**, SE1 7EH, ENG.
(T) 020 7922 8022 (F) 020 7922 8280
Speciality: Physiotherapy.
P S T (Ref:HM08664)

**GUYTON HOUSE**
**Guyton House**, 5 Vicarage St, North Walsham, **Norfolk**, NR28 9DQ, ENG.
(T) 01692 501042
Speciality: Complementary Medicines & Therapy.
● **Owner** Mr R Brown
C M (Ref:HM08665)

**GWENT CHIROPRACTIC CENTRE**
**Gwent Chiropractic Centre**, 77 Caerau Rd, Newport, NP20 4HJ, WAL.
(T) 01633 662022 (F) 01633 662202
Speciality: Chiropractic.
● **Owner** Dr B Bacon
P S T (Ref:HM08666)

**GWILLYM, ELAINE**
**Elaine Gwillym**, 24 Gillingham Cl, Kings Worthy, Winchester, **Hampshire**, SO23 7RL, ENG.
(T) 01962 885054
Speciality: Complementary Medicines & Therapy.
C M (Ref:HM08667)

**GWILT, ALAN**
**Alan Gwilt**, Laurel Cottage, Little Green, Mells, Frome, **Somerset**, BA11 3QZ, ENG.
(T) 01373 813118
Speciality: Complementary Medicines & Therapy.
● **Owner** A Gwilt
C M (Ref:HM08668)

**GWILT, ANNA**
**Anna Gwilt Osteopaths**, Little Green, Mells, Frome, **Somerset**, BA11 3QZ, ENG.
(T) 01373 812640 (F) 01373 813540
Speciality: Osteopathy.
● **Owner** Mrs A Gwilt
P S T (Ref:HM08669)

**GWYNEDD COMMUNITY TRUST**
**Gwynedd Community Trust**, Physiotherapy Clinic, Towyn Rd, Blaenau Ffestiniog, **Gwynedd**, LL41 3UR, WAL.
(T) 01766 830225
Speciality: Physiotherapy.
P S T (Ref:HM08670)

**GWYN-WILLIAMS, S**
**S Gwyn-Williams**, The Crane Surgery, Rectory Fields, Cranbrook, **Kent**, TN17 3JB, ENG.
(T) 01580 715992
Speciality: Osteopathy.
● **Owner** Mr S Gwyn-Williams
P S T (Ref:HM08671)

## GYALTSABJE BUDDHIST CENTRE

**Gyaltsabje Buddhist Centre**, 13 Sharrow View, Sheffield, **Yorkshire (South)**, S7 1ND, ENG.
(T) 01142 509663
(E) sally@sheffmeditation.org.uk
Speciality: Meditation.
● **Resident Teacher** Ani - La Shenyen
(T) 01142 585936 M: NKT.
● **Secretary** Mrs A Maxwell
● **Education Co-Ordinator** Ms S Bannister
(T) 01142 585936 M: NKT.
● **Admin Director** Ms L Williams
(T) 01442 205586 M: NKT.
H Yrs. Est.: 10 (Ref:HM08672)

## GYASI, A

**A Gyasi**, 25 Hemley Rd, Orsett, Grays, **Essex**, RM16 3DG, ENG.
(T) 01375 892491
Speciality: Chiropodists (Podiatrists).
● **Owner** Mrs A Gyasi
S (Ref:HM08673)

## H LEICESTER

**H Leicester**, 7 Cynthia Avenue, Woolston, Warrington, **Cheshire**, WA1 3UL, ENG.
(T) 01925 812689
Speciality: Hypnosis.
B (Ref:HM08674)

## H R CHINESE MEDICINE CENTRE

**H R Chinese Medicine Centre**, 155 Edgware Rd, London, **London (Greater)**, W2 2HR, ENG.
(T) 020 7258 3686
Speciality: Complementary Medicines & Therapy.
C M (Ref:HM08675)

## H R CHINESE MEDICINE CENTRE

**H R Chinese Medicine Centre**, 83 High St, London, **London (Greater)**, NW10 4NT, ENG.
(T) 020 8963 9166
Speciality: Complementary Medicines & Therapy.
● **Owner** Mr D Yu
C M (Ref:HM08676)

## H R CHINESE MEDICINE CENTRE

**H R Chinese Medicine Centre**, 132 High St, London, **London (Greater)**, E17 7JS, ENG.
(T) 020 8509 3868
Speciality: Complementary Medicines & Therapy.
● **Manageress** Mrs J Wang
C M (Ref:HM08677)

## HABERFELD, N

**N Haberfeld**, 55 Elm Drive, Hove, **Sussex (East)**, BN3 7JA, ENG.
(T) 01273 747043
Speciality: Chiropodists (Podiatrists).
S (Ref:HM08678)

## HACK, SHAMS Z E

**Shams Z E Hack**, 16 Hopkinsons Pl, London, **London (Greater)**, NW1 8TN, ENG.
(T) 020 7722 8673
Speciality: Homeopathy.
● **Owner** Ms S Hack
M (Ref:HM08679)

## HACKER, S M

**S M Hacker**, 9 High St, Newport, **Isle of Wight**, PO30 1SS, ENG.
(T) 01983 522396
Speciality: Chiropodists (Podiatrists).
● **Owner** Mrs S Hacker
S (Ref:HM08680)

## HACKETT, J

**J Hackett**, The Natural Way, 44 Victoria St, Paignton, **Devon**, TQ4 5DS, ENG.
(T) 01803 525279
Speciality: Reflexology.
S T (Ref:HM08681)

## HACKMAN, MARIE

**Marie Hackman**, 45 Wesley St, Kirkby-In-Ashfield, Nottingham, **Nottinghamshire**, NG17 9HN, ENG.
(T) 01623 720122
Speciality: Aromatherapy.
● **Owner** Ms M Hackman
M O (Ref:HM08682)

## HACKNEY & ISLINGTON PSYCHO

**Hackney & Islington Psychotherapy Practice (The)**, 46B Ferntower Rd, London, **London (Greater)**, N5 2JH, ENG.
(T) 020 7359 4943
Speciality: Psychotherapy.
● **Partner** Ms A Froshaug
B (Ref:HM08683)

## HACKNEY FOOT CLINIC

**Hackney Foot Clinic**, 56 Glyn Rd, London, **London (Greater)**, E5 0JD, ENG.
(T) 020 8985 8001
Speciality: Chiropodists (Podiatrists).
S (Ref:HM08684)

## HACKNEY HYPNOTHERAPY

**Hackney Hypnotherapy**, 16 Skipworth Rd, Victoria Park, London, **London (Greater)**, E9 7JH, ENG.
(T) 020 8525 0418
(E) simon.clarke2@btinternet.com
Speciality: Auto Suggestion, Cognitive Therapy, Counselling, Humanistic Psychology, Hypnosis, Hypnotherapy, Life Style Coaching, Psychotherapy, Stress Therapy. ✔
● **Hypno-Psychotherapist** Mr S Clarke Q: BA (Hons), DHP (NC), MNRHP, UKCP (Reg). M: NRHP, UKCP.
H Yrs. Est.: 4 (Ref:HM08685)

## HACKNEY, DAVID T

**David T Hackney**, 11 Bardney Rd, Hunmanby, Filey, **Yorkshire (North)**, YO14 0LX, ENG.
(T) 01723 890998
Speciality: Chiropodists (Podiatrists).
● **Owner** Mr D Hackney
S (Ref:HM08686)

## HADDEN, MARLENE

**Marlene Hadden**, 51 Newcastle Rd, Kilkeel, Newry, **County Down**, BT34 4ND, NIR.
(T) 028 4176 2023
Speciality: Acupressure, Aromatherapy, Bach Remedies, Bowen Therapy, Colour Therapy, Counselling, Dietician, Hay Diet, Indian Head Massage, Reflexology, Bone Therapy, Chinese Reflexology. ✔
● **Reflexologist** Mrs M Hadden Q: BT, IIHHT. M: IIHHT.
T Yrs. Est.: 6 (Ref:HM08687)

## HADDEN, ROGER

**Roger Hadden**, 115 Bitterne Drive, Woking, **Surrey**, GU21 3JX, ENG.
(T) 01483 764098
Speciality: Homeopathy.
● **Owner** Mr R Hadden
M (Ref:HM08688)

## HADDES

**Haddes**, 9 Briar Gr, Leigh, **Manchester (Greater)**, WN7 5QZ, ENG.
(T) 01942 700785
Speciality: Complementary Medicines & Therapy.
● **Owner** Miss M Webb
C M (Ref:HM08689)

## HADDOCK, WENDY

**Wendy Haddock**, Aldrens Lane, Lancaster, **Lancashire**, LA1 2DU, ENG.
(T) 01524 69864 (F) 01524 848155
Speciality: Complementary Medicines & Therapy.
M (Ref:HM08690)

## HADFIELD, ELIZABETH

**Hadfield Elizabeth**, 89 Coed Isaf Rd, Pontypridd, **Rhondda Cynon Taff**, CF37 1EN, WAL.
(T) 01443 486559
Speciality: Chiropodists (Podiatrists).
● **Owner** Ms E Hadfield
S (Ref:HM08691)

## HADFIELD, G T

**G T Hadfield**, Windmill Bank Cottage, Windmill Bank, Rugeley, **Staffordshire**, WS15 4NH, ENG.
(T) 01543 672221 (F) 01543 672221
Speciality: Hypnosis.
● **Owner** Mr G Hadfield
B (Ref:HM08692)

## HADFIELD, M D

**M D Hadfield**, 62 Grove Lane, Hale, Altrincham, **Cheshire**, WA15 8JG, ENG.
(T) 01619 049797
Speciality: Chiropodists (Podiatrists).
S (Ref:HM08693)

## HADFIELD, T

**T Hadfield**, 258 Hull Rd, Anlaby Common, Hull, **Humberside (North)**, HU4 7RR, ENG.
(T) 01482 572316 (F) 01482 572316
Speciality: Chiropodists (Podiatrists).
● **Owner** Miss T Hadfield
S (Ref:HM08694)

## HADLEIGH PODIATRY CLINIC

**Hadleigh Podiatry Clinic**, 281 London Rd, Hadleigh, Benfleet, **Essex**, SS7 2BN, ENG.
(T) 01702 551261 (F) 01702 551261
(W) www.aklein.co.uk
Speciality: Biomechanics, Chiropody, Nail Surgery. ✔
● **Chiropodist (Podiatrist)** Mr A Klein Q: S.R.Ch.
C Yrs. Est.: 10 (Ref:HM08695)

## HADLEY WOOD HEALTH CENTRE

**Hadley Wood Health Centre**, 28 Crescent West, Barnet, **Hertfordshire**, EN4 0EJ, ENG.
(T) 020 8441 8352
Speciality: Osteopathy.
P S T (Ref:HM08696)

## HADLEY, SUSAN

**Susan Hadley**, 37 Heather Gardens, Romford, **Essex**, RM1 4SS, ENG.
(T) 01708 744859
Speciality: Reflexology.
S T (Ref:HM08697)

## HAGGARD, CAROLINE

**Caroline Haggard**, 94 St James's St, Brighton, **Sussex (East)**, BN2 1TP, ENG.
(T) 01273 672952
Speciality: Alexander Technique.
● **Owner** Mr L Moore
M (Ref:HM08698)

## HAGGAS, ERNEST

**Ernest Haggas**, 21 Maes-Y-Llan, Dwygyfylchi, Penmaenmawr, **Conwy**, LL34 6RY, WAL.
(T) 01492 622454
Speciality: Chiropodists (Podiatrists).
● **Owner** Mr E Haggas
S (Ref:HM08699)

## HAGGIE, PATRICIA

**Patricia Haggie**, 3 Shaftoe Cres, Hexham, **Northumberland**, NE46 3DS, ENG.
(T) 01434 606162
Speciality: Homeopathy.
● **Owner** Mrs P Haggie
M (Ref:HM08700)

## HAGLEY CENTRE OF COMP MED

**Hagley Centre Of Complementary Medicine (The)**, 137 Worcester Rd, Hagley, Stourbridge, **Midlands (West)**, DY9 0NW, ENG.
(T) 01562 883699 (F) 01384 373582
Speciality: Acupuncture, Aromatherapy, Bach Remedies, Chiropractic, Complementary Therapy, Counselling, Flotation Therapy, Healer, Holistic Healing, Homeopathy, Hypnosis, Hypnotherapy, Indian Head Massage, Massage (Therapeutic). ✔
● **Hypnotherapist** Ms J Ward Q: Dip.Hyp. M: BSCH.
● **McTimoney Chiropractor** Ms H Jack Q: DC, MMCA. M: MCA.
● **Homeopath** Ms T Shipley Q: LCPH. M: HMA.
● **Acupuncturist** Ms L Bailey Q: Lic.Ac. M: BAcC.
B M S T Yrs. Est.: 3 (Ref:HM08701)

## HAHN, HERBERT

**Herbert Hahn**, Fairview Drive, Bristol, BS6 6PW, ENG.
(T) 01179 425078
Speciality: Psychology.
B (Ref:HM08702)

Key: B Mind-Body Medicine C Complementary Medicine H Self Help Treatment M Medicinal Therapy O Oriental Medicine P Postural Therapy S Manipulative Structural Therapy T Touch Therapy

### HAI TIAN HEALTH CENTRE

**Hai Tian Health Centre**, 88 Wilton Rd, London, **London (Greater)**, SW1V 1DN, ENG.
(T) 020 7630 6688
Speciality: Acupuncture.
● **Owner** Ms X Zhang
O (Ref:HM08703)

### HAI TIAN TRADING

**Hai Tian Trading Co Ltd**, 45A London Rd, Brighton, **Sussex (East)**, BN1 4JD, ENG.
(T) 01273 673888
Speciality: Complementary Medicines & Therapy.
C M (Ref:HM08704)

### HAIG, GEORGE

**George Haig**, 2 Torphichen Pl, Edinburgh, **Edinburgh (City of)**, EH3 8DU, SCO.
(T) 01312 282288 (F) 01312 284826
Speciality: Chiropractors.
● **Principal** Dr G Haig
P S T (Ref:HM08705)

### HAIGH, ALEXANDRA L

**Alexandra L Haigh**, 128 Longmoor Rd, Liphook, **Hampshire**, GU30 7NZ, ENG.
(T) 01428 723098
Speciality: Chiropodists (Podiatrists).
● **Owner** Alexandra Haigh
S (Ref:HM08706)

### HAIGH, ANNA-LOUISE

**Anna-Louise Haigh**, Lavender Court Therapy & Education Centre, 159 Kings Rd, Harrogate, **Yorkshire (North)**, HG1 5JQ, ENG.
(T) 01423 500494
Speciality: Aromatherapy.
● **Principal** Miss A Haigh
M O (Ref:HM08707)

### HAIGH, J

**J Haigh**, 91 Brecks Cr, Rotherham, **Yorkshire (South)**, S65 3HU, ENG.
(T) 01709 703505
Speciality: Chiropodists (Podiatrists).
● **Owner** Mrs J Haigh
S (Ref:HM08708)

### HAILSTONE, NEIL

**Neil Hailstone**, 7 Valley Rd, Buckingham, **Buckinghamshire**, MK18 7BW, ENG.
(T) 01280 817460
Speciality: Chiropodists (Podiatrists).
S (Ref:HM08709)

### HAILWOOD, ADRIAN

**Adrian Hailwood**, 23 Churchill Cres, Alrewas, Burton-On-Trent, **Staffordshire**, DE13 7EH, ENG.
(T) 01283 790188
Speciality: Homeopathy.
● **Owner** Mr A Hailwood
M (Ref:HM08710)

### HAILWOOD, ADRIAN

**Adrian Hailwood**, 9 Brewers Lane, Richmond, **Surrey**, TW9 1HH, ENG.
(T) 020 8332 6566
Speciality: Homeopathy.
● **Director** Mrs S Shingler
M (Ref:HM08711)

### HAIN, PATRICIA

**Patricia Hain**, 14 Brandlehow Rd, Putney, London, **London (Greater)**, SW15 2ED, ENG.
(T) 020 8874 2414 (F) 020 8874 2457
(E) phain@talk21.com
Speciality: Nutritional Therapy, Reflexology. ✓
● **Nutritional Therapist** Ms P Hain
Q: Dip.Nut.Th, Dip.Reflex. M: BANT, BRA.
B Yrs. Est.: 11 (Ref:HM08712)

### HAINES, C

**C Haines**, Watermouth Castle, Berrynarbor, Ilfracombe, **Devon**, EX34 9SL, ENG.
(T) 01271 867678
Speciality: Acupuncture.
O (Ref:HM08713)

### HAINES, N

**N Haines**, Nottingham Natural Health Centre, 354 Mansfield Rd, Nottingham, **Nottinghamshire**, NG5 2EF, ENG.
(T) 01159 608855
Speciality: Acupuncture.
O (Ref:HM08714)

### HAIR & BODY CARE CLINIC

**Hair & Body Care Clinic (The)**, 16A Front St, Hetton-Le-Hole, Houghton le Spring, **Tyne and Wear**, DH5 9PF, ENG.
(T) 01915 172577
Speciality: Complementary Medicines & Therapy.
C M (Ref:HM08715)

### HAIR FREE EPILIGHT CLINIC

**Hair Free Epilight Clinic**, 3 Stafford St, Eccleshall, Stafford, **Staffordshire**, ST21 6BL, ENG.
(T) 01785 859259 (F) 01785 859249
Speciality: Electrolysis.
● **Managing Director** Mr D Brough
T (Ref:HM08716)

### HAIR TOMMOROW GROUP

**Hair Tommorow Group**, Briarwood House, 11 College Avenue, Maidenhead, **Berkshire**, SL6 6AR, ENG.
(T) 01628 776587 (F) 01628 638810
Speciality: Complementary Medicines & Therapy.
● **Owner** Mrs A Bosworth
C M (Ref:HM08717)

### HAIR, LOUISE

**Louise Hair**, 14 Fiddlers Drive, Armthorpe, Doncaster, **Yorkshire (South)**, DN3 3TT, ENG.
(T) 01302 300835
Speciality: Reflexology.
● **Owner** Miss L Hair
S T (Ref:HM08718)

### HAIRSINE, P W

**P W Hairsine**, 78 Churchill Rd, Barnard Castle, **County Durham**, DL12 8LN, ENG.
(T) 01833 630640
Speciality: Osteopathy.
P S T (Ref:HM08719)

### HAISELDEN, JENNIE

**Jennie Haiselden**, 8 Hetton Cl, Heelands, **Buckinghamshire**, MK13 7NP, ENG.
(T) 01908 314199
Speciality: Reflexology.
S T (Ref:HM08720)

### HAJIOFF, RUTH

**Ruth Hajioff**, 6 Wildwood Gr, London, **London (Greater)**, NW3 7HU, ENG.
(T) 020 8731 7030 (F) 020 8731 7030
Speciality: Acupuncture.
● **Owner** Mrs R Hajioff
O (Ref:HM08721)

### HALAHAN, ELISABETH

**Elisabeth Halahan**, 12 Hillside Rd, St. Albans, **Hertfordshire**, AL1 3QL, ENG.
(T) 01727 857423 (F) 01727 837983
Speciality: Homeopathy. ✓
● **Owner** Mrs E Halahan Q: Dip.Hom. M: Soc.Hom.
M Yrs. Est.: 8 (Ref:HM08722)

### HALAS THERAPIES

**Halas Therapies**, Church Chambers, 26-32 High St, Halesowen, **Midlands (West)**, B63 3BB, ENG.
(T) 01215 501190
Speciality: Complementary Medicines & Therapy.
● **Partner** Mr R Priest
C M (Ref:HM08723)

### HALCYON AROMATICS

**Halcyon Aromatics**, 35 High St, Normanton, **Yorkshire (West)**, WF6 2AF, ENG.
(T) 01924 893059
Speciality: Aromatherapy.
● **Owner** Mrs A Close
M O (Ref:HM08724)

### HALCYON LIFESTYLE

**Halcyon Lifestyle Ltd**, 7a Hill Avenue, Amersham, **Buckinghamshire**, HP6 5BD, ENG.
(T) 01494 722707 (F) 01494 722707
Speciality: Complementary Medicines & Therapy.
● **Owner** Ms S Fowler
M (Ref:HM08725)

### HALCYON THERAPIES

**Halcyon Therapies**, Old Hall, Newtown, Leominster, **Herefordshire**, HR6 8QD, ENG.
(T) 01568 616090
Speciality: Physiotherapy.
● **Owner** Mrs H Thomas
P S T (Ref:HM08726)

### HALE ASSOCIATES

**Hale Associates**, 197 Tettenhall Rd, Wolverhampton, **Midlands (West)**, WV6 0BZ, ENG.
(T) 01902 429353
Speciality: Osteopathy. ✓
● **Osteopath** Mr G Hale Q: DO. M: GOsC.
S Yrs. Est.: 13 (Ref:HM08727)

### HALE CLINIC

**Hale Clinic (The)**, 7 Park Cres, London, **London (Greater)**, W1N 3HE, ENG.
(T) 020 7631 0156
Speciality: Osteopathy.
● **Therapist** Peter Bartlett
● **Therapist** Kenneth Underhill
P S T (Ref:HM08728)

### HALE, B E C (DR)

**Dr B E C Hale**, Thorpes, The Common, Galleywood, Chelmsford, **Essex**, CM2 8TN, ENG.
(T) 01245 352620
Speciality: Homeopathy.
● **Owner** Dr B Hale
M (Ref:HM08729)

### HALE, DAVID

**David Hale**, Dawley Medical Practice, Dawley, Telford, **Shropshire**, TF4 3AL, ENG.
(T) 01952 505213
Speciality: Acupuncture.
O (Ref:HM08730)

### HALE, FRANCIS R

**Francis R Hale**, 105 Grange Rd, Darlington, **County Durham**, DL1 5NN, ENG.
(T) 01325 464791
Speciality: Physiotherapy.
● **Owner** Mr F Hale
P S T (Ref:HM08731)

### HALE, GEOFF

**Geoff Hale**, 576 Bearwood Rd, Smethwick, **Midlands (West)**, B66 4BW, ENG.
(T) 01214 204340
Speciality: Osteopathy. ✓
● **Osteopath** Mr G Hale Q: DO. M: GOsC.
S Yrs. Est.: 13 (Ref:HM08732)

### HALE, J N

**J N Hale**, 75 Rose Lane, Biggleswade, **Bedfordshire**, SG18 0JY, ENG.
(T) 01767 316633
Speciality: Chiropodists (Podiatrists).
● **Owner** Mrs J Hale
S (Ref:HM08733)

### HALE, JO

**Jo Hale**, Queens Court, Woodland Rd, Derby, **Derbyshire**, DE22 1GR, ENG.
(T) 01332 299133
Speciality: Homeopathy.
M (Ref:HM08734)

### HALE, M

**M Hale**, 52 St Margaret's Rd, Swindon, **Wiltshire**, SN3 1RX, ENG.
(T) 01793 527851
Speciality: Osteopathy.
● **Owner** Mr M Hale
P S T (Ref:HM08735)

### HALE, M A

**M A Hale**, 44 North Rd, Midsomer Norton, Bath, **Somerset**, BA3 2QQ, ENG.
(T) 01761 414304
Speciality: Chiropodists (Podiatrists).
● **Owner** Mr M Hale
S (Ref:HM08736)

### HALE, MARTINE

**Martine Hale**, 56 Sistova Rd, London, **London (Greater)**, SW12 9QS, ENG.



Key continued: Yrs.Est: Years Established Q: Qualifications M: Professional Membership ✓ Indemnity Insurance Accept Credit Cards

(T) 020 8673 5116
Speciality: Physiotherapy.
● **Owner** Mrs M Hale
P S T (Ref:HM08737)

### HALE, MIKE
**Mike Hale**, Health Hydro, Milton Rd, Swindon, **Wiltshire**, SN1 5JA, ENG.
(T) 01793 465631
Speciality: Osteopathy.
P S T (Ref:HM08738)

### HALE, R C
**R C Hale**, 12 Moss Lane, Alderley Edge, **Cheshire**, SK9 7HN, ENG.
(T) 01625 582661
Speciality: Chiropodists (Podiatrists).
● **Owner** Mrs R Hale
S (Ref:HM08739)

### HALE, SHIRLEY
**Shirley Hale**, 24 Ross Court, Putney Hill, London, **London (Greater)**, SW15 3NY, ENG.
(T) 020 8789 0944
Speciality: Complementary Medicines & Therapy.
M (Ref:HM08740)

### HALE, STUART
**Stuart Hale**, 77 Fluin Lane, Frodsham, **Cheshire**, WA6 7QU, ENG.
(T) 01928 735689
Speciality: Osteopathy.
P S T (Ref:HM08741)

### HALE, SUE
**Sue Hale**, 20 Walter Rd, Swansea, SA1 5RS, WAL.
(T) 01792 234176
Speciality: Psychotherapy.
B (Ref:HM08742)

### HALES OSTEOPATHIC PRACTICE
**Janine Lees**, 8a Wilkinson Walk, Market Drayton, **Shropshire**, TF9 1PW, ENG.
(T) 01630 656546 (F) 01630 653533
Speciality: Acupuncture, Cranial Osteopathy, Family Planning (Natural), Hay Diet, Manipulation, Nutritional Therapy, Osteopathy, Vitamin Therapy. ✔
● **Therapist** Ms J Lees Q: DO. M: GOsC.
● **Therapist** Ms H Pass Q: Lic.Ac. M: BAcC.
● **Therapist** Ms S Jackson Q: B.Ed, Dip.ION. M: BANT.
S Yrs. Est.: 6 (Ref:HM08743)

### HALES, DIANE
**Diane Hales**, Chesworth House, Pound Green, Buxted, Uckfield, **Sussex (East)**, TN22 4JW, ENG.
(T) 01825 733766
Speciality: Osteopathy.
P S T (Ref:HM08744)

### HALES, G J
**G J Hales**, 1 North St, Castle Cary, **Somerset**, BA7 7AU, ENG.
(T) 01963 350618 (F) 01963 350618
Speciality: Chiropodists (Podiatrists).
● **Owner** Mr G Hales
S (Ref:HM08745)

### HALES, GERALD (DR)
**Dr Gerald Hales**, 19 Canon Harnett Court, Wolverton Mill, Milton Keynes, **Buckinghamshire**, MK12 5NF, ENG.
(T) 01908 312880 (F) 01908 317691
Speciality: Psychology.
● **Practice Manager** Miss D Smith
B (Ref:HM08746)

### HALES, J
**J Hales**, The Surgery, 20 Oxford St, Wellingborough, **Northamptonshire**, NN8 4HY, ENG.
(T) 01933 222418
Speciality: Chiropodists (Podiatrists).
S (Ref:HM08747)

### HALFORD, D
**D Halford**, 11 Wells Rd, Ilkley, **Yorkshire (West)**, LS29 9JB, ENG.
(T) 01943 816911
Speciality: Chiropodists (Podiatrists).
● **Chief Executive** Mr D Halford
S (Ref:HM08748)

### HALFORD, ELIZABETH
**Elizabeth Halford**, 145 Bengeo St, Hertford, **Hertfordshire**, SG14 3EY, ENG.
(T) 01992 586294
Speciality: Osteopathy.
P S T (Ref:HM08749)

### HALFORD, ELIZABETH
**Elizabeth Halford**, Cwmbychan, Ffostrasol, Llandysul, **Carmarthenshire**, SA44 5SB, WAL.
(T) 01239 851904 (F) 01239 851904
Speciality: Osteopathy.
● **Owner** Mr D Halford
P S T (Ref:HM08750)

### HALFORD, ELIZABETH
**Elizabeth Halford**, Watton Place Clinic, 60 High St, Watton At Stone, Hertford, **Hertfordshire**, SG14 3TA, ENG.
(T) 01992 586294
Speciality: Osteopathy.
P S T (Ref:HM08751)

### HALFORD, EVELYN
**Evelyn Halford**, 2 Woodland Cres, Bracknell, **Berkshire**, RG42 2LH, ENG.
(T) 01344 420099
Speciality: Chiropodists (Podiatrists).
● **Owner** Mrs E Halford
S (Ref:HM08752)

### HALFORD, ROBERT
**Robert Halford**, Cwmbychan, Ffostrasol, Llandysul, **Carmarthenshire**, SA44 5SB, WAL.
(T) 01239 851904 (F) 01239 851904
Speciality: Homeopathy.
● **Owner** Mr D Halford
M (Ref:HM08753)

### HALIFAX CHIROPODY CENTRE
**Halifax Chiropody Centre**, 8 King Cross St, Halifax, **Yorkshire (West)**, HX1 2SH, ENG.
(T) 01422 360421
Speciality: Chiropodists (Podiatrists).
S (Ref:HM08754)

### HALIFAX CHIROPRACTIC CLINIC
**Halifax Chiropractic Clinic**, 30 Prescott St, Halifax, **Yorkshire (West)**, HX1 2LG, ENG.
(T) 01422 252625
Speciality: Chiropractors.
● **Partner** Mrs D Cheung
P S T (Ref:HM08755)

### HALIFAX CLINIC OF NATURAL MED
**Halifax Clinic Of Natural Medicine**, 22 Clare Rd, Halifax, **Yorkshire (West)**, HX1 2HX, ENG.
(T) 01422 340919
Speciality: Hypnotherapy.
B (Ref:HM08756)

### HALISK ASSOCIATES
**Halisk Associates**, 63 Kooreman Avenue, Wisbech, **Cambridgeshire**, PE13 3HY, ENG.
(T) 01945 582493
Speciality: Complementary Medicines & Therapy.
● **Owner** Mrs M Fiske
M (Ref:HM08757)

### HALKYARD, STEVEN
**Steven Halkyard**, 29 Newlay Lane, Bramley, Leeds, **Yorkshire (West)**, LS13 2AL, ENG.
(T) 01132 299571
Speciality: Reflexology.
● **Owner** Mr S Halkyard
S T (Ref:HM08758)

### HALL & FORSTER
**Hall & Forster**, 27 New Green St, South Shields, **Tyne and Wear**, NE33 5DL, ENG.
(T) 01914 545701
Speciality: Electrolysis.
● **Owner** Mr J Larcombe
T (Ref:HM08759)

### HALL GREEN ALTERN PRACTICE
**Hall Green Alternative Practice**, 48 Kedleston Rd, Birmingham, **Midlands (West)**, B28 0NR, ENG.
(T) 01217 337170 (F) 01217 337170
(E) steve@skempson.freeserve.co.uk
Speciality: Bach Remedies, Holistic Healing, Homeopathy, Kinesiology, Australian flower remedies. ✔
● **Associate** Mr S Kempson
● **Owner** Ms J Wood Q: LCPH.
C Yrs. Est.: 6 (Ref:HM08760)

### HALL, A
**A Hall**, 51 Nottingham Rd, Derby, **Derbyshire**, DE1 3QT, ENG.
(T) 01773 822318
Speciality: Chiropodists (Podiatrists).
● **Owner** A Hall
S (Ref:HM08761)

### HALL, A M
**A M Hall**, Moortown Rd, Nettleton, Market Rasen, **Lincolnshire**, LN7 6HX, ENG.
(T) 01472 851230
Speciality: Homeopathy.
● **Owner** A Hall
M (Ref:HM08762)

### HALL, ALAN
**Alan Hall**, 12 Tudor Rd, Lincoln, **Lincolnshire**, LN6 3LL, ENG.
(T) 01522 884857
Speciality: Reflexology.
S T (Ref:HM08763)

### HALL, ALISON
**Alison Hall**, 10 Church St, Caernarfon, **Gwynedd**, LL55 1SW, WAL.
(T) 01286 678428
Speciality: Osteopathy.
P S T (Ref:HM08764)

### HALL, ANNIE
**Annie Hall**, 32 Eastgate, Louth, **Lincolnshire**, LN11 9NG, ENG.
(T) 01507 608166
Speciality: Homeopathy.
M (Ref:HM08765)

### HALL, ANNIE
**Annie Hall**, 26 West Prde, Lincoln, **Lincolnshire**, LN1 1JT, ENG.
(T) 01522 530530
Speciality: Homeopathy.
M (Ref:HM08766)

### HALL, BEVERLEY
**Beverley Hall**, 53 Albert Rd, Caversham Heights, Reading, **Berkshire**, RG4 7AW, ENG.
(T) 01189 463460
Speciality: Alexander Technique.
● **Teacher Of The Alexander Technique** Mrs B Hall Q: MSTAT. M: STAT.
P Yrs. Est.: 4 (Ref:HM08767)

### HALL, C
**C Hall**, The Southfields Clinic, 41 Southfields Rd, London, **London (Greater)**, SW18 1QW, ENG.
(T) 020 8874 4125
Speciality: Acupuncture.
O (Ref:HM08768)

### HALL, CHRISTINE
**Christine Hall**, 169 Elm Rd, New Malden, **Surrey**, KT3 3HX, ENG.
(T) 020 8942 1899
Speciality: Reflexology.
S T (Ref:HM08769)

### HALL, ELIZABETH
**Elizabeth Hall**, The Mount, Habberley Lane, Trimpley, Bewdley, **Worcestershire**, DY12 1NL, ENG.
(T) 01299 400545
Speciality: Complementary Medicines & Therapy.
C M (Ref:HM08770)

### HALL, G J
**G J Hall**, 15 Kingsley Rd, Norwich, **Norfolk**, NR1 3RB, ENG.
(T) 01603 624547
Speciality: Osteopathy.
● **Owner** Mr R Hall
P S T (Ref:HM08771)

### HALL, GERRY
**Gerry Hall**, The Old Post Office, Coates, Cirencester, **Gloucestershire**, GL7 6NW, ENG.
(T) 01285 770202

Speciality: Acupuncture.
O (Ref:HM08772)

**HALL, GRACE**

**Grace Hall**, 229B High St, Crowthorne, **Berkshire**, RG45 7AQ, ENG.
(T) 01344 761811 (F) 01344 751113
Speciality: Homeopathy, Nutritional Therapy.
✔
● **Partner/Nutritional Therapist**
Mrs G Hall
● **Natural Therapist** Mr M Hall Q: BA, MA.
C Yrs. Est.: 20 (Ref:HM08773)

**HALL, J**

**J Hall**, 12 Depmore Lane, Frodsham, **Cheshire**, WA6 6UB, ENG.
(T) 01928 787500
Speciality: Hypnosis.
● **Owner** Mrs J Hall
B (Ref:HM08774)

**HALL, J B**

**J B Hall**, 37 Bryntirion Hill, Bridgend, CF31 4BY, WAL.
(T) 01656 654932
Speciality: Physiotherapy.
P S T (Ref:HM08775)

**HALL, JACQUELINE**

**Jacqueline Hall**, Rowney Farm, Chaseways, Sawbridgeworth, **Hertfordshire**, CM21 0AS, ENG.
(T) 01279 725390
Speciality: Reflexology.
S T (Ref:HM08776)

**HALL, JOY**

**Joy Hall**, Timber Edge, Forge Rd, Naphill, High Wycombe, **Buckinghamshire**, HP14 4ST, ENG.
(T) 01494 565941 (F) 01494 565941
Speciality: Homeopathy.
● **Owner** Mrs J Hall
M (Ref:HM08777)

**HALL, JOY**

**Joy Hall**, St Margarets Vicarage, Hammersley Lane, Tylers Green, High Wycombe, **Buckinghamshire**, HP10 8HB, ENG.
(T) 01494 813367
Speciality: Homeopathy.
M (Ref:HM08778)

**HALL, KATHARINE**

**Katharine Hall**, 151-153 Clapham High St, London, **London (Greater)**, SW4 7SS, ENG.
(T) 020 7627 8890
Speciality: Complementary Medicines & Therapy.
● **Owner** Mr M Knight
M (Ref:HM08779)

**HALL, KATHRYN**

**Kathryn Hall**, 12 Binn Rd, Marsden, Huddersfield, **Yorkshire (West)**, HD7 6HF, ENG.
(T) 01484 840425
Speciality: Reflexology.
● **Owner** Mrs L Hall
S T (Ref:HM08780)

**HALL, KEN**

**Ken Hall**, 30 King St, Thorne, Doncaster, **Yorkshire (South)**, DN8 5BA, ENG.
(T) 01405 741996
Speciality: Complementary Medicines & Therapy.
C M (Ref:HM08781)

**HALL, LISA**

**Lisa Hall**, 5a Criterion Buildings, Portsmouth Rd, Thames Ditton, **Surrey**, KT7 0SS, ENG.
(T) 020 8786 8088
Speciality: Aromatherapy.
M O (Ref:HM08782)

**HALL, LYNN**

**Lynn Hall**, Ross-On-Wye, Hereford & Worcester, HR9, ENG.
(T) 01989 566214
Speciality: Bach Remedies.
M (Ref:HM08783)

**HALL, MANDY**

**Mandy Hall**, 57-63 Lea Rd, Northampton, **Northamptonshire**, NN1 4PE, ENG.
(T) 01604 460064
Speciality: Chiropodists (Podiatrists).
S (Ref:HM08784)

**HALL, MARGARET**

**Margaret Hall**, Scott St Complementary Therapy Centre, 58 Scott St, Barrow-in-Furness, **Cumbria**, LA14 1QE, ENG.
(T) 01229 826700
Speciality: Homeopathy.
M (Ref:HM08785)

**HALL, N S (DR)**

**Dr N S Hall**, 5 Cambridge Rd, Horsham, **Sussex (West)**, RH13 5ED, ENG.
(T) 01403 272559
Speciality: Hypnosis.
● **Owner** Dr N Hall
B (Ref:HM08786)

**HALL, PETER**

**Peter Hall**, Keswin, Longdowns, Penryn, **Cornwall**, TR10 9DR, ENG.
(T) 01209 861511
(E) peterhall@easicom.com
Speciality: Acupressure, Acupuncture, Cranial Osteopathy, Cupping, Dietician, Do-In, Electrotherapy, Macrobiotics, Meditation, Moxibustion, Oriental Diagnosis, Shiatsu, T'ai-Chi Ch'uan, Sports Therapy. ✔
● **Oriental Medical Practitioner**
Mr P Hall Q: Dip.Ac, Dip.Shiatsu. M: BAcC, Shiatsu Society UK.
C O S Yrs. Est.: 4 (Ref:HM08787)

**HALL, RICHARD**

**Richard Hall**, 15 Kingsley Rd, Norwich, **Norfolk**, NR1 3RB, ENG.
(T) 01603 736148
Speciality: Chiropodists (Podiatrists).
● **Owner** Mr R Hall
S (Ref:HM08788)

**HALL, SHEILA**

**Sheila Hall**, 12 High St, Haxey, Doncaster, **Yorkshire (South)**, DN9 2HX, ENG.
(T) 01302 842068
Speciality: Reflexology.
S T (Ref:HM08789)

**HALL, SUSAN**

**Susan Hall**, 39 Lower High St, Wednesbury, **Midlands (West)**, WS10 7AQ, ENG.
(T) 01215 053019
Speciality: Chiropody, Indian Head Massage, Hopi Ear Treatment. ✔
● **Chiropodist/Reflexologist**
Mrs S Hall Q: MBChA, MSSCh. M: B.A.Ch.P.
C Yrs. Est.: 10 (Ref:HM08790)

**HALL, SUSANNE**

**Susanne Hall**, 10 Boscastle Rd, London, **London (Greater)**, NW5 1EG, ENG.
(T) 020 7267 1519
Speciality: Alexander Technique.
● **Owner** Ms S Hall
P S (Ref:HM08791)

**HALL, VALERIE**

**Valerie Hall**, East Wing, Loton Hall, Alberbury, Shrewsbury, **Shropshire**, SY5 9AJ, ENG.
(T) 01743 884089
Speciality: Hypnosis.
B (Ref:HM08792)

**HALLACK, VIVIENNE**

**Vivienne Hallack**, 127 Merchants Quay, Salford, **Manchester (Greater)**, M5 2XQ, ENG.
(T) 01618 723945
Speciality: Homeopathy.
● **Owner** Miss V Hallack
M (Ref:HM08793)

**HALLAM CHIROPODY CLINIC**

**Hallam Chiropody Clinic**, 211 Oakbrook Rd, Sheffield, **Yorkshire (South)**, S11 7EB, ENG.
(T) 01142 630055
Speciality: Chiropodists (Podiatrists).
S (Ref:HM08794)

**HALLAM, CHRISTINA**

**Christina Hallam**, The Whitehouse, 282 St Johns Rd, Hemel Hempstead, **Hertfordshire**, HP1 1QG, ENG.
(T) 01442 265250
Speciality: Homeopathy.
M (Ref:HM08795)

**HALLAM, F E & M G**

**F E & M G Hallam**, 187 Queens Rd, Beeston, Nottingham, **Nottinghamshire**, NG9 2FE, ENG.
(T) 01159 255226
Speciality: Chiropodists (Podiatrists).
S (Ref:HM08796)

**HALLAM, JANET**

**Janet Hallam**, 61 Broad Hinton, Twyford, Reading, **Berkshire**, RG10 0LP, ENG.
(T) 01189 321693
Speciality: Chiropodists (Podiatrists).
S (Ref:HM08797)

**HALLAMSHIRE NATURAL HLTH CTRE**

**Hallamshire Natural Health Centre**, 10 Dover Rd, Hunters Bar, Sheffield, **Yorkshire (South)**, S11 8RH, ENG.
(T) 01142 662321
(E) hnhc@synergnet.co.uk
Speciality: Absent Healing, Alexander Technique, Aromatherapy, Bach Remedies, Bates Method, Bowen Therapy, Chiropractic, Complementary Therapy, Counselling, Crystal Healing, Dowsing, Healer, Healing Therapy, Herbal Medicine, Holistic Healing, Homeopathy, Indian Head Massage, Iridology, Manipulation, Massage (Therapeutic), Meditation, Nutritional Therapy, Psychotherapy, Reichian Therapy, Reiki, Tantra Therapy, Vitamin Therapy. ✔
● **Owner** Ms P Easten Q: MSTAT. M: STAT.
B Yrs. Est.: 10 (Ref:HM08798)

**HALLAMSHIRE PHYSIO/SPORTS CTRE**

**Hallamshire Physiotherapy & Sports Injury Centre**, Hallamshire Hospital, Glossop Rd, Sheffield, **Yorkshire (South)**, S10 2JF, ENG.
(T) 01142 798777
Speciality: Physiotherapy.
P S T (Ref:HM08799)

**HALLARD, SHARON**

**Sharon Hallard**, 31A St. Edward St, Leek, **Staffordshire**, ST13 5DN, ENG.
(T) 07831 295599
Speciality: Phytotherapy. ✔
● **Owner/Psychotherapist**
Mrs S Hallard Q: RGN, RMN. M: IGA, UKCP.
C Yrs. Est.: 10 (Ref:HM08800)

**HALLER, LYNN**

**Lynn Haller**, Clissold Park Health Centre, 154 Stoke Newington Church St, London, **London (Greater)**, N16 0JU, ENG.
(T) 020 7249 2990 (F) 020 7249 3977
Speciality: Osteopathy.
● **Owner** Mr D Berg
P S T (Ref:HM08801)

**HALLER, R L**

**R L Haller**, Sutherland House, 1a Ashbourne Avenue, London, **London (Greater)**, NW11 0DP, ENG.
(T) 020 8458 7869
Speciality: Osteopathy.
P S T (Ref:HM08802)

**HALLEWELL, LOUISA**

**Louisa Hallewell**, 12 Brackley Rd, Hazlemere, High Wycombe, **Buckinghamshire**, HP15 7EW, ENG.
(T) 07976 840978
Speciality: Reflexology.
● **Owner** Mrs L Halliwell
S T (Ref:HM08803)

**HALLIDAY, BRETT (DR)**

**Dr Brett Halliday**, Corner Church And Henry Streets, Tullamore, **County Offaly**, IRE.
(T) 05062 4570
Speciality: Complementary Medicines & Therapy.
M (Ref:HM08804)

**HALLIDAY, BRIAN M**

**Brian M Halliday**, St Johns Practice, 2 St. Johns Rd, Isleworth, **London (Greater)**, TW7 6NN, ENG.
(T) 020 8560 7073
Speciality: Osteopathy.




Key continued: Yrs.Est: Years Established Q: Qualifications M: Professional Membership ✔ Indemnity Insurance Accept Credit Cards

P S T (Ref:HM08805)

**HALLIDAY, C**

**C Halliday**, Oatlands Drive, Weybridge, **Surrey**, KT13 9DF, ENG.
(T) 01932 245855
Speciality: Aromatherapy.
● **Owner** Mrs C Halliday
M O (Ref:HM08806)

**HALLIDAY, J**

**J Halliday**, 98 Helmsley Rd, Newcastle Upon Tyne, **Tyne and Wear**, NE2 1RE, ENG.
(T) 01912 818500
Speciality: Psychotherapy.
B (Ref:HM08807)

**HALLIDAY, K J**

**K J Halliday**, 54 Thorpedene Gardens, Shoeburyness, Southend-On-Sea, **Essex**, SS3 9JD, ENG.
(T) 01702 295662
Speciality: Chiropodists (Podiatrists).
● **Owner** Mr K Halliday
S (Ref:HM08808)

**HALLIN, ANDREAS (DR)**

**Dr Andreas Hallin**, Blackberry Orthopaedic Clinic, Blackberry Court, Walnut Tree, Milton Keynes, **Buckinghamshire**, MK7 7PB, ENG.
(T) 01908 604666
Speciality: Chiropractors.
P S T (Ref:HM08809)

**HALLINAN, DEBORAH**

**Deborah Hallinan**, Weybank, 8 Riverside Gardens, Woking, **Surrey**, GU22 9LJ, ENG.
(T) 01483 763210
Speciality: Reflexology.
S T (Ref:HM08810)

**HALLOWELL, K**

**K Hallowell**, 34 Woodville Rd, Barnet, **Hertfordshire**, EN5 5HA, ENG.
(T) 020 8441 2188
Speciality: Physiotherapy.
P S T (Ref:HM08811)

**HALLS, D O**

**Mr D O Halls**, The Surgery, Old Bridge, Newlyn, Penzance, **Cornwall**, TR18 5PR, ENG.
(T) 01736 330588
Speciality: Hypnotherapy.
B (Ref:HM08812)

**HALLS, DENNIS**

**Dennis Halls**, The Surgery, Old Bridge, Newlyn, Penzance, **Cornwall**, TR18 5PR, ENG.
(T) 01736 330588
Speciality: Hypnotherapy.
B (Ref:HM08813)

**HALLS, R**

**R Halls**, 9 Beeches Avenue, Carshalton, **Surrey**, SM5 3LB, ENG.
(T) 020 8773 4508
Speciality: Homeopathy.
M (Ref:HM08814)

**HALPIN, P J**

**P J Halpin**, 112 Orsett Rd, Grays, **Essex**, RM17 5ES, ENG.
(T) 01375 370023
Speciality: Chiropodists (Podiatrists).
● **Owner** Mr P Halpin
S (Ref:HM08815)

**HALPIN, P J**

**P J Halpin**, Stonerunner, Rye Harbour Rd, Rye, **Sussex (East)**, TN31 7TT, ENG.
(T) 01797 224351
Speciality: Psychotherapy.
● **Owner** Mrs P Halpin
B (Ref:HM08816)

**HALSALL, JANET**

**Janet Halsall**, 14 Siskin Cl, Newton-Le-Willows, **Merseyside**, WA12 9XW, ENG.
(T) 01925 291146
Speciality: Reflexology.
S T (Ref:HM08817)

**HALSTEAD, DAVE**

**Dave Halstead**, Red Gables Mill Lane, Upton, Pontefract, **Yorkshire (West)**, WF9 1BZ, ENG.
(T) 01977 640565
Speciality: Physiotherapy.
P S T (Ref:HM08818)

**HALSTEAD, RITA**

**Rita Halstead**, 24 Parkstone Drive, Southend-On-Sea, **Essex**, SS2 6NX, ENG.
(T) 01702 337625
Speciality: Acupuncture.
● **Owner** Mrs R Halstead
O (Ref:HM08819)

**HALTEMPRICE CHIRO CLINIC**

**Haltemprice Chiropractic Clinic**, 4a Kingston Rd, Willerby, Hull, **Humberside (North)**, HU10 6BN, ENG.
(T) 01482 653255
Speciality: Chiropractic.
● **Owner** Mr D Grant
P S T (Ref:HM08820)

**HALTON, A**

**A Halton**, Bank Top Farm, Roston, Ashbourne, **Derbyshire**, DE6 2EH, ENG.
(T) 01335 324273
Speciality: Osteopathy.
● **Owner** A Halton
P S T (Ref:HM08821)

**HAM CHIROPRACTIC CLINIC**

**Ham Chiropractic Clinic**, 1 Dysart Avenue, Kingston Upon Thames, **Surrey**, KT2 5QZ, ENG.
(T) 020 8549 6696 (F) 020 8549 6696
(E) arek@btclick.com
Speciality: Chiropractic. ✔
● **Doctor** Dr S Nelson Q: BSc, DC. M: BCA, GCC.
● **Doctor** Dr A Mazur Q: BSc, DC. M: BCA, GCC.
S Yrs. Est.: 9 (Ref:HM08822)

**HAMAR, KLARE**

**Klare Hamar**, 27 Newington Cl, Frome, **Somerset**, BA11 1HW, ENG.
Speciality: Reflexology.
S T (Ref:HM08823)

**HAMBLEDON HOLISTIC HEALTH**

**Hambledon Holistic Health**, 1 Red Roofs, Malthouse Lane, Hambledon, Godalming, **Surrey**, GU8 4HH, ENG.
(T) 01428 684281
Speciality: Reflexology.
● **Owner** Ms R Clunie
S T (Ref:HM08824)

**HAMBLETT, J E**

**J E Hamblett**, 8 Henstead Rd, Southampton, **Hampshire**, SO15 2DD, ENG.
(T) 023 8033 1455
Speciality: Osteopathy.
● **Owner** Dr J Hamblett
P S T (Ref:HM08825)

**HAMBLETT, JOHN E (DR)**

**Dr John E Hamblett**, 30 Elgin Rd, Bournemouth, **Dorset**, BH4 9NL, ENG.
(T) 01202 764524
Speciality: Osteopathy.
● **Owner** Dr J Hamblett
P S T (Ref:HM08826)

**HAMBLETT, S P**

**S P Hamblett**, 3 Thirlmere Cl, Frodsham, **Cheshire**, WA6 7NA, ENG.
(T) 01928 733409
Speciality: Physiotherapy.
P S T (Ref:HM08827)

**HAMBLIN, PAT**

**Pat Hamblin**, 4 Lakeland Way, Walton, Wakefield, **Yorkshire (West)**, WF2 6TG, ENG.
(T) 01924 256796
Speciality: Reflexology.
● **Owner** Ms P Hamblin
S T (Ref:HM08828)

**HAMBLIN, R**

**R Hamblin**, 22 Streets Heath, West End, Woking, **Surrey**, GU24 9QY, ENG.
(T) 01276 858469
Speciality: Chiropodists (Podiatrists).
● **Owner** Mrs R Hamblin
S (Ref:HM08829)

**HAMBLY, PHILIP**

**Philip Hambly**, Imperial Centre, Grange Rd, Darlington, **County Durham**, DL1 5PE, ENG.
(T) 01325 381326
Speciality: Osteopathy.
P S T (Ref:HM08830)

**HAMBLY'S**

**Hambly's**, Durgates, Wadhurst, **Sussex (East)**, TN5 6DE, ENG.
(T) 01892 783027 (F) 01892 783027
Speciality: Herbalists.
● **Owner** Mrs F Hambley
M (Ref:HM08831)

**HAMER-BLOOM, S**

**S Hamer-Bloom**, Meadowcroft, 7a Lidgett Park Rd, Leeds, **Yorkshire (West)**, LS8 1EE, ENG.
(T) 01132 668069
Speciality: Chiropody, Podiatry. ✔
● **Owner/Chiropodist (Podiatrist)** Mrs S Hamer-Bloom Q: MBChA, MSSCh. M: B.A.Ch.P.
S Yrs. Est.: 15 (Ref:HM08832)

**HAMID, ALI**

**Ali Hamid**, 77 Carr Rd, Northolt, **London (Greater)**, UB5 4RB, ENG.
(T) 020 8422 7519
Speciality: Hypnotherapy.
● **Owner** A Hamid
B (Ref:HM08833)

**HAMID, M A**

**M A Hamid**, 595 Scott Hall Rd, Leeds, **Yorkshire (West)**, LS7 2NA, ENG.
(T) 01132 681326
Speciality: Hypnosis.
B (Ref:HM08834)

**HAMILTON FOOT CLINIC**

**Hamilton Foot Clinic (The)**, 11 Townhead St, Hamilton, **Lanarkshire (South)**, ML3 7BQ, SCO.
(T) 01698 428200
Speciality: Chiropodists (Podiatrists).
● **Owner** Ms A Inglis
S (Ref:HM08835)

**HAMILTON PSYCHIC FORUM**

**Hamilton Psychic Forum**, 25 Townhead St, Hamilton, **Lanarkshire (South)**, ML3 7BQ, SCO.
(T) 01698 423999 (F) 01698 891698
Speciality: Clairvoyants & Palmists.
● **Manager** Mrs C Halket
B (Ref:HM08836)

**HAMILTON, A**

**A Hamilton**, 22 Yew Tree Drive, Kingsteignton, Newton Abbot, **Devon**, TQ12 3SA, ENG.
(T) 01626 356203
Speciality: Chiropodists (Podiatrists).
● **Owner** A Hamilton
S (Ref:HM08837)

**HAMILTON, A**

**Mrs A Hamilton**, 157 Charles Avenue, Chichester, **Sussex (West)**, PO19 4HD, ENG.
(T) 01243 776555 (F) 01243 776555
Speciality: Herbalists.
● **Owner** Ms A Hamilton
M (Ref:HM08838)

**HAMILTON, A R**

**A R Hamilton**, 71A Hersham Rd, Walton-On-Thames, **Surrey**, KT12 1LL, ENG.
(T) 01932 227233 (F) 01932 252071
Speciality: Chiropodists (Podiatrists).
● **Owner** Mr A Hamilton
S (Ref:HM08839)

**HAMILTON, ALEX**

**Alex Hamilton**, The Surgery, 1 Leighton Rd, Leighton Buzzard, **Bedfordshire**, LU7 7LB, ENG.
(T) 01525 211444
Speciality: Osteopathy.
● **Owner** Mr J Batser
P S T (Ref:HM08840)

**HAMILTON, ANITA**

**Anita Hamilton**, 20 Broad Rig Avenue, Hove, **Sussex (East)**, BN3 8EW, ENG.
(T) 07880 964683
Speciality: Reflexology.
S T (Ref:HM08841)



Key: B Mind-Body Medicine C Complementary Medicine H Self Help Treatment M Medicinal Therapy O Oriental Medicine P Postural Therapy S Manipulative Structural Therapy T Touch Therapy

### HAMILTON, CYNTHIA

**Cynthia Hamilton**, 75 Leigh Rd, Leigh-On-Sea, **Essex**, SS9 1JN, ENG.
(T) 01702 714862 (F) 01702 716969
Speciality: Hypnotherapy.
● **Owner** Mrs C Merryfield
B (**Ref:**HM08842)

### HAMILTON, FIONA

**Fiona Hamilton**, 46 Durham Rd, Raynes Park, London, **London (Greater)**, SW20 0TW, ENG.
(T) 020 8946 3898 (F) 020 8688 9111
(E) f@fionahamilton.co.uk
(W) www.fionahamilton.co.uk
Speciality: Cranial Osteopathy, Osteopathy. ✓
● **Osteopath** Ms F Hamilton Q: DO, Reg.Osteopath. M: GOsC, RO.
S Yrs. Est.: 10 (**Ref:**HM08843)

### HAMILTON, JAMES

**James Hamilton**, 43 Kaimes View, Danderhall, Dalkeith, **Lothian (Mid)**, EH22 1QZ, SCO.
(T) 01316 630858
Speciality: Chiropody, Reflexology. ✓
● **Owner/Chiropodist/Reflexologist**
Mr J Hamilton Q: HND, M.S.C.P.
M T Yrs. Est.: 12 (**Ref:**HM08844)

### HAMILTON, MELANIE

**Melanie Hamilton**, 29 Breachfield, Burghclere, Newbury, **Berkshire**, RG20 9HZ, ENG.
(T) 01635 278636
Speciality: Chiropractic.
P S T (**Ref:**HM08845)

### HAMILTON, SAMANTHA

**Samantha Hamilton**, 613 Stonegate Rd, Leeds, **Yorkshire (West)**, LS17 6EJ, ENG.
(T) 01132 664913
Speciality: Clairvoyants & Palmists.
● **Owner** Mrs S Hamilton
B (**Ref:**HM08846)

### HAMILTON, W

**W Hamilton**, 240 Highbridge Rd, Sutton Coldfield, **Midlands (West)**, B73 5QU, ENG.
(T) 01213 553673
Speciality: Chiropodists (Podiatrists).
● **Owner** Mr W Hamilton
S (**Ref:**HM08847)

### HAMILTON-BAILY, ALISON E

**Alison E Hamilton-Baily**, 52 Haldon Rd, London, **London (Greater)**, SW18 1QG, ENG.
(T) 020 8333 4206
Speciality: Homeopathy.
M (**Ref:**HM08848)

### HAMILTON-PETERS, R & J A

**R & J A Hamilton-Peters**, 4 St Andrews Avenue, Harpenden, **Hertfordshire**, AL5 2RA, ENG.
(T) 01582 460051
(E) tojohp@cwcom.net
Speciality: Auto Suggestion, Autogenic Training, Complementary Therapy, Counselling, Healing Therapy, Holistic Healing, Hypnosis, Hypnotherapy, Psychotherapy, Stress Therapy. ✓
● **Principal** Mr R Hamilton-Peters Q: MA. M: ABCHyp, CAH.
● **Co-Principal**
Ms J Hamilton Peters Q: MA. M: ABCHyp, CAH.
B Yrs. Est.: 16 (**Ref:**HM08849)

### HAMILTON-PLANT, C A

**C A Hamilton-Plant**, The Radlett Practice, 107 Watling St, Radlett, **Hertfordshire**, WD7 7NG, ENG.
(T) 01923 855884
Speciality: Osteopathy.
P S T (**Ref:**HM08850)

### HAMILTON-WILSON, JOAN

**Joan Hamilton-Wilson**, 180 Old Bedford Rd, Luton, **Bedfordshire**, LU2 7HW, ENG.
(T) 01582 415494
Speciality: Chiropodists (Podiatrists).
● **Owner** Mrs J Hamilton-Wilson
S (**Ref:**HM08851)

### HAMLETT, ANN

**Ann Hamlett**, 11 Back Lane, Holmfirth, Huddersfield, **Yorkshire (West)**, HD7 1HG, ENG.
(T) 01484 686446
Speciality: Hypnotherapy.
● **Owner** Mrs A Hamlett
B (**Ref:**HM08852)

### HAMLIN, P W

**Hamlin P W**, Cornhill, Market Sq, Ilminster, **Somerset**, TA19 0AH, ENG.
(T) 01460 53921
Speciality: Chiropodists (Podiatrists).
● **Owner** Mr P Hamlin
S (**Ref:**HM08853)

### HAMLIN, P W

**P W Hamlin**, 38 North St, Langport, **Somerset**, TA10 9RQ, ENG.
(T) 01458 250793
Speciality: Chiropodists (Podiatrists).
● **Manager** Mr P Griffith
S (**Ref:**HM08854)

### HAMLIN, P W

**P W Hamlin**, Manor Lodge, Manor Lane, Wedmore, **Somerset**, BS28 4EL, ENG.
(T) 01934 712323
Speciality: Chiropodists (Podiatrists).
S (**Ref:**HM08855)

### HAMLIN-BRIGNALL, KATHRYN

**Kathryn Hamlin-Brignall**, Millfield, Stone, Tenterden, **Kent**, TN30 7JL, ENG.
(T) 01233 758318
Speciality: Hypnosis.
● **Owner** Ms K Hamlin-Brignall
B (**Ref:**HM08856)

### HAMLYN, EIRWEN

**Eirwen Hamlyn**, 1 Alexandra Pl, Sirhowy, Tredegar, **Blaenau Gwent**, NP22 4QA, WAL.
(T) 01495 722931
Speciality: Complementary Medicines & Therapy.
C M (**Ref:**HM08857)

### HAMLYNN HEALTH

**Hamlynn Health**, 7 Fulford Pk, Fulford, York, **Yorkshire (North)**, YO10 4QE, ENG.
(T) 01904 623840 (F) 01904 623840
Speciality: Complementary Medicines & Therapy.
● **Owner** Mrs L Byas
M (**Ref:**HM08858)

### HAMM, D R

**D R Hamm**, 70 Kiln Rd, Newbury, **Berkshire**, RG14 2LS, ENG.
(T) 01635 40800
Speciality: Osteopathy.
● **Owner** Mr D Hamm
P S T (**Ref:**HM08859)

### HAMM, D R

**D R Hamm**, The Croft, Hungerford, **Berkshire**, RG17 0HY, ENG.
(T) 01488 681695
Speciality: Osteopathy.
● **Owner** Mr D Hamm
P S T (**Ref:**HM08860)

### HAMMERSMITH ACUPUNCTURE

**Hammersmith Acupuncture & Chinese Herbal Clinic**, 3 Pleydell Avenue, Stamford Brook, Hammersmith, London, **London (Greater)**, W4 2NW, ENG.
(T) 020 8741 3556
Speciality: Herbalists.
M (**Ref:**HM08861)

### HAMMERSON, D

**D Hammerson**, 166 Packenham Rd, Basingstoke, **Hampshire**, RG21 8XY, ENG.
(T) 01256 321498
Speciality: Osteopathy.
● **Owner** Mrs D Hammerson
P S T (**Ref:**HM08862)

### HAMMET STREET PRACTICE

**Hammet Street Practice**, 2a Church Sq, Taunton, **Somerset**, TA1 1SA, ENG.
(T) 01823 254456 (F) 01823 254456
Speciality: Kinesiology, Osteopathy.
● **Owner** Mr P Walpole
P S T (**Ref:**HM08863)

### HAMMETT, JANET

**Janet Hammett**, 27 Selhurst Rd, London, **London (Greater)**, N9 9DB, ENG.
(T) 020 8803 7065
Speciality: Reflexology.
S T (**Ref:**HM08864)

### HAMMOND, ANNE

**Anne Hammond**, 39 Crossway, Manchester, **Manchester (Greater)**, M20 6TU, ENG.
(T) 01614 451018
Speciality: Aromatherapy.
M O (**Ref:**HM08865)

### HAMMOND, ANNE

**Anne Hammond**, Follifoot House, Leycester Rd, Knutsford, **Cheshire**, WA16 8QR, ENG.
(T) 01565 650645
Speciality: Reflexology.
S T (**Ref:**HM08866)

### HAMMOND, DIANNE

**Dianne Hammond**, 423 Wood Lane, Sheffield, **Yorkshire (South)**, S6 6AQ, ENG.
(T) 01142 336719
Speciality: Reflexology.
S T (**Ref:**HM08867)

### HAMMOND, RICHARD

**Richard Hammond**, 1 Clanricarde Gardens, Tunbridge Wells, **Kent**, TN1 1PE, ENG.
(T) 01892 783977
Speciality: Hypnotherapy.
● **Owner** Mr R Hammond
B (**Ref:**HM08868)

### HAMMONDS CHIROPODY

**Hammonds Chiropody**, 546 High Rd, London, **London (Greater)**, N17 9SY, ENG.
(T) 020 8808 3327
Speciality: Chiropodists (Podiatrists).
S (**Ref:**HM08869)

### HAMNETT, SHEILA

**Sheila Hamnett**, Kilnshaw Farm, Errington, Hebden Bridge, **Yorkshire (West)**, HX7 6JJ, ENG.
(T) 01422 844885
Speciality: Alexander Technique, Cranio-Sacral Therapy. ✓
● **Teacher of the Alexander Technique**
Ms S Hamnett M: STAT.
T Yrs. Est.: 5 (**Ref:**HM08870)

### HAMNETT-SADLER, G B

**G B Hamnett-Sadler**, 2 Park Avenue, Chadderton, Oldham, **Lancashire**, OL9 0AL, ENG.
(T) 01616 246716
Speciality: Chiropodists (Podiatrists).
● **Owner** Mr G Hamnett-Sadler
S (**Ref:**HM08871)

### HAMPDEN HOUSE CENTRE

**Hampden House Psychotherapy Centre**, 2 Palatine Rd, Manchester, **Manchester (Greater)**, M20 3JA, ENG.
(T) 01614 452099 (F) 01614 454399
Speciality: Psychotherapy.
● **Director** Dr J Bird
B (**Ref:**HM08872)

### HAMPEL, HILARY

**Hilary Hampel**, 19 Shrewsbury Avenue, Waterloo, Liverpool, **Merseyside**, L22 2AS, ENG.
(T) 01519 314116 (F) 01519 314116
Speciality: Homeopathy.
● **Owner** Mrs H Hampel
M (**Ref:**HM08873)

### HAMPER, JULIE

**Julie Hamper**, 141 Kipling Avenue, Goring-By-Sea, Worthing, **Sussex (West)**, BN12 6LL, ENG.
(T) 01903 505948
Speciality: Chiropodists (Podiatrists).
S (**Ref:**HM08874)

### HAMPSHAW, ANNA

**Anna Hampshaw**, 5 Park Trce, Leeds, **Yorkshire (West)**, LS6 4BB, ENG.
(T) 01132 957918
Speciality: Hypnotherapy.



Key continued: Yrs.Est: Years Established Q: Qualifications M: Professional Membership ✓ Indemnity Insurance Accept Credit Cards

● **Owner** Mrs A Hampshaw
**B** (**Ref:**HM08875)

**HAMPSHIRE MUSIC SPACE**

**Hampshire Music Space**, The Winchester Centre, 68 St. Georges St, Winchester, **Hampshire**, SO23 8AH, ENG.
(T) 01962 848036 (F) 01962 848029
Speciality: Complementary Medicines & Therapy.
● **Manager** Mrs B Read
**M** (**Ref:**HM08876)

**HAMPSHIRE THERAPY CENTRE**

**Hampshire Therapy Centre**, 21 Parkhouse Rd, Shipton Bellinger, Tidworth, **Hampshire**, SP9 7TW, ENG.
(T) 01980 843527 (F) 01980 843527
Speciality: Aromatherapy.
● **Partner** Mr P Dawson
**M** **O** (**Ref:**HM08877)

**HAMPSOM, JAMES**

**James Hampsom**, 83 The Esplanade, Fleetwood, **Lancashire**, FY7 7BG, ENG.
(T) 01253 872331
Speciality: Acupuncture. ✔
● **Acupuncturist** Mr J Hampson Q: MBAcC.
**O** (**Ref:**HM08878)

**HAMPSON, G C**

**G C Hampson**, 9 Recreation Ground Rd, Norwich, **Norfolk**, NR7 8EN, ENG.
(T) 01603 408138
Speciality: Physiotherapy.
● **Owner** Mr G Hampson
**P** **S** **T** (**Ref:**HM08879)

**HAMPSON, M R**

**M R Hampson**, 98 Union St, Oldham, **Lancashire**, OL1 1DU, ENG.
(T) 01616 286930
Speciality: Physiotherapy.
● **Owner** Ms M Hampson
**P** **S** **T** (**Ref:**HM08880)

**HAMPSTEAD ACU/CHINESE HBL MED**

**Hampstead Acupuncture & Chinese Herbal Medicine**, 1 Deansway, East Finchley, London, **London (Greater)**, N2 0NF, ENG.
(T) 020 8264 8074
(E) paul@taiji.net
(W) www.taiji.net
Speciality: Acupuncture. ✔
● **Director/Acupuncturist**
Mr P Brecher Q: BA.
**O** Yrs. Est.: 5 (**Ref:**HM08881)

**HAMPSTEAD ALTERNATIVE HEALTH**

**Hampstead Alternative Health**, 114 Heath St, Hampstead, London, **London (Greater)**, NW3 1DR, ENG.
(T) 020 8533 6476
Speciality: Complementary Medicines & Therapy.
● **Practitioner** Ms M Webb
**M** (**Ref:**HM08882)

**HAMPSTEAD CTRE-PSYCHOTHERAPY**

**Hampstead Centre For Psychotherapy**, 8 Willow Rd, London, **London (Greater)**, NW3 1TJ, ENG.
(T) 020 7794 8717
Speciality: Psychology.
● **Owner** Mr S Meyerson
**B** (**Ref:**HM08883)

**HAMPSTEAD WELL HEALING CENTRE**

**Hampstead Well Healing Centre (The)**, 16 Englands Lane, London, **London (Greater)**, NW3 4TG, ENG.
(T) 020 7722 9270 (F) 020 7722 5225
Speciality: Complementary Medicines & Therapy.
● **Director** Miss S Austin
**C** **M** (**Ref:**HM08884)

**HAMPTON CLINIC**

**Hampton Clinic**, 110 High St, Hampton, **London (Greater)**, TW12 2QR, ENG.
(T) 020 8979 3119
Speciality: Osteopathy.
**P** **S** **T** (**Ref:**HM08885)

**HAMPTON, ANNE**

**Anne Hampton**, 10 Wick Lane, Bournemouth, **Dorset**, BH6 4JU, ENG.
(T) 01202 422354
Speciality: Chiropody. ✔
● **Owner/Chiropodist** Ms A Hampton
**M** Yrs. Est.: 12 (**Ref:**HM08886)

**HAMPTON, ANTHONY**

**Anthony Hampton**, Broadeaves, 9 James St, Willenhall, **Midlands (West)**, WV13 1SS, ENG.
(T) 01902 606150
Speciality: Hopi Ear Candles, Reflexology.
**S** **T** (**Ref:**HM08887)

**HAMPTON, E M**

**E M Hampton**, Willow Hall, Willow Hall Lane, Wix, Manningtree, **Essex**, CO11 2UH, ENG.
(T) 01255 870349
Speciality: Complementary Medicines & Therapy.
● **Owner** Mr D Hampton
**C** **M** (**Ref:**HM08888)

**HAMPTON, KAREN**

**Karen Hampton**, 14 Thoroughfare, Halesworth, **Suffolk**, IP19 8AH, ENG.
(T) 01986 872899
Speciality: Aromatherapy.
● **Owner** Miss K Hampton
**M** **O** (**Ref:**HM08889)

**HANAM-CHAZ, CHAZ**

**Chaz Hanam-Chaz**, Kuching-Tidur, Walkampton, Yelverton, **Devon**, PL20 6JP, ENG.
(T) 01822 855177
Speciality: Hypnosis.
**B** (**Ref:**HM08890)

**HANCE, PETER**

**Peter Hance**, 68A High St, Dorking, **Surrey**, RH4 1AY, ENG.
(T) 01306 882044 (F) 01306 882044
Speciality: Chiropodists (Podiatrists).
● **Owner** Mr P Hance
**S** (**Ref:**HM08891)

**HANCHER, LYNNE**

**Lynne Hancher**, Ridgelands, Crateford Lane, Gailey, Stafford, **Staffordshire**, ST19 5PZ, ENG.
(T) 01902 850621
Speciality: Reflexology.
**S** **T** (**Ref:**HM08892)

**HANCOCK, C B**

**C B Hancock**, 28 Archer Rd, Penarth, **Glamorgan (Vale of)**, CF64 3HJ, WAL.
(T) 029 2070 8350
Speciality: Osteopathy.
● **Owner** Mr C Hancock
**P** **S** **T** (**Ref:**HM08893)

**HANCOCK, J**

**J Hancock**, 83 Talbot Rd, Hyde, **Cheshire**, SK14 4EX, ENG.
(T) 01613 660368
Speciality: Chiropodists (Podiatrists).
**S** (**Ref:**HM08894)

**HANCOCK, JOHN**

**John Hancock**, 51 Deer Pk Rd, Langtoft, Peterborough, **Cambridgeshire**, PE6 9RD, ENG.
(T) 01778 342816
Speciality: Chiropodists (Podiatrists).
**S** (**Ref:**HM08895)

**HANCOCK, PHILLIP**

**Phillip Hancock**, 24 Retiro St, Oldham, **Lancashire**, OL1 1SA, ENG.
(T) 01616 241785
Speciality: Chiropodists (Podiatrists).
**S** (**Ref:**HM08896)

**HANCOCK, S & NESS, A**

**Susan Hancock & Anjie Ness**, 20 Deuchar House, Sandyford Rd, Newcastle Upon Tyne, **Tyne and Wear**, NE2 1XG, ENG.
(T) 01912 617328
Speciality: Reflexology.
**S** **T** (**Ref:**HM08897)

**HANCOK, FIONA**

**Fiona Hancok**, New Cross Natural Therapy Centre, 394 New Cross Rd, London, **London (Greater)**, SE14 6TY, ENG.
(T) 020 8469 0858
Speciality: Complementary Medicines & Therapy.
**M** (**Ref:**HM08898)

**HAND, J**

**J Hand**, The Wellbeing Centre, 11 Musters Rd, West Bridgford, Nottingham, **Nottinghamshire**, NG2 7PP, ENG.
(T) 01159 825353
Speciality: Aromatherapy.
**M** **O** (**Ref:**HM08899)

**HANDFORD, RICHARD**

**Richard Handford**, 16 Hockerill St, Bishop's Stortford, **Hertfordshire**, CM23 2DW, ENG.
(T) 01279 652249 (F) 01279 652696
Speciality: Chiropodists (Podiatrists).
● **Owner** Mr R Handford
**S** (**Ref:**HM08900)

**HANDOLL & ASSOCIATES**

**Nicholas Handoll & Associates**, Holland House, 70 Belmont Rd, Hereford, **Herefordshire**, HR2 7JW, ENG.
(T) 01432 356655
Speciality: Osteopathy.
**P** **S** **T** (**Ref:**HM08901)

**HANDOLL, NICHOLAS & ASSOCIATES**

**Nicholas Handoll & Associates**, Priory House, New St, Ross-on-Wye, **Herefordshire**, HR9 7DA, ENG.
(T) 01989 563813
Speciality: Osteopathy.
**P** **S** **T** (**Ref:**HM08902)

**HAND-ON HEALING**

**Hand-On Healing**, 7 Lodge Rd, London, **London (Greater)**, NW4 4DD, ENG.
(T) 020 8203 7427
Speciality: Complementary Medicines & Therapy.
**C** **M** (**Ref:**HM08903)

**HANDS ACROSS THE VOID**

**Hands Across The Void**, 97 Inchbrae Drive, Aberdeen, **Aberdeenshire**, AB10 7AJ, SCO.
(T) 01224 208347
Speciality: Clairvoyants & Palmists, Spiritual Help.
● **Owner** Mrs A Smith
**B** Yrs. Est.: 1 (**Ref:**HM08904)

**HANDS FOR FEET**

**Hands For Feet**, 12 Hill St, Irvine, **Ayrshire (North)**, KA12 0DE, SCO.
(T) 01294 312305
Speciality: Chiropody. ✔
● **Chiropodist** Sonia Hands Q: M.S.C.P.
**M** Yrs. Est.: 5 (**Ref:**HM08905)

**HANDS OF HEALINGS**

**Hands Of Healings**, 310 Foeshill Rd, Coventry, **Midlands (West)**, CV6 5AJ, ENG.
(T) 024 7666 3309
Speciality: Complementary Medicines & Therapy.
● **Principal** Mrs J Hollister
**M** (**Ref:**HM08906)

**HANDS ON**

**Hands On**, Shop 3 Traitors Gate, St Marys Water Lane, Shrewsbury, **Shropshire**, SY1 2BX, ENG.
(T) 01743 355414
Speciality: Complementary Medicines & Therapy.
● **Owner** Ms B Hilton
**M** (**Ref:**HM08907)

**HANDS ON CLINIC**

**Hands On Clinic (The)**, Maltfield Rd, Headington, Oxford, **Oxfordshire**, OX3 9RG, ENG.
(T) 01865 744907
Speciality: Complementary Medicines & Therapy.
● **Partner** Mr T Marshall
**M** (**Ref:**HM08908)

**HANDS ON HEALTH**

**Hands On Health**, 180 Brighton Rd, Coulsdon, **London (Greater)**, CR5 2NF, ENG.
(T) 020 8660 3692



Key: **B** Mind-Body Medicine **C** Complementary Medicine **H** Self Help Treatment **M** Medicinal Therapy **O** Oriental Medicine **P** Postural Therapy **S** Manipulative Structural Therapy **T** Touch Therapy

Speciality: Aromatherapy.
● **Owner** Ms M Benson
M O (Ref:HM08909)

**HANDS ON HEALTH**

**Hands On Health**, Cobdown Sports Club, Station Rd, Ditton, Aylesford, **Kent**, ME20 6AU, ENG.
(T) 01622 719799 (F) 01622 719799
Speciality: Complementary Medicines & Therapy.
● **Partner** Mrs M Waters
M (Ref:HM08910)

**HANDS ON HEALTH**

**Hands On Health - Family Chiropractic**, Coltwood House, 2 Tongham Rd, Runfold, Farnham, **Surrey**, GU10 1PH, ENG.
(T) 01252 781474 (F) 01252 781474
(E) lara.young@talk21.com
Speciality: Chiropractic, Cranio-Sacral Therapy, Sacral Occipital Therapy, Chiropractic Paediatrics/Adults. ✓
● **Chiropractor** Ms L Young Q: BSc. M: SCA.
S Yrs. Est.: 1 (Ref:HM08911)

**HANDS ON HEALTH**

**Hands On Health**, 40 Fraser Rd, Carlton, Nottingham, **Nottinghamshire**, ENG.
Speciality: Massage (Therapeutic), Sports Massage. ✓
● **Sports Therapist** Ms S McKinnon Q: VTCT. M: FHT.
S (Ref:HM08912)

**HANDS ON PHYSIOTHERAPY**

**Hands On Physiotherapy**, 164 Wilmslow Rd, Handforth, Wilmslow, **Cheshire**, SK9 3LF, ENG.
(T) 01625 548409 (F) 01625 533898
Speciality: Acupuncture, Manipulation, Massage (Therapeutic), Physiotherapy. ✓
● **Physiotherapist** Mrs Widdowson Q: Grad Dip Phys, MCSP, SRP.
● **Partner/Physiotherapist**
Mrs A Wright Q: Grad Dip Phys, MCSP, SRP.
S Yrs. Est.: 8 (Ref:HM08913)

**HANDS ON THERAPY**

**Hands On Therapy**, 1 Parkway, London, **London (Greater)**, NW1 7AN, ENG.
(T) 020 7813 2655 (F) 020 7813 2789
Speciality: Complementary Medicines & Therapy.
● **Owner** Mr C Russell
C M (Ref:HM08914)

**HANDS ON THERAPY**

**Hands On Therapy**, 217 Whitecross, Wooton, Abingdon, **Oxfordshire**, OX13 6BW, ENG.
(T) 01235 539089 (F) 01235 522264
Speciality: Massage (Therapeutic), Rehabilitation Programmes, Ergonomics, Nutritional Advice. ✓
● **Sports Therapist** Mr J Hill Q: ISPI, ITEC. M: GCP.
C Yrs. Est.: 3 (Ref:HM08915)

**HANDS ON THERAPY CLINIC**

**Hands On Therapy Clinic**, Langman Chemists, Station St, Saltburn-by-the-Sea, **Cleveland**, TS12 1AE, ENG.
(T) 01287 625700
Speciality: Complementary Medicines & Therapy.
C M (Ref:HM08916)

**HANDS, ANNE**

**Anne Hands**, 394 Warwick Rd, Solihull, **Midlands (West)**, B91 1BB, ENG.
(T) 01217 050341 (F) 01217 114009
Speciality: Physiotherapy.
P S T (Ref:HM08917)

**HANDS, PETER**

**Peter Hands**, Byron House, 37 The Strand, Dawlish, **Devon**, EX7 9PT, ENG.
(T) 01626 863256
Speciality: Osteopathy.
● **Owner** Mr P Hands
P S T (Ref:HM08918)

**HANDS-ON-FEET**

**Hands-on-Feet**, Penwith, 9 Margaret Cl, Bicester, **Oxfordshire**, OX23 2DH, ENG.
(T) 01869 241296
Speciality: Reflexology.
S T (Ref:HM08919)

**HANDSWORTH CHIROPRACTIC CLINIC**

**Handsworth Chiropractic Clinic**, 269 Handsworth Rd, Handsworth, Sheffield, **Yorkshire (South)**, S13 9BN, ENG.
(T) 01142 812233
Speciality: Chiropractors.
P S T (Ref:HM08920)

**HANDY, SUSAN**

**Susan Handy**, 62 Green St, Hereford, **Herefordshire**, HR1 2QH, ENG.
(T) 01432 276814
Speciality: Psychotherapy.
● **Owner** Ms S Handy
B (Ref:HM08921)

**HANDYPERSON SCHEME**

**Handyperson Scheme**, 161 Cardigan Rd, Leeds, **Yorkshire (West)**, LS6 1LJ, ENG.
(T) 01132 756589
Speciality: Homeopathy.
● **Manager** Ms P Bainbridge
M (Ref:HM08922)

**HANEKE CHIROPRACTIC CLINIC**

**Haneke Chiropractic Clinic**, 55 Mill Cl, Wisbech, **Cambridgeshire**, PE13 3BD, ENG.
(T) 01945 582406
Speciality: Chiropractic.
● **Owner** Dr C Haneke
P S T (Ref:HM08923)

**HANFORD CHIROPODISTS**

**Hanford Chiropodists**, 10 Gateford Rd, Worksop, **Nottinghamshire**, S80 1EB, ENG.
(T) 01909 472611
Speciality: Chiropodists (Podiatrists).
● **Partner** Mrs R Hanford
S (Ref:HM08924)

**HANFORD, S P**

**S P Hanford**, 32 Mount Rd, Chessington, **Surrey**, KT9 1JG, ENG.
(T) 020 8397 6905
Speciality: Iridology, Reflexology. ✓
● **Reflexologist/Iridologist**
Ms S Hanford Q: Dip.Iridol, Dip.Reflex. M: IFR.
M Yrs. Est.: 3 (Ref:HM08925)

**HANKEY, DAVID**

**David Hankey Lic Ac**, 16 Reginald Sq, Dublin, **County Dublin**, IRE.
(T) 01453 3593
Speciality: Complementary Medicines & Therapy.
M (Ref:HM08926)

**HANKEY, DAVID**

**David Hankey LICAC C AC**, Green St, Dingle, **County Kerry**, IRE.
(T) 06691 59904
Speciality: Complementary Medicines & Therapy.
M (Ref:HM08927)

**HANKINS, SUSAN**

**Susan Hankins**, Charlton Cottage, 18 Copperkins Lane, Amersham, **Buckinghamshire**, HP6 5QF, ENG.
(T) 01494 725385 (F) 01494 729437
Speciality: Physiotherapy.
● **Owner** Mrs S Hankins
P S T (Ref:HM08928)

**HANLEY, I G**

**I G Hanley**, 7 Lynnehurst Drive, Comber, Newtownards, **County Down**, BT23 5LN, NIR.
(T) 028 9187 3644
Speciality: Psychology.
B (Ref:HM08929)

**HANNA, J**

**J Hanna**, 25 Chaerty Rd, Broughshane, Ballymena, **County Antrim**, BT42 4QA, NIR.
(T) 028 2586 1585
Speciality: Physiotherapy.
P S T (Ref:HM08930)

**HANNA, MARK**

**Mark Hanna**, The Coach House, 13 Langton Rd, Tunbridge Wells, **Kent**, TN4 8XA, ENG.
(T) 01892 543048 (F) 01892 543048
(E) help@stresshelp.co.uk
(W) www.stresshelp.co.uk
Speciality: Cognitive Therapy, Counselling, Dietician, Hay Diet, Holistic Healing, Hypnosis, Hypnotherapy, Postural Integration, Psychotherapy, Stress Therapy, Transactional Analysis, Vibrational Therapy, Yoga. ✓
● **Hypnotherapist/Stress Management**
Mr M Hanna Q: Dip.RSA, MA, MBA, MNCH.
H Yrs. Est.: 5 (Ref:HM08931)

**HANNA, MARK**

**Mark Hanna**, 5 Lime Hill Rd, Tunbridge Wells, **Kent**, TN1 1LL, ENG.
(T) 01892 543048
Speciality: Hypnosis.
B (Ref:HM08932)

**HANNA, MARY**

**Mary Hanna**, Fairfields Clinic, Skippetts Lane West, Basingstoke, **Hampshire**, RG21 3HP, ENG.
(T) 01256 326980
Speciality: Homeopathy.
M (Ref:HM08933)

**HANNAM, R J**

**R J Hannam**, South Green House, South Green, Dereham, **Norfolk**, NR19 1PU, ENG.
(T) 01362 690532
Speciality: Hypnotherapy.
● **Owner** Mr R Hannam
B (Ref:HM08934)

**HANNAN, TIM**

**Tim Hannan**, 11 Laurencebrook, Chapelizod, **County Dublin**, IRE.
(T) 01623 3490
Speciality: Complementary Medicines & Therapy.
M (Ref:HM08935)

**HANNEY, D**

**D Hanney**, Bridleholme, Bridle Path, East Boldon, **Tyne and Wear**, NE36 0AP, ENG.
(T) 01915 367756
Speciality: Physiotherapy.
P S T (Ref:HM08936)

**HANNEY, D**

**D Hanney**, The Newcastle Clinic, 52 Mitchell Avenue, Newcastle Upon Tyne, **Tyne and Wear**, NE2 3LA, ENG.
(T) 01912 810193
Speciality: Physiotherapy.
P S T (Ref:HM08937)

**HANNEY, DOROTHY**

**Dorothy Hanney**, Natural Therapy Centre, 7 Westgate Rd, Guisborough, **Cleveland**, TS14 6EA, ENG.
(T) 01287 633591
Speciality: Physiotherapy.
P S T (Ref:HM08938)

**HANSELL, A S**

**A S Hansell**, Exeter Physio & Sports Clinic, 11-15 Dixs Field, Exeter, **Devon**, EX1 1QA, ENG.
(T) 01392 211066
Speciality: Physiotherapy.
● **Owner** Mr A Hansell
P S T (Ref:HM08939)

**HANSEN, VIVI**

**Vivi Hansen**, 21 Birdworld Rd, Long Ashton, Bristol, BS41 9BA, ENG.
(T) 01275 394166
Speciality: Alexander Technique.
● **Owner** Ms V Hansen
P S (Ref:HM08940)

**HANSFORD & KAY**

**Hansford & Kay**, 199 Station Lane, Hornchurch, **Essex**, RM12 6LL, ENG.
(T) 01708 471111
Speciality: Chiropodists (Podiatrists).
S (Ref:HM08941)

**HANSFORD, JANE**

**Jane Hansford**, 1 Golflink Cottages, Downley Common, Downley, High Wycombe, **Buckinghamshire**, HP13 5YJ, ENG.
(T) 01494 451087
Speciality: Reflexology.



Key continued: Yrs.Est: Years Established Q: Qualifications M: Professional Membership ✓ Indemnity Insurance Accept Credit Cards

**S T** (Ref:HM08942)

**HANSFORD, LIZ**

**Liz Hansford**, 14 Arden Rd, Leckhampton, Cheltenham, **Gloucestershire**, GL53 0HH, ENG.
(T) 01242 526688
Speciality: Reflexology.
**S T** (Ref:HM08943)

**HANSON, S C**

**S C Hanson T/A Otley/Wetherby Chiropody Practice**, 28a New Market, Otley, **Yorkshire (West)**, LS21 3AE, ENG.
(T) 01943 463303 (F) 01943 463303
Speciality: Biomechanics, Cryo Surgery, Gait Analysis, Nail Surgery, Podiatry. ✓
● **Podiatrist** Mr S Hanson Q: S.R.Ch. M: S.C.P.
**M** Yrs. Est.: 15 (Ref:HM08944)

**HANSON, S C**

**S C Hanson**, 10 The Old Orchard, Pool In Wharfedale, Otley, **Yorkshire (West)**, LS21 1RY, ENG.
(T) 01132 843095
Speciality: Chiropodists (Podiatrists).
● **Partner** Mr S Hanson
**S** (Ref:HM08945)

**HANSSON CHIROPRACTIC CENTRE**

**Hansson Chiropractic Centre**, 16 Granby Court, Granby Industrial Estate, Weymouth, **Dorset**, DT4 9XB, ENG.
(T) 01305 761507
Speciality: Chiropractic.
● **Partner** Ms H Underwood
**P S T** (Ref:HM08946)

**HANTSCARE**

**Hampshire Sports Injury and Physiotherapy Clinic - D Newman**, 140 Lodge Rd, Southampton, **Hampshire**, SO14 6QR, ENG.
(T) 023 8033 0387 (F) 023 8063 1353
(E) pt@hantscare.softnet.co.uk
Speciality: Acupressure, Acupuncture, Biofeedback, Chiropractic, Electrotherapy, Manipulation, Massage (Therapeutic), Osteopathy, Physiotherapy, Podiatry. ✓
● **Practice Principal** Mr D Newman Q: Grad Dip Phys, MCSP, SRP. M: CSP, OCPPP.
**S** Yrs. Est.: 15 (Ref:HM08947)

**HANWELL, JULIET**

**Juliet Hanwell**, 109 High St, Berkhamsted, **Hertfordshire**, HP4 2DG, ENG.
(T) 01442 878900
Speciality: Osteopathy.
**P S T** (Ref:HM08948)

**HANWELL, TIM**

**Tim Hanwell**, 109 High St, Berkhamsted, **Hertfordshire**, HP4 2DG, ENG.
(T) 01442 878900
Speciality: Osteopathy.
**P S T** (Ref:HM08949)

**HAO (DR)**

**Dr Hao**, 16 Bingham St, Bangor, **County Down**, BT20 5DW, NIR.
(T) 028 9146 3888 (F) 028 9146 0888
Speciality: Complementary Medicines & Therapy.
● **Owner** Dr R Hao
**M** (Ref:HM08950)

**HAO CLINIC**

**Hao Clinic**, 189 Ballygomartin Rd, Belfast, **County Antrim**, BT13 3ND, NIR.
(T) 028 9071 8889 (F) 028 9080 7908
Speciality: Acupuncture.
● **Owner** Ms R Hao
**O** (Ref:HM08951)

**HAPPY FEET**

**Happy Feet**, 47 Dittisham Rd, London, **London (Greater)**, SE9 4BJ, ENG.
(T) 020 8851 3864
Speciality: Chiropodists (Podiatrists).
**S** (Ref:HM08952)

**HAPPY FEET**

**Happy Feet**, 4 Paddington St, London, **London (Greater)**, W1M 3LA, ENG.
(T) 020 7487 3998 (F) 020 8451 2648
Speciality: Reflexology.
● **Owner** Mrs J Drummond
**S T** (Ref:HM08953)

**HAPPY FEET**

**Happy Feet**, 29B Church St, Flint, **Flintshire**, CH6 5AD, WAL.
(T) 01352 763301
Speciality: Chiropodists (Podiatrists).
● **Owner** Mrs D Moorcroft
**S** (Ref:HM08954)

**HAPPY FEET CHIROPODY**

**Happy Feet Chiropody**, 1 Hickley Gardens, Brockworth, Gloucester, **Gloucestershire**, GL3 4QS, ENG.
(T) 01452 862825
Speciality: Chiropodists (Podiatrists).
**S** (Ref:HM08955)

**HAPPY FEET CHIROPODY SERVICE**

**Happy Feet Chiropody Service**, Prestberries Farm Surgery, Hartpury, Gloucester, **Gloucestershire**, GL19 3DB, ENG.
(T) 01452 700306
Speciality: Chiropractors.
**P S T** (Ref:HM08956)

**HAPPY SOLES MOBILE**

**Happy Soles Mobile**, 11 Crossfield Cl, Shaw, Oldham, **Lancashire**, OL2 8GB, ENG.
(T) 01706 299458
Speciality: Reflexology.
● **Owner** Mrs J Hodgkinson
**S T** (Ref:HM08957)

**HARBAGE, RALPH**

**Ralph Harbage**, The Sanctuary Of The Good Shepherd, Idless, Truro, **Cornwall**, TR4 9QS, ENG.
(T) 01872 273337
Speciality: Osteopathy.
● **Owner** Mr R Harbage
**P S T** (Ref:HM08958)

**HARBEN, PAM**

**Pam Harben**, 26 Hilldown Rd, Streatham, London, **London (Greater)**, SW16 3DZ, ENG.
(T) 020 8679 0330
Speciality: Reflexology.
**S T** (Ref:HM08959)

**HARBOROUGH OSTEOPATHIC CLINIC**

**Harborough Osteopathic Clinic**, 36 High St, Market Harborough, **Leicestershire**, LE16 7NL, ENG.
(T) 01858 410071
Speciality: Osteopathy.
**P S T** (Ref:HM08960)

**HARBOUR, ANNE**

**Anne Harbour**, 52 Thoresby Rd, Long Eaton, Nottingham, **Nottinghamshire**, NG10 3NP, ENG.
(T) 01159 731440
Speciality: Clairvoyants & Palmists.
● **Owner** Ms A Harbour
**B** (Ref:HM08961)

**HARCOMBE, LYDIA**

**Lydia Harcombe**, Wanstead Village Health Centre, 24 High St, London, **London (Greater)**, E11 2AQ, ENG.
(T) 020 8530 2126
Speciality: Aromatherapy.
**M O** (Ref:HM08962)

**HARCOMBE, PATRICIA**

**Patricia Harcombe**, 23 Conway Drive, Billinge, Wigan, **Lancashire**, WN5 7LH, ENG.
(T) 01744 603427
Speciality: Reflexology.
**S T** (Ref:HM08963)

**HARCOURT, A**

**A Harcourt**, 3 Horse St, Chipping Sodbury, Bristol, BS37 6DA, ENG.
(T) 01454 326256
Speciality: Osteopathy. ✓
● **Osteopath** Mr A Harcourt Q: DO. M: BAcC.
● **Osteopath** Mr T Sutcliffe Q: DO. M: BAcC.
**S** Yrs. Est.: 8 (Ref:HM08964)

**HARCOURT-RAY, JILL**

**Jill Harcourt-Ray**, Tybryn, Betws, Ammanford, **Carmarthenshire**, SA18 2PL, WAL.
(T) 01269 593017
Speciality: Aromatherapy.
**M O** (Ref:HM08965)

**HARDIE, ANNE**

**Anne Hardie MCSP SRP Sports Injury Clinic**, Woodcroft, 23 Midton Rd, Ayr, **Ayrshire (South)**, KA7 2SF, SCO.
(T) 01292 264383
Speciality: Aromatherapy, Physiotherapy. ✓
● **Aromatherapist/Physiotherpaist**
Mrs A Hardie M: CSP, SRP.
**C** Yrs. Est.: 30 (Ref:HM08966)

**HARDIE, LYNN**

**Lynn Hardie**, 16 Thorpe Gr, Stockport, **Cheshire**, SK4 5NB, ENG.
(T) 01614 321962
Speciality: Reflexology.
**S T** (Ref:HM08967)

**HARDING, AMANDA C**

**Amanda C Harding State Registered Chiropodist**, 90 Battersea Rise, London, **London (Greater)**, SW11 1EJ, ENG.
(T) 020 7228 8383
Speciality: Chiropodists (Podiatrists).
**S** (Ref:HM08968)

**HARDING, B J**

**B J Harding**, 26 Red Lion St, Boston, **Lincolnshire**, PE21 6PZ, ENG.
(T) 01205 354066
Speciality: Physiotherapy.
● **Owner** Mrs B Harding
**P S T** (Ref:HM08969)

**HARDING, H**

**H Harding**, 81 Entry Hill, Bath, **Somerset**, BA2 5LT, ENG.
(T) 01225 833853
Speciality: Chiropodists (Podiatrists).
● **Owner** Mrs H Harding
**S** (Ref:HM08970)

**HARDING, MANDY**

**Mandy Harding**, 144 Boulton Lane, Derby, **Derbyshire**, DE24 0FG, ENG.
(T) 01332 754403
Speciality: Chiropody. ✓
● **Owner/Chiropodist** Ms M Harding
Q: Inst.CH.P. M: Inst.CH.P.
**S** Yrs. Est.: 3 (Ref:HM08971)

**HARDING, S J**

**S J Harding**, 40 North Hinksey Lane, Oxford, **Oxfordshire**, OX2 0LY, ENG.
(T) 01865 200489
Speciality: Chiropractic.
**P S T** (Ref:HM08972)

**HARDISTY, CHRIS**

**Chris Hardisty**, 21 Richmond Avenue, Handforth, Wilmslow, **Cheshire**, SK9 3JD, ENG.
(T) 01625 522613 (F) 01625 522613
Speciality: Hypnosis.
● **Owner** Mrs C Hardisty
**B** (Ref:HM08973)

**HARDMAN, ALAN**

**Alan Hardman**, Calder House, Spring Lane, Colne, **Lancashire**, BB8 9BD, ENG.
(T) 01282 870973
Speciality: Chiropody. ✓
● **Chiropodist (Podiatrist)**
Mr A Hardman Q: DPodM, M.S.C.P. M: S.C.P.
**M** Yrs. Est.: 10 (Ref:HM08974)

**HARDMAN, CHRISTINE**

**Christine Hardman**, 2 Southend Court, Strathaven, **Lanarkshire (South)**, ML10 6QU, SCO.
(T) 01357 520315
Speciality: Hypnotherapy.
● **Owner** Mrs C Hardman
**B** (Ref:HM08975)

**HARDWICK, JUDITH**

**Judith Hardwick**, 4 St. Johns Rd, Smalley, Ilkeston, **Derbyshire**, DE7 6EG, ENG.
(T) 01332 880623
Speciality: Reflexology.
**S T** (Ref:HM08976)

**HARDWICKE, MICHAEL**

**Michael Hardwicke**, Newton Farm Cottage,



Key: **B** Mind-Body Medicine **C** Complementary Medicine **H** Self Help Treatment **M** Medicinal Therapy **O** Oriental Medicine **P** Postural Therapy **S** Manipulative Structural Therapy **T** Touch Therapy

Newton-In-Cartmel, Grange-over-Sands, **Cumbria**, LA11 6JJ, ENG.
(T) 01539 531781
(E) michaelhardwicke@compuserve.com
Speciality: Alexander Technique. ✓
● **Alexander Technique Teacher/Head of Training**
Mr M Hardwicke Q: BSc, MSTAT, PGCE. M: STAT.
P Yrs. Est.: 12 (Ref:HM08977)

## HARDY, CHRISTINE

**Christine Hardy**, 8 Kent Avenue, Cheadle Hulme, Cheadle, **Cheshire**, SK8 5QT, ENG.
(T) 01614 853929
Speciality: Complementary Medicines & Therapy.
● **Owner** Mrs C Hardy
C M (Ref:HM08978)

## HARDY, DIANE

**Diane Hardy**, 6 Martyns Gr, Westcliff-on-Sea, **Essex**, SS0 9XX, ENG.
(T) 01702 333134 (F) 01702 333134
Speciality: Homeopathy.
● **Owner** Ms D Hardy
M (Ref:HM08979)

## HARDY, ELIZABETH

**Elizabeth Hardy**, 2 Lotts Lane, Sompting, Lancing, **Sussex (West)**, BN15 9TX, ENG.
(T) 01903 755913
Speciality: Reflexology.
S T (Ref:HM08980)

## HARDY, JACK E

**Jack E Hardy**, 1 Blenheim Cres, South Croydon, **Surrey**, CR2 6BQ, ENG.
(T) 020 8688 2211
Speciality: Hypnosis, Hypnotherapy. ✓
● **Owner/Hypnotherapist** Mr J Hardy
B Yrs. Est.: 35 (Ref:HM08981)

## HARDY, JONATHAN

**Jonathan Hardy**, 13A North St, Havant, **Hampshire**, PO9 1PW, ENG.
(T) 023 9247 1757
Speciality: Homeopathy.
M (Ref:HM08982)

## HARDY, L M

**L M Hardy**, 67 Grenville Rd, Braintree, **Essex**, CM7 2PP, ENG.
(T) 01376 325630 (F) 01376 325630
Speciality: Reflexology.
● **Partner** Mr J Hardy
S T (Ref:HM08983)

## HARDY, MICHAEL

**Michael Hardy**, 8 The Cl, Tattingstone, Ipswich, **Suffolk**, IP9 2PD, ENG.
(T) 01473 328705
Speciality: Shiatsu. ✓
● **Owner/Shiatsu Therapist**
Mr M Hardy Q: MRSS.
C Yrs. Est.: 12 (Ref:HM08984)

## HARDY, S A

**S A Hardy**, 112 Chesterfield Rd North, Mansfield, **Nottinghamshire**, NG19 7HZ, ENG.
(T) 01623 420644
Speciality: Chiropodists (Podiatrists).
● **Owner** Mrs S Hardy
S (Ref:HM08985)

## HARDY, THEA

**Thea Hardy**, 151-153 Clapham High St, London, **London (Greater)**, SW4 7SS, ENG.
(T) 020 7627 8890
Speciality: Osteopathy.
● **Owner** Mr M Knight
P S T (Ref:HM08986)

## HARDYMAN, D

**D Hardyman**, 67 Richmond Park Avenue, Bournemouth, **Dorset**, BH8 9DN, ENG.
(T) 01202 394938
Speciality: Homeopathy.
M (Ref:HM08987)

## HARE, CAROL L

**Carol L Hare**, Rooms 11 - 12, 1st Floor Victoria Chambers, 60 London Rd, Derby, **Derbyshire**, DE1 2PA, ENG.
(T) 01332 344058
Speciality: Physiotherapy.
● **Owner** Mrs C Hare
P S T (Ref:HM08988)

## HAREFIELD CLINIC

**Harefield Clinic**, 60 Dean Rd, Southampton, **Hampshire**, SO18 6AP, ENG.
(T) 023 8068 5964
Speciality: Osteopathy.
● **Owner** Mr A Nelson
P S T (Ref:HM08989)

## HARES, GARRY

**Garry Hares**, 46 Theobalds Rd, London, **London (Greater)**, WC1X 8NW, ENG.
(T) 020 7831 1939 (F) 08701 218749
Speciality: Osteopathy.
● **Owner** Mr G Hares
P S T (Ref:HM08990)

## HAREWOOD, MARCIA M

**Marcia M Harewood Osteopath & Naturopath**, 255a Lavender Hill, Battersea, London, **London (Greater)**, SW11 1JD, ENG.
(T) 020 7498 9966
(E) marcia.harewood@virgin.net
Speciality: Cranial Osteopathy, Herbal Medicine, Iridology, Manipulation, Massage (Therapeutic), Naturopathy, Nutritional Therapy, Osteopathy, Vitamin Therapy. ✓ 💳
● **Osteopath/Naturopath**
Ms M Harewood Q: Dip.Herb.Med, Dip.Iridol, DO, MH, ND, RN. M: RoN.
S Yrs. Est.: 10 (Ref:HM08991)

## HARGHAM HALL OSTEO PRACTICE

**Hargham Hall Osteopathic Practice**, Hargham Hall Cottage, Hargham, Norwich, **Norfolk**, NR16 2JW, ENG.
(T) 01953 888363
(E) yayliffeost@talk21.com
Speciality: Cranial Osteopathy, Manipulation, Naturopathy, Osteopathy, Postural Integration. ✓
● **Registered Osteopath**
Arnaud Geanty Q: DO. M: GOsC.
● **Owner/Registered Osteopath**
Mrs Y Ayliffe Q: DO. M: GOsC.
P Yrs. Est.: 3 (Ref:HM08992)

## HARGREAVES, ALISON

**Alison Hargreaves**, School House, Milton On Stour, Gillingham, **Dorset**, SP8 5QD, ENG.
(T) 01747 823954
Speciality: Homeopathy.
M (Ref:HM08993)

## HARGREAVES, B

**B Hargreaves**, 25 Birch Avenue, Ashton-On-Ribble, Preston, **Lancashire**, PR2 1JU, ENG.
(T) 01772 728413
Speciality: Physiotherapy.
● **Owner** Mr B Hargreaves
P S T (Ref:HM08994)

## HARLAND, D S

**D S Harland**, The Surgery, 30 Lavington Rd, Croydon, **Surrey**, CR0 4PP, ENG.
(T) 020 8688 8517
Speciality: Chiropodists (Podiatrists).
● **Owner** Mr D Harland
S (Ref:HM08995)

## HARLAND, M

**M Harland**, The Wesley Lane Clinic, 6 Wesley Lane, Bicester, **Oxfordshire**, OX6 7JU, ENG.
(T) 01869 248538
Speciality: Chiropodists (Podiatrists).
S (Ref:HM08996)

## HARLEQUIN

**Harlequin**, Spindlewood, New St, Charfield, Wotton-under-Edge, **Gloucestershire**, GL12 8ES, ENG.
(T) 01453 521530 (F) 01453 521530
Speciality: Complementary Medicines & Therapy.
● **Owner** Mr D Woodhouse
C M (Ref:HM08997)

## HARLESTON CHIROPRACTIC CLINIC

**Harleston Chiropractic Clinic**, Clintergate Farm, Redenhall, Harleston, **Norfolk**, IP20 9PG, ENG.
(T) 01379 853149
Speciality: Chiropractic.
● **Owner** Ms J Rush
P S T (Ref:HM08998)

## HARLEY ST STRESS MNGMT

**Harley Street Stress Management Specialists Ltd**, 10 Harley St, London, **London (Greater)**, W1N 1AA, ENG.
(T) 020 7467 8404
(E) carolewan@aol.com
(W) www.harleystress.co.uk
Speciality: Auto Suggestion, Cognitive Therapy, Complementary Therapy, Counselling, Drama Therapy, Family Therapy, Group Therapy, Hypnosis, Hypnotherapy, Kinesiology, Life Style Coaching, Neuro-Linguistic Program, Psychotherapy, Stress Therapy, Visualisation Therapy, Sports Enhancement, Eye Movement Desensitisation & Reprocessing, Emotional Freedom Technique, Meridian Therapies. ✓
● **Therapist** Mr R Russell
● **Director** Ms C Wan Q: Dip.Hyp, EMDR L1-L2. M: HA, NRHP.
● **Therapist** Ms A Gnock-Shore
(T) 01932 883239
H Yrs. Est.: 5 (Ref:HM08999)

## HARLEY STREET ACADEMY

**Harley Street Academy Of Psychotherapists**, 142 Harley St, London, **London (Greater)**, W1N 1AH, ENG.
(T) 020 8346 0369 (F) 020 8346 0369
Speciality: Psychotherapy.
● **Principal** Mr C Constantino
B (Ref:HM09000)

## HARLEY STREET COMP MEDICINE

**Harley Street Complementary Medicine**, 1 Harley St, **London**, W1G 9QD, ENG.
(T) 08702 414025
(E) harleystreet@complementary.care.co.uk
(W) www.complementary-care.co.uk
Speciality: Homeopathy, Indian Head Massage, Nutritional Therapy, Reflexology, Reiki. ✓ 💳
● **Homeopath** Mr M Edwards Q: MAR. M: AoR, GCP.
● **Clinical Reflexologist**
Miss A Lehunte Q: MAR. M: AoR, GCP.
C Yrs. Est.: 3 (Ref:HM09001)

## HARLEY STREET PHYSIOTHERAPY

**Harley Street Physiotherapy**, 110 Harley St, London, **London (Greater)**, W1N 1AF, ENG.
(T) 020 7224 4588 (F) 020 7224 4588
Speciality: Physiotherapy.
P S T (Ref:HM09002)

## HARLEY STREET TCM FERTILITY

**TCM Healthcare**, 57 Harley St, London, **London (Greater)**, ENG.
(T) 020 8556 8843
(E) herb@tcm.uk.com
(W) www.tcm.uk.com
Speciality: Acupressure, Acupuncture, Herbal Medicine, Oriental Diagnosis. ✓
● **Medical Director** Yang Li M: ATCM UK.
● **Medical Practitioner** Hong Yang Q: BSc. M: RCHM.
● **Director** Shun Au Q: MBA.
O Yrs. Est.: 2 (Ref:HM09003)

## HARLEY, ANN

**Ann Harley**, 129 Rockmount Avenue, Orchard Park, Thornliebank, Glasgow, **Glasgow (City of)**, G46 7DR, SCO.
(T) 01416 203578
Speciality: Chiropodists (Podiatrists).
● **Owner** Miss A Harley
S (Ref:HM09004)

## HARLEY, D

**D Harley**, 30 Magdalen St, Norwich, **Norfolk**, NR3 1HU, ENG.
(T) 01603 620688
Speciality: Chiropodists (Podiatrists).
● **Owner** Mr D Harley
S (Ref:HM09005)

## HARLEY, KI

**Private Psychotherapy Practice**, 43 Ashley Gardens, Ambrosden Avenue, Victoria, London, **London (Greater)**, SW1P 1QF, ENG.
(T) 020 7630 8438



Key continued: Yrs.Est: Years Established Q: Qualifications M: Professional Membership ✓ Indemnity Insurance 💳 Accept Credit Cards

Speciality: Counselling, Psychotherapy, Transactional Analysis, Couples Therapy, Integrative Psychotherapy.
● **Psychotherapist** Mrs K Harley Q: MSc, UKCP (Reg). M: HA, UKCP.
[B] Yrs. Est.: 13 (**Ref:**HM09006)

## HARLEY, LIZ

**Harley Liz**, Rosemount Centre, 1c Mount St, Aberdeen, **Aberdeenshire**, AB25 2RA, **SCO**.
(T) 01224 636378
Speciality: Complementary Medicines & Therapy.
[M] (**Ref:**HM09007)

## HARLEY, LIZ

**Liz Harley**, Chelsea Lane, Inverurie, **Aberdeenshire**, AB51 3QQ, **SCO**.
(T) 01467 624888 (F) 01467 624888
Speciality: Complementary Medicines & Therapy.
● **Partner** Mrs C Craigmile
[C] [M] (**Ref:**HM09008)

## HARLING, KATRINA

**Katrina Harling**, 19b Connaught Rd, London, **London (Greater)**, NW10 9AJ, **ENG**.
(T) 020 8453 0900
Speciality: Complementary Medicines & Therapy.
[C] [M] (**Ref:**HM09009)

## HARLING, MARIANNE (DR)

**Dr Marianne Harling**, Flat 1, 24 Browning Avenue, Bournemouth, **Dorset**, BH5 1NN, **ENG**.
(T) 01202 395149
Speciality: Homeopathy. ✔
● **Owner** Dr M Harling Q: BA, Ch.B.
[C] Yrs. Est.: 43 (**Ref:**HM09010)

## HARLOW OSTEOPATHIC PRACTICE

**Harlow Osteopathic Practice**, 5-6 Second Floor, Market House, The High, Harlow, **Essex**, CM20 1BL, **ENG**.
(T) 01279 410136
Speciality: Acupuncture, Osteopathy. ✔
● **Osteopath** Mr G Attewell Q: BSc (Hons), DO, ND. M: GOsC.
● **Holistic Massage Therapist** Ms A Clayton
● **Osteopath** Ms C Gawlinska Q: BSc (Hons), DO. M: GOsC.
[S] Yrs. Est.: 15 (**Ref:**HM09011)

## HARMAN, ABIGAIL

**Abigail Harman**, 1 The Green, Foxton, Cambridge, **Cambridgeshire**, CB2 6ST, **ENG**.
(T) 01223 873086
Speciality: Reflexology.
[S] [T] (**Ref:**HM09012)

## HARMER, LESLEY

**Lesley Harmer**, 8 Willowside, London Colney, St. Albans, **Hertfordshire**, AL2 1EU, **ENG**.
(T) 01727 769251
Speciality: Chiropodists (Podiatrists).
[S] (**Ref:**HM09013)

## HARMON, MIKE

**Mike Harmon**, 13 Wellington House, 148 Peckham Rye, London, **London (Greater)**, SE22 9QP, **ENG**.
(T) 020 8693 6501
Speciality: Reflexology.
[S] [T] (**Ref:**HM09014)

## HARMONIOUS HEALTHCARE

**Harmonious Healthcare**, 1st Floor, 353 Preston Rd, Clayton-Le-Woods, Chorley, **Lancashire**, PR6 7PY, **ENG**.
(T) 01257 231232
(E) brian@reflexology100.fsnet.co.uk
(W) www.harmonioushealthcare.co.uk
Speciality: Aromatherapy, Hopi Ear Candles, Indian Head Massage, Massage (Therapeutic), Reflexology, Reiki, Remedial Massage, Soul Path Readings. ✔
● **Aromatherapist** Ms A Jeffrey Q: MICHT. M: ICHT.
● **Remedial Masseur** Ms J O'Dowd
● **Complementary Therapist** Mr B Jeffery Q: MBRA, MGCP. M: BRA, GCP.
● **Soul Path Reader** Ms E Slingsby
● **Remedial/Sports Masseur** Ms J Winter Q: MICHT. M: ICHT.
[C] Yrs. Est.: 1 (**Ref:**HM09015)

## HARMONIOUS HEALTHCARE

**Harmonious Healthcare**, 19 Pingle Croft, Clayton-Le-Woods, Chorley, **Lancashire**, PR6 7UL, **ENG**.
(T) 01772 620614
Speciality: Complementary Medicines & Therapy.
● **Director** Mr B Jeffery
[M] (**Ref:**HM09016)

## HARMONOLOGY CENTRE

**Harmonology Centre**, Culbokie, Culbokie, Dingwall, **Highland**, IV7 8JH, **SCO**.
(T) 01349 877828 (F) 01349 877818
(W) www.harmonology.co.uk
Speciality: Cranio-Sacral Therapy, Spiritual Healing, Swiss Bio Energy Massage. ✔
● **Owner** Mr H Valant
[C] Yrs. Est.: 12 (**Ref:**HM09017)

## HARMONY

**Harmony**, 3 Hatch Rd, Pilgrims Hatch, Brentwood, **Essex**, CM15 9PU, **ENG**.
(T) 01277 375751
Speciality: Complementary Medicines & Therapy.
● **Owner** Mrs S Coatrove
[M] (**Ref:**HM09018)

## HARMONY

**Harmony**, 90 Chatsworth Rd, Morecambe, **Lancashire**, LA3 1BL, **ENG**.
(T) 01524 831049
Speciality: Aromatherapy.
● **Owner** Mrs K Shaw
[M] [O] (**Ref:**HM09019)

## HARMONY

**Harmony**, 94 Golf Rd, New Inn, Pontypool, **Monmouthshire**, NP4 0QW, **WAL**.
(T) 01495 764764
Speciality: Aromatherapy, Reflexology, Reiki. ✔
● **Owner/Clinical Therapist** Mrs P Talbot Q: MRxS.
[C] Yrs. Est.: 1 (**Ref:**HM09020)

## HARMONY

**Harmony**, 69 Knowlton Rd, **Dorset**, BH17 9EE, **ENG**.
(T) 01202 698090
Speciality: Hypnosis.
[B] (**Ref:**HM09021)

## HARMONY & BALANCE CENTRE

**Harmony & Balance Centre**, Kia Islandvane Mungret Limk, **County Limerick**, **IRE**.
(T) 06130 4445
Speciality: Complementary Medicines & Therapy.
[M] (**Ref:**HM09022)

## HARMONY ACUPUNCTURE CLINIC

**Harmony Acupuncture Clinic**, Flood St, **County Galway**, **IRE**.
(T) 09156 8871
Speciality: Acupuncture.
[O] (**Ref:**HM09023)

## HARMONY CHINESE MED CTRE

**Harmony Chinese Medicine Centre**, 629 High Rd Leytonstone, London, **London (Greater)**, E11 4PA, **ENG**.
(T) 020 8518 7337 (F) 020 8556 5036
Speciality: Complementary Medicines & Therapy.
● **Director** Mr P Choy
[C] [M] (**Ref:**HM09024)

## HARMONY HEALING CENTRE

**Harmony Healing Centre**, 6 St Botolphs St, Colchester, **Essex**, CO2 7DU, **ENG**.
(T) 01206 364384
Speciality: Complementary Medicines & Therapy.
● **Owner** Mrs S Robinson
[M] (**Ref:**HM09025)

## HARMONY HOLISTICS

**Harmony Holistics**, 1 Charlwood Avenue, Liverpool, **Merseyside**, L36 5UH, **ENG**.
(T) 01514 899600
Speciality: Aromatherapy.
● **Owner** Mrs A Walker
[M] [O] (**Ref:**HM09026)

## HARMONY HYPNOTHERAPY CTRE

**Harmony Hypnotherapy & Natural Therapy Centre**, 7 Atherstone Cl, Canvey Island, **Essex**, SS8 7DG, **ENG**.
(T) 01268 692442
Speciality: Hypnosis.
● **Owner** Miss L Evans
[B] (**Ref:**HM09027)

## HARMONY IN HEALTH

**Harmony In Health**, Lasata, Laurels Avenue, Bangor On Dee, Wrexham, LL13 0BB, **WAL**.
(T) 01978 780121
(E) jenny.hargreaves@ukgateway.net
Speciality: Healer, Holistic Healing, Iridology, Naturopathy, Nutritional Therapy, Reiki, Spiritual Healing, Louise Hay Teacher.
● **Nutritionist/Healer** Ms J Hargreaves Q: D.Th.D, Dip.Iridol, Dip.N Med. M: BANT.
[B] [C] [T] Yrs. Est.: 8 (**Ref:**HM09028)

## HARMONY IN HEALTH

**Harmony In Health**, Hillside House, Bronwylfa, **Wrexham**, LL14 4LD, **WAL**.
(T) 01978 841626
Speciality: Complementary Medicines & Therapy.
[C] [M] (**Ref:**HM09029)

## HARMONY INDIAN HEAD MASS

**Harmony Indian Head Massage & Stress Counselling**, 3 Sedgefield Cl, Totton, Southampton, **Hampshire**, SO40 8GP, **ENG**.
(T) 023 8086 3605 (F) 023 8086 3605
Speciality: Complementary Medicines & Therapy.
● **Owner** Mr R Towler
[C] [M] (**Ref:**HM09030)

## HARMONY MASSAGE CENTRE

**Harmony Massage Centre (The)**, The Old Convent, Beeches Green, Stroud, **Gloucestershire**, GL5 4AD, **ENG**.
(T) 01453 884574
Speciality: Massage (Therapeutic).
● **Owner** Ms T Hefferman
[M] (**Ref:**HM09031)

## HARMONY PRODUCTS

**Harmony Products Ltd**, Po Box 2541, Saltdean, Brighton, **Sussex (East)**, BN2 8AA, **ENG**.
(T) 01273 305040
Speciality: Complementary Medicines & Therapy.
[M] (**Ref:**HM09032)

## HARMONY THERAPY & HEALING CTRE

**Harmony Therapy & Healing Centre (The)**, 486 Devizes Rd, Salisbury, **Wiltshire**, SP2 9LX, **ENG**.
(T) 01772 330113 (F) 01722 338251
Speciality: Complementary Medicines & Therapy.
● **Owner** Mrs V Thomas
[M] (**Ref:**HM09033)

## HARNWELL, J P

**J P Harnwell**, Tan Y Bryn, Llangwyfan, Denbigh, **Denbighshire**, LL16 4LU, **WAL**.
(T) 01824 790375
Speciality: Herbal Medicine, Nutritional Therapy, Psychotherapy.
[M] (**Ref:**HM09034)

## HARPENDEM OSTEOPATHIC PRACTICE

**Harpendem Osteopathic Practice (The)**, 58 Tennyson Rd, Harpenden, **Hertfordshire**, AL5 4BB, **ENG**.
(T) 01582 713648 (F) 01582 620355
Speciality: Acupuncture, Chiropody, Counselling, Cranial Osteopathy, Homeopathy, Manipulation, Osteopathy. ✔ CREDIT
● **Osteopath** Mr P Mitterhuber Q: BSc. M: GOsC.
● **Osteopath** Ms N Seager Q: BSc. M: GOsC.
● **Osteopath** Ms C Hamilton-Plant Q: DO.



Key: [B] Mind-Body Medicine [C] Complementary Medicine [H] Self Help Treatment [M] Medicinal Therapy [O] Oriental Medicine [P] Postural Therapy [S] Manipulative Structural Therapy [T] Touch Therapy

M: GOsC.
● **Osteopath** Mr P Colvin **Q:** DO. **M:** GOsC.
**S** **Yrs. Est.:** 30 (**Ref:**HM09035)

**HARPENDEN CHIROPRACTIC CLINIC**

**Harpenden Chiropractic Clinic**, 113 Southdown Rd, Harpenden, **Hertfordshire**, AL5 1QQ, ENG.
**(T)** 01582 766477
**Speciality:** Chiropractic, Herbal Medicine, Manipulation, Metamorphic Therapy. ✔
● **Chiropractor** Dr A Nelson **Q:** BSc (Chiro), DC.
**B H P S** **Yrs. Est.:** 7 (**Ref:**HM09036)

**HARPER, B**

**B Harper**, 2 Folly Lane, Swinton, Manchester, **Manchester (Greater)**, M27 0DW, ENG.
**(T)** 01617 947616
**Speciality:** Chiropodists (Podiatrists).
**S** (**Ref:**HM09037)

**HARPER, CHERYL**

**Cheryl Harper**, 15 Canterbury Avenue, Upminster, **Essex**, RM14 3LD, ENG.
**(T)** 01708 229749
**Speciality:** Reflexology.
**S T** (**Ref:**HM09038)

**HARPER, D**

**D Harper**, Gribble Bridge Lane, Biddenden, Ashford, **Kent**, TN27 8DH, ENG.
**(T)** 01580 291671
**Speciality:** Osteopathy.
● **Owner** Mrs D Harper
**P S T** (**Ref:**HM09039)

**HARPER, M B**

**M B Harper**, 162 Hawthorn Rd, Birmingham, **Midlands (West)**, B44 8PU, ENG.
**(T)** 01212 447485
**Speciality:** Chiropodists (Podiatrists).
● **Owner** Mrs M Harper
**S** (**Ref:**HM09040)

**HARPER, SUZANNE G**

**Suzanne G Harper**, 140 Harley St, London, **London (Greater)**, W1G 1AH, ENG.
**(T)** 020 7224 3387 **(F)** 020 7486 4080
**(E)** suzh@demon.co.uk
**(W)** www.wellbeing.co.uk
**Speciality:** Acupuncture, Bach Remedies, Counselling, Cranial Osteopathy, Hypnosis, Hypnotherapy, Life Style Coaching, Manipulation, Moxibustion, Naturopathy, Nutritional Therapy, Oriental Diagnosis, Osteopathy, Psychotherapy, Reiki, Vitamin Therapy. ✔ CREDIT
● **Osteopath/Therapist** Ms S Harper **Q:** DO, MBAcC, MGOsC, ND. **M:** ANLP, BAcC, GOsC.
**S** **Yrs. Est.:** 37 (**Ref:**HM09041)

**HARPER, SUZANNE G**

**Suzanne G Harper**, 32 Redriffe Rd, London, **London (Greater)**, E13 0JX, ENG.
**(T)** 020 8552 3397 **(F)** 020 8552 3397
**(E)** suza@demon.co.uk
**(W)** www.wellbeing.co.uk
**Speciality:** Acupuncture, Bach Remedies, Counselling, Cranial Osteopathy, Hypnosis, Hypnotherapy, Life Style Coaching, Manipulation, Moxibustion, Naturopathy, Nutritional Therapy, Oriental Diagnosis, Osteopathy, Psychotherapy, Reiki, Vitamin Therapy. ✔ CREDIT
● **Therapist** Ms S Harper **Q:** DO, MBAcC, MGOsC, ND. **M:** ANLP, BAcC, GOsC.
**S** **Yrs. Est.:** 27 (**Ref:**HM09042)

**HARPER, TOM**

**Tom Harper**, Natural Medicine Centre, 86 Queens Rd, Nuneaton, **Warwickshire**, CV11 5LE, ENG.
**(T)** 024 7634 3100
**Speciality:** Acupuncture.
**O** (**Ref:**HM09043)

**HARRINGTON, C V**

**C V Harrington**, 75 Woodthorpe Drive, Woodthorpe, Nottingham, **Nottinghamshire**, NG5 4GY, ENG.
**(T)** 01159 605206
**Speciality:** Physiotherapy.
● **Owner** Mrs C Harrington
**P S T** (**Ref:**HM09044)

**HARRINGTON, E**

**E Harrington**, 87 George St, Whithorn, Newton Stewart, **Dumfries and Galloway**, DG8 8PZ, SCO.
**(T)** 01988 500674
**Speciality:** Homeopathy.
**M** (**Ref:**HM09045)

**HARRINGTON, E**

**E Harrington**, 51 Henry Rd, West Bridgford, Nottingham, **Nottinghamshire**, NG2 7NB, ENG.
**(T)** 01159 812788
**Speciality:** Physiotherapy.
● **Owner** Mrs E Harrington
**P S T** (**Ref:**HM09046)

**HARRINGTON, ELIZABETH**

**Elizabeth Harrington**, 177 King St, Castle Douglas, **Dumfries and Galloway**, DG7 1DZ, SCO.
**(T)** 01556 504104 **(F)** 01556 504552
**Speciality:** Homeopathy.
● **Partner** Mr G Carlo
**M** (**Ref:**HM09047)

**HARRINGTON, MATTHEW**

**Matthew Harrington**, 26 Hopefield Avenue, London, **London (Greater)**, NW6 6LH, ENG.
**(T)** 020 8964 2765
**Speciality:** Complementary Medicines & Therapy.
**C M** (**Ref:**HM09048)

**HARRIS & ASSOCIATES**

**Paul A E Harris & Associates**, 34 Palmeira Sq, Hove, **Sussex (East)**, BN3 2JP, ENG.
**(T)** 01273 733469
**Speciality:** Chiropractors.
**P S T** (**Ref:**HM09049)

**HARRIS ELECTRONICS**

**Harris Electronics**, Clacton Rd, London, **London (Greater)**, N17 6UG, ENG.
**(T)** 020 8808 3655 **(F)** 020 8808 1431
**Speciality:** Electrolysis.
● **Owner** Mrs G Harris
**T** (**Ref:**HM09050)

**HARRIS, ANN**

**Ann Harris**, 7 Hopfield Gardens, Uckfield, **Sussex (East)**, TN22 1UU, ENG.
**(T)** 01825 767100
**Speciality:** Chiropodists (Podiatrists).
**S** (**Ref:**HM09051)

**HARRIS, ANTHONY S A**

**Anthony S A Harris**, 13 Connies House, Rhymney River Bridge Rd, Cardiff, **Glamorgan (Vale of)**, CF3 7YZ, WAL.
**(T)** 029 2045 1952
**Speciality:** Psychotherapy.
**B** (**Ref:**HM09052)

**HARRIS, ANYA**

**Anya Harris**, Nevill House, 164 Marine Prde, Brighton, **Sussex (East)**, BN2 1EJ, ENG.
**(T)** 01273 676032
**Speciality:** Complementary Medicines & Therapy.
**M** (**Ref:**HM09053)

**HARRIS, C**

**C Harris**, 21 Dendy Rd, Paignton, **Devon**, TQ4 5DB, ENG.
**(T)** 01803 527091
**Speciality:** Osteopathy.
● **Practice Manager** Mr C Goldsmith
**P S T** (**Ref:**HM09054)

**HARRIS, CAROLE**

**Carole Harris**, 26 Oliver Rd, Oxford, **Oxfordshire**, OX4 2JF, ENG.
**(T)** 01865 779732
**Speciality:** Reflexology.
**S T** (**Ref:**HM09055)

**HARRIS, CAROLINE**

**Caroline Harris**, 10 High St, Glastonbury, **Somerset**, BA6 9DU, ENG.
**(T)** 01458 834236
**Speciality:** Aromatherapy.
● **Director** Ms J Sanders
**M O** (**Ref:**HM09056)

**HARRIS, CHRIS**

**Chris Harris**, Natural Health Clinic, 98 Cathedral Rd, Cardiff, **Glamorgan (Vale of)**, CF11 9LP, WAL.
**(T)** 029 2022 2221
**Speciality:** Osteopathy.
● **Practice Manager** Mrs L Powell
**P S T** (**Ref:**HM09057)

**HARRIS, DAPHNE**

**Harris Daphne**, 5 Springback Way, Uppingham, Oakham, **Leicestershire**, LE15 9TT, ENG.
**(T)** 01572 823422 **(F)** 01572 822023
**Speciality:** Chiropodists (Podiatrists).
● **Owner** Mrs D Harris
**S** (**Ref:**HM09058)

**HARRIS, DAVID B**

**David B Harris**, 78 Broadfields Avenue, Edgware, **London (Greater)**, HA8 8SW, ENG.
**(T)** 020 8905 3565
**Speciality:** Chiropodists (Podiatrists).
● **Owner** Mr D Harris
**S** (**Ref:**HM09059)

**HARRIS, FRANCES E**

**Frances E Harris**, 26 Kingston Rd, New Malden, **Surrey**, KT3 3LS, ENG.
**(T)** 020 8942 3148 **(F)** 020 8949 7050
**Speciality:** Physiotherapy.
**P S T** (**Ref:**HM09060)

**HARRIS, FRANCIS**

**Francis Harris**, 18 Wolsey Cl, Coombe La West, Kingston Upon Thames, **Surrey**, KT2 7ER, ENG.
**(T)** 020 8336 2726
**Speciality:** Physiotherapy.
**P S T** (**Ref:**HM09061)

**HARRIS, G & J**

**G & J Harris**, Honeysuckle Cottage, Rixon, Sturminster Newton, **Dorset**, DT10 1BQ, ENG.
**(T)** 01258 472188
**Speciality:** Chiropodists (Podiatrists).
● **Owner** Mr G Harris
**S** (**Ref:**HM09062)

**HARRIS, GERALD**

**Gerald Harris**, 78 Park View Rd, Sutton Coldfield, **Midlands (West)**, B74 4PS, ENG.
**(T)** 01213 533131 **(F)** 01213 533131
**Speciality:** Hypnosis.
● **Owner** Mr G Harris
**B** (**Ref:**HM09063)

**HARRIS, J**

**Mrs J Harris**, 5 Mount Beacon, Bath, **Somerset**, BA1 5QP, ENG.
**(T)** 01225 312399
**Speciality:** Physiotherapy.
● **Partner** Mrs J Harris
**P S T** (**Ref:**HM09064)

**HARRIS, J**

**J Harris**, Rossmoyne, Ray Mill Rd East, Maidenhead, **Berkshire**, SL6 8TQ, ENG.
**(T)** 01628 621314
**Speciality:** Physiotherapy.
● **Owner** Mrs J Harris
**P S T** (**Ref:**HM09065)

**HARRIS, J**

**J Harris**, The Clinic, 37 St Peter St, Tiverton, **Devon**, EX16 6NW, ENG.
**(T)** 01884 255990
**Speciality:** Homeopathy.
**M** (**Ref:**HM09066)

**HARRIS, JANET**

**Janet Harris**, 16 Charlton Rd, Weston-Super-Mare, **Somerset**, BS23 4HQ, ENG.
**(T)** 01934 414104
**Speciality:** Chiropodists (Podiatrists).
● **Owner** Mrs J Harris
**S** (**Ref:**HM09067)

**HARRIS, JEANNE**

**Jeanne Harris**, Old Blundells Cottage, Lowman Green, Tiverton, **Devon**, EX16 4LB, ENG.
**(T)** 01884 256691
**Speciality:** Homeopathy.
**M** (**Ref:**HM09068)

**HARRIS, JEREMY**

**Jeremy Harris**, 56 Hatherall Rd, Maidstone, **Kent**, ME14 5HF, ENG.
**(T)** 01622 766073
**Speciality:** Chiropodists (Podiatrists).


Key continued: **Yrs.Est:** Years Established **Q:** Qualifications **M:** Professional Membership ✔ Indemnity Insurance CREDIT Accept Credit Cards

● **Owner** Mr J Harris
S (**Ref:**HM09069)

### HARRIS, JOANNA P
**Joanna P Harris**, Flat 4, 6 Holyrood Pl, Plymouth, **Devon**, PL1 2QB, ENG.
(T) 01752 601591
Speciality: Complementary Medicines & Therapy.
M (**Ref:**HM09070)

### HARRIS, JOHN
**John Harris**, 34 Hurst Rd, East Molesey, **Surrey**, KT8 9AF, ENG.
(T) 020 8979 0880
Speciality: Physiotherapy.
P S T (**Ref:**HM09071)

### HARRIS, JOHN A
**John A Harris**, 14 Springfield Park, Shrewsbury Rd, Market Drayton, **Shropshire**, TF9 3ET, ENG.
(T) 01630 652758
Speciality: Chiropodists (Podiatrists).
● **Owner** Mr J Harris
S (**Ref:**HM09072)

### HARRIS, JOHN R C
**John R C Harris**, 18 Burgh Heath Rd, Epsom, **Surrey**, KT17 4LS, ENG.
(T) 01372 728203 (F) 01372 722776
Speciality: Osteopathy.
● **Owner** Mr J Harris
P S T (**Ref:**HM09073)

### HARRIS, JONATHAN
**Jonathan Harris**, Odstone, Westcot Lane, Sparsholt, Wantage, **Oxfordshire**, OX12 9PZ, ENG.
(T) 01235 751573
Speciality: Psychotherapy.
● **Owner** Mr J Harris
B (**Ref:**HM09074)

### HARRIS, K R
**K R Harris**, The Surgery, 4 York Rd, Exeter, **Devon**, EX4 6PQ, ENG.
(T) 01392 254385
Speciality: Chiropractic.
P S T (**Ref:**HM09075)

### HARRIS, K R (DR)
**Dr K R Harris**, 24 St Peter St, Tiverton, **Devon**, EX16 6NU, ENG.
(T) 01884 253096
Speciality: Chiropractors.
P S T (**Ref:**HM09076)

### HARRIS, LESLEY
**Lesley Harris**, 68B Leicester Rd, Loughborough, **Leicestershire**, LE11 2AG, ENG.
(T) 01509 234522
Speciality: Herbal Medicine.
M (**Ref:**HM09077)

### HARRIS, LYN
**Lyn Harris**, Hook Barn, Chardstock, Axminster, **Devon**, EX13 7DD, ENG.
(T) 01460 220163
Speciality: Homeopathy.
● **Owner** Ms L Harris
M (**Ref:**HM09078)

### HARRIS, M M
**M M Harris**, 23 Manor Way, Harrow, **London (Greater)**, HA2 6BZ, ENG.
(T) 020 8863 2132
Speciality: Alexander Technique.
● **Owner** Miss M Harris
P S (**Ref:**HM09079)

### HARRIS, MICHAEL
**Michael Harris**, 2 Costly St, Ivybridge, **Devon**, PL21 0DB, ENG.
(T) 01752 896116
Speciality: Osteopathy.
P S T (**Ref:**HM09080)

### HARRIS, MICHAEL
**Michael Harris**, 59 Braymoor Rd, Birmingham, **Midlands (West)**, B33 0LR, ENG.
(T) 01217 882687
Speciality: Hypnosis.
● **Owner** Mr M Harris
B (**Ref:**HM09081)

### HARRIS, MICHELLE J
**Michelle J Harris**, 118 Belgrave Walk, Mitcham, **Surrey**, CR4 3QD, ENG.
(T) 020 8646 6053 (F) 020 8646 6053
Speciality: Hypnosis.
● **Owner** Mrs M Harris
B (**Ref:**HM09082)

### HARRIS, NESLI
**Nesli Harris**, 305 Great North Way, London, **London (Greater)**, NW4 1EU, ENG.
(T) 020 8203 0999
Speciality: Osteopathy.
P S T (**Ref:**HM09083)

### HARRIS, PAUL A E
**Paul A E Harris**, Warwick House Chiropractic Clinic, 4 Warwick Pl, Worthing, **Sussex (West)**, BN11 3EU, ENG.
(T) 01903 228040
Speciality: Chiropractic. ✔ CREDIT
● **Chiropractor** Mr P Harris **Q:** DC.
● **Chiropractor** Mr F Jenk **Q:** DC.
P Yrs. Est.: 10 (**Ref:**HM09084)

### HARRIS, PAUL H G
**Paul H G Harris**, 19 Gages Cl, Bristol, BS15 9UH, ENG.
(T) 01179 672216
Speciality: Chiropodists (Podiatrists).
S (**Ref:**HM09085)

### HARRIS, RACHEL
**Rachel Harris**, 34 Leicester St, Kettering, **Northamptonshire**, NN16 8EF, ENG.
(T) 01536 392267
Speciality: Chiropodists (Podiatrists).
S (**Ref:**HM09086)

### HARRIS, ROSE
**Rose Harris**, 54 The Avenue, Yeovil, **Somerset**, BA21 4BN, ENG.
(T) 01935 422488
Speciality: Acupuncture.
O (**Ref:**HM09087)

### HARRIS, S J
**S J Harris**, 407 Weddington Rd, Nuneaton, **Warwickshire**, CV10 0HA, ENG.
(T) 024 7634 3456
Speciality: Physiotherapy.
● **Owner** Mr S Harris
P S T (**Ref:**HM09088)

### HARRIS, STEVEN
**Steven Harris**, 5 Newman Passage, London, **London (Greater)**, W1P 3PF, ENG.
(T) 020 7637 7125
Speciality: Osteopathy.
P S T (**Ref:**HM09089)

### HARRIS-BEACH, JULIE
**Julie Harris-Beach**, Lannas House, 63 Meadrow, Godalming, **Surrey**, GU7 3HS, ENG.
(T) 01483 418000
Speciality: Hypnosis.
B (**Ref:**HM09090)

### HARRISON, A
**A Harrison**, 4 Browning Drive, Winchester, **Hampshire**, SO22 5AR, ENG.
(T) 01962 854625
Speciality: Chiropodists (Podiatrists).
● **Owner** A Harrison
S (**Ref:**HM09091)

### HARRISON, CHRISTINE
**Christine Harrison**, 118 Compton Rd, Wolverhampton, **Midlands (West)**, WV3 9PZ, ENG.
(T) 01902 424638
Speciality: Physiotherapy.
P S T (**Ref:**HM09092)

### HARRISON, DAVID
**David Harrison**, 22 Beast Banks, Kendal, **Cumbria**, LA9 4JW, ENG.
(T) 01539 740688
Speciality: Osteopathy.
● **Owner** Mr D Harrison
P S T (**Ref:**HM09093)

### HARRISON, DAVID
**David Harrison**, 36 Hook Bank Residential Mobile Homes, Hanley Castle, Worcester, **Worcestershire**, WR8 0BQ, ENG.
(T) 01684 594775
Speciality: Clairvoyants & Palmists.
● **Owner** Mr D Harrison
B (**Ref:**HM09094)

### HARRISON, DEBORAH
**Deborah Harrison**, 49 Goldsel Rd, Swanley, **Kent**, BR8 8HA, ENG.
(T) 01322 666427
Speciality: Chiropodists (Podiatrists).
● **Owner** Mrs D Harrison
S (**Ref:**HM09095)

### HARRISON, DENISE
**Denise Harrison**, 17 Sheldons Rd, Hook, **Hampshire**, RG27 9DL, ENG.
(T) 01256 764754
Speciality: Reflexology.
S T (**Ref:**HM09096)

### HARRISON, DUNCAN
**Duncan Harrison**, 8 Field Cl, Bollington, Macclesfield, **Cheshire**, SK10 5JG, ENG.
(T) 01625 575646
Speciality: Chiropodists (Podiatrists).
● **Owner** Mr D Harrison
S (**Ref:**HM09097)

### HARRISON, FIONA
**Fiona Harrison**, 7 High St, Thurlby, Bourne, **Lincolnshire**, PE10 0ED, ENG.
(T) 01778 423854
Speciality: Aromatherapy. ✔
● **Aromatherapist** Mrs F Harrison **Q:** Dip.Arom. **M:** FHT.
C Yrs. Est.: 7 (**Ref:**HM09098)

### HARRISON, GRETA
**Greta Harrison**, Windmill House, Grange Lane, Lichfield, **Staffordshire**, WS13 7ED, ENG.
(T) 01543 262853
Speciality: Reflexology.
S T (**Ref:**HM09099)

### HARRISON, IAN M
**Ian M Harrison**, The Hampshire Clinic, Basing Rd, Old Basing, Basingstoke, **Hampshire**, RG24 7AL, ENG.
(T) 01256 357111
Speciality: Osteopathy.
P S T (**Ref:**HM09100)

### HARRISON, J C
**J C Harrison**, 433 Aigburth Rd, Liverpool, **Merseyside**, L17 6BJ, ENG.
(T) 01514 271760 (F) 01514 275270
Speciality: Chiropodists (Podiatrists).
● **Owner** Mr J Harrison
S (**Ref:**HM09101)

### HARRISON, MALCOLM
**Malcolm Harrison**, 3 King Edward Rd, Watford, **Hertfordshire**, WD1 4DN, ENG.
(T) 01923 230148
Speciality: Physiotherapy.
P S T (**Ref:**HM09102)

### HARRISON, MANUELLA
**Manuella Harrison**, The Hanson Chiropractic Centre, Unit 16 Granby Court, Surrey Cl, Granby Industrial Estate, Weymouth, **Dorset**, DT4 9XB, ENG.
(T) 01305 761507
Speciality: Complementary Medicines & Therapy.
● **Partner** Mr D Groeger
M (**Ref:**HM09103)

### HARRISON, MONICA
**Monica Harrison**, 124 John St, Porthcawl, Bridgend, CF36 3DT, WAL.
(T) 01656 782440
Speciality: Reflexology.
S T (**Ref:**HM09104)

### HARRISON, R G
**R G Harrison**, 6 Bowling Court, Brighouse, **Yorkshire (West)**, HD6 2RL, ENG.
(T) 01484 717573
Speciality: Chiropodists (Podiatrists).
● **Owner** Mr R Harrison
S (**Ref:**HM09105)



Key: B Mind-Body Medicine C Complementary Medicine H Self Help Treatment M Medicinal Therapy O Oriental Medicine P Postural Therapy S Manipulative Structural Therapy T Touch Therapy

### HARRISON, RITA RGN
**Harrison Rita RGN**, Glor Na Mara Spanish Point Clare, **County Clare**, IRE.
(T) 06570 84589
Speciality: Complementary Medicines & Therapy.
**M** (**Ref:**HM09106)

### HARRISON, S
**S Harrison**, Bournehall Avenue, Bushey, Watford, **Hertfordshire**, WD2 3AU, ENG.
(T) 020 8950 0925
Speciality: Reflexology.
**S T** (**Ref:**HM09107)

### HARRISON, S
**S Harrison**, 86 Deerswood Avenue, Hatfield, **Hertfordshire**, AL10 8SA, ENG.
(T) 01707 265743
Speciality: Reflexology.
**S T** (**Ref:**HM09108)

### HARRISON, SUSAN
**Susan Harrison**, 49 Wilkins Cl, **Wiltshire**, SN2 7XW, ENG.
(T) 07715 048008
Speciality: Reflexology.
**S T** (**Ref:**HM09109)

### HARRISON, TIMOTHY M
**Timothy M Harrison**, 193 Harrow View, Harrow, **London (Greater)**, HA1 4SS, ENG.
(T) 020 8427 4287
Speciality: Hypnotherapy.
● **Owner** Mr T Harrison
**B** (**Ref:**HM09110)

### HARRISON, VALERIE
**Valerie Harrison**, Linden Hollow, Branksome Park Rd, Camberley, **Surrey**, GU15 2AQ, ENG.
(T) 01276 61711
Speciality: Chiropodists (Podiatrists).
**S** (**Ref:**HM09111)

### HARRISON, W L
**W L Harrison**, 4a Canada Rd, Walmer, Deal, **Kent**, CT14 7DZ, ENG.
(T) 01304 373007
Speciality: Chiropodists (Podiatrists).
● **Partner** Mr W Harrison
**S** (**Ref:**HM09112)

### HARRISON-WILLIAMS
**Harrison-Williams**, 36-38 Queen Mary Avenue, Cleethorpes, **Humberside (South)**, DN35 7ST, ENG.
(T) 01472 356884
Speciality: Chiropody. ✔
● **Owner/Chiropodist** Mrs B Williams
Q: M.S.C.P, S.R.Ch.
**M** (**Ref:**HM09113)

### HARRISON-WILLIAMS CHIROPODIST
**Harrison-Williams Chiropodist**, 41 St Peters Avenue, Cleethorpes, **Humberside (South)**, DN35 8HF, ENG.
(T) 01472 692514
Speciality: Chiropody. ✔
● **Chiropodist** Mr P Williams Q: Inst.CH.P.
**M** Yrs. Est.: 25 (**Ref:**HM09114)

### HARROGATE CHIROPRACTIC CLINIC
**Harrogate Chiropractic Clinic**, 1 Arthington Avenue, Harrogate, **Yorkshire (North)**, HG1 5NB, ENG.
(T) 01423 525863
Speciality: Chiropractic.
● **Partner** Mrs S Beer
**P S T** (**Ref:**HM09115)

### HARROGATE HOLISTIC HEALTH CTRE
**Harrogate Holistic Health Centre Ltd**, 45 Tower St, Harrogate, **Yorkshire (North)**, HG1 1HS, ENG.
(T) 01423 525556 (F) 01904 340159
(E) secondtonone@synergie.net
(W) www.dianaevans.co.uk
Speciality: Acupressure, Acupuncture, Allergy Testing, Aromatherapy, Cognitive Therapy, Complementary Therapy, Counselling, Cranial Osteopathy, Homeopathy, Hypnosis, Hypnotherapy, Iridology, Kinesiology, Nutritional Therapy, Psychotherapy, Reflexology, Reiki, Shiatsu, Colonic Irrigation.
● **Owner/Director** Ms Evans
**C** Yrs. Est.: 4 (**Ref:**HM09116)

### HARROGATE PODIATRY PRACTICE
**Harrogate Podiatry Practice**, 67 Kings Rd, Harrogate, **Yorkshire (North)**, HG1 5HJ, ENG.
(T) 01423 544004 (F) 01423 540041
Speciality: Chiropodists (Podiatrists).
● **Partner** Mr S Blower
**S** (**Ref:**HM09117)

### HARROGATE SCHOOL-AROMATHERAPY
**Harrogate School Of Aromatherapy**, Lavender Court Therapy &, Education Centre, 159 Kings Rd, Harrogate, **Yorkshire (North)**, HG1 5J2, ENG.
(T) 01423 500494
Speciality: Aromatherapy.
**M O** (**Ref:**HM09118)

### HARROP, S
**S Harrop**, 24-26 Old St, Ashton-under-Lyne, **Manchester (Greater)**, OL6 6LB, ENG.
(T) 01613 309853
Speciality: Herbal Medicine.
**M** (**Ref:**HM09119)

### HARROW CHIROPRACTIC CLINIC
**Harrow Chiropractic Clinic**, 4 Lime Court, Gayton Rd, Harrow, **London (Greater)**, HA1 2YD, ENG.
(T) 020 8427 2133
Speciality: Chiropractic.
**P S T** (**Ref:**HM09120)

### HARROW HEALTH CARE CENTRE
**Harrow Health Care Centre (The)**, 84-88 Pinner Rd, Harrow, **London (Greater)**, HA1 4LF, ENG.
(T) 020 8861 1221 (F) 020 8427 4915
Speciality: Acupressure, Acupuncture, Cranial Osteopathy, Cupping, Manipulation, Massage (Therapeutic), Naturopathy, Osteopathy, Rolfing, Stress Therapy, Vitamin Therapy, X-Ray. ✔
● **Osteopath/Acupuncturist** Mr J Thoeye Q: DO, MBAcC, MRO.
**C** Yrs. Est.: 10 (**Ref:**HM09121)

### HARRY, K M
**K M Harry**, 2 The Lawns, Melbourne, Melbourn, Royston, **Hertfordshire**, SG8 6BA, ENG.
(T) 01763 261716
Speciality: Osteopathy.
**P S T** (**Ref:**HM09122)

### HARRY, L M
**L M Harry**, Po Box 148, Cardiff, **Glamorgan (Vale of)**, CF4 9YS, WAL.
(T) 029 2075 9147 (F) 029 2075 9147
Speciality: Clairvoyants & Palmists.
● **Owner** Mr L Harry
**B** (**Ref:**HM09123)

### HART Z HYPNOTHERAPIST
**Hart Z Hypnotherapist**, 38A Campbell Rd, London, **London (Greater)**, E3 4DT, ENG.
(T) 020 8980 5162
Speciality: Hypnosis.
**B** (**Ref:**HM09124)

### HART, ELLEN
**Ellen Hart**, Montpelier Natural Health Clinic, 26 Picton St, Montpelier, Bristol, BS6 5QA, ENG.
(T) 01179 249353
Speciality: Osteopathy.
**P S T** (**Ref:**HM09125)

### HART, KAREN
**Karen Hart**, 7-9 Hawley Sq, Margate, **Kent**, CT9 1PF, ENG.
(T) 01843 292056 (F) 01843 299347
Speciality: Chiropodists (Podiatrists).
**S** (**Ref:**HM09126)

### HART, MARY
**Mary Hart**, 3 Sciennes Rd, Edinburgh, **Edinburgh (City of)**, EH9 1LE, SCO.
(T) 01316 683051
Speciality: Hypnosis.
**B** (**Ref:**HM09127)

### HART, OLIVIA
**Olivia Hart**, 16 Orchard Lane, Brampton, Huntingdon, **Cambridgeshire**, PE18 8TF, ENG.
(T) 01480 411382
Speciality: Electrolysis.
● **Owner** Mrs O Starky
**T** (**Ref:**HM09128)

### HART, P T
**P T Hart**, 23 Murrell Lock, Chelmsford, **Essex**, CM2 6SW, ENG.
(T) 01245 466345
Speciality: Chiropodists (Podiatrists).
● **Owner** Mr P Hart
**S** (**Ref:**HM09129)

### HART, RONALD
**Ronald Hart**, 29 Arundele Drive West, Saltdean, Brighton, **Sussex (East)**, BN2 8SJ, ENG.
(T) 01273 471565
Speciality: Chiropody, Nail Surgery. ✔
● **Owner/Chiropodist** Mr R Hart
(T) 01273 305342 M: S.C.P.
**M** Yrs. Est.: 31 (**Ref:**HM09130)

### HART, RONALD
**Ronald Hart**, 12 Malling St, Lewes, **Sussex (East)**, BN7 2RA, ENG.
(T) 01273 471565
Speciality: Chiropody, Nail Surgery. ✔
● **Chiropodist** Mr R Hart M: S.C.P.
**M** Yrs. Est.: 31 (**Ref:**HM09131)

### HART, S
**S Hart**, 3 Clevemede, Goring, Reading, **Berkshire**, RG8 9BU, ENG.
(T) 01491 873972 (F) 01491 873972
Speciality: Acupuncture.
● **Owner** Mrs S Hart
**O** (**Ref:**HM09132)

### HART, S
**S Hart**, 26 Grant St, Norwich, **Norfolk**, NR2 4HA, ENG.
(T) 01603 623795
Speciality: Psychotherapy.
**B** (**Ref:**HM09133)

### HARTBURN PHYSIOTHERAPY
**Hartburn Physiotherapy & Sports Injury Clinic**, 20 Hartburn Lane, Stockton-On-Tees, **Cleveland**, TS18 3QH, ENG.
(T) 01642 604106
Speciality: Physiotherapy.
● **Owner** Mrs K West
**P S T** (**Ref:**HM09134)

### HARTE, ELAINE
**Elaine Harte**, 80 Livingstone Rd, Kings Heath, Birmingham, **Midlands (West)**, B14 6DN, ENG.
(T) 01214 415848
Speciality: Chiropodists (Podiatrists).
**S** (**Ref:**HM09135)

### HARTER, J
**J Harter**, 44 Lauradale Rd, London, **London (Greater)**, N2 9LU, ENG.
(T) 020 8365 2564
Speciality: Homeopathy.
**M** (**Ref:**HM09136)

### HARTHEN, A
**A Harthen**, 72 Rider Haggard Rd, Norwich, **Norfolk**, NR7 9UQ, ENG.
(T) 01603 431315
Speciality: Chiropodists (Podiatrists).
● **Principal** Mr A Harthen
**S** (**Ref:**HM09137)

### HARTLEPOOL CHIROPRACTIC CLINIC
**Hartlepool Chiropractic Clinic**, 239 York Rd, Hartlepool, **Cleveland**, TS26 9AD, ENG.
(T) 01429 860460
Speciality: Chiropractic. ✔
● **Chiropractor** Mrs M Fletcher Q: DC. M: GCC.
**P** Yrs. Est.: 11 (**Ref:**HM09138)

### HARTLEY, ELAINE
**Elaine Hartley**, 39 Church Howle Cres, Marske-By-The-Sea, Redcar, **Cleveland**, TS11 7EJ, ENG.
(T) 01642 472305
Speciality: Physiotherapy.
● **Owner** Mrs E Hartley
**P S T** (**Ref:**HM09139)

### HARTLEY, GILL
**Gill Hartley**, 64 Frimley Grove Gardens, Frimley, Camberley, **Surrey**, GU16 7JY, ENG.



Key continued: **Yrs.Est:** Years Established **Q:** Qualifications **M:** Professional Membership ✔ Indemnity Insurance Accept Credit Cards

(T) 01276 64935
Speciality: Cranio-Sacral Therapy.
● **Therapist** Ms G Hartley M: CSTA, GCP.
T Yrs. Est.: 2 (**Ref:**HM09140)

**HARTLEY, H S**

**H S Hartley**, 87 Victory Rd, Beeston, Nottingham, **Nottinghamshire**, NG9 1LG, ENG.
(T) 01159 226666
Speciality: Chiropodists (Podiatrists).
S (**Ref:**HM09141)

**HARTLEY, J E**

**J E Hartley**, 1 Collets Court, Lansdown, Bourton-On-The-Water, Cheltenham, **Gloucestershire**, GL54 2AR, ENG.
(T) 01451 810086
Speciality: Osteopathy.
P S T (**Ref:**HM09142)

**HARTLEY, J E**

**J E Hartley**, 14 Clarence Sq, Cheltenham, **Gloucestershire**, GL50 4JN, ENG.
(T) 01242 516048
Speciality: Osteopathy.
● **Partner** Mr G Beresford
P S T (**Ref:**HM09143)

**HARTLEY, JANE E**

**Jane E Hartley**, 12 Windsor Rd, Evesham, **Worcestershire**, WR11 4QE, ENG.
(T) 01386 41219
Speciality: Osteopathy.
● **Owner** Mr G Beresford
P S T (**Ref:**HM09144)

**HARTLEY, JANET**

**Janet Hartley**, 20 Coppice Walk, Shirley, Solihull, **Midlands (West)**, B90 4HY, ENG.
(T) 01564 702186
Speciality: Homeopathy.
● **Partner** Mrs J Spence
M (**Ref:**HM09145)

**HARTLEY, P E**

**P E Hartley**, 2 Metcalf Mews, Uppermill, Oldham, **Lancashire**, OL3 6DN, ENG.
(T) 01457 820439
Speciality: Chiropodists (Podiatrists).
● **Owner** Mr P Hartley
C S (**Ref:**HM09146)

**HARTLEY, S**

**S Hartley**, 12 Stanley Rd, Sheffield, **Yorkshire (South)**, S8 9JB, ENG.
(T) 01142 507767
Speciality: Homeopathy.
● **Owner** Ms S Hartley
M (**Ref:**HM09147)

**HARTMAN, SUSAN**

**Susan Hartman**, 178 East Barnet Rd, Barnet, **Hertfordshire**, EN4 8RD, ENG.
(T) 020 8449 7754 (F) 020 8449 0174
Speciality: Complementary Medicines & Therapy.
● **Principal** Mr L Hartman
M (**Ref:**HM09148)

**HARTNESS, R**

**R Hartness**, Library Buildings, Regis Rd, Wolverhampton, **Midlands (West)**, WV6 8RU, ENG.
(T) 01902 741339
Speciality: Biomechanics, Chiropody, Cryo Surgery, Nail Surgery, Podiatry. ✔
● **Chiropodist (Podiatrist)**
Mr R Hartness Q: M.S.C.P, S.R.Ch. M: S.R.Ch.
M Yrs. Est.: 20 (**Ref:**HM09149)

**HARTSHORN, J**

**J Hartshorn**, Loughborough Physiotherapy Clinic, 3 The Coneries, Loughborough, **Leicestershire**, LE11 1DZ, ENG.
(T) 01509 263932
Speciality: Physiotherapy.
P S T (**Ref:**HM09150)

**HARTWELL, A E**

**A E Hartwell**, 53 Vicarage Avenue, Derby, **Derbyshire**, DE23 6TQ, ENG.
(T) 01332 383219
Speciality: Psychotherapy.
● **Owner** A Hartwell
B (**Ref:**HM09151)

**HARVEST CLINIC**

**Harvest Clinic Of Hypnotherapy (The)**, 201 St. Georges Rd, Glasgow, **Glasgow (City of)**, G3 6JD, SCO.
(T) 01413 330878 (F) 01413 330878
(E) gainhouse@supanet.com
(W) www.harvestclinic.co.uk
Speciality: Acupressure, Acupuncture, Aromatherapy, Bowen Therapy, Complementary Therapy, Counselling, Healer, Healing Therapy, Holistic Healing, Homeopathy, Hypnosis, Hypnotherapy, Indian Head Massage, Inhalation Therapy, Life Style Coaching, Massage (Therapeutic), Meditation, Polarity Therapy, Psychotherapy, Reflexology, Reiki, Rogerian Therapy, Stress Therapy, Vitamin Therapy. ✔
● **Therapist** Mr G Watts Q: Dip.Couns, L.C.C.H. M: L.C.C.H.
● **Therapist** Ms A Trainer Q: BA, Dip.Hyp, L.C.C.H. M: BSCH, L.C.C.H.
● **Therapist** Ms C Murdoch Q: L.C.C.H. M: L.C.C.H.
B Yrs. Est.: 16 (**Ref:**HM09152)

**HARVEST GRAIN**

**Harvest Grain Co (The)**, 3 The Covered Market, West Row, Darlington, **County Durham**, DL1 5PL, ENG.
(T) 01325 357788
Speciality: Complementary Medicines & Therapy.
● **Owner** Mrs V Rebel
M (**Ref:**HM09153)

**HARVEST GRAIN**

**Harvest Grain Co Ltd (The)**, 7 Farndale Gdns, Shildon, **County Durham**, DL4 2LZ, ENG.
(T) 01388 773063
Speciality: Complementary Medicines & Therapy.
● **Owner** Mrs V Revill
C M (**Ref:**HM09154)

**HARVEST MOON CENTRE**

**Harvest Moon Centre (The)**, 36 Bucklesbury, Hitchin, **Hertfordshire**, SG5 1BG, ENG.
(T) 01462 459020
Speciality: Complementary Medicines & Therapy.
● **Owner** Mr D Marshall
M (**Ref:**HM09155)

**HARVEST MOON CENTRE**

**Harvest Moon Centre**, 24 Lr Baggot St, Dublin, **County Dublin**, IRE.
(T) 01662 7556
(W) www.harvestmoon.ie
Speciality: Complementary Medicines & Therapy.
M (**Ref:**HM09156)

**HARVEY CLINIC**

**Harvey Clinic (The)**, 314 Kingston Rd, Willerby, Hull, **Humberside (North)**, HU10 6NF, ENG.
(T) 01482 651575 (F) 01482 651575
Speciality: Osteopathy.
● **Principal** Mr D Harvey
P S T (**Ref:**HM09157)

**HARVEY CLINIC**

**Harvey Clinic (The)**, 26 Cheriton Gardens, Folkestone, **Kent**, CT20 2AS, ENG.
(T) 01303 850077 (F) 01303 226225
Speciality: Osteopathy.
● **Owner** Mr T Drion
P S T (**Ref:**HM09158)

**HARVEY CLINIC**

**Harvey Clinic (The)**, 282 Kingston Rd, Willerby, Hull, **Humberside (North)**, HU10 6ND, ENG.
(T) 01482 651575
Speciality: Osteopathy.
P S T (**Ref:**HM09159)

**HARVEY, ALAN**

**Alan Harvey**, Natural Path Health Centre, 3 Holyrood St, Chard, **Somerset**, TA20 2AH, ENG.
(T) 01460 62953 (F) 01460 62953
Speciality: Homeopathy.
● **Owner** Mr M Newbound
M (**Ref:**HM09160)

**HARVEY, H**

**H Harvey**, 40 Beech Drive, Broadstairs, **Kent**, CT10 2LL, ENG.
(T) 01843 868640
Speciality: Electrolysis.
T (**Ref:**HM09161)

**HARVEY, K G**

**K G Harvey**, 49 Tenbury Rd, Birmingham, **Midlands (West)**, B14 6AH, ENG.
(T) 01214 442146 (F) 01214 442146
Speciality: Chiropodists (Podiatrists).
● **Partner** Mrs J Harvey
S (**Ref:**HM09162)

**HARVEY, LEE**

**Harvey Lee**, Essex House Medical Centre, Fore St, Chard, **Somerset**, TA20 1QA, ENG.
(T) 01460 65046
Speciality: Chiropractic.
P S T (**Ref:**HM09163)

**HARVEY, MARTIN**

**Martin Harvey**, Leominister Community Centre, School Rd, Leominster, **Herefordshire**, HR6 8NJ, ENG.
(T) 01568 614603
Speciality: Acupuncture.
O (**Ref:**HM09164)

**HARVEY, N J**

**Mrs N J Harvey**, Broomsquires Rd, Bagshot, **Surrey**, GU19 5NW, ENG.
(T) 01276 479051
Speciality: Chiropodists (Podiatrists).
S (**Ref:**HM09165)

**HARVEY, P C**

**Mrs P C Harvey**, The Bridgeman Centre, 18 Bridgeman Trce, Wigan, **Lancashire**, WN1 1TD, ENG.
(T) 01942 321235
Speciality: Physiotherapy.
P S T (**Ref:**HM09166)

**HARVEY, PETER**

**Peter Harvey**, 28 High St, Standish, Wigan, **Lancashire**, WN6 0HL, ENG.
(T) 01257 472661
Speciality: Physiotherapy.
● **Partner** Mr P Harvey
P S T (**Ref:**HM09167)

**HARVEY-KUMMER DIANNA**

**Harvey-Kummer Dianna**, Crouch End Health Centre, 50 Park Rd, London, **London (Greater)**, N8 8SU, ENG.
(T) 07957 634919
Speciality: Osteopathy.
● **Owner** Mrs D Harney-Kummer
P S T (**Ref:**HM09168)

**HARVEY-KUMMER, DIANNE**

**Dianne Harvey-Kummer**, 58 Malvern Rd, London, **London (Greater)**, N8 0LA, ENG.
(T) 020 8881 8976
Speciality: Osteopathy.
P S T (**Ref:**HM09169)

**HARVISON, K N**

**K N Harvison**, 115 Victoria Rd, Northwich, **Cheshire**, CW9 5RQ, ENG.
(T) 01606 43508
Speciality: Chiropodists (Podiatrists).
S (**Ref:**HM09170)

**HARWARD, M**

**M Harward**, 154 Evering Rd, London, **London (Greater)**, N16 7BD, ENG.
(T) 020 8525 9565 (F) 020 8525 9565
Speciality: Psychotherapy.
● **Owner** Mr M Harward
B (**Ref:**HM09171)

**HARWICH, ANDREW**

**Andrew Harwich**, 54 Northdown St, London, **London (Greater)**, N1 9BS, ENG.
(T) 020 7833 3748
Speciality: Osteopathy.
● **Owner** Mr A Harwich
P S T (**Ref:**HM09172)

**HARWOOD, B**

**B Harwood**, 28A Chatsworth Rd, London,



Key: B Mind-Body Medicine C Complementary Medicine H Self Help Treatment M Medicinal Therapy O Oriental Medicine P Postural Therapy S Manipulative Structural Therapy T Touch Therapy

**London (Greater)**, NW2 4BS, ENG.
(T) 020 8459 0397
Speciality: Homeopathy.
● **Owner** Mrs B Harwood
M (**Ref:**HM09173)

## HARWOOD, COLIN

**Colin Harwood**, Denison House, Hoo Rd, Wainscott, Rochester, **Kent**, ME3 8AA, ENG.
(T) 01634 722054
Speciality: Hypnosis.
B (**Ref:**HM09174)

## HARWOOD, J

**J Harwood**, 105 Parish Lane, London, **London (Greater)**, SE20 7NT, ENG.
(T) 020 8778 2959
Speciality: Acupuncture.
● **Owner** Mr J Harwood
O (**Ref:**HM09175)

## HARWOOD, KEITH J

**Keith J Harwood**, 930 Whalley New Rd, Wilpshire, Blackburn, **Lancashire**, BB1 9PH, ENG.
(T) 01254 247853
Speciality: Complementary Medicines & Therapy.
● **Owner** Mr K Harwood
C M (**Ref:**HM09176)

## HASAN, ZADI

**Zadi Hasan**, Fairway Avenue, Borehamwood, **Hertfordshire**, WD6 1PU, ENG.
(T) 07939 247627
Speciality: Acupuncture.
● **Owner** Mr Z Hasan
O (**Ref:**HM09177)

## HASAN, ZADI

**Zadi Hasan**, 38 Craig Mount, Radlett, **Hertfordshire**, WD7 7LW, ENG.
(T) 01923 853158
Speciality: Acupuncture.
O (**Ref:**HM09178)

## HASELDEN, MAXINE

**Maxine Haselden**, 21 Downton Cl, **Dorset**, BH8 0EP, ENG.
(T) 01202 519707
Speciality: Reflexology.
S T (**Ref:**HM09179)

## HASELTON, HOWARD

**Howard Haselton**, Harmony Health, 104 Whitley Wood Rd, Reading, **Berkshire**, RG2 8JG, ENG.
(T) 01189 872630
Speciality: Hypnosis, Nutritional Therapy, Reflexology, Yoga.
M (**Ref:**HM09180)

## HASKETT, CHRISTINE

**Christine Haskett**, Critchells, Upton Fort, Osmington Mills, Weymouth, **Dorset**, DT3 6HJ, ENG.
(T) 01305 834713
Speciality: Complementary Medicines & Therapy.
● **Owner** Ms C Haskett
C M (**Ref:**HM09181)

## HASLAM, ANTHONY

**Anthony Haslam**, 111 Lymington Rd, Torquay, **Devon**, TQ1 4BG, ENG.
(T) 01803 292131
Speciality: Chiropractic.
● **Owner** Mr A Haslam
P S T (**Ref:**HM09182)

## HASLAM, H

**H Haslam**, 9 Stirling Rd, Bolton, **Lancashire**, BL1 6RQ, ENG.
(T) 01204 304334
Speciality: Chiropodists (Podiatrists).
● **Owner** Mr H Haslam
S (**Ref:**HM09183)

## HASLAM, PENELOPE J

**Penelope J Haslam**, 146 Hurlingham Rd, London, **London (Greater)**, SW6 3NG, ENG.
(T) 020 7736 2013 (F) 020 7736 2013
Speciality: Osteopathy.
● **Owner** Mrs P Haslam
P S T (**Ref:**HM09184)

## HASLEMERE CHIROPRACTIC CLINIC

**Haslemere Chiropractic Clinic**, 40 West St, Haslemere, **Surrey**, GU27 2AB, ENG.
(T) 01428 642778
Speciality: Chiropractic.
P S T (**Ref:**HM09185)

## HASLEMERE SPORTS & PHYSIO

**Haslemere Sports & Physiotherapy Clinic**, 18 Clayhill House, Weyhill, Haslemere, **Surrey**, GU27 1DA, ENG.
(T) 01428 642577
Speciality: Physiotherapy.
P S T (**Ref:**HM09186)

## HASSETT, CHARLES

**Charles Hassett DO**, 21 Leicester St, Melton Mowbray, **Leicestershire**, LE13 0PP, ENG.
(T) 01664 480568
Speciality: Osteopathy. ✔
● **Osteopath** Mr C Hassett Q: DO. M: GOsC.
S Yrs. Est.: 8 (**Ref:**HM09187)

## HASTIE, A

**A Hastie**, 11 Rectory Lane, Guisborough, **Cleveland**, TS14 7DJ, ENG.
(T) 01287 610462
Speciality: Osteopathy.
● **Owner** A Hastie
P S T (**Ref:**HM09188)

## HASTIE, A

**Sandford Complementary Therapies - Alison Hastie**, Rowan House, 10 Ryarsh Rd, Birling, West Malling, **Kent**, ME19 5JW, ENG.
(T) 01732 872827
Speciality: Complementary Medicines & Therapy.
● **Owner** Mrs A Hastie
C M (**Ref:**HM09189)

## HASTINGS HOLISTIC HEALTH

**Hastings Holistic Health Clinic**, 44 North Trce, Hastings, **Sussex (East)**, TN34 3NR, ENG.
(T) 01424 427771
Speciality: Bach Remedies.
C (**Ref:**HM09190)

## HASTINGS, THERESA

**Theresa Hastings**, 8 Fennemore Cl, Oakley, Aylesbury, **Buckinghamshire**, HP18 9QW, ENG.
(T) 01844 237934
Speciality: Reflexology.
● **Owner** Mrs T Hastings
S T (**Ref:**HM09191)

## HASTRUP, ULLA

**Ulla Hastrup**, 42 Weymede, Byfleet, West Byfleet, **Surrey**, KT14 7DQ, ENG.
(T) 01932 353087
Speciality: Chiropodists (Podiatrists).
S (**Ref:**HM09192)

## HATCHARD, REBECCA

**Rebecca Hatchard**, 49 Broadmeadow, Walsall, **Midlands (West)**, WS9 8JB, ENG.
(T) 01922 459219
Speciality: Chiropodists (Podiatrists).
● **Owner** Mrs R Hatchard
S (**Ref:**HM09193)

## HATELY, S

**S Hately**, 2 East St, Bromley, **Kent**, BR1 1QU, ENG.
(T) 020 8402 5421
Speciality: Aromatherapy.
M O (**Ref:**HM09194)

## HATHA YOGA/COUNSELLING

**Elaine Savvides**, 35 Vernon Drive, Stanmore, **London (Greater)**, HA7 2BP, ENG.
(T) 020 8427 2667
Speciality: Counselling, Yoga. ✔
● **Owner** Mrs E Savvides Q: BWY.Teach.Dip, Dip.Couns. M: BACP, BWY.
H Yrs. Est.: 9 (**Ref:**HM09195)

## HATHAWAY, ELIZABETH

**Elizabeth Hathaway**, 55 Cannons Cl, Bishop's Stortford, **Hertfordshire**, CM23 2BQ, ENG.
(T) 01279 659540
Speciality: Alexander Technique. ✔
● **Owner** Ms E Hathaway M: STAT.
P Yrs. Est.: 8 (**Ref:**HM09196)

## HATHERLY, R M

**R M Hatherly**, 164 Whitby Rd, Ruislip, **London (Greater)**, HA4 9DR, ENG.
(T) 01895 635178
Speciality: Hypnotherapy.
B (**Ref:**HM09197)

## HATHERSAGE HEALTH & THRPY CTRE

**Hathersage Health & Therapy Centre (The)**, Bank House, Main Rd, Hathersage, Hope Valley, **Derbyshire**, S32 1BB, ENG.
(T) 01433 650369
Speciality: Aromatherapy, Massage (Therapeutic). ✔
● **Masseur** Mrs Judkins Q: Dip.Anat, Dip.Hol.Mass, Dip.Physi, ITEC. M: BABTAC.
B C Yrs. Est.: 5 (**Ref:**HM09198)

## HATTERSLEY, DAVID

**David Hattersley**, Southea House, Main Rd, Parson Drove, Wisbech, **Cambridgeshire**, PE13 4JA, ENG.
(T) 01945 700383
Speciality: Osteopathy.
P S T (**Ref:**HM09199)

## HATTERSLEY, LAURENCE

**Laurence Hattersley Osteopath**, 18 Georges Quay, Cork, **County Cork**, IRE.
(T) 021 4319 069
Speciality: Bach Remedies, Cranial Osteopathy, Electrotherapy, Manipulation, Osteopathy, Reiki. ✔
● **Osteopath** Mr L Hattersley Q: BSc (Hons), DO.
B S Yrs. Est.: 6 (**Ref:**HM09200)

## HATTON, JUNE

**June Hatton**, 97 Milton St, Brixham, **Devon**, TQ5 0AR, ENG.
(T) 01803 859418
Speciality: Chiropodists (Podiatrists).
● **Owner** Mrs J Hatton
S (**Ref:**HM09201)

## HAUGHTON, CATHERINE

**Catherine Haughton**, 18 Hillside Cl, Norwich, **Norfolk**, NR7 0QJ, ENG.
(T) 01603 439123
Speciality: Reflexology.
S T (**Ref:**HM09202)

## HAUGHTON, G W

**G W Haughton**, 52 Bewsey St, Warrington, **Cheshire**, WA2 7JE, ENG.
(T) 01925 652656
Speciality: Herbal Medicine.
● **Owner** Mr G Haughton
M (**Ref:**HM09203)

## HAUTHAL-SLEE, LORE

**Lore Hauthal-Slee**, 49 Kimberley Rd, Brighton, **Sussex (East)**, BN2 4EN, ENG.
(T) 01273 697533
Speciality: Complementary Medicines & Therapy.
● **Owner** Mrs L Hauthal-Slee
C M (**Ref:**HM09204)

## HAVELL, LINDA

**Linda Havell**, 312-314 Lewisham Rd, London, **London (Greater)**, SE13 7PA, ENG.
(T) 020 8244 0809
Speciality: Chiropodists (Podiatrists).
S (**Ref:**HM09205)

## HAVELOCK-SEARLE, PAULINE

**Mrs Pauline Havelock-Searle**, 73 Kempe Rd, Kensal Rise, London, **London (Greater)**, NW6 6SN, ENG.
(T) 020 8723 5840
Speciality: Counselling, Hypnosis, Hypnotherapy, Meditation, Yoga. ✔
● **Therapist** Mrs P Havelock-Searle Q: Dip.Hyp, MIAH, PGD.Add.Couns. M: IAH.
H Yrs. Est.: 12 (**Ref:**HM09206)

## HAVEN AROMATHERAPY CTRE

**Haven Aromatherapy Centre & Beauty Clinic (The)**, 78 Clapham Rd, Bedford, **Bedfordshire**, MK41 7PN, ENG.
(T) 01234 353001
Speciality: Aromatherapy.
M O (**Ref:**HM09207)


Key continued: Yrs.Est: Years Established Q: Qualifications M: Professional Membership ✔ Indemnity Insurance Accept Credit Cards

### HAVEN CLINIC
**Haven Clinic (The)**, 3 Violet Hill, London, **London (Greater)**, NW8 9EB, ENG.
(T) 020 7372 4880
Speciality: Chiropodists (Podiatrists).
● **Owner** Mrs J Bland
**S** (**Ref:**HM09208)

### HAVEN GREEN CLINIC
**Haven Green Clinic (The)**, 23 Haven Green, London, **London (Greater)**, W5 2UP, ENG.
(T) 020 8997 3181
Speciality: Acupuncture.
● **Manageress** Miss D Leavers
**O** (**Ref:**HM09209)

### HAVEN HYPNOTHERAPY
**Haven Hypnotherapy**, 35 Colesbourne Drive, Downhead Park, Milton Keynes, **Buckinghamshire**, MK15 9AL, ENG.
(T) 01908 232488
Speciality: Hypnosis.
**B** (**Ref:**HM09210)

### HAVERHILL CHIROPRACTIC CENTRE
**Haverhill Chiropractic Centre**, 1-2 Rose Cottages, Withersfield Rd, Haverhill, **Suffolk**, CB9 9LB, ENG.
(T) 01440 705020
Speciality: Chiropractic.
● **Owner** Dr I Garrod
**P S T** (**Ref:**HM09211)

### HAWARDEN PHYSIO PRACTICE
**Hawarden Physiotherapy Practice**, 117 The Highway, Hawarden, Deeside, **Flintshire**, CH5 3DL, WAL.
(T) 01244 532301 (F) 01244 520628
Speciality: Physiotherapy.
● **Principal** Mrs M Williams
**P S T** (**Ref:**HM09212)

### HAWE, R V
**R V Hawe**, The Lodge, Norney Grange, Shackleford Rd, Shackleford, Godalming, **Surrey**, GU8 6AE, ENG.
(T) 01483 426439
Speciality: Complementary Medicines & Therapy.
● **Owner** Mr R Hawe
**C M** (**Ref:**HM09213)

### HAWES, G M
**G M Hawes**, 25 Cartwright Rd, Charlton, Banbury, **Oxfordshire**, OX17 3DG, ENG.
(T) 01295 812327
Speciality: Chiropractic.
**P S T** (**Ref:**HM09214)

### HAWKE, J R
**J R Hawke**, The Lynwood Physiotherapy Clinic, 18 Lynwood Drive, Worcester Park, **Surrey**, KT4 7AB, ENG.
(T) 020 8337 8970
Speciality: Physiotherapy.
**P S T** (**Ref:**HM09215)

### HAWKHURST NATURAL THERAPIES
**Hawkhurst Natural Therapies**, 2 All Saints Lodge, Rye Rd, Hawkhurst, Cranbrook, **Kent**, TN18 4ET, ENG.
(T) 01580 754957
Speciality: Massage (Therapeutic), Reiki. ✔
● **Owner/Reiki Massage**
Mrs D Davidson **Q:** ITEC. **M:** ITEC.
**C** Yrs. Est.: 5 (**Ref:**HM09216)

### HAWKINS & FIELDING
**Anne Hawkins & Geoffrey Fielding**, 14 Breedon Hill Rd, Derby, **Derbyshire**, DE23 6TG, ENG.
(T) 01332 383951
Speciality: Osteopathy.
● **Partner** Mr G Fielding
**P S T** (**Ref:**HM09217)

### HAWKINS, CHARLOTTE
**Charlotte Hawkins**, 10 Harley St, London, **London (Greater)**, W1N 1AA, ENG.
(T) 020 7467 8318 (F) 020 7468 8312
Speciality: Chiropodists (Podiatrists).
● **Owner** Mrs C Hawkins
**S** (**Ref:**HM09218)

### HAWKINS, E
**E Hawkins**, 4 Rother View, Burwash, Etchingham, **Sussex (East)**, TN19 7BN, ENG.
(T) 01435 882523
Speciality: Chiropodists (Podiatrists).
● **Owner** Miss E Hawkins
**S** (**Ref:**HM09219)

### HAWKINS, JACKIE
**Jackie Hawkins**, 100 High St, Crediton, **Devon**, EX17 3LF, ENG.
(T) 01363 774175
Speciality: Aromatherapy.
**M O** (**Ref:**HM09220)

### HAWKINS, JAMES
**James Hawkins**, 78 Polwarth Trce, Edinburgh, **Edinburgh (City of)**, EH11 1NJ, SCO.
(T) 01313 378474
Speciality: Acupuncture.
**O** (**Ref:**HM09221)

### HAWKINS, JAN
**Jan Hawkins - Foundation for the Developing Person**, 376 Hale End Rd, Highams Park, London, **London (Greater)**, E4 9PB, ENG.
(T) 020 8531 9760 (F) 020 8531 9760
(W) www.thefdp.demon.co.uk
Speciality: Counselling, Encounter Groups, Group Therapy, Humanistic Psychology, Massage (Therapeutic), Psychotherapy, Rogerian Therapy, Stress Therapy. ✔
● **Psychotherapist/Trainer**
Ms J Hawkins **Q:** BSc (Hons), Cert.Ed, Dip.Psych. **M:** BPS.
**C** Yrs. Est.: 9 (**Ref:**HM09222)

### HAWKINS, LEONARD S
**Leonard S Hawkins**, Appledore, 93 Fenshurst Gardens, Long Ashton, Bristol, BS41 9AR, ENG.
(T) 01275 393058
Speciality: Psychotherapy.
**B** (**Ref:**HM09223)

### HAWKINS, LUKE
**Luke Hawkins**, Goodwood Court Surgery, 52 Cromwell Rd, Hove, **Sussex (East)**, BN3 3DX, ENG.
(T) 01273 770822
Speciality: Biomechanics, Chiropody, Nail Surgery, Podiatry. ✔
● **Chiropodist (Podiatrist)**
Mr L Hawkins **Q:** BSc, M.S.C.P, S.R.Ch. **M:** S.C.P.
**M** Yrs. Est.: 4 (**Ref:**HM09224)

### HAWKINS, M
**M Hawkins**, 25 Grove Rd, Fishponds, Bristol, BS16 2BJ, ENG.
(T) 01179 701539
Speciality: Chiropodists (Podiatrists).
● **Owner** Mrs M Hawkins
**S** (**Ref:**HM09225)

### HAWKINS, M E
**M E Hawkins**, 19 New Town, Uckfield, **Sussex (East)**, TN22 5DL, ENG.
(T) 01825 761163
Speciality: Chiropodists (Podiatrists).
**S** (**Ref:**HM09226)

### HAWKINS, R W
**R W Hawkins**, 15 East St, Weymouth, **Dorset**, DT4 8BW, ENG.
(T) 01305 789949
Speciality: Chiropodists (Podiatrists).
**S** (**Ref:**HM09227)

### HAWKINS, SHARON
**Sharon Hawkins**, 10 High St, Glastonbury, **Somerset**, BA6 9DU, ENG.
(T) 01458 834236
Speciality: Reflexology.
● **Director** Ms J Sanders
**S T** (**Ref:**HM09228)

### HAWKINS, SUZI
**Suzi Hawkins**, 31 Pembury Rd, Westcliff-on-Sea, **Essex**, SS0 8DU, ENG.
(T) 01702 338004
Speciality: Homeopathy.
● **Owner** Mrs S Hawkins
**M** (**Ref:**HM09229)

### HAWKINS, TINA
**Tina Hawkins**, 18-20 The Grove, London, **London (Greater)**, W5 5LH, ENG.
(T) 020 8566 3487
Speciality: Hypnosis.
**B** (**Ref:**HM09230)

### HAWKRIDGE, FRANCOISE
**Francoise Hawkridge**, 14 Redmayne Drive, Chelmsford, **Essex**, CM2 9AG, ENG.
(T) 01245 344375
Speciality: Acupuncture.
**O** (**Ref:**HM09231)

### HAWKSHAW FOOT CENTRE
**Hawkshaw Foot Centre**, Gean House, 3 Bolton Rd, Hawkshaw, Bury, **Lancashire**, BL8 4HZ, ENG.
(T) 01204 887573
Speciality: Chiropodists (Podiatrists).
**S** (**Ref:**HM09232)

### HAWKSLAND PHYSIOTHERAPY CENTRE
**Mrs Rosalind Boisseau**, Higher Hawksland Farm, St. Issey, Wadebridge, **Cornwall**, PL27 7RG, ENG.
(T) 01208 813199 (F) 01208 814724
(E) rossphysio@aol.com
Speciality: Acupuncture, Electrotherapy, Healer, Indian Head Massage, Manipulation, Massage (Therapeutic), Micro Manipulation, Ultrasonics. ✔
● **Physiotherapist** Mrs R Boisseau **Q:** MCSP, SRP. **M:** CSP.
● **Massage Practitioner/Healer**
Ms S Irwin **Q:** BSY. **M:** BSY.
**S** Yrs. Est.: 20 (**Ref:**HM09233)

### HAWLEY, DUNCAN
**Duncan Hawley**, 30 Walton Hall Avenue, Liverpool, **Merseyside**, L4 6UF, ENG.
(T) 01515 251822
Speciality: Chiropodists (Podiatrists).
**S** (**Ref:**HM09234)

### HAWLEY, KAREN
**Karen Hawley**, 59 School Lane, Egham, **Surrey**, TW20 9QJ, ENG.
(T) 01784 436790
Speciality: Chiropodists (Podiatrists).
**S** (**Ref:**HM09235)

### HAWNT, D W
**D W Hawnt**, 18 Albert Rd, Southsea, **Hampshire**, PO5 2SH, ENG.
(T) 023 9281 1395
Speciality: Chiropodists (Podiatrists).
● **Owner** Mr D Hawnt
**S** (**Ref:**HM09236)

### HAWORTH, DAVID
**David Haworth**, 22 Mythop Rd, Lytham St. Annes, **Lancashire**, FY8 4JD, ENG.
(T) 01253 739916
Speciality: Hypnosis.
● **Owner** Mr D Howarth
**B** (**Ref:**HM09237)

### HAWORTH, E
**Miss E Haworth**, Culver View Lodge, Carpenters Rd, St. Helens, Ryde, **Isle of Wight**, PO33 1YG, ENG.
(T) 01983 872808
Speciality: Chiropodists (Podiatrists).
**S** (**Ref:**HM09238)

### HAWORTH, JAMES
**James Haworth**, 26 Ribble Avenue, Darwen, **Lancashire**, BB3 0JR, ENG.
(T) 01254 775043
Speciality: Reflexology.
**S T** (**Ref:**HM09239)

### HAWORTH, JAN
**Jan Haworth**, 54 The Avenue, Yeovil, **Somerset**, BA21 4BN, ENG.
(T) 01935 422488
Speciality: Acupuncture.
**O** (**Ref:**HM09240)

### HAWORTH, ROBERT
**Robert Haworth**, Health Centre Complex, Cabourne Court, Lincoln, **Lincolnshire**, LN2 2JP, ENG.
(T) 01522 530645



Key: **B** Mind-Body Medicine **C** Complementary Medicine **H** Self Help Treatment **M** Medicinal Therapy **O** Oriental Medicine **P** Postural Therapy **S** Manipulative Structural Therapy **T** Touch Therapy

Speciality: Chiropodists (Podiatrists).
● **Practice Manager** Dr A Compton
S (Ref:HM09241)

### HAWTHORN CLINIC

**Hawthorn Clinic**, 14 Culverden Down, Tunbridge Wells, **Kent**, TN4 9SA, ENG.
(T) 01892 543033
Speciality: Osteopathy.
P S T (Ref:HM09242)

### HAWTHORN HOUSE AROMATHERAPY

**Hawthorn House Aromatherapy Clinic**, Station Works, Dyehouse Lane, Glastonbury, **Somerset**, BA6 9LZ, ENG.
(T) 01458 832980
Speciality: Aromatherapy.
● **Owner** Mrs S Knox
M O (Ref:HM09243)

### HAWTHORN LODGE PHYSIOTHERAPY

**Hawthorn Lodge Physiotherapy**, 87 Plough Hill Rd, Nuneaton, **Warwickshire**, CV10 9NY, ENG.
(T) 024 7639 2224
Speciality: Physiotherapy.
P S T (Ref:HM09244)

### HAWTIN, JANICE

**Janice Hawtin**, 9 Greenhill Park, London, **London (Greater)**, NW10 9AE, ENG.
(T) 020 8965 7026
Speciality: Reflexology.
S T (Ref:HM09245)

### HAXBY & HUNTINGTON ACUPUNCTURE

**Haxby & Huntington Acupuncture Clinic**, 2a Haxby Shopping Centre, The Village, Haxby, York, **Yorkshire (North)**, YO32 2LU, ENG.
(T) 01904 627807
Speciality: Complementary Medicines & Therapy.
● **Owner** Miss S Dixon
M (Ref:HM09246)

### HAXBY CHIROPRACTIC CLINIC

**Haxby Chiropractic Clinic**, 70 The Village, Haxby, York, **Yorkshire (North)**, YO32 2HX, ENG.
(T) 01904 766966
Speciality: Chiropractors.
● **Practice Manager** Dr S Forensen
P S T (Ref:HM09247)

### HAY LOFT CENTRE

**Hay Loft Centre For Healing & Meditation**, Hay Loft, Palmers Rd, Emsworth, **Hampshire**, PO10 7DL, ENG.
(T) 01243 370021
Speciality: Complementary Medicines & Therapy.
M (Ref:HM09248)

### HAY, PATRICIA

**Patricia Hay**, 4 Fairfield Rd, Ongar, **Essex**, CM5 9HJ, ENG.
(T) 01277 363675
Speciality: Reflexology.
S T (Ref:HM09249)

### HAYASHI, MIKI

**Miki Hayashi**, North Finchley, London, **London (Greater)**, N12, ENG.
Speciality: Bach Remedies.
M (Ref:HM09250)

### HAYDEN, C J

**C J Hayden**, 102 Chosen Drive, Churchdown, Gloucester, **Gloucestershire**, GL3 2QU, ENG.
(T) 01452 714511
Speciality: Osteopathy.
P S T (Ref:HM09251)

### HAYDEN, E C

**E C Hayden**, 102 Chosen Drive, Churchdown, Gloucester, **Gloucestershire**, GL3 2QU, ENG.
(T) 01452 714511 (F) 01452 541369
Speciality: Osteopathy.
● **Partner** Mr C Hayden
P S T (Ref:HM09252)

### HAYDEN, J T

**J T Hayden**, Eastfield Surgery, 4 Eastfield Rd, Birchington, **Kent**, CT7 9RH, ENG.
(T) 01843 841128
Speciality: Osteopathy.
P S T (Ref:HM09253)

### HAYDOCK, CLAIRE

**Claire Haydock**, 20A Church St, Great Harwood, Blackburn, **Lancashire**, BB6 7NF, ENG.
(T) 01254 876300
Speciality: Chiropody. ✔
● **Chiropodist** Claire Haydock Q: MBChA, MSSCh.
T Yrs. Est.: 7 (Ref:HM09254)

### HAYES HYPNOTHERAPY CENTRE

**Hayes Hypnotherapy Centre**, Point West Building, 1040 Uxbridge Rd, Hayes, **London (Greater)**, UB4 0RJ, ENG.
(T) 020 8561 5282
Speciality: Hypnosis.
● **Owner** Mrs S Rasala
B (Ref:HM09255)

### HAYES PHYSIOTHERAPY CLINIC

**Hayes Physiotherapy Clinic**, 246 Western Rd, Leigh-On-Sea, **Essex**, SS9 2QY, ENG.
(T) 01702 558069 (F) 01702 558069
Speciality: Physiotherapy.
● **Manager** Mr M Heardman
P S T (Ref:HM09256)

### HAYES, ANN

**Ann Hayes**, 5a Newton Rd, Great Barr, Birmingham, **Midlands (West)**, B43 6AA, ENG.
(T) 01213 585638
Speciality: Aromatherapy.
● **Owner** Mrs A Hayes
M O (Ref:HM09257)

### HAYES, CAROLE

**Carole Hayes**, 24 Sycamore Gr, Warwick, **Warwickshire**, CV34 5TL, ENG.
(T) 01926 407934
Speciality: Reflexology.
S T (Ref:HM09258)

### HAYES, GILL

**Gill Hayes**, 8 Rochford Walk, Wisbech, **Cambridgeshire**, PE13 3SU, ENG.
(T) 01945 463175
Speciality: Chiropodists (Podiatrists).
S (Ref:HM09259)

### HAYES, JACQUELINE

**Jacqueline Hayes BSc(Hons)Ost - TA - Osteopathic Principles**, Laurel Cottage, Main Rd, Knockholt, Sevenoaks, **Kent**, TN14 7NX, ENG.
(T) 01959 532714
Speciality: Cranial Osteopathy, Cupping, Osteopathy. ✔
● **Osteopath** Ms J Hayes Q: BSc, Hons (OST). M: GOsC.
S Yrs. Est.: 3 (Ref:HM09260)

### HAYES, L

**L Hayes**, 11 College Rd, Liverpool, **Merseyside**, L23 0RJ, ENG.
(T) 01519 284781
Speciality: Acupuncture.
● **Owner** Mr L Hayes
O (Ref:HM09261)

### HAYES, RORY

**Hayes Rory**, 3 Rosemount Tce, Dundrum Rd, Dublin, **County Dublin**, IRE.
(T) 01296 4438
Speciality: Chiropractors.
P S T (Ref:HM09262)

### HAYES, RORY (DR)

**Hayes, Dr Rory**, Wicklow Town, IRE.
(T) 04046 9267
Speciality: Chiropractors.
P S T (Ref:HM09263)

### HAYES, SUE

**Sue Hayes**, St Georges House, 56 Billing Rd, Northampton, **Northamptonshire**, NN1 5DB, ENG.
(T) 01604 601641 (F) 01604 601641
Speciality: Physiotherapy.
● **Partner** Mr P Whitty
P S T (Ref:HM09264)

### HAYES, VAL

**Val Hayes**, 31 Sundringham Drive, Crewe, **Cheshire**, CW2 8JF, ENG.
(T) 01270 665403
Speciality: Complementary Medicines & Therapy.
● **Owner** Val Hayes
M (Ref:HM09265)

### HAYHOE, A D

**A D Hayhoe**, 7 Rectory Rd, Newcastle Upon Tyne, **Tyne and Wear**, NE3 1XR, ENG.
(T) 01912 844039
Speciality: Chiropodists (Podiatrists).
S (Ref:HM09266)

### HAYHURST, GEOFFREY A

**Geoffrey A Hayhurst**, 207 Belmont Rd, Belfast, **County Antrim**, BT4 2AG, NIR.
(T) 028 9065 6664
Speciality: Osteopathy.
● **Owner** Mr G Hayhurst
P S T (Ref:HM09267)

### HAYLING ISLAND CHIRO CLINIC

**Chiropractic Clinic**, 17E Rails Lane, Hayling Island, **Hampshire**, PO11 9LG, ENG.
(T) 023 9246 7645
Speciality: Acupuncture, Chiropractic, Feldenkrais Methodology, Manipulation, Massage (Therapeutic), Postural Integration, Ultrasonics.
● **Chiropractor** Mr K Johnson Q: Dip.Chiro. M: BCA, GCC.
S Yrs. Est.: 12 (Ref:HM09268)

### HAYMAN, DOROTHY

**Dorothy Hayman**, Strawberry Cottage, Norton Rd, Tostock, Bury St. Edmunds, **Suffolk**, IP30 9PT, ENG.
(T) 01359 271390 (F) 01359 270360
Speciality: Electrolysis.
● **Owner** Mrs D Hayman
T (Ref:HM09269)

### HAYMAN-BUDDEN, G

**G Hayman-Budden**, The Priory, 32 Lower Odcombe, Lower Odcombe, Yeovil, **Somerset**, BA22 8TX, ENG.
(T) 01935 862433 (F) 01935 862433
Speciality: Physiotherapy.
● **Owner** Mrs G Hayman-Budden
P S T (Ref:HM09270)

### HAYNES, AVRIL

**Avril Haynes**, Field House, Fen Rd, Old Buckenham, Attleborough, **Norfolk**, NR17 1NP, ENG.
(T) 01953 456519
Speciality: Reflexology.
S T (Ref:HM09271)

### HAYNES, B P

**B P Haynes**, 19 Newsham Rd, Lancaster, **Lancashire**, LA1 4DG, ENG.
(T) 01524 383004
Speciality: Chiropodists (Podiatrists).
S (Ref:HM09272)

### HAYNES, E

**E Haynes**, 2 Crown Lane, Littleport, Ely, **Cambridgeshire**, CB6 1PP, ENG.
(T) 01353 863218
Speciality: Complementary Medicines & Therapy.
M (Ref:HM09273)

### HAYNES, ERIC

**Eric Haynes**, 33a Bridewell Rd, Cambridge, **Cambridgeshire**, CB1 4EN, ENG.
(T) 01223 214281
Speciality: Hypnosis.
B (Ref:HM09274)

### HAYNES, HILARY

**Hilary Haynes**, 55 Acacia Gr, New Malden, **Surrey**, KT3 3BU, ENG.
(T) 020 8408 4697
Speciality: Complementary Medicines & Therapy.
M (Ref:HM09275)

### HAYNES, S R

**S R Haynes**, Creeting Hills Farm, Creeting Hills, Creeting St. Mary, Ipswich, **Suffolk**, IP6 8PZ, ENG.
(T) 01449 722570
Speciality: Chiropodists (Podiatrists).
S (Ref:HM09276)



Key continued: Yrs.Est: Years Established Q: Qualifications M: Professional Membership ✔ Indemnity Insurance Accept Credit Cards

### HAYNES, SIOBHAN
**Siobhan Haynes**, 27 Portia Trce, Swansea, SA1 6XW, **WAL**.
(T) 01792 419699
Speciality: Homeopathy.
M (Ref:HM09277)

### HAYTER & OVERY
**Hayter & Overy**, Dunsham Farm, Aylesbury Rd, Bierton, Aylesbury, **Buckinghamshire**, HP22 5BU, ENG.
(T) 01296 428503
Speciality: Physiotherapy.
P S T (Ref:HM09278)

### HAYTER, HEATHER A
**Heather A Hayter**, 65 Edward Avenue, Eastleigh, **Hampshire**, SO50 6EE, ENG.
(T) 023 8064 2001
Speciality: Chiropodists (Podiatrists).
● **Owner** Mrs H Hayter
S (Ref:HM09279)

### HAYTER, M J
**M J Hayter**, 48 Brookley Rd, Brockenhurst, **Hampshire**, SO42 7RA, ENG.
(T) 01590 624126
Speciality: Complementary Medicines & Therapy.
● **Owner** Miss M Hayter
C M (Ref:HM09280)

### HAYWARD, HILARY
**Hilary Hayward**, 19 Balls Green, Withyham, Hartfield, **Sussex (East)**, TN7 4BU, ENG.
(T) 01892 770688 (F) 01892 770087
Speciality: Reflexology.
● **Owner** Mrs H Hayward
S T (Ref:HM09281)

### HAYWARD, JANET
**Janet Hayward**, 80 Plantation Rd, **Dorset**, BH17 9LP, ENG.
(T) 01202 698408
Speciality: Reflexology.
S T (Ref:HM09282)

### HAYWARD, LISA
**Lisa Hayward**, 1 Sheepwalk Cottages, School Rd, Kirby Cane, Bungay, **Suffolk**, NR35 2HL, ENG.
(T) 01508 518370
Speciality: Physiotherapy.
● **Owner** Mrs L Hayward
P S T (Ref:HM09283)

### HAYWARD, MONICA
**Monica Hayward**, Chy Gwin, Praa Lane, Germoe, Penzance, **Cornwall**, TR20 9AD, ENG.
(T) 01736 763696
Speciality: Homeopathy.
● **Owner** Mrs M Hayward
M (Ref:HM09284)

### HAYWARD, PERRIN
**Perrin Hayward**, 83 Whittaker Lane, Prestwich, Manchester, **Manchester (Greater)**, M25 1ET, ENG.
(T) 01617 730123
Speciality: Osteopathy.
● **Owner** Mr R Perrin
P S T (Ref:HM09285)

### HAYWARD, SOPHIE
**Sophie Hayward**, 11 Lymewood Drive, Disley, Stockport, **Cheshire**, SK12 2LD, ENG.
(T) 01663 764587
Speciality: Reflexology.
S T (Ref:HM09286)

### HAYWARD, ZENA
**Zena Hayward**, 5 Chapel Trce, Yarmouth Rd, Hemsby, Great Yarmouth, **Norfolk**, NR29 4NJ, ENG.
(T) 01493 732395
Speciality: Complementary Medicines & Therapy.
C M (Ref:HM09287)

### HAYWARDS HEATH NATURAL THRPY
**Haywards Heath Natural Therapy Rooms**, 55 Perrymount Rd, Haywards Heath, **Sussex (West)**, RH16 3BN, ENG.
(T) 01444 457889
Speciality: Complementary Medicines & Therapy.
● **Manager** Ms H Vintner
M (Ref:HM09288)

### HAYWOOD, T J
**T J Haywood**, 62 Moira Rd, Overseal, Swadlincote, **Derbyshire**, DE12 6JD, ENG.
(T) 01283 760656
Speciality: Hypnosis.
B (Ref:HM09289)

### HAZEL, J M
**J M Hazel**, 50 Learmonth Gr, Edinburgh, **Edinburgh (City of)**, EH4 1BN, SCO.
(T) 01313 328837
Speciality: Biomechanics, Chiropody, Nail Surgery. ✔
● **Chiropodist** Miss J Hazel Q: BSc, S.R.Ch. M: S.C.P.
● **Chiropodist (Podiatrist)**
Mr D Lowes Q: DPodM, S.R.Ch. M: S.C.P.
M Yrs. Est.: 14 (Ref:HM09290)

### HAZELBY, TRACY
**Tracy Hazelby**, Cae'r Felin, Brongest, Newcastle Emlyn, **Carmarthenshire**, SA38 9ES, WAL.
(T) 01239 858976
Speciality: Reflexology.
S T (Ref:HM09291)

### HAZELDENE, BARBARA
**Barbara Hazeldene**, Micklehurst Green, Stockport, **Cheshire**, SK2 5NU, ENG.
(T) 01614 565038
Speciality: Aromatherapy, Massage (Therapeutic), Reflexology. ✔
● **Reflexologist** Ms B Hazeldene Q: IIHHT, MICHT. M: ICHT.
C Yrs. Est.: 2 (Ref:HM09292)

### HAZELL, PRISCILLA
**Priscilla Hazell**, Moffat Cottage, Cokes Lane, Chalfont St. Giles, **Buckinghamshire**, HP8 4TX, ENG.
(T) 01494 762507
Speciality: Aromatherapy.
M O (Ref:HM09293)

### HAZEL'S HOLISTIC HEALTH CARE
**Hazel Holistic Health Care**, 61 Greenfields, Maidenhead, **Berkshire**, SL6 1BB, ENG.
(T) 01628 637275
Speciality: Reflexology, Shiatsu, On-Site Massage. ✔
● **Reflexologist** Ms H Irmak
C Yrs. Est.: 12 (Ref:HM09294)

### HAZELS PSYCHIC ADVISORY CENTRE
**Hazels Psychic Advisory Centre**, 28 Hillcrest Rd, Hornchurch, **Essex**, RM11 1EB, ENG.
(T) 07775 687653
Speciality: Clairvoyants & Palmists.
● **Owner** Mrs H Phillips
B (Ref:HM09295)

### HAZLEHURST, JEAN
**Jean Hazlehurst**, Grange Hall, Black Horse Hill, Wirral, **Merseyside**, CH48 7EF, ENG.
(T) 01516 251809
Speciality: Hypnotherapy.
● **Owner** Mrs J Hazelhurst
B (Ref:HM09296)

### HAZLEWOOD OSTEOPATHIC PRACTICE
**Hazlewood Osteopathic Practice (The)**, Hazelwood House, 197 Frindsbury Hill, Frindsbury, Rochester, **Kent**, ME2 4JS, ENG.
(T) 01634 710051
(E) robertburge@listmail.com
Speciality: Osteopathy. ✔
● **Osteopath** Mr R Burge Q: Adv.Dip.Ost, DO. M: GOsC.
S Yrs. Est.: 37 (Ref:HM09297)

### HEAD MASTER
**Head Master**, 19 Friars Walk, Lewes, **Sussex (East)**, BN7 2LF, ENG.
(T) 01273 487625 (F) 01273 483828
Speciality: Aromatherapy.
● **Partner** Mr G Wood
M O (Ref:HM09298)

### HEAD TO TOE THERAPY OLDHAM
**Head To Toe Therapy Oldham**, Mortimer St, Oldham, **Lancashire**, OL1 3JD, ENG.
(T) 07041 428166
Speciality: Complementary Medicines & Therapy.
● **Owner** Miss S Greaves
C M (Ref:HM09299)

### HEAD TO TOE WELL-BEING
**Head To Toe Well-Being**, 42 Station Approach Rd, Ramsgate, **Kent**, CT11 7RJ, ENG.
(T) 01843 590109
Speciality: Indian Head Massage, Reflexology.
● **Reflexologist** Ms T Dyson Q: Dip.Reflex, IIHHT. M: FHT.
T Yrs. Est.: 1 (Ref:HM09300)

### HEAD, BERYL
**Beryl Head**, 4 Longridge, Colchester, **Essex**, CO4 3FB, ENG.
(T) 01206 870756
Speciality: Hypnosis.
● **Owner** Mrs B Head
B (Ref:HM09301)

### HEAD, BERYL
**Beryl Head**, Hypnotherapy Cente, 29 Manor Rd, Colchester, **Essex**, CO3 3LX, ENG.
(T) 01206 578767
Speciality: Hypnotherapy.
● **Owner** Mrs B Head
B (Ref:HM09302)

### HEAD, J M
**J M Head**, 7 Gables Court, Kingfield Rd, Kingfield, Woking, **Surrey**, GU22 9EA, ENG.
(T) 01483 762003
Speciality: Chiropodists (Podiatrists).
● **Owner** Miss J Head
S (Ref:HM09303)

### HEAD, PAUL
**Paul Head**, 16 Church St, Crewkerne, **Somerset**, TA18 7HU, ENG.
(T) 01460 75580 (F) 01460 75580
Speciality: Chiropodists (Podiatrists).
● **Owner** Mr P Head
S (Ref:HM09304)

### HEADINGLEY CHIROPRACTIC CLINIC
**Headingley Chiropractic Clinic**, Inglebank, 174 Otley Rd, Leeds, **Yorkshire (West)**, LS16 5LG, ENG.
(T) 01132 289888
Speciality: Chiropractic.
P S T (Ref:HM09305)

### HEADINGTON ALEXANDER SCHOOL
**Headington Alexander Training School Oxford**, 10 York Rd, Headington, Oxford, **Oxfordshire**, OX3 8NW, ENG.
(T) 01865 454112 (F) 01865 454112
Speciality: Alexander Technique.
● **Principal** Mr S Cooper
P S (Ref:HM09306)

### HEADON, CHRISTOPHER
**Christopher Headon**, 79 Goodhart Way, West Wickham, **Kent**, BR4 0ET, ENG.
(T) 020 8777 6422
Speciality: Psychotherapy.
B (Ref:HM09307)

### HEADROW CHIROPODY & PODIATRY
**Headrow Chiropody & Podiatry (The)**, 21 Merrion St, Leeds, **Yorkshire (West)**, LS2 8JE, ENG.
(T) 01132 469600
Speciality: Chiropodists (Podiatrists).
● **Owner** Mr J Gohill
S (Ref:HM09308)

### HEADS & FACES
**Heads & Faces**, 39 Wide Bargate, Boston, **Lincolnshire**, PE21 6SR, ENG.
(T) 01205 369830
Speciality: Electrolysis.
● **Owner** Mrs S Edmonds
T (Ref:HM09309)

### HEAL ANN CARE
**Heal Ann Care**, 24 Green Terrace Sq, Saville Park, Halifax, **Yorkshire (West)**, HX1 3EP, ENG.

(T) 01422 354955
Speciality: Hypnosis.
B (Ref:HM09310)

**HEAL TO TOE**

**Heal To Toe**, 51 Cross Pit Lane, St. Helens, **Merseyside**, WA11 8AJ, ENG.
(T) 01744 886798 (F) 01744 886798
Speciality: Aromatherapy, Reflexology. ✔
● **Reflexologist** Mrs T Roberts Q: MICHT. M: ICHT.
C Yrs. Est.: 4 (Ref:HM09311)

**HEAL TRUST**

**Heal Trust (The)**, 375 Kennington Lane, London, **London (Greater)**, SE11 5QY, ENG.
(T) 020 7787 8158
Speciality: Complementary Medicines & Therapy.
C M (Ref:HM09312)

**HEAL, CHRISTIANNE**

**Christianne Heal**, 1 Petersfield, Cambridge, **Cambridgeshire**, CB1 1BB, ENG.
(T) 01223 319310
Speciality: Absent Healing, Bach Remedies, Counselling, Healer, Healing Therapy, Psychotherapy, Reflexology. ✔
● **Counsellor/Psychotherapist**
Ms C Heal Q: BA, Dip.Couns. M: BACP.
B Yrs. Est.: 20 (Ref:HM09313)

**HEAL, CHRISTIANNE**

**Christianne Heal**, 9 Cannon Pl, London, **London (Greater)**, NW3 1EH, ENG.
(T) 020 7435 5432
Speciality: Bach Remedies, Counselling, Healer, Psychotherapy, Reflexology. ✔
● **Counsellor/Psychotherapist**
Christianne Heal Q: BA, Dip.Couns. M: BACP.
B Yrs. Est.: 20 (Ref:HM09314)

**HEAL-ALL HERB AND ACU CTRE**

**Heal-All Herb And Acupuncture Centre**, 4 London Rd, North End, Portsmouth, **Hampshire**, PO2 0LH, ENG.
(T) 023 9267 0800 (F) 023 9267 0800
Speciality: Acupressure, Acupuncture, Cupping, Herbal Medicine, Moxibustion. ✔
● **Doctor** Hua Shang Q: MB. M: ATCM UK, BAcC, RCHM.
● **Doctor** Daian Zou Q: MB. M: ATCM UK.
● **Doctor** Jian Hong Guan Q: MB. M: ATCM UK.
C Yrs. Est.: 2 (Ref:HM09315)

**HEALD, M T**

**M T Heald**, 4 Victoria Rd, South Wirral, Ellesmere Port, **Cheshire**, CH65 8BS, ENG.
(T) 01513 552929
Speciality: Chiropody. ✔
● **Chiropodist** Mrs M Heald Q: L.C.C.H. M: Inst.CH.P.
M Yrs. Est.: 7 (Ref:HM09316)

**HEALE, SARA**

**Sara Heale**, 76 Greenway Rd, Taunton, **Somerset**, TA2 6LE, ENG.
(T) 01823 336581
Speciality: Homeopathy.
M (Ref:HM09317)

**HEALE, SARAH**

**Sarah Heale**, 6 Clarence Grove Rd, Weston-Super-Mare, **Somerset**, BS23 4AQ, ENG.
(T) 01934 626752
Speciality: Homeopathy.
● **Owner** Ms S Heal
M (Ref:HM09318)

**HEALER, ANDY JOHNSON**

**Andy Johnson Healer**, 12 Osterberg Rd, Dartford, **Kent**, DA1 5HE, ENG.
(T) 01474 871735
Speciality: Spiritual Healing.
B (Ref:HM09319)

**HEALERS WORLD**

**Healers World**, 7 Park Cresent, London, **London (Greater)**, W1N 3HE, ENG.
(T) 01425 461740 (F) 01428 727875
(E) drsharma@101clinic.co.uk
Speciality: Acupressure, Acupuncture, Alexander Technique, Aromatherapy, Art Therapy, Aversion Therapy, Ayurvedic Medicine, Bach Remedies, Bates Method, Bio-energetics, Biofeedback, Bowen Therapy, Chiropractic, Cognitive Therapy, Complementary Therapy, Counselling, Cranial Osteopathy, Cupping, Dietician, Faith Healing, Family Planning (Natural), Family Therapy, Group Therapy, Hay Diet, Healer, Healing Therapy, Herbal Medicine, Homeopathy, Hypnosis, Hypnotherapy, Indian Head Massage, Kinesiology, Kirlian Photography, Manipulation, Massage (Therapeutic), Meditation, Moxibustion, Mud Therapy, Naturopathy, Nutritional Therapy, Oriental Diagnosis, Colonic Irrigation. ✔ CREDIT
● **Medical Director** Dr R Sharma
(T) 01202 744747 Q: B.A.O, L.R.C.P&S (IRE), MB, MFHom, MRCH. M: FHom, GMC.
B Yrs. Est.: 40 (Ref:HM09320)

**HEALES CHIROPRACTIC CLINIC**

**Heales Chiropractic Clinic**, 146 Sundon Park Rd, Luton, **Bedfordshire**, LU3 3AH, ENG.
(T) 01582 579687 (F) 01582 493512
Speciality: Chiropractic. ✔ CREDIT
● **Chiropractor** Gutherie Steer Q: DC, MCC, MSc.
● **Principal** Mr G Heale Q: DC.
● **Chiropractor** Ms C Debrell Q: DC, MCC, MSc.
● **Chiropractor** Mr M Horrell Q: DC, MCC, MSc.
P Yrs. Est.: 20 (Ref:HM09321)

**HEALES CHIROPRACTIC CLINIC**

**Graham S Heale**, 133 Cambridge Rd, Hitchin, **Hertfordshire**, SG4 0JH, ENG.
(T) 01462 420077
Speciality: Chiropractic. ✔ CREDIT
● **Chiropractor** Ms C Debrell Q: BSc, DC. M: CC.
● **Chiropractor** Mr G Steer Q: DC, MSc.
● **Chiropractor** Mr M Horrell Q: BSc, DC. M: CC.
C Yrs. Est.: 9 (Ref:HM09322)

**HEALEY, NORMAN**

**Norman Healey**, Southgate, 20 Whitchurch Rd, Cublington, Leighton Buzzard, **Bedfordshire**, LU7 0LP, ENG.
(T) 01296 681394
Speciality: Osteopathy.
P S T (Ref:HM09323)

**HEALING & HYPNOTHERAPY CENTRE**

**Healing & Hypnotherapy Centre**, 12A Vista Drive, Ilford, **Essex**, IG4 5JE, ENG.
(T) 020 8550 4122
Speciality: Hypnosis.
● **Owner** Miss J Chilkes
C (Ref:HM09324)

**HEALING AND HERBS**

**Healing And Herbs**, 67 Rose Walk, West Wickham, Bromley, **Kent**, BR4 0SB, ENG.
(T) 020 8777 6769
Speciality: Absent Healing, Complementary Therapy, Crystal Healing, Dowsing, Faith Healing, Healer, Healing Therapy, Herbal Medicine, Indian Head Massage, Massage (Therapeutic), Meditation, Reiki, Seichem, Spiritual Healing, Stress Therapy, Touch Therapy, Karuna Reiki. ✔
● **Healer/Reiki Teacher**
Mr M Cardwell
(T) 020 8460 1173 Q: Karuna Master, MNFSH, Reiki Master. M: NFSH, Reiki Fed.
● **Herbalist** Ms K Hevezi Q: BSc, Dip.Herb.Med. M: NIMH.
M Yrs. Est.: 5 (Ref:HM09325)

**HEALING ARTS UK**

**Healing Arts UK Ltd**, 25 Shelley Avenue, Greenford, **London (Greater)**, UB6 8RX, ENG.
(T) 020 8575 6931
(W) www.healingartsuk.com
Speciality: Acupressure, Indian Head Massage, Massage (Therapeutic), Reiki, Sports Massage, Holistic Massage, & Remedial Massage. Also have on-site massage. ✔
● **Owner/Therapist** Mrs A Adamson Q: MTI. M: GCP.
S Yrs. Est.: 3 (Ref:HM09326)

**HEALING CENTRE**

**Healing Centre (The)**, 45 Studfield Rd, Sheffield, **Yorkshire (South)**, S6 4ST, ENG.
(T) 01142 347726 (F) 01142 347726
Speciality: Clairvoyants & Palmists.
● **Owner** Mr G Gilmour
B (Ref:HM09327)

**HEALING CLINIC**

**Natural Health Centre**, 33 Fulford Cross, York, **Yorkshire (North)**, YO10 4PB, ENG.
(T) 01904 679868 (F) 01904 679868
(W) www.thehealingclinic.co.uk
Speciality: Absent Healing, Acupressure, Acupuncture, Alexander Technique, Aromatherapy, Bach Remedies, Bowen Therapy, Chinese Herbal Medicine, Chiropractic, Complementary Therapy, Cranio-Sacral Therapy, Cupping, Family Planning (Natural), Herbal Medicine, Homeopathy, Kinesiology, Moxibustion, Nutritional Therapy, Oriental Diagnosis, Polarity Therapy, Reflexology, Reiki, Shiatsu, T'ai-Chi Ch'uan, Vitamin Therapy, McTimoney Chiropractic. ✔
● **Medical Herbalist** Mr D Purves Q: MNIMH. M: NIMH.
● **Reflexologist** Ms J McArthur M: AoR.
● **Reflexologist/Polarity Therapist**
Ms D Morar Q: BSR, Dip.Hyp, Dip.Psych, NLP. M: BCMA, BSR.
● **Acupuncturist/Kinesiologist**
Ms J Tramner Q: BA (Hons), Dip.Ac. M: BAcC.
● **Shiatsu Practitioner**
Mr P Chielmar Q: Dip.Shiatsu.
● **McTimoney Chiropractor**
Mr O Grant Q: DC, MMCA.
● **Teacher of the Alexander Technique**
Ms P Mason M: STAT.
● **Acupuncturist/Chinese Herbalist/Bowen Therapist**
Mr M Burgess M: BAcC, BTAA, RCHM.
● **Acupressure Massage Therapist**
Ms B Lawton
● **Acupressure Massage Therapist**
Mr J Robson Q: Cert.Massage.
● **Reiki Healer** Alexander Walker Q: Reiki 1, Reiki 2.
● **Homeopath/Cranio-Sacral Therapist**
Ms R Field Q: RSHom.
● **Reflexologist** Ms G Wallace M: AoR.
O Yrs. Est.: 9 (Ref:HM09328)

**HEALING CLINIC**

**Healing Clinic (The)**, 1190 Wimborne Rd, Bournemouth, **Dorset**, BH10 7AE, ENG.
(T) 01202 523500
Speciality: Complementary Medicines & Therapy.
C M (Ref:HM09329)

**HEALING CONNECTIONS**

**Healing Connections**, 197 Brunswick Rd, Ipswich, **Suffolk**, IP4 4DB, ENG.
(T) 01473 405958 (F) 01473 400337
Speciality: Aromatherapy, Indian Head Massage, Massage (Therapeutic), Reiki. ✔
● **Complementary Therapist**
Mr P Warnock Q: Reiki Master. M: IPTI.
C Yrs. Est.: 5 (Ref:HM09330)

**HEALING CONNECTIONS**

**Healing Connections**, 4 Bramford Lane, Ipswich, **Suffolk**, IP1 4DA, ENG.
(T) 01473 405958
Speciality: Complementary Medicines & Therapy.
C M (Ref:HM09331)

**HEALING CTRE NTRL ALT HLTHCARE**

**Healing Centre Natural Alternative Healthcare (The)**, Flat B, 176 Wightman Rd, London, **London (Greater)**, N8 0BT, ENG.
(T) 020 8372 5586
Speciality: Complementary Medicines & Therapy.
C M (Ref:HM09332)

**HEALING EARTH**

**Healing Earth**, 41-43 St. Owen St, Hereford, **Herefordshire**, HR1 2JB, ENG.
(T) 01432 342342
Speciality: Complementary Medicines & Therapy.
● **Owner** Mr N Heath
M (Ref:HM09333)

**HEALING FOUNDATION**

**Healing Foundation (The)**, Half Acre House, Upper Battlefield, Shrewsbury, **Shropshire**, SY4

4AA, ENG.
(T) 01939 210980 (F) 01939 210980
Speciality: Complementary Medicines & Therapy, Natural Healing.
● **Membership Secretary** Ms J Marston
● **Reflexologist** Ms D Manders
(T) 01743 247902 M: AoR.
● **Chairman** Mr M Webbern
C (Ref:HM09334)

### HEALING HANDS

**Healing Hands**, 13 Coventry Cres, Poole, **Dorset**, BH17 7HN, ENG.
(T) 01202 658616
Speciality: Complementary Medicines & Therapy.
● **Partner** Mr C Jackson
C M (Ref:HM09335)

### HEALING HANDS

**Healing Hands**, Woodside, Bures, **Suffolk**, CO8 5BN, ENG.
(T) 01787 228012
(E) jay@healinghands.screaming.net
Speciality: Aromatherapy, Bach Remedies, Complementary Therapy, Family Therapy, Healer, Healing Therapy, Holistic Healing, Hypnosis, Hypnotherapy, Indian Head Massage, Inhalation Therapy, Massage (Therapeutic), Reflexology, Reiki, Stress Therapy, Swedish Body Massage, Touch Therapy, Transactional Analysis, Visualisation Therapy. ✔
● **Multi Therapist** Mr J Phillips Q: ICHT, IIHHT. M: FHT.
C T Yrs. Est.: 3 (Ref:HM09336)

### HEALING HANDS

**Healing Hands**, The Stables, Leslie Mains, Leslie, Glenrothes, **Fife**, KY6 3EP, SCO.
(T) 01592 621758
Speciality: Massage (Therapeutic), Reflexology, Reiki.
● **Owner** Mr J Cromby
M (Ref:HM09337)

### HEALING HANDS

**Healing Hands**, Denbigh St, London, **London (Greater)**, SW1V 2EY, ENG.
(T) 020 7630 9690
Speciality: Complementary Medicines & Therapy.
● **Owner** Mrs V Morgan
C M (Ref:HM09338)

### HEALING HANDS

**Healing Hands**, 19A Bridge St, Kidwelly, **Carmarthenshire**, SA17 4UU, WAL.
(T) 01554 891114
Speciality: Massage (Therapeutic), Reiki, Spinal Touch therapy. ✔
● **Natural Therapist** Mrs G Jones Q: Dip.N Med. M: ALTT, BCMA, IFHB.
C T Yrs. Est.: 4 (Ref:HM09339)

### HEALING HANDS

**Healing Hands**, 12 High St, Brompton, Gillingham, **Kent**, ME7 5AE, ENG.
(T) 01634 848422 (F) 01634 848421
Speciality: Reflexology.
● **Owner** Mr R Rouse
S T (Ref:HM09340)

### HEALING HANDS

**Healing Hands**, 1 Station Approach, Heathfield, **Sussex (East)**, TN21 8LH, ENG.
(T) 01435 864183
Speciality: Complementary Medicines & Therapy.
C M (Ref:HM09341)

### HEALING HANDS NAT THERAPIES

**Healing Hands The Natural Therapies Clinic**, 9 Arthurs Hill, Shanklin, **Isle of Wight**, PO37 6EW, ENG.
(T) 01983 865649
Speciality: Complementary Medicines & Therapy.
C M (Ref:HM09342)

### HEALING HEART

**Healing Heart**, 3 Quantock Drive, Nuneaton, **Warwickshire**, CV10 8PU, ENG.
(T) 024 7635 6031
Speciality: Aromatherapy.
● **Owner** Ms M Lidster
M O (Ref:HM09343)

### HEALING HERBS

**Healing Herbs Ltd**, P O Box 65, Hereford, **Herefordshire**, HR2 0UW, ENG.
(T) 01873 890218
(E) jb@healing-herb.co.uk
(W) www.healing-herbs.co.uk
Speciality: Bach Remedies, Floral Essence Therapy. CREDIT
● **Owner** Mr J Barnard
H Yrs. Est.: 12 (Ref:HM09344)

### HEALING HOUSE

**Healing House**, 24 O'Connell Ave, Berkeley Rd, Dublin, **County Dublin**, IRE.
(T) 01830 6413 (F) 01830 6060
(E) info@healinghouse.ie
(W) www.healinghouse.ie
Speciality: Healing.
B (Ref:HM09345)

### HEALING LEAVES

**Healing Leaves**, 15 Chichester Park Central, Ballymena, **County Antrim**, BT42 4BE, NIR.
(T) 028 2563 2100 (F) 028 2563 2100
Speciality: Homeopathy.
M (Ref:HM09346)

### HEALING PLACE

**Healing Place (The)**, 61 Saint Assam's Way, Raheny, **County Dublin**, IRE.
(T) 01848 4270
(E) josephmcguire@iol.ie
Speciality: Cranio-Sacral Therapy, Shiatsu. ✔
● **Cranio-Sacral/Shiatsu Therapist** Mr J McGuire
B Yrs. Est.: 16 (Ref:HM09347)

### HEALING REFERALS

**Healing Referals**, 38 Oakdale Rd, London, **London (Greater)**, E11 4DL, ENG.
(T) 020 8558 2930
Speciality: Complementary Medicines & Therapy.
C M (Ref:HM09348)

### HEALING ROOM

**Healing Room (The)**, 3 Weir Pond Rd, Rochford, **Essex**, SS4 1AH, ENG.
(T) 01702 543943
Speciality: Absent Healing, Aromatherapy, Complementary Therapy, Healing Therapy, Holistic Healing, Indian Head Massage, Massage (Therapeutic), Reflexology, Reiki, Stress Therapy. ✔
● **Practitioner/Therapist** Ms P Fry M: ITEC.
● **Owner/Practitioner/Therapist** Ms J Gardner M: ANM, AOC, GCP.
M Yrs. Est.: 3 (Ref:HM09349)

### HEALING ROOM

**Healing Room**, 326 Clontarf Rd, Clontarf, Dublin, **County Dublin**, IRE.
(T) 01833 9646
Speciality: Healing.
B (Ref:HM09350)

### HEALING ROOM - DRUMCONDRA

**Healing Room - Drumcondra**, 13 Clonturk Pk, Drumcondra, **County Dublin**, IRE.
(T) 01836 8448
Speciality: Aromatherapy, Healing Therapy, Holistic Healing, Indian Head Massage, Massage (Therapeutic), Reflexology, Reiki, Shiatsu. ✔
● **Complementary Health Therapist** Ms N Daly
B Yrs. Est.: 4 (Ref:HM09351)

### HEALING STAR

**Healing Star (The)**, 6 Westmorland Way, Chandler's Ford, Eastleigh, **Hampshire**, SO53 2LA, ENG.
(T) 023 8026 7342
Speciality: Complementary Medicines & Therapy.
● **Owner** Mrs M Reid
C M (Ref:HM09352)

### HEALING STAR

**Healing Star (The)**, 35 Causeway Head, Penzance, **Cornwall**, TR18 2SP, ENG.
(T) 01736 330502
Speciality: Complementary Medicines & Therapy.
M (Ref:HM09353)

### HEALING THERAPIES

**Healing Therapies**, 9 Castleowen, Blarney, **County Cork**, IRE.
(T) 021 4382 235
(E) chspengeman@eircom.net
Speciality: Absent Healing, Aura Therapy, Healer, Healing Therapy, Meditation, Reiki, Seichem, Spiritual Healing, Stress Therapy, Tera-Mai, Touch Therapy, Visualisation Therapy. ✔
● **Healing Therapist** Ms C Spengeman Q: Masters Degree. M: ALTT, TMHA.
T Yrs. Est.: 5 (Ref:HM09354)

### HEALING TO WHOLENESS

**Healing To Wholeness**, 10 Cedar Rd, Tottenham, London, **London (Greater)**, N17 8NB, ENG.
(T) 020 8808 9562 (F) 020 8808 9562
Speciality: Complementary Medicines & Therapy.
● **Owner** Ms F McCallion
C M (Ref:HM09355)

### HEALING TOUCH

**Healing Touch**, 8 Lexham Gardens, London, **London (Greater)**, W8 5JH, ENG.
(T) 020 7373 6104
Speciality: Complementary Medicines & Therapy.
● **Owner** Mrs M Pherigo
C M (Ref:HM09356)

### HEALING TOUCH MASSAGE

**Healing Touch Massage**, Dublin, **County Dublin**, IRE.
(T) 01493 1485
Speciality: Healing.
B (Ref:HM09357)

### HEALING WAYS

**Healing Ways**, 14 Stanley St, Leek, **Staffordshire**, ST13 5HG, ENG.
(T) 01538 399526
Speciality: Complementary Medicines & Therapy.
● **Manager** Mrs H Pickford
C M (Ref:HM09358)

### HEALING WAYS

**Healing Ways**, 22 Chapel St, Llangollen, **Denbighshire**, LL20 8TH, WAL.
(T) 01691 773993 (F) 01691 773993
(E) joyb@constabfreeserve.co.uk
Speciality: Indian Head Massage, Manual Lymph Drainage, Reflexology, Stress Therapy, Magnified Healing, Diet/Nutrition Therapy. ✔
● **Complementary Therapist** Ms J Constable Q: MAR. M: AoR.
● **Complementary Therapist** Ms J Stone Q: MAR. M: AoR.
C Yrs. Est.: 1 (Ref:HM09359)

### HEALING WITH GABRIELLE TWINE

**Healing With Gabrielle Twine**, Court Farm, 14a Chapel Lane, Winford, Bristol, BS40 8EU, ENG.
(T) 01275 472335
Speciality: Absent Healing, Bach Remedies, Healer, Healing Therapy, Holistic Healing, Meditation, Spiritual Healing, Touch Therapy, Visualisation Therapy. ✔
● **Healer** Ms G Twine M: NFSH.
C T Yrs. Est.: 16 (Ref:HM09360)

### HEALING WORKSHOPS

**Healing Workshops**, 111 Queens Cresent, London, **London (Greater)**, NW5 4EY, ENG.
(T) 020 7482 4049 (F) 020 7813 0093
Speciality: Complementary Medicines & Therapy.
C M (Ref:HM09361)

### HEALING WORKSHOPS

**Healing Workshops**, P O Box 1678, London, **London (Greater)**, NW5 4EW, ENG.



Key: B Mind-Body Medicine C Complementary Medicine H Self Help Treatment M Medicinal Therapy O Oriental Medicine P Postural Therapy S Manipulative Structural Therapy T Touch Therapy

(T) 020 7482 4049
Speciality: Complementary Medicines & Therapy.
M (Ref:HM09362)

## HEALTH & BEAUTY CENTRE

**Health & Beauty Centre (The)**, 45-46 Market St, Haddington, **Lothian (East)**, EH41 3JE, SCO.
(T) 01620 825158
Speciality: Complementary Medicines & Therapy.
● **Owner** Miss S Haughey
M (Ref:HM09363)

## HEALTH & BEAUTY CENTRE

**Health & Beauty Centre**, 76 Hawthorn Ave, Woodlawn, Killarney, **County Kerry**, IRE.
(T) 06437 955
Speciality: Relaxation Technique.
H T (Ref:HM09364)

## HEALTH & BEAUTY CLINIC

**Health & Beauty Clinic**, 6 Hagley Rd, Stourbridge, **Midlands (West)**, DY8 1PS, ENG.
(T) 01384 372462
Speciality: Electrolysis.
T (Ref:HM09365)

## HEALTH & BEAUTY WISE

**Health & Beauty Wise**, 295 Robin Hood Lane, Blue Bell Hill, Chatham, **Kent**, ME5 9QU, ENG.
(T) 01634 200222
Speciality: Aromatherapy.
● **Owner** Mrs M Wise
M O (Ref:HM09366)

## HEALTH & FITNESS CLINIC

**Health & Fitness Clinic**, Physiotherapy Dept, Bristol Royal Infirmary, Upper Maudlin St, Bristol, BS2 8HW, ENG.
(T) 01179 282387
Speciality: Physiotherapy.
P S T (Ref:HM09367)

## HEALTH & HARMONY

**Health & Harmony (UK) Ltd**, 2 South Park Trce, Ilford, **Essex**, IG1 1YA, ENG.
(T) 020 8514 1286 (F) 020 8478 6075
Speciality: Complementary Medicines & Therapy.
● **Manager** Mrs J Pike
M (Ref:HM09368)

## HEALTH & HARMONY

**Health & Harmony Ltd**, 41B South Richmond St, Portobello, Dublin, **County Dublin**, IRE.
(T) 01475 9648
(E) health_harmony@yahoo.com
Speciality: Complementary Medicines & Therapy.
M (Ref:HM09369)

## HEALTH & HARMONY HOLISTIC

**Health & Harmony Holistic Healing**, Bonanza, Burgoyne Rd, Sunbury-On-Thames, **Surrey**, TW16 7PP, ENG.
(T) 01932 713606 (F) 01932 713606
Speciality: Complementary Medicines & Therapy.
● **Owner** Mrs C Francis-Lynch
C M (Ref:HM09370)

## HEALTH & HEALING

**Health & Healing**, 355-359 Two Mile Hill Rd, Bristol, BS15 1AF, ENG.
(T) 01179 145590
Speciality: Acupuncture, Allergy Testing, Aromatherapy, Bowen Therapy, Chiropractic, Counselling, Crystal Healing, Homeopathy, Hypnotherapy, Indian Head Massage, Manual Lymph Drainage, Neuro-Linguistic Program, Reflexology, Reiki, Shiatsu. ✓
● **Holistic Therapist** Lesley Taylor Q: MAR, RQA, TIDHA.
C Yrs. Est.: 4 (Ref:HM09371)

## HEALTH & HOLISTIC CENTRE

**Health & Holistic Centre**, 11 Queen St, Bath, **Somerset**, BA1 1HE, ENG.
(T) 01225 314795
Speciality: Complementary Medicines & Therapy.
● **Owner** Miss J Donson
M (Ref:HM09372)

## HEALTH & RELAXATION CENTRE

**Health & Relaxation Centre**, 30 Knowehead Rd, Broughshane, Ballymena, **County Antrim**, BT43 7LF, NIR.
(T) 028 2586 2060
Speciality: Complementary Medicines & Therapy.
● **Owner** Mrs L McOoke
M (Ref:HM09373)

## HEALTH & VITALITY

**Health & Vitality Ltd**, 5 Dowanside Rd, Glasgow, **Glasgow (City of)**, G12 9YB, SCO.
(T) 01413 391878 (F) 01419 502990
Speciality: Aromatherapy, Complementary Therapy, Reflexology, Reiki.
● **Sole Director** John G Williamson
M (Ref:HM09374)

## HEALTH ALLIANCE CENTRE

**Health Alliance Centre**, 9 Carliol Sq, Newcastle Upon Tyne, **Tyne and Wear**, NE1 6UF, ENG.
(T) 01912 453790
Speciality: Chiropractic, Manipulation, Massage (Therapeutic). ✓
● **Chiropractor** Mr S Henderson Q: B.App.Sc. M: GCC.
S Yrs. Est.: 1 (Ref:HM09375)

## HEALTH AT HOME

**Health At Home Ltd**, Polyne Farm, Sclerder Lane, Looe, **Cornwall**, PL13 2JD, ENG.
(T) 01503 272127 (F) 01503 272161
Speciality: Complementary Medicines & Therapy.
● **Owner** Mrs K Weiss
M (Ref:HM09376)

## HEALTH BARN CLINIC

**Health Barn Clinic**, 37 Abbey Avenue, St. Albans, **Hertfordshire**, AL3 4BH, ENG.
(T) 01727 833698 (F) 01727 844976
Speciality: Osteopathy.
P S T (Ref:HM09377)

## HEALTH CARE

**Health Care**, 2 Stocks Hill, Castor, Peterborough, **Cambridgeshire**, PE5 7AY, ENG.
(T) 01733 380631
Speciality: Complementary Medicines & Therapy.
● **Owner** Mrs K Barnes
M (Ref:HM09378)

## HEALTH CARE INTERNATIONAL

**Health Care International**, 27 Home Park, Plymouth, **Devon**, PL2 1BQ, ENG.
(T) 01752 607404
Speciality: Herbal Medicine.
● **Owner** Mr J Pomlett
M (Ref:HM09379)

## HEALTH CHAMBERS

**Health Chambers (The)**, 24a Trinity Church Gate, Wakefield, **Yorkshire (West)**, WF1 1TX, ENG.
(T) 01924 373353
Speciality: Acupuncture, Chinese Herbal Medicine, Herbal Medicine, Homeopathy, Indian Head Massage, Light Therapy, Massage (Therapeutic), Metamorphic Therapy, Osteopathy, Reflexology, Reiki, Swedish Body Massage.
P S T (Ref:HM09380)

## HEALTH CHECK

**Health Check**, 178 East Barnet Rd, Barnet, **Hertfordshire**, EN4 8RD, ENG.
(T) 020 8449 7754 (F) 020 8449 0174
Speciality: Complementary Medicines & Therapy.
● **Principal** Mr L Hartman
M (Ref:HM09381)

## HEALTH CONSULTANCY

**Health Consultancy (The)**, Spiral Lodge, Parkham Lane, Brixham, **Devon**, TQ5 9JR, ENG.
(T) 01803 859889 (F) 01803 857335
(E) schooladmin@gn.apc.org
Speciality: Counselling, Homeopathy, Manipulation, Massage (Therapeutic), Miasm Therapy, Psychotherapy, Reflexology, Stress Therapy, Oxygen Therapy. ✓

● **Therapist** Mr F Meredith Q: RSHom. M: HMA.
M Yrs. Est.: 8 (Ref:HM09382)

## HEALTH CORNER

**Health Corner Therapy Centre (The)**, 41B High St, Grantown-on-Spey, **Highland**, PH26 3EG, SCO.
(T) 01479 870400
(E) lorelan@easicom.com
Speciality: Acupuncture, Complementary Therapy, Counselling, Cranial Osteopathy, Electrotherapy, Indian Head Massage, Manipulation, Massage (Therapeutic), Moxibustion, Reflexology, Reiki, Shiatsu, Spiritual Healing, Stress Therapy, Yoga, Metamorphic Technique and Holistic Physiotherapy. ✓
● **Owner** Mr K Hummel
● **Therapist** Dr P Boxx M: BAcC.
● **Therapist** Ms C Hayes M: RSS.
● **Therapist** Ms B Hummel M: CSP, OCPPP.
● **Therapist** Ms L Claire-Mann Q: RGN.
B Yrs. Est.: 1 (Ref:HM09383)

## HEALTH COUNSEL

**Health Counsel**, 30 Kincora Court, Clontarf, **County Dublin**, IRE.
(T) 01833 8792
(E) health.counsel@oceanfree.net
Speciality: Auto Suggestion, Autogenic Training, Complementary Therapy, Gestalt Therapy, Healer, Healing Therapy, Hypnosis, Hypnotherapy, Massage (Therapeutic), Meditation, Silva Method, Stress Therapy, Emotional Freedom Therapy, Healing Through Hypnosis, Success Through Hypnosis, Stress Management Training, Assault Prevention for Health Workers, Past Life Regression Therapy. ✓
● **Hypnotherapist** Ms M Hickey Q: CIBTAC, ITEC, MICHP, RGN. M: ICHP.
B Yrs. Est.: 4 (Ref:HM09384)

## HEALTH EXPRESS

**Health Express**, 5 The High Parade, Streatham High Rd, London, **London (Greater)**, SW16 1EX, ENG.
(T) 020 8769 7543
Speciality: Complementary Medicines & Therapy.
● **Practice Manager** Mr H Patel
M (Ref:HM09385)

## HEALTH FOCUS

**Health Focus**, 3 Canal Yard Cottages, Canal Yard, Severn St, Welshpool, **Powys**, SY21 7AQ, WAL.
(T) 01938 556073
Speciality: Acupressure, Aromatherapy, Bowen Therapy, Chiropody, Homeopathy, Indian Head Massage, Massage (Therapeutic), Osteopathy, Reflexology, Reiki. ✓
● **Reflexologist** Ms K Evans Q: IIHHT. M: IIHHT.
● **Bowen Therapist** Ms D Fildes
● **Osteopath** Ms M Jones M: GOsC.
● **Chiropodist** Ms S Lindsey Q: M.S.C.P. M: S.C.P.
● **Reiki Master** Ms C Cumbe
● **Medical Herbalist/Homeopath** Dr A Hutchinson Q: BSc, LFHom.
C Yrs. Est.: 3 (Ref:HM09386)

## HEALTH FOOD CENTRE

**Health Food Centre**, 7 Warwick Rd, Carlisle, **Cumbria**, CA1 1DH, ENG.
(T) 01228 525228
Speciality: Complementary Medicines & Therapy.
C M (Ref:HM09387)

## HEALTH FOR ALL

**Health For All**, Flints, Rotten Row, Lewes, **Sussex (East)**, BN7 1TN, ENG.
(T) 01273 471543
Speciality: Complementary Medicines & Therapy.
C M (Ref:HM09388)

## HEALTH HYDRO

**Health Hydro**, Health Hydro, Milton Rd, Swindon, **Wiltshire**, SN1 5JA, ENG.
(T) 01793 465629 (F) 01793 465666
Speciality: Acupuncture, Alexander Technique, Aromatherapy, Chiropractic, Counselling, Homeopathy, Nutritional Therapy, Osteopathy, Postural Integration, Reflexology. ✓


Key continued: Yrs.Est: Years Established Q: Qualifications M: Professional Membership ✓ Indemnity Insurance Accept Credit Cards

● **Allergy Therapist** Mr C Mead **Q:** BIAT, D.Hom.Med.
● **Bach Remedy Therapist** Mr J Farrar
● **Remedial Sports Therapist** Mr G Pritchard
● **Clinic Manager** Ms L Belcher
C M Yrs. Est.: 30 (**Ref:**HM09389)

**HEALTH IS HAPPINESS REFLEX**

**Health Is Happiness Reflexology**, 3 Beedingwood Drive, Forest Rd, Colgate, Horsham, **Sussex (West)**, RH12 4TE, ENG.
(T) 01293 851760 (F) 01293 851760
Speciality: Reflexology. ✔
● **Reflexologist** Mr T Cullen **Q:** BCMA, BSR. M: GCP.
● **Reflexologist** Mrs J Cullen **Q:** BCMA, BSR. M: GCP.
C T Yrs. Est.: 9 (**Ref:**HM09390)

**HEALTH KINESIOLOGY**

**Health Kinesiology**, 47 Belgrave Avenue, Gidea Park, Romford, **Essex**, RM2 6QA, ENG.
(T) 01708 750818
Speciality: Kinesiology.
M (**Ref:**HM09391)

**HEALTH MAIL**

**Health Mail**, 19 Station Rd, Swanage, **Dorset**, BH19 1AB, ENG.
(T) 01929 422224 (F) 01929 427325
Speciality: Complementary Medicines & Therapy.
● **Owner** Mrs B Bartlett
M (**Ref:**HM09392)

**HEALTH MATTERS**

**Health Matters**, 31 Wansbeck Avenue, Stanley, **County Durham**, DH9 6HT, ENG.
(T) 01207 238103
Speciality: Aromatherapy.
M O (**Ref:**HM09393)

**HEALTH MATTERS**

**Health Matters**, 32A Cock Robin Lane, Catterall, Preston, **Lancashire**, PR3 1YL, ENG.
(T) 01995 602401 (F) 01995 602401
Speciality: Complementary Medicines & Therapy.
● **Owner** Ms A Scott
C M (**Ref:**HM09394)

**HEALTH MATTERS NATURAL HLTH**

**Health Matters Natural Health Centre**, Newton Green, Newton, Sudbury, **Suffolk**, CO10 0QL, ENG.
(T) 01787 310908
Speciality: Complementary Medicines & Therapy.
M (**Ref:**HM09395)

**HEALTH MATTERS WALES**

**Health Matters Wales**, Chez Nous, Llandevaud, Newport, NP18 2AF, WAL.
(T) 01633 400615
Speciality: Complementary Medicines & Therapy.
● **Owner** Mrs J Whitcombe
C M (**Ref:**HM09396)

**HEALTH POTENTIALS**

**Health Potentials**, 79 High St, Marlborough, **Wiltshire**, ENG.
(T) 01672 513656
Speciality: Complementary Medicines & Therapy.
● **Owner** Mr D Bainbridge
M (**Ref:**HM09397)

**HEALTH RELATED TRAINING**

**Health Related Training**, 8 Rains Rd, Bristol, BS3 2DL, ENG.
(T) 01179 637909
Speciality: Complementary Medicines & Therapy, Occupational Therapy.
M (**Ref:**HM09398)

**HEALTH SENSE**

**Health Sense**, Main St, Carrick-on-Shannon, **County Leitrim**, IRE.
(T) 07822 959
Speciality: Complementary Medicines & Therapy.
M (**Ref:**HM09399)

**HEALTH SERVICES**

**Health Services**, Millbrook Mental Health Unit, Mansfield Rd, Sutton-in-Ashfield, **Nottinghamshire**, NG17 4JT, ENG.
(T) 01623 784702
Speciality: Psychiatry.
B (**Ref:**HM09400)

**HEALTH SERVICES**

**Health Services In Cumbria & North Lancashire**, Owen Rd Centre, 69 Owen Rd, Lancaster, **Lancashire**, LA1 2LG, ENG.
(T) 01524 841660 (F) 01524 389484
Speciality: Psychotherapy.
● **Manager** Mr T Norton
B (**Ref:**HM09401)

**HEALTH SHOP**

**Health Shop (The)**, 3 Cross St, Willenhall, Wolverhampton, **Midlands (West)**, WV13 1PG, ENG.
(T) 01902 601035
Speciality: Aromatherapy, Bach Remedies, Homeopathy.
● **Owner** Ms H Codd
H Yrs. Est.: 20 (**Ref:**HM09402)

**HEALTH SHOP & HOMOEOPATHIC**

**Health Shop & Homoeopathic Clinic (The)**, 37 High St, Hornchurch, **Essex**, RM11 1TP, ENG.
(T) 01708 442677
Speciality: Homeopathy.
M (**Ref:**HM09403)

**HEALTH STRESS & INJURIES**

**Health Stress & Injuries Clinic**, Prestwick Airport, Glasgow Prestwick International Airport, Prestwick, **Ayrshire (South)**, KA9 2PL, SCO.
(T) 01292 678597 (F) 01292 678597
Speciality: Aromatherapy, Bowen Therapy, Chiropractic, Kinesiology, Laser Therapy. ✔
● **Therapist** Mr K Kilmurray M: BRA.
● **Therapist** Ms L Murray
● **Therapist** Ms J Walker **Q:** ITEC. M: IPTI.
P Yrs. Est.: 6 (**Ref:**HM09404)

**HEALTH STRESS & INJURIES CLNC**

**Health Stress & Injuries Clinic (The)**, 29 Castle St, Dumfries, **Dumfries and Galloway**, DG1 1DL, SCO.
(T) 01387 268725 (F) 01387 268725
Speciality: Bowen Therapy, Hypnotherapy, Psychotherapy, Spiritual Healing, Food Intolerences, Allergy Dowsing, NLP. ✔
● **Owner** Mr R McLernon **Q:** RMN. M: BTAA, NRHP.
C Yrs. Est.: 14 (**Ref:**HM09405)

**HEALTH TEAM**

**B L Beber and B H Kirsopp T/A The Health Team**, Crown Treatment Centre, Littleport, Ely, **Cambridgeshire**, CB6 1PP, ENG.
(T) 08707 898909 (F) 08707 898909
(E) thehealthteam@mail.com
(W) www.thehealthteam.uk.com
Speciality: Alexander Technique, Allergy Testing, Aromatherapy, Auto Suggestion, Bach Remedies, Bio-energetics, Chiropody, Clinical Ecology, Cognitive Therapy, Complementary Therapy, Dowsing, Electrotherapy, Floral Essence Therapy, Gait Analysis, Gestalt Therapy, Holistic Healing, Homeopathy, Humanistic Psychology, Hypnosis, Hypnotherapy, Indian Head Massage, Macrobiotics, Manipulation, Massage (Therapeutic), Meditation, Micro Manipulation, Naturopathy, Nutritional Therapy, Physiotherapy, Podiatry, Psychotherapy, Reflexology, Reichian Therapy, Reiki, Sound Therapy, Stress Therapy, Ultrasonics, Vibrational Therapy, Visualisation Therapy, Vitamin Therapy, Bio-Mechanical Assessment, Champisage, Educational Kinesiology, Manicure, Neuro-Psychology, Pedicure, Scenar, Sound Therapy, Sports Injury Therapy, Thought Field Therapy, Personal Fitness, Bush Flower Remedies, Orthotic Treatment, Neuro Developmental Delay Therapy, Allergy Therapy, Creative Healing, Alternative Medicine, Supplementary Medicine, Behavioural Psychotherapy, Child Psychology, Learning Difficulties and Expert Witness Advisors to the Courts and the Legal Profession. ✔
● **Nutritional Therapist** Ms J Green **Q:** MBSR, RNT. M: BANT, BSR.
● **Clinical Director** Mr B Beber **Q:** MAB Phys. M: AB Phys, BCA.
● **Neuro Psychologist** Ms F Blyde **Q:** BSc (Hons).
● **Sports Injury Therapist** Mr D Saint-Laurent **Q:** MIPTI. M: IPTI.
● **Aromatherapist/Reflexologist** Ms R Kirsopp **Q:** A.I.P.T.I, ITEC. M: IPTI.
● **Homeopath** Mr C Halls **Q:** LCPH, MHMA. M: HMA.
● **Chiropodist (Podiatrist)** Mr I Linane **Q:** MBChA, MBSR, MSSCh. M: B.A.Ch.P, BSR.
● **Manicurist/Pedicurist** Ms R McGowan **Q:** ITEC.
● **Teacher Of The Alexander Technique** Ms E Tarmy **Q:** MSTAT, PhD. M: STAT.
B C H M O P S T
Yrs. Est.: 5 (**Ref:**HM09406)

**HEALTH THERAPIES CLINIC**

**Health Therapies Clinic**, 13 Gladstone St, **County Waterford**, IRE.
(T) 05185 8584
Speciality: Complementary Medicines & Therapy.
M (**Ref:**HM09407)

**HEALTH WAVES**

**Health Waves**, 40 Lansdowne, Woodwater Lane, Exeter, **Devon**, EX2 5AR, ENG.
(T) 01392 496580 (F) 01392 496580
(E) martynrudin@yahoo.com
Speciality: Alexander Technique, Complementary Therapy, Dance Movement Therapy, Do-In, Healing Therapy, Massage (Therapeutic), Meditation, Nutritional Therapy, Reflexology, Sound Therapy, Stress Therapy, Tibetan Bowl Healing (Sound Healing), Contact Improvisation (Dance Movement Therapy). ✔
● **Practitioner** Mr M Rudin M: ITEC, STAT.
P Yrs. Est.: 10 (**Ref:**HM09408)

**HEALTH WORKS**

**Health Works**, 5 Bank Lane, Forres, **Moray**, SCO.
(T) 01309 641586
Speciality: Alexander Technique.
● **Therapist** Mr D Coppock
C P S (**Ref:**HM09409)

**HEALTHCARE INTERNATIONAL**

**Healthcare International**, Tyldesley, Manchester, **Manchester (Greater)**, M29 8PZ, ENG.
(T) 07071 223116
Speciality: Herbalists.
M (**Ref:**HM09410)

**HEALTHCARE INTERNATIONAL**

**Healthcare International**, 19 The Daglands, Camerton, Bath, **Somerset**, BA3 1PR, ENG.
(T) 01761 472265
Speciality: Complementary Medicines & Therapy.
● **Owner** Mrs V Gregory
C M (**Ref:**HM09411)

**HEALTHCARE INTERNATIONAL**

**Healthcare International**, 52 Graveleythorpe Rd, **Yorkshire (West)**, LS15 7EQ, ENG.
(T) 01132 604584
Speciality: Complementary Medicines & Therapy.
C M (**Ref:**HM09412)

**HEALTHPACK**

**Healthpack Ltd**, Langston Priory Workshops, Station Rd, Kingham, Chipping Norton, **Oxfordshire**, OX7 6UP, ENG.
(T) 01608 658862 (F) 01608 658816
(W) www.eastwestherbs.net
Speciality: Acupuncture, Aromatherapy, Chinese Herbal Medicine.
C (**Ref:**HM09413)

**HEALTHPOINT**

**Healthpoint**, 1 Watson Cl, Warwick, **Warwickshire**, CV34 5SW, ENG.
(T) 01926 497888



Key: B Mind-Body Medicine, C Complementary Medicine, H Self Help Treatment, M Medicinal Therapy, O Oriental Medicine, P Postural Therapy, S Manipulative Structural Therapy, T Touch Therapy

Speciality: Acupuncture.
● **Owner** Mr S Walsgrove
[M] (Ref:HM09414)

## HEALTHPOINT

**Healthpoint**, 12 Wolfe Cl, Parkgate Industrial Estate, Knutsford, **Cheshire**, WA16 8XJ, ENG.
(T) 01565 632000
Speciality: Complementary Medicines & Therapy.
[C] [M] (Ref:HM09415)

## HEALTHSHARE FOUNDATION

**Healthshare Foundation**, Bridge Cottage, Abbotskerswell, Newton Abbot, **Devon**, TQ12 5PE, ENG.
(T) 01626 367218
Speciality: Acupuncture.
● **Partner** Mrs B Williams
[O] (Ref:HM09416)

## HEALTHWISE

**Healthwise**, Chapel Market, London, **London (Greater)**, N1 9EZ, ENG.
(T) 020 7278 0788 (F) 020 8200 7653
Speciality: Acupuncture.
● **Doctor** Mrs S Xu
[O] (Ref:HM09417)

## HEALTHWISE

**Healthwise**, 44B Cooden Sea Rd, Bexhill-on-Sea, **Sussex (East)**, TN39 4SL, ENG.
(T) 01424 844075
(E) eileen.vaine@nationwideisp.net
Speciality: Bach Remedies, Counselling. [✔]
● **Owner** Mrs E Vaines **Q:** Dip.BFR, Dip.Couns, F.Inst.HFR, SRN. **M:** Inst.HFR.
[H] Yrs. Est.: 20 (Ref:HM09418)

## HEALTHWISE

**HealthWise**, 5 Midanbury Broadway, Witts Hill, Southampton, **Hampshire**, SO18 4QD, ENG.
(T) 023 0805 51818
Speciality: Acupuncture.
[O] (Ref:HM09419)

## HEALTHWISE

**HealthWise**, Rupert House, 70 Church Rd, Winterbourne Down, Bristol, BS36 1BY, ENG.
(T) 01454 850883
Speciality: Vitamin Therapy, Natural Skin Care.
[M] (Ref:HM09420)

## HEALTHWISE THERAPIES

**Healthwise Therapies**, 9 Brookvale Rd, Southampton, **Hampshire**, SO17 1QN, ENG.
(T) 023 8055 8921 (F) 023 8055 0948
Speciality: Physiotherapy.
● **Owner** Mrs J Hebbes
[P] [S] [T] (Ref:HM09421)

## HEALTHWORKS

**Holistic Health Care Ltd**, 5 Bank Lane, Forres, **Moray**, IV36 1NU, SCO.
(T) 01309 676691
Speciality: Acupressure, Acupuncture, Alexander Technique, Aromatherapy, Bach Remedies, Chiropractic, Counselling, Cranial Osteopathy, Family Planning (Natural), Healing Therapy, Herbal Medicine, Holistic Healing, Homeopathy, Hypnotherapy, Moxibustion, Naturopathy, Osteopathy, Reflexology, Reiki, Shiatsu, Spiritual Healing. [✔]
[C] Yrs. Est.: 8 (Ref:HM09422)

## HEALTHWORKS

**Healthworks**, 20 Ashford Drive, Kingswood, Maidstone, **Kent**, ME17 3PB, ENG.
(T) 01622 842311
Speciality: Homeopathy.
● **Employee** Mrs M Higgins
[M] (Ref:HM09423)

## HEALTHWORKS

**Healthworks**, 15 Great St Thomas Apostle, London, **London (Greater)**, EC4V 2BB, ENG.
(T) 020 7213 9833
Speciality: Psychotherapy.
● **Director** Mr J McCabe
[B] (Ref:HM09424)

## HEALTHY AND WISE

**Healthy and Wise**, 70 Watling St, Radlett, **Hertfordshire**, WD7, ENG.
(T) 01923 859919
(E) lowepath@aol.com
Speciality: Homeopathy. [✔]
● **Therapist** Mr A Lowe
[B] Yrs. Est.: 3 (Ref:HM09425)

## HEALTHY CHOICES

**Healthy Choices**, Muckno St, Castleblaney, **County Monaghan**, IRE.
(T) 04297 40555 (F) 04297 40555
(E) healthychoices@oceanfree.net
Speciality: Acupuncture, Aromatherapy, Bach Remedies, Colour Therapy, Complementary Therapy, Crystal Healing, Herbal Medicine, Holistic Healing, Hypnotherapy, Indian Head Massage, Massage (Therapeutic), Meditation, Nutritional Therapy, Postural Integration, Reflexology, Reiki, Spiritual Healing, Stress Therapy, Ultrasonics, Vitamin Therapy, Raycomp Allergy Testing and Desensitisation, Shamanic Healing, Physical/Sports Therapy. [✔]
● **Therapist** Gay Burnett **Q:** Dip.Arom, Dip.Reiki, Dip.Sports Therapy, RGN.
[B] Yrs. Est.: 2 (Ref:HM09426)

## HEALTHY FEET

**Healthy Feet**, 7 Charter Sq, Sheffield, **Yorkshire (South)**, S1 4HS, ENG.
(T) 01142 726688 (F) 01142 726688
(E) martyn-s@usa.net
(W) www.healthyfeet.co.uk
Speciality: Chiropractic, Complementary Therapy, Manipulation, Osteopathy, Reflexology. [✔]
● **Podiatrist** Mr M Sherman **Q:** BSc, DPodM, M.S.C.P, S.R.Ch. **M:** S.C.P.
[M] Yrs. Est.: 11 (Ref:HM09427)

## HEALTHY HOUSE

**Healthy House (The)**, Cold Harbour, Lower St, Ruscombe, Stroud, **Gloucestershire**, GL6 6DA, ENG.
(T) 01453 752216 (F) 01453 753533
Speciality: Complementary Medicines & Therapy.
● **Owner** Mr D Skelton
[M] (Ref:HM09428)

## HEALTHY LIVING CENTRE

**Healthy Living Centre**, 282 St. Pauls Rd, London, **London (Greater)**, N1 2LH, ENG.
(T) 020 7704 6900 (F) 020 7704 6050
Speciality: Floral Essence Therapy, Homeopathy, Nutritional Therapy. [✔]
● **Homeopath** Mr M Fernandez **Q:** MCPH. **M:** GCP, HMA.
● **Homeopath** Ms C Gaskin **Q:** LCPH. **M:** GCP, HMA.
● **Homeopath** Mr R Halford **M:** GCP, HMA.
● **Homeopath** Ms E Kramer **Q:** MCPH. **M:** GCP, HMA.
● **Homeopath** Ms A McGibbon **Q:** LCPH. **M:** GCP, HMA.
● **Homeopath** Ms E Woodward **Q:** LCPH. **M:** GCP, HMA.
● **Homeopath** Ms L Booth **Q:** LCPH. **M:** GCP, HMA.
[C] [M] Yrs. Est.: 5 (Ref:HM09429)

## HEALTHY OPTIONS

**Healthy Options**, 112A High St, Godalming, **Surrey**, GU7 1DW, ENG.
(T) 01483 427755
Speciality: Complementary Medicines & Therapy.
[C] [M] (Ref:HM09430)

## HEALY, DECLAN

**Healy Declan M S S Ch M B Ch A**, 45 Lr Dorset St, Dublin, **County Dublin**, IRE.
(T) 08681 37880
Speciality: Chiropodists (Podiatrists).
[S] (Ref:HM09431)

## HEALY, GERARD

**Gerard Healy D AP DHypt D It**, 126, Ranelagh, **County Dublin**, IRE.
(T) 08680 60259
Speciality: Acupuncture.
[O] (Ref:HM09432)

## HEALY, RICHARD

**Healy Richard Lic Ac RPN MBAcC**, Still Point Holistic Health Clinic, Ennis, **County Clare**, IRE.
(T) 06568 20454
Speciality: Acupuncture.
[O] (Ref:HM09433)

## HEALY, STEPHANIE

**Stephanie Healy**, High St, Sandwich, **Kent**, CT13 9EB, ENG.
(T) 01304 614000 (F) 01304 614000
Speciality: Physiotherapy.
● **Manager** Mr B Myers
[P] [S] [T] (Ref:HM09434)

## HEANEY, J

**J Heaney**, 23 East Trinity Rd, Edinburgh, **Edinburgh (City of)**, EH5 3DL, SCO.
(T) 01315 521510 (F) 01313 362907
Speciality: Chiropodists (Podiatrists).
● **Owner** Ms J Heaney
[S] (Ref:HM09435)

## HEANOR CHIROPRACTIC CLINIC

**Heanor Chiropractic Clinic**, 33 Mundy St, Heanor, **Derbyshire**, DE75 7EB, ENG.
(T) 01773 762346
Speciality: Chiropractic.
● **Owner** Mr S Knighton
[P] [S] [T] (Ref:HM09436)

## HEANOR PHYSIO & SPORTS

**Heanor Physiotherapy & Sports Injury Clinic**, 7 Mundy St, Heanor, **Derbyshire**, DE75 7EB, ENG.
(T) 01773 714020
Speciality: Physiotherapy.
[P] [S] [T] (Ref:HM09437)

## HEARN, JUNE

**June Hearn**, Tadworth, **Surrey**, KT20 5SA, ENG.
(T) 07889 428567
Speciality: Psychotherapy.
● **Owner** Mrs J Hearn
[B] (Ref:HM09438)

## HEARN, LORRAINE

**Lorraine Hearn**, 80 Beaconfield Rd, Plymouth, **Devon**, PL2 3LG, ENG.
(T) 01752 779635 (F) 01752 779635
Speciality: Chiropodists (Podiatrists).
● **Owner** Mrs L Hearn
[S] (Ref:HM09439)

## HEARNE, BRIAN

**Brian Hearne**, 5 Haywood Drive, Fleet, **Hampshire**, GU13 9SZ, ENG.
(T) 01252 617399
Speciality: Chiropody. [✔]
● **Chiropodist** Mr B Hearne **Q:** SMAE. **M:** B.A.Ch.P, SMAE.
[M] Yrs. Est.: 12 (Ref:HM09440)

## HEART & SOUL

**Heart & Soul**, 3 Stafford Hill Lane, Huddersfield, **Yorkshire (West)**, HD5 0EE, ENG.
(T) 01484 303264
Speciality: Complementary Medicines & Therapy.
● **Owner** Mrs J Booth
[C] [M] (Ref:HM09441)

## HEART OF ENGLAND SHIATSU

**Heart Of England Shiatsu**, 23 Albert St, Warwick, **Warwickshire**, CV34 4JX, ENG.
(T) 01926 492880
(E) heartofengland-shiatsu@yahoo.co.uk
Speciality: Counselling, Do-In, Macrobiotics, Nutritional Therapy, Oriental Diagnosis, Shiatsu, Yoga, Shiatsu Training, Meridian Exercise Classes, Lay Knowledge In Shiatsu. [✔]
● **Shiatsu Practitioner** Ms S Caunce **Q:** MRSS(t). **M:** Shiatsu Society UK.
[H] Yrs. Est.: 20 (Ref:HM09442)

## HEART TO HEART

**Heart To Heart**, 21 Norbeck Lane, Welton, Lincoln, **Lincolnshire**, LN2 3JP, ENG.
(T) 01673 862913
(E) beth@siriusconnection.com
(W) www.siriusconnection.com
Speciality: Bach Remedies, Crystal Healing, Healer, Holistic Healing, Homeopathy, Hypnotherapy, Paranormal Therapies, Reiki, Spiritual Healing, Stress Therapy, Astrology, Dreamwork, Soul Psychology. [✔]



Key continued: **Yrs.Est:** Years Established **Q:** Qualifications **M:** Professional Membership [✔] Indemnity Insurance [CREDIT] Accept Credit Cards

● **Healer/Therapist** Ms B Summers **Q:** NFSH. **M:** NFSH.
**B H P** Yrs. Est.: 15 (**Ref:**HM09443)

## HEARTLAKE PHYSIOTHERAPY
**Heartlake Physiotherapy**, 55 St Meddans St, Troon, **Ayrshire (South)**, KA10 6NN, SCO.
(T) 01292 318777
Speciality: Acupuncture, Physiotherapy. ✔
● **Physiotherapist/Owner** Mr A McLeod **Q:** MCSP, SRP. **M:** CSP.
**S** (**Ref:**HM09444)

## HEARTLANDS
**Anna-May Silvestro**, 28 Southlea Avenue, Leamington Spa, **Warwickshire**, CV31 3JN, ENG.
(T) 01926 883391
(E) annamay@easicom.com
Speciality: Acupressure, Acupuncture, Aversion Therapy, Counselling, Herbal Medicine, Meditation, Moxibustion, Music Therapy, Neuro-Linguistic Program, Nutritional Therapy, Oriental Diagnosis, Reiki, Seichem, Shiatsu, Silva Method, Stress Therapy, Visualisation Therapy, Vitamin Therapy, Ying & Yang, Yoga. ✔
● **Stress Consultant** Ms A Silvestro **Q:** Cert.Ed, Lic.Ac, MASC. **M:** ASC.
**C** Yrs. Est.: 10 (**Ref:**HM09445)

## HEATH HEALTH CARE
**Heath Health Care**, 5 Elm Ter, Constantine Rd, London, **London (Greater)**, NW3 2LL, ENG.
(T) 020 7267 4222
Speciality: Complementary Medicines & Therapy.
● **Owner** Ms L Greenwall
**M** (**Ref:**HM09446)

## HEATH HEALTH CARE CENTRE
**Heath Health Care Centre**, 5 Elm Trce, Constantine Rd, London, **London (Greater)**, NW3 2LL, ENG.
(T) 020 7267 4222
Speciality: Acupuncture, Chiropody, Chiropractic, Complementary Therapy, Osteopathy, Pilates.
● **Owner** Mr R Kiashek
**P S T** (**Ref:**HM09447)

## HEATH HEALTH CARE PHYSIO
**Heath Health Care Physiotherapy**, 5 Elm Trce, Constantine Rd, London, **London (Greater)**, NW3 2LL, ENG.
(T) 020 7267 8068
Speciality: Physiotherapy.
**P S T** (**Ref:**HM09448)

## HEATH MOUNT PHYSIOTHERAPY
**Heath Mount Physiotherapy**, 15 Heath Mount, Halifax, **Yorkshire (West)**, HX1 2YR, ENG.
(T) 01422 342649
Speciality: Physiotherapy.
● **Manager** Mr P Leary
**P S T** (**Ref:**HM09449)

## HEATH ROAD CLINIC
**Heath Road Clinic**, 53 Heath Rd, Maidstone, **Kent**, ME16 9LD, ENG.
(T) 01622 728306
Speciality: Physiotherapy.
**P S T** (**Ref:**HM09450)

## HEATH ROYD GARDEN PRACTICE
**Heath Royd Garden Practice**, 4 Toller Drive, Bradford, **Yorkshire (West)**, BD9 5NU, ENG.
(T) 01274 493125
Speciality: Alexander Technique.
● **Therapist** Dr C Heenan
**P S** (**Ref:**HM09451)

## HEATH, DAVID
**David Heath**, 2 Garfield Avenue, Stoke-On-Trent, **Staffordshire**, ST4 8ES, ENG.
(T) 01782 658555
Speciality: Osteopathy.
● **Partner** Mr D Heath
**P S T** (**Ref:**HM09452)

## HEATH, J
**Mrs J Heath**, 93 Loddon Bridge Rd, Woodley, Reading, **Berkshire**, RG5 4AE, ENG.
(T) 01189 697769
Speciality: Chiropractors.
● **Owner** Mr R Swaine
**P S T** (**Ref:**HM09453)

## HEATH, SUSAN
**Earth Wisdom**, Dolphin Pl, 41 Chenies Avenue, Little Chalfont, Amersham, **Buckinghamshire**, HP6 6PP, ENG.
(T) 01494 762029 (F) 01494 762029
(E) susiejheath@hotmail.com
Speciality: Absent Healing, Complementary Therapy, Dance Movement Therapy, Healing Therapy, Indian Head Massage, Life Style Coaching, Meditation, Music Therapy, Reiki, Personal, Professional/Corporate Life-Coaching. ✔
● **Director** Ms S Heath **Q:** Cert.Ed, Dip.Ed, Reiki Master.
**B** Yrs. Est.: 3 (**Ref:**HM09454)

## HEATHER MIXTURE
**Heather Mixture**, 10 Howard St, Kilmarnock, **Ayrshire (East)**, KA1 2BP, SCO.
(T) 01563 540819
Speciality: Complementary Medicines & Therapy.
**M** (**Ref:**HM09455)

## HEATHER, GRANT
**Grant Heather**, Cannon Sports Club, Odhams Walk, Endell St, London, **London (Greater)**, WC2H 9SA, ENG.
(T) 020 7497 8974
Speciality: Physiotherapy.
● **Principal** Ms H Grant
**P S T** (**Ref:**HM09456)

## HEATHER, LUCKY
**Lucky Heather**, 43 Chester Rd, Ilford, **Essex**, IG3 8PT, ENG.
(T) 020 8599 6013
Speciality: Clairvoyants & Palmists.
● **Owner** Miss K Murray
**B** (**Ref:**HM09457)

## HEATHFIELD CHIROPRACTIC CLINIC
**Heathfield Chiropractic Clinic**, Cave Cottage, Alexandra Rd, Heathfield, **Sussex (East)**, TN21 8EE, ENG.
(T) 01435 863212
Speciality: Chiropractic.
● **Owner** Mr R Rumary
**P S T** (**Ref:**HM09458)

## HEATHROW OSTEOPATHIC CLINIC
**Heathrow Osteopathic Clinic**, 47 Boltons Lane, Hayes, **London (Greater)**, UB3 5BS, ENG.
(T) 020 8564 9943
Speciality: Osteopathy.
**P S T** (**Ref:**HM09459)

## HEATH-RUMINSKA, PAULINE (DR)
**Dr Pauline Heath-Ruminska**, Flat D, 9 Elizabeth Court, Grove Rd, Bournemouth, **Dorset**, BH1 3DT, ENG.
(T) 01202 296269
Speciality: Acupuncture.
● **Owner** Dr P Heath-Ruminska
**O** (**Ref:**HM09460)

## HEATHSIDE CENTRE
**Heathside Centre For Health & Healing**, Heathside, 3 Hillcrest Rd, Dartford, **Kent**, DA1 3QN, ENG.
(T) 01322 524854 (F) 01322 524854
Speciality: Acupuncture, Aromatherapy, Chiropractic, Hopi Ear Candles, Indian Head Massage, Manual Lymph Drainage, Massage (Therapeutic), Reflexology, Reiki. ✔ CREDIT
● **Holistic Therapist** Ms J Quick
**C** Yrs. Est.: 3 (**Ref:**HM09461)

## HEATHSIDE PHYSIOTHERAPY DEPT
**Heathside Physiotherapy Department**, Heath Rd, Coxheath, Maidstone, **Kent**, ME17 4AH, ENG.
(T) 01622 741860 (F) 01622 749179
Speciality: Physiotherapy.
**P S T** (**Ref:**HM09462)

## HEATHVILLE CLINIC
**Heathville Clinic (The)**, 11 Heathville Rd, Gloucester, **Gloucestershire**, GL1 3DS, ENG.
(T) 01452 308799
Speciality: Osteopathy.
**P S T** (**Ref:**HM09463)

## HEATON PARK PHYSIO & SPORTS
**Heaton Park Physiotherapy & Sports Injury Clinic**, 121 Bury Old Rd, Prestwich, Manchester, **Manchester (Greater)**, M25 0EQ, ENG.
(T) 01617 731508
Speciality: Physiotherapy.
**P S T** (**Ref:**HM09464)

## HEATON, BARBARA
**Barbara Heaton**, 2 North St, Holywell Green, Halifax, **Yorkshire (West)**, HX4 9AX, ENG.
(T) 01422 371454
Speciality: Chiropodists (Podiatrists).
**S** (**Ref:**HM09465)

## HEATON, J
**J Heaton J**, Hailsham Lagoon Leisure Centre, Vicarage Lane, Hailsham, **Sussex (East)**, BN27 2AX, ENG.
(T) 01323 846755 (F) 01323 844731
Speciality: Complementary Medicines & Therapy.
● **Manager** Miss J Kelly
**M** (**Ref:**HM09466)

## HEATON, J M
**J M Heaton**, 41 Buckland Cres, London, **London (Greater)**, NW3 5DH, ENG.
(T) 020 7722 7428
Speciality: Psychiatry.
**B** (**Ref:**HM09467)

## HEATON, LYNDA
**Lynda Heaton**, 4 Milton Cl, Hawk Green, Marple, Stockport, **Cheshire**, SK6 7JT, ENG.
(T) 01614 277003
Speciality: Complementary Medicines & Therapy.
● **Owner** Ms L Heaton
**C M** (**Ref:**HM09468)

## HEATON, S
**S Heaton**, 1 Parkhills Rd, Bury, **Lancashire**, BL9 9AU, ENG.
(T) 01617 611835
Speciality: Physiotherapy.
● **Owner** Mrs S Heaton
**P S T** (**Ref:**HM09469)

## HEAVE, M & HUMPHREY, V
**Heavey M S Maeve Humphrey Val M R S**, Occupational Health Centre, Telford & District, Halesfield 13, Telford, **Shropshire**, TF7 4QP, ENG.
(T) 01952 581251
Speciality: Acupuncture.
**O** (**Ref:**HM09470)

## HEAVEN & EARTH
**Heaven & Earth**, Hexham Rd, Newcastle Upon Tyne, **Tyne and Wear**, NE15 9BT, ENG.
(T) 01912 646224
Speciality: Complementary Medicines & Therapy.
● **Owner** Mr W Scott
**M** (**Ref:**HM09471)

## HEAVEN MOUNTAIN TAIJI QUAN
**Heaven Mountain Taiji Quan**, P O Box 49, Tadworth, **Surrey**, KT20 5YP, ENG.
(T) 01737 813686
(E) paul@heavenmountain.co.uk
Speciality: Complementary Medicines & Therapy, Buqi - non contact energetic healing, Therapeutic exercise. ✔
● **Owner** Mr P Brewer **M:** TCUGB.
**C P** Yrs. Est.: 16 (**Ref:**HM09472)

## HEAVEN SCENT
**Heaven Scent**, 18A Pilkington Buildings, Roman Rd, Middlesbrough, **Cleveland**, TS5 6DY, ENG.
(T) 01642 650688
Speciality: Aromatherapy.
● **Owner** Ms H Forman
**M O** (**Ref:**HM09473)

## HEAVEN SCENT
**Heaven Scent (UK)**, 82 All Saints Rd, Kings Heath, Birmingham, **Midlands (West)**, B14 7LN, ENG.
(T) 01216 243422
Speciality: Aromatherapy.
**M O** (**Ref:**HM09474)



Key: **B** Mind-Body Medicine **C** Complementary Medicine **H** Self Help Treatment **M** Medicinal Therapy **O** Oriental Medicine **P** Postural Therapy **S** Manipulative Structural Therapy **T** Touch Therapy

## HEAVEN SCENT HOLISTIC THERAPY

**Heaven Scent Holistic Therapy Centre**, 11 Railway Rd, Darwen, **Lancashire**, BB3 2RG, ENG.
(T) 01254 763686 (F) 01254 763686
Speciality: Complementary Medicines & Therapy.
● **Owner** Mrs K Wiggans
M (Ref:HM09475)

## HEAVENLY BODIES

**Heavenly Bodies**, Marlwood Pl, Broughton, Chester, **Cheshire**, CH4 0PB, ENG.
(T) 01244 535444
Speciality: Aromatherapy.
● **Owner** Mrs L Rowley
M O (Ref:HM09476)

## HEAVENLY SPIRIT CENTRE

**Heavenly Spirit Centre**, 201 Seabourne Rd, Bournemouth, **Dorset**, BH5 2HJ, ENG.
(T) 01202 430781
Speciality: Complementary Medicines & Therapy.
● **Owner** Mrs H Saunders
M (Ref:HM09477)

## HEAVENS SCENT AROMATHERAPY

**Heavens Scent Aromatherapy**, 542A Chorley Old Rd, Bolton, **Lancashire**, BL11 6AB, ENG.
(T) 01204 494809
Speciality: Aromatherapy, Massage (Therapeutic). ✔
● **Aromatherapist** Ms J Oldroyd Q: Dip.Arom, NVQ L3. M: IFA.
T Yrs. Est.: 4 (Ref:HM09478)

## HEAVENS, SUSAN

**Susan Heavens**, 18 Lynton Avenue, London, **London (Greater)**, W13 0EB, ENG.
(T) 020 8998 1804
Speciality: Reflexology.
S T (Ref:HM09479)

## HEAVENZ AROMA HOME VISITING

**Heavenz Aroma Home Visiting & Mobile**, 17 Pembroke Rd, London, **London (Greater)**, N15 4NN, ENG.
(T) 020 8808 4445
Speciality: Aromatherapy.
M O (Ref:HM09480)

## HEAVEY, BRIDGET

**Heavey Bridget DIP AC LIC AC**, Lr Eyre St, Newbridge, **County Kildare**, IRE.
(T) 04543 1033
Speciality: Acupuncture.
O (Ref:HM09481)

## HEAVEY, MAEVE

**Heavey Ms Maeve**, Stanhope Surgery, Stanhope Rd, Waltham Cross, **Hertfordshire**, EN8 7DJ, ENG.
(T) 01992 635300
Speciality: Acupuncture.
O (Ref:HM09482)

## HEAVITREE CHIROPRACTIC CENTRE

**Heavitree Chiropractic Centre**, 15 Heavitree Rd, Exeter, **Devon**, EX1 2LD, ENG.
(T) 01392 421700
Speciality: Chiropractic.
P S T (Ref:HM09483)

## HEAYNS, C H

**C H Heayns**, Newport Pagnell Medical Centre, Queens Avenue, Newport Pagnell, **Buckinghamshire**, MK16 8QT, ENG.
(T) 01604 239385
Speciality: Chiropodists (Podiatrists).
● **Owner** Mr C Heayns
S (Ref:HM09484)

## HEBARIUM

**Hebarium (The)**, 3 Allport La Precinct, Wirral, **Merseyside**, CH62 7HH, ENG.
(T) 01513 349627
Speciality: Herbalists.
● **Owner** Mr H Griggs
M (Ref:HM09485)

## HEBBLETHWAITE, PRISCILLA

**Mrs Priscilla Hebblethwaite**, 40 The Southend, Ledbury, **Herefordshire**, HR8 2HD, ENG.
(T) 01531 632502
Speciality: Alexander Technique.
● **Owner** Mrs P Hebblethwaite
P S (Ref:HM09486)

## HEBDEN BRIDGE CENTRE

**Hebden Bridge Centre For Counselling And Psychotherapy (The)**, MacHpelah Works, Burnley Rd, Hebden Bridge, **Yorkshire (West)**, HX7 8AU, ENG.
(T) 01422 823828
(E) sue.canon@lineone.net
Speciality: Cognitive Therapy, Counselling, Gestalt Therapy, Group Therapy, Humanistic Psychology, Psychotherapy, Rogerian Therapy, Transactional Analysis. ✔
● **Therapist/Counsellor** Ms S Canon Q: Dip.Adv.Couns, MA. M: BACP, UKCP, UKRC.
● **Therapist/Counsellor** Ms D Farooq
(T) 01274 601850 Q: BA (Hons). M: BACP, SPTI.
H Yrs. Est.: 4 (Ref:HM09487)

## HEBDEN BRIDGE CHIROPODISTS

**Hebden Bridge Chiropodists**, Library Buildings, Hope St, Hebden Bridge, **Yorkshire (West)**, HX7 8AG, ENG.
(T) 01422 361971
Speciality: Chiropodists (Podiatrists).
● **Partner** Mrs E Hurst
S (Ref:HM09488)

## HEBDEN BRIDGE-REG CHIROP

**Hebden Bridge State Registered Chiropodists**, Hope St, Heptonstall, Hebden Bridge, **Yorkshire (West)**, HX7 7HA, ENG.
(T) 01422 846131
Speciality: Chiropodists (Podiatrists).
S (Ref:HM09489)

## HEDDLE, R

**R Heddle**, Ashford Clinic Of Complementary Medicine, 11 Western Avenue, Ashford, **Kent**, TN23 1LY, ENG.
(T) 01233 631530
Speciality: Complementary Medicines & Therapy.
M (Ref:HM09490)

## HEDERMAN, LINDA

**Hederman Linda**, Harolds X, Dublin, **County Dublin**, IRE.
(T) 01496 3843
Speciality: Complementary Medicines & Therapy.
M (Ref:HM09491)

## HEDGE END CHIROPRACTIC CLINIC

**Hedge End Chiropractic Clinic**, Unit 6, Hedge End Business Centre, Botley Rd, Hedge End, Southampton, **Hampshire**, SO30 2AU, ENG.
(T) 01489 797322 (F) 01489 797322
Speciality: Chiropractic.
● **Owner** Miss S Donald
P S T (Ref:HM09492)

## HEDGE, P

**P Hedge**, 3 Kennett, Lincombe Drive, Torquay, **Devon**, TQ1 2LP, ENG.
(T) 01803 211102
Speciality: Chiropodists (Podiatrists).
S (Ref:HM09493)

## HEDGEFIELD HOUSE

**Hedgefield House**, Stella Rd, Blaydon-on-Tyne, **Tyne and Wear**, NE21 4LR, ENG.
(T) 01914 136773
Speciality: Hypnotherapy.
● **Owner** Mr D Wood
B (Ref:HM09494)

## HEDGES, CECILY

**Cecily Hedges**, Cwmhawen Fach, Llangranog, Llandysul, **Carmarthenshire**, SA44 6AL, WAL.
(T) 01239 654386 (F) 01239 654386
Speciality: Psychotherapy.
● **Owner** Mrs C Hedges
B (Ref:HM09495)

## HEDLEY HILL HEALTH SERVICES

**Hedley Hill Health Services**, Hedley Hill Villa, Hedley Hill, Durham, **County Durham**, DH7 9EX, ENG.
(T) 01913 734376
Speciality: Osteopathy.
M (Ref:HM09496)

## HEDLEY, J H

**J H Hedley**, 1561 London Rd, London, **London (Greater)**, SW16 4AD, ENG.
(T) 020 8764 9284
Speciality: Chiropodists (Podiatrists).
● **Owner** Mr J Hedley
S (Ref:HM09497)

## HEELER CENTRE

**Heeler Centre (The)**, Bridge House, Station Approach East, Hassocks, **Sussex (West)**, BN6 8HN, ENG.
(T) 01273 843780 (F) 01273 843780
(E) paul@heeler.freeserve.co.uk
(W) www.heeler.co.uk
Speciality: Acupressure, Acupuncture, Aromatherapy, Bach Remedies, Bowen Therapy, Chiropody, Complementary Therapy, Counselling, Cranial Osteopathy, Cupping, Dietician, Homeopathy, Hypnosis, Hypnotherapy, Indian Head Massage, Manipulation, Massage (Therapeutic), Naturopathy, Nutritional Therapy, Osteopathy, Pilates, Podiatry, Postural Integration, Psychotherapy, Reflexology, Reiki, Shiatsu, Sports Massage, Vitamin Therapy, Yoga. ✔
● **Osteopath** Mr P Heeler
(T) 01273 843140 Q: BSc, Hons (OST). M: GOsC.
S Yrs. Est.: 4 (Ref:HM09498)

## HEENAN, M C

**M C Heenan**, 11 Milford Pl, Bradford, **Yorkshire (West)**, BD9 4RU, ENG.
(T) 01274 493125
Speciality: Psychotherapy.
B (Ref:HM09499)

## HEFFERNAN, EILEEN

**Eileen Heffernan**, 50 High St, Hastings, **Sussex (East)**, TN34 3EN, ENG.
(T) 01424 465050
Speciality: Reflexology.
● **Partner** Ms E Heffernan
S T (Ref:HM09500)

## HEFFERNAN, JOE

**Heffernan Joe BA MA Dip REM ED**, Glenside Boherbue, Mallow, **County Cork**, IRE.
(T) 029 7661 7
Speciality: Psychotherapy.
B (Ref:HM09501)

## HEFFERNAN, LINDA

**Heffernan Linda Lic Ac**, 6 St Brendans Rd, Woodquay, **County Galway**, IRE.
(T) 09156 1676
Speciality: Acupuncture.
O (Ref:HM09502)

## HEGARTY, TOM

**Hegarty Tom B A(Hons)(Psych) MA (Couns Psych)**, Douglas, **County Cork**, IRE.
(T) 021 4365 409
Speciality: Psychology.
B (Ref:HM09503)

## HEHIR, K

**K Hehir**, 6a Sloane Sq, London, **London (Greater)**, SW1W 8EE, ENG.
(T) 020 7730 8437
Speciality: Chiropodists (Podiatrists).
S (Ref:HM09504)

## HEHIR, S

**S Hehir**, 129 Sheen Rd, Richmond, **Surrey**, TW9 1YJ, ENG.
(T) 020 8332 2395
Speciality: Chiropractic.
P S T (Ref:HM09505)

## HEIB, L G

**L G Heib**, 51 Common Rd, Chandler's Ford, Eastleigh, **Hampshire**, SO53 1HG, ENG.
(T) 023 8026 9809
Speciality: Osteopathy.
● **Owner** Mr L Heib
P S T (Ref:HM09506)

## HEIMER, F

**F Heimer**, 353 Norton Rd, Stockton-On-Tees, **Cleveland**, TS20 2PH, ENG.


Key continued: Yrs.Est: Years Established Q: Qualifications M: Professional Membership ✔ Indemnity Insurance Accept Credit Cards

(T) 01642 360153
Speciality: Osteopathy.
P S T (Ref:HM09507)

## HEIMISCHE CLINIC

**Heimische Clinic**, 478 Great Cheetham St East, Salford, **Manchester (Greater)**, M7 4TW, ENG.
(T) 01617 080110 (F) 01617 080110
Speciality: Complementary Medicines & Therapy.
● **Partner** Mr M Liverman
C M (Ref:HM09508)

## HELEN BENFIELD HEALER & CLAIR

**Helen Benfield Healer & Clairvoyant**, Beggars Roost, Christchurch Rd, New Milton, **Hampshire**, BH25 6QF, ENG.
(T) 01425 612096
Speciality: Clairvoyants & Palmists.
B (Ref:HM09509)

## HELEN BENTLEY COMP THERAPIST

**Helen Bentley Complementary Therapist**, 41 Gladstone St, Normanton, **Yorkshire (West)**, WF6 2HJ, ENG.
(T) 01924 893983
Speciality: Aromatherapy, Indian Head Massage, Massage (Therapeutic), Reflexology.
M O (Ref:HM09510)

## HELEN BERNAT - FITNESS TRAINER

**Helen Bernat - Fitness Trainer**, 97 Grove Park Rd, Chiswick, London, **London (Greater)**, W4 3QD, ENG.
(T) 020 8995 7746 (F) 020 8995 7746
(E) fithelen@hotmail.com
Speciality: Massage (Therapeutic), Personal Training. ✓
● **Personal Trainer** Ms H Bernat Q: ITEC, RSA.
H Yrs. Est.: 6 (Ref:HM09511)

## HELEN C OTTAWAY-FOSTER

**Helen C Ottaway-Foster**, 2 Leyland Rd, Bulkington, Bedworth, **Warwickshire**, CV12 9LW, ENG.
(T) 024 7649 0149
Speciality: Hypnosis.
B (Ref:HM09512)

## HELEN MCCORMACK MED HERB

**Helen McCormack Medical Herbalist**, 186 Philipsburgh Ave, Marino, Dublin, **County Dublin**, IRE.
(T) 01836 8965
Speciality: Herbalists.
● **Medical Herbalist** Ms H McCormack Q: MNIMH.
M (Ref:HM09513)

## HELEN N SERVICE

**Helen N Service**, Bullburn, Drumnadrochit, Inverness, **Highland**, IV63 6XL, SCO.
(T) 01456 450556 (F) 01456 450109
Speciality: Chiropodists (Podiatrists).
● **Owner** Ms H Service
S (Ref:HM09514)

## HELEN SMITH CHIROPODIST

**Helen Smith Chiropodist**, The Surgery, Hillyfields Way, Winscombe, **Somerset**, BS25 1AF, ENG.
(T) 01934 842276
Speciality: Chiropody. ✓
● **Owner/Chiropodist** Ms H Smith Q: M.S.C.P, S.R.Ch. M: S.C.P.
M Yrs. Est.: 23 (Ref:HM09515)

## HELEN, MACAULAY

**MacAulay Helen**, 38 Prospect Lane, Solihull, **Midlands (West)**, B91 1HN, ENG.
(T) 01217 444240
Speciality: Reflexology.
● **Owner** Mrs H MacAuley
S T (Ref:HM09516)

## HELESFAY-EVANS, JO

**Jo Helesfay-Evans**, Pear Tree Barn, North Rd, Bodle St, Hailsham, **Sussex (East)**, BN27 4RH, ENG.
(T) 01323 831547
Speciality: Reflexology.
S T (Ref:HM09517)

## HELIANTHUS PRACTICE

**Marliese Symons**, 12 Farleigh Rd, Selsdon, Croydon, **Surrey**, CR2 8PB, ENG.
(T) 020 8651 6704 (F) 020 8651 6704
(E) m.symons@tesco.net
(W) www.helianthus.org
Speciality: Bach Remedies, Counselling, Herbal Medicine, Holistic Healing, Homeopathy, Nutritional Therapy, Phytotherapy. ✓
● **Homeopathic Practitioner**
Ms M Symons Q: BSc, RSHom. M: Soc.Hom.
B Yrs. Est.: 7 (Ref:HM09518)

## HELIOS CENTRE

**Helios Centre (The)**, 63 Collier St, London, **London (Greater)**, N1 9BE, ENG.
(T) 020 7713 7120 (F) 020 7837 1850
Speciality: Complementary Medicines & Therapy.
● **Director** Mr G Branson
C M (Ref:HM09519)

## HELIOS HOMOEOPATHIC CLINIC

**Helios Homoeopathic Clinic**, 97A Camden Rd, Tunbridge Wells, **Kent**, TN1 2QR, ENG.
(T) 01892 510950
Speciality: Homeopathy.
M (Ref:HM09520)

## HELIX CENTRE

**Helix Centre (The)**, 27 Bridge St, Loughborough, **Leicestershire**, LE11 1NH, ENG.
(T) 01162 838510
Speciality: Acupuncture, Alexander Technique, Aromatherapy, Cranio-Sacral Therapy, Healing Therapy, Herbal Medicine, Homeopathy, Hypnosis, Indian Head Massage, Iridology, Kinesiology, Massage (Therapeutic), McTimoney Chiropractic, Reflexology, Reiki, Remedial Massage, Spiritual Healing.
● **Administrator** Mr P Snow
C (Ref:HM09521)

## HELIX HOUSE

**Helix House**, Helix House, 15 Warwick St, Oxford, **Oxfordshire**, OX4 1SZ, ENG.
(T) 01865 243351
(E) helix@helixhouse.co.uk
(W) www.helixhouse.co.uk
Speciality: Cranial Osteopathy, Healing Therapy, Holistic Healing, Kinesiology, Neuro-Linguistic Program, Nutritional Therapy, Osteopathy, Psychotherapy, Spiritual Healing, Astrological Psychology, Transpersonal Psychotherapy/Counselling. ✓ CREDIT
● **Director/Practitioner**
Mr C Lindley-Jones Q: B.Ed, DIBAK, DO. M: GOsC.
● **Director/Practitioner**
Mrs K Lindley-Jones Q: MA. M: UKCP.
● **Osteopath** Mr T Bedford Q: BA (Hons), BSc, Hons (OST). M: GOsC.
● **Osteopath** Ms G Gautreau Q: DO. M: GOsC.
S Yrs. Est.: 18 (Ref:HM09522)

## HELLON-HARRIS, HUGH

**Hugh Hellon-Harris**, 21 Manor Rd North, Wallington, **Surrey**, SM6 7NS, ENG.
(T) 020 8647 2452 (F) 020 8669 7742
Speciality: Osteopathy.
● **Owner** Mr H Hellon-Harris
P S T (Ref:HM09523)

## HELLY'S HERBAL PRODUCTS

**Helly's Herbal Products**, Chandlers Yard, Ludhan Bridge Boatyard, Johnsons St, Ludham, Great Yarmouth, **Norfolk**, NR29 5NY, ENG.
(T) 01692 631170 (F) 01692 631172
Speciality: Aromatherapy.
● **Owner** Ms H Simons
M O (Ref:HM09524)

## HELM, HEATHER

**Heather Helm**, 35 Whittington Rd, Hutton, Brentwood, **Essex**, CM13 1JY, ENG.
(T) 01277 217847
Speciality: Complementary Medicines & Therapy.
● **Owner** Mrs H Helm
M (Ref:HM09525)

## HELSDON, E S

**E S Helsdon**, 53 York Rd, Tadcaster, **Yorkshire (North)**, LS24 8AE, ENG.
(T) 01937 834200
Speciality: Chiropodists (Podiatrists).
S (Ref:HM09526)

## HEMEL CHIROPRACTIC CLINIC

**Hemel Chiropractic Clinic**, 149 London Rd, Hemel Hempstead, **Hertfordshire**, HP3 9SQ, ENG.
(T) 01442 231500
Speciality: Chiropractic.
● **Owner** Dr D Cruzan
P S T (Ref:HM09527)

## HEMINGWAY, I

**I Hemingway**, 16 Brewerton Lane, Dewsbury, **Yorkshire (West)**, WF13 4PB, ENG.
(T) 01924 401807
Speciality: Chiropodists (Podiatrists).
S (Ref:HM09528)

## HEMINGWAY, IMOGEN

**Imogen Hemingway**, 7 Alexandra St, Eastwood, Nottingham, **Nottinghamshire**, NG16 3BD, ENG.
(T) 01773 530454
Speciality: Osteopathy.
P S T (Ref:HM09529)

## HEMINGWAY, JANET

**Janet Hemingway**, 8 Queen St, Horbury, Wakefield, **Yorkshire (West)**, WF4 6LP, ENG.
(T) 01924 264690
Speciality: Chiropodists (Podiatrists).
● **Owner** Mrs J Hemingway
S (Ref:HM09530)

## HEMINGWAY, JENNY

**Jenny Hemingway**, 262 Caledonian Rd, London, **London (Greater)**, N1 0NG, ENG.
(T) 020 7837 5045
Speciality: Osteopathy.
P S T (Ref:HM09531)

## HEMINGWAY, T

**T Hemingway**, 11 Clifton Hill, Exeter, **Devon**, EX1 2DL, ENG.
(T) 01392 279317
Speciality: Alexander Technique.
● **Partner** Mr R Wells
P S (Ref:HM09532)

## HEMMENS, JANE

**Jane Hemmens**, 68 Poynters Rd, Luton, **Bedfordshire**, LU4 0LA, ENG.
(T) 01582 606893
Speciality: Reflexology.
S T (Ref:HM09533)

## HEMMERMAN, I A

**I A Hemmerman**, 12 Fields Rd, Newport, NP20 4PJ, WAL.
(T) 01633 246821 (F) 01633 246821
Speciality: Homeopathy.
● **Practice Manager**
Mrs S Ambrozejczyk
M (Ref:HM09534)

## HEMMERMAN, J L

**J L Hemmerman**, 12 Fields Rd, Newport, NP20 4PJ, WAL.
(T) 01633 246821 (F) 01633 246821
Speciality: Physiotherapy.
● **Practice Manager**
Mrs S Ambrozejczyk
P S T (Ref:HM09535)

## HEMMINGS, RITA

**Rita Hemmings**, 396 Gloucester Rd, Cheltenham, **Gloucestershire**, GL51 7TB, ENG.
(T) 01242 513459
Speciality: Chiropractic.
● **Owner** Mrs R Hemmings
P S T (Ref:HM09536)

## HEMMINGWAY CHIROPODIST

**Hemmingway Chiropodist**, 9 Cotswold Cl, Eastbourne, **Sussex (East)**, BN23 8HH, ENG.
(T) 01323 460179
Speciality: Chiropody. ✓
● **Chiropodist (Podiatrist)**
Mrs S Hemmingway Q: MBChA, MSSCh.
M: S.C.P.
C M Yrs. Est.: 11 (Ref:HM09537)



Key: B Mind-Body Medicine C Complementary Medicine H Self Help Treatment M Medicinal Therapy O Oriental Medicine P Postural Therapy S Manipulative Structural Therapy T Touch Therapy

**HEMSLEY, SARAH**
**Sarah Hemsley**, Rushlye Oast, Bells Yew Green, Tunbridge Wells, **Kent**, TN3 9AP, ENG.
(T) 01892 750970
Speciality: Reflexology.
S T (Ref:HM09538)

**HEMSTEAD, JOHN S**
**Mr John S Hemstead**, 27 College Rd, Ringwood, **Hampshire**, BH24 1NU, ENG.
(T) 01425 479440
Speciality: Hypnosis.
B (Ref:HM09539)

**HENCHER, CAROLINE**
**Caroline Hencher**, 71 Leckhampton Rd, Cheltenham, **Gloucestershire**, GL53 0BS, ENG.
(T) 01242 572406
Speciality: Acupuncture.
● **Owner** Miss C Hencher
O (Ref:HM09540)

**HENCHER, CAROLINE**
**Caroline Hencher**, Cheltenham Holistic Centre, 66 Suffolk Rd, Cheltenham, **Gloucestershire**, GL50 2ED, ENG.
(T) 01242 584140
Speciality: Acupuncture.
O (Ref:HM09541)

**HENCHY, C L**
**C L Henchy**, Aluna Holistic Health Centre, Hescott House, 26 Lyndhurst Rd, Manchester, **Manchester (Greater)**, M20 6AA, ENG.
(T) 01614 453860
Speciality: Homeopathy.
M (Ref:HM09542)

**HENDEN, CHRIS**
**Chris Henden**, 84 Dunsmore Rd, Luton, **Bedfordshire**, LU1 5JY, ENG.
(T) 01582 454252
Speciality: Psychotherapy.
● **Owner** Mr C Henden
B (Ref:HM09543)

**HENDERSON, DAVID**
**David Henderson**, 116 Marlborough Rd, London, **London (Greater)**, N19 4NN, ENG.
(T) 020 7281 6219 (F) 020 7281 6219
Speciality: Psychotherapy.
● **Owner** Mr D Henderson
B (Ref:HM09544)

**HENDERSON, DAVID**
**David Henderson**, 1 Broadsands Walk, Gosport, **Hampshire**, PO12 2TS, ENG.
(T) 023 9258 6165
Speciality: Hypnosis.
B (Ref:HM09545)

**HENDERSON, DAVID**
**David Henderson**, Basement Flat, 16 Marlborough Rd, London, **London (Greater)**, N19 4NB, ENG.
(T) 020 7281 6219
Speciality: Psychotherapy.
B (Ref:HM09546)

**HENDERSON, H M**
**H M Henderson**, 80 Queens Rd, Penarth, **Glamorgan (Vale of)**, CF64 1DJ, WAL.
(T) 029 2070 7221
Speciality: Herbal Medicine.
● **Owner** Mrs H Henderson
M (Ref:HM09547)

**HENDERSON, I A**
**I A Henderson**, 17 Prestonhall Rd, Glenrothes, **Fife**, KY7 5RL, SCO.
(T) 01592 610940
Speciality: Chiropodists (Podiatrists).
● **Owner** Miss I Henderson
S (Ref:HM09548)

**HENDERSON, IRENE**
**Irene Henderson**, 84 Silver St, Newport Pagnell, **Buckinghamshire**, MK16 0EG, ENG.
(T) 01908 616840 (F) 01908 616840
Speciality: Physiotherapy.
● **Owner** Mrs I Henderson
P S T (Ref:HM09549)

**HENDERSON, MARGARET**
**Margaret Henderson**, 8 Elderslie Drive, Wallacestone, Falkirk, FK2 0DN, SCO.
(T) 01324 714250
Speciality: Physiotherapy.
P S T (Ref:HM09550)

**HENDON NATURAL HEALTH CENTRE**
**Hendon Natural Health Centre**, 12 Golders Rise, London, **London (Greater)**, NW4 2HR, ENG.
(T) 020 8202 9747 (F) 020 8202 3890
Speciality: Complementary Medicines & Therapy.
● **Owner** Miss K McCarroll
M (Ref:HM09551)

**HENDON TRAD CHINESE MED CTRE**
**Hendon Traditional Chinese Medicine Centre**, 56 Vivian Avenue, London, **London (Greater)**, NW4 3XH, ENG.
(T) 020 8202 1288 (F) 020 8202 2682
Speciality: Complementary Medicines & Therapy.
● **Director** Mr R Reitz
C M (Ref:HM09552)

**HENDRE SANCTUARY**
**Hendre Sanctuary (The)**, Unit 18, H T M Business Pk, Abergele Rd, Rhuddlan, Rhyl, **Denbighshire**, LL18 5UZ, WAL.
(T) 01745 590766 (F) 01745 590445
Speciality: Clairvoyants & Palmists.
● **Owner** Mrs M Maddocks
B (Ref:HM09553)

**HENDRICK, KEVIN**
**HENDRICK KEVIN ADHP MICHP BSc**, Albany Clinic Lr Fitzwilliam St, IRE.
(T) 01661 2222
(W) www.hypnosiseire.com
Speciality: Complementary Medicines & Therapy.
M (Ref:HM09554)

**HENDRY, ANGELA**
**Angela Hendry**, 7 Scott Cl, Taunton, **Somerset**, TA2 6UL, ENG.
(T) 01823 253720
Speciality: Complementary Medicines & Therapy.
● **Owner** Mrs A Hendry
C M (Ref:HM09555)

**HENDRY, FIONA & COLLEAGUES**
**Fiona Hendry & Colleagues**, 13 Stanton Rd, London, **London (Greater)**, SW13 0EY, ENG.
(T) 020 8878 8998
Speciality: Osteopathy.
P S T (Ref:HM09556)

**HENDRY, JUDITH**
**Judith Hendry**, 18 Nutfield Rd, Merstham, Redhill, **Surrey**, RH1 3EW, ENG.
(T) 01737 645352
Speciality: Chiropodists (Podiatrists).
● **Owner** Mrs J Hendry
S (Ref:HM09557)

**HENFREY, MICHELLE**
**Michelle Henfrey**, The Chris Lane Tennis Centre, Westfield Avenue, Woking, **Surrey**, GU22 9PF, ENG.
(T) 01483 722113
Speciality: Osteopathy.
● **Owner** Ms M Henfrey
P S T (Ref:HM09558)

**HENLEY CHIROPRACTIC & COMP**
**Henley Chiropractic & Complementary Health Clinic**, 1 West Lane, Henley-on-Thames, **Oxfordshire**, RG9 2DZ, ENG.
(T) 01491 578833
Speciality: Chiropractic.
P S T (Ref:HM09559)

**HENNEL, LIZ**
**Liz Hennel**, Natural Health Clinic, 177 Moorside Rd, Swinton, Manchester, **Manchester (Greater)**, M27 9LD, ENG.
(T) 01617 930091
Speciality: Homeopathy.
● **Partner** Mr G Jordan
M (Ref:HM09560)

**HENNEM, M E A**
**M E A Hennem**, 8 The Drive, Ilford, **Essex**, IG1 3HT, ENG.
(T) 020 8554 2792
Speciality: Chiropodists (Podiatrists).
● **Owner** Mrs M Hennem
S (Ref:HM09561)

**HENNESSY, MARGARET**
**Hennessy Margaret Dip Ac Lic**, 15 Old Rectory, Lucan, **County Dublin**, IRE.
(T) 01628 3795
Speciality: Acupuncture.
O (Ref:HM09562)

**HENNESSY, PIERCE**
**Hennessy Pierce &**, 7a Old Cork Rd, Midleton, **County Cork**, IRE.
(T) 021 4613 334
Speciality: Acupuncture.
O (Ref:HM09563)

**HENNESSY, PIERCE**
**Hennessy Pierce Lic A Dip AC**, Lr Windmill Hill, Youghal, **County Cork**, IRE.
(T) 024 9351 9
Speciality: Acupuncture.
O (Ref:HM09564)

**HENRIETTA CTRE FOR COMP THRPY**
**Henrietta Centre For Complementary Therapies (The)**, 21 Walter Road,, Swansea, **Glamorgan (Vale of)**, SA8 3BR, WAL.
(T) 01792 455364/411139
Speciality: Allergy Testing, Aromatherapy, Bach Remedies, Counselling, Homeopathy, Hypnotherapy, Meditation, Psychotherapy, Reflexology, Reiki, Shiatsu, Feng Shui. ✓ CREDIT
● **Astrology Consultant** Mr S Thomas
● **Psychotherapist** Mr Shrewsbury
(T) 01792 455364
● **Meditation Therapist** Mr J Gluck
● **Reflexologist** Ms L Aitchison Q: MIIR. M: AoR.
● **Counsellor** Inez Rowlands Q: BA, Dip.Couns.
● **Feng Shui Therapist** Ms E Bridle
● **Alexander Technique Therapist** Mr J Edwards
(T) 01792 428901 Q: MSTAT.
● **Aromatherapist/Reflexologist** Ms E Jenkins Q: MIFA.
● **Shiatsu Therapist** Ms J Andrewes
● **Homeopath** Ms J Johnson Q: BSc.
● **Bach Flower Therapist** Mr M Scott
(T) 01267 281761 Q: BA.
B C Yrs. Est.: 7 (Ref:HM09565)

**HENRIKSEN, HELLE**
**Helle Henriksen**, Ingledale, 1 Tanhouse Rd, Oxted, **Surrey**, RH8 9PE, ENG.
(T) 01883 717277
Speciality: Chiropractors.
P S T (Ref:HM09566)

**HENRY HOUSE HYDROTHERAPY CTRE**
**Henry House Hydrotherapy Centre**, 189 Heene Rd, Worthing, **Sussex (West)**, BN11 4NN, ENG.
(T) 01903 232875 (F) 01903 600044
Speciality: Complementary Medicines & Therapy.
● **Director** Mrs C Simporis
M (Ref:HM09567)

**HENRY, JOANNE**
**Joanne Henry**, 15 Fern Hill, Langdon Hills, Basildon, **Essex**, SS16 5UE, ENG.
(T) 01268 412388
Speciality: Aromatherapy.
M O (Ref:HM09568)

**HENRY, JOHN**
**John Henry**, 27 Elm Gr, London, **London (Greater)**, NW2 3AE, ENG.
(T) 020 8452 8865 (F) 020 8452 4956
Speciality: Psychotherapy.
B (Ref:HM09569)

**HENRY, MARTINE**
**Martine Henry**, 3 William St, London, **London (Greater)**, SW1X 9HL, ENG.
(T) 020 7235 0998


Key continued: **Yrs.Est:** Years Established **Q:** Qualifications **M:** Professional Membership ✓ Indemnity Insurance CREDIT Accept Credit Cards

Speciality: Electrolysis.
● **Owner** Ms M Henry
T (Ref:HM09570)

## HENRY, R H S

**R H S Henry**, 72 Kimberley Park Rd, Falmouth, **Cornwall**, TR11 2DF, ENG.
(T) 01326 312559
Speciality: Chiropodists (Podiatrists).
S (Ref:HM09571)

## HENSE, JOHN

**John Hense**, 6 Redstone Hill, Redhill, **Surrey**, RH1 4BP, ENG.
(T) 01737 763570
Speciality: Chiropodists (Podiatrists).
● **Principal** Mr J Hense
S (Ref:HM09572)

## HENSEY, C

**C Hensey**, 2 - 4 High St, Glastonbury, **Somerset**, BA6 9DU, ENG.
(T) 01458 833317
Speciality: Complementary Medicines & Therapy.
M (Ref:HM09573)

## HENSHAW, COLIN

**Colin Henshaw**, 140 Harley St, London, **London (Greater)**, W1N 1AH, ENG.
(T) 020 7487 4568 (F) 020 7486 4080
Speciality: Osteopathy.
● **Owner** Mr C Henshaw
P S T (Ref:HM09574)

## HENSHAW, S A

**S A Henshaw**, Verrington Lodge, Verrington, Wincanton, **Somerset**, BA9 8BN, ENG.
(T) 01963 32547
Speciality: Physiotherapy.
P S T (Ref:HM09575)

## HENSTAFF NATURAL HEALTH CLINIC

**Henstaff Natural Health Clinic**, Henstaff House, Llantrisant Rd, Groesfaen, Pontyclun, **Rhondda Cynon Taff**, CF72 8NG, WAL.
(T) 029 2089 1555
Speciality: Complementary Medicines & Therapy.
M (Ref:HM09576)

## HENSTRIDGE, EDWARD

**Edward Henstridge**, Bank House Clinic, 5 High St, Milford On Sea, Lymington, **Hampshire**, SO41 0QF, ENG.
(T) 01590 642749
Speciality: Chiropodists (Podiatrists).
● **Owner** Dr G Benes
S (Ref:HM09577)

## HENTHORN, L P

**Mrs L P Henthorn**, 15 Higher Rise, Shaw, Oldham, **Lancashire**, OL2 7QD, ENG.
(T) 01706 846064
Speciality: Chiropodists (Podiatrists).
● **Owner** Mrs L Henthorpe
S (Ref:HM09578)

## HENWOOD, CATHY

**Cathy Henwood**, 14 Birklands Rd, Shipley, **Yorkshire (West)**, BD18 3BY, ENG.
(T) 01274 593871
Speciality: Psychotherapy.
● **Owner** Mrs C Henwood
B (Ref:HM09579)

## HEPBURN, D

**D Hepburn**, 37 Sycamore Avenue, Lowestoft, **Suffolk**, NR33 9PH, ENG.
(T) 01502 563215
Speciality: Chiropodists (Podiatrists).
● **Owner** Mr D Hepburn
S (Ref:HM09580)

## HEPBURN, DAVID

**David Hepburn Visiting Chiropodists**, Ground Floor Surgery, 2 Stradbroke Rd, Lowestoft, **Suffolk**, NR33 7HT, ENG.
(T) 01502 512893
Speciality: Chiropodists (Podiatrists).
S (Ref:HM09581)

## HEPBURN, SUSAN

**Susan Hepburn**, 138 Harley St, London, **London (Greater)**, W1N 1AH, ENG.
(T) 020 7487 5200 (F) 020 7487 5200
Speciality: Hypnosis.
● **Owner** Mrs S Hepburn
B (Ref:HM09582)

## HEPPEL, V

**V Heppel**, Smithy Cottage, Kirkpatrick Durham, Castle Douglas, **Dumfries and Galloway**, DG7 3HT, SCO.
(T) 01556 650437
Speciality: Psychotherapy.
● **Owner** Dr V Heppel
B (Ref:HM09583)

## HEPWORTH, DAVID

**David Hepworth**, Broad Reach Clinic, 56 Alum Chine Rd, Bournemouth, **Dorset**, BH4 8DZ, ENG.
(T) 01202 769976
Speciality: Homeopathy.
M (Ref:HM09584)

## HEPWORTH, J P

**J P Hepworth**, 195 Chester Rd, Sunderland, **Tyne and Wear**, SR4 7TU, ENG.
(T) 01915 678926
Speciality: Chiropodists (Podiatrists).
S (Ref:HM09585)

## HERB & HEALTH

**Herb & Health**, 53 The Elmsleigh Centre, Staines, **Surrey**, TW18 4QF, ENG.
(T) 01784 462008 (F) 020 8868 1506
Speciality: Complementary Medicines & Therapy.
● **Owner** Mr T Dei
M (Ref:HM09586)

## HERB GARDEN

**Herb Garden (The)**, 125 Leigh Rd, Leigh-On-Sea, **Essex**, SS9 1BU, ENG.
(T) 01702 482178 (F) 01702 482178
Speciality: Acupuncture.
● **Owner** Mr J Barratt
O (Ref:HM09587)

## HERB HELPLINE

**Herb Helpline**, Unit 22, Spindus Rd, Speke Hall Industrial Estate, Liverpool, **Merseyside**, L24 1YA, ENG.
(T) 01514 489448 (F) 01514 489448
Speciality: Herbalists.
● **Owner** Mr J Nafr
M (Ref:HM09588)

## HERB HELPLINE

**Herb Helpline**, Bucksteep Manor, Bodle St, Hailsham, **Sussex (East)**, BN27 4RJ, ENG.
(T) 020 7357 0734
Speciality: Herbalists.
M (Ref:HM09589)

## HERB LEE

**Herb Lee**, 53A High St, Crawley, **Sussex (West)**, RH10 1BQ, ENG.
(T) 01293 539948
Speciality: Acupuncture.
O (Ref:HM09590)

## HERB LEE

**Herb Lee**, 775 London Rd, Westcliff-on-Sea, **Essex**, SS0 9SU, ENG.
(T) 01702 478988
Speciality: Complementary Medicines & Therapy.
● **Owner** Dr L Lee
M (Ref:HM09591)

## HERB MEDIC

**Herb Medic**, 38 Shirley High St, Southampton, **Hampshire**, SO15 3NG, ENG.
(T) 023 8077 8886
(W) www.herbmedic.co.uk
Speciality: Acupuncture, Chinese Herbal Medicine. ✔
● **Practitioner** Miss Nao
C O Yrs. Est.: 4 (Ref:HM09592)

## HERB ON LINE

**Herb On Line Ltd**, 3 Queen Charlotte Lane, Edinburgh, **Edinburgh (City of)**, EH6 6AY, SCO.
(T) 01315 555583 (F) 01315 533535
Speciality: Herbalists.
● **Manager** Mrs L Elder
M (Ref:HM09593)

## HERBAFAYRE

**Herbafayre**, 75 High St, Sheffield, **Yorkshire (South)**, S1 2GD, ENG.
(T) 01142 758064 (F) 01142 758064
Speciality: Complementary Medicines & Therapy.
● **Owner** Mr J Knight
C M (Ref:HM09594)

## HERBAL & ACUPUNCTURE

**Herbal & Acupuncture**, 15 Wicklow St, Dublin, **County Dublin**, IRE.
(T) 01677 1021 (F) 01677 1021
(E) josephinelynch@eircom.net
Speciality: Acupuncture, Herbal Medicine, Shiatsu.
● **Practitioner** Ms J Lynch M: RCHM.
O Yrs. Est.: 12 (Ref:HM09595)

## HERBAL & HOMEOPATHIC CLINIC

**Herbal & Homeopathic Clinic**, Unit 13 Deansgrange Ind Est Deansgrange, IRE.
(T) 01286 6280 (F) 01289 9722
(E) zota@iol.ie
Speciality: Herbalists.
M (Ref:HM09596)

## HERBAL APOTHECARY

**Herbal Apothecary (The)**, 103 High St, Syston, Leicester, **Leicestershire**, LE7 1GQ, ENG.
(T) 01162 602690
Speciality: Herbalists.
M (Ref:HM09597)

## HERBAL AUTHORITY

**Herbal Authority**, 1 High St, Brentwood, **Essex**, CM14 4RG, ENG.
(T) 01277 215030
Speciality: Acupuncture.
O (Ref:HM09598)

## HERBAL AUTHORITY

**Herbal Authority**, 192 King St, London, **London (Greater)**, W6 0RA, ENG.
(T) 020 8748 8868 (F) 020 8349 9804
Speciality: Herbal Medicine.
● **Chief Executive** Dr S Jiang
M (Ref:HM09599)

## HERBAL CARE

**Herbal Care**, 113 Hoe St, London, **London (Greater)**, E17 4RX, ENG.
(T) 020 8520 6688 (F) 020 7247 7085
Speciality: Acupuncture, Herbal Medicine. ✔
● **Complementary Therapist** Mr H Chen M: ATCM UK.
● **Complementary Therapist** Miss P Le M: ATCM UK.
C O Yrs. Est.: 2 (Ref:HM09600)

## HERBAL CARE

**Herbal Care**, 161 High St North, Eastham, London, **London (Greater)**, E6 1JB, ENG.
(T) 020 8592 4888 (F) 020 7247 7085
Speciality: Acupuncture, Herbal Medicine. ✔
● **Complementary Therapist** Mr H Chen M: ATCM UK.
● **Complementary Therapist** Miss P Le M: ATCM UK.
C O Yrs. Est.: 6 (Ref:HM09601)

## HERBAL CLINIC

**Herbal Clinic**, 1st Floor, 155 Belgrave Rd, Leicester, **Leicestershire**, LE4 6AS, ENG.
(T) 01162 661128 (F) 01162 661128
Speciality: Herbalists.
● **Owner** Mr H Jogiya
M (Ref:HM09602)

## HERBAL CLINIC

**Herbal Clinic**, 456 Stratford Rd, Sparkhill, Birmingham, **Midlands (West)**, B11 4AE, ENG.
(T) 01216 878788 (F) 01216 878789
Speciality: Complementary Medicines & Therapy.
● **Owner** Mrs N Khan
C M (Ref:HM09603)

## HERBAL CLINIC

**Herbal Clinic (The)**, 32 King Edward Rd, Swansea, SA1 4LL, WAL.
(T) 01792 474356
Speciality: Herbal Medicine.

Key: B Mind-Body Medicine; C Complementary Medicine; H Self Help Treatment; M Medicinal Therapy; O Oriental Medicine; P Postural Therapy; S Manipulative Structural Therapy; T Touch Therapy

● **Owner** Miss I James
M (Ref:HM09604)

**HERBAL CLINIC**

**Herbal Clinic (The)**, Pentland House, Garton-On-The-Wolds, Driffield, **Humberside (North)**, YO25 3EW, ENG.
(T) 01377 241800
Speciality: Herbalists.
● **Owner** Mrs M Garner
M (Ref:HM09605)

**HERBAL CLINIC**

**Herbal Clinic**, 11 Anglesea St, Dublin, **County Dublin**, IRE.
(T) 01672 5870
Speciality: Complementary Medicines & Therapy.
M (Ref:HM09606)

**HERBAL CLINIC**

**Herbal Clinic**, 236 Abbey Lane, **Leicestershire**, LE4 0DA, ENG.
(T) 01162 668193
Speciality: Complementary Medicines & Therapy.
C M (Ref:HM09607)

**HERBAL COTTAGE**

**Herbal Cottage**, 11 Vale Rd, Tunbridge Wells, **Kent**, TN1 1BS, ENG.
(T) 01892 619686 (F) 01892 619686
Speciality: Complementary Medicines & Therapy.
● **Owner** Mr J Guo
C M (Ref:HM09608)

**HERBAL DISPENSARY**

**Herbal Dispensary**, 148 Dumbarton Rd, Glasgow, **Glasgow (City of)**, G11 6XE, SCO.
(T) 01413 340705 (F) 01413 349789
Speciality: Complementary Medicines & Therapy.
C M (Ref:HM09609)

**HERBAL DISPENSARY**

**Herbal Dispensary**, Floraville, Bishopstown Rd, Cork, **County Cork**, IRE.
(T) 00353 214345955 (F) 00353 214345955
Speciality: Herbal Medicine. ✔ [credit card]
● **Consultant Herbalist**
Dr R Gleeson Q: BS, DipCH.P, DO.
M Yrs. Est.: 10 (Ref:HM09610)

**HERBAL GARDEN**

**Herbal Garden**, 258 High Rd Leyton, London, **London (Greater)**, E10 5PW, ENG.
(T) 020 8539 9577
Speciality: Herbal Medicine.
M (Ref:HM09611)

**HERBAL GARDEN AROMATHERAPY**

**Herbal Garden Aromatherapy**, 20 Eldon Gardens Shopping Centre, Percy St, Newcastle Upon Tyne, **Tyne and Wear**, NE1 7RA, ENG.
(T) 01912 303126
(E) suzanne@herbalgarden.co.uk
(W) www.herbalgarden.co.uk
Speciality: Aromatherapy, Bach Remedies, Complementary Therapy, Floral Essence Therapy, Herbal Medicine, Holistic Healing, Homeopathy, Inhalation Therapy, Music Therapy, Phytotherapy, Stress Therapy. ✔ [credit card]
● **Aromatherapist** Ms S Dinning Q: BSc.
● **Owner/Aromatherapist**
Mrs L Dinning M: IFA, ISPA.
M Yrs. Est.: 12 (Ref:HM09612)

**HERBAL GARDEN AROMATHERAPY**

**Herbal Garden Aromatherapy Centre**, 93 Rose St, Edinburgh, **Edinburgh (City of)**, EH2 3DT, SCO.
(T) 01312 200251
Speciality: Aromatherapy.
M O (Ref:HM09613)

**HERBAL HEALTH**

**Herbal Health**, Rosslyn, Oxford St, Rotherham, **Yorkshire (South)**, S65 2DJ, ENG.
(T) 01709 370447
Speciality: Herbalists.
● **Owner** Mrs G Mitchell
M (Ref:HM09614)

**HERBAL HEALTH**

**Herbal Health**, 5 Bank St, Rawtenstall, Rossendale, **Lancashire**, BB4 6QS, ENG.
(T) 01706 211152 (F) 01706 211152
Speciality: Herbal Medicine.
● **Partner** Mr J Spencer
M (Ref:HM09615)

**HERBAL HEALTH CLINIC**

**Herbal Health Clinic**, 39 Sussex Pl, Slough, **Berkshire**, SL1 1NH, ENG.
(T) 01753 791566
Speciality: Herbal Medicine.
● **Owner** Mrs L Bostock
M (Ref:HM09616)

**HERBAL HEALTH CLINIC**

**Ben Edwards**, 3 Place Farm Cottages, Fairlight Pl, Hastings, **Sussex (East)**, TN35 5DT, ENG.
(T) 01424 812761 (F) 01424 812761
(E) benedwards@tinyworld.co.uk
Speciality: Aromatherapy, Autogenic Training, Bach Remedies, Colour Therapy, Complementary Therapy, Counselling, Floral Essence Therapy, Healer, Healing Therapy, Herbal Medicine, Nutritional Therapy, Phytotherapy, Psychotherapy, Reflexology, Spiritual Healing, Stress Therapy, Visualisation Therapy, Vitamin Therapy. ✔
● **Therapist** Mr B Edwards Q: Dip.AP, Dip.Phyto, ITEC, MBAS, MNIMH. M: BAS, IFR, ITEC, NIMH.
M Yrs. Est.: 9 (Ref:HM09617)

**HERBAL HEALTH SERVICES**

**Herbal Health Company Services Ltd**, 100 Marlborough Rd, Dublin, **County Dublin**, IRE.
(T) 01496 3857
Speciality: Acupuncture, Herbal Medicine, Oriental Diagnosis, Medical Qi Gong. ✔
● **Practitioner** Ms K McBride Q: Lic.Ac.
O Yrs. Est.: 7 (Ref:HM09618)

**HERBAL HELPLINE**

**Herbal Helpline (The)**, Bear House, Trecastle, Brecon, **Powys**, LD3 8UH, WAL.
(T) 01874 638871 (F) 01874 638871
Speciality: Herbal Medicine. ✔
● **Owner** Mrs L Sanders
M Yrs. Est.: 16 (Ref:HM09619)

**HERBAL INN**

**Herbal Inn**, 9 Eld Lane, Colchester, **Essex**, CO1 1LS, ENG.
(T) 01206 368188
Speciality: Complementary Medicines & Therapy.
● **Manageress** Ms L Wang
M (Ref:HM09620)

**HERBAL INN**

**Herbal Inn**, 527 Kingsland Rd, **London**, E8 4AR, ENG.
(T) 020 7249 9888
Speciality: Complementary Medicines & Therapy.
C M (Ref:HM09621)

**HERBAL INN**

**Herbal Inn**, 556A High Rd, Wembley, **London (Greater)**, HA0 2AA, ENG.
(T) 020 8795 1883
Speciality: Herbal Medicine.
M (Ref:HM09622)

**HERBAL INN**

**Herbal Inn**, 63 Station Rd, Edgware, **London (Greater)**, HA8 7HX, ENG.
(T) 020 8381 1050 (F) 020 8349 9870
Speciality: Herbal Medicine.
● **Doctor** Mrs S Jaing
M (Ref:HM09623)

**HERBAL INN**

**Herbal Inn**, 81 Hammersmith Rd, London, **London (Greater)**, W14 8UZ, ENG.
(T) 020 7603 6151 (F) 020 8349 9804
Speciality: Complementary Medicines & Therapy.
● **Owner** Mrs S Jing
C M (Ref:HM09624)

**HERBAL INN**

**Herbal Inn (The)**, Unit 7a, 7 Eastgate, Basildon, **Essex**, SS14 1JJ, ENG.
(T) 01268 524896
Speciality: Herbalists.
M (Ref:HM09625)

**HERBAL INN**

**Herbal Inn (The)**, 15 East Sq, Basildon, **Essex**, SS14 1HT, ENG.
(T) 01268 286168
Speciality: Acupuncture.
O (Ref:HM09626)

**HERBAL INNOVATIONS**

**Herbal Innovations Ltd**, Po Box 537, Windsor, **Berkshire**, SL4 6XJ, ENG.
(T) 08707 873920 (F) 08707 873921
Speciality: Herbalists.
● **Director** Mr C Iradale
M (Ref:HM09627)

**HERBAL KING**

**Chinese Herbal Medicine & Healthcare Ltd**, 94 High St, Croydon, **Surrey**, CR9 1TN, ENG.
(T) 020 8649 8116
(W) www.herbalmed.org
Speciality: Acupuncture, Herbal Medicine, Massage (Therapeutic). ✔ [credit card]
● **Professor of Medicine** Dr W Zhu Q: DTCM.
O Yrs. Est.: 7 (Ref:HM09628)

**HERBAL MEDICINE & IRIDOLOGY**

**Herbal Medicine & Iridology**, 3c Eliot Hill, London, **London (Greater)**, SE13 7EB, ENG.
(T) 020 8852 7499
Speciality: Complementary Medicines & Therapy.
M (Ref:HM09629)

**HERBAL MEDICINE CLINIC**

**Herbal Medicine Clinic**, 14 Ray Drive, Maidenhead, **Berkshire**, SL6 8NG, ENG.
(T) 01628 778121 (F) 01628 785130
Speciality: Complementary Medicines & Therapy.
● **Owner** Mrs M Adejumo
C M (Ref:HM09630)

**HERBAL ONE**

**Herbal One**, Western Herbalists, 42 Bath St, Leamington Spa, **Warwickshire**, CV31 3AE, ENG.
(T) 01926 833368 (F) 01926 833368
(W) www.spiritmedicine.co.uk
Speciality: Acupuncture, Homeopathy, Iridology. ✔
● **Iridologist/Herbalist**
Ms A Francis
● **Homeopath/Herbalist** Mr T Bowler
(T) 01675 464247 Q: BSc (Hons), LCPH, MHMA. M: HMA.
● **Acupuncturist** Mr C Byrne Q: Lic.Ac. M: BAcC.
● **Acupuncturist** Ms C Perfitt Q: Lic.Ac, MBAcC. M: BAcC.
B Yrs. Est.: 1 (Ref:HM09631)

**HERBAL PHARMACY**

**Herbal Pharmacy**, 28 Ullenhall Rd, Sutton Coldfield, **Midlands (West)**, B76 2QG, ENG.
(T) 01213 131753 (F) 01213 131753
Speciality: Herbal Medicine. ✔ [credit card]
● **Owner** Mr C Rooker Q: MH.
C Yrs. Est.: 3 (Ref:HM09632)

**HERBAL SCHOOL**

**Herbal School The**, 24 Woods Rd, Caversham, Reading, **Berkshire**, RG4 6NA, ENG.
(T) 01189 475949
Speciality: Complementary Medicines & Therapy.
C (Ref:HM09633)

**HERBAL TINCTURES BY DR VOGEL**

**Herbal Tinctures By Dr Vogel**, 52 Stoke Newington Church St, London, **London (Greater)**, N16 0NB, ENG.
(T) 020 7249 9671
Speciality: Complementary Medicines & Therapy.
● **Senior Partner** Mrs J Sheridan
M (Ref:HM09634)

**HERBAL TREATMENT CENTRE**

**Herbal Treatment Centre**, 151 Billesley Lane, Moseley, Birmingham, **Midlands (West)**, B13



Key continued: Yrs.Est: Years Established Q: Qualifications M: Professional Membership ✔ Indemnity Insurance [credit card] Accept Credit Cards

9RW, ENG.
(T) 01214 494213
Speciality: Complementary Medicines & Therapy.
● **Owner** Mrs N Peterson
C M (Ref:HM09635)

**HERBAL TREATMENT CENTRE**
**Herbal Treatment Centre**, 163 Siddeley Avenue, Coventry, **Midlands (West)**, CV3 1GE, ENG.
(T) 024 7644 5441
Speciality: Herbal Medicine.
M (Ref:HM09636)

**HERBAL TREATMENT CLINIC**
**Herbal Treatment Clinic**, 21 High St, Caerleon, Newport, NP18 1AG, WAL.
(T) 01633 423401
Speciality: Homeopathy.
M (Ref:HM09637)

**HERBAL TREATMENT CLINIC**
**Medical Phytopath**, Suite 11, 38 Mount Pleasant, London, **London (Greater)**, WC1X 0AP, ENG.
(T) 020 7278 4954
Speciality: Herbal Medicine, Nutritional Therapy, Phytotherapy.
● **Medical Phytopath** Mr I McGregor
Q: Dip.Phyto, MCPP. M: C.Phyto.
M Yrs. Est.: 18 (Ref:HM09638)

**HERBAL WORLD**
**Herbal World**, 142 Kentish Town Rd, London, **London (Greater)**, NW1 9QB, ENG.
(T) 020 7482 6689
Speciality: Acupuncture.
● **Owner** Dr Y Shi
O (Ref:HM09639)

**HERBALIFE**
**Herbalife**, Low Lane, High Leven, Yarm, **Cleveland**, TS15 9JT, ENG.
(T) 01642 765203 (F) 01642 765203
Speciality: Complementary Medicines & Therapy.
● **Owner** Miss M Randall
C M (Ref:HM09640)

**HERBALIFE**
**Herbalife**, 37 Berkshire Gardens, London, **London (Greater)**, N13 6AA, ENG.
(T) 020 8889 0013
Speciality: Herbal Medicine.
M (Ref:HM09641)

**HERBALIFE INDEPENDENT DIST**
**Herbalife Independent Distributor**, 217 Church Rd, London, **London (Greater)**, NW10 9EP, ENG.
(T) 020 8830 0279
Speciality: Herbal Medicine.
M (Ref:HM09642)

**HERBALIST**
**Herbalist (The)**, 74 Lee High Rd, London, **London (Greater)**, SE13 5PT, ENG.
(T) 020 8852 9792
Speciality: Herbal Medicine.
M (Ref:HM09643)

**HERBALIST CENTRE**
**Herbalist Centre (The)**, 38 New Cavendish St, London, **London (Greater)**, W1M 7LH, ENG.
(T) 020 7935 0405 (F) 020 7935 0425
Speciality: Herbal Medicine.
M (Ref:HM09644)

**HERBALIST OF COLUMBIA RD**
**Herbalist Of Columbia Rd Ltd (The)**, 140 Columbia Rd, London, **London (Greater)**, E2 7RG, ENG.
(T) 020 7739 9344 (F) 020 7739 9378
Speciality: Herbalists.
● **Managing Director** Mr D Shaw
M (Ref:HM09645)

**HERBALIST, GODSHAER**
**Godshaer Herbalist**, The Old Stables, Ducking Stool Lane, Christchurch, **Dorset**, BH23 1DS, ENG.
(T) 01202 488122 (F) 01202 488121
Speciality: Herbal Medicine.
● **Owner** Mr A Hopking
M (Ref:HM09646)

**HERBALS**
**Herbals**, 23 Warramill Rd, Godalming, **Surrey**, GU7 1LU, ENG.
(T) 01483 428537
(E) cgalloway@nutritionist.freeserve.co.uk
Speciality: Herbal Medicine, Nutritional Therapy, Aromatic Medicine. ✔
● **Herbal Therapist**
Caroline Galloway Q: BSc. M: NIMH.
M Yrs. Est.: 2 (Ref:HM09647)

**HERBALWISE**
**Herbalwise**, Rockmarshall Jenkinstown, Dundalk, **County Louth**, IRE.
(T) 04293 76163
Speciality: Herbalists.
M (Ref:HM09648)

**HERBARIUM**
**Herbarium (The)**, 15 Bank St, Wrexham, LL11 1AH, WAL.
(T) 01978 364973 (F) 01978 364973
Speciality: Herbal Medicine.
● **Owner** Mrs J Griggs
M (Ref:HM09649)

**HERBARY CHINESE MEDICINE CTRE**
**Herbary Chinese Medicine Centre**, 26A Upper Tooting Rd, London, **London (Greater)**, SW17 7PG, ENG.
(T) 020 8672 3388
Speciality: Herbalists.
● **Manager** Miss H Lee
C M (Ref:HM09650)

**HERBARY CHINESE MEDICINE CTRE**
**Herbary Chinese Medicine Centre**, 31 Wellington St, Aldershot, **Hampshire**, GU11 1DX, ENG.
(T) 01252 333688
Speciality: Complementary Medicines & Therapy.
● **Manager** Mrs A Lee
M (Ref:HM09651)

**HERBAVET**
**Herbavet**, 21 Shirley Rd, Acocks Green, Birmingham, **Midlands (West)**, B27 7XU, ENG.
(T) 01216 931660 (F) 01217 069512
Speciality: Herbal Medicine.
● **Owner** Mr M Wooldridge
M (Ref:HM09652)

**HERBERT, DARYL**
**Daryl Herbert**, Churchill Medical Centre, 1 Churchill Ter, London, **London (Greater)**, E4 8DA, ENG.
(T) 020 8524 1505
Speciality: Osteopathy.
P S T (Ref:HM09653)

**HERBERT, P A**
**P A Herbert**, 202 Childwall Rd, Liverpool, **Merseyside**, L15 6UY, ENG.
(T) 01517 222793
Speciality: Physiotherapy.
P S T (Ref:HM09654)

**HERBERT, S J**
**S J Herbert**, 97 Shaftesbury Avenue, Waterlooville, **Hampshire**, PO7 5UU, ENG.
(T) 023 9223 1527
Speciality: Chiropractic.
● **Owner** Mr S Herbert
P S T (Ref:HM09655)

**HERBERT, STUART**
**Stuart Herbert**, 84 Fawcett Rd, Southsea, **Hampshire**, PO4 0DN, ENG.
(T) 023 9287 0707
Speciality: Chiropractic.
P S T (Ref:HM09656)

**HERBGARDEN CHINESE MED CTRE**
**Herbgarden Chinese Medical Centre**, 12 Gillygate, York, **Yorkshire (North)**, YO31 7EQ, ENG.
(T) 01904 678817
Speciality: Complementary Medicines & Therapy.
● **Manager** Mr W Zhuang
M (Ref:HM09657)

**HERBMEDIC**
**Herbmedic**, 162 Windmill St, Gravesend, **Kent**, DA12 1AH, ENG.
(T) 01474 335888
Speciality: Herbalists.
● **Manager** Mr M Mao
M (Ref:HM09658)

**HERBMEDIC**
**Herbmedic**, 168 Uxbridge Rd, London, **London (Greater)**, W12 8AA, ENG.
(T) 020 8740 9688
Speciality: Complementary Medicines & Therapy.
● **Partner** Mrs L Mao
C M (Ref:HM09659)

**HERBMEDIC**
**Herbmedic**, 1a Upper High St, Epsom, **Surrey**, KT17 4QY, ENG.
(T) 01372 726888
Speciality: Herbalists.
● **Owner** Ms L Mao
M (Ref:HM09660)

**HERBMEDIC**
**Herbmedic**, 21 Station Prde, Barking, **Essex**, IG11 8ED, ENG.
(T) 020 8591 6288 (F) 020 7511 5475
Speciality: Complementary Medicines & Therapy.
● **Manager** Miss L Mao
C M (Ref:HM09661)

**HERBMEDIC**
**Herbmedic**, 263 High St, Slough, **Berkshire**, SL1 1PH, ENG.
(T) 01753 551788
Speciality: Acupuncture.
O (Ref:HM09662)

**HERBMEDIC**
**Herbmedic Centre Ltd**, 22 Oliver St, London, **London (Greater)**, E6 5SE, ENG.
(T) 020 8511 5475 (F) 020 7511 6602
(E) ruoling@cwcoin.net
(W) www.herbmedic.co.uk
Speciality: Acupressure, Acupuncture, Complementary Therapy, Cupping, Herbal Medicine, Holistic Healing, Moxibustion, Oriental Diagnosis, Ying & Yang.
● **Manager/Practitioner** Ruoling Guo
Q: Dip.TCM, MSc. M: ATCM UK.
O Yrs. Est.: 4 (Ref:HM09663)

**HERBMEDIC**
**Herbmedic**, 9 High St North, London, **London (Greater)**, E6 1HS, ENG.
(T) 020 8552 8833
Speciality: Complementary Medicines & Therapy.
C M (Ref:HM09664)

**HERBMEDIC WEST TWO**
**Herbmedic West Two**, 37 Praed St, London, **London (Greater)**, W2 1NR, ENG.
(T) 020 7706 8866 (F) 020 7266 4808
Speciality: Complementary Medicines & Therapy.
C M (Ref:HM09665)

**HERBRIDGE**
**Herbridge**, 319 High St, Chatham, **Kent**, ME4 4BN, ENG.
(T) 01634 818198
Speciality: Acupuncture.
O (Ref:HM09666)

**HERBRIDGE CHINESE HEALTH CTRE**
**Herbridge Chinese Health Centre (The)**, 65 Mount Pleasant Rd, Tunbridge Wells, **Kent**, TN1 1PT, ENG.
(T) 01892 616828 (F) 020 7564 5834
Speciality: Complementary Medicines & Therapy.
● **Partner** Mrs C Zhang
M (Ref:HM09667)

**HERBS AND HELPERS**
**Herbs And Helpers**, Rear Of 64 Main St, Cockermouth, **Cumbria**, CA13 9LU, ENG.
(T) 01900 826392



Key: B Mind-Body Medicine C Complementary Medicine H Self Help Treatment M Medicinal Therapy O Oriental Medicine P Postural Therapy S Manipulative Structural Therapy T Touch Therapy

Speciality: Herbal Medicine, Iridology, Medical Herbalist, Western & Chinese Herbs. ✓
● **Medical Herbalist**
Mrs L Hodgekinson Q: Dip.TCM, MNIMH, MRCHM. M: NIMH, RCHM.
C O Yrs. Est.: 8 (Ref:HM09668)

## HERBS FOR EVERYONE
**Herbs For Everyone**, 25 Market St, Abergele, **Conwy**, LL22 7AG, WAL.
(T) 01745 833346 (F) 01745 826134
(E) leslaw@cwcom.net
(W) www.medicalherbalistsuk.com
Speciality: Acupuncture, Aromatherapy, Complementary Therapy, Counselling, Healer, Herbal Medicine, Iridology, Massage (Therapeutic), Nutritional Therapy, Osteopathy, Phytotherapy, Reflexology, Reiki, Remedial Massage, Sports Massage, Food Sensitivity Testing. ✓ [credit]
● **Aromatherapist** Ms R Fennell Q: IIHHT, IIST. M: CHAss.
● **Hypnotherapist** Mr M Gardner Q: IHT. M: IHT.
● **Herbalist** Dr L Bidzinski Q: MD(AM), MSc. M: BHMA, SNHS.
● **Therapist** Ms G Tudor Q: ITEC. M: AoR, ISPA, ITEC.
● **Acupuncturist** Ms C Davies Q: B.Ac, MBAcC. M: BAcC.
C M Yrs. Est.: 4 (Ref:HM09669)

## HERBS HANDS HEALING
**Herbs Hands Healing**, 2 Bridge Farm Cottage, Station Rd, Pulham Market, Diss, **Norfolk**, IP21 4TF, ENG.
(T) 01379 608201
Speciality: Herbal Medicine.
M (Ref:HM09670)

## HERBS KINGDOM
**Herbs Kingdom Co Ltd**, 132 Streatham Hill, **London**, SW2 4RS, ENG.
(T) 020 8671 7057 (F) 020 7738 7464
Speciality: Herbal Medicine.
M (Ref:HM09671)

## HERBS KINGDOM
**Herbs Kingdom Co Ltd**, Unit 13 Bessemer Park Trading Estate, 250 Milkwood Roa, London, **London (Greater)**, SE24 0HG, ENG.
(T) 020 7738 7474
Speciality: Herbalists.
M (Ref:HM09672)

## HERBS KINGDOM
**Herbs Kingdom Ltd**, 89C Church Rd, Hove, **Sussex (East)**, BN3 2BA, ENG.
(T) 01273 746484 (F) 01273 746484
Speciality: Complementary Medicines & Therapy.
● **Sole Director** Dr T Li
C M (Ref:HM09673)

## HERBS OF GRACE
**Herbs Of Grace**, 5a Lanwades Business Park, Kennett, Newmarket, **Suffolk**, CB8 7PN, ENG.
(T) 01638 750140 (F) 01638 552367
Speciality: Herbal Medicine.
● **Partner** Mr J Enkel
M (Ref:HM09674)

## HERBS SPECIALISTS
**Herbs Specialists**, 611b Lea Bridge Rd, Leyton, London, **London (Greater)**, E10 6AJ, ENG.
(T) 020 8521 2855
Speciality: Herbal Medicine.
● **Owner** Mr B Hoang
M (Ref:HM09675)

## HERDMAN, ALAN
**Alan Herdman**, 17 Homer Row, London, **London (Greater)**, W1H 1HU, ENG.
(T) 020 7723 9953
Speciality: Complementary Medicines & Therapy.
● **Owner** Mr A Herdman
M (Ref:HM09676)

## HEREFORD CENTRE
**Hereford Centre For Natural Health**, Belmont Medical Centre, Eastholme Avenue, Hereford, **Herefordshire**, HR2, ENG.
(T) 01432 279653
Speciality: Acupuncture, Alexander Technique, Allergy Testing, Aromatherapy, Chiropractic, Complementary Therapy, Counselling, Herbal Medicine, Homeopathy, Hypnotherapy, Kinesiology, Manipulation, Massage (Therapeutic), Naturopathy, Nutritional Therapy, Osteopathy, Psychotherapy, Reflexology, Shiatsu, Spiritual Healing, Stress Therapy, Visualisation Therapy. ✓
● **Director/Counsellor**
Collette Clements Q: Cert.Ed, Dip.HIC. M: COH.
● **Shiatsu Practitioner** Mr C Arroyo
● **Allergy Testing/Aromatherapist**
Ms L Thearle
● **Director/Therapist** Renske Tobyn Q: LLSA, MIFA, RGN.
● **Alexander Technique Therapist**
Ms J Vernon
● **Acupuncturist/Remedial Massage**
Ms D Pullen
● **Herbal Medicine** Mr G Tobyn
● **Acupuncturist/Chinese Herbalist**
Mr A Papier
● **Counsellor/Hypnotherapist**
Mr M Booth
● **Director/Osteopath/Naturopath**
Pushpa Rathod Q: DO, ND, Reg.Osteopath.
● **Spiritual Healer** Ms J Etheridge
S Yrs. Est.: 19 (Ref:HM09677)

## HEREFORD CHIROPRACTIC CLINIC
**Hereford Chiropractic Clinic**, Thornton House, 31 Southbank Rd, Hereford, **Herefordshire**, HR1 2TL, ENG.
(T) 01432 352928
Speciality: Chiropractic. ✓
● **Chiropractor** Dr N Nunn Q: BSc, DC, MSc (Chiro). M: BCA.
● **Chiropractor** Dr H Nunn Q: BSc, DC. M: BCA.
P Yrs. Est.: 11 (Ref:HM09678)

## HEREFORD HERBAL & NATURAL HLTH
**Hereford Herbal & Natural Health Centre**, 5a King St, Hereford, **Herefordshire**, HR4 9BW, ENG.
(T) 01432 354244
Speciality: Complementary Medicines & Therapy.
● **Director** Mr C Robbins
M (Ref:HM09679)

## HERFT, PATRICIA
**Patricia Herft**, 6 Lingrove Gardens, Buckhurst Hill, **Essex**, IG9 5HL, ENG.
(T) 020 8505 6484
Speciality: Reflexology.
S T (Ref:HM09680)

## HERIOT, LYNDA
**Lynda Heriot**, 17 Broad Park Rd, Bere Alston, Yelverton, **Devon**, PL20 7AH, ENG.
(T) 01822 840427
Speciality: Reflexology.
S T (Ref:HM09681)

## HERMANN, C
**C Hermann**, 20 Hillview Rd, Hucclecote, Gloucester, **Gloucestershire**, GL3 3LG, ENG.
(T) 01452 611854
Speciality: Chiropractic.
P S T (Ref:HM09682)

## HERMANN, CELIA
**Celia Hermann**, 16 Clarence Sq, Cheltenham, **Gloucestershire**, GL50 4JN, ENG.
(T) 01242 241933
Speciality: Chiropractors.
P S T (Ref:HM09683)

## HERMITAGE OILS
**Hermitage Oils**, The Hermitage, East Morton, Keighley, **Yorkshire (West)**, BD20 5UQ, ENG.
(T) 01274 565957 (F) 01274 569886
(E) ray@hermitageoils.com
(W) www.hermitageoils.com
Speciality: Aromatherapy. ✓ [credit]
● **Owner** Mr R Sherwin Q: Cert.Ed.
M Yrs. Est.: 11 (Ref:HM09684)

## HERRINGTON, I
**I Herrington**, St John Ambulance Centre, Station Rd, Hoveton, Norwich, **Norfolk**, NR12 8UR, ENG.
(T) 01603 784352
Speciality: Chiropodists (Podiatrists).
● **Owner** Mr I Herrington
S (Ref:HM09685)

## HERRINGTON, YVONNE
**Yvonne Herrington**, 16 Beane Avenue, Stevenage, **Hertfordshire**, SG2 7DL, ENG.
(T) 01438 314600
Speciality: Hypnosis.
● **Owner** Ms Y Herrington
B (Ref:HM09686)

## HERSBORG, TORBEN
**Hersborg Torben**, 342 Old St, London, **London (Greater)**, WC1N 2LD, ENG.
(T) 020 7404 7058
Speciality: Osteopathy.
P S T (Ref:HM09687)

## HERTERICH, NIGEL
**Nigel Herterich**, 204 Princes Rd, Dartford, **Kent**, DA1 3HR, ENG.
(T) 01322 279248 (F) 01322 279248
Speciality: Osteopathy. ✓
● **Osteopath** Mr N Herterich Q: BA, BSc. M: RoO.
S Yrs. Est.: 8 (Ref:HM09688)

## HERTFORD CENTRE
**Hertford Centre Of Acupuncture & Chinese Medicine**, 10 Parliament Sq, Hertford, **Hertfordshire**, SG14 1EY, ENG.
(T) 01992 536888
Speciality: Acupuncture.
● **Doctor** Dr M Xie
O (Ref:HM09689)

## HERTFORD NATURAL THERAPY CTRE
**Hertford Natural Therapy Centre**, 4 Old Cross, Hertford, **Hertfordshire**, SG14 1RB, ENG.
(T) 01992 589439
(W) www.goodfoodshop.co.uk
Speciality: Acupuncture, Aromatherapy, Chinese Herbal Medicine, Chiropractic, Counselling, Electrolipolysis, Homeopathy, Hypnotherapy, Indian Head Massage, Massage (Therapeutic), Nutritional Therapy, Physiotherapy, Reflexology, Reiki, Shiatsu, Stress Therapy, Traditional Chinese Medicine, Endermologie. ✓
● **Reflexologist/Aromatherapist**
Ms G Goodwin Q: BSc (Hons), MRQA.
M Yrs. Est.: 4 (Ref:HM09690)

## HERVE, JOYCE
**Joyce Herve**, 26 Abinger Avenue, Sutton, **Surrey**, SM2 7LJ, ENG.
(T) 020 8394 1533
Speciality: Chiropodists (Podiatrists).
● **Owner** Mrs J Herve
S (Ref:HM09691)

## HESCOTT, J D
**J D Hescott**, 49 Darlington Rd, Richmond, **Yorkshire (North)**, DL10 7BG, ENG.
(T) 01748 850020
Speciality: Biomechanics, Chiropody, Orthotics. ✓
● **Chiropodist** Mr J Hescott Q: MBChA. M: B.A.Ch.P.
M Yrs. Est.: 15 (Ref:HM09692)

## HESELDEN, TERESA E
**Teresa E Heselden**, Spring House, 28 West St, Faversham, **Kent**, ME13 7JG, ENG.
(T) 01795 591435
Speciality: Aromatherapy.
M O (Ref:HM09693)

## HESLOP, C
**C Heslop**, 4 Maypole Farm Estate, Manchester Rd, Carrington, Manchester, **Manchester (Greater)**, M31 4BD, ENG.
(T) 01617 762030
Speciality: Osteopathy.
P S T (Ref:HM09694)

## HESWALL HOLISTIC HEALTH CENTRE
**Heswall Holistic Health Centre**, 4 Milner Rd, Wirral, **Merseyside**, CH60 5RZ, ENG.
(T) 01513 427272
Speciality: Complementary Medicines & Therapy.
● **Managing Director** Miss M Wright
M (Ref:HM09695)


Key continued: Yrs.Est: Years Established Q: Qualifications M: Professional Membership ✓ Indemnity Insurance [credit] Accept Credit Cards

### HET UK
**HET UK**, 61 Juniper Way, Hayes, **London (Greater)**, UB3 1LF, ENG.
(T) 020 8581 3827
Speciality: Complementary Medicines & Therapy.
C M (**Ref:**HM09696)

### HETHERTON, ANNE
**Anne Hetherton**, 4 Royal Rd, Teddington, **London (Greater)**, TW11 0SB, ENG.
(T) 020 8977 7530
Speciality: Homeopathy.
● **Homeopath** Ms A Hetherton **Q:** L.C.C.H, RSHom. **M:** Soc.Hom.
B Yrs. Est.: 10 (**Ref:**HM09697)

### HEWERDINE, VICTORIA
**Victoria Hewerdine**, Flat E, 59 Springfield Rd, Brighton, **Sussex (East)**, BN1 6DF, ENG.
(T) 01273 550732
Speciality: Reflexology.
S T (**Ref:**HM09698)

### HEWETT, CHARMAIN
**Charmain Hewett**, 3 Hurst Rd, Eastbourne, **Sussex (East)**, BN21 2PJ, ENG.
(T) 01323 411900
Speciality: Chiropodists (Podiatrists).
● **Owner** Ms A Rambaut
S (**Ref:**HM09699)

### HEWETT, EMMA
**Emma Hewett**, 15 Halifax St, London, **London (Greater)**, SE26 6JA, ENG.
(T) 020 8699 3896
Speciality: Reflexology.
S T (**Ref:**HM09700)

### HEWISON, F
**F Hewison**, 10 Eldon Rd, Reading, **Berkshire**, RG1 4DH, ENG.
(T) 01189 502002
Speciality: Physiotherapy.
P S T (**Ref:**HM09701)

### HEWITT P & RUSHTON J
**P Hewitt & J Rushton**, 1 Traps Hill, Loughton, **Essex**, IG10 1SZ, ENG.
(T) 020 8508 9100
Speciality: Physiotherapy.
P S T (**Ref:**HM09702)

### HEWITT, ANDREW
**Andrew Hewitt**, Reflex Chiropractic Clinic, Archway Rd, Caversham, Reading, **Berkshire**, RG4 8HU, ENG.
(T) 01189 482970
Speciality: Acupuncture, Chiropractic, Massage (Therapeutic), Pilates.
● **Independent** Helen Chambers
● **Associate** Mary Tucker **Q:** DC. **M:** GCC.
● **Owner** Mrs V Lyle **Q:** DC. **M:** GCC.
P Yrs. Est.: 2 (**Ref:**HM09703)

### HEWITT, C A
**C A Hewitt**, 27-29 Manchester Rd, Knutsford, **Cheshire**, WA16 0LY, ENG.
(T) 01565 654425
Speciality: Osteopathy.
● **Owner** Mrs C Hewitt
P S T (**Ref:**HM09704)

### HEWITT, G
**G Hewitt**, 6 St. Mary St, Chepstow, **Monmouthshire**, NP16 5EU, WAL.
(T) 01291 627986
Speciality: Chiropodists (Podiatrists).
● **Owner** Mrs G Hewitt
S (**Ref:**HM09705)

### HEWITT, MAUREEN
**Maureen Hewitt**, 16 High St, Arnold, Nottingham, **Nottinghamshire**, NG5 7DZ, ENG.
(T) 01159 670128
Speciality: Chiropodists (Podiatrists).
S (**Ref:**HM09706)

### HEWITT, P M
**P M Hewitt**, 210A Harwoods Rd, Watford, **Hertfordshire**, WD1 7RT, ENG.
(T) 01923 231331
Speciality: Osteopathy.
● **Owner** Mr P Hewitt
P S T (**Ref:**HM09707)

### HEWITT, STEPHEN J
**Stephen J Hewitt**, The Valley Shopping Village, Team Valley Trading Estate, Gateshead, **Tyne and Wear**, NE11 0EN, ENG.
(T) 01914 915111
Speciality: Osteopathy.
P S T (**Ref:**HM09708)

### HEWORTH CHIROPODIST CLINIC
**Heworth Chiropodist Clinic**, 9 East Prde, York, **Yorkshire (North)**, YO31 7YB, ENG.
(T) 01904 438444
Speciality: Chiropody.
● **Owner** Mr M Pilmoor
S (**Ref:**HM09709)

### HEWSON, JAN
**Jan Hewson**, 31 Kings Cres, London, **London (Greater)**, N4 2SY, ENG.
(T) 020 7359 7671
Speciality: Reflexology.
S T (**Ref:**HM09710)

### HEXHAM CHIROPRACTIC CLINIC
**Hexham Chiropractic Clinic**, 26A Hallgate, Hexham, **Northumberland**, NE46 1XD, ENG.
(T) 01434 602666 (F) 01434 608079
Speciality: Chiropractic.
● **Director** Miss K Furness
P S T (**Ref:**HM09711)

### HEY, M J
**M J Hey**, 17A Brook St, Wakefield, **Yorkshire (West)**, WF1 1QW, ENG.
(T) 01924 373189
Speciality: Chiropodists (Podiatrists).
● **Owner** Mr M Hey
S (**Ref:**HM09712)

### HEYMANN, RUSSELL
**Russell Heymann**, 6 School Lane, Bricket Wood, St. Albans, **Hertfordshire**, AL2 3XU, ENG.
(T) 01923 674394
Speciality: Hypnosis.
● **Owner** Mr R Heymann
B (**Ref:**HM09713)

### HEYWARD, SHIRLEY
**Shirley Heyward**, 13 Leamington Avenue, Bromley, **Kent**, BR1 5BJ, ENG.
(T) 020 8402 1492
Speciality: Aromatherapy.
M O (**Ref:**HM09714)

### HEYWOODS
**Heywoods**, 327 High Rd, Woodford Green, **Essex**, IG8 9HQ, ENG.
(T) 020 8924 0088
Speciality: Complementary Medicines & Therapy.
C M (**Ref:**HM09715)

### HEYWORTH, S
**S Heyworth**, 166A Ivy Rd, Bolton, **Lancashire**, BL1 6EE, ENG.
(T) 01204 847166
Speciality: Chiropody, Podiatry.
● **Chiropodist (Podiatrist)** Mrs S Heyworth
M Yrs. Est.: 38 (**Ref:**HM09716)

### HIBBITT, L
**L Hibbitt**, 72 Abinger Rd, London, **London (Greater)**, W4 1EX, ENG.
(T) 020 8742 1608
Speciality: Complementary Medicines & Therapy.
M (**Ref:**HM09717)

### HICKEBOTTON, S
**S Hickebotton**, 1 Vineyard Cottage, East Clerklands, Melrose, **Scottish Borders**, TD6 9JR, SCO.
(T) 01835 870479
Speciality: Chiropractic.
P S T (**Ref:**HM09718)

### HICKEY, DAVID
**Hickey David**, 47 Dublin St, **County Longford**, IRE.
(T) 04348 500
Speciality: Chiropractors.
P S T (**Ref:**HM09719)

### HICKEY, T J
**T J Hickey**, 89 Pembroke Rd, Haverfordwest, **Pembrokeshire**, SA61 1LN, WAL.
(T) 01437 762189
Speciality: Chiropodists (Podiatrists).
● **Owner** Mr T Hickey
S (**Ref:**HM09720)

### HICKLING, KENNETH
**Kenneth Hickling**, 46 Cromwell Rd, Beeston, Nottingham, **Nottinghamshire**, NG9 1DP, ENG.
(T) 01159 254956
Speciality: Hypnosis.
● **Owner** Mr K Hickling
B (**Ref:**HM09721)

### HICKMAN, MARGARET GRACE
**Margaret Grace Hickman**, The Surgery, Victoria Cottage, 43 Watts Lane, Eastbourne, **Sussex (East)**, BN21 2LN, ENG.
(T) 01323 641706
Speciality: Chiropodists (Podiatrists).
● **Owner** Mrs M Hickman
S (**Ref:**HM09722)

### HICKS, C
**C Hicks**, Petworth Court, Felpham Rd, Bognor Regis, **Sussex (West)**, PO22 7PQ, ENG.
(T) 01243 868688
Speciality: Complementary Medicines & Therapy.
M (**Ref:**HM09723)

### HICKS, JACKIE
**Jackie Hicks**, 6 Combe Rd, Portishead, Bristol, BS20 6BJ, ENG.
(T) 01275 847886
Speciality: Chiropodists (Podiatrists).
● **Owner** Mrs J Hicks
S (**Ref:**HM09724)

### HICKS, KEVIN
**Kevin Hicks**, Ivy Cottage, High St, Bishops Itchington, Southam, **Warwickshire**, CV47 2QA, ENG.
(T) 01926 613700
Speciality: Clairvoyants & Palmists.
● **Owner** Mr K Hicks
B (**Ref:**HM09725)

### HICKS, SARA
**Sara Hicks**, 6 Spring St, Chipping Norton, **Oxfordshire**, OX7 5NL, ENG.
(T) 01608 643706
Speciality: Acupuncture.
O (**Ref:**HM09726)

### HIETT, ANNE
**Anne Hiett**, Little Hayes, Green Lane, Axminster, **Devon**, EX13 5TD, ENG.
(T) 01297 33370
Speciality: Reflexology.
S T (**Ref:**HM09727)

### HIGGINS, ADRIAN R
**Adrian R Higgins**, Bluntington Farm, Bluntington, Chaddesley Corbett, Kidderminster, **Worcestershire**, DY10 4NP, ENG.
(T) 01562 777666
Speciality: Osteopathy.
P S T (**Ref:**HM09728)

### HIGGINS, I
**I Higgins**, 10 Ainsdale Rd, Bolton, **Lancashire**, BL3 3BY, ENG.
(T) 01204 62595
Speciality: Chiropodists (Podiatrists).
S (**Ref:**HM09729)

### HIGGINS, I
**I Higgins**, 63 Aspin Park Rd, Knaresborough, **Yorkshire (North)**, HG5 8HG, ENG.
(T) 01423 860284
Speciality: Chiropodists (Podiatrists).
● **Owner** Mrs I Higgins
S (**Ref:**HM09730)

### HIGGINSON, ANN
**Ann Higginson**, 14 The Meadows, Hinckley, **Leicestershire**, LE10 2BU, ENG.
(T) 01455 610929
Speciality: Reflexology.
S T (**Ref:**HM09731)



Key: B Mind-Body Medicine; C Complementary Medicine; H Self Help Treatment; M Medicinal Therapy; O Oriental Medicine; P Postural Therapy; S Manipulative Structural Therapy; T Touch Therapy

### HIGGINSON, G & E
**Geoffrey & Elisabeth Higginson**, 27 St Kilda Rd, London, **London (Greater)**, W13 9DF, ENG.
(T) 020 8579 5209
Speciality: Alexander Technique.
● **Partner** Mrs E Higginson
P S (Ref:HM09732)

### HIGGINSON, S
**S Higginson**, Charlotte Sq, Newcastle Upon Tyne, **Tyne and Wear**, NE1 4XF, ENG.
(T) 01912 220305
Speciality: Alexander Technique.
P S (Ref:HM09733)

### HIGGS, ANN
**Ann Higgs**, Dove Cottage, 12 The Green Rd, Ashbourne, **Derbyshire**, DE6 1ED, ENG.
(T) 01335 344802
(E) ann.higgs@btinternet.com
Speciality: Reflexology. ✔
● **Reflexologist** Ann Higgs Q: MAR. M: AoR.
C Yrs. Est.: 7 (Ref:HM09734)

### HIGGS, E A C
**E A C Higgs**, 9 Poplar Court, Northampton, **Northamptonshire**, NN3 6SE, ENG.
(T) 01604 642398
Speciality: Chiropodists (Podiatrists).
● **Owner** Mr E Higgs
S (Ref:HM09735)

### HIGGS, M
**Mrs M Higgs**, 93 Castle St, Luton, **Bedfordshire**, LU1 3AJ, ENG.
(T) 01582 876866
Speciality: Chiropodists (Podiatrists).
S (Ref:HM09736)

### HIGGS, R W
**R W Higgs**, 8 Lonsdale Rd, Birmingham, **Midlands (West)**, B17 9RA, ENG.
(T) 01214 272970
Speciality: Chiropody. ✔
● **Chiropodist** Mr R Higgs Q: DPodM. M: S.C.P.
M (Ref:HM09737)

### HIGH PEAK HOLISTIC CENTRE
**High Peak Holistic Centre (The)**, Po Box 57, Wythenshawe, Manchester, **Manchester (Greater)**, M23 1TH, ENG.
(T) 01619 459202
(W) www.hphc.org.uk
Speciality: Aromatherapy, Counselling, Indian Head Massage, Massage (Therapeutic), Reflexology, Holistic Therapies, Management, Sports Therapy. ✔
● **Aromatherapist** Dr Most M: FHT.
C Yrs. Est.: 10 (Ref:HM09738)

### HIGH SPIRITS
**High Spirits**, Unit 9, Clements Arcade, 9- 11 Broadway, Leigh-On-Sea, **Essex**, SS9 1PA, ENG.
(T) 01702 527121
Speciality: Clairvoyants & Palmists.
● **Owner** Mr K Wade
B (Ref:HM09739)

### HIGH STREET CHIROPODY SURGERY
**High Street Chiropody Surgery (The)**, 93A High St, Edenbridge, **Kent**, TN8 5AU, ENG.
(T) 01732 865801
Speciality: Chiropodists (Podiatrists).
S (Ref:HM09740)

### HIGH STREET CLINIC
**High Street Clinic**, 62A High St, Hastings, **Sussex (East)**, TN34 3EW, ENG.
(T) 01424 431955
Speciality: Chiropodists (Podiatrists).
S (Ref:HM09741)

### HIGH STREET CLINIC
**High Street Clinic**, Flat 2, 6a High St, Fareham, **Hampshire**, PO16 7AN, ENG.
(T) 01329 285335
Speciality: Acupuncture, Aromatherapy, Chiropody, Chiropractic, Counselling, Homeopathy, Reflexology, Spiritual Healing. ✔
● **Owner** Mrs J Cooke
C Yrs. Est.: 10 (Ref:HM09742)

### HIGH STREET CLINIC MALBOROUGH
**High Street Clinic Malborough (The)**, 86 High St, Marlborough, **Wiltshire**, SN8 1HF, ENG.
(T) 01672 515151 (F) 01672 511919
Speciality: Complementary Medicines & Therapy.
● **Owner** Mrs J Parker
C M (Ref:HM09743)

### HIGH WYCOMBE CHIRO CLINIC
**High Wycombe Chiropractic Clinic**, 27 London Rd, High Wycombe, **Buckinghamshire**, HP11 1BJ, ENG.
(T) 01494 522368
Speciality: Chiropractic.
● **Partner** Miss A Marup
P S T (Ref:HM09744)

### HIGHAMS PARK NEURO PHYSIO CTRE
**Highams Park Neurological Physiotherapy Centre**, 211 Winchester Rd, London, **London (Greater)**, E4 9JW, ENG.
(T) 020 8531 1041
Speciality: Physiotherapy.
● **Owner** Mrs R Wharburton
P S T (Ref:HM09745)

### HIGHBURY CENTRE
**Highbury Centre (The)**, The Highbury Centre, 137 Grosvenor Avenue, London, **London (Greater)**, N5 2NH, ENG.
(T) 020 7226 1815
(E) alan.mars@virgin.net
Speciality: Alexander Technique, Cranio-Sacral Therapy, Communication Skills, Presentation Skills, Voice/Singing Therapy. Alexander Technique is for general good use and well being and can therefore be a help to many conditions but does not promise a cure for any.
● **Owner** Mr A Mars Q: MSTAT, NLP. M: STAT.
● **Teacher of the Alexander Technique** Refia Sacks Q: Cert.CST, MSTAT.
C Yrs. Est.: 17 (Ref:HM09746)

### HIGHBURY PARK CLINIC
**Highbury Park Clinic**, 111 Highbury Park, London, **London (Greater)**, N5 1UB, ENG.
(T) 020 7354 3020
Speciality: Osteopathy.
P S T (Ref:HM09747)

### HIGHCLIFFE CHIROPRACTIC CLINIC
**D C Allen**, Highcliffe Chiropractic Clinic, 415 Lymington Rd, Highcliffe, Christchurch, **Dorset**, BH23 5EN, ENG.
(T) 01425 277866
Speciality: Chiropractic. ✔
● **Chiropractor** Dr W Allen Q: BSc, DC. M: BCA.
● **Chiropractor** Dr D Allen Q: BSc, DC. M: BCA.
P Yrs. Est.: 14 (Ref:HM09748)

### HIGHCLIFFE CHIROPRACTIC CLINIC
**Highcliffe Chiropractic Clinic**, 45d Lymington Rd, Highcliffe, Christchurch, **Dorset**, BH23 5EN, ENG.
(T) 01425 277866
(E) dcallen.chiro@virgin.net
Speciality: Acupuncture, Chinese Herbal Medicine, Chiropractic, Kinesiology, Manipulation, Massage (Therapeutic), Nutritional Therapy, Vitamin Therapy. ✔
● **Partner** Weilin Allen Q: BSc (Hons), DC. M: BCA.
● **Principal** Mr D Allen Q: BSc (Hons), DC. M: BCA.
S Yrs. Est.: 13 (Ref:HM09749)

### HIGHCLIFFE OSTEOPATHIC CLINIC
**Highcliffe Osteopathic Clinic**, 278 Lymington Rd, Highcliffe, Christchurch, **Dorset**, BH23 5ET, ENG.
(T) 01425 271524
Speciality: Osteopathy.
● **Manager** Mrs S Temple
P S T (Ref:HM09750)

### HIGHGATE & HAMPSTEAD PHYSIO
**Highgate & Hampstead Physiotherapy Clinic**, 25 Cholmeley Cresent, London, **London (Greater)**, N6 5EZ, ENG.
(T) 020 8340 5414
Speciality: Physiotherapy.
P S T (Ref:HM09751)

### HIGHGATE HEALTH CENTRE
**Highgate Health Centre**, 31A Highgate, High St, London, **London (Greater)**, N6 5JT, ENG.
(T) 020 8348 5553
Speciality: Alexander Technique.
● **Therapist** Mr Smith
P S (Ref:HM09752)

### HIGHLAND CHIROPRACTIC CLINIC
**Highland Chiropractic Clinic**, 16 Francis St, Stornoway, **Western Isles**, HS1 2XB, SCO.
(T) 01851 701557 (F) 01851 706338
Speciality: Chiropractic.
P S T (Ref:HM09753)

### HIGHLAND CHIROPRACTIC CLINIC
**Highland Chiropractic Clinic (The)**, 8 Abban St, Inverness, **Highland**, IV3 8HH, SCO.
(T) 01463 717084
Speciality: Chiropractors.
P S T (Ref:HM09754)

### HIGHLAND COMM NHS TRUST
**Highland Communities NHS Trust Chiropody**, Fort William Clinic, Belford Rd, Fort William, **Highland**, PH33 6BS, SCO.
(T) 01397 702481
Speciality: Chiropodists (Podiatrists).
S (Ref:HM09755)

### HIGHLAND COMMUNITIES
**Highland Communities NHS Trust**, Craig Dunain Hospital, Inverness, **Highland**, IV3 8JU, SCO.
(T) 01463 704683 (F) 01463 716702
Speciality: Psychology.
● **Manager** Mr D Peck
B (Ref:HM09756)

### HIGHLEY, T J
**Christine Lambert**, 35 Cross St, Sale, **Cheshire**, M33 7FT, ENG.
(T) 01619 732743
Speciality: Chiropody. ✔
● **Owner** Ms C Lambert Q: M.S.C.P.
P Yrs. Est.: 6 (Ref:HM09757)

### HIGHSTEAD, KATE
**Kate Highstead**, 41 Station Rd, Woburn Sands, Milton Keynes, **Buckinghamshire**, MK17 8RX, ENG.
(T) 01908 583976
Speciality: Osteopathy.
● **Owner** Mrs K Highstead
P S T (Ref:HM09758)

### HIGHTHORN PHYSIOTHERAPY CLINIC
**Highthorn Physiotherapy Clinic**, 132 Lawrence St, York, **Yorkshire (North)**, YO10 3EB, ENG.
(T) 01904 431818 (F) 01904 431819
Speciality: Acupuncture, Alexander Technique, Homeopathy, Psychotherapy. ✔ [credit card]
● **Physiotherapist** Ms P Clarke Q: MCSP, SRP. M: CSP.
● **Teacher of the Alexander Technique** Ms G Freeman
● **Physiotherapist** Mr E Wilson Q: MCSP, SRP. M: CSP.
● **Physiotherapist** Ms C Parkinson Q: MCSP, SRP. M: CSP.
S Yrs. Est.: 16 (Ref:HM09759)

### HIGHWORTH CLINIC
**Highworth Clinic**, 15 Sheep St, Highworth, Swindon, **Wiltshire**, SN6 7AA, ENG.
(T) 01793 763752
Speciality: Chiropodists (Podiatrists).
S (Ref:HM09760)

### HIGHWORTH PHYSIOTHERAPY CLINIC
**Highworth Physiotherapy Clinic**, 22 Lechlade Rd, Highworth, Swindon, **Wiltshire**, SN6 7QR, ENG.
(T) 01793 763814 (F) 01793 763814
(E) sonya@highworth-physio.co.uk
Speciality: Acupuncture, Electrotherapy, Manipulation, Massage (Therapeutic), Postural Advice, Exercise Prescription, Hydrotherapy. ✔
● **Physiotherapist** Ms K Dack Q: MCSP, SRP.
● **Physiotherapist** Mrs S Nightingale Q: MCSP, SRP. M: CSP.
S Yrs. Est.: 13 (Ref:HM09761)


Key continued: Yrs.Est: Years Established Q: Qualifications M: Professional Membership ✔ Indemnity Insurance [credit card] Accept Credit Cards

## HILARY, MARTIN
**Martin Hilary**, Feet First, 161 Hook Rd, Surbiton, **Surrey**, KT6 5AR, ENG.
(T) 020 8397 6311
Speciality: Complementary Medicines & Therapy.
● **Owner** Mrs C Samson
C M (Ref:HM09763)

## HILDER, DEBORAH
**Deborah Hilder**, 3 Daws Meadow, Camelford, **Cornwall**, PL32 9PX, ENG.
(T) 01840 212345
Speciality: Reflexology.
S T (Ref:HM09764)

## HILDER, MONICA
**Monica Hilder**, 303 Findon Rd, Worthing, **Sussex (West)**, BN14 0HA, ENG.
(T) 01903 873625
Speciality: Reflexology.
S T (Ref:HM09765)

## HILDITCH, JUDITH
**Judith Hilditch**, The Carrs, Durham, **County Durham**, DH1 5HN, ENG.
(T) 01913 841408
Speciality: Complementary Medicines & Therapy.
● **Owner** Miss J Hilditch
M (Ref:HM09766)

## HILDRETH & COCKER
**Hildreth & Cocker Ltd**, Freepost, London, **London (Greater)**, SW12 0BR, ENG.
(T) 08003 166714 (F) 020 7274 2945
(E) orders@hildrethcocker.demon.co.uk
(W) www.naturallynatural.com
Speciality: Herbal Medicine, Naturopathy, Nutritional Therapy, Vitamin Therapy.
● **Practitioner** Mr R Allport
(T) 020 7274 0006 Q: MRCVS.
● **Nutritional Advisor** Dr R Newnham
(T) 020 7274 0006 Q: DO, ND, PhD.
● **Director** Mr H Cocker
(T) 020 7274 0006
H Yrs. Est.: 11 (Ref:HM09767)

## HILL CREST HEALING
**Hill Crest Healing**, 3 Hastings St, Castle Donington, Derby, **Derbyshire**, DE74 2LP, ENG.
(T) 01332 810560
Speciality: Complementary Medicines & Therapy.
C M (Ref:HM09768)

## HILL, ALISON
**Alison Hill**, 34 Church Path, Deal, **Kent**, CT14 9TH, ENG.
(T) 01304 362722
Speciality: Chiropodists (Podiatrists).
● **Owner** Mrs A Hill
S (Ref:HM09769)

## HILL, ANGELA
**Angela Hill**, 24 High St, Dronfield, **Derbyshire**, S18 1PY, ENG.
(T) 01246 411067
Speciality: Physiotherapy.
P S T (Ref:HM09770)

## HILL, ANTHONY W
**Anthony W Hill**, 129 Swanshurst Lane, Birmingham, **Midlands (West)**, B13 0AS, ENG.
(T) 01217 779440
Speciality: Chiropodists (Podiatrists).
S (Ref:HM09771)

## HILL, CAROLYN
**Carolyn Hill**, 138 Chilton St, Bridgwater, **Somerset**, TA6 3HZ, ENG.
(T) 01278 428458
Speciality: Complementary Medicines & Therapy.
● **Owner** Mrs C Hill
M (Ref:HM09772)

## HILL, CHARLOTTE
**Charlotte Hill**, Springbank House, 13 Pembroke Rd, Sevenoaks, **Kent**, TN13 1XR, ENG.
(T) 01732 453956
Speciality: Osteopathy.
● **Partner** Mrs P Pitcairn-Knowles
P S T (Ref:HM09773)

## HILL, CHARLOTTE
**Charlotte Hill**, Dexter House, 22 South End, Croydon, **Surrey**, CR0 1DN, ENG.
(T) 020 8240 4444 (F) 020 8240 4440
(E) charlotte@sixbones.fsnet.co.uk
Speciality: Osteopathy, Cranial. ✔
● **Osteopath** Ms C Hill Q: BSc, Hons (OST). M: CSP, GOsC.
S Yrs. Est.: 2 (Ref:HM09774)

## HILL, DAPHNE
**Daphne Hill**, 21 Ley Hey Rd, Marple, Stockport, **Cheshire**, SK6 6PQ, ENG.
(T) 01614 272243
Speciality: Homeopathy.
M (Ref:HM09775)

## HILL, ELIZABETH
**Elizabeth Hill**, 10 Oldfield Rd, Bishopdown, Salisbury, **Wiltshire**, SP1 3GQ, ENG.
(T) 01722 502609 (F) 01722 502609
Speciality: Reflexology.
● **Owner** Mrs E Hill
S T (Ref:HM09776)

## HILL, F S
**F S Hill**, 4 Ashley Rd, Epsom, **Surrey**, KT18 5AX, ENG.
(T) 01372 722092
Speciality: Chiropodists (Podiatrists).
● **Partner** Mr S Hill
S (Ref:HM09777)

## HILL, F S & M
**F S & M Hill Chiropodists**, 1 Spring Gdns, Dorking, **Surrey**, RH4 1EE, ENG.
(T) 01306 742900
Speciality: Chiropodists (Podiatrists).
S (Ref:HM09778)

## HILL, JANE
**Jane Hill**, Little Collingford, Collingford Lane, Danehill, Haywards Heath, **Sussex (West)**, RH17 7HZ, ENG.
(T) 01825 791301
Speciality: Physiotherapy.
● **Owner** Ms R Brown
P S T (Ref:HM09779)

## HILL, JULIE
**Julie Hill**, 93 New Forest Drive, Brockenhurst, **Hampshire**, SO42 7QT, ENG.
(T) 01590 623138 (F) 01590 623138
Speciality: Homeopathy.
● **Owner** Mrs J Hill
M (Ref:HM09780)

## HILL, LESLEY
**Lesley Hill**, 72 Christopher Way, Liverpool, **Merseyside**, L16 1JQ, ENG.
(T) 01517 381665
Speciality: Reflexology.
S T (Ref:HM09781)

## HILL, MARTIN
**Martin Hill**, 92 Chamberlin Rd, Norwich, **Norfolk**, NR3 3LN, ENG.
(T) 01603 488083
Speciality: Complementary Medicines & Therapy.
C M (Ref:HM09782)

## HILL, P
**P Hill**, Windmill Cottage, Laurel Lane, Weymouth, **Dorset**, DT3 5LZ, ENG.
(T) 01305 814428
Speciality: Chiropodists (Podiatrists).
● **Owner** Mrs P Hill
S (Ref:HM09783)

## HILL, PETER J
**Peter J Hill**, Prospect House, 4 Commercial Rd, Clayton West, Huddersfield, **Yorkshire (West)**, HD8 9PA, ENG.
(T) 01484 865279
Speciality: Aromatherapy.
M O (Ref:HM09784)

## HILL, PHILIP
**Philip Hill**, P O Box 616, London, **London (Greater)**, N6 5TS, ENG.
(T) 020 8340 9941
Speciality: Psychoanalysis.
● **Owner** Mr P Hill
B (Ref:HM09785)

## HILL, R B
**R B Hill**, The Doctors Surgery, Thorverton, Exeter, **Devon**, EX5 5NT, ENG.
(T) 01392 841022
Speciality: Acupuncture.
● **Partner** Mr R Hill
O (Ref:HM09786)

## HILL, R E
**R E Hill**, 9 Woody Bank, Cheslyn Hay, Walsall, **Midlands (West)**, WS6 7QA, ENG.
(T) 01922 419113
Speciality: Chiropodists (Podiatrists).
● **Owner** Ms R Hill
S (Ref:HM09787)

## HILL, REBECCA A
**Rebecca A Hill**, 19 Morestall Drive, Cirencester, **Gloucestershire**, GL7 1TF, ENG.
(T) 01285 640452
Speciality: Osteopathy.
● **Owner** Miss R Hill
P S T (Ref:HM09788)

## HILL, ROSIE
**Rosie Hill**, 80 Middle Way, Oxford, **Oxfordshire**, OX2 7LQ, ENG.
(T) 01865 511362
Speciality: Reflexology.
S T (Ref:HM09789)

## HILL, SARAH
**Sarah Hill**, 7 Sunnylaw Rd, Bridge Of Allan, Stirling, FK9 4QA, SCO.
(T) 01786 833759
Speciality: Acupuncture.
O (Ref:HM09790)

## HILL, SUSAN CLAIRE
**Susan Claire Hill**, The Casterbridge Chiropractic Clinic, 7 Icen Way, Dorchester, **Dorset**, DT1 1EW, ENG.
(T) 01305 263048 (F) 01305 251375
Speciality: Chiropractors.
● **Owner** Mr Q Standish-Hayes
P S T (Ref:HM09791)

## HILL, VIVIENNE
**Vivienne Hill**, 182A London Rd, Leicester, **Leicestershire**, LE2 1ND, ENG.
(T) 01162 544383
Speciality: Homeopathy.
M (Ref:HM09792)

## HILLBURY CHIROPRACTIC CLINIC
**Hillbury Chiropractic Clinic**, Hillbury, Old Salisbury Rd, Abbotts Ann, Andover, **Hampshire**, SP11 7NH, ENG.
(T) 01264 710811 (F) 01264 710811
Speciality: Chiropractors.
● **Owner** Mrs L Morley
P S T (Ref:HM09793)

## HILLER, STEPHANIE
**Stephanie Hiller**, 90 Carlton Rd, London, **London (Greater)**, E17 5RE, ENG.
(T) 020 8523 2203
Speciality: Reflexology.
S T (Ref:HM09794)

## HILLFIELDS HEALTH CENTRE
**Hillfields Health Centre**, 1 Howard St, Coventry, **Midlands (West)**, CV1 4GH, ENG.
(T) 024 7684 4161
Speciality: Chiropody.
S (Ref:HM09795)

## HILLIARD, N
**N Hilliard**, 7 Boskerris Trce, St Ives Rd, Carbis Bay, St. Ives, **Cornwall**, TR26 2SF, ENG.
(T) 01736 793733
Speciality: Osteopathy.
● **Owner** Mr N Hilliard
P S T (Ref:HM09796)

## HILLIARD, N & R
**N & R Hilliard**, 22 Chapel St, Camborne, **Cornwall**, TR14 8ED, ENG.
(T) 01209 612197
Speciality: Osteopathy.
P S T (Ref:HM09797)



Key: B Mind-Body Medicine; C Complementary Medicine; H Self Help Treatment; M Medicinal Therapy; O Oriental Medicine; P Postural Therapy; S Manipulative Structural Therapy; T Touch Therapy

**HILLIER, L V**

**L V Hillier**, 197 Norwood Rd, March, **Cambridgeshire**, PE15 8JJ, ENG.
(T) 01354 654757
Speciality: Chiropodists (Podiatrists).
● **Owner** Mrs L Hillier
S (Ref:HM09798)

**HILLMAN, M D T**

**M D T Hillman**, The Bourse, Delling Lane, Bosham, Chichester, **Sussex (West)**, PO18 8NR, ENG.
(T) 01243 572664
Speciality: Chiropodists (Podiatrists).
● **Owner** Mrs M Hillman
S (Ref:HM09799)

**HILLS & DE SOUSA**

**Hills A M D O & De Sousa R M G D O**, 107 Chalkwell Rd, Sittingbourne, **Kent**, ME10 2LP, ENG.
(T) 01795 477264
Speciality: Osteopathy.
P S T (Ref:HM09800)

**HILLS, MARGARET**

**Margaret Hills**, Tarquin, Roedean Rd, Tunbridge Wells, **Kent**, TN2 5JX, ENG.
(T) 01892 529730 (F) 01892 541131
Speciality: Osteopathy.
● **Owner** Mrs M Hills
P S T (Ref:HM09801)

**HILLS, MAURICE J**

**Maurice J Hills**, Tarquin, Roedean Rd, Tunbridge Wells, **Kent**, TN2 5JX, ENG.
(T) 01892 529730 (F) 01892 541131
Speciality: Osteopathy.
● **Owner** Mr M Hills
P S T (Ref:HM09802)

**HILLS, RUSSELL**

**Russell Hills**, Matthews House, 85 Epsom Rd, Guildford, **Surrey**, GU1 3PA, ENG.
(T) 01483 575876
Speciality: Physiotherapy.
P S T (Ref:HM09803)

**HILLSBOROUGH HEALTH CENTRE**

**Hillsborough Health Centre**, Chiropody Dept, Limbrick Rd, Sheffield, **Yorkshire (South)**, S6 2PE, ENG.
(T) 01142 716042
Speciality: Chiropodists (Podiatrists).
S (Ref:HM09804)

**HILLSIDE CHIROPODY SERVICES**

**Hillside Chiropody Services**, 75 Chequer Lane, Upholland, Skelmersdale, **Lancashire**, WN8 0DE, ENG.
(T) 01695 622394
Speciality: Chiropodists (Podiatrists).
● **Owner** Mr A Haslam
S (Ref:HM09805)

**HILLSIDE OSTEOPATHIC PRACTICE**

**Ms P M Crosbie**, 22 Hillside, Slough, **Berkshire**, SL1 2RW, ENG.
(T) 01753 715097
(E) pam.c@tesco.net
Speciality: Complementary Therapy, Cranial Osteopathy, Holistic Healing, Manipulation, Massage (Therapeutic), Osteopathy, Touch Therapy. ✔
● **Osteopath** Ms P Crosbie Q: BSc, Hons (OST). M: GOsC.
S Yrs. Est.: 1 (Ref:HM09806)

**HILLTOUT, S**

**S Hilltout**, 4 Meadow Way, South Cerney, Cirencester, **Gloucestershire**, GL7 6HY, ENG.
(T) 01285 861079
Speciality: Complementary Medicines & Therapy.
● **Owner** Mrs S Hilltout
C M (Ref:HM09807)

**HILLVIEW HOUSE HEALING CENTRE**

**Hillview House Healing Centre**, Killaready Castlemahon, **County Limerick**, IRE.
(T) 06972 249
Speciality: Healing.
B (Ref:HM09808)

**HILLVIEW PHYSIO & SPORTS CLNC**

**Hillview Physiotherapy & Sports Injury Clinic**, Hillview Medical Centre, Heathside Rd, Woking, **Surrey**, GU22 7QP, ENG.
(T) 01483 766668 (F) 01483 757067
Speciality: Physiotherapy. ✔
● **Physiotherapist** Ms A Grose Q: Grad Dip Phys, MCSP, SRP. M: CSP.
● **Physiotherapist** Mrs C Smith Q: Grad Dip Phys, MCSP, SRP. M: CSP.
● **Physiotherapist** Ms P Sacchi Q: Grad Dip Phys, MCSP, SRP. M: CSP.
S (Ref:HM09809)

**HILLYER, ANDREW**

**Andrew Hillyer**, Fleet, **Hampshire**, GU13, ENG.
(T) 01252 626434
Speciality: Bach Remedies.
M (Ref:HM09810)

**HILTON CLINIC**

**Hilton Clinic**, Hilton Clinic, Temple Cresent, Inverness, **Highland**, IV2 4TP, SCO.
(T) 01463 232856
Speciality: Chiropodists (Podiatrists).
S (Ref:HM09811)

**HILTON HEALTH CENTRE**

**Hilton Health Centre**, 26 Dartford Rd, Dartford, **Kent**, DA1 3DZ, ENG.
(T) 01322 227566
Speciality: Osteopathy.
● **Owner** Miss B Rankin
P S T (Ref:HM09812)

**HILTON HERBS**

**Hilton Herbs Ltd**, Downclose Farm, North Perrott, Crewkerne, **Somerset**, TA18 7SH, ENG.
(T) 01460 78300
Speciality: Complementary Medicines & Therapy.
C M (Ref:HM09813)

**HILTON, DAVID**

**David Hilton**, 30 Southgate Rd, Potters Bar, **Hertfordshire**, EN6 5DZ, ENG.
(T) 01707 652952
Speciality: Hypnosis.
● **Owner** Mr D Hilton
B (Ref:HM09814)

**HILTON, DOROTHY M**

**Dorothy M Hilton DO**, 28 Esher Rd, Walton-On-Thames, **Surrey**, KT12 4LG, ENG.
(T) 01372 464074
Speciality: Osteopathy.
● **Owner** Mrs D Hilton
P S T (Ref:HM09815)

**HILTON, KAREN**

**Karen Hilton**, 72 Shott Lane, Letchworth, **Hertfordshire**, SG6 1SE, ENG.
(T) 01462 486901
Speciality: Aromatherapy.
● **Owner** Ms K Hilton
M O (Ref:HM09816)

**HILTON, PETER**

**Peter Hilton**, 13 Hardhorn Rd, Poulton-le-Fylde, **Lancashire**, FY6 7SR, ENG.
(T) 01253 899778
Speciality: Psychotherapy.
● **Owner** Mr P Hilton
B (Ref:HM09817)

**HILTON, S P**

**S P Hilton**, 81 Palatine Rd, Goring-By-Sea, Worthing, **Sussex (West)**, BN12 6JR, ENG.
(T) 01903 504826
Speciality: Chiropodists (Podiatrists).
● **Owner** Mrs S Hilton
S (Ref:HM09818)

**HIMSWORTH, V**

**V Himsworth**, 12 Brinsworth Hall Cres, Brinsworth, Rotherham, **Yorkshire (South)**, S60 5EQ, ENG.
(T) 01709 369052
Speciality: Reflexology.
● **Owner** Mr V Himworth
S T (Ref:HM09819)

**HINCHCLIFFE, AMANDA**

**Amanda Hinchcliffe**, Manor Cottage, Brimington, Chesterfield, **Derbyshire**, S43 1QQ, ENG.
(T) 01246 211890
Speciality: Homeopathy.
M (Ref:HM09820)

**HINCHCLIFFE, SUSANNE**

**Susanne Hinchcliffe**, 54 Bramley Lane, Halifax, **Yorkshire (West)**, HX3 8NS, ENG.
(T) 01422 202003
Speciality: Chiropodists (Podiatrists).
● **Owner** Ms S Hinchcliffe
S (Ref:HM09821)

**HINCHLIFFE, JACKIE**

**Jackie Hinchliffe**, Westmoor, Main St, Ulley, Sheffield, **Yorkshire (South)**, S26 3YD, ENG.
(T) 01142 877449 (F) 01142 876343
Speciality: Absent Healing, Aromatherapy, Indian Head Massage, Massage (Therapeutic), Reflexology, Reiki, Paraffin Wax Therapy For Hands and Feet - good for aches, pains and arthritis. ✔
● **Owner** Mrs J Hinchliffe Q: City&Guilds (BTh & Electrol), Dip.Arom, Dip.SPA, GNSR. M: AoR, BABTAC, ISPA.
T Yrs. Est.: 14 (Ref:HM09822)

**HINCKLEY CHIROPRACTIC CLINIC**

**Hinckley Chiropractic Clinic**, 60 Hill St, Hinckley, **Leicestershire**, LE10 1DT, ENG.
(T) 01455 635488 (F) 01455 635488
Speciality: Chiropractic.
● **Director** Mr A Smycz
P S T (Ref:HM09823)

**HIND, CAROLE**

**Carole Hind**, 51 Eskdale Pl, Newton Aycliffe, **County Durham**, DL5 7DU, ENG.
(T) 01325 310758 (F) 01325 310758
Speciality: Indian Head Massage, Reflexology, Reiki.
● **Reflexologist** Ms C Hind Q: MBRA. M: BRA.
T Yrs. Est.: 10 (Ref:HM09824)

**HIND, SUSAN**

**Susan Hind**, 3 St. Georges Avenue, Havant, **Hampshire**, PO9 2RU, ENG.
(T) 023 9248 3658
Speciality: Reflexology.
S T (Ref:HM09825)

**HINDE, M J**

**M J Hinde**, Manor Lodge, Manor Park Cresent, Edgware, **London (Greater)**, HA8 7ND, ENG.
(T) 020 8952 5927
Speciality: Chiropodists (Podiatrists).
● **Owner** Mr M Hinde
S (Ref:HM09826)

**HINDE, TERESA**

**Teresa Hinde**, The Malt House, 34 Riverside, Eynsford, Dartford, **Kent**, DA4 0AE, ENG.
(T) 01322 863193
Speciality: Reflexology.
S T (Ref:HM09827)

**HINDLEY, DAVID**

**David Hindley**, 294 Buxton Rd, Stockport, **Cheshire**, SK2 7AN, ENG.
(T) 01614 569912
Speciality: Physiotherapy.
● **Owner** Mr D Hindley
P S T (Ref:HM09828)

**HINDMARCH, ANNE**

**Anne Hindmarch**, 40 Regent Pl, Rugby, **Warwickshire**, CV21 2PN, ENG.
(T) 01788 574870
Speciality: Chiropodists (Podiatrists).
S (Ref:HM09829)

**HINDMARSH, JULIE**

**Julie Hindmarsh**, 14 Falmouth Rd, London, **London (Greater)**, SE1 4JQ, ENG.
(T) 020 7403 7457
Speciality: Psychotherapy.
B (Ref:HM09830)

**HINDS, PATRICIA**

**Patricia Hinds**, 5 Royal Cl, Manor Rd, London, **London (Greater)**, N16 5SE, ENG.
(T) 020 8211 7057
Speciality: Reflexology.
S T (Ref:HM09831)


Key continued: Yrs.Est: Years Established Q: Qualifications M: Professional Membership ✔ Indemnity Insurance Accept Credit Cards

### HINES, STELLA
**Stella Hines**, 87 Godalming Avenue, Wallington, **Surrey**, SM6 8NT, ENG.
(T) 020 8686 8384
Speciality: Aromatherapy.
● **Owner** Mrs S Hines
M O (Ref:HM09832)

### HINGORANI, S
**S Hingorani**, 109-110 Bearwood Hill Rd, Burton-On-Trent, **Staffordshire**, DE15 0JW, ENG.
(T) 01283 566899
Speciality: Osteopathy.
P S T (Ref:HM09833)

### HINKS, MAXINE
**Maxine Hinks**, 340 Birmingham Rd, Lickey End, Bromsgrove, **Worcestershire**, B61 0HJ, ENG.
(T) 01527 836088
Speciality: Aromatherapy. ✔
● **Owner/Aromatherapist** Mrs M Hinks Q: Dip.Arom. M: IIHHT.
C Yrs. Est.: 3 (Ref:HM09834)

### HINKSMAN, DOROTHY
**Dorothy Hinksman**, 58 West St, Lilley, Luton, **Bedfordshire**, LU2 8LH, ENG.
(T) 01462 768601
Speciality: Chiropodists (Podiatrists).
● **Owner** Mrs D Hinksman
S (Ref:HM09835)

### HINTON, IAN
**Ian Hinton**, 787 Chigwell Rd, Woodford Green, **Essex**, IG8 8AU, ENG.
(T) 020 8559 0678
Speciality: Clairvoyants & Palmists.
● **Owner** Mr I Hinton
B (Ref:HM09836)

### HINTON, LYNN
**Lynn Hinton**, Reading, **Berkshire**, RG4, ENG.
(T) 01189 472830
Speciality: Bach Remedies.
M (Ref:HM09837)

### HINTON, NIKKI
**Nikki Hinton**, 23A Baalbec Rd, London, **London (Greater)**, N5 1QN, ENG.
(T) 020 7359 2350
Speciality: Reflexology.
● **Owner** Miss N Hinton
S T (Ref:HM09838)

### HIPKIN, B J
**B J Hipkin**, 242 Cathedral Rd, Cardiff, **Glamorgan (Vale of)**, CF11 9JG, WAL.
(T) 029 2023 3565
Speciality: Complementary Medicines & Therapy.
● **Owner** Mr B Hipkin
M (Ref:HM09839)

### HIPO-ANALYSIS CENTRE SALISBURY
**Hipo-Analysis Centre Salisbury**, The Old George, Middle Wallop, Stockbridge, **Hampshire**, SO20 8HN, ENG.
(T) 01264 781165
Speciality: Hypnosis.
● **Owner** Mr P Jaquiery
B (Ref:HM09840)

### HIROKO, KELLY
**Kelly Hiroko**, 46 Nursery Fields, Hythe, **Kent**, CT21 4DS, ENG.
(T) 01303 269452
Speciality: Reflexology.
S T (Ref:HM09841)

### HIRON, D
**D Hiron**, 99 St Johns Rd, Whitstable, **Kent**, CT5 2RZ, ENG.
(T) 01227 794798
Speciality: Aromatherapy.
● **Owner** Ms D Hiron
M O (Ref:HM09842)

### HIRST, B
**B Hirst**, 24 Wood St, Lytham St. Annes, **Lancashire**, FY8 1QR, ENG.
(T) 01253 780280
Speciality: Complementary Medicines & Therapy.
C M (Ref:HM09843)

### HIRST, FIONA
**Fiona Hirst**, Valley Medical Centre, Johnson St, Stocksbridge, Sheffield, **Yorkshire (South)**, S36 1BX, ENG.
(T) 01142 888338
Speciality: Herbalists.
● **Owner** Ms F Hirst
C M (Ref:HM09844)

### HIRST, MARY
**Mary Hirst**, Natural Path Health Centre, 3 Holyrood St, Chard, **Somerset**, TA20 2AH, ENG.
(T) 01460 62953 (F) 01460 63809
Speciality: Aromatherapy.
● **Owner** Mr M Newbound
M O (Ref:HM09845)

### HITCHINGS, CYNTHIA
**Cynthia Hitchings**, 85 North St, Nailsea, Bristol, BS48 4BS, ENG.
(T) 01275 855957
Speciality: Acupuncture.
● **Owner** Miss C Hitchings Q: Lic.Ac, MBAcC.
O (Ref:HM09846)

### HITCHINS, ROSIE
**Rosie Hitchins**, 72 Exeter Rd, Newmarket, **Suffolk**, CB8 8LR, ENG.
(T) 01638 603286
Speciality: Aromatherapy. ✔
● **Owner/Aromatherapist** Mrs R Hitchins Q: Dip.Arom.
C Yrs. Est.: 3 (Ref:HM09847)

### HO, ANNE-MARIE
**Mrs Anne-Marie Ho**, 199 County Rd, Walton, Liverpool, **Merseyside**, L4 5PB, ENG.
(T) 01512 877111 (F) 01517 220668
Speciality: Chiropodists (Podiatrists).
● **Owner** Mrs A Ho
S (Ref:HM09848)

### HOAD, A S
**A S Hoad**, Finchden Barn, Appledore Rd, Tenterden, **Kent**, TN30 7DD, ENG.
(T) 01580 764692 (F) 01580 764692
Speciality: Osteopathy.
● **Owner** Mr A Hoad
P S T (Ref:HM09849)

### HOAD, STUART
**Stuart Hoad**, Finchden Barn, Appledore Rd, Tenterden, **Kent**, TN30 7DD, ENG.
(T) 01233 640444
Speciality: Osteopathy.
● **Owner** Mr S Hoad
P S T (Ref:HM09850)

### HOARE, ELIZABETH
**Elizabeth Hoare**, 4 Cottenham Prde, London, **London (Greater)**, SW20 0BY, ENG.
(T) 020 8241 3842
Speciality: Reflexology.
S T (Ref:HM09851)

### HOARE, MICHAEL C
**Michael C Hoare**, Westmount, 10 Yarborough Rd, Wroxall, Ventnor, **Isle of Wight**, PO38 3EA, ENG.
(T) 01983 854178
Speciality: Homeopathy.
M (Ref:HM09852)

### HOBBS, CHRISTHEL
**Christhel Hobbs**, Hastings Chiropody Clinic, 25 Elphinstone Rd, Hastings, **Sussex (East)**, TN34 2EG, ENG.
(T) 01424 429042
Speciality: Chiropodists (Podiatrists).
S (Ref:HM09853)

### HOBBS, DIANA C
**Diana C Hobbs**, The Lanterns, Whitehouse Lane, Guildford, **Surrey**, GU4 7PT, ENG.
(T) 01483 571266
Speciality: Hypnosis.
B (Ref:HM09854)

### HOBBS, J M
**J M Hobbs**, Wellington Court, 416B High St, Lincoln, **Lincolnshire**, LN5 8HX, ENG.
(T) 01522 532061
Speciality: Osteopathy.
● **Owner** Mr J Hobbs
P S T (Ref:HM09855)

### HOBBS, S J
**S J Hobbs**, 16 Whitwell Rd, Bristol, BS14 9DP, ENG.
(T) 01179 719106
Speciality: Psychotherapy.
B (Ref:HM09856)

### HOBBS, SALLY
**Sally Hobbs**, 9 Church St, Chesham, **Buckinghamshire**, HP5 1HS, ENG.
(T) 01494 784945 (F) 01494 784945
Speciality: Naturopathy, Body Work. ✔
● **Owner** Ms S Hobbs Q: RN.
B S Yrs. Est.: 5 (Ref:HM09857)

### HOBBS, SALLY
**Sally Hobbs**, 84 Evelyn Drive, Pinner, **London (Greater)**, HA5 4RW, ENG.
(T) 020 8428 9926
Speciality: Naturopathy, Osteopathy, Body Work. ✔
● **Owner/Naturopath** Mrs S Hobbs Q: RN. M: BOA, RN.
C S Yrs. Est.: 12 (Ref:HM09858)

### HOBBS, SIMON
**Simon Hobbs**, Hastings Chiropractic Clinic, 25 Elphinstone Rd, Hastings, **Sussex (East)**, TN34 2EG, ENG.
(T) 01424 429042
Speciality: Chiropractic.
P S T (Ref:HM09859)

### HOBBS, T J
**T J Hobbs**, Jays, Old Vyne Lane, Baughurst, Tadley, **Hampshire**, RG26 5LF, ENG.
(T) 01256 850832
Speciality: Aromatherapy, Bowen Therapy, Reflexology. ✔
● **Therapist** Miss T Hobbs Q: BTER. M: BBA, BRA.
C Yrs. Est.: 10 (Ref:HM09860)

### HOBBY, B
**B Hobby**, 4a George St, Pocklington, York, **Yorkshire (North)**, YO42 2DF, ENG.
(T) 01759 302162
Speciality: Chiropodists (Podiatrists).
● **Owner** Mrs M Rimes
S (Ref:HM09861)

### HOBSON, ANNE
**Anne Hobson**, 17 Heaton Gr, Bradford, **Yorkshire (West)**, BD9 4DZ, ENG.
(T) 01274 545042
Speciality: Aromatherapy. ✔
● **Holistic Aromatherapist** Mrs A Hobson M: CSP, IFA, SRP.
C Yrs. Est.: 6 (Ref:HM09862)

### HOBSON, I K
**I K Hobson**, 76 Frenchgate, Richmond, **Yorkshire (North)**, DL10 7AG, ENG.
(T) 01748 822134 (F) 01748 826048
(E) ian-hobson@talk21.com
(W) www.darlingtonandrichmondchiropody.co.uk
Speciality: Biomechanics, Chiropody, Gait Analysis, Podiatry. ✔
● **Chiropodist (Podiatrist)** Mr I Hobson Q: DPodM, M.S.C.P. M: S.C.P.
P Yrs. Est.: 25 (Ref:HM09863)

### HOBSON, I K
**I K Hobson**, 85 West Auckland Rd, Darlington, **County Durham**, DL3 0LF, ENG.
(T) 01325 360152 (F) 01748 826048
(E) ianhobson@talk21.co.uk
(W) www.darlingtonandrichmondchiropody.co.uk
Speciality: Biomechanics, Chiropody, Gait Analysis, Podiatry. ✔
● **Owner** Mrs H Hobson
● **Chiropodist (Podiatrist)** Mr I Hobson Q: DPodM, M.S.C.P. M: S.C.P.
● **Chiropodist (Podiatrist)** Ms M Teasdale Q: BSc (Hons), M.S.C.P. M: S.C.P.
P Yrs. Est.: 9 (Ref:HM09864)

### HOBSON, L A
**L A Hobson**, Emily House, The St, Baconsthorpe, Holt, **Norfolk**, NR25 6AB, ENG.

Key: B Mind-Body Medicine · C Complementary Medicine · H Self Help Treatment · M Medicinal Therapy · O Oriental Medicine · P Postural Therapy · S Manipulative Structural Therapy · T Touch Therapy

(T) 01263 577398
Speciality: Chiropody, Nail Surgery. ✔
● Owner/Chiropodist Mrs L Hobson Q: BCA, MSSCh. M: B.A.Ch.P.
C Yrs. Est.: 6 (Ref:HM09865)

## HOBSON, N
**N Hobson**, 4 Grange Rd, Egham, **Surrey**, TW20 9QW, ENG.
(T) 01784 437219
Speciality: Osteopathy.
P S T (Ref:HM09866)

## HOBSON, RICHARD
**Richard Hobson**, 156A Huddersfield Rd, Mirfield, **Yorkshire (West)**, WF14 8AN, ENG.
(T) 01924 499681
(E) hypnosis@pastlifefsnet.co.uk
Speciality: Hypnosis, Hypnotherapy, Psychotherapy. ✔
● Owner/Hypnotherapist Mr R Hobson Q: C.Hyp, CMH.
B Yrs. Est.: 3 (Ref:HM09867)

## HOCK, GABRIELLE
**Gabrielle Hock**, 63 Warwick St, Oxford, **Oxfordshire**, OX4 1SZ, ENG.
(T) 01865 247851 (F) 01865 247851
Speciality: Acupuncture.
● Owner Miss G Hock
O (Ref:HM09868)

## HOCKEN, D E
**D E Hocken**, 183 Nottingham Rd, Stapleford, Nottingham, **Nottinghamshire**, NG9 8BE, ENG.
(T) 01159 397028 (F) 01159 397028
Speciality: Chiropodists (Podiatrists).
● Owner Mr D Hocken
S (Ref:HM09869)

## HODDELL, P J
**P J Hoddell**, Heath House, Heath House Lane, Codsall, Wolverhampton, **Midlands (West)**, WV8 2HW, ENG.
(T) 01902 842544
Speciality: Osteopathy.
● Owner Mr P Hoddell
P S T (Ref:HM09870)

## HODDES, S H (DR)
**Dr S H Hoddes**, 9 St. Andrews Rd, Liverpool, **Merseyside**, L23 7UP, ENG.
(T) 01519 244986
Speciality: Hypnosis.
B (Ref:HM09871)

## HODDINOTT, LAURA
**Laura Hoddinott**, 5 Brewery Lane, Lower Charlton, Shepton Mallet, **Somerset**, BA4 5QD, ENG.
(T) 01749 345832
Speciality: Aromatherapy.
● Owner Mrs L Hoddinott
M O (Ref:HM09872)

## HODGE CHIROPODIST
**Hodge Chiropodist**, 34 Glen Avenue, Batley, **Yorkshire (West)**, WF17 0ET, ENG.
(T) 01924 475338
Speciality: Chiropodists (Podiatrists).
● Owner Mr N Hodge
S (Ref:HM09873)

## HODGE, IAN
**Ian Hodge**, 19 Blackhouse Pl, Ayr, **Ayrshire (South)**, KA8 0HP, SCO.
(T) 01292 264960
Speciality: Absent Healing, Auto Suggestion, Autogenic Training, Cognitive Therapy, Complementary Therapy, Counselling, Dietician, Gestalt Therapy, Humanistic Psychology, Hypnosis, Hypnotherapy, Meditation, Paranormal Therapies, Psychotherapy, Rogerian Therapy, Stress Therapy, Visualisation Therapy, Yoga.
● Hypnotherapist Mr I Hodge Q: AMIH, BSY, CHP, FASC, PGD.Psychol. M: ASC, BSY, NRHP.
B H Yrs. Est.: 1 (Ref:HM09874)

## HODGE, S E
**S E Hodge**, 20 Holmbury Park, Bromley, **Kent**, BR1 2QS, ENG.
(T) 020 8295 0881
Speciality: Chiropodists (Podiatrists).
● Owner Mrs S Hodge
S (Ref:HM09875)

## HODGES, ANDREW
**Andrew Hodges**, 90 Ealing Village, London, **London (Greater)**, W5 2EA, ENG.
(T) 020 8566 9054 (F) 020 8248 5159
Speciality: Hypnotherapy.
● Owner Mr A Hodges
B (Ref:HM09876)

## HODGES, BILL (DR)
**Hodges Dr Bill**, 12 Clarinda Pk, Nth, Dun Laoghaire, **County Dublin**, IRE.
(T) 01280 0488
Speciality: Chiropodists (Podiatrists).
S (Ref:HM09877)

## HODGES, RAY
**Ray Hodges**, Stanton Cottage, Hempstead Lane, Potten End, Berkhamsted, **Hertfordshire**, HP4 2SD, ENG.
(T) 01442 864057
Speciality: Reflexology.
S T (Ref:HM09878)

## HODGINS, HELEN
**Helen Hodgins**, Nutshell Cottage, South Knighton, Newton Abbot, **Devon**, TQ12 6NT, ENG.
(T) 01626 821366
Speciality: Chiropodists (Podiatrists).
S (Ref:HM09879)

## HODGINS, HELEN
**Helen Hodgins**, 6 Queen St, Budleigh Salterton, **Devon**, EX9 6LB, ENG.
(T) 01395 446462
Speciality: Chiropodists (Podiatrists).
S (Ref:HM09880)

## HODGKINSON, ALISON
**Alison Hodgkinson**, 8 Luxemburg Gardens, London, **London (Greater)**, W6 7EA, ENG.
(T) 020 7602 7426 (F) 020 7602 7390
Speciality: Reflexology.
● Owner Mrs A Hodgkinson
S T (Ref:HM09881)

## HODGKINSON, JAMES R
**James R Hodgkinson**, 43 Caledonia Rd, Saltcoats, **Ayrshire (North)**, KA21 5AJ, SCO.
(T) 01294 466310
Speciality: Reflexology.
S T (Ref:HM09882)

## HODGSON, ANN
**Ann Hodgson**, 38 St. Marks Cr, Maidenhead, **Berkshire**, SL6 5DG, ENG.
(T) 01628 621157
Speciality: Aromatherapy.
M O (Ref:HM09883)

## HODGSON, BRIAN
**Brian Hodgson**, 52 Stoke Newington Church St, London, **London (Greater)**, N16 0NB, ENG.
(T) 020 7249 9671
Speciality: Hypnotherapy.
● Senior Partner Mrs J Sheridan
B (Ref:HM09884)

## HODGSON, DAPHNE
**Daphne Hodgson**, 17 Lancaster Park Rd, Harrogate, **Yorkshire (North)**, HG2 7SW, ENG.
(T) 01423 886766
Speciality: Osteopathy.
● Owner Mrs D Hodgson
P S T (Ref:HM09885)

## HODGSON, JENNIFER
**Jennifer Hodgson**, 71A St. Thomas St, Wells, **Somerset**, BA5 2UY, ENG.
(T) 01749 679014
Speciality: Osteopathy.
● Principal Ms J Hodgson
P S T (Ref:HM09886)

## HODGSON, M
**M Hodgson**, 1 Devas Gardens, Spondon, Derby, **Derbyshire**, DE21 7AD, ENG.
(T) 01332 670363
Speciality: Reflexology.
● Owner Mr M Hodgson
S T (Ref:HM09887)

## HODGSON, M
**M Hodgson**, The Bridge Clinic, 62 Flamborough Rd, Bridlington, **Humberside (North)**, YO15 2JL, ENG.
(T) 01262 401709
Speciality: Osteopathy.
● Owner Mr M Hodgson
P S T (Ref:HM09888)

## HODGSON, PATRICIA
**Patricia Hodgson**, 44 Papillon Rd, Colchester, **Essex**, CO3 3JG, ENG.
(T) 01206 575267
Speciality: Hypnosis.
● Owner Ms P Hodgson
B (Ref:HM09889)

## HODGSON, SALLY
**Sally Hodgson**, 20 Bedmond Rd, Hemel Hempstead, **Hertfordshire**, HP3 8LJ, ENG.
(T) 01442 257961
Speciality: Chiropodists (Podiatrists).
● Owner Ms S Hodgson
S (Ref:HM09890)

## HODKINSON, EDWINA
**Edwina Hodkinson**, 81 Bury And Bolton Rd, Radcliffe, Manchester, **Manchester (Greater)**, M26 4JY, ENG.
(T) 01617 972761 (F) 01617 972761
Speciality: Reflexology.
S T (Ref:HM09891)

## HODKINSON, J R
**J R Hodkinson**, 79C Hagley Rd, Halesowen, **Midlands (West)**, B63 4PY, ENG.
(T) 01215 500660
Speciality: Chiropodists (Podiatrists).
● Principal Mr J Hodkinson
S (Ref:HM09892)

## HODSDON, L M
**L M Hodsdon**, Rafton House, 9-11 Wellfield Rd, Hatfield, **Hertfordshire**, AL10 0BS, ENG.
(T) 01707 271858
Speciality: Chiropody. ✔
● Chiropodist Mrs L Hodsdon
M Yrs. Est.: 25 (Ref:HM09893)

## HODSON, D
**D Hodson**, 1 Upland Rd, South Croydon, **Surrey**, CR2 6RD, ENG.
(T) 020 8771 5665
Speciality: Hypnosis.
B (Ref:HM09894)

## HODSON, D
**D Hodson**, 46 Harley St, London, **London (Greater)**, W1N 1AD, ENG.
(T) 020 7631 5151
Speciality: Hypnosis.
B (Ref:HM09895)

## HODSON, P A
**P A Hodson**, 40 New Cheveley Rd, Newmarket, **Suffolk**, CB8 8BS, ENG.
(T) 01638 667589
Speciality: Acupuncture.
O (Ref:HM09896)

## HOEY JOE NATURAL HEALING CTRE
**Hoey Joe Natural Healing Centre**, 76 Nth Strand, Dublin, **County Dublin**, IRE.
(T) 01855 1009
Speciality: Healing.
B (Ref:HM09897)

## HOFFMAN INSTITUTE
**Hoffman Institute**, 66 Caistor Rd, London, **London (Greater)**, SW12 8PZ, ENG.
(T) 020 8333 2222
Speciality: Complementary Medicines & Therapy.
C M (Ref:HM09898)

## HOFFMAN, BERNIE
**Hoffman Bernie**, 6 Eyre Court Eyre St, Newbridge, **County Kildare**, IRE.
(T) 04543 7026
Speciality: Psychotherapy.
B (Ref:HM09899)

## HOFFMAN, BRIAN ASSOCIATES
**Brian Hoffman Associates**, 141 Southborough Lane, Bickley, Bromley, **Kent**, BR2 8AP, ENG.
(T) 020 8467 7363 (F) 020 8402 9744
(E) brianhoffman@uneone.net


Key continued: Yrs.Est: Years Established Q: Qualifications M: Professional Membership ✔ Indemnity Insurance Accept Credit Cards

(W) www.magnetic-power.co.uk
Speciality: Complementary Medicines & Therapy, Magno-Therapy.
● **Owner** Mr B Hoffman
C H Yrs. Est.: 2 (Ref:HM09900)

## HOFFMAN, W
**W Hoffman**, 19 Crow Wood Court, Crow Wood Avenue, Burnley, **Lancashire**, BB12 0LA, ENG.
(T) 01282 432938
Speciality: Clairvoyants & Palmists.
● **Owner** Mr W Hoffman
B (Ref:HM09901)

## HOFMAN, PETRA
**Petra Hofman**, Edinburgh, **Edinburgh (City of)**, EH13, SCO.
(T) 01314 411689
Speciality: Bach Remedies.
M (Ref:HM09902)

## HOFTON, EFFIE
**Effie Hofton**, 28 Oak Rd, Hale, Altrincham, **Cheshire**, WA15 9JA, ENG.
(T) 01619 277490
Speciality: Acupuncture.
O (Ref:HM09903)

## HOGAN, A
**A Hogan**, 78 Silhill Hall Rd, Solihull, **Midlands (West)**, B91 1JS, ENG.
(T) 01217 058686
Speciality: Chiropodists (Podiatrists).
● **Owner** A Hogan
S (Ref:HM09904)

## HOGAN, KATE
**Kate Hogan**, Cheviot Cres, Billingham, **Cleveland**, TS23 2PS, ENG.
(T) 01642 804070
Speciality: Chiropodists (Podiatrists).
● **Owner** Ms K Hogan
S (Ref:HM09905)

## HOGARTH CLINIC
**Hogarth Clinic**, 1a Airedale Avenue, Chiswick, London, **London (Greater)**, W4, ENG.
(T) 020 8742 7423
Speciality: Complementary Medicines & Therapy.
● **Therapist** Ms M Van Boetzelaer
M (Ref:HM09906)

## HOGARTH CLINIC
**Hogarth Clinic (The)**, 1a Airedale Avenue, Chiswick, London, **London (Greater)**, W4 2NW, ENG.
(T) 020 8742 7423 (F) 020 8742 1494
(E) clinic@thehogarth.co.uk
(W) www.hogarthgroup.co.uk
Speciality: Acupressure, Acupuncture, Alexander Technique, Bonesetting, Chiropractic, Complementary Therapy, Cranial Osteopathy, Cupping, Kinesiology, Manipulation, Massage (Therapeutic), Moxibustion, Naturopathy, Osteopathy, Physiotherapy, Postural Integration, Reflexology, Rolfing, Shiatsu, Stress Therapy, X-Ray. ✔
● **Osteopath/Acupuncturist**
Mr J Thoeye Q: DO, MBAcC, Reg.Acu, Reg.Osteopath. M: RN.
C Yrs. Est.: 10 (Ref:HM09907)

## HOGARTH, JAMES
**James Hogarth**, 47 High St, Hawick, **Scottish Borders**, TD9 9BU, SCO.
(T) 01450 372830
Speciality: Biomechanics, Chiropody. ✔
● **Chiropodist** Mr J Hogarth Q: Inst.CH.P, S.R.Ch.
C Yrs. Est.: 30 (Ref:HM09908)

## HOGARTH, L
**L Hogarth**, 9 West Albert Rd, Kirkcaldy, **Fife**, KY1 1DL, SCO.
(T) 01592 591111 (F) 01592 591111
Speciality: Chiropodists (Podiatrists).
● **Owner** Mr L Hogarth
S (Ref:HM09909)

## HOGBEN, A
**A Hogben**, 1 Station Approach, Worcester Park, **Surrey**, KT4 7NB, ENG.
(T) 020 8337 4486
Speciality: Chiropodists (Podiatrists).
S (Ref:HM09910)

## HOGG, B
**B Hogg**, 22 Christchurch St West, Frome, **Somerset**, BA11 1EE, ENG.
(T) 01373 467333
Speciality: Chiropodists (Podiatrists).
S (Ref:HM09911)

## HOGG, BRIAN
**Brian Hogg**, 37 King George Avenue, Droitwich, **Worcestershire**, WR9 7BB, ENG.
(T) 01905 778898
Speciality: Chiropodists (Podiatrists).
● **Owner** Mr B Hogg
S (Ref:HM09912)

## HOGG, DEBBI
**Debbi Hogg**, 37 Newton Rd, Great Barr, Birmingham, **Midlands (West)**, B43 6AD, ENG.
(T) 01213 586800 (F) 01213 583232
Speciality: Absent Healing, Allergy Testing, Bowen Therapy, Complementary Therapy, Holistic Healing, Reflexology, Reiki. ✔
● **Reflexologist** Mrs D Hogg Q: MBRA. M: BRA.
T Yrs. Est.: 7 (Ref:HM09913)

## HOGG, J S
**J S Hogg**, 23 Northumberland Sq, North Shields, **Tyne and Wear**, NE30 1PW, ENG.
(T) 01912 591400
Speciality: Chiropodists (Podiatrists).
● **Owner** Mr J Hogg
S (Ref:HM09914)

## HOGGARD, J
**J Hoggard**, 44 Westerham Rd, Sevenoaks, **Kent**, TN13 2PZ, ENG.
(T) 01732 454008
Speciality: Osteopathy.
P S T (Ref:HM09915)

## HOHLER, FRANK MICHAEL (DR)
**Hohler Dr Frank Michael**, Derryminihan West Castletownbe, **County Cork**, IRE.
(T) 027 7080 7
Speciality: Complementary Medicines & Therapy.
M (Ref:HM09916)

## HOLBEN, JENNY
**Jenny Holben**, 14 Chestnut Way, Brightlingsea, Colchester, **Essex**, CO7 0UA, ENG.
(T) 01206 304809
Speciality: Reflexology.
S T (Ref:HM09917)

## HOLBOROW, ROBERT
**Robert Holborow**, Gorseinon, Swansea, **Glamorgan (Vale of)**, SA4, WAL.
(T) 01792 897794
Speciality: Bach Remedies.
M (Ref:HM09918)

## HOLBURY CHIROPRACTIC CLINIC
**Holbury Chiropractic Clinic**, 177 Long Lane, Holbury, Southampton, **Hampshire**, SO45 2PA, ENG.
(T) 023 8089 0870
Speciality: Chiropractic.
● **Owner** Mr G Blomfiled
P S T (Ref:HM09919)

## HOLCOMBE, VAL
**Val Holcombe**, Broadwood Avenue, Ruislip, **London (Greater)**, HA4 7XR, ENG.
(T) 01895 633631
Speciality: Complementary Medicines & Therapy.
C M (Ref:HM09920)

## HOLDA-MARTIN, JACQUELINE
**Jacqueline Holda-Martin**, 30 Thorold Rd, Chatham, **Kent**, ME5 7EA, ENG.
(T) 01634 303990
Speciality: Hypnosis.
● **Owner** Ms J Holda-Martin
B (Ref:HM09921)

## HOLDAWAY, MICHELLE
**Michelle Holdaway**, 22 Hemdean Rd, Caversham, Reading, **Berkshire**, RG4 7SU, ENG.
(T) 01189 461306
Speciality: Alexander Technique.
● **Owner** Mrs M Holdaway
P S (Ref:HM09922)

## HOLDCOFT, LIA
**Lia Holdcoft**, 73 Hundred Acres Lane, Amersham, **Buckinghamshire**, HP7 9BX, ENG.
(T) 01494 725201
Speciality: Aromatherapy.
M O (Ref:HM09923)

## HOLDCROFT, P A
**P A Holdcroft**, 2 Stanley Rd, Newcastle, **Staffordshire**, ST5 0PE, ENG.
(T) 01782 619860
Speciality: Chiropodists (Podiatrists).
● **Owner** Mrs P Holdcroft
S (Ref:HM09924)

## HOLDCROFT, R A
**R A Holdcroft**, Fairport, Lid Lane, Cheadle, Stoke-On-Trent, **Staffordshire**, ST10 1PZ, ENG.
(T) 01538 753805
Speciality: Osteopathy.
P S T (Ref:HM09925)

## HOLDCROFT, ROSEMARIE A
**Rosemarie A Holdcroft (Mrs)**, Port Vale Football Club, Hamil Rd, Stoke-On-Trent, **Staffordshire**, ST6 1AW, ENG.
(T) 07973 261498
Speciality: Osteopathy.
P S T (Ref:HM09926)

## HOLDEN NATURAL HEALTH CLINIC
**Holden Natural Health Clinic**, The Bield, Lewes Rd, Forest Row, **Sussex (East)**, RH18 5AF, ENG.
(T) 01342 826899
(W) www.holherbs.com
Speciality: Colonic Hydrotherapy, Herbal Medicine, Iridology, Naturopathy, Reflexology, Colon Hydrotherapy and Jin Shin Jyutsu. ✔
● **Medical Herbalist** Ms K Holden Q: MHCT.
M Yrs. Est.: 15 (Ref:HM09927)

## HOLDEN NATURAL HEALTH CLINIC
**Holden Natural Health Clinic (The)**, 43 St Stephens Avenue, Ashtead, **Surrey**, KT21 1PJ, ENG.
(T) 01372 277779
Speciality: Complementary Medicines & Therapy.
C M (Ref:HM09928)

## HOLDEN, BERNARD
**Bernard Holden**, 107 Melton Rd, Wymondham, **Norfolk**, NR18 0DE, ENG.
(T) 01953 604428
Speciality: Chiropodists (Podiatrists).
● **Owner** Mr B Holden
S (Ref:HM09929)

## HOLDEN, ELFRIEDE
**Elfriede Holden**, 1 Semley Rd, Hassocks, **Sussex (West)**, BN6 8PD, ENG.
(T) 01273 842855
Speciality: Reflexology.
S T (Ref:HM09930)

## HOLDEN, G
**G Holden**, 5 Alderton Mews, Lambourn Cres, Leamington Spa, **Warwickshire**, CV31 1SX, ENG.
(T) 01926 337303
Speciality: Complementary Medicines & Therapy.
● **Owner** Mr G Holden
M (Ref:HM09931)

## HOLDEN, JOHN H
**John H Holden**, 72 Northgate, Blackburn, **Lancashire**, BB2 1AA, ENG.
(T) 01254 698311
Speciality: Chiropody. ✔
● **Chiropodist (Podiatrist)**
Mr J Holden Q: M.S.C.P, S.R.Ch.
B Yrs. Est.: 30 (Ref:HM09932)

## HOLDEN, NINA
**Nina Holden**, 18 Hunt End Lane, Redditch, **Worcestershire**, B97 5UW, ENG.
(T) 01527 458172
Speciality: Reflexology. ✔
● **Reflexologist** Ms N Holden Q: IIHHT. M: ICHT, IIHHT.



Key: B Mind-Body Medicine C Complementary Medicine H Self Help Treatment M Medicinal Therapy O Oriental Medicine P Postural Therapy S Manipulative Structural Therapy T Touch Therapy

M Yrs. Est.: 3 (Ref:HM09933)

**HOLDEN, SHEENA**

**Sheena Holden**, 10 Orchard Brae Gardens West, Edinburgh, **Edinburgh (City of)**, EH4 2HL, SCO.
(T) 01313 328590
Speciality: Reflexology. ✔
● **Reflexologist** Mrs S Holden Q: MBRA, RGN. M: BRA.
T Yrs. Est.: 35 (Ref:HM09934)

**HOLDENS HERBAL HEALTH**

**Holdens Herbal Health**, The Bield, Lewes Rd, Forest Row, **Sussex (East)**, RH18 5AF, ENG.
(T) 01342 826896 (F) 01342 826896
Speciality: Herbalists.
● **Sales Manager** Mr D Jonas
M (Ref:HM09935)

**HOLDERNESS CHIROPRACTIC CLINIC**

**Holderness Chiropractic Clinic**, 287-289 Holderness Rd, Hull, **Humberside (North)**, HU8 8TE, ENG.
(T) 01482 586605
Speciality: Chiropractic.
● **Owner** Mr D Grant
P S T (Ref:HM09936)

**HOLDING, MARTIN**

**Martin Holding**, 151 Hatch Lane, Windsor, **Berkshire**, SL4 3RL, ENG.
(T) 01753 862853
Speciality: Osteopathy.
P S T (Ref:HM09937)

**HOLDING, V T**

**V T Holding**, Kiran Virdee Medical Centre, Sultan Rd, Chatham, **Kent**, ME5 8TJ, ENG.
(T) 01634 687687
Speciality: Chiropodists (Podiatrists).
● **Owner** Miss V Holding
S (Ref:HM09938)

**HOLDON, P**

**P Holdon**, 5 Air St, Brighton, **Sussex (East)**, BN1 3FB, ENG.
(T) 01273 700888
Speciality: Hypnotherapy.
● **Owner** Mrs P Holdon
B (Ref:HM09939)

**HOLDSWORTH, HILARY**

**Hilary Holdsworth**, Dumfries Holistic Health Centre, 98 Loreburn St, Dumfries, **Dumfries and Galloway**, DG1 1HW, SCO.
(T) 01387 267617
Speciality: Reflexology.
S T (Ref:HM09940)

**HOLE, NIGEL**

**Nigel Hole**, 30 Eagle Lane, London, **London (Greater)**, E11 1PF, ENG.
(T) 020 8530 7337
Speciality: Osteopathy.
● **Owner** Mr N Hole
P S T (Ref:HM09941)

**HOLEN HOLISTICNERGY**

**Holen Holisticenergy**, 2 Rye River Pk, Dun Carraig, Leixlip, **County Kildare**, IRE.
(T) 01624 4604
Speciality: Complementary Medicines & Therapy.
M (Ref:HM09942)

**HOLFORD CHIROPODISTS**

**Holford Chiropodists**, 5 Lathkill Dale, Church Gresley, Swadlincote, **Derbyshire**, DE11 9RL, ENG.
(T) 01283 552535
Speciality: Chiropodists (Podiatrists).
● **Owner** Ms F Holford
S (Ref:HM09943)

**HOLISTIC**

**Holistic**, 18 Plover Drive, Broadheath, Altrincham, **Cheshire**, WA14 5NW, ENG.
(T) 01619 414462
Speciality: Complementary Medicines & Therapy.
● **Owner** Ms M Elmhirst
C M (Ref:HM09944)

**HOLISTIC APPROACH**

**Holistic Approach (The)**, 28 Hardhorn Rd, Poulton-le-Fylde, **Lancashire**, FY6 7SR, ENG.
(T) 01253 882245
Speciality: Aromatherapy.
● **Owner** Mrs C Haughton
M O (Ref:HM09945)

**HOLISTIC AROMATHERAPY**

**Holistic Aromatherapy**, 14 Stratheden Park, Cupar, **Fife**, KY15 5RP, SCO.
(T) 01334 655389
Speciality: Aromatherapy.
● **Owner** Mrs M Beattie
M O (Ref:HM09946)

**HOLISTIC AROMATHERAPY**

**Holistic Aromatherapy**, 15 East Prde, Hastings, **Sussex (East)**, TN34 3AL, ENG.
(T) 01424 719782
Speciality: Aromatherapy.
M O (Ref:HM09947)

**HOLISTIC ARTS STUDIOS**

**Holistic Art Studios**, 27 Cedar Cres, Horndean, Waterlooville, **Hampshire**, PO8 9EX, ENG.
(T) 07831 305512 (F) 023 9259 3822
(E) holisticartstudios@hotmail.com
Speciality: Complementary Therapy, Healer, Healing Therapy, Holistic Healing, Indian Head Massage, Massage (Therapeutic), Reflexology, Reiki, Spiritual Healing, Qualified in First Aid. ✔
● **Holistic Therapist** Ms D Paice
(T) 023 9259 3822 Q: IIHHT, ITEC. M: FHT, IPTI.
T Yrs. Est.: 1 (Ref:HM09948)

**HOLISTIC CENTRE**

**Holistic Centre (The)**, Wiggins Yard, Bridge St, Godalming, **Surrey**, GU7 1HL, ENG.
(T) 01483 418103
Speciality: Acupressure, Acupuncture, Aromatherapy, Chinese Herbal Medicine, Chiropody, Chiropractic, Counselling, Cranio-Sacral Therapy, Herbal Medicine, Homeopathy, Indian Head Massage, Massage (Therapeutic), Naturopathy, Osteopathy, Psychotherapy, Reflexology, Reiki, Shiatsu, Yoga, Allergy Freedom Programme, Applied Kinesiology, Bach Flower Remedies, Bowen Tehnique, Cranial Osteopathy, Therapy, Feldenkrais Method, Holistic Massage, Lymphatic Drainage, Pilates, Pre-natal and Birth Therapy. ✔
● **Reiki Therapist** Ms S Cameron
● **Therapist** Ms S Kypers
● **Psychologist** Ms L Kingston
● **Feldenkrais Method Therapist** Ms S Lemieux
● **Reflexologist/Yoga** Ms C Martin
● **Therapeutic Massage Therapist** Ms I Mariell
● **Medical Herbalist** Ms N Harding
● **Therapist** Mr D Haas
● **Cranio-Sacral Therapist/Homeopath** Ms A Williams
● **Acupuncturist** Jadwega Palmer
● **Bowen Technique Therapist** Ms J Ashford
● **Homeopath** Ms S Bogue
● **Chiropractor/Kinesiologist** Ms E Andrews
● **Shiatsu Therapist** Lee Breeze
● **Aromatherapist/Occupational Therapist** Ms K Broughton
● **Counsellor** Mr C Brown
● **Counsellor** Ms S Ballantyne
● **Cranial Osteopath/Osteopath** Mr C Grey
● **Meridian Therapist** Mr P Callaway
● **Kinesiologist** Ms J Phillips
● **Medical Herbalist** Mr T Carpenter
● **Therapist** Ms R Clunie
● **Facefirm Therapist** Ms S Collett
● **Chiropodist** Ms S Ward
● **Hypnotherapist** Mr D Sansom
● **Aromatherapist** Ms A Smith
● **Kinesiologist** Ms J Stephenson
● **Therapist** Mr D Stevens
● **Counsellor** Ms A Wallace
● **Osteopath** Mr A Beaumount
● **Therapist** Mr T Gauvain
C Yrs. Est.: 1 (Ref:HM09949)

**HOLISTIC CENTRE**

**Holistic Centre (The)**, 19 West St, Morecambe, **Lancashire**, LA3 1RB, ENG.
(T) 01524 823788
Speciality: Complementary Medicines & Therapy.
● **Owner** Mrs J Ferguson
M (Ref:HM09950)

**HOLISTIC CHIROPRACTOR**

**Adam Kaser - Holistic Chiropractor**, 42 Brighton Gr, Fenham, Newcastle Upon Tyne, **Tyne and Wear**, NE4 5NS, ENG.
(T) 01912 732040
Speciality: Acupressure, Chiropractic, Healer, Manipulation, Moxibustion, Postural Integration, T'ai-Chi Ch'uan. ✔
● **McTimoney-Corley Chiropractor** Mr A Kaser Q: BSc (Chiro). M: BAAC.
S Yrs. Est.: 15 (Ref:HM09951)

**HOLISTIC CLINIC/MYDDFAI HERBS**

**Holistic Clinic & Myddfai Herbs**, 1a King St, Llandeilo, **Carmarthenshire**, SA19 6AA, WAL.
(T) 01558 822199 (F) 01558 822199
Speciality: Complementary Medicines & Therapy.
● **Partner** Mr I Anderson
M (Ref:HM09952)

**HOLISTIC COUNS & HEALING CON**

**Holistic Counselling & Healing Consultancy**, 91 Stoke Rd, Gosport, **Hampshire**, PO12 1LR, ENG.
(T) 023 9235 8284
Speciality: Hypnotherapy.
B (Ref:HM09953)

**HOLISTIC ENERGY HEALING**

**Holistic Energy Healing Therapy**, Consillagh Newtownmountkennedy, **County Wicklow**, IRE.
(T) 01281 0143
Speciality: Complementary Medicines & Therapy.
M (Ref:HM09954)

**HOLISTIC FEMALE THERAPIST**

**Holistic Female Therapist**, 126 Heath Rd, London, **London (Greater)**, SW8 3AS, ENG.
(T) 020 7720 4415
Speciality: Complementary Medicines & Therapy.
● **Owner** Miss D McNicholls
M (Ref:HM09955)

**HOLISTIC FENG SHUI**

**Holistic Feng Shui**, P O Box 110, Seal, Sevenoaks, **Kent**, TN15 0ZQ, ENG.
(T) 01732 763792 (F) 01732 763914
Speciality: Complementary Medicines & Therapy.
● **Owner** Mrs P Penn
C M (Ref:HM09956)

**HOLISTIC HARMONY**

**Holistic Harmony**, 1st Floor, Queens Court, 39-41 Sandgate, Ayr, **Ayrshire (South)**, KA7 1BD, SCO.
(T) 01292 266261 (F) 01292 611294
Speciality: Complementary Medicines & Therapy.
● **Owner** Mrs H McLauchlen
M (Ref:HM09957)

**HOLISTIC HEALING**

**Holistic Healing**, Soundwell Rd, Bristol, BS16 4QH, ENG.
(T) 01179 092475
Speciality: Complementary Medicines & Therapy.
● **Owner** Mrs K Blackwell
M (Ref:HM09958)

**HOLISTIC HEALING**

**Holistic Healing-Pamela Edwards**, 11 Fieldhead Gardens, Bourne End, **Buckinghamshire**, SL8 5RN, ENG.
(T) 01628 526911
Speciality: Counselling, Indian Head Massage, Reflexology, Reiki. ✔
● **Holistic Therapist** Ms P Edwards Q: RGN. M: GCP.
C Yrs. Est.: 5 (Ref:HM09959)

**HOLISTIC HEALING**

**Geraldine Healing Clinic**, 22 Nessan Court,


Key continued: Yrs.Est: Years Established Q: Qualifications M: Professional Membership ✔ Indemnity Insurance Accept Credit Cards

Church Rd, Raheen, Limerick, **County Limerick**, IRE.
(T) 06130 8225
Speciality: Absent Healing, Acupressure, Aromatherapy, Bio-energetics, Healer, Healing Therapy, Holistic Healing, Indian Head Massage, Reflexology, Reiki, Seichem, Spiritual Healing. ✓
● **Acupuncturist** Marise McEldufe
(T) 08763 81963
T Yrs. Est.: 4 (**Ref:**HM09960)

## HOLISTIC HEALING & HYP

**Holistic Healing & Hypnotherapy Clinic**, 9 Clarkston Rd, Cathcart, Glasgow, **Glasgow (City of)**, G44 4EF, SCO.
(T) 01415 710040 (F) 01415 710041
(E) rizy.hypnotherapy@euphony.net
(W) www.hhhclinic.co.uk
Speciality: Bowen Therapy, Cognitive Therapy, Complementary Therapy, Healer, Healing Therapy, Herbal Medicine, Holistic Healing, Homeopathy, Humanistic Psychology, Hypnosis, Hypnotherapy, Indian Head Massage, Meditation, Psychotherapy, Reflexology, Reiki. ✓
● **Director** Rizy Mohammed
Q: Dip.Analytical.Hyp.Psych, Dip.Clin.Hyp, Dip.GPC, DipCH.P, MCPS, MHRS, MNCH, MNRSCT, NFSH, PICT. M: A.A.C.T, AGPC, Azeemi Federation UK, BHReg, CPS, HRS, HS, NCH, NFSH, NRSCT.
C H Yrs. Est.: 8 (**Ref:**HM09961)

## HOLISTIC HEALING CENTRE

**Holistic Healing Centre**, 25 Berrow Rd, Burnham-on-Sea, **Somerset**, TA8 2EY, ENG.
(T) 01278 780498
Speciality: Aromatherapy, Reflexology. ✓
● **Reflexologist** Ms E Ham Q: ITEC. M: IIHHT.
C Yrs. Est.: 6 (**Ref:**HM09962)

## HOLISTIC HEALING CENTRE

**Holistic Healing Centre**, 77 Bellwood St, Glasgow, **Glasgow (City of)**, G41 3EY, SCO.
(T) 01416 328291
Speciality: Complementary Medicines & Therapy.
● **Owner** Ms L Galloway
M (**Ref:**HM09963)

## HOLISTIC HEALING CENTRE

**Holistic Healing Centre**, 339 Clepington Rd, Dundee, **Angus**, DD3 8BA, SCO.
(T) 01382 819367
Speciality: Osteopathy. ✓
● **Osteopath** Mr Hewitt Q: DC. M: IBCA.
M Yrs. Est.: 41 (**Ref:**HM09964)

## HOLISTIC HEALING CENTRE

**Holistic Healing Ireland Ltd**, High St, Graiguenamanagh, **County Kilkenny**, IRE.
(T) 05032 4298 (F) 05032 5954
Speciality: Aromatherapy, Auto Suggestion, Counselling, Dowsing, Holistic Healing, Homeopathy, Hypnosis, Indian Head Massage, Massage (Therapeutic), Metamorphic Therapy, Polarity Therapy, Psychotherapy, Reflexology, Reiki, Touch Therapy, Quantum Touch Healing, Sand Therapy. ✓
● **Counsellor** Gene O'Sullivan Q: BSc.
● **Masseur** Joe Fox
● **Aromatherapist** Andrea Norton
● **Reiki Practitioner** Noeleen Mahon
T Yrs. Est.: 3 (**Ref:**HM09965)

## HOLISTIC HEALING CENTRE

**Holistic Healing Centre**, 38 Dame St, Dublin, **County Dublin**, IRE.
(T) 01671 0813
Speciality: Complementary Medicines & Therapy.
M (**Ref:**HM09966)

## HOLISTIC HEALING CLINICS

**Holistic Healing Clinics**, 103 Abbey Mill Business Centre, Paisley, **Renfrewshire**, PA1 1TJ, SCO.
(T) 01415 612400
Speciality: Complementary Medicines & Therapy.
● **Managing Director** Mr J Robertson
C M (**Ref:**HM09967)

## HOLISTIC HEALTH

**Holistic Health**, 12 May Bate Avenue, Kingston Upon Thames, **Surrey**, KT2 5UR, ENG.
(T) 020 8546 5600 (F) 020 8546 9006
Speciality: Acupuncture.
● **Owner** Ms M Aristidou
O (**Ref:**HM09968)

## HOLISTIC HEALTH

**Holistic Health**, 4 Upper Stoneborough Lane, Budleigh Salterton, **Devon**, EX9 6SU, ENG.
(T) 01395 442077
Speciality: Complementary Medicines & Therapy.
C M (**Ref:**HM09969)

## HOLISTIC HEALTH & BTY CLINIC

**Holistic Health & Beauty Clinic (The)**, 6a Alder Drive, Hoghton, Preston, **Lancashire**, PR5 0AD, ENG.
(T) 01254 852667
Speciality: Complementary Medicines & Therapy.
● **Owner** Mrs L Gornall
C M (**Ref:**HM09970)

## HOLISTIC HEALTH CENTRE

**Holistic Health Centre**, 1 Upland Rd, South Croydon, **Surrey**, CR2 6RD, ENG.
(T) 020 8760 0909
Speciality: Acupuncture, Allergy Testing, Homeopathy, Food Allergies. ✓
● **Acupuncturist** Dr N Raman Q: PhD.
C (**Ref:**HM09971)

## HOLISTIC HEALTH CENTRE

**Holistic Health Centre**, The Hollies, 9 Redhill, Stourbridge, **Midlands (West)**, DY8 1NA, ENG.
(T) 01384 379740
Speciality: Aura Therapy, Bach Remedies, Counselling, Floral Essence Therapy, Healer, Holistic Healing, Homeopathy, Spiritual Healing, Stress Therapy.
● **Holistic Physician** Dr H Ford Q: MA, MB, MRCP.
B C Yrs. Est.: 15 (**Ref:**HM09972)

## HOLISTIC HEALTH CENTRE

**Holistic Health Centre**, High Tor, Worgret Hill, Wareham, **Dorset**, DH20 6AD, ENG.
(T) 01929 556869 (F) 01929 555068
(E) jennie@innerpower.freeserve.co.uk
Speciality: Acupressure, Herbal Medicine, Homeopathy, Hypnotherapy, Kinesiology, Naturopathy, Shiatsu. ✓
● **Owner/Homeopath** Mr R Johnson
Q: D.Hom.Med, Dip.Hyp, Dip.Psych, ND.
M: BNA.
C Yrs. Est.: 10 (**Ref:**HM09973)

## HOLISTIC HEALTH CENTRE

**Holistic Health Centre (The)**, 37 North Rd, Kirkby Stephen, **Cumbria**, CA17 4RH, ENG.
(T) 01768 372482
Speciality: Complementary Medicines & Therapy.
● **Partner** Miss J Brown
C M (**Ref:**HM09974)

## HOLISTIC HEALTH CENTRE

**Holistic Health Centre**, 168 Roe Lane, Churchtown, Southport, **Merseyside**, PR9 7PN, ENG.
(T) 01704 212064
(E) garrettbernie@hotmail.co.uk
Speciality: Acupuncture, Bowen Therapy, Complementary Therapy, Electrotherapy, Homeopathy. ✓
● **Therapist** Mr B Garrett Q: BSc (Hons).
M: BTER, FFHom.
T Yrs. Est.: 12 (**Ref:**HM09975)

## HOLISTIC HEALTH CENTRE

**Holistic Health Centre (The)**, 50-52 High St, Overstrand, Cromer, **Norfolk**, NR27 0AB, ENG.
(T) 01263 579559
Speciality: Complementary Medicines & Therapy.
● **Owner** Mr S Langley
M (**Ref:**HM09976)

## HOLISTIC HEALTH CENTRE

**Holistic Health Centre**, 197 Lr Kimmage Rd, Kimmage Dublin 6W, IRE.
(T) 01492 9279
Speciality: Complementary Medicines & Therapy.
M (**Ref:**HM09977)

## HOLISTIC HEALTH CLINIC

**Holistic Health Clinic**, 56 Mansfield Rd, Ilford, **Essex**, IG1 3BD, ENG.
(T) 020 8554 6595 (F) 020 8554 1083
Speciality: Ayurvedic Medicine, Homeopathy, Nutritional Therapy, Botanical Medicine.
● **Principal Practitioner** M Iqbal Q: BSc, FRSH, ITEC, MGCP, MSc.
M S Yrs. Est.: 10 (**Ref:**HM09978)

## HOLISTIC HEALTH CONSULTANTS

**Holistic Health Consultants**, Rosenhill, Draughton Rd, Maidwell, Northampton, **Northamptonshire**, NN6 9JF, ENG.
(T) 01604 686678
Speciality: Complementary Medicines & Therapy.
C M (**Ref:**HM09979)

## HOLISTIC HEALTH FARM

**Holistic Health Farm & Reflexology Association/The Little House of Avalon Ltd**, The Little House Of Avalon, Taughmaconnell, Ballinasloe, **County Roscommon**, IRE.
(T) 00353 90583002
(E) littlehouseofavalon@eircom.net
(W) www.littlehouseofavalon.com
Speciality: Aromatherapy, Ayurvedic Medicine, Bach Remedies, Counselling, Crystal Healing, Healer, Herbal Medicine, Holistic Healing, Indian Head Massage, Iridology, Kinesiology, Life Style Coaching, Massage (Therapeutic), Meditation, Nutritional Therapy, Pattern Therapies, Reflexology, Reiki, Light Art Foot Reflexology, Foot Joint Mobilisation and Thai Bodywork. ✓
● **Therapist** Mr A Smith Q: Dip.Iridol, Reiki Master.
B Yrs. Est.: 3 (**Ref:**HM09980)

## HOLISTIC HEALTHCARE

**Holistic Healthcare**, 16 New Row, Dunfermline, **Fife**, KY12 7EF, SCO.
(T) 01383 736315
Speciality: Complementary Medicines & Therapy.
● **Owner** Mr J Wood
C M (**Ref:**HM09981)

## HOLISTIC HYPNOTHERAPY

**Holistic Hypnotherapy**, 2 Bern Links, Northampton, **Northamptonshire**, NN4 8SS, ENG.
(T) 01604 765749
Speciality: Hypnotherapy.
● **Owner** Mrs M Bell
B (**Ref:**HM09982)

## HOLISTIC HYPNOTHERAPY

**Holistic Hypnotherapy**, 42 The Spinney, Goldington, Bedford, **Bedfordshire**, MK41 0ET, ENG.
(T) 01234 341059
(E) enki@eridu.totalserve.co.uk
Speciality: Healer, Healing Therapy, Hypnosis, Hypnotherapy, Psychotherapy, Reiki, Stress Therapy, Visualisation Therapy, E.F.T - Emotional Freedom Therapy. ✓
● **Hypnotherapist** Mr M Newman
Q: Dip.Hol.Hyp. M: NAHH.
C Yrs. Est.: 9 (**Ref:**HM09983)

## HOLISTIC MATTERS

**Holistic Matters**, 20 Chatsworth Court, Stevenage, **Hertfordshire**, SG2 8DY, ENG.
(T) 01438 728589
Speciality: Reflexology.
● **Owner** Mrs J Matthias
S T (**Ref:**HM09984)

## HOLISTIC OPTIONS

**Holistic Options**, 3 Sydenham Mews, Bray, **County Wicklow**, IRE.
(T) 01286 6084
Speciality: Aromatherapy, Complementary Therapy, Holistic Healing, Indian Head Massage, Massage (Therapeutic), Reflexology, Stress Therapy. ✓



Key: B Mind-Body Medicine C Complementary Medicine H Self Help Treatment M Medicinal Therapy O Oriental Medicine P Postural Therapy S Manipulative Structural Therapy T Touch Therapy

● **Nurse/Therapist** Ms I Harvey Q: SRN.
B Yrs. Est.: 5 (Ref:HM09985)

**HOLISTIC PEACE**

**Holistic Peace**, 43 Brambles Enterprise Centre, Waterberry Drive, Waterlooville, **Hampshire**, PO7 7TH, ENG.
(T) 023 9223 1217
Speciality: Complementary Medicines & Therapy.
● **Owner** Mrs C Samuel
M (Ref:HM09986)

**HOLISTIC SCH OF REFLEX/MASSAGE**

**Holistic School of Reflexology And Massage**, City Centre D1, IRE.
(T) 01459 2460 (F) 01459 2460
Speciality: Reflexology.
S T (Ref:HM09987)

**HOLISTIC SCHOOL OF REFLEXOLOGY**

**Holistic School of Reflexology**, 2 Laurel Park, Clondalkin, **County Dublin**, IRE.
(T) 01459 2460
Speciality: Reflexology.
S T (Ref:HM09988)

**HOLISTIC SOL NTRL HEALING CTRE**

**Holistic Solutions Natural Healing Centre**, 15 Ascail Setanta, The Ferns, Blackrock, **County Louth**, IRE.
(T) 04293 22173
Speciality: Auto Suggestion, Healing Therapy, Hypnosis, Hypnotherapy, Psychotherapy, Reiki, Stress Therapy. ✓
● **Hypnotherapist/Psychotherapist** Ms A Finnerty M: ICHP.
B (Ref:HM09989)

**HOLISTIC SOURCING CENTRE**

**Holistic Sourcing Centre**, 67 Lr Camden St, Dublin, **County Dublin**, IRE.
(T) 01478 5022
Speciality: Complementary Medicines & Therapy.
M (Ref:HM09990)

**HOLISTIC SURGERY**

**Holistic Surgery (The)**, 79-81 Bowman St, Glasgow, **Glasgow (City of)**, G42 8LF, SCO.
(T) 01414 237648
Speciality: Complementary Medicines & Therapy.
M (Ref:HM09991)

**HOLISTIC THERAPEUTIC MASSAGE**

**Holistic Therapeutic Massage**, 55 Tysoe Avenue, Enfield, **London (Greater)**, EN3 6DZ, ENG.
(T) 020 8350 9214
Speciality: Massage (Therapeutic).
M (Ref:HM09992)

**HOLISTIC THERAPIES**

**Holistic Therapies**, 26 Sheerstone, Iwade, Sittingbourne, **Kent**, ME9 8RN, ENG.
(T) 01795 429946
Speciality: Aromatherapy, Indian Head Massage, Reflexology.
S T (Ref:HM09993)

**HOLISTIC THERAPIST**

**Holistic Therapist**, Harmony, 56 Arundel Rd, Worthing, **Sussex (West)**, BN13 3EQ, ENG.
(T) 01903 261449
Speciality: Aromatherapy.
M O (Ref:HM09994)

**HOLISTIC THERAPY CENTRE**

**Holistic Therapy Centre**, 40 Mannamead Rd, Plymouth, **Devon**, PL4 7AF, ENG.
(T) 01752 604211
Speciality: Complementary Medicines & Therapy.
M (Ref:HM09995)

**HOLISTIC THERAPY CENTRE**

**Holistic Therapy Centre (The)**, First Floor, 24 Reddish Rd, Stockport, **Cheshire**, SK5 7PE, ENG.
(T) 01612 921136
Speciality: Complementary Medicines & Therapy.
● **Manager** Ms R Devi
C M (Ref:HM09996)

**HOLISTIC THERAPY CENTRE**

**Holistic Therapy Centre**, Main St, Clarecastle, **County Clare**, IRE.
(T) 06568 44290
Speciality: Complementary Medicines & Therapy.
M (Ref:HM09997)

**HOLISTIC THERAPY CLINIC**

**Holistic Therapy Clinic**, 9 Stafford Rd, Newport, NP19 7DQ, WAL.
(T) 01633 264032 (F) 01633 264032
Speciality: Complementary Medicines & Therapy.
● **Chief Executive** Mr R Gardner
M (Ref:HM09998)

**HOLISTIC TRADING**

**Holistic Trading Co**, 1 Spring Cres, Southampton, **Hampshire**, SO17 2FZ, ENG.
(T) 023 8036 3026 (F) 023 8039 0983
Speciality: Aromatherapy.
● **Principal** Mr M McGinness
M O (Ref:HM09999)

**HOLISTIC TREATMENTS**

**Holistic Treatments By Fingertips**, 10 Marion Rd, Southsea, **Hampshire**, PO4 0QX, ENG.
(T) 023 9279 8253
Speciality: Aromatherapy.
M O (Ref:HM10000)

**HOLISTIC WAY**

**Holistic Way Ltd (The)**, 130 High St, Epping, **Essex**, CM16 4AG, ENG.
(T) 01992 571099
Speciality: Complementary Medicines & Therapy.
● **Director** Mrs S Haiden
M (Ref:HM10001)

**HOLISTICA**

**Holistica**, Flat 75/Newbank Tower, Bridgewater St, Salford, **Manchester (Greater)**, M3 7JZ, ENG.
(T) 01616 616936 (F) 07957 840168
Speciality: Complementary Medicines & Therapy.
● **Owner** Mr J Gilroy
C M (Ref:HM10002)

**HOLISTICLY YOURS**

**Holisticly Yours**, 61A Bourne St, Bilston, **Midlands (West)**, WV14 9HR, ENG.
(T) 01902 677677
Speciality: Aromatherapy.
● **Owner** Mrs A Weavers
M O (Ref:HM10003)

**HOLISTIX AROMATHERAPY**

**Holistix Aromatherapy**, 72A Mount Pleasant Rd, Tunbridge Wells, **Kent**, TN1 1RJ, ENG.
(T) 01892 535899
Speciality: Complementary Medicines & Therapy.
● **Partner** Ms J MacNay
M (Ref:HM10004)

**HOLLAND & ROBERTS**

**Holland & Roberts**, 36 Oxford Rd, Altrincham, **Cheshire**, WA14 2EB, ENG.
(T) 01619 281181
Speciality: Chiropodists (Podiatrists).
S (Ref:HM10005)

**HOLLAND PARK OSTEO PRACTICE**

**Holland Park Osteopathic Practice**, Basement Flat, 8 Holland Park Avenue, London, **London (Greater)**, W11 3QU, ENG.
(T) 020 7243 8005
Speciality: Osteopathy.
P S T (Ref:HM10006)

**HOLLAND, A G**

**A G Holland**, 84 Toll Bar Rd, Swinton, Mexborough, **Yorkshire (South)**, S64 8HH, ENG.
(T) 01709 582119
Speciality: Chiropodists (Podiatrists).
● **Owner** A Holland
S (Ref:HM10007)

**HOLLAND, G H R**

**G H R Holland**, Market Place Clinic, Commercial House, Market Pl, Easingwold, **Yorkshire (North)**, YO6 3AN, ENG.
(T) 01347 822805
Speciality: Chiropractic.
P S T (Ref:HM10008)

**HOLLAND, GLENYS**

**Glenys Holland**, Weir Cl, Hoyland, Barnsley, **Yorkshire (South)**, S74 9DB, ENG.
(T) 01226 742968
Speciality: Reflexology.
● **Owner** Mrs G Holland
S T (Ref:HM10009)

**HOLLAND, GLENYS J**

**Glenys J Holland**, 10 Fitzwilliam Drive, Harlington, Doncaster, **Yorkshire (South)**, DN5 7HY, ENG.
(T) 01709 896276
Speciality: Reflexology.
● **Owner** Mrs G Holland
S T (Ref:HM10010)

**HOLLAND, HELEN**

**Helen Holland**, 185a Torridon Rd, London, **London (Greater)**, SE6 1RG, ENG.
(T) 020 8480 9905
Speciality: Aromatherapy.
● **Owner** Ms L Griffin
M O (Ref:HM10011)

**HOLLAND, IAN**

**Ian Holland**, 26 Ashburton Rd, Glasgow, **Glasgow (City of)**, G12 0LZ, SCO.
(T) 01413 345846 (F) 01415 760323
Speciality: Complementary Medicines & Therapy.
● **Owner** Mr I Holland
C M (Ref:HM10012)

**HOLLAND, JACQUELINE**

**Jacqueline Holland**, Downacre, Doggetts Wood Lane, Chalfont St. Giles, **Buckinghamshire**, HP8 4TH, ENG.
(T) 01494 762311 (F) 01494 766968
Speciality: Aromatherapy.
● **Owner** Mrs J Holland
M O (Ref:HM10013)

**HOLLAND, R**

**R Holland**, Manor Walk Physiotherapy Centre, Manor Walk, Market Harborough, **Leicestershire**, LE16 9BP, ENG.
(T) 01858 431510
Speciality: Physiotherapy.
P S T (Ref:HM10014)

**HOLLAND-AVERY, H**

**H Holland-Avery**, 8 Rosefield Rd, Staines, **Surrey**, TW18 4NB, ENG.
(T) 01784 450666 (F) 01784 450666
Speciality: Acupuncture.
● **Owner** Mrs H Holland-Avery
O (Ref:HM10015)

**HOLLANDERS, HENRY (DR)**

**Dr Henry Hollanders**, 5 Barnoldswick Rd, Barrowford, Nelson, **Lancashire**, BB9 6BH, ENG.
(T) 01282 697211
Speciality: Psychotherapy.
● **Owner** Dr H Hollanders
B (Ref:HM10016)

**HOLLANDS, K M**

**K M Hollands**, 49 Hedgemans Rd, Dagenham, **Essex**, RM9 6HD, ENG.
(T) 020 8593 1057 (F) 020 8252 9567
Speciality: Hypnosis.
● **Owner** Mrs K Hollands
B (Ref:HM10017)

**HOLLANDS, P R**

**P R Hollands**, 21 Station Rd, Gidea Park, Romford, **Essex**, RM2 6BX, ENG.
(T) 01708 448125
Speciality: Chiropodists (Podiatrists).
S (Ref:HM10018)

**HOLLENBERY, S**

**S Hollenbery**, Lakeview, 5 Warren Rd, Bushey, Watford, **Hertfordshire**, WD2 1HU, ENG.
(T) 020 8421 9421 (F) 020 8387 0205
Speciality: Physiotherapy. ✓
● **Owner/Physiotherapist** Mrs S Hollinbery Q: MCSP, RCST, SRP. M: CSP.



Key continued: Yrs.Est: Years Established Q: Qualifications M: Professional Membership ✓ Indemnity Insurance Accept Credit Cards

S (Ref:HM10019)

## HOLLENBERY, SUSAN

**Susan Hollenbery**, 7 Wagon Rd, Barnet, **Hertfordshire**, EN4 0PW, ENG.
(T) 020 8440 8017 (F) 020 8440 4417
Speciality: Physiotherapy.
● **Owner** Ms S Hollenbery
P S T (Ref:HM10020)

## HOLLINGS, KATH

**Kath Hollings**, Aysgarth, St. Pauls Rd, Manningham, Bradford, **Yorkshire (West)**, BD8 7LU, ENG.
(T) 01274 773434 (F) 01274 493701
Speciality: Physiotherapy.
● **Owner** Mrs C Hollings
P S T (Ref:HM10021)

## HOLLINGSWORTH, ELAINE

**Elaine Hollingsworth**, Exeter, **Devon**, EX5, ENG.
(T) 01392 841434
Speciality: Bach Remedies.
M (Ref:HM10022)

## HOLLINGWORTH, SUSAN

**Susan Hollingworth**, Copthorne, Grafton, Marton Cum Grafton, York, **Yorkshire (North)**, YO51 9QJ, ENG.
(T) 01423 322225 (F) 01423 322205
Speciality: Homeopathy.
● **Owner** Ms S Hollingworth
M (Ref:HM10023)

## HOLLINSHEAD

**Hollinshead**, 104 Edleston Rd, Crewe, **Cheshire**, CW2 7HD, ENG.
(T) 01270 211466
Speciality: Chiropodists (Podiatrists).
S (Ref:HM10024)

## HOLLOWAY, JANE

**Jane Holloway**, 5 Coppice Gardens, Crowthorne, **Berkshire**, RG45 6EE, ENG.
(T) 01344 776886 (F) 01344 778615
Speciality: Aromatherapy.
● **Owner** Mrs J Holloway
M O (Ref:HM10025)

## HOLLOWAY, MICHAEL & AMANDA

**Michael & Amanda Holloway**, 56 New St, Burton-On-Trent, **Staffordshire**, DE14 3QY, ENG.
(T) 01283 543398
Speciality: Osteopathy.
P S T (Ref:HM10026)

## HOLLOWAY, P

**P Holloway**, Aba Therapy Centre, Merry Hill Shopping Centre, Brierley Hill, **Midlands (West)**, ENG.
(T) 01299 403309
(E) hollowaypaulaaba@aol.com
Speciality: Aromatherapy, Hypnotherapy, Reflexology, Stress Therapy.
● **Managing Director** Paula Holloway Q: IIHHT. M: HF.
B Yrs. Est.: 3 (Ref:HM10027)

## HOLLOWAY, P

**P Holloway**, 108 Abbeley Avenue, Stourport-on-Severn, **Worcestershire**, ENG.
(T) 01299 403309
Speciality: Complementary Medicines & Therapy.
● **Owner** Paula Holloway
M (Ref:HM10028)

## HOLLY COTTAGE CHIRO CLINIC

**Holly Cottage Chiropractic Clinic**, 58 Birmingham Rd, Sutton Coldfield, **Midlands (West)**, B72 1QJ, ENG.
(T) 01213 211755 (F) 01213 211766
(W) www.hollycottagechiropractic.co.uk
Speciality: Chiropractic. ✔
● **Owner/Chiropractor** Mr J Lange Q: CCEP, DC, FCC, MSc. M: BCA.
● **Chiropractor** Mr L Dawson Q: BA, CCSP, DC. M: BCA, CSP.
● **Chiropractor** Mr R Loatey Q: BSc (Hons), CCEP, DC, MSc (Chiro). M: BCA.
● **Chiropractor** Ms M Cook Q: BA (Hons), CCEP, DC, MSc. M: BCA.
P S Yrs. Est.: 12 (Ref:HM10029)

## HOLLYBANK NATURAL HEALTH CTRE

**Hollybank Natural Health Centre**, 22 Holly Bank Rd, Huddersfield, **Yorkshire (West)**, HD3 3LX, ENG.
(T) 01484 654751 (F) 01484 300163
Speciality: Complementary Medicines & Therapy.
● **Owner** Mrs C Garland
C M (Ref:HM10030)

## HOLM, KIRSTI

**Kirsti Holm**, Finchley Rd, London, **London (Greater)**, NW11 8RR, ENG.
(T) 020 8202 3654
Speciality: Hypnosis.
● **Owner** Mrs K Holm
B (Ref:HM10031)

## HOLM, M

**M Holm**, St Boswells Chiropractic Clinic, 16 Jenny Moores Rd, St. Boswells, Melrose, **Scottish Borders**, TD6 0AL, SCO.
(T) 01835 823645 (F) 01835 823930
Speciality: Chiropractors.
● **Partner** Dr C How
P S T (Ref:HM10032)

## HOLMAN, M J

**M J Holman**, Boldavon, Holbrook Rd, Stutton, Ipswich, **Suffolk**, IP9 2RY, ENG.
(T) 01473 327334
Speciality: Chiropodists (Podiatrists).
S (Ref:HM10033)

## HOLMDEN, JO-ANNE

**Jo-Anne Holmden**, 56 Crofton Rd, Orpington, **Kent**, BR6 8HY, ENG.
(T) 01689 897354
Speciality: Osteopathy.
● **Owner** Mrs J Holmden
P S T (Ref:HM10034)

## HOLME VALLEY CLINIC

**Holme Valley Clinic**, 16 Church St, Honley, Huddersfield, **Yorkshire (West)**, HD7 2AH, ENG.
(T) 01484 667761
Speciality: Physiotherapy.
● **Partner** Mr C Horner
P S T (Ref:HM10035)

## HOLME VALLEY SPORTS CLINIC

**Holme Valley Sports Injury Clinic**, 4 Brewery Drive, Huddersfield, **Yorkshire (West)**, HD4 6EN, ENG.
(T) 01484 541227
Speciality: Acupuncture, Physiotherapy. ✔
● **Physiotherapist** Mr J McLean Q: MCSP. M: CSP.
● **Sports Injury Therapist** Mr G Brook M: ICM.
S Yrs. Est.: 10 (Ref:HM10036)

## HOLME, CHRISTINE

**Christine Holme**, 8 Mill Lane, Wingerworth, Chesterfield, **Derbyshire**, S42 6NG, ENG.
(T) 01246 27243
Speciality: Chiropodists (Podiatrists).
● **Chiropodist** Ms C Holme Q: MBChA, MSSCh. M: B.A.Ch.P, SSCh.
S (Ref:HM10037)

## HOLMED CLINIC

**Holmed Clinic**, 665 Burnage Lane, Manchester, **Manchester (Greater)**, M19 1RR, ENG.
(T) 01614 428513
Speciality: Osteopathy. ✔
● **Osteopath** Mr T Green Q: DO. M: GOsC.
C Yrs. Est.: 13 (Ref:HM10038)

## HOLMES, A

**A Holmes**, Colbeck Rd, Harrow, **London (Greater)**, HA1 4BS, ENG.
(T) 020 8864 6199
Speciality: Hypnotherapy.
● **Owner** Mr A Holmes
B (Ref:HM10039)

## HOLMES, DAVID

**David Holmes**, 325 Willow Rd, Enfield, **London (Greater)**, EN1 3BX, ENG.
(T) 020 8364 6868
Speciality: Chiropody, Nail Surgery. ✔
● **Chiropodist** Mr D Holmes Q: MBChA, S.R.Ch.
M Yrs. Est.: 4 (Ref:HM10040)

## HOLMES, H J

**H J Holmes**, 2 Lime Gr, Kirby Muxloe, Leicester, **Leicestershire**, LE9 2DF, ENG.
(T) 01162 392024
Speciality: Chiropodists (Podiatrists).
● **Owner** Mrs H Holmes
S (Ref:HM10041)

## HOLMES, KYLIE

**Kylie Holmes**, Maurice Cl, Huntingdon, **Cambridgeshire**, PE18 0HD, ENG.
(T) 01480 356126 (F) 01480 356126
Speciality: Clairvoyants & Palmists.
● **Owner** Ms K Holmes
B (Ref:HM10042)

## HOLMES, M N & M

**M N & M Holmes**, 32 Holly Rd, Farnborough, **Hampshire**, GU14 0EA, ENG.
(T) 01252 542087 (F) 01252 542087
Speciality: Chiropodists (Podiatrists).
● **Senior Partner** Mr M Holmes
S (Ref:HM10043)

## HOLMES, PHILIP D

**Philip D Holmes**, 9 Kings Rd, St. Leonards-On-Sea, **Sussex (East)**, TN37 6EA, ENG.
(T) 01424 714800
Speciality: Acupuncture.
O (Ref:HM10044)

## HOLMES, S A

**Mrs S A Holmes**, 33 Sterling Avenue, Maidstone, **Kent**, ME16 0AX, ENG.
(T) 01622 763703
Speciality: Massage (Therapeutic), Reflexology, Spiritual Healing. ✔
● **Complementary Therapist** Mrs S Holmes Q: ITEC. M: IFR, ITEC, NFSH.
C Yrs. Est.: 10 (Ref:HM10045)

## HOLMES, STEPHEN

**Stephen Holmes**, 39 Trevelyan Cr, Stratford-Upon-Avon, **Warwickshire**, CV37 9LL, ENG.
(T) 01789 414578
Speciality: Chiropodists (Podiatrists).
S (Ref:HM10046)

## HOLMFIELD

**Holmfield**, 53 Front St, Sowerby, Thirsk, **Yorkshire (North)**, YO7 1JQ, ENG.
(T) 01845 524651 (F) 01845 525937
Speciality: Aromatherapy.
● **Owner** Mrs S Kendal
M O (Ref:HM10047)

## HOLMFIRTH PHYSIO/SPORTS INJURY

**Holmfirth Physiotherapy Sports Injury & Remedial Massage Clinic**, 6 Stable Court, Huddersfield Rd, Holmfirth, Huddersfield, **Yorkshire (West)**, HD7 1AZ, ENG.
(T) 01484 689808
Speciality: Aromatherapy, Biomechanics, Chiropody, Physiotherapy, Reflexology. ✔
● **Physiotherapist** Mr A Young Q: A.I.P.T.I, ITEC. M: IPTI.
● **Reflexologist** Ms J Young Q: ITEC, MAR. M: AoR.
S T (Ref:HM10048)

## HOLMS, JOHN

**John Holms**, 100 Station Prde, Harrogate, **Yorkshire (North)**, HG1 1HQ, ENG.
(T) 01423 561566 (F) 01423 567379
Speciality: Osteopathy.
● **Owner** Mr T Cree
P S T (Ref:HM10049)

## HOLOS COMP THERAPY CLINIC

**Holos Complementary Therapy Clinic**, 25B Strand St, Sandwich, **Kent**, CT13 9DT, ENG.
(T) 01304 620061
Speciality: Complementary Medicines & Therapy.
C M (Ref:HM10050)

## HOLOS MASSAGE SCHOOL & CLINIC

**Holos Massage School & Clinic (The)**, 36 Carden Rd, London, **London (Greater)**, SE15 3UD, ENG.
(T) 020 7732 9515
Speciality: Complementary Medicines &



Key: B Mind-Body Medicine  C Complementary Medicine  H Self Help Treatment  M Medicinal Therapy  O Oriental Medicine  P Postural Therapy  S Manipulative Structural Therapy  T Touch Therapy

Therapy.
● **Director** Ms I Leahy
C M (**Ref:**HM10051)

## HOLST MCQUAIG SYSTEMS

**Holst McQuaig Systems**, 3 Old Sneed Rd, Bristol, BS9 1ES, ENG.
(T) 01179 684836 (F) 01179 626916
Speciality: Psychology.
● **Principal** Mr J Marshall-Smith
B (**Ref:**HM10052)

## HOLT, M

**M Holt**, 45 Scotland Rd, Nelson, **Lancashire**, BB9 7UT, ENG.
(T) 01282 612366
Speciality: Chiropodists (Podiatrists).
S (**Ref:**HM10053)

## HOLT, PATRICIA

**Patricia Holt**, 30 Rumbold Rd, Huddersfield, **Yorkshire (West)**, HD3 3DB, ENG.
(T) 01484 451877
Speciality: Electrolysis.
T (**Ref:**HM10054)

## HOLT, R

**R Holt**, 1a Moore Avenue, Bradford, **Yorkshire (West)**, BD6 3HH, ENG.
(T) 01274 600659
Speciality: Osteopathy.
● **Owner** Mr H Floura
P S T (**Ref:**HM10055)

## HOLT, S L

**S L Holt**, South Warwickshire Chiropody Clinic, 3 Warwick Pl, Leamington Spa, **Warwickshire**, CV32 5BH, ENG.
(T) 01926 339817 (F) 01926 339817
Speciality: Chiropodists (Podiatrists).
● **Owner** Mr S Holt
S (**Ref:**HM10056)

## HOLT, TIM

**Tim Holt**, Canal Rd, Hereford, **Herefordshire**, HR1 2EA, ENG.
(T) 01432 279881
Speciality: Physiotherapy.
● **Manager** Mr J Wheadon
P S T (**Ref:**HM10057)

## HOLTHAM, W

**W Holtham**, 113 Otley Rd, Guiseley, Leeds, **Yorkshire (West)**, LS20 8AF, ENG.
(T) 01943 872278
Speciality: Osteopathy.
P S T (**Ref:**HM10058)

## HOLVEY, L I H

**L I H Holvey**, 5 York Rd, Woking, **Surrey**, GU22 7XE, ENG.
(T) 01483 720464
Speciality: Acupuncture.
O (**Ref:**HM10059)

## HOLYCOMBE

**Holycombe**, Holycombe, Whichford, Shipston on Stour, **Warwickshire**, CV36 5PH, ENG.
(T) 01608 684239 (F) 01608 684501
Speciality: Absent Healing, Complementary Therapy, Counselling, Gestalt Therapy, Healer, Healing Therapy, Holistic Healing, Psychotherapy, Reiki, Shiatsu, Spiritual Healing, Stress Therapy. ✔
● **Owner/Shiatsu Practitioner/Reiki Master** Mrs S Crofts Q: Reiki Master. M: Shiatsu Society UK.
● **Gestalt Practitioner (Training)** Mr A Birtwell M: GPTI.
B Yrs. Est.: 7 (**Ref:**HM10060)

## HOLYWELL ANNEXE CLINIC

**Holywell Annexe Clinic Ltd (The)**, Holywell Annexe, Holywell St, Chesterfield, **Derbyshire**, S41 7SH, ENG.
(T) 01246 273848 (F) 01246 273848
Speciality: Chiropodists (Podiatrists).
● **Owner** Mr V Fletcher
S (**Ref:**HM10061)

## HOLZAMER, MARIA

**Maria Holzamer**, 13 Carclew Ter, Truro, **Cornwall**, TR1 2EF, ENG.
(T) 01872 261516
Speciality: Herbalists.
● **Owner** Miss M Holzamer
M (**Ref:**HM10062)

## HOM/ACU PRACTITIONER

**Homoeopathic & Acupuncture Practitioners**, 5 York Rd, Batley, **Yorkshire (West)**, WF17 0LG, ENG.
(T) 01924 479251 (F) 01924 472846
Speciality: Complementary Medicines & Therapy.
● **Owner** Dr H Khan
C M (**Ref:**HM10063)

## HOME CHIROPODY SERVICE

**Home Chiropody Service**, 9 Chilston Cl, Tunbridge Wells, **Kent**, TN4 9LS, ENG.
(T) 01892 529672
Speciality: Chiropodists (Podiatrists).
S (**Ref:**HM10064)

## HOME FARMHOUSE

**Home Farmhouse**, Gun Green, Hawkhurst, Cranbrook, **Kent**, TN18 5DL, ENG.
(T) 01580 753055
Speciality: Physiotherapy.
P S T (**Ref:**HM10065)

## HOME HOLISTIC THERAPY

**Home Holistic Therapy**, 40 Lauderdale Avenue, Thornton, **Lancashire**, FY5 3JP, ENG.
(T) 01253 857134
Speciality: Aromatherapy.
● **Owner** Mr A Pearson
M O (**Ref:**HM10066)

## HOME VISIT CHIROPODISTS

**Home Visit Chiropodists**, 21 Brigstock House, Lilford Rd, London, **London (Greater)**, SE5 9QE, ENG.
(T) 020 7326 5224
Speciality: Chiropodists (Podiatrists).
● **Owner** Miss C Nasom
S (**Ref:**HM10067)

## HOME VISITING CHIROPODY SV

**Home Visiting Chiropody Service**, 25 Shalford Cl, Orpington, **Kent**, BR6 7UP, ENG.
(T) 01689 853347
Speciality: Chiropodists (Podiatrists).
● **Owner** Mr W McDermott
S (**Ref:**HM10068)

## HOME VISITING SERVICES

**Trina Ward MBACC MRCHM BSc (Hons)**, 1 Stephanie Court, Conewood St, Highbury, London, **London (Greater)**, N5 1DD, ENG.
(T) 020 7226 1143
(E) trina@sanbaedemon.co.uk
Speciality: Acupressure, Acupuncture, Complementary Therapy, Psychotherapy. ✔
● **Acupuncturist/Herbalist** Trina Ward Q: BSc (Hons), Dip.TCHM. M: BAcC, RCHM.
O Yrs. Est.: 8 (**Ref:**HM10069)

## HOME-A-THERAPY CLINIC

**Home-A-Therapy Clinic**, Fitzwilliam St, Lr, IRE.
(T) 08726 23266
Speciality: Aromatherapy.
M O (**Ref:**HM10070)

## HOMEOPATH AND NAT THERAPIST

**Homeopath and Natural Therapist**, Blind Pond Cottage, Castledon Rd, Billericay, **Essex**, CM11 1LH, ENG.
(T) 01268 560811
Speciality: Homeopathy.
● **Manager** Mrs Ashton
M (**Ref:**HM10071)

## HOMEOPATHIC CLINIC

**Homeopathic Clinic**, 1078-1080 Argyle St, Glasgow, **Glasgow (City of)**, G3 8LY, SCO.
(T) 01415 641207 (F) 01415 641519
Speciality: Homeopathy.
● **Owner** Mr G Anjum
M (**Ref:**HM10072)

## HOMEOPATHIC CLINIC

**Homeopathic Clinic**, 18 Rockland Drive, Stanmore, **London (Greater)**, HA7 2JE, ENG.
(T) 020 8930 2048
Speciality: Homeopathy.
● **Owner** Mrs P Honer
M (**Ref:**HM10073)

## HOMEOPATHIC CLINIC

**Natural Food Store**, 4 Exchange St, Norwich, **Norfolk**, NR2 1AT, ENG.
(T) 01603 613228 (F) 01603 455656
(E) pms@shop.naturally.com
(W) www.shop-naturally.com
Speciality: Aromatherapy, Bach Remedies, Complementary Therapy, Crystal Healing, Dietician, Faith Healing, Healer, Herbal Medicine, Homeopathy, Massage (Therapeutic), Reiki, Spiritual Healing. CREDIT
● **Director/Homeopath** Ms T Stephenson Q: LCPH, MHMA, RSHom. M: Soc.Hom.
M Yrs. Est.: 24 (**Ref:**HM10074)

## HOMEOPATHIC MEDICAL ASS

**Homeopathic Medical Association**, 6 Livingstone Rd, Gravesend, **Kent**, DA12 5DZ, ENG.
(T) 01474 560336 (F) 01474 327431
Speciality: Homeopathy.
● **Treasurer** Mr R Bains
M (**Ref:**HM10075)

## HOMEOPATHIC MEDICAL PRACTICE

**Homeopathic Medical Practice**, 30 Milford Pl, Bradford, **Yorkshire (West)**, BD9 4RU, ENG.
(T) 01274 774055
(E) gcrieb@doctors.org.uk
Speciality: Complementary Therapy, Holistic Healing, Homeopathy. ✔
● **Owner/Homeopathic Physician** Dr G Rieberer
C M Yrs. Est.: 7 (**Ref:**HM10076)

## HOMEOPATHIC MEDICINES

**Homeopathic Medicines**, 15 Duke St, Dublin, **County Dublin**, IRE.
(T) 01679 0451 (F) 01679 0457
Speciality: Homeopathy.
M (**Ref:**HM10077)

## HOMEOPATHIC PODIATRIST/REFLEX

**Margret M Robinson State Registered Chiropodist**, 38 Wilson St, Alexandria, **Argyll and Bute**, G83 0EF, SCO.
(T) 01389 751677
(E) maggiefeet@/cscotland.net
Speciality: Chiropody, Complementary Therapy, Homeopathy, Reflexology, Soft Tissue and Nail Management (especially feet). ✔
● **Owner/Chiropodist** Mrs M Robinson Q: BSc, DPodM, GSSR, LFHom. M: AoR, S.C.P.
M Yrs. Est.: 7 (**Ref:**HM10078)

## HOMEOPATHIC PRACTICE

**Homeopathic Practice (The)**, Bruiach, Church Trce, Newtonmore, **Highland**, PH20 1DT, SCO.
(T) 01540 673974 (F) 01540 673974
Speciality: Homeopathy.
● **Owner** Mrs J Willshunt
M (**Ref:**HM10079)

## HOMEOPATHY FOR CHILDREN

**Diana Seymour**, The Clare Centre, 27 Clare Rd, Halifax, **Yorkshire (West)**, HX7 6BY, ENG.
(T) 01422 846554
Speciality: Homeopathy. ✔
● **Owner/Homeopath** Mrs D Seymour (T) 01422 846554 or 366356 Q: RSHom. M: Soc.Hom.
B (**Ref:**HM10080)

## HOMEOPATHY HEALS

**Homeopathy Heals**, 70 Wimborne Rd, Poole, **Dorset**, BH15 2BZ, ENG.
(T) 01202 674956
(E) homeopath@keepwell.co.uk
Speciality: Homeopathy, Nutritional Therapy.
● **Homeopath** Mr I Roberts Q: BSc, PhD. M: Soc.Hom.
M Yrs. Est.: 1 (**Ref:**HM10081)

## HOMEWOOD CHIROPRACTIC CLINIC

**Homewood Chiropractic Clinic (The)**, 30 Osborn Rd, Fareham, **Hampshire**, PO16 7DS, ENG.
(T) 01329 280283 (F) 01329 829593
Speciality: Chiropractic.



Key continued: **Yrs.Est:** Years Established **Q:** Qualifications **M:** Professional Membership ✔ Indemnity Insurance CREDIT Accept Credit Cards

● **Owner** Mrs E Cook
P S T (**Ref:**HM10082)

## HOMOEOPATHIC ADVISORY CENTRE
**Homoeopathic Advisory Centre**, 130B Montague St, Worthing, **Sussex (West)**, BN11 3HG, ENG.
(T) 01903 237400
Speciality: Homeopathy.
M (**Ref:**HM10083)

## HOMOEOPATHIC CLINIC
**Homoeopathic Clinic**, 1 Cronshaw St, Manchester, **Manchester (Greater)**, M19 2TE, ENG.
(T) 01614 428861
Speciality: Homeopathy.
● **Owner** Mr M Zafar
M (**Ref:**HM10084)

## HOMOEOPATHIC CLINIC
**Homoeopathic Clinic**, 5 Robertson Pl, Forres, **Moray**, IV36 1EU, SCO.
(T) 01309 676871
Speciality: Complementary Medicines & Therapy.
M (**Ref:**HM10085)

## HOMOEOPATHIC CLINIC
**Homoeopathic Clinic**, 8 Doncaster Rd, Leicester, **Leicestershire**, LE4 6JH, ENG.
(T) 01162 662087
Speciality: Homeopathy.
● **Owner** Mrs N Amin
M (**Ref:**HM10086)

## HOMOEOPATHIC CLINIC
**Homoeopathic Clinic (The)**, The Physical Therapy Clinic, 1 South Bank Avenue, York, **Yorkshire (North)**, YO23 1DR, ENG.
(T) 01904 636778
Speciality: Complementary Medicines & Therapy.
● **Owner** Mr N Churchill
M (**Ref:**HM10087)

## HOMOEOPATHIC CLINIC
**Homoeopathic Clinic**, 13A North St, Havant, **Hampshire**, PO9 1PW, ENG.
(T) 023 9247 1757
Speciality: Acupressure, Chiropractic, Homeopathy, Manipulation, Massage (Therapeutic), Postural Integration. ✔
● **Chiropractor** Mr K Johnson M: BCA, GCC.
S Yrs. Est.: 12 (**Ref:**HM10088)

## HOMOEOPATHIC CLINIC
**Homoeopathic Clinic (The)**, Feasegate Healing Centre, 12 Feasegate, York, **Yorkshire (North)**, YO1 8SQ, ENG.
(T) 01904 636778
Speciality: Complementary Medicines & Therapy.
C M (**Ref:**HM10089)

## HOMOEOPATHIC CLINIC/PHARMACY
**Homoeopathic Private Clinic & Pharmacy**, 226 Portland Rd, Birmingham, **Midlands (West)**, B17 8LR, ENG.
Speciality: Homeopathy. ✔
C Yrs. Est.: 16 (**Ref:**HM10090)

## HOMOEOPATHIC CONSULTANCY
**Homoeopathic Consultancy (The)**, 41 Market Pl, Henley-on-Thames, **Oxfordshire**, RG9 2AA, ENG.
(T) 01491 410400
Speciality: Homeopathy.
M (**Ref:**HM10091)

## HOMOEOPATHIC GROUP
**Homoeopathic Group (The)**, 9 Min-Y-Nant, Cardiff, **Glamorgan (Vale of)**, CF14 6JR, WAL.
(T) 029 2061 3266
Speciality: Homeopathy.
● **Chairman** Mr C Shorrock
M (**Ref:**HM10092)

## HOMOEOPATHIC HEALTH CENTRE
**Homoeopathic Health Centre**, 5 Blackfen Rd, Sidcup, **Kent**, DA15 8QD, ENG.
(T) 020 8859 4028
Speciality: Homeopathy.
M (**Ref:**HM10093)

## HOMOEOPATHIC HEALTH CENTRE
**Homoeopathic Health Centre**, 9 Queen Anne St, London, **London (Greater)**, W1M 9FD, ENG.
(T) 020 7637 5466
Speciality: Complementary Medicines & Therapy.
C M (**Ref:**HM10094)

## HOMOEOPATHIC HEALTH CENTRE
**Homoeopathic Health Centre**, 342 Barking Rd, Plaistow, London, **London (Greater)**, E13 8HL, ENG.
(T) 020 7476 7263 (F) 020 7473 4610
Speciality: Homeopathy. ✔
● **Owner** Dr S Randhawa Q: D.Hom.Med. M: HMA.
M Yrs. Est.: 18 (**Ref:**HM10095)

## HOMOEOPATHIC HEALTH CLINIC
**Homoeopathic Health Clinic**, 44 Manor Green Rd, Epsom, **Surrey**, KT19 8RN, ENG.
(T) 01372 740214
Speciality: Homeopathy.
● **Owner** Mr P Evbenata
M (**Ref:**HM10096)

## HOMOEOPATHIC HEALTH CLINIC
**Homoeopathic Health Clinic**, 243 The Broadway, Southall, **London (Greater)**, UB1 1NF, ENG.
(T) 020 8574 2927 (F) 020 8843 9220
Speciality: Homeopathy.
● **Partner** Mrs H Sidhu
M (**Ref:**HM10097)

## HOMOEOPATHIC HOUSE
**Homoeopathic House (The)**, 35 Carlisle Rd, Hove, **Sussex (East)**, BN3 4FP, ENG.
(T) 01273 702070
Speciality: Homeopathy.
● **Owner** Mrs V Walton
M (**Ref:**HM10098)

## HOMOEOPATHIC MEDICINE
**Homoeopathic Medicine**, 12 Bispham Drive, Wirral, **Merseyside**, CH47 9SF, ENG.
(T) 01516 322784
Speciality: Homeopathy.
● **Owner** Mrs B Beechey
M (**Ref:**HM10099)

## HOMOEOPATHIC SUPPLY
**Homoeopathic Supply Co**, 4 Nelson Rd, Sheringham, **Norfolk**, NR26 8BU, ENG.
(T) 01263 824683 (F) 01263 821507
Speciality: Complementary Medicines & Therapy.
● **Owner** Mrs A Barker
C M (**Ref:**HM10100)

## HOMOEOPATHIC TRUST
**Homoeopathic Trust**, 15 Clerkenwell Cl, London, **London (Greater)**, EC1R 0AA, ENG.
(T) 020 7566 7800 (F) 020 7566 7815
Speciality: Complementary Medicines & Therapy.
● **Chief Executive** Ms S Penrose
M (**Ref:**HM10101)

## HOMOEOPATHIC VETERINARY CENTRE
**Homoeopathic Veterinary Centre**, 5 Burnley Avenue, Southport, **Merseyside**, PR8 3LS, ENG.
(T) 01704 572858 (F) 01704 572858
Speciality: Homeopathy.
● **Owner** Mrs D Willoughby
M (**Ref:**HM10102)

## HOMOEOPATHY
**Homoeopathy**, The Homoeopathy Clinic, 113 Lichfield St, Walsall, **Midlands (West)**, WS1 1SZ, ENG.
(T) 01922 621338
Speciality: Homeopathy.
● **Owner** Mrs D Reid
M (**Ref:**HM10103)

## HOMOEOPATHY CENTRE
**Homoeopathy Centre**, Wentworth Lodge, Wentworth Rd, Birmingham, **Midlands (West)**, B17 9SS, ENG.
(T) 01214 277366
Speciality: Homeopathy.
M (**Ref:**HM10104)

## HOMOEOPATHY CENTRE
**Homoeopathy Centre (The)**, 284 King's Gate, Aberdeen, **Aberdeenshire**, AB15 6AY, SCO.
(T) 01224 319643
Speciality: Homeopathy.
● **Owner** Mrs A Symonds
M (**Ref:**HM10105)

## HOMOEOPATHY CLINIC
**Homoeopathy Clinic**, Butterburn Clinic, Reid Sq, Dundee, **Angus**, DD3 6RP, SCO.
(T) 01382 884163
Speciality: Homeopathy.
● **Partner** Dr C Underwood
M (**Ref:**HM10106)

## HOMOEOPATHY CLINIC
**Homoeopathy Clinic**, 23 Wilbraham Rd, Manchester, **Manchester (Greater)**, M14 6FG, ENG.
(T) 01612 246809
Speciality: Homeopathy.
M (**Ref:**HM10107)

## HOMOEOPATHY IN BUCKINGHAM
**Homoeopathy In Buckingham**, 43 Kingfisher Rd, Buckingham, **Buckinghamshire**, MK18 7EX, ENG.
(T) 01280 817673
Speciality: Complementary Medicines & Therapy.
C M (**Ref:**HM10108)

## HOMOEOPATHY ONLINE
**Homoeopathy Online**, 5 Tannerbrook Cl, Clayton, Bradford, **Yorkshire (West)**, BD14 6ND, ENG.
(T) 08000 733633
Speciality: Homeopathy.
M (**Ref:**HM10109)

## HOMOEPATHY CENTRE
**Homoepathy Centre (The)**, 186 Wolverhampton St, Dudley, **Midlands (West)**, DY1 3AD, ENG.
(T) 01384 458634
Speciality: Homeopathy.
M (**Ref:**HM10110)

## HON, ARTHUR M R
**Arthur M R Hon**, East Quarter, Bingfield, Newcastle Upon Tyne, **Tyne and Wear**, NE19 2LH, ENG.
(T) 01434 672219 (F) 01434 672155
Speciality: Chiropractic. ✔
● **McTimoney Chiropractor** Mr R Arthur Q: AMC, DC, MMCA. M: GCC, MCA.
P S T Yrs. Est.: 25 (**Ref:**HM10111)

## HONES, JULIA
**Julia Hones**, 24 The Oaks, Swanley, **Kent**, BR8 7YQ, ENG.
(T) 01322 613943
Speciality: Complementary Medicines & Therapy.
C M (**Ref:**HM10112)

## HONEY B
**Honey B**, 16 Christchurch Rd, Tring, **Hertfordshire**, HP23 4EE, ENG.
(T) 01442 824067
Speciality: Electrolysis.
T (**Ref:**HM10113)

## HONEY, MICHAEL J
**Michael J Honey**, Trinity House, 150-152 Cumberland St, Macclesfield, **Cheshire**, SK10 1BP, ENG.
(T) 01625 615762
Speciality: Physiotherapy.
P S T (**Ref:**HM10114)

## HONEY, S L
**S L Honey**, Dalwood, Broxhill Rd, Havering-Atte-Bower, Romford, **Essex**, RM4 1QH, ENG.
(T) 01708 342416
Speciality: Physiotherapy.
P S T (**Ref:**HM10115)

## HONEYBOURNE, VANESSA
**Vanessa Honeybourne**, 10 Longhurst Rd, London, **London (Greater)**, SE13 5LP, ENG.
(T) 020 8297 1625
Speciality: Homeopathy.



Key: B Mind-Body Medicine C Complementary Medicine H Self Help Treatment M Medicinal Therapy O Oriental Medicine P Postural Therapy S Manipulative Structural Therapy T Touch Therapy

● **Owner** Miss V Honeybourne
**M** (**Ref:**HM10116)

### HONEYZ

**Honeyz**, 10 West St, Southend-On-Sea, **Essex**, SS2 6HJ, ENG.
(T) 01702 430800
Speciality: Complementary Medicines & Therapy.
● **Owner** Mrs T Paye
**M** (**Ref:**HM10117)

### HONG SOFTWARE & HERBAL CLINIC

**Hong Software & Herbal Clinic**, 16 Fulham High St, London, **London (Greater)**, SW6 3LQ, ENG.
(T) 07071 788888
Speciality: Herbal Medicine.
● **Owner** Ms A Bakewell
**M** (**Ref:**HM10118)

### HONG TAD ACUPUNCTURE & HERBAL

**Hong Tad Acupuncture & Chinese Herbal Clinic**, 21 St. Thomas Drive, Hatch End, Pinner, **London (Greater)**, HA5 4SX, ENG.
(T) 020 8421 2668
Speciality: Acupuncture, Bach Remedies, Crystal Healing, Cupping, Herbal Medicine, Holistic Healing, Massage (Therapeutic), Meditation, Moxibustion, Spiritual Healing, Stress Therapy, Vitamin Therapy. ✔
● **Consultant Acupuncturist/Herbalist** Ms L Shwe-Yin Clark Q: BSc, Lic.Ac. M: Ac.A.C, BAcC, RCHM.
**O** Yrs. Est.: 22 (**Ref:**HM10119)

### HONG, YUEN

**Hong Yuen Co**, 22 Rupert St, London, **London (Greater)**, W1V 7FN, ENG.
(T) 020 7439 2408 (F) 020 7439 0901
Speciality: Acupuncture.
● **Owner** Mr B Chan
**O** (**Ref:**HM10120)

### HONORE, NIKI

**Niki Honore**, Hendon Natural Health Centre, 12 Golders Rise, London, **London (Greater)**, NW4 2HR, ENG.
(T) 020 8202 9747 (F) 020 8202 3890
Speciality: Complementary Medicines & Therapy.
● **Owner** Ms K McCarroll
**M** (**Ref:**HM10121)

### HOOD, CHRISTINA

**Christina Hood**, Old Bank House, 59 High St, Odiham, Hook, **Hampshire**, RG29 1LF, ENG.
(T) 01256 702140 (F) 01256 704717
Speciality: Osteopathy.
● **Owner** Mrs C Hood
**P S T** (**Ref:**HM10122)

### HOOD, CHRISTINA

**Christina Hood**, 2 Bonsor Drive, Tadworth, **Surrey**, KT20 6HX, ENG.
(T) 01737 355114
Speciality: Osteopathy.
● **Owner** Miss C Hood
**P S T** (**Ref:**HM10123)

### HOOD, E

**E Hood**, 32 Wellington Gardens, London, **London (Greater)**, SE7 7PH, ENG.
(T) 020 8265 4333
Speciality: Reflexology.
**S T** (**Ref:**HM10124)

### HOOKER, J

**J Hooker**, 85 Vicarage Court, Vicarage Gate, London, **London (Greater)**, W8 4HG, ENG.
(T) 020 7937 0917
Speciality: Physiotherapy.
● **Owner** Miss J Hooker
**P S T** (**Ref:**HM10125)

### HOOL, MERYL

**Meryl Hool**, 8 Winch Cl, Cranbrook, **Kent**, TN17 3BW, ENG.
(T) 01580 712267
Speciality: Homeopathy.
**M** (**Ref:**HM10126)

### HOOLE, AVERIL

**Averil Hoole**, Brabant House, Portsmouth Rd, Thames Ditton, **Surrey**, KT7 0EY, ENG.
(T) 020 8398 7592
Speciality: Homeopathy.
**M** (**Ref:**HM10127)

### HOOPER, B

**B Hooper**, 65 Chantry Rd, Chessington, **Surrey**, KT9 1JT, ENG.
(T) 020 8397 4278
Speciality: Physiotherapy.
**P S T** (**Ref:**HM10128)

### HOOPER, HELEN

**Helen Hooper**, Chiropractic Clinic, 154 Leigh Rd, Wimborne, **Dorset**, BH21 2DB, ENG.
(T) 01202 880136
Speciality: Chiropractors.
**P S T** (**Ref:**HM10129)

### HOOPER, J A

**J A Hooper**, 1 Strawberry Avenue, Exeter, **Devon**, EX2 8GE, ENG.
(T) 01392 427757
Speciality: Osteopathy.
● **Owner** Ms J Hooper
**P S T** (**Ref:**HM10130)

### HOOPER, SARAH JANE

**Sarah Jane Hooper**, 1 Queens St, March, **Cambridgeshire**, PE15 8SN, ENG.
(T) 01354 651200
Speciality: Chiropodists (Podiatrists).
● **Owner** Mr S Hooper
**S** (**Ref:**HM10131)

### HOPCROFT, JULIE

**Julie Hopcroft**, Woodlow Guest House, 10 Parc Bean, St. Ives, **Cornwall**, TR26 1EA, ENG.
(T) 01736 797241
Speciality: Reflexology.
**S T** (**Ref:**HM10132)

### HOPE CHIROPRACTIC

**Hope Chiropractic**, 98 St. Stephens Rd, Canterbury, **Kent**, CT2 7JL, ENG.
(T) 01227 477004 (F) 01227 477005
(W) www.hopechiropractic.co.uk
Speciality: Chiropractic. ✔
● **Chiropractor** Mr V Hope Q: BSc (Chiro), DC. M: GCC.
● **Chiropractor** Mr C Farthing Q: B.App.Sc, BCSc, BSc, DC. M: GCC.
**P** Yrs. Est.: 2 (**Ref:**HM10133)

### HOPE CLINIC

**Hope Clinic (The)**, The Hope Clinic, 17 Star St, Ryde, **Isle of Wight**, PO33 2HX, ENG.
(T) 01983 563539
Speciality: Acupuncture, Aromatherapy, Chiropractic, Complementary Therapy, Counselling, Cranial Osteopathy, Homeopathy, Hypnotherapy, Indian Head Massage, Kinesiology, Manipulation, Massage (Therapeutic), Oriental Diagnosis, Reflexology. ✔ CREDIT
● **Hypnotherapist** Ms B Bailey Q: MIAH, MNCH.
● **Homeopath** Mr J Christopher Q: Dip.Ed, RSHom.
● **Massage and Reflexology** Ms T Skoludek Q: ICHT. M: IFHB.
● **Acupuncturist** Mr P Munt-Davies Q: Lic.Ac, MBAcC, MSc.
● **Acupunturist** Ms R Smith Q: BA (Hons), Dip.Ac, Lic.Ac, MBAcC.
● **Massage and Reflexology** Ms J Ham Q: ICHT, IHBC, IIST. M: IFHB.
● **Clinic Assistant** Mrs Yang
● **Owner/Chiropractor** Mr R Hope Q: BCA, DC, GCC (Reg). M: BCA, GCC.
**C** Yrs. Est.: 23 (**Ref:**HM10134)

### HOPE HEALING CLINIC

**Hope Healing Clinic**, The Birchcliff Centre, Birchcliff Rd, Hebden Bridge, **Yorkshire (West)**, HX7 8DG, ENG.
(T) 01422 844337
Speciality: Complementary Medicines & Therapy.
**M** (**Ref:**HM10135)

### HOPE STREET NATURAL HLTH CTRE

**Hope Street Natural Health Centre**, 37 Hope St, Liverpool, **Merseyside**, L1 9EA, ENG.
(T) 01517 071311
Speciality: Acupuncture. ✔
● **Owner** Mr K Milner Q: Dip.Ac. M: BAcC.
**S** (**Ref:**HM10136)

### HOPE, ANN

**Ann Hope**, Unit 1, 38 Copperfield St, London, **London (Greater)**, SE1 0EA, ENG.
(T) 020 7771 8934
Speciality: Chiropody, Podiatry.
● **Podiatrist** Ms A Hope Q: DPodM, MSc, S.R.Ch. M: S.C.P.
**M** Yrs. Est.: 2 (**Ref:**HM10137)

### HOPE, DAVID

**David Hope**, 40 The Quadrant, Sheffield, **Yorkshire (South)**, S17 4DB, ENG.
(T) 01142 361020 (F) 01142 362009
Speciality: Psychotherapy.
● **Owner** Mr D Hope
**B** (**Ref:**HM10138)

### HOPE, J A

**J A Hope**, St Johns Cross Farm, Main Rd, Marsh Lane, Sheffield, **Yorkshire (South)**, S21 5RH, ENG.
(T) 01246 432443 (F) 01246 432443
Speciality: Physiotherapy.
● **Owner** Mrs J Hope
**P S T** (**Ref:**HM10139)

### HOPE, JAMES

**James Hope**, 31 Regents Park Rd, London, **London (Greater)**, NW1 7TL, ENG.
(T) 020 7284 2309 (F) 020 7485 1521
Speciality: Hypnosis.
● **Owner** Mr J Hope
**B** (**Ref:**HM10140)

### HOPE-ALLAN, NICOLE

**Nicole Hope-Allan**, Battersea Back Clinic, 4 Ransomes Dock, Parkgate Rd, London, **London (Greater)**, SW11 4NP, ENG.
(T) 020 7223 7223
Speciality: Acupuncture.
**O** (**Ref:**HM10141)

### HOPEWELL, ALAN

**Alan Hopewell**, Natural Health Clinic, 177 Moorside Rd, Swinton, Manchester, **Manchester (Greater)**, M27 9LD, ENG.
(T) 01617 930091
Speciality: Complementary Medicines & Therapy.
● **Partner** Mr B Jordan
**M** (**Ref:**HM10142)

### HOPEWELL, G F

**G F Hopewell**, 13 Spilsby Rd, Boston, **Lincolnshire**, PE21 9NX, ENG.
(T) 01205 363452 (F) 01205 363452
Speciality: Chiropodists (Podiatrists).
● **Owner** Mr G Hopewell
**S** (**Ref:**HM10143)

### HOPKIN, A N L

**A N L Hopkin**, 74 Eastbury Rd, Northwood, **London (Greater)**, HA6 3AR, ENG.
(T) 01923 836624
Speciality: Psychotherapy.
● **Owner** Mrs A Hopkin
**B** (**Ref:**HM10144)

### HOPKINS, ALAN

**Alan Hopkins**, The Hanson Chiropractic Centre, Unit 16 Granby Court, Surrey Cl, Granby Industrial Estate, Weymouth, **Dorset**, DT4 9XB, ENG.
(T) 01305 761507
Speciality: Complementary Medicines & Therapy.
● **Partner** Mr D Groeger
**M** (**Ref:**HM10145)

### HOPKINS, B

**B Hopkins**, 56 High St, Prescot, **Merseyside**, L34 6HQ, ENG.
(T) 01514 932230
Speciality: Chiropodists (Podiatrists).
**S** (**Ref:**HM10146)

### HOPKINS, C J

**C J Hopkins**, Ford House, 2 High St, Wangford, Beccles, **Suffolk**, NR34 8RR, ENG.
(T) 01502 578271
(E) hopdoc@supanet.com



Key continued: **Yrs.Est:** Years Established **Q:** Qualifications **M:** Professional Membership ✔ Indemnity Insurance CREDIT Accept Credit Cards

Speciality: Acupuncture, Aversion Therapy, Complementary Therapy, Hypnosis, Hypnotherapy, Stress Therapy, Visualisation Therapy, EMDR- Eye Movement Desensitisation and Reprocessing.
✔
● **Therapist** Dr C Hopkins **Q:** BS, MB.
**B** Yrs. Est.: 20 (**Ref:**HM10147)

### HOPKINS, CAROL

**Carol Hopkins**, 35 Dryden Cr, Stevenage, **Hertfordshire**, SG2 0JH, ENG.
(T) 01438 725912
Speciality: Chiropodists (Podiatrists).
● **Owner** Ms C Hopkins
**S** (**Ref:**HM10148)

### HOPKINS, H G

**H G Hopkins**, 2 Roslin Gardens, Bournemouth, **Dorset**, BH3 7DR, ENG.
(T) 01202 536499
Speciality: Chiropractic. ✔
● **Owner/Chiropractor** Dr H Hodgkins **Q:** BCA, DC.
**P S T** Yrs. Est.: 12 (**Ref:**HM10149)

### HOPKINS, JILL

**Jill Hopkins**, Badgers Hay, Kingston St. Mary, Taunton, **Somerset**, TA2 8HU, ENG.
(T) 01823 451656
Speciality: Psychotherapy.
**B** (**Ref:**HM10150)

### HOPKINS, JUDY

**Judy Hopkins**, 14 West St, Geddington, Kettering, **Northamptonshire**, NN14 1BD, ENG.
(T) 01536 747577
Speciality: Hypnosis.
**B** (**Ref:**HM10151)

### HOPKINS, NORMAN

**Norman Hopkins**, 17 Heath Park Avenue, Cardiff, **Glamorgan (Vale of)**, CF14 3RF, WAL.
(T) 029 2075 1407
Speciality: Physiotherapy.
● **Owner** Mr N Hopkins
**P S T** (**Ref:**HM10152)

### HOPLEY, CHRISTINE

**Christine Hopley**, 41 Church Rd, Poole, **Dorset**, BH14 0NN, ENG.
(T) 01202 749514
Speciality: Physiotherapy.
**P S T** (**Ref:**HM10153)

### HOPLEY, DENISE

**Remedial Massage and Manipulative Therapy**, 6 Marissal Rd, Henbury, Bristol, BS10 7NN, ENG.
(T) 01179 501372
Speciality: Massage (Therapeutic), Remedial Massage, Manipulative Therapy.
● **Therapist** Ms D Hopley **Q:** Dip.Man.Th, Dip.Rem.Massage. **M:** SSM.
**S** Yrs. Est.: 12 (**Ref:**HM10154)

### HOPPER, ANN

**Ann Hopper**, 38 High St, Herne Bay, **Kent**, CT6 5LH, ENG.
(T) 01227 375686
Speciality: Physiotherapy.
● **Practice Manager** Ms A Hopper
**P S T** (**Ref:**HM10155)

### HOPPER, C A

**C A Hopper**, 91 New Cross Rd, Guildford, **Surrey**, GU2 9NU, ENG.
(T) 01483 822973
(E) c.hopper@ntlworld.com
Speciality: Counselling, Gestalt Therapy, Psychotherapy, Pyscho-Synthesis, Visualisation Therapy. ✔
● **Psychosynthesis Therapist** Mr C Hopper **Q:** Dip.Couns, Dip.P.E.T, Dip.Psych. **M:** BACP.
**C** Yrs. Est.: 7 (**Ref:**HM10156)

### HOPPER, K M

**Mrs K M Hopper**, 4 Lake Avenue, Bromley, **Kent**, BR1 4EN, ENG.
(T) 020 8464 8810
Speciality: Chiropodists (Podiatrists).
● **Owner** Mrs K Hopper
**S** (**Ref:**HM10157)

### HOPPERS

**Hoppers**, 77C Broadgate Lane, Horsforth, Leeds, **Yorkshire (West)**, LS18 5DU, ENG.
(T) 01132 798904 (F) 01132 583848
Speciality: Chiropodists (Podiatrists).
● **Owner** Mrs R Hopper
**S** (**Ref:**HM10158)

### HOPSON, A J

**A J Hopson**, 39 Prestbury Rd, Cheltenham, **Gloucestershire**, GL52 2PT, ENG.
(T) 01242 512601
Speciality: Chiropodists (Podiatrists).
● **Owner** A J Hopson
**S** (**Ref:**HM10159)

### HOPSON-SUGARS

**Hopson-Sugars**, The Corner House, 1 Hall Lane, Leicester, **Leicestershire**, LE2 8SF, ENG.
(T) 01162 837305
Speciality: Chiropodists (Podiatrists).
● **Owner** Mrs M Sugars
**S** (**Ref:**HM10160)

### HOPWOOD, S (DR)

**Dr S Hopwood**, 47 Fore St, Totnes, **Devon**, TQ9 5NJ, ENG.
(T) 01803 868282
Speciality: Acupuncture.
● **Owner** Dr S Hopwood
**O** (**Ref:**HM10161)

### HOPWOOD, S E

**S E Hopwood**, 10 Curzon Avenue, Birstall, Leicester, **Leicestershire**, LE4 4AA, ENG.
(T) 01162 671789
Speciality: Chiropodists (Podiatrists).
**S** (**Ref:**HM10162)

### HORAN, MARTIN

**Martin Horan**, 5 Abney Cl, Mickleover, Derby, **Derbyshire**, DE3 5DZ, ENG.
(T) 01332 511762
Speciality: Hypnosis.
**B** (**Ref:**HM10163)

### HORAN, THOMAS

**Horan Thomas BA Psych M Ed**, 59 Forster Ct Forster St, Galway, **County Galway**, IRE.
(T) 09156 7805
Speciality: Psychotherapy.
**B** (**Ref:**HM10164)

### HORBURY HYPNOTHERAPY CENTRE

**Horbury Hypnotherapy Centre**, 9a Westfield Rd, Horbury, Wakefield, **Yorkshire (West)**, WF4 6DN, ENG.
(T) 01924 363439
Speciality: Hypnosis.
**B** (**Ref:**HM10165)

### HORGAN, EILEEN

**Horgan Eileen**, 32 The Glen, **County Waterford**, IRE.
(T) 05187 9665
Speciality: Acupuncture.
**O** (**Ref:**HM10166)

### HORGAN, MARIE

**Marie Horgan**, Ardrum House, Bishopstown Rd, Cork, **County Cork**, IRE.
(T) 021 4343 791
Speciality: Counselling.
**B H** (**Ref:**HM10167)

### HORKEY, PHIL

**Phil Horkey**, 2 Barrett St, Oxford, **Oxfordshire**, OX2 0AT, ENG.
(T) 01865 245343
Speciality: Alexander Technique.
● **Owner** Mr P Horkey
**P S** (**Ref:**HM10168)

### HORMASJI, A & F

**A & F Hormasji**, 2a Cross Rd, Mawneys, Romford, **Essex**, RM7 8AT, ENG.
(T) 01708 764740
Speciality: Hypnotherapy.
● **Owner** Mr F Hormasji
**B** (**Ref:**HM10169)

### HORN, JEFFERY

**Mr Jeffery Horn**, 8 Arden Rd, London, **London (Greater)**, N3 3AN, ENG.
(T) 020 8346 5329
Speciality: Chiropodists (Podiatrists).
**S** (**Ref:**HM10170)

### HORNCASTLE REMEDIAL CENTRE

**Horncastle Remedial Centre**, Elmhurst, Lincoln Rd, Horncastle, **Lincolnshire**, LN9 5AW, ENG.
(T) 01507 525295
Speciality: Complementary Medicines & Therapy.
**C M** (**Ref:**HM10171)

### HORNCASTLE WAR MEMORIAL CENTRE

**Horncastle War Memorial Centre**, North St, Horncastle, **Lincolnshire**, LN9, ENG.
(T) 01507 525222
Speciality: Chiropractic. ✔
● **Partner** Dr C Ball **Q:** DC. **M:** GCC, SCA.
● **Owner** Ms K Royle
**P** Yrs. Est.: 1 (**Ref:**HM10172)

### HORNE, SUE

**Sue Horne**, Reflections Health, 14 Salisbury St, Fordingbridge, **Hampshire**, SP6 1AF, ENG.
(T) 01425 652297
Speciality: Acupuncture.
● **Owner** Mrs S Horne
**O** (**Ref:**HM10173)

### HORNE, SUE

**Sue Horne**, Unit 5 The Furlong, Ringwood, **Hampshire**, BH24 1AT, ENG.
(T) 01425 477507
Speciality: Acupuncture.
● **Owner** Mrs S Horne
**O** (**Ref:**HM10174)

### HORNE, SUE

**Sue Horne**, 13 Salisbury St, Cranborne, Wimborne, **Dorset**, BH21 5PU, ENG.
(T) 01725 517883 (F) 01725 517883
(E) suehorne@13cranborne.freeserve.co.uk
Speciality: Acupuncture, Massage (Therapeutic). ✔
● **Acupuncturist** Ms S Horne **Q:** ITEC, Lic.Ac, MBAcC. **M:** BAcC.
**O** Yrs. Est.: 5 (**Ref:**HM10175)

### HORNER, ANN

**Ann Horner**, Orion, 12 Moor Lane Cl, Torquay, **Devon**, TQ2 8PL, ENG.
(T) 01803 323772
Speciality: Reflexology.
**S T** (**Ref:**HM10176)

### HORNER, C

**Mrs C Horner**, 20A Rupert Avenue, High Wycombe, **Buckinghamshire**, HP12 3NG, ENG.
(T) 01494 445168
Speciality: Acupuncture.
**O** (**Ref:**HM10177)

### HORNER, L

**L Horner**, 37 Attwood Trce, Spennymoor, **County Durham**, DL16 6TD, ENG.
(T) 01388 815591
Speciality: Physiotherapy.
**P S T** (**Ref:**HM10178)

### HORNER, LINDLEY

**Lindley Horner**, 278 Main Rd, Sutton At Hone, Dartford, **Kent**, DA4 9HJ, ENG.
(T) 01322 860544
Speciality: Osteopathy.
**P S T** (**Ref:**HM10179)

### HORNER, MARGARET

**Margaret Horner**, 2 Kinsey St, Congleton, **Cheshire**, CW12 1ES, ENG.
(T) 01260 280444
Speciality: Osteopathy.
**P S T** (**Ref:**HM10180)

### HORNE-STANLEY, C

**C Horne-Stanley**, Flat 153 Ashley Gardens, Thirleby Rd, London, **London (Greater)**, SW1P 1HW, ENG.
(T) 020 7834 5696
Speciality: Hypnosis.
● **Owner** Ms C Horne-Stanley
**B** (**Ref:**HM10181)

### HORRIDGE, S P

**S P Horridge**, 56 Chorley Rd, Swinton,

Key: **B** Mind-Body Medicine **C** Complementary Medicine **H** Self Help Treatment **M** Medicinal Therapy **O** Oriental Medicine **P** Postural Therapy **S** Manipulative Structural Therapy **T** Touch Therapy

Manchester, **Manchester (Greater)**, M27 5AD, ENG.
(T) 01617 940004
Speciality: Chiropody. ✔
● **Continence Therapist**
Mrs M Horridge
● **Chiropodist (Podiatrist)**
Mr S Horridge Q: BSc, M.S.C.P, S.R.Ch.
M: S.R.Ch.
M Yrs. Est.: 15 (Ref:HM10182)

## HORROCKS
**Horrocks**, 5 West Kensington Mansions, Beaumont Cres, London, **London (Greater)**, W14 9PE, ENG.
(T) 020 7385 4091 (F) 020 7385 4091
Speciality: Psychotherapy.
● **Owner** Mr R Horrocks
B (Ref:HM10183)

## HORROCKS, JULIE
**Julie Horrocks**, 3 Town Hall Buildings, Princes St, Corbridge, **Northumberland**, NE45 5AD, ENG.
(T) 01434 633833
Speciality: Homeopathy.
● **Owner** Mrs J Horrocks
M (Ref:HM10184)

## HORSBURGH, E M
**E M Horsburgh**, 44 Sutton Rd, Terrington St. Clement, King's Lynn, **Norfolk**, PE34 4PQ, ENG.
(T) 01553 829630 (F) 01553 829630
Speciality: Chiropodists (Podiatrists).
● **Owner** Mr N Martin
S (Ref:HM10185)

## HORSBURGH, PENNY
**Penny Horsburgh**, 17 Mayfields, Sindlesham, Wokingham, **Berkshire**, RG41 5BY, ENG.
(T) 01189 773946
Speciality: Homeopathy.
● **Owner** Mrs P Horsburgh
M (Ref:HM10186)

## HORSBURGH, S J
**S J Horsburgh**, 44 Sutton Rd, Terrington St. Clement, King's Lynn, **Norfolk**, PE34 4PQ, ENG.
(T) 01553 829630 (F) 01553 829630
Speciality: Chiropodists (Podiatrists).
● **Owner** Mr N Martin
S (Ref:HM10187)

## HORSFIELD, FIONA
**Fiona Horsfield**, 1 Clayfield Mews, Newcomen Rd, Tunbridge Wells, **Kent**, TN4 9PA, ENG.
(T) 01892 545443
Speciality: Alexander Technique.
P S (Ref:HM10188)

## HORSFORD, HELENA
**Helena Horsford**, 21 Police Station Rd, Walton-On-Thames, **Surrey**, KT12 4JQ, ENG.
(T) 01932 246895
Speciality: Reflexology.
S T (Ref:HM10189)

## HORSFORTH PHYSIO & SPORTS
**Horsforth Physiotherapy & Sports Injury Clinic**, The Park Practice, Parkside, Horsforth, Leeds, **Yorkshire (West)**, LS18 4DJ, ENG.
(T) 01132 590343
Speciality: Physiotherapy.
● **Owner** Mrs P Smith
P S T (Ref:HM10190)

## HORSHAM CHIROPRACTIC CENTRE
**Horsham Chiropractic Centre**, Parkway, North Prde, Horsham, **Sussex (West)**, RH12 2BH, ENG.
(T) 01403 217557 (F) 01403 218401
Speciality: Chiropractic. ✔ CREDIT
● **Chiropractor** Dr S Bradford Q: B.App.Sc, BCA, DC. M: BCA.
● **Chiropractor** Dr S Fowle Q: BCA, DC.
M: BCA.
P Yrs. Est.: 11 (Ref:HM10191)

## HORSHAM OSTEOPATHS
**Horsham Osteopaths**, New St Clinic, 20 New St, Horsham, **Sussex (West)**, RH13 5DY, ENG.
(T) 01403 272788
Speciality: Osteopathy.
P S T (Ref:HM10192)

## HORSLEY, MARY E
**Mary E Horsley**, Bedcroft, Pitchcombe, Stroud, **Gloucestershire**, GL6 6LN, ENG.
(T) 01452 814422
Speciality: Acupuncture.
O (Ref:HM10193)

## HORSLEY, NICOLA
**Nicola Horsley**, 56 Valley Rd, Welwyn Garden City, **Hertfordshire**, AL8 7DN, ENG.
(T) 01707 334068
Speciality: Chiropodists (Podiatrists).
● **Owner** Mrs N Horsley
S (Ref:HM10194)

## HORTON, JONATHAN
**Jonathan Horton**, 107 Westgate, Chichester, **Sussex (West)**, PO19 3HB, ENG.
(T) 01243 786356
Speciality: Osteopathy.
P S T (Ref:HM10195)

## HORTON, R M
**R M Horton**, 46 Albion St, Exmouth, **Devon**, EX8 1JH, ENG.
(T) 01395 279634
Speciality: Physiotherapy.
P S T (Ref:HM10196)

## HORWICH SPORTS INJURY & PHYSIO
**Horwich Sports Injury & Physiotherapy Clinic**, The Consulting Rooms, Heaton Medical Centre, 2 Lucy St, Bolton, **Lancashire**, BL1 5PU, ENG.
(T) 01204 847616
Speciality: Physiotherapy.
P S T (Ref:HM10197)

## HORWICH, L
**L Horwich**, 1 Crabtree Lane, Harpenden, **Hertfordshire**, AL5 5TA, ENG.
(T) 01582 765121 (F) 01582 765121
Speciality: Reflexology.
● **Owner** Mrs L Horwich
S T (Ref:HM10198)

## HORWOOD, MARIE
**Marie Horwood**, 66 St Andrews Rd, Shoeburyness, Southend-On-Sea, **Essex**, SS3 9JJ, ENG.
(T) 01702 298902
Speciality: Chiropodists (Podiatrists).
● **Owner** Mrs M Horwood
S (Ref:HM10199)

## HOSGOOD, LYNN
**Lynn Hosgood**, 39 Glenville Rd, Walkford, Christchurch, **Dorset**, BH23 5PX, ENG.
(T) 01425 274486
Speciality: Electrolysis.
T (Ref:HM10200)

## HOSKINS, RAYMOND
**Raymond Hoskins**, 77 Redgate, Thetford, **Norfolk**, IP24 2HD, ENG.
(T) 01842 766500
Speciality: Hypnosis.
● **Owner** Mr R Hoskins
B (Ref:HM10201)

## HOSPICE INFORMATION SERVICE
**Hospice Information Service (The)**, St Christophers Hospice, 51-59 Lawrie Park Rd, London, **London (Greater)**, SE26 6DZ, ENG.
(T) 020 8778 9252
Speciality: Complementary Medicines & Therapy.
● **Information Officer** Ann Eve
M (Ref:HM10202)

## HOSSAIN, EVA N
**Eva N Hossain**, 17 Avenue Rd, Pinner, **London (Greater)**, HA5 3EZ, ENG.
(T) 020 8866 2913
Speciality: Chiropodists (Podiatrists).
S (Ref:HM10203)

## HOSSAIN, NATASHA
**Natasha Hossain**, 17 Avenue Rd, Pinner, **London (Greater)**, HA5 3EZ, ENG.
(T) 020 8866 9331
Speciality: Chiropodists (Podiatrists).
● **Owner** Ms N Hossain
S (Ref:HM10204)

## HOSWELL, CHRISTINE
**Christine Hoswell**, 14 Campbell Park Avenue, **County Antrim**, BT4 3FH, NIR.
(T) 028 9029 7111
Speciality: Reflexology.
S T (Ref:HM10205)

## HOT-PAK
**Hot-Pak 100% Natural**, Lonsdale House, 52 Blucher St, Birmingham, **Midlands (West)**, B1 1QU, ENG.
(T) 01216 888000 (F) 01216 881801
(W) www.hot-pak.com
Speciality: Complementary Medicines & Therapy, Hot-Pack's for Tension, Migraines, Neck and Back Injuries. CREDIT
● **Director** Mr P Gannon
B Yrs. Est.: 4 (Ref:HM10206)

## HOUE, DAVID
**David Houe**, 91A Lion Lane, Haslemere, **Surrey**, GU27 1JL, ENG.
(T) 01428 654446
Speciality: Osteopathy.
P S T (Ref:HM10207)

## HOUE, DAVID
**David Houe**, Natural Health York Clinic, Guildford Rd, Woking, **Surrey**, GU22 7QU, ENG.
(T) 01483 720464
Speciality: Complementary Medicines & Therapy.
M (Ref:HM10208)

## HOUGH, ALAN
**Alan Hough**, The Ridge, St. Leonards-On-Sea, **Sussex (East)**, TN37 7RE, ENG.
(T) 01424 757400 (F) 01424 757424
Speciality: Physiotherapy.
● **Owner** Mr A Hough
P S T (Ref:HM10209)

## HOUGH, TREVOR
**Trevor Hough**, The Clubhouse, Chester Rd, Mold, **Flintshire**, CH7 1UF, WAL.
(T) 01352 755730
Speciality: Physiotherapy.
● **Owner** Mr T Hough
P S T (Ref:HM10210)

## HOUGHTON, CHRISTINE
**Christine Houghton**, 55 Red Bank Rd, Blackpool, **Lancashire**, FY2 9HX, ENG.
(T) 01253 347438
Speciality: Chiropodists (Podiatrists).
● **Owner** Mrs C Houghton
S (Ref:HM10211)

## HOUGHTON, K E
**K E Houghton**, West Bracklesham Drive, Bracklesham Bay, Chichester, **Sussex (West)**, PO20 8PF, ENG.
(T) 01243 670938
Speciality: Physiotherapy.
● **Owner** Mrs K Houghton
P S T (Ref:HM10212)

## HOUGHTON, REBECCA
**Rebecca Houghton D O**, Downing, Smiths Lane, Snitterfield, Stratford-Upon-Avon, **Warwickshire**, CV37 0JZ, ENG.
(T) 01789 731144
Speciality: Osteopathy.
P S T (Ref:HM10213)

## HOUNSFIELD, BRIAN
**Brian Hounsfield**, 97 College Rd, Epsom, **Surrey**, KT17 4HY, ENG.
(T) 01372 726080
Speciality: Osteopathy.
● **Senior Partner** Mr B Hounsfield
P S T (Ref:HM10214)

## HOURIGAN, P
**P Hourigan**, 1 The Quadrant, Exeter, **Devon**, EX2 4LE, ENG.
(T) 01392 256774 (F) 01392 421662
Speciality: Physiotherapy.
P S T (Ref:HM10215)

## HOUSE OF AROMATHERAPY
**House Of Aromatherapy**, 262A Derby Rd, Ripley, **Derbyshire**, DE5 8JN, ENG.
(T) 01773 747347



Key continued: Yrs.Est: Years Established Q: Qualifications M: Professional Membership ✔ Indemnity Insurance CREDIT Accept Credit Cards

Speciality: Aromatherapy. ✔
● **Aromatherapist** Mrs P Bence Q: ITEC. M: GCP.
C Yrs. Est.: 8 (**Ref:**HM10216)

**HOUSE OF AROMATHERAPY**

**House Of Aromatherapy**, 87 London Rd, Derby, **Derbyshire**, DE1 2QS, ENG.
(T) 01332 202207
Speciality: Aromatherapy.
● **Owner** Mrs P Hayworth
M O (**Ref:**HM10217)

**HOUSE OF ASTROLOGY**

**House of Astrology**, 9 Parliament St, Temple Bar, Dublin, **County Dublin**, IRE.
(T) 01679 3404 (F) 01679 3411
(E) astrology@eircom.net
Speciality: Complementary Medicines & Therapy.
M (**Ref:**HM10218)

**HOUSE OF GOOD HEALTH**

**House Of Good Health (The)**, 6a Greys Rd, Henley-on-Thames, **Oxfordshire**, RG9 1RY, ENG.
(T) 01491 579204 (F) 01491 410195
Speciality: Chiropractic.
● **Owner** Dr J Poupel
P S T (**Ref:**HM10219)

**HOUSE OF MISTRY**

**House of Mistry Ltd**, 15-17 South End Rd, London, **London (Greater)**, NW3 2PT, ENG.
(T) 020 7794 0848 (F) 020 7431 5695
(E) carnvbia@yahoo.com
(W) www.mistry.co.uk
Speciality: Acupressure, Acupuncture, Aromatherapy, Ayurvedic Medicine, Bach Remedies, Chiropractic, Complementary Therapy, Counselling, Herbal Medicine, Homeopathy, Indian Head Massage, Massage (Therapeutic), Naturopathy, Reflexology, Shiatsu. ✔
● **Pharmacist** Mr R Mistry Q: BSc. M: RPS.
● **Manager/Homeopath** Mr C Mistry Q: BSc. M: Soc.Hom.
M Yrs. Est.: 25 (**Ref:**HM10220)

**HOUSE OF RAINBOWS**

**House Of Rainbows**, 37 Napton Drive, Leamington Spa, **Warwickshire**, CV32 7UX, ENG.
(T) 01926 337804
Speciality: Complementary Medicines & Therapy.
M (**Ref:**HM10221)

**HOUSE OF ZODIAC**

**House Of Zodiac (The)**, 59 Claremont North Avenue, Gateshead, **Tyne and Wear**, NE8 1RH, ENG.
(T) 01914 772087
Speciality: Clairvoyants & Palmists.
B (**Ref:**HM10222)

**HOUSTON, ANNE D**

**Anne D Houston**, Inchture, Perth, **Perth and Kinross**, PH14 9SE, SCO.
(T) 01828 686596
Speciality: Chiropodists (Podiatrists).
● **Owner** Dr A Houston
S (**Ref:**HM10223)

**HOUSTON, MOIRA**

**Moira Houston**, 5 Elm Ter, Constantine Rd, London, **London (Greater)**, NW3 2LL, ENG.
(T) 020 7267 4222
Speciality: Homeopathy.
● **Owner** Dr M Houston
M (**Ref:**HM10224)

**HOUSTOUN, J K**

**J K Houstoun**, 52A Magdalen St, Thetford, **Norfolk**, IP24 2BN, ENG.
(T) 01842 750555
Speciality: Chiropodists (Podiatrists).
S (**Ref:**HM10225)

**HOVE CHIROPODY CLINIC**

**Hove Chiropody Clinic**, 96 Goldstone Villas, Hove, **Sussex (East)**, BN3 3RU, ENG.
(T) 01273 328023
Speciality: Chiropodists (Podiatrists).
● **Owner** Mrs K Butterfill
S (**Ref:**HM10226)

**HOVE CHIROPRACTIC CLINIC**

**C Pearcey**, 2 West Way, Hove, **Sussex (East)**, BN3 8LD, ENG.
(T) 01273 733177 (F) 01273 888516
Speciality: Chiropractic, Massage (Therapeutic), McTimoney Chiropractic. ✔
● **Chiropractor** Mrs M Pearcey Q: DC. M: MCA.
● **Owner/Chiropractor** Mr C Pearcey Q: DC. M: MCA.
P Yrs. Est.: 21 (**Ref:**HM10227)

**HOVE OSTEOPATHIC CLINIC**

**Hove Osteopathic Clinic**, 24 Rutland Gardens, Hove, **Sussex (East)**, BN3 5PB, ENG.
(T) 01273 208410
Speciality: Cranial Osteopathy, Manipulation, Massage (Therapeutic), Osteopathy. ✔
● **Osteopath** Mr M Anderson Q: Reg.Osteopath. M: GOsC.
S Yrs. Est.: 12 (**Ref:**HM10228)

**HOW, C I**

**C I How**, St Boswells Chiropractic Clinic, 16 Jenny Moores Rd, St. Boswells, Melrose, **Scottish Borders**, TD6 0AL, SCO.
(T) 01835 823645 (F) 01835 823930
Speciality: Chiropractors.
● **Partner** Dr C How
P S T (**Ref:**HM10229)

**HOW, G**

**G How**, Doctors Surgery, 28 Beaumont St, Oxford, **Oxfordshire**, OX1 2NP, ENG.
(T) 01865 512673
Speciality: Homeopathy.
● **Principal** Dr D Curtin
M (**Ref:**HM10230)

**HOW, HELEN F**

**Helen F How**, 14 Craighall Gardens, Edinburgh, **Edinburgh (City of)**, EH6 4RJ, SCO.
(T) 01315 511044 (F) 01315 511044
Speciality: Osteopathy.
● **Owner** Mrs H How
P S T (**Ref:**HM10231)

**HOWAR, CHRIS**

**Chris Howar**, Newport Clinic Of Holistic Health, 36 Godfrey Rd, Newport, NP20 4PE, **WAL**.
(T) 01633 843333
Speciality: Complementary Medicines & Therapy.
● **Owner** Mr J Francis
M (**Ref:**HM10232)

**HOWARD AFFILIATES**

**Howard Affiliates**, P O Box 11, Linlithgow, **Lothian (West)**, EH49 6QH, SCO.
(T) 01506 842419
Speciality: Psychology.
B (**Ref:**HM10233)

**HOWARD, ELIZABETH**

**Elizabeth Howard**, Westmoreland House, Off Teall St, Wakefield, **Yorkshire (West)**, WF1 1PR, ENG.
(T) 01924 375410
Speciality: Electrolysis.
T (**Ref:**HM10234)

**HOWARD, G**

**G Howard**, 3 New House Trce, Station Rd, Edenbridge, **Kent**, TN8 6HJ, ENG.
(T) 01732 862225
Speciality: Clairvoyants & Palmists.
● **Owner** Miss G Howard
B (**Ref:**HM10235)

**HOWARD, JOHN & GAIL**

**John & Gail Howard**, 19 St Georges Avenue, Northampton, **Northamptonshire**, NN2 6JA, ENG.
(T) 01604 716817 (F) 01604 474599
Speciality: Hypnosis.
● **Partner** Mrs G Howard
B (**Ref:**HM10236)

**HOWARD, KAREN**

**Karen Howard**, 19 Balmoral Cl, Fernhill Heath, Worcester, **Worcestershire**, WR3 7XQ, ENG.
(T) 01905 454870
(W) www.complementary-healthcare.co.uk/info/howard
Speciality: Reflexology.
S T (**Ref:**HM10237)

**HOWARD, L**

**L Howard**, 161 Queens Rd, Buckhurst Hill, **Essex**, IG9 5AZ, ENG.
(T) 020 8505 8353
Speciality: Homeopathy.
M (**Ref:**HM10238)

**HOWARD, L**

**L Howard**, 15 Edge St, London, **London (Greater)**, W8 7PN, ENG.
(T) 020 7221 4602
Speciality: Homeopathy.
● **Manageress** Ms S Wilson
M (**Ref:**HM10239)

**HOWARD, LYNNE**

**Lynne Howard**, 123 Mildmay Rd, Islington, London, **London (Greater)**, N1 4PT, ENG.
(T) 020 7254 7621 (F) 020 7254 7621
Speciality: Bach Remedies, Complementary Therapy, Counselling, Floral Essence Therapy, Herbal Medicine, Homeopathy, Kinesiology. ✔
● **Homeopath** Ms L Howard Q: BA, MCH, RSHom. M: Soc.Hom.
B Yrs. Est.: 9 (**Ref:**HM10240)

**HOWARD, LYNNE**

**Lynne Howard**, 6 Erskine Rd, Primrose Hill, London, **London (Greater)**, NW3 3DJ, ENG.
(T) 020 7483 3344
Speciality: Homeopathy.
M (**Ref:**HM10241)

**HOWARD, T**

**T Howard**, 44 Southampton Rd, Fareham, **Hampshire**, PO16 7DY, ENG.
(T) 01329 281510
Speciality: Chiropodists (Podiatrists).
● **Owner** Mr T Howard
S (**Ref:**HM10242)

**HOWARD, TERRY**

**Terry Howard**, 133 Shepherds Lane, Dartford, **Kent**, DA1 2PA, ENG.
(T) 01322 273942
Speciality: Homeopathy.
● **Owner** Mr T Howard
M (**Ref:**HM10243)

**HOWARD, TERRY**

**Terry Howard**, Bexleyheath Natural Health Clinic, 284 Broadway, Bexleyheath, **Kent**, DA6 8AJ, ENG.
(T) 020 8303 6288 (F) 020 8303 6288
Speciality: Homeopathy.
● **Owner** Mr P Cousins
M (**Ref:**HM10244)

**HOWARD-BLOOD, LIBBY**

**Libby Howard-Blood**, 80 Spring Hill, Weston-Super-Mare, **Somerset**, BS22 9AZ, ENG.
(T) 01934 417160
Speciality: Complementary Medicines & Therapy.
● **Owner** Miss L Howard-Blood
C M (**Ref:**HM10245)

**HOWARD-PRAGER, JANET**

**Janet Howard-Prager**, 4 Greenhill Park, New Barnet, Barnet, **Hertfordshire**, EN5 1HG, ENG.
(T) 020 8440 1091
Speciality: Physiotherapy.
P S T (**Ref:**HM10246)

**HOWARTH, C D**

**C D Howarth**, 23 High St, Gosforth, Newcastle Upon Tyne, **Tyne and Wear**, NE3 4AD, ENG.
(T) 01912 851656
Speciality: Osteopathy.
P S T (**Ref:**HM10247)

**HOWARTH, D**

**D Howarth**, 33 Emblehope Drive, Gosforth, Newcastle Upon Tyne, **Tyne and Wear**, NE3 4RW, ENG.
(T) 01912 850293
Speciality: Acupuncture.
● **Owner** Mr D Howarth
O (**Ref:**HM10248)

**HOWARTH, D**

**D Howarth**, 91 Claypath, Durham, **County Durham**, DH1 1RG, ENG.



Key: B Mind-Body Medicine C Complementary Medicine H Self Help Treatment M Medicinal Therapy O Oriental Medicine P Postural Therapy S Manipulative Structural Therapy T Touch Therapy

(T) 01912 850293
Speciality: Acupuncture.
● **Owner** Mr D Howarth
O (Ref:HM10249)

## HOWARTH, JUNE

**June Howarth**, 15 Higher Dunscar, Egerton, Bolton, **Lancashire**, BL7 9TE, **ENG**.
(T) 01204 304413
Speciality: Electrolysis.
● **Owner** Mrs J Howarth
T (Ref:HM10250)

## HOWARTH, K

**K Howarth**, 11 The Ridgeway, Nelson, **Lancashire**, BB9 0DS, **ENG**.
(T) 01282 612907
Speciality: Psychotherapy.
● **Owner** Mrs K Howarth
B (Ref:HM10251)

## HOWARTH, LYNNE

**Lynne Howarth**, 17 De Ferrers Cl, East Leake, Loughborough, **Leicestershire**, LE12 6QD, **ENG**.
(T) 01509 820867
Speciality: Reflexology.
S T (Ref:HM10252)

## HOWARTH, M

**M Howarth**, 19 Burton Avenue, Timperley, Altrincham, **Cheshire**, WA15 6AQ, **ENG**.
(T) 01619 626234
Speciality: Complementary Medicines & Therapy.
● **Owner** Mr M Howarth
C M (Ref:HM10253)

## HOWARTH, M L

**M L Howarth**, 225 Lutterworth Rd, Nuneaton, **Warwickshire**, CV11 6PX, **ENG**.
(T) 024 7634 1204
Speciality: Chiropodists (Podiatrists).
S (Ref:HM10254)

## HOWARTH, R

**R Howarth**, 189 Fairlee Rd, Newport, **Isle of Wight**, PO30 2EP, **ENG**.
(T) 01983 520022 (F) 01983 528788
Speciality: Physiotherapy.
● **Managing Director** Mrs S Burton
P S T (Ref:HM10255)

## HOWAT, JONATHON

**Jonathon Howat**, 14 Holyoake Rd, Headington, Oxford, **Oxfordshire**, OX3 8AE, **ENG**.
(T) 01865 761802
Speciality: Chiropractors.
P S T (Ref:HM10256)

## HOWAT, MARGARET

**Margaret Howat**, Golders Hill Health Centre, North End Rd, London, **London (Greater)**, NW11 7UL, **ENG**.
(T) 020 8458 8822
Speciality: Physiotherapy.
● **Owner** Ms M Howat
P S T (Ref:HM10257)

## HOWCROFT, M

**Mrs M Howcroft**, Barrowby House, Hindon Lane, Tisbury, Salisbury, **Wiltshire**, SP3 6PZ, **ENG**.
(T) 01747 870286
Speciality: Physiotherapy.
● **Owner** Mrs M Howcroft
P S T (Ref:HM10258)

## HOWDEN, ELIZABETH

**Elizabeth Howden**, 2 Glebelands Rd, Knutsford, **Cheshire**, WA16 9DZ, **ENG**.
(T) 01565 650379
Speciality: Reflexology.
S T (Ref:HM10259)

## HOWDEN, LINDA

**Linda Howden**, 5 The Oval, Bradford, **Yorkshire (West)**, BD8 0AU, **ENG**.
(T) 01274 498954
Speciality: Acupuncture.
O (Ref:HM10260)

## HOWE, BARBARA

**Barbara Howe**, Springfield House, Newgate Rd, Wilmslow, **Cheshire**, SK9 5LL, **ENG**.
(T) 01625 523155
Speciality: Herbal Medicine, Naturopathy, Psychotherapy, Reflexology. ✔
● **Herbalist** Mrs B Howe **Q:** DBTh, FIRCH, MD(AM).
● **Psychologist** Mr K Howe **Q:** BSc, MD(AM), MSc, PhD. **M:** COH, RSA.
B Yrs. Est.: 60 (Ref:HM10261)

## HOWE, DENISE G

**Denise G Howe**, 135 Buckingham Rd, Bletchley, Milton Keynes, **Buckinghamshire**, MK3 5JD, **ENG**.
(T) 01908 366957
Speciality: Chiropodists (Podiatrists).
S (Ref:HM10262)

## HOWE, JAN

**Jan Howe**, Bradshawe Clinic Of Complementary Medicine, 5 Beech Lawns, Mullingar, **County Westmeath**, **IRE**.
(T) 08632 85856
Speciality: Acupressure, Do-In, Macrobiotics, Massage (Therapeutic), Moxibustion, Oriental Diagnosis, Shiatsu, Macrobiotic Dietary Advice. ✔
● **Shiatsu Therapist/Masseuse** Ms J Howe **Q:** ITEC, MRSS. **M:** Shiatsu Society UK.
O Yrs. Est.: 7 (Ref:HM10263)

## HOWE, KENNETH L

**Kenneth L Howe**, Springfield House, Newgate, Wilmslow, **Cheshire**, SK9 5LL, **ENG**.
(T) 01625 523155
Speciality: Complementary Medicines & Therapy.
C M (Ref:HM10264)

## HOWE, PAMELA

**Pamela Howe**, 106 Stockbridge Rd, Winchester, **Hampshire**, SO22 6RL, **ENG**.
(T) 01962 856310
Speciality: Reflexology.
S T (Ref:HM10265)

## HOWE, ROBERT

**Robert Howe**, 57 Romsey Cl, Rochester, **Kent**, ME2 3TJ, **ENG**.
(T) 01634 724365
Speciality: Chiropodists (Podiatrists).
S (Ref:HM10266)

## HOWELL, D B

**D B Howell**, 11 Heath Rd, Haywards Heath, **Sussex (West)**, RH16 3AX, **ENG**.
(T) 01444 450162 (F) 01444 459816
Speciality: Physiotherapy.
● **Practice Manager** Mrs W Langley
P S T (Ref:HM10267)

## HOWELL, JANE

**Jane Howell**, 3 Castelnau Gardens, London, **London (Greater)**, SW13 8DU, **ENG**.
(T) 020 8741 3415
Speciality: Reflexology.
S T (Ref:HM10268)

## HOWELL, N B

**N B Howell**, 11 Heath Rd, Haywards Heath, **Sussex (West)**, RH16 3AX, **ENG**.
(T) 01444 450162 (F) 01444 459816
Speciality: Physiotherapy.
● **Practice Manager** Mrs W Langley
P S T (Ref:HM10269)

## HOWELL, SHIRLEY

**Shirley Howell**, 1 Greenfield Park Drive, York, **Yorkshire (North)**, YO31 1JB, **ENG**.
(T) 01904 412337
Speciality: Psychotherapy.
● **Owner** Ms S Howell
B (Ref:HM10270)

## HOWELL, STEPHANIE

**Stephanie Howell**, 150 Crogen, Chirk, Wrexham, LL14 5BE, **WAL**.
(T) 01691 772729 (F) 01691 774676
Speciality: Aromatherapy.
● **Owner** Mrs S Howell
M O (Ref:HM10271)

## HOWELLS & BYTHEWAY

**Howells & Bytheway**, 22 King St, Dudley, **Midlands (West)**, DY2 8NY, **ENG**.
(T) 01384 250314
Speciality: Chiropodists (Podiatrists).
● **Partner** Mrs M Bytheway
S (Ref:HM10272)

## HOWELLS, G E

**G E Howells**, Tresaith, Cardigan, **Carmarthenshire**, SA43 2JH, **WAL**.
(T) 01239 811888
Speciality: Osteopathy.
● **Owner** Mrs G Howells
P S T (Ref:HM10273)

## HOWELLS, R (DR)

**Dr R Howells**, Consulting Rooms, 7 Radnor Walk, London, **London (Greater)**, SW3 4BP, **ENG**.
(T) 020 7349 3918
Speciality: Psychiatry.
● **Doctor** Dr R Howells
B (Ref:HM10274)

## HOWE'S HOLISTICS

**Howe's Holistics**, 70 Warburton Rd, Southampton, **Hampshire**, SO19 6HQ, **ENG**.
(T) 023 8040 6005
Speciality: Complementary Medicines & Therapy.
● **Owner** Ms M Howe
C M (Ref:HM10275)

## HOWES, GRAHAM

**Graham Howes**, 49 Heath Rd North, Locks Heath, Southampton, **Hampshire**, SO31 7PN, **ENG**.
(T) 01489 589654
Speciality: Chiropodists (Podiatrists).
● **Owner** Mr G Howes
S (Ref:HM10276)

## HOWETT, ROY

**Roy Howett**, 1 Cliffmere Cl, Cheadle Hulme, Cheadle, **Cheshire**, SK8 5JH, **ENG**.
(T) 01614 851585
Speciality: Hypnosis.
B (Ref:HM10277)

## HOWEY, ROSEMARY

**Rosemary Howey**, 14 Manor Cl, Droitwich, **Worcestershire**, WR9 8HG, **ENG**.
(T) 01905 770892 (F) 01905 770892
Speciality: Physiotherapy.
● **Owner** Mr R Howie
P S T (Ref:HM10278)

## HOWICK, E

**E Howick**, 25 Highland Rd, Southsea, **Hampshire**, PO4 9DA, **ENG**.
(T) 023 9283 2806
Speciality: Chiropodists (Podiatrists).
● **Owner** Mrs E Howick
S (Ref:HM10279)

## HOWIE & ASSOCIATES

**A S Howie & Associates**, 24 Billet St, Taunton, **Somerset**, TA1 3NG, **ENG**.
(T) 01823 272163
Speciality: Chiropodists (Podiatrists).
● **Owner** Mrs A Howie
S (Ref:HM10280)

## HOWIE, DAVID D

**David D Howie**, 9b Millburn St, Aberdeen, **Aberdeenshire**, AB11 6SS, **SCO**.
(T) 01224 574190
Speciality: Hypnosis.
B (Ref:HM10281)

## HOWIE, MARION

**Marion Howie**, Ridgeway, Latchingdon Rd, Cold Norton, Chelmsford, **Essex**, CM3 6HR, **ENG**.
(T) 01621 828839
Speciality: Homeopathy.
M (Ref:HM10282)

## HOWIE, TOM R

**Tom R Howie**, 7 Geddes Drive, Perth, **Perth and Kinross**, PH1 1QD, **SCO**.
(T) 01738 628275
Speciality: Chiropody, Podiatry. ✔
● **Chiropodist (Podiatrist)** Mr T Howie **Q:** MBChA, MSSCh. **M:** B.A.Ch.P, SSCh.
C Yrs. Est.: 15 (Ref:HM10283)

## HOWIE, TOM R

**Tom R Howie**, 3 Leonard St, Perth, **Perth and**



Key continued: **Yrs.Est:** Years Established **Q:** Qualifications **M:** Professional Membership ✔ Indemnity Insurance Accept Credit Cards

**Kinross**, PH2 8ET, SCO.
(T) 01738 622665
Speciality: Chiropody, Podiatry.
● **Chiropodist (Podiatrist)**
Mr T Howie Q: MBChA, MSSCh. M: B.A.Ch.P, SSCh.
C Yrs. Est.: 10 (Ref:HM10284)

### HOWLAND, ANN
**Ann Howland**, 14 Lancet Lane, Maidstone, **Kent**, ME15 9RX, ENG.
(T) 01622 743002
Speciality: Reflexology.
● **Owner** Mrs A Howland
S T (Ref:HM10285)

### HOWLE, E
**E Howle**, 8 Silver Cl, Biddulph, Stoke-On-Trent, **Staffordshire**, ST8 6JR, ENG.
(T) 01782 523429
Speciality: Chiropodists (Podiatrists).
● **Owner** Mrs E Howle
S (Ref:HM10286)

### HOWLE, E
**Mrs E Howle**, Victoria House, Victoria Rd, Newcastle, **Staffordshire**, ST5 1NN, ENG.
(T) 01782 710686
Speciality: Chiropodists (Podiatrists).
S (Ref:HM10287)

### HOWLETT & DICKINSON
**Howlett & Dickinson**, 25 Ashburton Rd, Newcastle Upon Tyne, **Tyne and Wear**, NE3 4XN, ENG.
(T) 01912 843698
Speciality: Chiropodists (Podiatrists).
● **Partner** Mrs C Howlett
S (Ref:HM10288)

### HOWLETT, DAVID
**David Howlett**, Flat 14 Block 1, Peabody Sq, London, **London (Greater)**, N1 8RW, ENG.
(T) 020 7354 9467
Speciality: Alexander Technique.
● **Owner** Mr D Howlett
P S (Ref:HM10289)

### HOWLETT, DAVID
**David Howlett**, Hanover House, Chard St, Axminster, **Devon**, EX13 5DZ, ENG.
(T) 01297 32331
Speciality: Alexander Technique.
● **Owner** Mr H Alldritt
P S (Ref:HM10290)

### HOWLETT, DAVID
**David Howlett**, Bodywise, 119 Roman Rd, London, **London (Greater)**, E2 0QN, ENG.
(T) 020 8981 6938
Speciality: Alexander Technique.
● **Owner** Mr D Howlett
P S (Ref:HM10291)

### HOWLEY & FIELD
**Howley L & Field P**, 130 Longbridge Rd, Barking, **Essex**, IG11 8SF, ENG.
(T) 020 8591 2406
Speciality: Osteopathy.
P S T (Ref:HM10292)

### HOWORTH, R
**R Howorth**, 64 High St, Porthmadog, **Gwynedd**, LL49 9LW, WAL.
(T) 01766 514680
Speciality: Acupuncture.
O (Ref:HM10293)

### HOWTH COUNSELLING SERVICE
**Howth Counselling Service**, The Burrows, Main St, Howth, **County Dublin**, IRE.
(T) 01832 3529
(E) cashell50@hotmail.com
Speciality: Art Therapy, Autogenic Training, Aversion Therapy, Cognitive Therapy, Colour Therapy, Counselling, Humanistic Psychology, Meditation, Psychotherapy, Rogerian Therapy, Stress Therapy. ✓
● **Psychologist** Pauline Walsh Q: BA, Dip.Couns, Dip.Psych. M: BPS.
H Yrs. Est.: 4 (Ref:HM10294)

### HOWTONE, CHRISTINA
**Christina Howtone**, 139 Sevenoaks Cl, Romford, **Essex**, RM3 7EF, ENG.
(T) 01708 373175
Speciality: Psychotherapy.
● **Owner** Mrs C Howtone
B (Ref:HM10295)

### HOYLAND, WISTY
**Wisty Hoyland**, 52 Stoke Newington Church St, London, **London (Greater)**, N16 0NB, ENG.
(T) 020 7249 9671
Speciality: Herbalists.
● **Senior Partner** Mrs J Sheridan
M (Ref:HM10296)

### HUA TUO HEALTH CLINIC
**Hua Tuo Health Clinic**, 9 Vernon Rd, London, **London (Greater)**, E11 4QT, ENG.
(T) 020 8558 6966
Speciality: Complementary Medicines & Therapy.
C M (Ref:HM10297)

### HUART, S C
**S C Huart**, Newhaven, Church End, Blewbury, Didcot, **Oxfordshire**, OX11 9QQ, ENG.
(T) 01235 850399
Speciality: Acupuncture.
O (Ref:HM10298)

### HUBBARD & PERKINS
**Hubbard & Perkins**, 178 Worcester Rd, Malvern, **Worcestershire**, WR14 1AG, ENG.
(T) 01684 569889
Speciality: Chiropodists (Podiatrists).
● **Employee** Mrs S Hubbard
S (Ref:HM10299)

### HUBBARD DIANETICS FOUNDATION
**Hubbard Dianetics Foundation (The)**, 5 St Georges Pl, Brighton, **Sussex (East)**, BN1 4GA, ENG.
(T) 01273 882697
Speciality: Complementary Medicines & Therapy.
M (Ref:HM10300)

### HUBBARD, LEE
**Lee Hubbard**, 17 Lester Gr, Hazlemere, High Wycombe, **Buckinghamshire**, HP15 7HW, ENG.
(T) 01494 711047
Speciality: Aromatherapy.
● **Owner** Miss L Hubbard
M O (Ref:HM10301)

### HUBBARD, NIK
**Nik Hubbard**, 'Beards', Tilbury Rd, Great Yeldham, Halstead, **Essex**, CO9 4JG, ENG.
(T) 01787 237282
Speciality: Reflexology.
S T (Ref:HM10302)

### HUBBARD-FORD, PATRICK
**Patrick Hubbard-Ford**, 24 Catherine St, Salisbury, **Wiltshire**, SP1 2DA, ENG.
(T) 01202 536599 (F) 01202 525636
Speciality: Chiropodists (Podiatrists).
● **Owner** Mr P Hubbard-Ford
S (Ref:HM10303)

### HUBBERS, HILARY
**Hilary Hubbers**, 106 Whitchurch Gardens, Edgware, **London (Greater)**, HA8 6PB, ENG.
(T) 020 8951 5900
Speciality: Osteopathy.
● **Owner** Mrs H Hubbers
P S T (Ref:HM10304)

### HUBBLE CLINIC OF OSTEO & ACU
**Hubble Clinic Of Osteopathy & Acupuncture (The)**, 193 Wickhay, Basildon, **Essex**, SS15 5AQ, ENG.
(T) 01268 451745
Speciality: Osteopathy.
● **Owner** Mr J Hubble
P S T (Ref:HM10305)

### HUDD, ALISON
**Alison Hudd**, Devizes, **Wiltshire**, SN10, ENG.
(T) 01380 860720
Speciality: Bach Remedies.
M (Ref:HM10306)

### HUDDERSFIELD PHYSIO UNIT
**Huddersfield Private Physio Unit**, 2 Murray Rd, Huddersfield, **Yorkshire (West)**, HD2 2AD, ENG.
(T) 01484 431972
Speciality: Physiotherapy.
● **Senior Partner** Mrs M Laycock
P S T (Ref:HM10307)

### HUDDLESTONE, BILL
**Bill Huddlestone**, 103 Victoria Rd, Fulwood, Preston, **Lancashire**, PR2 8NL, ENG.
(T) 01772 718307 (F) 01772 718307
Speciality: Hypnotherapy.
● **Owner** Mr B Huddleston
B (Ref:HM10308)

### HUDSON, ANNA
**Anna Hudson**, 81 St Johns Rd, Woking, **Surrey**, GU21 1QQ, ENG.
(T) 01483 722264 (F) 01483 730355
Speciality: Physiotherapy.
● **Owner** Mrs A Hudson
P S T (Ref:HM10309)

### HUDSON, ELIZABETH
**Elizabeth Hudson**, 14 The Glebe, Badby, Daventry, **Northamptonshire**, NN11 3AZ, ENG.
(T) 01327 877797
Speciality: Reflexology.
S T (Ref:HM10310)

### HUDSON, EMMA
**Emma Caroline Hudson**, The Wesley Lane Clinic, 6 Wesley Lane, Bicester, **Oxfordshire**, OX6 7JU, ENG.
(T) 01869 248538
Speciality: Manipulation, Osteopathy. ✓
● **Osteopath** Ms E Hudson Q: DO. M: GOsC.
S Yrs. Est.: 8 (Ref:HM10311)

### HUDSON, H
**H Hudson**, 2 Stable Court, Melbourne, Derby, **Derbyshire**, DE73 1LP, ENG.
(T) 01332 863114
Speciality: Chiropodists (Podiatrists).
S (Ref:HM10312)

### HUDSON, JOHN
**John Hudson**, 15 Hales Horn Cl, Bradley Stoke, Bristol, BS32 8AG, ENG.
(T) 01179 314300
Speciality: Hypnosis, Hypnotherapy, Psychotherapy, Stress Therapy. ✓ CREDIT
● **Hypnotherapist/Psychotherapist**
Mr J Hudson Q: BEd (Hons), Dip.Hyp, M.Ed, MBRCP. M: IAH, NCH.
B Yrs. Est.: 16 (Ref:HM10313)

### HUDSON, JOHN
**John Hudson**, Queen Anne House, 11 Charlotte St, Bath, **Somerset**, BA1 2NE, ENG.
(T) 01225 337992
Speciality: Hypnosis.
B (Ref:HM10314)

### HUDSON, JOHN
**John Hudson**, Bath Natural Health Clinic, Alexander House, James Street West, Bath, **Somerset**, BA1 2BP, ENG.
(T) 01225 313153
Speciality: Hypnotherapy, Psychotherapy.
✓ CREDIT
● **Hypnotherapist/Psychotherapist**
Mr J Hudson Q: BEd (Hons), Dip.Hyp, M.Ed. M: BRCP, IAH, NCH.
B Yrs. Est.: 16 (Ref:HM10315)

### HUDSON, M A
**M A Hudson**, 1 Heath Cresent, Norwich, **Norfolk**, NR6 6XD, ENG.
(T) 01603 425501 (F) 01603 425501
Speciality: Chiropodists (Podiatrists).
● **Owner** Mrs M Hudson
S (Ref:HM10316)

### HUDSON, MICHAEL B
**Michael B Hudson**, Hillview Clinic, Culcharry, Nairn, **Highland**, IV12 5QY, SCO.
(T) 01667 404373
Speciality: Osteopathy.
P S T (Ref:HM10317)

### HUDSON, ROSEMARY
**Rosemary Hudson**, Highcroft Cottage, Haslemere Rd, Milford, Godalming, **Surrey**, GU8 5BP, ENG.



Key: B Mind-Body Medicine C Complementary Medicine H Self Help Treatment M Medicinal Therapy O Oriental Medicine P Postural Therapy S Manipulative Structural Therapy T Touch Therapy

(T) 01483 425338 (F) 01483 425338
Speciality: Reflexology.
● **Owner** Mrs R Hudson
S T (Ref:HM10318)

## HUFTON, MARK
**Mark Hufton**, 1 Minto Rd, St Werbergs, Bristol, BS2 9YB, ENG.
(T) 01179 556524
Speciality: Aromatherapy.
M O (Ref:HM10319)

## HUGHAN, M J & D J
**M J & D J Hughan**, 13 Prestbury Rd, Macclesfield, **Cheshire**, SK10 1AU, ENG.
(T) 01625 424227
Speciality: Chiropodists (Podiatrists).
● **Partner** Mr M Hughan
S (Ref:HM10320)

## HUGH-BASSAM, O J (DR)
**Dr O J Hugh-Bassam**, 168 Christchurch Rd, Newport, NP19 8BD, WAL.
(T) 01633 669091 (F) 01633 282255
Speciality: Clairvoyants & Palmists.
● **Owner** Dr O Hugh-Bassam
B (Ref:HM10321)

## HUGHES, ANTHONY
**Hughes Anthony BSc LIC TCM**, 1 Leopardstown Dr, Stillorgan, **County Dublin**, IRE.
(T) 01288 0352
(E) natmed@iol.ie
Speciality: Complementary Medicines & Therapy.
M (Ref:HM10322)

## HUGHES, CARRIE
**Miss Carrie Hughes**, 59 Wimpole St, London, **London (Greater)**, W1M 7DE, ENG.
(T) 020 7935 7344
Speciality: Physiotherapy.
● **Owner** Miss C Hughes
P S T (Ref:HM10323)

## HUGHES, CLARE
**Clare Hughes**, 155 Ditchling Rise, Brighton, **Sussex (East)**, BN1 4QQ, ENG.
(T) 01273 623460
Speciality: Alexander Technique. ✓
● **Owner** Mrs C Hughes Q: MSTAT.
S Yrs. Est.: 22 (Ref:HM10324)

## HUGHES, DOREEN
**Doreen Hughes**, 2 Ash Rd, Onehouse, Stowmarket, **Suffolk**, IP14 3HB, ENG.
(T) 01449 770101
Speciality: Indian Head Massage, Reflexology.
S T (Ref:HM10325)

## HUGHES, HILARY
**Hilary Hughes**, 24 Smock Lane, Ashton-In-Makerfield, Wigan, **Lancashire**, WN4 0SN, ENG.
(T) 01942 511918
Speciality: Reflexology.
● **Owner** Mrs H Hughes
S T (Ref:HM10326)

## HUGHES, J
**J Hughes**, Muster Green, Haywards Heath, **Sussex (West)**, RH16 4AG, ENG.
(T) 01444 412863
Speciality: Chiropodists (Podiatrists).
● **Owner** Mr J Hughes
S (Ref:HM10327)

## HUGHES, J HACKER
**J Hacker Hughes**, 7 Rainsford Avenue, Chelmsford, **Essex**, CM1 2PJ, ENG.
(T) 01245 350923
Speciality: Psychotherapy.
B (Ref:HM10328)

## HUGHES, JANE CHRISTINE
**Jane Christine Hughes**, Whiteway Cottage, Horsley Bridge, Horsley, Stroud, **Gloucestershire**, GL6 0PN, ENG.
(T) 01453 833502
Speciality: Reflexology.
S T (Ref:HM10329)

## HUGHES, JEAN
**Jean Hughes**, 3 Pool Bank Rd, Wirral, **Merseyside**, CH62 4RR, ENG.
(T) 01516 448244
Speciality: Reflexology.
● **Owner** Ms J Hughes
S T (Ref:HM10330)

## HUGHES, JEAN
**Jean Hughes**, 48 Hibbert St, Luton, **Bedfordshire**, LU1 3UX, ENG.
(T) 01582 452096 (F) 01582 452096
Speciality: Complementary Medicines & Therapy.
● **Owner** Mrs J Hughes
C M (Ref:HM10331)

## HUGHES, LINDA
**Linda Hughes**, Foxhall, The Croft, Bures, **Suffolk**, CO8 5JB, ENG.
(T) 01787 227195
Speciality: Psychotherapy.
● **Owner** Mrs L Hughes
B (Ref:HM10332)

## HUGHES, LINDA
**Linda Hughes**, 16 Friends Field, Bures, **Suffolk**, CO8 5LH, ENG.
(T) 01787 227195
Speciality: Psychotherapy.
B (Ref:HM10333)

## HUGHES, M A
**M A Hughes**, 107 Highfields Rd, Witham, **Essex**, CM8 1LW, ENG.
(T) 01376 502600 (F) 01376 502600
Speciality: Hypnosis.
● **Owner** Mrs M Hughes
B (Ref:HM10334)

## HUGHES, MARGARET
**Margaret Hughes**, Pinfold Lane, Whitefield, Manchester, **Manchester (Greater)**, M45 7NY, ENG.
(T) 01617 665753
Speciality: Electrolysis.
● **Owner** Ms M Hughes
T (Ref:HM10335)

## HUGHES, MICHAEL
**Hughes Michael D H P M I A H**, Elm Pk, Clarina, **County Limerick**, IRE.
(T) 06135 5365 (F) 06135 3339
(E) hypnosis@writeme.com
(W) homepage.eircom.net/~mindmtrs
Speciality: Complementary Medicines & Therapy.
M (Ref:HM10336)

## HUGHES, PAMELA J
**Pamela J Hughes**, 19 Abbotsford Drive, Dudley, **Midlands (West)**, DY1 2HD, ENG.
(T) 01384 258590
Speciality: Chiropodists (Podiatrists).
● **Owner** Mrs P Hughes
S (Ref:HM10337)

## HUGHES, PAT
**Pat Hughes**, 20A Central Avenue, West Bridgeford, West Bridgford, Nottingham, **Nottinghamshire**, NG2 5GR, ENG.
(T) 01159 143311
Speciality: Aromatherapy.
M O (Ref:HM10338)

## HUGHES, PAUL
**Registered Homeopath**, 61A Garden Flat, Cathnor Rd, Shepherds Bush, London, **London (Greater)**, W12 9JB, ENG.
(T) 020 8749 3472
Speciality: Autogenic Training, Dowsing, Homeopathy. ✓
● **Homeopath** Mr P Hughes Q: RSHom.
B Yrs. Est.: 11 (Ref:HM10339)

## HUGHES, R L & J L
**R L & J L Hughes**, Bryn Hafod, Cerrigceinwen, Bodorgan, **Isle of Anglesey**, LL62 5PN, WAL.
(T) 01248 722170
Speciality: Chiropodists (Podiatrists).
● **Partner** Mrs J Hughes
S (Ref:HM10340)

## HUGHES, R T
**R T Hughes**, 50 Norton Lane, Burntwood, **Staffordshire**, WS7 0HN, ENG.
(T) 01543 684980
Speciality: Osteopathy.
● **Owner** Mr R Hughes
P S T (Ref:HM10341)

## HUGHES, SALLY-ANNE
**Sally-Anne Hughes**, The Old Cottage, Andrews Hill, Billingshurst, **Sussex (West)**, RH14 9JS, ENG.
(T) 01403 783912
Speciality: Chiropodists (Podiatrists).
● **Owner** Mrs S Hughes
S (Ref:HM10342)

## HUGHES, THERESA
**Theresa Hughes**, 3 Orchard Cl, Chorleywood, Rickmansworth, **Hertfordshire**, WD3 5QW, ENG.
(T) 01923 286727
Speciality: Homeopathy.
M (Ref:HM10343)

## HUGHES, VANESSA
**Vanessa Hughes**, Malvern, Worcester, **Worcestershire**, WR14, ENG.
(T) 01684 893495
Speciality: Bach Remedies.
M (Ref:HM10344)

## HUGHES-BARLOW, PAUL
**Paul Hughes-Barlow**, 259 Kings Rd Arches, Brighton, **Sussex (East)**, BN2 1TD, ENG.
(T) 01273 677206
Speciality: Clairvoyants & Palmists.
● **Owner** Mr P Hughes-Barlow
B (Ref:HM10345)

## HUGHGONSON, SUE
**Sue Hughgonson**, 2 Thornbarrow Hall, Thornbarrow Drive, Windermere, **Cumbria**, LA23 2EP, ENG.
(T) 01539 443004
Speciality: Hypnosis.
B (Ref:HM10346)

## HUGILL, JULET
**Julet Hugill**, Haggwood Farm, Wheldrake, York, **Yorkshire (North)**, YO19 6BE, ENG.
(T) 01904 449342
Speciality: Chiropodists (Podiatrists).
● **Owner** Miss J Hugill
S (Ref:HM10347)

## HUI CHUN CHINESE ACUPUNCTURE
**Hui Chun Chinese Acupuncture Clinic**, 54 Hill St, Glasgow, **Glasgow (City of)**, G3 6RH, SCO.
(T) 01413 321302
Speciality: Acupuncture.
O (Ref:HM10348)

## HUICHUN CLINIC OF T C M
**Huichun Clinic Of T C M (The)**, 325 Great Western Rd, Glasgow, **Glasgow (City of)**, G4 9HS, SCO.
(T) 01413 571313
Speciality: Complementary Medicines & Therapy.
● **Owner** Dr W Chen
M (Ref:HM10349)

## HUISMAN, MARTINE
**Martine Huisman**, 101 Watcombe Rd, Bournemouth, **Dorset**, BH6 5LP, ENG.
(T) 01202 427632
Speciality: Chiropractors.
P S T (Ref:HM10350)

## HULBERT, PENNY
**Penny Hulbert**, 44A Amherst Rd, Bexhill-on-Sea, **Sussex (East)**, TN40 1QW, ENG.
(T) 01424 223510
Speciality: Homeopathy.
● **Partner** Mr D Annetts
M (Ref:HM10351)

## HULCOTT END PRACTICE
**Hulcott End Practice**, Hulcott End, 204 Aylesbury Rd, Bierton, Aylesbury, **Buckinghamshire**, HP22 5DT, ENG.
(T) 01296 436638
Speciality: Acupressure, Acupuncture, Electrotherapy, Massage (Therapeutic), Physiotherapy, Reflexology. ✓
● **Physiotherapist/Reflexologist** Mrs L Padget Q: MCSP, MIFR, SRP.
P Yrs. Est.: 9 (Ref:HM10352)


Key continued: Yrs.Est: Years Established Q: Qualifications M: Professional Membership ✓ Indemnity Insurance Accept Credit Cards

## HULL CLINIC OF COMP MEDICINE
**Hull Clinic Of Complementary Medicine**, Holm Oak, 26 Heads Lane, Hessle, **Humberside (North)**, HU13 0JH, ENG.
(T) 01482 644848
Speciality: Chiropractic.
P S T (Ref:HM10353)

## HULL, TERRI
**Terri Hull**, Aberfoyle House, Stapley Rd, St. Albans, **Hertfordshire**, AL3 5EP, ENG.
(T) 01727 856687
Speciality: Aromatherapy.
● **Manager** Mrs S Bassett
M O (Ref:HM10354)

## HULLAND, ERIC
**Eric Hulland**, 26 Whinmoor Court, Leeds, **Yorkshire (West)**, LS14 1NX, ENG.
(T) 01132 650743
Speciality: Hypnosis.
● **Owner** Mr E Hulland
B (Ref:HM10355)

## HULME, A
**Mrs A Hulme**, Ravenscroft, Albaston, Gunnislake, **Cornwall**, PL18 9EZ, ENG.
(T) 01822 832268
Speciality: Chiropodists (Podiatrists).
S (Ref:HM10356)

## HULME, ALICE
**Alice Hulme**, Horndon House, Horndon, Peter Tavy, Tavistock, **Devon**, PL19 9NQ, ENG.
(T) 01822 810034
Speciality: Chiropodists (Podiatrists).
● **Owner** Mrs A Hulme
S (Ref:HM10357)

## HULME, J
**J Hulme**, 14 Jaffrey St, Leigh, **Manchester (Greater)**, WN7 1XX, ENG.
(T) 01942 608897
Speciality: Physiotherapy.
P S T (Ref:HM10358)

## HUMAN ASSETS
**Human Assets Ltd**, 19 Dunraven St, London, **London (Greater)**, W1Y 3FE, ENG.
(T) 020 7499 5630 (F) 020 7495 5868
Speciality: Psychology.
● **Managing Director** Dr C Woodruff
B (Ref:HM10359)

## HUMAN DEVELOPMENT & RELATIONS
**Human Development & Relations Practice**, Glencar Scotch, Letterkenny, **County Donegal**, IRE.
(T) 07426 405
Speciality: Complementary Medicines & Therapy.
M (Ref:HM10360)

## HUMAN FACTORS UK
**Human Factors UK Ltd**, 17 Portland Pl, London, **London (Greater)**, W1N 3AF, ENG.
(T) 020 7580 8754 (F) 020 7580 4531
Speciality: Psychology.
B (Ref:HM10361)

## HUMAN FOCUS RETURN TO WORK
**Human Focus Return To Work Ltd**, Unit A Mill Green Business Park, Mill Green Rd, Mitcham, **Surrey**, CR4 4HT, ENG.
(T) 020 8255 8182 (F) 020 8255 8172
(W) www.returntowork.co.uk
Speciality: Chiropractic, Cognitive Therapy, Counselling, Osteopathy, Physiotherapy, Phytotherapy, Occupational Therapy, Orthopaedic Specialist & Surgeon. ✔
● **Orthopaedic Surgeon**
Mr N Barton-Hanson M: BOrthA.
● **Physical Therapist** Kay Fitton Q: C.Psychol. M: CSP.
● **Clinical Psychologist**
Judith Crawford Q: BPS, C.Psychol. M: BPS.
H Yrs. Est.: 10 (Ref:HM10362)

## HUMAN I T
**Human I T Ltd**, Murdoch House, 40-44 Station Rd, Cambridge, **Cambridgeshire**, CB1 2JH, ENG.
(T) 01223 713640 (F) 01226 713641
Speciality: Psychoanalysis.
● **Sole Director**
Christopher John Barnett
B (Ref:HM10363)

## HUMAN PERFORMANCE CLINIC
**Human Performance Clinic (The)**, 3a Kirklee Trce, Kelvinside, Glasgow, **Glasgow (City of)**, G12 0TQ, SCO.
(T) 01413 373327or0800454770
Speciality: Hypnosis, Hypnotherapy, Neuro-Linguistic Program, Psychotherapy. ✔
● **Hypnotherapist/NLP Therapist**
Mr I Thomson
(T) 08004 547700
● **Hypnotherapist** Mr J McDonald
(T) 08004 547700 M: LCHyp.
● **NLP Practitioner** Ms L Henderson
(T) 08004 547700
B Yrs. Est.: 10 (Ref:HM10364)

## HUMAN RELATIONS SERVICES
**Human Relations Services**, Gables Farm, Higham, Alfreton, **Derbyshire**, DE55 6EH, ENG.
(T) 01773 833267
Speciality: Psychotherapy.
● **Owner** Mr J Baxter
B (Ref:HM10365)

## HUMAN TOUCH CENTRE
**Human Touch Complementary Holistic Therapy Centre**, 83A Great Stone Rd, Stretford, Manchester, **Manchester (Greater)**, M32 8GR, ENG.
(T) 01618 813421
Speciality: Aromatherapy, Counselling, Holistic Healing, Nutritional Therapy, Psychotherapy, Reflexology, Reiki.
● **Holistic Practitioner**
Ms J Thomason-Lynch Q: IIHHT, MAR. M: FHT, ICHT.
C (Ref:HM10366)

## HUMBERSTONE COUNSELLING
**Humberstone Counselling**, 189 Uppingham Rd, Leicester, **Leicestershire**, LE5 4BQ, ENG.
(T) 01162 764911 (F) 01162 764911
Speciality: Hypnosis.
● **Owner** Mr M Armstrong-Prior
B (Ref:HM10367)

## HUMBLE-JACKSON, S L
**S L Humble-Jackson**, 117 Pen-Y-Lan Rd, Cardiff, **Glamorgan (Vale of)**, CF23 5RB, WAL.
(T) 029 2049 3326
Speciality: Chiropodists (Podiatrists).
S (Ref:HM10368)

## HUMBLE-THOMAS, ELIZABETH
**Elizabeth Humble-Thomas**, 3 George St, Oxford, **Oxfordshire**, OX1 2AT, ENG.
(T) 01865 247377
Speciality: Chiropodists (Podiatrists).
● **Partner** Mrs F Lyon
S (Ref:HM10369)

## HUME, PETER D
**Peter D Hume**, 122 Dunraven Drive, Plymouth, **Devon**, PL6 6AT, ENG.
(T) 01752 702055 (F) 01752 702055
Speciality: Chiropody. ✔
● **Chiropodist (Podiatrist)**
Mr P Hume Q: MBChA, MSSCh. M: B.A.Ch.P, SSCh.
C Yrs. Est.: 4 (Ref:HM10370)

## HUMPHREY, A
**A Humphrey**, 17 Grafton Rd, London, **London (Greater)**, NW5 3DX, ENG.
(T) 020 7485 1167
Speciality: Psychotherapy.
● **Owner** Ms A Humphrey
B (Ref:HM10371)

## HUMPHREY, ALISON
**Alison Humphrey IIHHT Holistic Therapist**, 138 Shakespeare St, Coventry, **Midlands (West)**, CV2 4NG, ENG.
(T) 024 7644 0127
Speciality: Complementary Medicines & Therapy.
C M (Ref:HM10372)

## HUMPHREY, VAL
**Val Humphrey**, Telford & District Occupational Health Centre, Halesfield 13, Telford, **Shropshire**, TF7 4PL, ENG.
(T) 01952 581251 (F) 01952 581251
Speciality: Acupuncture.
● **Owner** Mrs V Humphrey
O (Ref:HM10373)

## HUMPHREYS, J E
**J E Humphreys**, Flat 2D Block, 2 Portman Mansions, Chiltern St, London, **London (Greater)**, W1M 1LE, ENG.
(T) 020 7486 7928
Speciality: Chiropodists (Podiatrists).
S (Ref:HM10374)

## HUMPHREYS, J E M
**J E M Humphreys**, 115 East Gomeldon Rd, Gomeldon, Salisbury, **Wiltshire**, SP4 6LZ, ENG.
(T) 01980 611764
Speciality: Chiropodists (Podiatrists).
● **Owner** Mrs J Humphreys
S (Ref:HM10375)

## HUMPHREYS, R
**R Humphreys**, 105 Weston Rd, Stoke-On-Trent, **Staffordshire**, ST3 6AN, ENG.
(T) 01782 316260
Speciality: Chiropodists (Podiatrists).
● **Owner** Mr R Humphreys
S (Ref:HM10376)

## HUMPHRIES, C
**C Humphries**, 13 London Rd, East Grinstead, **Sussex (West)**, RH19 1AL, ENG.
(T) 01342 325434 (F) 01342 325434
Speciality: Osteopathy.
● **Owner** Mr C Humphries
P S T (Ref:HM10377)

## HUMPHRIES, CARL
**Carl Humphries**, Butts Cottage, 149 High St, Uckfield, **Sussex (East)**, TN22 1HP, ENG.
(T) 01825 762657 (F) 01825 762657
Speciality: Osteopathy.
● **Owner** Mr C Humphries
P S T (Ref:HM10378)

## HUMPHRIES, JUDITH
**Judith Humphries**, 40 Elsham Rd, London, **London (Greater)**, W14 8HB, ENG.
(T) 020 7603 5127
Speciality: Reflexology.
S T (Ref:HM10379)

## HUMPHRIES, MARK
**Mark Humphries**, 4 Alexandra St, Eastwood, Nottingham, **Nottinghamshire**, NG16 3BD, ENG.
(T) 01773 763146
Speciality: Chiropodists (Podiatrists).
● **Owner** Mr M Humphries
S (Ref:HM10380)

## HUMPHRIES, MARK
**Mark Humphries**, 40 Humberston Rd, Nottingham, **Nottinghamshire**, NG8 2SZ, ENG.
(T) 01159 284904
Speciality: Chiropodists (Podiatrists).
● **Owner** Mr M Humphries
S (Ref:HM10381)

## HUMPHRIS, MANDY
**Mandy Humphris**, 47 Hilbre Rd, Wirral, **Merseyside**, CH48 3HB, ENG.
(T) 01516 251645
Speciality: Physiotherapy.
● **Owner** Mrs M Humphris
P S T (Ref:HM10382)

## HUMPHRY, S B
**S B Humphry**, The Old Vicarage, Church St, Hertford, **Hertfordshire**, SG14 1EJ, ENG.
(T) 01992 583415 (F) 01992 583415
Speciality: Osteopathy.
● **Owner** Mr S Humphry
P S T (Ref:HM10383)

## HUMPRIES-RILEY, B
**B Humpries-Riley**, Forge Rd, Machynlleth, **Powys**, SY20 8EQ, WAL.
(T) 01654 702959 (F) 01654 702220
Speciality: Chiropractors.
● **Owner** Mr J Riley

Key: B Mind-Body Medicine C Complementary Medicine H Self Help Treatment M Medicinal Therapy O Oriental Medicine P Postural Therapy S Manipulative Structural Therapy T Touch Therapy

P S T (Ref:HM10384)

### HUNN, MARGARET

**Margaret Hunn**, Ingledale, 1 Tanhouse Rd, Oxted, **Surrey**, RH8 9PE, ENG.
(T) 01883 717277
Speciality: Hypnotherapy.
B (Ref:HM10385)

### HUNT & ASSOCIATES

**E I Hunt & Associates**, Crispin House, 20 Wellington St, Blackburn, **Lancashire**, BB1 8AF, ENG.
(T) 01254 56991
Speciality: Chiropodists (Podiatrists).
S (Ref:HM10386)

### HUNT, A F

**A F Hunt**, 127 Staunton Rd, Headington, Oxford, **Oxfordshire**, OX3 7TN, ENG.
(T) 01865 762574
Speciality: Chiropodists (Podiatrists).
● Owner Mr A Hunt
S (Ref:HM10387)

### HUNT, A M

**A M Hunt**, 19 Layer Rd, Colchester, **Essex**, CO2 7HT, ENG.
(T) 01206 542580
Speciality: Physiotherapy.
● Owner A Hunt
P S T (Ref:HM10388)

### HUNT, C

**C Hunt**, 75 Leigh Rd, Leigh-On-Sea, **Essex**, SS9 1JN, ENG.
(T) 01702 714862 (F) 01702 716969
Speciality: Physiotherapy.
● Owner Mrs C Merryfield
P S T (Ref:HM10389)

### HUNT, C

**C Hunt**, Kent Clinic, 104 Walton Rd, East Molesey, **Surrey**, KT8 0DL, ENG.
(T) 020 8224 0200
Speciality: Complementary Medicines & Therapy.
M (Ref:HM10390)

### HUNT, CHARLES

**Charles Hunt**, 8 Fulmer Rd, Gerrards Cross, **Buckinghamshire**, SL9 7DT, ENG.
(T) 01753 887855 (F) 01753 887855
Speciality: Osteopathy.
● Owner Mr C Hunt
P S T (Ref:HM10391)

### HUNT, H

**H Hunt**, 3 Stable Cottages, Sutton Rd, Langley, Maidstone, **Kent**, ME17 3NQ, ENG.
(T) 01622 862254
Speciality: Chiropodists (Podiatrists).
● Owner Mrs H Hunt
S (Ref:HM10392)

### HUNT, J

**J Hunt**, 86 Babbacombe Rd, Torquay, **Devon**, TQ1 3SW, ENG.
(T) 01803 325657
Speciality: Chiropodists (Podiatrists).
● Owner Mrs W Evans
S (Ref:HM10393)

### HUNT, J H

**J H Hunt**, 1 Oak Drive, Hilton, Derby, **Derbyshire**, DE65 5GT, ENG.
(T) 01283 733073
Speciality: Chiropodists (Podiatrists).
● Owner Mrs J Hunt
S (Ref:HM10394)

### HUNT, JOHN

**John Hunt**, 2 Hollybush Villas, Church Village, Pontypridd, **Rhondda Cynon Taff**, CF38 1PU, WAL.
(T) 01443 204134 (F) 01443 209488
Speciality: Osteopathy.
● Owner Mr J Hunt
P S T (Ref:HM10395)

### HUNT, KEITH G

**Keith G Hunt**, 17 Vandyck Avenue, Keynsham, Bristol, BS31 2UH, ENG.
(T) 01179 867402
Speciality: Osteopathy.
P S T (Ref:HM10396)

### HUNT, M

**M Hunt**, 26 North St, Havant, **Hampshire**, PO9 1PR, ENG.
(T) 023 9248 4184
Speciality: Chiropodists (Podiatrists).
S (Ref:HM10397)

### HUNT, MAGGIE

**Maggie Hunt**, 79 Grange Park Avenue, London, **London (Greater)**, N21 2LN, ENG.
(T) 020 8360 1024
Speciality: Psychotherapy.
B (Ref:HM10398)

### HUNT, MARILYN

**Marilyn Hunt**, Oldham, **Manchester (Greater)**, OL3, ENG.
(T) 01457 820363
Speciality: Bach Remedies.
M (Ref:HM10399)

### HUNT, P

**P Hunt**, 2-4 High St, Glastonbury, **Somerset**, BA6 9DU, ENG.
(T) 01458 833317
Speciality: Acupuncture.
O (Ref:HM10400)

### HUNT, PATRICIA

**Patricia Hunt**, 37 Clockhouse Way, Braintree, **Essex**, CM7 3RD, ENG.
(T) 01376 325387
Speciality: Reflexology.
S T (Ref:HM10401)

### HUNT, PHILLIP R

**Phillip R Hunt**, 80 Burghley Rd, Peterborough, **Cambridgeshire**, PE1 2QE, ENG.
(T) 01733 347724 (F) 01733 347724
Speciality: Osteopathy.
● Owner Mr P Hunt
P S T (Ref:HM10402)

### HUNTE, H (DR)

**Dr H Hunte**, 379-381 Brixton Rd, London, **London (Greater)**, SW9 7DE, ENG.
(T) 020 7274 5820 (F) 020 7733 0005
Speciality: Homeopathy.
● Owner Dr H Hunte
M (Ref:HM10403)

### HUNTER, ALAN

**Alan Hunter**, 140 Marchmont Rd, Edinburgh, **Edinburgh (City of)**, EH9 1AQ, SCO.
(T) 01314 479440
Speciality: Complementary Medicines & Therapy.
● Owner Alan Hunter
C M (Ref:HM10404)

### HUNTER, CHRISTOPHER

**Christopher Hunter**, 75 Thornlaw Rd, London, **London (Greater)**, SE27 0SH, ENG.
(T) 020 8670 8917
Speciality: Chiropodists (Podiatrists).
● Owner Mr C Hunter
S (Ref:HM10405)

### HUNTER, HUGH

**Hugh Hunter**, 2 Paddock View, Thorntoun, Crosshouse, Kilmarnock, **Ayrshire (East)**, KA2 0BH, SCO.
(T) 01563 573920
Speciality: Physiotherapy.
● Owner Mr H Hunter
P S T (Ref:HM10406)

### HUNTER, PHILIPPA

**Philippa Hunter**, Unit F17 The Old Convent, Stroud, **Gloucestershire**, GL5 4AD, ENG.
(T) 01453 756143
Speciality: Aromatherapy.
M O (Ref:HM10407)

### HUNTER, REBECCA

**Rebecca Hunter**, The Westbourne Clinic, 112 Westbourne Rd, Huddersfield, **Yorkshire (West)**, HD1 4LF, ENG.
(T) 01484 542007 (F) 01484 542007
Speciality: Acupressure, Acupuncture, Aromatherapy, Herbal Medicine, Massage (Therapeutic), Nutritional Therapy. ✓
● Acupuncture Practitioner
Ms R Hunter Q: BA, Dip.Ac. M: BAcC.
O Yrs. Est.: 10 (Ref:HM10408)

### HUNTER, W

**W Hunter**, 35 Captain St Upper, Coleraine, **County Londonderry**, BT51 3LY, NIR.
(T) 028 7035 1877
Speciality: Chiropodists (Podiatrists).
● Owner Mrs W Hunter
S (Ref:HM10409)

### HUNTERS LODGE CLINIC

**Hunters Lodge Clinic (The)**, 3 Bond St, Redruth, **Cornwall**, TR15 2QB, ENG.
(T) 01209 214322
Speciality: Osteopathy.
● Owner Mr J Gillow
P S T (Ref:HM10410)

### HUNTINGDON COMPLEMENTARY

**Huntingdon Complementary Health Clinic**, 18 Ermine St, Huntingdon, **Cambridgeshire**, PE18 6EX, ENG.
(T) 01480 455221
Speciality: Osteopathy.
P S T (Ref:HM10411)

### HUNTLY CHIROPRACTIC CLINIC

**Huntly Chiropractic Clinic**, 20 Chapel St, Huntly, **Aberdeenshire**, AB54 8BS, SCO.
(T) 01466 792534
Speciality: Chiropractic. ✓
● Owner Mrs K Robertson Q: DC. M: BCA.
P Yrs. Est.: 20 (Ref:HM10412)

### HUNTS CLINICAL CARE

**Hunts Clinical Care**, Hinchingbrooke Hospital, Huntingdon, **Cambridgeshire**, PE18 8NT, ENG.
(T) 01480 363532
Speciality: Physiotherapy.
P S T (Ref:HM10413)

### HUNTSMAN, NATALIE

**Natalie Huntsman**, 44 Market Hill, Witham, **Essex**, CM8 2DE, ENG.
(T) 01376 514181
Speciality: Reflexology.
● Owner Miss N Huntsman
S T (Ref:HM10414)

### HUNWICK, JOSEPH

**Joseph Hunwick**, 10 High St, Glastonbury, **Somerset**, BA6 9DU, ENG.
(T) 01458 834236
Speciality: Herbalists.
● Director Ms J Sanders
M (Ref:HM10415)

### HURD, J V

**J V Hurd**, Flat 18, St. Johns Chambers, 2 Ashwell St, Leicester, **Leicestershire**, LE1 6JJ, ENG.
(T) 01162 545451
Speciality: Psychotherapy.
● Owner Ms J Hurd
B (Ref:HM10416)

### HURD, JOAN

**Joan Hurd**, Cwm Hardd, Nantyr, Llangollen, **Denbighshire**, LL20 7DD, WAL.
(T) 01691 718450
Speciality: Psychotherapy.
B (Ref:HM10417)

### HURFORD, A J

**A J Hurford**, 4 Clifton Hill, Bristol, BS8 1BN, ENG.
(T) 01179 736272
Speciality: Chiropodists (Podiatrists).
● Owner Mrs A Hurford
S (Ref:HM10418)

### HURLEY KATE LIC ACUP

**Hurley Kate Lic Acup**, Naas, Kildare, **County Kildare**, IRE.
(T) 04587 4640
Speciality: Acupuncture.
O (Ref:HM10419)

### HURLEY, DOT

**Dot Hurley**, 5 Corder Rd, Ipswich, **Suffolk**, IP4 2XD, ENG.
(T) 01473 251745
Speciality: Reflexology.
● Owner Mrs D Hurley
S T (Ref:HM10420)


Key continued: Yrs.Est: Years Established Q: Qualifications M: Professional Membership ✓ Indemnity Insurance Accept Credit Cards

## HURLEY, M
**M Hurley**, 30 Cedar Rd, Watford, **Hertfordshire**, WD1 4QW, ENG.
(T) 01923 240793
Speciality: Acupuncture.
● **Partner** Mrs M Hurley
O (Ref:HM10421)

## HURLFORD CHIROPODY CLINIC
**Hurlford Chiropody Clinic**, Union St, Hurlford, Kilmarnock, **Ayrshire (East)**, KA1 5BT, SCO.
(T) 01563 574897
Speciality: Chiropody.
S (Ref:HM10422)

## HURLSTON, DIANE
**Diane Hurlston**, 46 Oakham Cl, Redditch, **Worcestershire**, B98 7YG, ENG.
(T) 01527 401649
Speciality: Chiropodists (Podiatrists).
S (Ref:HM10423)

## HURRY, GEOFF
**Geoff Hurry**, The Linkmews Practice, 10A Charter Rd, Chippenham, **Wiltshire**, SN15 2RA, ENG.
(T) 01249 445880
Speciality: Hypnosis.
B (Ref:HM10424)

## HURSELL, BARRY
**Barry Hursell**, 35 City Rd, Norwich, **Norfolk**, NR1 3AP, ENG.
(T) 01603 623723
Speciality: Hypnosis.
B (Ref:HM10425)

## HURST, D M
**D M Hurst**, 32 Barnby Gate, Newark, **Nottinghamshire**, NG24 1PZ, ENG.
(T) 01636 704633
Speciality: Chiropodists (Podiatrists).
● **Owner** Mr D Hurst
S (Ref:HM10426)

## HURST, EDWARD ASSOCIATES
**Edward Hurst Associates**, 6 Crooms Hill, London, **London (Greater)**, SE10 8ER, ENG.
(T) 020 8858 4000
Speciality: Psychology.
B (Ref:HM10427)

## HURST, JEAN ANN
**Jean Ann Hurst**, 12 High St, Tattershall, Lincoln, **Lincolnshire**, LN4 4LE, ENG.
(T) 01526 342212
Speciality: Chiropractic.
P S T (Ref:HM10428)

## HURST, S
**Miss S Hurst**, 20 The Green, Twickenham, **London (Greater)**, TW2 5AB, ENG.
(T) 020 8893 3084
Speciality: Osteopathy.
P S T (Ref:HM10429)

## HUSBAND, B
**B Husband**, 26 Wake Green Rd, Birmingham, **Midlands (West)**, B13 9PA, ENG.
(T) 01214 499515
Speciality: Chiropractors.
P S T (Ref:HM10430)

## HUSBANDS, S
**S Husbands**, 38 Russell Trce, Leamington Spa, **Warwickshire**, CV31 1HE, ENG.
(T) 01926 337337
Speciality: Homeopathy.
M (Ref:HM10431)

## HUSBANDS, STEVE
**Steve Husbands**, 13 Frederick Rd, Stechford, Birmingham, **Midlands (West)**, B33 8AD, ENG.
(T) 01216 085848
Speciality: Holistic Healing, Homeopathy. ✔
● **Owner** Mr S Husbands Q: DSH.
C Yrs. Est.: 12 (Ref:HM10432)

## HUSEIN, JIWA (DR)
**Dr Jiwa Husein**, 102-104 Eastfield Rd, Peterborough, **Cambridgeshire**, PE1 4AX, ENG.
(T) 01733 554885
Speciality: Osteopathy.
P S T (Ref:HM10433)

## HUSKISSON, EILEEN
**Eileen Huskisson**, Station House, Station Rd, Sutton Weaver, Runcorn, **Cheshire**, WA7 3EP, ENG.
(T) 01928 714468
Speciality: Biomechanics, Chiropody. ✔
● **Owner/Chiropodist**
Mrs E Huskisson Q: Inst.CH.P. M: Inst.CH.P.
M Yrs. Est.: 7 (Ref:HM10434)

## HUSSAIN, M F
**M F Hussain**, 6 Cadnam Cl, Canterbury, **Kent**, CT2 7SD, ENG.
(T) 01227 762267 (F) 01227 455799
Speciality: Psychiatry.
● **Owner** Dr M Hussain
B (Ref:HM10435)

## HUSSAIN, S (DR)
**Dr S Hussain**, 6 Chad Rd, Birmingham, **Midlands (West)**, B15 3EN, ENG.
(T) 01214 561726
Speciality: Complementary Medicines & Therapy.
C M (Ref:HM10436)

## HUSSAIN-FARNSWORTH, R
**R Hussain-Farnsworth**, Bushmaster Natural Health Practice, 204 Uxbridge Rd, London, **London (Greater)**, W12 7JD, ENG.
(T) 020 8896 0697 (F) 020 8992 9621
Speciality: Homeopathy.
● **Owner** Ms R Hussain-Farnsworth
M (Ref:HM10437)

## HUSSEIN, ALLIDINA
**Hussein Allidina**, Fairway Avenue, Borehamwood, **Hertfordshire**, WD6 1PU, ENG.
(T) 020 8537 1486
Speciality: Chiropodists (Podiatrists).
● **Owner** Mr H Allidina
S (Ref:HM10438)

## HUSSEIN, I A
**I A Hussein**, 20 Upper Wimpole St, London, **London (Greater)**, W1M 7TA, ENG.
(T) 020 7486 1920
Speciality: Osteopathy.
● **Owner** Mrs I Hussein
P S T (Ref:HM10439)

## HUSSEY, DOMINICK
**Dominick Hussey**, 1 Harley St, London, **London (Greater)**, W1N 1DA, ENG.
(T) 020 7436 1446
Speciality: Osteopathy.
P S T (Ref:HM10440)

## HUSSEY, DOMINICK
**Dominick Hussey**, 112 Staveley Gardens, London, **London (Greater)**, W4 2SF, ENG.
(T) 020 8400 9619
Speciality: Osteopathy.
P S T (Ref:HM10441)

## HUSSEY, DOMINICK
**Dominick Hussey**, Aston Clinic, 26 Kingston Rd, New Malden, **Surrey**, KT3 3LS, ENG.
(T) 020 8942 3148 (F) 020 8949 7050
Speciality: Osteopathy.
P S T (Ref:HM10442)

## HUSTINGS, LESLEY
**Lesley Hustings**, Scott St Complementary Therapy Centre, 58 Scott St, Barrow-in-Furness, **Cumbria**, LA14 1QE, ENG.
(T) 01229 826700
Speciality: Complementary Medicines & Therapy.
M (Ref:HM10443)

## HUTCHENS, P W
**P W Hutchens**, 19 Claverley Gr, London, **London (Greater)**, N3 2DG, ENG.
(T) 020 8346 5903
Speciality: Chiropodists (Podiatrists).
● **Owner** Mr P Hutchens
S (Ref:HM10444)

## HUTCHESON, SALLY ANN
**Sally Ann Hutcheson**, 133 Wood St, Barnet, **Hertfordshire**, EN5 4BX, ENG.
(T) 020 8441 0231
Speciality: Homeopathy.
● **Owner** Mr M Cole
M (Ref:HM10445)

## HUTCHIN, MARK
**Mark Hutchin**, Oakwood, Bethersden, Ashford, **Kent**, TN26 3ED, ENG.
(T) 01233 820385
Speciality: Osteopathy.
● **Owner** Mr M Hutchin
P S T (Ref:HM10446)

## HUTCHINGS, D
**D Hutchings**, The Corner House, 6 Starmers Lane, Kislingbury, Northampton, **Northamptonshire**, NN7 4AE, ENG.
(T) 01604 831522
Speciality: Chiropodists (Podiatrists).
● **Owner** Mr D Hutchings
S (Ref:HM10447)

## HUTCHINGS, MARGARET
**Margaret Hutchings**, Southsea, Portsmouth, **Hampshire**, PO4 9DP, ENG.
(T) 023 9273 5585
Speciality: Aromatherapy, Massage (Therapeutic), Reflexology. ✔
● **Massage Therapist/Reflexologist**
Ms M Hutchings Q: Cert.Massage, IHBC, S.E.N, SSReflex. M: FHT.
T Yrs. Est.: 10 (Ref:HM10448)

## HUTCHINGS, MICHAEL
**Michael Hutchings**, Camberley Health Centre Frimley Rd, Camberley, **Surrey**, GU15 2PZ, ENG.
(T) 01276 64401
Speciality: Acupuncture.
O (Ref:HM10449)

## HUTCHINS, J R
**J R Hutchins**, 15 Bridge Rd, Park Gate, Southampton, **Hampshire**, SO31 7GD, ENG.
(T) 01489 584700
Speciality: Chiropodists (Podiatrists).
● **Owner** Mr J Hutchins
S (Ref:HM10450)

## HUTCHINSON, JANE
**Jane Hutchinson**, 2b Rochester Avenue, Luton, **Bedfordshire**, LU2 8EB, ENG.
(T) 01582 453390
Speciality: Reflexology.
S T (Ref:HM10451)

## HUTCHINSON, N
**N Hutchinson**, Pot House, The Avenue, Tisbury, Salisbury, **Wiltshire**, SP3 6JG, ENG.
(T) 01747 871264
Speciality: Aromatherapy.
● **Owner** Ms N Hutchinson
M O (Ref:HM10452)

## HUTCHISON, K C
**K C Hutchison**, 38 Greenside Lane, Lanark, **Lanarkshire (South)**, ML11 7PY, SCO.
(T) 01555 663203
Speciality: Chiropodists (Podiatrists).
S (Ref:HM10453)

## HUTHERT, J
**Mrs J Huthert**, 34 Pasture Rd, Letchworth, **Hertfordshire**, SG6 3LS, ENG.
(T) 01462 678142 (F) 01462 686560
Speciality: Hypnotherapy.
● **Owner** Mrs J Huthert
B (Ref:HM10454)

## HUTHERT, J
**J Huthert**, 8 Woolston Avenue, Letchworth, **Hertfordshire**, SG6 2ED, ENG.
(T) 01462 678142
Speciality: Hypnosis.
B (Ref:HM10455)

## HUTSON, ANNE
**Anne Hutson**, Bryants Arcade, Market Pl, Buxton, **Derbyshire**, SK17 6EB, ENG.
(T) 01298 72566
Speciality: Chiropodists (Podiatrists).
S (Ref:HM10456)

## HUTSON, JOHN
**John Hutson**, 5 The Twitchell, Baldock, **Hertfordshire**, SG7 6DN, ENG.
(T) 01462 894193
Speciality: Chiropodists (Podiatrists).

Key: B Mind-Body Medicine; C Complementary Medicine; H Self Help Treatment; M Medicinal Therapy; O Oriental Medicine; P Postural Therapy; S Manipulative Structural Therapy; T Touch Therapy

● **Owner** Mr J Hutson
S (**Ref:**HM10457)

### HUTTON, W

**W Hutton**, Two Hedges, Greenacres, Hemel Hempstead, **Hertfordshire**, HP2 4NA, ENG.
(T) 01442 214747 (F) 01442 214747
Speciality: Alexander Technique.
● **Owner** Mrs W Hutton
P S (**Ref:**HM10458)

### HUTTON, WILLIAM

**William Hutton**, 70 Burrelton Rd, Glasgow, **Glasgow (City of)**, G43 2LR, SCO.
(T) 01416 376273
Speciality: Chiropodists (Podiatrists).
● **Owner** Mr W Hutton
S (**Ref:**HM10459)

### HUXLEY, CAROL

**Carol Huxley**, 5 Elm Ter, Constantine Rd, London, **London (Greater)**, NW3 2LL, ENG.
(T) 020 7267 4222
Speciality: Aromatherapy.
● **Owner** Ms C Huxley
M O (**Ref:**HM10460)

### HUXTABLE, ALISON

**Alison Huxtable**, High Grove Clinic, 26 Grove Rd, Milton, Weston-Super-Mare, **Somerset**, BS22 8HE, ENG.
(T) 01934 419933
Speciality: Osteopathy. ✓
● **Osteopath** Miss B Mailang Q: BSc, Hons (OST). M: GOsC.
● **Osteopath** Mrs K Morrison Q: DO, ND. M: GOsC.
● **Owner** Miss A Huxtable Q: DO, ND, RN. M: GOsC.
S Yrs. Est.: 3 (**Ref:**HM10461)

### HUXTER, CHRISTINE

**Christine Huxter**, 5 Barrack Lane, Great Waltham, Chelmsford, **Essex**, CM3 1ES, ENG.
(T) 01245 361165
Speciality: Complementary Medicines & Therapy.
C M (**Ref:**HM10462)

### HUYTON, CHRISTOPHER

**Christopher Huyton**, 1 Moor Drive, Moor Rd, Leeds, **Yorkshire (West)**, LS6 4BY, ENG.
(T) 01132 786606
Speciality: Osteopathy.
P S T (**Ref:**HM10463)

### HUYTON, CHRISTOPHER P

**Christopher P Huyton**, 12A St Saviours Pl, York, **Yorkshire (North)**, YO1 7PJ, ENG.
(T) 01904 659588
Speciality: Osteopathy.
P S T (**Ref:**HM10464)

### HY (DR)

**Dr Hy**, 48 Edgware Rd, London, **London (Greater)**, W2 2EH, ENG.
(T) 020 7258 1538 (F) 020 7258 0083
Speciality: Complementary Medicines & Therapy.
● **Owner** Dr H Hy
C M (**Ref:**HM10465)

### HYANDS, TONI

**Toni Hyands**, Natural Health Clinic, 98 Cathedral Rd, Cardiff, **Glamorgan (Vale of)**, CF11 9LP, WAL.
(T) 029 2022 2221
Speciality: Hypnotherapy.
● **Practice Manager** Mrs L Powell
B (**Ref:**HM10466)

### HYATT, EDWARD B

**Edward B Hyatt**, 156 White Hill, Chesham, **Buckinghamshire**, HP5 1AT, ENG.
(T) 01494 784497
Speciality: Physiotherapy.
● **Owner** Mr E Hyatt
P S T (**Ref:**HM10467)

### HYDE ACUPUNCTURE & HERBALIST

**Hyde Acupuncture & Herbalist**, 14A Fore St, Yealmpton, Plymouth, **Devon**, PL8 2JN, ENG.
(T) 01752 881348
Speciality: Acupuncture.
O (**Ref:**HM10468)

### HYDE BARKER & ASSOCIATES

**P J Hyde Barker and Associates**, 217 Stoke Newington High St, London, **London (Greater)**, N16 0LH, ENG.
(T) 020 7275 0382
Speciality: Biomechanics, Chiropody, Podiatry. ✓
● **Chiropodist (Podiatrist)**
Mr P Hyde-Barker Q: BSc (Hons), DPodM.
P Yrs. Est.: 26 (**Ref:**HM10469)

### HYDE PHYSIOTHERAPY CENTRE

**Hyde Physiotherapy Centre**, Parsonage St, Hyde, **Cheshire**, SK14 1DP, ENG.
(T) 01613 683391 (F) 01613 669304
Speciality: Physiotherapy.
● **Manager** Mr S Adams
P S T (**Ref:**HM10470)

### HYDE, PHILIP

**Philip Hyde**, 43 Celandine Rise, Swinton, Mexborough, **Yorkshire (South)**, S64 8NZ, ENG.
(T) 01709 583715
Speciality: Osteopathy.
● **Owner** Mr P Hyde
P S T (**Ref:**HM10471)

### HYDEPARK SAUNA

**Hydepark Sauna**, 150 Hydepark St, Glasgow, **Glasgow (City of)**, G3 8BW, SCO.
(T) 01412 215991
Speciality: Aromatherapy.
● **Owner** Mrs K Fairnie
M O (**Ref:**HM10472)

### HYDES HERBAL CLINIC

**Hydes Herbal Clinic**, 68 London Rd, Leicester, **Leicestershire**, LE2 0QD, ENG.
(T) 01162 543178 (F) 01162 045930
Speciality: Herbal Medicine.
● **Owner** Mr J Hyde
M (**Ref:**HM10473)

### HYETT, SUE

**Sue Hyett**, Edwards House, 20 Shrub End Rd, Colchester, **Essex**, CO2 7XD, ENG.
(T) 01206 546319
Speciality: Homeopathy.
M (**Ref:**HM10474)

### HYGEIA CENTRE

**Hygeia Centre For Holistic Health & Wellbeing**, 7-9 Springfield Rd, Altrincham, **Cheshire**, WA14 1HE, ENG.
(T) 01619 415027
Speciality: Complementary Medicines & Therapy.
C M (**Ref:**HM10475)

### HYGEIA COLLEGE-COLOUR THERAPY

**Hygeia College Of Colour Therapy**, Brook House, Hampton Hill, Avening, Tetbury, **Gloucestershire**, GL8 8NS, ENG.
(T) 01453 832150 (F) 01453 835757
Speciality: Colour Therapy, Teaching and Treating Colour Therapy. ✓
● **Principal** Mr T Gimbel M: BRCP.
C Yrs. Est.: 44 (**Ref:**HM10476)

### HYLAND, RHONA

**Hyland Rhona**, 38 St Marys Rd, **County Galway**, IRE.
(T) 09152 2911
Speciality: Hypnotherapy.
B (**Ref:**HM10477)

### HYLTON, PENELOPE J

**Penelope J Hylton**, 36 Wilson Avenue, Henley-on-Thames, **Oxfordshire**, RG9 1ET, ENG.
(T) 01491 412322
Speciality: Complementary Medicines & Therapy.
C M (**Ref:**HM10478)

### HYMALAYAN INSTITUTE

**Hymalayan Institute For Yoga & Meditation**, 70 Claremont Rd, London, **London (Greater)**, W13 0DG, ENG.
(T) 020 8991 8090
Speciality: Relaxation Technique.
H T (**Ref:**HM10479)

### HYMAN, JOHN

**John Hyman**, 17 The Park, Newark, **Nottinghamshire**, NG24 1SD, ENG.
(T) 01636 702201
Speciality: Chiropodists (Podiatrists).
● **Owner** Mr J Hyman
S (**Ref:**HM10480)

### HYNDBURN PRIVATE CLINIC-OSTEO

**Hyndburn Private Clinic Of Osteopathy**, 5 Avenue Prde, Accrington, **Lancashire**, BB5 6PN, ENG.
(T) 01254 399915
Speciality: Osteopathy.
● **Director** Mr M Dixon
P S T (**Ref:**HM10481)

### HYNDLAND CLINIC

**Hyndland Clinic (The)**, 170 Hyndland Rd, Glasgow, **Glasgow (City of)**, G12 9HZ, SCO.
(T) 01413 391329
Speciality: Physiotherapy.
● **Owner** Mr G Allison
P S T (**Ref:**HM10482)

### HYNE, JOANNA E M

**Joanna E M Hyne**, 30 York St, Bedford, **Bedfordshire**, MK40 3RJ, ENG.
(T) 01234 211844 (F) 01234 348039
Speciality: Osteopathy.
● **Owner** Miss J Hyne
P S T (**Ref:**HM10483)

### HYNES, NANCY

**Nancy Hynes**, Derry City, Londonderry, **County Londonderry**, BT48, NIR.
(T) 028 7126 6047
Speciality: Bach Remedies.
M (**Ref:**HM10484)

### HYNOTHERAPY BY A J FOOTE

**Hynotherapy By A J Foote**, Waterloo Homeopathic Clinic, 67 St Johns Rd, Liverpool, **Merseyside**, L2 9QB, ENG.
(T) 01514 746020
Speciality: Hypnosis.
B (**Ref:**HM10485)

### HYNOTHERAPY SURGERY

**Hynotherapy Surgery**, 123 Hadham Rd, Bishop's Stortford, **Hertfordshire**, CM23 2QG, ENG.
(T) 01279 506476
Speciality: Hypnosis.
B (**Ref:**HM10486)

### HYP HEALING & REFLEX CTRE

**Hypnotherapy Healing & Reflexology Centre**, 5 Alexandra Trce, Truro, **Cornwall**, TR1 3HN, ENG.
(T) 01872 264205
Speciality: Hypnotherapy.
B (**Ref:**HM10489)

### HYPNO & PSYCHOTHERAPY PRACTICE

**Hypnotherapy & Psychotherapy Practice**, 11A Rostrevor Rd, London, **London (Greater)**, SW6 5AX, ENG.
(T) 020 7736 0567
Speciality: Psychotherapy.
B (**Ref:**HM10487)

### HYPNO CARE HEALTH CENTRE

**Hypno Care Health Centre**, 3 Market Sq, Northampton, **Northamptonshire**, NN1 2DL, ENG.
(T) 01604 601115
Speciality: Hypnotherapy.
B (**Ref:**HM10488)

### HYPNOCARE

**Hypnocare**, 32 Ferguson Avenue, Wirral, **Merseyside**, CH49 1RP, ENG.
(T) 01516 060259
Speciality: Neuro-Linguistic Program, Psychotherapy. ✓
● **Clinical Hypnotherapist**
Mr G Patrick Q: NLP.
B Yrs. Est.: 2 (**Ref:**HM10490)

### HYPNOCURE

**Hypnocure**, 128 Turners Hill, Cheshunt, Waltham Cross, **Hertfordshire**, EN8 9BN, ENG.
(T) 01992 460602



Key continued: Yrs.Est: Years Established Q: Qualifications M: Professional Membership ✓ Indemnity Insurance Accept Credit Cards

Speciality: Hypnosis.
B (Ref:HM10491)

## HYPNOS PRACTICE

**Hypnos Practice (The)**, 9 Simonside, Widnes, **Cheshire**, WA8 4YL, ENG.
(T) 01515 104285 (F) 01515 104285
(E) alanmccool@hypnospractice.demon.co.uk
Speciality: Auto Suggestion, Hypnosis, Hypnotherapy, Life Style Coaching, Stress Therapy, Visualisation Therapy. ✓
● **Consultant Hypnotherapist**
Mr A McCool Q: B.A.Th.H, Dip.Hyp, WFH.
M: B.A.Th.H, HF, HS, WFH.
B Yrs. Est.: 4 (Ref:HM10492)

## HYPNOSIS & PARAPSYCHOLOGY

**Hypnosis & Parapsychology**, 561 Trentham Rd, Stoke-On-Trent, **Staffordshire**, ST3 3BN, ENG.
(T) 01782 331807
Speciality: Hypnosis.
● **Owner** Mrs S Harding
B (Ref:HM10493)

## HYPNOSIS & STRESS COUNSELLING

**Clinical Hypnosis & Stress Counselling**, 14 Whitley Way, New Milton, **Hampshire**, BH25 5ET, ENG.
(T) 01425 627795
Speciality: Hypnosis, Hypnotherapy, Stress Therapy. ✓
● **Owner** Mrs A Newton Q: BSc, DHP (NC), DipCH.P, RGN.
B Yrs. Est.: 2 (Ref:HM10494)

## HYPNOSIS AND HEALTH

**Josephine P Teague**, 24 Milton Rd, Impington, Cambridge, **Cambridgeshire**, CB4 9NF, ENG.
(T) 01223 235127 (F) 01223 520162
(E) j.teague@ntlworld.com
Speciality: Biofeedback, Cognitive Therapy, Complementary Therapy, Counselling, Humanistic Psychology, Hypnosis, Hypnotherapy, Psychotherapy, Stress Therapy. ✓
● **Hypno-Analyst/Psychotherapist**
Mrs J Teague Q: BSc (Hons), Dip.Hyp, Dip.Psych, MSc. M: BPS, HRS, HS, NCH.
B H Yrs. Est.: 9 (Ref:HM10495)

## HYPNOSIS CENTRE

**Hypnosis Centre (The)**, Dolwion, Drefach Felindre, Velindre, Llandysul, **Carmarthenshire**, SA44 5UY, WAL.
(T) 01559 371495
Speciality: Hypnosis.
● **Partner** Mr A Wilson
B (Ref:HM10496)

## HYPNOSIS COUNSELLING CENTRE

**Hypnosis Counselling Centre**, 69 Wheatfield Way, Cranbrook, **Kent**, TN17 3NB, ENG.
(T) 01580 712141
Speciality: Hypnosis.
B (Ref:HM10497)

## HYPNOSIS HEALTH CLINIC

**Hypnosis Health Clinic**, Market House, Liverpool Rd, Luton, **Bedfordshire**, LU1 1HH, ENG.
(T) 01582 651199
Speciality: Hypnosis.
● **Director** Mr K MacRayne
B (Ref:HM10498)

## HYPNOSIS LEARNING CENTRE

**Hypnosis Learning Centre**, 7 Rockspring Gdns Belfield, Limerick, **County Limerick**, IRE.
(T) 08681 90351
Speciality: Hypnotherapy.
B (Ref:HM10499)

## HYPNOSIS WORKS

**Hypnosis Works**, 11A Cecil Rd, Weston-Super-Mare, **Somerset**, BS23 2NG, ENG.
(T) 01934 418007
Speciality: Hypnosis.
B (Ref:HM10500)

## HYPNOTHERAPIST

**Hypnotherapist**, 6 Kiln St, Aberdare, **Glamorgan (Vale of)**, CF44 6YW, WAL.
(T) 01685 883799
Speciality: Hypnosis.
● **Owner** Mr P Harper
B (Ref:HM10501)

## HYPNOTHERAPIST

**Hypnotherapist**, Martindale Rd, Hounslow, **London (Greater)**, TW4 7HG, ENG.
(T) 020 8577 6236
Speciality: Hypnotherapy.
● **Owner** Ms A Whitaker
B (Ref:HM10502)

## HYPNOTHERAPIST CENTRE-FYLDE

**Hypnotherapist Centre-Fylde**, 19 Queen St, Blackpool, **Lancashire**, FY1 1NL, ENG.
(T) 01253 751617
Speciality: Hypnosis.
● **Owner** Mr P Farnbank
B (Ref:HM10503)

## HYPNOTHERAPY

**Hypnotherapy**, Palmers Green, Enfield, **London (Greater)**, EN1 3TT, ENG.
(T) 020 8363 4808
Speciality: Hypnotherapy.
B (Ref:HM10504)

## HYPNOTHERAPY & ANALYSIS CENTRE

**Hypnotherapy & Analysis Centre**, Splinters, 5a Marvin Cl, Botley, Southampton, **Hampshire**, SO30 2EW, ENG.
(T) 01489 781076 (F) 01489 788472
Speciality: Hypnosis.
● **Owner** Mr P Cumner
B (Ref:HM10505)

## HYPNOTHERAPY & COUNSELLING

**Clinical Hypnotherapy & Counselling**, 47 Beechfield Rd, Swinton, Manchester, **Manchester (Greater)**, M27 5RA, ENG.
(T) 01617 947944
Speciality: Hypnotherapy.
● **Owner** Mr A Bergville
B (Ref:HM10506)

## HYPNOTHERAPY & COUNSELLING

**Hypnotherapy & Counselling**, 11 Chapelmere Cl, Sandbach, **Cheshire**, CW11 1TB, ENG.
(T) 01270 765359
Speciality: Hypnosis.
● **Owner** Mrs M Ward
B (Ref:HM10507)

## HYPNOTHERAPY & PSYCHO CONS

**Hypnotherapy & Psychotherapy Consultant**, 1 Apple Court, Waterhouse Lane, Chelmsford, **Essex**, CM1 2UD, ENG.
(T) 01245 269114
Speciality: Hypnosis, Hypnotherapy, Psychotherapy. ✓
● **Hypnotherapist/Psychotherapist**
Mr E Briggs Q: Dip.Hyp, Dip.Psych.
B Yrs. Est.: 20 (Ref:HM10508)

## HYPNOTHERAPY & PSYCHO PRACTICE

**Hypnotherapy & Psychotherapy Practice 1984**, 37 Orbain Rd, London, **London (Greater)**, SW6 7JZ, ENG.
(T) 020 7385 1166
Speciality: Hypnosis.
B (Ref:HM10509)

## HYPNOTHERAPY & RELAXATION CLNC

**Hypnotherapy & Relaxation Clinic**, 13 Fernlea, Risca, Newport, NP11 6FW, WAL.
(T) 01633 615050
Speciality: Hypnosis.
B (Ref:HM10510)

## HYPNOTHERAPY & TRAINING CENTRE

**Hypnotherapy & Training Centre**, Natural Therapy Centre, 7 Burges Rd, London, **London (Greater)**, E6 2BJ, ENG.
(T) 020 8472 7355
Speciality: Hypnotherapy.
● **Owner** Dr S Rehman
B (Ref:HM10511)

## HYPNOTHERAPY ADVICE CENTRE

**Hypnotherapy Advice Centre**, Second Floor, 117 Harley St, London, **London (Greater)**, W1N 1DH, ENG.
(T) 020 7224 7778
Speciality: Hypnotherapy.
● **Owner** Mr M Watson
B (Ref:HM10512)

## HYPNOTHERAPY ADVICE LINE

**Hypnotherapy Advice Line**, 16 Welbeck St, London, **London (Greater)**, W1M 7PF, ENG.
(T) 020 7224 7778
Speciality: Hypnosis.
B (Ref:HM10513)

## HYPNOTHERAPY AND COUNSELLING

**Hypnotherapy and Counselling**, Glendynn, Broomhill, Hetton-Le-Hole, Houghton le Spring, **Tyne and Wear**, DH5 9PT, ENG.
(T) 01915 260248
Speciality: Cognitive Therapy, Counselling, Hypnotherapy, Psychotherapy, Stress Therapy, Behavioural Therapy. ✓ CREDIT
● **Psychologist** Ms A Storey Q: BA (Hons) Psychol, MA, MSc. M: BPS.
H Yrs. Est.: 12 (Ref:HM10514)

## HYPNOTHERAPY CENTRE

**Hypnotherapy Centre (The)**, 68 Cusworth Lane, Doncaster, **Yorkshire (South)**, DN5 8JL, ENG.
(T) 01302 786977
(E) faith@hypnoticworld.co.uk
Speciality: Auto Suggestion, Autogenic Training, Complementary Therapy, Counselling, Hypnosis, Hypnotherapy, Psychotherapy, Past Life Therapy. ✓
● **Hypnotherapist** Ms F Waude Q: Dip.Hyp. M: HA.
B Yrs. Est.: 7 (Ref:HM10515)

## HYPNOTHERAPY CENTRE

**Hypnotherapy Centre**, 11 Kedleston Rise, Banbury, **Oxfordshire**, OX16 9TX, ENG.
(T) 01295 257353
Speciality: Absent Healing, Healer, Hypnosis, Hypnotherapy, Spiritual Healing. ✓
● **Spiritual Healer** Ms S Fry M: NFSH.
● **Owner/Hypnotherapist/Spiritual Healer**
Mr D Campbell M: NFSH.
H Yrs. Est.: 25 (Ref:HM10516)

## HYPNOTHERAPY CENTRE

**Hypnotherapy Centre**, 55 Liverpool Rd, Kidsgrove, Stoke-On-Trent, **Staffordshire**, ST7 1EA, ENG.
(T) 01782 784003
Speciality: Hypnotherapy.
● **Owner** Mr H Ravenscroft
B (Ref:HM10517)

## HYPNOTHERAPY CENTRE

**Hypnotherapy Centre**, The Science Village, Harrogate, **Yorkshire (North)**, HG1 4AG, ENG.
(T) 01423 500358
Speciality: Hypnosis.
B (Ref:HM10518)

## HYPNOTHERAPY CENTRE

**Hypnotherapy Centre**, Southern House, Hallfield Rd, Bradford, **Yorkshire (West)**, BD1 3RQ, ENG.
(T) 01274 307537
Speciality: Hypnosis.
B (Ref:HM10519)

## HYPNOTHERAPY CENTRE

**Hypnotherapy Centre**, Room 203 Miller House, Lancaster Rd, Preston, **Lancashire**, PR1 2RY, ENG.
(T) 01772 203565
Speciality: Hypnosis.
B (Ref:HM10520)

## HYPNOTHERAPY CENTRE

**Hypnotherapy Centre**, Flat 5 Dalboyne House, Belsize Rd, Lisburn, **County Antrim**, BT27 4AL, NIR.
(T) 028 9260 5462
(E) hypnotherapy.c.l@btclick.com
Speciality: Hypnosis, Hypnotherapy, Physiotherapy. ✓
● **Hypnotherapist** Mr A McCready Q: Dip.Hyp.
C Yrs. Est.: 5 (Ref:HM10521)

## HYPNOTHERAPY CENTRE

**Hypnotherapy Centre**, 8 Lidgett Lane, Garforth, Leeds, **Yorkshire (West)**, LS25 1EQ, ENG.
(T) 01132 868999 (F) 01132 877770
Speciality: Hypnosis.

● **Owner** Mr D McGinnity
B (**Ref:**HM10522)

### HYPNOTHERAPY CENTRE

**Hypnotherapy Centre**, 79 Hospital St, Nantwich, **Cheshire**, CW5 5RL, ENG.
(T) 01270 613009
Speciality: Hypnosis.
B (**Ref:**HM10523)

### HYPNOTHERAPY CENTRE

**Hypnotherapy Centre**, 3 Worsley Rd, Swinton, Manchester, **Manchester (Greater)**, M27 5WN, ENG.
(T) 01617 278551
Speciality: Hypnosis.
● **Owner** Mr A Sawyer
B (**Ref:**HM10524)

### HYPNOTHERAPY CENTRE

**Hypnotherapy Centre**, 16 Church Rd, Distington, Workington, **Cumbria**, CA14 5TE, ENG.
(T) 01946 830881
Speciality: Hypnosis, Hypnotherapy. ✔
● **Hypnotherapist** Mr J Lutton Q: Dip.Hyp. M: CAH.
B Yrs. Est.: 13 (**Ref:**HM10525)

### HYPNOTHERAPY CENTRE

**Hypnotherapy Centre**, 158 Lockerbie Rd, Dumfries, **Dumfries and Galloway**, DG1 3BW, SCO.
(T) 01387 251311
Speciality: Hypnosis.
B (**Ref:**HM10526)

### HYPNOTHERAPY CENTRE

**Hypnotherapy Centre**, 1 Wythburn Pl, London, **London (Greater)**, W1H 5WL, ENG.
(T) 020 7262 8852
Speciality: Hypnosis.
B (**Ref:**HM10527)

### HYPNOTHERAPY CENTRE

**Hypnotherapy Centre**, 104 High St, Mold, **Flintshire**, CH7 1BH, WAL.
(T) 01352 759962
Speciality: Hypnosis, Hypnotherapy, Psychotherapy.
● **Hypnotherapist** Mr K Clark Q: Dip.Hyp, Dip.Psych, MIAH, MNCH. M: IAH, NCH.
B Yrs. Est.: 10 (**Ref:**HM10528)

### HYPNOTHERAPY CENTRE

**Hypnotherapy Centre**, The Sanctuary, Kingsland Rd, Salisbury, **Wiltshire**, SP2 7DN, ENG.
(T) 01722 412486
Speciality: Absent Healing, Auto Suggestion, Cognitive Therapy, Counselling, Holistic Healing, Hypnosis, Hypnotherapy, Psychotherapy, Stress Therapy, Visualisation Therapy, Regression Therapy(Past Life).
H (**Ref:**HM10529)

### HYPNOTHERAPY CENTRE

**Hypnotherapy Centre (The)**, The Essex Golf & Country Club, Earls Colne, Colchester, **Essex**, CO6 2NS, ENG.
(T) 01787 220330
(E) beryl@owlsretreat.fsbusiness.co.uk
Speciality: Cognitive Therapy, Counselling, Hypnosis, Hypnotherapy, Psychotherapy. ✔
● **Owner/Hypno-Analyst** Mrs B Head Q: Dip.Hyp, MIAH.
B Yrs. Est.: 8 (**Ref:**HM10530)

### HYPNOTHERAPY CENTRE

**Hypnotherapy Centre**, 62 Catherine St, **County Limerick**, IRE.
(T) 06141 3500
Speciality: Hypnotherapy.
B (**Ref:**HM10531)

### HYPNOTHERAPY CENTRE

**Hypnotherapy Centre (The)**, Owls Retreat, 46 Firstore Drive, Lexden, Colchester, **Essex**, CO3 5EA, ENG.
(T) 01206 542577
(E) beryl@owlsretreat.fsbusiness.co.uk
Speciality: Cognitive Therapy, Counselling, Hypnosis, Hypnotherapy, Psychotherapy. ✔
● **Hypno-Analyst** Ms B Head Q: Dip.Hyp, MIAH. M: HA.
B Yrs. Est.: 8 (**Ref:**HM10532)

### HYPNOTHERAPY CENTRE BURNLEY

**Hypnotherapy Centre Burnley (The)**, 31 Hammerton St, Burnley, **Lancashire**, BB11 1LT, ENG.
(T) 01282 456796
Speciality: Hypnosis.
● **Owner** Mr L Carlin
B (**Ref:**HM10533)

### HYPNOTHERAPY CLINIC

**Hypnotherapy Clinic**, 6 Briarwood Drive, Cardiff, **Glamorgan (Vale of)**, CF23 6SR, WAL.
(T) 029 2075 8965
Speciality: Hypnosis.
● **Owner** Mrs B Roderick
B (**Ref:**HM10534)

### HYPNOTHERAPY CLINIC

**Hypnotherapy Clinic**, Kensington Court Clinic, 197 Chepstow Rd, Newport, NP19 8GH, WAL.
(T) 01633 277263
Speciality: Hypnotherapy.
B (**Ref:**HM10535)

### HYPNOTHERAPY CLINIC CORK

**Hypnotherapy Clinic Cork**, Therapy House, 6 Tuckey St, **County Cork**, IRE.
(T) 021 4273 575
Speciality: Hypnotherapy.
B (**Ref:**HM10536)

### HYPNOTHERAPY CONSULTANCY

**Hypnotherapy Consultancy**, 16 St Boniface Cliff Rd, Shanklin, **Isle of Wight**, PO37 6ET, ENG.
(T) 01983 866999 (F) 01983 866999
(E) denclare@shanklin1.freeserve
(W) www.uk-hypnotherapy.com
Speciality: Hypnotherapy.
● **Owner/Hypnotherapist** Mr D Clare Q: C.Hyp, CMH.
B Yrs. Est.: 20 (**Ref:**HM10537)

### HYPNOTHERAPY CONSULTANCY

**Hypnotherapy Consultancy**, 7 St Johns Cl, Rownhams, Southampton, **Hampshire**, SO16 8JW, ENG.
(T) 023 8073 3554
Speciality: Hypnosis.
B (**Ref:**HM10538)

### HYPNOTHERAPY FOR CHANGE

**Hypnotherapy For Change**, 1 Douglas Lane, Wraysbury, Staines, **Surrey**, TW19 5NF, ENG.
(T) 01784 483979
Speciality: Hypnosis.
● **Owner** Mrs M Cooper
B (**Ref:**HM10539)

### HYPNOTHERAPY IN HUTTON

**Hypnotherapy In Hutton**, 22 Manor Farm Cres, Weston-Super-Mare, **Somerset**, BS24 9XB, ENG.
(T) 01934 814953
(E) annemitchell@bushinternet.com
Speciality: Hypnosis, Hypnotherapy. ✔
● **Psychologist/Hypnotherapist** Ms A Mitchell Q: BSc (Hons), Dip.Ed, Dip.Hyp. M: CAH.
B (**Ref:**HM10540)

### HYPNOTHERAPY & STRESS CON

**Hypnotherapy & Stress Consultancy**, Rainbow Cottage, 30 Edward Way, Ashford, **Surrey**, TW15 3AY, ENG.
(T) 01784 642875
Speciality: Hypnosis.
B (**Ref:**HM10541)

### HYPNOTHRPY FOR POSITIVE CHANGE

**Hypnotherapy For Positive Change**, 185 Milton Rd, Milton, Portsmouth, **Hampshire**, PO3 6AJ, ENG.
(T) 023 9242 8140
Speciality: Aversion Therapy, Hypnosis, Hypnotherapy, Stress Therapy. ✔
● **Hypnotherapist** Ms S Dupont Q: Dip.Adv.Hyp. M: CRAH, NCH.
B Yrs. Est.: 4 (**Ref:**HM10542)

### HYSLOP, C P

**C P Hyslop**, 76 Beaconsfield Villas, Brighton, **Sussex (East)**, BN1 6HE, ENG.
(T) 01293 533449 (F) 021 9344 6244
Speciality: Herbal Medicine, Holistic Healing, Homeopathy, Neuro-Linguistic Program. ✔
● **Owner/Chartered Biologist** Mr C Hyslop Q: C.Biol, RSHom.
C Yrs. Est.: 12 (**Ref:**HM10543)

### HYTHE CHIROPODY SERVICES

**Hythe Chiropody Services**, 113 High St, Hythe, **Kent**, CT21 5JH, ENG.
(T) 01303 264800
Speciality: Chiropodists (Podiatrists).
● **Owner** Mr J Dorigan
S (**Ref:**HM10544)

### HYTHE CHIROPRACTIC CLINIC

**Hythe Chiropractic Clinic**, The Marsh, Hythe, Southampton, **Hampshire**, SO45 6AL, ENG.
(T) 023 8020 7826
Speciality: Chiropractic.
P S T (**Ref:**HM10545)

### HYTHE PHYSIOTHERAPY CENTRE

**Hythe Physiotherapy Centre**, 6 Stade St, Hythe, **Kent**, CT21 6BD, ENG.
(T) 01303 266470
Speciality: Physiotherapy.
P S T (**Ref:**HM10546)

### I A H

**I A H**, Po Box 180, Bournemouth, **Dorset**, BH3 7YR, ENG.
(T) 01202 589444
Speciality: Hypnotherapy.
B (**Ref:**HM10547)

### I C O M

**International College Of Oriental Medicine (UK) Ltd**, Green Hedges House, Green Hedges Avenue, East Grinstead, **Sussex (West)**, RH19 1DZ, ENG.
(T) 01342 313106/7 (F) 01342 318302
(W) www.orientalmed.ac.uk
Speciality: Acupuncture, Complementary Therapy, Massage (Therapeutic), Ying & Yang. ✔
● **Principal** Mrs P Giesberts
O Yrs. Est.: 27 (**Ref:**HM10548)

### I C S

**I C S**, P O Box 7806, Birmingham, **Midlands (West)**, B33 9UQ, ENG.
(T) 01217 898898
Speciality: Complementary Medicines & Therapy.
● **Owner** Mr P Mills
M (**Ref:**HM10549)

### I D AROMATICS

**I D Aromatics**, Poetview Trade Centre, Newtownards Rd, Belfast, **County Antrim**, BT4 1HE, NIR.
(T) 028 9073 9390
Speciality: Complementary Medicines & Therapy.
C M (**Ref:**HM10550)

### I MASTERSON PSYCHOANALYTIC

**I Masterson Psychoanalytic Psychotherapist**, Alberta, Ardtona Ave, Lr Church Rd, Dublin, **County Dublin**, IRE.
(T) 01298 8288
Speciality: Psychoanalysis.
B (**Ref:**HM10551)

### I P CONSULTANCIES

**I P Consultancies**, 8 Park Edge, Hathersage, Hope Valley, **Derbyshire**, S32 1BS, ENG.
(T) 01433 650395 (F) 01433 651995
Speciality: Psychology.
● **Owner** Mrs I Pilkington
B (**Ref:**HM10552)

### I P T I

**I P T I**, 58A Bridgegate, Retford, **Nottinghamshire**, DN22 7UZ, ENG.
(T) 01777 700383 (F) 01777 708741
Speciality: Complementary Medicines & Therapy.
● **Manager** Mr J Cragg
M (**Ref:**HM10553)

### I R C H

**International Register Of Consultant**


Key continued: **Yrs.Est:** Years Established **Q:** Qualifications **M:** Professional Membership ✔ Indemnity Insurance Accept Credit Cards

**Herbalists & Homeopaths**, 32 King Edward Rd, Swansea, SA1 4LL, **WAL**.
(T) 01792 655886 (F) 01792 655886
(E) office@irch.org
(W) www.irch.org
Speciality: Herbal Medicine, Homeopathy. ✔
● **Secretary** I H James Q: Dip.Hom. M: IRCH.
H M Yrs. Est.: 40 (Ref:HM10554)

## I Y S KEVALA CENTRE

**I Y S Kevala Centre**, Hunsdon Rd, Torquay, **Devon**, TQ1 1QB, **ENG**.
(T) 01803 215678 (F) 01803 215678
Speciality: Complementary Medicines & Therapy.
● **Owner** Mrs S White
C M (Ref:HM10555)

## IAIMI HEALTH STUDIOS

**Iaimi Health Studios**, 12 Parry Way, Arnold, Nottingham, **Nottinghamshire**, NG5 8DD, **ENG**.
(T) 01159 557039
Speciality: Complementary Medicines & Therapy.
● **Principal** Mr R Porter
C M (Ref:HM10556)

## IAN COLLANGE ASSOCIATES

**Ian Collange Associates**, 31C Market Hill, Royston, **Hertfordshire**, SG8 9JS, **ENG**.
(T) 01763 247440
Speciality: Osteopathy.
● **Owner** Mr I Collange
P S T (Ref:HM10557)

## IAN COLLANGE ASSOCIATES

**Ian Collange Associates**, 48 High St, Royston, **Hertfordshire**, SG8 9AW, **ENG**.
(T) 01763 246782
Speciality: Osteopathy.
P S T (Ref:HM10558)

## IAN LAWES ELECTRICAL

**Ian Lawes Electrical**, Belmont Leckwith Rd, Cardiff, **Glamorgan (Vale of)**, CF11 8HP, **WAL**.
(T) 029 2039 4573
Speciality: Electrolysis.
T (Ref:HM10559)

## IAN, MILNE

**Milne Ian DO MCO MICO**, Health Haven Lysaghts La, Ennis, **County Clare**, **IRE**.
(T) 08724 56213
Speciality: Complementary Medicines & Therapy.
M (Ref:HM10560)

## I'ANSON, K L

**K L I'anson**, Provident Buildings, The Green, Darwen, **Lancashire**, BB3 1PW, **ENG**.
(T) 01254 772990
Speciality: Osteopathy.
● **Owner** Miss K I'anson
P S T (Ref:HM10561)

## IBBETSON, A

**A Ibbetson**, 8 Highlea Cl, Yeadon, Leeds, **Yorkshire (West)**, LS19 7LU, **ENG**.
(T) 01132 503545
Speciality: Chiropodists (Podiatrists).
● **Owner** Mr A Ibbetson
S (Ref:HM10562)

## IBBETSON, JOHN A

**John A Ibbetson**, 57 Chorley New Rd, Bolton, **Lancashire**, BL1 4QR, **ENG**.
(T) 01204 523270
Speciality: Osteopathy.
P S T (Ref:HM10563)

## IBBETSON, JOHN A

**John A Ibbetson**, 349 Parrs Wood Rd, Manchester, **Manchester (Greater)**, M20 6JF, **ENG**.
(T) 01614 453615
Speciality: Osteopathy.
P S T (Ref:HM10564)

## IBBOTSON, GEOFF (DR)

**Dr Geoff Ibbotson**, Stubley House, 166 Featherstall Rd, Littleborough, **Manchester (Greater)**, OL15 8NZ, **ENG**.
(T) 01706 373825
(E) geoffibbotson@stubleyhouse.freeserve.co.uk
Speciality: Cognitive Therapy, Counselling, Hypnosis, Hypnotherapy, Psychotherapy. ✔
● **Independent Medical Practitioner**
Dr G Ibbotson Q: AKC, BS, BSc, D.Obst, MB, NLP. M: BSECH, RCOG.
B Yrs. Est.: 5 (Ref:HM10565)

## IBBS, ROGER

**Roger Ibbs**, 185 Hanley Rd, Stoke-On-Trent, **Staffordshire**, ST1 6BG, **ENG**.
(T) 01782 214559 (F) 01782 214559
Speciality: Chiropody, Podiatry. ✔
● **Owner/Chiropodist** Mr R Ibbs Q: S.R.Ch. M: S.R.Ch.
C Yrs. Est.: 33 (Ref:HM10566)

## ICE & FIRE

**Ice & Fire**, 7 Church St, Wolverton, Milton Keynes, **Buckinghamshire**, MK12 5LG, **ENG**.
(T) 01908 227977
Speciality: Aromatherapy.
● **Owner** Mrs N Sharpe
M O (Ref:HM10567)

## ICHP HEADQUARTERS

**ICHP Headquarters**, Curragh Camp Co, **County Kildare**, **IRE**.
(T) 04544 1814
Speciality: Hypnotherapy.
B (Ref:HM10568)

## ICHP HEADQUARTERS

**ICHP Headquarters**, Newbridge Co, **County Kildare**, **IRE**.
(T) 04543 3291
Speciality: Relaxation Technique.
H T (Ref:HM10569)

## ICHP HEADQUARTERS

**ICHP Headquarters**, Naas Co, **County Kildare**, **IRE**.
(T) 04587 4350
Speciality: Hypnotherapy.
B (Ref:HM10570)

## ICHP HEADQUARTERS

**ICHP Headquarters**, The Ferns B'rock Co, **County Louth**, **IRE**.
(T) 04293 22173
Speciality: Complementary Medicines & Therapy.
M (Ref:HM10571)

## IDESON, S M

**S M Ideson**, 52 Kirkby Lane, Great Broughton, Middlesbrough, **Cleveland**, TS9 7HG, **ENG**.
(T) 01642 712349
Speciality: Osteopathy.
● **Owner** Mrs S Ideson
P S T (Ref:HM10572)

## IDLE & ALLAN

**Ann F & Allan Idle**, 69 Hythe St, Dartford, **Kent**, DA1 1BG, **ENG**.
(T) 01322 224604
Speciality: Chiropodists (Podiatrists).
S (Ref:HM10573)

## IDLE AROMATHERAPY

**Idle Aromatherapy**, 5 Albion Rd, Bradford, **Yorkshire (West)**, BD10 9PY, **ENG**.
(T) 01274 620050
Speciality: Aromatherapy.
M O (Ref:HM10574)

## IFFLEY CLINIC

**Iffley Clinic (The)**, 68 Church Way, Iffley, Oxford, **Oxfordshire**, OX4 4EF, **ENG**.
(T) 01865 396939
Speciality: Complementary Medicines & Therapy.
● **Manageress** Ms V Greenwood
C M (Ref:HM10575)

## IFIELD CENTRE

**Ifield Centre For Physiotherapy & Sports Medicine**, Langley Corner, Ifield Green, Ifield, Crawley, **Sussex (West)**, RH11 0NF, **ENG**.
(T) 01293 618111 (F) 01293 538358
Speciality: Physiotherapy.
● **Manager** Mrs P Jordan
P S T (Ref:HM10576)

## IKEBANA SPIRIT MIND BODY CTRE

**Ikebana Spirit Mind Body Centre**, 4 Wynnefield Rd, (off, Rathmines, **County Dublin**, **IRE**.
(T) 01496 0948
Speciality: Complementary Medicines & Therapy.
M (Ref:HM10577)

## IKIN, SALLY

**Sally Ikin**, 37 High Town Rd, Maidenhead, **Berkshire**, SL6 1PA, **ENG**.
(T) 01628 788420
Speciality: Chiropodists (Podiatrists).
● **Owner** Mrs C Sanders
S (Ref:HM10578)

## IKIN, SALLY

**Sally Ikin**, 25 Gypsy Lane, Marlow, **Buckinghamshire**, SL7 3JT, **ENG**.
(T) 01628 474761 (F) 01628 474761
Speciality: Chiropodists (Podiatrists).
● **Owner** Mrs S Ikin
S (Ref:HM10579)

## ILKESTONE OSTEO & MED CTRE

**Ilkestone Osteopathy & Natural Medical Centre**, 18 Stanton Rd, Ilkeston, **Derbyshire**, DE7 5FQ, **ENG**.
(T) 01159 308255 (F) 01159 308225
Speciality: Aromatherapy, Herbal Medicine, Naturopathy, Osteopathy, Sports Massage. ✔
● **Reiki/Aromotherapist**
Ms P Westwood
● **Osteopath/Naturopath**
Mrs R Mallaband Q: BSc (Hons). M: GOsC.
● **Sports Massage/Herbalism**
Miss H Ryalls
S Yrs. Est.: 20 (Ref:HM10580)

## ILKLEY CHIROPODY CLINIC

**Ilkley Chiropody Clinic**, Springs Lane, Ilkley, **Yorkshire (West)**, LS29 8TQ, **ENG**.
(T) 01943 816122
Speciality: Chiropodists (Podiatrists).
S (Ref:HM10581)

## ILLUMINADA

**Illuminada**, 92 Camden Rd, Tunbridge Wells, **Kent**, TN1 2QP, **ENG**.
(T) 01892 616845
Speciality: Complementary Medicines & Therapy.
● **Partner** Mr R Dunkin
M (Ref:HM10582)

## ILSELEY, BERNARD

**Bernard Ilseley**, White House, 111 New St, Birmingham, **Midlands (West)**, B2 4EU, **ENG**.
(T) 01216 325576
Speciality: Clairvoyants & Palmists.
B (Ref:HM10583)

## ILSLEY, MARY

**Mary Ilsley**, 2 St Austins Croft, 28 Boscobel Rd, St. Leonards-On-Sea, **Sussex (East)**, TN38 0LX, **ENG**.
(T) 01424 718454
Speciality: Clairvoyants & Palmists.
● **Owner** Ms M Ilsley
B (Ref:HM10584)

## IM, KIM LAY

**Kim Lay Im**, 178 Grenville Rd, Plymouth, **Devon**, PL4 9QD, **ENG**.
(T) 01752 227841
Speciality: Acupuncture.
● **Owner** Mrs K Lay-Im
O (Ref:HM10585)

## IMAGES HEALTH & BEAUTY CLINIC

**Images Health & Beauty Clinic**, Main St, Ballinrobe, **County Mayo**, **IRE**.
(T) 09242 156 (F) 09242 073
(E) ryders@eircom.net
Speciality: Beauty Therapy.
H T (Ref:HM10586)

## IMAGE-STICS

**Image-Stics Ltd**, 811 Manchester Old Rd, Rhodes, Middleton, Manchester, **Manchester (Greater)**, M24 4RE, **ENG**.
(T) 01616 536073
Speciality: Complementary Medicines & Therapy.
C M (Ref:HM10587)

### IMMUNE DEVELOPMENT TRUST
**Immune Development Trust**, 90 Islington High St, London, **London (Greater)**, N1 8EG, ENG.
(T) 020 7704 1555 (F) 020 7226 9001
Speciality: Complementary Medicines & Therapy.
C M (Ref:HM10588)

### IMORTELLE
**Imortelle**, 66A York Rd, Weybridge, **Surrey**, KT13 9DY, ENG.
(T) 01932 847001
Speciality: Aromatherapy.
● **Owner** Miss L Spearing
M O (Ref:HM10589)

### IMPACT PHYSIO & SPORTS INJURIES
**Impact Physiotherapy & Sports Injuries Clinic (The)**, Station St, Long Eaton, Nottingham, **Nottinghamshire**, NG10 1GJ, ENG.
(T) 01159 721319 (F) 01159 460676
Speciality: Acupuncture, Physiotherapy. ✔
● **Owner/Physiotherapist**
Mrs R Royer Q: MCSP, SRP. M: CSP.
S Yrs. Est.: 18 (Ref:HM10590)

### IMPERIAL CHIROPODY SERVICES
**Imperial Chiropody Services**, 33 Rodney Rd, Cheltenham, **Gloucestershire**, GL50 1HX, ENG.
(T) 01242 227372
Speciality: Chiropodists (Podiatrists).
● **Owner** Miss J Holcroft
S (Ref:HM10591)

### IMPERIAL COLLEGE HEALTH CENTRE
**Imperial College Health Centre**, Southside, Watt's Way, Prince's Gardens, London, **London (Greater)**, SW7 1LU, ENG.
(T) 020 7584 6301
Speciality: Alexander Technique.
● **Therapist** Ms P Wetherell
P S (Ref:HM10592)

### IMPERIAL SCHOOL OF FENG SHUI
**Imperial School Of Feng Shui**, Po Box 135, Bushey, Watford, **Hertfordshire**, WD2 3YW, ENG.
(T) 020 8950 8282 (F) 020 8386 8041
Speciality: Complementary Medicines & Therapy.
● **Director** Mrs K Sheth
M (Ref:HM10593)

### IMPORT, SELINA
**Selina Import**, The Old Rectory, Dufton, Appleby-in-Westmorland, **Cumbria**, CA16 6DA, ENG.
(T) 01768 351635
Speciality: Complementary Medicines & Therapy.
● **Owner** Selina Import
M (Ref:HM10594)

### IN HARMONY AROMATHERAPY
**In Harmony Aromatherapy**, 24 Minto St, Edinburgh, **Edinburgh (City of)**, EH9 1SB, SCO.
(T) 01316 676296 (F) 01316 629933
(E) catherine@in-harmony.net
(W) www.in-harmony.net
Speciality: Aromatherapy. ✔
● **Aromatherapist** Mrs C Crawford Q: BSc, Dip.N Med, LLSA, MIFA. M: IFA.
C Yrs. Est.: 5 (Ref:HM10595)

### IN STEP CHIROPODY CLINIC
**In Step Chiropody Clinic Ltd**, 14 Halesworth Cl, Chesterfield, **Derbyshire**, S40 3LW, ENG.
(T) 01246 554788
Speciality: Complementary Medicines & Therapy.
● **Sole Director**
Margaret Florence Evelyn McCarthy
C M (Ref:HM10596)

### IN THE KNOW
**In The Know**, 12 Bank Pl, Pill, Bristol, BS20 0AQ, ENG.
(T) 01275 371100
Speciality: Complementary Medicines & Therapy.
● **Owner** Mr K Wellstead
M (Ref:HM10597)

### IN THE PINK
**In The Pink**, 20 Apple Tree Walk, Ombersley, Droitwich, **Worcestershire**, WR9 0HG, ENG.
(T) 01905 620729
Speciality: Aromatherapy, Indian Head Massage, Reflexology.
M O (Ref:HM10598)

### IN TOUCH
**In Touch**, 6 Hunts Lane, Desford, Leicester, **Leicestershire**, LE9 9LJ, ENG.
(T) 01455 828064
Speciality: Clairvoyants & Palmists.
● **Owner** Mrs P Blakewmore
B (Ref:HM10599)

### IN TOUCH MOBILE MASSAGE
**In Touch Mobile Theraupeutic Massage**, Longstowe Hall, Old North Rd, Longstowe, Cambridge, **Cambridgeshire**, CB3 7UH, ENG.
(T) 01954 719478
Speciality: Complementary Medicines & Therapy.
● **Owner** Mr P Kelly
M (Ref:HM10600)

### INCE, G A
**G A Ince**, 10 Colescroft Hill, Purley, **Surrey**, CR8 4BB, ENG.
(T) 020 8763 0972 (F) 020 8763 0973
Speciality: Homeopathy.
● **Partner** Mrs G Ince
M (Ref:HM10601)

### INCE, ROBERT J
**Robert J Ince**, 10 Colescroft Hill, Purley, **Surrey**, CR8 4BB, ENG.
(T) 020 8763 0972 (F) 020 8763 0972
Speciality: Homeopathy.
● **Owner** Mr R Ince
M (Ref:HM10602)

### INCH BY INCH TONING
**Inch By Inch Toning**, 24A Newtown Pk, Blackrock, **County Dublin**, IRE.
(T) 01288 9153
Speciality: Complementary Medicines & Therapy.
M (Ref:HM10603)

### INCHKEITH HOUSE
**Inchkeith House**, 139 Leith Walk, Edinburgh, **Edinburgh (City of)**, EH6 8NP, SCO.
(T) 01314 678530
Speciality: Chiropodists (Podiatrists).
S (Ref:HM10604)

### IND, A E
**A E Ind**, 48 Lansdown, Stroud, **Gloucestershire**, GL5 1BN, ENG.
(T) 01453 759768
Speciality: Chiropodists (Podiatrists).
● **Owner** A Ind
S (Ref:HM10605)

### INDEPENDANT MED PSYCH SVS
**Independant Medical Psychiatrist Services**, 2 Crawford Pl, London, **London (Greater)**, W1H 1JD, ENG.
(T) 020 8560 8728 (F) 020 8560 8728
Speciality: Psychiatry.
● **Doctor** Dr W Dzikowski
B (Ref:HM10606)

### INDEPENDENT CHILD PSYCHOL SVS
**Independent Child Psychology Services**, 56 Knighton Drive, Leicester, **Leicestershire**, LE2 3HB, ENG.
(T) 01162 448331
Speciality: Psychology.
B (Ref:HM10607)

### INDEPENDENT ED PSYCHOL SVS
**Independent Educational Psychology Services**, 16 The Bryn, Sketty, Swansea, SA2 8DD, WAL.
(T) 01792 208403
Speciality: Psychology.
B (Ref:HM10608)

### INDEPENDENT PSYCHOLOGICAL SVS
**Independent Psychological Services**, Care Of Media House, 16 Robertson St, Glasgow, **Glasgow (City of)**, G2 8DU, SCO.
(T) 01412 041549 (F) 01412 263744
Speciality: Psychology.
● **Partner** Mrs M Irvine
B (Ref:HM10609)

### INDEPENDENT PSYCHOLOGY SERVICE
**Independent Psychology Service**, 7 Lansdowne Rd, Muswell Hill, London, **London (Greater)**, N10 2AX, ENG.
(T) 020 8883 9685 (F) 020 8883 9685
Speciality: Art Therapy, Biofeedback, Cognitive Therapy, Counselling, Drama Therapy, Family Therapy, Gestalt Therapy, Psychotherapy, Rogerian Therapy, EMDR - Eye Movement Desensitisation and Reprocessing. ✔
● **Director** Ms M Roitt Q: BA (Hons) Psychol, MSc. M: BPS.
B Yrs. Est.: 11 (Ref:HM10610)

### INDIAN PALMIST RAI
**Indian Palmist Rai**, Palace Pier, Madeira Drive, Brighton, **Sussex (East)**, BN2 1TW, ENG.
(T) 01273 684868
Speciality: Clairvoyants & Palmists.
● **Owner** Mr N Mohamed
B (Ref:HM10611)

### INDIGO
**Indigo**, 2 Newlands Cl, Kidderminster, **Worcestershire**, DY11 5AR, ENG.
(T) 01562 745011
Speciality: Aromatherapy.
● **Partner** Mrs V Banner
M O (Ref:HM10612)

### INDIGO BAY AROMATHERAPY
**Indigo Bay Aromatherapy**, P O Box 4994, Lakes Rd, Braintree, **Essex**, CM7 3SS, ENG.
(T) 01376 328109 (F) 01376 328109
Speciality: Aromatherapy.
● **Owner** Mrs C Blake
M O (Ref:HM10613)

### INDIGO HEALTH CONSULTANCY
**Indigo Health Consultancy**, Rock Mount, Liverpool Rd, Chester, **Cheshire**, CH2 1AA, ENG.
(T) 01244 390800
Speciality: Complementary Medicines & Therapy.
● **Partner** Ms E Scott
C M (Ref:HM10614)

### INDIRA
**Indira**, 544 Green Lane, Ilford, **Essex**, IG3 9LL, ENG.
(T) 020 8599 2444
Speciality: Aromatherapy.
● **Partner** Ms T Couzens
M O (Ref:HM10615)

### INDRA RASTOGI
**Indra Rastogi**, 101 Westfield Rd, Edgbaston, Birmingham, **Midlands (West)**, B15 3JE, ENG.
(T) 01214 545943
Speciality: Chiropodists (Podiatrists).
S (Ref:HM10616)

### INDULGENCE
**Indulgence**, 145 Bradford Rd, Brighouse, **Yorkshire (West)**, HD6 4AD, ENG.
(T) 01484 402430
Speciality: Aromatherapy.
● **Owner** Miss J Telford
M O (Ref:HM10617)

### INGHAM, MARIE
**Marie Ingham**, 193B Brockley Rise, London, **London (Greater)**, SE23 1NL, ENG.
(T) 020 8690 8182
Speciality: Homeopathy.
● **Owner** Mr M Ingham
M (Ref:HM10618)

### INGHAM, NICHOLAS
**Nicholas Ingham**, 145A Huntingdon Rd, Cambridge, **Cambridgeshire**, CB3 0DH, ENG.
(T) 01223 358098
Speciality: Psychotherapy.
B (Ref:HM10619)

### INGLE, M T
**M T Ingle**, 335 Red Bank Rd, Blackpool, **Lancashire**, FY2 0HJ, ENG.
(T) 01253 351475


Key continued: Yrs.Est: Years Established Q: Qualifications M: Professional Membership ✔ Indemnity Insurance Accept Credit Cards

Speciality: Chiropodists (Podiatrists).
● **Owner** Mr M Ingle
S (Ref:HM10620)

## INGLEDALE NATURAL HEALTH CTRE

**Ingledale Natural Health Centre**, 1 Tanhouse Rd, Oxted, **Surrey**, RH8 9PE, ENG.
(T) 01883 717277
Speciality: Osteopathy, Ultrasonics. ✔
● **Osteopath** Ms K Nunn Q: DO. M: GOsC.
S Yrs. Est.: 16 (Ref:HM10621)

## INGLES

**Ingles**, 12 Crimicar Lane, Sheffield, **Yorkshire (South)**, S10 4FB, ENG.
(T) 01142 630641
Speciality: Chiropodists (Podiatrists).
● **Owner** Mr B Ingle
S (Ref:HM10622)

## INGRAM, C

**C Ingram**, 38 Bridge St, Andover, **Hampshire**, SP10 1BW, ENG.
(T) 01264 358466
Speciality: Osteopathy.
● **Owner** Mr C Ingram
P S T (Ref:HM10623)

## INGRAM, CLARE

**Clare Ingram**, 7 Pool Furlong, Clent, Stourbridge, **Midlands (West)**, DY9 9RE, ENG.
(T) 01562 777773
(E) ingrampcd@aol.com
Speciality: Acupressure, Acupuncture, Bach Remedies, Dowsing, Kinesiology. ✔
● **Acupuncturist** Mrs C Ingram Q: BIAT, Lic.Ac, MBAcC, SRN. M: BAcC, BIAET.
O Yrs. Est.: 10 (Ref:HM10624)

## INGRAM, NEIL

**Neil Ingram**, 68 The Avenue, Southampton, **Hampshire**, SO17 1XS, ENG.
(T) 023 8033 8863
Speciality: Osteopathy.
● **Owner** Mr N Ingram
P S T (Ref:HM10625)

## INGRAM, RACHAEL

**Rachael Ingram**, 3a Salterton Rd, Exmouth, **Devon**, EX8 2BJ, ENG.
(T) 01395 272918
Speciality: Chiropodists (Podiatrists).
● **Owner** Miss R Ingram
S (Ref:HM10626)

## INGRAM, S

**S Ingram**, 22 Eaton Village, Eaton, Abingdon, **Oxfordshire**, OX13 5PR, ENG.
(T) 01865 864053
Speciality: Osteopathy.
● **Owner** Mrs S Ingram
P S T (Ref:HM10627)

## INGRAMS, D (DR)

**Dr D Ingrams**, 130-132 Gloucester Rd, Bishopston, Bristol, BS7 8NL, ENG.
(T) 01179 245842
Speciality: Chiropractors.
P S T (Ref:HM10628)

## INGREY, DAVID

**David Ingrey**, 18 Fairlawn Rd, Bristol, BS6 5JS, ENG.
(T) 01179 556680
Speciality: Reflexology.
S T (Ref:HM10629)

## INGRID MASTERSON REG PSYCH

**Ingrid Masterson Reg Psychoanalytic Therapist**, 76a Castlewood Gardens, **County Carlow**, IRE.
(T) 01298 8288
Speciality: Psychoanalysis.
B (Ref:HM10630)

## INHEALTH CENTRE

**Inhealth Centre (The)**, 5 Dundonald St, Edinburgh, **Edinburgh (City of)**, EH3 6RX, SCO.
(T) 01314 774577
Speciality: Complementary Medicines & Therapy.
M (Ref:HM10631)

## INJURY TREATMENT CLINIC

**Injury Treatment Clinic**, 28 Ridings Cl, Doncaster, **Yorkshire (South)**, DN4 6UZ, ENG.
(T) 01302 537464
Speciality: Physiotherapy.
P S T (Ref:HM10632)

## INLPTA

**International NLP Trainers Association Ltd**, Po Box 288, Fareham, **Hampshire**, PO16 0YG, ENG.
(T) 01329 285353 (F) 01329 285757
(E) inlpta@btclick.com
(W) www.members.aol.com/inlpta/index.htm
Speciality: Auto Suggestion, Counselling, Hypnosis, Hypnotherapy, Neuro-Linguistic Program, Psychotherapy, Visualisation Therapy.
H (Ref:HM10633)

## INNER CALM

**Inner Calm**, 16 Sussex Cres, Castleford, **Yorkshire (West)**, WF10 3NX, ENG.
(T) 01977 559255
Speciality: Complementary Medicines & Therapy.
● **Owner** Miss T Braithwaite
M (Ref:HM10634)

## INNER CIRCLE HEALING CENTRE

**Inner Circle Healing Centre**, 1 Sutton Cross, Dublin, **County Dublin**, IRE.
(T) 01832 3777
(E) rhaada@hotmail.com
Speciality: Absent Healing, Acupuncture, Aromatherapy, Complementary Therapy, Crystal Healing, Dowsing, Healing Therapy, Holistic Healing, Hypnosis, Hypnotherapy, Indian Head Massage, Life Style Coaching, Massage (Therapeutic), Meditation, Paranormal Therapies, Pilates, Polarity Therapy, Psychotherapy, Reflexology, Reiki, Seichem, Spiritual Healing, Stress Therapy, Integrated Energy Therapy, Lymphatic Drainage, Pranic Healing, Rebirthing, NLP. ✔
● **Director** Magda Batista Q: Reiki Master.
● **Therapist** Ms A Obrien
● **Psychotherapist** Mr S Farrel M: ICHP.
T Yrs. Est.: 3 (Ref:HM10635)

## INNER HLTH & HEALING PRACTICE

**Inner Health & Healing Practice**, 49A High St, Yarm, **Cleveland**, TS15 9BH, ENG.
(T) 01642 785353
Speciality: Reflexology.
S T (Ref:HM10636)

## INNER PEACE

**Inner Peace**, The Courtyard, Dale Rd, Matlock, **Derbyshire**, DE4 3LT, ENG.
(T) 01629 760510
Speciality: Complementary Medicines & Therapy.
● **Owner** Mrs P Locke
C M (Ref:HM10637)

## INNER POTENTIAL CENTRE

**Inner Potential Centre (The)**, 36 Kelvedon Rd, London, **London (Greater)**, SW6 5BW, ENG.
(T) 020 7731 8822
Speciality: Complementary Medicines & Therapy.
C M (Ref:HM10638)

## INNER SENSE

**Inner Sense**, Yew Trees, Gloucestershire Lea, Warfield, Bracknell, **Berkshire**, RG42 3XQ, ENG.
(T) 01344 641846 (F) 01344 641846
Speciality: Hypnosis.
● **Owner** Mrs G Gardener
B (Ref:HM10639)

## INNER SPACE

**Inner Space**, 36 Shorts Gardens, London, **London (Greater)**, WC2H 9AB, ENG.
(T) 020 7836 6688 (F) 020 7836 6689
Speciality: Relaxation Technique.
● **Manageress** Miss A Lal
H T (Ref:HM10640)

## INNER SPACE SUFFOLK

**Dr David J Deacon**, Highdene, North Cliff, Kessingland, Lowestoft, **Suffolk**, NR33 7RA, ENG.
(T) 01502 742097 (F) 01502 742097
(E) david.deacon@which.net
Speciality: Acupuncture, Flotation Therapy, Hypnosis. ✔
● **Owner** Dr D Deacon Q: MA. M: BMAS.
M Yrs. Est.: 10 (Ref:HM10641)

## INNER VISION

**Inner Vision**, 100A Hamilton Rd, London, **London (Greater)**, NW11 9DY, ENG.
(T) 020 8458 3710
Speciality: Complementary Medicines & Therapy.
● **Owner** Miss S Brind
C M (Ref:HM10642)

## INNER WHISPERS & THERAPY CTRE

**Inner Whispers & Therapy Centre**, 37-39 Kingston Rd, Portsmouth, **Hampshire**, PO2 7DP, ENG.
(T) 023 9273 8388 (F) 023 9265 3061
Speciality: Indian Head Massage, Reiki, Crystal Workshops, Personal Growth, Physic Reading. ✔ CREDIT
● **Reiki Master** Mrs Cleuren Q: Dip.Hyp. M: HPG.
C Yrs. Est.: 2 (Ref:HM10643)

## INNERGY YOGA CENTRE

**Innergy Yoga Centre**, Acorn Hall, East Row, London, **London (Greater)**, W10 5AW, ENG.
(T) 020 8968 1178
Speciality: Yoga.
● **Director** Mr F Dorelli
H T (Ref:HM10644)

## INNERSANCTUM HOLISTIC HEALTH

**Innersanctum Holistic Health & Beauty Centre**, 42 St Lukes Rd, Old Windsor, Windsor, **Berkshire**, SL4 2QQ, ENG.
(T) 01753 832460
Speciality: Complementary Medicines & Therapy.
C M (Ref:HM10645)

## INNERSCENTS AROMATHERAPY

**Innerscents Aromatherapy**, 15 Prospect Rd, London, **London (Greater)**, NW2 2JT, ENG.
(T) 020 7435 1197 (F) 020 7432 1197
Speciality: Aromatherapy.
● **Partner** Mrs L Feldman
M O (Ref:HM10646)

## INNERSENSE

**Innersense**, 10 Vicarage Pl, Walsall, **Midlands (West)**, WS1 3NA, ENG.
(T) 01922 649142
Speciality: Aromatherapy, Beauty Therapy, Crystal Healing, Hopi Ear Candles, Reflexology, Reiki, Zero Balancing. ✔
● **Holistic Therapist** Ms C Prew M: BABTAC, IIHHT.
C Yrs. Est.: 4 (Ref:HM10647)

## INNERVISION HYPNOTHERAPY CTRE

**Innervision Hypnotherapy Centre**, 22 Laneham St, Scunthorpe, **Humberside**, DN15 6PB, ENG.
(T) 01724 277069
Speciality: Hypnosis.
● **Owner** Mr B Glenn
B (Ref:HM10648)

## INSCAPE

**Inscape**, 55 High St, Uppermill, Oldham, **Lancashire**, OL3 6AP, ENG.
(T) 01457 877659
Speciality: Psychotherapy.
● **Owner** Mr W Winter
B (Ref:HM10649)

## INS-CLINICAL HYP & PSYCHO

**Institute of Clinical Hypnotherapy & Psychotherapy**, Therapy House, 6 Tuckey St, **County Cork**, IRE.
(T) 021 4273 575 (F) 021 4275 785
(W) www.hypnosiseire.com
Speciality: Art Therapy, Auto Suggestion, Autogenic Training, Aversion Therapy, Biofeedback, Cognitive Therapy, Colour Therapy, Complementary Therapy, Counselling, Faith Healing, Healer, Healing Therapy, Hypnosis, Hypnotherapy, Life Style Coaching, Meditation, Psychotherapy, Spiritual Healing, Stress Therapy, Visualisation Therapy. ✔ CREDIT
● **Director ICHP/Hypnotherapist**

Dr J Keany Q: BA, MICHP, PhD. M: ACHE, ICHP, NCH.
M Yrs. Est.: 20 (Ref:HM10661)

**INS-COUNS & HYPNOTHERAPY**

**Institute of Counselling & Hypnotherapy (The)**, 118 Stillorgan Rd, IRE.
(T) 01260 0118
Speciality: Hypnotherapy.
B (Ref:HM10662)

**INS-CREATIVE COUNS & PSYCHO**

**Institute Of Creative Counselling & Psychotherapy**, 82 Upr Georges St, Dun Laoghaire, **County Dublin**, IRE.
(T) 01280 2523
Speciality: Psychotherapy.
B (Ref:HM10663)

**INSIDE STORY**

**Berrydales Publishers**, 5 Lawn Rd, London, **London (Greater)**, NW3 2XS, ENG.
(T) 020 7722 2866 (F) 020 7722 7685
(E) michelle@insidestory.com
(W) www.insidestory.com
Speciality: Complementary Medicines & Therapy.
● **Joint Director** Mr J Mallinson
● **Editor** Ms M Berriedale-Johnson
M Yrs. Est.: 8 (Ref:HM10650)

**INSIGHT**

**Insight**, 15 Pearson Avenue, Coventry, **Midlands (West)**, CV6 7DA, ENG.
(T) 01926 512000
Speciality: Clairvoyants & Palmists.
● **Owner** Mr K Richards
B (Ref:HM10651)

**INSIGHT**

**Insight**, 84 Earlham Gr, London, **London (Greater)**, E7 9AR, ENG.
(T) 020 8555 7992
Speciality: Clairvoyants & Palmists.
● **Owner** Mrs J Morris
B (Ref:HM10652)

**INSIGHT**

**Insight Ltd**, 6 Joan Avenue, Sunderland, **Tyne and Wear**, SR2 9TA, ENG.
(T) 01915 654485
Speciality: Clairvoyants & Palmists.
● **Owner** Miss J Mess
B (Ref:HM10653)

**INSIGHT NATURAL HEALTH CENTRE**

**Insight Natural Health Centre**, 131 Tuckton Rd, Bournemouth, **Dorset**, BH6 3JZ, ENG.
(T) 01202 418800
Speciality: Complementary Medicines & Therapy.
● **Owner** Mrs C Elkins
M (Ref:HM10654)

**INSIGHT PARTNERSHIP**

**Insight Partnership Ltd (The)**, 23 Bentinck St, London, **London (Greater)**, W1M 5RL, ENG.
(T) 020 7935 6887 (F) 020 7935 0255
Speciality: Psychology.
● **Director** Mr G Wilson
B (Ref:HM10655)

**INSIGHT PSYCHOLOGICAL SERVICES**

**Insight Psychological Services**, Maldwyn House, 13 Brigstocke Trce, Ferryside, **Carmarthenshire**, SA17 5SH, WAL.
(T) 01267 267526
Speciality: Psychology.
B (Ref:HM10656)

**INSIGHT THERAPIES**

**Insight Therapies**, 4 Green Croft, Romiley, Stockport, **Cheshire**, SK6 4LW, ENG.
(T) 01614 305229
Speciality: Reflexology.
S T (Ref:HM10657)

**INSIGHTS THERAPY CLINIC**

**Insights Therapy Clinic**, 88 Ridgeway Rd, Long Ashton, Bristol, BS41 9HA, ENG.
(T) 01275 393869 (F) 01275 393869
Speciality: Psychotherapy.
● **Principal** Mr C Ferguson
B (Ref:HM10658)

**INSPIRATIONS**

**Inspirations**, 180 High St, Enfield, **London (Greater)**, EN3 4EU, ENG.
(T) 020 8373 0171 (F) 020 8373 0171
Speciality: Complementary Medicines & Therapy.
● **Owner** Miss S Thompson
C M (Ref:HM10659)

**INSPIRED TECHNOLOGY**

**Inspired Technology Ltd**, Queens Chambers, 16 Queen St, Blackpool, **Lancashire**, FY1 1PD, ENG.
(T) 01253 753700 (F) 01253 290019
Speciality: Magnetic Therapy.
M (Ref:HM10660)

**INSTIT-DEVELOPMENTAL POTENTIAL**

**Institute For Developmental Potential (The)**, 6 Patna Pl, North Rd West, Plymouth, **Devon**, PL1 5AY, ENG.
(T) 01752 222188
Speciality: Hypnosis.
B (Ref:HM10664)

**INSTIT-TRAD HERBAL MED-ACUP**

**Institute Of Traditional Herbal Medicine & Aromatherapy**, 12 Prentices Lane, Woodbridge, **Suffolk**, IP12 4LF, ENG.
(T) 01394 388386 (F) 01394 388209
Speciality: Aromatherapy.
● **Owner** Mr G Mojay
M O (Ref:HM10665)

**INSTITUTE FOR COMP MEDICINE**

**Institute For Complementary Medicine**, 15 Tavern Quay, Sweden Gate, Off Plough Way, London, **London (Greater)**, SE16 7QZ, ENG.
(T) 020 7237 5165
Speciality: Complementary Medicines & Therapy.
M (Ref:HM10666)

**INSTITUTE FOR COMP MEDICINE**

**Institute For Complementary Medicine**, 15 Tavern Quay, Sweden Gate, Off Plough Way, London, **London (Greater)**, SE16 1QZ, ENG.
(T) 020 7237 5165
Speciality: Complementary Medicines & Therapy.
C M (Ref:HM10667)

**INSTITUTE OF BIO-ENERGETIC MED**

**Institute Of Bio-Energetic Medicine**, 103 North Rd, Poole, **Dorset**, BH14 0LU, ENG.
(T) 01202 733762 (F) 01202 733762
Speciality: Homeopathy.
● **Chief Executive** Dr A Scott-Morley
M (Ref:HM10668)

**INSTITUTE OF CHINESE MEDICINE**

**Institute Of Chinese Medicine**, 44 Chandos Pl, London, **London (Greater)**, WC2N 4HS, ENG.
(T) 020 7836 5220
Speciality: Complementary Medicines & Therapy.
C M (Ref:HM10669)

**INSTITUTE OF CHIROP & POD**

**Institute Of Chiropodists & Podiatrists (The)**, 11 Rockingham Gate, Sheffield, **Yorkshire (South)**, S1 4JD, ENG.
(T) 01142 727515
Speciality: Chiropodists (Podiatrists).
● **Manageress** Mrs L Wells
S (Ref:HM10670)

**INSTITUTE OF CHIROPODISTS**

**Institute Of Chiropodists (The)**, 27 Wright St, Southport, **Merseyside**, PR9 0TL, ENG.
(T) 01704 546141
Speciality: Chiropodists (Podiatrists).
S (Ref:HM10671)

**INSTITUTE OF CLINICAL HYPNOSIS**

**Institute Of Clinical Hypnosis (The)**, 28 Tantallon Rd, London, **London (Greater)**, SW12 8DG, ENG.
(T) 020 8675 1598 (F) 020 8673 2230
Speciality: Hypnosis.
B (Ref:HM10672)

**INSTITUTE OF DREAM ANALYSTS**

**Institute Of Dream Analysts**, 8 Willow Rd, London, **London (Greater)**, NW3 1TJ, ENG.
(T) 020 7794 8717
Speciality: Psychology.
● **Owner** Mr S Meyerson
B (Ref:HM10673)

**INSTITUTE OF ELECTROLYSIS**

**Institute Of Electrolysis**, 27 Bottesford Cl, Emerson Valley, Milton Keynes, **Buckinghamshire**, MK4 2AF, ENG.
(T) 01908 521511 (F) 01908 521511
Speciality: Electrolysis.
● **Administrator** Mrs J Jones
T (Ref:HM10674)

**INSTITUTE OF ELECTROLYSIS**

**Institute of Electrolysis (The)**, 138 Downs Barn Blvd, Downs Barn, Milton Keynes, **Buckinghamshire**, MK14 7RP, ENG.
(T) 01908 695297
Speciality: Electrolysis.
T (Ref:HM10675)

**INSTITUTE OF PAST LIFE**

**Institute Of Past Life Therapies Research**, 95 Prospect Rd, Woodford Green, **Essex**, IG8 7ND, ENG.
(T) 020 8505 8720
Speciality: Hypnosis.
B (Ref:HM10676)

**INSTITUTE OF PHYSICAL THERAPY**

**Institute Of Physical Therapy**, 18 Priory Hall, Stillorgan, **County Dublin**, IRE.
(T) 01283 5566 (F) 01283 5756
(E) iptas@iol.ie
Speciality: Complementary Medicines & Therapy.
M (Ref:HM10677)

**INSTITUTE OF PSYCHOSOCIAL MED**

**Institute of Psychosocial Medicine**, 2 Eden Pk, Summerhill Rd, Dun Laoghaire, **County Dublin**, IRE.
(T) 01280 0084
Speciality: Acupuncture, Counselling, Faith Healing, Massage (Therapeutic), Nutritional Therapy, Psychotherapy, Spiritual Healing, Christian Counselling, Herbal Detox, Psychology, Psychiatry. The institute offers these services of multiple alternative health practitioners, all work independently. ✔
● **Clinical Psychologist** Ms R Yoder Q: BA, MA, MSc. M: PSI.
B (Ref:HM10678)

**INSTITUTE OF PSYCHOTHERAPY**

**Institute of Psychotherapy**, 93 Alleyn Park, London, **London (Greater)**, SE21 8AA, ENG.
(T) 020 7284 4762
Speciality: Psychotherapy.
● **Psychotherapist** Mr D Grey
B (Ref:HM10679)

**INSTITUTE OF PSYCHOTHERAPY**

**Institute Of Psychotherapy & Social Studies**, West Hill House, 6 Swains Lane, London, **London (Greater)**, N6 6QS, ENG.
(T) 020 8314 1686
Speciality: Psychotherapy.
● **Administrator** Mr K Rose
B (Ref:HM10680)

**INSTITUTE OF TEAM PSYCHOLOGY**

**Institute Of Team Psychology**, 8 Willow Rd, London, **London (Greater)**, NW3 1TJ, ENG.
(T) 020 7794 8717
Speciality: Psychology.
● **Owner** Mr S Meyerson
B (Ref:HM10681)

**INSTITUTE-COSMIC/PSYCH STUDIES**

**Institute Of Cosmic & Psychic Studies (The)**, 10 Cleveland Way, London, **London (Greater)**, E1 4TR, ENG.
(T) 020 7790 2424 (F) 020 7790 2616
Speciality: Clairvoyants & Palmists.
B (Ref:HM10682)

**INT COLLEGE OF CRYSTAL HEALING**

**International College Of Crystal Healing**



Key continued: **Yrs.Est:** Years Established **Q:** Qualifications **M:** Professional Membership ✔ Indemnity Insurance ▬ Accept Credit Cards

**(The)**, 46 Lower Green Rd, Esher, **Surrey**, KT10 8HD, **ENG**.
**(T)** 020 8398 7252
**Speciality:** Complementary Medicines & Therapy.
**M** (**Ref:**HM10683)

### INT COLLEGE OF CRYSTAL HEALING
**International College Of Crystal Healing (The)**, P.O. Box 738, Canterbury, **Kent**, CT2 9GA, **ENG**.
**(T)** 01227 472435
**(W)** www.crystaltherapy.co.uk
**Speciality:** Crystal Healing.
**B** (**Ref:**HM10684)

### INT FEDERATION OF NEUROTHERAPY
**International Federation of Neurotherapy**, P.O Box 30419, London, **London (Greater)**, NW6 1GA, **ENG**.
**(T)** 07092 270519
**Speciality:** Ayurvedic Medicine, Neurotherapy.
**M** (**Ref:**HM10685)

### INT FLOWER ESSENCE REPERTOIRE
**International Flower Essence Repertoire**, The Living Tree, Milland, Liphook, **Hampshire**, GU30 7JS, **ENG**.
**(T)** 01428 741572 **(F)** 01428 741679
**Speciality:** Complementary Medicines & Therapy.
● **Managing Director** Mr D Dennis
**C** **M** (**Ref:**HM10686)

### INT INSTITUTE OF REFLEXOLOGY
**International Institute Of Reflexology (The)**, Hill House, 255 Turleigh, Bradford-on-Avon, **Wiltshire**, BA15 2HG, **ENG**.
**(T)** 01225 865899 **(F)** 01225 865899
**Speciality:** Reflexology.
● **Director** Mrs H Edwards
**S** **T** (**Ref:**HM10687)

### INT SOCIETY-AROMATHERAPY
**International Society of Professional Aromatherapy (The)**, 82 Ashby Rd, Hinckley, **Leicestershire**, LE10 1SN, **ENG**.
**(T)** 01455 637987 **(F)** 01455 890956
**Speciality:** Aromatherapy.
**M** **O** (**Ref:**HM10688)

### INTAHEALTH UK
**Crediton Complementary Health Centre**, 100 High St, Crediton, **Devon**, EX17 3LF, **ENG**.
**(T)** 01363 774175
**Speciality:** Holistic Healing, Homeopathy, Miasm Therapy, Nutritional Therapy, Vitamin Therapy, Electro Dermol Screening (Vega Testing).
● **Homeopath** Mr P Deem M: BANT, HMA.
**M** **Yrs. Est.:** 2 (**Ref:**HM10689)

### INTEGRAL HEALTH
**Integral Health**, 3a Oriental Rd, Woking, **Surrey**, GU22 7AH, **ENG**.
**(T)** 01483 726644 **(F)** 01483 764499
**(W)** www.integralhealth.org
**Speciality:** Acupuncture, Biomagnetic Therapy, Kinesiology, Nutritional Therapy, Functional Medicine, Emotional Therapy, Allergies and Toxicity. ✔
● **Functional Medicine Practitioner**
Mr S Shohet **Q:** Lic.Ac, MBAcC. **M:** GDS, ICAK, RCS (Eng).
**B** **C** **H** **M** **O** **P** **S** **T**
**Yrs. Est.:** 8 (**Ref:**HM10690)

### INTEGRATIVE COLLEGE
**Integrative College Of Holistic Medicine**, 14a Bar St, Scarborough, **Yorkshire (North)**, YO11 2HT, **ENG**.
**(T)** 01723 370478
**Speciality:** Complementary Medicines & Therapy.
● **Professor** Sir S Russell
**C** **M** (**Ref:**HM10691)

### INTEGRATIVE PSYCHOSYNTHESIS
**Integrative Psychosynthesis**, 1 Fairfax Rd, Teddington, **London (Greater)**, TW11 9DJ, **ENG**.
**(T)** 020 8943 3163
**Speciality:** Psychotherapy.
● **Owner** Mrs A Barfred-Dixon
**B** (**Ref:**HM10692)

### INTERNATIONAL COLLEGE
**International College Of Electric Therapies Ltd**, 808A High Rd, London, **London (Greater)**, N12 9QU, **ENG**.
**(T)** 020 8446 2210 **(F)** 020 8446 2210
**Speciality:** Hypnosis.
● **Owner** Mr G Philips
**B** (**Ref:**HM10693)

### INTERNATIONAL FED OF AROMA
**International Federation of Aromatherapists**, 4 Eastmearn Rd, West Deilwich, London, **London (Greater)**, SE21 8HA, **ENG**.
**(T)** 020 8874 22605
**Speciality:** Aromatherapy.
● **Therapist** Helena Trump
**M** **O** (**Ref:**HM10694)

### INTERNATIONAL FED OF REFLEX
**International Federation Of Reflexologists**, 76-78 Edridge Rd, Croydon, **Surrey**, CR0 1EF, **ENG**.
**(T)** 020 8667 9458 **(F)** 020 8649 9291
**Speciality:** Reflexology.
● **Owner** Mr D Tanner
**M** (**Ref:**HM10695)

### INTERNATIONAL INSTIT-REFLEX
**International Institute Of Reflexology**, 12 Elder Avenue, London, **London (Greater)**, N8 9TH, **ENG**.
**(T)** 020 8342 8208
**Speciality:** Reflexology.
● **Owner** Mr N Bunker
**S** **T** (**Ref:**HM10696)

### INTERNATIONAL MEDITATION CTRE
**International Meditation Centre**, Splatts House, Heddington, Calne, **Wiltshire**, SN11 0PE, **ENG**.
**(T)** 01380 850238 **(F)** 01380 850833
**Speciality:** Relaxation Technique.
● **Manager** Mr E Kilma
**H** **T** (**Ref:**HM10697)

### INTERNATIONAL PSYCHOLOGY SVS
**International Psychology Services**, 17 High St, Hurstpierpoint, Hassocks, **Sussex (West)**, BN6 9TT, **ENG**.
**(T)** 01273 835533 **(F)** 01273 833250
**Speciality:** Psychology.
● **Owner** Mr R Lion
**B** (**Ref:**HM10698)

### IN-THERAPY
**In-Therapy**, 13 Greenhill, Wembley, **London (Greater)**, HA9 9HS, **ENG**.
**(T)** 020 8904 3448
**Speciality:** Hypnosis.
**B** (**Ref:**HM10699)

### INTL INS OF REFLEX-WESTERN
**International Institute Of Reflexology (UK) Western**, 32 Priory Rd, Portbury, Bristol, BS20 7TH, **ENG**.
**(T)** 01275 373359
**Speciality:** Reflexology.
**S** **T** (**Ref:**HM10700)

### INTL PSYCHOANALYTICAL ASS
**International Psychoanalytical Association**, Broomhills, Woodside Lane, London, **London (Greater)**, N12 8UD, **ENG**.
**(T)** 020 8446 8324
**Speciality:** Psychoanalysis.
**B** (**Ref:**HM10701)

### INTRA
**Intra (Lifestyles)**, Laggaturrin Station Rd, Balla, **County Mayo**, **IRE**.
**(T)** 08728 28683
**Speciality:** Complementary Medicines & Therapy.
**M** (**Ref:**HM10702)

### INTUITION PSYCHIC CENTRE
**Intuition Psychic Centre**, 66 High St, Barkingside, Ilford, **Essex**, IG6 2DJ, **ENG**.
**(T)** 020 8551 9298
**Speciality:** Complementary Medicines & Therapy.
**C** **M** (**Ref:**HM10703)

### INVERCLYDE OSTEOPATHIC CLINIC
**Inverclyde Osteopathic Clinic**, 13 Union St, Greenock, **Inverclyde**, PA16 8JL, **SCO**.
**(T)** 01475 888132
**Speciality:** Acupuncture, Aromatherapy, Cranial Osteopathy, Homeopathy, Hypnotherapy, Indian Head Massage, Manipulation, Massage (Therapeutic), Osteopathy, Reflexology. ✔
● **Homeopath** Ms P Campbell
**(T)** 01294 822323 **Q:** Dip.Hom, MA.
● **Holistic Therapist**
Ms G Charleston
**(T)** 01475 716818 **Q:** MICHT. **M:** FHT.
● **Owner** Mr J Cleat **Q:** BSc (Hons), DO. **M:** GOsC.
● **Medical Practitioner/Acupuncturist/Hypnotherapist**
Dr M Robinson
**(T)** 01475 637968 **Q:** MB. **M:** BMAS.
**S** **Yrs. Est.:** 12 (**Ref:**HM10704)

### INVERNEILL HEALTH & SKIN CARE
**Inverneill Health & Skin Care**, Inverneil House, Inverneil, Ardrishaig, Lochgilphead, **Argyll and Bute**, PA30 8ES, **SCO**.
**(T)** 01546 603473
**Speciality:** Complementary Medicines & Therapy.
**C** **M** (**Ref:**HM10705)

### INVESTIGATIVE SCIENCE
**Investigative Science**, Wych End, The Spinney, Ford Lane, East Hendred, Wantage, **Oxfordshire**, OX12 8LS, **ENG**.
**(T)** 01235 833162
**Speciality:** Psychology.
● **Partner** Dr E Shepherd
**B** (**Ref:**HM10706)

### INWARD BOUND THERAPIES
**Inward Bound Therapies**, 10 Beaudesert, Leighton Buzzard, **Bedfordshire**, LU7 1HZ, **ENG**.
**(T)** 01525 851961
**Speciality:** Counselling, Hypnotherapy, Psychotherapy, Stress Therapy. ✔
● **Hypnotherapist** Mrs M Wilkinson **Q:** MABCH, MCAH, UKRC. **M:** BACP.
**B** **Yrs. Est.:** 12 (**Ref:**HM10707)

### IOKAI CENTRE FOR COMP MEDICINE
**Iokai Centre For Complementary Medicine**, 122 Boutport St, Barnstaple, **Devon**, EX31 1TD, **ENG**.
**(T)** 01271 371215
**Speciality:** Complementary Medicines & Therapy.
● **Owner** Mr S Firth
**M** (**Ref:**HM10708)

### IOKAI SHIATSU CLINIC
**Iokai Shiatsu Clinic**, 16 Watersmeet Rd, Lynmouth, **Devon**, EX35 6EP, **ENG**.
**(T)** 01598 752497
**Speciality:** Chinese Herbal Medicine, Shiatsu.
**M** (**Ref:**HM10709)

### IONS, ROBERT
**Robert Ions**, 28 Pashley Rd, Eastbourne, **Sussex (East)**, BN20 8DY, **ENG**.
**(T)** 01323 410050
**Speciality:** Chiropractic.
**P** **S** **T** (**Ref:**HM10710)

### IPHOFEN, R
**R Iphofen**, 64 High St, Porthmadog, **Gwynedd**, LL49 9LW, **WAL**.
**(T)** 01766 514680
**Speciality:** Hypnotherapy.
● **Partner** Ms S Foskett
**B** (**Ref:**HM10711)

### IPHOFEN, RON (DR)
**Ron Iphofen**, 9 Queens Pl, Chester, **Cheshire**, CH1 3LN, **ENG**.
**(T)** 01244 400771
**(E)** ron@iphofen.freeserve.co.uk
**Speciality:** Hypnosis, Hypnotherapy. ✔
● **Clinical Hypnotherapist**
Dr R Iphofen **Q:** B.Phil, BA, Dip.Clin.Hyp, MSc, PhD. **M:** BSCH.
**B** **Yrs. Est.:** 3 (**Ref:**HM10712)



Key: **B** Mind-Body Medicine **C** Complementary Medicine **H** Self Help Treatment **M** Medicinal Therapy **O** Oriental Medicine **P** Postural Therapy **S** Manipulative Structural Therapy **T** Touch Therapy

### IPRS
**IPRS**, 79 Dales Rd, Ipswich, **Suffolk**, IP1 4JR, ENG.
(T) 01473 463300 (F) 01473 463090
Speciality: Physiotherapy.
● **Managing Director** Mr D Eingham
P S T (Ref:HM10713)

### IPSWICH CHIROPRACTIC CLINIC
**Ipswich Chiropractic Clinic**, 338 Norwich Rd, Ipswich, **Suffolk**, IP1 4HD, ENG.
(T) 01473 463344
(E) jhawes@tesco.net
Speciality: Acupressure, Acupuncture, Aromatherapy, Biofeedback, Chiropractic, Complementary Therapy, Dietician, Holistic Healing, Hopi Ear Candles, Indian Head Massage, Manipulation, Massage (Therapeutic), Nutritional Therapy, Reflexology, Shiatsu, X-Ray, Non Invasive Acupuncture (Electro Acuscope). ✔
● **Chiropractor** Dr K Correll Q: DC. M: BCA, GCC.
● **Complementary Therapist** Ms J Hawes
(T) 01473 463344or01206394500 M: ITEC.
● **Acupuncturist/Nutritional Advisor** Ms M Patterson
● **Chiropractor** Dr J Wilhelm
(T) 01394 672019 Q: DC. M: BCA, GCC.
S Yrs. Est.: 22 (Ref:HM10714)

### IPSWICH PHYSIOTHERAPY PRACTICE
**Ipswich Physiotherapy Practice**, 82 Berners St, Ipswich, **Suffolk**, IP1 3LU, ENG.
(T) 01473 257555 (F) 01473 251313
Speciality: Acupuncture, Orthodontist, Physiotherapy and Gynaecology. ✔
● **Owner** Mr B Williams
● **Physiotherapist** Mr D Fraser Q: MCSP, SRP. M: CSP.
● **Physiotherapist** Ms G Yusaf Q: MCSP, SRP. M: CSP.
● **Physiotherapist** Ms C Wart Q: BSc, MCSP, SRP. M: CSP.
S (Ref:HM10715)

### IPSWICH PSYCHOTHERAPY/COUNS
**Ipswich Psychotherapy & Counselling Centre**, 10 St. Margarets St, Ipswich, **Suffolk**, IP4 2AT, ENG.
(T) 01473 216559
Speciality: Psychotherapy.
B (Ref:HM10716)

### IQBAL, Z
**Z Iqbal**, 76 Abington Avenue, Northampton, **Northamptonshire**, NN1 4PA, ENG.
(T) 01604 634903
Speciality: Chiropractic.
P S T (Ref:HM10717)

### IRELAND, MARIKA
**Marika Ireland**, 21 Etloe Rd, Bristol, BS6 7NZ, ENG.
(T) 01179 737588
Speciality: Chiropodists (Podiatrists).
S (Ref:HM10718)

### IRELAND, R B
**R B Ireland**, 39 Wilhelmina Avenue, Coulsdon, **London (Greater)**, CR5 1NL, ENG.
(T) 01737 557019
Speciality: Chiropodists (Podiatrists).
● **Owner** Mr R Ireland
S (Ref:HM10719)

### IRENE BAYLISS MCTIMONEY CHIRO
**Irene Bayliss McTimoney Chriopractor**, Simmonds, Fairford Rd, Lechlade, **Gloucestershire**, GL7 3AH, ENG.
(T) 01367 253304
Speciality: Chiropractic.
P S T (Ref:HM10720)

### IRIDOLOGY & HOLISTIC HLTH CLGE
**Iridology & Holistic Health College**, Grosvenor Lodge, 94 Grosvenor Rd, London, **London (Greater)**, SW1V 3LF, ENG.
(T) 020 7834 3579 (F) 020 7834 3579
Speciality: Herbal Medicine, Iridology, Naturopathy.
● **Partner** Mrs A Bradbury
M (Ref:HM10721)

### IRIDOLOGY & NATURAL HEALTH
**Iridology & Natural Health**, 62 New Rd, London, **London (Greater)**, SE2 0QG, ENG.
(T) 020 8311 1582
Speciality: Complementary Medicines & Therapy.
● **Owner** Ms A Holding
C M (Ref:HM10722)

### IRIDOLOGY/NUTRITIONAL THER
**Iridology/Nutritional Therapist**, Norwegian Wood, Berry Pomeroy, Totnes, **Devon**, TQ9 6LE, ENG.
(T) 01803 867462 (F) 01803 867462
(W) www.kevala.com
Speciality: Iridology, Nutritional Therapy. ✔
● **Therapist** Ms H Nicholson Q: DHD, Mir. M: BANT.
B Yrs. Est.: 12 (Ref:HM10723)

### IRIS RESEARCH & NUTRITION CTRE
**Iris Research & Nutrition Centre**, 62 Fairfield Rd, East Grinstead, **Sussex (West)**, RH19 4HB, ENG.
(T) 01342 325258
Speciality: Complementary Medicines & Therapy.
C M (Ref:HM10724)

### IRIS VON SASS-HYDE ART THRPY
**Iris Von Sass-Hyde Art Therapist**, Lindisfarne, Burton, Lincoln, **Lincolnshire**, LN1 2RD, ENG.
(T) 01522 538181
Speciality: Psychotherapy.
B (Ref:HM10725)

### IRISH ASS OF HYPNO-ANALYSTS
**Irish Association of Hypno-Analysts**, Therapy Hse, 6 Tuckey St, Cork, **County Cork**, IRE.
(T) 021 4275 785
(E) hypnosis@iol.ie
(W) www.hypnosiseire.com
Speciality: Hypnotherapy.
B (Ref:HM10726)

### IRISH ASS OF HYPNOTHERAPISTS
**Irish Association of Hypnotherapists**, 38 Park View Castleknock, IRE.
(T) 01821 2897
(W) www.hypnosiseire.com
Speciality: Hypnotherapy.
B (Ref:HM10727)

### IRISH CLGE OF TRAD CHINESE MED
**Irish College Of Traditional Chinese Medicine**, 100 Marlborough Rd, IRE.
(T) 01496 3857
Speciality: Complementary Medicines & Therapy.
M (Ref:HM10728)

### IRISH COLLEGE OF COMP MEDICINE
**Irish College Of Complementary Medicine**, 6 Main St, Donnybrook, **County Dublin**, IRE.
(T) 01269 6588
Speciality: Complementary Medicines & Therapy.
M (Ref:HM10729)

### IRISH COLLEGE-OSTEOPATHY
**Irish College Of Classical Osteopathy**, Coach House, 33 Terenure Rd, Dublin, **County Dublin**, IRE.
(T) 01490 4423
Speciality: Osteopathy.
P S T (Ref:HM10730)

### IRISH ESSENTIAL OIL
**Irish Essential Oil Co**, 43 The Green, Bray, **County Wicklow**, IRE.
(T) 01282 5583
Speciality: Complementary Medicines & Therapy.
M (Ref:HM10731)

### IRISH INS-COUNS & HYP
**Irish Institute of Counselling & Hypnotherapy**, 118 Stillorgan Rd, Dublin, **County Dublin**, IRE.
(T) 01260 0118
Speciality: Hypnotherapy.
B (Ref:HM10732)

### IRISH INSTIT-INTEGRATED PSYCHO
**Irish Institute For Integrated Psychotherapy**, 26 Longford Tce, Monkstown, **County Cork**, IRE.
(T) 01280 9313
Speciality: Psychotherapy.
B (Ref:HM10733)

### IRISH INSTIT-INTEGRATED PSYCHO
**Irish Institute For Integrated Psychotherapy**, 26 Longford Tce, Monkstown, **County Dublin**, IRE.
(T) 01280 9313
Speciality: Psychotherapy.
B (Ref:HM10734)

### IRISH PSYCHO-ANALYTICAL
**Irish Psycho-Analytical**, Grosvenor Sq, IRE.
(T) 01496 7288
Speciality: Psychoanalysis.
B (Ref:HM10735)

### IRISH SCHOOL OF FENG SHUI
**Feng Shui Irish School Of**, Milltownpark, Ranelagh, **County Dublin**, IRE.
(T) 01492 1534
(E) fengshui@ireland.com
Speciality: Complementary Medicines & Therapy.
M (Ref:HM10736)

### IRISH SCHOOL OF SHIATSU
**Irish School Of Shiatsu**, 22 Vernon Dr, Clontarf, **County Dublin**, IRE.
(T) 01833 7735
(E) shiatsu@eircom.net
Speciality: Complementary Medicines & Therapy.
M (Ref:HM10737)

### IRISH SCHOOL OF SHIATSU
**Shiatsu-Irish School Of**, 22 Vernon Dr, Clontarf, **County Dublin**, IRE.
(T) 01833 7735
(E) shiatsu@eircom.net
Speciality: Complementary Medicines & Therapy.
M (Ref:HM10738)

### IRISH SPIRITUAL HEALING CENTRE
**Irish Spiritual Healing Centre**, 30 Wicklow St, Dublin, **County Dublin**, IRE.
(T) 01671 5106
(W) www.irish-spiritual-centre.org
Speciality: Healing.
B (Ref:HM10739)

### IRNHAM LODGE COMP HEALTH CTRE
**Irnham Lodge Complementary Health Centre**, Townsend Rd, Minehead, **Somerset**, TA24 5RG, ENG.
(T) 01643 705020 (F) 01643 707921
Speciality: Complementary Medicines & Therapy.
● **Practice Manager** Mrs K Atkins
C M (Ref:HM10740)

### IRONS, FREDA
**Freda Irons**, 62 Wellingborough Rd, Northampton, **Northamptonshire**, NN1 4DN, ENG.
(T) 01604 639336
Speciality: Electrolysis.
● **Owner** Mrs F Irons
T (Ref:HM10741)

### IRONSIDE, YOLANDA
**Yolanda Ironside**, 31 Orchard Cres, Horsmonden, Tonbridge, **Kent**, TN12 8LG, ENG.
(T) 01892 723016
Speciality: Reflexology.
S T (Ref:HM10742)

### IRVINE, ALAN
**Alan Irvine**, 101 Lound Side, Chapeltown, Sheffield, **Yorkshire (South)**, S35 2US, ENG.
(T) 01142 468708
Speciality: Acupuncture.
● **Owner** Mr A Irvine
O (Ref:HM10743)

### IRVINE, MAURICE J
**Maurice J Irvine**, 9 St James St, Paisley, **Renfrewshire**, PA3 2HL, SCO.



Key continued: Yrs.Est: Years Established Q: Qualifications M: Professional Membership ✔ Indemnity Insurance Accept Credit Cards

(T) 01418 896550
Speciality: Chiropodists (Podiatrists).
S (Ref:HM10744)

## IRVINE, PHILLIPA

**Phillipa Irvine**, 41 Church Rd, Poole, **Dorset**, BH14 0NN, ENG.
(T) 01202 749514 (F) 01202 718906
Speciality: Physiotherapy.
● **Partner** Mrs C Swinhoe
P S T (Ref:HM10745)

## IRVING, GORDON R

**Gordon R Irving**, Cedar House, 4 Conway Rd, Bromsgrove, **Worcestershire**, B60 2AD, ENG.
(T) 01527 872291
Speciality: Osteopathy.
P S T (Ref:HM10746)

## IRVING, GORDON R

**Gordon R Irving**, 149 Ipsley St, Redditch, **Worcestershire**, B98 7AA, ENG.
(T) 01527 62221
Speciality: Osteopathy.
● **Owner** Mr G Irving
P S T (Ref:HM10747)

## IRVING, MARY

**Mary Irving**, 36 Gallows Hill Lane, Abbots Langley, **Hertfordshire**, WD5 0DA, ENG.
(T) 01923 263686
Speciality: Alexander Technique.
P S (Ref:HM10748)

## IRVING, MAUREEN V

**Maureen V Irving**, 1 Elm Avenue, Lenzie, Kirkintilloch, Glasgow, **Glasgow (City of)**, G66 4HJ, SCO.
(T) 01415 781598
Speciality: Hypnotherapy.
B (Ref:HM10749)

## IRWIN, A C

**A C Irwin**, 14-16 Swan St, West Malling, **Kent**, ME19 6LP, ENG.
(T) 01732 848460
Speciality: Chiropodists (Podiatrists).
● **Owner** Mr A Irwin
S (Ref:HM10750)

## IRWIN, CARL (DR)

**Dr Carl Irwin**, 174 Deans Lane, Edgware, **London (Greater)**, HA8 9NT, ENG.
(T) 020 8906 3323
Speciality: Chiropractors.
P S T (Ref:HM10751)

## IRWIN, MARY

**Irwin Mary Dip Aromatherapy/Reflexology**, 26 Lr, Salthill, **County Galway**, IRE.
(T) 09152 6880
Speciality: Aromatherapy, Reflexology.
M (Ref:HM10752)

## IRWIN, NICKY

**Nicky Irwin**, Natural Path Health Centre, 3 Holyrood St, Chard, **Somerset**, TA20 2AH, ENG.
(T) 01460 62953 (F) 01460 63809
Speciality: Reflexology.
● **Owner** Mr M Newbound
S T (Ref:HM10753)

## IRWIN, VICKY

**Vicky Irwin**, Care Of The Maple Clinic, 3-5 Horndean Rd, Bracknell, **Berkshire**, RG12 0XQ, ENG.
(T) 01344 862646
Speciality: Acupuncture.
● **Owner** Dr W Baker
O (Ref:HM10754)

## ISAAC, EVELYN

**Evelyn Isaac**, 32 South St, Bridport, **Dorset**, DT6 3NQ, ENG.
(T) 01308 427777 (F) 01308 427777
Speciality: Complementary Medicines & Therapy.
● **Practice Manager** Mrs S Marsh
M (Ref:HM10755)

## ISAAC, SUE

**Sue Isaac**, Park Hill Drive, Leicester, **Leicestershire**, LE2 8HR, ENG.
(T) 01162 838510
Speciality: Alexander Technique.
● **Owner** Ms S Isaac
P S (Ref:HM10756)

## ISAAC, TONI

**Toni Isaac**, 115A Lapwing Lane, Manchester, **Manchester (Greater)**, M20 6UR, ENG.
(T) 01619 736357
Speciality: Hypnosis.
● **Owner** Miss T Isaac
B (Ref:HM10757)

## ISABELLE DAVIDSON REFLEXOLOGY

**Isabelle Davidson Reflexology**, 10 Braemar Court, Glenco Rd, Bushey, Watford, **Hertfordshire**, WD2 3DT, ENG.
(T) 020 8950 0769
Speciality: Complementary Medicines & Therapy.
M (Ref:HM10758)

## ISHERWOOD, NIGEL

**Nigel Isherwood DHP MIAH**, Abbey Therapy Centre, River St, Bolton, **Lancashire**, BL2 1BX, ENG.
(T) 01204 524185
Speciality: Hypnosis.
B (Ref:HM10759)

## ISHERWOOD, SIMON

**Simon Isherwood**, Wesley Cottage, Chapel Lane, Maidford, Towcester, **Northamptonshire**, NN12 8HU, ENG.
(T) 01327 860495
Speciality: Chiropodists (Podiatrists).
● **Owner** Mr S Isherwood
S (Ref:HM10760)

## ISHTA CENTRE

**Ishta Centre (The)**, Ishta Centre, 26 Kings Avenue, Stone, **Staffordshire**, ST15 8HD, ENG.
(T) 01785 616010 (F) 01785 616010
(E) sue@ishta.co.uk
Speciality: Acupuncture, Aromatherapy, Bowen Therapy, Chiropractic, Counselling, Cranio-Sacral Therapy, Homeopathy, Kinesiology, Manipulation, Massage (Therapeutic), Meditation, Micro Manipulation, Moxibustion, Nutritional Therapy, Pilates, Reflexology, Reiki, Remedial Massage, Spiritual Healing, Vitamin Therapy, Pilates, Ishta Spinal Touch, McTimoney Chiropractic, Allergy Testing and Touch For Health. ✔
● **Practice Manager** Ms A Edwards
● **Reflexologist/Aromatherapist** Ms J Lanes Q: MBRA. M: BRA, BRCP.
● **Practice Manager** Ms S Weller
C S T Yrs. Est.: 5 (Ref:HM10761)

## ISIS

**ISIS**, 112a High St, Hythe, **Kent**, CT21 5LE, ENG.
(T) 01303 239580
Speciality: Clairvoyants & Palmists.
● **Owner** Ms S Aynsley
B (Ref:HM10762)

## ISIS

**ISIS**, 20 Albion Rd, Broadstairs, **Kent**, CT10 1LU, ENG.
(T) 01843 866860
Speciality: Absent Healing, Aromatherapy, Aura Therapy, Ayurvedic Medicine, Bach Remedies, Colour Therapy, Counselling, Crystal Healing, Faith Healing, Floral Essence Therapy, Gem Essence Therapy, Healer, Healing Therapy, Herbal Medicine, Homeopathy, Hypnotherapy, Indian Head Massage, Iridology, Kinesiology, Life Style Coaching, Meditation, Naturopathy, Psychotherapy, Pyramid Power, Reflexology, Spiritual Healing, Stress Therapy, Ying & Yang, Yoga, Zen Therapy. ✔ CREDIT
● **Manager** Mabel Gull Q: SRN. M: RCN.
B Yrs. Est.: 7 (Ref:HM10763)

## ISIS AROMATHERAPY

**Isis Aromatherapy**, 26 The Boulevard, Metrocentre, Gateshead, **Tyne and Wear**, NE11 9YN, ENG.
(T) 01914 932772 (F) 01912 243676
Speciality: Aromatherapy.
● **Owner** Mrs M Scott
M O (Ref:HM10764)

## ISIS CENTRE

**Isis Centre**, 2nd Floor Tawvale, Barnstaple, **Devon**, EX32 8NJ, ENG.
(T) 01271 375300
Speciality: Complementary Medicines & Therapy.
C M (Ref:HM10765)

## ISIS CENTRE

**Isis Centre**, Dartington House, 55 Little Clarendon St, Oxford, **Oxfordshire**, OX1 2HS, ENG.
(T) 01865 556648 (F) 01865 514538
Speciality: Psychotherapy.
● **Manager** Mr P Roys
B (Ref:HM10766)

## ISIS HEALING CENTRE

**Isis Healing Centre**, 3 Dorset St, Brighton, **Sussex (East)**, BN2 1WA, ENG.
(T) 01273 626644
Speciality: Complementary Medicines & Therapy.
C M (Ref:HM10767)

## ISIS HOUSE THERAPY CENTRE

**Isis House Therapy Centre**, 1 Broomstick Hall Rd, Waltham Abbey, **Essex**, EN9 1LN, ENG.
(T) 01992 715525
Speciality: Magnetic Therapy, Reflexology, Reiki, Full Body Massage. ✔
● **Director/Teacher** Ms B Nowopolski
Q: City&Guilds (Reflex), Dip.Reflex. M: FHT, IFR, IHBC.
C Yrs. Est.: 2 (Ref:HM10768)

## ISIS NATURAL THERAPIES

**Isis Natural Therapies**, 24 High St, Hythe, Southampton, **Hampshire**, SO45 6AH, ENG.
(T) 023 8084 3200
Speciality: Complementary Medicines & Therapy.
C M (Ref:HM10769)

## ISLAND HEALTH CENTRE

**Island Health Centre (The)**, 145 East Ferry Rd, London, **London (Greater)**, E14 3BQ, ENG.
(T) 020 8505 5078 (F) 020 8281 7746
Speciality: Hypnosis.
● **Owner** Ms M Johnson
B (Ref:HM10770)

## ISLE OF WIGHT LAVENDER

**Isle Of Wight Lavender Ltd**, Staplehurst Grange, Long Lane, Newport, **Isle of Wight**, PO30 2NQ, ENG.
(T) 01983 825272 (F) 01983 825272
Speciality: Aromatherapy.
● **Director** Mr P Abbott
M O (Ref:HM10771)

## ISLEWORTH HERBAL & OSTEO CLNC

**Isleworth Herbal & Osteopathic Clinic**, 171 Linkfield Rd, Isleworth, **London (Greater)**, TW7 6QY, ENG.
(T) 020 8568 0305 (F) 020 8568 0305
Speciality: Complementary Medicines & Therapy.
● **Owner** Mrs J Rhodes
C M (Ref:HM10772)

## ISLINGTON CHIROPRACTIC CLINIC

**Islington Chiropractic Clinic**, 5-6 The Precinct, Packington Sq, London, **London (Greater)**, N1 7UP, ENG.
(T) 020 7354 8883 (F) 020 7354 9798
Speciality: Acupuncture, Chiropractic, Massage (Therapeutic).
● **Manager** Mrs C O'Neill
P S T (Ref:HM10773)

## ISLINGTON CTRE FOR HOMOEOPATHY

**Islington Centre For Homoeopathy**, 44 Ellington St, London, **London (Greater)**, N7 8PL, ENG.
(T) 020 7700 4234
Speciality: Homeopathy.
M (Ref:HM10774)

## ISLINGTON PSYCHOTHERAPY

**Islington Psychotherapy Practice**, 25 Corsica St, London, **London (Greater)**, N5 1JT, ENG.
(T) 020 7354 0217
Speciality: Hypnosis, Psychotherapy, Yoga.
● **Owner** Ms E Rea



Key: B Mind-Body Medicine C Complementary Medicine H Self Help Treatment M Medicinal Therapy O Oriental Medicine P Postural Therapy S Manipulative Structural Therapy T Touch Therapy

B (Ref:HM10775)

### ISOBEL, GEMMELL
**Gemmell Isobel**, 45 Irvine Rd, Kilmarnock, **Ayrshire (East)**, KA1 2JN, SCO.
(T) 01563 544251
Speciality: Complementary Medicines & Therapy.
C M (Ref:HM10776)

### ISWARIAH, ROHAN
**Rohan Iswariah**, 8 High St, Benson, Wallingford, **Oxfordshire**, OX10 6RP, ENG.
(T) 01491 838866
Speciality: Osteopathy.
P S T (Ref:HM10777)

### IVERSON, B
**B Iverson**, 55 Tweedy Rd, Bromley, **Kent**, BR1 3NH, ENG.
(T) 020 8313 1577
Speciality: Complementary Medicines & Therapy.
M (Ref:HM10778)

### IVES, DENNIS
**Dennis Ives**, 7 Salisbury Cres, Oxford, **Oxfordshire**, OX2 7TJ, ENG.
(T) 01865 510069
Speciality: Hypnosis.
● **Owner** Mr D Ives
B (Ref:HM10779)

### IVES, R
**R Ives**, 28 Athenlay Rd, London, **London (Greater)**, SE10 9JB, ENG.
(T) 020 8858 8557
Speciality: Osteopathy.
P S T (Ref:HM10780)

### IVES, R
**R Ives**, 174 Ifield Rd, London, **London (Greater)**, SW10 9AF, ENG.
(T) 020 7373 8575
Speciality: Osteopathy.
P S T (Ref:HM10781)

### IVESON
**Mr Iveson**, 1 High St, Newmarket, **Suffolk**, CB8 8LX, ENG.
(T) 01638 662475
Speciality: Chiropractic.
P S T (Ref:HM10782)

### IVILL, WENDY
**Wendy Ivill**, 5 Hermes Cl, Helston, **Cornwall**, TR13 8DA, ENG.
(T) 01326 561583 (F) 01326 561583
Speciality: Aromatherapy.
● **Owner** Mrs W Ivill
M O (Ref:HM10783)

### IVINS, V J
**V J Ivins**, 3 Gustavus Rd, Camborne, **Cornwall**, TR14 7LL, ENG.
(T) 01209 710370 (F) 01209 710370
Speciality: Physiotherapy.
● **Owner** Miss V Ivins
P S T (Ref:HM10784)

### IVORY, BRIAN S
**Brian S Ivory**, Castle Gayer, Leys Lane, Marazion, **Cornwall**, TR17 0AQ, ENG.
(T) 01736 711548 (F) 01736 711110
Speciality: Chiropodists (Podiatrists).
● **Partner** Mr J Trewhella
S (Ref:HM10785)

### IVY HOUSE CLINIC
**Ivy House Clinic (The)**, 41 Station Rd, Woburn Sands, Milton Keynes, **Buckinghamshire**, MK17 8RX, ENG.
(T) 01908 281608 (F) 01908 587258
Speciality: Complementary Medicines & Therapy.
● **Owner** Mrs J Stanley
M (Ref:HM10786)

### IVYBRIDGE CHIROPRACTIC CENTRE
**Ivybridge Chiropractic Centre (The)**, Moorhaven, Ivybridge, **Devon**, PL21 0EX, ENG.
(T) 01752 698063
Speciality: Chiropractic.
● **Manageress** Mrs F Verwey
P S T (Ref:HM10787)

### IYE
**Imrye**, 1 Aqua Trce, Newbiggin-by-the-Sea, **Northumberland**, NE64 6PB, ENG.
(T) 01670 856801
Speciality: Complementary Medicines & Therapy.
● **Owner** Mr N Imrye
C M (Ref:HM10788)

### IYENGAR YOGA INSTITUTE
**Iyengar Yoga Institute**, 223a Randolph Avenue, London, **London (Greater)**, W9 1NL, ENG.
(T) 020 7624 3080
Speciality: Relaxation Technique.
H T (Ref:HM10789)

### IZOD, M A
**M A Izod**, 80 Stortford Hall Park, Bishop's Stortford, **Hertfordshire**, CM23 5AN, ENG.
(T) 01279 651063
Speciality: Complementary Medicines & Therapy.
● **Owner** Mrs M Izod
C M (Ref:HM10790)

### IZZARD, SARA
**Sara Izzard**, The Natural Health Centre, 46 Park Pl, Leeds, **Yorkshire (West)**, LS1 2RY, ENG.
(T) 01132 436066
Speciality: Osteopathy.
● **Owner** Ms S Izzard
P S T (Ref:HM10791)

### J & J HARROP
**J & J Harrop**, 3 Sackville St, Bradford, **Yorkshire (West)**, BD1 2AJ, ENG.
(T) 01274 727949
Speciality: Chiropody. ✓
● **Chiropodist (Podiatrist)**
Mr J Harrop
● **Chiropodist (Podiatrist)**
Mrs J Harrop
M Yrs. Est.: 26 (Ref:HM10792)

### J BENSON CHIROPODIST
**Mrs J Benson Chiropodist**, 327 Holyhead Rd, Coventry, **Midlands (West)**, CV5 8JQ, ENG.
(T) 024 7659 3415
(E) jane.e.benson@btinternet.com
Speciality: Chiropody. ✓
● **Chiropodist** Mrs J Benson Q: MBChA, MSSCh. M: B.A.Ch.P, SMAE.
C Yrs. Est.: 15 (Ref:HM10793)

### J BIRD AUTOGENIC TRAINING
**J Bird Autogenic Training**, All Hallows House, Idol Lane, London, **London (Greater)**, EC3R 5DD, ENG.
(T) 020 7283 8908
Speciality: Complementary Medicines & Therapy.
M (Ref:HM10794)

### J C A PSYCHIC CENTRE
**J C A Psychic Centre**, 1a High St East, Wallsend, **Tyne and Wear**, NE28 8PA, ENG.
(T) 01912 955016
Speciality: Clairvoyants & Palmists.
● **Owner** Miss J Ness
B (Ref:HM10795)

### J H SPORTS INJURIES CLINIC
**J H Sports Injuries Clinic**, 7 Cambrian Drive, Yate, Bristol, BS37 5TR, ENG.
(T) 01454 322134
Speciality: Physiotherapy.
● **Owner** Mr J Higgs
P S T (Ref:HM10796)

### J H W PSYCHOLOGICAL SERVICES
**J H W Psychological Services**, 126 Whalley Rd, Accrington, **Lancashire**, BB5 1BS, ENG.
(T) 01254 395443
Speciality: Hypnosis.
B (Ref:HM10797)

### J J COUNSELLING SERVICES
**J J Counselling Services**, Acorn Cottage, Bigmore Lane, Eadmore End, High Wycombe, **Buckinghamshire**, HP14 3UR, ENG.
(T) 01494 882692 (F) 01494 882692
(E) counselling@jojackson.fsnet.co.uk
Speciality: Counselling, Family Therapy, Psychotherapy, Stress Therapy. ✓
● **Systemic Psychotherapist**
Ms J Jackson Q: MSc, S.C.M, SRN. M: AFT, UKCP.
C Yrs. Est.: 6 (Ref:HM10798)

### J J CREDLAND CHIROPODIST
**J J Credland Chiropodist**, 31 High St, Hatfield, Doncaster, **Yorkshire (South)**, DN7 6RS, ENG.
(T) 01302 351545
Speciality: Chiropodists (Podiatrists).
S (Ref:HM10799)

### J R G THERAPY SERVICES
**J R G Therapy Services**, 22 Woodhill Cr, Leeds, **Yorkshire (West)**, LS16 7BX, ENG.
(T) 01132 269084 (F) 01132 269084
Speciality: Complementary Medicines & Therapy.
● **Owner** Mrs J Gibson
M (Ref:HM10800)

### J SIMMONDS LIFESTYLE PRODUCTS
**Jenni Simmonds Lifestyle Products Ltd**, Priory Shopping Centre, Dartford, **Kent**, DA1 2HS, ENG.
(T) 01322 281292
Speciality: Aromatherapy.
M O (Ref:HM10801)

### J T SERVICES
**J T Services**, 16 Longpark Hill, Maidencombe, Torquay, **Devon**, TQ1 4TL, ENG.
(T) 01803 313386 (F) 01803 313376
(E) john.jtservices@virginnet
Speciality: Complementary Medicines & Therapy, Magno-Therapy.
● **Executive** Mr J Todd
C H Yrs. Est.: 4 (Ref:HM10802)

### J V ASSOCIATES
**J V Associates**, 43 Middlefield, Farnham, **Surrey**, GU9 8QA, ENG.
(T) 01252 710986
Speciality: Complementary Medicines & Therapy, Magno-Therapy.
● **Magnotherapist** Mr J Fitzpatrick
C Yrs. Est.: 3 (Ref:HM10803)

### J W PHYSIOTHERAPY & SPORTS
**J W Physiotherapy & Sports Injury Clinic**, 27 High St, South Queensferry, Edinburgh, **Edinburgh (City of)**, EH30 9PP, SCO.
(T) 01313 315802
(E) jwphysio@aol
Speciality: Acupuncture, Manipulation, Massage (Therapeutic), Podiatry, Ultrasonics. ✓
● **Owner** Ms J Winning Q: Grad Dip Phys, MCSP, SRP. M: CSP.
S Yrs. Est.: 4 (Ref:HM10804)

### J W PHYSIOTHERAPY & SPORTS
**J W Physiotherapy & Sports Injury Clinic**, Ladywell Medical Centre, Corstorphine, Edinburgh, **Edinburgh (City of)**, EH12 7TB, SCO.
(T) 01313 164816 (F) 01313 343602
(E) jwphysio@aol
Speciality: Acupuncture, Manipulation, Massage (Therapeutic), Podiatry, Ultrasonics, Strapping. ✓
● **Owner** Ms J Winning Q: Grad Dip Phys, MCSP, SRP. M: CSP.
S Yrs. Est.: 4 (Ref:HM10805)

### JABBAR, A
**A Jabbar**, 1 Palatine Rd, Southport, **Merseyside**, PR8 2BS, ENG.
(T) 01704 569145
Speciality: Osteopathy.
● **Owner** Mr A Jabbar
P S T (Ref:HM10806)

### JABBAR, ABDUL
**Abdul Jabbar**, 8 Sutton Rd, Kirk Sandall, Doncaster, **Yorkshire (South)**, DN3 1NY, ENG.
(T) 01302 884719
Speciality: Chiropodists (Podiatrists).
● **Owner** Mr A Jabbar
S (Ref:HM10807)

### JABROO, C
**C Jabroo**, Manchester House, Bridge St, Cardigan, **Carmarthenshire**, SA43 1HY, WAL.
(T) 01239 614102



Key continued: Yrs.Est: Years Established Q: Qualifications M: Professional Membership ✓ Indemnity Insurance Accept Credit Cards

Speciality: Herbal Medicine, Diagnosis and Treatment. ✔
● **Herbalist** Mr C Jaboo
M Yrs. Est.: 10 (Ref:HM10808)

**JABROO, C**

**C Jabroo**, Morfa Farm, Blaenffos, Boncath, **Pembrokeshire**, SA37 0HX, WAL.
(T) 01239 841462
Speciality: Herbal Medicine, Diagnosis and Treatment. ✔
● **Herbalist** Mrs C Jabroo
C Yrs. Est.: 10 (Ref:HM10809)

**JACALAN ESSENTIAL OILS**

**Jacalan Essential Oils Ltd**, The New Stables Bull Lane, Maldon, **Essex**, CM9 4QB, ENG.
(T) 01621 840491
Speciality: Aromatherapy.
● **Sole Director**
Jack Andrew Ransome
M O (Ref:HM10810)

**JACCQUELINE ELLISON PRACTICE**

**Jacqueline Ellison**, 81 Cedars Rd, Beckenham, **Kent**, BR3 4JQ, ENG.
(T) 020 8650 3831
Speciality: Cranial Osteopathy, Manipulation, Massage (Therapeutic), Osteopathy. ✔
● **Osteopath** Miss J Ellison Q: BSc (Hons). M: GOsC.
S Yrs. Est.: 2 (Ref:HM10811)

**JACK, R A F**

**R A F Jack**, Catshill Village Surgery, 36 Woodrow Lane, Catshill, Bromsgrove, **Worcestershire**, B61 0PU, ENG.
(T) 01527 877144
Speciality: Complementary Medicines & Therapy.
C M (Ref:HM10812)

**JACK, S A**

**S A Jack**, 4 Pensfield, Benson, Wallingford, **Oxfordshire**, OX10 6PD, ENG.
(T) 01491 834124 (F) 01491 834124
Speciality: Chiropodists (Podiatrists).
● **Owner** Mrs S Jack
S (Ref:HM10813)

**JACKAMAN, SUSAN**

**Susan Jackaman**, 37 Cedar Court, Grove Park Rd, Weston-Super-Mare, **Somerset**, BS23 2LB, ENG.
(T) 01934 645186
Speciality: Chiropodists (Podiatrists).
● **Owner** Mrs S Jackaman
S (Ref:HM10814)

**JACKMAN, K**

**K Jackman**, 21 Beach Rd, Severn Beach, Bristol, BS35 4PE, ENG.
(T) 01454 632735
Speciality: Chiropodists (Podiatrists).
● **Owner** Mrs K Jackman
S (Ref:HM10815)

**JACKSON & RUDLAND**

**Jackson & Rudland**, St. Marys House, 55-56 Cheap St, Newbury, **Berkshire**, RG14 5DH, ENG.
(T) 01635 30252
Speciality: Chiropodists (Podiatrists).
S (Ref:HM10816)

**JACKSON, A E**

**A E Jackson**, 4 Lansdowne Sq, Weymouth, **Dorset**, DT4 9QT, ENG.
(T) 01305 784986
Speciality: Acupuncture, Allergy Testing, Clinical Ecology, Counselling, Homeopathy, Iridology, Osteopathy, Reflexology. ✔
● **Holistic Therapist**
Mrs A Langstone Wring Q: ITEC, MRxS.
P Yrs. Est.: 25 (Ref:HM10817)

**JACKSON, ALISON**

**Alison Jackson**, Cushag, Brasswell, Dumfries, **Dumfries and Galloway**, DG1 3JY, SCO.
(T) 01387 252142
Speciality: Chiropodists (Podiatrists).
● **Owner** Mrs A Jackson
S (Ref:HM10818)

**JACKSON, ALISON**

**Alison Jackson**, Braemar Rd, Brentford, **London (Greater)**, TW8 0NR, ENG.
(T) 020 8400 1951
Speciality: Acupuncture.
O (Ref:HM10819)

**JACKSON, ALISON**

**Alison Jackson**, 71 Greenway Cl, London, **London (Greater)**, N11 3NT, ENG.
(T) 020 8361 2940
Speciality: Reflexology.
S T (Ref:HM10820)

**JACKSON, AMANDA**

**Amanda Jackson**, 40 Sandringham Way, Market Harborough, **Leicestershire**, LE16 8EP, ENG.
(T) 01858 410552
Speciality: Homeopathy.
● **Owner** Mrs A Jackson
M (Ref:HM10821)

**JACKSON, ANDREA**

**Andrea Jackson**, 1 New Cottages, Castle Lane, Exmouth, **Devon**, EX8 2RG, ENG.
(T) 01395 270303
Speciality: Osteopathy.
P S T (Ref:HM10822)

**JACKSON, ANDREA**

**Andrea Jackson**, 1 Hylton Surgery, Seafield Lane, Sidmouth, **Devon**, EX10 8HF, ENG.
(T) 01395 577473 (F) 01395 577473
Speciality: Osteopathy.
● **Partner** Mrs A Jackson
P S T (Ref:HM10823)

**JACKSON, ANDREW**

**Andrew Jackson**, Blackberry Orthopaedic Clinic, Blackberry Court, Walnut Tree, Milton Keynes, **Buckinghamshire**, MK7 7PB, ENG.
(T) 01908 604666
Speciality: Osteopathy.
P S T (Ref:HM10824)

**JACKSON, ANDREW**

**Andrew Jackson**, 37 Coley Avenue, Reading, **Berkshire**, RG1 6LL, ENG.
(T) 01189 572882
Speciality: Osteopathy.
● **Owner** Mr A Jackson
P S T (Ref:HM10825)

**JACKSON, ANGELA**

**Angela Jackson**, 4 George St, Alderley Edge, **Cheshire**, SK9 7EJ, ENG.
(T) 01625 590444
Speciality: Physiotherapy.
P S T (Ref:HM10826)

**JACKSON, APRIL H A**

**April H A Jackson**, 46 Grosvenor Pl, Newcastle Upon Tyne, **Tyne and Wear**, NE2 2RE, ENG.
(T) 01912 818225
Speciality: Homeopathy.
M (Ref:HM10827)

**JACKSON, B**

**B Jackson**, 96 Harrington Rd, Workington, **Cumbria**, CA14 2UW, ENG.
(T) 01900 603034
Speciality: Osteopathy.
● **Owner** Mr B Jackson
P S T (Ref:HM10828)

**JACKSON, B**

**B Jackson**, 215 Kingsway, Dunmurry, Belfast, **County Antrim**, BT17 9SB, NIR.
(T) 028 9030 1202
Speciality: Osteopathy.
P S T (Ref:HM10829)

**JACKSON, BARBARA**

**Barbara Jackson**, 7 Purkiss Rd, Hertford, **Hertfordshire**, SG13 8JA, ENG.
(T) 01992 422207
Speciality: Counselling, Solution Focus Therapy. ✔
● **Counsellor** Mrs B Jackson Q: MA. M: BACP.
C Yrs. Est.: 17 (Ref:HM10830)

**JACKSON, CELIA**

**Celia Jackson**, 25 Upton Rd, Bexleyheath, **Kent**, DA6 8LH, ENG.
(T) 020 8301 0972
Speciality: Hypnosis.
● **Owner** Ms C Jackson
B (Ref:HM10831)

**JACKSON, CYRIL**

**Cyril Jackson**, 208 Westborough Rd, Westcliff-on-Sea, **Essex**, SS0 9PR, ENG.
(T) 01702 353006
Speciality: Hypnosis, Hypnotherapy. ✔
● **Owner** Mr C Jackson Q: DCH, Dip.StM, NLP. M: NCH.
B Yrs. Est.: 3 (Ref:HM10832)

**JACKSON, D M**

**D M Jackson**, 80 Vicarage Drive, Kendal, **Cumbria**, LA9 5BA, ENG.
(T) 01539 740452
Speciality: Osteopathy.
● **Owner** Mrs D Jackson
P S T (Ref:HM10833)

**JACKSON, D M**

**D M Jackson**, 114 Windermere Rd, Kendal, **Cumbria**, LA9 5EZ, ENG.
(T) 01539 740452
Speciality: Osteopathy.
P S T (Ref:HM10834)

**JACKSON, DEREK**

**Derek Jackson**, 14 Gresham Gardens, Woodthorpe, Nottingham, **Nottinghamshire**, NG5 4LU, ENG.
(T) 01159 263797
Speciality: Hypnosis.
● **Owner** Mr D Jackson
B (Ref:HM10835)

**JACKSON, F N**

**F N Jackson**, 19 Priory Rd, High Wycombe, **Buckinghamshire**, HP13 6SL, ENG.
(T) 01494 438554
Speciality: Physiotherapy.
P S T (Ref:HM10836)

**JACKSON, FRANCISCA-IRENE**

**Francisca-Irene Jackson**, Flat 7, 5 Lambolle Rd, London, **London (Greater)**, NW3 4HS, ENG.
(T) 020 7431 5790
Speciality: Reflexology.
S T (Ref:HM10837)

**JACKSON, G P**

**G P Jackson**, 7 Stanhope Trce, Bideford, **Devon**, EX39 3JZ, ENG.
(T) 01237 472271
Speciality: Chiropodists (Podiatrists).
S (Ref:HM10838)

**JACKSON, J**

**J Jackson**, 16 King St, Richmond, **Surrey**, TW9 1ND, ENG.
(T) 020 8332 1132
Speciality: Physiotherapy.
P S T (Ref:HM10839)

**JACKSON, J**

**Mrs J Jackson**, 9 Beech Gr, Gosport, **Hampshire**, PO12 2EJ, ENG.
(T) 023 9251 0824
Speciality: Chiropody.
● **Owner** Mrs J Jackson
S (Ref:HM10840)

**JACKSON, J M M**

**J M M Jackson**, 1 Spring Drive, Balderton, Newark, **Nottinghamshire**, NG24 3JS, ENG.
(T) 01636 677844
Speciality: Chiropodists (Podiatrists).
● **Owner** Mrs J Jackson
S (Ref:HM10841)

**JACKSON, J W**

**Mr J W Jackson**, 47 Maxwood Rd, Galston, **Ayrshire (East)**, KA4 8JN, SCO.
(T) 01563 821102
Speciality: Chiropodists (Podiatrists).
S (Ref:HM10842)

**JACKSON, JANICE**

**Janice Jackson**, 78 Countisbury Avenue, Enfield, **London (Greater)**, EN1 2NN, ENG.
(T) 020 8360 7686
Speciality: Chiropodists (Podiatrists).
S (Ref:HM10843)



Key: B Mind-Body Medicine C Complementary Medicine H Self Help Treatment M Medicinal Therapy O Oriental Medicine P Postural Therapy S Manipulative Structural Therapy T Touch Therapy

### JACKSON, M W
**M W Jackson**, 4 Swiss Heights, Stourport-on-Severn, **Worcestershire**, DY13 0LJ, ENG.
(T) 01299 878661
Speciality: Chiropodists (Podiatrists).
● **Owner** Mr M Jackson
S (Ref:HM10844)

### JACKSON, MICHAEL
**Michael Jackson**, 36 Eclipse Rd, Alcester, **Warwickshire**, B49 5EH, ENG.
(T) 01789 764084
Speciality: Hypnosis.
● **Sole Director**
Michael William Jackson
B (Ref:HM10845)

### JACKSON, NIGEL
**Nigel Jackson**, Arena Leisure Centre, Grand Avenue, Camberley, **Surrey**, GU15 3QH, ENG.
(T) 01276 25752
Speciality: Chiropodists (Podiatrists).
● **Manager** Mr K Ryan
S (Ref:HM10846)

### JACKSON, P G
**P G Jackson**, 1 Chaseville Prde, Chaseville Park Rd, London, **London (Greater)**, N21 1PG, ENG.
(T) 020 8360 6658
Speciality: Chiropodists (Podiatrists).
S (Ref:HM10847)

### JACKSON, R M & P M
**R M & P M Jackson**, 15 Yarm Rd, Stockton-On-Tees, **Cleveland**, TS18 3NJ, ENG.
(T) 01642 678196
Speciality: Chiropodists (Podiatrists).
S (Ref:HM10848)

### JACKSON, ROBIN
**Robin Jackson**, Roseneath Dental Surgery, Mount Ararat Rd, Richmond, **Surrey**, TW10 6PA, ENG.
(T) 020 8948 0371
Speciality: Osteopathy.
● **Osteopath** Robin Jackson Q: DO.
P S T (Ref:HM10849)

### JACKSON, ROGER D
**Roger D Jackson**, 5 Parkinson Lane, Halifax, **Yorkshire (West)**, HX1 3XA, ENG.
(T) 01422 364070
Speciality: Electrotherapy, Manipulation, Massage (Therapeutic), Osteopathy, Physiotherapy. ✔
● **Osteopath** Mr R Jackson Q: DO. M: BOA.
S Yrs. Est.: 16 (Ref:HM10850)

### JACKSON, RYAN
**Ryan Jackson**, Blackberry Orthopaedic Clinic, Blackberry Court, Walnut Tree, Milton Keynes, **Buckinghamshire**, MK7 7PB, ENG.
(T) 01908 604666
Speciality: Physiotherapy.
P S T (Ref:HM10851)

### JACKSON, W D & SONS
**W D Jackson & Sons**, 34 Printing Office St, Doncaster, **Yorkshire (South)**, DN1 1TR, ENG.
(T) 01302 323508
Speciality: Herbal Medicine.
● **Owner** Mr J Shepherd
M (Ref:HM10852)

### JACKSON-BASS, ALISON
**Alison Jackson-Bass**, 1 King St, Bakewell, **Derbyshire**, DE45 1DZ, ENG.
(T) 01298 812669
Speciality: Acupuncture.
● **Owner** Ms A Jackson-Bass
O (Ref:HM10853)

### JACKSONS
**Jacksons**, 118 St. Pauls Rd, Wallasey, **Merseyside**, CH44 7AW, ENG.
(T) 01512 010920 (F) 01516 910994
Speciality: Hypnosis, Hypnotherapy, Phytotherapy, Medical Herbalist. ✔
● **Owner/Chemist** Mr B Jackson
B Yrs. Est.: 15 (Ref:HM10854)

### JACKYS ALTERNATIVE THERAPIES
**Jackys Alternative Therapies**, Old Court Studio, Upper Bray Rd, Bray, Maidenhead, **Berkshire**, SL6 2DB, ENG.
(T) 01628 784914
Speciality: Complementary Medicines & Therapy.
C M (Ref:HM10855)

### JACOB, SIMON
**Simon Jacob**, 101 Elstree Rd, Hemel Hempstead, **Hertfordshire**, HP2 7QN, ENG.
(T) 07970 920240
Speciality: Psychotherapy.
● **Owner** Mr S Jacob
B (Ref:HM10856)

### JACOBS, B L
**B L Jacobs**, The Radlett Practice, 107 Watling St, Radlett, **Hertfordshire**, WD7 7NG, ENG.
(T) 01923 855884
Speciality: Osteopathy.
P S T (Ref:HM10857)

### JACOBS, BRIAN M
**Brian M Jacobs**, 5 Great Bushey Drive, London, **London (Greater)**, N20 8QN, ENG.
(T) 020 8446 8061
Speciality: Hypnotherapy. ✔
● **Hypnotherapist** Mr B Jacobs Q: UKRAH. M: GHR, NRAH.
B (Ref:HM10858)

### JACOBS, F (DR)
**Dr F Jacobs**, 110a Northgate St, Bury St. Edmunds, **Suffolk**, IP33 1HP, ENG.
(T) 01284 702155 (F) 01284 702155
Speciality: Chiropractic.
● **Practice Manager** Mrs M Stevenson
P S T (Ref:HM10859)

### JACOBS, FREDERICK
**Frederick Jacobs**, 6 Lessingham Avenue, Ilford, **Essex**, IG5 0BJ, ENG.
(T) 020 8550 2844
Speciality: Chiropodists (Podiatrists).
● **Partner** Mr F Jacobs
S (Ref:HM10860)

### JACOBS, K A
**K A Jacobs**, 12 Toley Avenue, Wembley, **London (Greater)**, HA9 9TB, ENG.
(T) 020 8904 3739
Speciality: Chiropodists (Podiatrists).
S (Ref:HM10861)

### JACOBS, MARION
**Marion Jacobs**, 30 Kensington Drive, Bury, **Lancashire**, BL8 2DE, ENG.
(T) 01617 970945 (F) 01617 970945
Speciality: Reflexology.
● **Owner** Mr C Jacobs
S T (Ref:HM10862)

### JACQUELINE
**Jacqueline**, 17 Empress Avenue, Farnborough, **Hampshire**, GU14 8LU, ENG.
(T) 01252 521931
Speciality: Clairvoyants & Palmists.
● **Owner** Mrs J Cook
B (Ref:HM10863)

### JACQUES, I M
**I M Jacques**, 38 Green Park, Bath, **Somerset**, BA1 1HZ, ENG.
(T) 01225 424784
Speciality: Chiropodists (Podiatrists).
● **Owner** Mrs I Jacques
S (Ref:HM10864)

### JACQUI
**Jacqui**, 20 Bridge Rd, Crosby, Liverpool, **Merseyside**, L23 6SG, ENG.
(T) 01519 320844
Speciality: Clairvoyants & Palmists.
● **Owner** Ms J Williams
B (Ref:HM10865)

### JACQUI BATES COUNSELLING
**Jacqui Bates Counselling**, 10 Greenhill Drive, Barwell, Leicester, **Leicestershire**, LE9 8BW, ENG.
(T) 01455 843440
Speciality: Counselling, Hypnosis, Hypnotherapy. ✔
● **Counsellor/Hypnotherapist**
Mrs J Bates M: HS.
B Yrs. Est.: 7 (Ref:HM10866)

### JADE COLLEGE-NATURAL THERAPY
**Jade College Of Natural Therapy**, 12 Jenkyn Rd, Wootton, Bedford, **Bedfordshire**, MK43 9HE, ENG.
(T) 01234 767619 (F) 01234 766528
(E) avil@jadecollege.demom.co.uk
Speciality: Aromatherapy, Indian Head Massage, Nutritional Therapy, Physiotherapy, Reflexology, Sports Massage, Sports Therapy.
● **Princpal of the College**
Ms Hamilton M: ITEC.
● **Principal** Mrs A McOnnell
C Yrs. Est.: 12 (Ref:HM10867)

### JADE HEALTH & BEAUTY
**Jade Health & Beauty**, 36 Barnstaple Rd, Southend-On-Sea, **Essex**, SS1 3PA, ENG.
(T) 01702 582131
Speciality: Electrolysis.
● **Owner** Mrs J Jane
T (Ref:HM10868)

### JAFARI, CAROLINE
**Caroline Jafari**, 155 London Rd, Hazel Gr, Stockport, **Cheshire**, SK7 4HH, ENG.
(T) 01614 561689
Speciality: Chiropodists (Podiatrists).
S (Ref:HM10869)

### JAFFEY, JOEL
**Joel Jaffey**, 12 High St, Oakington, Cambridge, **Cambridgeshire**, CB4 5AG, ENG.
(T) 01223 237459 (F) 01223 237459
Speciality: Homeopathy.
● **Partner** Mr G Giddings
M (Ref:HM10870)

### JAG, SONEJI
**Soneji Jag**, 54 Sheepcote Rd, Harrow, **London (Greater)**, HA1 2JF, ENG.
(T) 020 8427 1149
Speciality: Homeopathy.
M (Ref:HM10871)

### JAGER THERAPY CENTRE
**Jager Therapy Centre**, 1 Osborne Rd, Newcastle Upon Tyne, **Tyne and Wear**, NE2 2AA, ENG.
(T) 01912 091336
Speciality: Hypnosis.
● **Owner** Mr M Thomson
B (Ref:HM10872)

### JAGER, KURT W
**Kurt W Jager**, 1-2a Clay Hill House, Weyhill, Haslemere, **Surrey**, GU27 1DA, ENG.
(T) 01428 651067 (F) 01428 653001
Speciality: Osteopathy.
● **Owner** Mr K Jager
P S T (Ref:HM10873)

### JAGO, W (DR)
**Dr W Jago**, 11 West Hill St, Brighton, **Sussex (East)**, BN1 3RR, ENG.
(T) 01273 326134
Speciality: Hypnotherapy.
B (Ref:HM10874)

### JAKINGS, S
**S Jakings**, Pengelstein, Robbs Chase, Outwell, Wisbech, **Cambridgeshire**, PE14 8TD, ENG.
(T) 01945 772130
Speciality: Chiropodists (Podiatrists).
S (Ref:HM10875)

### JAKUBOWSKI & AST
**Dr Antony Jakubowski & Associates**, Gonstead Clinic Uk, 22 Harley St, London, **London (Greater)**, W1N 1AP, ENG.
(T) 020 7637 2920
Speciality: Chiropractic.
P S T (Ref:HM10876)

### JAKUBOWSKI, ANNE
**Anne Jakubowski Consultant Clinical Hypnotherapist**, Holmed Clinic, 665 Burnage Lane, Manchester, **Manchester (Greater)**, M19 1RR, ENG.
(T) 01614 421296
Speciality: Hypnotherapy.
● **Owner** Mrs A Jacubowski
B (Ref:HM10877)


Key continued: Yrs.Est: Years Established Q: Qualifications M: Professional Membership ✔ Indemnity Insurance Accept Credit Cards

## JAMES OF ROTHERHITHE
**James Of Rotherhithe**, 182-184 Lower Rd, London, **London (Greater)**, SE16 2UN, ENG.
(T) 020 7237 1896 (F) 020 7231 3520
Speciality: Chiropodists (Podiatrists).
● **Owner** Mr I Schlazer
S (Ref:HM10878)

## JAMES STREET CLINIC
**James Street Clinic**, 49 James St, Louth, **Lincolnshire**, LN11 0JW, ENG.
(T) 01507 610007
Speciality: Chiropractors.
● **Owner** Dr M Broe
P S T (Ref:HM10879)

## JAMES, ANN
**Ann James Chiropody/Podiatry Practice**, 270 Heath Rd, Higher Bebington, Wirral, **Merseyside**, CH63 2HQ, ENG.
(T) 01516 080927 (F) 01516 080927
(E) ann.james@ic24.net
Speciality: Aromatherapy, Biomechanics, Complementary Therapy, Massage (Therapeutic), Nail Surgery, Orthotics, Ultrasonics, Sports Therapies, Cryotherapy, Essential Oil Therapies, Dermatoligical Assessments, Foot Prosthetics, Diabetic Assessments and Management. Overpronation (Rollingin), Supination (Rollingout) Feet. ✔
● **Podiatrist** Ms A James Q: BSc, DPodM, M.S.C.P, S.R.Ch. M: S.C.P.
● **Podiatrist** Mr K Price Q: BSc, M.S.C.P, S.R.Ch. M: S.C.P.
C Yrs. Est.: 8 (Ref:HM10880)

## JAMES, CHRIS
**James Chris**, 8 Woodstock Drive, Hasland, Chesterfield, **Derbyshire**, S41 0EU, ENG.
(T) 01246 230998
Speciality: Chiropodists (Podiatrists).
● **Owner** Miss C James
S (Ref:HM10881)

## JAMES, CHRISTINE
**Christine James**, St. Albans, **Hertfordshire**, AL3, ENG.
(T) 01582 842178
Speciality: Aromatherapy.
M O (Ref:HM10882)

## JAMES, DANIEL D
**Daniel D James**, 26 St Johns Trce, Aberdeen, **Aberdeenshire**, AB15 7PH, SCO.
(T) 01224 317531
Speciality: Hypnosis.
● **Owner** Mr J Daniel
B (Ref:HM10883)

## JAMES, DEE
**Dee James**, Gentleman Farm, Bardfield Saling, **Essex**, CM7 5ED, ENG.
(T) 01378 50414
Speciality: Complementary Medicines & Therapy.
● **Owner** D James
M (Ref:HM10884)

## JAMES, DIANNE
**Dianne James**, Cheltenham, **Gloucestershire**, GL53, ENG.
(T) 01242 512385
Speciality: Bach Remedies.
M (Ref:HM10885)

## JAMES, HELEN
**Helen James**, Elton Holme, Bottom St, Northend, Southam, **Warwickshire**, CV47 2TH, ENG.
(T) 01295 770369
Speciality: Chiropractic.
● **Owner** Mrs H James
P S T (Ref:HM10886)

## JAMES, JAMESON
**Jameson James ADHP MICHP**, Bray, **County Wicklow**, IRE.
(T) 08628 35758
(W) www.hypnosiseire.com
Speciality: Complementary Medicines & Therapy.
M (Ref:HM10887)

## JAMES, JAMESON
**Jameson James MIAH ADHP**, Holistic Health Clinic, Bray, **County Wicklow**, IRE.
(T) 08628 35758
Speciality: Complementary Medicines & Therapy.
M (Ref:HM10888)

## JAMES, KEITH
**Keith James**, Bristol Lawn Tennis Club, Redland Green, Bristol, BS6 7HF, ENG.
(T) 01179 741444
Speciality: Physiotherapy.
P S T (Ref:HM10889)

## JAMES, LINDA
**Linda James**, 94 Riverside Rd, Gorleston, Great Yarmouth, **Norfolk**, NR31 6PX, ENG.
(T) 01493 442236
Speciality: Aromatherapy. ✔
● **Owner/Aromatherapist** Mrs L James
Q: Dip.Arom.
C Yrs. Est.: 7 (Ref:HM10890)

## JAMES, M
**M James Ltd**, 14 Cedars Rd, London, **London (Greater)**, SW4 0QB, ENG.
(T) 020 7787 9898 (F) 07970 762373
Speciality: Complementary Medicines & Therapy.
● **Owner** Mr J Murphy
M (Ref:HM10891)

## JAMES, MALCOLM
**Malcolm James**, Newbridge House, 117 Lynn Rd, Snettisham, King's Lynn, **Norfolk**, PE31 7QG, ENG.
(T) 01485 541210
Speciality: Osteopathy.
P S T (Ref:HM10892)

## JAMES, MALCOLM (DR)
**Dr Malcolm James**, 6a Jubilee Court, Hunstanton Rd, Dersingham, King's Lynn, **Norfolk**, PE31 6HH, ENG.
(T) 01485 541210 (F) 01485 541210
Speciality: Osteopathy.
● **Doctor** Dr M James
P S T (Ref:HM10893)

## JAMES, MAURICE
**Maurice James**, 116 - 118 Elderfield Rd, London, **London (Greater)**, E5 0LE, ENG.
(T) 020 8533 7918
Speciality: Reflexology.
S T (Ref:HM10894)

## JAMES, OLIVER
**Oliver James**, Grosvenor Avenue, London, **London (Greater)**, N5 2NL, ENG.
(T) 020 7690 4278
Speciality: Complementary Medicines & Therapy.
● **Owner** Mr O James
M (Ref:HM10895)

## JAMES, PETER
**Peter James**, 86 Happaway Rd, Torquay, **Devon**, TQ2 8EU, ENG.
(T) 01803 311305
Speciality: Hypnotherapy.
B (Ref:HM10896)

## JAMES, R
**R James**, All Hallows House, Idol Lane, London, **London (Greater)**, EC3R 5DD, ENG.
(T) 020 7283 8908
Speciality: Complementary Medicines & Therapy.
M (Ref:HM10897)

## JAMES, RONAN
**Ronan James**, 52A Main St, Swords, **County Dublin**, IRE.
(T) 01840 4161 (F) 01840 9130
Speciality: Complementary Medicines & Therapy.
M (Ref:HM10898)

## JAMES, RUTH
**Ruth James**, 91 Greenlaw Cres, Glenrothes, **Fife**, KY6 1JG, SCO.
(T) 01592 612738
Speciality: Chiropodists (Podiatrists).
● **Owner** Mrs R James
S (Ref:HM10899)

## JAMES, STEPHANIE
**Stephanie James**, Stable Court, Huddersfield Rd, Holmfirth, Huddersfield, **Yorkshire (West)**, HD7 1AZ, ENG.
(T) 01484 689808
Speciality: Chiropodists (Podiatrists).
● **Owner** Miss S James
S (Ref:HM10900)

## JAMES, SUSAN
**Susan James**, 22 Tall Pines, Stafford, **Staffordshire**, ST17 4QF, ENG.
(T) 01785 614771
Speciality: Clairvoyants & Palmists.
B (Ref:HM10901)

## JAMES, SUSAN
**Susan James**, 16 Haddon Court, Shakespeare Rd, Harpenden, **Hertfordshire**, AL5 5NB, ENG.
(T) 01582 763374
Speciality: Alexander Technique.
P S (Ref:HM10902)

## JAMESON PERSONAL EXCELLENCE
**Jameson Personal Excellence**, 11 Rose Hill, Wicklow, **County Wicklow**, IRE.
(T) 04046 6749 (F) 04046 6749
(E) jameson@oceanfree.net
(W) www.jamesonpersonalexcellence.com
Speciality: Absent Healing, Auto Suggestion, Aversion Therapy, Cognitive Therapy, Complementary Therapy, Counselling, Gestalt Therapy, Healer, Healing Therapy, Humanistic Psychology, Hypnosis, Hypnotherapy, Psychotherapy, Reiki, Seichem, Spiritual Healing, Stress Therapy, Touch Therapy, Visualisation Therapy.
● **Owner** Mr J Jameson Q: MICHP, NLP. M: ICHP.
B Yrs. Est.: 3 (Ref:HM10903)

## JAMESON, BARBARA
**Barbara Jameson**, 640 Bramford Rd, Ipswich, **Suffolk**, IP1 5BQ, ENG.
(T) 01473 745646
Speciality: Acupuncture.
● **Owner** Mrs B Jameson
O (Ref:HM10904)

## JAMESON, JAMES
**Jameson James**, 11 Rose Hill, **County Wicklow**, IRE.
(T) 04046 6749
Speciality: Complementary Medicines & Therapy.
M (Ref:HM10905)

## JAMIESON, ANGELA C
**Angela C Jamieson**, 12 Charters Court, Dalbeattie, **Dumfries and Galloway**, DG5 4DD, SCO.
(T) 01556 611315
Speciality: Chiropodists (Podiatrists).
S (Ref:HM10906)

## JAMIESON, M
**M Jamieson**, 10 Ropery St, London, **London (Greater)**, E3 4QF, ENG.
(T) 020 8983 0103
Speciality: Complementary Medicines & Therapy.
● **Owner** Ms M Jamieson
C M (Ref:HM10907)

## JAMIESON, TOM
**Tom Jamieson**, 109 Ennerdale Rd, Newcastle Upon Tyne, **Tyne and Wear**, NE6 4DL, ENG.
(T) 01912 620774
Speciality: Homeopathy.
M (Ref:HM10908)

## JAMIL, M T (DR)
**Dr M T Jamil**, 29A Broadway, Maidenhead, **Berkshire**, SL6 1LY, ENG.
(T) 01628 771766 (F) 01628 771766
Speciality: Acupuncture.
● **Manager** Mr J Coffey
O (Ref:HM10909)

## JAMOOJI, MEHRU
**Mehru Jamooji**, Brabant House, Portsmouth Rd, Thames Ditton, **Surrey**, KT7 0EY, ENG.



Key: B Mind-Body Medicine C Complementary Medicine H Self Help Treatment M Medicinal Therapy O Oriental Medicine P Postural Therapy S Manipulative Structural Therapy T Touch Therapy

(T) 020 8398 7592
Speciality: Reflexology.
S T (Ref:HM10910)

### JAMSHID, ZADEH HASHEMI
**Zadeh Hashemi Jamshid**, 23 Whitethorn Pk, Letterkenny, **County Donegal**, IRE.
(T) 07427 164
Speciality: Complementary Medicines & Therapy.
M (Ref:HM10911)

### JAN DE VRIES HEALTH CARE
**Jan De Vries Health Care**, 20 Wellington Sq, Ayr, **Ayrshire (South)**, KA7 1EZ, SCO.
(T) 01292 886650
Speciality: Complementary Medicines & Therapy.
● **Director** Mrs A Laurie
C M (Ref:HM10912)

### JAN LLOYD AROMATHERAPY
**Jan Lloyd Aromatherapy**, 2 Hunt Cl, Hampton Magna, Warwick, **Warwickshire**, CV35 8SW, ENG.
(T) 01926 498949
Speciality: Aromatherapy, Massage (Therapeutic), Meditation, Reiki. ✔
● **Owner/Clinical Aromatherapist/Reiki Master**
Mrs J Lloyd Q: BEd (Hons). M: IFA.
B Yrs. Est.: 2 (Ref:HM10913)

### JANE ANNE'S ELECTROLYSIS
**Jane Anne's Electrolysis & Beauty Clinic**, 29 High St, Kington, **Herefordshire**, HR5 3BJ, ENG.
(T) 01544 230551
Speciality: Electrolysis.
● **Owner** Mrs J Rogers
T (Ref:HM10914)

### JANE EVEREST SHIATSU PRACT
**Jane Everest Shiatsu Practitioner**, 20A Central Avenue, West Bridgeford, West Bridgford, Nottingham, **Nottinghamshire**, NG2 5GR, ENG.
(T) 01159 143311
Speciality: Complementary Medicines & Therapy.
M (Ref:HM10915)

### JANE HAMMOND THERAPY
**Jane Hammond Therapy**, 6 Norbury St, Northwich, **Cheshire**, CW9 7AL, ENG.
(T) 01606 44577
(E) info@janehammondtherapy.co.uk
(W) www.janehammondtherapy.co.uk
Speciality: Cognitive Therapy, Counselling, Psychotherapy, Rogerian Therapy, Transactional Analysis. ✔
● **Psychotherapist** Ms J Hammond M: EATA, ITA.
B Yrs. Est.: 7 (Ref:HM10916)

### JANE HYDE CHRTRD PHYSIO
**Mrs Jane Hyde Chartered Physiotherapist**, Down Farm, Lamerton, Tavistock, **Devon**, PL19 8QA, ENG.
(T) 01822 613838 (F) 01822 616122
Speciality: Manipulation, Phytotherapy, Pilates, Ultrasonics. ✔
● **Physiotherapist** Mrs J Hyde Q: Grad Dip Phys. M: CSP.
H P S Yrs. Est.: 11 (Ref:HM10917)

### JANE'S, BEVERLEY
**Beverley Jane's**, 38 Blakenall Lane, Walsall, **Midlands (West)**, WS3 1HG, ENG.
(T) 01922 475111
Speciality: Chiropodists (Podiatrists).
S (Ref:HM10918)

### JANES, G
**G Janes**, 4 Chelsea Gdns, Stockton-On-Tees, **Cleveland**, TS20 1RZ, ENG.
(T) 01642 879545
Speciality: Reflexology.
● **Owner** Mrs G Janes
S T (Ref:HM10919)

### JANET MARTIN BEAUTY SPECIALIST
**Janet Martin Beauty Specialist**, 69 Castle St, Cambridge, **Cambridgeshire**, CB3 0AH, ENG.
(T) 01223 353340
Speciality: Electrolysis.
T (Ref:HM10920)

### JANOWSKI, ANNE
**Anne Janowski**, 3 Laburnum Cl, Cambridge, **Cambridgeshire**, CB4 1BB, ENG.
(T) 01223 564681
Speciality: Chiropodists (Podiatrists).
S (Ref:HM10921)

### JANQUILLITY
**Janquillity**, 25-27 Cranleigh Court Rd, Yate, Bristol, BS37 5DQ, ENG.
(T) 01454 321757
Speciality: Aromatherapy.
● **Owner** Mrs J Richards
M O (Ref:HM10922)

### JANSEN, W
**W Jansen**, Dunsthorpe House, 33 St Dunstans St, Canterbury, **Kent**, CT2 8BZ, ENG.
(T) 01227 768886 (F) 01227 768896
Speciality: Osteopathy.
● **Owner** Mr W Jansen
P S T (Ref:HM10923)

### JANSEN, W
**W Jansen**, 42 South Eastern Rd, Ramsgate, **Kent**, CT11 9QF, ENG.
(T) 01843 585477
Speciality: Osteopathy.
● **Partner** Mr W Jansen
P S T (Ref:HM10924)

### JAPAN NATURAL
**Japan Natural Ltd**, 59 Brewer St, London, **London (Greater)**, W1R 3FB, ENG.
(T) 020 7287 1499 (F) 020 7287 3466
Speciality: Complementary Medicines & Therapy.
● **Managing Director** Mr T Yashida
M (Ref:HM10925)

### JAQUELINE MASSAGE
**Jaqueline Massage**, 25a Connaught St, London, **London (Greater)**, W2 2AY, ENG.
(T) 020 7402 7949
Speciality: Complementary Medicines & Therapy.
C M (Ref:HM10926)

### JARMAN, C
**C Jarman**, 8 Elgin St, Preston, **Lancashire**, PR1 6BH, ENG.
(T) 01772 823749
Speciality: Reflexology.
● **Owner** Mrs C Jarman
S T (Ref:HM10927)

### JARMAN, JANET
**Janet Jarman**, 8 Rothschild Rd, Wing, Leighton Buzzard, **Bedfordshire**, LU7 0NL, ENG.
(T) 01296 688114
Speciality: Reflexology.
S T (Ref:HM10928)

### JARMAN, RON
**Ron Jarman**, 12 St Albans Drive, Sheffield, **Yorkshire (South)**, S10 4DL, ENG.
(T) 01142 306878
Speciality: Reflexology.
● **Owner** Mr R Jarman
S T (Ref:HM10929)

### JARRETT, EMMA
**Emma Jarrett**, Flat 3, 22 Victoria Sq, Bristol, BS8 4ES, ENG.
(T) 01179 741216
Speciality: Alexander Technique.
P S (Ref:HM10930)

### JARROLD, RICHARD
**Richard Jarrold**, 13 Northweald Lane, Kingston Upon Thames, **Surrey**, KT2 5GL, ENG.
(T) 020 8404 0673
Speciality: Complementary Medicines & Therapy.
● **Owner** Mr R Jarrold
C M (Ref:HM10931)

### JARVIS, DIANE
**Diane Jarvis**, 66 Barbara Avenue, Leicester Forest East, Leicester, **Leicestershire**, LE3 3HD, ENG.
(T) 01162 339133 (F) 01162 339133
Speciality: Aromatherapy.
● **Owner** Ms D Jarvis
M O (Ref:HM10932)

### JARVIS, JUNE
**June Jarvis**, 54 The Avenue, Yeovil, **Somerset**, BA21 4BN, ENG.
(T) 01935 422488
Speciality: Relaxation Technique.
H T (Ref:HM10933)

### JARVIS, K R
**K R Jarvis**, 30 Old Chester Rd, Bebington, Wirral, **Merseyside**, CH63 7LQ, ENG.
(T) 01516 454495
Speciality: Biomechanics, Chiropody, Cryo Surgery, Orthotics, Podiatry. ✔
● **Chiropodist (Podiatrist)**
Mr K Jarvis
M Yrs. Est.: 40 (Ref:HM10934)

### JARVIS, MAGGIE
**Maggie Jarvis**, 14A New Rd, Marlow, **Buckinghamshire**, SL7 3NG, ENG.
(T) 01628 473309
Speciality: Chiropodists (Podiatrists).
● **Owner** Mrs M Jarvis
S (Ref:HM10935)

### JARVIS, PETER
**Peter Jarvis**, 63 Collingwood Rd, Witham, **Essex**, CM8 2EE, ENG.
(T) 01376 512188 (F) 01376 510256
Speciality: Osteopathy.
● **Owner** Mr P Jarvis
P S T (Ref:HM10936)

### JASMINE HOLISTIC HEALTH
**Jasmine Holistic Health & Beauty Therapy**, 61 Old Fosse Rd, Bath, **Somerset**, BA2 2SP, ENG.
(T) 01225 830436
Speciality: Aromatherapy, Indian Head Massage, Reflexology.
S T (Ref:HM10937)

### JASMINE ROOM
**Jasmine Room**, 43 West Portland St, Troon, **Ayrshire (South)**, KA10 6AB, SCO.
(T) 01292 310606
Speciality: Reflexology.
● **Owner** Miss L Jamieson
S T (Ref:HM10938)

### JAVIAD, M A
**M A Javiad**, 28 Avenue Rd, Doncaster, **Yorkshire (South)**, DN2 4AQ, ENG.
(T) 01302 321816 (F) 01302 342731
Speciality: Physiotherapy.
● **Owner** Mr M Javiad
P S T (Ref:HM10939)

### JAY, D
**D Jay Ltd**, 113 Pope St, Birmingham, **Midlands (West)**, B1 3AG, ENG.
(T) 01212 362073 (F) 01212 334516
Speciality: Complementary Medicines & Therapy.
● **Joint Director** Mr D Jehan
● **Joint Director**
Dominique Elaine Jehan
● **Owner** Mr D Jay
C Yrs. Est.: 20 (Ref:HM10940)

### JAY, TIMOTHY C
**Timothy C Jay**, 6 Woodstock Rd, Taunton, **Somerset**, TA1 1EJ, ENG.
(T) 01823 333973 (F) 01823 335169
Speciality: Chiropractic.
● **Senior Partner** Mr T Jay
P S T (Ref:HM10941)

### JAYASINGHE, MIGEL
**Migel Jayasinghe**, 1 Waddon Cl, Croydon, **Surrey**, CR0 4JT, ENG.
(T) 020 8688 9010
Speciality: Psychology.
● **Owner** Mr M Jayasinghe
B (Ref:HM10942)

### JAYAWARDENA, A A
**A A Jayawardena**, 9 Stockbridge Gardens, Chichester, **Sussex (West)**, PO19 2RL, ENG.
(T) 01243 771720
Speciality: Chiropodists (Podiatrists).



Key continued: **Yrs.Est:** Years Established **Q:** Qualifications **M:** Professional Membership ✔ Indemnity Insurance Accept Credit Cards

● **Owner** Mr A Jayawardena
S (Ref:HM10943)

## JAYCOCK, SUE
**Sue Jaycock**, 14 Brookside, Woodford Halse, Daventry, **Northamptonshire**, NN11 3RU, ENG.
(T) 01327 261347
Speciality: Complementary Medicines & Therapy.
● **Owner** S Jaycock
M (Ref:HM10944)

## JAYES, CERI
**Ceri Jayes**, 187 Halstead Rd, Mountsorrel, Loughborough, **Leicestershire**, LE12 7HE, ENG.
(T) 01162 374566
Speciality: Reflexology.
S T (Ref:HM10945)

## JAYNE & PAYNE
**Jayne & Payne**, 98 Kiln Rd, Benfleet, **Essex**, SS7 1TE, ENG.
(T) 01268 793854
Speciality: Physiotherapy.
● **Partner** Mr M Payne
P S T (Ref:HM10946)

## JDS
**JDs**, Bourne House, Morrison St, Castleford, **Yorkshire (West)**, WF10 4BE, ENG.
(T) 01977 558882
Speciality: Relaxation Technique.
H T (Ref:HM10947)

## JEAN, DALY
**Daly Jean N I S A T**, Patrickswell, IRE.
(T) 06135 5171
Speciality: Psychotherapy.
B (Ref:HM10948)

## JEANES, P J
**P J Jeanes**, 27 London Rd, Marlborough, **Wiltshire**, SN8 2AA, ENG.
(T) 01672 512530
Speciality: Chiropodists (Podiatrists).
● **Owner** Mr P Jeanes
S (Ref:HM10949)

## JEANNE
**Jeanne**, 61 Brindley Cres, Cannock, **Staffordshire**, WS12 4DT, ENG.
(T) 01543 876280
Speciality: Clairvoyants & Palmists.
B (Ref:HM10950)

## JEANNE OF KENT
**Jeanne Of Kent**, 46 Belmont Rd, Ramsgate, **Kent**, CT11 7QG, ENG.
(T) 01843 587929 (F) 01843 587830
Speciality: Clairvoyants & Palmists.
● **Owner** Ms J Murton
B (Ref:HM10951)

## JEANNET, ELIZABETH
**Elizabeth Jeannet**, 10 Harley St, London, **London (Greater)**, W1N 1AA, ENG.
(T) 020 7431 3918
Speciality: Alexander Technique.
● **Practitioner** Ms E Jeannet
P S (Ref:HM10952)

## JEANS, SIMON
**Simon Jeans**, Castleton House, Castle St, Mere, Warminster, **Wiltshire**, BA12 6JE, ENG.
(T) 01747 860161
Speciality: Chiropodists (Podiatrists).
S (Ref:HM10953)

## JEANS, SIMON N
**Simon N Jeans**, 2 Glencairn, South St, Sherborne, **Dorset**, DT9 3NQ, ENG.
(T) 01935 812472
Speciality: Chiropodists (Podiatrists).
● **Owner** Mr S Jeans
S (Ref:HM10954)

## JEAVONS, JO
**Jo Jeavons**, **Yorkshire (West)**, LS6, ENG.
(T) 01132 780916
Speciality: Bach Remedies.
M (Ref:HM10955)

## JEENA
**Jeena**, 47 Gregory Cresent, London, **London (Greater)**, SE9 5RZ, ENG.
(T) 020 8859 4337
Speciality: Clairvoyants & Palmists.
B (Ref:HM10956)

## JEFFARIES, PHILIP
**Philip Jeffaries**, Lower King St, Wexford, **County Wexford**, IRE.
(T) 05321 482 (F) 05436 661
(E) philjeffaries@unison.ie
Speciality: Osteopathy.
● **Osteopath** Mr P Jeffaries Q: BSc, Reg.Osteopath. M: GOsC.
S Yrs. Est.: 4 (Ref:HM10957)

## JEFFARIES, PHILIP
**Philip Jeffaries**, Slaney Medical Centre, Temple Shannon, Enniscorthy, **County Wexford**, IRE.
(T) 05436 663 (F) 05436 661
(E) philjeffaries@unison.ie
Speciality: Osteopathy. ✔
● **Osteopath** Mr P Jeffaries Q: BSc, Reg.Osteopath. M: GOsC.
S Yrs. Est.: 2 (Ref:HM10958)

## JEFFERIES, TREVOR
**Trevor Jefferies**, Waytefield Clinic, Preston Drove, Brighton, **Sussex (East)**, BN1 6LA, ENG.
(T) 01273 550727
Speciality: Osteopathy.
● **Owner** Mr T Jefferies
P S T (Ref:HM10959)

## JEFFERIS, PATRICIA
**Jefferis Patricia**, Southview Cottage, Main Rd, Hutton, Weston-Super-Mare, **Somerset**, BS24 9SR, ENG.
(T) 01934 813171
Speciality: Complementary Medicines & Therapy.
C M (Ref:HM10960)

## JEFFERSON, CARLTON
**Carlton Jefferson**, 188A Rye Lane, London, **London (Greater)**, SE15 4NF, ENG.
(T) 020 7639 0699
Speciality: Chiropodists (Podiatrists).
● **Owner** Mr C Jefferson
S (Ref:HM10961)

## JEFFERSON, JOHN
**John Jefferson**, 26 Whitley Rd, Whitley Bay, **Tyne and Wear**, NE26 2NF, ENG.
(T) 01912 525650
Speciality: Osteopathy.
● **Owner** Mr J Jefferson
P S T (Ref:HM10962)

## JEFFERY & ASSOCIATES
**K R Jeffery & Associates**, Highfield Chiropractic Clinic, 48 Kedleston Rd, Derby, **Derbyshire**, DE22 1GW, ENG.
(T) 01332 346760 (F) 01332 291786
Speciality: Chiropractic.
● **Owner** Mr K Jeffrey
P S T (Ref:HM10963)

## JEFFERY, HELEN
**Helen Jeffery**, 3 Beaulands Cl, Cambridge, **Cambridgeshire**, CB4 1JA, ENG.
(T) 01223 316096
Speciality: Alexander Technique.
P S (Ref:HM10964)

## JEFFERY, JO
**Jo Jeffery**, 4 Colles Rd, Wells, **Somerset**, BA5 3JZ, ENG.
(T) 01749 671528
Speciality: Reflexology.
S T (Ref:HM10965)

## JEFFERYS, SIMON
**Simon Jefferys**, 13 Dee Fords Avenue, Chester, **Cheshire**, CH3 5UP, ENG.
(T) 01244 347279
Speciality: Hypnosis.
B (Ref:HM10966)

## JEFFFEREY, P J
**P J Jeffferey**, 27 Bath New Rd, Radstock, Bath, **Somerset**, BA3 3ED, ENG.
(T) 01761 434611
Speciality: Chiropodists (Podiatrists).
● **Owner** Mrs P Jefferey
S (Ref:HM10967)

## JEFFREY & ASSOCIATES
**Miss A B Jeffrey & Associates**, 55 Clay Avenue, Mitcham, **Surrey**, CR4 1BT, ENG.
(T) 020 8648 4535
Speciality: Osteopathy.
P S T (Ref:HM10968)

## JEFFREY, C E
**C E Jeffrey**, Dental Surgery, 17 Monton Green, Eccles, Manchester, **Manchester (Greater)**, M30 9LE, ENG.
(T) 01617 893770
Speciality: Chiropodists (Podiatrists).
● **Partner** Miss J Cavanagh
S (Ref:HM10969)

## JEFFREY, G M
**G M Jeffrey**, 20 Crowhill Rd, Bishopbriggs, Glasgow, **Glasgow (City of)**, G64 1QY, SCO.
(T) 01417 624834
Speciality: Physiotherapy.
P S T (Ref:HM10970)

## JEFFREY, R
**R Jeffrey**, 1 Sefton Paddock, Stoke Poges, Slough, **Berkshire**, SL2 4PT, ENG.
(T) 01753 662346
Speciality: Electrolysis.
● **Owner** Miss R Jeffrey
T (Ref:HM10971)

## JEFFRIES, BARBARA
**Barbara Jeffries**, 5 Priory Park Rd, Dawlish, **Devon**, EX7 9LX, ENG.
(T) 01626 862542
Speciality: Counselling, Psychotherapy. ✔
● **Psychotherapist/Counsellor** Ms B Jeffries Q: Dip.Int.Psych, MA. M: BACP.
B Yrs. Est.: 2 (Ref:HM10972)

## JEFFS, K A
**K A Jeffs**, Ben Knowle, Worth, Wookey, Wells, **Somerset**, BA5 1LW, ENG.
(T) 01749 675352
Speciality: Herbal Medicine.
● **Owner** Mrs K Jeffs
M (Ref:HM10973)

## JEFFS, PAULINE
**Pauline Jeffs**, 11 Woodside Drive, Wrenthorpe, Wakefield, **Yorkshire (West)**, WF2 0NA, ENG.
(T) 01924 365633
Speciality: Reflexology.
● **Owner** Mrs P Jeffs
S T (Ref:HM10974)

## JELFS, MARTIN
**Martin Jelfs**, 56 Alum Chine Rd, Bournemouth, **Dorset**, BH4 8DZ, ENG.
(E) martinj@dircon.co.uk
Speciality: Bio-energetics, Counselling, Gestalt Therapy, Humanistic Psychology, Massage (Therapeutic), Psychotherapy, Reichian Therapy, Rogerian Therapy, Stress Therapy, Tantra Therapy, Mind-Body Healing. ✔
● **Psychotherapist** Mr M Jelfs Q: BSc, MA, UKCP (Reg). M: BACP, UKCP.
B Yrs. Est.: 18 (Ref:HM10975)

## JELFS, MARTIN
**Martin Jelfs**, 14 Chesterton Rd, London, **London (Greater)**, E13 8BA, ENG.
(T) 07973 504121
(E) martinj@dircon.co.uk
Speciality: Bio-energetics, Counselling, Gestalt Therapy, Humanistic Psychology, Massage (Therapeutic), Psychotherapy, Reichian Therapy, Rogerian Therapy, Tantra Therapy, Mind-Body Healing. ✔
● **Psychotherapist** Mr M Jelfs Q: BSc, MA, UKCP (Reg). M: BACP, UKCP.
B Yrs. Est.: 18 (Ref:HM10976)

## JELFS, MARTIN
**Martin Jelfs**, Eden Medical Centre, 63A Kings Rd, Chelsea, London, **London (Greater)**, SW3 4WT, ENG.
(T) 07973 504121
(E) martinj@dircon.co.uk
Speciality: Bio-energetics, Counselling, Gestalt Therapy, Humanistic Psychology, Massage (Therapeutic), Psychotherapy, Reichian Therapy, Rogerian Therapy, Stress Therapy, Tantra Therapy,



Key: B Mind-Body Medicine, C Complementary Medicine, H Self Help Treatment, M Medicinal Therapy, O Oriental Medicine, P Postural Therapy, S Manipulative Structural Therapy, T Touch Therapy

Mind-Body Healing. ✔
● **Psychotherapist** Mr M Jelfs **Q:** BSc, MA, UKCP (Reg). **M:** BACP, UKCP.
**B** Yrs. Est.: 18 (**Ref:**HM10977)

## JEMPSON, NICOLA

**Nicola Jempson**, 30 High St, Battle, **Sussex (East)**, TN33 0AF, ENG.
(T) 01424 774987
Speciality: Complementary Medicines & Therapy, McTimoney Chiropractic. ✔
● **Chiropractor** Nicola Jempson **Q:** DC, MMCA. **M:** CC, GCC.
● **Homeopath** Pam Fore
**C** Yrs. Est.: 6 (**Ref:**HM10978)

## JEMSON, SANDRA

**Sandra Jemson**, 12 Falklands Cl, Marske-By-The-Sea, Redcar, **Cleveland**, TS11 6DN, ENG.
(T) 01642 481849
Speciality: Complementary Medicines & Therapy.
● **Owner** Mrs S Jemson
**C M** (**Ref:**HM10979)

## JENAI

**Jenai**, 3 Sunnybank Pl, Edinburgh, **Edinburgh (City of)**, EH7 5TJ, SCO.
(T) 01316 595412 (F) 01315 563345
Speciality: Reflexology. ✔
● **Owner/Holistic Therapist**
Miss P North **Q:** Dip.Hom. **M:** IPA.
**C** Yrs. Est.: 12 (**Ref:**HM10980)

## JENKINS, CHARLES (DR)

**Jenkins Dr Charles**, Foxford Rd, Ballina, **County Mayo**, IRE.
(T) 09670 664
Speciality: Chiropractors.
**P S T** (**Ref:**HM10981)

## JENKINS, DAVID

**David Jenkins**, 97 College Rd, Epsom, **Surrey**, KT17 4HY, ENG.
(T) 01372 726080
Speciality: Osteopathy.
● **Senior Partner** Mr B Hounsfield
**P S T** (**Ref:**HM10982)

## JENKINS, E A

**E A Jenkins**, 65 Prettygate Rd, Colchester, **Essex**, CO3 4ED, ENG.
(T) 01206 575790
Speciality: Chiropodists (Podiatrists).
**S** (**Ref:**HM10983)

## JENKINS, G & G

**G & G Jenkins**, 167 North Rd, Ferndale, **Rhondda Cynon Taff**, CF43 4RA, WAL.
(T) 01443 732037
Speciality: Chiropodists (Podiatrists).
● **Owner** Mrs G Jenkins
**S** (**Ref:**HM10984)

## JENKINS, G M

**G M Jenkins**, 86 Oak Lane, Norwich, **Norfolk**, NR6 7DD, ENG.
(T) 01603 482951
Speciality: Osteopathy.
**P S T** (**Ref:**HM10985)

## JENKINS, HUGH

**Hugh Jenkins**, Exeter Physio & Sports Clinic, 11-15 Dixs Field, Exeter, **Devon**, EX1 1QA, ENG.
(T) 01392 211066
Speciality: Physiotherapy.
**P S T** (**Ref:**HM10986)

## JENKINS, JOHN

**John Jenkins**, 21 Highfields, Brackla, Bridgend, CF31 2PA, WAL.
(T) 01656 649715
Speciality: Hypnotherapy. ✔
● **Hypnotherapist** Mr J Jenkins **M:** BIH.
**B** Yrs. Est.: 2 (**Ref:**HM10987)

## JENKINS, JUDITH

**Judith Jenkins**, 11 Railway Rd, Ormskirk, **Lancashire**, L39 2DN, ENG.
(T) 01695 570488
Speciality: Osteopathy.
● **Owner** Miss J Jenkins
**P S T** (**Ref:**HM10988)

## JENKINS, JUDITH

**Judith Jenkins**, Southport Osteopathic, Clinic 67 Liverpool Rd, Southport, **Merseyside**, PR8 4PG, ENG.
(T) 01704 550694
Speciality: Osteopathy.
**P S T** (**Ref:**HM10989)

## JENKINS, K J

**K J Jenkins**, Vine Cottage, 11A School Lane, North Hykeham, Lincoln, **Lincolnshire**, LN6 9QS, ENG.
(T) 01522 685613
Speciality: Homeopathy.
● **Owner** Dr K Jenkins
**M** (**Ref:**HM10990)

## JENKINS, KATHERINE

**Katherine Jenkins**, Halscombe Farm Cottage, Halscombe Lane, Ide, Exeter, **Devon**, EX2 9TQ, ENG.
(T) 01392 811836
Speciality: Hypnosis.
● **Partner** Mrs K Jenkins
**B** (**Ref:**HM10991)

## JENKINS, MARY (DR)

**Dr Mary Jenkins**, 117 Cathedral Rd, Cardiff, **Glamorgan (Vale of)**, CF11 9PH, WAL.
(T) 029 2022 4422
Speciality: Hypnosis.
**B** (**Ref:**HM10992)

## JENKINS, R W

**R W Jenkins**, 540 Green St, London, **London (Greater)**, E13 9DA, ENG.
(T) 020 8472 0057
Speciality: Physiotherapy.
● **Owner** Mr R Jenkins
**P S T** (**Ref:**HM10993)

## JENKINS, RUSSELL

**Russell Jenkins**, 32 Lorne Rd, Southsea, **Hampshire**, PO5 1RR, ENG.
(T) 023 9282 0304
Speciality: Aromatherapy, Bach Remedies, Counselling, Cranial Osteopathy, Indian Head Massage, Kinesiology, Manual Lymph Drainage, Metamorphic Therapy, Polarity Therapy, Reflexology, Integration Healing, Chakra Balance, Massage, NLP. ✔
● **Holistic Therapist** Mr R Jenkins **M:** IPTI, ISPA, ITEC.
**C** Yrs. Est.: 92 (**Ref:**HM10994)

## JENKINS, RUSSELL

**Russell Jenkins**, 122 The Grove, Moordown, Bournemouth, **Dorset**, BH9 2UA, ENG.
(T) 01202 518152
Speciality: Complementary Medicines & Therapy.
● **Owner** Russell Jenkins
**M** (**Ref:**HM10995)

## JENKINS, RUSSELL S

**Russell S Jenkins L C S P (Phys)**, 60 Upham Rd, Swindon, **Wiltshire**, SN3 1DN, ENG.
(T) 01793 496547
(E) rphysio2000@aol.com
Speciality: Electrotherapy, Kinesiology, Manipulation, Massage (Therapeutic). ✔
● **Physiologist** Mr R Jenkins **Q:** LCSP. **M:** LCSP.
**S** Yrs. Est.: 8 (**Ref:**HM10996)

## JENKINS, SARA

**Sara Jenkins**, 57 Fleetwood Cl, Tadworth, **Surrey**, KT20 5QH, ENG.
(T) 01737 363058
Speciality: Aromatherapy.
**M O** (**Ref:**HM10997)

## JENKINSON, CLIFF

**Cliff Jenkinson**, 11 Victoria Rd, Dorchester, **Dorset**, DT1 1SB, ENG.
(T) 01308 427777 (F) 01305 257551
Speciality: Complementary Medicines & Therapy.
● **Owner** Mr C Jenkinson
**M** (**Ref:**HM10998)

## JENKINSON, LEILA

**Leila Jenkinson**, 8 Plover Drive, Broadheath, Altrincham, **Cheshire**, WA14 5NW, ENG.
(T) 01619 290359
Speciality: Reflexology. ✔
● **Owner/Reflexologist**
Mrs L Jenkinson **Q:** IIHHT. **M:** ICHT.
**C** Yrs. Est.: 2 (**Ref:**HM10999)

## JENKINSON, TRISHA

**Trisha Jenkinson**, 11 Lower Northend, Batheaston, Bath, **Somerset**, BA1 7EZ, ENG.
(T) 01225 852473
Speciality: Reflexology.
**S T** (**Ref:**HM11000)

## JENKS, B R

**B R Jenks**, 2 Quarry Rd, Broseley Wood, Broseley, **Shropshire**, TF12 5QF, ENG.
(T) 01952 883892
Speciality: Hypnosis.
● **Owner** Mr B Jenks
**B** (**Ref:**HM11001)

## JENNER, ROSEMARY

**Rosemary Jenner**, Kennaways, Ospringe, Faversham, **Kent**, ME13 0HA, ENG.
(T) 01795 532906
Speciality: Aromatherapy.
● **Owner** Miss R Jenner
**M O** (**Ref:**HM11002)

## JENNER, SUE

**Sue Jenner**, 42 Portland Avenue, Gravesend, **Kent**, DA12 5HE, ENG.
(T) 01474 324908 (F) 01474 331335
Speciality: Psychology.
● **Owner** Ms S Jenner
**B** (**Ref:**HM11003)

## JENNIFER K HOUGH - PHYSIO

**Jennifer K Hough**, 4 Collings Weels Cl, Caddington, **Bedfordshire**, LU1 4BG, ENG.
(T) 01582 418159 (F) 08701 210873
(E) mailbox@jhough.fsbusiness.co.uk
(W) www.jhough.fsbusiness.co.uk
Speciality: Manipulation, Massage (Therapeutic), Physiotherapy. ✔
● **Owner** Ms J Hough **Q:** MAB Phys, SMAE. **M:** AB Phys.
**S** Yrs. Est.: 8 (**Ref:**HM11004)

## JENNIFER SAJIR PAED PHYSIO

**Jennifer Sajir Paediatric Physiotherapist**, Hook End, 29 The Hook, New Barnet, Barnet, **Hertfordshire**, EN5 1LQ, ENG.
(T) 020 8275 0402
(E) jennifersajir@supanet.com
Speciality: Physiotherapy, Paediatric Physiotherapy, Neurodevelopmental Physiotherapy, Hydrotherapy(for children). ✔
● **Senior Paediatric Physiotherapist**
Mrs J Sajir **Q:** Grad Dip Phys, MCSP, SRP. **M:** CSP.
**P** (**Ref:**HM11005)

## JENNINGS, DONAL

**Jennings Donal**, Coaldwood, Craughwell, **County Galway**, IRE.
(T) 09184 6034
Speciality: Complementary Medicines & Therapy.
**M** (**Ref:**HM11006)

## JENNINGS-BROWN, S

**Mrs S Jennings-Brown**, 27 Moorside Rd, Stockport, **Cheshire**, SK4 4DT, ENG.
(T) 01614 319635
Speciality: Chiropodists (Podiatrists).
**S** (**Ref:**HM11007)

## JENNY HOK

**Jenny Hok**, Middle Old Park, Farnham, **Surrey**, GU10 5EA, ENG.
(T) 01252 715092
Speciality: Reflexology.
**S T** (**Ref:**HM11008)

## JENNY, FRANCIS

**Francis Jenny**, 10 Lynton Cl, Hurstpierpoint, Hassocks, **Sussex (West)**, BN6 9AN, ENG.
(T) 01273 835742
Speciality: Reflexology.
● **Owner** Ms J Francius
**S T** (**Ref:**HM11009)

## JENNY'S

**Jenny's**, 97 Richmond Hill, Luton,



Key continued: **Yrs.Est:** Years Established **Q:** Qualifications **M:** Professional Membership ✔ Indemnity Insurance Accept Credit Cards

**Bedfordshire**, LU2 7JQ, ENG.
(T) 01582 429263
Speciality: Electrolysis.
● **Owner** Mrs J Dale
[T] (Ref:HM11010)

## JENSEN, A J
**A J Jensen**, 1 South St, West Butterwick, Scunthorpe, **Humberside**, DN17 3JT, ENG.
(T) 01724 783276
Speciality: Chiropodists (Podiatrists).
● **Owner** A J Jensen
[S] (Ref:HM11011)

## JENTERPRISES
**Jenterprises Ltd**, P O Box 2405, Bath, **Somerset**, BA1 5ZB, ENG.
(T) 01225 331521
Speciality: Clairvoyants & Palmists.
● **Managing Director** Ms J Nicholson
[B] (Ref:HM11012)

## JEOFFROY, ANNA
**Anna Jeoffroy**, 83 Margaret Rd, Barnet, **Hertfordshire**, EN4 9NX, ENG.
(T) 020 8440 2694
Speciality: Reflexology.
[S] [T] (Ref:HM11013)

## JEPSON, S L
**S L Jepson**, 20 Prospect Avenue, Shipley, **Yorkshire (West)**, BD18 2LW, ENG.
(T) 01274 589111
Speciality: Chiropodists (Podiatrists).
● **Owner** Ms S Jepson
[S] (Ref:HM11014)

## JEREMY, C
**C Jeremy**, 33 The Parade, Roath, Cardiff, **Glamorgan (Vale of)**, CF24 3AD, WAL.
(T) 029 2048 0619
Speciality: Reflexology.
[S] [T] (Ref:HM11015)

## JEREMY, SARAH
**Sarah Jeremy**, 7 Harebell Cl, Littlehampton, **Sussex (West)**, BN17 6WE, ENG.
(T) 01903 719401
Speciality: Physiotherapy.
● **Owner** Mrs S Jemery
[P] [S] [T] (Ref:HM11016)

## JERONIMUS & HUGHES
**Jeronimus Dr J & Hughes Dr S**, The Octagon Chiropractic Clinic, 2 St Peter's Rd, London, **London (Greater)**, W6 9LZ, ENG.
(T) 020 8563 2608
Speciality: Chiropractors.
[P] [S] [T] (Ref:HM11017)

## JERRETT, CHRIS
**Chris Jerrett**, Access House, Great Western St, Wednesbury, **Midlands (West)**, WS10 7LE, ENG.
(T) 01215 052785 (F) 01215 052785
Speciality: Physiotherapy.
● **Owner** Mr R Jerrett
[P] [S] [T] (Ref:HM11018)

## JESKINS, J
**J Jeskins**, 73 Ilges Lane, Cholsey, Wallingford, **Oxfordshire**, OX10 9PA, ENG.
(T) 01491 651579
Speciality: Physiotherapy.
[P] [S] [T] (Ref:HM11019)

## JESSIE
**Jessie**, 158 Harborough Avenue, Sheffield, **Yorkshire (South)**, S2 1QU, ENG.
(T) 01142 641009
Speciality: Clairvoyants & Palmists.
● **Owner** Mrs J Smith
[B] (Ref:HM11020)

## JESSOP CLINIC
**Jessop Clinic**, 93 High Rd, Gorleston, Great Yarmouth, **Norfolk**, NR31 0PE, ENG.
(T) 01493 443095 (F) 01493 650044
(E) acupuncture@jessupclinic.co.uk
Speciality: Acupuncture, Electrotherapy, Manipulation, Massage (Therapeutic), Osteopathy. ✔
● **Massage Therapist** Mr J Holmes Q: ITEC.
● **Acupuncturist** Ms M Grimson Q: Lic.Ac. M: BAcC.
● **Osteopath** Mr M Jessup Q: DO. M: GOsC.
[S] Yrs. Est.: 18 (Ref:HM11021)

## JESSOP, ELAINE
**Elaine Jessop**, Munro Medical Centre, West Elloe Avenue, Spalding, **Lincolnshire**, PE11 2BY, ENG.
(T) 01775 821480
Speciality: Acupuncture.
[O] (Ref:HM11022)

## JET FORM IRELAND
**Jet Form Ireland**, Main St, Tyrellspass, **County Westmeath**, IRE.
(T) 04423 975
Speciality: Complementary Medicines & Therapy.
[M] (Ref:HM11023)

## JEVON, NICKY & DENIS
**Nicky & Denis Jevon**, Tan Y Marian, High St, Glyn Ceiriog, Llangollen, **Denbighshire**, LL20 7EH, WAL.
(T) 01691 718256
Speciality: Herbal Medicine.
[M] (Ref:HM11024)

## JEWERS, M S
**M S Jewers**, The Bedford Park Surgery, 55 South Prde, London, **London (Greater)**, W4 5LH, ENG.
(T) 020 8742 1331
(E) mattjewers@hotmail/.com
Speciality: Biomechanics, Chiropody, Nail Surgery, Podiatry. ✔ [CREDIT]
● **Chiropodist (Podiatrist)**
Mr M Jewers Q: DPodM, M.S.C.P.
[C] Yrs. Est.: 10 (Ref:HM11025)

## JEWERS, T
**T Jewers**, 2a Guildford Pk Rd, Guildford, **Surrey**, GU2 7ND, ENG.
(T) 01483 579500
Speciality: Osteopathy.
[P] [S] [T] (Ref:HM11026)

## JEWRY, PATRICIA
**Patricia Jewry (Mobile)**, 11 Bridle Cl, Paignton, **Devon**, TQ4 7SL, ENG.
(T) 01803 842481
Speciality: Chiropodists (Podiatrists).
● **Owner** Mrs P Jewry
[S] (Ref:HM11027)

## JIANG CLINIC HERBAL INN
**Jiang Clinic Herbal Inn**, 191 Regents Park Rd, London, **London (Greater)**, N3 3PA, ENG.
(T) 020 8349 0640 (F) 020 8349 9804
Speciality: Acupuncture.
[O] (Ref:HM11028)

## JILL HENDRY ASS PHYSIOTHERAPY
**Jill Hendry Associates Physiotherapy**, Cannons Health Club & Spa, Cousin Lane, London, **London (Greater)**, EC4R 3TE, ENG.
(T) 020 7283 0108
Speciality: Physiotherapy.
[P] [S] [T] (Ref:HM11029)

## JILLEY, W
**W Jilley**, 2 Crown Lane, Littleport, Ely, **Cambridgeshire**, CB6 1PP, ENG.
(T) 01353 863218
Speciality: Herbalists.
[M] (Ref:HM11030)

## JILLINS, BOB
**Bob Jillins**, Acacia House, 104 Fronks Rd, Harwich, **Essex**, CO12 3RY, ENG.
(T) 01255 242445
Speciality: Reflexology.
[S] [T] (Ref:HM11031)

## JIM MARSH & STEPHANIE STOCK
**Jim Marshall & Stephanie Stocker**, Weston Surgery, 36 Combe Park, Bath, **Somerset**, BA1 3NR, ENG.
(T) 01225 446089
Speciality: Chiropodists (Podiatrists).
[S] (Ref:HM11032)

## JIMENEZ, HILARY
**Hilary Jimenez**, 34 Green Avenue, London, **London (Greater)**, W13 9RW, ENG.
(T) 020 8566 1953
Speciality: Reflexology.
[S] [T] (Ref:HM11033)

## JING YING WANG
**Mrs Jing Ying Wang**, 1 Kernthorpe Rd, Birmingham, **Midlands (West)**, B14 6RA, ENG.
(T) 01214 433093
Speciality: Acupuncture.
[O] (Ref:HM11034)

## JINKS, BARBARA
**Barbara Jinks**, 198 Battersea Bridge Rd, London, **London (Greater)**, SW11 3AE, ENG.
(T) 020 7228 4832
Speciality: Osteopathy.
● **Owner** Mrs B Jinks
[P] [S] [T] (Ref:HM11035)

## JIVRAJ, T H
**T H Jivraj**, 286 Preston Rd, Harrow, **London (Greater)**, HA3 0QA, ENG.
(T) 020 8908 4272
Speciality: Chiropodists (Podiatrists).
● **Owner** Mr D Jivraj
[S] (Ref:HM11036)

## JIWA, A
**A Jiwa**, 107 Wrythe Lane, Carshalton, **Surrey**, SM5 2RR, ENG.
(T) 020 8644 8972
Speciality: Chiropodists (Podiatrists).
● **Owner** Mrs A Jiwa
[S] (Ref:HM11037)

## JOAN ELIZABETH CLAIRVOYANT
**Joan Elizabeth Clairvoyant**, 2a Harewood Gardens, Peterborough, **Cambridgeshire**, PE3 9NF, ENG.
(T) 01733 265314 (F) 01733 265314
Speciality: Clairvoyants & Palmists.
● **Partner** Mrs J Turner
[B] (Ref:HM11038)

## JOAN PEARNE CHIROPODY CLINIC
**Joan Pearne Chiropody Clinic**, 3 Applegarth, Godalming, **Surrey**, GU7 2BU, ENG.
(T) 01483 414688
Speciality: Chiropodists (Podiatrists).
[S] (Ref:HM11039)

## JOANNA SMITH AROMATHERAPY
**Joanna Smith Aromatherapy**, 1st Floor High St, Chipping Campden, **Gloucestershire**, GL55 6AT, ENG.
(T) 01386 840727
Speciality: Aromatherapy, Bach Remedies, Bowen Therapy, Reflexology.
● **Accredited Journey Therapist**
Brandon Bays
● **Owner/Therapist** Mrs J Smith Q: ITEC, MBSR. M: BSR, BTER, ISPA.
[M] [O] Yrs. Est.: 12 (Ref:HM11040)

## JOBAIRE, MELANIE
**Melanie Jobaire**, Apple Tree Chiropractic Clinic, 4 High St, Steyning, **Sussex (West)**, BN44 3GG, ENG.
(T) 01903 814005
Speciality: Chiropractic.
[P] [S] [T] (Ref:HM11041)

## JOBBER, J V
**J V Jobber**, 39 Upper Lichfield St, Willenhall, **Midlands (West)**, WV13 1PT, ENG.
(T) 01902 607090
Speciality: Chiropodists (Podiatrists).
[S] (Ref:HM11042)

## JOCHIM, ANDREAS
**Andreas Jochim**, The Albany Clinic, 11 Station Rd, Sidcup, **Kent**, DA15 7EN, ENG.
(T) 020 8300 4361
Speciality: Osteopathy.
[P] [S] [T] (Ref:HM11043)

## JOCHIM, ANDREAS
**Andreas Jochim**, 50 Scotts Lane, Bromley, **Kent**, BR2 0LL, ENG.
(T) 020 8650 0509
Speciality: Osteopathy.
● **Owner** Mr A Jochim
[P] [S] [T] (Ref:HM11044)

## JOE MILLER SPORTS INJURY
**Joe Miller Sports Injury Clinic**, Lodge Farm



Key: [B] Mind-Body Medicine [C] Complementary Medicine [H] Self Help Treatment [M] Medicinal Therapy [O] Oriental Medicine [P] Postural Therapy [S] Manipulative Structural Therapy [T] Touch Therapy

Cottage, Furneux, Pelham, Buntingford, **Hertfordshire**, SG9 0LD, ENG.
(T) 01279 777893
(E) joe@physio2.k.freeserve.co.uk
Speciality: Chiropractic, Cupping, Electrotherapy, Kinesiology, Manipulation, Osteopathy, Ultrasonics. ✔
● **Sole Practitioner** Mr J Miller Q: Dip.Sports Therapy, MSST. M: SST.
S Yrs. Est.: 16 (Ref:HM11045)

## JOE, GRIFFIN

**Griffin Joe BSC PSYCH DIP HYP**, 30 Forest Pk, Athy, **County Kildare**, IRE.
(T) 05073 8663
Speciality: Complementary Medicines & Therapy.
M (Ref:HM11046)

## JOHANSON, CAROL

**Carol Johanson**, 21 Dunblane Rd, Sunderland, **Tyne and Wear**, SR6 8EU, ENG.
(T) 01915 489457
Speciality: Chiropodists (Podiatrists).
● **Owner** Ms C Johanson
S (Ref:HM11047)

## JOHANSSON, BERIT

**Berit Johansson**, 11 Leith Mansions, Grantully Rd, London, **London (Greater)**, W9 1LQ, ENG.
(T) 020 7286 3350
Speciality: Reflexology.
S T (Ref:HM11048)

## JOHARI, ULLA

**Ulla Johari**, The Copse, School Lane, West Lulworth, Wareham, **Dorset**, BH20 5SA, ENG.
(T) 01929 400581 (F) 01929 400581
Speciality: Acupuncture.
● **Owner** Mrs U Johari
O (Ref:HM11049)

## JOHN COOPER ASSOCIATES

**John Cooper Associates**, West One House, 17 St Georges Rd, Cheltenham, **Gloucestershire**, GL50 3DT, ENG.
(T) 01242 239238 (F) 01242 222665
Speciality: Psychology.
● **Owner** Mr J Cooper
B (Ref:HM11050)

## JOHN HOLDEN ASSOCIATES

**John Holden Associates**, 72 Northgate, Blackburn, **Lancashire**, BB2 1AA, ENG.
(T) 01254 698311
Speciality: Biomechanics, Chiropody, Nail Surgery, Podiatry. ✔
● **Chiropodist (Podiatrist)** Mary Almond Q: M.S.C.P, S.R.Ch.
● **Chiropodist (Podiatrist)** Mr J Holden Q: M.S.C.P, S.R.Ch.
● **Owner** Mrs P Holden
M Yrs. Est.: 31 (Ref:HM11051)

## JOHN PATTISON CHIROPODIST

**John Pattison Chiropodist**, 11 Elmfield Cl, Gravesend, **Kent**, DA11 0LP, ENG.
(T) 01474 567283
Speciality: Chiropodists (Podiatrists).
● **Owner** Mr J Pattison
S (Ref:HM11052)

## JOHN ROBERTS-JAMES CLINIC

**John Roberts-James Clinic**, 25 Southend Avenue, Darlington, **County Durham**, DL3 7HW, ENG.
(T) 01325 463766
Speciality: Osteopathy.
P S T (Ref:HM11053)

## JOHN, JACQUELINE

**Jacqueline John**, Blackheath Osteopathy & Acupuncture Clinic, 19 Tranquil Vale, London, **London (Greater)**, SE3 0BU, ENG.
(T) 020 8852 1706
Speciality: Osteopathy.
P S T (Ref:HM11054)

## JOHN, KEITH

**Keith John**, 68 Park St, Tonna, Neath, **Glamorgan (Vale of)**, SA11 3JQ, WAL.
(T) 01639 631918
Speciality: Physiotherapy.
● **Owner** Mr K John
P S T (Ref:HM11055)

## JOHN, PETER

**Peter John**, 21 Kashmir Rd, London, **London (Greater)**, SE7 8QN, ENG.
(T) 020 8856 5865
Speciality: Clairvoyants & Palmists.
B (Ref:HM11056)

## JOHN, RUSSELL

**Russell John**, 10A McCurtain St, **County Cork**, IRE.
(T) 021 4503 711
Speciality: Complementary Medicines & Therapy.
M (Ref:HM11057)

## JOHN, S U

**S U John**, 127 Hart Rd, Benfleet, **Essex**, SS7 3QP, ENG.
(T) 01268 774249 (F) 01268 779454
Speciality: Osteopathy.
● **Owner** Mrs S John
P S T (Ref:HM11058)

## JOHN, T

**T John**, Sutherland House, 1a Ashbourne Avenue, London, **London (Greater)**, NW11 0DP, ENG.
(T) 020 8458 7869
Speciality: Osteopathy.
P S T (Ref:HM11059)

## JOHNS, DAVID M

**David M Johns**, Cornerstone, 8 Borovere Lane, Alton, **Hampshire**, GU34 1PD, ENG.
(T) 01420 83296
Speciality: Chiropodists (Podiatrists).
● **Owner** Mr D Johns
S (Ref:HM11060)

## JOHNSON FOOTCARE

**Johnson Footcare**, 11 Hollyfield Rd South, Sutton Coldfield, **Midlands (West)**, B76 1NY, ENG.
(T) 01213 781710 (F) 01213 781710
Speciality: Chiropody. ✔
● **Owner/Chiropodist** Ms E Johnson Q: MSSCh. M: B.A.Ch.P.
M Yrs. Est.: 2 (Ref:HM11061)

## JOHNSON S & O'BRIEN A

**S Johnson & A O'Brien**, Star Yard, Horsemarket, Barnard Castle, **County Durham**, DL12 8LY, ENG.
(T) 01833 690887
Speciality: Physiotherapy.
● **Owner** Ms A O'Brien
P S T (Ref:HM11062)

## JOHNSON, A

**A Johnson**, Bannercross Osteopathic Practice, 939 Ecclesall Rd, Sheffield, **Yorkshire (South)**, S11 8TL, ENG.
(T) 01142 685664
Speciality: Osteopathy.
P S T (Ref:HM11063)

## JOHNSON, A E

**A E Johnson**, 8 Norman Rd, Northfield, Birmingham, **Midlands (West)**, B31 2EW, ENG.
(T) 01214 760217
Speciality: Physiotherapy.
● **Owner** Mr A Johnson
P S T (Ref:HM11064)

## JOHNSON, ANDREW

**Andrew Johnson**, 10 High St, Glastonbury, **Somerset**, BA6 9DU, ENG.
(T) 01458 834236
Speciality: Herbal Medicine.
● **Director** Ms J Sanders
M (Ref:HM11065)

## JOHNSON, ANDREW N

**Andrew N Johnson**, Williams Osteopathic Clinic, 64 Marsland Rd, Sale, **Cheshire**, M33 3HG, ENG.
(T) 01619 696555
Speciality: Osteopathy.
P S T (Ref:HM11066)

## JOHNSON, ANNE

**Anne Johnson**, 2 Manor Way, Deeping St. James, Peterborough, **Cambridgeshire**, PE6 8PT, ENG.
(T) 01778 344517
Speciality: Osteopathy.
P S T (Ref:HM11067)

## JOHNSON, ANNE

**Anne Johnson**, 6 Moor End, Eaton Bray, Dunstable, **Bedfordshire**, LU6 2HN, ENG.
(T) 01525 221958
(E) anne-johnson@lineone.net
Speciality: Cranial Osteopathy, Osteopathy. ✔
● **Osteopath** Mrs A Johnson Q: DO. M: GOsC.
S Yrs. Est.: 10 (Ref:HM11068)

## JOHNSON, BERNADETTE

**Bernadette Johnson**, 11 Fourth Avenue, Wickford, **Essex**, SS11 8RQ, ENG.
(T) 01268 734327 (F) 01268 734327
Speciality: Reflexology.
● **Owner** Mrs B Johnson
S T (Ref:HM11069)

## JOHNSON, C

**C Johnson**, 84 Llangranog Rd, Llanishen, Cardiff, **Glamorgan (Vale of)**, CF14 5BQ, WAL.
(T) 029 2075 2199
Speciality: Reflexology.
S T (Ref:HM11070)

## JOHNSON, CAROL

**Carol Johnson**, 28 Muriel Rd, Beeston, Nottingham, **Nottinghamshire**, NG9 2HH, ENG.
(T) 01159 170464
Speciality: Chiropodists (Podiatrists).
● **Owner** Mrs C Johnson
S (Ref:HM11071)

## JOHNSON, CELIA

**Celia Johnson**, 33 New Inn Lane, Burpham, Guildford, **Surrey**, GU4 7HN, ENG.
(T) 01483 573281
Speciality: Complementary Medicines & Therapy.
C M (Ref:HM11072)

## JOHNSON, G

**G Johnson**, 1 Glenlyon Rd, London, **London (Greater)**, SE9 1AL, ENG.
(T) 020 8859 8006
Speciality: Chiropodists (Podiatrists).
S (Ref:HM11073)

## JOHNSON, HELEN

**Helen Johnson**, Sunnyside, Bovingdon Green, Marlow, **Buckinghamshire**, SL7 2JH, ENG.
(T) 01628 477779
Speciality: Clinical Ecology, Cranial Osteopathy, Floral Essence Therapy, Gem Essence Therapy, Homeopathy, Naturopathy, Osteopathy.
● **Therapist** Ms H Johnson Q: DO, Lic.Hom, ND. M: GOsC, LCH, RN.
B Yrs. Est.: 10 (Ref:HM11074)

## JOHNSON, HELEN JANE

**Helen Jane Johnson**, Holmers Farm, Holmer Lane, Booker, High Wycombe, **Buckinghamshire**, HP12 4QA, ENG.
(T) 01494 473414
Speciality: Homeopathy.
M (Ref:HM11075)

## JOHNSON, HETTY

**Hetty Johnson**, 13 Beech Gr, Northampton, **Northamptonshire**, NN3 6JX, ENG.
(T) 01604 643380
Speciality: Hypnosis.
B (Ref:HM11076)

## JOHNSON, IAN RICHARD

**Ian Richard Johnson**, 22 Baldock St, Ware, **Hertfordshire**, SG12 9DZ, ENG.
(T) 01920 486100
Speciality: Hypnotherapy.
● **Owner** Mr I Johnson
B (Ref:HM11077)

## JOHNSON, JAMES D

**James D Johnson**, 30 Cumberland Mansions, Seymour Pl, London, **London (Greater)**, W1H 5TF, ENG.
(T) 020 7262 3022
Speciality: Osteopathy.
P S T (Ref:HM11078)

## JOHNSON, JANICE

**Janice Johnson**, 7 Vicars Croft, St Augustines

Green, Rugeley, **Staffordshire**, WS15 3JU, ENG.
(T) 01889 575505
Speciality: Absent Healing, Auto Suggestion, Cognitive Therapy, Counselling, Healer, Healing Therapy, Hypnosis, Hypnotherapy, Life Style Coaching, Meditation, Psychotherapy, Reiki, Spiritual Healing, Stress Therapy, Visualisation Therapy. ✔
● **Hypnotherapist/Psychotherapist**
Mrs J Johnson Q: BSc (Hons), DHP (NC).
M: BPS, NRHP.
[H] Yrs. Est.: 6 (Ref:HM11079)

### JOHNSON, JOHN R
**John R Johnson**, 177 Upper Richmond Rd West, London, **London (Greater)**, SW14 8DU, ENG.
(T) 020 8876 2604
Speciality: Chiropodists (Podiatrists).
● **Owner** Mr J Johnson
[S] (Ref:HM11080)

### JOHNSON, JUDITH
**Judith Johnson**, 21A Walter Rd, Swansea, SA1 5NQ, WAL.
(T) 01792 874237
Speciality: Homeopathy.
● **Owner** Mrs J Johnson
[M] (Ref:HM11081)

### JOHNSON, L
**L Johnson**, 74 Broadmead, London, **London (Greater)**, SE6 3SD, ENG.
(T) 020 8695 5364
Speciality: Complementary Medicines & Therapy.
● **Owner** Mrs L Johnson
[M] (Ref:HM11082)

### JOHNSON, LINDA
**Linda Johnson**, Natural Therapy Centre, 7 Westgate Rd, Guisborough, **Cleveland**, TS14 6EA, ENG.
(T) 01287 633591
Speciality: Reflexology.
[S] [T] (Ref:HM11083)

### JOHNSON, LOUISE
**Louise Johnson**, 215C Carshalton Rd, Carshalton, **Surrey**, SM5 3PZ, ENG.
(T) 020 8661 0751
Speciality: Reflexology.
[S] [T] (Ref:HM11084)

### JOHNSON, MARCIA
**Marcia Johnson**, 18 Palmerston Rd, Buckhurst Hill, **Essex**, IG9 5LT, ENG.
(T) 020 8505 5078
Speciality: Hypnotherapy.
[B] (Ref:HM11085)

### JOHNSON, MELVYN
**Melvyn Johnson**, 33 Drummond Rd, Ilkeston, **Derbyshire**, DE7 5HA, ENG.
(T) 01159 306582
Speciality: Osteopathy. ✔
● **Osteopath** Mr M Johnson Q: DO. M: GOsC.
[S] Yrs. Est.: 15 (Ref:HM11086)

### JOHNSON, MICHAEL
**Michael Johnson**, 8 Huxnor Rd, Kingskerswell, Newton Abbot, **Devon**, TQ12 5DX, ENG.
(T) 01803 872741
Speciality: Acupuncture, Bach Remedies, Complementary Therapy, Cupping, Dowsing, Homeopathy, Indian Head Massage, Massage (Therapeutic), Moxibustion, Oriental Diagnosis, Reflexology, Ying & Yang. ✔
● **Acupuncturist/Homeopath/Reflexologist**
Mr M Johnson Q: Dip.Hom, Dip.Reflex, Lic.Ac.
M: BAcC, ICHT.
[O] Yrs. Est.: 18 (Ref:HM11087)

### JOHNSON, P
**P Johnson**, Dunsthorpe House, 33 St Dunstans St, Canterbury, **Kent**, CT2 8BZ, ENG.
(T) 01227 768886 (F) 01227 768896
Speciality: Hypnotherapy.
● **Owner** Mr W Jansen
[B] (Ref:HM11088)

### JOHNSON, P
**P Johnson**, 10 High Rd East, Felixstowe, **Suffolk**, IP11 9JT, ENG.
(T) 01394 285776
Speciality: Chiropodists (Podiatrists).
● **Owner** Mr P Johnson
[S] (Ref:HM11089)

### JOHNSON, P A
**P A Johnson**, 60 Durham Cl, Grantham, **Lincolnshire**, NG31 8RL, ENG.
(T) 01476 563236
Speciality: Physiotherapy.
[P] [S] [T] (Ref:HM11090)

### JOHNSON, PAM
**Pam Johnson**, 457 London Rd, Hemel Hempstead, **Hertfordshire**, HP3 9BE, ENG.
(T) 01442 249998
Speciality: Reflexology.
● **Owner** Mrs P Johnson
[S] [T] (Ref:HM11091)

### JOHNSON, PAUL J
**Paul J Johnson**, 11 Heath Rd, Haywards Heath, **Sussex (West)**, RH16 3AX, ENG.
(T) 01444 450162 (F) 01444 459816
Speciality: Physiotherapy.
● **Practice Manager** Mrs W Langley
[P] [S] [T] (Ref:HM11092)

### JOHNSON, PETER
**Peter Johnson**, 16 Wells Rd, Radstock, Bath, **Somerset**, BA3 3RH, ENG.
(T) 01761 439530
Speciality: Chiropodists (Podiatrists).
● **Owner** Mr P Johnson
[S] (Ref:HM11093)

### JOHNSON, ROSS
**Ross Johnson**, 56 Hinkler Rd, Southampton, **Hampshire**, SO19 6FT, ENG.
(T) 023 8046 3907
Speciality: Chiropodists (Podiatrists).
[S] (Ref:HM11094)

### JOHNSON, SARAH
**Sarah Johnson**, 89 Millhouses Lane, Sheffield, **Yorkshire (South)**, S7 2HD, ENG.
(T) 01142 368483
Speciality: Reflexology.
[S] [T] (Ref:HM11095)

### JOHNSON, STEVEN R
**Steven R Johnson**, College Of Oriental Medicine, 2 Grove Rd, Retford, **Nottinghamshire**, DN22 6NA, ENG.
(T) 01777 701509
Speciality: Acupuncture.
[O] (Ref:HM11096)

### JOHNSON, STUART
**Stuart Johnson**, 7 Swift St, Barnsley, **Yorkshire (South)**, S75 2SN, ENG.
(T) 01226 240335
Speciality: Hypnosis.
● **Owner** Mr S Johnson
[B] (Ref:HM11097)

### JOHNSON, SUE
**Sue Johnson**, 174 Ifield Rd, London, **London (Greater)**, SW10 9AF, ENG.
(T) 020 7373 8575
Speciality: Acupuncture.
[O] (Ref:HM11098)

### JOHNSON, SUE
**Sue Johnson**, Wanstead Dental And Health Centre, 24 High Rd, London, **London (Greater)**, E11 2AQ, ENG.
(T) 020 8530 2126
Speciality: Acupuncture.
[O] (Ref:HM11099)

### JOHNSON, SUE
**Sue Johnson**, Womens Health Centre, 107-109 The Grove, London, **London (Greater)**, E15 1HP, ENG.
(T) 020 8221 0311
Speciality: Acupuncture.
[O] (Ref:HM11100)

### JOHNSON, SUSAN
**Susan Johnson**, 5 Pump Sq, Boston, **Lincolnshire**, PE21 6QW, ENG.
(T) 01205 358749
Speciality: Physiotherapy.
[P] [S] [T] (Ref:HM11101)

### JOHNSTON, J M
**J M Johnston**, Safron Court, Saffron Walden, **Essex**, CB11 3HB, ENG.
(T) 01799 500540
Speciality: Hypnotherapy.
● **Owner** Mrs J Johnston
[B] (Ref:HM11102)

### JOHNSTON, NORA
**Nora Johnston**, 5 Leighwood Avenue, Leigh-On-Sea, **Essex**, SS9 4LF, ENG.
(T) 01702 529880
Speciality: Chiropodists (Podiatrists).
● **Owner** Mrs N Johnston
[S] (Ref:HM11103)

### JOHNSTON, SALLY
**Sally Johnston**, 21 Parkholme Rd, London, **London (Greater)**, E8 3AG, ENG.
(T) 020 7254 1746
Speciality: Osteopathy.
[P] [S] [T] (Ref:HM11104)

### JOHNSTONE, ALLAN
**Allan Johnstone**, Sun & Moon Cottage, Elworthy, Lydeard St. Lawrence, Taunton, **Somerset**, TA4 3PX, ENG.
(T) 01984 656692
Speciality: Acupuncture.
● **Owner** Mr A Johnstone
[O] (Ref:HM11105)

### JOHNSTONE, CHRISTOPHER
**Christopher Johnstone**, Health Hydro, Milton Rd, Swindon, **Wiltshire**, SN1 5JA, ENG.
(T) 01793 465631
Speciality: Chiropractors.
[P] [S] [T] (Ref:HM11106)

### JOHNSTONS CHIROPODIST
**Johnstons Chiropodist**, 23 Upper George St, Luton, **Bedfordshire**, LU1 2RD, ENG.
(T) 01582 731033
Speciality: Chiropody, Indian Head Massage, Reflexology, Reiki. ✔
● **Owner/Chiropodist**
Miss R Johnston Q: M.S.C.P., S.R.Ch.
[T] Yrs. Est.: 100 (Ref:HM11107)

### JOINTS & POINTS
**Joints & Points**, 27b Church Rd, Bebington, Wirral, **Merseyside**, CH63 7PG, ENG.
(T) 01516 453534
Speciality: Physiotherapy.
● **Partner** Mr A Bursar
[P] [S] [T] (Ref:HM11108)

### JOLLIFFEE, PAM
**Pam Jolliffee**, 1 Purewell Cross Rd, Christchurch, **Dorset**, BH23 3AF, ENG.
(T) 01202 499518 (F) 01202 475706
Speciality: Physiotherapy.
● **Senior Partner** Mrs D Todd
[P] [S] [T] (Ref:HM11109)

### JOLLY, G M
**G M Jolly**, 69 Millcroft, Carlisle, **Cumbria**, CA3 0HT, ENG.
(T) 01228 524811
Speciality: Hypnosis.
● **Owner** Mr G Jolly
[B] (Ref:HM11110)

### JOLY, S
**S Joly**, The Old Vicarage, Somerset Sq, Nailsea, Bristol, BS48 1RN, ENG.
(T) 01275 857912
Speciality: Osteopathy.
[P] [S] [T] (Ref:HM11111)

### JONATHANS
**Jonathans**, 19 Burrill Avenue, York, **Yorkshire (North)**, YO30 6HP, ENG.
(T) 01904 655683
Speciality: Aromatherapy.
[M] [O] (Ref:HM11112)

### JONES B D L
**Jones B D L**, 79B High St, Pwllheli, **Gwynedd**, LL53 5RR, WAL.
(T) 01758 613211
Speciality: Chiropodists (Podiatrists).
[S] (Ref:HM11113)

**JONES, A C**

**A C Jones**, Pampas, Broadclyst, Exeter, **Devon**, EX5 3EJ, ENG.
(T) 01392 464878
Speciality: Chiropractors.
P S T (Ref:HM11114)

**JONES, ALAN**

**Alan Jones**, 161 Kimbolton Cres, Stevenage, **Hertfordshire**, SG2 8RN, ENG.
(T) 01438 239646
Speciality: Chiropody, Nail Surgery. ✔
● **Chiropodist** Mr A Jones Q: MBChA, MSSCh. M: B.A.Ch.P.
C Yrs. Est.: 6 (Ref:HM11115)

**JONES, ALISON**

**Alison Jones**, 58 Coventry Rd, Burbage, Hinckley, **Leicestershire**, LE10 2HP, ENG.
(T) 01455 233171
Speciality: Hypnotherapy.
B (Ref:HM11116)

**JONES, ALISON**

**Alison Jones**, Clissold Park Health Centre, 154 Stoke Newington Church St, London, **London (Greater)**, N16 0JU, ENG.
(T) 020 7249 2990 (F) 020 7249 3977
Speciality: Complementary Medicines & Therapy.
● **Director** Mr D Berg
M (Ref:HM11117)

**JONES, ALISON**

**Alison Jones**, The Worcester Chiropody & Podiatry Clinic, 23 Bransford Rd, Worcester, **Worcestershire**, WR2 4EW, ENG.
(T) 01905 428434
Speciality: Chiropodists (Podiatrists).
S (Ref:HM11118)

**JONES, ANN**

**Ann Jones**, 14 Trenant Cl, Polzeath, Wadebridge, **Cornwall**, PL27 6SW, ENG.
(T) 01208 863258
Speciality: Complementary Medicines & Therapy.
● **Owner** Ms A Jones
C M (Ref:HM11119)

**JONES, B A**

**B A Jones**, 8 Ellis St, Barnoldswick, **Lancashire**, BB18 5AD, ENG.
(T) 01282 813065
Speciality: Chiropodists (Podiatrists).
S (Ref:HM11120)

**JONES, B A**

**B A Jones**, Kendall House, Chatburn Rd, Clitheroe, **Lancashire**, BB7 2AP, ENG.
(T) 01200 424901
Speciality: Chiropodists (Podiatrists).
S (Ref:HM11121)

**JONES, B E**

**B E Jones**, 13 Elm Tree Avenue, Aberystwyth, **Ceredigion**, SY23 1LP, WAL.
(T) 01970 617269 (F) 01970 617269
(E) bridgetjones@onetel.net.uk
Speciality: Chiropody. ✔
● **Chiropodist** Ms B Jones Q: S.R.Ch. M: S.C.P.
S Yrs. Est.: 33 (Ref:HM11122)

**JONES, BARBARA**

**Barbara Jones**, Dorset Stores, Holyhead, **Isle of Anglesey**, LL65 2SY, WAL.
(T) 01407 763011
Speciality: Chiropodists (Podiatrists).
● **Partner** Mr H Jones
S (Ref:HM11123)

**JONES, BARBARA A**

**Barbara A Jones**, 34 Kings Gardens, Upminster, **Essex**, RM14 1JX, ENG.
(T) 01708 226605
Speciality: Chiropractors.
P S T (Ref:HM11124)

**JONES, BECKY**

**Becky Jones**, Hackswood House, Clevedon Rd, Walton-in-Gordano, **Somerset**, BS21 7AJ, ENG.
(T) 01275 872002 (F) 01275 872002
Speciality: Hypnosis, Hypnotherapy, Past Life Therapy. ✔
● **Hypnotherapist** Ms B Jones Q: MNSPH. M: GHR, NSPH.
B Yrs. Est.: 5 (Ref:HM11125)

**JONES, CAROLYN**

**Carolyn Jones**, Tegfan, Heol Derwen, New Inn, Pontypool, **Monmouthshire**, NP4 0QS, WAL.
(T) 01495 763694
Speciality: Complementary Medicines & Therapy.
● **Owner** Mrs C Jones
C M (Ref:HM11126)

**JONES, CHERYL**

**Cheryl Jones**, 310 Gloucester Rd, Horfield, Bristol, BS7 8TJ, ENG.
(T) 01179 444448
Speciality: Osteopathy.
P S T (Ref:HM11127)

**JONES, CHRISTINE**

**Christine Jones**, 5 Church St, Warwick, **Warwickshire**, CV34 4AB, ENG.
(T) 01926 491071
Speciality: Physiotherapy.
P S T (Ref:HM11128)

**JONES, CHRISTINE**

**Christine Jones**, 82 Haydock St, Newton-Le-Willows, **Merseyside**, WA12 9DJ, ENG.
(T) 01925 220930
Speciality: Chiropodists (Podiatrists).
S (Ref:HM11129)

**JONES, COLEEN**

**Jones Coleen B A (Psych)**, South Trce, **County Cork**, IRE.
(T) 021 4813 285
Speciality: Psychology.
B (Ref:HM11130)

**JONES, COLEEN**

**Coleen Jones**, Suite 2, South Terrace Medical Centre, Infirmary Rd, **County Cork**, IRE.
(T) 021 4813 285
Speciality: Counselling, Family Therapy, Gestalt Therapy, Group Therapy, Humanistic Psychology, Psychotherapy. ✔
● **Psychotherapist/Counsellor** Ms C Jones Q: BA, MA. M: IACT.
B Yrs. Est.: 7 (Ref:HM11131)

**JONES, D A**

**D A Jones**, Tyldesley House, 48 Clarence Rd, Llandudno, **Conwy**, LL30 1TW, WAL.
(T) 01492 871285
Speciality: Psychiatry.
B (Ref:HM11132)

**JONES, D E F**

**D E F Jones**, The Physiotherapy Clinic, 29 High St, Merthyr Tydfil, **Glamorgan (Vale of)**, CF47 8DP, WAL.
(T) 01685 723456
Speciality: Physiotherapy.
● **Principal** Mr D Jones
P S T (Ref:HM11133)

**JONES, DARCY**

**Darcy Jones**, North Hampshire Osteopathic Clinic, 27 Chequers Rd, Basingstoke, **Hampshire**, RG21 7PT, ENG.
(T) 01256 352241
Speciality: Osteopathy.
P S T (Ref:HM11134)

**JONES, DAVE**

**Dave Jones**, 8 Forest Glade, London, **London (Greater)**, E11 1LU, ENG.
(T) 020 8989 6565
Speciality: Psychotherapy.
B (Ref:HM11135)

**JONES, DAVID**

**David Jones**, 47 Sutton Rd, Walsall, **Midlands (West)**, WS1 2PQ, ENG.
(T) 01922 622521
Speciality: Osteopathy.
P S T (Ref:HM11136)

**JONES, DAVID**

**David Jones**, 14 Carrwood, Knutsford, **Cheshire**, WA16 8NB, ENG.
(T) 01565 633967
Speciality: Acupuncture.
● **Owner** Mr D Jones
O (Ref:HM11137)

**JONES, EILEEN**

**Eileen Jones**, Ackroyd St, Morley, Leeds, **Yorkshire (West)**, LS27 8PZ, ENG.
(T) 01132 380330
Speciality: Chiropodists (Podiatrists).
● **Owner** Mrs E Jones
S (Ref:HM11138)

**JONES, EILUNED**

**Eiluned Jones**, 32 Samels Court, South Black Lion Lane, London, **London (Greater)**, W6 9TL, ENG.
(T) 020 8748 8148
Speciality: Reflexology.
S T (Ref:HM11139)

**JONES, ELIZABETH**

**Elizabeth Jones**, 326 Southampton Rd, Titchfield, Fareham, **Hampshire**, PO14 4AZ, ENG.
(T) 01329 841204
Speciality: Chiropodists (Podiatrists).
● **Owner** Ms E Jones
S (Ref:HM11140)

**JONES, ELIZABETH M**

**Elizabeth M Jones**, 6 Dovedale Rise, Mitcham, **Surrey**, CR4 3JN, ENG.
(T) 020 8648 2679
Speciality: Chiropodists (Podiatrists).
S (Ref:HM11141)

**JONES, ERIKA**

**Erika Jones**, Martindale House, Lombard St, Newark, **Nottinghamshire**, NG24 1XG, ENG.
(T) 01636 611150
Speciality: Acupuncture.
● **Administrator** Mr S Taylor
O (Ref:HM11142)

**JONES, F J**

**Mrs F J Jones**, 48 Bridge St, Berwick-Upon-Tweed, **Northumberland**, TD15 1AQ, SCO.
(T) 01289 307749 (F) 01289 307749
Speciality: Complementary Medicines & Therapy.
● **Owner** Mrs F Jones
C M (Ref:HM11143)

**JONES, G M E**

**G M E Jones**, 26 Cranworth Rd, Winchester, **Hampshire**, SO22 6SE, ENG.
(T) 01962 854657 (F) 01962 854657
Speciality: Physiotherapy.
● **Owner** Mrs G Jones
P S T (Ref:HM11144)

**JONES, GILL**

**Gill Jones**, Chanslys, Halfway House, Shrewsbury, **Shropshire**, SY5 9EA, ENG.
(T) 01743 885155
Speciality: Chiropodists (Podiatrists).
● **Owner** Mrs G Jones
S (Ref:HM11145)

**JONES, GLENNIS**

**Mrs Glennis Jones**, 88 Rodney St, Liverpool, **Merseyside**, L1 9AR, ENG.
(T) 01517 086070 (F) 01517 097279
Speciality: Physiotherapy.
P S T (Ref:HM11146)

**JONES, H A P**

**H A P Jones**, Bron Haul, High St, Bala, **Gwynedd**, LL23 7AE, WAL.
(T) 01678 520543
Speciality: Chiropodists (Podiatrists).
● **Owner** Mrs S Jones
S (Ref:HM11147)

**JONES, IAN**

**Ian Jones**, The Castle Clinic, 18-20The Ropewalk, Nottingham, **Nottinghamshire**, NG1 5DT, ENG.
(T) 01159 472263 (F) 01159 556306
Speciality: Physiotherapy.
● **Owner** Mr M Pook
P S T (Ref:HM11148)

**JONES, IAN G**

**Ian G Jones**, 3 Spanish Pl, London, **London (Greater)**, W1M 5AN, ENG.
(T) 020 7486 6001



Key continued: **Yrs.Est:** Years Established **Q:** Qualifications **M:** Professional Membership ✔ Indemnity Insurance Accept Credit Cards

YOUR
HORSE
Includes over
1000 saddleries
3000 Riding Schools,
and over1200 breeders
The Ultimate
Guide
to over
8,000
Equestrian
Services
in the UK & Ireland
www.hccyourhorse.com
Also known as
HORSE
RESOURCE
Publishing
HCC
An HCC Next Generation Directory

<u>Speciality:</u> Chiropodists (Podiatrists).
● **Owner** Mr I Jones
S (**Ref:**HM11149)

**JONES, J**

**J Jones**, Hill Cottage, Coventry Rd, Berkswell, Coventry, **Midlands (West)**, CV7 7AZ, ENG.
(T) 01676 532320
<u>Speciality:</u> Herbal Medicine.
M (**Ref:**HM11150)

**JONES, J A**

**J A Jones**, 28 Marine Cres, Goring-By-Sea, Worthing, **Sussex (West)**, BN12 4JF, ENG.
(T) 01903 244655 (F) 01903 244655
<u>Speciality:</u> Chiropodists (Podiatrists).
● **Owner** Mrs J Jones
S (**Ref:**HM11151)

**JONES, J A**

**J A Jones**, 28A Low Skellgate, Ripon, **Yorkshire (North)**, HG4 1BG, ENG.
(T) 01765 607265
<u>Speciality:</u> Chiropodists (Podiatrists).
● **Owner** Mrs J Jones
S (**Ref:**HM11152)

**JONES, J G**

**J G Jones**, Clyn-Coch, Alltwalis, Carmarthen, **Carmarthenshire**, SA32 7EA, WAL.
(T) 01559 384382
<u>Speciality:</u> Osteopathy.
● **Owner** Mr J Jones
P S T (**Ref:**HM11153)

**JONES, J M**

**J M Jones**, 3 Park Villas, Ruthin Rd, Mold, **Flintshire**, CH7 1QG, WAL.
(T) 01352 756981
<u>Speciality:</u> Acupuncture.
● **Owner** Mrs J Jones
O (**Ref:**HM11154)

**JONES, J W**

**J W Jones**, 16 Darley Cl, Widnes, **Cheshire**, WA8 4EB, ENG.
(T) 01514 204572
(E) jwejones@bushinternet.com
<u>Speciality:</u> Chiropody, Podiatry. ✔
● **Owner/Chiropodist/Podiatrist**
Mr J Jones Q: MBChA, MSSCh. M: B.A.Ch.P.
M <u>Yrs. Est.:</u> 10 (**Ref:**HM11155)

**JONES, JACQUELINE A**

**Jacqueline A Jones**, Suite 2 Thatcham House, Turners Drive, Thatcham, **Berkshire**, RG19 4QB, ENG.
(T) 01635 871677
<u>Speciality:</u> Physiotherapy.
● **Owner** Miss J Jones
P S T (**Ref:**HM11156)

**JONES, JANET**

**Janet Jones**, 10 Burr Cl, Sutton, Witney, **Oxfordshire**, OX8 1SJ, ENG.
(T) 01865 883801
<u>Speciality:</u> Reflexology.
S T (**Ref:**HM11157)

**JONES, JEAN**

**Jean Jones**, 1 The Bight, South Woodham Ferrers, Chelmsford, **Essex**, CM3 5GJ, ENG.
(T) 01245 323408
<u>Speciality:</u> Reflexology.
S T (**Ref:**HM11158)

**JONES, JENNIFER**

**Jennifer Jones**, 19 Armthorpe Drive, Little Sutton, Ellesmere Port, **Merseyside**, CH66 4NN, ENG.
(T) 01513 394764
<u>Speciality:</u> Acupuncture.
● **Owner** Ms J Jones
O (**Ref:**HM11159)

**JONES, JOYCE**

**Joyce Jones**, 41 Riddings Rd, Timperley, Altrincham, **Cheshire**, WA15 6BW, ENG.
(T) 01619 627570
<u>Speciality:</u> Reflexology.
S T (**Ref:**HM11160)

**JONES, JULIE**

**Julie Jones**, 125 Powder Mill Lane, Twickenham, **London (Greater)**, TW2 6EG, ENG.
(T) 020 8755 1576
<u>Speciality:</u> Reflexology.
S T (**Ref:**HM11161)

**JONES, KATHY**

**Kathy Jones**, 101 Canonbury Rd, London, **London (Greater)**, N1 2XB, ENG.
(T) 020 7226 0804
<u>Speciality:</u> Chiropodists (Podiatrists).
S (**Ref:**HM11162)

**JONES, KELLIE**

**Kellie Jones**, 22 Waterson Vale, Chelmsford, **Essex**, CM2 9PB, ENG.
(T) 07775 858037
<u>Speciality:</u> Reflexology.
S T (**Ref:**HM11163)

**JONES, KELLIE A**

**Kellie A Jones**, 11 Colyers Reach, Chelmsford, **Essex**, CM2 6RW, ENG.
(T) 01245 451662
<u>Speciality:</u> Reflexology.
● **Owner** Ms K Jones
S T (**Ref:**HM11164)

**JONES, KEVIN D G**

**Kevin D G Jones**, 45 Barrs Court Rd, Aylestone Hill, Hereford, **Herefordshire**, HR1 1EQ, ENG.
(T) 01432 266986
(E) kevin.jones@virgin.net
<u>Speciality:</u> Osteopathy. ✔
● **Osteopath** Mr K Jones Q: DO. M: GOsC.
S <u>Yrs. Est.:</u> 12 (**Ref:**HM11165)

**JONES, L R**

**L R Jones**, 26 Clarence St, Gloucester, **Gloucestershire**, GL1 1DP, ENG.
(T) 01452 523164
<u>Speciality:</u> Chiropodists (Podiatrists).
S (**Ref:**HM11166)

**JONES, LYNDA**

**Lynda Jones**, 36 Murray Court, Ascot, **Berkshire**, SL5 9BP, ENG.
(T) 01344 625526
<u>Speciality:</u> Homeopathy.
● **Owner** Mrs L Jones
M (**Ref:**HM11167)

**JONES, M**

**M Jones**, 126 Ferry Lane, Stanley, Wakefield, **Yorkshire (West)**, WF3 4LH, ENG.
(T) 01924 364039
<u>Speciality:</u> Reflexology.
S T (**Ref:**HM11168)

**JONES, M**

**M Jones**, 55A Comber Rd, Dundonald, Belfast, **County Antrim**, BT16 0BJ, NIR.
(T) 028 9048 2337 (F) 028 9048 2337
<u>Speciality:</u> Physiotherapy.
● **Owner** Mr M Jones
P S T (**Ref:**HM11169)

**JONES, M E**

**Mrs M E Jones**, Dan Y Cefn, Manordeilo, Llandeilo, **Carmarthenshire**, SA19 7BD, WAL.
(T) 01550 777448 (F) 01550 777067
<u>Speciality:</u> Physiotherapy.
● **Owner** Mrs M Jones
P S T (**Ref:**HM11170)

**JONES, MARGARET**

**Margaret Jones**, Fairfields Clinic, Skippetts Lane West, Basingstoke, **Hampshire**, RG21 3HP, ENG.
(T) 01256 326980
<u>Speciality:</u> Reflexology.
● **Owner** Ms M Jones
S T (**Ref:**HM11171)

**JONES, MARGARET**

**Margaret Jones**, 11 Norwich Avenue, Rochdale, **Lancashire**, OL11 5JZ, ENG.
(T) 01706 356456
<u>Speciality:</u> Reflexology.
S T (**Ref:**HM11172)

**JONES, MARILYN**

**Marilyn Jones**, Maple Beck, Cl Lane, Alsager, **Cheshire**, ST7 2TY, ENG.
(T) 01270 873214
<u>Speciality:</u> Acupuncture.
O (**Ref:**HM11173)

**JONES, MARILYN D**

**Marilyn D Jones**, Hillsea, Scredda, St. Austell, **Cornwall**, PL25 5RY, ENG.
(T) 01726 70252
<u>Speciality:</u> Hypnosis.
B (**Ref:**HM11174)

**JONES, MARION**

**Marion Jones**, Natural Health Clinic, 98 Cathedral Rd, Cardiff, **Glamorgan (Vale of)**, CF11 9LP, WAL.
(T) 029 2022 2221
<u>Speciality:</u> Aromatherapy.
M O (**Ref:**HM11175)

**JONES, MARION**

**Marion Jones**, 10 Pen-Y-Graig, Cardiff, **Glamorgan (Vale of)**, CF14 6SU, WAL.
(T) 029 2061 0433
<u>Speciality:</u> Aromatherapy.
● **Owner** Mrs M Jones
M O (**Ref:**HM11176)

**JONES, MARION**

**Marion Jones**, Bryn-Eithin, Brithdir, Llanfyllin, **Powys**, SY22 5HD, WAL.
(T) 01691 648061
<u>Speciality:</u> Osteopathy.
● **Owner** Mrs M Jones
P S T (**Ref:**HM11177)

**JONES, MARTIN**

**Martin Jones**, The Tonbridge Clinic, 339 Shipbourne Rd, Tonbridge, **Kent**, TN10 3ET, ENG.
(T) 01732 350255 (F) 01732 362343
<u>Speciality:</u> Acupuncture.
O (**Ref:**HM11178)

**JONES, MICHAEL A**

**Michael A Jones**, 143 Farren Rd, Birmingham, **Midlands (West)**, B31 5HL, ENG.
(T) 01216 089262
<u>Speciality:</u> Reflexology.
● **Owner** Mr M Jones
S T (**Ref:**HM11179)

**JONES, MONICA**

**Monica Jones**, 80 Elers Rd, London, **London (Greater)**, W13 9QD, ENG.
(T) 020 8579 9785
<u>Speciality:</u> Hypnosis.
● **Owner** Mrs M Jones
B (**Ref:**HM11180)

**JONES, NEIL**

**Neil Jones**, 139 Wolverhampton Rd, Burgess Bridge, Codsall, Wolverhampton, **Midlands (West)**, WV8 1PD, ENG.
(T) 01902 844030 (F) 01902 845177
<u>Speciality:</u> Physiotherapy.
● **Partner** Mr J Barnes
P S T (**Ref:**HM11181)

**JONES, NIGEL**

**Osteopath**, Littlehampton Natural Health Centre, 10C Granville Rd, Littlehampton, **Sussex (West)**, BN17 5JU, ENG.
(T) 01903 734373 (F) 01903 734373
(E) nigeljone@yahoo.co.uk
<u>Speciality:</u> Manipulation, Osteopathy. ✔
● **Owner/Osteopath** Mr N Jones Q: DO, MICO. M: GOsC.
S <u>Yrs. Est.:</u> 12 (**Ref:**HM11182)

**JONES, P**

**P Jones**, 13 New St, Stourport-on-Severn, **Worcestershire**, DY13 8UW, ENG.
(T) 01299 878058
<u>Speciality:</u> Chiropodists (Podiatrists).
● **Owner** Miss P Jones
S (**Ref:**HM11183)

**JONES, P**

**P Jones**, 16 Snowgatehead, New Mill, Huddersfield, **Yorkshire (West)**, HD7 7DH, ENG.
(T) 01484 682196
<u>Speciality:</u> Herbal Medicine.
M (**Ref:**HM11184)

**JONES, P R**

**P R Jones**, 9 Sussex Pl, Slough, **Berkshire**, SL1 1NH, ENG.
(T) 01753 522077
<u>Speciality:</u> Chiropodists (Podiatrists).



Key: B Mind-Body Medicine C Complementary Medicine H Self Help Treatment M Medicinal Therapy O Oriental Medicine P Postural Therapy S Manipulative Structural Therapy T Touch Therapy

● **Owner** Mr P Jones
**S** (**Ref:**HM11185)

## JONES, PAT
**Pat Jones**, The Halifax Clinic Of Natural Medicine, 22 Clare Rd, Halifax, **Yorkshire (West)**, HX1 2HX, ENG.
(T) 01422 340919
Speciality: Herbalists.
**M** (**Ref:**HM11186)

## JONES, PATRICIA JEAN
**Patricia Jean Jones**, Penwith, 9 Margaret Cl, Bicester, **Oxfordshire**, OX6 8DH, ENG.
(T) 01869 241290
Speciality: Reflexology.
**S T** (**Ref:**HM11187)

## JONES, PAULA
**Paula Jones**, RCBC Sports Injury & Physiotherapy Clinic, Royal County, Bracknell, **Berkshire**, RG12 7PB, ENG.
(T) 01344 869066
Speciality: Physiotherapy.
**P S T** (**Ref:**HM11188)

## JONES, PAULINE
**Pauline Jones**, The Cranleigh Chiropractic Clinic, Ruffold Lodge, Cranleigh, **Surrey**, GU6 8LT, ENG.
(T) 01483 274002
Speciality: Chiropractors.
**P S T** (**Ref:**HM11189)

## JONES, RAYMOND
**Raymond Jones**, 55 High St, Midsomer Norton, Bath, **Somerset**, BA3 2DQ, ENG.
(T) 01373 463098
Speciality: Allergy Testing, Chiropractic. ✓
● **Chiropractor** Dr H Jones **Q:** DC.
● **Chiropractor** Dr R Jones **Q:** DC.
**P** Yrs. Est.: 19 (**Ref:**HM11190)

## JONES, ROSALIND
**Rosalind Jones**, 137 Magdalen Rd, Oxford, **Oxfordshire**, OX4 1RJ, ENG.
(T) 01865 396939
Speciality: Osteopathy.
● **Owner** Mr M Franklin
**P S T** (**Ref:**HM11191)

## JONES, RUTH C
**Ruth C Jones**, Hampshire Tennis & Health Club, Botley Rd, West End, Southampton, **Hampshire**, SO30 3HA, ENG.
(T) 023 8036 3009 (F) 023 8036 1100
Speciality: Physiotherapy.
● **Owner** Miss R Jones
**P S T** (**Ref:**HM11192)

## JONES, S
**S Jones**, 1a Coniston Rd, Astley, Tyldesley, Manchester, **Manchester (Greater)**, M29 7AS, ENG.
(T) 01942 887881
Speciality: Chiropodists (Podiatrists).
● **Owner** Mrs S Jones
**S** (**Ref:**HM11193)

## JONES, S
**S Jones**, Norris Rd Surgery, 356 Norris Rd, Sale, **Cheshire**, M33 2RL, ENG.
(T) 01619 625464
Speciality: Chiropodists (Podiatrists).
● **Doctor** Dr G Platt
**S** (**Ref:**HM11194)

## JONES, SARAH
**Sarah Jones**, 22 Botany Drive, Dudley, **Midlands (West)**, DY3 3XT, ENG.
(T) 01902 679266
Speciality: Reflexology.
**S T** (**Ref:**HM11195)

## JONES, SHARON
**Mrs Sharon Jones**, 7 Orchard Prde, Eastbourne, **Sussex (East)**, BN20 9JP, ENG.
(T) 01323 484455
Speciality: Chiropodists (Podiatrists).
● **Owner** Mrs S Jones **Q:** Inst.CH.P.
**S** (**Ref:**HM11196)

## JONES, SHEILA
**Sheila Jones**, 1 University Approach, Birmingham, **Midlands (West)**, B15 2SB, ENG.
(T) 01214 727989
Speciality: Hypnotherapy.
● **Owner** Mrs S Jones
**B** (**Ref:**HM11197)

## JONES, SHIRLEY
**Shirley Jones**, 6 New Rd, Castlethorpe, Milton Keynes, **Buckinghamshire**, MK19 7EH, ENG.
(T) 01908 510634
Speciality: Chiropodists (Podiatrists).
**S** (**Ref:**HM11198)

## JONES, STEVE
**Steve Jones**, 39 Tydfil Pl, Cardiff, **Glamorgan (Vale of)**, CF23 5HP, WAL.
(T) 029 2048 4555
Speciality: Acupuncture.
**O** (**Ref:**HM11199)

## JONES, VAL
**Val Jones**, 53 Fairfield Rd, Bournheath, Bromsgrove, **Worcestershire**, B61 9JL, ENG.
(T) 01527 878611
Speciality: Chiropody. ✓
● **Owner/Chiropodist** Mrs V Jones **Q:** MSc (Chiro).
**M** Yrs. Est.: 15 (**Ref:**HM11200)

## JONES, VALERIE I
**Valerie I Jones**, Halkyn House, 19 Rhosddu Rd, Wrexham, LL11 1NE, **WAL**.
(T) 01978 353565
Speciality: Chiropodists (Podiatrists).
● **Owner** Miss V Jones
**S** (**Ref:**HM11201)

## JONES, W PRITCHARD
**W Pritchard Jones**, East View, East St, Llantwit Major, **Glamorgan (Vale of)**, CF61 1XY, WAL.
(T) 01446 796077
Speciality: Chiropodists (Podiatrists).
**S** (**Ref:**HM11202)

## JONES, WENDY
**Broadwater Osteopathic Practice**, 2 Sompting Rd, Broadwater, Worthing, **Sussex (West)**, BN14 9EP, ENG.
(T) 01903 203360
Speciality: Electrotherapy, Massage (Therapeutic). ✓
● **Remedial Masseuse** Ms W Jones **Q:** LCSP. **M:** LCSP.
**S** Yrs. Est.: 12 (**Ref:**HM11203)

## JONES-GRIFFITHS, A M
**Mrs A M Jones-Griffiths**, Hill Farm, Penhow, Caldicot, **Monmouthshire**, NP26 3AE, WAL.
(T) 01633 820321
Speciality: Physiotherapy.
● **Owner** Mrs A Jones-Griffiths
**P S T** (**Ref:**HM11204)

## JONSON, RONALD
**Ronald Jonson**, Natural Health York Clinic, Guildford Rd, Woking, **Surrey**, GU22 7QU, ENG.
(T) 01483 720464
Speciality: Osteopathy.
**P S T** (**Ref:**HM11205)

## JOOP TANIS
**Joop Tanis**, Cambridge City Football Club, The Long Room, Milton Rd, Cambridge, **Cambridgeshire**, CB4 1UY, ENG.
(T) 01223 368886
Speciality: Physiotherapy.
**P S T** (**Ref:**HM11206)

## JORDAN & ASSOCIATES
**Gill Jordan & Associates**, 120 Church Lane, London, **London (Greater)**, N2 0TB, ENG.
(T) 020 8883 7828
Speciality: Physiotherapy.
**P S T** (**Ref:**HM11207)

## JORDAN, A I
**A I Jordan**, 43 Mayfield Gardens, London, **London (Greater)**, W7 3RB, ENG.
(T) 020 8578 4431
Speciality: Psychotherapy.
● **Owner** Mrs A Jordan
**B** (**Ref:**HM11208)

## JORDAN, J P
**J P Jordan**, 15 Ingram Cl, Horsham, **Sussex (West)**, RH12 1JU, ENG.
(T) 01403 267454
Speciality: Physiotherapy.
● **Owner** Mr J Jordan
**P S T** (**Ref:**HM11209)

## JORDAN, PAMELA
**Pamela Jordan**, Aylesbury, **Buckinghamshire**, HP20, ENG.
(T) 01296 425365
Speciality: Bach Remedies.
**M** (**Ref:**HM11210)

## JORDAN, S E
**S E Jordan**, Station Rd, Sidcup, **Kent**, DA15 7DU, ENG.
(T) 020 8300 9233
Speciality: Chiropodists (Podiatrists).
● **Owner** Mrs S Jordan
**S** (**Ref:**HM11211)

## JORDAN, TESSA
**Tessa Jordan**, Ipswich, **Suffolk**, IP4, ENG.
(T) 01473 728498
Speciality: Bach Remedies.
**M** (**Ref:**HM11212)

## JORGENSEN, ANNE
**Anne Jorgensen**, Petersham Physiotherapy Clinic, 1 Ashley Gardens, Richmond, **Surrey**, TW10 7BU, ENG.
(T) 020 8940 0075
Speciality: Physiotherapy.
**P S T** (**Ref:**HM11213)

## JOS, SHANAHAN THOS
**Shanahan Thos Jos**, 5 Devon Pl, The Cresent, **County Galway**, IRE.
(T) 09158 1575
Speciality: Acupuncture.
**O** (**Ref:**HM11214)

## JOSEPH CLINIC
**Joseph Clinic**, 3 Bedford Rd, South Woodford, London, **London (Greater)**, E18 2AQ, ENG.
(T) 020 8989 7569 (F) 020 8989 8143
(E) eftekhar@
Speciality: Acupuncture, Osteopathy. ✓
● **Osteopath** Dr F Eftekhari **M:** GOsC.
**S** Yrs. Est.: 36 (**Ref:**HM11215)

## JOSEPH, A
**A Joseph**, 52 Criffel Avenue, London, **London (Greater)**, SW2 4BN, ENG.
(T) 020 8674 1233 (F) 020 8674 1543
Speciality: Hypnotherapy.
● **Owner** Mr A Joseph
**B** (**Ref:**HM11216)

## JOSEPH, BRIAN
**Brian Joseph**, Finchley House, 858 Finchley Rd, London, **London (Greater)**, NW11 6AB, ENG.
(T) 020 8458 2586
Speciality: Osteopathy.
**P S T** (**Ref:**HM11217)

## JOSEPH, EMMA
**Emma Joseph**, Finchley House, 858 Finchley Rd, London, **London (Greater)**, NW11 6AB, ENG.
(T) 020 8201 9201
Speciality: Chiropodists (Podiatrists).
● **Owner** Miss E Joseph
**S** (**Ref:**HM11218)

## JOSEPHINE, LYNCH
**Lynch Josephine A C M O**, The Odyssey Ctr 15A Wicklow St, Dublin, **County Dublin**, IRE.
(T) 01467 0116
Speciality: Herbalists.
**M** (**Ref:**HM11219)

## JOSHI, NICK
**Nick Joshi (Surbiton Chiropody)**, 26c Cottage Gr, Surbiton, **Surrey**, KT6 4JH, ENG.
(T) 020 8390 2700
Speciality: Chiropodists (Podiatrists).
● **Owner** Mr N Joshi
**S** (**Ref:**HM11220)

## JOSLING, A
**A Josling**, 41 Terminus Rd, Eastbourne, **Sussex (East)**, BN21 3QL, ENG.
(T) 01323 430025 (F) 01323 648452
Speciality: Homeopathy.
● **Partner** Mrs S Josling

B (Ref:HM11221)

## JOURNAL OF ORIGINAL IDEAS
**Journal Of Original Ideas**, 8 Willow Rd, London, **London (Greater)**, NW3 1TJ, ENG.
(T) 020 7794 8717
Speciality: Psychology.
● **Owner** Mr S Meyerson
B (Ref:HM11222)

## JOURNEY SEMINARS
**Journey Seminars Ltd (The)**, Po Box 1992, Iver, **Buckinghamshire**, SL0 0XX, ENG.
(T) 01753 630060 (F) 01753 630063
Speciality: Complementary Medicines & Therapy.
● **Managing Director** Mr K Billett
M (Ref:HM11223)

## JOWETT, G M
**G M Jowett**, 4 St Johns Rd, Taunton, **Somerset**, TA1 4AZ, ENG.
(T) 01823 277287
Speciality: Physiotherapy.
● **Owner** Mr G Jowett
P S T (Ref:HM11224)

## JOWETT, R S J
**R S J Jowett**, Unit 2 Realtex House, Leeds Rd, Rawdon, Leeds, **Yorkshire (West)**, LS19 6AX, ENG.
(T) 01132 501999 (F) 01132 501505
Speciality: Hypnosis.
● **Principal** Mr R Jowett
B (Ref:HM11225)

## JOWETT, R S J
**R S J Jowett**, Suite 1, 12 Oxford St, Harrogate, **Yorkshire (North)**, HG1 1PU, ENG.
(T) 01423 530505
Speciality: Hypnotherapy.
● **Owner** Mr R Jowett
B (Ref:HM11226)

## JOWETT, R S J
**R S J Jowett**, Royal Chambers, 110 Station Prde, Harrogate, **Yorkshire (North)**, HG1 1EP, ENG.
(T) 01423 530505
Speciality: Hypnosis.
B (Ref:HM11227)

## JOWSEY, J E
**J E Jowsey**, 428B Ecclesall Rd, Sheffield, **Yorkshire (South)**, S11 8PX, ENG.
(T) 01142 301597
Speciality: Physiotherapy.
P S T (Ref:HM11228)

## JOY WALTER CHARTERED PHYSIO
**Joy Walter Chartered Physiotherapist**, Hinchley Wood Practice, Woodside House, Station Approach, Esher, **Surrey**, KT10 0WQ, ENG.
(T) 020 8398 5588
Speciality: Physiotherapy.
P S T (Ref:HM11229)

## JOY, ALAN
**Alan Joy**, 318 Oldham Rd, Royton, Oldham, **Lancashire**, OL2 5AS, ENG.
(T) 01616 526781
Speciality: Osteopathy.
P S T (Ref:HM11230)

## JOY, JANET
**Janet Joy**, 27 Darwell Drive, Stone Cross, Pevensey, **Sussex (East)**, BN24 5PG, ENG.
(T) 01323 461889
Speciality: Cognitive Therapy, Colour Therapy, Complementary Therapy, Counselling, Healing Therapy, Humanistic Psychology, Hypnosis, Hypnotherapy, Neuro-Linguistic Program, Psychotherapy, Stress Therapy, Visualisation Therapy. ✔
● **Ericksonian Psychotherapist**
Mrs J Joy Q: BEd (Hons), Dip.EH, NLP. M: BPS, NCH, NCP.
B Yrs. Est.: 12 (Ref:HM11231)

## JOY, M E
**M E Joy**, Shockerwick Cottage, Upper Shockerwick, Bath, **Somerset**, BA1 7LH, ENG.
(T) 01225 742960
Speciality: Physiotherapy.
● **Owner** Mrs M Joy
P S T (Ref:HM11232)

## JOY, NICOLA & TOMMY
**Nicola & Tommy Joy Merchants**, 80 Churchfield Rd, Houghton Regis, Dunstable, **Bedfordshire**, LU5 5HW, ENG.
(T) 01582 866348
Speciality: Clairvoyants & Palmists.
● **Partner** Mr T Joy
B (Ref:HM11233)

## JOYCE BURTON PHYSIO CLINIC
**Joyce Burton Physiotherapy Clinic**, 48B Main St, Burton Joyce, Nottingham, **Nottinghamshire**, NG14 5DZ, ENG.
(T) 01159 312336
Speciality: Physiotherapy.
P S T (Ref:HM11234)

## JOYCE, EDWIN
**Edwin Joyce**, 52 York Rd, Watford, **Hertfordshire**, WD1 8BE, ENG.
(T) 01923 773060
Speciality: Chiropractic.
P S T (Ref:HM11235)

## JOYCE, HELEN G M
**Helen G M Joyce Osteopath**, 21 High St, Botley, Southampton, **Hampshire**, SO30 2EA, ENG.
(T) 01489 786383
Speciality: Osteopathy. ✔
● **Osteopath** Mrs H Joyce Q: DO. M: GOsC.
S Yrs. Est.: 13 (Ref:HM11236)

## JOYCE, JAMES
**James Joyce**, 93 Henderson Rd, Southsea, **Hampshire**, PO4 9JE, ENG.
(T) 023 9273 8320
Speciality: Physiotherapy.
P S T (Ref:HM11237)

## JOYCE, PHILIP
**Philip Joyce**, 49 Ashton Gardens, Romford, **Essex**, RM6 6RT, ENG.
(T) 020 8491 5427
Speciality: Reflexology.
S T (Ref:HM11238)

## JOYNES, IAN
**Ian Joynes**, 21 Wingrave Cres, Brentwood, **Essex**, CM14 5PA, ENG.
(T) 01422 359597
Speciality: Biomechanics, Chiropody, Nail Surgery, Orthotics, Podiatry. ✔
● **Chiropodist (Podiatrist)**
Mr I Joynes Q: BSc (Hons), DPodM, M.S.C.P, S.R.Ch.
M Yrs. Est.: 20 (Ref:HM11239)

## JOYNES, IAN
**Ian Joynes**, 38 Clare Rd, Halifax, **Yorkshire (West)**, HX1 2HX, ENG.
(T) 01422 359597
Speciality: Chiropodists (Podiatrists).
S (Ref:HM11240)

## JOYOUS FEET
**Joyous Feet**, 59 Heanor Rd, Ilkeston, **Derbyshire**, DE7 8DY, ENG.
(T) 01159 321117
Speciality: Reflexology.
● **Owner** Mrs J Nottingham
S T (Ref:HM11241)

## JUBILEE COMP THERAPY CENTRE
**Jubilee Complementary Therapy Centre**, 31 Jubilee Business Park, Jubilee Cl, Weymouth, **Dorset**, DT4 7BG, ENG.
(T) 01305 766755
Speciality: Complementary Medicines & Therapy.
● **Partner** Mrs A Neil
M (Ref:HM11242)

## JUBY, P
**P Juby**, 35 Tuddenham Rd, Ipswich, **Suffolk**, IP4 2SN, ENG.
(T) 01473 254729
Speciality: Osteopathy.
● **Owner** Mr J Juby
P S T (Ref:HM11243)

## JUDAH, ALISON
**Alison Judah**, Ealing YMCA, 14 Bond St, London, **London (Greater)**, W5 5AA, ENG.
(T) 07956 287776
Speciality: Osteopathy.
P S T (Ref:HM11244)

## JUDD, J R
**J R Judd**, Sharon, First Avenue, Hook End, Brentwood, **Essex**, CM15 0HL, ENG.
(T) 01277 823332
Speciality: Chiropodists (Podiatrists).
S (Ref:HM11245)

## JUDGE, BRENDA
**Brenda Judge**, 16 Clarence Sq, Cheltenham, **Gloucestershire**, GL50 4JN, ENG.
(T) 01242 241933
Speciality: Hypnotherapy.
B (Ref:HM11246)

## JUDGE, J P
**J P Judge**, 43 London Rd, Rainham, Gillingham, **Kent**, ME8 7RG, ENG.
(T) 01634 361720
Speciality: Chiropodists (Podiatrists).
● **Owner** Mr J Judge
S (Ref:HM11247)

## JUDITH CARLYLE HYPNOTHERAPIST
**Judith Carlyle Hypnotherapist**, 14 West Cl, Pontefract, **Yorkshire (West)**, WF8 3NR, ENG.
(T) 01977 702651
Speciality: Hypnotherapy.
B (Ref:HM11248)

## JUDY COURIE - REFLEX & AROMA
**Judy Courie - Reflexology**, The Anstees, Duffryn Cres, Peterston-Super-Ely, Cardiff, **Glamorgan (Vale of)**, CF5 6NF, WAL.
(T) 01446 760633
Speciality: Aromatherapy, Reflexology, Sports Massage. ✔
● **Reflexologist/Aromatherapist**
Ms J Courie Q: ITEC, NVQ L3. M: AoR, GCP.
T Yrs. Est.: 3 (Ref:HM11250)

## JUFFS, C
**C Juffs**, 128 Lower Sandford St, Lichfield, **Staffordshire**, WS13 6RA, ENG.
(T) 01543 262346
Speciality: Alexander Technique.
● **Owner** Ms C Juffs
P S (Ref:HM11251)

## JUKES, CLARE
**Clare Jukes**, 4 Colnbrook Court, Old Bath Rd, Colnbrook, Slough, **Berkshire**, SL3 0NN, ENG.
(T) 01753 686244
Speciality: Reflexology.
S T (Ref:HM11252)

## JUKES, M
**M Jukes**, Chesnuts, 72 Chalfont Rd, Seer Green, Beaconsfield, **Buckinghamshire**, HP9 2QP, ENG.
(T) 01494 670038
Speciality: Osteopathy.
P S T (Ref:HM11253)

## JULAILA, A
**A Julaila**, 62 Elsenham Rd, London, **London (Greater)**, E12 6LA, ENG.
(T) 020 8478 7366
Speciality: Osteopathy.
P S T (Ref:HM11254)

## JULIA GREAVES NEW IMAGE
**Julia Greaves New Image**, 95 Kirkgate, Shipley, **Yorkshire (West)**, BD18 3LR, ENG.
(T) 01274 591789
Speciality: Aromatherapy.
M O (Ref:HM11255)

## JULIE ADAMS REFLEXOLOGIST
**Julie Adams Reflexologist**, Old Saddlery, Bratton Fleming, Barnstaple, **Devon**, EX31 4RN, ENG.
(T) 01598 710642
Speciality: Reflexology. ✔
● **Reflexologist** Ms J Adams Q: MBRA. M: BRA.
T Yrs. Est.: 9 (Ref:HM11256)

## JULIE ROSE STADIUM
**Julie Rose Stadium**, Kennington Rd, Kennington, Ashford, **Kent**, TN24 9QP, ENG.
(T) 01233 613131 (F) 01233 613130

Key: B Mind-Body Medicine  C Complementary Medicine  H Self Help Treatment  M Medicinal Therapy  O Oriental Medicine  P Postural Therapy  S Manipulative Structural Therapy  T Touch Therapy

Speciality: Physiotherapy.
● **Owner** Mrs U Martindale
P S T (Ref:HM11257)

**JULIEN, M**
**M Julien**, 497 Aldborough Rd North, Ilford, **Essex**, IG2 7SY, **ENG**.
(T) 020 8599 0625
Speciality: Psychotherapy.
● **Owner** Mr M Julien
B (Ref:HM11258)

**JULIEN-LAFERRIER, CHRISTINE**
**Christine Julien-Laferrier**, The Chelsea Practice, 186 Fulham Rd, London, **London (Greater)**, SW10 9PN, **ENG**.
(T) 020 7351 9918 (F) 020 7352 3359
Speciality: Physiotherapy.
● **Partner** Mrs H Chesser
P S T (Ref:HM11259)

**JULIES**
**Julies**, 16 Firwood Cl, Neath, **Glamorgan (Vale of)**, SA10 7UR, **WAL**.
(T) 01639 632309
Speciality: Aromatherapy.
● **Owner** Mrs J Cross
M O (Ref:HM11260)

**JULLINGS, ANGELA**
**Angela Jullings**, The Hogarth Clinic, Airedale Avenue, London, **London (Greater)**, W4 2NW, **ENG**.
(T) 020 8723 0528
Speciality: Hypnotherapy.
B (Ref:HM11261)

**JUNA, F**
**F Juna**, 10 Eldon Rd, Reading, **Berkshire**, RG1 4DH, **ENG**.
(T) 01189 502002
Speciality: Homeopathy.
M (Ref:HM11262)

**JUNE NORMAN BEAUTY CLINIC**
**June Norman Beauty Clinic**, 4 The Sq, Lightwater, **Surrey**, GU18 5SS, **ENG**.
(T) 01276 475511
Speciality: Electrolysis.
● **Owner** Mrs J Norman
T (Ref:HM11263)

**JUNE PLATTS ASSOCIATES**
**June Platts Associates**, 24 Telegraph Lane, Four Marks, Alton, **Hampshire**, GU34 5AX, **ENG**.
(T) 01420 561797
Speciality: Psychotherapy.
● **Owner** Mrs J Platts
B (Ref:HM11264)

**JUNE, LUCINDA**
**Lucinda June**, 24 Bluebell Avenue, Penistone, Sheffield, **Yorkshire (South)**, S36 6LQ, **ENG**.
(T) 01226 766709
Speciality: Clairvoyants & Palmists.
● **Owner** Mrs L June
B (Ref:HM11265)

**JUNG CENTRE**
**Jung Centre**, 29 Manor St, Dublin, **County Dublin**, **IRE**.
(T) 01868 4363
Speciality: Complementary Medicines & Therapy.
M (Ref:HM11266)

**JUNIPA SALES**
**Junipa Sales**, The Vines, Robbs Lane, Outwell, Wisbech, **Cambridgeshire**, PE14 8PN, **ENG**.
(T) 01945 773806
Speciality: Complementary Medicines & Therapy.
C M (Ref:HM11267)

**JUNIPER BERRY**
**Juniper Berry Co**, Woodlands, Trinity Wood Rd, Hockley, **Essex**, SS5 5JW, **ENG**.
(T) 01702 204264 (F) 01702 204264
Speciality: Aromatherapy.
● **Partner** Mrs M Juniper
M O (Ref:HM11268)

**JUNNER, ROSEMARY**
**Rosemary Junner**, 62 Galbraith Drive, Milngavie, Glasgow, **Glasgow (City of)**, G62 6NE, **SCO**.
(T) 01419 564004
Speciality: Chiropodists (Podiatrists).
● **Owner** Mrs R Junner
S (Ref:HM11269)

**JU-PIERRE, FRANK**
**Frank Ju-Pierre**, 459 Green Lanes, London, **London (Greater)**, N13 4BS, **ENG**.
(T) 020 8882 4262
Speciality: Chiropodists (Podiatrists).
● **Owner** Mr F Ju-Pierre
S (Ref:HM11270)

**JUPP, DAVID M**
**David M Jupp**, The Old Nursery Office, Rock Rd, Storrington, Pulborough, **Sussex (West)**, RH20 3JL, **ENG**.
(T) 01903 892081
Speciality: Chiropodists (Podiatrists).
S (Ref:HM11271)

**JUPP, DAVID M**
**David M Jupp**, Horstmanns Opticians Ltd, 18 Carfax, Horsham, **Sussex (West)**, RH12 1ED, **ENG**.
(T) 01403 265287
Speciality: Chiropodists (Podiatrists).
S (Ref:HM11272)

**JUPP, J**
**J Jupp**, 86 Longbrook St, Exeter, **Devon**, EX4 6AP, **ENG**.
(T) 01392 434074
Speciality: Reflexology.
S T (Ref:HM11273)

**JURIANSZ, ALAN & JENNIFER**
**Juriansz Alan & Jennifer**, 88 Heath Rd, Twickenham, **London (Greater)**, TW1 4BW, **ENG**.
(T) 020 8892 2356
Speciality: Chiropractic.
P S T (Ref:HM11274)

**JURY, CATHY**
**Cathy Jury**, 2 Mill Lane, Bluntisham, Huntingdon, **Cambridgeshire**, PE28 3LR, **ENG**.
(T) 01487 841804
Speciality: Reflexology.
S T (Ref:HM11275)

**JURY, YAEL**
**Yael Jury**, 87 Tumulus Rd, Saltdean, Brighton, **Sussex (East)**, BN2 8FR, **ENG**.
(T) 01273 390151
Speciality: Reflexology.
S T (Ref:HM11276)

**JUST 4 U**
**Just 4 U**, The Kiosk, Midland Rd, Swadlincote, **Derbyshire**, DE11 0AN, **ENG**.
(T) 01283 211900 (F) 01283 229273
Speciality: Aromatherapy.
● **Owner** Mrs L Fearn
M O (Ref:HM11277)

**JUST ESSENTIALS**
**Just Essentials**, 88 High St, Needham Market, Ipswich, **Suffolk**, IP6 8DG, **ENG**.
(T) 01449 720724 (F) 01449 720724
Speciality: Aromatherapy.
● **Owner** Miss A Deakin
M O (Ref:HM11278)

**JUST FEET CHIROPODY CLINICS**
**Just Feet Chiropody Clinics**, 227B Walworth Rd, London, **London (Greater)**, SE17 1RL, **ENG**.
(T) 020 7277 2229
Speciality: Chiropractors.
P S T (Ref:HM11279)

**JUST FOR FEET**
**Just For Feet**, 22 Glenkirk Drive, Glasgow, **Glasgow (City of)**, G15 6DH, **SCO**.
(T) 01419 490254
Speciality: Chiropodists (Podiatrists).
● **Owner** Mrs E Fraser
S (Ref:HM11280)

**JUST IMAGINE**
**Just Imagine**, 18 Matthew St, Dunstable, **Bedfordshire**, LU6 1SD, **ENG**.
(T) 01582 665400
Speciality: Complementary Medicines & Therapy.
C M (Ref:HM11281)

**JUST JILLS**
**Just Jills**, 12 The Broadway, Woodhall Spa, **Lincolnshire**, LN10 6ST, **ENG**.
(T) 01526 353794
(E) justjill@ntlworld.com
Speciality: Bach Remedies, Counselling, Homeopathy, Reflexology. ✔
● **Homeopath/Reflexologist/Counsellor** Mrs G Robinson **Q:** BIH, HMD, ITEC. **M:** ASC, BSY.
C Yrs. Est.: 4 (Ref:HM11282)

**JUST MAGNOTHERAPY**
**Just Magnotherapy**, 19 Lowcroft, Woodthorpe, Nottingham, **Nottinghamshire**, NG5 4JR, **ENG**.
(T) 01159 202810
Speciality: Magnetic Therapy.
M (Ref:HM11283)

**JUST MASSAGE**
**Just Massage**, 52 Tavistock St, Leamington Spa, **Warwickshire**, CV32 5PW, **ENG**.
(T) 01926 311414
Speciality: Massage (Therapeutic).
M (Ref:HM11284)

**JUST RELAX**
**Just Relax**, The New Parsonage, 47 Moorend Rd, Yardley Gobion, Towcester, **Northamptonshire**, NN12 7UF, **ENG**.
(T) 01908 542201
Speciality: Indian Head Massage, Reflexology, Swedish Body Massage. ✔
● **Owner/Reflexologist** Ms H Jones **Q:** MIFR. **M:** IFR.
C T Yrs. Est.: 6 (Ref:HM11285)

**JUSTRICH SWISS HRBL BODY CARE**
**Justrich Swiss Herbal Body Care**, 4 Bramble Walk, Roundswell, Barnstaple, **Devon**, EX31 3RF, **ENG**.
(T) 01271 375095
Speciality: Complementary Medicines & Therapy.
C M (Ref:HM11286)

**JUSTRICH UK**
**Justrich UK**, Station Rd, Aslacton, Norwich, **Norfolk**, NR15 2DU, **ENG**.
(T) 01379 677556 (F) 01379 677556
Speciality: Complementary Medicines & Therapy.
● **Owner** Mrs E Goody
M (Ref:HM11287)

**K BANFIELD NATUROPATHY/OSTEO**
**Katie Banfield Osteopathy And Naturopathy**, Horn St Surgery, 24 Horn St, Winslow, **Buckinghamshire**, HK18 3AL, **ENG**.
(F) 0870 1313965
(E) katie.banfield@btinternet.com
Speciality: Aromatherapy, Cranial Osteopathy, Manipulation, Massage (Therapeutic), Naturopathy, Nutritional Therapy, Osteopathy, Vitamin Therapy, Visceral Osteopathy. ✔
● **Osteopath/Naturopath**
Ms K Banfield
(T) 01296 612361 **Q:** BSc (Hons), ND. **M:** BNA, GOsC.
S Yrs. Est.: 8 (Ref:HM11288)

**K I FED GB PURE HEALTH**
**K I Federation Of GBPure Health**, 80 St Albans Rd, Lytham St. Annes, **Lancashire**, FY8 1XD, **ENG**.
(T) 01253 712417
Speciality: Relaxation Technique.
H T (Ref:HM11289)

**K I FEDERATION OF GB**
**K I Federation Of Great Britain**, The Causeway, Mark, Highbridge, **Somerset**, TA9 4PZ, **ENG**.
(T) 01278 641166
Speciality: Relaxation Technique.
H T (Ref:HM11290)

**K L WRIGHT CHIROPODY SERVICES**
**K L Wright Chiropody Services**, April Cottage, 2 The Green, Havering-Atte-Bower, Romford, **Essex**, RM4 1PL, **ENG**.



Key continued: **Yrs.Est:** Years Established **Q:** Qualifications **M:** Professional Membership ✔ Indemnity Insurance [card] Accept Credit Cards

(T) 01708 757537
Speciality: Chiropodists (Podiatrists).
S (Ref:HM11291)

**KACHA-STONES.COM**

**Kacha Stones**, Glasfryn, Capel Iwan, Newcastle Emlyn, **Carmarthenshire**, SA38 9LT, WAL.
(T) 01559 371503
(E) info@kacha-stones.com
(W) www.kacha-stones.com
Speciality: Aura Therapy, Crystal Healing, Dowsing, Floral Essence Therapy, Gem Essence Therapy, Holistic Healing, Naturopathy, Paranormal Therapies, Pyramid Power, Stress Therapy, Yoga.
● **Owner/Crystal Healer** Mr S Wells
B Yrs. Est.: 8 (Ref:HM11292)

**KADRI, KALPNA**

**Kalpna Kadri**, 75 Blake Hall Rd, London, **London (Greater)**, E11 3QX, ENG.
(T) 020 8989 1678 (F) 020 8928 0699
Speciality: Homeopathy.
● **Owner** Ms K Kadri
M (Ref:HM11293)

**KAGYU SAMYE DZONG LONDON**

**Kagyu Samye Dzong London Rokpa Trust Registered Charity**, Carlisle Lane, Lambeth, London, **London (Greater)**, SE1 7LG, ENG.
(T) 020 7928 5447 (F) 020 7633 9339
(E) london@samye.org
(W) www.samye.org/london
Speciality: Herbal Medicine, Oriental Diagnosis. ✓
● **Director** Ms A Zangmo
C O Yrs. Est.: 3 (Ref:HM11294)

**KALDESIC, J A**

**J A Kaldesic**, Homelands, Weddington Lane, Caldecote, Nuneaton, **Warwickshire**, CV10 0TS, ENG.
(T) 024 7632 0030
Speciality: Physiotherapy.
● **Owner** Mrs J Kaldesic
P S T (Ref:HM11295)

**KALISCH, DAVID**

**David Kalisch**, The Terrace, 35 Staplegrove Rd, Taunton, **Somerset**, TA1 1DG, ENG.
(T) 01823 338968
Speciality: Psychotherapy.
● **Owner** Ms J Gotto
B (Ref:HM11296)

**KALLAS, JEMIMA**

**Jemima Kallas**, Brondesbury Rd, London, **London (Greater)**, NW6 6BA, ENG.
Speciality: Homeopathy. ✓
● **Homeopath** Ms J Kallas Q: BA, LCH, MBA, RSHom. M: Soc.Hom.
B Yrs. Est.: 4 (Ref:HM11297)

**KALLAWAY, KATHLEEN**

**Kathleen Kallaway**, Crosses Farm, Clayhidon, Cullompton, **Devon**, EX15 3QB, ENG.
(T) 01823 680384
Speciality: Complementary Medicines & Therapy.
C M (Ref:HM11298)

**KALM PHYSIOTHERAPY SERVICES**

**Kalm Physiotherapy Services**, Kalm House, Rotherham, **Yorkshire (South)**, S60 2TR, ENG.
(T) 01709 370654
Speciality: Physiotherapy.
P S T (Ref:HM11299)

**KALTCHEVA-HICKS, DANIELA**

**Daniela Kaltcheva-Hicks**, 27 Beltwood Rd, Belvedere, **Kent**, DA17 6DS, ENG.
(T) 01322 439654
Speciality: Reflexology.
S T (Ref:HM11300)

**KAM, ADELINE K C**

**Adeline K C Kam**, 8 High Ridge, Sydney Rd, London, **London (Greater)**, N10 2LX, ENG.
(T) 020 8883 3282 (F) 020 8883 3282
Speciality: Hypnotherapy.
● **Owner** Ms A Kam
B (Ref:HM11301)

**KAMLASHANTI CHIRO CLINIC**

**Kamlashanti Chiropractic Clinic**, 84 Draycott Avenue, Harrow, **London (Greater)**, HA3 0BY, ENG.
(T) 020 8907 6542
Speciality: Chiropractic.
● **Doctor** Dr I Patel
P S T (Ref:HM11302)

**KANAKAM, JONATHAN**

**Kanakam Jonathan**, 50 Farnham Rd, Slough, **Berkshire**, SL1 3TA, ENG.
(T) 01753 552976
Speciality: Osteopathy.
P S T (Ref:HM11303)

**KANANI, ALPESH**

**Alpesh Kanani**, 98 Central Rd, Worcester Park, **Surrey**, KT4 8HU, ENG.
(T) 020 8335 3433
Speciality: Osteopathy.
P S T (Ref:HM11304)

**KANANI, ALPESH**

**Alpesh Kanani**, 1-3 Rectory Rd, Beckenham, **Kent**, BR3 1HL, ENG.
(T) 020 8663 6110
Speciality: Osteopathy.
P S T (Ref:HM11305)

**KANANI, ALPESH**

**Alpesh Kanani**, 25 Henrietta St, London, **London (Greater)**, WC2E 8NA, ENG.
(T) 020 7836 1505
Speciality: Osteopathy.
P S T (Ref:HM11306)

**KANDOLA, PEARN**

**Pearn Kandola**, 76 Banbury Rd, Oxford, **Oxfordshire**, OX2 6JT, ENG.
(T) 01865 516202 (F) 01865 510812
Speciality: Psychology.
B (Ref:HM11307)

**KANDOLA, PEARN**

**Pearn Kandola**, 18/19 Harcourt St, Dublin, **County Dublin**, IRE.
(T) 01475 3931 (F) 01475 3215
(E) mail@dublin.pearnkandola.com
(W) www.pearnkandola.com
Speciality: Psychology.
B (Ref:HM11308)

**KANE AND ROSS CLINICS**

**Kane And Ross Clinics**, 9 Upper Wimpole St, London, **London (Greater)**, W1G 6LJ, ENG.
(T) 020 7486 9588
(E) kanem@wmin.ac.uk
Speciality: Acupuncture, Cranial Osteopathy, Herbal Medicine, Manipulation, Naturopathy, Osteopathy, Stress Therapy. ✓
● **Practitioner** Mr M Kane Q: DO, MA. M: BAcC, GNC, GOsC.
● **Osteopath** Ms S Robinson Q: BSc, Hons (OST). M: GOsC.
● **Osteopath** Simone Ross Q: B.Phil, BSc, Hons (OST), RGN.
S Yrs. Est.: 12 (Ref:HM11309)

**KANE, MARK**

**Mark Kane**, 9 Upper Wimpole St, London, **London (Greater)**, W1M 7TD, ENG.
(T) 020 7486 9588
Speciality: Complementary Medicines & Therapy.
C M (Ref:HM11310)

**KANE, T**

**T Kane**, 127A Clepington Rd, Dundee, **Angus**, DD3 7PA, SCO.
(T) 01382 826441
Speciality: Chiropodists (Podiatrists).
● **Owner** Mr T Kane
S (Ref:HM11311)

**KANELLAKIS, P**

**P Kanellakis**, 174 Boleyn Rd, London, **London (Greater)**, E7 9QJ, ENG.
(T) 020 8472 2622
Speciality: Psychology.
● **Owner** Mr P Kanellakis
B (Ref:HM11312)

**KANG DA CLINIC**

**Kang Da Clinic**, 245 Manningham Lane, Bradford, **Yorkshire (West)**, BD8 7ER, ENG.
(T) 01274 484514
(E) sfswitala@aol.com
Speciality: Acupressure, Acupuncture, Bach Remedies, Chiropractic, Complementary Therapy, Cranial Osteopathy, Cupping, Herbal Medicine, Kinesiology, Massage (Therapeutic), Moxibustion, Osteopathy. ✓
● **Therapist** Mr G Watts Q: BA, Dip.Ac. M: BAcC.
● **Therapist** Dr L Han Q: B.Ac. M: BAcC, RCHM.
● **Chiropractor** Dr C Waterner Q: DC. M: MCA.
● **Therapist** Dr S Switala Q: BSc, Dip.Ac, Dip.Herb.Med, DO, ND, PhD. M: BAcC, RCHM.
O P S Yrs. Est.: 12 (Ref:HM11313)

**KANUTIN, A**

**A Kanutin**, 19 High St, Chelmsford, **Essex**, CM1 1BE, ENG.
(T) 01245 353779
Speciality: Osteopathy.
● **Owner** A Kanutin
P S T (Ref:HM11314)

**KANUTIN, ANTHONY**

**Anthony Kanutin**, Ground Floor Suite, 51 Milton Rd, Westcliff-on-Sea, **Essex**, SS0 7JP, ENG.
(T) 01702 332424
Speciality: Osteopathy.
● **Owner** Mr A Kanutin
P S T (Ref:HM11315)

**KARADIA, V**

**V Karadia**, Gloucester Park Swimming Pool, Broadmayne, Basildon, **Essex**, SS14 2EB, ENG.
(T) 01268 273343 (F) 01268 280881
Speciality: Osteopathy.
● **Owner** Mr V Karadia
P S T (Ref:HM11316)

**KARAGIANNI, CHRISTINA**

**Christina Karagianni**, Stockport, **Cheshire**, SK12, ENG.
(T) 01663 766789
Speciality: Bach Remedies.
M (Ref:HM11317)

**KARAVANSERIA**

**Karavanseria**, 18 Station Rd, Milngavie, Glasgow, **Glasgow (City of)**, G62 8AB, SCO.
(T) 01419 565500
Speciality: Aromatherapy.
● **Owner** Miss D Lockhart
M O (Ref:HM11318)

**KARDAHJI, F C**

**F C Kardahji**, The Cairn, Palace Rd, Buxton, **Derbyshire**, SK17 6AF, ENG.
(T) 01298 23715
(E) sue.kardahji@which.net
Speciality: Chiropody, Gait Analysis, Podiatry. ✓
● **Chiropodist (Podiatrist)** Farouk Kardahji Q: S.R.Ch. M: S.C.P.
M Yrs. Est.: 18 (Ref:HM11319)

**KAREN**

**Karen**, 26 Chestnut Gr, Barnet, **Hertfordshire**, EN4 8PU, ENG.
(T) 020 8440 2081
Speciality: Clairvoyants & Palmists.
● **Owner** Miss K Porter
B (Ref:HM11320)

**KAREN SLATER AROMATHERAPIST**

**Karen Slater Aromatherapist**, 76 Castle Court, Broomburn Dr, Newton Mearns, Glasgow, **Glasgow (City of)**, G77 5JE, SCO.
(T) 01416 397989
Speciality: Aromatherapy.
M (Ref:HM11321)

**KAREN, CUDWORTH**

**Cudworth Karen**, 3 Dale Croft, Ilkley, **Yorkshire (West)**, LS29 9NS, ENG.
(T) 01943 609952
Speciality: Chiropodists (Podiatrists).
S (Ref:HM11322)

**KAREN, PEARSON**

**Karen Pearson**, Blackbrook Chartered



Key: B Mind-Body Medicine C Complementary Medicine H Self Help Treatment M Medicinal Therapy O Oriental Medicine P Postural Therapy S Manipulative Structural Therapy T Touch Therapy

Physiotherapy Clinic, Scamells Corner, Dorking, **Surrey**, RH5 4DU, ENG.
(T) 01306 888992
Speciality: Physiotherapy.
P S T (Ref:HM11323)

**KARIM, M**

**M Karim**, Bridgend Health Care Centre, Sir Georges St, Thurso, **Highland**, KW14 7AW, SCO.
(T) 01847 896363
Speciality: Acupuncture.
O (Ref:HM11324)

**KARIM, S**

**S Karim**, 785 Whalley New Rd, Blackburn, **Lancashire**, BB1 9BE, ENG.
(T) 07976 501349
Speciality: Hypnosis.
B (Ref:HM11325)

**KARMA COMMUNICATIONS**

**Karma Communications Ltd**, P O Box 6, Stalybridge, **Manchester (Greater)**, SK15 2FD, ENG.
(T) 01613 048444
Speciality: Clairvoyants & Palmists.
● **Owner** Mrs G Edwards
B (Ref:HM11326)

**KARMANIE HOLISTIC THERAPIES**

**Karmanie Holistic Therapies**, 16 Souchenford, Plean, Stirling, FK7 8AP, SCO.
(T) 01786 812899
Speciality: Complementary Medicines & Therapy.
M (Ref:HM11327)

**KARMERS CLINIQUE**

**Karmers Clinique**, Black Rock Mews, Rear Of 220-224 Chatham Hill, Chatham, **Kent**, ME5 7BA, ENG.
(T) 01634 852714 (F) 01634 577384
(E) claire@karmers-clinique.co.uk
Speciality: Aromatherapy, Auricular Therapy, Manual Lymph Drainage, Reflexology, Thermo-Hydrotherapy with essentials oils, Rodder Method. ✔
● **Owner** Mrs C Higglesdon Q: ITEC, TATQ. M: IFA, IFR.
C M Yrs. Est.: 3 (Ref:HM11328)

**KARN, M**

**M Karn**, 32-34 Market St, Southport, **Merseyside**, PR8 1HJ, ENG.
(T) 01704 570655
Speciality: Complementary Medicines & Therapy.
● **Owner** Mrs M Karn
M (Ref:HM11329)

**KARRAN, MARGARETTE**

**Margarette Karran**, 134 Mather Avenue, Liverpool, **Merseyside**, L18 7HB, ENG.
(T) 01517 242765
Speciality: Reflexology.
S T (Ref:HM11330)

**KARRENBAUER, MONIKA**

**Monika Karrenbauer**, Henley-on-Thames, **Oxfordshire**, RG9, ENG.
(T) 01189 403915
Speciality: Bach Remedies.
M (Ref:HM11331)

**KARUNA CENTRE**

**Karuna Centre**, 2 Stafford Gardens, West Stafford, Dorchester, **Dorset**, DT2 8XA, ENG.
(T) 01305 266607
Speciality: Complementary Medicines & Therapy.
● **Practitioner** Mrs E Robinson
M (Ref:HM11332)

**KARYM**

**Karym**, Starley Rd, Coventry, **Midlands (West)**, CV1 3JU, ENG.
(T) 024 7655 0683
Speciality: Clairvoyants & Palmists.
● **Owner** Miss M Lewis
B (Ref:HM11333)

**KATE**

**Kate**, 3 Bird St, Dudley, **Midlands (West)**, DY3 2LX, ENG.
(T) 01384 233303
Speciality: Clairvoyants & Palmists.
● **Owner** Mrs K Parker
B (Ref:HM11334)

**KATE CLEGG REMEDIAL CLINIC**

**Kate Clegg Remedial Clinic**, Market Pl, Garstang, Preston, **Lancashire**, PR3 1ZA, ENG.
(T) 01995 601711
Speciality: Aromatherapy.
M O (Ref:HM11335)

**KATERYNA**

**Kateryna**, 92 Portobello High St, Edinburgh, **Edinburgh (City of)**, EH15 1AN, SCO.
(T) 01314 680712 (F) 01314 680712
Speciality: Clairvoyants & Palmists.
● **Owner** Mrs K Lauder
B (Ref:HM11336)

**KATESMARK, R**

**R Katesmark**, Cheyham Lodge Osteopath Clinic, 11 Cheam Rd, Epsom, **Surrey**, KT17 1ST, ENG.
(T) 020 8393 3038
Speciality: Osteopathy.
● **Principal** Mr R Katesmark
P S T (Ref:HM11337)

**KATHEKE, K**

**K Katheke**, 7 Carnarvon Drive, Hayes, **London (Greater)**, UB3 1PT, ENG.
(T) 020 8573 4747
Speciality: Physiotherapy.
● **Owner** Ms K Kathoke
P S T (Ref:HM11338)

**KATHERINE'S THERAPIES**

**Katherine's Therapies**, 99 Ewell Rd, Surbiton, **Surrey**, KT6 6AH, ENG.
(T) 020 8390 4474
Speciality: Aromatherapy, Massage (Therapeutic), Reflexology, Swedish Body Massage.
M O (Ref:HM11339)

**KATI, NINA**

**Kati Nina**, Clondonnell Rathgormath, **County Waterford**, IRE.
(T) 05164 6273
Speciality: Complementary Medicines & Therapy.
M (Ref:HM11340)

**KATSIS, HAYLEY**

**Katsis Mrs Hayley**, 39 Main Rd, Longfield, **Kent**, DA3 7QT, ENG.
(T) 01474 702895
Speciality: Chiropodists (Podiatrists).
S (Ref:HM11341)

**KATZ, JANICE**

**Janice Katz**, 29 King St, Luton, **Bedfordshire**, LU1 2DW, ENG.
(T) 01582 482220
Speciality: Psychotherapy.
● **Owner** Ms J Katz
B (Ref:HM11342)

**KAUFMANN & MCROBBIE**

**Kaufmann & McRobbie**, 1279 High Rd, London, **London (Greater)**, N20 9HS, ENG.
(T) 020 8446 1900 (F) 020 8446 1900
Speciality: Chiropodists (Podiatrists).
● **Owner** Mr K Garber
S (Ref:HM11343)

**KAULA, CAROLYN M**

**Carolyn M Kaula**, Woodlands, 103 High St, Bembridge, **Isle of Wight**, PO35 5SF, ENG.
(T) 01983 875177
Speciality: Physiotherapy.
P S T (Ref:HM11344)

**KAULA, CAROLYN M**

**Carolyn M Kaula**, Victoria House Physiotherapy Clinic, 102 George St, Ryde, **Isle of Wight**, PO33 2JE, ENG.
(T) 01983 812576
Speciality: Physiotherapy.
P S T (Ref:HM11345)

**KAVANAGH, N**

**N Kavanagh**, 92 Bewdley Rd North, Stourport-on-Severn, **Worcestershire**, DY13 8PS, ENG.
(T) 01299 877774
Speciality: Osteopathy.
P S T (Ref:HM11346)

**KAVANAGH, NIGEL**

**Nigel Kavanagh**, 22 Church St, Kidderminster, **Worcestershire**, DY10 2AW, ENG.
(T) 01562 822115
Speciality: Osteopathy.
● **Principal** Mr N Kavanagh
P S T (Ref:HM11347)

**KAVANAGH, TERESA**

**Kavanagh Teresa**, 9 Hill Court, Portmarnock, **County Dublin**, IRE.
(T) 01846 0390
Speciality: Acupuncture.
O (Ref:HM11348)

**KAY SILVER HYPNOTHERAPY**

**Kay Silver T/A Hypnotherapy**, 22 Chetwode Trce, Aldershot, **Hampshire**, GU11 3NR, ENG.
(T) 01252 676770
Speciality: Hypnosis, Hypnotherapy, Visualisation Therapy, Natural Vision Training. ✔
● **Owner** Ms K Silver Q: BSc (Hons), Dip.EH, Dip.Psych, NLP. M: BPS.
B Yrs. Est.: 4 (Ref:HM11349)

**KAY, ANDREA**

**Andrea Kay**, 53 Whitefield Avenue, Purley, **Surrey**, CR8 4BP, ENG.
(T) 020 8763 8987 (F) 020 8763 8987
Speciality: Hypnosis.
● **Owner** Mrs A Kay
B (Ref:HM11350)

**KAY, DAVID**

**David Kay**, 5 Whiteford Rd, Plymouth, **Devon**, PL3 5LU, ENG.
(T) 01752 662954
Speciality: Physiotherapy.
P S T (Ref:HM11351)

**KAY, ELIZABETH**

**Elizabeth Kay**, 8 Panmure Trce, Dundee, **Angus**, DD3 6HP, SCO.
(T) 01382 226426
Speciality: Complementary Medicines & Therapy.
● **Owner** Ms E Kay
M (Ref:HM11352)

**KAY, P**

**P Kay**, 10 Rydal Cl, Dronfield Woodhouse, Dronfield, **Derbyshire**, S18 8PU, ENG.
(T) 01246 290779
Speciality: Acupuncture, Herbal Medicine.
● **Owner** Mr P Kay
O (Ref:HM11353)

**KAY, PAUL**

**Paul Kay**, Unit 22, Greenfield Business Pk 1, Bagillt Rd, Greenfield, Holywell, **Flintshire**, CH8 7HW, WAL.
(T) 01352 711164
Speciality: Physiotherapy.
● **Owner** Mr P Kay
P S T (Ref:HM11354)

**KAY, R M**

**R M Kay**, 10 Rydal Cl, Dronfield Woodhouse, Dronfield, **Derbyshire**, S18 8PU, ENG.
(T) 01246 418522
Speciality: Chiropodists (Podiatrists).
● **Owner** Ms R Kay
S (Ref:HM11355)

**KAY, SHELIA**

**Shelia Kay**, 411 Revidge Rd, Blackburn, **Lancashire**, BB1 8DF, ENG.
(T) 01254 698495
Speciality: Complementary Medicines & Therapy.
● **Owner** Miss S Kay
C M (Ref:HM11356)

**KAYE, ANDREW**

**Andrew Kaye**, 225 Bury New Rd, Whitefield, Manchester, **Manchester (Greater)**, M45 6AA, ENG.
(T) 01617 961414
Speciality: Physiotherapy.
P S T (Ref:HM11357)



Key continued: Yrs.Est: Years Established Q: Qualifications M: Professional Membership ✔ Indemnity Insurance Accept Credit Cards

### KAYE, COLIN
**Colin Kaye**, 917 Harrogate Rd, Bradford, **Yorkshire (West)**, BD10 0QY, ENG.
(T) 01274 611844
Speciality: Physiotherapy.
P S T (Ref:HM11358)

### KAYE, JANET
**Janet Kaye**, 2a Bankfield Rd, Cheadle Hulme, Cheadle, **Cheshire**, SK8 6EY, ENG.
(T) 01614 852667
Speciality: Reflexology.
S T (Ref:HM11359)

### KAYE, M P
**Kaye M P**, 20 Goda Rd, Littlehampton, **Sussex (West)**, BN17 6AS, ENG.
(T) 01903 715865
Speciality: Chiropodists (Podiatrists).
● **Owner** Mr C Kaye
S (Ref:HM11360)

### KAYIZA, M S
**M S Kayiza**, 116A Lawrence Rd, Southsea, **Hampshire**, PO5 1NZ, ENG.
(T) 023 9286 2414
Speciality: Chiropractic.
● **Owner** Miss M Kayiza
P S T (Ref:HM11361)

### KAY'S
**Kay's**, 50 Cromwell Rd, Feltham, **London (Greater)**, TW13 5AT, ENG.
(T) 020 8890 2885
Speciality: Chiropodists (Podiatrists).
● **Owner** Mrs J Komornicka
S (Ref:HM11362)

### KD PHYSIOTHERAPY
**KD Physiotherapy**, 157b Havant Rd, Drayton, Portsmouth, **Hampshire**, PO6 2AA, ENG.
(T) 023 9238 1089 (F) 023 9238 1089
Speciality: Acupuncture, Manipulation, Physiotherapy. ✔
● **Owner/Physiotherapist**
Mr K Dunleavy Q: Grad Dip Phys, MCSP, SRP. M: CSP.
S Yrs. Est.: 1 (Ref:HM11363)

### KEADY, SUSAN M
**Susan M Keady**, Towngate Healthcare Clinic, 102 Towngate, Leyland, Preston, **Lancashire**, PR5 1LQ, ENG.
(T) 01772 456657
Speciality: Acupuncture.
● **Practice Manager** Ms S Keady
O (Ref:HM11364)

### KEANE, DANIEL (DR)
**Dr Daniel Keane**, Lucys Lane, Barretts Pl, Macroom, **County Cork**, IRE.
(T) 026 4211 6
Speciality: Chiropractors.
● **Chiropractor** Dr D Keane
P S T (Ref:HM11365)

### KEANE, ISOBEL
**Isobel Keane**, 8 Lichfield Gr, Harrogate, **Yorkshire (North)**, HG3 2UA, ENG.
(T) 07939 230741
Speciality: Chiropodists (Podiatrists).
● **Owner** Ms I Keane
S (Ref:HM11366)

### KEANE, JERRY
**Keane Jerry LIC AC**, Riverside Clinic Penrose Quay, IRE.
(T) 021 4551 747
Speciality: Acupuncture.
O (Ref:HM11367)

### KEANE, JERRY
**Keane Jerry LIC AC CAC (China) M**, 19 Inchvale Rd, Shamrock Lawn Douglas, Cork, **County Cork**, IRE.
(T) 021 4891 138
Speciality: Acupuncture.
O (Ref:HM11368)

### KEANE, NOELETTE R G N
**Keane Noelette R G N**, Slainte, Abbey St, Car Park, Ennis, **County Clare**, IRE.
(T) 06568 42019
Speciality: Complementary Medicines & Therapy.
M (Ref:HM11369)

### KEARNEY, JOHN
**John Kearney**, Flat 6, 47 St. John's Villas, London, **London (Greater)**, N19 3EE, ENG.
(T) 020 7272 7264
Speciality: Reflexology.
S T (Ref:HM11370)

### KEARNEY, V L
**Kearney V L**, Cinder Lane, Liverpool, **Merseyside**, L18 2HD, ENG.
(T) 01517 380379
Speciality: Chiropodists (Podiatrists).
S (Ref:HM11371)

### KEARNS, ANTHONY P
**Anthony P Kearns**, 43 Cecil Rd, Weston-Super-Mare, **Somerset**, BS23 2NY, ENG.
(T) 01934 624307
Speciality: Osteopathy.
P S T (Ref:HM11372)

### KEATES, BECKY
**Becky Keates**, 1 Purewell Cross Rd, Christchurch, **Dorset**, BH23 3AF, ENG.
(T) 01202 499518 (F) 01202 475706
Speciality: Physiotherapy.
● **Senior Partner** Mrs D Todd
P S T (Ref:HM11373)

### KEATING, B G
**B G Keating**, 28 Brookside Cres, Greenmount, Bury, **Lancashire**, BL8 4BG, ENG.
(T) 01204 888070 (F) 01204 888070
Speciality: Reflexology.
● **Owner** Mrs B Keating
S T (Ref:HM11374)

### KEATING, J
**J Keating**, Corner Cottage, Willington Corner, Willington, Tarporley, **Cheshire**, CW6 0NE, ENG.
(T) 01829 752472
Speciality: Acupuncture.
O (Ref:HM11375)

### KEATING, J
**Keating J**, 84 Congleton Rd, Sandbach, **Cheshire**, CW11 1HG, ENG.
(T) 01270 763926
Speciality: Acupuncture.
● **Partner** Mrs J Keating
O (Ref:HM11376)

### KEATING, JAMES
**James Keating**, 34 Brancaster Lane, Purley, **Surrey**, CR8 1HF, ENG.
(T) 020 8660 7076
Speciality: Alexander Technique.
● **Owner** Mr J Keating
P S (Ref:HM11377)

### KEATING, KEVIN
**Keating Kevin**, Clonagoose Mullinahone, **County Tipperary**, IRE.
(T) 05253 169
Speciality: Hypnotherapy.
B (Ref:HM11378)

### KEATING, MARY
**Mary Keating Acupuncture**, Coolaleen, Broadford, Charleville, **County Cork**, IRE.
(T) 00353 6384040
(E) mgcremin@eircom.net
Speciality: Acupuncture, Cupping, Holistic Healing, Moxibustion, Reiki. ✔
● **Acupuncturist** Ms M Keating Q: BSc. M: AIA.
O Yrs. Est.: 7 (Ref:HM11379)

### KEEFE, VIRGINIA
**Virginia Keefe**, Waytefield Clinic, Preston Drove, Brighton, **Sussex (East)**, BN1 6LA, ENG.
(T) 01273 550727
Speciality: Osteopathy.
● **Owner** Ms V Keefe
P S T (Ref:HM11380)

### KEEFE, VIRGINIA
**Virginia Keefe**, 35 Montreal Rd, Brighton, **Sussex (East)**, BN2 2UY, ENG.
(T) 01273 698498
Speciality: Osteopathy.
● **Owner** Mrs V Keefe
P S T (Ref:HM11381)

### KEEFER, W B
**W B Keefer**, 1 South Bank Avenue, York, **Yorkshire (North)**, YO23 1DR, ENG.
(T) 01904 612203
Speciality: Physiotherapy.
● **Owner** Ms W Keefer
P S T (Ref:HM11382)

### KEEL, JULIAN
**Julian Keel**, 41 Eastern Avenue, Reading, **Berkshire**, RG1 5RX, ENG.
(T) 01189 267438
Speciality: Chiropractors.
● **Senior Partner** Mr S Carpenter
P S T (Ref:HM11383)

### KEELER, THELMA
**Thelma Keeler**, 134-136 Delce Rd, Rochester, **Kent**, ME1 2DT, ENG.
(T) 01634 847273
Speciality: Electrolysis.
T (Ref:HM11384)

### KEELING, E F
**Keeling E F**, 7 Park Cres, London, **London (Greater)**, W1N 3HE, ENG.
(T) 020 7435 1740
Speciality: Osteopathy.
P S T (Ref:HM11385)

### KEELING, ERNEST
**Ernest Keeling**, 55 Belsize Lane, London, **London (Greater)**, NW3 5AU, ENG.
(T) 020 7435 1740
Speciality: Osteopathy.
P S T (Ref:HM11386)

### KEELING, SHEILA
**Sheila Keeling**, 8 Hooton Rd, Carlton, Nottingham, **Nottinghamshire**, NG4 1FZ, ENG.
(T) 01159 652030
Speciality: Complementary Medicines & Therapy.
● **Bowen Therapist** Ms S Keeling
M (Ref:HM11387)

### KEELY, JANETTE
**Janette Keely**, Bryn Moel, Clawddnewydd Rd, Ruthin, **Denbighshire**, LL15 2LR, WAL.
(T) 01824 750463
Speciality: Chiropractic.
P S T (Ref:HM11388)

### KEEMAN, MARGOT A
**Keeman Margot A MRSI**, 15 Birch Field Loretto Rd, Killarney, **County Kerry**, IRE.
(T) 06436 648
Speciality: Complementary Medicines & Therapy.
M (Ref:HM11389)

### KEEN, ANDREW R
**Andrew R Keen**, 66 Calbroke Rd, Slough, **Berkshire**, SL2 2HH, ENG.
(T) 01753 525131 (F) 01753 525131
Speciality: Chiropodists (Podiatrists).
● **Owner** Mr A Keene Q: MBChA, MSSCh.
S (Ref:HM11390)

### KEEN, STEVE
**Steve Keen**, Bishops Lodge, Oakley Green Rd, Oakley Green, Windsor, **Berkshire**, SL4 5UL, ENG.
(T) 01753 869755
Speciality: Psychology.
B (Ref:HM11391)

### KEENA, KEN
**Keena Ken ADHP MICHP**, 160 Cappaghmore, IRE.
(T) 01457 3607
(W) www.hypnosisire.com
Speciality: Relaxation Technique.
H T (Ref:HM11392)

### KEENAN RESEARCH
**Keenan Research Ltd**, Queen Ann House, 11 Charlotte St, Bath, **Somerset**, BA1 2NE, ENG.
(T) 01225 336569 (F) 01225 442685
Speciality: Psychology.
● **Managing Director** Mr K Keenan
B (Ref:HM11393)



Key: B Mind-Body Medicine C Complementary Medicine H Self Help Treatment M Medicinal Therapy O Oriental Medicine P Postural Therapy S Manipulative Structural Therapy T Touch Therapy

### KEEP IN STEP
**Keep In Step**, 134 High St, Leslie, Glenrothes, **Fife**, KY6 3DB, **SCO**.
(T) 01592 745485
Speciality: Chiropody. ✔
● **Chiropodist** Mrs M Davidson M: SCA.
[M] Yrs. Est.: 25 (**Ref:**HM11394)

### KEET CLINIC
**Keet Clinic (The)**, 15 King St, Covent Garden, London, **London (Greater)**, WC2E 8HN, **ENG**.
(T) 020 7836 4446 (F) 020 8340 2303
Speciality: Complementary Medicines & Therapy.
● **Owner** Mr M Campion
[C] [M] (**Ref:**HM11395)

### KEET, MICHAEL
**Keet Michael**, 15 King St, Covent Garden, London, **London (Greater)**, WC2E 8HN, **ENG**.
(T) 020 7240 1438
Speciality: Chiropodists (Podiatrists).
[S] (**Ref:**HM11396)

### KEETCH, KIT
**Kit Keetch**, Leigh-On-Sea, **Essex**, SS9, **ENG**.
(T) 01702 511752
Speciality: Bach Remedies.
[M] (**Ref:**HM11397)

### KEETON, JOE
**Joe Keeton**, 194 Birkenhead Rd, Meols, Wirral, **Merseyside**, CH47 0NF, **ENG**.
(T) 01516 326346
Speciality: Hypnotherapy.
[B] (**Ref:**HM11398)

### KEEVIL, P A
**P A Keevil**, 2b Honey Lane, Cholsey, Wallingford, **Oxfordshire**, OX10 9NP, **ENG**.
(T) 01491 652574
Speciality: Chiropodists (Podiatrists).
[S] (**Ref:**HM11399)

### KEEVIL, P A
**P A Keevil**, Penhurst, York Rd, West Hagbourne, Didcot, **Oxfordshire**, OX11 0NG, **ENG**.
(T) 01235 850077
Speciality: Chiropodists (Podiatrists).
● **Owner** Mrs P Keevil
[S] (**Ref:**HM11400)

### KEHOE, JOANNA
**Joanna Kehoe**, 4 Scotland Bridge Rd, New Haw, Addlestone, **Surrey**, KT15 3HD, **ENG**.
(T) 01932 342202
Speciality: Chiropodists (Podiatrists).
[S] (**Ref:**HM11401)

### KEIGHLEY CHIROPODY CLINIC
**Keighley Chiropody Clinic**, Keighley Health Centre, Oakworth Rd, Keighley, **Yorkshire (West)**, BD21 1SA, **ENG**.
(T) 01535 606111
Speciality: Chiropodists (Podiatrists).
[S] (**Ref:**HM11402)

### KEIGHLEY CHIROPRACTOR CLINIC
**Keighley Chiropractor Clinic**, 3 Granby Drive, Riddlesden, Keighley, **Yorkshire (West)**, BD20 5AU, **ENG**.
(T) 01535 603100
Speciality: Chiropractors.
● **Partner** Ms J Beer
[P] [S] [T] (**Ref:**HM11403)

### KEIGHLEY, S J
**S J Keighley**, 14 Highgate, Bradford, **Yorkshire (West)**, BD9 4BB, **ENG**.
(T) 01274 545551
Speciality: Chiropodists (Podiatrists).
● **Owner** Mrs S Keighley
[S] (**Ref:**HM11404)

### KEIL CENTRE
**Keil Centre (The)**, 5 South Lauder Rd, Edinburgh, **Edinburgh (City of)**, EH9 2LJ, **SCO**.
(T) 01316 678059 (F) 01316 677946
Speciality: Psychology.
● **Partner** Mr I Teirney
[B] (**Ref:**HM11405)

### KEIL CENTRE
**Keil Centre (The)**, 3 Fitzroy Pl, Glasgow, **Glasgow (City of)**, G3 7RH, **SCO**.
(T) 01412 212893 (F) 01412 213450
Speciality: Psychology.
● **Manager** Mrs V Gray
[B] (**Ref:**HM11406)

### KEILBART, P A
**P A Keilbart**, 60 Charlestown Rd, St. Austell, **Cornwall**, PL25 3NN, **ENG**.
(T) 01726 67788
Speciality: Osteopathy.
● **Owner** Mrs P Keilbart
[P] [S] [T] (**Ref:**HM11407)

### KEILDSON, HANNAH
**Hannah Keildson**, 80 Micklefield Rd, High Wycombe, **Buckinghamshire**, HP13 7EY, **ENG**.
(T) 01494 443579
Speciality: Reflexology.
[S] [T] (**Ref:**HM11408)

### KEILLER, S T B
**S T B Keiller**, 7 Victoria Pl, Prom, Kingsbridge, **Devon**, TQ7 1JG, **ENG**.
(T) 01548 852042
Speciality: Chiropodists (Podiatrists).
● **Owner** Mr S Keiller
[S] (**Ref:**HM11409)

### KEISNER, MICHAEL
**Michael Keisner**, Edgware Centre For Natural Health, 128 High St, Edgware, **London (Greater)**, HA8 7EL, **ENG**.
(T) 020 8951 3475
Speciality: Acupuncture.
[O] (**Ref:**HM11410)

### KEISNER, MICHAEL
**Michael Keisner**, 36 Park Gr, Edgware, **London (Greater)**, HA8 7SJ, **ENG**.
(T) 07956 119559
Speciality: Acupuncture.
● **Owner** Mr M Keisner
[O] (**Ref:**HM11411)

### KEITH EGLETON HYPNOTHERAPY
**Keith Egleton Hypnotherapy**, Ottershaw, 10 Belmont Cl, Uxbridge, **London (Greater)**, UB8 1RF, **ENG**.
(T) 01895 274249
(E) k.egl@virgin.net
(W) www.keithegleton.co.uk
Speciality: Hypnosis, Hypnotherapy. [Credit Card]
● **Hypnotherapist** Mr K Egleton Q: MCAH, MIAH, MNCH. M: NCH.
[B] Yrs. Est.: 11 (**Ref:**HM11412)

### KEITH LINLEY HYPNOTHERAPY
**Keith Linley Hypnotherapy**, 155 Laithes Lane, Barnsley, **Yorkshire (South)**, S71 3AH, **ENG**.
(T) 01226 283962
Speciality: Hypnosis.
[B] (**Ref:**HM11413)

### KEITH LORD TAROT READER
**Keith Lord Tarot Reader & Psychic Counsellor**, 50 Ermine Rd, Rectory Farm, Northampton, **Northamptonshire**, NN3 5ES, **ENG**.
(T) 01604 412542
Speciality: Clairvoyants & Palmists.
[B] (**Ref:**HM11414)

### KEITH, GILL
**Gill Keith**, Stepping Stones, 11 Royal Trce, Glasgow, **Glasgow (City of)**, G3 7NT, **SCO**.
(T) 01419 469330
Speciality: Homeopathy.
● **Owner** Ms G Keith
[M] (**Ref:**HM11415)

### KELIMAR CLINIC
**Kelimar Clinic**, Glen Rd, Torwood, Larbert, **Falkirk**, FK5 4SN, **SCO**.
(T) 01324 557057
Speciality: Remedial Massage. ✔
● **Owner** Miss M Osborne M: LCSP.
[C] [T] Yrs. Est.: 10 (**Ref:**HM11416)

### KELLEHER, COLETTE
**Kelleher Colette M MISCP LIC AC**, 4 The Crescent, **County Galway**, **IRE**.
(T) 09158 4916
Speciality: Complementary Medicines & Therapy.
[M] (**Ref:**HM11417)

### KELLERMANS
**Kellermans**, The New Surgery, 8 Bridge Of Weir Rd, Kilmacolm, **Inverclyde**, PA13 4AT, **SCO**.
(T) 01505 874999
Speciality: Acupuncture, Aromatherapy, Bowen Therapy, Chiropody, Counselling, Cranio-Sacral Therapy, Healing Therapy, Homeopathy, Hypnotherapy, Indian Head Massage, Life Style Coaching, Massage (Therapeutic), Neuro-Linguistic Program, Osteopathy, Phytotherapy, Psychotherapy, Reflexology, Reiki, Shiatsu, Spiritual Healing, Stress Therapy. ✔
● **Therapist** Mr T Verdat Q: NFSH. M: BCHE.
● **Therapist** Ms E Leitch M: IPTI.
[C] Yrs. Est.: 9 (**Ref:**HM11418)

### KELLETT, DAVID
**David Kellett**, 28 Hallowell Rd, Northwood, **London (Greater)**, HA6 1DN, **ENG**.
(T) 01923 827833
Speciality: Osteopathy.
[P] [S] [T] (**Ref:**HM11419)

### KELLETT, DAVID & ASSOCIATES
**David Kellett & Associates**, 118 Whinbush Rd, Hitchin, **Hertfordshire**, SG5 1PN, **ENG**.
(T) 01462 438622
Speciality: Osteopathy.
● **Owner** Mr D Kellett
[P] [S] [T] (**Ref:**HM11420)

### KELLETT-HARRISON, ELAINE
**Elaine Kellett-Harrison**, Hyde Park Therapy Centre, Calder House, Spring Lane, Colne, **Lancashire**, BB8 9BD, **ENG**.
(T) 01282 867392
Speciality: Reflexology.
● **Owner** Mrs E Kellett-Harrison
[S] [T] (**Ref:**HM11421)

### KELLEY, M P
**M P Kelley**, 20 Medina Villas, Hove, **Sussex (East)**, BN3 2RL, **ENG**.
(T) 01273 202701 (F) 01273 202701
Speciality: Chiropodists (Podiatrists).
● **Owner** Mr M Kelley
[S] (**Ref:**HM11422)

### KELLY & ASSOCIATES
**Kelly Teresa & Associates**, Village Green House, Douglas West,, Cork, **County Cork**, **IRE**.
(T) 021 4896 161
Speciality: Osteopathy.
[P] [S] [T] (**Ref:**HM11423)

### KELLY CHIROPODY
**Kelly Chiropody**, 536 Burnley Rd, Rossendale, **Lancashire**, BB4 8NE, **ENG**.
(T) 01706 211419
(E) kelly.chiropody@talk21.com
Speciality: Biomechanics, Chiropody, Indian Head Massage, Osteopathy, Psychotherapy, Reflexology. ✔
● **Reflexologist/Chiropodist**
Mr S Kelly Q: MBChA, MICHT, MSSCh.
M: B.A.Ch.P, IIHHT.
[M] Yrs. Est.: 16 (**Ref:**HM11424)

### KELLY HYPNOTHERAPY CLINIC
**Kelly Hypnotherapy Clinic**, Main St, Camolin, Enniscorthy, **County Wexford**, **IRE**.
(T) 05483 425
Speciality: Hypnotherapy.
[B] (**Ref:**HM11425)

### KELLY, ALISON
**Kelly Alison**, Tullyallen, Drogheda, **County Louth**, **IRE**.
(T) 04198 45691
Speciality: Hypnotherapy.
[B] (**Ref:**HM11426)

### KELLY, ANGELINA
**Angelina Kelly ITEC MIRI BFRP MGCP**, 20 Forest Pk, Kingswood Est, Dublin, **County Dublin**, **IRE**.
(T) 01451 9283
Speciality: Bach Remedies, Phytotherapy, Reflexology, T'ai-Chi Ch'uan, Cellular Healing. ✔
● **Manager** Angelina Kelly Q: BFRP, ITEC, MGCP,


Key continued: **Yrs.Est:** Years Established **Q:** Qualifications **M:** Professional Membership ✔ Indemnity Insurance [Credit Card] Accept Credit Cards

MIRI. M: DrEBF, IRI.
B Yrs. Est.: 5 (Ref:HM11427)

## KELLY, ANNETTE M
**Annette M Kelly**, Railway Cottage, Kilwinning, **Ayrshire (North)**, KA13 7RF, SCO.
(T) 01294 557131
Speciality: Complementary Medicines & Therapy.
● **Owner** Ms A Kelly
C M (Ref:HM11428)

## KELLY, C
**C Kelly**, 2c Grosvenor Rd, Urmston, Manchester, **Manchester (Greater)**, M41 5AQ, ENG.
(T) 01612 807482
Speciality: Chiropodists (Podiatrists).
● **Owner** Mrs J Collier
S (Ref:HM11429)

## KELLY, EILEEN
**Eileen Kelly**, 11 Lancaster Cl, Stevenage, **Hertfordshire**, SG1 4RX, ENG.
(T) 01438 214277
Speciality: Reflexology.
S T (Ref:HM11430)

## KELLY, GILLIAN
**Gillian Kelly**, 31 Shenfield Rd, Brentwood, **Essex**, CM15 8AG, ENG.
(T) 01277 260080
Speciality: Acupuncture. ✔
● **Acupuncturist** Gillian Kelly Q: Lic.Ac, MBA, MRCHM.
● **Acupuncturist** Daniella Matal Q: Dip.Ac, Dip.TCM, MBAcC, MRCHM.
C Yrs. Est.: 13 (Ref:HM11431)

## KELLY, JOHN
**Kelly John J DHP, M I A H**, Main St, Camolin E'corthy, IRE.
(T) 05483 425
Speciality: Hypnotherapy.
B (Ref:HM11432)

## KELLY, KEITH
**Kelly Keith PV**, 147 River Forest, Leixlip, **County Kildare**, IRE.
(T) 01624 7300
Speciality: Acupuncture.
O (Ref:HM11433)

## KELLY, KEVIN
**Kevin Kelly**, 49 Ganna Park Rd, Plymouth, **Devon**, PL3 4NN, ENG.
(T) 01752 253777
Speciality: Chiropractic.
P S T (Ref:HM11434)

## KELLY, L
**L Kelly**, 109 Eastgate Centre, Basildon, **Essex**, SS14 1AG, ENG.
(T) 01268 530789
Speciality: Chiropodists (Podiatrists).
● **Owner** Mrs L Kelly
S (Ref:HM11435)

## KELLY, L V
**L V Kelly**, 6 Redlands, Tiverton, **Devon**, EX16 4DH, ENG.
(T) 01884 256170 (F) 01884 242550
Speciality: Hypnosis.
● **Owner** Mr L Kelly
B (Ref:HM11436)

## KELLY, MARY
**Mary Kelly**, 4 Steel Court, Longwell Green, Bristol, BS30 7DU, ENG.
(T) 01179 329110
Speciality: Clairvoyants & Palmists.
● **Owner** Miss S Callaway
B (Ref:HM11437)

## KELLY, MAUREEN
**Maureen Kelly**, 48 Highbury Trce, Leeds, **Yorkshire (West)**, LS6 4ET, ENG.
(T) 01132 741773
Speciality: Chiropodists (Podiatrists).
● **Owner** Ms M Kelly
S (Ref:HM11438)

## KELLY, O H
**O H Kelly**, 70 Suffolk Cres, Belfast, **County Antrim**, BT11 9JT, NIR.
(T) 028 9061 4075
Speciality: Chiropodists (Podiatrists).
S (Ref:HM11439)

## KELLY, PENNY
**Penny Kelly**, 72 Windsor Rd, London, **London (Greater)**, E10 5LR, ENG.
(T) 020 8558 6841
Speciality: Osteopathy.
P S T (Ref:HM11440)

## KELLY, ROBERT
**Robert Kelly**, 41 Hills Rd, Cambridge, **Cambridgeshire**, CB2 1NT, ENG.
(T) 01223 301577
Speciality: Hypnosis.
B (Ref:HM11441)

## KELLY, ROSALEEN
**Kelly Rosaleen R P N , M S R I**, Kiltaboe Ballyhaunis, **County Mayo**, IRE.
(T) 09073 0022
Speciality: Complementary Medicines & Therapy.
M (Ref:HM11442)

## KELLY, S
**S Kelly**, 1b Station Rd, Grotton, Oldham, **Lancashire**, OL4 5SF, ENG.
(T) 01616 273356
Speciality: Chiropodists (Podiatrists).
S (Ref:HM11443)

## KELLY, SHEILA
**Sheila Kelly**, 18 High St, Uppermill, Oldham, **Lancashire**, OL3 6HX, ENG.
(T) 01457 875565
Speciality: Chiropodists (Podiatrists).
S (Ref:HM11444)

## KELLY, SUSAN
**Susan Kelly**, 38 Duchess Drive, Blackpool, **Lancashire**, FY2 9PH, ENG.
(T) 01253 352596
Speciality: Electrolysis.
● **Owner** Mrs S Kelly
T (Ref:HM11445)

## KELLY, T G
**T G Kelly**, 123 Drum Brae South, Edinburgh, **Edinburgh (City of)**, EH12 8TL, SCO.
(T) 01313 395428
Speciality: Biomechanics, Chiropody, Nail Surgery. ✔
● **Chiropodist** Mr T Kelly Q: DPodM, S.R.Ch. M: S.C.P.
M Yrs. Est.: 21 (Ref:HM11446)

## KELLY, T G
**T G Kelly**, 90 Leamington Trce, Edinburgh, **Edinburgh (City of)**, EH10 4JU, SCO.
(T) 01312 295986
Speciality: Biomechanics, Chiropody, Nail Surgery. ✔
● **Chiropodist** Mr T Kelly Q: DPodM, S.R.Ch. M: S.C.P.
M Yrs. Est.: 21 (Ref:HM11447)

## KELLY'S FOOTCARE
**Kelly's Footcare**, 67 High St, Bentley, Doncaster, **Yorkshire (South)**, DN5 0AA, ENG.
(T) 01302 820160
Speciality: Chiropodists (Podiatrists).
S (Ref:HM11448)

## KELSALE PHYSIOTHERAPY CENTRE
**Kelsale Physiotherapy Centre**, Old Manor House, Bridge St, Kelsale, Saxmundham, **Suffolk**, IP17 2PG, ENG.
(T) 01728 604403 (F) 01728 604405
Speciality: Physiotherapy.
● **Owner** Ms M Taylor
P S T (Ref:HM11449)

## KELSALL, D
**D Kelsall**, The Greenhouse, 19 Newry Park, Chester, **Cheshire**, CH2 2AR, ENG.
(T) 01244 375458
Speciality: Reflexology.
● **Owner** Mrs D Kelsall
S T (Ref:HM11450)

## KELSALL, PETER T
**Peter T Kelsall**, 2 Burlington St, Blackburn, **Lancashire**, BB2 6ES, ENG.
(T) 01254 52726
Speciality: Osteopathy.
P S T (Ref:HM11451)

## KELSEY, L R
**L R Kelsey**, 6 Trendlewood Park, Bristol, BS16 1TE, ENG.
(T) 01179 650138
Speciality: Chiropodists (Podiatrists).
● **Owner** Mrs L Kelsey
S (Ref:HM11452)

## KELSH, C M E
**C M E Kelsh**, 3 Hayes Mead Rd, Bromley, **Kent**, BR2 7HR, ENG.
(T) 020 8462 1703
Speciality: Physiotherapy.
● **Owner** Mrs C Kelsh
P S T (Ref:HM11453)

## KELTIE, ANNE
**Anne Keltie**, 103 Regal Way, Harrow, **London (Greater)**, HA3 0SG, ENG.
(T) 020 8907 3983 (F) 020 8907 3983
Speciality: Physiotherapy.
● **Owner** Mrs A Keltie
P S T (Ref:HM11454)

## KEMATEN
**Kematen**, 3 High St, Tattershall, Lincoln, **Lincolnshire**, LN4 4LE, ENG.
(T) 01526 345471
Speciality: Complementary Medicines & Therapy.
● **Owner** Mr A Franklin
M (Ref:HM11455)

## KEMBER, J M
**J M Kember**, The Elgin Physiotherapy Clinic, 4 Elgin Rd, London, **London (Greater)**, N22 7UE, ENG.
(T) 020 8889 4505
Speciality: Physiotherapy.
● **Owner** Mrs J Kember
P S T (Ref:HM11456)

## KEMP, E A
**E A Kemp**, 3 Little Dockray, Penrith, **Cumbria**, CA11 7HL, ENG.
(T) 01768 867843
Speciality: Complementary Medicines & Therapy.
M (Ref:HM11457)

## KEMP, G
**G Kemp**, 25 Cooks Meadow, Edlesborough, Dunstable, **Bedfordshire**, LU6 2RP, ENG.
(T) 01525 222396 (F) 01525 222396
Speciality: Clairvoyants & Palmists.
● **Owner** Miss G Kemp
B (Ref:HM11458)

## KEMP, G (DR)
**Dr G Kemp**, 150 Brackens Lane, Alvaston, Derby, **Derbyshire**, DE24 0AL, ENG.
(T) 01332 571531 (F) 01332 736428
Speciality: Physiotherapy.
● **Owner** Mr G Kemp
P S T (Ref:HM11459)

## KEMP, G D
**Surgical Chiropodist**, 87-150 Brackens Lane, Alvaston, Derby, **Derbyshire**, DE24 0AL, ENG.
(T) 01332 571531
Speciality: Chiropody, Nutritional Therapy. ✔
● **Surgical Chiropodist** Mr G Kemp Q: MBChA, MSSCh. M: B.A.Ch.P.
M Yrs. Est.: 15 (Ref:HM11460)

## KEMP, GILLIAN
**Complementary Therapy Centre**, 87-150 Brackens Lane, Alvaston, Derby, **Derbyshire**, DE24 0AL, ENG.
(T) 01332 571531 (F) 01332 571531
Speciality: Acupressure, Aromatherapy, Complementary Therapy, Counselling, Dietician, Hypnosis, Hypnotherapy, Manipulation, Massage (Therapeutic), Nutritional Therapy, Psychotherapy, Reflexology, Stress Therapy, Swedish Body Massage, Chinese Massage, Non Surgical Face Lift. ✔
● **Physiotherapist/Hypnotherapist** Dr G Kemp Q: AccHyp, BPS, MAB Phys. M: BPA, BPS.
B T Yrs. Est.: 15 (Ref:HM11461)



Key: B Mind-Body Medicine C Complementary Medicine H Self Help Treatment M Medicinal Therapy O Oriental Medicine P Postural Therapy S Manipulative Structural Therapy T Touch Therapy

**KEMP, JANET**

**Janet Kemp**, 22 London Rd, Stapeley, Nantwich, **Cheshire**, CW5 7JL, ENG.
(T) 01270 627055
Speciality: Reflexology.
● **Owner** Mrs J Kemp
S T (**Ref:**HM11462)

**KEMP, N J**

**N J Kemp**, Saracens House Business Centre, 25 St Margarets Green, Ipswich, **Suffolk**, IP4 2BN, ENG.
(T) 01473 218005
Speciality: Osteopathy.
● **Owner** Mr N Kemp
P S T (**Ref:**HM11463)

**KEMP, R**

**R Kemp**, 27 Oaks Drive, Colchester, **Essex**, CO3 3QZ, ENG.
(T) 01206 711044
Speciality: Osteopathy.
● **Owner** Mr R Kemp
P S T (**Ref:**HM11464)

**KEMP, SANDRA**

**Sandra Kemp**, 16 Sunnyhill Rd, Herne Bay, **Kent**, CT6 8LT, ENG.
(T) 01227 362727
Speciality: Complementary Medicines & Therapy.
● **Owner** Mrs S Kemp
C M (**Ref:**HM11465)

**KEMP, SHELAGH**

**Shelagh Kemp**, Coppins, Kiln Cl, Prestwood, Great Missenden, **Buckinghamshire**, HP16 9DJ, ENG.
(T) 01494 863806
Speciality: Chiropodists (Podiatrists).
● **Owner** Ms S Kemp
S (**Ref:**HM11466)

**KEMP, VALERIE**

**Valerie Kemp L C P H , M H M A , (U K )**, 18 Livingstone St, Leicester, **Leicestershire**, LE3 0QY, ENG.
(T) 01162 220739
Speciality: Homeopathy.
M (**Ref:**HM11467)

**KEMPSON, STEVE**

**Steve Kempson**, Hall Green Alternative Practice, Kedleston Rd, Birmingham, **Midlands (West)**, B28 0NR, ENG.
(T) 01217 337170 (F) 01217 337170
Speciality: Kinesiology. ✔
● **Owner/Kinesiologist** Mr S Kempson **Q:** CKCS. **M:** KFRP.
B Yrs. Est.: 4 (**Ref:**HM11468)

**KEMPSTON CHIROPRACTIC CLINIC**

**Kempston Chiropractic Clinic**, 160 Bedford Rd, Kempston, Bedford, **Bedfordshire**, MK42 8BH, ENG.
(T) 01234 853444
Speciality: Chiropractic. ✔
● **Doctor** Mr F So **Q:** DC. **M:** BCA, GCC.
P Yrs. Est.: 2 (**Ref:**HM11469)

**KEMP-WHEELER, S (DR)**

**Dr S Kemp-Wheeler**, 10 Eldon Rd, Reading, **Berkshire**, RG1 4DH, ENG.
(T) 01189 502002
Speciality: Psychology.
B (**Ref:**HM11470)

**KEN, HOWARD**

**Howard Ken**, 150 Lovely Lane, Warrington, **Cheshire**, WA5 1PH, ENG.
(T) 01925 240411
Speciality: Hypnotherapy.
B (**Ref:**HM11471)

**KENDAL, D J**

**D J Kendal (Mobile)**, 7 Hamilton Rd, Exmouth, **Devon**, EX8 2LD, ENG.
(T) 01395 277894
Speciality: Chiropodists (Podiatrists).
● **Owner** Mr D Kendall
S (**Ref:**HM11472)

**KENDAL, ELIZABETH J**

**Elizabeth J Kendal**, 22 Cheltenham Rd, Gloucester, **Gloucestershire**, GL2 0LS, ENG.
(T) 01452 308799
Speciality: Osteopathy.
P S T (**Ref:**HM11473)

**KENDAL, S L**

**S L Kendal**, Blade Mill, Yarde, Williton, Taunton, **Somerset**, TA4 4HW, ENG.
(T) 01984 640270
Speciality: Chiropractic.
● **Owner** Miss S Kendal
P S T (**Ref:**HM11474)

**KENDALL, CHEW**

**Kendall Chew**, 19 Lichfield St, Stone, **Staffordshire**, ST15 8NA, ENG.
(T) 01785 816481
Speciality: Osteopathy.
● **Practice Manager** Mrs W Mellor
P S T (**Ref:**HM11475)

**KENDALL, DINA**

**Dina Kendall**, The Helix Centre, Woodbrook House, 27 Bridge St, Loughborough, **Leicestershire**, LE11 1NH, ENG.
(T) 01509 230200
Speciality: Complementary Medicines & Therapy.
M (**Ref:**HM11476)

**KENDALL, P**

**P Kendall**, 27a Harley Pl, London, **London (Greater)**, W1N 1HB, ENG.
(T) 020 7637 3177
Speciality: Psychology.
● **Owner** Mr P Kendall
B (**Ref:**HM11477)

**KENDALL, SALLY**

**Sally Kendall**, 2 Glasslyn Rd, London, **London (Greater)**, N8 8RH, ENG.
(T) 020 8340 3278
Speciality: Homeopathy.
M (**Ref:**HM11478)

**KENDEL HOUSE CLINIC**

**Kendel House Clinic**, 24 Chatburn Rd, Clitheroe, **Lancashire**, BB7 2AP, ENG.
(T) 01200 424901
Speciality: Acupuncture, Chiropody, Cranial Osteopathy, Homeopathy, Hypnotherapy, Osteopathy, Reflexology, Spiritual Healing. ✔
● **Osteopath** Ms H Alison **M:** GOsC.
● **General Practitioner** Dr S Donnelly
● **Osteopath** Mrs H Percival **M:** GOsC.
● **Osteopath** Mr R Percival **M:** GOsC.
S Yrs. Est.: 10 (**Ref:**HM11479)

**KENDRICK, C A**

**C A Kendrick**, 44 High St, Coedpoeth, Wrexham, LL11 3SB, **WAL**.
(T) 01978 756593
Speciality: Chiropodists (Podiatrists).
● **Owner** Mrs C Kendrick
S (**Ref:**HM11480)

**KENDRICK, DIANE**

**Diane Kendrick**, 11 Springfield Rd, **Dorset**, BH14 0LG, ENG.
(T) 01202 740392
Speciality: Reflexology.
S T (**Ref:**HM11481)

**KENDRICK, MARGARET**

**Margaret Kendrick**, 3 Sea View Prde, Mayland, Chelmsford, **Essex**, CM3 6EL, ENG.
(T) 01621 742745
Speciality: Hypnosis.
B (**Ref:**HM11482)

**KENEE, HAZEL**

**Mrs Hazel Kenee**, 41 Castlefield Cl, Eastleaze, Swindon, **Wiltshire**, SN5 7EG, ENG.
(T) 01793 871248
Speciality: Chiropodists (Podiatrists).
S (**Ref:**HM11483)

**KENILWORTH CHIROPODY SURGERY**

**Kenilworth Chiropody Surgery**, 6 Station Rd, Kenilworth, **Warwickshire**, CV8 1JJ, ENG.
(T) 01926 856471
Speciality: Chiropodists (Podiatrists).
S (**Ref:**HM11484)

**KENILWORTH PHYSIOTHERAPY**

**Kenilworth Physiotherapy**, 10 Inverary Cl, Kenilworth, **Warwickshire**, CV8 2NZ, ENG.
(T) 01926 512507
Speciality: Physiotherapy.
P S T (**Ref:**HM11485)

**KENNAN, PHILIPPA**

**Philippa Kennan**, The Rigg, Hatching Green, Harpenden, **Hertfordshire**, AL5 2JP, ENG.
(T) 01582 765471
Speciality: Reflexology.
S T (**Ref:**HM11486)

**KENNARD, S**

**S Kennard**, Westbourne House, Westbourne Trce, Shuttern, Taunton, **Somerset**, TA1 4ES, ENG.
(T) 01823 332871
Speciality: Osteopathy.
P S T (**Ref:**HM11487)

**KENNEDY CASEY, BRIDGET**

**Bridget Kennedy Casey**, 22 Carabullaun Lr Park Rd, Corbally, **County Limerick**, IRE.
(T) 06131 6273
Speciality: Complementary Medicines & Therapy.
M (**Ref:**HM11488)

**KENNEDY, CLAIRE**

**Claire Kennedy**, 463 Chorley Old Rd, Bolton, **Lancashire**, BL1 6AH, ENG.
(T) 01204 841003
Speciality: Chiropodists (Podiatrists).
S (**Ref:**HM11489)

**KENNEDY, E**

**E Kennedy**, 126 High St, Lymington, **Hampshire**, SO41 9AQ, ENG.
(T) 01590 679560
Speciality: Osteopathy.
● **Senior Partner** Dr P Hardy
P S T (**Ref:**HM11490)

**KENNEDY, EDWARD**

**Edward Kennedy**, 16 Richmond Park Cres, Bournemouth, **Dorset**, BH8 9BU, ENG.
(T) 01202 304382
Speciality: Osteopathy. ✔
● **Owner/Osteopath** Mr E Kennedy **Q:** BSc, DO. **M:** GOsC.
S Yrs. Est.: 5 (**Ref:**HM11491)

**KENNEDY, GRAHAM**

**Graham Kennedy**, 37 High Town Rd, Maidenhead, **Berkshire**, SL6 1PA, ENG.
(T) 01628 788420
Speciality: Complementary Medicines & Therapy.
● **Owner** Mrs C Sanders
M (**Ref:**HM11492)

**KENNEDY, J**

**J Kennedy**, 1 Crossfield Rd, Hale, Altrincham, **Cheshire**, WA15 8DU, ENG.
(T) 01619 039191
Speciality: Physiotherapy.
● **Owner** Mr J Kennedy
P S T (**Ref:**HM11493)

**KENNEDY, JASMINE**

**Jasmine Kennedy**, 52 Seaview Rd, Gillingham, **Kent**, ME7 4NH, ENG.
(T) 01634 577915
Speciality: Complementary Medicines & Therapy.
M (**Ref:**HM11494)

**KENNEDY, JOHN M**

**John M Kennedy**, 6 Gregory Avenue, Mapperley, Nottingham, **Nottinghamshire**, NG3 6BW, ENG.
(T) 01159 609825
Speciality: Acupuncture.
O (**Ref:**HM11495)

**KENNEDY, SARAH**

**Sarah Kennedy**, Abbey View Medical Centre, Salisbury Rd, Shaftesbury, **Dorset**, SP7 8DH, ENG.
(T) 01747 856719
Speciality: Reflexology.
S T (**Ref:**HM11496)



Key continued: **Yrs.Est:** Years Established **Q:** Qualifications **M:** Professional Membership ✔ Indemnity Insurance Accept Credit Cards

## KENNEDY, SHIRLEY
**Shirley Kennedy**, 86 Newbridge Rd, Ballymoney, **County Antrim**, BT53 6QS, NIR.
(T) 028 2766 5000
Speciality: Electrolysis.
● **Owner** Mrs S Kennedy
T (Ref:HM11497)

## KENNERLEY, JUNE
**June Kennerley**, 97 Dunelm South, Sunderland, **Tyne and Wear**, SR2 7QX, ENG.
(T) 01915 282574
Speciality: Acupuncture.
O (Ref:HM11498)

## KENNERLEY, MAGGIE
**Maggie Kennerley**, Flint Cottage, Whitepost Lane, Meopham, Gravesend, **Kent**, DA13 0TZ, ENG.
(T) 01732 822346
Speciality: Reflexology.
S T (Ref:HM11499)

## KENNETH ATHERTON HOMOEOPATH
**Kenneth Atherton Homoeopath**, 14 Derby Lane, Liverpool, **Merseyside**, L13 3HS, ENG.
(T) 01512 200243
Speciality: Homeopathy.
M (Ref:HM11500)

## KENNETH C HUGGINS HYPNOTHERAPY
**Kenneth C Huggins Hypnotherapy**, 12 Toulsons Croft, Nottingham, **Nottinghamshire**, NG6 0QS, ENG.
(T) 01159 193690
Speciality: Hypnosis, Hypnotherapy. ✔
● **Hypnotherapist** Mr K Huggins Q: Dip.Hyp. M: BSCH, HA.
B Yrs. Est.: 2 (Ref:HM11501)

## KENNING, GILLIAN
**Gillian Kenning**, Little Orchard, Brentmoor Rd, West End, Woking, **Surrey**, GU24 9QG, ENG.
(T) 01276 855529
Speciality: Hypnosis.
● **Owner** Mrs G Kenning
B (Ref:HM11502)

## KENNINGTON CHIROPODY SURGERY
**Kennington Chiropody Surgery (The)**, 304 Kennington Rd, London, **London (Greater)**, SE11 4LD, ENG.
(T) 020 7735 4303
Speciality: Chiropodists (Podiatrists).
S (Ref:HM11503)

## KENNON, SUSAN
**Susan Kennon**, 10 Fouracres, Letchworth, **Hertfordshire**, SG6 3UF, ENG.
(T) 01462 682268
Speciality: Reflexology.
S T (Ref:HM11504)

## KENNY, A
**A Kenny**, 4th Floor, Hepworth Chambers, Church St, Liverpool, **Merseyside**, L1 3BG, ENG.
(T) 01517 092995
Speciality: Chiropodists (Podiatrists).
● **Owner** Mrs A Kenny
S (Ref:HM11505)

## KENNY, D J
**D J Kenny**, 8 St Marks Cl, Bexhill-on-Sea, **Sussex (East)**, TN39 4PW, ENG.
(T) 01424 844469
Speciality: Hypnosis.
● **Owner** Mr D Kenny
B (Ref:HM11506)

## KENNY, DESMOND
**Desmond Kenny**, 9 Kings Rd, St. Leonards-On-Sea, **Sussex (East)**, TN37 6EA, ENG.
(T) 01424 714800
Speciality: Hypnotherapy.
B (Ref:HM11507)

## KENNY, HELEN
**Kenny Helen**, The Medical Ctr 14 New St, **County Longford**, IRE.
(T) 04348 788
Speciality: Complementary Medicines & Therapy.
M (Ref:HM11508)

## KENNY, MARGARET
**Margaret Kenny Homoeopathy**, 92 Connolly St, Nenagh, **County Tipperary**, IRE.
(T) 06734 677
Speciality: Homeopathy.
M (Ref:HM11509)

## KENSHALL, ABIGAL
**Abigal Kenshall**, 337-339 Norwich Rd, Ipswich, **Suffolk**, IP1 4BN, ENG.
(T) 01473 464300
Speciality: Hypnotherapy.
● **Owner** A Kenshall
B (Ref:HM11510)

## KENSINGTON CLINIC
**Kensington Clinic (The)**, 65 Marloes Rd, London, **London (Greater)**, W8 6LE, ENG.
(T) 020 7938 3730 (F) 020 7938 3730
Speciality: Physiotherapy.
P S T (Ref:HM11511)

## KENSINGTON COURT CLINIC
**Kensington Court Clinic**, 197 Chepstow Rd, Newport, NP19 8GH, WAL.
(T) 01633 277068
Speciality: Osteopathy.
P S T (Ref:HM11512)

## KENSINGTON THERAPY CENTRE
**Kensington Therapy Centre**, 213 Kensington High St, London, **London (Greater)**, W8 6BD, ENG.
(T) 020 7376 1199 (F) 020 7938 3155
Speciality: Complementary Medicines & Therapy.
M (Ref:HM11513)

## KENT CLINIC OF NATURAL MED
**Kent Chemist**, 104 Walton Rd, East Molesey, **Surrey**, KT8 0DL, ENG.
(T) 01344 646423
Speciality: Absent Healing, Acupressure, Acupuncture, Aromatherapy, Aversion Therapy, Bach Remedies, Chiropractic, Colour Therapy, Counselling, Cranial Osteopathy, Dowsing, Faith Healing, Family Therapy, Hay Diet, Healer, Healing Therapy, Herbal Medicine, Holistic Healing, Homeopathy, Humanistic Psychology, Hypnosis, Hypnotherapy, Kinesiology, Life Style Coaching, Manipulation, Massage (Therapeutic), Meditation, Miasm Therapy, Nutritional Therapy, Polarity Therapy, Psychotherapy, Reflexology, Reiki, Spiritual Healing, Stress Therapy, T'ai-Chi Ch'uan, Touch Therapy, Yoga. ✔
● **Reflexologist** Ms V Woolley
(T) 020 8241 6197 Q: MAR.
● **Hypnotherapist/Life Coach** Ms C McMillan
(T) 020 8941 3060 Q: Reiki 2.
● **Homeopath** Mr A Dipple Q: Dip.Hom, RSHom. M: Soc.Hom.
● **Counsellor/Psychotherapist** Liesbet Plissart
(T) 07808 295520 Q: BA (Hons), Dip.Couns, MSc.
● **Chiropodist (Podiatrist)** Mr R Littlewood
(T) 020 8941 6923 Q: MBChA, MSSCh.
● **Chiropractor** Dr M Boles
(T) 01372 37443 Q: BA, BSc, DC, MCC.
● **Acupuncturist** Mr M Weiland
(T) 020 8876 7360 Q: B.Ac, MBAcC.
● **Counsellor/Spiritual Healer** Ms R Hill
(T) 020 8979 3717 Q: Dip.Couns, RGN. M: NFSH.
● **Polarity Therapist** Mr T Grant
(T) 07887 884926 Q: BSc.
● **Homeopath** Ms A Van Haeften
(T) 01306 742901 Q: LCH. M: Soc.Hom.
● **Aromatherapist/Therapeutic Massage Therapist** Ms S Hall
(T) 07930 137543 Q: BA (Hons), ITEC.
● **Reiki Healer** Ms C Weiland
(T) 020 8876 7360
● **Medical Herbalist** Ms G Robson
(T) 020 8364 6167 Q: BSc (Hons), MNIMH.
M Yrs. Est.: 5 (Ref:HM11514)

## KENT COUNS PSYCHOTHPY UNION
**Kent Counselling Psychotherapists Union**, 19 Birling Rd, Tunbridge Wells, **Kent**, TN2 5LX, ENG.
(T) 01892 529903
Speciality: Psychotherapy.
B (Ref:HM11515)

## KENT CURATIVE HYPNOTHERAPY
**Kent Curative Hypnotherapy Centre**, 23 The Downs, Beacon Hill, Herne Bay, **Kent**, CT6 6BA, ENG.
(T) 01227 360710
Speciality: Hypnosis.
● **Partner** Mrs A Kyne
B (Ref:HM11516)

## KENT HOUSE CHIROPRACTIC CLINIC
**Kent House Chiropractic Clinic**, 10 High St, Orpington, **Kent**, BR6 0JG, ENG.
(T) 01689 873130
Speciality: Chiropractic. ✔
● **Chiropractor** Dr J De Graas Q: DC.
● **Chiropractor** Dr M Chippendale Q: BSc, DC.
P Yrs. Est.: 18 (Ref:HM11517)

## KENT HOUSE CHIROPRACTIC CLINIC
**Kent House Chiropractic Clinic**, 366 Croydon Rd, Beckenham, **Kent**, BR3 4EX, ENG.
(T) 020 8663 3878 (F) 020 8663 3878
Speciality: Chiropractic. ✔
● **Chiropractor** Dr J Hollstorm Q: BSc, DC.
● **Chiropractor** Dr A Lavery Q: BSc (Chiro), DC.
P Yrs. Est.: 18 (Ref:HM11518)

## KENT HOUSE CHIROPRACTIC CLINIC
**Mr & Mrs Chippendale**, 10 High St, Orpington, **Kent**, BR6 0JG, ENG.
(T) 01689 873130
Speciality: Chiropractic. ✔
● **Owner/Chiropractor** Dr A Stick Q: BSc, DC. M: SCA.
● **Associate/Chiropractor** Dr M Duperron Q: BSc, DC.
P Yrs. Est.: 18 (Ref:HM11519)

## KENT HOUSE CHIROPRACTIC CLINIC
**Kent House Chiropractic Clinic**, Westfield Cottage, Morants Court Rd, Upper Dunton Green, Sevenoaks, **Kent**, TN13 2TR, ENG.
(T) 01732 742120
Speciality: Chiropractic.
● **Chiropractor** Dr A Stick Q: DC, MCC.
● **Chiropractor** Dr M Chippendale Q: BSc, DC.
● **Chiropractor** Dr M Duperron Q: DC.
C Yrs. Est.: 18 (Ref:HM11520)

## KENT INSTITUTE OF COMP MED
**Kent Institute Of Complementary Medicine**, P O Box 114, Sheldwich Lees, Faversham, **Kent**, ME13 0ER, ENG.
(T) 01795 533133
Speciality: Aromatherapy.
M O (Ref:HM11521)

## KENT OSTEOPATHIC CLINIC
**Kent Osteopathic Clinic**, 33 High St, Gillingham, **Kent**, ME7 1BQ, ENG.
(T) 01634 855224
Speciality: Osteopathy.
● **Owner** Mr G Miller
P S T (Ref:HM11522)

## KENT, E
**E Kent**, 1 Church Lane, Towersey, Thame, **Oxfordshire**, OX9 3QL, ENG.
(T) 01844 216033
Speciality: Physiotherapy.
● **Owner** Mrs E Kent
P S T (Ref:HM11523)

## KENT, JANET
**Janet E Kent**, 12 Shepherds Lane, Caversham, Reading, **Berkshire**, RG4 7JH, ENG.
(T) 01189 464085
(E) janetkent@virgin.net
Speciality: Psychotherapy. ✔
● **Psychotherapist/Counsellor** Ms J Kent Q: Dip.Adv.Couns, MSc. M: BACP, UKRC.
B Yrs. Est.: 6 (Ref:HM11524)



Key: B Mind-Body Medicine C Complementary Medicine H Self Help Treatment M Medicinal Therapy O Oriental Medicine P Postural Therapy S Manipulative Structural Therapy T Touch Therapy

**KENT, JOAN**
**Joan Kent**, 24 Burrows Way, Rayleigh, **Essex**, SS6 7DG, ENG.
(T) 01268 775732 (F) 01268 775732
Speciality: Reflexology.
● **Owner** Mrs J Kent
B (Ref:HM11525)

**KENT, JOANNE**
**Joanne Kent**, 4 Highgate Heights, 77 Shepherds Hill, London, **London (Greater)**, N6 5RF, ENG.
(T) 020 8374 0287
Speciality: Reflexology.
S T (Ref:HM11526)

**KENT, JOY**
**Joy Kent**, 19 Lydiard Way, Trowbridge, **Wiltshire**, BA14 0UN, ENG.
(T) 01225 765168
Speciality: Electrolysis.
● **Owner** Mrs J Kent
T (Ref:HM11527)

**KENT, MATTHEW**
**Matthew Kent**, Ely Complementary Health Centre, 29a St Marys St, Ely, **Cambridgeshire**, CB7 4HF, ENG.
(T) 01353 664476
Speciality: Acupuncture.
O (Ref:HM11528)

**KENT, PATRICIA**
**Patricia Kent**, 2 Briar Cl, Oving, Chichester, **Sussex (West)**, PO20 6BY, ENG.
(T) 01243 781977
Speciality: Complementary Medicines & Therapy.
● **Owner** Miss P Kent
C M (Ref:HM11529)

**KENTES PHYSIOTHERAPY CLINIC**
**Kentes Physiotherapy Clinic**, 38 Barnstaple Rd, Southend-On-Sea, **Essex**, SS1 3PA, ENG.
(T) 01702 588831 (F) 01702 588831
Speciality: Physiotherapy.
● **Manager** Mrs P Clawson
P S T (Ref:HM11530)

**KENTISH, LORNE**
**Lorne Kentish**, 15 Baring Rd, Beaconsfield, **Buckinghamshire**, HP9 2NB, ENG.
(T) 01494 672112
Speciality: Chiropody. ✔
● **Chiropodist/Reflexologist**
Mrs L Kentish Q: MBChA, MBRA. M: B.A.Ch.P, BRA.
M Yrs. Est.: 13 (Ref:HM11531)

**KENTON BRIDGE PHYSIO PRACTICE**
**Kenton Bridge Physiotherapy Practice**, 155-175 Kenton Rd, Harrow, **London (Greater)**, HA3 0YX, ENG.
(T) 020 8907 4001
Speciality: Physiotherapy.
● **Manager** Mr S Abrahams
P S T (Ref:HM11532)

**KENTON, JEREMY**
**Jeremy Kenton**, 49-51 High St, Dunmow, **Essex**, CM6 1AE, ENG.
(T) 01371 876661
Speciality: Osteopathy.
● **Owner** Mr J Kenton
P S T (Ref:HM11533)

**KENT-PAYNE, J**
**J Kent-Payne**, Larkhall Post Office, 6 Lambridge Buildings, Bath, **Somerset**, BA1 6RS, ENG.
(T) 01225 312183
Speciality: Chiropodists (Podiatrists).
● **Owner** Mr B Kent-Payne
S (Ref:HM11534)

**KENWARD, SANDRA**
**Sandra Kenward**, 15 Hilltop, Llanelli, **Carmarthenshire**, SA14 8DF, WAL.
(T) 01554 780179
Speciality: Reflexology.
S T (Ref:HM11535)

**KENYON, JACELYN**
**Jacelyn Kenyon**, 33 Willow Tree Rd, Altrincham, **Cheshire**, WA14 2EQ, ENG.
(T) 07931 183513
Speciality: Reflexology.
S T (Ref:HM11536)

**KEOGH, DAVID**
**David Keogh**, 834 Fishponds Rd, Fishponds, Bristol, BS16 3XA, ENG.
(T) 01179 491290
Speciality: Complementary Medicines & Therapy.
M (Ref:HM11537)

**KEOGH, DAVID**
**David Keogh**, 18 Hillside View, Peasedown St John, Bath, **Somerset**, BA2 8ES, ENG.
(T) 01761 437890
Speciality: Herbal Medicine.
M (Ref:HM11538)

**KEOGH, JENNY**
**Jenny Keogh**, Craniosacral Therapy, 52 Stoke Newington Church St, London, **London (Greater)**, N16 0NB, ENG.
(T) 020 7241 5033
Speciality: Complementary Medicines & Therapy.
C M (Ref:HM11539)

**KEOGH, MARTIN**
**Martin Keogh**, The Topsham Surgery, The White House, Holman Way, Topsham, Exeter, **Devon**, EX3 0EN, ENG.
(T) 01392 875552
Speciality: Osteopathy.
● **Owner** Mr M Keogh
P S T (Ref:HM11540)

**KEPPENS, I**
**Mrs I Keppens**, Flat 10 Lemna Court, Lemna Rd, London, **London (Greater)**, E11 1HU, ENG.
(T) 020 8539 5087
Speciality: Psychotherapy.
B (Ref:HM11541)

**KERFOOT OWEN, RITA**
**Rita Kerfoot Owen**, Denbigh, **Denbighshire**, LL16, WAL.
(T) 01745 816559
Speciality: Bach Remedies.
M (Ref:HM11542)

**KERLEY, JEAN**
**Jean Kerley**, 8 Tidworth Rd, Porton, Salisbury, **Wiltshire**, SP4 0NG, ENG.
(T) 01980 610721
Speciality: Psychotherapy.
B (Ref:HM11543)

**KERN, MICHAEL**
**Michael Kern**, 29 Dollis Park, Finchley Central, London, **London (Greater)**, N3 1HJ, ENG.
(T) 020 8349 0297 (F) 020 8349 0297
Speciality: Cranial Osteopathy, Cranio-Sacral Therapy, Naturopathy, Osteopathy. ✔
● **Osteopath/Naturopath/Cranio-Sacral Therapist**
Mr M Kern Q: DO, ND, RCST. M: GOsC, RCST.
S Yrs. Est.: 15 (Ref:HM11544)

**KERNOHAN, SARA**
**Sara Kernohan**, Jura, Youngs Walk, Catterick, Richmond, **Yorkshire (North)**, DL10 7PT, ENG.
Speciality: Healing Therapy.
M O (Ref:HM11545)

**KERNOHAN, SARA**
**Sara Kernohan**, The Treatment Room, The Hair & Beauty Company, Watchfield, **Oxfordshire**, SN6 8TE, ENG.
(T) 01793 784555
Speciality: Aromatherapy.
M O (Ref:HM11546)

**KERR, A N F**
**A N F Kerr**, 36 Altrincham Rd, Wilmslow, **Cheshire**, SK9 5ND, ENG.
(T) 01625 530977
Speciality: Osteopathy.
● **Owner** A Kerr
P S T (Ref:HM11547)

**KERR, J A**
**J A Kerr**, 7 Brandreth Rd, Plymouth, **Devon**, PL3 5HQ, ENG.
(T) 01752 662641
Speciality: Homeopathy.
● **Owner** Mr J Kerr
M (Ref:HM11548)

**KERR, JAMES**
**James Kerr**, 180 Quarry St, Hamilton, **Lanarkshire (South)**, ML3 6QR, SCO.
(T) 01698 285102
Speciality: Chiropodists (Podiatrists).
S (Ref:HM11549)

**KERR, JAMES**
**James Kerr**, Glen House, 200 Tottenham Court Rd, London, **London (Greater)**, W1P 9LA, ENG.
(T) 020 8870 2552
Speciality: Hypnotherapy.
● **Owner** Mr J Kerr
B (Ref:HM11550)

**KERR, R**
**R Kerr**, 8 Irish St, Whitehaven, **Cumbria**, CA28 7BU, ENG.
(T) 01946 61950
Speciality: Chiropodists (Podiatrists).
S (Ref:HM11551)

**KERRIDGE, B W**
**B W Kerridge**, 22 Mill Rd, Loddon, Norwich, **Norfolk**, NR14 6DR, ENG.
(T) 01508 528211
Speciality: Chiropodists (Podiatrists).
● **Owner** Mr B Kerridge
S (Ref:HM11552)

**KERRIDGE, SARAH**
**Sarah Kerridge**, East London Homoeopathic Group Practice, 18 Martello St, London, **London (Greater)**, E8 3PE, ENG.
(T) 020 7241 2171
Speciality: Reflexology.
S T (Ref:HM11553)

**KERRISON, KEITH**
**Keith Kerrison**, 275 Knightsfield, Welwyn Garden City, **Hertfordshire**, AL8 7RA, ENG.
(T) 01707 338279
Speciality: Psychotherapy.
● **Owner** Mr K Kerrison
B (Ref:HM11554)

**KERRY, LIZ**
**Liz Kerry**, 102 Southbourne Rd, Bournemouth, **Dorset**, BH6 3QQ, ENG.
(T) 01202 424833
Speciality: Complementary Medicines & Therapy.
● **Owner** Mr J Milward
M (Ref:HM11555)

**KERSEY, M D**
**M D Kersey**, 5 The Limes, Stony Stratford, Milton Keynes, **Buckinghamshire**, MK11 1ET, ENG.
(T) 01908 564442
Speciality: Chiropodists (Podiatrists).
● **Owner** Mr M Kersey
S (Ref:HM11556)

**KERSHAW, ALAN DAVID**
**Alan David Kershaw**, Carlton House, Wakefield, **Yorkshire (West)**, WF1 2DJ, ENG.
(T) 01924 360706
Speciality: Hypnotherapy.
● **Owner** A Kershaw
B (Ref:HM11557)

**KERSHNER, F**
**F Kershner**, 36 Market St, Mottram, Hyde, **Cheshire**, SK14 6JG, ENG.
(T) 01457 765213
Speciality: Herbal Medicine.
● **Owner** Ms F Kershner
M (Ref:HM11558)

**KERSTIN HEALTH & BEAUTY**
**Kerstin Health & Beauty**, 155 The Ryde, Hatfield, **Hertfordshire**, AL9 5DQ, ENG.
(T) 01707 251453
Speciality: Reflexology, Holistic Massage. ✔
● **Therapist** Mrs K Schmidt Q: IHBC, IIHHT. M: BABTAC, BAE, FHT.
C Yrs. Est.: 6 (Ref:HM11559)

**KESAVAN, S K**
**S K Kesavan**, 48 Long Meadows, Bramhope, Leeds, **Yorkshire (West)**, LS16 9DS, ENG.
(T) 01132 673063


Key continued: Yrs.Est: Years Established Q: Qualifications M: Professional Membership ✔ Indemnity Insurance Accept Credit Cards

Speciality: Homeopathy.
● **Owner** Dr S Kesavan
M (Ref:HM11560)

## KESGRAVE CHIROPRACTIC CLINIC
**Kesgrave Chiropractic Clinic**, 313 Main Rd, Kesgrave, Ipswich, **Suffolk**, IP5 2PT, ENG.
(T) 01473 624345 (F) 01473 624345
Speciality: Chiropractic.
● **Partner** Mr R Martin
P S T (Ref:HM11561)

## KESHET-ORR, J
**J Keshet-Orr**, 181 Hampstead Way, London, **London (Greater)**, NW11 7YA, ENG.
(T) 020 8455 4511 (F) 020 8455 4514
Speciality: Psychotherapy.
● **Owner** Mrs J Kershet-Orr
B (Ref:HM11562)

## KESSLER, GABRIEL
**Kessler Mr Gabriel**, Flat 16, 8 Newton St, London, **London (Greater)**, WC2B 5EG, ENG.
(T) 020 7404 5534 (F) 020 7404 5534
Speciality: Homeopathy.
M (Ref:HM11563)

## KESTEVEN NATURAL HEALTH CENTRE
**Kesteven Natural Health Centre**, Church Farm, Church Walk, Great Hale, Sleaford, **Lincolnshire**, NG34 9LL, ENG.
(T) 01529 460536
Speciality: Bach Remedies, Bio-energetics, Counselling. ✔
● **Partner** Mr N Fuller Q: LFHom, MNRHP.
● **Homeopath** Mrs S Fuller Q: LFHom.
C Yrs. Est.: 32 (Ref:HM11564)

## KESTREL
**Kestrel**, Sibbards Cottage, Debden Green, Saffron Walden, **Essex**, CB11 3LX, ENG.
(T) 01371 830302 (F) 01371 830302
Speciality: Physiotherapy.
● **Owner** Mrs T Preasgood
P S T (Ref:HM11565)

## KESTREL
**Kestrel**, Saffran Walden Hospital, Radwinter Rd, Saffron Walden, **Essex**, CB11 3HY, ENG.
(T) 01799 523396 (F) 01799 523396
Speciality: Physiotherapy.
● **Owner** Mrs T Peasgood
P S T (Ref:HM11566)

## KETTERING CHIROPRACTIC CLINIC
**Kettering Chiropractic Clinic**, 20 Headlands, Kettering, **Northamptonshire**, NN15 7HP, ENG.
(T) 01536 510998
Speciality: Chiropractors.
● **Owner** Dr Z Iqbal
P S T (Ref:HM11567)

## KETTERING OSTEOPATH
**Kettering Osteopath**, 32 Headlands, Kettering, **Northamptonshire**, NN15 7HP, ENG.
(T) 01536 512927 (F) 01536 516000
Speciality: Chiropractic, Osteopathy.
P S T (Ref:HM11568)

## KETTLE, JONATHAN
**Jonathan Kettle**, 75 Risbygate St, Bury St. Edmunds, **Suffolk**, IP33 3AQ, ENG.
(T) 01284 769153
Speciality: Osteopathy.
P S T (Ref:HM11569)

## KETTLE, LESLEY
**Lesley Kettle**, 6 Parkside Drive, Exmouth, **Devon**, EX8 4LA, ENG.
(T) 01395 278680
Speciality: Chiropodists (Podiatrists).
● **Owner** Mrs L Kettle
S (Ref:HM11570)

## KETTLE, NIGEL
**Nigel Kettle**, 9 Beeches Avenue, Carshalton, **Surrey**, SM5 3LB, ENG.
(T) 020 8773 4508
Speciality: Aromatherapy.
M O (Ref:HM11571)

## KEVAN, ROBERT
**Robert Kevan**, 4 Ravenshoe Cl, Bourne End, **Buckinghamshire**, SL8 5QP, ENG.
(T) 01628 530464
Speciality: Chiropodists (Podiatrists).
● **Owner** Mr R Kevan
S (Ref:HM11572)

## KEVIN FISHER CHIROPODY
**Kevin Fisher Chiropody**, 32A Queen St, Wolverhampton, **Midlands (West)**, WV1 3JW, ENG.
(T) 01902 681166
Speciality: Chiropody. ✔
● **Chiropodist** Mr K Fisher Q: MBChA. M: B.A.Ch.P.
C Yrs. Est.: 9 (Ref:HM11573)

## KEVIN POWER PSYCHOTHERAPY
**Kevin Power Psychotherapy**, Church Hill House, Church Hill, Eythorne, Dover, **Kent**, CT15 4AQ, ENG.
(T) 01304 830488
Speciality: Psychotherapy.
● **Owner** Mr K Power
B (Ref:HM11574)

## KEW CHIROPRACTIC CLINIC
**Kew Chiropractic Clinic**, 157a Kew Rd, Richmond, **Surrey**, TW9 2PN, ENG.
(T) 020 8948 0679 (F) 020 8332 2526
(E) mrcharliejonyd@hotmail
Speciality: Chiropractic, Electrotherapy, Kinesiology, Manipulation, Massage (Therapeutic), X-Ray. ✔
● **Chiropractor** Mr M Polland
(T) 020 8948 2744 Q: DC. M: BCA, EChiroU.
● **Clinic Director** Mr P Danford
(T) 020 8948 2744 Q: DC. M: ACA, BCA, CC, EChiroU, GCC, ICA.
● **Chiropractor** Mr C Ross
(T) 020 8948 2744 Q: DC. M: BCA, CC, EChiroU.
S Yrs. Est.: 35 (Ref:HM11575)

## KEW, DEREK
**Derek Kew**, 29 Elm Cl, Elsenham, Bishop's Stortford, **Hertfordshire**, CM22 6LE, ENG.
(T) 01279 812200
(E) derekkew@clara.co.uk
(W) www.derek-kew.co.uk
Speciality: Counselling, Hypnosis, Hypnotherapy, Psychotherapy, Rogerian Therapy, Stress Therapy, Transactional Analysis, Visualisation Therapy. ✔
● **Counsellor/Therapist** Mr D Kew Q: BA, Dip.Hyp, Dip.Psych. M: BACP, NCH.
B Yrs. Est.: 10 (Ref:HM11576)

## KEY CENTRE FOR HOMOEOPATHY
**Key Centre For Homoeopathy (The)**, 2 North Parade Passage, Bath, **Somerset**, BA1 1NX, ENG.
(T) 01225 420953
Speciality: Homeopathy.
M (Ref:HM11577)

## KEYE, C
**C Keye**, 20 Goda Rd, Littlehampton, **Sussex (West)**, BN17 6AS, ENG.
(T) 01903 715865
Speciality: Physiotherapy.
● **Owner** Mr C Kaye
P S T (Ref:HM11578)

## KEYES, SUSAN
**Susan Keyes**, 15 Munnoch Cr, Ardrossan, **Ayrshire (North)**, KA22 7PW, SCO.
(T) 01294 461226
Speciality: Reflexology.
● **Owner** Mrs S Keyes
S T (Ref:HM11579)

## KEYNSHAM CHIROPRACTIC CLINIC
**Keynsham Chiropractic Clinic**, Keynsham Chiropractic Clinic, 2 Temple Court, Keynsham, Bristol, BS31 1HA, ENG.
(T) 01179 866578 (F) 01179 861578
Speciality: Chiropractic. ✔
● **Chiropractor** Ms D Spree Q: DC, MSc. M: BCA.
● **Owner/Chiropractor** Dr K Fohlmann Q: DC. M: BCA.
● **Chiropractor** Mr D Morley Q: DC, MSc. M: BCA.
P Yrs. Est.: 11 (Ref:HM11580)

## KEYS
**Keys**, 131A Alcester Rd, Birmingham, **Midlands (West)**, B13 8JP, ENG.
(T) 01214 498122
Speciality: Psychotherapy.
B (Ref:HM11581)

## KEYS, J
**J Keys**, 5 Leslie Pl, Edinburgh, **Edinburgh (City of)**, EH4 1NG, SCO.
(T) 01313 321182
Speciality: Physiotherapy.
● **Owner** Ms J Keys
P S T (Ref:HM11582)

## KHAFAF, TARA
**Tara Khafaf**, 52 Combe Park, Bath, **Somerset**, BA1 3NH, ENG.
(T) 01225 443744
Speciality: Reflexology.
S T (Ref:HM11583)

## KHALED, BEN MOUSSA
**Ben Moussa Khaled**, The Crawford St.Centre, 27-79 Crawford St, London, **London (Greater)**, W1H 1PL, ENG.
(T) 020 7723 5676
Speciality: Osteopathy.
P S T (Ref:HM11584)

## KHALSA, S S
**S S Khalsa Homeopath**, 14 Glen Court, Avenue Rd, Wolverhampton, **Midlands (West)**, WV3 9JW, ENG.
(T) 01902 681778
Speciality: Homeopathy.
M (Ref:HM11585)

## KHAN, D
**D Khan**, 87 Northcote Rd, London, **London (Greater)**, SW11 6PL, ENG.
(T) 020 7223 2417
Speciality: Chiropractic.
P S T (Ref:HM11586)

## KHAN, FARIDA
**Farida Khan**, Audley Cottage, Slanting Hill, Hermitage, Thatcham, **Berkshire**, RG18 9QG, ENG.
(T) 01635 200353
Speciality: Aromatherapy.
● **Owner** Mrs F Khan
M O (Ref:HM11587)

## KHAN, H
**H Khan**, Health Centre Valley Rd, Liversedge, **Yorkshire (West)**, WF15 6DF, ENG.
(T) 01924 407771
Speciality: Homeopathy.
● **Manager** Mr H Khan
M (Ref:HM11588)

## KHAN, M A
**M A Khan**, Flat 32 Matlock Court, 46 Kensington Park Rd, London, **London (Greater)**, W11 3BS, ENG.
(T) 020 7727 4662
Speciality: Acupuncture.
O (Ref:HM11589)

## KHEIR, DIANE
**Kheir Diane**, 58 Tennyson Rd, Harpenden, **Hertfordshire**, AL5 4BB, ENG.
(T) 01582 713648
Speciality: Osteopathy.
P S T (Ref:HM11590)

## KI CLINIC
**Ki Clinic (The)**, The Old Stables, Hallgate, Hexham, **Northumberland**, NE46 1XD, ENG.
(T) 01434 608189 (F) 01434 608189
(E) info@thekiclinic.co.uk
(W) www.thekiclinic.co.uk
Speciality: Acupressure, Acupuncture, Aromatherapy, Bach Remedies, Complementary Therapy, Counselling, Hay Diet, Herbal Medicine, Indian Head Massage, Iridology, Kinesiology, Massage (Therapeutic), Moxibustion, Nutritional Therapy, Reflexology, Vitamin Therapy, Detoxification Programmes. ✔
● **Medical Herbalist** Mr R Menzies Q: BSc, DBTh. M: IRCH.
● **Reflexologist/Health Kinesiologist**



Key: B Mind-Body Medicine C Complementary Medicine H Self Help Treatment M Medicinal Therapy O Oriental Medicine P Postural Therapy S Manipulative Structural Therapy T Touch Therapy

Mr M Costar **Q:** Cert.Couns, Cert.Couns.Groupwork, Cert.Ed, ITEC, MAMA, MAR. **M:** AoR.
**B** Yrs. Est.: 10 (**Ref:**HM11591)

### KIDDLE, B E

**B E Kiddle**, The Willows, Fishers Lane, Mark, Highbridge, **Somerset**, TA9 4LZ, ENG.
(T) 01452 720929
Speciality: Complementary Medicines & Therapy, Trichology.
**M** (**Ref:**HM11592)

### KIDLINGTON CHIROPRACTIC

**Kidlington Chiropractic**, Jacobean House, Glebe St, East Kilbride, Glasgow, **Glasgow (City of)**, G74 4LY, SCO.
(T) 01355 330121
Speciality: Complementary Medicines & Therapy.
● **Owner** Mrs A Flemming
**M** (**Ref:**HM11593)

### KIDLINGTON CHIROPRACTIC

**Kidlington Chiropractic**, 18 High St, Kidlington, **Oxfordshire**, OX5 1EH, ENG.
(T) 01865 377877 (F) 01865 377877
(E) kcc@networkchiropractic.co.uk
(W) www.networkchiropractic.co.uk
Speciality: Chiropractic, Specialises in Network Spinal Analysis. ✓
● **Chiropractor** Dr S Rynsburger **Q:** B.App.Sc, BSc. **M:** GCC, SCA.
**C** Yrs. Est.: 10 (**Ref:**HM11594)

### KIDLINGTON HERBAL PRACTICE

**Kidlington Herbal Practice**, 71 Benmead Rd, Kidlington, **Oxfordshire**, OX5 2AX, ENG.
(T) 01865 842260 (F) 01865 842260
(E) mohi@therapist.net
Speciality: Herbal Medicine, Naturopathy. ✓
● **Practitioner** Mr M Rezvani **Q:** BSc, MNIMH, MSc, PhD. **M:** NIMH.
**M** Yrs. Est.: 10 (**Ref:**HM11595)

### KIDLINGTON OSTEO PRACTICE

**Kidlington Osteopathic Practice**, 330 Oxford Rd, Kidlington, Oxon, Oxford, **Oxfordshire**, OX5 1DA, ENG.
(T) 01865 378803
Speciality: Acupressure, Aromatherapy, Electrotherapy, Massage (Therapeutic), Osteopathy, Rolfing, Ultrasonics. ✓
● **Osteopath** Mr J Leaman **Q:** ND. **M:** GOsS.
**S** Yrs. Est.: 10 (**Ref:**HM11596)

### KIDSON, J H P

**J H P Kidson**, 90 Lustrells Cres, Saltdean, Brighton, **Sussex (East)**, BN2 8FL, ENG.
(T) 01273 307787
Speciality: Homeopathy.
● **Owner** Mr J Kidson
**M** (**Ref:**HM11597)

### KIKAI SHIATSU CENTRE

**Kikai Shiatsu Centre**, 172a Arlington Rd, Camden, London, **London (Greater)**, NW1 7HL, ENG.
(T) 020 8368 9050
(E) chris@kikaifreeserve.co.uk
(W) www.kikai.freeserve.co.uk
Speciality: Moxibustion, Oriental Diagnosis, Shiatsu, Chi Kung (Qi Gong). ✓
● **Shiatsu Practitioner/Teacher**
Mr C Osborne
(T) 01342 823516 **Q:** MRSS(t). **M:** RSS.
● **Shiatsu Practitioner/Teacher**
Mr G Crisp **Q:** BA, MRSS(t). **M:** RSS.
**C O** Yrs. Est.: 13 (**Ref:**HM11598)

### KILBEY, ALISON

**Alison Kilbey**, 61 Olympia Cl, Northampton, **Northamptonshire**, NN4 0RU, ENG.
(T) 01604 702501 (F) 01604 702501
Speciality: Electrolysis.
● **Owner** Mrs A Kilbey
**T** (**Ref:**HM11599)

### KILBRIDE, PETER

**KPF Services**, 83 Argyle Avenue, Hounslow, **London (Greater)**, TW3 2LL, ENG.
(T) 08008 984279 (F) 020 8898 0414
(E) hyponoses@bt2online.co.uk
Speciality: Aversion Therapy, Cognitive Therapy, Complementary Therapy, Counselling, Hypnosis, Hypnotherapy, Psychotherapy, Stress Therapy, Visualisation Therapy, Regression, Past life aggression. ✓
● **Owner/Hypnotherapist/Psychotherapist**
Mr P Kilbride **Q:** Dip.Clin.Hyp. **M:** BSCH.
**B** Yrs. Est.: 5 (**Ref:**HM11600)

### KILGALLON, P

**P Kilgallon**, 12 York Rd, Stoke-On-Trent, **Staffordshire**, ST3 6NW, ENG.
(T) 01782 595390 (F) 01782 595390
Speciality: Homeopathy.
● **Owner** Mrs P Kilgallon
**M** (**Ref:**HM11601)

### KILGOUR, ALEXANDRA

**Alexandra Kilgour**, 17 Carlisle Rd, Hove, **Sussex (East)**, BN3 4FP, ENG.
(T) 01273 747058
Speciality: Complementary Medicines & Therapy.
● **Owner** Miss A Kilgour
**C M** (**Ref:**HM11602)

### KILKENNY CHIROPRACTIC CLINIC

**Kilkenny Chiropractic Clinic**, U1 Priory Hse, Dean St, **County Kilkenny**, IRE.
(T) 05651 959
Speciality: Chiropractors.
**P S T** (**Ref:**HM11603)

### KILKENNY, STEPHANIE

**Kilkenny Stephanie MISPA ITEC**, Pond Rd, Castlebar, **County Mayo**, IRE.
(T) 09423 945
Speciality: Aromatherapy.
**M O** (**Ref:**HM11604)

### KILLAMARSH OSTEOPATHY PRACTICE

**Killamarsh Osteopathy Practice**, 4 Kirkcroft Lane, Killamarsh, Sheffield, **Yorkshire (South)**, S21 1BS, ENG.
(T) 01142 480524 (F) 01142 480524
Speciality: Osteopathy.
● **Partner** Mrs G Eakins
**P S T** (**Ref:**HM11605)

### KILLEEN, OLIVER

**Killeen Oliver Ph D**, 14 Wayburn Cl, Earlscourt, Waterford, **County Waterford**, IRE.
(T) 05185 8297 (F) 05185 8298
(E) ojk@indigo.ie
Speciality: Counselling.
**B H** (**Ref:**HM11606)

### KILLORAN-GANNON, SHEILA

**Killoran-Gannon Sheila B A**, 43 Belgrave Sq, Rathmines, **County Dublin**, IRE.
(T) 01496 0545
Speciality: Psychotherapy.
**B** (**Ref:**HM11607)

### KILLOUGH, D

**Killough D SR CH**, 139 Falls Rd, Belfast, **County Antrim**, BT12 6AF, NIR.
(T) 028 9024 2452
Speciality: Chiropodists (Podiatrists).
● **Owner** Mrs F Killough
**S** (**Ref:**HM11608)

### KILLYNURE THERAPY CENTRE

**Killynure Therapy Centre**, 79 Tempo Rd, Enniskillen, **County Fermanagh**, BT74 6HR, NIR.
(T) 028 6632 8200
Speciality: Physiotherapy.
● **Owner** Ms L Burke
**P S T** (**Ref:**HM11609)

### KILNER, FELICIA

**Felicia Kilner**, 41 Eastern Avenue, Reading, **Berkshire**, RG1 5RX, ENG.
(T) 01189 267438
Speciality: Chiropractic.
● **Senior Partner** Mr S Carpenter
**P S T** (**Ref:**HM11610)

### KILTALOWN HSE HOLISTIC HEALING

**Kiltalown House Creativity Holistic Healing Centre**, Blessington Rd, Jobstown, Tallaght, **County Dublin**, IRE.
(T) 01452 2466
Speciality: Complementary Medicines & Therapy.
**M** (**Ref:**HM11611)

### KILVINGTON & ASSOCIATES

**Kilvington & Associates**, 44 - 46 Fitzwilliam Rd, Rotherham, **Yorkshire (South)**, S65 1PT, ENG.
(T) 01709 364466
Speciality: Hypnosis.
**B** (**Ref:**HM11612)

### KILWORTH CHIROPRACTIC CLINIC

**Kilworth Chiropractic Clinic**, The Market House Kilworth Village, **County Cork**, IRE.
(T) 025 2743 6
Speciality: Chiropractors.
**P S T** (**Ref:**HM11613)

### KIM PERRY QUALIFIED CHIROP

**Kim Perry Qualified Chiropodist**, Maywood, Beaconsfield, **Buckinghamshire**, HP9 2BU, ENG.
(T) 01494 670793
Speciality: Chiropodists (Podiatrists).
**S** (**Ref:**HM11614)

### KIMBLE, A H

**A H Kimble**, 73 Station Rd, Burgess Hill, **Sussex (West)**, RH15 9DY, ENG.
(T) 01444 881523
Speciality: Physiotherapy.
● **Owner** Mr A Kimble
**P S T** (**Ref:**HM11615)

### KIMIA HEALTH CLINIC

**Kimia Health Clinic**, Britannia House, 1-11 Glenthorne Rd, London, **London (Greater)**, W6 0LH, ENG.
(T) 020 8741 2722 (F) 020 8748 9898
Speciality: Psychotherapy.
● **Owner** Dr B Baluchi
**B** (**Ref:**HM11616)

### KIMS

**Kims**, 9 Woodthorpe Rd, Ashford, **Surrey**, TW15 2RL, ENG.
(T) 01784 248090
Speciality: Complementary Medicines & Therapy.
**M** (**Ref:**HM11617)

### KIN HON CLINIC

**Kin Hon Clinic**, 37 Charter House, Lord Montgomery Way, Portsmouth, **Hampshire**, PO1 2SU, ENG.
(T) 023 9282 3454
Speciality: Acupuncture.
● **Owner** Ms G Kispal
**O** (**Ref:**HM11618)

### KINCORTH CLINIC

**Kincorth Clinic**, Chiropody Department, Provost Watt Drive, Aberdeen, **Aberdeenshire**, AB12 5BT, SCO.
(T) 01224 872384
Speciality: Chiropodists (Podiatrists).
● **Owner** Mrs A Lindsey
**S** (**Ref:**HM11619)

### KINESIOLOGIST

**Kinesiologist**, 7 Charlestown, Ackworth, Pontefract, **Yorkshire (West)**, WF7 7DU, ENG.
(T) 01977 616901
Speciality: Complementary Medicines & Therapy.
● **Owner** Ms T Hinchcliffe
**C M** (**Ref:**HM11620)

### KINESIOLOGY & COMP HEALTH CTRE

**Kinnesiology & Complementary Health Centre**, 81 Lancashire St, Leicester, **Leicestershire**, LE4 7AF, ENG.
(T) 01162 661962
Speciality: Kinesiology.
**C** (**Ref:**HM11621)

### KINESIOLOGY FEDERATION

**Kinesiology Federation**, Po Box 17, Woolmer Green, Knebworth, **Hertfordshire**, SG3 6UF, ENG.
(T) 01438 817998 (F) 01438 817998
Speciality: Complementary Medicines & Therapy.
● **Chairman** Mrs P Roberts



Key continued: **Yrs.Est:** Years Established **Q:** Qualifications **M:** Professional Membership ✓ Indemnity Insurance Accept Credit Cards

M (Ref:HM11622)

### KINESIOLOGY FEDERATION

**Kinesiology Federation (The)**, Po Box 83, Sheffield, **Yorkshire (South)**, S7 2AW, ENG.
(T) 01142 814064
Speciality: Complementary Medicines & Therapy.
M (Ref:HM11623)

### KING & MCDONALD

**King & McDonald**, Meadow View Farm, Kinwalsey Lane, Meriden, Coventry, **Midlands (West)**, CV7 7HT, ENG.
(T) 01676 540274
Speciality: Physiotherapy.
P S T (Ref:HM11624)

### KING, A

**Mrs A King**, 48 Church Rd, Malvern, **Worcestershire**, WR14 1NG, ENG.
(T) 01684 568744 (F) 01684 568744
Speciality: Osteopathy.
● **Owner** Mr K Smith
P S T (Ref:HM11625)

### KING, ANDREA

**Andrea King**, 23 Broome Gr, Wivenhoe, Colchester, **Essex**, CO7 9QB, ENG.
(T) 01206 824565
Speciality: Reflexology.
S T (Ref:HM11626)

### KING, DERRELL

**Derrell King**, 68 Gloucester Rd, Barnet, **Hertfordshire**, EN5 1NB, ENG.
(T) 020 8441 7441 (F) 020 8441 7461
Speciality: Alexander Technique.
● **Owner** Ms D King
P S (Ref:HM11627)

### KING, G Y

**G Y King**, 38 Lark Rise, Liphook, **Hampshire**, GU30 7QT, ENG.
(T) 01428 722225
Speciality: Chiropodists (Podiatrists).
● **Owner** Mrs G King
S (Ref:HM11628)

### KING, HEATHER

**Heather King**, 56 Midhope Way, Barnsley, **Yorkshire (South)**, S75 2LS, ENG.
(T) 01226 770800
Speciality: Complementary Medicines & Therapy.
C M (Ref:HM11629)

### KING, HILARY

**Hilary King**, 13 Aden Gr, London, **London (Greater)**, N16 9NP, ENG.
(T) 020 7254 9206
Speciality: Alexander Technique.
● **Owner** Ms H King
P S (Ref:HM11630)

### KING, J R

**J R King**, 30 Cedar Rd, Watford, **Hertfordshire**, WD1 4QW, ENG.
(T) 01923 240793
Speciality: Acupuncture.
● **Partner** Mr J King
O (Ref:HM11631)

### KING, K M

**K M King**, 115 North End Rd, London, **London (Greater)**, NW11 7TA, ENG.
(T) 020 8455 5998
Speciality: Physiotherapy.
● **Owner** Mr K King
P S T (Ref:HM11632)

### KING, KAREN

**Karen King**, Stafford, **Staffordshire**, ST16, ENG.
(T) 07970 936247
Speciality: Bach Remedies.
M (Ref:HM11633)

### KING, LESLEY

**Lesley King**, 62 Paynton Rd, St. Leonards-On-Sea, **Sussex (East)**, TN37 7DZ, ENG.
(T) 01424 441397
Speciality: Homeopathy.
● **Owner** Mrs L King
M (Ref:HM11634)

### KING, LESLEY J

**Lesley J King**, 30 The Piazza, Covent Garden, London, **London (Greater)**, WC2E 8BE, ENG.
(T) 020 7836 4835
Speciality: Physiotherapy.
P S T (Ref:HM11635)

### KING, LIZ

**Liz King**, Whiteways, 89 Guildford Rd, Bagshot, **Surrey**, GU19 5NS, ENG.
(T) 01276 472291
Speciality: Chiropodists (Podiatrists).
S (Ref:HM11636)

### KING, M T

**M T King**, 1 Forsters Lane, Bridport, **Dorset**, DT6 3HY, ENG.
(T) 01308 425107
Speciality: Complementary Medicines & Therapy.
● **Owner** Mrs M King
C M (Ref:HM11637)

### KING, R

**R King**, 30 Cedar Rd, Watford, **Hertfordshire**, WD1 4QW, ENG.
(T) 01923 240793
Speciality: Acupuncture.
O (Ref:HM11638)

### KING, S

**S King**, 112 Ellis Rd, Crowthorne, **Berkshire**, RG45 6PH, ENG.
(T) 01344 773810
Speciality: Chiropodists (Podiatrists).
● **Owner** Mrs S King
S (Ref:HM11639)

### KING, S

**S King**, 1st Floor Woburn Court, 8 Guildhall Hill, Norwich, **Norfolk**, NR2 1JG, ENG.
(T) 01603 219254
Speciality: Homeopathy.
● **Partner** Mr S King
M (Ref:HM11640)

### KING, S

**S King**, 2 South View, Sandford, Crediton, **Devon**, EX17 4LP, ENG.
(T) 01363 777833
Speciality: Complementary Medicines & Therapy.
C M (Ref:HM11641)

### KING, SANDRA

**Sandra King**, 19 Missden Drive, Hemel Hempstead, **Hertfordshire**, HP3 8QR, ENG.
(T) 01442 217238
Speciality: Reflexology.
S T (Ref:HM11642)

### KING, SIMON

**Simon King**, Temple St Clinic, 18 Temple St, Sidmouth, **Devon**, EX10 9AY, ENG.
(T) 01395 516529
Speciality: Acupuncture.
O (Ref:HM11643)

### KING, SIMON

**Simon King**, 227 St Leonards Rd, Norwich, **Norfolk**, NR1 4JN, ENG.
(T) 01603 466092
(E) simon-king@cwcom.net
(W) www.simon-king.com
Speciality: Ayurvedic Medicine, Bach Remedies, Family Therapy, Floral Essence Therapy, Gem Essence Therapy, Hay Diet, Healing Therapy, Herbal Medicine, Holistic Healing, Homeopathy, Macrobiotics, Naturopathy, Nutritional Therapy, Pattern Therapies, Phytotherapy, Sensitivity Training, Stress Therapy, Vibrational Therapy, Vitamin Therapy, Exercises. ✔
● **Homeopath** Mr S King Q: LCPH, MHMA. M: HMA.
B Yrs. Est.: 10 (Ref:HM11644)

### KING, STELLA

**Stella King**, 6 White Hart Fold, Todmorden, **Yorkshire (West)**, OL14 7BD, ENG.
(T) 01706 813527
Speciality: Acupuncture.
● **Partner** Ms A Rotheram
O (Ref:HM11645)

### KING, VERONICA

**Veronica King**, Scott St Complementary Therapy Centre, 58 Scott St, Barrow-in-Furness, **Cumbria**, LA14 1QE, ENG.
(T) 01229 826700
Speciality: Homeopathy.
M (Ref:HM11646)

### KINGCROSS PRACTICE

**Kingcross Practice (The)**, 97 Judd St, London, **London (Greater)**, WC1H 9NE, ENG.
(T) 020 7209 1564 (F) 020 7383 5068
Speciality: Complementary Medicines & Therapy.
● **Partner** Mr A Syrimas
M (Ref:HM11647)

### KINGFISHER CHIROP & HYP

**Kingfisher Chiropody & Hypnotherapy Clinic**, Kingfisher Surgery, Elthorne Way, Newport Pagnell, **Buckinghamshire**, MK16 0JR, ENG.
(T) 01908 615566
Speciality: Chiropody, Hypnotherapy.
P S T (Ref:HM11648)

### KINGFISHER HOL HEALING CTRE

**Kingfisher Holistic Healing Centre (The)**, 9 Valley Rd, Hebden Bridge, **Yorkshire (West)**, HX7 7BZ, ENG.
(T) 01422 842424
Speciality: Complementary Medicines & Therapy.
● **Director** Mrs M Philcox
M (Ref:HM11649)

### KINGFISHERS COMP HEALTH CARE

**Kingfishers Complementary Health Care**, 2 Kingfisher Cl, The Wharf, Reading, **Berkshire**, RG7 4UY, ENG.
(T) 01189 713875 (F) 08701 606947
(E) admin@kchc.fsbusiness.co.uk
(W) www.kchc.fsbusiness.co.uk
Speciality: Aromatherapy, Bach Remedies, Complementary Therapy, Indian Head Massage, Kinesiology, Reflexology, Reiki, Shiatsu. ✔
● **Reflexologist** Ms D Wiltshire
(T) 01189 812988 Q: ITEC. M: BABTAC.
● **Shiatsu Practitioner** Ms C Memory
● **Aromatherapist/Manager**
Mr J Nixon Q: ITEC. M: GCP.
T Yrs. Est.: 2 (Ref:HM11650)

### KINGHAM, D

**D Kingham**, 2 Clifton Pk, Bristol, BS8 3BS, ENG.
(T) 01179 737371 (F) 01179 730887
Speciality: Psychiatry.
● **Senior Partner** Dr M Sternberg
B (Ref:HM11651)

### KINGS CLINIC

**Kings Clinic (The)**, 48 Fenton Rd, Bournemouth, **Dorset**, BH6 5BT, ENG.
(T) 01202 420751
Speciality: Chiropractic.
P S T (Ref:HM11652)

### KINGS HILL REFLEXOLOGY

**Kings Hill Reflexology**, 5 Saxon Cl, Kings Hill, West Malling, **Kent**, ME19 4SA, ENG.
(T) 01732 874984
Speciality: Reflexology.
● **Owner** Mrs P McPartlin
S T (Ref:HM11653)

### KINGS LANGLEY OSTEO PRACTICE

**Kings Langley Osteopathic Practice**, 40 Vicarage Lane, Kings Langley, **Hertfordshire**, WD4 9HR, ENG.
(T) 01923 260535
Speciality: Osteopathy.
P S T (Ref:HM11654)

### KINGS LANGLEY PHYSIO CLINIC

**Kings Langley Physiotherapy Clinic**, 34 High St, Kings Langley, **Hertfordshire**, WD4 9HT, ENG.
(T) 01923 261974 (F) 01923 261974
Speciality: Physiotherapy.
● **Partner** Ms J Moore
P S T (Ref:HM11655)



Key: B Mind-Body Medicine C Complementary Medicine H Self Help Treatment M Medicinal Therapy O Oriental Medicine P Postural Therapy S Manipulative Structural Therapy T Touch Therapy

**KINGS PHYSIOTHERAPY CENTRE**

**Kings Physiotherapy Centre**, The Barn, Moat House Works, Kings Coughton, Alcester, **Warwickshire**, B49 5QF, ENG.
(T) 01789 766100
Speciality: Physiotherapy.
● **Senior Partner** Dr H Keene
P S T (**Ref:**HM11656)

**KINGS ROAD CLINIC**

**Kings Road Clinic**, 9 Kings Rd, St. Leonards-On-Sea, **Sussex (East)**, TN37 6EA, ENG.
(T) 01424 714800
Speciality: Complementary Medicines & Therapy.
M (**Ref:**HM11657)

**KINGSBRIDGE COMP HLTH PRACTICE**

**Nicholsons Wholefoods**, 12 Fore St, Kingsbridge, **Devon**, TQ7 4LY, ENG.
(T) 01548 560847
Speciality: Absent Healing, Acupressure, Acupuncture, Complementary Therapy, Counselling, Healer, Healing Therapy, Herbal Medicine, Holistic Healing, Homeopathy, Hypnotherapy, Manipulation, Massage (Therapeutic), Meditation, Miasm Therapy, Nutritional Therapy, Oriental Diagnosis, Psychotherapy, Reflexology, Reiki, Shiatsu, Spiritual Healing, Stress Therapy, Touch Therapy, Vitamin Therapy, Yoga. ✔
● **Medical Herbalist** Ms A Seal
(T) 01548 511347 Q: BSc, MNIMH.
● **Practice Co-Ordinator** Ms J Hunn
Q: Dip.Hom, DSH. M: Soc.Hom.
● **Healer/Counsellor** Mr M Pringle
(T) 01548 580251
● **Acupuncturist** Dom Eccles
(T) 01803 732458 Q: Lic.Ac, MBAcC.
B Yrs. Est.: 8 (**Ref:**HM11658)

**KINGSBRIDGE PHYSICAL THERAPY**

**Kingsbridge Physical Therapy Clinic**, 6 Derby Rd, Kingsbridge, **Devon**, TQ7 1JJ, ENG.
(T) 01548 854324
Speciality: Acupressure, Electrotherapy, Manipulation, Massage (Therapeutic), Osteopathy, Food Sensitivity Blood Test and Diet - Run Nutron South West Franchise. Physiotherapy - Muscle Energy - Neuromuscular Inhibition Computerised Lymphatic Drainage Based on Systolic Heart Rate. ✔
● **Physiotherapist/Osteopath**
Mr D Barrow Q: MA, MAB Phys, MAO, MBA.
M Yrs. Est.: 4 (**Ref:**HM11659)

**KINGSBURY PSYCHOTHERAPY PRAC**

**Kingsbury Psychotherapy Practice**, 19 Winston Avenue, Kingsbury, London, **London (Greater)**, NW9 7LA, ENG.
(T) 020 8200 7725 (F) 08701 629145
(E) satguru@hotmail.com
Speciality: Absent Healing, Cognitive Therapy, Counselling, Group Therapy, Healer, Healing Therapy, Hypnosis, Hypnotherapy, Paranormal Therapies, Psychotherapy, Reiki, Seichem, Stress Therapy. ✔
● **Psychotherapist** Mr D Howard Q: C.Hyp, Dip.Couns, MNCH, Reiki Master. M: BACP.
B Yrs. Est.: 10 (**Ref:**HM11660)

**KINGSCOTT, DAVID**

**David Kingscott**, 2 Rodbury Court, Station Rd, Backwell, Bristol, BS19 3NW, ENG.
(T) 01275 463758
Speciality: Chiropodists (Podiatrists).
S (**Ref:**HM11661)

**KINGSFIELD CTRE-PHYSIOTHERAPY**

**Kingsfield Centre For Physiotherapy**, 2 Kingsfield Rd, Watford, **Hertfordshire**, WD1 4PS, ENG.
(T) 01923 218082
Speciality: Physiotherapy.
● **Partner** Mrs K Hine
P S T (**Ref:**HM11662)

**KINGSGATE ACUPUNCTURE PRACTICE**

**Kingsgate Acupuncture Practice**, 80 Kingsgate Rd, West Hampstead, London, **London (Greater)**, NW6 4LA, ENG.
(T) 020 7419 1211
(E) marion@mfixlerfreeserve.co.uk
Speciality: Acupressure, Acupuncture, Cupping, Moxibustion, Oriental Diagnosis, Japanese Acupuncture. ✔
● **Acupuncturist** Ms M Fixler Q: Dip.Ac. M: BAcC.
O Yrs. Est.: 10 (**Ref:**HM11663)

**KINGSLAND, S A**

**S A Kingsland**, 11 Blackwood Cl, West Byfleet, **Surrey**, KT14 6PW, ENG.
(T) 01932 341484
Speciality: Electrolysis.
● **Owner** Mrs S Kingsland
T (**Ref:**HM11664)

**KINGSLEIGH CLINIC**

**Kingsleigh Clinic**, 98 High St, Rayleigh, **Essex**, SS6 7BY, ENG.
(T) 01268 741000
Speciality: Homeopathy.
● **Principal** Mr G Johnson
M (**Ref:**HM11665)

**KINGSLEY, JOSIE**

**Josie Kingsley**, 65 Meadow St, Preston, **Lancashire**, PR1 1TS, ENG.
(T) 01772 250189
Speciality: Chiropodists (Podiatrists).
● **Owner** Ms J Kinglsey
S (**Ref:**HM11666)

**KINGSLEY, NOEL**

**Alexander Technique**, 21 Harcourt House, 19 Cavendish Sq, London, **London (Greater)**, W1M 9AB, ENG.
(T) 020 7491 3505
(E) noel@alex-tech.co.uk
(W) www.alexander-technique.com
Speciality: Alexander Technique. ✔
● **Practitioner/Teacher**
Mr N Kingsley M: STAT.
P Yrs. Est.: 7 (**Ref:**HM11667)

**KINGSLEY, V**

**V Kingsley**, 4 Brunton St, Darlington, **County Durham**, DL1 4EN, ENG.
(T) 01325 284247
Speciality: Clairvoyants & Palmists.
B (**Ref:**HM11668)

**KINGSLEY-HOLT, MIRANDA**

**Miranda Kingsley-Holt**, Unit 2, Cobblestone Walk, 74 High St, Steyning, **Sussex (West)**, BN44 3RD, ENG.
(T) 01903 879323
Speciality: Homeopathy.
● **Owner** Ms M Kingsleyholt
M (**Ref:**HM11669)

**KINGSLEY-THOMAS, FERNANDA**

**Fernanda Kingsley-Thomas**, Caterham, **Surrey**, CR3, ENG.
(T) 01883 344330
Speciality: Bach Remedies.
M (**Ref:**HM11670)

**KINGSMEAD PHYSIOTHERAPY CLINIC**

**Kingsmead Physiotherapy Clinic**, 224 Pollards Oak Rd, Oxted, **Surrey**, RH8 0JP, ENG.
(T) 01883 712987 (F) 01883 712987
Speciality: Physiotherapy.
P S T (**Ref:**HM11671)

**KINGSMILL, STEPHEN**

**Stephen Kingsmill**, 144 Miller Drive, Fareham, **Hampshire**, PO16 7LW, ENG.
(T) 01329 232373
Speciality: Hypnotherapy.
● **Owner** Mr S Kingsmill
B (**Ref:**HM11672)

**KINGSMITH, ANNE-MARIE**

**Anne-Marie Kingsmith**, 7 Spring Avenue, Gildersome, Morley, Leeds, **Yorkshire (West)**, LS27 7BS, ENG.
(T) 01132 525616
Speciality: Chiropody, Podiatry. ✔
● **Owner/Chiropodist**
Mrs A Kingsmith Q: Inst.CH.P, L.I.S.Ch.
T Yrs. Est.: 20 (**Ref:**HM11673)

**KINGSTON & RICHMOND HYNO CTRE**

**Kingston & Richmond Hynotherapy Centre**, 15 Uxbridge Rd, Kingston Upon Thames, **Surrey**, KT1 2LH, ENG.
(T) 020 8546 8122
Speciality: Hypnosis.
B (**Ref:**HM11674)

**KINGSTON CHIROPRACTIC CLINIC**

**Kingston Chiropractic Clinic**, 1 Surbiton Cres, Kingston Upon Thames, **Surrey**, KT1 2JP, ENG.
(T) 020 8549 7655
Speciality: Chiropractic.
P S T (**Ref:**HM11675)

**KINGSTON HYPNOTHERAPY CENTRE**

**Kingston Hypnotherapy Centre**, 27 Broomwood Rd, Kingston Upon Thames, **Surrey**, KT1 4ER, ENG.
(T) 020 8943 4794
Speciality: Hypnotherapy.
B (**Ref:**HM11676)

**KINGSTON NATURAL HEALING CTRE**

**Kingston Natural Healing Centre**, 40 Eastbury Rd, Kingston Upon Thames, **Surrey**, KT2 5AN, ENG.
(T) 020 8546 5793
Speciality: Acupressure, Acupuncture, Alexander Technique, Aromatherapy, Bach Remedies, Counselling, Cranial Osteopathy, Family Therapy, Healer, Homeopathy, Hypnotherapy, Kinesiology, Massage (Therapeutic), Osteopathy, Psychotherapy, Reflexology, Reiki, Shiatsu, Spiritual Healing, Stress Therapy, Buteyko Asthma Treatment, Chinese Herbalism, Health & Beauty, High Touch Jin Shin Jitsu. ✔
● **Hypnotherapist/Psychotherapist/Counsellor**
Ms J Marshall Q: BRCP, DHP (NC), NRHP (Assoc), UKCP (Reg). M: BACP, BRCP, NRHP, UKCP.
● **Acupuncturist** Ms J Fraser Q: Dip.Ac, MA, MBAcC. M: BAcC.
● **Owner** Ms L Kukowski
● **Osteopath** Ms A Peacock Q: DO. M: GOsC.
● **Owner** Mrs A Chalfont
M Yrs. Est.: 17 (**Ref:**HM11677)

**KINGSTON NATUROPATHIC CENTRE**

**Kingston Naturopathic Centre**, 25 Woodbines Avenue, Kingston Upon Thames, **Surrey**, KT1 2AX, ENG.
(T) 020 8547 1259
Speciality: Complementary Medicines & Therapy.
C M (**Ref:**HM11678)

**KINGSTON OSTEOPATHS**

**Kingston Osteopaths**, Chichester House, 145A London Rd, Kingston Upon Thames, **Surrey**, KT2 6NH, ENG.
(T) 020 8546 5995
Speciality: Cranial Osteopathy, Manipulation, Massage (Therapeutic), Osteopathy. ✔
● **Osteopath** Ms R Morrison Q: BSc, MSc. M: GOsC.
● **Osteopath** Ms P Guildford Q: BSc, Hons (OST). M: GOsC.
S Yrs. Est.: 6 (**Ref:**HM11679)

**KINGSTON, J H**

**J H Kingston**, Crofton Physiotherapy Clinic, Starts Hill Rd, Orpington, **Kent**, BR6 7AR, ENG.
(T) 01689 853863
Speciality: Physiotherapy.
P S T (**Ref:**HM11680)

**KINGSTON, PATRICIA**

**Patricia Kingston**, 16 Pelham Gardens, Folkestone, **Kent**, CT20 2LF, ENG.
(T) 01303 241011
Speciality: Reflexology.
S T (**Ref:**HM11681)

**KINGSWOOD CHIROPRACTIC CLINIC**

**Kingswood Chiropractic Clinic**, The Orchard Medical Centre, MacDonald Walk, Kingswood, Bristol, BS15 8NJ, ENG.
(T) 01179 612060 (F) 01179 353428
Speciality: Chiropractic. ✔
● **Chiropractor** Mr D Morley Q: DC, MSc. M: BCA.
● **Practice Manager** Dr K Fohlmann Q: DC. M: BCA.


Key continued: Yrs.Est: Years Established Q: Qualifications M: Professional Membership ✔ Indemnity Insurance Accept Credit Cards

P Yrs. Est.: 3 (Ref:HM11682)

**KINGTON PHYSIOTHERAPY DEPT**

**Kington Physiotherapy Department**, Kington Cottage Hospital, Victoria Rd, Kington, **Herefordshire**, HR5 3BX, ENG.
(T) 01544 230583
Speciality: Physiotherapy.
P S T (Ref:HM11683)

**KING-TURNER, P**

**Miss P King-Turner**, 36A London Rd, Blackwater, Camberley, **Surrey**, GU17 9AA, ENG.
(T) 01276 36475
Speciality: Osteopathy.
P S T (Ref:HM11684)

**KINLOCH, DEBORAH**

**Deborah Kinloch**, 11 Wick Rd, Wigginton, Tring, **Hertfordshire**, HP23 6EL, ENG.
(T) 01442 827557
Speciality: Herbalists.
● **Owner** Mr D Kinloch
M (Ref:HM11685)

**KINNAIRD, F M**

**F M Kinnaird**, 92 Whitcliffe Rd, Cleckheaton, **Yorkshire (West)**, BD19 3DR, ENG.
(T) 01535 647065 (F) 01535 679104
(E) psychsolution@msn.com
Speciality: Aversion Therapy, Biofeedback, Cognitive Therapy, Counselling, Gestalt Therapy, Humanistic Psychology, Hypnosis, Hypnotherapy, Life Style Coaching, Meditation, Psychotherapy, Rogerian Therapy, Stress Therapy, Transactional Analysis, Rational emotional behavioural therapy, post trauma counselling therapy.
● **Owner/Chartered Psychologist**
Mr F Kinnaird Q: BSc (Hons). M: BPS.
B Yrs. Est.: 18 (Ref:HM11686)

**KINNAIRD, S H**

**S H Kinnaird**, Redacre Pressmennan, Dunbar, **Lothian (East)**, EH42 1TF, SCO.
(T) 01368 850229
Speciality: Physiotherapy.
● **Senior Partner** Mr J Kinnaird
P S T (Ref:HM11687)

**KINNEAR, E M L**

**E M L Kinnear**, 42 Alexandra Rd, Richmond, **Surrey**, TW9 2BS, ENG.
(T) 020 8940 7662
Speciality: Physiotherapy.
P S T (Ref:HM11688)

**KINNEAR, MARGARET**

**Margaret Kinnear**, Maple House, 50A Ivry St, Ipswich, **Suffolk**, IP1 3QP, ENG.
(T) 01473 214981
Speciality: Reflexology.
S T (Ref:HM11689)

**KINNEY, CAROL**

**Carol Kinney Holistic Therapist**, 31 Briarfield Rd, Ellesmere Port, **Merseyside**, CH65 8BE, ENG.
(T) 01512 015534
Speciality: Complementary Medicines & Therapy.
M (Ref:HM03716)

**KINSALE CHIROPRACTIC CLINIC**

**Kinsale Chiropractic Clinic**, O'Connell St, Kinsale, **County Cork**, IRE.
(T) 021 4773 617
Speciality: Chiropractors.
P S T (Ref:HM11690)

**KINSELLA, DENIS**

**Kinsella Denis L C S P (Phys)**, The Sq, Ferns, **County Wexford**, IRE.
(T) 05466 442
Speciality: Complementary Medicines & Therapy.
M (Ref:HM11691)

**KINSELLA, KARLA**

**Karla Kinsella**, 205 Buchanan St, Glasgow, **Glasgow (City of)**, G1 2JZ, SCO.
(T) 01413 321835
Speciality: Clairvoyants & Palmists.
B (Ref:HM11692)

**KINSELLA, MARIE**

**Marie Kinsella**, Tickincor, Clonmel, **County Tipperary**, IRE.
(T) 05223 073
Speciality: Cognitive Therapy, Counselling, Gestalt Therapy, Group Therapy, Humanistic Psychology, Stress Therapy, Relationship Therapy. ✓
● **Counselling Psychotherapist**
Ms M Kinsella Q: BSc (Hons), Dip.Couns.
M: IACT, PSI.
H Yrs. Est.: 4 (Ref:HM11693)

**KINSEY, G C**

**G C Kinsey**, 60 Lodge Rd, Walsall, **Midlands (West)**, WS5 3LA, ENG.
(T) 01213 575096
Speciality: Chiropodists (Podiatrists).
● **Owner** Mrs G Kinsey
S (Ref:HM11694)

**KIOTECH**

**Kiotech Ltd**, 11 St James Sq, London, **London (Greater)**, SW1Y 4LB, ENG.
(T) 020 7577 7505 (F) 020 7389 0798
Speciality: Complementary Medicines & Therapy.
● **Managing Director** Mr H Goldin
M (Ref:HM11695)

**KIPPAX, JANET**

**Janet Kippax**, 240 Sidegate Lane, Ipswich, **Suffolk**, IP4 3DH, ENG.
(T) 01473 726902
Speciality: Homeopathy.
M (Ref:HM11696)

**KIPPAX, STEPHEN**

**Stephen Kippax**, 240 Sidegate Lane, Ipswich, **Suffolk**, IP4 3DH, ENG.
(T) 01473 726902
Speciality: Herbal Medicine.
M (Ref:HM11697)

**KIPPAX-CHUI, JANE**

**Jane Kippax-Chui**, Chiswick Bridge Golf Range, Dukes Meadows, London, **London (Greater)**, W4 2SH, ENG.
(T) 020 8995 3952
Speciality: Physiotherapy.
P S T (Ref:HM11698)

**KIPPING, NICOLA**

**Nicola Kipping**, 41 Church Rd, Poole, **Dorset**, BH14 0NN, ENG.
(T) 01202 749514 (F) 01202 718906
Speciality: Physiotherapy.
● **Partner** Mrs C Swinhoe
P S T (Ref:HM11699)

**KIRBY, ANNIE**

**Annie Kirby**, 1 Hawthorne Rd, Radlett, **Hertfordshire**, WD7 7BJ, ENG.
(T) 01923 857674
Speciality: Reflexology.
S T (Ref:HM11700)

**KIRBY, DAVE**

**Dave Kirby**, 360 Icknield Way, Luton, **Bedfordshire**, LU3 2JU, ENG.
(T) 01582 595058 (F) 01582 595058
Speciality: Physiotherapy.
● **Owner** Mr D Kirby
P S T (Ref:HM11701)

**KIRBY, M**

**Miranda Kirby**, Derriman Cl, Sheffield, **Yorkshire (South)**, S11 9LB, ENG.
(T) 01142 364017
Speciality: Reflexology, Reiki. ✓
● **Owner** Ms M Kirby Q: MIIR.
C Yrs. Est.: 3 (Ref:HM11702)

**KIRCHER, T**

**T Kircher**, New Cross Natural Therapy Centre, 394 New Cross Rd, London, **London (Greater)**, SE14 6TY, ENG.
(T) 020 8469 0858
Speciality: Acupuncture.
O (Ref:HM11703)

**KIRK, A**

**A Kirk**, 50 Plungington Rd, Preston, **Lancashire**, PR1 7RB, ENG.
(T) 01772 556520
Speciality: Chiropodists (Podiatrists).
● **Partner** Mr I Cuerden
S (Ref:HM11704)

**KIRK, A S**

**A S Kirk**, 1 Kenilworth Rd, Lytham St. Annes, **Lancashire**, FY8 1TZ, ENG.
(T) 01253 723254 (F) 01253 723254
Speciality: Chiropodists (Podiatrists).
● **Owner** Mr A Kirk
S (Ref:HM11705)

**KIRK, DONNA**

**Donna Kirk**, 11 Barclay Manor, Dromore, **County Down**, BT25 2HX, NIR.
(T) 028 9753 3116
Speciality: Reflexology.
S T (Ref:HM11706)

**KIRK, DONNA**

**Donna Kirk**, 179 Telscombe Way, Luton, **Bedfordshire**, LU2 8QP, ENG.
(T) 01582 614105
Speciality: Reflexology.
S T (Ref:HM11707)

**KIRK, J**

**J Kirk**, 154 Drymen Rd, Bearsden, Glasgow, **Glasgow (City of)**, G61 3RE, SCO.
(T) 01419 423145
Speciality: Chiropodists (Podiatrists).
S (Ref:HM11708)

**KIRK, J**

**J Kirk**, 7 Robin Hill Drive, Chislehurst, **Kent**, BR7 5ER, ENG.
(T) 020 8467 6827
Speciality: Chiropodists (Podiatrists).
● **Owner** Mrs J Kirk
S (Ref:HM11709)

**KIRK, LAURENCE**

**Laurence Kirk**, Avon House, 29 New Broad St, Stratford-Upon-Avon, **Warwickshire**, CV37 6HW, ENG.
(T) 01789 204803
Speciality: Osteopathy.
P S T (Ref:HM11710)

**KIRK, ROBIN**

**Kirk Robin**, Bank Chambers, 10 Borough High St, London, **London (Greater)**, SE1 9QQ, ENG.
(T) 020 7378 0850
Speciality: Osteopathy.
P S T (Ref:HM11711)

**KIRKCALDY CHIROPRACTIC CLINIC**

**Kirkcaldy Chiropractic Clinic**, 42 Townsend Pl, Kirkcaldy, **Fife**, KY1 1HB, SCO.
(T) 01592 260791
Speciality: Chiropractors.
● **Owner** Dr E Leerberg
P S T (Ref:HM11712)

**KIRKE, STEPHANIE**

**Stephanie Kirke**, 40 Rowan Drive, Newbury, **Berkshire**, RG14 1LY, ENG.
(T) 01635 820580
Speciality: Psychotherapy.
B (Ref:HM11713)

**KIRKEVOLL, SHEY**

**Shey Kirkevoll**, 52 Waldemar Avenue, London, **London (Greater)**, SW6 5NA, ENG.
(T) 020 7731 7069
Speciality: Electrolysis.
● **Owner** Mrs S Kirkevoll
T (Ref:HM11714)

**KIRKHAM CHIROPODY PRACTICE**

**Kirkham Chiropody Practice**, 5 Freckleton St, Kirkham, Preston, **Lancashire**, PR4 2SN, ENG.
(T) 01772 685909
Speciality: Chiropodists (Podiatrists).
● **Partner** Ms S Fowler
S (Ref:HM11715)

**KIRKHAM PHYSIOTHERAPY CENTRE**

**Kirkham Physiotherapy Centre**, Ash Tree House, Church St, Kirkham, Preston, **Lancashire**, PR4 2SE, ENG.
(T) 01772 672202
Speciality: Physiotherapy.
● **Owner** Mrs L Jonson



Key: B Mind-Body Medicine C Complementary Medicine H Self Help Treatment M Medicinal Therapy O Oriental Medicine P Postural Therapy S Manipulative Structural Therapy T Touch Therapy

P S T (Ref:HM11716)

## KIRKINTILLOCH FOOT CLINIC

**Kirkintilloch Foot Clinic**, 4 Freeland Pl, Kirkintilloch, Glasgow, **Glasgow (City of)**, G66 1ND, SCO.
(T) 01417 752932
Speciality: Chiropodists (Podiatrists).
S (Ref:HM11717)

## KIRKMEAD CENTRE

**Kirkmead Centre**, Flat 3 Holland Court, The Mead, Street, **Somerset**, BA16 0AQ, ENG.
(T) 01458 448434
Speciality: Aromatherapy, Reflexology. ✔
● **Owner/Aromatherapist** Mrs H Grint
Q: Dip.Arom. M: IFR, ITEC.
C Yrs. Est.: 7 (Ref:HM11718)

## KIRKPATRICK, IAN

**Ian Kirkpatrick**, 35 Chester Rd, Chigwell, **Essex**, IG7 6AH, ENG.
(T) 020 8500 5298
Speciality: Reflexology.
S T (Ref:HM11719)

## KIRKPATRICK, W H

**W H Kirkpatrick**, 70 Oldfield Lane South, Greenford, **London (Greater)**, UB6 9LD, ENG.
(T) 020 8575 0388
Speciality: Osteopathy.
● **Owner** Mr W Kirkpatrick
P S T (Ref:HM11720)

## KIRKSOPP, B K

**B K Kirksopp**, 2 Crown Lane, Littleport, Ely, **Cambridgeshire**, CB6 1PP, ENG.
(T) 01353 863218
Speciality: Reflexology.
S T (Ref:HM11721)

## KIRKUP, KEVIN

**Kevin Kirkup**, 1 Hartside, Birtley, Chester Le Street, **County Durham**, DH3 2EW, ENG.
(T) 01914 921448
Speciality: Osteopathy.
P S T (Ref:HM11722)

## KIRRIEMUIR PHYSIO CLINIC

**Kirriemuir Physiotherapy Clinic**, 17 School Wynd, Kirriemuir, **Angus**, DD8 4BQ, SCO.
(T) 01575 575616
Speciality: Acupuncture, Physiotherapy. ✔
● **Owner** Mrs D Roberts Q: MCSP, SRP. M: CSP.
S Yrs. Est.: 6 (Ref:HM11723)

## KIRSH, MALCOLM (DR)

**Dr Malcolm Kirsh**, 57 Hall Lane, London, **London (Greater)**, NW4 4TJ, ENG.
(T) 020 8203 7355 (F) 020 8203 9732
Speciality: Hypnosis, Hypnotherapy, Psychotherapy, Psychology. ✔
● **Psychotherapist/Hypnotherapist**
Mr M Kirsh Q: PhD. M: ANLP, BACP, NCH, NCP.
B Yrs. Est.: 20 (Ref:HM11724)

## KIRSH, MALCOLM (DR)

**Dr Malcolm Kirsh**, The Hale Clinic, 7 Park Cres, London, **London (Greater)**, W1N 3HE, ENG.
(T) 020 8230 7355
Speciality: Hypnosis, Hypnotherapy, Psychotherapy, Psychology. ✔
● **Psychotherapist/Hypnotherapist**
Dr M Kirsh Q: PhD. M: ANLP, BABCP, NCH, NCP.
B Yrs. Est.: 20 (Ref:HM11725)

## KIRTON, CHRISTINE

**Christine Kirton**, 10 Chargate Cl, Walton-On-Thames, **Surrey**, KT12 5DN, ENG.
(T) 01932 225374
Speciality: Psychotherapy.
● **Owner** Mrs C Kirton
B (Ref:HM11726)

## KIRWAN, A M & S P

**A M & S P Kirwan**, 6 Langham Pl, Northampton, **Northamptonshire**, NN2 6AA, ENG.
(T) 01604 630649
Speciality: Chiropodists (Podiatrists).
S (Ref:HM11727)

## KITCHEN, H J (DR)/KITCHEN, J A

**Dr Hugo J Kitchen & Mr James A Kitchen**, Fightback UK, 6 Mansell St, Stratford-Upon-Avon, **Warwickshire**, CV37 6NR, ENG.
(T) 01789 414289 (F) 01789 299003
Speciality: Osteopathy.
● **Senior Partner** Dr H Kitchen
P S T (Ref:HM11728)

## KITSON OSTEOPATH

**Kitson Osteopath**, 1 Bromsgrove Rd, Halesowen, **Midlands (West)**, B63 3JQ, ENG.
(T) 01215 011111
Speciality: Osteopathy.
P S T (Ref:HM11729)

## KITSON, P

**P Kitson**, 62 St. Georges Rd, Redditch, **Worcestershire**, B98 8ED, ENG.
(T) 01527 596619
Speciality: Acupuncture, Aromatherapy, Osteopathy, Reflexology. ✔ [credit card]
● **Therapist** Mrs H Kitson M: IIHHT.
● **Osteopath** Mr P Kitson Q: DO.
C Yrs. Est.: 22 (Ref:HM11730)

## KITSON, PAUL

**Paul Kitson**, 84 New Rd, Kidderminster, **Worcestershire**, DY10 1AE, ENG.
(T) 01562 861717
Speciality: Osteopathy.
● **Owner** Mr F Kitson
P S T (Ref:HM11731)

## KITSON, PAUL

**Paul Kitson**, 45 Bull St, West Bromwich Ringway, West Bromwich, **Midlands (West)**, B70 6EU, ENG.
(T) 01215 536679
Speciality: Osteopathy.
● **Owner** Mr P Kitson
P S T (Ref:HM11732)

## KITSON, PAUL

**Paul Kitson**, 10A Worcester St, Stourbridge, **Midlands (West)**, DY8 1AN, ENG.
(T) 01384 443388 (F) 01384 394904
Speciality: Osteopathy.
● **Owner** Mr P Kitson
P S T (Ref:HM11733)

## KJAERVIK, SUSANNE

**Susanne Kjaervik**, The Surgery, 1 Leighton Rd, Leighton Buzzard, **Bedfordshire**, LU7 7LB, ENG.
(T) 01525 211444
Speciality: Physiotherapy.
● **Owner** Mr J Betser
P S T (Ref:HM11734)

## KJAERVIK, SUSANNE

**Susanne Kjaervik**, Woodside Clinic, 88 Great Northern Rd, Dunstable, **Bedfordshire**, LU5 4BT, ENG.
(T) 01582 608400
Speciality: Physiotherapy.
P S T (Ref:HM11735)

## KJELDSEN, TIM

**Tim Kjeldsen**, 34A Amesbury Rd, Cardiff, **Glamorgan (Vale of)**, CF23 5DW, WAL.
(T) 029 2045 8988
Speciality: Alexander Technique.
P S (Ref:HM11736)

## KLEIN, JEMMA

**Jemma Klein**, 32 Manor Hall Avenue, London, **London (Greater)**, NW4 1NX, ENG.
(T) 020 8203 3078 (F) 020 8203 3078
Speciality: Chiropody. ✔
● **Chiropodist (Podiatrist)**
Mrs J Klein Q: BSc (Hons), M.S.C.P, S.R.Ch.
C Yrs. Est.: 2 (Ref:HM11737)

## KLEINMANN, SHIELA

**Shiela Kleinmann**, 19 Oxford St, Leamington Spa, **Warwickshire**, CV32 4RA, ENG.
(T) 01926 337362
Speciality: Complementary Medicines & Therapy.
● **Owner** Mrs S Kleinmann
C M (Ref:HM11738)

## KLUG, H S

**H S Klug**, Sutherland House, 1a Ashbourne Avenue, London, **London (Greater)**, NW11 0DP, ENG.
(T) 020 8458 7869
Speciality: Osteopathy.
P S T (Ref:HM11739)

## KNAPMAN, D J

**D J Knapman**, 7 Fons George Rd, Taunton, **Somerset**, TA1 3JU, ENG.
(T) 01823 335303
Speciality: Psychology.
● **Owner** Mr D Knapman
B (Ref:HM11740)

## KNAPP, SALLY

**Sally Knapp**, 12 Tower St, Cirencester, **Gloucestershire**, GL7 1EF, ENG.
(T) 01285 653855
Speciality: Hypnosis.
● **Owner** Ms S Knapp
B (Ref:HM11741)

## KNEBWORTH PHYSIO CLINIC

**K C S Ltd**, 3a Kenilworth Cl, Stevenage, **Hertfordshire**, SG2 8TB, ENG.
(T) 01438 812258 (F) 01438 812258
Speciality: Electrotherapy, Manipulation, Massage (Therapeutic), Physiotherapy, Stress Therapy, Ultrasonics. ✔
● **Physiotherapist** Ms S Right M: CPSM.
● **Physiotherapist** Ms R Cluff Q: MCSP, SRP. M: CPSM, CSP.
● **Owner/Physiotherapist**
Mrs D Seller Q: MCSP, SRP. M: CPSM, CSP.
● **Physiotherapist** Ms J Watson Q: MCSP, SRP. M: CPSM, CSP.
S Yrs. Est.: 18 (Ref:HM11742)

## KNIGHT & ASSOCIATES

**C Knight & Associates**, 39 The Market Sq, London, **London (Greater)**, N9 0TZ, ENG.
(T) 020 8803 2915
Speciality: Chiropodists (Podiatrists).
S (Ref:HM11743)

## KNIGHT, A

**A Knight**, 12 Tiverton Rd, London, **London (Greater)**, NW10 3HL, ENG.
(T) 020 8964 9836
Speciality: Complementary Medicines & Therapy.
● **Owner** A Knight
C M (Ref:HM11744)

## KNIGHT, ALICE

**Alice Knight**, 170 North Rd, Combe Down, Bath, **Somerset**, BA2 5DL, ENG.
(T) 01225 833184
Speciality: Alexander Technique.
P S (Ref:HM11745)

## KNIGHT, ANDREW

**Andrew Knight**, Hawkers Cottage, West St, Somerton, **Somerset**, TA11 6NA, ENG.
(T) 01458 272082
Speciality: Osteopathy.
P S T (Ref:HM11746)

## KNIGHT, ANDREW M

**Andrew M Knight**, Woodcock House, Woodcock St, Castle Cary, **Somerset**, BA7 7BW, ENG.
(T) 01963 351477
Speciality: Osteopathy.
● **Owner** Mr A Knight
P S T (Ref:HM11747)

## KNIGHT, ANNA

**Anna Knight**, 188 Victoria Rd, Ferndown, **Dorset**, BH22 9JE, ENG.
(T) 01202 861513
Speciality: Complementary Medicines & Therapy.
● **Owner** Mrs A Knight
C M (Ref:HM11748)

## KNIGHT, C E

**C E Knight**, 48 Silver St, Dursley, **Gloucestershire**, GL11 4NA, ENG.
(T) 01453 547012
Speciality: Chiropodists (Podiatrists).
● **Owner** Mrs C Knight
S (Ref:HM11749)

## KNIGHT, E

**E Knight**, 129 Upper Bridge Rd, Chelmsford, **Essex**, CM2 0BA, ENG.
(T) 01245 345654
Speciality: Complementary Medicines &



Key continued: **Yrs.Est:** Years Established **Q:** Qualifications **M:** Professional Membership ✔ Indemnity Insurance [credit card] Accept Credit Cards

Therapy.
● **Owner** Miss E Knight
C M (Ref:HM11750)

## KNIGHT, J M

**J M Knight**, 121 Mythop Rd, Lytham St. Annes, **Lancashire**, FY8 4HJ, ENG.
(T) 01253 734601
Speciality: Complementary Medicines & Therapy.
● **Owner** Mrs J Knight
C M (Ref:HM11751)

## KNIGHT, JAYNE

**Jayne Knight**, 35 Sorrel Drive, Woodville, Swadlincote, **Derbyshire**, DE11 7JS, ENG.
(T) 01283 221214
Speciality: Reflexology.
S T (Ref:HM11752)

## KNIGHT, KAY

**Kay Knight**, 27 Frys Lane, Yateley, **Hampshire**, GU46 7TJ, ENG.
(T) 01252 870760
Speciality: Chiropodists (Podiatrists).
● **Owner** Mrs K Knight
S (Ref:HM11753)

## KNIGHT, MICHELLE

**Michelle Knight**, 60 Neal St, London, **London (Greater)**, WC2H 9PA, ENG.
(T) 020 7497 2423
Speciality: Clairvoyants & Palmists.
B (Ref:HM11754)

## KNIGHT, ROWENA

**Rowena Knight**, Keys Counselling & Psychotherapy, 131A Alcester Rd, Birmingham, **Midlands (West)**, B13 8JP, ENG.
(T) 01214 431580
Speciality: Alexander Technique.
● **Doctor** Mr D King
P S (Ref:HM11755)

## KNIGHT, S L

**S L Knight**, 93 Byng Drive, Potters Bar, **Hertfordshire**, EN6 1UJ, ENG.
(T) 01707 658636
Speciality: Aromatherapy, Reflexology.
● **Owner** Mrs S Knight
B (Ref:HM11756)

## KNIGHT, S R

**S R Knight**, 48 Silver St, Dursley, **Gloucestershire**, GL11 4NA, ENG.
(T) 01453 547012
Speciality: Chiropodists (Podiatrists).
● **Owner** Mrs C Knight
S (Ref:HM11757)

## KNIGHT, SYLVIA

**Sylvia Knight**, 14 Millfield Drive, Camblesforth, Selby, **Yorkshire (North)**, YO8 8JY, ENG.
(T) 01757 617186
Speciality: Reflexology.
S T (Ref:HM11758)

## KNIGHT, TOM

**Tom Knight**, 160 Station Rd, Ratby, Leicester, **Leicestershire**, LE6 0JP, ENG.
(T) 01162 387425
Speciality: Complementary Medicines & Therapy.
● **Owner** Mr T Knight
C M (Ref:HM11759)

## KNIGHTS, VALERIE

**Valerie Knights**, 91 Park Rd, Bolton, **Lancashire**, BL1 4RQ, ENG.
(T) 01204 392250
Speciality: Hypnotherapy.
B (Ref:HM11760)

## KNIGHTSBRIDGE CHIROPRACTIC

**Knightsbridge Chiropractic Clinic (The)**, 50 Hans Cres, 1st Floor Knightsbridge Business Centre, London, **London (Greater)**, SW1P 1SB, ENG.
(T) 020 7222 3456
Speciality: Chiropractic.
● **Manager** Ms K Nelson
P S T (Ref:HM11761)

## KNIGHTSWOOD CLINIC

**Knightswood Clinic**, 33 Oxbarton, Stoke Gifford, Bristol, BS34 8RP, ENG.
(T) 01179 095361
Speciality: Physiotherapy. ✔
● **Owner/Physiotherapist** Mr M Lewis Q: LCSP. M: LCSP.
S Yrs. Est.: 15 (Ref:HM11762)

## KNISZ, P

**P Knisz**, 6 Ashfield Trce, Bradford Rd, Bingley, **Yorkshire (West)**, BD16 1EQ, ENG.
(T) 01274 562311
Speciality: Chiropodists (Podiatrists).
● **Owner** Mr P Knisz
S (Ref:HM11763)

## KNOTT, ELIZABETH

**Elizabeth Knott**, Ivy Bank, Chapel St, Hazel Gr, Stockport, **Cheshire**, SK7 4JH, ENG.
(T) 01614 566535
Speciality: Aromatherapy.
● **Owner** Miss E Knott
M O (Ref:HM11764)

## KNOWD, KAREN

**Karen Knowd**, 135 Newcomen Rd, Wellingborough, **Northamptonshire**, NN8 1JP, ENG.
(T) 01933 380592
Speciality: Complementary Medicines & Therapy.
● **Owner** Ms L Smart
M (Ref:HM11765)

## KNOWLAND, VIVIEN

**Vivien Knowland**, 32 Dryburgh Rd, London, **London (Greater)**, SW15 1BL, ENG.
(T) 020 8788 8788
Speciality: Reflexology.
S T (Ref:HM11766)

## KNOWLE HOUSE

**Knowle House**, 4 Meavy Way, Plymouth, **Devon**, PL5 3JB, ENG.
(T) 01752 793152
Speciality: Chiropodists (Podiatrists).
S (Ref:HM11767)

## KNOWLES, BARBARA

**Barbara Knowles**, 4a Burlington Drive, Stockport, **Cheshire**, SK3 8UE, ENG.
(T) 01614 562241
Speciality: Aromatherapy.
M O (Ref:HM11768)

## KNOWLES, BERNARD

**Bernard Knowles**, Brighton Marina Village, Brighton, **Sussex (East)**, BN2 5UF, ENG.
(T) 01273 818177
Speciality: Complementary Medicines & Therapy.
● **Owner** Mr B Knowles
M (Ref:HM11769)

## KNOWLES, J

**J Knowles**, 8 Shambles, York, **Yorkshire (North)**, YO1 7LZ, ENG.
(T) 01904 629128
Speciality: Biomechanics, Chiropody, Nail Surgery. ✔
● **Chiropodist** Mr A Ferguson Q: BSc, DPodM, M.S.C.P.
● **Chiropodist** J Knowles Q: DPodM, M.S.C.P.
C Yrs. Est.: 20 (Ref:HM11770)

## KNOWLES, JANICE

**Janice Knowles**, 95 High St, Newton-Le-Willows, **Merseyside**, WA12 9SL, ENG.
(T) 01925 220044
Speciality: Biomechanics, Chiropody, Nail Surgery, Podiatry. ✔
● **Owner/Chiropodist** Mrs J Knowles Q: M.S.C.P.
S Yrs. Est.: 13 (Ref:HM11771)

## KNOX, DAWN

**Dawn Knox**, 14 Eccleston Rd, Higher Kinnerton, Chester, **Cheshire**, CH4 9DY, ENG.
(T) 01244 660117
Speciality: Homeopathy.
● **Owner** Mrs D Knox
M (Ref:HM11772)

## KNOX, HELEN

**Helen Knox**, 50 Springcroft Cres, Baillieston, Glasgow, **Glasgow (City of)**, G69 6SB, SCO.
(T) 01417 719205
Speciality: Reflexology.
S T (Ref:HM11773)

## KNUDSEN, KIM

**Kim Knudsen**, The Little Venice Psychotherapy Practice, 45 Warwick Cres, London, **London (Greater)**, W2 6NE, ENG.
(T) 020 7286 5355
Speciality: Psychotherapy.
● **Psychotherapist** Mrs K Knudsen Q: BSc, Dip.Psych.
B Yrs. Est.: 40 (Ref:HM11774)

## KNUTSFORD CHIROPRACTIC CLINIC

**Dr E Heinonen T/A Knutsford Chiropractic Clinic**, 15 King St, Knutsford, **Cheshire**, WA16 6DW, ENG.
(T) 01565 651133 (F) 01565 755837
(E) info@health-select.com
Speciality: Absent Healing, Aromatherapy, Chiropractic, Complementary Therapy, Counselling, Healer, Healing Therapy, Holistic Healing, Hypnosis, Indian Head Massage, Manipulation, Massage (Therapeutic), Meditation, Reflexology, Reiki, Spiritual Healing, Visualisation Therapy, X-Ray, Yoga, Zero Balancing, Thero-Auricular, Emotional Therapy. ✔
● **Owner/Chiropractor** Dr E Heinonen Q: BSc, DC. M: BCA, GCC.
● **Chiropractor** Mr K Haslam Q: BSc, DC. M: BCA, GCC.
● **Therapist** Ms P Hardy Q: Dip.StM. M: FHT, ZBA(UK).
● **Associate** Ms J Twist Q: BA (Hons). M: NRHP.
O S T Yrs. Est.: 10 (Ref:HM11775)

## KOBASHI

**Kobashi**, 2 Fore St, Ide, Exeter, **Devon**, EX2 9RQ, ENG.
(T) 01392 217628 (F) 01392 427090
Speciality: Aromatherapy.
● **Owner** Mrs L Ballard
M O (Ref:HM11776)

## KOCH, H C H

**H C H Koch**, Wellington Mews, Wellington St, Cheltenham, **Gloucestershire**, GL50 1XY, ENG.
(T) 01242 263715
Speciality: Psychology.
● **Owner** Dr H Koch
B (Ref:HM11777)

## KOHLER, SUE

**Sue Kohler**, 43 Alexandria Drive, Surbiton, **Surrey**, KT5 9AD, ENG.
(T) 020 8390 1859
Speciality: Indian Head Massage, Reflexology.
S T (Ref:HM11778)

## KOLTHAMMER, J

**J Kolthammer**, New Cross Natural Therapy Centre, 394 New Cross Rd, London, **London (Greater)**, SE14 6TY, ENG.
(T) 020 8469 0858
Speciality: Chiropractors.
P S T (Ref:HM11779)

## KOLTHAMMER, JOHN

**John Kolthammer DC, MMCA**, 151 Cardinal Avenue, Morden, **Surrey**, SM4 4ST, ENG.
(T) 020 8335 0544
(E) john@kolthammer.freeserve.co.uk
Speciality: Chiropractic, Manipulation. ✔
● **McTimoney Chiropractor** Mr J Kolthammer Q: Dip.Chiro. M: MCA.
S Yrs. Est.: 7 (Ref:HM11780)

## KONDIC, CHRIS

**Chris Kondic**, 133 Wood St, Barnet, **Hertfordshire**, EN5 4BX, ENG.
(T) 020 8449 7656
Speciality: Complementary Medicines & Therapy.
M (Ref:HM11781)

## KONRAD, GABRIEL

**Gabriel Konrad**, 4 Elm Park Rd, Havant, **Hampshire**, PO9 2AD, ENG.
(T) 023 9248 6957 (F) 023 9248 6957
Speciality: Osteopathy.
● **Owner** Mr G Konrad



Key: B Mind-Body Medicine C Complementary Medicine H Self Help Treatment M Medicinal Therapy O Oriental Medicine P Postural Therapy S Manipulative Structural Therapy T Touch Therapy

P S T (Ref:HM11782)

## KONTOS, A
**A Kontos**, 6a Sloane Sq, London, **London (Greater)**, SW1W 8EE, ENG.
(T) 020 7730 8437
Speciality: Chiropodists (Podiatrists).
● **Owner** A Kontos
S (Ref:HM11783)

## KONTOU, F
**F Kontou**, 11 Mercers Avenue, Bishop's Stortford, **Hertfordshire**, CM23 4AG, ENG.
(T) 01279 658626
Speciality: Reflexology.
● **Owner** Mrs F Kontou
S T (Ref:HM11784)

## KOPELOWITZ, C A
**C A Kopelowitz**, 40 Woodhall Gate, Pinner, **London (Greater)**, HA5 4TL, ENG.
(T) 020 8866 3863
Speciality: Physiotherapy.
● **Owner** Ms C Kopelowitz
P S T (Ref:HM11785)

## KORTH & ASSOCIATES
**Stuart Korth & Associates**, Wenvoe, 159 St Johns Rd, Tunbridge Wells, **Kent**, TN4 9UP, ENG.
(T) 01892 521134
Speciality: Osteopathy.
P S T (Ref:HM11786)

## KORTH, STUART
**Stuart Korth**, 27 Bickenhall Mansions, Bickenhall St, London, **London (Greater)**, W1H 3LE, ENG.
(T) 020 7935 0844
Speciality: Osteopathy.
P S T (Ref:HM11787)

## KORYO SOOJI CLINIC
**Koryo Sooji Clinic**, 2b Alleyn Park, Southall, **London (Greater)**, UB2 5QT, ENG.
(T) 020 8571 4536 (F) 020 8571 4536
Speciality: Complementary Medicines & Therapy.
● **Owner** Mr Y Wong
C M (Ref:HM11788)

## KOS, JARMILA
**Jarmila Kos**, 8 Ridings Cl, London, **London (Greater)**, N6 5XE, ENG.
(T) 020 8341 9880
Speciality: Reflexology.
S T (Ref:HM11789)

## KOSEFF, S S
**S S Koseff**, 19 Glebe Rd, Stanmore, **London (Greater)**, HA7 4EJ, ENG.
(T) 020 8954 7533
Speciality: Complementary Medicines & Therapy.
C M (Ref:HM11790)

## KOSMEA
**Kosmea**, Top Farm, Silver St, Benniworth, Market Rasen, **Lincolnshire**, LN8 6JR, ENG.
(T) 01507 313861
Speciality: Aromatherapy.
● **Partner** Mrs R Loughton
M O (Ref:HM11791)

## KOTEN, SUSAN
**Susan Koten**, 14 Corbets Avenue, Upminster, **Essex**, RM14 2EQ, ENG.
(T) 01708 223524 (F) 01708 223524
Speciality: Herbal Medicine.
● **Owner** Mrs S Koten
M (Ref:HM11792)

## KOZUBIK, IVA
**Iva Kozubik**, 16 Clarence Sq, Cheltenham, **Gloucestershire**, GL50 4JN, ENG.
(T) 01242 241933
Speciality: Acupuncture.
O (Ref:HM11793)

## KRAFT, T
**T Kraft**, 80 Harley St, London, **London (Greater)**, W1N 1AE, ENG.
(T) 020 7580 2692
Speciality: Psychotherapy.
● **Owner** Dr T Kraft
B (Ref:HM11794)

## KRAFT, T
**T Kraft**, 9 The Fairway, New Barnet, Barnet, **Hertfordshire**, EN5 1HH, ENG.
(T) 020 8440 3434
Speciality: Psychotherapy.
B (Ref:HM11795)

## KRAMER, STUART
**Stuart Kramer**, B U P A Alexandra Hospital, Impton Lane, Chatham, **Kent**, ME5 9PG, ENG.
(T) 01634 687166
Speciality: Osteopathy.
P S T (Ref:HM11796)

## KRAUS, R A
**R A Kraus**, 18 Dyserth Rd, Rhyl, **Denbighshire**, LL18 4DP, WAL.
(T) 01745 337980
Speciality: Chiropodists (Podiatrists).
● **Owner** Mr R Kraus
S (Ref:HM11797)

## KRAWCHENKO, LOUISE A V
**Louise A V Krawchenko**, Tavistock Complementary Health Care Centre, 7a Market St, Tavistock, **Devon**, PL19 0DA, ENG.
(T) 01822 616103 (F) 01822 616103
Speciality: Osteopathy.
● **Owner** Ms L Krawchenko
P S T (Ref:HM11798)

## KREY, JOHN
**John Krey**, 68 Newport Rd, Barnstaple, **Devon**, EX32 9BG, ENG.
(T) 01271 344958
Speciality: Chiropractic.
P S T (Ref:HM11799)

## KRILL, W E
**W E Krill**, Chiropody Surgery, Chart Lane, Reigate, **Surrey**, RH2 7BN, ENG.
(T) 01737 243643
Speciality: Chiropodists (Podiatrists).
● **Owner** Mr W Krill
S (Ref:HM11800)

## KRIR, J
**J Krir**, 23c Goat Lane, Basingstoke, **Hampshire**, RG21 7PZ, ENG.
(T) 01256 326590
Speciality: Chiropractors.
● **Doctor** Mrs J Krir
P S T (Ref:HM11801)

## KRISHNA RAMAMOURTHY MNIMH
**Krishna Ramamourthy Mnimh**, 28 Hanover Rd, London, **London (Greater)**, N15 4DL, ENG.
(T) 020 8808 7744
Speciality: Herbal Medicine.
M (Ref:HM11802)

## KRISS, ADRIAN D
**Kriss Adrian D**, Perry Cottage, 11 Perry Lane, Bromsgrove, **Worcestershire**, B61 7JL, ENG.
(T) 01527 832263 (F) 07971 11620
Speciality: Chiropody. ✔
● **Chiropodist (Podiatrist)** Mr A Kriss Q: DPodM, M.S.C.P.
M Yrs. Est.: 18 (Ref:HM11803)

## KRISS, PAULINE
**Pauline Kriss (Mobile)**, 6 Thornley Cl, Birmingham, **Midlands (West)**, B13 9UQ, ENG.
(T) 07713 248585
Speciality: Chiropodists (Podiatrists).
● **Owner** Mrs P Kriss
S (Ref:HM11804)

## KRISS, STEPHEN
**Stephen Kriss**, Ravenscroft Medical Centre, 166-168 Golders Green Rd, London, **London (Greater)**, NW11 8BB, ENG.
(T) 020 8209 0922
Speciality: Chiropodists (Podiatrists).
S (Ref:HM11805)

## KRISTANA
**Kristana**, 139A Green St, Eastbourne, **Sussex (East)**, BN21 1SB, ENG.
(T) 01323 644149
Speciality: Absent Healing, Counselling, Spiritual Healing, Clairvoyant Mediumship.
● **Clairvoyant Medium/Healer** Ms K
B Yrs. Est.: 20 (Ref:HM11806)

## KRISTENSEN, MARIANNE
**Marianne Kristensen**, Keynsham Chiropractic Clinic, 2 Temple Court, Keynsham, Bristol, BS31 1HA, ENG.
(T) 01179 866578
Speciality: Chiropractors.
P S T (Ref:HM11807)

## KRISTIN, BONNEY
**Bonney Kristin**, Doonavanig Roberts Cove, **County Cork**, IRE.
(T) 021 4887 440
Speciality: Complementary Medicines & Therapy.
M (Ref:HM11808)

## KROPP, I E E
**I E E Kropp**, 29 Halstead Rd, Mountsorrel, Loughborough, **Leicestershire**, LE12 7HD, ENG.
(T) 01162 302232
Speciality: Chiropodists (Podiatrists).
S (Ref:HM11809)

## KRYPCZYK, ANNA
**Anna Krypczyk**, 166 Tulketh Rd, Ashton-On-Ribble, Preston, **Lancashire**, PR2 1ER, ENG.
(T) 01772 761166
Speciality: Acupuncture.
● **Owner** Ms A Krypczyk
O (Ref:HM11810)

## KRYSTYNA, KRZYZAK
**Krzyzak Krystyna**, 30 Litchdon St, Barnstaple, **Devon**, EX32 8ND, ENG.
(T) 01271 345733
Speciality: Herbalists.
● **Owner** Ms K Krzyzak
M (Ref:HM11811)

## KSC
**KSC**, 20 Canterbury Rd, Herne Bay, **Kent**, CT6 5DJ, ENG.
(T) 01227 363066 (F) 01227 366038
Speciality: Aromatherapy, Counselling, Cranial Osteopathy, Massage (Therapeutic), Nutritional Therapy, Osteopathy, Psychotherapy, Reflexology, Sports Massage. ✔
● **Chiropodist** Ms P Forbes-Rawle Q: BSc (Hons), DPodM, S.R.Ch.
● **Counsellor** Ms D Wells Q: Dip.Couns.
● **Medical Herbalist/Teacher** Ms V Ridley Q: MNIMH.
● **Therapist** Ms A McGuire Q: BA (Hons), IIST, MICHT, MIFA, MIFR. M: ICHT, IFA, IFR.
● **Administrator** Mrs F Dixon Q: BSc.
● **Osteopath/Cranial Osteopath** Mr T Greenfield Q: DO, RCST.
● **Owner** Mr R Dixon
C Yrs. Est.: 20 (Ref:HM11812)

## KUA, R P
**R P Kumra**, 22 Derby Lane, Liverpool, **Merseyside**, L13 3DL, ENG.
(T) 01512 594423 (F) 01514 868775
Speciality: Acupuncture.
● **Owner** Mr R Kumra
O (Ref:HM11813)

## KUAN YING, LIM
**Lim Kuan Ying**, 101 Woden Avenue, Wolverhampton, **Midlands (West)**, WV11 1PS, ENG.
(T) 01902 728686
Speciality: Acupuncture.
● **Owner** Miss K Lim
O (Ref:HM11814)

## KUDZI C K Y
**Kudzi C K Y**, 312 Brownhill Rd, London, **London (Greater)**, SE6 1AX, ENG.
(T) 020 8697 2037
Speciality: Chiropodists (Podiatrists).
S (Ref:HM11815)

## KUHN, SUE
**Sue Kuhn**, 13 Belgrave Cres, Bath, **Somerset**, BA1 5JU, ENG.
(T) 01225 465846
Speciality: Psychotherapy.
B (Ref:HM11816)

## KULKARNI, P S
**P S Kulkarni**, 83 London Rd, Rayleigh, **Essex**,




Key continued: Yrs.Est: Years Established Q: Qualifications M: Professional Membership ✔ Indemnity Insurance Accept Credit Cards

SS6 9HR, ENG.
(T) 01268 784003 (F) 01268 782131
Speciality: Acupuncture.
● **Practice Manager** Mrs R Redfern
O (Ref:HM11817)

## KULWINDER, S
**S Kulwinder**, 45 Osborne St, Slough, **Berkshire**, SL1 1TT, ENG.
(T) 01753 528010
Speciality: Osteopathy.
● **Principal** Mr K Bajwa
P S T (Ref:HM11818)

## KUMAR, NIRDOSH
**Nirdosh Kumar**, 35 Abbotsford Rd, Ilford, **Essex**, IG3 9QX, ENG.
(T) 020 8270 1517
Speciality: Hypnosis.
● **Owner** Mr N Kumar
B (Ref:HM11819)

## KUMARESAN, S
**S Kumaresan**, 8 Alderleys, Benfleet, **Essex**, SS7 3QY, ENG.
(T) 01268 747349 (F) 01268 747349
Speciality: Physiotherapy.
● **Owner** Mr S Kumaresan
P S T (Ref:HM11820)

## KUMARIS, BRAHMA
**Brahma Kumaris**, 20 Polwarth Cr, Edinburgh, **Edinburgh (City of)**, EH11 1HW, SCO.
(T) 01312 297220 (F) 01312 297220
Speciality: Complementary Medicines & Therapy.
● **Manager** Mrs L Gupta
C M (Ref:HM11821)

## KUNDAIKER, J
**J Kundaiker**, The Surgery, 297 Greenford Rd, Greenford, **London (Greater)**, UB6 8RE, ENG.
(T) 020 8575 0174
Speciality: Chiropodists (Podiatrists).
S (Ref:HM11822)

## KUNZ, RICHARD
**Richard Kunz**, Poplar House, 6 Ashfield Trce, Bradford Rd, Bingley, **Yorkshire (West)**, BD16 1EQ, ENG.
(T) 01274 561225
Speciality: Physiotherapy.
● **Owner** Mr R Kunz
P S T (Ref:HM11823)

## KUPRADZE, NADINE
**Nadine Kupradze**, Ground Floor Flat, 2 Dancer Rd, London, **London (Greater)**, SW6 4DX, ENG.
(T) 020 7731 7210
Speciality: Reflexology.
S T (Ref:HM11824)

## KURANCHIE, CLAUDETTE
**Claudette Kuranchie**, 23 Chartwell Court, 9 Broomhill Walk, Woodford Green, **Essex**, IG8 9HF, ENG.
(T) 07957 347688
Speciality: Reflexology.
S T (Ref:HM11825)

## KURIAN, M
**M Kurian**, Heath Lane Consulting Rooms, 7 Heath Lane, Stourbridge, **Midlands (West)**, DY8 1RF, ENG.
(T) 01384 379111
Speciality: Psychiatry.
B (Ref:HM11826)

## KURIAN, M (DR)
**Dr M Kurian**, Summerfield Rd Consulting Rooms, 8 Summerfield Rd, Wolverhampton, **Midlands (West)**, WV1 4PR, ENG.
(T) 01902 429044 (F) 01902 710290
Speciality: Psychiatry.
● **Chairman** Mr S Taylor
B (Ref:HM11827)

## KUSIAR, BILL
**Bill Kusiar**, 36 Church St, Oswestry, **Shropshire**, SY11 2SP, ENG.
(T) 01691 671413
Speciality: Chiropractic.
● **Practice Manager** Mrs J Gill
P S T (Ref:HM11828)

## KUSIAR, C W
**C W Kusiar**, 1 Pepper St, Nantwich, **Cheshire**, CW5 5AB, ENG.
(T) 01270 610640
Speciality: Chiropractic.
● **Owner** Dr C Kusiar
P S T (Ref:HM11829)

## KUSIAR, C W
**C W Kusiar**, 148 Sutton Rd, Shrewsbury, **Shropshire**, SY2 6QT, ENG.
(T) 01743 343926
Speciality: Chiropractic.
P S T (Ref:HM11830)

## KWENORA HERBAL HEALTH
**Kwenora Herbal Health**, 8 River Rd, Littlehampton, **Sussex (West)**, BN17 5BN, ENG.
(T) 01903 713315 (F) 01903 713315
Speciality: Herbal Medicine.
● **Owner** Mrs G Nairne
M (Ref:HM11831)

## KYPERS, SARAH
**Sarah Kypers**, Healthy Options, 112A High St, Godalming, **Surrey**, GU7 1DW, ENG.
(T) 01483 427755
Speciality: Homeopathy.
M (Ref:HM11832)

## KYPERS, SARAH
**Sarah Kypers**, 3 Crundles, Petersfield, **Hampshire**, GU31 4PJ, ENG.
(T) 01730 265808
Speciality: Homeopathy, Hypnosis, Life Style Coaching.
● **Owner** Ms S Kypers
M (Ref:HM11833)

## KYPERS, SARAH
**Sarah Kypers**, 2 Eastrop Lane, Basingstoke, **Hampshire**, RG21 4AR, ENG.
(T) 01256 321099
Speciality: Herbal Medicine, Homeopathy.
● **Owner** Ms S Kypers
M (Ref:HM11834)

## KYPHI
**Kyphi**, The Emporium, 8-10 Oldham St, Manchester, **Manchester (Greater)**, M1 1JQ, ENG.
(T) 01612 780650
Speciality: Aromatherapy.
● **Owner** Miss H Smith
M O (Ref:HM11835)

## KYRIA, S
**S Kyria**, 10 Bromley Common, Bromley, **Kent**, BR2 9PD, ENG.
(T) 020 8466 6657
Speciality: Osteopathy.
● **Owner** Mr S Kyria
P S T (Ref:HM11836)

## KYRIAKI PEROS
**Kyriaki Peros**, 47B Mason St, London, **London (Greater)**, SE17 1HF, ENG.
(T) 020 7252 5091
Speciality: Reflexology.
S T (Ref:HM11837)

## KYRIAKOS KAPLANIS
**Kyriakos Kaplanis**, 46A Moor Rd, Manchester, **Manchester (Greater)**, M23 9BG, ENG.
(T) 01619 987068
Speciality: Reflexology.
S T (Ref:HM11838)

## KYRIAKOS, GEORGE
**George Kyriakos**, 179 West Rd, Westcliff-on-Sea, **Essex**, SS0 9DH, ENG.
(T) 01702 333749
Speciality: Hypnosis.
B (Ref:HM11839)

## L A M A S HEALTH THERAPEUTICS
**L A M A S Health Therapeutics**, 25 Watson Rd, Worksop, **Nottinghamshire**, S80 2BA, ENG.
(T) 01909 482190 (F) 01909 482190
Speciality: Complementary Medicines & Therapy.
● **Owner** Mr A Lowe
C M (Ref:HM11840)

## L A ROSS - ACUPUNCTURIST
**Mrs L A Ross - Acupuncturist**, The Birches, Shadoxhurst, Ashford, **Kent**, TN26 1LZ, ENG.
(T) 01233 733387
Speciality: Acupuncture.
O (Ref:HM11841)

## L C I STRESS MANAGEMENT
**L C I Stress Management**, 5 Carmichael Cl, Lichfield, **Staffordshire**, WS14 9YW, ENG.
(T) 01543 419491
Speciality: Hypnosis.
B (Ref:HM11842)

## L C M CLINIC
**L C M Clinic**, 5 Newman Passage, London, **London (Greater)**, W1P 3PF, ENG.
(T) 020 7637 7125
Speciality: Complementary Medicines & Therapy.
C M (Ref:HM11843)

## L W FOOTCARE
**L W Footcare**, 19 Bourtree Pl, Hawick, **Scottish Borders**, TD9 9HL, SCO.
(T) 01450 376937
Speciality: Biomechanics, Chiropody, Podiatry.
✔
● **Owner/Chiropodist** Ms L Wood **Q:** MBChA, MSSCh.
C Yrs. Est.: 7 (Ref:HM11844)

## LA BELLE SANTE NATURELLE
**La Belle Sante Naturelle**, Jarvis Cooden Beach Hotel, Cooden Sea Rd, Bexhill-on-Sea, **Sussex (East)**, TN39 4TT, ENG.
(T) 01424 845025
Speciality: Hypnosis.
● **Owner** Ms J Rossi
B (Ref:HM11845)

## LA CREME HAIR & BEAUTY
**La Creme Hair & Beauty**, 12 Earl St, Sheffield, **Yorkshire (South)**, S1 4PY, ENG.
(T) 01142 701874
Speciality: Electrolysis.
T (Ref:HM11846)

## LA TOUCHE, ROBERT
**Robert La Touche**, 15 Sheeplands Avenue, Guildford, **Surrey**, GU1 2SG, ENG.
(T) 01483 827039
Speciality: Chiropractic.
● **Owner** Mr R Latouche
P S T (Ref:HM11847)

## LAC, J
**J Lac**, 36 Ticonderoga Gdns, Southampton, **Hampshire**, SO19 9HB, ENG.
(T) 023 8034 8367
Speciality: Reflexology.
● **Owner** Mrs J Lac
S T (Ref:HM11848)

## LACEY, K
**K Lacey**, 43 Castle St, Trowbridge, **Wiltshire**, BA14 8AY, ENG.
(T) 01225 763898
Speciality: Chiropodists (Podiatrists).
S (Ref:HM11849)

## LACK, J E J
**J E J Lack**, The Cottage, 1 Albion Villas, Folkestone, **Kent**, CT20 1RP, ENG.
(T) 01303 254431
Speciality: Electrolysis.
T (Ref:HM11850)

## LACKFORD, M
**M Lackford**, Barfield Rd, York, **Yorkshire (North)**, YO31 9AW, ENG.
(T) 01904 426486
Speciality: Chiropodists (Podiatrists).
● **Owner** Mrs M Lackford
S (Ref:HM11851)

## LACOCK PHYSIO & SPORTS
**Lacock Physiotherapy & Sports Injury Clinic**, Raycroft, Cantax Hill, Lacock, Chippenham, **Wiltshire**, SN15 2JZ, ENG.
(T) 01249 730132
Speciality: Physiotherapy.
P S T (Ref:HM11852)



Key: B Mind-Body Medicine, C Complementary Medicine, H Self Help Treatment, M Medicinal Therapy, O Oriental Medicine, P Postural Therapy, S Manipulative Structural Therapy, T Touch Therapy

**LACY, MELANIE DE**

**Melanie De Lacy**, Harriers, Hunters Way, Chichester, **Sussex (West)**, PO19 4RB, ENG.
(T) 01243 527827
Speciality: Physiotherapy.
P S T (Ref:HM11853)

**LADY BAY**

**Lady Bay**, 5 Trent Blvd, West Bridgford, Nottingham, **Nottinghamshire**, NG2 5BB, ENG.
(T) 01159 821782
Speciality: Chiropodists (Podiatrists).
● **Owner** Mr A Sain
S (Ref:HM11854)

**LADY FAYRE**

**Lady Fayre**, 22 St Johns St, York, **Yorkshire (North)**, YO31 7QT, ENG.
(T) 01904 635053
Speciality: Electrolysis.
T (Ref:HM11855)

**LADY GREYSTONES BEAUTY SALON**

**Lady Greystones Beauty Salon**, Church Rd, Greystones, **County Wicklow**, IRE.
(T) 01287 2311
Speciality: Beauty Therapy.
H T (Ref:HM11856)

**LADYBIRD HEALTHCARE**

**Ladybird Healthcare**, 15 Holland Rd, Felixstowe, **Suffolk**, IP11 2BA, ENG.
(T) 01394 285246 (F) 01394 276875
Speciality: Complementary Medicines & Therapy.
● **Partner** Mrs J Driver
C M (Ref:HM11857)

**LADYCARE ALLERGY**

**Ladycare Allergy**, 18 Upr Abbeygate St, **County Galway**, IRE.
(T) 09156 8995
Speciality: Complementary Medicines & Therapy.
M (Ref:HM11858)

**LAFFERTY, C**

**Mrs C Lafferty**, 49A Park Lane, Poynton, Stockport, **Cheshire**, SK12 1RD, ENG.
(T) 01625 877970
Speciality: Chiropodists (Podiatrists).
● **Owner** Mrs C Lafferty
S (Ref:HM11859)

**LAFFERTY, FRANCIS**

**Francis Lafferty**, 22 Glendyke Rd, Liverpool, **Merseyside**, L18 6JR, ENG.
(T) 01517 241427
Speciality: Chiropodists (Podiatrists).
● **Owner** Mr F Lafferty
S (Ref:HM11860)

**LAFITTE, J L**

**J L Lafitte**, 13 Park Cres, Forest Row, **Sussex (East)**, RH18 5ED, ENG.
(T) 01342 822639
Speciality: Chiropractic.
P S T (Ref:HM11861)

**LAHER, RICHARD JOHN**

**Richard John Laher**, Flat C, 28 Odhams Walk, London, **London (Greater)**, WC2H 9SA, ENG.
(T) 020 7836 7156
Speciality: Alexander Technique.
● **Owner** Mr J Laher
P S (Ref:HM11862)

**LAIDLAW, PAUL**

**Paul Laidlaw**, 3 Ledsham Park, St. Leonards-On-Sea, **Sussex (East)**, TN37 7LQ, ENG.
(T) 01424 753993 (F) 01424 753993
Speciality: Physiotherapy.
● **Director** Mr P Laidlaw
P S T (Ref:HM11863)

**LAIFER, D**

**D Laifer**, 13 Bromefield, Stanmore, **London (Greater)**, HA7 1AA, ENG.
(T) 020 8952 4238
Speciality: Chiropodists (Podiatrists).
S (Ref:HM11864)

**LAING, RICHARD**

**Richard Laing**, 58A Heath Rd, Colchester, **Essex**, CO3 4DJ, ENG.
(T) 01206 575581
Speciality: Homeopathy.
M (Ref:HM11865)

**LAING, RICHARD (DR)**

**Dr Richard Laing**, 20 Drury Rd, Colchester, **Essex**, CO2 7UX, ENG.
(T) 01206 575581
(E) richardlaing@ntlworld.com
Speciality: Bach Remedies, Homeopathy. ✔
● **Homeopathic Physician** Dr R Laing Q: MB, MFHom. M: FHom.
M Yrs. Est.: 20 (Ref:HM11866)

**LAISTER, MARTIN**

**Laister Martin**, 13 Mansfield Rd, Rotherham, **Yorkshire (South)**, S60 2DR, ENG.
(T) 01709 369420
Speciality: Chiropodists (Podiatrists).
S (Ref:HM11867)

**LAISTER, MARTIN**

**Martin Laister**, 13 Mansfield Rd, Rotherham, **Yorkshire (South)**, S60 2DR, ENG.
(T) 01709 369420
Speciality: Chiropody. ✔
● **Owner/Chiropodist** Mr M Laister Q: DPodM, M.S.C.P, S.R.Ch.
C Yrs. Est.: 15 (Ref:HM11868)

**LAISTER, PAMELA**

**Pamela Laister**, Mariners, Gorse Way, Hartley, Longfield, **Kent**, DA3 8AE, ENG.
(T) 01474 705288 (F) 01474 705288
Speciality: Electrolysis.
● **Owner** Mrs P Laister
T (Ref:HM11869)

**LAKE, D**

**D Lake**, The Devon Parade Clinic, 322 Wellingborough Rd, Northampton, **Northamptonshire**, NN1 4EP, ENG.
(T) 01604 622999
Speciality: Physiotherapy.
● **Owner** Mr A Costain
P S T (Ref:HM11870)

**LAKE, DORRIE**

**Lake Dorrie**, The Wellbeing Centre, 11 Musters Rd, West Bridgford, Nottingham, **Nottinghamshire**, NG2 7PP, ENG.
(T) 01159 825353
Speciality: Psychotherapy.
B (Ref:HM11871)

**LAKELAND AROMATICS**

**Lakeland Aromatics**, Unit 34, Warwick Mill Business Park, Warwick Bridge, Carlisle, **Cumbria**, CA4 8RR, ENG.
(T) 01228 561444 (F) 01228 561626
Speciality: Aromatherapy.
● **Owner** Mrs F Whealan
M O (Ref:HM11872)

**LAKELAND CHIROPRACTIC CENTRE**

**Lakeland Chiropractic Centre**, 71A Highgate, Kendal, **Cumbria**, LA9 4ED, ENG.
(T) 01539 721796
Speciality: Chiropractic.
P S T (Ref:HM11873)

**LAKELAND HYPNOTHERAPY CENTRE**

**Lakeland Hypnotherapy Centre**, 3 Yard, 89 Stricklandgate, Kendal, **Cumbria**, LA9 4RA, ENG.
(T) 01539 732244
Speciality: Hypnosis.
B (Ref:HM11874)

**LAKESIDE PHYSIO CLINIC**

**Lakeside Physiotherapy Clinic**, Festival Way, Festival Park, Stoke-On-Trent, **Staffordshire**, ST1 5PU, ENG.
(T) 01782 205707
Speciality: Physiotherapy.
● **Physiotherapist** Mr M Copeland
P S T (Ref:HM11875)

**LAKHAMI, A**

**A Lakhami**, 119 Munster Rd, London, **London (Greater)**, SW6 6DH, ENG.
(T) 020 7736 1670
Speciality: Chiropodists (Podiatrists).
● **Owner** Ms L Sheen
S (Ref:HM11876)

**LAKHANI, B V**

**B V Lakhani**, 40 Hilton Avenue, London, **London (Greater)**, N12 9HB, ENG.
(T) 020 8445 7008
Speciality: Osteopathy.
● **Owner** Mr H Lakhani
P S T (Ref:HM11877)

**LAKHANI, B V**

**B V Lakhani**, 1 Manor Rd, Rugby, **Warwickshire**, CV21 2SX, ENG.
(T) 01788 542628
Speciality: Osteopathy.
P S T (Ref:HM11878)

**LAKSIMI, T**

**T Laksimi**, 68 Streatham Hill, London, **London (Greater)**, SW2 4RD, ENG.
(T) 020 8674 3799 (F) 020 8674 3799
Speciality: Acupuncture.
● **Manager** Mr P Goss
O (Ref:HM11879)

**LAL, VALERIE**

**Valerie Lal**, 12 Station Rd, Epping, **Essex**, CM16 4HN, ENG.
(T) 01992 573452
Speciality: Chiropodists (Podiatrists).
● **Owner** Mrs V Lal
S (Ref:HM11880)

**LALLOO'S ACUPUNCTURE CLINIC**

**Lalloo's Acupuncture Clinic Ltd**, Unit 6 Phibsboro S.C, Dublin, **County Dublin**, IRE.
(T) 01830 9551
(E) rlalloo@indigo.ie
Speciality: Absent Healing, Acupressure, Acupuncture, Aromatherapy, Bach Remedies, Colour Therapy, Complementary Therapy, Electrotherapy, Healer, Healing Therapy, Herbal Medicine, Holistic Healing, Homeopathy, Indian Head Massage, Kinesiology, Moxibustion, Naturopathy, Polarity Therapy, Reflexology, Reiki, Stress Therapy, Tera-Mai, Touch Therapy, Vitamin Therapy, Ying & Yang. ✔
● **Acupuncturist/Reflexologist** Ms J Hancock
● **Reiki Healer** Ms E Lalloo Q: Reiki Master. M: Reiki Association.
● **Acupuncturist/Allergist** Mr R Lalloo Q: PhD.
O Yrs. Est.: 15 (Ref:HM11881)

**LALLY, KAREN**

**Karen Lally**, 103 Grange Lane, Winsford, **Cheshire**, CW7 2QX, ENG.
(T) 01606 592233
Speciality: Hypnosis.
● **Owner** Miss K Lally
B (Ref:HM11882)

**LAM RIM CTRE FOR WHOLE HEALTH**

**Lam Rim Centre for Whole Health**, 12 Victoria Pl, Bristol, BS3 3BP, ENG.
(T) 01179 231138
Speciality: Acupuncture, Aromatherapy, Counselling, Dance Movement Therapy, Homeopathy, Osteopathy, Reflexology, Shiatsu, Holistic Massage, Movement Psychotherapy, Thai Yoga Massage. ✔
● **Shiatsu Practitioner** Ms J MacDonald
● **Psychotherapist/Counsellor** Ms S Groves Q: BA (Hons), Dip.HIP. M: UKCP.
● **Holistic Massage Therapist** Mr D Wood Q: Dip.MTI.
● **Osteopath** Ms J Briggs Q: DO. M: GOsC.
● **Acupuncturist** Mr A Peck Q: Lic.Ac, MBAcC.
● **Shiatsu Practitioner** Ms M Whiting Q: Dip.Shiatsu.
● **Reflexologist/Aromatherapist** Nix James
● **Psychotherapist/Counsellor** Ms G Smith
(T) 01225 334624 Q: BSc, Dip.Int.Psych, MA. M: UKCP.
● **Acupuncturist** Ms J Glover Q: Lic.Ac, MBAcC.
● **Osteopath** Satyen Gadher Q: DO, MRO. M: RoO.
● **Osteopath** Ms K Knight Q: BSc, Hons (OST).



Key continued: Yrs.Est: Years Established Q: Qualifications M: Professional Membership ✔ Indemnity Insurance Accept Credit Cards

M: BOA, GOsC.
● **Acupuncturist** Mr R Parnell Q: BA, Lic.Ac, MBAcC.
● **Dance Movement Therapist** Ms E Goldhahn
(T) 01364 72687 Q: ADMT UK.Sen, BA (Hons).
● **Holistic Massage Therapist** Ms C Storer Q: BA, ITEC, MTI.
● **Teacher** Ms L Rose
● **Teacher** Mr S Yandell
● **Homeopath** Ms L Clark Q: BA, Dip.Couns, L.C.C.H, RSHom. M: BACP.
● **Shiatsu Practitioner** Mr K Phillips
● **Osteopath** Ms C Howard Q: DO.
● **Counsellor** Ms S Hobbs
(T) 01179 719106 Q: Dip.Couns. M: BACP.
C Yrs. Est.: 12 (Ref:HM11883)

## LAMB CHIROPRATIC CLINIC
**Lamb Chiropratic Clinic**, Mill Farm, Harlington Rd, Sharpenhoe, Bedford, **Bedfordshire**, MK45 4SJ, ENG.
(T) 01525 876727
Speciality: Chiropractic.
P S T (Ref:HM11884)

## LAMB, BRIAN V
**Brian V Lamb**, Quarryside, Castletown, Thurso, **Highland**, KW14 8SS, SCO.
(T) 01847 821721 (F) 01847 821721
Speciality: Herbalists.
● **Owner** Mr B Lamb
M (Ref:HM11885)

## LAMB, D
**D Lamb**, 127 Stamford Drive, Stalybridge, **Manchester (Greater)**, SK15 1QT, ENG.
(T) 01612 922660
Speciality: Complementary Medicines & Therapy.
● **Owner** Mrs D Lamb
M (Ref:HM11886)

## LAMB, G
**G Lamb**, 28 Hallowell Rd, Northwood, **London (Greater)**, HA6 1DN, ENG.
(T) 01923 827833
Speciality: Osteopathy.
P S T (Ref:HM11887)

## LAMB, G BRIAN
**G Brian Lamb**, Top Flat, 13 Castle Hill Avenue, Folkestone, **Kent**, CT20 2TD, ENG.
(T) 01303 851294 (F) 01303 851294
(E) lambofkent@cs.com
Speciality: Alexander Technique, Bach Remedies, Bates Method, Complementary Therapy, Counselling, Cupping, Dietician, Hay Diet, Healing Therapy, Herbal Medicine, Holistic Healing, Manipulation, Massage (Therapeutic), Music Therapy, Naturopathy, Nutritional Therapy, Osteopathy, Psychotherapy, Stress Therapy, Vitamin Therapy, Eeman Technique of Relaxation, Hypericum.
● **Naturopath** Mr B Lamb Q: DO, ND.
C H Yrs. Est.: 37 (Ref:HM11888)

## LAMB, H (DR)
**Dr H Lamb**, The Lamb Chiropractic Clinic, 48 Marsh Rd, Pinner, **London (Greater)**, HA5 5NQ, ENG.
(T) 020 8866 3230
Speciality: Chiropractors.
P S T (Ref:HM11889)

## LAMB, VICTORIA
**Victoria Lamb**, 67 Church Hill, Cheddington, Leighton Buzzard, **Bedfordshire**, LU7 0SX, ENG.
(T) 01296 661970
Speciality: Aromatherapy.
● **Owner** Ms V Lamb
M O (Ref:HM11890)

## LAMB, W G
**W G Lamb**, 61 Albany Rd, Chatham, **Kent**, ME4 5DN, ENG.
(T) 01634 405796
Speciality: Chiropodists (Podiatrists).
● **Partner** Mr G Lamb
S (Ref:HM11891)

## LAMBDA HEALTHCARE
**Lambda Healthcare**, 7 Farringford Cl, Cambridge, **Cambridgeshire**, CB4 3LU, ENG.
(T) 01223 312830
Speciality: Complementary Medicines & Therapy.
C M (Ref:HM11892)

## LAMBE, BARRY
**Barry Lambe DIP ACU**, 12 Abbey Ct, Naas, **County Kildare**, IRE.
(T) 04589 6895
Speciality: Acupuncture.
O (Ref:HM11893)

## LAMBERT, B
**B Lambert**, 3 Chapel Pl, Fore St, Topsham, Exeter, **Devon**, EX3 0HS, ENG.
(T) 01392 877628
Speciality: Chiropodists (Podiatrists).
S (Ref:HM11894)

## LAMBERT, C W
**C W Lambert**, 1603 Great Western Rd, Glasgow, **Glasgow (City of)**, G13 1LT, SCO.
(T) 01419 506677 (F) 01419 506677
Speciality: Biomechanics, Chiropody, Nail Surgery, Orthotics, Podiatry. ✔
● **Owner/Chiropodist** Mr C Lambert Q: BSc, S.R.Ch. M: S.C.P.
M Yrs. Est.: 24 (Ref:HM11895)

## LAMBERT, H M
**H M Lambert**, Lomond House, Raikes Rd, Great Eccleston, Preston, **Lancashire**, PR3 0ZA, ENG.
(T) 01995 671633
Speciality: Complementary Medicines & Therapy.
C M (Ref:HM11896)

## LAMBERT, IAN
**Ian Lambert**, 31 Elcho St, Peebles, **Scottish Borders**, EH45 8LQ, SCO.
(T) 01721 722301
Speciality: Osteopathy.
● **Owner** Mr I Lambert
P S T (Ref:HM11897)

## LAMBERT, KAREN
**Karen Lambert**, 127 Beechburn Park, Crook, **County Durham**, DL15 8SA, ENG.
(T) 01388 768725
Speciality: Aromatherapy.
● **Owner** Mrs K Lambert
M O (Ref:HM11898)

## LAMBERT, M J
**M J Lambert**, Woodnuts Cottage, Duver Rd, St. Helens, Ryde, **Isle of Wight**, PO33 1XY, ENG.
(T) 01983 874641
Speciality: Hypnotherapy.
B (Ref:HM11899)

## LAMBERT, MARGARET
**Margaret Lambert**, 6 Shalcross Drive, Cheshunt, Waltham Cross, **Hertfordshire**, EN8 8UX, ENG.
(T) 01992 632040
Speciality: Homeopathy.
● **Owner** Mrs M Lambert
M (Ref:HM11900)

## LAMBERT, RACHEL
**Rachel Lambert**, 77 Belmont Rd, Belfast, **County Antrim**, BT4 2AA, NIR.
(T) 028 9047 1905
Speciality: Aromatherapy, Reflexology, Reiki. ✔
● **Aromatherapist** Miss R Lambert Q: Dip.Arom. M: RQA.
C Yrs. Est.: 5 (Ref:HM11901)

## LAMBON, MICHELE
**Michele Lambon**, 14 Wensleydale, Droitwich, **Worcestershire**, WR9 8PF, ENG.
(T) 01905 776616
Speciality: Reflexology.
S T (Ref:HM11902)

## LAMBOURN COURT
**Lambourn Court**, Eaton Railway Crossing, Church Lane, Eaton, Norwich, **Norfolk**, NR4 6NN, ENG.
(T) 01603 503333
Speciality: Hypnosis.
B (Ref:HM11903)

## LAMBOURN COURT INTERNATIONAL
**Lambourn Court International**, 32 Milesmere, Two Mile Ash, Milton Keynes, **Buckinghamshire**, MK8 8DP, ENG.
(T) 01908 265815 (F) 01908 569503
Speciality: Hypnosis, Neuro-Linguistic Program, Personal Development.
● **Owner** Mr T Bezchi
B (Ref:HM11904)

## LAMBOURN COURT INTERNATIONAL
**Lambourn Court International**, 41 Hall Park Avenue, Westcliff-on-Sea, **Essex**, SS0 8NP, ENG.
(T) 01702 475437
Speciality: Hypnosis.
● **Partner** Mrs C Degroot
B (Ref:HM11905)

## LAMBOURN COURT STRESS MNGMT
**Lambourn Court Stress Management Consultants**, 5 Lower Meadow, Edgworth, Turton, Bolton, **Lancashire**, BL7 0DQ, ENG.
(T) 01204 853761
Speciality: Hypnosis.
B (Ref:HM11906)

## LAMBTON PLACE HEALTH CLUB
**Lambton Place Health Club**, Lambton Pl, London, **London (Greater)**, W11 2SH, ENG.
(T) 020 7229 2291
Speciality: Alexander Technique.
● **Therapist** Mrs C Fish
P S (Ref:HM11907)

## LAMH IOMLANE TEO
**Lamh Iomlane Teo**, The Coast Guard Ctge Cooleen, Dingle, **County Kerry**, IRE.
(T) 06691 52474
Speciality: Complementary Medicines & Therapy.
M (Ref:HM11908)

## LAMKIN, CARLA
**Carla Lamkin**, 36 Fitzroy Rd, London, **London (Greater)**, NW1 8TY, ENG.
(T) 020 7483 3215
Speciality: Osteopathy.
● **Owner** Ms C Lamkin
P S T (Ref:HM11909)

## LAMONT, KEITH
**Keith Lamont**, South View Cottage, 33 Oakley Lane, Oakley, Basingstoke, **Hampshire**, RG23 7JZ, ENG.
(T) 01256 782000 (F) 01256 782000
Speciality: Acupuncture.
● **Owner** Mr K Lamont
O (Ref:HM11910)

## LAMORISSE, JEANNE
**Jeanne Lamorisse**, Aberfoyle House, Stapley Rd, St. Albans, **Hertfordshire**, AL3 5EP, ENG.
(T) 01727 856687
Speciality: Complementary Medicines & Therapy.
● **Manager** Mrs S Bassett
M (Ref:HM11911)

## LAMPARD, J L
**J L Lampard**, First Floor, Rumford Shopping Hall, Market Pl, Romford, **Essex**, RM1 3AT, ENG.
(T) 01708 734888
Speciality: Chiropodists (Podiatrists).
● **Owner** Mrs J Lampard
S (Ref:HM11912)

## LAMS, M A
**M A Lams**, 10 Tannsfeld Rd, London, **London (Greater)**, SE26 5DF, ENG.
(T) 020 8244 7610
Speciality: Hypnotherapy.
● **Owner** Mr M Lams
B (Ref:HM11913)

## LANCASHIRE EPILIGHT CLINIC
**Lancashire Epilight Clinic Ltd (The)**, Victoria House, 3 Chorley New Rd, Bolton, **Lancashire**, BL1 4QR, ENG.
(T) 01204 369100 (F) 01204 369101
Speciality: Electrolysis.
● **Practice Manager** Ms J Carr



Key: B Mind-Body Medicine C Complementary Medicine H Self Help Treatment M Medicinal Therapy O Oriental Medicine P Postural Therapy S Manipulative Structural Therapy T Touch Therapy

T (Ref:HM11914)

**LANCASHIRE, A W**

**A W Lancashire**, 31B Market Pl, Ripley, **Derbyshire**, DE5 3HA, ENG.
(T) 01773 512249
Speciality: Chiropody, Osteopathy. ✔
● **Chiropodist** Justin Forsyth Q: DPodM, S.R.Ch.
● **Osteopath** Mr A Lancashire Q: DO. M: GOsC.
S Yrs. Est.: 10 (Ref:HM11915)

**LANCASHIRE, LINDA**

**Linda Lancashire**, 63 Belper Lane, Belper, **Derbyshire**, DE56 2UQ, ENG.
(T) 01773 824222
Speciality: Clairvoyants & Palmists.
B (Ref:HM11916)

**LANCASTER, L**

**L Lancaster**, Brooklands, North Rd, Holme, Carnforth, **Lancashire**, LA6 1QA, ENG.
(T) 01524 781032 (F) 01524 781032
Speciality: Hypnosis.
● **Owner** Mrs L Lancaster
B (Ref:HM11917)

**LANCASTER, PAULA**

**Paula Lancaster**, 2 Glebe Field Drive, Wetherby, **Yorkshire (West)**, LS22 6WG, ENG.
(T) 01937 580835
Speciality: Chiropodists (Podiatrists).
● **Owner** Miss P Lancaster
S (Ref:HM11918)

**LANCELOT, M M**

**M M Lancelot**, 5c Chapel Lane, Bingley, **Yorkshire (West)**, BD16 2NG, ENG.
(T) 01274 531607
Speciality: Psychotherapy.
● **Owner** Ms M Lanceleot
B (Ref:HM11919)

**LANCEY, V H**

**V H Lancey**, 14 Llyswen Rd, Cardiff, **Glamorgan (Vale of)**, CF23 6NG, WAL.
(T) 029 2075 8566
Speciality: Physiotherapy.
P S T (Ref:HM11920)

**LAND, D F**

**D F Land**, 7 Rowan Tree Cl, Liss, **Hampshire**, GU33 7JU, ENG.
(T) 01730 894097
Speciality: Chiropodists (Podiatrists).
● **Owner** Mrs D Land
S (Ref:HM11921)

**LANDALE, J B (DR)**

**Dr J B Landale**, Morningside, Savile Rd, Hebden Bridge, **Yorkshire (West)**, HX7 6ND, ENG.
(T) 01422 843123
Speciality: Acupuncture.
O (Ref:HM11922)

**LANDER, EILEEN**

**Eileen Lander**, Gym N. Slim, R/O 208 Stratford Rd, Shirley, Solihull, **Midlands (West)**, B90 3AG, ENG.
(T) 01217 224003
Speciality: Aromatherapy.
M O (Ref:HM11923)

**LANDER, H J**

**H J Lander**, 43 Hazelhurst Rd, Kings Heath, Birmingham, **Midlands (West)**, B14 7PH, ENG.
(T) 01214 443193
Speciality: Physiotherapy.
● **Owner** Mrs H Lander
P S T (Ref:HM11924)

**LANDO, AGNETA**

**Agneta Lando**, 81 Queens Rd, London, **London (Greater)**, SW19 8NR, ENG.
(T) 020 8879 1567
Speciality: Physiotherapy.
● **Owner** A Lando
P S T (Ref:HM11925)

**LANDON, IAN**

**Ian Landon**, Wessex House, Upper Market St, Eastleigh, **Hampshire**, SO50 9FD, ENG.
(T) 023 8062 0800
Speciality: Hypnotherapy.
● **Owner** Mr I Landon
B (Ref:HM11926)

**LANDSDOWNE COLLEGE OF ACU**

**Landsdowne College of Acupuncture & Complementary Medicine**, Fairfield House, Newbridge Ave, IRE.
(T) 01660 1487
Speciality: Acupuncture.
O (Ref:HM11927)

**LANDSKER CHIROPRACTIC CLINIC**

**Landsker Chiropractic Clinic**, The Old Corn Store, Northfield Rd, Narberth, **Pembrokeshire**, SA67 7AR, WAL.
(T) 01834 860200 (F) 01834 860140
Speciality: Chiropractors.
● **Senior Partner** Mr A Glaister
P S T (Ref:HM11928)

**LANE, A**

**A Lane**, 23 Hoskins Rd, Oxted, **Surrey**, RH8 9HT, ENG.
(T) 01883 716395
Speciality: Physiotherapy.
● **Owner** A Lane
P S T (Ref:HM11929)

**LANE, ANNA**

**Anna Lane**, The Practice, 43 Hagley Rd, Stourbridge, **Midlands (West)**, DY8 1QR, ENG.
(T) 01384 376359
Speciality: Hypnotherapy.
B (Ref:HM11930)

**LANE, CORINNE**

**Corinne Lane**, 5 Lorne St, Reading, **Berkshire**, RG1 7YW, ENG.
(T) 01189 576864
Speciality: Counselling, Psychotherapy. ✔
● **Psychotherapist** Ms C Lane Q: BA (Hons), Cert.Couns, Cert.Couns.Groupwork, CHP. M: BPS, NRHP, UKRC.
B Yrs. Est.: 9 (Ref:HM11931)

**LANE, DANIEL**

**Lane Daniel**, Knocknenaugh Kiskeam, Mallow, **County Cork**, IRE.
(T) 06451 127
Speciality: Complementary Medicines & Therapy.
M (Ref:HM11932)

**LANE, DANIEL P**

**Daniel P Lane**, North Hinksey Lane, Oxford, **Oxfordshire**, OX2 0JW, ENG.
(T) 01865 204246
Speciality: Chiropractors.
P S T (Ref:HM11933)

**LANE, DAVID**

**David Lane**, 369 High St, Rochester, **Kent**, ME1 1DD, ENG.
(T) 01634 404671
Speciality: Hypnosis.
B (Ref:HM11934)

**LANE, F C**

**F C Lane**, 18 Collingwood Rd, Horsham, **Sussex (West)**, RH12 2QW, ENG.
(T) 01403 253639
Speciality: Chiropodists (Podiatrists).
● **Owner** Mr F Lane
S (Ref:HM11935)

**LANE, JEFF**

**Jeff Lane**, Portsmouth Natural Health Centre, 20 Landport Trce, Portsmouth, **Hampshire**, PO1 2RG, ENG.
(T) 023 9283 0558
Speciality: Complementary Medicines & Therapy.
M (Ref:HM11936)

**LANE, MARGARET J**

**Margaret J Lane**, Broomfield Lodge, Common Lane, Dartford, **Kent**, DA2 7BA, ENG.
(T) 01322 224532
Speciality: Chiropodists (Podiatrists).
● **Owner** Mrs M Lane
S (Ref:HM11937)

**LANE, R A**

**R A Lane**, 169 Westwood Rd, Sutton Coldfield, **Midlands (West)**, B74 3SY, ENG.
(T) 01213 539046
Speciality: Chiropodists (Podiatrists).
S (Ref:HM11938)

**LANE, T A**

**Mrs T A Lane**, 4 Elsworthy, Thames Ditton, **Surrey**, KT7 0YP, ENG.
(T) 020 8398 3377
Speciality: Chiropodists (Podiatrists).
S (Ref:HM11939)

**LANES CLINIC**

**Lanes Clinic Of Complementary Health**, 4 Bartholomews, Brighton, **Sussex (East)**, BN1 1HG, ENG.
(T) 08000 358359
Speciality: Complementary Medicines & Therapy.
● **Practice Manager** Ms M Tasou
M (Ref:HM11940)

**LANES MEDICAL PRACTICE**

**Lanes Medical Practice (The)**, Plough Lane, Stoke Poges, Slough, **Berkshire**, SL2 4JW, ENG.
(T) 01753 663617
Speciality: Complementary Medicines & Therapy.
● **Manager**
M (Ref:HM11941)

**LANES, TESSA**

**Tessa Lanes**, Aston Clinic, 26 Kingston Rd, New Malden, **Surrey**, KT3 3LS, ENG.
(T) 020 8942 3148 (F) 020 8949 7050
Speciality: Chiropodists (Podiatrists).
S (Ref:HM11942)

**LANE-WILLAM, AVIS**

**Avis Lane-Willam**, 310 Gloucester Rd, Horfield, Bristol, BS7 8TJ, ENG.
(T) 01179 444448
Speciality: Acupuncture.
● **Owner** Ms A Lane-Willam
O (Ref:HM11943)

**LANE-WILLAN, AVIS**

**Avis Lane-Willan**, Roseway Cottage, Clevedon Rd, Walton In Gordano, Clevedon, **Somerset**, BS21 7AW, ENG.
(T) 01275 873793
Speciality: Acupuncture.
O (Ref:HM11944)

**LANEY, RANDELL**

**Randell Laney**, Wood Dene, Golf Club Rd, Woking, **Surrey**, GU22 0LS, ENG.
(T) 01483 768587
Speciality: Physiotherapy.
P S T (Ref:HM11945)

**LANG, GILL**

**Gill Lang**, 4 St. James Gardens, Westcliff-on-Sea, **Essex**, SS0 0BU, ENG.
(T) 01702 347154
Speciality: Reflexology.
S T (Ref:HM11946)

**LANG, GLORIA**

**Gloria Lang**, 7 Millhouse Villas, Chelmsford Rd, Barnston, Dunmow, **Essex**, CM6 1LS, ENG.
(T) 01371 870273
Speciality: Reflexology.
S T (Ref:HM11947)

**LANG, RICHARD**

**Richard Lang**, Clissold Park Health Centre, 154 Stoke Newington Church St, London, **London (Greater)**, N16 0JU, ENG.
(T) 020 7249 2990 (F) 020 7249 3977
Speciality: Psychotherapy.
● **Owner** Mr D Berg
B (Ref:HM11948)

**LANGDALE-KING, ROSIE**

**Rosie Langdale-King**, 87 Victor Rd, Teddington, **London (Greater)**, TW11 8SP, ENG.
(T) 020 8977 7098
Speciality: Reflexology.
● **Owner** Mrs R Langdale-King
S T (Ref:HM11949)

**LANGDON, E M**

**E M Langdon**, Court Farm, Clovelly, Bideford, **Devon**, EX39 5TA, ENG.
(T) 01237 431305
Speciality: Physiotherapy.
P S T (Ref:HM11950)



Key continued: Yrs.Est: Years Established Q: Qualifications M: Professional Membership ✔ Indemnity Insurance ▬ Accept Credit Cards

## LANGE, MAXINE
**Maxine Lange**, 3rd Floor, Victory House, 99-101 Regent St, London, **London (Greater)**, W1R 7HB, ENG.
(T) 020 7434 2992 (F) 020 7434 2994
Speciality: Psychology.
● **Owner** Ms M Lange
B (Ref:HM11951)

## LANGHORNE, CAROLINE
**Caroline Langhorne**, 68 Herne Rd, Surbiton, **Surrey**, KT6 5BP, ENG.
(T) 020 8397 0162
Speciality: Chiropodists (Podiatrists).
S (Ref:HM11952)

## LANGLEY CHIROPRACTORS CLINIC
**Langley Chiropractors Clinic**, 218 High St, Langley, Slough, **Berkshire**, SL3 8LL, ENG.
(T) 01753 545805
Speciality: Chiropractic. ✔
● **Owner** Helen Turndale Q: BSc, DC.
● **Chiropractor** Rebecca Rees Q: BSc, DC.
P S T Yrs. Est.: 16 (Ref:HM11953)

## LANGLEY, ALLEN
**Allen Langley**, Bryn Hyfryd, Trearddur Bay, Holyhead, **Isle of Anglesey**, LL65 2UD, WAL.
(T) 01407 861258
Speciality: Hypnotherapy.
B (Ref:HM11954)

## LANGLEY, CHRISTINA
**Christina Langley**, 16A Cannon Hill Lane, London, **London (Greater)**, SW20 9EP, ENG.
(T) 020 8542 9476
Speciality: Clairvoyants & Palmists.
● **Owner** Ms C Langley
B (Ref:HM11955)

## LANGLEY, CHRISTINE
**Christine Langley**, 26 Wycombe Rd, Princes Risborough, **Buckinghamshire**, HP27 0DH, ENG.
(T) 01844 275055
Speciality: Osteopathy.
● **Owner** Mrs C Langley
P S T (Ref:HM11956)

## LANGLEY, LYNNE
**Lynne Langley**, Scunthorpe, **Humberside**, DN17, ENG.
(T) 01724 849530
Speciality: Bach Remedies.
M (Ref:HM11957)

## LANGRIDGE, LORRAINE
**Lorraine Langridge**, 47 Lawrence Hill Rd, Dartford, **Kent**, DA1 3AG, ENG.
(T) 01322 220928
Speciality: Acupuncture.
O (Ref:HM11958)

## LANGSIDE PSYCHOLOGICAL SVS
**Langside Psychological Services**, Battlefield Primary School, 44 Carmichael Pl, Glasgow, **Glasgow (City of)**, G42 9SY, SCO.
(T) 01416 320638
Speciality: Psychology.
B (Ref:HM11959)

## LANGSLEY, T
**T Langsley**, 97 Little Norton Lane, Sheffield, **Yorkshire (South)**, S8 8GB, ENG.
(T) 01142 746479
Speciality: Chiropodists (Podiatrists).
S (Ref:HM11960)

## LANKESTER, CHARLES
**Charles Lankester**, Equilibrium Centre, 117 Granville Rd, London, **London (Greater)**, SW18 5SF, ENG.
(T) 020 8870 8761
Speciality: Osteopathy.
P S T (Ref:HM11961)

## LANNER NATURAL HEALTH CLINIC
**Lanner Natural Health Clinic**, Cleveland House, The Sq, Lanner, Redruth, **Cornwall**, TR16 6EJ, ENG.
(T) 01209 314300
Speciality: Complementary Medicines & Therapy.
C M (Ref:HM11962)

## LANSDOWN CLNC OF PHYS MED
**Lansdown Clinic Of Physical Medicine (The)**, 10 Lansdown, Stroud, **Gloucestershire**, GL5 1BB, ENG.
(T) 01453 755799
Speciality: Chiropractic.
P S T (Ref:HM11963)

## LANSDOWN PHYSIOTHERAPY CLINIC
**Lansdown Physiotherapy Clinic**, Sulis Manor Rd, Bath, **Somerset**, BA2 2AL, ENG.
(T) 01225 830038 (F) 01225 833102
Speciality: Manipulation, Ultrasonics. ✔
● **Physiotherapist** Mr C Youngs Q: MCSP, SRP. M: CSP.
S Yrs. Est.: 1 (Ref:HM11964)

## LANSMAN, ROBIN J
**Robin J Lansman**, Kings Corner Surgery, Kings Rd, Ascot, **Berkshire**, SL5 0AE, ENG.
(T) 01628 624544 (F) 01628 540990
Speciality: Osteopathy.
P S T (Ref:HM11965)

## LANSMAN, ROBIN J
**Robin J Lansman**, 8a Moor Lane, Maidenhead, **Berkshire**, SL6 7JU, ENG.
(T) 01628 624544
Speciality: Osteopathy.
● **Owner** Mr R Lansman
P S T (Ref:HM11966)

## LANT, JOHN & PARTNERS
**John Lant & Partners**, 206 Chesterton Rd, Cambridge, **Cambridgeshire**, CB4 1NE, ENG.
(T) 01223 367661
Speciality: Osteopathy.
● **Senior Partner** Mr J Lant
P S T (Ref:HM11967)

## LAPKA, M S L
**M S L Lapka**, 12 Wheatley Cl, Exeter, **Devon**, EX4 1NT, ENG.
(T) 01392 218183
Speciality: Chiropodists (Podiatrists).
● **Owner** Mr M Lapka
S (Ref:HM11968)

## LAPPIN, MARY
**Mary Lappin**, 61 Victoria Rd, Bangor, **County Down**, BT20 5ER, NIR.
(T) 028 9146 4000 (F) 028 9146 4000
Speciality: Complementary Medicines & Therapy.
● **Owner** Mrs M Lappin
C M (Ref:HM11969)

## LARCOMBE, J
**J Larcombe**, 35 Station Rd, Frimley, Camberley, **Surrey**, GU16 5HE, ENG.
(T) 01276 684297 (F) 01276 684297
Speciality: Chiropodists (Podiatrists).
● **Owner** Mrs P Larcombe
S (Ref:HM11970)

## LARDER-SMITH, JANE
**Jane Larder-Smith**, Westfield, Mead Lane, Sandford, Winscombe, **Somerset**, BS25 5RG, ENG.
(T) 01934 823084
Speciality: Physiotherapy.
● **Owner** Mrs J Larder-Smith
P S T (Ref:HM11971)

## LARGS NATURAL HEALTH CLINIC
**Largs Natural Health Clinic**, 106 Greenock Rd, Largs, **Ayrshire (North)**, KA30 8PG, SCO.
(T) 01475 673162
Speciality: Homeopathy.
M (Ref:HM11972)

## LARHOLT, A
**A Larholt**, 52 Queens Rd, Southend-On-Sea, **Essex**, SS1 1NL, ENG.
(T) 01702 348221
Speciality: Osteopathy.
P S T (Ref:HM11973)

## LARKIN, CATHERINE (DR)
**Larkin Catherine Dr**, 61 Wilfield Rd, Sandymount, Dublin, **County Dublin**, IRE.
(T) 01260 0826
Speciality: Complementary Medicines & Therapy.
M (Ref:HM11974)

## LARKIN, H
**H Larkin**, Four Fells, Town Head, Hawes, **Yorkshire (North)**, DL8 3RG, ENG.
(T) 01969 667425
Speciality: Homeopathy.
● **Owner** Ms H Larkin
M (Ref:HM11975)

## LARKIN, JILL
**Jill Larkin**, Chanctonbury, 2 St Johns Rd, Haywards Heath, **Sussex (West)**, RH16 4EH, ENG.
(T) 01444 412191
Speciality: Crystal Healing, Reiki.
M (Ref:HM11976)

## LARKMAN, K
**K Larkman**, 5 Ditton Grange Cl, Surbiton, **Surrey**, KT6 5HQ, ENG.
(T) 020 8398 4351
Speciality: Homeopathy.
M (Ref:HM11977)

## LAROUCHE, NADINE
**Nadine Larouche**, Blackheath Therapy Centre, 184-186 Westcombe Hill, London, **London (Greater)**, SE3 7DH, ENG.
(T) 020 8691 3506 (F) 020 8691 3506
Speciality: Complementary Medicines & Therapy.
● **Owner** Mrs N Larouche
C M (Ref:HM11978)

## LAROUCHE, PIERRE
**Pierre Larouche**, 13 Nelson Rd, London, **London (Greater)**, SE10 9JB, ENG.
(T) 020 8858 8557
Speciality: Osteopathy.
● **Partner** Mr A Parr
P S T (Ref:HM11979)

## LARWOOD SURGERY
**Larwood Surgery**, Worksop, **Nottinghamshire**, S81 0HH, ENG.
(T) 01142 508882
Speciality: Alexander Technique.
● **Practitioner** Mr G Crewe
P S (Ref:HM11980)

## LA-SANTE AROMATHERAPY
**La-Sante Aromatherapy**, 10 Harold Rd, Clacton-On-Sea, **Essex**, CO15 6AJ, ENG.
(T) 01255 431265 (F) 01255 431265
Speciality: Aromatherapy. ✔
● **Aromatherapist** Mrs A Daws Q: GIA. M: GIA.
C Yrs. Est.: 3 (Ref:HM11981)

## LASER THERAPY
**Laser Therapy**, 158 Queens Drive, Glasgow, **Glasgow (City of)**, G42 8QN, SCO.
(T) 01414 236647 (F) 01414 236647
Speciality: Acupuncture.
● **Owner** Mr R Penman
O (Ref:HM11982)

## LASER THERAPY
**Laser Therapy**, Suite 12 Enterprise House, South Bank Business Park, Kirkintilloch, Glasgow, **Glasgow (City of)**, G66 1XQ, SCO.
(T) 01415 780058
Speciality: Complementary Medicines & Therapy.
C M (Ref:HM11983)

## LASER THERAPY CENTRE
**Laser Therapy Centre**, McGregor House, 10 Donaldson Cresent, Kirkintilloch, Glasgow, **Glasgow (City of)**, G66 1XF, SCO.
(T) 01415 780058
Speciality: Complementary Medicines & Therapy, Laser Therapy.
● **Owner** Miss S Shanks
B Yrs. Est.: 4 (Ref:HM11984)

## LASERTROLYSIS UK
**Lasertrolysis UK Ltd**, Hill Rd, Eccleston, Chester, **Cheshire**, CH4 9HQ, ENG.
(T) 01244 680214
Speciality: Electrolysis.
● **Owner** Mr J Bills
T (Ref:HM11985)

Key: B Mind-Body Medicine, C Complementary Medicine, H Self Help Treatment, M Medicinal Therapy, O Oriental Medicine, P Postural Therapy, S Manipulative Structural Therapy, T Touch Therapy

## LASSMAN, J
**J Lassman**, 13-14 St. Georges Mews, London, **London (Greater)**, NW1 8XE, **ENG**.
(T) 020 8203 7298
Speciality: Acupuncture. ✔
● **Owner** Ms J Lassman **Q:** Lic.Ac. **M:** BAcC.
O Yrs. Est.: 2 (**Ref:**HM11986)

## LAST, ALISON
**Alison Last**, 85 Middleton Hall Rd, Birmingham, **Midlands (West)**, B30 1AG, **ENG**.
(T) 07973 209630 (F) 01216 285009
Speciality: Physiotherapy.
● **Owner** Mrs A Last
P S T (**Ref:**HM11987)

## LAST, CHRISTINE
**Christine Last**, 5 Villa Rd, Stanway, Colchester, **Essex**, CO3 5RH, **ENG**.
(T) 01206 560146
Speciality: Reflexology.
S T (**Ref:**HM11988)

## LAST, MARIANNE
**Marianne Last**, 98 Cathedral Rd, Cardiff, **Glamorgan (Vale of)**, CF11 9LP, **WAL**.
(T) 01600 716641
Speciality: Herbalists.
● **Owner** Ms M Last
M (**Ref:**HM11989)

## LAST, MARIANNE
**Marianne Last**, Newport Clinic Of Holistic Health, 36 Godfrey Rd, Newport, NP20 4PE, **WAL**.
(T) 01633 843333
Speciality: Complementary Medicines & Therapy.
● **Owner** Mr J Francis
M (**Ref:**HM11990)

## LATCHEM, V
**V Latchem**, Station House, Staverton, Totnes, **Devon**, TQ9 6AG, **ENG**.
(T) 01803 762772
Speciality: Osteopathy.
P S T (**Ref:**HM11991)

## LATCHFORD, A
**A Latchford**, 10 Eldon Rd, Reading, **Berkshire**, RG1 4DH, **ENG**.
(T) 01189 502002
Speciality: Physiotherapy.
● **Owner** A Latchford
P S T (**Ref:**HM11992)

## LATHAM, E
**Mrs E Latham**, 399 West Wycombe Rd, High Wycombe, **Buckinghamshire**, HP12 4AE, **ENG**.
(T) 01494 523753
Speciality: Chiropodists (Podiatrists).
● **Owner** Mrs E Latham
S (**Ref:**HM11993)

## LATHAM, P
**P Latham**, 3 St Loyes Trce, Exeter, **Devon**, EX2 5DD, **ENG**.
(T) 01392 422386
Speciality: Chiropodists (Podiatrists).
S (**Ref:**HM11994)

## LATHAM, PATRICIA
**Patricia Latham**, 49 Percy Rd, **Wrexham**, LL13 7EB, **WAL**.
(T) 01978 350542
Speciality: Reflexology.
S T (**Ref:**HM11995)

## LATHAM, R
**R Latham**, Vale Edge, Bath Rd, Blagdon, Bristol, BS40 7XY, **ENG**.
(T) 01934 852994
Speciality: Physiotherapy.
P S T (**Ref:**HM11996)

## LATTER, J E
**Latter J E**, Pasadena, Galsworthy Rd, Chertsey, **Surrey**, KT16 8EP, **ENG**.
(T) 01932 565319
Speciality: Chiropodists (Podiatrists).
S (**Ref:**HM11997)

## LATTER, STEVEN
**Latter Steven**, Deale House, 16 Lavant St, Petersfield, **Hampshire**, GU32 3EW, **ENG**.
(T) 01730 269095
Speciality: Hypnotherapy.
● **Owner** Mr S Latter
B (**Ref:**HM11998)

## LATTIMER SPORTS INJURIES
**Lattimer Sports Injuries Clinic (The)**, 123 Eastern Avenue, Southend-On-Sea, **Essex**, SS2 4DX, **ENG**.
(T) 01702 611098 (F) 01702 612092
Speciality: Physiotherapy.
P S T (**Ref:**HM11999)

## LATTIMORE, GILLIAN
**Lattimore Gillian**, 93A Hillcrest Dr, Lucan, **County Dublin**, **IRE**.
(T) 01624 1214
Speciality: Acupuncture.
O (**Ref:**HM12000)

## LATTY & ASSOCIATES
**H J Latty & Associates**, 38 Green Park, Bath, **Somerset**, BA1 1HZ, **ENG**.
(T) 01225 424784
Speciality: Chiropodists (Podiatrists).
S (**Ref:**HM12001)

## LAUDER, STEVE
**Steve Lauder**, 15 Fitzilian Avenue, Romford, **Essex**, RM3 0QS, **ENG**.
(T) 01708 348826
Speciality: Hypnotherapy.
● **Owner** Mr S Lauder
B (**Ref:**HM12002)

## LAUGH THERAPY & HAPINESS
**Laughter Therapy and the Hapiness Project**, The Deep And Meaningful Training Co. Ltd, Elms Court, Botley, Oxford, **Oxfordshire**, OX2 9LP, **ENG**.
(T) 01865 244414
Speciality: Complementary Medicines & Therapy, Laughter Therapy.
M (**Ref:**HM12003)

## LAUNAY, C
**C Launay**, 90 Sloane St, London, **London (Greater)**, SW1X 9PQ, **ENG**.
(T) 020 7259 5667
Speciality: Physiotherapy.
P S T (**Ref:**HM12004)

## LAUNDON, J
**J Laundon**, 37A South St, Lancing, **Sussex (West)**, BN15 8AN, **ENG**.
(T) 01903 750770
Speciality: Osteopathy.
● **Owner** Mr J Laundon
P S T (**Ref:**HM12005)

## LAUNER, M
**M Launer**, Burnley General Hospital, Casterton Avenue, Burnley, **Lancashire**, BB10 2PQ, **ENG**.
(T) 01282 420906
Speciality: Psychiatry.
B (**Ref:**HM12006)

## LAURANT, PIERRE
**Pierre Laurant**, Unit 31 The Mill, Mill Lane, Coppull, Chorley, **Lancashire**, PR7 5BW, **ENG**.
(T) 01257 794442 (F) 01257 794551
Speciality: Aromatherapy.
● **Managing Director** Mr B O'Dwyer
M O (**Ref:**HM12007)

## LAUREL FARM CLINIC
**Laurel Farm Clinic & School Of Complementary Medicine**, 17 Carlingcott, Peasedown St. John, Bath, **Somerset**, BA2 8AN, **ENG**.
(T) 01761 434098 (F) 01761 434905
Speciality: Complementary Medicines & Therapy.
● **Owner** Mrs H Adler-Collins
C M (**Ref:**HM12008)

## LAUREL PLACE
**Laurel Place**, New Rd, Churchill, Winscombe, **Somerset**, BS25 5NW, **ENG**.
(T) 01934 853396
Speciality: Acupuncture, Aromatherapy, Chiropractic, Healing Therapy, Homeopathy, Hypnosis, Kinesiology, Life Style Coaching, McTimoney Chiropractic, Meditation, Neuro-Linguistic Program, Nutritional Therapy, Psychotherapy, Reflexology, Reiki, Shiatsu, Spiritual Healing, Personal Development.
● **Owner** Mr R Ford
C (**Ref:**HM12009)

## LAUREL, MARTIN
**Martin Laurel**, Farm Castlerea, **County Galway**, **IRE**.
(T) 09074 3235
Speciality: Chiropractors.
P S T (**Ref:**HM12010)

## LAUREL'S
**Laurel's**, 3 Queens Parade Mansions, Brownlow Rd, London, **London (Greater)**, N11 2DL, **ENG**.
(T) 020 8881 1596
Speciality: Complementary Medicines & Therapy.
● **Owner** Miss L Hopkins
C M (**Ref:**HM12011)

## LAURENS HOLVE
**Laurens Holve**, 55 Dartmouth Park Rd, London, **London (Greater)**, NW5 1SL, **ENG**.
(T) 020 7482 1248 (F) 020 7916 6619
Speciality: Osteopathy.
● **Owner** Mr L Holve
P S T (**Ref:**HM12012)

## LAURENT, PIERRE
**Pierre Laurent (UK) Ltd**, 22 Tweedsmuir Cl, Basingstoke, **Hampshire**, RG22 5DP, **ENG**.
(T) 01256 414040
Speciality: Aromatherapy.
M O (**Ref:**HM12013)

## LAURIDSEN, H
**H Lauridsen**, 106 Stockbridge Rd, Winchester, **Hampshire**, SO22 6RL, **ENG**.
(T) 01962 864701
Speciality: Chiropractic.
P S T (**Ref:**HM12014)

## LAURIE, A
**A Laurie**, 68 Torbrex Rd, Cumbernauld, Glasgow, **Glasgow (City of)**, G67 2LE, **SCO**.
(T) 01236 730403
Speciality: Chiropody. ✔
● **Chiropodist** Mr A Laurie **Q:** DPodM.
M Yrs. Est.: 6 (**Ref:**HM12015)

## LAURIE, ANGELA
**Angela Laurie**, 1a Blenheim Rd, Minehead, **Somerset**, TA24 5PY, **ENG**.
(T) 01643 704737
Speciality: Hypnotherapy.
● **Owner** Mrs A Lorrie
B (**Ref:**HM12016)

## LAUS, ROBERT
**Mr Robert Laus**, 174 Woodseer St, London, **London (Greater)**, E1 5HQ, **ENG**.
(T) 020 7377 1367
Speciality: Physiotherapy.
● **Owner** Mr R Laus
P S T (**Ref:**HM12017)

## LAVELETTE, PETER
**Peter Lavelette**, Parkwood Chiropractic Clinic, 189 Fidlas Rd, Llanishen, Cardiff, **Glamorgan (Vale of)**, CF14 5LZ, **WAL**.
(T) 029 2076 6777 (F) 029 2076 6777
Speciality: Chiropractors.
● **Senior Partner** Ms L Sasse
P S T (**Ref:**HM12018)

## LAVENANT, M
**M Lavenant**, Flat 9, 9 Second Avenue, Hove, **Sussex (East)**, BN3 2LH, **ENG**.
(T) 01273 220651 (F) 01273 220651
Speciality: Herbal Medicine.
● **Owner** Mr M Lavenant
M (**Ref:**HM12019)

## LAVENANT, MAURICE
**Maurice Lavenant**, The Acupuncture Practice, 16 Ferry Rd, Rye, **Sussex (East)**, TN31 7DN, **ENG**.
(T) 01797 225099
Speciality: Acupuncture.
O (**Ref:**HM12020)

## LAVENDER HILL HOMEOPATHIC CTRE
**Lavender Hill Homeopathic Centre**, 33


Key continued: **Yrs.Est:** Years Established **Q:** Qualifications **M:** Professional Membership ✔ Indemnity Insurance Accept Credit Cards

Ilminster Gardens, London, **London (Greater)**, SW11 1PJ, ENG.
(T) 020 7978 4519
Speciality: Homeopathy.
● **Owner** Mr M Strange
M (Ref:HM12021)

## LAVENDER HOUSE

**Lavender House Aromatherapy & Shiatsu Centre**, 30-31 Henley St, Stratford-Upon-Avon, **Warwickshire**, CV37 6QW, ENG.
(T) 01789 204775
Speciality: Aromatherapy, Shiatsu.
M (Ref:HM12022)

## LAVENDER LODGE CLINIC

**Lavender Lodge Clinic**, The St, Hacheston, Woodbridge, **Suffolk**, IP13 0DT, ENG.
(T) 01728 747933
(E) kjpepps@hotmailcom
Speciality: Absent Healing, Acupressure, Aromatherapy, Colour Therapy, Counselling, Crystal Healing, Electrotherapy, Healing Therapy, Holistic Healing, Homeopathy, Manipulation, Massage (Therapeutic), Meditation, Osteopathy, Paranormal Therapies, Psychotherapy, Reflexology, Reiki, Spiritual Healing, This company supplies all complementary therapies. It has healing workshops and training workshops. Meditation and visualisation workshops. Circle/Intution training work and complete mind/body/spirit attunement. ✔
● **Practitioner/Circle Work** Mr K Pepper
● **Owner/Practitioner** Miss T Brewer Q: Dip.Hom, Dip.Man.Th, Dip.Massage, Dip.Phys, Dip.Psych, Dip.Reflex, DO. M: SMAE.
C Yrs. Est.: 5 (Ref:HM12023)

## LAVENDER ROOMS

**Lavender Rooms (The)**, Savile Centre, The Town, Dewsbury, **Yorkshire (West)**, WF12 0QY, ENG.
(T) 01924 458115
Speciality: Aromatherapy.
● **Owner** Mrs J Speight
M O (Ref:HM12024)

## LAVENDER ROOMS

**Lavender Rooms (The)**, 82a Edge Top Rd, Dewsbury, **Yorkshire (West)**, WF12 0BH, ENG.
(T) 01924 458115
Speciality: Aromatherapy.
M O (Ref:HM12025)

## LAVENDER, M J

**M J Lavender**, 88 Rodney St, Liverpool, **Merseyside**, L1 9AR, ENG.
(T) 01517 096639 (F) 01517 097279
Speciality: Osteopathy.
P S T (Ref:HM12026)

## LAVENDER, M J

**M J Lavender**, 87 Thingwall Rd, Wirral, **Merseyside**, CH61 3UB, ENG.
(T) 01516 486870
Speciality: Osteopathy.
P S T (Ref:HM12027)

## LAVENDER, PAUL

**Paul Lavender**, 83 The Vale, Golders Green, London, **London (Greater)**, NW11 8TJ, ENG.
(T) 020 8922 6779
Speciality: Complementary Medicines & Therapy.
● **Bowen Therapist** Mr P Lavender
● **Bowen Therapist** Ms C Collenette
M (Ref:HM12028)

## LAVENDER, S

**Mrs S Lavender**, 32 Chiltern Rd, Maidenhead, **Berkshire**, SL6 1XA, ENG.
(T) 01628 628727
Speciality: Bowen Therapy, Meditation, Reiki, Spiritual Healing, Past Life Regression, Spirt Release.
● **Holistic Therapist** Mrs S Lavender Q: MBChA, Reiki Master. M: B.A.Ch.P.
C Yrs. Est.: 15 (Ref:HM12029)

## LAVERSTOCK PHYSIO PRACTICE

**Laverstock Physiotherapy Practice**, Halliwell, Kingswood Rd, Tunbridge Wells, **Kent**, TN2 4UJ, ENG.
(T) 01892 546657
Speciality: Physiotherapy.
P S T (Ref:HM12030)

## LAVERTY, J Y

**J Y Laverty**, 4 Bentinck St, London, **London (Greater)**, W1M 5RJ, ENG.
(T) 020 7224 0171
Speciality: Physiotherapy.
P S T (Ref:HM12031)

## LAVERTY, SUSIE

**Susie Laverty**, 12 Bradley Rd, Winchester, **Hampshire**, SO22 6LG, ENG.
(T) 01962 884028
Speciality: Bach Remedies, Crystal Healing, Healing Therapy, Meditation, Reiki, Spiritual Healing, Chi Kung.
C (Ref:HM12032)

## LAVERTY, SUSIE

**Susie Laverty**, Winchester, **Hampshire**, SO22, ENG.
(T) 01962 884028
Speciality: Bach Remedies.
M (Ref:HM12033)

## LAVINGOTN, A

**A Lavington**, Woodcut, Peneden Heath, Maidstone, **Kent**, ME14 2EQ, ENG.
(T) 01622 693460
Speciality: Aromatherapy, Infant Massage Instructor. ✔
● **Aromatherapist** Mrs A Lavington Q: Dip.Arom. M: IFA.
C Yrs. Est.: 5 (Ref:HM12034)

## LAVIS, G J & H M

**G J & H M Lavis**, 14 Newbury St, Wantage, **Oxfordshire**, OX12 8DA, ENG.
(T) 01235 760186 (F) 01235 760186
Speciality: Chiropodists (Podiatrists).
● **Director** Mr G Lavis
S (Ref:HM12035)

## LAW, DEREK T

**Derek T Law**, 23 Poole Rd, Bournemouth, **Dorset**, BH4 9DF, ENG.
(T) 01202 764161
Speciality: Osteopathy.
● **Owner** Mr D Law
P S T (Ref:HM12036)

## LAW, J REYNOLDS

**J Reynolds Law**, 36 St Andrews St South, Bury St. Edmunds, **Suffolk**, IP33 3PH, ENG.
(T) 01284 752176
Speciality: Chiropodists (Podiatrists).
S (Ref:HM12037)

## LAW, MARIE

**Marie Law**, 2 Walpole St, Wolverhampton, **Midlands (West)**, WV6 0AT, ENG.
(T) 01902 312133
Speciality: Clairvoyants & Palmists.
B (Ref:HM12038)

## LAW, MARY

**Mrs Mary Law**, Flat 9, Pebble Court, 114 Southwood Rd, Hayling Island, **Hampshire**, PO11 9QF, ENG.
(T) 023 9246 1584 (F) 023 9246 1584
Speciality: Clairvoyants & Palmists.
● **Owner** Mrs M Law
B (Ref:HM12039)

## LAWES, JENNIFER

**Jennifer Lawes**, 24 Catherine St, Salisbury, **Wiltshire**, SP1 2DA, ENG.
(T) 01722 322138 (F) 01722 322138
Speciality: Reflexology.
● **Owner** Mrs J Lawes
S T (Ref:HM12040)

## LAWLER, R & G

**Roger & Gillian Lawler**, The Ibis Centre, 18 Hampton St, Tetbury, **Gloucestershire**, GL8 8JN, ENG.
(T) 01666 502898
(E) ibiscentre@amserve.net
Speciality: Crystal Healing, Floral Essence Therapy, Massage (Therapeutic), Reflexology, Clairvoyant, Muscle Toning. ✔
● **Reflexologist** Ms G Lawler Q: MBRA. M: BRA.
● **Owner/Reflexologist** Mr R Lawler Q: MBRA. M: BRA.
T Yrs. Est.: 15 (Ref:HM12041)

## LAWLER-DOCHERTY, JANIS

**Janis Lawler-Docherty**, 8 Arthurlie Drive, Newton Mearns, Glasgow, **Glasgow (City of)**, G77 5AF, SCO.
(T) 01416 398446
Speciality: Chiropodists (Podiatrists).
● **Owner** Mrs J Lawler-Docherty
S (Ref:HM12042)

## LAWLESS, D

**D Lawless**, 150 Seabrook Rd, Hythe, **Kent**, CT21 5RA, ENG.
(T) 01303 264190
Speciality: Chiropodists (Podiatrists).
● **Owner** Mrs D Lawless
S (Ref:HM12043)

## LAWLESS, GIULIA

**Giulia Lawless**, Kimberley Pl, Cannons Lane, Hatfield Broad Oak, Bishop's Stortford, **Hertfordshire**, CM22 7HX, ENG.
(T) 01279 718882
Speciality: Aromatherapy.
● **Owner** Ms G Lawless
M O (Ref:HM12044)

## LAWLOR, M

**M Lawlor**, 20A Central Avenue, West Bridgford, Nottingham, **Nottinghamshire**, NG2 5GR, ENG.
(T) 01159 143311
Speciality: Complementary Medicines & Therapy.
● **Practice Manager** Mrs S Peacock
M (Ref:HM12045)

## LAWRANCE, ELIZABETH A

**Elizabeth A Lawrance**, Woodside Lodge, Furnace Lane, Broad Oak, Rye, **Sussex (East)**, TN31 6ES, ENG.
(T) 01424 883135
Speciality: Physiotherapy.
P S T (Ref:HM12046)

## LAWRENCE, J M

**J M Lawrence**, 26 Monmouth St, Bath, **Somerset**, BA1 2AP, ENG.
(T) 01225 448993 (F) 01225 333866
Speciality: Osteopathy.
● **Owner** Mr J Lawrence
P S T (Ref:HM12047)

## LAWRENCE, J M

**J M Lawrence**, Catkins, Brayford, Barnstaple, **Devon**, EX32 7QN, ENG.
(T) 01598 710008 (F) 01598 710008
Speciality: Osteopathy.
● **Owner** Mr J Lawrence
P S T (Ref:HM12048)

## LAWRENCE, JESSE (DR)

**Lawrence Dr Jesse**, Old Cratloe Rd, **County Limerick**, IRE.
(T) 06132 7716
Speciality: Chiropractors.
P S T (Ref:HM12049)

## LAWRENCE, JILLIAN

**Jillian Lawrence**, Woodbridge, **Suffolk**, IP13, ENG.
(T) 01473 738104
Speciality: Hypnotherapy.
B (Ref:HM12050)

## LAWRENCE, M A

**M A Lawrence**, North Calvadnack, Polgear, Redruth, **Cornwall**, TR16 6PS, ENG.
(T) 01209 861369
Speciality: Chiropodists (Podiatrists).
● **Owner** Mrs M Lawrence
S (Ref:HM12051)

## LAWRENCE, MICHAEL W

**Michael W Lawrence**, 23 Merley Ways, Wimborne, **Dorset**, BH21 1QN, ENG.
(T) 01202 882062
Speciality: Chiropodists (Podiatrists).
● **Owner** Mr M Lawrence

S (Ref:HM12052)

**LAWRENCE, P F**

**P F Lawrence**, The Surgery, Ivy Court, Tenterden, **Kent**, TN30 6RB, ENG.
(T) 01580 763666 (F) 01580 766194
Speciality: Physiotherapy.
P S T (Ref:HM12053)

**LAWRENCE, P F**

**P F Lawrence**, 9 Romney Rd, Hamstreet, Ashford, **Kent**, TN26 2JB, ENG.
(T) 01233 732657 (F) 01580 766194
Speciality: Physiotherapy.
● **Principal** Mrs P Lawrence
P S T (Ref:HM12054)

**LAWRENCE, R E**

**R E Lawrence**, 96 Harley St, London, **London (Greater)**, W1N 1AF, ENG.
(T) 020 7486 0506 (F) 020 7487 4146
Speciality: Psychiatry.
B (Ref:HM12055)

**LAWRENCE, S**

**S Lawrence**, 5 Whinyates Rd, London, **London (Greater)**, SE9 6NW, ENG.
(T) 020 8319 4661
Speciality: Reflexology.
● **Owner** Ms S Lawrence
S T (Ref:HM12056)

**LAWRENSON, MONICA M**

**Lawrenson Monica M**, Chalfont St. Peter, Gerrards Cross, **Buckinghamshire**, SL9 9BG, ENG.
(T) 07711 143080
Speciality: Chiropodists (Podiatrists).
S (Ref:HM12057)

**LAWRIE, A**

**A Lawrie**, 11A Station Rd, Invergowrie, Dundee, **Angus**, DD2 5AP, SCO.
(T) 01382 562493
Speciality: Hypnotherapy.
● **Owner** Mrs A Lawrie
B (Ref:HM12058)

**LAWRIE, CAROLINE**

**Caroline Lawrie**, 157 Harringay Rd, London, **London (Greater)**, N15 3HP, ENG.
(T) 020 8881 9785
Speciality: Crystal Healing, Reflexology.
● **Owner** Ms C Lawrie
S T (Ref:HM12059)

**LAW'S**

**Law's**, 270 High St, Gateshead, **Tyne and Wear**, NE8 1EL, ENG.
(T) 01914 772649
Speciality: Herbal Medicine.
● **Owner** Mr W Law
M (Ref:HM12060)

**LAWS, F J**

**F J Laws**, Chygathow, Green Lane, Portreath, Redruth, **Cornwall**, TR16 4NT, ENG.
(T) 01209 842509
Speciality: Hypnosis.
● **Owner** Mrs F Laws
B (Ref:HM12061)

**LAWS, VICKY**

**Vicky Laws**, Heavenly Soles Reflexology Clinic, 20B Bridge St, Killamarsh, Sheffield, **Yorkshire (South)**, S21 1AH, ENG.
(T) 01142 513351
Speciality: Reflexology.
S T (Ref:HM12062)

**LAWSON, HEATHER**

**Heather Lawson**, 2 The Orchards, Little Kingshill, Great Missenden, **Buckinghamshire**, HP16 0EA, ENG.
(T) 01494 891005
Speciality: Reflexology.
S T (Ref:HM12063)

**LAWSON, J A**

**J A Lawson**, 2 Newland St, Worthing, **Sussex (West)**, BN11 1JU, ENG.
(T) 01903 520534
Speciality: Chiropodists (Podiatrists).
S (Ref:HM12064)

**LAWSON, JANET**

**Janet Lawson**, Brackley Health Centre, Halse Rd, Brackley, **Northamptonshire**, NN13 6EJ, ENG.
(T) 01280 701956
Speciality: Osteopathy.
● **Owner** Mrs J Lawson
P S T (Ref:HM12065)

**LAWSON, JANET**

**Janet Lawson**, Chantry House, Ground Floor, West St, Buckingham, **Buckinghamshire**, MK18 1HL, ENG.
(T) 01280 823033
Speciality: Osteopathy.
● **Owner** Mrs J Lawson
P S T (Ref:HM12066)

**LAWSON, JANET**

**Janet Lawson**, Lactodorum, 38 Brackley Rd, Towcester, **Northamptonshire**, NN12 6DJ, ENG.
(T) 01327 358515 (F) 01280 700155
Speciality: Osteopathy.
● **Owner** Mrs J Lawson
P S T (Ref:HM12067)

**LAWSON, JOSEPHINE**

**Josephine Lawson**, Bankside House, 107-112 Leadenhall St, London, **London (Greater)**, EC3A 4AF, ENG.
(T) 020 7929 0983 (F) 020 7220 7556
Speciality: Physiotherapy.
● **Owner** Ms J Lawson
P S T (Ref:HM12068)

**LAWSON, PETER R**

**Peter R Lawson**, Woodheath, 215 Hadlow Rd, Tonbridge, **Kent**, TN10 4LP, ENG.
(T) 01732 358403
Speciality: Chiropodists (Podiatrists).
S (Ref:HM12069)

**LAWSON, R J**

**R J Lawson**, 447A Linthorpe Rd, Middlesbrough, **Cleveland**, TS5 6HX, ENG.
(T) 01642 812703
Speciality: Chiropodists (Podiatrists).
● **Owner** Mr R Lawson
S (Ref:HM12070)

**LAWSON, R O L**

**R O L Lawson**, Oakdene, 7 Milton Avenue, Wellingborough, **Northamptonshire**, NN8 3RD, ENG.
(T) 01933 224465
Speciality: Osteopathy.
● **Owner** Mr R Lawson
P S T (Ref:HM12071)

**LAWTON, D V**

**D V Lawton**, 74 Livingstone Drive, East Kilbride, Glasgow, **Glasgow (City of)**, G75 0EL, SCO.
(T) 01355 266011
Speciality: Complementary Medicines & Therapy.
● **Owner** Mr D Lawton
M (Ref:HM12072)

**LAWTON, HELEN**

**Helen Lawton**, **County Durham**, DL3, ENG.
(T) 01325 467413
Speciality: Bach Remedies.
M (Ref:HM12073)

**LAXTON, R**

**R Laxton**, 71 Elder Rd, London, **London (Greater)**, SE27 9NB, ENG.
(T) 020 8670 0831
Speciality: Chiropodists (Podiatrists).
S (Ref:HM12074)

**LAY, VIVIEN & PARTNERS**

**Vivien Lay & Partners**, 5 Sittingbourne Avenue, Enfield, **London (Greater)**, EN1 2DA, ENG.
(T) 020 8360 4739
Speciality: Osteopathy.
● **Owner** Ms V Lay
P S T (Ref:HM12075)

**LAYLAND, ROSALIND**

**Rosalind Layland**, 38 The Drive, Collier Row, Romford, **Essex**, RM5 3TR, ENG.
(T) 01708 753342
Speciality: Reflexology.
S T (Ref:HM12076)

**LAYNE, SUSAN G**

**Susan G Layne**, 143 Bloomfield Rd, Blackpool, **Lancashire**, FY1 6JN, ENG.
(T) 01253 348435
Speciality: Bach Remedies, Complementary Therapy, Dowsing, Massage (Therapeutic), Meditation, Metamorphic Therapy, Reflexology.
✔
● **Practitioner** Mrs S Layne Q: MAR, MGCP, MIPTI. M: IPTI.
T Yrs. Est.: 10 (Ref:HM12077)

**LAZARUS NONO**

**Lazarus Nono**, 102 Geary Rd, Dollis Hill, London, **London (Greater)**, NW10 1HR, ENG.
(T) 020 8450 8688
Speciality: Osteopathy.
● **Owner** Mr J Dela-Cruz
P S T (Ref:HM12078)

**LAZARUS, GAIL**

**Gail Lazarus**, 38 Charmouth Rd, St. Albans, **Hertfordshire**, AL1 4SN, ENG.
(T) 01727 836495
Speciality: Acupuncture.
● **Owner** Ms G Lazarus
O (Ref:HM12079)

**LAZENBY, D**

**D Lazenby**, 4a George St, Pocklington, York, **Yorkshire (North)**, YO42 2DF, ENG.
(T) 01759 302162
Speciality: Complementary Medicines & Therapy.
● **Owner** Mrs M Rimes
M (Ref:HM12080)

**LAZUREK, DONNA**

**Donna Lazurek**, 2 The Avenue, Alsager, Stoke-On-Trent, **Staffordshire**, ST7 2AN, ENG.
(T) 01270 873569
Speciality: Complementary Medicines & Therapy.
C M (Ref:HM12081)

**LE BAS, ROSS**

**Ross Le Bas**, 116 Old London Rd, St. Albans, **Hertfordshire**, AL1 1PU, ENG.
(T) 01727 811716
Speciality: Physiotherapy.
P S T (Ref:HM12082)

**LE BON, JOHATHAN**

**Johathan Le Bon**, The Old Fire Station Surgery, 68A Portsmouth Rd, Southampton, **Hampshire**, SO19 9AN, ENG.
(T) 023 8044 8901
Speciality: Osteopathy.
P S T (Ref:HM12083)

**LE BROCQ**

**Mr Le Brocq**, Windwhistle, High St, Shirrell Heath, Southampton, **Hampshire**, SO32 2JN, ENG.
(T) 01329 832432
Speciality: Physiotherapy.
P S T (Ref:HM12084)

**LE CUC, KIM**

**Kim Le Cuc**, 29B Fayland Avenue, London, **London (Greater)**, SW16 1TG, ENG.
(T) 020 8769 6927
Speciality: Acupuncture.
● **Owner** Ms C Le
O (Ref:HM12085)

**LE HUNTE, ASHIKA**

**Ashika Le Hunte**, 14 Finnamore Wood Camp, Frieth Rd, Marlow, **Buckinghamshire**, SL7 2HU, ENG.
Speciality: Reflexology.
S T (Ref:HM12086)

**LE, J**

**J Le**, Cassidy Rd Medical Centre, 651A Fulham Rd, London, **London (Greater)**, SW6 5PX, ENG.
(T) 020 7731 2511 (F) 020 7371 7857
Speciality: Acupuncture.
● **Manager** Mr L McNulty
O (Ref:HM12087)

**LEACH HEALTH CLINIC**

**Leach Health Clinic**, Tyock Business Centre, Grampian Rd, Elgin, **Moray**, IV30 1XN, SCO.



Key continued: Yrs.Est: Years Established Q: Qualifications M: Professional Membership ✔ Indemnity Insurance Accept Credit Cards

(T) 01343 549510 (F) 01343 548743
Speciality: Complementary Medicines & Therapy.
M (Ref:HM12088)

**LEACH, JANINE**

**Janine Leach**, 24 Blenheim Gardens, Wallington, **Surrey**, SM6 9PP, ENG.
(T) 020 8773 1106
Speciality: Osteopathy.
P S T (Ref:HM12089)

**LEACH, P**

**P Leach**, 35 Aylesbury St, Bletchley, Milton Keynes, **Buckinghamshire**, MK2 2BQ, ENG.
(T) 01908 647351
Speciality: Osteopathy.
P S T (Ref:HM12090)

**LEACH, TRICIA**

**Tricia Leach**, 243 Peartree Avenue, Southampton, **Hampshire**, SO19 7RD, ENG.
(T) 023 8044 7555
Speciality: Reiki.
● **Reiki Therapist** Ms T Leach Q: Reiki 1, Reiki 2.
C Yrs. Est.: 7 (Ref:HM12091)

**LEACH, VANDRA**

**Vandra Leach**, 126 High St, Lymington, **Hampshire**, SO41 9AQ, ENG.
(T) 01590 679560
Speciality: Chiropodists (Podiatrists).
● **Senior Partner** Dr P Hardy
S (Ref:HM12092)

**LEACOCK, S D**

**S D Leacock**, 97 Hempstead Rd, Watford, **Hertfordshire**, WD1 3HE, ENG.
(T) 01923 222936
Speciality: Osteopathy.
● **Owner** Mr S Leacock
P S T (Ref:HM12093)

**LEADBETTER, E D J**

**E D J Leadbetter**, 148 Crowmarsh Hill, Crowmarsh Gifford, Wallingford, **Oxfordshire**, OX10 8EQ, ENG.
(T) 01491 824463
Speciality: Physiotherapy.
P S T (Ref:HM12094)

**LEADER, D G**

**D G Leader**, 584 City Way, Rochester, **Kent**, ME1 2TW, ENG.
(T) 01634 848557
Speciality: Chiropodists (Podiatrists).
● **Owner** Mr D Leader
S (Ref:HM12095)

**LEADER, S**

**S Leader**, New Cross Natural Therapy Centre, 394 New Cross Rd, London, **London (Greater)**, SE14 6TY, ENG.
(T) 020 8469 0858
Speciality: Homeopathy.
M (Ref:HM12096)

**LEAH CHIROPRACTIC CLINIC**

**Leah Chiropractic Clinic**, 50 Grahams Rd, Falkirk, FK1 1HN, SCO.
(T) 01324 621677 (F) 01324 621676
Speciality: Chiropractors.
● **Owner** Mr D Niewald
P S T (Ref:HM12097)

**LEAH CHIROPRACTIC CLINIC**

**Leah Chiropractic Clinic**, 28 Grahams Rd, **Falkirk**, FK1 1HR, SCO.
(T) 01324 621676
Speciality: Chiropractic.
P S T (Ref:HM12098)

**LEAH CLINIC**

**Leah Clinic**, 4 Park Circus Pl, Glasgow, **Glasgow (City of)**, G3 6AN, SCO.
(T) 01413 310898 (F) 01413 533031
Speciality: Chiropractors.
● **Director** Dr A Hager
P S T (Ref:HM12099)

**LEAHY, TONY**

**Tony Leahy**, 144 Great Spenders, Basildon, **Essex**, SS14 2NT, ENG.
(T) 01268 521882
Speciality: Clairvoyants & Palmists.
B (Ref:HM12100)

**LEAKE, DIANE**

**Diane Leake**, 30 The Centre, Evenwood, Bishop Auckland, **County Durham**, DL14 9QF, ENG.
(T) 01388 832112
Speciality: Complementary Medicines & Therapy.
M (Ref:HM12101)

**LEAL, DOUGLAS**

**Douglas Leal**, Denview Rd, Potterton, Aberdeen, **Aberdeenshire**, AB23 8ZJ, SCO.
(T) 01358 742620
Speciality: Chiropody. ✔
● **Owner/Chiropodist** Mr D Leal Q: M.S.C.P, MBChA, MSSCh.
M Yrs. Est.: 3 (Ref:HM12102)

**LEALAN, HEATHER**

**Heather Lealan**, 13 Springfield Cottages, Heybridge, Maldon, **Essex**, CM9 4LZ, ENG.
(T) 01621 857678
Speciality: Complementary Medicines & Therapy.
● **Owner** Mrs H Lealan
M (Ref:HM12103)

**LEAMINGTON SPA CHIRO CLINIC**

**Dr Elizabeth Laverick**, 4 Warwick New Rd, Leamington Spa, **Warwickshire**, CV32 5JF, ENG.
(T) 01926 427354
Speciality: Allergy Testing, Chiropractic, Homeopathy, Nutritional Therapy. ✔
● **Owner** Dr E Laverick Q: DC. M: BCA.
● **Associate/Chiropractor**
Dr P Charley Q: BSc (Chiro), BSc (Hons), DC, MSc (Chiro). M: BCA.
P Yrs. Est.: 11 (Ref:HM12104)

**LEAMINGTON SPA PHYSIOTHERAPY**

**Leamington Spa Physiotherapy**, Out Patients, Court St, Leamington Spa, **Warwickshire**, CV31 2BB, ENG.
(T) 01926 421142 (F) 01926 330323
Speciality: Physiotherapy.
● **Manager** Mrs S Cook
P S T (Ref:HM12105)

**LEAN, C**

**C Lean**, 34 Princes St, Southport, **Merseyside**, PR8 1EQ, ENG.
(T) 01704 544927 (F) 01704 544124
Speciality: Chiropodists (Podiatrists).
● **Owner** Mrs C Lean
S (Ref:HM12106)

**LEANE, MAURICE**

**Maurice Leane**, 133 Wood St, Barnet, **Hertfordshire**, EN5 4BX, ENG.
(T) 020 8441 0231
Speciality: Chiropodists (Podiatrists).
● **Owner** Mr M Cole
S (Ref:HM12107)

**LEARMAN, A B**

**A B Learman**, 45 Oakdene Drive, Leeds, **Yorkshire (West)**, LS17 8XW, ENG.
(T) 01132 695232
Speciality: Chiropodists (Podiatrists).
● **Owner** Mr A Learman
S (Ref:HM12108)

**LEARNIT**

**Learnit Ltd**, Rose Bank, Sutton, Thirsk, **Yorkshire (North)**, YO7 2PR, ENG.
(T) 01845 597097
Speciality: Psychology.
B (Ref:HM12109)

**LEARY, MARINA T**

**Marina T Leary**, 21 Oakhill, Claygate, Esher, **Surrey**, KT10 0TG, ENG.
(T) 01372 465878
Speciality: Physiotherapy.
P S T (Ref:HM12110)

**LEARY, PAUL**

**Paul Leary**, Edgerton Clinic, 89 New North Rd, Huddersfield, **Yorkshire (West)**, HD1 5ND, ENG.
(T) 01484 548134
Speciality: Physiotherapy.
● **Owner** Mr P Leary
P S T (Ref:HM12111)

**LEASK, ANDREW**

**Andrew Leask**, Guildhall Building, Navigation St, Birmingham, **Midlands (West)**, B2 4BT, ENG.
(T) 01216 325332
Speciality: Osteopathy.
● **Owner** Mr A Leask
P S T (Ref:HM12112)

**LEATHERBARROW, G L**

**G L Leatherbarrow**, 44 Whittaker Lane, Prestwich, Manchester, **Manchester (Greater)**, M25 1FX, ENG.
(T) 01617 735225
Speciality: Chiropodists (Podiatrists).
● **Owner** Ms P Madeley
S (Ref:HM12113)

**LEATHERHEAD CHIRO CLINIC**

**Leatherhead Chiropractic Clinic**, 8 The Crescent, Leatherhead, **Surrey**, KT22 8EE, ENG.
(T) 01372 370043 (F) 01372 386386
(W) www.vitalbody.co.uk
Speciality: Chiropractic, Allergies, Cancer Support.
● **Owner/Holistic Therapy**
Mr D Stevens Q: Dip.Chiro. M: BAcC.
M Yrs. Est.: 4 (Ref:HM12114)

**LEBOR, JILL**

**Jill Lebor**, 24 Watling St, Canterbury, **Kent**, CT1 2UB, ENG.
(T) 01227 452202
(E) jilllebor@ukonline.co.uk
Speciality: Bowen Therapy, Reiki, Shiatsu, Hopi Ear Candles. ✔
● **Shiatsu Practitioner** Ms J Lebor
(T) 01227 750294 Q: BTAA, MRSS. M: Shiatsu Society UK.
O Yrs. Est.: 8 (Ref:HM12115)

**LEBRET, A F**

**A F Lebret**, 18 Kingswood Avenue, Bromley, **Kent**, BR2 0NY, ENG.
(T) 020 8464 6709
Speciality: Osteopathy.
● **Owner** Mr A Lebret
P S T (Ref:HM12116)

**LEBRET, A F**

**A F Lebret**, 16 Beckenham Rd, Beckenham, **Kent**, BR3 4LS, ENG.
(T) 020 8650 4313
Speciality: Osteopathy, Structural Medicine. ✔
● **Osteopath** Mrs A Percival Q: DO. M: BOA, GOsC.
S Yrs. Est.: 49 (Ref:HM12117)

**LEBROOY, W**

**W Lebrooy (RGN MGCP ITEC)**, 24A Parkhurst Rd, Bexhill-on-Sea, **Sussex (East)**, TN40 1DF, ENG.
(T) 01424 733028
Speciality: Complementary Medicines & Therapy.
C M (Ref:HM12118)

**LECKHAMPTON CHIROPRACTIC CLNC**

**Leckhampton Chiropractic Clinic**, 2 Brunswick Buildings, Bethesda St, Leckhampton, Cheltenham, **Gloucestershire**, GL50 2AZ, ENG.
(T) 01242 227440
Speciality: Chiropractic, Manipulation, Massage (Therapeutic). ✔
● **Chiropractor** Ms A Shaw Q: DC. M: BCA, GCC.
S Yrs. Est.: 6 (Ref:HM12119)

**LECKIE, STEVEN**

**Steven Leckie**, 13C Elmbourne Rd, London, **London (Greater)**, SW17 8JS, ENG.
(T) 020 8772 1851
Speciality: Chiropodists (Podiatrists).
● **Owner** Mr S Leckie
S (Ref:HM12120)

**LECOINTE, PETER**

**Peter Lecointe**, 21 Southern Gardens, Totton, Southampton, **Hampshire**, SO40 8RW, ENG.
(T) 023 8086 1191
Speciality: Chiropodists (Podiatrists).
● **Owner** Mr P Lecointe
S (Ref:HM12121)



Key: B Mind-Body Medicine C Complementary Medicine H Self Help Treatment M Medicinal Therapy O Oriental Medicine P Postural Therapy S Manipulative Structural Therapy T Touch Therapy

### LEDBURY NATURAL HEALTH CENTRE
**Ledbury Natural Health Centre For Holistic Therapist**, 1st Floor The Old Post Office, Bank Cresent, Ledbury, **Herefordshire**, HR8 1AA, ENG.
(T) 01531 634220 (F) 01531 634220
Speciality: Alexander Technique, Allergy Testing, Aromatherapy, Bach Remedies, Chiropractic, Counselling, Healing Therapy, Herbal Medicine, Homeopathy, Hypnotherapy, Indian Head Massage, Massage (Therapeutic), Reflexology, Reiki, Zero Balancing, NLP. ✓
● **Therapist** Mrs Brown
C Yrs. Est.: 10 (Ref:HM12122)

### LEDBURY OSTEOPATHIC PRACTICE
**Ledbury Osteopathic Practice**, 2 Conigree Villas, Woodleigh Rd, Ledbury, **Herefordshire**, HR8 2BL, ENG.
(T) 01531 635080
Speciality: Osteopathy.
● **Owner** Ms B Gyde
P S T (Ref:HM12123)

### LEDBURY WHOLEFOODS
**Ledbury Wholefoods**, 82 The Homend, Ledbury, **Herefordshire**, HR8 1BX, ENG.
(T) 01531 632889
Speciality: Complementary Medicines & Therapy.
● **Owner** Ms S Burns
C (Ref:HM12124)

### LEDDINGTON-WRIGHT, S
**S Leddington-Wright**, 71 Mayfield Rd, Coventry, **Midlands (West)**, CV5 6PL, ENG.
(T) 024 7667 3741
Speciality: Physiotherapy.
P S T (Ref:HM12125)

### LEDDY, GILLIAN
**Gillian Leddy**, 29 Warwick Gardens, Ilford, **Essex**, IG1 4LE, ENG.
(T) 020 8518 1442
Speciality: Herbal Medicine.
● **Owner** Mrs G Leddy
M (Ref:HM12126)

### LEDERMAN, E (DR)
**Dr E Lederman**, 98B Hazellville Rd, London, **London (Greater)**, N19 3NA, ENG.
(T) 020 7263 8551
Speciality: Osteopathy.
● **Owner** Dr E Lederman
P S T (Ref:HM12127)

### LEDGER, DIANE
**Diane Ledger**, 2 Monmouth Rd, Harlington, Dunstable, **Bedfordshire**, LU5 6NE, ENG.
(T) 01525 873602
Speciality: Reflexology.
S T (Ref:HM12128)

### LEDLIE, C
**C Ledlie**, 3 St. Johns Pl, Larne, **County Antrim**, BT40 1TB, NIR.
(T) 028 2826 0167
Speciality: Chiropodists (Podiatrists).
● **Owner** Mrs C Ledlie
S (Ref:HM12129)

### LEE COMPLEMENTARY HEALTH CTRE
**Lee Complementary Health Centre**, 172-174 Manor Lane, Lee, London, **London (Greater)**, SE12 8LP, ENG.
(T) 020 8858 5969 (F) 020 8297 8887
(E) nikki@ssom.co.uk
Speciality: Acupuncture, Alexander Technique, Aromatherapy, Cognitive Therapy, Complementary Therapy, Counselling, Cranial Osteopathy, Herbal Medicine, Homeopathy, Manipulation, Massage (Therapeutic), Moxibustion, Naturopathy, Nutritional Therapy, Oriental Diagnosis, Osteopathy, Phytotherapy, Pilates, Reflexology, Reiki, T'ai-Chi Ch'uan, Ultrasonics, Vitamin Therapy, Yoga. ✓
● **Traditional Chinese Acupuncturist** Mary Dobbing Q: BSc, Dip.Ac. M: BAcC.
● **Homeopath** Pat Macrae Q: LCH, RSHom. M: Soc.Hom.
● **Owner** Ms G Howells Q: DO, MCSP, Reg.Osteopath, SRP.
● **Osteopath** Nikki Moss Q: DO, Reg.Osteopath.
S Yrs. Est.: 25 (Ref:HM12130)

### LEE GATE REMEDIAL CLINIC
**Lee Gate Remedial Clinic**, 149 Lee Gate, Bolton, **Lancashire**, BL2 4BQ, ENG.
(T) 01204 597587
Speciality: Physiotherapy.
P S T (Ref:HM12131)

### LEE, ADELINE
**Adeline Lee**, Astro Lodge, 16 South Prde, Skegness, **Lincolnshire**, PE25 3HW, ENG.
(T) 01754 763725
Speciality: Clairvoyants & Palmists.
● **Owner** Mrs A Lee
B (Ref:HM12132)

### LEE, ALAN
**Alan Lee**, 111 Graiglwyd Rd, Cockett, Swansea, SA2 0UZ, WAL.
(T) 01792 207463
Speciality: Physiotherapy.
● **Owner** Mr A Lee
P S T (Ref:HM12133)

### LEE, ELAINE
**Elaine Lee**, 3 Mill St, Eynsham, Witney, **Oxfordshire**, OX8 1JX, ENG.
(T) 01865 880325
Speciality: Chiropractic.
● **Owner** Mrs E Lee
P S T (Ref:HM12134)

### LEE, FELICITY
**Felicity Lee**, 13 Everswell Rd, Cardiff, **Glamorgan (Vale of)**, CF5 3DH, WAL.
(T) 029 2056 8786
Speciality: Homeopathy.
M (Ref:HM12135)

### LEE, FRANK
**Frank Lee**, 17 Wimborne Avenue, Ipswich, **Suffolk**, IP3 8QW, ENG.
(T) 01473 724722
Speciality: Physiotherapy.
● **Owner** Mr F Lee
P S T (Ref:HM12136)

### LEE, H (DR)
**Dr H Lee**, 31A First Avenue, Wembley, **London (Greater)**, HA9 8QG, ENG.
(T) 020 8908 1233
Speciality: Acupuncture.
O (Ref:HM12137)

### LEE, HENRY
**Henry Lee**, 5a Park Pl, Horsham, **Sussex (West)**, RH12 1DF, ENG.
(T) 01403 272788
Speciality: Osteopathy.
P S T (Ref:HM12138)

### LEE, K (DR)
**Dr K Lee**, 31A First Avenue, Wembley, **London (Greater)**, HA9 8QG, ENG.
(T) 020 8908 1233
Speciality: Acupuncture.
O (Ref:HM12139)

### LEE, KEN
**Ken Lee**, 3 Baroness Pl, Penarth, **Glamorgan (Vale of)**, CF64 3UL, WAL.
(T) 029 2070 4116
Speciality: Hypnosis.
● **Owner** Mr K Lee
B (Ref:HM12140)

### LEE, LAURA
**Laura Lee**, 21 Annie Taylor House, Walton Rd, London, **London (Greater)**, E12 5RG, ENG.
(T) 020 8514 5095
Speciality: Clairvoyants & Palmists.
● **Owner** Miss L Lee
B (Ref:HM12141)

### LEE, MAUREEN
**Maureen Lee**, 8 Orion Rd, Weymouth, **Dorset**, DT4 8LG, ENG.
(T) 01305 784231
Speciality: Aromatherapy.
● **Owner** Mrs M Lee
M O (Ref:HM12142)

### LEE, NICOLA
**Nicola Lee**, 42 Cumberland Rd, London, **London (Greater)**, W3 6EY, ENG.
(T) 020 8896 9128
Speciality: Reflexology.
S T (Ref:HM12143)

### LEE, PATRICK (DR)
**Lee Dr Patrick MB DCH D OBS MRCGP M**, 1 The Sq, Ballincollig, **County Cork**, IRE.
(T) 021 4875 353
Speciality: Acupuncture.
O (Ref:HM12144)

### LEE, ROBIN
**Robin Lee**, Garden Croft, Beech Lawn, Guildford, **Surrey**, GU1 3PE, ENG.
(T) 01483 455764
Speciality: Hypnosis.
● **Principal** Mr R Lee
B (Ref:HM12145)

### LEE, STEPHEN
**Stephen Lee**, 136 Birchfield Rd, Northampton, **Northamptonshire**, NN1 4RH, ENG.
(T) 01604 717585
Speciality: Acupuncture. ✓
● **Owner/Acupuncturist** Mr S Lee Q: BA, Lic.Ac, MRCHM. M: BAcC.
C (Ref:HM12146)

### LEE, VICKY
**Vicky Lee**, 102 Southbourne Rd, Bournemouth, **Dorset**, BH6 3QQ, ENG.
(T) 01202 424833
Speciality: Complementary Medicines & Therapy.
● **Owner** Mr J Milward
M (Ref:HM12147)

### LEE, W E
**W E Lee**, 16 Norfolk Way, Bishop's Stortford, **Hertfordshire**, CM23 3PW, ENG.
(T) 01279 654051
Speciality: Chiropodists (Podiatrists).
● **Owner** Mrs W Lee
S (Ref:HM12148)

### LEE-BARBER, S
**S Lee-Barber**, Flat 2, 59 Huddleston Rd, London, **London (Greater)**, N7 0AD, ENG.
(T) 020 7700 5893
Speciality: Alexander Technique.
● **Owner** Miss S Lee-Barber
P S (Ref:HM12149)

### LEECE, M
**M Leece**, 21 Bronte Old Rd, Thornton, Bradford, **Yorkshire (West)**, BD13 3HN, ENG.
(T) 01274 833038
Speciality: Chiropodists (Podiatrists).
● **Owner** Mrs M Leece
S (Ref:HM12150)

### LEECH, JUNE & EASTAUGH, MIRIAM
**June Leech & Miriam Eastaugh**, Lower Floor Offices, 79 High St, Hastings, **Sussex (East)**, TN34 3EL, ENG.
(T) 01424 719455
Speciality: Osteopathy.
P S T (Ref:HM12151)

### LEE-CROWTHER, CATHRYN
**Cathryn Lee-Crowther**, 5 Sheridan Rd, Colne, **Lancashire**, BB8 7HW, ENG.
(T) 01282 868787
Speciality: Reflexology.
S T (Ref:HM12152)

### LEEDS ACUPUNCTURE CLINIC
**Leeds Acupuncture Clinic**, 179 St Lane, Leeds, **Yorkshire (West)**, LS8 1AA, ENG.
(T) 01132 664102
Speciality: Acupuncture.
● **Owner** Dr G Broch
O (Ref:HM12153)

### LEEDS CHINESE MEDICAL CENTRE
**Chinese Medical Academy UK**, Leeds Chinese Medical Centre, 217 Stainbeck Rd, Leeds, **Yorkshire (West)**, LS7 2LR, ENG.
(T) 01132 886688 (F) 08707 468866
(E) info@cmauk.org
Speciality: Acupressure, Acupuncture, Herbal Medicine, Holistic Healing, Moxibustion.
● **Owner/Doctor Of TCM** Dr D Xiu M: BRCP.
O (Ref:HM12154)



Key continued: **Yrs.Est:** Years Established **Q:** Qualifications **M:** Professional Membership ✓ Indemnity Insurance ▬ Accept Credit Cards

**LEEDS CHIROPODY CLINIC**

**Leeds Chiropody Clinic**, 159 Beeston Rd, Leeds, **Yorkshire (West)**, LS11 6AW, ENG.
(T) 01132 703330 (F) 01132 946556
Speciality: Chiropodists (Podiatrists).
S (Ref:HM12155)

**LEEDS CHIROPRACTIC CENTRE**

**Leeds Chiropractic Centre**, 305 Harrogate Rd, Leeds, **Yorkshire (West)**, LS17 6PA, ENG.
(T) 01132 370026
Speciality: Chiropractic.
P S T (Ref:HM12156)

**LEEDS COMP THERAPY CENTRE**

**Leeds Complementary Therapy Centre**, 249A Otley Rd, Leeds, **Yorkshire (West)**, LS16 5LQ, ENG.
(T) 01132 781267
Speciality: Complementary Medicines & Therapy.
C M (Ref:HM12157)

**LEEDS COUNSELLING & PSYCHO SVS**

**Leeds Counselling & Psychotherapy Services**, Victoria Buildings, 14 Weetwood Lane, Headingley, **Yorkshire (West)**, LS16 5LX, ENG.
(T) 01132 789953
(E) walford@u.genie.co.uk
Speciality: Cognitive Therapy, Counselling, Group Therapy, Humanistic Psychology, Psychotherapy, Sensitivity Training, Transactional Analysis. ✔
● **Owner/Director** Ms J Walford Q: UKCP (Reg).
● **Director** Mr R Walford Q: UKCP (Reg).
H Yrs. Est.: 10 (Ref:HM12158)

**LEEDS PHYSIOTHERAPY CLINIC**

**Leeds Physiotherapy Clinic**, 38 Park Sq, Leeds, **Yorkshire (West)**, LS1 2NY, ENG.
(T) 01132 457800
Speciality: Physiotherapy.
P S T (Ref:HM12159)

**LEEDS PSYCHOTHERAPY SERVICES**

**Leeds Psychotherapy Services**, 2a Weetwood Lane, Headingley, **Yorkshire (West)**, LS16 5LS, ENG.
(T) 01132 789953
Speciality: Psychotherapy.
B (Ref:HM12160)

**LEEDS RUGBY CLUB REHAB CTRE**

**Leeds Rugby Club Rehabilitation Centre**, Chandos Avenue, Leeds, **Yorkshire (West)**, LS8 1QX, ENG.
(T) 01132 668288
Speciality: Physiotherapy.
P S T (Ref:HM12161)

**LEEDS SCH OF NATURAL THERAPIES**

**Leeds School Of Natural Therapies**, 198 Low Lane, Horsforth, Leeds, **Yorkshire (West)**, LS18 5QW, ENG.
(T) 01132 586337
Speciality: Complementary Medicines & Therapy.
M (Ref:HM12162)

**LEEDS SPORTS INJURY CLINIC**

**Leeds Sports Injury Clinic**, 4 Greenock Rd, Leeds, **Yorkshire (West)**, LS12 3JQ, ENG.
(T) 01132 799279
Speciality: Physiotherapy.
P S T (Ref:HM12163)

**LEEDS TRICHOLOGY CONSULTANCY**

**Leeds Trichology Consultancy**, 8 New Adel Avenue, **Yorkshire (West)**, LS16 6BE, ENG.
(T) 01132 676601
(W) www.complementary-healthcare.co.uk/info/leeds-tric
Speciality: Complementary Medicines & Therapy, Trichology.
M (Ref:HM12164)

**LEEK HOMOEOPATHIC PRACTICE**

**Leek Homoeopathic Practice**, 16 Moorhouse St, Leek, **Staffordshire**, ST13 5NB, ENG.
(T) 01538 385346
Speciality: Homeopathy.
M (Ref:HM12165)

**LEEMING, C**

**C Leeming**, 1 Mornington Villas, Bradford, **Yorkshire (West)**, BD8 7HB, ENG.
(T) 01274 546861 (F) 01274 487705
Speciality: Physiotherapy.
● **Secretary** Mr A Harley
P S T (Ref:HM12166)

**LEEMING, C**

**C Leeming**, The Gables, Cecil Avenue, Halifax, **Yorkshire (West)**, HX3 8SN, ENG.
(T) 01422 202392
Speciality: Physiotherapy.
● **Owner** Mrs C Leeming
P S T (Ref:HM12167)

**LEEPER, SARAH**

**Sarah Leeper**, 5 Sayerland Rd, Polegate, **Sussex (East)**, BN26 6NU, ENG.
(T) 01323 487689
Speciality: Physiotherapy.
● **Owner** Mrs S Leeper
P S T (Ref:HM12168)

**LEES, J D**

**J D Lees**, 37 High St, Amblecote, Stourbridge, **Midlands (West)**, DY8 4DG, ENG.
(T) 01384 390000
Speciality: Chiropodists (Podiatrists).
S (Ref:HM12169)

**LEES, PATRICIA**

**Patricia Lees**, 19 Stonehouse Rd, Sandford, Strathaven, **Lanarkshire (South)**, ML10 6PD, SCO.
(T) 01357 520788
Speciality: Hypnosis.
● **Owner** Mrs P Lees
B (Ref:HM12170)

**LEESON, CHRISTINE**

**Christine Leeson**, 34 Penns Lane, Coleshill, Birmingham, **Midlands (West)**, B46 1BA, ENG.
(T) 01675 464369
Speciality: Acupuncture.
● **Owner** Mrs C Leeson
O (Ref:HM12171)

**LEESON, D J**

**D J Leeson**, Ashmount, Lower Northdown Avenue, Margate, **Kent**, CT9 2NJ, ENG.
(T) 01843 223274
Speciality: Chiropodists (Podiatrists).
● **Owner** Mr D Leeson
S (Ref:HM12172)

**LEFEBVRE, COLLETTE**

**Collette Lefebvre**, 21 Hampton Pk, Bristol, BS6 6LG, ENG.
(T) 01179 731397
Speciality: Acupuncture.
● **Owner** Ms C Lefebvre
O (Ref:HM12173)

**LEFEVER, M E**

**Mrs M E Lefever**, 2a Pelham St, London, **London (Greater)**, SW7 2NG, ENG.
(T) 020 7584 6511 (F) 020 7225 1147
Speciality: Physiotherapy.
● **Owner** Mrs M Lefever
P S T (Ref:HM12174)

**LEGG, PAM**

**Pam Legg**, 32 Calland, Smeeth, Ashford, **Kent**, TN25 6QD, ENG.
(T) 01303 812732
Speciality: Reflexology.
S T (Ref:HM12175)

**LEGGE, PAT**

**Pat Legge**, Green Cottage, Huxley Lane, Huxley, Chester, **Cheshire**, CH3 9BG, ENG.
(T) 01829 781429
Speciality: Aromatherapy. ✔
● **Owner/Aromatherapist** Mrs P Legge Q: ITEC. M: IFA.
C Yrs. Est.: 3 (Ref:HM12176)

**LEGGETT, JANET**

**Janet Leggett**, 92 Church La East, Aldershot, **Hampshire**, GU11 3HJ, ENG.
(T) 01252 317421
Speciality: Chiropodists (Podiatrists).
● **Owner** Ms J Leggett
S (Ref:HM12177)

**LEGGETTER, D**

**D Leggetter**, 12 Thamesgate Cl, Richmond, **Surrey**, TW10 7YS, ENG.
(T) 020 8332 1482 (F) 020 8948 6651
Speciality: Hypnosis.
● **Owner** Ms D Leggetter
B (Ref:HM12178)

**LEGGOTT, C**

**C Leggott**, 17 Laburnum Way, Yeovil, **Somerset**, BA20 2PL, ENG.
(T) 01935 425951
Speciality: Chiropodists (Podiatrists).
● **Owner** Mrs C Leggott
S (Ref:HM12179)

**LEHAIN, DAN**

**Dan Lehain**, 34 Beverley Parklands, Beverley, **Humberside (North)**, HU17 0RA, ENG.
(T) 01482 870458
Speciality: Psychotherapy.
B (Ref:HM12180)

**LEHNERT, MANFRED L**

**Manfred L Lehnert**, 14 The Crescent, Nantwich, **Cheshire**, CW5 5ND, ENG.
(T) 01270 623433
Speciality: Chiropodists (Podiatrists).
● **Owner** Mr M Lehnert
S (Ref:HM12181)

**LEIBBRANDT**

**Leibbrandt**, 29 Chesil St, Winchester, **Hampshire**, SO23 0HU, ENG.
(T) 01962 851951 (F) 01962 851951
Speciality: Herbal Medicine.
● **Owner** Ms D Leibbrandt
M (Ref:HM12182)

**LEICESTER ACUPUNCTURE & HERBAL**

**Leicester Acupuncture & Herbal Clinic**, 196 Clarendon Park Rd, Leicester, **Leicestershire**, LE2 3AF, ENG.
(T) 01162 708149
Speciality: Acupuncture.
● **Owner** Dr S Patel
O (Ref:HM12183)

**LEIGH HOUSE NAT HEALTH CLINIC**

**Leigh House Natural Health Clinic**, Dunsthorpe House, 33 St Dunstans St, Canterbury, **Kent**, CT2 8BZ, ENG.
(T) 01227 768886 (F) 01227 768896
Speciality: Osteopathy.
● **Owner** Mr W Jansen
P S T (Ref:HM12184)

**LEIGH SANCTUARY**

**Leigh Sanctuary,The**, Stable Mws, The Broadway, Leigh-On-Sea, **Essex**, SS9 1RW, ENG.
(T) 01702 482224
Speciality: Complementary Medicines & Therapy.
C M (Ref:HM12185)

**LEIGH, ANNA**

**Anna Leigh**, Flat 6 River Court, Minster Rd, Coventry, **Midlands (West)**, CV1 3AF, ENG.
(T) 024 7663 4900 (F) 024 7663 4900
Speciality: Clairvoyants & Palmists.
● **Owner** Mrs A Leigh
B (Ref:HM12186)

**LEIGH, JON**

**Jon Leigh**, 15 Ethelbert Rd, Canterbury, **Kent**, CT1 3ND, ENG.
(T) 01227 766797
Speciality: Osteopathy.
● **Director** Mrs J Pelham
P S T (Ref:HM12187)

**LEIGH, JON H**

**Jon H Leigh**, 46 Broadway, Sheerness, **Kent**, ME12 1TR, ENG.
(T) 01795 663481 (F) 01795 663221
Speciality: Osteopathy.
● **Owner** Mr J Leigh
P S T (Ref:HM12188)

**LEIGH, MARTIN**

**Leigh Martin**, 8 Fitzilian Avenue, Harold Wood, Romford, **Essex**, RM3 0QS, ENG.
(T) 01708 377667



Key: B Mind-Body Medicine C Complementary Medicine H Self Help Treatment M Medicinal Therapy O Oriental Medicine P Postural Therapy S Manipulative Structural Therapy T Touch Therapy

Speciality: Aromatherapy, Cranio-Sacral Therapy, Healing Therapy, Manipulation, Massage (Therapeutic), Osteopathy, Osteomyology. ✓
● **Osteomyologist** Mr L Martin Q: BSc, CMT, DM, DO. M: TAO.
● **Aromatherapist/Beauty Therapist** Irene Milton Q: CIBTAC. M: BABTAC.
S Yrs. Est.: 18 (Ref:HM12189)

## LEIGH, NIGEL

**Nigel Leigh**, 177 Longfield Rd, Darlington, **County Durham**, DL3 0HS, ENG.
(T) 01325 269602
Speciality: Clairvoyants & Palmists.
B (Ref:HM12190)

## LEIGH, P

**P Leigh**, 16 Ferry Rd, Rye, **Sussex (East)**, TN31 7DN, ENG.
(T) 01797 225099
Speciality: Chiropodists (Podiatrists).
S (Ref:HM12191)

## LEIGH, P A

**P A Leigh**, 1 The Firs, Barley Lane, Hastings, **Sussex (East)**, TN35 5PA, ENG.
(T) 01424 443097
Speciality: Chiropodists (Podiatrists).
● **Owner** Mrs P Leigh
S (Ref:HM12192)

## LEIGH, PETER A

**Peter A Leigh**, 34 Kings Rd, Fleet, **Hampshire**, GU13 9AQ, ENG.
(T) 01252 625359
Speciality: Osteopathy.
P S T (Ref:HM12193)

## LEIGH, SUSAN

**Susan Leigh**, 3 Alstone Drive, Altrincham, **Cheshire**, WA14 4LD, ENG.
(T) 01619 287880
Speciality: Hypnosis.
● **Owner** Mrs S Leigh
B (Ref:HM12194)

## LEIGHTON CHIROPODY PRACTICE

**Leighton Chiropody Practice**, Old Bank House, 16-18 Lake St, Leighton Buzzard, **Bedfordshire**, LU7 8RT, ENG.
(T) 01525 382900
Speciality: Chiropodists (Podiatrists).
S (Ref:HM12195)

## LEIGHTON REFLEXOLOGY CLINIC

**Leighton Reflexology Clinic**, The Old Laundry, 15 Wellhead Lane, Westbury, **Wiltshire**, BA13 3PW, ENG.
(T) 01373 858380
(E) sarahreflex@fsmail.net
(W) www.theoldlaundry.freeserve.co.uk
Speciality: Complementary Therapy, Healing Therapy, Holistic Healing, Indian Head Massage, Massage (Therapeutic), Reflexology, Reiki, Stress Therapy, Touch Therapy, Ying & Yang. ✓
● **Owner/Reflexologist/Masseuse** Ms S Wiseman Q: IIHHT. M: ICHT.
T Yrs. Est.: 5 (Ref:HM12196)

## LEIGHTON, A

**A Leighton**, 133 Wood St, Barnet, **Hertfordshire**, EN5 4BX, ENG.
(T) 020 8449 7656
Speciality: Acupuncture.
● **Owner** A Leighton
O (Ref:HM12197)

## LEIPER, B

**B Leiper**, Ashdown Osteopathic Centre, The Sq, Lewes Rd, Forest Row, **Sussex (East)**, RH18 5ES, ENG.
(T) 01342 822505 (F) 01342 822505
Speciality: Osteopathy.
● **Owner** Mr T Strutt
P S T (Ref:HM12198)

## LEIPER, BRUCE M

**Bruce M Leiper Osteopath**, 126 Ashford Rd, Bearsted, Maidstone, **Kent**, ME14 4LX, ENG.
(T) 01622 735568
Speciality: Osteopathy.
P S T (Ref:HM12199)

## LEIRE PHYSIOTHERAPY PRACTICE

**Leire Physiotherapy Practice**, Leire Mill, Dunton Rd, Leire, Lutterworth, **Leicestershire**, LE17 5HQ, ENG.
(T) 01455 209813
Speciality: Physiotherapy.
● **Owner** Mrs S Harris
P S T (Ref:HM12200)

## LEJEUNE, LIZ

**Liz Lejeune**, Cheltenham Holistic Centre, 66 Suffolk Rd, Cheltenham, **Gloucestershire**, GL50 2ED, ENG.
(T) 01242 584140
Speciality: Psychotherapy.
B (Ref:HM12201)

## LELJEVAHL, KARIN

**Karin Leljevahl**, Richmond Homoeopathic Clinic, St Matthieas Centre, Church Rd, Richmond, **Surrey**, TW10 6PN, ENG.
(T) 020 8940 9949
Speciality: Homeopathy.
● **Owner** Mrs K Leljevahl
M (Ref:HM12202)

## LELLIOTT, P E

**P E Lelliott**, 4 Warnham Gardens, Bexhill-on-Sea, **Sussex (East)**, TN39 3SP, ENG.
(T) 01424 843770
Speciality: Chiropodists (Podiatrists).
S (Ref:HM12203)

## LEMM, D M

**D M Lemm**, 80 Ashley Rd, Bloxwich, Walsall, **Midlands (West)**, WS3 2QF, ENG.
(T) 01922 421234
Speciality: Hypnosis.
B (Ref:HM12204)

## LEMMON, LINDA

**Linda Lemmon**, 31 Shenfield Rd, Brentwood, **Essex**, CM15 8AG, ENG.
(T) 01277 210664
Speciality: Homeopathy.
● **Partner** Mrs L Lemmon
M (Ref:HM12205)

## LEMON ST NTRL HLTH PRACTICE

**Lemon Street Natural Health Practice (The)**, 66 Lemon St, Truro, **Cornwall**, TR1 2PN, ENG.
(T) 01872 264064
Speciality: Acupuncture, Aromatherapy, Bach Remedies, Chinese Herbal Medicine, Chiropractic, Complementary Therapy, Herbal Medicine, Holistic Healing, Homeopathy, Hypnosis, Kinesiology, Massage (Therapeutic), Metamorphic Therapy, Psychotherapy, Reflexology, Reiki, Shiatsu, Vitamin Therapy.
● **Partner** Mr P Smith
C (Ref:HM12206)

## LEMON TREE TREATMENT ROOM

**Lemon Tree Treatment Room (The)**, Care Of Touche Hair Dressing Salon, 26 Woodcote Rd, Wallington, **Surrey**, SM6 0NN, ENG.
(T) 020 8647 2949
Speciality: Complementary Medicines & Therapy.
● **Owner** Ms T Luck
C M (Ref:HM12207)

## LEMON, RORY

**Rory Lemon**, 169 Elm Rd, New Malden, **Surrey**, KT3 3HX, ENG.
(T) 020 8942 1899
Speciality: Indian Head Massage, Massage (Therapeutic).
M (Ref:HM12208)

## LENA

**Lena**, 17 Barward Rd, Galston, **Ayrshire (East)**, KA4 8BX, SCO.
(T) 01563 822684
Speciality: Clairvoyants & Palmists.
● **Owner** Mrs J McEwan
B (Ref:HM12209)

## LENDRICK LODGE

**Lendrick Lodge & Yoga Healing Centre**, Brig 'O' Turk, Callander, **Perth and Kinross**, FK17 8HR, SCO.
(T) 01877 376263
(E) enquiries@lendricklodge.com
(W) www.lendricklodge.com
Speciality: Acupuncture, Aromatherapy, Massage (Therapeutic), Meditation, Reiki, Yoga, Shamanism, Colour Therapy and Mantra Sound Healing. ✓ CREDIT
● **Manager** Mr S Mulhearn
B C H S T
Yrs. Est.: 14 (Ref:HM12210)

## LENG, N R C

**N R C Leng**, 136 Harley St, London, **London (Greater)**, W1N 1AH, ENG.
(T) 020 7224 3513
Speciality: Psychology.
B (Ref:HM12211)

## LENNAN, CHRIS

**Chris Lennan**, 10 Springfield, Lightwater, **Surrey**, GU18 5XP, ENG.
(T) 01276 476551
Speciality: Reflexology.
● **Owner** Mrs C Lennan
S T (Ref:HM12212)

## LENNICK, JOY

**Joy Lennick**, 5 Belgravia Gardens, Hereford, **Herefordshire**, HR1 1RB, ENG.
(T) 01432 354058 (F) 01432 261346
Speciality: Chiropodists (Podiatrists).
● **Owner** Mrs J Lennick
S (Ref:HM12213)

## LENNIE, ANNE

**Anne Lennie**, 44 Bisley Rd, Stroud, **Gloucestershire**, GL5 1HF, ENG.
(T) 01453 750791
Speciality: Homeopathy.
● **Owner** Mrs A Lennie
M (Ref:HM12214)

## LENNON, JOY

**Joy Lennon**, Ashfield 66 Kincora Rd, Dublin, **County Dublin**, IRE.
(T) 01833 4356
Speciality: Complementary Medicines & Therapy.
M (Ref:HM12215)

## LENNON, MICHAEL

**Michael Lennon**, Galway Rd, Roscommon, **County Roscommon**, IRE.
(T) 09032 6023
Speciality: Acupuncture.
O (Ref:HM12216)

## LENNOX, CHRISTOPHER

**Christopher Lennox**, 32 Cordville Cl, Chaddesden, Derby, **Derbyshire**, DE21 6WX, ENG.
(T) 01332 609093
Speciality: Chiropodists (Podiatrists).
● **Owner** Mr C Lennox
S (Ref:HM12217)

## LENWORTH DAY THERAPY SERVICE

**Lenworth Day Therapy Service**, 135 Beaver Lane, Ashford, **Kent**, TN23 5NX, ENG.
(T) 01233 664229 (F) 01233 664229
Speciality: Complementary Medicines & Therapy.
● **Employee** Mrs V Booth
M (Ref:HM12218)

## LENZIE CLINIC

**Lenzie Clinic (The)**, The Tower, Garngaber Avenue, Kirkintilloch, Glasgow, **Glasgow (City of)**, G66 4LJ, SCO.
(T) 01417 761704
Speciality: Osteopathy.
● **Owner** Mr L Lowdin
P S T (Ref:HM12219)

## LEO FORTUNE TELLER

**Leo Fortune Teller**, 47 Prospect Drive, Ashgill, Larkhall, **Lanarkshire (South)**, ML9 3AJ, SCO.
(T) 01698 883327
Speciality: Clairvoyants & Palmists.
B (Ref:HM12220)

## LEOMINSTER OSTEOPATHS

**Leominster Osteopaths**, 6 Chapel Walk, Burgess St, Leominster, **Herefordshire**, HR6

8DE, ENG.
(T) 01568 610610 (F) 01568 610610
(E) lich22@hotmail.com
Speciality: Cranial Osteopathy, Macrobiotics, Naturopathy, Osteopathy, Buteyko Technique. ✓
● **Osteopath/Naturopath** Mr S Lichtenstein Q: DO, ND, RN. M: GOsC, RoN.
● **Osteopath** Ms P Kavallares Q: DO. M: GOsC.
● **Osteopath** Ms S Lansdale Q: DO. M: GOsC.
S Yrs. Est.: 17 (Ref:HM12221)

### LEON
**Leon**, 22 Market St, Southport, **Merseyside**, PR8 1HJ, ENG.
(T) 01704 544930
Speciality: Clairvoyants & Palmists.
● **Owner** Mr L Cohen
B (Ref:HM12222)

### LEONARD, CELINE
**Leonard Celine Ph D , Lic Ac**, 24 Hamilton St, Dublin, **County Dublin**, IRE.
(T) 01454 2140
Speciality: Complementary Medicines & Therapy.
M (Ref:HM12223)

### LEONARD, CHRIS
**Chris Leonard**, 108 Haverstock Hill, London, **London (Greater)**, NW3 2BD, ENG.
(T) 020 7485 1520
Speciality: Osteopathy.
P S T (Ref:HM12224)

### LEOPOLD MULLER REHAB CTRE
**Leopold Muller Rehabilitation Centre**, 7-9 Darlaston Rd, London, **London (Greater)**, SW19 4LF, ENG.
(T) 020 8947 5050 (F) 020 8947 5050
Speciality: Physiotherapy.
● **Owner** Ms A Ottie
P S T (Ref:HM12225)

### LERA, LOUISA
**Louisa Lera**, Nottingham Natural Health Centre, 354 Mansfield Rd, Nottingham, **Nottinghamshire**, NG5 2EF, ENG.
(T) 01159 608855
Speciality: Homeopathy.
M (Ref:HM12226)

### LERA, LOUISA
**Louisa Lera**, The Castle Clinic, 18-20 The Ropewalk, Nottingham, **Nottinghamshire**, NG1 5DT, ENG.
(T) 01159 472263 (F) 01159 556306
Speciality: Homeopathy.
● **Owner** Mr M Pook
M (Ref:HM12227)

### LERIGO, SYLVIA
**Sylvia Lerigo**, 2 Berryfield, Long Buckby, Northampton, **Northamptonshire**, NN6 7RQ, ENG.
(T) 01327 844100 (F) 01327 842427
Speciality: Hypnosis.
● **Owner** Mrs S Lerigo
B (Ref:HM12228)

### LEROUX
**Miss LeRoux**, Hillrise, Bramble Hill, Balcombe, Haywards Heath, **Sussex (West)**, RH17 6HR, ENG.
(T) 01444 811207
Speciality: Physiotherapy.
● **Owner** Miss B Leroux
P S T (Ref:HM12229)

### LEROY, C
**C Leroy**, 1 Roydon Rd, Diss, **Norfolk**, IP22 4LN, ENG.
(T) 01379 640370 (F) 01379 650020
Speciality: Chiropodists (Podiatrists).
● **Owner** Mrs C Leroy
S (Ref:HM12230)

### LERWICK CHIROPRACTIC CLINIC
**Lerwick Chiropractic Clinic**, 47 North Rd, Lerwick, **Shetland Islands**, ZE1 0NX, SCO.
(T) 01595 690500
Speciality: Chiropractic, Healing Therapy, Herbal Medicine, Postural Integration, Vitamin Therapy. ✓
● **Chiropractor** Dr E Madsen Q: BSc (Chiro), DC, MCC.
P Yrs. Est.: 8 (Ref:HM12231)

### LERWILL, SARAH
**Sarah Lerwill**, Holdstone Farm, Combe Martin, Ilfracombe, **Devon**, EX34 0PE, ENG.
(T) 01271 883423
Speciality: Chiropodists (Podiatrists).
S (Ref:HM12232)

### LESADD, JENNY
**Jenny Lesadd**, 56 Bruswick St, Walthamstow, London, **London (Greater)**, E17 9NB, ENG.
(T) 020 8520 1779
Speciality: Psychotherapy.
B (Ref:HM12233)

### LESKIN, RICHARD
**Richard Leskin**, The Haelan Clinic, 41 The Broadway, Crouch End, London, **London (Greater)**, N8 8DT, ENG.
(T) 020 8340 1518
Speciality: Complementary Medicines & Therapy.
● **Manager** Mr J Krahn
M (Ref:HM12234)

### LESKIN, RICHARD
**Richard Leskin**, 332 Long Lane, London, **London (Greater)**, N2 8JP, ENG.
(T) 020 8346 2285
Speciality: Complementary Medicines & Therapy.
● **Owner** Mr R Leskin
C M (Ref:HM12235)

### LESLEY WEIGHT MOBILE THERAPIST
**Lesley Weight Mobile Therapist**, 86 The Hoo, Harlow, **Essex**, CM17 0HR, ENG.
(T) 01279 304721
Speciality: Aromatherapy.
M O (Ref:HM12236)

### LESLEY'S REFLEXOLOGY
**Lesley's Reflexology**, Unit S13, West Midlands House, Gipsy Lane, Willenhall, **Midlands (West)**, WV13 2HA, ENG.
(T) 01902 482421
Speciality: Complementary Medicines & Therapy.
M (Ref:HM12237)

### LESLIE CLIFF
**Leslie Cliff**, 3 The Park, East Harling, Norwich, **Norfolk**, NR16 2LY, ENG.
(T) 01953 718374
Speciality: Hypnosis.
● **Owner** Mr L Cliff
B (Ref:HM12238)

### LESLIE MAYNERD
**Leslie Maynerd**, The Oakhouse Clinic, 80 Woodcote Rd, Caversham, Reading, **Berkshire**, RG4 7EX, ENG.
(T) 01189 476067 (F) 01189 475110
Speciality: Aromatherapy.
● **Owner** Mrs L Maynerd
M O (Ref:HM12239)

### LESLIE, CAROL
**Carol Leslie**, 21 Edinburgh Cl, Southwater, Horsham, **Sussex (West)**, RH13 7XB, ENG.
(T) 01403 732428
Speciality: Chiropodists (Podiatrists).
● **Employee** Mrs C Leslie
S (Ref:HM12240)

### LESLIE, PAM
**Pam Leslie**, 13A Weston Park, London, **London (Greater)**, N8 9SY, ENG.
(T) 020 8341 1543
Speciality: Aromatherapy.
● **Owner** Ms P Leslie
M O (Ref:HM12241)

### LESSELL, C B
**C B Lessell**, 122 High St, Kempston, Bedford, **Bedfordshire**, MK42 7BN, ENG.
(T) 01234 851775 (F) 01234 856572
Speciality: Homeopathy.
● **Owner** Dr C Lessell
M (Ref:HM12242)

### LESTER, JOHN
**John Lester**, 32 Derwent Rd, Basingstoke, **Hampshire**, RG22 5JB, ENG.
(T) 01256 327465
Speciality: Osteopathy.
● **Partner** Mr M Lester
P S T (Ref:HM12243)

### LESTER, MARK
**Mark Lester**, 32 Derwent Rd, Basingstoke, **Hampshire**, RG22 5JB, ENG.
(T) 01256 327465
Speciality: Osteopathy.
● **Partner** Mr M Lester
P S T (Ref:HM12244)

### LESZCZUK, PAULA
**Paula Leszczuk**, 22A Fishergate, York, **Yorkshire (North)**, YO10 4AB, ENG.
(T) 01904 641981
(E) leszczukpaula@aol
Speciality: Homeopathy. ✓
● **Homeopath** Ms P Leszczuk
(T) 01759 372563 Q: BSc (Hons), Dip.Hom. M: Soc.Hom.
B Yrs. Est.: 1 (Ref:HM12245)

### LESZCZUK, PAULA
**Paula Leszczuk**, The Market Place Clinic, Easingwold, **Yorkshire (North)**, ENG.
(T) 01759 372563
(E) leszczukpaula@aol
Speciality: Homeopathy. ✓
● **Homeopath** Ms P Leszczuk Q: BSc, Dip.Hom. M: Soc.Hom.
B Yrs. Est.: 1 (Ref:HM12246)

### LETCHWORTH CENTRE
**Letchworth Centre For Homoeopathy & Complementary Medicine**, Rosehill Hospital, Hitchin Rd, Letchworth, **Hertfordshire**, SG6 3NA, ENG.
(T) 01462 678804
Speciality: Osteopathy.
P S T (Ref:HM12247)

### LETCHWORTH-PHYSIOTHERAPY
**Letchworth Private Physiotherapy & Sports Injuries Clinic (The)**, 56A Station Rd, Letchworth, **Hertfordshire**, SG6 3BE, ENG.
(T) 01462 482009
Speciality: Physiotherapy. ✓
● **Owner/Physiotherapist** Mr G Smith Q: MCSP, SRP. M: CSP.
S Yrs. Est.: 10 (Ref:HM12248)

### LETHERBY, S
**S Letherby**, Boulevard Pharmacy, 23 Waterloo St, Weston-Super-Mare, **Somerset**, BS23 1LS, ENG.
(T) 01934 623898
Speciality: Chiropodists (Podiatrists).
S (Ref:HM12249)

### LETHEREN, V A
**V A Letheren**, 26 Amersham Rd, High Wycombe, **Buckinghamshire**, HP13 6QU, ENG.
(T) 01494 528691
Speciality: Physiotherapy.
P S T (Ref:HM12250)

### LETTERKENNY & CHINESE HERBAL
**Letterkenny & Chinese Herbal Clinic**, Ramelton Rd, Ballyraine, Letterkenny, **County Donegal**, IRE.
(T) 07424 559
Speciality: Complementary Medicines & Therapy.
M (Ref:HM12251)

### LETTERKENNY CHIROPRACTIC
**Letterkenny Chiropractic Clinic**, Glencar Rd, Letterkenny, **County Donegal**, IRE.
(T) 07425 207
Speciality: Chiropractors.
P S T (Ref:HM12252)

### LEVENE & ASSOCIATES
**B Levene & Associates**, 51 Milton Rd, Westcliff-on-Sea, **Essex**, SS0 7JP, ENG.
(T) 01702 337311
Speciality: Chiropodists (Podiatrists).
● **Owner** Mr B Levene
S (Ref:HM12253)

### LEVENE & ASSOCIATES
**B Levene & Associates**, 9 East St, Southend-



Key: B Mind-Body Medicine  C Complementary Medicine  H Self Help Treatment  M Medicinal Therapy  O Oriental Medicine  P Postural Therapy  S Manipulative Structural Therapy  T Touch Therapy

On-Sea, **Essex**, SS2 6LQ, ENG.
**(T)** 01702 467585
Speciality: Chiropodists (Podiatrists).
● **Manager** Mr B Levene
S (Ref:HM12254)

**LEVENE, L**

**L Levene**, 11 Rathbone Rd, Wavertree, Liverpool, **Merseyside**, L15 4HG, ENG.
**(T)** 01514 752323
Speciality: Hypnosis.
● **Owner** Mr L Levene
B (Ref:HM12255)

**LEVER CLINIC**

**Lever Clinic (The)**, 29 Fyfield Rd, Enfield, **London (Greater)**, EN1 3TT, ENG.
**(T)** 020 8366 0666 **(F)** 020 8366 0666
Speciality: Acupressure, Acupuncture, Electrotherapy, Manipulation, Massage (Therapeutic), Micro Manipulation, Nutritional Therapy, Osteopathy, Polarity Therapy, Postural Integration, Reflexology, Stress Therapy, Touch Therapy, Ultrasonics. ✔
● **Therapist** Mr D Van Wyk Q: Grad Dip Phys, MCSP. M: CSP.
S Yrs. Est.: 40 (Ref:HM12256)

**LEVER CLINIC**

**Lever Clinic**, 10 St Brelades Pl, St. Albans, **Hertfordshire**, AL4 9RG, ENG.
**(T)** 01727 868839
Speciality: Acupuncture.
● **Owner** Mr G Lever
O (Ref:HM12257)

**LEVER CLINIC**

**Lever Clinic (The)**, 5 St John's Church Rd, London, **London (Greater)**, E9 6EJ, ENG.
**(T)** 020 8985 4079
Speciality: Physiotherapy.
P S T (Ref:HM12258)

**LEVER CLINIC-ACU & OSTEOPATHY**

**Lever Clinic Of Acupuncture & Osteopathy**, 10 St Brelades Pl, Jersey Farm, St. Albans, **Hertfordshire**, AL3 5RA, ENG.
**(T)** 01727 868839
Speciality: Acupuncture.
O (Ref:HM12259)

**LEVER, A**

**A Lever**, 1 Vicarage Lane, Highworth, Swindon, **Wiltshire**, SN6 7AD, ENG.
**(T)** 01793 762734
Speciality: Clairvoyants & Palmists.
● **Owner** Mrs A Ades
B (Ref:HM12260)

**LEVER, I J**

**I J Lever**, 182A Dorchester Rd, Weymouth, **Dorset**, DT3 5HU, ENG.
**(T)** 01305 786893
Speciality: Osteopathy. ✔
● **Osteopath** Mr I Lever Q: DO. M: GOsC.
S Yrs. Est.: 24 (Ref:HM12261)

**LEVER, IAN J**

**Ian J Lever**, Old Stables, Grange Rd, Wareham, **Dorset**, BH20 5AL, ENG.
**(T)** 01929 551320
Speciality: Osteopathy.
P S T (Ref:HM12262)

**LEVER, JUDITH**

**Judith Lever**, 28 Hallowell Rd, Northwood, **London (Greater)**, HA6 1DN, ENG.
**(T)** 01923 827833
Speciality: Alexander Technique.
P S (Ref:HM12263)

**LEVER, R**

**R Lever**, 28 Hallowell Rd, Northwood, **London (Greater)**, HA6 1DN, ENG.
**(T)** 01923 827833
Speciality: Osteopathy.
P S T (Ref:HM12264)

**LEVICK, JENNIFER**

**Jennifer Levick**, Green Care Clinic, 146 Upperthorpe, Sheffield, **Yorkshire (South)**, S6 3NF, ENG.
**(T)** 01142 812100
Speciality: Reflexology.
S T (Ref:HM12265)

**LEVY, DAVID**

**David Levy**, 19 Woollards Lane, Great Shelford, Cambridge, **Cambridgeshire**, CB2 5LZ, ENG.
**(T)** 01223 834634
Speciality: Chiropodists (Podiatrists).
S (Ref:HM12266)

**LEVY, M**

**M Levy**, 155-175 Kenton Rd, Harrow, **London (Greater)**, HA3 0YX, ENG.
**(T)** 020 8907 6989
Speciality: Physiotherapy.
P S T (Ref:HM12267)

**LEVY, PAUL**

**Paul Levy**, 8 Micawber Way, Chelmsford, **Essex**, CM1 4UG, ENG.
**(T)** 01245 441745
Speciality: Chiropodists (Podiatrists).
● **Owner** Mr P Levy
S (Ref:HM12268)

**LEVY, PAUL**

**Paul Levy**, Unit 18 Bentalls Shopping Centre, Colchester Rd, Heybridge, Maldon, **Essex**, CM9 4GD, ENG.
**(T)** 01621 857931 **(F)** 01621 857931
**(W)** www.yell.co.uk/sites/chiroplevyp/
Speciality: Biomechanics, Chiropody, Cryo Surgery, Homeopathy, Nail Surgery, Orthotics, Podiatry. ✔
● **Owner/Chiropodist** Mr P Levy Q: DPodM, M.S.C.P, S.R.Ch.
M Yrs. Est.: 30 (Ref:HM12269)

**LEWES CHIROPODY**

**Lewes Chiropody (The)**, St Andrews Mews, St Andrews Lane, Lewes, **Sussex (East)**, BN7 1UW, ENG.
**(T)** 01273 475000
Speciality: Chiropodists (Podiatrists).
S (Ref:HM12270)

**LEWES CHIROPRACTIC CLINIC**

**Lewes Chiropractic Clinic**, St Andrews Mews, St Andrews Lane, Lewes, **Sussex (East)**, BN7 1UW, ENG.
**(T)** 01273 483327
Speciality: Chiropractic, Manipulation, X-Ray.
● **Chiropractor** Ms J Layton Q: DC. M: BCA.
● **Chiropractor** Mrs H Henriksen Q: CCSP, DC. M: BCA.
P Yrs. Est.: 10 (Ref:HM12271)

**LEWES THERAPY ROOMS**

**Lewes Therapy Rooms (The)**, St Andrews Mews, St Andrews Lane, Lewes, **Sussex (East)**, BN7 1UW, ENG.
**(T)** 01273 474450
Speciality: Complementary Medicines & Therapy.
● **Owner** Mrs S Bramsden
M (Ref:HM12272)

**LEWIN, ROCHELLE**

**Rochelle Lewin**, 43 Milton Drive, Borehamwood, **Hertfordshire**, WD6 2BA, ENG.
**(T)** 020 8207 1670
Speciality: Art Therapy, Counselling, Dance Movement Therapy, Drama Therapy, Group Therapy, Life Style Coaching, Visualisation Therapy, Elements of the therapies marked are used as and when they are needed.
● **Personal Development Consultant** Ms R Lewin
H Yrs. Est.: 12 (Ref:HM12273)

**LEWIN, SANDRA**

**Sandra Lewin**, 22 Cranwell Gr, Shepperton, **Surrey**, TW17 0JR, ENG.
**(T)** 01932 889787
Speciality: Reflexology.
S T (Ref:HM12274)

**LEWINTON, EVELYN**

**Evelyn Lewinton**, 15 Hamilton Rd, Evesham, **Worcestershire**, WR11 6XE, ENG.
**(T)** 01386 45948
Speciality: Reflexology.
S T (Ref:HM12275)

**LEWIS ANDERSON ASSOCIATES**

**Lewis Anderson Associates**, 28 Grosvenor St, London, **London (Greater)**, W1X 9FE, ENG.
**(T)** 020 7917 9656 **(F)** 020 7917 6002
Speciality: Psychology.
● **Partner** Ms P Anderson
B (Ref:HM12276)

**LEWIS CLINIC**

**Lewis Clinic For Counselling & Hypnotherapy (The)**, 1-7 Harley St, London, **London (Greater)**, W1N 1DA, ENG.
**(T)** 020 7636 1820
Speciality: Complementary Medicines & Therapy.
C M (Ref:HM12277)

**LEWIS, ALUN**

**Alun Lewis**, 4 Lewis Cres, Llanelli, **Carmarthenshire**, SA14 9EW, WAL.
**(T)** 01554 773586
Speciality: Physiotherapy.
● **Owner** Mr A Lewis
P S T (Ref:HM12278)

**LEWIS, ANDREW J**

**Andrew J Lewis**, Greyhill Surgery, Woodstock Way, Caldicot, **Monmouthshire**, NP26 5DB, WAL.
**(T)** 01291 424833
Speciality: Osteopathy.
● **Owner** Mr A Lewis
P S T (Ref:HM12279)

**LEWIS, B**

**B Lewis**, Fleetwood, Poplar Gr, Woking, **Surrey**, GU22 7SD, ENG.
**(T)** 01483 830908
Speciality: Physiotherapy.
● **Owner** Mr B Lewis
P S T (Ref:HM12280)

**LEWIS, BERYL**

**Beryl Lewis**, 12 Highlands, 131 Oakleigh Rd North, London, **London (Greater)**, N20 9HA, ENG.
**(T)** 020 8445 1615
Speciality: Reflexology.
S T (Ref:HM12281)

**LEWIS, BRIAN**

**Brian Lewis**, 16 Glamis Cl, Woodhall Farm, Hemel Hempstead, **Hertfordshire**, HP2 7QB, ENG.
**(T)** 01442 211223
Speciality: Osteopathy.
P S T (Ref:HM12282)

**LEWIS, C**

**C Lewis**, 6 Laustan Cl, Guildford, **Surrey**, GU1 2TS, ENG.
**(T)** 01483 569637
Speciality: Acupuncture.
O (Ref:HM12283)

**LEWIS, CAROL**

**Carol Lewis**, 10 Balgowan St, London, **London (Greater)**, SE18 1ED, ENG.
**(T)** 020 8855 9266
Speciality: Homeopathy.
● **Owner** Mrs C Lewis
M (Ref:HM12284)

**LEWIS, CARYN**

**Caryn Lewis**, 9 Kipling Drive, Larkfield, Aylesford, **Kent**, ME20 6UJ, ENG.
**(T)** 01732 844441
Speciality: Osteopathy.
P S T (Ref:HM12285)

**LEWIS, CATERINA**

**Caterina Lewis**, 8 Robin Hill, Dinas Powys, **Glamorgan (Vale of)**, CF64 4TF, WAL.
**(T)** 029 2051 5248
Speciality: Aromatherapy.
● **Partner** Mrs C Lewis
M O (Ref:HM12286)

**LEWIS, CHRISTIAN**

**Christian Lewis**, Physiotherapy Clinic, 10 Elm Rd, Bishop's Stortford, **Hertfordshire**, CM23 2SS, ENG.
**(T)** 01279 657558
Speciality: Physiotherapy.



Key continued: Yrs.Est: Years Established Q: Qualifications M: Professional Membership ✔ Indemnity Insurance Accept Credit Cards

● **Owner** Mr C Lewis
**P S T** (**Ref:**HM12287)

### LEWIS, D J S

**D J S Lewis**, Sandford House, 3 Tranmere Cl, Lymington, **Hampshire**, SO41 3QQ, ENG.
(T) 01590 670033
(E) lewisdhom@aol.com
Speciality: Bach Remedies, Homeopathy, Kinesiology, Reiki. ✔
● **Classical Homeopath** Mr D Lewis
Q: Dip.Hom. M: Soc.Hom.
**M** Yrs. Est.: 5 (**Ref:**HM12288)

### LEWIS, D MICHAEL

**D Michael Lewis**, 34 Portland St, Aberystwyth, **Ceredigion**, SY23 2DX, WAL.
(T) 01970 615153
Speciality: Chiropody. ✔
● **Chiropodist** Mr D Lewis Q: M.S.C.P, S.R.Ch.
**C M** Yrs. Est.: 25 (**Ref:**HM12289)

### LEWIS, DAVID

**David Lewis**, Lymington, **Hampshire**, SO41, ENG.
(T) 01590 670033
Speciality: Homeopathy.
**M** (**Ref:**HM12290)

### LEWIS, ERIC R

**Eric R Lewis**, 11 Station Rd, London, **London (Greater)**, N21 3SB, ENG.
(T) 020 8360 2717
Speciality: Physiotherapy.
**P S T** (**Ref:**HM12291)

### LEWIS, F M K

**F M K Lewis**, 19 Shelvers Hill, Tadworth, **Surrey**, KT20 5PU, ENG.
(T) 01737 813115
Speciality: Physiotherapy.
● **Owner** Mr A Kirby
**P S T** (**Ref:**HM12292)

### LEWIS, GERRY

**Gerry Lewis**, 6 Chapel Cl, Pwllmeyric, Chepstow, **Monmouthshire**, NP16 6HW, WAL.
(T) 01291 626037
Speciality: Physiotherapy.
● **Owner** Mr G Lewis
**P S T** (**Ref:**HM12293)

### LEWIS, GILL

**Gill Lewis**, 15 Beech Rd, Purley On Thames, Reading, **Berkshire**, RG8 8DR, ENG.
(T) 01189 843473 (F) 01189 843473
Speciality: Chiropractic.
● **Owner** Ms G Lewis
**P S T** (**Ref:**HM12294)

### LEWIS, HELEN

**Helen Lewis**, 22 Little Common, Stanmore, **London (Greater)**, HA7 3BZ, ENG.
(T) 020 8954 7251
Speciality: Clairvoyants & Palmists.
● **Owner** Mrs H Lewis
**B** (**Ref:**HM12295)

### LEWIS, JACQUELINE

**Jacqueline Lewis**, 29 Claremont Drive, Market Harborough, **Leicestershire**, LE16 8BX, ENG.
(T) 01858 433020
Speciality: Massage (Therapeutic). ✔
● **Owner/Therapeutic Massage**
Mrs J Lewis Q: MIPTI. M: IPTI.
**C** Yrs. Est.: 8 (**Ref:**HM12296)

### LEWIS, JACQUELINE

**Jacqueline Lewis**, 19 Logan St, Market Harborough, **Leicestershire**, LE16 9AW, ENG.
(T) 01858 433020
Speciality: Complementary Medicines & Therapy.
**C M** (**Ref:**HM12297)

### LEWIS, JAN

**Jan Lewis**, The Terrace, 35 Staplegrove Rd, Taunton, **Somerset**, TA1 1DG, ENG.
(T) 01823 322032
Speciality: Homeopathy.
**M** (**Ref:**HM12298)

### LEWIS, JANET

**Janet Lewis**, 43 Fieldhead Gardens, Bourne End, **Buckinghamshire**, SL8 5RN, ENG.
(T) 01628 810187
Speciality: Reflexology.
● **Owner** Ms J Lewis
**S T** (**Ref:**HM12299)

### LEWIS, JULIE

**Julie Lewis**, Blackheath Osteopathy & Acupuncture Clinic, 19 Tranquil Vale, London, **London (Greater)**, SE3 0BU, ENG.
(T) 020 8852 1706
Speciality: Osteopathy.
**P S T** (**Ref:**HM12300)

### LEWIS, K

**K Lewis**, 4 Crofts Cl, Chiddingfold, Godalming, **Surrey**, GU8 4SG, ENG.
(T) 01428 684674
Speciality: Physiotherapy.
● **Owner** Mrs K Lewis
**P S T** (**Ref:**HM12301)

### LEWIS, KEN

**Ken Lewis**, 7 Brown Heath Rd, Waverton, Chester, **Cheshire**, CH3 7PP, ENG.
(T) 01244 336744
Speciality: Psychology.
● **Principal** Mr K Lewis
**B** (**Ref:**HM12302)

### LEWIS, MAGGIE

**Maggie Lewis**, 32 Oxford Rd, Cowley, Oxford, **Oxfordshire**, OX4 2DS, ENG.
(T) 01865 718059
Speciality: Psychotherapy.
**B** (**Ref:**HM12303)

### LEWIS, MARK

**Mark Lewis**, 185a Torridon Rd, London, **London (Greater)**, SE6 1RG, ENG.
(T) 020 8480 9905
Speciality: Hypnotherapy.
● **Owner** Ms L Griffin
**B** (**Ref:**HM12304)

### LEWIS, MYRA

**Myra Lewis**, Starley Rd, Coventry, **Midlands (West)**, CV1 3JU, ENG.
(T) 024 7655 0683
Speciality: Aromatherapy. ✔
● **Aromatherapist** Myra Lewis Q: IIHHT.
M: IIHHT.
**C** Yrs. Est.: 7 (**Ref:**HM12305)

### LEWIS, P J

**P J Lewis**, 21 High St, Shepperton, **Surrey**, TW17 9AJ, ENG.
(T) 01932 786473 (F) 01932 230900
Speciality: Chiropodists (Podiatrists).
● **Owner** Mr P Lewis
**S** (**Ref:**HM12306)

### LEWIS, P M

**P M Lewis**, 1 Somerset Pl, Merthyr Tydfil, **Glamorgan (Vale of)**, CF47 0DU, WAL.
(T) 01685 722137
Speciality: Physiotherapy.
● **Practice Manager** Mr P Lewis
**P S T** (**Ref:**HM12307)

### LEWIS, PETER

**Peter Lewis**, 8 Robin Hill, Dinas Powys, **Glamorgan (Vale of)**, CF64 4TF, WAL.
(T) 029 2051 5248
Speciality: Reflexology.
● **Partner** Mr P Lewis
**S T** (**Ref:**HM12308)

### LEWIS, REBECCA

**Rebecca Lewis**, 53A Washway Rd, Sale, **Cheshire**, M33 7AB, ENG.
(T) 01619 052134
Speciality: Chiropodists (Podiatrists).
**S** (**Ref:**HM12309)

### LEWIS, RHODA

**Rhoda Lewis**, St Bedes Chambers, Albert Rd, Jarrow, **Tyne and Wear**, NE32 5RR, ENG.
(T) 01914 220209
Speciality: Homeopathy.
● **Owner** Mrs R Lewis
**M** (**Ref:**HM12310)

### LEWIS, RICHARD

**Richard Lewis**, 63 Franciscan Rd, Tooting Bec, London, **London (Greater)**, SW17 8EA, ENG.
(T) 020 8672 5035
Speciality: Psychotherapy.
● **Owner** Mr R Lewis
**B** (**Ref:**HM12311)

### LEWIS, S M

**S M Lewis**, 64 Walter Rd, Swansea, SA1 4PT, WAL.
(T) 01792 643815
Speciality: Physiotherapy.
● **Owner** Mrs S Lewis
**P S T** (**Ref:**HM12312)

### LEWIS, SARAH

**Sarah Lewis**, 7 Fyfield Way, Littleton, Winchester, **Hampshire**, SO22 6PB, ENG.
(T) 01962 882304
Speciality: Reflexology.
**S T** (**Ref:**HM12313)

### LEWIS-FRY, K E

**K E Lewis-Fry**, 22 Carbery Avenue, Bournemouth, **Dorset**, BH6 3LF, ENG.
(T) 01202 420919
Speciality: Chiropodists (Podiatrists).
● **Owner** Mrs K Lewis-Fry
**S** (**Ref:**HM12314)

### LEWISHAM FOOT CLINIC

**Lewisham Foot Clinic (The)**, 3 Courthill Rd, London, **London (Greater)**, SE13 6DN, ENG.
(T) 020 8297 9631 (F) 020 8852 3507
Speciality: Chiropodists (Podiatrists).
● **Practice Manager**
Mrs D McCullough
**S** (**Ref:**HM12315)

### LEWISHAM OSTEOPATHIC PRACTICE

**Lewisham Osteopathic Practice**, 312-314 Lewisham Rd, London, **London (Greater)**, SE13 7PA, ENG.
(T) 020 8852 5577
Speciality: Osteopathy.
**P S T** (**Ref:**HM12316)

### LEWORTHY, M

**M Leworthy**, Ashdown Osteopathic Centre, The Sq, Lewes Rd, Forest Row, **Sussex (East)**, RH18 5ES, ENG.
(T) 01342 822505 (F) 01342 822505
Speciality: Osteopathy.
● **Owner** Mr T Strutt
**P S T** (**Ref:**HM12317)

### LEY, ALISON

**Alison Ley**, 33 Northgate, Canterbury, **Kent**, CT1 1BL, ENG.
(T) 01227 451317
Speciality: Osteopathy.
**P S T** (**Ref:**HM12318)

### LEYLAND PHYSIOTHERAPY CENTRE

**Leyland Physiotherapy Centre (The)**, 83 Bow Lane, Leyland, **Lancashire**, PR25 4YB, ENG.
(T) 01772 435235
Speciality: Acupuncture, Physiotherapy. ✔
● **Physiotherapist** Mrs L Lea Q: MCSP, SRP.
M: CSP.
● **Physiotherapist** Ms M Horton Q: MCSP, SRP.
M: CSP.
**S** (**Ref:**HM12319)

### LEYSON, S & I

**I M U & S M D Leyson**, Coachhouse, Ynysllynlladd, Cadoxton, Neath, **Glamorgan (Vale of)**, SA10 8DA, WAL.
(T) 01639 643233
Speciality: Chiropractic.
**P S T** (**Ref:**HM12320)

### LEYSON, S & I

**I M U & S M D Leyson**, Gwendwr, 16 Uplands Cresent, Uplands, Swansea, SA2 0PB, WAL.
(T) 01792 476644
Speciality: Chiropractic.
**P S T** (**Ref:**HM12321)

### LI (PROFESSOR)

**Professor Li**, 62 Hughenden Rd, High Wycombe, **Buckinghamshire**, HP13 5DU, ENG.
(T) 01494 531164
Speciality: Acupuncture.
● **Owner** Mr G Li
**O** (**Ref:**HM12322)

Key: **B** Mind-Body Medicine **C** Complementary Medicine **H** Self Help Treatment **M** Medicinal Therapy **O** Oriental Medicine **P** Postural Therapy **S** Manipulative Structural Therapy **T** Touch Therapy

## LI, G Q (DR)

**Dr G Q Li**, 2 Boyn Valley Rd, Maidenhead, **Berkshire**, SL6 4ED, ENG.
(T) 01628 672005
Speciality: Acupuncture.
● **Owner** Mr H Lye
O (Ref:HM12323)

## LIBERTY CLINIC

**Liberty Clinic (The)**, 394 Romford Rd, London, **London (Greater)**, E7 8DF, ENG.
(T) 020 8552 6063 (F) 020 8470 6250
Speciality: Osteopathy.
● **Practice Manager** Mr L Bennett
P S T (Ref:HM12324)

## LIBRA AROMATICS

**Libra Aromatics**, 34 Holme Ter, Wigan, **Lancashire**, WN1 2HG, ENG.
(T) 01942 239794
Speciality: Aromatherapy.
● **Owner** Mr A McKann
M O (Ref:HM12325)

## LIBRA HEALTH BACK PAIN CENTRE

**Libra Health Back Pain Centre Sketchley Hall**, Manor Way, Burbage, Hinckley, **Leicestershire**, LE10 3HT, ENG.
(T) 01455 890023 (F) 01455 636282
Speciality: Physiotherapy.
● **General Manager** Mrs C Starkey
P S T (Ref:HM12326)

## LIBRA HOLISTIC THERAPY

**Libra Holistic Therapy**, 8 Market St, Kirkby Lonsdale, Carnforth, **Lancashire**, LA6 2AU, ENG.
(T) 01524 271208
Speciality: Complementary Medicines & Therapy.
● **Owner** Mrs A Blackmore-Tucker
C M (Ref:HM12327)

## LIBRA THERAPY CENTRE

**Libra Therapy Centre**, 153 Queen St, Whitehaven, **Cumbria**, CA28 7BA, ENG.
(T) 01946 599611
Speciality: Acupressure, Aromatherapy, Osteopathy, Reflexology, Lecture of Complementary Therapy. ✓
● **Owner/Complementary Therapist** Mr P Barry Q: BSc. M: IHBC.
● **Osteopath** Mr Q Howarth
C S Yrs. Est.: 12 (Ref:HM12328)

## LICHFIELD ELECTROLYSIS CLINIC

**Lichfield Electrolysis Clinic**, 30A Bird St, Lichfield, **Staffordshire**, WS13 6PR, ENG.
(T) 01543 250192
Speciality: Electrolysis.
● **Owner** Mrs R Bayliss
T (Ref:HM12329)

## LIDDELL, D

**D Liddell**, 6 Westbourne Rd, Hartlepool, **Cleveland**, TS25 5RE, ENG.
(T) 01429 861339
Speciality: Osteopathy.
P S T (Ref:HM12330)

## LIDDELL-SMITH, P J

**P J Liddell-Smith**, 3 Briarwood, Finchampstead, Wokingham, **Berkshire**, RG40 4XA, ENG.
(T) 01189 328511
Speciality: Chiropodists (Podiatrists).
● **Owner** Mrs P Liddell-Smith
S (Ref:HM12331)

## LIDSTER, CAROL

**Carol Lidster**, 25 Lower Gungate, Tamworth, **Staffordshire**, B79 7AT, ENG.
(T) 01827 68374
Speciality: Acupuncture.
O (Ref:HM12332)

## LIEBERMAN, JACOB

**Jacob Lieberman**, 13 Kinburn St, London, **London (Greater)**, SE16 6DN, ENG.
(T) 020 7252 0936 (F) 020 7252 0936
Speciality: Osteopathy.
● **Partner** Mr J Lieberman
P S T (Ref:HM12333)

## LIEGIS-JOHNSTON, S

**S Liegis-Johnston**, 16 Hextol Trce, Hexham, **Northumberland**, NE46 2DF, ENG.
(T) 01434 601368
Speciality: Complementary Medicines & Therapy.
C M (Ref:HM12334)

## LIFE

**Life Pregnancy Care Service**, 26A Guildhall St, Lincoln, **Lincolnshire**, LN1 1TR, ENG.
(T) 01522 527040
Speciality: Counselling, Pre and Post Abortion Counselling, Miscarriage Counselling.
H (Ref:HM12335)

## LIFE & HEALTH MANAGEMENT

**Life & Health Management**, 5 Mayfield Avenue, Southgate, London, **London (Greater)**, N14 6DY, ENG.
(T) 020 8886 4774
Speciality: Physiotherapy.
● **Director** Ms C Adams
P S T (Ref:HM12336)

## LIFE BY DESIGN

**Life By Design**, St Georges House, 44 Hatton Garden, London, **London (Greater)**, EC1N 8ER, ENG.
(T) 020 7242 1422
Speciality: Hypnotherapy.
● **Director** Mr P Phillips
B (Ref:HM12337)

## LIFE CARING CENTRE

**Pontypridd Life Group**, 2 Church St, Pontypridd, **Rhondda Cynon Taff**, CF37 4DD, WAL.
(T) 01443 402051
(W) www.lifeuk.org
Speciality: Counselling.
H (Ref:HM12338)

## LIFE CENTRE

**Life Centre (The)**, 15 Edge St, London, **London (Greater)**, W8 7PM, ENG.
(T) 020 7221 4602
Speciality: Acupuncture.
● **Manageress** Miss S Wilson
O (Ref:HM12339)

## LIFE CHANGES

**Life Changes**, 72 Cole Park Rd, Twickenham, **London (Greater)**, TW1 1HU, ENG.
(T) 020 8395 7977
Speciality: Hypnosis.
B (Ref:HM12340)

## LIFE CRYSTALS

**Life Crystals (UK) Ltd**, 156 Camden High St, London, **London (Greater)**, NW1 0NE, ENG.
(T) 020 7267 2112
Speciality: Complementary Medicines & Therapy.
C M (Ref:HM12341)

## LIFE FOUNDATION SCHOOL

**Life Foundation School Of Therapeutics**, Maristowe, Dover St, Bilston, **Midlands (West)**, WV14 6AL, ENG.
(T) 01902 409164 (F) 01902 497362
Speciality: Complementary Medicines & Therapy.
● **Accountant** Mr G Turner
C M (Ref:HM12342)

## LIFE FOUNDATION SCHOOL

**Life Foundation School Of Theraputics**, 1 Harden Pl, Edinburgh, **Edinburgh (City of)**, EH11 1JD, SCO.
(T) 01312 293591
Speciality: Complementary Medicines & Therapy.
● **Manager** Mrs E Rowans
C M (Ref:HM12343)

## LIFE GUIDANCE

**Life Guidance**, Berkley House, 31 Bower Way, Slough, **Berkshire**, SL1 5HW, ENG.
(T) 01628 660899
(W) www.lifeguidance.co.uk
Speciality: Cognitive Therapy, Counselling, Dowsing, Hypnosis, Hypnotherapy, Psychotherapy, Reiki, Stress Therapy, Visualisation Therapy, Tarot and Astrology. ✓
● **Hypnotherapist** Ms A Jirschitzka Q: Dip.Hyp, Reiki Master. M: HA.
B Yrs. Est.: 12 (Ref:HM12344)

## LIFE 'N' LIMB

**Life 'N' Limb**, Lormore, Eastcliff, Porthtowan, Truro, **Cornwall**, TR4 8AW, ENG.
(T) 01209 890910
Speciality: Aromatherapy, Massage (Therapeutic), Tui Na. ✓
● **Owner/Holistic Aromatherapist** Ms N Mitchell Q: AOC, ITEC. M: GCP.
C Yrs. Est.: 3 (Ref:HM12345)

## LIFE 'N' LIMB

**Life 'N' Limb**, 3 Bond St, Redruth, **Cornwall**, TR15 2QA, ENG.
(T) 01209 215012
Speciality: Acupressure, Aromatherapy, Complementary Therapy, Holistic Healing, Inhalation Therapy, Manipulation, Massage (Therapeutic), Stress Therapy, Touch Therapy, Tui Na. ✓ CREDIT
● **Holistic Aromatherapist** Ms N Mitchell
(T) 01209 890910 Q: ITEC. M: AOC, GCP.
T Yrs. Est.: 3 (Ref:HM12346)

## LIFE NATURAL THERAPY CENTRE

**Life Natural Therapy Centre**, Lindum House, High St, Barrow-upon-Humber, **Humberside**, DN19 7AA, ENG.
(T) 01469 532399 (F) 01469 532132
Speciality: Complementary Medicines & Therapy.
● **Owner** Mrs R Crampin
M (Ref:HM12347)

## LIFE PREGNANCY CARE CENTRE

**Life Pregnancy Care Centre**, 22a St Andrews St, Cambridge, **Cambridgeshire**, CB2 3AX, ENG.
(T) 01223 316300
Speciality: Complementary Medicines & Therapy.
M (Ref:HM12348)

## LIFE STYLE NATURAL HEALTH CTRE

**Life Style Natural Health Centre**, The Hersham Centre, Hersham, Walton-On-Thames, **Surrey**, KT12 4HL, ENG.
(T) 01932 254624
Speciality: Aromatherapy, Chiropody, Herbal Medicine, Homeopathy, Iridology, Massage (Therapeutic), Nutritional Therapy, Psychotherapy, Reflexology, Remedial Massage, Swedish Body Massage, Bioresonence Therapy.
C (Ref:HM12349)

## LIFE TREE

**Life Tree**, 37 Spencer Rd, Derry, **County Londonderry**, BT47 6AA, NIR.
(T) 028 7134 2865 (F) 028 7134 7880
(E) shop@tinyworld.co.uk
(W) www.goodhealth-lifetree.co.uk
Speciality: Allergy Testing, Aromatherapy, Bach Remedies, Hay Diet, Herbal Medicine, Homeopathy, Indian Head Massage, Kinesiology. ✓ CREDIT
● **Natural Therapist** Mrs A Munro Q: LLSA. M: BIAET, IFA, IScB.
M Yrs. Est.: 15 (Ref:HM12350)

## LIFECHANGERS

**Lifechangers**, 87 Station Rd, Ilkeston, **Derbyshire**, DE7 5LJ, ENG.
(T) 01159 321537
Speciality: Psychotherapy.
● **Owner** Mr S Hellen
B (Ref:HM12351)

## LIFE-ENERGIES

**Life-Energies International Plc**, The Coach House, The Avenue, Odstock, Salisbury, **Wiltshire**, SP5 4JA, ENG.
(T) 01722 340221 (F) 01722 349468
(E) tecvet@life-energies.com
(W) www.life-energies.com
Speciality: Aromatherapy, Bio-energetics, Holistic Healing, Indian Head Massage, Kinesiology, Massage (Therapeutic), Nutritional Therapy, Orgone Therapy, Reflexology, Stress Therapy, Vitamin Therapy, Yoga, Skenar Therapy. ✓ CREDIT
● **Director** Gillian Barker



Key continued: Yrs.Est: Years Established Q: Qualifications M: Professional Membership ✓ Indemnity Insurance CREDIT Accept Credit Cards

- **Director** Mr R Meacock **Q:** BVSc, MRCVS. **M:** BVA.
- **Therapist** Thelma Judson
- **Therapist** Jo Vere Nicoll

**B** Yrs. Est.: 3 (**Ref:**HM12352)

## LIFELINE

**Lifeline**, 29 St Edwen Gardens, Cardiff, **Glamorgan (Vale of)**, CF14 4JZ, **WAL**.
(T) 029 2062 0123
Speciality: Reflexology.
- **Owner** Mrs H Venn

**S T** (**Ref:**HM12353)

## LIFELINE

**Lifeline**, 23 Osprey, Orton Goldhay, Peterborough, **Cambridgeshire**, PE2 5FW, **ENG**.
(T) 01733 238676 (F) 01733 361554
Speciality: Cognitive Therapy, Counselling, Gestalt Therapy, Group Therapy, Life Style Coaching, Music Therapy, Psychotherapy, Spiritual Healing, Stress Therapy.
- **Psychologist** Mr L Phillips **Q:** BA (Hons).

**B** Yrs. Est.: 15 (**Ref:**HM12354)

## LIFELINES

**Lifelines**, The Ridgeway, St. Albans, **Hertfordshire**, AL4 9NR, **ENG**.
(T) 01727 760781 (F) 01727 866022
(E) daphane@lifelines.fsnet.co.uk
Speciality: Spiritual Healing, Stress Therapy, Relaxation, Assertiveness Training. ✔
- **Owner/Spiritual Healer** Mrs D Harris **Q:** Cert.Ed, MISMA. **M:** NFSH.

**C** Yrs. Est.: 8 (**Ref:**HM12355)

## LIFEQUEST

**Lifequest**, Sevendale House, 7 Dale St, Manchester, **Manchester (Greater)**, M1 1JA, **ENG**.
(T) 01612 280220
Speciality: Complementary Medicines & Therapy.
- **Director** Mr J Callaghan

**C M** (**Ref:**HM12356)

## LIFE'S ESSENTIALS

**Life's Essentials**, 20 Duart Drive, East Kilbride, Glasgow, **Glasgow (City of)**, G74 4BJ, **SCO**.
(T) 01355 579770
Speciality: Aromatherapy.

**M O** (**Ref:**HM12357)

## LIFE'S OPTION

**Life's Option**, 51 Foxland Cl, Shirley, Solihull, **Midlands (West)**, B90 4HL, **ENG**.
(T) 01564 703408
Speciality: Aromatherapy. ✔
- **Aromatherapist** Susie Pierce **Q:** ITEC. **M:** ITEC.

**C** Yrs. Est.: 10 (**Ref:**HM12358)

## LIFESOLUTIONS

**Lifesolutions**, 8 Balmoral Cres, Dronfield Woodhouse, Dronfield, **Derbyshire**, S18 8ZY, **ENG**.
(T) 01246 416544 (F) 01246 416544
(E) carolewan@aol.com
(W) www.lifesolutions.org.uk
Speciality: Auto Suggestion, Autogenic Training, Cognitive Therapy, Complementary Therapy, Counselling, Hypnosis, Hypnotherapy, Life Style Coaching, Neuro-Linguistic Program, Psychotherapy, Stress Therapy, Visualisation Therapy, Eye Movement Desensitisation & Reprocessing (EMDR), Meridian Therapies, Emotional Freedom Technique (EFT). ✔
- **Partner** Ms C Wan **Q:** Dip.Hyp, EMDR L1-L2. **M:** HA, NHR.
- **Partner** Mr R Russell

(T) 01476 585898
**H** Yrs. Est.: 9 (**Ref:**HM12359)

## LIFESOURCE

**Lifesource Ltd**, Old Acres, Station Lane, Farnsfield, Newark, **Nottinghamshire**, NG22 8LB, **ENG**.
(T) 01623 883319
Speciality: Complementary Medicines & Therapy.
- **Marketing Director** Sarah Louise Illingworth

**C M** (**Ref:**HM12360)

## LIFESPRING PRODUCTS

**Lifespring Products**, 111 Cliftonville Rd, Belfast, **County Antrim**, BT14 6JQ, **NIR**.
(T) 028 9075 3658 (F) 028 9074 8236
Speciality: Complementary Medicines & Therapy.
- **Managing Director** Mr D Baulter

**C M** (**Ref:**HM12361)

## LIFESTYLE

**Lifestyle**, 15 Mary Rd, Wells, **Somerset**, BA5 2NF, **ENG**.
(T) 01749 674818
Speciality: Complementary Medicines & Therapy.
- **Owner** Mrs M Duncan

**C M** (**Ref:**HM12362)

## LIFESTYLE FOOTCARE

**Lifestyle Footcare**, Alder House, Station Rd, Endon, Stoke-On-Trent, **Staffordshire**, ST9 9DR, **ENG**.
(T) 01782 503002
Speciality: Chiropodists (Podiatrists).
- **Senior Partner** Mr A Hulm

**S** (**Ref:**HM12363)

## LIFESTYLE MANAGEMENT

**Lifestyle Management**, 58A Wimpole St, London, **London (Greater)**, W1M 7DE, **ENG**.
(T) 020 7935 1965
Speciality: Hypnosis.

**B** (**Ref:**HM12364)

## LIFESTYLE MEDICINE

**Lifestyle Medicine**, 11 Tarbolton Rd, Dundonald, Kilmarnock, **Ayrshire (East)**, KA2 9HQ, **SCO**.
(T) 01563 850263
Speciality: Osteopathy.
- **Owner** Mr A Lee

**P S T** (**Ref:**HM12365)

## LIFESUPPORT

**Lifesupport**, Kirkbymoorside Natural Health Centre, Tinley Garth, Kirkbymoorside, York, **Yorkshire (North)**, YO62 6AR, **ENG**.
(T) 01751 430335 (F) 01751 430335
(E) angieatlifesupport@care4free.net
Speciality: Absent Healing, Acupressure, Acupuncture, Alexander Technique, Aromatherapy, Auto Suggestion, Chiropractic, Counselling, Crystal Healing, Healer, Hypnotherapy, Indian Head Massage, Kinesiology, Macrobiotics, Massage (Therapeutic), Metamorphic Therapy, Moxibustion, Nutritional Therapy, Oriental Diagnosis, Reflexology, Reiki, Seichem, Stress Therapy, Tera-Mai, Visualisation Therapy, Yoga, Feng Shui, Emotional Freedom Technique. ✔
- **Owner/Reflexologist** Ms J Sampson **Q:** Dip.Reflex. **M:** RxS.

**B** Yrs. Est.: 1 (**Ref:**HM12366)

## LIFE-WAYS

**Life-Ways**, 30 Albany Rd, Stratford-Upon-Avon, **Warwickshire**, CV37 9LB, **ENG**.
(T) 01789 292052
Speciality: Homeopathy. ✔
- **Homeopath** Ms A McIntyre **Q:** LCPH. **M:** HMA.

**M** Yrs. Est.: 6 (**Ref:**HM12367)

## LIFE-WORK POTENTIAL

**Jane Thurnell-Read T/A Life-Work Potential**, Sea View House, Long Rock, Penzance, **Cornwall**, TR20 8JF, **ENG**.
(T) 01736 719030 (F) 01736 719040
(E) jane@lifeworkpotential.com
(W) www.healthk.co.uk
Speciality: Kinesiology. ✔
- **Health Kinesiologist** Ms J Thernell-Read **M:** KFRP.

**B C** Yrs. Est.: 18 (**Ref:**HM12368)

## LIGHT TOUCH THERAPY TRAINING

**Susanna Terry - Light Touch Therapy Training**, Well Park, Belstone, Okehampton, **Devon**, EX20 1QZ, **ENG**.
(T) 01837 840718 (F) 01837 840718
(E) susanna@lightouch.co.uk
(W) www.lightouch.co.uk
Speciality: Complementary Therapy, Counselling, Homeopathy, Rogerian Therapy, Stress Therapy, Touch Therapy, Vitamin Therapy, Zero Balancing, Spiritual Touch Therapy, Body Release,. ✔
- **Homeopath/Counsellor/Therapist** Mrs S Terry **Q:** Dip.Couns, RSHom. **M:** Soc.Hom.

**B P T** Yrs. Est.: 12 (**Ref:**HM12369)

## LIGHT UP YOUR LIFE

**Light up your Life**, 10 Westminster Avenue, Kirkby-In-Ashfield, Nottingham, **Nottinghamshire**, NG17 7HY, **ENG**.
(T) 01623 755891
Speciality: Absent Healing, Crystal Healing, Healing Therapy, Holistic Healing, Meditation, Pyramid Power, Reiki, Seichem, Shiatsu, Tera-Mai, Painless spinal touch. ✔
- **Reiki/Seichem Master** Mrs W Walker **Q:** BA, Reiki Master. **M:** BEST.

**T** Yrs. Est.: 5 (**Ref:**HM12370)

## LIGHT WAYS

**Light Ways**, 4 Eling Lane, Totton, Southampton, **Hampshire**, SO40 9GA, **ENG**.
(T) 023 8086 3758
Speciality: Clairvoyants & Palmists.
- **Owner** Mr R Witcher

**B** (**Ref:**HM12371)

## LIGHTBODY, STEWART

**Stewart Lightbody**, The Halifax Clinic Of Natural Medicine, 22 Clare Rd, Halifax, **Yorkshire (West)**, HX1 2HX, **ENG**.
(T) 01422 340919
Speciality: Acupuncture.

**O** (**Ref:**HM12372)

## LIGHTENED PATHWAYS

**Lightened Pathways**, Law Farm Cottage, Dechmont, Broxburn, **Lothian (West)**, EH52 6NB, **SCO**.
(T) 01506 811445
Speciality: Clairvoyants & Palmists.

**B** (**Ref:**HM12373)

## LIGHTFOOT, ANNA

**Anna Lightfoot**, 173B Southfield Rd, London, **London (Greater)**, W4 5LB, **ENG**.
(T) 07931 464986
Speciality: Reflexology.

**S T** (**Ref:**HM12374)

## LIGHTWOOD, P E

**P E Lightwood**, 127 Ford Rd, Newport, **Shropshire**, TF10 7UL, **ENG**.
(T) 01952 812070
Speciality: Chiropodists (Podiatrists).
- **Owner** Mrs S Lightwood

**S** (**Ref:**HM12375)

## LIKISMA

**Likisma**, 17 Lyndale Rd, Hapton, Burnley, **Lancashire**, BB11 5RD, **ENG**.
(T) 01282 777066 (F) 01282 777066
Speciality: Aromatherapy.
- **Partner** Mr K Ratcliffe

**M O** (**Ref:**HM12376)

## LIKISMA

**Likisma**, Thrift St, Wollaston, Wellingborough, **Northamptonshire**, NN29 7QJ, **ENG**.
(T) 01933 665088
Speciality: Aromatherapy.

**M O** (**Ref:**HM12377)

## LIKISMA

**Likisma**, Po Box 4870, Lower Earley, Reading, **Berkshire**, RG6 4FJ, **ENG**.
(T) 01189 873377
Speciality: Aromatherapy.
- **Owner** Mrs D Hindle

**M O** (**Ref:**HM12378)

## LIKISMA

**Likisma**, Po Box 122, Mansfield, **Nottinghamshire**, NG19 6SD, **ENG**.
(T) 01623 515541 (F) 01623 515541
Speciality: Aromatherapy.
- **Owner** Mr P Noke

**M O** (**Ref:**HM12379)

## LIKISMA

**Likisma**, 31 Leighfield Cl, Bedford, **Bedfordshire**, MK41 0AG, **ENG**.
(T) 01234 343725



Key: **B** Mind-Body Medicine **C** Complementary Medicine **H** Self Help Treatment **M** Medicinal Therapy **O** Oriental Medicine **P** Postural Therapy **S** Manipulative Structural Therapy **T** Touch Therapy

Speciality: Aromatherapy.
● **Owner** Ms M Eaton
M O (Ref:HM12380)

**LIKISMA**
**Likisma**, 25 Gathorne Rd, London, **London (Greater)**, N22 5ND, ENG.
(T) 020 8881 8317 (F) 020 8881 1164
Speciality: Aromatherapy.
● **Owner** Mrs R Clancy
M O (Ref:HM12381)

**LIKISMA**
**Likisma**, 10 Longbridge, Willesborough, Ashford, **Kent**, TN24 0TA, ENG.
(T) 01233 665199 (F) 01233 637390
Speciality: Aromatherapy.
● **Partner** Mr T Sansom
M O (Ref:HM12382)

**LIKISMA**
**Likisma**, 3 Fraser Rd, Calverley, Pudsey, **Yorkshire (West)**, LS28 5RU, ENG.
(T) 01274 612422 (F) 01274 612422
Speciality: Aromatherapy.
● **Owner** Mrs A Greenhough
M O (Ref:HM12383)

**LIKISMA**
**Likisma**, 62 Hastings Cl, Breedon-On-The-Hill, Derby, **Derbyshire**, DE73 1BN, ENG.
(T) 01332 863752
Speciality: Complementary Medicines & Therapy.
● **Owner** Mrs J Baldwin
C M (Ref:HM12384)

**LIKISMA**
**Likisma**, 67 Firsdown, Stevenage, **Hertfordshire**, SG2 9EL, ENG.
(T) 01438 239871
Speciality: Complementary Medicines & Therapy.
C M (Ref:HM12385)

**LIKISMA AROMATHERAPY**
**Likisma Aromatherapy**, 7 Manor Lane, Hawarden, Deeside, **Flintshire**, CH5 3PP, WAL.
(T) 01244 538241 (F) 01244 538241
Speciality: Aromatherapy.
● **Partner** Mr D Mackey
M O (Ref:HM12386)

**LIKISMA PRESENTATIONS**
**Likisma Presentations**, 26 Kickdom Cl, Amesbury, Salisbury, **Wiltshire**, SP4 7XB, ENG.
(T) 01980 622216 (F) 01980 622216
Speciality: Aromatherapy.
● **Partner** Mr K Walsh
M O (Ref:HM12387)

**LIKISMA PRESENTATIONS**
**Likisma Presentations Ltd**, 55 Park Rd, Sittingbourne, **Kent**, ME10 1DY, ENG.
(T) 01795 436451
Speciality: Aromatherapy.
M O (Ref:HM12388)

**LIKISMA PRESENTATIONS**
**Likisma Presentations Ltd**, 9-11 Denington Rd, Denington Industrial Estate, Wellingborough, **Northamptonshire**, NN8 2QH, ENG.
(T) 01933 440727 (F) 01933 440733
Speciality: Aromatherapy.
● **Director** Mrs L Birk
M O (Ref:HM12389)

**LILBURN, JESSICA**
**Jessica Lilburn**, 47 Hunters Court, Newcastle Upon Tyne, **Tyne and Wear**, NE3 1SP, ENG.
(T) 01912 847787
Speciality: Reflexology.
S T (Ref:HM12390)

**LILLESHALL SPORTS INJURY CTRE**
**Lilleshall Sports Injury Centre**, Lilleshall National Sports Centre, Lilleshall, Newport, **Shropshire**, TF10 9AT, ENG.
(T) 01952 605828 (F) 01952 820924
Speciality: Physiotherapy.
P S T (Ref:HM12391)

**LILLEY CLINIC**
**Lilley Clinic (The)**, The Courtyard, Lowerslope End Farm, Stype, Hungerford, **Berkshire**, RG17 0RE, ENG.
(T) 01488 685320
Speciality: Physiotherapy.
P S T (Ref:HM12392)

**LILLEY, PENNY**
**Penny Lilley**, Dumfries Holistic Health Centre, 98 Loreburn St, Dumfries, **Dumfries and Galloway**, DG1 1HW, SCO.
(T) 01387 267617
Speciality: Complementary Medicines & Therapy.
M (Ref:HM12393)

**LILLEY, PENNY**
**Penny Lilley**, Ridgeway, Hadrian Way, Chilworth, Southampton, **Hampshire**, SO16 7HY, ENG.
(T) 023 8076 9679
Speciality: Physiotherapy.
● **Owner** Mrs P Lilley
P S T (Ref:HM12394)

**LILLIE, FRANCIS J**
**Francis J Lillie**, 27A Harley Pl, London, **London (Greater)**, W1N 1HB, ENG.
(T) 020 7323 2370 (F) 020 7637 5227
Speciality: Psychology.
● **Owner** Mr F Lillie
B (Ref:HM12395)

**LILWALL, EMMA**
**Emma Lilwall**, 33 Pound St, Newbury, **Berkshire**, RG14 6AE, ENG.
(T) 01635 580200
Speciality: Homeopathy.
● **Partner** Ms E Lilwall
M (Ref:HM12396)

**LIME STREET OSTEOPATHIC**
**Lime Street Osteopathic Clinic**, 1 Lime St, London, **London (Greater)**, EC3M 7HA, ENG.
(T) 020 7327 5341
Speciality: Osteopathy.
P S T (Ref:HM12397)

**LIMERICK COLLEGE**
**Limerick College Of Beauty Therapy**, 123 O'Connell St, **County Limerick**, IRE.
(T) 06141 0628
Speciality: Beauty Therapy.
H T (Ref:HM12398)

**LIMERICK HEALING CENTRE**
**Limerick Healing Centre of Colour & Light**, 65 Catherine St, **County Limerick**, IRE.
(T) 06140 0431
Speciality: Healing.
B (Ref:HM12399)

**LIMERICK HEALTH**
**Limerick Health & Injury Services**, South Court Hotel Raheen, **County Limerick**, IRE.
(T) 06148 7430
Speciality: Complementary Medicines & Therapy.
M (Ref:HM12400)

**LIMERICK INSTITUTE OF MASSAGE**
**Limerick Institute of Massage**, Ballyhane Birdhill, IRE.
(T) 06137 9079
Speciality: Complementary Medicines & Therapy.
M (Ref:HM12401)

**LIMERICK OSTEOPATHIC CENTRE**
**Limerick Osteopathic Centre**, 19 Catherine St, **County Limerick**, IRE.
(T) 06131 8558
Speciality: Osteopathy.
P S T (Ref:HM12402)

**LIMETREE CENTRE**
**Limetree Centre (The)**, Fitzroy House, Lynwood Drive, Worcester Park, **Surrey**, KT4 7AD, ENG.
(T) 020 8330 0100
Speciality: Reflexology.
S T (Ref:HM12403)

**LINANE, IAN**
**Ian Linane**, 79 Leafields, Houghton Regis, Dunstable, **Bedfordshire**, LU5 5LU, ENG.
(T) 01582 862627
Speciality: Chiropodists (Podiatrists).
● **Owner** Mr I Linane
S (Ref:HM12404)

**LINCOLN CLINIC-PSYCHOTHERAPY**
**Lincoln Clinic & Centre For Psychotherapy (The)**, 19 Abbeyville Mews, 88 Clapham Park Rd, London, **London (Greater)**, SW4 7BX, ENG.
(T) 020 7978 1545 (F) 020 7720 4721
Speciality: Psychotherapy.
● **Accountant** Mr J Adam
B (Ref:HM12405)

**LINCOLN COUTTS**
**Lincoln Coutts**, 585 Holburn St, Aberdeen, **Aberdeenshire**, AB10 7LH, SCO.
(T) 01224 211517
Speciality: Complementary Medicines & Therapy.
M (Ref:HM12406)

**LINCOLN HERBAL TREATMENT CTRE**
**Lincoln Herbal Treatment Centre (The)**, 64-68 The Park, West Prde, Lincoln, **Lincolnshire**, LN1 1XS, ENG.
(T) 01522 543207
Speciality: Bach Remedies, Herbal Medicine. ✔
● **Medical Herbalist**
Mr A Stableford Q: BSc, MNIMH. M: NIMH.
M Yrs. Est.: 16 (Ref:HM12407)

**LINCOLN LAWSON, B**
**B Lincoln Lawson**, 11A Gro Rd, Seaford, **Sussex (East)**, BN25 1TT, ENG.
(T) 01323 898881
Speciality: Chiropodists (Podiatrists).
● **Owner** Mrs B Shenton
S (Ref:HM12408)

**LINCOLN PSYCHOTHERAPY PRACTICE**
**Lincoln Psychotherapy Practice (The)**, 8 Church Drive, Lincoln, **Lincolnshire**, LN6 7AX, ENG.
(T) 01522 526777
Speciality: Psychotherapy.
● **Owner** Mrs J Flannery
B (Ref:HM12409)

**LINCOLN, FRED**
**Fred Lincoln**, Plowmans, Yeomans Meadows, Sevenoaks, **Kent**, TN13 2LS, ENG.
(T) 01732 461194
Speciality: Reflexology.
S T (Ref:HM12410)

**LINDA PULLAN CHIROPODIST**
**Linda Pullan Chiropodist**, The Harrow Health Care Centre, 84-88 Pinner Rd, Harrow, **London (Greater)**, HA1 4JN, ENG.
(T) 020 8861 1221
Speciality: Chiropodists (Podiatrists).
S (Ref:HM12411)

**LINDA, FULTON**
**Fulton Linda M I A H I P**, 46 Elmwood Ave, Lr, Ranelagh, **County Dublin**, IRE.
(T) 01497 1188
Speciality: Complementary Medicines & Therapy.
M (Ref:HM12412)

**LINDA'S AQUA-AURA**
**Linda's Aqua-Aura**, 22B High St, Hastings, **Sussex (East)**, TN34 3EY, ENG.
(T) 01424 718104
Speciality: Clairvoyants & Palmists.
● **Owner** Mrs L Leselleur
B (Ref:HM12413)

**LINDBERG FITNESS**
**Lindberg Fitness For Body & Mind**, 40 Margaret St, London, **London (Greater)**, W1N 7FB, ENG.
(T) 020 7629 4040
(E) info@studiolindberg.com
(W) www.studiolindberg.com
Speciality: Pilates. ✔
● **Mind Body Fitness Consultant**
Ms A Lindberg Q: BA (Hons).
P Yrs. Est.: 1 (Ref:HM12414)

**LINDEMAN, A J**
**Tree of Life Clinic (The)**, 54 Barrington St, Tiverton, **Devon**, EX16 6QP, ENG.
(T) 01884 258143 (F) 01884 258143


Key continued: Yrs.Est: Years Established Q: Qualifications M: Professional Membership ✔ Indemnity Insurance Accept Credit Cards

Speciality: Homeopathy, Iridology, Miasm Therapy, Naturopathy, Phytotherapy, B.F.O (Bio-Electric Function Diagnostics A.K.N Electro-Acupuncture). ✔
- **Homeopath** Mr A Lindeman
- **Owner** Mrs J Seeley

M Yrs. Est.: 15 (**Ref:**HM12415)

**LINDEN HOUSE PSYCHOLOGICAL SVS**

**Linden House Psychological Services**, 2 Baird Rd, Ratho, Newbridge, **Edinburgh (City of)**, EH28 8RA, SCO.
(T) 01313 331365 (F) 01313 330999
Speciality: Psychology.
- **Owner** Mrs B Robson

B (**Ref:**HM12416)

**LINDISFARNE CENTRE**

**Lindisfarne Centre**, 71 Westgate Rd, Newcastle Upon Tyne, **Tyne and Wear**, NE1 1SG, ENG.
(T) 01912 617643
Speciality: Homeopathy.
M (**Ref:**HM12417)

**LINDLEY, CLAIRE**

**Claire Lindley**, 9 Montgomery Rd, Caversfield, Bicester, **Oxfordshire**, OX6 9FG, ENG.
(T) 01869 321893
Speciality: Physiotherapy.
- **Owner** Mrs C Lindley

P S T (**Ref:**HM12418)

**LINDLEY, E A**

**Mrs E A Lindley**, Audlem Lodge, 2 Ridgeway, Broadstone, **Dorset**, BH18 8EA, ENG.
(T) 01202 693199
Speciality: Physiotherapy.
P S T (**Ref:**HM12419)

**LINDOS PSYCHOTHERAPY CENTRE**

**Lindos Psychotherapy Centre**, Saddlemakers Lane, Melton, Woodbridge, **Suffolk**, IP12 1PP, ENG.
(T) 01394 380100 (F) 01394 380111
Speciality: Psychotherapy.
- **Principal** Ms L Skirroy

B (**Ref:**HM12420)

**LINDQUIST, I**

**I Lindquist**, Raycroft, Ray Mill Rd East, Maidenhead, **Berkshire**, SL6 8TB, ENG.
(T) 01628 626857
Speciality: Physiotherapy.
P S T (**Ref:**HM12421)

**LINDSAY, ANNE**

**Anne Lindsay**, **Yorkshire (West)**, LS6, ENG.
(T) 01132 691564
Speciality: Reflexology.
S T (**Ref:**HM12422)

**LINDSAY, DAVID**

**David Lindsay**, 13 Craigie Rd, Ayr, **Ayrshire (South)**, KA8 0EZ, SCO.
(T) 01292 610780 (F) 01292 610780
Speciality: Chiropodists (Podiatrists).
- **Owner** Mr D Lindsay

S (**Ref:**HM12423)

**LINDSAY, LISA F**

**Lisa F Lindsay**, Calda, Wood Lane, Knaphill, Woking, **Surrey**, GU21 2AD, ENG.
(T) 01483 489501
Speciality: Osteopathy.
- **Owner** Mrs L Lindsay

P S T (**Ref:**HM12424)

**LINDSAY, MARGARET**

**Margaret Lindsay**, Dumfries Holistic Health Centre, 98 Loreburn St, Dumfries, **Dumfries and Galloway**, DG1 1HW, SCO.
(T) 01387 267617
Speciality: Complementary Medicines & Therapy.
M (**Ref:**HM12425)

**LINDY, D**

**D Lindy**, Bishops Pk Centre, Lancaster Way, Bishop's Stortford, **Hertfordshire**, CM23 4DA, ENG.
(T) 01279 651859
Speciality: Cranial Osteopathy, Osteopathy.
✔
- **Osteopath** Miss V Aldridge Q: Ost.Med. M: GOsC.
- **Osteopath** Miss A Lovell Q: BSc (Hons). M: GOsC.
- **Osteopath** Mr D Lindy Q: DO, FRSH. M: GOsC.

S Yrs. Est.: 30 (**Ref:**HM12426)

**LINDY, DAVID**

**David Lindy**, Loverings, Beaumont Hill, Dunmow, **Essex**, CM6 2AW, ENG.
(T) 01371 872269
Speciality: Osteopathy.
P S T (**Ref:**HM12427)

**LINFIELD, P**

**P Linfield**, 25 Lansdowne Rd, Angmering, Littlehampton, **Sussex (West)**, BN16 4JX, ENG.
(T) 01903 784682
Speciality: Physiotherapy.
- **Owner** Mrs P Lindfield

P S T (**Ref:**HM12428)

**LINFORD, ANITA**

**Anita Linford**, Barnita, Shalstone, Buckingham, **Buckinghamshire**, MK18 5DZ, ENG.
(T) 01280 850639
Speciality: Complementary Medicines & Therapy.
- **Owner** Mrs A Linford

C M (**Ref:**HM12429)

**LINFORTH, A E**

**A E Linforth**, 61 Breck Rd, Anfield, Liverpool, **Merseyside**, L4 2QS, ENG.
(T) 01512 631668
Speciality: Chiropodists (Podiatrists).
- **Owner** Mr A Linforth

S (**Ref:**HM12430)

**LING**

**Ling (The)**, 28 Crow La West, Newton-Le-Willows, **Merseyside**, WA12 9YG, ENG.
(T) 01925 225547
Speciality: Physiotherapy.
- **Owner** Mr M Stabler

P S T (**Ref:**HM12431)

**LING, E**

**E Ling**, 19 Applegarth Drive, Ilford, **Essex**, IG2 7TQ, ENG.
(T) 020 8590 5162
Speciality: Psychotherapy.
- **Owner** Ms E Ling

B (**Ref:**HM12432)

**LING, J**

**J Ling**, 59 Albert Rd, Tamworth, **Staffordshire**, B79 7JN, ENG.
(T) 01827 65568
Speciality: Acupuncture.
- **Owner** Dr J Ling

O (**Ref:**HM12433)

**LING, STEPHEN W**

**Stephen W Ling**, 59 Albert Rd, Tamworth, **Staffordshire**, B79 7JN, ENG.
(T) 01827 65568
Speciality: Osteopathy.
- **Owner** Mr S Ling

P S T (**Ref:**HM12434)

**LINGWOOD CLINIC**

**Lingwood Clinic**, 20 Victoria Rd, Stanford-Le-Hope, **Essex**, SS17 0HS, ENG.
(T) 01375 361011
(W) www.lingwoodclinic.co.uk
Speciality: Acupuncture, Aromatherapy, Homeopathy, Kinesiology, Osteopathy, Shiatsu.
✔
- **Osteopath** Mr P Murphy Q: DO.
- **Shiatsu/Acupressure Therapist** Mr J McAllister Q: ITEC.
- **Homeopath** Jag Ram Q: Dip.Hom, DNM, PGD.Hom.
- **Osteopath** Mr D Moore Q: Dip.Ac, Dip.Hom, DO.
- **Aromatherapist/Kinesiologist/Reiki** Ms J Hodge Q: Dip.Anat, Dip.Arom, Dip.Kines, Dip.Massage, Reiki 1, Reiki 2.
- **Osteopath** Mr P Naisbitt Q: BSc (Hons), Dip.Sports Massage.
- **Acupuncturist/Sports Massage** Ms K Brunt Q: Dip.Ac, Dip.Sports Massage.
- **Osteopath** Ms S Lovett Q: BSc (Hons). M: GOsC.
- **Massage Assistant** Ms J Hewing Q: Dip.Manag.Treat, Dip.Sports Massage, Dip.Sports Therapy.

P S T (**Ref:**HM12435)

**LINKMAN, BEVERLEY**

**Beverley Linkman**, 66 Marland Fold, Rochdale, **Lancashire**, OL11 4RF, ENG.
(T) 01706 340320
Speciality: Chiropodists (Podiatrists).
S (**Ref:**HM12436)

**LINKS CLINIC**

**Links Clinic (The)**, 78A Stockport Rd, Marple, Stockport, **Cheshire**, SK6 6AH, ENG.
(T) 01614 278577
Speciality: Osteopathy.
- **Owner** Mr B Walker

P S T (**Ref:**HM12437)

**LINLITHGOW PHYSIO PRACTICE**

**Linlithgow Physiotherapy Practice**, Lingate, Falkirk Rd, Linlithgow, **Lothian (West)**, EH49 7PG, SCO.
(T) 01506 847101
Speciality: Acupuncture, Physiotherapy. ✔
- **Practice Manager** Ms I Reed
- **Owner/Physiotherapist** Ms H Thomson Q: MCSP, SRP. M: CSP.

S Yrs. Est.: 10 (**Ref:**HM12438)

**LINN, DUBH**

**Dubh Linn - Counselling**, 16 Prospect Rd, Glasnevin, **County Dublin**, IRE.
(T) 01830 2358
(E) dubhl@indigo.ie
Speciality: Counselling.
B H (**Ref:**HM12439)

**LINN, PAMELA**

**Pamela Linn**, 75 Leigh Rd, Leigh-On-Sea, **Essex**, SS9 1JN, ENG.
(T) 01702 714862 (F) 01702 716969
Speciality: Homeopathy.
- **Owner** Mrs C Merryfield

M (**Ref:**HM12440)

**LINSTEAD, J**

**J Linstead**, 130 High St, Wivenhoe, Colchester, **Essex**, CO7 9AF, ENG.
(T) 01206 827355
Speciality: Complementary Medicines & Therapy.
- **Owner** Mrs J Linstead

C M (**Ref:**HM12441)

**LINTON, CHERRIE**

**Cherrie Linton**, 10 Houndean Rise, Lewes, **Sussex (East)**, BN7 1EG, ENG.
(T) 01273 487706
Speciality: Reflexology.
S T (**Ref:**HM12442)

**LINTON, THERESA**

**Theresa Linton**, Blackmill Bay, Toberonochy, Oban, **Argyll and Bute**, PA34 4TZ, SCO.
(T) 01852 314366
Speciality: Reflexology.
S T (**Ref:**HM12443)

**LINTON, UNNA**

**Unna Linton**, 10 Shuttle St, Paisley, **Renfrewshire**, PA1 1YD, SCO.
(T) 01418 480004
Speciality: Chiropody. ✔
- **Owner/Chiropodist** Mrs U Linton Q: MBChA. M: B.A.Ch.P.

C Yrs. Est.: 10 (**Ref:**HM12444)

**LINTONBON, DAVID**

**David Lintonbon**, 24 Gloucester Avenue, London, **London (Greater)**, NW1 7BG, ENG.
(T) 020 7485 1048
Speciality: Osteopathy.
P S T (**Ref:**HM12445)

**LION HOUSE SURGERY**

**Vinewood Healthcare**, 28 Castle St, Tiverton, **Devon**, EX16 6RG, ENG.
(T) 01884 257444
Speciality: Acupuncture, Chiropractic, Remedial Massage.



Key: B Mind-Body Medicine, C Complementary Medicine, H Self Help Treatment, M Medicinal Therapy, O Oriental Medicine, P Postural Therapy, S Manipulative Structural Therapy, T Touch Therapy

● **Osteopath** Dr G Gallacher
● **Naturopath/Osteopath** Dr J Vine M: BCA.
● **Chiropractor** Dr A Stewart Q: DC. M: BCA.
● **Remedial Massage Therapist**
Mrs T Bayly Q: LCSP.
● **Owner/Osteopath** Dr S Woods Q: DO.
P S T Yrs. Est.: 25 (Ref:HM12446)

## LIONHEART PHYSIO & SPORTS

**Lionheart Physiotherapy & Sports Injury Clinic**, 16 St Johns Rd, Leatherhead, **Surrey**, KT22 8SE, **ENG**.
(T) 01372 374612
Speciality: Physiotherapy.
P S T (Ref:HM12447)

## LIP ONG

**Lip Ong**, Pavilion Clinic, Plough Lane, Stoke Poges, Slough, **Berkshire**, SL2 4JR, **ENG**.
(T) 01753 663617
Speciality: Complementary Medicines & Therapy.
C M (Ref:HM12448)

## LIPKIN, F J

**F J Lipkin**, Daresbury Lodge, Chester Rd, Daresbury, Warrington, **Cheshire**, WA4 5LR, **ENG**.
(T) 01925 740510
Speciality: Chiropodists (Podiatrists).
● **Owner** Miss F Lipkin
S (Ref:HM12449)

## LIPKIN, FENELLA

**Fenella Lipkin**, Allerton Health Centre, 615 Smithdown Rd, Liverpool, **Merseyside**, L15 5AG, **ENG**.
(T) 01517 345909
Speciality: Chiropodists (Podiatrists).
S (Ref:HM12450)

## LISA MCDONNELL CHIROPODIST

**Lisa McDonnell Chiropodist**, 26 Stillorgan Hth Stillorgan, Dublin, **County Dublin**, **IRE**.
(T) 01278 1440
Speciality: Chiropodists (Podiatrists).
S (Ref:HM12451)

## LISBURN CHIROPRACTIC CLINIC

**Lisburn Chiropractic Clinic**, 28A Bachelors Walk, Lisburn, **County Antrim**, BT28 1XN, **NIR**.
(T) 028 9266 5405
Speciality: Chiropractic. ✓ [credit card]
● **Owner/Chiropractor** Dr N Maurice Q: BSc, DC, MCC. M: SCA.
P Yrs. Est.: 6 (Ref:HM12452)

## LISKEARD CHIROPRACTIC CLINIC

**Liskeard Chiropractic Clinic**, 18 Dean St, Liskeard, **Cornwall**, PL14 4AA, **ENG**.
(T) 01579 340654
Speciality: Chiropractic. ✓
● **Associate** Dr R Southam Q: DC. M: BCA.
● **Owner** Dr B Whittingham Q: DC. M: BCA.
P Yrs. Est.: 3 (Ref:HM12453)

## LISLE, T

**T Lisle**, 1 Station Approach, Worcester Park, **Surrey**, KT4 7NB, **ENG**.
(T) 020 8337 4486
Speciality: Chiropodists (Podiatrists).
S (Ref:HM12454)

## LISLE, THOMAS

**Mr Thomas Lisle**, 36 Alexandra Rd, Farnborough, **Hampshire**, GU14 6DA, **ENG**.
(T) 01252 545454
Speciality: Biomechanics, Chiropody, Cryo Surgery, Orthotics, Podiatry. ✓
● **Chiropodist (Podiatrist)**
Mr T Lisle Q: BSc (Hons), DPodM, S.R.Ch.
M: S.C.P.
M Yrs. Est.: 16 (Ref:HM12455)

## LISON, CAROLINE

**Caroline Lison**, 11 Fairford Cl, Redditch, **Worcestershire**, B98 9LU, **ENG**.
(T) 07768 363885
Speciality: Reflexology.
S T (Ref:HM12456)

## LISSADELL HOUSE PRACTICE

**Lissadell House Practice (The)**, 8 Holford Cl, Tilehurst, Reading, **Berkshire**, RG31 5PB, **ENG**.
(T) 01189 426192
Speciality: Chiropractic, Homeopathy, Massage (Therapeutic), Nutritional Therapy. ✓
● **Owner** Mrs K Ryan Q: DC, MA. M: CC, GCC, MCA.
P Yrs. Est.: 10 (Ref:HM12457)

## LISTCARD CHIROPODY CENTRE

**Listcard Chiropody Centre**, Sherlock House, 6 Manor Rd, Wallasey, **Merseyside**, CH45 4JB, **ENG**.
(T) 01515 122799
Speciality: Chiropodists (Podiatrists).
S (Ref:HM12458)

## LISTENING CENTRE

**Listening Centre (Lewes) Ltd (The)**, 16A Station St, Lewes, **Sussex (East)**, BN7 2DB, **ENG**.
(T) 01273 474877 (F) 01273 487500
Speciality: Complementary Medicines & Therapy.
● **Director** Mr A Smith
C M (Ref:HM12459)

## LISTENING CENTRE

**Listening Centre (London) Ltd (The)**, 26 Eccleston Sq, London, **London (Greater)**, SW1V 1NS, **ENG**.
(T) 020 7821 9862
Speciality: Complementary Medicines & Therapy.
M (Ref:HM12460)

## LISTER NATURAL HEALTH PRACTICE

**Lister Natural Health Practice**, Admiralty House, 2 Bank Pl, Arwenack St, Falmouth, **Cornwall**, TR11 4AT, **ENG**.
(T) 01326 210202 (F) 01326 210199
(E) enquiries@lister-natural-health.co.uk
(W) www.lister-natural-health.co.uk
Speciality: Absent Healing, Acupressure, Acupuncture, Aromatherapy, Auto Suggestion, Aversion Therapy, Bach Remedies, Chinese Herbal Medicine, Chiropractic, Cognitive Therapy, Complementary Therapy, Counselling, Cranial Osteopathy, Cranio-Sacral Therapy, Cupping, Encounter Groups, Family Therapy, Gestalt Therapy, Group Therapy, Hay Diet, Healer, Healing Therapy, Herbal Medicine, Holistic Healing, Homeopathy, Humanistic Psychology, Hypnosis, Hypnotherapy, Indian Head Massage, Life Style Coaching, Massage (Therapeutic), Meditation, Moxibustion, Nutritional Therapy, Oriental Diagnosis, Paranormal Therapies, Postural Integration, Primal Therapy, Neuro-Linguistic Programming, (Free) Financial Counselling, Paediatric, Chiropractic, Regression, Feng Shui Massage, Numerology Consultancy, I Ching, Chi Kung. Also able to cross-refer to Specialists, Consultants and Doctors in Cornwall and Devon. ✓
● **Executive Administrator/Partner**
Mr D Snow
● **Owner** Ms Y Burdekin
(T) 01326 318180 Q: IIHHT, MICHT. M: FHT.
● **Medical Hynotherapist/Counsellor**
Ms M Snow Q: MHA, MISMA. M: HA.
B C H M O P S T
Yrs. Est.: 4 (Ref:HM12461)

## LISTER, CHRISTINE

**Christine Lister**, 37 Erlesmere Gardens, London, **London (Greater)**, W13 9TZ, **ENG**.
(T) 020 8567 4044
Speciality: Osteopathy.
P S T (Ref:HM12462)

## LITCHFIELD, P

**P Litchfield**, 20 Harmans Way, Weedon, Northampton, **Northamptonshire**, NN7 4PB, **ENG**.
(T) 01327 341497
Speciality: Chiropodists (Podiatrists).
● **Owner** Mrs P Litchfield
S (Ref:HM12463)

## LITHERLAND, C B

**C B Litherland**, 76 Town St, Horsforth, Leeds, **Yorkshire (West)**, LS18 4AP, **ENG**.
(T) 01132 589987
Speciality: Chiropodists (Podiatrists).
S (Ref:HM12464)

## LITTERICK, GILLIAN

**Gillian Litterick**, 21 Harcourt House, 19 Cavendish Sq, London, **London (Greater)**, W1M 9AB, **ENG**.
(T) 020 7409 3216
Speciality: Physiotherapy.
P S T (Ref:HM12465)

## LITTLE HERBAL

**Little Herbal Co (The)**, 35 St Georges Rd, Holmfirth, Huddersfield, **Yorkshire (West)**, HD7 1UQ, **ENG**.
(T) 01484 685100 (F) 01484 685100
Speciality: Herbalists.
M (Ref:HM12466)

## LITTLE LONDON HERBAL STORE

**Little London Herbal Store**, 4 Kings Walk, Nottingham, **Nottinghamshire**, NG1 2AE, **ENG**.
(T) 01159 472854
Speciality: Herbal Medicine.
● **Owner** Mrs H Mitchell
M (Ref:HM12467)

## LITTLE SANCTUARY

**Little Sanctuary (The)**, 187 Watling St, Radlett, **Hertfordshire**, WD7 7NQ, **ENG**.
(T) 01923 856088
Speciality: Complementary Medicines & Therapy.
● **Owner** Ms A Green
C M (Ref:HM12468)

## LITTLE VENICE CHIROPODY

**Miss M Maghami**, The Little Venice Medical Centre, 2 Crompton St, London, **London (Greater)**, W2 1ND, **ENG**.
(T) 020 7724 7767 (F) 020 7723 8580
Speciality: Acupuncture, Biomechanics, Chiropody, Counselling, Podiatry.
● **Chiropodist (Podiatrist)**
Miss M Maghami Q: BSc (Hons), M.S.C.P., S.R.Ch.
M: S.C.P.
M Yrs. Est.: 4 (Ref:HM12469)

## LITTLEHAMPTON NAT HLTH CTRE

**Littlehampton Natural Health Centre**, 10C Granville Rd, Littlehampton, **Sussex (West)**, BN17 5JU, **ENG**.
(T) 01903 734373
(W) www.lnhc.co.uk
Speciality: Absent Healing, Acupuncture, Alexander Technique, Aromatherapy, Art Therapy, Auto Suggestion, Bach Remedies, Bowen Therapy, Chiropody, Chiropractic, Clinical Ecology, Colour Therapy, Counselling, Cranial Osteopathy, Cranio-Sacral Therapy, Dietician, Faith Healing, Healer, Healing Therapy, Herbal Medicine, Holistic Healing, Homeopathy, Hypnosis, Hypnotherapy, Indian Head Massage, Iridology, Kinesiology, Manipulation, Massage (Therapeutic), McTimoney Chiropractic, Meditation, Metamorphic Therapy, Miasm Therapy, Micro Manipulation, Moxibustion, Music Therapy, Naturopathy, Nutritional Therapy, Oriental Diagnosis, Osteopathy, Aura Soma Colour, Trager, Qi Gong, Substance Abuse Counselling, Chinese Herbalism, Chi Kung, Thai Massage, Trager. ✓
● **McTimoney/Network Chiropractor**
Mr J Mason Q: DC. M: GCC.
● **Osteopath/Homeopath**
Ms L Cooksley Q: DO. M: GOsC, ICO.
● **Osteopath** Mr N Jones Q: DO. M: GOsC, ICO.
● **Partner** Ms R Rowley
● **Osteopath** Ms L Donald Q: DO. M: GOsC.
B C H M O P S T
Yrs. Est.: 9 (Ref:HM12470)

## LITTLEJOHN CLINIC

**Littlejohn Clinic (The)**, 27 Sandown Rd, Sandown, **Isle of Wight**, PO36 9JL, **ENG**.
(T) 01983 408833
Speciality: Osteopathy.
● **Owner** Mr B Howard
P S T (Ref:HM12471)

## LITTLEJOHN CLINIC

**The LittleJohn Clinic**, 122A Cromwellsfort Rd, Walkinstown, Dublin, **County Dublin**, **IRE**.
(T) 01456 0300 (F) 01455 6665
Speciality: Counselling, Cranial Osteopathy, Osteopathy. ✓ [credit card]



Key continued: Yrs.Est: Years Established Q: Qualifications M: Professional Membership ✓ Indemnity Insurance [credit card] Accept Credit Cards

● **Clinic Director** Mr C Cambell M: GOsC.
● **Supervisor** Mr J Fiel
● **Chief Executive Officer**
Ms F Moore
**B** Yrs. Est.: 3 (**Ref:**HM12472)

## LITTLEJOHN, S

**S Littlejohn**, 5 Barrhill Trce, Cumnock, **Ayrshire (East)**, KA18 1PT, SCO.
(T) 01290 425996
Speciality: Nail Surgery, Podiatry, Bio-Mechanical Evaluations, Orthosis Manufacture. ✓
● **Chiropodist (Podiatrist)**
Mr S Littlejohn Q: BSc, DPodM. M: S.C.P.
**S** Yrs. Est.: 8 (**Ref:**HM12473)

## LITTLEMORE, JAN

**Jan Littlemore**, 24 Daybrook Rd, London, **London (Greater)**, SW19 3DH, ENG.
(T) 020 8287 5703
Speciality: Aromatherapy.
● **Owner** Ms J Littlemole
**M** **O** (**Ref:**HM12474)

## LITTLER, J M

**J M Littler**, 71 Henrietta St, Leigh, **Manchester (Greater)**, WN7 1LH, ENG.
(T) 01942 608459
Speciality: Chiropodists (Podiatrists).
**S** (**Ref:**HM12475)

## LITTLEWOOD, JULIE

**Julie Littlewood**, 7 Essex Rd, Lowestoft, **Suffolk**, NR32 2HQ, ENG.
(T) 01502 589831
Speciality: Aromatherapy.
● **Owner** Mrs J Littlewood
**M** **O** (**Ref:**HM12476)

## LIU CLINIC

**Liu Clinic (The)**, 13 Gunnersbury Avenue, London, **London (Greater)**, W5 3XD, ENG.
(T) 020 8993 2549
Speciality: Acupuncture.
● **Manager** Mr P Ashmore
**O** (**Ref:**HM12477)

## LIU, K H (DR)

**Dr K H Liu**, 292 Park Rd, London, **London (Greater)**, N8 8JY, ENG.
(T) 020 8340 9625 (F) 020 8340 9625
Speciality: Acupuncture.
● **Owner** Mr K Liu
**O** (**Ref:**HM12478)

## LIVE PSYCHIC LINE

**Live Psychic Line**, 16 Croham Rd, South Croydon, **Surrey**, CR2 7BA, ENG.
(T) 020 8649 8622
Speciality: Clairvoyants & Palmists.
**B** (**Ref:**HM12479)

## LIVERPOOL CENTRE FOR HEALTH

**Liverpool Centre For Health**, 123 Netherfield Rd North, Liverpool, **Merseyside**, L5 3NW, ENG.
(T) 01512 073263 (F) 01512 982192
Speciality: Complementary Medicines & Therapy.
● **Manager** Mrs K Sheerin
**C** **M** (**Ref:**HM12480)

## LIVESEY, PAULE

**Paule Livesey**, 2 Sacombe Cottages, Church Hill, Harbledown, Canterbury, **Kent**, CT2 9AE, ENG.
(T) 01227 459777
Speciality: Complementary Medicines & Therapy.
● **Owner** Ms P Livesey
**M** (**Ref:**HM12481)

## LIVESEY, SUSAN

**Susan Livesey**, 33 Belgrave Court, Wellesley Rd, London, **London (Greater)**, W4 4LG, ENG.
(T) 020 8987 9424
Speciality: Electrolysis.
● **Owner** Mrs S Livesey
**T** (**Ref:**HM12482)

## LIVING CENTRE CLINIC

**Living Centre Clinic**, 32 Durham Rd, Raynes Park, London, **London (Greater)**, SW20 0TW, ENG.
(T) 020 8946 2331
(E) info@living-centre-clinic.co.uk
(W) www.living-centre-clinic.co.uk
Speciality: Acupressure, Acupuncture, Alexander Technique, Aromatherapy, Bach Remedies, Chinese Herbal Medicine, Chiropody, Chiropractic, Complementary Therapy, Counselling, Herbal Medicine, Holistic Healing, Homeopathy, Hypnosis, Hypnotherapy, Indian Head Massage, Iridology, Kinesiology, Magnetic Therapy, Massage (Therapeutic), McTimoney Chiropractic, Meditation, Moxibustion, Nutritional Therapy, Osteopathy, Physiotherapy, Psychotherapy, Reflexology, Reiki, Remedial Massage, Shiatsu, Spiritual Healing, Vitamin Therapy, Chinese Massage, Emotional Freedom Techniques. ✓
● **Osteopath** Mr V Jamooji Q: DO. M: GOsC.
● **Private G.P** Dr A Darr
**C** (**Ref:**HM12483)

## LIVING HARMONY

**Living Harmony**, 18 Edendale Rd, Bexleyheath, **Kent**, DA7 6RW, ENG.
(T) 01322 403656 (F) 020 8402 5710
Speciality: Aromatherapy.
● **Owner** Mrs T Edge
**M** **O** (**Ref:**HM12484)

## LIVING HEALTH

**Living Health**, 2-6 North Prde, Grantham, **Lincolnshire**, NG31 8AN, ENG.
(T) 01476 400100 (F) 01476 400101
Speciality: Chiropractic, Kinesiology. ✓ CREDIT
● **Chiropractor** Mr A Hesseltine Q: BS, DC. M: GCC.
● **Chiropractor** Lois Hickling Q: DC. M: GCC.
● **Chiropractor** Mr T Jeppisen Q: DC. M: GCC.
● **Owner** Mr S King Q: BSc (Chiro), DIBAK. M: BCA, GCC.
**P** Yrs. Est.: 6 (**Ref:**HM12485)

## LIVING HEALTHILY

**Living Healthily**, 30a Church St, Great Burstead, Billericay, **Essex**, CM11 2SY, ENG.
(T) 01277 636567
Speciality: Complementary Medicines & Therapy.
● **Owner** Shirley Goddard
**M** (**Ref:**HM12486)

## LIVING MIND

**Living Mind**, 12 Kilmaurs Rd, Edinburgh, **Edinburgh (City of)**, EH16 5DA, SCO.
(T) 01316 679541 (F) 01316 675057
(E) sichel@dircon.co.uk
Speciality: Absent Healing, Auto Suggestion, Aversion Therapy, Complementary Therapy, Healer, Holistic Healing, Hypnosis, Hypnotherapy, Stress Therapy, Colourpuncture, Sekhem. ✓
● **Owner/Hypnotherapist** Dr M Sichel Q: BSCH, MSc, PgDCH. M: BSCH.
**B** Yrs. Est.: 3 (**Ref:**HM12487)

## LIVING WELL CLINIC

**Living Well Clinic**, 22 Church Rd, Bromley, **Kent**, BR2 0EG, ENG.
(T) 020 8466 8283 (F) 020 8325 2649
Speciality: Chiropractic. ✓
● **Chiropractor** Ms S Carless Q: BS. M: BAS.
**P** Yrs. Est.: 2 (**Ref:**HM12488)

## LIVINGSTON, J

**J Livingston**, Old School House, Somerford Keynes, Cirencester, **Gloucestershire**, GL7 6DJ, ENG.
(T) 01285 861420
Speciality: Osteopathy.
**P** **S** **T** (**Ref:**HM12489)

## LIVINGSTON, RONALD (DR)

**Dr Ronald Livingston**, 2 Ashton Court, 46 Western Rd, Poole, **Dorset**, BH13 6EU, ENG.
(T) 01202 763384 (F) 01202 707982
Speciality: Homeopathy.
● **Owner** Dr R Livingston
**M** (**Ref:**HM12490)

## LIVINGSTONE, J L

**J L Livingstone**, The Woodberry Clinic, 351 Muswell Hill Broadway, London, **London (Greater)**, N10 1BX, ENG.
(T) 020 8883 6079
Speciality: Chiropodists (Podiatrists).
**S** (**Ref:**HM12491)

## LIVINGSTONE, R K

**R K Livingstone**, Cowick Lodge, New Cross Rd, Stamford, **Lincolnshire**, PE9 1AJ, ENG.
(T) 01780 766862 (F) 01780 755878
Speciality: Acupuncture.
● **Owner** Mrs R Livingstone
**O** (**Ref:**HM12492)

## LIVINGSTONE, SHIRLEY

**Shirley Livingstone**, 46 Chapeldown Rd, Torpoint, **Cornwall**, PL11 2HU, ENG.
(T) 01752 813416
Speciality: Chiropodists (Podiatrists).
● **Owner** Mrs S Livingstone
**S** (**Ref:**HM12493)

## LIZ DAWSON - PSYCHOTHERAPIST

**Liz Dawson - Psychotherapist**, 48A Overdale Rd, Ealing, London, **London (Greater)**, W5 4TT, ENG.
(T) 020 8840 1441
(E) lizdawson@sonow.com
Speciality: Art Therapy, Cognitive Therapy, Counselling, Family Therapy, Group Therapy, Humanistic Psychology, Psychotherapy, Rogerian Therapy. ✓
● **Psychotherapist/Counsellor**
Ms L Dawson Q: Dip.Couns, MSc. M: UKCP.
**B** Yrs. Est.: 3 (**Ref:**HM12494)

## LIZ HALE HANDSON HEALTH

**Liz Hale**, 4 Hunting Gr, Boxworth, Cambridge, **Cambridgeshire**, CB3 8NE, ENG.
(T) 01954 267034
Speciality: Aromatherapy, Bach Remedies, Bowen Therapy, Complementary Therapy, Crystal Healing, Dowsing, Electrotherapy, Healer, Holistic Healing, Indian Head Massage, Massage (Therapeutic), Reflexology, Reiki, Seichem, Vibrational Therapy, Thermal Treatments. ✓
● **Therapist** Ms L Hale Q: APNT, ITEC. M: BTER.
**T** Yrs. Est.: 7 (**Ref:**HM12495)

## LJUBO, JACIC

**Ljubo Jacic**, 24 Marmion Rd, Battersea, London, **London (Greater)**, SW11 5PA, ENG.
(T) 020 7223 9899
Speciality: Indian Head Massage, Massage (Therapeutic), Reflexology.
**S** **T** (**Ref:**HM12496)

## LLANDEILO ACUPUCTURE CLINIC

**Llandeilo Acupucture Clinic**, 27 Carmarthen St, Llandeilo, **Carmarthenshire**, SA19 6AN, WAL.
(T) 01558 824235
Speciality: Acupuncture.
● **Partner** Mrs K Morgan
**O** (**Ref:**HM12497)

## LLANDINAM COUNSELLING

**Llandinam Counselling**, Lower Cwmffrwdd, Llandinam, **Powys**, SY17 5AH, WAL.
(T) 01686 688862
Speciality: Psychotherapy.
**B** (**Ref:**HM12498)

## LLANDRINDOD WELLS SPA TOWN

**Llandrindod Wells Spa Town Trust**, Rock Park Spa Centre, Rock Park, Llandrindod Wells, **Powys**, LD1 6AE, WAL.
(T) 01597 822997 (F) 01597 824102
Speciality: Acupuncture, Allergy Testing, Chiropody, Counselling, Homeopathy, Hypnotherapy, Kinesiology, Osteopathy, Psychotherapy, Reiki, Energy Balancing, Manual Lymphatic Drainage. ✓
● **Therapist** Ms M Hardy Q: BA, KFRP.
● **Allergy Therapist** Ms S Hough
● **Osteopath** Ms E Davies Q: BA, DO, ND.
● **Chairman of Llandridod Wells Trust**
Mr D Baird-Murray
● **Consultant Medical Herbalist**
Ms S Owen Q: MNIMH.
● **Therapist** Ms S Peace Q: BA, MBChA, MSSCh.
● **Osteopath** Genevieve Brown Q: DO.
● **Holistic/Remedial Massage Therapist**
Ms C Williams Q: ITEC.
● **Remedial Massage/Manual Lymphatic Drainage**

Key: **B** Mind-Body Medicine **C** Complementary Medicine **H** Self Help Treatment **M** Medicinal Therapy **O** Oriental Medicine **P** Postural Therapy **S** Manipulative Structural Therapy **T** Touch Therapy

Mr A Stott M: LCSP.
● **Homeopath** Ms K Biggs Q: RGN.
● **Acupuncturist** Ms J Flinning Q: Lic.Ac, MBAcC.
● **Reiki Master/Aromatherapist** Assara Richardson Q: MIFA, Reiki 3.
**C** Yrs. Est.: 6 (**Ref:**HM12499)

### LLANISHEN CHIROPODY CLINIC

**Llanishen Chiropody Clinic**, 17 Station Rd, Llanishen, Cardiff, **Glamorgan (Vale of)**, CF14 5LS, **WAL**.
(T) 029 2076 2419
Speciality: Chiropodists (Podiatrists).
**S** (**Ref:**HM12500)

### LLANISHEN PHYSIOTHERAPY CLINIC

**Llanishen Physiotherapy Clinic**, 17A Station Rd, Llanishen, Cardiff, **Glamorgan (Vale of)**, CF14 5LS, **WAL**.
(T) 029 2075 5775
Speciality: Physiotherapy. ✔
● **Owner/Physiotherapist** Mrs B Reed Q: MCSP, SRP. M: CSP.
**S** Yrs. Est.: 11 (**Ref:**HM12501)

### LLEWELLYN CONSULTANCY

**Llewellyn Consultancy**, Ty Goch, 4 St Mary's Mews, Tickhill, Doncaster, **Yorkshire (South)**, DN11 9LR, **ENG**.
(T) 01302 743113 (F) 01302 742346
(E) mairll@aol.com
(W) www.members.aol.com/tickhillhealth
Speciality: Absent Healing, Acupressure, Aromatherapy, Art Therapy, Auto Suggestion, Bach Remedies, Biofeedback, Cognitive Therapy, Complementary Therapy, Counselling, Dietician, Family Therapy, Gestalt Therapy, Group Therapy, Healer, Healing Therapy, Holistic Healing, Homeopathy, Hypnosis, Hypnotherapy, Kinesiology, Reflexology, Stress Therapy. ✔
● **Hypnotherapist** Ms M Llewellyn Q: BSc. M: CPS, HA, HS.
● **Homeopath** Dr T Llewellyn-Edwards Q: PhD. M: HMA.
**B** Yrs. Est.: 25 (**Ref:**HM12502)

### LLEWELLYN, MARGARET

**Margaret Llewellyn**, 7 Glebeland Drive, Bredon, Tewkesbury, **Gloucestershire**, GL20 7QF, **ENG**.
(T) 01684 773957
Speciality: Reflexology.
**S** **T** (**Ref:**HM12503)

### LLEWELLYN, MARY

**Mary Llewellyn**, 7 Kingsley Rd, Horley, **Surrey**, RH6 8HP, **ENG**.
(T) 01293 783379
Speciality: Chiropodists (Podiatrists).
**S** (**Ref:**HM12504)

### LLEWELLYN, TAM (DR)

**Dr Tam Llewellyn**, 4 St Marys Mews, St Marys Rd, Tickhill, Doncaster, **Yorkshire (South)**, DN11 9LR, **ENG**.
(T) 01302 743113
Speciality: Homeopathy.
**M** (**Ref:**HM12505)

### LLEWELLYN, V J

**V J Llewellyn**, 51 Houndiscombe Rd, Plymouth, **Devon**, PL4 6EX, **ENG**.
(T) 01752 670707
Speciality: Physiotherapy.
● **Owner** Mrs V Llewellyn
**P** **S** **T** (**Ref:**HM12506)

### LLKLEY HEALING CENTRE

**Ilkley Healing Centre**, 8 Nelson Rd, Llkley, **Yorkshire (West)**, LS29 8HN, **ENG**.
(T) 01423 507856
Speciality: Alexander Technique.
● **Therapist** Ms S Firth
**P** **S** (**Ref:**HM12507)

### LLOYD, A

**A Lloyd**, Little Court, Conyngham Rd, Herne Bay, **Kent**, CT6 6PT, **ENG**.
(T) 01227 743150
Speciality: Acupuncture.
● **Owner** Mr A Lloyd
**O** (**Ref:**HM12508)

### LLOYD, C

**C Lloyd**, The Natural Health Centre, 46 Park Pl, Leeds, **Yorkshire (West)**, LS1 2RY, **ENG**.
(T) 01132 436066
Speciality: Homeopathy.
● **Owner** Ms C Lloyd
**M** (**Ref:**HM12509)

### LLOYD, CAROLINE

**Caroline Lloyd**, 4 Athlone Ter, Leeds, **Yorkshire (West)**, LS12 1UA, **ENG**.
(T) 01132 799074 (F) 01132 799074
Speciality: Homeopathy.
● **Owner** Ms C Lloyd
**M** (**Ref:**HM12510)

### LLOYD, D E

**D E Lloyd**, 41A The Tything, Worcester, **Worcestershire**, WR1 1JT, **ENG**.
(T) 01905 22172
Speciality: Chiropodists (Podiatrists).
**S** (**Ref:**HM12511)

### LLOYD, H

**H Lloyd**, 26 Warren Hall Court, Broughton, Chester, **Cheshire**, CH4 0SD, **ENG**.
(T) 01244 661115
Speciality: Chiropodists (Podiatrists).
● **Owner** Mrs H Lloyd
**S** (**Ref:**HM12512)

### LLOYD, N

**N Lloyd**, 44 Bliss Way, Cambridge, **Cambridgeshire**, CB1 9YE, **ENG**.
(T) 07801 866779
Speciality: Reflexology.
● **Owner** Miss N Lloyd
**S** **T** (**Ref:**HM12513)

### LLOYD, PETER R

**Mr Peter R Lloyd**, 12 Regent Rd, Wallasey, **Merseyside**, CH45 8JU, **ENG**.
(T) 01516 389132
Speciality: Osteopathy.
**P** **S** **T** (**Ref:**HM12514)

### LLOYD, R N

**R N Lloyd**, 5 Warwick Sq, Carlisle, **Cumbria**, CA1 1LB, **ENG**.
(T) 01228 524701
Speciality: Osteopathy.
● **Owner** Mr R Lloyd
**P** **S** **T** (**Ref:**HM12515)

### LLOYD, SANDRA

**Sandra Lloyd**, 33 Etchingham Park Rd, London, **London (Greater)**, N3 2DU, **ENG**.
(T) 020 8349 1758
Speciality: Reflexology.
**S** **T** (**Ref:**HM12516)

### LLOYD, TIM

**Tim Lloyd**, Warblington St, Portsmouth, **Hampshire**, PO1 2EX, **ENG**.
(T) 07071 221562
Speciality: Homeopathy.
● **Owner** Mr T Lloyd
**M** (**Ref:**HM12517)

### LLOYD, TIM

**Tim Lloyd**, Portsmouth Natural Health Centre, 20 Landport Trce, Portsmouth, **Hampshire**, PO1 2RG, **ENG**.
(T) 023 9283 0558
Speciality: Homeopathy.
**M** (**Ref:**HM12518)

### LLOYD-BOTTING, N

**N Lloyd-Botting**, 12 Mill Rd, Cambridge, **Cambridgeshire**, CB1 2AD, **ENG**.
(T) 01223 566122
Speciality: Aromatherapy.
**C** **M** **O** (**Ref:**HM12519)

### LLOYD-DAVIES, T

**T Lloyd-Davies**, 27 Friar Gate, Derby, **Derbyshire**, DE1 1ZW, **ENG**.
(T) 01332 385861
Speciality: Chiropodists (Podiatrists).
● **Owner** Mr T Lloyd-Davies
**S** (**Ref:**HM12520)

### LLOYD-JONES, J

**Mrs J Lloyd-Jones**, Flat 2, 2 Market St, Nailsworth, Stroud, **Gloucestershire**, GL6 0BX, **ENG**.
(T) 01453 835582
Speciality: Acupuncture.
**O** (**Ref:**HM12521)

### LLOYD-JONES, M A

**M A Lloyd-Jones**, Halifax Cottage, St Marys Lane, Tewkesbury, **Gloucestershire**, GL20 5SF, **ENG**.
(T) 01684 294368
Speciality: Osteopathy.
**P** **S** **T** (**Ref:**HM12522)

### LLOYD-JONES, M A

**Mr M A Lloyd-Jones**, Flat 2, 2 Market St, Nailsworth, Stroud, **Gloucestershire**, GL6 0BX, **ENG**.
(T) 01453 835582
Speciality: Osteopathy.
**P** **S** **T** (**Ref:**HM12523)

### LLOYD-OWEN CONSULTANCY

**Lloyd-Owen Consultancy**, Lloyd-Owen Stress Clinic, 17 Cowlersley Lane, Huddersfield, **Yorkshire (West)**, HD4 5TY, **ENG**.
(T) 01484 460333 (F) 01484 460333
Speciality: Hypnosis.
● **Owner** Mrs M Lloyd-Owen
**B** (**Ref:**HM12524)

### LLOYD-WILLIAMS, KATHLEEN

**Kathleen Lloyd-Williams**, 125 Westernmoor, Washington, **Tyne and Wear**, NE37 1LT, **ENG**.
(T) 01914 167324
Speciality: Complementary Medicines & Therapy.
● **Owner** Mrs K Lloyd-Williams
**C** **M** (**Ref:**HM12525)

### LOADER, JANE

**Jane Loader**, 31 Abbey Cl, Axminster, **Devon**, EX13 5QU, **ENG**.
(T) 01297 32403 (F) 01297 32403
Speciality: Aromatherapy.
● **Owner** Mrs J Loader
**M** **O** (**Ref:**HM12526)

### LOBASHER, M

**M Lobasher**, 234 Great Portland St, London, **London (Greater)**, W1N 5HG, **ENG**.
(T) 020 7486 6630
Speciality: Psychology.
● **Owner** Mrs M Lobasher
**B** (**Ref:**HM12527)

### LOBB, BRIAN W

**Brian W Lobb**, 6 Arran Cl, Erith, **Kent**, DA8 3SL, **ENG**.
(T) 01322 337812
(E) brian.1066@bti
Speciality: Cognitive Therapy, Counselling, Family Therapy, Gestalt Therapy, Humanistic Psychology, Hypnosis, Hypnotherapy, Psychotherapy, Rogerian Therapy, Stress Therapy, Transactional Analysis, Visualisation Therapy. ✔
● **Psychotherapist/Hypnotherapist** Mr B Lobb Q: BSc, C.Hyp, NRHP (Assoc). M: NRHP.
**B** Yrs. Est.: 10 (**Ref:**HM12528)

### LOBB, JUDY

**Judy Lobb**, Penvercoe Farm, Ruthern Bridge, Bodmin, **Cornwall**, PL30 5LY, **ENG**.
(T) 01208 831300
Speciality: Homeopathy.
● **Senior Partner** Mr T Lobb
**M** (**Ref:**HM12529)

### LOBO, GLENN P

**Glenn P Lobo**, 12 Ashburnham Rd, Luton, **Bedfordshire**, LU1 1JP, **ENG**.
(T) 01582 721531
Speciality: Acupuncture.
● **Owner** Mr G Lobo
**O** (**Ref:**HM12530)

### LOBO, MARIETTE

**Mariette Lobo**, Flat 2, 10 Fortingall Avenue, Glasgow, **Glasgow (City of)**, G12 0LR, **SCO**.
(T) 01413 395591
Speciality: Reflexology.
**S** **T** (**Ref:**HM12531)



Key continued: Yrs.Est: Years Established Q: Qualifications M: Professional Membership ✔ Indemnity Insurance ▬ Accept Credit Cards

### LOCHRIE, JANE
**Jane Lochrie**, 95 Lavender Drive, East Kilbride, Glasgow, **Glasgow (City of)**, G75 9JH, SCO.
(T) 01355 261540
Speciality: Chiropodists (Podiatrists).
● **Owner** Ms J Lochrie
[S] (Ref:HM12532)

### LOCK, ALISON
**Alison Lock**, 78 Brookmead Drive, Wallingford, **Oxfordshire**, OX10 9BJ, ENG.
(T) 01491 839229
Speciality: Reflexology.
[S] [T] (Ref:HM12533)

### LOCK, ALISON
**Alison Lock**, Wallingford, **Oxfordshire**, OX10, ENG.
(T) 01491 839229
Speciality: Bach Remedies, Counselling, Reflexology.
[S] [T] (Ref:HM12534)

### LOCK, J D
**J D Lock**, 20 Thoresby Rd, Rainworth, Mansfield, **Nottinghamshire**, NG21 0DS, ENG.
(T) 01623 798205
Speciality: Chiropodists (Podiatrists).
[S] (Ref:HM12535)

### LOCK, M J
**M J Lock**, 124 Wellesley Rd, Clacton-On-Sea, **Essex**, CO15 3PT, ENG.
(T) 01255 422337
Speciality: Chiropractors.
[P] [S] [T] (Ref:HM12536)

### LOCK, MICHAEL
**Michael Lock**, 9-10 Havelock St, Ilkeston, **Derbyshire**, DE7 5RJ, ENG.
(T) 01159 308900 (F) 01159 301769
Speciality: Psychology.
● **Owner** Mr M Lock
[B] (Ref:HM12537)

### LOCK, ROBERT
**Beltain Centre of Natural Therapies**, Courtyard, 1 Colliton Walk, Dorchester, **Dorset**, DT1 1TZ, ENG.
(T) 01305 267069
Speciality: Acupuncture, Complementary Therapy, Hypnosis, Hypnotherapy, Magnetic Therapy, Moxibustion, Oriental Diagnosis. ✔
● **Reiki Master** Ms P Garland Q: Reiki Master.
● **Acupuncturist/Hypnotherapist** Mr R Lock Q: Lic.Ac, MBAcC. M: BAcC, BBA, INT.
[C] [O] Yrs. Est.: 4 (Ref:HM12538)

### LOCKE, ANNA
**Anna Locke**, 16 Ferdinand House, Ferdinand Pl, London, **London (Greater)**, NW1 8EB, ENG.
(T) 020 7482 1437/07946228110
(W) www.mineraltest.co.uk
Speciality: Indian Head Massage, Reflexology.
[S] [T] (Ref:HM12539)

### LOCKE, PETER A
**Peter A Locke**, 4 Elmsleigh Park, Paignton, **Devon**, TQ4 5AT, ENG.
(T) 01803 559916
Speciality: Chiropractors.
[P] [S] [T] (Ref:HM12540)

### LOCKE, SUSAN
**Susan Locke**, 10 Heaton Cl, Peterborough, **Cambridgeshire**, PE3 9QA, ENG.
(T) 01733 262130
Speciality: Reflexology.
● **Owner** Ms S Locke
[S] [T] (Ref:HM12541)

### LOCKER, KAY
**Kay Locker**, 145 Marlborough Hill, Harrow, **London (Greater)**, HA1 1UG, ENG.
(T) 020 8863 6529
Speciality: Hypnosis.
● **Owner** Ms K Locker
[B] (Ref:HM12542)

### LOCKETT, EMMA
**Emma Lockett**, 12 Millcrest Cl, Worsley, Manchester, **Manchester (Greater)**, M28 1YE, ENG.
(T) 01617 037159
Speciality: Reflexology.
● **Owner** Ms E Thomas
[S] [T] (Ref:HM12543)

### LOCKETT, LEIGH
**Leigh Lockett**, 2 Foxglove Cl, Crewe, **Cheshire**, CW2 6UD, ENG.
(T) 01270 568990
Speciality: Electrolysis.
● **Owner** Mrs G Andrews
[T] (Ref:HM12544)

### LOCKHAMS THERAPY CENTRE
**Lockhams Therapy Centre**, Lockhams Lake Rd, Curdridge, Southampton, **Hampshire**, SO32 2HH, ENG.
(T) 01489 785125
(E) lockhams@bigfoot.com
Speciality: Absent Healing, Dowsing, Indian Head Massage, Massage (Therapeutic), Reflexology, Reiki. ✔
● **Assistant Tutor** Mr P Allison Q: Reiki Master. M: IPTI, ITEC.
● **Owner** Mrs T Allison Q: ITEC, Reiki Master. M: IPTI, ITEC.
[P] Yrs. Est.: 8 (Ref:HM12545)

### LOCKHART, A R
**A R Lockhart**, The Pavilion, Abbots Leigh Rd, Abbots Leigh, Bristol, BS8 3QD, ENG.
(T) 01179 238165 (F) 01179 238165
Speciality: Physiotherapy.
● **Owner** Mr A Lockhart
[P] [S] [T] (Ref:HM12546)

### LOCKHART, CLAIRE
**Claire Lockhart**, 32 Glen Side, Birmingham, **Midlands (West)**, B32 3RU, ENG.
(T) 01214 265327
Speciality: Reflexology.
[S] [T] (Ref:HM12547)

### LOCKHART, M D
**M D Lockhart**, 15 Crescent Rd, Lundin Links, Leven, **Fife**, KY8 6AE, SCO.
(T) 01333 320265
Speciality: Physiotherapy.
● **Principal** Mrs M Lockhart
[P] [S] [T] (Ref:HM12548)

### LOCKIE, A H
**A H Lockie**, 4 Waterden Rd, Guildford, **Surrey**, GU1 2AW, ENG.
(T) 01483 503240 (F) 01483 531177
Speciality: Homeopathy.
● **Practice Manager** Mrs C Don
[M] (Ref:HM12549)

### LOCKINGTON & ASSOCIATES
**H K Lockington & Associates**, 3 Hook Lane, Welling, **Kent**, DA16 2DH, ENG.
(T) 020 8303 8254
Speciality: Chiropodists (Podiatrists).
[S] (Ref:HM12550)

### LOCKINGTON, W M
**W M Lockington**, Acupuncture Clinic, Market St, Penkridge, Stafford, **Staffordshire**, ST19 5DH, ENG.
(T) 01785 713371
Speciality: Acupuncture.
● **Owner** Mrs W Lockington
[O] (Ref:HM12551)

### LOCKLEY, J
**J Lockley**, Woodside Clinic, 88 Great Northern Rd, Dunstable, **Bedfordshire**, LU5 4BT, ENG.
(T) 01582 608400
Speciality: Physiotherapy.
[P] [S] [T] (Ref:HM12552)

### LOCKWOOD, A
**A Lockwood**, 20 Sude Hill, New Mill, Huddersfield, **Yorkshire (West)**, HD7 7BZ, ENG.
(T) 01484 687632
Speciality: Chiropodists (Podiatrists).
● **Owner** Mr A Lockwood
[S] (Ref:HM12553)

### LOCKWOOD, CHARLES M A
**Charles M A Lockwood**, 9 Washbourne Cl, Brixham, **Devon**, TQ5 9TG, ENG.
(T) 01803 854735
Speciality: Chiropodists (Podiatrists).
● **Owner** Mr C Lockwood
[S] (Ref:HM12554)

### LOCKYER, ROSEMARY
**Rosemary Lockyer**, 27 Craven Rd, Newbury, **Berkshire**, RG14 5NG, ENG.
(T) 01635 31679
Speciality: Reflexology.
[S] [T] (Ref:HM12555)

### LODDER, JENNY
**Jenny Lodder**, Crouch Hall Rd Surgery, 48 Crouch Hall Rd, London, **London (Greater)**, N8 8HJ, ENG.
(T) 020 8340 7736 (F) 020 8340 3384
Speciality: Complementary Medicines & Therapy.
● **Practice Manager** Mrs M Maciesczek
[C] [M] (Ref:HM12556)

### LODER, H
**H Loder**, Whitehayes, Riddlecombe, Chulmleigh, **Devon**, EX18 7NY, ENG.
(T) 01769 520319 (F) 01769 520319
Speciality: Herbal Medicine.
● **Owner** Mrs H Loder
[M] (Ref:HM12557)

### LODGE FARM CHIROPRACTIC CENTRE
**Lodge Farm Chiropractic Centre**, Lodge Farm, Tilford Rd, Farnham, **Surrey**, GU9 8HU, ENG.
(T) 01252 716403
Speciality: Chiropractic.
[P] [S] [T] (Ref:HM12558)

### LODGE, ANGELA H
**Angela H Lodge**, 12 Northolmby St, Howden, Goole, **Humberside (North)**, DN14 7JL, ENG.
(T) 01430 410473
Speciality: Hypnotherapy.
● **Senior Partner** Mrs A Lodge
[B] (Ref:HM12559)

### LOEWENTHAL, DEL
**Del Loewenthal**, 70 Kenilworth Avenue, London, **London (Greater)**, SW19 7LR, ENG.
(T) 020 8947 7085 (F) 020 8947 7085
Speciality: Psychotherapy.
● **Owner** Dr D Loewenthal
[B] (Ref:HM12560)

### LOFT SUITE
**Loft Suite (The)**, Christchurch Medical Centre, 1 Purewell Cross Rd, Christchurch, **Dorset**, BH23 3AF, ENG.
(T) 01202 486948
Speciality: Chiropodists (Podiatrists).
[S] (Ref:HM12561)

### LOFTUS, J
**Mr J Loftus**, Sutton Osteopathy & Natural Health Clinic, 22 Throwley Way, Sutton, **Surrey**, SM1 4AF, ENG.
(T) 020 8642 2307
Speciality: Osteopathy.
[P] [S] [T] (Ref:HM12562)

### LOFTUS, N
**N Loftus**, 123 Royd St, Slaithwaite, Huddersfield, **Yorkshire (West)**, HD7 5DX, ENG.
(T) 01484 846409 (F) 01484 847486
Speciality: Chiropodists (Podiatrists).
● **Partner** Mr D Loftus
[S] (Ref:HM12563)

### LOFTUS-BAKER, LYNNE
**Lynne Loftus-Baker**, Rosalie Cosheston, Pembroke, **Pembrokeshire**, SA72 4SS, WAL.
(T) 01646 621461
Speciality: Bach Remedies.
[M] (Ref:HM12564)

### LOGAN, CAROL
**Carol Logan**, 7 Alderbank Pl, Shandon, Edinburgh, **Edinburgh (City of)**, EH11 1SZ, SCO.
(T) 01313 376752 (F) 01314 784780
(E) carollogan@shentherapy.abel.co.uk
Speciality: Counselling, Nutritional Therapy, Psychotherapy, Rogerian Therapy, Shen Therapy, Physio-Emotional Release Therapy. ✔
● **Instructor/Practitioner**



Key: [B] Mind-Body Medicine [C] Complementary Medicine [H] Self Help Treatment [M] Medicinal Therapy [O] Oriental Medicine [P] Postural Therapy [S] Manipulative Structural Therapy [T] Touch Therapy

Ms C Logan Q: BA (Hons), CSI, Dip.Adv Couns&Therapy Skills, Dip.Diet, MCSP. M: ISTA.
T Yrs. Est.: 6 (Ref:HM12565)

**LOGAN, DAVID**

**David Logan**, 9 Beaufort East, Bath, **Somerset**, BA1 6QD, ENG.
(T) 01225 423599
Speciality: Counselling, Hypnosis, Hypnotherapy, Reiki, Stress Therapy, Life Style Management. ✔
● **Hypnotherapist** Mr D Logan Q: BA (Hons), Dip.Hyp.
B H Yrs. Est.: 8 (Ref:HM12566)

**LOGAN, K**

**K Logan**, 7 Eastfield Rd, North Berwick, **Lothian (East)**, EH39 4EW, SCO.
(T) 01620 894028
Speciality: Reflexology.
● **Owner** Kelly Logan
S T (Ref:HM12567)

**LOGAN, ROBIN**

**Robin Logan**, 1 Waterloo Rd, Epsom, **Surrey**, KT19 8AY, ENG.
(T) 01372 729100
Speciality: Homeopathy.
M (Ref:HM12568)

**LOGUE, JOHN**

**John Logue**, 76 Purley Rise, Purley On Thames, Reading, **Berkshire**, RG8 8DH, ENG.
(T) 01189 843158 (F) 01189 843039
Speciality: Complementary Medicines & Therapy.
● **Owner** Mr J Logue
C M (Ref:HM12569)

**LOGUE, MARTIN**

**Martin Logue**, 265 Green Lanes, London, **London (Greater)**, N13 4XE, ENG.
(T) 020 8886 9977
Speciality: Herbalists.
● **Owner** Mr S Thurgood
M (Ref:HM12570)

**LOGUE, MARTIN**

**Martin Logue**, 235 Cowley Rd, Oxford, **Oxfordshire**, OX4 1XG, ENG.
(T) 01865 790235
Speciality: Herbalists.
● **Owner** Miss N Plested
M (Ref:HM12571)

**LOGUE, ROSE**

**Rose Logue**, 85 Kensington Rd, Northolt, **London (Greater)**, UB5 6AW, ENG.
(T) 020 8842 4382
Speciality: Reflexology.
S T (Ref:HM12572)

**LOMAS, CHRISTINA**

**Christina Lomas**, Scarroway, Hillswood Avenue, Leek, **Staffordshire**, ST13 8EG, ENG.
(T) 01538 373292
Speciality: Reflexology.
S T (Ref:HM12573)

**LOMAS, CLIFFORD**

**Clifford Lomas - Osteopath**, 316B Buxton Rd, Stockport, **Cheshire**, SK2 7DD, ENG.
(T) 01614 562087
Speciality: Bowen Therapy, Manipulation, Massage (Therapeutic), Naturopathy, Osteopathy. ✔
● **Osteopath/Naturopath** Mr C Lomas Q: DO. M: GOsC.
S Yrs. Est.: 14 (Ref:HM12574)

**LOMAS, V**

**V Lomas**, 25 Hallcroft Drive, Horbury, Wakefield, **Yorkshire (West)**, WF4 5DQ, ENG.
(T) 01924 277987
Speciality: Chiropodists (Podiatrists).
S (Ref:HM12575)

**LOMAS-HARRIS, ELISABETH**

**Elisabeth Lomas-Harris**, 48 Teapot Lane, Aylesford, **Kent**, ME20 7JT, ENG.
(T) 01622 715597
Speciality: Reflexology.
S T (Ref:HM12576)

**LOMAX, JAMES**

**James Lomax**, 43-45 Clyde Rd, Manchester, **Manchester (Greater)**, M20 2JJ, ENG.
(T) 01614 481057
Speciality: Alexander Technique.
P S (Ref:HM12577)

**LOMAX, KATE**

**Kate Lomax**, 2 Elm Lane, Havant, **Hampshire**, PO9 1HL, ENG.
(T) 023 9247 6488
Speciality: Clairvoyants & Palmists.
B (Ref:HM12578)

**LOMAX, PETER J**

**Peter J Lomax**, 4 Highbury, Newcastle Upon Tyne, **Tyne and Wear**, NE2 3BX, ENG.
(T) 01912 813711
Speciality: Chiropractors.
● **Partner** Dr M Bailey
P S T (Ref:HM12579)

**LOMAX, T**

**T Lomax**, 29 Hersham Rd, Walton-On-Thames, **Surrey**, KT12 1LF, ENG.
(T) 01932 227360 (F) 01932 254395
Speciality: Osteopathy.
● **Principal** Mr S Barron
P S T (Ref:HM12580)

**LOMOND, MARSHA**

**Marsha Lomond**, 97 Ladyshot, Harlow, **Essex**, CM20 3EW, ENG.
(T) 01279 413716
Speciality: Psychotherapy.
B (Ref:HM12581)

**LONDON ACADEMY OF ORIENTAL MED**

**London Academy Of Oriental Medicine**, Priorsfield, Priory Rd, Forest Row, **Sussex (East)**, RH18 5HR, ENG.
(T) 01342 826811 (F) 01342 826027
Speciality: Herbalists.
M (Ref:HM12582)

**LONDON ASS OF PRIMAL PSYCHO**

**Human Question Ltd (The)**, West Hill House, 6 Swains Lane, London, **London (Greater)**, N6 6QS, ENG.
(T) 020 7267 9616 (F) 020 7482 0858
(E) sue@lapp.org
(W) www.lapp.org
Speciality: Primal Therapy, Psychotherapy. ✔
● **Senior Psychotherapist** Ms S Jenssen Q: BA (Hons), Dip.Ath. M: UKCP.
B Yrs. Est.: 15 (Ref:HM12583)

**LONDON CENTRE OF TRICHOLOGY**

**London Centre Of Trichology**, 74 Wigmore St, London, **London (Greater)**, W1H 9DL, ENG.
(T) 020 7935 1935
Speciality: Complementary Medicines & Therapy, Trichology.
M (Ref:HM12584)

**LONDON CLGE OF AC/ORIENTAL MED**

**London College of Acupuncture & Oriental Medicine**, Hr House, 447 High Rd, North Finchley, London, **London (Greater)**, N12 0AZ, ENG.
(T) 020 8371 0810
Speciality: Acupuncture, Chinese Herbal Medicine, Complementary Therapy.
● **Practitioner** Ruth Paeton
M (Ref:HM12585)

**LONDON CLINIC OF PHYSIOTHERAPY**

**London Clinic Of Physiotherapy & Herbal Medicine (The)**, Gemini House, 180-182 Bermondsey St, London, **London (Greater)**, SE1 3TQ, ENG.
(T) 020 7378 8888 (F) 020 7378 1666
Speciality: Herbal Medicine.
M (Ref:HM12586)

**LONDON COLLEGE OF CLINICAL HYP**

**London College Of Clinical Hypnosis**, 17 Hallmeadow Rd, Glossop, **Derbyshire**, SK13 7RE, ENG.
(T) 01457 861151 (F) 01457 852301
Speciality: Hypnotherapy.
● **Owner** Mrs J Bannister
B (Ref:HM12587)

**LONDON COLLEGE OF CLINICAL HYP**

**London College Of Clinical Hypnosis Ltd**, 15 Connaught Sq, London, **London (Greater)**, W2 2HG, ENG.
(T) 020 7706 1346 (F) 020 7262 1237
Speciality: Hypnotherapy.
● **Principal** Mr M Joseph
B (Ref:HM12588)

**LONDON COLLEGE OF OSTEO MED**

**London College Of Osteopathic Medicine**, 8-10 Boston Pl, London, **London (Greater)**, NW1 6QH, ENG.
(T) 020 7262 5250 (F) 020 7723 7492
Speciality: Osteopathy.
● **Manager** Mrs A Dalby
P S T (Ref:HM12589)

**LONDON COLLEGE OF SHIATSU**

**London College Of Shiatsu (The)**, 25-27 Dalling Rd, London, **London (Greater)**, W6 0JD, ENG.
(T) 020 8741 3323
Speciality: Complementary Medicines & Therapy.
● **Manager** Mr N Kyriacou
C M (Ref:HM12590)

**LONDON COLLEGE-CLINICAL HYP**

**London College Of Clinical Hypnotherapists**, Norman Court Lodge, Upper Clatford, Andover, **Hampshire**, SP11 7HB, ENG.
(T) 01264 335855 (F) 01264 358800
Speciality: Hypnosis.
● **Manager** Mr M Joseph
B (Ref:HM12592)

**LONDON COLLEGE-CLNC HYPNOSIS**

**London College Of Clinical Hypnosis Ltd**, 229a Sussex Gardens, London, **London (Greater)**, W2 2RL, ENG.
(T) 020 7402 9037
Speciality: Hypnosis.
B (Ref:HM12591)

**LONDON COLLEGE-HOMEOPATHY**

**London College Of Classical Homoeopathy**, Hahnemann House, 32 Welbeck St, London, **London (Greater)**, W1M 7PG, ENG.
(T) 020 7487 4322 (F) 020 7487 4299
Speciality: Complementary Medicines & Therapy.
● **Director** Mrs M Hood
M (Ref:HM12593)

**LONDON COLLEGE-HYPNOTHERAPY**

**London College Of Clinical Hypnotherapy**, Kamdaris, Harrowbeer Lane, Yelverton, **Devon**, PL20 6DY, ENG.
(T) 01822 853086 (F) 01822 853086
Speciality: Hypnosis.
● **Director** Dr C McKinnon
B (Ref:HM12594)

**LONDON COUNSELLING CENTRE**

**London Counselling Centre (The)**, 47A Golders Green Rd, London, **London (Greater)**, NW11 8EL, ENG.
(T) 020 8201 8526
Speciality: Psychotherapy.
B (Ref:HM12595)

**LONDON CTRE FOR PSYCHOTHERAPY**

**London Centre For Psychotherapy**, 32 Leighton Rd, London, **London (Greater)**, NW5 2QE, ENG.
(T) 020 7482 2002 (F) 020 7482 4222
Speciality: Psychotherapy.
● **Office Manager** Mrs J Wilby
B (Ref:HM12596)

**LONDON FLOAT CENTRE**

**London Float Centre (The)**, 7a Clapham Common, South Side, London, **London (Greater)**, SW4 7AA, ENG.
(T) 020 7720 4952 (F) 020 7627 3381
Speciality: Acupressure, Acupuncture, Alexander Technique, Aromatherapy, Ayurvedic Medicine, Bach Remedies, Chinese Herbal Medicine, Chiropractic, Colonic Hydrotherapy, Complementary Therapy, Cranio-Sacral Therapy, Crystal Healing, Herbal Medicine, Homeopathy, Hopi Ear Candles, Hypnosis, Indian Head



Key continued: Yrs.Est: Years Established Q: Qualifications M: Professional Membership ✔ Indemnity Insurance Accept Credit Cards

Massage, Iridology, Kinesiology, Massage (Therapeutic), McTimoney Chiropractic, Meditation, Metamorphic Therapy, Naturopathy, Nutritional Therapy, Osteopathy, Pilates, Polarity Therapy, Reflexology, Reiki, Remedial Massage, Shiatsu, Stress Therapy, Swedish Body Massage, T'ai-Chi Ch'uan, Tui-na, Yoga, Chi Kung, Chinese Massage, Thai Massage.
● **Manager** Emma Arden
[C] (**Ref:**HM12597)

### LONDON FOOT CLINIC
**London Foot Clinic**, 180 High Rd, London, **London (Greater)**, NW10 2PB, **ENG**.
(T) 020 8459 3375
Speciality: Chiropodists (Podiatrists).
[S] (**Ref:**HM12598)

### LONDON INDIAN CHAMPISSAGE CTRE
**London Centre Of Indian Champissage**, 136 Holloway Rd, London, **London (Greater)**, N7 8DD, **ENG**.
(T) 020 7609 3590 (F) 020 7607 4228
(E) mehta@indianchampissage.com
(W) www.indianchampissage.com
Speciality: Bowen Therapy, Indian Head Massage, Manipulation, Massage (Therapeutic), Osteopathy, Reiki, Facial Rejuvenation. ✔
● **Therapist** Mrs K Mehta
(T) 020 7607 3331 Q: BA, BT, MIPTI. M: GCP, IPTI.
● **Owner/Therapist/Tutor** Mr N Mehta Q: BA, DO, LCSP, MCO. M: GCP.
[T] (**Ref:**HM12599)

### LONDON INS OF STRESS MNGMT
**London Institute Of Stress Management**, 336 Lisburn Rd, Belfast, **County Antrim**, BT9 6GH, **NIR**.
(T) 028 9066 3414
Speciality: Hypnosis.
[B] (**Ref:**HM12600)

### LONDON INSTITUTE FOR TRAINING
**London Institute For Training Of Complementary Acupuncture**, 379-381 Brixton Rd, London, **London (Greater)**, SW9 7DE, **ENG**.
(T) 020 7978 8705
Speciality: Acupuncture.
[O] (**Ref:**HM12601)

### LONDON ROAD CHIROPODY CLINIC
**London Road Chiropody Clinic**, 116 London Rd, Maidstone, **Kent**, ME16 0DJ, **ENG**.
(T) 01622 693514 (F) 01622 681088
Speciality: Chiropodists (Podiatrists).
● **Owner** Mr I Lenehan
[S] (**Ref:**HM12602)

### LONDON ROAD PHYSIO PRACTICE
**London Road Physiotherapy Practice**, 70 London Rd, Wickford, **Essex**, SS12 0AN, **ENG**.
(T) 01268 561696
Speciality: Chiropody, Physiotherapy. ✔
● **Physiotherapist** Ms T Phillips Q: MCSP, SRP.
● **Physiotherapist** Mrs J Snape Q: MCSP, SRP. M: CSP.
● **Physiotherapist** Mr R Alasi Q: MCSP, SRP.
● **Chiropodist** Ms A Patel Q: DPodM, S.R.Ch.
● **Physiotherapist** Ms E Jones Q: MCSP, SRP.
● **Practice Manager** Ms L Bowers
● **Physiotherapist** Mr A McGregor Q: MCSP, SRP. M: CSP.
● **Physiotherapist** Ms C Bissett Q: MCSP, SRP.
[S] Yrs. Est.: 11 (**Ref:**HM12603)

### LONDON SCHOOL OF OSTEOPATHY
**London School of Osteopathy**, 56-60 Nelson St, London, **London (Greater)**, E1 2DE, **ENG**.
(T) 020 7265 9777 (F) 020 7515 5285
(E) sharon@londonschoolofosteopathy.com
(W) www.londonschoolofosteopathy.com
Speciality: Osteopathy, Childrens Osteopathic Clinic. ✔
● **Assistant** Ms S Robinson
● **Registrar** Ms Y D'souza M: GOsC.
[H] [S] Yrs. Est.: 52 (**Ref:**HM12604)

### LONDON SCHOOL OF OSTEOPATHY
**London School Of Osteopathy**, 11 Selsdon Way, London, **London (Greater)**, E14 9GL, **ENG**.
(T) 020 7538 8334 (F) 020 7515 5285
Speciality: Osteopathy.
[P] [S] [T] (**Ref:**HM12605)

### LONDON SCHOOL OF SPRTS MASSAGE
**London School Of Sports Massage Ltd**, Suite 5, Battle, **Sussex (East)**, TN33 0AQ, **ENG**.
(T) 01424 774459
(W) www.lsfm.com
Speciality: Sports Massage. ✔
● **Principal Tutor/Director** Mr M Cash
● **Administrator** Ms H Stewart
[P] [T] Yrs. Est.: 10 (**Ref:**HM12606)

### LONDON SHIATSU CENTRE
**London Shiatsu Centre**, 25-27 Dalling Rd, London, **London (Greater)**, W6 0JD, **ENG**.
(T) 020 8741 3323
Speciality: Complementary Medicines & Therapy.
● **Manager** Mr N Kyriacou
[M] (**Ref:**HM12607)

### LONDON SHYNESS CENTRE
**London Shyness Centre**, 55B Blomfield Rd, London, **London (Greater)**, W9 2PD, **ENG**.
(T) 020 7289 4317
Speciality: Homeopathy.
[C] (**Ref:**HM12608)

### LONDON SMOKING CESSATION CTRE
**London Smoking Cessation Centre (The)**, 31 Church St, Enfield, **London (Greater)**, EN2 6AJ, **ENG**.
(T) 020 8342 0999 (F) 020 8366 0101
Speciality: Complementary Medicines & Therapy.
● **Director** Mrs N Trip
[M] (**Ref:**HM12609)

### LONDON SPINE AND JOINT CLINIC
**London Spine And Joint Clinic (Morden)**, First Floor, 7-11 London Rd, Morden, **Surrey**, SM4 5HT, **ENG**.
(T) 020 8646 3139 (F) 020 8646 3139
Speciality: Aromatherapy, Chiropractic, Complementary Therapy, Homeopathy, Indian Head Massage, Manipulation, Massage (Therapeutic), Reflexology, Rehabilitation, Myofacial Trigger Point Therapy. ✔
● **Clinic Director** Dr G Van Der Walt Q: Ch.B, DC. M: BCA.
[S] Yrs. Est.: 1 (**Ref:**HM12610)

### LONDON SPINE AND JOINT CLINIC
**London Spine And Joint Clinic**, 14 Norfolk Pl, London, **London (Greater)**, W2 1QJ, **ENG**.
(T) 020 7706 7003 (F) 020 7706 7003
(E) reidchiropractic@yahoo.com
Speciality: Acupressure, Acupuncture, Aromatherapy, Chiropractic, Complementary Therapy, Electrotherapy, Indian Head Massage, Life Style Coaching, Manipulation, Massage (Therapeutic), Phytotherapy, Reflexology, X-Ray, Foot Assessment Correction, Orthotic Manufacture.
● **Chiropractor** Dr R Reid Q: CCEP, DC. M: BCA, GCC.
● **Massage Therapist** Nicky Reid Q: ITEC. M: GCP.
● **Chiropractor** Dr A Vice Q: BSc, DC. M: BCA, GCC.
● **Sports Therapist** Bharti Odedra M: GCT.
[S] (**Ref:**HM12611)

### LONDT, CYPRIAN
**Cyprian Londt**, The Peckham Pulse, 10 Melon Rd, London, **London (Greater)**, SE15 5QN, **ENG**.
(T) 020 7701 2535
Speciality: Osteopathy.
● **Owner** Mr C Londt
[P] [S] [T] (**Ref:**HM12612)

### LONERGAN, BARRY
**Barry Lonergan**, Somerton, Elysian Fields, Sidmouth, **Devon**, EX10 8UH, **ENG**.
(T) 01395 516845 (F) 01395 512010
Speciality: Osteopathy.
● **Owner** Mr B Lonergan
[P] [S] [T] (**Ref:**HM12613)

### LONG CRENDON OSTEOPATHS
**Long Crendon Osteopaths**, 14 Bicester Rd, Long Crendon, Aylesbury, **Buckinghamshire**, HP18 9BP, **ENG**.
(T) 01844 202090
(E) robert@pettingell.fsnet.co.uk
Speciality: Manipulation, Massage (Therapeutic), Osteopathy. ✔
● **Osteopath** Mr R Pettingell Q: DO. M: GOsC.
[S] Yrs. Est.: 3 (**Ref:**HM12614)

### LONG LIFE CHINESE HERBAL MED
**Long Life Chinese Herbal Medicine**, 99 High St, Stourbridge, **Midlands (West)**, DY8 1EQ, **ENG**.
(T) 01384 390088
Speciality: Herbalists.
● **Owner** Mr S Gao
[M] (**Ref:**HM12615)

### LONG LIFE CHINESE HERBAL MED
**Long Life Chinese Herbal Medicine**, 9 Carters Green, West Bromwich, **Midlands (West)**, B70 9QP, **ENG**.
(T) 01215 804592
Speciality: Complementary Medicines & Therapy.
● **Owner** Mr S Gao
[M] (**Ref:**HM12616)

### LONG RIVER TAI CHI CIRCLE
**Long River Tai Chi Circle**, 23 Napiershall St, Glasgow, **Glasgow (City of)**, G20 6EZ, **SCO**.
(T) 01413 575102
(W) www.immediatearts.com
Speciality: T'ai-Chi Ch'uan.
● **Tai Chi Teacher** Mr J Kauskas
[C] [O] Yrs. Est.: 10 (**Ref:**HM12617)

### LONG TUONG VAN
**Long Tuong Van**, 168 Burton Rd, Derby, **Derbyshire**, DE1 1TQ, **ENG**.
(T) 01332 380100
Speciality: Acupuncture.
[O] (**Ref:**HM12618)

### LONG, A
**A Long**, 53 Queen St, Cardiff, **Glamorgan (Vale of)**, CF10 2AS, **WAL**.
(T) 029 2022 2697
Speciality: Chiropodists (Podiatrists).
● **Owner** A Long
[S] (**Ref:**HM12619)

### LONG, C
**C Long**, 19 Wellington Avenue, Bristol, BS6 5HP, **ENG**.
(T) 01179 429744
Speciality: Homeopathy.
● **Owner** Mrs C Long
[M] (**Ref:**HM12620)

### LONG, R E
**R E Long**, 35 Queen St, Louth, **Lincolnshire**, LN11 9BJ, **ENG**.
(T) 01507 603927
Speciality: Chiropodists (Podiatrists).
● **Owner** Mr R Long
[S] (**Ref:**HM12621)

### LONG, SUSAN
**Susan Long**, 4 Jorvik Cl, York, **Yorkshire (North)**, YO26 5HD, **ENG**.
(T) 01904 784752
Speciality: Chiropodists (Podiatrists).
● **Owner** Miss S Long
[S] (**Ref:**HM12622)

### LONGARETTI, ANTHONY
**Anthony Longaretti DO**, 130 Victoria Rd, Queens Park, London, **London (Greater)**, NW6 6QB, **ENG**.
(T) 020 7328 7269
(E) tony@tlongaretti.freeserve.co.uk
(W) www.tlongaretti.freeserve.co.uk
Speciality: Osteopathy. ✔
● **Osteopath** Mr A Longaretti Q: DO. M: GOsC.
[S] Yrs. Est.: 4 (**Ref:**HM12623)

### LONGBROOK CENTRE
**Longbrook Centre (The)**, 86 Longbrook St, Exeter, **Devon**, EX4 6AP, **ENG**.
(T) 01392 434074
Speciality: Complementary Medicines & Therapy.
[C] [M] (**Ref:**HM12624)



Key: [B] Mind-Body Medicine [C] Complementary Medicine [H] Self Help Treatment [M] Medicinal Therapy [O] Oriental Medicine [P] Postural Therapy [S] Manipulative Structural Therapy [T] Touch Therapy

## LONGFIELD, MARK
**Longfield Mark**, Natural Healing Centre Thompson House McCurtain St, **County Cork**, IRE.
(T) 021 4501 600
(E) healingt@gofree.indigo.ie
Speciality: Healing.
B (Ref:HM12625)

## LONGFORD BEAUTY CLINIC
**Longford Beauty Clinic**, Dublin St, **County Longford**, IRE.
(T) 04345 590
Speciality: Aromatherapy, Dermalogical Spa Body Therapy, Classic European Skin Care Treatment, Express Skin Care Treatment, Back Facial Treatment, Revitalising Eye Treatment.
✔ CREDIT
● **Beauty Therapist** Ms L Tiernan M: ITEC.
● **Beauty Therapist** Ms B O'Connor Kelly M: ITEC.
T Yrs. Est.: 6 (Ref:HM12626)

## LONGFORD PHYSIO & SPORTS
**Longford Physiotherapy & Sports Injury Clinic**, 2 Pembury Avenue, Coventry, **Midlands (West)**, CV6 6JT, ENG.
(T) 024 7636 7918
(E) pabla@onetel.nat.uk
Speciality: Acupuncture, Electrotherapy, Massage (Therapeutic), Physiotherapy, Phytotherapy, Postural Integration. ✔
● **Physiotherapist** Mrs K Pabla Q: Chartered Physio, Grad Dip Phys, MCSP, SRP. M: CPS, CSP, OCPPP.
M P S Yrs. Est.: 19 (Ref:HM12627)

## LONGLEY, JOANNA
**Joanna Longley**, 52A Wardo Avenue, London, **London (Greater)**, SW6 6RE, ENG.
(T) 020 7731 3942
Speciality: Hypnosis.
● **Owner** Ms J Longley
B (Ref:HM12628)

## LONGTHORP, S V
**S V Longthorp**, 184 London Rd, Headington, Oxford, **Oxfordshire**, OX3 9EE, ENG.
(T) 01865 763530
Speciality: Chiropodists (Podiatrists).
S (Ref:HM12629)

## LONGTON, PATRICIA M
**Patricia M Longton**, 155 Breck Rd, Poulton-le-Fylde, **Lancashire**, FY6 7HJ, ENG.
(T) 01253 883559
Speciality: Chiropodists (Podiatrists).
● **Owner** Mrs P Longton
S (Ref:HM12630)

## LONGWORTH, WENDY
**Wendy Longworth**, East Finchley Clinic, Cory Pharmacy, 166-168 High Rd, London, **London (Greater)**, N2 9AS, ENG.
(T) 020 8883 5888
Speciality: Physiotherapy.
P S T (Ref:HM12631)

## LONSDALE, FIONA
**Fiona Lonsdale**, Doctors Surgery, 138 Harley St, London, **London (Greater)**, W1N 1AH, ENG.
(T) 020 7486 3155 (F) 020 7486 3155
Speciality: Physiotherapy.
● **Owner** Ms F Lonsdale
P S T (Ref:HM12632)

## LOOK 2 NATURE
**Look 2 Nature**, P O Box 30, Riverhead, Sevenoaks, **Kent**, TN13 2TT, ENG.
(T) 08003 285453
Speciality: Complementary Medicines & Therapy.
M (Ref:HM12633)

## LOOKERS NATURAL THERAPY CLINIC
**Lookers Natural Therapy Clinic**, 3 Church St, Hereford, **Herefordshire**, HR1 2LT, ENG.
(T) 01432 271528
Speciality: Aromatherapy.
M O (Ref:HM12634)

## LOOMS, DAVID W
**David W Looms**, 22 Langdale Drive, Nuneaton, **Warwickshire**, CV11 6EY, ENG.
(T) 024 7634 7768
Speciality: Physiotherapy.
● **Owner** Mr D Looms
P S T (Ref:HM12635)

## LOPATO, G E
**G E Lopato**, 339 Lytham Rd, Blackpool, **Lancashire**, FY4 1DS, ENG.
(T) 01253 400606
Speciality: Chiropodists (Podiatrists).
● **Owner** Mrs G Lopato
S (Ref:HM12636)

## LOPES, ROBYN
**Robyn Lopes**, Downhorn Farm, Horn Lane, Plymouth, **Devon**, PL9 9BR, ENG.
(T) 01752 407698
Speciality: Chiropractic.
● **Owner** Mrs R Lopes
P S T (Ref:HM12637)

## LORAM, CHARLES
**Charles Loram**, 51 Waterloo St, Hove, **Sussex (East)**, BN3 1AH, ENG.
(T) 01273 725469
Speciality: Alexander Technique.
● **Owner** Mr C Loram
P S (Ref:HM12638)

## LORD, K H
**K H Lord**, 42 Warwick Avenue, Coventry, **Midlands (West)**, CV5 6DG, ENG.
(T) 024 7667 3940
Speciality: Osteopathy.
P S T (Ref:HM12639)

## LORD, LESLEY
**Miss Lesley Lord**, 28 Angel Cres, Bridgwater, **Somerset**, TA6 3EW, ENG.
(T) 01278 433077
Speciality: Chiropodists (Podiatrists).
● **Owner** Mrs L Lord
S (Ref:HM12640)

## LORD, WENDY
**Wendy Lord**, Glyder, Mount St, Menai Bridge, **Isle of Anglesey**, LL59 5BW, WAL.
(T) 01248 713921
Speciality: Reflexology.
S T (Ref:HM12641)

## LORDAN, KATHERINE
**Katherine Lordan**, 16 Anstey Cl, Waddesdon, Aylesbury, **Buckinghamshire**, HP18 0NB, ENG.
(T) 01296 658162
Speciality: Hypnosis.
B (Ref:HM12642)

## LORENZ, BERNICE
**Bernice Lorenz**, The Spinney, Magpie Lane, Coleshill, Amersham, **Buckinghamshire**, HP7 0LS, ENG.
(T) 01494 722618
Speciality: Chiropodists (Podiatrists).
● **Owner** Mrs B Lorenz
S (Ref:HM12643)

## LORETTE PARK
**Lorette Park**, 68c St Michaels Gr, Fareham, **Hampshire**, PO14 1DS, ENG.
(T) 01329 317132
Speciality: Reflexology.
S T (Ref:HM12644)

## LORIAN CLINIC FOR COMP MED
**Lorian Clinic For Complementary Medicine (The)**, Peachey House, Bepton Rd, Midhurst, **Sussex (West)**, GU29 9LU, ENG.
(T) 01730 810540 (F) 01730 812248
Speciality: Complementary Medicines & Therapy.
● **Secretary** Ms S Upfold
C M (Ref:HM12645)

## LORRAINE DOCHERTY HOL PRACT
**Lorraine Docherty Holistic Practitioner**, Ferndale House, Gutterscroft, Haslington, Crewe, **Cheshire**, CW1 5RJ, ENG.
(T) 01270 584048
Speciality: Complementary Medicines & Therapy.
● **Owner** Mrs L Docherty
C M (Ref:HM12646)

## LORRIMAN, MARGARET
**Margaret Lorriman**, 1 Orchard Way, Wymeswold, Loughborough, **Leicestershire**, LE12 6SW, ENG.
(T) 01509 880442
Speciality: Reflexology.
S T (Ref:HM12647)

## LOSANG DRAGPA BUDDHIST CENTRE
**Losang Dragpa Buddhist Centre**, Dobroyd Castle, Pexwood Rd, Todmorden, **Yorkshire (West)**, OL14 7JJ, ENG.
(T) 01706 812247
Speciality: Complementary Medicines & Therapy.
C M (Ref:HM12648)

## LOTERY, FRANCOISE
**Francoise Lotery**, 113 Quebec Rd, Ilford, **Essex**, IG2 6AW, ENG.
(T) 020 8518 3741 (F) 020 8518 3741
Speciality: Hypnosis.
● **Owner** Ms F Lotery
B (Ref:HM12649)

## LOTHIAN HERBS
**Lothian Herbs (Edinburgh) Ltd**, Peffermill Industrial Estate, Peffermill Rd, Edinburgh, **Edinburgh (City of)**, EH16 5UY, SCO.
(T) 01316 619803
Speciality: Aromatherapy.
M O (Ref:HM12650)

## LOTIONS & POTIONS
**Lotions & Potions**, 7 West St, Dorking, **Surrey**, RH4 1BL, ENG.
(T) 01306 740955
Speciality: Complementary Medicines & Therapy.
● **Managing Director** Ms R Kaye
M (Ref:HM12651)

## LOTUS CLINIC
**Lotus Clinic**, 49 Housley Park, Chapeltown, Sheffield, **Yorkshire (South)**, S35 2UE, ENG.
(T) 01142 400366
Speciality: Reflexology.
● **Owner** Mrs S Price
S T (Ref:HM12652)

## LOTUS CLINIC
**Lotus Educational Health Clinic**, 19 Upper Berkeley St, London, **London (Greater)**, W1H 7PF, ENG.
(T) 020 7724 4004 (F) 020 7724 3003
Speciality: Homeopathy. ✔
● **Homeopath** Ms J Kallas Q: BA (Hons), LCH, MBA, RSHom. M: Soc.Hom.
B C Yrs. Est.: 2 (Ref:HM12653)

## LOTUS EMPORIUM
**Lotus Emporium**, 39A Sydney St, Brighton, **Sussex (East)**, BN1 4EP, ENG.
(T) 01273 674742 (F) 01273 674742
Speciality: Aromatherapy.
● **Manager** Ms V Crawford
M O (Ref:HM12654)

## LOTUS EMPORIUM
**Lotus Emporium**, Unit 9 Guildhall Market, High St, Bath, **Somerset**, BA1 5AW, ENG.
(T) 01225 448011 (F) 01225 448011
Speciality: Aromatherapy.
M O (Ref:HM12655)

## LOTUS HEALING CENTRE
**Lotus Healing Centre**, White House Farm, Saxtead, Woodbridge, **Suffolk**, IP13 9QT, ENG.
(T) 01728 724606
Speciality: Complementary Medicines & Therapy.
C M (Ref:HM12656)

## LOTUS HERBS
**Lotus Herbs**, 15 Church St, Beaumaris, **Isle of Anglesey**, LL58 8AB, WAL.
(T) 01248 811330
Speciality: Herbalists.
● **Owner** Mrs G Harvach
M (Ref:HM12657)

## LOTUS LODGE
**Lotus Lodge**, Lady Chapel, Maynooth, **County Kildare**, IRE.



Key continued: Yrs.Est: Years Established Q: Qualifications M: Professional Membership ✔ Indemnity Insurance CREDIT Accept Credit Cards

(T) 01628 6027
(E) m.e.m.@hotmail.com
Speciality: Healing.
B (Ref:HM12658)

**LOUGHBOROUGH CHIRO CLINIC**

**Loughborough Chiropractic Clinic**, 25 Park Rd, Loughborough, **Leicestershire**, LE11 2ED, ENG.
(T) 01509 219800 (F) 01509 210336
Speciality: Chiropractors.
● **Owner** Mr J Hammond
P S T (Ref:HM12659)

**LOUGHBOROUGH OSTEOPATHIC**

**Loughborough Osteopathic Clinic**, 95 Ashby Rd, Loughborough, **Leicestershire**, LE11 3AB, ENG.
(T) 01509 262880 (F) 01509 262880
(W) www.loughboroughosteopath.co.uk
Speciality: Osteopathy. ✓
● **Owner** Mr J Butler Q: Reg.Osteopath.
M: GOsC.
S Yrs. Est.: 18 (Ref:HM12660)

**LOUGHLIN, N**

**N Loughlin**, 37 Northwood Avenue, Knaphill, Woking, **Surrey**, GU21 2ES, ENG.
(T) 01483 473554
Speciality: Chiropodists (Podiatrists).
● **Owner** Mrs S Loughlin
S (Ref:HM12661)

**LOUGHRAN, MARGARETA**

**Margareta Loughran**, 91 Cheyne Walk, London, **London (Greater)**, SW10 0DQ, ENG.
(T) 020 7352 8458
Speciality: Psychoanalysis.
B (Ref:HM12662)

**LOUGHTON, ANDREA**

**Andrea Loughton**, 33 Jubilee Rd, Gosforth, Newcastle Upon Tyne, **Tyne and Wear**, NE3 3EU, ENG.
(T) 01912 851333
Speciality: Reflexology.
S T (Ref:HM12663)

**LOUIS, L**

**L Louis**, 18A Church St, Oswestry, **Shropshire**, SY11 2SP, ENG.
(T) 01691 670307
Speciality: Osteopathy.
P S T (Ref:HM12664)

**LOUISA-JAYNE HILL M INST CH P**

**Louisa-Jayne Hill M Inst Ch P**, 150 Sundridge Drive, Chatham, **Kent**, ME5 8HG, ENG.
Speciality: Chiropodists (Podiatrists).
S (Ref:HM12665)

**LOUISE**

**Louise**, Rosedale Clinic, 48 Redlands Rd, Reading, **Berkshire**, RG1 5HR, ENG.
(T) 01189 314682
Speciality: Clairvoyants & Palmists.
B (Ref:HM12666)

**LOUISE BRITTLE**

**Louise Brittle**, 26 Lincolncroft, Shenstone, Lichfield, **Staffordshire**, WS14 0ND, ENG.
(T) 01543 480840
Speciality: Biomechanics, Chiropody, Cryo Surgery, Gait Analysis, Nail Surgery, Podiatry, Sports Medicine. ✓
● **Chiropodist (Podiatrist)**
Ms L Brittle Q: BSc (Hons). M: S.C.P, S.R.Ch.
C Yrs. Est.: 3 (Ref:HM12667)

**LOUISE HEALING CENTRE**

**Louise Healing Centre**, 47 Newmarket St, Grimsby, **Humberside (South)**, DN32 7BP, ENG.
(T) 01472 242545
Speciality: Absent Healing, Acupressure, Aromatherapy, Auto Suggestion, Complementary Therapy, Counselling, Faith Healing, Healer, Healing Therapy, Herbal Medicine, Holistic Healing, Homeopathy, Hypnotherapy, Indian Head Massage, Massage (Therapeutic), Meditation, Reflexology, Spiritual Healing, T'ai-Chi Ch'uan, Yoga. ✓
● **Therapist** Ms Wilkins M: AoR.
● **Therapist** Ms Horsefall M: AoR.
● **Therapist** Ms M Griffin
● **Owner** Ms S Thomas Q: RGN.
B C Yrs. Est.: 3 (Ref:HM12668)

**LOUTH CHIROPRACTIC CLINIC**

**Louth Chiropractic Clinic**, 35 Eastgate, Louth, **Lincolnshire**, LN11 9NH, ENG.
(T) 01507 600644
Speciality: Chiropractic.
P S T (Ref:HM12669)

**LOVE, CLAIRE**

**Claire Love**, 3a Agincourt St, Monmouth, **Monmouthshire**, NP25 3DZ, WAL.
(T) 01600 716880 (F) 01600 716880
Speciality: Osteopathy.
● **Principal** Ms C Love
P S T (Ref:HM12670)

**LOVEDAY, J A**

**J A Loveday**, 28 York Rd, Worthing, **Sussex (West)**, BN11 3EN, ENG.
(T) 01903 217048
Speciality: Chiropodists (Podiatrists).
● **Owner** Mrs J Loveday
S (Ref:HM12671)

**LOVEGROVE, SHERINE**

**Sherine Lovegrove**, 52 Stoke Newington Church St, London, **London (Greater)**, N16 0NB, ENG.
(T) 020 7241 5033 (F) 020 7502 1182
Speciality: Hypnotherapy.
● **Senior Partner** Mrs J Sharidan
B (Ref:HM12672)

**LOVELACE, KIM PAUL**

**Kim Paul Lovelace**, 1 Hope Villas, Yapton Rd, Barnham, Bognor Regis, **Sussex (West)**, PO22 0BB, ENG.
(T) 01243 555476
Speciality: Complementary Medicines & Therapy.
C M (Ref:HM12673)

**LOVELADY, B M**

**B M Lovelady**, 13 Western Avenue, Bournemouth, **Dorset**, BH10 5BN, ENG.
(T) 01202 517843
Speciality: Chiropodists (Podiatrists).
● **Owner** Mrs B Lovelady
S (Ref:HM12674)

**LOVELAND, SYLVIA**

**Sylvia Loveland**, 9 Amshurst Villas, Gallants Lane, East Farleigh, Maidstone, **Kent**, ME15 0LQ, ENG.
(T) 01622 747816
Speciality: Clairvoyants & Palmists.
● **Owner** Mrs S Loveland
B (Ref:HM12675)

**LOVELL, A G**

**A G Lovell**, Bishops Pk Centre, Lancaster Way, Bishop's Stortford, **Hertfordshire**, CM23 4DA, ENG.
(T) 01279 651859
Speciality: Osteopathy.
● **Owner** Mr D Lindy
P S T (Ref:HM12676)

**LOVELL, JENNY**

**Jenny Lovell**, 21 Oxford Rd, Colchester, **Essex**, CO3 3HT, ENG.
(T) 01206 764083
Speciality: Acupuncture.
● **Owner** Ms J Lovell
O (Ref:HM12677)

**LOVELL, P**

**P Lovell**, 1 New St, Wells, **Somerset**, BA5 2LA, ENG.
(T) 01749 674716
Speciality: Chiropractors.
P S T (Ref:HM12678)

**LOVELL, PETER**

**Peter Lovell**, 123 Beeleigh Link, Chelmsford, **Essex**, CM2 6PH, ENG.
(T) 01245 252177
Speciality: Complementary Medicines & Therapy.
● **Owner** Peter Lovell
M (Ref:HM12679)

**LOVERIDGE, KATHY**

**Kathy Loveridge**, 34 The Avenue, Watford, **Hertfordshire**, WD1 3NS, ENG.
(T) 01923 225646
Speciality: Complementary Medicines & Therapy.
M (Ref:HM12680)

**LOVESEY, R M**

**R M Lovesey**, Holly House, 6 Barncroft, Berkhamsted, **Hertfordshire**, HP4 3NL, ENG.
(T) 01442 864243 (F) 01442 878548
Speciality: Acupuncture.
● **Owner** Mrs R Lovesey
O (Ref:HM12681)

**LOVETT, PAULINE**

**Pauline Lovett**, 75 Leigh Rd, Leigh-On-Sea, **Essex**, SS9 1JN, ENG.
(T) 01702 714862 (F) 01702 716969
Speciality: Homeopathy.
● **Owner** Mrs C Merryfield
M (Ref:HM12682)

**LOVITT, ANGELA**

**Angela Lovitt**, 18 Jolliffe Rd, Poole, **Dorset**, BH15 2HB, ENG.
(T) 01202 386703
Speciality: Reflexology.
● **Owner** Mrs A Lovitt
S T (Ref:HM12683)

**LOW, A**

**A Low**, The Sydney Fisher Clinic, 81 Tressillian Rd, London, **London (Greater)**, SE4 1XZ, ENG.
(T) 020 8694 2714 (F) 020 8694 2714
Speciality: Osteopathy.
● **Partner** Mrs J Mitchell
P S T (Ref:HM12684)

**LOW, C J**

**C J Low**, 34 Rustat Rd, Cambridge, **Cambridgeshire**, CB1 3QT, ENG.
(T) 01223 415117 (F) 01223 240750
Speciality: Acupuncture.
● **Owner** Mr C Low
O (Ref:HM12685)

**LOW, JANET (DR)**

**Dr Janet Low**, Flat 6, St. Martins Court, Ullswater Rd, London, **London (Greater)**, SE27 0AN, ENG.
(T) 020 8244 4549
(E) janet.low@lineone,net
Speciality: Counselling, Psychotherapy. ✓
● **Owner/Psychoanalytic Therapist**
Dr J Low Q: BA (Hons), MA, PhD.
H (Ref:HM12686)

**LOW, LORNA**

**Lorna Low**, 5 Damers Rd, Dorchester, **Dorset**, DT1 2JX, ENG.
(T) 01305 263430
Speciality: Osteopathy.
P S T (Ref:HM12687)

**LOW, ROYSTON**

**Royston Low**, 118 Foley Rd, Claygate, Esher, **Surrey**, KT10 0NA, ENG.
(T) 01372 464171
Speciality: Acupuncture, Osteopathy. ✓
● **Doctor of Acupuncture/Osteopath**
Mr R Low Q: DO, Dr.Ac, ND, PhD. M: AACP, BAcC, BOsC.
O Yrs. Est.: 40 (Ref:HM12688)

**LOW-BEER, F E**

**F E Low-Beer**, 1 Pullens Lane, Headington, Oxford, **Oxfordshire**, OX3 0BX, ENG.
(T) 01865 761429
Speciality: Psychotherapy.
B (Ref:HM12689)

**LOWDE, JANIE**

**Janie Lowde**, 1 Purewell Cross Rd, Christchurch, **Dorset**, BH23 3AF, ENG.
(T) 01202 499518 (F) 01202 475706
Speciality: Physiotherapy.
● **Senior Partner** Mrs D Todd
P S T (Ref:HM12690)

**LOWDE, JANIE**

**Janie Lowde**, 41 Church Rd, Poole, **Dorset**, BH14 0NN, ENG.
(T) 01202 749514 (F) 01202 718906
Speciality: Physiotherapy.
● **Partner** Mrs C Swinhoe



Key: B Mind-Body Medicine C Complementary Medicine H Self Help Treatment M Medicinal Therapy O Oriental Medicine P Postural Therapy S Manipulative Structural Therapy T Touch Therapy

P S T (Ref:HM12691)

**LOWE, ANDREA**

**Andrea Lowe**, Derby Chambers, 6 The Rock, Bury, **Lancashire**, BL9 0NT, ENG.
(T) 01617 641440
Speciality: Hypnotherapy.
● **Owner** Ms A Lowe
B (Ref:HM12692)

**LOWE, CATHIE**

**Cathie Lowe**, Health Hydro, Milton Rd, Swindon, **Wiltshire**, SN1 5JA, ENG.
(T) 01793 465631
Speciality: Aromatherapy.
M O (Ref:HM12693)

**LOWE, D L**

**D L Lowe**, 17 Ashley Rd, Altrincham, **Cheshire**, WA14 2DT, ENG.
(T) 01619 285033
Speciality: Chiropodists (Podiatrists).
● **Owner** Miss D Lowe
S (Ref:HM12694)

**LOWE, IRENE**

**Irene Lowe**, 5 Wantage, Telford, **Shropshire**, TF7 5PA, ENG.
(T) 01952 582001
Speciality: Reflexology.
S T (Ref:HM12695)

**LOWE, JANET**

**Janet Lowe**, Cleomone, Tenterden Rd, Biddenden, Ashford, **Kent**, TN27 8BL, ENG.
(T) 01580 291024
Speciality: Reflexology.
S T (Ref:HM12696)

**LOWE, JOHN**

**John Lowe**, First Floor, 85 Stricklandgate, Kendal, **Cumbria**, LA9 4RA, ENG.
(T) 01539 733882
Speciality: Chiropodists (Podiatrists).
S (Ref:HM12697)

**LOWE, K**

**K Lowe**, Packhams, North St, Midhurst, **Sussex (West)**, GU29 9DJ, ENG.
(T) 01730 813911
Speciality: Complementary Medicines & Therapy.
● **Owner** Mr K Lowe
C M (Ref:HM12698)

**LOWE, KENNETH**

**Naturopathic Surgery**, 26 Meadow Cl, Liphook, **Hampshire**, GU30 7BJ, ENG.
(T) 01428 723355
Speciality: Acupressure, Acupuncture, Bonesetting, Clinical Ecology, Complementary Therapy, Dietician, Electrotherapy, Hay Diet, Homeopathy, Kinesiology, Manipulation, Massage (Therapeutic), Naturopathy, Nutritional Therapy, Postural Integration, Shiatsu, Vitamin Therapy, Electro-Acupuncture, Auricular Acupuncture. ✓
● **Naturopath** Mr K Lowe Q: DO, ND, RN.
M: BNA, SAAc.
S Yrs. Est.: 45 (Ref:HM12699)

**LOWE, RACHEL**

**Rachel Lowe**, Hebden Bridge Centre For Natural Medicine, 33 West End, Hebden Bridge, **Yorkshire (West)**, HX7 8UQ, ENG.
(T) 01422 843017
Speciality: Homeopathy.
M (Ref:HM12700)

**LOWER, P R**

**P R Lower**, 61 Rotherfield Cres, Brighton, **Sussex (East)**, BN1 8FH, ENG.
(T) 01273 880269
Speciality: Chiropodists (Podiatrists).
● **Owner** Mr P Lower
S (Ref:HM12701)

**LOWES, D N**

**D N Lowes**, 50 Learmonth Gr, Edinburgh, **Edinburgh (City of)**, EH4 1BN, SCO.
(T) 01313 328837
Speciality: Chiropodists (Podiatrists).
● **Partner** Miss J Hazel
S (Ref:HM12702)

**LOWESTOFT TRAD ACUPUNTURE CLNC**

**Lowestoft Traditional Acupunture Clinic**, 59A High St, Lowestoft, **Suffolk**, NR32 1JA, ENG.
(T) 01502 580520
Speciality: Acupuncture.
● **Owner** Mrs M Spearing
O (Ref:HM12703)

**LOWETH, DEBORAH**

**Deborah Loweth**, 14 Knights Cl, Buntingford, **Hertfordshire**, SG9 9SE, ENG.
(T) 01763 272008
Speciality: Chiropodists (Podiatrists).
S (Ref:HM12704)

**LOWICK, DELIA**

**Delia Lowick**, 51 Palmerston Rd, Northampton, **Northamptonshire**, NN1 5EU, ENG.
(T) 01604 631507
Speciality: Complementary Medicines & Therapy.
C M (Ref:HM12705)

**LOWINGER, LEAH**

**Leah Lowinger**, 12 Ashford Rd, Fordingbridge, **Hampshire**, SP6 1BZ, ENG.
(T) 01425 657615
Speciality: Psychology.
● **Owner** Ms L Lowinger
B (Ref:HM12706)

**LOWIS, PETER**

**Peter Lowis**, Clissold Park Health Centre, 154 Stoke Newington Church St, London, **London (Greater)**, N16 0JU, ENG.
(T) 020 7249 2990 (F) 020 7249 3977
Speciality: Psychotherapy.
● **Owner** Mr D Berg
B (Ref:HM12707)

**LOWMAN, V**

**V Lowman**, 5 Mason Rd, Kidderminster, **Worcestershire**, DY11 6AF, ENG.
(T) 01562 824440 (F) 01562 824440
Speciality: Chiropodists (Podiatrists).
S (Ref:HM12708)

**LOWRY, H M**

**H M Lowry**, 8 Orchard Way, Stratford-Upon-Avon, **Warwickshire**, CV37 9QE, ENG.
(T) 01789 262010
Speciality: Physiotherapy.
● **Owner** Mr H Lowry
P S T (Ref:HM12709)

**LOWSON, H**

**H Lowson**, Alberta House, Kings Park Drive, Bournemouth, **Dorset**, BH7 7AG, ENG.
(T) 01202 396282
Speciality: Psychotherapy.
B (Ref:HM12710)

**LOWTHER, MAVIS**

**Mavis Lowther**, 1 Boswell Rd, Doncaster, **Yorkshire (South)**, DN4 7BJ, ENG.
(T) 01302 539681
Speciality: Reflexology.
S T (Ref:HM12711)

**LOXTON, K**

**K Loxton**, 2a Guildford Park Rd, Guildford, **Surrey**, GU2 7ND, ENG.
(T) 01483 579500
Speciality: Reflexology.
S T (Ref:HM12712)

**LPS TRAINING & CONSULTANCY**

**Lps Training & Consultancy**, 7 Kirkstall Avenue, Leeds, **Yorkshire (West)**, LS5 3DN, ENG.
(T) 01132 755774 (F) 01132 556069
(W) www.lpstraining.com
Speciality: Manipulation, Mobilisation. ✓
● **Physiotherapist** Mr S Love Q: BA, Grad Dip Phys, MCSP.
● **Nurse** Julie Love Q: RGN.
S (Ref:HM12713)

**LU, X**

**X Lu**, 1 Upland Rd, South Croydon, **Surrey**, CR2 6RD, ENG.
(T) 020 8681 8665
Speciality: Herbalists.
M (Ref:HM12714)

**LUBBOCK, BRIDGET**

**Ms Bridget Lubbock**, Centre For Complementary Medicine, 20 Lavant St, Petersfield, **Hampshire**, GU32 3EW, ENG.
(T) 01730 266539
Speciality: Acupuncture.
O (Ref:HM12715)

**LUBBOCK, R W H**

**R W H Lubbock**, 19 Adelaide Rd, Walton-On-Thames, **Surrey**, KT12 1NB, ENG.
(T) 01932 229131 (F) 01932 229131
Speciality: Psychology.
● **Owner** Mr R Lubbock
B (Ref:HM12716)

**LUCAN FAMILY CENTRE**

**Lucan Family Centre**, 2 Hanbury La, Lucan, **County Dublin**, IRE.
(T) 01621 7022
Speciality: Counselling.
B H (Ref:HM12717)

**LUCAN NATURAL HEALING CENTRE**

**Lucan Natural Healing Centre**, 12 Rochfort Gr, Lucan, **County Dublin**, IRE.
(T) 01624 0050
Speciality: Healing.
B (Ref:HM12718)

**LUCAS, JANICE T**

**Janice T Lucas**, 21 Middlemead, Folkestone, **Kent**, CT19 5UB, ENG.
(T) 01303 244491
Speciality: Complementary Medicines & Therapy.
● **Owner** Mrs J Lucas
C M (Ref:HM12719)

**LUCAS, P**

**Mrs P Lucas**, 2 St Johns Rd, Isleworth, **London (Greater)**, TW7 6NN, ENG.
(T) 020 8560 7073
Speciality: Chiropodists (Podiatrists).
S (Ref:HM12720)

**LUCCHETTI, C A**

**C A Lucchetti**, 4 Brewery Lane, Wymondham, **Norfolk**, NR18 0AZ, ENG.
(T) 01953 606660 (F) 01953 606660
Speciality: Chiropractic.
● **Owner** Mr C Lucchetti
P S T (Ref:HM12721)

**LUCE, PETER J**

**Peter J Luce**, 269 New Rd, Saltash, **Cornwall**, PL12 6HQ, ENG.
(T) 01752 844777
Speciality: Hypnosis.
B (Ref:HM12722)

**LUCK, MARGARET**

**Margaret Luck**, 9 Hazel Copse, Chippenham, **Wiltshire**, SN14 0PD, ENG.
(T) 01249 444857
Speciality: Aromatherapy.
● **Owner** Mrs M Luck
M O (Ref:HM12723)

**LUCKOCK, M**

**M Luckock**, 224 Western Avenue, Dagenham, **Essex**, RM10 8UP, ENG.
(T) 07050 333845
Speciality: Hypnotherapy.
● **Owner** Mr M Luckock
B (Ref:HM12724)

**LUCY, IRENE**

**Irene Lucy**, 65 Ashley Rd, New Milton, **Hampshire**, BH25 6AZ, ENG.
(T) 01425 611559
Speciality: Complementary Medicines & Therapy.
● **Partner** Mrs I Lucy
C M (Ref:HM12725)

**LUDKINS, P**

**P Ludkins**, 3 Radnor Park West, Folkestone, **Kent**, CT19 5HH, ENG.
(T) 01303 254733
Speciality: Acupuncture.
● **Owner** Mr P Ludkins
O (Ref:HM12726)



Key continued: **Yrs.Est:** Years Established **Q:** Qualifications **M:** Professional Membership ✓ Indemnity Insurance Accept Credit Cards

### LUDLOW OSTEOPATHIC CLINIC
**Ludlow Osteopathic Clinic**, 125 Corve St, Ludlow, **Shropshire**, SY8 2PG, ENG.
(T) 01584 877869 (F) 01432 355585
Speciality: Allergy Testing, Naturopathy, Osteopathy. ✔
● **Osteopath** Ms P Rathod **Q:** BSc (Hons), DO, ND. **M:** RO, RoN.
S Yrs. Est.: 11 (**Ref:**HM12727)

### LUFF, JIM
**Jim Luff D C H**, Quarrendon Lincoln Rd, Glinton, Peterborough, **Cambridgeshire**, PE6 7JR, ENG.
(T) 01733 253545
Speciality: Hypnotherapy.
B (**Ref:**HM12728)

### LUFF, ROBIN R
**Robin R Luff**, 26 Charlesworth Drive, Waterlooville, **Hampshire**, PO7 6AX, ENG.
(T) 023 9225 3252
Speciality: Chiropodists (Podiatrists).
● **Managing Director** Mr R Luff
S (**Ref:**HM12729)

### LUFFINGHAM, D & E
**D & E Luffingham**, 1 Grange House, Grange Rd, Midhurst, **Sussex (West)**, GU29 9LS, ENG.
(T) 01730 812312
Speciality: Chiropodists (Podiatrists).
● **Owner** Mr D Luffingham
S (**Ref:**HM12730)

### LUFFINGHAM, D & E
**Luffingham D & E**, 12 West St, Haslemere, **Surrey**, GU27 2AB, ENG.
(T) 01428 643788
Speciality: Chiropodists (Podiatrists).
S (**Ref:**HM12731)

### LUGG, G
**G Lugg**, 134-136 Delce Rd, Rochester, **Kent**, ME1 2DT, ENG.
(T) 01634 847254
Speciality: Chiropody. ✔
● **Owner/Chiropodist** Mrs G Lugg **Q:** M.S.C.P, MAR, S.R.Ch.
T Yrs. Est.: 10 (**Ref:**HM12732)

### LUKEHURST, DAVID
**David Lukehurst**, 87 Victoria Rd, Nottingham, **Nottinghamshire**, NG5 2NL, ENG.
(T) 01159 602266
Speciality: Homeopathy.
● **Partner** Mrs L Lukehurst
M (**Ref:**HM12733)

### LUKEHURST, LINDSAY
**Lindsay Lukehurst**, 87 Victoria Rd, Nottingham, **Nottinghamshire**, NG5 2NL, ENG.
(T) 01159 602266
Speciality: Acupuncture.
● **Partner** Mrs L Lukehurst
O (**Ref:**HM12734)

### LUKER, RONALD H
**Ronald H Luker**, 3 Catherine Wayte Cl, Greenmeadow, Swindon, **Wiltshire**, SN2 3PG, ENG.
(T) 01793 722230
Speciality: Complementary Medicines & Therapy.
● **Owner** Mr R Luker
C M (**Ref:**HM12735)

### LUKLINSKI, B M (DR)
**Dr B M Luklinski**, 31 Merrow Woods, Guildford, **Surrey**, GU1 2LQ, ENG.
(T) 01483 300812
Speciality: Physiotherapy.
P S T (**Ref:**HM12736)

### LUMB, JANE
**Jane Lumb**, 15 Chancery Trce, Halifax, **Yorkshire (West)**, HX3 0SB, ENG.
(T) 01422 330796
Speciality: Chiropodists (Podiatrists).
● **Owner** Ms J Lumb
S (**Ref:**HM12737)

### LUMINI POTENTIAL
**Lumini Potential**, 25 Pine Vale Cres, Bournemouth, **Dorset**, BH10 6BG, ENG.
(T) 01202 515952
Speciality: Complementary Medicines & Therapy.
● **Owner** Mrs S Stefan
C M (**Ref:**HM12738)

### LUMLEY, S J
**Mrs S J Lumley**, 15 Grove Avenue, London, **London (Greater)**, W7 3ER, ENG.
(T) 020 8840 7365
Speciality: Physiotherapy.
P S T (**Ref:**HM12739)

### LUMSDEN, D
**D Lumsden**, 1 Chalton Rd, Bridge Of Allan, Stirling, FK9 4DX, SCO.
(T) 01786 833230
Speciality: Chiropodists (Podiatrists).
● **Owner** Mrs D Ferguson
S (**Ref:**HM12740)

### LUNT, CELIA
**Celia Lunt**, 141 Church Rd, Combe Down, Bath, **Somerset**, BA2 5JL, ENG.
(T) 01225 834527
Speciality: Chiropodists (Podiatrists).
● **Owner** Mrs C Lunt
S (**Ref:**HM12741)

### LUNT, JULIE
**Julie Lunt**, The Firs, 1 Barrs Wood Rd, New Milton, **Hampshire**, BH25 5HS, ENG.
(T) 01425 610398
Speciality: Aromatherapy.
M O (**Ref:**HM12742)

### LURIE, DAVID
**David Lurie**, 98B Hazellville Rd, London, **London (Greater)**, N19 3NA, ENG.
(T) 020 7281 5869
Speciality: Herbal Medicine.
M (**Ref:**HM12743)

### LUSCHER INS-COLOUR PSYCHOL
**Luscher Institute Of Colour Psychology**, 35 Landsdowne Park, Templeogue, Dublin, **County Dublin**, IRE.
(T) 01493 5577
Speciality: Psychology.
B (**Ref:**HM12744)

### LUSH, AUDREY
**Audrey Lush**, 15 Cairngorm Cres, Barrhead, Glasgow, **Glasgow (City of)**, G78 2AW, SCO.
(T) 01418 816764
Speciality: Chiropractic.
P S T (**Ref:**HM12745)

### LUTHER, R E
**R E Luther**, 161 Erith Rd, Bexleyheath, **Kent**, DA7 6HX, ENG.
(T) 01322 551688
Speciality: Chiropodists (Podiatrists).
● **Owner** Mr R Luther
S (**Ref:**HM12746)

### LUTON PHYSIO SPORTS INJURY
**Luton Physiotherapy Sports Injury Clinic**, 154 Ashcroft Rd, Luton, **Bedfordshire**, LU2 9AU, ENG.
(T) 01582 416619
Speciality: Physiotherapy.
● **Owner** Mrs L Waddell
P S T (**Ref:**HM12747)

### LUTZ, GARY
**Gary Lutz**, 853 Finchley Rd, London, **London (Greater)**, NW11 8LX, ENG.
(T) 020 8455 5646
Speciality: Osteopathy.
P S T (**Ref:**HM12748)

### LUTZ, PERRY
**Perry Lutz**, 171A High St, Hampton Hill, Hampton, **London (Greater)**, TW12 1NL, ENG.
(T) 020 8979 4519
Speciality: Osteopathy.
P S T (**Ref:**HM12749)

### LUTZ, PERRY
**Perry Lutz**, 48 Taylor Cl, Hampton, **London (Greater)**, TW12 1LF, ENG.
(T) 020 8783 1295
Speciality: Osteopathy.
P S T (**Ref:**HM12750)

### LUXTON, PAT
**Miss Pat Luxton**, 25 Lower Gungate, Tamworth, **Staffordshire**, B79 7AT, ENG.
(T) 01827 68374
Speciality: Complementary Medicines & Therapy.
M (**Ref:**HM12751)

### LUXTON, PAULINE
**Pauline Luxton**, 109 Fairdene Rd, Coulsdon, **London (Greater)**, CR5 1RH, ENG.
(T) 01737 554086
Speciality: Biomechanics, Chiropody, Reiki, Seichem, Tera-Mai. ✔
● **Chiropodist/Healer** Ms P Luxton **Q:** MBChA, MSSCh. **M:** B.A.Ch.P, Reiki Association, RSAss.
T Yrs. Est.: 6 (**Ref:**HM12752)

### LVJ COUNSELLING & HYPNOTHERAPY
**LVJ Counselling & Hypnotherapy**, 150 Norton Lane, Hammerwich, Burntwood, **Staffordshire**, WS7 0HE, ENG.
(T) 01543 674332
Speciality: Hypnotherapy.
● **Owner** Mrs L Joyce
B (**Ref:**HM12753)

### LY, THI PHUNG (DR)
**Dr Thi Phung Ly**, 12 Radegund Rd, Cambridge, **Cambridgeshire**, CB1 3RL, ENG.
(T) 01223 242824
Speciality: Acupuncture, Counselling, Meditation, Moxibustion. ✔
● **Acupuncture Practitioner** Hong-Phuuc Ho **M:** BAcC.
● **Acupuncture Practitioner** Thi-Phung Ly **Q:** LRCP, MD. **M:** BAcC, BMA, RCS (Eng).
O Yrs. Est.: 18 (**Ref:**HM12754)

### LYCIUM CENTRE
**Lycium Centre (The)**, 12 Hamilton Rd, Bangor, **County Down**, BT20 4LE, NIR.
(T) 028 9146 7467
Speciality: Acupuncture, Aromatherapy, Cupping, Herbal Medicine, Indian Head Massage, Massage (Therapeutic), Meditation, Oriental Diagnosis, Reflexology. ✔
● **Therapist** Ms C Megrath **Q:** Dip.Arom, Dip.Reflex. **M:** IIHHT.
● **Therapist** Mr M Megrath **Q:** Dip.Ac, Dip.TCM, ITEC, MRCHM. **M:** RCHM.
C O Yrs. Est.: 6 (**Ref:**HM12755)

### LYE, JENNY
**Jenny Lye**, Brook End House, Spelders Hill, Brook, Ashford, **Kent**, TN25 5PB, ENG.
(T) 01233 812058
Speciality: Reflexology.
S T (**Ref:**HM12756)

### LYKISMA
**Lykisma**, Tenby House, Keycol Hill, Newington, Sittingbourne, **Kent**, ME9 7LG, ENG.
(T) 01795 844179
Speciality: Aromatherapy.
● **Partner** Mr B Beer
M O (**Ref:**HM12757)

### LYLEE, URWIN
**Urwin Lylee**, 35 Jane St, Workington, **Cumbria**, CA14 3BS, ENG.
(T) 01900 607300
Speciality: Chiropractic.
P S T (**Ref:**HM12758)

### LYMINGTON CHIROPRACTIC CLINIC
**Lymington Chiropractic Clinic (The)**, 126 High St, Lymington, **Hampshire**, SO41 9AQ, ENG.
(T) 01590 679560 (F) 01189 761703
Speciality: Chiropody, Chiropractic, Counselling, Cranial Osteopathy, Electrotherapy, Herbal Medicine, Manipulation, Massage (Therapeutic), Nutritional Therapy, Osteopathy, Postural Integration, Psychotherapy, Ultrasonics, X-Ray. ✔
● **Chiropractor/Clinic Principal** Dr P Hardy **Q:** BCA, DC, MCC. **M:** BCA.
● **Chiropractor** Ms F Marshall **Q:** BCA, BSc, DC. **M:** BCA.
● **Chiropractor** Mr C Wood **Q:** BCA, BSc, DC, MCC.



Key: B Mind-Body Medicine C Complementary Medicine H Self Help Treatment M Medicinal Therapy O Oriental Medicine P Postural Therapy S Manipulative Structural Therapy T Touch Therapy

**S** Yrs. Est.: 13 (Ref:HM12759)

## LYMINGTON PLATING

**Lymington Plating**, 22-31 Harwell Rd, Poole, **Dorset**, BH17 0GE, ENG.
(T) 01202 676069 (F) 01202 665564
Speciality: Electrolysis.
● **Director** Mr P Holloway
**T** (Ref:HM12760)

## LYNCH, A MASSEY

**A Massey Lynch**, 21 Akenside Trce, Newcastle Upon Tyne, **Tyne and Wear**, NE2 1TN, ENG.
(T) 01912 817723
Speciality: Alexander Technique.
**P** **S** (Ref:HM12761)

## LYNCH, GERALDINE

**Lynch Geraldine L M A C N F S H**, 62 Kevin Barry Vlas, Tralee, **County Kerry**, IRE.
(T) 06671 22554
Speciality: Healing.
**B** (Ref:HM12762)

## LYNCH, JEREMIAH

**Lynch Jeremiah**, Carberytown Glounthaune, **County Cork**, IRE.
(T) 021 4354 605
Speciality: Counselling.
**B** **H** (Ref:HM12763)

## LYNCH, SEAMUS

**Lynch Seamus Lic Ac M B Acc**, 17 Alma Rd, Monkstown, **County Dublin**, IRE.
(T) 01284 6073
Speciality: Acupuncture.
**O** (Ref:HM12764)

## LYNCH, STEPHEN

**Stephen Lynch**, 205 Green Meadow Rd, Birmingham, **Midlands (West)**, B29 4EF, ENG.
(T) 01214 781665
Speciality: Hypnosis.
● **Owner** Mr S Lynch
**B** (Ref:HM12765)

## LYNCH, SUZANNE

**Lynch Suzanne**, Middleton Pk, Castletowngeoghegan, **County Westmeath**, IRE.
(T) 04426 253
Speciality: Complementary Medicines & Therapy.
**M** (Ref:HM12766)

## LYNDA

**Lynda**, 25 Ryeleaze, Potterne, Devizes, **Wiltshire**, SN10 5NJ, ENG.
(T) 01380 721239
Speciality: Clairvoyants & Palmists.
● **Owner** Ms L Light
**B** (Ref:HM12767)

## LYNDA CROFT REIKI MASTER

**Lynda Croft Reiki Master**, Reiki Teaching & Healing For Animals, Burnham-on-Crouch, **Essex**, ENG.
Speciality: Reiki.
**M** (Ref:HM12768)

## LYNDEN SCHOOL OF REFLEXOLOGY

**Lynden School Of Reflexology (The)**, 22A Lakewood Rd, Highcliffe, Christchurch, **Dorset**, BH23 5NX, ENG.
(T) 01425 276351 (F) 01425 271257
Speciality: Reflexology.
● **Principal** Mrs J Hopespencer
**S** **T** (Ref:HM12769)

## LYNDHURST HOUSE

**Lyndhurst House**, Cleddau House, The Marina, Milford Haven, **Pembrokeshire**, SA73 3AF, WAL.
(T) 01646 695310
Speciality: Aromatherapy.
● **Owner** Mrs C Cleecley
**M** **O** (Ref:HM12770)

## LYNN

**Lynn**, 11A Aigburth Vale, Liverpool, **Merseyside**, L17 0DE, ENG.
(T) 01517 274296
Speciality: Clairvoyants & Palmists.
● **Owner** Miss E Brookes
**B** (Ref:HM12771)

## LYNN BROWN CLINICAL AROM

**Lynn Brown Clinical Aromatherapist**, 36 Campbell St, Darvel, **Ayrshire (East)**, KA17 0DA, SCO.
(T) 01560 322208
(E) lynnbrown.therapy@virgin.net
Speciality: Aromatherapy, Complementary Therapy, Holistic Healing, Massage (Therapeutic), Reflexology. ✔
● **Clinical Therapist** Ms L Brown
Q: Dip.Clin.Arom. M: AOC, GCP.
**C** Yrs. Est.: 5 (Ref:HM12772)

## LYNN REFLEXOLOGY CLINIC

**Lynn Reflexology Clinic**, Middleton, King's Lynn, **Norfolk**, PE32 1EZ, ENG.
(T) 01553 691269 (F) 01553 691269
Speciality: Reflexology.
● **Owner** Mrs L Simons
**S** **T** (Ref:HM12773)

## LYNOSIS

**Lynosis**, 22 Thorney La South, Iver, **Buckinghamshire**, SL0 9AE, ENG.
(T) 01753 654286
Speciality: Hypnotherapy.
● **Owner** Mrs L Cooper
**B** (Ref:HM12774)

## LYNWOOD PHYSIO & SPORTS

**Lynwood Physiotherapy & Sports Injury Clinic (The)**, 18 Lynwood Drive, Worcester Park, **Surrey**, KT4 7AB, ENG.
(T) 020 8337 8970
Speciality: Physiotherapy.
**P** **S** **T** (Ref:HM12775)

## LYON & JOHNSTON

**Lyon & Johnston**, Station Rd, Grangemouth, **Falkirk**, FK3 8DG, SCO.
(T) 01324 483327
Speciality: Chiropodists (Podiatrists).
**S** (Ref:HM12776)

## LYON, A

**A Lyon**, 509 Warrington Rd, Rainhill, Prescot, **Merseyside**, L35 4LP, ENG.
(T) 01514 311700
Speciality: Osteopathy.
● **Osteopath** Jonathon Bell
**P** **S** **T** (Ref:HM12777)

## LYON, ANDREW

**Andrew Lyon**, 36C London Rd, Alderley Edge, **Cheshire**, SK9 7DZ, ENG.
(T) 01625 585458
Speciality: Osteopathy.
● **Owner** Mr A Lyon
**P** **S** **T** (Ref:HM12778)

## LYON, F A

**F A Lyon**, 3 George St, Oxford, **Oxfordshire**, OX1 2AT, ENG.
(T) 01865 247377
Speciality: Chiropodists (Podiatrists).
● **Partner** Mrs F Lyon
**S** (Ref:HM12779)

## LYON, HARRIETTE

**Harriette Lyon**, 215 Princess Way, Portadown, Craigavon, **County Armagh**, BT63 5EN, NIR.
(T) 028 3835 0042
Speciality: Chiropody. ✔
● **Owner/Chiropodist** Mrs H Lyon Q: SMAE. M: SMAE.
**M** Yrs. Est.: 32 (Ref:HM12780)

## LYON, JAN

**Jan Lyon**, 1 Oban Rd, Beeston, Nottingham, **Nottinghamshire**, NG9 4FX, ENG.
(T) 01159 224819
Speciality: Aromatherapy.
● **Owner** Ms J Lyon
**M** **O** (Ref:HM12781)

## LYON, JOSEPHINE

**Josephine Lyon**, 15 Brunswick Court, Regency St, London, **London (Greater)**, SW1P 4AE, ENG.
(T) 020 7834 7418
Speciality: Hypnotherapy.
● **Owner** Ms J Lyon
**B** (Ref:HM12782)

## LYON, P

**P Lyon**, Guilder Lane, Salisbury, **Wiltshire**, ENG.
(T) 01794 340664
Speciality: Alexander Technique, Postural Integration, Re-education. ✔
● **Alexander Technique Teacher**
Ms P Lyon Q: MSTAT.
**P** Yrs. Est.: 5 (Ref:HM12783)

## LYONS, A J

**A J Lyons**, 184 Longsight, Bolton, **Lancashire**, BL2 3JA, ENG.
(T) 01204 596420
Speciality: Electrolysis.
● **Owner** A J Lyons
**T** (Ref:HM12784)

## LYONS, A R & G B

**A R & G B Lyons**, 4 Compton Cl, Shepton Mallet, **Somerset**, BA4 5QZ, ENG.
(T) 01749 342377
Speciality: Chiropodists (Podiatrists).
● **Owner** Mr A Lyons
**S** (Ref:HM12785)

## LYONS, FERGUS

**Lyons Fergus D H P M I A H H**, Bluepool, Kanturk, **County Cork**, IRE.
(T) 08624 60465
Speciality: Complementary Medicines & Therapy.
**M** (Ref:HM12786)

## LYONS, JACQUELINE

**Jacqueline Lyons**, Amberley, Hawley Lane, Halebarns, Altrincham, **Cheshire**, WA15 0DR, ENG.
(T) 01619 805896
Speciality: Chiropodists (Podiatrists).
● **Owner** Maj J Lyons
**S** (Ref:HM12787)

## LYONS, STEVEN

**Steven Lyons**, 56 Blackburn Rd, Accrington, **Lancashire**, BB5 1LE, ENG.
(T) 01254 383440
Speciality: Chiropodists (Podiatrists).
**S** (Ref:HM12788)

## LYONS, STEVEN

**Steven Lyons**, Richmond House Clinic, Stockport Rd, Hyde, **Cheshire**, SK14 5QT, ENG.
(T) 01613 682496
Speciality: Chiropodists (Podiatrists).
**S** (Ref:HM12789)

## LYONS, VERA

**Vera Lyons**, The Den, 118 Bexley Rd, London, **London (Greater)**, SE9 2PG, ENG.
(T) 020 8333 1191
Speciality: Reflexology.
**S** **T** (Ref:HM12790)

## LYTHGOE, A G

**A G Lythgoe**, 44 Lavender Drive, Rudheath, Northwich, **Cheshire**, CW9 7EQ, ENG.
(T) 01606 49100
Speciality: Chiropodists (Podiatrists).
● **Owner** Mr A Lythgoe
**S** (Ref:HM12791)

## LYTHGOE, J C

**J C Lythgoe**, 63 Runcorn Rd, Moore, Warrington, **Cheshire**, WA4 6TX, ENG.
(T) 01925 740335
Speciality: Chiropodists (Podiatrists).
● **Owner** Mr J Lythgoe
**S** (Ref:HM12792)

## LYTTLE, DEBBIE

**Debbie Lyttle**, Flat 3D, 210 Walm Lane, London, **London (Greater)**, NW2 3BP, ENG.
(T) 020 8208 0868
Speciality: Reflexology.
**S** **T** (Ref:HM12793)

## M & B SERVICES

**M & B Services Reflexology & Personal Counselling**, 76 Northfield Lane, Wickersley, Rotherham, **Yorkshire (South)**, S66 2HW, ENG.
(T) 01709 540308
Speciality: Counselling, Reflexology, Shiatsu. ✔
● **Owner/Senior Practitioner**


Key continued: Yrs.Est: Years Established Q: Qualifications M: Professional Membership ✔ Indemnity Insurance Accept Credit Cards

Mr M Bird Q: Guild of Reflexologists. M: Guild of Reflexologists.
C Yrs. Est.: 7 (Ref:HM12794)

**M & M DELIGHTS**

**M & M Delights**, Unit 15 South Mall, London, **London (Greater)**, N9 0TT, ENG.
(T) 020 8351 6112
Speciality: Complementary Medicines & Therapy.
● **Partner** Ms M De-Freitas
C M (Ref:HM12795)

**M C COPELAND-GRIFFITHS & AST**

**M C Copeland-Griffiths & Associates**, Blandford Chiropractic Clinic, Damory Court St, Blandford Forum, **Dorset**, DT11 7QU, ENG.
(T) 01258 455214
Speciality: Chiropractic.
P S T (Ref:HM12796)

**M C S P**

**M C S P**, 24 St Leonards Rd, Ayr, **Ayrshire (South)**, KA7 2PT, SCO.
(T) 01292 262587
Speciality: Physiotherapy.
● **Owner** Mr J Diell
P S T (Ref:HM12797)

**M CULLINGWORTH SHIATSU**

**M Cullingworth Shiatsu**, All Hallows House, Idol Lane, London, **London (Greater)**, EC3R 5DD, ENG.
(T) 020 7283 8908
Speciality: Complementary Medicines & Therapy.
M (Ref:HM12798)

**M H B ASSOCIATES**

**M H B Associates**, 40A Glasgow St, Helensburgh, **Argyll and Bute**, G84 8DA, SCO.
(T) 01436 679922
Speciality: Hypnosis.
B (Ref:HM12799)

**M I G'S NATURAL HEATHCARE CTRE**

**M I G's Natural Heathcare Centre**, Chriton House, Mount Stuart Sq, Cardiff, **Glamorgan (Vale of)**, CF10 5LR, WAL.
(T) 029 2051 5816
Speciality: Complementary Medicines & Therapy.
C M (Ref:HM12800)

**M J BRADLEY - KINESIOLOGIST**

**M J Bradley - Kinesiologist**, Grasmere, 26 Darlingscott Rd, Shipston on Stour, **Warwickshire**, CV36 4DR, ENG.
(T) 01608 661283
Speciality: Chiropractors.
P S T (Ref:HM12801)

**M J HAYLETT - PHYSIOTHERAPIST**

**M J Haylett - Physiotherapist**, 17 Timperley Lane, Leigh, **Manchester (Greater)**, WN7 3DZ, ENG.
(T) 01942 675241
Speciality: Manipulation, Massage (Therapeutic), Stress Therapy, Ultrasonics. ✔
● **Owner/Physiotherapist**
Mrs M Haylett Q: MAB Phys. M: SMAE.
S Yrs. Est.: 9 (Ref:HM12802)

**M K CLINIC**

**M K Clinic**, 15 Glyn St, New Bradwell, Milton Keynes, **Buckinghamshire**, MK13 0DF, ENG.
(T) 01908 320418 (F) 01908 316566
Speciality: Osteopathy.
● **Senior Partner** Mr C Parish
P S T (Ref:HM12803)

**M L C DISABILITY SERVICES**

**M L C Disability Services**, 26 Cedar Rd, London, **London (Greater)**, NW2 6SR, ENG.
(T) 020 8208 2298
Speciality: Complementary Medicines & Therapy, Occupational Therapy.
M (Ref:HM12804)

**M M AFRIN JUNIOR**

**M M Afrin Junior**, 38 Church St, Stornoway, **Western Isles**, HS1 2JE, SCO.
(T) 01851 704363
Speciality: Chiropodists (Podiatrists).
● **Owner** Mr M Afrin
S (Ref:HM12805)

**M MAGDALENE HEALING/MEDITATION**

**Mary Magdalene Healing & Meditation Centre (The)**, 6 Henshaw Cr, Newbury, **Berkshire**, RG14 6ES, ENG.
(T) 01635 37707
Speciality: Complementary Medicines & Therapy.
● **Owner** Ms V Radford
M (Ref:HM12806)

**M S THERAPY CENTRE**

**M S Therapy Centre**, Unit 7, Rosebery Ind Pk, Rosebery Avenue, London, **London (Greater)**, N17 9SR, ENG.
(T) 020 8885 2332
Speciality: Complementary Medicines & Therapy.
C M (Ref:HM12807)

**M SUTTON-COULSON SOLENT PHYSIO**

**M Sutton-Coulson Solent Physiotherapy & Sports Injuries**, 14 Russell Rd, Lee-On-The-Solent, **Hampshire**, PO13 9HP, ENG.
(T) 023 9255 0301
Speciality: Physiotherapy.
● **Owner** Mrs M Sutton-Cou
P S T (Ref:HM12808)

**M T DANCE**

**M T Dance**, 68 Glasgow Rd, Edinburgh, **Edinburgh (City of)**, EH12 8LN, SCO.
(T) 01313 341966
Speciality: Chiropodists (Podiatrists).
S (Ref:HM12809)

**M THORLOW CHIROPODY**

**M Thorlow Chiropody**, 11 Broad St, Pershore, **Worcestershire**, WR10 1BB, ENG.
(T) 01386 553883
Speciality: Biomechanics, Chiropody. ✔
● **Chiropodist** Mr M Thorlow Q: MBChA, SSChA. M: B.A.Ch.P.
C Yrs. Est.: 10 (Ref:HM12810)

**M, JACKSON A**

**Jackson A M**, Herbal Treatment Centre, Cheltenham, **Gloucestershire**, GL53 0LW, ENG.
(T) 01242 238440
Speciality: Complementary Medicines & Therapy.
M (Ref:HM12811)

**MABBERLEY, KATHIE**

**Kathie Mabberley**, Dayden's Healthcare Centre, 42 High St, Ashford, **Kent**, TN, ENG.
(T) 01233 660882
(E) mabbscylinder@virgin.net
Speciality: Aromatherapy, Bowen Therapy, Indian Head Massage, Reflexology.
● **Therapist** Ms K Mabberley Q: ART(Reg), BTER, ISPA, ITEC, MAR.
T Yrs. Est.: 12 (Ref:HM12812)

**MABBERLEY, KATHIE**

**Kathie Mabberley**, Cylinder House, Freshfield Lane, Saltwood, Hythe, **Kent**, CT21 4QH, ENG.
(T) 01303 268745
Speciality: Reflexology.
S T (Ref:HM12813)

**MACALEVEY, MIKE**

**Mike MacAlevey**, 76 Hartfield Rd, Forest Row, **Sussex (East)**, RH18 5BZ, ENG.
(T) 01342 824339
Speciality: Osteopathy.
● **Owner** Mr M MacAlevey
P S T (Ref:HM12814)

**MACALLAN, STEPHEN**

**Weaver House Clinic**, 19a Pillory St, Nantwich, **Cheshire**, CW2 6PF, ENG.
(T) 01270 629933 (F) 01270 626711
(E) stephenmacallan@ukonline.co.uk
(W) www.stephenmacallan.co.uk
Speciality: Acupuncture, Dietician, Herbal Medicine, Holistic Healing, Moxibustion, Naturopathy, Nutritional Therapy, Oriental Diagnosis, Kosmed Treatment, Vega Testing. ✔
● **Practitioner** Mr S MacAllan Q: B.Ac, Lic.Ac, M.Ac, MH. M: AMH, BAcC.
C Yrs. Est.: 20 (Ref:HM12815)

**MACALLAN, STEPHEN**

**Stephen Macallan**, The Weaver House Clinic, 19A Pillory St, Nantwich, **Cheshire**, CW5 5BZ, ENG.
(T) 01270 629933
Speciality: Acupuncture.
O (Ref:HM12816)

**MACARI, SALVINA**

**Salvina Macari**, 7 Addiscombe Rd, Margate, **Kent**, CT9 2SF, ENG.
(T) 01843 295910
Speciality: Reflexology.
S T (Ref:HM12817)

**MACARTHUR, JACKIE**

**Jackie MacArthur**, 8 Wheatcroft Cl, Burntwood, **Staffordshire**, WS7 8SX, ENG.
(T) 01543 686652
Speciality: Electrolysis.
T (Ref:HM12818)

**MACARTHUR, T**

**T MacArthur**, 12A St Saviours Pl, York, **Yorkshire (North)**, YO1 7PJ, ENG.
(T) 01904 659588
Speciality: Osteopathy.
● **Owner** Mr T MacArthur
P S T (Ref:HM12819)

**MACARTHUR, T**

**T Macarthur**, The Old Health Centre, Church Lane, Boroughbridge, York, **Yorkshire (North)**, YO51 9BD, ENG.
(T) 01423 323969
Speciality: Osteopathy.
P S T (Ref:HM12820)

**MACARTNEY HOUSE PSYCHOTHERAPY**

**Macartney House Psychotherapy Service**, Beech Mount, Manchester, **Manchester (Greater)**, M9 5XS, ENG.
(T) 01612 057555 (F) 01612 035731
Speciality: Psychotherapy.
● **Manageress** Dr L Ivanson
B (Ref:HM12821)

**MACBRAYNE, KEITH**

**Keith MacBrayne**, 17 Bedford Rd, Northill, Biggleswade, **Bedfordshire**, SG18 9AH, ENG.
(T) 01767 627010
Speciality: Hypnotherapy.
● **Owner** Mr K MacBrayne
B (Ref:HM12822)

**MACCARTHY, BRIAN (DR)**

**MacCarthy Brian Dr**, James St, Westport Mayo, **County Mayo**, IRE.
(T) 09829 555
Speciality: Chiropractors.
P S T (Ref:HM12823)

**MACDERMOTT, S**

**S MacDermott**, 24 Raleigh St, London, **London (Greater)**, N1 8NP, ENG.
(T) 020 7226 9584
Speciality: Alexander Technique.
● **Owner** Mrs S MacDermott
P S (Ref:HM12824)

**MACDONALD, JANICE**

**Janice MacDonald**, 4 MacDonald Court, Beith, **Ayrshire (North)**, KA15 1BW, SCO.
(T) 01505 504204
Speciality: Chiropodists (Podiatrists).
S (Ref:HM12825)

**MACDONALD, KATHRYN**

**Kathryn MacDonald**, 1 Puddingmoor, Beccles, **Suffolk**, NR34 9PL, ENG.
(T) 01502 712505
Speciality: Osteopathy.
● **Owner** Mr M James
P S T (Ref:HM12826)

**MACDONALD, R S J**

**R S J Macdonald**, 11 Lower Meddon St, Bideford, **Devon**, EX39 2BL, ENG.
(T) 01237 475023
Speciality: Acupuncture.
O (Ref:HM12827)

**MACDONALD, R S J**

**R S J MacDonald**, The Mews, 43 Clifton Rd,



Key: B Mind-Body Medicine C Complementary Medicine H Self Help Treatment M Medicinal Therapy O Oriental Medicine P Postural Therapy S Manipulative Structural Therapy T Touch Therapy

London, **London (Greater)**, SE25 6PX, ENG.
(T) 020 8653 2941
Speciality: Herbal Medicine.
M (Ref:HM12828)

## MACDONALD, RODERIC

**Roderic MacDonald**, 106 Wellesley Rd, London, **London (Greater)**, W4 3AP, ENG.
(T) 020 8994 1701
Speciality: Osteopathy.
● **Owner** Mr R MacDonald
P S T (Ref:HM12829)

## MACDONALD-INGLE, HAZEL

**Hazel Macdonald-Ingle**, 19 Saffron Cl, Wootton Bassett, Swindon, **Wiltshire**, SN4 7JA, ENG.
(T) 01793 850453
Speciality: Chiropodists (Podiatrists).
S (Ref:HM12830)

## MACDONNELL, MICHELLE

**Michelle MacDonnell**, 98 Kensington Church St, London, **London (Greater)**, W8 4BU, ENG.
(T) 020 7792 5287 (F) 020 7792 5287
Speciality: Alexander Technique.
● **Owner** Miss M MacDonnell
P S (Ref:HM12831)

## MACE, CHRISTOPHER J

**Christopher J Mace**, Wellspring, 61A Hartland Way, Croydon, **Surrey**, CR0 8RJ, ENG.
(T) 020 8777 5409 (F) 020 8777 5409
Speciality: Osteopathy.
● **Owner** Mr C Mace
P S T (Ref:HM12832)

## MACEOIN, BETH

**Beth Maceoin**, 11 Osborne Avenue, Newcastle Upon Tyne, **Tyne and Wear**, NE2 1JQ, ENG.
(T) 01912 816667
Speciality: Homeopathy.
M (Ref:HM12833)

## MACFARLANE, CLARE

**Clare Macfarlane**, 32 Falkenham Rd, Kirton, Ipswich, **Suffolk**, IP10 0NW, ENG.
(T) 01394 448620
Speciality: Reflexology.
S T (Ref:HM12834)

## MACFARLANE, GEORGE R

**George R MacFarlane**, 15 Kensington High St, London, **London (Greater)**, W8 5NP, ENG.
(T) 020 7937 4846
Speciality: Chiropodists (Podiatrists).
S (Ref:HM12835)

## MACFARLANE, T D

**T D MacFarlane**, 2 The Avenue, West Moors, Ferndown, **Dorset**, BH22 0LT, ENG.
(T) 01202 872237
Speciality: Chiropodists (Podiatrists).
● **Owner** Mr T MacFarlane
S (Ref:HM12836)

## MACHA, FREDDY

**Freddy Macha**, Clissold Park Health Centre, 154 Stoke Newington Church St, London, **London (Greater)**, N16 0JU, ENG.
(T) 020 7249 2990 (F) 020 7249 3977
Speciality: Reflexology.
● **Director** Mr D Berg
S T (Ref:HM12837)

## MACHADO, LOUISA

**Louisa Machado**, 82 Sutherland St, **Yorkshire (North)**, YO23 1HQ, ENG.
(T) 01904 620898
Speciality: Reflexology.
S T (Ref:HM12838)

## MACHIN, KAREN

**Karen Machin**, Coneymore, The Plantation, Storrington, Pulborough, **Sussex (West)**, RH20 4JG, ENG.
(T) 01903 742677
Speciality: Reflexology.
S T (Ref:HM12839)

## MACHOVER, ILANA

**Ilana Machover**, 5 Milman Rd, London, **London (Greater)**, NW6 6EN, ENG.
(T) 020 8969 5356
Speciality: Alexander Technique.
● **Owner** Ms I Machover
P S (Ref:HM12840)

## MACINNES, BERYL

**Beryl MacInnes**, 22 Chase Lane, Harwich, **Essex**, CO12 4NB, ENG.
(T) 01255 551399
Speciality: Bach Remedies.
M (Ref:HM12841)

## MACINTYRE-THOMSON, MARIE

**Marie MacIntyre-Thomson**, 17 Lulworth Walk, Leeds, **Yorkshire (West)**, LS15 8NZ, ENG.
(T) 01132 601594
Speciality: Hypnosis.
● **Owner** Mrs M MacIntyre-Thomson
B (Ref:HM12842)

## MACK, DEREK

**Derek Mack**, Matthews House, 85 Epsom Rd, Guildford, **Surrey**, GU1 3PA, ENG.
(T) 01483 575876
Speciality: Physiotherapy.
P S T (Ref:HM12843)

## MACKAY, BILL

**Bill Mackay**, St Georges House, 56 Billing Rd, Northampton, **Northamptonshire**, NN1 5DB, ENG.
(T) 01604 601641 (F) 01604 601641
Speciality: Physiotherapy.
● **Partner** Mr P Whitty
P S T (Ref:HM12844)

## MACKAY, I

**I Mackay**, May Cottage, Birnie, Elgin, **Moray**, IV30 8SR, SCO.
(T) 01343 860578
Speciality: Hypnosis.
● **Owner** Mr I Mackay
B (Ref:HM12845)

## MACKAY, J M

**J M Mackay**, 42A King St, Bathgate, **Lothian (West)**, EH48 1AX, SCO.
(T) 01506 652847
Speciality: Chiropodists (Podiatrists).
● **Owner** Mr J Mackay
S (Ref:HM12846)

## MACKAY, JOHN

**John Mackay**, 45 Milton Avenue, Eaton Ford, St Neots, Huntingdon, **Cambridgeshire**, PE19 3LH, ENG.
(T) 01480 476325 (F) 01480 215969
Speciality: Psychology.
● **Owner** Mr J Mackay
B (Ref:HM12847)

## MACKAY, SUSIE

**Susie Mackay**, 337-339 Norwich Rd, Ipswich, **Suffolk**, IP1 4BN, ENG.
(T) 01473 464300
Speciality: Complementary Medicines & Therapy.
M (Ref:HM12848)

## MACKELLAR, D

**D Mackellar**, 78 Hall Rd, Norwich, **Norfolk**, NR1 3HP, ENG.
(T) 01603 219899 (F) 01603 219899
Speciality: Osteopathy.
● **Owner** Mr D MacKellar
P S T (Ref:HM12849)

## MACKENZIE, BOYD

**Boyd Mackenzie**, 30 Kinnoull Causeway, Perth, **Perth and Kinross**, PH2 8HQ, SCO.
(T) 01738 622864
Speciality: Osteopathy.
P S T (Ref:HM12850)

## MACKENZIE, D, HATFIELD, J

**Mackenzie Davey Hatfield Jefferies & Co**, Cardinal House, The Green, Hampton Court, East Molesey, **Surrey**, KT8 9BW, ENG.
(T) 020 8979 6921
Speciality: Psychology.
B (Ref:HM12851)

## MACKENZIE, J D

**J D MacKenzie**, Cameron & Carabine Building, North Rd, Fort William, **Highland**, PH33 6PP, SCO.
(T) 01599 534141
Speciality: Osteopathy.
P S T (Ref:HM12852)

## MACKENZIE, J D

**J D MacKenzie**, The Osteopaths Surgery, Station Rd, Kyle of Lochalsh, **Highland**, IV40 8AE, SCO.
(T) 01599 534141
Speciality: Osteopathy.
P S T (Ref:HM12853)

## MACKENZIE, J D

**J D MacKenzie**, 1a Wentworth St, Portree, **Highland**, IV51 9EJ, SCO.
(T) 01599 534141
Speciality: Osteopathy.
P S T (Ref:HM12854)

## MACKENZIE, R

**R MacKenzie**, 6 Balhousie St, Perth, **Perth and Kinross**, PH1 5HJ, SCO.
(T) 01738 621321
Speciality: Chiropodists (Podiatrists).
S (Ref:HM12855)

## MACKEY, D

**D Mackey**, Glanfield Cl, Bishops Lydeard, Taunton, **Somerset**, TA4 3BH, ENG.
(T) 01823 433619
Speciality: Hypnosis.
● **Owner** Mr D Mackey
B (Ref:HM12856)

## MACKEY, D

**Mr D Mackey**, Flat 3, 95 Lausanne Rd, London, **London (Greater)**, SE15 2HY, ENG.
(T) 020 7358 9577
Speciality: Complementary Medicines & Therapy.
M (Ref:HM12857)

## MACKIE, A A

**A A Mackie**, 24 Mardale Cres, Edinburgh, **Edinburgh (City of)**, EH10 5AG, SCO.
(T) 01312 292946
Speciality: Chiropodists (Podiatrists).
S (Ref:HM12858)

## MACKIE, CHERYL

**Cheryl Mackie**, 20 St. Stephens Rd, West Drayton, **London (Greater)**, UB7 7RL, ENG.
(T) 01895 859083
Speciality: Reflexology.
S T (Ref:HM12859)

## MACKINTOSH, SUSAN

**Susan Mackintosh**, 59A Abbey Rd, Scone, Perth, **Perth and Kinross**, PH2 6LL, SCO.
(T) 01738 550055 (F) 01738 550055
Speciality: Homeopathy.
● **Owner** Mrs S Mackintosh
M (Ref:HM12860)

## MACLAREN, ALISON

**Alison Maclaren**, 30 St Georges Trce, Jesmond, Newcastle Upon Tyne, **Tyne and Wear**, NE2 2SY, ENG.
(T) 01912 810670
Speciality: Psychology.
B (Ref:HM12861)

## MACLAVERTY, RUTH

**Ruth MacLaverty**, Kirby Cottage, Kirby Mount, Wirral, **Merseyside**, CH48 2HU, ENG.
(T) 01516 256392
Speciality: Chiropodists (Podiatrists).
● **Owner** Mrs R MacLaverty
S (Ref:HM12862)

## MACLEAN, JANE FERGUSON

**Jane Ferguson MacLean**, The Tall House, Gough Rd, Sandgate, Folkestone, **Kent**, CT20 3BE, ENG.
(T) 01303 243526
Speciality: Reflexology.
S T (Ref:HM12863)

## MACLEAN, LAURA

**Laura Maclean**, Ardencaple, Burnett Park East, Banchory, **Aberdeenshire**, AB31 4AE, SCO.
(T) 01330 825517 (F) 01330 825517
Speciality: Chiropodists (Podiatrists).
● **Owner** Mrs L Maclean
S (Ref:HM12864)



Key continued: **Yrs.Est:** Years Established **Q:** Qualifications **M:** Professional Membership ✔ Indemnity Insurance ▬ Accept Credit Cards

### MACLEOD, KENNETH
**Kenneth MacLeod**, 1328 Shettleston Rd, Glasgow, **Glasgow (City of)**, G32 7YS, SCO.
(T) 01417 789291
Speciality: Chiropodists (Podiatrists).
S (Ref:HM12865)

### MACLEOD, S R M
**S R M MacLeod**, Westacre, Southampton Rd, Hythe, Southampton, **Hampshire**, SO45 5AB, ENG.
(T) 023 8084 4730
Speciality: Osteopathy.
● **Owner** Mr S MacLeod
P S T (Ref:HM12866)

### MACLIAM, FIONNULA
**Dynamics-Interpersonal Skills Training**, 4 Wynnefield Rd, Rathmines, **County Dublin**, IRE.
(T) 00353 14973498
(E) fmacliam@iol.ie
Speciality: Cognitive Therapy, Psychotherapy. ✔
● **Cognitive Behavioural Psychotherapist** Fionnula MacLiam Q: BA, Dip.Psych, RMN. M: BACP.
B Yrs. Est.: 10 (Ref:HM12867)

### MACLURE, IAN (DR)
**Dr Ian Maclure**, The Weaver House Clinic, 19A Pillory St, Nantwich, **Cheshire**, CW5 5BZ, ENG.
(T) 01270 629933
Speciality: Homeopathy.
M (Ref:HM12868)

### MACLUSKY, K A
**K A Maclusky**, Kilchoan, Thorncote Green, Hatch, Sandy, **Bedfordshire**, SG19 1PU, ENG.
(T) 01767 627689
Speciality: Complementary Medicines & Therapy.
C M (Ref:HM12869)

### MACMILLAN, JOHN
**John MacMillan**, Scott St Complementary Therapy Centre, 58 Scott St, Barrow-in-Furness, **Cumbria**, LA14 1QE, ENG.
(T) 01229 826700
Speciality: Chiropodists (Podiatrists).
S (Ref:HM12870)

### MACNAMARA, MARY V
**MacNamara Mary V RGN Dip PH Ed Lic TCM MR CM**, The Bungalow Turn Pike Rd, Ennis, **County Clare**, IRE.
(T) 06568 41280
Speciality: Complementary Medicines & Therapy.
M (Ref:HM12871)

### MACNEILL, E M
**E M Macneill**, 21 Knaresborough Rd, Sheffield, **Yorkshire (South)**, S7 2LA, ENG.
(T) 01142 364349
Speciality: Psychology.
B (Ref:HM12872)

### MACNIVEN, S
**S MacNiven**, 4 Treelands Drive, Cheltenham, **Gloucestershire**, GL53 0DB, ENG.
(T) 01242 256542
Speciality: Complementary Medicines & Therapy.
● **Owner** Mrs S MacNiven
C M (Ref:HM12873)

### MACONOCHIE, A J
**A J MacOnochie**, 27 Woodyard Rd, Dumbarton, **Argyll and Bute**, G82 4BG, SCO.
(T) 01389 768768
Speciality: Chiropodists (Podiatrists).
● **Owner** Mrs A MacOnoche
S (Ref:HM12874)

### MACONOCHIE, A J
**A J MacOnochie**, Shore Rd, Cove, Helensburgh, **Argyll and Bute**, G84 0NX, SCO.
(T) 01436 842517
Speciality: Chiropodists (Podiatrists).
● **Owner** A J MacOnochie
S (Ref:HM12875)

### MACPHERSON, IAN R
**Ian R MacPherson**, 5 Castlehill Drive, Largs, **Ayrshire (North)**, KA30 9NA, SCO.
(T) 01475 675942
Speciality: Chiropodists (Podiatrists).
● **Owner** Mr I Macpherson
S (Ref:HM12876)

### MACPHERSON, R G
**R G MacPherson**, 38 Braid Rd, Edinburgh, **Edinburgh (City of)**, EH10 6AD, SCO.
(T) 01314 475197
Speciality: Biomechanics, Chiropody, Nail Surgery. ✔
● **Owner/Chiropodist**
Mr R Macpherson Q: LCH, M.S.C.P.
M Yrs. Est.: 40 (Ref:HM12877)

### MACPHERSON, VIVIEN M
**Vivien M MacPherson**, 20 Shavinbrae, Ayr, **Ayrshire (South)**, KA7 3NQ, SCO.
(T) 01292 269553 (F) 01292 269553
Speciality: Physiotherapy.
● **Owner** Mrs V Macpherson
P S T (Ref:HM12878)

### MACQUIRE-SAMSON, P
**P Macquire-Samson**, 2 Clifton Pk, Bristol, BS8 3BS, ENG.
(T) 01179 737371 (F) 01179 730887
Speciality: Psychiatry.
● **Senior Partner** Dr M Sternberg
B (Ref:HM12879)

### MACRAE, BARBARA
**Barbara Macrae**, 36 Chazey Rd, Caversham, Reading, **Berkshire**, RG4 7DS, ENG.
(T) 01189 470040
Speciality: Physiotherapy.
P S T (Ref:HM12880)

### MACRAE, V C
**V C MacRae**, 13 Condor Gr, Blackpool, **Lancashire**, FY1 5NA, ENG.
(T) 01253 763916
Speciality: Chiropodists (Podiatrists).
● **Owner** Ms V Macrae
S (Ref:HM12881)

### MACWHINNIE, IAN
**Ian Macwhinnie**, Creative Health Centre, 39A Regent St, Leamington Spa, **Warwickshire**, CV33 5EE, ENG.
(T) 01926 316500
Speciality: Shiatsu.
M (Ref:HM12882)

### MADAM MORGANA & MERLIN
**Madam Morgana & Merlin**, 33 Jacobs Cl, Stantonbury, Milton Keynes, **Buckinghamshire**, MK14 6EJ, ENG.
(T) 01908 315042 (F) 01908 579363
Speciality: Clairvoyants & Palmists.
● **Owner** Mr R Griffiths
B (Ref:HM12883)

### MADAM RIO
**Madam Rio**, 96 Cowick St, Exeter, **Devon**, EX4 1JF, ENG.
(T) 01392 213186
Speciality: Clairvoyants & Palmists.
● **Owner** Ms M Rio
B (Ref:HM12884)

### MADAM ROSINA
**Madam Rosina**, Pier Approach, Bournemouth, **Dorset**, BH2 5AA, ENG.
(T) 01202 554176
Speciality: Clairvoyants & Palmists.
B (Ref:HM12885)

### MADAM SIAN
**Madam Sian**, 29 Penhill Cl, Ouston, Chester Le Street, **County Durham**, DH2 1SF, ENG.
(T) 01914 108290
Speciality: Clairvoyants & Palmists.
B (Ref:HM12886)

### MADAM VALMA
**Madam Valma**, 9 Regent St, Weston-Super-Mare, **Somerset**, BS23 1SE, ENG.
(T) 01934 622599
Speciality: Clairvoyants & Palmists.
● **Owner** Mrs V Pucci
B (Ref:HM12887)

### MADAM VERITY
**Madam Verity**, 28 Hyde Rd, Paignton, **Devon**, TQ4 5BY, ENG.
(T) 01803 844192
Speciality: Clairvoyants & Palmists.
● **Owner** Mrs M Geoffries
B (Ref:HM12888)

### MADAM ZENA
**Madam Zena**, 39 Brooksbank Avenue, Redcar, **Cleveland**, TS10 1HW, ENG.
(T) 01642 482045
Speciality: Clairvoyants & Palmists.
● **Owner** Mrs Z Ramsey
B (Ref:HM12889)

### MADAME MOONA
**Madame Moona**, Gingerbread Cottage, Wickham Rd, Fareham, **Hampshire**, PO17 5BT, ENG.
(T) 01329 833997
Speciality: Clairvoyants & Palmists.
● **Owner/Clairvoyant**
Mrs D Redet-Smith
C (Ref:HM12890)

### MADAME VALMA
**Madame Valma**, Flat 6, 18 Shrubbery Rd, Weston-Super-Mare, **Somerset**, BS23 2JH, ENG.
(T) 01934 645197
Speciality: Clairvoyants & Palmists.
● **Owner** Ms V Pucci
B (Ref:HM12891)

### MADAN DE MOHAN
**Madan De Mohan**, 396 High St, Lincoln, **Lincolnshire**, LN5 7SS, ENG.
(T) 01522 887887
Speciality: Chiropractors.
● **Owner** Dr M Mohan
P S T (Ref:HM12892)

### MADDEN, BRENDAN
**MADDEN BRENDAN MA Psych, Dip Psych, MIAHM**, 1 Chelmsford Rd, Ranelagh, **County Dublin**, IRE.
(T) 01491 3033
Speciality: Psychotherapy.
B (Ref:HM12893)

### MADDERN, WENDY
**Wendy Maddern**, Park Clinic, Earl Rd, Mold, **Flintshire**, CH7 1AX, WAL.
(T) 01352 757697
Speciality: Homeopathy.
● **Owner** Mrs W Maddern
M (Ref:HM12894)

### MADDICK, ELAINE
**Elaine Maddick**, 10 Charles Avenue, Ancaster, Grantham, **Lincolnshire**, NG32 3QH, ENG.
(T) 01400 230638
Speciality: Reflexology.
S T (Ref:HM12895)

### MADDISON-PETTS, CHRISTINE
**Christine Maddison-Petts**, 21 Riverwell, Northampton, **Northamptonshire**, NN3 5EG, ENG.
(T) 01604 411640
Speciality: Chiropodists (Podiatrists).
S (Ref:HM12896)

### MADDOCK, L
**L Maddock**, Bridge House, Crudwell, Malmesbury, **Wiltshire**, SN16 9EY, ENG.
(T) 01666 577397
Speciality: Physiotherapy.
P S T (Ref:HM12897)

### MADDOCKS CLINIC
**Maddocks Clinic (The)**, Villa Court, Madeley, Telford, **Shropshire**, TF7 5AG, ENG.
(T) 01952 585556 (F) 01952 585556
(E) t.pirie@virgin.net
Speciality: Acupuncture, Healing Therapy, Homeopathy, Kinesiology, Physiotherapy, Reiki. ✔
● **Physiotherapist** Ms H Adams Q: MCSP, SRP. M: CSP.
● **Classical Homeopath**
Ms D McClaughlin
(T) 01630 657642 Q: L.C.C.H.

Key: B Mind-Body Medicine · C Complementary Medicine · H Self Help Treatment · M Medicinal Therapy · O Oriental Medicine · P Postural Therapy · S Manipulative Structural Therapy · T Touch Therapy

● **Physiotherapist** Mr J Pirie **Q:** MCSP, SRP. **M:** CSP.
● **Physiotherapist** Mrs T Pirie **Q:** MCSP, SRP. **M:** CSP.
[C] Yrs. Est.: 8 (**Ref:**HM12898)

## MADELEY, P A

**P A Madeley**, 44 Whittaker Lane, Prestwich, Manchester, **Manchester (Greater)**, M25 1FX, ENG.
(T) 01617 735225
Speciality: Chiropodists (Podiatrists).
[S] (**Ref:**HM12899)

## MADHU, ANHES

**Anhes Madhu**, 8 Fairfield Rd, Montpelier, Bristol, BS6 5JP, ENG.
(T) 01179 466606
Speciality: Homeopathy.
● **Owner** Mrs M Anhes
[M] (**Ref:**HM12900)

## MADIGAN, CARMEL

**Madigan Carmel S E N O N C M N H**, School Rd, Whitechurch, **County Cork**, IRE.
(T) 021 4385 942
Speciality: Aromatherapy.
[M] [O] (**Ref:**HM12901)

## MADSEN, N P C

**N P C Madsen**, White Lodge, Bridge Rd, Bursledon, Southampton, **Hampshire**, SO31 8AL, ENG.
(T) 023 8040 2365
Speciality: Osteopathy.
[P] [S] [T] (**Ref:**HM12902)

## MAECHLER, R P

**R P Maechler**, 71 Pembroke Cres, Hove, **Sussex (East)**, BN3 5DF, ENG.
(T) 01273 736489
Speciality: Chiropodists (Podiatrists).
● **Owner** Mr R Maechler
[S] (**Ref:**HM12903)

## MAGEE, MAUREEN

**Maureen Magee**, 51 Cambridge Gr, London, **London (Greater)**, W6 0LB, ENG.
(T) 020 8748 8926
Speciality: Clairvoyants & Palmists.
● **Owner** Ms K Magee
[B] (**Ref:**HM12904)

## MAGENTA THERAPIES

**Magenta Therapies**, 16-18 Newington Buildings, Liverpool, **Merseyside**, L12 1LN, ENG.
(T) 01512 818816
Speciality: Complementary Medicines & Therapy.
● **Owner** Miss F Crossland
[C] [M] (**Ref:**HM12905)

## MAGHERAFELT CHIRO CLINIC

**Magherafelt Chiropractic Clinic**, 4 Hospital Rd, Magherafelt, **County Londonderry**, BT45 5DG, NIR.
(T) 028 7963 4676
Speciality: Chiropractic. ✓
● **Chiropractor** Dr E Keenan **Q:** DO. **M:** SCA.
[S] Yrs. Est.: 8 (**Ref:**HM12906)

## MAGHULL PHYSIOTHERAPY CLINIC

**Maghull Physiotherapy Clinic**, 160 Liverpool Rd North, Liverpool, **Merseyside**, L31 2HP, ENG.
(T) 01515 318941
Speciality: Physiotherapy.
[P] [S] [T] (**Ref:**HM12907)

## MAGIC POTIONS BY POST

**Magic Potions By Post**, 27 Gloucester Rd, London, **London (Greater)**, WC1N 3XX, ENG.
(T) 08703 219885 (F) 08701 255400
Speciality: Clairvoyants & Palmists.
● **Owner** Mr D Goodman
[B] (**Ref:**HM12908)

## MAGIC TOUCH

**Magic Touch**, 67 Bevisland, Swindon, **Wiltshire**, SN3 6AN, ENG.
(T) 01793 693946
Speciality: Complementary Medicines & Therapy.
[C] [M] (**Ref:**HM12909)

## MAGIC TOUCH

**Magic Touch (The)**, 5 Wharfside, Bletchley, Milton Keynes, **Buckinghamshire**, MK2 2AZ, ENG.
(T) 01908 648489 (F) 01908 648491
Speciality: Complementary Medicines & Therapy.
● **Owner** Mr L Delisser
[M] (**Ref:**HM12910)

## MAGIDOV, MISHA & JUDITH

**Misha & Judith Magidov**, 10 Elmcroft Avenue, London, **London (Greater)**, NW11 0RR, ENG.
(T) 020 8455 3938 (F) 020 8455 3938
Speciality: Alexander Technique.
● **Partner** Mrs J Magidov
[P] [S] (**Ref:**HM12911)

## MAGILL, HEATHER

**Heather Magill**, 2 Samphire Cl, Lymington, **Hampshire**, SO41 9LR, ENG.
(T) 01590 678199
Speciality: Chiropodists (Podiatrists).
● **Owner** Mrs H Magill
[S] (**Ref:**HM12912)

## MAGNA JEWELLERY

**Magna Jewellery Ltd**, Po Box 338, Edgware, **London (Greater)**, HA8 8HZ, ENG.
(T) 020 8958 9719 (F) 020 8958 9719
Speciality: Magnetic Therapy.
● **Owner** Mr J Frankel
[C] (**Ref:**HM12913)

## MAGNAFLOW

**Magnaflow**, 2 Oaksmoor Cl, Wheaton Aston, Stafford, **Staffordshire**, ST19 9PE, ENG.
(T) 01785 840204 (F) 01785 840204
(E) scottwarton@ic24.net
Speciality: Complementary Medicines & Therapy, Bioflow Products.
● **Owner** Mr S Wharton
[C] Yrs. Est.: 3 (**Ref:**HM12914)

## MAGNET THERAPY

**Magnet Therapy**, 91 Dacy Rd, Liverpool, **Merseyside**, L5 6RZ, ENG.
(T) 01512 609819
Speciality: Complementary Medicines & Therapy.
● **Owner** Mr I Derbyshire
[M] (**Ref:**HM12915)

## MAGNETIC PAIN RELIEF SYSTEMS

**Magnetic Pain Relief Systems**, 110 Fog Lane, Manchester, **Manchester (Greater)**, M20 6SP, ENG.
(T) 01614 452634 (F) 01614 451965
Speciality: Complementary Medicines & Therapy.
● **Owner** Mr L Gorham
[C] [M] (**Ref:**HM12916)

## MAGNETIC THERAPY

**Magnetic Therapy Ltd**, Freepost 9954, Worsley, Manchester, **Manchester (Greater)**, M28 2GA, ENG.
(T) 01617 935110 (F) 01617 285055
Speciality: Magnetic Therapy.
● **Joint Director** Mr J Whitehead
● **Director** Mrs C Whitehead
[C] Yrs. Est.: 5 (**Ref:**HM12917)

## MAGNETS 4 HEALTH

**Magnets 4 Health**, 1 Brook Cottages, Ivinghoe Aston, Leighton Buzzard, **Bedfordshire**, LU7 9DG, ENG.
(T) 01525 229666 (F) 01525 229666
(E) melvyn@magnets4health.co.uk
(W) www.magnets4health.co.uk
Speciality: Magnetic Therapy. ✓
● **Acupuncturist/Herbalist** Mr M Epstein **Q:** BSc, Dip.Ac, Dip.CHM. **M:** BAcC, BBA.
[H] Yrs. Est.: 6 (**Ref:**HM12918)

## MAGNO PULSE

**Magno Pulse**, Cromhall Farm, Easton Piercy, Kington St. Michael, Chippenham, **Wiltshire**, SN14 6JU, ENG.
(T) 01179 710710 (F) 01179 720720
(W) www.magnopulse.com
Speciality: Complementary Therapy, Magnetic Therapy, Polarity Therapy, Healing with the use of magnets for humans and animals. ✓
● **Owner** Mr D Price
[C] [H] Yrs. Est.: 6 (**Ref:**HM12919)

## MAGNO-PULSE

**Magno-Pulse**, 24 Emery Rd, Bristol, BS4 5PF, ENG.
(T) 01179 710710 (F) 01179 720720
Speciality: Magnetic Therapy.
● **Owner** Mr D Price
[M] (**Ref:**HM12920)

## MAGNOTHERAPY

**Magnotherapy (UK)**, Whernside House, Whernside Rd, Woodthorpe, Nottingham, **Nottinghamshire**, NG5 4LD, ENG.
(T) 01159 531798
Speciality: Complementary Medicines & Therapy.
● **Owner** Mr G Clifford
[M] (**Ref:**HM12921)

## MAGNOTHERAPY PRODUCTS

**Magnotherapy Products**, 4 Athelstan Cl, Quarrington, Sleaford, **Lincolnshire**, NG34 8UY, ENG.
(T) 01529 304222
Speciality: Complementary Medicines & Therapy.
[C] [M] (**Ref:**HM12922)

## MAGNUS, CHRIS

**Chris Magnus**, 18 Chilburn Rd, Clacton-On-Sea, **Essex**, CO15 4NX, ENG.
(T) 01255 436216
Speciality: Chiropodists (Podiatrists).
● **Owner** Mr C Magnus
[S] (**Ref:**HM12923)

## MAGOVERN, PATK (DR)

**Magovern Dr Patk MB Dobst RCPI, Dip Med Acp**, 12 Herbert Pl, Dublin, **County Dublin**, IRE.
(T) 01678 5388
Speciality: Homeopathy.
[M] (**Ref:**HM12924)

## MAGUIRE, KEVIN

**Kevin Maguire**, 16 Ducie Rd, Staple Hill, Bristol, BS16 5JY, ENG.
(T) 01179 572223
Speciality: Chiropodists (Podiatrists).
[S] (**Ref:**HM12925)

## MAHARISHI AYUR VEDA HLTH CTRE

**Maharishi Ayur Veda Health Centre**, Gostins Building, 32-34 Hanover St, Liverpool, **Merseyside**, L1 4LN, ENG.
(T) 01517 099504
Speciality: Complementary Medicines & Therapy.
[M] (**Ref:**HM12926)

## MAHARISHI AYUR-VEDA HLTH CARE

**Maharishi Ayur-Veda Health Care Ltd**, 9 Wilfred Rd, Bournemouth, **Dorset**, BH5 1ND, ENG.
(T) 01202 392700 (F) 01202 303315
Speciality: Complementary Medicines & Therapy.
● **Manager** Mr I Heywood
[C] [M] (**Ref:**HM12927)

## MAHARISHI AYUR-VEDA HLTH CTRE

**Maharishi Ayur-Veda Health Centre**, The Golden Dome, Woodley Park Rd, Skelmersdale, **Lancashire**, WN8 6UQ, ENG.
(T) 01695 51008 (F) 01695 720325
Speciality: Complementary Medicines & Therapy.
● **Manager** Mr F Chalmers
[C] [M] (**Ref:**HM12928)

## MAHBOOBANI, KATHY

**Kathy Mahboobani**, Coast Hill Cottage, Coast Hill, Westcott, Dorking, **Surrey**, RH4 3LH, ENG.
(T) 01306 877238
Speciality: Reflexology.
[S] [T] (**Ref:**HM12929)

## MAHER, CARRON

**Carron Maher**, 13 Whitby Green, Caversham, Reading, **Berkshire**, RG4 6SL, ENG.
(T) 01189 476764


Key continued: **Yrs.Est:** Years Established **Q:** Qualifications **M:** Professional Membership ✓ Indemnity Insurance Accept Credit Cards

Speciality: Chiropodists (Podiatrists).
S (Ref:HM12930)

**MAHER, J HYPNOTHERAPY**

**J Maher Hypnotherapy**, Flat 1, 4 The Glebe, London, **London (Greater)**, SE3 9TT, ENG.
(T) 020 8318 6949
Speciality: Hypnosis.
B (Ref:HM12931)

**MAHIEU, M L**

**M L Mahieu**, 28 Abingdon Villas, London, **London (Greater)**, W8 6BX, ENG.
(T) 020 7584 3424
Speciality: Osteopathy.
P S T (Ref:HM12932)

**MAIDENHEAD CHIROPRACTIC**

**Maidenhead Chiropractic**, Maidenhead Chiropractice, 7 Bridge Avenue, Maidenhead, **Berkshire**, SL6 1RR, ENG.
(T) 01628 629236 (F) 01628 542772
Speciality: Chiropractic, Massage (Therapeutic), Exercise Rehabilitation. ✓
- **Chiropractor** Dr B Neilson Q: DC. M: BCA.
- **Chiropractor** Dr R Rees Q: BSc, DC. M: BCA.
- **Owner** Dr C Turner Q: DC. M: BCA.
- **Chiropractor** Dr G Rockman Q: DC. M: SCA.

P Yrs. Est.: 12 (Ref:HM12933)

**MAIDENHEAD PHYSIO & SPORTS**

**Maidenhead Physiotherapy & Sports Injury Clinic**, 55 Switchback Rd South, Maidenhead, **Berkshire**, SL6 7QF, ENG.
(T) 01628 629638 (F) 01628 629191
Speciality: Acupuncture, Manipulation, Physiotherapy. ✓
- **Owner** Mrs C Price Q: Grad Dip Phys, MCSP, SRP. M: CSP.

S Yrs. Est.: 15 (Ref:HM12934)

**MAIDSTONE ACUPUNCTURE CLINIC**

**Maidstone Acupuncture Clinic**, 13 Boughton Lane, Loose, Maidstone, **Kent**, ME15 9QN, ENG.
(T) 01622 741598
Speciality: Acupuncture. ✓
- **Acupuncturist** Mr P Hammond Q: Lic.Ac, MBAcC. M: BAcC.

O Yrs. Est.: 22 (Ref:HM12935)

**MAIDSTONE CHIROPODY PRACTICE**

**Maidstone Chiropody Practice**, 22 Church St, Maidstone, **Kent**, ME14 1EN, ENG.
(T) 01622 762628
Speciality: Chiropodists (Podiatrists).
S (Ref:HM12936)

**MAIDSTONE COLLEGE-OSTEOPATHY**

**Maidstone College Of Osteopathy (The)**, 28-30 Tonbridge Rd, Maidstone, **Kent**, ME16 8RT, ENG.
(T) 01622 752375
Speciality: Osteopathy.
P S T (Ref:HM12937)

**MAIDSTONE SCHOOL-MASS/AROMA**

**Maidstone School Of Massage & Aromatherapy**, 14 Sheppey Rd, Maidstone, **Kent**, ME15 9SL, ENG.
(T) 01622 744796 (F) 01622 744796
Speciality: Complementary Medicines & Therapy.
- **Partner** Mr A Chell

M (Ref:HM12938)

**MAIN, BOB**

**Bob Main**, 12 High St, Galashiels, **Scottish Borders**, TD1 1SD, SCO.
(T) 01896 751588
Speciality: Chiropractic.
- **Owner** Mr R Main

P S T (Ref:HM12939)

**MAIN, ERIC G**

**Eric G Main**, 33 Bonnygate, Cupar, **Fife**, KY15 4BU, SCO.
(T) 01334 655618
Speciality: Chiropodists (Podiatrists).
S (Ref:HM12940)

**MAIN, J**

**J Main**, 33 Causewayside, Edinburgh, **Edinburgh (City of)**, EH9 1QF, SCO.
(T) 01316 629686
Speciality: Chiropodists (Podiatrists).
S (Ref:HM12941)

**MAIN, ROBERT J**

**Robert J Main**, Main Office, Abbey St, Melrose, **Scottish Borders**, TD6 9PX, SCO.
(T) 01896 823704
Speciality: Chiropodists (Podiatrists).
- **Owner** Mr R Main

S (Ref:HM12942)

**MAIN, ROBERT J**

**Robert J Main**, Working Mens Club, Market Sq, Duns, **Scottish Borders**, TD11 3BY, SCO.
(T) 01361 810411
Speciality: Chiropodists (Podiatrists).
- **Owner** Mr R Main

S (Ref:HM12943)

**MAINES, C**

**C Maines**, 43 Waggs Rd, Congleton, **Cheshire**, CW12 4BP, ENG.
(T) 01260 277918
Speciality: Physiotherapy.
- **Owner** Mrs C Maines

P S T (Ref:HM12944)

**MAINEY, V D**

**V D Mainey**, Landau, Chapel Lane, Hoghton, Preston, **Lancashire**, PR5 0RY, ENG.
(T) 01254 853605
Speciality: Acupuncture.
- **Owner** Dr V Mainey

O (Ref:HM12945)

**MAINI, Y P**

**Y P Maini**, 21 Latham Rd, Bexleyheath, **Kent**, DA6 7NN, ENG.
(T) 01322 408184
Speciality: Homeopathy.
M (Ref:HM12946)

**MAIR, L L**

**Miss L L Mair**, 76 Radnor Rd, Twickenham, **London (Greater)**, TW1 4ND, ENG.
(T) 020 8892 3259
Speciality: Chiropodists (Podiatrists).
S (Ref:HM12947)

**MAIR, MARGARET**

**Margaret Mair**, 6 Coull Green, Kingswells, Aberdeen, **Aberdeenshire**, AB15 8TR, SCO.
(T) 01224 744943
Speciality: Complementary Medicines & Therapy.
- **Owner** Mrs M Mair

C M (Ref:HM12948)

**MAIREAD, RYAN**

**Ryan Mairead**, Clifton Ct Lr Fitzwilliam St, Dublin, **County Dublin**, IRE.
(T) 01661 4828
Speciality: Psychology.
B (Ref:HM12949)

**MAISNER CTRE-EATING DISORDERS**

**Maisner Centre For Eating Disorders**, 48 Clarendon Villas, Hove, **Sussex (East)**, BN3 3RA, ENG.
(T) 01273 729818
Speciality: Hypnotherapy.
- **Owner** Mrs P Maiser

B (Ref:HM12950)

**MAITLAND, J**

**J Maitland**, 17 High St, Airdrie, **Lanarkshire (North)**, ML6 0DT, SCO.
(T) 01236 768736
Speciality: Chiropodists (Podiatrists).
- **Owner** Mr J Maitland

S (Ref:HM12951)

**MAITLAND-TITTERTON, SARAH**

**Sarah Maitland-Titterton**, Hook, **Hampshire**, RG27, ENG.
(T) 01256 882393
Speciality: Bach Remedies.
M (Ref:HM12952)

**MAJOR, EMMA**

**Emma Major**, 97 White Horse Lane, London Colney, St. Albans, **Hertfordshire**, AL2 1JW, ENG.
(T) 01727 822276
Speciality: Chiropractic.
P S T (Ref:HM12953)

**MAJOR, ROSEMARY**

**Rosemary Major**, 14 Meadowsweet, Eaton Ford, St. Neots, **Cambridgeshire**, PE19 7GR, ENG.
Speciality: Reflexology.
S T (Ref:HM12954)

**MAKIN, HOLY**

**Holy Makin**, 62 Paul St, London, **London (Greater)**, EC2A 4NA, ENG.
(T) 020 7251 4429 (F) 020 7613 4737
Speciality: Complementary Medicines & Therapy.
M (Ref:HM12955)

**MAKINSON, MAUREEN ANNE**

**Maureen Anne Makinson**, 38 Weymouth Drive, Hindley, Wigan, **Lancashire**, WN2 4QX, ENG.
(T) 01942 259038
Speciality: Chiropodists (Podiatrists).
- **Owner** Mrs M Makinson

S (Ref:HM12956)

**MAKRAND, HOWARD**

**Howard Makrand**, 11 Heaton House, Heaton Rd, Lancaster, **Lancashire**, LA1 4SU, ENG.
(T) 01524 849938
Speciality: Herbal Medicine.
- **Owner** Mr M Howard

M (Ref:HM12957)

**MAKURAH, LILY**

**Lily Makurah**, 12 Lombard Court, Crown St, London, **London (Greater)**, W3 8SA, ENG.
(T) 020 8993 3488
Speciality: Reflexology.
S T (Ref:HM12958)

**MALACHOWSKI, P**

**P Malachowski**, 1st Floor Woburn Court, 8 Guildhall Hill, Norwich, **Norfolk**, NR2 1JG, ENG.
(T) 01603 219254
Speciality: Complementary Medicines & Therapy.
- **Partner** Mr P Malachowski

M (Ref:HM12959)

**MALAK, NAJI**

**Naji Malak**, 64 Bethel St, Norwich, **Norfolk**, NR2 1NR, ENG.
(T) 01603 666546
Speciality: Acupuncture.
- **Manager** Mr B Almond

O (Ref:HM12960)

**MALAROC**

**Mr M Grimmer**, 21 Prospect Pl, Pakefield, Lowestoft, **Suffolk**, NR33 7DA, ENG.
(T) 01502 563602
Speciality: Manipulation, Massage (Therapeutic), Osteopathy, Phytotherapy, Ultrasonics, Vibrational Therapy. ✓
- **Physiotherapist** Mr M Grimmer Q: MAB Phys, SMAE. M: SMAE.

S Yrs. Est.: 35 (Ref:HM12961)

**MALCOLM H BROWN CHIROPODIST**

**Malcolm H Brown Chiropodist**, 81 West Gate, Mansfield, **Nottinghamshire**, NG18 1RT, ENG.
(T) 01623 623376
Speciality: Chiropodists (Podiatrists).
S (Ref:HM12962)

**MALCOLM SMITH ASSOCIATES**

**Malcolm Smith Associates**, Elms Arcade, High St, Stevenage, **Hertfordshire**, SG1 3EF, ENG.
(T) 01438 318988 (F) 01438 724974
Speciality: Chiropodists (Podiatrists).
- **Principal** Mr M Smith

S (Ref:HM12963)

**MALCOLM, HANNE**

**Hanne Malcolm**, 29 Bell St, Tayport, **Fife**, DD6 9AP, SCO.
(T) 01382 553596
Speciality: Hypnosis.
B (Ref:HM12964)

**MALCOLM, JOYCE**

**Joyce Malcolm**, The Natural Health Practice, Spicer Rd, Exeter, **Devon**, EX1 1SX, ENG.
(T) 01392 499364
Speciality: Complementary Medicines & Therapy.

C M (Ref:HM12965)

**MALCOLM, M J**

**M J Malcolm**, 27 Boutport St, Barnstaple, **Devon**, EX31 1RP, ENG.
(T) 01271 323392
Speciality: Chiropodists (Podiatrists).
S (Ref:HM12966)

**MALDON ACUPUNCTURE & HOM**

**Maldon Acupuncture & Homeopathic Clinic**, 2nd Floor, 50 High St, Maldon, **Essex**, CM9 5PN, ENG.
(T) 01621 850505
Speciality: Complementary Medicines & Therapy.
● **Partner** Mr S Thomas
M (Ref:HM12967)

**MALDON HOMOEOPATHIC CLINIC**

**Maldon Homoeopathic Clinic**, Oakwood House, 2 High St, Maldon, **Essex**, CM9 5PJ, ENG.
(T) 01621 851741
Speciality: Homeopathy.
● **Partner** Mrs B O'Brien
M (Ref:HM12968)

**MALDON HYPNOTHERAPY CLINIC**

**Maldon Hypnotherapy Clinic**, First Floor, 52A High St, Maldon, **Essex**, CM9 5PN, ENG.
(T) 01621 859007
Speciality: Hypnosis.
● **Owner** Mr A Dale
B (Ref:HM12969)

**MALDWYN-EVANS, M**

**M Maldwyn-Evans**, The Priory, Worcester Rd, Ledbury, **Herefordshire**, HR8 1PL, ENG.
(T) 01531 634238
Speciality: Reflexology.
S T (Ref:HM12970)

**MALE, R S**

**R S Male**, 22 Dean St, Aberdare, **Glamorgan (Vale of)**, CF44 7BN, WAL.
(T) 01685 886400
Speciality: Chiropodists (Podiatrists).
S (Ref:HM12971)

**MALHOTRA, A K**

**A K Malhotra**, 51 Redbridge La East, Ilford, **Essex**, IG4 5EU, ENG.
(T) 020 8551 3550
Speciality: Chiropodists (Podiatrists).
● **Owner** A K Malhotra
S (Ref:HM12972)

**MALIN, C J**

**C J Malin**, The Village Studio, Attleborough Rd, Nuneaton, **Warwickshire**, CV11 4HZ, ENG.
(T) 024 7632 7401
Speciality: Chiropodists (Podiatrists).
● **Owner** Miss C Malin
S (Ref:HM12973)

**MALIPHANT, JACKIE**

**Jackie Maliphant**, Seale, **Surrey**, GU10, ENG.
(T) 01252 782724
Speciality: Reflexology.
S T (Ref:HM12974)

**MALKIN, DK, MANIP THERAPY**

**D K Malkin Manipulative Therapy Clinic**, Rooms 3 & 4, 330 Lytham Rd, Blackpool, **Lancashire**, FY4 1DW, ENG.
(T) 01253 346115
Speciality: Aromatherapy, Complementary Therapy, Cupping, Electrotherapy, Manipulation, Massage (Therapeutic), Osteopathy, Stress Therapy, Ultrasonics. ✔ CREDIT
● **Remedial Massage Therapist** C. S Taylor M: LCSP.
● **Manipulative Therapist** Mrs D Malkin M: LCSP.
S Yrs. Est.: 30 (Ref:HM12975)

**MALLARD, CAROLE**

**Carole Mallard**, 77 Betjeman Way, Hemel Hempstead, **Hertfordshire**, HP1 3HJ, ENG.
(T) 01442 211797
Speciality: Reflexology.
S T (Ref:HM12976)

**MALLARDO, RENEE**

**Renee Mallardo**, Old Forge Cottage, 39 Ringmore Rd, Shaldon, Shaldon, **Devon**, TQ14 0AG, ENG.
(T) 01626 873881
Speciality: Absent Healing, Auto Suggestion, Aversion Therapy, Cognitive Therapy, Counselling, Family Therapy, Group Therapy, Hypnosis, Hypnotherapy, Psychotherapy, Reiki, Rogerian Therapy, Stress Therapy. ✔
● **Psychotherapist** Renee Mallardo Q: DHP (NC). M: NRHP, UKCP.
H Yrs. Est.: 11 (Ref:HM12977)

**MALLION, CAROLINE E**

**Caroline E Mallion**, Luxistore, 232 Stockport Rd, Timperley, Altrincham, **Cheshire**, WA15 7UN, ENG.
(T) 01619 801558
Speciality: Chiropodists (Podiatrists).
● **Owner** Mrs C Mallion
S (Ref:HM12978)

**MALLION, CHRISTINE**

**Christine Mallion**, 68 Barrington Rd, Altrincham, **Cheshire**, WA14 1JB, ENG.
(T) 01619 294744 (F) 01619 295677
Speciality: Physiotherapy.
● **Practice Manager** Mrs C Mallion
P S T (Ref:HM12979)

**MALLON, B**

**B Mallon**, 7 Didsbury Park, Manchester, **Manchester (Greater)**, M20 5LH, ENG.
(T) 01614 488780
Speciality: Complementary Medicines & Therapy.
● **Owner** Ms B Mallon
C M (Ref:HM12980)

**MALLOWS, J**

**J Mallows**, Bridgend Health Care Centre, Sir Georges St, Thurso, **Highland**, KW14 7AW, SCO.
(T) 01847 896363
Speciality: Osteopathy.
P S T (Ref:HM12981)

**MALMESBURY CHIROPRACTIC CLINIC**

**Malmesbury Chiropractic Clinic**, Cross Hayes, Malmesbury, **Wiltshire**, SN16 9BG, ENG.
(T) 01666 824884 (F) 01666 822688
(W) www.skelian.co.uk
Speciality: Chiropractic. ✔
● **Chiropractor** Mr Smelle Q: BCA, BSc, DC. M: BCA.
● **Chiropractor** Louise Hopkins Q: BCA, DC. M: BCA, CC.
● **Chiropractor** Mr K Walker
S Yrs. Est.: 10 (Ref:HM12982)

**MALONE, P**

**P Malone**, 15 Windsor Avenue, Lurgan, Craigavon, **County Armagh**, BT67 9BG, NIR.
(T) 028 3832 2696
Speciality: Chiropodists (Podiatrists).
● **Owner** Mr P Malone
S (Ref:HM12983)

**MALONE, PATRICIA**

**Malone B A Cert Counselling NLP Practitioner Patricia**, 70 Rosemount Estate, Dundrum, **County Dublin**, IRE.
(T) 01298 9552
Speciality: Counselling.
B H (Ref:HM12984)

**MALONEY, M**

**M Maloney**, 168 High St, Maldon, **Essex**, CM9 5BX, ENG.
(T) 01621 859094
Speciality: Osteopathy.
● **Owner** Mrs M Maloney
P S T (Ref:HM12985)

**MALONEY, M P**

**M P Maloney**, 66 High St, Great Baddow, Chelmsford, **Essex**, CM2 7HH, ENG.
(T) 01245 476677 (F) 01245 473433
Speciality: Osteopathy.
● **Owner** Mr M Maloney
P S T (Ref:HM12986)

**MALONEY, MAUREEN**

**Maloney Maureen**, 73 Claremont, **County Galway**, IRE.
(T) 09152 5941
Speciality: Complementary Medicines & Therapy.
M (Ref:HM12987)

**MALONEY, MONICA**

**Maloney Monica**, Moycullen, **County Galway**, IRE.
(T) 09155 5144
Speciality: Aromatherapy.
M O (Ref:HM12988)

**MALONNE, MARIANNE**

**Marianne Malonne**, 37 The Towers, Lower Mortlake Rd, Richmond, **Surrey**, TW9 2JR, ENG.
(T) 020 8948 8561
Speciality: Reflexology.
S T (Ref:HM12989)

**MALOY, ALISON**

**Alison Maloy**, Hasler House, 90 High St, Dunmow, **Essex**, CM6 1AP, ENG.
(T) 01371 875217
Speciality: Osteopathy.
● **Owner** Mrs A Maloy
P S T (Ref:HM12990)

**MALOY, ALISON**

**Alison Maloy**, 15 Oakroyd Avenue, Dunmow, **Essex**, CM6 1HG, ENG.
(T) 01371 875217
Speciality: Osteopathy.
P S T (Ref:HM12991)

**MALTINGS NATURAL THERAPIES**

**Maltings Natural Therapies (The)**, The Maltings, West End, Bruton, **Somerset**, BA10 0BB, ENG.
(T) 01749 813814
Speciality: Complementary Medicines & Therapy.
● **Owner** Mrs D Nunn
C M (Ref:HM12992)

**MALTINGS PHYSIO & CHIROPODY**

**Maltings Physiotherapy & Chiropody Clinic (The)**, 40A Flaxley Rd, Selby, **Yorkshire (North)**, YO8 4BG, ENG.
(T) 01757 213236 (F) 01977 676695
Speciality: Physiotherapy.
● **Owner** Mr A Drewitt
P S T (Ref:HM12993)

**MALVERN CHIROPODY SURGERY**

**Malvern Chiropody Surgery (The)**, 64 Worcester Rd, Malvern, **Worcestershire**, WR14 4AB, ENG.
(T) 01684 561342
Speciality: Chiropodists (Podiatrists).
● **Owner** Mr D Williams
S (Ref:HM12994)

**MALVERN HILLS HOMOEOPATHIC**

**Malvern Hills Homoeopathic Clinic**, Ground Floor, 52 Priory Rd, Malvern, **Worcestershire**, WR14 3DB, ENG.
(T) 01684 563192
Speciality: Homeopathy.
M (Ref:HM12995)

**MALVERN HILLS PHYSIO CLINIC**

**Malvern Hills Physiotherapy Clinic**, 127 Church St, Malvern, **Worcestershire**, WR14 2BA, ENG.
(T) 01684 574053 (F) 01684 574053
Speciality: Physiotherapy.
● **Owner** Mr S Montgomery
P S T (Ref:HM12996)

**MALVERN HILLS REMEDIES**

**Malvern Hills Remedies**, Seaford House, 365 Worcester Rd, Malvern, **Worcestershire**, WR14 1AR, ENG.
(T) 01684 891656 (F) 01684 891687
Speciality: Complementary Medicines & Therapy.
● **Employee** Mr R Drury
M (Ref:HM12997)

**MALVERN NATURAL HEALTH CENTRE**

**Malvern Natural Health Centre**, 15 Abbey Rd, Malvern, **Worcestershire**, WR14 3ES, ENG.
(T) 01684 893238
Speciality: Acupuncture, Aromatherapy, Bowen Therapy, Crystal Healing, Herbal Medicine,


Key continued: Yrs.Est: Years Established Q: Qualifications M: Professional Membership ✔ Indemnity Insurance CREDIT Accept Credit Cards

Homeopathy, Hypnotherapy, Reflexology, Reiki, Seichem, T'ai-Chi Ch'uan, Zero Balancing. ✓
● **Partner** Mrs K Sinclair
C Yrs. Est.: 15 (Ref:HM12998)

## MALVERN OSTEOPATHIC CLINIC

**Malvern Osteopathic Clinic**, 8 Tibberton Rd, Malvern, **Worcestershire**, WR14 3AN, ENG.
(T) 01684 575379 (F) 01684 564350
(E) ie@malvernosteo.co.uk
(W) www.malvernosteo.co.uk
Speciality: Acupuncture, Manipulation, Massage (Therapeutic), Osteopathy, Ultrasonics. ✓
● **Osteopath/Acupuncturist**
Mr I Elias Q: DO, Lic.Ac. M: GOsC.
● **Osteopath** Ms H Yeoman Q: DO. M: GOsC.
S Yrs. Est.: 16 (Ref:HM12999)

## MANA MANAGEMENT

**Mana Management Ltd**, 29 Woodsford Sq, London, **London (Greater)**, W14 8DP, ENG.
(T) 020 7603 6165 (F) 020 7602 9473
Speciality: Complementary Medicines & Therapy.
● **Owner** Mrs E Fieldgrass
M (Ref:HM13000)

## MANCHESTER GESTALT CENTRE

**Manchester Gestalt Centre**, 7 Norman Rd, Manchester, **Manchester (Greater)**, M14 5LF, ENG.
(T) 01612 572202 (F) 01612 572202
Speciality: Psychotherapy.
B (Ref:HM13001)

## MANCHESTER HOMOEOPATHIC CLINIC

**Manchester Homoeopathic Clinic (The)**, Brunswick St, Manchester, **Manchester (Greater)**, M13 9ST, ENG.
(T) 01612 732446 (F) 01612 732446
Speciality: Homeopathy.
● **Owner** Dr G Burns
M (Ref:HM13002)

## MANCHESTER INSTITUTE-PSYCHO

**Manchester Institute For Psychotherapists**, 454 Barlow Moor Rd, Manchester, **Manchester (Greater)**, M21 0BQ, ENG.
(T) 01618 629456
Speciality: Psychotherapy.
B (Ref:HM13003)

## MANCHESTER SCHOOL OF MASSAGE

**Manchester School Of Massage**, 77 Russell Rd, Manchester, **Manchester (Greater)**, M16 8AR, ENG.
(T) 01618 629752
Speciality: Aromatherapy, Indian Head Massage, Massage (Therapeutic), Reflexology, Radionics.
C (Ref:HM13004)

## MANCHESTER SPORT INJURIES

**Manchester Sport Injuries Clinic**, 30 The Crescent, Salford, **Manchester (Greater)**, M5 4FP, ENG.
(T) 01617 457551 (F) 01617 430703
Speciality: Physiotherapy.
● **Owner** Mrs L Atherton
P S T (Ref:HM13005)

## MANCHESTER THERAPY CENTRE

**Manchester Therapy Centre (The)**, 199 Monton Rd, Monton, Eccles, Manchester, **Manchester (Greater)**, M30 9PN, ENG.
(T) 01617 888760
Speciality: Physiotherapy.
● **Practitioner** Ms J Gill
P S T (Ref:HM13006)

## MANDALAY HOTEL

**Mandalay Hotel**, 7 Cleveland Rd, Paignton, **Devon**, TQ4 6EN, ENG.
(T) 01803 525653
Speciality: Complementary Medicines & Therapy.
C M (Ref:HM13007)

## MANDARIN THERAPIES

**Mandarin Therapies**, 48 Station Rd, Bardney, Lincoln, **Lincolnshire**, LN3 5UD, ENG.
(T) 01526 399121
Speciality: Complementary Medicines & Therapy.
C M (Ref:HM13008)

## MANDY BALDWIN - TRICHOLOGIST

**Mandy Baldwin - Trichologist**, 51 Pickford Lane, Bexleyheath, **Kent**, DA7 4QU, ENG.
(T) 020 8301 1888
Speciality: Complementary Medicines & Therapy, Trichology.
M (Ref:HM13009)

## MANGAN PETER & CRAVEN CLAIRE

**Peter Mangan & Claire Craven**, 11-13 Woodcote Rd, Wallington, **Surrey**, SM6 0LH, ENG.
(T) 020 8669 5075
Speciality: Osteopathy.
P S T (Ref:HM13010)

## MANGAN, ANNE

**Anne Mangan RGN DO MGO**, 18 Priory Hall, Stillorgan, **County Dublin**, IRE.
(T) 01283 5566 (F) 01283 5756
(E) iptas@iol.ie
Speciality: Osteopathy.
P S T (Ref:HM13011)

## MANGLES, DENISE

**Denise Mangles**, 16 Veasy Park, Wembury, Plymouth, **Devon**, PL9 0ES, ENG.
(T) 01752 863255
Speciality: Aromatherapy, Reflexology, Swedish Body Massage.
M O (Ref:HM13012)

## MANGNALL, J

**J Mangnall**, 107 Walmsley St, Fleetwood, **Lancashire**, FY7 6LL, ENG.
(T) 01253 872464
Speciality: Chiropodists (Podiatrists).
● **Owner** Mrs J Mangnall
S (Ref:HM13013)

## MANION, D

**D Manion**, 59 Bellevue, Stourbridge, **Midlands (West)**, DY8 5DB, ENG.
(T) 01384 291721
Speciality: Acupuncture.
O (Ref:HM13014)

## MANKOO, KAREN

**Karen Mankoo**, 37 St Dunstans Rd, London, **London (Greater)**, W7 2EY, ENG.
(T) 020 8566 2489
Speciality: Aromatherapy.
● **Owner** Ms K Mankoo
M O (Ref:HM13015)

## MANLEY CLINIC

**Manley Clinic (The)**, Flat 2, 35A Welbeck St, London, **London (Greater)**, W1M 7PG, ENG.
(T) 020 8977 7530
Speciality: Homeopathy, Osteopathy. ✓
● **Homeopath** Ms A Hetherton Q: L.C.C.H, RSHom. M: Soc.Hom.
B Yrs. Est.: 10 (Ref:HM13016)

## MANN, ALAN

**Alan Mann**, 94 Woodcote Grove Rd, Coulsdon, **London (Greater)**, CR5 2AE, ENG.
(T) 020 8763 1787 (F) 020 8407 2415
Speciality: Chiropodists (Podiatrists).
● **Owner** Mr A Mann
S (Ref:HM13017)

## MANN, G C & DAVID, R T

**G C Mann & R T David**, 97 South St, Dorking, **Surrey**, RH4 2JU, ENG.
(T) 01306 883332
Speciality: Chiropodists (Podiatrists).
● **Practice Manager** Mrs L Dymott
S (Ref:HM13018)

## MANN, H S

**H S Mann**, 290 London Rd, Slough, **Berkshire**, SL3 7HT, ENG.
(T) 01753 580420
Speciality: Osteopathy.
● **Owner** Mr H Mann
P S T (Ref:HM13019)

## MANN, LESLEY

**Lesley Mann**, 80 The Warren, West Dean, Chichester, **Sussex (West)**, PO18 0RP, ENG.
(T) 01243 811509
Speciality: Alexander Technique.
P S (Ref:HM13020)

## MANN, NEIL

**Mr Neil Mann**, 8 Becmead Avenue, London, **London (Greater)**, SW16 1UQ, ENG.
(T) 020 8769 3267
Speciality: Osteopathy.
● **Owner** Mr N Mann
P S T (Ref:HM13021)

## MANN, PATRICIA

**Patricia Mann**, 3 Greenbank, Kennington, Ashford, **Kent**, TN24 9NJ, ENG.
(T) 01233 627500
Speciality: Complementary Medicines & Therapy.
● **Owner** Mrs P Mann
C M (Ref:HM13022)

## MANN, PAUL

**Paul Mann**, 37 Clover Rd, Timperley, Altrincham, **Cheshire**, WA15 7NG, ENG.
(T) 01619 803290 (F) 01619 803290
Speciality: Hypnosis.
● **Owner** Mr P Mann
B (Ref:HM13023)

## MANN, RICHARD

**Mann Richard Osteopath**, 1 Rus-In-Urbe Tce, Dun Laoghaire, **County Dublin**, IRE.
(T) 01280 3890
Speciality: Osteopathy.
P S T (Ref:HM13024)

## MANN, SUSAN

**Susan Mann**, 44 Elvaston Pl, London, **London (Greater)**, SW7 5NP, ENG.
(T) 020 7581 2548
Speciality: Psychology.
● **Doctor** Dr S Mann
B (Ref:HM13025)

## MANNERING, PAM

**Pam Mannering**, 25 Sedgmoor Rd, Flackwell Heath, High Wycombe, **Buckinghamshire**, HP10 9AW, ENG.
(T) 01628 525317
Speciality: Chiropodists (Podiatrists).
● **Owner** Mrs P Mannering
S (Ref:HM13026)

## MANNING, D J

**D J Manning**, 14 Sutherland Avenue, Bexhill-on-Sea, **Sussex (East)**, TN39 3QR, ENG.
(T) 01424 216549
Speciality: Hypnotherapy.
● **Owner** Mr D Manning
B (Ref:HM13027)

## MANNING, D J (DR)

**Dr D J Manning**, 12 Fiennes Rd, Herstmonceux, Hailsham, **Sussex (East)**, BN27 4LN, ENG.
(T) 01323 831677
(W) www.complementary-healthcare.co.uk/info/dmanning
Speciality: Hypnosis.
B (Ref:HM13028)

## MANNING, FRANCES

**Frances Manning**, 66 Woodbastwick Rd, London, **London (Greater)**, SE26 5LH, ENG.
(T) 020 8778 6402
Speciality: Reflexology.
S T (Ref:HM13029)

## MANNING, JONATHAN

**Jonathan Manning**, 1 Castle Rd, Southampton, **Hampshire**, SO18 1QP, ENG.
(T) 023 8058 2219
Speciality: Hypnosis.
● **Owner** Mr J Manning
B (Ref:HM13030)

## MANNING, MATTHEW

**Matthew Manning**, Sturgeons Hall, The Green, Hartest, Bury St. Edmunds, **Suffolk**, IP29 4DH, ENG.
(T) 01284 830222 (F) 01284 830228
Speciality: Complementary Medicines & Therapy.
● **Owner** Mr M Manning
C M (Ref:HM13031)



Key: B Mind-Body Medicine, C Complementary Medicine, H Self Help Treatment, M Medicinal Therapy, O Oriental Medicine, P Postural Therapy, S Manipulative Structural Therapy, T Touch Therapy

**MANNING, PAMELA**

**Pamela Manning**, 37 High Town Rd, Maidenhead, **Berkshire**, SL6 1PA, ENG.
(T) 01628 788420
Speciality: Chiropodists (Podiatrists).
● **Owner** Mrs C Sanders
S (Ref:HM13032)

**MANNING, PAUL**

**Paul Manning**, 8 Regent Pl, Rugby, **Warwickshire**, CV21 2PN, ENG.
(T) 01788 568410
Speciality: Chiropodists (Podiatrists).
● **Owner** Mr P Manning
S (Ref:HM13033)

**MANNING-PHILLIPS, J**

**J Manning-Phillips**, 9 Malvern Way, Porton, Salisbury, **Wiltshire**, SP4 0NL, ENG.
(T) 01980 610219
Speciality: Physiotherapy.
P S T (Ref:HM13034)

**MANOGUE, ANNIE**

**Annie Manogue**, 58 St. Georges Rd, Manchester, **Manchester (Greater)**, M14 6SZ, ENG.
(T) 01612 257352
Speciality: Homeopathy.
M (Ref:HM13035)

**MANOR CHIROPODY CLINIC**

**Manor Chiropody Clinic**, 6 Manor Rd, Wallasey, **Merseyside**, CH45 4JB, ENG.
(T) 01516 399100 (F) 01516 912009
Speciality: Chiropodists (Podiatrists).
● **Owner** Miss S Swindlehurst
S (Ref:HM13036)

**MANOR GROVE CLINIC**

**Manor Grove Clinic (The)**, Scott Park Surgery, 205 Western Approaches, Southend-On-Sea, **Essex**, SS2 6XY, ENG.
(T) 01702 420858
Speciality: Complementary Medicines & Therapy.
● **Principal** Mr A Ratcliff
M (Ref:HM13037)

**MANOR HLTH FOOD/NUTRITION CTRE**

**Health Food**, 93 Victoria Rd, Ruislip, **London (Greater)**, HA4 9BH, ENG.
(T) 01895 672386
Speciality: Complementary Medicines & Therapy.
C (Ref:HM13038)

**MANOR HOUSE**

**Manor House**, Suite 1 Gosford House, Gosford Rd, Beccles, **Suffolk**, NR34 9QW, ENG.
(T) 01502 717779
Speciality: Acupuncture, Chiropody, Herbal Medicine, Nutritional Therapy, Osteopathy, Podiatry. ✔
● **Osteopath** Mr M James Q: DO. M: GOsC.
● **Osteopath** Kathrine McDonald Q: BSc. M: GOsC.
● **Chiropodist** Mr D Measer Q: MBChA, MSSCh.
S Yrs. Est.: 3 (Ref:HM13039)

**MANOR HOUSE CENTRE**

**Manor House Centre**, 80 East End Rd, London, **London (Greater)**, E3 2SY, ENG.
(T) 020 8371 0180
Speciality: Psychotherapy.
● **Therapist** Judith Dell
B (Ref:HM13040)

**MANOR WALK PHYSIO CENTRE**

**Manor Walk Physiotherapy Centre**, Manor Walk, Market Harborough, **Leicestershire**, LE16 9BP, ENG.
(T) 01858 431510
Speciality: Physiotherapy.
P S T (Ref:HM13041)

**MANSBRIDGE PHYSIO PRACTICE**

**Mansbridge Physiotherapy Practice**, 1 Mansbridge Cottages, Mansbridge Rd, Southampton, **Hampshire**, SO18 2NH, ENG.
(T) 023 8058 1586
Speciality: Physiotherapy.
● **Owner** Mrs M Mortimer
P S T (Ref:HM13042)

**MANSBRIDGE, SANDRA**

**Sandra Mansbridge**, The Hope Clinic, 17 Star St, Ryde, **Isle of Wight**, PO33 2HX, ENG.
(T) 01983 563539
Speciality: Reflexology.
S T (Ref:HM13043)

**MANSELL**

**Mansell**, 11 The Arcade, Leicester Rd, Wigston, **Leicestershire**, LE18 1NZ, ENG.
(T) 01162 880440
Speciality: Chiropodists (Podiatrists).
S (Ref:HM13044)

**MANSELL-HOPE, CAROLE**

**Carole Mansell-Hope**, The Weaver House Clinic, 19A Pillory St, Nantwich, **Cheshire**, CW5 5BZ, ENG.
(T) 01270 629933
Speciality: Hypnotherapy.
B (Ref:HM13045)

**MANSFIELD CHIROPODY**

**Mansfield Chiropody**, Care Of Boots, 39 Four Seasons Shopping Centre, Mansfield, **Nottinghamshire**, NG18 1SU, ENG.
(T) 01623 422522
Speciality: Chiropody. ✔
● **Owner/Chiropodist** Mr G Pointing
Q: Inst.CH.P. M: Inst.CH.P.
C Yrs. Est.: 3 (Ref:HM13046)

**MANSFIELD CHIROPRACTIC CLINIC**

**Mansfield Chiropractic Clinic**, 40A Rosemary St, Mansfield, **Nottinghamshire**, NG19 6AB, ENG.
(T) 01623 635333
Speciality: Chiropractic.
● **Owner** Dr P Welsh
P S T (Ref:HM13047)

**MANSFIELD, ANGELA**

**Angela Mansfield**, 52 Stoke Newington Church St, London, **London (Greater)**, N16 0NB, ENG.
(T) 020 7249 9671 (F) 020 7502 1182
Speciality: Acupuncture.
● **Principal** Mrs J Sheridan
O (Ref:HM13048)

**MANSFIELD, PETER**

**Peter Mansfield**, 3 St. Aubyns Rd, Portslade, Brighton, **Sussex (East)**, BN41 1AB, ENG.
(T) 01273 424752
Speciality: Alexander Technique.
P S (Ref:HM13049)

**MANSTON, N**

**N Manston**, 56 Gidley Way, Horspath, Oxford, **Oxfordshire**, OX33 1RG, ENG.
(T) 01865 875854
Speciality: Osteopathy.
P S T (Ref:HM13050)

**MANT, I**

**I Mant**, Loughborough Physiotherapy Clinic, 3 The Coneries, Loughborough, **Leicestershire**, LE11 1DZ, ENG.
(T) 01509 263932 (F) 01509 263932
Speciality: Physiotherapy.
P S T (Ref:HM13051)

**MANTLE & WHITE ELECTRICAL**

**Mantle & White Electrical**, 166 Withern Rd, Nottingham, **Nottinghamshire**, NG8 6FQ, ENG.
(T) 01159 199992
Speciality: Electrolysis.
T (Ref:HM13052)

**MANTLE, FIONA**

**Fiona Mantle**, 30C Sycamore Gr, New Malden, **Surrey**, KT3 3DQ, ENG.
(T) 020 8942 9593
Speciality: Bach Remedies, Hypnosis.
● **Owner** Ms F Mantle
B (Ref:HM13053)

**MANTLE, FIONA**

**Fiona Mantle**, New Malden, **Surrey**, KT3, ENG.
(T) 020 8942 9593
Speciality: Hypnotherapy.
B (Ref:HM13054)

**MANTON, JOSEPHINE**

**Josephine Manton**, The College Practice, 60 Highgate Rd, London, **London (Greater)**, NW5 1PA, ENG.
(T) 020 7267 6445 (F) 020 7267 6445
Speciality: Osteopathy.
● **Partner** Ms J Manton
P S T (Ref:HM13055)

**MAOUDIS, P G**

**P G Maoudis**, Intershop, 1a Warwick Row, Coventry, **Midlands (West)**, CV1 1EX, ENG.
(T) 024 7622 0185
Speciality: Chiropodists (Podiatrists).
S (Ref:HM13056)

**MAOUDIS, P G**

**P G Maoudis**, 15 Lant Cl, Coventry, **Midlands (West)**, CV4 9TG, ENG.
(T) 024 7647 1033 (F) 024 7647 1033
Speciality: Chiropodists (Podiatrists).
● **Owner** Mr P Maoudis
S (Ref:HM13057)

**MAPERTON TRUST**

**Maperton Trust (The)**, Maperton, Wincanton, **Somerset**, BA9 8EH, ENG.
(T) 01963 32651 (F) 01963 32626
Speciality: Holistic Healing.
● **Secretary** Ms J Heath
(T) 01963 32657
C (Ref:HM13058)

**MAPES, JANET**

**Janet Mapes**, 66 Elmtree Rd, Sutton Coldfield, **Midlands (West)**, B74 3RX, ENG.
(T) 01213 533668
Speciality: Aromatherapy, Bach Remedies, Yoga, Bach Centre-Reg practitioner. ✔
● **Owner** Mrs J Mapes Q: ISPA.
C Yrs. Est.: 15 (Ref:HM13059)

**MAPLE LEAF CLINIC**

**Maple Leaf Clinic (The)**, 20 The Green, Twickenham, **London (Greater)**, TW2 5AB, ENG.
(T) 020 8892 6909 (F) 020 8894 5034
Speciality: Chiropodists (Podiatrists).
● **Owner** Mr G Rosenberg
S (Ref:HM13060)

**MAPLE TREE OSTEO PRACTICE**

**Maple Tree Osteopathic Practice**, 322 Wellingborough Rd, Northampton, **Northamptonshire**, NN1 4EP, ENG.
(T) 01604 628151
(E) becquereau@maple-osteo.freeserve.co.uk
Speciality: Healer, Osteopathy. ✔
● **Owner** Mr C Becquereau Q: BSc (Hons). M: GOsC.
S Yrs. Est.: 3 (Ref:HM13061)

**MAPLE TREE PRACTICE**

**Maple Tree Practice**, 2a Leyton Rd, Harpenden, **Hertfordshire**, AL5 2TL, ENG.
(T) 01582 760781
Speciality: Osteopathy.
● **Partner** Ms M Lacey
P S T (Ref:HM13062)

**MAPLES PHYSIO & REFLEXTHERAPY**

**Maples Physiotherapy & Reflextherapy**, 103 Navigation Rd, Altrincham, **Cheshire**, WA14 1LJ, ENG.
(T) 01619 416588
Speciality: Reflexology.
S T (Ref:HM13063)

**MAPPERLEY, B S**

**B S Mapperley**, 15 Cromer Rd, Overstrand, Cromer, **Norfolk**, NR27 0NT, ENG.
(T) 01263 579463
Speciality: Chiropodists (Podiatrists).
S (Ref:HM13064)

**MARAR, N Z**

**N Z Marar**, 1 Middle St, Taunton, **Somerset**, TA1 1SU, ENG.
(T) 01823 326261
Speciality: Homeopathy.
● **Owner** Mr N Marar
M (Ref:HM13065)

**MARCER, NICHOLAS**

**Nicholas Marcer**, 59 Church St, Boughton



Key continued: Yrs.Est: Years Established Q: Qualifications M: Professional Membership ✔ Indemnity Insurance Accept Credit Cards

Monchelsea, Maidstone, **Kent**, ME17 4HN, ENG.
(T) 01622 744992
Speciality: Osteopathy.
P S T (**Ref:**HM13066)

## MARCH CENTRE
**March Centre (The)**, 52 Egerton Avenue, Leicester, **Leicestershire**, LE4 0DN, ENG.
(T) 01162 665239
Speciality: Complementary Medicines & Therapy.
M (**Ref:**HM13067)

## MARCH, JANIS
**Janis March**, Home Farm, Stockport Rd, Thelwall, Warrington, **Cheshire**, WA4 2TQ, ENG.
(T) 01925 754389
Speciality: Reflexology.
S T (**Ref:**HM13068)

## MARCH, THIERRY
**Thierry March**, Brabant House, Portsmouth Rd, Thames Ditton, **Surrey**, KT7 0EY, ENG.
(T) 020 8398 7592
Speciality: Herbal Medicine.
M (**Ref:**HM13069)

## MARCHAL, ALISON
**Alison Marchal**, 5 Sandpiper Cl, Ifield, Crawley, **Sussex (West)**, RH11 0SB, ENG.
(T) 01293 527858
Speciality: Chiropodists (Podiatrists).
● **Owner** Ms A Marchal
S (**Ref:**HM13070)

## MARCHANT, SUE
**Sue Marchant**, 37 Park Lane, Tilehurst, Reading, **Berkshire**, RG31 5DP, ENG.
(T) 01189 426202
Speciality: Chiropodists (Podiatrists).
● **Owner** Mrs S Marchant
S (**Ref:**HM13071)

## MARCHANT-JONES, ALISON
**Alison Marchant-Jones**, 6 Coleswood Rd, Harpenden, **Hertfordshire**, AL5 1EQ, ENG.
(T) 01582 467736
Speciality: Complementary Medicines & Therapy, Trichology.
M (**Ref:**HM13072)

## MARCHMONT PHYSIOTHERAPY CLINIC
**Marchmont Physiotherapy Clinic**, 24 Biggar Rd, Edinburgh, **Edinburgh (City of)**, EH10 7BH, SCO.
(T) 01314 777774 (F) 01314 777774
Speciality: Physiotherapy. ✔
● **Owner/Physiotherapist**
Mrs M McAinsh **Q:** MCSP, SRP.
S Yrs. Est.: 10 (**Ref:**HM13073)

## MARCH-SMITH, ROSIE
**Rosie March-Smith**, Ellerslie, Cattistock, Dorchester, **Dorset**, DT2 0JL, ENG.
(T) 01300 321355
Speciality: Psychotherapy.
● **Owner** Mrs R March-Smith
B (**Ref:**HM13074)

## MARCO, ALAN
**Alan Marco**, Plascelyn Cottage, Ystradgynlais, Swansea, **Glamorgan (Vale of)**, SA9 1QB, WAL.
(T) 01639 843885
Speciality: Hypnotherapy.
● **Owner** Alan Marco
B (**Ref:**HM13075)

## MARCONI, L R
**L R Marconi**, 246A London Rd, Stoke-On-Trent, **Staffordshire**, ST4 5RH, ENG.
(T) 01782 744179
Speciality: Biomechanics, Chiropody. ✔
● **Chiropodist** Mrs L Marconi **Q:** MBChA, MSSCh.
C Yrs. Est.: 13 (**Ref:**HM13076)

## MARCOULLIDES, A G
**A G Marcoullides A G**, Cannon Hill Clinic, 16 Cannon Hill, London, **London (Greater)**, N14 7HD, ENG.
(T) 020 8882 2131
Speciality: Osteopathy.
P S T (**Ref:**HM13077)

## MARCUS, CLAIRE HANNAH
**Claire Hannah Marcus**, 36 Novello Way, Borehamwood, **Hertfordshire**, WD6 5RT, ENG.
(T) 020 8207 3115
Speciality: Reflexology.
S T (**Ref:**HM13078)

## MARCUS, M
**M Marcus**, 14 Kingsland, Newcastle Upon Tyne, **Tyne and Wear**, NE2 3AL, ENG.
(T) 01912 818032
Speciality: Alexander Technique.
P S (**Ref:**HM13079)

## MARCUS, MARY
**Mary Marcus**, Alington House, 4 North Bailey, Durham, **County Durham**, DH1 3ET, ENG.
(T) 01642 644067
Speciality: Alexander Technique.
● **Partner** Ms M Marcus
P S (**Ref:**HM13080)

## MARDEL, JEREMY
**Jeremy Mardel**, 46 St Johns Rd, Farnham, **Surrey**, GU9 8NU, ENG.
(T) 01252 727077 (F) 01252 727077
Speciality: Homeopathy.
● **Owner** Mr J Mardel
M (**Ref:**HM13081)

## MARDEL, JEREMY
**Jeremy Mardel**, 111 West St, Farnham, **Surrey**, GU9 7HH, ENG.
(T) 01252 713785
Speciality: Homeopathy.
M (**Ref:**HM13082)

## MARFLEET, RACHAEL
**Rachael Marfleet**, 6 Manton Drive, Luton, **Bedfordshire**, LU2 7DH, ENG.
(T) 01582 411223 (F) 01582 411223
Speciality: Acupuncture.
● **Owner** Ms R Marfleet
O (**Ref:**HM13083)

## MARFLEET, RACHAEL DE VERE
**Rachael D E Vere Marfleet**, The Shen Tao Clinic, 4 The Shires Old Bedford Rd, **Bedfordshire**, LU2 7QA, ENG.
(T) 01582 411223
Speciality: Acupuncture.
O (**Ref:**HM13084)

## MARGA, ANANDA
**Ananda Marga**, 3a Cazenove Rd, London, **London (Greater)**, N16 6PA, ENG.
(T) 020 8806 4250 (F) 020 8806 4250
Speciality: Relaxation Technique.
H T (**Ref:**HM13085)

## MARGARET HILLS CLINIC
**Margaret Hills Clinic (The)**, 1 Oaks Precinct, Caesar Rd, Kenilworth, **Warwickshire**, CV8 1DP, ENG.
(T) 01926 854783 (F) 01926 513133
Speciality: Complementary Medicines & Therapy.
● **Partner** Mr G Hills
C M (**Ref:**HM13086)

## MARGARET, DEFFELY
**Deffely Margaret P D C R**, 15 New Line, Castlebar, **County Mayo**, IRE.
(T) 09422 940
Speciality: Complementary Medicines & Therapy.
M (**Ref:**HM13087)

## MARGARET, HILL
**Hill Margaret ADHP MICHP**, Castleknock, IRE.
(T) 01821 2974
(W) www.hypnosiseire.com
Speciality: Complementary Medicines & Therapy.
M (**Ref:**HM13088)

## MARGARET, KENNELLY
**Kennelly Margaret**, Colgate Kilcock, **County Meath**, IRE.
(T) 01628 4465
Speciality: Psychoanalysis.
B (**Ref:**HM13089)

## MARGARET'S AROMA/HEALING
**Margaret's Aromatherapy & Healing Ltd**, Ansdell Rd, Blackpool, **Lancashire**, FY1 6PZ, ENG.
(T) 01253 768997
Speciality: Aromatherapy.
● **Owner** Ms M Evans
M O (**Ref:**HM13090)

## MARGE THE HAMLET
**Marge The Hamlet**, 16 Hawthorn Rd, Denton, Manchester, **Manchester (Greater)**, M34 3QP, ENG.
(T) 01613 209831 (F) 01613 209831
Speciality: Clairvoyants & Palmists.
● **Owner** Mrs M Prop
B (**Ref:**HM13091)

## MARGO, SAMMY
**Sammy Margo**, 444 Finchley Rd, London, **London (Greater)**, NW2 2HY, ENG.
(T) 020 7435 4910 (F) 020 7435 0461
Speciality: Physiotherapy.
● **Owner** Miss S Margo
P S T (**Ref:**HM13092)

## MARHSALL, E
**E Marhsall**, 2 Kenwood Rd, Sheffield, **Yorkshire (South)**, S7 1NP, ENG.
(T) 01142 552048
Speciality: Acupuncture.
● **Owner** Mr D Wainwright
O (**Ref:**HM13093)

## MARIA
**Maria**, 28 Whiteapron St, South Kirkby, Pontefract, **Yorkshire (West)**, WF9 3LH, ENG.
(T) 01977 609311
Speciality: Clairvoyants & Palmists.
B (**Ref:**HM13094)

## MARIAN ASSOCIATION
**Marian Association (The)**, West Hill House, 6 Swains Lane, Highgate, London, **London (Greater)**, N6 6QS, ENG.
(T) 020 8340 1306 (F) 020 8348 3210
Speciality: Psychotherapy.
● **Director** Ms B Martin
B (**Ref:**HM13095)

## MARIANNE, RALPH
**Ralph Marianne**, 13 Fourth Avenue, Garston Park, Tilehurst, Reading, **Berkshire**, RG31 4TG, ENG.
(T) 01189 456269
Speciality: Homeopathy.
M (**Ref:**HM13096)

## MARIA'S AROMATHERAPY CENTRE
**Maria's Aromatherapy Centre**, 11 Whittingham Rd, Longridge, Preston, **Lancashire**, PR3 2AA, ENG.
(T) 01772 785747
Speciality: Aromatherapy.
M O (**Ref:**HM13097)

## MARIE, PRENDERGAST
**Prendergast Marie LIC TCM AI ACU**, Caherdean Ballyhar, Killarney, **County Kerry**, IRE.
(T) 06697 64114
Speciality: Complementary Medicines & Therapy.
M (**Ref:**HM13098)

## MARIE, SOUTA
**Marie Souta**, 25 Point Hill, Greenwich, London, **London (Greater)**, SE10 8QW, ENG.
(T) 020 8692 0628
Speciality: Counselling, Psychotherapy. ✔
● **Counsellor/Psychotherapist**
Ms M Souta **Q:** Dip.Psych, MA. **M:** UKCP.
B Yrs. Est.: 2 (**Ref:**HM13099)

## MARIE-FRANCE BEAUTY CLINIC
**Marie-France Beauty Clinic**, 56 Brookwood Rd, London, **London (Greater)**, SW18 5BY, ENG.
(T) 020 8874 2021
Speciality: Electrolysis.
T (**Ref:**HM13100)

## MARILINA
**Marilina**, Hern Farm, Moggs Mead, Petersfield, **Hampshire**, GU31 4PY, ENG.
(T) 01730 268019



Key: B Mind-Body Medicine C Complementary Medicine H Self Help Treatment M Medicinal Therapy
O Oriental Medicine P Postural Therapy S Manipulative Structural Therapy T Touch Therapy

Speciality: Clairvoyants & Palmists.
● **Owner** Ms M Durant
B (Ref:HM13101)

## MARINE CLINIC

**Marine Clinic**, 12 Marine Drive, Rottingdean, Brighton, **Sussex (East)**, BN2 7HQ, ENG.
(T) 01273 307001
Speciality: Acupuncture.
O (Ref:HM13102)

## MARIPOSA AROMATHERAPY

**Mariposa Aromatherapy**, 91 Bellevue Rd, Edinburgh, **Edinburgh (City of)**, EH7 4DH, SCO.
(T) 01315 579916
Speciality: Aromatherapy, Massage (Therapeutic). ✔
● **Aromatherapist** Genni Poole Q: Dip.Arom. M: IFA.
C Yrs. Est.: 5 (Ref:HM13103)

## MARISCOTTI, SHEILA

**Sheila Mariscotti**, 24 Lindford Chase, Lindford, Bordon, **Hampshire**, GU35 0TB, ENG.
(T) 01420 475872
Speciality: Herbal Medicine.
M (Ref:HM13104)

## MARITAL & COUPLES THERAPY CTRE

**Marital & Couples Therapy Centre**, 8 Willow Rd, London, **London (Greater)**, NW3 1TJ, ENG.
(T) 020 7794 8717
Speciality: Psychology.
● **Owner** Mr S Meyerson
B (Ref:HM13105)

## MARK CHURCH AROMATHERAPY

**Mark Church Aromatherapy**, 23 High St, Southwold, **Suffolk**, IP18 6AD, ENG.
(T) 01502 722144
Speciality: Aromatherapy. ✔
● **Aromatherapist** Mr M Church Q: RQA, T.I.Dip.
C Yrs. Est.: 7 (Ref:HM13106)

## MARK GOULDING - ACUPUNCTURIST

**Mark Goulding - Acupuncturist**, The Hollies, Glen Of The Downs, **County Wicklow**, IRE.
(T) 00353 12873378
(E) mgoulding@eircom.net
Speciality: Acupressure, Acupuncture, Complementary Therapy, Cupping, Electrotherapy, Herbal Medicine, Holistic Healing, Homeopathy, Moxibustion, Naturopathy, Oriental Diagnosis, Stress Therapy. ✔
● **Acupuncturist** Mr M Goulding Q: Cert.Ac, Dip.Ac, Lic.Ac.
O Yrs. Est.: 3 (Ref:HM13107)

## MARK RIDDLE HYPNOTHERAPY

**Mark Riddle Hypnotherapy**, Church Farmhouse, Middle St, Corringham, Gainsborough, **Lincolnshire**, DN21 5QY, ENG.
(T) 01427 839190 (F) 01427 838634
(E) enquires@hypnotherapy-uk.co.uk
Speciality: Auto Suggestion, Aversion Therapy, Biofeedback, Complementary Therapy, Counselling, Dietician, Family Therapy, Holistic Healing, Humanistic Psychology, Hypnosis, Hypnotherapy, Life Style Coaching, Meditation, Phytotherapy, Stress Therapy, Visualisation Therapy, Voice Therapy, Stop Smoking Clinic. ✔
● **Owner/Hypnotherapy Consultant**
Mr M Riddle Q: BHA, Dip.Hyp. M: IAH.
B H Yrs. Est.: 4 (Ref:HM13108)

## MARK, ELLISON

**Ellison Mark**, 10 Dover Rd, Sheffield, **Yorkshire (South)**, S11 8RH, ENG.
(T) 01142 662321
Speciality: Hypnotherapy.
B (Ref:HM13109)

## MARKANDAY, A

**A Markanday**, 577 Uxbridge Rd, Pinner, **London (Greater)**, HA5 4RD, ENG.
(T) 020 8428 0272
Speciality: Acupuncture.
● **Owner** A Markanday
O (Ref:HM13110)

## MARKBY, S B

**S B Markby**, Curtle House, High St, Beaulieu, Brockenhurst, **Hampshire**, SO42 7YB, ENG.
(T) 01590 612451
Speciality: Physiotherapy.
● **Owner** Mrs S Markby
P S T (Ref:HM13111)

## MARKET DRAYTON COTTAGE HOSP

**Market Drayton Cottage Hospital**, Shropshire St, Market Drayton, **Shropshire**, TF9 3DQ, ENG.
(T) 01630 652057 (F) 01630 652057
Speciality: Physiotherapy.
● **Manager** Mrs A Turslow
P S T (Ref:HM13112)

## MARKET STREET CHIROPODY CLINIC

**Market Street Chiropody Clinic**, Les Fairclough, 47 Market St, Birkenhead, **Merseyside**, CH41 5BS, ENG.
(T) 01516 500770
Speciality: Biomechanics, Chiropody, Nail Surgery. ✔
● **Owner/Chiropodist**
Mr L Fairclough M: SMAE.
M Yrs. Est.: 5 (Ref:HM13113)

## MARKET STREET CLINIC

**Market Street Clinic**, 11 Market St, Launceston, **Cornwall**, PL15 8EP, ENG.
(T) 01566 777600
Speciality: Chiropodists (Podiatrists).
● **Owner** Mrs S McCutcheon
S (Ref:HM13114)

## MARKHAM, I

**I Markham**, 8 Westbury Lane, Newport Pagnell, **Buckinghamshire**, MK16 8JA, ENG.
(T) 01908 618994
Speciality: Electrolysis.
● **Owner** Mrs I Markham
T (Ref:HM13115)

## MARKHAM, IAN

**Ian Markham**, 8 Riverside, Churnet View Rd, Oakamoor, Stoke-On-Trent, **Staffordshire**, ST10 3AE, ENG.
(T) 01538 702956
Speciality: Acupuncture.
● **Owner** Mr I Markham
O (Ref:HM13116)

## MARKLAND COMP THERAPY CENTRE

**Markland Complementary Therapy Centre**, Dalton House, 33 Leigh Rd, Bolton, **Lancashire**, BL1 4BD, ENG.
(T) 01942 841088
Speciality: Complementary Medicines & Therapy.
C M (Ref:HM13117)

## MARKS TEY HEALTH CENTRE

**Marks Tey Health Centre**, 31a London Rd, Marks Tey, Colchester, **Essex**, CO6 1DZ, ENG.
(T) 01206 21022
Speciality: Complementary Medicines & Therapy.
C M (Ref:HM13118)

## MARKS, DARREN HYPNOTHERAPY

**Darren Marks Hypnotherapy**, The Hale Clinic, 7 Park Cres, London, **London (Greater)**, W1N 3HE, ENG.
(T) 020 8581 3614
Speciality: Hypnosis, Hypnotherapy, Reiki. ✔
● **Hypnotherapist** Mr D Marks Q: BHA, DHP (NC), DipCH.P. M: ICHP.
B Yrs. Est.: 5 (Ref:HM13119)

## MARKS, DARREN HYPNOTHERAPY

**Darren Marks Hypnotherapy**, The South East Cancer Help Centre, 2 Purley Road(Tesco Development), Purley, **Surrey**, CR8 2HA, ENG.
(T) 020 8581 3614
(E) hypnohealing@yahoo.com
(W) www.hypnohealing.fsnet.co.uk
Speciality: Hypnosis, Hypnotherapy, Reiki, Mind-Body Healing. ✔
● **Hypnotherapist** Mr D Marks Q: Dip.Hyp, Dip.Psych, DipCH.P, MHA. M: HA, ICHP.
B Yrs. Est.: 5 (Ref:HM13120)

## MARKS, S

**S Marks**, Natural Medicine Centre, 86 Queens Rd, Nuneaton, **Warwickshire**, CV11 5LE, ENG.
(T) 024 7634 3100
Speciality: Aromatherapy.
M O (Ref:HM13121)

## MARLBOROUGH CHIRO CLINIC

**Marlborough Chiropractic Clinic**, 99a High St, Marlborough, **Wiltshire**, SN8 1HD, ENG.
(T) 01672 511599
Speciality: Chiropractic, Manipulation, Massage (Therapeutic), Trigger Point Therapy, Proprioceptive Neurological Facilitation, Rehabilitative Training. ✔
● **Chiropractor** Mr R Smith Q: BSc (Chiro). M: BCA, EChiroU, GCC.
S Yrs. Est.: 5 (Ref:HM13122)

## MARLBOROUGH NATURAL HLTH CTRE

**Marlborough Natural Health Centre (The)**, 47 Kingsbury St, Marlborough, **Wiltshire**, SN8 1JE, ENG.
(T) 01672 515051
(W) www.marlboroughnaturalhealth.com
Speciality: Acupuncture, Aromatherapy, Bach Remedies, Bates Method, Counselling, Crystal Healing, Hypnotherapy, Indian Head Massage, Kinesiology, Psychotherapy, Shiatsu, Dream Work, Tarot, Vision Batch Method, NLP, Angel Therapy, Astrology. ✔
B C O T Yrs. Est.: 2 (Ref:HM13123)

## MARLBOROUGH PHYSIO CLINIC

**Marlborough Physiotherapy Clinic**, 3 New Rd, Marlborough, **Wiltshire**, SN8 1BU, ENG.
(T) 01672 516182
Speciality: Physiotherapy.
P S T (Ref:HM13124)

## MARLBOROUGH THERAPY PRACTICE

**Marlborough Therapy Practice**, Flat 2, 69 Marlborough Pl, St Johns Wood, London, **London (Greater)**, NW8 0PT, ENG.
(T) 020 7328 6224
(E) sachakhan@hotmail.com
Speciality: Auto Suggestion, Autogenic Training, Cognitive Therapy, Counselling, Hypnosis, Hypnotherapy, Psychotherapy, Stress Therapy, Visualisation Therapy, Rational Emotive Behaviour Therapy. ✔
● **Psychotherapist** Sacha Khan Q: BSc (Hons), CHP, DHP (NC). M: NRHP.
B Yrs. Est.: 3 (Ref:HM13125)

## MARLING CLINIC

**Marling Clinic**, Stanley Mill Lodge, Ryeford, Stonehouse, **Gloucestershire**, GL10 3HH, ENG.
(T) 01453 823100
Speciality: Acupuncture.
O (Ref:HM13126)

## MARLOR, J

**J Marlor**, 86 Cramore Lane, Aldershot, **Hampshire**, GU11 3BB, ENG.
(T) 01252 323673
Speciality: Biomechanics, Chiropody. ✔
● **Chiropodist** Mr J Marlor Q: S.R.Ch. M: S.C.P.
M Yrs. Est.: 33 (Ref:HM13127)

## MARLOW HOMOEOPATHIC CLINIC

**Marlow Homoeopathic Clinic (The)**, 55A Glade Rd, Marlow, **Buckinghamshire**, SL7 1DQ, ENG.
(T) 01628 476200
Speciality: Homeopathy.
● **Practice Manager**
Mrs J Lipton-Rose
M (Ref:HM13128)

## MARLOW OSTEOPATHIC CLINIC

**Marlow Osteopathic Clinic**, The Annexe, The Doctors' House, Victoria Rd, Marlow, **Buckinghamshire**, SL7 1DN, ENG.
(T) 01628 477466
Speciality: Osteopathy.
P S T (Ref:HM13129)

## MARLOW PHYSIO & SPORTS INJURY

**Marlow Physiotherapy & Sports Injury Clinic**, Pavilion Ground, Pound Lane, Marlow, **Buckinghamshire**, SL7 2AE, ENG.
(T) 01628 898140
Speciality: Physiotherapy.
P S T (Ref:HM13130)

## MARNEY, KATE

**Kate Marney**, 15 Lower St, Stroud, **Gloucestershire**, GL5 2HT, ENG.



Key continued: Yrs.Est: Years Established Q: Qualifications M: Professional Membership ✔ Indemnity Insurance Accept Credit Cards

(T) 01453 765508
Speciality: Homeopathy.
M (Ref:HM13131)

**MARREN, PAULA**
**Marren Paula**, 48 Fair St, Drogheda, **County Louth**, IRE.
(T) 04198 31620
Speciality: Osteopathy.
P S T (Ref:HM13132)

**MARREN, PAULA**
**Marren Paula**, 1 Merrion Sq, Dublin, **County Dublin**, IRE.
(T) 01661 6143
Speciality: Osteopathy.
P S T (Ref:HM13133)

**MARRIOTT, D A**
**D A Marriott**, 70 Monarch Prde, London Rd, Mitcham, **Surrey**, CR4 3HB, ENG.
(T) 020 8648 4280
Speciality: Chiropodists (Podiatrists).
S (Ref:HM13134)

**MARRIOTT, D A**
**D A Marriott**, 79 Brigstock Rd, Thornton Heath, **Surrey**, CR7 7JH, ENG.
(T) 020 8689 7143
Speciality: Chiropodists (Podiatrists).
● **Owner** Mr D Marriott
S (Ref:HM13135)

**MARRIOTT, F**
**F Marriott**, Castle Clinic, 23 St Marys St, Bridgnorth, **Shropshire**, WV16 4DW, ENG.
(T) 01746 768366
Speciality: Complementary Medicines & Therapy.
● **Owner** Mrs F Marriott
C M (Ref:HM13136)

**MARRIOTT, HELEN**
**Helen Marriott**, Scarborough, **Yorkshire (North)**, YO12, ENG.
(T) 01723 365148
Speciality: Bach Remedies.
H T (Ref:HM13137)

**MARRIOTT, HUGH**
**Hugh Marriott**, 41 New St, Chipping Norton, **Oxfordshire**, OX7 5LL, ENG.
(T) 01608 643149
(E) hughmarriott@lineone.net
Speciality: Cranial Osteopathy, Osteopathy. ✔
● **Osteopath** Mr H Marriott **Q:** BSc, DO.
M: GOsC.
S Yrs. Est.: 12 (Ref:HM13138)

**MARRIOTT, HUGH**
**Hugh Marriott**, 15a Parsons St, Banbury, **Oxfordshire**, OX16 8LY, ENG.
(T) 01295 272903
Speciality: Osteopathy.
P S T (Ref:HM13139)

**MARRIS, TIMOTHY**
**Timothy Marris**, The Old Mill Therapy Centre, North Rd, Ambleside, **Cumbria**, LA22 9DT, ENG.
(T) 01539 433220
Speciality: Osteopathy.
● **Partner** Mr T Marris
P S T (Ref:HM13140)

**MARSDEN, P**
**Mr P Marsden**, Santamaria, Doncaster Rd, Finningley, Doncaster, **Yorkshire (South)**, DN9 3BN, ENG.
(T) 01302 771295
Speciality: Chiropodists (Podiatrists).
S (Ref:HM13141)

**MARSDEN, S A**
**S A Marsden**, 37 The Heathers, Bamber Bridge, Preston, **Lancashire**, PR5 8LL, ENG.
(T) 01772 316402
Speciality: Chiropodists (Podiatrists).
● **Owner** Mrs S Marsden
S (Ref:HM13142)

**MARSDEN-RYLE, D**
**D Marsden-Ryle**, Little Swallows, Blackstone, Ipplepen, Newton Abbot, **Devon**, TQ12 5QN, ENG.
(T) 01803 812223 (F) 01803 813564
Speciality: Complementary Medicines & Therapy.
● **Owner** Mr D Marsden-Ryle
C M (Ref:HM13143)

**MARSH, A**
**A Marsh**, The Joseph Clinic, 3 Bedford Rd, London, **London (Greater)**, E18 2AQ, ENG.
(T) 020 8989 7569
Speciality: Osteopathy.
● **Doctor** Dr Eftekari
P S T (Ref:HM13144)

**MARSH, ANDREW**
**Andrew Marsh**, 32 South St, Bridport, **Dorset**, DT6 3NQ, ENG.
(T) 01308 427777 (F) 01308 427777
Speciality: Complementary Medicines & Therapy.
● **Practice Manager** Mrs S Marsh
C M (Ref:HM13145)

**MARSH, E C**
**E C Marsh**, 67 Charles St, St. Helens, **Merseyside**, WA10 1LJ, ENG.
(T) 01744 22664
Speciality: Chiropody. ✔
● **Owner/Chiropodist** Mrs E Marsh
C Yrs. Est.: 30 (Ref:HM13146)

**MARSH, F W**
**F W Marsh**, Dental Surgery, 2-4 Heath Rd, Penketh, Warrington, **Cheshire**, WA5 2BS, ENG.
(T) 01925 791909
Speciality: Chiropody. ✔
● **Chiropodist** Mr F Marsh **Q:** Inst.CH.P.
M: Inst.CH.P.
C Yrs. Est.: 11 (Ref:HM13147)

**MARSH, F W**
**F W Marsh**, 41 Vine St, Widnes, **Cheshire**, WA8 6DW, ENG.
(T) 01514 207385
Speciality: Chiropodists (Podiatrists).
S (Ref:HM13148)

**MARSH, OLIVE**
**Olive Marsh**, 45 Napier Cres, Fareham, **Hampshire**, PO15 5BL, ENG.
(T) 01329 846219
Speciality: Chiropodists (Podiatrists).
● **Owner** Mrs O Marsh
S (Ref:HM13149)

**MARSH, PAMELA J**
**Pamela J Marsh**, 8 Oxford St, Nottingham, **Nottinghamshire**, NG1 5BH, ENG.
(T) 01159 417714
Speciality: Physiotherapy.
● **Owner** Mrs P Marsh
P S T (Ref:HM13150)

**MARSH, PAMELA J**
**Pamela J Marsh**, Clifton Lodge, 1 Long Acre East, Bingham, Nottingham, **Nottinghamshire**, NG13 8BY, ENG.
(T) 01949 839069
Speciality: Physiotherapy.
● **Owner** Mrs P Marsh
P S T (Ref:HM13151)

**MARSHALL & STOCKER**
**Marshall & Stocker**, 518 Gloucester Rd, Horfield, Bristol, BS7 8UF, ENG.
(T) 01179 520771
Speciality: Chiropodists (Podiatrists).
S (Ref:HM13152)

**MARSHALL, ALEXANDER**
**Alexander Marshall**, 258A Elgin Avenue, London, **London (Greater)**, W9 1JD, ENG.
(T) 020 7289 3582
Speciality: Alexander Technique.
P S (Ref:HM13153)

**MARSHALL, ANGELA**
**Angela Marshall**, 51-53 London Rd, Croydon, **Surrey**, CR0 2RF, ENG.
(T) 020 8645 0094
Speciality: Hypnotherapy.
● **Owner** Mrs A Marshall
B (Ref:HM13154)

**MARSHALL, ANNE**
**Anne Marshall**, 43 Swinburne Rd, Darlington, **County Durham**, DL3 7TD, ENG.
(T) 01325 489780 (F) 01325 364144
Speciality: Physiotherapy.
● **Owner** Mrs A Marshall
P S T (Ref:HM13155)

**MARSHALL, C A**
**C A Marshall**, 6 West Prde, Norwich, **Norfolk**, NR2 3DW, ENG.
(T) 01603 625944
Speciality: Hypnosis.
● **Owner** Mr C Marshall
B (Ref:HM13156)

**MARSHALL, CAROLYN**
**Carolyn Marshall**, 2 Rhoscolyn Drive, Tattenhoe, Milton Keynes, **Buckinghamshire**, MK4 3AE, ENG.
(T) 01908 503982
Speciality: Reflexology.
S T (Ref:HM13157)

**MARSHALL, E**
**E Marshall**, 34 Lon Ceredigion, Pwllheli, **Gwynedd**, LL53 5PP, WAL.
(T) 01758 701636
Speciality: Chiropodists (Podiatrists).
● **Owner** Mrs E Marshall
S (Ref:HM13158)

**MARSHALL, E**
**E Marshall**, 77 Iscoed Rd, Pontarddulais, Swansea, **Glamorgan (Vale of)**, SA4 1UP, WAL.
(T) 01792 883133
Speciality: Chiropodists (Podiatrists).
S (Ref:HM13159)

**MARSHALL, FIONA S**
**Fiona S Marshall**, 18 Caledonian Rd, Edinburgh, **Edinburgh (City of)**, EH11 2DF, SCO.
(T) 01316 230356
Speciality: Aromatherapy.
● **Owner** Mrs F Marshall
M O (Ref:HM13160)

**MARSHALL, G**
**G Marshall**, The Cottage, Woodland Head, Yeoford, Crediton, **Devon**, EX17 5HE, ENG.
(T) 01647 24050
Speciality: Chiropodists (Podiatrists).
● **Owner** Mrs G Marshall
S (Ref:HM13161)

**MARSHALL, HENRY**
**Henry Marshall**, Huntingdon House, Huntingdon St, Nottingham, **Nottinghamshire**, NG1 3LY, ENG.
(T) 01159 550283
Speciality: Hypnotherapy.
● **Owner** Mr H Marshall
B (Ref:HM13162)

**MARSHALL, IAN**
**Ian Marshall**, 160C Tressillian Rd, London, **London (Greater)**, SE4 1XY, ENG.
(T) 020 8692 1426
Speciality: Hypnosis.
B (Ref:HM13163)

**MARSHALL, JILL**
**Jill Marshall**, Moonraker, Hadham Rd, Standon, Ware, **Hertfordshire**, SG11 1LH, ENG.
(T) 01920 822487
Speciality: Physiotherapy.
● **Owner** Mrs J Marshall
P S T (Ref:HM13164)

**MARSHALL, JILL**
**Jill Marshall**, 11 Montserrat Rd, Putney, London, **London (Greater)**, SW15 2LD, ENG.
(T) 020 8789 2548
Speciality: Hypnosis.
B (Ref:HM13165)

**MARSHALL, KAREN**
**Karen Marshall**, 26 Roxburgh St, Galashiels, **Scottish Borders**, TD1 1PF, SCO.
(T) 01896 752285
Speciality: Chiropodists (Podiatrists).
● **Owner** Mrs K Marshall
S (Ref:HM13166)

**MARSHALL, LESLIE**
**Leslie Marshall**, 20 Marshall Pl, Perth, **Perth**



Key: B Mind-Body Medicine C Complementary Medicine H Self Help Treatment M Medicinal Therapy O Oriental Medicine P Postural Therapy S Manipulative Structural Therapy T Touch Therapy

**and Kinross**, PH2 8AG, SCO.
(T) 01738 445945
Speciality: Chiropractic.
● **Owner** Dr I Hodgson
P S T (Ref:HM13167)

## MARSHALL, LYNN

**Lynn Marshall**, Hay Lane Cottage, Longdon Green, Rugeley, **Staffordshire**, WS15 4QQ, ENG.
(T) 01543 490381
Speciality: Reflexology.
S T (Ref:HM13168)

## MARSHALL, MICHAEL

**Michael Marshall**, 4 Bentinck Cl, Nuncargate, Kirkby-In-Ashfield, Nottingham, **Nottinghamshire**, NG17 9ET, ENG.
(T) 01623 721870
Speciality: Complementary Medicines & Therapy.
C M (Ref:HM13169)

## MARSHALL, S A

**S A Marshall**, 1 Butler Rd, Newton Aycliffe, **County Durham**, DL5 5LU, ENG.
(T) 01325 313654
Speciality: Chiropodists (Podiatrists).
● **Owner** Miss S Marshall
S (Ref:HM13170)

## MARSHALL, S C

**S C Marshall**, 185 Granton Rd, Edinburgh, **Edinburgh (City of)**, EH5 3RQ, SCO.
(T) 01315 525088
Speciality: Chiropody. ✓
● **Owner/Chiropodist** Mrs S Marshall Q: S.R.Ch. M: S.C.P.
M Yrs. Est.: 30 (Ref:HM13171)

## MARSHALL, STEVE

**Steve Marshall**, 49 Paget Rd, Cambridge, **Cambridgeshire**, CB2 2JF, ENG.
(T) 01223 506252
Speciality: Hypnosis.
● **Owner** Mr S Marshall
B (Ref:HM13172)

## MARSHALL-MANIFOLD, T

**T Marshall-Manifold**, 1 Evelyn Rd, London, **London (Greater)**, SW19 8NU, ENG.
(T) 020 8543 5477
Speciality: Homeopathy.
M (Ref:HM13173)

## MARSHALL-RAVEN, L

**L Marshall-Raven**, 5 Market Pl, Stowmarket, **Suffolk**, IP14 1DT, ENG.
(T) 01449 675600 (F) 01449 675600
Speciality: Chiropodists (Podiatrists).
● **Owner** Mrs L Marshall-Raven
S (Ref:HM13174)

## MARSLAND PRIVATE CTRE OF ACU

**Marsland Private Treatment Centre Of Acupuncture**, 406 Bolton Rd, Blackburn, **Lancashire**, BB2 4JQ, ENG.
(T) 01254 678791
Speciality: Acupuncture.
O (Ref:HM13175)

## MARSLAND, L

**L Marsland**, 4 Stamford End, Exton, Oakham, **Leicestershire**, LE15 8BQ, ENG.
(T) 01572 812063
Speciality: Chiropodists (Podiatrists).
● **Owner** Mrs L Marsland
S (Ref:HM13176)

## MARSLAND, MICHELLE

**Michelle Marsland**, Lilac Cottage, Askett, Princes Risborough, **Buckinghamshire**, HP27 9LT, ENG.
(T) 01844 347792
Speciality: Acupuncture.
O (Ref:HM13177)

## MARSON, JOY

**Joy Marson**, Bullbeggars, Church Hill, Woking, **Surrey**, GU21 4QE, ENG.
(T) 01483 763318 (F) 01483 829618
(E) joymarson@nth.ndo.co.uk
(W) www.nutritionaltherapy.org.uk
Speciality: Iridology, Nutritional Therapy. ✓
● **Nutritional Therapist** Mrs J Marson Q: Dip.Iridol, Dip.N Med, Dip.Nut.Th, MA. M: BANT.
M Yrs. Est.: 2 (Ref:HM13178)

## MARSTON, SUE

**Sue Marston**, 106 Minster Rd, Stourport-on-Severn, **Worcestershire**, DY13 8AB, ENG.
(T) 01562 742628
Speciality: Acupuncture, Hypnotherapy, Reiki. ✓
● **Owner** Ms S Marston Q: Lic.Ac. M: BAcC.
O Yrs. Est.: 10 (Ref:HM13179)

## MARSTON, ZENA

**Zena Marston**, 834 Fishponds Rd, Fishponds, Bristol, BS16 3XA, ENG.
(T) 01179 491290
Speciality: Chiropodists (Podiatrists).
S (Ref:HM13180)

## MARTIN REGINA PSYCHOLOGIST

**Martin Regina Psychologist**, Ashbrook House, 10 Main St, Raheny, **County Dublin**, IRE.
(T) 01851 1320
Speciality: Psychology.
B (Ref:HM13181)

## MARTIN ST JAMES THERAPY CTRE

**Martin St James Therapy Centre**, 25 Mackenzie Cres, Burncross, Sheffield, **Yorkshire (South)**, S35 1UR, ENG.
(T) 01142 460457
Speciality: Hypnotherapy.
B (Ref:HM13182)

## MARTIN WILLEY ASS OF ST MNGMT

**Martin Willey Association Of Stress Management**, 45 Woodvale Avenue, Cardiff, **Glamorgan (Vale of)**, CF23 6SP, WAL.
(T) 029 2075 0060
Speciality: Hypnosis.
● **Owner** Mr M Willey
B (Ref:HM13183)

## MARTIN, AHERNE

**Martin Aherne**, Cosmona, Loughrea, **County Galway**, IRE.
(T) 09184 2762
Speciality: Acupuncture.
O (Ref:HM13184)

## MARTIN, ALISON

**Alison Martin**, Castleton House, Castle St, Mere, Warminster, **Wiltshire**, BA12 6JE, ENG.
(T) 01747 860161
Speciality: Osteopathy.
P S T (Ref:HM13185)

## MARTIN, ANNE

**Anne Martin**, 137 Brent St, London, **London (Greater)**, NW4 2DJ, ENG.
(T) 020 8457 2643
Speciality: Psychotherapy.
B (Ref:HM13186)

## MARTIN, ANNE

**Anne Martin**, 11 Rymer St, London, **London (Greater)**, SE24 0NQ, ENG.
(T) 020 7738 6202
Speciality: Indian Head Massage, Massage (Therapeutic).
● **Owner** Ms A Martin
M (Ref:HM13187)

## MARTIN, BARBARA

**Barbara Martin**, 12 Helmingham, Tamworth, **Staffordshire**, B79 7UA, ENG.
(T) 01827 61369
Speciality: Aromatherapy.
● **Owner** Mrs B Martin
M O (Ref:HM13188)

## MARTIN, C M

**C M Martin**, 6 Randolph Pl, Edinburgh, **Edinburgh (City of)**, EH3 7TE, SCO.
(T) 01312 262524
Speciality: Chiropodists (Podiatrists).
● **Owner** Mrs C Martin
S (Ref:HM13189)

## MARTIN, CHERIE (DR)

**Dr Cherie Martin**, 1 Kenmure Rd, Giffnock, Glasgow, **Glasgow (City of)**, G46 6TU, SCO.
(T) 01415 775030 (F) 01415 775030
Speciality: Psychotherapy.
B (Ref:HM13190)

## MARTIN, D

**D Martin**, Preston Medical Centre, Wembley, **London (Greater)**, HA9 8JZ, ENG.
(T) 020 8904 4344
Speciality: Osteopathy.
P S T (Ref:HM13191)

## MARTIN, HILARY

**Hilary Martin**, 11 The Crescent, West Molesey, **Surrey**, KT8 1RB, ENG.
(T) 020 8979 9352
Speciality: Reflexology.
S T (Ref:HM13192)

## MARTIN, I F

**I F Martin**, Oakburn House, 49 William St, Helensburgh, **Argyll and Bute**, G84 8XY, SCO.
(T) 01436 673085
Speciality: Physiotherapy.
P S T (Ref:HM13193)

## MARTIN, J

**J Martin**, 21 Burrough St, Ash, Martock, **Somerset**, TA12 6NZ, ENG.
(T) 01935 823706
Speciality: Physiotherapy.
● **Owner** Mrs J Martin
P S T (Ref:HM13194)

## MARTIN, J

**J Martin**, 8 Robslee Drive, Giffnock, Glasgow, **Glasgow (City of)**, G46 7BA, SCO.
(T) 01416 387140
Speciality: Physiotherapy.
● **Owner** Mr J Martin
P S T (Ref:HM13195)

## MARTIN, J H

**J H Martin**, Queen St, Exeter, **Devon**, EX4 3SP, ENG.
(T) 01392 273963 (F) 01392 273963
Speciality: Chiropodists (Podiatrists).
● **Owner** Mrs J Martin
S (Ref:HM13196)

## MARTIN, J J

**J J Martin**, 101 Lawson Rd, Norwich, **Norfolk**, NR3 4LE, ENG.
(T) 01603 423800
Speciality: Complementary Medicines & Therapy.
● **Owner** Mr J Martin
M (Ref:HM13197)

## MARTIN, J R

**J R Martin**, 1 Station Rd, Okehampton, **Devon**, EX20 1DY, ENG.
(T) 01837 53973
Speciality: Chiropodists (Podiatrists).
S (Ref:HM13198)

## MARTIN, J V

**J V Martin**, 35 St Andrews Rd, Worthing, **Sussex (West)**, BN13 1HW, ENG.
(T) 01903 266139 (F) 01903 266139
Speciality: Physiotherapy.
● **Owner** Miss J Martin
P S T (Ref:HM13199)

## MARTIN, JEAN

**Jean Martin**, 94 Parkhill Rd, Birkenhead, **Merseyside**, CH42 9JD, ENG.
(T) 01516 088601
Speciality: Reflexology.
S T (Ref:HM13200)

## MARTIN, KIELY

**Kiely Martin C Hyp A C H E**, 37 Daffodil Fields Carrigrohane, Cork, **County Cork**, IRE.
(T) 021 4870 870
Speciality: Hypnotherapy.
B (Ref:HM13201)

## MARTIN, LEIGH

**Leigh Martin**, Unit 29, 167b Old Rd, Clacton-On-Sea, **Essex**, CO15 3AU, ENG.
(T) 01255 433120
Speciality: Aromatherapy, Cranio-Sacral Therapy, Healing Therapy, Manipulation, Massage (Therapeutic), Osteomyology. ✓
● **Osteomyologist** Mr L Martin Q: BSc, DM, DO. M: TAO.
● **Aromatherapist/Beauty Therapist**



Key continued: Yrs.Est: Years Established Q: Qualifications M: Professional Membership ✓ Indemnity Insurance ▭ Accept Credit Cards

Irene Milton Q: CIBTAC. M: BABTAC.
S Yrs. Est.: 18 (Ref:HM13202)

## MARTIN, LYN
**Lyn Martin**, 9 Kings Barn Lane, Steyning, **Sussex (West)**, BN44 3YR, ENG.
(T) 01903 813992
Speciality: Reflexology.
S T (Ref:HM13203)

## MARTIN, MARIA
**Maria Martin**, 4 Queen Annes Gr, Enfield, **London (Greater)**, EN1 2JP, ENG.
(T) 020 8364 2115
Speciality: Reflexology.
S T (Ref:HM13204)

## MARTIN, P
**P Martin**, Adams Chemists, 33 Morley Avenue, Churchdown, Gloucester, **Gloucestershire**, GL3 2BL, ENG.
(T) 01452 712422
Speciality: Chiropodists (Podiatrists).
S (Ref:HM13205)

## MARTIN, PAULA
**Paula Martin**, Bretland House, Bretland Rd, Tunbridge Wells, **Kent**, TN4 8PB, ENG.
(T) 01892 548840
Speciality: Aromatherapy.
● **Owner** Mrs P Martin
M O (Ref:HM13206)

## MARTIN, R J
**R J Martin**, 55 Villa Cres, Bulkington, Bedworth, **Warwickshire**, CV12 9NF, ENG.
(T) 024 7631 4630
Speciality: Chiropodists (Podiatrists).
● **Owner** Mr R Martin
S (Ref:HM13207)

## MARTIN, RHUNA
**Rhuna Martin**, 13 St Peters Sq, London, **London (Greater)**, W6 9AB, ENG.
(T) 020 8748 3691 (F) 020 8748 3691
Speciality: Alexander Technique. ✔
● **Teacher of the Alexander Technique**
Ms R Martin Q: MSTAT. M: STAT.
H Yrs. Est.: 20 (Ref:HM13208)

## MARTIN, S & N
**S & N Martin**, Wolverton Drive, Windmill Hill, Runcorn, **Cheshire**, WA7 6PQ, ENG.
(T) 01928 718889
Speciality: Hypnotherapy.
● **Owner** Mrs S Tuck
B (Ref:HM13209)

## MARTIN, SANDIE
**Sandie Martin**, Physiotherapy Clinic, 79 New Market Rd, Norwich, **Norfolk**, NR2 2HW, ENG.
(T) 01603 625959
Speciality: Physiotherapy.
P S T (Ref:HM13210)

## MARTIN, T C
**T C Martin**, 82 Walsall St, Willenhall, **Midlands (West)**, WV13 2EU, ENG.
(T) 01902 607543
Speciality: Physiotherapy.
P S T (Ref:HM13211)

## MARTIN, TONY
**Tony Martin**, 25 Helmsdale, Woking, **Surrey**, GU21 3HT, ENG.
(T) 01483 721695
Speciality: Complementary Medicines & Therapy.
● **Owner** Mr T Martin
C M (Ref:HM13212)

## MARTIN, WHYTE
**Whyte Martin**, Woodtown Drumconrath, Navan, **County Meath**, IRE.
(T) 04168 54107
Speciality: Complementary Medicines & Therapy.
M (Ref:HM13213)

## MARTINEAU, M
**M Martineau**, 1 Fairpark Rd, Exeter, **Devon**, EX2 4HL, ENG.
(T) 01392 271835
Speciality: Chiropractic.
● **Owner** Dr M Martineau
P S T (Ref:HM13214)

## MARTINEAU, M (DR)
**Dr M Martineau**, 53 Imperial Rd, Exmouth, **Devon**, EX8 1DQ, ENG.
(T) 01395 222656
Speciality: Chiropractic.
● **Owner** Mr M Martineau
P S T (Ref:HM13215)

## MARTINEAU, RACHEL
**Rachel Martineau**, 168 Carlyle Rd, London, **London (Greater)**, W5 4BJ, ENG.
(T) 020 8560 5738
Speciality: Osteopathy.
● **Owner** Miss R Martineau
P S T (Ref:HM13216)

## MARTINS, P
**P Martins**, 6 Myrtle Pl, Pershore Rd, Selly Oak, Birmingham, **Midlands (West)**, B29 7NA, ENG.
(T) 01214 725741
Speciality: Alexander Technique.
P S (Ref:HM13217)

## MARTLAND, ANNE
**Anne Martland**, 122 Church Rd, Formby, Liverpool, **Merseyside**, L37 3NH, ENG.
(T) 01704 834903
Speciality: Reflexology.
S T (Ref:HM13218)

## MARTLAND, B
**B Martland**, 5 King St West, Wigan, **Lancashire**, WN1 1LP, ENG.
(T) 01942 245372
Speciality: Electrolysis.
● **Owner** Mrs B Lindley
T (Ref:HM13219)

## MARY
**Mary**, 14 Essex St, Walsall, **Midlands (West)**, WS2 7AU, ENG.
(T) 01922 636683
Speciality: Clairvoyants & Palmists.
● **Owner** Mrs M Hoffman
B (Ref:HM13220)

## MARY CANNON - CLINICAL NUTRI
**Mary Cannon - Clinical Nutritionist**, 81 High St, Bridge, Canterbury, **Kent**, CT4 5AR, ENG.
(T) 01227 830596
(E) mary-cannon@virgin.net
Speciality: Clinical Ecology, Complementary Therapy, Dietician, Hay Diet, Herbal Medicine, Holistic Healing, Macrobiotics, Nutritional Therapy, Orthomolecular Medicine, Phytotherapy, Stress Therapy, Vitamin Therapy. ✔
● **Clinical Nutritionist**
Mrs M Cannon Q: Cert.Ed, Dip.ION, MSc. M: BANT.
C H Yrs. Est.: 11 (Ref:HM13221)

## MARY HERAGHTY AT HEALTHY FEET
**Healthy Feet**, 52 St Enoch Sq, Glasgow, **Glasgow (City of)**, G1 4AA, SCO.
(T) 01412 045414
(E) mary@healthy-feet.co.uk
Speciality: Aromatherapy, Chiropody, Reflexology. ✔
● **Owner/Therapist** Ms M Heraghty Q: GSSR, L.V.Ch.C. M: SCA, SIR.
B Yrs. Est.: 15 (Ref:HM13222)

## MARY MARTIN SCHOOL - REFLEX
**Mary Martin School Of Reflexology**, 72B Sharps Lane, Ruislip, **London (Greater)**, HA4 7JQ, ENG.
(T) 01895 635621
Speciality: Reflexology.
● **Owner** Ms M Martin
S T (Ref:HM13223)

## MARY STREET CHIRO CLINIC
**Mary Street Chiropractic Clinic**, 13 Mary St, Sunderland, **Tyne and Wear**, SR1 3NH, ENG.
(T) 01915 653335
Speciality: Chiropractic.
● **Senior Partner** Mr G Leef
P S T (Ref:HM13224)

## MARY WILKINSON - MCTIMONEY
**Mary Wilkinson - McTimoney Chiropractor**, 1 Middle St, Taunton, **Somerset**, TA1 1SH, ENG.
(T) 01823 272227
Speciality: Complementary Medicines & Therapy, Chiropractic McTimoney. ✔
● **McTimoney Chiropractor**
Mrs M Wilkinson Q: AMC, DC. M: CC, MCA.
● **Owner** Mrs J Drewitt
S Yrs. Est.: 6 (Ref:HM13225)

## MARY WILKINSON - MCTIMONEY
**Mary Wilkinson - McTimoney Chiropractor**, Higher Putham, Wheddon Cross, Minehead, **Somerset**, TA24 7AS, ENG.
(T) 01643 841660 (F) 01643 841660
Speciality: Chiropractic, McTimoney Chiropractic. ✔
● **McTimoney Chiropractor**
Ms M Wilkinson Q: AMC, DC. M: CC, MCA.
S Yrs. Est.: 6 (Ref:HM13226)

## MARY, KELLY
**Kelly Mary**, Hilltown, Buncrana, **County Donegal**, IRE.
(T) 07762 484
Speciality: Aromatherapy.
M O (Ref:HM13227)

## MARYANNE
**Maryanne**, 97 Boxley Rd, Chatham, **Kent**, ME5 9JD, ENG.
(T) 01634 311614
Speciality: Clairvoyants & Palmists.
B (Ref:HM13228)

## MARYGOLD AROMATHERAPY CLINIC
**Marygold Aromatherapy Clinic**, 90 Bridge St, Dundalk, **County Louth**, IRE.
(T) 04293 32154
Speciality: Aromatherapy.
M O (Ref:HM13229)

## MARY'S PALMIST
**Mary's Palmist**, 1b Tower Court, West St, Carlisle, **Cumbria**, CA3 8TP, ENG.
(T) 01228 595573
Speciality: Clairvoyants & Palmists.
● **Owner** Mrs M Swale
B (Ref:HM13230)

## MASKERY, M
**M Maskery**, 8 Pinecroft Rd, Ipswich, **Suffolk**, IP1 6BW, ENG.
(T) 01473 741023 (F) 01473 422223
Speciality: Reflexology.
● **Owner** Mr M Maskery
S T (Ref:HM13231)

## MASON & ASSOCIATES
**G N G Mason & Associates**, 94 Parrock St, Gravesend, **Kent**, DA12 1EX, ENG.
(T) 01474 326657
Speciality: Osteopathy. ✔
● **Osteopath** Mr G Mason Q: DO. M: GOsC.
S Yrs. Est.: 35 (Ref:HM13232)

## MASON & ASSOCIATES
**G N G Mason & Associates**, 240 Maidstone Rd, Chatham, **Kent**, ME4 6JN, ENG.
(T) 01634 842583
Speciality: Osteopathy. ✔
● **Osteopath** Mr G Mason Q: DO. M: GOsC.
S Yrs. Est.: 35 (Ref:HM13233)

## MASON GOODMAN NAT MEDICINE
**Mason Goodman Natural Medicine Clinic (The)**, 66 High St, Barnet, **Hertfordshire**, EN5 5SY, ENG.
(T) 020 8441 5844
Speciality: Osteopathy.
P S T (Ref:HM13234)

## MASON, A
**A Mason**, 39 Saffron Cres, Tickhill, Doncaster, **Yorkshire (South)**, DN11 9RX, ENG.
(T) 01302 743451
Speciality: Physiotherapy.
● **Owner** A Mason
P S T (Ref:HM13235)

## MASON, CAROLINE A
**Caroline A Mason**, 157A Trysyll Rd, Wolverhampton, **Midlands (West)**, WV3 7JP, ENG.
(T) 01902 335194
Speciality: Chiropodists (Podiatrists).

S (Ref:HM13236)

**MASON, D**

**D Mason**, 4 Selborne Rd, London, **London (Greater)**, N14 7DH, ENG.
(T) 020 8882 3411
Speciality: Chiropodists (Podiatrists).
● **Owner** Mr D Mason
S (Ref:HM13237)

**MASON, D H**

**D H Mason**, 54 Christiemiller Avenue, Edinburgh, **Edinburgh (City of)**, EH7 6AZ, SCO.
(T) 01316 692067
Speciality: Chiropodists (Podiatrists).
S (Ref:HM13238)

**MASON, DAVID**

**David Mason**, 52 Westbrook End, Newton Longville, Milton Keynes, **Buckinghamshire**, MK17 0DF, ENG.
(T) 01908 373652 (F) 01908 373652
Speciality: Hypnosis.
● **Owner** Mr Mason
B (Ref:HM13239)

**MASON, DAVID**

**David Mason**, Roundstone Surgery, Polebarn Rd, Trowbridge, **Wiltshire**, BA14 7EG, ENG.
(T) 01225 752752
Speciality: Chiropodists (Podiatrists).
S (Ref:HM13240)

**MASON, DIANE**

**Diane Mason**, 75 Clay Lane, Clay Cross, Chesterfield, **Derbyshire**, S45 9AW, ENG.
(T) 01246 866836
Speciality: Chiropodists (Podiatrists).
S (Ref:HM13241)

**MASON, J R**

**J R Mason**, 8 Wrotham Rd, Gravesend, **Kent**, DA11 0PA, ENG.
(T) 01474 355400
Speciality: Chiropodists (Podiatrists).
S (Ref:HM13242)

**MASON, J W**

**J W Mason**, 216 Coates Rd, Whittlesey, Peterborough, **Cambridgeshire**, PE7 2BE, ENG.
(T) 01733 840881
Speciality: Osteopathy.
● **Owner** Mr J Mason
P S T (Ref:HM13243)

**MASON, JAY**

**Jay Mason**, 7 Tavy Rd, Saltash, **Cornwall**, PL12 6DE, ENG.
(T) 01752 846096
Speciality: Psychotherapy.
● **Owner** Mr J Mason
B (Ref:HM13244)

**MASON, JOHN**

**John Mason**, Angels Rest, Rectory Cl, Ashington, Pulborough, **Sussex (West)**, RH20 3LP, ENG.
(T) 01903 892171
Speciality: Chiropractic.
● **Owner** Mr J Mason
P S T (Ref:HM13245)

**MASON, KEITH**

**Keith Mason**, Hope Cottages, Upper St, Breamore, Fordingbridge, **Hampshire**, SP6 2BX, ENG.
(T) 01725 513018
Speciality: Homeopathy.
M (Ref:HM13246)

**MASON, L C**

**Mason Hypnotherapy Clinic (The)**, 92 The Paddocks, Stevenage, **Hertfordshire**, SG2 9UB, ENG.
(T) 01438 359632
Speciality: Hypnosis, Hypnotherapy, Psychotherapy, Visualisation Therapy. ✔
● **Hypnotherapist** Mr L Mason Q: FNCP. M: NCP.
B Yrs. Est.: 33 (Ref:HM13247)

**MASON, MARCUS**

**Marcus Mason**, Centre For Healing Arts, 5a South St, Totnes, **Devon**, TQ9 5DZ, ENG.
(E) starfire@ic24.net
Speciality: Acupuncture, Cupping, Healing Therapy, Moxibustion, Oriental Diagnosis. ✔
● **Acupuncturist** Mr M Mason Q: Lic.Ac, MBAcC. M: BAcC.
O Yrs. Est.: 14 (Ref:HM13248)

**MASON, MARK**

**Mason Mark**, 86 Marmion Rd, Southsea, **Hampshire**, PO5 2BB, ENG.
(T) 023 9286 3099
Speciality: Chiropractors.
● **Partner** Mrs G Blackman
P S T (Ref:HM13249)

**MASON, P R**

**P R Mason**, 1 Eastbrook Cl, Dinas Powys, **Glamorgan (Vale of)**, CF64 4DB, WAL.
(T) 029 2051 2541
Speciality: Chiropodists (Podiatrists).
● **Owner** Mrs P Mason
S (Ref:HM13250)

**MASON, SARAH**

**Sarah Mason**, The Long House, Dunsfold, Godalming, **Surrey**, GU8 4LH, ENG.
(T) 01483 200823
Speciality: Reflexology.
S T (Ref:HM13251)

**MASON, T G**

**T G Mason**, 1 Leeds House, Cypress Court, Rochester, **Kent**, ME2 4PU, ENG.
(T) 01634 727301
Speciality: Hypnosis.
B (Ref:HM13252)

**MASON, W J**

**W J Mason**, Guan Soon, Field Lane, Friskney, Boston, **Lincolnshire**, PE22 8RL, ENG.
(T) 01754 820447
Speciality: Osteopathy.
● **Owner** Mr W Mason
P S T (Ref:HM13253)

**MASON, YVONNE**

**Yvonne Mason**, 41 Church Rd, Poole, **Dorset**, BH14 0NN, ENG.
(T) 01202 749514 (F) 01202 718906
Speciality: Physiotherapy.
● **Partner** Mrs C Swinhoe
P S T (Ref:HM13254)

**MASSAGE & REFLEXOLOGY**

**Massage & Reflexology**, Glenamour House, Park Rd, Waterloo, Liverpool, **Merseyside**, L22 3XG, ENG.
(T) 01519 491303
Speciality: Massage (Therapeutic), Reflexology.
M (Ref:HM13255)

**MASSAGE & REFLEXOLOGY CENTRE**

**Massage & Reflexology Centre**, 2 Lees Rd, Mossley, Ashton-under-Lyne, **Manchester (Greater)**, OL5 0PF, ENG.
(T) 01457 835491 (F) 01457 835491
Speciality: Reflexology.
● **Owner** Miss K Probert
S T (Ref:HM13256)

**MASSAGE AROMA THAI ORIENTAL**

**Massage Aromatherapy Thai Oriental**, 50 Hans Cres, London, **London (Greater)**, SW1X 0NA, ENG.
(T) 020 7584 4447
Speciality: Aromatherapy.
M O (Ref:HM13257)

**MASSAGE AROMATHERAPY ORIENTAL**

**Massage Aromatherapy Oriental**, Office 26, 7-11 Kensington High St, London, **London (Greater)**, W8 5NP, ENG.
(T) 020 7938 3259
Speciality: Complementary Medicines & Therapy.
● **Owner** Mrs Z Starace
M (Ref:HM13258)

**MASSAGE BY ISOBEL**

**Massage By Isobel**, Holme Valley Clinic, 16 Church St, Honley, Huddersfield, **Yorkshire (West)**, HD7 2AH, ENG.
(T) 01484 688739
Speciality: Aromatherapy.
● **Owner** Mrs I Healy
M O (Ref:HM13259)

**MASSAGE FOR HEALTH**

**Massage For Health**, 2 Church Path, Rattlesden, Bury St. Edmunds, **Suffolk**, IP30 0RG, ENG.
(T) 01449 737510
(E) unicale@aol.com
Speciality: Cupping, Healer, Healing Therapy, Holistic Healing, Massage (Therapeutic), Spiritual Healing, Ying & Yang, Tui Na Chinese Massage. ✔
● **Owner** Ms M Storer Q: ITEC.
S Yrs. Est.: 3 (Ref:HM13260)

**MASSAGE MARIORA**

**Massage Mariora**, 16 Balderton St, London, **London (Greater)**, W1Y 1TF, ENG.
(T) 020 7355 4036
Speciality: Complementary Medicines & Therapy.
● **Employee** Mrs M Massage
M (Ref:HM13261)

**MASSAGE RELAXING THERAPEUTIC**

**Massage Relaxing Therapeutic**, Fern, Morebath, Tiverton, **Devon**, EX16 9AL, ENG.
(T) 01398 332104
Speciality: Massage (Therapeutic), Relaxing Therapeutic Massage, Teaches Tai-Chi Ch'uan.
● **Partner** Mr A Bladbey M: ITEC.
B C P T Yrs. Est.: 10 (Ref:HM13262)

**MASSAGE THERAPEUTIC**

**Massage Therapeutic**, 40 St Johns Drive, London, **London (Greater)**, SW18 4UN, ENG.
(T) 020 8488 2575 (F) 020 8488 2575
Speciality: Complementary Medicines & Therapy.
● **Owner** Mr F Santiago
C M (Ref:HM13263)

**MASSAGE THERAPY & REFLEXOLOGY**

**Massage Therapy & Reflexology**, Green Lane, London, **London (Greater)**, W7 2PA, ENG.
(T) 020 8840 0809
Speciality: Reflexology.
● **Owner** Ms T Mekonnen
S T (Ref:HM13264)

**MASSAGE TRAINING INSTITUTE**

**Massage Training Institute (The)**, 22-24 Highbury Gr, London, **London (Greater)**, N5 2DQ, ENG.
(T) 020 7226 5313
Speciality: Complementary Medicines & Therapy.
M (Ref:HM13265)

**MASSAGE-AROMATHERAPY**

**Massage-Aromatherapy**, 2 Old Brompton Rd, Chelsea, London, **London (Greater)**, SW7 3DQ, ENG.
(T) 020 7370 4588
Speciality: Aromatherapy.
M O (Ref:HM13266)

**MASSEY, JANET**

**Janet Massey**, Park Ter West, Horsham, **Sussex (West)**, RH12 1HY, ENG.
(T) 01403 242545 (F) 01482 266902
Speciality: Hypnotherapy.
● **Owner** Mrs J Massey
B (Ref:HM13267)

**MASSEY, JANET**

**Janet Massey**, Horsham Golf & Fitness, Denne Park, Horsham, **Sussex (West)**, RH13 7AX, ENG.
(T) 01403 242545
Speciality: Hypnosis.
B (Ref:HM13268)

**MASSEY, JULIA**

**Julia Massey**, Upminster Complementary Healing Centre, Pea Lane, Upminster, **Essex**, RM14 2XH, ENG.
(T) 01708 251124
Speciality: Reflexology.
S T (Ref:HM13269)

**MASSEY, RAYMOND**

**Raymond Massey**, 5 Lon Gardener, Pendyffryn, Valley, Holyhead, **Isle of Anglesey**, LL65 3DN, WAL.



Key continued: Yrs.Est: Years Established Q: Qualifications M: Professional Membership ✔ Indemnity Insurance Accept Credit Cards

(T) 01407 741974
Speciality: Chiropodists (Podiatrists).
● **Owner** Mr R Massey
S (Ref:HM13270)

## MASSINGHAM CHIROPRACTIC CLINIC

**Massingham Chiropractic Clinic**, Station House, Little Massingham, King's Lynn, **Norfolk**, PE32 2JU, ENG.
(T) 01485 520123
Speciality: Chiropractors.
● **Chiropractor** Sheila Lake
P S T (Ref:HM13271)

## MASSON, C R

**C R Masson**, 14 The Oaks, Yeoford, Crediton, **Devon**, EX17 5PP, ENG.
(T) 01363 84149
Speciality: Chiropodists (Podiatrists).
● **Owner** Mrs C Masson
S (Ref:HM13272)

## MASTERS, B

**B Masters**, Bank House, 9 Exeter St, Launceston, **Cornwall**, PL15 9EQ, ENG.
(T) 01566 773671
Speciality: Chiropractic, Applied Neurology. ✔
● **Chiropractor** Dr B Masters Q: BEd (Hons), DC, PhD. M: BCA, CC.
P Yrs. Est.: 20 (Ref:HM13273)

## MASTERS, DAVID

**David Masters**, 11 Avenue Prde, Accrington, **Lancashire**, BB5 6PN, ENG.
(T) 01254 872442
Speciality: Hypnosis.
● **Owner** Mr D Masters
B (Ref:HM13274)

## MASTERS, LEE

**Lee Masters**, 591 London Rd, Westcliff-on-Sea, **Essex**, SS0 9PQ, ENG.
(T) 01702 346816
Speciality: Osteopathy.
P S T (Ref:HM13275)

## MASTERS, PAUL

**Paul Masters**, 591 London Rd, Westcliff-on-Sea, **Essex**, SS0 9PQ, ENG.
(T) 01702 346816
Speciality: Osteopathy.
P S T (Ref:HM13276)

## MATHARU, M K

**M K Matharu**, 47 Courtenay Gardens, Upminster, **Essex**, RM14 1DH, ENG.
(T) 01708 640670
Speciality: Chiropodists (Podiatrists).
S (Ref:HM13277)

## MATHER, A R

**A R Mather**, 41 Chorley Rd, Blackrod, Bolton, **Lancashire**, BL6 5JR, ENG.
(T) 01204 692318
Speciality: Chiropodists (Podiatrists).
S (Ref:HM13278)

## MATHER, JANINE

**Janine Mather**, Clissold Park Health Centre, 154 Stoke Newington Church St, London, **London (Greater)**, N16 0JU, ENG.
(T) 020 7249 2990 (F) 020 7249 3977
Speciality: Complementary Medicines & Therapy.
● **Director** Mr D Berg
M (Ref:HM13279)

## MATHER, PAULINE

**Pauline Mather DO**, Health Hydro And Baths, Milton Rd, Swindon, **Wiltshire**, SN1 5JA, ENG.
(T) 01793 465629 (F) 01793 465666
(E) pmather@aol.com
Speciality: Acupressure, Bach Remedies, Cranial Osteopathy, Dietician, Hay Diet, Herbal Medicine, Kinesiology, Manipulation, Massage (Therapeutic), Moxibustion, Nutritional Therapy, Osteopathy, Pilates, Stress Therapy, Vitamin Therapy. ✔ CREDIT
● **Osteopath** Ms P Mather Q: BSc (Hons), DIBAK, DO. M: GOsC.
S Yrs. Est.: 14 (Ref:HM13280)

## MATHER, SUE

**Sue Mather MSECH MHMA**, The Retreat, Nickley Wood, Shadoxhurst, Ashford, **Kent**, TN26 1LZ, ENG.
(T) 01233 731071
(E) susie.mather@virgin.net
Speciality: Homeopathy. ✔
● **Homeopath** Ms S Mather Q: MHMA. M: HMA.
M Yrs. Est.: 2 (Ref:HM13281)

## MATHERS, SHONA

**Shona Mathers**, 43A Argyle St, St. Andrews, **Fife**, KY16 9BX, SCO.
(T) 01334 479755
Speciality: Hypnosis.
● **Owner** Ms S Mathers
B (Ref:HM13282)

## MATHESON, B & P

**B & P Matheson**, Glencove, Dizzard, Bude, **Cornwall**, EX23 0NX, ENG.
(T) 01840 230322
Speciality: Acupuncture.
● **Partner** Mrs P Matheson
O (Ref:HM13283)

## MATHESON, CHRISTINE

**Christine Matheson**, 10B Manley St, London, **London (Greater)**, NW1 8LT, ENG.
(T) 020 7209 4026
Speciality: Alexander Technique.
● **Owner** Ms C Matheson
P S (Ref:HM13284)

## MATHESON, P A

**Mrs P A Matheson**, Trelash Cottage, Warbstow, Launceston, **Cornwall**, PL15 8RL, ENG.
(T) 01840 261412
Speciality: Acupuncture.
● **Owner** Mrs P Matheson
O (Ref:HM13285)

## MATHEW HUNT CHIROPODIST

**Mathew Hunt Chiropodist**, 76 The Broadway, Chesham, **Buckinghamshire**, HP5 1EG, ENG.
(T) 01494 786723
Speciality: Chiropody.
P S T (Ref:HM13286)

## MATHEWS, ANGELA

**Angela Mathews**, 100 Western Rd, Hove, **Sussex (East)**, BN3 1FA, ENG.
(T) 01273 737173
Speciality: Homeopathy.
● **Owner** Mrs A Mathews
M (Ref:HM13287)

## MATHEWS, F G & M D

**F G & M D Mathews**, 83 Chichester Rd, Portsmouth, **Hampshire**, PO2 0AG, ENG.
(T) 023 9266 0652
Speciality: Chiropodists (Podiatrists).
● **Partner** Mrs M Mathews
S (Ref:HM13288)

## MATHEWS, T

**T Mathews**, 2 Broad Oak Rd, Canterbury, **Kent**, CT2 7PW, ENG.
(T) 01227 458430
Speciality: Osteopathy.
● **Owner** Mr T Matthews
P S T (Ref:HM13289)

## MATHIESON, M A

**Miss M A Mathieson**, 35 New Sq, Cambridge, **Cambridgeshire**, CB1 1EZ, ENG.
(T) 01223 464699
Speciality: Chiropody, Podiatry. ✔
● **Chiropodist** Miss M Mathieson Q: DPodM, S.R.Ch. M: S.C.P.
M Yrs. Est.: 10 (Ref:HM13290)

## MATKIN, CHARLES

**Charles Matkin**, 15 Church St, Hunstanton, **Norfolk**, PE36 5HA, ENG.
(T) 01485 532318
Speciality: Chiropodists (Podiatrists).
S (Ref:HM13291)

## MATLOCK CHIROPRACTIC CLINIC

**Matlock Chiropractic Clinic**, 28 Bank Rd, Matlock, **Derbyshire**, DE4 3NF, ENG.
(T) 01629 57951 (F) 01629 57951
Speciality: Chiropractors.
● **Owner** Mr D Allen
P S T (Ref:HM13292)

## MATLOCK PHYSIOTHERAPY CENTRE

**Matlock Physiotherapy Centre**, Edgefold Rd, Matlock, **Derbyshire**, DE4 3NJ, ENG.
(T) 01629 580380
(E) petebailey@synergynet.co.uk
Speciality: Floral Essence Therapy, Herbal Medicine, Homeopathy. CREDIT
● **Homeopath** Mr P Bailey Q: LCPH, RGN. M: HMA.
M (Ref:HM13293)

## MATOL

**Matol**, 3a Hartley Business Park, Selborne Rd, Alton, **Hampshire**, GU34 3HP, ENG.
(T) 01420 511576 (F) 01420 511777
Speciality: Complementary Medicines & Therapy.
● **General Manager** Mrs A Graham
M (Ref:HM13294)

## MATOL HERBAL BEVERAGE

**Matol Herbal Beverage Co**, 83 Lumley Flats, Holbein Pl, London, **London (Greater)**, SW1W 8LU, ENG.
(T) 020 7730 2203
Speciality: Complementary Medicines & Therapy.
C M (Ref:HM13295)

## MATRAVES, SUE

**Matraves Sue**, 9 Lock Avenue, Maidenhead, **Berkshire**, SL6 8JW, ENG.
(T) 01628 627225
Speciality: Complementary Medicines & Therapy.
C M (Ref:HM13296)

## MATTHEW DAV & SAMANTHA TAY

**Matthew Davies D O & Samantha Taylor D O**, Surrey House, 114 Tilt Rd, Cobham, **Surrey**, KT11 3JH, ENG.
(T) 01932 866852
Speciality: Osteopathy.
P S T (Ref:HM13297)

## MATTHEW, MARY

**Mary Matthew**, 16 Darroch Brae, Alness, **Highland**, IV17 0SD, SCO.
(T) 01349 882457
Speciality: Chiropodists (Podiatrists).
● **Owner** Mrs M Matthew
S (Ref:HM13298)

## MATTHEWS, A

**A Matthews**, Hefren House, 1 Cressy Rd, Alfreton, **Derbyshire**, DE55 7BR, ENG.
(T) 01773 832158
Speciality: Chiropody, Reflexology. ✔
● **Chiropodist/Reflexologist**
Ms A Matthews Q: M.Ch.A. M: B.A.Ch.P, SSChA.
P (Ref:HM13299)

## MATTHEWS, ALLEN

**Allen Matthews**, 60 Woodbridge Rd, Guildford, **Surrey**, GU1 4RF, ENG.
(T) 01483 571783
Speciality: Physiotherapy.
P S T (Ref:HM13300)

## MATTHEWS, AMANDA

**Amanda Matthews**, 34 Northern Common, Dronfield Woodhouse, Dronfield, **Derbyshire**, S18 8XJ, ENG.
(T) 01142 890433
Speciality: Chiropody, Reflexology. ✔
● **Chiropodist/Reflexologist**
Miss A Matthews Q: MSSCh.
P Yrs. Est.: 5 (Ref:HM13301)

## MATTHEWS, DIANE

**Diane Matthews**, 118A North St, Romford, **Essex**, RM1 1DL, ENG.
(T) 01708 727239
Speciality: Electrolysis.
T (Ref:HM13302)

## MATTHEWS, E G

**E G Matthews**, Matthews House, 85 Epsom Rd, Guildford, **Surrey**, GU1 3PA, ENG.
(T) 01483 575876

Speciality: Physiotherapy.
P S T (Ref:HM13303)

## MATTHEWS, ERIC

**Eric Matthews**, 16 Ashley St, Carlisle, **Cumbria**, CA2 7BD, **ENG**.
(T) 01228 593473
Speciality: Complementary Medicines & Therapy.
● **Owner** Mr E Matthews
M (Ref:HM13304)

## MATTHEWS, FIONA

**Fiona Matthews**, Sunnydale Natural Health Centre, Cornwood Rd, Ivybridge, **Devon**, PL21 9JJ, **ENG**.
(T) 01752 895401
Speciality: Acupuncture.
● **Owner** Mrs F Matthes
O (Ref:HM13305)

## MATTHEWS, FRANK

**Frank Matthews**, 94 Springfield Blvd, Springfield, Milton Keynes, **Buckinghamshire**, MK6 3HY, **ENG**.
(T) 01908 607677
Speciality: Hypnosis, Hypnotherapy. ✓
● **Hypnotherapist** Mr F Matthews Q: Dip.Hyp, MHA. M: ASC.
B Yrs. Est.: 6 (Ref:HM13306)

## MATTHEWS, G

**G Matthews**, 37 Slate St, Morriston, Swansea, SA6 8AA, **WAL**.
(T) 01792 781097
Speciality: Chiropodists (Podiatrists).
● **Partner** Mr G Matthews
S (Ref:HM13307)

## MATTHEWS, J

**Mr J Matthews**, 60 Woodbridge Rd, Guildford, **Surrey**, GU1 4RF, **ENG**.
(T) 01483 571783
Speciality: Physiotherapy.
P S T (Ref:HM13308)

## MATTHEWS, JAN

**Jan Matthews**, 38 Taylors Rd, Chesham, **Buckinghamshire**, HP5 3BU, **ENG**.
(T) 01494 792342
Speciality: Hypnosis.
● **Owner** Mrs J Matthews
B (Ref:HM13309)

## MATTHEWS, M

**M Matthews**, 21 St Albans Rd, Bristol, BS6 7SF, **ENG**.
(T) 01179 232802 (F) 01179 232802
Speciality: Acupuncture.
● **Owner** Mr M Matthews
O (Ref:HM13310)

## MATTHEWS, MAX

**Max Matthews**, 5 South St, Torrington, **Devon**, EX38 8HE, **ENG**.
(T) 01805 622591
Speciality: Chiropodists (Podiatrists).
S (Ref:HM13311)

## MATTHEWS, ROBERT

**Robert Matthews**, 66h Windsor Rd, Ealing, London, **London (Greater)**, W5 5PH, **ENG**.
(T) 020 8840 9961
Speciality: Complementary Therapy, Counselling, Healer, Hypnosis, Hypnotherapy, Psychotherapy. ✓
● **Hypnotherapist** Mr R Matthews Q: BSCH, DipCH.P. M: BSCH.
B Yrs. Est.: 6 (Ref:HM13312)

## MATTHEWS, ROGER

**Roger Matthews**, 30 Albany Rd, Stratford-Upon-Avon, **Warwickshire**, CV37 6PG, **ENG**.
(T) 01789 292052
Speciality: Chiropodists (Podiatrists).
S (Ref:HM13313)

## MATTHEWS, S

**S Matthews**, The Atman Clinic, 108 St Johns Rd, Tunbridge Wells, **Kent**, TN4 9PH, **ENG**.
(T) 01892 544783
Speciality: Osteopathy.
P S T (Ref:HM13314)

## MATTHEWS, SUSAN

**Susan Matthews**, Whistlers End, Rodways Bank, Upper Colwall, Malvern, **Worcestershire**, WR13 6PU, **ENG**.
(T) 01684 540127
Speciality: Osteopathy.
P S T (Ref:HM13315)

## MATTHEWS, V

**V Matthews**, 14 Fusehill St, Carlisle, **Cumbria**, CA1 2ES, **ENG**.
(T) 01228 536233
Speciality: Osteopathy.
● **Owner** Mr V Matthews
P S T (Ref:HM13316)

## MATTHEWS, V

**V Matthews**, 66 Brunel Rd, Paignton, **Devon**, TQ4 6HP, **ENG**.
(T) 01803 842182
Speciality: Physiotherapy.
● **Owner** Mrs V Matthews
P S T (Ref:HM13317)

## MATTINSON, LESLEY

**Lesley Mattinson**, 24 Lord St, Little Lever, Bolton, **Lancashire**, BL3 1JA, **ENG**.
(T) 01204 706930
Speciality: Reflexology.
S T (Ref:HM13318)

## MAUGER, GILLY

**Gilly Mauger**, 23 Lennard Rd, Dunton Green, Sevenoaks, **Kent**, TN13 2UU, **ENG**.
(T) 01732 465266
Speciality: Chiropractors.
● **Owner** Mrs G Mauger
P S T (Ref:HM13319)

## MAUGHAM, ANNE

**Anne Maugham**, 34 Grove Avenue, Beeston, Nottingham, **Nottinghamshire**, NG9 4DZ, **ENG**.
(T) 01159 430949
Speciality: Electrolysis.
● **Owner** Mrs A Maugham
T (Ref:HM13320)

## MAUGHAN, ANNA

**Anna Maughan**, Natural Therapy Centre, 7 Westgate Rd, Guisborough, **Cleveland**, TS14 6EA, **ENG**.
(T) 01287 633591
Speciality: Homeopathy.
M (Ref:HM13321)

## MAUGHAN, E

**E Maughan**, Chiropodist Surgery, 75 Attwood Trce, Spennymoor, **County Durham**, DL16 6TE, **ENG**.
(T) 01388 819026
Speciality: Chiropodists (Podiatrists).
● **Owner** Mrs E Maughan
S (Ref:HM13322)

## MAULE, A A

**A A Maule**, 44 Bushey Wood Rd, Sheffield, **Yorkshire (South)**, S17 3QB, **ENG**.
(T) 01142 351759
Speciality: Physiotherapy.
P S T (Ref:HM13323)

## MAULE, V

**V Maule**, Chelsea Lane, Inverurie, **Aberdeenshire**, AB51 3QQ, **SCO**.
(T) 01467 624888 (F) 01467 624888
Speciality: Homeopathy.
● **Partner** Mrs C Craigmile
M (Ref:HM13324)

## MAUNDER, TRACY

**Tracy Maunder**, Portland Physiotherapy Practice, 7 Devonshire St, London, **London (Greater)**, W1N 1FT, **ENG**.
(T) 020 7486 0886
Speciality: Physiotherapy.
● **Manager** Mrs T Maunder
P S T (Ref:HM13325)

## MAUREEN

**Maureen**, 4 Ruskin Cl, Coventry, **Midlands (West)**, CV6 1PN, **ENG**.
(T) 024 7659 2740 (F) 024 7660 0697
Speciality: Clairvoyants & Palmists.
● **Owner** Mrs M Butler
B (Ref:HM13326)

## MAUREEN

**Maureen**, 38 Main Rd, Meriden, Coventry, **Midlands (West)**, CV7 7LU, **ENG**.
(T) 01676 521123 (F) 01676 521123
Speciality: Clairvoyants & Palmists.
● **Owner** Mrs M Shakespeare
B (Ref:HM13327)

## MAUREEN PRIDDLE

**Maureen Priddle**, 41 Cambridge Rd, Sawbridgeworth, **Hertfordshire**, CM21 9JP, **ENG**.
(T) 01279 724963 (F) 01279 600525
Speciality: Aromatherapy, Reflexology. ✓
● **Aromatherapist/Reflexologist**
Mrs M Priddle Q: Dip.Arom, Dip.Reflex. M: BSR, IFA.
C Yrs. Est.: 12 (Ref:HM13328)

## MAW, M

**M Maw**, 55 East St, Seaford, **Sussex (East)**, BN25 1SE, **ENG**.
(T) 01323 894336
Speciality: Chiropodists (Podiatrists).
S (Ref:HM13329)

## MAWDITT, ELIZABETH

**Elizabeth Mawditt**, 4 Station Rd, Warminster, **Wiltshire**, BA12 9BR, **ENG**.
(T) 01985 213927
Speciality: Osteopathy.
● **Partner** Mr J Penny
P S T (Ref:HM13330)

## MAWDSLEY, JEAN

**Jean Mawdsley**, 173 Mount Rd, Higher Bebington, Wirral, **Merseyside**, CH63 8PJ, **ENG**.
(T) 01516 087690
Speciality: Chiropodists (Podiatrists).
● **Owner** Mrs J Mawdsley
S (Ref:HM13331)

## MAWSON, MARY M

**Mary M Mawson**, 9 Railway Trce, Kings Langley, **Hertfordshire**, WD4 8JB, **ENG**.
(T) 01923 266577
Speciality: Homeopathy.
● **Owner** Mrs M Mawson
M (Ref:HM13332)

## MAXIM, L

**L Maxim**, Lower St, St. Asaph, **Denbighshire**, LL17 0SG, **WAL**.
(T) 01745 584994
Speciality: Chiropodists (Podiatrists).
● **Owner** Mrs L Maxim
S (Ref:HM13333)

## MAXWELL BRIAR

**Maxwell Briar**, 72 Leathwaite Rd, London, **London (Greater)**, SW11 6RT, **ENG**.
(T) 020 7223 1766
Speciality: Alexander Technique.
● **Owner** Mrs B Maxwell
P S (Ref:HM13334)

## MAXWELL SMITH, FIONA

**Maxwell Smith Fiona**, Old Market Lane, /glebe Lane, Killarney, **County Kerry**, **IRE**.
(T) 06435 995
Speciality: Herbalists.
M (Ref:HM13335)

## MAXWELL, A T

**Mrs A T Maxwell**, 9 Bradgate, Cuffley, Potters Bar, **Hertfordshire**, EN6 4RW, **ENG**.
(T) 01707 874501
Speciality: Physiotherapy.
● **Owner** Mrs A Maxwell Q: BSc, Grad Dip Phys, MCSP, SRP.
P S T (Ref:HM13336)

## MAXWELL, MARY

**Mary Maxwell**, 229 Upper Newtownards Rd, Belfast, **County Antrim**, BT4 3JF, **NIR**.
(T) 028 9042 6426
Speciality: Chiropody, Reflexology. ✓
● **Chiropodist/Reflexologist**
Mrs M Maxwell M: Inst.CH.P.
M T Yrs. Est.: 27 (Ref:HM13337)

## MAXWELL, P S

**P S Maxwell**, 121 Westgate, Guisborough, **Cleveland**, TS14 6AH, **ENG**.




Key continued: Yrs.Est: Years Established Q: Qualifications M: Professional Membership ✓ Indemnity Insurance Accept Credit Cards

(T) 01287 632204
Speciality: Chiropodists (Podiatrists).
● **Owner** Mr P Maxwell
S (Ref:HM13338)

## MAXWELL-WEIR, CHRISTINE

**Christine Maxwell-Weir**, 40 Kixley Lane, Knowle, Solihull, **Midlands (West)**, B93 0JG, ENG.
(T) 01564 771297
Speciality: Chiropodists (Podiatrists).
● **Owner** Ms C Maxwell-Weir
S (Ref:HM13339)

## MAY, ADAM

**Adam May**, Cefn Cana, Llanddaniel, Gaerwen, **Isle of Anglesey**, LL60 6EF, WAL.
(T) 01248 421015
Speciality: Psychotherapy.
● **Owner** Mr A May
B (Ref:HM13340)

## MAY, AMANDA

**Amanda May**, The Fairbourne Clinic, 17 Wendan Rd, Newbury, **Berkshire**, RG14 7AG, ENG.
(T) 01635 44200
Speciality: Chiropodists (Podiatrists).
S (Ref:HM13341)

## MAY, CELIA

**Celia May**, 8 Meadow Rise, Iwade, Sittingbourne, **Kent**, ME9 8SB, ENG.
(T) 01795 424467
Speciality: Hypnosis.
● **Owner** Ms C May
B (Ref:HM13342)

## MAY, CLAIRE

**Claire May**, 57 Shaldon Drive, Ruislip, **London (Greater)**, HA4 0UJ, ENG.
(T) 020 8582 2723
Speciality: Reflexology.
S T (Ref:HM13343)

## MAY, DAISY

**Daisy May**, 2 Thackeray Rd, Southampton, **Hampshire**, SO17 2GT, ENG.
(T) 023 8055 2346
Speciality: Clairvoyants & Palmists.
B (Ref:HM13344)

## MAY, HELEN

**Helen May**, 106 Dixon St, Swindon, **Wiltshire**, SN1 3PJ, ENG.
(T) 01793 528328
Speciality: Complementary Medicines & Therapy.
● **Owner** Miss H May
C M (Ref:HM13345)

## MAY, IAN

**Ian May**, 135 Sandridge Rd, St. Albans, **Hertfordshire**, AL1 4AH, ENG.
(T) 01727 852811 (F) 01727 852811
Speciality: Chiropodists (Podiatrists).
● **Owner** Mr I May
S (Ref:HM13346)

## MAY, S

**S May**, Chelsea Lane, Inverurie, **Aberdeenshire**, AB51 3QQ, SCO.
(T) 01467 624888 (F) 01467 624888
Speciality: Acupuncture.
● **Partner** Mrs C Craigmile
O (Ref:HM13347)

## MAY, S P

**S P May**, Bonnyton Croft, Bonnyton, Old Rayne, Insch, **Aberdeenshire**, AB52 6TD, SCO.
(T) 01464 851444
Speciality: Acupuncture.
O (Ref:HM13348)

## MAY, SUSAN

**Susan May**, 6 Woodland Cl, Hatfield Peverel, Chelmsford, **Essex**, CM3 2DA, ENG.
(T) 01245 381920
Speciality: Reflexology.
S T (Ref:HM13349)

## MAYERS, AMANDA

**Amanda Mayers**, 4 Arlies Lane, Stalybridge, **Manchester (Greater)**, SK15 3PZ, ENG.
(T) 01613 386735
Speciality: Complementary Medicines & Therapy.
● **Owner** Mrs A Mayers
M (Ref:HM13350)

## MAYERSBACH, ANN C

**Ann C Mayersbach**, 343 Eastcote Lane, Harrow, **London (Greater)**, HA2 8RY, ENG.
(T) 020 8866 9795
Speciality: Osteopathy.
● **Owner** Ms A Mayersbach
P S T (Ref:HM13351)

## MAYFAIR GROUP

**Mayfair Group (The)**, 120 The Worthys, Bradley Stoke, Bristol, BS32 8DQ, ENG.
(T) 01179 312661 (F) 01179 312661
Speciality: Aromatherapy.
M O (Ref:HM13352)

## MAYFIELD ACUPUNCTURE CLINIC

**Mayfield Acupuncture Clinic**, 13 Mayfield Gardens, Brentwood, **Essex**, CM14 4UJ, ENG.
(T) 01277 223894
Speciality: Acupuncture.
● **Manager** Mr G Bartlett
O (Ref:HM13353)

## MAYHEW, C

**C Mayhew**, 11 Lavender Court, Ashington, **Northumberland**, NE63 9FE, ENG.
(T) 01670 819756
Speciality: Chiropodists (Podiatrists).
● **Owner** Mrs C Meyhew
S (Ref:HM13354)

## MAYHEW, PAMELA

**Ms Pamela Mayhew**, 145 Cyril St West, Taunton, **Somerset**, TA2 6JD, ENG.
(T) 01823 327636
Speciality: Reflexology.
S T (Ref:HM13355)

## MAYNARD, CLIVE

**Clive Maynard**, Bank House Clinic, 5 High St, Milford On Sea, Lymington, **Hampshire**, SO41 0QF, ENG.
(T) 01590 642749
Speciality: Chiropractors.
● **Owner** Dr G Benes
P S T (Ref:HM13356)

## MAYNARD, MARTIN A

**Martin A Maynard**, 22 Forestfield, Horsham, **Sussex (West)**, RH13 6DZ, ENG.
(T) 01403 262961
Speciality: Chiropody. ✔
● **Chiropodist** Mr M Maynard Q: MBChA, MSSCh. M: B.A.Ch.P.
S Yrs. Est.: 3 (Ref:HM13357)

## MAYNARD, SUSANNE

**Susanne Maynard**, 72 The Lane, Hauxton, Cambridge, **Cambridgeshire**, CB2 5HP, ENG.
(T) 01223 871645 (F) 01223 871645
Speciality: Physiotherapy, Stroke Rehabilitation. ✔
● **Physiotherapist** Ms S Maynard Q: Grad Dip Phys, MCSP, SRP. M: CSP.
P S T (Ref:HM13358)

## MAYOR, DAVID F

**David F Mayor**, 86 Handside Lane, Welwyn Garden City, **Hertfordshire**, AL8 6SJ, ENG.
(T) 01707 320782
Speciality: Acupressure, Acupuncture, Cupping, Electrolipolysis, Massage (Therapeutic), Moxibustion, Nutritional Therapy, Vibrational Therapy, Vitamin Therapy. ✔
● **Acupuncturist** Mr D Mayor Q: B.Ac. M: BAcC.
H O T Yrs. Est.: 18 (Ref:HM13359)

## MAYS, ELLIE

**Ellie Mays**, 6 Partridge Cl, Chippenham, **Wiltshire**, SN14 6XY, ENG.
(T) 01249 463104
Speciality: Clairvoyants & Palmists.
● **Owner** Miss E Phillips
B (Ref:HM13360)

## MAYWAY UK

**Mayway UK Ltd**, The Waterside Trading Centre, Trumpers Way, London, **London (Greater)**, W7 2QD, ENG.
(T) 020 8893 6873
Speciality: Herbal Medicine.
M (Ref:HM13361)

## MAZUR, ARTUR

**Artur Mazur**, Ham Chiropractic Clinic, 8 Dukes Avenue, Kingston Upon Thames, **Surrey**, KT2 5QY, ENG.
(T) 020 8549 6696
Speciality: Chiropractic.
P S T (Ref:HM13362)

## MAZURKE, B A

**B A Mazurke**, 101 Woodkirk Gardens, Dewsbury, **Yorkshire (West)**, WF12 7JA, ENG.
(T) 01924 476653
Speciality: Reflexology.
● **Owner** Mr B Mazurke
S T (Ref:HM13363)

## MCALLISTER, C

**C McAllister**, 4 Lakenfields, Norwich, **Norfolk**, NR1 2HB, ENG.
(T) 01603 760450
Speciality: Complementary Medicines & Therapy.
● **Owner** Mrs C McAllister
C M (Ref:HM13364)

## MCALLISTER, C (DR)

**Dr C McAllister**, 255 New Bedford Rd, Luton, **Bedfordshire**, LU3 1LW, ENG.
(T) 01582 876800 (F) 01582 876800
Speciality: Psychotherapy.
● **Principal** Dr C McAllister
B (Ref:HM13365)

## MCALLISTER, G C

**G C McAllister**, McAllisters Physio & Sports Medical Clinic, 31 Pickford St, Huddersfield, **Yorkshire (West)**, HD3 4LG, ENG.
(T) 01484 650464
Speciality: Physiotherapy.
P S T (Ref:HM13366)

## MCALLISTER, LIN

**Lin McAllister**, 13 New Rd, Weybridge, **Surrey**, KT13 9BW, ENG.
(T) 01932 842539
Speciality: Hypnosis.
● **Owner** Ms L McAllister
B (Ref:HM13367)

## MCANELLY, J L

**J L McAnelly**, 9 Bedeburn Rd, Newcastle Upon Tyne, **Tyne and Wear**, NE5 4JL, ENG.
(T) 01912 861161
(E) joeleo@btinternet.com
Speciality: Counselling, Hypnosis, Hypnotherapy. ✔
● **Owner/Hynotherapist** Mr J McAnelly Q: BA (Hons) Psychol, NCP (Acc). M: MPNLP, NCH.
C Yrs. Est.: 22 (Ref:HM13368)

## MCARTHUR, JILL

**Jill McArthur**, 3 Scaife St, York, **Yorkshire (North)**, YO31 8HP, ENG.
(T) 01904 625542
Speciality: Reflexology.
S T (Ref:HM13369)

## MCATEER, K

**K McAteer**, 12 Pennine Prde, Pennine Drive, London, **London (Greater)**, NW2 1NT, ENG.
(T) 020 8455 6652
Speciality: Chiropodists (Podiatrists).
● **Owner** Ms K McAteer
S (Ref:HM13370)

## MCATEER, MARK

**Mark McAteer**, 43 Plantation Avenue, Carrickfergus, **County Antrim**, BT38 9BJ, NIR.
(T) 028 9335 0162 (F) 028 9336 5622
Speciality: Electrolysis.
● **Owner** Mr M MacAteer
T (Ref:HM13371)

## MCATHEY, CAROLE

**Carole McAthey**, 42 Hampton Ct Avenue, East Molesey, **Surrey**, KT8 0BQ, ENG.
(T) 020 8398 3293
Speciality: Physiotherapy.
● **Owner** Ms C McAthey



Key: B Mind-Body Medicine C Complementary Medicine H Self Help Treatment M Medicinal Therapy O Oriental Medicine P Postural Therapy S Manipulative Structural Therapy T Touch Therapy

P S T (Ref:HM13372)

**MCAVOY, JAMES**

**James McAvoy**, 22 Lancaster Rd, St. Albans, **Hertfordshire**, AL1 4ET, ENG.
(T) 01727 856852 (F) 01727 868799
Speciality: Osteopathy.
● **Owner** Mr J McAvoy
P S T (Ref:HM13373)

**MCBRINE, HAZEL**

**Hazel McBrine**, 39 Seapark, Castlerock, Coleraine, **County Londonderry**, BT51 4TH, NIR.
(T) 028 7084 8870
Speciality: Reflexology.
S T (Ref:HM13374)

**MCCABE, MARY**

**McCabe Mary M I Ch O**, "ashleigh" Ballyroan, **County Laois**, IRE.
(T) 05023 1752
Speciality: Chiropodists (Podiatrists).
S (Ref:HM13375)

**MCCABE, P J**

**P J McCabe**, 10 Charles St, Kilmarnock, **Ayrshire (East)**, KA1 2DX, SCO.
(T) 01563 532313
Speciality: Biomechanics, Chiropody, Nail Surgery. ✔
● **Chiropodist** Mr P McCabe Q: DPodM, S.R.Ch. M: S.C.P.
M Yrs. Est.: 40 (Ref:HM13376)

**MCCABE, PAULINE J**

**Pauline J McCabe**, 40 Glastonbury Drive, Poynton, Stockport, **Cheshire**, SK12 1EN, ENG.
(T) 01625 630501
Speciality: Chiropodists (Podiatrists).
● **Owner** Mrs P McCabe
S (Ref:HM13377)

**MCCABE, VINCENT**

**McCabe Vincent**, 41 Thornville Rd, Kilbarrack, Dublin, **County Dublin**, IRE.
(T) 01839 2133
Speciality: Aromatherapy.
M O (Ref:HM13378)

**MCCAFFERTY, SUSANNE**

**Susanne McCafferty**, 39 Greenway, Great Horwood, **Buckinghamshire**, MK17 0QR, ENG.
(T) 01296 712705
Speciality: Reflexology.
S T (Ref:HM13379)

**MCCAFFREY, GERARDINE**

**Gerardine McCaffrey**, 2 Dukes Avenue, Chiswick, London, **London (Greater)**, W4 2AF, ENG.
(T) 020 8742 2989
Speciality: Chiropody, Massage (Therapeutic), Reflexology, Bach Flower Therapy.
● **Holistic Therapist**
Ms G McCaffrey M: IIR, SMAE.
B Yrs. Est.: 3 (Ref:HM13380)

**MCCAFFREY, J E**

**J E McCaffrey**, 15 Blackfriars St, King's Lynn, **Norfolk**, PE30 1NN, ENG.
(T) 01553 691574
Speciality: Chiropodists (Podiatrists).
● **Owner** Mr J McCaffrey
S (Ref:HM13381)

**MCCALL, LYNN**

**Lynn McCall**, 37 Westbourne Cres, Bearsden, Glasgow, **Glasgow (City of)**, G61 4HB, SCO.
(T) 01419 429865
Speciality: Physiotherapy.
● **Owner** Mrs L McCall
P S T (Ref:HM13382)

**MCCALL, N**

**N McCall**, Ashdown Osteopathic Centre, The Sq, Lewes Rd, Forest Row, **Sussex (East)**, RH18 5ES, ENG.
(T) 01342 822505 (F) 01342 822505
Speciality: Osteopathy.
● **Owner** Mr T Strutt
P S T (Ref:HM13383)

**MCCALL, P W**

**P W McCall**, 12 Lugley St, Newport, **Isle of Wight**, PO30 5HD, ENG.
(T) 01983 529339
Speciality: Chiropodists (Podiatrists).
S (Ref:HM13384)

**MCCANCE, A B**

**A B McCance**, 4 Annick Cottage, Kingsford, Stewarton, Kilmarnock, **Ayrshire (East)**, KA3 5JS, SCO.
(T) 01560 484321 (F) 01560 484321
Speciality: Hypnotherapy.
● **Owner** Ms N McCance
B (Ref:HM13385)

**MCCANCE, H M**

**H M Mccance**, 104A Upper Parliament St, Nottingham, **Nottinghamshire**, NG1 6LF, ENG.
(T) 01159 413085
Speciality: Chiropodists (Podiatrists).
● **Partner** Mrs A Rockley
S (Ref:HM13386)

**MCCANN, ALEXANDRA**

**Alexandra McCann**, Flat 1 36 Oxford Rd, Altrincham, **Cheshire**, WA14 2EB, ENG.
(T) 01619 296288
Speciality: Osteopathy.
P S T (Ref:HM13387)

**MCCANN, ANGELA**

**Angela McCann**, 25 Slievemoyne Park, Belfast, **County Antrim**, BT15 5GZ, NIR.
(T) 028 9077 6647
Speciality: Physiotherapy.
P S T (Ref:HM13388)

**MCCANN, JACQUI**

**Jacqui McCann**, Flat 5, Victoria Pl, Hollycombe, Liphook, **Hampshire**, GU30 7LP, ENG.
(T) 01428 725474
Speciality: Acupuncture.
O (Ref:HM13389)

**MCCANN, VICTORIA**

**Victoria McCann**, 6 Haslett Avenue West, Crawley, **Sussex (West)**, RH10 1HS, ENG.
(T) 01293 525969
Speciality: Chiropodists (Podiatrists).
● **Owner** Ms V McCann
S (Ref:HM13390)

**MCCAREY, J**

**J McCarey**, Berkhamsted Chiropractice Clinic, 69 High St, Berkhamsted, **Hertfordshire**, HP4 2DE, ENG.
(T) 01442 863800
Speciality: Chiropractic.
P S T (Ref:HM13391)

**MCCARTAN, DEBORAH**

**Deborah McCartan**, 60B Mill St, Newry, **County Down**, BT34 1AJ, NIR.
(T) 028 3026 4121
Speciality: Biomechanics, Chiropody, Nail Surgery, Podiatry. ✔
● **Chiropodist (Podiatrist)**
Mrs D McCartan Q: DPodM, S.R.Ch. M: S.C.P.
M Yrs. Est.: 6 (Ref:HM13392)

**MCCARTHY, A**

**A McCarthy**, 18 Meetinghouse Lane, Newtownards, **County Down**, BT23 7AA, NIR.
(T) 028 9182 2354
Speciality: Chiropodists (Podiatrists).
● **Owner** A McCarthy
S (Ref:HM13393)

**MCCARTHY, C R**

**C R McCarthy**, The Old Barn, Marshside, Canterbury, **Kent**, CT3 4EE, ENG.
(T) 01227 860696
Speciality: Psychotherapy.
B (Ref:HM13394)

**MCCARTHY, J P**

**J P McCarthy**, Sotwell Hill Lodge, High Rd, Brightwell-Cum-Sotwell, Wallingford, **Oxfordshire**, OX10 0PS, ENG.
(T) 01491 836386
Speciality: Chiropodists (Podiatrists).
● **Owner** Mr J McCarthy
S (Ref:HM13395)

**MCCARTHY, JANE**

**Jane McCarthy**, 42 Salters Rd, Newcastle Upon Tyne, **Tyne and Wear**, NE3 1DX, ENG.
(T) 01912 843558 (F) 01912 843558
Speciality: Psychology.
● **Owner** Mrs J McCarthy
B (Ref:HM13396)

**MCCARTHY, JOHN**

**John McCarthy**, 28 Weymouth St, London, **London (Greater)**, W1N 3FA, ENG.
(T) 020 7436 6567
Speciality: Chiropodists (Podiatrists).
S (Ref:HM13397)

**MCCARTHY, PAUL**

**McCarthy Paul**, Sunnyside Seafield Ave, Monkstown, **County Dublin**, IRE.
(T) 01280 1950
Speciality: Acupuncture.
O (Ref:HM13398)

**MCCARTHY, ROSALYN**

**Rosalyn McCarthy**, 17 Brightwell Avenue, Totternhoe, Dunstable, **Bedfordshire**, LU6 1QT, ENG.
(T) 01582 608517
Speciality: Psychology.
● **Owner** Mrs R McCarthy
B (Ref:HM13399)

**MCCARTHY, SUSAN**

**Susan McCarthy**, Waltham St Lawrence, **Berkshire**, RG10, ENG.
(T) 01189 343423
Speciality: Bach Remedies.
M (Ref:HM13400)

**MCCARTNEY, W J**

**W J McCartney**, 20 Smithfield, Lisburn, **County Antrim**, BT28 1TH, NIR.
(T) 028 9266 5802 (F) 028 9266 2261
Speciality: Biomechanics, Chiropody, Nail Surgery, Podiatry. ✔
● **Owner** Mr W McCartney
● **Chiropodist (Podiatrist)**
Mr D Smith Q: DPodM, S.R.Ch. M: S.C.P.
M Yrs. Est.: 30 (Ref:HM13401)

**MCCATTY, RONALD R**

**Ronald R McCatty**, 39 Durdham Park, Bristol, BS6 6XF, ENG.
(T) 01179 736768
Speciality: Osteopathy.
● **Owner** Mr R McCatty
P S T (Ref:HM13402)

**MCCAULEY, R**

**R McCauley**, Cromac House, 137 Warwick New Rd, Leamington Spa, **Warwickshire**, CV32 6AB, ENG.
(T) 01926 882230 (F) 01926 882230
Speciality: Osteopathy.
● **Owner** Miss R McCauley
P S T (Ref:HM13403)

**MCCAUSLAND, C**

**C McCausland**, 153 Nevill Rd, London, **London (Greater)**, N16 0SU, ENG.
(T) 020 7249 2768
Speciality: Acupuncture.
● **Owner** Mrs C McCausland
O (Ref:HM13404)

**MCCLARNON, S A**

**S A McClarnon**, 21 York Cl, Southwater, Horsham, **Sussex (West)**, RH13 7XJ, ENG.
(T) 01403 731970 (F) 01403 731970
Speciality: Chiropodists (Podiatrists).
● **Owner** Mrs S McClarnon
S (Ref:HM13405)

**MCCLEARY, ROBERT (DR)**

**Dr Robert McCleary**, 126 Clontarf Rd, **County Dublin**, IRE.
(T) 01833 6183
Speciality: Chiropractors.
P S T (Ref:HM13406)

**MCCLELLAND, S M**

**S M McClelland**, The Coach House, Flaunden Lane, Bovingdon, Hemel Hempstead, **Hertfordshire**, HP3 0PA, ENG.
(T) 01442 833136
Speciality: Physiotherapy.
● **Owner** Mrs S McClelland


Key continued: **Yrs.Est:** Years Established **Q:** Qualifications **M:** Professional Membership ✔ Indemnity Insurance Accept Credit Cards

P S T (Ref:HM13407)

## MCCLEMENT, SHIRLEY

**Shirley McClement**, 1 Gladstone Rd, Hoddesdon, **Hertfordshire**, EN11 0JN, ENG.
(T) 01992 467844
Speciality: Reflexology.
S T (Ref:HM13408)

## MCCLOSKEY, P J

**P J McCloskey**, 234 Northfield Avenue, London, **London (Greater)**, W13 9SJ, ENG.
(T) 020 8567 0910
(E) foothealthcentre@netnetscapeonline.co.uk
Speciality: Chiropody, Podiatry, Ultrasonics, X-Ray. ✔
● **Podiatrist/Podiatric Surgeon** Mr P McCloskey Q: B.A.Ch.P, BSc, DPodM, FCPod(s), S.R.Ch.
P Yrs. Est.: 22 (Ref:HM13409)

## MCCLUNE, LORNA

**Lorna McClune**, 30 Galloway St, Dumfries, **Dumfries and Galloway**, DG2 7TN, SCO.
(T) 01387 268381
Speciality: Biomechanics, Chiropody, Nail Surgery. ✔
● **Chiropodist** Mr L McClune Q: DPodM, M.S.C.P. M: S.C.P, S.R.Ch.
C Yrs. Est.: 9 (Ref:HM13410)

## MCCLUNG, KENNETH

**Kenneth McClung**, 59 Heath Rd East, Petersfield, **Hampshire**, GU31 4HN, ENG.
(T) 01730 263683
Speciality: Chiropodists (Podiatrists).
● **Owner** Mr K McClung
S (Ref:HM13411)

## MCCLURG, T A

**Podiatrist**, 28 Hamilton Rd, Bangor, **County Down**, BT20 4LE, NIR.
(T) 028 9145 4799 (F) 028 9145 4799
Speciality: Acupressure.
● **Podiatrist** Mr T McClurg Q: DPodM, S.R.Ch. M: S.C.P.
M Yrs. Est.: 40 (Ref:HM13412)

## MCCLUSKEY, J

**J McCluskey**, Bridge St Chiropody Clinic, 31 Bridge St, Strathaven, **Lanarkshire (South)**, ML10 6AN, SCO.
(T) 01357 520446
Speciality: Chiropodists (Podiatrists).
● **Owner** Mr J McCluskey
S (Ref:HM13413)

## MCCLUSKEY, J

**J McCluskey**, 40 Torranyard Ter, Hamilton, **Lanarkshire (South)**, ML3 8XG, SCO.
(T) 01698 826093
Speciality: Chiropodists (Podiatrists).
● **Owner** Mr J McCluskey
S (Ref:HM13414)

## MCCLUSKEY, JEAN E

**Mrs Jean E McCluskey**, Windle Cottage, Plough Lane, Lathom, Ormskirk, **Lancashire**, L40 6JL, ENG.
(T) 01695 729019
Speciality: Physiotherapy.
P S T (Ref:HM13415)

## MCCLYMOUNT, JENNIFER

**Jennifer McClymount**, Omega Leswalt, High Rd, Stranraer, **Dumfries and Galloway**, DG9 0AA, SCO.
(T) 01776 702881
Speciality: Chiropody, Podiatry. ✔
● **Chiropodist** Mrs J McClymount Q: DPodM, S.R.Ch. M: S.C.P.
M Yrs. Est.: 22 (Ref:HM13416)

## MCCOLE, D

**D McCole**, 5a Esplanade, Whitley Bay, **Tyne and Wear**, NE26 2AG, ENG.
(T) 01912 523129
Speciality: Chiropodists (Podiatrists).
● **Owner** Mr D McCole
S (Ref:HM13417)

## MCCOLGAN, NEWTON

**Newton McColgan**, 24 The Cross, Lymm, **Cheshire**, WA13 0HU, ENG.
(T) 01925 754366
Speciality: Chiropodists (Podiatrists).
S (Ref:HM13418)

## MCCONAGHY, M G

**M G McConaghy**, 16 Sandon St, Waterloo, Liverpool, **Merseyside**, L22 5NW, ENG.
(T) 01514 745430
Speciality: Reflexology.
● **Owner** Mr M McConaghy
S T (Ref:HM13419)

## MCCONNELL, JULIE

**Julie McConnell**, Apex House Business Centre, Wonastow Rd, Monmouth, **Monmouthshire**, NP25 5JB, WAL.
(T) 01600 719300 (F) 01600 714234
Speciality: Physiotherapy.
● **Owner** Mrs J McConnell
P S T (Ref:HM13420)

## MCCORMAC, LOUISE

**Louise McCormac**, 55 Bridge St, Banbridge, **County Down**, BT32 3JL, NIR.
(T) 028 4062 4309
Speciality: Physiotherapy.
P S T (Ref:HM13421)

## MCCORMICK PHYSIO & SPORTS

**McCormick Physiotherapy & Sports Injury Clinic**, 8 Osborne Trce, Edinburgh, **Edinburgh (City of)**, EH12 5HG, SCO.
(T) 01313 133252 (F) 01313 133252
Speciality: Physiotherapy.
● **Owner** Mrs K Pearce
P S T (Ref:HM13422)

## MCCORMICK, BRIAN

**Brian McCormick**, 466-472 Warrington Rd, Culcheth, Warrington, **Cheshire**, WA3 5QX, ENG.
(T) 01925 765839
Speciality: Osteopathy.
● **Owner** Dr M Nabi
P S T (Ref:HM13423)

## MCCORMICK, FRANCES

**Frances McCormick**, 37 Ruskin Rd, Southsea, **Hampshire**, PO4 8RQ, ENG.
(T) 023 9281 8768
Speciality: Reflexology.
S T (Ref:HM13424)

## MCCORMICK, KITTY

**Kitty McCormick**, Brighton, **Sussex (West)**, BN2, ENG.
(T) 01273 703741
Speciality: Reflexology.
S T (Ref:HM13425)

## MCCORRIE, JOHN

**John McCorrie**, Martindale House, Lombard St, Newark, **Nottinghamshire**, NG24 1XG, ENG.
(T) 01636 611150
Speciality: Herbalists.
● **Administrator** Mrs S Taylor
M (Ref:HM13426)

## MCCORRIE, LISA

**Lisa McCorrie**, Well Natural Health Centre, 89 Institute Rd, Birmingham, **Midlands (West)**, B14 7EU, ENG.
(T) 01214 431580
Speciality: Reflexology.
S T (Ref:HM13427)

## MCCOY, DOLORES

**Dolores McCoy**, 3 Croft Park, Holywood, **County Down**, BT18 0PF, NIR.
(T) 028 9042 4604
Speciality: Reflexology.
S T (Ref:HM13428)

## MCCOY, ROBERT J

**Robert J McCoy**, 127 High St, Edenbridge, **Kent**, TN8 5AX, ENG.
(T) 01732 865444
Speciality: Osteopathy.
● **Owner** Mr R McCoy
P S T (Ref:HM13429)

## MCCREA, SUE

**Sue McCrea**, 19 Thackeray Cl, Rugby, **Warwickshire**, CV22 5RN, ENG.
(T) 01788 817966
Speciality: Reflexology.
S T (Ref:HM13430)

## MCCREADY, KEN

**McCREADY KEN ADHP MICHP**, 117-119, Ranelagh, **County Dublin**, IRE.
(T) 01491 0689
(W) www.hypnosiseire.com
Speciality: Complementary Medicines & Therapy.
M (Ref:HM13431)

## MCCREADY, M D (DR)

**McCready Dr M D**, 29 Pembroke Pk, Donnybrook, **County Dublin**, IRE.
(T) 01668 0342
Speciality: Complementary Medicines & Therapy.
M (Ref:HM13432)

## MCCRORIE, MARTIN

**Martin McCrorie**, 14 Arundel Drive East, Saltdean, Brighton, **Sussex (West)**, BN2 8SL, ENG.
(T) 01273 309795
Speciality: Physiotherapy.
P S T (Ref:HM13433)

## MCCRORY, GERALDINE

**Geraldine McCrory**, 10 Cathedral Villas, Cathedral Rd, Armagh, **County Armagh**, BT61 7QX, NIR.
(T) 028 3752 7978
Speciality: Reflexology.
S T (Ref:HM13434)

## MCCROSSAN ASSOCIATES

**McCrossan Associates**, Mason St, Motherwell, **Lanarkshire (North)**, ML1 1YE, SCO.
(T) 01698 327373
Speciality: Chiropodists (Podiatrists).
● **Partner** Mrs M McCrossan
S (Ref:HM13435)

## MCCRYSTALS NATUROPATHIC CENTRE

**Brian McCrystal**, Pentagon House, George St, Ballymena, **County Antrim**, BT43 5AP, NIR.
(T) 028 2564 9701 (F) 028 2564 9701
Speciality: Acupressure, Anthroposohical Medicine, Aromatherapy, Bach Remedies, Complementary Therapy, Counselling, Herbal Medicine, Holistic Healing, Homeopathy, Indian Head Massage, Massage (Therapeutic), Naturopathy, Nutritional Therapy, Reflexology, Stress Therapy, Touch Therapy, Vitamin Therapy. ✔
● **Owner** Mr B McCrystal Q: MH. M: BRCP.
C T Yrs. Est.: 17 (Ref:HM13436)

## MCCULLY, JOAN

**Miss Joan McCully**, 18 Irwin Avenue, Belfast, **County Antrim**, BT4 3AF, NIR.
(T) 028 9065 4230
Speciality: Chiropody. ✔
● **Chiropodist** Miss J McCully Q: S.R.Ch. M: S.C.P.
M Yrs. Est.: 20 (Ref:HM13437)

## MCCURRICH, J

**J McCurrich**, 130-132 Gloucester Rd, Bishopston, Bristol, BS7 8NL, ENG.
(T) 01179 245842
Speciality: Chiropractors.
● **Doctor** Mr J Jensen
P S T (Ref:HM13438)

## MCCUTCHEON, IAN

**Ian McCutcheon**, Wharton Cottage, Main St, Burton, Carnforth, **Lancashire**, LA6 1NA, ENG.
(T) 01524 781383
Speciality: Chiropodists (Podiatrists).
● **Owner** Mr I McCutcheon
S (Ref:HM13439)

## MCCUTCHEON, R M

**R M McCutcheon**, 150 High St, Holywood, **County Down**, BT18 9HS, NIR.
(T) 028 9042 5953 (F) 028 9042 5953
Speciality: Osteopathy.
● **Owner** Mr R McCutcheon
P S T (Ref:HM13440)

## MCCUTCHEON, TINA

**Tina McCutcheon**, White House, 22B Springvale Rd, Balywater, Newtownards, **County**

**Down**, BT22 2PE, **NIR**.
**(T)** 028 4275 8069 **(F)** 028 4275 8069
**(E)** tmccutch@aol.com
**Speciality:** Acupuncture, Bach Remedies, Cranial Osteopathy, Herbal Medicine, Homeopathy, Kinesiology, Manipulation, Nutritional Therapy, Osteopathy.
● **Complementary Therapist**
Ms T McCutcheon **Q:** DO, Lic.Ac, PhD.
**M** Yrs. Est.: 16 (**Ref:**HM13441)

## MCDAID, M S

**M S McDaid**, 1 Mill View, Clifford St, Chudleigh, Newton Abbot, **Devon**, TQ13 0LQ, **ENG**.
**(T)** 01626 853873
**Speciality:** Osteopathy.
**P S T** (**Ref:**HM13442)

## MCDERMOTT AROMATHERAPY

**McDermott Aromatherapy**, 21 Furness Avenue, Ormskirk, **Lancashire**, L39 4TT, **ENG**.
**(T)** 01695 575294
**Speciality:** Aromatherapy.
● **Owner** Mrs F McDermott
**M O** (**Ref:**HM13443)

## MCDERMOTT, ADRIAN

**Adrian McDermott**, Clocktower Practice, 50 Park Rd, London, **London (Greater)**, N8 9SU, **ENG**.
**(T)** 020 8341 7425
**Speciality:** Herbal Medicine.
● **Practice Manager** Mr A McDermott
**M** (**Ref:**HM13444)

## MCDERMOTT, ADRIAN

**Adrian McDermott Medical Herbalist**, 24 High St, London, **London (Greater)**, E11 2AQ, **ENG**.
**(T)** 020 8530 2126
**Speciality:** Herbal Medicine.
**M** (**Ref:**HM13445)

## MCDERMOTT, CLARA

**Clara Mcdermott**, 14B Esterbrooke St, London, **London (Greater)**, SW1P 4NW, **ENG**.
**(T)** 020 7233 9903
**Speciality:** Psychotherapy.
● **Owner** Miss C McDermott
**B** (**Ref:**HM13446)

## MCDERMOTT, J V

**J V McDermott**, 567 Warwick Rd, Solihull, **Midlands (West)**, B91 1AW, **ENG**.
**(T)** 01217 058353
**Speciality:** Osteopathy. ✔
● **Osteopath** Mr J Patel **Q:** DO. **M:** GOsC.
● **Owner** Mrs S McDermott
**S** Yrs. Est.: 30 (**Ref:**HM13447)

## MCDERMOTT, MARY

**McDermott Mary MAIC**, The Sq, Castlerea, **County Roscommon**, **IRE**.
**(T)** 09072 1168
**Speciality:** Acupuncture.
**O** (**Ref:**HM13448)

## MCDERMOTT, P

**P McDermott**, 2 Springfield Rd, Kings Heath, Birmingham, **Midlands (West)**, B14 7DS, **ENG**.
**(T)** 01214 413228
**Speciality:** Chiropodists (Podiatrists).
**S** (**Ref:**HM13449)

## MCDERMOTT, T P

**T P McDermott**, 24 Eastlands Rd, Rugby, **Warwickshire**, CV21 3RP, **ENG**.
**(T)** 01788 571407
**Speciality:** Psychotherapy.
● **Owner** Mr T McDermott
**B** (**Ref:**HM13450)

## MCDEVITT, ANNE

**Anne McDevitt**, 13 Wicklow St, Dublin, **County Dublin**, **IRE**.
**(T)** 01677 7962 **(F)** 01677 7061
**Speciality:** Complementary Medicines & Therapy.
**M** (**Ref:**HM13451)

## MCDONALD PARTNERSHIP

**McDonald Partnership**, 16 Fitzroy Pl, Glasgow, **Glasgow (City of)**, G3 7RW, **SCO**.
**(T)** 01412 043455
**Speciality:** Psychotherapy.
**B** (**Ref:**HM13452)

## MCDONALD, ALASTAIR

**Alastair McDonald**, 150 Railway St, Cardiff, **Glamorgan (Vale of)**, CF24 2NH, **WAL**.
**(T)** 029 2048 4833
**Speciality:** Alexander Technique.
● **Owner** Mr A McDonald
**P S** (**Ref:**HM13453)

## MCDONALD, D W

**D W McDonald**, 2 Church Lane, Donaghadee, **County Down**, BT21 0AJ, **NIR**.
**(T)** 028 9188 3616
**Speciality:** Chiropodists (Podiatrists).
**S** (**Ref:**HM13454)

## MCDONALD, D W

**D W McDonald**, 32 Abbey St, Bangor, **County Down**, BT20 4JB, **NIR**.
**(T)** 028 9127 0310
**Speciality:** Chiropodists (Podiatrists).
● **Owner** Mr D McDonald
**S** (**Ref:**HM13455)

## MCDONALD, DAVID S

**David S Mcdonald**, 22 Brunton Pl, Edinburgh, **Edinburgh (City of)**, EH7 5EJ, **SCO**.
**(T)** 01316 521806
**Speciality:** Biomechanics, Chiropody, Nail Surgery, Podiatry. ✔
● **Owner/Chiropodist** Mr D McDonald
**Q:** DPodM, M.S.C.P, S.R.Ch.
**M** Yrs. Est.: 14 (**Ref:**HM13456)

## MCDONALD, EILEEN

**Eileen McDonald**, 3 Elmwood Avenue, Newton Mearns, Glasgow, **Glasgow (City of)**, G77 6EH, **SCO**.
**(T)** 01416 398748
**Speciality:** Chiropodists (Podiatrists).
**S** (**Ref:**HM13457)

## MCDONALD, JEANETTE

**Jeanette McDonald**, 49 Pembridge Rd, Bovingdon, Hemel Hempstead, **Hertfordshire**, HP3 0QN, **ENG**.
**(T)** 01442 834373
**Speciality:** Aromatherapy.
**M O** (**Ref:**HM13458)

## MCDONALD, M

**Miss M McDonald**, 42 Ashcroft Rd, Cirencester, **Gloucestershire**, GL7 1QX, **ENG**.
**(T)** 01285 643958
**Speciality:** Osteopathy.
**P S T** (**Ref:**HM13459)

## MCDONALD, MARGARET

**Margaret McDonald**, Tipping Brow House, Tipping Brow, Mobberley, Knutsford, **Cheshire**, WA16 7JE, **ENG**.
**(T)** 01565 873145
**Speciality:** Reflexology.
**S T** (**Ref:**HM13460)

## MCDONNELL, ANN MARIE

**Ann Marie McDonnell**, 7 Southvale Rd, London, **London (Greater)**, SE3 0TP, **ENG**.
**(T)** 020 8852 5369
**Speciality:** Chiropractors.
**P S T** (**Ref:**HM13461)

## MCDONNELL, P

**P McDonnell**, 2 Holbeck, Astley, Tyldesley, Manchester, **Manchester (Greater)**, M29 7DU, **ENG**.
**(T)** 01942 894672
**Speciality:** Chiropodists (Podiatrists).
**S** (**Ref:**HM13462)

## MCDONOUGH, TRAVIS (DR)

**McDonough Dr Travis B Sc , D C**, The Surgery Springfield Court, Ennis, **County Clare**, **IRE**.
**(T)** 06568 28288
**Speciality:** Chiropractors.
**P S T** (**Ref:**HM13463)

## MCDOUALL, VERONICA

**Veronica McDouall**, 71 Bridge St, Cambridge, **Cambridgeshire**, CB2 1UR, **ENG**.
**(T)** 01223 313515
**Speciality:** Psychotherapy.
**B** (**Ref:**HM13464)

## MCDOUGALL, NORRIE

**Norrie McDougall**, The Vines, 2 Trinity Rd, Sheerness, **Kent**, ME12 2PQ, **ENG**.
**(T)** 01795 871871
**Speciality:** Chiropodists (Podiatrists).
**S** (**Ref:**HM13465)

## MCDOWALL, SANDRA

**Sandra McDowall**, 1 Quintons Corner, East Bergholt, Colchester, **Essex**, CO7 6RD, **ENG**.
**(T)** 01206 298465
**Speciality:** Chiropodists (Podiatrists).
● **Owner** Mrs S McDowall
**S** (**Ref:**HM13466)

## MCDOWELL, S

**S McDowell**, 153 Hastings Rd, Tunbridge Wells, **Kent**, TN2 4JU, **ENG**.
**(T)** 01892 823275
**Speciality:** Chiropractic. ✔
● **Chiropractor** Mr S McDowell **Q:** DC. **M:** BCA.
**P** (**Ref:**HM13467)

## MCDOWELL, STEPHEN

**Stephen McDowell**, 1 Birling Rd, Tunbridge Wells, **Kent**, TN2 5LX, **ENG**.
**(T)** 01892 549714
**Speciality:** Chiropractic.
**P S T** (**Ref:**HM13468)

## MCELDUFF, M

**McELDUFF M Lic Ac M A I A C**, **County Limerick**, **IRE**.
**(T)** 06122 7601
**Speciality:** Acupuncture.
**O** (**Ref:**HM13469)

## MCELROY, BEVERLY

**Beverly McElroy**, 362-364 Goldington Rd, Bedford, **Bedfordshire**, MK41 9NT, **ENG**.
**(T)** 01234 351411 **(F)** 01234 273694
**Speciality:** Chiropodists (Podiatrists).
● **Manager** Mrs K Duffell
**S** (**Ref:**HM13470)

## MCENTEE, DOLORES

**McEntee Dolores**, Crickstown Curragha Ashbourne, **County Meath**, **IRE**.
**(T)** 01835 2409
**Speciality:** Complementary Medicines & Therapy.
**M** (**Ref:**HM13471)

## MCENTYRE, NUALA

**Nuala McEntyre**, 9 Eldon St, Bury, **Lancashire**, BL9 5AZ, **ENG**.
**(T)** 01617 976564
**Speciality:** Chiropodists (Podiatrists).
● **Owner** Ms N McEntyre
**S** (**Ref:**HM13472)

## MCEVOY, RACHEL ANN

**Rachel Ann McEvoy**, 456 Chester Rd, Sutton Coldfield, **Midlands (West)**, B73 5BP, **ENG**.
**(T)** 01213 739235
**Speciality:** Chiropodists (Podiatrists).
● **Owner** Ms R McEvoy
**S** (**Ref:**HM13473)

## MCFADYEN, J

**J McFadyen**, 8 Joydon Drive, Romford, **Essex**, RM6 4SU, **ENG**.
**(T)** 020 8590 3131
**Speciality:** Hypnotherapy.
● **Owner** Mr J McFadyen
**B** (**Ref:**HM13474)

## MCFARLANE, BILL

**Bill McFarlane**, 2 Corporation St, Chesterfield, **Derbyshire**, S41 7TP, **ENG**.
**(T)** 01246 540010
**Speciality:** Hypnosis.
● **Owner** Mr W McFarlane
**B** (**Ref:**HM13475)

## MCFARLANE, JOAN

**Joan McFarlane**, 166 Loxley Rd, Stratford-Upon-Avon, **Warwickshire**, CV37 7DT, **ENG**.
**(T)** 01789 298040 **(F)** 01789 298040
**Speciality:** Physiotherapy.
● **Owner** Ms J McFarlane
**P S T** (**Ref:**HM13476)



Key continued: **Yrs.Est:** Years Established **Q:** Qualifications **M:** Professional Membership ✔ Indemnity Insurance Accept Credit Cards

## MCFARLANE, R L

**R L McFarlane**, 264 Bath St, Glasgow, **Glasgow (City of)**, G2 4JP, SCO.
(T) 01413 312361
Speciality: Physiotherapy.
P S T (Ref:HM13477)

## MCGARAHAN, C

**C McGarahan**, 41 Rose St, Condorrat, Cumbernauld, Glasgow, **Glasgow (City of)**, G67 4ET, SCO.
(T) 01236 720505
Speciality: Chiropodists (Podiatrists).
S (Ref:HM13478)

## MCGARRELL, L

**L McGarrell**, 58 Central Avenue, Hayes, **London (Greater)**, UB3 2BY, ENG.
(T) 020 8561 0003
Speciality: Chiropodists (Podiatrists).
● **Owner** Mr L McGarrell
S (Ref:HM13479)

## MCGARVEY, LINDA

**Linda McGarvey**, Aldrens Lane, Lancaster, **Lancashire**, LA1 2DU, ENG.
(T) 01524 69864 (F) 01524 848155
Speciality: Complementary Medicines & Therapy.
M (Ref:HM13480)

## MCGEE, GABRIELLE

**Gabrielle McGee**, 38 Fellows Rd, London, **London (Greater)**, NW3 3LH, ENG.
(T) 020 7916 4204
Speciality: Psychotherapy.
● **Owner** Mrs G McGee
B (Ref:HM13481)

## MCGHIE, PETER M

**Peter M McGhie**, 32 Tivoli Rd, Brighton, **Sussex (East)**, BN1 5BH, ENG.
(T) 01273 555593
Speciality: Hypnosis.
B (Ref:HM13482)

## MCGIBBON, KAREN

**Karen McGibbon**, School Lane, Upholland, Skelmersdale, **Lancashire**, WN8 0LW, ENG.
(T) 01695 625064
Speciality: Chiropodists (Podiatrists).
● **Owner** Mrs K McGibbon
S (Ref:HM13483)

## MCGILL, L

**Clairvoyant & Therapist**, Fron Uchaf, Llangwm, Corwen, **Denbighshire**, LL21 0RD, WAL.
(T) 01490 460460
Speciality: Counselling, Homeopathy, Kinesiology, Reiki, Spiritual Healing, SPR Massage. ✔
● **Kinesiologist** Mrs L McGill
C Yrs. Est.: 8 (Ref:HM13484)

## MCGILLIGAN, DOLORES

**McGilligan Dolores M I I R M I R I**, 15 Pembroke Cottages, Donnybrook, **County Dublin**, IRE.
(T) 01269 5629
Speciality: Reflexology.
S T (Ref:HM13485)

## MCGINLEY, TONY

**McGinley Tony M A I A**, 9 Westcourt, Tralee, **County Kerry**, IRE.
(T) 06671 24694
Speciality: Acupuncture.
O (Ref:HM13486)

## MCGINTY, J

**J McGinty**, 170 Altyre Avenue, Glenrothes, **Fife**, KY7 4PZ, SCO.
(T) 01592 771001
Speciality: Reflexology.
● **Owner** Mrs J McGinty
S T (Ref:HM13487)

## MCGLADE, CHRIS

**Chris McGlade**, 19 Burgess Drive, Fleet Hargate, Holbeach, Spalding, **Lincolnshire**, PE12 8NR, ENG.
(T) 01406 426249
Speciality: Chiropodists (Podiatrists).
● **Owner** Mr C McGlade
S (Ref:HM13488)

## MCGLOIN, TARJA

**Tarja McGloin**, 71 Mora Rd, London, **London (Greater)**, NW2 6TB, ENG.
(T) 020 8208 0401
Speciality: Reflexology.
S T (Ref:HM13489)

## MCGORRIN, RICHARD

**Richard McGorrin**, 3 Glebe Parc, St. Tudy, Bodmin, **Cornwall**, PL30 3AS, ENG.
(T) 01208 851059
Speciality: Chiropodists (Podiatrists).
● **Owner** Mr R McGorrin
S (Ref:HM13490)

## MCGOVEN, J

**J McGoven**, 243 Chester Rd, Whitby, Ellesmere Port, **Merseyside**, CH66 2LJ, ENG.
(T) 01513 568269
Speciality: Osteopathy.
P S T (Ref:HM13491)

## MCGOVERN, FIONA

**Fiona McGovern**, **Ayrshire (North)**, KA27, SCO.
(T) 01770 600135
Speciality: Bach Remedies.
M (Ref:HM13492)

## MCGOVERN, RITA

**Rita McGovern**, Lifestyle Natural Health Centre, Hersham Green Shopping Centre, Walton-On-Thames, **Surrey**, KT12 4HU, ENG.
(T) 01932 248824
Speciality: Complementary Medicines & Therapy.
M (Ref:HM13493)

## MCGRAIL, SARAH

**Sarah McGrail**, 1 Bacup Rd, Rossendale, **Lancashire**, BB4 7NG, ENG.
(T) 01706 240034
Speciality: Physiotherapy.
● **Owner** Mrs S McGrail
P S T (Ref:HM13494)

## MCGRATH, JOE

**McGrath Joe**, 22 Gulistan Tce, Rathmines, **County Dublin**, IRE.
(T) 01497 9273
Speciality: Chiropractors.
P S T (Ref:HM13495)

## MCGRAW, LIZZIE

**Lizzie McGraw**, Wanakar Lodge, Ashfield, Dunblane, **Perth and Kinross**, FK15 0JS, SCO.
(T) 01786 822364
Speciality: Complementary Medicines & Therapy.
● **Owner** Mrs L McGraw
M (Ref:HM13496)

## MCGRAW, LIZZIE

**Lizzie McGraw**, Old Glassingall, Glassingall, Dunblane, **Perth and Kinross**, FK15 0JG, SCO.
(T) 01786 822364
Speciality: Complementary Medicines & Therapy.
C M (Ref:HM13497)

## MCGREADY, NORMA

**Norma McGready**, 66 Erleigh Court Gardens, Earley, Reading, **Berkshire**, RG6 1EJ, ENG.
(T) 01189 662828
Speciality: Electrolysis.
T (Ref:HM13498)

## MCGREGOR, CAROLYN

**Carolyn Mcgregor**, Wenvoe, 159 St Johns Rd, Tunbridge Wells, **Kent**, TN4 9UP, ENG.
(T) 01892 521134
Speciality: Osteopathy.
P S T (Ref:HM13499)

## MCGREGOR, J

**J McGregor**, 11 St John St, Manchester, **Manchester (Greater)**, M3 4DW, ENG.
(T) 01618 328797
Speciality: Physiotherapy.
● **Owner** Mr J McGregor
P S T (Ref:HM13500)

## MCGREGOR, S

**S McGregor**, Bridle Way, North Heath, Chieveley, Newbury, **Berkshire**, RG20 8UD, ENG.
(T) 01635 248048
Speciality: Osteopathy.
P S T (Ref:HM13501)

## MCGREGOR, SHERRY

**Sherry McGregor**, 49 Etterby St, Carlisle, **Cumbria**, CA3 9JD, ENG.
(T) 01228 546588 (F) 01228 546588
Speciality: Osteopathy.
● **Partner** Miss S McGregor
P S T (Ref:HM13502)

## MCGREGOR, STUART

**Stuart McGregor**, 5a Grove St, Wantage, **Oxfordshire**, OX12 7AB, ENG.
(T) 01235 768033
Speciality: Osteopathy.
● **Partner** Mr S McGregor
P S T (Ref:HM13503)

## MCGREGOR, TONY

**Tony McGregor**, 127 Kingsley Cl, Shaw, Newbury, **Berkshire**, RG14 2EB, ENG.
(T) 01635 34231
Speciality: Counselling, Hypnosis, Hypnotherapy, Psychotherapy, Stress Therapy. ✔
● **Hypnotherapist/Psychotherapist** Mr T McGregor Q: BSc, Dip.Hyp, Dip.Psych, MNRHP M: UKCP
B Yrs. Est.: 15 (Ref:HM13504)

## MCGUCKEN, LORNA N

**Lorna N McGucken**, 28 Court Yard, London, **London (Greater)**, SE9 5QA, ENG.
(T) 020 8850 7623
Speciality: Chiropodists (Podiatrists).
● **Owner** Miss L McGucken
S (Ref:HM13505)

## MCGUIGGAN, MARY

**Mary McGuiggan**, 16 Edenavaddy Rd, Ballynahinch, **County Down**, BT24 8JJ, NIR.
(T) 028 9756 1345
Speciality: Reflexology.
S T (Ref:HM13506)

## MCGUINNESS, MICHEAL

**McGUINNESS MICHAEL ADHP MICHP**, Maynooth Co, **County Kildare**, IRE.
(T) 01628 9946
(W) www.hypnosiseire.com
Speciality: Complementary Medicines & Therapy.
M (Ref:HM13507)

## MCGUIRE, MICK

**Mick McGuire**, 44 Christ Church Rd, Doncaster, **Yorkshire (South)**, DN1 2QL, ENG.
(T) 01302 341514
Speciality: Physiotherapy.
● **Owner** Mr M McGuire
P S T (Ref:HM13508)

## MCHUGH HYPNOSIS & REFLEXOLOGY

**McHugh Hypnosis and Reflexology**, 15 Westbury Park, Westbury Court, Lucan, **County Dublin**, IRE.
(T) 00353 16241035
(E) hypnomike@oceanfree.net
(W) www.mchughhypnosis.com
Speciality: Cognitive Therapy, Counselling, Hypnosis, Hypnotherapy, Psychotherapy, Reflexology. ✔
● **Hypnotist/Reflexologist** Mr M McHugh Q: Dip.Hyp, Dip.Reflex, ITEC. M: ICHP
● **Hypnotist** Ms R Gerrard Q: Dip.Hyp. M: ICHP
● **Reflexologist** Ms O Gentleman M: IRI, ITEC.
● **Hypnotist/Teacher** Mr J Keaney Q: Dip.Hyp. M: ICHP
B Yrs. Est.: 6 (Ref:HM13509)

## MCILWRAITH, B G

**B G Mcilwraith**, 72 Lochalsh Rd, Inverness, **Highland**, IV3 8HW, SCO.
(T) 01463 222839 (F) 01463 222839
Speciality: Osteopathy.
● **Owner** Mr B Mcllwraith
P S T (Ref:HM13510)



Key: B Mind-Body Medicine C Complementary Medicine H Self Help Treatment M Medicinal Therapy O Oriental Medicine P Postural Therapy S Manipulative Structural Therapy T Touch Therapy

**MCINTOSH, A**

**A McIntosh**, Gilliat Drive, Guildford, **Surrey**, GU4 7EN, ENG.
(T) 01483 502961
Speciality: Aromatherapy.
● **Owner** Mrs A McIntosh
M O (Ref:HM13511)

**MCINTOSH, G**

**G McIntosh**, 30-32 Battlefield Rd, Glasgow, **Glasgow (City of)**, G42 9QH, SCO.
(T) 01416 321266
Speciality: Osteopathy.
● **Owner** Ms C Anderson
P S T (Ref:HM13512)

**MCINTOSH, GILLIAN**

**Gillian Mcintosh**, 9 Bell St, Renfrew, **Renfrewshire**, PA4 8PP, SCO.
(T) 01418 866930
Speciality: Osteopathy.
P S T (Ref:HM13513)

**MCINTOSH, GILLIAN**

**Gillian McIntosh**, 76A Causeyside St, Paisley, **Renfrewshire**, PA1 1YP, SCO.
(T) 01418 898416
Speciality: Osteopathy.
P S T (Ref:HM13514)

**MCINTOSH, IAIN**

**Iain McIntosh**, 10 Harley St, London, **London (Greater)**, W1N 1AA, ENG.
(T) 020 7467 8342 (F) 020 7467 8312
Speciality: Hypnosis.
● **Owner** Mr I McIntosh
B (Ref:HM13515)

**MCINTOSH, IRENE**

**Irene McIntosh**, 88 Desswood Pl, Aberdeen, **Aberdeenshire**, AB15 4DQ, SCO.
(T) 01224 639784 (F) 01224 635587
Speciality: Hypnosis.
● **Owner** Mrs I McIntosh
B (Ref:HM13516)

**MCINTOSH, MAUREEN**

**Maureen McIntosh**, 32 Cornerswell Rd, Penarth, **Glamorgan (Vale of)**, CF64 2WA, WAL.
(T) 029 2070 0124
Speciality: Chiropractic.
● **Owner** Mr B O'Donnell
P S T (Ref:HM13517)

**MCIVOR, K**

**K McIvor**, New Dundas Clinic, 28J Dundas St, Bonnyrigg, **Lothian (Mid)**, EH19 3AS, SCO.
(T) 01316 633331
Speciality: Physiotherapy.
● **Owner** Mr K McIvor
P S T (Ref:HM13518)

**MCKAY & ASSOCIATES**

**Andrea McKay & Associates**, 7 Bold St, Warrington, **Cheshire**, WA1 1DN, ENG.
(T) 01925 573233
Speciality: Chiropodists (Podiatrists).
S (Ref:HM13519)

**MCKAY, B**

**B McKay**, New Cross Natural Therapy Centre, 394 New Cross Rd, London, **London (Greater)**, SE14 6TY, ENG.
(T) 020 8469 0858
Speciality: Osteopathy.
P S T (Ref:HM13520)

**MCKAY, GAIL**

**Gail McKay**, Health Hydro, Milton Rd, Swindon, **Wiltshire**, SN1 5JA, ENG.
(T) 01793 465631
Speciality: Aromatherapy.
M O (Ref:HM13521)

**MCKAY, MARIA**

**Maria McKay**, West Arlehaven, Blanefield, Glasgow, **Glasgow (City of)**, G63 9AW, SCO.
(T) 01416 360387
Speciality: Homeopathy.
● **Owner** Mrs M McKay
M (Ref:HM13522)

**MCKAY, MARIA**

**Maria McKay**, 10 Mansionhouse Rd, Glasgow, **Glasgow (City of)**, G41 3DN, SCO.
(T) 01416 360387
Speciality: Homeopathy.
M (Ref:HM13523)

**MCKEAG, JULIE**

**Julie McKeag**, 3 Chatsworth Avenue, Bishop Auckland, **County Durham**, DL14 6AX, ENG.
(T) 01388 601899
Speciality: Complementary Medicines & Therapy.
● **Owner** Ms J McKeag
C M (Ref:HM13524)

**MCKEEVER, L**

**L McKeever**, 95 Green Rd, Kidlington, **Oxfordshire**, OX5 2HA, ENG.
(T) 01865 375399
Speciality: Chiropodists (Podiatrists).
● **Owner** Mr L McKeever
S (Ref:HM13525)

**MCKELLAR, ROSE**

**Rose McKellar**, 116 Evenlode Rd, Southampton, **Hampshire**, SO16 9EG, ENG.
(T) 023 8078 1067
Speciality: Complementary Medicines & Therapy.
● **Owner** Miss R McKellar
C M (Ref:HM13526)

**MCKENNA, L**

**L McKenna (Remedial Massage)**, Towngate Health Clinic, 102 Towngate, Leyland, Preston, **Lancashire**, PR5 1LQ, ENG.
(T) 01772 456657
Speciality: Complementary Medicines & Therapy.
● **Owner** Miss L McKenna
M (Ref:HM13527)

**MCKENNA, M**

**M McKenna**, 1 Dalhousie Gardens, Bishopbriggs, Glasgow, **Glasgow (City of)**, G64 3DL, SCO.
(T) 01417 723132
Speciality: Chiropodists (Podiatrists).
● **Owner** Mrs M McKenna
S (Ref:HM13528)

**MCKENZIE, GEORGE**

**George McKenzie**, 18 Nuthurst Cres, Ansley, Nuneaton, **Warwickshire**, CV10 9PJ, ENG.
(T) 024 7639 5757
Speciality: Chiropodists (Podiatrists).
● **Partner** Mr G McKenzie
S (Ref:HM13529)

**MCKENZIE, PENELOPE**

**Penelope McKenzie**, 18 Nuthurst Cres, Ansley, Nuneaton, **Warwickshire**, CV10 9PJ, ENG.
(T) 024 7639 5757
Speciality: Chiropodists (Podiatrists).
● **Partner** Mrs P McKenzie
S (Ref:HM13530)

**MCKEOWN & ASSOCIATES**

**John McKeown & Associates**, 17 Prince Albert St, Brighton, **Sussex (East)**, BN1 1HF, ENG.
(T) 01273 821402 (F) 01273 203800
Speciality: Psychology.
● **Owner** Mr J McKeown
B (Ref:HM13531)

**MCKEOWN, KAY**

**Mrs Kay McKeown**, 62 Dean Court Rd, Rotting Dean, Brighton, **Sussex (East)**, BN2 7DJ, ENG.
(T) 01270 3306616
Speciality: Alexander Technique. ✔
● **Owner** Mrs K McKeown M: STAT.
B H P S T
Yrs. Est.: 2 (Ref:HM13532)

**MCKIE, IAN**

**Ian McKie**, 13 Queens Dr West, Peterborough, **Cambridgeshire**, PE1 2UR, ENG.
(T) 01733 566042
Speciality: Hypnotherapy.
B (Ref:HM13533)

**MCKINNA, ANNE**

**Anne McKinna**, Baredown Cottage, The Baredown, Nately Scures, Hook, **Hampshire**, RG27 9JT, ENG.
(T) 01256 765522
Speciality: Electrolysis.
● **Owner** Mrs A McKinna
T (Ref:HM13534)

**MCKINNEY, G H**

**G H McKinney**, 20 Central Avenue, Portstewart, **County Londonderry**, BT55 7BS, NIR.
(T) 028 7083 3878
Speciality: Chiropodists (Podiatrists).
● **Principal** Mr P McKinney
S (Ref:HM13535)

**MCKINNON, A**

**A McKinnon**, 28 Hillend Rd, Arbroath, **Angus**, DD11 2AR, SCO.
(T) 01241 877100
Speciality: Chiropodists (Podiatrists).
S (Ref:HM13536)

**MCKIRDY, GILLIAN**

**Gillian McKirdy**, 2 Manse Rd, Newmains, Wishaw, **Lanarkshire (North)**, ML2 9AX, SCO.
(T) 01698 386884
Speciality: Aromatherapy.
● **Owner** Mrs G McKirdy
M O (Ref:HM13537)

**MCKITTRICK, S J**

**S J McKittrick**, 50 Dover Rd, Southport, **Merseyside**, PR8 4TD, ENG.
(T) 01704 564775
Speciality: Chiropodists (Podiatrists).
● **Owner** Mr S McKittrick
S (Ref:HM13538)

**MCLAREN, CATH RENA**

**Cath Rena McLaren**, 92 Balmalloch Rd, Kilsyth, Glasgow, **Glasgow (City of)**, G65 9NW, SCO.
(T) 01236 824523
Speciality: Acupressure, Aromatherapy, Bowen Therapy, Reflexology, Reiki, Acupressure, On-site Massage. ✔
● **Practitioner** Ms C McLaren Q: GSSR, MBPA. M: BPA.
C Yrs. Est.: 4 (Ref:HM13539)

**MCLAREN, LESLEY**

**Lesley McLaren**, 14 Edendale Rd, Cheltenham, **Gloucestershire**, GL51 0TY, ENG.
(T) 01242 583155
Speciality: Reflexology.
S T (Ref:HM13540)

**MCLAREN, LINDA**

**Linda McLaren**, 16 Clarence Sq, Cheltenham, **Gloucestershire**, GL50 4JN, ENG.
(T) 01242 241933
Speciality: Homeopathy.
M (Ref:HM13541)

**MCLAREN, M**

**M McLaren**, 26 The Meadows, Halstead, Sevenoaks, **Kent**, TN14 7HD, ENG.
(T) 01959 533028 (F) 01959 534351
Speciality: Acupuncture.
● **Owner** Mrs M McLaren
O (Ref:HM13542)

**MCLAREN, PETER**

**Peter McLaren**, 52 Woods Avenue, Hatfield, **Hertfordshire**, AL10 8LY, ENG.
(T) 01707 264513
Speciality: Hypnosis.
● **Owner** Mr P McLaren
B (Ref:HM13543)

**MCLAUGHLIN, AIMEE**

**Aimee Mclaughlin**, 9 Brackley Cl, Peterborough, **Cambridgeshire**, PE3 6LH, ENG.
(T) 01733 551881
Speciality: Complementary Medicines & Therapy.
● **Owner** A McLaughlin
C M (Ref:HM13544)

**MCLAUGHLIN, E**

**E McLaughlin**, 40 Carlisle Rd, Londonderry, **County Londonderry**, BT48 6JW, NIR.
(T) 028 7137 4097
Speciality: Chiropodists (Podiatrists).
● **Owner** Miss E McLaughlin



Key continued: **Yrs.Est:** Years Established Q: Qualifications M: Professional Membership ✔ Indemnity Insurance Accept Credit Cards

S (Ref:HM13545)

## MCLAUGHLIN, K D

**K D McLaughlin**, 79 Cockton Hill Rd, Bishop Auckland, **County Durham**, DL14 6HS, ENG.
(T) 01388 605056
Speciality: Chiropodists (Podiatrists).
S (Ref:HM13546)

## MCLAUGHLIN, L

**L McLaughlin**, Chesterfield Clinic, Holywell Annexe, Holywell St, Chesterfield, **Derbyshire**, S41 7SH, ENG.
(T) 01246 200311
Speciality: Chiropractors.
P S T (Ref:HM13547)

## MCLAUGHLIN, M C

**M C McLaughlin**, 1048 Tollcross Rd, Glasgow, **Glasgow (City of)**, G32 8UW, SCO.
(T) 01417 782829
Speciality: Chiropodists (Podiatrists).
S (Ref:HM13548)

## MCLAUGHLIN, SANDRA

**Sandra McLaughlin**, 64 Springdale Avenue, Broadstone, **Dorset**, BH18 9EX, ENG.
(T) 01202 602239
Speciality: Reflexology.
S T (Ref:HM13549)

## MCLAY, G

**G McLay**, 30 Southfield Rd, Cumbernauld, Glasgow, **Glasgow (City of)**, G68 9DZ, SCO.
(T) 01236 731247
Speciality: Chiropodists (Podiatrists).
S (Ref:HM13550)

## MCLEAN, A M

**Mrs Anne Margaret McLean**, Bonhill, 33 Brouster Hill, East Kilbride, Glasgow, **Glasgow (City of)**, G74 1AG, SCO.
(T) 01355 226742 (F) 01335 900501
(E) annem@cableinet.co.uk
Speciality: Herbal Medicine, Homeopathy, Magnetic Therapy. ✔
● **Chiropodist (Podiatrist)**
Mrs A McLean Q: BSc, DPodM, M.S.C.P, S.R.Ch. M: S.C.P.
M Yrs. Est.: 20 (Ref:HM13551)

## MCLEAN, JIM

**Jim McLean**, 68B Leicester Rd, Loughborough, **Leicestershire**, LE11 2AG, ENG.
(T) 01509 234522
Speciality: Hypnotherapy.
B (Ref:HM13552)

## MCLEAN, JOHN

**John McLean**, Business Centre, 120 West Heath Rd, London, **London (Greater)**, NW3 7TY, ENG.
(T) 020 8731 6500
Speciality: Psychotherapy.
● **Owner** Mr J McLean
B (Ref:HM13553)

## MCLEAN, TERRI

**Terri Mclean**, 17 Rugby Rd, Clifton Upon Dunsmore, Rugby, **Warwickshire**, CV23 0DE, ENG.
(T) 01788 565669
Speciality: Complementary Medicines & Therapy.
M (Ref:HM13554)

## MCLEAVY, CANDY

**Candy McLeavy**, 2 Walsingham Pl, Truro, **Cornwall**, TR1 2RP, ENG.
(T) 01872 263163
Speciality: Acupuncture.
● **Owner** Mrs C McLeavy
O (Ref:HM13555)

## MCLEISH, JACQUI

**Jacqui McLeish**, County Health, 15 High St, Holt, **Norfolk**, NR25 6BN, ENG.
(T) 01263 713974
Speciality: Complementary Medicines & Therapy.
M (Ref:HM13556)

## MCLEOD ST PHYSIO CLINIC

**McLeod Street Physiotherapy Clinic**, 22b McLeod St, Edinburgh, **Edinburgh (City of)**, EH11 2NH, SCO.
(T) 01313 374981 (F) 01313 379822
Speciality: Physiotherapy.
P S T (Ref:HM13557)

## MCLEOD, S

**S McLeod**, Kingarth, Wadeslea, Elie, Leven, **Fife**, KY9 1EA, SCO.
(T) 01333 330275
Speciality: Osteopathy.
● **Owner** Miss S McLeod
P S T (Ref:HM13558)

## MCLOUGHLIN, BRENDAN

**B McLoughlin MA FPC UKCP**, The Open House Centre, Manvers St, Bath, **Somerset**, BA1 1JW, ENG.
(T) 01225 481297
Speciality: Counselling, Psychotherapy. ✔
● **Psychotherapist** Mr B McLoughlin Q: MA, UKCP (Reg). M: FPC.
B Yrs. Est.: 18 (Ref:HM13559)

## MCLOUGHLIN, CLAIRE

**Claire McLoughlin**, 3 Martins Lane, Wallasey, **Merseyside**, CH44 1BA, ENG.
(T) 01516 911463 (F) 01516 305565
Speciality: Biomechanics, Chiropody, Nail Surgery, Orthotics, Podiatry. ✔
● **Chiropodist (Podiatrist)**
Miss C McLoughlin Q: DPodM, M.S.C.P, S.R.Ch.
M Yrs. Est.: 14 (Ref:HM13560)

## MCLOUGHLIN, F

**F Mcloughlin**, 68 Church St, Portadown, Craigavon, **County Armagh**, BT62 3EU, NIR.
(T) 028 3833 2612
Speciality: Chiropodists (Podiatrists).
● **Owner** Mr F McLoughlin
S (Ref:HM13561)

## MCLUCKIE, ALEXANDER

**Alexander McLuckie**, Surgery Premier House, 15 Wheeler Gate, Nottingham, **Nottinghamshire**, NG1 2AQ, ENG.
(T) 01159 484525
Speciality: Chiropodists (Podiatrists).
S (Ref:HM13562)

## MCMAHON MOUGHTIN CONSULTANCY

**McMahon Moughtin Consultancy**, 1 Yeomans Court, Clumber Rd West, The Park, Nottingham, **Nottinghamshire**, NG7 1EU, ENG.
(T) 01159 472933
Speciality: Psychotherapy.
B (Ref:HM13563)

## MCMAHON, GLADEANA

**Gladeana McMahon**, 11 Streetfield Mews, London, **London (Greater)**, SE3 0ER, ENG.
(T) 020 8852 4854
Speciality: Psychotherapy.
B (Ref:HM13564)

## MCMAHON, K

**K McMahon**, 22 Belfast Rd, Lisburn, **County Antrim**, BT27 4AS, NIR.
(T) 028 9266 6837
Speciality: Chiropodists (Podiatrists).
● **Owner** Mr K McMahon
S (Ref:HM13565)

## MCMAHON, ROSEMARY

**Rosemary McMahon**, 16 High View Avenue, Grays, **Essex**, RM17 6RU, ENG.
(T) 01375 380473
Speciality: Homeopathy.
● **Owner** Mrs R McMahon
M (Ref:HM13566)

## MCMAHON, STEPHANIE

**Stephanie McMahon**, 160 St Albans Rd, Sandridge, St. Albans, **Hertfordshire**, AL4 9LP, ENG.
(T) 01727 842393
Speciality: Osteopathy.
P S T (Ref:HM13567)

## MCMANUS, E

**E McManus**, Chiropody Surgery, 158 Putney High St, London, **London (Greater)**, SW15 1RT, ENG.
(T) 020 8788 0820
Speciality: Chiropodists (Podiatrists).
S (Ref:HM13568)

## MCMANUS, EILEEN

**Eileen McManus**, 29 Sangers Drive, Horley, **Surrey**, RH6 8AH, ENG.
(T) 01293 782527
Speciality: Acupuncture.
● **Owner** Miss E McManus
O (Ref:HM13569)

## MCMANUS, MARIE

**Marie McManus**, 77 Station Rd, Kings Norton, Birmingham, **Midlands (West)**, B30 1DE, ENG.
(T) 01214 597844
Speciality: Osteopathy.
P S T (Ref:HM13570)

## MCMANUS, RAYMOND

**Raymond McManus**, 124 Westfield Rd, Kings Heath, Birmingham, **Midlands (West)**, B14 7SU, ENG.
(T) 01216 243410
Speciality: Hypnosis.
B (Ref:HM13571)

## MCMILLAN ANIMAL HEALTH

**McMillan Animal Health**, 29 Salmon Leap, Chester, **Cheshire**, CH4 7JJ, ENG.
(T) 01244 629090 (F) 01244 629090
Speciality: Homeopathy.
● **Owner** Mr J McMillan
M (Ref:HM13572)

## MCMILLAN, D

**D McMillan Mrs**, Pendee, Aingers Green, Weeley Rd, Great Bentley, Colchester, **Essex**, CO7 8NE, ENG.
(T) 01206 251773
Speciality: Chiropodists (Podiatrists).
● **Owner** Mrs D McMillan
S (Ref:HM13573)

## MCMULLAN, J

**J McMullan**, 8c Brampton Rd, Huntingdon, **Cambridgeshire**, PE18 6BQ, ENG.
(T) 01480 453592
Speciality: Chiropodists (Podiatrists).
● **Owner** Mr J McMullan
S (Ref:HM13574)

## MCMULLAN, MARITA

**Marita McMullan**, 7 Royal Lodge Rd, **County Antrim**, BT8 7UL, NIR.
(T) 028 9040 2042
Speciality: Reflexology.
S T (Ref:HM13575)

## MCNAMARA, MARY

**McNamara Mary V R G N Dip P H Ed**, The Bungalow Turnpike Rd, Ennis, **County Clare**, IRE.
(T) 06568 41280
Speciality: Acupuncture.
O (Ref:HM13576)

## MCNAMEE, BRIAN

**McNamee Brian M Sc C A S**, 31 Taney Ave, Dublin, **County Dublin**, IRE.
(T) 01296 0773
Speciality: Complementary Medicines & Therapy.
M (Ref:HM13577)

## MCNAMEE, THERESE

**Therese McNamee ADHP MICHP**, Templeogue, **County Dublin**, IRE.
(T) 01494 5835
(W) www.hypnosiseire.com
Speciality: Complementary Medicines & Therapy.
M (Ref:HM13578)

## MCNAUGHTON PHYSIO CLINIC

**McNaughton Physiotherapy Clinic**, Doctors Surgery, 14 Moray Pl, Edinburgh, **Edinburgh (City of)**, EH3 6DT, SCO.
(T) 01312 255320
Speciality: Physiotherapy.
P S T (Ref:HM13579)

## MCNAUGHTON PHYSIO CLINIC

**McNaughton Physiotherapy Clinic**, 81 Colinton Rd, Edinburgh, **Edinburgh (City of)**, EH10 5DF, SCO.
(T) 01313 375135
Speciality: Physiotherapy.
P S T (Ref:HM13580)



Key: B Mind-Body Medicine C Complementary Medicine H Self Help Treatment M Medicinal Therapy O Oriental Medicine P Postural Therapy S Manipulative Structural Therapy T Touch Therapy

**MCNEIL, D A**
**D A McNeil**, 56 Queens Avenue, London, **London (Greater)**, N10 3NU, ENG.
(T) 020 8442 0582
Speciality: Psychotherapy.
B (Ref:HM13581)

**MCNEIL, R D**
**R D McNeil**, 56 Queens Avenue, London, **London (Greater)**, N10 3NU, ENG.
(T) 020 8442 0582
Speciality: Homeopathy.
M (Ref:HM13582)

**MCNEILL, MARGARET**
**Margaret McNeill**, Steth's, 113 High St, Coleshill, Birmingham, **Midlands (West)**, B46 3BP, ENG.
(T) 01675 465726
Speciality: Acupuncture.
● **Owner** Ms M McNeill
O (Ref:HM13583)

**MCNEILL, MARGARET**
**Margaret McNeill**, 4 The Crescent, Solihull, **Midlands (West)**, B91 1JP, ENG.
(T) 01675 465726
Speciality: Acupuncture.
● **Owner** Mrs M McNeill
O (Ref:HM13584)

**MCNICHOL CHIROPODY CLINIC**
**McNichol Chiropody Clinic**, 289A High St, West Bromwich, **Midlands (West)**, B70 8ND, ENG.
(T) 01215 532251
Speciality: Chiropodists (Podiatrists).
S (Ref:HM13585)

**MCNICHOLAS, JOAN**
**McNicholas Joan**, Westport, **County Mayo**, IRE.
(T) 09827 127
Speciality: Complementary Medicines & Therapy.
M (Ref:HM13586)

**MCNICOL, KIRSTY**
**Kirsty McNicol**, Gazelda Industrial Estate, 212 Lower High St, Watford, **Hertfordshire**, WD1 2JL, ENG.
(T) 01923 460089
Speciality: Reflexology.
● **Owner** Miss K McNichol
S T (Ref:HM13587)

**MCNULTY, RAAKHEE**
**Raakhee McNulty**, 46 Manor Drive, **Leicestershire**, LE4 1BL, ENG.
(T) 01162 367759
Speciality: Reflexology.
S T (Ref:HM13588)

**MCPHERSON, MALCOLM**
**Malcolm McPherson**, 15-17 Belmont St, Aberdeen, **Aberdeenshire**, AB10 1JR, SCO.
(T) 01224 620495
Speciality: Psychotherapy.
● **Owner** Mr M McPherson
B (Ref:HM13589)

**MCPHERSON, PATRICIA**
**Patricia McPherson**, 5 Kilvey Trce, St. Thomas, Swansea, SA1 8BA, WAL.
(T) 01792 421225
Speciality: Complementary Medicines & Therapy.
● **Owner** Ms P McPherson
C M (Ref:HM13590)

**MCPHIE, SUSAN**
**Susan McPhie**, 26 Fore St, Okehampton, **Devon**, EX20 1HB, ENG.
(T) 01837 55398
Speciality: Complementary Medicines & Therapy.
● **Manager** Mrs B King
C M (Ref:HM13591)

**MCQUEEN, DAVID**
**David McQueen**, 6 Gainburn Court, Cumbernauld, Glasgow, **Glasgow (City of)**, G67 4QG, SCO.
(T) 01236 612141
Speciality: Hypnosis.
B (Ref:HM13592)

**MCQUILLAN, D**
**D McQuillan**, 15 Windsor St, Bletchley, Milton Keynes, **Buckinghamshire**, MK2 2LN, ENG.
(T) 01908 372265
Speciality: Chiropodists (Podiatrists).
● **Partner** Mr R East
S (Ref:HM13593)

**MCQUILLAN, JANE**
**Jane McQuillan**, 31 Prince's St, Ulverston, **Cumbria**, LA12 7NQ, ENG.
(T) 01229 588404
Speciality: Psychotherapy.
B (Ref:HM13594)

**MCQUINN, S**
**S McQuinn**, 5a Buxton Old Rd, Disley, Stockport, **Cheshire**, SK12 2BB, ENG.
(T) 01663 764864 (F) 01663 763792
Speciality: Physiotherapy.
● **Owner** Mrs S McQuinn
P S T (Ref:HM13595)

**MCROBBIE, DAVINA**
**Davina McRobbie**, 161 Westbury Avenue, London, **London (Greater)**, N22 6RX, ENG.
(T) 020 8881 3479
Speciality: Chiropodists (Podiatrists).
● **Owner** Ms D McRobbie
S (Ref:HM13596)

**MCSHANE, M**
**M McShane**, 29 Sutton St, Durham, **County Durham**, DH1 4BW, ENG.
(T) 01913 848590
Speciality: Chiropodists (Podiatrists).
S (Ref:HM13597)

**MCSHANE, MCSWEENEY, FRANKLIN**
**McShane, McSweeney, Franklin**, 2 Stratton Pines, Bishopstown, **County Cork**, IRE.
(T) 021 4543 803
Speciality: Complementary Medicines & Therapy.
M (Ref:HM13598)

**MCTEAGUE, S**
**S McTeague**, 213 Sangley Rd, London, **London (Greater)**, SE6 2DY, ENG.
(T) 020 8698 6138
Speciality: Psychology.
B (Ref:HM13599)

**MCTIMONEY CHIROPRACTIC**
**McTimoney Chiropractic**, Unit 2 Home Buildings, Great Barrington, Burford, **Oxfordshire**, OX18 4UR, ENG.
(T) 01451 844684
Speciality: Chiropractic.
● **Owner** Ms L Miller
P S T (Ref:HM13600)

**MCTIMONEY CHIROPRACTIC**
**McTimoney Chiropractic**, The Cl, Chipping Warden, Banbury, **Oxfordshire**, OX17 1LP, ENG.
(T) 01295 660291
Speciality: Chiropractic.
● **Owner** Mrs P Platt
P S T (Ref:HM13601)

**MCTIMONEY CHIROPRACTIC**
**McTimoney Chiropractic**, Hillcrest, Pontymason Lane, Rogerstone, Newport, NP10 9GH, WAL.
(T) 01633 891969
Speciality: Chiropractic.
● **Owner** Mrs E Collins
P S T (Ref:HM13602)

**MCTIMONEY CHIROPRACTIC**
**McTimoney Chiropractic**, 48 Village Rd, London, **London (Greater)**, N3 1TJ, ENG.
(T) 020 8371 0522
Speciality: Chiropractors.
● **Owner** Mrs J Griffiths
P S T (Ref:HM13603)

**MCTIMONEY CHIROPRACTIC CLINIC**
**McTimoney Chiropractic Clinic**, Holly Tree Cottage, Forebridge, Little Bedwyn, Marlborough, **Wiltshire**, SN8 3JS, ENG.
(T) 01672 870391
Speciality: Chiropractic. ✓
● **Chiropractor** Ms M Woollhead Q: AMCA, DC, GCC (Reg), MMCA. M: GCC, MCA.
● **Chiropractor** Mrs P Allinson Q: DC, MMCA, Reg.Chiropractor. M: GCC, MCA.
S Yrs. Est.: 11 (Ref:HM13604)

**MCTIMONEY CHIROPRACTIC CLINIC**
**McTimoney Chiropractic Clinic**, 198 Stirling Rd, Larbert, **Falkirk**, FK5 4SQ, SCO.
(T) 01324 557628
Speciality: Chiropractors.
● **Practice Manager** Mrs C Ellis
P S T (Ref:HM13605)

**MCTIMONEY CHIROPRACTIC CLINIC**
**McTimoney Chiropractic Clinic**, 8 Taylor Rd, Norwich, **Norfolk**, NR5 8LY, ENG.
(T) 01603 455240
Speciality: Chiropractic.
● **Owner** Mr M Baron
P S T (Ref:HM13606)

**MCTIMONEY CHIROPRACTIC CLINIC**
**McTimoney Chiropractic Clinic**, Unit 1&2 Earl Soham Business Centre, Earl Soham, Woodbridge, **Suffolk**, IP13 7SA, ENG.
(T) 01728 685960
Speciality: Chiropractic, Manipulation, Massage (Therapeutic). ✓
● **Chiropractor** Ms C Keeble Q: C of C, DC, RN. M: MCA.
● **Chiropractor** Ms R Cowley Q: C of C, DC. M: MCA.
S Yrs. Est.: 5 (Ref:HM13607)

**MCTIMONEY CHIROPRACTIC CLINIC**
**McTimoney Chiropractic Clinic**, 32 Hulham Rd, Exmouth, **Devon**, EX8 3HS, ENG.
(T) 01395 269996
Speciality: Chiropractic.
● **Owner** Ms A Strickland
P S T (Ref:HM13608)

**MCTIMONEY CHIROPRACTIC CLINIC**
**McTimoney Chiropractic Clinic**, 22 Viewforth, Edinburgh, **Edinburgh (City of)**, EH10 4JG, SCO.
(T) 01312 289215
Speciality: Chiropractors.
● **Owner** Mrs C Ellis
P S T (Ref:HM13609)

**MCTIMONEY CHIROPRACTIC CLINIC**
**McTimoney Chiropractic Clinic**, 6 Woodburn Avenue, Clarkston, Glasgow, **Glasgow (City of)**, G76 7TZ, SCO.
(T) 01416 441111
Speciality: Chiropractors.
● **Practice Manager** Mr A Dalziel
P S T (Ref:HM13610)

**MCTIMONEY CHIROPRACTIC CLINIC**
**McTimoney Chiropractic Clinic**, 432 Shields Rd, Pollokshields, Glasgow, **Glasgow (City of)**, G41 1NS, SCO.
(T) 01414 293164 (F) 01414 293164
Speciality: Chiropractic, Cranio-Sacral Therapy, Specialising in Paediatrics. ✓
● **Chiropractor** Ms T Naddell Q: DC.
S Yrs. Est.: 10 (Ref:HM13611)

**MCTIMONEY CHIROPRACTIC CLINIC**
**McTimoney Chiropractic Clinic**, Davenport House, Bowers Way, Harpenden, **Hertfordshire**, AL5 4HX, ENG.
(T) 01582 713464
(E) liserose@compuserve.com
Speciality: Aromatherapy, Chiropractic, Reflexology, On-Site Massage(Seated Massage). ✓
● **Chiropractor** Ms L Rose Q: DC, MMCA. M: MCA.
S Yrs. Est.: 20 (Ref:HM13612)

**MCTIMONEY CHIROPRACTIC CLINIC**
**McTimoney Chiropractic Clinic (The)**, 17 Alexandra Rd, Malvern, **Worcestershire**, WR14 1HA, ENG.
(T) 01684 567480
Speciality: Chiropractors.
P S T (Ref:HM13613)


Key continued: Yrs.Est: Years Established Q: Qualifications M: Professional Membership ✓ Indemnity Insurance Accept Credit Cards

**MCTIMONEY CHIROPRACTIC COLLEGE**

**McTimoney Chiropractic College**, The Clock House, Abingdon, **Oxfordshire**, OX14 5SH, ENG.
(T) 01235 523336
Speciality: Chiropractic, Complementary Therapy, McTimoney Chiropractic.
P S T (Ref:HM13614)

**MCTIMONEY CHIROPRACTICE**

**McTimoney Chiropractice**, Hillbury, Old Salisbury Rd, Abbotts Ann, Andover, **Hampshire**, SP11 7NH, ENG.
(T) 01264 710811
Speciality: Chiropractors.
● **Owner** Miss L Morley
P S T (Ref:HM13615)

**MCTIMONEY CHIROPRACTICE**

**McTimoney Chiropractice**, 18a Junction Rd, Andover, **Hampshire**, SP10 3QU, ENG.
(T) 01264 353322
Speciality: Chiropractic.
P S T (Ref:HM13616)

**MCTIMONEY CHIROPRACTOR**

**McTimoney Chiropractor**, Gardeners Cottage, Alscot Pk, Atherstone On Stour, Stratford-Upon-Avon, **Warwickshire**, CV37 8BL, ENG.
(T) 01789 450052
Speciality: Chiropractic.
● **Owner** Mrs C Dickin
P S T (Ref:HM13617)

**MCTIMONEY DIRECTORY**

**McTimoney Directory**, Maypole Oak, Monmouth, **Monmouthshire**, NP25 5QH, WAL.
(T) 01600 713527
Speciality: Chiropractic, McTimoney Chiropractic.
P S T (Ref:HM13618)

**MCTIMONEY, R**

**R McTimoney**, 18 Sandown Rd, Sandown, **Isle of Wight**, PO36 9JP, ENG.
(T) 01983 403518
Speciality: Chiropractic.
● **Owner** Mr R McTimoney
P S T (Ref:HM13619)

**MCVEIGH, R G**

**R G McVeigh**, 11 Spinney Avenue, Countesthorpe, Leicester, **Leicestershire**, LE8 5RJ, ENG.
(T) 01162 771754
Speciality: Chiropodists (Podiatrists).
● **Owner** Mr R McVeigh
S (Ref:HM13620)

**MCVEY, JOHN**

**John McVey**, 537 Welford Rd, Leicester, **Leicestershire**, LE2 6FN, ENG.
(T) 01162 705590 (F) 01162 705590
Speciality: Physiotherapy.
P S T (Ref:HM13621)

**MCVEY, S A**

**S A McVey**, 21 South St, Greenock, **Inverclyde**, PA16 8UA, SCO.
(T) 01475 888696
Speciality: Chiropodists (Podiatrists).
S (Ref:HM13622)

**MCVITTIE, D**

**D McVittie**, 11 Buckstone Lea, Edinburgh, **Edinburgh (City of)**, EH10 6XE, SCO.
(T) 01314 454593
(E) mcvittie@mcvittie.worldonline.co.uk
Speciality: Reflexology.
● **Reflexologist** Ms D McVittie Q: BA (Hons), MBRA. M: BRA.
T Yrs. Est.: 4 (Ref:HM13623)

**MCWATT, LIZ**

**Liz McWatt**, 18 West St, Kendal, **Cumbria**, LA9 5QL, ENG.
(T) 01539 728188
(E) liz.mcwatt@tinyworld.co.uk
Speciality: Aromatherapy, Bach Remedies, Complementary Therapy, Floral Essence Therapy, Holistic Healing, Massage (Therapeutic), Meditation, Nutritional Therapy. ✓
● **Nutritional Therapist/Aromatherapist** Ms L McWatt Q: Dip.Arom, Dip.Nut.Med, RGN. M: BANT, IFA.
B C Yrs. Est.: 4 (Ref:HM13624)

**MCWHITER, J**

**J McWhiter**, All Hallows House, Idol Lane, London, **London (Greater)**, EC3R 5DD, ENG.
(T) 020 7283 8908
Speciality: Chiropractors.
P S T (Ref:HM13625)

**MEAD, BRUCE**

**Bruce Mead**, Poplar Buildings, Woodhorn Rd, Ashington, **Northumberland**, NE63 0BA, ENG.
(T) 01670 813324
Speciality: Chiropody. ✓
● **Chiropodist** Mr B Mead Q: MBChA. M: S.C.P.
S Yrs. Est.: 20 (Ref:HM13626)

**MEAD, KATHY**

**Kathy Mead**, 19 Woodland Way, Stevenage, **Hertfordshire**, SG2 8BU, ENG.
(T) 01438 747648
Speciality: Reflexology.
● **Owner** Ms K Mead
S T (Ref:HM13627)

**MEADE, SADIE**

**Meade Sadie**, 19 The Castlelands Castleside, Rathfarnham, **County Dublin**, IRE.
(T) 01492 4278
(W) www.cablenet.ie/reflexology
Speciality: Reflexology.
S T (Ref:HM13628)

**MEADEN, C A**

**C A Meaden**, 9 Bloomfield Rd, Maidenhead, **Berkshire**, SL6 4NS, ENG.
(T) 01628 629601
Speciality: Physiotherapy.
● **Owner** Mrs C Meaden
P S T (Ref:HM13629)

**MEADOWS**

**Meadows of Canterbury Ltd**, Unit 2, Stour Valley Business Park, Ashford Rd, Canterbury, **Kent**, CT4 7HF, ENG.
(T) 01227 731489
Speciality: Aromatherapy.
● **Sales/Promotions** Ms S Devey Q: CIBTAC, IHBC.
M (Ref:HM13630)

**MEADOWS**

**Meadows**, 50 Palace St, Canterbury, **Kent**, CT1 2DY, ENG.
(T) 01227 784844
Speciality: Aromatherapy.
M O (Ref:HM13631)

**MEADOWS, ERIC**

**Eric Meadows**, 27 Rodmell Avenue, Saltdean, Brighton, **Sussex (East)**, BN2 8LT, ENG.
(T) 01273 305718
Speciality: Reflexology.
S T (Ref:HM13632)

**MEADOWS, LINDSEY**

**Lindsey Meadows**, 11 Hurst Park, Penwortham, Preston, **Lancashire**, PR1 9BD, ENG.
(T) 01772 746163
Speciality: Chiropodists (Podiatrists).
● **Owner** Miss L Meadows
S (Ref:HM13633)

**MEADOWSWEET**

**Meadowsweet**, 18 Wellington Sq, Hastings, **Sussex (East)**, TN34 1PB, ENG.
(T) 01424 722466 (F) 01424 722466
Speciality: Massage (Therapeutic), Physio Massage (Using Aromatherapy Oils). ✓
● **Owner/Sports Therapist** Mrs A Karhunen M: IIHFT.
C Yrs. Est.: 2 (Ref:HM13634)

**MEADS, A E**

**A E Meads**, 2 St Philips Rd, Leicester, **Leicestershire**, LE5 5TQ, ENG.
(T) 01162 738256
Speciality: Physiotherapy.
● **Owner** Mr J Thomas
P S T (Ref:HM13635)

**MEADWAY, SUE**

**Sue Meadway**, 45 Meadowridge, Hatch Warren, Basingstoke, **Hampshire**, RG22 4QH, ENG.
(T) 01256 329940
Speciality: Chiropodists (Podiatrists).
S (Ref:HM13636)

**MEAKIN, D W**

**D W Meakin**, 175 Bromsgrove Rd, Redditch, **Worcestershire**, B97 4SQ, ENG.
(T) 01527 69328
Speciality: Naturopathy, Osteopathy. ✓
● **Owner** Mr D Meakin Q: DO, ND. M: BNA, BOA.
S Yrs. Est.: 12 (Ref:HM13637)

**MEAKIN, JACKIE**

**Jackie Meakin**, 24 High St, Dronfield, **Derbyshire**, S18 1PY, ENG.
(T) 01246 411067
Speciality: Herbalists.
M (Ref:HM13638)

**MEAKIN, JACKIE**

**Jackie Meakin**, Dog Hole Farm, 126 Holymoor Rd, Holymoorside, Chesterfield, **Derbyshire**, S42 7DU, ENG.
(T) 01246 567202
Speciality: Herbal Medicine.
M (Ref:HM13639)

**MEAKIN, R J**

**R J Meakin**, The Old Bakery, High St, Wadhurst, **Sussex (East)**, TN5 6AA, ENG.
(T) 01892 782674
Speciality: Chiropodists (Podiatrists).
S (Ref:HM13640)

**MEANEY-PRICE, SHELIA**

**Shelia Meaney-Price**, Rutland House Clinic, George St, Teignmouth, **Devon**, TQ14 8AG, ENG.
(T) 01626 774665
Speciality: Chiropodists (Podiatrists).
S (Ref:HM13641)

**MEARE, RACHAEL**

**Rachael Meare**, Sunrise, Stembridge, Martock, **Somerset**, TA12 6BW, ENG.
(T) 01460 242669
Speciality: Complementary Medicines & Therapy.
● **Owner** Mrs R Meare
C M (Ref:HM13642)

**MECHEN, M**

**M Mechen**, 546 Lytham Rd, Blackpool, **Lancashire**, FY4 1RE, ENG.
(T) 01253 345210
Speciality: Aromatherapy.
● **Owner** Mrs M Mechen
M O (Ref:HM13643)

**MEDAYD PHYSIOTHERAPY**

**Medayd Physiotherapy**, 7 Dawley Rd, Arleston, Telford, **Shropshire**, TF1 2HW, ENG.
(T) 01952 247894
Speciality: Physiotherapy. ✓
● **Owner/Physiotherapist** Mrs A Day Q: Grad Dip Phys, MCSP, SRP. M: CSP.
S (Ref:HM13644)

**MEDAYD PHYSIOTHERAPY**

**Medayd Physiotherapy**, 52 Stafford St, Market Drayton, **Shropshire**, TF9 1JB, ENG.
(T) 01630 652304
Speciality: Physiotherapy. ✓
● **Physiotherapist** Ms L Bickerstaffe Q: Grad Dip Phys, MCSP, SRP. M: CSP.
● **Physiotherapist** Ms E Needs Q: Grad Dip Phys, MCSP, SRP. M: CSP.
● **Physiotherapist** Mr M Watton Q: MCSP, SRP. M: CSP.
● **Owner/Physiotherapist** Mrs A Day Q: Grad Dip Phys, MCSP, SRP. M: CSP.
S Yrs. Est.: 20 (Ref:HM13645)

**MEDDINGS, GLORIA**

**Gloria Meddings**, Keston, North Greenlands, Pennington, Lymington, **Hampshire**, SO41 8BB, ENG.
(T) 01590 677546
Speciality: Chiropodists (Podiatrists).
● **Owner** Ms G Meddings
S (Ref:HM13646)

**MEDELY CLINIC**

**Medely Clinic**, 114 Long Lane, Grays, **Essex**,

RM16 2PP, ENG.
(T) 01375 374982 (F) 01375 374982
(E) medely-clinic@yahoo.co.uk
Speciality: Aromatherapy, Complementary Therapy, Indian Head Massage, Massage (Therapeutic), Reflexology, Sports Injuries. ✓
● **Owner** Mr M Medlock Q: AOC, BA (Hons), ISPA, ITEC, MIFA. M: AOC, IFA, ISPA.
C T Yrs. Est.: 4 (Ref:HM13647)

## MEDHURST, REBECCA
**Rebecca Medhurst**, 9 Chesterton Rd, Ladbrook Gr, London, **London (Greater)**, W10 5LY, ENG.
(T) 020 8964 8693
Speciality: Reflexology.
C S T (Ref:HM13648)

## MEDICAL ACUPUNCTURE CENTRE
**Medical Acupuncture Centre**, 12 Barns St, Ayr, **Ayrshire (South)**, KA7 1XA, SCO.
(T) 01292 260024
Speciality: Acupuncture.
● **Manageress** Mrs A Smith
O (Ref:HM13649)

## MEDICAL ALTERNATIVES
**Medical Alternatives**, 1 Marlborough Studio, 12 Finchley Rd, St John's Wood, London, **London (Greater)**, NW8 6EB, ENG.
(T) 020 7586 6543
Speciality: Alexander Technique.
● **Therapist** Ms K Borang
P S (Ref:HM13650)

## MEDICAL HERBALIST
**Medical Herbalist**, 59 Valley Rise, Dersingham, King's Lynn, **Norfolk**, PE31 6PT, ENG.
(T) 01485 540332
Speciality: Herbal Medicine.
● **Owner** Ms W Jilly
M (Ref:HM13651)

## MEDICAL HERBALIST
**Medical Herbalist**, 76 Southgrove Rd, Sheffield, **Yorkshire (South)**, S10 2NQ, ENG.
(T) 01142 669293
Speciality: Herbal Medicine. ✓
● **Owner/Medical Herbalist**
Mrs V Miles Q: Dip.Herb.Med. M: NIMH.
C Yrs. Est.: 18 (Ref:HM13652)

## MEDICAL HYPNOTHERAPY CLINIC
**Medical Hypnotherapy Clinic (The)**, Longdene House, Doric Drive, Tadworth, **Surrey**, KT20 6HH, ENG.
(T) 01737 351833
Speciality: Hypnosis, Brief Strategic Therapy, Clinical Hypnosis. ✓
● **Medical Director** Dr R Dupe
(T) 020 7351 8321 Q: BSc, MA, PhD.
B Yrs. Est.: 10 (Ref:HM13653)

## MEDICAL SCIENCES TECH CORP
**Medical Sciences Technology Corporation**, The Integrated Medical Centre, Vita Clinics, 97 Harley St, London, **London (Greater)**, W1G 6AG, ENG.
(T) 020 7486 1123
(W) www.complementary-healthcare.co.uk/vitaclinics
Speciality: Complementary Therapy, Herbal Medicine, Holistic Healing, Nutritional Therapy, Phytotherapy, Stress Therapy, Vitamin Therapy, Chelation and Auto-Haemotherapy.
C (Ref:HM13654)

## MEDICAL SCIENCES TECHNOLOGY
**Medical Sciences Technology U K Ltd**, Bedford House, 81 Bedford Pl, Southampton, **Hampshire**, SO15 2DF, ENG.
(T) 023 8022 5722 (F) 023 8022 5725
Speciality: Complementary Medicines & Therapy.
● **Owner** Ms C Sheheh
M (Ref:HM13655)

## MEDI-CALL ASSISTANCE
**Medi-Call Assistance**, 183-185 Church Rd, Hove, **Sussex (East)**, BN3 2AB, ENG.
(T) 01273 321976 (F) 01273 731261
Speciality: Complementary Medicines & Therapy.
● **Managing Director** Mr F White
M (Ref:HM13656)

## MEDICINE
**Medicine**, 29 Old Bakehouse Yard, Morpeth, **Northumberland**, NE61 1AT, ENG.
(T) 01670 511084
Speciality: Complementary Medicines & Therapy.
C M (Ref:HM13657)

## MEDICINE GARDEN
**Medicine Garden (The)**, 46a High St, Emsworth, **Hampshire**, PO10 7AW, ENG.
(T) 01243 378555
Speciality: Complementary Medicines & Therapy.
● **Manager** Mrs J Smith
C M (Ref:HM13658)

## MEDICINE ORGANISATION
**Medicine Organisation**, Cunningham Fahy Carol Lic. Acu. Tcm Menlo Pk, Menlo, **County Galway**, IRE.
(T) 09176 1487
Speciality: Hypnotherapy.
B (Ref:HM13659)

## MEDICINE ORGANISATION
**Medicine Organisation**, Castlebar Co, **County Mayo**, IRE.
(T) 09422 940
Speciality: Complementary Medicines & Therapy.
M (Ref:HM13660)

## MEDICINE ORGANISATION
**Medicine Organisation**, Barna Co, **County Galway**, IRE.
(T) 09159 1894
Speciality: Acupuncture.
O (Ref:HM13661)

## MEDICINE ORGANISATION
**Medicine Organisation**, 33 Shantalla Rd, **County Galway**, IRE.
(T) 09152 2631
Speciality: Osteopathy.
P S T (Ref:HM13662)

## MEDICINE ORGANISATION
**Medicine Organisation**, Claregalway Co, **County Galway**, IRE.
(T) 09179 9124
Speciality: Acupuncture.
O (Ref:HM13663)

## MEDICINE ORGANISATION
**Medicine Organisation**, Galway Rd, **County Roscommon**, IRE.
(T) 09032 6023
Speciality: Reflexology.
S T (Ref:HM13664)

## MEDICINE ORGANISATION
**Medicine Organisation**, Co, **County Galway**, IRE.
(T) 09159 1937
Speciality: Acupuncture.
O (Ref:HM13665)

## MEDICINE ORGANISATION
**Medicine Organisation**, Lr Abbeygate St, **County Galway**, IRE.
(T) 09156 3329
Speciality: Acupuncture.
O (Ref:HM13666)

## MEDICINE ORGANISATION
**Medicine Organisation**, Murrisk Westport Co, **County Mayo**, IRE.
(T) 09864 829
Speciality: Acupuncture.
O (Ref:HM13667)

## MEDICINE SHOP
**Medicine Shop Ltd (The)**, 48B London Rd, Alderley Edge, **Cheshire**, SK9 7DZ, ENG.
(T) 01625 582900
Speciality: Complementary Medicines & Therapy.
C M (Ref:HM13668)

## MEDICINE WHEEL
**Medicine Wheel (The)**, 216 Limestone Rd, Belfast, **County Antrim**, BT15 3AP, NIR.
(T) 028 9075 1577
Speciality: Complementary Medicines & Therapy.
● **Partner** Mrs D Burke
C M (Ref:HM13669)

## MEDICINE WHEEL
**Medicine Wheel (The)**, 42A Bramhall Lane South, Bramhall, Stockport, **Cheshire**, SK7 1AH, ENG.
(T) 01614 390777 (F) 01614 390777
Speciality: Healing Therapy, Holistic Healing.
✓ CREDIT
● **Pharmacist** Mr H Minton
C Yrs. Est.: 1 (Ref:HM13670)

## MEDICINE, JOE
**Medicine Joe Ltd**, 33 Butterfield Orchard, Dublin, **County Dublin**, IRE.
(T) 01493 1787
Speciality: Complementary Medicines & Therapy.
M (Ref:HM13671)

## MEDINATURALS
**Medinaturals**, 37 Limpsfield Rd, South Croydon, **Surrey**, CR2 9LA, ENG.
(T) 020 8657 0401 (F) 020 8657 2203
Speciality: Complementary Medicines & Therapy.
● **Partner** Mr D Patel
C M (Ref:HM13672)

## MEDITATION
**Meditation**, Wellington Court, 53 Chivalry Rd, London, **London (Greater)**, SW11 1HX, ENG.
(T) 020 7350 2676
Speciality: Complementary Medicines & Therapy.
● **Owner** Mr P Sharda
M (Ref:HM13673)

## MEDWAY ACUPUNCTURE CLINIC
**Medway Acupuncture Clinic**, 28 Watling St, Gillingham, **Kent**, ME7 2YH, ENG.
(T) 01634 574432
Speciality: Acupuncture.
O (Ref:HM13674)

## MEDWAY ALTERNATIVE HEALTH CTRE
**Medway Alternative Health Centre**, 16 Kingswood Rd, Gillingham, **Kent**, ME7 1DZ, ENG.
(T) 01634 854823
Speciality: Complementary Medicines & Therapy.
● **Owner** Mrs E McShane
C M (Ref:HM13675)

## MEDWAY CHIROPRACTIC CLINIC
**Medway Chiropractic Clinic**, 168 Frindsbury Hill, Rochester, **Kent**, ME2 4JR, ENG.
(T) 01634 723878
Speciality: Chiropractors.
P S T (Ref:HM13676)

## MEDWAY OSTEOPATHIC CLINIC
**Medway Osteopathic Clinic**, 36 City Way, Rochester, **Kent**, ME1 2AB, ENG.
(T) 01634 814700
Speciality: Osteopathy.
P S T (Ref:HM13677)

## MEEHAN, ANNE
**Meehan Anne**, 54 Ashbury Lawn, Ballinode, **County Sligo**, IRE.
(T) 07171 624
Speciality: Counselling.
B H (Ref:HM13678)

## MEEHAN, SIOBHAN
**Meehan Siobhan**, The Acupuncture Clinic Church St, Athlone, **County Westmeath**, IRE.
(T) 09023 7454
Speciality: Acupuncture.
O (Ref:HM13679)

## MEEK, LISA
**Lisa Meek**, 1 Westbrook Cl, Barnet, **Hertfordshire**, EN4 9AU, ENG.
(T) 020 8441 9605
Speciality: Chiropractic.
P S T (Ref:HM13680)

## MEEK, LISA
**Lisa Meek**, 52 Stoke Newington Church St,




Key continued: Yrs.Est: Years Established Q: Qualifications M: Professional Membership ✓ Indemnity Insurance CREDIT Accept Credit Cards

London, **London (Greater)**, N16 0NB, ENG.
(T) 020 7241 5033 (F) 020 7502 1182
Speciality: Chiropodists (Podiatrists).
● **Senior Partner** Mrs J Sharidan
S (**Ref:**HM13681)

## MEEK, ROSLYN

**Roslyn Meek**, 47 Clydesdale St, Hamilton, **Lanarkshire (South)**, ML3 0DD, SCO.
(T) 01698 891262
Speciality: Osteopathy.
P S T (**Ref:**HM13682)

## MEEKS, FIONA

**Fiona Meeks**, 73 Richmond St, East Sheen, Barnes, Richmond, **Surrey**, SW14 8JY, ENG.
(T) 020 8876 3010
Speciality: Bowen Therapy. ✓
● **Bowen Therapist** Fiona Meeks Q: ECBS, MAR, RGN. M: BTER.
C Yrs. Est.: 4 (**Ref:**HM13683)

## MEENA'S

**Meena's**, 1 Chaucer Avenue, Hayes, **London (Greater)**, UB4 0AP, ENG.
(T) 020 8561 0632
Speciality: Electrolysis.
● **Owner** Mrs M Malkani
T (**Ref:**HM13684)

## MEENEGHAN, TOM

**Tom Meeneghan**, The Practice, Charter House, 29A London Rd, Croydon, **Surrey**, CR0 2RE, ENG.
(T) 020 8868 87588
Speciality: Herbal Medicine, Homeopathy, Miasm Therapy, Stress Therapy. ✓
● **Homeopath** Mr T Meeneghan Q: RSHom. M: Soc.Hom.
B M Yrs. Est.: 12 (**Ref:**HM13685)

## MEERAN, M

**M Meeran**, 30-32 Lismore Rd, South Croydon, **Surrey**, CR2 7QA, ENG.
(T) 020 8680 0774
Speciality: Acupuncture.
O (**Ref:**HM13686)

## MEESON, LINDA

**Linda Meeson**, 27 North Rd, Dewsbury, **Yorkshire (West)**, WF13 3AB, ENG.
(T) 01924 464492
Speciality: Chiropodists (Podiatrists).
S (**Ref:**HM13687)

## MEFFAN, JOHN

**John Meffan**, 5 Church St, Ewell, Epsom, **Surrey**, KT17 2AU, ENG.
(T) 020 8393 3441
Speciality: Osteopathy.
● **Owner** Mr J Meffan
P S T (**Ref:**HM13688)

## MEFFAN, W

**W Meffan**, The Lynwood Physiotherapy Clinic, 18 Lynwood Drive, Worcester Park, **Surrey**, KT4 7AB, ENG.
(T) 020 8337 8970
Speciality: Physiotherapy.
P S T (**Ref:**HM13689)

## MEGAVITAMIN THERAPY

**Megavitamin Therapy**, The Institute For Optimum Nutrition, 5 Jerdan Pl, London, **London (Greater)**, SW6 1BE, ENG.
(T) 020 8877 9993
Speciality: Complementary Medicines & Therapy.
● **Manager** Dr Fourial
M (**Ref:**HM13690)

## MEGSON, BARBARA

**Barbara Megson**, 63 Bywell Rd, Dewsbury, **Yorkshire (West)**, WF12 7LH, ENG.
(T) 01924 458337
Speciality: Reflexology.
S T (**Ref:**HM13691)

## MEHMET, SUSAN

**Susan Mehmet**, 39 Pirbright Rd, London, **London (Greater)**, SW18 5ND, ENG.
(T) 020 8871 1482
Speciality: Reflexology.
● **Owner** Mrs S Mehmet
S T (**Ref:**HM13692)

## MEHREZ, ANITA

**Anita Mehrez**, 5 Brookfold Rd, Stockport, **Cheshire**, SK4 5EJ, ENG.
(T) 01614 327381
Speciality: Reflexology.
S T (**Ref:**HM13693)

## MEHRTENS, HELEN

**Helen Mehrtens**, Hart Leisure Centre, Hitches Lane, Fleet, **Hampshire**, GU13 8HZ, ENG.
(T) 01252 811773 (F) 01252 620414
Speciality: Physiotherapy.
● **Owner** Mrs H Mehrten
P S T (**Ref:**HM13694)

## MEHTA HYPNOTHERAPY

**Mehta Hypnotherapy**, 48 Troutbeck Rd, Gatley, Cheadle, **Cheshire**, SK8 4RR, ENG.
(T) 01614 289666 (F) 01612 051678
(E) hypnotherapy@manish-mehta.co.uk
(W) www.manish-mehta.co.uk
Speciality: Auto Suggestion, Complementary Therapy, Hypnosis, Hypnotherapy, Neuro-Linguistic Program.
● **Pharmacist/Hypnotherapist** Manish S Mehta Q: BSc (Hons), Dip.CAH, MBHReg, MNCH. M: GHR, RPS.
B Yrs. Est.: 8 (**Ref:**HM13695)

## MEHTA, P

**P Mehta**, Ravenscroft Medical Centre, 166-168 Golders Green Rd, London, **London (Greater)**, NW11 8BB, ENG.
(T) 020 8209 0922
Speciality: Chiropodists (Podiatrists).
S (**Ref:**HM13696)

## MEIGHAN, JUDITH

**Judith Meighan**, 120 Risborough Rd, Bedford, **Bedfordshire**, MK41 9QP, ENG.
(T) 01234 306158 (F) 01234 306158
Speciality: Reflexology.
● **Owner** Mrs J Meighan
S T (**Ref:**HM13697)

## MEIRA, A P

**A P Meira**, 14 Welham Rd, Retford, **Nottinghamshire**, DN22 6TN, ENG.
(T) 01777 860599
Speciality: Chiropodists (Podiatrists).
● **Owner** A Meira
S (**Ref:**HM13698)

## MEISE, LINDA

**Linda Meise**, 2 Howard Rd, Broadstairs, **Kent**, CT10 1QX, ENG.
(T) 01843 860895
Speciality: Hypnosis.
B (**Ref:**HM13699)

## MEISHA SKIN CARE

**Meisha Skin Care & Aromatherapy Supplies**, 5a Orrisdale Trce, Cheltenham, **Gloucestershire**, GL53 7HZ, ENG.
(T) 01242 222636
Speciality: Aromatherapy.
M O (**Ref:**HM13700)

## MEJLAENDER, KARIN

**Karin Mejlaender**, 137 Magdalen Rd, Oxford, **Oxfordshire**, OX4 1RJ, ENG.
(T) 01865 396939
Speciality: Acupuncture.
● **Owner** Mr M Franklin
O (**Ref:**HM13701)

## MELA CENTRE OF OSTEOPATHY

**Mela Centre of Osteopathy (The)**, 141-145 Trinity Avenue, Llandudno, **Conwy**, LL30 2UZ, WAL.
(T) 01492 872604 (F) 01492 872604
Speciality: Complementary Therapy, Electrotherapy, Manipulation, Massage (Therapeutic), Osteopathy, Postural Integration, Stretching. ✓
● **Osteomyologist/Osteopath** Ms M Bellenand Q: BA (Hons), DO, MAO. M: TAO.
S Yrs. Est.: 6 (**Ref:**HM13702)

## MELDGAARD, E

**E Meldgaard**, Beech House Surgery, Station Rd, Ilminster, **Somerset**, TA19 9BE, ENG.
(T) 01460 54888
Speciality: Chiropractors.
P S T (**Ref:**HM13703)

## MELHUISH, J I

**J I Melhuish**, 70 Canford Bottom, Colehill, Wimborne, **Dorset**, BH21 2HF, ENG.
(T) 01202 882166
Speciality: Chiropractic.
P S T (**Ref:**HM13704)

## MELHUISH, J I (DR)

**Dr J I Melhuish**, 13A Whitefield Rd, New Milton, **Hampshire**, BH25 6DE, ENG.
(T) 01425 620222
Speciality: Chiropractic, Reflexology, Remedial Massage, Orthopaedic. ✓
P Yrs. Est.: 10 (**Ref:**HM13705)

## MELIA, KAY

**Kay Melia**, 41 Park Avenue, Shelley, Huddersfield, **Yorkshire (West)**, HD8 8JY, ENG.
(T) 01484 606139
Speciality: Hypnosis.
● **Owner** Mrs K Melia
B (**Ref:**HM13706)

## MELIOR

**Melior Ltd**, 29 Marlowe Rd, Cambridge, **Cambridgeshire**, CB3 9JW, ENG.
(T) 01223 304777 (F) 01223 303870
Speciality: Complementary Medicines & Therapy.
● **Owner** Mr S Beyers
M (**Ref:**HM13707)

## MELLERICK, N D

**N D Mellerick**, Sayesbury Manor, Bell St, Sawbridgeworth, **Hertfordshire**, CM21 9AW, ENG.
(T) 01279 723790 (F) 01279 723817
Speciality: Osteopathy. ✓
● **Osteopath** Mr N Mellerick Q: DO. M: GOsC.
● **Osteopath** Mrs C Cousins Q: BSc (Hons). M: GOsC.
S Yrs. Est.: 24 (**Ref:**HM13708)

## MELLOR, J SIMON

**J Simon Mellor**, 6 Coleridge Drive, Cheadle, Stoke-On-Trent, **Staffordshire**, ST10 1XA, ENG.
(T) 01538 754835
Speciality: Biomechanics, Chiropody, Nail Surgery, Podiatry. ✓
● **Chiropodist (Podiatrist)** Mr J Mellor Q: BSc (Hons), DPodM, M.S.C.P, S.R.Ch.
C Yrs. Est.: 19 (**Ref:**HM13709)

## MELLOR, RACHAEL

**Rachael Mellor**, 8 Honeycomb Cl, Narborough, Leicester, **Leicestershire**, LE9 5PS, ENG.
(T) 01162 864435
Speciality: Chiropodists (Podiatrists).
S (**Ref:**HM13710)

## MELLOR, SARA L

**Sara L Mellor**, Wentworth House, West Sq, 1 London Rd, Maldon, **Essex**, CM9 6HD, ENG.
(T) 01621 856262
Speciality: Osteopathy.
P S T (**Ref:**HM13711)

## MELLOR, V

**V Mellor**, Roselands, 4 Middleton Rd, Manchester, **Manchester (Greater)**, M8 5DS, ENG.
(T) 01617 959111 (F) 01616 549591
Speciality: Psychology.
B (**Ref:**HM13712)

## MELLOR-FRITH BRIDGET

**Mellor-Frith Bridget**, 17 Meadows Lane, Darton, Barnsley, **Yorkshire (South)**, S75 5PF, ENG.
(T) 028 2538 2270
Speciality: Chiropodists (Podiatrists).
S (**Ref:**HM13713)

## MELLOW MOMENTS

**Mellow Moments**, 72 High St, Skipton, **Yorkshire (North)**, BD23 1JJ, ENG.
(T) 01756 790300
Speciality: Aromatherapy.
M O (**Ref:**HM13714)

**MELROSE, DAVID**

**David Melrose**, 1 Harley St, London, **London (Greater)**, W1N 1DA, ENG.
(T) 020 7436 1446
Speciality: Osteopathy.
P S T (Ref:HM13715)

**MELT/TEMPLE BAR NATURAL**

**MELT/Temple Bar Natural Healing Centre**, 2 Temple Lane, Dublin, **County Dublin**, IRE.
(T) 01679 8786
(E) info@2melt.com
(W) www.2melt.com
Speciality: Acupressure, Acupuncture, Aromatherapy, Art Therapy, Aura Therapy, Bach Remedies, Colour Therapy, Counselling, Cupping, Dance Movement Therapy, Healer, Healing Therapy, Herbal Medicine, Holistic Healing, Homeopathy, Indian Head Massage, Kinesiology, Macrobiotics, Massage (Therapeutic), Meditation, Moxibustion, Oriental Diagnosis, Pilates, Polarity Therapy, Reflexology, Reiki, Seichem, Shiatsu, Stress Therapy, T'ai-Chi Ch'uan, Vibrational Therapy, Vitamin Therapy, Yoga, Aura Soma, Tuina Massage, Thai Massage, Yoga, Astanga, Lyengar - Yoganidra. ✓ CREDIT
● **Therapist** Ms M Huges Q: Dip.Massage. M: ITEC.
● **Manager/Therapist** Ms M Magill Q: Lic.Ac.
● **Therapist** Mr S Hughes Q: Lic.Ac.
● **Therapist** Ms S Laurette M: ITEC.
M Yrs. Est.: 5 (Ref:HM13716)

**MELTON MOWBRAY PHYSIO CLINIC**

**Melton Mowbray Physiotherapy & Sports Injury Clinic**, 36A Leicester St, Melton Mowbray, **Leicestershire**, LE13 0PP, ENG.
(T) 01664 480037
(E) knightphysio@aol.com
Speciality: Acupuncture, Physiotherapy. ✓
● **Physiotherapist** Ms K Knight Q: MCSP. M: SRP.
S Yrs. Est.: 7 (Ref:HM13717)

**MELVILL, R H**

**R H Melvill**, Dene Cottage, Oak Grange Rd, West Clandon, Guildford, **Surrey**, GU4 7TZ, ENG.
(T) 01483 222474
Speciality: Chiropractic.
P S T (Ref:HM13718)

**MELZACK, D**

**D Melzack**, 31 Oxenpark Avenue, Wembley, **London (Greater)**, HA9 9SY, ENG.
(T) 020 8904 4656
Speciality: Chiropodists (Podiatrists).
S (Ref:HM13719)

**MEMBERS OF NAT INS OF MED HERB**

**Members Of National Institute Of Medical Herbalist**, Kensington Court Clinic, 197 Chepstow Rd, Newport, NP19 8GH, WAL.
(T) 01633 277263
Speciality: Herbal Medicine.
M (Ref:HM13720)

**MEMORIES HEALTH CENTRE**

**Memories Health Centre**, 1st Floor, 14 High St, Stoke-On-Trent, **Staffordshire**, ST6 5TF, ENG.
(T) 01782 811487
Speciality: Aromatherapy.
M O (Ref:HM13721)

**MENDES DA COSTA, P J**

**P J Mendes Da Costa**, 124 Oatlands Drive, Weybridge, **Surrey**, KT13 9HL, ENG.
(T) 01932 858284
Speciality: Chiropodists (Podiatrists).
S (Ref:HM13722)

**MENDOZA, ALISON**

**Alison Mendoza**, 46 Nelsons Row, Clapham, London, **London (Greater)**, SW4 7JH, ENG.
(T) 020 7627 8509
Speciality: Reflexology, Shiatsu, Spiritual Healing.
S T (Ref:HM13723)

**MENELAUS, CHERYL T (DR)**

**Dr Cheryl T Menelaus**, 5 Milland Mews, Hailsham, **Sussex (East)**, BN27 1TZ, ENG.
(T) 01323 848818
Speciality: Psychotherapy.
● **Owner** Dr C Menelaus
B (Ref:HM13724)

**MENEZES, A**

**A Menezes**, 89 Ringwood Rd, Ferndown, **Dorset**, BH22 9AA, ENG.
Speciality: Chiropractic.
P S T (Ref:HM13725)

**MENEZES, ROYCE**

**Royce Menezes**, 105 St. Thomas Rd, Trowbridge, **Wiltshire**, BA14 7LT, ENG.
(T) 01225 777377
Speciality: Complementary Medicines & Therapy.
● **Partner** Mrs C Menezes
C M (Ref:HM13726)

**MENIER, BEA**

**Bea Menier**, 91 Croft Rd, Swindon, **Wiltshire**, SN1 4DN, ENG.
(T) 01793 694943
Speciality: Reflexology.
● **Owner** Ms B Menier
S T (Ref:HM13727)

**MENSANA PSYCHOLOGICAL THRP**

**Mensana Psychological Therapies**, 5 Lardon Cottages, Wallingford Rd, Streatley, Reading, **Berkshire**, RG8 9JU, ENG.
(T) 01491 875794
Speciality: Psychotherapy.
B (Ref:HM13728)

**MENZIES, AVERIL**

**Averil Menzies**, 6 Westwood Cl, Emsworth, **Hampshire**, PO10 7QL, ENG.
(T) 01243 375506
Speciality: Chiropodists (Podiatrists).
● **Owner** Mrs A Menzies
S (Ref:HM13729)

**MENZIES, S J**

**S J Menzies**, Rookswood, Chestnut Cl, Peakirk, Peterborough, **Cambridgeshire**, PE6 7NW, ENG.
(T) 01733 252086
Speciality: Acupuncture.
O (Ref:HM13730)

**MENZIES-TRULL, CHRISTOPHER**

**Christopher Menzies-Trull**, 16 Grosvenor Rd, Newcastle, **Staffordshire**, ST5 1LW, ENG.
(T) 01782 713977 (F) 01782 713977
Speciality: Herbal Medicine.
M (Ref:HM13731)

**MEOPHAM CLINIC**

**Meopham Clinic (The)**, Coningsby, Wrotham Rd, Meopham, Gravesend, **Kent**, DA13 0HN, ENG.
(T) 01474 812135
Speciality: Acupuncture, Aromatherapy, Auricular Therapy, Bowen Therapy, Chiropody, Counselling, Herbal Medicine, Homeopathy, Massage (Therapeutic), Osteomyology, Osteopathy, Podiatry. ✓
● **Chiropodist (Podiatrist)** Mr S Gray Q: BSc (Hons), M.S.C.P, S.R.Ch.
● **Practitioner** Ms P Holden Q: L.C.C.H, MHMA.
● **Therapist** Ms A Coslett-Derby Q: DO, TATQ.
● **Osteopath** Mr S Prideaux Q: DO, MBAcC, MRCHM. M: GOsC.
● **Aromatherapist/Sports Massage Therapist** Ms C Young Q: RQA, TIDHA.
● **Osteopath** Ms S Sedgwick Q: DO. M: GOsC.
● **Counsellor** Ms N Perl Q: Dip.Couns.
● **Acupuncturist** Mr P Blacker Q: Dip.Ac. M: BAcC.
C Yrs. Est.: 13 (Ref:HM13732)

**MEPHISTO**

**Mephisto**, 22 Denman St, London, **London (Greater)**, W1V 7RJ, ENG.
(T) 020 7434 2208 (F) 020 7734 9098
Speciality: Chiropodists (Podiatrists).
● **Owner** Mr M Sanders
S (Ref:HM13733)

**MERCER, HAYLEY**

**Hayley Mercer**, 16 Witham Way, Upper Stratton, Swindon, **Wiltshire**, SN2 6NN, ENG.
(T) 01793 832168
Speciality: Aromatherapy.
M O (Ref:HM13734)

**MERE PRACTICE**

**Mere Practice**, Castleton House, Castle St, Mere, Warminster, **Wiltshire**, BA12 6JE, ENG.
(T) 01747 860161
Speciality: Complementary Medicines & Therapy.
M (Ref:HM13735)

**MEREDITH, C A**

**C A Meredith**, Clippenham Cottage, Cowbeech, Hailsham, **Sussex (East)**, BN27 4JJ, ENG.
(T) 01323 832395
Speciality: Osteopathy.
● **Owner** Ms C Meredith
P S T (Ref:HM13736)

**MEREDITH, DAVID**

**David Meredith**, 2 Shavington Avenue, Chester, **Cheshire**, CH2 3RD, ENG.
(T) 01244 322762
Speciality: Osteopathy.
● **Owner** Mr D Meredith
P S T (Ref:HM13737)

**MEREDITH, P R**

**P R Meredith**, 6 Derby St West, Ormskirk, **Lancashire**, L39 3NH, ENG.
(T) 01695 578435
Speciality: Chiropodists (Podiatrists).
● **Owner** Mr P Meredith
S (Ref:HM13738)

**MEREDITH, P R**

**P R Meredith**, 62 Cleveleys Rd, Southport, **Merseyside**, PR9 9SP, ENG.
(T) 01704 231339
Speciality: Chiropodists (Podiatrists).
S (Ref:HM13739)

**MERIDIAN CLINIC**

**Meridian Clinic (The)**, 8 Bank St, Bury, **Lancashire**, BL9 0DL, ENG.
(T) 01617 631700 (F) 01617 631700
Speciality: Chiropractic.
● **Owner** Mrs C Shanks
P S T (Ref:HM13740)

**MERIDIAN COUNS & PSYCHO SVS**

**Meridian Counselling & Psychotherapy Services**, Mycenae House, 90 Mycenae Rd, London, **London (Greater)**, SE3 7SE, ENG.
(T) 020 8293 5223
Speciality: Psychotherapy.
B (Ref:HM13741)

**MERIDIAN HEALTH**

**Meridian Health**, 1 North Rd, Holsworthy, **Devon**, EX22 6EJ, ENG.
(T) 01409 254305 (F) 01409 254305
Speciality: Complementary Medicines & Therapy.
● **Owner** Ms Y King
M (Ref:HM13742)

**MERIDIAN HEALTHCARE**

**Meridian Healthcare**, 37 Station Rd, Hinckley, **Leicestershire**, LE10 1AP, ENG.
(T) 01455 233484
Speciality: Osteopathy.
● **Partner** Mr J Lloyd-Paine
P S T (Ref:HM13743)

**MERIDIAN MASSAGE & REFLEXOLOGY**

**Meridian Massage & Reflexology**, 10 Fenwick Trce, Durham, **County Durham**, DH1 4JJ, ENG.
(T) 01913 843337
Speciality: Massage (Therapeutic), Reflexology.
● **Owner** Mr S Hill
M (Ref:HM13744)

**MERIDIAN RADIONICS**

**Meridian Radionics**, Lanzeague, St. Just In Roseland, Truro, **Cornwall**, TR2 5JD, ENG.
(T) 01326 270990 (F) 01326 270591
Speciality: Complementary Medicines & Therapy.
● **Owner** Mrs A Davy
M (Ref:HM13745)

**MERIDIAN THERAPY**

**Meridian Therapy**, 48 High St, Lowestoft, **Suffolk**, NR32 1HZ, ENG.
(T) 01502 563300



Key continued: Yrs.Est: Years Established Q: Qualifications M: Professional Membership ✓ Indemnity Insurance CREDIT Accept Credit Cards

Speciality: Complementary Medicines & Therapy.
● **Owner** Mr H Khalil
**C** **M** (**Ref:**HM13746)

## MERILAHT, R

**R Merilaht**, Woodrise, Graig Penllyn, Cowbridge, **Glamorgan (Vale of)**, CF71 7RT, WAL.
(T) 01446 774221
Speciality: Chiropodists (Podiatrists).
● **Owner** Mr P Merilaht
**S** (**Ref:**HM13747)

## MERLIN ENTERTAINMENT

**Merlin Entertainment**, Suite 14A 30-31 Wicklow St, Dublin, **County Dublin**, IRE.
(T) 01670 5016
Speciality: Hypnotherapy.
**B** (**Ref:**HM13748)

## MERMAID CHIROPRACTIC PRACTICE

**Mermaid Chiropractic Practice**, 158a York Rd, Hartlepool, **Cleveland**, TS26 9DT, ENG.
(T) 01429 296766 (F) 01429 296788
Speciality: Chiropractic. ✔
● **Owner/Chiropractor** Dr K Rose Q: DC, MSc. M: GCC.
**P** Yrs. Est.: 1 (**Ref:**HM13749)

## MERRIEN, A

**A Merrien**, Petworth Court, Felpham Rd, Bognor Regis, **Sussex (West)**, PO22 7PQ, ENG.
(T) 01243 868688
Speciality: Chiropodists (Podiatrists).
● **Owner** Mrs A Shelley
**S** (**Ref:**HM13750)

## MERRION SQUARE OSTEOPATHS

**Merrion Square Osteopaths**, 1 Merrion Sq, Dublin, **County Dublin**, IRE.
(T) 01661 6143
Speciality: Osteopathy.
**P** **S** **T** (**Ref:**HM13751)

## MERRIOTT, SUSAN J

**Susan J Merriott**, 25 King St, Worthing, **Sussex (West)**, BN14 7BN, ENG.
(T) 01903 206575
Speciality: Homeopathy.
**M** (**Ref:**HM13752)

## MERRY, EWEN

**Ewen Merry**, Worcester Chiropractic Clinic, 102 Bromyard Rd, Worcester, **Worcestershire**, WR2 5DJ, ENG.
(T) 01905 428956 (F) 01905 748907
Speciality: Chiropractic.
● **Owner** Mr E Merry
**P** **S** **T** (**Ref:**HM13753)

## MERRYDOWN CENTRE

**Merrydown Centre**, Broomleaf Rd, Farnham, **Surrey**, GU9 8DH, ENG.
(T) 01252 737107 (F) 01252 737107
Speciality: Psychotherapy.
● **Practice Manager** Mrs D Johnen
**B** (**Ref:**HM13754)

## MERRYFIELD, C

**C Merryfield**, 75 Leigh Rd, Leigh-On-Sea, **Essex**, SS9 1JN, ENG.
(T) 01702 714862 (F) 01702 716969
Speciality: Chiropodists (Podiatrists).
● **Owner** Mrs C Merryfield
**S** (**Ref:**HM13755)

## MERSEYSIDE SCHOOL OF MASSAGE

**Merseyside School of Massage**, 66A Lord St, Liverpool, **Merseyside**, L2 1TD, ENG.
(T) 01517 099701
Speciality: Complementary Medicines & Therapy.
**M** (**Ref:**HM13756)

## MERSH, J M

**J M Mersh**, Greenhill Physiotherapy & Sports Injury Clinic, 165 Hemper Lane, Sheffield, **Yorkshire (South)**, S8 7FB, ENG.
(T) 01142 373006
Speciality: Physiotherapy.
● **Partner** Mr J Mersh
**P** **S** **T** (**Ref:**HM13757)

## MERTON ACUPUNCTURE & HERBAL

**Merton Acupuncture & Herbal Clinic**, 396-398 Stanley Rd, Bootle, **Merseyside**, L20 5AB, ENG.
(T) 01519 222873 (F) 01519 222873
Speciality: Acupuncture.
● **Owner** Mr P Pang
**O** (**Ref:**HM13758)

## MESGER-SCHOFIELD, FIONA

**Fiona Mesger-Schofield**, Apple Cottages, Old Dean, Bovingdon, Hemel Hempstead, **Hertfordshire**, HP3 0EZ, ENG.
(T) 01442 834627
Speciality: Aromatherapy.
**M** **O** (**Ref:**HM13759)

## MESSENGER, DENISE

**Denise Messenger**, 17 Carey Way, Olney, **Buckinghamshire**, MK46 4DR, ENG.
(T) 01234 713425
Speciality: Hypnosis.
**B** (**Ref:**HM13760)

## MESSINGHAM CHIROPODIST SURGERY

**Messingham Chiropodist Surgery (The)**, Wendover Rd, Messingham, Scunthorpe, **Humberside**, DN17 3SN, ENG.
(T) 01724 764430
Speciality: Chiropody. ✔
● **Chiropodist** Mrs D Stevenson Q: MBChA, MSSCh. M: B.A.Ch.P.
**M** Yrs. Est.: 6 (**Ref:**HM13761)

## MESSOM, C A

**C A Messom**, Bridge House, Enborne Row, Wash Water, Newbury, **Berkshire**, RG20 0LX, ENG.
(T) 01635 45281
Speciality: Chiropodists (Podiatrists).
● **Owner** Mrs C Messom
**S** (**Ref:**HM13762)

## METABOLICS

**Metabolics Ltd**, 5 Eastcott Common, Eastcott, Devizes, **Wiltshire**, SN10 4PL, ENG.
(T) 01380 812799 (F) 01380 813078
(W) www.metabolics.co.uk
Speciality: Nutritional Therapy.
● **Joint Director**
Christopher Robin Astill-Smith
● **Manager** Mr R Kite
● **Joint Director**
Alison Claire Astill-Smith
**C** Yrs. Est.: 9 (**Ref:**HM13763)

## METAFORCE

**Metaforce Ltd**, 2 Nursery Gardens, Chilworth, Guildford, **Surrey**, GU4 8PA, ENG.
(T) 01483 571551
Speciality: Hypnosis.
**B** (**Ref:**HM13764)

## METAGENICS UK

**Metagenics UK Ltd**, 16A St Marys St, Wallingford, **Oxfordshire**, OX10 0EW, ENG.
(T) 01491 833243 (F) 01491 833254
Speciality: Complementary Medicines & Therapy.
**C** **M** (**Ref:**HM13765)

## METAMORPHIC ASSOCIATION

**Metamorphic Association (The)**, 67 Ritherdon Rd, London, **London (Greater)**, SW17 8QE, ENG.
(T) 020 8672 5951
Speciality: Complementary Medicines & Therapy.
● **Practitioner** G Saint-Pierre
**M** (**Ref:**HM13766)

## METCALF, JOHN

**John Metcalf**, 153 Radcliffe Rd, Bolton, **Lancashire**, BL2 1NZ, ENG.
(T) 01204 409220
Speciality: Osteopathy.
● **Owner** Mr J Metcalf
**P** **S** **T** (**Ref:**HM13767)

## METCALF, M F

**M F Metcalf**, 2a Bassett Crescent West, Southampton, **Hampshire**, SO16 7DZ, ENG.
(T) 023 8078 4367
Speciality: Chiropodists (Podiatrists).
**S** (**Ref:**HM13768)

## METCALF, RICHARD

**Richard Metcalf**, The Elmwood Health Centre, Huddersfield Rd, Holmfirth, Huddersfield, **Yorkshire (West)**, HD7 2TT, ENG.
(T) 01484 688359
Speciality: Osteopathy.
● **Owner** Mr R Metcalf
**P** **S** **T** (**Ref:**HM13769)

## METCALF, Y

**Y Metcalf**, Community Centre, Hill Top, West Bromwich, **Midlands (West)**, B70 0RZ, ENG.
(T) 01215 568038 (F) 01215 564322
Speciality: Chiropodists (Podiatrists).
● **Owner** Mrs Y Metcalf
**S** (**Ref:**HM13770)

## METCALFE, D (DR)

**Dr D Metcalfe**, 157 Burlington Rd, New Malden, **Surrey**, KT3 4LU, ENG.
(T) 020 8942 0962
Speciality: Chiropractors.
● **Owner** Dr D Metcalfe
**P** **S** **T** (**Ref:**HM13771)

## METCALFE, MANDY

**Mandy Metcalfe**, 1 Crosby Rd, Northallerton, **Yorkshire (North)**, DL6 1AA, ENG.
(T) 01609 783600 (F) 01609 783600
Speciality: Acupuncture.
● **Owner** Miss J Waterworth
**O** (**Ref:**HM13772)

## METCALFF, L

**L Metcalff**, 30A Front St East, Bedlington, **Northumberland**, NE22 5AA, ENG.
(T) 01670 531110
Speciality: Chiropody.
● **Owner** Mrs L Metcalff
**S** (**Ref:**HM13773)

## METFORD, TIM

**Tim Metford**, Natural Medicine Centre, 86 Queens Rd, Nuneaton, **Warwickshire**, CV11 5LE, ENG.
(T) 024 7634 3351
Speciality: Acupuncture.
**O** (**Ref:**HM13774)

## METHANANDA, S P

**S P Methananda**, 75 Canterbury Rd, Margate, **Kent**, CT9 5AS, ENG.
(T) 01843 228828 (F) 01843 228828
Speciality: Physiotherapy.
● **Owner** Mr S Methananda
**P** **S** **T** (**Ref:**HM13775)

## METRO ELECTROLYSIS CLINIC

**Metro Electrolysis Clinic**, 29 Ropergate, Pontefract, **Yorkshire (West)**, WF8 1LY, ENG.
(T) 01977 703999
Speciality: Electrolysis.
● **Owner** Mrs V Nicholls
**T** (**Ref:**HM13776)

## METSON, R K

**R K Metson**, 68A Church Rd, Tiptree, Colchester, **Essex**, CO5 0HB, ENG.
(T) 01621 816285 (F) 01621 816285
Speciality: Chiropodists (Podiatrists).
● **Owner** Mrs S Metson-Caylor
**S** (**Ref:**HM13777)

## METTE MARUP & MIKKELSEN

**Anne Mette Marup & Gitte B Mikkelsen**, High Wycombe Chiropractic Clinic, 27 London Rd, High Wycombe, **Buckinghamshire**, HP11 1BJ, ENG.
(T) 01494 524194
Speciality: Chiropractic.
**P** **S** **T** (**Ref:**HM13778)

## METUS, M L

**M L Metus**, 48A Barton Hill Rd, Torquay, **Devon**, TQ2 8JD, ENG.
(T) 01803 329799
Speciality: Chiropractors.
**P** **S** **T** (**Ref:**HM13779)

## MEULENBROEKS, ROSE

**Rose Meulenbroeks**, 8 Dunstable Mews, London, **London (Greater)**, W1G 6BT, ENG.
(T) 020 7935 4763
Speciality: Reflexology.

Key: **B** Mind-Body Medicine **C** Complementary Medicine **H** Self Help Treatment **M** Medicinal Therapy **O** Oriental Medicine **P** Postural Therapy **S** Manipulative Structural Therapy **T** Touch Therapy

S T (Ref:HM13780)

**MEW, JILL**

**Jill Mew**, 44 Westerham Rd, Sevenoaks, **Kent**, TN13 2PZ, ENG.
(T) 01732 450979
Speciality: Osteopathy.
● **Owner** Mrs J Mew
P S T (Ref:HM13781)

**MEWIS, R J**

**R J Mewis**, 293 Conway Rd, Colwyn Bay, **Conwy**, LL28 5AA, WAL.
(T) 01495 46045
Speciality: Chiropractic, McTimoney Therapy. ✓
● **Owner** Mr R Mewis Q: DC. M: GCC.
P Yrs. Est.: 15 (Ref:HM13782)

**MEWS CLINIC HOLISTIC HEALTH**

**Mews Clinic Holistic Health For Mind & Body (The)**, 5 Watts Lane, Eastbourne, **Sussex (East)**, BN21 1NP, ENG.
(T) 01323 733743
Speciality: Complementary Medicines & Therapy.
● **Partner** Mrs J Richardson
M (Ref:HM13783)

**MEWS PHYSIOTHERAPY CLINIC**

**Mews Physiotherapy Clinic (The)**, 41-43 Gosport St, Lymington, **Hampshire**, SO41 9BB, ENG.
(T) 01590 688788
Speciality: Physiotherapy.
P S T (Ref:HM13784)

**MEYER, A**

**A Meyer**, Woodland Rd, Derby, **Derbyshire**, DE22 1GR, ENG.
(T) 01332 299133
Speciality: Homeopathy.
M (Ref:HM13785)

**MEYER, ANDREA**

**Andrea Meyer**, 14 Sansome Walk, Worcester, **Worcestershire**, WR1 1LP, ENG.
(T) 01905 26450
Speciality: Osteopathy.
P S T (Ref:HM13786)

**MEYER, LEO**

**Leo Meyer**, 25 Moore Park Rd, London, **London (Greater)**, SW6 2HU, ENG.
(T) 020 7731 3876
Speciality: Reflexology.
S T (Ref:HM13787)

**MEYERS, K L C**

**K L C Meyers**, 12A St Thomas Rd, Newquay, **Cornwall**, TR7 1RS, ENG.
(T) 01637 876554
Speciality: Osteopathy.
P S T (Ref:HM13788)

**MEYERSON, SIMON**

**Simon Meyerson**, 8 Willow Rd, London, **London (Greater)**, NW3 1TJ, ENG.
(T) 020 7794 8717
Speciality: Psychotherapy, Psychology, Sports Psychology. ✓ CREDIT
● **Psychologist** Mr S Meyerson Q: BA (Hons), BPS, MA.
B Yrs. Est.: 30 (Ref:HM13789)

**MHB ASSOCIATES**

**MHB Associates**, 25A Suffolk St, Helensburgh, **Argyll and Bute**, G84 9PD, SCO.
(T) 01436 679922
Speciality: Hypnotherapy.
● **Owner** Mr J Hunter
B (Ref:HM13790)

**MICALLEF, JANICE**

**Janice Micallef**, 136 North Cray Rd, Bexley, **Kent**, DA5 3NB, ENG.
(T) 01322 558334 (F) 01322 558334
Speciality: Homeopathy.
● **Owner** Mrs J Micallef
M (Ref:HM13791)

**MICHAEL INSTITUTE-SPATIAL DYN**

**Michael Institute Of Spatial Dynamics (The)**, 2 Cheverils, Priory Rd, Forest Row, **Sussex (East)**, RH18 5HR, ENG.
(T) 01342 826677 (F) 01342 826677
Speciality: Complementary Medicines & Therapy.
● **Director** Mr M Baker
C M (Ref:HM13792)

**MICHAEL, DAVID**

**David Michael**, Frankleigh House, 75 Bath Rd, Bradford-on-Avon, **Wiltshire**, BA15 2PB, ENG.
(T) 01225 867896
Speciality: Psychotherapy.
● **Owner** Mr D Michael
B (Ref:HM13793)

**MICHAEL, G**

**G Michael**, 52-54 Wigmore St, London, **London (Greater)**, W1H 0AU, ENG.
(T) 020 7935 7877
Speciality: Chiropodists (Podiatrists).
● **Practice Manager** Miss G Michael
S (Ref:HM13794)

**MICHAEL, J**

**J Michael**, 6 Clifton Rd, London, **London (Greater)**, N8 8HY, ENG.
(T) 020 8340 0378
Speciality: Chiropodists (Podiatrists).
● **Owner** Mr J Michael
S (Ref:HM13795)

**MICHAEL, MARIE**

**Marie Michael**, 6 Pavilion Mews, London, **London (Greater)**, N3 3QD, ENG.
(T) 020 8343 3423
Speciality: Hypnosis.
B (Ref:HM13796)

**MICHELL, C**

**C Michell**, 19 Lulworth Cl, Paignton, **Devon**, TQ4 7RG, ENG.
(T) 01803 553024
Speciality: Chiropodists (Podiatrists).
S (Ref:HM13797)

**MICHELLE PEARSON AT HARMONY**

**Michelle Pearson At Harmony**, 4-6 Ashford Rd, Tenterden, **Kent**, TN30 6QU, ENG.
(T) 01580 764434
Speciality: Aromatherapy.
● **Partner** Miss J Ludford
M O (Ref:HM13798)

**MICHELOTTI, ALAN**

**Alan Michelotti**, The Gate House, 1 Abbotswood, Guildford, **Surrey**, GU1 1NZ, ENG.
(T) 01483 562830 (F) 01483 304856
Speciality: Chiropractors.
● **Owner** Mr R Bennett
P S T (Ref:HM13799)

**MICHIE, A**

**A Michie**, 3a Agincourt St, Monmouth, **Monmouthshire**, NP25 3DZ, WAL.
(T) 01600 716880
Speciality: Osteopathy.
● **Principal** Ms C Love
P S T (Ref:HM13800)

**MICHIE, CAROL A**

**Carol A Michie**, 3 Clavadel Rd, Paddock Wood, Tonbridge, **Kent**, TN12 6EW, ENG.
(T) 01892 836089
Speciality: Osteopathy.
P S T (Ref:HM13801)

**MICHIE, CATRIONA**

**Catriona Michie**, Homestead Cottage, Feathers Lane, Wraysbury, Staines, **Surrey**, TW19 5AN, ENG.
(T) 01784 483741
Speciality: Reflexology.
S T (Ref:HM13802)

**MICKELBOROUGH, ESTELLE**

**Estelle Mickelborough**, 22 Keats Way, Wickford, **Essex**, SS12 0BU, ENG.
(T) 01268 766007
Speciality: Hypnosis.
● **Owner** Ms E Mickelborough
B (Ref:HM13803)

**MICKLEBURGH, P**

**P Mickleburgh**, 8 Bingham Rd, Croydon, **Surrey**, CR0 7EB, ENG.
(T) 020 8656 0548
Speciality: Chiropodists (Podiatrists).
● **Owner** Mr P Mickleburgh
S (Ref:HM13804)

**MID SUSSEX CHIROPRACTIC CLINIC**

**Mid Sussex Chiropractic Clinic**, 66A Church Walk, Burgess Hill, **Sussex (West)**, RH15 9AS, ENG.
(T) 01444 257555
Speciality: Chiropractic, Cranial Osteopathy, Hypnotherapy, Kinesiology, Life Style Coaching, Manipulation, Meditation, Nutritional Therapy, Vitamin Therapy, X-Ray. ✓
● **Chiropractor** Dr R White Q: B.App.Sc, DC. M: BCA.
S Yrs. Est.: 2 (Ref:HM13805)

**MID SUSSEX HOMEOPATHIC CLINIC**

**Mid Sussex Homeopathic Group Clinic**, 9 Mill Rd, Burgess Hill, **Sussex (West)**, RH15 8DN, ENG.
(T) 01444 239498 (F) 01444 236848
(E) homeopathy@platform11.org.uk
Speciality: Homeopathy. ✓
● **Consultant** D Roche Q: Ch.B, DRCOG, MB, MFHom, MRCGP. M: BMA, FHom.
● **Assistant Consultant** Mr D Ferme-Woods Q: BS, MB, MFHom. M: BMA, FHom.
M Yrs. Est.: 18 (Ref:HM13806)

**MID SUSSEX HOMEOPATHIC CLINIC**

**Mid Sussex Homoeopathic Group Clinic**, 11 Wingle Tye Rd, Burgess Hill, **Sussex (West)**, RH15 9HR, ENG.
(T) 01444 239498 (F) 01444 236848
Speciality: Homeopathy.
● **Practice Manager** Mrs M Mitchell
M (Ref:HM13807)

**MIDAS TOUCH**

**Midas Touch**, 29 Sandpit Lane, St. Albans, **Hertfordshire**, AL1 4EW, ENG.
(T) 020 8372 8491
Speciality: Acupressure, Aromatherapy, Massage (Therapeutic), Reiki. ✓
● **Sole Trader** Miss D Robbins Q: ITHMA. M: RQA.
T Yrs. Est.: 2 (Ref:HM13808)

**MIDAS TOUCH**

**Midas Touch**, Windmill Hill, Enfield, **London (Greater)**, EN2 7AF, ENG.
(T) 020 8372 8491
Speciality: Acupressure, Aromatherapy, Indian Head Massage, Reiki, Chakra and Aura Healing.
● **Owner** Miss D Robbins
M O (Ref:HM13809)

**MID-CHESHIRE HOM GRP**

**Mid-Cheshire Homoeopathic Group**, 2 Watling St, Northwich, **Cheshire**, CW9 5EX, ENG.
(T) 01606 45984
Speciality: Homeopathy.
● **Practice Manager** Mrs Y Lawrence
M (Ref:HM13810)

**MIDDA, JULIAN OST & SPORTS THER**

**Midda Julian Osteopath & Sports Therapist**, 2 Winchester Avenue, Bristol, BS4 3NA, ENG.
(T) 01179 724755
Speciality: Osteopathy.
P S T (Ref:HM13811)

**MIDDLE EARTH AROMA SUPPLIES**

**Middle Earth Aromatherapy Supplies**, Unit 24 Trago Mills Shopping Centre, Liverton, Newton Abbot, **Devon**, TQ12 6JD, ENG.
(T) 01626 824830
Speciality: Aromatherapy.
M O (Ref:HM13812)

**MIDDLE WAY RE-EDUCATION CTRE**

**Middle Way Re-Education Centre (The)**, 5 Chiltern Cl, Stone, Aylesbury, **Buckinghamshire**, HP17 8RA, ENG.
(T) 01296 748109
(E) crossma@compuserve.com
(W) www.the-middle-way.com
Speciality: Alexander Technique, Meditation, Sound Therapy, Zen Therapy, Neuro Development Therapy. ✓




Key continued: Yrs.Est: Years Established Q: Qualifications M: Professional Membership ✓ Indemnity Insurance CREDIT Accept Credit Cards

- **Teacher** Mr M Cross Q: MSTAT. M: STAT.
- **Teacher of the Alexander Technique** Chie Cross Q: MSTAT. M: STAT.

H Yrs. Est.: 3 (Ref:HM13813)

## MIDDLEMARSH CLINIC

**Middlemarsh Clinic**, 1a Acland Rd, Dorchester, **Dorset**, DT1 1EF, ENG.
(T) 01305 262626 (F) 01305 250153
Speciality: Complementary Medicines & Therapy.
- **Director** Mr K Slowe

M (Ref:HM13814)

## MIDDLES PICCADILLY CTRE

**Middles Piccadilly Natural Healing Centre**, Middle Piccadilly, Holwell, Sherborne, **Dorset**, DT9 5LW, ENG.
(T) 01963 23468 (F) 01963 23764
Speciality: Acupressure, Alexander Technique, Aromatherapy, Bach Remedies, Cranio-Sacral Therapy, Homeopathy, Indian Head Massage, Kinesiology, Reflexology, Reiki, Shiatsu.
- **Director** Mr D Harvey

C (Ref:HM13815)

## MIDDLESEX SCHOOL OF COMP MED

**Middlesex School Of Complementary Medicine**, Victoria House, 18 Dalston Gdns, Stanmore, **London (Greater)**, HA7 1BU, ENG.
(T) 020 8204 4477
Speciality: Complementary Medicines & Therapy.

M (Ref:HM13816)

## MIDDLETON & ASSOCIATES

**Scot Middleton & Associates**, Wilmslow Chiropractic Clinic, 15 Lindow Prde, Chapel Lane, Wilmslow, **Cheshire**, SK9 5JL, ENG.
(T) 01625 531164 (F) 01625 549616
Speciality: Chiropractic, Homeopathy, Physiotherapy. ✓
- **Chiropractor** Dr G Robinson Q: DC, MSc.
- **Physiotherapist/Homeopathy** Dr A Brito-Babapulle
- **Chiropractor** Dr E Davies Q: DC, MSc.
- **Chiropractor** Dr S Bird Q: DC, MSc.
- **Owner** Dr S Middleton Q: DC.
- **Chiropractor** Mrs A Roach

P Yrs. Est.: 15 (Ref:HM13817)

## MIDDLETON HOM & NAT THRPY CTRE

**Middleton Homoeopathy & Natural Therapy Centre**, 14B Middleton Gardens, Middleton, Manchester, **Manchester (Greater)**, M24 4DF, ENG.
(T) 01616 537772
Speciality: Complementary Medicines & Therapy.
- **Owner** Ms D Selwesiukownn

C M (Ref:HM13818)

## MIDDLETON, AUDREY

**Audrey Middleton**, 24 Sandringham Rd, Doncaster, **Yorkshire (South)**, DN2 5HU, ENG.
(T) 01302 341595
Speciality: Psychotherapy.

B (Ref:HM13819)

## MIDDLETON, CAROLE

**Carole Middleton**, 14 Channel View, St. Ives, **Cornwall**, TR26 1RG, ENG.
(T) 01736 799308
Speciality: Homeopathy.
- **Owner** Mrs C Middleton

M (Ref:HM13820)

## MIDDLETON, IAN W

**Consultant Medical Herbalist**, 128 High St, Edgware, **London (Greater)**, HA8 7EL, ENG.
(T) 020 8951 3475
Speciality: Dietician, Herbal Medicine, Massage (Therapeutic), Phytotherapy. ✓
- **Consultant Medical Herbalist** Mr I Middleton Q: Cert.Phyto. M: NIMH.

M Yrs. Est.: 13 (Ref:HM13821)

## MIDDLETON, SCOTT (DR)

**Dr Scott Middleton**, Langworthy Medical Centre, 250 Langworthy Rd, Salford, **Manchester (Greater)**, M6 5WW, ENG.
(T) 01617 369855
Speciality: Chiropractic.

P S T (Ref:HM13822)

## MIDDLETON, VALERIE

**Valerie Middleton**, 12 Simpson Rd, Richmond, **Surrey**, TW10 7TU, ENG.
(T) 020 8948 1570
Speciality: Reflexology.

S T (Ref:HM13823)

## MID-GLAMORGAN HEALTH AUTHORITY

**Mid-Glamorgan Health Authority**, Chiropody Dept, Berry Sq, Dowlais, Merthyr Tydfil, **Glamorgan (Vale of)**, CF48 3RL, WAL.
(T) 01685 722383
Speciality: Chiropractic.

P S T (Ref:HM13824)

## MIDGLEY & ASSOCIATES

**Midgley D J & Associates**, 143 Cheam Rd, Cheam, Sutton, **Surrey**, SM1 2BP, ENG.
(T) 020 8643 3990
Speciality: Osteopathy.

P S T (Ref:HM13825)

## MIDGLEY, CLARE

**Clare Midgley**, Newton Aycliffe, **County Durham**, DL5, ENG.
(T) 01325 317378
Speciality: Bach Remedies.

M (Ref:HM13826)

## MID-HERTS ALEXANDER CENTRE

**Mid-Herts Alexander Centre**, 15 Springfields, Welwyn Garden City, **Hertfordshire**, AL8 6XS, ENG.
(T) 01707 331391
Speciality: Alexander Technique, Complementary Therapy, Life Style Coaching, Stress Therapy, Voice Therapy. ✓
- **Manager** Mr B Bagenal Q: MSTAT.

P Yrs. Est.: 12 (Ref:HM13827)

## MIDHURST CHIROPRACTIC CLINIC

**Midhurst Chiropractic Clinic**, Flat 2, Hamlyn House, Rumbolds Hill, Midhurst, **Sussex (West)**, GU29 9ND, ENG.
(T) 01730 817711
Speciality: Chiropractors.
- **Manager** Mr S Procter

P S T (Ref:HM13828)

## MIDLAND ALOE VERA CENTRE

**Midland Aloe Vera Centre**, The Cottage, Longbridge, Warwick, **Warwickshire**, CV34 6RB, ENG.
(T) 01926 411710 (F) 01926 403299
Speciality: Complementary Medicines & Therapy.
- **Owner** Mr B Parker

C M (Ref:HM13829)

## MIDLAND HYPNOTHERAPY CENTRE

**Midland Hypnotherapy Centre**, 10 Balaclava Rd, Birmingham, **Midlands (West)**, B14 7SG, ENG.
(T) 01214 445435
(W) www.aqch.org
Speciality: Hypnosis, Curative Hypnotherapy. ✓ CREDIT
- **Owner/Curative Hypnotherapist** Miss H Lesser Q: Dip.Hyp. M: AQCH.

B Yrs. Est.: 18 (Ref:HM13830)

## MIDLAND HYPNOTHERAPY CENTRE

**Midland Hypnotherapy Centre**, 10 Balaclava Rd, Kings Heath, Birmingham, **Midlands (West)**, B14 7SG, ENG.
(T) 01214 445435
(E) hypnohel@aol.com
Speciality: Auto Suggestion, Autogenic Training, Counselling, Hypnosis, Hypnotherapy, Stress Therapy, Curative Hypnotherapy, Lesserian(TM) Curative Hypnotherapy. ✓ CREDIT
- **Curative Hypnotherapist** Ms H Lesser Q: Dip.Hyp, MAQCH. M: AQCH.

B Yrs. Est.: 19 (Ref:HM13831)

## MIDLAND MEDICAL HOM PRACTICE

**Midland Medical Homeopath Practice**, 681a Warwick Rd, Solihull, **Midlands (West)**, B91 3DA, ENG.
(T) 01213 552155 (F) 07092 230859
(E) david@myspine.org.uk
Speciality: Homeopathy. ✓
- **Homeopathic Physician** Dr D Smith Q: Ch.B, MB, MFHom, MRCGP. M: FHom, GMC.

M Yrs. Est.: 17 (Ref:HM13832)

## MIDLAND MEDICAL HOM PRACTICE

**Midland Medical Homeopathic Practice**, 162 Jockey Rd, Boldmere, Sutton Coldfield, **Midlands (West)**, B73 5PP, ENG.
(T) 01213 552155 (F) 07092 230859
(E) david@myspine.org.uk
Speciality: Homeopathy. ✓
- **Homeopathic Physician** Dr D Smith Q: Ch.B, MB, MFHom, MRCGP. M: FHom, GMC.

M Yrs. Est.: 17 (Ref:HM13833)

## MIDLAND MEDICAL HOM PRACTICE

**Midland Medical Homeopathic Practice**, Birmingham Nuffield Hospital, 22 Somerset Rd, Edgbaston, Birmingham, **Midlands (West)**, B15 2QQ, ENG.
(T) 01213 552155 (F) 07092 230859
(E) david@myspine.org.uk
Speciality: Homeopathy. ✓
- **Homeopathic Physician** Dr D Smith Q: Ch.B, MB, MFHom, MRCGP. M: FHom, GMC.

M Yrs. Est.: 17 (Ref:HM13834)

## MIDLAND MEDICAL OSTEO PRACTICE

**Midland Medical Osteopathic Practice**, 162 Jockey Rd, Boldmore, Sutton Coldfield, **Midlands (West)**, B73 5PP, ENG.
(T) 01213 552155 (F) 07092 230859
(E) david@myspine.org.uk
(W) www.myspine.org.uk
Speciality: Acupuncture, Homeopathy, Manipulation, Massage (Therapeutic), Osteopathy, Ultrasound. ✓
- **Medical Osteopath** Dr D Smith Q: Ch.B, MB, MLCOM, MRCGP. M: GMC, GOsC.

S Yrs. Est.: 17 (Ref:HM13835)

## MIDLAND MEDICAL OSTEO PRACTICE

**Midland Medical Osteopathic Practice**, The Birmingham Nuffield Hospital, 22 Somerset Rd, Edgbaston, Birmingham, **Midlands (West)**, B15 2QQ, ENG.
(T) 01213 552155
(E) david@myspine.org.uk
Speciality: Acupuncture, Homeopathy, Manipulation, Massage (Therapeutic), Osteopathy, Ultrasound. ✓
- **Medical Homeopath** Dr D Smith Q: Ch.B, MB, MRCGP. M: GMC, GOsC.

S Yrs. Est.: 17 (Ref:HM13836)

## MIDLAND MEDICAL OSTEO PRACTICE

**Midland Medical Osteopathic Practice**, 681a Warwick Rd, Solihull, **Midlands (West)**, B91 3DA, ENG.
(T) 01213 552155 (F) 07092 230859
(E) david@myspine.org.uk
(W) www.myspine.org.uk
Speciality: Acupuncture, Homeopathy, Manipulation, Massage (Therapeutic), Osteopathy, Ultrasound. ✓
- **Medical Osteopath** Dr D Smith Q: Ch.B, MB, MLCOM, MRCGP. M: GMC, GOsC.

S Yrs. Est.: 17 (Ref:HM13837)

## MIDLAND PHYSIOTHERAPY CLINIC

**Midland Physiotherapy Clinic**, 10 Mere Green Cl, Sutton Coldfield, **Midlands (West)**, B75 5BZ, ENG.
(T) 01213 233707
Speciality: Physiotherapy.

P S T (Ref:HM13838)

## MIDLAND PHYSIOTHERAPY CLINICS

**Midland Physiotherapy Clinics**, Harcourt House, Harrison Rd, Sutton Coldfield, **Midlands (West)**, B74 4JL, ENG.
(T) 01215 809828 (F) 01215 809838
Speciality: Physiotherapy.
- **Partner** Mr A Hunter

P S T (Ref:HM13839)

## MIDLAND PSYCHOLOGICAL SERVICE

**Midland Psychological Service**, 27 Gate Lane, Sutton Coldfield, **Midlands (West)**, B73 5TR, ENG.
(T) 01213 542638 (F) 01213 542611
Speciality: Psychology.
- **Senior Partner** Dr D Trent

B (Ref:HM13840)

## MIDLAND REFLEXOLOGY

**Midland Reflexology Register Training Centre**, 413 Harborne Rd, Birmingham, **Midlands (West)**, B15 3LB, ENG.
(T) 01216 289900 (F) 01216 289900
Speciality: Reflexology.
● **Owner** Mrs D Wilson
M (Ref:HM13841)

## MIDLANDS HOM CONSULTANTS

**Midlands Homoeopathic Consultants**, 285 Dudley Rd, Wolverhampton, **Midlands (West)**, WV2 3JU, ENG.
(T) 01902 339900
Speciality: Homeopathy.
● **Owner** Mr B Yadav
M (Ref:HM13842)

## MIDNIGHT OIL JOURNEYMAN

**Midnight Oil Journeyman**, 3a Magdalene St, Glastonbury, **Somerset**, BA6 9EW, ENG.
(T) 01458 835970 (F) 01458 831361
Speciality: Aromatherapy.
● **Manageress** Miss J Bailey
M O (Ref:HM13843)

## MIDSOMER NORTON CHIROPRACTIC

**Midsomer Norton Chiropractic Clinic**, St Chads Surgery, Gullock Tyning, Midsomer Norton, Bath, **Somerset**, BA3 2UH, ENG.
(T) 01761 411412 (F) 01179 861578
Speciality: Acupuncture, Chiropractic. ✔
● **Chiropractor** Mr D Morley Q: DC, MSc.
● **Chiropractor** Ms D Spree
● **Chiropractor** Mr K Fohlnann Q: DC.
P Yrs. Est.: 10 (Ref:HM13844)

## MIDSUMMER COTTAGE CLINIC

**Midsummer Cottage Clinic**, Midsummer Cottage, Nether Westcote, Chipping Norton, **Oxfordshire**, OX7 6SD, ENG.
(T) 01993 830419 (F) 01993 830957
(E) ehp@globalnet.co.uk
Speciality: Acupuncture, Herbal Medicine. ✔
● **Owner** Mr M McIntyre M: BAcC, NIMH, RCHM.
O Yrs. Est.: 22 (Ref:HM13845)

## MIDWINTER, L

**L Midwinter**, 3 King St, Todmorden, **Yorkshire (West)**, OL14 5SL, ENG.
(T) 01706 819464
Speciality: Physiotherapy.
P S T (Ref:HM13846)

## MIERS, IRENE

**Irene Miers**, 13 Aelybryn Rd, Colwyn Bay, **Conwy**, LL29 7HD, WAL.
(T) 01492 533263
Speciality: Electrolysis.
● **Owner** Mrs I Mier
T (Ref:HM13847)

## MIGGIN, EMILY

**Miggin Emily A A D CIBTAC**, Basement Office 5 Morehampton Rd, Dublin, **County Dublin**, IRE.
(T) 08727 03119
Speciality: Complementary Medicines & Therapy.
M (Ref:HM13848)

## MIJATOVICH, NICOLA

**Nicola Mijatovich**, Ground Floor Flat, 5 Barry Rd, London, **London (Greater)**, SE22 0HX, ENG.
(T) 020 8299 6635
Speciality: Reflexology.
S T (Ref:HM13849)

## MIKE L'S SMOKING CESSATION

**Mike L's Smoking Cessation Consultancy**, 15 Penshurst Cl, Canterbury, **Kent**, CT2 7RA, ENG.
(T) 01227 450897
Speciality: Complementary Medicines & Therapy.
● **Owner** Mr M Long
M (Ref:HM13850)

## MIKE, MARY

**Mary Mike**, British Acupuncture Association, 34 Alderney St, London, **London (Greater)**, SW1V 4EU, ENG.
(T) 020 7834 1012
Speciality: Acupuncture.
O (Ref:HM13851)

## MILBORNE, JOHN

**John Milborne**, Burnawn House, The Sq, Raunds, Wellingborough, **Northamptonshire**, NN9 6HP, ENG.
(T) 01933 626584
Speciality: Osteopathy.
● **Owner** Mr J Milborne
P S T (Ref:HM13852)

## MILENKOVIC, S

**S Milenkovic**, 10 Loganbarns Rd, Dumfries, **Dumfries and Galloway**, DG1 4BU, SCO.
(T) 01387 250047
Speciality: Chiropodists (Podiatrists).
● **Owner** Miss S Milenkovic
S (Ref:HM13853)

## MILES, ANDREW

**Andrew Miles**, Llandaff Chiropractic Clinic, 116 Station Rd, Llandaff North, Cardiff, **Glamorgan (Vale of)**, CF14 2FH, WAL.
(T) 029 2055 2299 (F) 029 2055 2299
Speciality: Allergy Testing, Chiropractic, Kinesiology.
● **Owner/Chiropractor** Mr A Miles Q: DC, MCC. M: BCA, GCC.
P Yrs. Est.: 7 (Ref:HM13854)

## MILES, C J

**C J Miles**, 84 Eastern Rd, Romford, **Essex**, RM1 3QA, ENG.
(T) 01708 745381
Speciality: Biomechanics, Chiropody, Nail Surgery, Podiatry. ✔
● **Owner/Chiropodist** Miss C Miles Q: BSc, DPodM, S.R.Ch.
C Yrs. Est.: 9 (Ref:HM13855)

## MILES, DOROTHEA

**Dorothea Miles**, 444 Knutsford Rd, Warrington, **Cheshire**, WA4 1DU, ENG.
(T) 01925 487204
Speciality: Clairvoyants & Palmists.
● **Owner** Mrs D Miles
B (Ref:HM13856)

## MILES, E J

**E J Miles**, Poynters, Effingham Rd, Copthorne, Crawley, **Sussex (West)**, RH10 3HY, ENG.
(T) 01342 714376
Speciality: Chiropodists (Podiatrists).
● **Owner** Mrs E Miles
S (Ref:HM13857)

## MILES, JAMES

**James Miles**, 1 Puddingmoor, Beccles, **Suffolk**, NR34 9PL, ENG.
(T) 01502 712505
Speciality: Osteopathy.
● **Owner** Mr M James
P S T (Ref:HM13858)

## MILES, JENNIFER

**Jennifer Miles**, 97-99 Seven Sisters Rd, London, **London (Greater)**, N7 7QP, ENG.
(T) 020 7609 7764 (F) 020 7609 7764
Speciality: Acupuncture.
● **Owner** Miss J Miles
O (Ref:HM13859)

## MILES, JENNIFER

**Jennifer Miles**, 14 Beacon Hill, London, **London (Greater)**, N7 9LY, ENG.
(T) 020 7609 7764
Speciality: Complementary Medicines & Therapy.
C M (Ref:HM13860)

## MILES, NATALIE

**Natalie Miles**, 7 The Lane, London, **London (Greater)**, SE3 9SL, ENG.
(T) 020 8318 3423
Speciality: Psychotherapy.
● **Owner** Mrs N Miles
B (Ref:HM13861)

## MILES, R W

**R W Miles**, 39 Coalford, Jackfield, Telford, **Shropshire**, TF8 7NA, ENG.
(T) 01952 882683
Speciality: Chiropodists (Podiatrists).
● **Owner** Mr R Miles
S (Ref:HM13862)

## MILFORD MASSAGE PRACTICE

**Milford Massage Practice**, 6 Swallow Cl, Milford, Godalming, **Surrey**, GU8 5DJ, ENG.
(T) 01483 860485
Speciality: Manipulation, Remedial Massage. ✔
● **Owner/Back Therapist** Mrs R Bryson Q: A.I.P.T.I, ITEC. M: IPTI.
C Yrs. Est.: 16 (Ref:HM13863)

## MILFORD STREET CHIROPODY

**Milford Street Chiropody Clinic**, 57 Milford St, Salisbury, **Wiltshire**, SP1 2BP, ENG.
(T) 01722 414214
Speciality: Chiropodists (Podiatrists).
● **Partner** Mr J Barnes
S (Ref:HM13864)

## MILL BANK OSTEOPATHIC CLINIC

**Mill Bank Osteopathic Clinic**, Mill Bank, Stafford, **Staffordshire**, ST16 2QT, ENG.
(T) 01785 226848
Speciality: Cranial Osteopathy, Osteopathy. ✔
● **Osteopath** Mr Corson Q: DO, MSc. M: GOsC.
S Yrs. Est.: 15 (Ref:HM13865)

## MILL HILL

**Mill Hill**, 1 Kings Rd, Blackburn, **Lancashire**, BB2 4PX, ENG.
(T) 01254 200662
Speciality: Chiropody.
● **Owner** Miss N Walsh
S (Ref:HM13866)

## MILL HILL PHYSIO & SPORT

**Mill Hill Physiotherapy & Sport Injury Clinic**, 8 Flower Lane, London, **London (Greater)**, NW7 2JB, ENG.
(T) 020 8959 6443 (F) 020 8959 6443
Speciality: Physiotherapy.
● **Employee** Miss B Witham
P S T (Ref:HM13867)

## MILL ST CHIROPRACTIC

**Mill St Chiropractic**, 127 Mill St, Kidlington, **Oxfordshire**, OX5 2EE, ENG.
(T) 01865 460495 (F) 01865 376555
Speciality: Chiropractors.
● **Owner** Dr C Perkins
P S T (Ref:HM13868)

## MILL, DAVID

**David Mill**, 16 Church St, Bridgwater, **Somerset**, TA6 5AS, ENG.
(T) 01278 455955 (F) 01278 457036
Speciality: Chiropodists (Podiatrists).
● **Owner** Mr D Mill
S (Ref:HM13869)

## MILLARD, PETER M J

**Peter M J Millard**, 157A New Rd, Rubery, Rednal, Birmingham, **Midlands (West)**, B45 9JW, ENG.
(T) 01216 836996
Speciality: Chiropodists (Podiatrists).
● **Owner** Mr P Millard
S (Ref:HM13870)

## MILLBANK, SALLY ANN

**Sally Ann Millbank**, Castleton House, Castle St, Mere, Warminster, **Wiltshire**, BA12 6JE, ENG.
(T) 01747 860161
Speciality: Aromatherapy.
M O (Ref:HM13871)

## MILLBANK, SALLY-ANN

**Sally-Ann Millbank**, Abbey View Complementary Clinic, Abbey View Medical Centre, Shaftesbury, **Dorset**, SP7 8DH, ENG.
(T) 01747 856719 (F) 01747 856701
Speciality: Reflexology.
S T (Ref:HM13872)

## MILLBROOK HEALTH & BEAUTY

**Millbrook Health & Beauty**, 5 King St, Millbrook, Torpoint, **Cornwall**, PL10 1AP, ENG.
(T) 01752 822391 (F) 01752 822391
Speciality: Aromatherapy.
● **Owner** Mr L Brown
M O (Ref:HM13873)



Key continued: Yrs.Est: Years Established Q: Qualifications M: Professional Membership ✔ Indemnity Insurance ▬ Accept Credit Cards

## MILLEN, CAROL
**Carol Millen**, 12 Wordsworth Rise, East Grinstead, **Sussex (West)**, RH19 1TW, ENG.
(T) 01342 311017
Speciality: Aromatherapy.
● **Owner** Mrs C Millen
[M] [O] (**Ref:**HM13874)

## MILLENNIUM COMP HEALTH CLINIC
**Millennium Complementary Health Clinic**, Richford Gate Primary Care Centre, London, **London (Greater)**, W6 7HY, ENG.
(T) 020 8846 7539
Speciality: Aromatherapy.
[P] [S] [T] (**Ref:**HM13875)

## MILLENNIUM HEALTHCARE
**Millennium Healthcare**, 8 Park Rd, Sittingbourne, **Kent**, ME10 1DR, ENG.
(T) 01795 439922 (F) 01795 439933
Speciality: Complementary Medicines & Therapy.
● **Partner** Mrs E Cruise
[C] [M] (**Ref:**HM13876)

## MILLENNIUM HOMEOPATHY
**Millennium Homeopathy**, 14 Oakcroft Gardens, Littlehampton, **Sussex (West)**, BN17 6LT, ENG.
(T) 01903 739187
(W) www.mil-hom.co.uk
Speciality: Homeopathy.
● **Homeopath** Mrs C Moss Q: LCPH. M: HMA.
[C] Yrs. Est.: 3 (**Ref:**HM13877)

## MILLENNIUM STRESS MANAGEMENT
**Millennium Stress Management**, 40 Malthouse Lane, Burgess Hill, **Sussex (West)**, RH15 9XA, ENG.
(T) 01444 258123 (F) 01444 258123
Speciality: Hypnosis.
● **Owner** Mrs S Elsey
[B] (**Ref:**HM13878)

## MILLER & ASSOCIATES
**C A Miller & Associates**, 20 Churton St, London, **London (Greater)**, SW1V 2LL, ENG.
(T) 020 7834 3149
Speciality: Chiropodists (Podiatrists).
● **Owner** Mrs C Miller
[S] (**Ref:**HM13879)

## MILLER CONSULTANCY
**Miller Consultancy (The)**, Room 15, U R C Building, Eden St, Kingston Upon Thames, **Surrey**, KT1 1HZ, ENG.
(T) 020 8974 6111 (F) 020 8974 6111
Speciality: Healing Therapy, Hypnosis, Hypnotherapy, Magnetic Therapy, Psychotherapy, Spiritual Healing.
● **Owner/Hypnotherapist/Psychotherapist** Mr M Miller
(T) 028 0974 6111 Q: DHP (NC), MNRHP. M: NRHP.
● **Assistant** Mrs G Miller
[B] [C] Yrs. Est.: 1 (**Ref:**HM13880)

## MILLER, ADELE
**Adele Miller**, 37 High Town Rd, Maidenhead, **Berkshire**, SL6 1PA, ENG.
(T) 01628 788420
Speciality: Homeopathy.
● **Owner** Mrs C Sanders
[M] (**Ref:**HM13881)

## MILLER, C A
**C A Miller**, 35 The St, Manuden, Bishop's Stortford, **Hertfordshire**, CM23 1DF, ENG.
(T) 01279 812167
Speciality: Chiropodists (Podiatrists).
[S] (**Ref:**HM13882)

## MILLER, D
**D Miller**, 1 Elmfield Avenue, London, **London (Greater)**, N8 8QG, ENG.
(T) 020 8348 8045 (F) 020 8348 8045
Speciality: Alexander Technique.
● **Owner** Mrs D Miller
[P] [S] (**Ref:**HM13883)

## MILLER, D
**D Miller**, 80A Southampton Row, London, **London (Greater)**, WC1B 4BB, ENG.
(T) 020 7404 5348
Speciality: Alexander Technique.
● **Partner** Mrs D Miller
[P] [S] (**Ref:**HM13884)

## MILLER, GAIL
**Gail Miller**, 127 Embleton Rd, **Yorkshire (West)**, LS26 9DA, ENG.
(T) 01977 510866
Speciality: Indian Head Massage.
[M] (**Ref:**HM13885)

## MILLER, HELENE
**Helene Miller**, 20 Audley Gr, Bath, **Somerset**, BA1 3BT, ENG.
(T) 01225 422930
Speciality: Reflexology.
[S] [T] (**Ref:**HM13886)

## MILLER, IAN A
**Ian A Miller**, 12 Kingswood Cl, Guildford, **Surrey**, GU1 2SD, ENG.
(T) 01483 304744
Speciality: Chiropractic.
[P] [S] [T] (**Ref:**HM13887)

## MILLER, J
**J Miller**, 2a Corry St, Newtownards, **County Down**, BT23 4AF, NIR.
(T) 028 9181 8251
Speciality: Complementary Medicines & Therapy.
[C] [M] (**Ref:**HM13888)

## MILLER, J
**J Miller**, 16 Newry Park, Chester, **Cheshire**, CH2 2AR, ENG.
(T) 01244 371114 (F) 01244 371114
Speciality: Herbal Medicine.
● **Owner** Ms J Miller
[M] (**Ref:**HM13889)

## MILLER, J F
**J F Miller**, 19 Stanley Rd, Oxford, **Oxfordshire**, OX4 1QY, ENG.
(T) 01865 725203
Speciality: Psychotherapy.
● **Owner** Mr J Miller
[B] (**Ref:**HM13890)

## MILLER, JENNY
**Jenny Miller**, 37 Rock Rd, Sittingbourne, **Kent**, ME10 1JF, ENG.
(T) 01795 478599
Speciality: Reflexology.
[S] [T] (**Ref:**HM13891)

## MILLER, JONATHAN
**Jonathan Miller**, 7 Fleece Rd, Surbiton, **Surrey**, KT6 5JP, ENG.
(T) 020 8873 7189
Speciality: Chiropodists (Podiatrists).
● **Owner** Mr J Miller
[S] (**Ref:**HM13892)

## MILLER, JULIE A
**Julie A Miller**, 36 Norwood Cres, Stanningley, Pudsey, **Yorkshire (West)**, LS28 6NG, ENG.
(T) 01132 363804 (F) 01132 363804
Speciality: Aromatherapy.
● **Owner** Mrs J Miller
[M] [O] (**Ref:**HM13893)

## MILLER, MORRIS
**Morris Miller**, 7 Hawthorn Drive, Sway, Lymington, **Hampshire**, SO41 6DX, ENG.
(T) 01590 682235
Speciality: Hypnosis.
● **Owner** Mr M Miller
[B] (**Ref:**HM13894)

## MILLER, NORMAN
**Norman Miller**, 5 Grosvenor Mansions, Church St, Sidmouth, **Devon**, EX10 8NB, ENG.
(T) 01395 513547
Speciality: Chiropodists (Podiatrists).
● **Owner** Mr N Miller
[S] (**Ref:**HM13895)

## MILLER, P J (DR)
**Dr P J Miller**, 67 Mersea Rd, Colchester, **Essex**, CO2 7QR, ENG.
(T) 01206 549809 (F) 01206 549852
Speciality: Chiropractors.
● **Principal** Dr I Garrod
[P] [S] [T] (**Ref:**HM13896)

## MILLER, P M
**P M Miller**, 36 Belle Vue St, Filey, **Yorkshire (North)**, YO14 9HY, ENG.
(T) 01723 513778
Speciality: Physiotherapy.
● **Owner** Mrs P Miller
[P] [S] [T] (**Ref:**HM13897)

## MILLER, PAM
**Pam Miller**, Winston, 120 Woodbridge Rd East, Ipswich, **Suffolk**, IP4 5QJ, ENG.
(T) 01473 719889
Speciality: Reflexology.
[S] [T] (**Ref:**HM13898)

## MILLER, R
**R Miller**, 21 Railway St, Gillingham, **Kent**, ME7 1XF, ENG.
(T) 01634 852169
Speciality: Chiropodists (Podiatrists).
● **Owner** Mr R Miller
[S] (**Ref:**HM13899)

## MILLER, R W
**R W Miller**, 94 Parrock St, Gravesend, **Kent**, DA12 1EX, ENG.
(T) 01474 326657
Speciality: Chiropodists (Podiatrists).
[S] (**Ref:**HM13900)

## MILLER, SANDRA
**Sandra Miller**, 11 Limes Way, Shabbington, Aylesbury, **Buckinghamshire**, HP18 9HB, ENG.
(T) 01844 201709 (F) 01844 201709
Speciality: Chiropodists (Podiatrists).
● **Owner** Mrs S Miller
[S] (**Ref:**HM13901)

## MILLER, SUE
**Sue Miller**, 21 The Elms, Woodbine Cl, Waltham Abbey, **Essex**, EN9 3RF, ENG.
(T) 01992 768649
Speciality: Reflexology.
[S] [T] (**Ref:**HM13902)

## MILLER, SUSAN
**Susan Miller**, 49 Ashworth Lane, Bolton, **Lancashire**, BL1 8RD, ENG.
(T) 01204 594419
Speciality: Reflexology.
● **Owner** Mrs S Miller
[S] [T] (**Ref:**HM13903)

## MILLER, TRISH
**Trish Miller**, Springers Croft, Coldharbour Rd, Lower Dicker, Hailsham, **Sussex (East)**, BN27 3PS, ENG.
(T) 01323 848227
Speciality: Complementary Medicines & Therapy.
● **Owner** Mrs T Miller
[C] [M] (**Ref:**HM13904)

## MILLER, VALERIE
**Valerie Miller**, Walsall, **Midlands (West)**, WS4, ENG.
(T) 01922 620373
Speciality: Bach Remedies.
[M] (**Ref:**HM13905)

## MILLER-ROLT, SUE
**Sue Miller-Rolt**, 27 Hardel Walk, London, **London (Greater)**, SW2 2QG, ENG.
(T) 020 8671 0725
Speciality: Clairvoyants & Palmists.
● **Owner** Miss S Miller-Rolt
[B] (**Ref:**HM13906)

## MILLETT, HUGH
**Hugh Millett**, 18 Shirley Cl, Malvern, **Worcestershire**, WR14 2NH, ENG.
(T) 01684 567056
Speciality: Psychotherapy.
● **Owner** Rev H Millett
[B] (**Ref:**HM13907)

## MILLETT, HUGH
**Hugh Millett**, Malvern Natural Health Centre, 15 Abbey Rd, Malvern, **Worcestershire**, WR14 3ES, ENG.
(T) 01684 893238
Speciality: Psychotherapy.
● **Owner** Mr H Millett
[B] (**Ref:**HM13908)

Key: [B] Mind-Body Medicine [C] Complementary Medicine [H] Self Help Treatment [M] Medicinal Therapy [O] Oriental Medicine [P] Postural Therapy [S] Manipulative Structural Therapy [T] Touch Therapy

**MILLETT-DEW, ROBERT**
**Robert Millett-Dew**, 33 Silver St, Warminster, **Wiltshire**, BA12 8PT, ENG.
(T) 01985 219614 (F) 01985 219614
Speciality: Hypnosis.
● **Owner** Mr R Millett-Dew
B (Ref:HM13909)

**MILLHOUSE**
**Mrs Millhouse**, 43 High Rd, Wormley, Broxbourne, **Hertfordshire**, EN10 6HT, ENG.
(T) 01992 443026
Speciality: Osteopathy.
P S T (Ref:HM13910)

**MILLICAN, JO**
**Jo Millican**, 17 Montserrat Rd, London, **London (Greater)**, SW15 2LD, ENG.
(T) 020 8785 0790 (F) 020 8789 3910
Speciality: Homeopathy.
● **Owner** Mrs J Millican
M (Ref:HM13911)

**MILLICAN, JO**
**Jo Millican**, 11 Montserrat Rd, Putney, London, **London (Greater)**, SW15 2LD, ENG.
(T) 020 8789 2548
Speciality: Homeopathy.
M (Ref:HM13912)

**MILLICAN, SALLY**
**Sally Millican**, Pen Pynfarch, Llandysul, **Carmarthenshire**, SA44 4RU, WAL.
(T) 01559 384832
Speciality: Herbal Medicine.
● **Owner** Ms S Millican
M (Ref:HM13913)

**MILLIGAN & HILL**
**Milligan & Hill**, 16 St. Helen's Pl, London, **London (Greater)**, EC3A 6DF, ENG.
(T) 020 7628 3575 (F) 020 7628 0798
Speciality: Physiotherapy.
● **Partner** Ms H Milligan
P S T (Ref:HM13914)

**MILLIGAN, RICHARD**
**Richard Milligan**, 25 Waterpark Rd, Birkenhead, **Merseyside**, CH42 8PJ, ENG.
(T) 01516 082507
Speciality: Reflexology.
S T (Ref:HM13915)

**MILLINGTON, EDDIE**
**Eddie Millington**, 20 Murton St, Sunderland, **Tyne and Wear**, SR1 2QY, ENG.
(T) 01915 656498
Speciality: Clairvoyants & Palmists.
B (Ref:HM13916)

**MILLINGTON, JANET**
**Janet Millington**, 115 Greaves Lane, Stannington, Sheffield, **Yorkshire (South)**, S6 6BD, ENG.
(T) 01142 340697
Speciality: Hypnosis, Hypnotherapy. ✔
● **Hypnotherapist** Ms J Millington Q: Cert.Ed. M: APHP.
B Yrs. Est.: 8 (Ref:HM13917)

**MILLINGTON, P**
**P Millington**, 40 Chaplin Rd, East Bergholt, Colchester, **Essex**, CO7 6SR, ENG.
(T) 01206 298658
Speciality: Chiropodists (Podiatrists).
S (Ref:HM13918)

**MILLINGTON, P**
**P Millington**, 82 Old Rd, Frinton-on-Sea, **Essex**, CO13 9BY, ENG.
(T) 01255 678600
Speciality: Chiropodists (Podiatrists).
S (Ref:HM13919)

**MILLINGTON, P**
**P Millington**, Friars Clinic, 56 Friars St, Sudbury, **Suffolk**, CO10 2AG, ENG.
(T) 01787 374964 (F) 01787 374964
Speciality: Chiropodists (Podiatrists).
● **Partner** Mrs D Durrant
S (Ref:HM13920)

**MILLMAN & ASSOCIATES**
**Rachel Millman & Associates**, 5 Accommodation Rd, London, **London (Greater)**, NW11 8ED, ENG.
(T) 020 8731 8484
Speciality: Hypnosis.
● **Owner** Miss R Millman
B (Ref:HM13921)

**MILLS DE-WIN STUDIOS**
**Mills De-Win Studios**, 4 Crescent Prde, Uxbridge Rd, Hillingdon, **London (Greater)**, UB10 0LG, ENG.
(T) 01895 233871
(E) millsdewinstudios@rjnewman.demon.co.uk
Speciality: Aromatherapy, Bowen Therapy, Electrolysis, Massage (Therapeutic). ✔ CREDIT
● **Therapist** Ms J Mills Q: BABTAC, ECBS. M: BABTAC, BTER.
P Yrs. Est.: 11 (Ref:HM13922)

**MILLS, A**
**A Mills**, 3 Highmount Cl, Winchester, **Hampshire**, SO23 0JT, ENG.
(T) 01962 841145 (F) 01962 841145
Speciality: Alexander Technique.
● **Owner** Mr A Mills
P S (Ref:HM13923)

**MILLS, A R**
**A R Mills**, Awelon, Pentraeth, **Isle of Anglesey**, LL75 8AQ, WAL.
(T) 01248 450621
Speciality: Osteopathy.
● **Owner** Mr A Mills
P S T (Ref:HM13924)

**MILLS, ANDREW D**
**Andrew D Mills**, 105 Stock Rd, Billericay, **Essex**, CM12 0RP, ENG.
(T) 01277 634080 (F) 01277 634080
Speciality: Osteopathy.
● **Owner** Mr A Mills
P S T (Ref:HM13925)

**MILLS, B J**
**B J Mills**, 29 Lashmere, Copthorne, Crawley, **Sussex (West)**, RH10 3RR, ENG.
(T) 01342 713883
Speciality: Osteopathy.
● **Owner** Mrs B Mills
P S T (Ref:HM13926)

**MILLS, C A**
**C A Mills**, 57 Horsley Vale, South Shields, **Tyne and Wear**, NE34 6LA, ENG.
(T) 01914 542209
Speciality: Complementary Medicines & Therapy.
M (Ref:HM13927)

**MILLS, CLARE**
**Clare Mills**, 16 Nunney Cl, Keynsham, Bristol, BS31 1XF, ENG.
(T) 01179 868184
Speciality: Reflexology.
S T (Ref:HM13928)

**MILLS, D**
**D Mills**, Coppers, 56 London Rd, Hailsham, **Sussex (East)**, BN27 3DD, ENG.
(T) 01323 843924
Speciality: Complementary Medicines & Therapy.
C M (Ref:HM13929)

**MILLS, K**
**K Mills**, Oakhurst, Church Rd, Hockley, **Essex**, SS5 4SS, ENG.
(T) 01702 205290
Speciality: Physiotherapy.
● **Owner** Mrs K Mills
P S T (Ref:HM13930)

**MILLS, M**
**M Mills**, 5 Langholm Rd, East Boldon, **Tyne and Wear**, NE36 0ED, ENG.
(T) 01915 190977
Speciality: Homeopathy.
● **Owner** Mrs M Mills
M (Ref:HM13931)

**MILLS, MARGARET**
**Margaret Mills**, Mapleheath, 15 Parsonage Lane, Farnham Common, Slough, **Berkshire**, SL2 3NZ, ENG.
(T) 01753 642330 (F) 01753 645939
Speciality: Homeopathy.
● **Owner** Mrs M Mills
M (Ref:HM13932)

**MILLS, STEPHANIE**
**Stephanie Mills**, 39 Browns Rd, Surbiton, **Surrey**, KT5 8ST, ENG.
(T) 020 8399 3215 (F) 020 8390 1010
Speciality: Acupuncture.
● **Owner** Miss S Mills
O (Ref:HM13933)

**MILLS, SUE**
**Sue Mills**, 267 Dales Rd, Ipswich, **Suffolk**, IP1 4LR, ENG.
(T) 01473 221386
Speciality: Reflexology.
S T (Ref:HM13934)

**MILLS, SUSAN**
**Susan Mills**, 61A Overhill Rd, London, **London (Greater)**, SE22 0PH, ENG.
(T) 020 8299 0593
Speciality: Hypnosis.
B (Ref:HM13935)

**MILLSMITH, SELBY**
**Selby MillSmith Ltd**, 30 Circus Mews, Bath, **Somerset**, BA1 2PW, ENG.
(T) 01225 446655 (F) 01225 446643
Speciality: Psychology.
● **Office Manager** Miss S Francis
B (Ref:HM13936)

**MILLSTREAM**
**Millstream**, Old Mill Lane, Camborne, **Cornwall**, TR14 0DX, ENG.
(T) 01209 610287
Speciality: Complementary Medicines & Therapy.
● **Owner** Mrs K Cox
M (Ref:HM13937)

**MILLSTREAM MEDICAL CENTRE**
**Millstream Medical Centre**, North St, Storrington, Pulborough, **Sussex (West)**, RH20 4DH, ENG.
(T) 01903 744602 (F) 01903 744602
Speciality: Physiotherapy.
● **Owner** Miss K Notman
P S T (Ref:HM13938)

**MILLWARD, FRAN**
**Fran Millward**, Flat C, 16 Earlham St, London, **London (Greater)**, WC2H 9LN, ENG.
(T) 020 7379 0775
Speciality: Reflexology.
S T (Ref:HM13939)

**MILNE, ALEC**
**Alec Milne**, 257 Renfrew St, Glasgow, **Glasgow (City of)**, G3 6TT, SCO.
(T) 01413 320229
Speciality: Complementary Medicines & Therapy.
● **Owner** Alec Milne
C M (Ref:HM13940)

**MILNE, ALEXANDER**
**Alexander Milne**, New St Clinic, 20 New St, Horsham, **Sussex (West)**, RH12 1DF, ENG.
(T) 01403 272788
Speciality: Osteopathy.
P S T (Ref:HM13941)

**MILNE, P M**
**P M Milne**, Ceann Na Coille, 9 Lawson Avenue, Banchory, **Aberdeenshire**, AB31 5TW, SCO.
(T) 01330 825405
Speciality: Physiotherapy.
P S T (Ref:HM13942)

**MILO**
**Milo**, 19 Meath Rd, Preston, **Lancashire**, PR1 8EP, ENG.
(T) 01772 257681
Speciality: Clairvoyants & Palmists.
● **Owner** Mr F Willis
B (Ref:HM13943)

**MILSOM STREET CLINIC**
**Milsom Street Clinic**, 28 Milsom St, Bath, **Somerset**, BA1 1DG, ENG.
(T) 01225 463502


Key continued: Yrs.Est: Years Established Q: Qualifications M: Professional Membership ✔ Indemnity Insurance CREDIT Accept Credit Cards

Speciality: Acupuncture, Alexander Technique, Aromatherapy, Counselling, Cranio-Sacral Therapy, Indian Head Massage, Osteopathy, Reflexology, Shiatsu. ✔
● **Counsellor** Ms A Cameron Q: BA, Dip.Couns. M: BCPC.
● **Osteopath** Mr Bodle Q: DO. M: GOsC.
C Yrs. Est.: 10 (Ref:HM13944)

### MILSOM, CAROLINE
**Caroline Milsom**, 19 The Fairway, Braunton, **Devon**, EX33 1DZ, ENG.
(T) 01271 814418
Speciality: Chiropodists (Podiatrists).
● **Owner** Mrs C Milsom
S (Ref:HM13945)

### MILTON HEALTH
**Milton Health Ltd**, 36 Wheatlands Rd East, Harrogate, **Yorkshire (North)**, HG2 8QS, ENG.
(T) 01423 521194 (F) 01423 502428
Speciality: Complementary Medicines & Therapy.
M (Ref:HM13946)

### MILTON HOUSE SURGERY
**Milton House Surgery**, Doctors Commons Rd, Berkhamsted, **Hertfordshire**, HP4 3BY, ENG.
(T) 01442 871311
Speciality: Physiotherapy.
● **Owner** Mrs M Watts
P S T (Ref:HM13947)

### MILTON KEYNES CHIRO CLINIC
**Milton Keynes Chiropractic Clinic**, Blackberry Court, Walnut Tree, Milton Keynes, **Buckinghamshire**, MK7 7PB, ENG.
(T) 01908 677719
Speciality: Chiropractic.
P S T (Ref:HM13948)

### MILTON KEYNES HOMEOPATHIC
**Milton Keynes Homeopathic Clinic**, 18 Walney Pl, Tattenhoe, Milton Keynes, **Buckinghamshire**, MK4 3BG, ENG.
(T) 01908 522171
Speciality: Homeopathy.
M (Ref:HM13949)

### MILTON KEYNES SPORTS INJURY
**Milton Keynes Sports Injury Clinic**, Blackberry Orthopaedic Clinic, Blackberry Court, Walnut Tree, Milton Keynes, **Buckinghamshire**, MK7 7PB, ENG.
(T) 01908 604666
Speciality: Osteopathy.
P S T (Ref:HM13950)

### MILTON, CHRIS
**Chris Milton**, 8 Peerley Cl, East Wittering, Chichester, **Sussex (West)**, PO20 8PB, ENG.
(T) 01243 671806
Speciality: Aromatherapy.
● **Owner** Mrs C Milton
M O (Ref:HM13951)

### MILTON, R J
**R J Milton**, Melbury Cottage, Melbury Rd, London, **London (Greater)**, W14 8LP, ENG.
(T) 020 7603 8823 (F) 020 7603 0040
Speciality: Physiotherapy.
● **Owner** Mrs R Milton
P S T (Ref:HM13952)

### MILTON, RHONA M
**Rhona M Milton**, 17 Eastwick Park Avenue, Bookham, Leatherhead, **Surrey**, KT23 3LY, ENG.
(T) 01372 454346
Speciality: Complementary Medicines & Therapy.
C M (Ref:HM13953)

### MILTON, S & C
**Simeon Milton & Carolynn Milton**, Epsom Downs Osteopathic Clinic, 128 Great Tattenhams, Epsom, **Surrey**, KT18 5SE, ENG.
(T) 01737 353660
Speciality: Osteopathy.
P S T (Ref:HM13954)

### MILWARD, S J
**S J Milward**, 54 Rosedale Avenue, Atherton, Manchester, **Manchester (Greater)**, M46 0EA, ENG.
(T) 01942 892289 (F) 01942 892289
Speciality: Osteopathy.
● **Owner** Mr S Milward
P S T (Ref:HM13955)

### MINCHINHAMPTON PHYSIO SVS
**Minchinhampton Physiotherapy Services**, Windmill Rd, Minchinhampton, Stroud, **Gloucestershire**, GL6 9EE, ENG.
(T) 01453 882917
Speciality: Physiotherapy.
P S T (Ref:HM13956)

### MIND & BODY NATURAL THERAPIES
**Mind & Body Natural Therapies**, 105 Meadow View, Higham Ferrers, Rushden, **Northamptonshire**, NN10 8EN, ENG.
(T) 01933 313202
Speciality: Complementary Medicines & Therapy.
M (Ref:HM13957)

### MIND AND BODY
**Lesley McDonald T/A Mind And Body**, 8 George St, Croydon, **Surrey**, CR0 1PA, ENG.
(T) 020 8681 8877
(E) mindandbody@btinternet.com
Speciality: Aromatherapy, Bach Remedies, Cranio-Sacral Therapy, Homeopathy, Hypnotherapy, Indian Head Massage, Iridology, Kinesiology, Massage (Therapeutic), Reflexology, Reiki.
● **Therapist** Ms V Buck M: Soc.SM.
● **Owner/Therapist** Ms L McDonald Q: BSYA (Ad Reflex), Dip.Arom.
● **Owner/Therapist** Ms T Munro M: ISPA.
B Yrs. Est.: 8 (Ref:HM13958)

### MIND AND BODY
**Mind And Body**, 31 West St, Buckingham, **Buckinghamshire**, MK18 1HE, ENG.
(T) 01280 812022
Speciality: Absent Healing, Aromatherapy, Aura Therapy, Complementary Therapy, Counselling, Dowsing, Healer, Healing Therapy, Holistic Healing, Indian Head Massage, Meditation, Reiki, Spiritual Healing, Stress Therapy, Touch Therapy, Visualisation Therapy. ✔
● **Holistic Therapist** Ms S Hampton M: BRCP.
B Yrs. Est.: 5 (Ref:HM13959)

### MIND BODY SOUL & ASSOCIATES
**Mind Body Soul & Associates**, Scottish Office, Po Box 10027, Dundee, **Angus**, DD2 4YJ., SCO.
(T) 020 85571207
Speciality: Acupuncture, Alexander Technique, Aromatherapy, Holistic Healing, Homeopathy, Hopi Ear Candles, Indian Head Massage, Kinesiology, Massage (Therapeutic), Meditation, Naturopathy, Nutritional Therapy, Osteopathy, Reflexology, Reiki, Remedial Massage, Shiatsu, Stress Therapy, Swedish Body Massage, Hypericum, Personal Development, Sports Therapy/Personal Fitness Training.
C (Ref:HM13960)

### MIND BODY SOUL DEVELOPMENT ORG
**Mind Body Soul Development Organisation**, Hill Farm, Penhow, Caldicot, **Monmouthshire**, NP26 3AE, WAL.
(T) 01633 400072
Speciality: Physiotherapy. ✔
● **Partner** Mrs Cinganelli
● **Clairvoyant/Medium** Mr Cinganelli
C Yrs. Est.: 5 (Ref:HM13961)

### MIND BODY SOUL DEVELOPMNT ORG
**Mind Body Soul Development Organisation**, 45 High St, Rochester, **Kent**, ME1 1LP, ENG.
(T) 01634 817819 (F) 01634 817819
Speciality: Clairvoyants & Palmists.
● **Owner** Mr M Cinganelli
B (Ref:HM13962)

### MIND MATTERS
**Mind Matters**, 11 Eshe Rd, Liverpool, **Merseyside**, L23 3AR, ENG.
(T) 01514 769624
Speciality: Hypnosis.
B (Ref:HM13963)

### MIND MATTERS
**Mind Matters**, 81 Aldermans Drive, Peterborough, **Cambridgeshire**, PE3 6AX, ENG.
(T) 01733 313204
Speciality: Hypnotherapy.
B (Ref:HM13964)

### MIND MATTERS
**Mind Matters**, 9 Priory Cl, Deeping St. James, Peterborough, **Cambridgeshire**, PE6 8PR, ENG.
(T) 01778 342958 (F) 01778 341320
Speciality: Hypnosis.
● **Partner** Mr C Fincham
B (Ref:HM13965)

### MIND TRAIN
**Mind Train**, 145 East Ferry Rd, London, **London (Greater)**, E14 3BQ, ENG.
(T) 020 8505 5078
Speciality: Hypnotherapy.
B (Ref:HM13966)

### MIND WORK SOLUTIONS
**Angus Ewing**, 46 Queen St, Broadwater, **Sussex (West)**, BN14 7BJ, ENG.
(T) 01903 203034 (F) 01903 535934
(E) clanotter@freeuk.com
(W) www.mindworksolutions.co.uk
Speciality: Holistic Healing, Hypnotherapy. ✔
● **Owner** Mr A Ewing Q: C.Hyp, CMH, NLP, TLT. M: HA, NCH, NGH(US), UKGHE.
C Yrs. Est.: 13 (Ref:HM13967)

### MINDA'S BEAUTY PARLOUR
**Minda's Beauty Parlour**, 22 Ashford Rd, London, **London (Greater)**, E6 2AW, ENG.
(T) 020 8471 0532
Speciality: Electrolysis.
● **Owner** Mrs M Nandra
T (Ref:HM13968)

### MINDWORKS HYPNOTHERAPY CLINIC
**Mindworks Hypnotherapy Clinic**, 179 Stubbington Avenue, Northend, Portsmouth, **Hampshire**, PO2 0JJ, ENG.
(T) 08000 925758 (F) 08000 925758
(E) mary@lineone.net
Speciality: Cognitive Therapy, Counselling, Hypnosis, Hypnotherapy, Life Style Coaching, Psychotherapy, Stress Therapy, Voice Therapy, Self-Hypnosis. ✔
● **Hypnotherapist/Psychotherapist** Mrs M Burgess
(T) 023 9242 2637 Q: A Level(Psychol), Dip.Clin.Hyp/Psych, RSA Cert(Couns). M: HA, Ukreg.Pract.GPs.Hosp.
B Yrs. Est.: 3 (Ref:HM13969)

### MINERVA HOMEOPATHIC CENTRE
**Minerva Homeopathic Centre**, 173 Fulham Palace Rd, London, **London (Greater)**, W6 8QT, ENG.
(T) 020 7385 3512
Speciality: Homeopathy.
M (Ref:HM13970)

### MING HERBAL CLINIC
**Ming Herbal Clinic**, 41 Mill Lane, London, **London (Greater)**, NW6 1NB, ENG.
(T) 020 7431 0548
Speciality: Complementary Medicines & Therapy.
● **Owner** Mr M Li
C M (Ref:HM13971)

### MING IMPERIAL HERBAL MEDICINE
**Ming Imperial Herbal Medicine**, 43 Highgate High St, London, **London (Greater)**, N6 5JX, ENG.
(T) 020 8347 6188 (F) 020 8349 9804
Speciality: Complementary Medicines & Therapy.
● **Manager** Dr S Jaing
C M (Ref:HM13972)

### MINGS CHINESE HERBALISTS
**Mings Chinese Herbalists**, Bristol Rd, Erdington, Birmingham, **Midlands (West)**, B23 6AD, ENG.
(T) 01214 765423
Speciality: Herbalists.
● **Manager** Mr O Su
M (Ref:HM13973)



Key: B Mind-Body Medicine C Complementary Medicine H Self Help Treatment M Medicinal Therapy O Oriental Medicine P Postural Therapy S Manipulative Structural Therapy T Touch Therapy

**MINGUY, CHANTEL**

**Chantel Minguy**, 52 Arnewood Rd, Bournemouth, **Dorset**, BH6 5DJ, ENG.
(T) 01202 434422
Speciality: Reflexology.
S T (Ref:HM13974)

**MINIHAN-CRANE, BAIRBRE**

**Bairbre Minihan-Crane**, Victoria House, Portsmouth Rd, Esher, **Surrey**, KT10 9JB, ENG.
(T) 01372 467140
Speciality: Physiotherapy.
P S T (Ref:HM13975)

**MINIHANE, LIZ**

**Liz Minihane**, 36 Leighton Rd, Birmingham, **Midlands (West)**, B13 8HD, ENG.
(T) 01214 499237
Speciality: Homeopathy.
M (Ref:HM13976)

**MINISTER, COLIN**

**Colin Minister**, Pickering Merdical Practice, Southgate, Pickering, **Yorkshire (North)**, YO18 8BL, ENG.
(T) 01751 477772
Speciality: Osteopathy.
● **Owner** Mr C Minister
P S T (Ref:HM13977)

**MINNERY, PATRICIA**

**Patricia Minnery**, 21 King St, Newmilns, **Ayrshire (East)**, KA16 9DN, SCO.
(T) 01560 323896
Speciality: Aromatherapy.
M O (Ref:HM13978)

**MINNERY, SHEILA**

**Sheila Minnery**, Lancaster, **Lancashire**, LA1, ENG.
(T) 01524 69300
Speciality: Bach Remedies.
M (Ref:HM13979)

**MINNS, DANIELE**

**Daniele Minns**, 51 Agar Gr, London, **London (Greater)**, NW1 9UE, ENG.
(T) 020 7267 6781
Speciality: Reflexology.
S T (Ref:HM13980)

**MINTZ, J**

**J Mintz**, 12A Kings Rd, Prestwich, Manchester, **Manchester (Greater)**, M25 0LE, ENG.
(T) 01617 733087
Speciality: Chiropodists (Podiatrists).
S (Ref:HM13981)

**MINTZ, J**

**Mr J Mintz**, 253 Manchester Rd, Droylsden, Manchester, **Manchester (Greater)**, M43 6HE, ENG.
(T) 01613 700344
Speciality: Chiropodists (Podiatrists).
S (Ref:HM13982)

**MIQUEL, SHEILA**

**Sheila Miquel**, 44 Gorton St, Blackpool, **Lancashire**, FY1 3HP, ENG.
(T) 01253 620273
Speciality: Clairvoyants & Palmists.
● **Owner** Mrs S Miquel
B (Ref:HM13983)

**MIRAGE BEAUTY ROOMS**

**Mirage Beauty Rooms**, Worthing Leisure Centre, Shaftesbury Avenue, Goring-By-Sea, Worthing, **Sussex (West)**, BN12 4ET, ENG.
(T) 01903 244404
Speciality: Electrolysis.
T (Ref:HM13984)

**MIRANDA, FRANCES**

**Frances Miranda**, 35 Cypress Cl, Desborough, Kettering, **Northamptonshire**, NN14 2XU, ENG.
(T) 01536 760241 (F) 01536 760241
Speciality: Clairvoyants & Palmists.
● **Owner** Mrs F Burnham
B (Ref:HM13985)

**MIRFIELD NATURAL HEALTH CENTRE**

**Mirfield Natural Health Centre**, 4 Town Hall St, Mirfield, **Yorkshire (West)**, WF14 8DH, ENG.
(T) 01924 498946
Speciality: Complementary Medicines & Therapy.
● **Owner** Mrs M Scott
C M (Ref:HM13986)

**MIRZA, (PROFESSOR)**

**Professor Mirza**, 216 Kings Rd Arches, Brighton, **Sussex (East)**, BN1 1NB, ENG.
(T) 01273 721859
Speciality: Clairvoyants & Palmists.
B (Ref:HM13987)

**MIRZA, A (DR)**

**Dr A Mirza**, Symbiosis Health Clinic, 66 Vernon Drive, Stanmore, **London (Greater)**, HA7 2BT, ENG.
(T) 020 8427 3268
Speciality: Osteopathy.
P S T (Ref:HM13988)

**MIRZA, ALEEM**

**Aleem M Mirza**, Hornsey Rd, London, **London (Greater)**, N7 7NY, ENG.
(T) 020 7609 2166 (F) 020 7700 3094
Speciality: Osteopathy.
● **Chief Executive** Mr M Tebett
P S T (Ref:HM13989)

**MIRZA, ISHRET**

**Ishret Mirza**, 4a Kingfield Trce, Kingfield Rd, Woking, **Surrey**, GU22 9EE, ENG.
(T) 01483 771821
Speciality: Herbal Medicine.
● **Owner** Ms I Mirza
M (Ref:HM13990)

**MIRZA, ISHRET**

**Ishret Mirza**, Natural Health York Clinic, Guildford Rd, Woking, **Surrey**, GU22 7QU, ENG.
(T) 01483 720464 (F) 01483 723844
Speciality: Herbalists.
● **Owner** Ms I Mirza
M (Ref:HM13991)

**MIRZOEFF, PETER**

**Peter Mirzoeff**, The Old Barn, Town Farm, Beacon Hill, Penn, **Buckinghamshire**, HP10 8NJ, ENG.
(T) 01494 817207 (F) 01494 817447
Speciality: Hypnosis, Hypnotherapy, Neuro-Linguistic Program, Psychotherapy. ✔
● **Hypnotherapist** Mr P Mirzoeff Q: BHReg, Dip.EH, NLP M: BIH.
B Yrs. Est.: 9 (Ref:HM13992)

**MISRA, P C**

**P C Misra**, 21 Onslow Drive, Glasgow, **Glasgow (City of)**, G31 2LY, SCO.
(T) 01415 519366
Speciality: Hypnosis.
● **Owner** Dr P Misra
B (Ref:HM13993)

**MISSELBROOK, JILL**

**Jill Misselbrook**, 5 Monterey Pines, Bognor Regis, **Sussex (West)**, PO22 7LA, ENG.
(T) 01243 869453
Speciality: Physiotherapy.
● **Owner** Ms J Misselbrook
P S T (Ref:HM13994)

**MISSION, CHAITANYA**

**Chaitanya Mission**, Station Rd, Cheadle Hulme, Cheadle, **Cheshire**, SK8 7BG, ENG.
(T) 01614 828448 (F) 01614 858984
Speciality: Meditation, Inner peace.
● **Teacher Of Meditation** Mrs S Dasi
C Yrs. Est.: 4 (Ref:HM13995)

**MIST, CORINNE**

**Corinne Mist**, 62 Buckingham Way, Frimley, Camberley, **Surrey**, GU16 8FX, ENG.
(T) 01252 654293
Speciality: Aromatherapy, Indian Head Massage, Massage (Therapeutic), Reflexology, Reiki, Holistic Therapy. ✔
● **Holistic Therapist** Ms C Mist Q: IIHHT, ITEC, MICHT. M: FHT, ITEC.
C Yrs. Est.: 3 (Ref:HM13996)

**MIST, JULIA**

**Julia Mist**, The White House, Tilthams Green, Godalming, **Surrey**, GU7 3BT, ENG.
(T) 01483 423100 (F) 01483 423100
Speciality: Aromatherapy.
● **Owner** Mrs J Mist
M O (Ref:HM13997)

**MISTELY, SONIA**

**Sonia Mistely**, 26 Brunswick St, Teignmouth, **Devon**, TQ14 8AF, ENG.
(T) 01626 773339 (F) 01626 777811
Speciality: Osteopathy.
● **Practice Manager** Mrs L Westlake
P S T (Ref:HM13998)

**MISTRAL, J**

**J Mistral**, 37 Alexandra Rd, Frome, **Somerset**, BA11 1LX, ENG.
(T) 01373 463368
Speciality: Homeopathy.
● **Owner** Mrs J Mistral
M (Ref:HM13999)

**MITCHELL, AIDAN (DR)**

**Mitchell Dr Aidan Bsc Msc, D C**, Tobin's Medical Hall O'Neill St, Carrickmacross, **County Monaghan**, IRE.
(T) 04296 61217
Speciality: Chiropractors.
P S T (Ref:HM14000)

**MITCHELL, AIDAN (DR)**

**Mitchell, Dr Aidan**, 12 Watergate St, Navan, **County Meath**, IRE.
(T) 07767 4277
Speciality: Chiropractors.
P S T (Ref:HM14001)

**MITCHELL, AMY**

**Amy Mitchell**, 179 Northfield Avenue, London, **London (Greater)**, W13 9QT, ENG.
(T) 020 8567 2403
Speciality: Osteopathy.
P S T (Ref:HM14002)

**MITCHELL, CAROLE**

**Carole Mitchell**, 9 Bell St, Renfrew, **Renfrewshire**, PA4 8PP, SCO.
(T) 01418 866930
Speciality: Osteopathy.
P S T (Ref:HM14003)

**MITCHELL, DEIRDRE**

**Deirdre Mitchell**, 7 Turmoyra Court, Lough Rd, Lurgan, Craigavon, **County Armagh**, BT66 6SD, NIR.
(T) 028 3834 6076
Speciality: Reflexology.
S T (Ref:HM14004)

**MITCHELL, EMMA**

**Emma Mitchell**, Three Acres, Chapel Lane, Easton, Winchester, **Hampshire**, SO21 1HQ, ENG.
(T) 01962 861378
Speciality: Reflexology.
S T (Ref:HM14005)

**MITCHELL, G D**

**G D Mitchell**, 5 Church Rd, Woolton, Liverpool, **Merseyside**, L25 5JE, ENG.
(T) 01514 284637
Speciality: Chiropodists (Podiatrists).
S (Ref:HM14006)

**MITCHELL, GILLIAN M**

**Gillian M Mitchell**, 10A Albert St, Aberdeen, **Aberdeenshire**, AB25 1XQ, SCO.
(T) 01224 643803
Speciality: Osteopathy.
● **Employee** Mr G Mitchell
P S T (Ref:HM14007)

**MITCHELL, GRACE**

**Grace Mitchell**, 68 Iona Way, Kirkintilloch, Glasgow, **Glasgow (City of)**, G66 3PY, SCO.
(T) 01417 750510
Speciality: Reflexology.
● **Owner** Mrs G Mitchell
S T (Ref:HM14008)

**MITCHELL, J**

**J Mitchell**, The Sydney Fisher Clinic, 81 Tressillian Rd, London, **London (Greater)**, SE4 1XZ, ENG.
(T) 020 8694 2714 (F) 020 8694 2714
Speciality: Osteopathy.
● **Partner** Mrs J Mitchell


Key continued: Yrs.Est: Years Established Q: Qualifications M: Professional Membership ✔ Indemnity Insurance Accept Credit Cards

P S T (Ref:HM14009)

**MITCHELL, JANE**

**Jane Mitchell**, 41 Overdale Avenue, Glenfield, Leicester, **Leicestershire**, LE3 8GQ, ENG.
(T) 01162 878567
Speciality: Hypnotherapy.
● **Partner** Mrs J Pollard
B (Ref:HM14010)

**MITCHELL, JANE**

**Jane Mitchell**, 13 Selwood Rd, Chessington, **Surrey**, KT9 2QT, ENG.
(T) 020 8287 6577
Speciality: Herbal Medicine.
● **Owner** Mrs J Mitchell
M (Ref:HM14011)

**MITCHELL, JOANNA**

**Miss Joanna Mitchell**, 105 Langthorne St, London, **London (Greater)**, SW6 6JU, ENG.
(T) 020 7381 3328
Speciality: Osteopathy.
P S T (Ref:HM14012)

**MITCHELL, JOY**

**Joy Mitchell**, 112 Manor Lane, Halesowen, **Midlands (West)**, B62 8QW, ENG.
(T) 01215 591324
Speciality: Chiropodists (Podiatrists).
● **Owner** Mrs J Mitchell
S (Ref:HM14013)

**MITCHELL, VICTORIA**

**Victoria Mitchell**, Crowsheath Farm, Hawkswood Rd, Downham, Billericay, **Essex**, CM11 1JT, ENG.
(T) 01268 711744 (F) 01268 711707
Speciality: Complementary Medicines & Therapy.
● **Partner** Ms V Mitchell
M (Ref:HM14014)

**MITCHELL, VIRGINIA**

**Virginia Mitchell**, 6b Slocum Cl, London, **London (Greater)**, SE28 8LQ, ENG.
Speciality: Reflexology.
S T (Ref:HM14015)

**MITCHER, D A**

**D A Mitcher**, 7 Fern Cl, Eastbourne, **Sussex (East)**, BN23 8AQ, ENG.
(T) 01323 766830
Speciality: Complementary Medicines & Therapy.
● **Owner** Mr D Mitcher
C M (Ref:HM14016)

**MITCHESON, D**

**D Mitcheson**, 5 Walworth Gr, Middlesbrough, **Cleveland**, TS5 8AN, ENG.
(T) 01642 282113
Speciality: Complementary Medicines & Therapy.
● **Owner** Diane Mitcheson
M (Ref:HM14017)

**MITRE HOUSE CENTRE**

**Mitre House Centre**, Room 102 Mitre House, 149 Western Rd, Brighton, **Sussex (East)**, BN1 2DD, ENG.
(T) 01273 778148
Speciality: Complementary Medicines & Therapy.
● **Partner** Ms B Smale
M (Ref:HM14018)

**MITTAL, A**

**A Mittal B A W A**, 34 Roe Lane, Southport, **Merseyside**, PR9 9DZ, ENG.
(T) 01704 533846
Speciality: Acupuncture.
O (Ref:HM14019)

**MITTAL, R (DR)**

**Dr R Mittal**, 10 Eldon Rd, Reading, **Berkshire**, RG1 4DH, ENG.
(T) 01189 502002
Speciality: Acupuncture.
O (Ref:HM14020)

**MITTERHUBER, P F**

**P F Mitterhuber**, The Radlett Practice, 107 Watling St, Radlett, **Hertfordshire**, WD7 7NG, ENG.
(T) 01923 855884
Speciality: Osteopathy.
P S T (Ref:HM14021)

**MM MOBILE MASSAGE**

**MM Mobile Massage**, Tregorran, Marshgate, Camelford, **Cornwall**, PL32 9YN, ENG.
(T) 01840 261738
Speciality: Complementary Medicines & Therapy.
● **Partner** Mr A Burgess
C M (Ref:HM14022)

**MO, JOSEPH**

**Joseph Mo**, 3 Kingston Rd, Taunton, **Somerset**, TA2 7SA, ENG.
(T) 01823 334143
Speciality: Acupuncture.
● **Owner** Mr J Mo
O (Ref:HM14023)

**MOAT, ANTOINETTE**

**Antoinette Moat**, Crenham Mill, Hartland, Bideford, **Devon**, EX39 6HN, ENG.
(T) 01288 331261 (F) 01288 331261
Speciality: Alexander Technique.
● **Owner** Mrs A Moat
P S (Ref:HM14024)

**MOBBERLEY COMP HEALTHCARE**

**Mobberley Complementary Healthcare**, Eden House, Ivy Bank Trading Estate, Town Lane, Mobberley, Knutsford, **Cheshire**, WA16 7HP, ENG.
(T) 01656 873624 (F) 01565 873624
Speciality: Complementary Medicines & Therapy.
● **Owner** Mrs J Parkes
M (Ref:HM14025)

**MOBILE CHIROPODIST**

**Mobile Chiropodist**, 12 Cemetery Rd, Cannock, **Staffordshire**, WS11 2QH, ENG.
(T) 01543 469358
Speciality: Chiropodists (Podiatrists).
S (Ref:HM14026)

**MOBILE CHIROPODIST**

**Mobile Chiropodist**, 23 Newton St, Darwen, **Lancashire**, BB3 0HG, ENG.
(T) 01254 706961
Speciality: Chiropody. ✔
● **Chiropodist** Mrs E Cocker Q: MSSCh. M: B.A.Ch.P.
M Yrs. Est.: 1 (Ref:HM14027)

**MOBILE CHIROPODY SERVICES**

**Mobile Chiropody Services**, 28 Warriston Drive, Edinburgh, **Edinburgh (City of)**, EH3 5LY, SCO.
(T) 01315 523302
Speciality: Biomechanics, Chiropody, Podiatry. ✔
● **Chiropodist** Miss J Hook Q: DPodM, S.R.Ch. M: S.C.P.
M Yrs. Est.: 2 (Ref:HM14028)

**MOBILE COMPLEMENTARY THERAPIES**

**Julie Richards Complementary Therapies**, 3 Cleveleys Avenue, Chorlton, Manchester, **Manchester (Greater)**, M21 8TS, ENG.
(T) 01618 607982
(E) julierichards@freeuk.com
(W) www.julierichards.freeuk.com
Speciality: Aromatherapy, Complementary Therapy, Indian Head Massage, Manipulation, Massage (Therapeutic), Nutritional Therapy, Remedial Massage, Stress Therapy, Remedial Exercise. ✔
● **Sports Therapist** Ms J Richards Q: Dip.Sports Therapy. M: FHT.
C S Yrs. Est.: 4 (Ref:HM14029)

**MOBILE FEEL GOOD**

**Mobile Feel Good Co**, 1 Monkfrith Way, London, **London (Greater)**, N14 5LG, ENG.
(T) 08007 315100
Speciality: Complementary Medicines & Therapy.
● **Director** Miss J Cambell
M (Ref:HM14030)

**MOBILE FOOTWORKS**

**Mobile Footworks**, 23 Emanuel Cl, Caerphilly, **Glamorgan (Vale of)**, CF83 1SG, WAL.
(T) 029 2088 7421 (F) 07989 013044
(E) paulandtracygill@net.co.uk
Speciality: Acupressure, Aromatherapy, Chiropody, Complementary Therapy, Holistic Healing, Massage (Therapeutic), Reflexology. ✔
● **Foot Therapist** Tracy Gill M: IHBC, SMAE.
M Yrs. Est.: 5 (Ref:HM14031)

**MOBILE PHYSIO**

**Mobile Physio**, 72A Wightman Rd, London, **London (Greater)**, N4 1RW, ENG.
(T) 020 8340 0099 (F) 020 8341 6007
Speciality: Physiotherapy.
● **Managing Director** Mr G Wilson
P S T (Ref:HM14032)

**MOBILE PHYSIOTHERAPY ASS**

**Mobile Physiotherapy Association**, 2 Marsland Avenue, Wakefield, **Yorkshire (West)**, WF1 4NT, ENG.
(T) 01924 373083
Speciality: Physiotherapy.
● **Chief Executive** Mrs D Finneymore
P S T (Ref:HM14033)

**MOBILE PHYSIOTHERAPY SERVICE**

**Mobile Physiotherapy Service**, 856A Woodborough Rd, Nottingham, **Nottinghamshire**, NG3 5QQ, ENG.
(T) 01159 606408
Speciality: Physiotherapy.
P S T (Ref:HM14034)

**MOFFAT, C**

**C Moffat**, Southwood, Burchetts Green, Maidenhead, **Berkshire**, SL6 6QS, ENG.
(T) 01628 823340
Speciality: Alexander Technique.
● **Owner** Ms C Moffatt
P S (Ref:HM14035)

**MOFFATT, M H**

**M H Moffatt**, 20 Shaldon Avenue, Stockton Brook, Stoke-On-Trent, **Staffordshire**, ST9 9PU, ENG.
(T) 01782 543965
Speciality: Chiropodists (Podiatrists).
● **Owner** Mr M Moffatt
S (Ref:HM14036)

**MOFFITT, JOHN**

**Moffitt John ADHP MICHP BA HDE**, 12 Main St, Lucan, **County Dublin**, IRE.
(T) 08682 01267
(W) www.hypnosiseire.com
Speciality: Complementary Medicines & Therapy.
M (Ref:HM14037)

**MOGENSEN, C**

**C Mogensen**, Old Hall, Rectory Hill, East Bergholt, Colchester, **Essex**, CO7 6TG, ENG.
(T) 01206 298402
Speciality: Osteopathy.
● **Owner** Mr C Mogensen
P S T (Ref:HM14038)

**MOGENSEN, K**

**K Mogensen**, Old Hall, Rectory Hill, East Bergholt, Colchester, **Essex**, CO7 6TG, ENG.
(T) 01206 298402
Speciality: Reflexology.
S T (Ref:HM14039)

**MOGEY, E**

**E Mogey**, 523 Blackpool Rd, Ashton-On-Ribble, Preston, **Lancashire**, PR2 1EQ, ENG.
(T) 01772 727814
Speciality: Chiropodists (Podiatrists).
S (Ref:HM14040)

**MOHAMED, ALNOOR**

**Alnoor Mohamed**, 15 Canfield Gardens, London, **London (Greater)**, NW6 3JT, ENG.
(T) 020 7328 1430
Speciality: Acupuncture.
O (Ref:HM14041)

**MOHAMMED (PROFESSOR)**

**Professor Mohammed**, 68 Goodramgate, York, **Yorkshire (North)**, YO1 7LF, ENG.
(T) 01904 651622
Speciality: Clairvoyants & Palmists.
● **Professor** Mr N Mohammed



Key: B Mind-Body Medicine C Complementary Medicine H Self Help Treatment M Medicinal Therapy O Oriental Medicine P Postural Therapy S Manipulative Structural Therapy T Touch Therapy

B (Ref:HM14042)

**MOHAMMED, CHARLES**

**Charles Mohammed**, 73 Upper High St, Epsom, **Surrey**, KT17 4RA, ENG.
(T) 01372 725770
Speciality: Chiropodists (Podiatrists).
● **Owner** Mr C Mohammed
S (Ref:HM14043)

**MOHAN, BERNADETTE**

**Bernadette Mohan**, The Wesley Lane Clinic, 6 Wesley Lane, Bicester, **Oxfordshire**, OX6 7JU, ENG.
(T) 01869 248538
Speciality: Acupuncture.
O (Ref:HM14044)

**MOHAN, M T(DR)**

**Dr M T Mohan**, 396 High St, Lincoln, **Lincolnshire**, LN5 7SS, ENG.
(T) 01522 887887
Speciality: Physiotherapy.
● **Owner** Dr M Mohan
P S T (Ref:HM14045)

**MOHAN, TERRY**

**Terence Mohan**, 20 Nelson Rd, Bury St. Edmunds, **Suffolk**, IP33 3AG, ENG.
(T) 01284 701505
(E) terry.mohan@easynet.co.uk
Speciality: Autogenic Training, Cognitive Therapy, Counselling, Hypnosis, Hypnotherapy, Psychotherapy, Rogerian Therapy, Stress Therapy, Visualisation Therapy, EMDR (Eye Movement Desensitisation and Reprocessing), CBT (Cognitive Behavioural Therapy), Neuro Linguistic Psychotherapy, Couple Counselling. ✔
● **Therapist** Mr T Mohan Q: Dip.EH, EMDR L1-L2. M: NCH, UKCP.
B Yrs. Est.: 10 (Ref:HM14046)

**MOIR, GILL**

**Gill Moir**, 6 Abingdon Gardens, Bath, **Somerset**, BA2 2UY, ENG.
(T) 01225 834883
Speciality: Aromatherapy, Baby Massage, Indian Head Massage, Massage (Therapeutic), Reflexology, Reiki, Stress Therapy, Swedish Body Massage.
S T (Ref:HM14047)

**MOISHE, LEWIS**

**Moishe Lewis**, 21 Cranwich Rd, Stamford Hill, London, **London (Greater)**, N16 5HZ, ENG.
(T) 020 8802 8500
Speciality: Osteopathy.
P S T (Ref:HM14048)

**MOLE, DEBBIE**

**Debbie Mole**, 4 The Crescent, Solihull, **Midlands (West)**, B91 1JP, ENG.
(T) 01217 056036 (F) 01217 111267
Speciality: Hypnotherapy.
● **Partner** Mrs J Smillie
B (Ref:HM14049)

**MOLES, SUZSI**

**Suzsi Moles**, 20 Treeton Rd, Howden, Goole, **Humberside (North)**, DN14 7DQ, ENG.
(T) 01430 430661 (F) 01430 430077
Speciality: Reflexology.
● **Owner** Mrs S Moles
S T (Ref:HM14050)

**MOLESWORTH, ROGER**

**Roger Molesworth**, Little Jordans, Blackhouse Rd, Colgate, Horsham, **Sussex (West)**, RH13 6HS, ENG.
(T) 01293 851465
Speciality: Aromatherapy.
● **Owner** Mr R Molesworth
M O (Ref:HM14051)

**MOLLEREAU, ANNE MARIE**

**Mollereau Anne Marie I C C A M**, Kilbline, Thomastown, **County Kilkenny**, IRE.
(T) 01 562 7313
Speciality: Acupuncture.
O (Ref:HM14052)

**MOLLOY, PAULINE**

**Pauline Molloy**, 37 Greenstead Avenue, Woodford Green, **Essex**, IG8 7HE, ENG.
(T) 020 8505 5485
Speciality: Reflexology.
S T (Ref:HM14053)

**MOLLOY, RUPERT**

**Rupert Molloy**, 24 Hensington Rd, Woodstock, **Oxfordshire**, OX20 1JL, ENG.
(T) 01993 811815
Speciality: Chiropractic.
● **Owner** Dr R Molloy
P S T (Ref:HM14054)

**MOLONEY, KATE**

**Kate Moloney**, 11 Brownhill Rd, Batley, **Yorkshire (West)**, WF17 0QZ, ENG.
(T) 01924 443874
Speciality: Hypnosis.
B (Ref:HM14055)

**MOLONEY, MARY JOE**

**Moloney Mary Joe ADHP MICHP**, Donaghmede, IRE.
(T) 08682 52316
(W) www.hypnosiseire.com
Speciality: Complementary Medicines & Therapy.
M (Ref:HM14056)

**MOLYNEUX, DAVID J**

**David J Molyneux**, 1105A Bristol Rd South, Northfield, Birmingham, **Midlands (West)**, B31 2QP, ENG.
(T) 01214 769143
Speciality: Chiropodists (Podiatrists).
● **Owner** Mr D Molyneux
S (Ref:HM14057)

**MOMENTA**

**Momenta**, Stanhope House, 1a Station Rd, Cippenham, Slough, **Berkshire**, SL1 6JJ, ENG.
(T) 01628 667267
Speciality: Hypnosis, Neuro-Linguistic Program, Psychotherapy, Stress Therapy, Personal Development.
B (Ref:HM14058)

**MONAGHAN**

**Monaghan**, Lough Egish, Castleblayney, **County Monaghan**, IRE.
(T) 04297 45546
Speciality: Homeopathy.
M (Ref:HM14059)

**MONAGHAN CHIROPRACTIC CLINIC**

**Monaghan Chiropractic Clinic**, Lough Egish, Castleblayney, **County Monaghan**, IRE.
(T) 04297 45070
Speciality: Chiropractors.
P S T (Ref:HM14060)

**MONAGHAN, CIARAN**

**Ciaran Monaghan**, 33 Abbeydale Cres, The Oaks, Lucan, **County Dublin**, IRE.
(T) 01624 9934
Speciality: Complementary Medicines & Therapy.
M (Ref:HM14061)

**MONAS, MARIAN**

**Marian Monas**, 12 Mill Rd, Cambridge, **Cambridgeshire**, CB1 2AD, ENG.
(T) 01223 566122
Speciality: Acupuncture.
O (Ref:HM14062)

**MONAS, MARIAN**

**Marian Monas**, 119 Roman Rd, Bethnal Green, London, **London (Greater)**, E2 0QN, ENG.
(T) 020 8981 6938
Speciality: Acupuncture.
O (Ref:HM14063)

**MONCK, LORRAINE**

**Lorraine Monck**, 76 Church St, Tewkesbury, **Gloucestershire**, GL20 5RX, ENG.
(T) 01684 296884
Speciality: Chiropodists (Podiatrists).
S (Ref:HM14064)

**MONCRIEFF, CILLA**

**Cilla Moncrieff**, 30 West Way, Clevedon, **Somerset**, BS21 7XN, ENG.
(T) 01275 879810
Speciality: Complementary Medicines & Therapy.
M (Ref:HM14065)

**MONIQUES HOLISTIC CLINIC**

**Moniques Holistic Clinic**, 8 Drogheda St, Balbriggan, **County Dublin**, IRE.
(T) 01841 3161
Speciality: Complementary Medicines & Therapy.
M (Ref:HM14066)

**MONK, MICHAEL**

**Michael Monk**, Brewers Cottage, 35 London Rd, Copford, Colchester, **Essex**, CO6 1LG, ENG.
(T) 01206 211370
Speciality: Osteopathy.
● **Owner** Mr M Monk
P S T (Ref:HM14067)

**MONK, PETER**

**Peter Monk**, 45 Oxhey Rd, Watford, **Hertfordshire**, WD1 4QG, ENG.
(T) 01923 254259
Speciality: Hypnosis.
● **Owner** Mr P Monk
B (Ref:HM14068)

**MONKSTOWN AROMA & REFLEX**

**Monkstown Aromatherapy & Reflexology**, Parkgarriff Cottage, Monkstown, **County Cork**, IRE.
(T) 021 4841 793
Speciality: Aromatherapy.
M O (Ref:HM14069)

**MONKSTOWN COUNSELLING SVCE**

**Monkstown Counselling Svce**, St Judes 72 Monkstown Rd, Monkstown, Dublin, **County Dublin**, IRE.
(T) 01280 7237
Speciality: Counselling.
B H (Ref:HM14070)

**MONMOUTH HERBAL CLINIC**

**Monmouth Herbal Clinic**, 16 Agincourt Sq, Monmouth, **Monmouthshire**, NP25 3DY, WAL.
(T) 01600 719497 (F) 01600 719497
Speciality: Herbalists.
● **Practice Manager** Ms M Last
M (Ref:HM14071)

**MONMOUTH NATURAL HEALTH CENTRE**

**Monmouth Natural Health Centre**, Chippenham House, Monmouth, **Monmouthshire**, NP25 3NY, WAL.
(T) 01600 772622
Speciality: Complementary Medicines & Therapy.
● **Teacher** Mrs B Ridley
C M (Ref:HM14072)

**MONROE, T**

**T Monroe**, 75 Slough Rd, Datchet, Slough, **Berkshire**, SL3 9AL, ENG.
(T) 01753 580598
Speciality: Osteopathy.
● **Manager** Mrs M Monroe
P S T (Ref:HM14073)

**MONSAL HEAD NATURAL THRPY CTRE**

**Monsal Head Natural Therapy Centre**, Monsal Head, Bakewell, **Derbyshire**, DE45 1NL, ENG.
(T) 01629 640376 (F) 01629 640376
Speciality: Complementary Medicines & Therapy.
● **Partner** Mrs S Harman
C M (Ref:HM14074)

**MONSHIN, DEBORAH J**

**Deborah J Monshin**, Virginia House Settlement,, Looe St, Plymouth, **Devon**, PL4 0EB, ENG.
(T) 01752 880880
Speciality: Auto Suggestion, Aversion Therapy, Bach Remedies, Hypnosis, Hypnotherapy, Meditation, Psychotherapy, Stress Therapy, Visualisation Therapy, Past Life Regression Therapy. EMDR (Eye Movement Desensitisation and Reprocessing). ✔
● **Owner/Clinical Therapist**
Ms D Monshin Q: MNSPH. M: NSPH.
B Yrs. Est.: 1 (Ref:HM14075)



Key continued: Yrs.Est: Years Established Q: Qualifications M: Professional Membership ✔ Indemnity Insurance Accept Credit Cards

## MONSON, J L B
**J L B Monson**, The Elements Of Health, Complementary Medical Centre, 64 Basil St, Norwich, **Norfolk**, NR1 1LU, ENG.
(T) 01603 621001 (F) 01603 665759
Speciality: Counselling, Hypnotherapy. ✔
● **Sole Owner** Mrs J Monson M: BACP.
C Yrs. Est.: 13 (**Ref:**HM14076)

## MONT, K
**K Mont**, Millbrook Farm, Millbrook Hill, Nutley, Uckfield, **Sussex (East)**, TN22 3PJ, ENG.
(T) 01825 712242 (F) 01825 712242
Speciality: Homeopathy.
● **Owner** Mrs K Mont
M (**Ref:**HM14077)

## MONTAGU CLINIC
**Montagu Clinic (The)**, Clay St, London, **London (Greater)**, W1H 3FS, ENG.
(T) 020 7935 4315
Speciality: Chiropodists (Podiatrists).
S (**Ref:**HM14078)

## MONTAGUE, D E
**D E Montague**, 6a Sloane Sq, London, **London (Greater)**, SW1W 8EE, ENG.
(T) 020 7730 8437
Speciality: Physiotherapy.
P S T (**Ref:**HM14079)

## MONTAGUE-COOK, B
**Mr B Montague Cook**, 168 Westmount Rd, London, **London (Greater)**, SE9 1XA, ENG.
(T) 020 8294 0097
Speciality: Osteopathy.
P S T (**Ref:**HM14080)

## MONTAGUE-SMITH, G
**G Montague-Smith**, The Atman Clinic, 108 St. Johns Rd, Tunbridge Wells, **Kent**, TN4 9PH, ENG.
(T) 01892 544783
Speciality: Osteopathy.
P S T (**Ref:**HM14081)

## MONTAGUE-SMITH, T
**T Montague-Smith**, The Atman Clinic, 108 St. Johns Rd, Tunbridge Wells, **Kent**, TN4 9PH, ENG.
(T) 01892 544783
Speciality: Complementary Medicines & Therapy.
M (**Ref:**HM14082)

## MONTAGUE-THOMAS, A
**A Montague-Thomas**, 58 Fairmantle St, Truro, **Cornwall**, TR1 2EG, ENG.
(T) 01872 222699
Speciality: Herbal Medicine.
● **Medical Herbalist**
Ms A Montague-Thomas
M (**Ref:**HM14083)

## MONTANARO TRUST
**Montanaro Trust (The)**, 41 Berks Hill, Chorleywood, Rickmansworth, **Hertfordshire**, WD3 5AJ, ENG.
(T) 01923 286741 (F) 01923 286742
Speciality: Complementary Medicines & Therapy.
● **Director** Ms C Montanaro
M (**Ref:**HM14084)

## MONTE, KEN (DR)
**Ken Monte Dr**, Unit 5 Tara Court Main St, Portlaoise, **County Laois**, IRE.
(T) 05026 2106
Speciality: Chiropractors.
P S T (**Ref:**HM14085)

## MONTEIRO, B T
**B T Monteiro**, 11 Moor Park Avenue, Preston, **Lancashire**, PR1 6AS, ENG.
(T) 01772 251507 (F) 01772 558761
Speciality: Psychiatry.
● **Manager** Mr F Iddon
B (**Ref:**HM14086)

## MONTROSE CHIROP & POD PRAC
**Montrose Chiropody & Podiatry Practice**, 134 Montrose Avenue, Edgware, **London (Greater)**, HA8 0DR, ENG.
(T) 020 8959 5421
Speciality: Chiropodists (Podiatrists).
S (**Ref:**HM14087)

## MONTROSE CHIROPODY CLINIC
**Montrose Chiropody Clinic**, 9 Murray St, Montrose, **Angus**, DD10 8LH, SCO.
(T) 01674 678979
Speciality: Chiropodists (Podiatrists).
S (**Ref:**HM14088)

## MONTROSE NATURAL HEALTH CARE
**Montrose Natural Health Care**, Cockleton Lane, Cowes, **Isle of Wight**, PO31 8QE, ENG.
(T) 01983 294509
Speciality: Reflexology.
● **Owner** Mrs C Hurley
S T (**Ref:**HM14089)

## MONTSERRAT CLINIC
**Montserrat Clinic**, 17 Montserrat Rd, Putney, London, **London (Greater)**, SW15 2LD, ENG.
(T) 020 8780 2727 (F) 020 8784 3910
Speciality: Acupuncture, Electrotherapy, Homeopathy, Manipulation, Massage (Therapeutic), Osteopathy, PAMS (Power Assisted Micro Manipulation). ✔
● **Homeopath** Jo Millican Q: LCPH. M: HMA.
● **Osteopath** Mr J Prescott Q: BSc, DO. M: GOsC.
B P S Yrs. Est.: 5 (**Ref:**HM14090)

## MONYPENNY, HELEN
**Helen Monypenny**, Garden Flats, 7 Upper Gr, London, **London (Greater)**, SE25 6JX, ENG.
(T) 020 8653 1646
Speciality: Psychotherapy.
● **Owner** Ms H Monypenny
B (**Ref:**HM14091)

## MOODIE, A
**A Moodie**, Aldrens Lane, Lancaster, **Lancashire**, LA1 2DU, ENG.
(T) 01524 69864 (F) 01524 848155
Speciality: Homeopathy.
● **Owner** A Moodie
M (**Ref:**HM14092)

## MOODMAKERS
**Moodmakers**, 34 Glasgow Rd, Denny, **Stirling**, FK6 6BA, SCO.
(T) 01324 825060
Speciality: Clairvoyants & Palmists.
B (**Ref:**HM14093)

## MOODY, C B
**Mrs C B Moody**, St Peters Sq Surgery, 3 St Peters Sq, Hereford, **Herefordshire**, HR1 2PG, ENG.
(T) 01432 272202
Speciality: Chiropodists (Podiatrists).
S (**Ref:**HM14094)

## MOODY, DAVID
**David Moody**, Sunnydale, Cornwood Rd, Ivybridge, **Devon**, PL21 9JJ, ENG.
(T) 01752 893253
Speciality: Osteopathy.
P S T (**Ref:**HM14095)

## MOODY, DONALD A
**Donald A Moody**, Sunnydale Natural Health Centre, Cornwood Rd, Ivybridge, **Devon**, PL21 9JJ, ENG.
(T) 01752 893253 (F) 01752 893253
Speciality: Osteopathy.
● **Owner** Mr D Moody
P S T (**Ref:**HM14096)

## MOODY, PAUL
**Paul Moody**, Ingledale, 1 Tanhouse Rd, Oxted, **Surrey**, RH8 9PE, ENG.
(T) 01883 717277
Speciality: Osteopathy.
P S T (**Ref:**HM14097)

## MOON, BARBARA
**Barbara Moon**, 90 Watkin Rd, Clayton-Le-Woods, Chorley, **Lancashire**, PR6 7PX, ENG.
(T) 01257 275169 (F) 01257 231799
Speciality: Psychotherapy.
● **Owner** Mrs B Moon
B (**Ref:**HM14098)

## MOON, BARBARA
**Barbara Moon**, 7 Brinklow Cl, Southport, **Merseyside**, PR8 2SL, ENG.
(T) 01704 576901
Speciality: Reflexology.
S T (**Ref:**HM14099)

## MOON, EDWARD
**Edward Moon**, Brabant House, Portsmouth Rd, Thames Ditton, **Surrey**, KT7 0EY, ENG.
(T) 020 8398 7592
Speciality: Complementary Medicines & Therapy.
M (**Ref:**HM14100)

## MOONBEAMS
**Moonbeams**, London Rd, Purfleet, **Essex**, RM19 1RJ, ENG.
(T) 01708 862206
Speciality: Clairvoyants & Palmists.
● **Owner** Mrs S Prentiss
B (**Ref:**HM14101)

## MOONCIE, BENEDICT
**Benedict Mooncie**, 50 High St, Hastings, **Sussex (East)**, TN34 3EN, ENG.
(T) 01424 465050
Speciality: Psychotherapy.
● **Partner** Mr B Mooncie
B (**Ref:**HM14102)

## MOONE, ROSEMARY
**Moone Rosemary MSTAT**, 8 Knockrea Dr Ballinlough, Cork, **County Cork**, IRE.
(T) 021 4311 411
Speciality: Alexander Technique.
P S (**Ref:**HM14103)

## MOONEEGAN, V
**V Mooneegan**, 140 Matlock Rd, Chaddesden, Derby, **Derbyshire**, DE21 4QB, ENG.
(T) 01332 677410
Speciality: Chiropodists (Podiatrists).
● **Owner** Mr V Mooneegan
S (**Ref:**HM14104)

## MOONEY, ALAN
**Mooney Alan MIACT MIAHIP**, 14 Upr Clanbrassil St, IRE.
(T) 01453 8356
Speciality: Complementary Medicines & Therapy.
M (**Ref:**HM14105)

## MOONEY, ANN
**Ann Mooney**, 10 Finsbury Avenue, Sileby, Loughborough, **Leicestershire**, LE12 7PJ, ENG.
(T) 01509 816397
Speciality: Hypnotherapy.
● **Owner** Mrs A Mooney
B (**Ref:**HM14106)

## MOONEY, K
**K Mooney**, 1 Carron House, Carron Way, Cumbernauld, Glasgow, **Glasgow (City of)**, G67 1ER, SCO.
(T) 01236 781958
Speciality: Aromatherapy.
M O (**Ref:**HM14107)

## MOONEY-DANIEL, G C
**G C Mooney-Daniel**, 219 Annesley Rd, Hucknall, Nottingham, **Nottinghamshire**, NG15 7DB, ENG.
(T) 01159 529067
Speciality: Reflexology.
● **Owner** Mrs G Mooney-Daniel
S T (**Ref:**HM14108)

## MOONFLEET CLINIC
**Moonfleet Clinic (The)**, The Lodge, Terregles, Dumfries, **Dumfries and Galloway**, DG2 9RT, SCO.
(T) 01387 720328
Speciality: Complementary Medicines & Therapy.
C M (**Ref:**HM14109)

## MOON-STONE
**Mrs Moon-Stone**, Mead End Farm, Waterlooville, **Hampshire**, PO7 6UX, ENG.
(T) 023 9226 4397
Speciality: Clairvoyants & Palmists.
● **Owner** Mrs S Moon-Stone
B (**Ref:**HM14110)

## MOONSTONE HEALING CENTRE
**Moonstone Healing Centre**, 2 Moores Pl, Brentwood, **Essex**, CM14 4AG, ENG.



Key: B Mind-Body Medicine C Complementary Medicine H Self Help Treatment M Medicinal Therapy O Oriental Medicine P Postural Therapy S Manipulative Structural Therapy T Touch Therapy

(T) 01277 222341
Speciality: Absent Healing, Acupuncture, Aromatherapy, Aura Therapy, Bach Remedies, Bowen Therapy, Cognitive Therapy, Complementary Therapy, Counselling, Crystal Healing, Dowsing, Healer, Healing Therapy, Holistic Healing, Hypnosis, Hypnotherapy, Indian Head Massage, Kirlian Photography, Manipulation, Massage (Therapeutic), Meditation, Psychotherapy, Reflexology, Reiki, Shiatsu, Spiritual Healing, Sports Massage, Stress Therapy, Transactional Analysis, Visualisation Therapy, Sport Injury Therapy, Past Life Regression. ✔
● **Crystal Healer/Business Manager** Mr S Flack M: BSY.
● **Owner** Mrs S Flack
B Yrs. Est.: 1 (Ref:HM14111)

**MOONSTONES**

**Moonstones**, Evenlode Cres, Coventry, **Midlands (West)**, CV6 1BY, ENG.
(T) 024 7659 2700
Speciality: Clairvoyants & Palmists.
B (Ref:HM14112)

**MOONSTONES NAT THERAPY CLINIC**

**Moonstones Natural Therapy Clinic**, 31c-31d Holton Rd, Barry, **Glamorgan (Vale of)**, CF63 4LA, WAL.
(T) 01446 733122
Speciality: Complementary Medicines & Therapy.
M (Ref:HM14113)

**MOORE GROARKE, GILLIAN (DR)**

**Dr Gillian Moore Groarke**, Suite 21 Cork Clinic Western Rd, Cork, **County Cork**, IRE.
(T) 021 4343 073
(E) gmg@corkclinic.com
(W) www.corkclinic.com
Speciality: Complementary Medicines & Therapy.
M (Ref:HM14114)

**MOORE, ANGELA**

**Angela Moore**, 57 Melbourne Rd, London, **London (Greater)**, SW19 3BB, ENG.
(T) 020 8543 2518
Speciality: Reflexology.
S T (Ref:HM14115)

**MOORE, BEVERLEY**

**Beverley Moore**, New Grange, Lyme Rd, Axminster, **Devon**, EX13 5BH, ENG.
(T) 01297 35727 (F) 01297 35727
Speciality: Aromatherapy.
● **Owner** Mrs B Moore
M O (Ref:HM14116)

**MOORE, C**

**C Moore**, 9 Lilac Cl, Anston, Sheffield, **Yorkshire (South)**, S25 5GN, ENG.
(T) 01909 560988
Speciality: Complementary Medicines & Therapy.
● **Owner** Mr C Moore
C M (Ref:HM14117)

**MOORE, C A**

**C A Moore**, Carlton Chambers, Queen St, Wellington, Telford, **Shropshire**, TF1 1EW, ENG.
(T) 01952 223219
Speciality: Chiropodists (Podiatrists).
● **Owner** Mr C Moore
S (Ref:HM14118)

**MOORE, CAROL**

**Carol Moore**, 1st Floor Woburn Court, 8 Guildhall Hill, Norwich, **Norfolk**, NR2 1JG, ENG.
(T) 01603 219254
Speciality: Homeopathy.
● **Partner** Mrs C Moore
M (Ref:HM14119)

**MOORE, CHRIS**

**Chris Moore**, Kenilworth Lodge, 126 Kenilworth Gardens, Westcliff-on-Sea, **Essex**, SS0 0BT, ENG.
(T) 01702 392266
Speciality: Homeopathy.
M (Ref:HM14120)

**MOORE, CHRISTINE**

**Christine Moore**, Copper Beech, 3 Kittersley Drive, Liverton, Newton Abbot, **Devon**, TQ12 6YX, ENG.
(T) 01626 821153
Speciality: Reflexology.
S T (Ref:HM14121)

**MOORE, DENIS**

**Denis Moore**, 7 Parkland Avenue, Romford, **Essex**, RM1 4EL, ENG.
(T) 01708 741601
Speciality: Chiropodists (Podiatrists).
● **Owner** Mr D Moore
S (Ref:HM14122)

**MOORE, GINA**

**Gina Moore**, 110 Kirkby Rd, Barwell, **Leicestershire**, LE9 8FN, ENG.
(T) 01455 842603
Speciality: Reflexology.
S T (Ref:HM14123)

**MOORE, J**

**J Moore**, 1 Stoneshey Gate, Widdop Rd, Hebden Bridge, **Yorkshire (West)**, HX7 7HD, ENG.
(T) 01422 846736
Speciality: Complementary Medicines & Therapy.
● **Owner** Ms J Moore
C M (Ref:HM14124)

**MOORE, JACKIE**

**Jackie Moore**, 43 Highfield Avenue, Chesterfield, **Derbyshire**, S41 7AU, ENG.
(T) 01246 204296 (F) 01246 232282
Speciality: Reflexology.
S T (Ref:HM14125)

**MOORE, LEONARD J**

**Leonard J Moore**, 52 Thornford Gardens, Southend-On-Sea, **Essex**, SS2 6PY, ENG.
(T) 01702 345010
Speciality: Chiropodists (Podiatrists).
● **Owner** Mr L Moore
S (Ref:HM14126)

**MOORE, M**

**M Moore**, Mountview, Brughas, Enniskillen, **County Fermanagh**, BT74 5DQ, NIR.
(T) 028 6634 1576
Speciality: Chiropodists (Podiatrists).
S (Ref:HM14127)

**MOORE, M H**

**M H Moore**, 27 Broom Gardens, Kirkcaldy, **Fife**, KY2 6YZ, SCO.
(T) 01592 206353
Speciality: Physiotherapy.
● **Owner** Mrs M Moore
P S T (Ref:HM14128)

**MOORE, M J**

**M J Moore**, 11a Dean Trce, Ryton, **Tyne and Wear**, NE40 3HQ, ENG.
(T) 01914 134003
Speciality: Acupuncture.
● **Owner** Miss N Moore
O (Ref:HM14129)

**MOORE, MAGGIE**

**Maggie Moore**, St Marys Rd, Birnam, Dunkeld, **Perth and Kinross**, PH8 0BJ, SCO.
(T) 01350 728800
Speciality: Acupuncture.
O (Ref:HM14130)

**MOORE, ROBERT P**

**Robert P Moore**, 18 Dean Row Rd, Wilmslow, **Cheshire**, SK9 2PL, ENG.
(T) 08007 312954 (F) 01625 523091
Speciality: Hypnotherapy.
● **Owner** Mr R Moore
B (Ref:HM14131)

**MOORE, S**

**S Moore**, Little Spark, Sparkford Rd, Winchester, **Hampshire**, SO22 4NN, ENG.
(T) 01962 849247
Speciality: Osteopathy.
● **Owner** Miss S Moore
P S T (Ref:HM14132)

**MOORE, SARAH**

**Sarah Moore**, Park Pharmacy, Pilgrims Cl, Chandler's Ford, Eastleigh, **Hampshire**, SO53 4ST, ENG.
(T) 023 8026 5055
Speciality: Osteopathy.
P S T (Ref:HM14133)

**MOORE, SUSAN**

**Susan Moore**, 13 Sowerberry Cl, Chelmsford, **Essex**, CM1 4YB, ENG.
(T) 01245 440021 (F) 01245 440021
Speciality: Chiropody, Podiatry, Reflexology, Reiki. ✔
● **Chiropodist/Reflexologist** Mrs S Moore Q: MAR, MSSCh. M: AoR, B.A.Ch.P, MSSCh.
M T Yrs. Est.: 6 (Ref:HM14134)

**MOORE, TERESA**

**Teresa Moore**, Rose Farm, Streamcross, Claverham, Bristol, BS49 4QD, ENG.
(T) 01934 838282
Speciality: Homeopathy.
● **Owner** Ms T Moor
M (Ref:HM14135)

**MOORE-GROACKE, GILLIAN (DR)**

**Consultant Psychologist**, Suite 21, Cork Clinic, Western Rd, **County Cork**, IRE.
(T) 021 4343 073 (F) 021 4343 073
(E) gmg@corkclinic.com
(W) www.corkclinic.com
Speciality: Cognitive Therapy, Counselling, Family Therapy, Feldenkrais Methodology, Gestalt Therapy, Hypnosis, Hypnotherapy, Psychotherapy. ✔
● **Consultant Psychologist** Dr G Moore-Groacke Q: PhD.
H (Ref:HM14136)

**MOORFIELD FLOATATION**

**Moorfield Floatation**, 81 Moorfield, Oldtown, Wadsworth, Hebden Bridge, **Yorkshire (West)**, HX7 8SG, ENG.
(T) 01422 846389
(W) www.moorfieldfloatation.connectfree.co.uk
Speciality: Flotation Therapy, Massage (Therapeutic).
● **Owner** Ms S Carr M: FTA.
H (Ref:HM14137)

**MOORGATE NATURAL HEALING CTRE**

**Moorgate Natural Healing Centre**, 3 Moorgate Rd, Rotherham, **Yorkshire (South)**, S60 2EN, ENG.
(T) 01709 375100
(E) info@mnch.co.uk
(W) www.mnhc.co.uk
Speciality: Absent Healing, Aromatherapy, Auto Suggestion, Aversion Therapy, Complementary Therapy, Gestalt Therapy, Humanistic Psychology, Hypnosis, Hypnotherapy, Massage (Therapeutic), Meditation, Psychotherapy, Reiki, Seichem, Spiritual Healing, Tera-Mai, Transactional Analysis, Visualisation Therapy. ✔
● **Complementary Therapist** Ms S Holland
B C Yrs. Est.: 3 (Ref:HM14138)

**MOORHOUSE, R C**

**R C Moorhouse**, 8 Longhurst Cl, Leicester, **Leicestershire**, LE4 7WA, ENG.
(T) 01162 611600
Speciality: Chiropodists (Podiatrists).
S (Ref:HM14139)

**MOORTHY, N S**

**N S Moorthy**, 1079 Garratt Lane, London, **London (Greater)**, SW17 0LN, ENG.
(T) 020 8682 3876 (F) 020 8333 7904
Speciality: Acupuncture.
● **Doctor** Dr N Moorthy
O (Ref:HM14140)

**MOORTHY, N S (DR)**

**Dr N S Moorthy**, 59 Dulverton Rd, South Croydon, **Surrey**, CR2 8PJ, ENG.
(T) 020 8657 6147
Speciality: Acupuncture.
● **Owner** Dr M Moorthy
O (Ref:HM14141)

**MORAN, ANGELA**

**Angela Moran**, 17 Sutherland Rd, London, **London (Greater)**, E17 6BJ, ENG.
(T) 020 8531 0531
Speciality: Chiropodists (Podiatrists).
● **Owner** Mrs A Moran



Key continued: Yrs.Est: Years Established Q: Qualifications M: Professional Membership ✔ Indemnity Insurance Accept Credit Cards

S (Ref:HM14142)

## MORAN, CARMEL

**Carmel Moran**, 5 Winchester Rd, Walton-On-Thames, **Surrey**, KT12 2RG, ENG.
(T) 01932 248264
Speciality: Reflexology, Reiki.
S T (Ref:HM14143)

## MORAN, CIARAN

**Ciaran Moran**, Avonlee O'Rahilly Row, Fermoy, **County Cork**, IRE.
(T) 025 3121 6
(E) cpmoran@indigo.ie
Speciality: Acupuncture.
O (Ref:HM14144)

## MORAN, DAVID

**David Moran**, 21 Edelvale Rd, Southampton, **Hampshire**, SO18 5PQ, ENG.
(T) 023 8036 8945 (F) 023 8036 8945
Speciality: Hypnosis.
● **Owner** Mr D Moran
B (Ref:HM14145)

## MORAN, MARY

**Mary Moran**, Rowestown Barntown, **County Wexford**, IRE.
(T) 05320 704
Speciality: Counselling.
B H (Ref:HM14146)

## MORAN, S M F

**S M F Moran**, 38 Wenlock Rd, Beechwood, Runcorn, **Cheshire**, WA7 3JB, ENG.
(T) 01928 714531
Speciality: Chiropodists (Podiatrists).
● **Owner** Mr S Moran
S (Ref:HM14147)

## MORAN, SUSAN

**Susan Moran**, 39 Westvale Rd, Timperley, Altrincham, **Cheshire**, WA15 7RL, ENG.
(T) 01619 291241
Speciality: Electrolysis.
T (Ref:HM14148)

## MORAY CHANONRY CENTRE

**Moray Chanonry Centre**, Grampian Rd, Elgin, **Moray**, IV30 1XJ, SCO.
(T) 01343 543780
Speciality: Complementary Medicines & Therapy.
C M (Ref:HM14149)

## MORBEY, PETER

**Peter Morbey**, 1 Meadow Villas, Weston-Super-Mare, **Somerset**, BS23 1RN, ENG.
(T) 01934 416640
Speciality: Chiropodists (Podiatrists).
● **Partner** Mrs M Morbey
S (Ref:HM14150)

## MORDEN CLINIC

**Morden Clinic**, 105 London Rd, Morden, **Surrey**, SM4 5HP, ENG.
(T) 020 8288 9038
Speciality: Complementary Medicines & Therapy.
M (Ref:HM14151)

## MORDIN, MARK

**Mark Mordin**, 33 Milton Avenue, London, **London (Greater)**, N6 5QF, ENG.
(T) 020 8340 7062
Speciality: Complementary Medicines & Therapy.
● **Owner** Mr M Mordin Q: MA, MBRA, MRSS, RNT.
C M (Ref:HM14152)

## MORE, JO

**Jo More**, 14 Allerton Grange Vale, Leeds, **Yorkshire (West)**, LS17 6LT, ENG.
(T) 01132 697850
Speciality: Homeopathy.
M (Ref:HM14153)

## MOREL, SUZIE

**Suzie Morel**, St Brides Alexander Centre, St. Brides-Super-Ely, Cardiff, **Glamorgan (Vale of)**, CF5 6EY, WAL.
(T) 01446 760813
Speciality: Alexander Technique.
P S (Ref:HM14154)

## MORETON CHIROPRACTIC CLINIC

**Moreton Chiropractic Clinic**, 15 Orchard Rd, Wirral, **Merseyside**, CH46 8TR, ENG.
(T) 01516 770123
Speciality: Chiropractors.
● **Owner** Mr D Darwent
P S T (Ref:HM14155)

## MORETON REMEDIAL CLINIC

**Moreton Remedial Clinic**, 168 Hoylake Rd, Wirral, **Merseyside**, CH46 8TQ, ENG.
(T) 01516 061211 (F) 01516 061211
Speciality: Osteopathy.
● **Owner** Mr L Davies
P S T (Ref:HM14156)

## MORETON, JUNE

**June Moreton**, 1 Woodlands, Paddock Wood, Tonbridge, **Kent**, TN12 6AR, ENG.
(T) 01892 833900 (F) 01892 833900
Speciality: Aromatherapy.
● **Owner** Mrs J Moreton
M O (Ref:HM14157)

## MORGAN, A

**A Morgan**, 7 Holly Rd, Northampton, **Northamptonshire**, NN1 4QL, ENG.
(T) 01604 231088
Speciality: Acupuncture.
● **Owner** Mr A Morgan
O (Ref:HM14158)

## MORGAN, C

**C Morgan**, 39 Tydfil Pl, Penylan, Cardiff, **Glamorgan (Vale of)**, CF23 5HA, WAL.
(T) 029 2048 4555
Speciality: Acupuncture.
O (Ref:HM14159)

## MORGAN, CLIVE

**Clive Morgan**, Gaer Llwydd, Lamb Lane, Ponthir, Newport, NP18 1HA, WAL.
(T) 01633 421599 (F) 01633 421599
Speciality: Chiropodists (Podiatrists).
● **Owner** Mr C Morgan
S (Ref:HM14160)

## MORGAN, D

**D Morgan**, Dalriada House, Coleraine Rd, Ballycastle, **County Antrim**, BT54 6BA, NIR.
(T) 028 2076 9478
Speciality: Chiropractic.
P S T (Ref:HM14161)

## MORGAN, F C

**F C Morgan**, 2 Stornoway Cres, Wishaw, **Lanarkshire (North)**, ML2 8XS, SCO.
(T) 01698 382593
Speciality: Chiropodists (Podiatrists).
● **Owner** Miss F Morgan
S (Ref:HM14162)

## MORGAN, GILLIAN

**Gillian Morgan**, Cornflower, 49 High St, Brightlingsea, Colchester, **Essex**, CO7 0AQ, ENG.
(T) 01206 305581
Speciality: Aromatherapy.
● **Owner** Ms G Morgan
M O (Ref:HM14163)

## MORGAN, GILLIAN

**Gillian Morgan**, 53 Station Rd, Princes Risborough, **Buckinghamshire**, HP27 9DE, ENG.
(T) 01844 345652
Speciality: Chiropodists (Podiatrists).
S (Ref:HM14164)

## MORGAN, J D

**J D Morgan**, 9 Richmond Pl, Ilkley, **Yorkshire (West)**, LS29 8TJ, ENG.
(T) 01943 603170
Speciality: Hypnosis.
B (Ref:HM14165)

## MORGAN, J D

**J D Morgan**, Suite 5 Floor 6 Manor Building, Manor Row, Bradford, **Yorkshire (West)**, BD1 4NL, ENG.
(T) 01274 370890
Speciality: Hypnosis.
B (Ref:HM14166)

## MORGAN, J D (DR)

**Dr J D Morgan**, Leeds Complementary Therapy Centre, 249A Otley Rd, Leeds, **Yorkshire (West)**, LS16 5LQ, ENG.
(T) 01132 306333
(W) www.morganic.org
Speciality: Humanistic Psychology, Hypnosis, Hypnotherapy, Psychotherapy. ✔
● **Hypnotherapist** Dr J Morgan Q: MA, PhD. M: HA, HS, NCP, NHR.
● **Hypnotherapist** Mrs R Griffiths M: HA.
B Yrs. Est.: 18 (Ref:HM14167)

## MORGAN, JANE

**Jane Morgan**, 1 Ridge Avenue, Halebarns, Altrincham, **Cheshire**, WA15 0AY, ENG.
(T) 01619 805462
Speciality: Physiotherapy.
● **Owner** Mrs J Morgan
P S T (Ref:HM14168)

## MORGAN, JO

**Jo Morgan**, 6 Silver Birch Cl, Caerleon, Newport, NP18 3RX, WAL.
(T) 01633 420847
Speciality: Hypnotherapy.
● **Owner** Mrs J Morgan
B (Ref:HM14169)

## MORGAN, JOANNA

**Joanna Morgan**, 1 St Johns Mead, Beggars Lane, Winchester, **Hampshire**, SO23 0HE, ENG.
(T) 01962 853450
Speciality: Physiotherapy.
● **Owner** Mrs J Morgan
P S T (Ref:HM14170)

## MORGAN, M

**M Morgan**, 14 Bruce Rd, Kidderminster, **Worcestershire**, DY10 2TY, ENG.
(T) 01562 67228
Speciality: Complementary Medicines & Therapy.
● **Owner** Mr M Morgan
C M (Ref:HM14171)

## MORGAN, MARTYN

**Martyn Morgan**, 834 Fishponds Rd, Fishponds, Bristol, BS16 3XA, ENG.
(T) 01179 491290
Speciality: Osteopathy.
P S T (Ref:HM14172)

## MORGAN, P D

**P D Morgan**, 342 Bolton Rd, Kearsley, Bolton, **Lancashire**, BL4 8NQ, ENG.
(T) 01204 707335
Speciality: Physiotherapy.
● **Owner** Mr P Morgan
P S T (Ref:HM14173)

## MORGAN, SANDRA

**Sandra Morgan**, 15 Burges Rd, London, **London (Greater)**, E6 2BJ, ENG.
(T) 020 8472 9496
Speciality: Physiotherapy.
P S T (Ref:HM14174)

## MORGAN, TINA

**Tina Morgan**, 5 Mountain Rd, Upper Brynamman, Ammanford, **Carmarthenshire**, SA18 1BT, WAL.
(T) 01269 826882
Speciality: Clairvoyants & Palmists.
B (Ref:HM14175)

## MORGAN, V

**V Morgan**, Chesterfield Hospital, 3 Clifton Hill, Bristol, BS8 1BP, ENG.
(T) 01179 730391
Speciality: Physiotherapy.
P S T (Ref:HM14176)

## MORGAN, VALERIE

**Valerie Morgan**, Rozel House, Tenterfields, Halesowen, **Midlands (West)**, B63 3LH, ENG.
(T) 01215 501533 (F) 01215 501533
(E) valerieannmorgan@cs.com
Speciality: Acupuncture, Bach Remedies, Bowen Therapy, Homeopathy, Naturopathy, Reflexology. ✔
● **Owner/Natural Medicine Consultant** Mrs V Morgan Q: BTER, Dip.Ac, Dip.Hom, DO, ND.

Key: B Mind-Body Medicine, C Complementary Medicine, H Self Help Treatment, M Medicinal Therapy, O Oriental Medicine, P Postural Therapy, S Manipulative Structural Therapy, T Touch Therapy

M: ATCM UK, BTER.
M Yrs. Est.: 10 (Ref:HM14177)

## MORGAN-AYRES, PAUL (PROF)

**Paul S Morgan-Ayres**, 234 Coed-Y-Gores, Cardiff, **Glamorgan (Vale of)**, CF23 9NL, WAL.
(T) 08707 424121
(E) counselling@ntlworld.com
Speciality: Absent Healing, Autogenic Training, Aversion Therapy, Cognitive Therapy, Complementary Therapy, Counselling, Encounter Groups, Faith Healing, Group Therapy, Healer, Healing Therapy, Holistic Healing, Hypnosis, Hypnotherapy, Life Style Coaching, Meditation, Paranormal Therapies, Psychotherapy, Spiritual Healing, Stress Therapy, Transactional Analysis, Visualisation Therapy, Analysis, NLP, Prayer Healing, Clinical Hypnosis, Psychic Counselling and Therapeutic Martial Arts. ✔
● **Therapist** Mr P Morgan-Ayres Q: BSc, Dip.Couns, Dip.Psych, MASC. M: CPS, HS.
B H Yrs. Est.: 8 (Ref:HM14178)

## MORLAND-AUSTIN, FIONA

**Fiona Morland-Austin**, Farnborough, **Hampshire**, GU14, ENG.
(T) 01252 545455
Speciality: Bach Remedies.
M (Ref:HM14179)

## MORLEY ACUPUNCTURE CLINIC

**Morley Acupuncture Clinic & Complementary Therapy Centre**, 1 Queen St, Morley, Leeds, **Yorkshire (West)**, LS27 8EG, ENG.
(T) 01132 380208 (F) 01132 380208
(E) john@mac-tcm.demon.co.uk
(W) www.mac-tcm.demon.co.uk
Speciality: Acupuncture, Complementary Therapy, Cupping, Dowsing, Hay Diet, Healing Therapy, Herbal Medicine, Moxibustion, Naturopathy, Nutritional Therapy, Oriental Diagnosis, Spiritual Healing, Ying & Yang. ✔
● **Director** Mr J Heptonstall Q: BSc (Hons), MBAcC. M: BAcC.
C O Yrs. Est.: 14 (Ref:HM14180)

## MORLEY, C

**C Morley**, 31 Wicklow St, Dublin, **County Dublin**, IRE.
(T) 01671 3467
Speciality: Complementary Medicines & Therapy.
M (Ref:HM14181)

## MORLEY, HAZEL

**Hazel Morley**, 19 Bentley Court, Finedon Rd Industrial Estate, Wellingborough, **Northamptonshire**, NN8 4BQ, ENG.
(T) 01933 279815 (F) 01933 279815
Speciality: Physiotherapy.
● **Partner** Mrs J White
P S T (Ref:HM14182)

## MORLEY, JOHN

**John Morley**, 140 Harley St, London, **London (Greater)**, W1N 1AH, ENG.
(T) 020 7487 2617
Speciality: Complementary Medicines & Therapy.
C M (Ref:HM14183)

## MORLEY, KAREN

**Karen Morley**, 182 Hill Lane, Southampton, **Hampshire**, SO15 5DB, ENG.
(T) 023 8022 0770
Speciality: Aromatherapy.
● **Owner** Mrs K Morley
M O (Ref:HM14184)

## MORLEY, M E

**M E Morley**, Mill Cottage, 7 Birmingham Rd, Blakedown, Kidderminster, **Worcestershire**, DY10 3JD, ENG.
(T) 01562 700899
Speciality: Physiotherapy.
● **Owner** Mrs M Morley
P S T (Ref:HM14185)

## MORLEY, VALERIE

**Valerie Morley**, 834 Fishponds Rd, Fishponds, Bristol, BS16 3XA, ENG.
(T) 01179 491290
Speciality: Reflexology.
S T (Ref:HM14186)

## MORLEY-KIRK, JOHN

**John Morley-Kirk**, The Lindum Medical Practice, 1 Cabourne Court, Cabourne Avenue, Lincoln, **Lincolnshire**, LN2 2JP, ENG.
(T) 01522 569033 (F) 01949 850068
(E) jmk@electricmed.com
(W) www.electricmed.com
Speciality: Complementary Therapy, Hypnotherapy, Reflexology, Electronic Vibrational Medicine. ✔
● **Therapist** Mr J Morley-Kirk Q: ART(Reg), MAR, MIIR. M: IIR.
C Yrs. Est.: 10 (Ref:HM14187)

## MORLEY-KIRK, JOHN

**John Morley-Kirk**, The Clinic Of Natural Therapies, 14a Main Rd, Radcliffe-On-Trent, **Nottinghamshire**, NG12 2FH, ENG.
(T) 01159 332773 (F) 01949 850068
(E) jmk@electricmed.com
(W) www.electricmed.com
Speciality: Complementary Therapy, Hypnotherapy, Reflexology, Electronic Vibrational Medicine. ✔
● **Therapist** Mr J Morley-Kirk Q: ART(Reg), MAR, MIIR. M: IIR.
C Yrs. Est.: 10 (Ref:HM14188)

## MORNING LIGHT

**Morning Light**, Mandally Rd, Invergarry, **Highland**, PH35 4HP, SCO.
(T) 01809 501282
Speciality: Psychotherapy.
● **Owner** Mr C Malcouronne
B (Ref:HM14189)

## MORNINGSIDE HEALTH CLINIC

**Morningside Health Clinic**, 135 Buckingham Rd, Bletchley, Milton Keynes, **Buckinghamshire**, MK3 5JD, ENG.
(T) 01908 366957
Speciality: Chiropractic.
P S T (Ref:HM14190)

## MORNINGSIDE NATURAL HLTH CTRE

**Morningside Natural Health Centre**, 5 Millar Cr, Edinburgh, **Edinburgh (City of)**, EH10 5HN, SCO.
(T) 01314 528964
Speciality: Complementary Medicines & Therapy.
● **Owner** Mr J MacLeash
M (Ref:HM14191)

## MORNINGSIDE PODIATRY SERVICE

**Morningside Podiatry Service**, 73 Morningside Rd, Edinburgh, **Edinburgh (City of)**, EH10 4AY, SCO.
(T) 01314 529064
(E) nfernando@bigfoot.com
Speciality: Biomechanics, Chiropody, Nail Surgery, Podiatry. ✔ CREDIT
● **Chiropodist (Podiatrist)**
Mrs G Fernando Q: DPodM, S.R.Ch. M: S.C.P.
● **Chiropodist (Podiatrist)**
Mr N Fernando Q: DPodM, S.R.Ch. M: S.C.P.
S Yrs. Est.: 12 (Ref:HM14192)

## MORNINGTON PHYSIOTHERAPY

**Mornington Physiotherapy**, 5 Mornington Villas, Manningham Lane, Bradford, **Yorkshire (West)**, BD8 7JX, ENG.
(T) 01274 544000 (F) 01274 824300
(W) www.morningtonphysiotherapy.co.uk
Speciality: Alexander Technique, Chiropody, Electrotherapy, Manipulation, Massage (Therapeutic), Micro Manipulation, Osteopathy, Physiotherapy, Pilates, Podiatry, Ultrasonics.
✔ CREDIT
● **Chartered Physiotherapist**
Mr D Ramsbottom Q: MCSP, SRP. M: CSP.
S Yrs. Est.: 19 (Ref:HM14193)

## MOROZ, CAROLYN

**Carolyn Moroz**, 1 Springbank, Unstone, Dronfield, **Derbyshire**, S18 4AD, ENG.
(T) 01246 411643
Speciality: Chiropodists (Podiatrists).
● **Owner** Mrs C Moroz
S (Ref:HM14194)

## MOROZZO, RUTH

**Ruth Morozzo**, 4 Eden Rd, Ednam, Kelso, **Scottish Borders**, TD5 7QG, SCO.
(T) 01573 226645
Speciality: Reflexology.
S T (Ref:HM14195)

## MORPHEW, JOHN (DR)

**Dr John Morphew**, Lindis Farn, Penrose, Wadebridge, **Cornwall**, PL27 7TB, ENG.
(T) 01841 540737
Speciality: Acupuncture.
● **Owner** Dr J Morphew
O (Ref:HM14196)

## MORRELL, C

**C Morrell**, 159 Hope Farm Rd, Great Sutton, Ellesmere Port, **Merseyside**, CH66 2TJ, ENG.
(T) 01513 393856
Speciality: Chiropodists (Podiatrists).
S (Ref:HM14197)

## MORRIS & ASSOCIATES

**Jane Morris & Associates**, 18 Ermine St, Huntingdon, **Cambridgeshire**, PE18 6EX, ENG.
(T) 01480 455221
Speciality: Acupressure, Acupuncture, Alexander Technique, Cranial Osteopathy, Homeopathy, Osteopathy, Physiotherapy, Phytotherapy, Pilates, Psychotherapy, Reflexology.
P S T (Ref:HM14198)

## MORRIS, A E

**A E Morris**, 2a-3a Station Chambers, Station Rd, Biggleswade, **Bedfordshire**, SG18 8AH, ENG.
(T) 01767 600758
Speciality: Physiotherapy.
● **Owner** Miss A Morris
P S T (Ref:HM14199)

## MORRIS, A P

**A P Morris**, 4 Powells Pl, Porth, **Rhondda Cynon Taff**, CF39 9RW, WAL.
(T) 01443 687848
Speciality: Herbal Medicine.
● **Owner** Mr A Morris
M (Ref:HM14200)

## MORRIS, C B

**C B Morris**, 370 Hoe St, London, **London (Greater)**, E17 9AA, ENG.
(T) 020 8520 6016
Speciality: Chiropodists (Podiatrists).
S (Ref:HM14201)

## MORRIS, CLAIRE

**Claire Morris**, 44 Hewell Rd, Barnt Green, Birmingham, **Midlands (West)**, B45 8NF, ENG.
(T) 01214 456016
Speciality: Chiropody. ✔
● **Chiropodist (Podiatrist)**
Claire Morris Q: BSc (Hons), M.S.C.P, S.R.Ch.
M Yrs. Est.: 13 (Ref:HM14202)

## MORRIS, CLIFFORD A

**Clifford A Morris**, Chyme Cottage, Crowan, Praze, Camborne, **Cornwall**, TR14 9NB, ENG.
(T) 01209 831854
Speciality: Chiropodists (Podiatrists).
● **Owner** Mr C Morris
S (Ref:HM14203)

## MORRIS, CYNTHIA

**Cynthia Morris**, 136A Holbrook Lane, Coventry, **Midlands (West)**, CV6 4BN, ENG.
(T) 024 7668 1239
Speciality: Aromatherapy.
● **Owner** Mrs C Morris
M O (Ref:HM14204)

## MORRIS, HENRY

**Henry Morris**, 161 High St, Barnet, **Hertfordshire**, EN5 5SU, ENG.
(T) 020 8440 8977
Speciality: Chiropodists (Podiatrists).
● **Owner** Mr H Morris
S (Ref:HM14205)

## MORRIS, J K

**Mrs J K Morris**, 9 Warren Drive, Wickford, **Essex**, SS11 8NE, ENG.
(T) 01268 562277
Speciality: Hypnosis.
● **Owner** Mrs J Morris


Key continued: Yrs.Est: Years Established Q: Qualifications M: Professional Membership ✔ Indemnity Insurance CREDIT Accept Credit Cards

B (Ref:HM14206)

### MORRIS, JENNIFER

**Jennifer Morris**, 45 Western Rd, Chandler's Ford, Eastleigh, **Hampshire**, SO53 5DD, ENG.
(T) 023 8027 1206
Speciality: Chiropodists (Podiatrists).
● **Owner** Mrs J Morris
S (Ref:HM14207)

### MORRIS, JOHN

**John Morris**, 40 High St, Pelsall, Walsall, **Midlands (West)**, WS3 4LT, ENG.
(T) 01922 682906
Speciality: Chiropodists (Podiatrists).
● **Owner** Mr J Morris
S (Ref:HM14208)

### MORRIS, MARGARET

**Margaret Morris**, 49 Sunningvale Avenue, Biggin Hill, Westerham, **Kent**, TN16 3BX, ENG.
(T) 01959 572868
Speciality: Complementary Medicines & Therapy.
M (Ref:HM14209)

### MORRIS, MICHELLE

**Michelle Morris**, Eltham Health Clinic, 93 Eltham Hill, London, **London (Greater)**, SE9 5SU, ENG.
(T) 020 8294 1113
Speciality: Homeopathy.
M (Ref:HM14210)

### MORRIS, PENNY

**Penny Morris**, 28 Martins Walk, London, **London (Greater)**, N10 1JT, ENG.
(T) 020 8883 7595
Speciality: Reflexology.
S T (Ref:HM14211)

### MORRIS, PETER

**Peter Morris**, 38 Nettlecombe Cl, Sutton, **Surrey**, SM2 6TR, ENG.
(T) 020 8408 3683
Speciality: Chiropodists (Podiatrists).
S (Ref:HM14212)

### MORRIS, RACHEL T

**Rachel T Morris**, 236D Manley Rd, Manchester, **Manchester (Greater)**, M21 0RU, ENG.
(T) 01618 600636
Speciality: Hypnosis.
● **Owner** Mrs R Morris
B (Ref:HM14213)

### MORRIS, S

**S Morris**, 31 Ifield Rd, London, **London (Greater)**, SW10 9AZ, ENG.
(T) 020 7351 1788
Speciality: Alexander Technique.
● **Owner** Miss S Morris
P S (Ref:HM14214)

### MORRIS, STEPHEN

**Stephen Morris**, 58 New Church Rd, Hove, **Sussex (East)**, BN3 4FL, ENG.
(T) 01273 725667 (F) 01273 208015
Speciality: Osteopathy.
● **Owner** Mr S Morris
P S T (Ref:HM14215)

### MORRIS, STEPHEN

**Stephen Morris**, 11 New Church Rd, Hove, **Sussex (East)**, BN3 4AA, ENG.
(T) 01273 725667
Speciality: Osteopathy.
P S T (Ref:HM14216)

### MORRIS, T J

**T J Morris**, 18 New Buildings, Hinckley, **Leicestershire**, LE10 1HW, ENG.
(T) 01455 619757
Speciality: Physiotherapy.
● **Owner** Mr T Morris
P S T (Ref:HM14217)

### MORRIS, TIMOTHY

**Timothy Morris**, 2a Mandalay Rd, London, **London (Greater)**, SW4 9ED, ENG.
(T) 020 8675 1294 (F) 020 8675 0635
Speciality: Osteopathy.
● **Owner** Mr T Morris
P S T (Ref:HM14218)

### MORRISH, MO

**Mo Morrish**, Southern Hay Lodge, 1 Barnfield Cres, Exeter, **Devon**, EX1 1QT, ENG.
(T) 01392 214074
Speciality: Homeopathy.
● **Manager** Mr M Morrish
M (Ref:HM14219)

### MORRISON, ANTHONY

**Anthony Morrison**, 72 Mill St, Kidderminster, **Worcestershire**, DY11 6XJ, ENG.
(T) 01562 755833
Speciality: Complementary Medicines & Therapy.
● **Owner** Mr A Morrison
C M (Ref:HM14220)

### MORRISON, C H

**C H Morrison**, 11 Clarence Trce, Chester Le Street, **County Durham**, DH3 3DG, ENG.
(T) 01913 883196
Speciality: Chiropodists (Podiatrists).
S (Ref:HM14221)

### MORRISON, CAROLE

**Carole Morrison**, Gills Cottage, 366 Pensby Rd, Heswall, Wirral, **Merseyside**, CH61 9NQ, ENG.
(T) 01516 486225
Speciality: Chiropodists (Podiatrists).
S (Ref:HM14222)

### MORRISON, D C

**D C Morrison**, 113 Warwick Rd, Carlisle, **Cumbria**, CA1 1JY, ENG.
(T) 01228 511446
Speciality: Chiropodists (Podiatrists).
S (Ref:HM14223)

### MORRISON, G N

**G N Morrison**, 85 Epsom Rd, Guildford, **Surrey**, GU1 3PA, ENG.
(T) 01483 564109
Speciality: Chiropodists (Podiatrists).
● **Principal** Mr G Morrison
S (Ref:HM14224)

### MORRISON, JOHN D

**John D Morrison**, 2 Ure Court, Grangemouth, **Falkirk**, FK3 9DS, SCO.
(T) 01324 486708
Speciality: Chiropodists (Podiatrists).
S (Ref:HM14225)

### MORRISON, L

**L Morrison**, 27b Mill Lane, Wigginton, York, **Yorkshire (North)**, YO32 2PU, ENG.
(T) 01904 750096
Speciality: Chiropodists (Podiatrists).
● **Owner** Mrs L Morrison
S (Ref:HM14226)

### MORRISON, L

**L Morrison**, 4-6 Gillygate, York, **Yorkshire (North)**, YO31 7EQ, ENG.
(T) 01904 628047
Speciality: Chiropodists (Podiatrists).
● **Owner** Mrs L Morrison
S (Ref:HM14227)

### MORRISON, LIBBY (DR)

**Dr Libby Morrison**, 4 Belgrave Rd, Rathmines, **County Dublin**, IRE.
(T) 01497 0174
Speciality: Chiropractors.
P S T (Ref:HM14228)

### MORRISON, R

**R Morrison**, New Cross Natural Therapy Centre, 394 New Cross Rd, London, **London (Greater)**, SE14 6TY, ENG.
(T) 020 8469 0858
Speciality: Complementary Medicines & Therapy.
M (Ref:HM14229)

### MORRISON, R D

**R D Morrison**, 1 Sycamore Gr, Winchburgh, Broxburn, **Lothian (West)**, EH52 6SX, SCO.
(T) 01506 890541
Speciality: Osteopathy.
● **Owner** Mr R Morrison
P S T (Ref:HM14230)

### MORRISON, SANDRA

**Sandra Morrison**, 54 Garscube Trce, Edinburgh, **Edinburgh (City of)**, EH12 6BN, SCO.
(T) 01313 132373
Speciality: Reflexology.
S T (Ref:HM14231)

### MORRISON, SUSAN

**Susan Morrison**, 75 Risbygate St, Bury St. Edmunds, **Suffolk**, IP33 3AQ, ENG.
(T) 01284 769153
Speciality: Osteopathy.
P S T (Ref:HM14232)

### MORRISS, C

**C Morriss**, 10 Eldon Rd, Reading, **Berkshire**, RG1 4DH, ENG.
(T) 01189 502002
Speciality: Osteopathy.
P S T (Ref:HM14233)

### MORRISS, CHRISTOPHER J

**Christopher J Morriss**, 18 Morgan Rd, Reading, **Berkshire**, RG1 5HG, ENG.
(T) 01189 753893
Speciality: Osteopathy.
P S T (Ref:HM14234)

### MORRISSEY TRADITIONAL ACU

**Morrissey Traditional Acupuncture**, 16 Lr George St, Crossabeg, **County Wexford**, IRE.
(T) 05328 408
Speciality: Acupuncture.
O (Ref:HM14235)

### MORRISSEY, BLANCHE

**Blanche Morrissey**, Conkers, Wendover Rd, Bourne End, **Buckinghamshire**, SL8 5NT, ENG.
(E) blanchemorrissey@hotmail.com
(W) www.zyworld.com/blanchef
Speciality: Biomechanics, Chiropody, Cryo Surgery, Orthotics, Podiatry, Sports Injury Therapy.
✔
● **Podiatrist** Ms B Morrissey Q: FSSCh, MBChA.
M: B.A.Ch.P.
C Yrs. Est.: 6 (Ref:HM14236)

### MORRISSEY, PAUL

**Paul Morrissey**, Addington Palace Country Club, Gravel Hill, Croydon, **Surrey**, CR0 5BB, ENG.
(T) 020 8686 8181 (F) 020 8686 8181
Speciality: Osteopathy.
● **Owner** Mr P Morrisey
P S T (Ref:HM14237)

### MORROW, CARYS

**Morrow Carys BA M Psych Sc**, 2 Hanbury La, Lucan, **County Dublin**, IRE.
(T) 01621 7022
Speciality: Complementary Medicines & Therapy.
M (Ref:HM14238)

### MORSE, EMMA

**Emma Morse A N M**, 17 Hillside Parc, Madron, Penzance, **Cornwall**, TR20 8RU, ENG.
(T) 01736 350174
(E) nicky.morse@virgin.net
Speciality: Aromatherapy.
● **Aromatherapist** Ms E Morse Q: ANM.
M: ANM.
C Yrs. Est.: 2 (Ref:HM14239)

### MORTIMER WHITE, E

**E Mortimer White**, 219 Greenway Rd, Taunton, **Somerset**, TA2 6LN, ENG.
(T) 01823 333041
Speciality: Physiotherapy.
P S T (Ref:HM14240)

### MORTIMER, GERALDINE

**Geraldine Mortimer**, 60 Elmbridge, Harlow, **Essex**, CM17 0JX, ENG.
(T) 01279 300036
Speciality: Reflexology.
S T (Ref:HM14241)

### MORTIMER, HANNAH

**Hannah Mortimer**, Pill Rigg, Sowerby Under Cotcliffe, Northallerton, **Yorkshire (North)**, DL6 3RH, ENG.
(T) 01609 771441 (F) 01609 771441
Speciality: Psychology.
● **Owner** Mrs H Mortimer



Key: B Mind-Body Medicine C Complementary Medicine H Self Help Treatment M Medicinal Therapy O Oriental Medicine P Postural Therapy S Manipulative Structural Therapy T Touch Therapy

B (Ref:HM14242)

## MORTIMER, PHILIP

**Philip Mortimer**, 19 Yalding Gardens, Nottingham, **Nottinghamshire**, NG8 2PZ, ENG.
(T) 01159 285703
Speciality: Osteopathy.
● **Owner** Mr P Mortimer
P S T (Ref:HM14243)

## MORTIMER, VICTORIA

**Victoria Mortimer**, 66 Brick Kiln Way, Braintree, **Essex**, CM7 3FP, ENG.
(T) 01376 342602
Speciality: Reflexology.
S T (Ref:HM14244)

## MORTIMORE & STUDART

**Mortimore & Studart**, 7 Pembroke Rd, Sevenoaks, **Kent**, TN13 1XR, ENG.
(T) 01732 453995
Speciality: Chiropodists (Podiatrists).
S (Ref:HM14245)

## MORTIMORE, P G

**P G Mortimore**, 3 Hoskins Rd, Oxted, **Surrey**, RH8 9HT, ENG.
(T) 01883 713979
Speciality: Chiropodists (Podiatrists).
● **Owner** Mrs C Mortimore
S (Ref:HM14246)

## MORTON, A P

**A P Morton**, 202 Peverell Park Rd, Plymouth, **Devon**, PL3 4QE, ENG.
(T) 01752 783873
Speciality: Physiotherapy.
● **Owner** A Morton
P S T (Ref:HM14247)

## MORTON, ALEX

**Alex Morton**, 22 Farley Rd, Malvern, **Worcestershire**, WR14 1NF, ENG.
(T) 01684 566646
Speciality: Chiropractors.
● **Owner** Mr A Morton
P S T (Ref:HM14248)

## MORTON, H

**H Morton**, 29 Bryony Gr, Marton-In-Cleveland, Middlesbrough, **Cleveland**, TS7 8SW, ENG.
(T) 01642 318807
Speciality: Chiropodists (Podiatrists).
● **Owner** Mrs H Morton
S (Ref:HM14249)

## MORTON, J V

**J V Morton**, Body Scene, 3 Princess St, Knutsford, **Cheshire**, WA16 6BY, ENG.
(T) 01565 621008
Speciality: Chiropodists (Podiatrists).
● **Owner** Mrs J Morton
S (Ref:HM14250)

## MORTON, J V

**Mrs J V Morton**, 2 Beach Rd, Hartford, Northwich, **Cheshire**, CW8 4BA, ENG.
(T) 01606 79269
Speciality: Chiropody, Podiatry.
● **Owner/Chiropodist/Podiatrist**
Mrs J Morton
S Yrs. Est.: 25 (Ref:HM14251)

## MORTON, P J

**P J Morton**, 33 High St, Northallerton, **Yorkshire (North)**, DL7 8EE, ENG.
(T) 01609 771138
Speciality: Osteopathy.
● **Owner** Mr P Morton
P S T (Ref:HM14252)

## MORTON, PETER J

**Peter J Morton**, Galtres House, 3 Lysander Cl, York, **Yorkshire (North)**, YO30 4GE, ENG.
(T) 01904 693863
Speciality: Osteopathy.
● **Owner** Mr P Morton
P S T (Ref:HM14253)

## MORTON, PHILLIPA

**Phillipa Morton**, 41 Ynyscedwyn Rd, Ystradgynlais, Swansea, **Glamorgan (Vale of)**, SA9 1BH, WAL.
(T) 01639 845980
Speciality: Aromatherapy.
● **Owner** Mrs P Morton
M O (Ref:HM14254)

## MORTON, WILLIAM

**William Morton**, 4 Delamere Rd, London, **London (Greater)**, W5 3JR, ENG.
(T) 020 8567 9759
Speciality: Alexander Technique.
● **Owner** Mr W Morton
P S (Ref:HM14255)

## MOSBOROUGH PHYSIO & SPORTS

**Mosborough Physiotherapy & Sports Injury Clinic**, 97 High St, Mosborough, Sheffield, **Yorkshire (South)**, S19 5AF, ENG.
(T) 01142 511304
Speciality: Physiotherapy.
● **Partner** Mr J Mersh
P S T (Ref:HM14256)

## MOSELEY, ANNIE

**Annie Moseley**, 94 St James's St, Brighton, **Sussex (East)**, BN2 1TP, ENG.
(T) 01273 672952
Speciality: Complementary Medicines & Therapy.
● **Owner** Mr L Moore
M (Ref:HM14257)

## MOSELEY, B

**B Moseley**, 18 High St, Uppermill, Oldham, **Lancashire**, OL3 6HX, ENG.
(T) 01457 875565
Speciality: Chiropodists (Podiatrists).
S (Ref:HM14258)

## MOSELEY, B

**B Moseley**, 1b Station Rd, Grotton, Oldham, **Lancashire**, OL4 5SF, ENG.
(T) 01616 273356
Speciality: Chiropodists (Podiatrists).
S (Ref:HM14259)

## MOSHTAEL, O

**O Moshtael**, 11B King George Avenue, Bushey, Watford, **Hertfordshire**, WD2 3NT, ENG.
(T) 020 8950 2561
Speciality: Chiropodists (Podiatrists).
S (Ref:HM14260)

## MOSS & ASSOCIATES

**Juliet Moss & Associates**, Quantock Lodge, 67 Nightingale Lane, London, **London (Greater)**, SW12 8ST, ENG.
(T) 020 8675 5633 (F) 020 8675 9434
Speciality: Physiotherapy.
● **Owner** Ms J Moss
P S T (Ref:HM14261)

## MOSS PHARMACY

**Scholl Centre**, 225 Union St, Aberdeen, **Aberdeenshire**, AB11 6BQ, SCO.
(T) 01224 590146
Speciality: Chiropody. ✔
● **Chiropodist** Mrs S Jolly Q: S.R.Ch. M: S.R.Ch.
● **Manageress** Mrs D Bakker
M Yrs. Est.: 8 (Ref:HM14262)

## MOSS PHARMACY PODIATRY

**Orthoticity Ltd**, 34-36 High St, Godalming, **Surrey**, GU7 1DZ, ENG.
(T) 01483 425437 (F) 01483 861118
(E) info@surrey-foot-health.co.uk
(W) www.surrey-foot-health.co.uk
Speciality: Cryo Surgery, Homeopathic Podiatry and foot massage. ✔ CREDIT
● **Director** Mr M Swindon Q: SRPod. M: S.C.P.
M Yrs. Est.: 2 (Ref:HM14263)

## MOSS, GRAEME

**Graeme Moss**, 13 Dunspring Lane, Ilford, **Essex**, IG5 0UA, ENG.
(T) 020 8550 0212
Speciality: Remedial Massage. ✔
● **Owner/Remedial Physical Therapist**
Mr G Moss Q: LCSP.
C Yrs. Est.: 17 (Ref:HM14264)

## MOSS, JANICE

**Janice Moss**, Runnymede Health & Fitness Spa, Runnymede Hotel, Windsor Rd, Englefield Green, Egham, **Surrey**, TW20 0AG, ENG.
(T) 01784 470099
Speciality: Osteopathy.
P S T (Ref:HM14265)

## MOSS, OLGA

**Olga Moss**, 2 Milldene Avenue, North Shields, **Tyne and Wear**, NE30 2PS, ENG.
(T) 01912 577078
(W) website.lineone.net/~olga.moss
Speciality: Reflexology.
S T (Ref:HM14266)

## MOSS, PAUL

**Paul Moss**, 46 Lambs Conduit St, London, **London (Greater)**, WC1N 3LJ, ENG.
(T) 020 7404 3312
Speciality: Osteopathy.
P S T (Ref:HM14267)

## MOSS, PAUL W

**Paul W Moss**, 5 Briardale Gardens, London, **London (Greater)**, NW3 7PN, ENG.
(T) 020 7435 5549
Speciality: Osteopathy.
P S T (Ref:HM14268)

## MOSS, RACHAEL

**Rachael Moss**, 38 Dilbridge Rd West, Colchester, **Essex**, CO4 4BJ, ENG.
(T) 01206 520001
Speciality: Reflexology.
S T (Ref:HM14269)

## MOSSHILL HOLISTIC CENTRE

**Mosshill Holistic Centre**, Moss Hill, Penmachno, Betws-y-Coed, **Gwynedd**, LL24 0PW, WAL.
(T) 01690 710198
Speciality: Meditation, Teaches Reduction & Meditation. ✔
● **Spiritual Master Holistic Practitioner**
Mr V Thompson
B C Yrs. Est.: 50 (Ref:HM14270)

## MOSSMAN, CELIA

**Celia Mossman**, 38 Ouseley Cl, Marston, Oxford, **Oxfordshire**, OX3 0JS, ENG.
(T) 01865 240703
Speciality: Reflexology.
S T (Ref:HM14271)

## MOSSO, MARINA

**Marina Mosso**, 137 Magdalen Rd, Oxford, **Oxfordshire**, OX4 1RJ, ENG.
(T) 01865 396939
Speciality: Complementary Medicines & Therapy.
● **Owner** Mr M Franklin
M (Ref:HM14272)

## MOTCOMBE PARK PHYSIOTHERAPY

**Motcombe Park Physiotherapy & Sports Injury Clinic**, Westfields, New Rd, Shaftesbury, **Dorset**, SP7 8QH, ENG.
(T) 01747 850328 (F) 01747 850328
Speciality: Acupuncture, Physiotherapy. ✔
● **Owner/Physiotherapist**
Mrs C Worrall Q: MCSP, SRP. M: CSP.
S Yrs. Est.: 10 (Ref:HM14273)

## MOTE, CHRISTOPHER C

**C Christopher Mote**, Riverside Cottage, 15 Eastcote Rd, Pinner, **London (Greater)**, HA5 1EA, ENG.
(T) 020 8868 9315
Speciality: Osteopathy.
P S T (Ref:HM14274)

## MOTHER EARTH

**Mother Earth**, Harbour St, Tullamore, **County Offaly**, IRE.
(T) 05062 3499
Speciality: Complementary Medicines & Therapy.
M (Ref:HM14275)

## MOTHERSOLE, VINETA

**Vineta Mothersole - Chiropodist/Podiatrist**, 67 Quentin Rd, Blackheath, London, **London (Greater)**, SE13 5DG, ENG.
(T) 020 8852 4366
Speciality: Chiropody, Chiropody using natural products, essential oils and herbs. ✔
● **Chiropodist** Vinita Mothersole Q: BSc, M.S.C.P., S.R.Ch. M: S.C.P.



Key continued: **Yrs.Est:** Years Established **Q:** Qualifications **M:** Professional Membership ✔ Indemnity Insurance CREDIT Accept Credit Cards

**M** Yrs. Est.: 3 (**Ref:**HM20682)

## MOTIVATIONAL RESEARCH & DVPT

**Motivational Research & Development**, 4 Ladywood Rd, Four Oaks, Sutton Coldfield, **Midlands (West)**, B74 2SN, ENG.
(T) 01213 233350
Speciality: Hypnosis.
**B** (**Ref:**HM14276)

## MOTLEY, MAUREEN

**Maureen Motley**, 14 Queenswood Avenue, Northampton, **Northamptonshire**, NN3 6JU, ENG.
(T) 01604 491533
Speciality: Aromatherapy. ✔
● **Owner/Aromatherapist**
Mrs M Motley M: ISPA.
**C** Yrs. Est.: 10 (**Ref:**HM14277)

## MOTT, DAVID

**David Mott**, 2 Clarendon Rd, Bournemouth, **Dorset**, BH4 8AH, ENG.
(T) 01202 768638 (F) 01202 751038
Speciality: Physiotherapy.
● **Practice Manager** Mrs D Amar
**P S T** (**Ref:**HM14278)

## MOTTINGHAM HYPNOTHERAPY CTRE

**Mottingham Hypnotherapy & Primary Cause Analysis Centre**, Greet, Mottingham Lane, London, **London (Greater)**, SE9 4RX, ENG.
(T) 020 8851 0302 (F) 020 8851 0302
(E) edithbird49@hotmail.com
Speciality: Counselling, Hypnosis, Hypnotherapy, Hypno Analysis. ✔
● **Owner** Mrs E Bird Q: MCPS. M: CPS, HRS, HS.
**B** Yrs. Est.: 11 (**Ref:**HM14279)

## MOTTRAM, ANN

**Ann Mottram**, 75 Dunholme Rd, London, **London (Greater)**, N9 9QT, ENG.
(T) 020 8803 5932
Speciality: Psychotherapy.
● **Owner** Mrs A Mottram
**B** (**Ref:**HM14280)

## MOTTRAM, ROB

**Rob Mottram**, 42 Lichfield Gardens, Richmond, **Surrey**, TW9 1AP, ENG.
(T) 020 8332 6036 (F) 020 8332 1773
Speciality: Complementary Medicines & Therapy.
**M** (**Ref:**HM14281)

## MOUCHET, F

**F Mouchet**, 134 Thaxted Rd, Saffron Walden, **Essex**, CB11 3BJ, ENG.
(T) 01799 528323
Speciality: Counselling, Psychotherapy. ✔
● **Psychotherapist** Mrs F Mouchet
Q: Cert.Adv.Gestalt Therapy, Dip.Couns.Psychosthis.
**B** Yrs. Est.: 13 (**Ref:**HM14282)

## MOULDING, ANNE

**Anne Moulding**, W E I Clinic, 57A Garland St, Bury St. Edmunds, **Suffolk**, IP33 1EZ, ENG.
(T) 01284 704228
Speciality: Aromatherapy.
**M O** (**Ref:**HM14283)

## MOULE, TERRY G

**Terry G Moule**, Cheapside Farmhouse, Sandridgebury Lane, Sandridge, St. Albans, **Hertfordshire**, AL3 6JF, ENG.
(T) 01727 857714
Speciality: Osteopathy.
**P S T** (**Ref:**HM14284)

## MOULE, TERRY G

**Terry G Moule**, 1 The Stables, Walwyn Rd, Colwall Green, **Herefordshire**, WR13 6QX, ENG.
(T) 01684 541262
Speciality: Naturopathy, Osteopathy.
**P S T** (**Ref:**HM14285)

## MOULT, MICHAEL A

**Michael A Moult**, 4 Scafell Cl, Weston-Super-Mare, **Somerset**, BS23 2XF, ENG.
(T) 01934 643336
Speciality: Hypnotherapy.
**B** (**Ref:**HM14286)

## MOULTON, JAMES

**James Moulton**, 125 Albert Rd, Harrogate, **Yorkshire (North)**, HG1 4HT, ENG.
(T) 01423 505384
Speciality: Chiropodists (Podiatrists).
● **Owner** Mr J Moulton
**S** (**Ref:**HM14287)

## MOUNSEY, L A

**L A Mounsey**, 56 Witham Rd, Woodhall Spa, **Lincolnshire**, LN10 6RD, ENG.
(T) 01526 353968
Speciality: Chiropodists (Podiatrists).
**S** (**Ref:**HM14288)

## MOUNT ALVERNIA PHYSIOTHERAPY

**Mount Alvernia Physiotherapy & Sports Medicine Clinic**, Mt Alvernia Hospital, Harvey Rd, Guildford, **Surrey**, GU1 3LX, ENG.
(T) 01483 570122
Speciality: Physiotherapy.
**P S T** (**Ref:**HM14289)

## MOUNT SOUTHWELL CLINIC

**Mount Southwell Clinic**, Market Sq, Letterkenny, **County Donegal**, IRE.
(T) 07428 588
Speciality: Hypnotherapy.
**B** (**Ref:**HM14290)

## MOUNT STREET COMP THERAPIES

**Mount Street Complementary Therapies**, 6 Mount St, Manchester, **Manchester (Greater)**, M2 5NS, ENG.
(T) 01618 347899
Speciality: Acupuncture, Allergy Testing, Aromatherapy, Homeopathy, Massage (Therapeutic), Reflexology, Shiatsu. ✔
● **Owner/Acupuncturist** Mrs J Sweet Q: BSc, Lic.Ac. M: BAcC.
● **Homeopath** Ms C Searson Q: BSc.
● **Acupuncturist** Ms J Dale Q: BA, Lic.Ac. M: BAcC.
● **Complementary Therapist**
Ms A Martinsen Q: IIHHT, ITEC, VTCT.
**C** Yrs. Est.: 7 (**Ref:**HM14291)

## MOUNTCASTLE CLINIC

**Mountcastle Clinic**, Milton Surgery, 132 Mountcastle Drive South, Edinburgh, **Edinburgh (City of)**, EH15 3LL, SCO.
(T) 01316 573613 (F) 01316 690269
Speciality: Chiropodists (Podiatrists).
**S** (**Ref:**HM14292)

## MOUNTFORD, CAROLINE

**Caroline Mountford**, 18 Cliddesden Rd, Basingstoke, **Hampshire**, RG21 3DU, ENG.
(T) 01256 479500 (F) 01256 479500
Speciality: Acupuncture.
● **Owner** Ms C Mountford
**O** (**Ref:**HM14293)

## MOUNTFORD, PAUL

**Paul Mountford**, 3 Parker Trce, Ferryhill, **County Durham**, DL17 8JY, ENG.
(T) 01740 656855
Speciality: Chiropodists (Podiatrists).
**S** (**Ref:**HM14294)

## MOUNTFORT, KATRINA

**Katrina Mountfort**, 7D Wolsley Rd, London, **London (Greater)**, N8 8RR, ENG.
(T) 020 8341 4462
Speciality: Bach Remedies.
**M** (**Ref:**HM14295)

## MOUNTVIEW NTRL HEALTH CLINIC

**Mountview Natural Health Clinic**, 76 Mountview Rd, London, **London (Greater)**, N4 4JR, ENG.
(T) 020 8348 7457
Speciality: Psychotherapy.
**B** (**Ref:**HM14296)

## MOUNTWAY

**Mountway Ltd**, Unit 7 Tafarnaubach Industrial Estate, Tafarnaubach, Tredegar, **Blaenau Gwent**, NP22 3AA, WAL.
(T) 01495 723300 (F) 01495 723360
Speciality: Complementary Medicines & Therapy.
● **Managing Director** Mr R Watkinson
**M** (**Ref:**HM14297)

## MOURANT, JENNIFER L

**Jennifer L Mourant**, 146 Trowbridge Rd, Bradford-on-Avon, **Wiltshire**, BA15 1EW, ENG.
(T) 01225 866789
Speciality: Bach Remedies, Indian Head Massage, Massage (Therapeutic). ✔
● **Owner/Bach Practitioner**
Mrs J Mourant Q: IHBC, IIHHT, ITEC. M: BFIR.
**C H** Yrs. Est.: 11 (**Ref:**HM14298)

## MOURTON, JEAN

**Jean Mourton**, 8 Patriot Cl, Spalding, **Lincolnshire**, PE11 1YA, ENG.
(T) 01775 713754
Speciality: Reflexology.
**S T** (**Ref:**HM14299)

## MOUZOURIDES, S

**S Mouzourides**, 35 Hawthorn Avenue, London, **London (Greater)**, N13 4JS, ENG.
(T) 020 8886 7546
Speciality: Complementary Medicines & Therapy.
**C M** (**Ref:**HM14300)

## MOVEMENT CENTRE

**Movement Centre (The)**, Robert Jones & Agnes Hunt Orthopaedic Hospital, Gobowen, Oswestry, **Shropshire**, SY10 7AG, ENG.
(T) 01691 404248 (F) 01691 404248
Speciality: Physiotherapy.
● **Director** Mrs P Butler
**P S T** (**Ref:**HM14301)

## MOWBRAY, ALISON

**Alison Mowbray**, Martindale House, Lombard St, Newark, **Nottinghamshire**, NG24 1XG, ENG.
(T) 01636 611150
Speciality: Acupuncture.
● **Administrator** Mrs S Taylor
**O** (**Ref:**HM14302)

## MOWLEM, BRENDA

**Brenda Mowlem**, Skirbeck, Tibberton, Newport, **Shropshire**, TF10 8NL, ENG.
(T) 01952 550400 (F) 01952 550400
Speciality: Chiropodists (Podiatrists).
● **Owner** Mrs B Mowlem
**S** (**Ref:**HM14303)

## MOXLEY, SHIRLEY

**Shirley Moxley**, 51 Trinity View, Caerleon, Newport, NP18 3SU, WAL.
(T) 01633 421496
Speciality: Reflexology. ✔
● **Reflexologist** Ms S Moxley Q: BRCP.
**C** Yrs. Est.: 7 (**Ref:**HM14304)

## MOYLES, JOHN

**Moyles John**, Annagh Beg Ballycastle, **County Mayo**, IRE.
(T) 09643 068
Speciality: Complementary Medicines & Therapy.
**M** (**Ref:**HM14305)

## MOYNIHAN, T

**T Moynihan**, 24A Orchard Rd, Melbourn, Royston, **Hertfordshire**, SG8 6HH, ENG.
(T) 01763 260900
Speciality: Osteopathy.
**P S T** (**Ref:**HM14306)

## MOYNIHAN, T

**T Moynihan**, 33 High St, Ashwell, Baldock, **Hertfordshire**, SG7 5NP, ENG.
(T) 01462 742942
Speciality: Osteopathy.
**P S T** (**Ref:**HM14307)

## M-POWER

**Tadeusz Klepacz**, 6 Highview Rd, London, **London (Greater)**, W13 0HB, ENG.
(T) 020 8997 1913
(E) tjk@stdoms.ac.uk
Speciality: Auto Suggestion, Cognitive Therapy, Counselling, Humanistic Psychology, Hypnotherapy, Life Style Coaching, Psychotherapy, Stress Therapy. ✔
● **Psychotherapist** Mr T Klepacz
Q: Dip.Adv.Hyp, NLP. M: ANLP, CRAH.
**B** Yrs. Est.: 3 (**Ref:**HM14308)



Key: **B** Mind-Body Medicine **C** Complementary Medicine **H** Self Help Treatment **M** Medicinal Therapy **O** Oriental Medicine **P** Postural Therapy **S** Manipulative Structural Therapy **T** Touch Therapy

### MR THERAPY
**Mr Therapy**, 5 Dent Drive, Wakefield, **Yorkshire (West)**, WF1 4JG, ENG.
(T) 01924 372193
Speciality: Aromatherapy.
M O (Ref:HM14309)

### MSM INFORMATION
**MSM Information**, Maypole Oak, Monmouth, **Monmouthshire**, NP25 5QH, WAL.
(T) 01600 713527
Speciality: Nutritional Therapy.
M (Ref:HM14310)

### MUCKLEY, ALBERT
**Muckley Albert Lic Ac T A S UK**, East Ferry, Midleton, **County Cork**, IRE.
(T) 021 4652 678
Speciality: Acupuncture.
O (Ref:HM14311)

### MUDDLE & ASSOCIATES
**Simon Muddle & Associates**, Leisure Centre, Stone Cross, Northallerton, **Yorkshire (North)**, DL6 2UZ, ENG.
(T) 01609 778888
Speciality: Complementary Medicines & Therapy.
C M (Ref:HM14312)

### MUDDLE & ASSOCIATES
**Simon Muddle & Associates**, 5 Ingramgate, Thirsk, **Yorkshire (North)**, YO7 1DD, ENG.
(T) 01845 525600 (F) 01845 525600
Speciality: Complementary Medicines & Therapy.
● **Owner** Mr S Muddle
C M (Ref:HM14313)

### MUDDLE & ASSOCIATES
**Simon Muddle & Associates**, 7a Finkle St, Richmond, **Yorkshire (North)**, DL10 4QA, ENG.
(T) 01748 822111
Speciality: Osteopathy.
● **Owner** Mr S Muddle
C P S T (Ref:HM14314)

### MUDDLE, SIMON & ASSOCIATES
**Muddle Simon & Associates**, 5 Victoria Rd, Darlington, **County Durham**, DL1 5SJ, ENG.
(T) 01325 488500
Speciality: Osteopathy.
C P S T (Ref:HM14315)

### MUGAN, D R
**D R Mugan**, 137 Kings Rd, London Colney, St. Albans, **Hertfordshire**, AL2 1ER, ENG.
(T) 01727 825971
Speciality: Aromatherapy.
M O (Ref:HM14316)

### MUGHAL, JAVED
**Javed Mughal**, 7 Maidstone Rd, Gillingham, **Kent**, ME8 0DH, ENG.
(T) 01634 377638
Speciality: Physiotherapy.
● **Owner** Mr J Mughal
P S T (Ref:HM14317)

### MUIR, BEVERLEY
**Beverley Muir**, 59 The Woodlands, Esher, **Surrey**, KT10 8BZ, ENG.
(T) 020 8398 1572
Speciality: Aromatherapy.
M O (Ref:HM14318)

### MUIR, MARGARET
**Margaret Muir**, 13 Longcraigs Avenue, Ardrossan, **Ayrshire (North)**, KA22 7PU, SCO.
(T) 01294 468931
Speciality: Complementary Medicines & Therapy.
● **Owner** Mrs M Muir
C M (Ref:HM14319)

### MUIR, P M
**P M Muir**, Putnoe Lane, Bedford, **Bedfordshire**, MK41 9AB, ENG.
(T) 01234 261846
Speciality: Physiotherapy.
● **Partner** Mrs P Muir
P S T (Ref:HM14320)

### MUIREND CHIROPRACTIC CLINIC
**Muirend Chiropractic Clinic**, 455 Clarkston Rd, Glasgow, **Glasgow (City of)**, G44 3LW, SCO.
(T) 01416 370220
Speciality: Chiropractic.
P S T (Ref:HM14321)

### MUIRHEAD ROBERTS
**Muirhead Roberts**, 280 Balham High Rd, London, **London (Greater)**, SW17 7AL, ENG.
(T) 020 8682 1800
Speciality: Physiotherapy.
P S T (Ref:HM14322)

### MUIRHEAD, MARGARET
**Margaret Muirhead**, 2 Nargate Cl, Littlebourne, Canterbury, **Kent**, CT3 1UL, ENG.
(T) 01227 720971
Speciality: Counselling, Herbal Medicine, Nutritional Therapy, Vitamin Therapy, Use of a pendulum for guidence in any life questions patients may have. ✔
● **Owner/Medical Herbalist**
Ms M Muirhead Q: Dip.Herb.Med. M: NIMH.
M Yrs. Est.: 4 (Ref:HM14323)

### MUIR'S NATURAL HEALTH CENTRE
**Muir's Natural Health Centre (The)**, Muirs Busines Centre, Kinross, **Perth and Kinross**, KY13 8AU, SCO.
(T) 01577 865665
Speciality: Complementary Medicines & Therapy.
● **Director** Miss J Abberton
M (Ref:HM14324)

### MUISE, D W
**D W Muise**, 305A Cavehill Rd, Belfast, **County Antrim**, BT15 5EY, NIR.
(T) 028 9039 1411
Speciality: Chiropodists (Podiatrists).
S (Ref:HM14325)

### MUISE, DAVID
**David Muise**, 1 Serpentine Rd, Newtownabbey, **County Antrim**, BT36 7HA, NIR.
(T) 028 9077 7525
Speciality: Chiropodists (Podiatrists).
S (Ref:HM14326)

### MUKHERJI, P S
**P S Mukherji**, 66 Pentland Trce, Edinburgh, **Edinburgh (City of)**, EH10 6HE, SCO.
(T) 01314 455668 (F) 01314 455668
Speciality: Bach Remedies, Homeopathy.
● **Owner** Dr P Mukherji
M (Ref:HM14327)

### MUKHERJI, PURNENDU
**Purnendu Mukherji**, Edinburgh, **Edinburgh (City of)**, EH10, SCO.
(T) 01314 455668
Speciality: Bach Remedies.
M (Ref:HM14328)

### MULA, ANIA
**Ania Mula**, 66 Church St, Croydon, **Surrey**, CR0 1RB, ENG.
(T) 020 8688 0888
Speciality: Osteopathy.
P S T (Ref:HM14329)

### MULCAHY, ML (DR)
**Mulcahy Dr Ml**, 73 Merrion Rd, Dublin, **County Dublin**, IRE.
(T) 01269 4706
Speciality: Psychiatry.
B (Ref:HM14330)

### MULCAHY, SANDIE
**Sandie Mulcahy**, Health Hydro, Milton Rd, Swindon, **Wiltshire**, SN1 5JA, ENG.
(T) 01793 465629
Speciality: Aromatherapy.
M O (Ref:HM14331)

### MULCAHY, TRICIA
**Tricia Mulcahy**, 34 Kitchener Rd, London, **London (Greater)**, N2 8AS, ENG.
(T) 020 8883 7716
Speciality: Psychotherapy.
B (Ref:HM14332)

### MULCHINOCK, PENNY
**Penny Mulchinock**, 115 Fernlea Rd, London, **London (Greater)**, SW12 9RP, ENG.
(T) 020 8673 6931
Speciality: Psychotherapy.
B (Ref:HM14333)

### MULCHRONE, SUSANNE
**Susanne Mulchrone (Mobile)**, 20 Selangor Avenue, Emsworth, **Hampshire**, PO10 7LT, ENG.
(T) 01243 375019
Speciality: Aromatherapy.
● **Owner** Mrs S Mulchrone
M O (Ref:HM14334)

### MULHOLLAND, ANDREA
**Andrea Mulholland**, 141 Lodge Lane, Dukinfield, **Cheshire**, SK16 5JF, ENG.
(T) 01613 032806
Speciality: Chiropodists (Podiatrists).
● **Owner** Mrs A Mulholland
S (Ref:HM14335)

### MULLALLY, K
**K Mullally**, 3rd Floor, 57a Wimpole St, London, **London (Greater)**, W1M 7DF, ENG.
(T) 020 7486 1095
Speciality: Osteopathy.
P S T (Ref:HM14336)

### MULLALLY, K
**K Mullally**, 47 Leam Trce, Leamington Spa, **Warwickshire**, CV31 1BQ, ENG.
(T) 01926 425441
Speciality: Osteopathy.
● **Owner** Mr K Mullally
P S T (Ref:HM14337)

### MULLALLY, MICHAEL
**Michael Mullally**, 40 Williams St, **County Galway**, IRE.
(T) 09156 8449
Speciality: Psychology.
B (Ref:HM14338)

### MULLAN, JENNIFER
**Jennifer Mullan**, 22 Dowthorpe End, Earls Barton, Northampton, **Northamptonshire**, NN6 0NH, ENG.
(T) 01604 811942
Speciality: Reflexology.
S T (Ref:HM14339)

### MULLAN, PETER
**Peter Mullan**, 28 Bryce Avenue, Carron, Falkirk, FK2 8JA, SCO.
(T) 01324 553853
Speciality: Physiotherapy.
● **Owner** Mr P Mullen
P S T (Ref:HM14340)

### MULLEN, ANDREW C D
**Andrew C D Mullen**, 182 Kensington Church St, London, **London (Greater)**, W8 4DP, ENG.
(T) 020 7262 4507
Speciality: Osteopathy.
P S T (Ref:HM14341)

### MULLEN, ANDREW T W
**Andrew T W Mullen**, 46 Martin Way, Morden, **Surrey**, SM4 5AH, ENG.
(T) 020 8540 0210
Speciality: Osteopathy.
P S T (Ref:HM14342)

### MULLER, GLYNIS
**Glynis Muller**, 2 Beechams Cottages, Spring Gardens Rd, Chappel, Colchester, **Essex**, CO6 2DW, ENG.
(T) 01206 241731
Speciality: Reflexology.
S T (Ref:HM14343)

### MULLIGAN, JEAN H
**Jean H Mulligan**, 55 Bridge St, Banbridge, **County Down**, BT32 3JL, NIR.
(T) 028 4062 4309
Speciality: Physiotherapy.
P S T (Ref:HM14344)

### MULLIGAN, R
**R Mulligan**, Ederney, Enniskillen, **County Fermanagh**, BT93 1HW, NIR.
(T) 028 6863 2207



Key continued: **Yrs.Est:** Years Established **Q:** Qualifications **M:** Professional Membership ✔ Indemnity Insurance Accept Credit Cards

Speciality: Complementary Medicines & Therapy.
● **Owner** Mr R Mulligan
C M (Ref:HM14345)

## MULLINGAR CHIROPRACTORS CLINIC
**Mullingar Chiropractors Clinic**, 60 Austin Friar, Mullingar, **County Westmeath**, IRE.
(T) 04448 374
Speciality: Chiropractors.
P S T (Ref:HM14346)

## MULLINGAR THERAPEUTIC CLINIC
**Mullingar Therapeutic Clinic**, 39 Austin Friar St, Mullingar, **County Westmeath**, IRE.
(T) 04447 277
Speciality: Complementary Medicines & Therapy.
M (Ref:HM14347)

## MULLINS, JOHN
**John Mullins**, Therapy Health Education Centre, 33 The Parade, Roath, Cardiff, **Glamorgan (Vale of)**, CF24 3AD, WAL.
(T) 029 2048 2682
(E) jmullins@cwcom.net
Speciality: Acupuncture, Chiropody, Counselling, Cranial Osteopathy, Hay Diet, Hypnotherapy, Physiotherapy, Shiatsu, Sports Massage. ✓
● **Osteopath** Mr J Mullins Q: BSc, DO, ND, PhD. M: RN, RoN, RoO.
S Yrs. Est.: 3 (Ref:HM14348)

## MULLINS, MARJORIE
**Marjorie Mullins**, 80 Birchwood Avenue, North Gosforth, Newcastle Upon Tyne, **Tyne and Wear**, NE13 6QA, ENG.
(T) 01912 921926
Speciality: Reflexology.
S T (Ref:HM14349)

## MULROY CHIROPODIST
**Mulroy Chiropodist**, 33B Inkerman St, Llanelli, **Carmarthenshire**, SA15 1RY, WAL.
(T) 01554 778575
Speciality: Chiropodists (Podiatrists).
● **Owner** Mr M Mulroy
S (Ref:HM14350)

## MULTIPLE SCLEROSIS THRPY CTRE
**Multiple Sclerosis Therapy Centre**, Bradbury House, 155 Barkers Lane, Bedford, **Bedfordshire**, MK41 9RX, ENG.
(T) 01234 325781 (F) 01234 365242
Speciality: Aromatherapy, Chiropody, Counselling, Dietician, Reflexology, Shiatsu, M S Theory, Nurse Speech Therapist. ✓
● **Manager** Ms V Woods
● **Therapist** Margaret Wilson
C Yrs. Est.: 5 (Ref:HM14351)

## MULTI-THERAPY CENTRE
**Multi-Therapy Centre**, 1 Savernake Cres, Marlborough, **Wiltshire**, SN8 4BJ, ENG.
(T) 01672 512807
Speciality: Acupressure, Bach Remedies, Kinesiology, Massage (Therapeutic), Oriental Diagnosis, Reflexology, Reiki, T'ai-Chi Ch'uan, Ortho-Bionamy. ✓
● **Owner** Mrs C Higley M: ANM, BRA, IIR.
B Yrs. Est.: 16 (Ref:HM14352)

## MULVANEY, ALISTAIR
**Alistair Mulvaney**, 34 Landon Rd, Herne Bay, **Kent**, CT6 6HP, ENG.
(T) 01227 360940
Speciality: Biomechanics, Chiropody, Podiatry. ✓
● **Chiropodist (Podiatrist)**
Mrs E Mulvaney Q: M.S.C.P, S.R.Ch. M: S.C.P.
● **Chiropodist (Podiatrist)**
Mr A Mulvaney Q: S.R.Ch. M: S.C.P.
C Yrs. Est.: 15 (Ref:HM14353)

## MULVANEY, E J
**E J Mulvaney**, 34 Landon Rd, Herne Bay, **Kent**, CT6 6HP, ENG.
(T) 01227 360940
Speciality: Chiropodists (Podiatrists).
● **Partner** Mrs E Mulvaney
S (Ref:HM14354)

## MUMBRAY, LINDA
**Linda Mumbray**, 214 Wolverton Rd, Blakelands, **Buckinghamshire**, MK14 5AB, ENG.
(T) 01908 610395
Speciality: Reflexology.
S T (Ref:HM14355)

## MUMBY, HELEN
**Helen Mumby**, Martindale House, Lombard St, Newark, **Nottinghamshire**, NG24 1XG, ENG.
(T) 01636 611150
Speciality: Aromatherapy.
● **Administrator** Mrs S Taylor
M O (Ref:HM14356)

## MUMBY-CROFT, HELEN
**Helen Mumby-Croft**, 12 Market Pl, Spalding, **Lincolnshire**, PE11 1SL, ENG.
(T) 01775 711822 (F) 01775 711822
Speciality: Physiotherapy.
● **Owner** Mrs H Mumby-Croft
P S T (Ref:HM14357)

## MUNCEY, ALAN
**Alan Muncey**, 9 Church Rd, Chavey Down, Ascot, **Berkshire**, SL5 8RR, ENG.
(T) 01344 883662
Speciality: Hypnotherapy.
● **Hypnotherapist** Alan Muncey
B (Ref:HM14358)

## MUNCEY, J
**Miss J Muncey**, 78 Fencepiece Rd, Ilford, **Essex**, IG6 2JY, ENG.
(T) 020 8501 4647
Speciality: Physiotherapy.
P S T (Ref:HM14359)

## MUNDAY S S C
**Munday S S C**, 14 High Rd Leyton, London, **London (Greater)**, E15 2BP, ENG.
(T) 020 8519 9447
Speciality: Chiropodists (Podiatrists).
● **Owner** Mr S Munday
S (Ref:HM14360)

## MUNDAY, SARA DE LACEY
**Sara De Lacey Munday**, The Castle Clinic, 18-20 The Ropewalk, Nottingham, **Nottinghamshire**, NG1 5DT, ENG.
(T) 01159 472263 (F) 01159 556306
Speciality: Osteopathy.
● **Owner** Mr M Pook
P S T (Ref:HM14361)

## MUNGUR, K
**K Mungur**, 165 Highfield Rd, Blackpool, **Lancashire**, FY4 2HG, ENG.
(T) 01253 406353
Speciality: Chiropodists (Podiatrists).
● **Owner** Mr K Mungur
S (Ref:HM14362)

## MUNRO, EVELYN
**Evelyn Munro**, Inverurie, **Aberdeenshire**, AB51, SCO.
(T) 01651 873014
Speciality: Bach Remedies.
M (Ref:HM14363)

## MUNRO, I J
**I J Munro**, Glenbrook Rd, Balerno, **Edinburgh (City of)**, EH14 7BE, SCO.
(T) 01314 515655 (F) 01314 494828
Speciality: Reflexology.
● **Owner** Mrs I Rae
S T (Ref:HM14364)

## MUNRO, JANE
**Jane Munro**, 89 York Rd, Kings Heath, Birmingham, **Midlands (West)**, B14 7RY, ENG.
(T) 01214 440803
Speciality: Complementary Medicines & Therapy.
● **Owner** Miss J Munro
C M (Ref:HM14365)

## MUNRO, LESLEY
**Lesley Munro**, 26 Kirkhill Rd, Edinburgh, **Edinburgh (City of)**, EH16 5DD, SCO.
(T) 01316 628925 (F) 01316 628925
Speciality: Homeopathy.
● **Owner** Ms L Munro
M (Ref:HM14366)

## MUNRO, PAULINE A
**Pauline A Munro**, Queensway Medical Centre, Queensway, Poulton-le-Fylde, **Lancashire**, FY6 7ST, ENG.
(T) 01253 893139
Speciality: Physiotherapy.
● **Owner** Mrs P Munro
P S T (Ref:HM14367)

## MUNTING, E
**E Munting**, 4 Old Hall Gardens, Brooke, Norwich, **Norfolk**, NR15 1JZ, ENG.
(T) 01508 550523
Speciality: Physiotherapy.
P S T (Ref:HM14368)

## MURAYAMA, YOSHIHIRO
**Yoshihiro Murayama**, 42 Prospect Rd, Southborough, Tunbridge Wells, **Kent**, TN4 0EN, ENG.
(T) 01892 548879 (F) 01892 680664
Speciality: Acupuncture.
● **Owner** Mr Y Murayama
O (Ref:HM14369)

## MURDOCH, M
**M Murdoch**, 35 Sandford Avenue, Church Stretton, **Shropshire**, SY6 6BH, ENG.
(T) 01694 724152
Speciality: Physiotherapy.
P S T (Ref:HM14370)

## MURDOCH, R J
**R J Murdoch**, Somnes Avenue, Canvey Island, **Essex**, SS8 9RA, ENG.
(T) 01268 694342 (F) 01268 682920
Speciality: Physiotherapy.
● **Manager** Mr G Short
P S T (Ref:HM14371)

## MURDOCH, R J
**R J Murdoch**, 220 Eastwood Rd North, Leigh-On-Sea, **Essex**, SS9 4LU, ENG.
(T) 01702 421467
Speciality: Physiotherapy.
● **Owner** Ms R Murdoch
P S T (Ref:HM14372)

## MURFIN, PAUL
**Paul Murfin**, 208 Banstead Rd, Banstead, **Surrey**, SM7 1QG, ENG.
(T) 020 8786 7604
Speciality: Hypnotherapy.
B (Ref:HM14373)

## MURPHY & ASSOCIATES
**M Murphy & Associates**, Colville Health Centre, 51 Kensington Park Rd, London, **London (Greater)**, W11 1PA, ENG.
(T) 020 7727 6827 (F) 020 7243 1882
Speciality: Chiropodists (Podiatrists).
● **Owner** Ms M Murphy
S (Ref:HM14374)

## MURPHY, A M
**A M Murphy**, 79 St Georges Rd, Stourbridge, **Midlands (West)**, DY8 3DU, ENG.
(T) 01384 835486
Speciality: Chiropodists (Podiatrists).
● **Owner** Miss A Murphy
S (Ref:HM14375)

## MURPHY, ALAN
**Alan Murphy**, 42 Georgiana St, London, **London (Greater)**, NW1 0EB, ENG.
(T) 020 7485 0358
Speciality: Psychotherapy. ✓
● **Psychotherapist** Mr A Murphy Q: Dip.Psych. M: UKCP.
B Yrs. Est.: 5 (Ref:HM14376)

## MURPHY, ANNE
**Murphy Anne**, 18 Market St, **County Monaghan**, IRE.
(T) 04783 109
Speciality: Complementary Medicines & Therapy.
M (Ref:HM14377)

## MURPHY, BERNADETTE
**Murphy Bernadette**, Stavsnas Coolcotts, **County Wexford**, IRE.
(T) 05342 269
Speciality: Hypnotherapy.

B (Ref:HM14378)

**MURPHY, BOB**

**Bob Murphy**, 94 St James's St, Brighton, **Sussex (West)**, BN2 1TP, ENG.
(T) 01273 672952
Speciality: Reflexology.
● **Owner** Mr L Moore
S T (Ref:HM14379)

**MURPHY, BRENDAN**

**Murphy Brendan MIACT**, 377 Clontarf Rd, Dublin, **County Dublin**, IRE.
(T) 01833 1758
Speciality: Counselling.
B H (Ref:HM14380)

**MURPHY, CYNTHIA**

**Cynthia Murphy**, Fairfields Clinic, Skippetts Lane West, Basingstoke, **Hampshire**, RG21 3HP, ENG.
(T) 01256 326980
Speciality: Complementary Medicines & Therapy.
M (Ref:HM14381)

**MURPHY, ELIZABETH**

**Murphy Elizabeth**, Fitzgerald Hse, 74 Grand Prde, **County Cork**, IRE.
(T) 021 4272 100
Speciality: Complementary Medicines & Therapy.
M (Ref:HM14382)

**MURPHY, GARY**

**Murphy Gary P Lic Ac AMTAS MAI A**, U1 Rossdale Hse, Medical Cntr Bishopstown, Cork, **County Cork**, IRE.
(T) 021 4342 000
Speciality: Acupuncture.
O (Ref:HM14383)

**MURPHY, GERARD (DR)**

**Murphy Dr Gerard MB MRCGP MICGP**, Gleann An Oir Main Rd, Ballincollig, **County Cork**, IRE.
(T) 021 4873 640
Speciality: Acupuncture.
O (Ref:HM14384)

**MURPHY, J E**

**J E Murphy**, 12 Barn Green, Wolverhampton, **Midlands (West)**, WV3 7AY, ENG.
(T) 01902 343882
Speciality: Chiropodists (Podiatrists).
S (Ref:HM14385)

**MURPHY, K**

**K Murphy**, 376 Washway Rd, Sale, **Cheshire**, M33 4HF, ENG.
(T) 01619 731603 (F) 01619 731603
Speciality: Physiotherapy.
● **Owner** Mr K Murphy
P S T (Ref:HM14386)

**MURPHY, KEVIN**

**Kevin Murphy DC**, The Professional Centre For Holistic Health, 50 High St, Hastings, **Sussex (East)**, TN34 3RU, ENG.
(T) 01424 465050
(E) kevin@chiromurph.worldonline.co.uk
(W) www.professionalcentre.com
Speciality: Chiropractic, Cranial Osteopathy, Healer, Kinesiology, Massage (Therapeutic).
● **McTimoney Chiropractor**
Mr K Murphy Q: Dip.Chiro. M: GCC.
S Yrs. Est.: 3 (Ref:HM14387)

**MURPHY, MARY**

**Mary Murphy - Psychotherapy & Hypnotherapy**, Coolhull, Duncormick, **County Wexford**, IRE.
(T) 05156 1132
(E) marysol@eircom.net
Speciality: Cognitive Therapy, Counselling, Encounter Groups, Gestalt Therapy, Group Therapy, Humanistic Psychology, Hypnosis, Hypnotherapy, Life Style Coaching, Pattern Therapies, Psychotherapy, Rogerian Therapy, Sensitivity Training, Stress Therapy, Transactional Analysis. ✔
● **Psychotherapist/Hypnotherapist/Counsellor**
Ms M Murphy Q: BA.
B Yrs. Est.: 10 (Ref:HM14388)

**MURPHY, MARY**

**Murphy Mary D H P C M A P T**, Coolhull Duncormick, IRE.
(T) 05156 1132
Speciality: Psychotherapy.
B (Ref:HM14389)

**MURPHY, MAUREEN**

**Maureen Murphy**, 425 Nottingham Rd, Mansfield, **Nottinghamshire**, NG18 4SU, ENG.
(T) 01623 620128
Speciality: Herbal Medicine.
M (Ref:HM14390)

**MURPHY, MAUREEN**

**Maureen Murphy**, Dollis Hill, London, **London (Greater)**, NW2, ENG.
(T) 020 8452 7559
Speciality: Bach Remedies.
M (Ref:HM14391)

**MURPHY, RORY (DR)**

**Murphy Dr Rory**, 60 Austin Friar St, Mullingar, **County Westmeath**, IRE.
(T) 04448 374
Speciality: Chiropractors.
P S T (Ref:HM14392)

**MURPHY, SHARON**

**Murphy Sharon**, Navan Rd, Dublin, **County Dublin**, IRE.
(T) 01868 2180
Speciality: Complementary Medicines & Therapy.
M (Ref:HM14393)

**MURPHY, TERESA**

**MURPHY TERESA S R N Lic Ac**, Coolnaha Sth Ballyhaunis, IRE.
(T) 09073 0670
Speciality: Acupuncture.
O (Ref:HM14394)

**MURPHY, TERRY**

**Terry Murphy**, 59 Frogmore Park Drive, Blackwater, Camberley, **Surrey**, GU17 0PJ, ENG.
(T) 01276 34181 (F) 01276 35606
Speciality: Chiropractic.
● **Partner** Mr T Murphy
P S T (Ref:HM14395)

**MURRAY, A**

**A Murray**, Standalane House, Kincardine, Alloa, **Clackmannanshire**, FK10 4NX, SCO.
(T) 01259 730785
Speciality: Psychology.
● **Owner** A Murray
B (Ref:HM14396)

**MURRAY, A G**

**A G Murray**, 89 Viney Bank, Court Wood Lane, Croydon, **Surrey**, CR0 9JU, ENG.
(T) 020 8651 5100
Speciality: Chiropody.
● **Owner** Mr A Murray
S (Ref:HM14397)

**MURRAY, ANN**

**Ann Murray**, 7 Shaw Cres, Hutton, Brentwood, **Essex**, CM13 1JD, ENG.
(T) 01277 226613
Speciality: Reflexology.
S T (Ref:HM14398)

**MURRAY, ARLENE**

**Arlene Murray**, 9 Grindle Cl, Fareham, **Hampshire**, PO16 8EF, ENG.
(T) 01329 310180
Speciality: Complementary Medicines & Therapy.
● **Owner** Mrs A Murray
C M (Ref:HM14399)

**MURRAY, C O**

**C O Murray**, 3 Lucerne Rd, Thornton Heath, **Surrey**, CR7 7BB, ENG.
(T) 020 8683 2649 (F) 020 8683 2649
Speciality: Psychology.
● **Owner** Dr C Murray
B (Ref:HM14400)

**MURRAY, CATHERINE**

**Murray Catherine M I A C T M U K C P**, Newtown House Centre, Doneraile, **County Cork**, IRE.
(T) 022 2411 7
Speciality: Psychotherapy.
B (Ref:HM14401)

**MURRAY, DECLAN (DR)**

**Murray Dr Declan M R C Psych**, Curam Town Mall, Swords, **County Dublin**, IRE.
(T) 01840 3391
(E) 100074.1540@compuserve.com
Speciality: Psychiatry.
B (Ref:HM14402)

**MURRAY, DORIS**

**Doris Murray**, 12 Sun St, Sunniside, Newcastle Upon Tyne, **Tyne and Wear**, NE16 5LR, ENG.
(T) 01914 881388
Speciality: Chiropodists (Podiatrists).
S (Ref:HM14403)

**MURRAY, DOROTHY**

**Dorothy Murray**, 68B Leicester Rd, Loughborough, **Leicestershire**, LE11 2AG, ENG.
(T) 01509 234522
Speciality: Chiropodists (Podiatrists).
S (Ref:HM14404)

**MURRAY, GILLIAN E**

**Gillian E Murray**, 25 Heathfield Rd, Southampton, **Hampshire**, SO19 1DL, ENG.
(T) 023 8044 9781
Speciality: Chiropodists (Podiatrists).
S (Ref:HM14405)

**MURRAY, HEATHER**

**Heather Murray**, Rogers Cottage, Forest Green, Dorking, **Surrey**, RH5 5SQ, ENG.
(T) 01306 621268
Speciality: Complementary Medicines & Therapy.
C M (Ref:HM14406)

**MURRAY, K**

**K Murray**, Chelsea Lane, Inverurie, **Aberdeenshire**, AB51 3QQ, SCO.
(T) 01467 624888 (F) 01467 624888
Speciality: Hypnotherapy.
● **Partner** Mrs C Craigmile
B (Ref:HM14407)

**MURRAY, KAREN**

**Miss Karen Murray**, 43 Chester Rd, Ilford, **Essex**, IG3 8PT, ENG.
(T) 07050 622844
Speciality: Hypnotherapy.
● **Owner** Miss K Murray
B (Ref:HM14408)

**MURRAY, LESLEY**

**Lesley Murray**, Sierras, Ospringe Pla, Faversham, **Kent**, ME13 8TB, ENG.
(T) 01795 537159
Speciality: Homeopathy.
M (Ref:HM14409)

**MURRAY, P**

**P Murray**, 27 St Edmunds Rd, Northampton, **Northamptonshire**, NN1 5DY, ENG.
(T) 01604 624594
Speciality: Chiropodists (Podiatrists).
● **Owner** Mr P Murray
S (Ref:HM14410)

**MURRAY, R**

**R Murray**, 18 Lansdowne Rd, London, **London (Greater)**, W11 3LL, ENG.
(T) 020 7727 7222
Speciality: Alexander Technique.
● **Employee** Mr J Brown
P S (Ref:HM14411)

**MURRAY, R H**

**R H Murray**, 4 Gainsborough Cl, Cherry Garden Avenue, Folkestone, **Kent**, CT19 5NB, ENG.
(T) 01303 278319
Speciality: Hypnosis.
B (Ref:HM14412)

**MURRAY, S L**

**S L Murray**, Arden House, Alexandra Rd, Sudbury, **Suffolk**, CO10 2RY, ENG.
(T) 01787 319931
Speciality: Chiropodists (Podiatrists).
S (Ref:HM14413)



Key continued: Yrs.Est: Years Established Q: Qualifications M: Professional Membership ✔ Indemnity Insurance Accept Credit Cards

**MURRAY, T A (DR)**

**Dr T A Murray**, 28 Grendon Gardens, Wembley, **London (Greater)**, HA9 9NE, ENG.
(T) 020 8904 5801
Speciality: Osteopathy.
P S T (Ref:HM14414)

**MURRAY, TERESA**

**Teresa Murray**, 60 Beechwood Rise, Watford, **Hertfordshire**, WD2 5SG, ENG.
(T) 01923 460536
Speciality: Reflexology.
● **Owner** Mrs T Murray
S T (Ref:HM14415)

**MURRAY, VICTORIA**

**Victoria Murray**, Aston Clinic, 26 Kingston Rd, New Malden, **Surrey**, KT3 3LS, ENG.
(T) 020 8942 3148 (F) 020 8949 7050
Speciality: Reflexology.
S T (Ref:HM14416)

**MURRAY, WILFRID**

**Wilfrid Murray**, 121 Replingham Rd, London, **London (Greater)**, SW18 5LX, ENG.
(T) 020 8870 7643
Speciality: Alexander Technique.
● **Owner** Mr W Murray
P S (Ref:HM14417)

**MURRELL, CHARLES**

**Charles Murrell**, 67A Old Tovil Rd, Maidstone, **Kent**, ME15 6PU, ENG.
(T) 01622 754648
Speciality: Reflexology.
S T (Ref:HM14418)

**MURRELL, JANE**

**Jane Murrell**, Whitwell Farm, Long Marston, Tring, **Hertfordshire**, HP23 4RA, ENG.
(T) 01296 668190
Speciality: Reflexology.
S T (Ref:HM14419)

**MURRELL, JOHN**

**John Murrell**, 17 Lincoln Rd, Oxford, **Oxfordshire**, OX1 4TB, ENG.
(T) 01865 794292
Speciality: Complementary Medicines & Therapy.
C M (Ref:HM14420)

**MURRELL, PAULINE**

**Pauline Murrell**, Bexleyheath Natural Health Clinic, 284 Broadway, Bexleyheath, **Kent**, DA6 8AJ, ENG.
(T) 020 8303 6288 (F) 020 8303 6288
Speciality: Physiotherapy.
● **Owner** Mr P Cousins
P S T (Ref:HM14421)

**MURRELL, R J**

**R J Murrell**, 1 Eastfield, Chirnside, Duns, **Scottish Borders**, TD11 3XF, SCO.
(T) 01890 818960
Speciality: Osteopathy.
P S T (Ref:HM14422)

**MURRIN, P**

**P Murrin**, 1 Fern Bank, High St, Eynsford, Dartford, **Kent**, DA4 0AU, ENG.
(T) 01322 864613
Speciality: Chiropodists (Podiatrists).
S (Ref:HM14423)

**MURRIN, P M**

**P M Murrin**, 43 Evans St, Barry, **Glamorgan (Vale of)**, CF62 8DU, WAL.
(T) 01446 733805
Speciality: Chiropodists (Podiatrists).
● **Owner** Mrs P Murrin
S (Ref:HM14424)

**MUSCATY, J**

**J Muscaty**, Sherbourne House, 32 Woodhill Rd, Portishead, Bristol, BS20 7EZ, ENG.
(T) 01275 843482
Speciality: Osteopathy.
P S T (Ref:HM14425)

**MUSCLE EFFECT THERAPY**

**Muscle Effect Therapy**, 33 Wellington La, Dublin, **County Dublin**, IRE.
(T) 01668 0316
(W) www.catalase.com/met.htm
Speciality: Complementary Medicines & Therapy.
M (Ref:HM14426)

**MUSGRAVE-BROWN, LYLEEN**

**Lyleen Musgrave-Brown**, Hardings, Norwich Rd, Scole, Diss, **Norfolk**, IP21 4DY, ENG.
(T) 01379 741198
Speciality: Reflexology.
S T (Ref:HM14427)

**MUSTAFA, S**

**S Mustafa**, The Academy Health & Fitness Centre, 16 Hoxton Sq, London, **London (Greater)**, N1 6NT, ENG.
(T) 020 7729 5789 (F) 020 7739 4753
Speciality: Osteopathy.
● **Owner** Mr B Brain
P S T (Ref:HM14428)

**MUSTARD SEED CLINIC**

**Mustard Seed Clinic (The)**, 22 McDonough Cl, Chessington, **Surrey**, KT9 1ER, ENG.
(T) 020 8391 2190 (F) 020 8391 9061
Speciality: Physiotherapy.
● **Owner** Mr R Howlett
P S T (Ref:HM14429)

**MUSTARD SEED HEALTH**

**Mustard Seed Health**, 13 Burnside Pl, Irvine, **Ayrshire (North)**, KA12 0UN, SCO.
(T) 01294 272312
Speciality: Reflexology.
● **Owner** Mrs R Thomson
S T (Ref:HM14430)

**MUSWELL HILL CHIROPRACTIC**

**Muswell Hill Chiropractic Clinic**, 130 Colney Hatch Lane, Muswell Hill, London, **London (Greater)**, N10 1ER, ENG.
(T) 020 8442 0008
Speciality: Chiropractic.
P S T (Ref:HM14431)

**MYATT, ANITA**

**Anita Myatt**, The Health Centre, 564 Penn Rd, Wolverhampton, **Midlands (West)**, WV4 4HU, ENG.
(T) 01902 343616
Speciality: Allergy Testing, Aromatherapy, Crystal Healing, Herbal Medicine, Hopi Ear Candles, Nutritional Therapy, Pyramid Power, Reflexology, Shiatsu, Organ function testing, Mercury test, Relaxation wave and crystal therapy. ✓
● **Medical Herbalist** Anita Myatt M: BHMA.
C Yrs. Est.: 18 (Ref:HM14432)

**MYATT, R**

**R Myatt**, Po Box 2, Sidmouth, **Devon**, EX10 9ZY, ENG.
(T) 01395 513803
Speciality: Psychology.
● **Doctor** Dr R Myatt
B (Ref:HM14433)

**MYDDLETON, TRACY**

**Tracy Myddleton**, 35 Pentridge Drive, Ilkeston, **Derbyshire**, DE7 9HT, ENG.
(T) 01159 443025
Speciality: Chiropodists (Podiatrists).
● **Owner** Mrs T Myddleton
S (Ref:HM14434)

**MYERS, H**

**H Myers**, 34 Tacklee Rd, Yapton, Arundel, **Sussex (West)**, BN18 0HB, ENG.
(T) 01243 551581
Speciality: Chiropodists (Podiatrists).
S (Ref:HM14435)

**MYERS, LINDA**

**Linda Myers**, 6 Osprey Cl, Dukinfield, **Cheshire**, SK16 5QE, ENG.
(T) 01613 384745
Speciality: Complementary Medicines & Therapy.
● **Owner** Mrs L Myers
C M (Ref:HM14436)

**MYERS, MARION**

**Analytical Psychotherapy**, 44 St Marys Rd, Leamington Spa, **Warwickshire**, CV31 1JP, ENG.
(T) 01926 425403 (F) 08707 34403
Speciality: Psychotherapy. ✓
● **Analytical Psychotherapist**
Ms M Myers Q: BCP (Reg), UKCP (Reg).
M: BACP, BAP.
H Yrs. Est.: 10 (Ref:HM14437)

**MYERS, MERRILYN**

**Merrilyn Myers**, 7 Skillicorne Mews, Queens Rd, Cheltenham, **Gloucestershire**, GL50 2NJ, ENG.
(T) 01242 529700 (F) 01242 516227
Speciality: Bach Remedies, Bach Flower Therapy. ✓
● **Owner/Bach Flower Remedies**
Mrs M Myers M: BHMA.
B C Yrs. Est.: 20 (Ref:HM14438)

**MYERS, R J L**

**R J L Myers**, 36 Doncaster Rd, Scunthorpe, **Humberside**, DN15 7RQ, ENG.
(T) 01724 842054
Speciality: Chiropodists (Podiatrists).
S (Ref:HM14439)

**MYERS, RHONA**

**Mrs Rhona Myers**, 127 Stonegrove, Edgware, **London (Greater)**, HA8 7TJ, ENG.
(T) 020 8958 7117
Speciality: Homeopathy.
● **Owner** Mrs R Myers
M (Ref:HM14440)

**MYERS, WENDY**

**Wendy Myers**, 24 High St, Dronfield, **Derbyshire**, S18 1PY, ENG.
(T) 01246 411067
Speciality: Reflexology.
S T (Ref:HM14441)

**MYLES, JOHN**

**John Myles**, 20A Abbotswood, Guildford, **Surrey**, GU1 1UX, ENG.
(T) 01483 577834 (F) 01483 562499
Speciality: Hypnosis.
● **Owner** Mr J Myles
B (Ref:HM14442)

**MYOGENICS**

**Myogenics**, 30 Fieldhead Gdns, Bourne End, **Buckinghamshire**, SL8 5RN, ENG.
(T) 01628 810981
Speciality: Complementary Medicines & Therapy.
● **Owner** Mr C Revans
M (Ref:HM14443)

**MYSTIC FRAGRANCE**

**Mystic Fragrance**, 145B Stoke Newington Rd, London, **London (Greater)**, N16 8BP, ENG.
(T) 020 8965 7610 (F) 020 7254 4776
Speciality: Complementary Medicines & Therapy.
● **Owner** Mr J Shah
C M (Ref:HM14444)

**MYSTIC SCHEHERAZADE**

**Mystic Scheherazade**, 47 Argyll View, Larne, **County Antrim**, BT40 2JS, NIR.
(T) 028 2827 7009
(E) mysticscheherazade@ukf.co.uk
Speciality: Counselling, Spiritual Healing, Phsychic, Clairvoyant. ✓
● **Owner/Psychic Clairvoyant**
Mrs S Al-Tellawy
B Yrs. Est.: 11 (Ref:HM14445)

**MYSTICAL PATHWAYS**

**Mystical Pathways**, 25 Morlais, Emmer Green, Reading, **Berkshire**, RG4 8PQ, ENG.
(T) 01189 464561
Speciality: Clairvoyants & Palmists.
● **Owner** Mrs M Pollard
B (Ref:HM14446)

**MYSTICAL PATHWAYS**

**Mystical Pathways**, 3 Crown Cottages, Swinley Rd, Ascot, **Berkshire**, SL5 8AS, ENG.
(T) 01344 626786
Speciality: Clairvoyants & Palmists.
● **Owner** Mr M Pollard
B (Ref:HM14447)

**N A P A**

**N A P A**, 39 Flitwick Rd, Ampthill, Bedford,

Key: B Mind-Body Medicine C Complementary Medicine H Self Help Treatment M Medicinal Therapy O Oriental Medicine P Postural Therapy S Manipulative Structural Therapy T Touch Therapy

**Bedfordshire**, MK45 2NS, ENG.
(T) 01525 403833 (F) 01525 403833
Speciality: Complementary Medicines & Therapy.
● **Owner** Mr R Dutton
M (Ref:HM14448)

## N H S

**Springwell House Chiropody Clinic**, 26 Ardmillan Trce, Edinburgh, **Edinburgh (City of)**, EH11 2JL, SCO.
(T) 01315 377469
Speciality: Chiropody.
● **Chiropodist** Mr M Lobjoie Q: BSc, S.R.Ch. M: S.R.Ch.
M Yrs. Est.: 6 (Ref:HM14449)

## N H S TRUST CHIROPODY CLINIC

**N H S Trust Chiropody Clinic**, 7 Burn St, Dalbeattie, **Dumfries and Galloway**, DG5 4AE, SCO.
(T) 01556 611163
Speciality: Chiropodists (Podiatrists).
S (Ref:HM14450)

## N I HOMOEOPATHIC SOCIETY

**N I Homoeopathic Society**, 1 Cranmore Park, Belfast, **County Antrim**, BT9 6JF, NIR.
(T) 028 9066 2942
Speciality: Homeopathy.
M (Ref:HM14451)

## N J HARRISON CHIROPODY SERVICE

**N J Harrison Chiropody Service**, 25 Dunsfold Way, New Addington, Croydon, **Surrey**, CR0 0TP, ENG.
(T) 020 8240 7634
Speciality: Chiropractors.
● **Owner** Miss N Harrison
P S T (Ref:HM14452)

## N L P ACADEMY

**N L P Academy**, 35-37 East St, Bromley, **Kent**, BR1 1QE, ENG.
(T) 020 8402 1120 (F) 020 8402 1130
Speciality: Hypnotherapy.
● **Principal** Mr M Carroll
B (Ref:HM14453)

## N P PHYSIOTHERAPY SERVICES

**N P Physiotherapy Services**, Newport Pagnell Medical Centre, Queens Avenue, Newport Pagnell, **Buckinghamshire**, MK16 8QT, ENG.
(T) 01908 619901 (F) 01908 615099
Speciality: Physiotherapy.
● **Partner** Mr N Campbell
P S T (Ref:HM14454)

## NAARIS BEAUTY PARLOUR

**Naaris Beauty Parlour**, Unit 1, 124 Hanworth Rd, Hounslow, **London (Greater)**, TW3 1UG, ENG.
(T) 020 8577 1142
Speciality: Electrolysis.
● **Owner** Miss N Reel
T (Ref:HM14455)

## NAAS ACUPUNCTURE

**Naas Acupuncture**, Rathasker Sq, Kilcullen Rd, Naas Co, **County Kildare**, IRE.
(T) 04587 6687
Speciality: Acupuncture.
O (Ref:HM14456)

## NAAS CHIROPRACTIC CLINIC

**Naas Chiropractic Clinic**, 4 New Row, Naas, **County Kildare**, IRE.
(T) 04587 6355
Speciality: Chiropractors.
P S T (Ref:HM14457)

## NAFSIYAT-INTER CULTURAL THRPY

**Nafsiyat-Inter Cultural Therapy Centre**, 278 Seven Sisters Rd, London, **London (Greater)**, N4 2HY, ENG.
(T) 020 7263 6394 (F) 020 7561 1870
Speciality: Psychotherapy.
B (Ref:HM14458)

## NAGLA, P A

**P A Nagla**, 12 Rankin Avenue, Hesketh Bank, Preston, **Lancashire**, PR4 6PA, ENG.
(T) 01772 815486
Speciality: Chiropodists (Podiatrists).
● **Owner** Mrs P Nagla
S (Ref:HM14459)

## NAILSEA CHIROPRACTIC CLINIC

**Nailsea Chiropractic Clinic**, 22 Colliers Walk, Nailsea, Bristol, BS48 2XH, ENG.
(T) 01275 810296 (F) 01275 810296
(E) leroux@msn.com
Speciality: Aromatherapy, Chiropractic, Complementary Therapy, Electrotherapy, Manipulation, Massage (Therapeutic), Ultrasonics, X-Ray. ✔
● **Chiropractor** Ms E Donovan M: CC.
● **Chiropractor** Ms D Le Roux Q: BSc (Chiro), DC, FCC, MSc (Chiro). M: BCA, CC.
S Yrs. Est.: 9 (Ref:HM14460)

## NAILSWORTH NATURAL HLTH CTRE

**Nailsworth Natural Health Centre**, George St, Nailsworth, Stroud, **Gloucestershire**, GL6 0AG, ENG.
(T) 01453 872229
Speciality: Complementary Medicines & Therapy.
● **Owner** Mrs S Johns
M (Ref:HM14461)

## NAIRN HYDROTHERAPY POOL

**Nairn Hydrotherapy Pool**, Cawdor Rd, Nairn, **Highland**, IV12 5ED, SCO.
(T) 01667 455351 (F) 01667 456883
Speciality: Complementary Medicines & Therapy.
● **Manager** Mrs J McIver
C M (Ref:HM14462)

## NAISH, P

**P Naish**, 10 Eldon Rd, Reading, **Berkshire**, RG1 4DH, ENG.
(T) 01189 502002
Speciality: Psychology.
B (Ref:HM14463)

## NAISH, P

**P Naish**, Low Lane House, Middleham Rd, Leyburn, **Yorkshire (North)**, DL8 5HD, ENG.
(T) 01969 623354 (F) 01969 623800
Speciality: Physiotherapy.
● **Owner** Mrs P Naish
P S T (Ref:HM14464)

## NAMREE FARM

**Namree Farm (Holistic Healing Ctr)**, Cappagh, Inistioge, **County Kilkenny**, IRE.
(T) 05658 722
Speciality: Healing.
B (Ref:HM14465)

## NANCHOLAS, DAPHNE

**Daphne Nancholas**, 39 Nutgrove Avenue, Bristol, BS3 4QF, ENG.
(T) 01179 660393
Speciality: Homeopathy.
● **Owner** Ms D Nancholas
M (Ref:HM14466)

## NANCOLLAS, C M

**C M Nancollas**, The Bridgeman Centre, 18 Bridgeman Trce, Wigan, **Lancashire**, WN1 1TD, ENG.
(T) 01942 321235
Speciality: Physiotherapy.
P S T (Ref:HM14467)

## NANCY METCALFE MOBILE CONSULT

**Nancy Metcalfe Mobile Consultant**, 4 Station Cottages, Huttons Ambo, York, **Yorkshire (North)**, YO60 7HQ, ENG.
(T) 01653 694831
Speciality: Massage (Therapeutic), Music Therapy, Stress Therapy, Touch Therapy, Vibrational Therapy. ✔
● **Massage Therapist** Ms N Metcalfe Q: IIHHT, VAI.Dip. M: FHT.
T Yrs. Est.: 3 (Ref:HM14468)

## NANDLAL, J A

**J A Nandlal**, 14 Eastcote Lane, Harrow, **London (Greater)**, HA2 8BP, ENG.
(T) 020 8422 1411
Speciality: Chiropodists (Podiatrists).
S (Ref:HM14469)

## NANDLAL, J A

**J A Nandlal**, 72 Longmore Avenue, Barnet, **Hertfordshire**, EN5 1JX, ENG.
(T) 020 8449 3620
Speciality: Chiropodists (Podiatrists).
S (Ref:HM14470)

## NANTWICH CHIROPODY CLINIC

**Nantwich Chiropody Clinic (The)**, 10 Mill St, Nantwich, **Cheshire**, CW5 5ST, ENG.
(T) 01270 627118 (F) 01270 627118
Speciality: Chiropodists (Podiatrists).
● **Owner** Mrs A Lynch
S (Ref:HM14471)

## NAOMI, ELIA

**Elia Naomi**, 3 Selborne Cl, Petersfield, **Hampshire**, GU32 2JB, ENG.
(T) 01730 261256
Speciality: Physiotherapy.
P S T (Ref:HM14472)

## NAPIER, WILLIAM J M

**William J M Napier**, Belsize Park Chiropractic Clinic, 18 Lambolle Pl, London, **London (Greater)**, NW3 4PG, ENG.
(T) 020 7483 1022
Speciality: Chiropractic.
P S T (Ref:HM14473)

## NAPIERS CLINIC & DISPENSARY

**Napiers Clinic & Dispensary**, 18 Bristo Pl, Edinburgh, **Edinburgh (City of)**, EH1 1EZ, SCO.
(T) 01312 255542
Speciality: Herbal Medicine.
● **Teacher** Mr R Harrower
M (Ref:HM14474)

## NAPIER'S DISPENSARY & CLINIC

**Napier's Dispensary & Clinic**, 61 Cresswell St, Hillhead, Glasgow, **Glasgow (City of)**, G12 8AD, SCO.
(T) 01413 395859
Speciality: Alexander Technique.
● **Teacher** Miss C Stewart
P S (Ref:HM14475)

## NAPIERS DISPENSARY STOCKBRIDGE

**Napiers Dispensary Stockbridge**, 35 Hamilton Pl, Edinburgh, **Edinburgh (City of)**, EH3 5BA, SCO.
(T) 01313 152130 (F) 01313 431152
Speciality: Herbal Medicine.
● **Owner** Miss D Atkinson
M (Ref:HM14476)

## NAPIERS HERBS

**Napiers Herbs**, Napiers Farm, Colchester Rd, Tiptree, Colchester, **Essex**, CO5 0EX, ENG.
(T) 01621 815238
Speciality: Complementary Medicines & Therapy.
● **Partner** Mrs R Adams
M (Ref:HM14477)

## NAPIERS MAIL ORDER

**Napiers Mail Order Ltd**, 35 Hamilton Pl, Edinburgh, **Edinburgh (City of)**, EH3 5BA, SCO.
(T) 01313 436683 (F) 01313 436683
Speciality: Complementary Medicines & Therapy.
● **Manageress** Ms A McQuirter
M (Ref:HM14478)

## NAPLES, EILEEN

**Eileen Naples**, 57 Crown Rd, Wheatley, Oxford, **Oxfordshire**, OX33 1UL, ENG.
(T) 01865 873218
Speciality: Chiropractic.
P S T (Ref:HM14479)

## NAPLES, EILEEN

**Eileen Naples**, Ryecroft, Plantation Rd, Leighton Buzzard, **Bedfordshire**, LU7 7HT, ENG.
(T) 01525 377384
Speciality: Chiropractic.
● **Owner** Mrs E Naples
P S T (Ref:HM14480)

## NAPPER, RICHARD

**Richard Napper**, Stillpoint, Broad St Pl, Bath, **Somerset**, BA1 5LH, ENG.
(T) 01225 460106
Speciality: Homeopathy.



Key continued: Yrs.Est: Years Established Q: Qualifications M: Professional Membership ✔ Indemnity Insurance Accept Credit Cards

M (Ref:HM14481)

**NAPPER, RICHARD**

**Richard Napper**, Newport Clinic Of Holistic Health, 36 Godfrey Rd, Newport, NP20 4PE, **WAL**.
(T) 01633 843333
Speciality: Complementary Medicines & Therapy.
● **Owner** Mr J Francis
C M (Ref:HM14482)

**NAPPER, WENDY**

**Wendy Napper**, 15A Binghams Rd, Crossways, Dorchester, **Dorset**, DT2 8BW, ENG.
(T) 01305 852424
Speciality: Chiropodists (Podiatrists).
● **Owner** Mrs W Napper
S (Ref:HM14483)

**NAPTHINE, MARYANNE**

**Maryanne Napthine**, 76 Private Rd, Mapperley, Nottingham, **Nottinghamshire**, NG3 5FQ, ENG.
(T) 01159 857893
Speciality: Chiropodists (Podiatrists).
● **Owner** Mrs M Napthine
S (Ref:HM14484)

**NARAYAN, M**

**M Narayan**, 30 Rotten Row, Lichfield, **Staffordshire**, WS13 6JB, ENG.
(T) 01543 252673
Speciality: Osteopathy.
● **Senior Partner** Ms J Scratchley
P S T (Ref:HM14485)

**NARAYAN, MAMTA**

**Mamta Narayan**, 25 Lower Gungate, Tamworth, **Staffordshire**, B79 7AT, ENG.
(T) 01827 68374
Speciality: Osteopathy.
● **Osteopath** Mamta Narayan Q: DO. M: GOsC.
S Yrs. Est.: 8 (Ref:HM14486)

**NASEBY ACUPUNCTURE CLINIC**

**Naseby Acupuncture Clinic**, 25 Naseby Rise, Newbury, **Berkshire**, RG14 2SF, ENG.
(T) 01635 48452
(E) julia@naseby-acupuncture.fsnet.co.uk
(W) www.naseby-acupuncture.fsnet.co.uk
Speciality: Acupuncture. ✔
● **Acupuncturist** Ms J Sommerville Q: Lic.Ac, MBAcC. M: BAcC.
O Yrs. Est.: 4 (Ref:HM14487)

**NASH, A**

**A Nash**, 60 Woodbridge Rd, Guildford, **Surrey**, GU1 4RF, ENG.
(T) 01483 571783
Speciality: Physiotherapy.
P S T (Ref:HM14488)

**NASH, B**

**B Nash**, 11 Biscoe Court, Wheatley, Oxford, **Oxfordshire**, OX33 1YX, ENG.
(T) 01865 874312
Speciality: Complementary Medicines & Therapy.
C M (Ref:HM14489)

**NASH, KATE**

**Kate Nash**, Clissold Park Health Centre, 154 Stoke Newington Church St, London, **London (Greater)**, N16 0JU, ENG.
(T) 020 7249 2990 (F) 020 7249 3977
Speciality: Osteopathy.
● **Owner** Mr D Berg
P S T (Ref:HM14490)

**NASH, LARAINE S**

**Mrs Laraine S Nash**, 2 Goring Rd, Staines, **Surrey**, TW18 3EH, ENG.
(T) 01784 463447
Speciality: Osteopathy.
P S T (Ref:HM14491)

**NASH, MONICA**

**Monica Nash**, Timbers, Forge Lane, Egerton, Ashford, **Kent**, TN27 9EJ, ENG.
(T) 01233 756331
Speciality: Reflexology.
S T (Ref:HM14492)

**NASH, RICHARD**

**Richard Nash**, Doctors House Annexe, Victoria Rd, Marlow, **Buckinghamshire**, SL7 1DS, ENG.
(T) 01628 481333
Speciality: Physiotherapy.
P S T (Ref:HM14493)

**NASH, S**

**S Nash**, 8 Godwin Rd, London, **London (Greater)**, E7 0LE, ENG.
(T) 020 8536 1536
Speciality: Psychotherapy.
● **Owner** Ms S Nash
B (Ref:HM14494)

**NASTRUCCI, SUSAN**

**Susan Nastrucci**, 101 Monkhams Avenue, Woodford Green, **Essex**, IG8 0ER, ENG.
(T) 020 8505 2302
Speciality: Osteopathy.
P S T (Ref:HM14495)

**NAT COLLEGE-HYPNOSIS/PSYCHO**

**National College Of Hypnosis & Psychotherapy (The)**, 12 Cross St, Nelson, **Lancashire**, BB9 7EN, ENG.
(T) 01282 699378
Speciality: Hypnosis.
B (Ref:HM14496)

**NAT COUNCIL-PSYCHOTHERAPISTS**

**National Council Of Psychotherapists (The)**, Hazelwood, Broadmead, Lymington, **Hampshire**, SO41 6DH, ENG.
(T) 01590 683770
Speciality: Hypnosis, Psychotherapy.
B (Ref:HM14497)

**NAT FED OF SPIRITUAL HEALERS**

**National Federation Of Spiritual Healers**, Old Manor Farm Studio, Church St, Sunbury-on-Thames, **Surrey**, TW16 6RG, ENG.
(T) 01932 783164
Speciality: Complementary Medicines & Therapy.
● **Healer** Mr R Hutchingson
M (Ref:HM14498)

**NAT FED OF SPIRITUAL HEALERS**

**National Federation Of Spiritual Healers**, Tweenways, School Lane, Lower Bourne, Farnham, **Surrey**, GU10 3PE, ENG.
(T) 01252 722292
Speciality: Complementary Medicines & Therapy.
● **Owner** Mrs E Selby-Short
C M (Ref:HM14499)

**NAT FED OF SPIRITUAL HEALERS**

**National Federation Of Spiritual Healers**, 3 Hardcourts Cl, West Wickham, **Kent**, BR4 9LG, ENG.
(T) 020 8777 8482
Speciality: Complementary Medicines & Therapy.
C M (Ref:HM14500)

**NAT INSTITUTE OF MED HERBAL**

**National Institute Of Medical Herbalists**, 56 Longbrook St, Exeter, **Devon**, EX4 6AH, ENG.
(T) 01392 426022 (F) 01392 498962
Speciality: Herbal Medicine.
● **Information Officer** Trudy Norris
M (Ref:HM14501)

**NATCARE MEDICINE CENTRE**

**Natcare Medicine Centre**, 188 Elm Park Avenue, Elm Park, Hornchurch, **Essex**, RM12 4SD, ENG.
(T) 01708 453888
Speciality: Complementary Medicines & Therapy.
M (Ref:HM14502)

**NATHAN, HARRY**

**Harry Nathan**, Mulburry Clinic, 3A High St, Slough, **Berkshire**, SL1 1DY, ENG.
(T) 01753 551156 (F) 01753 551156
Speciality: Aromatherapy.
M O (Ref:HM14503)

**NATHAN, K**

**K Nathan**, Edgware Physiotherapy Sports Injury Clinic, 10 The Drive, Edgware, **London (Greater)**, HA8 8PT, ENG.
(T) 020 8958 9820
Speciality: Physiotherapy.
P S T (Ref:HM14504)

**NATHAN, ROBERT D**

**Robert D Nathan**, 225 Bury New Rd, Whitefield, Manchester, **Manchester (Greater)**, M45 8GW, ENG.
(T) 01617 662766
Speciality: Chiropodists (Podiatrists).
● **Owner** Mr R Nathan
S (Ref:HM14505)

**NATIONAL COUNCIL OF PSYCHO**

**National Council Of Psychotherapists**, Vine Cottage, 35 Old Lane, Cobham, **Surrey**, KT11 1NW, ENG.
(T) 01483 283592
Speciality: Psychotherapy.
● **Owner** Mrs A Cousins
B (Ref:HM14506)

**NATIONAL COUNCIL-HYPNOTHERAPY**

**National Council For Hypnotherapy**, P O Box 779, Burton-On-The-Wolds, Loughborough, **Leicestershire**, LE12 5ZF, ENG.
(T) 08009 520545 (F) 01509 881477
Speciality: Hypnotherapy.
● **Secretary** Mrs F Biddle
B (Ref:HM14507)

**NATIONAL HOMEOPATHIC SERVICE**

**National Homeopathic Service**, 191A Kentish Town Rd, London, **London (Greater)**, NW5 2JU, ENG.
(T) 020 7482 0432
Speciality: Complementary Medicines & Therapy.
C M (Ref:HM14508)

**NATURA**

**Natura**, 1436A London Rd, Leigh-On-Sea, **Essex**, SS9 2UL, ENG.
(T) 01702 478228 (F) 01702 713408
Speciality: Complementary Medicines & Therapy.
● **Owner** Mrs C Cottridge
M (Ref:HM14509)

**NATURAL & HOLISTIC CENTRE**

**Natural & Holistic Centre (The)**, 508 Aureole Walk, Newmarket, **Suffolk**, CB8 7BH, ENG.
(T) 01638 661466
Speciality: Complementary Medicines & Therapy.
● **Owner** Miss C Corton
M (Ref:HM14510)

**NATURAL & HOLISTIC THRPY CTRE**

**Natural & Holistic Therapy Centre**, 8 Welcomes Rd, Kenley, **Surrey**, CR8 5HD, ENG.
(T) 020 8763 9699
Speciality: Complementary Medicines & Therapy.
C M (Ref:HM14511)

**NATURAL ALTERNATIVES**

**Natural Alternatives**, 14a Bar St, Scarborough, **Yorkshire (North)**, YO11 2HT, ENG.
(T) 01723 353308
Speciality: Complementary Medicines & Therapy.
● **Owner** Mrs B Hurd
C M (Ref:HM14512)

**NATURAL APPROACH**

**Natural Approach (The)**, Mona St, Amlwch, **Isle of Anglesey**, LL68 9AN, WAL.
(T) 07714 273786 (F) 07714 273786
Speciality: Complementary Medicines & Therapy.
● **Owner** Mrs J Lawson
M (Ref:HM14513)

**NATURAL BACK CARE CLINIC**

**Natural Back Care Clinic**, 24 Worcester Rd, Malvern, **Worcestershire**, WR14 4QW, ENG.
(T) 01684 573247
Speciality: Chiropractic.
● **Partner** Ms K Hooley
P S T (Ref:HM14514)

**NATURAL BALANCE**

**Natural Balance Massage and Aromatherapy**, 13 The Briars, Knaresborough, **Yorkshire (North)**, HG5 0PG, ENG.



Key: B Mind-Body Medicine C Complementary Medicine H Self Help Treatment M Medicinal Therapy O Oriental Medicine P Postural Therapy S Manipulative Structural Therapy T Touch Therapy

(T) 01423 861421
Speciality: Aromatherapy, Massage (Therapeutic), Specialises in backs ✓
● **Owner/Massage Therapist**
Miss T Gray Q: CIBTAC. M: BABTAC.
T Yrs. Est.: 3 (Ref:HM14515)

## NATURAL BALANCE
**Natural Balance**, 183 Victoria Rd, Swindon, **Wiltshire**, SN1 3DF, ENG.
(T) 01793 435058
Speciality: Aromatherapy.
M O (Ref:HM14516)

## NATURAL BALANCE
**Natural Balance**, 93 Bailielands, Linlithgow, **Lothian (West)**, EH49 7SY, SCO.
(T) 01506 843113
Speciality: Complementary Medicines & Therapy.
● **Owner** Mrs H Boyd
M (Ref:HM14517)

## NATURAL BODY TREATMENTS
**Natural Body Treatments**, 7 Bastable Avenue, Barking, **Essex**, IG11 0NF, ENG.
(T) 020 8270 2708
Speciality: Complementary Medicines & Therapy.
C M (Ref:HM14518)

## NATURAL BY NATURE OILS
**Natural By Nature Oils Ltd**, 9 Vivian Avenue, London, **London (Greater)**, NW4 3UT, ENG.
(T) 020 8202 5718 (F) 020 8202 1439
Speciality: Aromatherapy.
● **Manager** Mr D Watson
M O (Ref:HM14519)

## NATURAL CARE
**Natural Care**, 35 Rainnieshill Gardens, Newmachar, Aberdeen, **Aberdeenshire**, AB21 0XZ, SCO.
(T) 01651 862528 (F) 01651 862528
Speciality: Reflexology.
● **Owner** Mrs C Mair
S T (Ref:HM14520)

## NATURAL CHOICE
**Natural Choice**, 22 Burn Estate, Huntington, York, **Yorkshire (North)**, YO32 9PZ, ENG.
(T) 01904 761029
Speciality: Complementary Medicines & Therapy.
● **Owner** Mrs M Edwards
M (Ref:HM14521)

## NATURAL CHOICE
**Natural Choice**, 152 Birmingham Rd, Sutton Coldfield, **Midlands (West)**, B72 1LY, ENG.
(T) 01213 555522 (F) 01214 495591
Speciality: Aromatherapy.
● **Manager** Mrs M Price
C (Ref:HM14522)

## NATURAL CHOICE AROMATHERAPY
**Natural Choice Aromatherapy**, 39 Bakewell Drive, Wigan, **Lancashire**, WN6 8QH, ENG.
(T) 01942 324654 (F) 01942 324654
Speciality: Aromatherapy.
● **Owner** Mrs M McGovern
M O (Ref:HM14523)

## NATURAL CHOICE HEALTH FOODS
**Natural Choice Health Foods**, 96 High St, Alfreton, **Derbyshire**, DE55 7BE, ENG.
(T) 01773 833226
Speciality: Herbal Medicine.
● **Owner** Mr D Pennington
C (Ref:HM14524)

## NATURAL CHOICE HEALTH FOODS
**Natural Choice Health Foods**, 5 Long Shambles, Chesterfield, **Derbyshire**, S40 1PX, ENG.
(T) 01773 833226
Speciality: Herbal Medicine.
C (Ref:HM14525)

## NATURAL CHOICE HEALTH FOODS
**Natural Choice Health Foods**, 44 Oxford St, Ripley, **Derbyshire**, DE5 3AP, ENG.
(T) 01773 833226
Speciality: Herbal Medicine.
● **Owner** Mr P Pennington
C (Ref:HM14526)

## NATURAL CLINIC
**Natural Clinic (The)**, Bretland House, Bretland Rd, Tunbridge Wells, **Kent**, TN4 8PB, ENG.
(T) 01892 548840 (F) 01892 536832
Speciality: Electrolysis.
● **Owner** Mrs P Martin
T (Ref:HM14527)

## NATURAL ELEMENTS
**Natural Elements**, 19B Newbottle St, Houghton le Spring, **Tyne and Wear**, DH4 4AP, ENG.
(T) 01915 126310
Speciality: Complementary Medicines & Therapy.
● **Owner** Miss D Herkes
M (Ref:HM14528)

## NATURAL ELEMENTS
**Natural Elements**, 209 Willesden Lane, London, **London (Greater)**, NW6 7YR, ENG.
(T) 020 8451 5501
Speciality: Complementary Medicines & Therapy.
● **Owner** Mr M Shepherd
C M (Ref:HM14529)

## NATURAL ENERGY HEALTH SERVICES
**Natural Energy Health Services**, 117 Burdyke Avenue, York, **Yorkshire (North)**, YO30 6JX, ENG.
(T) 01904 636723
Speciality: Complementary Medicines & Therapy.
● **Owner** Mr D Erikson
C M (Ref:HM14530)

## NATURAL HARMONY
**Natural Harmony**, Eldon House, 11A King St, Wolverhampton, **Midlands (West)**, WV1 1ST, ENG.
(T) 01902 820844
Speciality: Acupuncture.
● **Partner** Mrs C Barker-Hall
O (Ref:HM14531)

## NATURAL HARMONY
**Natural Harmony**, Conygre Family Centre, Sedgley Rd East, Tipton, **Midlands (West)**, DY4 8UH, ENG.
(T) 01215 571538
Speciality: Reflexology.
● **Owner** Mrs L Main
S T (Ref:HM14532)

## NATURAL HEALERS
**Natural Healers**, 28 Newman Drive, Branston, Burton-On-Trent, **Staffordshire**, DE14 3DZ, ENG.
(T) 01283 568838
Speciality: Complementary Medicines & Therapy.
C M (Ref:HM14533)

## NATURAL HEALING
**Natural Healing**, Lychgate House, High St, Pattingham, Wolverhampton, **Midlands (West)**, WV6 7BQ, ENG.
(T) 01902 701983
Speciality: Complementary Medicines & Therapy.
● **Employee** Ms A Dunning
M (Ref:HM14534)

## NATURAL HEALING AND REIKI CTRE
**Natural Healing Teaching Therapy And Reiki Centre**, 9 High St, Addlestone, **Surrey**, KT15 1TL, ENG.
(T) 01932 883523
Speciality: Complementary Medicines & Therapy.
● **Partner** Mrs J Gill
C M (Ref:HM14535)

## NATURAL HEALING CENTRE
**Natural Healing Centre (The)**, 111 Greenbank Rd, Darlington, **County Durham**, DL3 6EN, ENG.
(T) 01325 486263 (F) 01325 263743
(E) allisonagius@hotmail.com
Speciality: Absent Healing, Alexander Technique, Aromatherapy, Bach Remedies, Beauty Therapy, Bowen Therapy, Complementary Therapy, Counselling, Cranial Osteopathy, Dietician, Dowsing, Healer, Healing Therapy, Holistic Healing, Homeopathy, Hypnotherapy, Indian Head Massage, Kinesiology, Massage (Therapeutic), Meditation, Nutritional Therapy, Reflexology, Reiki, Shiatsu, Spiritual Healing, Stress Therapy, Skeletal Balancing, Results, Re-birthing. ✓
● **Owner** Ms A Agius Q: Reiki Master. M: GCP.
B Yrs. Est.: 2 (Ref:HM14536)

## NATURAL HEALING CENTRE
**Natural Healing Centre**, High St, Penrhyndeudraeth, **Gwynedd**, LL48 6BL, WAL.
(T) 01766 770899
Speciality: Complementary Medicines & Therapy.
M (Ref:HM14537)

## NATURAL HEALING CENTRE
**Natural Healing Centre**, 1 Church Sq, Bodmin, **Cornwall**, PL31 2DP, ENG.
(T) 01208 79666
Speciality: Complementary Medicines & Therapy.
● **Owner** Mrs S Claridge
M (Ref:HM14538)

## NATURAL HEALING CENTRE
**Natural Healing Centre**, 27 Braintree Rd, Witham, **Essex**, CM8 2DD, ENG.
(T) 01376 511069
Speciality: Complementary Medicines & Therapy.
● **Manager** Mr N Brunton
C M (Ref:HM14539)

## NATURAL HEALING CENTRE
**Natural Healing Centre**, 27 Wells St, Scunthorpe, **Humberside**, DN15 6HL, ENG.
(T) 01724 872056
Speciality: Complementary Medicines & Therapy.
C M (Ref:HM14540)

## NATURAL HEALING CENTRE
**Natural Healing Centre**, 39 Station Rd, Sutton, **Surrey**, SM2 6DF, ENG.
(T) 020 8770 3765 (F) 020 8287 7008
Speciality: Aromatherapy, Beauty Therapy, Hopi Ear Candles, Indian Head Massage, Reflexology, Reiki, Spiritual Healing. ✓
● **Reflexologist** Mrs M Rudenko Q: IIHHT, MAR, Reiki Master, RGN.
C Yrs. Est.: 12 (Ref:HM14541)

## NATURAL HEALING CENTRE
**Natural Healing Centre**, 72 Pasture Rd, Goole, **Humberside (North)**, DN14 6HE, ENG.
(T) 01405 769119 (F) 01405 769119
Speciality: Complementary Medicines & Therapy.
● **Owner** Mrs K Huddlestone
C M (Ref:HM14542)

## NATURAL HEALING CENTRE
**Natural Healing Centre (The)**, 3 Dundee Court, Falkirk, FK1 1PW, SCO.
(T) 01324 882559
Speciality: Absent Healing, Aromatherapy, Reiki. ✓
● **Clinical Aromatherapist/Reiki Healer**
Mrs C Reid Q: Dip.Clin.Arom, Reiki 1, Reiki 2. M: AOC, ISPA.
M Yrs. Est.: 1 (Ref:HM14543)

## NATURAL HEALING CENTRE
**Natural Healing Centre (The)**, 76 Berkeley Cl, Ruislip, **London (Greater)**, HA4 6LF, ENG.
(T) 01895 675464 (F) 01895 675464
Speciality: Complementary Medicines & Therapy.
● **Owner** Mrs E Findlow
M (Ref:HM14544)

## NATURAL HEALING CENTRE
**Natural Healing Centre Of Woodbridge (The)**, 24 Thoroughfare, Woodbridge, **Suffolk**, IP12 1AQ, ENG.
(T) 01394 380580
Speciality: Complementary Medicines & Therapy.
● **Partner** Mrs S Allen
M (Ref:HM14545)



Key continued: Yrs.Est: Years Established Q: Qualifications M: Professional Membership ✓ Indemnity Insurance Accept Credit Cards

### NATURAL HEALING CENTRE
**Natural Healing Centre**, Ballinamore, Leitrim, **County Leitrim**, IRE.
(T) 07844 923
Speciality: Healing.
B (Ref:HM14546)

### NATURAL HEALING CENTRE
**Natural Healing Centre**, Corclough West, Belmullet, **County Mayo**, IRE.
(T) 09782 065
(E) naturalhealing@eircom.net
Speciality: Absent Healing, Acupressure, Aura Therapy, Bach Remedies, Bates Method, Colour Therapy, Complementary Therapy, Counselling, Crystal Healing, Dance Movement Therapy, Family Therapy, Floral Essence Therapy, Group Therapy, Healer, Healing Therapy, Herbal Medicine, Holistic Healing, Indian Head Massage, Kinesiology, Life Style Coaching, Massage (Therapeutic), Meditation, Postural Integration, Psychotherapy, Reflexology, Reiki, Sensitivity Training, Sound Therapy, Spiritual Healing, Stress Therapy, Touch Therapy, Visualisation Therapy, Voice Therapy, Ying & Yang, Natural Vision Improvement.
● **Natural Healing Teacher** Ms G Jurgens Q: Reiki Master.
H Yrs. Est.: 9 (Ref:HM14547)

### NATURAL HEALING CENTRE
**Natural Healing Centre**, Thompson Hse, McCurtain St, Cork, **County Cork**, IRE.
(T) 021 4501 600
(E) healingt@gofree.indigo.ie
Speciality: Healing.
B (Ref:HM14548)

### NATURAL HEALING CLINIC
**Natural Healing Clinic**, 7 Rushfield Vale, Fenay Bridge, Huddersfield, **Yorkshire (West)**, HD8 0BX, ENG.
(T) 01484 609615 (F) 01484 609615
Speciality: Complementary Medicines & Therapy.
● **Owner** Ms R McKenzie
M (Ref:HM14549)

### NATURAL HEALING CLINIC
**P R Underwoods T/A The Natural Healing Clinic**, 30 The Ridgeway, Waddon Ponds, Croydon, **Surrey**, CR0 4AE, ENG.
(T) 020 8688 1347
Speciality: Bowen Therapy, Complementary Therapy, Electrolipolysis, Massage (Therapeutic), Reflexology, Reiki, Stress Therapy, Neways Independent Distributor for Health and Personal Care Products. Gaia Form Therapist - Body Contouring, Toning, Physiostimulation, Lymphatic Drainage, Pain Relief. On-Site Massage-Head, Neck Shoulder Massage for Stress and Tension Relief in the Home or Workplace. Massage through Clothing. ✔
● **Owner/Therapist** Ms T Underwood Q: ITEC, Reiki 2, Reiki 3. M: BTER.
C T Yrs. Est.: 5 (Ref:HM14550)

### NATURAL HEALING ROOMS
**Natural Healing Rooms**, 8 Wolfe Tone St, Clonakilty, **County Cork**, IRE.
(T) 023 3474 8
Speciality: Healing.
B (Ref:HM14551)

### NATURAL HEALTH
**Natural Health**, 27A Frogmore Rd, Westbury, **Wiltshire**, BA13 3AT, ENG.
(T) 01373 826166
Speciality: Complementary Medicines & Therapy.
● **Owner** Mr M Cuthbert
C M (Ref:HM14552)

### NATURAL HEALTH
**Natural Health**, 339 Ballards Lane, North Finchley, London, **London (Greater)**, N12 8LT, ENG.
(T) 020 8445 4397
Speciality: Complementary Medicines & Therapy.
C M (Ref:HM14553)

### NATURAL HEALTH
**Natural Health-Newark Ltd**, Martindale House, Lombard St, Newark, **Nottinghamshire**, NG24 1XG, ENG.
(T) 01636 611150 (F) 01636 613605
(E) rw-physio@yahoo.co.uk
Speciality: Absent Healing, Acupuncture, Aromatherapy, Art Therapy, Bach Remedies, Bowen Therapy, Colour Therapy, Complementary Therapy, Counselling, Crystal Healing, Dietician, Gestalt Therapy, Healer, Healing Therapy, Herbal Medicine, Holistic Healing, Homeopathy, Hypnotherapy, Indian Head Massage, Iridology, Kinesiology, Manipulation, Massage (Therapeutic), Miasm Therapy, Nutritional Therapy, Pilates, Psychotherapy, Reflexology, Reiki, Shiatsu, Stress Therapy, Yoga, Hopi Ear Candles. ✔
● **Director** Mr M Rowlinson Q: BSc, D.Hom.Med. M: Soc.Hom.
● **Director** Ms R White Q: Grad Dip Phys, MCSP, SRP. M: CSP, SRP.
M Yrs. Est.: 5 (Ref:HM14554)

### NATURAL HEALTH
**Natural Health Co (The)**, 44 Chipchase, Washington, **Tyne and Wear**, NE38 0NQ, ENG.
(T) 01914 170765
Speciality: Complementary Medicines & Therapy.
● **Owner** Ms P Appleton
M (Ref:HM14555)

### NATURAL HEALTH
**Natural Health**, St Marks House, Lombard St, Newark, **Nottinghamshire**, NG24 1XX, ENG.
(T) 01636 611150
Speciality: Complementary Medicines & Therapy.
C M (Ref:HM14556)

### NATURAL HEALTH & BEAUTY SALON
**Natural Health & Beauty Salon (The)**, 146 Lower High St, Merthyr Tydfil, **Glamorgan (Vale of)**, CF47 8EB, WAL.
(T) 01685 721861
Speciality: Complementary Medicines & Therapy.
M (Ref:HM14557)

### NATURAL HEALTH & CHIROPODY
**Margaret L Foggie**, 135 Nethergate, Dundee, **Angus**, DD1 4DP, SCO.
(T) 01382 221275
Speciality: Indian Head Massage. ✔
● **Chiropodist (Podiatrist)** Ms M Foggie Q: MBChA, MSSCh. M: B.A.Ch.P, FHT, SSCh.
T Yrs. Est.: 4 (Ref:HM14558)

### NATURAL HEALTH & HEALING
**Natural Health & Healing**, 2 Hazel Gr, Rockbeare, Exeter, **Devon**, EX5 2HH, ENG.
(T) 01404 822687
Speciality: Complementary Medicines & Therapy.
● **Owner** Mrs P Clarke
C M (Ref:HM14559)

### NATURAL HEALTH CARE
**Natural Health Care**, 32 South Tay St, Dundee, **Angus**, DD1 1PD, SCO.
(T) 01382 200419 (F) 01382 200419
Speciality: Hypnosis.
● **Owner** Mrs V MacLeod
B (Ref:HM14560)

### NATURAL HEALTH CARE
**Natural Health Care**, 46B Park St, Camberley, **Surrey**, GU15 3PL, ENG.
(T) 01276 678400
Speciality: Complementary Medicines & Therapy.
C M (Ref:HM14561)

### NATURAL HEALTH CENTRE
**Natural Health Centre**, Chislehurst Natural Health Centre, 40 High St, Chislehurst, **Kent**, BR7 5AQ, ENG.
(T) 020 8687 1749
(E) andri@pete.fsbusiness.co.uk
Speciality: Counselling, Psychotherapy, Management Therapy. ✔
● **Physiotherapist** Ms A Pete Q: Dip.Hyp, Dip.Psych.
C Yrs. Est.: 2 (Ref:HM14562)

### NATURAL HEALTH CENTRE
**Natural Health Centre**, 1 St Andrews St, Dumfries, **Dumfries and Galloway**, DG1 1DE, SCO.
(T) 01556 502982
Speciality: Physiotherapy.
P S T (Ref:HM14563)

### NATURAL HEALTH CENTRE
**Natural Health Centre**, 22 Church St, Kidderminster, **Worcestershire**, DY10 2AW, ENG.
(T) 01562 67629
Speciality: Acupuncture. ✔
● **Acupuncturist** Mr T Concannon Q: Lic.Ac, MBAcC.
O (Ref:HM14564)

### NATURAL HEALTH CENTRE
**Natural Health Centre**, 33 Pound St, Newbury, **Berkshire**, RG14 6AE, ENG.
(T) 01635 580200
Speciality: Complementary Medicines & Therapy.
M (Ref:HM14565)

### NATURAL HEALTH CENTRE
**Natural Health Centre**, 78 Meadow St, Preston, **Lancashire**, PR1 1TS, ENG.
(T) 01772 825177 (F) 01772 825177
(W) www.jolanta.co.uk
Speciality: Acupuncture, Aromatherapy, Electrotherapy, Homeopathy, Indian Head Massage, Massage (Therapeutic), Nutritional Therapy, Reflexology, Reiki. ✔
● **Owner** Ms J Basnyet Q: BA (Hons), BSc, ITEC. M: AoR, IFA.
C S Yrs. Est.: 18 (Ref:HM14566)

### NATURAL HEALTH CENTRE
**Natural Health Centre**, The Way Of Life, New Century Way, Nuneaton, **Warwickshire**, CV11 5NE, ENG.
(T) 024 7634 3100
(E) tmetford@aol.com
(W) www.naturalhealth-centre.co.uk
Speciality: Acupuncture, Aromatherapy, Bach Remedies, Bowen Therapy, Complementary Therapy, Cranial Osteopathy, Crystal Healing, Herbal Medicine, Homeopathy, Hypnotherapy, Massage (Therapeutic), Naturopathy, Oriental Diagnosis, Osteopathy, Reflexology, Reiki, Seichem, Sports Massage, Stress Therapy, Medical Herbalist. ✔
● **Medical Herbalist** Tunde Checklin Q: MNIMH, RM.
● **Acupuncturist** Lois Francis Q: Adv.Lic.Ac, MBAcC. M: BAcC.
● **Acupuncturist** Mr T Metford Q: Lic.Ac, MBAcC. M: BAcC.
● **Homeopath** Ms A Devenport M: HMA.
● **Osteopath** Mr T Harper Q: BSc, DO, Hons (OST), ND, RN. M: GOsC.
● **Reflexologist** Ms J Stammers Q: MIFR. M: BCMA.
● **Sports Massage Therapist** Ms J Richards
B C Yrs. Est.: 3 (Ref:HM14567)

### NATURAL HEALTH CENTRE
**Natural Health Centre**, 72 High St, West Wickham, **Kent**, BR4 0NH, ENG.
(T) 020 8776 0444
Speciality: Acupuncture, Alexander Technique, Aromatherapy, Bach Remedies, Bowen Therapy, Chiropody, Complementary Therapy, Counselling, Healing Therapy, Herbal Medicine, Holistic Healing, Homeopathy, Indian Head Massage, Massage (Therapeutic), Meditation, Nutritional Therapy, Podiatry, Reflexology, Reiki, Shiatsu, Spiritual Healing. ✔
● **Owner** Ms P Bromley Q: MCH, RSHom.
C Yrs. Est.: 13 (Ref:HM14568)

### NATURAL HEALTH CENTRE
**Natural Health Centre (The)**, 86 The Green, Kings Norton, Birmingham, **Midlands (West)**, B38 8RS, ENG.
(T) 01214 593535
Speciality: Complementary Medicines & Therapy.
● **Owner** Mr K Saunders



Key: B Mind-Body Medicine C Complementary Medicine H Self Help Treatment M Medicinal Therapy O Oriental Medicine P Postural Therapy S Manipulative Structural Therapy T Touch Therapy

C M (Ref:HM14569)

**NATURAL HEALTH CENTRE**

**Natural Health Centre (The)**, Unit 4, Bank Farm Rd, Radbrook Green, Shrewsbury, **Shropshire**, SY3 6DU, ENG.
(T) 01743 248878
Speciality: Complementary Medicines & Therapy.
● **Partner** Mrs H Foxwell
C M (Ref:HM14570)

**NATURAL HEALTH CENTRE**

**Natural Health Centre**, 54 Patrick St, (over Burger King), **County Cork**, IRE.
(T) 021 4273 008
Speciality: Complementary Medicines & Therapy.
M (Ref:HM14571)

**NATURAL HEALTH CENTRE**

**Natural Health Centre**, Ashdale House, Blarney, **County Cork**, IRE.
(T) 021 4382 151
Speciality: Complementary Medicines & Therapy.
M (Ref:HM14572)

**NATURAL HEALTH CENTRE**

**Natural Health Centre (The)**, 57-59 High St, Dalkeith, **Lothian (Mid)**, EH22 1JA, SCO.
(T) 01620 892353
(E) af1557@aol.com
Speciality: Aromatherapy, Holistic Healing, Homeopathy, Hypnotherapy, Iridology, Reiki, Remedial Massage, Shiatsu, Sports Massage, Needle free Acupuncture(laser). ✔ CREDIT
● **Owner** Mr D Coward
(T) 01316 542495 Q: SPMRS. M: PMAS.
● **Complementary Therapist** Mr G Fraser Q: IHT. M: IHT.
C Yrs. Est.: 10 (Ref:HM14573)

**NATURAL HEALTH CENTRE**

**Natural Health Centre (The)**, 18 Cotswold Drive, Finham, Coventry, **Midlands (West)**, CV3 6EY, ENG.
(T) 024 7641 1646
(W) www.naturalhealth-centre.co.uk
Speciality: Acupuncture. ✔
● **Acupuncturist** Mrs L Metford Q: Adv.Lic.Ac, MBAcC. M: BAcC.
● **Acupuncturist** Mr T Metford Q: Lic.Ac, MBAcC. M: BAcC.
C (Ref:HM14574)

**NATURAL HEALTH CLINIC**

**Natural Health Clinic**, 286 Preston Rd, Harrow, **London (Greater)**, HA3 0B2, ENG.
(T) 020 8908 4272
(E) tazdin@jivrajfreeserve.co.uk
Speciality: Acupressure, Autogenic Training, Counselling, Healing Therapy, Homeopathy, Kinesiology, Nutritional Therapy, Reflexology, Shiatsu, Touch Therapy, Vitamin Therapy. ✔
● **Homeopath** Mr T Jivraj Q: BSc (Hons), D.Hom.Med, MBChA, MSSCh. M: HMA.
M Yrs. Est.: 20 (Ref:HM14575)

**NATURAL HEALTH CLINIC**

**Natural Health Clinic**, 16 Leyland St, Prescot, **Merseyside**, L34 5QP, ENG.
(T) 01514 309223
Speciality: Acupuncture, Aromatherapy, Counselling, Homeopathy, Hypnosis, Hypnotherapy, Reflexology. ✔
● **Therapist** Dr S Chana Q: Dip.Med.Ac, MFHom. M: GMC.
● **Therapist** Mr B McMinn Q: MA.
● **Therapist** Ms P Denton
(T) 01744 751114 Q: ICHT, IIHHT, ITEC. M: FHT.
M Yrs. Est.: 14 (Ref:HM14576)

**NATURAL HEALTH CLINIC**

**Natural Health Clinic**, 168 Burton Rd, Derby, **Derbyshire**, DE1 1TQ, ENG.
(T) 01332 349493
Speciality: Acupressure, Acupuncture, Aromatherapy, Auto Suggestion, Bach Remedies, Cognitive Therapy, Counselling, Dowsing, Electrotherapy, Healer, Holistic Healing, Hypnosis, Hypnotherapy, Manipulation, Massage (Therapeutic), Psychotherapy, Stress Therapy, Yoga.
● **Therapist** Ms D Richardson
S Yrs. Est.: 12 (Ref:HM14577)

**NATURAL HEALTH CLINIC**

**Natural Health Clinic**, 141A Harrowden Rd, Bedford, **Bedfordshire**, MK42 0RU, ENG.
(T) 01234 217100
Speciality: Complementary Medicines & Therapy.
● **Partner** Ms S Harper
M (Ref:HM14578)

**NATURAL HEALTH CLINIC**

**Natural Health Clinic**, Chanters Lodge, Hind St, Ottery St. Mary, **Devon**, EX11 1QR, ENG.
(T) 01404 815925
Speciality: Complementary Medicines & Therapy.
C M (Ref:HM14579)

**NATURAL HEALTH CLINIC**

**Natural Health Clinic**, 99 George St, Stranraer, **Dumfries and Galloway**, DG9 7JP, SCO.
(T) 01776 702052
Speciality: Complementary Medicines & Therapy.
● **Owner** Mrs J McQuistin
C M (Ref:HM14580)

**NATURAL HEALTH CLINIC**

**Natural Health Clinic**, 73 Thorne Rd, Doncaster, **Yorkshire (South)**, DN1 2EX, ENG.
(T) 01302 322697
Speciality: Complementary Medicines & Therapy.
● **Owner** Mrs B Grashion
C M (Ref:HM14581)

**NATURAL HEALTH CLINIC**

**Natural Health Clinic**, 39 Cotham Hill, Bristol, BS6 6JY, ENG.
(T) 01179 741199 (F) 01179 237266
Speciality: Complementary Medicines & Therapy.
● **Director** Mr T Harrison
C M (Ref:HM14582)

**NATURAL HEALTH CLINIC**

**Natural Health Clinic**, 26 Market St, Carnforth, **Lancashire**, LA5 9JX, ENG.
(T) 01524 720916
Speciality: Complementary Medicines & Therapy.
C M (Ref:HM14583)

**NATURAL HEALTH CLINIC**

**Natural Health Clinic**, 133 Gatley Rd, Gatley, Cheadle, **Cheshire**, SK8 4PD, ENG.
(T) 01614 284980
Speciality: Osteopathy.
P S T (Ref:HM14584)

**NATURAL HEALTH CLINIC**

**Natural Health Clinic**, 1a Norwood Avenue, Blackpool, **Lancashire**, FY3 7DJ, ENG.
(T) 01253 302799
Speciality: Complementary Medicines & Therapy.
● **Owner** Mrs S Cousins
C M (Ref:HM14585)

**NATURAL HEALTH CLINIC**

**Natural Health Clinic (The)**, 3 Borough Fields Shopping Centre, Wootton Bassett, Swindon, **Wiltshire**, SN4 7AX, ENG.
(T) 01793 849393 (F) 01793 849393
Speciality: Complementary Medicines & Therapy.
● **Owner** Miss J Baker
C M (Ref:HM14586)

**NATURAL HEALTH CLINIC**

**Natural Health Clinic (The)**, 35C Bear St, Barnstaple, **Devon**, EX32 7DZ, ENG.
(T) 01271 328228 (F) 01271 372003
Speciality: Complementary Medicines & Therapy.
● **Owner** Mr E Tyas
C M (Ref:HM14587)

**NATURAL HEALTH CLINIC**

**Natural Health Clinic (The)**, 72A Market Pl, Warwick, **Warwickshire**, CV34 4SD, ENG.
(T) 01926 400558
Speciality: Acupuncture.
● **Partner** Ms J Still
O (Ref:HM14588)

**NATURAL HEALTH CLINIC**

**Natural Health Clinic**, 10C High St, Buntingford, **Hertfordshire**, SG9 9AG, ENG.
(T) 01763 274760 (F) 01763 274768
Speciality: Herbal Medicine, Homeopathy, Osteopathy. ✔
● **Secretary** Ms H Julian
● **Osteopath** Ms K Prince Q: DO.
● **Homeopath** Ms C Kowalski Q: RSHom.
C Yrs. Est.: 2 (Ref:HM14589)

**NATURAL HEALTH CLINIC**

**Natural Health Clinic**, The Mews 154 Leinster Rd, Rathmines, **County Dublin**, IRE.
(T) 01496 1316
Speciality: Complementary Medicines & Therapy.
M (Ref:HM14590)

**NATURAL HEALTH CONSULTANCY**

**Natural Health Consultancy Ltd**, Stratfield House, 188 Dukes Ride, Crowthorne, **Berkshire**, RG45 6DS, ENG.
(T) 01344 771212
(E) nhc@ukonline.co.uk
Speciality: Acupuncture, Alexander Technique, Allergy Testing, Aromatherapy, Auricular Therapy, Bach Remedies, Bowen Therapy, Chiropractic, Colour Therapy, Complementary Therapy, Counselling, Cranio-Sacral Therapy, Crystal Healing, Dance Movement Therapy, Healer, Holistic Healing, Homeopathy, Hypnotherapy, Indian Head Massage, Life Style Coaching, Massage (Therapeutic), Meditation, Miasm Therapy, Osteopathy, Pilates, Psychotherapy, Reflexology, Reiki, Shiatsu, Stress Therapy, Tantra Therapy, Yoga, Past Life Regression, Soul Retrieval. ✔ CREDIT
● **Osteopath** Mr D Herson Q: BSc, Hons (OST).
● **Reiki Practitioner** Mr A Dean
● **Homeopath** Ms K Lethbridge Q: LCH.
● **McTimoney Chiropractor** Mr J Gorman Q: MMCA.
B (Ref:HM14591)

**NATURAL HEALTH CONSULTANCY**

**Natural Health Consultancy**, 23C Church Rd, Poole, **Dorset**, BH14 8UF, ENG.
(T) 01202 747063
Speciality: Aromatherapy, Feldenkrais Methodology, Herbal Medicine, Holistic Healing, Homeopathy, Indian Head Massage, Massage (Therapeutic), Metamorphic Therapy, Nutritional Therapy, Reiki, Feldenkrais Teacher Practitioner, Hydrotherm Massage, Shamanism - South American. ✔
● **Administrator** Ms M Wyld
● **Director** Mr W Van-Dorp Q: BSc (Hons), D.Hom.Med.
● **Administrator** Ms E Miller
C Yrs. Est.: 22 (Ref:HM14592)

**NATURAL HEALTH NEWARK**

**Natural Health Newark Ltd**, Martindale House, Lombard St, Newark, **Nottinghamshire**, NG24 1XG, ENG.
(T) 01636 611150
Speciality: Complementary Medicines & Therapy.
● **Owner** Ms R White
M (Ref:HM14593)

**NATURAL HEALTH PRACTICE**

**Natural Health Practice**, 93 Parkhurst Rd, Horley, **Surrey**, RH6 8EX, ENG.
(T) 01293 775467
Speciality: Massage (Therapeutic), Naturopathy, Osteopathy. ✔
● **Osteopath/Naturopath** Mr M Cassar Q: DO, ND. M: GOsC.
S Yrs. Est.: 10 (Ref:HM14594)

**NATURAL HEALTH SERVICE**

**Natural Health Service**, 3 Hazel Farm Rd, Totton, Southampton, **Hampshire**, SO40 8WU, ENG.
(T) 023 8042 8420 (F) 023 8042 8421
(E) adam@tnhs.fsnet.co.uk



Key continued: Yrs.Est: Years Established Q: Qualifications M: Professional Membership ✔ Indemnity Insurance CREDIT Accept Credit Cards

Speciality: Aromatherapy, Chiropractic, Counselling, Homeopathy, Indian Head Massage, Reflexology, Reiki, Sports Massage, Bioresonance, Counselling, Body Massage. ✔
● **Chiropractor** Mr P Connery Q: BSc (Hons). M: GCC.
● **Complementary Therapist** Ms L Stephens Q: ITEC, MFHT, MICHT, MRxS. M: SVA.
● **Homeopath Therapist** Mr A Hardyman Q: Dip.Hom, MBPA.
C Yrs. Est.: 5 (Ref:HM14595)

## NATURAL HEALTH SERVICE

**Natural Health Service (The)**, 270 High St, Glasgow, **Glasgow (City of)**, G4 0QT, SCO.
(T) 01415 524420
Speciality: Osteopathy.
P S T (Ref:HM14596)

## NATURAL HEALTH STORE

**Natural Health Store**, Queen St, Tramore, **County Waterford**, IRE.
(T) 05139 0991
Speciality: Complementary Medicines & Therapy.
M (Ref:HM14597)

## NATURAL HEALTH THERAPIES

**Natural Health Therapies**, Elphin, **County Roscommon**, IRE.
(T) 07835 784
Speciality: Reflexology.
S T (Ref:HM14598)

## NATURAL HEALTH THERAPY

**Natural Health Therapy**, 31 Langford Cres, Benfleet, **Essex**, SS7 3JP, ENG.
(T) 01268 795620
Speciality: Complementary Medicines & Therapy.
● **Owner** Mrs D Tracey
C M (Ref:HM14599)

## NATURAL HEALTH THERAPY CENTRE

**Natural Health Therapy Centre**, Douglas Vlge, East, **County Cork**, IRE.
(T) 021 4892 133
Speciality: Complementary Medicines & Therapy.
M (Ref:HM14600)

## NATURAL HEALTHCARE

**Natural Healthcare**, 10 St Fagans St, Cardiff, **Glamorgan (Vale of)**, CF11 7LG, WAL.
(T) 029 2025 2086 (F) 029 2025 2086
(W) www.aura-spiritual.com
Speciality: Indian Head Massage, Massage (Therapeutic), Meditation, Reflexology, Reiki, Yoga, Sound Therapy, Steam Therapy. ✔
● **Alternative Therapist** Mr S Sabir M: FHT.
B C H S T
Yrs. Est.: 2 (Ref:HM14601)

## NATURAL HEALTHCARE

**Natural Healthcare**, 69B Redbrink Cres, Barry, **Glamorgan (Vale of)**, CF62 5TT, WAL.
(T) 01446 742727
Speciality: Herbal Medicine.
● **Owner** Mrs G Murphy
M (Ref:HM14602)

## NATURAL HLTH & IRIDOLOGY CTRE

**Natural Health & Iridology Centre**, 25 Curzon St, Newcastle, **Staffordshire**, ST5 0PD, ENG.
(T) 01782 711592
Speciality: Complementary Medicines & Therapy.
M (Ref:HM14603)

## NATURAL HLTH AND HEALING CTRE

**Natural Health and Healing Centre**, 204 Ukbridge Rd, London, **London (Greater)**, W12 7JD, ENG.
(T) 020 8749 3792
Speciality: Complementary Medicines & Therapy.
● **Practice Manager** Mr A Stafford
M (Ref:HM14604)

## NATURAL HOLISTIC THERAPIES

**Natural Holistic Therapies**, 400 Tilehouse Lane, Tidbury Green, Solihull, **Midlands (West)**, B90 1PX, ENG.
(T) 01564 824656
Speciality: Aromatherapy.
● **Owner** Ms E Davies
M O (Ref:HM14605)

## NATURAL HOLISTIC THERAPIES

**Natural Holistic Therapies**, 1 The Pines, Midgery Lane, Fulwood, Preston, **Lancashire**, PR2 9SX, ENG.
(T) 01772 703393
Speciality: Complementary Medicines & Therapy.
● **Owner** Mrs M Dorgu
C M (Ref:HM14606)

## NATURAL HOUSE & BEAUTY CLINIC

**Natural House & Beauty Clinic**, Damar, Post Office Lane, Broad Hinton, Swindon, **Wiltshire**, SN4 9PB, ENG.
(T) 01793 731442
Speciality: Aromatherapy.
M O (Ref:HM14607)

## NATURAL LIFE AROMATHERAPY

**Natural Life Aromatherapy Ltd**, 4 Hersham Centre, Hersham Green, Hersham, Walton-On-Thames, **Surrey**, KT12 4HL, ENG.
(T) 01932 269245
Speciality: Acupuncture, Aromatherapy, Chiropody, Herbal Medicine, Homeopathy, Iridology, Massage (Therapeutic), Nutritional Therapy, Psychotherapy, Reflexology, Remedial Massage, Swedish Body Massage, Bioresonance Therapy.
C (Ref:HM14608)

## NATURAL MEDICINE CENTRE

**Natural Medicine Centre Ltd**, 72 High St, West Wickham, **Kent**, BR4 0NH, ENG.
(T) 020 8776 1525
Speciality: Complementary Medicines & Therapy.
● **Administrator** Sally Louise Bromley
C M (Ref:HM14609)

## NATURAL MEDICINE CENTRE

**Natural Medicine Centre**, Kells Rd, Navan, **County Meath**, IRE.
(T) 04627 156 (F) 04627 156
Speciality: Acupressure, Acupuncture, Bach Remedies, Cupping, Herbal Medicine, Homeopathy, Moxibustion, Vega Testing. ✔
● **Acupuncturist** Ms G Dillon Q: Dip.Ac, Lic.Ac.
O Yrs. Est.: 12 (Ref:HM14610)

## NATURAL MEDICINE CENTRE

**Natural Medicine Centre**, 14 Ludlow St, Navan, **County Meath**, IRE.
(T) 04627 156
Speciality: Complementary Medicines & Therapy.
M (Ref:HM14611)

## NATURAL MEDICINE SOCIETY

**Natural Medicine Society**, Po Box 232, West Molesey, **Surrey**, KT8 1YF, ENG.
(T) 020 8974 1166 (F) 020 8974 1166
Speciality: Complementary Medicines & Therapy.
● **Director** Mrs S Liu
M (Ref:HM14612)

## NATURAL OPTIONS

**Natural Options**, 85A Glasnevin Ave, Dublin, **County Dublin**, IRE.
(T) 01862 2258
Speciality: Complementary Medicines & Therapy.
M (Ref:HM14613)

## NATURAL ORGANICS

**Natural Organics**, 32-34 High St, Croydon, **Surrey**, CR0 1YA, ENG.
(T) 020 8667 0989
Speciality: Aromatherapy.
● **Owner** Mr J Perry
M O (Ref:HM14614)

## NATURAL ORIGINS

**Natural Origins**, 5a Skinner St, Whitby, **Yorkshire (North)**, YO21 3AH, ENG.
(T) 01947 825127
Speciality: Complementary Medicines & Therapy.
● **Owner** Mrs A Black
C M (Ref:HM14615)

## NATURAL PARTNERS

**Natural Partners**, Jopes Pk, Luckett, Callington, **Cornwall**, PL17 8LG, ENG.
(T) 01579 370807 (F) 01579 370807
Speciality: Herbal Medicine.
● **Owner** Mr M Brockmann
M (Ref:HM14616)

## NATURAL PATH

**Natural Path**, 9 Corporation St, Taunton, **Somerset**, TA1 4AJ, ENG.
(T) 01823 325111
Speciality: Complementary Medicines & Therapy.
C M (Ref:HM14617)

## NATURAL PATH TO RADIANT HEALTH

**Natural Path To Radiant Health (The)**, College Town, Sandhurst, **Berkshire**, GU47 0QF, ENG.
(T) 01276 609771
Speciality: Complementary Medicines & Therapy.
● **Owner** Ms H Goodman-Payne
M (Ref:HM14618)

## NATURAL REMEDIES

**Natural Remedies**, 35A Brecknock Rd, London, **London (Greater)**, N7 0BT, ENG.
(T) 020 7267 3884 (F) 020 7267 3884
Speciality: Complementary Medicines & Therapy.
● **Manager** Mr I Ogilvy
C M (Ref:HM14619)

## NATURAL REMEDY CENTRE

**Natural Remedy Centre**, 39 Ripple Rd, Barking, **Essex**, IG11 7NT, ENG.
(T) 020 8594 3016 (F) 020 8594 3018
(E) saramzeb@virgin.net
(W) www.naturalremedycentre.co.uk
Speciality: Absent Healing, Acupressure, Acupuncture, Aromatherapy, Bach Remedies, Chinese Herbal Medicine, Chiropody, Cupping, Herbal Medicine, Homeopathy, Hypnotherapy, Indian Head Massage, Massage (Therapeutic), Moxibustion, Oriental Diagnosis, Reflexology, Reiki, Spinal Touch. ✔
● **Chinese Herbalist** Huang Li Fang
● **Homeopathic Doctor** Saran Zeb Q: Dip.Hom.Med.Sc, HMD. M: HMA.
● **Owner** Mrs C Yee Q: SRN. M: ISPA.
B C O T Yrs. Est.: 11 (Ref:HM14620)

## NATURAL REMEDY CLINIC

**Natural Remedy Clinic**, 90 Main St, Thornton, Kirkcaldy, **Fife**, KY1 4AG, SCO.
(T) 01592 773303
Speciality: Absent Healing, Aromatherapy, Bach Remedies, Bio-energetics, Cranial Osteopathy, Cupping, Faith Healing, Healer, Healing Therapy, Manipulation, Osteopathy, Reflexology, Reiki, Spiritual Healing, Stress Therapy.
● **Owner/Therapist** Miss J Tiernan
C S (Ref:HM14621)

## NATURAL SCIENCE COM

**Natural Science Com Ltd**, Lindslade, Middleton St, Llandrindod Wells, **Powys**, LD1 5ET, WAL.
(T) 01597 825966 (F) 01597 825215
Speciality: Complementary Medicines & Therapy.
● **Director** Mr S Hopkins
M (Ref:HM14622)

## NATURAL SELECTION

**Natural Selection**, 3 Esplanade Mews, Sunderland, **Tyne and Wear**, SR2 7DY, ENG.
(T) 01915 659171
(E) klaire@natural-selection.freeserve.co.uk
Speciality: Aromatherapy, Bio-energetics, Complementary Therapy, Holistic Healing, Indian Head Massage, Massage (Therapeutic). ✔
● **Therapist** Ms K Ferry Q: Dip.Arom, Dip.Body Massage, Dip.BT. M: ICHT, IFHB.
H Yrs. Est.: 4 (Ref:HM14623)



Key: B Mind-Body Medicine C Complementary Medicine H Self Help Treatment M Medicinal Therapy O Oriental Medicine P Postural Therapy S Manipulative Structural Therapy T Touch Therapy

## NATURAL SLEEP FOUNDATION

**Natural Sleep Foundation (The)**, The Pink House, 81 Downs Rd, Sutton, **Surrey**, SM2 5PR, ENG.
(T) 020 8642 3780
Speciality: Complementary Medicines & Therapy.
● **Director** Mr I Gulvin
C Yrs. Est.: 30 (Ref:HM14624)

## NATURAL SOLUTIONS

**Natural Solutions**, Holistic Sourcing Centre, 67 Lower Camden St, **County Dublin**, IRE.
(T) 01 280 5506
(E) alisterbredee@dol.ie
Speciality: Absent Healing, Complementary Therapy, Counselling, Dietician, Healer, Healing Therapy, Hypnosis, Hypnotherapy, Kinesiology, Life Style Coaching, Naturopathy, Nutritional Therapy, Psychotherapy, Reiki, Voice Therapy, Meridian Therapies. ✓
● **Therapist** Mr A Bredee Q: Reiki Master.
B Yrs. Est.: 16 (Ref:HM14625)

## NATURAL SPIRITUAL HEALING

**Natural Spiritual Healing**, 42 Ridge Green Cl, Sulis Meadows, Bath, **Somerset**, BA2 2EG, ENG.
(T) 01225 833563
(E) ivanna@kalinka.freeserve.co.uk
Speciality: Absent Healing, Healer, Healing Therapy. ✓
● **Spiritual Healer** Ms I James Q: Dip.Spiritual Healing. M: ISRHA.
B Yrs. Est.: 4 (Ref:HM14626)

## NATURAL STUFF HEALTH SHOP

**Natural Stuff Health Shop**, O'Connor Sq, Tullamore, **County Offaly**, IRE.
(T) 05064 1308
Speciality: Complementary Medicines & Therapy.
M (Ref:HM14627)

## NATURAL THERAPEUTICS

**Natural Therapeutics**, 18 Regent St, Cheltenham, **Gloucestershire**, GL50 1HE, ENG.
(T) 01242 221526
Speciality: Bach Remedies.
C (Ref:HM14628)

## NATURAL THERAPIES

**Natural Therapies**, 79 Newbegin, Hornsea, **Humberside (North)**, HU18 1PA, ENG.
(T) 01964 536416
Speciality: Acupressure, Acupuncture, Family Planning (Natural), Hypnotherapy, Massage (Therapeutic), Moxibustion, Music Therapy, Visualisation Therapy, Ying & Yang. ✓
● **Acupuncturist** Ms D Sutcliffe Q: Dip.Ac. M: BAcC.
O Yrs. Est.: 10 (Ref:HM14629)

## NATURAL THERAPIES

**Natural Therapies**, 1st Floor, 3 High St, Congleton, **Cheshire**, CW12 1BN, ENG.
(T) 01260 270888
Speciality: Complementary Medicines & Therapy.
● **Partner** Mrs B Walsh
M (Ref:HM14630)

## NATURAL THERAPIES

**Natural Therapies**, 6a Linskill Sq, Baxtergate, Whitby, **Yorkshire (North)**, YO21 1DA, ENG.
(T) 01947 820623
Speciality: Complementary Medicines & Therapy.
C M (Ref:HM14631)

## NATURAL THERAPIES

**Angela Riste - Natural Health Therapist**, Chantings, Old Town, Chard, **Somerset**, TA20 2BD, ENG.
(T) 01460 61733
Speciality: Aromatherapy, Colour Therapy, Crystal Healing, Floral Essence Therapy, Gem Essence Therapy, Indian Head Massage, Massage (Therapeutic), Metamorphic Therapy, Reiki, Seichem. ✓
● **Natural Health Therapist**
Ms A Riste Q: Dip.Arom, Dip.Indian Head Massage, Reiki Master.
T Yrs. Est.: 1 (Ref:HM14632)

## NATURAL THERAPIES CLINIC

**Natural Therapies Clinic**, Natural Therapies Clinic, Grays Lane House, Old Town, Moreton-in-Marsh, **Gloucestershire**, GL56 0LP, ENG.
(T) 01608 650077
(W) www.natural-therapies-clinic.co.uk
Speciality: Acupuncture, Alexander Technique, Aromatherapy, Chiropractic, Homeopathy, Naturopathy, Nutritional Therapy, Reflexology, Remedial Massage, Sound Therapy. ✓
● **Aromatherapist** Ms S Franklin Q: ITEC, MGCP. M: GCP.
● **Homeopath** Ms S Treanor
● **Reflexologist** Mrs J Morris Q: BEd (Hons), MA, MBChA, MBRA. M: B.A.Ch.P, BRA.
● **Nutritional/Sound Therapist/Naturopath** Ms H Green Q: Dip.ION, Dip.SPLD, RSA. M: DPA.
● **McTimoney Chiropractor**
Ms S Hemming Q: DC, MMCA. M: MCA.
● **Alexander Technique Therapist**
Ms J Sampson Q: MSTAT. M: STAT.
● **Owner/Acupuncturist** Ms C Edwards Q: BA (Hons), Lic.Ac. M: BAcC.
C Yrs. Est.: 12 (Ref:HM14633)

## NATURAL THERAPIES CLINIC

**Natural Therapies Clinic**, **County Westmeath**, IRE.
(T) 08681 22861
Speciality: Acupuncture.
O (Ref:HM14634)

## NATURAL THERAPIST

**Susan Howes**, 41 Montrose Avenue, Sidcup, **Kent**, DA15 9DT, ENG.
(T) 020 8300 7904
Speciality: Aromatherapy, Holistic Healing, Manipulation, Massage (Therapeutic), Reiki, Stress Therapy. ✓
● **Owner/Therapist** Mrs S Howes M: ITEC.
H P S T Yrs. Est.: 4 (Ref:HM14635)

## NATURAL THERAPY & BEAUTY

**Natural Therapy & Beauty Clinic**, Coolmine Sports Complex, Clonsilla, **County Dublin**, IRE.
(T) 01820 7172
Speciality: Complementary Medicines & Therapy.
M (Ref:HM14636)

## NATURAL THERAPY CENTRE

**Natural Therapy Centre**, 7 Westgate Rd, Guisborough, **Cleveland**, TS14 6EA, ENG.
(T) 01287 633591
Speciality: Acupuncture, Aromatherapy, Beauty Therapy, Chiropody, Homeopathy, Hypnotherapy, Osteopathy, Reflexology, Oriental Health. ✓
● **Remedial Massage** Ms J Russell Q: LCSP, RGN. M: LCSP.
C Yrs. Est.: 15 (Ref:HM14637)

## NATURAL THERAPY CENTRE

**Natural Therapy Centre**, 23 Trinity House Lane, Hull, **Humberside (North)**, HU1 2JA, ENG.
(T) 01482 326408
Speciality: Hypnosis.
B (Ref:HM14638)

## NATURAL THERAPY CENTRE

**Natural Therapy Centre**, The Bentley Centre, Stratton Rd, Marshgate, Swindon, **Wiltshire**, SN1 2SH, ENG.
(T) 01793 495551
(E) pennie@astbury.net
Speciality: Absent Healing, Complementary Therapy, Herbal Medicine, Hypnosis, Hypnotherapy, Life Style Coaching, Massage (Therapeutic), Neuro-Linguistic Program, Nutritional Therapy, Phytotherapy, Postural Integration, Reflexology, Reiki, Spiritual Healing, Stress Therapy, Touch Therapy, Visualisation Therapy, Trager Approach, EMAR - Ear Movement Desensitisation and Reprocessing, Relaxation, Food Sensitivity Testing and Vertical Reflex Therapy (a form of reflexology) - VRT. ✓
● **Hypnotherapist** Ms M Nicholls
(T) 01793 763378 Q: C.Hyp, CMH, NLP. M: UKGHE.
● **Manager/Practitioner**
Ms J Nicholls Q: LCSP, RGN. M: LCSP, Trager UK.
● **Holistic Therapist** Ms P Astbury Q: Reiki Master. M: AoR.
B C H Yrs. Est.: 8 (Ref:HM14639)

## NATURAL THERAPY CENTRE

**Natural Therapy Centre**, Lower Catherine St, Newry, **County Down**, BT35 6BE, NIR.
(T) 028 3026 2567
Speciality: Complementary Medicines & Therapy.
● **Owner** Mrs K Pickett
C M (Ref:HM14640)

## NATURAL THERAPY CENTRE

**Natural Therapy Centre**, Gaunts House, Petersham Lane, Wimborne, **Dorset**, BH21 4JQ, ENG.
(T) 01202 841522 (F) 01202 841959
Speciality: Complementary Medicines & Therapy.
● **Owner** Sir R Glyn
C M (Ref:HM14641)

## NATURAL THERAPY CENTRE

**Natural Therapy Centre**, 21A Southampton St, Farnborough, **Hampshire**, GU14 6AU, ENG.
(T) 01252 545837 (F) 01252 545837
Speciality: Complementary Medicines & Therapy.
● **Owner** Mrs E Cobb
C M (Ref:HM14642)

## NATURAL THERAPY CENTRE

**Natural Therapy Centre**, 11 London Rd, Tonbridge, **Kent**, TN10 3AB, ENG.
(T) 01732 355868
Speciality: Acupuncture, Herbal Medicine, Allergy Therapy, Skenar Practitioner. ✓
● **Acupuncturist** Susan Tosoni Q: BSc, MNIMH.
● **Owner/Medical Herblist**
Mrs D Benjamin Q: MNIMH.
C Yrs. Est.: 15 (Ref:HM14643)

## NATURAL THERAPY CENTRE

**Natural Therapy Centre**, 106A Denmark Hill, London, **London (Greater)**, SE5 8RX, ENG.
(T) 020 7738 3133
Speciality: Complementary Medicines & Therapy.
M (Ref:HM14644)

## NATURAL THERAPY CENTRE

**Natural Therapy Centre**, 10 New St, Chipping Norton, **Oxfordshire**, OX7 5LJ, ENG.
(T) 01608 641995
Speciality: Complementary Medicines & Therapy.
M (Ref:HM14645)

## NATURAL THERAPY CENTRE

**Natural Therapy Centre (The)**, 10 Bank St, Inverness, **Highland**, IV1 1QY, SCO.
(T) 01463 711060
Speciality: Complementary Medicines & Therapy.
C M (Ref:HM14646)

## NATURAL THERAPY CENTRE

**Natural Therapy Centre (The)**, 12A North Bridge St, Hawick, **Scottish Borders**, TD9 9QW, SCO.
(T) 01450 370403
Speciality: Osteopathy.
● **Owner** Mr S Carson
C (Ref:HM14647)

## NATURAL THERAPY CENTRE

**Natural Therapy Centre (The)**, 81 East Clyde St, Helensburgh, **Argyll and Bute**, G84 7PF, SCO.
(T) 01436 672389
Speciality: Alexander Technique, Aromatherapy, Cranial Osteopathy, Naturopathy, Osteopathy, Reflexology, Stress Therapy. ✓
● **Aromatherapist/Reflexologist**
Ms A Puedie M: AoA, AoR.
● **Aromatherapist/Reflexologist**
Mrs L Duncan M: AoA, AoR.
● **Consultant** Mr D Scott Q: Reg.Osteopath. M: BOsC.
S Yrs. Est.: 15 (Ref:HM14648)

## NATURAL THERAPY CENTRE

**Natural Therapy Centre (The)**, 29 Long St, Dursley, **Gloucestershire**, GL11 4HR, ENG.
(T) 01453 545066 (F) 01453 861068

(E) mlsutton@talk21.com
Speciality: Acupuncture, Aromatherapy, Cranio-Sacral Therapy, Homeopathy, Indian Head Massage, Massage (Therapeutic), Nutritional Therapy, Reflexology, Reiki, Shiatsu, Holistic Massage. ✔
- **Reflexologist** Ms C Hughes Q: MAR. M: AoR.
- **Reiki Master** Ms D Bladek Q: Reiki Master.
- **Owner** Mrs M Sutton Q: ANM. M: ANM.
- **Aromatherapist** Ms C Bonney Q: ITEC. M: ITEC.
- **Cranio-Sacral Therapist** Mr P Tucker Q: RCST.
- **Nutritional Therapist** Ms S Mason
- **Remedial Massage Therapist** Ms M Staddon
- **Homeopath** Ms H Judd Q: L.C.C.H. M: L.C.C.H.

C Yrs. Est.: 2 (Ref:HM14649)

## NATURAL THERAPY CENTRE

**Natural Therapy Centre (The)**, 5 Normandy St, Alton, **Hampshire**, GU34 1DD, ENG.
(T) 01420 82356
Speciality: Hypnosis.
B (Ref:HM14650)

## NATURAL THERAPY CENTRE

**Hureston Homoeopathic Practice (The)**, 3 Newquay Cl, Hureston Grange, Nuneaton, **Warwickshire**, CV11 6FH, ENG.
(T) 024 7632 5450
Speciality: Bowen Therapy, Floral Essence Therapy, Homeopathy, Manipulation. ✔
- **Homeopath/Bowen Practitioner** Ms J Hartley Q: BTER, LCPH, MHMA. M: BA UK, BTER, HMA.
- **Homeopath** Mr M Byng Q: BTER, LCPH, MHMA. M: BA UK, BTER, HMA.

M S Yrs. Est.: 9 (Ref:HM14651)

## NATURAL THERAPY CENTRE

**Natural Therapy Centre**, 15/16 West End, Mallow, **County Cork**, IRE.
(T) 022 5159 5
Speciality: Complementary Medicines & Therapy.
M (Ref:HM14652)

## NATURAL THERAPY CENTRE

**Natural Therapy Centre**, Custom House Buildings, Whitefriargate, Hull, **Humberside (North)**, HU1 2ER, ENG.
(T) 01482 326408 (F) 01482 609884
Speciality: Autogenic Training, Hypnotherapy, Stress Therapy, Past Life Regression Therapy. ✔
- **Hypnotherapist** Mr S Burgess M: NCH, UKGHE.

B Yrs. Est.: 9 (Ref:HM14653)

## NATURAL THERAPY CLINIC

**Natural Therapy Clinic**, 138 Oak Tree Lane, Mansfield, **Nottinghamshire**, NG18 3HR, ENG.
(T) 01623 626842 (F) 01623 651580
Speciality: Acupuncture, Aromatherapy, Herbal Medicine, Psychotherapy, Reflexology, Reiki. ✔
- **Osteopath/Acupuncturist** Mr H Cooke Q: Chart.Psych. M: State.Reg.Psych.
- **Medical Herbalist** Ms B Cooke Q: MNIMH. M: NIMH.

C Yrs. Est.: 40 (Ref:HM14654)

## NATURAL THERAPY CLINIC

**Dr Mark Pollard**, 2 Boyn Valley Rd, Maidenhead, **Berkshire**, SL6 4ED, ENG.
(T) 01628 672005
(W) www.naturaltherapyclinic.co.uk
Speciality: Acupuncture, Alexander Technique, Aromatherapy, Bach Remedies, Chiropractic, Counselling, Crystal Healing, Herbal Medicine, Holistic Healing, Homeopathy, Hypnotherapy, Indian Head Massage, Iridology, Kinesiology, Manipulation, Massage (Therapeutic), Meditation, Nutritional Therapy, Polarity Therapy, Reflexology, Reiki, Seichem, Stress Therapy, Touch Therapy, Vitamin Therapy, Spagyria. ✔
- **Reflexologist** Louise Prince Q: MAR.
- **Practitioner** Dr S Cheung Q: MSc. M: RCHM.
- **Teacher of the Alexander Technique** Mr M Jones Q: MSTAT.
- **Associate** Dr G Li M: ATCM UK.
- **Practice Manager** Francis Dashwood Evans Q: DO. M: BOA.
- **Therapist** Dr E Gheorghiu Q: DM. M: FHom.
- **Owner** Dr M Pollard Q: DC. M: BCA.

P Yrs. Est.: 17 (Ref:HM14655)

## NATURAL THERAPY CLINIC

**Natural Therapy Clinic**, 2 Boyn Valley Rd, Maidenhead, **Berkshire**, SL6 4ED, ENG.
(T) 01628 672005 (F) 01628 672005
Speciality: Acupuncture, Alexander Technique, Aromatherapy, Bach Remedies, Chinese Herbal Medicine, Chiropractic, Cognitive Therapy, Complementary Therapy, Counselling, Healing Therapy, Herbal Medicine, Homeopathy, Hypnotherapy, Indian Head Massage, Iridology, Kinesiology, Manipulation, Massage (Therapeutic), Moxibustion, Oriental Diagnosis, Osteopathy, Psychotherapy, Reflexology, Seichem, Spagyria. ✔
- **Homeopath** Dr E Gheorghiu M: FHom.
- **Acupuncturist** Dr S Cheung M: BAcC.
- **Acupuncturist** Dr G Li
- **Therapist** Ms L Prince M: AoR.
- **Chiropractor** Dr M Pollard M: BCA.
- **Therapist** Ms L Barnes Q: ITEC.
- **Psychotherapist/Hypnotherapist** Ms J Thams M: NCH, NCP.
- **Reiki Master** Cornelius
- **Chiropractor** Dr C Ross M: BCA.
- **Therapist** Mr M Jones
- **Practice Manager** Francis Dashwood-Evans

M Yrs. Est.: 11 (Ref:HM14656)

## NATURAL THERAPY CLINIC

**Natural Therapy Clinic**, The Lodge Surgery, 59 Whitham Rd, Sheffield, **Yorkshire (South)**, S10 2SL, ENG.
(T) 01142 678900
Speciality: Complementary Medicines & Therapy.
- **Owner** Mr S Johnstone

C M (Ref:HM14657)

## NATURAL THERAPY CLINIC

**Natural Therapy Clinic**, Bainton Balk Farm, Bainton, Driffield, **Humberside (North)**, YO25 9EQ, ENG.
(T) 01377 217237
Speciality: Complementary Medicines & Therapy.
- **Owner** Ms J Hepworth

C M (Ref:HM14658)

## NATURAL THERAPY CLINIC

**Natural Therapy Clinic**, 2 Stoke Rd, Bishops Cleeve, Cheltenham, **Gloucestershire**, GL52 4RP, ENG.
(T) 01242 676951
Speciality: Complementary Medicines & Therapy.
C M (Ref:HM14659)

## NATURAL THERAPY CLINIC

**Natural Therapy Clinic (The)**, 25 Bingham St, Bangor, **Gwynedd**, BT20 5DW, WAL.
(T) 028 9146 4847
Speciality: Alexander Technique, Aromatherapy, Bowen Therapy, Counselling, Crystal Healing, Hypnotherapy, Indian Head Massage, Kinesiology, Reflexology, Reiki, Shiatsu, Bowen Technique. ✔
- **Kinesiologist** Miss S McCaig
- **Therapist** Ms J Irving Q: BSc (Hons), MNCH.
- **Counsellor** Miss D Smithwood
- **Teacher of the Alexander Technique** Mr D White Q: BSc, MSTAT.
- **Crystal/Reiki Therapist** Miss R Law Q: BA (Hons), Reiki 2.
- **Therapist** Ms D Leslie Q: MICHT.

C Yrs. Est.: 6 (Ref:HM14660)

## NATURAL THERAPY CLINIC

**Natural Therapy Clinic (The)**, 150-152 Grange Rd, Blackpool, **Lancashire**, FY3 8PG, ENG.
(T) 01253 394383
Speciality: Physiotherapy.
P S T (Ref:HM14661)

## NATURAL THERAPY CLINIC

**Natural Therapy Clinic**, 36 Main St, Letterkenny, **County Donegal**, IRE.
(T) 07429 300
Speciality: Complementary Medicines & Therapy.
M (Ref:HM14662)

## NATURAL THERAPY PRACTICE

**Natural Therapy Practice**, 109 Blindmans Lane, Cheshunt, Waltham Cross, **Hertfordshire**, EN8 9DN, ENG.
(T) 01992 621110
Speciality: Osteopathy.
P S T (Ref:HM14663)

## NATURAL THERAPY SERVICES

**Natural Therapy Services**, 45 High St, Swanwick, Alfreton, **Derbyshire**, DE55 1AA, ENG.
(T) 01773 603880
Speciality: Complementary Medicines & Therapy.
C M (Ref:HM14664)

## NATURAL THRPY CLNC/TRNING CTRE

**Natural Therapy Clinic & Training Centre**, 3a The Parade, Ringwood Rd, Verwood, **Dorset**, BH31 7AA, ENG.
(T) 01202 827811 (F) 01202 827811
Speciality: Complementary Medicines & Therapy.
- **Owner** Miss K Keane

C M (Ref:HM14665)

## NATURAL TOUCH

**Natural Touch (The)**, 176 Sherrards Way, Barnet, **Hertfordshire**, EN5 2BS, ENG.
(T) 020 8441 2687
Speciality: Aromatherapy.
M O (Ref:HM14666)

## NATURAL TOUCH THERAPY

**Natural Touch Therapy**, Flat 8, Lincoln Court, Rockhurst Drive, Eastbourne, **Sussex (East)**, BN20 8UY, ENG.
(T) 01323 411461
Speciality: Complementary Medicines & Therapy.
- **Owner** Miss T Cleverly

M (Ref:HM14667)

## NATURAL WAY AROMATHERAPY

**Natural Way Aromatherapy (The)**, 16 Melstock Cl, Tipton, **Midlands (West)**, DY4 8AY, ENG.
(T) 01215 303651
Speciality: Aromatherapy.
- **Owner** Mrs C Boden

M O (Ref:HM14668)

## NATURAL WAY HEALTH CENTRE

**Natural Way Health Centre (The)**, 253 Alen Moss Rd, Loughborough, **Leicestershire**, LE11 4LU, ENG.
(T) 01509 261131
Speciality: Acupuncture, Counselling, Reiki, Shiatsu. ✔
- **Acupuncturist** Mr N Pomfrett Q: Lic.Ac, MBAcC. M: BAcC.
- **Reiki/Shiatsu Therapist** Ms J Lewis Q: MRSS, Reiki Master.

C (Ref:HM14669)

## NATURAL WAYS

**Natural Ways**, 28 Laburnum Rd, London, **London (Greater)**, SW19 1BQ, ENG.
(T) 020 8540 0158
Speciality: Complementary Medicines & Therapy.
M (Ref:HM14670)

## NATURAL WHEAT BAG

**Natural Wheat Bag Co Ltd (The)**, Unit 10 Emley Moor Business Park, Leys Lane, Emley, Huddersfield, **Yorkshire (West)**, HD8 9QY, ENG.
(T) 01924 840504 (F) 01924 840648
Speciality: Complementary Medicines & Therapy.
- **Managing Director** Mrs S Wymer

C M (Ref:HM14671)

## NATURAL-BALANCE CO UK

**Gail Wieringa - Homeopath**, Quickmoor Cottage, Common Wood, Chipperfield, Kings Langley, **Hertfordshire**, WD4 9BB, ENG.
(T) 01923 268993 (F) 01923 264873



Key: B Mind-Body Medicine C Complementary Medicine H Self Help Treatment M Medicinal Therapy O Oriental Medicine P Postural Therapy S Manipulative Structural Therapy T Touch Therapy

(E) gail@natural-balance.co.uk
(W) www.natural-balance.co.uk
Speciality: Bach Remedies, Complementary Therapy, Homeopathy. ✔
● **Homeopath** Ms G Weirenga Q: BSc (Hons), PHSH. M: Soc.Hom.
B Yrs. Est.: 2 (Ref:HM14672)

## NATURALLY NUTRITION

**Naturally Nutrition**, Natural Therapy Centre, The Bentley Centre, Stratton Rd, Marshgate, Swindon, **Wiltshire**, SN1 2SH, ENG.
(T) 07818 400910
Speciality: Nutritional Therapy. ✔
● **Nutrition Consultant** Mrs Gibson Q: BSc (Hons), Lic.ION.
C Yrs. Est.: 1 (Ref:HM14673)

## NATURE CARE CLINIC

**Nature Care Clinic**, 3b Broadway North, High Rd, Pitsea, Basildon, **Essex**, SS13 3AT, ENG.
(T) 01268 584080
Speciality: Chiropractors.
● **Practice Manager** Ms V Watkins
C P S T (Ref:HM14674)

## NATURE CARE COLLEGE

**Nature Care College**, 3a Broadway, High Rd, Pitsea, Basildon, **Essex**, SS13 3AT, ENG.
(T) 01268 553600
Speciality: Complementary Medicines & Therapy.
● **Owner** Mr P McIntyre
M (Ref:HM14675)

## NATURE CURES

**Nature Cures**, 8 Magdalen St, Colchester, **Essex**, CO1 2JT, ENG.
(T) 01206 571794
Speciality: Complementary Medicines & Therapy.
C M (Ref:HM14676)

## NATURE HEALTH CENTRE

**Nature Health Centre (The)**, 354 Uxbridge Rd, London, **London (Greater)**, W12 7LL, ENG.
(T) 020 8743 5665 (F) 020 8743 5665
Speciality: Complementary Medicines & Therapy.
● **Partner** Mrs A Mohammad
C M (Ref:HM14677)

## NATURE SECRETS

**Nature Secrets**, 46 Harley St, London, **London (Greater)**, W1N 1AD, ENG.
(T) 020 7436 7436 (F) 020 7436 7436
Speciality: Complementary Medicines & Therapy.
● **Owner** Dr N Eccles
M (Ref:HM14678)

## NATURE SUN SHINE HERBS

**Nature Sun Shine Herbs**, 24 Woods Rd, Caversham, Reading, **Berkshire**, RG4 6NA, ENG.
(T) 01189 475949
Speciality: Complementary Medicines & Therapy.
● **Owner** Ms L Roffey
M (Ref:HM14679)

## NATURE SUNSHINE DISTRIBUTOR

**Nature Sunshine Distributor**, 134 Fairlight Rd, Hastings, **Sussex (East)**, TN35 5EL, ENG.
(T) 01424 422433 (F) 01424 436553
Speciality: Complementary Medicines & Therapy.
● **Owner** Mr G Ingamells
C M (Ref:HM14680)

## NATURE SUNSHINE PRODUCTS

**Nature Sunshine Products**, 21 Thatchers Piece, Droitwich, **Worcestershire**, WR9 9EF, ENG.
(T) 01905 771362
Speciality: Complementary Medicines & Therapy.
● **Partner** Mrs A Browning
C M (Ref:HM14681)

## NATURE WORKS

**Nature Works**, 16 Balderton St, London, **London (Greater)**, W1Y 1TF, ENG.
(T) 020 7355 4036
Speciality: Alexander Technique.
● **Manager** Mr A Maunder
P S (Ref:HM14682)

## NATURECARE

**Naturecare**, 92 Mina Rd, Bristol, BS2 9XW, ENG.
(T) 01179 552117
Speciality: Acupuncture.
● **Partner** Ms J Pollard
O (Ref:HM14683)

## NATURECURES

**R Graham T/A Naturecures**, Hill House, Ellis St, Boxford, Sudbury, **Suffolk**, CO10 5HP, ENG.
(T) 01787 210005
(E) richard@natramed.freeserve.co.uk
(W) www.natramed.freeserve.co.uk
Speciality: Acupressure, Acupuncture, Manipulation, Massage (Therapeutic), Moxibustion, Nutritional Therapy, Oriental Diagnosis, Shiatsu. ✔
● **Manager** Mr R Graham Q: LCSP, MBAcC. M: BAcC, LCSP.
O S Yrs. Est.: 10 (Ref:HM14684)

## NATURELIEF

**Naturelief**, 1 Meadow Lane, Up Hatherley, Cheltenham, **Gloucestershire**, GL51 5NP, ENG.
(T) 01242 513699
Speciality: Complementary Medicines & Therapy.
C M (Ref:HM14685)

## NATURES COMFORTS HEATPACKS

**Natures Comforts Heatpacks**, 78 Stanstead Cr, Brighton, **Sussex (East)**, BN2 6TQ, ENG.
(T) 01273 301114
Speciality: Aromatherapy.
● **Owner** Ms M Southwell
M O (Ref:HM14686)

## NATURES ENERGY

**Natures Energy**, 542 Chorley Old Rd, Bolton, **Lancashire**, BL1 6AB, ENG.
(T) 01204 465192
Speciality: Complementary Medicines & Therapy.
● **Owner** Ms L Birchall
M (Ref:HM14687)

## NATURES GATE

**Natures Gate**, Po Box 371, Basingstoke, **Hampshire**, RG24 8GD, ENG.
(T) 01256 346060 (F) 01256 346050
(E) natures.gate@virgin.net
(W) www.naturesgatetens.com
Speciality: Complementary Medicines & Therapy, TENS - Trans Electrical Nerve Stimulation. ✔ [credit card]
● **Marketing Director** Ms T Dundovic Q: RGN. M: RCN.
C H Yrs. Est.: 8 (Ref:HM14688)

## NATURE'S GIFT

**Nature's Gift**, 2 The Colonnade, High St, Maidenhead, **Berkshire**, SL6 1QL, ENG.
(T) 01628 674414
Speciality: Complementary Medicines & Therapy.
● **Owner** Mr P Bishop
M (Ref:HM14689)

## NATURES GIFT AROMATHERAPY

**Natures Gift Aromatherapy - Celia Clegg**, 96 Park Rd, Wigan, **Lancashire**, WN6 7AQ, ENG.
(T) 01942 324759
Speciality: Aromatherapy.
● **Aromatherapist** Ms C Clegg Q: IIHHT, MICHT.
M O (Ref:HM14690)

## NATURE'S HEALING

**Nature's Healing**, 17 Fairholme Drive, Mansfield, **Nottinghamshire**, NG19 6DN, ENG.
(T) 01623 634444
Speciality: Aromatherapy.
M O (Ref:HM14691)

## NATURES NECTAR

**Natures Nectar**, 31 High St, Seaford, **Sussex (East)**, BN25 1PA, ENG.
(T) 01323 873176
Speciality: Aromatherapy.
M O (Ref:HM14692)

## NATURES PATH

**Natures Path**, 64 Fowler Rd, Coventry, **Midlands (West)**, CV6 1ND, ENG.
(T) 024 7659 0794
Speciality: Complementary Medicines & Therapy.
C M (Ref:HM14693)

## NATURES REMEDIES

**Natures Remedies**, 32 South Clerk St, Edinburgh, **Edinburgh (City of)**, EH8 9PR, SCO.
(T) 01316 227192
Speciality: Herbal Medicine.
● **Owner** Mr M Mohammed
M (Ref:HM14694)

## NATURE'S REMEDIES

**Nature's Remedies**, 36 Longfield Drive, Amersham, **Buckinghamshire**, HP6 5HE, ENG.
(T) 01494 727888 (F) 01494 722545
Speciality: Complementary Medicines & Therapy.
● **Owner** Mr B Ouvery
M (Ref:HM14695)

## NATURES SUNSHINE DISTRIBUTOR

**Natures Sunshine Distributor**, 5 Dale House Lane, Kenilworth, **Warwickshire**, CV8 2HW, ENG.
(T) 01926 856219
Speciality: Complementary Medicines & Therapy.
C M (Ref:HM14696)

## NATURES SUNSHINE PRODUCTS

**Natures Sunshine Products**, 84 Stoneleigh Rd, Solihull, **Midlands (West)**, B91 1DJ, ENG.
(T) 01217 050939
Speciality: Complementary Medicines & Therapy.
C M (Ref:HM14697)

## NATURES TOUCH

**Natures Touch**, Buccleuch St, Melrose, **Scottish Borders**, TD6 9LB, SCO.
(T) 01896 823782 (F) 01896 823782
Speciality: Aromatherapy. ✔
● **Owner/Aromatherapist** Ms Y Hodgson Q: ISPA.
C Yrs. Est.: 3 (Ref:HM14698)

## NATURES TREASURES

**Natures Treasures Ltd**, New Portreath Rd, Redruth, **Cornwall**, TR16 4QL, ENG.
(T) 01209 843881 (F) 01209 843882
Speciality: Aromatherapy.
● **Managing Director** Mrs M Nelson
M O (Ref:HM14699)

## NATURES WAY

**Natures Way**, 6 Wistaria Avenue, Chipping Sodbury, Bristol, BS37 6LE, ENG.
(T) 01454 320679 (F) 01454 320679
Speciality: Complementary Medicines & Therapy.
● **Owner** Mr P Warren
C M (Ref:HM14700)

## NATURES WAY

**Natures Way**, 396 High St, Lincoln, **Lincolnshire**, LN5 7SS, ENG.
(T) 01522 887887
Speciality: Hypnotherapy.
● **Owner** Ms A White
B (Ref:HM14701)

## NATURES WAY

**Natures Way**, 22 Woodmarket, Kelso, **Scottish Borders**, TD5 7AX, SCO.
(T) 01573 224080
Speciality: Aromatherapy, Bach Remedies. ✔
● **Manageress** Mrs J Miller
● **Owner** Mr J Miller
C H Yrs. Est.: 5 (Ref:HM14702)

## NATURE'S WAY

**Nature's Way**, 14 Chelsea House, London Rd, Bath, **Somerset**, BA1 6DA, ENG.
(T) 01225 444786
Speciality: Complementary Medicines & Therapy.
● **Therapist** Mr P Warren
M (Ref:HM14703)


Key continued: Yrs.Est: Years Established Q: Qualifications M: Professional Membership ✔ Indemnity Insurance [credit card] Accept Credit Cards

### NATURES WAY CLINIC

**Natures Way Clinic**, Colne Commercial Centre, Exchange St, Colne, **Lancashire**, BB8 0SQ, ENG.
(T) 01422 844885
Speciality: Complementary Medicines & Therapy.
● **Therapist** Ms S Hamnett
**C** **M** (Ref:HM14704)

### NATURES WORKROOM

**Natures Workroom**, 86B Fenay Bridge Rd, Fenay Bridge, Huddersfield, **Yorkshire (West)**, HD8 0AY, ENG.
(T) 01484 559551
Speciality: Aromatherapy, Indian Head Massage, Massage (Therapeutic), Reflexology. ✔
● **Aromatherapist** Ms J Booth Q: ITEC. M: GCP.
● **Aromatherapist** Mrs M Maule Q: ITEC. M: GCP.
**C** Yrs. Est.: 2 (Ref:HM14705)

### NATURES WORLD

**Natures World**, 1 Orchard Avenue, Bolton Le Sands, Carnforth, **Lancashire**, LA5 8HP, ENG.
(T) 01524 732502 (F) 01524 732502
Speciality: Aromatherapy.
● **Owner** Mrs S Knight
**M** **O** (Ref:HM14706)

### NATUREWORKS

**Natureworks**, 16 Balderton St, London, **London (Greater)**, W1Y 1TF, ENG.
(T) 020 7355 4036 (F) 020 7499 9087
Speciality: Complementary Medicines & Therapy.
● **Office Manager** Mr S Emmerson
**M** (Ref:HM14707)

### NATUROPATHIC HEALTH & BEAUTY

**Naturopathic Health & Beauty Co Ltd**, Willow Tree Marina, West Quay Drive, Hayes, **London (Greater)**, UB4 9TA, ENG.
(T) 020 8842 3956 (F) 020 8841 7557
Speciality: Complementary Medicines & Therapy.
● **Managing Director** Mr N Pearce
**C** **M** (Ref:HM14708)

### NATUROPATHIC HEALTH CENTRE

**Naturopathic Health Centre**, 7 Rutland Rd, Southport, **Merseyside**, PR8 6PB, ENG.
(T) 01704 530574
Speciality: Chiropractic, Cranial Osteopathy, Crystal Healing, Hay Diet, Herbal Medicine, Holistic Healing, Homeopathy, Manipulation, Massage (Therapeutic), Naturopathy, Nutritional Therapy, Osteopathy, Reflexology, Rolfing, Ultrasonics, Colonic Hydrotherapy. ✔
● **Naturopath** Miss N Barbasch Q: DO, ND, RN.
**P** **S** Yrs. Est.: 35 (Ref:HM14709)

### NAUGHTON, G

**G Naughton**, 29 Borough Hill, Petersfield, **Hampshire**, GU32 3LQ, ENG.
(T) 01730 262095
Speciality: Psychotherapy.
**B** (Ref:HM14710)

### NAYDLER, NICK

**Nick Naydler**, 4 Seddon Rd, St Werburghs, Bristol, BS2 9YA, ENG.
(T) 01179 550752
Speciality: Counselling, Psychotherapy. ✔
● **Psychotherapist** Mr N Naydler Q: BACP, IP, MA (Hons). M: UKCP.
**P** **S** **T** Yrs. Est.: 12 (Ref:HM14711)

### NAYLOR & ASSOCIATES

**D J Naylor & Associates**, 106 Fenchurch St, London, **London (Greater)**, EC3M 5JB, ENG.
(T) 020 7481 3132 (F) 020 7481 3132
Speciality: Physiotherapy.
● **Manager** Mr C Warwick
**P** **S** **T** (Ref:HM14712)

### NAYLOR, ANTHEA

**Anthea Naylor**, 71 Lee St, Horley, **Surrey**, RH6 8HD, ENG.
(T) 01293 772127
Speciality: Chiropodists (Podiatrists).
**S** (Ref:HM14713)

### NAYLOR, DIANA

**Diana Naylor**, Bellstone Court, Shrewsbury, **Shropshire**, SY1 1JB, ENG.
(T) 01743 362787
Speciality: Chiropodists (Podiatrists).
**S** (Ref:HM14714)

### NAYLOR, ESTER

**Ester Naylor**, Birmingham, **Midlands (West)**, B11, ENG.
(T) 01212 420824
Speciality: Bach Remedies.
**M** (Ref:HM14715)

### NAYLOR, JOHN

**John Naylor**, 50 Weston Way, Northampton, **Northamptonshire**, NN3 3BN, ENG.
(T) 01604 401862 (F) 01604 401862
Speciality: Alexander Technique.
● **Owner** Mr J Naylor
**P** **S** (Ref:HM14716)

### NE LONDON PSYCHO COUNS ASS

**North East London Psychotherapy Counselling Association**, 24 Kyverdale Rd, London, **London (Greater)**, N16 7AH, ENG.
(T) 020 7502 7536
Speciality: Psychotherapy.
● **Owner** Mr F Dalal
**B** (Ref:HM14717)

### NEAL, JULIE

**Julie Neal**, Manor House, Barton Hartshorn, Buckingham, **Buckinghamshire**, MK18 4JU, ENG.
(T) 01280 848943 (F) 01892 667525
Speciality: Acupuncture.
● **Manager** Ms S Petszaft
**O** (Ref:HM14718)

### NEAL, KATE

**Kate Neal**, 5 Elm Ter, Constantine Rd, London, **London (Greater)**, NW3 2LL, ENG.
(T) 020 7267 4222
Speciality: Complementary Medicines & Therapy.
● **Owner** Ms K Neal
**M** (Ref:HM14719)

### NEAL, MARIA

**Maria Neal**, 2 Wallwork Cl, Rochdale, **Lancashire**, OL11 5FB, ENG.
(T) 01706 654752
Speciality: Complementary Medicines & Therapy.
● **Owner** Mrs M Neal
**C** **M** (Ref:HM14720)

### NEALE, ALISON

**Alison Neale**, 5 The Hythe, Chickerell, Weymouth, **Dorset**, DT3 4NE, ENG.
(T) 01305 783565
Speciality: Complementary Medicines & Therapy.
**C** **M** (Ref:HM14721)

### NEALE, CLIVE & LYNNE

**Clive & Lynne Neale**, 14 Park Hall Rd, London, **London (Greater)**, N2 9PU, ENG.
(T) 020 8444 9732
Speciality: Alexander Technique.
● **Partner** Mrs L Aserappa-Neale
**P** **S** (Ref:HM14722)

### NEALE, EDWARD

**Edward Neale**, 24 West Rd, Tallington, Stamford, **Lincolnshire**, PE9 4RS, ENG.
(T) 01780 740448
Speciality: Chiropodists (Podiatrists).
● **Partner** Mrs J Neale
**S** (Ref:HM14723)

### NEALE, JOAN E

**Joan E Neale**, 24 West Rd, Tallington, Stamford, **Lincolnshire**, PE9 4RS, ENG.
(T) 01780 740448
Speciality: Reflexology.
● **Partner** Mrs J Neale
**S** **T** (Ref:HM14724)

### NEALE-BROWN, CLAIRE

**Claire Neale-Brown**, 8 Littledown Rd, Cheltenham, **Gloucestershire**, GL53 9LP, ENG.
(T) 01242 529592
Speciality: Alexander Technique.
● **Owner** Mrs C Neale-Brown
**P** **S** (Ref:HM14725)

### NEALS YARD

**Neals Yard (Natural Remedies) Ltd**, 23-25 Morgan Arcade, Cardiff, **Glamorgan (Vale of)**, CF10 1AF, WAL.
(T) 029 2023 5721
Speciality: Complementary Medicines & Therapy.
● **Manager** Mrs E Manns
**M** (Ref:HM14726)

### NEALS YARD NATURAL REMEDIES

**Neals Yard Natural Remedies**, 9 Elgin Cres, London, **London (Greater)**, W11 2JA, ENG.
(T) 020 7727 3998
Speciality: Complementary Medicines & Therapy.
**M** (Ref:HM14727)

### NEALS YARD REMEDIES

**Neals Yard Remedies**, 29 John Dalton St, St. James's Sq, Manchester, **Manchester (Greater)**, M2 6DS, ENG.
(T) 01618 351713 (F) 01618 359322
Speciality: Complementary Medicines & Therapy.
● **Manager** Miss S Yarnell
**C** **M** (Ref:HM14728)

### NEALS YARD REMEDIES

**Neals Yard Remedies**, 2a Kensington Gardens, Brighton, **Sussex (East)**, BN1 4AL, ENG.
(T) 01273 601464 (F) 01273 601464
Speciality: Complementary Medicines & Therapy.
● **Owner** Mr N Campeau
**C** **M** (Ref:HM14729)

### NEALS YARD REMEDIES

**Neals Yard Remedies**, 46A George St, Edinburgh, **Edinburgh (City of)**, EH2 2LE, SCO.
(T) 01312 263223 (F) 01312 263223
Speciality: Complementary Medicines & Therapy.
● **Manager** Ms J Hames
**M** (Ref:HM14730)

### NEAL'S YARD REMEDIES

**Neal's Yard Remedies**, 15 Neals Yard, London, **London (Greater)**, WC2H 9DP, ENG.
(T) 020 7379 7222 (F) 020 7379 0705
Speciality: Complementary Medicines & Therapy.
● **Manager** Ms C Twohig
**C** **M** (Ref:HM14731)

### NEAL'S YARD REMEDIES

**Neal's Yard Remedies**, Chelsea Farmers Market, 125 Sydney St, London, **London (Greater)**, SW3 6NR, ENG.
(T) 020 7351 6380 (F) 020 7376 7245
Speciality: Complementary Medicines & Therapy.
● **Manager** Miss K Wilford
**C** **M** (Ref:HM14732)

### NEAL'S YARD REMEDIES

**Neal's Yard Remedies**, 68 Chalk Farm Rd, London, **London (Greater)**, NW1 8AN, ENG.
(T) 020 7284 2039 (F) 020 7284 2039
Speciality: Complementary Medicines & Therapy.
● **Partner** Mrs M Rodriques
**C** **M** (Ref:HM14733)

### NEAL'S YARD REMEDIES

**Neal's Yard Remedies**, 5 Golden Cross, Oxford, **Oxfordshire**, OX1 3EU, ENG.
(T) 01865 245436 (F) 01865 245436
Speciality: Herbal Medicine.
● **Owner** Mr M Higgins
**M** (Ref:HM14734)

### NEAL'S YARD REMEDIES

**Neal's Yard Remedies**, 37 The Glades Shopping Centre, High St, Bromley, **Kent**, BR1 1DD, ENG.
(T) 020 8313 9898
Speciality: Complementary Medicines & Therapy.
**C** **M** (Ref:HM14735)

Key: **B** Mind-Body Medicine **C** Complementary Medicine **H** Self Help Treatment **M** Medicinal Therapy **O** Oriental Medicine **P** Postural Therapy **S** Manipulative Structural Therapy **T** Touch Therapy

**NEAL'S YARD REMEDIES**

**Neal's Yard Remedies**, 19 Central Arcade, Newcastle Upon Tyne, **Tyne and Wear**, NE1 5BP, ENG.
(T) 01912 322525
Speciality: Complementary Medicines & Therapy.
● **Owner** Mrs J Wakefield
C M (Ref:HM14736)

**NEAL'S YARD REMEDIES**

**Neal's Yard Remedies**, 126 Whiteladies Rd, Bristol, BS8 2RP, ENG.
(T) 01179 466034 (F) 01179 741350
Speciality: Complementary Medicines & Therapy.
● **Director** Mr G Meanwell
C M (Ref:HM14737)

**NEAL'S YARD REMEDIES**

**Neal's Yard Remedies**, 26 Lower Goat Lane, Norwich, **Norfolk**, NR2 1EL, ENG.
(T) 01603 766681
Speciality: Complementary Medicines & Therapy.
C M (Ref:HM14738)

**NEAL'S YARD REMEDIES**

**Neal's Yard Remedies Ltd**, 26-34 Ingate Pl, London, **London (Greater)**, SW8 3NS, ENG.
(T) 020 7498 1686 (F) 020 7498 2505
Speciality: Complementary Medicines & Therapy.
● **Managing Director** Ms A Purvis
M (Ref:HM14739)

**NEAL'S YARD THERAPY ROOMS**

**Neal's Yard Therapy Rooms**, 2 Neal's Yard, Convent Garden, London, **London (Greater)**, WC2H 9DP, ENG.
(T) 020 7379 7662
Speciality: Complementary Medicines & Therapy.
● **Manager** Miss I Weskin
● **Psychotherapist** Josefine Speyer
M (Ref:HM14740)

**NEASMITH, PAULINE**

**Pauline Neasmith**, 16 Clarence Sq, Cheltenham, **Gloucestershire**, GL50 4JN, ENG.
(T) 01242 241933
Speciality: Complementary Medicines & Therapy.
M (Ref:HM14741)

**NEAT FEET**

**Neat Feet Ltd**, 108 High St, Rottingdean, Brighton, **Sussex (East)**, BN2 7HF, ENG.
(T) 01273 302830
Speciality: Biomechanics, Chiropody, Laser Treatment, Nail Surgery, Podiatry. ✔
● **Chiropodist** Ms K Glennon Q: BSc, M.S.C.P, S.R.Ch.
● **Owner/Chiropodist** Mr D Spellman Q: BSc, DPodM, M.S.C.P, S.R.Ch.
M Yrs. Est.: 15 (Ref:HM14742)

**NEAT FEET**

**Neat Feet**, Room 8, 5 South Fergus Pl, Kirkcaldy, **Fife**, KY1 1YA, SCO.
(T) 01592 644464
(W) www.neatfeetreflexology.co.uk
Speciality: Alexander Technique, Indian Head Massage, Kinesiology, Massage (Therapeutic), Reflexology, Reiki. ✔
● **Practitioner** Ms J Birnie M: IPTI, SNHS.
● **Massage Therapist** Ms L Campbell M: PMAS.
● **Reflexologist** Mr J Baker
S Yrs. Est.: 2 (Ref:HM14743)

**NEATH CHIROPODY CLINIC**

**Neath Chiropody Clinic**, 108 London Rd, Neath, **Glamorgan (Vale of)**, SA11 1HL, WAL.
(T) 01639 763102
Speciality: Chiropodists (Podiatrists).
● **Owner** Mr A Prowse
S (Ref:HM14744)

**NEATH HERBAL CLINIC**

**Neath Herbal Clinic**, 7c The Parade, Neath, **Glamorgan (Vale of)**, SA11 1RB, WAL.
(T) 01639 645141
Speciality: Herbalists.
M (Ref:HM14745)

**NEEDFUL THINGS**

**Needful Things**, 74 Shaftesbury Drive, Wardle, Rochdale, **Lancashire**, OL12 9LS, ENG.
(T) 01706 372764
Speciality: Clairvoyants & Palmists.
● **Owner** Miss J Kenworthy
B (Ref:HM14746)

**NEEDHAM, A**

**A Needham**, Cassidy Rd Medical Centre, 651A Fulham Rd, London, **London (Greater)**, SW6 5PX, ENG.
(T) 020 7731 2511 (F) 020 7371 7857
Speciality: Psychotherapy.
● **Manager** Mr L McNulty
B (Ref:HM14747)

**NEEDHAM, ALIX**

**Alix Needham**, 13 Merton Hall Rd, London, **London (Greater)**, SW19 3PP, ENG.
(T) 020 8543 2086
Speciality: Hypnotherapy.
B (Ref:HM14748)

**NEEDHAM, ANGELA**

**Angela Needham RSHom Homeopath**, 46 Panton Rd, Hoole, Chester, **Cheshire**, CH2 3HX, ENG.
(T) 01244 311952
(E) angelan@madasafish.com
Speciality: Holistic Healing, Homeopathy. ✔
● **Homeopath** Ms A Needham Q: BA, MCH, RSHom. M: Soc.Hom.
C M Yrs. Est.: 16 (Ref:HM14749)

**NEEDHAM, ANN**

**Ann Needham**, 109 Mill Gate, Ackworth, Pontefract, **Yorkshire (West)**, WF7 7PJ, ENG.
(T) 01977 615231
Speciality: Psychotherapy.
B (Ref:HM14750)

**NEEDHAM, LYNDA M**

**Advanced Hypnosis & Hypnotherapy Consultancy**, 5 Broad Oaks, Randley, Telford, **Shropshire**, TF3 2LJ, ENG.
(T) 08707 407566 (F) 08707 407566
(E) lmn@advancedhypnosis.co.uk
(W) www.advancedhypnosis.co.uk
Speciality: Acupuncture, Cognitive Therapy, Counselling, Humanistic Psychology, Hypnosis, Hypnotherapy, Life Style Coaching, Stress Therapy, Auricular Acupuncture. ✔ [credit card]
● **Psychotherapist** Ms L Needham Q: BA, C.Hyp, CMH. M: SAAc.
B C Yrs. Est.: 6 (Ref:HM14751)

**NEEDHAM, P E**

**P E Needham**, 12 South Prde, Northallerton, **Yorkshire (North)**, DL7 8SE, ENG.
(T) 01748 834008
Speciality: Hypnosis.
● **Owner** Mr P Needham
B (Ref:HM14752)

**NEEDLEMAN, DAVID**

**David Needleman**, Cory Pharmcy, 166-168 High Rd, London, **London (Greater)**, N2 9AS, ENG.
(T) 020 8444 9966
Speciality: Homeopathy.
● **Owner** Mr D Needleman
M (Ref:HM14753)

**NEEDS, S J**

**S J Needs**, 39 Rotherslade Rd, Langland, Swansea, SA3 4QW, WAL.
(T) 01792 361449
Speciality: Physiotherapy.
P S T (Ref:HM14754)

**NEELS AROMATHERAPY**

**Neels Aromatherapy**, 54 Greenmarket, Newcastle Upon Tyne, **Tyne and Wear**, NE1 7YA, ENG.
(T) 01912 331199 (F) 01912 331199
Speciality: Aromatherapy. ✔ [credit card]
● **Owner/Aromatherapist** Mrs N Jassal Q: ISPA, MSc. M: IFA.
C Yrs. Est.: 11 (Ref:HM14755)

**NEELY, P**

**P Neely**, 121 Malone Rd, Belfast, **County Antrim**, BT9 6SP, NIR.
(T) 028 9066 0349
Speciality: Physiotherapy.
● **Owner** Mrs P Neely
P S T (Ref:HM14756)

**NEEPHA**

**Neepha Ltd**, 572 Durham Rd, Gateshead, **Tyne and Wear**, NE9 6HX, ENG.
(T) 01914 911808 (F) 01914 871475
Speciality: Physiotherapy.
● **Practice Manager** Mrs S Cramb
P S T (Ref:HM14757)

**NEEPHA**

**Neepha Ltd**, Mercantile House, 10 Lapwing Lane, Manchester, **Manchester (Greater)**, M20 2WS, ENG.
(T) 01614 346664 (F) 01614 345187
Speciality: Physiotherapy.
● **Manager** Miss A Hewitt
P S T (Ref:HM14758)

**NEIJIA**

**Neijia Acupunture**, Boscombe Manor Medical Centre, 40 Florence Rd, Bournemouth, **Dorset**, BH5 1HQ, ENG.
(T) 01202 512394 (F) 01444 811413
(E) neijia@feng-shui-medicine.com
(W) www.feng-shui-medicine.com
Speciality: Acupressure, Acupuncture, Aromatherapy, Cupping, Massage (Therapeutic), Moxibustion, Oriental Diagnosis, T'ai-Chi Ch'uan. ✔
● **Acupunturist** Mr M Edmondson Q: Lic.Ac. M: BAcC.
O Yrs. Est.: 5 (Ref:HM14759)

**NEIL, ERIC G**

**Eric G Neil**, 106 Gunnersbury Avenue, London, **London (Greater)**, W5 4HB, ENG.
(T) 020 8992 4204
Speciality: Osteopathy.
● **Owner** Mr E Neil
P S T (Ref:HM14760)

**NEIL-ASHER, S**

**S Neil-Asher**, 108 Swains Lane, Highgate Village, London, **London (Greater)**, N6 6BS, ENG.
(T) 020 8347 6160 (F) 020 8348 1777
(W) www.frozenshoulder.com
Speciality: Naturopathy, Osteopathy. ✔ [credit card]
● **Osteopath** Mr S Neil-Asher Q: BS, Hons (OST). M: GOsC.
● **Osteopath** Ms M Vizincey-Lambert Q: BSc, Hons (OST). M: GOsC.
● **Osteopath/Naturopath** Efthimi Lazarou Q: BSc, ND.
S Yrs. Est.: 7 (Ref:HM14761)

**NEILL, BOB**

**Bob Neill**, 41 St. Lukes Rd, Maidstone, **Kent**, ME14 5AS, ENG.
(T) 01622 753600
Speciality: Hypnosis.
B (Ref:HM14762)

**NEILL, R**

**R Neill**, 147 Thorne Rd, Doncaster, **Yorkshire (South)**, DN2 5BH, ENG.
(T) 01302 366258
Speciality: Physiotherapy.
● **Owner** Mr R Neill
P S T (Ref:HM14763)

**NEILL, VICTORIA**

**Victoria Neill**, 17 Earlsfield Rd, London, **London (Greater)**, SW18 3DB, ENG.
(T) 020 8874 2895 (F) 020 8870 3205
(E) victoria.neill@btconnect.com
Speciality: Acupressure, Acupuncture, Electrotherapy, Kinesiology, Manipulation, Massage (Therapeutic), Micro Manipulation, Pilates, Postural Integration, Stress Therapy, Ultrasonics, Visualisation Therapy, Relaxation Techniques, Breathing Control, Spinal Mobilisation, Back Care, Manual Handling Training. ✔
● **Physiotherapist** Ms V Neill Q: Dip.Sports.Med, MCSP. M: CSP, MACP, SRP.



Key continued: Yrs.Est: Years Established Q: Qualifications M: Professional Membership ✔ Indemnity Insurance [credit card] Accept Credit Cards

M **Yrs. Est.:** 20 (**Ref:**HM14764)

## NEILL-HIGGINS, CHRISTINA

**Christina Neill-Higgins**, East House, 45 New St, Pudsey, **Yorkshire (West)**, LS28 8PE, ENG.
(T) 01132 040663 (F) 01132 040663
(E) footfiddler@tesco.net
**Speciality:** Homeopathy, Reflexology, Reiki. ✔
● **Complementary Therapist**
Ms C Neill-Higgins Q: Dip.Hom, MBSR, Reiki Master, RGN. M: BSR, GCP, HAR, UKCC.
B M **Yrs. Est.:** 5 (**Ref:**HM14765)

## NEILSEN, R

**R Neilsen**, 13 Thrale Rd, Streatham, London, **London (Greater)**, SW16 1NS, ENG.
(T) 020 8677 3838
**Speciality:** Reflexology.
S T (**Ref:**HM14766)

## NEILSON, J R

**J R Neilson**, 67 Fisher St, Broughty Ferry, Dundee, **Angus**, DD5 1EF, SCO.
(T) 01382 779138
**Speciality:** Psychotherapy.
● **Owner** Mrs J Neilson
B (**Ref:**HM14767)

## NEL, C A

**C A Nel**, 124A The Hundred, Romsey, **Hampshire**, SO51 8BY, ENG.
(T) 01794 514087 (F) 01794 514087
**Speciality:** Chiropodists (Podiatrists).
● **Owner** Mr C Nel
S (**Ref:**HM14768)

## NELLIS, RAYMOND

**Raymond Nellis**, 4 Scalby Avenue, Scarborough, **Yorkshire (North)**, YO12 6HP, ENG.
(T) 01723 366972
**Speciality:** Reflexology.
● **Owner** Mr R Nellis
S T (**Ref:**HM14769)

## NELLIS, S

**S Nellis**, Oakthorpe Rd, Palmers Green, London, **London (Greater)**, N13 5HY, ENG.
(T) 020 8805 5445
**Speciality:** Reflexology.
● **Owner** Mrs S Nellis
S T (**Ref:**HM14770)

## NELMES CHIROPRACTIC CLINIC

**Nelmes Chiropractic Clinic**, 25 St Stephens Lane, Verwood, **Dorset**, BH31 7BQ, ENG.
(T) 01202 823043
**Speciality:** Chiropractic.
● **Director** Mr C Nelmes
P S T (**Ref:**HM14771)

## NELSON, A

**A Nelson & Co Ltd**, 11 Hawkins Way, Bovingdon, Hemel Hempstead, **Hertfordshire**, HP3 0UB, ENG.
(T) 01442 831441 (F) 01442 831295
**Speciality:** Complementary Medicines & Therapy.
● **Manager** Mr C Turner
C M (**Ref:**HM14772)

## NELSON, A

**A Nelson & Co Ltd**, Broadheath House, 83 Wimbledon Park Side, London, **London (Greater)**, SW19 5LP, ENG.
(T) 020 8780 4200 (F) 020 8780 5871
**Speciality:** Complementary Medicines & Therapy.
● **Managing Director** Mr R Wilson
M (**Ref:**HM14773)

## NELSON, ANDREW

**Andrew Nelson Hypnosis & Acupuncture**, 54-56 Moss Rd, Stretford, Manchester, **Manchester (Greater)**, M32 0AY, ENG.
(T) 01618 658640
**Speciality:** Hypnotherapy.
B (**Ref:**HM14774)

## NELSON, CHRIS

**Chris Nelson**, 161 Goosemoor Lane, Birmingham, **Midlands (West)**, B23 5QG, ENG.
(T) 01213 864600 (F) 01213 864600
**Speciality:** Chiropodists (Podiatrists).
● **Owner** Mr C Nelson
S (**Ref:**HM14775)

## NELSON, CHRISTINE

**Christine Nelson**, 1 Bowling Green Lane, Combe Martin, Ilfracombe, **Devon**, EX34 0LG, ENG.
(T) 01271 883724
**Speciality:** Reflexology.
S T (**Ref:**HM14776)

## NELSON, DANIEL

**Daniel Nelson**, St Cross Osteopathic Clinic, 1 Norman Rd, Winchester, **Hampshire**, SO23 9PW, ENG.
(T) 01962 866329
**Speciality:** Osteopathy.
● **Owner** Mr D Nelson
P S T (**Ref:**HM14777)

## NELSON, GAN

**Gan Nelson**, 194 Welling Way, Welling, **Kent**, DA16 2RS, ENG.
(T) 020 8856 1928
**Speciality:** Physiotherapy.
P S T (**Ref:**HM14778)

## NELSON, LISA

**Lisa Nelson**, 114B West Green Rd, London, **London (Greater)**, N15 5AA, ENG.
(T) 020 8800 8819
**Speciality:** Aromatherapy.
● **Owner** Ms L Nelson
M O (**Ref:**HM14779)

## NELSON, PATRICIA

**Patricia Nelson**, 26 Loomsway, Wirral, **Merseyside**, CH61 4UD, ENG.
(T) 01516 483154
**Speciality:** Chiropody. ✔
● **Owner** Mrs P Nelson
M **Yrs. Est.:** 5 (**Ref:**HM14780)

## NELSON, PAUL

**Paul Nelson**, Litchdon Medical Centre, Landkey Rd, Barnstaple, **Devon**, EX32 9LL, ENG.
(T) 01271 323443
**Speciality:** Complementary Therapy, Counselling, Dietician, Hay Diet, Holistic Healing, Homeopathy, Nutritional Therapy, Psychotherapy, Rogerian Therapy, Stress Therapy, Vitamin Therapy. ✔
● **Practitioner/Counsellor**
Mr P Nelson
(T) 01598 710010 Q: MCH, RSHom. M: BACP, Soc.Hom.
H M **Yrs. Est.:** 4 (**Ref:**HM14781)

## NELSON, S

**S Nelson**, 10 Lynfield Rd, Great Harwood, Blackburn, **Lancashire**, BB6 7TS, ENG.
(T) 01254 886108
(W) www.sheilanelson.co.uk
**Speciality:** Bach Remedies, Holistic Healing, Reflexology, Registered in Bach Flower Remedies ✔
● **Owner** Mrs S Nelson Q: ITEC.
C **Yrs. Est.:** 9 (**Ref:**HM14782)

## NELSONS HOM & BACH REMEDIES

**Nelsons Homoeopathy & Bach Remedies**, 73 Duke St, London, **London (Greater)**, W1M 6BY, ENG.
(T) 020 7495 2404
**Speciality:** Homeopathy.
M (**Ref:**HM14783)

## NELSONS HOMOEOPATHIC PHARMACY

**Nelsons Homoeopathic Pharmacy Ltd**, 15 Duke St, Dublin, **County Dublin**, IRE.
(T) 01679 0451 (F) 01679 0457
**Speciality:** Homeopathy.
M (**Ref:**HM14784)

## NENE VALLEY COMP THERAPIES

**Nene Valley Complementary Therapies**, 3 Pytchley Cl, Brixworth, Northampton, **Northamptonshire**, NN6 9EW, ENG.
(T) 01604 881390
**Speciality:** Aromatherapy, Indian Head Massage, Reflexology, Reiki. ✔
● **Holistic Therapist** Mrs L Parrott
C **Yrs. Est.:** 5 (**Ref:**HM14785)

## NERVA, VALERIE

**Valerie Nerva**, Lavinia, Providence Pl, Calstock, **Cornwall**, PL18 9RW, ENG.
(T) 01822 832214
**Speciality:** Hypnosis, Psychotherapy.
B (**Ref:**HM14786)

## NESS, DIEUDONNEE

**Dieudonnee Ness**, Flat 6, Keats House, Churchill Gdns, London, **London (Greater)**, SW1V 3HY, ENG.
(T) 020 7834 6938
**Speciality:** Physiotherapy.
● **Owner** Mrs D Ness
P S T (**Ref:**HM14787)

## NETHERCLIFT, CAROLYN

**Carolyn Netherclift**, 8 Eastgate Sq, Pickering, **Yorkshire (North)**, YO18 7DP, ENG.
(T) 01751 477439
**Speciality:** Acupuncture.
O (**Ref:**HM14788)

## NETHERWAY, JEAN

**Mrs Jean Netherway**, Roots, Higher Westaland, Marldon, Paignton, **Devon**, TQ3 1RR, ENG.
(T) 01803 525447
**Speciality:** Shiatsu. ✔
● **Owner/Shiatsu** Mrs J Netherway Q: MRSS(t).
C **Yrs. Est.:** 7 (**Ref:**HM14789)

## NEUBACHER, SYLVIA

**Sylvia Neubacher**, 2 Pemberton Rd, East Molesey, **Surrey**, KT8 9LH, ENG.
(T) 020 8941 4334
**Speciality:** Homeopathy.
M (**Ref:**HM14790)

## NEUBERT, CHRISTINA

**Christina Neubert**, Harriers, Hunters Way, Chichester, **Sussex (West)**, PO19 4RB, ENG.
(T) 01243 527827
**Speciality:** Physiotherapy.
P S T (**Ref:**HM14791)

## NEUDEGG, KENNETH

**Kenneth Neudegg**, 14 Langdon Shaw, Sidcup, **Kent**, DA14 6AU, ENG.
(T) 020 8302 6696
**Speciality:** Reflexology.
S T (**Ref:**HM14792)

## NEUFELDT, BEATRICE (DR)

**Neufeldt Dr Beatrice Psychosomatic Medici**, Ballina, **County Mayo**, IRE.
(T) 06137 6301
**Speciality:** Complementary Medicines & Therapy.
M (**Ref:**HM14793)

## NEURO PHYSIOTHERAPY

**Neuro Physiotherapy**, 4 St Helens Lane, Leeds, **Yorkshire (West)**, LS16 8AB, ENG.
(T) 01132 676365
**Speciality:** Physiotherapy.
● **Owner** Mrs J Fisher
P S T (**Ref:**HM14794)

## NEURURER, MARIANNA

**Marianna Neururer**, 75A Choumert Rd, Peckham Rye, London, **London (Greater)**, SE15 4AR, ENG.
(T) 020 7635 9137
**Speciality:** Alexander Technique.
● **Owner** Mrs M Neururer
P S (**Ref:**HM14795)

## NEVER FELT BETTER

**Never Felt Better**, 25 Catherine Ford Rd, Dinton, Salisbury, **Wiltshire**, SP3 5HB, ENG.
(T) 01722 716110
**Speciality:** Complementary Medicines & Therapy.
● **Partner** Miss S Gibb
M (**Ref:**HM14796)

## NEVIES, ALAN

**Alan Nevies**, 44 Hoop Lane, London, **London (Greater)**, NW11 7NH, ENG.
(T) 020 8458 3874
**Speciality:** Osteopathy.
● **Owner** Mr A Nevies
P S T (**Ref:**HM14797)



Key: B Mind-Body Medicine | C Complementary Medicine | H Self Help Treatment | M Medicinal Therapy | O Oriental Medicine | P Postural Therapy | S Manipulative Structural Therapy | T Touch Therapy

**NEVILLE, PAMELA**

**Pamela Neville**, 26 Dunbottle Lane, Mirfield, **Yorkshire (West)**, WF14 9JJ, ENG.
(T) 01924 495446
Speciality: Hypnotherapy.
● **Owner** Mrs P Neville
B (Ref:HM14798)

**NEVILLE, PAMELA**

**Pamela Neville**, 4 Town Hall St, Mirfield, **Yorkshire (West)**, WF14 8DH, ENG.
(T) 01924 495446
Speciality: Hypnosis.
● **Owner** Mrs M Scott
B (Ref:HM14799)

**NEVILLE-TOWLE, E**

**E Neville-Towle**, 353 Upper Richmond Rd, London, **London (Greater)**, SW15 5QJ, ENG.
(T) 020 8876 2998
Speciality: Physiotherapy.
P S T (Ref:HM14800)

**NEVILLE-TOWLE, V**

**V Neville-Towle**, 35 Downshire Sq, Reading, **Berkshire**, RG1 6NH, ENG.
(T) 01189 573440
Speciality: Osteopathy.
● **Owner** Mr V Neville-Towle
P S T (Ref:HM14801)

**NEVIN, ANTHONY**

**Anthony Nevin**, The Old Convent, Beeches Green, Stroud, **Gloucestershire**, GL5 4AD, ENG.
(T) 01453 766394
Speciality: Osteopathy.
P S T (Ref:HM14802)

**NEVIN, ANTHONY R**

**Anthony R Nevin**, The Vineyard, Berkeley St, Cheltenham, **Gloucestershire**, GL52 2SX, ENG.
(T) 01242 221153
Speciality: Osteopathy.
P S T (Ref:HM14803)

**NEVITT, NEIL**

**Neil Nevitt**, 183 Queens Drive, Wavertree, Liverpool, **Merseyside**, L15 6XU, ENG.
(T) 01517 223840
Speciality: Chiropodists (Podiatrists).
● **Owner** Mr N Nevitt
S (Ref:HM14804)

**NEW AGE FOUNDATION**

**New Age Foundation (The)**, 61 Collier St, London, **London (Greater)**, N1 9BE, ENG.
(T) 020 7713 7122
Speciality: Complementary Medicines & Therapy.
C M (Ref:HM14805)

**NEW AGE HOLISTIC & MASSAGE**

**New Age Holistic & Massage**, Apt 4 Phoenix Vw James St, Dublin, **County Dublin**, IRE.
(T) 01454 9373
Speciality: Complementary Medicines & Therapy.
M (Ref:HM14806)

**NEW AVALONIA DESIGNS**

**New Avalonia Designs**, Wellhouse Lane, Glastonbury, **Somerset**, BA6 8BJ, ENG.
(T) 01458 834214
Speciality: Complementary Medicines & Therapy.
C M (Ref:HM14807)

**NEW BEGINNINGS**

**New Beginnings**, 87 Gloucester Rd, Bishopston, Bristol, BS7 8AS, ENG.
(T) 01179 075884
Speciality: Complementary Medicines & Therapy.
● **Owner** Ms B Tyrrell
M (Ref:HM14808)

**NEW BEGINNINGS**

**New Beginnings**, 3 Weavers Court, Linfield Rd, Belfast, **County Antrim**, BT12 5NS, NIR.
(T) 028 9022 4008
Speciality: Hypnosis.
B (Ref:HM14809)

**NEW BEGINNINGS**

**New Beginnings**, Little Trees Cottage Cortober, Carrick-on-Shannon, **County Leitrim**, IRE.
(T) 07821 451
Speciality: Complementary Medicines & Therapy.
M (Ref:HM14810)

**NEW BEGINNINGS HYPNOTHERAPY**

**New Beginnings Hypnotherapy Clinic**, Drim Rd, Glencolumbcille, **County Donegal**, IRE.
(T) 07330 311
Speciality: Hypnotherapy.
B (Ref:HM14811)

**NEW BROOK OILS**

**New Brook Oils**, Nuthurst Rd, Maplehurst, Horsham, **Sussex (West)**, RH13 6RB, ENG.
(T) 01403 864879 (F) 01403 864879
Speciality: Aromatherapy.
● **Owner** Mrs D Phillips
M O (Ref:HM14812)

**NEW CONTEMPORARY AROMATHERAPY**

**New Contemporary Aromatherapy**, 171A Kings Rd, Cardiff, **Glamorgan (Vale of)**, CF11 9DE, WAL.
(T) 029 2033 1256
Speciality: Aromatherapy.
● **Owner** Ms N Marchant
M O (Ref:HM14813)

**NEW CROSS NATURAL THRPY CTRE**

**New Cross Natural Therapy Centre Ltd**, 394 New Cross Rd, London, **London (Greater)**, SE14 6TY, ENG.
(T) 020 8469 0858
(E) michael@yogaturkey.co.uk
Speciality: Acupuncture, Alexander Technique, Aromatherapy, Chiropractic, Complementary Therapy, Counselling, Cranial Osteopathy, Cranio-Sacral Therapy, Feldenkrais Methodology, Gestalt Therapy, Group Therapy, Healer, Homeopathy, Kinesiology, Massage (Therapeutic), Nutritional Therapy, Osteopathy, Postural Integration, Psychotherapy, Reflexology, Reiki, Shiatsu.
● **Director** Mr M Cullingworth Q: MRSS. M: Shiatsu Society UK.
C Yrs. Est.: 25 (Ref:HM14814)

**NEW DAY NATURAL THERAPY CTRE**

**New Day Natural Therapy Centre**, Castle Moat Chambers, Bath Pl, Taunton, **Somerset**, TA1 4EP, ENG.
(T) 01823 325365
Speciality: Complementary Medicines & Therapy.
● **Owner** Mrs W Stark
C M (Ref:HM14815)

**NEW DIRECTIONS**

**New Directions**, 13 Barker Rd, Middlesbrough, **Cleveland**, TS5 5EW, ENG.
(T) 01642 821254
Speciality: Psychotherapy.
● **Owner** Mr D Midgley
B (Ref:HM14816)

**NEW DUNDAS CLINIC**

**New Dundas Clinic**, Lothian St, Bonnyrigg Rose F.C., Bonnyrigg, **Lothian (Mid)**, EH19 3AE, SCO.
(T) 01316 633331
Speciality: Acupressure, Cupping, Electrotherapy, Magnetic Therapy, Manipulation, Massage (Therapeutic). ✓
● **Sports Physiotherapist** K McIvor Q: LVMC, MSST. M: SMTO.
S Yrs. Est.: 6 (Ref:HM14817)

**NEW HORIZON AROMATICS**

**New Horizon Aromatics**, 44 Queens Way, Southampton, **Hampshire**, SO14 3GT, ENG.
(T) 023 8039 9664
Speciality: Aromatherapy.
● **Owner** Mr C Ockendon
M O (Ref:HM14818)

**NEW IMAGE SELF-HEALTH CLINIC**

**New Image Self-Health Clinic**, 46 Lambs Conduit St, London, **London (Greater)**, WC1N 3LJ, ENG.
(T) 020 7404 2500 (F) 020 7404 3312
Speciality: Complementary Medicines & Therapy.
● **Owner** Miss J Parekh
C M (Ref:HM14819)

**NEW LIFE NATURAL HEALTH CARE**

**New Life Trust**, 27 Northumberland Sq, North Shields, **Tyne and Wear**, NE30 1PW, ENG.
(T) 01912 960026 (F) 01912 578713
(E) newlifetrust@lineone.net
Speciality: Aromatherapy, Art Therapy, Bach Remedies, Bowen Therapy, Chiropractic, Clinical Ecology, Complementary Therapy, Counselling, Herbal Medicine, Holistic Healing, Homeopathy, Indian Head Massage, Kinesiology, Manipulation, Massage (Therapeutic), Miasm Therapy, Naturopathy, Nutritional Therapy, Pilates, Reflexology, Lymphatic Drainage. ✓
● **Director/Consultant Homeopathy** Annie Gray Q: MNCHM, RSHom. M: Soc.Hom.
C M Yrs. Est.: 6 (Ref:HM14820)

**NEW LIFE NATURAL HEALTH CARE**

**New Life Products Ltd**, 20 Green Lane, Poynton, Stockport, **Cheshire**, SK12 1TJ, ENG.
(T) 01625 850994 (F) 01625 850605
Speciality: Aromatherapy, Art Therapy, Bach Remedies, Bowen Therapy, Chiropractic, Clinical Ecology, Complementary Therapy, Counselling, Herbal Medicine, Holistic Healing, Homeopathy, Indian Head Massage, Kinesiology, Manipulation, Massage (Therapeutic), Miasm Therapy, Naturopathy, Nutritional Therapy, Pilates, Reflexology, Lymphatic Drainage. ✓
● **Managing Director** Mr B Johnson
M Yrs. Est.: 6 (Ref:HM14821)

**NEW LIFE NATURAL HEALTH CENTRE**

**New Life Natural Health Centre**, 3 St Mary St, Cardiff, **Glamorgan (Vale of)**, CF10 1AT, WAL.
(T) 029 2025 1071
Speciality: Complementary Medicines & Therapy.
● **Director** Mr K Bowles
M (Ref:HM14822)

**NEW MAGICK**

**New Magick Co Ltd**, 3-7 Temple Avenue, London, **London (Greater)**, EC4Y 0HP, ENG.
(T) 020 7583 6336
Speciality: Relaxation Technique.
● **Managing Director** Mr L Alexander
H T (Ref:HM14823)

**NEW MARKET RD PHYSIO PRACTICE**

**New Market Road Physiotherapy Practice**, 79 New Market Rd, Norwich, **Norfolk**, NR2 2HW, ENG.
(T) 01603 625959 (F) 01603 625959
Speciality: Acupuncture, Physiotherapy. ✓
● **Practice Manager** Jill Tubby
● **Physiotherapist** Patrica Phillips Q: MCSP, SRP.
● **Physiotherapist** Jane Bevington Q: MCSP, SRP.
● **Physiotherapist** Alexandra Martin Q: MCSP, SRP.
S Yrs. Est.: 10 (Ref:HM14824)

**NEW MILTON CHIROPRACTIC CLINIC**

**New Milton Chiropractic Clinic**, 13A Whitefield Rd, New Milton, **Hampshire**, BH25 6DE, ENG.
(T) 01425 620222
(E) jonandjane@madasafish.com
Speciality: Acupuncture, Chiropractic, Complementary Therapy, Hay Diet, Manipulation, Massage (Therapeutic), Micro Manipulation, Nutritional Therapy, Reflexology, Vitamin Therapy, X-Ray, Spinal Rehabilitation Therapy. ✓
● **Chiropractor** Mr J Melhuish Q: BSc (Chiro), CCEP, DC, MCC. M: BCA.
● **Chiropractor** Mr N Hudson-Cook Q: BCA, DC.
P S Yrs. Est.: 20 (Ref:HM14825)

**NEW OXFORD HOUSE CLINICS**

**New Oxford House Clinics**, 5a Cheapside, Reading, **Berkshire**, RG1 7AG, ENG.
(T) 01189 391361
Speciality: Osteopathy.
● **Owner** Mr R Pearcey
M (Ref:HM14826)

**NEW PINES PRIVATE NURSING HOME**

**New Pines Private Nursing Home (The)**, 1



Key continued: Yrs.Est: Years Established Q: Qualifications M: Professional Membership ✓ Indemnity Insurance Accept Credit Cards

Station Rd, Wesham, Preston, **Lancashire**, PR4 3AA, ENG.
(T) 01772 686343
Speciality: Physiotherapy.
P S T (Ref:HM14827)

## NEW POSSIBILITIES NHS TRUST
**New Possibilities NHS Trust**, Clinical Psychology Service, 114 Ipswich Rd, Colchester, **Essex**, CO4 4AA, ENG.
(T) 01206 864198
Speciality: Psychology.
B (Ref:HM14828)

## NEW ROAD NATURAL HEALTH CLINIC
**New Road Natural Health Clinic**, 128 New Rd, Portsmouth, **Hampshire**, PO2 7RJ, ENG.
(T) 023 9282 8998
Speciality: Chiropodists (Podiatrists).
● **Practice Manager** Mr J Preston
S (Ref:HM14829)

## NEW ROAD SPORT & REMEDIAL
**New Road Sport & Remedial Massage Clinic**, New Rd, Halifax, **Yorkshire (West)**, HX1 2LH, ENG.
(T) 01422 253996
Speciality: Complementary Medicines & Therapy.
● **Owner** Mrs J Pilling
M (Ref:HM14830)

## NEW ROCK HEALING ARTS CENTRE
**New Rock Healing Arts Centre**, Kempley Rd, Dymock, **Gloucestershire**, GL18 2BB, ENG.
(T) 01531 890366
Speciality: Complementary Medicines & Therapy.
● **Principal** Mr G Dinnen
C M (Ref:HM14831)

## NEW SEASONS
**New Seasons**, The Old Post Office, Lockinge, Wantage, **Oxfordshire**, OX12 8PA, ENG.
(T) 01235 835133 (F) 01235 834294
Speciality: Aromatherapy.
● **Partner** Mrs A Breakspeare
M O (Ref:HM14832)

## NEW SILHOUETTE
**New Silhouette**, 265 Main Rd, Sidcup, **Kent**, DA14 6QL, ENG.
(T) 020 8308 0715
Speciality: Complementary Medicines & Therapy.
● **Manager** Susanne Prentice
M (Ref:HM14833)

## NEW SNEDDON STREET CLINIC
**New Sneddon Street Clinic**, 8 New Sneddon St, Paisley, **Renfrewshire**, PA3 2AD, SCO.
(T) 01418 877771
Speciality: Chiropodists (Podiatrists).
S (Ref:HM14834)

## NEW SPIRIT NATURALS
**New Spirit Naturals Ltd**, Sandy Lane, Wokingham, **Berkshire**, RG41 4DB, ENG.
(T) 01189 892511
(W) www.newspirit.com
Speciality: Herbal Medicine.
● **Operations Manager** Mrs B Adcock
C (Ref:HM14835)

## NEW VICTORIA HOSPITAL
**New Victoria Hospital**, 184 Coombe La West, Kingston Upon Thames, **Surrey**, KT2 7EG, ENG.
(T) 020 8949 9000
Speciality: Physiotherapy.
P S T (Ref:HM14836)

## NEW VISTAS HEALTHCARE
**New Vistas Healthcare Ltd**, Plassey Technological Pk, **County Limerick**, IRE.
(T) 06133 4455
(E) newvista@iol.ie
Speciality: Homeopathy.
M (Ref:HM14837)

## NEW WEALDEN CLINIC
**New Wealden Clinic**, 1 Clayfield Mews, Newcomen Rd, Tunbridge Wells, **Kent**, TN4 9PA, ENG.
(T) 01892 545443
Speciality: Complementary Medicines & Therapy.
● **Therapist** Ms F Horsfield
M (Ref:HM14838)

## NEW, G S
**G S New**, 10 Waterlakes, Edenbridge, **Kent**, TN8 5BX, ENG.
(T) 01732 862738
Speciality: Physiotherapy.
P S T (Ref:HM14839)

## NEWALL, K
**K Newall**, The John Wright Sports Centre, Calderwood Rd, East Kilbride, Glasgow, **Glasgow (City of)**, G74 3EU, SCO.
(T) 01355 279068
Speciality: Aromatherapy.
● **Owner** Mrs K Newall
M O (Ref:HM14840)

## NEWARK CHIROPRACTIC CLINIC
**Newark Chiropractic Clinic**, 30 Castle Gate, Newark, **Nottinghamshire**, NG24 1BG, ENG.
(T) 01636 605815
Speciality: Chiropractic.
● **Owner** Mr R Banker
P S T (Ref:HM14841)

## NEWARK OSTEOPATHIC CLINIC
**Newark Osteopathic Clinic**, 64 Harcourt St, Newark, **Nottinghamshire**, NG24 1RF, ENG.
(T) 01636 611644
Speciality: Osteopathy.
● **Principal** Mr J Nissim
P S T (Ref:HM14842)

## NEWARK PHYSIOTHERAPY CLINIC
**Newark Physiotherapy Clinic**, 2 Carter Gate, Newark, **Nottinghamshire**, NG24 1UB, ENG.
(T) 01636 610142 (F) 01636 610142
Speciality: Physiotherapy.
● **Owner** Mr M Wilson
P S T (Ref:HM14843)

## NEWAYS INDEPENDENT CONSULTANT
**Neways Independent Consultant**, 1 Kilberry St, Dundee, **Angus**, DD3 6DE, SCO.
(T) 01382 644410
Speciality: Holistic Healing, Vitamin Therapy.
M (Ref:HM14844)

## NEWBERRY, JOHN L
**John L Newberry**, 72 Cotterells, Hemel Hempstead, **Hertfordshire**, HP1 1JG, ENG.
(T) 01442 255098
Speciality: Chiropodists (Podiatrists).
● **Owner** Mr J Newberry
S (Ref:HM14845)

## NEWBERRY, JOYCE
**Joyce Newberry**, 9 North Rd, West Wickham, **Kent**, BR4 0JS, ENG.
(T) 020 8776 0964
Speciality: Complementary Medicines & Therapy.
M (Ref:HM14846)

## NEWBOLD CHIROPODY CENTRE
**Newbold Chiropody Centre**, Newbold Surgery, 3 Windermere Rd, Chesterfield, **Derbyshire**, S41 8DU, ENG.
(T) 01246 277381
Speciality: Chiropodists (Podiatrists).
● **Manager** Mrs M Murphy
S (Ref:HM14847)

## NEWBOLD, A G
**A G Newbold**, 34 Browsfield Rd, Addingham, Ilkley, **Yorkshire (West)**, LS29 0TF, ENG.
(T) 01943 830714
Speciality: Chiropodists (Podiatrists).
● **Owner** Mr A Newbold
S (Ref:HM14848)

## NEWBON, B
**B Newbon**, 91 Millfield Rd, West Kingsdown, Sevenoaks, **Kent**, TN15 6BX, ENG.
(T) 01474 853611 (F) 01474 853611
Speciality: Physiotherapy.
● **Owner** Mrs B Newbon
P S T (Ref:HM14849)

## NEWBRIDGE PHARMACY
**Kiddem Ltd**, 325 Tettenhall Rd, Newbridge, Wolverhampton, **Midlands (West)**, WV6 0JZ, ENG.
(T) 01902 752868 (F) 01902 752868
(E) dmillard@supanet.com
Speciality: Acupuncture, Anthroposohical Medicine, Aromatherapy, Bach Remedies, Bowen Therapy, Complementary Therapy, Electrotherapy, Herbal Medicine, Homeopathy, Indian Head Massage, Nutritional Therapy, Reflexology, Ultrasonics. ✔
● **Acupuncturist** Mr D Millard
(T) 01926 491689 Q: Lic.Ac. M: BAcC.
● **Reflexologist/Aromatherapist** Ms S Jones Q: Dip.Arom, Dip.Indian Head Massage, Dip.Reflex. M: AoR, ISPA.
● **Physiotherapist/Bowen Therapist** Ms S Lewis Q: BTER, MCSP. M: BTER, CSP.
● **Manager** Mr A Lewis Q: B.Pharm, LCPH, M.R.Pharm.S, MHMA. M: HMA.
C Yrs. Est.: 6 (Ref:HM14850)

## NEWBURY CHIROPRACTIC CENTRE
**Newbury Chiropractic Centre**, 6 Cheap St, Newbury, **Berkshire**, RG14 5DD, ENG.
(T) 01635 48088
Speciality: Chiropractic.
● **Owner** Dr B Norton Q: BCA, DC.
P Yrs. Est.: 10 (Ref:HM14851)

## NEWBURY PHYSIOTHERAPY
**Newbury Physiotherapy**, 73 Enborne Rd, Newbury, **Berkshire**, RG14 6AP, ENG.
(T) 01635 44882
Speciality: Acupuncture, Physiotherapy. ✔
● **Physiotherapist** Ms M Jones Q: MCSP, SRP. M: CSP.
● **Physiotherapist** Ms S Smith Q: MCSP, SRP. M: CSP.
● **Physiotherapist** Ms K Donato Q: MCSP, RGRT, SRP. M: CSP.
S (Ref:HM14852)

## NEWBURY PRACTICE
**Newbury Practice Of Natural Therapy**, St. Marys House, 55-56 Cheap St, Newbury, **Berkshire**, RG14 5DH, ENG.
(T) 01635 30252
Speciality: Osteopathy.
P S T (Ref:HM14853)

## NEWCASTLE CLINIC
**Newcastle Clinic (The)**, 52 Mitchell Avenue, Newcastle Upon Tyne, **Tyne and Wear**, NE2 3LA, ENG.
(T) 01912 810193
Speciality: Osteopathy.
P S T (Ref:HM14854)

## NEWCASTLE SPRTS INJ/THRPY CTRE
**Newcastle Sports Injury Clinic & Therapy Centre**, The City Pool, Northumberland Rd, Newcastle Upon Tyne, **Tyne and Wear**, NE1 8SE, ENG.
(T) 01912 330500 (F) 01912 116249
Speciality: Acupuncture, Chiropody, Physiotherapy, Remedial Massage, Chi-Kung, Tuina Massage. ✔
● **Physiotherapist** Ms F Ritson Q: MCSP, SRP. M: CSP.
● **Chiropodist** Ms A Lynagh Q: Grad.Dip.Pod, S.R.Ch.
● **Owner/Physiotherapist** Mrs K Dearden Q: MCSP, SRP. M: CSP.
● **Physiotherapist** Mr D Deas Q: MCSP, SRP. M: CSP.
● **Physiotherapist** Ms K Parry Q: MCSP, SRP. M: CSP.
S Yrs. Est.: 5 (Ref:HM14855)

## NEWCASTLE/NE TRANS MEDITA CTRE
**Local Association of the Maharishi Foundation Education**, Maharishi Vedic Centre, 27 South Trce, Esh Winning, Durham, **County Durham**, DH7 9PR, ENG.
(T) 01913 732000
(E) meditation@ne-england.freeserve.co.uk
(W) www.t-m.org.uk
Speciality: Ayurvedic Medicine, Herbal Medicine, Meditation, Stress Therapy, Transcendental Meditation. ✔
● **Chairman** Mr P Kember
● **TM Teacher** Ms J Kember



Key: B Mind-Body Medicine, C Complementary Medicine, H Self Help Treatment, M Medicinal Therapy, O Oriental Medicine, P Postural Therapy, S Manipulative Structural Therapy, T Touch Therapy

B Yrs. Est.: 5 (Ref:HM14856)

## NEWCOMBE-JONES, ELAINE

**Elaine Newcombe-Jones**, 41A Great Pulteney St, Bath, **Somerset**, BA2 4DP, ENG.
(T) 01225 464420
Speciality: Reflexology.
S T (Ref:HM14857)

## NEWCOME, ROBERT

**Robert Newcome**, 31 Ray Park Avenue, Maidenhead, **Berkshire**, SL6 8DZ, ENG.
(T) 01628 671146 (F) 01628 671146
Speciality: Hypnosis.
● **Owner** Mr R Newcome
B (Ref:HM14858)

## NEWELL, A J

**A J Newell**, 166 Old Bedford Rd, Luton, **Bedfordshire**, LU2 7HN, ENG.
(T) 01582 734080
Speciality: Complementary Medicines & Therapy.
C M (Ref:HM14859)

## NEWELL, JOHN

**John Newell**, 55 Market St, Ashby-de-la-Zouch, **Leicestershire**, LE65 1AH, ENG.
(T) 01530 412281
Speciality: Osteopathy.
● **Owner** Mr J Newell
M (Ref:HM14860)

## NEWELL, JOHN

**John Newell**, Abbots Hill Chambers, Gower St, Derby, **Derbyshire**, DE1 1SD, ENG.
(T) 01332 368195
Speciality: Osteopathy.
P S T (Ref:HM14861)

## NEWEY, RACHEL

**Rachel Newey**, Hill House, 2 Hawksworth Drive, Kenilworth, **Warwickshire**, CV8 2GP, ENG.
(T) 01926 854094
Speciality: Chiropractic, Reiki. ✔
● **Chiropractor** Mrs R Newey Q: DC, GCC (Reg), MCC, MMCA. M: GCC, MCA.
S Yrs. Est.: 6 (Ref:HM14862)

## NEWHAM, DAVID

**David Newham**, 12 St. Helens Park Rd, Hastings, **Sussex (East)**, TN34 2ER, ENG.
(T) 01424 430516
Speciality: Reflexology.
S T (Ref:HM14863)

## NEWHAVEN OSTEOPATHIC CLINIC

**Newhaven Osteopathic Clinic (The)**, 65 Brighton Rd, Newhaven, **Sussex (East)**, BN9 9NG, ENG.
(T) 01273 611474
Speciality: Osteopathy.
P S T (Ref:HM14864)

## NEWICK PHYSIOTHERAPY CLINIC

**Newick Physiotherapy Clinic**, 1 Newick Hill, Newick, Lewes, **Sussex (East)**, BN8 4QR, ENG.
(T) 01825 721000 (F) 01825 721000
Speciality: Acupuncture, Physiotherapy. ✔
● **Owner/Physiotherapist** Mrs J Laidlaw Q: MCSP, SRP. M: CSP.
S Yrs. Est.: 2 (Ref:HM14865)

## NEWLAND CHIROPRACTIC CLINIC

**Newland Chiropractic Clinic**, 82 Newland, St James Trce, Lincoln, **Lincolnshire**, LN1 1YA, ENG.
(T) 01522 538450 (F) 01522 538450
Speciality: Chiropractic, Manipulation, Massage (Therapeutic), X-Ray. ✔
● **Chiropractor** Mr D Clark Q: BSc (Chiro), DC. M: BCA.
● **Chiropractor** Ms A Hensman Q: BSc (Hons), MSc (Chiro). M: BCA.
● **Chiropractor** Mr D Barnes-Heath Q: BSc, CCEP, DC. M: BCA.
S Yrs. Est.: 3 (Ref:HM14866)

## NEWLANDS INSTITUTE FOR

**Newlands Institute For**, 2 Monastery Rd, Clondalkin, **County Dublin**, IRE.
(T) 01459 4573
Speciality: Complementary Medicines & Therapy.
M (Ref:HM14867)

## NEWLANDS PARK NTRL HEALTHCARE

**Newlands Park Natural Healthcare Centre**, 48 Newlands Park, London, **London (Greater)**, SE26 5NE, ENG.
(T) 020 8659 5001
Speciality: Homeopathy.
M (Ref:HM14868)

## NEWLIFE, A

**A Newlife**, 19 Devon Way, Harwich, **Essex**, CO12 4RB, ENG.
(T) 01255 502302 (F) 01255 502023
Speciality: Complementary Medicines & Therapy.
● **Manager** Mr M Davison
M (Ref:HM14869)

## NEWMAN, BARBARA

**Barbara Newman**, 25 Pastern Pl, Downs Barn, Milton Keynes, **Buckinghamshire**, MK14 7RB, ENG.
(T) 01908 397069
(W) www.complementary-healthcare.co.uk/info/newman
Speciality: Reflexology, Reiki.
S T (Ref:HM14870)

## NEWMAN, JANE

**Jane Newman**, 5 Elm Trce, Constantine Rd, London, **London (Greater)**, NW3 2LL, ENG.
(T) 020 7267 4222
Speciality: Physiotherapy.
● **Owner** Ms J Newman
P S T (Ref:HM14871)

## NEWMAN, M A

**M A Newman**, 112 Toms Lane, Kings Langley, **Hertfordshire**, WD4 8NR, ENG.
(T) 01923 265315
Speciality: Physiotherapy.
P S T (Ref:HM14872)

## NEWMAN, SOGRA

**Sogra Newman**, The Old Rectory, Old Rectory Lane, Rivenhall, Witham, **Essex**, CM8 3HJ, ENG.
(T) 01376 517004
Speciality: Osteopathy.
P S T (Ref:HM14873)

## NEWMAN, TANYA

**Tanya Newman**, 18 The Avenue, Bromley, **Kent**, BR1 2BT, ENG.
(T) 020 8460 1646
Speciality: Osteopathy.
P S T (Ref:HM14874)

## NEWMAN, TURNER R

**Turner R Newman**, Letchworth Natural Therapy Clinic, 111 Norton Way South, Letchworth, **Hertfordshire**, SG6 1NY, ENG.
(T) 01462 684232
Speciality: Osteopathy.
P S T (Ref:HM14875)

## NEWMARK, JOSPEHINE

**Josephine Newmark**, 18 Caythorpe Rd, Leeds, **Yorkshire (West)**, LS16 5HW, ENG.
(T) 01132 755576
Speciality: Alexander Technique.
● **Owner** Mrs J Newmark
P S (Ref:HM14876)

## NEWMARKET CHIROPRACTIC CLINIC

**Newmarket Chiropractic Clinic**, 1 High St, Newmarket, **Suffolk**, CB8 8LX, ENG.
(T) 01638 665858
Speciality: Chiropractic.
P S T (Ref:HM14877)

## NEWNS, DAVID

**David Newns**, 110 Waterloo Rd, Uxbridge, **London (Greater)**, UB8 2QY, ENG.
(T) 01895 467046
Speciality: Psychotherapy.
B (Ref:HM14878)

## NEWPORT ACUPUNCTURE CLINIC

**Newport Acupuncture Clinic**, 6a Union St, Newport Pagnell, **Buckinghamshire**, MK16 8ET, ENG.
(T) 01908 216637
Speciality: Acupuncture.
O (Ref:HM14879)

## NEWPORT CHIROPRACTIC CLINIC

**Newport Chiropractic Clinic**, Albany Chambers, Skinner St, Newport, NP20 1HD, WAL.
(T) 01633 243533
Speciality: Chiropractic.
P S T (Ref:HM14880)

## NEWPORT POWER & LIGHTING

**Newport Power & Lighting**, P O Box 248, Mill St, Newport, NP9 2YT, WAL.
(T) 01633 275566 (F) 01633 275665
Speciality: Electrolysis.
● **Owner** Mr A Parsons
T (Ref:HM14881)

## NEWPORT, JANE

**Jane Newport**, Wisucote, Bristol Rd, Wraxall, **Somerset**, BS48 1LE, ENG.
(T) 01275 858865
Speciality: Complementary Medicines & Therapy.
● **Owner** Jane Newport
M (Ref:HM14882)

## NEWQUAY CHIROPRACTIC CLINIC

**Newquay Chiropractic Clinic**, 1 Chester Rd, Newquay, **Cornwall**, TR7 2RT, ENG.
(T) 01637 878788 (F) 01637 878788
Speciality: Acupuncture, Aromatherapy, Chiropractic, Complementary Therapy, Herbal Medicine, Homeopathy, Indian Head Massage, Kinesiology, Manipulation, Massage (Therapeutic), Moxibustion, Nutritional Therapy, Reflexology, Shiatsu. ✔
● **Chiropractor** Mr M Noone Q: BSc (Chiro), DC. M: BCA, GCC.
S Yrs. Est.: 5 (Ref:HM14883)

## NEWQUAY FOOT CLINIC

**Newquay Foot Clinic (The)**, The Surgery, Chapel Hill, Newquay, **Cornwall**, TR7 1ND, ENG.
(T) 01637 880968 (F) 01637 880968
Speciality: Chiropodists (Podiatrists).
● **Owner** Mr R Goulding
S (Ref:HM14884)

## NEWQUAY PHYSIOTHERAPY CENTRE

**Newquay Physiotherapy Centre**, 12A St Thomas Rd, Newquay, **Cornwall**, TR7 1RS, ENG.
(T) 01637 852500 (F) 01637 852500
Speciality: Physiotherapy.
● **Manager** Mr G Gilchrist
P S T (Ref:HM14885)

## NEWRY CHIROPRACTIC CLINIC

**Newry Chiropractic Clinic**, 36 Merchants Quay, Newry, **County Down**, BT35 8HF, NIR.
(T) 028 3026 6166
Speciality: Chiropractic. ✔
● **Chiropractor** Dr T Tuira Q: BSc, DC.
● **Manager** Mrs B Mallon
P Yrs. Est.: 7 (Ref:HM14886)

## NEWRY CHIROPRACTIC CLINIC

**Newry Chiropractic Clinic**, 37A Thomas St, Armagh, IRE.
(T) 04851 1955
Speciality: Chiropractors.
P S T (Ref:HM14887)

## NEWRY CHIROPRACTIC CLINIC

**Newry Chiropractic Clinic**, 122 Upr Lisburn Rd, Belfast, IRE.
(T) 04860 4294
Speciality: Chiropractors.
P S T (Ref:HM14888)

## NEWSHAM ASS URMSTON REMEDIAL

**Newsham Associates Urmston Remedial Clinic**, 6 Church Rd, Urmston, Manchester, **Manchester (Greater)**, M41 9BU, ENG.
(T) 01617 553993
Speciality: Osteopathy.
P S T (Ref:HM14889)

## NEWSHAM, R W

**R W Newsham**, 2 Knowlys Rd, Heysham, Morecambe, **Lancashire**, LA3 2PE, ENG.
(T) 01524 852244
Speciality: Chiropodists (Podiatrists).
● **Owner** Mr R Newsham
S (Ref:HM14890)



Key continued: **Yrs.Est:** Years Established **Q:** Qualifications **M:** Professional Membership ✔ Indemnity Insurance Accept Credit Cards

### NEWSOM-DAVIS, R
**R Newsom-Davis**, London Medical Centre, 144 Harley St, London, **London (Greater)**, W1N 1AH, ENG.
(T) 020 7935 0023 (F) 020 7935 5972
Speciality: Psychology.
● **Manager** Mr P Gainsborough
B (Ref:HM14891)

### NEWTON CLINIC
**Newton Clinic**, 1a East Churchfield Rd, London, **London (Greater)**, W3 7LL, ENG.
(T) 020 8749 3799
Speciality: Hypnosis.
● **Owner** Mrs S Newton
B (Ref:HM14892)

### NEWTON HOUSE
**Newton House**, Newton Lane, Lower Whitley, Warrington, **Cheshire**, WA4 4JA, ENG.
(T) 01925 730527
Speciality: Acupuncture.
O (Ref:HM14893)

### NEWTON, A C
**A C Newton**, Hollybank, Kingsland, Leominster, **Herefordshire**, HR6 9SE, ENG.
(T) 01568 709005
Speciality: Physiotherapy.
● **Owner** A C Newton
P S T (Ref:HM14894)

### NEWTON, C
**C Newton**, 2-4 High St, Glastonbury, **Somerset**, BA6 9DU, ENG.
(T) 01458 833317
Speciality: Chiropractors.
P S T (Ref:HM14895)

### NEWTON, DON
**Don Newton**, Consulting Rooms, 1 Station Rd, Okehampton, **Devon**, EX20 1ED, ENG.
(T) 01837 53972
Speciality: Osteopathy.
P S T (Ref:HM14896)

### NEWTON, J
**J Newton**, 515 Coopers Building, Church St, Liverpool, **Merseyside**, L1 3AA, ENG.
(T) 01517 099154
Speciality: Electrolysis.
● **Owner** Ms J Newton
T (Ref:HM14897)

### NEWTON, J C
**J C Newton**, 78 Knutsford Rd, Grappenhall, Warrington, **Cheshire**, WA4 2PJ, ENG.
(T) 01925 265765
Speciality: Biomechanics, Chiropody, Nail Surgery, Podiatry. ✔
● **Chiropodist (Podiatrist)**
Mr J Newton Q: M.S.C.P, S.R.Ch. M: S.C.P, S.R.Ch.
C Yrs. Est.: 20 (Ref:HM14898)

### NEWTON, JULIE
**Julie Newton**, The Nook, 2 Cam Green, Cam, Dursley, **Gloucestershire**, GL11 5HN, ENG.
(T) 01453 543914
Speciality: Electrolysis.
● **Owner** Miss J Newton
T (Ref:HM14899)

### NEWTON, KAREN
**Karen Newton**, 17 Downs Cl, Bradford-on-Avon, **Wiltshire**, BA15 1PR, ENG.
(T) 01225 863601
Speciality: Reflexology.
S T (Ref:HM14900)

### NEWTON, PAULINE
**Pauline Newton**, 26 Rowley Mead, Thornwood, Epping, **Essex**, CM16 6NH, ENG.
(T) 01992 573844
Speciality: Reflexology.
● **Owner** Ms P Newton
S T (Ref:HM14901)

### NEWTONS TRADITIONAL REMEDIES
**Newtons Traditional Remedies Ltd**, 5 High St, Shirley, Solihull, **Midlands (West)**, B90 1HA, ENG.
(T) 01214 366753 (F) 01214 366688
Speciality: Herbal Medicine.
● **Manageress** Mrs V Harris
M (Ref:HM14902)

### NEWTOWN CHIROPRACTIC SURGERY
**Newtown Chiropractic Surgery**, 69 Dundas St, Edinburgh, **Edinburgh (City of)**, EH3 6RS, SCO.
(T) 01315 564288 (F) 01315 564326
Speciality: Chiropractic.
P S T (Ref:HM14903)

### NEYLON, MARIAN
**Neylon Marian RGN LIC AC**, Lisheen Ballynacally, Ennis, **County Clare**, IRE.
(T) 08764 24510
Speciality: Complementary Medicines & Therapy.
M (Ref:HM14904)

### NI NARAIGH, JAYAVATI
**Ni Naraigh Jayavati Dip Psychth**, Ballydehob, Cork, **County Cork**, IRE.
(T) 028 3736 0
Speciality: Psychotherapy.
B (Ref:HM14905)

### NICE, P
**P Nice**, The Therapy Suite, 92B Broad St, Canterbury, **Kent**, CT1 2LU, ENG.
(T) 01304 842343
Speciality: Acupuncture.
O (Ref:HM14906)

### NICHOLAS, YVONNE
**Yvonne Nicholas**, 80 Minerva Cl, Warrington, **Cheshire**, WA4 2XN, ENG.
(T) 01925 571887
Speciality: Chiropodists (Podiatrists).
● **Owner** Mrs H Nicholas
S (Ref:HM14907)

### NICHOLDS, PATRICIA
**Patricia Nicholds**, Houndown Cottage, Ivy Mill Lane, Godstone, **Surrey**, RH9 8NF, ENG.
(T) 01883 742626
Speciality: Complementary Medicines & Therapy.
C M (Ref:HM14908)

### NICHOLLS, FRANK
**Frank Nicholls**, 4 Cowper Rd Carpark, Dereham, **Norfolk**, NR19 2BX, ENG.
(T) 01362 697274
Speciality: Chiropodists (Podiatrists).
● **Owner** Mr F Nicholls
S (Ref:HM14909)

### NICHOLLS, JOHN
**John Nicholls**, Towngate Healthcare Clinic, 102 Towngate, Leyland, Preston, **Lancashire**, PR5 1LQ, ENG.
(T) 01772 456657
Speciality: Complementary Medicines & Therapy.
● **Practice Manager** Ms S Keady
M (Ref:HM14910)

### NICHOLLS, JONATHAN
**Jonathan Nicholls**, The Worcester Chiropody & Podiatry Clinic, 23 Bransford Rd, Worcester, **Worcestershire**, WR2 4EW, ENG.
(T) 01905 428434
Speciality: Chiropodists (Podiatrists).
S (Ref:HM14911)

### NICHOLLS, PAUL
**Paul Nicholls**, Godswell House, Church St, Bloxham, Banbury, **Oxfordshire**, OX15 4ES, ENG.
(T) 01295 721472
Speciality: Physiotherapy.
P S T (Ref:HM14912)

### NICHOLLS, SOPHIA
**Sophia Nicholls**, 8 St. Helens Way, Benson, Wallingford, **Oxfordshire**, OX10 6SW, ENG.
(T) 01491 833395
Speciality: Chiropodists (Podiatrists).
● **Owner** Mrs S Nicholls
S (Ref:HM14913)

### NICHOLLS, SUE
**Sue Nicholls**, 2 Westhill, St. Austell, **Cornwall**, PL25 5ET, ENG.
(T) 01726 61191
Speciality: Chiropodists (Podiatrists).
S (Ref:HM14914)

### NICHOLLS, VERITY
**Verity Nicholls**, 55 Deepdene Vale, Dorking, **Surrey**, RH4 1NJ, ENG.
(T) 01306 884723
Speciality: Chiropody. ✔
● **Chiropodist** Ms V Nicholls Q: MBChA, MSSCh. M: B.A.Ch.P.
C Yrs. Est.: 6 (Ref:HM14915)

### NICHOLS, JONATHAN
**Jonathan Nichols**, 7 Percival Rd, Bristol, BS8 3LE, ENG.
(T) 01179 237705 (F) 01179 733809
Speciality: Osteopathy.
P S T (Ref:HM14916)

### NICHOLS, JONATHAN
**Jonathan Nichols**, Beachley Rd, Sedbury, Chepstow, **Monmouthshire**, NP16 7AA, WAL.
(T) 01291 627374
Speciality: Osteopathy.
● **Owner** Mr J Nichols
P S T (Ref:HM14917)

### NICHOLS, SYLVIA
**Sylvia Nichols**, 9 Northdown, Ashford, **Kent**, TN24 8RB, ENG.
(T) 01233 626206
Speciality: Aromatherapy, Reflexology, Reiki.
● **Owner** Mrs S Nichols
M O (Ref:HM14918)

### NICHOLSON, ROSIE
**Rosie Nicholson**, 18 Harrison Avenue, **Dorset**, BH1 4NT, ENG.
(T) 01202 301961
Speciality: Complementary Medicines & Therapy.
C M (Ref:HM14919)

### NICHOLSON, SHEILA
**Sheila Nicholson**, Castleton House, Castle St, Mere, Warminster, **Wiltshire**, BA12 6JE, ENG.
(T) 01747 860161
Speciality: Physiotherapy.
P S T (Ref:HM14920)

### NICHOLSON, V E
**V E Nicholson**, 57 Basterfield House, Golden Lane Estate, London, **London (Greater)**, EC1Y 0TR, ENG.
(T) 020 7490 2310
Speciality: Hypnotherapy.
B (Ref:HM14921)

### NICKALLS, JILL
**Jill Nickalls**, Bay Tree House, 87 Crown Rd, Twickenham, **London (Greater)**, TW1 3EX, ENG.
(T) 020 8892 8434
Speciality: Osteopathy.
P S T (Ref:HM14922)

### NICKI HAVES PHYSIO CLINIC
**Nicki Haves Physiotherapy Clinic**, 99 Flixton Rd, Urmston, Manchester, **Manchester (Greater)**, M41 5BF, ENG.
(T) 01617 487272
Speciality: Physiotherapy. ✔
● **Practice Manager** Ms A Haves
● **Owner/Physiotherapist** Ms N Haves Q: BSc, MCSP, SRP. M: CSP.
S (Ref:HM14923)

### NICOL, A
**A Nicol**, 1 Heath Rd, Ripley, **Derbyshire**, DE5 3EN, ENG.
(T) 01773 749155
Speciality: Chiropodists (Podiatrists).
● **Owner** Mrs A Nicol
S (Ref:HM14924)

### NICOL, L
**L Nicol**, Chelsea Lane, Inverurie, **Aberdeenshire**, AB51 3QQ, SCO.
(T) 01467 624888 (F) 01467 624888
Speciality: Reflexology.
● **Partner** Mrs C Craigmile
S T (Ref:HM14925)

### NICOLA @ HOLISTIC HOUSE
**Nicola**, 24 Guildford Rd West, Farnborough, **Hampshire**, GU14 6PU, ENG.
(T) 01252 650968

Key: B Mind-Body Medicine, C Complementary Medicine, H Self Help Treatment, M Medicinal Therapy, O Oriental Medicine, P Postural Therapy, S Manipulative Structural Therapy, T Touch Therapy

**Speciality:** Aromatherapy, Indian Head Massage, Massage (Therapeutic), Reflexology, Stress Therapy, Swedish Body Massage.
**C** (Ref:HM14926)

## NICOLA FRY-HEALTH & BEAUTY
**Nicola Fry-Health & Beauty**, 1 Hatchlands Rd, Redhill, **Surrey**, RH1 6AA, ENG.
(T) 01737 765640
**Speciality:** Aromatherapy, Beauty Therapy, Complementary Therapy, Electrotherapy, Indian Head Massage, Manual Lymph Drainage, Massage (Therapeutic), Reflexology, Reiki, (Vodder), Red Vein Removal. ✔
- **Owner** Ms N Fry Q: IHBC. M: BABTAC, IFHB.
- **Therapist** Ms J Nightingale Q: CIBTAC. M: BABTAC.
- **Head Therapist** Ms L Hargreaves Q: IHBC. M: BABTAC.

**M** Yrs. Est.: 12 (Ref:HM14927)

## NICOLL, ANGELA
**Angela Nicoll**, 10 Tillybrake Rd, Banchory, **Aberdeenshire**, AB31 5UN, SCO.
(T) 01330 824505 (F) 01330 824505
**Speciality:** Hypnotherapy.
- **Owner** Mrs A Nicoll

**B** (Ref:HM14928)

## NICOLL, ELAINE
**Elaine Nicoll**, 17 West High St, Forfar, **Angus**, DD8 1BE, SCO.
(T) 01307 465181
**Speciality:** Biomechanics, Chiropody, Nail Surgery, Podiatry. ✔
- **Chiropodist (Podiatrist)** Ms A Geddes Q: BSc, S.R.Ch. M: S.C.P.
- **Chiropodist (Podiatrist)** Ms J Bell Q: BSc, S.R.Ch. M: S.C.P.
- **Chiropodist (Podiatrist)** Ms E Nicoll Q: BSc, S.R.Ch. M: S.C.P.

**M** Yrs. Est.: 10 (Ref:HM14929)

## NICOLLE, J
**J Nicolle**, Holmdale, Sidmouth, **Devon**, EX10 8DQ, ENG.
(T) 01395 578757
**Speciality:** Chiropodists (Podiatrists).
- **Owner** Mr J Nicolle

**S** (Ref:HM14930)

## NIEBOER, SARAH
**Sarah Nieboer**, 8 Kinnoul Rd, London, **London (Greater)**, W6 8NQ, ENG.
(T) 020 7385 7123
**Speciality:** Psychotherapy.
- **Owner** Mrs S Nieboer

**B** (Ref:HM14931)

## NIEHORSTER, R
**R Niehorster**, Stratford House, Maldon Rd, Danbury, Chelmsford, **Essex**, CM3 4QW, ENG.
(T) 01245 224447
**Speciality:** Homeopathy.
- **Owner** Mrs R Niehorster

**M** (Ref:HM14932)

## NIEL-ASHER, S
**S Niel-Asher**, Bressey Osteopathic Clinic, 30 Bressey Gr, London, **London (Greater)**, E18 2HU, ENG.
(T) 020 8532 9889 (F) 028 0989 9164
(W) www.frozenshoulder.com
**Speciality:** Osteopathy. ✔
- **Owner/Osteopath** Mr S Neil-Asher Q: BSc. M: GOsC.

**S** Yrs. Est.: 9 (Ref:HM14933)

## NIELD, HELEN
**Helen Nield**, 32 The Avenue, Caldicot, **Monmouthshire**, NP26 4AB, WAL.
(T) 01291 641622
**Speciality:** Hypnotherapy.
- **Owner** Mrs H Nield

**B** (Ref:HM14934)

## NIELSEN, RITA C
**Rita C Nielsen MD**, Natural Therapy Clinic, 127 Moyser Rd, London, **London (Greater)**, SW16 6SJ, ENG.
(T) 020 8769 5652
**Speciality:** Aromatherapy, Nutritional Therapy, Reflexology. ✔
- **Owner/Natural Therapist** Mrs R Nielsen Q: ISPA. M: IFR, ISPA.

**C** Yrs. Est.: 10 (Ref:HM14935)

## NIGEL DE SALENGRE
**Nigel de Salengre**, 7 Bedford Row, Barnstaple, **Devon**, EX32 8NR, ENG.
(T) 01271 373346
**Speciality:** Osteopathy.
**P** **S** **T** (Ref:HM14936)

## NIGHTINGALE PHYSIO PRACTICE
**Nightingale Physiotherapy Practice**, 2-2A Turner Lane, Whiston, Rotherham, **Yorkshire (South)**, S60 4HY, ENG.
(T) 01709 371190 (F) 01709 371190
**Speciality:** Acupuncture, Manipulation, Physiotherapy. ✔
- **Physiotherapist** Mr G Hill Q: MCSP, SRP. M: CSP.
- **Physiotherapist** Mr J Isaacs Q: MCSP, MSc, SRP. M: CSP.

**S** Yrs. Est.: 6 (Ref:HM14937)

## NIGHTINGALE, J
**J Nightingale**, 86 Longbrook St, Exeter, **Devon**, EX4 6AP, ENG.
(T) 01392 434074
**Speciality:** Alexander Technique.
**P** **S** (Ref:HM14938)

## NIGHTINGALE, JERRY
**Nightingale Jerry**, 2 Budleigh Cottages, Kenn, Exeter, **Devon**, EX6 7XQ, ENG.
(T) 01392 832829
**Speciality:** Alexander Technique.
**P** **S** (Ref:HM14939)

## NIGHTINGALE, JOANNA
**Joanna Nightingale**, Terling, Oakley Rd, Harwich, **Essex**, CO12 5DR, ENG.
(T) 01255 554855
**Speciality:** Hypnosis.
**B** (Ref:HM14940)

## NIGHTINGALE, N C
**Mr N C Nightingale**, Seven Trees, Ockham Rd North, East Horsley, Leatherhead, **Surrey**, KT24 6NU, ENG.
(T) 01483 284604
**Speciality:** Chiropodists (Podiatrists).
**S** (Ref:HM14941)

## NIGHTINGALE, ROSE
**Rose Nightingale**, 16 Church Avenue, Leighton Buzzard, **Bedfordshire**, LU7 7AD, ENG.
(T) 01525 379224
**Speciality:** Homeopathy.
- **Owner** Mrs R Nightingale

**M** (Ref:HM14942)

## NIJSSEN, M C
**M C Nijssen**, 171 Wokingham Rd, Reading, **Berkshire**, RG6 1LT, ENG.
(T) 01189 268840
**Speciality:** Chiropodists (Podiatrists).
- **Owner** Ms M Nijssen

**S** (Ref:HM14943)

## NIKKEN INDEPENDENT DISTRIBUTOR
**Nikken Independent Distributor**, 340 Outwood Common Rd, Billericay, **Essex**, CM11 2LT, ENG.
(T) 07966 197248 (F) 01708 551577
**Speciality:** Complementary Medicines & Therapy.
- **Owner** Mr K Gilliham

**C** **M** (Ref:HM14944)

## NIKKEN INDEPENDENT DISTRIBUTOR
**Nikken Independent Distributor**, New Rd, Rainham, **Kent**, RM13 8ES, ENG.
(T) 01708 522235 (F) 01708 551577
**Speciality:** Complementary Medicines & Therapy.
- **Owner** Mr K Gilliham

**M** (Ref:HM14945)

## NIMAN, GEORGE
**George Niman**, Broxholme, 112 Conway Rd, Colwyn Bay, **Conwy**, LL29 7LL, WAL.
(T) 01492 534328
**Speciality:** Acupuncture.
- **Principal** Dr G Niman

**O** (Ref:HM14946)

## NINA, ANNE
**Anne Nina**, 12 Gordon Rd, Brighton, **Sussex (East)**, BN1 6PD, ENG.
(T) 01273 232616
**Speciality:** Clairvoyants & Palmists.
**B** (Ref:HM14947)

## NINO, CAFOLLA
**Cafolla Nino Dip HP MNACHP**, 40 Bolton St, IRE.
(T) 01872 6915
**Speciality:** Complementary Medicines & Therapy.
**M** (Ref:HM14948)

## NIPA DAS
**Nipa Das**, Thorncombe, Church Rd, Windlesham, **Surrey**, GU20 6BT, ENG.
(T) 01276 473371
**Speciality:** Complementary Medicines & Therapy.
**M** (Ref:HM14949)

## NIRVANA
**Nirvana**, Stoneleigh Park Rd, Epsom, **Surrey**, KT19 0QT, ENG.
(T) 020 8393 7500
**Speciality:** Aromatherapy.
- **Partner** Miss C Wheller

**M** **O** (Ref:HM14950)

## NISSIM & ASSOCIATES
**M J Nissim & Associates**, 64 Harcourt St, Newark, **Nottinghamshire**, NG24 1RF, ENG.
(T) 01636 611644
**Speciality:** Osteopathy.
- **Principal** Mr J Nissim

**P** **S** **T** (Ref:HM14951)

## NITHSDALE, DIANA
**Diana Nithsdale**, The Cottage, Carr Lane, Wansford, Driffield, **Humberside (North)**, YO25 8NP, ENG.
(T) 01377 254220
**Speciality:** Homeopathy.
- **Owner** Mrs D Nithsdale

**M** (Ref:HM14952)

## NITTY GRITTY WHOLEFOODS
**Nitty Gritty Wholefoods**, 24 West St, Leominster, **Herefordshire**, HR6 8ES, ENG.
(T) 01568 611600
**Speciality:** Aromatherapy, Bach Remedies, Herbal Medicine, Homeopathy.
- **Shop Assistant** Ms S Cleary Q: BA (Hons), MCH, RSHom. M: RSoH.
- **Shop Owner** Mrs P Hackett Q: BSc (Hons).

**H** Yrs. Est.: 26 (Ref:HM14953)

## NIVERN, D
**Diane Nivern Centre for Aromatherapy & Complementary Therapy**, The Treatment Rooms, 406 Bury New Rd, Whitefield, Manchester, **Manchester (Greater)**, M45 7SX, ENG.
(T) 01617 961169 (F) 01619 596753
(E) therapt@dianenivern.com
(W) www.dianenivern.com
**Speciality:** Absent Healing, Acupressure, Aromatherapy, Bach Remedies, Chiropractic, Complementary Therapy, Counselling, Dowsing, Floral Essence Therapy, Healer, Healing Therapy, Holistic Healing, Indian Head Massage, Inhalation Therapy, Manipulation, Massage (Therapeutic), Meditation, Mud Therapy, Reflexology, Reiki, Shiatsu, Stress Therapy, Vitamin Therapy, Ying & Yang, Natural Beauty Therapy, Kombucha. ✔
- **Senior Therapist** Ms D Nivern Q: LLSA, MIFA. M: IFA.

**C** **S** Yrs. Est.: 7 (Ref:HM14954)

## NIXON, LOUISE
**Louise Nixon**, Barracks Cottage, Badger, Wolverhampton, **Midlands (West)**, WV6 7JU, ENG.
(T) 01746 783517
**Speciality:** Chiropodists (Podiatrists).
**S** (Ref:HM14955)

## NIXON, M
**M Nixon**, 358 Old Glenarm Rd, Larne, **County Antrim**, BT40 2LG, NIR.
(T) 028 2826 0066
**Speciality:** Physiotherapy.

● **Owner** Mr M Nixon
P S T (**Ref:**HM14956)

## NIXON, MICHAEL
**Michael Nixon**, 20 Brackendale, London, **London (Greater)**, N21 3DG, ENG.
(T) 020 8886 3274
Speciality: Osteopathy.
P S T (**Ref:**HM14957)

## NIXON, MICHAEL
**Michael Nixon**, Morris House Surgery, Waltheof Gdns, London, **London (Greater)**, N17 7EB, ENG.
(T) 020 8801 1277
Speciality: Osteopathy.
● **Senior Partner** Dr G Amato
P S T (**Ref:**HM14958)

## NIXON, S
**S Nixon**, 43 Weymouth St, London, **London (Greater)**, W1N 3LD, ENG.
(T) 020 7935 9558 (F) 020 7935 9558
Speciality: Complementary Medicines & Therapy.
● **Owner** Mrs S Nixon
C M (**Ref:**HM14959)

## N'KABU, UCHE
**N'kabu Uche**, The Hale Clinic, 7 Park Cresent, London, **London (Greater)**, W1N 3HE, ENG.
(T) 020 7631 0156
Speciality: Chiropodists (Podiatrists).
S (**Ref:**HM14960)

## NLF CHIROPODY
**NLF Chiropody**, The Health Station, 21 Brand St, Hitchin, **Hertfordshire**, SG5 1JE, ENG.
(T) 01462 435409
Speciality: Chiropodists (Podiatrists).
● **Owner** Mr N Farmer
S (**Ref:**HM14961)

## NLP THERAPY
**NLP Therapy**, 66 Cwmcuddy Drive, Bassaleg, Newport, NP10 8JB, WAL.
(T) 01633 897978
Speciality: Hypnosis.
B (**Ref:**HM14962)

## NOAD, SARA
**Sara Noad**, 25 Croydon Rd, Westerham, **Kent**, TN16 1TS, ENG.
(T) 01959 562658
Speciality: Reflexology.
S T (**Ref:**HM14963)

## NOAH'S ARK PSYCHOTHERAPY
**Noah's Ark Psychotherapy**, The Lodge, Wilby Rd, Stradbroke, Eye, **Suffolk**, IP21 5JN, ENG.
(T) 01379 384707
(E) noahs.ark@breathemail.net
Speciality: Cognitive Therapy, Counselling, Family Therapy, Humanistic Psychology, Hypnotherapy, Psychotherapy, Stress Therapy, Transactional Analysis. ✔
● **Psychotherapist/Hypnotherapist** Mr B Threadgall **Q:** Dip.Couns, Dip.Hyp, Dip.Psych. **M:** NCP.
B Yrs. Est.: 9 (**Ref:**HM14964)

## NOAKES, STEVE
**Steve Noakes**, 70 Milward Rd, Hastings, **Sussex (East)**, TN34 3RR, ENG.
(T) 01424 443856
Speciality: Herbal Medicine.
M (**Ref:**HM14965)

## NOBES, PETER
**Peter Nobes**, 79 Elliscombe Rd, London, **London (Greater)**, SE7 7PD, ENG.
(T) 020 8858 8742
Speciality: Alexander Technique.
● **Owner** Mr P Nobes
P S (**Ref:**HM14966)

## NOBLE CLINIC
**Noble Clinic (The)**, The White House, High St, Brenchley, Tonbridge, **Kent**, TN12 7NQ, ENG.
(T) 01892 722251 (F) 01892 722251
Speciality: Chiropodists (Podiatrists).
● **Owner** Mrs D Hanger
S (**Ref:**HM14967)

## NOBLE, ANDREW (DR)
**DR Andrew Noble**, 19 Hamilton Rd, Bangor, **County Down**, BT20 4LL, **NIR**.
(T) 028 9147 1200
Speciality: Chiropractic. ✔
● **Chiropractor** Dr A Noble **Q:** DC.
P Yrs. Est.: 27 (**Ref:**HM14968)

## NOBLE, CAROLINE
**Caroline Noble**, 19 Lawn Rd, Milford On Sea, Lymington, **Hampshire**, SO41 0QZ, ENG.
(T) 01590 643098
Speciality: Chiropodists (Podiatrists).
● **Owner** Mrs C Noble
S (**Ref:**HM14969)

## NOBLE, J D
**J D Noble WMSCH (hons) MACP**, Gilead, Shipston Rd, Stratford-Upon-Avon, **Warwickshire**, CV37 8LZ, ENG.
(T) 01789 293210
Speciality: Chiropodists (Podiatrists).
● **Owner** Mr J Noble
S (**Ref:**HM14970)

## NOBLE, SUE
**Sue Noble**, 41 Church Rd, Poole, **Dorset**, BH14 0NN, ENG.
(T) 01202 749514 (F) 01202 718906
Speciality: Physiotherapy.
● **Partner** Mrs C Swinhoe
P S T (**Ref:**HM14971)

## NOBLE, SUZANNE
**Suzanne Noble**, Chapel House, Pudleston, Leominster, **Herefordshire**, HR6 0RE, ENG.
(T) 01568 750462
Speciality: Homeopathy.
M (**Ref:**HM14972)

## NOBLE, TERRY D
**Terry D Noble**, 6 Merland Rise, Epsom, **Surrey**, KT18 5RZ, ENG.
(T) 01737 371134
Speciality: Chiropodists (Podiatrists).
● **Owner** Mr T Noble
S (**Ref:**HM14973)

## NOBLETT, ANN
**Ann Noblett**, 10 Victoria House, 84 Kings Avenue, London, **London (Greater)**, SW4 8BN, ENG.
(T) 020 7313 4934
Speciality: Reflexology.
S T (**Ref:**HM14974)

## NOBREGA, M J N
**M J N Nobrega**, 171 Ecclesall Rd South, Sheffield, **Yorkshire (South)**, S11 9PN, ENG.
(T) 01142 361066
Speciality: Physiotherapy.
P S T (**Ref:**HM14975)

## NOCKOLDS, JENNY
**Jenny Nockolds**, 35 Wodeland Avenue, Guildford, **Surrey**, GU2 4JZ, ENG.
(T) 01483 576385
Speciality: Homeopathy.
● **Owner** Mrs J Nockolds
M (**Ref:**HM14976)

## NOCKOLDS, JENNY
**Jenny Nockolds**, The Reve Pavilion, 2a Guildford Park Rd, Guildford, **Surrey**, GU2 7ND, ENG.
(T) 01483 579500
Speciality: Homeopathy.
M (**Ref:**HM14977)

## NOIRET, C J P
**Mrs C J P Noiret**, Toad Hall, Brook, Newport, **Isle of Wight**, PO30 4EU, ENG.
(T) 01983 740678
Speciality: Osteopathy.
● **Owner** Mrs C Noiret
P S T (**Ref:**HM14978)

## NOLAN FINBARR
**Nolan Finbarr**, 12 Trafalgar Tce, Monkstown, **County Dublin**, IRE.
(T) 01280 2542
Speciality: Healing.
B (**Ref:**HM14979)

## NOLAN, BERNADETTE
**Bernadette Nolan**, 1 Cavendish Rd, Middlesbrough, **Cleveland**, TS4 3BZ, ENG.
(T) 01642 273439
Speciality: Chiropodists (Podiatrists).
● **Owner** Miss B Nolan
S (**Ref:**HM14980)

## NOLAN, CAROL
**Carol Nolan**, 74E Tisbury Rd, Hove, **Sussex (East)**, BN3 5AD, ENG.
(T) 01273 553327
Speciality: Chiropodists (Podiatrists).
● **Owner** Mrs C Nolan
S (**Ref:**HM14981)

## NOLAN, CLAIRE
**Claire Nolan**, 19 Millfields, Stansted, **Essex**, CM24 8AT, ENG.
(T) 01279 812443
Speciality: Reflexology.
S T (**Ref:**HM14982)

## NOLAN, DOROTHY J
**Mrs Dorothy J Nolan**, 28 Market St, Wigan, **Lancashire**, WN1 1HX, ENG.
(T) 01942 826305
Speciality: Chiropodists (Podiatrists).
S (**Ref:**HM14983)

## NOLAN, J A
**J A Nolan**, 56 Church Rd, Gatley, Cheadle, **Cheshire**, SK8 4NQ, ENG.
(T) 01614 910781
Speciality: Chiropodists (Podiatrists).
S (**Ref:**HM14984)

## NOLAN, JOHN
**John Nolan**, Broomhill Medical Centre, 183 Whitham, Sheffield, **Yorkshire (South)**, S10 2SN, ENG.
(T) 07641 112223
Speciality: Complementary Medicines & Therapy.
● **Owner** Mr J Nolan
C M (**Ref:**HM14985)

## NOLAN, SARAH
**Sarah Nolan**, 74 Avenue Hill, Leeds, **Yorkshire (West)**, LS8 4EZ, ENG.
(T) 01132 350003
Speciality: Acupuncture.
O (**Ref:**HM14986)

## NOMA
**Noma (Complex Homeopathy) Ltd**, Unit 3 Hollybrook Rd, Southampton, **Hampshire**, SO16 6RB, ENG.
(T) 023 8077 0513 (F) 023 8070 2459
(W) www.complementary-medicine.com/1
Speciality: Acupuncture, Herbal Medicine, Homeopathy. ✔
● **Managing Director** Mrs S Austen
● **Joint Director** Mr A Kelly
● **Secretary** Ms M McCaffery
C Yrs. Est.: 20 (**Ref:**HM14987)

## NOONEY, MICHAEL
**Michael Nooney Osteopath**, 75 Monread Hgts, Naas, **County Kildare**, IRE.
(T) 04589 6597
Speciality: Osteopathy.
P S T (**Ref:**HM14988)

## NORBURY COMP THERAPY CLINIC
**Norbury Complementary Therapy Clinic**, 1490-1492 London Rd, London, **London (Greater)**, SW16 4BT, ENG.
(T) 020 8764 7888 (F) 020 8764 7888
Speciality: Complementary Medicines & Therapy.
● **Principal** Dr O Chang
C M (**Ref:**HM14989)

## NORBURY, SUSAN
**Susan Norbury**, Wincote Farm, Wincote, Eccleshall, Stafford, **Staffordshire**, ST21 6JE, ENG.
(T) 01785 850337 (F) 01785 850337
(E) wincotefarm@lineone.net
(W) www.wincotefarm.co.uk
Speciality: Aromatherapy, Reflexology. ✔
● **Reflexologist** Mr S Norbury **Q:** ITEC, MAR.



Key: B Mind-Body Medicine, C Complementary Medicine, H Self Help Treatment, M Medicinal Therapy, O Oriental Medicine, P Postural Therapy, S Manipulative Structural Therapy, T Touch Therapy

H Yrs. Est.: 5 (Ref:HM14990)

## NORDIC
**Nordic**, Cullen Upr, **County Wicklow**, IRE.
(T) 04044 8204
(E) ciaran@nordic.ie
Speciality: Complementary Medicines & Therapy.
M (Ref:HM14991)

## NORDOFF-ROBBINS MUSIC THERAPY
**Nordoff-Robbins Music Therapy In Scotland**, 8 Academy Lane, Loanhead, **Lothian (Mid)**, EH20 9RP, SCO.
(T) 01314 404822
Speciality: Complementary Medicines & Therapy.
● **Accountant** Sam George Alder
C M (Ref:HM14992)

## NORFOLK CLINIC
**Norfolk Clinic (The)**, 38-40 Magdalen Rd, Norwich, **Norfolk**, NR3 4AG, ENG.
(T) 01603 660792
Speciality: Acupuncture, Alexander Technique, Aromatherapy, Complementary Therapy, Counselling, Cranial Osteopathy, Cupping, Healer, Herbal Medicine, Homeopathy, Hypnotherapy, Massage (Therapeutic), Nutritional Therapy, Osteopathy, Reflexology.
● **Osteopath** Mr M Booth Q: DO, Reg.Osteopath. M: GOsC.
● **Medical Herbalist** Mr T Lane Q: Dip.Herb.Med, MNIMH. M: AMH.
● **Acupuncturist** Mr G Palmer Q: MBAcC, Reg.Acu.
● **Homeopath** Mr S Gordon Q: RSHom. M: Soc.Hom.
S Yrs. Est.: 25 (Ref:HM14993)

## NORFOLK ESSENTIAL OILS
**Norfolk Essential Oils**, Pates Farm, Wisbech Rd, Tipsend, Welney, Wisbech, **Cambridgeshire**, PE14 9SQ, ENG.
(T) 01354 638065 (F) 01354 638065
Speciality: Aromatherapy.
M O (Ref:HM14994)

## NORFOLK NATURAL HEALTH SERVICE
**Norfolk Natural Health Service**, 6b Raymound St, Thetford, **Norfolk**, IP24 2EA, ENG.
(T) 01842 820121 (F) 01842 764647
(E) jmountjo@uk.packardbell.org
Speciality: Absent Healing, Acupressure, Acupuncture, Aromatherapy, Bach Remedies, Bowen Therapy, Complementary Therapy, Counselling, Healing Therapy, Herbal Medicine, Homeopathy, Hypnotherapy, Indian Head Massage, Iridology, Life Style Coaching, Massage (Therapeutic), Meditation, Moxibustion, Nutritional Therapy, Phytotherapy, Psychotherapy, Reflexology, Reiki, Shiatsu, Spiritual Healing, T'ai-Chi Ch'uan, Ying & Yang. ✔ CREDIT
● **Owner/Herbalist** Mrs J Mountjoy-Roost Q: Dip.Nutrition, MH. M: BHMA.
M Yrs. Est.: 3 (Ref:HM14995)

## NORFOLK, JILL
**Jill Norfolk**, 'Firs', Emmets Park, Binfield, Bracknell, **Berkshire**, RG42 4HQ, ENG.
(T) 01344 302555
Speciality: Aromatherapy.
M O (Ref:HM14996)

## NORGAARD, IDA
**Ida Norgaard**, 21 Thurloe Pl, London, **London (Greater)**, SW7 2SP, ENG.
(T) 020 7591 1929 (F) 020 7591 1912
Speciality: Chiropractors.
● **Owner** Dr I Norgaard
P S T (Ref:HM14997)

## NORITEX
**Noritex (Woolana) Ltd**, 48 Seagoe Industrial Area, Portadown, Craigavon, **County Armagh**, BT63 5QE, NIR.
(T) 028 3833 5060 (F) 028 3836 1885
Speciality: Complementary Medicines & Therapy, Warmth Therapy.
● **Managing Director** Mrs G Scholz
M (Ref:HM14998)

## NORMAN, A J
**A J Norman**, John Kennedy Rd, King's Lynn, **Norfolk**, PE30 2AA, ENG.
(T) 01553 772512 (F) 01553 775546
Speciality: Chiropractic, Homeopathy, Massage (Therapeutic), Stress Therapy. ✔
● **Chiropractor** Dr S Chirila Q: BSc, BSc (Hons), MSc (Chiro).
● **Chiropractor** Dr S Sandhu Q: BSc, BSc (Hons), MSc (Chiro).
● **Owner** Dr A Norman Q: BSc, DC.
P Yrs. Est.: 18 (Ref:HM14999)

## NORMAN, ANNE
**Anne Norman**, Old Mill House, Harwich Rd, Wix, Manningtree, **Essex**, CO11 2RY, ENG.
(T) 01255 870750
Speciality: Psychotherapy.
● **Owner** Ms A Norman
B (Ref:HM15000)

## NORMAN, CATHERINE
**Catherine Norman**, 6 Prince William Cl, Worthing, **Sussex (West)**, BN14 0AZ, ENG.
(T) 01903 267287
Speciality: Chiropodists (Podiatrists).
● **Owner** Ms C Norman
S (Ref:HM15001)

## NORMAN, HILARY
**Hilary Norman**, Stoneleigh, Southwaite, Carlisle, **Cumbria**, CA4 0NA, ENG.
(T) 01768 885304
Speciality: Complementary Medicines & Therapy.
C M (Ref:HM15002)

## NORMAN, I
**I Norman**, 88 Great Northern Rd, Dunstable, **Bedfordshire**, LU5 4BT, ENG.
(T) 01582 608400 (F) 01582 471371
Speciality: Osteopathy.
● **Owner** Mr J Betser
P S T (Ref:HM15003)

## NORMAN, J M
**J M Norman**, 35 Egbert Rd, Winchester, **Hampshire**, SO23 7EB, ENG.
(T) 01962 841084
Speciality: Chiropody, Reflexology. CREDIT
● **Reflexologist** Mrs J Norman Q: MIFR. M: SMAE.
T Yrs. Est.: 5 (Ref:HM15004)

## NORMAN, KATHY
**Kathy Norman**, 9 Crantock Cl, Essington, Wolverhampton, **Midlands (West)**, WV11 2ED, ENG.
(T) 01922 475968
Speciality: Hopi Ear Candles, Indian Head Massage, Reflexology, Reiki.
S T (Ref:HM15005)

## NORMAN, NANCY
**Nancy Norman**, Cheops, Egypt Hill, Cowes, **Isle of Wight**, PO31 8BP, ENG.
(T) 01983 280159
Speciality: Aromatherapy, Crystal Healing, Meditation, Reiki.
C (Ref:HM15006)

## NORMAN, PETER
**Peter Norman**, The Montagu Clinic, Clay St, London, **London (Greater)**, W1H 3FS, ENG.
(T) 020 7935 4315
Speciality: Chiropodists (Podiatrists).
S (Ref:HM15007)

## NORRIS ASSOCIATES
**Norris Associates**, 1 Barkers Lane, Sale, **Cheshire**, M33 6RP, ENG.
(T) 01619 720512
Speciality: Physiotherapy.
P S T (Ref:HM15008)

## NORRIS ASSOCIATES
**Norris Associates**, 9a High St, Congleton, **Cheshire**, CW12 1BN, ENG.
(T) 01260 290564
Speciality: Physiotherapy.
P S T (Ref:HM15009)

## NORRIS, A H
**A H Norris**, The Hermitage, 42 Alexandra Rd, Scunthorpe, **Humberside**, DN16 2SF, ENG.
(T) 01724 860384 (F) 01724 860384
Speciality: Clairvoyants & Palmists.
● **Owner** Mrs P Warrington
B (Ref:HM15010)

## NORRIS, A J (DR)
**Norris Dr A J**, 55 Moor Green Lane, Birmingham, **Midlands (West)**, B13 8NE, ENG.
(T) 01214 499683
Speciality: Psychology.
B (Ref:HM15011)

## NORRIS, JANINE
**Janine Norris**, 18 Lambolle Pl, London, **London (Greater)**, NW3 4PG, ENG.
(T) 020 7483 3568 (F) 020 7483 3568
Speciality: Acupuncture.
● **Owner** Ms J Norris
O (Ref:HM15012)

## NORRIS, MARIA
**Maria Norris**, 7 The Rise, East Grinstead, **Sussex (West)**, RH19 4DS, ENG.
(T) 01342 328905
Speciality: Psychotherapy.
● **Owner** Mrs M Norris
B (Ref:HM15013)

## NORRIS, Q
**Q Norris**, 15 Lambourne Drive, Bagshot, **Surrey**, GU19 5BY, ENG.
(T) 01276 472329
Speciality: Alexander Technique.
● **Owner** Mr Q Norris
P S (Ref:HM15014)

## NORRIS, T
**T Norris**, 48 West Avenue, Clacton-On-Sea, **Essex**, CO15 1HA, ENG.
(T) 01255 425995 (F) 01255 425995
Speciality: Chiropodists (Podiatrists).
● **Owner** Mr T Norris
S (Ref:HM15015)

## NORSO BIOMAGNETICS UK
**Norso Biomagnetics UK**, 15 Cotswold View, Bath, **Somerset**, BA2 1HA, ENG.
(T) 01225 314096 (F) 01225 316397
(E) norsouk@aol.com
(W) www.norso-biomagnetics.co.uk
Speciality: Biomagnetic Therapy, Magnetic Therapy. CREDIT
● **Accredited Therapist/Owner** Ms G Vergari Q: CMA. M: BIMT, CMA.
H Yrs. Est.: 6 (Ref:HM15016)

## NORSWORTHY, CLAIRE
**Claire Norsworthy**, 121 Kings Rd, Fleet, **Hampshire**, GU13 9DR, ENG.
(T) 01252 810113
Speciality: Reflexology, Reiki, Touch For Health. ✔
● **Owner** Ms C Norsworthy Q: RGN.
C T Yrs. Est.: 6 (Ref:HM15017)

## NORTH & SOUTH
**North & South**, 19 Otley Rd, Leeds, **Yorkshire (West)**, LS6 3AA, ENG.
(T) 01132 758741
Speciality: Aromatherapy.
M O (Ref:HM15018)

## NORTH AREA COLLEGE STOCKPORT
**North Area College Stockport**, Buckingham Rd, Heaton Manor, Stockport, **Cheshire**, SK4 4RA, ENG.
(T) 01625 871140
Speciality: Complementary Medicines & Therapy.
M (Ref:HM15019)

## NORTH BAR CLINIC
**North Bar Clinic**, 57 North Bar Within, Beverley, **Humberside (North)**, HU17 8DG, ENG.
(T) 01482 861083
Speciality: Complementary Medicines & Therapy.
C M (Ref:HM15020)

## NORTH BEDS OSTEOPATHIC CLINIC
**North Bedfordshire Osteopathic Clinic**, Molivers Lane, Bromham, Bedford, **Bedfordshire**, MK43 8JT, ENG.

(T) 01234 823621
Speciality: Osteopathy.
P S T (Ref:HM15021)

## NORTH COLLEGE OSTEO PRACTICE

**North College Osteopathic Practice**, North College House, King St, Elgin, **Moray**, IV30 1HU, SCO.
(T) 01343 550382 (F) 01343 551405
Speciality: Osteopathy.
● **Partner** Mrs E Robinson
P S T (Ref:HM15022)

## NORTH DOWN CLINIC

**North Down Clinic**, 41-43 Castle St, Comber, **County Down**, BT23 4DY, NIR.
(T) 028 9187 1334 (F) 028 9187 0838
(E) cedosteopath@onetel.net.uk
(W) www.biocranial.org
Speciality: Cranial Osteopathy, Osteopathy, Bio-Cranial Therapy.
● **Principal** Mr R Boyd Q: DO, MNIMH, Reg.Osteopath.
● **Associate** Mr C Delepoulle Q: BSc, Hons (OST), Reg.Osteopath.
S Yrs. Est.: 30 (Ref:HM15023)

## NORTH DOWN CLINIC

**North Down Clinic**, 15 Farnham Rd, Bangor, **Gwynedd**, BT20 3SP, WAL.
(T) 028 9127 0626
Speciality: Osteopathy.
P S T (Ref:HM15024)

## NORTH DOWNS PHYSIOTHERAPY

**North Downs Physiotherapy & Sports Injury Clinic**, North Downs Hospital, 46 Tupwood Lane, Caterham, **Surrey**, CR3 6DP, ENG.
(T) 01883 345202
Speciality: Physiotherapy.
P S T (Ref:HM15025)

## NORTH EAST FIFE CHIROPODY PRAC

**North East Fife Chiropody Practice**, 44 Inverie St, St. Monans, Anstruther, **Fife**, KY10 2BW, SCO.
(T) 01333 730494
Speciality: Chiropodists (Podiatrists).
● **Senior Partner** Mr J Chance
S (Ref:HM15026)

## NORTH END CHIROPRACTIC CLINIC

**North End Chiropractic Clinic**, 285 London Rd, Portsmouth, **Hampshire**, PO2 9HE, ENG.
(T) 023 9265 4758
Speciality: Chiropractic.
● **Owner** Mrs C Horsfield
P S T (Ref:HM15027)

## NORTH END PRACTICE

**North End Practice**, 8a Burghley Rd, London, **London (Greater)**, NW5 1UE, ENG.
(T) 020 7485 9362 (F) 020 7485 6395
Speciality: Osteopathy.
● **Owner** Mr D Sharlaff
P S T (Ref:HM15028)

## NORTH END ROAD PSYCHO PRACTICE

**North End Road Psychotherapy Practice (The)**, 18B North End Rd, London, **London (Greater)**, NW11 7PH, ENG.
(T) 020 8905 5937
Speciality: Psychotherapy.
B (Ref:HM15029)

## NORTH HAMPS OSTEOPATHIC CLINIC

**North Hampshire Osteopathic Clinic**, 2 Eastrop Lane, Basingstoke, **Hampshire**, RG21 4AR, ENG.
(T) 01256 324555
Speciality: Osteopathy.
● **Osteopath** Miss J Bond
P S T (Ref:HM15030)

## NORTH KENT CHIROPRACTIC CLINIC

**North Kent Chiropractic Clinic**, 126 Maidstone Rd, Chatham, **Kent**, ME4 6DQ, ENG.
(T) 01634 828559 (F) 01634 407059
Speciality: Chiropractic.
● **Practice Manager** Mr G Bjarnason
P S T (Ref:HM15031)

## NORTH LONDON BACK PAIN CLNC

**North London Back Pain Sports Injury Clinic**, 69A Brent St, Hendon, London, **London (Greater)**, NW4 2EA, ENG.
(T) 020 8203 6652
Speciality: Osteopathy.
P S T (Ref:HM15032)

## NORTH LONDON CTRE-GROUP THRPY

**North London Centre For Group Therapy (The)**, 138 Bramley Rd, London, **London (Greater)**, N14 4HU, ENG.
(T) 020 8440 1451
Speciality: Psychotherapy.
B (Ref:HM15033)

## NORTH LONDON LINK CONSULTANCY

**North London Link Consultancy & Psychotherapy Practice**, 25 Grove Avenue, London, **London (Greater)**, N3 1QS, ENG.
(T) 020 8349 9827
Speciality: Psychotherapy.
B (Ref:HM15034)

## NORTH LONDON PHYSIO CENTRE

**North London Physiotherapy Centre (The)**, The North Middlesex Hospital Trust, Sterling Way, London, **London (Greater)**, N18 1QX, ENG.
(T) 020 8887 4147
Speciality: Physiotherapy.
P S T (Ref:HM15035)

## NORTH POLE SCH OF T'AI-CHI

**North Pole School of T'ai-Chi Ch'uan (The)**, 83 St Quintin Avenue, London, **London (Greater)**, W10 6PB, ENG.
(T) 020 8960 2141
(E) richard@richardbebb.freeserve.co.uk
Speciality: T'ai-Chi Ch'uan.
● **Manager/Teacher** Mr R Bebb
O Yrs. Est.: 5 (Ref:HM15094)

## NORTH SHROPSHIRE PHYSIO CENTRE

**North Shropshire Physiotherapy Centre**, 39 Church St, Oswestry, **Shropshire**, SY11 2SZ, ENG.
(T) 01691 670006
Speciality: Physiotherapy.
● **Owner** Ms J Lawrence
P S T (Ref:HM15037)

## NORTH WALES PHYSIO & SPORTS

**North Wales Physiotherapy Sports Injury Clinic**, Care Of Deeside Leisure Centre, Chester Rd West, Queensferry, Deeside, **Flintshire**, CH5 1SA, WAL.
(T) 01244 830429 (F) 01244 836511
Speciality: Physiotherapy.
● **Owner** Mr R Davieson
P S T (Ref:HM15038)

## NORTH WALES YOGA/NAT THRPY

**North Wales Yoga & Natural Therapy Centre**, 2a Erskine Rd, Colwyn Bay, **Conwy**, LL29 8EU, WAL.
(T) 01492 533961
Speciality: Yoga.
C (Ref:HM15039)

## NORTH WALSHAM CHIROPRACTIC

**North Walsham Chiropractic Clinic**, Kings Arms Loke, North Walsham, **Norfolk**, NR28 9JX, ENG.
(T) 01692 500600
Speciality: Chiropractic.
P S T (Ref:HM15040)

## NORTH WEST ACUPUNCTURE CLINIC

**North West Acupuncture Clinic**, 1 York Chambers, Wallgate, Wigan, **Lancashire**, WN1 1BG, ENG.
(T) 01942 230458
Speciality: Acupuncture.
● **Partner** Mrs S Dootson
O (Ref:HM15041)

## NORTH WEST COMP THERAPY CTRE

**North West Complementary Therapy Centre**, 28 Dudley Rd, Manchester, **Manchester (Greater)**, M16 8DE, ENG.
(T) 01612 260953 (F) 01612 260953
Speciality: Complementary Medicines & Therapy.
● **Manager** Dr M Abeelaal
C M (Ref:HM15042)

## NORTH WEST LIFESTYLE MNGMT

**North West Lifestyle Management**, Camborne Rd, Burtonwood, Warrington, **Cheshire**, WA5 4LX, ENG.
(T) 01925 290812
Speciality: Life Style Coaching, Massage (Therapeutic), Nutritional Therapy, Stress Therapy, Personal Development, Sports Therapy/Personal Fitness Training.
M (Ref:HM15043)

## NORTH, JUDITH

**Judith North**, 23 West St, Long Buckby, Northampton, **Northamptonshire**, NN6 7QF, ENG.
(T) 01327 843867
Speciality: Aromatherapy.
M O (Ref:HM15044)

## NORTH, L W

**L W North**, 189A Richmond Rd, Twickenham, **London (Greater)**, TW1 2NJ, ENG.
(T) 020 8892 2308
Speciality: Chiropractors.
P S T (Ref:HM15045)

## NORTH, SARAH

**Sarah North**, The Old Bakery, High St, Wadhurst, **Sussex (East)**, TN5 6AA, ENG.
(T) 01892 782674
Speciality: Homeopathy.
M (Ref:HM15046)

## NORTH, SARAH

**Sarah North**, 21 Broadwater Down, Tunbridge Wells, **Kent**, TN2 5NL, ENG.
(T) 01892 520659
Speciality: Homeopathy.
● **Owner** Ms S Noth
M (Ref:HM15047)

## NORTHALL, ANNE

**Anne Northall**, 105 Rectory Lane, Surbiton, **Surrey**, KT6 5HP, ENG.
(T) 020 8398 5354
Speciality: Acupuncture.
● **Owner** Mrs A Northall
O (Ref:HM15048)

## NORTHALLERTON PHYSIOTHERAPY

**Northallerton Physiotherapy**, 162 Bankhead Rd, Northallerton, **Yorkshire (North)**, DL6 1JD, ENG.
(T) 01609 777644
Speciality: Physiotherapy.
P S T (Ref:HM15049)

## NORTHAMBER

**Kathleen Ward Clinic**, Readuff, Loughmourne, Castleblayney, **County Monaghan**, IRE.
(T) 04297 45070 (F) 04297 45958
Speciality: Acupressure, Acupuncture, Bach Remedies, Chiropractic, Complementary Therapy, Counselling, Cupping, Herbal Medicine, Holistic Healing, Homeopathy, Hypnosis, Hypnotherapy, Manipulation, Massage (Therapeutic), Meditation, Naturopathy, Nutritional Therapy, Osteopathy, Psychotherapy, Reflexology, Stress Therapy, Vibrational Therapy, Vitamin Therapy.
● **Acupuncturist/Therapist** Prekop
● **Chiropractor** McGrath
● **Chiropodist (Podiatrist)** Brennan
● **Physical Therapist** McKenna
● **Acupuncturist/Therapist** Herron
● **Physical Therapist** Markey
● **Chiropractor** Smyth
● **Complementary Practitioner** Ms K Ward Q: Dip.Nutrition, Dip.Reflex, RGN, S.C.M. M: RxS.
● **Chiropodist (Podiatrist)** Dunwoody
M Yrs. Est.: 17 (Ref:HM15050)

## NORTHAMPTON CHIROPRACTIC

**Northampton Chiropractic Clinic**, 53c Main Rd, Duston, Northampton, **Northamptonshire**, NN5 6JN, ENG.
(T) 01604 759740
Speciality: Chiropractic, Rehabilitation Gym.
● **Chiropractor** Dr S Sunil Q: DC, MSc. M: BCA, GCC.
● **Associate** Mr P Kleberg Q: BSc, DC. M: BCA,



Key: B Mind-Body Medicine C Complementary Medicine H Self Help Treatment M Medicinal Therapy O Oriental Medicine P Postural Therapy S Manipulative Structural Therapy T Touch Therapy

GCC.
● **Chiropractor** Dr Y Oweyomi **Q:** DC, MSc. M: BCA, GCC.
P Yrs. Est.: 12 (**Ref:**HM15051)

### NORTHAMPTON CLINIC

**Northampton Clinic (The)**, 72 Abington Avenue, Northampton, **Northamptonshire**, NN1 4PA, ENG.
(T) 01604 632232
Speciality: Kinesiology, Nutritional Therapy. ✔ CREDIT
● **Nutritionist** Mrs Parker **Q:** Dip.Nutrition. M: ION.
C Yrs. Est.: 4 (**Ref:**HM15052)

### NORTHAMPTON SCHOOL OF PODIATRY

**Northampton School Of Podiatry**, Cliftonville, Northampton, **Northamptonshire**, NN1 5BD, ENG.
(T) 01604 627303 (F) 01604 622317
Speciality: Chiropodists (Podiatrists).
● **Principal** Mr W Turner
S (**Ref:**HM15053)

### NORTHCROFT CLINIC

**Northcroft Clinic**, 1818 Pershore Rd, Kings Norton, Birmingham, **Midlands (West)**, B30 3AU, ENG.
(T) 01214 863444
Speciality: Osteopathy.
P S T (**Ref:**HM15054)

### NORTHDOWN CLINIC

**Northdown Clinic**, 2 Ballybunden Rd, Killinchy, **County Down**, BT23 6RB, NIR.
(T) 028 9754 2838
Speciality: Complementary Medicines & Therapy.
● **Practitioner** Robert Boyd
M (**Ref:**HM15055)

### NORTHERN ACU & OSTEO MED CTRE

**Northern Acupuncture & Osteopathic Medical Centre**, 1st Floor Carne House, Parsons Lane, Bury, **Lancashire**, BL9 0JT, ENG.
(T) 01617 973607
Speciality: Osteopathy.
P S T (**Ref:**HM15056)

### NORTHERN COLLEGE CLINIC

**Northern College Clinic**, Swinburne House, Swinburne St, Gateshead, **Tyne and Wear**, NE8 1AX, ENG.
(T) 01914 900274 (F) 01914 900276
Speciality: Homeopathy.
C (**Ref:**HM15057)

### NORTHERN COLLEGE OF ACU

**Northern College of Acupuncture**, 61 Micklegate, York, **Yorkshire (North)**, YO1 6LJ, ENG.
(T) 01904 343305
Speciality: Complementary Medicines & Therapy.
● **Marketing** Ali Coles
M (**Ref:**HM15058)

### NORTHERN COLLEGE OF ACUP

**Northern College Of Acupuncture (The)**, 124 Acomb Rd, York, **Yorkshire (North)**, YO24 4EY, ENG.
(T) 01904 785120 (F) 01904 780386
Speciality: Acupuncture.
● **Principal** Mr R Blackwell
O (**Ref:**HM15059)

### NORTHERN COLLEGE OF HOM MED

**Northern College Of Homeopathic Medicine**, 1st Floor Swinburne House, Swinburne St, Gateshead, **Tyne and Wear**, NE8 1AX, ENG.
(T) 01914 900276
Speciality: Complementary Medicines & Therapy.
M (**Ref:**HM15060)

### NORTHERN GUILD-PSYCHOTHERAPY

**Northern Guild For Psychotherapy**, 77 Acklam Rd, Stockton-On-Tees, **Cleveland**, TS20 1SY, ENG.
(T) 01642 649004
(W) www.northern-guild.co.uk
Speciality: Cognitive Therapy, Counselling, Drama Therapy, Family Therapy, Gestalt Therapy, Group Therapy, Nutritional Therapy, Psychotherapy, Stress Therapy, Transactional Analysis. ✔
● **Director** Ms C Lister-Ford M: UKCP.
C Yrs. Est.: 18 (**Ref:**HM15061)

### NORTHERN GUILD-PSYCHOTHERAPY

**Northern Guild For Psychotherapy (The)**, 83 Jesmond Rd, Newcastle Upon Tyne, **Tyne and Wear**, NE2 1NH, ENG.
(T) 01912 098383 (F) 01912 098383
Speciality: Psychotherapy.
● **Director** Mrs C Lister-Ford
B (**Ref:**HM15062)

### NORTHERN INS OF ORIENTAL MED

**Northern Institute Of Oriental Medicine (The)**, 178 St Albans Rd, Lytham St. Annes, **Lancashire**, FY8 3NQ, ENG.
(T) 01253 728035 (F) 01253 728035
Speciality: Complementary Medicines & Therapy.
● **Owner** Mr J Brazier
C M (**Ref:**HM15063)

### NORTHERN REIKI PARTNERSHIP

**Northern Reiki Partnership**, 1 Upper Wortley Drive, Leeds, **Yorkshire (West)**, LS12 4JA, ENG.
(T) 01132 793279
Speciality: Complementary Medicines & Therapy.
● **Partner** Mr M Webb
M (**Ref:**HM15064)

### NORTHERN SCHOOL-AROMATHERAPY

**Northern School Of Aromatherapy**, 23 Huddersfield Rd, Mirfield, **Yorkshire (West)**, WF14 8AE, ENG.
(T) 01924 498507
Speciality: Aromatherapy.
M O (**Ref:**HM15065)

### NORTHFIELDS PSYCHOTHERAPY SV

**Northfields Psychotherapy Service (The)**, Lansdowne Drive, London, **London (Greater)**, E8 3EP, ENG.
(T) 020 7683 0476
Speciality: Psychotherapy.
B (**Ref:**HM15066)

### NORTHWOOD CLINIC

**Northwood Clinic**, 36 Westow St, Crystal Palace, London, **London (Greater)**, SE19 3AH, ENG.
(T) 020 8653 5646
(W) www.northwoodclinic.co.uk
Speciality: Biomechanics, Chiropody, Osteopathy, Phytotherapy, Podiatry. ✔ CREDIT
● **Podiatrist** Ms C Tye **Q:** S.R.Ch. M: S.R.Ch.
C Yrs. Est.: 5 (**Ref:**HM15067)

### NORTHWOOD, R S

**R S Northwood**, 59 Vicarage Rd, Kings Heath, Birmingham, **Midlands (West)**, B14 7QA, ENG.
(T) 01214 434696
Speciality: Osteopathy.
● **Owner** Mr R Northwood
P S T (**Ref:**HM15068)

### NORTON HOMOEOPATHIC PRACTICE

**Norton Homoeopathic Practice (The)**, 105 Worcester St, Stourbridge, **Midlands (West)**, DY8 1AX, ENG.
(T) 01384 440811
Speciality: Homeopathy.
M (**Ref:**HM15069)

### NORTON, CHRIS

**Chris Norton**, 11/Oakdale, Thornhill Rd, Sutton Coldfield, **Midlands (West)**, B74 2LH, ENG.
(T) 01213 843284
Speciality: Chiropodists (Podiatrists).
● **Owner** Mr C Norton
S (**Ref:**HM15070)

### NORTON, DAVID

**David Norton**, Southmead Clinic, Blackpond Lane, Farnham Common, Slough, **Berkshire**, SL2 3ER, ENG.
(T) 01753 646381 (F) 01753 646381
Speciality: Osteopathy.
● **Owner** Mr D Norton
P S T (**Ref:**HM15071)

### NORTON, ROSEMARY

**Norton Rosemary**, Upper Holway Rd, Taunton, **Somerset**, TA1 2HF, ENG.
(T) 01823 282147
Speciality: Acupuncture.
O (**Ref:**HM15072)

### NORTON, ROSEMARY

**Rosemary Norton**, Natural Path Health Centre, 3 Holyrood St, Chard, **Somerset**, TA20 2AH, ENG.
(T) 01460 62953 (F) 01460 63809
Speciality: Acupuncture.
● **Owner** Mr M Newbound
O (**Ref:**HM15073)

### NORTON, STEVE

**Steve Norton**, 11A Otterburn Gardens, Middlesbrough, **Cleveland**, TS5 8DE, ENG.
(T) 01642 590365
Speciality: Hypnosis.
B (**Ref:**HM15074)

### NORWELL, M

**M Norwell**, Norfields, Luncarty, Perth, **Perth and Kinross**, PH1 3HZ, SCO.
(T) 01738 583613
Speciality: Physiotherapy.
● **Owner** Mrs M Norwell
P S T (**Ref:**HM15075)

### NORWICH CENTRE

**Norwich Centre**, 7 Earlham Rd, Norwich, Norwich, **Norfolk**, NR2 3RA, ENG.
(T) 01603 617709
Speciality: Complementary Medicines & Therapy.
● **Centre Director** Caroline Kitcatt
M (**Ref:**HM15076)

### NORWICH SPINAL/SPORTS INJ PRAC

**Norwich Spinal & Sports Injury Practice**, 302 Bowthorpe Rd, Norwich, **Norfolk**, NR5 8AB, ENG.
(T) 01603 763455
Speciality: Physiotherapy.
● **Owner** Mr K Tomes
P S T (**Ref:**HM15077)

### NORWOOD & STEPHENSON

**Norwood & Stephenson**, 6 Limes Rd, Folkestone, **Kent**, CT19 4AU, ENG.
(T) 01303 276721
Speciality: Chiropodists (Podiatrists).
S (**Ref:**HM15078)

### NOTIONS

**Notions**, 45 Sheaf St, Daventry, **Northamptonshire**, NN11 4AA, ENG.
(T) 01327 301865
Speciality: Electrolysis.
● **Owner** Mrs G Wensley
T (**Ref:**HM15079)

### NOTMAN, JACKIE

**Jackie Notman**, 14 Ridgemead, Calne, **Wiltshire**, SN11 9EL, ENG.
(T) 01249 821249
Speciality: Aromatherapy.
M O (**Ref:**HM15080)

### NOTTING HILL TRAD ACU CTRE

**Notting Hill Traditional Acupuncture Centre (The)**, 21 Ladbroke Gr, London, **London (Greater)**, W11 3AY, ENG.
(T) 020 7221 1326
Speciality: Acupuncture, Homeopathy, Osteopathy. ✔
● **Acupunturist** Ms S Davidson M: BAcC.
● **Homeopath** Robin Logan
● **Acupuncturist** Mr D Cocks M: BAcC.
● **Acupuncturist** Mr G Woods M: BAcC.
● **Osteopath** Eyal Ledarman
● **Acupuncturist** Ms D Cook M: BAcC.
● **Acupuncturist** Ms S Cheetham M: BAcC.
● **Acupuncturist** Mr T Laurence M: BAcC.
● **Acupuncturist** Naji Malak M: BAcC.
C Yrs. Est.: 10 (**Ref:**HM15081)

### NOTTINGHAM BACK PAIN CLINIC

**Nottingham Back Pain Clinic**, 2b Thackerays Lane, Woodthorpe, Nottingham, **Nottinghamshire**, NG5 4HP, ENG.
(T) 01159 676699



Key continued: **Yrs.Est:** Years Established **Q:** Qualifications **M:** Professional Membership ✔ Indemnity Insurance CREDIT Accept Credit Cards

Speciality: Osteopathy.
● **Owner** Mr K Booth
P S T (Ref:HM15082)

## NOTTINGHAM M S THERAPY CTRE

**Nottingham Multiple Sclerosis Therapy Centre**, Unit H2, Trent Park Ind Estate, Little Tennis Street South, Nottingham, **Nottinghamshire**, NG2 4EU, ENG.
(T) 01159 505991
Speciality: Aromatherapy, Reflexology, Oxygen Therapy and Neuro Physiotherapy. ✓
● **Reflexologist** Mrs T Cassidy Q: ITEC.
● **Neuro Therapist** Mrs J Light
● **Centre Manager** Mrs G Cant
C Yrs. Est.: 16 (Ref:HM15083)

## NOTTINGHAM NATURAL HEALTH CTRE

**Nottingham Natural Health Centre**, 354 Mansfield Rd, Nottingham, **Nottinghamshire**, NG5 2EF, ENG.
(T) 01159 608855
(W) www.webhealth.co.uk
Speciality: Acupuncture, Alexander Technique, Aromatherapy, Bates Method, Bowen Therapy, Chiropractic, Counselling, Cranio-Sacral Therapy, Herbal Medicine, Homeopathy, Hypnotherapy, Iridology, Kinesiology, Massage (Therapeutic), Naturopathy, Nutritional Therapy, Osteopathy, Psychotherapy, Reflexology, Reiki, Shiatsu, Zero Balancing, Metamorphic Technique, Radionics, Healing, Rebirthing, Anthroposophical Medicine, Management, Remedial Massge, Vibrational Medicine. ✓
● **Receptionist** Mrs P Haverkhap
C (Ref:HM15084)

## NOTTINGHAM SPORTS INJURY

**Nottingham Sports Injury Clinic**, 736 Manfield Rd, Woodthorpe, Nottingham, **Nottinghamshire**, NG5 3FZ, ENG.
(T) 01159 609553 (F) 01159 856842
Speciality: Physiotherapy. ✓
● **Physiotherapist** Mrs H Tomlinson Q: MCSP, SRP. M: CSP.
● **Owner** Mr I Tomlinson
S (Ref:HM15085)

## NOTTINGHAM, STUART

**Stuart Nottingham - Chartered Physiotherapist**, 38 Station Rd, Fernhill Heath, Worcester, **Worcestershire**, WR3 7UP, ENG.
(T) 01905 452144 (F) 01905 452144
(E) sjnott@physiofirst.org.uk
Speciality: Acupressure, Acupuncture, Electrotherapy, Manipulation, Massage (Therapeutic), Pilates, Ultrasonics, Vibrational Therapy. ✓
● **Physiotherapist** Mr S Nottingham Q: MCSP, SRP. M: CSP.
S Yrs. Est.: 8 (Ref:HM15086)

## NOTTRET, K

**K Nottret**, 30 Rotten Row, Lichfield, **Staffordshire**, WS13 6JB, ENG.
(T) 01543 252673
Speciality: Osteopathy.
● **Senior Partner** Ms J Scratchley
P S T (Ref:HM15087)

## NOYCE, T J

**T J Noyce**, Fairford Frith Hill Rd, Godalming, **Surrey**, GU7 2ED, ENG.
(T) 01483 414798
Speciality: Chiropodists (Podiatrists).
● **Owner** Mr T Noyce
S (Ref:HM15088)

## NOYES, DEIDRE

**Deidre Noyes**, 26 Mulberry Way, London, **London (Greater)**, E18 1ED, ENG.
(T) 020 8530 8804
Speciality: Hypnotherapy.
● **Owner** Mr D Noyes
B (Ref:HM15089)

## NOYS, ALISON

**Alison Noys**, Flat 19 Harold Court, 64 Harold Court Rd, Romford, **Essex**, RM3 0LA, ENG.
(T) 01708 342148
Speciality: Reflexology.
S T (Ref:HM15090)

## NRTH LEEDS PHYSIO/SPRTS INJ

**North Leeds Physiotherapy & Sports Injuries Centre**, 112 Long Row, Horsforth, Leeds, **Yorkshire (West)**, LS18 5AT, ENG.
(T) 01132 582204
Speciality: Acupuncture, Electrotherapy, Manipulation, Massage (Therapeutic). ✓
● **Physiotherapist** Ms S Beldon Q: BSc (Hons). M: CPSM, CSP, OCPPP.
S Yrs. Est.: 1 (Ref:HM15091)

## NRTH LONDON ALEXANDER PRACTICE

**North London Alexander Practice**, 8 Courthope Rd, London, **London (Greater)**, NW3 2LB, ENG.
(T) 020 7284 4298
(E) amastertontr@aol.com
Speciality: Alexander Technique. ✓
● **Teacher of the Alexander Technique** Ms A Masterton Q: MSTAT. M: STAT.
C P Yrs. Est.: 4 (Ref:HM15092)

## NRTH LONDON PSYCHO COUNS ASS

**North London Psychotherapy & Counselling Association**, 15 Gresley Rd, London, **London (Greater)**, N19 3LA, ENG.
(T) 020 7272 4133
Speciality: Psychotherapy.
B (Ref:HM15093)

## NRTH OF ENGLAND STRESS MNGMT

**North Of England Stress Management**, 5 Westmoreland St, Darlington, **County Durham**, DL3 0NX, ENG.
(T) 01325 460061
Speciality: Complementary Medicines & Therapy.
● **Owner** Mr F Serra
C M (Ref:HM15036)

## NRTH WALES CLI OF RELAXATION

**North Wales Clinic Of Relaxation**, Roslyn, Promenade, Llanfairfechan, **Conwy**, LL33 0BU, WAL.
(T) 01248 680706
Speciality: Complementary Medicines & Therapy.
C M (Ref:HM15095)

## NRTH WARWICKSHIRE NHS CHIROP

**North Warwickshire NHS Trust Chiropody Service**, Camphill Clinic, 43 Ramsden Avenue, Nuneaton, **Warwickshire**, CV10 9EB, ENG.
(T) 024 7639 2784
Speciality: Chiropodists (Podiatrists).
S (Ref:HM15096)

## NRTH WEST ALLERGY & NUTRITION

**North West Allergy & Nutrition**, 30 Greenmount Lane, Bolton, **Lancashire**, BL1 5JF, ENG.
(T) 01204 496678
Speciality: Complementary Medicines & Therapy.
● **Owner** Mrs E Betley
M (Ref:HM15097)

## NRTH WST LONDON PSYCHOTHY CTRE

**North West London Psychotherapy Centre**, 7 Rudall Cr, London, **London (Greater)**, NW3 1RR, ENG.
(T) 020 7431 5192
Speciality: Psychotherapy.
B (Ref:HM15098)

## NS3UK NUTRITION SERVICES

**Nutrition Services Supplies Support**, 51 Trevelyan, Bracknell, **Berkshire**, RG12 8YD, ENG.
(T) 01344 360033 (F) 01344 360033
(E) kate@ns3.co.uk
(W) www.ns3.co.uk
Speciality: Nutritional Therapy. ✓
● **Owner/Managing Director** Mrs K Neil Q: Dip.ION, RM, RN. M: BANT.
M Yrs. Est.: 3 (Ref:HM15099)

## NTH IRELAND MUSIC THER TRUST

**Northern Ireland Music Therapy Trust**, Knockbracken Healthcare Park, Saintfield Rd, Belfast, **County Antrim**, BT8 8BH, NIR.
(T) 028 9070 5854 (F) 028 9070 5854
Speciality: Music Therapy. ✓
● **Therapist** Ms K Diamond Q: SRAaT(M).
● **Therapist** Mr B Smith Q: SRAaT(M).
● **Therapist** Ms N Murray Q: SRAaT(M).
C Yrs. Est.: 10 (Ref:HM15100)

## NUALA WOULFE BEAUTY SALON

**Nuala Woulfe Beauty Salon Ltd**, 4c Glasthule Rd, Sandycove, **County Dublin**, IRE.
(T) 01230 0244 (F) 01230 4882
(E) nualawoulfebeautysalon@eircom.net
(W) www.nualawoulfebeautysalon.ie
Speciality: Acupressure, Aromatherapy, Electrotherapy, Holistic Healing, Magnetic Therapy, Massage (Therapeutic), Mud Therapy, Reflexology, Light Therapy, Lymphatic Drainage Treatments, Magno Plus. ✓ CREDIT
● **Beauty Therapist** Nuala Woulfe M: IRI, SAC.
C Yrs. Est.: 7 (Ref:HM15101)

## NUGENT, L C

**L C Nugent**, 27 Oaks Drive, Colchester, **Essex**, CO3 3QZ, ENG.
(T) 01206 572761
Speciality: Osteopathy.
● **Partner** Mr L Nugent
P S T (Ref:HM15102)

## NUMBER 11 THERAPY CENTRE

**Number 11 Therapy Centre**, 11 Mickleburgh Hill, Herne Bay, **Kent**, CT6 6AA, ENG.
(T) 01227 360294 (F) 01227 360294
Speciality: Complementary Medicines & Therapy.
● **Owner** Mr G Davies
M (Ref:HM15103)

## NUNEATON CHIROPRACTIC CLINIC

**Nuneaton Chiropractic Clinic**, 29 Attleborough Rd, Nuneaton, **Warwickshire**, CV11 4HZ, ENG.
(T) 024 7638 3138
Speciality: Chiropractic, Reiki. ✓
● **Chiropractor** Dr L Dawson Q: BSc, DC. M: BCA, GCC.
● **Owner** Dr R Hatfield Q: BSc, DC. M: BCA, GCC.
P Yrs. Est.: 100 (Ref:HM15104)

## NUNN, BARBARA

**Barbara Nunn**, 118 Clacton Rd, St. Osyth, Clacton-On-Sea, **Essex**, CO16 8PF, ENG.
(T) 01255 820677
Speciality: Complementary Medicines & Therapy.
● **Owner** Mrs B Nunn
C M (Ref:HM15105)

## NUNN, KATIE

**Katie Nunn**, The Goodlife Natural Health Centre, 207 High St, Sutton, **Surrey**, SM1 1JU, ENG.
(T) 020 8770 1156
Speciality: Osteopathy.
P S T (Ref:HM15106)

## NUNN, PAULINE

**Pauline Nunn**, 7 Ludham Cl, Chesterfield, **Derbyshire**, S41 8SB, ENG.
(T) 01246 211053
Speciality: Reflexology.
● **Owner** Mrs P Nunn
S T (Ref:HM15107)

## NUNN, SALLY

**Sally Nunn**, Bow Window, 59 High St, Arundel, **Sussex (West)**, BN18 9AJ, ENG.
(T) 01903 884466
Speciality: Homeopathy, Holistic Therapy. ✓
● **Owner** Ms S Nunn Q: L.C.C.H, RSHom.
C Yrs. Est.: 4 (Ref:HM15108)

## NUNNS, PATRICIA

**Patricia Nunns**, 46 Culver Rd, Basingstoke, **Hampshire**, RG21 3LT, ENG.
(T) 01256 842048
Speciality: Reflexology.
● **Owner** Mrs P Nunns
S T (Ref:HM15109)

## NURCHIR

**Mr Carl R Burrows**, 29 Hampden Rd, Malvern Link, **Worcestershire**, WR14 1NB, ENG.
(T) 01684 561168
(E) carl@footaid.u-net.com
Speciality: Biomechanics, Chiropody, Electrotherapy, Manipulation, Massage

Key: B Mind-Body Medicine; C Complementary Medicine; H Self Help Treatment; M Medicinal Therapy; O Oriental Medicine; P Postural Therapy; S Manipulative Structural Therapy; T Touch Therapy

(Therapeutic), Ultrasonics, Orthotic Therapy. ✔
● **Chiropodist** Mr C Burrows M: Inst.CH.P, S.C.P.
C Yrs. Est.: 34 (Ref:HM15110)

**NURSE, SUE**

**Sue Nurse**, 3 Clandon Rd, Ilford, **Essex**, IG3 8BB, ENG.
(T) 020 8491 5797
Speciality: Reflexology.
● **Owner** Ms S Nurse
S T (Ref:HM15111)

**NURTURED BY NATURE**

**Nurtured By Nature**, 28 Wilford Lane, West Bridgford, Nottingham, **Nottinghamshire**, NG2 7QX, ENG.
(T) 01159 810745 (F) 01159 240307
Speciality: Aromatherapy.
● **Owner** Mrs C Price
M O (Ref:HM15112)

**NUTE, JANET**

**Janet Nute**, 23 Pen-Y-Wain Rd, Cardiff, **Glamorgan (Vale of)**, CF24 4GF, WAL.
(T) 029 2033 1927
Speciality: Chiropodists (Podiatrists).
● **Owner** Mrs J Nute
S (Ref:HM15113)

**NUTE, JANET**

**Janet Nute**, 36 Dogfield St, Off Crwys Rd, Cardiff, **Glamorgan (Vale of)**, CF24 4QZ, WAL.
(T) 029 2022 3086
Speciality: Chiropodists (Podiatrists).
S (Ref:HM15114)

**NUTMEG CLINIC**

**Nutmeg Clinic**, 1 Maypole St, Wombourne, Wolverhampton, **Midlands (West)**, WV5 9JB, ENG.
(T) 01902 324952
Speciality: Aromatherapy.
● **Owner** Mrs J Granger
M O (Ref:HM15115)

**NUTRAMIST**

**Nutramist**, 235a Golders Green Rd, London, **London (Greater)**, NW11 9ES, ENG.
(T) 020 8455 1400 (F) 020 8201 8924
Speciality: Complementary Medicines & Therapy.
● **Manager** Mr D Rokach
C M (Ref:HM15116)

**NUTRI CENTRE**

**Nutri Centre (The)**, 7 Park Cres, London, **London (Greater)**, W1N 3HE, ENG.
(T) 020 7436 5122 (F) 020 7436 5171
Speciality: Complementary Medicines & Therapy.
● **Owner** Mr R Metha
C M (Ref:HM15117)

**NUTRIMED**

**Nutrimed**, 57 Hales Park, Bewdley, **Worcestershire**, DY12 2HU, ENG.
(T) 01299 405219
Speciality: Herbal Medicine, Nutritional Therapy.
C (Ref:HM15118)

**NUTRI-SOL**

**Nutri-Sol**, 79 University Avenue, Belfast, **County Antrim**, BT7 1GX, NIR.
(T) 028 9039 2484
Speciality: Complementary Medicines & Therapy.
M (Ref:HM15119)

**NUTRITION & HEALTH**

**Nutrition & Health Co Ltd (The)**, Church View, 3 Knockhundred Row, Midhurst, **Sussex (West)**, GU29 9DQ, ENG.
(T) 01730 814943 (F) 01730 810467
Speciality: Complementary Medicines & Therapy.
● **Owner** Ms L Barr
M (Ref:HM15120)

**NUTRITION AND ALLERGY CLINIC**

**Nutrition and Allergy Clinic**, 11 Mauldeth Cl, Heaton Merpeg, Stockport, **Cheshire**, SK4 3NP, ENG.
(T) 01614 320964
(E) mmoss.nutrition@ukonline.co.uk
Speciality: Clinical Ecology, Complementary Therapy, Counselling, Dowsing, Healer, Healing Therapy, Herbal Medicine, Holistic Healing, Nutritional Therapy, Orthomolecular Medicine, Vitamin Therapy. ✔
● **Nutritionist** Ms M Moss Q: Dip.ION, MA, UCTD. M: BANT.
C Yrs. Est.: 8 (Ref:HM15121)

**NUTRITION CLINIC**

**Nutrition Clinic (The)**, 9 Upper Hill St, Blaenavon, Pontypool, **Monmouthshire**, NP4 9NN, WAL.
(T) 01495 790170 (F) 01495 790170
(E) caroline.nutri.clin@talkzi.com
Speciality: Nutritional Therapy, Scenar Therapy. ✔
● **Nutrition Consultant**
Mrs C Edwards Q: Dip.ION. M: BANT.
H M P S Yrs. Est.: 5 (Ref:HM15122)

**NUTRITION FOR LIFE**

**Nutrition For Life International**, The Hay Barn, Brinsea, Congresbury, **Somerset**, BS49 5JL, ENG.
(T) 01934 853319 (F) 01934 853319
(E) roberton@brinseahaybarn.freeserve.co.uk
Speciality: Complementary Therapy, Nutritional Therapy. ✔
● **Owner** Ms M Lorang-Roberton
B C H Yrs. Est.: 18 (Ref:HM15123)

**NUTRITION FOR LIFE INT**

**Val & Sons**, 37 Iberia House, Hornsey Rise, London, **London (Greater)**, N19 3TY, ENG.
(T) 020 7686 1108
Speciality: Family Planning (Natural), Herbal Medicine, Nutritional Therapy, Vitamin Therapy.
● **Executive Distributor**
Mrs V Graham
H (Ref:HM15124)

**NUTRITION PLUS**

**Nutrition Plus**, Watersedge, Church End, Blewbury, Didcot, **Oxfordshire**, OX11 9QH, ENG.
(T) 01235 851650
Speciality: Complementary Medicines & Therapy.
C M (Ref:HM15125)

**NUTRITION WORLD**

**Nutrition World**, 45 McKinley Pl, Newton Mearns Shopping Centre, Newton Mearns, **Glasgow (City of)**, G77 6EZ, SCO.
(T) 01416 397770 (F) 01355 579546
(E) caroline raff@hotmail.com
Speciality: Acupressure, Aromatherapy, Bach Remedies, Bowen Therapy, Cranial Osteopathy, Hay Diet, Herbal Medicine, Indian Head Massage, Kinesiology, Manipulation, Massage (Therapeutic), Physiotherapy, Reflexology, Shiatsu, Vitamin Therapy, Yoga, Lymphatic Drainage. ✔ [credit card]
● **Healthcare Consultant**
Ms C Rafferty
● **Aromatherapist/Yoga Therapist**
Ms S Scott
● **Reflexologist** Ms L Trecher
● **Physiotherapist/Cranial-Sacral Therapist**
Ms L Renfrew Q: MCSP.
M Yrs. Est.: 6 (Ref:HM15126)

**NUTRITIONAL THERAPY**

**Nutritional Therapy**, 1 The Crescent, Mottram St. Andrew, Macclesfield, **Cheshire**, SK10 4QW, ENG.
(T) 01625 586219
Speciality: Complementary Medicines & Therapy.
● **Owner** Ms S Dixon
M (Ref:HM15127)

**NUTRITIONIST**

**Nutritionist**, 1 Horley Cl, Bexleyheath, **Kent**, DA6 7HS, ENG.
(T) 01322 554798
Speciality: Complementary Medicines & Therapy.
C M (Ref:HM15128)

**NUTRON FOOD SENSITIVITY**

**Nutron Food Sensitivity**, The Old Mill, The St, Albury, Guildford, **Surrey**, GU5 9AZ, ENG.
(T) 01483 203666 (F) 01483 203456
Speciality: Complementary Medicines & Therapy.
● **Chief Executive** Mr J Bradney
M (Ref:HM15129)

**NUTRON WEIGHT & HEALTH CLINIC**

**Nutron Weight & Health Clinic**, Unit 3 Canada St, **County Waterford**, IRE.
(T) 05185 6185
Speciality: Complementary Medicines & Therapy.
M (Ref:HM15130)

**NUTT, N**

**N Nutt**, 32 New Row, Coleraine, **County Londonderry**, BT52 1AF, NIR.
(T) 028 7034 2589
Speciality: Chiropodists (Podiatrists).
S (Ref:HM15131)

**NUTTALL, A J**

**A J Nuttall**, 6 Anson Rd, Wilmslow, **Cheshire**, SK9 2HE, ENG.
(T) 01625 533729
Speciality: Chiropodists (Podiatrists).
● **Owner** Mrs A Nuttall
S (Ref:HM15132)

**NUTTELL, DAVE**

**Dave Nuttell**, 34 Harpers Lane, Bolton, **Lancashire**, BL1 6HR, ENG.
(T) 01204 844290 (F) 01204 844290
Speciality: Hypnosis.
● **Owner** Mr D Nuttall
B (Ref:HM15133)

**NUTTER, D**

**D Nutter**, 65 Cleaver St, Burnley, **Lancashire**, BB10 3BS, ENG.
(T) 01282 454563
Speciality: Acupuncture.
O (Ref:HM15134)

**NW COLLEGE-HOMOEOPATHY**

**North West College Of Homoeopathy**, 23 Wilbraham Rd, Manchester, **Manchester (Greater)**, M14 6FG, ENG.
(T) 01612 572445
Speciality: Homeopathy.
M (Ref:HM15135)

**O & L WOMENS HEALTH PHYSIO**

**O & L Womens Health Physiotherapy Clinic**, Fortis Green Health Centre, 150 Fortis Green, London, **London (Greater)**, N10 3PA, ENG.
(T) 020 8365 7247 (F) 020 8365 7247
Speciality: Physiotherapy.
● **Owner** Ms O Lawal
P S T (Ref:HM15136)

**O C G**

**O C G Ltd**, 7 Fenlock Court, Fenlock Rd, Blenheim Office Pk, Long Hanborough, Witney, **Oxfordshire**, OX8 8LN, ENG.
(T) 01993 880304 (F) 01993 880618
Speciality: Psychology.
● **Manager** Mrs J Walliker
B (Ref:HM15137)

**O MAILLE, SEAN**

**O Maille Sean B A (Psych )**, 22 College Rd, **County Galway**, IRE.
(T) 09156 6879
Speciality: Complementary Medicines & Therapy.
M (Ref:HM15138)

**O Z**

**O Z**, Relexation Centre, Marple Rd, Chisworth, Broadbottom, Hyde, **Cheshire**, SK14 6DH, ENG.
(T) 01457 863267
Speciality: Complementary Medicines & Therapy.
C M (Ref:HM15139)

**OADBY HOUSE**

**Oadby House Physiotherapy & Sports Injury Clinic**, 21 Wigston Rd, Oadby, Leicester, **Leicestershire**, LE2 5QF, ENG.
(T) 01162 710723



Key continued: Yrs.Est: Years Established Q: Qualifications M: Professional Membership ✔ Indemnity Insurance [credit card] Accept Credit Cards

Speciality: Acupuncture, Physiotherapy. ✓
● **Physiotherapist** Ms C Turner Q: MCSP, SRP. M: CSP.
● **Physiotherapist** Ms S Hazeldine Q: MCSP, SRP. M: CSP.
S Yrs. Est.: 10 (Ref:HM15140)

**OADBY THERAPY CENTRE**

**Oadby Therapy Centre**, 79 Wigston Rd, Oadby, Leicester, **Leicestershire**, LE2 5QG, ENG.
(T) 01162 712987
Speciality: Hypnosis.
B (Ref:HM15141)

**OADES, JANET**

**Janet Oades**, Mulberry Cottage, 33 Sunderland St, Tickhill, Doncaster, **Yorkshire (South)**, DN11 9PT, ENG.
(T) 01302 745828
Speciality: Acupuncture.
O (Ref:HM15142)

**OAK HOUSE THERAPY CENTRE**

**Oak House Therapy Centre**, Halberry Lane, Newport, **Isle of Wight**, PO30 2ER, ENG.
(T) 01983 526333
Speciality: Physiotherapy.
P S T (Ref:HM15143)

**OAK TREES CLINIC**

**Oak Trees Clinic**, 31 The Mall, London, **London (Greater)**, W5 2PX, ENG.
(T) 020 8566 2920
Speciality: Complementary Medicines & Therapy.
C M (Ref:HM15144)

**OAKENFOLD, L**

**L Oakenfold**, Ashdown Osteopathic Centre, The Sq, Lewes Rd, Forest Row, **Sussex (East)**, RH18 5ES, ENG.
(T) 01342 822505 (F) 01342 822505
Speciality: Osteopathy.
● **Owner** Mr T Strutt
P S T (Ref:HM15145)

**OAKES, JILL**

**Jill Oakes**, Chester Rd, Grappenhall, Warrington, **Cheshire**, WA4 2QG, ENG.
(T) 01925 861713 (F) 01925 861713
Speciality: Aromatherapy.
● **Owner** Mr K Oakes
M O (Ref:HM15146)

**OAKES, R & GUL, MARGARET**

**Russell Oakes & Margaret Gul**, The Oakland Clinic, 18C High St, Standish, Wigan, **Lancashire**, WN6 0HL, ENG.
(T) 01257 405406
Speciality: Osteopathy.
P S T (Ref:HM15147)

**OAKES, ROBERT**

**Robert Oakes**, 10 Harley St, London, **London (Greater)**, W1N 1AA, ENG.
(T) 020 7580 2424 (F) 01214 561736
Speciality: Psychology.
● **Owner** Dr R Oakes
B (Ref:HM15148)

**OAKEY, D C**

**D C Oakey**, 41 Robert Franklin Way, South Cerney, Cirencester, **Gloucestershire**, GL7 5UD, ENG.
(T) 01285 861005
Speciality: Chiropodists (Podiatrists).
● **Owner** Mr D Oakey
S (Ref:HM15149)

**OAKFIELD CLINIC**

**Oakfield Clinic (The)**, Wood Farm House, Marlbank Rd, Welland, Malvern, **Worcestershire**, WR13 6NA, ENG.
(T) 01684 311534 (F) 01684 311534
(E) john@health-naturally.co.uk
(W) www.health-naturally.com
Speciality: Complementary Medicines & Therapy, Buteyko Breathing Method.
● **Teacher** Mr J Mackisack
H Yrs. Est.: 2 (Ref:HM15150)

**OAKFIELD NATURAL HEALTH CENTRE**

**Oakfield Natural Health Centre**, 16 Penallta Rd, Ystrad Mynach, Hengoed, **Caerphilly**, CF82 7AP, WAL.
(T) 01443 862157
Speciality: Aromatherapy, Chiropody, Counselling, Homeopathy, Hypnotherapy, Reflexology. ✓
● **Chairman** Mrs M Liphard
(T) 01443 812117
● **Beighton** Mr J
C Yrs. Est.: 4 (Ref:HM15151)

**OAKHAM OSTEOPATHIC CLINIC**

**Oakham Osteopathic Clinic**, Oakham Medical Centre, Cold Overton Rd, Oakham, **Leicestershire**, LE15 6NT, ENG.
(T) 01162 571234
Speciality: Osteopathy.
P S T (Ref:HM15152)

**OAKHAM PHYSIOTHERAPY CLINIC**

**Oakham Physiotherapy Clinic**, 21 Burley Rd, Oakham, **Leicestershire**, LE15 6DH, ENG.
(T) 01572 756726
Speciality: Physiotherapy.
● **Owner** Mr K Carter
P S T (Ref:HM15153)

**OAKLEIGH THERAPY CENTRE**

**Oakleigh Therapy Centre**, 253 Oakleigh Rd North, London, **London (Greater)**, N20 0TX, ENG.
(T) 020 8361 8681 (F) 020 8361 8681
Speciality: Physiotherapy.
● **Owner** Mr A Shah
P S T (Ref:HM15154)

**OAKLEY, IAN**

**Ian Oakley**, Glen Royd, Birchcliffe Rd, Hebden Bridge, **Yorkshire (West)**, HX7 8DB, ENG.
(T) 01422 843563
Speciality: Psychotherapy.
B (Ref:HM15155)

**OAKLEY, STEVEN**

**Steven Oakley**, 75 Leigh Rd, Leigh-On-Sea, **Essex**, SS9 1JN, ENG.
(T) 01702 714862 (F) 01702 716969
Speciality: Physiotherapy.
● **Owner** Mrs C Merryfield
P S T (Ref:HM15156)

**OAKS PHYSIO & ACUPUNTURE**

**Oaks Physiotherapy Acupunture Sports Injuries Clinic (The)**, 13 The Oaks, Sunderland, **Tyne and Wear**, SR2 8EX, ENG.
(T) 01915 142136
Speciality: Physiotherapy.
P S T (Ref:HM15157)

**OAKTREE COMP HEALTH PRACTICE**

**Oaktree Complementary Health Practice**, 26 Victoria St, Cambridge, **Cambridgeshire**, CB1 1JP, ENG.
(T) 01223 319155 (F) 01223 319155
Speciality: Complementary Medicines & Therapy.
● **Senior Partner** Mr P Kimber
M (Ref:HM15158)

**OAKWOOD OSTEOPATHS**

**Oakwood Osteopaths**, 166 Bramley Rd, London, **London (Greater)**, N14 4HX, ENG.
(T) 020 8350 0036
Speciality: Osteopathy.
P S T (Ref:HM15159)

**OASIS CENTRE**

**Oasis Centre**, 12 Eastwood Cl, London, **London (Greater)**, E18 1BX, ENG.
(T) 020 8532 9800
Speciality: Psychotherapy.
B (Ref:HM15160)

**OASIS CLINIC**

**Oasis Clinic**, 43 Busdens Way, Milford, Godalming, **Surrey**, GU8 5JP, ENG.
(T) 01483 860360 (F) 01483 860360
Speciality: Osteopathy.
● **Manager** Mrs J Hamilton
P S T (Ref:HM15161)

**OASIS CLINICS**

**Oasis Clinics**, The Ark, Mount Lane, Turners Hill, Crawley, **Sussex (West)**, RH10 4RA, ENG.
(T) 01342 712266
Speciality: Osteopathy.
● **Owner** Mr M Jones
P S T (Ref:HM15162)

**OASIS COMPLEMENTARY THERAPIES**

**Oasis Complementary Therapies Ltd**, Dee Hills Park, Chester, **Cheshire**, CH3 5AX, ENG.
(T) 01244 342424
Speciality: Complementary Medicines & Therapy.
● **Partner** Mrs C Elliott
C M (Ref:HM15163)

**OASIS NATURAL THERAPY CLINIC**

**Oasis Natural Therapy Clinic (The)**, Fieldhouse Lane, Globe Park, Marlow, **Buckinghamshire**, SL7 1LU, ENG.
(T) 01628 488988
Speciality: Complementary Medicines & Therapy.
C M (Ref:HM15164)

**OATHALL PHYSIOTHERAPY CLINIC**

**Oathall Physiotherapy Clinic**, 41-43 Boltro Rd, Haywards Heath, **Sussex (West)**, RH16 1BJ, ENG.
(T) 01444 413743
Speciality: Physiotherapy.
● **Owner** Mrs T Carter
P S T (Ref:HM15165)

**OATLANDS OSTEOPATHIC CLINIC**

**Oatlands Osteopathic Clinic**, 20 Oatlands Drive, Weybridge, **Surrey**, KT13 9JL, ENG.
(T) 01932 887111
Speciality: Osteopathy.
P S T (Ref:HM15166)

**OATS, A J**

**A J Oats**, 20 Victoria Rd, Devizes, **Wiltshire**, SN10 1ET, ENG.
(T) 01380 721949
Speciality: Osteopathy.
● **Owner** Mrs A Oats
P S T (Ref:HM15167)

**OBANYE, A I (DR)**

**Dr A I Obanye**, Flat 1, 16 High Lane, Manchester, **Manchester (Greater)**, M21 9DF, ENG.
(T) 01618 819106
Speciality: Hypnotherapy.
B (Ref:HM15168)

**OBEARA, REA**

**Obeara Rea PH D**, 10 Montpelier Tce, **County Galway**, IRE.
(T) 09158 9330
Speciality: Complementary Medicines & Therapy.
M (Ref:HM15169)

**OBONYO, T J**

**T J Obonyo**, 1 Kingsway, Dalry, **Ayrshire (North)**, KA24 5HE, SCO.
(T) 01294 835449
Speciality: Physiotherapy.
● **Owner** Mr T Obonyo
P S T (Ref:HM15170)

**O'BRIAN, D**

**D O'Brian**, 41 Golfdrum St, Dunfermline, **Fife**, KY12 8DZ, SCO.
(T) 01383 733376
Speciality: Chiropody. ✓
● **Chiropodist** Mr D O'Brian Q: M.S.C.P.
M Yrs. Est.: 13 (Ref:HM15171)

**O'BRIEN FAHEY, ANNETTE**

**O'Brien Fahey Annette DHP AH MIAHH RT**, The Bramble Rose, Clonmel, **County Tipperary**, IRE.
(T) 05227 250
Speciality: Hypnotherapy.
B (Ref:HM15172)

**O'BRIEN, ANN**

**Ann O'Brien**, 88B Antill Rd, London, **London (Greater)**, E3 5BP, ENG.
(T) 020 8981 3082
Speciality: Hypnotherapy.
● **Owner** Miss A O'Brien
B (Ref:HM15173)

**O'BRIEN, ANN**

**Ann O'Brien**, Bodywise, 119 Roman Rd, London,



Key: B Mind-Body Medicine | C Complementary Medicine | H Self Help Treatment | M Medicinal Therapy | O Oriental Medicine | P Postural Therapy | S Manipulative Structural Therapy | T Touch Therapy

**London (Greater)**, E2 0QN, ENG.
(T) 020 8981 6938
Speciality: Hypnotherapy.
[B] (Ref:HM15174)

### O'BRIEN, BRIDGET
**O'Brien Bridget**, 519 S. C. Rd, Dublin, **County Dublin**, IRE.
(T) 01454 1170
Speciality: Complementary Medicines & Therapy.
[M] (Ref:HM15175)

### O'BRIEN, CARMEL
**O'Brien Carmel**, Fernbank Point Rd, Crosshaven, **County Cork**, IRE.
(T) 021 4831 991
Speciality: Complementary Medicines & Therapy.
[M] (Ref:HM15176)

### O'BRIEN, DAVID
**O'Brien David**, 2 Beechwalk Brookwood Scholars, Rathfarnham, **County Dublin**, IRE.
(T) 08722 15837
Speciality: Complementary Medicines & Therapy.
[M] (Ref:HM15177)

### O'BRIEN, EAMONN
**Eamonn O'Brien**, 37 Upper Duke St, Liverpool, **Merseyside**, L1 9DY, ENG.
(T) 01517 091195
Speciality: Hypnosis.
● **Owner** Mr E O'Brien
[B] (Ref:HM15178)

### O'BRIEN, FRANCES
**Frances O'Brien**, 1 Tarrant Avenue, Witney, **Oxfordshire**, OX8 6EE, ENG.
(T) 01993 704607
Speciality: Acupuncture. ✔
● **Owner/Acupuncturist** Ms F O'Brien
M: BAcC.
[C] Yrs. Est.: 15 (Ref:HM15179)

### O'BRIEN, HANNAH
**O'Brien Hannah M I R I**, Inchnagree Buttevant, **County Cork**, IRE.
(T) 022 2428 6
Speciality: Complementary Medicines & Therapy.
[M] (Ref:HM15180)

### O'BRIEN, HELEN
**Helen O'Brien**, 1 Furzen Cl, Dunstable, **Bedfordshire**, LU6 3EN, ENG.
(T) 01582 696053
Speciality: Physiotherapy.
● **Owner** Mrs H O'Brien
[P] [S] [T] (Ref:HM15181)

### O'BRIEN, J
**J O'Brien**, 59 School Rd, Pontefract, **Yorkshire (West)**, WF8 2AJ, ENG.
(T) 01977 707951 (F) 01977 707951
Speciality: Chiropodists (Podiatrists).
● **Owner** Mr J O'Brien
[S] (Ref:HM15182)

### O'BRIEN, JAMES
**James O'Brien**, 54A Lower Addiscombe Rd, Croydon, **Surrey**, CR0 6AA, ENG.
(T) 020 8240 7059
Speciality: Acupuncture.
● **Principal** Mr J O'Brien
[O] (Ref:HM15183)

### O'BRIEN, JANE
**Jane O'Brien**, 22 Hollies Avenue, West Byfleet, **Surrey**, KT14 6AJ, ENG.
(T) 01932 344391
Speciality: Homeopathy.
● **Owner** Mrs J O'Brien
[M] (Ref:HM15184)

### O'BRIEN, JILL
**Jill O'Brien**, Lavenders, 61 Headley Rd, Liphook, **Hampshire**, GU30 7PR, ENG.
(T) 01428 722417
Speciality: Reflexology.
[S] [T] (Ref:HM15185)

### O'BRIEN, JOHN
**John O'Brien**, 271 Banbury Rd, Oxford, **Oxfordshire**, OX2 7JF, ENG.
(T) 01865 556954
Speciality: Osteopathy.
● **Owner** Mr J O'Brien
[P] [S] [T] (Ref:HM15186)

### O'BRIEN, JOHN C
**John C O'Brien**, 33 Crouch St, Banbury, **Oxfordshire**, OX16 9PR, ENG.
(T) 01295 261228
Speciality: Osteopathy.
● **Owner** Mr J O'Brian
[P] [S] [T] (Ref:HM15187)

### O'BRIEN, MARY KENNEDY
**Kennedy O'Brien Mary D O**, 41 Glenthorn Killarney Rd, Bray, **County Wicklow**, IRE.
(T) 01286 2054
Speciality: Osteopathy.
[P] [S] [T] (Ref:HM15188)

### O'BRIEN, THERESE
**O'Brien Therese I T E C**, 45 Bulfin Rd, Inchicore, Dublin, **County Dublin**, IRE.
(T) 01454 0709
Speciality: Aromatherapy.
[M] [O] (Ref:HM15189)

### OBSERVATORY
**Observatory (The)**, 4 Archfield Rd, Bristol, BS6 6BE, ENG.
(T) 01179 426070
Speciality: Complementary Medicines & Therapy.
● **Owner** Mrs S Papier
[C] [M] (Ref:HM15190)

### O'BYRNE, A
**A O'Byrne**, Westholme Lodge, Winston, Darlington, **County Durham**, DL2 3QL, ENG.
(T) 01325 730799
Speciality: Chiropodists (Podiatrists).
● **Owner** A O'Byrne
[S] (Ref:HM15191)

### O'CALLAGHAN, JOHN
**O'Callaghan John REIKI Natural Healing R M P T**, 12 Willbrook Rd, Rathfarnham, **County Dublin**, IRE.
(T) 01493 4563
Speciality: Healing.
[B] (Ref:HM15192)

### O'CALLAGHAN, STEVE
**Therapeutic Massage**, The Ishta Natural Health Centre, 26 Kings Avenue, Stone, **Staffordshire**, ST15 8HD, ENG.
(T) 01785 616010
(E) steveocall@bigfoot.com
Speciality: Indian Head Massage, Massage (Therapeutic). ✔
● **Massage Therapist**
Mr S O'Callaghan Q: Dip.Th.Massage. M: SHP.
[S] Yrs. Est.: 1 (Ref:HM15193)

### OCCUPATION/PERSONALITY TESTING
**Occupational & Personality Testing**, 14 Gwynne Park Avenue, Woodford Green, **Essex**, IG8 8AB, ENG.
(T) 020 8505 8453
Speciality: Psychology.
● **Owner** Mr M Brandon
[B] (Ref:HM15194)

### OCCUPATIONAL CONSULTANCY SVS
**Occupational Consultancy Services**, 106 Starbold Cres, Knowle, Solihull, **Midlands (West)**, B93 9LA, ENG.
(T) 01564 770071 (F) 01564 770071
Speciality: Psychology.
● **Owner** Mr A Scott
[B] (Ref:HM15195)

### OCCUPATIONAL PSYCHOL SOLUTIONS
**Occupational Psychology Solutions**, 47 Compton Avenue, Aston-On-Trent, Derby, **Derbyshire**, DE72 2AU, ENG.
(T) 01332 799007
Speciality: Psychology.
[B] (Ref:HM15196)

### OCCUPATIONAL PSYCHOLOGY SVS
**Occupational Psychology Services Ltd**, Townsend Chambers, Amherst Hill, Sevenoaks, **Kent**, TN13 2EL, ENG.
(T) 01732 742544
Speciality: Psychology.
[B] (Ref:HM15197)

### OCEAN ALTERNATIVE LIFESTYLE
**Ocean Alternative Lifestyle**, 30-31 Byram Arcade, Huddersfield, **Yorkshire (West)**, HD1 1ND, ENG.
(T) 01484 435232
Speciality: Complementary Medicines & Therapy.
● **Employee** Mr G Isaacs
[M] (Ref:HM15198)

### OCEAN BREEZE SANCTUARY
**Ocean Breeze Sanctuary**, 54 Harpenden Lane, Redbourn, St. Albans, **Hertfordshire**, AL3 7PB, ENG.
(T) 01582 792665
Speciality: Complementary Medicines & Therapy.
[C] [M] (Ref:HM15199)

### OCEAN SUN
**Ocean Sun**, 515 Charlton House, 687 Chester Rd, Manchester, **Manchester (Greater)**, M16 0GW, ENG.
(T) 01618 770408
Speciality: Hypnotherapy.
● **Owner** Mr M Gaynor
[B] (Ref:HM15200)

### OCEANFLOOD COMPUTERS
**Oceanflood Computers Ltd**, 35A Moorlands Rd, Camberley, **Surrey**, GU15 3AG, ENG.
(T) 01252 333738
Speciality: Osteopathy.
[P] [S] [T] (Ref:HM15201)

### OCHANDO, MARI-TRINI
**Mari-Trini Ochando**, Clissold Park Health Centre, 154 Stoke Newington Church St, London, **London (Greater)**, N16 0JU, ENG.
(T) 020 7249 2990 (F) 020 7249 3977
Speciality: Reflexology.
● **Director** Ms D Berg
[S] [T] (Ref:HM15202)

### O'COLMAIN, AIDAN (DR)
**Dr Aidan O'Colmain**, Medical Centre, 6 Plunkett Avenue, Mervue, Galway, **County Galway**, IRE.
(T) 09173 5727
(E) aocolmain@eircom.net
Speciality: Acupuncture. ✔
● **Owner** Dr A O'Colmain Q: DipCH.P, MB.
[O] Yrs. Est.: 2 (Ref:HM15203)

### O'CONNELL, KATHRYNE R G N
**O'Connell Kathryne R G N**, Tienaboul, Killarney, **County Kerry**, IRE.
(T) 06435 263
Speciality: Complementary Medicines & Therapy.
[M] (Ref:HM15204)

### O'CONNELL, RYAN (DR)
**O'Connell Dr & Ryan Dr**, Belvedere Surgery Douglas Rd, Cork, **County Cork**, IRE.
(T) 021 4294 777 (F) 021 4294 056
Speciality: Acupuncture.
[O] (Ref:HM15205)

### O'CONNOR & ASSOCIATES
**O'Connor Noel & Ass**, Kilross Clinic Bishopstown Rd, **County Cork**, IRE.
(T) 021 4342 042
Speciality: Osteopathy.
[P] [S] [T] (Ref:HM15206)

### O'CONNOR, AINE
**O'Connor Aine**, 45 Huntstown Ct, Clonsilla, **County Dublin**, IRE.
(T) 01821 6163
Speciality: Complementary Medicines & Therapy.
[M] (Ref:HM15207)

### O'CONNOR, AMANDA
**Amanda O'Connor**, 21 Curzon Rd, London, **London (Greater)**, W5 1NE, ENG.
(T) 07956 444385
Speciality: Osteopathy.
● **Owner** Mrs A O'Connor


Key continued: Yrs.Est: Years Established Q: Qualifications M: Professional Membership ✔ Indemnity Insurance Accept Credit Cards

P S T (Ref:HM15208)

**O'CONNOR, BARBARA**

**Barbara O'Connor**, Martindale House, Lombard St, Newark, **Nottinghamshire**, NG24 1XG, ENG.
(T) 01636 611150
Speciality: Complementary Medicines & Therapy.
● **Administrator** Mrs S Taylor
M (Ref:HM15209)

**O'CONNOR, CELINE CASEY**

**O'Connor Casey Celine**, Foxgrove Hse, Rockbarton, Bruff, **County Limerick**, IRE.
(T) 06138 2151
(E) celinecasey@eircom.net
Speciality: Acupuncture.
O (Ref:HM15210)

**O'CONNOR, COLM (DR)**

**O'Connor Dr Colm M A , M Clin Psych ,**, 50 Manor Hill, Ballincollig, **County Cork**, IRE.
(T) 021 4870 410
Speciality: Psychology.
B (Ref:HM15211)

**O'CONNOR, LYNDA-ANN**

**Lynda-Ann O'Connor**, 4 Hestan Pl, Kilmarnock, **Ayrshire (East)**, KA3 2JR, SCO.
(T) 01563 520178
Speciality: Reflexology.
S T (Ref:HM15212)

**O'CONNOR, MARY**

**Mary O'Connor**, 92 Wilton Court, **County Cork**, IRE.
Speciality: Complementary Medicines & Therapy.
● **Owner** Mrs M O'Connor
(T) 021 4546 827
M (Ref:HM15213)

**O'CONNOR, PENNY**

**Penny O'Connor**, 111 Godfrey House, Bath St, London, **London (Greater)**, EC1V 9ET, ENG.
(T) 020 7253 2022
(E) penny@messages.co.uk
(W) www.oxenburgh.com/alexander
Speciality: Alexander Technique. ✔
● **Teacher of the Alexander Technique** Ms P O'Connor Q: MSTAT. M: STAT.
C Yrs. Est.: 8 (Ref:HM15214)

**O'CONNOR, R**

**R O'Connor**, 47 Moira Rd, Woodville, Swadlincote, **Derbyshire**, DE11 8DG, ENG.
(T) 01283 211229
Speciality: Chiropodists (Podiatrists).
● **Owner** Mr P Oconnor
S (Ref:HM15215)

**OCTAGON PRIVATE CLINIC**

**Octagon Private Clinic**, 2 St Peters Rd, Hammersmith, London, **London (Greater)**, W6 9BD, ENG.
(T) 020 8563 2608
Speciality: Chiropractors.
● **Therapist** Stephen Hughes
P S T (Ref:HM15216)

**O'DEA, CATHERINE**

**Catherine O'Dea Dip Psychotherapy**, Eglinton Hse, Eglinton Tce, Dundrum, **County Dublin**, IRE.
(T) 01298 6204
Speciality: Psychotherapy.
● **Psychotherapist** Ms C O Dea Q: Dip.Psych.
B (Ref:HM15217)

**O'DEA, EDMOND (DR)**

**O'Dea Dr Edmond**, 19 Barrington St, **County Limerick**, IRE.
(T) 06131 2442
Speciality: Complementary Medicines & Therapy.
M (Ref:HM15218)

**O'DELL, ANNIE**

**Annie O'Dell**, 192 Beechcroft Rd, London, **London (Greater)**, SW17 7DG, ENG.
(T) 020 8682 3516
Speciality: Reflexology.
S T (Ref:HM15219)

**ODOM, S A**

**S A Odom**, Sarsden Halt Cottage, Sarsden Halt, Churchill, Chipping Norton, **Oxfordshire**, OX7 6NT, ENG.
(T) 01608 658664
Speciality: Chiropodists (Podiatrists).
S (Ref:HM15220)

**O'DONAGHUE, SHIRLEY**

**Shirley O'Donaghue**, The Coach House, 38 Knoll Rd, Dorking, **Surrey**, RH4 3EP, ENG.
(T) 01306 882291
Speciality: Complementary Medicines & Therapy.
C M (Ref:HM15221)

**O'DONNELL, ANGELA**

**Angela O'Donnell**, 16 Brandon Cl, Chafford Hundred, Grays, **Essex**, RM16 6QX, ENG.
(T) 01375 480533
Speciality: Electrolysis.
T (Ref:HM15222)

**O'DONNELL, ANNEGRET**

**Annegret O'Donnell**, 9 Lynton Rd, Hythe, **Kent**, CT21 6DB, ENG.
(T) 01303 267081
Speciality: Reflexology.
S T (Ref:HM15223)

**O'DONNELL, C M**

**Mrs C M O'Donnell**, 1 Cayton Drive, Middlesbrough, **Cleveland**, TS5 7NJ, ENG.
(T) 01642 815417
Speciality: Chiropodists (Podiatrists).
● **Owner** Mrs C O'Donnell
S (Ref:HM15224)

**O'DONNELL, ELSPETH**

**Elspeth O'Donnell**, 42 Foliat Drive, Wantage, **Oxfordshire**, OX12 7AL, ENG.
(T) 01235 760460 (F) 01235 760460
Speciality: Acupressure, Massage (Therapeutic), Shiatsu. ✔
● **Physiotherapist** Ms E O'Donnell Q: MCSP. M: CSP.
P Yrs. Est.: 12 (Ref:HM15225)

**O'DONOGHUE, AILEEN**

**O'Donoghue Aileen**, 9 The Cooperage Bohereencael, Killarney, **County Kerry**, IRE.
(T) 06437 159
Speciality: Healing.
B (Ref:HM15226)

**O'DONOGHUE, ANNE**

**O'Donoghue Anne**, 26 Upr John St, **County Kilkenny**, IRE.
(T) 05662 196
Speciality: Acupuncture.
O (Ref:HM15227)

**O'DONOGHUE, CHRISTINE**

**Christine O'Donoghue**, Orchard Clinic, Holywell Hill, St. Albans, **Hertfordshire**, AL1 1BX, ENG.
(T) 01727 855414 (F) 01727 835131
Speciality: Physiotherapy.
● **Owner** Mrs C O'Donoghue
P S T (Ref:HM15228)

**O'DOWD, MARY**

**O Dowd Mary**, 5 Thorndale Ballyclough, **County Limerick**, IRE.
(T) 06122 9818
Speciality: Counselling.
B H (Ref:HM15229)

**O'DRISCOLL, PAULINE**

**Pauline O'Driscoll**, 43 Rasper Rd, London, **London (Greater)**, N20 0LU, ENG.
(T) 020 8446 3339
Speciality: Homeopathy.
M (Ref:HM15230)

**ODSAL HEALTH CENTRE**

**Odsal Health Centre**, Chiropodists, 55 Odsal Rd, Bradford, **Yorkshire (West)**, BD6 1PR, ENG.
(T) 01274 691996
Speciality: Chiropodists (Podiatrists).
S (Ref:HM15231)

**O'DWYER, ANNEGRET**

**Annegret O'Dwyer**, Brabant House, Portsmouth Rd, Thames Ditton, **Surrey**, KT7 0EY, ENG.
(T) 020 8398 7592
Speciality: Psychotherapy.
B (Ref:HM15232)

**O'DWYER, LINDA**

**O'Dwyer Linda Lic Ac M A I Ac**, 5 Mount Russell Fr Russell Rd, **County Limerick**, IRE.
(T) 06130 3728
Speciality: Complementary Medicines & Therapy.
M (Ref:HM15233)

**O'DWYER, MARY**

**Mary O'Dwyer**, Prospect House, Lower Dicker, Hailsham, **Sussex (East)**, BN27 4BT, ENG.
(T) 01323 844449
Speciality: Physiotherapy.
● **Owner** Mrs M O'Dwyer
P S T (Ref:HM15234)

**ODYSSEY FOUNDATION**

**Odyssey Foundation (The)**, Westfield Lakes, Far Ings Rd, Barton-Upon-Humber, **Humberside**, DN18 5RG, ENG.
(T) 01652 633133
Speciality: Complementary Medicines & Therapy.
C M (Ref:HM15235)

**O'FARRELL, MAGDA**

**Magda O'Farrell**, Springfield Lodge, Ballybride Rd, Rathmichael, IRE.
(T) 01282 2893
Speciality: Psychotherapy.
● **Psychotherapist** Magda OFarrell Q: Dip.Psych.
B (Ref:HM15236)

**O'FARRELL, MARY**

**O'Farrell Mary**, 2 Main St, Midleton, **County Cork**, IRE.
(T) 021 4632 937
Speciality: Complementary Medicines & Therapy.
M (Ref:HM15237)

**O'FLAHERTY, CHRISTINE**

**Christine O'Flaherty**, Barbican Physiotherapy Clinic, 1 The Postern, Wood St, London, **London (Greater)**, EC2Y 8BJ, ENG.
(T) 020 7628 4182
Speciality: Physiotherapy.
P S T (Ref:HM15238)

**O'FLYNN, DERMOT (DR)**

**Dr Dermot O'Flynn**, 17 Shakespeare Rd, London, **London (Greater)**, SE24 0LA, ENG.
(T) 020 7733 8070
Speciality: Acupuncture.
O (Ref:HM15239)

**O'FLYNN, DERMOT (DR)**

**Dr Dermot O'Flynn**, 57 Milton Rd, London, **London (Greater)**, SE24 0NW, ENG.
(T) 020 7733 8070
Speciality: Acupuncture.
O (Ref:HM15240)

**OGDEN, GEOFF**

**Geoff Ogden**, Rusty Tiles, Crathorne, Yarm, **Cleveland**, TS15 0BA, ENG.
(T) 01642 701436
Speciality: Psychology.
B (Ref:HM15241)

**O'GRADY, MARGARET**

**Margaret O'Grady**, 'The Bungalow', 91 Baldwins Lane, Birmingham, **Midlands (West)**, B28 0PX, ENG.
(T) 01217 455826
Speciality: Reflexology.
S T (Ref:HM15242)

**O'GRADY, TANYA**

**O'Grady Tanya Dip Nut**, Cooldrinagh, Leixlip, **County Kildare**, IRE.
(T) 01624 5546
Speciality: Complementary Medicines & Therapy.
M (Ref:HM15243)

**O'HARA, CARMEL**

**O'Hara Carmel M Med Sc (Psych)**, Dublin, **County Dublin**, IRE.



Key: B Mind-Body Medicine, C Complementary Medicine, H Self Help Treatment, M Medicinal Therapy, O Oriental Medicine, P Postural Therapy, S Manipulative Structural Therapy, T Touch Therapy

(T) 01660 1192
Speciality: Psychotherapy.
B (Ref:HM15244)

**O'HARA, CHRISTINE**

**Christine O'Hara**, 3 Phoenix Pk, Skelton, Penrith, **Cumbria**, CA11 9SD, ENG.
(T) 01768 484208
Speciality: Homeopathy.
● **Owner** Ms C O'Hara
M (Ref:HM15245)

**O'HARA, JOHN**

**John O'Hara**, 52 Oakwood Rd, Bricket Wood, St. Albans, **Hertfordshire**, AL2 3PX, ENG.
(T) 01923 674908 (F) 01923 674908
(E) john@reflexology33.fsnet.co.uk
Speciality: Reflexology. ✔
● **Reflexologist** Mr J O'Hara Q: MBRA. M: BRA.
C Yrs. Est.: 9 (Ref:HM15246)

**O'HARA, SIMON**

**Simon O'Hara**, The Clocktower Practice, 50-66 Park Rd, London, **London (Greater)**, N8 8SU, ENG.
(T) 020 8967 3614
Speciality: Chiropodists (Podiatrists).
S (Ref:HM15247)

**OHUCHE, MARGARET**

**Margaret OHuche**, 19 Cambridge Rd, London, **London (Greater)**, SE20 7XJ, ENG.
(T) 020 8778 9468
Speciality: Osteopathy.
P S T (Ref:HM15248)

**OISIN CENTRE**

**Oisin Centre Of Natural Healing**, Killare Ballinea, **County Westmeath**, IRE.
(T) 04456 495
Speciality: Healing.
B (Ref:HM15249)

**O'KANE, B A**

**B A O'Kane**, 36 Main St, Garvagh, Coleraine, **County Londonderry**, BT51 5AD, NIR.
(T) 028 2955 7304
Speciality: Chiropodists (Podiatrists).
● **Owner** Mrs B O'Kane
S (Ref:HM15250)

**O'KANE, C**

**C O'Kane**, The Clinic, 36 Knockbreda Rd, Belfast, **County Antrim**, BT6 0JB, NIR.
(T) 028 9064 1089
Speciality: Chiropractors.
P S T (Ref:HM15251)

**O'KEEFE, C S**

**C S O'Keefe**, 37 Newnham Green, Gorleston, Great Yarmouth, **Norfolk**, NR31 7JS, ENG.
(T) 01493 604548
Speciality: Chiropodists (Podiatrists).
● **Owner** Mr C O'Keefe
S (Ref:HM15252)

**O'KEEFFE, BRIAN**

**O'Keeffe Brian**, 19 Barrington St, **County Limerick**, IRE.
(T) 06131 3811
Speciality: Psychology.
B (Ref:HM15253)

**O'KELL, DAVID S**

**David S O'Kell**, The Surgery 452 Leeds Rd, Dewsbury, **Yorkshire (West)**, WF12 7QE, ENG.
(T) 01924 450183
Speciality: Acupuncture.
● **Owner** Mr D O'Kell
O (Ref:HM15254)

**OLD CONVENT**

**McTimoney Chiropractor**, Beeches Green, Stroud, **Gloucestershire**, GL5 5PW, ENG.
(T) 01453 872229 (F) 01453 872229
(E) paul@maunsell-mctimoney.com
(W) www.healthyback.co.uk
Speciality: Absent Healing, Anthroposohical Medicine, Chiropractic, Faith Healing, Healer, Healing Therapy, Manipulation, Spiritual Healing, Stress Therapy, McTimoney Chiropractic. ✔
● **Chiropractor** Mr P Maunsell Q: DC. M: GCC.
S (Ref:HM15255)

**OLD HALL CLINIC**

**Old Hall Clinic (The)**, 14 Old Hall Rd, Gatley, **Cheshire**, SK8 4BE, ENG.
(T) 01614 284222
Speciality: Acupuncture, Counselling, Homeopathy, Osteopathy, Psychotherapy. CREDIT
● **Practitioner** Mr P Owen Q: BSc (Hons), DO.
● **Homeopathic Physician** Dr P Caville
C Yrs. Est.: 18 (Ref:HM15256)

**OLD HALL CLINIC**

**Old Hall Clinic**, 14 Old Hall Rd, Gatley, Manchester, **Manchester (Greater)**, SK8 4BE, ENG.
(T) 01614 284222
Speciality: Complementary Medicines & Therapy.
● **Therapist** Mrs B King
M (Ref:HM15257)

**OLD HOUSE CLINIC**

**Old House Clinic (The)**, 660 Allesley Old Rd, Coventry, **Midlands (West)**, CV5 8GB, ENG.
(T) 024 7671 2083 (F) 024 7671 2083
Speciality: Acupuncture.
● **Partner** Mr A Connor
O (Ref:HM15258)

**OLD ORCHARD SURGERY**

**Old Orchard Surgery**, South St, Wilton, Salisbury, **Wiltshire**, ENG.
(T) 01722 744775
Speciality: Alexander Technique.
● **Practitioner** Mr R Smith
P S (Ref:HM15259)

**OLD PIT PRACTICE**

**Old Pit Practice (The)**, 21 Front St, Framwellgate Moor, Durham, **County Durham**, DH1 5EJ, ENG.
(T) 01913 842549 (F) 01913 842549
Speciality: Acupuncture, Physiotherapy, Podiatry, Psychotherapy, Reflexology, Sports Massage. ✔
● **Owner/Physiotherapist** Mr D Linton Q: MCSP, SRP. M: CSP.
S Yrs. Est.: 10 (Ref:HM15260)

**OLD RECTORY**

**Old Rectory (The)**, Rectory Lane, Saltwood, Hythe, **Kent**, CT21 4QA, ENG.
(T) 01303 267374 (F) 01580 763368
Speciality: Homeopathy.
● **Owner** Mr J Stevens
M (Ref:HM15261)

**OLD SURGERY**

**Old Surgery (The)**, Hungerford Rd, Crewe, **Cheshire**, CW1 5EQ, ENG.
(T) 01270 211100
Speciality: Complementary Medicines & Therapy.
● **Practice Manager** Mr P Brammer
M (Ref:HM15262)

**OLD TOWN CHIROPRACTIC CLINIC**

**Robert J Ions**, 24 Church St, Old Town, Eastbourne, **Sussex (East)**, BN21 1HS, ENG.
(T) 01323 410050
(E) chiropractor@supanet.com
Speciality: Chiropractic, Manipulation. ✔
● **Chiropractor** Mr R Ions Q: DO. M: CC, GCC, MCA.
S Yrs. Est.: 4 (Ref:HM15263)

**OLD WOKING GRANGE**

**Old Woking Grange**, High St, Old Woking, Woking, **Surrey**, GU22 8LB, ENG.
(T) 01483 772269 (F) 01483 772761
(E) enquries@oldwokinggrange.co.uk
(W) www.oldwokinggrange.co.uk
Speciality: Acupressure, Acupuncture, Alexander Technique, Aromatherapy, Art Therapy, Auto Suggestion, Autogenic Training, Bach Remedies, Bowen Therapy, Chiropractic, Cognitive Therapy, Colour Therapy, Cranial Osteopathy, Dance Movement Therapy, Dowsing, Drama Therapy, Feldenkrais Methodology, Floral Essence Therapy, Healer, Healing Therapy, Holistic Healing, Homeopathy, Hypnosis, Hypnotherapy, Indian Head Massage, Iridology, Kinesiology, Life Style Coaching, Macrobiotics, Massage (Therapeutic), Meditation, Metamorphic Therapy, Music Therapy, Naturopathy, Nutritional Therapy, Osteopathy, Pilates, Reflexology, Reiki, Shiatsu. ✔ CREDIT
● **Partner** Mrs J Bailey
● **Clinic Manager** Ms P MacGregor
C Yrs. Est.: 1 (Ref:HM15264)

**OLDACRE, RAY**

**Ray Oldacre**, 4 Kingsley Rd, Stafford, **Staffordshire**, ST17 9BZ, ENG.
(T) 01784 256635
Speciality: Hypnosis.
B (Ref:HM15265)

**OLDHAM AROMATICS**

**Oldham Aromatics**, Unit 21 Market Hall, Albion St, Oldham, **Lancashire**, OL1 3BG, ENG.
(T) 01616 286961
Speciality: Aromatherapy.
● **Owner** Mr D Freer
M O (Ref:HM15266)

**OLDHAM PHYSIO & CHIROP CTRE**

**Oldham Physiotherapy & Chiropodist Centre**, Kirkstyle House, 79-81 Huddersfield Rd, Oldham, **Lancashire**, OL1 3NQ, ENG.
(T) 01616 271187 (F) 01616 270052
Speciality: Physiotherapy.
● **Owner** Mrs C Wiseman
P S T (Ref:HM15267)

**OLDHAM, P A**

**P A Oldham**, 6 Fairfax Court, Yarm, **Cleveland**, TS15 9QZ, ENG.
(T) 01642 787272
Speciality: Aromatherapy.
● **Owner** Mrs P Oldham
M O (Ref:HM15268)

**OLDHAM, P A**

**P A Oldham**, 8 Prestwick Court, Eaglescliffe, Stockton-On-Tees, **Cleveland**, TS16 9ED, ENG.
(T) 01642 780645 (F) 01642 780645
Speciality: Reflexology.
● **Owner** Mrs P Oldham
S T (Ref:HM15269)

**OLDHAM, TERRY**

**Terry Oldham**, 15 Ladysmith St, Stockport, **Cheshire**, SK3 8DY, ENG.
(T) 01614 809373
Speciality: Reflexology.
S T (Ref:HM15270)

**OLDHAM, VALERIE**

**Valerie Oldham**, 1 Lavender Cl, Manchester, **Manchester (Greater)**, M23 9SH, ENG.
(T) 01619 454195
Speciality: Electrolysis.
● **Owner** Mrs V Oldham
T (Ref:HM15271)

**OLDING, R D**

**R D Olding**, 10 Harley St, London, **London (Greater)**, W1N 1AA, ENG.
(T) 020 7467 8300 (F) 020 7467 8312
Speciality: Acupuncture.
O (Ref:HM15272)

**OLDROYD, B K**

**B K Oldroyd**, 1 Murray Rd, Northwood, **London (Greater)**, HA6 2YP, ENG.
(T) 01923 823222
Speciality: Physiotherapy.
P S T (Ref:HM15273)

**OLDROYD, B K**

**Mrs B K Oldroyd**, 33 Halland Way, Northwood, **London (Greater)**, HA6 2BY, ENG.
(T) 01923 823222
Speciality: Physiotherapy.
● **Physiotherapist** Mrs Oldroyd
P S T (Ref:HM15274)

**OLDROYD, P J**

**Mrs P J Oldroyd**, Lower Grange Farmhouse, Chester Rd, Kelsall, Tarporley, **Cheshire**, CW6 0RJ, ENG.
(T) 01829 751205
Speciality: Physiotherapy.
P S T (Ref:HM15275)

**O'LEARY, MARTINA**

**O'Leary Martina**, Pembroke Hse, Pembroke St, **County Cork**, IRE.



Key continued: Yrs.Est: Years Established Q: Qualifications M: Professional Membership ✔ Indemnity Insurance CREDIT Accept Credit Cards

**(T)** 021 4279 912
**Speciality:** Psychotherapy.
**B** (**Ref:**HM15276)

## O'LEARY, MARTINA

**O'Leary Martina**, Pembroke Hse, **IRE**.
**(T)** 08687 05708
**Speciality:** Complementary Medicines & Therapy.
**M** (**Ref:**HM15277)

## O'LEARY, MARY

**O'Leary Mary D O M G O**, Knocknagree, **County Cork**, **IRE**.
**(T)** 06456 010
**Speciality:** Osteopathy.
**P S T** (**Ref:**HM15278)

## OLESEN, ANNE-GRETE

**Anne-Grete Olesen**, Oxford, **Oxfordshire**, OX2, **ENG**.
**(T)** 01865 556789
**Speciality:** Bach Remedies.
**M** (**Ref:**HM15279)

## OLIVE BRANCH

**Olive Branch (The)**, 18 Wheatsheaf Cl, Horsham, **Sussex (West)**, RH12 5TH, **ENG**.
**(T)** 01403 255903
**Speciality:** Complementary Medicines & Therapy.
● **Owner** Mrs L Alison
**C M** (**Ref:**HM15280)

## OLIVE GROVE BODY SCIENCE

**Olive Grove Body Science**, 4 Drayton Gr, Drayton, Norwich, **Norfolk**, NR8 6PU, **ENG**.
**(T)** 01603 868135
**Speciality:** Biomechanics, Chiropody. ✔
● **Chiropodist** Mrs F Bailey
**C** **Yrs. Est.:** 25 (**Ref:**HM15281)

## OLIVE TRUST NATURAL THRPY CTRE

**Olive Trust Natural Therapy Centre (The)**, 24A Castle St, Cirencester, **Gloucestershire**, GL7 1QH, **ENG**.
**(T)** 07885 862728
**Speciality:** Chiropractic.
● **Practice Manager** Mrs D Leek
**P S T** (**Ref:**HM15282)

## OLIVELLE, J S

**J S Olivelle**, Chingford Foot Clinic, 66 Station Rd, London, **London (Greater)**, E4 7BA, **ENG**.
**(T)** 020 8524 8433
**Speciality:** Chiropodists (Podiatrists).
**S** (**Ref:**HM15283)

## OLIVELLE, JOSEPH

**Joseph Olivelle**, 2 Lodge Avenue, Chelmsford, **Essex**, CM2 7EA, **ENG**.
**(T)** 01245 473762
**Speciality:** Chiropodists (Podiatrists).
**S** (**Ref:**HM15284)

## OLIVER & STODDARD

**Oliver & Stoddard**, 8 St Bernards Cres, Edinburgh, **Edinburgh (City of)**, EH4 1NP, **SCO**.
**(T)** 01313 431111 **(F)** 01313 329957
**Speciality:** Nutritional Therapy.
● **Nutritional Health Care** Miss H Narracott
**C** **Yrs. Est.:** 2 (**Ref:**HM15285)

## OLIVER ASSOCIATES

**Oliver Associates**, 3 Longmeade Gardens, Wilmslow, **Cheshire**, SK9 1DA, **ENG**.
**(T)** 01625 539108 **(F)** 01625 535877
**Speciality:** Hypnotherapy.
● **Owner** Mr L Oliver
**B** (**Ref:**HM15286)

## OLIVER, BETTY

**Betty Oliver**, Leamington Rd, Coventry, **Midlands (West)**, CV3 6HZ, **ENG**.
**(T)** 024 7650 5342
**Speciality:** Aromatherapy.
● **Owner** Ms B Oliver
**M O** (**Ref:**HM15287)

## OLIVER, D

**D Oliver**, 1 Hornes Field Court, Church Crookham, Fleet, **Hampshire**, GU13 0XT, **ENG**.
**(T)** 01252 626427
**Speciality:** Herbal Medicine.
● **Owner** Mr D Oliver
**M** (**Ref:**HM15288)

## OLIVER, EDWARD

**Edward Oliver**, 78 Fernside Rd, Poole, **Dorset**, BH15 2JL, **ENG**.
**(T)** 01202 681457
**Speciality:** Chiropodists (Podiatrists).
● **Owner** Mr E Oliver
**S** (**Ref:**HM15289)

## OLIVER, G C

**G C Oliver**, The Glen, Stonehills, Fawley, Southampton, **Hampshire**, SO45 1DU, **ENG**.
**(T)** 023 8089 8682
**Speciality:** Complementary Medicines & Therapy.
● **Owner** Mrs G Oliver
**C M** (**Ref:**HM15290)

## OLIVER, J P

**J P Oliver**, 6 Springfield, Bushey Heath, Watford, **Hertfordshire**, WD2 3JL, **ENG**.
**(T)** 020 8421 9130
**Speciality:** Hypnosis.
● **Owner** Mr J Oliver
**B** (**Ref:**HM15291)

## OLIVER, JENNY

**Jenny Oliver**, Priory House, New St, Ross-on-Wye, **Herefordshire**, HR9 7DA, **ENG**.
**(T)** 01989 564082
**Speciality:** Psychotherapy.
**B** (**Ref:**HM15292)

## OLIVER, KATE

**Kate Oliver**, 3 Uplands Rd, London, **London (Greater)**, N8 9NN, **ENG**.
**(T)** 020 8347 9608
**Speciality:** Hypnosis.
● **Owner** Ms K Oliver
**B** (**Ref:**HM15293)

## OLIVER, MARION

**Marion Oliver**, Catsash House, Catsash, Newport, NP18 1JQ, **WAL**.
**(T)** 01633 423284
**Speciality:** Reflexology. ✔
● **Owner/Reflexologist** Mrs M Oliver **Q:** MAR.
**C** **Yrs. Est.:** 8 (**Ref:**HM15294)

## OLIVER, P H

**P H Oliver**, 24 North Hill Cl, Brixham, **Devon**, TQ5 8RY, **ENG**.
**(T)** 01803 857134
**Speciality:** Chiropodists (Podiatrists).
**S** (**Ref:**HM15295)

## OLIVER, PETER

**Peter Oliver**, Alpha House, H Granville St, Peterborough, **Cambridgeshire**, PE1 2QJ, **ENG**.
**(T)** 01733 566033
**Speciality:** Hypnotherapy.
**B** (**Ref:**HM15296)

## OLIVER-CARTER, JOAN

**Joan Oliver-Carter**, 82 Urmston Lane, Stretford, Manchester, **Manchester (Greater)**, M32 9BQ, **ENG**.
**(T)** 01618 643305
**Speciality:** Hypnosis.
**B** (**Ref:**HM15297)

## OLIVIA, S

**S Olivia**, 1 Upland Rd, South Croydon, **Surrey**, CR2 6RD, **ENG**.
**(T)** 020 8681 8665
**Speciality:** Acupuncture.
**P S T** (**Ref:**HM15298)

## OLIVIER, JONATHAN

**Jonathan Olivier**, Natural Therapy Centre, 7 Westgate Rd, Guisborough, **Cleveland**, TS14 6EA, **ENG**.
**(T)** 01287 633591
**Speciality:** Chiropodists (Podiatrists).
**S** (**Ref:**HM15299)

## OLLIVIER, D R

**D R Ollivier**, 22 Thrush Rd, Redcar, **Cleveland**, TS10 2AT, **ENG**.
**(T)** 01642 481980
**Speciality:** Chiropodists (Podiatrists).
**S** (**Ref:**HM15300)

## OLLIVIER, J P

**J P Ollivier**, 22 Thrush Rd, Redcar, **Cleveland**, TS10 2AT, **ENG**.
**(T)** 01642 481980
**Speciality:** Chiropodists (Podiatrists).
**S** (**Ref:**HM15301)

## OLNEY OSTEOPATHIC SURGERY

**Olney Osteopathic Surgery**, 1 Rose Court, Olney, **Buckinghamshire**, MK46 4BY, **ENG**.
**(T)** 01234 712003 **(F)** 01234 712003
**Speciality:** Osteopathy.
● **Partner** Mr P Mason
**P S T** (**Ref:**HM15302)

## OLORENSHAW, A J

**A J Olorenshaw**, Fairlead, Chart Lane, Reigate, **Surrey**, RH2 7EG, **ENG**.
**(T)** 01737 245041
**Speciality:** Osteopathy.
● **Owner** A Olorenshaw
**P S T** (**Ref:**HM15303)

## O'LOUGHLIN, ANNE

**Anne O'Loughlin ADHP**, 214 South Circular Rd, Dublin, **County Dublin**, **IRE**.
**(T)** 01454 4181
**(W)** www.hypnosiseire.com
**Speciality:** Complementary Medicines & Therapy.
● **Therapist** Ms A OLoughlin **Q:** MICHP.
**M** (**Ref:**HM15304)

## OLSEN, G J D

**G J D Olsen**, 21 Old Rd, Tiverton, **Devon**, EX16 4HJ, **ENG**.
**(T)** 01884 256952
**Speciality:** Chiropodists (Podiatrists).
● **Owner** Mr G Olsen
**S** (**Ref:**HM15305)

## OLSSON, J D

**J D Olsson**, 2a Mayfield Avenue, Blackpool, **Lancashire**, FY4 2NT, **ENG**.
**(T)** 01253 348926
**Speciality:** Physiotherapy.
● **Owner** Mr J Olsson
**P S T** (**Ref:**HM15306)

## O'MAHONY, JERRY

**Jerry O'Mahony**, 51 Henrys Avenue, Woodford Green, **Essex**, IG8 9RB, **ENG**.
**(T)** 020 8504 2462
**Speciality:** Physiotherapy.
● **Owner** Mr J O'Mahony
**P S T** (**Ref:**HM15307)

## O'MAHONY, JOHN & BEATE

**John & Beate O'Mahony**, 13 Tircur Rd, Omagh, **County Tyrone**, BT79 7TY, **NIR**.
**(T)** 028 8164 8153
**Speciality:** Acupuncture.
**O** (**Ref:**HM15308)

## O'MAHONY, REGINA

**O'Mahony Regina**, 8 Elm Cl, Rosebank Douglas, Cork, **County Cork**, **IRE**.
**(T)** 08726 48339
**(E)** fengshuimasterint@email.net
**Speciality:** Complementary Medicines & Therapy.
**M** (**Ref:**HM15309)

## O'MALLEY, DERRY

**O'Malley Derry**, Cabury House Catherine Pl, Limerick, **County Limerick**, **IRE**.
**(T)** 06131 7670
**Speciality:** Complementary Medicines & Therapy.
**M** (**Ref:**HM15310)

## O'MALLEY, JOHN

**John O'Malley**, 4 Queens Rd, Mumbles, Swansea, SA3 4AN, **WAL**.
**(T)** 01792 368858
**Speciality:** Chiropodists (Podiatrists).
● **Owner** Mr J O'Malley
**S** (**Ref:**HM15311)

## O'MALLEY, M J

**M J O'Malley**, 176 Drake St, Rochdale, **Lancashire**, OL16 1UP, **ENG**.
**(T)** 01706 655110
**Speciality:** Chiropodists (Podiatrists).

Key: **B** Mind-Body Medicine **C** Complementary Medicine **H** Self Help Treatment **M** Medicinal Therapy **O** Oriental Medicine **P** Postural Therapy **S** Manipulative Structural Therapy **T** Touch Therapy

● **Owner** Mr M O'Malley
**S** (**Ref:**HM15312)

**O'MALLEY, M J**

**M J O'Malley**, Dental Surgery, 27 York St, Heywood, **Manchester (Greater)**, OL10 4NN, ENG.
(T) 01706 360176
Speciality: Chiropodists (Podiatrists).
● **Senior Partner** Mr B Wallis
**S** (**Ref:**HM15313)

**O'MALLEY, MOIRA**

**Moira O'Malley**, The Arches, Park Rd, Hartlepool, **Cleveland**, TS26 9HU, ENG.
(T) 01429 862242
Speciality: Chiropodists (Podiatrists).
● **Owner** Mrs M O'Malley
**S** (**Ref:**HM15314)

**O'MARA, MARY**

**O'Mara Mary**, Crookstown Lr Ballytore, Athy, **County Kildare**, IRE.
(T) 05072 3231
Speciality: Complementary Medicines & Therapy.
**M** (**Ref:**HM15315)

**O'MEARA, MAURA**

**O'Meara Maura M Ed , M Sc , D A C**, 20, Alphonsus Rd, , Lr Newtown, **County Waterford**, IRE.
(T) 05187 7050
Speciality: Complementary Medicines & Therapy.
**M** (**Ref:**HM15316)

**O'MEARA, WILLIAM**

**William O'Meara**, 10 Willow Drive, Seaford, **Sussex (East)**, BN25 4BZ, ENG.
(T) 01323 873617
Speciality: Homeopathy.
● **Owner** Mr W Omeara
**M** (**Ref:**HM15317)

**O'MEARA, WILLIAM J**

**William J O'Meara**, 6a Stanley Rd, Peacehaven, **Sussex (East)**, BN10 7SP, ENG.
(T) 01273 587382
Speciality: Homeopathy.
**M** (**Ref:**HM15318)

**OMICRON**

**Omicron (UK) Ltd**, Kynance House, Verney Junction, Buckingham, **Buckinghamshire**, MK18 2JZ, ENG.
(T) 01296 714433 (F) 01296 714455
Speciality: Complementary Medicines & Therapy.
● **Director** Mr C Mistry
**C** **M** (**Ref:**HM15319)

**ONE HEALTH**

**One Health**, 13 Princes Rd, Newcastle Upon Tyne, **Tyne and Wear**, NE3 5TT, ENG.
(T) 01912 362776
Speciality: Complementary Medicines & Therapy.
● **Owner** Dr G Carey
**M** (**Ref:**HM15320)

**ONE STEP**

**One Step**, Alberta House, Kings Park Drive, Bournemouth, **Dorset**, BH7 7AG, ENG.
(T) 01202 396282
Speciality: Psychotherapy.
**B** (**Ref:**HM15321)

**ONE STEP FOOTCARE**

**One Step Footcare**, 9 Waters Rd, Kingston Upon Thames, **Surrey**, KT1 3LW, ENG.
(T) 020 8549 4260 (F) 020 8408 1258
Speciality: Chiropodists (Podiatrists).
● **Owner** Mr R Montgomery
**S** (**Ref:**HM15322)

**ONE STOP HEALTH & BEAUTY**

**O S H B Complementary Therapists**, Cambridge House, Cambridge St, Accrington, **Lancashire**, BB5 6ED, ENG.
(T) 01254 351215
Speciality: Absent Healing, Acupressure, Aromatherapy, Bach Remedies, Complementary Therapy, Faith Healing, Floral Essence Therapy, Healer, Holistic Healing, Homeopathy, Indian Head Massage, Life Style Coaching, Manipulation, Massage (Therapeutic), Meditation, Paranormal Therapies, Polarity Therapy, Postural Integration, Reflexology, Reiki, Rolfing, Spiritual Healing, Stress Therapy, Touch Therapy, Vibrational Therapy, Sports Injury Clinic and Fitness Testing. ✓
● **Complementary Health Therapist** Ms S Akhtar Q: ICHT, IIHHT. M: ICHT.
● **Holistic Therapist** Mr M Aspin M: FHT.
● **Homeopath** Ms W Stone Q: Dip.Hom, MSc. M: Soc.Hom.
**B** (**Ref:**HM15323)

**ONE TO ONE**

**One To One**, 16 High March, High March Industrial Estate, Daventry, **Northamptonshire**, NN11 4HB, ENG.
(T) 01327 871118
Speciality: Physiotherapy.
● **Administrator** Mrs D Smith
**P** **S** **T** (**Ref:**HM15324)

**O'NEIL, L**

**L O'Neil**, Bryn Melyn Trce, Rhostryfan, Caernarfon, **Gwynedd**, LL54 7LY, WAL.
(T) 01286 831777
(E) admin@therapy4-u.co.uk
(W) www.therapy4-u.co.uk
Speciality: Counselling, Hypnotherapy, Psychotherapy. ✓
● **Owner/Hypnotherapist/Counsellor** Mrs L O'Neil Q: BA (Hons) Psychol, Dip.Hyp. M: HA.
**C** Yrs. Est.: 5 (**Ref:**HM15325)

**O'NEIL, PAULA**

**Paula O'Neil**, 5 Heathway, Iver, **Buckinghamshire**, SL0 0BX, ENG.
(T) 01753 651852
Speciality: Reflexology, Vacuflex Reflexology. ✓
● **Owner/Reflexologist** Miss P O'Neil Q: MIIR. M: IIR.
**O** Yrs. Est.: 2 (**Ref:**HM15326)

**O'NEILL, E**

**E O'neill**, 27A-29 Huntingdon Rd, Leicester, **Leicestershire**, LE4 9GG, ENG.
(T) 01162 766770 (F) 01162 877272
Speciality: Chiropodists (Podiatrists).
● **Owner** Ms E Stretton
**S** (**Ref:**HM15327)

**O'NEILL, ELIZABETH**

**O'Neill Elizabeth**, Walkinstown Osteopathic Clinic Walkinstown, Dublin, **County Dublin**, IRE.
(T) 01450 4438
Speciality: Complementary Medicines & Therapy.
**M** (**Ref:**HM15328)

**O'NEILL, H**

**H O'Neill**, 42 Mansfield St, Glasgow, **Glasgow (City of)**, G11 5QW, SCO.
(T) 01413 344136
Speciality: Chiropodists (Podiatrists).
● **Owner** Mr H O'Neill
**S** (**Ref:**HM15329)

**O'NEILL, KATE**

**O'Neill Kate BA MA PSYCH**, Drummin East Delgany, **County Wicklow**, IRE.
(T) 01287 1090
Speciality: Complementary Medicines & Therapy.
**M** (**Ref:**HM15330)

**O'NEILL, LIZ**

**Liz O'Neill**, 177 Cemetery Rd, Sheffield, **Yorkshire (South)**, S11 8FQ, ENG.
(T) 01142 509242
Speciality: Reflexology.
**S** **T** (**Ref:**HM15331)

**O'NEILL, M P & S J**

**M P & S J O'Neill**, 39 High St, Hounslow, **London (Greater)**, TW3 1RH, ENG.
(T) 020 8570 1759
Speciality: Chiropodists (Podiatrists).
**S** (**Ref:**HM15332)

**O'NEILL, MARIA**

**Maria O'Neill**, 20 Main St, Laurelvale, Tandragee, Craigavon, **County Armagh**, BT62 2LN, NIR.
(T) 028 3884 1524
Speciality: Reflexology.
**S** **T** (**Ref:**HM15333)

**O'NEILL, MARLENE**

**Marlene O'Neill**, 15 Gatefield Cl, Radcliffe, Manchester, **Manchester (Greater)**, M26 3UY, ENG.
(T) 01617 234115
Speciality: Reflexology.
● **Owner** Mrs M O'Neill
**S** **T** (**Ref:**HM15334)

**O'NEILL, P J**

**O'Neill P J MASC(PTh), RET(PC), DPSYCHOL(ADV)**, 2 Denny St, Tralee, **County Kerry**, IRE.
(T) 06671 20121
Speciality: Complementary Medicines & Therapy.
**M** (**Ref:**HM15335)

**O'NEILL, REGINA**

**Regina O'Neill Consultant Hypnotherapist**, 243 Warsash Rd, Locks Heath, **Hampshire**, SO31 6TN, ENG.
(T) 01489 576735
Speciality: Chiropractic.
**P** **S** **T** (**Ref:**HM15336)

**O'NEILL, RICHARD**

**Richard O'Neill**, 6 Tamworth Drive, Bury, **Lancashire**, BL8 1DP, ENG.
(T) 01617 637416
Speciality: Hypnosis.
● **Owner** Mr R O'Neill
**B** (**Ref:**HM15337)

**O'NEILL, SUSAN**

**Susan O'Neill**, St. Michaels Croft, Durrants Lane, Berkhamsted, **Hertfordshire**, HP4 3PJ, ENG.
(T) 01442 872770
Speciality: Reflexology.
**S** **T** (**Ref:**HM15338)

**O'NEILL, TESS**

**Tess O'Neill**, The Waldegrave Clinic, 82 Waldegrave Rd, Teddington, **London (Greater)**, TW11 8LG, ENG.
(T) 020 8943 2424
Speciality: Chiropodists (Podiatrists).
**S** (**Ref:**HM15339)

**ONLY NATURAL TREATMENT CENTRE**

**Only Natural Treatment Centre**, Unit H1C, Chester Enterprise Centre, Hoole Bridge, Chester, **Cheshire**, CH2 3NE, ENG.
(T) 01244 320546 (F) 01244 310690
Speciality: Complementary Medicines & Therapy.
● **Owner** Mr G Floyd
**C** **M** (**Ref:**HM15340)

**ONSLOW, H**

**Miss H Onslow**, 60 Woodbridge Rd, Guildford, **Surrey**, GU1 4RF, ENG.
(T) 01483 571783
Speciality: Physiotherapy.
**P** **S** **T** (**Ref:**HM15341)

**OPEN CENTRE**

**Open Centre (The)**, 188 Old St, London, **London (Greater)**, EC1V 9BP, ENG.
(T) 020 7251 1504
Speciality: Complementary Medicines & Therapy.
● **Psychotherapist** Guy Gladstone
**M** (**Ref:**HM15342)

**OPEN MINDS**

**Open Minds**, 25 Milton Rd, Harpenden, **Hertfordshire**, AL5 5LA, ENG.
(T) 01582 762914
Speciality: Healer, Healing Therapy, Shiatsu. ✓
● **Shiatsu Practitioner** Mrs Gray
● **Healer** Mr Gray Q: NFSH. M: NFSH.
**B** **C** Yrs. Est.: 10 (**Ref:**HM15343)



Key continued: **Yrs.Est:** Years Established **Q:** Qualifications **M:** Professional Membership ✓ Indemnity Insurance Accept Credit Cards

## O'PRESCO, MARGARET

**Margaret O'Presco**, 2 De Vere Cl, Wivenhoe, Colchester, **Essex**, CO7 9AX, ENG.
(T) 01206 822601 (F) 01206 822601
Speciality: Homeopathy.
● **Owner** Mrs M O'Presco
M (Ref:HM15344)

## O'PREY, M

**M O'Prey**, 4 The Sq, Ballynahinch, **County Down**, BT24 8AP, NIR.
(T) 028 9756 1159
Speciality: Chiropodists (Podiatrists).
S (Ref:HM15345)

## O'PREY, M J

**M J O'Prey**, First Floor, 46D High St, Lurgan, Craigavon, **County Armagh**, BT66 8AU, NIR.
(T) 028 3832 1442
Speciality: Chiropodists (Podiatrists).
● **Owner** Mrs M O'Prey
S (Ref:HM15346)

## OPTIMUM HEALTH

**Optimum Health**, Suite 1 Oak House Brunswick St, Macclesfield, **Cheshire**, SK10 1ER, ENG.
(T) 01625 433444
Speciality: Complementary Medicines & Therapy.
● **Owner** Mrs C Tharpe
C M (Ref:HM15347)

## OPTIMUM HEALTH

**Optimum Health**, 26a Central Avenue, West Bridgford, Nottingham, **Nottinghamshire**, NG2 5GR, ENG.
(T) 01159 143311 (F) 01159 143312
(E) james.booth3@ntlworld.com
(W) www.optimum-health.couk.com
Speciality: Absent Healing, Acupressure, Acupuncture, Allergy Testing, Aromatherapy, Auricular Therapy, Bach Remedies, Colonic Hydrotherapy, Complementary Therapy, Counselling, Cranial Osteopathy, Floral Essence Therapy, Gestalt Therapy, Group Therapy, Healer, Homeopathy, Hopi Ear Candles, Hypnosis, Hypnotherapy, Indian Head Massage, Kinesiology, Massage (Therapeutic), Neuro-Linguistic Program, Nutritional Therapy, Osteopathy, Reflexology, Reiki, Shiatsu, Sound Therapy, Spiritual Healing, Stress Therapy, Vitamin Therapy. ✔
● **Osteopath** Mr J Booth Q: DO. M: GOsC.
● **Aromatherapist/Masseur** Ms L Silveston Q: ITEC, TATQ. M: ISPA.
● **Shiatsu Practitioner** Mr T Tyson
● **Reflexologist** Mr T Henderson Q: MIIR. M: IIR.
● **Homeopath** Ms J Masters Q: LCPH, MHMA. M: HMA.
C M Yrs. Est.: 5 (Ref:HM15348)

## OPTIMUM HEALTHCARE

**Optimum Healthcare**, Ranlagh, Dublin, **County Dublin**, IRE.
(T) 01660 7903
Speciality: Complementary Medicines & Therapy.
M (Ref:HM15349)

## OPTIMUM NUTRITION & ALOE VERA

**Optimum Nutrition & Aloe Vera**, 82 Broomside Lane, Durham, **County Durham**, DH1 2QT, ENG.
(T) 01913 847049 (F) 01913 847049
Speciality: Complementary Medicines & Therapy.
C M (Ref:HM15350)

## OPTIONS FOR CHANGE

**Options For Change**, 12 Seyton Avenue, Giffnock, Glasgow, **Glasgow (City of)**, G46 6QA, SCO.
(T) 01416 380903 (F) 01416 380903
(W) www.ofc-coaching.com
Speciality: Hypnosis, Neuro-Linguistic Program, Life Coaching, Developmental Behavioural Modelling. ✔ CREDIT
● **Life Coach** Ms S Lyons
M Yrs. Est.: 5 (Ref:HM15351)

## OPTIVAVA

**Optivava**, The Coachhouse Clinic, 155 High St, Tenterden, **Kent**, TN30 6JS, ENG.
(T) 01580 763481
(W) www.optiviva.com
Speciality: Osteopathy. ✔ CREDIT
● **Osteopath** Rebecca Krebs Q: BSc, DO.
● **Osteopath** Thiboutt Chatognon Q: BSc.
● **Owner/Osteopath** Mr J Stevens
C Yrs. Est.: 10 (Ref:HM15352)

## OPUS STOOL

**Opus Stool Co**, Main St, Swinton, Duns, **Scottish Borders**, TD11 3JJ, SCO.
(T) 01890 860254
Speciality: Complementary Medicines & Therapy.
● **Owner** Mrs H Hastings
M (Ref:HM15353)

## ORACLE HEALING CENTRE & SHOP

**Oracle Healing Centre & Shop**, 12 Market St, Watford, **Hertfordshire**, WD1 7AD, ENG.
(T) 01923 249464 (F) 01923 249464
Speciality: Complementary Medicines & Therapy.
● **Owner** Mrs F Cullen
C M (Ref:HM15354)

## ORAM & ASSOCIATES

**John Oram & Associates**, 13 Rustlings Rd, Sheffield, **Yorkshire (South)**, S11 7AA, ENG.
(T) 01142 663910
Speciality: Psychotherapy.
B (Ref:HM15355)

## ORANGE TREE

**Orange Tree**, 8 The Crescent, Hyde Park, Leeds, **Yorkshire (West)**, LS6 2NW, ENG.
(T) 01132 169888
Speciality: Aromatherapy.
● **Manager** Miss C Swain
M O (Ref:HM15356)

## ORANMORE ACCUPUNCTURE CLINIC

**Oranmore Accupuncture Clinic**, Oranmore, **County Galway**, IRE.
(T) 09179 2002
Speciality: Acupuncture.
O (Ref:HM15357)

## O'RAWE, IVY

**Ivy O'Rawe**, 53 Castle Gardens, **County Antrim**, BT15 4GB, NIR.
(T) 028 9077 1944
Speciality: Reflexology.
S T (Ref:HM15358)

## ORCHARD CENTRE

**Orchard Centre (The)**, 15 Cedar Cl, Chard, **Somerset**, TA20 1DB, ENG.
(T) 01460 61777
Speciality: Hypnotherapy.
B (Ref:HM15359)

## ORCHARD CLINIC

**Vinewood Healthcare**, The Mount, 21 High St, Wellington, **Somerset**, TA21 8QT, ENG.
(T) 01823 662149
Speciality: Acupuncture, Chiropractic, Remedial Massage. ✔
● **Associate** Mrs J Baily Q: LCSP.
● **Owner** Dr S Woods Q: DO. M: BAcC.
● **Associate** Dr G Gallagher Q: BDS.
● **Chiropractor** Dr A Stewart Q: DC. M: BCA.
C Yrs. Est.: 25 (Ref:HM15360)

## ORCHARD CLNC CTRE FOR COMP MED

**Orchard Clinic Centre For Complementary Medicine**, 4 Orchard Lane, Amersham, **Buckinghamshire**, HP6 5AB, ENG.
(T) 01494 726228
Speciality: Osteopathy.
● **Therapist** Mrs M Sadler
P S T (Ref:HM15361)

## ORCHARD HSE SGY-DAVID MANDER

**Orchard House Surgery-David Mander**, 8 Orchard Way, Stratford-Upon-Avon, **Warwickshire**, CV37 9QE, ENG.
(T) 01789 415647
Speciality: Chiropractic.
● **Owner** Mr D Mander
P S T (Ref:HM15362)

## ORCHARD LODGE CLINIC

**Orchard Lodge Clinic**, 48 Church Rd, Malvern Link, **Worcestershire**, WR14 1NG, ENG.
(T) 01684 568744
Speciality: Complementary Medicines & Therapy.
● **Partner** Mr K Smith
M (Ref:HM15363)

## ORCHARD MEDICAL CENTRE

**Orchard Medical Centre**, MacDonald Walk, Kingswood, Bristol, BS15 8NJ, ENG.
(T) 01179 604006 (F) 01179 604006
(E) gramhammid@aol.com
Speciality: Biomechanics, Chiropody, Chiropractic, Nail Surgery, Reflexology. ✔
● **Chiropractor** Mr K Fohlmann Q: DC. M: BCA.
● **Chiropractor** Davina Spree Q: DC, MSc. M: BCA.
● **Owner/Chiropodist** Mr G Middleton Q: BSc (Hons), M.S.C.P, S.R.Ch.
● **Reflexologist** Mr A Mason
● **Chiropractor** Mr D Morley Q: DC. M: BCA.
M Yrs. Est.: 2 (Ref:HM15364)

## ORCHARD RESOURCE CENTRE

**Orchard Resource Centre**, Hill St, Hinckley, **Leicestershire**, LE10 1DS, ENG.
(T) 01455 443950 (F) 01455 443944
Speciality: Psychiatry.
● **Administrator** Ms M Hatcher
B (Ref:HM15365)

## ORCHARD SURGERY CHIRO CLINIC

**Orchard Surgery Chiropractic Clinic**, Baldock Rd, Buntingford, **Hertfordshire**, SG9 9DL, ENG.
(T) 01763 274646
Speciality: Chiropractic.
● **Owner** Ms A Harris
P S T (Ref:HM15366)

## ORCHARD THERAPIES PORTSWOOD

**Orchard Therapies Portswood Chiropractic Clinic**, 52 Portswood Rd, Southampton, **Hampshire**, SO17 2FW, ENG.
(T) 023 8055 3000 (F) 023 8058 5436
Speciality: Reflexology.
● **Partner** Miss S Keenan
S T (Ref:HM15367)

## ORCHARD, DAVID

**David Orchard**, 33 Northgate, Canterbury, **Kent**, CT1 1BL, ENG.
(T) 01227 451317
Speciality: Chiropodists (Podiatrists).
S (Ref:HM15368)

## ORCHARD, H

**H Orchard**, 62 St Briavels Drive, Yate, Bristol, BS37 4HP, ENG.
(T) 01454 311775
Speciality: Chiropodists (Podiatrists).
● **Owner** Mrs H Orchard
S (Ref:HM15369)

## O'REGAN, NOEL (DR)

**O'Regan Dr Noel Ac**, 8 Langford Row, **County Cork**, IRE.
(T) 021 4964 470
Speciality: Physiotherapy.
P S T (Ref:HM15370)

## O'REILLY, A

**A O'Reilly**, 111 Strouden Rd, Bournemouth, **Dorset**, BH9 1QW, ENG.
(T) 01202 532896
Speciality: Chiropodists (Podiatrists).
● **Owner** Miss A O'Reilly
S (Ref:HM15371)

## O'REILLY, FRANCES

**Frances O'Reilly**, Coppertrees, Forest Rd, Effingham Junction, Leatherhead, **Surrey**, KT24 5HE, ENG.
(T) 01483 281632
Speciality: Reflexology.
S T (Ref:HM15372)

## O'REILLY, JULIA

**Julia O'Reilly**, Natural Health Clinic, 177 Moorside Rd, Swinton, Manchester, **Manchester (Greater)**, M27 9LD, ENG.
(T) 01617 930091
Speciality: Reflexology.
● **Partner** Mr B Jordan



Key: B Mind-Body Medicine C Complementary Medicine H Self Help Treatment M Medicinal Therapy O Oriental Medicine P Postural Therapy S Manipulative Structural Therapy T Touch Therapy

S T (Ref:HM15373)

## O'REILLY, MARK (DR)

**O'Reilly Dr Mark Ph D C Psychol**, Harristown Brannockstown, Naas, **County Kildare**, IRE.
(T) 04548 3615
Speciality: Complementary Medicines & Therapy.
M (Ref:HM15374)

## O'REILLY, SALLY M A

**O'Reilly Sally M A Couns Psych M N H I I**, **County Cork**, IRE.
(T) 021 4276 367
Speciality: Complementary Medicines & Therapy.
M (Ref:HM15375)

## O'REILLY, TREENA

**Treena O'Reilly**, 15 Adelaide Rd, Leamington Spa, **Warwickshire**, CV31 3PN, ENG.
(T) 01926 450633 (F) 01926 450633
Speciality: Chiropodists (Podiatrists).
● **Owner** Mr T O'Reilly
S (Ref:HM15376)

## ORGANISATIONAL HEALING

**Organisational Healing Ltd**, 48 Walton Rd, Stockton Heath, Warrington, **Cheshire**, WA4 6NL, ENG.
(T) 01925 861600
Speciality: Complementary Medicines & Therapy.
C M (Ref:HM15377)

## ORGANISATION-CHARTERED PHYSIO

**Organisation Of Chartered Physiotherapists**, Suite 8 Weston Chambers, Weston Rd, Southend-On-Sea, **Essex**, SS1 1AT, ENG.
(T) 01702 393578
Speciality: Physiotherapy.
P S T (Ref:HM15378)

## ORGASMATRON UK

**Orgasmatron UK**, 102 Downs Rd, Coulsdon, **London (Greater)**, CR5 1AE, ENG.
(T) 01737 558755 (F) 01737 558755
Speciality: Aromatherapy.
● **Director** Mrs P Smith
M O (Ref:HM15379)

## ORIEL METHUEN

**Oriel Methuen**, Spectrum, 7 Endymion Rd, London, **London (Greater)**, N4 1EE, ENG.
(T) 020 8348 3006
Speciality: Psychotherapy.
● **Owner** Ms O Muthuen
B (Ref:HM15380)

## ORIENTAL HEALTH CENTRE

**Oriental Health Centre**, 3 Alloway Pl, Ayr, **Ayrshire (South)**, KA7 2AA, SCO.
(T) 01292 880355 (F) 01292 618366
Speciality: Acupuncture, Bonesetting, Herbal Medicine, Chinese Traditional Therapy. ✔
● **Acupunturist** Dr Peng
● **Owner** Mr M McColm
C Yrs. Est.: 1 (Ref:HM15381)

## ORIENTAL HERBALISTS

**Oriental Herbalists**, Unit 7 Tanners Court, The Friars, Newcastle Upon Tyne, **Tyne and Wear**, NE1 5XE, ENG.
(T) 01912 320178
Speciality: Complementary Medicines & Therapy.
C M (Ref:HM15382)

## ORIENTAL MEDICAL CENTRE

**Oriental Medical Centre**, 2-4 Kenway Rd, Earls Court, London, **London (Greater)**, SW5 0RR, ENG.
(T) 020 7296 0012
Speciality: Complementary Medicines & Therapy.
C M (Ref:HM15383)

## ORIENTAL MEDICAL CENTRE

**Oriental Medical Centre**, 12 The Woolmead, Farnham, **Surrey**, GU9 7TX, ENG.
(T) 01252 718888 (F) 01483 416876
Speciality: Complementary Medicines & Therapy.
● **Owner** Mr E Fink
C M (Ref:HM15384)

## ORIENTAL MEDICAL CENTRE

**Oriental Medical Centre (The)**, 31 High St, Godalming, **Surrey**, GU7 1AU, ENG.
(T) 01483 860353
Speciality: Complementary Medicines & Therapy.
● **Manageress** Mrs L Fink
C M (Ref:HM15385)

## ORIENTAL MEDICINE

**Dr E Chang Chinese Herbal Medicine and Acupuncture**, 4 Chase Side, Southgate, London, **London (Greater)**, N14 5BP, ENG.
(T) 020 8886 5391 (F) 020 8886 5391
Speciality: Acupressure, Acupuncture, Cupping, Herbal Medicine, Massage (Therapeutic), Moxibustion, Oriental Diagnosis, Reflexology. ✔
● **Herbal Doctor and Acupuncturist** Ms E Change M: BAcC, RCHM.
● **Company Secretary** Mr R James
O Yrs. Est.: 8 (Ref:HM15386)

## ORIENTAL MEDICINE PRACTICE

**Oriental Medicine Practice (The)**, 35 North View, Westbury Park, Bristol, BS6 7PY, ENG.
(T) 01179 078890 (F) 01179 078860
(E) keith@swcom.org.uk
(W) www.orientalmedicine.co.uk
Speciality: Acupuncture, Cupping, Dietician, Herbal Medicine, Life Style Coaching, Massage (Therapeutic), Moxibustion, Nutritional Therapy, Oriental Diagnosis, Shiatsu, Vitamin Therapy, Cellular Health Analysis, Allergy Testing. ✔ [credit card]
● **Shiatsu Practitioner/Therapist** Ms E Ferris Q: BA (Hons), MRSS(t). M: BRCP, Shiatsu Society UK.
● **Acupuncturist/Chinese Herbalist** Ms H Fielding Q: Dip.CHM, Lic.Ac. M: BAcC, RCHM.
● **Acupuncturist/Nutritionalist** Mr K Ferris Q: Dip.Ac, Dip.Nutrition, Dip.Shiatsu. M: BRCP.
● **Acupuncturist** Mr H McGrath Q: Dip.Ac. M: BRCP.
C O Yrs. Est.: 15 (Ref:HM15387)

## ORIENTAL MEDICINE PRACTICE

**Oriental Medicine Practice (The)**, 6 Alexandra Rd, Burton-On-Trent, **Staffordshire**, DE15 0JE, ENG.
(T) 01283 516443 (F) 01283 516443
Speciality: Acupuncture.
● **Partner** Mr G Gargini
O (Ref:HM15388)

## ORIENTAL THERAPY INTERNATIONAL

**Oriental Therapy International**, Limetree Trce, 2 Highfields, Burwash, Etchingham, **Sussex (East)**, TN19 7HE, ENG.
(T) 01435 883808
Speciality: Complementary Medicines & Therapy.
C M (Ref:HM15389)

## ORIGINAL CUTTING EDGE

**Original Cutting Edge Co (The)**, Intrument Servicing, 14 Tolworth Rise South, Surbiton, **Surrey**, KT5 9NN, ENG.
(T) 020 8241 0970 (F) 020 8296 0230
Speciality: Chiropodists (Podiatrists).
● **Owner** Mr J Haines
S (Ref:HM15390)

## ORIGINAL WHEAT BAG

**Original Wheat Bag Co Ltd**, P O Box 437, Woking, **Surrey**, GU21 4FU, ENG.
(T) 01483 598483 (F) 01276 855564
Speciality: Complementary Medicines & Therapy.
● **Partner** Mrs K Millman
C M (Ref:HM15391)

## ORIGINALS

**Originals**, Wallerscote House, Winnington Lane, Northwich, **Cheshire**, CW8 4EG, ENG.
(T) 01606 782233
Speciality: Aromatherapy.
M O (Ref:HM15392)

## ORMAY, A P

**A P Ormay**, 113 Goldhurst Trce, London, **London (Greater)**, NW6 3HA, ENG.
(T) 020 7625 6576
Speciality: Psychotherapy.
● **Owner** A Ormay
B (Ref:HM15393)

## ORME, ELIZABETH

**Elizabeth Orme**, 54 The Avenue, Yeovil, **Somerset**, BA21 4BN, ENG.
(T) 01935 422488
Speciality: Complementary Medicines & Therapy.
M (Ref:HM15394)

## ORME, RUTH

**Ruth Orme**, 11 Sandhurst Avenue, Stourbridge, **Midlands (West)**, DY9 0XG, ENG.
(T) 01562 884491
Speciality: Chiropodists (Podiatrists).
● **Owner** Mrs R Orme
S (Ref:HM15395)

## ORME, SUE

**Sue Orme**, 16 Forgefield, Biggin Hill, Westerham, **Kent**, TN16 3DS, ENG.
(T) 01959 700813
Speciality: Reflexology.
S T (Ref:HM15396)

## ORMEROD

**Ormerod**, 5 Sq St, Ramsbottom, Bury, **Lancashire**, BL0 9BE, ENG.
(T) 01706 826320
Speciality: Chiropodists (Podiatrists).
S (Ref:HM15397)

## ORMROD, KEN

**Ken Ormrod**, 35 Fir Rd, Liverpool, **Merseyside**, L22 4QL, ENG.
(T) 01519 200008 (F) 01519 200008
Speciality: Complementary Medicines & Therapy.
● **Owner** Mr K Ormrod
C M (Ref:HM15398)

## ORMSBY, NEIL

**Neil Ormsby**, 56 Church Hill, Two Mile Ash, Milton Keynes, **Buckinghamshire**, MK8 8JE, ENG.
(T) 01908 569987
Speciality: Spiritual Healing. ✔
● **Owner/Astrologer** Mr N Ormsby
B Yrs. Est.: 14 (Ref:HM15399)

## ORMSKIRK PHYSIO CENTRE

**Ormskirk Physiotherapy Centre & Sports Injury Clinic**, 75 Aughton St, Ormskirk, **Lancashire**, L39 3BN, ENG.
(T) 01695 570002 (F) 01695 581121
Speciality: Physiotherapy.
● **Partner** Mr J Hall
P S T (Ref:HM15400)

## O'ROURKE, LESLEY

**Lesley O'Rourke**, 166 Coombfield Drive, Dartford, **Kent**, DA2 7LH, ENG.
(T) 01474 702661
Speciality: Reflexology.
S T (Ref:HM15401)

## ORPINGTON CHIROPRACTIC CLINIC

**Orpington Chiropractic Clinic**, St. Botolphs Rd, Orpington, **Kent**, BR6 0JG, ENG.
(T) 020 8663 3878
Speciality: Chiropractors.
P S T (Ref:HM15402)

## ORPINGTON CHIROPRACTICE CLINIC

**Orpington Chiropractice Clinic**, 29 St Botolphs Rd, Sevenoaks, **Kent**, TN13 3AQ, ENG.
(T) 01732 742120
Speciality: Chiropractic.
P S T (Ref:HM15403)

## ORR, JOSCELYNE

**Joscelyne Orr**, 35 Main St, Cottesmore, Oakham, **Leicestershire**, LE15 7DH, ENG.
(T) 01572 813264
Speciality: Aromatherapy.
● **Owner** Mrs J Orr
M O (Ref:HM15404)

## ORR, WILLIAM A

**William A Orr**, 12 Rodney St, Liverpool, **Merseyside**, L1 2TE, ENG.


Key continued: **Yrs.Est:** Years Established **Q:** Qualifications **M:** Professional Membership ✔ Indemnity Insurance [credit card] Accept Credit Cards

(T) 01517 090479
Speciality: Acupuncture, Manipulation, Physiotherapy.
O (Ref:HM15405)

### ORRELL CHIROPODY PRACTICE
**Orrell Chiropody Practice**, 8 Gathurst Rd, Orrell, Wigan, **Lancashire**, WN5 8QH, ENG.
(T) 01942 215391
Speciality: Chiropodists (Podiatrists).
● **Owner** Mr S Turton
S (Ref:HM15406)

### ORRIDGE, T
**T Orridge**, Nottingham Natural Health Centre, 354 Mansfield Rd, Nottingham, **Nottinghamshire**, NG5 2EF, ENG.
(T) 01159 608855
Speciality: Complementary Medicines & Therapy.
M (Ref:HM15407)

### ORRISS, GEOFF
**Geoff Orriss**, 15 Kings Rd, Walton-On-Thames, **Surrey**, KT12 2RA, ENG.
(T) 01932 254391
Speciality: Hypnosis.
● **Owner** Mr G Orriss
B (Ref:HM15408)

### ORSACKOVA, HELENA
**Helena Orsackova**, 96A Burnt Ash Hill, London, **London (Greater)**, SE12 0HT, ENG.
(T) 020 8857 9964
Speciality: Complementary Medicines & Therapy.
C M (Ref:HM15409)

### ORTHOAED
**Orthoaed**, Hivron, Bleddfa, Knighton, **Powys**, LD7 1NY, WAL.
(T) 01547 550245
Speciality: Physiotherapy.
● **Partner** Mrs A Green Price
P S T (Ref:HM15410)

### ORTHOMOL
**Orthomol Ltd**, Unit 9, Berkshire Business Centre, Berkshire Drive, Thatcham, **Berkshire**, RG19 4EW, ENG.
(T) 01635 866333 (F) 01635 866555
Speciality: Complementary Medicines & Therapy.
● **Technical Manager** Mr M Greiner
M (Ref:HM15411)

### ORTHOTICITY
**Orthoticity Ltd**, 71 Oxted Green, Milford, Godalming, **Surrey**, GU8 5DD, ENG.
(T) 01483 861118 (F) 01483 861118
Speciality: Chiropodists (Podiatrists).
● **Owner** Mr M Swindon
S (Ref:HM15412)

### ORTON, G
**G Orton**, 39 Knoll Drive, Styvechale, Coventry, **Midlands (West)**, CV3 5BU, ENG.
(T) 024 7641 5983
Speciality: Reflexology.
● **Owner** Gill Orton
S T (Ref:HM15413)

### ORTON, S
**S Orton**, St Thomas Clinic, St Thomas Park, Lymington, **Hampshire**, SO41 9NF, ENG.
(T) 01590 674477
Speciality: Osteopathy.
P S T (Ref:HM15414)

### ORTON, S
**S Orton**, Salisbury Neck & Back Pain Clinic, 57 Milford St, Salisbury, **Wiltshire**, SP1 2BP, ENG.
(T) 01722 414214
Speciality: Osteopathy.
● **Partner** Mr J Barnes
P S T (Ref:HM15415)

### ORWELL COUNSELLING GROUP
**Orwell Counselling Group**, Iris Cottage, Benhall Green, Benhall, Saxmundham, **Suffolk**, IP17 1HL, ENG.
(T) 01728 603515
Speciality: Psychotherapy.
B (Ref:HM15416)

### OSBORN, AMY
**Amy Osborn**, Old Bank House, 59 High St, Odiham, Hook, **Hampshire**, RG29 1LF, ENG.
(T) 01256 702140 (F) 01256 704717
Speciality: Chiropodists (Podiatrists).
● **Owner** Mrs C Hood
S (Ref:HM15417)

### OSBORN, HELEN
**Helen Osborn**, 12 Shaftesbury Avenue, Bedford, **Bedfordshire**, MK40 3SA, ENG.
(T) 01234 216889
Speciality: Alexander Technique. ✔
● **Owner** Ms H Osborn **Q:** BA (Hons). **M:** STAT.
P S Yrs. Est.: 5 (Ref:HM15418)

### OSBORN, TERRI
**Terri Osborn**, 5 Hornet Rd, Emsworth, **Hampshire**, PO10 8EL, ENG.
(T) 01243 374542
Speciality: Reflexology.
S T (Ref:HM15419)

### OSBORNE CLINIC
**Osborne Clinic (The)**, 22 Osborne Avenue, Jesmond, Newcastle Upon Tyne, **Tyne and Wear**, NE2 1JQ, ENG.
(T) 01912 813379 (F) 01912 815952
(E) physio@osbourneclinic.demon.co.uk
(W) www.osborneclinic.co.uk
Speciality: Acupuncture, Aromatherapy, Biofeedback, Complementary Therapy, Counselling, Electrotherapy, Manipulation, Massage (Therapeutic), Osteopathy, Pilates, Reflexology, Stress Therapy, Ultrasonics. ✔
● **Aromatherapist/Therapeutic Massage Therapist** Ms L Adams **Q:** ISPA, SRN.
● **Physiotherapist** Miss C Fitch **Q:** BSc (Hons), MCSP, SRP.
● **Reflexologist** Ms A Lightfoot **Q:** IIHHT.
● **Practice Principal** Mrs A Moodie **Q:** MCSP, SRP. **M:** AACP, ACA.
● **Physiotherapist** Mrs P Leggett **Q:** MCSP, SRP.
● **Physiotherapist** Mrs G Cameron **Q:** MCSP, SRP.
● **Sports and Remedial Massage Therapist** Jo Richardson **M:** GCP, PMBCA.
S Yrs. Est.: 22 (Ref:HM15420)

### OSBORNE, CHRISTINE
**Christine Osborne**, 15 Dyfrig St, Barry, **Glamorgan (Vale of)**, CF62 5TW, WAL.
(T) 01446 733108
Speciality: Reflexology.
S T (Ref:HM15421)

### OSBORNE, D
**D Osborne**, 77A Upper Sandhurst Rd, Bristol, BS4 3RU, ENG.
(T) 01179 777145
Speciality: Chiropodists (Podiatrists).
S (Ref:HM15422)

### OSBORNE, HOLLY
**Holly Osborne**, 725A Garratt Lane, London, **London (Greater)**, SW17 0PD, ENG.
(T) 020 8879 0322
Speciality: Reflexology.
S T (Ref:HM15423)

### OSBORNE, JEAN
**Jean Osborne**, 11 Pittlesden, Tenterden, **Kent**, TN30 6HJ, ENG.
(T) 01580 765116
Speciality: Homeopathy.
● **Owner** Mrs J Osborne
M (Ref:HM15424)

### OSBORNE, JEAN
**Jean Osborne**, 30 High St, Tenterden, **Kent**, TN30 6AR, ENG.
(T) 01580 766424
Speciality: Homeopathy.
M (Ref:HM15425)

### OSBORNE, JO
**Jo Osborne**, 42 Parkland Avenue, Slough, **Berkshire**, SL3 7LQ, ENG.
(T) 01753 541818 (F) 01753 541818
Speciality: Complementary Medicines & Therapy.
● **Owner** Mrs J Osborne
M (Ref:HM15426)

### OSBORNE, M
**M Osborne**, 77A Upper Sandhurst Rd, Bristol, BS4 3RU, ENG.
(T) 01179 777145
Speciality: Chiropodists (Podiatrists).
S (Ref:HM15427)

### OSBORNE, P
**P Osborne**, 10 All Saints Rd, Kings Heath, Birmingham, **Midlands (West)**, B14 7LL, ENG.
(T) 01214 442366
Speciality: Chiropodists (Podiatrists).
● **Owner** Mrs P Osborne
S (Ref:HM15428)

### OSBORNE, R
**R Osborne**, 180 Southmead Rd, Westbury-On-Trym, Bristol, BS10 5DR, ENG.
(T) 01179 592000
Speciality: Osteopathy.
● **Partner** Miss R Osborne
P S T (Ref:HM15429)

### OSBORNE, R
**R Osborne**, Flat 3, 12 Sunnyside Rd, Clevedon, **Somerset**, BS21 7TA, ENG.
(T) 01275 340360
Speciality: Osteopathy.
● **Owner** Mr M Morgan
P S T (Ref:HM15430)

### OSGOOD, JANE
**Jane Osgood**, 39 Crossway, Manchester, **Manchester (Greater)**, M20 6TU, ENG.
(T) 01614 451018
Speciality: Alexander Technique.
P S (Ref:HM15431)

### O'SHEA, A C
**A C O'shea**, 9 Tudor Cl, Grayshott, Hindhead, **Surrey**, GU26 6HP, ENG.
(T) 01428 607947
Speciality: Chiropodists (Podiatrists).
● **Owner** Mrs A O'Shea
S (Ref:HM15432)

### O'SHEA, LESLEY
**Lesley O'Shea**, 54 St. Peters Cl, Flitwick, Bedford, **Bedfordshire**, MK45 1EZ, ENG.
(T) 01525 751975
Speciality: Reflexology.
S T (Ref:HM15433)

### O'SHEA, SHEILA & PARTNERS
**Sheila O'Shea & Partners**, 130 Devonshire Rd, Chorley, **Lancashire**, PR7 2BY, ENG.
(T) 01257 260520
Speciality: Osteopathy.
● **Partner** Mr E O'Shea
P S T (Ref:HM15434)

### OSMAN, BRIAN
**Brian Osman**, 70 Langham Rd, Boxted, Colchester, **Essex**, CO4 5HT, ENG.
(T) 01206 272534
Speciality: Psychology, Psychology. ✔
● **Psychologist** Mr B Osman **Q:** BA, BA (Hons), C.Psychol.
B Yrs. Est.: 10 (Ref:HM15435)

### OSMAN, ELIZABETH
**Elizabeth Osman**, The Maple Clinic, 3-5 Horndean Rd, Bracknell, **Berkshire**, RG12 0XQ, ENG.
(T) 01344 862646
Speciality: Aromatherapy.
● **Owner** Dr W Baker
M O (Ref:HM15436)

### OSMAN, JO
**Jo Osman**, 308 Markhouse Rd, London, **London (Greater)**, E17 8EF, ENG.
(T) 020 8923 8513 (F) 020 8923 8513
Speciality: Hypnosis.
● **Owner** Mr J Osman
B (Ref:HM15437)

### OSMAN, SARA
**Sara Osman**, 72 High St, Alton, **Hampshire**, GU34 1EX, ENG.
(T) 01420 543334
Speciality: Complementary Medicines & Therapy.

- **Owner** Mrs L Vallati
M (**Ref:**HM15438)

**OSMAN, SARA**

**Sara Osman**, Peachey House, Bepton Rd, Midhurst, **Sussex (West)**, GU29 9LU, ENG.
(T) 01730 810540 (F) 01730 812248
Speciality: Complementary Medicines & Therapy.
- **Secretary** Ms S Upfold
M (**Ref:**HM15439)

**OSMAN, SARAH**

**Sarah Osman**, 1st Floor 20 Lavant St, Petersfield, **Hampshire**, GU32 3EW, ENG.
(T) 01730 231655
Speciality: Complementary Medicines & Therapy.
- **Manager** Ms G Silverthorn
M (**Ref:**HM15440)

**OSMER PSYCHIC CENTRE**

**Osmer Psychic Centre**, 30 Piquet Rd, London, **London (Greater)**, SE20 7XZ, ENG.
(T) 020 8778 9667
Speciality: Clairvoyants & Palmists.
- **Owner** Mrs S Knell
B (**Ref:**HM15441)

**O'SOBANDE, RICHARD**

**Richard O'Sobande**, 6 Cameron Pk, Edinburgh, **Edinburgh (City of)**, EH16 5JY, SCO.
(T) 01316 673027 (F) 01316 673027
Speciality: Osteopathy.
- **Owner** Mr R Sobande
P S T (**Ref:**HM15442)

**OSTEO CLINIC & HEALING CENTRE**

**Osteopathic Clinic & Healing Centre**, 70 Mayfield Rd, South Croydon, **Surrey**, CR2 0BF, ENG.
(T) 020 8651 4071
Speciality: Osteopathy.
- **Owner** Mr K Haq
P S T (**Ref:**HM15443)

**OSTEO-MEDIC SERVICES**

**Osteo-Medic Services**, Lambworth Lodge, Main St, Great Hatfield, Hull, **Humberside (North)**, HU11 4US, ENG.
(T) 01964 534681
Speciality: Osteopathy.
- **Owner** Mr S Wilkinson
P S T (**Ref:**HM15444)

**OSTEOPATH**

**Osteopath**, 9 Winfield, Newent, **Gloucestershire**, GL18 1QB, ENG.
(T) 01531 822392 (F) 01531 822392
(E) seden@ttclick.co.uk
Speciality: Manipulation, Massage (Therapeutic), Naturopathy, Osteopathy. ✓
- **Osteopath** Miss S Eden Q: DO. M: GOsC.
S Yrs. Est.: 11 (**Ref:**HM15445)

**OSTEOPATH CLINIC**

**Osteopath Clinic**, 168A Bramcote Lane, Nottingham, **Nottinghamshire**, NG8 2QP, ENG.
(T) 01332 762576
Speciality: Osteopathy.
- **Owner** Mr S Gandhi
P S T (**Ref:**HM15446)

**OSTEOPATH CLINIC**

**Osteopath Clinic**, 56 Derby Lane, Derby, **Derbyshire**, DE23 8UA, ENG.
(T) 01332 762576
Speciality: Osteopathy.
- **Owner** Mr S Gandhi
P S T (**Ref:**HM15447)

**OSTEOPATH SPORTS CARE ASS**

**Osteopath Sports Care Association (The)**, P O Box 221, London, **London (Greater)**, WC2B 4EJ, ENG.
(T) 08706 010031
Speciality: Osteopathy.
P S T (**Ref:**HM15448)

**OSTEOPATHIC**

**Osteopathic**, 101 Ludlow Rd, Church Stretton, **Shropshire**, SY6 6RA, ENG.
(T) 01694 724866
Speciality: Counselling, Cranial Osteopathy, Cupping, Massage (Therapeutic), Osteopathy, Rolfing, Celloid Mineral Therapy. ✓
- **Osteopath** Ms E Keeling-Howard
S Yrs. Est.: 2 (**Ref:**HM15449)

**OSTEOPATHIC & PHYSICAL CLINIC**

**Osteopathic & Physical Therapies Clinic**, Church View House, Church Gate, Moffat, **Dumfries and Galloway**, DG10 9EG, SCO.
(T) 01683 221815
Speciality: Osteopathy.
- **Owner** Mr J McLeish
P S T (**Ref:**HM15450)

**OSTEOPATHIC & SPORTS CLINIC**

**Osteopathic & Sports Injury Clinic**, 42 The Broadway, London, **London (Greater)**, E15 4QS, ENG.
(T) 020 8522 1034
Speciality: Osteopathy.
P S T (**Ref:**HM15451)

**OSTEOPATHIC & SPORTS CLINIC**

**Osteopathic & Sports Therapy Clinic**, Rear Of Crown House, High St, Hungerford, **Berkshire**, RG17 0NF, ENG.
(T) 01488 686195
Speciality: Osteopathy.
- **Owner** Mrs J Hutchings
P S T (**Ref:**HM15452)

**OSTEOPATHIC ASSOCIATION CLINIC**

**Osteopathic Association Clinic**, 8-10 Boston Pl, London, **London (Greater)**, NW1 6QH, ENG.
(T) 020 7262 1128 (F) 020 7723 7492
Speciality: Manipulation, Osteopathy.
- **Manager** Ms A Dalby
S Yrs. Est.: 74 (**Ref:**HM15453)

**OSTEOPATHIC CENTRE**

**Osteopathic Centre**, 34 Alderney St, London, **London (Greater)**, SW1V 4EU, ENG.
(T) 020 7834 1012
Speciality: Complementary Medicines & Therapy.
- **Osteopath** Mr G Hughes
M (**Ref:**HM15454)

**OSTEOPATHIC CENTRE**

**Osteopathic Centre**, 3 Martin Gr, Morden, **Surrey**, SM4 5AJ, ENG.
(T) 020 8543 4463
Speciality: Osteopathy.
P S T (**Ref:**HM15455)

**OSTEOPATHIC CENTRE**

**Osteopathic Centre (The)**, 51 High St, Menai Bridge, **Isle of Anglesey**, LL59 5EF, WAL.
(T) 01248 716297
Speciality: Osteopathy.
- **Partner** Mrs J Griffiths
P S T (**Ref:**HM15456)

**OSTEOPATHIC CENTRE**

**Osteopathic Centre (The)**, 9a Mansfield Rd, Chessington, **Surrey**, KT9 2PJ, ENG.
(T) 020 8397 8629
Speciality: Osteopathy.
P S T (**Ref:**HM15457)

**OSTEOPATHIC CENTRE**

**Osteopathic Centre For Family & Children (The)**, 349 Hills Rd, Cambridge, **Cambridgeshire**, CB2 2QT, ENG.
(T) 01223 242828
Speciality: Osteopathy.
- **Manager** Mrs S Deora
P S T (**Ref:**HM15458)

**OSTEOPATHIC CLINIC**

**Osteopathic Clinic (The)**, The Osteopathic Clinic, 178 East Barnet Rd, New Barnet, Barnet, **Hertfordshire**, EN4 8RD, ENG.
(T) 020 8449 754 (F) 020 8449 0174
Speciality: Acupressure, Acupuncture, Aromatherapy, Bach Remedies, Chiropody, Complementary Therapy, Counselling, Cranial Osteopathy, Herbal Medicine, Indian Head Massage, Manipulation, Massage (Therapeutic), Osteopathy, Physiotherapy, Podiatry, Reflexology, Reiki, Musculo-Skeletal Physician. ✓
- **Reflexologist** Ms J Kember
- **Practice Manager** Mrs D Evans
- **Osteopath** Mr C Evans Q: DO. M: GOsC.
- **Chiropodist (Podiatrist)** Mrs T Dawes
- **Counsellor** Mr I D'souza
- **Osteopath** Miss T Knock
- **Reiki/Bach Flower Practitioner** Ms M Drake
- **Physiotherapist** Mr R Mallick
- **Consultant Osteopath/Musculo-Skeletal Physician** Dr J Griffiths
- **Acupuncturist** Ms T Pui Ling Chan
- **Principal** Mr L Hartman
S Yrs. Est.: 30 (**Ref:**HM15459)

**OSTEOPATHIC CLINIC**

**Osteopathic Clinic (The)**, Unit 9 Clover House, Boston Rd, Cranwell, Sleaford, **Lincolnshire**, NG34 8HD, ENG.
(T) 01529 414894
Speciality: Osteopathy.
P S T (**Ref:**HM15460)

**OSTEOPATHIC CLINIC**

**Osteopathic Clinic (The)**, 2 Echo Sq, Gravesend, **Kent**, DA12 1NP, ENG.
(T) 01474 321631
Speciality: Osteopathy. ✓
- **Osteopath** Mr K Fadil Q: BSc (Hons). M: GOsC.
S Yrs. Est.: 1 (**Ref:**HM15461)

**OSTEOPATHIC CLINIC**

**Osteopathic Clinic (The)**, 21 Enterprise House, Kingsway North, Team Valley Trading Estate, Gateshead, **Tyne and Wear**, NE11 0SR, ENG.
(T) 01914 915111 (F) 01914 872503
Speciality: Osteopathy.
- **Practice Manager** Mrs S Robson
P S T (**Ref:**HM15462)

**OSTEOPATHIC CTRE FOR CHILDREN**

**Osteopathic Centre For Children**, 109 Harley St, London, **London (Greater)**, W1N 1DG, ENG.
(T) 020 7486 6160 (F) 020 7925 0019
Speciality: Osteopathy.
- **Manager** Mrs P Ferrell
P S T (**Ref:**HM15463)

**OSTEOPATHIC EMERGENCY SERVICE**

**Osteopathic Emergency Service**, 30 Cumberland Mansions, Seymour Pl, London, **London (Greater)**, W1H 5TF, ENG.
(T) 020 7262 3022
(E) richard_stubs@btinternet.com
(W) www.starosteopath.com
Speciality: Osteopathy.
- **Osteopath** Mr R Stubbs Q: DO. M: GOsC.
S Yrs. Est.: 21 (**Ref:**HM15464)

**OSTEOPATHIC FAMILY CENTRE**

**Osteopathic Family Centre**, 14 Lemon St, Truro, **Cornwall**, TR1 2LS, ENG.
(T) 01872 275880 (F) 01872 275880
Speciality: Cranial Osteopathy, Manipulation, Osteopathy.
- **Osteopath** Mr D Evans Q: DO. M: GOsC.
S T (**Ref:**HM15465)

**OSTEOPATHIC PRACTICE**

**Osteopathic Practice**, 10A High St, Tunbridge Wells, **Kent**, TN1 1UX, ENG.
(T) 01892 514112 (F) 01892 530778
Speciality: Cranial Osteopathy, Osteopathy. ✓
- **Osteopath** Mrs C Huggett Q: DO. M: GOsC.
S Yrs. Est.: 8 (**Ref:**HM15466)

**OSTEOPATHIC PRACTICE**

**Osteopathic Practice (The)**, 17 Charlton Rd, Blackheath, London, **London (Greater)**, SE3 7EU, ENG.
(T) 020 8853 2275 (F) 020 3051 353
(E) contact@theosteopathicpractice.co.uk
(W) www.osteopathicpractice.co.uk
Speciality: Cranial Osteopathy, Osteopathy. ✓
- **Osteopath** Mr D Ayres Q: BSc, Hons (OST). M: BOA, GOsC.
- **Osteopath** Mr D Kean Q: DO. M: GOsC.
S Yrs. Est.: 6 (**Ref:**HM15467)

**OSTEOPATHIC PRACTICE**

**Osteopathic Practice**, 47 Campion Trce, Leamington Spa, **Warwickshire**, CV32 4SU,


Key continued: **Yrs.Est:** Years Established **Q:** Qualifications **M:** Professional Membership ✓ Indemnity Insurance Accept Credit Cards

ENG.
(T) 01926 335932 (F) 01926 339574
Speciality: Osteopathy.
● **Osteopath** Miss J O'Connor Q: DO. M: GOsC.
● **Osteopath** Mr N Lunt Q: BSc (Hons), MA. M: GOsC.
● **Osteopath** Mr C McCann Q: BSc (Hons). M: GOsC.
P S T (Ref:HM15468)

## OSTEOPATHIC PRACTICE

**Osteopathic Practice**, High St, Tisbury, **Wiltshire**, SP2 9LT, ENG.
(T) 01747 871044
Speciality: Alexander Technique.
● **Osteopath** Mrs S MacDermot
P S (Ref:HM15469)

## OSTEOPATHIC PRACTICE

**Robi Persad Registered Osteopath**, 4 Batholomew Villas, London, **London (Greater)**, NW5 2LL, ENG.
(T) 020 7209 3243
(E) rsvp@devvers.co.uk
(W) www.osteopathicpractice.com
Speciality: Acupressure, Acupuncture, Cranial Osteopathy, Cupping, Healing Therapy, Homeopathy, Manipulation, Massage (Therapeutic), Osteopathy, Shiatsu, Ultrasonics, Yoga.
● **Osteopath** Mr R Persad Q: BSc, Hons (OST). M: GOsC.
S Yrs. Est.: 7 (Ref:HM15470)

## OSTEOPATHIC PRACTICE

**Sue Philbey - Osteopath**, 71 Fieldview, Earlsfield, London, **London (Greater)**, SW18 3HF, ENG.
(T) 020 8870 7345 (F) 020 8870 7345
Speciality: Manipulation, Massage (Therapeutic), Naturopathy, Osteopathy. ✔
● **Osteopath/Naturopath** Ms S Philbey Q: BSc, DO, Hons (OST), ND. M: BNA, GOsC.
S Yrs. Est.: 1 (Ref:HM15471)

## OSTEOPATHIC PRACTICE

**Osteopathic Practice (The)**, Wrekin Professional Centre, Holyhead Rd, Wellington, Telford, **Shropshire**, TF1 2ED, ENG.
(T) 01952 641418 (F) 01952 641418
Speciality: Osteopathy.
P S T (Ref:HM15472)

## OSTEOPATHIC PRACTICE

**Osteopathic Practice (The)**, 161 Leathwaite Rd, London, **London (Greater)**, SW11 6RW, ENG.
(T) 020 7801 0662
Speciality: Cranial Osteopathy, Osteopathy. ✔
● **Osteopath** Mr A Beaumont Q: BA, DO. M: GOsC.
S Yrs. Est.: 4 (Ref:HM15473)

## OSTEOPATHIC PRACTICE

**Osteopathic Practice**, Cinema Lane, Wexford Town, Wexford, **County Wexford**, IRE.
(T) 05324 890
(E) mporter@eircom.net
Speciality: Manipulation, Massage (Therapeutic), Osteopathy. ✔
● **Osteopath** Mr M Porter Q: BSc (Hons), RGN. M: GOsS.
S Yrs. Est.: 2 (Ref:HM15474)

## OSTEOPATHS

**Osteopaths**, 39 St Marks Rd, Salisbury, **Wiltshire**, SP1 3AY, ENG.
(T) 01722 331317
Speciality: Cranial Osteopathy, Osteopathy. ✔
● **Osteopath** Mr Browning Q: DO. M: GOsC.
S Yrs. Est.: 25 (Ref:HM15475)

## OSTEOPATHS FOR INDUSTRY

**Osteopaths For Industry Ltd**, 1 Grove Way, Esher, **Surrey**, KT10 8HH, ENG.
(T) 020 8398 7533 (F) 020 8398 4864
Speciality: Osteopathy.
● **Managing Director** Mrs J Kaye
P S T (Ref:HM15476)

## OSTEOPATHY

**Osteopathy**, 36A London Rd, Blackwater, Camberley, **Surrey**, GU17 9AA, ENG.
(T) 01276 36475
Speciality: Acupuncture, Cranial Osteopathy, Manipulation, Osteopathy. ✔
● **Osteopath** Ms K Benstead Q: BSc, DO. M: GOsC.
● **Owner** Mrs J Coulsting
S (Ref:HM15477)

## OSTEOPATHY & ACUPUNCTURE

**Osteopathy & Acupuncture Clinic**, Bromfield Medical Centre, Bryn Hilyn Lane, Mold, **Flintshire**, CH7 1JY, WAL.
(T) 01352 754195 (F) 01325 754195
Speciality: Osteopathy.
● **Owner** Mrs B Cordwell
P S T (Ref:HM15478)

## OSTEOPATHY AT ESQUIRE'S

**Bee Musson**, Esquire's Barbers, 8 Station Prde, South St, Lancing, **Sussex (West)**, BN15 8AA, ENG.
(T) 01903 761596 (F) 01903 761596
Speciality: Complementary Therapy, Cranial Osteopathy, Manipulation, Massage (Therapeutic), Osteopathy. ✔
● **Registered Osteopath** Bee Musson Q: Reg.Osteopath. M: GOsC.
● **Owner** Mr G Brennan
S Yrs. Est.: 1 (Ref:HM15479)

## OSTLE, SAMANTHA

**Samantha Ostle**, The Conifers, Preston, Telford, **Shropshire**, TF6 6DH, ENG.
(T) 01952 677062
Speciality: Chiropractic. ✔
● **McTimoney Chiropractor** Ms S Ostle Q: AMC, DC, MMCA. M: GCC, MCA.
S Yrs. Est.: 5 (Ref:HM15480)

## O'SULLIVAN, A

**A O'Sullivan**, 89 St. Agnes Pl, London, **London (Greater)**, SE11 4BB, ENG.
(T) 020 7820 9551
Speciality: Acupuncture.
● **Owner** A O'Sullivan
O (Ref:HM15481)

## O'SULLIVAN, FRANCES

**Frances O'Sullivan**, **Yorkshire (West)**, LS6, ENG.
(T) 01132 740509
Speciality: Bach Remedies.
M (Ref:HM15482)

## O'SULLIVAN, JOHN

**O'Sullivan John**, 17 Bonaventure Pl, **County Cork**, IRE.
(T) 021 4318 179
Speciality: Acupuncture.
O (Ref:HM15483)

## O'SULLIVAN, KEVIN

**Kevin O'Sullivan**, 111 Manfield, Skelmersdale, **Lancashire**, WN8 6SU, ENG.
(T) 01695 728133 (F) 01695 728133
Speciality: Chiropodists (Podiatrists).
● **Owner** Mr K O'Sullivan
S (Ref:HM15484)

## O'SULLIVAN, KEVIN (DR)

**O'Sullivan Dr Kevin**, The Surgery South Douglas Rd, **County Cork**, IRE.
(T) 021 4365 013
Speciality: Osteopathy.
P S T (Ref:HM15485)

## O'SULLIVAN, M

**M O'Sullivan**, 25 Inverleith Row, Edinburgh, **Edinburgh (City of)**, EH3 5QH, SCO.
(T) 01315 516624
Speciality: Chiropodists (Podiatrists).
● **Owner** Ms M O'Sullivan
S (Ref:HM15486)

## O'SULLIVAN, M

**M O'Sullivan**, 52 Stoke Newington Church St, London, **London (Greater)**, N16 0NB, ENG.
(T) 020 7249 9671
Speciality: Hypnotherapy.
● **Senior Partner** Mrs J Sheridan
B (Ref:HM15487)

## O'SULLIVAN, MARY

**O'Sullivan Mary P DIP N H I I M I R I**, Acra Hse, Maylor St, Cork, **County Cork**, IRE.
(T) 021 4274 645
Speciality: Complementary Medicines & Therapy.
M (Ref:HM15488)

## O'SULLIVAN, MARYCH

**O'Sullivan Marych M Sc**, 33 Woodquay, **County Galway**, IRE.
(T) 09156 7511
Speciality: Complementary Medicines & Therapy.
M (Ref:HM15489)

## O'SULLIVAN, PAM

**Pam O'Sullivan**, Richborough Cottage, Ash Rd, Sandwich, **Kent**, CT13 9JA, ENG.
(T) 01304 611963
Speciality: Osteopathy.
P S T (Ref:HM15490)

## O'SULLIVAN, SHEILA

**Sheila O'Sullivan**, Brambleside, High Wycombe, **Buckinghamshire**, HP11 1JE, ENG.
(T) 01494 459517
Speciality: Psychotherapy.
● **Owner** Ms S O'Sullivan
B (Ref:HM15491)

## O'SULLIVAN, TANYA

**Tanya O'Sullivan**, Matthews House, 85 Epsom Rd, Guildford, **Surrey**, GU1 3PA, ENG.
(T) 01483 575876
Speciality: Physiotherapy.
P S T (Ref:HM15492)

## OTHEN, FIONA

**Fiona Othen**, 80 Hullbridge Rd, Rayleigh, **Essex**, SS6 9QL, ENG.
(T) 01268 784929
Speciality: Chiropractic.
● **Owner** Mrs F Othen
P S T (Ref:HM15493)

## OTLEY PHYSIOTHERAPISTS CLINIC

**Otley Physiotherapists Clinic**, 4 Carr Bank Cottages, Otley, **Yorkshire (West)**, LS21 2AJ, ENG.
(T) 01943 850723
Speciality: Physiotherapy.
● **Owner** Mrs W Carswell
P S T (Ref:HM15494)

## O'TOOLE, ALAN

**Alan O'Toole**, 2 North Parade Passage, Bath, **Somerset**, BA1 1NX, ENG.
(T) 01225 426171
Speciality: Osteopathy.
● **Owner** A O'Toole
P S T (Ref:HM15495)

## OTREMBA, KATHARINA

**Katharina Otremba**, 19 Bonser Rd, Strawberry Hill, Twickenham, **London (Greater)**, TW1 4RQ, ENG.
(T) 020 8891 6969
(E) katharinaotrenmba@btinternet.com
Speciality: Aversion Therapy, Bach Remedies, Biofeedback, Cognitive Therapy, Complementary Therapy, Counselling, Dowsing, Floral Essence Therapy, Gem Essence Therapy, Holistic Healing, Hypnosis, Hypnotherapy, Kinesiology, Nutritional Therapy, Psychotherapy, Stress Therapy, Visualisation Therapy, Vitamin Therapy, Positive Thinking and Park's Inner Child Therapy. ✔
● **Hypnotherapist/Kinesiologist** Ms K Otremba M: KFRP, NCH.
B H T Yrs. Est.: 5 (Ref:HM15496)

## OTTERSHAW OSTEOPATHIC PRACTICE

**Ottershaw Osteopathic Practice**, 2 Brox Rd, Ottershaw, Chertsey, **Surrey**, KT16 9PF, ENG.
(T) 01932 873180
Speciality: Osteopathy.
P S T (Ref:HM15497)

## OUILLON-PALMER, LAURENCE

**Laurence Ouillon-Palmer**, 10 Geralds Rd, High Wycombe, **Buckinghamshire**, HP13 6BW, ENG.
(T) 01494 534055



Key: B Mind-Body Medicine C Complementary Medicine H Self Help Treatment M Medicinal Therapy O Oriental Medicine P Postural Therapy S Manipulative Structural Therapy T Touch Therapy

Speciality: Reflexology.
S T (Ref:HM15498)

### OULTON FOOT CLINIC

**Oulton Foot Clinic (The)**, 151 Warwick Rd, Solihull, **Midlands (West)**, B92 7HN, ENG.
(T) 01217 063162
Speciality: Chiropody. ✔
● **Chiropodist (Podiatrist)**
Mr F Harris Q: BSc, DPodM. M: S.C.P.
● **Chiropodist (Podiatrist)**
N J Harris Q: BSc, DPodM. M: S.C.P.
M Yrs. Est.: 40 (Ref:HM15499)

### OUNDLE COMMUNITY CARE UNIT

**Oundle Community Care Unit**, Mason House, Glapthorn Rd, Oundle, Peterborough, **Cambridgeshire**, PE8 4JA, ENG.
(T) 01832 274255 (F) 01832 274705
Speciality: Psychiatry.
B (Ref:HM15500)

### OUSEBANK HYPNOTHERAPY

**Ousebank Hypnotherapy**, 66 Calverton Rd, Stony Stratford, Milton Keynes, **Buckinghamshire**, MK11 1HL, ENG.
(T) 01908 260091
Speciality: Hypnosis.
● **Owner** Mr V Stone
B (Ref:HM15501)

### OUTCOMES

**Outcomes Ltd**, 4 Ravenslea Rd, Wandsworth Common, London, **London (Greater)**, SW12 8SB, ENG.
(T) 020 8673 2719 (F) 020 8673 0933
(E) mick@outcomes.ndo.co.uk
(W) www.nlp-international.co.uk
Speciality: Aromatherapy, Auto Suggestion, Autogenic Training, Cognitive Therapy, Complementary Therapy, Counselling, Dowsing, Family Therapy, Gestalt Therapy, Group Therapy, Healer, Healing Therapy, Holistic Healing, Humanistic Psychology, Hypnosis, Hypnotherapy, Indian Head Massage, Kinesiology, Life Style Coaching, Massage (Therapeutic), Meditation, Psychotherapy, Reflexology, Reiki, Stress Therapy, Visualisation Therapy. ✔
● **Director** Mr M Lawrence Q: CMH, ITEC, NLP. M: HA.
B Yrs. Est.: 7 (Ref:HM15502)

### OUTEN, PAULINE

**Pauline Outen**, 132 West Dean, West Dean, Chichester, **Sussex (West)**, PO18 0RX, ENG.
(T) 01243 811344
Speciality: Reflexology.
S T (Ref:HM15503)

### OUTRAM, ANDREA F

**Andrea F Outram**, 10 Mowbray Cl, Sunderland, **Tyne and Wear**, SR2 8JA, ENG.
(T) 01915 650479
Speciality: Chiropodists (Podiatrists).
● **Owner** Mrs A Outram
S (Ref:HM15504)

### OUTREACH CLUB

**Outreach Club**, 7 Gayford Rd, London, **London (Greater)**, W12 9BY, ENG.
(T) 020 8932 2715
Speciality: Complementary Medicines & Therapy.
● **Partner** Mrs S Lynch
C M (Ref:HM15505)

### OUTRIDGE, M

**Mrs M Outridge**, 12 Boundary Rd, Farnborough, **Hampshire**, GU14 6SF, ENG.
(T) 01252 546630
Speciality: Chiropodists (Podiatrists).
● **Owner** Mrs M Outridge
S (Ref:HM15506)

### OUTSIDE IN

**Outside In (Cambridge) Ltd**, Unit 21 Scotland Rd Estate, Dry Drayton, Cambridge, **Cambridgeshire**, CB3 8AT, ENG.
(T) 01954 211955 (F) 01954 211956
(E) info@outsidein.co.uk
(W) www.outsidein.co.uk
Speciality: Light Therapy. ✔
● **Sole Director** Mr S Hayes
H Yrs. Est.: 9 (Ref:HM15507)

### OVENDEN, ANDREW

**Andrew Ovenden**, 2 Godstone Rd, Oxted, **Surrey**, RH8 9JT, ENG.
(T) 01883 714036
Speciality: Homeopathy.
M (Ref:HM15508)

### OVENDEN, ANDREW

**Andrew Ovenden**, 411A London Rd, Camberley, **Surrey**, GU15 3HZ, ENG.
(T) 01276 691946
Speciality: Homeopathy.
M (Ref:HM15509)

### OVENS, M

**M Ovens**, 20 James St, Llanbradach, Caerphilly, **Glamorgan (Vale of)**, CF83 3LJ, WAL.
(T) 029 2086 7587
Speciality: Psychiatry.
B (Ref:HM15510)

### OVER, C J A

**C J A Over**, 59 College Rd, Cheshunt, Waltham Cross, **Hertfordshire**, EN8 9LS, ENG.
(T) 01992 621122
Speciality: Chiropodists (Podiatrists).
● **Principal** Mr C Over
S (Ref:HM15511)

### OVERINGTON, KEL

**Kel Overington**, 76 High Avenue, Letchworth, **Hertfordshire**, SG6 3QW, ENG.
(T) 01462 483860
(E) keloverington@ntlworl.com.
Speciality: Shiatsu. ✔
● **Owner** Mr K Overington Q: ITEC, MRSS.
C Yrs. Est.: 4 (Ref:HM15512)

### OVERTON OSTEOPATHIC CLINIC

**Overton Osteopathic Clinic**, 25B High St, Overton, Basingstoke, **Hampshire**, RG25 3HB, ENG.
(T) 01256 770022
Speciality: Osteopathy.
● **Owner** Mr I Harrison
P S T (Ref:HM15513)

### OVERTON, PETER J

**Peter J Overton**, Springfield House, Shipston Rd, Stratford-Upon-Avon, **Warwickshire**, CV37 7LN, ENG.
(T) 01789 205900
Speciality: Osteopathy.
P S T (Ref:HM15514)

### OVERTONES

**Overtones**, 87 New Rd, Woodston, Peterborough, **Cambridgeshire**, PE2 9HD, ENG.
(T) 01733 569910
Speciality: Physiotherapy.
● **Owner** Mr J Hale
P S T (Ref:HM15515)

### OVERY, J

**J Overy**, 12 Camperdown, Great Yarmouth, **Norfolk**, NR30 3JB, ENG.
(T) 01493 331149
Speciality: Complementary Medicines & Therapy.
C M (Ref:HM15516)

### OVESEN, PEER B K

**Peer B K Ovesen**, 164 Nimrod Rd, London, **London (Greater)**, SW16 6TL, ENG.
(T) 07939 226332
Speciality: Reflexology.
S T (Ref:HM15517)

### OWEN ROAD SURGERY

**Owen Road Surgery**, Owen Rd Centre, 69 Owen Rd, Lancaster, **Lancashire**, LA1 2LG, ENG.
(T) 01524 846293
Speciality: Physiotherapy.
● **Manager** Mrs J Edwards
P S T (Ref:HM15518)

### OWEN, D

**D Owen**, 142 Hampton Rd, Twickenham, **London (Greater)**, TW2 5QR, ENG.
(T) 020 8898 1287
Speciality: Homeopathy.
M (Ref:HM15519)

### OWEN, D K

**D K Owen**, 14 Woodside Rd, Poole, **Dorset**, BH14 9JJ, ENG.
(T) 01202 739730
Speciality: Homeopathy.
M (Ref:HM15520)

### OWEN, DAVID A

**David A Owen**, 3 Wingfield Mansions, 137 Wingfield Rd, Plymouth, **Devon**, PL3 4ER, ENG.
(T) 01752 563640
Speciality: Hypnotherapy.
● **Owner** Mr D Owen
B (Ref:HM15521)

### OWEN, DAVID A

**David A Owen**, 3 Membland Court, Newton Ferrers, Plymouth, **Devon**, PL8 1HR, ENG.
(T) 01752 872278
Speciality: Alexander Technique.
P S (Ref:HM15522)

### OWEN, GEORGE

**George Owen**, 169 Drake St, Rochdale, **Lancashire**, OL11 1EF, ENG.
(T) 01706 633169
Speciality: Osteopathy.
P S T (Ref:HM15523)

### OWEN, JOE

**Joe Owen**, Unit 7 Kingsgate Workshops, 110-116 Kingsgate Rd, London, **London (Greater)**, NW6 2JG, ENG.
(T) 020 7328 7667 (F) 020 7328 7878
Speciality: Reflexology.
● **Owner** Mr J Owen
S T (Ref:HM15524)

### OWEN, L J

**L J Owen**, 5 Claremont St, Bilston, **Midlands (West)**, WV14 6BA, ENG.
(T) 01902 496460
Speciality: Chiropodists (Podiatrists).
S (Ref:HM15525)

### OWEN, LIBBY

**Libby Owen**, Swale Chiropractic Clinic, 167A London Rd, Sittingbourne, **Kent**, ME10 1PA, ENG.
(T) 01795 520707 (F) 01795 520799
Speciality: Chiropractors.
● **Owner** Mr K Cullen
P S T (Ref:HM15526)

### OWEN, M

**M Owen**, 36 Westminster Cl, Feltham, **London (Greater)**, TW14 9XD, ENG.
(T) 020 8867 0241
Speciality: Reflexology.
● **Owner** Ms M Owen
S T (Ref:HM15527)

### OWEN, PAM

**Pam Owen**, 16 Old Acres, Woodborough, Nottingham, **Nottinghamshire**, NG14 6ES, ENG.
(T) 01159 652994
Speciality: Reflexology.
● **Owner** Mrs P Owen
S T (Ref:HM15528)

### OWEN, RACHEL

**Rachel Owen**, 22 Spencer Gardens, Rochford, **Essex**, SS4 1TJ, ENG.
(T) 01702 531058
Speciality: Reflexology.
S T (Ref:HM15529)

### OWEN, T

**T Owen**, 4 Wellington Rd, Prenton, **Merseyside**, CH43 2JE, ENG.
(T) 01516 521328
Speciality: Osteopathy.
● **Owner** Mr T Owen
P S T (Ref:HM15530)

### OWEN, VICTOR

**Victor Owen**, 8 Grasmere Cl, Kempston, Bedford, **Bedfordshire**, MK42 8JG, ENG.
(T) 01234 852799
Speciality: Clairvoyants & Palmists.
B (Ref:HM15531)

### OWEN-JONES, JOY

**Joy Owen-Jones**, Fairfields Clinic, Skippetts Lane West, Basingstoke, **Hampshire**, RG21 3HP,



Key continued: Yrs.Est: Years Established Q: Qualifications M: Professional Membership ✔ Indemnity Insurance Accept Credit Cards

ENG.
(T) 01256 326980
Speciality: Relaxation Technique.
● **Owner** Ms J Owen-Jones
H T (Ref:HM15532)

## OWENS, PAULINE

**Pauline Owens**, 28 Laurel Cres, Halifax, **Yorkshire (West)**, HX2 8DF, ENG.
(T) 01422 357093
Speciality: Reflexology, Spiritual Healing. ✔
● **Reflexologist** Mrs P Owens Q: MBRA, MSSCh.
B T Yrs. Est.: 8 (**Ref:**HM15533)

## OWENS, SPENCER

**Spencer Owens**, 70 Elkington Rd, Burry Port, **Carmarthenshire**, SA16 0AA, WAL.
(T) 01554 834291
Speciality: Physiotherapy.
● **Owner** Mr S Owens
P S T (**Ref:**HM15534)

## OWERS, DONALD M

**Donald M Owers**, 75 Tillmouth Avenue, Holywell, Whitley Bay, **Tyne and Wear**, NE25 0NR, ENG.
(T) 01912 374525
Speciality: Chiropodists (Podiatrists).
● **Owner** Mr D Owers
S (**Ref:**HM15535)

## OXBOROUGH, JOY

**Joy Oxborough**, 35 Eires Croft, Bretton, Peterborough, **Cambridgeshire**, PE3 8YE, ENG.
(T) 01733 330697
Speciality: Herbal Medicine, Indian Head Massage, Massage (Therapeutic), Nutritional Therapy, Reflexology. ✔
● **Owner** Mrs J Oxborough M: IIHHT.
C H Yrs. Est.: 4 (**Ref:**HM15536)

## OXFORD ALLERGY TESTING SVS

**Oxford Allergy Testing Services (Oats) U K Ltd**, Deddington Health Centre, Earls Lane, Deddington, Banbury, **Oxfordshire**, OX15 0TQ, ENG.
(T) 01869 337323 (F) 01869 337592
Speciality: Complementary Medicines & Therapy.
● **Owner** Mr S Weygan
M (**Ref:**HM15537)

## OXFORD CHIROPRACTIC CLINIC

**Oxford Chiropractic Clinic**, 14 Holyoake Rd, Headington, Oxford, **Oxfordshire**, OX3 8AE, ENG.
(T) 01865 761802
Speciality: Chiropractic.
P S T (**Ref:**HM15538)

## OXFORD CLINIC

**Oxford Clinic (The)**, 33 Oxford St, Barrow-in-Furness, **Cumbria**, LA14 5QJ, ENG.
(T) 01229 827717
Speciality: Physiotherapy.
P S T (**Ref:**HM15539)

## OXFORD NATURAL HEALTH CENTRE

**Oxford Natural Health Centre**, 3 Church Cowley Rd, Iffley, Oxford, **Oxfordshire**, OX4 3JR, ENG.
(T) 01865 715615
Speciality: Complementary Medicines & Therapy.
● **Therapist** Mrs M Storrs
M (**Ref:**HM15540)

## OXFORD NUTRITION & ALLRGY CTRE

**Oxford Nutrition And Allergy Centre**, 137 Magdalen Rd, Oxford, **Oxfordshire**, OX4 1RJ, ENG.
(T) 01865 459553
Speciality: Clinical Ecology, Complementary Therapy, Dietician, Hay Diet, Herbal Medicine, Holistic Healing, Naturopathy, Nutritional Therapy, Sports Nutrition. ✔
● **Nutritionist** Mr M Franklin Q: Dip.NS, MA. M: BANT.
M Yrs. Est.: 12 (**Ref:**HM15541)

## OXFORD SCHOOL OF MASSAGE

**Oxford School of Massage**, 17 Lakeside, Oxford, **Oxfordshire**, OX2 8JF, ENG.
(T) 01865 510245
Speciality: Complementary Medicines & Therapy.
C M (**Ref:**HM15542)

## OXFORD STREET THERAPY CENTRE

**Oxford Street Therapy Centre**, Oxford House, 35-36 Oxford St, Southampton, **Hampshire**, SO14 3DS, ENG.
(T) 023 8036 5100
Speciality: Hypnosis.
B (**Ref:**HM15543)

## OXFORD TRANSCENDTL MEDITA CTRE

**Oxford Transcendental Meditation Centre**, 76 Church Rd, Sandford-On-Thames, Oxford, **Oxfordshire**, OX4 4YB, ENG.
(T) 01865 777046 (F) 01865 777046
(E) tmoxford@cwcom.net
Speciality: Ayurvedic Medicine, Herbal Medicine, Meditation, Stress Therapy. CREDIT
● **Partner/T M Teacher** Mrs C Lambert Q: TM Teacher. M: Maharishi Foundation.
● **Partner/T M Teacher** Mr G Lambert Q: TM Teacher. M: Maharishi Foundation.
B C Yrs. Est.: 13 (**Ref:**HM15544)

## OXFORDSHIRE BOWEN CLINIC

**Oxfordshire Bowen Clinic**, 127 Sheerstock, Haddenham, Aylesbury, **Buckinghamshire**, HP17 8EY, ENG.
(T) 07802 800511
(E) oxford.bowen@ntlworld.com
(W) homepage.ntlworld.com/ian.jones13
Speciality: Bowen Therapy, Massage (Therapeutic). ✔
● **Therapist** Mr I Jones Q: Cert.ECBS, ITEC. M: BTER.
T Yrs. Est.: 2 (**Ref:**HM15545)

## OZ

**Oz**, Relaxation Centre, Marple Rd, Chisworth, Glossop, **Derbyshire**, SK13 5DH, ENG.
(T) 01457 863267
Speciality: Complementary Medicines & Therapy.
M (**Ref:**HM15546)

## P A AROMATHERAPY

**P A Aromatherapy**, 7 Crossley St, Wetherby, **Yorkshire (West)**, LS22 6RT, ENG.
(T) 01977 672188 (F) 01937 589187
Speciality: Aromatherapy. ✔ CREDIT
● **Aromatherapist** Ms P Northern Q: MIFA. M: ATC, IFA.
C (**Ref:**HM15547)

## P B AROMATHERAPY

**P B Aromatherapy**, 233 Edge Green Lane, Golborne, Warrington, **Cheshire**, WA3 3UZ, ENG.
(T) 01942 510918
Speciality: Aromatherapy.
M O (**Ref:**HM15548)

## P C S

**P C S Ltd**, Pearl Assurance House, 43 Princess Way, Swansea, SA1 5DJ, WAL.
(T) 01792 464614 (F) 01792 652719
Speciality: Psychology.
● **Office Manager** Mrs M Bevan
B (**Ref:**HM15549)

## P D W PRAGNELL SPINAL THRP

**P D W Pragnell Spinal Therapist**, Douglas House, Seaview, **Isle of Wight**, PO34 5HB, ENG.
(T) 01983 613368
Speciality: Osteopathy.
● **Owner** Mr P Pragnell
P S T (**Ref:**HM15550)

## P M ASSOCIATES

**P M Associates**, 1 St Marys Cl, Appleton, Warrington, **Cheshire**, WA4 5DD, ENG.
(T) 01925 262510 (F) 01925 262510
Speciality: Psychology.
● **Owner** Mr P Matthews
B (**Ref:**HM15551)

## P MATTHEWS STRESS MNGMT

**Peter Matthews Stress Management**, 10 Wimborne Avenue, Chadderton, Oldham, **Lancashire**, OL9 0RN, ENG.
(T) 01616 522284
Speciality: Hypnosis.
● **Owner** Mr P Mathews
B (**Ref:**HM16072)

## P OF SPIRITUAL HEART

**Miss P Of Spiritual Heart**, 88 Sheep St, Bicester, **Oxfordshire**, OX6 7LP, ENG.
(T) 01869 248388
Speciality: Clairvoyants & Palmists.
B (**Ref:**HM15552)

## PACIFIC WAVES PRODUCTIONS

**Sha R Le Wilante**, 42 Daintry Cl, Harrow, **London (Greater)**, HA3 8PT, ENG.
(T) 020 8907 7702
(E) pwp@sha01.globalnet.co.uk
Speciality: Auto Suggestion, Cognitive Therapy, Complementary Therapy, Counselling, Family Therapy, Gestalt Therapy, Group Therapy, Hypnosis, Hypnotherapy, Psychotherapy, Stress Therapy, Transactional Analysis, Visualisation Therapy. ✔ CREDIT
● **Director** Ms S Lé Wilante Q: BA (Hons), Dip.Couns, Dip.Psych. M: ETSI, NCH.
H Yrs. Est.: 6 (**Ref:**HM15553)

## PACKARD, JOY

**Joy Packard**, 137 Magdalen Rd, Oxford, **Oxfordshire**, OX4 1RJ, ENG.
(T) 01865 396939
Speciality: Alexander Technique.
● **Owner** Mr M Franklin
P S (**Ref:**HM15554)

## PACKARD, JOY

**Joy Packard**, 47 Divinity Rd, Oxford, **Oxfordshire**, OX4 1LH, ENG.
(T) 01865 798246
Speciality: Alexander Technique.
● **Owner** Mrs J Packard
P S (**Ref:**HM15555)

## PACKER, COLIN

**Colin Packer**, 4 Croft Rd, Brighton, **Sussex (East)**, BN1 5JJ, ENG.
(T) 01273 508322
Speciality: Reflexology.
S T (**Ref:**HM15556)

## PACKER, RACHEL

**Rachel Packer**, 353 Baslow Rd, Sheffield, **Yorkshire (South)**, S17 3BH, ENG.
(T) 01142 351044
Speciality: Homeopathy.
● **Owner** Mrs R Packer
M (**Ref:**HM15557)

## PADAYACHI, ANASUYA (DR)

**Dr Anasuya Padayachi**, 18C High St, Standish, Wigan, **Lancashire**, WN6 0HL, ENG.
(T) 01257 405406
Speciality: Homeopathy.
● **Owner** Ms A Padayachi
M (**Ref:**HM15558)

## PADBURY, F

**Padbury F**, 11 Musters Rd, West Bridgford, Nottingham, **Nottinghamshire**, NG2 7PP, ENG.
(T) 01159 825353
Speciality: Reflexology.
● **Owner** Ms F Padbury
S T (**Ref:**HM15559)

## PADBURY, S

**S Padbury**, The Wellbeing Centre, 11 Musters Rd, West Bridgford, Nottingham, **Nottinghamshire**, NG2 7PP, ENG.
(T) 01159 825353
Speciality: Reflexology.
S T (**Ref:**HM15560)

## PADBURY, STEPHANIE

**Stephanie Padbury**, 57 Gladstone St, Loughborough, **Leicestershire**, LE11 1NR, ENG.
(T) 01509 218043
Speciality: Reflexology.
S T (**Ref:**HM15561)

## PADDOCK, MADELINE

**Madeline Paddock**, 3 Sycamore Drive, Kings Worthy, Winchester, **Hampshire**, SO23 7NW, ENG.
(T) 01962 884092
Speciality: Aromatherapy.
M O (**Ref:**HM15562)

**PADDOCKS PHYSIO/SPORT INJ CTRE**

**Paddocks Physiotherapy & Sport Injuries Centre**, The Old Cross Keys House, New Rd, Princes Risborough, **Buckinghamshire**, HP27 0LF, ENG.
(T) 01844 275167
Speciality: Physiotherapy.
● **Manager** Mrs D Cliffe
P S T (Ref:HM15563)

**PADDON-ROW, J**

**J Paddon-Row**, Flat 7, Grosvenor Court, Grosvenor Rd, Southampton, **Hampshire**, SO17 1UJ, ENG.
(T) 023 8055 8855
Speciality: Physiotherapy.
● **Owner** Miss J Paddon-Row
P S T (Ref:HM15564)

**PADGET, CHRIS**

**Chris Padget**, 1 Northside, Middridge, Newton Aycliffe, **County Durham**, DL5 7JF, ENG.
(T) 01325 316968
Speciality: Complementary Medicines & Therapy.
● **Owner** Ms C Padget
C M (Ref:HM15565)

**PADGETT, NATALIE**

**Natalie Padgett**, 38 Thorn Lane, Bradford, **Yorkshire (West)**, BD9 6NB, ENG.
(T) 01274 543785
Speciality: Reflexology.
S T (Ref:HM15566)

**PADWICK, J**

**J Padwick**, 20 Newtons Rd, Kewstoke, Weston-Super-Mare, **Somerset**, BS22 9LP, ENG.
(T) 01934 516805
Speciality: Chiropodists (Podiatrists).
● **Owner** Mrs J Padwick
S (Ref:HM15567)

**PAGE, B**

**B Page**, 48 Goss Drive, Street, **Somerset**, BA16 0RR, ENG.
(T) 01458 443891
Speciality: Chiropodists (Podiatrists).
S (Ref:HM15568)

**PAGE, BARBARA E**

**Barbara E Page**, Daymer, Pettycur Rd, Kinghorn, Burntisland, **Fife**, KY3 9RW, SCO.
(T) 01592 890480
Speciality: Reflexology.
● **Owner** Mrs B Page
S T (Ref:HM15569)

**PAGE, COLIN J**

**Colin J Page MAHA**, 4 The Graylings, Carlton Colville, Lowestoft, **Suffolk**, NR33 8ND, ENG.
(T) 01502 512939
Speciality: Hypnosis, Hypnotherapy, Relaxation.
● **Hypnotherapist** Mr C Page Q: Dip.Hyp. M: AHA.
B Yrs. Est.: 17 (Ref:HM15570)

**PAGE, F T**

**F T Page**, Mount Farm, Stainsacre Lane, Whitby, **Yorkshire (North)**, YO22 4HU, ENG.
(T) 01947 605632
Speciality: Chiropractic.
P S T (Ref:HM15571)

**PAGE, FAYE**

**Faye Page**, Seaford Lodge, Peopleton, Pershore, **Worcestershire**, WR10 2LF, ENG.
(T) 01905 840622 (F) 01905 840580
Speciality: Psychology.
● **Owner** Mrs F Page
B (Ref:HM15572)

**PAGET P & MORTON H**

**P Paget & H Morton**, Park View, 276 Marton Rd, Middlesbrough, **Cleveland**, TS4 2NS, ENG.
(T) 01642 242357
Speciality: Chiropodists (Podiatrists).
S (Ref:HM15573)

**PAGET, P**

**Mrs P Paget**, 21 Balmoral Rd, Middlesbrough, **Cleveland**, TS3 0NF, ENG.
(T) 01642 311172
Speciality: Chiropodists (Podiatrists).
● **Owner** Mrs P Paget
S (Ref:HM15574)

**PAIGNTON NATURAL HEALTH CENTRE**

**Paignton Natural Health Centre**, Bay Tree House, 6 Fisher St, Paignton, **Devon**, TQ4 5EL, ENG.
(T) 01803 522009
Speciality: Complementary Medicines & Therapy.
C M (Ref:HM15575)

**PAIGNTON PHYSIOTHERAPY**

**Paignton Physiotherapy & Sports Injury Clinic**, 27 Morin Rd, Paignton, **Devon**, TQ3 2PN, ENG.
(T) 01803 522480
Speciality: Acupuncture, Physiotherapy. ✔
● **Physiotherapist** Mr S Davies Q: MCSP, SRP. M: CSP.
S Yrs. Est.: 11 (Ref:HM15576)

**PAIN & INJURY CLINIC**

**Pain & Injury Clinic (The)**, 114 Westbourne Rd, Huddersfield, **Yorkshire (West)**, HD1 4LF, ENG.
(T) 01484 423918
Speciality: Physiotherapy.
● **Owner** Mr C Hewitson
P S T (Ref:HM15577)

**PAIN & PARALYSIS SPECIALIST**

**A W Cropley**, 3 Northgate, Chichester, **Sussex (West)**, PO19 1BA, ENG.
(T) 01243 537364
(E) anthony.@btinternet.com
Speciality: Absent Healing, Aura Therapy, Bio-energetics, Complementary Therapy, Healer, Holistic Healing, Manipulation, Massage (Therapeutic), Nutritional Therapy, Reiki, Stress Therapy, Vitamin Therapy, Scenar Therapy, for pain and paralysis treatment. ✔
● **Owner** Mr A Cropley M: ICHT.
C S Yrs. Est.: 5 (Ref:HM15578)

**PAIN CLINIC**

**Pain Clinic**, Kingston Hospital, Galsworthy Rd, Kingston Upon Thames, **Surrey**, KT2 7QB, ENG.
(T) 020 8546 7711
Speciality: Alexander Technique.
● **Therapist** Mr S Scott
P S (Ref:HM15579)

**PAIN RELIEF CENTRE**

**Pain Relief Centre (The)**, Willesden Green Sports Centre, Donnington Rd, London, **London (Greater)**, NW10 3QX, ENG.
(T) 020 8450 8688
Speciality: Complementary Medicines & Therapy.
M (Ref:HM15580)

**PAIN RELIEF THERAPIST**

**Pain Relief Therapist**, 107 Victoria Rd, Southend-On-Sea, **Essex**, SS1 2TF, ENG.
(T) 01702 461666 (F) 01702 461666
Speciality: Complementary Medicines & Therapy.
C M (Ref:HM15581)

**PAIN, JEAN**

**Jean Pain**, 7 Way Lane, Waterbeach, Cambridge, **Cambridgeshire**, CB5 9NQ, ENG.
(T) 01223 860356
Speciality: Psychotherapy.
● **Owner** Mrs J Pain
B (Ref:HM15582)

**PAIN, S R**

**S R Pain**, 37 Algitha Rd, Skegness, **Lincolnshire**, PE25 2AJ, ENG.
(T) 01754 766489
Speciality: Chiropodists (Podiatrists).
● **Owner** Mr S Pain
S (Ref:HM15583)

**PAIN, SALLY**

**Sally Pain**, 28 Carlisle Cl, Colchester, **Essex**, CO1 2YT, ENG.
(T) 01206 865582 (F) 01206 863432
Speciality: Complementary Medicines & Therapy.
● **Owner** Mrs S Pain
C M (Ref:HM15584)

**PAINSOOTHER HEALTH PRODUCTS**

**Painsoother Health Products**, 13 High Tarth, Kendal, **Cumbria**, LA9 5NR, ENG.
(T) 01539 720401
Speciality: Complementary Medicines & Therapy.
● **Owner** Mrs A Williams
M (Ref:HM15585)

**PAINTER, R F**

**R F Painter**, 224A High St, Berkhamsted, **Hertfordshire**, HP4 1AG, ENG.
(T) 01442 862858
Speciality: Chiropodists (Podiatrists).
● **Owner** Mr R Painter
S (Ref:HM15586)

**PAISLEY CHIROPRACTIC CLINIC**

**Anthonisz Alternative Healthcare Ltd**, 2 Glasgow Rd, Paisley, **Renfrewshire**, PA1 3QA, SCO.
(T) 01418 875770
(E) paisleychiroclinic@tinyworld.co.uk
Speciality: Acupressure, Bach Remedies, Chiropractic, Clinical Ecology, Complementary Therapy, Family Planning (Natural), Holistic Healing, Kinesiology, Manipulation, Nutritional Therapy, Stress Therapy, Vitamin Therapy, X-Ray, Neuro Emotional Technique, Cranial Therapy. ✔
● **Chiropractor** Kingsley Anthonisz Q: BSc, BSc (Chiro). M: SCA.
● **Chiropractor** Mrs V Anthonisz Q: BSc, BSc (Chiro). M: SCA.
S Yrs. Est.: 2 (Ref:HM15587)

**PAISLEY NATURAL THERAPY CENTRE**

**C M Mitchell DO(Hons) MRO**, 76A Causeyside St, Paisley, **Renfrewshire**, PA1 1YP, SCO.
(T) 01418 898416
Speciality: Acupuncture, Aromatherapy, Bach Remedies, Counselling, Cranial Osteopathy, Herbal Medicine, Homeopathy, Hypnotherapy, Indian Head Massage, Manipulation, Massage (Therapeutic), Osteopathy, Polarity Therapy, Reflexology, Reiki. ✔ CREDIT
● **Osteopath** Ms Mitchell Q: DO (Hons). M: GOsC.
S Yrs. Est.: 21 (Ref:HM15588)

**PAISLEY PHYSIOTHERAPY CENTRE**

**A & L B P S Ltd**, 13 Old Sneddon St, Paisley, **Renfrewshire**, PA3 2AG, SCO.
(T) 01415 610358 (F) 01418 841676
(E) abphysio@hotmail.com
Speciality: Acupuncture, Biofeedback, Complementary Therapy, Electrotherapy, Manipulation, Massage (Therapeutic), Micro Manipulation, Osteopathy, Sound Therapy, Ultrasonics, Interferential Therapy, Combination Therapy, Rehabilitation, Exercise Regimes, Stroke Rehab, Prevention/Prophylax's.
● **Physiotherapist/Director**
Mr A Benning Q: BSc, MCSP, SRP. M: CSP.
S (Ref:HM15589)

**PALACE ROAD OSTEOPATHIC CLINIC**

**Palace Road Osteopathic Clinic**, 68 Palace Rd, London, **London (Greater)**, N8 8QP, ENG.
(T) 020 8348 7432
(E) palost@pa68.demon.co.uk
Speciality: Osteopathy.
● **Osteopath** Mr A Marsh Q: BSc, DO. M: GOsC.
C Yrs. Est.: 12 (Ref:HM15590)

**PALFREY, MIKE**

**Mike Palfrey**, The Wellbeing Centre, 11 Musters Rd, Nottingham, **Nottinghamshire**, NG5 3GQ, ENG.
(T) 01159 825353
Speciality: Osteopathy.
P S T (Ref:HM15591)

**PALFREYMAN, SUE**

**Sue Palfreyman**, 42d Elder Avenue, Crouch End, London, **London (Greater)**, N8 8PS, ENG.
(T) 020 8348 3600
Speciality: Manipulation, Osteopathy, Postural Advice. ✔ CREDIT
● **Osteopath** Ms S Palfreyman Q: BSc, MA. M: GOsC.
S Yrs. Est.: 7 (Ref:HM15592)


Key continued: Yrs.Est: Years Established Q: Qualifications M: Professional Membership ✔ Indemnity Insurance CREDIT Accept Credit Cards

## PALIN, J M

**J M Palin**, Bonfield Farm, Catfoss Lane, Seaton, Hull, **Humberside (North)**, HU11 5SN, ENG.
(T) 01964 533776
Speciality: Chiropodists (Podiatrists).
S (Ref:HM15593)

## PALK, RICHARD

**Richard Palk**, 3 Ashdon Cl, Woodford Green, **Essex**, IG8 0EF, ENG.
(T) 020 8505 3547 (F) 020 8505 3547
Speciality: Homeopathy.
● **Owner** Mr R Palk
M (Ref:HM15594)

## PALLAS, ANDREW

**Andrew Pallas - Osteopath**, 17 Moorway, Guiseley, Leeds, **Yorkshire (West)**, LS20 8LD, ENG.
(T) 01943 878363
Speciality: Cranial Osteopathy, Naturopathy, Neuro-Linguistic Program, Osteopathy. ✔
● **Osteopath/Naturopath** Mr A Pallas Q: DO, ND, NLP. M: GCRN, GOsC.
S Yrs. Est.: 10 (Ref:HM15595)

## PALLISTER, TRUDY C

**Trudy C Pallister**, 42 Coquet Drive, Pelton, Chester Le Street, **County Durham**, DH2 1EW, ENG.
(T) 01914 100393
Speciality: Chiropodists (Podiatrists).
● **Owner** Miss T Pallister
S (Ref:HM15596)

## PALMER, BARBARA J

**Barbara J Palmer**, 81 Orton Lane, Wolverhampton, **Midlands (West)**, WV4 4XA, ENG.
(T) 01902 898431
Speciality: Electrolysis.
● **Owner** Mrs B Palmer
T (Ref:HM15597)

## PALMER, CHRISTINE

**Christine Palmer**, 6 Oakfield Rd, Harpenden, **Hertfordshire**, AL5 2NE, ENG.
(T) 01582 761822 (F) 01582 467580
Speciality: Physiotherapy.
● **Owner** Mrs C Palmer
P S T (Ref:HM15598)

## PALMER, CLARE

**Clare Palmer**, Clissold Park Health Centre, 154 Stoke Newington Church St, London, **London (Greater)**, N16 0JU, ENG.
(T) 020 7249 2990 (F) 020 7249 3977
Speciality: Homeopathy.
● **Owner** Mr D Berg
M (Ref:HM15599)

## PALMER, DAVID J

**Bowen Practitioner**, 12 Woodberry Cl, Leigh-On-Sea, **Essex**, SS9 4QT, ENG.
(T) 01702 526047
Speciality: Bowen Therapy, Massage (Therapeutic), A sequence of precise and gentle moves over soft tissue, for all ages. It is a treatment suitable whatever your level of fitness. ✔
● **Bowen Practitioner** Mr D Palmer M: BTER.
P S Yrs. Est.: 2 (Ref:HM15600)

## PALMER, E J

**E J Palmer**, 144 Crookes, Sheffield, **Yorkshire (South)**, S10 1UH, ENG.
(T) 01142 682162
Speciality: Chiropodists (Podiatrists).
● **Owner** Mrs E Palmer
S (Ref:HM15601)

## PALMER, ELEANOR

**Eleanor Palmer**, 6 Hill Rise, Rickmansworth, **Hertfordshire**, WD3 7NZ, ENG.
(T) 01923 776922
Speciality: Reflexology.
S T (Ref:HM15602)

## PALMER, FIONA

**Fiona Palmer**, 11 Portpool Lane, London, **London (Greater)**, EC1N 7UJ, ENG.
(T) 020 7405 4870
Speciality: Osteopathy.
● **Owner** Miss A Salih
P S T (Ref:HM15603)

## PALMER, G A PETER

**G A Peter Palmer**, Care Of Lewis Opticians, 5 Bartlett St, Caerphilly, **Glamorgan (Vale of)**, CF83 1JS, WAL.
(T) 029 2088 8100
Speciality: Osteopathy.
P S T (Ref:HM15604)

## PALMER, GAYLE

**Gayle Palmer DO**, 5 City Business Centre, Basin Rd, Chichester, **Sussex (West)**, PO19 2DU, ENG.
(T) 01243 786946
Speciality: Complementary Therapy, Counselling, Cranial Osteopathy, Dowsing, Healer, Healing Therapy, Osteopathy, Postural Integration, Reiki, Stress Therapy, Vitamin Therapy. ✔
● **Osteopath** Ms G Palmer Q: DO. M: GOsC.
P S T Yrs. Est.: 10 (Ref:HM15605)

## PALMER, GAYLE

**Gayle Palmer DO**, Pescott's Cl, Birdham, Chichester, **Sussex (West)**, PO20 7HD, ENG.
(T) 01243 512522 (F) 01243 512522
(E) gayle_palmer@hotmail.com
Speciality: Biofeedback, Bonesetting, Complementary Therapy, Counselling, Cranial Osteopathy, Dowsing, Healing Therapy, Homeopathy, Kinesiology, Manipulation, Massage (Therapeutic), Osteopathy, Reiki, Stress Therapy, Vitamin Therapy. ✔
● **Osteopath** Ms G Palmer Q: DO. M: GOsC.
S Yrs. Est.: 10 (Ref:HM15606)

## PALMER, JONATHAN C

**Jonathan C Palmer**, 39 Northernhay St, Exeter, **Devon**, EX4 3ER, ENG.
(T) 01392 259101
Speciality: Chiropodists (Podiatrists).
● **Owner** Mr J Palmer
S (Ref:HM15607)

## PALMER, JUNE

**June Palmer**, 193 Barnett Wood Lane, Ashtead, **Surrey**, KT21 2LP, ENG.
(T) 01372 275675
Speciality: Hypnosis.
● **Owner** Mrs J Palmer
B (Ref:HM15608)

## PALMER, LORRAINE

**Lorraine Palmer**, Rodina, Partridge Hill, Landford, Salisbury, **Wiltshire**, SP5 2BB, ENG.
(T) 01794 324407
Speciality: Reflexology.
S T (Ref:HM15609)

## PALMER, LUCILLE

**Lucille Palmer**, 1 Gloucester Trce, Southend-On-Sea, **Essex**, SS1 3AZ, ENG.
(T) 01702 585463
Speciality: Physiotherapy.
● **Partner** Mrs L Palmer
P S T (Ref:HM15610)

## PALMER, LYNDA M A

**Lynda M A Palmer**, 15 Granville Dene, Bovingdon, Hemel Hempstead, **Hertfordshire**, HP3 0JE, ENG.
(T) 01442 832967
Speciality: Reflexology.
S T (Ref:HM15611)

## PALMER, PETER G A

**Peter G A Palmer**, 116 Cathedral Rd, Cardiff, **Glamorgan (Vale of)**, CF11 9LP, WAL.
(T) 029 2064 0474
Speciality: Osteopathy.
P S T (Ref:HM15612)

## PALMER, ROY

**Roy Palmer**, 362-364 Goldington Rd, Bedford, **Bedfordshire**, MK41 9NT, ENG.
(T) 01234 351411 (F) 01234 273694
Speciality: Alexander Technique.
● **Manager** Mrs K Duffell
P S (Ref:HM15613)

## PALMER, S F

**S F Palmer**, Old Vicarage House, Vicarage Lane, Bramham, Wetherby, **Yorkshire (West)**, LS23 6QG, ENG.
(T) 01937 842850
Speciality: Chiropractic.
● **Owner** Mr S Palmer
S (Ref:HM15614)

## PALMER, SIMON

**Simon Palmer**, Reynolds Barn, Farm Cl, Chichester, **Sussex (West)**, PO18 8AW, ENG.
(T) 01243 784500
Speciality: Osteopathy.
● **Owner** Mr S Palmer
P S T (Ref:HM15615)

## PALMER, STEPHEN

**Stephen Palmer**, 3 Southvale Rd, London, **London (Greater)**, SE3 0TP, ENG.
(T) 020 8852 6165
Speciality: Psychotherapy.
B (Ref:HM15616)

## PALMER, STEPHEN R

**Stephen R Palmer**, Crawley Leisure Centre, Haslett Avenue, Crawley, **Sussex (West)**, RH10 1TS, ENG.
(T) 01293 537431
Speciality: Osteopathy.
P S T (Ref:HM15617)

## PALMER, SUSAN

**Susan Palmer**, Brokeswood Lodge, The Ridgewaye, Tunbridge Wells, **Kent**, TN4 0AD, ENG.
(T) 01892 521290
Speciality: Homeopathy.
● **Owner** Mrs S Palmer
M (Ref:HM15618)

## PALMER, T J

**T J Palmer**, The Therapy Centre, 92B Broad St, Canterbury, **Kent**, CT1 2LU, ENG.
(T) 01227 452202
Speciality: Hypnosis.
B (Ref:HM15619)

## PALMIST

**Palmist**, 6 Alexandra Rd, Colchester, **Essex**, CO3 3DB, ENG.
(T) 01206 769121
Speciality: Complementary Medicines & Therapy, Palmistry.
● **Palmist** Mrs L Bates
B Yrs. Est.: 10 (Ref:HM15620)

## PALMIST & TAROT READING

**Palmist & Tarot Reading**, Pewterspear Lane, Appleton, Warrington, **Cheshire**, WA4 5DY, ENG.
(T) 01925 265343
Speciality: Clairvoyants & Palmists.
● **Owner** Mrs A Ogden
B (Ref:HM15621)

## PALMISTRY BY SARAH

**Palmistry By Sarah**, 146 Oldwood Pl, Livingston, **Lothian (West)**, EH54 6UX, SCO.
(T) 01506 417710
Speciality: Clairvoyants & Palmists.
B (Ref:HM15622)

## PALOMBELLA, SARAH

**Sarah Palombella**, St Ives, 175 Main St, Halton, Runcorn, **Cheshire**, WA7 2PP, ENG.
(T) 01928 573745
Speciality: Reflexology.
S T (Ref:HM15623)

## PAMFLETT, E C

**E C Pamflett**, 5 Marlborough Court, Hungerford, **Berkshire**, RG17 0DT, ENG.
(T) 01488 684615
Speciality: Chiropodists (Podiatrists).
● **Owner** Mr E Pamflett
S (Ref:HM15624)

## PAMO, NORDZIN

**Nordzin Pamo**, 5 Court Cl, Whitchurch, Cardiff, **Glamorgan (Vale of)**, CF14 1JR, WAL.
(T) 029 2021 7517
Speciality: Homeopathy.
● **Owner** Mrs N Pamo
M (Ref:HM15625)

## PAM'S CHIROPODY SERVICE

**Pam's Chiropody Service**, 31 Trinity Rd, Rothwell, Kettering, **Northamptonshire**, NN14 6HY, ENG.



Key: B Mind-Body Medicine C Complementary Medicine H Self Help Treatment M Medicinal Therapy O Oriental Medicine P Postural Therapy S Manipulative Structural Therapy T Touch Therapy

(T) 01536 712907
Speciality: Chiropodists (Podiatrists).
● **Owner** Miss P Whymant
[S] (**Ref:**HM15626)

### PAMS HOLISTIC THERAPY CENTRE

**Pams Holistic Therapy Centre**, The Herons, Church St, Shoreham, Sevenoaks, **Kent**, TN14 7RY, ENG.
(T) 01959 524309 (F) 01959 524309
Speciality: Complementary Medicines & Therapy.
● **Owner** Mrs P Murphy
[C] [M] (**Ref:**HM15627)

### PANACEA ACUPUNCTURE CLINIC

**Panacea Acupuncture Clinic (The)**, 29a George Hudson St, York, **Yorkshire (North)**, YO1 6JL, ENG.
(T) 01904 654906
Speciality: Acupuncture.
● **Acupuncturist/Herbalist** Mr Chi
[O] (**Ref:**HM15628)

### PANAYIOTOU, ANTOINETTE

**Antoinette Panayiotou**, 203 Bracknell Cl, London, **London (Greater)**, N22 5TA, ENG.
(T) 020 8881 7713
Speciality: Complementary Medicines & Therapy.
● **Owner** Mrs A Panayiotou
[C] [M] (**Ref:**HM15629)

### PANDIT, HELEN

**Helen Pandit**, 51 Langley Rd, Watford, **Hertfordshire**, WD1 3PB, ENG.
(T) 01923 232056 (F) 01923 232056
Speciality: Chiropodists (Podiatrists).
● **Owner** Mrs H Pandit
[S] (**Ref:**HM15630)

### PANESAR, G

**G Panesar**, 14 St Michaels Trce, London, **London (Greater)**, N22 7SJ, ENG.
(T) 020 8889 1610
Speciality: Osteopathy.
[P] [S] [T] (**Ref:**HM15631)

### PANGBOURNE CHIROPODY CLINIC

**Pangbourne Chiropody Clinic**, The Quantocks, North St, Theale, Reading, **Berkshire**, RG7 5EX, ENG.
(T) 01189 305338
Speciality: Chiropodists (Podiatrists).
● **Owner** Ms J Reid
[S] (**Ref:**HM15632)

### PANIGRAHI, P

**P Panigrahi**, 13 Radcliffe Rd, Healing, Grimsby, **Humberside (South)**, DN41 7NQ, ENG.
(T) 01472 882578
Speciality: Acupuncture.
● **Doctor** Dr P Panigrahi
[O] (**Ref:**HM15633)

### PANK, SARAH

**Sarah Pank**, Williams Osteopathic Clinic, 64 Marsland Rd, Sale, **Cheshire**, M33 3HG, ENG.
(T) 01619 696555
Speciality: Osteopathy.
[P] [S] [T] (**Ref:**HM15634)

### PANK, SARAH

**Sarah Pank**, 2 Crescent Rd, Hale, Altrincham, **Cheshire**, WA15 9NA, ENG.
(T) 01619 298101
Speciality: Osteopathy.
● **Owner** Mrs C Morley
[P] [S] [T] (**Ref:**HM15635)

### PANNELL, R J

**R J Pannell**, 8 Burleigh Park Rd, Plymouth, **Devon**, PL3 4QH, ENG.
(T) 01752 776136
Speciality: Chiropody, Podiatry, Rolfing. ✓
● **Complementary Therapist** Mr R Pannell **Q:** S.R.Ch. **M:** S.R.Ch.
[B] [C] [H] [P] [S] [T]
Yrs. Est.: 30 (**Ref:**HM15636)

### PANSY POTTERS CLOUD 9

**Pansy Potters Cloud 9**, 9 Queensway Mall, Cornbow Centre, Halesowen, **Midlands (West)**, B63 4AZ, ENG.
(T) 01215 013099
Speciality: Complementary Medicines & Therapy.
● **Owner** Ms S Lacy
[M] (**Ref:**HM15637)

### PANTALL, A L

**A L Pantall**, 35A High St, Snodland, **Kent**, ME6 5AG, ENG.
(T) 01634 245303
Speciality: Osteopathy.
● **Owner** A L Pantall
[P] [S] [T] (**Ref:**HM15638)

### PANTELI, H

**H Panteli**, 103 Kevington Drive, Chislehurst, **Kent**, BR7 6RW, ENG.
(T) 01689 823077
Speciality: Reflexology.
● **Owner** Mrs H Panteli
[S] [T] (**Ref:**HM15639)

### PAOLA WEINBERG SYLT

**Paola Weinberg Sylt**, 10 Woodham Cl, Hartford, Northwich, **Cheshire**, CW8 1SG, ENG.
(T) 01606 76422
Speciality: Reflexology.
[S] [T] (**Ref:**HM15640)

### PAOLUCCI, ANNA

**Anna Paolucci**, 51 Gwynne Rd, **Dorset**, BH12 2AR, ENG.
(T) 01202 736435
Speciality: Reflexology.
[S] [T] (**Ref:**HM15641)

### PAPOUTSIS, MARGARET

**Mrs Margaret Papoutsis**, 20 Sundial Avenue, London, **London (Greater)**, SE25 4BX, ENG.
(T) 020 8653 8785 (F) 020 8653 9852
(E) papoutsis@aol.com
Speciality: Osteopathy. ✓
● **Osteopath** Mrs M Papoutsis **Q:** DO. **M:** GOsC.
[S] Yrs. Est.: 30 (**Ref:**HM15642)

### PAPWORTH, H A

**Mrs H A Papworth**, 29 Nursery Gardens, Purley On Thames, Reading, **Berkshire**, RG8 8AS, ENG.
(T) 01189 844283
Speciality: Chiropodists (Podiatrists).
[S] (**Ref:**HM15643)

### PARADAEMA, PAULA

**Paula Paradaema**, 7 Romney Avenue, Blackpool, **Lancashire**, FY4 3AH, ENG.
(T) 01253 344334 (F) 01253 341717
Speciality: Clairvoyants & Palmists.
● **Owner** Mrs P Paradaema
[B] (**Ref:**HM15644)

### PARADISE, PAM

**Pam Paradise**, Endlesham Rd, London, **London (Greater)**, SW12 8LA, ENG.
(T) 020 8675 1447
Speciality: Hypnosis.
[B] (**Ref:**HM15645)

### PARCHMENT STREET CLINIC

**Parchment Street Clinic**, 53 Parchment St, Winchester, **Hampshire**, SO23 8BA, ENG.
(T) 01962 853984 (F) 01489 877689
(E) pakarmapa@aol.com
(W) www.parchmentclinic.co.uk
Speciality: Acupuncture, Aromatherapy, Chiropractic, Complementary Therapy, Counselling, Herbal Medicine, Manipulation, Massage (Therapeutic), Oriental Diagnosis, Phytotherapy, Reflexology, X-Ray. ✓
● **Acupuncturist** Ms J Coleman **Q:** B.Ac, Lic.Ac.
● **Chiropractor** Dr M Hutchinson **Q:** DC. **M:** BCA, CC.
● **Acupuncturist** Ms D Hamilton Cousins
(T) 01962 860659 **Q:** Dip.Ac, MBAcC. **M:** BAcC.
● **Reflexologist** Peggah Wheeler **Q:** ITEC. **M:** GCP.
● **Medical Herbalist** Ms L Breeze
(T) 01962 735950 **Q:** MNIMH. **M:** NIMH.
[M] [O] [S] Yrs. Est.: 22 (**Ref:**HM15646)

### PARDOE, CHRISTOPHER

**Pardoe Christopher N D ,D O**, 29 Castle Cl, Dr, Blarney, **County Cork**, IRE.
(T) 021 4381 173
Speciality: Osteopathy.
[P] [S] [T] (**Ref:**HM15647)

### PARDOE, DIANA T

**Diana T Pardoe**, Pixie Cottage, 47 Churchfields, Bromsgrove, **Worcestershire**, B61 8DX, ENG.
(T) 01527 870085
Speciality: Complementary Therapy, Holistic Healing, Hypnosis, Hypnotherapy, Indian Head Massage.
● **Owner** Ms D Pardoe **Q:** BA (Hons), Dip.Indian Head Massage. **M:** HA.
[B] Yrs. Est.: 20 (**Ref:**HM15648)

### PARDOE, IAN S (DR)

**Dr Ian S Pardoe**, 81 Harborne Rd, Birmingham, **Midlands (West)**, B15 3HG, ENG.
(T) 01214 559496 (F) 01214 550288
Speciality: Acupuncture.
● **Senior Partner** Dr G Oates
[O] (**Ref:**HM15649)

### PARDOE, L

**L Pardoe**, 36 Abbotts Cl, Romford, **Essex**, RM7 8QU, ENG.
(T) 01708 762953
Speciality: Complementary Medicines & Therapy.
● **Owner** Mrs L Pardoe
[M] (**Ref:**HM15650)

### PARE, KAREN

**Karen Pare**, Rickyard Farmhouse, Foscot, Chipping Norton, **Oxfordshire**, OX7 6RL, ENG.
(T) 01608 659955
Speciality: Aromatherapy.
[M] [O] (**Ref:**HM15651)

### PARFETT, G

**G Parfett**, 9 Witheys Yard, High St, Stroud, **Gloucestershire**, GL5 1AP, ENG.
(T) 01453 750796
Speciality: Osteopathy.
[P] [S] [T] (**Ref:**HM15652)

### PARFETT, GORDON

**Gordon Parfett**, Ty Hareth, School Meadow, Ffynnongynydd, Hereford, **Herefordshire**, HR3 5LX, ENG.
(T) 01497 847043
Speciality: Acupuncture.
[O] (**Ref:**HM15653)

### PARFITT, A J

**A J Parfitt**, 22 Den Hill, Eastbourne, **Sussex (East)**, BN20 8SZ, ENG.
(T) 01323 649439
Speciality: Acupuncture.
● **Owner** Mr A Parfitt
[O] (**Ref:**HM15654)

### PARFITT, ALISTAIR H

**Alistair H Parfitt**, 575 Wimborne Rd, Bournemouth, **Dorset**, BH9 2AR, ENG.
(T) 01202 528942
Speciality: Chiropodists (Podiatrists).
● **Owner** Mr A Parfitt
[S] (**Ref:**HM15655)

### PARFITT, STEVE

**Steve Parfitt**, 7 Nelson St, Stroud, **Gloucestershire**, GL5 2HL, ENG.
(T) 01453 759444 (F) 01453 759444
Speciality: Acupuncture.
● **Owner** Mr S Parfitt
[O] (**Ref:**HM15656)

### PARIS, ANNA

**Anna Paris**, Southertons Farmhouse, Westleigh, Tiverton, **Devon**, EX16 7HY, ENG.
(T) 01823 672728 (F) 01823 672728
Speciality: Acupuncture.
● **Owner** Mrs A Paris
[O] (**Ref:**HM15657)

### PARIS, LINDA

**Linda Paris**, 137 Magdalen Rd, Oxford, **Oxfordshire**, OX4 1RJ, ENG.
(T) 01865 396939
Speciality: Acupuncture.
● **Owner** Mr M Franklin
[O] (**Ref:**HM15658)


Key continued: **Yrs.Est:** Years Established **Q:** Qualifications **M:** Professional Membership ✓ Indemnity Insurance [card] Accept Credit Cards

## PARIS, LYN
**Lyn Paris**, Newbury Practice Of Natural Therapy, 55-56 Cheap St, Newbury, **Berkshire**, RG14 5DH, ENG.
(T) 01635 30252
Speciality: Acupuncture.
O (Ref:HM15659)

## PARISH, ANN
**Ann Parish**, 57 Newstead Avenue, Orpington, **Kent**, BR6 9RW, ENG.
(T) 01689 853143 (F) 01689 853143
Speciality: Aromatherapy.
● **Owner** Mrs A Parish
M O (Ref:HM15660)

## PARISH, CHRISTOPHER
**Christopher Parish**, 90 College Rd, Liverpool, **Merseyside**, L23 0RP, ENG.
(T) 01519 244784 (F) 01512 263034
Speciality: Chiropodists (Podiatrists).
● **Owner** Mrs S Jones
S (Ref:HM15661)

## PARK ATTWOOD CLINIC
**Park Attwood Clinic**, Trimpley Lane, Shatterford, Bewdley, **Worcestershire**, DY12 1RE, ENG.
(T) 01299 861444
Speciality: Complementary Medicines & Therapy.
C M (Ref:HM15662)

## PARK CLINIC
**Park Clinic**, Banbury Rugby Union Football Club, Oxford Rd, Bodicote, Banbury, **Oxfordshire**, OX15 4AF, ENG.
(T) 01295 253622 (F) 01295 253622
Speciality: Physiotherapy.
● **Owner** Mrs S Bolton
P S T (Ref:HM15663)

## PARK FARM CHIROPODY SERVICES
**Park Farm Chiropody Services**, 115 Birchover Way, Allestree, Derby, **Derbyshire**, DE22 2QH, ENG.
(T) 01332 551593 (F) 01332 551593
Speciality: Chiropody.
● **Partner** Mrs L McCann
S (Ref:HM15664)

## PARK GATE CHIROPRACTIC CENTRE
**Park Gate Chiropractic Centre**, 1-1A Middle Rd, Park Gate, Southampton, **Hampshire**, SO31 7GH, ENG.
(T) 01489 578733
Speciality: Chiropractic.
● **Partner** Dr J Bearling
P S T (Ref:HM15665)

## PARK HOUSE CLINIC
**Park House Clinic**, St Chads Green, Midsomer Norton, Bath, **Somerset**, BA3 2JT, ENG.
(T) 01761 416614 (F) 01761 416614
(E) stanley.l.hicks@which.net
Speciality: Acupuncture, Cranial Osteopathy, Electrotherapy, Osteopathy, PAM, Ultrasonics, Vibrational Therapy. ✔
● **Osteopath/Acupuncturist**
Mr S Hicks Q: BSc, DO. M: BOA.
S Yrs. Est.: 3 (Ref:HM15666)

## PARK LANE CLINIC
**Park Lane Clinic**, 10 Thornhill Gardens, Sunderland, **Tyne and Wear**, SR2 7LD, ENG.
(T) 01915 144100
Speciality: Hypnosis.
B (Ref:HM15667)

## PARK LANE COMP HEALTH CENTRE
**Park Lane Complementary Health Centre**, 70D Park Lane, Chippenham, **Wiltshire**, SN15 1LW, ENG.
(T) 01249 655088
Speciality: Complementary Medicines & Therapy.
● **Owner** Mr Z Bozic
M (Ref:HM15668)

## PARK PHYSIOTHERAPY
**Park Physiotherapy**, Weston Park, Weston Longville, Norwich, **Norfolk**, NR9 5JW, ENG.
(T) 01603 872335
Speciality: Acupuncture, Cranial Osteopathy, Cranio-Sacral Therapy, Electrotherapy, Manipulation, Massage (Therapeutic), Myofascial and Muscle Balance. ✔
● **Physiotherapist** Ms S Mayfield Q: MCSP, SRP. M: CSP.
● **Physiotherapist** Ms J Byrne Q: MCSP, SRP. M: CSP.
● **Physiotherapist** Ms E Palmer Q: Grad Dip Phys, MCSP, SRP. M: CSP.
S Yrs. Est.: 11 (Ref:HM15669)

## PARK PHYSIOTHERAPY & SPORTS
**Park Physiotherapy & Sports Injury Clinic**, 29 Rickmansworth Rd, Watford, **Hertfordshire**, WD1 7HL, ENG.
(T) 01923 222436
Speciality: Physiotherapy.
P S T (Ref:HM15670)

## PARK PLACE HEALTH CLINIC
**Park Place Health Clinic**, Chiropdy, Park Pl, Darlington, **County Durham**, DL1 5LW, ENG.
(T) 01325 480038 (F) 01325 483818
Speciality: Chiropodists (Podiatrists).
● **Manager** Mr G Cowley Q: S.R.Ch. M: S.C.P.
S (Ref:HM15671)

## PARK PRACTICE
**Park Practice (The)**, 10 Park Rd, Coventry, **Midlands (West)**, CV1 2LA, ENG.
(T) 024 7655 5114
Speciality: Acupuncture, Aromatherapy, Chiropody, Homeopathy, Hypnotherapy, Osteopathy, Reflexology, Bowen Technique, Management. ✔ CREDIT
● **Osteopath** Ms J Sheridan Q: BSc (Hons), DO (Hons).
● **Osteopath/Naturopath** Mr T Harper Q: BSc, Hons (OST), RN.
● **Acupuncturist** Mr B Clensy Q: B.Ac, MBAcC.
● **Homeopathic Medical Practitioner**
Dr M Curley Q: DRCOG, MFHom.
● **Homeopath** Ms P Mitchell Q: LCPH, MHMA.
● **Homeopath/Pharmacist**
Desiree Holloway Q: LFHom, M.R.Pharm.S, MHMA.
● **Chiropodist** Ms A Mofid Q: BSc, M.S.C.P.
● **Registered Practitioner**
Dr S Charles-Holmes Q: ECBS, FRCP.
● **Aromatherapist** Ms C Cowley Q: MGCP.
● **Holistic Medical Practitioner**
Dr B King Q: BS, MB, MRCGP, MRCP.
● **Reflexologist** Ms B Merriman Q: IIHHT. M: ICHT.
C Yrs. Est.: 7 (Ref:HM15672)

## PARK PRACTICE
**Park Practice (The)**, 13 Nelson Rd, London, **London (Greater)**, SE10 9JB, ENG.
(T) 020 8858 8557
Speciality: Homeopathy.
● **Partner** Mr A Parr
M (Ref:HM15673)

## PARK PRACTICE OSTEOPATH CLINIC
**Park Practice Osteopath Clinic**, 13 Nelson Rd, London, **London (Greater)**, SE10 9JB, ENG.
(T) 07956 628998
Speciality: Osteopathy.
P S T (Ref:HM15674)

## PARK REHABILITATION CENTRE
**Park Rehabilitation Centre (The)**, Badsley Moor Lane, Rotherham, **Yorkshire (South)**, S65 2QL, ENG.
(T) 01709 302323 (F) 01709 302312
Speciality: Physiotherapy.
● **Manager** Mrs S York
P S T (Ref:HM15675)

## PARK ROAD SURGERY
**Park Road Surgery**, 31 Park Rd, Burgess Hill, **Sussex (West)**, RH15 8EU, ENG.
(T) 01444 232251
Speciality: Acupuncture.
● **Owner** Dr D Soper
O (Ref:HM15676)

## PARK VIEW CHIROPRACTIC
**Park View Chiropractic Clinic**, Park View, Church Lane, Toddington, Cheltenham, **Gloucestershire**, GL54 5DQ, ENG.
(T) 01242 621429
Speciality: Chiropractors.
● **Owner** Mrs L Rolfe
P S T (Ref:HM15677)

## PARK, ANGELA
**Angela Park**, The Lupins, Wycombe Rd, Studley Green, High Wycombe, **Buckinghamshire**, HP14 3UY, ENG.
(T) 01494 482605
Speciality: Chiropodists (Podiatrists).
S (Ref:HM15678)

## PARK, D
**D Park**, 95 Woone Lane, Clitheroe, **Lancashire**, BB7 1BJ, ENG.
(T) 01200 423181
Speciality: Physiotherapy.
P S T (Ref:HM15679)

## PARK, JAMES
**James Park**, 13 Streatley Rd, London, **London (Greater)**, NW6 7LJ, ENG.
(T) 020 7328 3284 (F) 020 7328 2461
Speciality: Psychotherapy.
● **Owner** Mr J Park
B (Ref:HM15680)

## PARK, MARY T
**Mary T Park**, 12 Norfolk Rd, Walton-Le-Dale, Preston, **Lancashire**, PR5 4GB, ENG.
(T) 01772 338358
Speciality: Chiropodists (Podiatrists).
S (Ref:HM15681)

## PARK, N
**N Park**, 76 Copley Rd, Doncaster, **Yorkshire (South)**, DN1 2QW, ENG.
(T) 01302 368200
Speciality: Chiropodists (Podiatrists).
S (Ref:HM15682)

## PARKER CLINIC
**Parker Clinic (The)**, 130-132 Gloucester Rd, Bishopston, Bristol, BS7 8NL, ENG.
(T) 01179 245842 (F) 01179 246310
Speciality: Chiropractic, Massage (Therapeutic), Physiotherapy. ✔ CREDIT
● **Chiropractor** D Smink Q: B.App.Sc, BSc (Chiro).
● **Chiropractor** E Meldegard Q: DC.
● **Therapist** Mr B Turner Q: DC, MSc, SRP.
● **Chiropractor** Dr J Jensen Q: DC.
P Yrs. Est.: 15 (Ref:HM15683)

## PARKER, ANTHONY
**Anthony Parker**, 33 Woodbridge Rd, Guildford, **Surrey**, GU1 1ED, ENG.
(T) 01483 888900
Speciality: Chiropractic.
P S T (Ref:HM15684)

## PARKER, BRIAN
**Brian Parker**, 2 Mark Cl, Bexleyheath, **Kent**, DA7 5JX, ENG.
(T) 020 8304 5446
Speciality: Physiotherapy.
● **Owner** Mr B Parker
P S T (Ref:HM15685)

## PARKER, CAROL
**Carol Parker**, Watchbell House, 8 Lugley St, Newport, **Isle of Wight**, PO30 5HD, ENG.
(T) 01983 522477
Speciality: Acupuncture.
● **Owner** Mr G Creed
O (Ref:HM15686)

## PARKER, CAROL J
**Carol J Parker**, 175 Batten Avenue, Woking, **Surrey**, GU21 1UP, ENG.
(T) 01483 488003
Speciality: Chiropodists (Podiatrists).
S (Ref:HM15687)

## PARKER, DIANA
**Diana Parker**, Innstep, 4 Bateman Drive, Aylesbury, **Buckinghamshire**, HP21 8AF, ENG.
(T) 01296 422340
Speciality: Chiropodists (Podiatrists).
S (Ref:HM15688)

## PARKER, EDMUND
**D Edmund Parker**, Hafan, Hardwick Hill Lane, Chepstow, **Monmouthshire**, NP16 5PP, WAL.



Key: B Mind-Body Medicine, C Complementary Medicine, H Self Help Treatment, M Medicinal Therapy, O Oriental Medicine, P Postural Therapy, S Manipulative Structural Therapy, T Touch Therapy

(T) 01291 623792
Speciality: Osteopathy.
P S T (Ref:HM15689)

**PARKER, ERIC J**

**Eric J Parker**, 6 Merchiston Pl, Edinburgh, **Edinburgh (City of)**, EH10 4NR, SCO.
(T) 01312 286629
Speciality: Chiropodists (Podiatrists).
S (Ref:HM15690)

**PARKER, G**

**G Parker**, The Surgery, 20 Oxford St, Wellingborough, **Northamptonshire**, NN8 4HY, ENG.
(T) 01933 222418
Speciality: Chiropodists (Podiatrists).
S (Ref:HM15691)

**PARKER, J M**

**J M Parker**, Old Mill House, Rowfant, Crawley, **Sussex (West)**, RH10 4TB, ENG.
(T) 01293 884493
Speciality: Physiotherapy.
P S T (Ref:HM15692)

**PARKER, JAMES**

**James Parker**, 16 Hickman St, Gainsborough, **Lincolnshire**, DN21 2DZ, ENG.
(T) 01427 616984 (F) 01427 616984
Speciality: Chiropodists (Podiatrists).
● **Owner** Mr J Parker
S (Ref:HM15693)

**PARKER, JENNY**

**Jenny Parker**, 40 St Margarets Rd, London, **London (Greater)**, E12 5DP, ENG.
(T) 020 8989 4823
Speciality: Physiotherapy.
● **Owner** Mrs J Parker
P S T (Ref:HM15694)

**PARKER, JOHN**

**John Parker**, 9 Kensington Cl, London, **London (Greater)**, N11 3PU, ENG.
(T) 020 8368 2706
Speciality: Psychotherapy.
● **Owner** Mr J Parker
B (Ref:HM15695)

**PARKER, JONATHAN**

**Jonathan Parker**, Kelm's House, 8 Plymouth Rd, Totnes, **Devon**, TQ9 5PH, ENG.
(T) 01803 865841
Speciality: Osteopathy.
P S T (Ref:HM15696)

**PARKER, KATHY**

**Kathy Parker**, 9 Fettes Row, Edinburgh, **Edinburgh (City of)**, EH3 6SE, SCO.
(T) 01315 578286
Speciality: Homeopathy.
● **Owner** Ms K Parker
M (Ref:HM15697)

**PARKER, L**

**L Parker**, Sandy Gates, North Stoke, Bath, **Somerset**, BA1 9AS, ENG.
(T) 01179 324985 (F) 01179 324985
Speciality: Chiropodists (Podiatrists).
● **Owner** Mr T Parker
S (Ref:HM15698)

**PARKER, NIESJE**

**Niesje Parker**, 26 Victena Rd, Fair Oak, Eastleigh, **Hampshire**, SO50 7FX, ENG.
(T) 023 8069 4727
Speciality: Psychotherapy.
● **Owner** Mrs N Parker
B (Ref:HM15699)

**PARKER, PHILIP**

**Philip Parker**, 1st Floor Austin House, Queen St, Hitchin, **Hertfordshire**, SG4 9TS, ENG.
(T) 01462 437757
Speciality: Osteopathy.
P S T (Ref:HM15700)

**PARKER, R M**

**R M Parker**, 4 Royal Rd, Ramsgate, **Kent**, CT11 9LE, ENG.
(T) 01843 582773
Speciality: Complementary Medicines & Therapy.
C M (Ref:HM15701)

**PARKER, RAY**

**Ray Parker**, 15 Lowther Rd, **Dorset**, BH8 8NG, ENG.
(T) 01202 391794
Speciality: Reflexology.
S T (Ref:HM15702)

**PARKER, RAYMOND**

**Raymond Parker**, 2 Meadowcroft, Lower Darwen, Darwen, **Lancashire**, BB3 0RU, ENG.
(T) 01254 673584
Speciality: Physiotherapy.
P S T (Ref:HM15703)

**PARKER, RICHARD**

**Richard Parker**, The Rolle Clinic, 6 Rolle Rd, Exmouth, **Devon**, EX8 2AB, ENG.
(T) 01395 222666
Speciality: Chiropodists (Podiatrists).
● **Owner** Mr A Smith
S (Ref:HM15704)

**PARKER, SARAH**

**Sarah Parker**, Flat 2, 2 Market St, Nailsworth, Stroud, **Gloucestershire**, GL6 0BX, ENG.
(T) 01453 835582
Speciality: Acupuncture.
O (Ref:HM15705)

**PARKER, SUSAN**

**Susan Parker**, 24 High St, Welford, Northampton, **Northamptonshire**, NN6 6HT, ENG.
(T) 01858 575675
Speciality: Hypnosis.
B (Ref:HM15706)

**PARKER, SUZY**

**Suzy Parker**, 10 High St, Glastonbury, **Somerset**, BA6 9DU, ENG.
(T) 01458 834236
Speciality: Homeopathy.
● **Director** Ms J Sanders
M (Ref:HM15707)

**PARKER, SUZY**

**Suzy Parker**, Chestnuts, Bove Town, Glastonbury, **Somerset**, BA6 8JG, ENG.
(T) 01458 832582
Speciality: Homeopathy.
● **Owner** Ms S Parker
M (Ref:HM15708)

**PARKER, WILLIAM**

**William Parker**, 6 Blakeney Court, Maidenhead, **Berkshire**, SL6 7ER, ENG.
(T) 01628 542942
Speciality: Complementary Medicines & Therapy.
C M (Ref:HM15709)

**PARKES, J**

**J Parkes**, 106 Knightlow Rd, Birmingham, **Midlands (West)**, B17 8QA, ENG.
(T) 01214 344010
Speciality: Aromatherapy.
● **Owner** Mr J McCormick
M O (Ref:HM15710)

**PARKES, JOHN**

**John Parkes**, 26 Thickthorn Cl, Kenilworth, **Warwickshire**, CV8 2AF, ENG.
(T) 01926 864900
Speciality: Chiropodists (Podiatrists).
● **Principal** Mr J Parkes
S (Ref:HM15711)

**PARKES, MAURA**

**Parkes Maura**, 575 Woodview, Rathfarnham, **County Dublin**, IRE.
(T) 01493 0063
Speciality: Complementary Medicines & Therapy.
M (Ref:HM15712)

**PARKES, VAL**

**Val Parkes**, 28A Marlpit Lane, Sutton Coldfield, **Midlands (West)**, B75 5PN, ENG.
(T) 01213 084803
Speciality: Psychotherapy.
● **Owner** Mrs V Parkes
B (Ref:HM15713)

**PARKGATE CLINIC**

**Parkgate Clinic**, Tilanto, North Prde, Parkgate, Neston, **Cheshire**, CH64 6RL, ENG.
(T) 01513 363392 (F) 01513 363392
Speciality: Complementary Medicines & Therapy.
● **Owner** Mrs D Barry
C M (Ref:HM15714)

**PARKHOUSE, R**

**R Parkhouse**, Bryn Tirion, Penmaen Park, Llanfairfechan, **Conwy**, LL33 0RN, WAL.
(T) 01248 680514
Speciality: Osteopathy.
P S T (Ref:HM15715)

**PARKIN, A G**

**A G Parkin**, 14 Craneshaugh Cl, Hexham, **Northumberland**, NE46 2PG, ENG.
(T) 01434 600627
Speciality: Homeopathy.
● **Owner** A Parkin
M (Ref:HM15716)

**PARKIN, EVELYN**

**Evelyn Parkin**, 63 Wansunt Rd, Bexley, **Kent**, DA5 2DJ, ENG.
(T) 01322 525432
Speciality: Reflexology.
S T (Ref:HM15717)

**PARKIN, JANE**

**Jane Parkin**, 67 Huddleston Rd, London, **London (Greater)**, N7 0AE, ENG.
(T) 020 7609 2069
Speciality: Homeopathy.
● **Owner** Ms J Parkin
M (Ref:HM15718)

**PARKINSON, JUDI**

**Judi Parkinson**, 48 Newlands Park, London, **London (Greater)**, SE26 5NE, ENG.
(T) 020 8659 5001
Speciality: Psychotherapy.
B (Ref:HM15719)

**PARKS, HILARY**

**Hilary Parks**, 3 Wilderness Rd, Elland, **Yorkshire (West)**, HX5 9PQ, ENG.
(T) 01422 374446
(W) www.reflexions-uk.co.uk
Speciality: Indian Head Massage, Reflexology, Body Massage. ✓
● **Complementary Therapist**
Mrs H Parks Q: IIHHT, ITEC. M: FHT.
C T Yrs. Est.: 2 (Ref:HM15720)

**PARKS, L A**

**L A Parks**, Lower Ground Floor, 21 Gildredge Rd, Eastbourne, **Sussex (East)**, BN21 4RU, ENG.
(T) 01323 646611 (F) 01323 648611
Speciality: Chiropodists (Podiatrists).
● **Owner** Mrs L Parks
S (Ref:HM15721)

**PARKSIDE STRESS MANAGEMENT**

**Parkside Stress Management**, 6 Oxford St, Nottingham, **Nottinghamshire**, NG1 5BH, ENG.
(T) 01159 550777
Speciality: Absent Healing, Allergy Testing, Aromatherapy, Aura Therapy, Bach Remedies, Colour Therapy, Complementary Therapy, Counselling, Crystal Healing, Dietician, Healer, Healing Therapy, Holistic Healing, Indian Head Massage, Inhalation Therapy, Kinesiology, Meditation, Nutritional Therapy, Reiki, Visualisation Therapy, Vitamin Therapy, Yoga, Aura Soma.
● **Therapist** Ms S Taylor M: GCP.
● **Therapist** Mr A Ward
B Yrs. Est.: 19 (Ref:HM15722)

**PARKWOOD CHIROPRACTIC CLINIC**

**Parkwood Chiropractic Clinic**, The Sq, Aberconway Pl, Oakdale, Blackwood, **Caerphilly**, NP12 0LR, WAL.
(T) 01495 225388 (F) 01495 225388
Speciality: Chiropractic. ✓ [credit card]
● **Chiropractor** Mr G Norman Q: BSc (Chiro), DC. M: BCA.
● **Clinic Manager** Mr S Keel
S Yrs. Est.: 3 (Ref:HM15723)



Key continued: Yrs.Est: Years Established Q: Qualifications M: Professional Membership ✓ Indemnity Insurance [credit card] Accept Credit Cards

### PARKWOOD CHIROPRACTIC CLINIC
**Parkwood Chiropractic Clinic**, 93 Cathedral Rd, Cardiff, **Glamorgan (Vale of)**, CF11 9PG, WAL.
(T) 029 2022 8889 (F) 029 2022 8889
Speciality: Chiropractic. ✔
● **Chiropractor** Dr P Lavalette Q: BCA, BSc (Chiro). M: GCC.
● **Senior Partner** Ms L Sasse Q: BCA, BSc (Chiro), DC. M: GCC.
● **Chiropractor** Dr M Patel Q: BCA, BSc (Chiro). M: GCC.
P Yrs. Est.: 5 (Ref:HM15724)

### PARKWOOD CHIROPRACTIC CLINIC
**Parkwood Chiropractic Clinic**, 10 Whitethorn Drive, Brackla, Bridgend, CF31 2PQ, WAL.
(T) 01656 767588
Speciality: Chiropractic. ✔
● **Owner** Dr M Weiner Q: BSc (Chiro), DC. M: GCC, SCA.
● **Chiropractor** Dr L Di Fiore Q: BSc (Chiro), DC. M: GCC, SCA.
P Yrs. Est.: 4 (Ref:HM15725)

### PARKWOOD CHIROPRACTIC CLINIC
**Parkwood Chiropractic Clinic**, 189 Fidlas Rd, Llanishen, Cardiff, **Glamorgan (Vale of)**, CF14 5LZ, WAL.
(T) 029 2076 6777 (F) 029 2076 6777
Speciality: Chiropractic. ✔
● **Senior Partner** Ms L Sasse Q: BCA, BSc (Chiro). M: GCC.
● **Chiropractor** Dr G Norman Q: BSc (Chiro), DC. M: BCA, GCC.
● **Chiropractor** Dr M Patel M: BCA, GCC.
P Yrs. Est.: 5 (Ref:HM15726)

### PARNELL, R H
**R H Parnell**, 71A St. Thomas St, Wells, **Somerset**, BA5 2UY, ENG.
(T) 01749 679014
Speciality: Acupuncture. ✔
● **Acupuncturist** Mr R Parnell Q: Cert.Ac, Lic.Ac. M: BAcC.
O Yrs. Est.: 15 (Ref:HM15727)

### PAROLIN, PAUL
**Paul Parolin RCSTA**, Woodbridge Complementary Health Centre, Sandy Lane, Martlesham, Woodbridge, **Suffolk**, IP12 4SD, ENG.
(T) 01394 388234
Speciality: Chiropractic, Cranial Osteopathy, Cranio-Sacral Therapy, Yoga. ✔
● **Chiropractor** Mr P Porolin Q: DC, Dip.Chiro, Dip.CSTh. M: CSTA, GCC.
B P S T Yrs. Est.: 4 (Ref:HM15728)

### PARR, ANDREW
**Andrew Parr**, 13 Nelson Rd, London, **London (Greater)**, SE10 9JB, ENG.
(T) 020 8293 4323 (F) 020 8293 4323
Speciality: Hypnotherapy.
● **Partner** Mr A Parr
B (Ref:HM15729)

### PARR, CAROL
**Carol Parr**, 4 Knowlesley Meadows, Darwen, **Lancashire**, BB3 2UP, ENG.
(T) 01254 761549
Speciality: Chiropodists (Podiatrists).
S (Ref:HM15730)

### PARR, JIM
**Jim Parr**, 8 Corner Gate, Westhoughton, Bolton, **Lancashire**, BL5 2SE, ENG.
(T) 01942 813525
Speciality: Chiropodists (Podiatrists).
S (Ref:HM15731)

### PARRETTI, ROSEMARY
**Rosemary Parretti**, 7 Heath Lane, Stourbridge, **Midlands (West)**, DY8 1RF, ENG.
(T) 01384 396146 (F) 01384 441931
Speciality: Homeopathy.
● **Owner** Mrs R Parretti
M (Ref:HM15732)

### PARROTT, C J
**C J Parrott**, 47 Quest Hills Rd, Malvern, **Worcestershire**, WR14 1RL, ENG.
(T) 01684 567095
Speciality: Hypnosis.
B (Ref:HM15733)

### PARROTT, J M
**J M Parrott**, 1 West Common, Harpenden, **Hertfordshire**, AL5 2JG, ENG.
(T) 01582 461949
Speciality: Physiotherapy.
● **Owner** Mrs J Parrott
P S T (Ref:HM15734)

### PARROTT, LINDA
**Linda Parrott**, Nene Valley Complementary Therapies, Northampton, **Northamptonshire**, NN6, ENG.
(T) 01604 881390
Speciality: Aromatherapy, Indian Head Massage, Massage (Therapeutic), Reflexology, Reiki.
C (Ref:HM15735)

### PARRY & MCCAFFERY
**Parry & McCaffery**, 64A Old Milton Rd, New Milton, **Hampshire**, BH25 6DX, ENG.
(T) 01425 611089
Speciality: Osteopathy.
P S T (Ref:HM15736)

### PARRY, CATHERYN
**Catheryn Parry**, 308 Linthorpe Rd, Middlesbrough, **Cleveland**, TS1 3QX, ENG.
(T) 01642 240090
Speciality: Hypnotherapy.
B (Ref:HM15737)

### PARRY, J M
**J M Parry**, Boat House Cottage, 3 Esplanade Lane, Watchet, **Somerset**, TA23 0AH, ENG.
(T) 01984 631632
Speciality: Chiropody. ✔
● **Chiropodist** Ms J Parry Q: DPodM, S.R.Ch. M: S.C.P, S.R.Ch.
M Yrs. Est.: 10 (Ref:HM15738)

### PARRY, LIZA
**Liza Parry**, 36 Fields Rd, Alsager, Stoke-On-Trent, **Staffordshire**, ST7 2NA, ENG.
(T) 01270 882351
Speciality: Acupuncture.
● **Owner** Miss L Parry
O (Ref:HM15739)

### PARRY, N J
**N J Parry**, 73 Christchurch Rd, Ringwood, **Hampshire**, BH24 1DH, ENG.
(T) 01425 476930
Speciality: Osteopathy.
● **Owner** Mrs N Parry
P S T (Ref:HM15740)

### PARRY, PHIL
**Phil Parry**, 93 Blackoak Rd, Cardiff, **Glamorgan (Vale of)**, CF23 6QW, WAL.
(T) 029 2076 5522
Speciality: Osteopathy.
P S T (Ref:HM15741)

### PARRY, SHEILA
**Sheila Parry**, Little Whitehouse, Whitehouse Cross, Porchfield, **Isle of Wight**, PO30 4LG, ENG.
(T) 01983 520211
Speciality: Alexander Technique.
P S (Ref:HM15742)

### PARRY, SHELLA
**Shella Parry**, Porchfield, **Isle of Wight**, PO30, ENG.
(T) 01983 520211
Speciality: Alexander Technique.
P S (Ref:HM15743)

### PARRY-ELLIS, MARGARET
**Margaret Parry-Ellis**, 15 Lycroft Cl, Goring, Reading, **Berkshire**, RG8 0AT, ENG.
(T) 01491 873119 (F) 01491 873119
Speciality: Hypnosis.
● **Owner** Mrs M Parry-Ellis
B (Ref:HM15744)

### PARSIFAL OSTEOPATHIC CLINIC
**Parsifal Osteopathic Clinic**, 5 Parsifal Rd, West Hamptsead, London, **London (Greater)**, NW6 1UG, ENG.
(T) 020 7431 8831
Speciality: Osteopathy.
P S T (Ref:HM15745)

### PARSON, SYLVIA A
**Sylvia A Parson**, Bethany House Surgery, 85 Battle Rd, Hailsham, **Sussex (East)**, BN27 1UA, ENG.
(T) 01323 848485
Speciality: Chiropodists (Podiatrists).
S (Ref:HM15746)

### PARSONS STREET CLINIC
**Parsons Street Clinic (The)**, 15A Parsons St, Banbury, **Oxfordshire**, OX16 5LY, ENG.
(T) 01295 272903
Speciality: Acupuncture, Aromatherapy, Bach Remedies, Chiropractic, Complementary Therapy, Counselling, Cranial Osteopathy, Encounter Groups, Group Therapy, Herbal Medicine, Homeopathy, Manipulation, Massage (Therapeutic), Moxibustion, Osteopathy. ✔
● **Medical Herbalist** Ms R Evans Q: BSc (Hons), MNIMH. M: NIMH.
● **Owner/Osteopath** Mr H Marriott Q: BSc (Hons), DO. M: GOsC.
● **Acupuncturist** Ms C Brannigan Q: BSc, Lic.Ac. M: BAcC.
● **Homeopath** Ms S Treanor M: Soc.Hom.
M Yrs. Est.: 8 (Ref:HM15747)

### PARSONS, BRONDA
**Bronda Parsons**, Averbury House, Poachers Gate, Dawley, Telford, **Shropshire**, TF4 3PZ, ENG.
(T) 01952 597568
Speciality: Reflexology.
S T (Ref:HM15748)

### PARSONS, C A
**C A Parsons**, 88 Rodney St, Liverpool, **Merseyside**, L1 9AR, ENG.
(T) 01517 096639 (F) 01517 097279
Speciality: Osteopathy.
P S T (Ref:HM15749)

### PARSONS, CAROL
**Carol Parsons**, Coromandel, Lower Farm Rd, Ringshall, Stowmarket, **Suffolk**, IP14 2JE, ENG.
(T) 01473 658718
Speciality: Reflexology.
S T (Ref:HM15750)

### PARSONS, CHRIS
**Chris Parsons**, 238B Kingston Rd, Staines, **Surrey**, TW18 1PG, ENG.
(T) 01784 453814
Speciality: Physiotherapy.
● **Owner** Mrs C Parsons
P S T (Ref:HM15751)

### PARSONS, CHRISTINA
**Christina Parsons**, 18 Deansgate, Leek, **Staffordshire**, ST13 6JF, ENG.
(T) 01538 388176 (F) 01538 388176
Speciality: Osteopathy.
● **Owner** Miss C Parsons
P S T (Ref:HM15752)

### PARSONS, G
**Mrs G Parsons**, 90 York Rd, Teddington, **London (Greater)**, TW11 8SN, ENG.
(T) 020 8287 4787
Speciality: Chiropodists (Podiatrists).
S (Ref:HM15753)

### PARSONS, G H
**G H Parsons**, Ayando, Cold Ash Hill, Cold Ash, Thatcham, **Berkshire**, RG18 9NX, ENG.
(T) 01635 864630
Speciality: Chiropodists (Podiatrists).
● **Owner** Mr G Parsons
S (Ref:HM15754)

### PARSONS, IAN H
**Ian H Parsons**, Matlock Physiotherapy Centre, Lime Grove Walk, Matlock, **Derbyshire**, DE4 3FD, ENG.
(T) 01629 580380
Speciality: Physiotherapy.
P S T (Ref:HM15755)

### PARSONS, J
**J Parsons**, 20 Burnby Lane, Pocklington, York, **Yorkshire (North)**, YO42 2QD, ENG.
(T) 01759 303491
Speciality: Complementary Medicines &

Therapy.
C M (Ref:HM15756)

## PARSONS, JEFF
**Jeff Parsons**, The Clinic, 37 St Peter St, Tiverton, **Devon**, EX16 6NW, ENG.
(T) 01884 255990
Speciality: Complementary Medicines & Therapy.
M (Ref:HM15757)

## PARSONS, JOHN
**John Parsons**, 11 Sylvan Way, Gillingham, **Dorset**, SP8 4EQ, ENG.
(T) 01747 825763
Speciality: Chiropodists (Podiatrists).
● **Owner** Mr J Parsons
S (Ref:HM15758)

## PARSONS, PETER
**Peter Parsons**, 20 Wood St, Lytham St. Annes, **Lancashire**, FY8 1QS, ENG.
(T) 01253 725947
Speciality: Chiropodists (Podiatrists).
● **Owner** Mr P Mathews
S (Ref:HM15759)

## PARSONS, ROBERT
**Robert Parsons**, 5 Elm Ter, Constantine Rd, London, **London (Greater)**, NW3 2LL, ENG.
(T) 020 7267 4222
Speciality: Hypnotherapy.
● **Owner** Mr R Parson
B (Ref:HM15760)

## PARTINGTON, NICHOLAS
**Nicholas Partington**, 40 Daniells, Welwyn Garden City, **Hertfordshire**, AL7 1QX, ENG.
(T) 01707 326666
Speciality: Chiropodists (Podiatrists).
● **Owner** Mr N Partington
S (Ref:HM15761)

## PARTINGTON, T
**T Partington**, Ashford Clinic Of Complementary Medicine, Western Avenue, Ashford, **Kent**, TN23 1LY, ENG.
(T) 01233 631530
Speciality: Homeopathy.
M (Ref:HM15762)

## PARTLAN, ROBERT
**Robert Partlan**, 197 Old St, Ashton-under-Lyne, **Manchester (Greater)**, OL6 7SR, ENG.
(T) 01613 437571
Speciality: Hypnosis.
B (Ref:HM15763)

## PARTNERSHIP, BAKER (DR)
**Dr Baker Partnership**, 10 Elgin Rd, Bournemouth, **Dorset**, BH4 9NL, ENG.
(T) 01202 763836 (F) 01202 761766
Speciality: Cognitive Therapy, Counselling, Psychotherapy, Rogerian Therapy, Stress Therapy, Emotional Processing Therapy. ✔
● **Clinical Psychologist**
Professor R Baker Q: BA, PhD. M: BPS.
● **Administrator** Mrs A Baker Q: BSc, Cert.Management, MSc.
B Yrs. Est.: 14 (Ref:HM15764)

## PARTON, KAY
**Kay Parton**, Cottonstones, 68 Burkes Rd, Beaconsfield, **Buckinghamshire**, HP9 1EW, ENG.
(T) 01494 681457 (F) 01494 681457
Speciality: Aromatherapy.
● **Owner** Mrs K Parton
M O (Ref:HM15765)

## PARTON, S R
**S R Parton**, 231 Clarendon Park Rd, Leicester, **Leicestershire**, LE2 3AN, ENG.
(T) 01162 707145
Speciality: Chiropodists (Podiatrists).
● **Senior Partner** Mr S Parton
S (Ref:HM15766)

## PARTRIDGE, DEIRDRE
**Deirdre Partridge**, 516 Earlham Rd, Norwich, **Norfolk**, NR4 7HR, ENG.
(T) 01603 504379
Speciality: Reflexology.
S T (Ref:HM15767)

## PARTRIDGE, JENNY
**Jenny Partridge**, Tapwood Cottages, Buckland, Betchworth, **Surrey**, RH3 7BG, ENG.
(T) 01737 242341
Speciality: Aromatherapy.
M O (Ref:HM15768)

## PARTRIDGE, VERONICA
**Veronica Partridge**, Sampsons Hall, Kersey, Ipswich, **Suffolk**, IP7 6EL, ENG.
(T) 01473 823188
Speciality: Reflexology.
S T (Ref:HM15769)

## PARVEEN, ASMA
**Asma Parveen**, 8 Sarsfield Rd, Greenford, **London (Greater)**, UB6 7AB, ENG.
(T) 020 8810 7098
Speciality: Homeopathy.
● **Owner** Mrs A Parveen
M (Ref:HM15770)

## PARVEZ, SHAUKAT
**Shaukat Parvez**, 328 Cranbrook Rd, Ilford, **Essex**, IG2 6EP, ENG.
(T) 020 8554 1738
Speciality: Acupuncture, Chiropractic, Osteopathy.
● **Owner** Mr S Parvez Q: B.Ac, BSc (Hons), DC, DO, FRSH. M: BAcC, GOsC.
P S T Yrs. Est.: 15 (Ref:HM15771)

## PARZIALE, BARBARA
**Mrs Barbara Parziale**, 2 Third Avenue, Blackpool, **Lancashire**, FY4 2EU, ENG.
(T) 01253 347075
Speciality: Physiotherapy.
● **Owner** Mrs B Parziale
P S T (Ref:HM15772)

## PASCOE & ASSOCIATES
**M G Pascoe & Associates**, 23 Quarry Hill Rd, Tonbridge, **Kent**, TN9 2RN, ENG.
(T) 01732 355634
Speciality: Osteopathy.
P S T (Ref:HM15773)

## PASCOE, J E
**J E Pascoe**, 6 Tresahar Rd, Falmouth, **Cornwall**, TR11 4EE, ENG.
(T) 01326 315164
Speciality: Physiotherapy.
● **Owner** Mrs J Pascoe
P S T (Ref:HM15774)

## PASHLEY, MAGGIE
**Maggie Pashley**, 72 Broxholm Rd, London, **London (Greater)**, SE27 0BT, ENG.
(T) 020 8670 0477
Speciality: Crystal Healing, Indian Head Massage, Magnetic Therapy, Reflexology, Reiki, Shiatsu.
S T (Ref:HM15775)

## PASK, PHIL
**Phil Pask**, St Georges House, 56 Billing Rd, Northampton, **Northamptonshire**, NN1 5DB, ENG.
(T) 01604 601641 (F) 01604 601641
Speciality: Physiotherapy.
● **Partner** Mr P Witty
P S T (Ref:HM15776)

## PASS, MARGARET
**Margaret Pass**, 3 Castle View Rd, Clevedon, **Somerset**, BS21 7EP, ENG.
(T) 01275 878137
Speciality: Chiropodists (Podiatrists).
● **Owner** Mrs M Pass
S (Ref:HM15777)

## PASSCHIER, CORNELIUS
**Cornelius Passchier**, 7 Elwill Way, Beckenham, **Kent**, BR3 3AB, ENG.
(T) 020 8658 7827
Speciality: Homeopathy, Psychotherapy.
B (Ref:HM15778)

## PASSCHIER, MAREANNE SASSEN
**Mareanne Sassen Passchier**, 7 Elwill Way, Beckenham, **Kent**, BR3 3AB, ENG.
(T) 020 8658 6454
(E) mareanne@mapshomeopath.co.uk
Speciality: Bach Remedies, Counselling, Healer, Holistic Healing, Homeopathy, Meditation. ✔
● **Owner** Mrs M Passchier
C Yrs. Est.: 13 (Ref:HM15779)

## PASSEY, F
**F Passey**, 38 Harborne Rd, Birmingham, **Midlands (West)**, B15 3HE, ENG.
(T) 01214 541390
Speciality: Osteopathy.
● **Chairman** Mr R Priest
P S T (Ref:HM15780)

## PASSEY, FIONA
**Fiona Passey**, 186 Wolverhampton St, Dudley, **Midlands (West)**, DY1 3AD, ENG.
(T) 01384 458634
Speciality: Osteopathy.
P S T (Ref:HM15781)

## PAT, ELLIOTT
**Elliott Pat**, 44 Whitebarn Lane, Dagenham, **Essex**, RM10 9LH, ENG.
(T) 020 8517 1836
Speciality: Reflexology.
S T (Ref:HM15782)

## PATEL, AARAS
**Aaras Patel**, Arden House, 15 Harrington Villas, Brighton, **Sussex (East)**, BN1 6RG, ENG.
(T) 01273 507412 (F) 01273 507412
Speciality: Osteopathy.
● **Owner** Ms D Bell
P S T (Ref:HM15783)

## PATEL, AKKIK
**Akkik Patel**, Arden House, 15 Harrington Villas, Brighton, **Sussex (East)**, BN1 6RG, ENG.
(T) 01273 507412 (F) 01273 507412
Speciality: Homeopathy.
● **Owner** Ms D Bell
M (Ref:HM15784)

## PATEL, ANITA M
**Anita M Patel**, 2 Surman Trce, Princes Rd, Romford, **Essex**, RM1 2TB, ENG.
(T) 01708 728498
Speciality: Chiropodists (Podiatrists).
S (Ref:HM15785)

## PATEL, DIPTI
**Dipti Patel**, 12 Oakmeadow Way, Groby, **Leicestershire**, LE6 0YN, ENG.
(T) 01162 312059
Speciality: Reflexology.
S T (Ref:HM15786)

## PATEL, J (DR)
**Dr J Patel**, 154 Clifton Rd, London, **London (Greater)**, SE25 6QA, ENG.
(T) 020 8653 0831
Speciality: Chiropractic.
P S T (Ref:HM15787)

## PATEL, J C
**J C Patel**, 329 Baring Rd, London, **London (Greater)**, SE12 0DU, ENG.
(T) 020 8851 7500
Speciality: Biomechanics, Chiropody, Nail Surgery, Podiatry. ✔
● **Chiropodist (Podiatrist)**
Nita Patel Q: BSc (Hons), M.S.C.P, S.R.Ch. M: S.C.P.
● **Chiropodist (Podiatrist)**
Mr J Patel Q: M.S.C.P, S.R.Ch. M: S.C.P.
M Yrs. Est.: 10 (Ref:HM15788)

## PATEL, K
**K Patel**, 84 Netheravon Rd, London, **London (Greater)**, W4 2NB, ENG.
(T) 020 8400 3776
Speciality: Chiropodists (Podiatrists).
● **Owner** Ms K Patel
S (Ref:HM15789)

## PATEL, K M
**K M Patel**, Carewell Medical Centre, 74 Kenton Rd, Harrow, **London (Greater)**, HA3 8AE, ENG.
(T) 020 8909 1990 (F) 020 8909 1901
Speciality: Chiropodists (Podiatrists).
● **Senior Partner** Dr P Vakil
S (Ref:HM15790)

## PATEL, K M
**K M Patel**, 54 Joel St, Northwood, **London**


Key continued: Yrs.Est: Years Established Q: Qualifications M: Professional Membership ✔ Indemnity Insurance Accept Credit Cards

(Greater), HA6 1PA, ENG.
(T) 020 8907 1130
Speciality: Chiropodists (Podiatrists).
S (Ref:HM15791)

## PATEL, LINA
**Lina Patel**, The Arena, Stockley Park, Heathrow, **London (Greater)**, UB11 1AA, ENG.
(T) 020 8881 36842/07941070668
(W) www.complementary-healthcare.co.uk/info/lpatel
Speciality: Healing Therapy, Indian Head Massage, Reflexology.
S T (Ref:HM15792)

## PATEL, M
**M Patel**, 30 Chaucer Way, Hoddesdon, **Hertfordshire**, EN11 9QP, ENG.
(T) 01992 461746
Speciality: Chiropodists (Podiatrists).
S (Ref:HM15793)

## PATEL, MANESH
**Manesh Patel**, 126 The Ridgeway, North Harrow, Harrow, **London (Greater)**, HA2 7PZ, ENG.
(T) 020 8868 5692
Speciality: Chiropodists (Podiatrists).
S (Ref:HM15794)

## PATEL, N
**N Patel**, 53 Friern Barnet Rd, London, **London (Greater)**, N11 3EG, ENG.
(T) 020 8368 0924
Speciality: Chiropodists (Podiatrists).
S (Ref:HM15795)

## PATEL, NEIL
**Neil Patel**, 73 Constance Rd, Isleworth, **London (Greater)**, TW7 6ER, ENG.
(T) 020 8758 9478 (F) 020 8847 4857
Speciality: Osteopathy.
● **Owner** Mr N Patel
P S T (Ref:HM15796)

## PATEL, P
**Miss P Patel**, 171 St. John's Hill, London, **London (Greater)**, SW11 1TQ, ENG.
(T) 020 7228 8563
Speciality: Osteopathy.
● **Owner** Miss P Patel
P S T (Ref:HM15797)

## PATEL, PRAGNA
**Mrs Pragna Patel**, 130 Watford Rd, Wembley, **London (Greater)**, HA0 3HF, ENG.
(T) 020 8908 2979
Speciality: Osteopathy.
P S T (Ref:HM15798)

## PATEL, PRATIKSHA
**Pratiksha Patel**, 62 Richmond Rd, Worthing, **Sussex (West)**, BN11 4AF, ENG.
(T) 01903 210175
Speciality: Chiropractic.
● **Manager** Miss F Freest
P S T (Ref:HM15799)

## PATEL, RIMA
**Rima Patel**, 3 Rensburg Villas, Rensburg Rd, London, **London (Greater)**, E17 7HW, ENG.
(T) 020 8520 9233
Speciality: Homeopathy.
M (Ref:HM15800)

## PATEL, S
**S Patel**, 28 Joel St, Northwood, **London (Greater)**, HA6 1PF, ENG.
(T) 020 8909 2949
Speciality: Chiropodists (Podiatrists).
● **Owner** Mrs S Patel
S (Ref:HM15801)

## PATEL, S A
**S A Patel**, 3 Grove Rd, Sutton, **Surrey**, SM1 1BB, ENG.
(T) 020 8642 7299
Speciality: Chiropodists (Podiatrists).
● **Owner** Mrs S Patel
S (Ref:HM15802)

## PATEL, SHILPA
**Shilpa Patel**, 24 Hiliary Gdns, Stanmore, **London (Greater)**, HA7 2NQ, ENG.
(T) 020 8933 5417
Speciality: Complementary Medicines & Therapy.
C M (Ref:HM15803)

## PATEL, SHITAL
**Shital Patel**, Mountfield Surgery, 55 Mountfield Rd, London, **London (Greater)**, N3 3NR, ENG.
(T) 020 8343 0847
Speciality: Osteopathy.
P S T (Ref:HM15804)

## PATEL, SURENDRAKUMAR
**Surendrakumar Patel**, Hayes Cottage Hospital, Grange Rd, Hayes, **London (Greater)**, UB3 2RR, ENG.
(T) 020 8848 9457
Speciality: Acupuncture.
● **Practice Manager** Mr L Harris
O (Ref:HM15805)

## PATEL, SUSHILA
**Sushila Patel**, 731 Clay Hill Rd, Basildon, **Essex**, SS16 4NH, ENG.
(T) 01268 553653
Speciality: Chiropodists (Podiatrists).
S (Ref:HM15806)

## PATEMAN, A R & H G
**A R & H G Pateman**, 1 Whitecroft Way, Beckenham, **Kent**, BR3 3AQ, ENG.
(T) 020 8650 5000
Speciality: Osteopathy.
● **Partner** Mr A Pateman
P S T (Ref:HM15807)

## PATERSON, E C
**E C Paterson**, 4 Mark Lane, Eastbourne, **Sussex (East)**, BN21 4RJ, ENG.
(T) 01323 730960
Speciality: Chiropodists (Podiatrists).
S (Ref:HM15808)

## PATERSON, J
**J Paterson**, 11 Ferndale Rd, Chichester, **Sussex (West)**, PO19 4QJ, ENG.
(T) 01243 527901
Speciality: Chiropodists (Podiatrists).
● **Owner** Mrs J Paterson
S (Ref:HM15809)

## PATERSON, KARETH
**Kareth Paterson**, 29 River Cl, Ruislip, **London (Greater)**, HA4 7UY, ENG.
(T) 01895 677755
Speciality: Indian Head Massage, Reflexology, Reiki.
S T (Ref:HM15810)

## PATERSON, LINDA
**Linda Paterson**, 7 Bazley Rd, Lytham St. Annes, **Lancashire**, FY8 1AJ, ENG.
(T) 01253 733272
Speciality: Chiropodists (Podiatrists).
● **Owner** Mrs L Paterson
S (Ref:HM15811)

## PATERSON, MARGARET
**Margaret Paterson**, 72-74 Abington Avenue, Northampton, **Northamptonshire**, NN1 4PA, ENG.
(T) 01604 632232
Speciality: Reflexology.
● **Owner** Mrs M Paterson
S T (Ref:HM15812)

## PATERSON, MARGARET
**Margaret Paterson**, Craniosacral Therapy Clinic, 73 Queens Park Prde, Northampton, **Northamptonshire**, NN2 6LR, ENG.
(T) 01604 891296
Speciality: Bach Remedies.
● **Owner** Mrs M Paterson
C (Ref:HM15813)

## PATERSON, MARGARET
**Margaret Paterson**, 11 Gleeson Drive, Orpington, **Kent**, BR6 9LJ, ENG.
(T) 01689 858991
(E) mags.paterson@virgin.net
Speciality: Absent Healing, Indian Head Massage, Reflexology, Spiritual Healing. ✔
● **Reflexologist/Healer**
Mrs M Paterson Q: MBRA, MNFSH. M: BRA, NFSH.
T Yrs. Est.: 7 (Ref:HM15814)

## PATERSON, NINA S
**Nina S Paterson**, 14 Gladstone Pl, Stirling, FK8 2NN, SCO.
(T) 01786 472444
Speciality: Chiropodists (Podiatrists).
● **Owner** Mrs N Paterson
S (Ref:HM15815)

## PATHAK, J
**J Pathak**, Strode House, 301A Kingsbury Rd, London, **London (Greater)**, NW9 9PE, ENG.
(T) 020 8203 8977
Speciality: Homeopathy.
● **Owner** Mr P Godfrey
M (Ref:HM15816)

## PATHAN, A S
**A S Pathan**, 539 High Rd, London, **London (Greater)**, E11 4PB, ENG.
(T) 020 8558 7224
Speciality: Homeopathy.
M (Ref:HM15817)

## PATHS TO MASTERY
**Paths To Mastery**, 31 Forest Gr, Eccleston Park, Prescot, **Merseyside**, L34 2RY, ENG.
(T) 01514 932323 (F) 01514 932323
Speciality: Complementary Medicines & Therapy.
● **Owner** Mr L Allen
C M (Ref:HM15818)

## PATHWAYS HYPNOTHERAPY
**Pathways Hypnotherapy**, 64 Knights Manor Way, Dartford, **Kent**, DA1 5SP, ENG.
(T) 01322 275848
Speciality: Hypnotherapy.
B (Ref:HM15819)

## PATHWAYS TO HEALTH
**Pathways To Health**, 12 St. Georges Pl, Brighton, **Sussex (East)**, BN1 4GB, ENG.
(T) 01273 686586
Speciality: Acupuncture.
● **Director** Ms J Painter
O (Ref:HM15820)

## PATHWAYS TO HEALTH
**Pathways To Health**, 39 Town End Rd, Holmfirth, Huddersfield, **Yorkshire (West)**, HD7 1AH, ENG.
(T) 01484 683917
Speciality: Complementary Medicines & Therapy.
● **Accountant** Mr C Jane
● **Director** Andrew John Porter
● **Owner/Spiritual Healer**
Ms M Vasey
● **Project Manager**
Kathleen Jane Painter
C (Ref:HM15821)

## PATHWAYS TRUST CTRE - COMP MED
**Pathways Trust Centre For Complementary Medicine**, 110 Salmon Lane, London, **London (Greater)**, E14 7PQ, ENG.
(T) 020 7515 6115
Speciality: Complementary Medicines & Therapy.
C M (Ref:HM15822)

## PATON, BARBARA
**Barbara Paton**, Wickets, Wilton Lane, Jordans, Beaconsfield, **Buckinghamshire**, HP9 2TB, ENG.
(T) 01494 873272
Speciality: Alexander Technique, Phytotherapy. ✔
● **Teacher of the Alexander Technique/Physiotherapist**
Mrs B Paton M: CSP, STAT.
B P Yrs. Est.: 5 (Ref:HM15823)

## PATON, MARY S
**Mary S Paton Chiropodist**, 94 Waterside, Irvine, **Ayrshire (North)**, KA12 8QL, SCO.
(T) 01294 279270
Speciality: Chiropody. ✔
● **Practice Manager** Mr A Paton
● **Chiropodist** Ms M Paton Q: M.S.C.P, S.R.Ch. M: S.C.P.
M Yrs. Est.: 30 (Ref:HM15824)



Key: B Mind-Body Medicine C Complementary Medicine H Self Help Treatment M Medicinal Therapy O Oriental Medicine P Postural Therapy S Manipulative Structural Therapy T Touch Therapy

### PATON, W A
**W A Paton**, Lower House, Oldcastle Lane, Threapwood, Malpas, **Cheshire**, SY14 7BA, ENG.
(T) 01948 770687 (F) 01948 770480
Speciality: Physiotherapy. ✔
● **Physiotherapist** Mrs W Paton Q: MCSP, RGRT. M: CSP.
S Yrs. Est.: 20 (Ref:HM15825)

### PATON-SMITH, ARLEEN
**Arleen Paton-Smith**, 57 Maydowns Rd, Chestfield, Whitstable, **Kent**, CT5 3LN, ENG.
(T) 01227 792578 (F) 01227 792578
Speciality: Complementary Medicines & Therapy.
● **Owner** Mrs A Paton-Smith
C M (Ref:HM15826)

### PATTERSON, I D
**I D Patterson**, 6b St Marys Pl, Aberdeen, **Aberdeenshire**, AB11 6HL, SCO.
(T) 01224 575571 (F) 01651 851272
Speciality: Psychology.
● **Owner** Mr I Patterson
B (Ref:HM15827)

### PATTERSON, J W
**J W Patterson**, 18 Macclesfield Rd, Holmes Chapel, Crewe, **Cheshire**, CW4 7NF, ENG.
(T) 01477 544383
Speciality: Chiropodists (Podiatrists).
S (Ref:HM15828)

### PATTERSON, JUDY
**Judy Patterson**, 20A Central Avenue, West Bridgeford, West Bridgford, Nottingham, **Nottinghamshire**, NG2 5GR, ENG.
(T) 01159 143311
Speciality: Herbal Medicine.
M (Ref:HM15829)

### PATTERSON, L F
**L F Patterson**, Above M F Pharmacy, Four Lane Ends, Newcastle Upon Tyne, **Tyne and Wear**, NE7 7UJ, ENG.
(T) 01912 660625
Speciality: Chiropodists (Podiatrists).
● **Owner** Mr L Patterson
S (Ref:HM15830)

### PATTERSON, R
**R Patterson**, 15 Beatrice Trce, Shiney Row, Houghton le Spring, **Tyne and Wear**, DH4 4QW, ENG.
(T) 01913 853321
Speciality: Chiropodists (Podiatrists).
S (Ref:HM15831)

### PATTERSON, VICKY
**Vicky Patterson**, 27 Queen Mary Avenue, Glasgow, **Glasgow (City of)**, G42 8DS, SCO.
(T) 01414 243490 (F) 01414 243490
Speciality: Hypnosis.
● **Owner** Ms V Patterson
B (Ref:HM15832)

### PATTERSON, YVONNE
**Yvonne Patterson**, 110 St Stephens St, Edinburgh, **Edinburgh (City of)**, EH3 5AQ, SCO.
(T) 07801 225944
Speciality: Aromatherapy. ✔
● **Aromatherapist** Yvonne Patterson Q: Dip.Arom. M: IFA.
C Yrs. Est.: 4 (Ref:HM15833)

### PATTINSON, C J (DR)
**Dr C J Pattinson**, 16 Woodcote Park Rd, Epsom, **Surrey**, KT18 7EX, ENG.
(T) 01372 812985
Speciality: Hypnotherapy.
● **Owner** Dr C Pattinson
B (Ref:HM15834)

### PATTON, MICHAEL
**Michael Patton**, 8 Kings Rd, Birmingham, **Midlands (West)**, B14 6TG, ENG.
(T) 01212 443386
Speciality: Complementary Medicines & Therapy.
C M (Ref:HM15835)

### PATTONY HYPNOTHERAPY GROUP
**Pattony Hypnotherapy Group**, 17 Greysham Court, Demesne Rd, Manchester, **Manchester (Greater)**, M16 8PF, ENG.
(T) 01618 680900
Speciality: Hypnotherapy.
B (Ref:HM15836)

### PAUC, R A
**R A Pauc**, Andover Chiropractic Clinic, 2 Church Cl, Andover, **Hampshire**, SP10 1DP, ENG.
(T) 01264 358760
Speciality: Chiropractic.
P S T (Ref:HM15837)

### PAUL BOIZOT AROMATHERAPY
**Paul Boizot**, 9 Sturton Rd, Syresham, Brackley, **Northamptonshire**, NN13 5HL, ENG.
(T) 01280 850313
Speciality: Complementary Medicines & Therapy.
M (Ref:HM15838)

### PAUL BOIZOT AROMATHERAPY
**Paul Boizot**, 9 Sturton Rd, Sheffield, **Yorkshire (South)**, S4 7DE, ENG.
(T) 01142 561708
(E) paulboizot@synergynet.co.uk
Speciality: Aromatherapy. ✔
● **Sole Trader** Mr P Boizot M: ISPA.
B Yrs. Est.: 9 (Ref:HM15839)

### PAUL BURKE ASSOCIATES
**Paul Burke Associates**, 422 Firth Park Rd, Sheffield, **Yorkshire (South)**, S5 6HH, ENG.
(T) 01142 426726
Speciality: Chiropodists (Podiatrists).
● **Owner** Mr P Burke
S (Ref:HM15840)

### PAUL CHEDGEY MEDICAL HERBALIST
**Paul Chedgey Medical Herbalist MNIMH**, Paydens Natural Health Centre, 126 Ashford Rd, Bearsted, Maidstone, **Kent**, ME14 4LX, ENG.
(T) 01622 630603
Speciality: Complementary Medicines & Therapy.
● **Manager** Miss L Johnson
● **Medical Herbalist** Mr P Chedgey
C M (Ref:HM15841)

### PAUL DENNEHY - HYPNOTHERAPIST
**Paul Dennehy - Hypnotherapist/Psychotherapist**, 113 Commons Rd, Cork, **County Cork**, IRE.
(T) 021 4362 793 (F) 021 4362 793
(E) pauldee@eircom.net
Speciality: Auto Suggestion, Autogenic Training, Aversion Therapy, Complementary Therapy, Counselling, Drama Therapy, Faith Healing, Gestalt Therapy, Group Therapy, Healer, Healing Therapy, Holistic Healing, Hypnosis, Hypnotherapy, Inhalation Therapy, Kinesiology, Meditation, Music Therapy, Polarity Therapy, Psychotherapy, Pyscho-Synthesis, Rogerian Therapy, Sensitivity Training, Sound Therapy, Spiritual Healing, Stress Therapy, Touch Therapy, Transactional Analysis, Voice Therapy, Ying & Yang, Emotional Freedom Therapy. ✔ 💳
● **Hypnotherapist/Psychotherapist** Mr P Dennehy M: ICHP.
B Yrs. Est.: 3 (Ref:HM15842)

### PAUL MAWER PSYCHOLGICAL SVS
**Paul Mawer Psycholgical Services**, 671 Chester Rd, Aldridge, Walsall, **Midlands (West)**, WS9 0LT, ENG.
(T) 01922 458298
Speciality: Psychology, Bupa Provider, Psychology. ✔
● **Chartered Psychologist** Mr A Mawer Q: BSc. M: BPS.
C Yrs. Est.: 24 (Ref:HM15843)

### PAUL MCCARTHY ACUPUNCTURE
**Paul McCarthy Acupuncture**, Sunnyside Seafield Ave, Monkstown, **County Cork**, IRE.
(T) 01280 1950
Speciality: Acupuncture.
O (Ref:HM15844)

### PAUL MURFIN HYPNOTHERAPIST
**Paul Murfin Hypnotherapist**, 51 George St, Brighton, **Sussex (East)**, BN2 1RJ, ENG.
(T) 01273 622990
Speciality: Hypnosis.
B (Ref:HM15845)

### PAUL TAYLOR HYPNOTHERAPY
**Paul Taylor Hypnotherapy**, 175 Padgate Lane, Warrington, **Cheshire**, WA1 3SW, ENG.
(T) 01925 244666
Speciality: Hypnosis.
B (Ref:HM15846)

### PAUL, EDWINA
**Edwina Paul**, 51 Clarendon Rd, Borehamwood, **Hertfordshire**, WD6 1BD, ENG.
(T) 020 8953 9052
Speciality: Chiropodists (Podiatrists).
S (Ref:HM15847)

### PAUL, MARSDEN
**Marsden Paul ADHP MICHP**, 2a Eglinton Park Dunlaoire, IRE.
(T) 01280 5821
(W) www.hypnosiseire.com
Speciality: Complementary Medicines & Therapy.
M (Ref:HM15848)

### PAULA LESZCZUK
**Paula Leszczuk**, Thirsk Natural Health Clinic, Thirsk, **Yorkshire (North)**, ENG.
(T) 01759 372563
(E) leszczukpaula@aol
Speciality: Homeopathy. ✔
● **Homeopath** Ms P Leszczuk Q: BSc (Hons), Dip.Hom. M: Soc.Hom.
B Yrs. Est.: 1 (Ref:HM15849)

### PAULO, EMMA
**Emma Paulo**, 227 New Kings Rd, London, **London (Greater)**, SW6 4XE, ENG.
(T) 020 7371 9028
Speciality: Reflexology.
S T (Ref:HM15850)

### PAUL'S
**Paul's**, Dunimarle Lodge Kirkton, Culross, Dunfermline, **Fife**, KY12 8EW, SCO.
(T) 01383 882394
Speciality: Psychotherapy.
● **Owner** Mr P Anderson
B (Ref:HM15851)

### PAULS, A
**A Pauls**, 49 Pear Tree Walk, Cheshunt, Waltham Cross, **Hertfordshire**, EN7 6RG, ENG.
(T) 01992 633604
Speciality: Osteopathy.
● **Owner** Mrs A Pauls
P S T (Ref:HM15852)

### PAVEL VITEK
**Pavel Vitek**, New England House, New England Lane, Sedlescombe, Battle, **Sussex (East)**, TN33 0RP, ENG.
(T) 01424 870029
Speciality: Reflexology.
S T (Ref:HM15853)

### PAVEY, M F
**M F Pavey**, 25 Gillian Avenue, St. Albans, **Hertfordshire**, AL1 2QH, ENG.
(T) 01727 830555
Speciality: Chiropodists (Podiatrists).
S (Ref:HM15854)

### PAVILION, REVE
**Reve Pavilion (The)**, 2a Guildford Park Rd, Guildford, **Surrey**, GU2 7ND, ENG.
(T) 01483 579500 (F) 01483 456611
Speciality: Osteopathy.
● **Owner** Mr M Mathews
P S T (Ref:HM15855)

### PAWLEY, PHILIP
**Philip Pawley**, Strathnaver, High Lane, Burscough, Ormskirk, **Lancashire**, L40 7SL, ENG.
(T) 01695 574069
Speciality: Alexander Technique.
P S (Ref:HM15856)

### PAWLEY, PHILIP
**Philip Pawley**, 12 Rodney St, Liverpool, **Merseyside**, L1 2TE, ENG.
(T) 01517 086172
Speciality: Alexander Technique.
P S (Ref:HM15857)



Key continued: **Yrs.Est:** Years Established **Q:** Qualifications **M:** Professional Membership ✔ Indemnity Insurance 💳 Accept Credit Cards

### PAWSEY, SUSAN
**Susan Pawsey**, 45 Slayleigh Lane, Sheffield, **Yorkshire (South)**, S10 3RG, ENG.
(T) 01142 303201
Speciality: Osteopathy.
● **Owner** Mr S Pawsey
P S T (Ref:HM15858)

### PAXTON, JACQUELINE
**Jacqueline Paxton**, Jays Nest, 67 Rosebery Rd, Epsom, **Surrey**, KT18 6AB, ENG.
(T) 01372 277336
Speciality: Reflexology.
S T (Ref:HM15859)

### PAYMENT BY RESULTS
**Payment By Results**, 4 Ravenslea Rd, London, **London (Greater)**, SW12 8SB, ENG.
(T) 020 8673 2719 (F) 020 8673 2719
Speciality: Hypnotherapy.
● **Director** Mr M Lawrence
B (Ref:HM15860)

### PAYNE, AUDREY
**Audrey Payne**, 39 Springs Lane, Ilkley, **Yorkshire (West)**, LS29 8TE, ENG.
(T) 01943 601921
Speciality: Complementary Therapy, Reflexology, Reiki, Eastern Head Massage. ✔
● **Reflexologist** Audrey Payne Q: Cert.EHM, MBRA, Reiki 2. M: BRA.
T Yrs. Est.: 4 (Ref:HM15861)

### PAYNE, C
**Mrs C Payne**, Beamends, Burnhams Rd, Bookham, Leatherhead, **Surrey**, KT23 3AU, ENG.
(T) 01372 457282
Speciality: Chiropodists (Podiatrists).
S (Ref:HM15862)

### PAYNE, I J
**I J Payne**, 18 Kingsdown Rd, Epsom, **Surrey**, KT17 3PU, ENG.
(T) 01372 723452
Speciality: Osteopathy.
● **Owner** Mrs I Payne
P S T (Ref:HM15863)

### PAYNE, I J
**I J Payne**, Bridge Cottage, 9 Madrepore Rd, Torquay, **Devon**, TQ1 1EY, ENG.
(T) 01803 298982
Speciality: Acupuncture.
O (Ref:HM15864)

### PAYNE, JULIE
**Julie Payne**, Ambridge, Lower Quinton, Stratford-Upon-Avon, **Warwickshire**, CV37 8SG, ENG.
(T) 01789 721273
Speciality: Homeopathy.
● **Owner** Ms J Payne
M (Ref:HM15865)

### PAYNE, MAXINE
**Maxine Payne**, 16 East Bank, Selsey, Chichester, **Sussex (West)**, PO20 0SP, ENG.
(T) 01243 605090
Speciality: Chiropodists (Podiatrists).
● **Partner** Mr L Payne
S (Ref:HM15866)

### PAYNE, MICHAEL
**Michael Payne**, 11 Hazelville Cl, Harwich, **Essex**, CO12 3TQ, ENG.
(T) 01255 554013
Speciality: Chiropodists (Podiatrists).
● **Owner** Mr M Payne
S (Ref:HM15867)

### PAYNE, MICHAEL
**Michael Payne**, Suite 3 Rectory Court, 143 Hythe Hill, Colchester, **Essex**, CO1 2NF, ENG.
(T) 07802 987455
Speciality: Chiropodists (Podiatrists).
● **Owner** Mr M Payne
S (Ref:HM15868)

### PAYNE, R
**R Payne**, Central Car Park, Limavady, **County Londonderry**, BT49 0HW, NIR.
(T) 028 7776 5208
Speciality: Chiropodists (Podiatrists).
● **Owner** Mrs R Payne
S (Ref:HM15869)

### PAYNE, R A
**R A Payne**, 1 St Michaels Rd, Cardiff, **Glamorgan (Vale of)**, CF5 2AL, WAL.
(T) 029 2056 3826
Speciality: Physiotherapy.
P S T (Ref:HM15870)

### PAYNE, SUZANNE
**Suzanne Payne**, 102 Southbourne Rd, Bournemouth, **Dorset**, BH6 3QQ, ENG.
(T) 01202 424833
Speciality: Complementary Medicines & Therapy.
● **Owner** Mr J Milward
M (Ref:HM15871)

### PAYNE, V A
**V A Payne**, 4 Warwick Court, 75 Station Rd, New Barnet, Barnet, **Hertfordshire**, EN5 1PT, ENG.
(T) 020 8449 6477
Speciality: Chiropodists (Podiatrists).
● **Owner** Mr V Payne
S (Ref:HM15872)

### PAYNE, VERONICA
**Veronica Payne**, 94 St James's St, Brighton, **Sussex (East)**, BN2 1TP, ENG.
(T) 01273 672952
Speciality: Homeopathy.
● **Owner** Mr L Moore
M (Ref:HM15873)

### PAYNTON, M G
**M G Paynton**, Suite 4 Borough House, Marlborough Rd, Banbury, **Oxfordshire**, OX16 5TH, ENG.
(T) 01295 273073
Speciality: Chiropodists (Podiatrists).
● **Owner** Mr M Paynton
S (Ref:HM15874)

### PAYTON, ANTHONY
**Anthony Payton**, 5 Orchard Pl, Barlaston, Stoke-On-Trent, **Staffordshire**, ST12 9DL, ENG.
(T) 01782 372897 (F) 01782 372897
(E) safefeet@aol.com
(W) www.safefeet.co.uk
Speciality: Biomechanics, Chiropody, Nail Surgery. ✔
● **Owner/Chiropodist** Mr A Payton Q: M.S.C.P. M: S.C.P.
C Yrs. Est.: 3 (Ref:HM15875)

### PEACE CLINIC
**Peace Clinic (The)**, Cwm Mellion, Llangammarch Wells, **Powys**, LD4 4EN, WAL.
(T) 01591 620339 (F) 01591 620339
(E) peacesusan@hotmail.com
Speciality: Counselling, Humanistic Psychology, Hypnosis, Hypnotherapy, Psychotherapy. ✔
● **Owner/Hypnotherapist/Psychotherapist** Ms S Peace Q: BA (Hons), DHP (NC), FHA, FHRS, MBChA, MNRHP, MSSCh. M: UKCP.
M Yrs. Est.: 32 (Ref:HM15876)

### PEACEHAVEN AROMATHERAPY
**Peacehaven Aromatherapy**, 4 Moorland Rd, Leek, **Staffordshire**, ST13 5BW, ENG.
(T) 01538 382986 (F) 01538 382986
(E) peacehavenok@hotmail.com
Speciality: Aromatherapy. ✔
● **Owner/Clinical Aromatherapist** Mrs L Robinson
T Yrs. Est.: 10 (Ref:HM15877)

### PEACH, A
**A Peach**, 132 Tettenhall Rd, Wolverhampton, **Midlands (West)**, WV6 0BL, ENG.
(T) 01902 757003
Speciality: Physiotherapy.
● **Owner** Mr A Peach
P S T (Ref:HM15878)

### PEACH, F J
**F J Peach**, 5 Church Lane, Stafford, **Staffordshire**, ST16 2AW, ENG.
(T) 01785 258522
Speciality: Biomechanics, Chiropody, Nail Surgery, Podiatry. ✔
● **Chiropodist** Ms A Upton Q: M.S.C.P.
● **Chiropodist** Mr M Blank Q: M.S.C.P.
● **Chiropodist** Mr F Peach Q: M.S.C.P.
● **Chiropodist** Ms H Keyse Q: M.S.C.P.
C Yrs. Est.: 50 (Ref:HM15879)

### PEACH, LYN
**Lyn Peach**, 26 Denton Rd, Burton-On-Trent, **Staffordshire**, DE13 0QA, ENG.
(T) 01283 535820
Speciality: Chiropodists (Podiatrists).
● **Owner** Mrs L Peach
S (Ref:HM15880)

### PEACOCK, ALISON
**Alison Peacock**, 11 Castle Cl, Henley-In-Arden, Solihull, **Warwickshire**, B95 5LR, ENG.
(T) 01564 792182
Speciality: Hypnotherapy.
B (Ref:HM15881)

### PEACOCK, ANGELA
**Angela Peacock**, 3 Quarry House Lane, Durham, **County Durham**, DH1 4JA, ENG.
(T) 01913 849557
Speciality: Reflexology.
S T (Ref:HM15882)

### PEACOCK, EMMA
**Emma Peacock**, Chantry Medical Practice, South Park, Sevenoaks, **Kent**, TN13 1ED, ENG.
(T) 01732 742529
Speciality: Chiropodists (Podiatrists).
● **Owner** Miss E Peacock
S (Ref:HM15883)

### PEACOCK, J W
**J W Peacock**, 8 Strathmore St, Perth, **Perth and Kinross**, PH2 7HP, SCO.
(T) 01738 627917
Speciality: Physiotherapy.
● **Owner** Mr J Peacock
P S T (Ref:HM15884)

### PEACOCK, K
**K Peacock**, 28 Highland Avenue, London, **London (Greater)**, W7 3RF, ENG.
(T) 020 8575 3000
Speciality: Alexander Technique.
P S (Ref:HM15885)

### PEACOCK, P
**P Peacock**, 218 Abbots Rd, Abbots Langley, **Hertfordshire**, WD5 0BP, ENG.
(T) 01923 490375
Speciality: Reflexology.
S T (Ref:HM15886)

### PEACOCK, R
**R Peacock**, 9 Beeches Avenue, Carshalton, **Surrey**, SM5 3LB, ENG.
(T) 020 8773 4508
Speciality: Hypnotherapy.
B (Ref:HM15887)

### PEACOCK, SALLY
**Sally Peacock**, 60D High St, Caterham, **Surrey**, CR3 5UB, ENG.
(T) 01883 347478
Speciality: Chiropodists (Podiatrists).
S (Ref:HM15888)

### PEAK PERFORMANCE CONSULTANCY
**Peak Performance Consultancy**, 8 Willow Rd, London, **London (Greater)**, NW3 1TJ, ENG.
(T) 020 7794 8717
Speciality: Psychology.
● **Owner** Mr S Meyerson
B (Ref:HM15889)

### PEAK PSYCHOLOGY SERVICE
**Peak Psychology Service**, Suite 5G & 5H Business Centre, North Mill, Belper, **Derbyshire**, DE56 1YD, ENG.
(T) 01773 880222 (F) 01773 880703
Speciality: Psychology.
● **Partner** Mr T Birkin
B (Ref:HM15890)

### PEAKE, A C
**A C Peake**, Ash Marsh, Mill Lane, Wellington, Telford, **Shropshire**, TF1 1PF, ENG.
(T) 01952 223648
Speciality: Chiropodists (Podiatrists).
● **Owner** Mr A Peake
S (Ref:HM15891)



Key: B Mind-Body Medicine C Complementary Medicine H Self Help Treatment M Medicinal Therapy O Oriental Medicine P Postural Therapy S Manipulative Structural Therapy T Touch Therapy

**PEAKE, C F**
**C F Peake**, 2 Brookside, Longclough Drive, Glossop, **Derbyshire**, SK13 8HN, ENG.
(T) 01457 862796
Speciality: Chiropodists (Podiatrists).
S (Ref:HM15892)

**PEAPER, C**
**C Peaper**, 192 Dore Avenue, Fareham, **Hampshire**, PO16 8EP, ENG.
(T) 01329 288006
Speciality: Chiropodists (Podiatrists).
● **Owner** Mrs C Peaper
S (Ref:HM15893)

**PEARCE, BRIAN S**
**Brian S Pearce**, 23 Bretlands Way, Burton-On-Trent, **Staffordshire**, DE15 9SH, ENG.
(T) 01283 564194
Speciality: Chiropodists (Podiatrists).
● **Owner** Mr B Pearce
S (Ref:HM15894)

**PEARCE, G**
**G Pearce**, 152 Turners Rd North, Luton, **Bedfordshire**, LU2 9AH, ENG.
(T) 01582 726744
Speciality: Psychotherapy.
● **Owner** Mr G Pearce
B (Ref:HM15895)

**PEARCE, JOAN**
**Joan Pearce**, 101 Fairlight Rd, Hastings, **Sussex (East)**, TN35 5EJ, ENG.
(T) 01424 421053
Speciality: Aromatherapy.
● **Owner** Mrs J Pearce
M O (Ref:HM15896)

**PEARCE, KEITH**
**Keith Pearce**, 90 Viceroy Cl, Bristol Rd, Birmingham, **Midlands (West)**, B5 7UU, ENG.
(T) 01214 406129
Speciality: Complementary Medicines & Therapy.
● **Owner** Mr K Pearce
C M (Ref:HM15897)

**PEARCE, L**
**L Pearce**, Harlequin House, 43 Chester Rd, Ilford, **Essex**, IG3 8PT, ENG.
(T) 020 8599 6013
Speciality: Psychotherapy.
B (Ref:HM15898)

**PEARCE, P J**
**P J Pearce**, 39 Meadow Walk, Gosport, **Hampshire**, PO13 0YN, ENG.
(T) 01329 237221
Speciality: Chiropodists (Podiatrists).
● **Owner** Mr P Pearce
S (Ref:HM15899)

**PEARCE, R P**
**R P Pearce**, 8 Lebanon Avenue, Feltham, **London (Greater)**, TW13 6RS, ENG.
(T) 020 8898 1146 (F) 020 8898 1146
Speciality: Osteopathy.
● **Owner** Mrs R Pearce
P S T (Ref:HM15900)

**PEARCE, V**
**V Pearce**, 3 St Michaels Rd, Wareham, **Dorset**, BH20 4QU, ENG.
(T) 01929 553672
Speciality: Complementary Medicines & Therapy.
● **Owner** Mrs V Pearce
C M (Ref:HM15901)

**PEARCE, YVONNE**
**Yvonne Pearce**, 9 Pickton Cl, Chesterfield, **Derbyshire**, S40 2DE, ENG.
(T) 01246 202219
Speciality: Reflexology.
S T (Ref:HM15902)

**PEARCEY, M**
**M Pearcey**, 2 West Way, Hove, **Sussex (East)**, BN3 8LD, ENG.
(T) 01273 733177
Speciality: Chiropractic.
P S T (Ref:HM15903)

**PEARL AROMATHERAPY**
**Pearl Aromatherapy**, Marbury Dale, Bannel Lane, Buckley, **Flintshire**, CH7 3AP, WAL.
(T) 01244 547424
Speciality: Aromatherapy.
M O (Ref:HM15904)

**PEARL AROMATICS**
**Pearl Aromatics**, 4 Market St, Widnes, **Cheshire**, WA8 7SN, ENG.
(T) 01514 207266
Speciality: Aromatherapy.
● **Owner** Ms J Edwards
M O (Ref:HM15905)

**PEARL LAMONT**
**Pearl Lamont**, The Limes Cottage, Great Ashfield, Bury St. Edmunds, **Suffolk**, IP31 3HA, ENG.
(T) 01359 259761
Speciality: Hypnosis.
B (Ref:HM15906)

**PEARSON & MARKLOVE**
**J Pearson & A Marklove**, 128 New Rd, Portsmouth, **Hampshire**, PO2 7RJ, ENG.
(T) 023 9282 8998
Speciality: Acupuncture.
● **Partner** Mr J Pearson
O (Ref:HM15907)

**PEARSON, A V A (DR)**
**Dr A V A Pearson**, 49 High Bannerdown, Batheaston, Bath, **Somerset**, BA1 7JZ, ENG.
(T) 01225 858293
Speciality: Complementary Medicines & Therapy.
● **Owner** Dr A Pearson
C M (Ref:HM15908)

**PEARSON, B J**
**B J Pearson**, 95 Dunraven St, Tonypandy, **Rhondda Cynon Taff**, CF40 1AR, WAL.
(T) 01443 439018
Speciality: Chiropodists (Podiatrists).
● **Owner** Mr B Pearson
S (Ref:HM15909)

**PEARSON, C**
**C Pearson**, 3 Linen Yard, South St, Crewkerne, **Somerset**, TA18 8AB, ENG.
(T) 01460 78068
Speciality: Osteopathy.
● **Owner** Mrs B Harrison
P S T (Ref:HM15910)

**PEARSON, CHRISTINE**
**Christine Pearson**, 34 Underdale Rd, Shrewsbury, **Shropshire**, SY2 5DW, ENG.
(T) 01743 366628
Speciality: Counselling, Reflexology, Reiki. ✔
● **Counselling Therapist** Mrs C Pearson Q: Dip.Couns. M: BACP.
C Yrs. Est.: 7 (Ref:HM15911)

**PEARSON, E**
**E Pearson**, Honeymead, Bekesbourne, Canterbury, **Kent**, CT4 5DZ, ENG.
(T) 01227 831593
Speciality: Reflexology.
● **Reflexologist** Eve Pearson
S T (Ref:HM15912)

**PEARSON, EILEEN**
**Eileen Pearson**, 7 Northumberland Avenue, London, **London (Greater)**, E12 5HF, ENG.
(T) 020 8989 3070
Speciality: Psychology.
B (Ref:HM15913)

**PEARSON, K J**
**K J Pearson**, 22 Osborne Avenue, Newcastle Upon Tyne, **Tyne and Wear**, NE2 1JQ, ENG.
(T) 01912 813379
Speciality: Physiotherapy.
● **Owner** Mrs A Moodie
P S T (Ref:HM15914)

**PEARSON, K J**
**K J Pearson**, 33 Devon Sq, Newton Abbot, **Devon**, TQ12 2HH, ENG.
(T) 01626 354507
Speciality: Chiropodists (Podiatrists).
● **Owner** Mr K Pearson
S (Ref:HM15915)

**PEARSON, NINA**
**Nina Pearson**, 34 Downside Rd, Sutton, **Surrey**, SM2 5HP, ENG.
(T) 020 8643 1609
Speciality: Reflexology.
S T (Ref:HM15916)

**PEARSON, VIVIENNE**
**Vivienne Pearson**, The Physiotherapy Centre, 7 Church Drive, Daybrook, Nottingham, **Nottinghamshire**, NG5 6JD, ENG.
(T) 01159 267052
Speciality: Physiotherapy.
● **Owner** Mrs V Pearson
P S T (Ref:HM15917)

**PEARSON, YASMIN**
**Yasmin Pearson**, 5 Summerlea Gardens, Church St, Littlehampton, **Sussex (West)**, BN17 5PT, ENG.
(T) 01903 715985
Speciality: Reflexology.
S T (Ref:HM15918)

**PEARTON, GILL**
**Gill Pearton**, 16 Crow Lane, Rochester, **Kent**, ME1 1RF, ENG.
(T) 01634 403535
Speciality: Bowen Therapy, Reflexology. ✔
● **Reflexologist** Gill Pearton Q: MAR. M: AoR.
C Yrs. Est.: 5 (Ref:HM15919)

**PEASTON, S**
**S Peaston**, 52 Main St, Roslin, **Lothian (Mid)**, EH25 9LS, SCO.
(T) 01314 482122
Speciality: Reflexology.
● **Owner** Mrs S Peaston
S T (Ref:HM15920)

**PEAT, J**
**J Peat**, 9 Aintree Cl, Doncaster, **Yorkshire (South)**, DN5 8UA, ENG.
(T) 01302 783394
Speciality: Chiropodists (Podiatrists).
● **Owner** Mrs J Peat
S (Ref:HM15921)

**PEATFIELD, K J**
**K J Peatfield**, 8 Elm Trce, Pontefract, **Yorkshire (West)**, WF8 1DG, ENG.
(T) 01977 704508
Speciality: Chiropodists (Podiatrists).
S (Ref:HM15922)

**PECK, GORDON**
**Gordon Peck**, 8 Chilston Rd, Tunbridge Wells, **Kent**, TN4 9LT, ENG.
(T) 01892 546237
Speciality: Acupuncture.
O (Ref:HM15923)

**PECK, S K**
**S K Peck**, Garden Farm, The Town, Great Staughton, St Neots, Huntingdon, **Cambridgeshire**, PE19 4BE, ENG.
(T) 01480 861456 (F) 01480 861947
Speciality: Physiotherapy.
● **Owner** Mrs S Peck
P S T (Ref:HM15924)

**PECK, SUE**
**Sue Peck**, 38 Armshead Rd, Werrington, Stoke-On-Trent, **Staffordshire**, ST9 0HJ, ENG.
(T) 01782 304106 (F) 01782 303789
Speciality: Aromatherapy.
● **Owner** Mrs S Peck
M O (Ref:HM15925)

**PEDEN, ANDREW**
**Andrew Peden**, 177 Main St, Prestwick, **Ayrshire (South)**, KA9 1AA, SCO.
(T) 01292 479406
Speciality: Chiropodists (Podiatrists).
S (Ref:HM15926)

**PEDEN, G J**
**G J Peden**, Poke Logan, Liphill Quay, Bere Ferrers, Yelverton, **Devon**, PL20 7JY, ENG.
(T) 01822 840696
Speciality: Chiropodists (Podiatrists).
S (Ref:HM15927)



Key continued: **Yrs.Est:** Years Established **Q:** Qualifications **M:** Professional Membership ✔ Indemnity Insurance Accept Credit Cards

**PEDEN, JOYCE**

**Joyce Peden**, 2 Pym St, Tavistock, **Devon**, PL19 0AW, ENG.
(T) 01822 617482
Speciality: Chiropodists (Podiatrists).
● **Owner** Miss K Williams
S (**Ref:**HM15928)

**PEDERSEN, GITTE**

**Gitte Pedersen**, Wallingford Therapy Clinic, 9 St. Leonards Sq, Wallingford, **Oxfordshire**, OX10 0AR, ENG.
(T) 01491 824724
Speciality: Complementary Medicines & Therapy.
● **Manager** Mrs M Stokes
M (**Ref:**HM15929)

**PEDERSEN, PALLE**

**Palle Pedersen**, Hale Clinic, 7 Park Cresent, London, **London (Greater)**, W1N 3HE, ENG.
(T) 020 7631 0156
Speciality: Chiropractors.
P S T (**Ref:**HM15930)

**PEDIWEAR SHOE CENTRE**

**Pediwear Shoe Centre**, 24 Westgate, Halifax, **Yorkshire (West)**, HX1 1DJ, ENG.
(T) 01422 331009
Speciality: Chiropodists (Podiatrists).
● **Owner** Mr B Small
S (**Ref:**HM15931)

**PEDLER, FAY**

**Fay Pedler**, 5 Whiteford Rd, Plymouth, **Devon**, PL3 5LU, ENG.
(T) 01752 664519
Speciality: Physiotherapy.
● **Owner** Mrs F Pedler
P S T (**Ref:**HM15932)

**PEDLEY, ANNE**

**Anne Pedley**, Natural Therapy Centre, 10 Holmgate Rd, Clay Cross, Chesterfield, **Derbyshire**, S45 9PH, ENG.
(T) 01246 866947
Speciality: Osteopathy.
● **Owner** Mrs A Pedley
P S T (**Ref:**HM15933)

**PEDLEY, S & D E**

**S & D E Pedley**, 100 The Boulevard, Stoke-On-Trent, **Staffordshire**, ST6 6DW, ENG.
(T) 01782 838444
Speciality: Chiropodists (Podiatrists).
● **Owner** Mrs D Pedley
S (**Ref:**HM15934)

**PEDORTHICS FOOT SGY PRACTICE**

**Pedorthics Foot Surgery Practice**, 6 Le Breos Avenue, Uplands, **Swansea**, SA2 0LB, WAL.
(T) 07774 782469
Speciality: Biomechanics, Gait Analysis.
● **Chiropodist (Podiatrist)**
Mr R David Q: DPodM, FCPod(s), S.R.Ch, SRN.
S Yrs. Est.: 16 (**Ref:**HM15935)

**PEEBLES, P M**

**Mrs P M Peebles**, 15 Holly Avenue, Breaston, Derby, **Derbyshire**, DE72 3BG, ENG.
(T) 01332 873748
Speciality: Reflexology.
● **Owner** Mrs P Peebles
S T (**Ref:**HM15936)

**PEEDLE, DAVID**

**David Peedle**, 27 The Hyde, Ware, **Hertfordshire**, SG12 0ER, ENG.
(T) 01920 460182
Speciality: Chiropodists (Podiatrists).
● **Owner** Mr D Peele
S (**Ref:**HM15937)

**PEEDLE, DAVID R**

**David R Peedle**, 6 The Cheshunt Centre, 58 High St, Cheshunt, Waltham Cross, **Hertfordshire**, EN8 0AQ, ENG.
(T) 01992 636665
Speciality: Chiropody. ✓
● **Chiropodist** Mr D Peedle Q: MBChA, MSSCh.
M Yrs. Est.: 6 (**Ref:**HM15938)

**PEEL, DENNIS**

**Dennis Peel**, 4 Penparc, Tumble, Llanelli, **Carmarthenshire**, SA14 6EP, WAL.
(T) 01269 841644
Speciality: Physiotherapy.
● **Owner** Mr D Peel
P S T (**Ref:**HM15939)

**PEER, MARISA**

**Marisa Peer**, 25 Cloncurry St, London, **London (Greater)**, SW6 6DR, ENG.
(T) 020 7371 9367 (F) 020 7736 4370
Speciality: Hypnosis.
● **Owner** Miss M Peer
B (**Ref:**HM15940)

**PEERLESS, M J**

**M J Peerless**, Waterhouse Farm, Exbourne, Okehampton, **Devon**, EX20 3QY, ENG.
(T) 01837 851276
Speciality: Chiropodists (Podiatrists).
S (**Ref:**HM15941)

**PEERS, C**

**C Peers**, 40 Eastlake St, Plymouth, **Devon**, PL1 1BE, ENG.
(T) 01752 225567
Speciality: Osteopathy.
● **Owner** Mr C Peers
P S T (**Ref:**HM15942)

**PEERS-JOHNSON, D R**

**D R Peers-Johnson**, 79 Marlow Bottom, Marlow, **Buckinghamshire**, SL7 3NA, ENG.
(T) 01628 487720 (F) 01628 472197
Speciality: Osteopathy.
● **Owner** Mr D Peers-Johnson
P S T (**Ref:**HM15943)

**PEET, SANDRA**

**Sandra Peet**, 31 Firfield Rd, Addlestone, **Surrey**, KT15 1QU, ENG.
(T) 01932 853667 (F) 01932 853667
Speciality: Psychotherapy.
● **Owner** Mrs S Peet
B (**Ref:**HM15944)

**PEGASUS CENTRE**

**Pegasus Centre**, Byways, Altwood Cl, Maidenhead, **Berkshire**, SL6 4PP, ENG.
(T) 01628 778820
Speciality: Psychotherapy.
● **Partner** Mr D England
B (**Ref:**HM15945)

**PEGG, M G**

**M G Pegg**, 64 High St, Snainton, Scarborough, **Yorkshire (North)**, YO13 9AL, ENG.
(T) 01723 859605
Speciality: Physiotherapy.
● **Owner** Mr M Pegg
P S T (**Ref:**HM15946)

**PEHRSON, S**

**S Pehrson**, The Coach House, Paradise Rd, Henley-on-Thames, **Oxfordshire**, RG9 1UB, ENG.
(T) 01491 574267
Speciality: Alexander Technique.
P S (**Ref:**HM15947)

**PEKING HERBAL & ACU CENTRE**

**Peking Herbal & Acupuncture Centre (The)**, 230 Streatham High Rd, London, **London (Greater)**, SW16 1BB, ENG.
(T) 020 8677 6066 (F) 020 8677 6066
Speciality: Acupuncture.
● **Manager** Mr Y Yao
O (**Ref:**HM15948)

**PELE, ANDRI**

**Andri Pele**, East London Homoeopathic Group Practice, 18 Martello St, London, **London (Greater)**, E8 3PE, ENG.
(T) 020 7241 2171
Speciality: Hypnotherapy.
B (**Ref:**HM15949)

**PELE, ANDRI**

**Ms Andri Pele**, 24 Rowden Rd, Beckenham, **Kent**, BR3 4NA, ENG.
(T) 020 8697 1749
Speciality: Counselling, Hypnotherapy, Psychotherapy. ✓
● **Hypnotherapist/Pyschotherapist**
Ms A Pele Q: Dip.Hyp, Dip.Psych.
C Yrs. Est.: 4 (**Ref:**HM15950)

**PELHAM, P H**

**P H Pelham**, 15 Ethelbert Rd, Canterbury, **Kent**, CT1 3ND, ENG.
(T) 01227 766797
Speciality: Herbalists.
● **Director** Mrs J Pelham
M (**Ref:**HM15951)

**PELL, KAREN**

**Karen Pell**, 16 Cromwells Meadow, Lichfield, **Staffordshire**, WS14 9EW, ENG.
(T) 01543 262704
Speciality: Reflexology.
● **Owner** Ms K Pell
S T (**Ref:**HM15952)

**PELLIN INSTITUTE**

**Pellin Institute**, 15 Killyon Rd, London, **London (Greater)**, SW8 2XS, ENG.
(T) 020 7720 4499
Speciality: Psychotherapy.
B (**Ref:**HM15953)

**PELLING, K**

**Miss K Pelling**, Trevone, 52 Copthorne Rd, Felbridge, East Grinstead, **Sussex (West)**, RH19 2NS, ENG.
(T) 01342 321526
Speciality: Osteopathy.
P S T (**Ref:**HM15954)

**PELLING, KAREN**

**Karen Pelling**, 77 Woodford Rd, London, **London (Greater)**, E18 2EA, ENG.
(T) 020 8532 2922 (F) 020 8989 4508
Speciality: Osteopathy.
● **Owner** Miss K Pelling
P S T (**Ref:**HM15955)

**PEMBERY, S**

**S Pembery**, 48 The Grove, St Margarets Rd, Twickenham, **London (Greater)**, TW1 1RB, ENG.
(T) 020 8744 1694
Speciality: Chiropodists (Podiatrists).
● **Owner** Ms S Pembery
S (**Ref:**HM15956)

**PEMBERY, SALLY**

**Sally Pembery**, Fairoak, Portsmouth Rd, Esher, **Surrey**, KT10 9PJ, ENG.
(T) 01372 460031
Speciality: Chiropodists (Podiatrists).
● **Owner** Ms S Pembery
S (**Ref:**HM15957)

**PEMBURY, SALLY**

**Sally Pembury**, Woodside House, Station Approach, Hinchley Wood, Esher, **Surrey**, KT10 0SR, ENG.
(T) 020 8398 7744 (F) 020 8398 9922
Speciality: Chiropodists (Podiatrists).
● **Owner** Mrs S Pembry
S (**Ref:**HM15958)

**PEN Y LON**

**Pen Y Lon**, The Barn, Clwyd St, Ruthin, **Denbighshire**, LL15 1HH, WAL.
(T) 01824 707738
Speciality: Physiotherapy.
● **Owner** Ms J Wilkinson
P S T (**Ref:**HM15959)

**PENACHE**

**Penache**, 8 Canons Drive, St. Johns Priory, Lechlade, **Gloucestershire**, GL7 3HP, ENG.
(T) 01367 252106
Speciality: Aromatherapy. ✓
● **Owner/Aromatherapist** Mrs S Astle
Q: Dip.Arom. M: IIHHT.
C Yrs. Est.: 3 (**Ref:**HM15960)

**PENARTH CHIROPRACTIC CLINIC**

**Penarth Chiropractic Clinic**, 32 Cornerswell Rd, Penarth, **Glamorgan (Vale of)**, CF64 2WA, WAL.
(T) 029 2070 0124
Speciality: Chiropractic, Manipulation, Massage (Therapeutic).
● **Owner/Chiropractor**
Mr B O'Donnell Q: DC, FCC, MMCA. M: CC, MCA.
● **Chiropractor** Maureen McIntosh Q: DC, FCC, MMCA. M: MCA.

Key: B Mind-Body Medicine C Complementary Medicine H Self Help Treatment M Medicinal Therapy O Oriental Medicine P Postural Therapy S Manipulative Structural Therapy T Touch Therapy

S Yrs. Est.: 10 (Ref:HM15961)

**PENARTH HOMEOPATHY CLINIC**
**D E Jenkins**, 149 Plymouth Rd, Penarth, **Glamorgan (Vale of)**, CF64 5DG, WAL.
(T) 029 2070 8967
Speciality: Homeopathy. ✓
● **Owner** Mr D Jenkins Q: BSc.
C Yrs. Est.: 16 (Ref:HM15962)

**PENDER, CHRISTINE**
**Christine Pender**, 63 Princes St, Cardiff, **Glamorgan (Vale of)**, CF24 3SL, WAL.
(T) 029 2049 3852
Speciality: Bach Remedies, Herbal Medicine.
M (Ref:HM15963)

**PENDER, CHRISTINE**
**Christine Pender**, 63 Princes St, Roath, Cardiff, **Glamorgan (Vale of)**, CF24 3SL, WAL.
(T) 029 2049 3852
Speciality: Bach Remedies.
M (Ref:HM15964)

**PENDERGAST, ANN**
**Pendergast Ann**, Betaghstown Cottage Betaghstow Clane, **County Kildare**, IRE.
(T) 08720 69642
Speciality: Complementary Medicines & Therapy.
M (Ref:HM15965)

**PENDERGAST, E A**
**E A Pendergast**, 43 Brynrhyg, Colwyn Bay, **Conwy**, LL29 6DP, WAL.
(T) 01492 531007
Speciality: Chiropodists (Podiatrists).
● **Owner** Mr E Pendergast
S (Ref:HM15966)

**PENDLE NATURAL HEALING CENTRE**
**Pendle Natural Healing Centre**, Unit 17, Colne Commercial Centre, Exchange St, Colne, **Lancashire**, BB8 0SQ, ENG.
(T) 01282 864154
Speciality: Hypnotherapy.
● **Director** Mr M Storey
B (Ref:HM15967)

**PENDLETON, LINDA**
**Linda Pendleton**, 166 Blaguegate Lane, Skelmersdale, **Lancashire**, WN8 8TY, ENG.
(T) 01695 727657
Speciality: Reflexology.
S T (Ref:HM15968)

**PENDRY, ANNA**
**Anna Pendry**, Queens Quay, 58 Upper Thames St, London, **London (Greater)**, EC4V 3EH, ENG.
(T) 020 7329 1282
Speciality: Hypnotherapy.
B (Ref:HM15969)

**PENDRY, BARBARA**
**Barbara Pendry BSc (Hons) MNIMH**, 2 Cavendish Rd, Barnet, **Hertfordshire**, EN5 4DZ, ENG.
(T) 020 8906 4841
Speciality: Herbal Medicine.
M (Ref:HM15970)

**PENFOLD, CHRISTINE**
**Christine Penfold**, 40 Green Dragon Lane, Brentford, **London (Greater)**, TW8 0EN, ENG.
(T) 020 8758 0323
Speciality: Reflexology.
S T (Ref:HM15971)

**PENFOLD, LYN**
**Lyn Penfold**, 29 St Annes Rd East, Lytham St. Annes, **Lancashire**, FY8 1TA, ENG.
(T) 01253 720464
Speciality: Reflexology.
S T (Ref:HM15972)

**PENFOLD, NICOLA**
**Nicola Penfold**, 52 Tanyard Way, Horley, **Surrey**, RH6 9PG, ENG.
(T) 01293 783547
Speciality: Complementary Medicines & Therapy.
C M (Ref:HM15973)

**PENGELLY, D W**
**D W Pengelly**, Pigmeadow Lane, Liskeard, **Cornwall**, PL14 6AT, ENG.
(T) 01579 344090
Speciality: Chiropodists (Podiatrists).
● **Owner** Mrs T Teasdale
S (Ref:HM15974)

**PENISTONE**
**Penistone**, Stoneleigh, High Bank, Thurlstone, Sheffield, **Yorkshire (South)**, S36 9QH, ENG.
(T) 01226 766139
Speciality: Homeopathy.
● **Owner** Mrs L Kenyon
M (Ref:HM15975)

**PENISTONE PHYSIO/CHIROP CTRE**
**Penistone Physiotherapy & Chiropody Centre**, 2-4 Bridge St, Penistone, Sheffield, **Yorkshire (South)**, S36 6AJ, ENG.
(T) 01226 761616
Speciality: Physiotherapy.
● **Owner** Ms J Ellingsworth
P S T (Ref:HM15976)

**PENMAN, ANNE**
**Penman Anne Laser Therapy**, 69 Main St, Blackrock, **County Dublin**, IRE.
(T) 01278 0028
Speciality: Complementary Medicines & Therapy.
M (Ref:HM15977)

**PENMAN, TONY**
**Tony Penman**, Newport Clinic Of Holistic Health, 36 Godfrey Rd, Newport, NP20 4PE, WAL.
(T) 01633 843333
Speciality: Complementary Medicines & Therapy.
● **Owner** Mr J Francis
M (Ref:HM15978)

**PENN CLINIC**
**Penn Clinic**, Hayes Cottage Hospital, Grange Rd, Hayes, **London (Greater)**, UB3 2RR, ENG.
(T) 020 8848 9457
Speciality: Osteopathy.
● **Practice Manager** Mr L Harris
P S T (Ref:HM15979)

**PENN COUNSELLING/PSYCHOTHERAPY**
**Penn Counselling & Psychotherapy**, 28 Carter Walk, Penn, High Wycombe, **Buckinghamshire**, HP10 8ER, ENG.
(T) 01494 814164
Speciality: Psychotherapy.
B (Ref:HM15980)

**PENN, CAROLINE M**
**Caroline M Penn**, 40 Crawford Rd, Hatfield, **Hertfordshire**, AL10 0PE, ENG.
(T) 01707 274148
Speciality: Osteopathy.
P S T (Ref:HM15981)

**PENN, D E**
**D E Penn**, Hayes Cottage Hospital, Grange Rd, Hayes, **London (Greater)**, UB3 2RR, ENG.
(T) 020 8848 9457
Speciality: Physiotherapy.
● **Practice Manager** Mr L Harris
P S T (Ref:HM15982)

**PENN, J T**
**Mrs J T Penn**, 213 York Rd, Southend-On-Sea, **Essex**, SS1 2RU, ENG.
(T) 01702 462191
Speciality: Hypnosis.
● **Owner** Mrs J Penn
B (Ref:HM15983)

**PENN, NICOLA**
**Nicola Penn**, 14 Fairhaven Rd, Redhill, **Surrey**, RH1 2LA, ENG.
(T) 01737 212372
Speciality: Osteopathy.
P S T (Ref:HM15984)

**PENNANT VALLEY**
**Pennant Valley**, Herberdeg Rd, Pontyates, Llanelli, **Carmarthenshire**, SA15 5UR, WAL.
(T) 01269 861707 (F) 01269 861707
Speciality: Aromatherapy.
● **Owner** Mr P Bowen
M O (Ref:HM15985)

**PENNEFATHER, R J**
**R J Pennefather**, By Ways, Altwood Cl, Maidenhead, **Berkshire**, SL6 4PP, ENG.
(T) 01628 635807
Speciality: Osteopathy.
P S T (Ref:HM15986)

**PENNINE INS-PSYCHOTHERAPY**
**Pennine Institute Of Psychotherapy**, 27 Clare Rd, Halifax, **Yorkshire (West)**, HX1 2WQ, ENG.
(T) 01422 366356
Speciality: Psychotherapy.
B (Ref:HM15987)

**PENNINE NATURAL HEALING CENTRE**
**Pennine Natural Healing Centre**, 13 Burnley Rd, Luddendenfoot, Halifax, **Yorkshire (West)**, HX2 6AA, ENG.
(T) 01422 882791
Speciality: Complementary Medicines & Therapy.
C M (Ref:HM15988)

**PENNINGTON, BERNARD**
**Bernard Pennington**, 27A Peartree Way, Elm, Wisbech, **Cambridgeshire**, PE14 0BS, ENG.
(T) 01945 860429
Speciality: Chiropodists (Podiatrists).
● **Owner** Mr B Pennington
S (Ref:HM15989)

**PENNINGTON, PAM**
**Pam Pennington**, St Chiropractic Clinic, 74A High St, Street, **Somerset**, BA16 0EN, ENG.
(T) 01458 840490
Speciality: Chiropody, Podiatry. ✓
● **Chiropodist (Podiatrist)** Ms P Pennington
C M Yrs. Est.: 15 (Ref:HM15990)

**PENNINGTON, PAM V**
**Pam V Pennington**, South View, Lower New Rd, Cheddar, **Somerset**, BS27 3DZ, ENG.
(T) 01934 744161
Speciality: Chiropody, Podiatry. ✓
● **Owner/Chiropodist** Mrs P Pennington Q: M.S.C.P, MBChA, MSSCh.
M Yrs. Est.: 15 (Ref:HM15991)

**PENNINGTON, ZIGGY**
**Ziggy Pennington**, 2 Town Hall Rd, Havant, **Hampshire**, PO9 1AN, ENG.
(T) 023 9248 3316
Speciality: Electrolysis.
● **Owner** Mrs Z Pennington
T (Ref:HM15992)

**PENNY**
**Penny**, 12 Hornby Rd, Liverpool, **Merseyside**, L9 3DD, ENG.
(T) 01515 255925
Speciality: Clairvoyants & Palmists.
B (Ref:HM15993)

**PENNY, BARBARA**
**Barbara Penny**, 31 Danefield Trce, Otley, **Yorkshire (West)**, LS21 1HU, ENG.
(T) 01943 461730
Speciality: Reflexology.
● **Owner** Mrs B Penny
S T (Ref:HM15994)

**PENNY, NICOLA**
**Nicola Penny**, 105 Havelock Rd, Brighton, **Sussex (East)**, BN1 6GL, ENG.
(T) 01273 565212
Speciality: Physiotherapy.
● **Senior Partner** Mrs S Foulds
P S T (Ref:HM15995)

**PENNYCOOK, AMANDA**
**Amanda Pennycook**, Edleston Clinic, 68 Edleston Rd, Crewe, **Cheshire**, CW2 7HD, ENG.
(T) 01270 251484
Speciality: Biomechanics, Chiropody. ✓
● **Owner/Chiropodist** Mrs A Pennycook Q: M.S.C.P, S.R.Ch.
M Yrs. Est.: 11 (Ref:HM15996)

**PENNY'S PEDICURE PARLOUR**
**Penny's Pedicure Parlour**, 279 Blackmoorfoot Rd, Huddersfield, **Yorkshire (West)**, HD4 5RL, ENG.



Key continued: Yrs.Est: Years Established Q: Qualifications M: Professional Membership ✓ Indemnity Insurance Accept Credit Cards

(T) 01484 460491
Speciality: Chiropodists (Podiatrists).
● **Owner** Mrs P Reeves
S (Ref:HM15997)

## PENWARDEN, DAVID
**David Penwarden**, 66 Amberley Gardens, Epsom, **Surrey**, KT19 0NG, ENG.
(T) 020 8394 0704
Speciality: Osteopathy.
● **Owner** Mr D Penwarden
P S T (Ref:HM15998)

## PENWARDEN, DAVID
**Mr David Penwarden**, 18 Warren Avenue, Sutton, **Surrey**, SM2 7QL, ENG.
(T) 020 8642 6639 (F) 020 8642 6639
Speciality: Osteopathy.
● **Owner** Mr D Penwarden
P S T (Ref:HM15999)

## PENWARDEN, F
**Mrs F Penwarden**, 18 Warren Avenue, Sutton, **Surrey**, SM2 7QL, ENG.
(T) 020 8642 6639 (F) 020 8642 6639
Speciality: Homeopathy.
● **Owner** Mr D Penwarden
M (Ref:HM16000)

## PENWETHERS HOLISTIC CARE CTRE
**Penwethers Holistic Care Centre Ltd**, 57 Killerton Rd, Bude, **Cornwall**, EX23 8EW, ENG.
(T) 01288 354256 (F) 01288 354256
Speciality: Complementary Medicines & Therapy.
● **Director** Dr L Bowden
M (Ref:HM16001)

## PENWORTHAM CHIROPODY SERVICE
**Penwortham Chiropody Service**, 36C Liverpool Rd, Penwortham, Preston, **Lancashire**, PR1 0DQ, ENG.
(T) 01772 751750
Speciality: Chiropodists (Podiatrists).
● **Owner** Mrs P Broughton
S (Ref:HM16002)

## PEN-Y-BRYN HOLISTIC THERAPY
**Pen-Y-Bryn Holistic Therapy Clinic**, 5 Liverpool Rd, Ashton-In-Makerfield, Wigan, **Lancashire**, WN4 0YT, ENG.
(T) 01942 728956
Speciality: Aromatherapy, Healing Therapy, Hopi Ear Candles, Indian Head Massage, Kinesiology, Massage (Therapeutic), Reflexology, Reiki, Remedial Massage, Stress Therapy, Sports Therapy, Personal Fitness Training.
C (Ref:HM16003)

## PENYLAN CLINIC
**Penylan Clinic Of Natural Health**, 70 Colchester Avenue, Penylan, Cardiff, **Glamorgan (Vale of)**, CF23 9AZ, WAL.
(T) 029 2049 3756
Speciality: Complementary Medicines & Therapy.
● **Owner** Mrs N Sandhu
C M (Ref:HM16004)

## PENYLAN PODIATRIC CENTRE
**Penylan Podiatric Centre (The)**, 63 Waterloo Rd, Penylan, Cardiff, **Glamorgan (Vale of)**, CF23 9BL, WAL.
(T) 029 2048 2383
Speciality: Aromatherapy, Biomechanics, Chiropody, Nail Surgery, Physiotherapy, Podiatry. ✔ CREDIT
● **Chiropodist (Podiatrist)**
Mr S Coombe Q: DPodM, MSc, S.R.Ch. M: S.C.P.
● **Chiropodist (Podiatrist)**
Mr D Thomas Q: DPodM, S.R.Ch. M: S.C.P.
M Yrs. Est.: 10 (Ref:HM16005)

## PENZANCE NATURAL HEALTH CENTRE
**Penzance Natural Health Centre**, 5 Morrab Rd, Penzance, **Cornwall**, TR18 4EL, ENG.
(T) 01736 360522
Speciality: Acupuncture, Alexander Technique, Aromatherapy, Bach Remedies, Counselling, Cranial Osteopathy, Healer, Herbal Medicine, Homeopathy, Hypnosis, Indian Head Massage, Massage (Therapeutic), Meditation, Psychotherapy, Reflexology, Reiki, Shiatsu, Spiritual Healing. ✔
● **Co-ordinator** Mrs C Savage
● **Medical Herbalist** Mrs N Green M: NIMH.
C Yrs. Est.: 18 (Ref:HM16006)

## PEOPLE CONSULTING
**People Consulting Ltd**, 19 Brandreth Rd, London, **London (Greater)**, SW17 8ER, ENG.
(T) 020 8672 2174 (F) 020 8672 2174
Speciality: Psychology.
B (Ref:HM16007)

## PEOPLEWISE
**Peoplewise**, 1 Bellevue Rd, London, **London (Greater)**, SW13 0BJ, ENG.
(T) 020 8876 7382 (F) 020 8876 7082
Speciality: Psychology.
● **Director** Mrs L Board
B (Ref:HM16008)

## PEPPER, JOHN
**John Pepper Change & Stress Management**, Flat One, 2 Laurel Bank, Lancaster, **Lancashire**, LA1 5LN, ENG.
(T) 01524 60157 (F) 01524 60157
Speciality: Counselling, Healer, Life Style Coaching, Meditation, Psychotherapy, Rogerian Therapy, Spiritual Healing, Stress Therapy, Visualisation Therapy. ✔
● **Counsellor/Healer** Mr J Pepper
Q: Dip.Adv.Couns, MNFSH. M: BACP, NFSH.
M Yrs. Est.: 5 (Ref:HM16009)

## PEPPER, SUSAN
**Susan Pepper**, 57 Hazeldene Rd, Goodmayes, Ilford, **Essex**, IG3 9RA, ENG.
(T) 020 8599 6979
Speciality: Alexander Technique. ✔
● **Teacher of the Alexander Technique**
Ms S Pepper Q: MSTAT. M: STAT.
P Yrs. Est.: 17 (Ref:HM16010)

## PEPPLER, EILEEN
**Eileen Peppler**, 18 Anstey Cl, Waddesdon, Aylesbury, **Buckinghamshire**, HP18 0NB, ENG.
(T) 01296 658798
Speciality: Aromatherapy.
M O (Ref:HM16011)

## PERCEPTION BUSINESS PSYCHOL
**Perception Business Psychologists**, Faircross, 1 North Rd, Gloucester, **Gloucestershire**, GL1 3JX, ENG.
(T) 01452 303319 (F) 01452 533660
Speciality: Psychology.
B (Ref:HM16012)

## PERCIVAL, A A
**A A Percival**, 6 First Avenue, Havant, **Hampshire**, PO9 2QN, ENG.
(T) 023 9245 4393
Speciality: Chiropodists (Podiatrists).
S (Ref:HM16013)

## PERCIVAL, ANN
**Ann Percival**, Cheltenham, **Gloucestershire**, GL52, ENG.
(T) 01242 221526
Speciality: Bach Remedies.
M (Ref:HM16014)

## PERCIVAL, C
**C Percival**, The Surgery, 4 York Rd, Exeter, **Devon**, EX4 6PQ, ENG.
(T) 01392 254385
Speciality: Chiropodists (Podiatrists).
S (Ref:HM16015)

## PERCIVAL, JO
**Jo Percival**, 8 Stanhope Gardens, London, **London (Greater)**, NW7 2JD, ENG.
(T) 020 8906 4623
Speciality: Homeopathy.
● **Owner** Mrs J Percival
M (Ref:HM16016)

## PERCIVAL, PAMELA
**Pamela Percival**, 14 Palmerston Rd, Shanklin, **Isle of Wight**, PO37 6AS, ENG.
(T) 01983 862347
Speciality: Hypnosis.
B (Ref:HM16017)

## PERCIVAL, R W & H A
**R W & H A Percival**, 24 Chatburn Rd, Clitheroe, **Lancashire**, BB7 2AP, ENG.
(T) 01200 424901
Speciality: Osteopathy.
P S T (Ref:HM16018)

## PEREIRA, L
**L Pereira**, 12 Market Sq, Horsham, **Sussex (West)**, RH12 1EU, ENG.
(T) 01403 252228
Speciality: Osteopathy.
● **Senior Partner** Mr K Beckwith
P S T (Ref:HM16019)

## PERELES, JUDE
**Jude Pereles**, 10 Wenning Avenue, Bentham, Lancaster, **Lancashire**, LA2 7LR, ENG.
(T) 01524 261750
Speciality: Complementary Medicines & Therapy.
● **Owner** Mrs J Pereles
M (Ref:HM16020)

## PERFECT OILS
**Perfect Oils**, Treetops, Rayners Avenue, Loudwater, High Wycombe, **Buckinghamshire**, HP10 9SN, ENG.
(T) 01494 815003
Speciality: Aromatherapy.
● **Owner** Mrs J Perfect
M O (Ref:HM16021)

## PERFECT, CATHY
**Cathy Perfect**, Unit 8, Coldart Business Centre, 3 King Edward Avenue, Dartford, **Kent**, DA1 2HZ, ENG.
(T) 01322 294442
Speciality: Complementary Medicines & Therapy.
● **Owner** Miss C Perfect
M (Ref:HM16022)

## PERFORMANCE PHYSIOTHERAPY
**Performance Physiotherapy**, Richmond Athletic Ground, Kew Foot Rd, Richmond, **Surrey**, TW9 2SS, ENG.
(T) 020 8332 2467
Speciality: Physiotherapy.
● **Owner** Mrs M Pearson
P S T (Ref:HM16023)

## PERICLEOUS, CHRISTINE
**Christine Pericleous**, 47 Ecclesbourne Gdns, London, **London (Greater)**, N13 5JD, ENG.
(T) 020 8372 8760
Speciality: Psychotherapy.
● **Owner** Ms C Pericleous
B (Ref:HM16024)

## PERINGER, EVA
**Eva Peringer**, 23 St. Marys St, Bridgnorth, **Shropshire**, WV16 4DW, ENG.
(T) 01746 768196
Speciality: Complementary Medicines & Therapy.
M (Ref:HM16025)

## PERKINS, L
**L Perkins**, 29 King George Rd, Minehead, **Somerset**, TA24 5JD, ENG.
(T) 01643 702685
Speciality: Chiropody. ✔
● **Chiropodist** L Perkins Q: DPodM, M.S.C.P.
C Yrs. Est.: 22 (Ref:HM16026)

## PERKINS, SYBIL
**Sybil Perkins**, 2a Tudor Way, Uxbridge, **London (Greater)**, UB10 9AB, ENG.
(T) 01895 239966
Speciality: Electrolysis.
● **Owner** Mrs S Perkins
T (Ref:HM16027)

## PERKS, R
**R Perks**, 76 St John St, Lichfield, **Staffordshire**, WS14 9DX, ENG.
(T) 01543 268044
Speciality: Acupuncture.
O (Ref:HM16028)

## PERLMAN, M (DR)
**Dr M Perlman**, 3 Wellington Rd, Bournemouth, **Dorset**, BH8 8AD, ENG.
(T) 01202 557170 (F) 01202 296047
Speciality: Chiropractors.

● **Owner** Mr D Perlman
P S T (Ref:HM16029)

## PERMA-JEUNE
**Perma-Jeune Ltd**, 45 Mortimer St, London, **London (Greater)**, W1N 7TD, ENG.
(T) 020 7580 6900 (F) 020 7580 5538
Speciality: Complementary Medicines & Therapy.
M (Ref:HM16030)

## PERPETUAL INNOVATIONS
**Perpetual Innovations**, Lodge House, Lodge Sq, Cow Lane, Burnley, **Lancashire**, BB11 1NN, ENG.
(T) 01282 459494 (F) 01282 459001
Speciality: Complementary Medicines & Therapy.
● **Director** Mr D Shaw
C M (Ref:HM16031)

## PERRET, NICOLE
**Nicole Perret**, 577 Dunstable Rd, Luton, **Bedfordshire**, LU4 8QW, ENG.
(T) 01582 575045
Speciality: Osteopathy.
P S T (Ref:HM16032)

## PERRET, NICOLE (DR)
**Dr Nicole Perret**, Lisieux Way, Taunton, **Somerset**, TA1 2LB, ENG.
(T) 01823 259444 (F) 01823 322715
Speciality: Osteopathy.
● **Practice Manager** Mrs G Berriman
P S T (Ref:HM16033)

## PERRETT, J R
**J R Perrett**, 1492 Greenford Rd, Greenford, **London (Greater)**, UB6 0HP, ENG.
(T) 020 8422 5785
Speciality: Chiropodists (Podiatrists).
S (Ref:HM16034)

## PERRIN & ASSOCIATES
**Raymond N Perrin & Associates**, 11 St John St, Manchester, **Manchester (Greater)**, M3 4DW, ENG.
(T) 01617 730123
Speciality: Osteopathy.
P S T (Ref:HM16035)

## PERRIN, M
**M Perrin**, Bramble Chine, Charterhouse Rd, Godalming, **Surrey**, GU7 2AT, ENG.
(T) 01483 424544
Speciality: Physiotherapy.
● **Owner** Mrs M Perrin
P S T (Ref:HM16036)

## PERRINA, MARIE
**Marie Perrina**, 8 Grenville Rd, London, **London (Greater)**, N19 4EH, ENG.
(T) 020 7263 4841
Speciality: Reflexology.
S T (Ref:HM16037)

## PERRINS, JOSEPH
**Joseph Perrins**, 9 Stonehills Mansions, 8 Streatham High Rd, London, **London (Greater)**, SW16 1DD, ENG.
(T) 020 8769 2118
Speciality: Hypnosis.
● **Owner** Mr J Perrins
B (Ref:HM16038)

## PERRY
**Mr Perry**, 17 Hellesdon Rd, Norwich, **Norfolk**, NR6 5EB, ENG.
(T) 01603 630103
Speciality: Hypnosis.
B (Ref:HM16039)

## PERRY, ALICIA
**Alicia Perry**, 175 The Fairway, Kings Norton, Birmingham, **Midlands (West)**, B38 8YN, ENG.
(T) 01214 591359
Speciality: Reflexology.
S T (Ref:HM16040)

## PERRY, DANIEL L
**Daniel L Perry**, 212 Preston Rd, Wembley, **London (Greater)**, HA9 8PB, ENG.
(T) 020 8904 3334
Speciality: Chiropodists (Podiatrists).
S (Ref:HM16041)

## PERRY, DANIEL L
**Daniel L Perry**, 90 Battersea Rise, London, **London (Greater)**, SW11 1EJ, ENG.
(T) 020 7223 4437
Speciality: Chiropodists (Podiatrists).
S (Ref:HM16042)

## PERRY, ELAINE
**Elaine Perry**, 16 Runnemede Rd, Egham, **Surrey**, TW20 9BD, ENG.
(T) 01784 433891
Speciality: Reflexology.
S T (Ref:HM16043)

## PERRY, JANET
**Janet Perry**, The Llwyn, Clun, Craven Arms, **Shropshire**, SY7 8NB, ENG.
(T) 01588 640749
Speciality: Alexander Technique.
P S (Ref:HM16044)

## PERRY, JANET
**Janet Perry**, Chapel House, 16 Old St, Ludlow, **Shropshire**, SY8 1NP, ENG.
(T) 01584 876153
Speciality: Alexander Technique.
● **Owner** Mr J Shelton
P S (Ref:HM16045)

## PERRY, JEAN
**Jean Perry**, 19 Hall Cl, Stanford-Le-Hope, **Essex**, SS17 8HJ, ENG.
(T) 01375 675945
Speciality: Hypnosis.
● **Owner** Ms J Perry
B (Ref:HM16046)

## PERRY, JEAN
**Jean Perry**, 15 York Cres, Loughton, **Essex**, IG10 1RW, ENG.
(T) 020 8508 2770
Speciality: Reflexology.
S T (Ref:HM16047)

## PERRY, JUDITH
**Judith Perry**, 17 Bramley Avenue, Upper Halliford Rd, Shepperton, **Surrey**, TW17 8TF, ENG.
(T) 01932 781836
Speciality: Homeopathy.
● **Owner** Mrs J Perry
M (Ref:HM16048)

## PERRY, KAREN
**Karen Perry**, 49 Bush Spring, Baldock, **Hertfordshire**, SG7 6QT, ENG.
(T) 01462 895789
Speciality: Chiropody. ✓
● **Owner/Chiropodist** Mrs K Perry Q: MBChA, MSSCh. M: B.A.Ch.P, SSCh.
S Yrs. Est.: 4 (Ref:HM16049)

## PERRY, L
**L Perry**, 54 Lawrence Avenue, New Malden, **Surrey**, KT3 5NA, ENG.
(T) 020 8337 7500 (F) 020 8337 6777
Speciality: Complementary Medicines & Therapy.
● **Owner** Ms L Perry
C M (Ref:HM16050)

## PERRY, SJ & GRACE, B
**Perry Stephen J & Grace Barbara**, 53 Longcroft Lane, Welwyn Garden City, **Hertfordshire**, AL8 6EB, ENG.
(T) 01707 334902
Speciality: Osteopathy.
P S T (Ref:HM16051)

## PERRY, VIC
**Vic Perry**, 9 Highgrove Drive, Chellaston, Derby, **Derbyshire**, DE73 1XA, ENG.
(T) 01332 701448
Speciality: Aromatherapy.
M O (Ref:HM16052)

## PERSAD, ROBI
**Robi Persad**, Clissold Park Health Centre, 154 Stoke Newington Church St, London, **London (Greater)**, N16 0JU, ENG.
(T) 020 7249 2990 (F) 020 7249 3977
Speciality: Osteopathy.
● **Owner** Mr D Berg
P S T (Ref:HM16053)

## PERSAD, ROBI
**Robi Persad**, 14 Patshull Rd, London, **London (Greater)**, NW5 2LB, ENG.
(T) 020 7209 3243
Speciality: Osteopathy.
P S T (Ref:HM16054)

## PERSAUD, PENNEY & PARTNERS
**Penney Persaud & Partners**, The Surgery, 73 Brougham St, Skipton, **Yorkshire (North)**, BD23 2HD, ENG.
(T) 01756 792610
Speciality: Osteopathy.
P S T (Ref:HM16055)

## PERSHORE
**Pershore**, Crown House, 2 Church Row, Pershore, **Worcestershire**, WR10 1BL, ENG.
(T) 01386 561951
Speciality: Homeopathy.
M (Ref:HM16056)

## PERSHORE NAT THERAPY CLINIC
**Pershore Natural Therapy Clinic**, 24C Broad St, Pershore, **Worcestershire**, WR10 1AY, ENG.
(T) 01386 552874
Speciality: Acupuncture, Aromatherapy, Bach Remedies, Cupping, Herbal Medicine, Homeopathy, Hypnotherapy, Indian Head Massage, Kinesiology, Moxibustion, Reflexology, Reiki, Spiritual Healing, Emotional Therapy. ✓
● **Homeopath** Ms R Hermolle Q: LCPH.
● **Reflexologist** Ms L Long
(T) 01242 604609 Q: A.I.P.T.I, ITEC. M: GCP.
● **Kinesiologist** Chris Robinson Q: BA, KFRP, PGCE.
● **Holistic Therapist** Jaki Allen
(T) 01386 710678 Q: ITEC.
C Yrs. Est.: 5 (Ref:HM16057)

## PERSHORE PHYSIOTHERAPY CLINIC
**Pershore Physiotherapy Clinic**, Allesborough Farm, Allesborough Hill, Pershore, **Worcestershire**, WR10 2AB, ENG.
(T) 01386 555551
Speciality: Physiotherapy.
P S T (Ref:HM16058)

## PERSON TO PERSON
**Person To Person**, 5 Mountside, Stanmore, **London (Greater)**, HA7 2DS, ENG.
(T) 020 8422 8045
Speciality: Psychotherapy.
B (Ref:HM16059)

## PERSONAL READINGS
**Personal Readings**, 142 Richmond Rd, Accrington, **Lancashire**, BB5 0JN, ENG.
(T) 01254 394338
Speciality: Clairvoyants & Palmists.
● **Owner** Mrs M Cowell
B (Ref:HM16060)

## PERSONAL REFLECTIONS
**Personal Reflections Ltd**, 21 Bucklersbury, Hitchin, **Hertfordshire**, SG5 1BG, ENG.
(T) 01462 630301 (F) 01462 630302
(E) amandawatkin@personal-reflections.co.uk
(W) www.personal-reflections.co.uk
Speciality: Absent Healing, Aromatherapy, Complementary Therapy, Counselling, Crystal Healing, Dowsing, Healer, Healing Therapy, Holistic Healing, Indian Head Massage, Meditation, Reflexology, Reiki, Spiritual Healing, Stress Therapy, Swedish Body Massage, Personal Development Workshops, Person Centered Counselling, Career & Life Strategies. ✓
● **Therapist** Valerie Thompson M: IIHHT.
● **Therapist** Jenny Sheach M: IIHHT.
● **Director/Therapist**
Miss A Watkins Q: IIHHT, MAR, Reiki Master. M: AoR, FHT.
● **Director/Counsellor** Ms E Webber
B C Yrs. Est.: 2 (Ref:HM16061)

## PERSONAL/RELATIONSHIP THERAPY
**Personal & Relationship Therapy**, 12 Springfield Rd, Kingston Upon Thames, **Surrey**, KT1 2SA, ENG.
(T) 020 8549 2334
Speciality: Psychotherapy.
B (Ref:HM16062)



Key continued: Yrs.Est: Years Established Q: Qualifications M: Professional Membership ✓ Indemnity Insurance Accept Credit Cards

**PERSONNEL DECISIONS INT UK**

**Personnel Decisions International UK Ltd**, Dalkeith House, 7 Clarendon Pl, Leamington Spa, **Warwickshire**, CV32 5QL, ENG.
(T) 01926 334114
Speciality: Psychology.
● **Financial Director**
John Gamble Tynan
B (Ref:HM16063)

**PERSPECTIVES CLINIC**

**Complementary Therapies At Perspectives Clinic**, 68 Campfield Rd, St. Albans, **Hertfordshire**, AL1 5HZ, ENG.
(T) 01727 861441
Speciality: Complementary Medicines & Therapy.
● **Partner** Miss M Ciaccio
C M (Ref:HM16064)

**PERTH & KINROSS N H S TRUST**

**Perth & Kinross N H S Trust**, Chiropody Ladywalk Clinic, Ladywalk, Anstruther, **Fife**, KY10 3EX, SCO.
(T) 01333 312595
Speciality: Chiropodists (Podiatrists).
● **Manager** Mr C Parton
S (Ref:HM16065)

**PERTH BACK PAIN CLINIC**

**Perth Back Pain Clinic**, 137 Glasgow Rd, Perth, **Perth and Kinross**, PH2 0LU, SCO.
(T) 01738 626833
Speciality: Physiotherapy.
● **Owner** Mr P Murrie
P S T (Ref:HM16066)

**PERTH CHIRO & OSTEO CENTRE**

**Perth Chiropractic & Osteopathic Centre**, The Lodge, Osla Rd, Perth, **Perth and Kinross**, PH2 7HG, SCO.
(T) 01738 442012 (F) 01738 445645
Speciality: Chiropractic.
● **Owner** Dr D Lennyhan
P S T (Ref:HM16067)

**PERTH, F**

**F Perth**, Vicarage Rd, Newmarket, **Suffolk**, CB8 8HP, ENG.
(T) 01638 561680
Speciality: Chiropractic.
P S T (Ref:HM16068)

**PESTER, ROSLYN**

**Roslyn Pester**, 22 Elgin Rd, Bournemouth, **Dorset**, BH4 9NL, ENG.
(T) 01202 751755
Speciality: Electrolysis.
● **Owner** Mrs R Pester
T (Ref:HM16069)

**PETCH, MARIAN**

**Marian Petch**, Glenshee, 3 Mile Bridge, Great North Rd, Gosforth, Newcastle Upon Tyne, **Tyne and Wear**, NE3 2DS, ENG.
(T) 01912 843334
Speciality: Reflexology.
S T (Ref:HM16070)

**PETER & CAROLINE**

**Peter Bland & Caroline Allington**, 3 Burnivale, Malmesbury, **Wiltshire**, SN16 0BL, ENG.
(T) 01666 829293
Speciality: Absent Healing, Acupressure, Aromatherapy, Art Therapy, Aura Therapy, Colour Therapy, Complementary Therapy, Counselling, Healer, Healing Therapy, Holistic Healing, Massage (Therapeutic), Meditation, Music Therapy, Nutritional Therapy, Spiritual Healing, Vibrational Therapy, Visualisation Therapy.
● **Complementary Therapist**
Ms C Allington Q: BSc, MA. M: ARMT.
● **Psychic/Healer** Mr P Bland
B Yrs. Est.: 18 (Ref:HM16071)

**PETER PSYCHIC CLAIRVOYANT**

**Peter Psychic Clairvoyant**, 41 Court Way, Twickenham, **London (Greater)**, TW2 7SA, ENG.
(T) 020 8892 7794
Speciality: Clairvoyants & Palmists.
B (Ref:HM16073)

**PETER SADLER NATURAL MED CTRE**

**Peter Sadler Natural Medicine Centre**, Lullington Rd, Rosliston, Swadlincote, **Derbyshire**, DE12 8HZ, ENG.
(T) 01283 760522 (F) 01283 760522
Speciality: Osteopathy.
● **Owner** Mr P Sadler
P S T (Ref:HM16074)

**PETER STREET CLINIC**

**Peter Street Clinic**, 4 Peter St, Workington, **Cumbria**, CA14 3DA, ENG.
(T) 01900 607300
Speciality: Chiropody. ✔
● **Owner** Mrs L Urwin Q: MSSCh.
S Yrs. Est.: 12 (Ref:HM16075)

**PETER THERAPEUTIC MASSEUR**

**Peter Therapeutic Masseur**, 38 Harrogate Rd, Caversham, Reading, **Berkshire**, RG4 7PN, ENG.
(T) 01189 470623
Speciality: Complementary Medicines & Therapy.
C M (Ref:HM16076)

**PETER WANLESS & BETTY HOLTROP**

**Peter Wanless & Betty Anne Holtrop**, Flat 1, 170 Goldhurst Trce, London, **London (Greater)**, NW6 3HN, ENG.
(T) 020 7328 7641
Speciality: Psychotherapy.
B (Ref:HM16077)

**PETER, CURRAN**

**Curran Peter**, Creevaghbeg Quin, **County Clare**, IRE.
(T) 06568 25801
Speciality: Complementary Medicines & Therapy.
M (Ref:HM16078)

**PETER, MARTIN**

**Martin Peter**, 11 Nightingale Way, Midsomer Norton, Bath, **Somerset**, BA3 4NL, ENG.
(T) 01761 419299
Speciality: Chiropodists (Podiatrists).
S (Ref:HM16079)

**PETERPAN & TINKERBELL**

**Peterpan & Tinkerbell**, 8 Abbotshill Pk, Totnes Rd, Abbotskerswell, Newton Abbot, **Devon**, TQ12 5NG, ENG.
(T) 01626 362514 (F) 01626 362514
Speciality: Hypnosis.
● **Partner** Mr S Gibbons
B (Ref:HM16080)

**PETERS, A J**

**A J Peters**, 99 Horseshoe Lane East, Guildford, **Surrey**, GU1 2TW, ENG.
(T) 01483 570921
Speciality: Osteopathy.
● **Owner** A Peters
P S T (Ref:HM16081)

**PETERS, CAROL**

**Carol Peters**, 16 Lyndale Rd, Redhill, **Surrey**, RH1 2HA, ENG.
(T) 01737 761671
Speciality: Hypnosis.
● **Owner** Mrs C Peters
B (Ref:HM16082)

**PETERS, CAROLINE**

**Caroline Peters**, 79 The St, West Horsley, Leatherhead, **Surrey**, KT24 6BG, ENG.
(T) 01483 283717 (F) 01483 281287
Speciality: Complementary Medicines & Therapy.
● **Owner** Mrs C Peters
M (Ref:HM16083)

**PETERS, DAVID (DR)**

**Dr David Peters**, 17 Marylebone Rd, London, **London (Greater)**, NW1 4PR, ENG.
(T) 020 7935 6328
Speciality: Homeopathy.
M (Ref:HM16084)

**PETERS, EVERARD**

**Everard Peters - Osteopath/Alexander Technique**, 16 Avenue Rd, Leamington Spa, **Warwickshire**, CV31 3PQ, ENG.
(T) 01926 338168
Speciality: Alexander Technique, Cranial Osteopathy, Osteopathy. ✔
● **Osteopath/Alexander Teacher**
Mr E Peters Q: BSc, DO, MSTAT. M: GOsC, STAT.
P S Yrs. Est.: 22 (Ref:HM16085)

**PETERS, JEAN**

**Jean Peters**, 47 Ditton Rd, Datchet, Slough, **Berkshire**, SL3 9LJ, ENG.
(T) 01753 582522
Speciality: Aromatherapy, Chiropody, Massage (Therapeutic), Podiatry, Reflexology, Reiki, Shiatsu. ✔
● **Chiropodist (Podiatrist)**
Mrs J Peters Q: BSc (Hons), DPodM. M: ITEC.
C M Yrs. Est.: 6 (Ref:HM16086)

**PETERS, KAREN**

**Karen Peters**, 54 High St, West Mersea, Colchester, **Essex**, CO5 8JE, ENG.
(T) 01206 384862
Speciality: Chiropodists (Podiatrists).
● **Practice Manager** Mr J Parr
S (Ref:HM16087)

**PETERS, LIN**

**Lin Peters**, Flat 21, The Alexandra, 32-35 Eversfield Pl, St. Leonards-On-Sea, **Sussex (East)**, TN37 6QP, ENG.
(T) 01424 424376
Speciality: Osteopathy.
● **Owner** Mrs L Peters
P S T (Ref:HM16088)

**PETERS, MATTHEW**

**Matthew Peters**, Alva House, Valley Drive, Marling Cross, Gravesend, **Kent**, DA12 5UE, ENG.
(T) 01474 331120
Speciality: Osteopathy.
P S T (Ref:HM16089)

**PETHER, ANNE**

**Anne Pether**, Tower Hill Farm House, Tower Hill Drive, Costessey, Norwich, **Norfolk**, NR8 5AX, ENG.
(T) 01603 745215
Speciality: Reflexology.
S T (Ref:HM16090)

**PETLEY, KIRSTIE**

**Kirstie Petley**, 4 Ham Lane, Gosport, **Hampshire**, PO12 4AN, ENG.
(T) 023 9279 6541
Speciality: Physiotherapy.
P S T (Ref:HM16091)

**PETRAMAN, FRANCOISE**

**Francoise Petraman**, Arc-En-Ciel, 2 Fieldside, High St, West Lavington, Devizes, **Wiltshire**, SN10 4HQ, ENG.
(T) 01380 813406
Speciality: Reflexology.
S T (Ref:HM16092)

**PETT, DIANA**

**Diana Pett**, 2 Hankham St, Hankham, Pevensey, **Sussex (East)**, BN24 5BG, ENG.
(T) 01323 766766
Speciality: Homeopathy.
● **Owner** Mr S Pett
M (Ref:HM16093)

**PETTER, C**

**C Petter**, 1st Floor, 20 Lavant St, Petersfield, **Hampshire**, GU32 3EW, ENG.
(T) 01730 231655
Speciality: Osteopathy.
P S T (Ref:HM16094)

**PETTIFER, JUSTINA**

**Justina Pettifer**, 2 Shelburne Rd, Calne, **Wiltshire**, SN11 8EW, ENG.
(T) 01249 811024
(E) justina@zeronet.co.uk
Speciality: Aromatherapy, Aversion Therapy, Cognitive Therapy, Counselling, Gestalt Therapy, Humanistic Psychology, Hypnosis, Hypnotherapy, Life Style Coaching, Psychotherapy, Reiki, Shiatsu, Stress Therapy. ✔
● **Shiatsu Practitioner/Aromatherapist**
Comfort Q: Dip.Shiatsu, ITEC. M: IPTI.
● **Hypnotherapist/Hypno-Psychotherapist**
Ms J Pettifer Q: Dip.Hyp. M: NRHP.
B H Yrs. Est.: 3 (Ref:HM16095)

**PETTIGREW, MICHAEL**

**Michael Pettigrew**, 244 Ramsgreave Drive, Blackburn, **Lancashire**, BB1 8RW, ENG.
(T) 01254 245215
Speciality: Physiotherapy.
P S T (Ref:HM16096)

**PETTIGREW, N**

**N Pettigrew**, 38 Cardwell Rd, Gourock, **Inverclyde**, PA19 1UH, SCO.
(T) 01475 632028
Speciality: Homeopathy.
● **Manager** Mr N Pettigrew
M (Ref:HM16097)

**PETTIT, M J**

**M J Pettit**, Westbrook House, 30 High St, Stanford-Le-Hope, **Essex**, SS17 0HQ, ENG.
(T) 01375 673671
Speciality: Physiotherapy.
P S T (Ref:HM16098)

**PETTMAN, JENNIFER**

**Jennifer Pettman**, Fishers Farm, Fontridge Lane, Etchingham, **Sussex (East)**, TN19 7DD, ENG.
(T) 01580 819421
Speciality: Complementary Medicines & Therapy.
C M (Ref:HM16099)

**PETTS WOOD CHIROPODY-PODIATRY**

**Petts Wood Chiropody & Podiatry**, 1 Fairway, Orpington, **Kent**, BR5 1EF, ENG.
(T) 01689 828000 (F) 01689 822795
Speciality: Chiropodists (Podiatrists).
● **Partner** Mrs V Jones
S (Ref:HM16100)

**PETTS, PHILIP**

**Philip Petts**, Evegate Clinic, The Old Barn, Station Rd, Smeeth, Ashford, **Kent**, TN25 6SX, ENG.
(T) 01303 813712
Speciality: Chiropractic.
P S T (Ref:HM16101)

**PETULENGRO**

**Petulengro**, 1a Fleet St, Torquay, **Devon**, TQ1 1BX, ENG.
(T) 01803 291380
Speciality: Clairvoyants & Palmists.
B (Ref:HM16102)

**PETULENGRO, LEAH**

**Leah Petulengro**, Coral Island, Prom, Blackpool, **Lancashire**, FY1 5DW, ENG.
(T) 01253 290462
Speciality: Clairvoyants & Palmists.
● **Owner** Mrs L Petulengro
B (Ref:HM16103)

**PETULENGRO, LEE**

**Lee Petulengro**, 75 Pasture St, Grimsby, **Humberside (South)**, DN32 9AB, ENG.
(T) 01472 210717 (F) 01472 210717
Speciality: Clairvoyants & Palmists.
● **Owner** Mr L Petulengro
B (Ref:HM16104)

**PEVENSEY BAY NTRL HEALING**

**Pevensey Bay Natural Healing Clinic**, 6 Maresfield Drive, Pevensey Bay, Pevensey, **Sussex (East)**, BN24 6RU, ENG.
(T) 01323 761114
Speciality: Aromatherapy, Healing Therapy, Reflexology, Remedial Massage.
M O (Ref:HM16105)

**PFEFFER, JEREMY M**

**Jeremy M Pfeffer**, 97 Harley St, London, **London (Greater)**, W1N 1DF, ENG.
(T) 020 7935 3878
Speciality: Psychiatry.
● **Practice Manager** Dr J Pfeffer
B (Ref:HM16106)

**PFEIFFER, MARIANNA**

**Marianna Pfeiffer**, 30 West Hill Rd, St. Leonards-On-Sea, **Sussex (East)**, TN38 0NB, ENG.
(T) 01424 445527
Speciality: Aromatherapy.
● **Owner** Mrs M Pfeiffer
M O (Ref:HM16107)

**PG SALES**

**PG Sales**, Plantation Rd, **County Monaghan**, IRE.
(T) 08727 64990
Speciality: Herbalists.
M (Ref:HM16108)

**PHARMACARE**

**Pharmacare Pharmacy**, 84 Bridgwater Drive, Westcliff-on-Sea, **Essex**, SS0 0DH, ENG.
(T) 01702 344569
(E) enquiries@pharmacy2k.co.uk
(W) www.pharmacy2k.co.uk
Speciality: Allergy Testing, Aromatherapy, Complementary Therapy, Herbal Medicine, Homeopathy, Massage (Therapeutic), Phytotherapy, Vitamin Therapy. ✓ [credit card]
● **Owner/Pharmacist/Trainee Medical Herbalist**
Mr J Tang Q: BSc. M: RPS.
● **Therapist** Ms D Fairey Q: ITEC. M: ITEC.
M Yrs. Est.: 4 (Ref:HM16109)

**PHEBY, JACQUELINE**

**Jacqueline Pheby**, 2 Augustus Walk, Andover, **Hampshire**, SP10 5JS, ENG.
(T) 01264 391322
Speciality: Complementary Medicines & Therapy.
● **Owner** Mrs J Pheby
C M (Ref:HM16110)

**PHELAN, ALAN**

**Alan Phelan**, 10 Merthyr Rd, Cardiff, **Glamorgan (Vale of)**, CF14 3JP, WAL.
(T) 029 2062 7177
Speciality: Chiropodists (Podiatrists).
● **Owner** Mr A Phelan
S (Ref:HM16111)

**PHELAN, ALAN**

**Alan Phelan**, 22 Cornerswell Rd, Penarth, **Glamorgan (Vale of)**, CF64 3LQ, WAL.
(T) 029 2070 4515
Speciality: Chiropodists (Podiatrists).
S (Ref:HM16112)

**PHELAN, ALAN**

**Alan Phelan**, 28 High St, Barry, **Glamorgan (Vale of)**, CF62 7EB, WAL.
(T) 01446 734064
Speciality: Chiropodists (Podiatrists).
S (Ref:HM16113)

**PHIL FOGGITT**

**Phil Foggitt**, 2 Bridge Cottages, Feniton, Honiton, **Devon**, EX14 3BR, ENG.
(T) 01404 851048
Speciality: Homeopathy.
● **Owner** Mr P Foggitt
M (Ref:HM16114)

**PHIL SEAL PSYCHOTHERAPY**

**Phil Seal Psychotherapy**, 59 Victory Way, Cottenham, Cambridge, **Cambridgeshire**, CB4 8TG, ENG.
(T) 01954 251250
Speciality: Complementary Therapy, Hypnosis, Hypnotherapy, Neuro-Linguistic Program, Psychotherapy, Stress Therapy, Visualisation Therapy, Dream Therapy, Past Life Regression. ✓
● **Owner** Mr P Seal Q: C.Hyp, CMH, NLP. M: UKGHE.
H Yrs. Est.: 6 (Ref:HM16115)

**PHILADELPHIA ASSOCIATION**

**Philadelphia Association**, 4 Martys Yard, Off 17 Hampstead High St, London, **London (Greater)**, NW3 1QW, ENG.
(T) 020 7794 2652 (F) 020 7794 2652
Speciality: Psychotherapy.
B (Ref:HM16116)

**PHILBRICK, G**

**G Philbrick**, Welbeck House, 69 Porchester Rd, Fareham, **Hampshire**, PO16 8AP, ENG.
(T) 01329 280502
Speciality: Chiropodists (Podiatrists).
S (Ref:HM16117)

**PHILIP D HOLMES**

**Philip D Holmes**, Ashfield House, 15A Upper Avenue, Eastbourne, **Sussex (East)**, BN21 3XR, ENG.
(T) 01323 738784
(W) www.acupuncture-eastbourne.co.uk
Speciality: Acupuncture, Herbal Medicine, Moxibustion, Oriental Diagnosis.
● **Acupuncturist** Mr P Holmes Q: B.Ac, LCSP, MBAcC.
O (Ref:HM16118)

**PHILIP KINGSLEY TRICHOLOGICAL**

**Philip Kingsley Trichological Clinic (The)**, 54 Green St, London, **London (Greater)**, W1Y 3RH, ENG.
(T) 020 7629 4004
Speciality: Complementary Medicines & Therapy, Trichology.
M (Ref:HM16119)

**PHILIP STOCK - PHYSIOTHERAPIST**

**Philip Stock - Physiotherapist Clinic**, 3 George St, Glossop, **Derbyshire**, SK13 8AY, ENG.
(T) 01457 865063
Speciality: Chiropractic, Electrotherapy, Holistic Healing, Kinesiology, Manipulation, Massage (Therapeutic), Osteopathy, Phytotherapy, Ultrasonics. ✓
● **Physiotherapist** Mr P Stock Q: BA (Hons), Grad Dip Phys, MCSP, MSc, SRP. M: CSP.
S Yrs. Est.: 7 (Ref:HM16120)

**PHILIP, AARONS**

**Aarons Philip**, 38 Church St, Rickmansworth, **Hertfordshire**, WD3 1DJ, ENG.
(T) 01923 840098
Speciality: Osteopathy.
P S T (Ref:HM16121)

**PHILIP, HELEN**

**Helen Philip**, Anvil Rise, High St, Hempstead, Saffron Walden, **Essex**, CB10 2PD, ENG.
(T) 01799 599701 (F) 01799 599006
Speciality: Complementary Medicines & Therapy.
● **Owner** Mrs H Philip
C M (Ref:HM16122)

**PHILIPS, J**

**J Philips**, Woodside Clinic, 88 Great Northern Rd, Dunstable, **Bedfordshire**, LU5 4BT, ENG.
(T) 01582 608400
Speciality: Osteopathy.
P S T (Ref:HM16123)

**PHILLIPS, ANN**

**Ann Phillips**, 13 Silvermere Pk, Shifnal, **Shropshire**, TF11 9BN, ENG.
(T) 01952 462209 (F) 01952 462209
Speciality: Aromatherapy, Reflexology, Reiki. ✓
● **Owner** Mrs A Phillips M: BCMA, IPTI.
C Yrs. Est.: 6 (Ref:HM16124)

**PHILLIPS, C**

**C Phillips**, 60 Woodbridge Rd, Guildford, **Surrey**, GU1 4RF, ENG.
(T) 01483 571783
Speciality: Physiotherapy.
P S T (Ref:HM16125)

**PHILLIPS, C**

**C Phillips**, 542 Banbury Rd, Oxford, **Oxfordshire**, OX2 8EG, ENG.
(T) 01865 552564
Speciality: Physiotherapy.
● **Owner** Mrs C Phillips
P S T (Ref:HM16126)

**PHILLIPS, CAROL**

**Carol Phillips**, 92 Morehall Avenue, Folkestone, **Kent**, CT19 4EE, ENG.
(T) 01303 279106
Speciality: Reflexology.
S T (Ref:HM16127)

**PHILLIPS, DAVID**

**David Phillips**, Rose Cottage, Landimore, Swansea, SA3 1HD, WAL.
(T) 01792 390703
Speciality: Chiropractic.
P S T (Ref:HM16128)



Key continued: Yrs.Est: Years Established Q: Qualifications M: Professional Membership ✓ Indemnity Insurance [credit card] Accept Credit Cards

**PHILLIPS, DAWN**

**Dawn Phillips**, 7 Tilmore Gardens, Petersfield, **Hampshire**, GU32 2JQ, ENG.
(T) 023 8023 3217
Speciality: Homeopathy.
● **Owner** Ms D Phillips
M (Ref:HM16129)

**PHILLIPS, HARRY (DR)**

**Dr Harry Phillips**, 30 The Piazza, Covent Garden, London, **London (Greater)**, WC2E 8BE, ENG.
(T) 020 7836 4835
Speciality: Osteopathy.
P S T (Ref:HM16130)

**PHILLIPS, HILLARY**

**Hillary Phillips**, 140 Harley St, London, **London (Greater)**, W1N 1AH, ENG.
(T) 020 7486 8687 (F) 020 7486 4080
Speciality: Complementary Medicines & Therapy.
● **Partner** Mrs H Phillips
M (Ref:HM16131)

**PHILLIPS, J A**

**J A Phillips**, 5 Hilltop Rd, Earley, Reading, **Berkshire**, RG6 1BY, ENG.
(T) 01189 667366
Speciality: Chiropodists (Podiatrists).
S (Ref:HM16132)

**PHILLIPS, JEAN**

**Jean Phillips**, Ely Complementary Health Centre, 29a St Marys St, Ely, **Cambridgeshire**, CB7 4HF, ENG.
(T) 01353 664476
Speciality: Hypnotherapy.
● **Owner** Mr A Spence
B (Ref:HM16133)

**PHILLIPS, JOAN**

**Joan Phillips**, 36 Tollard Cl, **Dorset**, BH12 4AU, ENG.
(T) 01202 736510
Speciality: Reflexology.
S T (Ref:HM16134)

**PHILLIPS, K**

**K Phillips**, 47 Azalea Walk, Pinner, **London (Greater)**, HA5 2EH, ENG.
(T) 020 8868 0338 (F) 020 8868 7426
Speciality: Hypnotherapy.
● **Owner** Dr K Phillips
B (Ref:HM16135)

**PHILLIPS, L**

**L Phillips**, 11 Viking Way, Christchurch, **Dorset**, BH23 4AQ, ENG.
(T) 01425 276417 (F) 01425 276278
Speciality: Psychotherapy.
● **Owner** Mr L Phillips
B (Ref:HM16136)

**PHILLIPS, L**

**L Phillips**, 3-4 Hunter St, Whitby, **Yorkshire (North)**, YO21 3DA, ENG.
(T) 01947 820319
Speciality: Chiropodists (Podiatrists).
● **Owner** Mr L Phillips
S (Ref:HM16137)

**PHILLIPS, LORRAINE**

**Lorraine Phillips**, 453 Barlow Moor Rd, Manchester, **Manchester (Greater)**, M21 8AU, ENG.
(T) 01618 812128 (F) 01618 812128
Speciality: Aromatherapy.
● **Owner** Mr N Bell
M O (Ref:HM16138)

**PHILLIPS, LORRAINE**

**Lorraine Phillips**, 32 Deyne St, Salford, **Manchester (Greater)**, M6 5WT, ENG.
(T) 01612 880784
Speciality: Reflexology.
S T (Ref:HM16139)

**PHILLIPS, ROSALYN**

**Rosalyn Phillips**, Edgware Clinic For Natural Health, 128 High St, Edgware, **London (Greater)**, HA8 7EL, ENG.
(T) 020 8951 3475
Speciality: Reflexology.
S T (Ref:HM16140)

**PHILLIPS, SAMANTHA**

**Samantha Phillips**, 52 Dollis Pk, London, **London (Greater)**, N3 1BS, ENG.
(T) 020 8346 5766
Speciality: Homeopathy.
● **Owner** Ms S Phillips
M (Ref:HM16141)

**PHILLIPS, SANDRA**

**Sandra Phillips**, 42 Brookside, St. Dials, Cwmbran, **Torfaen**, NP44 4NB, WAL.
(T) 01633 866756
Speciality: Hypnosis.
● **Owner** Mrs S Phillips
B (Ref:HM16142)

**PHILLIPS, STAN**

**Phillips Stan**, 15 Broad St, **County Waterford**, IRE.
(T) 05184 4300
Speciality: Complementary Medicines & Therapy.
M (Ref:HM16143)

**PHILLIPS, T G**

**T G Phillips**, 59 Clos Cilsaig, Dafen, Llanelli, **Carmarthenshire**, SA14 8QY, WAL.
(T) 01554 759559
Speciality: Chiropodists (Podiatrists).
● **Owner** Mr T Phillips
S (Ref:HM16144)

**PHILLIPSON, B J**

**B J Phillipson**, High Grendon, 2 Easton Way, Grendon, Northampton, **Northamptonshire**, NN7 1JQ, ENG.
(T) 01933 663894
Speciality: Herbal Medicine.
M (Ref:HM16145)

**PHILLPOT, ANN**

**Ann Phillpot**, 159 Merry Hill Rd, Bushey, **Herefordshire**, WD23 1DF, ENG.
(T) 020 8386 0571
Speciality: Reflexology.
S T (Ref:HM16146)

**PHILP, CHRISTINE**

**Christine Philp**, Glenrae, Oak Tree Rd, Milford, Godalming, **Surrey**, GU8 5JJ, ENG.
(T) 01483 429290
Speciality: Aromatherapy, Bach Remedies, Massage (Therapeutic), Reiki. ✔
● **Aromatherapist** Mrs C Philp Q: GIA. M: GCP.
C Yrs. Est.: 6 (Ref:HM16147)

**PHILPOTT, J**

**J Philpott**, 3 Blackmore Mews, Exeter, **Devon**, EX2 5SA, ENG.
(T) 01392 430130 (F) 01392 494500
Speciality: Chiropodists (Podiatrists).
● **Owner** Mrs J Philpott
S (Ref:HM16148)

**PHILPOTT, MONIQUE**

**Monique Philpott**, Tibenham, Bunwell, Norwich, **Norfolk**, NR16 1SU, ENG.
(T) 01379 677897
Speciality: Reflexology, Reiki.
S T (Ref:HM16149)

**PHILPS, A**

**A Philps**, 18 Lansdowne Rd, London, **London (Greater)**, W11 3LL, ENG.
(T) 020 7727 7222
Speciality: Alexander Technique.
● **Employee** Mr J Brown
P S (Ref:HM16150)

**PHOENIX**

**Phoenix**, 1 Wellington Rd, Horsham, **Sussex (West)**, RH12 1DD, ENG.
(T) 01403 274799
Speciality: Complementary Medicines & Therapy.
● **Partner** Mr K Burgess
C M (Ref:HM16151)

**PHOENIX**

**Phoenix**, 67 Chertsey Cr, New Addington, Croydon, **Surrey**, CR0 0DE, ENG.
(T) 020 8660 4406
Speciality: Counselling, Clairvoyant. CREDIT
● **Owner/Counsellor** Mrs J Connor
B Yrs. Est.: 25 (Ref:HM16152)

**PHOENIX ACUPUNCTURE CLINIC**

**Phoenix Acupuncture Clinic**, 81 Lincoln Rd, Peterborough, **Cambridgeshire**, PE1 2SH, ENG.
(T) 07887 525218
Speciality: Acupuncture.
O (Ref:HM16153)

**PHOENIX CENTRE**

**Phoenix Centre**, 26 Knutsford Avenue, Heaton Chapel, Stockport, **Cheshire**, SK4 5LQ, ENG.
(T) 01614 323022
Speciality: Absent Healing, Healer, Hypnosis, Hypnotherapy, Spiritual Healing, Emotional Freedom Technique (EFT), Meridian Therapy, Management. ✔
● **Owner** Ms C Leybourne Q: MACH. M: ACH, HA.
B Yrs. Est.: 8 (Ref:HM16154)

**PHOENIX FOOT HEALTH**

**Phoenix Foot Health**, Essex House, Worting Rd, Basingstoke, **Hampshire**, RG21 8SU, ENG.
(T) 01256 470464
Speciality: Chiropodists (Podiatrists).
S (Ref:HM16155)

**PHOENIX HOLISTIC CENTRE**

**Joseph Carey Psychic Foundation**, 85-85a College St, Portsea, Portsmouth, **Hampshire**, PO1 3HB, ENG.
(T) 023 9283 0500 (F) 023 9269 3169
(E) phoenixcentre@pgen.net
(W) www.phoenixcentre.co.uk
Speciality: Absent Healing, Acupuncture, Aromatherapy, Art Therapy, Complementary Therapy, Counselling, Crystal Healing, Flotation Therapy, Group Therapy, Healer, Healing Therapy, Herbal Medicine, Holistic Healing, Hypnotherapy, Indian Head Massage, Massage (Therapeutic), Meditation, Nutritional Therapy, Paranormal Therapies, Reflexology, Reiki, Spiritual Healing, Chi-Kung(Qi-Gong). ✔
● **President** Mr A Ashenden
(T) 023 9269 3169 M: BAHA, CHO.
B Yrs. Est.: 6 (Ref:HM16156)

**PHOENIX HOM/ALLGY TESTING CTRE**

**Phoenix Homoeopathy & Allergy Testing Centre**, 1 Queensbridge Rd, London, **London (Greater)**, E2 8NP, ENG.
(T) 020 7613 4309
Speciality: Homeopathy.
● **Owner** Mr C Sanders
M (Ref:HM16157)

**PHOENIX THERAPY CENTRE**

**Phoenix Therapy Centre**, 1 Wellington Rd, Horsham, **Sussex (West)**, RH12 1DD, ENG.
(T) 01403 274799
Speciality: Alexander Technique.
● **Therapist** Ms S Geiges
P S (Ref:HM16158)

**PHOKOU, PERI P**

**Peri P Phokou**, 29 Totteridge Lane, London, **London (Greater)**, N20 0EX, ENG.
(T) 020 8343 8587
Speciality: Osteopathy.
P S T (Ref:HM16159)

**PHOMBEAH, JULIA**

**Julia Phombeah**, Hendon Natural Health Centre, 12 Golders Rise, London, **London (Greater)**, NW4 2HR, ENG.
(T) 020 8202 9747 (F) 020 8202 3890
Speciality: Aromatherapy.
● **Owner** Ms K McCarroll
M O (Ref:HM16160)

**PHONE A PSYCHIC**

**Phone A Psychic**, Po Box 6632, London, **London (Greater)**, E8 2QP, ENG.
(T) 020 7690 9667
Speciality: Clairvoyants & Palmists.
B (Ref:HM16161)

**PHYSIC SUPPER CLUB**

**Physic Supper Club**, 9 Kings Cr, Poole, **Dorset**, BH14 9PR, ENG.
(T) 01202 715269
Speciality: Clairvoyants & Palmists.
● **Owner** Mrs D Plattern



Key: B Mind-Body Medicine C Complementary Medicine H Self Help Treatment M Medicinal Therapy O Oriental Medicine P Postural Therapy S Manipulative Structural Therapy T Touch Therapy

B (Ref:HM16162)

**PHYSICAL EVALUATION SYSTEMS**

**Physical Evaluation Systems Ltd**, Ingram House, 227 Ingram St, Glasgow, **Glasgow (City of)**, G1 1DA, SCO.
(T) 01412 432342
Speciality: Physiotherapy.
● **Owner** Mrs N Ferry
P S T (Ref:HM16163)

**PHYSICAL THERAPY CLINIC**

**Physical Therapy Clinic**, 127A Main St, Garforth, Leeds, **Yorkshire (West)**, LS25 1AF, ENG.
(T) 07957 365092
Speciality: Complementary Medicines & Therapy.
C M (Ref:HM16164)

**PHYSICAL THERAPY CLINIC**

**Physical Therapy Clinic**, 16 Downs Pk Rd, Totton, Southampton, **Hampshire**, SO40 9GJ, ENG.
(T) 023 8086 3854
Speciality: Complementary Medicines & Therapy.
● **Owner** Mr D Cooke
M (Ref:HM16165)

**PHYSICAL THERAPY CLINIC**

**Physical Therapy Clinic (The)**, 10 Guild St, Stratford-Upon-Avon, **Warwickshire**, CV37 6RE, ENG.
(T) 01789 267765
Speciality: Physiotherapy.
● **Owner** Ms J Ivings
P S T (Ref:HM16166)

**PHYSICAL THERAPY CLINIC**

**Physical Therapy Clinic (The)**, Hale Station, 1 Victoria Rd, Hale, Altrincham, **Cheshire**, WA15 9AF, ENG.
(T) 01619 295402 (F) 01619 295402
Speciality: Physiotherapy.
● **Practice Manager** Mrs S Tilton
P S T (Ref:HM16167)

**PHYSICAL THERAPY STORE**

**Physical Therapy Store**, 8 Shillingford St, London, **London (Greater)**, N1 2DP, ENG.
(T) 020 7354 2002 (F) 020 7354 2002
Speciality: Physiotherapy.
● **Owner** Mr J Shotbolt
P S T (Ref:HM16168)

**PHYSICARE**

**Physicare**, Po Box 8988, Lanark, **Lanarkshire (South)**, ML11 7QD, SCO.
(T) 01555 664053 (F) 01555 664058
Speciality: Physiotherapy.
● **Managing Director** Mr D Scott
P S T (Ref:HM16169)

**PHYSICARE**

**Physicare**, Atrium Business Centre, North Caldeen Rd, Coatbridge, **Lanarkshire (North)**, ML5 4EF, SCO.
(T) 01236 702055 (F) 01555 664058
Speciality: Physiotherapy.
P S T (Ref:HM16170)

**PHYSIO**

**Physio & Co Ltd**, 29 Malone Rd, Belfast, **County Antrim**, BT9 6RU, NIR.
(T) 028 9038 2828 (F) 028 9038 2828
Speciality: Physiotherapy.
● **Director** Mr P McOrmac
P S T (Ref:HM16171)

**PHYSIO & ACUPUNCTURIST CENTRE**

**Physiotherapy & Acupuncturist Centre**, 544 Green Lane, Ilford, **Essex**, IG3 9LL, ENG.
(T) 020 8599 2444
Speciality: Complementary Medicines & Therapy.
● **Partner** Ms T Couzens
M (Ref:HM16172)

**PHYSIO & BACK CARE CLINIC**

**Physiotherapy & Back Care Clinic (The)**, 288 North Rd, Cardiff, **Glamorgan (Vale of)**, CF14 3BN, WAL.
(T) 029 2052 9688
Speciality: Physiotherapy.
P S T (Ref:HM16173)

**PHYSIO & MANIPULATION CLINIC**

**Physiotherapy (Manipulation Clinic)**, 41 Rectory Lane, Loughton, **Essex**, IG10 1NZ, ENG.
(T) 020 8502 0029
Speciality: Acupuncture.
O (Ref:HM16174)

**PHYSIO & SPORTS CLINIC**

**Physiotherapist & Sports Clinic (The)**, Luton Regional Sports Centre, St Thomas's Rd, Luton, **Bedfordshire**, LU2 7XP, ENG.
(T) 07961 197443
Speciality: Physiotherapy.
P S T (Ref:HM16175)

**PHYSIO & SPORTS INJURIES**

**Physiotherapy & Sports Injuries Clinic**, 7 Grange Trce, Sunderland, **Tyne and Wear**, SR2 7DF, ENG.
(T) 01915 101913
Speciality: Physiotherapy.
P S T (Ref:HM16176)

**PHYSIO & SPORTS INJURIES CLNC**

**Physiotherapy And Sports Injuries Clinic**, 13 Ravenscroft Park, Barnet, **Hertfordshire**, EN5 4ND, ENG.
(T) 020 8441 4499 (F) 020 8441 4499
(E) broadoak@msn.com
Speciality: Biofeedback, Electrotherapy, Manipulation, Massage (Therapeutic), Ultrasonics. ✔
● **Physiotherapist** Ms J Eaton Q: MCSP, SRP. M: CSP.
S Yrs. Est.: 18 (Ref:HM16177)

**PHYSIO & SPORTS INJURY**

**Physiotherapy & Sports Injury Clinic**, West Midlands Hospital, Colman Hill, Halesowen, **Midlands (West)**, B63 2AH, ENG.
(T) 01384 560123 (F) 01384 411103
Speciality: Physiotherapy.
● **Manager** Mr D Jones
P S T (Ref:HM16178)

**PHYSIO & SPORTS INJURY CENTRE**

**Physiotherapy & Sports Injury Centre**, 252 Leyland Lane, Leyland, Preston, **Lancashire**, PR5 3HL, ENG.
(T) 01772 458387
Speciality: Physiotherapy.
P S T (Ref:HM16179)

**PHYSIO & SPORTS INJURY CENTRE**

**Physiotherapy & Sports Injury Centre**, 544 Green Lane, Ilford, **Essex**, IG3 9LL, ENG.
(T) 020 8590 5909 (F) 020 8599 2444
Speciality: Physiotherapy.
● **Owner** Mrs R Chandresinghe
P S T (Ref:HM16180)

**PHYSIO & SPORTS INJURY CLINIC**

**Macclesfield Physiotherapy & Sports Injury Clinic**, Bollin House, Sunderland St, Macclesfield, **Cheshire**, SK11 6JL, ENG.
(T) 01260 252205 (F) 01260 253030
Speciality: Acupressure, Alexander Technique, Bach Remedies, Electrolipolysis, Manipulation, Massage (Therapeutic), Ultrasonics. ✔
● **Physiotherapist** Ms I Menaged Q: Grad Dip Phys, MCSP, SRP. M: CSP.
H P S T Yrs. Est.: 18 (Ref:HM16181)

**PHYSIO & SPORTS INJURY CLINIC**

**Physiotherapy & Sports Injury Clinic**, 26 Rondini Avenue, Luton, **Bedfordshire**, LU3 1RR, ENG.
(T) 01582 594940
Speciality: Physiotherapy.
P S T (Ref:HM16182)

**PHYSIO & SPORTS INJURY CLINIC**

**Physiotherapy & Sports Injury Clinic**, 27 Bancroft Rd, Maidenbower, Crawley, **Sussex (West)**, RH10 7WS, ENG.
(T) 01293 887270
Speciality: Physiotherapy.
● **Owner** Mrs K Jenkins
P S T (Ref:HM16183)

**PHYSIO & SPORTS INJURY CLINIC**

**Physiotherapy & Sports Injury Clinic**, 31 South St, Epsom, **Surrey**, KT18 7PJ, ENG.
(T) 01372 745477
Speciality: Physiotherapy.
P S T (Ref:HM16184)

**PHYSIO & SPORTS INJURY CLINIC**

**Physiotherapy And Sports Injury Clinic**, 28 Station Rd, Whalley, Clitheroe, **Lancashire**, BB7 9RH, ENG.
(T) 01254 823183 (F) 01254 823834
Speciality: Physiotherapy.
● **Owner** Mrs W Douglas
P S T (Ref:HM16185)

**PHYSIO & SPORTS INJURY CLINIC**

**Colchester Physiotherapy & Sports Injury Clinic (The)**, 97 Crouch St, Colchester, **Essex**, CO3 3HA, ENG.
(T) 01206 579631 (F) 01206 579682
Speciality: Biofeedback, Electrotherapy, Manipulation, Massage (Therapeutic), Micro Manipulation, Physiotherapy, Ultrasonics, Postural Control. ✔
● **Physiotherapist** Ms H Ayache Q: MCSP, SRP. M: CSP, OCPPP, SRP.
● **Physiotherapist** Ms J Grant Q: MCSP, SRP. M: CSP, OCPPP, SRP.
● **Physiotherapist** Ms J Peacock Q: Dip.CM, MCSP, PGD.App.PSp, SRP. M: CSP, OCPPP, SRP.
● **Physiotherapist** Mrs J Mitchell Q: MCSP, SRP. M: CSP, OCPPP, SRP.
S Yrs. Est.: 27 (Ref:HM16186)

**PHYSIO & SPORTS INJURY CLNC**

**Physiotherapy & Sports Injury Clinic**, 43 Hammerton St, Burnley, **Lancashire**, BB11 1LT, ENG.
(T) 01282 450204
Speciality: Physiotherapy.
P S T (Ref:HM16187)

**PHYSIO & SPORTS INJURY CLNC**

**Physiotherapy & Sports Injury Clinic**, Summerlands Lodge, 123 Canterbury Rd, Westgate-on-Sea, **Kent**, CT8 8LY, ENG.
(T) 01843 833166 (F) 01843 832736
Speciality: Physiotherapy.
● **Owner** Mrs A Nicholass
P S T (Ref:HM16188)

**PHYSIO & SPORTS INJURY CLNC**

**Physiotherapy & Sports Injury Clinic**, Langford Medical Practice, 9 Nightingale Pl, Bicester, **Oxfordshire**, OX6 0XX, ENG.
(T) 01869 249749 (F) 01869 249749
Speciality: Physiotherapy.
● **Owner** Mrs D Elder
P S T (Ref:HM16189)

**PHYSIO & SPORTS INJURY CLNC**

**Physiotherapy & Sports Injury Clinic**, 38 Between Streets, Cobham, **Surrey**, KT11 1AF, ENG.
(T) 01932 862370 (F) 01932 862370
Speciality: Physiotherapy.
● **Owner** Mrs S Beer
P S T (Ref:HM16190)

**PHYSIO & SPORTS INJURY CLNC**

**Physiotherapy & Sports Injury Clinic**, 11 Heath Rd, Haywards Heath, **Sussex (West)**, RH16 3AX, ENG.
(T) 01444 450162 (F) 01444 459816
Speciality: Physiotherapy.
● **Practice Manager** Mrs W Langley
P S T (Ref:HM16191)

**PHYSIO & SPORTS INJURY CLNC**

**Physiotherapy & Sports Injury Clinic**, 21A Abington Gr, Northampton, **Northamptonshire**, NN1 4QW, ENG.
(T) 01604 713374
Speciality: Physiotherapy.
● **Owner** Mr E Palmer-Jeffrey
P S T (Ref:HM16192)

**PHYSIO ACTIVE**

**Glossop Physiotherapy & Sports Injuries Clinic**, 88 High St West, Glossop, **Derbyshire**, SK13 8BB, ENG.
(T) 01457 860978



Key continued: **Yrs.Est:** Years Established **Q:** Qualifications **M:** Professional Membership ✔ Indemnity Insurance Accept Credit Cards

(E) jackie.stanton@tesco.net
Speciality: Acupressure, Acupuncture, Aromatherapy, Counselling, Electrotherapy, Homeopathy, Indian Head Massage, Kinesiology, Manipulation, Massage (Therapeutic), Oriental Diagnosis, Osteopathy, Physiotherapy, Postural Integration, Psychotherapy, Reflexology, Reiki, Shiatsu, Ultrasonics, Postural Restabilisation. ✓
● **Physiotherapist** Mr C Lee Q: Dip.Phys, MCSP, SRP. M: CSP.
● **Osteopath** Mr D Ellwood Q: BSc, DCR(R), Hons (OST). M: BOA, GOsC.
● **Counsellor/Psychotherapist** Ms H Holland
(T) 01457 766866 M: BACP.
● **Aromatherapist** Ms A Wilkie
(T) 01457 855916 M: ISPA.
● **Homeopath** Ms J Stanton
(T) 01457 861940 Q: BA (Hons), RSHom. M: Soc.Hom.
M Yrs. Est.: 8 (**Ref:**HM16193)

## PHYSIO ACUPUNCTURE CLINIC

**Physiotherapy Acupuncture Clinic**, 128 Christchurch Rd, London, **London (Greater)**, SW2 3DF, **ENG**.
(T) 020 8671 5583
Speciality: Acupuncture.
O (**Ref:**HM16194)

## PHYSIO AND SPORTS INJURIES

**Physiotherapy And Sports Injuries Clinic (The)**, Market Chambers, Market Pl, Ramsbottom, Bury, **Lancashire**, BL0 9AJ, **ENG**.
(T) 01706 827748
Speciality: Cognitive Therapy, Electrolipolysis, Kinesiology, Manipulation, Massage (Therapeutic), Micro Manipulation, Postural Integration, Ergonomic Advice. ✓
● **Physiotherapist** Mr R Mandel Q: BA, MCSP, SRP. M: CSP.
S Yrs. Est.: 10 (**Ref:**HM16195)

## PHYSIO CENTRAL

**Physio Central**, 145 Bath St, Glasgow, **Glasgow (City of)**, G2 4SQ, **SCO**.
(T) 01415 723323 (F) 01415 721010
Speciality: Physiotherapy.
● **Owner** Mrs A Barraclough
P S T (**Ref:**HM16196)

## PHYSIO DIRECT

**Physio Direct**, 27-29 Herbert Rd, Nottingham, **Nottinghamshire**, NG5 1BS, **ENG**.
(T) 01158 417474 (F) 01159 610062
Speciality: Physiotherapy. ✓
● **Physiotherapist** Mr O Robinson Q: BSc (Hons), MCSP, SRP. M: CSP.
S Yrs. Est.: 2 (**Ref:**HM16197)

## PHYSIO FIRST CENTRE

**Physio First Centre**, Park Rd, Whitchurch, Cardiff, **Glamorgan (Vale of)**, CF14 7EZ, **WAL**.
(T) 07071 880189
Speciality: Acupuncture. ✓
● **Physiotherapist** Mr A Seary Q: MCSP, SRP. M: CSP.
S Yrs. Est.: 14 (**Ref:**HM16198)

## PHYSIO FIRST PRACTICE

**Physio First Practice**, Lyndhurst, 47 Straight Bit, Flackwell Heath, High Wycombe, **Buckinghamshire**, HP10 9NE, **ENG**.
(T) 01628 522399
Speciality: Electrotherapy, Manipulation, Massage (Therapeutic), Physiotherapy, Mobilisation. ✓
● **Physiotherapist** Ms A Turley Q: MCSP, SRP. M: CSP.
● **Physiotherapist** Ms R Clarkson Q: MCSP, SRP. M: CSP.
S Yrs. Est.: 19 (**Ref:**HM16199)

## PHYSIO FOCUS

**Physio Focus**, Pirnhall Rd, Bannockburn, Stirling, FK7 8EH, **SCO**.
(T) 01786 480048 (F) 01786 489849
Speciality: Physiotherapy.
● **Owner** Miss S Airth
P S T (**Ref:**HM16200)

## PHYSIO MED

**Physio Med**, 159 Beeston Rd, Leeds, **Yorkshire (West)**, LS11 6AW, **ENG**.
(T) 01132 703330 (F) 01132 946556
Speciality: Physiotherapy.
● **Dentist** Mr D Brown
P S T (**Ref:**HM16201)

## PHYSIO ONE

**Physio One**, 16 Balderton St, London, **London (Greater)**, W1Y 1TF, **ENG**.
(T) 020 7355 4036 (F) 08701 693296
Speciality: Acupuncture, Dance Movement Therapy, Manipulation, Massage (Therapeutic), Phytotherapy, Friction Massage, Therapeutic Exercise, Mobilisation, Soft Connective Tissue Mobilisation. CREDIT
● **Physiotherapist** Mr S Monfared Q: Grad Dip Phys, SRP. M: CSP, SOM, SRP.
P S Yrs. Est.: 1 (**Ref:**HM16202)

## PHYSIO PLUS

**Physio Plus**, Progress House, 17 Cecil Rd, Hale, Altrincham, **Cheshire**, WA15 9NZ, **ENG**.
(T) 01619 291030 (F) 01619 294116
Speciality: Aromatherapy, Biomechanics, Chinese Herbal Medicine, Nutritional Therapy, Physiotherapy, Podiatry. ✓
● **Podiatrist** Mr C Parish Q: DPodM, M.S.C.P., S.R.Ch.
● **Owner** Ms J Clark
C S (**Ref:**HM16203)

## PHYSIO PLUS

**Physio Plus**, Que Bella, Green Acre, Nottingham, **Nottinghamshire**, NG8 4DT, **ENG**.
(T) 01159 169192
Speciality: Physiotherapy.
● **Owner** Miss A Smith
P S T (**Ref:**HM16204)

## PHYSIO SOLUTIONS

**H Skehan TA Physio Solutions Physiotherapy and Sports Injury Clinic**, 23 Baron St, Islington, London, **London (Greater)**, N1 9ET, **ENG**.
(T) 020 7713 7780 (F) 020 7713 7323
(E) hs@physiosolutions.co.uk
Speciality: Acupuncture, Physiotherapy. ✓ CREDIT
● **Physiotherapist** Ms H Skehan Q: MCSP, MMACP, MSc, SRP. M: CSP.
P S T Yrs. Est.: 3 (**Ref:**HM16205)

## PHYSIO SPORT

**Physio Sport**, 97-99 Great Portwood St, Stockport, **Cheshire**, SK1 2AS, **ENG**.
(T) 01614 801800 (F) 01614 801800
Speciality: Physiotherapy.
● **Owner** Mr G Heward
P S T (**Ref:**HM16206)

## PHYSIO SPORTS & DANCE INJURY

**Physiotherapy Sports & Dance Injury Clinic (The)**, New River Sports Centre, White Hart Lane, London, **London (Greater)**, N22 5QW, **ENG**.
(T) 020 8889 8459
Speciality: Physiotherapy.
● **Owner** Miss A Blackshaw
P S T (**Ref:**HM16207)

## PHYSIO SPORTS & SPINAL CLINIC

**Physiotherapy Sports & Spinal Clinic**, 35A Russell Drive, Ampthill, Bedford, **Bedfordshire**, MK45 2TX, **ENG**.
(T) 01525 841845 (F) 01525 841845
Speciality: Physiotherapy.
● **Partner** Mrs A Chick
P S T (**Ref:**HM16208)

## PHYSIO SPORTS INJURY CLINIC

**Physiotherapy Sports Injury & Fitness Clinic**, Wallerscote House, Winnington Lane, Northwich, **Cheshire**, CW8 4EG, **ENG**.
(T) 01606 871618
Speciality: Physiotherapy. ✓
● **Owner** Ms S Storah Q: Dip.RG&RT, MCSP, SRP.
● **Physiotherapist** Fiona Chesworth Q: MCSP, SRP. M: CSP.
● **Physiotherapist** Ann Mayfield Q: MCSP, SRP. M: CSP.
S Yrs. Est.: 16 (**Ref:**HM16209)

## PHYSIO, MASSAGE & PR ACU

**Chartered Society Of Physiotherapy**, 12 Dolphin Avenue, Bournemouth, **Dorset**, BH10 6DU, **ENG**.
(T) 01202 574949
Speciality: Acupuncture, Art Therapy, Colour Therapy, Complementary Therapy, Counselling, Electrotherapy, Healing Therapy, Massage (Therapeutic), Stress Therapy, Touch Therapy, Ultrasonics, Breathing Exercises. ✓
● **Physio-Assistant/Masseur** Sabatini Jacqui M: CSP.
● **Owner/Masseur/Physiotherapist** Mr K Pritchard Q: MCSP, S.R.Ch, SRP. M: CSP.
M Yrs. Est.: 40 (**Ref:**HM16210)

## PHYSIOCARE

**Physiocare**, 226 Wokingham Rd, Reading, **Berkshire**, RG6 1JS, **ENG**.
(T) 01189 664585 (F) 01189 664585
Speciality: Physiotherapy.
● **Senior Partner** Mrs E Jones
P S T (**Ref:**HM16211)

## PHYSIOCARE

**Physiocare**, 27 Station Rd, Twyford, Reading, **Berkshire**, RG10 9NS, **ENG**.
(T) 01189 344055 (F) 01189 664585
Speciality: Physiotherapy.
● **Partner** Mrs E Jones
P S T (**Ref:**HM16212)

## PHYSIODIRECT

**Physiodirect**, 334 Mansfield Rd, Nottingham, **Nottinghamshire**, NG5 2EF, **ENG**.
(T) 01159 691528
Speciality: Physiotherapy.
● **Licensee** Mr T Ricard
P S T (**Ref:**HM16213)

## PHYSIODIRECT

**PhysioDirect**, Shakespeare St, Nottingham, **Nottinghamshire**, **ENG**.
(T) 01158 477770
Speciality: Physiotherapy. ✓
● **Owner/Physiotherapist** Mr O Robinson Q: BSc (Hons), MCSP, SRP. M: CSP.
S (**Ref:**HM16214)

## PHYSIODIRECT SPORTS INJURY

**Physiodirect Sports Injury Clinic**, Main Rd, Radcliffe-On-Trent, Nottingham, **Nottinghamshire**, NG12 2GD, **ENG**.
(T) 01159 333181
Speciality: Physiotherapy.
● **Owner** Mrs B Bilkhu
P S T (**Ref:**HM16215)

## PHYSIODIRECT WEST BRIDGFORD

**PhysioDirect West Bridgford**, Boundary Rd, West Bridgford, Nottingham, **Nottinghamshire**, NG2 7BW, **ENG**.
(T) 01159 743203
Speciality: Physiotherapy.
● **Licensee** Mr T Ricard
P S T (**Ref:**HM16216)

## PHYSIOFIRST

**PhysioFirst**, Cedar House, The Bell Plantation, Watling St, Towcester, **Northamptonshire**, NN12 6HN, **ENG**.
(T) 01327 354441
Speciality: Physiotherapy.
P S T (**Ref:**HM16217)

## PHYSIOFIT

**PhysioFit**, 252-258 North End Rd, Fulham, London, **London (Greater)**, SW6 1NN, **ENG**.
(T) 020 7385 1288
Speciality: Physiotherapy.
● **Owner** Miss V Roe
P S T (**Ref:**HM16218)

## PHYSIOPLUS

**Physioplus**, 28 Harborough Rd, Northampton, **Northamptonshire**, NN2 7AZ, **ENG**.
(T) 01604 722372 (F) 01604 722472
Speciality: Physiotherapy.
● **Principal** Mrs S Southam
P S T (**Ref:**HM16219)

## PHYSIOTHERAPY & ACUPUNCTURE

**Physiotherapy & Acupuncture**, McCauley Chemists, **County Wexford**, **IRE**.
(T) 05322 666

Key: B Mind-Body Medicine C Complementary Medicine H Self Help Treatment M Medicinal Therapy O Oriental Medicine P Postural Therapy S Manipulative Structural Therapy T Touch Therapy

Speciality: Acupuncture.
O (Ref:HM16220)

### PHYSIOTHERAPY & FITNESS CENTRE

**Physiotherapy & Fitness Centre**, 12 High St, Bottesford, Nottingham, **Nottinghamshire**, NG13 0AA, ENG.
(T) 01949 843106
Speciality: Physiotherapy.
● **Owner** Mrs A Eaton
P S T (Ref:HM16221)

### PHYSIOTHERAPY & REHAB PRACTICE

**Physiotherapy & Rehabilitation Practice**, 1-4 Harbour Yard, Chelsea Harbour, London, **London (Greater)**, SW10 0XD, ENG.
(T) 020 7349 9996 (F) 020 7349 9997
Speciality: Physiotherapy.
● **Owner** Mr D Bolton
P S T (Ref:HM16222)

### PHYSIOTHERAPY & SPORTS CLINIC

**Physiotherapy & Sports Clinic (The)**, Fawcett House, Fawcett Yard, Morpeth, **Northumberland**, NE61 1BG, ENG.
(T) 01670 513205
Speciality: Acupuncture, Manipulation, Physiotherapy. ✔
● **Physiotherapist/Owner**
Mr Clunies-Ross Q: MCSP, SRP. M: CSP.
● **Physiotherapist** Ms Z Stimpson Q: MCSP, SRP. M: CSP.
S (Ref:HM16223)

### PHYSIOTHERAPY ASSOCIATES

**Physiotherapy Associates**, Valley Business Centre, 67 Church Rd, Newtownabbey, **County Antrim**, BT36 7LS, NIR.
(T) 028 9055 2655
Speciality: Physiotherapy.
P S T (Ref:HM16224)

### PHYSIOTHERAPY CENTRE

**Physiotherapy Centre**, Rectory Lane Health Centre, Rectory Lane, Loughton, **Essex**, IG10 3RU, ENG.
(T) 020 8281 7612
Speciality: Physiotherapy.
P S T (Ref:HM16225)

### PHYSIOTHERAPY CENTRE

**Physiotherapy Centre (The)**, Annexe, The Manor House, High St, Rothwell, Kettering, **Northamptonshire**, NN14 6BQ, ENG.
(T) 01536 418404 (F) 01536 418404
Speciality: Physiotherapy.
● **Owner** Mr S McKee
P S T (Ref:HM16226)

### PHYSIOTHERAPY CENTRE

**Physiotherapy Centre (The)**, 28 Roundhill Rd, Torquay, **Devon**, TQ2 6TH, ENG.
(T) 01803 606021
Speciality: Physiotherapy.
● **Owner** Mr I Gray
P S T (Ref:HM16227)

### PHYSIOTHERAPY CENTRE

**Physiotherapy Centre (The)**, 37 Chesterfield Rd, Dronfield, **Derbyshire**, S18 2XA, ENG.
(T) 01246 290190
Speciality: Physiotherapy.
● **Owner** Ms V Roberts
P S T (Ref:HM16228)

### PHYSIOTHERAPY CENTRE

**Physiotherapy Centre (The)**, 39 Harwood Rd, London, **London (Greater)**, SW6 4QP, ENG.
(T) 020 7736 0193
Speciality: Physiotherapy.
● **Owner** Mr M Gleeson
P S T (Ref:HM16229)

### PHYSIOTHERAPY CENTRE

**Physiotherapy Centre (The)**, Brenchley House, 75-77 High St, Sittingbourne, **Kent**, ME10 4AW, ENG.
(T) 01795 435060
Speciality: Biomechanics, Chiropody, Nail Surgery, Physiotherapy. ✔
● **Chiropodist** Mr A Mulvaney Q: S.R.Ch. M: S.C.P.
● **Physiotherapist** Mrs P Bartley Q: SRP. M: SRP.
B Yrs. Est.: 5 (Ref:HM16230)

### PHYSIOTHERAPY CENTRE

**Physiotherapy Centre (The)**, Woodcocks Court, Queen St, Gillingham, **Dorset**, SP8 4DZ, ENG.
(T) 01747 822277
Speciality: Physiotherapy.
● **Owner** Mrs J Flexney-Briscoe
P S T (Ref:HM16231)

### PHYSIOTHERAPY CENTRE

**Physiotherapy Centre (The)**, Viscount Way, London Heathrow Airport, Hounslow, **London (Greater)**, TW6 2JR, ENG.
(T) 020 8562 2352 (F) 020 8562 2352
Speciality: Physiotherapy.
● **Owner** Mrs S Aujla
P S T (Ref:HM16232)

### PHYSIOTHERAPY CENTRE

**Physiotherapy Centre (The)**, 96 London Rd, Waterlooville, **Hampshire**, PO7 5AB, ENG.
(T) 023 9221 5050 (F) 023 9234 2198
Speciality: Physiotherapy, Podiatry. ✔ [credit card]
● **Physiotherapist** Mr P Foster Q: MCSP, SRP. M: CSP.
● **Practice Manager**
Ms S Marshallsea
● **Podiatrist** Mr P Harradine Q: MSc, S.R.Ch.
S Yrs. Est.: 15 (Ref:HM16233)

### PHYSIOTHERAPY CLINIC

**Physiotherapy Clinic**, Saunders Business Centre, Victoria St, Ipswich, **Suffolk**, IP1 2JX, ENG.
(T) 01473 215905 (F) 01473 219419
Speciality: Physiotherapy.
● **Owner** Mr B Simpson
P S T (Ref:HM16234)

### PHYSIOTHERAPY CLINIC

**Physiotherapy Clinic**, Dalziel Workspace, Mason St, Motherwell, **Lanarkshire (North)**, ML1 5RZ, SCO.
(T) 01698 381910
Speciality: Physiotherapy.
P S T (Ref:HM16235)

### PHYSIOTHERAPY CLINIC

**Physiotherapy Clinic**, 27 Lyman Drive, Wishaw, **Lanarkshire (North)**, ML2 8TQ, SCO.
(T) 01698 381916
Speciality: Physiotherapy.
P S T (Ref:HM16236)

### PHYSIOTHERAPY CLINIC

**Physiotherapy clinic (The)**, 18B Collingwood Rd, Northampton, **Northamptonshire**, NN1 4RD, ENG.
(T) 01604 719290 (F) 01604 719449
Speciality: Physiotherapy.
● **Principal** Mrs S Rodley
P S T (Ref:HM16237)

### PHYSIOTHERAPY CLINIC

**Physiotherapy Clinic (The)**, 44 Plymouth Rd, Tavistock, **Devon**, PL19 8BU, ENG.
(T) 01822 616900 (F) 01822 616900
Speciality: Physiotherapy.
● **Partner** Mrs B Endacott
P S T (Ref:HM16238)

### PHYSIOTHERAPY CLINIC

**Physiotherapy Clinic (The)**, 700 Chigwell Rd, Woodford Green, **Essex**, IG8 8AL, ENG.
(T) 020 8506 0326
Speciality: Physiotherapy.
P S T (Ref:HM16239)

### PHYSIOTHERAPY CLINIC

**Physiotherapy Clinic (The)**, Golders Hill Health Centre, 151 North End Rd, London, **London (Greater)**, NW11 7FE, ENG.
(T) 020 8455 7809 (F) 020 8458 2003
Speciality: Physiotherapy.
● **Owner** Ms S Julka
P S T (Ref:HM16240)

### PHYSIOTHERAPY CLINIC

**Physiotherapy Clinic (The)**, Coppertrees House, 84A Market St, Kingswinford, **Midlands (West)**, DY6 9LN, ENG.
(T) 01384 280081 (F) 01384 270746
Speciality: Acupuncture, Physiotherapy.
● **Physiotherapist** Mr J Behari Q: MCSP, MSc, SRP. M: CSP.
S (Ref:HM16241)

### PHYSIOTHERAPY CLINIC

**Physiotherapy Clinic (The)**, Cannons Health Club, Newbury Racecourse, Newbury, **Berkshire**, RG14 7PN, ENG.
(T) 01635 569977
Speciality: Physiotherapy.
● **Partner** Mrs H Armitage
P S T (Ref:HM16242)

### PHYSIOTHERAPY CLINIC

**Physiotherapy Clinic (The)**, 96A Wilderspool Causeway, Warrington, **Cheshire**, WA4 6PU, ENG.
(T) 01925 575066
Speciality: Physiotherapy.
● **Partner** Mr B Burke
P S T (Ref:HM16243)

### PHYSIOTHERAPY CLINIC

**Physiotherapy Clinic (The)**, 78 Fencepiece Rd, Ilford, **Essex**, IG6 2JY, ENG.
(T) 020 8501 4647
Speciality: Physiotherapy.
P S T (Ref:HM16244)

### PHYSIOTHERAPY CLINIC

**Physiotherapy Clinic (The)**, 25 Coventry Rd, Hinckley, **Leicestershire**, LE10 0JR, ENG.
(T) 01455 632623
Speciality: Physiotherapy.
P S T (Ref:HM16245)

### PHYSIOTHERAPY CLINIC

**Physiotherapy Clinic Ltd (The)**, 55 Oakleigh Pk North, London, **London (Greater)**, N20 9AT, ENG.
(T) 020 8446 9633 (F) 020 8458 2003
Speciality: Physiotherapy.
● **Managing Director** Mr S Kapoor
P S T (Ref:HM16246)

### PHYSIOTHERAPY CLINIC

**Physiotherapy Clinic (The)**, Olympiad Leisure Centre, Monkton Park, Chippenham, **Wiltshire**, SN15 3PE, ENG.
(T) 01249 444144 (F) 01249 443648
Speciality: Acupuncture, Physiotherapy.
✔ [credit card]
● **Physiotherapist** Ms S Gillard Q: Grad Dip Phys, SRP. M: CSP.
● **Owner** Mr A Baldwin Q: BSc (Hons). M: SRP.
● **Associate** Mr C Smith
S Yrs. Est.: 5 (Ref:HM16247)

### PHYSIOTHERAPY CONSULTANCY SVS

**Physiotherapy Consultancy Services**, 4 Alexandra Rd, Reading, **Berkshire**, RG1 5PD, ENG.
(T) 01189 353020 (F) 01189 353040
Speciality: Physiotherapy.
P S T (Ref:HM16248)

### PHYSIOTHERAPY DEPARTMENT

**Physiotherapy Department**, Didcot Hospital, Didcot, **Oxfordshire**, OX11 0AG, ENG.
(T) 01235 816734
Speciality: Physiotherapy.
P S T (Ref:HM16249)

### PHYSIOTHERAPY DEPARTMENT

**Physiotherapy Department**, Rushden Memorial Clinic, Hayway, Rushden, **Northamptonshire**, NN10 6AG, ENG.
(T) 01933 410445
Speciality: Physiotherapy.
P S T (Ref:HM16250)

### PHYSIOTHERAPY DEPARTMENT

**Physiotherapy Department**, The Old Stennack School, Stennack, St. Ives, **Cornwall**, TR26 1RU, ENG.
(T) 01736 799085
Speciality: Physiotherapy.
● **Manager** Mrs G Ellis
P S T (Ref:HM16251)

### PHYSIOTHERAPY DEPT WELLINGTON

**Physiotherapy Department Wellington**, Wellington & District Hospital, Bulford,



Key continued: **Yrs.Est:** Years Established **Q:** Qualifications **M:** Professional Membership ✔ Indemnity Insurance [credit card] Accept Credit Cards

Wellington, **Somerset**, TA21 8QQ, ENG.
(T) 01823 666077
Speciality: Physiotherapy.
P S T (Ref:HM16252)

## PHYSIOTHERAPY PRACTICE
**Physiotherapy Practice**, 12 Clive Rd, West Dulwich, London, **London (Greater)**, SE21 8BY, ENG.
(T) 020 8670 3763 (F) 020 8670 3763
Speciality: Complementary Therapy, Electrotherapy, Manipulation, Massage (Therapeutic), Nutritional Therapy, Phytotherapy, Remedial Massage, Stress Therapy, Ultrasonics, Vitamin Therapy, Exercise Therapy, Gen Spirits Massage. ✔
● **Physiotherapist** Dr K Wright M: SMAE.
S Yrs. Est.: 11 (Ref:HM16253)

## PHYSIOTHERAPY PRACTICE
**Physiotherapy Practice (The)**, 105 Havelock Rd, Brighton, **Sussex (East)**, BN1 6GL, ENG.
(T) 01273 565212
Speciality: Physiotherapy.
● **Senior Partner** Mrs S Foulds
P S T (Ref:HM16254)

## PHYSIOTHERAPY SERVICES
**Physiotherapy Services**, 23 Greenwell St, Fauldhouse, Bathgate, **Lothian (West)**, EH47 9ET, SCO.
(T) 01501 770940
Speciality: Physiotherapy.
P S T (Ref:HM16255)

## PHYSIOTHERAPY SERVICES
**Physiotherapy Services**, 31 Market St, Tottington, Bury, **Lancashire**, BL8 4AA, ENG.
(T) 01204 880400
Speciality: Physiotherapy.
P S T (Ref:HM16256)

## PHYSIOTHERAPY SERVICES
**Physiotherapy Services**, 12 Station Trce, Caerphilly, **Glamorgan (Vale of)**, CF83 1HD, WAL.
(T) 029 2086 2137 (F) 029 2088 2817
Speciality: Physiotherapy.
● **Owner** Mrs D Hughes
P S T (Ref:HM16257)

## PHYSIOTHERAPY TREATMENT CLINIC
**Physiotherapy Treatment Clinic**, Stonecroft, Glebe Cl, Barton, Richmond, **Yorkshire (North)**, DL10 6JZ, ENG.
(T) 01325 377900
Speciality: Physiotherapy.
P S T (Ref:HM16258)

## PHYSIOTHERAPY, S K
**S K Physiotherapy**, 14 Lesbourne Rd, Reigate, **Surrey**, RH2 7LD, ENG.
(T) 07041 380194 (F) 07041 380194
Speciality: Osteopathy.
● **Owner** Mr K Blackburn
P S T (Ref:HM16259)

## PHYSIOWORKS
**Physioworks**, 1st Floor Avery House, 1-3 Avery Row, London, **London (Greater)**, W1X 9HF, ENG.
(T) 020 7409 1539
Speciality: Physiotherapy.
P S T (Ref:HM16260)

## PHYTHIAN, KATHLEEN
**Kathleen Phythian**, 55 Rodney St, Liverpool, **Merseyside**, L1 9ER, ENG.
(T) 01512 847318 (F) 01512 847318
Speciality: Hypnosis.
● **Owner** Ms K Phythian
B (Ref:HM16261)

## PICHLER, JOHN
**John Pichler**, 78 High St, Hurstpierpoint, Hassocks, **Sussex (West)**, BN6 9RQ, ENG.
(T) 01273 834211
Speciality: Osteopathy.
● **Owner** Mrs S Daillie
P S T (Ref:HM16262)

## PICHLER, JOHN F
**John F Pichler**, Horsted Green Health Centre, Horsted Pond Cottage, Little Horsted, Uckfield, **Sussex (East)**, TN22 5TR, ENG.
(T) 01825 760264 (F) 01825 760264
Speciality: Osteopathy.
● **Owner** Mr J Pichler
P S T (Ref:HM16263)

## PICKANCE, GEOFF S
**Geoff S Pickance**, 13 Ashfield Rd, Nottingham, **Nottinghamshire**, NG2 4LR, ENG.
(T) 01159 583686
Speciality: Complementary Medicines & Therapy.
● **Owner** Mr G Pickance
C M (Ref:HM16264)

## PICKARD, OWEN
**Owen Pickard**, 41 Cedar Gr, Roundswell, Barnstaple, **Devon**, EX31 3QT, ENG.
(T) 01271 328004
Speciality: Chiropractic.
● **Owner** Mr O Pickard
P S T (Ref:HM16265)

## PICKARD, ROBIN
**Robin Pickard**, Health Works Fitness Studio, Western Rd, Stratford-Upon-Avon, **Warwickshire**, CV37 0AH, ENG.
(T) 01789 262725
Speciality: Physiotherapy.
P S T (Ref:HM16266)

## PICKEN, M
**M Picken**, 11 Bunkley Meadow, Hamstreet, Ashford, **Kent**, TN26 2HQ, ENG.
(T) 01233 733212 (F) 01233 733212
Speciality: Chiropodists (Podiatrists).
● **Owner** Mrs M Picken
S (Ref:HM16267)

## PICKEN, M
**M Picken**, Ashford Clinic Of Complementary Medicine, Western Avenue, Ashford, **Kent**, TN23 1LY, ENG.
(T) 01233 631530
Speciality: Complementary Medicines & Therapy.
M (Ref:HM16268)

## PICKERDEN, P
**P Pickerden**, 475 Grimsby Rd, Cleethorpes, **Humberside (South)**, DN35 8AJ, ENG.
(T) 01472 600539
Speciality: Chiropodists (Podiatrists).
● **Owner** Mrs P Pickerden
S (Ref:HM16269)

## PICKERING, JO
**Jo Pickering**, The Manor House, Gaulby Rd, Kings Norton, Leicester, **Leicestershire**, LE7 9BA, ENG.
(T) 01162 596633 (F) 01162 596633
Speciality: Homeopathy.
● **Owner** Mrs J Pickering
M (Ref:HM16270)

## PICKETT, L
**L Pickett**, 9 Fairview, Weston-Super-Mare, **Somerset**, BS22 6UP, ENG.
(T) 01934 512973
Speciality: Reflexology.
● **Owner** Mrs L Pickett
S T (Ref:HM16271)

## PICKFORD, J K
**J K Pickford**, 39 Masefield Way, Northampton, **Northamptonshire**, NN2 7JT, ENG.
(T) 01604 710439
Speciality: Chiropodists (Podiatrists).
● **Owner** Mr J Pickford
S (Ref:HM16272)

## PICKIN, N & R J
**N & R J Pickin**, 24 Coronation Rd, Crosby, Liverpool, **Merseyside**, L23 5RQ, ENG.
(T) 01519 247238
Speciality: Chiropodists (Podiatrists).
● **Owner** Mr N Pickin
S (Ref:HM16273)

## PICKWOAD, BIRTHE H
**Birthe H Pickwoad, D O**, Brackenbury Natural Health Clinic, 30 Brackenbury Rd, London, **London (Greater)**, W6 0BA, ENG.
(T) 020 8741 9264 (F) 020 8748 6511
Speciality: Osteopathy.
● **Owner** Ms B Pickwoad
P S T (Ref:HM16274)

## PIDD, MARTIN
**Martin Pidd Registered Osteopath**, 19 Rodborough Rd, London, **London (Greater)**, NW11 8SA, ENG.
(T) 020 8455 2675
Speciality: Osteopathy.
P S T (Ref:HM16275)

## PIDDUCK, J
**J Pidduck**, 90 Ivy St, Rainham, Gillingham, **Kent**, ME8 8BH, ENG.
(T) 01634 387631
Speciality: Chiropodists (Podiatrists).
● **Owner** Mrs J Pidduck
S (Ref:HM16276)

## PIDGLEY, S
**S Pidgley**, 11 Clifton Rd, Llandudno, **Conwy**, LL30 2YH, WAL.
(T) 01492 548487
Speciality: Hypnosis.
B (Ref:HM16277)

## PIENAAR, DOROTHY
**Dorothy Pienaar**, 29 Grantham Rd, Reading, **Berkshire**, RG30 3NJ, ENG.
(T) 01189 583985
Speciality: Osteopathy.
● **Owner** Mrs D Pienaar
P S T (Ref:HM16278)

## PIERCEY, MICHAEL
**Michael Piercey Muswell Healing Arts**, 169 Avenue Mews, London, **London (Greater)**, N10 3NN, ENG.
(T) 020 8365 3545
Speciality: Complementary Medicines & Therapy.
● **Manager** Mrs D Sequoia
C M (Ref:HM16279)

## PIERRE, LINDA
**Linda Pierre J**, 155c Upland Rd, London, **London (Greater)**, SE22 0DF, ENG.
(T) 020 8299 2275 (F) 020 8299 2275
Speciality: Reflexology.
● **Owner** Ms L Pierre
S T (Ref:HM16280)

## PIGGOTT, R S
**R S Piggott**, 212 Porchester Rd, Nottingham, **Nottinghamshire**, NG3 6LH, ENG.
(T) 01159 504511
Speciality: Psychotherapy.
● **Owner** Mr R Piggott
B (Ref:HM16281)

## PIGHTLING, PATRICIA
**Patricia Pightling**, 34 Dunstall Avenue, Leicester, **Leicestershire**, LE3 3DN, ENG.
(T) 01162 993912
Speciality: Clairvoyants & Palmists.
● **Owner** Mrs P Pightling
B (Ref:HM16282)

## PIGOTT, MARJORIE
**Marjorie Pigott**, 36 Freelands Rd, Bromley, **Kent**, BR1 3HY, ENG.
(T) 020 8464 9330
Speciality: Chiropodists (Podiatrists).
● **Owner** Mrs M Pigott
S (Ref:HM16283)

## PIKE, BEA
**Bea Pike**, 84 Kempe Rd, London, **London (Greater)**, NW6 6SL, ENG.
(T) 020 8969 1247
Speciality: Osteopathy.
P S T (Ref:HM16284)

## PIKE, DAVINA
**Davina Pike**, 4 Hollydale Drive, Bromley, **Kent**, BR2 8QL, ENG.
(T) 01689 858308
Speciality: Reflexology.
S T (Ref:HM16285)

## PIKE, ELIZABETH G & J K
**Elizabeth G & J K Pike**, 52 High St, Shirley, Solihull, **Midlands (West)**, B90 1EY, ENG.
(T) 01214 302828



Key: B Mind-Body Medicine C Complementary Medicine H Self Help Treatment M Medicinal Therapy O Oriental Medicine P Postural Therapy S Manipulative Structural Therapy T Touch Therapy

Speciality: Chiropody. ✔
● **Partner** Mrs E Pike
● **Owner/Chiropractor** Mr J Pike Q: Inst.CH.P. LCH. M: Inst.CH.P.
M Yrs. Est.: 30 (Ref:HM16286)

## PIKE, R P
**R P Pike**, 7 Pelham Rd, Southsea, **Hampshire**, PO5 3DT, ENG.
(T) 023 9282 1711
Speciality: Chiropodists (Podiatrists).
S (Ref:HM16287)

## PIKE, RALPH
**Ralph Pike**, 73 Endowood Rd, Sheffield, **Yorkshire (South)**, S7 2LY, ENG.
(T) 01142 363043
Speciality: Complementary Medicines & Therapy.
C M (Ref:HM16288)

## PIKE, ROGER
**Roger Pike**, 4 Mayfield Rd, Girton, Cambridge, **Cambridgeshire**, CB3 0PH, ENG.
(T) 01223 277355
Speciality: Osteopathy.
● **Owner** Mr R Pike
P S T (Ref:HM16289)

## PIKE, S
**S Pike**, 48 Church Rd, Malvern, **Worcestershire**, WR14 1NG, ENG.
(T) 01684 568744
Speciality: Osteopathy.
P S T (Ref:HM16290)

## PIKE, STUART
**Stuart Pike**, 1 Oswald Ter South, Sunderland, **Tyne and Wear**, SR5 3BG, ENG.
(T) 01915 499664
Speciality: Hypnosis.
B (Ref:HM16291)

## PILATES FOUNDATION UK
**Pilates Foundation UK Ltd**, 16 Canning St, Edinburgh, **Edinburgh (City of)**, EH3 8EG, SCO.
(T) 01312 211131
Speciality: Complementary Medicines & Therapy.
● **Partner** Mr P Charlton
M (Ref:HM16292)

## PILATES FOUNDATION UK
**Pilates foundation UK Ltd**, 185 Ladybank Rd, Mickleover, Derby, **Derbyshire**, DE3 5QL, ENG.
(T) 01332 521270
Speciality: Complementary Medicines & Therapy.
● **Manager** Ms Y White
M (Ref:HM16293)

## PILATES STUDIO
**Pilates Studio Ltd (The)**, 116 Great Portland St, London, **London (Greater)**, W1N 5PG, ENG.
(T) 020 7636 2636
Speciality: Complementary Medicines & Therapy.
● **Joint Director** Ms S Parravicini
M (Ref:HM16294)

## PILGRIM, N M
**N M Pilgrim**, 71 Mayfield Rd, Coventry, **Midlands (West)**, CV5 6PL, ENG.
(T) 024 7667 3741
Speciality: Physiotherapy.
P S T (Ref:HM16295)

## PILKINGTON, MICHAEL
**Michael Pilkington**, 18 Mead Walk, Burton-On-Trent, **Staffordshire**, DE15 9SJ, ENG.
(T) 01283 541223
Speciality: Chiropodists (Podiatrists).
● **Owner** Mr M Pilkington
S (Ref:HM16296)

## PILLATH, CHRISTINE
**Christine Pillath**, 58 Holifast Rd, Sutton Coldfield, **Midlands (West)**, B72 1AE, ENG.
(T) 01213 731069
Speciality: Alexander Technique. ✔
● **Owner** Ms C Pillath Q: MSTAT.
C Yrs. Est.: 2 (Ref:HM16297)

## PILLING, M
**M Pilling**, 34 Elmsleigh Gardens, Southampton, **Hampshire**, SO16 3GF, ENG.
(T) 023 8067 9408
Speciality: Reflexology.
● **Owner** Mrs M Pilling
S T (Ref:HM16298)

## PILTON PHYSIOTHERAPY CENTRE
**Pilton Physiotherapy Centre**, 20 Pilton St, Barnstaple, **Devon**, EX31 1PJ, ENG.
(T) 01271 379789
Speciality: Physiotherapy.
P S T (Ref:HM16299)

## PIM CHIROPRACTIC CLINIC
**Pim Chiropractic Clinic**, 29 Kendrick Rd, Reading, **Berkshire**, RG1 5DU, ENG.
(T) 01189 752153 (F) 01189 874514
Speciality: Chiropractic.
● **Owner** Ms F Pim
P S T (Ref:HM16300)

## PIM HEALTH CLINIC
**Pim Health Clinic (The)**, 29 Kendrick Rd, Reading, **Berkshire**, RG1 5DU, ENG.
(T) 01189 872313
Speciality: Chiropractic, Herbal Medicine, Osteopathy, Stress Therapy. ✔ [Credit card]
● **Owner** Dr D Pim Q: DC, DO, ND. M: GCC, NIMH.
P Yrs. Est.: 37 (Ref:HM16301)

## PIM, MICHAEL (DR)
**Dr Michael Pim**, 76 New Wokingham Rd, Crowthorne, **Berkshire**, RG45 6JP, ENG.
(T) 01344 762777
Speciality: Chiropractic.
● **Owner** Dr M Pimm
P S T (Ref:HM16302)

## PIM, R D
**R D Pim**, 29 Kendrick Rd, Reading, **Berkshire**, RG1 5DU, ENG.
(T) 01189 872313
Speciality: Chiropractors.
● **Principal** Dr D Pim
P S T (Ref:HM16303)

## PINCHES, CHRISTOPHER
**Christopher Pinches**, 146 High St, Banstead, **Surrey**, SM7 2NZ, ENG.
(T) 01737 373684
Speciality: Osteopathy.
P S T (Ref:HM16304)

## PINCHES, CHRISTOPHER
**Christopher Pinches**, 2 Bishops Rd, Farnham, **Surrey**, GU9 0JA, ENG.
(T) 01252 722912
Speciality: Osteopathy.
● **Osteopath** Mr C Pinches Q: DO.
P S T (Ref:HM16305)

## PINDER CENTRE
**Pinder Centre For Hydrotherapy & Physiotherapy (The)**, Avington, Winchester, **Hampshire**, SO21 1DD, ENG.
(T) 01962 779498
Speciality: Physiotherapy.
P S T (Ref:HM16306)

## PINDER, F C
**F C Pinder**, 2 Bramble Cl, Hildenborough, Tonbridge, **Kent**, TN11 9HG, ENG.
(T) 01732 833115 (F) 01732 833115
Speciality: Hypnosis.
● **Owner** Ms F Pinder
B (Ref:HM16307)

## PINDER, M
**M Pinder**, 40A Ringwood Rd, London, **London (Greater)**, E17 8PP, ENG.
(T) 020 8925 9314 (F) 020 8521 2944
Speciality: Homeopathy.
● **Owner** Ms M Pinder
M (Ref:HM16308)

## PINE & ASSOCIATES
**Louise Pine & Associates**, St Mary's Medical Centre, Vicarage Rd, Strood, Rochester, **Kent**, ME2 4DG, ENG.
(T) 01634 294884
Speciality: Chiropodists (Podiatrists).
S (Ref:HM16309)

## PINE LODGE
**Pine Lodge**, 79 Liverpool Rd, Chester, **Cheshire**, CH2 1AW, ENG.
(T) 01244 364776 (F) 01244 364778
Speciality: Psychiatry.
● **Director** Dr A Cotgrove
B (Ref:HM16310)

## PINEHURST
**Pinehurst**, 3 Avondale Rd, St. Leonards-On-Sea, **Sussex (East)**, TN38 0SA, ENG.
(T) 01424 423687 (F) 01424 429984
Speciality: Complementary Medicines & Therapy.
● **Owner** Mrs S Lyle
C M (Ref:HM16311)

## PINEWOOD CHIROPODY PRACTICE
**Anthony H Mason**, Maythorne Cottage, Pinewood Rd, Iver, **Buckinghamshire**, SL0 0NL, ENG.
(T) 01753 652754 (F) 01753 655161
(E) nicola-segrott@virginnet.co.uk
Speciality: Biomechanics, Chiropody, Podiatry. ✔
● **Chiropodist (Podiatrist)** Mr A Mason Q: MBChA, MSSCh. M: B.A.Ch.P.
● **Chiropodist** Nicola Segrott (T) 01753 655161 Q: MBChA, MSSCh. M: B.A.Ch.P.
S Yrs. Est.: 15 (Ref:HM16312)

## PINEWOOD PHYSIOTHERAPY CLINIC
**Pinewood Physiotherapy Clinic**, 8 Barbour Gardens, Colchester, **Essex**, CO2 9SA, ENG.
(T) 01206 545557
Speciality: Bonesetting, Electrotherapy, Manipulation, Massage (Therapeutic), Osteopathy, Phytotherapy, Stress Therapy, Ultrasonics, Rehabilitation Exercises. ✔
● **Physiotherapist** Mr T Treharne M: SMAE.
S Yrs. Est.: 12 (Ref:HM16313)

## PINKNEY, J G
**J G Pinkney**, 3 Southfields Rd, Eastbourne, **Sussex (East)**, BN21 1BU, ENG.
(T) 01323 645210
Speciality: Chiropodists (Podiatrists).
● **Owner** Mr J Pinkney
S (Ref:HM16314)

## PINNER HLTH FOODS & THRPY CTRE
**Pinner Health Foods & Therapy Centre**, 65 Bridge St, Pinner, **London (Greater)**, HA5 3HZ, ENG.
(T) 020 8429 1336
Speciality: Complementary Medicines & Therapy.
● **Director** Mr S Bilakhia
C M (Ref:HM16315)

## PINNER ROAD PHYSIOTHERAPY
**Pinner Road Physiotherapy**, 97 Pinner Rd, Harrow, **London (Greater)**, HA1 4ET, ENG.
(T) 020 8861 6001
Speciality: Acupuncture, Physiotherapy. ✔ [Credit card]
● **Physiotherapist** Kate Crotty Q: MCSP, SRP. M: AACP, CSP.
S Yrs. Est.: 10 (Ref:HM16316)

## PINNY, JASON
**Jason Pinny**, 247 Watling St, Radlett, **Hertfordshire**, WD7 7AL, ENG.
(T) 01923 853689
Speciality: Osteopathy.
● **Owner** Mr J Pinny
P S T (Ref:HM16317)

## PINSENT, MARIA
**Maria Pinsent**, Flat 5, 162 Randolph Avenue, London, **London (Greater)**, W9 1PG, ENG.
(T) 020 7266 5762
Speciality: Reflexology.
S T (Ref:HM16318)

## PINSKER, SUZANNE
**Suzanne Pinsker**, The Chelsea Practice, 186 Fulham Rd, London, **London (Greater)**, SW10 9PN, ENG.
(T) 020 7352 9385
Speciality: Osteopathy.
P S T (Ref:HM16319)


Key continued: Yrs.Est: Years Established Q: Qualifications M: Professional Membership ✔ Indemnity Insurance [Credit card] Accept Credit Cards

## PINTO, RANDAL P
**Randal P Pinto**, Hertford Natural Therapy Centre, 4 Old Cross, Hertford, **Hertfordshire**, SG14 1PY, ENG.
(T) 01992 589439
Speciality: Acupuncture.
O (Ref:HM16320)

## PIPER CHIROPODY
**Piper Chiropody**, 3 Bystock Ter, Exeter, **Devon**, EX4 4HY, ENG.
(T) 01392 217333
Speciality: Chiropodists (Podiatrists).
● **Owner** Mr D Piper
S (Ref:HM16321)

## PIPER, C
**C Piper**, 3 Battle Rd, St. Leonards-On-Sea, **Sussex (East)**, TN37 7AA, ENG.
(T) 01424 440898
Speciality: Osteopathy.
● **Owner** Miss C Piper
P S T (Ref:HM16322)

## PIPER, CLAIRE
**Claire Piper**, 3 Battle Rd, St. Leonards-On-Sea, **Sussex (East)**, TN38 0TU, ENG.
(T) 01424 713643
Speciality: Osteopathy.
P S T (Ref:HM16323)

## PIPER, KARREN
**Karren Piper**, 53 The St, Brandeston, Woodbridge, **Suffolk**, IP13 7AA, ENG.
(T) 01728 685688
Speciality: Reflexology.
S T (Ref:HM16324)

## PIPER, MARK W
**Mark W Piper**, 17A High St, Manningtree, **Essex**, CO11 1AG, ENG.
(T) 01206 392458 (F) 01206 392458
Speciality: Osteopathy.
● **Partner** Mr M Piper
P S T (Ref:HM16325)

## PIPER, ROBIN
**Robin Piper**, 148 Mercers Rd, London, **London (Greater)**, N19 4PX, ENG.
(T) 020 7272 4002
Speciality: Psychotherapy.
B (Ref:HM16326)

## PIRAINO, MARK
**Piraino Mark**, Somers House, Linkfield Corner, Redhill, **Surrey**, RH1 2JB, ENG.
(T) 01737 766659
Speciality: Osteopathy.
P S T (Ref:HM16327)

## PIRANTY, AVERIL
**Averil Piranty**, Staunton Lodge, Gloucester Rd, Staunton, Gloucester, **Gloucestershire**, GL19 3RD, ENG.
(T) 01452 840103
Speciality: Complementary Medicines & Therapy.
M (Ref:HM16328)

## PIRIE, STEPHEN
**Stephen Pirie**, 17 Park Rd, London, **London (Greater)**, NW1 6XN, ENG.
(T) 020 7935 3207
Speciality: Osteopathy.
P S T (Ref:HM16329)

## PISCES NATURAL THERAPY CENTRE
**Pisces Natural Therapy Centre (The)**, 7 Shakespeare Rd, Romford, **Essex**, RM1 2QD, ENG.
(T) 01708 724474
Speciality: Auto Suggestion, Aversion Therapy, Bach Remedies, Biofeedback, Complementary Therapy, Counselling, Hypnosis, Hypnotherapy, Naturopathy, Psychotherapy, Reflexology, Stress Therapy. ✔
● **Owner/Hypno-Analyst**
Mrs A Malenoir Q: PhD. M: NCH.
B Yrs. Est.: 18 (Ref:HM16330)

## PITAMBER, NADINE
**Nadine Pitamber**, 54 Norbury Court Rd, London, **London (Greater)**, SW16 4HT, ENG.
(T) 07909 960759
Speciality: Reflexology.
S T (Ref:HM16331)

## PITCAIRN, TONY
**Tony Pitcairn**, 7 Middleton Avenue, Ilkley, **Yorkshire (West)**, LS29 0AD, ENG.
(T) 01943 609066
Speciality: Hypnosis.
B (Ref:HM16332)

## PITCAIRN-KNOWLES, M
**M Pitcairn-Knowles**, Springbank House, 13 Pembroke Rd, Sevenoaks, **Kent**, TN13 1XR, ENG.
(T) 01732 453956
Speciality: Osteopathy.
● **Partner** Mrs P Pitcairn-Knowles
P S T (Ref:HM16333)

## PITCAIRN-KNOWLES, R
**R Pitcairn-Knowles**, Springbank House, 13 Pembroke Rd, Sevenoaks, **Kent**, TN13 1XR, ENG.
(T) 01732 453956
Speciality: Osteopathy.
● **Partner** Mrs P Pitcairn-Knowles
P S T (Ref:HM16334)

## PITE, J
**J Pite**, 26 Harold Rd, London, **London (Greater)**, E11 4QY, ENG.
(T) 020 8558 8958
Speciality: Alexander Technique.
P S (Ref:HM16335)

## PITHER, ANNE
**Anne Pither**, 29 Weare Gifford, Shoeburyness, Southend-On-Sea, **Essex**, SS3 8AB, ENG.
(T) 01702 586036 (F) 01702 586036
Speciality: Physiotherapy.
● **Owner** Mrs A Pither
P S T (Ref:HM16336)

## PITHER'S YARD CLINIC
**Pither's Yard Clinic**, High St, Castle Cary, **Somerset**, BA7 7AN, ENG.
(T) 01963 350405
Speciality: Complementary Medicines & Therapy.
● **Director** Mrs C Whiticombe
M (Ref:HM16337)

## PITMAN, CLARE
**Clare Pitman**, 102 Chosen Drive, Churchdown, Gloucester, **Gloucestershire**, GL3 2QU, ENG.
(T) 01452 714511 (F) 01452 541369
Speciality: Osteopathy.
● **Partner** Mr C Hayden
P S T (Ref:HM16338)

## PITMAN, DIANE
**Diane Pitman**, 125 Carlton Rd, Redhill, **Surrey**, RH1 2DE, ENG.
(T) 01737 779931
Speciality: Homeopathy.
M (Ref:HM16339)

## PITMAN, LOU
**Lou Pitman**, 5 Gundreda Rd, Lewes, **Sussex (East)**, BN7 1PT, ENG.
(T) 01273 472775
Speciality: Complementary Medicines & Therapy.
● **Owner** Ms L Pitman
C M (Ref:HM16340)

## PITMAN, SUE
**Sue Pitman**, 36 Haverhill Rd, Stapleford, Cambridge, **Cambridgeshire**, CB2 5BX, ENG.
(T) 01223 843164
Speciality: Complementary Medicines & Therapy.
● **Owner** Mrs S Pitman
C M (Ref:HM16341)

## PITMAN, VICKI
**Vicki Pitman**, 54 The Avenue, Yeovil, **Somerset**, BA21 4BN, ENG.
(T) 01935 422488
Speciality: Aromatherapy.
M O (Ref:HM16342)

## PITMAN, VICTORIA
**Victoria Pitman**, Hayes Corner, South Cheriton, Templecombe, **Somerset**, BA8 0BR, ENG.
(T) 01963 370300
Speciality: Reflexology.
S T (Ref:HM16343)

## PITSTOW, S P
**S P Pitstow**, 25 Bath St, Rhyl, **Denbighshire**, LL18 3EB, WAL.
(T) 01745 339314
Speciality: Osteopathy.
P S T (Ref:HM16344)

## PITT, D
**D Pitt**, 9 Gatefield Lane, Faversham, **Kent**, ME13 8NX, ENG.
(T) 01795 591337
Speciality: Osteopathy.
● **Owner** Miss D Pitt
P S T (Ref:HM16345)

## PITT, HARRY
**Harry Pitt**, 117 High St, Kinver, Stourbridge, **Midlands (West)**, DY7 6HL, ENG.
(T) 07071 224275
Speciality: Chiropodists (Podiatrists).
● **Owner** Mr H Pitt
S (Ref:HM16346)

## PITT, I T
**I T Pitt Osteopath**, 127 Milton Rd, Weston-Super-Mare, **Somerset**, BS23 2UY, ENG.
(T) 01934 629116
Speciality: Acupuncture, Bonesetting, Chiropractic, Cranial Osteopathy, Cupping, Dietician, Electrotherapy, Homeopathy, Manipulation, Massage (Therapeutic), Micro Manipulation, Moxibustion, Nutritional Therapy, Osteopathy, Postural Integration.
● **Osteopath** Mr I Pitt Q: DO, Lic.Ac. M: GOsC.
S Yrs. Est.: 17 (Ref:HM16347)

## PITT, KATHLEEN
**Kathleen Pitt**, 79 Clare St, Northampton, **Northamptonshire**, NN1 3JE, ENG.
(T) 01604 631806
Speciality: Reflexology.
S T (Ref:HM16348)

## PITT, KATHY
**Kathy Pitt**, 32A East St, Shoreham-by-Sea, **Sussex (West)**, BN43 5ZD, ENG.
(T) 01273 454310
Speciality: Holistic Healing, Homeopathy. ✔
● **Homeopath/Holistic Healer**
Ms K Pitt Q: BA, LCH, RSHom.
C Yrs. Est.: 12 (Ref:HM16349)

## PITT, S E
**S E Pitt**, Suite 1 Worthington House, 146 High St, Burton-On-Trent, **Staffordshire**, DE14 1JE, ENG.
(T) 01283 536309
Speciality: Physiotherapy.
● **Owner** Ms S Pitt
P S T (Ref:HM16350)

## PITT, S E
**S E Pitt**, White Gables, 104 Walsall Rd, Lichfield, **Staffordshire**, WS13 8AF, ENG.
(T) 01543 258382
Speciality: Physiotherapy.
P S T (Ref:HM16351)

## PITTAM, C
**C Pittam**, 3 Pleydell Avenue, London, **London (Greater)**, W6 0XX, ENG.
(T) 020 8741 3404
Speciality: Chiropractic.
● **Practice Manager** Dr C Pittam
P S T (Ref:HM16352)

## PITTS, RICHARD
**Richard Pitts**, 22 Stirling Cl, Carterton, **Oxfordshire**, OX18 3PH, ENG.
(T) 01993 846046
Speciality: Reflexology.
S T (Ref:HM16353)

## PIZER, ISAAC
**Isaac Pizer**, Bishops Drive, Oakwood, Derby, **Derbyshire**, DE21 2DF, ENG.
(T) 01332 281607
Speciality: Psychotherapy.
● **Owner** Mr I Pizer
B (Ref:HM16354)

## PLAINS PHYSIO & BACK PAIN
**Plains Physiotherapy & Back Pain Clinic**, 856A Woodborough Rd, Nottingham,



Key: B Mind-Body Medicine C Complementary Medicine H Self Help Treatment M Medicinal Therapy O Oriental Medicine P Postural Therapy S Manipulative Structural Therapy T Touch Therapy

**Nottinghamshire**, NG3 5QQ, ENG.
(T) 01159 606408 (F) 01159 606408
Speciality: Physiotherapy. ✔
● **Physiotherapist** Reuben Crossley Q: MCSP, SRP. M: CSP.
● **Owner** Mr I Tomlinson
S (Ref:HM16355)

## PLANT CHIROPODY
**Plant Chiropody**, 8 Parkway, Wilmslow, **Cheshire**, SK9 1LS, ENG.
(T) 01625 526875
Speciality: Chiropodists (Podiatrists).
● **Owner** Mrs R Plant
S (Ref:HM16356)

## PLANT, BELINDA
**Belinda Plant**, 1 Broadham Pl, Hall Hill, Oxted, **Surrey**, RH8 9PD, ENG.
(T) 01883 730766
Speciality: Reflexology.
S T (Ref:HM16357)

## PLANT, R M
**R M Plant**, 19A High St, Burton-On-Trent, **Staffordshire**, DE14 1HU, ENG.
(T) 01283 566129
Speciality: Chiropodists (Podiatrists).
● **Owner** Mr R Plant
S (Ref:HM16358)

## PLANT, R M
**R M Plant**, 21 Birch Trce, Stoke-On-Trent, **Staffordshire**, ST1 3JN, ENG.
(T) 01782 215504
Speciality: Biomechanics, Chiropody, Nail Surgery. ✔
● **Owner/Chiropodist** Miss R Plant Q: M.S.C.P.
C Yrs. Est.: 12 (Ref:HM16359)

## PLANT, R M
**R M Plant**, Uttoxeter Town Hall, High St, Uttoxeter, **Staffordshire**, ST14 7HN, ENG.
(T) 01889 563645
Speciality: Chiropodists (Podiatrists).
● **Owner** Mrs R Plant
S (Ref:HM16360)

## PLANT, R M
**R M Plant**, Marsh Farm, Sugnall, Stafford, **Staffordshire**, ST21 6NF, ENG.
(T) 01785 850346
Speciality: Chiropodists (Podiatrists).
● **Owner** Miss R Plant
S (Ref:HM16361)

## PLATINGS, T N
**T N Platings**, Veldon, Holden Rd, Tunbridge Wells, **Kent**, TN4 0QD, ENG.
(T) 01892 533187
Speciality: Chiropodists (Podiatrists).
● **Owner** Mrs T Platings
S (Ref:HM16362)

## PLATT, DEE
**Dee Platt**, 30 Glycena Rd, London, **London (Greater)**, SW11 5TR, ENG.
(T) 020 7223 6795 (F) 020 7223 6795
Speciality: Kinesiology, Reflexology, High Touch Jin Shin.
● **Owner** Miss D Platt
C (Ref:HM16363)

## PLATT, JOHN
**John Platt**, 22 Canterbury Avenue, Ilford, **Essex**, IG1 3NA, ENG.
(T) 020 8554 9536
Speciality: Physiotherapy.
● **Owner** Mr J Platt
P S T (Ref:HM16364)

## PLAYERS, MEGAN
**Megan Players**, Eastcove House, Tiverton, **Devon**, EX16 6RS, ENG.
(T) 01398 331973
Speciality: Shiatsu, Palm Readings. ✔
● **Shiatsu Practitioner**
Megan Players Q: BA (Hons), MRSS. M: RSS.
C Yrs. Est.: 5 (Ref:HM16365)

## PLAYLE, A
**A Playle**, 23E Dulwich Rd, London, **London (Greater)**, SE24 0NT, ENG.
(T) 020 7737 1225
Speciality: Chiropodists (Podiatrists).
● **Owner** A Playle
S (Ref:HM16366)

## PLESHETTE, JANET
**Janet Pleshette**, 27 Connaught Rd, Barnet, **Hertfordshire**, EN5 2PX, ENG.
(T) 020 8440 5341
Speciality: Reflexology.
S T (Ref:HM16367)

## PLESTED, JOHN
**John Plested**, 9 Stubbs Avenue, Headington, Oxford, **Oxfordshire**, OX3 8RT, ENG.
(T) 01865 777592
Speciality: Complementary Medicines & Therapy, Holistic Massage. ✔
● **Owner/Massage** Mr J Plested Q: ITEC.
C Yrs. Est.: 9 (Ref:HM16368)

## PLESTED, NICOLA
**Nicola Plested**, Cogges Surgery, Cogges Hill Rd, Witney, **Oxfordshire**, OX8 6FP, ENG.
(T) 01993 709966
Speciality: Chiropractic.
● **Principal** Ms N Plested
P S T (Ref:HM16369)

## PLEWS, BARBARA
**Barbara Plews**, 2 St Peters Lane, Canterbury, **Kent**, CT1 2BP, ENG.
(T) 01227 454354
Speciality: Physiotherapy.
● **Owner** Mrs B Plew
P S T (Ref:HM16370)

## PLEXUS BIO ENERGY
**Plexus Bio Energy**, 74 Bridgewater Drive, Northampton, **Northamptonshire**, NN3 3AG, ENG.
(T) 01604 603057 (F) 01604 629016
Speciality: Complementary Medicines & Therapy.
● **Manager** Mr G Odocherty
C M (Ref:HM16371)

## PLEXUS BIO ENERGY
**Plexus Bio Energy**, Market St, Ennis, **County Clare**, IRE.
(T) 06568 41844
Speciality: Complementary Medicines & Therapy.
M (Ref:HM16372)

## PLEXUS BIO ENERGY
**Plexus Bio Energy (Irl) Ltd**, Lismoyle Hse, Merchants Rd, **County Galway**, IRE.
(T) 09156 8855
Speciality: Complementary Medicines & Therapy.
M (Ref:HM16373)

## PLEXUS BIO-ENERGY
**Plexus Bio-Energy & Therapeutic Massage**, 28 Garden Vlge, Cres, Kilpeddar, Wicklow, **County Wicklow**, IRE.
(T) 01281 1194
Speciality: Complementary Medicines & Therapy.
M (Ref:HM16374)

## PLEXUS BIO-ENERGY HEALING
**Plexus Bio-Energy Healing**, 9 Dargle View, Rathfarnham, **County Dublin**, IRE.
(T) 01298 6878
(W) www.avcweb.com/bioenergy
Speciality: Complementary Medicines & Therapy.
M (Ref:HM16375)

## PLOWMAN, JOHN (DR)
**Dr John Plowman**, Beeston House, Goldcroft Common, Caerleon, Newport, NP18 1NG, WAL.
(T) 01633 420095
Speciality: Hypnotherapy.
B (Ref:HM16376)

## PLOWMAN, JOHN (DR)
**Dr John Plowman**, 22 Goldcroft Common, Newport, NP18 1, WAL.
(T) 01633 420095
Speciality: Hypnosis.
B (Ref:HM16377)

## PLUCKROSE, S N
**S N Pluckrose**, Croham Lodge, Croham Rd, Crowborough, **Sussex (East)**, TN6 2RH, ENG.
(T) 01892 665291
Speciality: Osteopathy.
● **Partner** Ms S Pluckrose
P S T (Ref:HM16378)

## PLUIDGE, MARK
**Mark Plumridge**, 6 Highburgh Rd, Glasgow, **Glasgow (City of)**, G12 9YD, SCO.
(T) 01413 390523
Speciality: Biomechanics, Chiropody, Nail Surgery, Podiatry. ✔
● **Chiropodist (Podiatrist)**
Mr M Plumridge Q: DPodM, S.R.Ch. M: S.C.P.
M Yrs. Est.: 17 (Ref:HM16379)

## PLUMB, STEPHEN
**Stephen Plumb**, 18 Christchurch St West, Frome, **Somerset**, BA11 1EG, ENG.
(T) 01373 463548
Speciality: Osteopathy.
● **Owner** Mr S Plumb
P S T (Ref:HM16380)

## PLUMMER, ANNE
**Anne Plummer**, Cleveland Homoepathic Clinic, 72A Parliament Rd, Middlesbrough, **Cleveland**, TS1 4JS, ENG.
(T) 01642 244337
Speciality: Homeopathy.
● **Partner** Mrs A Plummer
M (Ref:HM16381)

## PLUMMER, FRANK
**Frank Plummer**, 16 Hillside Avenue, Silverstone, Towcester, **Northamptonshire**, NN12 8UR, ENG.
(T) 01327 857495
Speciality: Electrolysis.
T (Ref:HM16382)

## PLUMMER, HOWARD G
**Howard G Plummer**, 206 Newport Rd, Cardiff, **Glamorgan (Vale of)**, CF24 1DL, WAL.
(T) 029 2048 4683
Speciality: Complementary Medicines & Therapy.
● **Owner** Mr H Plummer
C M (Ref:HM16383)

## PLUMMER, VALERIE
**Valerie Plummer**, May Cottage, Grubwood Lane, Cookham, Maidenhead, **Berkshire**, SL6 9UD, ENG.
(T) 01628 475582
Speciality: Aromatherapy, Bach Remedies.
M O (Ref:HM16384)

## PLUMMER, VALERIE
**Valerie Plummer**, Cookham Dean, **Berkshire**, SL6, ENG.
(T) 01628 475582
Speciality: Aromatherapy.
M O (Ref:HM16385)

## PLYMOUTH CHIROPODY PRACTICE
**Plymouth Chiropody Practice**, 5 Cornwall St, Plymouth City Centre, Plymouth, **Devon**, PL1 1NL, ENG.
(T) 01752 661700
Speciality: Chiropodists (Podiatrists).
● **Owner** Miss K George
S (Ref:HM16386)

## PLYMOUTH IND COMP PSYCH NURS
**Plymouth Independent Community Psychiatric Nursing**, Courtyard Barn, Bephillick, Duloe, Liskeard, **Cornwall**, PL14 4QA, ENG.
(T) 01503 264380
Speciality: Psychiatry.
B (Ref:HM16387)

## PLYMOUTH OSTEOPATHS
**Plymouth Osteopaths**, 13 Peverell Park Rd, Peverell, Plymouth, **Devon**, PL3 4LS, ENG.
(T) 01752 667581
(W) www.plymouthosteopaths.co.uk
Speciality: Kinesiology, Osteopathy. ✔
● **Owner** Mr J Doddrell Q: DO. M: GOsC.
● **Osteopath** Mr A Banbury Q: DO. M: GOsC.



Key continued: Yrs.Est: Years Established Q: Qualifications M: Professional Membership ✔ Indemnity Insurance Accept Credit Cards

● **Osteopath** Mr J Oldham **Q:** BSc, Hons (OST). **M:** GOsC.
● **Osteopath** Pia Mudaciar **Q:** BSc. **M:** GOsC.
**S** Yrs. Est.: 20 (**Ref:**HM16388)

## PLYMPTON OSTEOPATHIC CLINIC

**Plympton Osteopathic Clinic**, 70 Ridgeway, Plymouth, **Devon**, PL7 2AL, ENG.
(T) 01752 347663
Speciality: Chiropodists (Podiatrists).
● **Owner** Mrs H Robinson
**S** (**Ref:**HM16389)

## POCKETT, MARGARET

**Margaret Pockett**, 16 Clarence Sq, Cheltenham, **Gloucestershire**, GL50 4JN, ENG.
(T) 01242 241933
Speciality: Acupuncture.
**C** **O** (**Ref:**HM16390)

## POCOCK, A

**A Pocock**, 2 Broad Oak Rd, Bristol, BS13 9DG, ENG.
(T) 01179 644145
Speciality: Chiropody. ✔
● **Chiropodist (Podiatrist)**
Avril Pocock **Q:** SMAE. **M:** SMAE.
**M** Yrs. Est.: 9 (**Ref:**HM16391)

## POD NHS/PRIVATE FOOT HLTH SVS

**Podiatry NHS & Private Foot Health Services**, St Barnabas Clinic, Albert St, Oxford, **Oxfordshire**, OX2 6AY, ENG.
(T) 01865 311312 (F) 01865 311676
Speciality: Chiropodists (Podiatrists).
● **Manager** Mr P Joyce
**S** (**Ref:**HM16392)

## PODIATRY CLINIC

**Podiatry Clinic (The)**, The Clinic, 198 New North Rd, London, **London (Greater)**, N1 7BJ, ENG.
(T) 020 7354 8820
(E) rfp@thepodiatryclinic.com
Speciality: Biomechanics, Chiropody, Postural Integration. ✔
● **Chiropodist (Podiatrist)**
Mr R Pearce **Q:** BSc (Hons). **M:** S.C.P.
**S** Yrs. Est.: 5 (**Ref:**HM16393)

## PODIATRY CLINIC

**Podiatry Clinic (The)**, 23 St Peter St, Peterhead, **Aberdeenshire**, AB42 1QB, SCO.
(T) 01779 477576 (F) 01779 477476
Speciality: Chiropodists (Podiatrists).
● **Owner** Ms F Sutherland
**S** (**Ref:**HM16394)

## PODIATRY SERVICES

**Podiatry Services**, 7 Drake Cl, Horsham, **Sussex (West)**, RH12 5UB, ENG.
(T) 01403 211944 (F) 01403 254604
Speciality: Chiropodists (Podiatrists).
● **Owner** Mr A Jenkins
**S** (**Ref:**HM16395)

## PODICARE CHIROPODY

**Podicare Chiropody**, 4 The Gallery, Letchworth, **Hertfordshire**, SG6 3BL, ENG.
(T) 01462 670900
Speciality: Chiropodists (Podiatrists).
● **Owner** Ms E Wade
**S** (**Ref:**HM16396)

## PODO KARE

**Podo Kare Ltd**, 3 Cheadle Cl, Penkridge, Stafford, **Staffordshire**, ST19 5SZ, ENG.
(T) 01785 715568
Speciality: Chiropodists (Podiatrists).
**S** (**Ref:**HM16397)

## POINTER, TERESA

**Teresa Pointer**, 185 Hungate St, Aylsham, Norwich, **Norfolk**, NR11 6JX, ENG.
(T) 01263 733916
Speciality: Reflexology.
**S** **T** (**Ref:**HM16398)

## POINTON, RICHARD

**Richard Pointon**, Mitre House, 149 Western Rd, Brighton, **Sussex (East)**, BN1 2DB, ENG.
(T) 01273 326622
Speciality: Osteopathy.
● **Owner** Mr R Pointon
**P** **S** **T** (**Ref:**HM16399)

## POLAK, CAROL

**Carol Polak**, 67 Evendons Lane, Wokingham, **Berkshire**, RG41 4AD, ENG.
(T) 01189 770258
Speciality: Reflexology.
**S** **T** (**Ref:**HM16400)

## POLAND STREET PRACTICE

**Poland Street Practice**, 38 Poland St, London, **London (Greater)**, W1V 3DA, ENG.
(T) 020 7437 6383
Speciality: Osteopathy.
● **Owner** Margaret Neary
**P** **S** **T** (**Ref:**HM16401)

## POLE, G

**G Pole**, 14 Brownlow Rd, Croydon, **Surrey**, CR0 5JT, ENG.
(T) 020 8688 1415
Speciality: Chiropodists (Podiatrists).
● **Owner** Mrs G Pole
**S** (**Ref:**HM16402)

## POLLARD, B

**B Pollard**, The Basement, 6 Wells Promenade, Ilkley, **Yorkshire (West)**, LS29 9LF, ENG.
(T) 01943 817191
Speciality: Osteopathy.
**P** **S** **T** (**Ref:**HM16403)

## POLLARD, CYNTHIA

**Cynthia Pollard**, Mill End, Mill Lane, Gerrards Cross, **Buckinghamshire**, SL9 8AZ, ENG.
(T) 01753 885164 (F) 01753 885526
Speciality: Psychology.
● **Owner** Mrs C Pollard
**B** (**Ref:**HM16404)

## POLLARD, ELIZABETH

**Elizabeth Pollard**, 23 Horsendale Avenue, Nuthall, Nottingham, **Nottinghamshire**, NG16 1AQ, ENG.
(T) 01159 272156
Speciality: Chiropodists (Podiatrists).
**S** (**Ref:**HM16405)

## POLLARD, JACQUELINE

**Jacqueline Pollard**, 16 Lawnside Mews, Palatine Rd, Manchester, **Manchester (Greater)**, M20 3YD, ENG.
(T) 01614 487570
Speciality: Reflexology.
**S** **T** (**Ref:**HM16406)

## POLLARD, JOY

**Joy Pollard**, 41 Overdale Avenue, Glenfield, Leicester, **Leicestershire**, LE3 8GQ, ENG.
(T) 01162 878567
Speciality: Hypnosis.
**B** (**Ref:**HM16407)

## POLLARD, M

**M Pollard**, 157A Kew Rd, Richmond, **Surrey**, TW9 2PN, ENG.
(T) 020 8948 2744
Speciality: Chiropractors.
**P** **S** **T** (**Ref:**HM16408)

## POLLARD, SALLY

**Sally Pollard**, 250B Brighton Rd, Worthing, **Sussex (West)**, BN11 2EY, ENG.
(T) 01903 823172
Speciality: Psychotherapy.
● **Owner** Mrs S Pollard
**B** (**Ref:**HM16409)

## POLLARD, SALLY

**Sally Pollard**, 40 Riverbank, Lower Beach Rd, Shoreham-by-Sea, **Sussex (West)**, BN43 5YH, ENG.
(T) 01273 463607
Speciality: Psychotherapy.
**B** (**Ref:**HM16410)

## POLLENDINE, I

**I Pollendine**, 20 High St, Patrington, Hull, **Humberside (North)**, HU12 0RE, ENG.
(T) 01964 630340
Speciality: Chiropodists (Podiatrists).
**S** (**Ref:**HM16411)

## POLLEY, JOHN G

**John G Polley**, 32A Cardiff Rd, Caerphilly, **Glamorgan (Vale of)**, CF83 1JP, WAL.
(T) 029 2086 6213
Speciality: Chiropodists (Podiatrists).
● **Partner** Mr L Polley
**S** (**Ref:**HM16412)

## POLLEY, LYNDON

**Lyndon Polley**, 25 Romilly Cres, Cardiff, **Glamorgan (Vale of)**, CF11 9NP, WAL.
(T) 029 2023 3587 (F) 029 2049 3964
Speciality: Biomechanics, Chiropody, Nail Surgery, Podiatry. ✔
● **Owner/Chiropodist** Mr L Polley **Q:** DPodM, M.S.C.P, S.R.Ch.
**M** Yrs. Est.: 20 (**Ref:**HM16413)

## POLLEY, LYNDON

**Lyndon Polley**, 32A Cardiff Rd, Caerphilly, **Glamorgan (Vale of)**, CF83 1JP, WAL.
(T) 029 2086 6213
Speciality: Biomechanics, Chiropody, Nail Surgery, Podiatry. ✔
● **Chiropodist (Podiatrist)**
Mr L Polley **Q:** DPodM, S.R.Ch. **M:** S.C.P.
**M** Yrs. Est.: 20 (**Ref:**HM16414)

## POLLEY, LYNDON

**Lyndon Polley**, 3 Minian Rd, Roath Park, Cardiff, **Glamorgan (Vale of)**, CF23 5EE, WAL.
(T) 029 2049 3964
Speciality: Biomechanics, Chiropody, Nail Surgery, Podiatry. ✔
● **Chiropodist (Podiatrist)**
Mr L Polley **Q:** DPodM, S.R.Ch. **M:** S.C.P.
**M** Yrs. Est.: 20 (**Ref:**HM16415)

## POLLEY, LYNDON

**Lyndon Polley**, 20 Taff St, Pontypridd, **Rhondda Cynon Taff**, CF37 4UA, WAL.
(T) 01443 480244
Speciality: Biomechanics, Chiropody, Nail Surgery, Podiatry. ✔
● **Chiropodist (Podiatrist)**
Mr L Polley **Q:** DPodM, S.R.Ch. **M:** S.C.P.
**M** Yrs. Est.: 20 (**Ref:**HM16416)

## POLLOCK & SIMPSON

**Julian Pollock & Cathy Simpson Hypnotherapy**, 44 The Ham, Westbury, **Wiltshire**, BA13 4HD, ENG.
(T) 01373 300254
Speciality: Hypnosis.
**B** (**Ref:**HM16417)

## POLLOCK, SUSAN

**Susan Pollock**, 45 Aylesbury Rd, Thame, **Oxfordshire**, OX9 3AU, ENG.
(T) 01844 216933
Speciality: Aromatherapy, Biomechanics, Chiropody, Holistic Healing, Laser Treatment, Massage (Therapeutic), Podiatry, Reflexology, Stress Therapy. ✔
● **Chiropodist (Podiatrist)**
Susan Pollock **Q:** Inst.CH.P, MSTAT.
**M** Yrs. Est.: 25 (**Ref:**HM16418)

## POLLOK PSYCHOLOGICAL SERVICES

**Pollok Psychological Services**, 75 Househillwood Cres, Glasgow, **Glasgow (City of)**, G53 6BG, SCO.
(T) 01418 815502
Speciality: Psychology.
**B** (**Ref:**HM16419)

## POLSON, KIRSTEN E

**Kirsten E Polson**, 76A Causeyside St, Paisley, **Renfrewshire**, PA1 1YP, SCO.
(T) 01418 898416
Speciality: Osteopathy.
**P** **S** **T** (**Ref:**HM16420)

## POMEGRANATE PRODUCTS

**Pomegranate Products Ltd**, 2 Westfield Farm Cottage, Front St, Chedzoy, Bridgwater, **Somerset**, TA7 8RE, ENG.
(T) 01278 433084
Speciality: Aromatherapy.
**M** **O** (**Ref:**HM16421)

## POMFRET HERBALIST

**Pomfret Herbalist**, Unit 2 Market Hall, Pontefract, **Yorkshire (West)**, WF8 1AU, ENG.
(T) 01977 791925 (F) 01977 706619
Speciality: Herbal Medicine.



Key: **B** Mind-Body Medicine **C** Complementary Medicine **H** Self Help Treatment **M** Medicinal Therapy **O** Oriental Medicine **P** Postural Therapy **S** Manipulative Structural Therapy **T** Touch Therapy

● **Owner** Mr M Wilson
M (Ref:HM16422)

**PONTEFRACT CHIROPODY SERVICES**

**Pontefract Chiropody Services**, Danes Court, Philips Lane, Darrington, Pontefract, **Yorkshire (West)**, WF8 3BH, ENG.
(T) 01977 706820
Speciality: Chiropodists (Podiatrists).
● **Owner** Mr A Taylor-Meek
S (Ref:HM16423)

**PONTEFRACT CHIROPRACTIC CLINIC**

**Pontefract Chiropractic Clinic**, 21A Cornmarket, Pontefract, **Yorkshire (West)**, WF8 1AN, ENG.
(T) 01977 690333
Speciality: Chiropractic.
● **Owner** Ms A Byrgren
P S T (Ref:HM16424)

**PONTESBURY PHYSIO PRACTICE**

**Pontesbury Physiotherapy Practice**, Nags Head Cottage, Shrewsbury Rd, Pontesbury, Shrewsbury, **Shropshire**, SY5 0QD, ENG.
(T) 01743 790036
Speciality: Physiotherapy.
P S T (Ref:HM16425)

**PONTYPRIDD TRAD CHINESE MED**

**Pontypridd Traditional Chinese Medicine Clinic (The)**, 30 Gelliwastad Rd, Pontypridd, **Rhondda Cynon Taff**, CF37 2BN, WAL.
(T) 01443 403886
Speciality: Complementary Medicines & Therapy.
C M (Ref:HM16426)

**POOL, J M**

**Mrs J M Pool**, 221 Desborough Avenue, High Wycombe, **Buckinghamshire**, HP11 2TW, ENG.
(T) 01494 461042
Speciality: Chiropodists (Podiatrists).
S (Ref:HM16427)

**POOL, NICKY**

**Nicky Pool**, Purton House, Purton Lane, Farnham Royal, Slough, **Berkshire**, SL2 3LY, ENG.
(T) 01753 01753644541
Speciality: Homeopathy.
M (Ref:HM16428)

**POOLE, P J**

**P J Poole**, 7 Strathmore Rd, Worthing, **Sussex (West)**, BN13 1PJ, ENG.
(T) 01903 504247
Speciality: Chiropodists (Podiatrists).
● **Owner** Mrs P Poole
S (Ref:HM16429)

**POOLE, R L**

**R L Poole**, 7b York St, Stourport-on-Severn, **Worcestershire**, DY13 9EQ, ENG.
(T) 01299 825602
Speciality: Chiropodists (Podiatrists).
S (Ref:HM16430)

**POOLER, ADENEY**

**Adeney Pooler**, Treverbyn, Bagbury Rd, Bude, **Cornwall**, EX23 8QJ, ENG.
(T) 01288 354587
Speciality: Chiropractic.
● **Owner** Mr A Pooler
P S T (Ref:HM16431)

**POOLEY, ALISON**

**Alison Pooley**, Chyvale, Lower Albion Row, Carharrack, Redruth, **Cornwall**, TR16 5RB, ENG.
(T) 01209 820695
Speciality: Reflexology.
S T (Ref:HM16432)

**POPE, ANGELA**

**Angela Pope**, Anyards Rd, Cobham, **Surrey**, KT11 2LH, ENG.
(T) 01932 868940
Speciality: Reflexology.
S T (Ref:HM16433)

**POPE, THOMAS**

**Thomas Pope**, 4 Corinne Rd, London, **London (Greater)**, N19 5EY, ENG.
(T) 020 7607 2825
Speciality: Alexander Technique.
P S (Ref:HM16434)

**POPLE, S R**

**S R Pople**, 15 North View, Staple Hill, Bristol, BS16 5RU, ENG.
(T) 01179 560614
Speciality: Chiropodists (Podiatrists).
S (Ref:HM16435)

**POPOVIC, M**

**M Popovic**, 66 Bandley Rise, Stevenage, **Hertfordshire**, SG2 9NS, ENG.
(T) 01438 727941
Speciality: Complementary Medicines & Therapy.
C M (Ref:HM16436)

**POPPLEWELL, MARK**

**Mark Popplewell**, 16 Laithe Croft Rd, Batley, **Yorkshire (West)**, WF17 6LY, ENG.
(T) 01924 443527
(E) markpoptcm@yahoo.co.uk
Speciality: Acupressure, Acupuncture, Cupping, Massage (Therapeutic), Moxibustion, Oriental Diagnosis, T'ai-Chi Ch'uan, Diet, Lifestyle Advice, Chinese Food Energetics, Qi Gong, Chinese Yoga. ✔
● **Acupuncturist** Mr M Popplewell Q: Dip.Ac. M: BAcC.
O Yrs. Est.: 2 (Ref:HM16437)

**POPPLEWELL, REBECCA**

**Rebecca Popplewell**, Molford House, 27 South St, South Molton, **Devon**, EX36 4AA, ENG.
(T) 01769 574830 (F) 01769 574830
Speciality: Osteopathy.
● **Partner** Mrs R Popplewell
P S T (Ref:HM16438)

**POPPLEWELL, SALLY**

**Sally Popplewell**, 33 Chamberlain Rd, Birmingham, **Midlands (West)**, B13 0QP, ENG.
(T) 01214 442676
Speciality: Reflexology, Shiatsu.
S T (Ref:HM16439)

**PORCHESTER SPORTS CLINIC**

**Porchester Sports Injury Clinic**, Porchester Centre, Queensway, London, **London (Greater)**, W2 5HS, ENG.
(T) 020 7792 1275
Speciality: Physiotherapy.
● **Owner** Mr G Lindsay
P S T (Ref:HM16440)

**PORDAGE, ELIZABETH**

**Elizabeth Pordage**, 4 Broadlands, Hanworth, Feltham, **London (Greater)**, TW13 6HF, ENG.
(T) 020 8979 7940
Speciality: Complementary Medicines & Therapy.
C M (Ref:HM16441)

**PORRITT, M**

**M Porritt**, 450 Blackburn Rd, Bolton, **Lancashire**, BL1 8NL, ENG.
(T) 01204 308320
Speciality: Electrolysis.
T (Ref:HM16442)

**PORTAL, MEG**

**Meg Portal**, 88 Cecilia Rd, London, **London (Greater)**, N1 1RL, ENG.
(T) 020 7254 2867
Speciality: Homeopathy.
M (Ref:HM16443)

**PORTAL, MEG**

**Meg Portal**, 11-13 Strutton Ground, Off Victoria St, London, **London (Greater)**, SW1P 2HY, ENG.
(T) 020 7254 2867
Speciality: Homeopathy.
● **Owner** Ms M Portal
M (Ref:HM16444)

**PORTEOUS, TRISH**

**Trish Porteous**, Mayo Farm, Cann, Shaftesbury, **Dorset**, SP7 0EF, ENG.
(T) 01747 852051
Speciality: Psychotherapy.
● **Owner** Mrs T Porteous
B (Ref:HM16445)

**PORTER, A J**

**A J Porter**, 28 Hollyfield Avenue, London, **London (Greater)**, N11 3BY, ENG.
(T) 020 8368 0865
Speciality: Complementary Medicines & Therapy.
● **Owner** A Porter
C M (Ref:HM16446)

**PORTER, ANTHONY**

**Anthony Porter**, Two Oaks, Halterworth Lane, Romsey, **Hampshire**, SO51 9AD, ENG.
(T) 01794 516317
Speciality: Chiropodists (Podiatrists).
● **Owner** Mr A Porter
S (Ref:HM16447)

**PORTER, CHRISTINE**

**Christine Porter**, 9 Thompson Drive, Hatfield, Doncaster, **Yorkshire (South)**, DN7 6JX, ENG.
(T) 01302 842406
Speciality: Reflexology.
● **Owner** Mrs C Porter
S T (Ref:HM16448)

**PORTER, M S**

**M S Porter**, 16 Watercombe Heights, Yeovil, **Somerset**, BA20 2TA, ENG.
(T) 01935 477653
Speciality: Chiropodists (Podiatrists).
● **Owner** Mrs M Porter
S (Ref:HM16449)

**PORTER, MARK**

**Porter Mark Bsc(hons) Ost RGN LSSM(Dip)**, Cinema La, **County Wexford**, IRE.
(T) 05324 890
Speciality: Osteopathy.
P S T (Ref:HM16450)

**PORTLAND PHYSIOTHERAPY CLINIC**

**Portland Physiotherapy Clinic**, Wilmington House, Portland Rd, East Grinstead, **Sussex (West)**, RH19 4EB, ENG.
(T) 01342 327246
Speciality: Acupuncture, Physiotherapy. ✔
● **Physiotherapist** Mrs J West Q: Grad Dip Phys, MCSP, SRP. M: CSP.
● **Physiotherapist** Mrs S Moore Q: Grad Dip Phys, MCSP, SRP. M: CSP.
S Yrs. Est.: 7 (Ref:HM16451)

**PORTLAOISE FAMILY CHIROPRACTIC**

**Portlaoise Family Chiropractic**, Unit 5 Tara Court Main St, Portlaoise, **County Laois**, IRE.
(T) 05026 2106
Speciality: Chiropractors.
P S T (Ref:HM16452)

**PORTMAN LODGE**

**Portman Lodge**, Portman Lodge, Durweston, Blandford Forum, **Dorset**, DT11 0QA, ENG.
(T) 01258 452168 (F) 01258 450456
Speciality: Complementary Medicines & Therapy.
● **Manager** Ms A Black
C M (Ref:HM16453)

**PORTSMOUTH MEDICAL HERBALIST**

**Portsmouth Medical Herbalist Ltd (The)**, 83 Kingston Cres, Portsmouth, **Hampshire**, PO2 8AA, ENG.
(T) 023 9266 3445
Speciality: Herbal Medicine.
● **Sole Director**
Geoffrey Stuart Stevenson
M (Ref:HM16454)

**POSITIVE HEALING ROOM**

**Positive Healing Room (The)**, Suite 12, 904 Warwick Rd, Acocks Green, Birmingham, **Midlands (West)**, B27 6QG, ENG.
(T) 01217 076309
Speciality: Complementary Medicines & Therapy.
● **Owner** Mr P Whittingham
M (Ref:HM16455)

**POSITIVE LIVING**

**Positive Living**, Greenmantle, Bayleys Hill, Sevenoaks, **Kent**, TN14 6HS, ENG.
(T) 01732 458540
Speciality: Complementary Medicines & Therapy.
C M (Ref:HM16456)

## POSTER, C

**C Poster**, 339 Ballards Lane, London, **London (Greater)**, N12 8LJ, ENG.
(T) 020 8445 4397
Speciality: Complementary Medicines & Therapy.
● **Director** Mr E Thankey
M (Ref:HM16457)

## POSTLETHWAITE, CAROLINE

**Caroline Postlethwaite**, 23 Forewood Rise, Crowhurst, Battle, **Sussex (East)**, TN33 9AH, ENG.
(T) 01424 830545 (F) 01424 830720
Speciality: Osteopathy.
● **Owner** Mrs C Postlethwaite
P S T (Ref:HM16458)

## POSTON, JONATHAN

**Jonathan Poston**, Prestwich Physical Therapy Centre, 497 Bury New Rd, Prestwich, Manchester, **Manchester (Greater)**, M25 1AD, ENG.
(T) 01617 986352
Speciality: Osteopathy.
P S T (Ref:HM16459)

## POST-TRAUMATIC STRESS CLINIC

**Post-Traumatic Stress Clinic**, 8 Willow Rd, London, **London (Greater)**, NW3 1TJ, ENG.
(T) 020 7794 8717
Speciality: Psychology.
● **Owner** Mr S Meyerson
B (Ref:HM16460)

## POSTURITEBACK CARE PRODUCTS

**Posturiteback Care Products**, Beeches Rd, London, **London (Greater)**, SW17 7LZ, ENG.
(T) 020 8767 5889
Speciality: Physiotherapy.
P S T (Ref:HM16461)

## POT POURRI PRETTIES

**Pot Pourri Pretties**, 7 Regent St, Runcorn, **Cheshire**, WA7 1LJ, ENG.
(T) 01928 772054
Speciality: Aromatherapy.
● **Owner** Mrs S Johnson
M O (Ref:HM16462)

## POTHECARY, I C (DR)

**Dr I C Pothecary**, 31 Hurst Avenue, Horsham, **Sussex (West)**, RH12 2EL, ENG.
(T) 01403 253146
Speciality: Osteopathy.
● **Owner** Mr I Pothecary
P S T (Ref:HM16463)

## POTTER, CHRISTINE

**Christine Potter**, 18 Wesley St, Sabden, Clitheroe, **Lancashire**, BB7 9EH, ENG.
(T) 01282 776189
Speciality: Herbal Medicine.
● **Owner** Miss C Potter
M (Ref:HM16464)

## POTTER, DEREK

**Derek Potter**, Lowcroft House, Church Rd, Wombourne, Wolverhampton, **Midlands (West)**, WV5 9EZ, ENG.
(T) 01902 898256
Speciality: Physiotherapy.
● **Owner** Mr D Potter
P S T (Ref:HM16465)

## POTTER, J

**J Potter**, 323 Pinhoe Rd, Exeter, **Devon**, EX4 8AD, ENG.
(T) 01392 467438
Speciality: Chiropractors.
P S T (Ref:HM16466)

## POTTER, J

**J Potter**, 38 Hurford Drive, Thatcham, **Berkshire**, RG19 4WA, ENG.
(T) 01635 872231
Speciality: Physiotherapy.
P S T (Ref:HM16467)

## POTTER, MARK

**Mark Potter**, Injury Treatment Centre, 20 New St, Worthing, **Sussex (West)**, BN11 3BT, ENG.
(T) 01903 205599
Speciality: Physiotherapy.
P S T (Ref:HM16468)

## POTTER, MICHAEL

**Michael Potter**, Blackheath Osteopathy & Acupuncture Clinic, 19 Tranquil Vale, London, **London (Greater)**, SE3 0BU, ENG.
(T) 020 8852 1706
Speciality: Acupuncture.
O (Ref:HM16469)

## POTTER, MICHAEL

**Michael Potter**, Imladris, Fallowfields, Lower Broomborough, Plymouth Road, Totnes, **Devon**, TQ9 5LX, ENG.
(T) 01803 867726
Speciality: Acupuncture.
● **Owner** Mr M Potter
O (Ref:HM16470)

## POTTERGATE PSYCHOTHRPY PRACTCE

**Pottergate Psychotherapy Practice**, 11 Pottergate, Norwich, **Norfolk**, NR2 1DS, ENG.
(T) 01603 629576
Speciality: Psychotherapy.
● **Employee** Mrs J Harrison
B (Ref:HM16471)

## POTTERTON, DAVID

**David Potterton**, 27 Lower Elmstone Drive, Tilehurst, Reading, **Berkshire**, RG31 5EB, ENG.
(T) 01189 454040 (F) 01189 454040
Speciality: Herbal Medicine.
● **Owner** Mr D Potterton
M (Ref:HM16472)

## POTTINGER, MARGARET

**Margaret Pottinger**, Fairfields Clinic, Skippetts Lane West, Basingstoke, **Hampshire**, RG21 3HP, ENG.
(T) 01256 326980
Speciality: Complementary Medicines & Therapy.
M (Ref:HM16473)

## POTTLE, C J

**C J Pottle**, 2 Eastwood Avenue, Grimsby, **Humberside (South)**, DN34 5BE, ENG.
(T) 01472 878551 (F) 01472 878551
Speciality: Physiotherapy.
● **Owner** Mrs C Pottle
P S T (Ref:HM16474)

## POTTS, DEBORAH

**Deborah Potts**, 30 Park Rd, Disley, Stockport, **Cheshire**, SK12 2NA, ENG.
(T) 01663 764155
Speciality: Chiropodists (Podiatrists).
● **Owner** Mrs D Potts
S (Ref:HM16475)

## POTTS, J

**J Potts**, 17 Broad St, Bromyard, **Herefordshire**, HR7 4BT, ENG.
(T) 01885 488608
Speciality: Chiropodists (Podiatrists).
● **Owner** Mr J Potts
S (Ref:HM16476)

## POTTS, J

**J Potts**, 25 Brockington Rd, Bodenham, Hereford, **Herefordshire**, HR1 3LR, ENG.
(T) 01568 797413
Speciality: Chiropodists (Podiatrists).
S (Ref:HM16477)

## POTTS, M C

**M C Potts**, 201 Northgate St, Great Yarmouth, **Norfolk**, NR30 1DH, ENG.
(T) 01493 844577
Speciality: Chiropodists (Podiatrists).
● **Owner** Mr M Potts
S (Ref:HM16478)

## POTTS, ROY

**Roy Potts**, Harwood Cottage, Withywood Lane, Cranmore, Shepton Mallet, **Somerset**, BA4 4QR, ENG.
(T) 01749 880478 (F) 01749 880478
Speciality: Chiropodists (Podiatrists).
● **Owner** Mr R Potts
S (Ref:HM16479)

## POULSEN, P (DR)

**Dr P Poulsen**, Castleton Health Centre, 2 Elizabeth St, Rochdale, **Lancashire**, OL11 3HY, ENG.
(T) 01706 658905
Speciality: Chiropractic.
P S T (Ref:HM16480)

## POULTON, J

**J Poulton**, 66 King St, Ramsgate, **Kent**, CT11 8NY, ENG.
(T) 01843 593997
Speciality: Chiropodists (Podiatrists).
● **Owner** Mr J Poulton
S (Ref:HM16481)

## POURAMINI, A

**A Pouramini**, The Gate House, 1 Abbotswood, Guildford, **Surrey**, GU1 1UN, ENG.
(T) 01483 562830 (F) 01483 304856
Speciality: Chiropractic.
● **Owner** Mr R Bennett
P S T (Ref:HM16482)

## POVEY, JILL

**Jill Povey**, 16 Moorhouse St, Leek, **Staffordshire**, ST13 5NB, ENG.
(T) 01538 385346
Speciality: Homeopathy.
● **Owner** Mrs J Povey
M (Ref:HM16483)

## POW, SUE

**Sue Pow**, 53 St. John St, Bridgwater, **Somerset**, TA6 5HR, ENG.
(T) 01278 445439
Speciality: Reflexology.
● **Owner** Mrs S Pow
S T (Ref:HM16484)

## POWE, M

**M Powe**, 4 Epsom Rd, Beeston, Nottingham, **Nottinghamshire**, NG9 6HQ, ENG.
(T) 01159 721957 (F) 01159 721957
Speciality: Chiropodists (Podiatrists).
● **Owner** Mr M Powe
S (Ref:HM16485)

## POWELL & GILCHRIST

**Powell & Gilchrist**, 36 Eslington Trce, Newcastle Upon Tyne, **Tyne and Wear**, NE2 4RN, ENG.
(T) 01912 811755
Speciality: Chiropodists (Podiatrists).
● **Partner** Mr J Powell
S (Ref:HM16486)

## POWELL, ANNE-MARIE

**Anne-Marie Powell**, 208A Tankerton Rd, Tankerton, Whitstable, **Kent**, CT5 2AT, ENG.
(T) 01227 264123
Speciality: Reflexology.
S T (Ref:HM16487)

## POWELL, AUDREY E

**Audrey E Powell**, 5 Montpelier, Weston-Super-Mare, **Somerset**, BS23 2RH, ENG.
(T) 01934 418075
Speciality: Chiropodists (Podiatrists).
S (Ref:HM16488)

## POWELL, C R

**C R Powell**, 43 Salford Rd, Southport, **Merseyside**, PR8 3JX, ENG.
(T) 01704 576285 (F) 01704 576285
Speciality: Hypnotherapy.
● **Owner** Mrs C Powell
B (Ref:HM16489)

## POWELL, G E

**G E Powell**, 9 Devonshire Pl, London, **London (Greater)**, W1N 1PB, ENG.
(T) 020 7487 4112 (F) 020 7935 3235
Speciality: Psychology.
● **Doctor** Dr G Powell
B (Ref:HM16490)

## POWELL, GRAHAM

**Graham Powell**, Surgery, Minster House, Church St, Kidderminster, **Worcestershire**, DY10 2AD, ENG.
(T) 01562 751911
Speciality: Chiropodists (Podiatrists).
● **Owner** Mr G Powell
S (Ref:HM16491)

## POWELL, GRAHAM

**Graham Powell**, 33 Low Habberley, Kidderminster, **Worcestershire**, DY11 5RA, ENG.



Key: B Mind-Body Medicine | C Complementary Medicine | H Self Help Treatment | M Medicinal Therapy | O Oriental Medicine | P Postural Therapy | S Manipulative Structural Therapy | T Touch Therapy

(T) 01562 823094
Speciality: Chiropodists (Podiatrists).
● **Owner** Mr G Powell
S (Ref:HM16492)

**POWELL, IANTO D**
**Ianto D Powell**, Park Clinic, Earl Rd, Mold, **Flintshire**, CH7 1AX, WAL.
(T) 01352 753331
Speciality: Osteopathy.
P S T (Ref:HM16493)

**POWELL, IANTO D**
**Ianto D Powell Osteopath**, Park Clinic, Park St, Denbigh, **Denbighshire**, LL16 3DE, WAL.
(T) 01745 813718
Speciality: Osteopathy.
P S T (Ref:HM16494)

**POWELL, IANTO D**
**Ianto D Powell Osteopath**, Earl Chambers, Earl Rd, Mold, **Flintshire**, CH7 1AL, WAL.
(T) 01352 753331
Speciality: Osteopathy.
P S T (Ref:HM16495)

**POWELL, J**
**J Powell**, 24 Union St, Hereford, **Herefordshire**, HR1 2BT, ENG.
(T) 01432 272913
Speciality: Chiropodists (Podiatrists).
● **Owner** Mr J Powell
S (Ref:HM16496)

**POWELL, JEANNE**
**Jeanne Powell**, 15 Rye Walk, Ingatestone, **Essex**, CM4 9AL, ENG.
(T) 01277 352606
Speciality: Chiropodists (Podiatrists).
● **Owner** Mrs J Powell
S (Ref:HM16497)

**POWELL, JUDITH**
**Judith Powell**, 30 Chepstow Villas, London, **London (Greater)**, W11 2QZ, ENG.
(T) 020 7221 9279
Speciality: Physiotherapy.
● **Owner** Mrs J Powell
P S T (Ref:HM16498)

**POWELL, MARTIN**
**Martin Powell**, Health Hydro, Milton Rd, Swindon, **Wiltshire**, SN1 5JA, ENG.
(T) 01793 465631
Speciality: Acupuncture.
O (Ref:HM16499)

**POWER & SERCOMBE PRACTICE**
**Power & Sercombe Practice**, 51 The Avenue, Southampton, **Hampshire**, SO17 1XQ, ENG.
(T) 023 8022 8430 (F) 023 8063 4918
Speciality: Osteopathy.
● **Partner** Mr M Power
P S T (Ref:HM16500)

**POWER, ANNE**
**Anne Power**, 5 Elm Ter, Constantine Rd, London, **London (Greater)**, NW3 2LL, ENG.
(T) 020 7267 4222
Speciality: Physiotherapy.
● **Owner** Ms A Power
P S T (Ref:HM16501)

**POWER, CLIVE**
**Clive Power**, 11 Upper Cres, Minster Lovell, Witney, **Oxfordshire**, OX8 5RT, ENG.
(T) 01993 776225 (F) 01993 708862
Speciality: Osteopathy.
● **Owner** Mr C Power
P S T (Ref:HM16502)

**POWER, DAVID J**
**David J Power**, Bardney, 6 Grapsome Cl, Chessington, **Surrey**, KT9 2SG, ENG.
(T) 020 8391 1997
Speciality: Chiropody. ✔
● **Chiropodist** Mr D Power Q: M.S.C.P, MSSCh.
M Yrs. Est.: 9 (Ref:HM16503)

**POWER, NICHOLAS**
**Power Nicholas Lic Ac D Ac**, 50 Sandycove Rd, Dun Laoire, Dublin, **County Dublin**, IRE.
(T) 01280 3505
Speciality: Complementary Medicines & Therapy.
M (Ref:HM16504)

**POWER, PATRICK**
**Power Patrick D O**, 5 Shandon St, Dungarvan, **County Waterford**, IRE.
(T) 05842 903
Speciality: Complementary Medicines & Therapy.
M (Ref:HM16505)

**POWER, RICHARD**
**Power Richard**, 26 Fitzwilliam Sq, Dublin, **County Dublin**, IRE.
(T) 01676 3036
Speciality: Complementary Medicines & Therapy.
M (Ref:HM16506)

**POWER, RICHENDA**
**Richenda Power**, Hillside, Church Lane, Worting, Basingstoke, **Hampshire**, RG23 8PX, ENG.
(T) 01256 322959
Speciality: Osteopathy.
● **Owner** Dr R Power
P S T (Ref:HM16507)

**POWER-ASHMAN, LINDA**
**Linda Power-Ashman**, 12 The Broadway, Dudley, **Midlands (West)**, DY1 4AR, ENG.
(T) 01384 254044
Speciality: Chiropodists (Podiatrists).
● **Owner** Mrs L Power-Ashman
S (Ref:HM16508)

**POWNALL & ASSOCIATES**
**Pownall Gordon & Associates**, Inworth Hall Villa Barn, Kelvedon Rd, Inworth, Colchester, **Essex**, CO5 9SN, ENG.
(T) 01376 572051
Speciality: Hypnotherapy.
● **Owner** Mr G Pownall
B (Ref:HM16509)

**POWNALL & ASSOCIATES**
**Pownall Gordon & Associates**, 2 Fiddlers Hall, Tollesbury Rd, Tollesbury, Maldon, **Essex**, CM9 8RP, ENG.
(T) 01621 868184
Speciality: Hypnotherapy.
● **Owner** Mr G Pownall
B (Ref:HM16510)

**POWNALL, C J**
**C J Pownall**, 152 Bent Lane, Culcheth, Warrington, **Cheshire**, WA3 5ES, ENG.
(T) 01925 766735
Speciality: Chiropodists (Podiatrists).
S (Ref:HM16511)

**POWNALL, JILL**
**Jill Pownall**, The Paddocks, 6 Green Acres Cl, Whitchurch, Aylesbury, **Buckinghamshire**, HP22 4JP, ENG.
(T) 01296 641920 (F) 01296 641920
Speciality: Physiotherapy.
● **Owner** Mrs J Pownall
P S T (Ref:HM16512)

**POWNER, CLIVE**
**Clive Powner**, 180 Hednesford Rd, Heath Hayes, Cannock, **Staffordshire**, WS12 5DZ, ENG.
(T) 01543 459862
Speciality: Hypnotherapy.
● **Owner** Mr C Powner
B (Ref:HM16513)

**POWNER, MARGARET**
**Margaret Powner**, Brynhowell, Glandwr, Whitland, **Carmarthenshire**, SA34 0UD, WAL.
(T) 01994 419738
Speciality: Reflexology.
S T (Ref:HM16514)

**POWRIE, S**
**S Powrie**, 9 The Birches, Formby, Liverpool, **Merseyside**, L37 7HX, ENG.
(T) 01704 831085
Speciality: Chiropodists (Podiatrists).
● **Owner** Mrs S Powrie
S (Ref:HM16515)

**POWYS HEALTH CARE TRUST**
**Powys Health Care Trust**, Chiropodists & Dieticians, Bronllys Hospital, Bronllys, Brecon, **Powys**, LD3 0LU, WAL.
(T) 01874 711111
Speciality: Chiropodists (Podiatrists).
S (Ref:HM16516)

**POXON, ANJU**
**Anju Poxon**, Bradley Stoke, **Gloucestershire**, BS32, ENG.
(T) 01179 699326
Speciality: Reflexology.
S T (Ref:HM16517)

**POYNTER, K J**
**K J Poynter**, 1 Bunyan Rd, Biggleswade, **Bedfordshire**, SG18 8QQ, ENG.
(T) 01767 601879
Speciality: Osteopathy.
P S T (Ref:HM16518)

**POYNTON CHIROPRACTIC CLINIC**
**David Middleton**, Poynton Chiropractic Clinic, 52A Clifford Rd, Poynton, Stockport, **Cheshire**, SK12 1JA, ENG.
(T) 01625 850300 (F) 01625 850300
(E) poynton.chiro@btinternet.com
(W) www.poynton.chiro.btinternet.co.uk
Speciality: Chiropractic, Manipulation, Massage (Therapeutic). ✔
● **Chiropractor** Dr D Middleton Q: BSc (Chiro), DC, MCC. M: BCA, CC.
● **Masseuse/Practice Manager** Ms S Middleton Q: IHBC. M: IMM.
P S Yrs. Est.: 8 (Ref:HM16519)

**PRACTICE**
**Practice (The)**, 17 Sussex Pl, Slough, **Berkshire**, SL1 2RL, ENG.
(T) 01753 820303
Speciality: Psychotherapy.
B (Ref:HM16520)

**PRACTICE**
**Practice (The)**, 28 High St, Banchory, **Aberdeenshire**, AB31 5SR, SCO.
(T) 01330 825234
Speciality: Complementary Medicines & Therapy.
● **Owner** Mrs L MacPhee
C M (Ref:HM16521)

**PRACTICE OF HYPNOTHERAPY**
**Practice Of Hypnotherapy**, 6 Supple Park S.C, Dunshaughlin, **County Meath**, IRE.
(T) 01825 8557
Speciality: Hypnotherapy.
B (Ref:HM16522)

**PRACTICE WORKS**
**Practice Works**, 17 The Cedars, Albert Park Rd, Malvern, **Worcestershire**, WR14 1HW, ENG.
(T) 01684 576649
Speciality: Complementary Medicines & Therapy.
● **Owner** Mr D Powell
C M (Ref:HM16523)

**PRACTITONERS SCHOOL**
**Practitioners School of Reflexology**, 47 Leyborne Park, Kew, Richmond, **Surrey**, TW9 3HB, ENG.
(T) 020 8948 2380
(W) www.handsonreflexology.com
Speciality: Reflexology.
S T (Ref:HM16524)

**PRAFULBALA**
**Prafulbala**, 9a Birkbeck Rd, London, **London (Greater)**, W3 6BG, ENG.
(T) 020 8992 8261
Speciality: Complementary Medicines & Therapy.
● **Owner** Ms P Parmer
M (Ref:HM16525)

**PRAGNELL, C A**
**C A Pragnell**, 4 Crown St, Harrow, **London (Greater)**, HA2 0HR, ENG.
(T) 020 8864 4878
Speciality: Osteopathy.
● **Owner** Dr C Pragnell
P S T (Ref:HM16526)

**PRASAD, B**
**B Prasad**, Middleton Rd, Leeds, **Yorkshire**


Key continued: Yrs.Est: Years Established Q: Qualifications M: Professional Membership ✔ Indemnity Insurance Accept Credit Cards

**(West)**, LS10 3DZ, ENG.
(T) 01132 709139 (F) 01132 709139
Speciality: Acupuncture.
● **Owner** Dr B Prasad
O (Ref:HM16527)

## PREBBLE, PETER
**Peter Prebble**, 11 Tannery Wharf, Newark, **Nottinghamshire**, NG24 4US, ENG.
(T) 01636 681856 (F) 01636 681856
Speciality: Psychology.
● **Owner** Mr P Prebble
B (Ref:HM16528)

## PREDICTIONS
**Predictions**, 24 Princes St, Southport, **Merseyside**, PR8 1EQ, ENG.
(T) 01704 543810
Speciality: Clairvoyants & Palmists.
● **Owner** Ms M Woods
B (Ref:HM16529)

## PREECE, ELLA
**Ella Preece**, 1 Barnfield Gardens, Brighton, **Sussex (East)**, BN2 2HQ, ENG.
(T) 01273 700452
Speciality: Reflexology.
S T (Ref:HM16530)

## PREECE, MARGARET
**Margaret Preece**, 26 Cheston Avenue, Croydon, **Surrey**, CR0 8DA, ENG.
(T) 020 8777 4742
Speciality: Reflexology.
● **Owner** Mrs M Preece
S T (Ref:HM16531)

## PREECE, R E
**R E Preece**, 30 High St, Burnham, Slough, **Berkshire**, SL1 7JP, ENG.
(T) 01628 603977
Speciality: Chiropodists (Podiatrists).
S (Ref:HM16532)

## PREES COMPLEMENTARY THERAPIES
**Prees Complementary Therapies**, Prees House, Prees, Whitchurch, **Shropshire**, SY13 2DG, ENG.
(T) 01948 840398
Speciality: Aromatherapy, Hypnosis, Hypnotherapy, Reflexology. ✔
● **Owner** Mr R Bonfield Q: Dip.(GC), Dip.Hyp. M: HRS, NCH, NRSCT, SSM.
● **Reflexologist** Ms J Bonfield Q: Cert.Ed, IHBC, IIHHT. M: IIHHT.
B C Yrs. Est.: 6 (Ref:HM16533)

## PREISLER, TONI TYE
**Toni Tye Preisler**, 99 Radford Rd, Leamington Spa, **Warwickshire**, CV31 1JZ, ENG.
(T) 01926 882494
Speciality: Psychotherapy.
B (Ref:HM16534)

## PREMADASA, L (DR)
**Dr L Premadasa**, Woodside Osteopathic Clinic, 47A Bancroft, Hitchin, **Hertfordshire**, SG5 1LA, ENG.
(T) 01462 452929
Speciality: Osteopathy.
● **Senior Partner** Mr A El-Sayed
P S T (Ref:HM16535)

## PREMAL SHAH
**Premal Shah**, 126 Mayfair Avenue, Ilford, **Essex**, IG1 3DH, ENG.
(T) 020 8220 1876
Speciality: Physiotherapy.
● **Owner** Mr P Shah
P S T (Ref:HM16536)

## PREMIER AROMATHERAPY
**Premier Aromatherapy**, 28 Caledonian Way, Belton, Great Yarmouth, **Norfolk**, NR31 9PQ, ENG.
(T) 01493 781439
Speciality: Aromatherapy.
M O (Ref:HM16537)

## PREMIER ELECTRICS
**Premier Electrics**, 33 New Barn Rd, Shoreham-by-Sea, **Sussex (West)**, BN43 6HN, ENG.
(T) 01273 452363
Speciality: Electrolysis.
T (Ref:HM16538)

## PREMIER HEALTH-SPORTS THERAPY
**Premier Health & Sports Therapy Ltd**, 17-21 Hatton Wall, London, **London (Greater)**, EC1N 8JE, ENG.
(T) 020 7209 0229 (F) 020 7209 0229
Speciality: Physiotherapy.
● **Director** Mr R Lial
P S T (Ref:HM16539)

## PREMIER PHYSIOTHERAPY CENTRE
**Premier Physiotherapy Centre**, Unit 2 Granary Court, High Rd, Chadwell Heath, Romford, **Essex**, RM6 6PY, ENG.
(T) 07000 782218
Speciality: Physiotherapy.
● **Owner** Mr J Green
P S T (Ref:HM16540)

## PRENDERGAST, BREDA
**Prendergast Breda**, Natural Therapy Centre 15/16 West End, Mallow, **County Cork**, IRE.
(T) 08682 46475
Speciality: Complementary Medicines & Therapy.
M (Ref:HM16541)

## PRENDERGAST, KARL
**Osteopathic Clinic**, 5 Devon Pl, The Crescent, **County Galway**, IRE.
(T) 09158 9417
(E) karlh@iolfree.ie
Speciality: Cranial Osteopathy, Manipulation, Osteopathy. ✔
● **Osteopath** Mr K Prendergast Q: BSc, Hons (OST).
S Yrs. Est.: 5 (Ref:HM16542)

## PRENDERGAST, LILY
**Prendergast Lily**, 21 Truman St, Bentley, Doncaster, **Yorkshire (South)**, DN5 0BZ, ENG.
(T) 01302 873326
Speciality: Chiropodists (Podiatrists).
S (Ref:HM16543)

## PRESSURE WORKS
**Pressure Works**, 63 Silverberry Rd, Weston-Super-Mare, **Somerset**, BS22 6RY, ENG.
(T) 01934 516886 (F) 01934 513268
Speciality: Acupressure, Massage (Therapeutic). ✔
● **Owner** Mrs L Bailey
● **Masseur** Mr D Bailey Q: IIST, ITEC.
M Yrs. Est.: 2 (Ref:HM16544)

## PREST, C
**C Prest**, 513 Hempshaw Lane, Stockport, **Cheshire**, SK1 3AB, ENG.
(T) 01614 833173
Speciality: Chiropodists (Podiatrists).
S (Ref:HM16545)

## PREST, CAROLINE
**Caroline Prest**, 848 Chester Rd, Stretford, Manchester, **Manchester (Greater)**, M32 0QJ, ENG.
(T) 01618 643245
Speciality: Chiropodists (Podiatrists).
S (Ref:HM16546)

## PRESTBERRIES FARM
**Prestberries Farm Natural Therapy & Teaching Centre**, Blackwells End, Hartpury, Gloucester, **Gloucestershire**, GL19 3DB, ENG.
(T) 01452 700306
Speciality: Complementary Medicines & Therapy.
C M (Ref:HM16547)

## PRESTON CLINIC OF HERBAL MED
**Preston Clinic Of Herbal Medicine**, 5-7 St Wilfred St, Preston, **Lancashire**, PR1 2TE, ENG.
(T) 01772 252526
Speciality: Herbal Medicine.
M (Ref:HM16548)

## PRESTON PHYSIOTHERAPY CENTRE
**Preston Physiotherapy Centre (The)**, 7 Moor Park Avenue, Preston, **Lancashire**, PR1 6AS, ENG.
(T) 01772 204690
Speciality: Physiotherapy.
P S T (Ref:HM16549)

## PRESTON THERAPY CENTRE
**Preston Therapy Centre**, 57 Garstang Rd, Preston, **Lancashire**, PR1 1LB, ENG.
(T) 01772 886994
Speciality: Psychotherapy.
B (Ref:HM16550)

## PRESTON, CATHY
**Cathy Preston**, 15 Ned Lane, Slaithwaite, Huddersfield, **Yorkshire (West)**, HD7 5HQ, ENG.
(T) 01484 844588
Speciality: Auto Suggestion, Complementary Therapy, Counselling, Hypnosis, Hypnotherapy, Psychotherapy, Stress Therapy. ✔
● **Hypnotherapist/Psychotherapist** Ms C Preston Q: BHA.
H Yrs. Est.: 13 (Ref:HM16551)

## PRESTON, GEORGE
**George Preston**, 185 Scraptoft Lane, Leicester, **Leicestershire**, LE5 2HS, ENG.
(T) 01162 418309
Speciality: Physiotherapy.
● **Partner** Mrs J Preston
P S T (Ref:HM16552)

## PRESTON, LINDA
**Linda Preston**, Woodlyn, Tockholes Rd, Darwen, **Lancashire**, BB3 1JY, ENG.
(T) 01254 704801
Speciality: Clairvoyants & Palmists.
● **Owner** Mrs L Preston
B (Ref:HM16553)

## PRESTON, M E
**M E Preston**, Upper Nordens Clinic, Royal Oak Lane, High Hurstwood, Uckfield, **Sussex (East)**, TN22 4AN, ENG.
(T) 01825 732681
Speciality: Physiotherapy.
● **Owner** Mrs M Preston
P S T (Ref:HM16554)

## PRESTON, MARK
**Mark Preston**, 228 South Ealing Rd, London, **London (Greater)**, W5 4RP, ENG.
(T) 07020 973780
Speciality: Acupuncture.
O (Ref:HM16555)

## PRESTON, MARTIN
**Martin Preston**, Marlborough Leisure Centre, Marlborough, **Wiltshire**, SN8 1PB, ENG.
(T) 01672 513161
Speciality: Osteopathy.
P S T (Ref:HM16556)

## PRESTON, MARTIN
**Martin Preston**, Pewsey Osteopathic Clinic, 9 High St, Pewsey, **Wiltshire**, SN9 5AF, ENG.
(T) 01672 564646
Speciality: Osteopathy.
P S T (Ref:HM16557)

## PRESTON, S F
**S F Preston**, 156 Hermon Hill, London, **London (Greater)**, E18 1QH, ENG.
(T) 020 8989 5876
Speciality: Chiropodists (Podiatrists).
● **Owner** Ms S Preston
S (Ref:HM16558)

## PRESTON, ZINA
**Zina Preston**, Scott St Complementary Therapy Centre, 58 Scott St, Barrow-in-Furness, **Cumbria**, LA14 1QE, ENG.
(T) 01229 826700
Speciality: Aromatherapy.
● **Owner** Z Preston
M O (Ref:HM16559)

## PRESTONS CHRTRD PHYSIOTHERAPY
**Prestons Chartered Physiotherapy Clinic**, 29 Alexandra Rd, Peterborough, **Cambridgeshire**, PE1 3DE, ENG.
(T) 01733 565911
Speciality: Physiotherapy. ✔
● **Physiotherapist/Owner** Mr W Preston Q: Grad Dip Phys, MCSP, SRP. M: CSP.
● **Physiotherapist** Ms H Preston Q: BSc (Hons), MCSP, SRP. M: CSP.
S Yrs. Est.: 30 (Ref:HM16560)



Key: B Mind-Body Medicine C Complementary Medicine H Self Help Treatment M Medicinal Therapy O Oriental Medicine P Postural Therapy S Manipulative Structural Therapy T Touch Therapy

## PRESTWICH PHYSIOTHERAPY CLINIC

**Prestwich Physiotherapy Sports Injury Clinic**, 119 Heywood Rd, Prestwich, Manchester, **Manchester (Greater)**, M25 1LP, ENG.
(T) 01617 733034 (F) 01617 733034
Speciality: Physiotherapy.
P S T (Ref:HM16561)

## PRESTWOOD PHYSIOTHERAPY CLINIC

**Prestwood Physiotherapy & Sports Injuries Clinic**, Pankridge Farm, Moat Lane, Prestwood, Great Missenden, **Buckinghamshire**, HP16 9DA, ENG.
(T) 01494 891919 (F) 01494 891990
Speciality: Physiotherapy. ✔
● **Owner** Mrs C Heaton Q: MCSP, SRP. M: AACP.
● **Physiotherapist** Carol Parr Q: MCSP, SRP. M: CSP.
● **Physiotherapist** Elizabeth Deacon Q: MCSP, SRP. M: CSP.
● **Physiotherapist** Julie Copping Q: BSc, MCSP, SRP. M: CSP.
S Yrs. Est.: 22 (Ref:HM16562)

## PRETLOVE, ANN

**Ann Pretlove**, Green Ridges, 3 The Meadow, Chislehurst, **Kent**, BR7 6AA, ENG.
(T) 020 8467 2719
Speciality: Physiotherapy.
P S T (Ref:HM16563)

## PRETORIUS, C

**C Pretorius**, 60 Woodbridge Rd, Guildford, **Surrey**, GU1 4RF, ENG.
(T) 01483 571783
Speciality: Physiotherapy.
P S T (Ref:HM16564)

## PRETTY, RUTH

**Ruth Pretty**, Edgewood, Sale Green, Droitwich, **Worcestershire**, WR9 7LN, ENG.
(T) 01905 391551
Speciality: Reflexology.
S T (Ref:HM16565)

## PREW, BEVERLEY

**Beverley Prew**, 1 Ealing Cl, Norton, Runcorn, **Cheshire**, WA7 6QU, ENG.
(T) 01928 713881 (F) 01928 713881
(E) beverleyprew@yahoo.com
Speciality: Complementary Therapy, Indian Head Massage, Massage (Therapeutic), Reiki, Remedial Massage. ✔
● **Therapist** Ms B Prew Q: ITEC. M: GCP.
C Yrs. Est.: 1 (Ref:HM16566)

## PRICE, ANNE

**Anne Price**, Natural Ways, 6 Market St, Southport, **Merseyside**, PR8 1HH, ENG.
(T) 01704 545210
Speciality: Hypnotherapy.
B (Ref:HM16567)

## PRICE, D E

**D E Price**, 1a The Grove, Burnham-on-Sea, **Somerset**, TA8 2PA, ENG.
(T) 01278 780630
Speciality: Reflexology.
S T (Ref:HM16568)

## PRICE, ELIZABETH

**Elizabeth Price**, Redwall Farm House, Redwall Lane, Linton, Maidstone, **Kent**, ME17 4AX, ENG.
(T) 01622 743682
Speciality: Reflexology.
● **Owner** Mrs E Price
S T (Ref:HM16569)

## PRICE, ELIZABETH

**Elizabeth Price**, 32 South St, Bridport, **Dorset**, DT6 3NQ, ENG.
(T) 01308 427777 (F) 01308 427777
Speciality: Complementary Medicines & Therapy.
● **Practice Manager** Mrs S Marsh
M (Ref:HM16570)

## PRICE, G

**G Price**, Chelsea Lane, Inverurie, **Aberdeenshire**, AB51 3QQ, SCO.
(T) 01467 624888 (F) 01467 624888
Speciality: Chiropodists (Podiatrists).
● **Partner** Mrs C Craigmile
S (Ref:HM16571)

## PRICE, G J

**G J Price**, 35 Mount Rd, Wickford, **Essex**, SS11 8HJ, ENG.
(T) 01268 733181 (F) 08701 343750
(W) www.dietv.kngt/5275
Speciality: Chiropractic, Dietician, Electrotherapy, Herbal Medicine, Life Style Coaching, Manipulation, Osteopathy, Ultrasonics, Vitamin Therapy.
● **Owner** Nina Price
● **Owner** Mr J Price Q: LCSP. M: LCSP.
O Yrs. Est.: 27 (Ref:HM16572)

## PRICE, GILLIAN

**Gillian Price**, 212 Upper St, London, **London (Greater)**, N1 1RL, ENG.
(T) 020 8802 2311
Speciality: Acupuncture.
● **Owner** Ms G Price
O (Ref:HM16573)

## PRICE, GILLIAN

**Gillian Price**, Clissold Park Health Centre, 154 Stoke Newington Church St, London, **London (Greater)**, N16 0JU, ENG.
(T) 020 7249 2990 (F) 020 7249 3977
Speciality: Acupuncture.
● **Owner** Mr D Berg
O (Ref:HM16574)

## PRICE, GILLIAN

**Gillian Price**, 360 Green Lanes, Harringay, London, **London (Greater)**, N4 1DA, ENG.
(T) 020 8802 2311
(E) gillian_price@yahoo.com
Speciality: Acupuncture, Cupping, Moxibustion, Electro-Acupuncture - with or without needles. ✔
● **Acupuncturist** Ms G Price Q: Dip.Ac, MBAcC. M: BAcC.
O Yrs. Est.: 7 (Ref:HM16575)

## PRICE, GILLIAN

**Gillian Price**, 15 Malvern Avenue, Bexleyheath, **Kent**, DA7 5LE, ENG.
(T) 020 8310 9276
Speciality: Reflexology.
● **Owner** Mrs G Price
S T (Ref:HM16576)

## PRICE, GRAHAM

**Graham Price**, 52 Bank Rd, Matlock, **Derbyshire**, DE4 3GL, ENG.
(T) 01629 580996
Speciality: Osteopathy.
● **Owner** Mr G Price
P S T (Ref:HM16577)

## PRICE, H M

**H M Price**, 8 Brooklyn Rd, Cheadle, **Cheshire**, SK8 1BS, ENG.
(T) 01614 912938
Speciality: Chiropodists (Podiatrists).
S (Ref:HM16578)

## PRICE, J

**J Price**, 3 Ham Barn Cottage, Welsh Rd, Cubbington, Leamington Spa, **Warwickshire**, CV33 9AD, ENG.
(T) 01926 430052
Speciality: Chiropodists (Podiatrists).
● **Owner** Mr J Price
S (Ref:HM16579)

## PRICE, J

**J Price**, 32 The Avenue, Caldicot, **Monmouthshire**, NP26 4AB, WAL.
(T) 01633 880004
Speciality: Chiropodists (Podiatrists).
S (Ref:HM16580)

## PRICE, J A J

**J A J Price**, 42A Station Avenue, Coventry, **Midlands (West)**, CV4 9HS, ENG.
(T) 024 7646 6053
Speciality: Chiropodists (Podiatrists).
● **Owner** Mr J Price
S (Ref:HM16581)

## PRICE, JACKIE

**Jackie Price**, 65 Cowpen Lane, Billingham, **Cleveland**, TS23 4AT, ENG.
(T) 01642 562625
Speciality: Chiropodists (Podiatrists).
S (Ref:HM16582)

## PRICE, JAMES

**James Price**, 116 Nevill Avenue, Hove, **Sussex (East)**, BN3 7ND, ENG.
(T) 01273 774086
Speciality: Chiropody. ✔
● **Owner/Chiropodist** Mr J Price Q: M.S.C.P, MBChA.
M Yrs. Est.: 12 (Ref:HM16583)

## PRICE, JILL

**Jill Price**, Bienvenu, Parkend Rd, Coalway, Coleford, **Gloucestershire**, GL16 7HX, ENG.
(T) 01594 833372
Speciality: Complementary Medicines & Therapy.
C M (Ref:HM16584)

## PRICE, LYDIA

**Lydia Price**, The McTimoney Chiropractic Clinic, Stiffords Bridge, Cradley, Malvern, **Worcestershire**, WR13 5NL, ENG.
(T) 01886 880085
Speciality: Chiropractic.
P S T (Ref:HM16585)

## PRICE, M J

**M J Price**, 111 Congleton Rd, Biddulph, Stoke-On-Trent, **Staffordshire**, ST8 6EF, ENG.
(T) 01782 523763
Speciality: Hypnosis.
B (Ref:HM16586)

## PRICE, M P

**M P Price**, 5 Dunbar Drive, Woodley, Reading, **Berkshire**, RG5 4HA, ENG.
(T) 01189 697153
Speciality: Chiropodists (Podiatrists).
● **Owner** Mrs M Price
S (Ref:HM16587)

## PRICE, MARTHA

**Martha Price**, Westbourne House, Westbourne Trce, Shuttern, Taunton, **Somerset**, TA1 4ES, ENG.
(T) 01823 332871
Speciality: Osteopathy.
P S T (Ref:HM16588)

## PRICE, NICOLA

**Nicola Price**, 3 Middle Lane, Cherhill, Calne, **Wiltshire**, SN11 8XX, ENG.
(T) 01249 816935
Speciality: Chiropodists (Podiatrists).
S (Ref:HM16589)

## PRICE, R

**R Price**, 37 Slate St, Morriston, Swansea, SA6 8AA, WAL.
(T) 01792 781097
Speciality: Chiropodists (Podiatrists).
● **Partner** Mr G Matthews
S (Ref:HM16590)

## PRICE, ROGER

**Roger Price**, The McTimoney Chiropractic Clinic, Stiffords Bridge, Cradley, Malvern, **Worcestershire**, WR13 5NL, ENG.
(T) 01886 880085
Speciality: Chiropractors.
P S T (Ref:HM16591)

## PRICE, S C

**S C Price**, 1a The Grove, Burnham-on-Sea, **Somerset**, TA8 2PA, ENG.
(T) 01278 780630
Speciality: Homeopathy.
M (Ref:HM16592)

## PRICE, SANDRA

**Sandra Price**, 12 Fitzjames Avenue, Croydon, **Surrey**, CR0 5DH, ENG.
(T) 020 8654 3862
Speciality: Osteopathy. ✔
● **Owner/Osteopath** Ms S Price Q: DO. M: GOsC.
C S Yrs. Est.: 12 (Ref:HM16593)

## PRICE, SANDRA

**Sandra Price**, London Medical Centre, 144 Harley St, London, **London (Greater)**, W1N 1AH, ENG.


Key continued: Yrs.Est: Years Established Q: Qualifications M: Professional Membership ✔ Indemnity Insurance Accept Credit Cards

(T) 020 7935 0023 (F) 020 7935 5972
Speciality: Osteopathy. ✔
● **Osteopath** Ms S Price Q: DO. M: GOsC.
C S Yrs. Est.: 12 (Ref:HM16594)

**PRICE, SANDRA**

**Sandra Price**, 71b Sutherland, Maidavale, London, **London (Greater)**, W9 2HS, ENG.
(T) 020 7266 0758
Speciality: Osteopathy. ✔
● **Osteopath** Ms S Price Q: DO. M: GOsC.
C S Yrs. Est.: 12 (Ref:HM16595)

**PRICE, SARAH**

**Sarah Price**, 16 Whitworth Way, Wilstead, Bedford, **Bedfordshire**, MK45 3DX, ENG.
(T) 01234 741462 (F) 01234 741462
Speciality: Aromatherapy, Massage (Therapeutic). ✔
● **Aromatherapist** Ms S Price Q: MIFA. M: IFA.
T Yrs. Est.: 9 (Ref:HM16596)

**PRICE, TRACY**

**Tracy Price**, 166 Heath Lane, Blackfordby, Swadlincote, **Derbyshire**, DE11 8AA, ENG.
(T) 01283 211593
Speciality: Reflexology.
S T (Ref:HM16597)

**PRICE, VICTORIA**

**Victoria Price**, 28 New Rd, Brynteg, **Wrexham**, LL11 6PD, WAL.
(T) 07887 556022
Speciality: Reflexology.
S T (Ref:HM16598)

**PRICE-PULMAN**

**Price-Pulman**, Ty Ceffyl Bach, Abercanaid, Merthyr Tydfil, **Glamorgan (Vale of)**, CF48 1YS, WAL.
(T) 01685 376380
Speciality: Complementary Medicines & Therapy.
● **Owner** Mrs M Pulman
C M (Ref:HM16599)

**PRIDDLE, M**

**M Priddle**, 29 High St, Harlow, **Essex**, CM17 0DN, ENG.
(T) 01279 438444
Speciality: Aromatherapy.
● **Partner** Mr N Bruce
M O (Ref:HM16600)

**PRIDDLE, P**

**P Priddle**, 29 High St, Harlow, **Essex**, CM17 0DN, ENG.
(T) 01279 438444
Speciality: Hypnotherapy.
● **Partner** Mr N Bruce
B (Ref:HM16601)

**PRIDDLE, PATRICK**

**Patrick Priddle**, 41 Cambridge Rd, Sawbridgeworth, **Hertfordshire**, CM21 9JP, ENG.
(T) 01279 724963 (F) 01279 600525
Speciality: Hypnosis, Hypnotherapy. ✔
● **Hypnotherapist** Mr P Priddle Q: Dip.Hyp.
M: BIH, NCH, NCP.
C Yrs. Est.: 9 (Ref:HM16602)

**PRIDDY, G**

**G Priddy**, Market St, Bromsgrove, **Worcestershire**, B61 8AQ, ENG.
(T) 01527 872365
Speciality: Physiotherapy.
P S T (Ref:HM16603)

**PRIDEAUX-BRUNE, COLETTE**

**Colette Prideaux-Brune**, Hartfield Cottage, Packers Hill, Holwell, Sherborne, **Dorset**, DT9 5LN, ENG.
(T) 01963 23204
Speciality: Aromatherapy, Reflexology, La Stone Therapy and Hot Rock Massage. ✔
● **Therapist** Mrs C Prideaux-Brune Q: ITEC, MIIR.
M: IFA.
C Yrs. Est.: 17 (Ref:HM16604)

**PRIDMORE, JOSEPHINE**

**Josephine Pridmore**, Magna House, 81 Merley Lane, Merley, Wimborne, **Dorset**, BH12 2NW, ENG.
(T) 01202 739868
Speciality: Shiatsu, Yoga. ✔
● **Shiatsu Practitioner**
Ms J Pridmore Q: Dip.Shiatsu, MRSS(t).
M: Shiatsu Society UK.
C Yrs. Est.: 12 (Ref:HM16605)

**PRIEDE, C L**

**C L Priede**, 235 Leagrave High St, Luton, **Bedfordshire**, LU4 0NA, ENG.
(T) 01582 574441
Speciality: Chiropodists (Podiatrists).
S (Ref:HM16606)

**PRIEST, JILLIAN**

**Jillian Priest**, 148 Cheam Rd, Sutton, **Surrey**, SM1 2EB, ENG.
(T) 020 8642 2165
Speciality: Homeopathy.
M (Ref:HM16607)

**PRIEST, NIGEL**

**Nigel Priest**, 54 Dyas Rd, Hollywood, Birmingham, **Midlands (West)**, B47 5LJ, ENG.
(T) 01214 305298
Speciality: Hypnotherapy.
● **Owner** Mr N Priest
B (Ref:HM16608)

**PRIEST, NIGEL**

**Nigel Priest**, 1 Fawnbrake Avenue, London, **London (Greater)**, SE24 0BE, ENG.
(T) 020 7733 0848
Speciality: Hypnosis.
B (Ref:HM16609)

**PRIEST, ROSIE**

**Rosie Priest DC**, Seedbed Centre, Loughton, **Essex**, IG10 3TQ, ENG.
(T) 020 8508 5600
Speciality: Chiropractic.
P S T (Ref:HM16610)

**PRIESTLEY, E**

**E Priestley**, 115 Birchover Way, Allestree, Derby, **Derbyshire**, DE22 2QH, ENG.
(T) 01332 551593 (F) 01332 551593
Speciality: Chiropodists (Podiatrists).
● **Partner** Mrs L McCann
S (Ref:HM16611)

**PRIESTLEY, E**

**E Priestley**, 243 Lambourn Drive, Allestree, Derby, **Derbyshire**, DE22 2UR, ENG.
(T) 01332 551892
Speciality: Chiropodists (Podiatrists).
● **Owner** Mrs E Priestley
S (Ref:HM16612)

**PRIMAL INTEGRATION PROGRAMME**

**Primal Integration Programme (The)**, 36 Womersley Rd, Crouch End, London, **London (Greater)**, N89 AN, ENG.
(T) 020 8341 7226
Speciality: Complementary Medicines & Therapy.
● **Therapist** Juliana Brown
M (Ref:HM16613)

**PRIMARY HOUSE PROMOTION SVS**

**Primary House Promotion Services**, Centurian House, Centurian Way, Leyland, Preston, **Lancashire**, PR5 1TZ, ENG.
(T) 01772 454454 (F) 01772 422666
Speciality: Acupuncture.
● **Owner** Mr K Dennis
O (Ref:HM16614)

**PRIMECARE**

**Primecare**, 131 Rotton Park Rd, Birmingham, **Midlands (West)**, B16 0LJ, ENG.
(T) 01214 546829
Speciality: Hypnosis.
● **Owner** Mrs S Lewis
B (Ref:HM16615)

**PRIMROSE HEALING CENTRE**

**Primrose Healing Centre**, 9-10 St Georges Mews, London, **London (Greater)**, NW1 8XE, ENG.
(T) 020 7586 0148
(E) firstpath@btinternet.com
(W) www.firstpathbtinternet.co.uk
Speciality: Hypnotherapy, Osteopathy. ✔
● **Hypnotherapist** Ms N Zaman Q: NLP.
M: NCH.
B Yrs. Est.: 3 (Ref:HM16616)

**PRINCE**

**Prince**, Ty Capel, Penmynydd Rd, Llangefni, **Isle of Anglesey**, LL77 7HR, WAL.
(T) 01248 722957
Speciality: Chiropodists (Podiatrists).
● **Partner** Mr R Prince
S (Ref:HM16617)

**PRINCE**

**Prince**, 486 Harrow Rd, London, **London (Greater)**, W9 3QA, ENG.
(T) 020 8969 8959
Speciality: Chiropractic.
P S T (Ref:HM16618)

**PRINCE, KAREN**

**Karen Prince**, 10C High St, Buntingford, **Hertfordshire**, SG9 9AG, ENG.
(T) 01763 274760 (F) 01763 271149
Speciality: Osteopathy.
● **Owner** Ms K Prince
P S T (Ref:HM16619)

**PRINCE, KAREN**

**Karen Prince**, Oakington Therapy Centre, 12 High St, Oakington, Cambridge, **Cambridgeshire**, CB4 5AG, ENG.
(T) 01223 237459 (F) 01223 237459
Speciality: Osteopathy.
● **Director** Mr R Giddings
P S T (Ref:HM16620)

**PRINCE, R**

**R Prince**, Damon, Old Hillside Rd, Winchester, **Hampshire**, SO22 5LN, ENG.
(T) 01962 861184
Speciality: Clairvoyants & Palmists.
B (Ref:HM16621)

**PRINCE, TANIA A**

**Tania A Prince**, 20 Cumberland St, Macclesfield, **Cheshire**, SK10 1DD, ENG.
(T) 01625 520016
(W) www.nlp-hypnotherapy.com
Speciality: Counselling, Hypnosis, Hypnotherapy, Neuro-Linguistic Program, Meridian Therapy, Timeline Therapy. ✔
● **Hypnotherapist/Psychotherapist**
Ms T Prince Q: Dip.Hyp, NLP (Master). M: AMT, NRHP, TTA, UKCP.
B Yrs. Est.: 8 (Ref:HM16622)

**PRINCES AVENUE OSTEOPATHIC**

**Princes Avenue Osteopathic Clinic**, 60 Princes Avenue, Walderslade, Chatham, **Kent**, ME5 8AH, ENG.
(T) 01634 681138
(E) jean.hopkins@tinyworld.co.uk
Speciality: Osteopathy.
● **Osteopath** Ms J Hopkins Q: DO. M: GOsC.
S Yrs. Est.: 10 (Ref:HM16623)

**PRINCESS MARGARET HOSPITAL**

**Princess Margaret Hospital (The)**, Physiotherapy Department, Osborne Rd, Windsor, **Berkshire**, SL4 3SJ, ENG.
(T) 01753 743344
Speciality: Physiotherapy.
● **Manager** Ms T Playle
P S T (Ref:HM16624)

**PRING, R**

**R Pring**, 2 Crown Lane, Littleport, Ely, **Cambridgeshire**, CB6 1PP, ENG.
(T) 01353 863218
Speciality: Chiropodists (Podiatrists).
S (Ref:HM16625)

**PRINGLE CHIROPRACTIC**

**Pringle Chiropractic**, 41-43 Church View, Holywood, **County Down**, BT18 9DP, NIR.
(T) 028 9042 3232
(E) pringle@iol.ie
Speciality: Acupressure, Acupuncture, Alexander Technique, Bonesetting, Bowen Therapy, Chiropractic, Complementary Therapy, Feldenkrais Methodology, Hay Diet, Kinesiology, Manipulation, Massage (Therapeutic), Nutritional Therapy, Pilates, Reflexology, Reiki, Rolfing, Shiatsu, T'ai-Chi Ch'uan, X-Ray, Ying & Yang, High Maintenance Care. ✔



Key: B Mind-Body Medicine C Complementary Medicine H Self Help Treatment M Medicinal Therapy O Oriental Medicine P Postural Therapy S Manipulative Structural Therapy T Touch Therapy

● **Clinic Director** Dr P Pringle Q: DC.
● **Chiropractor** Dr S Pinkerton Q: DC. M: SCA.
● **Clinic Massage Therapist** Mr H Jamshidi
● **Chiropractor** Dr M Harris Q: DC. M: ICA.
P S Yrs. Est.: 39 (Ref:HM16626)

## PRINGLE, AMANDA

**Amanda Pringle**, 6 Hinchley Cl, Esher, **Surrey**, KT10 0BY, ENG.
(T) 020 8398 3598
Speciality: Reflexology.
S T (Ref:HM16627)

## PRIOR, CYNTHIA

**Cynthia Prior**, Brocks Hollow, Vann Rd, Fernhurst, Haslemere, **Surrey**, GU27 3NL, ENG.
(T) 01428 658780
Speciality: Reflexology.
S T (Ref:HM16628)

## PRIORS PODIATRY PRACTICE

**Priors Podiatry Practice**, The Priors, Pinfold Lane, Penkridge, **Staffordshire**, ST19 5AP, ENG.
(T) 01785 714867 (F) 01785 714795
(E) mark@dynastat.org.uk
(W) www.dynastat.org.uk
Speciality: Acupuncture, Biomechanics, Hypnosis, X-Ray, Ambulatory Foot Surgery. ✔
● **Owner** Mr M Emms
● **Podiatric Surgeon** Mr M Price Q: BSc (Hons), S.R.Ch.
M Yrs. Est.: 2 (Ref:HM16629)

## PRIOR-SANDERSON, SARA

**Sara Prior-Sanderson**, Flintstones, 2 The Loke, East Beckham, Norwich, **Norfolk**, NR11 8RP, ENG.
(T) 01263 823726
Speciality: Reflexology.
S T (Ref:HM16630)

## PRIORY CENTRE

**Priory Centre (The)**, The Dover Business Centre, 151-153 Folkestone Rd, Dover, **Kent**, CT17 9SG, ENG.
(T) 01304 210004 (F) 01304 214163
Speciality: Complementary Medicines & Therapy.
● **Practice Manager** Miss V West
M (Ref:HM16631)

## PRIORY CLINIC OSTEOPATHS

**Priory Clinic Osteopaths**, 18 Priory Hall, Stillorgan, **County Dublin**, IRE.
(T) 18002 54642 (F) 18002 835756
(E) iptas@iol.ie
Speciality: Osteopathy.
P S T (Ref:HM16632)

## PRIORY HEIGHTS

**Priory Heights**, 20 Priory Heights, Eastbourne, **Sussex (East)**, BN20 8SR, ENG.
(T) 01323 641929
Speciality: Acupuncture. ✔
● **Owner** Mr T Tamplin Q: Lic.Ac. M: BAcC.
O Yrs. Est.: 14 (Ref:HM16633)

## PRIORY PRACTICE

**Priory Practice (The)**, 11 Prince Avenue, Southend-On-Sea, **Essex**, SS2 6RL, ENG.
(T) 01702 300302 (F) 01702 300302
Speciality: Hypnosis.
● **Owner** Mr D Lovegrove
B (Ref:HM16634)

## PRIOSE COLES

**Primrose Coles**, Hillcrest, Dragonby, Scunthorpe, **Humberside**, DN15 0BE, ENG.
(T) 01724 858505
Speciality: Aromatherapy, Bach Remedies, Counselling, Crystal Healing, Healing Therapy, Herbal Medicine, Holistic Healing, Homeopathy, Kinesiology, Massage (Therapeutic), Naturopathy, Nutritional Therapy, Reflexology, Vitamin Therapy.
● **Naturopath** Ms P Coles Q: ND, SPNT. M: SPNT.
B C Yrs. Est.: 17 (Ref:HM16635)

## PRISM THERAPIES

**Prism Hypnotherapy (Jayne Whitehouse)**, 23 Stanmore Gr, Halesowen, **Midlands (West)**, B62 0HG, ENG.
(T) 01214 211552 (F) 01214 211552
(E) jaynewhitehouse@hotmail.com
(W) www.creativehealth.co.uk
Speciality: Acupressure, Hypnosis, Hypnotherapy, Reiki, Stress Therapy, Tui Na Acupressure Massage. ✔
● **Clinical Hypnotherapist** Ms J Whitehouse Q: BA (Hons), BSCH, Dip.Hyp, Reiki Master. M: BSCH, HS.
B Yrs. Est.: 4 (Ref:HM16636)

## PRITCHARD, AUDREY

**Audrey Pritchard**, Spring Bank, Aberhafesp, Newtown, **Powys**, SY16 3HH, WAL.
(T) 01686 622067
Speciality: Reflexology.
S T (Ref:HM16637)

## PRITCHARD, JEAN

**Jean Pritchard**, 71 Pengam Rd, Aberbargoed, Bargoed, **Caerphilly**, CF81 9FT, WAL.
(T) 01443 834878
Speciality: Complementary Medicines & Therapy.
● **Owner** Ms J Pritchard
C M (Ref:HM16638)

## PRITCHARD, MAUREEN

**Maureen Pritchard**, 6 Harding Cl, Redbourn, St. Albans, **Hertfordshire**, AL3 7NT, ENG.
(T) 01582 792129
Speciality: Complementary Medicines & Therapy.
● **Bowen Therapist** Mrs M Pritchard
M (Ref:HM16639)

## PRIVATE ACUPUNCTURE CLINIC

**Private Acupuncture Clinic (The)**, 41 Rectory Lane, Loughton, **Essex**, IG10 1NZ, ENG.
(T) 020 8502 0029
Speciality: Acupuncture.
O (Ref:HM16640)

## PRIVATE CLINIC OF NAT THRPY

**Private Clinic Of Natural Therapeutics (The)**, Chesnuts, 72 Chalfont Rd, Seer Green, Beaconsfield, **Buckinghamshire**, HP9 2QP, ENG.
(T) 01494 670038
Speciality: Osteopathy.
P S T (Ref:HM16641)

## PRIVATE CTRE-CRISIS PSYCHOLOGY

**Private Centre For Crisis Psychology**, Pinetum, Broughton Hall, Broughton, Skipton, **Yorkshire (North)**, BD23 3AE, ENG.
(T) 01756 796383 (F) 01756 796384
Speciality: Psychology.
● **Director** Mrs B Wright
B (Ref:HM16642)

## PRIVATE HEALTH CENTRE CLINIC

**Private Health Centre Branch Clinic**, 41 Rectory Lane, Loughton, **Essex**, IG10 1NZ, ENG.
(T) 020 8502 0029
(E) info@privatehealthcentre.org.uk
(W) www.privatehealthcentre.org.uk
Speciality: Acupuncture, Herbal Medicine, Homeopathy, Occupational Therapy. ✔
● **Complementary Therapist** Mr Pahwa Q: B.Ac, DPT, MCSP, OTD. M: BAcC.
C M O S Yrs. Est.: 21 (Ref:HM16643)

## PRIVATE HEALTH CLINIC

**Private Health Clinic**, 37a Green St, Forest Gate, London, **London (Greater)**, E7 8DA, ENG.
(T) 020 8472 0170 (F) 020 8471 5693
(E) jagdishpahwa@privatehealthcentre.org.uk
(W) www.privatehealthcentre.org.uk
Speciality: Acupuncture, Ayurvedic Medicine, Chiropody, Counselling, Herbal Medicine, Homeopathy, Hypnosis, Osteopathy, Physiotherapy, Polarity Therapy, Reflexology, Yoga, Occupational Therapy. ✔
● **Therapist** Mr J Pahwa Q: B.Ac, DPT, OTD. M: AACP, BAcC, CSP, FIH, OCPPP, PA, RCHM, SOM.
C M O S Yrs. Est.: 26 (Ref:HM16644)

## PRIVATE LINES

**Private Lines**, 319 Gallowgate, Glasgow, **Glasgow (City of)**, G40 2EF, SCO.
(T) 01415 561206
Speciality: Herbal Medicine.
● **Managing Director** Mr J Reece
M (Ref:HM16645)

## PRIVATE MEDICAL ACUPUNCTURE

**Private Medical Acupuncture**, Brooke Rd, Grays, **Essex**, RM17 5BY, ENG.
(T) 01375 372555
Speciality: Acupuncture.
O (Ref:HM16646)

## PRIVATE PHYSIOTHERAPY CLINIC

**Private Physiotherapy Clinic (The)**, The Riverside Surgery, Waterside, Evesham, **Worcestershire**, WR11 6JP, ENG.
(T) 01386 422421
Speciality: Physiotherapy.
P S T (Ref:HM16647)

## PRIVATE POLYCLINIC

**Private Polyclinic (The)**, 41 Rectory Lane, Loughton, **Essex**, IG10 1QN, ENG.
(T) 020 8502 0029
Speciality: Acupuncture.
O (Ref:HM16648)

## PRIVATE PRACTICE

**Private Practice**, 10 The Avenue, London, **London (Greater)**, N8 0JR, ENG.
(T) 020 8888 7104
Speciality: Psychotherapy.
● **Psychologist/Psychotherapist** Hara Pepeli M: BPS, UKCP.
M Yrs. Est.: 10 (Ref:HM16649)

## PRO PHYSIO CLINIC

**Pro Physio Clinic**, 152 Dover Rd, Walmer, Deal, **Kent**, CT14 7JQ, ENG.
(T) 01304 375253
Speciality: Physiotherapy.
● **Owner** Mr L Westbrook
P S T (Ref:HM16650)

## PROBERT, DIANA

**Diana Probert**, Elements, Newcastle Drive, Orton Longueville, Peterborough, **Cambridgeshire**, PE2 7AU, ENG.
(T) 01733 361116
Speciality: Reiki.
M (Ref:HM16651)

## PROCESS ORIENTED PSYCHOLOGY

**Process Oriented Psychology**, 10 Gillespie St, Edinburgh, **Edinburgh (City of)**, EH3 9NH, SCO.
(T) 01312 293096 (F) 01312 293096
Speciality: Psychotherapy.
B (Ref:HM16652)

## PROCTER, SHARON

**Sharon Procter**, 1 Harley St, London, **London (Greater)**, W1N 1DA, ENG.
(T) 020 7436 1446
Speciality: Osteopathy.
P S T (Ref:HM16653)

## PROCTER, SHARON

**Sharon Procter**, 97 College Rd, Epsom, **Surrey**, KT17 4HY, ENG.
(T) 01372 726080
Speciality: Osteopathy.
● **Senior Partner** Mr B Hounsfield
P S T (Ref:HM16654)

## PROCTOR, LYNDA

**Lynda Proctor**, 1 St Elmo Gr, Leeds, **Yorkshire (West)**, LS9 9BT, ENG.
(T) 01132 482243
Speciality: Chiropodists (Podiatrists).
S (Ref:HM16655)

## PROF ASS OF ALEXANDER TEACHERS

**Professional Association Of Alexander Teachers**, 17 Earls Hill View, Bicton Heath, Shrewsbury, **Shropshire**, SY3 5HA, ENG.
(T) 01743 246136
Speciality: Alexander Technique.
● **Partner** Mrs D Burnicle
P S (Ref:HM16656)

## PROF REGISTER OF ACUPUNCTURE

**Prof Register of Acupuncture**, 2-5 Johnsons Pl, South King St, IRE.
(T) 01679 4216
Speciality: Acupuncture.
O (Ref:HM16657)

## PROFESSIONAL HYP CTRE

**Professional Hypnotherapist Centre**, 28


Key continued: Yrs.Est: Years Established Q: Qualifications M: Professional Membership ✔ Indemnity Insurance Accept Credit Cards

Lakeside Cres, Barnet, **Hertfordshire**, EN4 8QJ, ENG.
(T) 020 8441 9685
Speciality: Hypnosis.
B (Ref:HM16658)

**PROFESSIONAL HYPNOTHERAPY**

**Professional Hypnotherapy Services**, 285 Dover Rd, Folkestone, **Kent**, CT19 6NT, ENG.
(T) 01303 253343
Speciality: Hypnosis.
B (Ref:HM16659)

**PROFESSIONAL PHYSIO CARE**

**Professional Physiotherapy Care Ltd**, 7 Grosvenor Trce, Wetherby, **Yorkshire (West)**, LS22 6PF, ENG.
(T) 01937 587006
Speciality: Physiotherapy.
P S T (Ref:HM16660)

**PROFESSIONAL PSYCHO CENTRE**

**Professional Psychotherapy Centre (The)**, Abington Medical Centre, 51A Beech Avenue, Northampton, **Northamptonshire**, NN3 2JG, ENG.
(T) 01604 231599
Speciality: Psychotherapy.
● **Owner** Mr A Symeou
B (Ref:HM16661)

**PROFESSIONAL REGISTER**

**Professional Register of Traditional Chinese Medicine**, 100 Marlborough Rd, Dublin, **County Dublin**, IRE.
(T) 01496 7830
Speciality: Complementary Medicines & Therapy.
M (Ref:HM16662)

**PROFIT, GILL**

**Gill Profit**, 1 Church St, Braunston, Oakham, **Leicestershire**, LE15 8QT, ENG.
(T) 01572 722347
Speciality: Physiotherapy.
● **Owner** Mrs G Profit
P S T (Ref:HM16663)

**PROGRAMME HEALTH/HEALING CTRE**

**Progressive Health & Healing Centre**, 44-46 Ryder Rd, Plymouth, **Devon**, PL2 1JA, ENG.
(T) 01752 606001 (F) 01752 606002
Speciality: Complementary Medicines & Therapy.
C M (Ref:HM16664)

**PROGRESSIVE HYPNOTHERAPY**

**Progressive Hypnotherapy Clinic**, 63 Clanbrassil St, Dundalk, **County Louth**, IRE.
(T) 04293 31406
Speciality: Hypnotherapy.
B (Ref:HM16665)

**PROPERT, DAVID**

**David Propert**, Dolpin Sq Health Club, Dolphin Sq, London, **London (Greater)**, SW1V 3LX, ENG.
(T) 020 7798 8685
(W) www.davidpropert.com
Speciality: Osteopathy. ✓
● **Principal Osteopath** Mr D Propert **Q:** BSc (Hons). **M:** GOsC.
S Yrs. Est.: 8 (**Ref:**HM16666)

**PROSPECT HEALTH**

**Prospect Health Ltd**, Prospect House, 13 Carlton Rd South, Weymouth, **Dorset**, DT4 7PL, ENG.
(T) 01305 780565 (F) 01305 780566
Speciality: Aromatherapy, Auto Suggestion, Beauty Therapy, Bowen Therapy, Chiropractic, Counselling, Faith Healing, Healing Therapy, Homeopathy, Hypnosis, Hypnotherapy, Manipulation, Massage (Therapeutic), Nutritional Therapy, Reflexology, Vibrational Therapy, Physio/Sports Injuries Clinic, Holistic Dentistry, Non Surgical Face Lift. ✓
● **Director/Hygienist** Ms K Weller
C Yrs. Est.: 2 (**Ref:**HM16667)

**PROTEC PHYSIO & ACUPUNCTURE**

**Protec Physiotherapy & Acupuncture Clinic**, 16 Penlan St, Pwllheli, **Gwynedd**, LL53 5DE, WAL.
(T) 01758 701667
Speciality: Physiotherapy.
● **Manager** Mr J Cooper
P S T (Ref:HM16668)

**PROTEC PHYSIO & ACUPUNCTURE**

**Protec Physiotherapy & Acupuncture Clinic**, Pwll Brwyn, Lon Uchaf, Morfa Nefyn, Pwllheli, **Gwynedd**, LL53 6AD, WAL.
(T) 01758 720039 (F) 01758 720039
Speciality: Physiotherapy.
P S T (Ref:HM16669)

**PROTEC PHYSIO & ACUPUNCTURE**

**Protec Physiotherapy & Acupuncture Clinic (The)**, 1 Railway Trce, Criccieth, **Gwynedd**, LL52 0HF, WAL.
(T) 01766 522167 (F) 01758 720039
Speciality: Physiotherapy.
● **Owner** Mrs K Cooper
P S T (Ref:HM16670)

**PROTEC PHYSIO & ACUPUNCTURE**

**Protec Physiotherapy & Acupuncture Clinic (The)**, 46 Bridge St, Caernarfon, **Gwynedd**, LL55 1AF, WAL.
(T) 01286 674173
Speciality: Physiotherapy.
P S T (Ref:HM16671)

**PROTHERO, PEGGY**

**Peggy Prothero**, 26 Parkgate Rd, Neston, **Cheshire**, CH64 9XE, ENG.
(T) 01513 362423
Speciality: Psychotherapy.
● **Partner** Mrs P Prothero
B (Ref:HM16672)

**PROUD, N R**

**N R Proud**, 26 Mansfield Rd, Skegby, Sutton-in-Ashfield, **Nottinghamshire**, NG17 3EQ, ENG.
(T) 01623 556971
Speciality: Complementary Medicines & Therapy.
C M (Ref:HM16673)

**PROUDFOOT SCHOOL**

**Proudfoot School Of Hypnosis & Psychotherapy**, Caxton Way, Eastfield, Scarborough, **Yorkshire (North)**, YO11 3YT, ENG.
(T) 01723 585960
(W) www.proudfoothypnosis.com
Speciality: Hypnosis.
● **Hypnotherapist** Mr W Proudfoot
B Yrs. Est.: 20 (**Ref:**HM16674)

**PROUDFOOT, WILF**

**Wilf Proudfoot**, 278 Scalby Rd, Scarborough, **Yorkshire (North)**, YO12 6EA, ENG.
(T) 01723 367027
(W) www.ukguild.com
Speciality: Hypnotherapy. ✓
● **Hypnotherapist** Mr W Proudfoot
C Yrs. Est.: 20 (**Ref:**HM16675)

**PROUDMAN CHIROPRACTIC CLINIC**

**Proudman Chiropractic Clinic**, 20 Lodge Manor, Coleraine, **County Londonderry**, BT52 1JX, NIR.
(T) 028 7035 2008
Speciality: Chiropractors.
● **Owner** Dr K Proudman
P S T (Ref:HM16676)

**PROWER, JANET**

**Janet Prower**, 116 Dartmouth Rd, London, **London (Greater)**, NW2 4HB, ENG.
(T) 020 8452 7517
Speciality: Osteopathy.
P S T (Ref:HM16677)

**PRUDEN, J F**

**J F Pruden**, 34 College Rd, Liverpool, **Merseyside**, L23 0RW, ENG.
(T) 01519 282120
Speciality: Chiropodists (Podiatrists).
● **Owner** Mr J Pruden
S (Ref:HM16678)

**PRUE BRAND**

**Prue Brand**, 15F Cambridge Pk, Twickenham, **London (Greater)**, TW1 2JE, ENG.
(T) 020 8891 3501
Speciality: Reflexology.
● **Owner** Ms P Brand
S T (Ref:HM16679)

**PRYCE, JOHN**

**John Pryce**, 10 North Prde, Penzance, **Cornwall**, TR18 4SH, ENG.
(T) 01736 363122
Speciality: Chiropodists (Podiatrists).
● **Owner** Mr J Pryce
S (Ref:HM16680)

**PSARADELIS, T**

**T Psaradelis**, Chota Koti, Crowhurst Lane, West Kingsdown, Sevenoaks, **Kent**, TN15 6JE, ENG.
(T) 01474 854099
Speciality: Aromatherapy.
● **Owner** Ms T Psaradelis
M O (Ref:HM16681)

**PSL**

**PSL**, Letchford House, Headstone Lane, Harrow, **London (Greater)**, HA3 6PE, ENG.
(T) 020 8421 0115 (F) 020 8421 6966
Speciality: Psychology.
● **Director** Mr R Alburgh
B (Ref:HM16682)

**PSYCHIATRIC CONSULT PRACTICE**

**Psychiatric Consulting Practice**, 5 Walton St, Oxford, **Oxfordshire**, OX1 2HG, ENG.
(T) 01865 554754
Speciality: Psychiatry.
● **Professor** Mr R Tilleard-Cole
B (Ref:HM16683)

**PSYCHIC & HEALING CENTRE**

**Psychic & Healing Centre In Scotland (The)**, 82 Victoria Rd, Glasgow, **Glasgow (City of)**, G42 7AA, SCO.
(T) 01415 751205
Speciality: Reiki, Psychic Therapy. ✓
● **Owner** Mr A Lynas
C Yrs. Est.: 3 (**Ref:**HM16684)

**PSYCHIC AND LIFE SOLUTIONS**

**Tarot And Psychic Agency**, 24 Burgess St, Edinburgh, **Edinburgh (City of)**, EH6 6RD, SCO.
(T) 01315 544486
(E) pegasus@easynet.co.uk
(W) www.scotlandthehive.com
Speciality: Counselling, Drama Therapy, Encounter Groups, Group Therapy, Humanistic Psychology, Sound Therapy, Spiritual Healing, Career Therapy, Psychic Life Analysis, Mediumship, Psychic Linking. ✓
● **Energy Work Counsellor** Ms L Brzoska **Q:** BSc.
● **Tarot/Career Counsellor** Mr A Hennessey **Q:** HND.
H Yrs. Est.: 3 (**Ref:**HM16685)

**PSYCHIC CIRCLE**

**Psychic Circle Ltd (The)**, Kingfisher Court, Newbury, **Berkshire**, RG14 5SJ, ENG.
(T) 01635 36335 (F) 01635 36336
Speciality: Clairvoyants & Palmists.
● **Manager** Mrs B Kepe
B (Ref:HM16686)

**PSYCHIC CLAIRVOYANT**

**Psychic Clairvoyant Tarot Readings**, 18 St Michaels Rd, Preston, **Lancashire**, PR1 6LY, ENG.
(T) 01772 556235
Speciality: Clairvoyants & Palmists.
● **Owner** Mrs J Hutchins
B (Ref:HM16687)

**PSYCHIC CONSULTANTS**

**Psychic Consultants**, 61 Cresswell St, Glasgow, **Glasgow (City of)**, G12 8AD, SCO.
(T) 01413 331418 (F) 01413 331418
Speciality: Clairvoyants & Palmists.
● **Owner** Mr J Book
B (Ref:HM16688)

**PSYCHIC FRIENDS NETWORK**

**Psychic Friends Network**, 234 Lower Twydall Lane, Gillingham, **Kent**, ME8 6QP, ENG.
(T) 01634 310361
Speciality: Clairvoyants & Palmists.
● **Owner** Ms I Knox
B (Ref:HM16689)



Key: B Mind-Body Medicine C Complementary Medicine H Self Help Treatment M Medicinal Therapy O Oriental Medicine P Postural Therapy S Manipulative Structural Therapy T Touch Therapy

## PSYCHIC INT AWARENESS SOCIETY
**Psychic International Awareness Society**, Room 208, Imex House, 40 Princess St, Manchester, **Manchester (Greater)**, M1 6DE, ENG.
(T) 01616 617654
Speciality: Clairvoyants & Palmists.
● **Director** Mrs C Japzon
B (Ref:HM16690)

## PSYCHIC READERS
**Psychic Readers**, 599 Holloway Rd, London, **London (Greater)**, N19 4DJ, ENG.
(T) 020 7263 5913
Speciality: Clairvoyants & Palmists.
● **Owner** Mrs L Williams
B (Ref:HM16691)

## PSYCHIC SHOP
**Psychic Shop (The)**, 124 Albert Rd, Plymouth, **Devon**, PL2 1AQ, ENG.
(T) 01752 551919
Speciality: Clairvoyants & Palmists.
● **Owner** Miss S Hatch
B (Ref:HM16692)

## PSYCHIC SOLUTIONS INT
**Psychic Solutions International Ltd**, 6 Camden Pl, Preston, **Lancashire**, PR1 3JL, ENG.
(T) 07071 601701
Speciality: Clairvoyants & Palmists.
B (Ref:HM16693)

## PSYCHIC THOUGHTS
**Psychic Thoughts**, 25 Orchard St, Falkirk, FK1 1RF, SCO.
(T) 01324 625001
Speciality: Clairvoyants & Palmists.
● **Partner** Mrs I Reilly
B (Ref:HM16694)

## PSYCHICS, SAM
**Sam Psychics**, Sycamore Avenue, Knottingley, **Yorkshire (West)**, WF11 0PL, ENG.
(T) 01977 674249
Speciality: Clairvoyants & Palmists.
● **Owner/Clairvoyant** Ms S Amos
B (Ref:HM16695)

## PSYCHO & COUNSELLING CENTRE
**North Staffs Centre For Psychotherapy & Counselling**, 2 Gower St, Newcastle, **Staffordshire**, ST5 1JQ, ENG.
(T) 01782 719705
Speciality: Psychotherapy.
● **Owner** Mr A Hassall
B (Ref:HM16696)

## PSYCHO & HYPNOTHERAPY CLINIC
**Psychotherapy & Hypnotherapy Clinic**, 50 Bell St, Sawbridgeworth, **Hertfordshire**, CM21 9AN, ENG.
(T) 01279 726662
Speciality: Psychotherapy.
● **Owner** Mrs C Judd
B (Ref:HM16697)

## PSYCHO ASS & CONSULTING
**Psychological Assessment & Consulting**, 2b South Trce, Court West South Trce, Cork, **County Cork**, IRE.
(T) 021 4314 505
(E) info@psyassess.com
(W) www.psyassess.com
Speciality: Psychology.
B (Ref:HM16698)

## PSYCHOL & FAMILY THRPY PRACT
**Delahunty Psychological & Family Therapy Practice**, 6 Snipe Lawn, Newcastle, Galway, **County Galway**, IRE.
(T) 08723 09037
Speciality: Counselling, Family Therapy, Psychotherapy, Marital Therapy. ✔
● **Psychotherapist** Mr A Delahunty
Q: Deg(Hons)Psychol. M: FTAI.
M Yrs. Est.: 6 (Ref:HM16699)

## PSYCHOLOGICAL & COUNS SVS
**Psychological & Counselling Services**, 26 Bloxworth Cl, Wallington, **Surrey**, SM6 7NL, ENG.
(T) 020 8647 7901 (F) 020 8647 7901
Speciality: Psychotherapy.
● **Owner** Ms C Hobson
B (Ref:HM16700)

## PSYCHOLOGICAL ADVANTAGE
**Psychological Advantage (The)**, 24 Croft Pl, Livingston, **Lothian (West)**, EH54 6RJ, SCO.
(T) 01506 461241
Speciality: Psychology.
● **Owner** Mr S Watkins
B (Ref:HM16701)

## PSYCHOLOGICAL CONSULTANCY
**Psychological Consultancy Services Ltd**, 101 Sorrento Rd, Dalkey, **County Dublin**, IRE.
(T) 01285 9400 (F) 01285 9632
Speciality: Psychology.
B (Ref:HM16702)

## PSYCHOLOGICAL CONSULTANCY SVS
**Psychological Consultancy Services Ltd**, 223-231 Old Marylebone Rd, London, **London (Greater)**, NW1 5QT, ENG.
(T) 020 7402 3363
Speciality: Psychology.
● **Accountant** Robert Michael Coe
B (Ref:HM16703)

## PSYCHOLOGICAL CONSULTING SVS
**Psychological Consulting Services**, 38 Bold Business Centre, Bold Lane, St. Helens, **Merseyside**, WA9 4TX, ENG.
(T) 01925 224192 (F) 01925 224192
Speciality: Psychotherapy.
● **Director** Mr L Veale
B (Ref:HM16704)

## PSYCHOLOGICAL SERVICE
**Psychological Service**, 13 Abbey Park Pl, Dunfermline, **Fife**, KY12 7PT, SCO.
(T) 01383 312800
Speciality: Psychology.
B (Ref:HM16705)

## PSYCHOLOGICAL SERVICE
**Psychological Service**, 5 Bedford Pl, Maidstone, **Kent**, ME16 8JB, ENG.
(T) 01622 679085 (F) 01622 679670
Speciality: Psychology.
● **Owner** Mrs H Flatman
B (Ref:HM16706)

## PSYCHOLOGICAL SERVICE
**Psychological Service**, Matthew St, Kirkcaldy, **Fife**, KY2 5AT, SCO.
(T) 01592 412500
Speciality: Psychology.
B (Ref:HM16707)

## PSYCHOLOGICAL SERVICE
**Psychological Service**, Queen Mary Avenue, Clydebank, **Argyll and Bute**, G81 2LR, SCO.
(T) 01419 520311 (F) 01419 518213
Speciality: Psychology.
● **Principal** Mrs C Basaie
B (Ref:HM16708)

## PSYCHOLOGICAL SERVICE
**Psychological Service**, St Aloysius School, Main St, Chapelhall, Airdrie, **Lanarkshire (North)**, ML6 8SF, SCO.
(T) 01236 764135 (F) 01236 747292
Speciality: Psychology.
● **Manager** Mrs C Munroe
B (Ref:HM16709)

## PSYCHOLOGICAL SERVICE
**Psychological Service**, Woodend Rd, Cardenden, Lochgelly, **Fife**, KY5 0NE, SCO.
(T) 01592 414752 (F) 01592 414759
Speciality: Psychology.
● **Director** Mr B Kirkaldy
B (Ref:HM16710)

## PSYCHOLOGICAL SERVICES
**Psychological Services**, St Brides High School, Platthorn Drive, East Kilbride, Glasgow, **Glasgow (City of)**, G74 1NL, SCO.
(T) 01355 236984 (F) 01355 276598
Speciality: Psychology.
● **Manager** Dr F Murphy
B (Ref:HM16711)

## PSYCHOLOGICAL SERVICES
**Psychological Services**, 2 Woodside Trce, Glasgow, **Glasgow (City of)**, G3 7UY, SCO.
(T) 01412 118000
Speciality: Psychology.
B (Ref:HM16712)

## PSYCHOLOGICAL SERVICES
**Psychological Services**, 562A Scott Hall Rd, Leeds, **Yorkshire (West)**, LS7 3RD, ENG.
(T) 01132 370524
Speciality: Psychology.
● **Director** Dr D Duckworth
B (Ref:HM16713)

## PSYCHOLOGICAL SERVICES
**Psychological Services**, St Mary's Primary School, Whitelees Rd, Lanark, **Lanarkshire (South)**, ML11 7RX, SCO.
(T) 01555 661673
Speciality: Psychology.
B (Ref:HM16714)

## PSYCHOLOGICAL SERVICES
**Psychological Services**, St Josephs Primary School, Joanna Trce, Blantyre, Glasgow, **Glasgow (City of)**, G72 0YJ, SCO.
(T) 01698 710568
Speciality: Psychology.
B (Ref:HM16715)

## PSYCHOLOGICAL SERVICES
**Psychological Services To Industry Education**, Tirley Lane, Utkinton, Tarporley, **Cheshire**, CW6 0JZ, ENG.
(T) 01829 752862 (F) 01829 752666
Speciality: Psychology.
● **Manager** Mr K Lindley
B (Ref:HM16716)

## PSYCHOLOGICAL/THERAPEUTIC CONS
**Psychological & Therapeutic Consultancy**, 57 Western Rd, Leigh-On-Sea, **Essex**, SS9 2PT, ENG.
(T) 01702 472183
Speciality: Psychology.
● **Partner** Mr G Wilson
B (Ref:HM16717)

## PSYCHOLOGIST NORTH WEST
**Psychologist North West**, 1 Nansen Rd, Gatley, Cheadle, **Cheshire**, SK8 4JL, ENG.
(T) 01614 284855 (F) 01614 284855
Speciality: Psychology.
● **Owner** Mr S Lewis
B (Ref:HM16718)

## PSYCHOLOGIST-HYPNOTHERAPIST
**Psychologist-Hypnotherapist**, Holistic Psychotherapy, 16 Brackendene, Bricket Wood, St. Albans, **Hertfordshire**, AL2 3SX, ENG.
(T) 01923 672880 (F) 01923 672880
Speciality: Hypnosis.
● **Owner** Dr S Timmann
B (Ref:HM16719)

## PSYCHOLOGY CONSULTANCY SERVICE
**Psychology Consultancy Service**, Chadeslode House, 130 Abbey Foregate, Shrewsbury, **Shropshire**, SY2 6AX, ENG.
(T) 01743 343633 (F) 01743 352210
Speciality: Psychology.
● **Director** Mr C Newnes
B (Ref:HM16720)

## PSYCHOLOGY IN PRACTICE
**Psychology In Practice Ltd**, 20 The Drive, Roundhay, Leeds, **Yorkshire (West)**, LS8 1JF, ENG.
(T) 01132 370309
Speciality: Psychology.
B (Ref:HM16721)

## PSYCHOLOGY OF VISION
**Psychology Of Vision**, France Farm, Upavon, Pewsey, **Wiltshire**, SN9 6DR, ENG.
(T) 01980 635199 (F) 01980 635101
Speciality: Complementary Medicines & Therapy.
● **Managing Director** Mr J Allen
C M (Ref:HM16722)

## PSYCHOLOGY SERVICES INT
**Psychology Services International Ltd**, Westleigh, Broomfield, Bridgwater, **Somerset**, TA5 2EH, ENG.
(T) 08009 754579


Key continued: Yrs.Est: Years Established Q: Qualifications M: Professional Membership ✔ Indemnity Insurance Accept Credit Cards

Speciality: Psychology.
● **Owner** Dr R Sharpe
B (Ref:HM16723)

## PSYCHOLOGY SPECIALIST INPUT

**Psychology Specialist Input**, Foresterseat, Cothal, Dyce, Aberdeen, **Aberdeenshire**, AB21 0HX, SCO.
(T) 01224 791751 (F) 01224 791751
Speciality: Psychology.
● **Owner** Mr F Woods
B (Ref:HM16724)

## PSYCHOSYNTH AND ED TRUST

**Psychosynthesis and Education Trust**, 92-94 Tooley St, London, **London (Greater)**, SE1 2TH, ENG.
(T) 020 7403 2100
Speciality: Complementary Medicines & Therapy.
● **Administrator** Robert Mason
M (Ref:HM16725)

## PSYCHOTHERAPY

**Psychotherapy**, 12 Sheraton Cl, Elstree, Borehamwood, **Hertfordshire**, WD6 3PZ, ENG.
(T) 020 8905 1565
Speciality: Psychotherapy. ✔
● **Owner** Ms A Wiser M: AHPP, BACP.
B Yrs. Est.: 8 (Ref:HM16726)

## PSYCHOTHERAPY

**Psychotherapy**, 15 Tuesday Market Pl, King's Lynn, **Norfolk**, PE30 1JN, ENG.
(T) 01553 773854
Speciality: Psychotherapy.
B (Ref:HM16727)

## PSYCHOTHERAPY & COUNS PRACTICE

**Psychotherapy & Counselling Practice (The)**, 11 Linksview, Dollis Rd, London, **London (Greater)**, N3 1RN, ENG.
(T) 020 8371 0443 (F) 020 8371 0606
Speciality: Psychotherapy.
● **Owner** Mr R Swynnerton
B (Ref:HM16728)

## PSYCHOTHERAPY & COUNS SVS

**Psychotherapy & Counselling Services**, St Pirans, 31 Upton Rd, Callow End, Worcester, **Worcestershire**, WR2 4TY, ENG.
(T) 01905 830316
Speciality: Psychotherapy.
B (Ref:HM16729)

## PSYCHOTHERAPY & COUNSELLING SV

**Confidential Psychotherapy & Counselling Service**, 14 New Parks Cres, Scarborough, **Yorkshire (North)**, YO12 5JZ, ENG.
(T) 01723 379715
Speciality: Psychotherapy.
B (Ref:HM16730)

## PSYCHOTHERAPY & HYPNOTHERAPY

**Psychotherapy & Hypnotherapy**, 58 Gurney Avenue, Hereford, **Herefordshire**, HR1 1XW, ENG.
(T) 01432 350738
Speciality: Psychotherapy.
● **Owner** Mr B Cornick
B (Ref:HM16731)

## PSYCHOTHERAPY ASSOCIATES INT

**Psychotherapy Associates International Ltd**, 81-83 Villa Rd, Birmingham, **Midlands (West)**, B19 1NH, ENG.
(T) 01215 230145 (F) 01215 235062
Speciality: Psychotherapy.
● **Managing Director** Mrs N Johnson
B (Ref:HM16732)

## PSYCHOTHERAPY CENTRE

**Psychotherapy Centre (The)**, 1 Wythburn Pl, London, **London (Greater)**, W1H 5WL, ENG.
(T) 020 7723 6173
Speciality: Psychotherapy.
● **Principal** Mr R Brian
B (Ref:HM16733)

## PSYCHOTHERAPY CENTRE

**Psychotherapy Centre (The)**, 67 Upper Berkeley St, London, **London (Greater)**, W1H 7QX, ENG.
(T) 020 7723 6173
Speciality: Hypnotherapy, Psychotherapy, Psycho-Analysis, TNT(Therapy not Theory), Psychodynamic Psychotherapy, Hypno-Analysis. ✔
● **Psychotherapist** Nick Morley
● **Psychotherapist** Ms E Scott
● **Psychotherapist** Mr S Pilkington-Miksa
● **Principal** Mr R Brian
B Yrs. Est.: 40 (Ref:HM16734)

## PSYCHOTHERAPY REFERRAL SERVICE

**Psychotherapy Referral Service**, 74 Lincoln Avenue, Twickenham, **London (Greater)**, TW2 6NP, ENG.
(T) 020 8898 2522
Speciality: Psychotherapy.
● **Owner** Mrs S Dean
B (Ref:HM16735)

## PSYCHOTHERAPY REFERRAL SERVICE

**Psychotherapy Referral Service**, 222 South Norwood Hill, London, **London (Greater)**, SE25 6AS, ENG.
(T) 020 8771 2311
Speciality: Psychotherapy.
B (Ref:HM16736)

## PSYCHOTHERAPY SERVICES

**Margaret Comport**, 41 Cubitt Trce, London, **London (Greater)**, SW4 6AU, ENG.
(T) 020 7720 5170
Speciality: Counselling, Hypnotherapy, Psychotherapy. ✔
● **Counsellor/Psychotherapist/Hypnotherapist** Ms M Comport Q: MNCH. M: GHR, NCH, NCP.
B H Yrs. Est.: 10 (Ref:HM16737)

## PSYCHOTHERAPY UNIT

**Psychotherapy Unit**, 4 Shide Rd, Newport, **Isle of Wight**, PO30 1YQ, ENG.
(T) 01983 521511 (F) 01983 533134
Speciality: Psychotherapy.
B (Ref:HM16738)

## PSYCHOTHERAPY/HYPNOTHERAPY

**Psychotherapy/Hypnotherapy**, The Chalet, Trood Stables, Trood Lane, Matford, Exeter, **Devon**, EX2 8XX, ENG.
(T) 01392 215430
Speciality: Counselling, Gestalt Therapy, Group Therapy, Psychotherapy. ✔
● **Psychotherapist** G Knowles Q: Dip.Hyp, Dip.Psych. M: BACP, GASW, HA.
B Yrs. Est.: 16 (Ref:HM16739)

## PSYCLOPS

**Psyclops Ltd**, 200-202 High St, Bromley, **Kent**, BR1 1PW, ENG.
(T) 020 8249 2747 (F) 020 8249 2747
Speciality: Psychology.
● **Owner** Miss S Izzard
B (Ref:HM16740)

## PUCZYNSKI, JOHN

**John Puczynski**, 3 Heath Lane, Hemel Hempstead, **Hertfordshire**, HP1 1TS, ENG.
(T) 01442 263581 (F) 01442 263581
Speciality: Complementary Medicines & Therapy.
● **Owner** Mr J Puczynski
C M (Ref:HM16741)

## PUDSEY CLINIC OF ALT MEDICINE

**Pudsey Clinic Of Alternative Medicine**, 46 Chapeltown, Pudsey, **Yorkshire (West)**, LS28 8BS, ENG.
(T) 01132 393396 (F) 01132 293443
Speciality: Complementary Medicines & Therapy.
● **Manageress** Mrs L Hector
C M (Ref:HM16742)

## PUFFIN HYDROTHERAPY POOL

**Puffin Hydrotherapy Pool**, Ferry Rd, Dingwall, **Highland**, IV15 9QS, SCO.
(T) 01349 864414 (F) 01349 864414
Speciality: Physiotherapy, Hydrotherapy. ✔
● **Physiotherapist** Fran Bowen Q: MCSP, SRP. M: CSP.
● **Manager** Mrs M Hayden
● **Physiotherapist** Mr J Woodham Q: MCSP, SRP. M: CSP.
S (Ref:HM16743)

## PUGH, ANNE W

**Anne W Pugh**, 6 Fairhaven Rd, Southport, **Merseyside**, PR9 9UJ, ENG.
(T) 01704 226383
Speciality: Chiropodists (Podiatrists).
S (Ref:HM16744)

## PUGH, CHERYL

**Cheryl Pugh**, 20 Hatfield Cl, Rainworth, Mansfield, **Nottinghamshire**, NG21 0LL, ENG.
(T) 01623 798119
Speciality: Hypnosis.
● **Owner** Mrs C Pugh
B (Ref:HM16745)

## PUGH, CHERYL

**Cheryl Pugh**, The Wellbeing Centre, 11 Musters Rd, West Bridgford, Nottingham, **Nottinghamshire**, NG2 7PP, ENG.
(T) 01159 825353
Speciality: Hypnotherapy.
● **Partner** Mrs C Pugh
B (Ref:HM16746)

## PUGH, G

**G Pugh**, 44 Groombridge Rd, London, **London (Greater)**, E9 7DP, ENG.
(T) 020 8985 7440
Speciality: Psychotherapy.
● **Owner** Dr G Pugh
B (Ref:HM16747)

## PUGH, JANE

**Miss Jane Pugh**, 60 Lascotts Rd, London, **London (Greater)**, N22 8JN, ENG.
(T) 020 8881 7008
Speciality: Alexander Technique.
● **Owner** Miss J Pugh
P S (Ref:HM16748)

## PUGH, VIV

**Viv Pugh**, 32 Garth Rd, T.Y. Coch, Cwmbran, **Torfaen**, NP44 7AB, WAL.
(T) 01633 484042
Speciality: Osteopathy.
P S T (Ref:HM16749)

## PULHAM MARKET THERAPY CLINIC

**Pulham Market Therapy Clinic**, Rockaway, Tattlepot Rd, Pulham Market, Diss, **Norfolk**, IP21 4TL, ENG.
(T) 01379 608382
Speciality: Complementary Medicines & Therapy.
● **Owner** Mr P Turner
C M (Ref:HM16750)

## PULLAN, LINDA

**Linda Pullan**, Harrow Health Care Centre, 84-88 Pinner Rd, Harrow, **London (Greater)**, HA1 4YX, ENG.
(T) 020 8427 4915
Speciality: Chiropodists (Podiatrists).
S (Ref:HM16751)

## PULLEN, AUDREY M

**Audrey M Pullen**, 60 Sheals Cres, Maidstone, **Kent**, ME15 6TJ, ENG.
(T) 01622 765520
Speciality: Chiropodists (Podiatrists).
● **Owner** Mrs A Pullen
S (Ref:HM16752)

## PULLEN, JOHN D

**John D Pullen**, 26 Longmoore St, London, **London (Greater)**, SW1V 1JF, ENG.
(T) 020 7233 9030
Speciality: Chiropodists (Podiatrists).
● **Owner** Mr J Pullen
S (Ref:HM16753)

## PULLEN, R W

**R W Pullen**, The Physiotherapy & Sports Injury Clinic, 6 Saint Marys St, Shrewsbury, **Shropshire**, SY1 1EB, ENG.
(T) 01743 271975
Speciality: Physiotherapy.
● **Owner** Mr R Pullen
P S T (Ref:HM16754)

## PULLMAN, JUDITH

**Judith Pullman Clinical Hypnotherapist**, 24



Key: B Mind-Body Medicine, C Complementary Medicine, H Self Help Treatment, M Medicinal Therapy, O Oriental Medicine, P Postural Therapy, S Manipulative Structural Therapy, T Touch Therapy

Templar Rd, Oxford, **Oxfordshire**, OX2 8LT, ENG.
(T) 01865 513536
Speciality: Hypnosis.
B (Ref:HM11249)

### PULMAN, SUZETTE
**Suzette Pulman**, 16 Grammar School Rd, Lymm, **Cheshire**, WA13 0BQ, ENG.
(T) 01925 752264
Speciality: Osteopathy.
P S T (Ref:HM16755)

### PUMO, AMANDA
**Amanda Pumo**, 13 Ford St North, Nottingham, **Nottinghamshire**, NG7 7BB, ENG.
(T) 01159 613237
Speciality: Hypnosis.
B (Ref:HM16756)

### PUMO, AMANDA
**Amanda Pumo**, Nottingham Natural Health Centre, 354 Mansfield Rd, Nottingham, **Nottinghamshire**, NG5 2EF, ENG.
(T) 01159 608855
Speciality: Hypnotherapy.
B (Ref:HM16757)

### PUNDYKE, MARIA
**Maria Pundyke**, 15 Chatsworth, Bangor, **County Down**, BT19 7WA, NIR.
(T) 028 9146 6995
Speciality: Reflexology.
S T (Ref:HM16758)

### PUNNI, R
**R Punni**, 49 High St, Cheshunt, Waltham Cross, **Hertfordshire**, EN8 0BS, ENG.
(T) 01992 622471 (F) 01992 622471
Speciality: Chiropodists (Podiatrists).
● **Manager** Mr H Punni
S (Ref:HM16759)

### PUNTER, EDWARD
**Edward Punter**, Naish Estate, Christchurch Rd, New Milton, **Hampshire**, BH25 7RE, ENG.
(T) 01425 278035
Speciality: Homeopathy.
● **Owner** Mr E Punter
M (Ref:HM16760)

### PUNTER, WENDY
**Wendy Punter**, 10 Arne Gr, Orpington, **Kent**, BR6 9TT, ENG.
(T) 01689 876316
Speciality: Homeopathy.
M (Ref:HM16761)

### PURCELL, AMANDA
**Amanda Purcell**, 96 Manchester Rd, Bury, **Lancashire**, BL9 0TH, ENG.
(T) 01617 644278
Speciality: Osteopathy. ✔
● **Osteopath** Miss A Purcell Q: DO. M: GOsC.
S Yrs. Est.: 16 (Ref:HM16762)

### PURE ESSENCE
**Pure Essence**, Six Score Rd, Langtoft, Peterborough, **Cambridgeshire**, PE6 9QF, ENG.
(T) 01778 341101
Speciality: Complementary Medicines & Therapy.
● **Owner** Mrs A Etherington
M (Ref:HM16763)

### PURE ESSENTIALS DIRECT
**Pure Essentials Direct L'Aroma Aromatherapy**, Rich View, Prenton, **Merseyside**, CH43 5SZ, ENG.
(T) 01516 520050 (F) 01516 520051
(E) laura@laroma.freeserve.co.uk
(W) www.merseyworld.com/laroma
Speciality: Aromatherapy.
● **Director** Ms L Drane M: ATC, NORA.
M O (Ref:HM16764)

### PURE HEALTH
**Pure Health**, 80 St Albans Rd, Lytham St. Annes, **Lancashire**, FY8 1XD, ENG.
(T) 01253 712417
Speciality: Aromatherapy, Bach Remedies, Herbal Medicine, Homeopathy, Life Style Coaching, Manipulation, Massage (Therapeutic), Naturopathy, Nutritional Therapy, Reflexology, Remedial Massage, Stress Therapy, Natural Skin Care.
C (Ref:HM16765)

### PURLEY CHIROPODY PRACTICE
**Purley Chiropody Practice (The)**, 5 Russell Hill Prde, Russell Hill Rd, Purley, **Surrey**, CR8 2LE, ENG.
(T) 020 8660 3091
Speciality: Chiropodists (Podiatrists).
● **Practice Manager** Mrs M Winders
S (Ref:HM16766)

### PURLEY CHIROPRACTIC CLINIC
**Purley Chiropractic Clinic**, 140 Brighton Rd, Purley, **Surrey**, CR8 4HA, ENG.
(T) 020 8763 2629
Speciality: Chiropractic.
P S T (Ref:HM16767)

### PURLEY OSTEOPATHIC CLINIC
**Purley Osteopathic Clinic**, 206 Brighton Rd, Purley, **Surrey**, CR8 4HB, ENG.
(T) 020 8763 0071
Speciality: Osteopathy.
P S T (Ref:HM16768)

### PURLYS
**Dental Surgery**, 185 Nevells Rd, Garden City, Letchworth, **Hertfordshire**, SG6 4TS, ENG.
(T) 01462 684350 (F) 01462 670095
Speciality: Acupuncture, Homeopathy, Hypnosis, Dental surgery especially for Mercury Toxicity, ie: removal of Amalgam fillings under a strict protocol, found useful for various conditions. Especially ME and MS. ✔ CREDIT
● **Dental Surgeon** Nitin Kotecha Q: BDS.
● **Dental Surgeon** Ajay Gulati Q: BDS, MSc.
● **Dental Surgeon/Hypnotherapist** Mr M Menczykowski Q: Dip.Clin.Hyp.
● **Dental Surgeon** Alison Stroomer Q: BDS.
M Yrs. Est.: 40 (Ref:HM16769)

### PURPLE FLAME AROMATHERAPY
**Purple Flame Aromatherapy**, St Johns Spinney, Gunhill, Coventry, **Midlands (West)**, CV7 8BR, ENG.
(T) 01676 542542 (F) 01676 540777
(E) purple.flame@zetnet.co.uk
(W) www.purpleflame.co.uk
Speciality: Aromatherapy. ✔
● **Manager** Mr R Stapsford
● **Aromatherapy Teacher** Mr J Murray Q: ISPA. M: EOTA, IFA, ISPA.
● **Principle** Ms C Sapsford M: IFA, ISPA.
M O Yrs. Est.: 20 (Ref:HM16770)

### PURPLE FLAME AROMATHERAPY
**Purple Flame Aromatherapy**, 61 Clinton Lane, Kenilworth, **Warwickshire**, CV8 1AS, ENG.
(T) 01926 855980
Speciality: Aromatherapy.
M O (Ref:HM16771)

### PURPLE HAZE
**Purple Haze**, 178 Kirkgate, Bradford, **Yorkshire (West)**, BD1 1QT, ENG.
(T) 01274 393695
Speciality: Aromatherapy.
● **Owner** Mr R Clegg
M O (Ref:HM16772)

### PURPLE HAZE AROMATHERAPY
**Purple Haze Aromatherapy**, 26 Kemton Cl, Alton, **Hampshire**, GU34 2TY, ENG.
(T) 01420 86760
Speciality: Aromatherapy.
● **Owner** Mrs J Durn
M O (Ref:HM16773)

### PURRETT-SMITH, DEE
**Dee Purrett-Smith**, Aston Clinic, 26 Kingston Rd, New Malden, **Surrey**, KT3 3LS, ENG.
(T) 020 8942 3148 (F) 020 8949 7050
Speciality: Alexander Technique.
P S (Ref:HM16774)

### PURTON HOUSE HOMEOPATHIC CTRE
**Purton House Homeopathic Centre**, Penley Grange, Marlow Rd, Stokenchurch, **Buckinghamshire**, HP14 3UW, ENG.
(T) 01494 485952 (F) 01494 484668
(W) www.purtonhouse.com
Speciality: Complementary Therapy, Homeopathy, Psychotherapy. ✔ CREDIT
● **Partner** Ms N Pool Q: A.T.Psych, RSHom, SRN. M: Soc.Hom, UKCP.
M Yrs. Est.: 16 (Ref:HM16775)

### PURVES, DONALD A
**Donald A Purves**, 52 Hill Top Mount, Leeds, **Yorkshire (West)**, LS8 4EW, ENG.
(T) 01132 491711
Speciality: Herbal Medicine.
● **Owner** Mr D Purves
M (Ref:HM16776)

### PURVES, SHIRLEY A
**Shirley A Purves**, 38 Fore St, Topsham, Exeter, **Devon**, EX3 0HR, ENG.
(T) 01392 876116
Speciality: Physiotherapy.
P S T (Ref:HM16777)

### PU-SHAN CHINESE
**PU-Shan Chinese**, Suite 14 24/26 Dame St, IRE.
(T) 01679 9753
Speciality: Acupuncture.
O (Ref:HM16778)

### PUSHPA, NANA
**Nana Pushpa**, 2 Deanhill Rd, London, **London (Greater)**, SW14 7DF, ENG.
(T) 020 8876 2424
Speciality: Acupuncture.
● **Owner** Dr N Pushpa
O (Ref:HM16779)

### PUTNEY CHIROPRACTIC
**Putney Chiropractic**, 32 Bective Rd, Putney, London, **London (Greater)**, SW15 2QA, ENG.
(T) 020 8877 0377
Speciality: Chiropractic, X-Ray. ✔ CREDIT
● **Chiropractor** Dr Potter Q: B.App.Sc. M: GCC.
● **Chiropractor** Dr Wenban Q: B.App.Sc. M: GCC.
● **Chiropractor** Dr McLean Q: B.App.Sc. M: GCC.
S Yrs. Est.: 13 (Ref:HM16780)

### PUTNEY HYPNOTHERAPY CLINIC
**Putney Hypnotherapy Clinic**, 251 Upper Richmond Rd, London, **London (Greater)**, SW15 6SW, ENG.
(T) 020 8780 0255
Speciality: Hypnosis.
B (Ref:HM16781)

### PUTNEY NATURAL THERAPY CLINIC
**Putney Natural Therapy Clinic**, 11 Montserrat Rd, London, **London (Greater)**, SW15 2LD, ENG.
(T) 020 8789 2548
Speciality: Chiropodists (Podiatrists).
S (Ref:HM16782)

### PYE, MICHAEL
**Michael Pye**, 6 Romney Pl, Maidstone, **Kent**, ME15 6LE, ENG.
(T) 01622 690039 (F) 01622 201568
Speciality: Osteopathy.
● **Owner** Mr M Pye
P S T (Ref:HM16783)

### PYLE, G J
**G J Pyle**, 43B Wood St, Stratford-Upon-Avon, **Warwickshire**, CV37 6JG, ENG.
(T) 01789 292841
Speciality: Chiropodists (Podiatrists).
● **Owner** Mrs G Pyle
S (Ref:HM16784)

### PYLE, M W
**M W Pyle**, 12 Victoria Mews, Saltisford, Warwick, **Warwickshire**, CV34 4TE, ENG.
(T) 01926 492826
Speciality: Chiropodists (Podiatrists).
● **Owner** Mr M Pyle
S (Ref:HM16785)

### PYLE, RAYMOND
**Raymond Pyle**, 39 Lansdowne Rd, Luton, **Bedfordshire**, LU3 1EE, ENG.
(T) 01582 452985
Speciality: Osteopathy.
● **Owner** Mr R Pyle
P S T (Ref:HM16786)



Key continued: Yrs.Est: Years Established Q: Qualifications M: Professional Membership ✔ Indemnity Insurance CREDIT Accept Credit Cards

### PYNE, BERNADETTE
**Bernadette Pyne**, 8 Mossway, Middleton, Manchester, **Manchester (Greater)**, M24 1NS, ENG.
(T) 01616 535505
Speciality: Physiotherapy.
● **Owner** Mrs B Pyne
P S T (Ref:HM16787)

### PYNE, MICHELE
**Michele Pyne**, 24 London Rd, Brentwood, **Essex**, CM14 4QG, ENG.
(T) 01277 213826
Speciality: Chiropodists (Podiatrists).
● **Owner** Ms M Pyne
S (Ref:HM16788)

### QI SHEN NATURAL HEALING CENTRE
**Qi Shen Natural Healing Centre**, 21 Bridge Rd, Market Drayton, **Shropshire**, TF9 3UN, ENG.
(T) 01630 658999
Speciality: Complementary Medicines & Therapy.
● **Owner** Ms J Hankins
C M (Ref:HM16789)

### QUALITY ANALYSIS
**Quality Analysis Ltd**, 16 Crittall Rd, Witham, **Essex**, CM8 3DR, ENG.
(T) 01376 511773 (F) 01376 511368
Speciality: Aromatherapy.
● **Office Manager** Mrs S Bliss
M O (Ref:HM16790)

### QUARRY, PHILLIP
**Phillip Quarry**, 63 Stonechat Avenue, Abbeydale, Gloucester, **Gloucestershire**, GL4 4XE, ENG.
(T) 01452 301887
Speciality: Acupuncture.
O (Ref:HM16791)

### QUATTRO PARTNERSHIP
**Quattro Partnership (The)**, Seymour Lodge, 47 East Park Prde, Northampton, **Northamptonshire**, NN1 4LA, ENG.
(T) 01604 620652
Speciality: Psychology.
● **Partner** Ms A Edmonds
B (Ref:HM16792)

### QUEEN ELIZABETH'S FOUNDATION
**Queen Elizabeth's Foundation For Disabled People**, Bridge Ct Resource Centre, Brent Way, Dartford, **Kent**, DA2 6DA, ENG.
(T) 01322 229820 (F) 01322 279904
Speciality: Complementary Medicines & Therapy.
● **Manager** Mr M Bishop
M (Ref:HM16793)

### QUEEN STREET HERBAL CLINIC
**Queen Street Herbal Clinic (The)**, 21A Plashet Gr, London, **London (Greater)**, E6 1AD, ENG.
(T) 020 8552 4600
Speciality: Complementary Medicines & Therapy.
● **Director** Mr M Rana
C M (Ref:HM16794)

### QUEEN VICTORIA MEMORIAL HOSP
**Queen Victoria Memorial Hospital (The)**, Enquiries, King Edward Avenue, Herne Bay, **Kent**, CT6 6EB, ENG.
(T) 01227 594821 (F) 01227 594799
Speciality: Chiropodists (Podiatrists).
S (Ref:HM16795)

### QUEENS SQUARE SURGERY
**Stephen Gordon**, Queens Sq, Attleborough, **Norfolk**, NR17, ENG.
(T) 01953 453166
Speciality: Homeopathy. ✔
● **Homeopath** Mr S Gordon Q: MCH, RSHom. M: Soc.Hom.
M Yrs. Est.: 20 (Ref:HM16796)

### QUEENSBURY PHYSIO PRACTICE
**Queensbury Physiotherapy Practice**, 1 Russell Avenue, Queensbury, Bradford, **Yorkshire (West)**, BD13 2AL, ENG.
(T) 01274 814961
Speciality: Physiotherapy.
P S T (Ref:HM16797)

### QUENTIN-HICKS, M
**M Quentin-Hicks**, 35 Norwich Rd, Lowestoft, **Suffolk**, NR32 2BJ, ENG.
(T) 01502 500374
Speciality: Osteopathy.
● **Owner** Mr M Quentin-Hicks
P S T (Ref:HM16798)

### QUEST THERAPY
**Quest Therapy**, 8 Westbourne Park, Urmston, Manchester, **Manchester (Greater)**, M41 0XS, ENG.
(T) 01617 471188 (F) 01617 498536
Speciality: Hypnosis.
● **Director** Mr T Allen
B (Ref:HM16799)

### QUICK, JULIA
**Julia Quick**, Garden Flat, 13 Park Hall Rd, West Dulwich, London, **London (Greater)**, SE21 8EH, ENG.
(T) 020 8766 7324
Speciality: Acupuncture.
O (Ref:HM16800)

### QUICKSTROM, BETH
**Beth Quickstrom**, 5 Westbury Lane, Newport Pagnell, **Buckinghamshire**, MK16 8JA, ENG.
(T) 01908 210471
Speciality: Psychology.
B (Ref:HM16801)

### QUIESSENSE
**Quiessense**, Wellcroft House, Church St, High St, Royston, Barnsley, **Yorkshire (South)**, S71 4RF, ENG.
(T) 01226 727555
Speciality: Complementary Medicines & Therapy.
● **Partner** Mrs E Allen
C M (Ref:HM16802)

### QUIGLEY, CAROLINE
**Caroline Quigley**, 61 Waverley Rd, St. Albans, **Hertfordshire**, AL3 5PH, ENG.
(T) 01727 840682
Speciality: Osteopathy.
P S T (Ref:HM16803)

### QUILTER, ALISON J
**Alison J Quilter**, Old Plough House, Plough Lane, Sarratt, Rickmansworth, **Hertfordshire**, WD3 4NN, ENG.
(T) 01923 260525
Speciality: Chiropodists (Podiatrists).
● **Owner** Mrs A Quilter
S (Ref:HM16804)

### QUIN, JENNIFER A
**Jennifer A Quin**, 3 Hamilton Avenue, Glasgow, **Glasgow (City of)**, G41 4JG, SCO.
(T) 01414 273711
Speciality: Complementary Medicines & Therapy.
C M (Ref:HM16805)

### QUINESSENCE
**Quinessence**, Unit 1 Linden Way, Coalville, **Leicestershire**, LE67 3JY, ENG.
(T) 01530 838358 (F) 01530 814171
Speciality: Aromatherapy.
● **Owner** Mr G Lith
M O (Ref:HM16806)

### QUINLAN, ANNE-MARIA
**Quinlan Anne-Maria**, Castleview Ballincrossig, Glanmire, **County Cork**, IRE.
(T) 021 4822 352
Speciality: Complementary Medicines & Therapy.
M (Ref:HM16807)

### QUINN, BARBARA
**Barbara Quinn - Osteopath**, 2 Catherine St, Killyleagh, Downpatrick, **County Down**, BT30 9QQ, NIR.
(T) 028 4482 8358
Speciality: Cranial Osteopathy, Manipulation, Osteopathy. ✔
● **Owner/Osteopath** Ms B Quinn Q: BSc, Hons (OST), ND. M: GOsC.
S Yrs. Est.: 4 (Ref:HM16808)

### QUINN, G A W
**Mrs G A W Quinn**, Dodington Hall, Dodington, Nether Stowey, Bridgwater, **Somerset**, TA5 1LF, ENG.
(T) 01278 741400
Speciality: Hypnosis.
B (Ref:HM16809)

### QUINN, JIM
**Jim Quinn**, 14 Brechame Rd, Chapelton, Strathaven, **Lanarkshire (South)**, ML10 6SP, SCO.
(T) 08000 744289
(E) jimqhom@lineone.net
Speciality: Homeopathy. ✔
● **Homeopath** Mr J Quinn Q: L.C.C.H. M: Soc.Hom.
M Yrs. Est.: 4 (Ref:HM16810)

### QUINN, LEN
**Len Quinn**, Health Hydro, Milton Rd, Swindon, **Wiltshire**, SN1 5JA, ENG.
(T) 01793 465629
Speciality: Physiotherapy.
P S T (Ref:HM16811)

### QUINN, P
**P Quinn**, 80 Worthington Rd, Surbiton, **Surrey**, KT6 7RX, ENG.
(T) 020 8399 7260
Speciality: Physiotherapy.
P S T (Ref:HM16812)

### QUINN, PHILLIP D R
**Phillip D R Quinn**, 21B High Holme Rd, Louth, **Lincolnshire**, LN11 0EX, ENG.
(T) 01507 607336
Speciality: Hypnosis.
B (Ref:HM16813)

### QUINN-BERGER, JUNE
**Quinn-Berger June P H D Psych**, 40 Lansdowne Rd, Dublin, **County Dublin**, IRE.
(T) 01660 9454
Speciality: Complementary Medicines & Therapy.
M (Ref:HM16814)

### QUINN-COTTER, BONNIE
**Quinn-Cotter Bonnie**, Inniskean Victoria Ave, Cork, **County Cork**, IRE.
(T) 021 4310 380
Speciality: Counselling.
B H (Ref:HM16815)

### QUINTARELLI, G
**G Quintarelli**, 64A Castle Rd, London, **London (Greater)**, NW1 8SN, ENG.
(T) 020 7267 8847
Speciality: Osteopathy.
P S T (Ref:HM16816)

### QUINTESSENCE AROMATHERAPY
**Quintessence Aromatherapy**, 37 The Farthings, Kingston Upon Thames, **Surrey**, KT2 7PT, ENG.
(T) 020 8546 0532
Speciality: Aromatherapy.
● **Partner** Mrs M Bowers-Clark
M O (Ref:HM16817)

### QUINTON, R M
**R M Quinton**, 50 Waters Green, Macclesfield, **Cheshire**, SK11 6JT, ENG.
(T) 01625 427069 (F) 01625 427069
Speciality: Osteopathy.
● **Owner** Mr R Quinton
P S T (Ref:HM16818)

### QUINTON, R M
**R M Quinton**, 1b Wain Lea, Harriseahead, Stoke-On-Trent, **Staffordshire**, ST7 4LG, ENG.
(T) 01782 513379
Speciality: Acupuncture.
● **Owner** Mr R Quinton
O (Ref:HM16819)

### QUIRKE, G
**G Quirke**, Tisere, Tuckingmill, Tisbury, Salisbury, **Wiltshire**, SP3 6JA, ENG.
(T) 01747 871306
(E) gjq@globalnet.co.uk
Speciality: Auto Suggestion, Aversion Therapy,

Key: B Mind-Body Medicine C Complementary Medicine H Self Help Treatment M Medicinal Therapy O Oriental Medicine P Postural Therapy S Manipulative Structural Therapy T Touch Therapy

Complementary Therapy, Hypnosis, Hypnotherapy. ✓
● **Hypnotherapist** Gerry Quirke M: CAH.
B Yrs. Est.: 12 (Ref:HM16820)

## QUIT SMOKING CENTRE
**Lodge Hypnotherapy Centre (The)**, Stifford Hill, North Stifford, Grays, **Essex**, RM16 5UJ, ENG.
(T) 01375 396900 (F) 01375 396900
(E) lodge@hypnosis.uk.net
(W) www.hypnosis.uk.net
Speciality: Hypnosis, Hypnotherapy, Psychotherapy. ✓
● **Hypnotherapist** Mr C Cowin Q: Dip.Hom, Dip.Hyp, Dip.Psych, MIAH. M: IAH.
● **Hypnotherapist** Mrs J Cowin Q: Dip.Hyp, Dip.Psych, MIAH. M: IAH.
B Yrs. Est.: 8 (Ref:HM16821)

## QURBAN, AMIR
**Amir Qurban**, Pear Tree Rd, Derby, **Derbyshire**, DE23 6QD, ENG.
(T) 01332 345405
Speciality: Acupuncture.
● **Partner** Mr A Qurban
O (Ref:HM16822)

## QURESHI, JOHN
**John Qureshi**, 47 Bell Lane, Eton Wick, Windsor, **Berkshire**, SL4 6LQ, ENG.
(T) 01753 857095
Speciality: Osteopathy.
● **Owner** Mr J Quershi
P S T (Ref:HM16823)

## QURESHI, M J H
**M J H Qureshi**, 321 Tettenhall Rd, Wolverhampton, **Midlands (West)**, WV6 0JZ, ENG.
(T) 01902 742270 (F) 01902 740256
Speciality: Psychiatry.
● **Owner** Dr M Qureshi
B (Ref:HM16824)

## QURESHI, S
**S Qureshi**, 30 The Drive, Hove, **Sussex (East)**, BN3 3JD, ENG.
(T) 01273 778123 (F) 01273 776266
Speciality: Physiotherapy.
● **Practice Manager** Mrs M Ward
P S T (Ref:HM16825)

## QURESHI, SABREEN
**Sabreen Qureshi**, 25-27 Castle St, Brighton, **Sussex (East)**, BN1 2HD, ENG.
(T) 01273 739606 (F) 01273 324075
Speciality: Physiotherapy.
● **Owner** Ms S Qureshi
P S T (Ref:HM16826)

## QUYE, KARINA
**Karina Quye**, 16 Daneland, Barnet, **Hertfordshire**, EN4 8PY, ENG.
(T) 020 8440 3768
Speciality: Reflexology.
● **Owner** Mrs K Quye
S T (Ref:HM16827)

## R & M TRADING
**R & M Trading**, 142 High Northgate, **County Durham**, DL1 1UW, ENG.
(T) 01325 241322
Speciality: Aromatherapy.
M O (Ref:HM16828)

## R C C M
**R C C M**, Millstream Surgery, Cherry Tree Walk, Redditch, **Worcestershire**, B97 6PB, ENG.
(T) 01527 60790
Speciality: Acupuncture, Aromatherapy, Counselling, Osteopathy, Reflexology. ✓ CREDIT
● **G.P** Dr S Ananthram
● **Practitioner** Mrs W Hooper Q: Lic.Ac, MBAcC, MICHT.
● **Osteopath** Mr D Evans Q: BSc, Hons (OST).
C Yrs. Est.: 8 (Ref:HM16829)

## R C G FOOTCARE
**R C G Footcare**, 514 Welford Rd, Leicester, **Leicestershire**, LE2 6EN, ENG.
(T) 01162 811921
Speciality: Chiropodists (Podiatrists).
S (Ref:HM16830)

## R D C PHYSIOTHERAPY CLINIC
**R D C Physiotherapy Clinic**, 32 Wimpole St, London, **London (Greater)**, W1M 7AE, ENG.
(T) 020 7580 1650
Speciality: Physiotherapy.
P S T (Ref:HM16831)

## R L A
**R L A**, 96 Queens Rd, Buckhurst Hill, **Essex**, IG9 5BS, ENG.
(T) 020 8504 1341
Speciality: Chiropodists (Podiatrists).
● **Partner** Mr R Carr
S (Ref:HM16832)

## RABAYA HOMOEOPATHIC CLINIC
**Rabaya Homoeopathic Clinic**, 14 Sutton St, London, **London (Greater)**, E1 0BB, ENG.
(T) 020 7790 1897
Speciality: Homeopathy.
● **Owner** Ms R Islam
M (Ref:HM16833)

## RABESS, ANGELA
**Angela Rabess**, 12 Dorchester Cl, Basingstoke, **Hampshire**, RG23 8EX, ENG.
(T) 01256 467395
Speciality: Reflexology.
S T (Ref:HM16834)

## RABLEY, M
**M Rabley**, Brookeswood, Loperwood Lane, Calmore, Southampton, **Hampshire**, SO40 2RR, ENG.
(T) 023 8081 2361
Speciality: Chiropractic.
● **Owner** Dr M Rabley
P S T (Ref:HM16835)

## RACHAEL, MANNING
**Manning Rachael ADHP MICHP**, 91 Terenure Rd, Nth 6W, IRE.
(T) 01492 9077
(W) www.hypnosiseire.com
Speciality: Hypnotherapy.
B (Ref:HM16836)

## RACHEL YOUNG - HYPNOTHERAPIST
**Rachel Young - Hypnotherapist**, Brecon Cottage, Oakhill Avenue, Pinner, **London (Greater)**, HA5 3DL, ENG.
(T) 020 8866 3737 (F) 020 8868 4515
Speciality: Absent Healing, Aversion Therapy, Colour Therapy, Complementary Therapy, Counselling, Crystal Healing, Dietician, Dowsing, Faith Healing, Gestalt Therapy, Healer, Healing Therapy, Holistic Healing, Humanistic Psychology, Hypnosis, Hypnotherapy, Life Style Coaching, Meditation, Psychotherapy, Reiki, Spiritual Healing, Stress Therapy, Touch Therapy, Visualisation Therapy, Ying & Yang, Hypno Healing.
● **Hypnotherapist/Complementary Therapist**
Ms S Young Q: NFSH, Reiki 2, SRN. M: ABCHyp, BACP, NFSH, RCN, UKCC.
B Yrs. Est.: 4 (Ref:HM16837)

## RACLE, P
**P Racle**, 2 Bowers Avenue, Urmston, Manchester, **Manchester (Greater)**, M41 5TG, ENG.
(T) 01617 484419
Speciality: Physiotherapy.
● **Owner** Mr P Racle
P S T (Ref:HM16838)

## RADAN, P J
**P J Radan**, 12 High Park Avenue, Stourbridge, **Midlands (West)**, DY8 3NH, ENG.
(T) 01384 374291
Speciality: Chiropodists (Podiatrists).
S (Ref:HM16839)

## RADFORD, ANDREA
**Arena Sports Injury & Physiotherapy Centre (The)**, 3 Fromer Rd, Wooburn Green, High Wycombe, **Buckinghamshire**, HP10 0PR, ENG.
(T) 01628 527280
Speciality: Physiotherapy.
P S T (Ref:HM16840)

## RADFORD, C
**C Radford**, 76 Bridge St, Swindon, **Wiltshire**, SN1 1BT, ENG.
(T) 01793 511284
Speciality: Chiropodists (Podiatrists).
● **Owner** Mr C Radford
S (Ref:HM16841)

## RADFORD, CAROLE A
**Carole A Radford**, 30 Stone Quarry Rd, Burniston, Scarborough, **Yorkshire (North)**, YO13 0DF, ENG.
(T) 01723 870018
Speciality: Chiropodists (Podiatrists).
● **Partner** Mr M Radford
S (Ref:HM16842)

## RADFORD, CATHERINE
**Catherine Radford**, 1 Clarkson St, Worsbrough, Barnsley, **Yorkshire (South)**, S70 4SJ, ENG.
(T) 01226 239052 (F) 01226 239052
Speciality: Hypnotherapy.
● **Owner** Mrs C Radford
B (Ref:HM16843)

## RADFORD, CHRISTOPHER
**Christopher Radford**, 116 London Rd, Marlborough, **Wiltshire**, SN8 1LH, ENG.
(T) 01672 516006
Speciality: Chiropodists (Podiatrists).
S (Ref:HM16844)

## RADFORD, PAULINE
**Pauline Radford**, Visiting Practice, Valley Rd, Burghfield Common, Reading, **Berkshire**, RG7 3NF, ENG.
(T) 01189 832800 (F) 01189 832800
Speciality: Chiropodists (Podiatrists).
● **Owner** Mrs P Radford
S (Ref:HM16845)

## RADHA, CELIA
**Celia Radha**, 203 Hills Rd, Cambridge, **Cambridgeshire**, CB2 2RN, ENG.
(T) 01223 210585
Speciality: Complementary Medicines & Therapy.
C M (Ref:HM16846)

## RADIANT COLOUR
**Radiant Colour**, Firth Lodge, Firth Rd, Roslin, **Lothian (Mid)**, EH25 9QJ, SCO.
(T) 01968 678789 (F) 01968 678789
(E) info@radiantcolour.co.uk
(W) www.radiantcolour.co.uk
Speciality: Colour Therapy, Complementary Therapy, Counselling, Natural Healing. ✓ CREDIT
● **Colour Health Practitioner**
Alison Demarco M: BRCP, CTA, IAC, ICM.
B Yrs. Est.: 12 (Ref:HM16847)

## RADIANT HEALTH
**Radiant Health**, 21a Salisbury Rd, Edinburgh, **Edinburgh (City of)**, EH16 5AA, SCO.
(T) 01316 673133
Speciality: T'ai-Chi Ch'uan.
● **Manager** Mr V Spence
M (Ref:HM16848)

## RADIANT HEALTH CLINIC
**Radiant Health Clinic**, Albion Chambers, 1 High St, Leighton Buzzard, **Bedfordshire**, LU7 7DN, ENG.
(T) 01525 372311
Speciality: Acupuncture.
O (Ref:HM16849)

## RADIN, J
**J Radin**, St James Chiropractic Clinic, 158 Winchester Rd, Southampton, **Hampshire**, SO16 6UE, ENG.
(T) 023 8078 8111
Speciality: Chiropractic.
P S T (Ref:HM16850)

## RADIONIC ASSOCIATION
**Radionic Association (The)**, Baerlein House, Goose Green, Deddington, Banbury, **Oxfordshire**, OX15 0SZ, ENG.
(T) 01869 338852
Speciality: Complementary Medicines & Therapy, Radionics.
C (Ref:HM16851)



Key continued: Yrs.Est: Years Established Q: Qualifications M: Professional Membership ✓ Indemnity Insurance CREDIT Accept Credit Cards

## RADIVAN, B A
**B A Radivan**, 198 Bury New Rd, Whitefield, Manchester, **Manchester (Greater)**, M45 6QF, ENG.
(T) 01617 665564
Speciality: Chiropodists (Podiatrists).
S (Ref:HM16852)

## RADIVAN, B A
**B A Radivan**, Irlam Clinic, 125 Liverpool Rd, Irlam, Manchester, **Manchester (Greater)**, M44 6DP, ENG.
(T) 01617 751679
Speciality: Chiropodists (Podiatrists).
S (Ref:HM16853)

## RADIVAN, BARRY
**Barry Radivan**, 26 Higher Market St, Farnworth, Bolton, **Lancashire**, BL4 9DJ, ENG.
(T) 01204 572338
Speciality: Chiropodists (Podiatrists).
● **Partner** Mr B Radivan
S (Ref:HM16854)

## RADLETT PRACTICE
**Radlett Practice (The)**, 107 Watling St, Radlett, **Hertfordshire**, WD7 7NG, ENG.
(T) 01923 855884
Speciality: Osteopathy.
P S T (Ref:HM16855)

## RADONS-HARRIS
**Radons-Harris**, 138 Fog Lane, Manchester, **Manchester (Greater)**, M20 6SW, ENG.
(T) 01614 344332
Speciality: Complementary Medicines & Therapy.
● **Owner** Mrs A Harris
M (Ref:HM16856)

## RADWAN, R
**R Radwan**, 57 Heath Lane, Bladon, Woodstock, **Oxfordshire**, OX20 1RZ, ENG.
(T) 01993 813221 (F) 01993 813221
Speciality: Reflexology.
● **Owner** Mrs R Radwan
S T (Ref:HM16857)

## RAE, A D
**A D Rae**, 9 Park Gardens, Edinburgh, **Edinburgh (City of)**, EH16 6JF, SCO.
(T) 01316 649628 (F) 01316 649628
Speciality: Physiotherapy.
● **Partner** Mrs A Rae
P S T (Ref:HM16858)

## RAE, FRED K
**Fred K Rae**, South Pilmuir Rd, Clackmannan, **Clackmannanshire**, FK10 4ET, SCO.
(T) 01259 214463
Speciality: Chiropodists (Podiatrists).
S (Ref:HM16859)

## RAE, J S (DR)
**Dr J S Rae**, 12 Church Rd, Wembury, Plymouth, **Devon**, PL9 0JE, ENG.
(T) 01752 862169
Speciality: Homeopathy.
M (Ref:HM16860)

## RAE, M
**M Rae**, 169 Valley Rd, Kenley, **Surrey**, CR8 5BZ, ENG.
(T) 020 8660 6910
Speciality: Physiotherapy.
P S T (Ref:HM16861)

## RAE, M S
**M S Rae**, Fairfield, Cavendish Rd, Weybridge, **Surrey**, KT13 0JN, ENG.
(T) 01932 849868
Speciality: Chiropodists (Podiatrists).
● **Owner** Mrs M Rae
S (Ref:HM16862)

## RAE, S M
**S M Rae**, 9 Park Gardens, Edinburgh, **Edinburgh (City of)**, EH16 6JF, SCO.
(T) 01316 649628 (F) 01316 649628
Speciality: Physiotherapy.
● **Partner** Mrs A Rae
P S T (Ref:HM16863)

## RAE, Y
**Y Rae**, 6 Heaps Farm Court, Stalybridge, **Manchester (Greater)**, SK15 2RN, ENG.
(T) 01613 038141
Speciality: Clairvoyants & Palmists.
● **Owner** Mrs Y Rae
B (Ref:HM16864)

## RAEBURN, JO
**Jo Raeburn**, Waxwell Cottage, 548 Uxbridge Rd, Pinner, **London (Greater)**, HA5 3QA, ENG.
(T) 020 8429 8239
(E) pj@raeburn.worldonline.co.uk
Speciality: Aromatherapy, Indian Head Massage, Reiki. ✔
● **Therapist/Healer** Ms J Raeburn Q: BSc (Hons), Dip.L.C.I.C, TIDHA. M: RQA.
T Yrs. Est.: 1 (Ref:HM16865)

## RAFFIT, PHILIPPE
**Philippe Raffit**, 10 Chorley Rd, Blackrod, Bolton, **Lancashire**, BL6 5JS, ENG.
(T) 01204 668686
Speciality: Osteopathy.
● **Owner** Mr P Raffit
P S T (Ref:HM16866)

## RAFTERY, LUKE
**Mr Luke Raftery**, 48 Newlands Park, London, **London (Greater)**, SE26 5NE, ENG.
(T) 020 8659 5001
Speciality: Chiropodists (Podiatrists).
S (Ref:HM16867)

## RAGGETT, JANET
**Janet Raggett**, 27 Alder Way, Swanley, **Kent**, BR8 7XD, ENG.
(T) 01322 407493
Speciality: Chiropodists (Podiatrists).
● **Owner** Mrs J Raggett
S (Ref:HM16868)

## RAGLAN PRECINCT SALON
**Raglan Precinct Salon**, 15 Raglan Precinct, Chaldon Rd, Caterham, **Surrey**, CR3 5UG, ENG.
(T) 01883 342264
Speciality: Complementary Medicines & Therapy.
C M (Ref:HM16869)

## RAHENY TCM & ACUPUNCTURE
**Raheny TCM & Acupuncture Clinic**, 436 Howth Rd, Dublin, **County Dublin**, IRE.
(T) 01832 8491
Speciality: Acupuncture.
O (Ref:HM16870)

## RAHMAN, AKHLAQUE
**Akhlaque Rahman**, Stoke Damerel Business Centre, 5 Church St, Plymouth, **Devon**, PL3 4DT, ENG.
(T) 01752 607008
Speciality: Chiropractic.
P S T (Ref:HM16871)

## RAHS, EFFIE
**Effie Rahs**, 14 The Spinney, London, **London (Greater)**, N21 1LH, ENG.
(T) 020 8245 0958
Speciality: Reflexology.
S T (Ref:HM16872)

## RAILTON, CAROLE
**Carole Railton**, Flat 7, Elm Quay Court, 30 Nine Elms Lane, London, **London (Greater)**, SW8 5DE, ENG.
(T) 020 7627 4053
Speciality: Reflexology.
S T (Ref:HM16873)

## RAINBOW ALTERNATIVES
**Rainbow Alternatives**, 23 North Main St, Wigtown, Newton Stewart, **Dumfries and Galloway**, DG8 9HL, SCO.
(T) 01988 402410
Speciality: Complementary Medicines & Therapy.
● **Owner** Mrs F Clements-Russell
C M (Ref:HM16874)

## RAINBOW BRIDGE SCHOOL
**Rainbow Bridge School Of Aromatherapy**, Woodlands Centre, Newby Village, Middlesbrough, **Cleveland**, TS8 0AH, ENG.
(T) 01642 313454
(E) joyburnett@rbsa.freeserve.co.uk
Speciality: Aromatherapy, Reflexology. ✔
● **Owner** Ms J Burnett Q: Dip.BSA, ITEC.A&P, RBS.H.A.D, SPClinDip.A. M: ASC, BCMA, BSY, ISPA.
● **Aromatherapist** Ms K Almond Q: ISPA, ITEC.A&P. M: ISPA.
C Yrs. Est.: 6 (Ref:HM16875)

## RAINBOW BRIDGE STUDIO
**Rainbow Bridge Studio**, 7 Hastings Rd, Crawley, **Sussex (West)**, RH10 7AL, ENG.
(T) 01293 408554 (F) 01293 418520
Speciality: Clairvoyants & Palmists.
● **Partner** Mr K Smith
B (Ref:HM16876)

## RAINBOW CENTRE
**Rainbow Centre (The)**, 15 High St, Sutton-On-Sea, Mablethorpe, **Lincolnshire**, LN12 2EZ, ENG.
(T) 01507 441230
Speciality: Complementary Medicines & Therapy.
C M (Ref:HM16877)

## RAINBOW GROUP
**Rainbow Group (The)**, 84 Wood Rd, Shepperton, **Surrey**, TW17 0DP, ENG.
(T) 01932 568862
Speciality: Complementary Medicines & Therapy.
● **Owner** Ms E Coleman
C M (Ref:HM16878)

## RAINBOW NATURAL HEALTH CENTRE
**Rainbow Natural Health Centre (The)**, 83 Brighton Rd, Redhill, **Surrey**, RH1 6PS, ENG.
(T) 01737 770289
Speciality: Homeopathy.
● **Owner** Mr D Kemp
M (Ref:HM16879)

## RAINBOW NATURAL THERAPIES
**Rainbow Natural Therapies**, 8 High St, Calne, **Wiltshire**, SN11 0BS, ENG.
(T) 01249 817789
Speciality: Counselling, Massage (Therapeutic). ✔
● **Owner/Therapist** Mr T Page Q: MTI.
C Yrs. Est.: 10 (Ref:HM16880)

## RAINBOW PATHWAYS
**Rainbow Pathways**, 22B High St, Hastings, **Sussex (East)**, TN34 3EY, ENG.
(T) 01424 446880
Speciality: Complementary Medicines & Therapy.
● **Partner** Ms M Anderson
M (Ref:HM16881)

## RAINBOW PATHWAYS
**Rainbow Pathways**, 7 Old Humphrey Avenue, Hastings, **Sussex (East)**, TN34 3BT, ENG.
(T) 01424 719116
Speciality: Complementary Therapy, Crystal Healing, Reflexology, Reiki, Regression Therapy, Therapy Tables.
C (Ref:HM16882)

## RAINBOW PREGNANCY ADVICE
**Rainbow Pregnancy Advice**, Bolton Pentecostal Church, Bury New Rd, Bolton, **Lancashire**, BL2 2BD, ENG.
(T) 01204 522002 (F) 01204 522732
Speciality: Counselling, Pregnancy Testing, Pregnancy Advice. ✔
● **Co-ordinator** Ms D Carr
(T) 01617 648350
C Yrs. Est.: 5 (Ref:HM16883)

## RAINBOW STAR HEALING
**Rainbow Star Healing & Training Centre**, 37 Castle Rd, Hadleigh, Ipswich, **Suffolk**, IP7 6JP, ENG.
(T) 01473 823371
Speciality: Complementary Medicines & Therapy.
● **Managing Director** Mrs A Bingham
C M (Ref:HM16884)

## RAINBOW TREE CENTRE
**Rainbow Tree Centre (The)**, 75 Knowles Hill Cr, London, **London (Greater)**, SE13 6DT, ENG.



Key: B Mind-Body Medicine C Complementary Medicine H Self Help Treatment M Medicinal Therapy O Oriental Medicine P Postural Therapy S Manipulative Structural Therapy T Touch Therapy

(T) 020 8852 9788
Speciality: Psychotherapy.
● **Owner** Ms L Wildwood
B (Ref:HM16885)

## RAINBOW WORLD HEALING CENTRE

**Rainbow World Healing Centre**, 104 St. Helens St, Ipswich, **Suffolk**, IP4 2LB, ENG.
(T) 01473 231134
Speciality: Complementary Medicines & Therapy.
● **Owner** Mrs G Taylor
M (Ref:HM16886)

## RAINBOW, RICHARD S

**Richard S Rainbow**, 27 St Pauls Gardens, Whitley Bay, **Tyne and Wear**, NE25 8RG, ENG.
(T) 01912 529133
(E) rainbow.hypnosis@byinternet.com
Speciality: Auto Suggestion, Cognitive Therapy, Hypnosis, Hypnotherapy, Psychotherapy, Stress Therapy, Visualisation Therapy. ✓
● **Director/Therapist** Mr R Rainbow Q: Cert.Ed, Dip.EH, NLP. M: HA.
B H Yrs. Est.: 10 (Ref:HM16887)

## RAINBOWS AROMATHERAPY CLINIC

**Rainbows Aromatherapy Clinic**, Hillside, St. Issey, Wadebridge, **Cornwall**, PL27 7QF, ENG.
(T) 01841 540666
Speciality: Complementary Medicines & Therapy.
● **Owner** Miss M Baldwin
C M (Ref:HM16888)

## RAINEY, C

**C Rainey**, 33 Bynghams, Harlow, **Essex**, CM19 5NR, ENG.
(T) 01279 415453
Speciality: Chiropodists (Podiatrists).
● **Owner** Mr C Rainey
S (Ref:HM16889)

## RAINEY, MARTHA

**Martha Rainey**, 79 Mains River, Erskine, **Renfrewshire**, PA8 7JF, SCO.
(T) 01418 126045 (F) 01418 126045
Speciality: Reflexology. ✓
● **Owner/Reflexologist** Mrs M Rainey Q: MAR.
C Yrs. Est.: 3 (Ref:HM16890)

## RAINS, KEN

**Ken Rains**, 24 Northcombe Rd, Stockport, **Cheshire**, SK3 8RD, ENG.
(T) 01614 564349
Speciality: Clairvoyants & Palmists.
● **Owner** Mr K Rains
B (Ref:HM16891)

## RAINSFORD, JOSEPHINE

**Josephine Rainsford**, 106 Aberdale Gardens, Potters Bar, **Hertfordshire**, EN6 2JF, ENG.
(T) 01707 658499
Speciality: Homeopathy.
● **Owner** Mrs J Rainsford
M (Ref:HM16892)

## RAINTREE HEALTH

**Raintree Health (UK) Ltd**, 12 Thornton, Bradford, **Yorkshire (West)**, BD13 3YD, ENG.
(T) 07811 904159
(E) admin@raintree-health.co.uk
(W) www.raintree-health.co.uk
Speciality: Herbal Medicine.
● **Director** Mr L Martin
C Yrs. Est.: 2 (Ref:HM16893)

## RAITHATHA, MAHENDRA

**Mahendra Raithatha**, 59 Kensington Avenue, Watford, **Hertfordshire**, WD1 7RZ, ENG.
(T) 01923 240462
Speciality: Reflexology.
● **Owner** Mr M Raithatha
S T (Ref:HM16894)

## RAITZ, SOPHIE

**Sophie Raitz**, 13 Kinburn St, London, **London (Greater)**, SE16 6DN, ENG.
(T) 020 7252 0936 (F) 020 7252 0936
Speciality: Osteopathy.
● **Partner** Mr J Lieberman
P S T (Ref:HM16895)

## RAJA YOGA BRAMA KUMARIS CENTRE

**Raja Yoga Brama Kumaris Centre**, 1 Richmond Villas, Chilkwell St, Glastonbury, **Somerset**, BA6 8DF, ENG.
(T) 01458 834537
Speciality: Relaxation Technique.
H T (Ref:HM16896)

## RAJA YOGA MEDITATION

**Raja Yoga Meditation**, 8 Haxby Court, Felbridge Cl, Cardiff, **Glamorgan (Vale of)**, CF10 4BH, WAL.
(T) 029 2048 0557
Speciality: Meditation, Yoga.
M (Ref:HM16897)

## RAJA YOGA MEDITATION

**Raja Yoga Meditation**, 2 Northbrook Rd, Ilford, **Essex**, IG1 3BS, ENG.
(T) 020 8478 6451 (F) 020 8478 6451
Speciality: Meditation, Yoga.
● **Director** Mrs B Manju
C (Ref:HM16898)

## RAJA, AMITA (DR)

**Dr Amita Raja**, Narborough Health Centre, Thornton Drive, Narborough, Leicester, **Leicestershire**, LE9 5GX, ENG.
(T) 01162 862386
Speciality: Homeopathy.
M (Ref:HM16899)

## RAJA, AMITA S

**Amita S Raja**, 3 Teasel Cl, Narborough, Leicester, **Leicestershire**, LE9 5DZ, ENG.
(T) 01162 750601 (F) 01162 750601
Speciality: Homeopathy.
● **Owner** Dr A Raja
M (Ref:HM16900)

## RAJA, AMITA S

**Amita S Raja**, 193 Narborough Rd, Leicester, **Leicestershire**, LE3 0PE, ENG.
(T) 01162 548593
Speciality: Homeopathy.
M (Ref:HM16901)

## RAJAGOPALAN, J

**J Rajagopalan**, 11 Crecy Walk, Hensington Gate, Woodstock, **Oxfordshire**, OX20 1UT, ENG.
(T) 01993 812370
Speciality: Acupuncture.
● **Owner** Mrs J Rajagopalan
O (Ref:HM16902)

## RAJENDRAN, D

**D Rajendran**, Strood Sports Centre, Watling St, Rochester, **Kent**, ME2 3JQ, ENG.
(T) 01634 717171
Speciality: Osteopathy.
● **Owner** Mr D Rajendran
P S T (Ref:HM16903)

## RAJGURU, RASIK

**Rasik Rajguru**, 147 King's Cross Rd, London, **London (Greater)**, WC1X 9BN, ENG.
(T) 020 7833 8733
Speciality: Complementary Medicines & Therapy.
C M (Ref:HM16904)

## RALLEY, JANE

**Jane Ralley**, The Haelan Clinic, 41 The Broadway, Crouch End, London, **London (Greater)**, N8 8DT, ENG.
(T) 020 8340 1518
Speciality: Complementary Medicines & Therapy.
● **Manager** Mr J Krahn
C M (Ref:HM16905)

## RALPH & EVANS

**Ralph & Evans**, 11 Best Lane, Canterbury, **Kent**, CT1 2JB, ENG.
(T) 01227 471771
Speciality: Herbal Medicine. ✓ [credit card]
● **Medical Herbalist** Mr P Evans Q: MNIMH. M: NIMH.
M Yrs. Est.: 10 (Ref:HM16906)

## RALPH SUTTON

**Ralph Sutton**, 166 Tulketh Rd, Ashton-On-Ribble, Preston, **Lancashire**, PR2 1ER, ENG.
(T) 01772 761166
Speciality: Osteopathy.
● **Owner** Mrs D Griffiths
P S T (Ref:HM16907)

## RALPH, ANITA

**Anita Ralph**, 8 West St, West Malling, **Kent**, ME19 6QX, ENG.
(T) 01732 871818
Speciality: Herbalists.
● **Partner** Ms A Ralph
M (Ref:HM16908)

## RALPH, ANITA

**Anita Ralph**, The West Malling Clinic, 23 Swan St, West Malling, **Kent**, ME19 6JU, ENG.
(T) 01732 871818
Speciality: Herbal Medicine.
M (Ref:HM16909)

## RAM, J

**J Ram**, 164 Ballards Rd, Dagenham, **Essex**, RM10 9AB, ENG.
(T) 020 8984 9240 (F) 020 8984 9240
Speciality: Complementary Medicines & Therapy.
● **Owner** Dr J Ram
C M (Ref:HM16910)

## RAMA

**Rama (The)**, 9 Lynton Cl, Chadderton, Oldham, **Lancashire**, OL9 0RD, ENG.
(T) 01616 334392
Speciality: Clairvoyants & Palmists.
● **Owner** Mr R Rama
B (Ref:HM16911)

## RAMAKRISHNA VEDANTA CENTRE

**Ramakrishna Vedanta Centre**, Vendanta Centre, Blind Lane, Bourne End, **Buckinghamshire**, SL8 5LF, ENG.
(T) 01628 526464
Speciality: Relaxation Technique.
H T (Ref:HM16912)

## RAMAYA, K

**K Ramaya**, 16 Bridge St, Lampeter, **Carmarthenshire**, SA48 7AA, WAL.
(T) 01570 422109
Speciality: Chiropodists (Podiatrists).
S (Ref:HM16913)

## RAMBAUT, ANN

**Ann Rambaut**, 3 Hurst Rd, Eastbourne, **Sussex (East)**, BN21 2PJ, ENG.
(T) 01323 411900
Speciality: Physiotherapy.
● **Owner** Ms A Rambaut
P S T (Ref:HM16914)

## RAMONA

**Ramona**, The Cottage, 30 Moor Lane, Hutton, Preston, **Lancashire**, PR4 5SE, ENG.
(T) 01772 614441
Speciality: Clairvoyants & Palmists.
● **Owner** Mrs A Ramona
B (Ref:HM16915)

## RAMONA, SUE

**Sue Ramona**, Psychotherapy Practice, 230 Langlands Rd, Glasgow, **Glasgow (City of)**, G51 4AQ, SCO.
(T) 01414 451722
Speciality: Psychotherapy.
● **Owner** Dr R Sue
B (Ref:HM16916)

## RAMSAY & ASSOCIATES

**Dr L R Ramsay & Associates**, 21a Northumberland Sq, North Shields, **Tyne and Wear**, NE30 1PW, ENG.
(T) 01912 964004 (F) 01912 587640
Speciality: Chiropractic.
● **Practice Manager** Mrs A Ramsay
P S T (Ref:HM16917)

## RAMSAY, A R

**A R Ramsay**, 31 Linefield Rd, Carnoustie, **Angus**, DD7 6DP, SCO.
(T) 01241 853634
Speciality: Chiropodists (Podiatrists).
● **Owner** Mr A Ramsay
S (Ref:HM16918)

## RAMSBOTTOM PHYSIO CLINIC

**Ramsbottom Physiotherapy Clinic**, 138



Key continued: Yrs.Est: Years Established Q: Qualifications M: Professional Membership ✓ Indemnity Insurance [credit card] Accept Credit Cards

Bolton Rd West, Ramsbottom, Bury, **Lancashire**, BL0 9NB, ENG.
**(T)** 01706 825727
Speciality: Acupuncture, Manipulation, Massage (Therapeutic), Physiotherapy, Mobilisation. ✔
- **Physiotherapist/Owner** Mr A Raw **M:** SST.
- **Physiotherapist** Mr Wilcock **M:** SST.

**S** (**Ref:**HM16919)

### RAMSEY, CAROLYN
**Carolyn Ramsey**, 1 Perkins Cl, Hornton, Banbury, **Oxfordshire**, OX15 6BP, ENG.
**(T)** 01295 670719
Speciality: Chiropodists (Podiatrists).
**S** (**Ref:**HM16920)

### RAMSEY, G D
**G D Ramsey**, 191 Green Lane Rd, Leicester, **Leicestershire**, LE5 4PD, ENG.
**(T)** 01162 769420
Speciality: Chiropodists (Podiatrists).
**S** (**Ref:**HM16921)

### RAMSEY, L
**L Ramsey**, 11 Longsight, Bolton, **Lancashire**, BL2 3HS, ENG.
**(T)** 01204 308908
Speciality: Chiropodists (Podiatrists).
**S** (**Ref:**HM16922)

### RAMSEYER, GEORGINA
**Georgina Ramseyer**, 16 Broomfield View, Leeds, **Yorkshire (West)**, LS6 3DH, ENG.
**(T)** 01132 741540
Speciality: Homeopathy.
- **Owner** Ms G Ramseyer

**M** (**Ref:**HM16923)

### RAMSGATE PHYSIO & SPORTS
**Ramsgate Physiotherapy & Sports Injuries Clinic**, 33 St. Mildreds Avenue, Ramsgate, **Kent**, CT11 0HS, ENG.
**(T)** 01843 852853
Speciality: Physiotherapy.
- **Owner** Mr F Fraser

**P S T** (**Ref:**HM16924)

### RAND, E
**E Rand**, Beverley Clinic, 362 Coombe Lane, London, **London (Greater)**, SW20 0RJ, ENG.
**(T)** 020 8241 2515
Speciality: Aromatherapy.
**M O** (**Ref:**HM16925)

### RANDALL, CAROLINE
**Caroline Randall**, 69 Boyton Rd, London, **London (Greater)**, N8 7AE, ENG.
**(T)** 020 8348 0537
Speciality: Holistic Healing, Massage (Therapeutic), Phytotherapy, Bio-Dynamic Technique. ✔
- **Owner** Mrs C Randell **Q:** BDI. **M:** B.A.Ch.P, BDI.

**C** Yrs. Est.: 9 (**Ref:**HM16926)

### RANDALL, JULIA
**Julia Randall**, 19 Cambrian Rd, Richmond, **Surrey**, TW10 6JQ, ENG.
**(T)** 020 8940 2432 **(F)** 020 8332 7790
Speciality: Reflexology.
- **Owner** Mrs J Randall

**S T** (**Ref:**HM16927)

### RANDALL, MARGARET
**Margaret Randall**, 61 The Paddock, Bishop's Stortford, **Hertfordshire**, CM23 4JW, ENG.
**(T)** 01279 507998
Speciality: Reflexology.
- **Owner** Mrs M Randall

**S T** (**Ref:**HM16928)

### RANDALL, PATRICK
**Randall Patrick**, 52 Ryecroft, Bray, **County Wicklow**, IRE.
**(T)** 01276 1390
Speciality: Complementary Medicines & Therapy.
**M** (**Ref:**HM16929)

### RANDALL, PAUL
**Paul Randall**, Martindale House, Lombard St, Newark, **Nottinghamshire**, NG24 1XG, ENG.
**(T)** 01636 611150
Speciality: Osteopathy.
- **Employee** Mrs S Taylor

**P S T** (**Ref:**HM16930)

### RANDALL-WOOD, MELANIE
**Mrs Melanie Randall-Wood**, 10 Hillcroft Cres, London, **London (Greater)**, W5 2SQ, ENG.
**(T)** 020 8997 5907
Speciality: Physiotherapy.
**P S T** (**Ref:**HM16931)

### RANDELL, BELINDA
**Belinda Randell**, 128 Straight Bit, Flackwell Heath, High Wycombe, **Buckinghamshire**, HP10 9NH, ENG.
**(T)** 01628 528248
Speciality: Chiropractic.
**P S T** (**Ref:**HM16932)

### RANDELL, K M & S P
**K M & S P Randell**, Clarges, High St, Uckfield, **Sussex (East)**, TN22 1AT, ENG.
**(T)** 01825 766656
Speciality: Chiropodists (Podiatrists).
- **Partner** Mr S Randell

**S** (**Ref:**HM16933)

### RANDELL, KAREN & STEPHEN
**Karen & Stephen Randell**, 25 Dudley Rd, Tunbridge Wells, **Kent**, TN1 1LE, ENG.
**(T)** 01892 523939
Speciality: Chiropodists (Podiatrists).
**S** (**Ref:**HM16934)

### RANDELL, KAREN & STEPHEN
**Karen & Stephen Randell**, The Chiropody Clinic, The Cross, London Rd, Crowborough, **Sussex (East)**, TN6 2TT, ENG.
**(T)** 01892 654978
Speciality: Chiropodists (Podiatrists).
**S** (**Ref:**HM16935)

### RANDERIA, JAMSHED (DR)
**Dr Jamshed Randeria**, 26 Farm Cl, Hoylake Cresent, Uxbridge, **London (Greater)**, UB10 8JB, ENG.
**(T)** 01895 630549
Speciality: Homeopathy.
**M** (**Ref:**HM16936)

### RANDHAWA, PAL
**Pal Randhawa**, 19 Brookside Avenue, Wollaton, Nottingham, **Nottinghamshire**, NG8 2RD, ENG.
**(T)** 01159 855726
Speciality: Reflexology.
**S T** (**Ref:**HM16937)

### RANKIN, PAM
**Pam Rankin**, Natural Health Clinic, 177 Moorside Rd, Swinton, Manchester, **Manchester (Greater)**, M27 9LD, ENG.
**(T)** 01617 930091
Speciality: Aromatherapy.
- **Partner** Mr G Jordan

**M O** (**Ref:**HM16938)

### RANKINE, VANORA
**Vanora Rankine**, Tathhill, Beattock, Moffat, **Dumfries and Galloway**, DG10 9RH, **SCO**.
**(T)** 01683 300695 **(F)** 01683 300324
Speciality: Chiropody. ✔
- **Owner/Chiropodist** Ms V Rankine **Q:** DPodM.

**M** Yrs. Est.: 11 (**Ref:**HM16939)

### RANSOME, JENNIFER
**Jennifer Ransome**, 31 Weymouth St, London, **London (Greater)**, W1N 3FJ, ENG.
**(T)** 020 7580 1391
Speciality: Chiropodists (Podiatrists).
- **Owner** Ms J Ransome

**S** (**Ref:**HM16940)

### RAO, R S
**R S Rao**, The Longmead Centre, Sefton Rd, Epsom, **Surrey**, KT19 9HG, ENG.
**(T)** 01372 745150
Speciality: Chiropodists (Podiatrists).
**S** (**Ref:**HM16941)

### RAOUX, PHILIPPE
**Philippe Raoux**, Blackheath Osteopathy & Acupuncture Clinic, 19 Tranquil Vale, London, **London (Greater)**, SE3 0BU, ENG.
**(T)** 020 8852 1706
Speciality: Osteopathy.
**P S T** (**Ref:**HM16942)

### RAPHAEL ALT THERAPY PRACTICE
**Raphael Alternative Therapy Practice**, Hawley Green, Blackwater, Camberley, **Surrey**, GU17 9BW, ENG.
**(T)** 01276 38122
Speciality: Complementary Medicines & Therapy.
- **Owner** Mrs P Jenkins

**M** (**Ref:**HM16943)

### RAPHAEL, L G
**L G Raphael**, 27 Beehive Lane, Ilford, **Essex**, IG1 3RG, ENG.
**(T)** 020 8554 5412 **(F)** 020 8554 5412
Speciality: Chiropodists (Podiatrists).
- **Owner** Mr L Raphael

**S** (**Ref:**HM16944)

### RASHBROOKE, K M
**K M Rashbrooke**, Tregonhay, Baber Lane, St. Dominick, Saltash, **Cornwall**, PL12 6TE, ENG.
**(T)** 01579 350162
Speciality: Physiotherapy.
**P S T** (**Ref:**HM16945)

### RASMUSSEN, A C
**A C Rasmussen**, 1 Westfield Rd, Woking, **Surrey**, GU22 9LZ, ENG.
**(T)** 01483 768810 **(F)** 01483 821549
Speciality: Osteopathy.
- **Owner** Miss A Rasmussen

**P S T** (**Ref:**HM16946)

### RATCLIFF, SUSAN
**Susan Ratcliff**, 48 The Grove, St Margarets Rd, Twickenham, **London (Greater)**, TW1 1RB, ENG.
**(T)** 020 8744 1694
Speciality: Hypnosis.
- **Owner** Ms S Pembrey

**B** (**Ref:**HM16947)

### RATCLIFFE & STINSON
**Ratcliffe & Stinson**, 97 Victoria Rd, Scarborough, **Yorkshire (North)**, YO11 1SP, ENG.
**(T)** 01723 372540
Speciality: Chiropodists (Podiatrists).
- **Owner** Ms T Stinson

**S** (**Ref:**HM16948)

### RATCLIFFE, MARK
**Mark Ratcliffe**, 147 St James St, Burnley, **Lancashire**, BB11 1PD, ENG.
**(T)** 01282 450850 **(F)** 01282 455038
Speciality: Manipulation, Naturopathy, Osteopathy. ✔
- **Therapist** Mr M Ratcliffe **Q:** DO. **M:** GOsC.
- **Therapist** Mr S Murray **Q:** DO, ND.

**S** Yrs. Est.: 10 (**Ref:**HM16949)

### RATCLIFFE, MARK
**Mark Ratcliffe**, 365 Accrington Rd, Blackburn, **Lancashire**, BB1 3NN, ENG.
**(T)** 01254 55529
Speciality: Osteopathy.
**P S T** (**Ref:**HM16950)

### RATCLIFFE, P
**P Ratcliffe**, 26 West Prde, Lincoln, **Lincolnshire**, LN1 1JT, ENG.
**(T)** 01522 530530
Speciality: Chiropodists (Podiatrists).
**S** (**Ref:**HM16951)

### RATCLIFFE, PAULINE
**Pauline Ratcliffe**, 36 Southerndown Avenue, The Mayals, Mayals, Swansea, SA3 5EL, **WAL**.
**(T)** 01792 406307
Speciality: Homeopathy.
**M** (**Ref:**HM16952)

### RATH, MATTHIAS
**Matthias Rath Ltd**, 17 Liverpool Rd, Slough, **Berkshire**, SL1 4QZ, ENG.
**(T)** 01753 690000
Speciality: Complementary Medicines & Therapy.
- **Manager** Mr N Hoss

**M** (**Ref:**HM16953)

### RATHBONE CHIROPODY CLINIC
**Rathbone Chiropody Clinic**, 12 Rathbone Market, London, **London (Greater)**, E16 1EH,

Key: **B** Mind-Body Medicine **C** Complementary Medicine **H** Self Help Treatment **M** Medicinal Therapy **O** Oriental Medicine **P** Postural Therapy **S** Manipulative Structural Therapy **T** Touch Therapy

ENG.
(T) 020 7474 6718
Speciality: Chiropodists (Podiatrists).
S (Ref:HM16954)

**RATHBONE, DONNA**

**Donna Rathbone**, Overdale, 35 West End, Osmotherley, Northallerton, **Yorkshire (North)**, DL6 3AE, ENG.
(T) 01609 883437
Speciality: Chiropody, Reiki. ✔
● **Owner/Chiropodist** Mrs D Rathbone
Q: DPodM, Inst.CH.P. M: GCP.
M Yrs. Est.: 11 (Ref:HM16955)

**RATHBONE, M J**

**M J Rathbone**, 41 Hills Rd, Cambridge, **Cambridgeshire**, CB2 1NT, ENG.
(T) 01223 314434
Speciality: Osteopathy.
P S T (Ref:HM16956)

**RATHMINES CHIROPRACTIC CENTRE**

**Rathmines Chiropractic Centre**, 22 Gulistan Trce, Rathmines, **County Dublin**, 6, IRE.
(T) 4979273
Speciality: Chiropractic, Cranial Osteopathy, Manipulation. ✔
● **Chiropractor** Mr J McGrath Q: BSc, Dip.Chiro. M: BAAC.
S Yrs. Est.: 2 (Ref:HM16957)

**RATIGAN, SARAH**

**Sarah Ratigan**, 82 Gayford Rd, London, **London (Greater)**, W12 9BW, ENG.
(T) 020 8740 9997
Speciality: Reflexology.
S T (Ref:HM16958)

**RATLEY LODGE CLINIC**

**Ratley Lodge Clinic**, Ratley, Banbury, **Oxfordshire**, OX15 6OT, ENG.
(T) 01295 670536
Speciality: Complementary Medicines & Therapy.
● **Therapist** Jean Thorne
M (Ref:HM16959)

**RATNAYAKE, MALINI**

**Malini Ratnayake**, 16 Westmead Avenue, Wisbech, **Cambridgeshire**, PE13 2SL, ENG.
(T) 01945 584221
Speciality: Acupuncture.
● **Owner** Mrs M Ratnayake Q: AACP, MCSP, SRP.
O (Ref:HM16960)

**RATNAYAKE, MIKE**

**Mike Ratnayake**, 16 Westmead Avenue, Wisbech, **Cambridgeshire**, PE13 2SL, ENG.
(T) 01945 584221
Speciality: Physiotherapy.
● **Owner** Mr M Raynayake
P S T (Ref:HM16961)

**RATSEY, DAVID**

**David Ratsey**, 2 Harley St, London, **London (Greater)**, W1N 1AA, ENG.
(T) 020 7589 2776
Speciality: Homeopathy.
M (Ref:HM16962)

**RATTI, D**

**Mrs D Ratti**, 45 The Gallop, Sutton, **Surrey**, SM2 5RY, ENG.
(T) 020 8642 1105
Speciality: Chiropodists (Podiatrists).
● **Owner** Mrs D Ratti
S (Ref:HM16963)

**RAVEN HILL CHIROPRACTIC CLINIC**

**Raven Hill Chiropractic Clinic**, Raven Hill, Tivoli Estate, Cork, **County Cork**, IRE.
(T) 021 4566 515
Speciality: Chiropractic, Homeopathy, Massage (Therapeutic), Nutritional Therapy. ✔
● **Chiropractor** Ms K Ryan Q: DC, MA. M: CC, GCC, MCA.
P Yrs. Est.: 10 (Ref:HM16964)

**RAVEN, JANE M**

**Jane M Raven**, 1 Old Surgery, Rumbolds Hill, Midhurst, **Sussex (West)**, GU29 9BY, ENG.
(T) 01730 812320
Speciality: Chiropodists (Podiatrists).
S (Ref:HM16965)

**RAVENSARA THERAPIES**

**Ravensara Therapies**, 8 Links Avenue, Mablethorpe, **Lincolnshire**, LN12 1QL, ENG.
(T) 01507 479137
Speciality: Complementary Medicines & Therapy.
● **Owner** Ms S Goodley
C M (Ref:HM16966)

**RAVENSCROFT CENTRE**

**Ravenscroft Centre (The)**, 6 Ravenscroft Avenue, London, **London (Greater)**, NW11 0RY, ENG.
(T) 020 8455 3743 (F) 020 8201 8319
(E) ravenscroft@easynet.co.uk
Speciality: Aromatherapy, Complementary Therapy, Counselling, Healing Therapy, Holistic Healing, Life Style Coaching, Massage (Therapeutic), Psychotherapy, Reflexology, Spiritual Healing, Stress Therapy, Ravenscroft approach to psycho-spiritual integration. ✔
● **Director** Mr C Digby-Jones M: ANLP.
● **Director** Mrs E Watkins-Seymour
B Yrs. Est.: 20 (Ref:HM16967)

**RAVENSCROFT, GINNY**

**Ginny Ravenscroft**, Lower End Farm, Eastington, Cheltenham, **Gloucestershire**, GL54 3PN, ENG.
(T) 01451 860257
Speciality: Reflexology.
S T (Ref:HM16968)

**RAWLINGS, B T**

**B T Rawlings**, 34 Bevington Cres, Coventry, **Midlands (West)**, CV6 1PE, ENG.
(T) 024 7659 8578
Speciality: Chiropodists (Podiatrists).
S (Ref:HM16969)

**RAWLINGS, MAXINE**

**Maxine Rawlings**, 23 Tillstone St, Brighton, **Sussex (East)**, BN2 2BD, ENG.
(T) 01273 692944
Speciality: Reflexology.
S T (Ref:HM16970)

**RAWLINGS, S**

**S Rawlings**, 18 Poplar Gr, Kennington, Oxford, **Oxfordshire**, OX1 5QW, ENG.
(T) 01865 735432
Speciality: Chiropodists (Podiatrists).
● **Owner** Mrs S Rawlings
S (Ref:HM16971)

**RAWLINS, E G**

**E G Rawlins**, 18 Wimpole St, London, **London (Greater)**, W1M 7AD, ENG.
(T) 020 7631 0724
Speciality: Chiropodists (Podiatrists).
S (Ref:HM16972)

**RAWLINS, JANET**

**Janet Rawlins**, Caige Bush Farm, Wood Rd, Ashill, Ilminster, **Somerset**, TA19 9NR, ENG.
(T) 01823 480155
Speciality: Aromatherapy.
M O (Ref:HM16973)

**RAWLINSON, KATE**

**Kate Rawlinson**, 6 Ranelagh Drive South, Liverpool, **Merseyside**, L19 9DR, ENG.
(T) 01514 279248
Speciality: Hypnosis.
● **Owner** Mrs K Rawlinson
B (Ref:HM16974)

**RAWLINSON, MARGARET**

**Margaret Rawlinson**, Cedar Lodge, 48 Sheephouse Rd, Maidenhead, **Berkshire**, SL6 8HH, ENG.
(T) 01628 770796
Speciality: Acupuncture, Shiatsu, Yoga.
O (Ref:HM16975)

**RAWORTH CENTRE**

**Raworth Centre (East Anglia)**, Bealings Holt Martlesham Rd, Little Bealings, Woodbridge, **Suffolk**, IP13 6LX, ENG.
(T) 01473 630303
Speciality: Complementary Medicines & Therapy.
C M (Ref:HM16976)

**RAWORTH CLINIC**

**Raworth Clinic**, 20-26 South St, Dorking, **Surrey**, RH4 2HQ, ENG.
(T) 020 8878 7896
Speciality: Alexander Technique.
● **Therapist** Mr S Baxter
P S (Ref:HM16977)

**RAWORTH, SUZANNE**

**Suzanne Raworth**, 27 Burncrooks Avenue, Bearsden, Glasgow, **Glasgow (City of)**, G61 4NL, SCO.
(T) 01415 700110
Speciality: Complementary Medicines & Therapy, Trichology.
M (Ref:HM16978)

**RAWSON, JUDITH**

**Judith Rawson**, Willow Dene, Denholme Gate Rd, Hipperholme, Halifax, **Yorkshire (West)**, HX3 8HX, ENG.
(T) 01422 202118
Speciality: Chiropodists (Podiatrists).
S (Ref:HM16979)

**RAY, F**

**F Ray**, 9 Dunheved Rd, Saltash, **Cornwall**, PL12 4BW, ENG.
(T) 01752 846610 (F) 01752 846610
Speciality: Physiotherapy.
● **Owner** Mrs F Ray
P S T (Ref:HM16980)

**RAYBOULD, J**

**J Raybould**, 64 Burford, Telford, **Shropshire**, TF3 1LH, ENG.
(T) 01952 592439
Speciality: Chiropodists (Podiatrists).
● **Owner** Mr J Raybould
S (Ref:HM16981)

**RAYMER, RUTH**

**Ruth Raymer**, New House, Clacton Rd, Wix, Harwich, **Essex**, CO11 2RU, ENG.
(T) 01255 871069
Speciality: Complementary Medicines & Therapy.
● **Owner** Ruth Raymer
M (Ref:HM16982)

**RAYMOND, GEOFF**

**Geoff Raymond**, 3 The Greenway, Middleton St George, **County Durham**, DL2 1EB, ENG.
(T) 01325 332495
Speciality: Complementary Medicines & Therapy.
C M (Ref:HM16983)

**RAYNER, BEN**

**Ben Rayner**, 19 Newcastle Rd, Reading, **Berkshire**, RG2 7TN, ENG.
(T) 01189 622100
Speciality: Homeopathy.
● **Owner** Mr B Rayner
M (Ref:HM16984)

**RAYNER, J D**

**J D Rayner**, Southbourne Rd, Bournemouth, **Dorset**, BH6 3QQ, ENG.
(T) 01202 425793
Speciality: Chiropodists (Podiatrists).
● **Owner** Mr J Rayner
S (Ref:HM16985)

**RAYNER, MARY M (DR)**

**Dr Mary M Rayner**, 33 Meadow Hill Rd, Birmingham, **Midlands (West)**, B38 8DF, ENG.
(T) 01214 586595 (F) 01214 586595
Speciality: Homeopathy.
● **Owner** Dr M Rayner
M (Ref:HM16986)

**RAYNER, SALLY**

**Sally Rayner**, 14 Colwyn Avenue, Rhos On Sea, Colwyn Bay, **Conwy**, LL28 4RB, WAL.
(T) 01492 549520
Speciality: Reflexology.
S T (Ref:HM16987)

**RAYNOR, JOHN**

**John Raynor**, 102 Southbourne Rd, Bournemouth, **Dorset**, BH6 3QQ, ENG.
(T) 01202 424833



Key continued: Yrs.Est: Years Established Q: Qualifications M: Professional Membership ✔ Indemnity Insurance ▬ Accept Credit Cards

Speciality: Complementary Medicines & Therapy.
● **Owner** Mr J Milward
M (Ref:HM16988)

### RAZZMATAZZ INTERNATIONAL

**Razzmatazz International Ltd**, 6a Roxby Rd Industrial Estate, Winterton, Scunthorpe, **Humberside**, DN15 9SX, ENG.
(T) 01724 735000 (F) 01724 735555
Speciality: Aromatherapy.
M O (Ref:HM16989)

### REA, J

**J Rea**, 28 North End, Ballyclare, **County Antrim**, BT39 9BN, NIR.
(T) 028 9334 1715
Speciality: Chiropractors.
● **Owner** Miss J Rea
P S T (Ref:HM16990)

### REACH DIRECT

**Reach Direct Ltd**, The Coach House, Puxton Rd, Hewish, Weston-Super-Mare, **Somerset**, BS24 6UE, ENG.
(T) 01934 820620 (F) 01934 820984
Speciality: Complementary Medicines & Therapy.
● **Accountant** Geoffrey Michael Say
M (Ref:HM16991)

### READ, B

**B Read**, 4 White Hart St, Aylsham, Norwich, **Norfolk**, NR11 6HG, ENG.
(T) 01263 734533
Speciality: Chiropodists (Podiatrists).
● **Owner** Mr B Read
S (Ref:HM16992)

### READ, CHARLES

**Charles R S Read DO & Associates**, 10 Harley St, London, **London (Greater)**, W1N 1AA, ENG.
(T) 020 8467 4451 (F) 020 8467 8312
Speciality: Cranial Osteopathy, Manipulation, Osteopathy. ✔
● **Osteopath** Ms S Dempster Q: DO. M: GOsC.
● **Osteopath** Mr C Read Q: DO. M: GOsC.
S Yrs. Est.: 12 (Ref:HM16993)

### READ, CHARLES REG OSTEOPATH

**Charles R S Read DO & Associates**, 13 Claremont Rd, Bickley, Bromley, **Kent**, BR1 2JL, ENG.
(T) 020 8467 4451 (F) 020 7467 8312
Speciality: Cranial Osteopathy, Manipulation, Osteopathy. ✔
● **Osteopath** Mr C Read Q: DO. M: GOsC.
● **Osteopath** Ms S Dempster Q: BSc, Hons (OST). M: GOsC.
S Yrs. Est.: 12 (Ref:HM16994)

### READ, GRAHAM

**Graham Read**, 79 Histon Rd, Cambridge, **Cambridgeshire**, CB4 3JD, ENG.
(T) 01223 322636
Speciality: Chiropodists (Podiatrists).
● **Owner** Mr G Read
S (Ref:HM16995)

### READ, MATTHEW J

**Matthew J Read**, 248 Hillside Rd, Castle Gresley, Swadlincote, **Derbyshire**, DE11 9HE, ENG.
(T) 01283 216752
Speciality: Chiropodists (Podiatrists).
● **Owner** Mr M Read
S (Ref:HM16996)

### READ, S R

**S R Read**, 40 Langley Avenue, Brixham, **Devon**, TQ5 9JG, ENG.
(T) 01803 855502
Speciality: Chiropodists (Podiatrists).
S (Ref:HM16997)

### READ, SANDRA

**Sandra Read**, 8 Whitebeam Cl, Waltham Cross, **Hertfordshire**, EN7 6NH, ENG.
(T) 01992 632959 (F) 01992 632959
Speciality: Complementary Medicines & Therapy.
● **Owner** Ms S Read
C M (Ref:HM16998)

### READE COLLEGE

**Reade College (The)**, 48 Victoria Avenue, Hunstanton, **Norfolk**, PE36 6BX, ENG.
(T) 01485 532840
Speciality: Complementary Medicines & Therapy.
● **Principal** Mr A Besgrove
C M (Ref:HM16999)

### READHEAD, DIANA

**Diana Readhead**, 29 Crawford St, London, **London (Greater)**, W1H 1PL, ENG.
(T) 020 7723 5676
Speciality: Alexander Technique.
● **Owner** Miss D Readhead
P S (Ref:HM17000)

### READING CHIROPRACTIC CLINIC

**Reading Chiropractic Clinic**, 41 Eastern Avenue, Reading, **Berkshire**, RG1 5RX, ENG.
(T) 01189 267438
Speciality: Chiropractors.
● **Senior Partner** Mr S Carpenter
P S T (Ref:HM17001)

### READING, JENNIE

**Jennie Reading**, 1 Denstead Oast, Denstead Lane, Chartham Hatch, Canterbury, **Kent**, CT4 7SH, ENG.
(T) 01227 730808 (F) 01227 730808
Speciality: Reflexology.
● **Owner** Mrs J Reading
S T (Ref:HM17002)

### REANEY, L

**L Reaney**, Mazda Buildings, Campo Lane, Sheffield, **Yorkshire (South)**, S1 2EF, ENG.
(T) 01142 759333
Speciality: Chiropodists (Podiatrists).
● **Owner** Ms L Reaney
S (Ref:HM17003)

### REAY, H

**H Reay**, 94 Upper Newtownards Rd, Belfast, **County Antrim**, BT4 3EN, NIR.
(T) 028 9065 5468
Speciality: Chiropody, Nail Surgery. ✔
● **Owner/Chiropodist** Mrs H Reay Q: M.S.C.P, S.R.Ch.
M Yrs. Est.: 43 (Ref:HM17004)

### REAY, MARIA

**Maria Reay**, Tracey Hill Cottage, Roborough, Winkleigh, **Devon**, EX19 8TG, ENG.
(T) 01805 603297
Speciality: Chiropodists (Podiatrists).
● **Owner** Mrs M Reay
S (Ref:HM17005)

### REDBRIDGE HEALING CENTRE

**Redbridge Healing Centre**, I R S D A Hall Craven Gardens, Ilford, **Essex**, IG5 0BP, ENG.
(T) 020 8550 5650
Speciality: Complementary Medicines & Therapy.
C M (Ref:HM17006)

### REDCAR PHYSIO & SPORTS

**Redcar Physiotherapy & Sports Injury Clinic**, 14 Park Avenue, Redcar, **Cleveland**, TS10 3JZ, ENG.
(T) 01642 490110 (F) 01642 476913
Speciality: Acupuncture, Manipulation, Massage (Therapeutic), Physiotherapy. ✔
● **Owner/Physiotherapist** Mr P Chinn Q: Grad Dip Phys, MCSP, SRP. M: CSP.
● **Physiotherapist** Mrs C Chinn Q: Grad Dip Phys, MCSP, SRP. M: CSP.
S Yrs. Est.: 14 (Ref:HM17007)

### REDCROFT CLINIC

**Redcroft Clinic**, 12 Barham Cl, Weybridge, **Surrey**, KT13 9PR, ENG.
(T) 01932 851372 (F) 01932 851372
Speciality: Physiotherapy.
● **Owner** Mrs P Varney
P S T (Ref:HM17008)

### REDDEN, REBECCA

**Rebecca Redden**, Stock, Ingatestone, **Essex**, CM4 9NA, ENG.
(T) 01277 841843
Speciality: Hypnosis.
● **Partner** Ms R Redden
B (Ref:HM17009)

### REDDING-THOMAS, K

**K Redding-Thomas**, 259 Wells Rd, Bristol, BS4 2PH, ENG.
(T) 01179 770572
Speciality: Chiropodists (Podiatrists).
● **Owner** Mr K Redding-Thomas
S (Ref:HM17010)

### REDDING-THOMAS, K

**K Redding-Thomas**, 5 St Leonards Rd, Windsor, **Berkshire**, SL4 3BN, ENG.
(T) 01753 863688
Speciality: Chiropodists (Podiatrists).
● **Owner** Mr K Redding-Thomas
S (Ref:HM17011)

### REDDING-THOMAS, K

**K Redding-Thomas**, 27 The Arcade, Bristol, BS1 3JD, ENG.
(T) 01179 273698
Speciality: Chiropodists (Podiatrists).
● **Manager** Mrs M Tait
S (Ref:HM17012)

### REDDITCH CHIROPRACTIC CLINIC

**Redditch Chiropractic Clinic**, 137 Evesham Rd, Redditch, **Worcestershire**, B97 4JX, ENG.
(T) 01527 402762
Speciality: Chiropractic. ✔
● **Associate/Chiropractor**
Mr P Chorley Q: BSc (Chiro), BSc (Hons), MSc (Chiro). M: BCA.
● **Owner/Chiropractor** Ms E Laverick Q: DC. M: BCA.
P S T Yrs. Est.: 5 (Ref:HM17013)

### REDDITCH FOOTCARE SURGERY

**Redditch Footcare Surgery**, 149 Ipsley St, Redditch, **Worcestershire**, B98 7AA, ENG.
(T) 01527 584224
Speciality: Biomechanics, Chiropody, Nail Surgery, Orthosis. ✔
● **Chiropodist** Ms S Fell Q: BSc. M: S.C.P.
M Yrs. Est.: 10 (Ref:HM17014)

### REDDY, ANNE

**Anne Reddy**, 9 Kings Rd, St. Leonards-On-Sea, **Sussex (East)**, TN37 6EA, ENG.
(T) 01424 714800
Speciality: Complementary Medicines & Therapy.
M (Ref:HM17015)

### REDFEARN, C M & D R

**C M & D R Redfearn**, 75 Cromwell Rd, Risca, Newport, NP11 7AD, WAL.
(T) 01633 601513
Speciality: Complementary Medicines & Therapy.
C M (Ref:HM17016)

### REDFERN - MEDICAL HERBALIST

**Susan Redfern BA NIMH - Medical Herbalist**, 46 Hamilton Rd, Southville, Bristol, BS3 1PB, ENG.
(T) 01179 538198
Speciality: Herbal Medicine.
M (Ref:HM17017)

### REDFERN, AMANDA

**Amanda Redfern**, 8 Birch Vale, Belper, **Derbyshire**, DE56 1BR, ENG.
(T) 01773 827632
(W) www.complementary-healthcare.co.uk/info/redfern
Speciality: Reflexology.
S T (Ref:HM17018)

### REDFERN, D J

**D J Redfern**, 5 Rosedale, Worksop, **Nottinghamshire**, S81 0TB, ENG.
(T) 01909 473107
Speciality: Chiropodists (Podiatrists).
● **Owner** Mr D Redfern
S (Ref:HM17019)

### REDFERN, JANE

**Jane Redfern**, Chetnole, Sherborne, **Dorset**, DT9 6HH, ENG.
(T) 01935 872833 (F) 01935 873669
Speciality: Physiotherapy.

● **Owner** Ms J Redfern
P S T (Ref:HM17020)

**REDFERN, JOY**

**Joy Redfern**, Lower End Cottage, Lower End, Priors Hardwick, Southam, **Warwickshire**, CV47 7SP, ENG.
(T) 01327 261834
Speciality: Reflexology.
S T (Ref:HM17021)

**REDFORD, SARAH**

**Sarah Redford**, 185 Elm Drive, Hove, **Sussex (East)**, BN3 7JD, ENG.
(T) 01273 746110
Speciality: Reflexology.
S T (Ref:HM17022)

**REDGRAVE CLINIC**

**Redgrave Clinic**, 3 Station Rd, Bourne End, **Buckinghamshire**, SL8 5QD, ENG.
(T) 01628 533200
Speciality: Osteopathy.
P S T (Ref:HM17023)

**REDGRAVE, ANN**

**Ann Redgrave**, School House, Station Rd, Bourne End, **Buckinghamshire**, SL8 5QD, ENG.
(T) 01628 533200
Speciality: Osteopathy.
P S T (Ref:HM17024)

**REDGRAVE, KENNETH**

**Kenneth Redgrave**, 11 Parker Avenue, Hartford, Northwich, **Cheshire**, CW8 3AH, ENG.
(T) 01606 74874
Speciality: Cognitive Therapy, Counselling, Hypnotherapy, Psychotherapy.
● **Psychotherapist** Mr K Redgrave Q: BA, Dip.Psych. M: UKCP.
B Yrs. Est.: 12 (Ref:HM17025)

**REDGROVE, N**

**N Redgrove**, Old Wood Stables, The Old Wood, Skellingthorpe, Lincoln, **Lincolnshire**, LN6 5UA, ENG.
(T) 01522 824739
Speciality: Complementary Medicines & Therapy.
● **Owner** Nick Redgrove
M (Ref:HM17026)

**REDHOUSE**

**Redhouse**, 78 Manchester Rd, Swinton, Manchester, **Manchester (Greater)**, M27 5FG, ENG.
(T) 01617 940875 (F) 01617 278661
Speciality: Psychotherapy.
● **Manager** Mr M Fisher
B (Ref:HM17027)

**REDLANDS HOUSE CLINIC**

**Redlands House Clinic**, Redland House Clinic, 118 Redland Rd, Bristol, BS6 6QT, ENG.
(T) 01179 420200
Speciality: Chiropractic, Physiotherapy.
✔
● **Owner** Mr J Cook Q: DC.
● **Physiotherapist** Ms J Lott Q: MCSP, SRP.
● **Chiropractor** J D Scrimshaw Q: DC.
● **Chiropractor** R.C Grace Q: DC.
● **Chiropractor** M Mc Ginn Q: DC, MSc.
P Yrs. Est.: 12 (Ref:HM17028)

**REDLER, LEON (DR)**

**Dr Leon Redler**, Care Of Diorama Arts, 34 Osnaburgh St, London, **London (Greater)**, NW1 3ND, ENG.
(T) 020 7916 5191
Speciality: Psychotherapy.
B (Ref:HM17029)

**REDMAN, L**

**L Redman**, The Devon Parade Clinic, 322 Wellingborough Rd, Northampton, **Northamptonshire**, NN1 4EP, ENG.
(T) 01604 622999
Speciality: Homeopathy.
● **Owner** Mr A Costain
M (Ref:HM17030)

**REDMOND, CAROLINE**

**Caroline Redmond**, 60 Seymour Avenue, Bristol, BS7 9HN, ENG.
(T) 01179 244084
Speciality: Homeopathy, Holistic Therapy. ✔
● **Owner** Ms C Redmond Q: BA. M: HMA.
C Yrs. Est.: 7 (Ref:HM17031)

**REDMOND, JO**

**Jo Redmond**, 62 Paul St, London, **London (Greater)**, EC2A 4NA, ENG.
(T) 020 7251 4429 (F) 020 7613 4737
Speciality: Complementary Medicines & Therapy.
M (Ref:HM17032)

**REDWELL PHYSIO CLINIC**

**Redwell Physiotherapy Clinic**, Redwell Medical Centre, 1 Turner Rd, Wellingborough, **Northamptonshire**, NN8 4UT, ENG.
(T) 01933 400777 (F) 01933 402869
Speciality: Physiotherapy.
● **Practice Manager** Mr D Winter
P S T (Ref:HM17033)

**REDWOOD, DAWN**

**Dawn Redwood**, Winswood House, Park Rd, Crediton, **Devon**, EX17 3BS, ENG.
(T) 01363 773375
Speciality: Reflexology.
S T (Ref:HM17034)

**REDWOOD, SARAH**

**Sarah Redwood**, 8 Tidworth Avenue, Runwell, Wickford, **Essex**, SS11 7JB, ENG.
(T) 01268 762204
Speciality: Reflexology.
S T (Ref:HM17035)

**REDWOOD-COUNS/ PSYCHOTHERAPY**

**Redwood Counselling & Psychotherapy**, 55 Lanbourne Wd, Dublin, **County Dublin**, IRE.
(T) 01235 2034
Speciality: Psychotherapy.
B (Ref:HM17036)

**REECE, EMMA**

**Emma Reece**, 38 Ullswater Avenue, Crewe, **Cheshire**, CW2 8QQ, ENG.
(T) 01270 664809
Speciality: Reflexology.
● **Owner** Mr E Reece
S T (Ref:HM17037)

**REECE, JULIE**

**Julie Reece**, Rose View, High St, Bagillt, **Flintshire**, CH6 6HE, WAL.
(T) 01352 719222
Speciality: Biomechanics, Chiropody, Orthotics. ✔
● **Owner/Chiropodist** Mrs J Reece Q: DPodM, M.S.C.P. M: S.C.P.
M Yrs. Est.: 8 (Ref:HM17038)

**REECE, P & BRADSHAW, J**

**P Reece & J Bradshaw**, 18 Rosslyn Rd, Stoke-On-Trent, **Staffordshire**, ST3 4JD, ENG.
(T) 01782 599883
(E) paulreece@feetfirst.fsbusiness.co.uk
Speciality: Biomechanics, Chiropody, Cryo Surgery, Gait Analysis, Nail Surgery. ✔
● **Chiropodist** Mrs J Bradshaw Q: DPodM. M: S.R.Ch.
● **Chiropodist** Mr P Reece Q: BSc (Hons). M: S.R.Ch.
S Yrs. Est.: 12 (Ref:HM17039)

**REED, ANN**

**Ann Reed**, Natural Path Health Centre, 3 Holyrood St, Chard, **Somerset**, TA20 2AH, ENG.
(T) 01460 62953 (F) 01460 63809
Speciality: Chiropodists (Podiatrists).
● **Owner** Mr M Newbound
S (Ref:HM17040)

**REED, G W**

**G W Reed**, 65 Newland St, Rugby, **Warwickshire**, CV22 7BJ, ENG.
(T) 01788 579334
Speciality: Chiropodists (Podiatrists).
● **Owner** Mr G Reed
S (Ref:HM17041)

**REED, JEAN**

**Jean Reed**, 13 Esmond Rd, London, **London (Greater)**, W4 1JG, ENG.
(T) 020 8742 0001
Speciality: Reflexology.
S T (Ref:HM17042)

**REED, PHILIP**

**Philip Reed**, 18 Cranborne Avenue, Hitchin, **Hertfordshire**, SG5 2BS, ENG.
(T) 01462 440048
Speciality: Hypnosis.
B (Ref:HM17043)

**REED, SUZANNE**

**Suzanne Reed**, 11 Forest Court, Dorridge, Solihull, **Midlands (West)**, B93 8HN, ENG.
(T) 01564 771071
Speciality: Chiropodists (Podiatrists).
● **Owner** Mrs S Reed
S (Ref:HM17044)

**REED, TED**

**Ted Reed**, 48 Park Cres, Sunningdale, **Berkshire**, SL5 0AZ, ENG.
(T) 01344 625566
Speciality: T'ai-Chi Ch'uan. ✔
● **Tai Chi Chuan Instructor** Mr T Reed M: BCCMA.
O Yrs. Est.: 11 (Ref:HM17045)

**REED, W A**

**W A Reed**, 16 Leagrove Rd, Clevedon, **Somerset**, BS21 7QR, ENG.
(T) 01275 877840 (F) 01275 877840
Speciality: Aromatherapy, Sports Massage. ✔
● **Aromatherapist** Mrs W Reed Q: Dip.Arom. M: IFA.
C Yrs. Est.: 11 (Ref:HM17046)

**REEL, SARAH**

**Sarah Reel**, 24 Wayside Cres, Harrogate, **Yorkshire (North)**, HG2 8NJ, ENG.
(T) 01423 881179
Speciality: Chiropodists (Podiatrists).
● **Professor** Mrs S Reel
S (Ref:HM17047)

**REES, JACQUELINE**

**Jacqueline Rees**, 29 Park Rd, Stanton, Burton-On-Trent, **Staffordshire**, DE15 9TW, ENG.
(T) 01283 211832
Speciality: Chiropodists (Podiatrists).
S (Ref:HM17048)

**REES, L E**

**L E Rees**, The Hawthorns, Reynoldston, Swansea, SA3 1AA, WAL.
(T) 01792 391395 (F) 01792 391395
Speciality: Hypnosis.
● **Owner** Mrs L Rees
B (Ref:HM17049)

**REES, MARGARET**

**Margaret Rees**, Physiotherapy & Sports Injury Clinic, 3 Franchise St, Kidderminster, **Worcestershire**, DY11 6RE, ENG.
(T) 01562 67129
Speciality: Physiotherapy.
● **Senior Partner** Mrs R Watson
P S T (Ref:HM17050)

**REES, MAUREEN E**

**Maureen E Rees**, Selsdon Osteopathic Practice, 1 Upper Selsdon Rd, South Croydon, **Surrey**, CR2 8DD, ENG.
(T) 020 8651 3315 (F) 020 8651 3315
Speciality: Osteopathy.
● **Owner** Ms M Rees
P S T (Ref:HM17051)

**REES, PAULINE**

**Pauline Rees**, 1 Downside, Southdown Avenue, Lewes, **Sussex (East)**, BN7 1EE, ENG.
(T) 01273 487290
Speciality: Reflexology.
S T (Ref:HM17052)

**REES, R**

**R Rees**, Gwendwr, 16 Uplands Cresent, Uplands, Swansea, SA2 0PB, WAL.
(T) 01792 476644
Speciality: Chiropractors.
P S T (Ref:HM17053)

**REES, R**

**R Rees**, Coachhouse, Ynysllynlladd, Cadoxton, Neath, **Glamorgan (Vale of)**, SA10 8DA, WAL.



Key continued: Yrs.Est: Years Established Q: Qualifications M: Professional Membership ✔ Indemnity Insurance Accept Credit Cards

(T) 01639 643233
Speciality: Chiropractors.
P S T (Ref:HM17054)

**REES, ROSEMARY**

**Rosemary Rees**, Bridport Complementary Medicine Centre, 32 South St, Bridport, **Dorset**, DT6 3NQ, ENG.
(T) 01305 871079
Speciality: Homeopathy.
● **Owner** Mrs R Rees
M (Ref:HM17055)

**REES, TREVOR**

**Trevor Rees**, 7 Calvert Trce, Swansea, SA1 6AY, WAL.
(T) 01792 641967
Speciality: Chiropodists (Podiatrists).
● **Owner** Mr T Rees
S (Ref:HM17056)

**REESE, M M**

**M M Reese**, 73 Llantrisant Rd, Pontyclun, **Rhondda Cynon Taff**, CF72 9DP, WAL.
(T) 01443 222810
Speciality: Chiropodists (Podiatrists).
● **Owner** Mr M Reese
S (Ref:HM17057)

**REEVE, ANNA C**

**Anna C Reeve**, 1 Les Maisonettes, Smarden Rd, Headcorn, Ashford, **Kent**, TN27 9TA, ENG.
(T) 01622 890803
Speciality: Osteopathy.
P S T (Ref:HM17058)

**REEVE, ANNE**

**Anne Reeve**, 1 Redshank Drive, Heybridge, Maldon, **Essex**, CM9 4UE, ENG.
(T) 01621 854129
Speciality: Reflexology.
S T (Ref:HM17059)

**REEVE, MALCOLM**

**Malcolm Reeve**, The Park Practice, 13 Nelson Rd, Greenwich, London, **London (Greater)**, SE10 9JB, ENG.
(T) 020 8692 0628 (F) 020 8293 4323
Speciality: Acupuncture, Cranio-Sacral Therapy. ✔
● **Acupuncturist** Mr M Reeve Q: Lic.Ac. M: BAcC.
O (Ref:HM17060)

**REEVES, ALAN**

**Alan Reeves**, 83 Shaftesbury Rd, Brighton, **Sussex (East)**, BN1 4NG, ENG.
(T) 01273 695390
Speciality: Psychotherapy.
● **Owner** Mr A Reeves
B (Ref:HM17061)

**REEVES, ALAN**

**Alan Reeves**, 213B Ditchling Rd, Brighton, **Sussex (East)**, BN1 6JD, ENG.
(T) 01273 541194
Speciality: Counselling, Psychotherapy. ✔
● **Owner/Psychotherapist**
Mr A Reeves Q: BSc, Dip.Psych. M: UKCP.
B Yrs. Est.: 5 (Ref:HM17062)

**REEVES, BOB**

**Bob Reeves**, 221 New Church Rd, Hove, **Sussex (East)**, BN3 4ED, ENG.
(T) 01273 385115
Speciality: Complementary Medicines & Therapy.
M (Ref:HM17063)

**REEVES, ELAINE**

**Elaine Reeves**, 72 Amberley Way, Wickwar, Wotton-under-Edge, **Gloucestershire**, GL12 8LP, ENG.
(T) 01454 299229
Speciality: Chiropodists (Podiatrists).
● **Owner** Mrs E Reeves
S (Ref:HM17064)

**REEVES, J**

**J Reeves**, 12 Fore St, Saltash, **Cornwall**, PL12 6JL, ENG.
(T) 01752 845005
Speciality: Chiropodists (Podiatrists).
S (Ref:HM17065)

**REEVES, J**

**J Reeves**, 21 Hazelwood Rd, Callington, **Cornwall**, PL17 7EU, ENG.
(T) 01579 382537
Speciality: Chiropody. ✔
● **Owner/Chiropodist** Mr J Reeves Q: MBChA, MSSCh. M: B.A.Ch.P, SSCh.
C Yrs. Est.: 20 (Ref:HM17066)

**REEVES, MICHAEL**

**Michael Reeves**, 42 Pembroke Park, Marldon, Paignton, **Devon**, TQ3 1NL, ENG.
(T) 01803 859313
Speciality: Chiropodists (Podiatrists).
S (Ref:HM17067)

**REEVES, SUSAN**

**Susan Reeves**, Larch Cottage, 3 Sportsfield, Maidstone, **Kent**, ME14 5LR, ENG.
(T) 01622 764344
Speciality: Reflexology.
S T (Ref:HM17068)

**REFERRAL CENTRE**

**Referral Centre (The)**, Equine Services, Tall Trees, Longburton, Sherborne, **Dorset**, DT9 5PH, ENG.
(T) 01963 210609
Speciality: Complementary Medicines & Therapy.
● **Owner** Mr C Dyer
C M (Ref:HM17069)

**REFLECTED HEALTH**

**Reflected Health**, 132 Green Lane, Sandown, **Isle of Wight**, PO36 9NL, ENG.
(T) 01983 402208
Speciality: Reflexology.
S T (Ref:HM17070)

**REFLECTIONS REFLEXOLOGISTS**

**Reflections Reflexologists**, 19 Burton Avenue, Timperley, Altrincham, **Cheshire**, WA15 6AQ, ENG.
(T) 01619 626234
Speciality: Reflexology.
S T (Ref:HM17071)

**REFLECTIVE PRACTICE**

**Reflective Practice**, 203 Rugby Rd, Leamington Spa, **Warwickshire**, CV32 6DY, ENG.
(T) 01926 885033
Speciality: Psychology.
B (Ref:HM17072)

**REFLEXIONS**

**Reflexions**, Cheltenham Recreation Centre, Tommy Taylors Lane, Cheltenham, **Gloucestershire**, GL50 4RN, ENG.
(T) 01242 251500
Speciality: Reflexology.
● **Owner** Mrs J Rayner
S T (Ref:HM17073)

**REFLEXOLOGY**

**Reflexology**, 25 High St, Avening, Tetbury, **Gloucestershire**, GL8 8NF, ENG.
(T) 01453 836029 (F) 01453 836028
Speciality: Reflexology.
● **Owner** Mrs R Cartwright
S T (Ref:HM17074)

**REFLEXOLOGY**

**Reflexology**, Springfield, 366 Billing Rd East, Northampton, **Northamptonshire**, NN3 3LJ, ENG.
(T) 01604 632885
Speciality: Reflexology.
● **Owner** Mrs D Millin
S T (Ref:HM17075)

**REFLEXOLOGY**

**Reflexology**, 7 Leach Rd, Aylesbury, **Buckinghamshire**, HP21 8LG, ENG.
(T) 01296 339741
Speciality: Reflexology.
● **Owner** Mrs M Day
S T (Ref:HM17076)

**REFLEXOLOGY**

**Reflexology**, 77 Chestnut Rd, Enfield, **London (Greater)**, EN3 6SY, ENG.
(T) 01992 761074
Speciality: Reflexology. ✔
● **Reflexologist** Mrs C Sharp M: BRA.
C Yrs. Est.: 12 (Ref:HM17077)

**REFLEXOLOGY & ALLERGY THERAPY**

**Reflexology & Allergy Therapy**, Arosfa, Groesffordd, Brecon, **Powys**, LD3 7SN, WAL.
(T) 01874 665495 (F) 01874 665495
Speciality: Reflexology, Allergy Therapy. ✔
● **Reflexologist/Allergy Therapist**
Mrs J Abbott Q: ITEC, MRxS. M: IET, ITEC, RxS.
C Yrs. Est.: 10 (Ref:HM17078)

**REFLEXOLOGY & CHIROPODY**

**Reflexology & Chiropody**, 2 Winmarleigh Gardens, Pennington, Leigh, **Manchester (Greater)**, WN7 3JF, ENG.
(T) 01942 671506
Speciality: Complementary Therapy, Homeopathy, Reflexology, Stress Therapy. ✔
● **Nurse** Mrs S Mellor Q: MBRA, MFHom, MSSCh, SRN. M: FHom.
B T Yrs. Est.: 26 (Ref:HM17079)

**REFLEXOLOGY & STRESS CLINIC**

**Reflexology & Stress Clinic**, 36 Tudor Way, Uxbridge, **London (Greater)**, UB10 0BE, ENG.
(T) 01895 239049
Speciality: Reflexology.
S T (Ref:HM17080)

**REFLEXOLOGY BY DEBORAH**

**Reflexology By Deborah**, 9 Stonedale Rd, Kempston, Bedford, **Bedfordshire**, MK42 8NE, ENG.
(T) 01234 302698
Speciality: Reflexology.
● **Owner** Ms D Creaney
S T (Ref:HM17081)

**REFLEXOLOGY BY ROSALEEN**

**Reflexology By Rosaleen**, 103 Ridgeway, Welwyn Garden City, **Hertfordshire**, AL7 2DB, ENG.
(T) 01707 376080
Speciality: Reflexology.
● **Owner** Mrs R Dicks
S T (Ref:HM17082)

**REFLEXOLOGY CENTRE**

**Reflexology Centre (The)**, 2 Bridge Chambers, Barnstaple Sq, Barnstaple, **Devon**, EX31 1HB, ENG.
(T) 01271 343896
Speciality: Reflexology. ✔
● **Manager/Practitioner**
Mrs S Bailey Q: ITEC, MRxS, RGN. M: RxS.
T Yrs. Est.: 9 (Ref:HM17083)

**REFLEXOLOGY CLINIC**

**Reflexology Clinic (The)**, St Andrews House, Cornwall St, Kirton Lindsey, **Lincolnshire**, DN21 4PP, ENG.
(T) 01652 640016
Speciality: Aromatherapy, Complementary Therapy, Indian Head Massage, Reflexology, Reiki. ✔
● **Clinical Reflexologist**
Ms M Kerss Q: ITEC, MCSR, MRxS, ONC, RGN. M: RxS.
● **Assistant Clinical Reflexologist**
Ms D Winter Q: ITEC, MAR, MIPTI. M: AoR.
● **Assistant Clinical Reflexologist**
Ms B Batty Q: MAR.
T Yrs. Est.: 5 (Ref:HM17084)

**REFLEXOLOGY CLINIC**

**Reflexology Clinic**, Silverbirch House, 122 Obelisk Rise, Kingsthorpe, **Northamptonshire**, NN2 8QU, ENG.
(T) 01604 842000 (F) 01604 842000or01604842001
(E) junfalk@skynet.co.uk
Speciality: Dowsing, Indian Head Massage, Reflexology, Reiki, Teaches Baby Massage to parents. Healing (not spiritual healing just healing). ✔
● **Consultant/Reflexologist**
Mrs E Jungfalk-Down M: AoR, BCMA, GCP.
B T Yrs. Est.: 10 (Ref:HM17085)

**REFLEXOLOGY CLINIC**

**Reflexology Clinic**, 4 Brock St, Bath,



Key: B Mind-Body Medicine C Complementary Medicine H Self Help Treatment M Medicinal Therapy O Oriental Medicine P Postural Therapy S Manipulative Structural Therapy T Touch Therapy

**Somerset**, BA1 2LN, **ENG**.
(T) 01225 442811
Speciality: Reflexology.
S T (Ref:HM17086)

## REFLEXOLOGY CLINIC

**Reflexology Clinic**, 35 Holyhead Rd, Bangor, **Gwynedd**, LL57 2EU, **WAL**.
(T) 01248 354203 (F) 01248 370076
Speciality: Reflexology.
● **Owner** Miss N Waters
S T (Ref:HM17087)

## REFLEXOLOGY CLINIC

**Reflexology Clinic (The)**, 204 High St, Hornchurch, **Essex**, RM12 6QP, **ENG**.
(T) 01708 476677
Speciality: Counselling, Hypnotherapy, Indian Head Massage, Massage (Therapeutic), Nutritional Therapy, Reflexology, Reiki. ✔
● **Reflexology/Massage Therapist**
Ms J Acteson Q: ITEC, MCSR. M: RxS.
C Yrs. Est.: 7 (Ref:HM17088)

## REFLEXOLOGY CLINIC

**Reflexology Clinic**, 18 Starfield Rd, London, **London (Greater)**, W12 9SW, **ENG**.
(T) 020 8740 8700
(E) corinnajantiz@breathemail.net
Speciality: Massage (Therapeutic), Reflexology, Reiki. ✔
● **Massage Therapist** Corinna Javitz M: AoR, IIR.
T Yrs. Est.: 15 (Ref:HM17089)

## REFLEXOLOGY CLINIC

**Reflexology Clinic (The)**, 310 Great Western Rd, Aberdeen, **Aberdeenshire**, AB10 6PL, **SCO**.
(T) 01651 842928
Speciality: Reflexology.
S T (Ref:HM17090)

## REFLEXOLOGY CLINIC

**J C F Moorhouse**, 68 Avon Cres, Stratford-Upon-Avon, **Warwickshire**, CV37 7EZ, **ENG**.
(T) 01789 268983
(E) john@reflexologyclinic.co.uk
(W) www.reflexologyclinic.co.uk
Speciality: Reflexology. ✔
● **Director** Mr J Moorhouse Q: MAR, MBRA. M: AoR, BRA.
M Yrs. Est.: 11 (Ref:HM17091)

## REFLEXOLOGY CLINIC

**Reflexology Clinic (The)**, 13 Lower Catherine St, Newry, **County Down**, BT35 6BE, **NIR**.
(T) 028 3025 2950
(E) patreflex@bush
Speciality: Aromatherapy, Indian Head Massage, Massage (Therapeutic), Reflexology.
✔ CREDIT
● **Aromatherapist** Anne Blair M: BABTAC.
● **Owner/Reflexologist**
Mr P Thornton M: AoR, IRI.
T Yrs. Est.: 4 (Ref:HM17092)

## REFLEXOLOGY CLINIC

**Reflexology Clinic (The)**, 12B Bittacy Hill, London, **London (Greater)**, NW7 1LB, **ENG**.
(T) 020 8343 0222 (F) 020 8343 0222
Speciality: Reflexology.
● **Owner** Mr A Hall
S T (Ref:HM17093)

## REFLEXOLOGY CLINIC

**Reflexology Clinic (The)**, 117 Hartfield Rd, Forest Row, **Sussex (East)**, RH18 5LY, **ENG**.
(T) 01342 824549
Speciality: Reflexology.
S T (Ref:HM17094)

## REFLEXOLOGY FOR HEALTH

**Reflexology For Health & Reflexology**, 12 Milton Rd, Eastbourne, **Sussex (East)**, BN21 1SJ, **ENG**.
(T) 01323 417040
(E) thebrownings_uk@yahoo.co.uk
Speciality: Reflexology. ✔
● **Reflexologist** Mrs K Browning Q: Dip.Reflex, IIHHT. M: FHT.
T Yrs. Est.: 2 (Ref:HM17095)

## REFLEXOLOGY THERAPY

**Reflexology Therapy**, 127 Orford Lane, Warrington, **Cheshire**, WA2 7AR, **ENG**.
(T) 01925 445076
Speciality: Complementary Medicines & Therapy.
M (Ref:HM17096)

## REG CHIROPRACTIC CLINIC

**Regis Chiropractic Clinic**, 56 Aldwick Rd, Bognor Regis, **Sussex (West)**, PO21 2PN, **ENG**.
(T) 01243 860088
Speciality: Chiropractors.
● **Owner** Miss G Blackman
P S T (Ref:HM17102)

## REGAN & ASSOCIATES

**Regan Stephanie & Associates**, Coonann 91 Raheny Rd, Raheny, Dublin, **County Dublin**, **IRE**.
(T) 01831 4812 (F) 01851 1201
(E) l:stephanie.regan@indigo.ie
Speciality: Psychotherapy.
B (Ref:HM17097)

## REGAN, ANNE MARIE

**Regan Anne Marie**, Lynn Medical Ctr, Cong, **County Mayo**, **IRE**.
(T) 09156 6998 (F) 09156 6992
Speciality: Complementary Medicines & Therapy.
M (Ref:HM17098)

## REGENCY ELECTROLYSIS

**Regency Electrolysis**, 2 Regent Chambers, Regent Rd, Blackpool, **Lancashire**, FY1 4LY, **ENG**.
(T) 01253 626142
Speciality: Electrolysis.
● **Owner** Miss B Hindle
T (Ref:HM17099)

## REGENT HEALTH

**Regent Health**, 12 Albert Rd, Belvedere, **Kent**, DA17 5LJ, **ENG**.
(T) 01322 446244
Speciality: Complementary Medicines & Therapy.
M (Ref:HM17100)

## REGENTS CLINIC

**Regents Clinic**, 14 St Georges Mews, London, **London (Greater)**, NW1 8XE, **ENG**.
(T) 020 7722 8898
Speciality: Osteopathy.
● **Owner** Mr D Mundy
P S T (Ref:HM17101)

## REGISTERED HOMEOPATH

**Registered Homeopath**, 4 Faskine Cres, Airdrie, **Lanarkshire (North)**, ML6 9EB, **SCO**.
(T) 01236 754935
(E) john@carlin47.freeserve.co.uk
Speciality: Bach Remedies, Homeopathy. ✔
● **Homeopath** Mr J Carlin Q: RSHom. M: Soc.Hom.
M Yrs. Est.: 9 (Ref:HM17103)

## REGISTERED OSTEOPATHS

**Registered Osteopaths**, 8a Montgomery Trce, Ayr, **Ayrshire (South)**, KA7 1JL, **SCO**.
(T) 01413 390894
Speciality: Osteopathy.
P S T (Ref:HM17104)

## REGUVA-CELL

**Reguva-Cell**, Unit 5 George V Pl, Thames Avenue, Windsor, **Berkshire**, SL4 1QP, **ENG**.
(T) 01753 833322
Speciality: Complementary Medicines & Therapy.
C M (Ref:HM17105)

## REHAB

**Rehab**, 21 Higham Rd, Chesham, **Buckinghamshire**, HP5 2AF, **ENG**.
(T) 01494 776307
Speciality: Complementary Medicines & Therapy.
M (Ref:HM17106)

## REHAB WITHOUT WALLS

**Rehab Without Walls**, 27 Presley Way, Crownhill, Milton Keynes, **Buckinghamshire**, MK8 0ES, **ENG**.
(T) 01908 560041 (F) 07002 329799
Speciality: Complementary Medicines & Therapy.
● **Director** Mrs C Johnson
C M (Ref:HM17107)

## REHABFIRST

**RehabFirst**, Plantation House, Watling St, Towcester, **Northamptonshire**, NN12 6HN, **ENG**.
(T) 01327 352555 (F) 01327 354476
Speciality: Physiotherapy.
P S T (Ref:HM17108)

## REHMAN, S (DR)

**Dr S Rehman**, 2 St John St, Manchester, **Manchester (Greater)**, M3 4DA, **ENG**.
(T) 01618 195559
Speciality: Hypnotherapy.
● **Doctor** Dr S Reyman
B (Ref:HM17109)

## REI KI SEMINARS

**Rei Ki Seminars Ltd**, Po Box 321, Watford, **Hertfordshire**, WD1 4RZ, **ENG**.
(T) 01923 242093
Speciality: Complementary Medicines & Therapy.
C M (Ref:HM17110)

## REIBL, TINA

**Tina Reibl**, 37 High Town Rd, Maidenhead, **Berkshire**, SL6 1PA, **ENG**.
(T) 01628 788420
Speciality: Hypnotherapy.
● **Owner** Mrs C Sanders
B (Ref:HM17111)

## REID, A

**A Reid**, 41 Templehill, Troon, **Ayrshire (South)**, KA10 6BQ, **SCO**.
(T) 01292 311554
Speciality: Biomechanics, Chiropody, Nail Surgery, Nailbrace Technique. ✔
● **Chiropodist** Mr A Reid Q: DPodM.
M Yrs. Est.: 11 (Ref:HM17112)

## REID, BARBARA

**Barbara Reid**, 55 Littleover Lane, **Derbyshire**, DE23 6JH, **ENG**.
(T) 01332 730135
Speciality: Reflexology.
S T (Ref:HM17113)

## REID, BOSCO

**Reid Bosco DOMCO MIOA**, Donegal Rd, Ballybofey, **County Donegal**, **IRE**.
(T) 07430 020
Speciality: Complementary Medicines & Therapy.
M (Ref:HM17114)

## REID, C R

**C R Reid**, 24 Quebec Rd, Dereham, **Norfolk**, NR19 2DR, **ENG**.
(T) 01362 696079 (F) 01362 696079
Speciality: Osteopathy.
● **Owner** Mr C Reid
P S T (Ref:HM17115)

## REID, E

**E Reid**, 64 Bowfield Rd, West Kilbride, **Ayrshire (North)**, KA23 9JZ, **SCO**.
(T) 01294 823417 (F) 01294 823417
Speciality: Chiropody, Reflexology. ✔
● **Chiropodist/Reflexologist**
Mrs E Reid Q: MBChA, MSSCh. M: S.C.P.
M T Yrs. Est.: 10 (Ref:HM17116)

## REID, ELIZABETH

**Mrs Elizabeth Reid**, 4 South Dean Rd, Kilmarnock, **Ayrshire (East)**, KA3 7RE, **SCO**.
(T) 01563 543882 (F) 01563 543882
Speciality: Absent Healing, Complementary Therapy, Healing Therapy, Indian Head Massage, Reflexology, Reiki, Stress Therapy, Polarity Healing, Hopi Ear Candles. ✔
● **Therapist** Mrs E Reid Q: GSSR. M: SIR.
C H T Yrs. Est.: 9 (Ref:HM17117)

## REID, K

**K Reid**, 3 Barnes Rd, Darlington, **County Durham**, DL3 9BH, **ENG**.
(T) 01325 483724
Speciality: Physiotherapy.
● **Owner** Mr K Reid
P S T (Ref:HM17118)


Key continued: Yrs.Est: Years Established Q: Qualifications M: Professional Membership ✔ Indemnity Insurance CREDIT Accept Credit Cards

## REID, MEG
**Meg Reid**, 5 Station Rd, Wivenhoe, Colchester, **Essex**, CO7 9DH, **ENG**.
(T) 01206 823723
Speciality: Reflexology.
S T (Ref:HM17119)

## REID, R H
**R H Reid**, 19 Southchurch Rd, Southend-On-Sea, **Essex**, SS1 2NG, **ENG**.
(T) 01702 467717 (F) 01702 615751
Speciality: Chiropodists (Podiatrists).
● **Owner** Mr R Reid
S (Ref:HM17120)

## REID, SUSAN
**Susan Reid**, Ilex, Fendyke Rd, Emneth, Wisbech, **Cambridgeshire**, PE14 8BA, **ENG**.
(T) 01945 464822
(W) www.stat.org
Speciality: Alexander Technique, Stress Therapy, Touch Therapy. ✔
● **Owner** Mrs S Reid Q: B.Ed. M: STAT.
S Yrs. Est.: 2 (Ref:HM17121)

## REIGATE CHIROPRACTIC CLINIC
**Reigate Chiropractic Clinic (The)**, The Wall House, Yorke Rd, Reigate, **Surrey**, RH2 9HG, **ENG**.
(T) 01737 247171
Speciality: Chiropractic.
P S T (Ref:HM17122)

## REIGATE OSTEOPATHIC
**Reigate General Osteopathic & Childrens Clinic**, Ringley Park, 59 Reigate Rd, Reigate, **Surrey**, RH2 0QT, **ENG**.
(T) 01737 240123
Speciality: Osteopathy.
P S T (Ref:HM17123)

## REIGATE OSTEOPATHIC CLINIC
**Reigate Osteopathic Clinic**, Fairlead, Chart Lane, Reigate, **Surrey**, RH2 7EG, **ENG**.
(T) 01737 245041
Speciality: Osteopathy.
P S T (Ref:HM17124)

## REIKI
**Reiki**, 27 Lavington Rd, London, **London (Greater)**, W13 9NN, **ENG**.
(T) 020 8579 3813 (F) 020 8579 3813
Speciality: Complementary Medicines & Therapy.
● **Partner** Miss M Pauffley
C M (Ref:HM17125)

## REIKI
**Reiki**, 19 Salts Rd, West Walton, Wisbech, **Cambridgeshire**, PE14 7EJ, **ENG**.
(T) 01945 584640 (F) 01945 584640
(E) mason2@tinyworld.co.uk
Speciality: Absent Healing, Complementary Therapy, Healer, Healing Therapy, Reiki. ✔
● **Reiki Master/Teacher** Ms M Mason
M: Reiki Fed.
C T Yrs. Est.: 5 (Ref:HM17126)

## REIKI
**Reiki**, 36 Barthomley Cres, Crewe, **Cheshire**, CW2 8TW, **ENG**.
(T) 01270 212863
Speciality: Hypnosis, Neuro-Linguistic Program, Reiki.
M (Ref:HM17127)

## REIKI & SEICHEM
**Reiki & Seichem**, 25 Fore St, Lostwithiel, **Cornwall**, PL22 0BL, **ENG**.
(T) 01208 873785
Speciality: Complementary Medicines & Therapy.
● **Owner** Mr J Wainwright
M (Ref:HM17128)

## REIKI ASSOCIATION
**Reiki Association**, 10 Sylvan Way, West Wickham, **Kent**, BR4 9HB, **ENG**.
(T) 020 8462 5842
Speciality: Reiki.
● **Owner** Mrs I Jenner
M (Ref:HM17129)

## REIKI CENTRE
**Reiki Centre (The)**, 9a Adie Rd, London, **London (Greater)**, W6 0PW, **ENG**.
(T) 020 8563 7590
Speciality: Complementary Medicines & Therapy.
C M (Ref:HM17130)

## REIKI HEALING
**Reiki Healing**, 27 Cranston Drive, Sale, **Cheshire**, M33 2PB, **ENG**.
(T) 01619 739953
Speciality: Complementary Medicines & Therapy.
C M (Ref:HM17131)

## REIKI HEALING & TRAINING CTRE
**Delphiris at the Centre for Reiki Healing & Training**, 11 Welshside, Fryent Gr, London, **London (Greater)**, NW9 7RU, **ENG**.
(T) 020 8200 5985
(W) www.complementary-healthcare.co.uk/info/delphiris
Speciality: Complementary Medicines & Therapy, Ocean Therapy.
M (Ref:HM17132)

## REIKI HEALING & TRAINING CTRE
**Centre for Reiki Healing & Training (The)**, 11 Welshside, Freyent Gr, London, **London (Greater)**, NW3 7RU, **ENG**.
(T) 020 8200 5985
(W) www.complementary-healthcare.co.uk/info/crht
Speciality: Indian Head Massage, Meditation, Reiki.
C (Ref:HM17133)

## REIKI HEALING & YOGA
**Reiki Healing & Yoga**, Larksfield, Englefield Green, Egham, **Surrey**, TW20 0RB, **ENG**.
(T) 01784 433634
Speciality: Complementary Medicines & Therapy.
M (Ref:HM17134)

## REIKI HEALING BY TRICIA
**Reiki Healing By Tricia**, 74 Ombersley Cl, Redditch, **Worcestershire**, B98 7UT, **ENG**.
(T) 01527 458853
Speciality: Reiki.
● **Owner** Mrs T Sawyer
M (Ref:HM17135)

## REIKI HEALING CENTRE
**Reiki Healing Centre**, 189A Petts Wood Rd, Orpington, **Kent**, BR5 1JZ, **ENG**.
(T) 01689 817589
Speciality: Reiki.
M (Ref:HM17136)

## REIKI HEALTH CENTRE
**Reiki Health Centre**, 16 Hilltop, Long Crendon, Aylesbury, **Buckinghamshire**, HP18 9AT, **ENG**.
(T) 01844 201338
Speciality: Aromatherapy, Healing Therapy, Reiki, Training (student) in Hypnotherapy and Psychotherapy. ✔
● **Reiki/Seichem Master**
Mr J Harrison Q: ITEC. M: IPTI, ITEC.
C Yrs. Est.: 10 (Ref:HM17137)

## REIKI LIGHT
**Reiki Light**, 14d Eastfield Cres, Dumbarton, **Argyll and Bute**, G82 1DU, **SCO**.
(T) 01389 765547
(W) www.reikilight.co.uk
Speciality: Reiki. ✔
● **Owner/Reiki Master** Mrs J Niven Q: Reiki Master. M: Reiki Association.
B Yrs. Est.: 4 (Ref:HM17138)

## REIKI LIGHT SELF HEALING CTRE
**Reiki Light Self Healing Centre (The)**, 15 Gloucester Rd, London, **London (Greater)**, E11 2ED, **ENG**.
(T) 020 8530 3166
Speciality: Reiki.
M (Ref:HM17139)

## REIKI MASTER
**Reiki Master**, 35 Ewart St, Brighton, **Sussex (East)**, BN2 2UP **ENG**.
(T) 01273 272774
Speciality: Reiki, Chakra and Aura Healing.
● **Owner** Miss C Moore
M (Ref:HM17140)

## REIKI MASTER & HEALER
**Reiki Master & Healer**, 3 Appletree Cl, Southend-On-Sea, **Essex**, SS2 4QX, **ENG**.
(T) 01702 616988
Speciality: Complementary Medicines & Therapy.
● **Owner** Mrs C Bampton
C M (Ref:HM17141)

## REIKI NATURAL HEALING CENTRE
**Reiki Natural Healing Centre**, 128 West St, Portchester, Fareham, **Hampshire**, PO16 9XE, **ENG**.
(T) 023 9232 1287 (F) 023 9264 7111
Speciality: Reiki. ✔
● **Owner/Reiki Master** Ms H Buglear Q: Reiki Master.
C Yrs. Est.: 6 (Ref:HM17142)

## REIKI PRACTITIONER
**Reiki Practitioner**, 16 Kenbury St, London, **London (Greater)**, SE5 9BS, **ENG**.
(T) 020 7737 1952
Speciality: Complementary Medicines & Therapy.
C M (Ref:HM17143)

## REIKI PRACTITONER
**Reiki Practitoner**, Flat 1, 75 Castelnau, London, **London (Greater)**, SW13 9RT, **ENG**.
(T) 020 8741 4907
Speciality: Complementary Medicines & Therapy.
C M (Ref:HM17144)

## REIKI ROOM
**Reiki Room (The)**, 24 New Pk Rd, Newgate St, Hertford, **Hertfordshire**, SG13 8RF, **ENG**.
(T) 01707 872147
Speciality: Complementary Medicines & Therapy.
● **Owner** Miss M Scott
M (Ref:HM17145)

## REIKI SCHOOL
**Reiki School (The)**, Budworth, Shay Lane, Halebarns, Altrincham, **Cheshire**, WA15 8UE, **ENG**.
(T) 01619 806453 (F) 01619 806453
Speciality: Complementary Medicines & Therapy.
● **Owner** Mr C Parkes
C M (Ref:HM17146)

## REIKI SEICHEM
**Reiki Seichem**, 3 Cott Rd, Lostwithiel, **Cornwall**, PL22 0ET, **ENG**.
(T) 01208 873785
Speciality: Complementary Medicines & Therapy.
C M (Ref:HM17147)

## REIKI THERAPY CENTRE
**Reiki Therapy Centre**, 120 St. Peters St, Lowestoft, **Suffolk**, NR32 1UD, **ENG**.
(T) 01502 538659
Speciality: Complementary Medicines & Therapy.
● **Practice Manager** Mrs R Kent
M (Ref:HM17148)

## REIKI TRAINING CENTRE
**Reiki Training Centre**, Millwood, Pitcaple, Inverurie, **Aberdeenshire**, AB51 5DX, **SCO**.
(T) 01467 681259 (F) 01467 681259
(E) elizabeth@reikitraining.org.uk
(W) www.reikitraining.org.uk
Speciality: Absent Healing, Aromatherapy, Metamorphic Therapy, Reiki. ✔
● **Reiki Master** Ms E Harley Q: ITEC, Karuna Master, Reiki Master. M: ISPA, RGN.
B Yrs. Est.: 7 (Ref:HM17149)

## REIKI-4-LIFE
**Reiki-4-Life**, 129 Asbridge St, Windsor, Liverpool, **Merseyside**, L8 0UG, **ENG**.
(T) 07715 006290
Speciality: Crystal Healing, Healing Therapy, Massage (Therapeutic), Reiki, Chakra and Aura Healing.
M (Ref:HM17150)



Key: B Mind-Body Medicine C Complementary Medicine H Self Help Treatment M Medicinal Therapy O Oriental Medicine P Postural Therapy S Manipulative Structural Therapy T Touch Therapy

**REILLY, DANIEL**
**Daniel Reilly**, 12 Bon Accord Trce, Aberdeen, **Aberdeenshire**, AB11 6DP, SCO.
(T) 01224 574616
Speciality: Alexander Technique.
P S (Ref:HM17151)

**REILLY, MERVYN**
**Mervyn Reilly**, 116 Cambridge Avenue, Whitley Bay, **Tyne and Wear**, NE26 1BA, ENG.
(T) 01912 533669
Speciality: Hypnosis.
B (Ref:HM17152)

**REITER, NED**
**Ned Reiter**, 54 The Avenue, Yeovil, **Somerset**, BA21 4BN, ENG.
(T) 01935 422488
Speciality: Herbalists.
M (Ref:HM17153)

**REJUVENATION**
**Rejuvenation**, Cariocca Business Park, Hellidon Cl, Ardwick, Manchester, **Manchester (Greater)**, M12 4AH, ENG.
(T) 01612 738216
Speciality: Holistic Healing. ✓
● **Complementary Therapist** Ms B
(T) 01612 73826 Q: IIHHT. M: IIHHT.
C Yrs. Est.: 5 (Ref:HM17154)

**REJUVENATION**
**Rejuvenation**, 76 Reddish Rd, Stockport, **Cheshire**, SK5 7QU, ENG.
(T) 01614 800843
Speciality: Reflexology.
● **Owner** Mrs E Armstead
S T (Ref:HM17155)

**RELATIONAL THERAPY**
**Relational Therapy**, 54 Sunnybank Rd, Brighouse, **Yorkshire (West)**, HD6 2AE, ENG.
(T) 01484 721365
Speciality: Psychotherapy.
● **Owner** Mrs K Squires
B (Ref:HM17156)

**RELAX**
**Relax**, Damon House, Mowbray St, Stockport, **Cheshire**, SK1 3EJ, ENG.
(T) 01614 761117
Speciality: Aromatherapy.
● **Owner** Mr G Smith
M O (Ref:HM17157)

**RELAX**
**Relax**, 5 Granville Gr, Stockton-On-Tees, **Cleveland**, TS20 2EP, ENG.
(T) 01642 559948
Speciality: Reflexology.
S T (Ref:HM17158)

**RELAX AROMA/REFLEXOLOGY**
**Relax Aromatherapy & Reflexology**, 183 Chalkwell Rd, Sittingbourne, **Kent**, ME10 1BJ, ENG.
(T) 01795 472869
Speciality: Complementary Medicines & Therapy.
● **Owner** Mrs C Atkins
C M (Ref:HM17159)

**RELAX AROMATHERAPY**
**Relax Aromatherapy**, 37 Clare Rd, Maidenhead, **Berkshire**, SL6 4DW, ENG.
(T) 01628 625452
Speciality: Aromatherapy.
M O (Ref:HM17160)

**RELAX NOW**
**Relax Now**, 50 Reeves Avenue, London, **London (Greater)**, NW9 8LP, ENG.
(T) 020 8200 5985
Speciality: Complementary Medicines & Therapy.
● **Owner** Miss I Hoffmann
M (Ref:HM17161)

**RELAX THERAPY**
**Relax Therapy**, 221 Broad St, Bromsgrove, **Worcestershire**, B61 8NL, ENG.
(T) 01527 559054 (F) 01527 559054
Speciality: Aromatherapy.
● **Owner** Miss B Andrews
M O (Ref:HM17162)

**RELAXAROMA**
**Relaxaroma**, 9 Feversham Avenue, Bournemouth, **Dorset**, BH8 9NH, ENG.
(T) 01202 398001 (F) 01202 398001
Speciality: Aromatherapy.
● **Owner** Mr S Sherman
M O (Ref:HM17163)

**RELAXATION CENTRE**
**Relaxation Centre**, 7 Waddington Rd, St. Albans, **Hertfordshire**, AL3 5EX, ENG.
(T) 01727 867071
Speciality: Complementary Medicines & Therapy.
● **Owner** Mrs V Spence
C M (Ref:HM17164)

**RELAXATION PHYSICAL**
**Relaxation Physical & Natural Therapies**, Cauldwell Hall Rd, Ipswich, **Suffolk**, IP4 5BN, ENG.
(T) 01473 270120
Speciality: Complementary Medicines & Therapy.
C M (Ref:HM17165)

**RELAXATION PLACE**
**Relaxation Place (The)**, 740a High Rd, Leytonstone, London, **London (Greater)**, E11 3AW, ENG.
(T) 020 8539 0001
(E) therelaxationplace@talk21.com
Speciality: Aromatherapy. ✓ [credit card]
● **Aromatherapist** Ms M Glover Q: HND. M: BABTAC.
C Yrs. Est.: 9 (Ref:HM17166)

**RELAXATION REMEDIAL THERAPIES**
**Relaxation Remedial Therapies**, 60 Place Farm Way, Monks Risborough, Princes Risborough, **Buckinghamshire**, HP27 9JY, ENG.
(T) 01844 347098
Speciality: Complementary Medicines & Therapy.
● **Owner** Ms J Durrant
C M (Ref:HM17167)

**RELAXATION STUDIO**
**Relaxation Studio (The)**, 103 Arleston Drive, Nottingham, **Nottinghamshire**, NG8 2GB, ENG.
(T) 01159 280700
Speciality: Complementary Medicines & Therapy.
● **Owner** Mrs S Peck
C M (Ref:HM17168)

**RELAXING HEALTHY OPTIONS**
**Relaxing Healthy Options**, St Stephens Rd, Hounslow, **London (Greater)**, TW3 2BW, ENG.
(T) 020 8572 1053 (F) 020 8572 1053
Speciality: Acupressure, Aromatherapy, Indian Head Massage, Massage (Therapeutic), Polarity Therapy, Reflexology.
● **Owner** Mrs J Sibley
S T (Ref:HM17169)

**RELEASE COUNS & TRAINING SVS**
**Release Counselling & Training Services**, 62 Station Rd, Amersham, **Buckinghamshire**, HP7 0BD, ENG.
(T) 01494 434077
Speciality: Psychotherapy.
● **Owner** Mrs L Nankin
B (Ref:HM17170)

**RELF, M J**
**M J Relf**, 116 Barkham Rd, Wokingham, **Berkshire**, RG41 2RP, ENG.
(T) 01189 891226
Speciality: Osteopathy.
P S T (Ref:HM17171)

**REMAS CLINIC**
**Remas Clinic**, 3 Jocelyn Pl, Dundalk, **County Louth**, IRE.
(T) 04293 52115
Speciality: Complementary Medicines & Therapy.
M (Ref:HM17172)

**REMEDIAL MASSAGE**
**Remedial Massage**, 93 Crookings Lane, Penwortham, Preston, **Lancashire**, PR1 0HX, ENG.
(T) 01772 741776
Speciality: Complementary Medicines & Therapy.
● **Owner** Ms C Hope
M (Ref:HM17173)

**REMEDIAL MASSAGE THERAPY**
**Remedial Massage Therapy**, Little Garth, Rowney Green Lane, Alvechurch, Birmingham, **Midlands (West)**, B48 7QS, ENG.
(T) 01214 456364 (F) 01214 456364
Speciality: Manipulation, Massage (Therapeutic), Deep Lymphatic Drainage. ✓
● **Owner/Remedial Massage Therapist** Mrs L Friedlander-Small Q: Dip.Rem.Massage. M: LCSP.
S Yrs. Est.: 5 (Ref:HM17174)

**REMEDIAL MASSAGE/SPORTS**
**Remedial Massage & Sports Therapy**, 303-307 Bury Old Rd, Heap, Bury, **Lancashire**, BL9 7JG, ENG.
(T) 01617 646729
Speciality: Physiotherapy, Remedial Massage. ✓
● **Complementary Therapist** Mr M Taylor M: LCSP.
P S T Yrs. Est.: 2 (Ref:HM17175)

**REMEDIES**
**Remedies**, 4 South St, Horncastle, **Lincolnshire**, LN9 6DT, ENG.
(T) 01507 524096 (F) 01790 754173
Speciality: Remedial Massage. ✓
● **Owner/Remedial Massage Therapist** Mrs V Smith M: LCSP.
C P Yrs. Est.: 12 (Ref:HM17176)

**REMEDIES ELECTROLYSIS**
**Remedies Electrolysis**, 97 Fore St, Topsham, Exeter, **Devon**, EX3 0HQ, ENG.
(T) 01392 877221
Speciality: Electrolysis.
T (Ref:HM17177)

**REMEDIES HEALTH CARE**
**Remedies Health Care**, 26 Bridge St, Dunfermline, **Fife**, KY12 8DA, SCO.
(T) 01383 721444
Speciality: Aromatherapy.
M O (Ref:HM17178)

**REMEDY BOX**
**Remedy Box (The)**, 16 Memorial Rd, Worsley, Manchester, **Manchester (Greater)**, M28 3AG, ENG.
(T) 01617 993971
Speciality: Complementary Medicines & Therapy.
● **Owner** Miss A Cassar
M (Ref:HM17179)

**RENAISSANCE HOLISTIC THRPY**
**Renaissance Holistic Therapy Centre**, 160 Gordon Rd, Harborne, Birmingham, **Midlands (West)**, B17 9EY, ENG.
(T) 01214 281449
Speciality: Aromatherapy.
M O (Ref:HM17180)

**RENDELL, MARCIA**
**Marcia Rendell**, 41 Church Rd, Poole, **Dorset**, BH14 0NN, ENG.
(T) 01202 749514
Speciality: Physiotherapy.
P S T (Ref:HM17181)

**RENDLE, S**
**S Rendle**, 37 Upland Drive, Plymouth, **Devon**, PL6 6BE, ENG.
(T) 01752 766399
Speciality: Chiropody, Nail Surgery. ✓
● **Surgical Chiropodist** S Rendle Q: MBChA, MSSCh. M: B.A.Ch.P, SSCh.
S Yrs. Est.: 25 (Ref:HM17182)

**RENFIELD CLINIC-HYPNOTHERAPY**
**Renfield Clinic Of Hypnotherapy**, 83 Renfield St, Glasgow, **Glasgow (City of)**, G2 1LP, SCO.
(T) 01413 531899
Speciality: Hypnotherapy.
● **Owner** Mr A Stewart


Key continued: Yrs.Est: Years Established Q: Qualifications M: Professional Membership ✓ Indemnity Insurance [credit card] Accept Credit Cards

B (Ref:HM17183)

**RENJI CHINESE MEDICINE CENTRE**

**Renji Chinese Medicine Centre**, 18-20 Sunbridge Rd, Bradford, **Yorkshire (West)**, BD1 2AY, ENG.
(T) 01274 731888
Speciality: Complementary Medicines & Therapy.
M (Ref:HM17184)

**RENJI CHINESE MEDICINE CENTRE**

**Renji Chinese Medicine Centre**, 11 Radcliffe St, Wolverton, Milton Keynes, **Buckinghamshire**, MK12 5DQ, ENG.
(T) 01908 316688
Speciality: Acupuncture.
● **Owner** Mr Z Yongzong
O (Ref:HM17185)

**RENMAN, TONY**

**Tony Renman**, Natural Health Clinic, 98 Cathedral Rd, Cardiff, **Glamorgan (Vale of)**, CF11 9LP, WAL.
(T) 029 2022 2221
Speciality: Complementary Medicines & Therapy.
● **Practice Manager** Mrs L Powell
M (Ref:HM17186)

**RENNIE, KATHRYN**

**Kathryn Rennie**, 7 Guillemot Gardens, Gosport, **Hampshire**, PO13 0RG, ENG.
(T) 01329 319263
Speciality: Reflexology.
● **Owner** Mrs K Rennie
S T (Ref:HM17187)

**RENSHAW, SARAH J**

**Sarah J Renshaw**, 316B Buxton Rd, Stockport, **Cheshire**, SK2 7DD, ENG.
(T) 01614 561793
Speciality: Chiropodists (Podiatrists).
● **Owner** Miss S Renshaw
S (Ref:HM17188)

**RENTON, ANGELA**

**Angela Renton**, 54 The Avenue, Yeovil, **Somerset**, BA21 4BN, ENG.
(T) 01935 422488
Speciality: Aromatherapy.
M O (Ref:HM17189)

**RENTOUL, J W**

**J W Rentoul**, 36 Fore St, Tregony, Truro, **Cornwall**, TR2 5RN, ENG.
(T) 01872 530233
Speciality: Acupuncture.
● **Owner** Dr J Rentoul
O (Ref:HM17190)

**RENTOUL, R W**

**R W Rentoul**, 3 The Orchard, Wolverhampton, **Midlands (West)**, WV6 9PF, ENG.
(T) 01902 758504
Speciality: Psychotherapy.
● **Owner** Mr R Rentoul
B (Ref:HM17191)

**RENWICK, SARAH NADINE**

**Alternative Medical Centre**, 55 High St, Cowbridge, **Glamorgan (Vale of)**, CF71 7AE, WAL.
(T) 01446 775066
(W) www.sarahrenwick.co.uk
Speciality: Acupressure, Acupuncture, Anthroposohical Medicine, Aromatherapy, Ayurvedic Medicine, Bach Remedies, Bowen Therapy, Complementary Therapy, Counselling, Cranial Osteopathy, Crystal Healing, Cupping, Dietician, Do-In, Dowsing, Faith Healing, Family Planning (Natural), Family Therapy, Feldenkrais Methodology, Floral Essence Therapy, Gem Essence Therapy, Gestalt Therapy, Hay Diet, Healer, Healing Therapy, Herbal Medicine, Holistic Healing, Indian Head Massage, Life Style Coaching, Macrobiotics, Manipulation, Massage (Therapeutic), Meditation, Moxibustion, Mud Therapy, Music Therapy, Nutritional Therapy, Oriental Diagnosis. ✔
● **Owner** Ms S Renwick Q: BABTAC.
O Yrs. Est.: 12 (Ref:HM17192)

**REN-YI**

**Ren-Yi**, Mercers Yard, High St East, Uppingham, Oakham, **Leicestershire**, LE15 9PY, ENG.
(T) 01572 822221 (F) 01572 822221
Speciality: Complementary Medicines & Therapy.
● **Partner** Mr N Hamilton
C M (Ref:HM17193)

**RENZO, REINALDO**

**Reinaldo Renzo**, 27 Buckland Cres, London, **London (Greater)**, NW3 5DH, ENG.
(T) 020 7722 2441 (F) 020 7722 2441
Speciality: Alexander Technique.
● **Owner** Mr R Renzo
P S (Ref:HM17194)

**REPLINGHAM CLINIC**

**Replingham Clinic (The)**, 95 Replingham Rd, Southfields, London, **London (Greater)**, SW18 5LU, ENG.
(T) 020 8875 1101
(W) www.replinghamclinic.co.uk
Speciality: Acupressure, Acupuncture, Alexander Technique, Aromatherapy, Bach Remedies, Chiropody, Complementary Therapy, Counselling, Cranial Osteopathy, Herbal Medicine, Homeopathy, Hypnosis, Hypnotherapy, Indian Head Massage, Massage (Therapeutic), Naturopathy, Osteopathy, Psychotherapy, Reflexology, Shiatsu, Visualisation Therapy, Emotional Freedom Technique (EFT), Past Life Regression. ✔
● **Osteopath** Mr S Byrne Q: DO. M: GOsC.
● **Chinese Doctor** Dr Y Zheng M: ATCM UK.
● **Owner** Ms S Chambers
● **Therapist/Counsellor** Dominic Carmel Boland Q: MNCH, MNCP. M: NCH, NCP.
● **Osteopath** Ms A Judah Q: BSc, DO.
● **Homeopath/Shiatsu Practitioner** Ms J McDonnell M: HMA.
● **Osteopath** Mr P Mason Q: DO.
● **Therapist** Ms J Sutherland Q: ITEC, MIPTI. M: IPTI.
● **Psychotherapist** Mr A Nneke Q: BA (Hons).
● **Practitioner** Mr P Cousin Q: B.Ac, BSc, Dip.CHM.
● **Homeopath/Therapist** Ms J Robinson Q: ITEC, MIFA. M: IFA.
● **Acupuncturist** Mr M Barry Q: LCSP, Lic.Ac, MBAcC. M: BAcC.
● **Counsellor/Hypnotherapist** Ms R Armitage Q: Dip.EH, NLP.
● **Homeopath** Ms B Geraghty Q: BA (Hons), RSHom. M: L.C.C.H.
● **Practitioner** Dr M Xie M: ATCM UK, RCHM.
● **Osteopath** Ms J Borsattino Q: DO.
C Yrs. Est.: 7 (Ref:HM17195)

**RESEK, G**

**G Resek**, 135 Harley St, London, **London (Greater)**, W1N 1DJ, ENG.
(T) 020 7935 6032
Speciality: Psychiatry.
B (Ref:HM17196)

**RESPIRATORY/ALLERGY DIAGNOSTIC**

**Respiratory & Allergy Diagnostic Services**, Charlemont Clinic Charlemont M, Dublin, **County Dublin**, IRE.
(T) 01418 8482
Speciality: Complementary Medicines & Therapy.
M (Ref:HM17197)

**RESTAN, L**

**Miss L Restan**, Devonshire Hospital, 29-31 Devonshire St, London, **London (Greater)**, W1N 1RF, ENG.
(T) 020 7486 2494
Speciality: Chiropodists (Podiatrists).
S (Ref:HM17198)

**RESTAN, LEILA**

**Miss Leila Restan**, 130 Harley St, London, **London (Greater)**, W1N 1AH, ENG.
(T) 020 7935 6558 (F) 020 7935 2385
Speciality: Chiropodists (Podiatrists).
● **Owner** Miss L Restan
S (Ref:HM17199)

**RETFORD CHIROPRACTIC CLINIC**

**Retford Chiropractic Clinic Ltd**, 67 Grove St, Retford, **Nottinghamshire**, DN22 6LA, ENG.
(T) 01777 710720 (F) 01777 710920
(E) simon@retfordchiro.co.uk
(W) www.retfordchiro.co.uk
Speciality: Aromatherapy, Chiropractic, Complementary Therapy, Cranial Osteopathy, Indian Head Massage, Kinesiology, Manipulation, Nutritional Therapy, Reflexology. ✔ CREDIT
● **Aromatherapist** Ms M King M: IFA.
● **Chiropractor** Mr S King Q: B.App.Sc. M: BCA.
P S Yrs. Est.: 10 (Ref:HM17200)

**RETIEF & ASSOCIATES**

**Derrick M Retief & Associates**, The Lewes Osteopathic Clinic, Fullers Passage, 19b High St, Lewes, **Sussex (East)**, BN7 2LN, ENG.
(T) 01273 474428
Speciality: Osteopathy.
P S T (Ref:HM17201)

**RETREAT**

**Retreat (The)**, Grafton, Hereford, **Herefordshire**, HR2 8BN, ENG.
(T) 01432 277644
Speciality: Complementary Medicines & Therapy.
● **Owner** Mrs S Dakin
M (Ref:HM17202)

**RETREAT**

**Retreat (The)**, 5 Corporation Buildings, Back Row, Denbigh, **Denbighshire**, LL16 3TE, WAL.
(T) 01745 817600
Speciality: Aromatherapy.
● **Owner** Mrs C Jones
M O (Ref:HM17203)

**REVEREND CAROL HADDERSLEY**

**Reverend Carol Haddersley**, 49 Tyler Drive, Rainham, **Kent**, ME8 9LU, ENG.
(T) 01634 370717 (F) 01634 235602
(E) carol@caheddersley.fsnet.co.uk
Speciality: Healer. ✔
● **Healer/Practitioner** Rev C Haddersley M: CHA.
C Yrs. Est.: 10 (Ref:HM17204)

**REVITALIZE**

**Revitalize**, 4 Fryer Avenue, Leamington Spa, **Warwickshire**, CV32 6HY, ENG.
(T) 01926 427684
Speciality: Aromatherapy. ✔
● **Owner/Aromatherapist** Mrs E Beddow Q: IIHHT, IIST. M: FHT, ICHT.
C Yrs. Est.: 3 (Ref:HM17205)

**REVIVAL HOLISTIC THERAPY CTRE**

**Revival Holistic Therapy Centre**, 45 Avery Rd, Sutton Coldfield, **Midlands (West)**, B73 6QB, ENG.
(T) 01213 551554
Speciality: Aromatherapy, Bach Remedies.
● **Owner** Mrs V Hinks
M O (Ref:HM17206)

**REYNOLDS, A R**

**A R Reynolds**, 25 Curlew Drive, Hythe, Southampton, **Hampshire**, SO45 3GB, ENG.
(T) 023 8084 1148
Speciality: Osteopathy.
● **Owner** Mr A Reynolds
P S T (Ref:HM17207)

**REYNOLDS, C**

**C Reynolds**, 6 Manor Avenue, Lyme Regis, **Dorset**, DT7 3AU, ENG.
(T) 01297 443814
Speciality: Herbalists.
● **Owner** Mrs C Reynolds
M (Ref:HM17208)

**REYNOLDS, CAROL**

**Carol Reynolds**, Morningside Health Clinic, 135 Buckingham Rd, Bletchley, Milton Keynes, **Buckinghamshire**, MK3 5JD, ENG.
(T) 01908 366957
Speciality: Homeopathy.
● **Partner** Mrs L Warr
M (Ref:HM17209)



Key: B Mind-Body Medicine C Complementary Medicine H Self Help Treatment M Medicinal Therapy O Oriental Medicine P Postural Therapy S Manipulative Structural Therapy T Touch Therapy

## REYNOLDS, DAVID
**David Reynolds**, 32 Station Rd, Marlow, **Buckinghamshire**, SL7 1NE, ENG.
(T) 01628 476443 (F) 01628 476443
Speciality: Osteopathy.
● **Owner** Mr D Reynolds
P S T (**Ref:**HM17210)

## REYNOLDS, DAVID
**David Reynolds**, 63a Smithbrook Kilns, Cranleigh, **Surrey**, GU6 8JJ, ENG.
(T) 01483 275500
Speciality: Acupuncture.
O (**Ref:**HM17211)

## REYNOLDS, HELEN
**Helen Reynolds**, 8a Cooper St, Bideford, **Devon**, EX39 2DA, ENG.
(T) 01237 422226
Speciality: Chiropodists (Podiatrists).
● **Owner** Mrs H Reynolds
S (**Ref:**HM17212)

## REYNOLDS, MARION
**Marion Reynolds**, 3 White Court, Kings Ride, Alfriston, **Sussex (East)**, BN26 5XP, ENG.
(T) 01323 871668
Speciality: Reflexology.
● **Owner** Ms M Reynolds Q: BTER, MAR.
S T (**Ref:**HM17213)

## REYNOLDS, NATHAN
**Nathan Reynolds**, 249A Otley Rd, Leeds, **Yorkshire (West)**, LS16 5LQ, ENG.
(T) 01132 745126
Speciality: Osteopathy.
● **Partner** Mrs N Sell
P S T (**Ref:**HM17214)

## REYNOLDS, PAULA
**Paula Reynolds**, 101 Eastwood Rd, Rayleigh, **Essex**, SS6 7LA, ENG.
(T) 01268 778894
Speciality: Complementary Medicines & Therapy.
C M (**Ref:**HM17215)

## REYNOLDS, TESS
**Tess Reynolds**, 14 St Johns Hill, Ellesmere, **Shropshire**, SY12 0HA, ENG.
(T) 01691 622006
Speciality: Acupuncture. ✔
● **Acupuncturist** Ms T Reynolds Q: Lic.Ac. M: BAcC.
O Yrs. Est.: 10 (**Ref:**HM17216)

## RHAM, TRICIA
**Tricia Rham**, 2 Castlegate, Cockermouth, **Cumbria**, CA13 9EU, ENG.
(T) 01900 825332
(E) triciabgc@aol.com
Speciality: Chiropractic, Counselling, Cranio-Sacral Therapy, McTimoney Chiropractic, Metamorphic Therapy. ✔
● **Owner** Miss T Rham Q: CST, DC.
S Yrs. Est.: 12 (**Ref:**HM17217)

## RHIANNON'S CAT
**Rhiannon's Cat**, G24 Pyke Aisle, Main Hall, Grange Precinct, Birkenhead, **Merseyside**, CH41 2YL, ENG.
(T) 01516 447915 (F) 01516 447915
Speciality: Aromatherapy.
● **Owner** Ms A Mackenzie
M O (**Ref:**HM17218)

## RHIANS BEAUTY & THERAPY CENTRE
**Rhians Beauty & Therapy Centre**, 53 Teme St, Tenbury Wells, **Worcestershire**, WR15 8AE, ENG.
(T) 01584 811898
Speciality: Aromatherapy.
● **Owner** Mrs R Robinson
M O (**Ref:**HM17219)

## RHIDIAN & COLLEAGUES
**E Rhidian & Colleagues**, Farnham Physiotherapy & Sports Clinic, 5 Hart House, The Hart, Farnham, **Surrey**, GU9 7HA, ENG.
(T) 01252 726479
Speciality: Physiotherapy.
P S T (**Ref:**HM17220)

## RHODES HOUSE NATURAL HEALTH
**Rhodes House Natural Health Clinic**, Rhodes House, 112 St Leonards Gate, Lancaster, **Lancashire**, LA1 1NN, ENG.
(T) 01524 848106
Speciality: Complementary Medicines & Therapy.
C M (**Ref:**HM17221)

## RHODES, B
**B Rhodes**, 28 Stanley St, Bourne, **Lincolnshire**, PE10 9BL, ENG.
(T) 01778 426101
Speciality: Chiropodists (Podiatrists).
● **Owner** Mr B Rhodes
S (**Ref:**HM17222)

## RHODES, E A
**E A Rhodes**, 39 Carleton View, Pontefract, **Yorkshire (West)**, WF8 2SD, ENG.
(T) 01977 701457
Speciality: Chiropodists (Podiatrists).
● **Owner** Mrs E Rhodes
S (**Ref:**HM17223)

## RHODES, GEORGINA
**Georgina Rhodes**, Croft Barton, Bishops Caundle, Sherborne, **Dorset**, DT9 5NG, ENG.
(T) 01963 23444
Speciality: Acupuncture.
● **Owner** Miss G Rhodes
O (**Ref:**HM17224)

## RHODES, GEORGINA
**Georgina Rhodes**, 10 Redwing St, Milborne Port, Sherborne, **Dorset**, DT9 5AR, ENG.
(T) 01963 251316
Speciality: Acupuncture.
O (**Ref:**HM17225)

## RHODES, J D & E M
**J D & E M Rhodes**, Edward House, 217A King Cross Rd, Halifax, **Yorkshire (West)**, HX1 3JL, ENG.
(T) 01422 353866
Speciality: Chiropodists (Podiatrists).
S (**Ref:**HM17226)

## RHODES, P
**P Rhodes**, 140 West End Avenue, Harrogate, **Yorkshire (North)**, HG2 9BT, ENG.
(T) 01423 506893
Speciality: Chiropodists (Podiatrists).
● **Owner** Ms P Rhodes
S (**Ref:**HM17227)

## RHODES, RACHEL MISPA
**Rachel Mispa Rhodes M R X S**, Maybush Medical Centre, Belle Isle Health Park, Potobello Rd, Wakefield, **Yorkshire (West)**, WF1 5PN, ENG.
(T) 01924 328143
Speciality: Complementary Medicines & Therapy.
C M (**Ref:**HM17228)

## RHODES, SIMON
**Simon Rhodes**, 3 Queens Cl, Edgware, **London (Greater)**, HA8 7PU, ENG.
(T) 020 8905 3264
Speciality: Chiropodists (Podiatrists).
● **Owner** Mr S Rhodes
S (**Ref:**HM17229)

## RHODES, SIMON P
**Simon P Rhodes**, 67 Kilburn High Rd, London, **London (Greater)**, NW6 6HY, ENG.
(T) 020 7624 1576
Speciality: Chiropodists (Podiatrists).
S (**Ref:**HM17230)

## RHODIE, ANDREA
**Andrea Rhodie**, 210 Battlefield Rd, Glasgow, **Glasgow (City of)**, G42 9HN, SCO.
(T) 01416 498947
Speciality: Aromatherapy. ✔
● **Clinical Aromatherapist** Ms A Rhodie M: HAF.
C Yrs. Est.: 2 (**Ref:**HM17231)

## RHONA INGLIS AROMATHERAPY
**Rhona Inglis Aromatherapy**, 11A Grange Pl, Kilmarnock, **Ayrshire (East)**, KA1 2AB, SCO.
(T) 01563 525207
Speciality: Aromatherapy.
M O (**Ref:**HM17232)

## RHONE, B
**B Rhone**, 4 Offa, Chirk, Wrexham, LL14 5BP, WAL.
(T) 01691 773203
Speciality: Osteopathy.
P S T (**Ref:**HM17233)

## RHYS, BILL
**Bill Rhys**, 6 Church St, Poole, **Dorset**, BH15 1JP, ENG.
(T) 01202 678947
Speciality: Complementary Medicines & Therapy.
● **Owner** Mr B Rhys
C M (**Ref:**HM17234)

## RHYTHMIC MASSAGE PRACTICE
**Rhythmic Massage Practice**, 1 Medway Cottages, Lower Rd, Forest Row, **Sussex (East)**, RH18 5HE, ENG.
(T) 01342 823558
Speciality: Complementary Medicines & Therapy.
● **Owner** Mrs R Gilde
C M (**Ref:**HM17235)

## RIBBINS, K J
**K J Ribbins**, Lutterworth Physiotherapy Practice, 7 High St, Lutterworth, **Leicestershire**, LE17 4AT, ENG.
(T) 01455 550270
Speciality: Physiotherapy.
● **Owner** Mrs K Ribbins
P S T (**Ref:**HM17236)

## RICARDO, D R
**D R Ricardo**, Saddlers House, Princes St, Montgomery, **Powys**, SY15 6PY, WAL.
(T) 01686 668753
Speciality: Homeopathy.
M (**Ref:**HM17237)

## RICARDO, LINDA
**Linda Ricardo**, 11 The Gardens, Brookmans Park, Hatfield, **Hertfordshire**, AL9 7UL, ENG.
(T) 01707 650521
Speciality: Reflexology.
S T (**Ref:**HM17238)

## RICE, LAVINIA
**Lavinia Rice**, 16 Worthing Rd, Ingol, Preston, **Lancashire**, PR2 3UQ, ENG.
(T) 01772 732430
Speciality: Clairvoyants & Palmists.
● **Owner** Mrs L Rice
B (**Ref:**HM17239)

## RICE, LOUISE
**Louise Rice**, Church Cl, Gnosall, Stafford, **Staffordshire**, ST20 0DD, ENG.
(T) 07966 213805
Speciality: Chiropodists (Podiatrists).
● **Owner** Ms L Rice
S (**Ref:**HM17240)

## RICE, OWEN
**Owen Rice**, 9 Firlee, East Kilbride, Glasgow, **Glasgow (City of)**, G75 8SZ, SCO.
(T) 01355 234779
Speciality: Chiropodists (Podiatrists).
S (**Ref:**HM17241)

## RICH, ELIZABETH
**Elizabeth Rich**, The Camellias, 364 London Rd, Slough, **Berkshire**, SL3 7HX, ENG.
(T) 01753 543500
Speciality: Chiropodists (Podiatrists).
S (**Ref:**HM17242)

## RICHARD ANDREWS HAIR & BEAUTY
**Richard Andrews Hair & Beauty**, 15 Stanley Way, Orpington, **Kent**, BR5 2HE, ENG.
(T) 01689 829042
Speciality: Complementary Medicines & Therapy.
● **Owner** Mr R Andrews
M (**Ref:**HM17243)

## RICHARD GIBBONS - ACUPUNCT
**Richard Gibbons - Acupuncturist**, Bristol Natural Health Service, 310 Gloucester Rd, Horfield, Bristol, BS7 8TJ, ENG.
(T) 01179 444448



Key continued: **Yrs.Est:** Years Established **Q:** Qualifications **M:** Professional Membership ✔ Indemnity Insurance ▭ Accept Credit Cards

(E) richardgibbons@beeb.net
Speciality: Acupuncture.
● **Acupuncturist** Mr R Gibbons
(T) 01179 739541 Q: Lic.Ac. M: BAcC.
O Yrs. Est.: 6 (Ref:HM17244)

## RICHARD JUDD CHIROPODIST

**Richard Judd Chiropodist**, 31 Hambledon Rd, Clanfield, Waterlooville, **Hampshire**, PO8 0QU, ENG.
(T) 023 9259 5217
Speciality: Chiropodists (Podiatrists).
S (Ref:HM17245)

## RICHARDS OSTEOPATHIC CLINIC

**Richards Osteopathic Clinic & Natural Health Centre**, 67 Three Bridges Rd, Crawley, **Sussex (West)**, RH10 1JJ, ENG.
(T) 01293 562601
Speciality: Osteopathy.
● **Partner** Mr J Richards
P S T (Ref:HM17246)

## RICHARDS, B

**B Richards**, 44 Sadler St, Middleton, Manchester, **Manchester (Greater)**, M24 5DJ, ENG.
(T) 01616 430867
Speciality: Chiropodists (Podiatrists).
S (Ref:HM17247)

## RICHARDS, CARMEL

**Carmel Richards**, Pembrey Physiotherapy Clinic, Plas Carmel, Heo Y Mynydd, Pembrey, Burry Port, **Carmarthenshire**, SA16 0AZ, **WAL**.
(T) 01554 834241 (F) 01554 834051
Speciality: Physiotherapy.
● **Owner** Ms C Richards
P S T (Ref:HM17248)

## RICHARDS, CLAIRE

**Claire Richards**, Ben Venuto, Pitmore Lane, Pennington, Lymington, **Hampshire**, SO41 8LL, ENG.
(T) 01590 683322
Speciality: Aura Therapy, Bach Remedies, Colour Therapy, Crystal Healing, Dowsing, Faith Healing, Healer, Healing Therapy, Holistic Healing, Indian Head Massage, Massage (Therapeutic), Reflexology, Reiki, Spiritual Healing, Reflexology with specific colour application with a crystal torch to the reflexes of the feet.
● **Reflexologist/Masseuse**
Ms C Richards Q: IIHHT. M: FHT.
T Yrs. Est.: 5 (Ref:HM17249)

## RICHARDS, DAVID

**David Richards**, 13 Kingsley Rd, Chester, **Cheshire**, CH3 5RR, ENG.
(T) 01244 314875
Speciality: Chiropody.
● **Chiropodist (Podiatrist)**
Mr D Richards Q: MBChA, MSSCh.
M Yrs. Est.: 2 (Ref:HM17250)

## RICHARDS, GERALDINE

**Geraldine Richards**, 10 Jezreels Rd, Gillingham, **Kent**, ME7 5NF, ENG.
(T) 01634 570223
Speciality: Chiropodists (Podiatrists).
S (Ref:HM17251)

## RICHARDS, HILARY

**Hilary Richards**, 214 Thirlmere Avenue, Tilehurst, Reading, **Berkshire**, RG30 6XJ, ENG.
(T) 01189 412547
Speciality: Chiropodists (Podiatrists).
S (Ref:HM17252)

## RICHARDS, J

**J Richards**, Newman Turner Practice, 111 Norton Way South, Letchworth, **Hertfordshire**, SG6 1NY, ENG.
(T) 01462 684232
Speciality: Hypnotherapy.
B (Ref:HM17253)

## RICHARDS, J

**Richards J**, Windmill Hill Clinic, Whinbush Rd, Hitchin, **Hertfordshire**, SG5 1PJ, ENG.
(T) 01462 450264
Speciality: Hypnotherapy.
B (Ref:HM17254)

## RICHARDS, JESSICA

**Jessica Richards**, Crofts Natural Health, 16A High St, Hitchin, **Hertfordshire**, SG5 1AT, ENG.
(T) 07071 223661
Speciality: Hypnosis.
● **Owner** Ms J Richards
B (Ref:HM17255)

## RICHARDS, JESSICA

**Jessica Richards**, London Medical Centre, 144 Harley St, London, **London (Greater)**, W1N 1AH, ENG.
(T) 020 7935 0023 (F) 020 7935 5972
Speciality: Hypnosis.
● **Manager** Mr P Gainsborough
B (Ref:HM17256)

## RICHARDS, JONATHAN

**Jonathan Richards**, 48 Bendysh Rd, Bushey, Watford, **Hertfordshire**, WD2 2HY, ENG.
(T) 01923 213174
Speciality: Chiropodists (Podiatrists).
● **Owner** Mr M Hinde
S (Ref:HM17257)

## RICHARDS, KATHY

**Kathy Richards**, 88 Wroxham Gardens, Potters Bar, **Hertfordshire**, EN6 3DL, ENG.
(T) 01707 850034
Speciality: Reflexology.
S T (Ref:HM17258)

## RICHARDS, KERRY

**Kerry Richards**, 97 Town Lane, Mobberley, Knutsford, **Cheshire**, WA16 7HH, ENG.
(T) 01565 872157
Speciality: Chiropodists (Podiatrists).
● **Owner** Mrs K Perry
S (Ref:HM17259)

## RICHARDS, KERRY L

**Kerry L Richards**, 84 Congleton Rd, Sandbach, **Cheshire**, CW11 1HG, ENG.
(T) 01270 763926
Speciality: Chiropody, Podiatry.
● **Chiropodist (Podiatrist)**
Ms K Richards Q: DPodM, S.R.Ch. M: S.C.P.
M Yrs. Est.: 6 (Ref:HM17260)

## RICHARDS, M J

**M J Richards**, 71 Woodbury Avenue, Wells, **Somerset**, BA5 2XP, ENG.
(T) 01749 677482
Speciality: Chiropody.
● **Chiropodist** Ms M Richards Q: MSSCh, SRN, SRNHV. M: B.A.Ch.P, SRNHV, SSCh.
M Yrs. Est.: 12 (Ref:HM17261)

## RICHARDS, P

**P Richards**, 60 Castle Rd, Worthing, **Sussex (West)**, BN13 1DQ, ENG.
(T) 01903 262826
Speciality: Chiropodists (Podiatrists).
S (Ref:HM17262)

## RICHARDS, PAUL

**Paul Richards**, 12A Alexandra St, Nottingham, **Nottinghamshire**, NG5 1AY, ENG.
(T) 01159 857372
Speciality: Psychotherapy.
● **Owner** Mr P Richards
B (Ref:HM17263)

## RICHARDS, R

**R Richards**, University Of Research International, 9 Alliston Gardens, Northampton, **Northamptonshire**, NN2 6DS, ENG.
(T) 01604 604542
Speciality: Psychology.
B (Ref:HM17264)

## RICHARDS, VERONICA

**Veronica Richards**, 4 Evesham Rd, Cleeve Prior, Evesham, **Worcestershire**, WR11 5JX, ENG.
(T) 01789 778543
Speciality: Homeopathy.
● **Owner** Miss V Richards
M (Ref:HM17265)

## RICHARDSON CLINIC

**Richardson Clinic (The)**, 37 Westgate, Heckmondwike, **Yorkshire (West)**, WF16 0HE, ENG.
(T) 01924 402763 (F) 01924 500025
Speciality: Acupuncture, Aromatherapy, Chiropody, Counselling, Homeopathy, Hypnosis, Massage (Therapeutic), Physiotherapy, Psychotherapy, Vega Test, Full Body Screening Medical Check, Bio-Energetic Testing, Colonic Hydrotherapy.
● **Therapist** Miss Jaikaran Q: RGN.
C Yrs. Est.: 15 (Ref:HM17266)

## RICHARDSON, A

**A Richardson**, Far End, Pyebush Lane, Acle, Norwich, **Norfolk**, NR13 3QZ, ENG.
(T) 01493 751544
Speciality: Hypnotherapy.
● **Owner** Mr A Richardson
B (Ref:HM17267)

## RICHARDSON, ALAN

**Complementary Medicine Group**, 24 St Stephens Rd, Norwich, **Norfolk**, NR1 3QU, ENG.
(T) 01603 768511
(E) alanr@clara.co.uk
(W) www.kinesiology-east.co.uk
Speciality: Bio-energetics, Complementary Therapy, Counselling, Hypnotherapy, Kinesiology, Massage (Therapeutic), Nutritional Therapy, Phytotherapy, Psychotherapy, Stress Therapy, Vitamin Therapy.
● **Complementary Therapist**
Mr A Richardson Q: NLP.
● **Clinical Psychologist**
Mr R Barnes
(T) 01603 614914
B C Yrs. Est.: 15 (Ref:HM17268)

## RICHARDSON, BRIAN J

**Brian J Richardson**, Mapleleaf Podiatry, 124 St Pancras, Chichester, **Sussex (West)**, PO19 4LH, ENG.
(T) 01243 538535
(E) b.j.richardson@talk21.com
Speciality: Biomechanics, Gait Analysis, Orthotics, Standard medical treatment. Biomechanical Analysis and Bespoke Biomechanical, Sport injuries.
● **Owner/Podiatrist** Mr B Richardson Q: B.Ed, BA, DPodM, M.S.C.P.
S Yrs. Est.: 10 (Ref:HM17269)

## RICHARDSON, C E

**C E Richardson**, 197A Shirley Rd, Croydon, **Surrey**, CR0 8SB, ENG.
(T) 020 8654 4670
Speciality: Chiropodists (Podiatrists).
● **Owner** Miss C Richardson
S (Ref:HM17270)

## RICHARDSON, CAROL

**Carol Richardson**, 4 Old Foundry Court, Old Rd, Acle, Norwich, **Norfolk**, NR13 3QG, ENG.
(T) 01493 751544
Speciality: Bach Remedies.
M (Ref:HM17271)

## RICHARDSON, CHRIS

**Chris Richardson**, The Swan Clinic, Vicarage St, Warminster, **Wiltshire**, BA12 8JE, ENG.
(T) 01985 217158
Speciality: Chiropractic.
P S T (Ref:HM17272)

## RICHARDSON, CYRIL

**Cyril Richardson**, 6 Harpur Rd, Walsall, **Midlands (West)**, WS4 2DN, ENG.
(T) 01922 614294
Speciality: Chiropody, Podiatry.
● **Chiropodist** Mr C Richardson Q: BA. M: B.A.Ch.P.
C Yrs. Est.: 12 (Ref:HM17273)

## RICHARDSON, D L

**D L Richardson**, Cornerways, 121 Torquay Rd, Paignton, **Devon**, TQ3 2SF, ENG.
(T) 01803 557766
Speciality: Chiropodists (Podiatrists).
S (Ref:HM17274)

## RICHARDSON, DAVID

**David Richardson**, 253 Wells Rd, Bristol, BS4 2PH, ENG.
(T) 01179 710221
Speciality: Osteopathy.



Key: B Mind-Body Medicine C Complementary Medicine H Self Help Treatment M Medicinal Therapy O Oriental Medicine P Postural Therapy S Manipulative Structural Therapy T Touch Therapy

● **Partner** Mr D Richardson
**P S T** (**Ref:**HM17275)

### RICHARDSON, DEBORAH

**Deborah Richardson**, The Chiropody And Podiatry Clinic, Rydal Mount, St Mary's Trce, Heworth, Gateshead, **Tyne and Wear**, NE10 0NY, ENG.
**(T)** 01914 695035
**Speciality:** Chiropody, Podiatry.
● **Owner/Chiropodist**
Mrs D Richardson **Q:** DPodM, M.S.C.P, S.R.Ch. **M:** S.C.P.
**S** (**Ref:**HM17276)

### RICHARDSON, DIANA

**Diana Richardson**, 95 Goddard Avenue, Swindon, **Wiltshire**, SN1 4HT, ENG.
**(T)** 01793 695185
**Speciality:** Aromatherapy.
**M O** (**Ref:**HM17277)

### RICHARDSON, ELAINE

**Elaine Richardson**, Karuna, 2 Stafford Gardens, West Stafford, Dorchester, **Dorset**, DT2 8XA, ENG.
**(T)** 01305 266607
**Speciality:** Alexander Technique.
● **Owner** Mrs E Richardson
**P S** (**Ref:**HM17278)

### RICHARDSON, J

**J Richardson**, 26 Belle Vue, Bude, **Cornwall**, EX23 8JS, ENG.
**(T)** 01288 355451
**Speciality:** Chiropodists (Podiatrists).
**S** (**Ref:**HM17279)

### RICHARDSON, J

**J Richardson**, The Devon Parade Clinic, 322 Wellingborough Rd, Northampton, **Northamptonshire**, NN1 4EP, ENG.
**(T)** 01604 622999
**Speciality:** Reflexology.
● **Owner** Mr A Costain
**S T** (**Ref:**HM17280)

### RICHARDSON, JACQUI

**Jacqui Richardson**, 111 Lynmouth Cres, Furzton, **Buckinghamshire**, MK4 1JZ, ENG.
**(T)** 01908 503213
**Speciality:** Reflexology.
**S T** (**Ref:**HM17281)

### RICHARDSON, JANET

**Janet Richardson**, Honeywood Cottage, Sunset Lane, West Chiltington, Pulborough, **Sussex (West)**, RH20 2NY, ENG.
**(T)** 01798 812102
**Speciality:** Biomechanics, Chiropody. ✔
● **Owner/Chiropodist**
Mrs J Richardson **Q:** MBChA, MSSCh.
**C** **Yrs. Est.:** 11 (**Ref:**HM17282)

### RICHARDSON, JILL

**Jill Richardson**, Blackberry Orthopaedic Clinic, Blackberry Court, Walnut Tree, Milton Keynes, **Buckinghamshire**, MK7 7PB, ENG.
**(T)** 01908 604666
**Speciality:** Physiotherapy.
**P S T** (**Ref:**HM17283)

### RICHARDSON, MARTIN

**Martin Richardson**, 18 Addison Rd, Chesham, **Buckinghamshire**, HP5 2BD, ENG.
**(T)** 01494 771789
**Speciality:** Complementary Medicines & Therapy.
● **Owner** Mr M Richardson
**C M** (**Ref:**HM17284)

### RICHARDSON, NAOMI

**Naomi Richardson**, 2 Farfield, Kidderminster, **Worcestershire**, DY10 1UG, ENG.
**(T)** 01562 829297
**Speciality:** Psychotherapy.
● **Owner** Mrs N Richardson
**B** (**Ref:**HM17285)

### RICHARDSON, P

**P Richardson**, 59 Queen St, Great Harwood, Blackburn, **Lancashire**, BB6 7NH, ENG.
**(T)** 01254 876022
**Speciality:** Chiropodists (Podiatrists).
● **Owner** Mr P Richardson
**S** (**Ref:**HM17286)

### RICHARDSON, R F

**R F Richardson**, 126 Haydon Park Rd, London, **London (Greater)**, SW19 8JT, ENG.
**(T)** 020 8542 0854
**Speciality:** Physiotherapy.
● **Owner** Mr R Richardson
**P S T** (**Ref:**HM17287)

### RICHARDSON, ROSEMARY

**Rosemary Richardson**, 2 Craigdam Cottages, Tarves, Ellon, **Aberdeenshire**, AB41 7NR, SCO.
**(T)** 01651 851612
**Speciality:** Reflexology.
**S T** (**Ref:**HM17288)

### RICHARDSON, S M W

**S M W Richardson**, 30 Salop Rd, Oswestry, **Shropshire**, SY11 2NU, ENG.
**(T)** 01691 671171
**Speciality:** Homeopathy.
**M** (**Ref:**HM17289)

### RICHARDSON, SALLY

**Sally Richardson**, 255/3 Canongate, Edinburgh, **Edinburgh (City of)**, EH8 8BQ, SCO.
**(T)** 01315 583167
**Speciality:** Reflexology.
**S T** (**Ref:**HM17290)

### RICHARDSON, SARAH

**Sarah Richardson**, 37 Brookly Gardens, Fleet, **Hampshire**, GU13 9BU, ENG.
**(T)** 01252 684751
**Speciality:** Reflexology.
**S T** (**Ref:**HM17291)

### RICHARDSON, SHEILA

**Sheila Richardson**, The Homoepathic Centre, 13A North St, Havant, **Hampshire**, PO9 1PW, ENG.
**(T)** 023 9247 1757
**Speciality:** Acupuncture.
**O** (**Ref:**HM17292)

### RICHARDSON, SUSAN

**Susan Richardson**, 25 Cypress Cl, Taverham, Norwich, **Norfolk**, NR8 6QG, ENG.
**(T)** 01603 861019
**Speciality:** Hypnosis.
**B** (**Ref:**HM17293)

### RICHARDSON, T G

**T G Richardson**, 4 Buttermere Gr, West Auckland, Bishop Auckland, **County Durham**, DL14 9LG, ENG.
**(T)** 01388 832040
**Speciality:** Hypnosis.
**B** (**Ref:**HM17294)

### RICHFIELD, MARISE

**Marise Richfield**, Slaid Hill Medical Centre, 18-24 Slaid Hill Court, Leeds, **Yorkshire (West)**, LS17 8TJ, ENG.
**(T)** 01132 888282
**Speciality:** Osteopathy.
● **Owner** Miss M Richfield
**P S T** (**Ref:**HM17295)

### RICHIE, ELIZABETH

**Elizabeth Richie**, Axe View, Axmouth, Seaton, **Devon**, EX12 4BQ, ENG.
**(T)** 01297 21443
**Speciality:** Acupuncture.
**O** (**Ref:**HM17296)

### RICHMOND CHIROPRACTIC CLINIC

**Richmond Chiropractic Clinic**, 349 Richmond Rd, Twickenham, **London (Greater)**, TW1 2ES, ENG.
**(T)** 020 8744 9117
**Speciality:** Chiropractic.
**P S T** (**Ref:**HM17297)

### RICHMOND HEALING CENTRE

**Richmond Healing Centre (The)**, Retreat Rd, Richmond, **Surrey**, TW9 1NN, ENG.
**(T)** 07071 881120
**Speciality:** Complementary Medicines & Therapy.
● **Owner** Ms S Powell
**C M** (**Ref:**HM17298)

### RICHMOND HOUSE PHYSIO

**Richmond House Private Physiotherapy Clinic**, Richmond House, Stockport Rd, Hyde, **Cheshire**, SK14 5QT, ENG.
**(T)** 01613 682496
**Speciality:** Physiotherapy.
**P S T** (**Ref:**HM17299)

### RICHMOND OSTEOPATHIC

**Richmond Osteopathic & Sports Clinic**, Richmond Athletic Ground, Kew Foot Rd, Richmond, **Surrey**, TW9 2SS, ENG.
**(T)** 020 8940 2336
**Speciality:** Osteopathy.
**P S T** (**Ref:**HM17300)

### RICHMOND PHYSIOTHERAPY

**Richmond Physiotherapy**, 16 King St, Richmond, **Surrey**, TW9 1ND, ENG.
**(T)** 020 8332 1132 **(F)** 020 8948 7906
**Speciality:** Massage (Therapeutic), Physiotherapy, Reflexology, Sports Massage, Cranial Therapy. ✔ CREDIT
● **Physiotherapist** Ms K Sheehy **Q:** Grad Dip Phys, MCSP, SRP. **M:** CSP.
**S** **Yrs. Est.:** 5 (**Ref:**HM17301)

### RICHMOND REFLEXOLOGY

**Richmond Reflexology**, 16 King St, Richmond, **Surrey**, TW9 1ND, ENG.
**(T)** 020 8322 1132 **(F)** 020 8948 7906
**Speciality:** Reflexology.
● **Partner** Mrs E Wall
**S T** (**Ref:**HM17302)

### RICHMOND, CLAIRE

**Claire Richmond**, The Radlett Practice, 107 Watling St, Radlett, **Hertfordshire**, WD7 7NG, ENG.
**(T)** 01923 855884
**Speciality:** Osteopathy.
**P S T** (**Ref:**HM17303)

### RICHMOND, CLARE

**Clare Richmond**, Treatment Centre, Portmill Lane, Hitchin, **Hertfordshire**, SG4 9TH, ENG.
**(T)** 01462 713031
**Speciality:** Osteopathy.
**P S T** (**Ref:**HM17304)

### RICHMOND, E A

**E A Richmond**, 198 Kilraughts Rd, Ballymoney, **County Antrim**, BT53 8NW, NIR.
**(T)** 028 2766 2981
**Speciality:** Chiropodists (Podiatrists).
● **Owner** Mrs E Richmond
**S** (**Ref:**HM17305)

### RICHMOND, G R

**G R Richmond**, The Cottage, Little London, Heathfield, **Sussex (East)**, TN21 0NU, ENG.
**(T)** 01435 862091
**Speciality:** Physiotherapy.
● **Owner** Mr G Richmond
**P S T** (**Ref:**HM17306)

### RICHMOND, T J

**T J Richmond**, 101 Fydell St, Boston, **Lincolnshire**, PE21 8LG, ENG.
**(T)** 01205 311786
**Speciality:** Osteopathy.
● **Owner** Mr T Richmond
**P S T** (**Ref:**HM17307)

### RICHMOND-SMITH, P

**Miss P Richmond-Smith**, 158 Knollmead, Surbiton, **Surrey**, KT5 9QW, ENG.
**(T)** 020 8337 2581
**Speciality:** Osteopathy.
**P S T** (**Ref:**HM17308)

### RICKARD, CLIVE

**Clive Rickard**, 38 Moorgate Rd, Rotherham, **Yorkshire (South)**, S60 2AG, ENG.
**(T)** 01709 828868
**Speciality:** Osteopathy.
● **Owner** Mr C Rickard
**P S T** (**Ref:**HM17309)

### RICKARD, CLIVE A

**Clive A Rickard**, 45 Clarence Rd, Chesterfield, **Derbyshire**, S40 1LQ, ENG.
**(T)** 01246 277711
**Speciality:** Osteopathy.



Key continued: **Yrs.Est:** Years Established **Q:** Qualifications **M:** Professional Membership ✔ Indemnity Insurance CREDIT Accept Credit Cards

● **Owner** Mr C Rickard
P S T (Ref:HM17310)

**RICKETT, MARION**

**Marion Rickett**, 40 High St, Hemel Hempstead, **Hertfordshire**, HP1 3AE, ENG.
(T) 01442 250294
Speciality: Psychotherapy.
B (Ref:HM17311)

**RICKETTS, ANNE**

**Anne Ricketts**, 6 Yolsum Cl, Haddenham, Aylesbury, **Buckinghamshire**, HP17 8DG, ENG.
(T) 01844 292069
Speciality: Chiropodists (Podiatrists).
S (Ref:HM17312)

**RIDDELL, CAROLINE**

**Caroline Riddell**, 239 Balham High Rd, London, **London (Greater)**, SW17 7BD, ENG.
(T) 020 8682 4849
Speciality: Hypnosis.
● **Owner** Mrs C Riddell
B (Ref:HM17313)

**RIDER, J**

**J Rider**, 33 Severn Rd, Aveley, South Ockendon, **Essex**, RM15 4NR, ENG.
(T) 01708 864831
Speciality: Chiropodists (Podiatrists).
● **Owner** Mrs J Rider
S (Ref:HM17314)

**RIDGE, D**

**D Ridge Osteopath**, 10 Canon St, Aberdare, **Glamorgan (Vale of)**, CF44 7AT, WAL.
(T) 01685 870000
Speciality: Manipulation, Massage (Therapeutic), Osteopathy. ✔
● **Osteopath** Mr D Ridge Q: DO. M: GOsC.
S Yrs. Est.: 10 (Ref:HM17315)

**RIDGE, D**

**D Ridge Osteopath**, 14 Church St, Merthyr Tydfil, **Glamorgan (Vale of)**, CF47 0AY, WAL.
(T) 01685 388111
Speciality: Manipulation, Massage (Therapeutic), Osteopathy. ✔
● **Osteopath** Mr D Ridge Q: DO. M: GOsC.
S Yrs. Est.: 2 (Ref:HM17316)

**RIDGEWAY CHIROPRACTIC CLINIC**

**Ridgeway Chiropractic Clinic**, First Floor Fairwater Stables, Fairwater House, High St, Wroughton, Swindon, **Wiltshire**, SN4 9JX, ENG.
(T) 01793 845300 (F) 01793 845155
Speciality: Chiropractic.
● **Sole Director**
Mark Philip Blokland
P S T (Ref:HM17317)

**RIDGUARD, YVONNE**

**Yvonne Ridguard**, Fairfields Clinic, Skippetts Lane West, Basingstoke, **Hampshire**, RG21 3HP, ENG.
(T) 01256 326980
Speciality: Osteopathy.
● **Owner** Mrs Y Ridguard
P S T (Ref:HM17318)

**RIDLER, PATRICIA**

**Patricia Ridler**, Cowley Clinic, 2 Cowleys Way, Pershore, **Worcestershire**, WR10 1EY, ENG.
(T) 01386 554209
Speciality: Chiropractic.
● **Owner** Miss P Ridler
P S T (Ref:HM17319)

**RIDLER, SHIRLEY**

**Shirley Ridler**, Parkway, West Down, Ilfracombe, **Devon**, EX34 8NF, ENG.
(T) 01271 864062
Speciality: Complementary Medicines & Therapy.
● **Owner** Shirley Ridler
M (Ref:HM17320)

**RIDLEY MEWS COMP HEALTH CTRE**

**Ridley Mews Complementary Health Centre**, 8 Ridley Mews, Stockton-On-Tees, **Cleveland**, TS20 1DW, ENG.
(T) 01642 533004
Speciality: Homeopathy.
M (Ref:HM17321)

**RIDLEY, ANDREW**

**Andrew Ridley**, 25 Richmond Rd, Thornton Heath, **Surrey**, CR7 7QE, ENG.
(T) 020 8689 4353
Speciality: Chiropodists (Podiatrists).
S (Ref:HM17322)

**RIDLEY, STELLA**

**Stella Ridley**, 1 Solent House, Harbour Rd, Gosport, **Hampshire**, PO12 1BG, ENG.
(T) 023 9258 6889
Speciality: Psychotherapy.
● **Owner** Miss S Ridley
B (Ref:HM17323)

**RIDLEY, VICKY**

**Medical Herbalist**, The Watling St Therapy Centre, 24 Watling St, Canterbury, **Kent**, CT1 2UB, ENG.
(T) 01227 452202
(E) vickyridley@yahoo.com
Speciality: Herbal Medicine. ✔
● **Medical Herbalist** Ms V Ridley
(T) 01227 720952 Q: Dip.Phyto. M: CPP, NIMH.
M Yrs. Est.: 6 (Ref:HM17324)

**RIDSDALE, J S**

**J S Ridsdale**, 7 Brookfield Rd, Bury, **Lancashire**, BL9 5LA, ENG.
(T) 01617 641077
Speciality: Chiropodists (Podiatrists).
● **Owner** Mrs J Ridsdale
S (Ref:HM17325)

**RIES, GIDEON**

**Gideon Ries**, 72 Abbeville Rd, London, **London (Greater)**, SW4 9NA, ENG.
(T) 020 7622 7797
Speciality: Osteopathy.
P S T (Ref:HM17326)

**RIES, GIDEON S**

**Gideon S Ries**, 10 High St, Glastonbury, **Somerset**, BA6 9DU, ENG.
(T) 01458 834236 (F) 01458 834236
Speciality: Osteopathy.
● **Practice Manager** Mr G Ries
P S T (Ref:HM17327)

**RIES, JOAN L**

**Joan L Ries**, 42 Codsall Rd, Wolverhampton, **Midlands (West)**, WV6 9ED, ENG.
(T) 01902 755407
Speciality: Physiotherapy.
● **Owner** Ms J Ries
P S T (Ref:HM17328)

**RIETCHEL, F**

**F Rietchel**, 6 Hatfield Buildings, Widcombe Hill, Bath, **Somerset**, BA2 6AF, ENG.
(T) 01225 331136
Speciality: Alexander Technique.
P S (Ref:HM17329)

**RIGAL, M**

**Miss M Rigal**, 412A Ewell Rd, Tolworth, Surbiton, **Surrey**, KT6 7HF, ENG.
(T) 020 8390 6456
(E) podiatrist@mayrigal.com.uk
Speciality: Chiropody, Reflexology.
● **Podiatrist** Miss M Rigal Q: S.R.Ch. M: S.C.P.
● **Reflexologist** Ms R Heathe Q: Dip.Reflex, ITEC.
● **Podiatrist** Worrall Q: S.R.Ch. M: S.C.P.
M Yrs. Est.: 10 (Ref:HM17330)

**RIGBY COURT CLINIC**

**Rigby Court Clinic & Chinese Dispensary**, 6 Rigby's Court, St Giles St, Norwich, **Norfolk**, NR2 1NT, ENG.
(T) 01603 616126
Speciality: Acupressure, Acupuncture, Aromatherapy, Autogenic Training, Biofeedback, Cognitive Therapy, Complementary Therapy, Counselling, Cupping, Floral Essence Therapy, Herbal Medicine, Homeopathy, Hypnotherapy, Indian Head Massage, Kinesiology, Life Style Coaching, Massage (Therapeutic), Moxibustion, Nutritional Therapy, Oriental Diagnosis, Psychotherapy, Reflexology, Reiki, Shiatsu, Stress Therapy, Tuina, Stress Management. ✔
● **Clinic Manager/Practitioner**
Miss L Dover Q: Dip.Arom, Dip.StM. M: IFA, ISMA.
● **Clinic Manager/Practitioner**
Ms E Farrant Q: Dip.TCM. M: BAcC, RCHM.
B C Yrs. Est.: 5 (Ref:HM17331)

**RIGBY, JACQUI**

**Jacqui Rigby**, 49B Maldon Rd, London, **London (Greater)**, W3 6SZ, ENG.
(T) 020 8248 4806
Speciality: Alexander Technique.
● **Owner** Ms J Rigby
P S (Ref:HM17332)

**RIGBY, T L**

**T L Rigby**, The Oxford Practice, 5 Oxford St, Malmesbury, **Wiltshire**, SN16 9AX, ENG.
(T) 01666 824560
Speciality: Osteopathy.
P S T (Ref:HM17333)

**RIGG, SUSAN**

**Susan Rigg**, Norwich, **Norfolk**, NR4, ENG.
(T) 01603 457393
Speciality: Bach Remedies.
M (Ref:HM17334)

**RIGLEY, T**

**T Rigley**, 46 Rowditch Avenue, Derby, **Derbyshire**, DE22 3LD, ENG.
(T) 01332 344034
Speciality: Complementary Medicines & Therapy.
● **Owner** Mr T Rigley
C M (Ref:HM17335)

**RIHAL, PAMELA**

**Pamela Rihal**, Primrose Cottage, Sandy Cross Lane, Heathfield, **Sussex (East)**, TN21 8QL, ENG.
(T) 01435 862947
Speciality: Reflexology.
S T (Ref:HM17336)

**RIJSKIJK, CAROLE**

**Carole Rijskijk**, The Moorings, Salisbury Rd, St. Margarets Bay, Dover, **Kent**, CT15 6DP, ENG.
(T) 01304 853131
Speciality: Osteopathy.
P S T (Ref:HM17337)

**RILEY CHIROPRACTIC CLINIC**

**Riley Chiropractic Clinic**, Unit 1, 86 Clonbrassil St, Dundalk, **County Louth**, IRE.
(T) 04293 28699
Speciality: Chiropractors.
P S T (Ref:HM17338)

**RILEY FLETCHER FOUNDATION**

**Riley Fletcher Foundation (The)**, Phoenix, Church St, Hampton Lucy, Warwick, **Warwickshire**, CV35 8BE, ENG.
(T) 01789 470787 (F) 01789 470858
Speciality: Complementary Medicines & Therapy.
● **Partner** Ms J Fletcher
C M (Ref:HM17339)

**RILEY, BERNADETTE**

**Bernadette Riley**, 22 Rossall Rd, Lytham St. Annes, **Lancashire**, FY8 4ES, ENG.
(T) 01253 739107
Speciality: Homeopathy.
● **Owner** Mrs B Riley
M (Ref:HM17340)

**RILEY, CHASE (DR)**

**Riley, Dr Chase**, 28 Fair St, Drogheda, **County Louth**, IRE.
(T) 04198 30599
Speciality: Chiropractors.
P S T (Ref:HM17341)

**RILEY, JANE**

**Jane Riley**, 54 Rosedale Avenue, Atherton, Manchester, **Manchester (Greater)**, M46 0EA, ENG.
(T) 01942 892289
Speciality: Herbalists.
M (Ref:HM17342)

**RILEY, JANE E**

**Jane E Riley**, 15 Mount St, Liverpool, **Merseyside**, L1 9HD, ENG.
(T) 01517 092324
Speciality: Herbal Medicine.
● **Owner** Mrs J Riley



Key: B Mind-Body Medicine C Complementary Medicine H Self Help Treatment M Medicinal Therapy O Oriental Medicine P Postural Therapy S Manipulative Structural Therapy T Touch Therapy

M (Ref:HM17343)

## RILEY, LYNN

**Lynn Riley**, Dill Hall Lane, Church, Accrington, **Lancashire**, BB5 4DR, ENG.
(T) 01254 234884
Speciality: Chiropodists (Podiatrists).
● **Owner** Mrs L Riley
S (Ref:HM17344)

## RILEY, S

**S Riley**, 4a George St, Pocklington, York, **Yorkshire (North)**, YO42 2DF, ENG.
(T) 01759 302162
Speciality: Homeopathy.
● **Owner** Mrs M Rimes
M (Ref:HM17345)

## RILEY, S

**S Riley**, 31 Old Rd, Holme-On-Spalding-Moor, York, **Yorkshire (North)**, YO43 4AD, ENG.
(T) 01430 860690
Speciality: Homeopathy.
● **Owner** Mrs S Riley
M (Ref:HM17346)

## RILEY, S

**S Riley**, 4a George St, Pocklington, **Humberside**, YO4 2DF, ENG.
(T) 01759 302162
Speciality: Homeopathy.
M (Ref:HM17347)

## RILEY, SUSAN M

**Susan M Riley**, 65 Belgrave Rd, Darwen, **Lancashire**, BB3 2SF, ENG.
(T) 01254 771782
Speciality: Homeopathy.
M (Ref:HM17348)

## RIMES, S C

**S C Rimes**, 41 Mill Lane, Chinnor, **Oxfordshire**, OX9 4QU, ENG.
(T) 01844 353036
Speciality: Chiropodists (Podiatrists).
● **Owner** Mrs S Rimes
S (Ref:HM17349)

## RIMMER, CHRISTINE

**Christine Rimmer**, 12 Woodshaw Gr, Worsley, Manchester, **Manchester (Greater)**, M28 7XX, ENG.
(T) 01617 901607
Speciality: Reflexology.
● **Owner** Mrs C Rimmer
S T (Ref:HM17350)

## RINALDINI, RENATA

**Renata Rinaldini**, 19 Rochford Drive, Luton, **Bedfordshire**, LU2 8SS, ENG.
(T) 01582 695168
Speciality: Homeopathy.
● **Owner** Ms R Rinaldini
M (Ref:HM17351)

## RINDER, TONY

**Tony Rinder**, 8 Deansgate, Blackpool, **Lancashire**, FY1 1BN, ENG.
(T) 01253 295354 (F) 01253 295354
Speciality: Physiotherapy.
● **Manager** Mr F Rinder
P S T (Ref:HM17352)

## RINEEN NATURAL HEALING CENTRE

**Rineen Natural Healing Centre**, Rineen Castlehaven, Skibbereen, **County Cork**, IRE.
(T) 028 3632 6
Speciality: Healing.
B (Ref:HM17353)

## RING, MARY

**Ring Mary Bio-Energy**, 1 Douglas Hall Ave, Douglas, Cork, **County Cork**, IRE.
(T) 021 4364 048
Speciality: Complementary Medicines & Therapy.
M (Ref:HM17354)

## RINGWOOD CHIROPRACTIC CLINIC

**Dr M Browning**, 39A Southampton Rd, Ringwood, **Hampshire**, BH24 1HE, ENG.
(T) 01425 473093 (F) 01425 473093
Speciality: Chiropractic. ✔
● **Owner** Dr M Browning Q: BCA, DC.
P Yrs. Est.: 2 (Ref:HM17355)

## RINGWOOD FOOT SHOP

**Ringwood Foot Shop**, 1 Northumberland Court, Ringwood, **Hampshire**, BH24 1AY, ENG.
(T) 01425 470142
Speciality: Chiropodists (Podiatrists).
● **Owner** Mr M Moore
S (Ref:HM17356)

## RINGWOOD NATURAL HEALTH CLINIC

**Ringwood Natural Health Clinic (The)**, 11 Meeting House Lane, Ringwood, **Hampshire**, BH24 1AY, ENG.
(T) 01425 471947
Speciality: Acupuncture, Alexander Technique, Aromatherapy, Bowen Therapy, Chiropractic, Cranial Osteopathy, Gestalt Therapy, Homeopathy, Hypnotherapy, Indian Head Massage, Kinesiology, Massage (Therapeutic), Metamorphic Therapy, Moxibustion, Reflexology, Reiki, Shiatsu, La Stone Therapy, McTimoney Chiropractic, Medi Scan, Sports & Remedial Massage Therapy, Skenar. ✔
● **Owner/Manager** Ms A Finn Q: ITEC, L.C.C.H.
B C Yrs. Est.: 2 (Ref:HM17357)

## RINGWOOD PHYSIOTHERAPY CENTRE

**Ringwood Physiotherapy Centre**, 56 Southampton Rd, Ringwood, **Hampshire**, BH24 1JD, ENG.
(T) 01425 472202 (F) 01425 472202
Speciality: Acupuncture, Physiotherapy. ✔
● **Physiotherapist** Mrs F Allen Q: MCSP, SRP. M: AACP.
● **Physiotherapist** Ms M Q: MCSP, SRP. M: AACP.
S Yrs. Est.: 4 (Ref:HM17358)

## RINGWOOD, JAN

**Jan Ringwood**, 6 Asket Gardens, Oakwood, Leeds, **Yorkshire (West)**, LS8 2NW, ENG.
(T) 01132 659019
Speciality: Homeopathy.
M (Ref:HM17359)

## RINSKE, BARTSTRA

**Bartstra Rinske**, Hexham Swimming Pool, Gilesgate, Hexham, **Northumberland**, NE46 3NP, ENG.
(T) 01434 600088
Speciality: Osteopathy.
P S T (Ref:HM17360)

## RINTU, BASU

**Basu Rintu**, 19 Manor Park Cl, Tilehurst, Reading, **Berkshire**, RG30 4PS, ENG.
(T) 01189 451500
Speciality: Hypnosis.
B (Ref:HM17361)

## RIORDAN, SHAYLA

**Riordan Shayla**, 1 Lansdowne Tce, Patricks Hill, **County Cork**, IRE.
(T) 021 4500 509
Speciality: Psychotherapy.
B (Ref:HM17362)

## RIPLEY THERAPY CENTRE

**Ripley Therapy Centre**, 51 Wall St, Ripley, **Derbyshire**, DE5 3DE, ENG.
(T) 01773 747164
Speciality: Osteopathy.
● **Owner** Mrs D Walker
P S T (Ref:HM17363)

## RIPON COMP THERAPY CENTRE

**Ripon Complementary Therapy Centre**, 1a North St, Ripon, **Yorkshire (North)**, HG4 1JY, ENG.
(T) 01765 607836
Speciality: Complementary Medicines & Therapy.
● **Owner** Miss A Harrison
M (Ref:HM17364)

## RIPON NATURAL HEALTH CENTRE

**Ripon Natural Health Centre**, 27 Market Pl, Ripon, **Yorkshire (North)**, HG4 1BN, ENG.
(T) 01765 601447 (F) 01765 601447
(E) riponnaturalhealthcentre@hotmail.com
Speciality: Acupressure, Acupuncture, Aromatherapy, Ayurvedic Medicine, Bach Remedies, Bates Method, Complementary Therapy, Cranial Osteopathy, Cupping, Family Therapy, Healer, Healing Therapy, Herbal Medicine, Holistic Healing, Homeopathy, Indian Head Massage, Manipulation, Miasm Therapy, Massage (Therapeutic), Meditation, Moxibustion, Nutritional Therapy, Osteopathy, Reiki, Shiatsu, Stress Therapy, Touch Therapy. ✔
● **Aromatherapist** Ms B Askew Q: Dip.SPA, Reiki Master. M: ISPA.
● **Homeopath** Ms J Young Q: RSHom. M: Soc.Hom.
● **Osteopath/Homeopath/Acupuncturist** Mr M Young Q: DO, MBAcC, RSHom. M: BACP, GOsC, Soc.Hom.
● **Osteopath** Ms C MacDonald Q: DO. M: GOsC.
M Yrs. Est.: 18 (Ref:HM17365)

## RIPPER, JULIE

**Julie Ripper**, 37 Churchill Rd, St. Albans, **Hertfordshire**, AL1 4HH, ENG.
(T) 07973 345468
Speciality: Hypnosis.
B (Ref:HM17366)

## RIPPONDEN THERAPY CENTRE

**Ripponden Therapy Centre (The)**, Apartment 60, Rishworth Palace, Rishworth Mill Lane, Rishworth, Sowerby Bridge, **Yorkshire (West)**, HX6 4RZ, ENG.
(T) 01422 825122
Speciality: Physiotherapy.
P S T (Ref:HM17367)

## RISING CRANE CENTRE

**Rising Crane Centre**, Stuart Court, 51 Stuart Rd, Kempston, Bedford, **Bedfordshire**, MK42 8HS, ENG.
(T) 01234 855527
Speciality: Acupuncture.
O (Ref:HM17368)

## RISING DRAGON TAI CHI

**Rising Dragon Tai Chi**, Bishopston, Bristol, BS3, ENG.
(T) 01179 832982
(W) www.risingdragontaichi.com
Speciality: Meditation, T'ai-Chi Ch'uan, Teaches Tai Chi Chuan and Meditation does not actually practice. ✔
● **Teacher** Ms G Minter M: TCUGB.
H Yrs. Est.: 17 (Ref:HM17369)

## RISING DRAGON TAI CHI SCHOOL

**Rising Dragon Tai Chi School**, Clifton, Bristol, ENG.
(T) 01179 832982
(W) www.risingdragontaichi.com
Speciality: Meditation, T'ai-Chi Ch'uan, Teaches Tai Chi and Meditation does not practice. ✔
● **Teacher** Ms G Minter M: TCUGB.
H Yrs. Est.: 17 (Ref:HM17370)

## RITA

**Rita**, 66 Taylor Rd, Birmingham, **Midlands (West)**, B13 0PG, ENG.
(T) 01212 421474
Speciality: Aromatherapy.
M O (Ref:HM17371)

## RITCHIE, DOROTHY

**Dorothy Ritchie**, 15 Preston Rd, Lytham St. Annes, **Lancashire**, FY8 5BL, ENG.
(T) 01253 730671
Speciality: Physiotherapy.
P S T (Ref:HM17372)

## RITZ CHIROPODIST

**Ritz Chiropodist (The)**, 30 Forest Hall Rd, Newcastle Upon Tyne, **Tyne and Wear**, NE12 9AL, ENG.
(T) 01912 169094
Speciality: Chiropodists (Podiatrists).
● **Owner** Mrs L Foley
S (Ref:HM17373)

## RIVENDELL CENTRE

**Rivendell Centre**, Mores Lane, Warley, Brentwood, **Essex**, CM14 5UA, ENG.
(T) 01277 375797 (F) 01277 375979
Speciality: Complementary Medicines & Therapy.
● **Owner** Mrs S Lewin


Key continued: Yrs.Est: Years Established Q: Qualifications M: Professional Membership ✔ Indemnity Insurance Accept Credit Cards

M (Ref:HM17374)

## RIVENDELL NAT THERAPY CLINIC

**Rivendell Natural Therapy Clinic**, Rivendell, Cwmbach Rd, Aberdare, **Glamorgan (Vale of)**, CF44 0NF, **WAL**.
(T) 01685 875237
Speciality: Aromatherapy, Reflexology, Reiki.
M (Ref:HM17375)

## RIVER-MOON

**River-Moon**, 67 Southfield Rd, Birmingham, **Midlands (West)**, B16 0JP, **ENG**.
(T) 01214 201900 (F) 07070 713898
Speciality: Aromatherapy.
● **Owner** Mrs G Lovatt
M O (Ref:HM17376)

## RIVERS, PATRICIA

**Patricia Rivers**, North Drive, Fakenham, **Norfolk**, NR21 8HA, **ENG**.
(T) 01328 856348
Speciality: Aromatherapy.
M O (Ref:HM17377)

## RIVERSIDE CHIROPRACTIC CLINIC

**Riverside Chiropractic Clinic**, 585 Holburn St, Aberdeen, **Aberdeenshire**, AB10 7LH, **SCO**.
(T) 01224 211517
Speciality: Chiropractic, Healing Therapy, Herbal Medicine, Postural Integration, Vitamin Therapy. ✔
● **Chiropractor** Dr E Madsen **Q:** BSc (Chiro), DC, MCC. **M:** CC.
H P S T Yrs. Est.: 8 (Ref:HM17378)

## RIVERSIDE CHIROPRACTIC CLINIC

**Riverside Chiropractic Clinic**, 30 Litchdon St, Barnstaple, **Devon**, EX32 8ND, **ENG**.
(T) 01271 345142
(W) www.riversidechiropracticclinic.co.uk
Speciality: Chiropractic, Manipulation, Massage (Therapeutic), Ultrasonics, X-Ray. ✔
● **Chiropractor** Dixon **Q:** BSc, DC. **M:** BCA.
● **Chiropractor** Dr S Masters **Q:** BSc, DC. **M:** BCA.
S Yrs. Est.: 8 (Ref:HM17379)

## RIVERSIDE PRACTICE

**Riverside Practice**, 13-14 Okehampton St, Exeter, **Devon**, EX4 1DU, **ENG**.
(T) 01392 254510
Speciality: Osteopathy.
● **Owner** Mrs F Schaznick
P S T (Ref:HM17380)

## RIVETT, DOREEN

**Doreen Rivett**, 13 Anchor Reach, South Woodham Ferrers, Chelmsford, **Essex**, CM3 5GS, **ENG**.
(T) 01245 322997
Speciality: Reflexology.
● **Owner** Miss D Rivett
S T (Ref:HM17381)

## RIVETT, LYNN

**Lynn Rivett**, Hungerford, **Berkshire**, RG17, **ENG**.
(T) 01488 658261
Speciality: Aromatherapy.
M O (Ref:HM17382)

## RIVIERA OSTEOPATHIC CLINIC

**Riviera Osteopathic Clinic**, 21 Dendy Rd, Paignton, **Devon**, TQ4 5DB, **ENG**.
(T) 01803 550539 (F) 01803 665080
Speciality: Osteopathy.
● **Owner** Mrs C Harris
P S T (Ref:HM17383)

## RIVIERE, SUSANNA

**Susanna Riviere**, 56 Ridgway Pl, London, **London (Greater)**, SW19 4SW, **ENG**.
(T) 020 8946 2308
Speciality: Reflexology.
S T (Ref:HM17384)

## ROARTY, JULIE D

**Julie D Roarty**, Albyn Cottage, 6 Corstorphine High St, Edinburgh, **Edinburgh (City of)**, EH12 7ST, **SCO**.
(T) 01313 341769
Speciality: Chiropodists (Podiatrists).
S (Ref:HM17385)

## ROBARK CENTRE

**Robark Centre (The)**, 2 Baughton Hall Cottage, Baughton, Earls Croome, Worcester, **Worcestershire**, WR8 9DQ, **ENG**.
(T) 01684 593049
Speciality: Hypnosis.
● **Owner** Mrs A Procter
B (Ref:HM17386)

## ROBB, A (DR)

**Dr A Robb**, 29 Hope St, Lanark, **Lanarkshire (South)**, ML11 7NE, **SCO**.
(T) 01555 662812
Speciality: Acupuncture, Homeopathy.
✔
● **Doctor** Dr A Robb **Q:** Ch.B, Dip.Med.Ac, MB, MFHom. **M:** BMAS, FFHom.
C Yrs. Est.: 11 (Ref:HM17387)

## ROBB, S J

**S J Robb**, 91 Westfields, St. Albans, **Hertfordshire**, AL3 4LY, **ENG**.
(T) 01727 863927
Speciality: Chiropodists (Podiatrists).
● **Owner** Mrs S Robb
S (Ref:HM17388)

## ROBBERTS, VIVIEN

**Vivien Robberts**, Orchard House, The Green, Luddington, Stratford-Upon-Avon, **Warwickshire**, CV37 9SJ, **ENG**.
(T) 01789 750364 (F) 01789 750364
Speciality: Physiotherapy.
● **Owner** Mrs V Robberts
P S T (Ref:HM17389)

## ROBBINS, A L

**A L Robbins**, 1a Castle St, Launceston, **Cornwall**, PL15 8AZ, **ENG**.
(T) 01566 776342
Speciality: Chiropodists (Podiatrists).
● **Owner** Mr A Robins
S (Ref:HM17390)

## ROBBINS, C A

**C A Robbins**, 2b Honey Lane, Cholsey, Wallingford, **Oxfordshire**, OX10 9NP, **ENG**.
(T) 01491 652574
Speciality: Chiropodists (Podiatrists).
S (Ref:HM17391)

## ROBBINS, CAROLINE

**Caroline Robbins**, Parkfield Surgeries, 13 Parkfield Rd, Taunton, **Somerset**, TA1 4RL, **ENG**.
(T) 01823 254642
Speciality: Acupuncture.
● **Owner** Mr C Robbins
O (Ref:HM17392)

## ROBBINS, CHRISTOPHER

**Christopher Robbins Medical Herbalist**, 6 Cantilupe Rd, Ross-on-Wye, **Herefordshire**, HR9 7AN, **ENG**.
(T) 01989 768437
Speciality: Herbalists.
M (Ref:HM17393)

## ROBBINS, JAMES H

**James H Robbins**, 79 Garden Suburb, Dursley, **Gloucestershire**, GL11 4EN, **ENG**.
(T) 01453 545084
Speciality: Hypnosis.
B (Ref:HM17394)

## ROBE-QUINN, BERNICE

**Bernice Robe-Quinn**, 168 Duke St, Southport, **Merseyside**, PR8 5EL, **ENG**.
(T) 01704 548915
Speciality: Clairvoyants & Palmists.
B (Ref:HM17395)

## ROBERT BIRD REFLEXOLOGIST

**Robert Bird Reflexologist**, 153 Queens Rd, Yardley, Birmingham, **Midlands (West)**, B26 2AS, **ENG**.
(T) 01216 289178
Speciality: Reflexology.
S T (Ref:HM17396)

## ROBERT CRAIG THERAPY

**Robert Craig Therapy Ltd**, 67 Callender St, Ramsbottom, Bury, **Lancashire**, BL0 9DX, **ENG**.
(T) 01706 829857 (F) 01706 829857
Speciality: Complementary Medicines & Therapy.
● **Owner** Mr R Craig
M (Ref:HM17397)

## ROBERT STONE THERAPEUTICS

**Robert Stone Therapeutics**, 153 Broughton Rd, Edinburgh, **Edinburgh (City of)**, EH7 4JJ, **SCO**.
(T) 01315 540445
(E) robstm@yahoo.co.uk
Speciality: Aromatherapy, Homeopathy, Indian Head Massage, Massage (Therapeutic), Meditation, Reflexology. ✔
● **Massage Therapist** Mr R McNicholls **Q:** ITEC. **M:** GCP.
S Yrs. Est.: 4 (Ref:HM17398)

## ROBERTON, JILL

**Jill Roberton**, 59 Old Compton Lane, Farnham, **Surrey**, GU9 8EG, **ENG**.
(T) 01252 727183 (F) 01252 727183
Speciality: Reflexology.
● **Owner** Ms J Roberton
S T (Ref:HM17399)

## ROBERTS & LEAHY

**Roberts & Leahy**, 45 Rodney Rd, Cheltenham, **Gloucestershire**, GL50 1HX, **ENG**.
(T) 01242 226414
Speciality: Chiropodists (Podiatrists).
S (Ref:HM17400)

## ROBERTS, A J

**A J Roberts**, Lombard House, 12-17 Upper Bridge St, Canterbury, **Kent**, CT1 2NF, **ENG**.
(T) 01227 462152
Speciality: Osteopathy.
● **Owner** Mrs A Roberts
P S T (Ref:HM17401)

## ROBERTS, ADRIAN

**Adrian Roberts**, Solihull Pain Clinic, 308 Blossomfield Rd, Solihull, **Midlands (West)**, B91 1TF, **ENG**.
(T) 01217 050101
Speciality: Physiotherapy.
P S T (Ref:HM17402)

## ROBERTS, ALISON

**Alison Roberts**, Old Convent, Moat Rd, East Grinstead, **Sussex (West)**, RH19 3RS, **ENG**.
(T) 01342 328296
Speciality: Aromatherapy.
● **Owner** Mrs A Roberts
M O (Ref:HM17403)

## ROBERTS, ANN

**Ann Roberts**, 3 Holly Cl, Hale Village, Liverpool, **Merseyside**, L24 4BY, **ENG**.
(T) 01514 254682
Speciality: Chiropodists (Podiatrists).
S (Ref:HM17404)

## ROBERTS, C M

**C M Roberts**, The Pilates Studio, 5 The Stables, 7 Weyhill, Haslemere, **Surrey**, GU27 1PY, **ENG**.
(T) 01428 654252 (F) 01428 654252
Speciality: Complementary Medicines & Therapy.
● **Owner** Mrs C Roberts
M (Ref:HM17405)

## ROBERTS, CATHERINE

**Catherine Roberts**, 140 Lyham Rd, London, **London (Greater)**, SW2 5QD, **ENG**.
(T) 020 8671 3655
Speciality: Hypnosis.
B (Ref:HM17406)

## ROBERTS, CATHERINE

**Catherine Roberts**, Clevedale, The Shallows, Saltford, Bristol, BS31 3EX, **ENG**.
(T) 01225 400236 (F) 01225 401500
Speciality: Acupuncture.
● **Owner** Mrs C Roberts
O (Ref:HM17407)

## ROBERTS, CLARE

**Clare Roberts**, 27 Pottersfield Rd, Woodmancote, Cheltenham, **Gloucestershire**, GL52 4PY, **ENG**.
(T) 01242 672836
Speciality: Chiropodists (Podiatrists).
S (Ref:HM17408)



Key: B Mind-Body Medicine C Complementary Medicine H Self Help Treatment M Medicinal Therapy O Oriental Medicine P Postural Therapy S Manipulative Structural Therapy T Touch Therapy

### ROBERTS, EMMA
**Emma Roberts**, 1 Grove Cottage, Orange Hill, Binfield, Bracknell, **Berkshire**, RG42 5PR, ENG.
(T) 01344 482851
Speciality: Chiropractors.
● **Owner** Miss E Roberts
P S T (Ref:HM17409)

### ROBERTS, FIONA
**Fiona Roberts**, 66 Busbridge Lane, Godalming, **Surrey**, GU7 1QQ, ENG.
(T) 01483 422733
Speciality: Physiotherapy.
P S T (Ref:HM17410)

### ROBERTS, FRANK
**Roberts Frank Herbal Dispensers Ltd**, Dean St, Bristol, BS2 8FR, ENG.
(T) 01179 428704 (F) 01179 441297
Speciality: Herbal Medicine.
● **Managing Director** Mr D Hennessy
M (Ref:HM17411)

### ROBERTS, GARRY
**Garry Roberts**, Scott St Complementary Therapy Centre, 58 Scott St, Barrow-in-Furness, **Cumbria**, LA14 1QE, ENG.
(T) 01229 826700
Speciality: Complementary Medicines & Therapy.
M (Ref:HM17412)

### ROBERTS, GRAHAM
**Graham Roberts**, 83 Harvest Rd, Englefield Green, Egham, **Surrey**, TW20 0QR, ENG.
(T) 01784 454422
Speciality: Chiropractors.
● **Owner** Mr G Roberts
P S T (Ref:HM17413)

### ROBERTS, GRAHAM J
**Graham J Roberts**, Orchard View, Martley Rd, Lower Broadheath, Worcester, **Worcestershire**, WR2 6QG, ENG.
(T) 01905 640133
Speciality: Complementary Medicines & Therapy.
● **Owner** Mr G Roberts
C M (Ref:HM17414)

### ROBERTS, J
**J Roberts**, Middle Walton, Walton, Worthen, Shrewsbury, **Shropshire**, SY5 9JN, ENG.
(T) 01743 891277
Speciality: Reflexology.
● **Partner** Mrs J Roberts
S T (Ref:HM17415)

### ROBERTS, J R
**J R Roberts**, The Abbey Clinic, 6a Albert Rd, Belvedere, **Kent**, DA17 5LJ, ENG.
(T) 01322 436436
Speciality: Osteopathy.
P S T (Ref:HM17416)

### ROBERTS, JILL
**Jill Roberts**, 79 Springfield Rd, Sheffield, **Yorkshire (South)**, S7 2GG, ENG.
(T) 01142 363614
Speciality: Chiropodists (Podiatrists).
● **Owner** Mrs J Roberts
S (Ref:HM17417)

### ROBERTS, KATE
**Kate Roberts**, 1 Basford Villas, Etruria Rd, Newcastle, **Staffordshire**, ST5 0TQ, ENG.
(T) 01782 627276
Speciality: Counselling, Humanistic Psychology, Meditation, Psychotherapy, Pyscho-Synthesis, Rogerian Therapy, Stress Therapy, Psychodynamic Therapy, Inner Child Therapy. ✔
● **Counsellor** Ms K Roberts Q: BA (Hons), Dip.Couns. M: BACP, UKRC.
B Yrs. Est.: 7 (Ref:HM17418)

### ROBERTS, KATE
**Kate Roberts**, 131 Chislehurst Rd, Orpington, **Kent**, BR6 0DR, ENG.
(T) 01689 827936
Speciality: Reflexology.
S T (Ref:HM17419)

### ROBERTS, MATT
**Matt Roberts At The Royal Garden**, The Royal Garden, 2-24 Kensington High St, London, **London (Greater)**, W8 4PT, ENG.
(E) firstpath@btinternet.com
Speciality: Hypnotherapy. ✔
● **Owner** Ms N Zaman Q: DipCH.P, NLP. M: NCH.
B Yrs. Est.: 3 (Ref:HM17420)

### ROBERTS, P
**P Roberts**, Three Oaks, Dean Oak Lane, Leigh, Reigate, **Surrey**, RH2 8PZ, ENG.
(T) 01293 862012
Speciality: Complementary Medicines & Therapy.
C M (Ref:HM17421)

### ROBERTS, R J (DR)
**Dr R J Roberts**, 8 Mill Cl, East Coker, Yeovil, **Somerset**, BA22 9LF, ENG.
(T) 01935 862832
Speciality: Psychotherapy.
B (Ref:HM17422)

### ROBERTS, R N
**R N Roberts**, 80 Snakes Lane, Woodford Green, **Essex**, IG8 7QQ, ENG.
(T) 020 8504 6388
Speciality: Chiropodists (Podiatrists).
● **Owner** Mr R Roberts
S (Ref:HM17423)

### ROBERTS, S
**Mrs S Roberts**, The Coach House, 66 Northfield End, Henley-on-Thames, **Oxfordshire**, RG9 2JN, ENG.
(T) 01491 577129 (F) 01491 577129
Speciality: Physiotherapy.
P S T (Ref:HM17424)

### ROBERTS, S
**S Roberts**, Idris House, Abbey Rd, Llangollen, **Denbighshire**, LL20 8SS, WAL.
(T) 01978 861800
Speciality: Chiropractic.
● **Owner** Mr S Roberts
P S T (Ref:HM17425)

### ROBERTS, S
**S Roberts**, Cae Glas House, 36 Church St, Oswestry, **Shropshire**, SY11 2SP, ENG.
(T) 01691 672909
Speciality: Chiropractic.
P S T (Ref:HM17426)

### ROBERTS, S (DR)
**Dr S Roberts**, 87 Palatine Rd, Manchester, **Manchester (Greater)**, M20 3JQ, ENG.
(T) 01614 462009
Speciality: Chiropractic.
● **Doctor** Dr S Roberts
P S T (Ref:HM17427)

### ROBERTS, S A
**S A Roberts**, Grey Friars, Hill Foot Lane, Pannal, Harrogate, **Yorkshire (North)**, HG3 1NT, ENG.
(T) 01423 871419 (F) 01423 873781
Speciality: Physiotherapy.
● **Owner** Mrs S Roberts
P S T (Ref:HM17428)

### ROBERTS, SALLY
**Sally Roberts**, 125 Stansted Rd, Bishop's Stortford, **Hertfordshire**, CM23 2AL, ENG.
(T) 01279 832283
Speciality: Chiropodists (Podiatrists).
● **Owner** Mrs S Roberts
S (Ref:HM17429)

### ROBERTS, T J
**T J Roberts**, 2 West Hill, St. Austell, **Cornwall**, PL25 5ET, ENG.
(T) 01726 74578
Speciality: Chiropodists (Podiatrists).
● **Owner** Mr T Roberts
S (Ref:HM17430)

### ROBERTS, TRACEY
**Tracey Roberts**, 4 Mosley Cl, Timperley, Altrincham, **Cheshire**, WA15 6LB, ENG.
(T) 01619 807152
Speciality: Reflexology.
S T (Ref:HM17431)

### ROBERTS, V
**V Roberts**, Paultons Sq Practice, 5 Paultons Sq, London, **London (Greater)**, SW3 5AP, ENG.
(T) 020 7352 5172
Speciality: Physiotherapy.
P S T (Ref:HM17432)

### ROBERTSHAW, A
**A Robertshaw**, 20 High St, Albrighton, Wolverhampton, **Midlands (West)**, WV7 3JB, ENG.
(T) 01902 374697
Speciality: Complementary Medicines & Therapy.
● **Owner** Mrs A Robertshaw
C M (Ref:HM17433)

### ROBERTSON & ASSOCIATES
**Stuart Robertson & Associates**, 31 Chandos Rd South, Manchester, **Manchester (Greater)**, M21 0TH, ENG.
(T) 01618 810353 (F) 01618 606683
Speciality: Psychology.
● **Partner** Dr D Wilkie
B (Ref:HM17434)

### ROBERTSON & ASSOCIATES
**Stuart Robertson & Associates**, Empress Business Centre, Chester Rd, Manchester, **Manchester (Greater)**, M16 9EA, ENG.
(T) 01618 773277 (F) 01618 774500
Speciality: Psychology.
● **Senior Partner** Mr S Robertson
B (Ref:HM17435)

### ROBERTSON, A
**A Robertson**, Westbridge Mill, Bridge St, Kirkcaldy, **Fife**, KY1 1TE, SCO.
(T) 01592 643600
Speciality: Physiotherapy.
● **Owner** Mr A Robertson
P S T (Ref:HM17436)

### ROBERTSON, ANGUS
**Angus Robertson**, 6 Broughton Rd, Salford, **Buckinghamshire**, MK17 8BJ, ENG.
(T) 01908 582967
Speciality: Reflexology.
S T (Ref:HM17437)

### ROBERTSON, FIONA
**Fiona Robertson**, Highbury Park Clinic, 111 Highbury Pk, London, **London (Greater)**, N5 1UB, ENG.
(T) 020 7704 6704
Speciality: Osteopathy.
● **Owner** Mrs F Robertson
P S T (Ref:HM17438)

### ROBERTSON, FIONA
**Fiona Robertson**, 1 Mount Pleasant, Middletown, Welshpool, **Powys**, SY21 8DH, WAL.
(T) 01938 570556
Speciality: Complementary Medicines & Therapy.
● **Owner** Ms F Robertson
M (Ref:HM17439)

### ROBERTSON, FIONA
**Fiona Robertson**, Alternatives Complementary Therapy Centre, 118 High St, Northwood, **London (Greater)**, HA6 2NT, ENG.
(T) 01923 828832
Speciality: Naturopathy, Osteopathy, Reflexology.
S T (Ref:HM17440)

### ROBERTSON, IAN R
**Ian R Robertson**, 16 De Parys Avenue, Bedford, **Bedfordshire**, MK40 2TW, ENG.
(T) 01234 351250
Speciality: Chiropodists (Podiatrists).
● **Owner** Mr I Robertson
S (Ref:HM17441)

### ROBERTSON, IAN R
**Ian R Robertson**, Rothschild House, Chapel St, Tring, **Hertfordshire**, HP23 6PU, ENG.
(T) 01442 822468
Speciality: Chiropodists (Podiatrists).
S (Ref:HM17442)

### ROBERTSON, JENNIFER
**Jennifer Robertson**, 27 Cedar Rd, Kilmarnock,



Key continued: Yrs.Est: Years Established Q: Qualifications M: Professional Membership ✔ Indemnity Insurance CREDIT Accept Credit Cards

# garden answers

Includes over 8,800 Garden Centres

# The Ultimate Guide

to over

30,000

Garden Services

in the UK & Ireland

www.go4gardens.com

Also known as

Go4gardens

Publishing HCC

An HCC Next Generation Directory

**Ayrshire (East)**, KA1 2HP, SCO.
(T) 01563 525087
Speciality: Aromatherapy.
● **Owner** Miss J Robertson
M O (Ref:HM17443)

## ROBERTSON, JULIET

**Juliet Robertson**, 109 Rosewell Court, Bath, **Somerset**, BA1 2AH, ENG.
(T) 01225 420834
Speciality: Reflexology.
S T (Ref:HM17444)

## ROBERTSON, K

**K Robertson**, 10 Pitt Trce, Stirling, FK8 2EZ, SCO.
(T) 01786 479832
Speciality: Osteopathy.
P S T (Ref:HM17445)

## ROBERTSON, K & ROWLAND, D

**Karen Robertson & David Rowland**, 47 Murray Rd, London, **London (Greater)**, SW19 4PF, ENG.
(T) 020 8946 6103 (F) 020 8947 0907
Speciality: Osteopathy.
● **Partner** Mr D Rowland
P S T (Ref:HM17446)

## ROBERTSON, KEITH

**Keith Robertson**, 270 High St, Glasgow, **Glasgow (City of)**, G4 0QT, SCO.
(T) 01415 524420
Speciality: Herbal Medicine.
M (Ref:HM17447)

## ROBERTSON, KENNETH P

**Kenneth P Robertson**, 11 Amersham Hill, High Wycombe, **Buckinghamshire**, HP13 6NR, ENG.
(T) 01494 527954
Speciality: Chiropodists (Podiatrists).
S (Ref:HM17448)

## ROBERTSON, M

**M Robertson**, 30A Windsor St, Edinburgh, **Edinburgh (City of)**, EH7 5JR, SCO.
(T) 01315 570279
Speciality: Complementary Medicines & Therapy.
● **Owner** Mrs M Robertson
C M (Ref:HM17449)

## ROBERTSON, MAUREEN

**Maureen Robertson**, 270 High St, Glasgow, **Glasgow (City of)**, G4 0QT, SCO.
(T) 01415 524420
Speciality: Aromatherapy.
M O (Ref:HM17450)

## ROBERTSON, MAUREEN & KEITH

**Maureen & Keith Robertson**, P O Box 52, Glasgow, **Glasgow (City of)**, G52 3RZ, SCO.
(T) 01418 827001
Speciality: Herbal Medicine.
● **Partner** Mrs M Robertson
M (Ref:HM17451)

## ROBERTSON, MICHAEL

**Michael Robertson**, 36 Thorngrove Avenue, Aberdeen, **Aberdeenshire**, AB15 7XR, SCO.
(T) 01224 316398 (F) 01224 316398
Speciality: Reflexology.
● **Owner** Mr M Roberston
S T (Ref:HM17452)

## ROBERTSON, MING CHEN

**Ming Chen Robertson**, 24 Bernard St, Edinburgh, **Edinburgh (City of)**, EH4 2LS, SCO.
(T) 01239 831742
Speciality: Chiropodists (Podiatrists).

● **Owner** Mrs M Robertson-Williams
S (Ref:HM17455)

## ROBIN LANE MEDICAL CENTRE

**Robin Lane Medical Centre**, Pudsey, Leeds, **Yorkshire (West)**, LS28 7BR, ENG.
(T) 01132 566017
Speciality: Alexander Technique.
● **Teacher** Mrs H Gretton
P S (Ref:HM17456)

## ROBINIA COMP HEALTH CLINIC

**Robinia Complemetary Health Clinic**, Wey House, Norton Fitzwarren, Taunton, **Somerset**, TA4 1BT, ENG.
(T) 01823 321332
Speciality: Complementary Medicines & Therapy.
● **Director** Mr B Groves
C M (Ref:HM17457)

## ROBINSON & PIERCE PODIATISTS

**Robinson & Pierce Podiatists**, 70 Ridgeway, Plymouth, **Devon**, PL7 2AL, ENG.
(T) 01752 347663
Speciality: Chiropodists (Podiatrists).
● **Owner** Mrs H Robinson
S (Ref:HM17458)

## ROBINSON & SONS

**J Robinson & Sons (Bradford) Ltd**, P O Box 236, Bradford, **Yorkshire (West)**, BD9 6UT, ENG.
(T) 01274 409937
Speciality: Herbal Medicine.
● **Owner** Mr W Carnelley
M (Ref:HM17459)

## ROBINSON, ANN

**Ann Robinson**, 11 Cedar Cl, Lincoln, **Lincolnshire**, LN5 9BG, ENG.
(T) 01522 722560
Speciality: Reflexology.
S T (Ref:HM17460)

## ROBINSON, B J

**B J Robinson**, 68 Liverpool Rd, Longton, Preston, **Lancashire**, PR4 5HA, ENG.
(T) 01772 614965
Speciality: Chiropodists (Podiatrists).
S (Ref:HM17461)

## ROBINSON, C

**C Robinson**, Brookside, Well Being Centre, Whiston, Rotherham, **Yorkshire (South)**, S60 4HX, ENG.
(T) 01142 470389
Speciality: Hypnosis.
B (Ref:HM17462)

## ROBINSON, C Z

**C Z Robinson**, The Radlett Practice, 107 Watling St, Radlett, **Hertfordshire**, WD7 7NG, ENG.
(T) 01923 855884
Speciality: Osteopathy.
P S T (Ref:HM17463)

## ROBINSON, CHARLOTTE

**Charlotte Robinson**, 50 Woodstock Rd North, St. Albans, **Hertfordshire**, AL1 4QF, ENG.
(T) 01727 837661
Speciality: Chiropodists (Podiatrists).
S (Ref:HM17464)

## ROBINSON, CLARE

**Clare Robinson**, Friars Rd Chiropody & Therapy Centre, 22 Friars Rd, Coventry, **Midlands (West)**, CV1 2LL, ENG.

HP15 7DT, ENG.
(T) 01494 711497

Speciality: Reflexology.
S T (Ref:HM17467)

## ROBINSON, DENISE

**Denise Robinson**, 19 Northfield Avenue, Orpington, **Kent**, BR5 4JQ, ENG.
(T) 01689 896475
Speciality: Complementary Medicines & Therapy.
M (Ref:HM17468)

## ROBINSON, ELIZABETH

**Elizabeth Robinson**, Chelsea House, Chelsea Lane, West High St, Inverurie, **Aberdeenshire**, AB51 3QQ, SCO.
(T) 01467 625460
Speciality: Osteopathy.
● **Owner** Mr N Robinson
P S T (Ref:HM17469)

## ROBINSON, ELIZABETH

**Elizabeth Robinson**, Glenroyd House, Boroughbridge Rd, Bishop Monkton, Harrogate, **Yorkshire (North)**, HG3 3QN, ENG.
(T) 01765 677827
Speciality: Chiropodists (Podiatrists).
S (Ref:HM17470)

## ROBINSON, ELIZABETH

**Elizabeth Robinson**, 5 Bank Lane, Forres, **Moray**, IV36 1NU, SCO.
(T) 01309 671413
Speciality: Osteopathy.
● **Owner** Mr N Robinson
P S T (Ref:HM17471)

## ROBINSON, ELLIE

**Ellie Robinson**, 834 Fishponds Rd, Fishponds, Bristol, BS16 3XA, ENG.
(T) 01179 491290
Speciality: Acupuncture.
O (Ref:HM17472)

## ROBINSON, GABIE

**Gabie Robinson**, 11 Landseer Rd, Enfield, **London (Greater)**, EN1 1DP, ENG.
(T) 020 8364 6167
(E) gabierobson@ntlworld.com
Speciality: Herbal Medicine. ✓
● **Medical Herbalist** Ms G Robson Q: BSc (Hons). M: NIMH.
C Yrs. Est.: 1 (Ref:HM17473)

## ROBINSON, GRAHAM

**Graham Robinson**, 31 Lichfield Rd, Burntwood, **Staffordshire**, WS7 0HQ, ENG.
(T) 01543 677095
Speciality: Complementary Medicines & Therapy.
C M (Ref:HM17474)

## ROBINSON, H

**H Robinson**, Rose Tree House, Durham, **County Durham**, DH1 4JF, ENG.
(T) 01913 864280
Speciality: Chiropodists (Podiatrists).
S (Ref:HM17475)

## ROBINSON, IRIS E M

**Iris E M Robinson**, 12 Princes Sq, Exeter, **Devon**, EX2 9AN, ENG.
(T) 01392 433365 (F) 01392 433365
Speciality: Acupuncture.
● **Owner** Mrs I Robinson
O (Ref:HM17476)

(T) 01208 72025

Key: B Mind-Body Medicine  O Oriental Medicine  C Complementary Medicine  P Postural Therapy  H Self Help Treatment  S Manipulative Structural Therapy  M Medicinal Therapy  T Touch Therapy

Towcester, **Northamptonshire**, NN12 6DJ, ENG

Speciality: Chiropodists (Podiatrists).
● **Owner** Mr J Robinson
**S** (**Ref:**HM17479)

**ROBINSON, JACKIE**

**Jackie Robinson**, 126 Radlett Rd, Frogmore, St. Albans, **Hertfordshire**, AL2 2LB, ENG.
(T) 01727 872826
Speciality: Reflexology.
● **Owner** Ms J Robinson
**S** **T** (**Ref:**HM17480)

**ROBINSON, JACQUELINE**

**Jacqueline Robinson**, 74 Marmion Rd, Hove, **Sussex (East)**, BN3 5FT, ENG.
(T) 01273 882652
Speciality: Reflexology.
**S** **T** (**Ref:**HM17481)

**ROBINSON, JAMES**

**James Robinson**, 50 Plymouth Rd, Penarth, **Glamorgan (Vale of)**, CF64 3DB, WAL.
(T) 029 2070 1323
Speciality: Psychology.
**B** (**Ref:**HM17482)

**ROBINSON, JAQUELINE**

**Jaqueline Robinson**, 23 Old Palace Lane, Richmond, **Surrey**, TW9 1PG, ENG.
(T) 020 8948 3652
Speciality: Aromatherapy.
● **Owner** Ms J Robinson
**M** **O** (**Ref:**HM17483)

**ROBINSON, JOHN**

**John Robinson**, 62 Acres Rd, Brierley Hill, **Midlands (West)**, DY5 2XY, ENG.
(T) 01384 484945 (F) 01384 4484945
Speciality: Chiropody. ✓
● **Chiropodist** Mr J Robinson Q: S.R.Ch. M: S.C.P.
**M** (**Ref:**HM17484)

**ROBINSON, K**

**K Robinson**, 42 Armond Rd, Witham, **Essex**, CM8 2HA, ENG.
(T) 01376 511627
Speciality: Chiropodists (Podiatrists).
**S** (**Ref:**HM17485)

**ROBINSON, KAREN**

**Karen Robinson**, 26 Greenways, Flitwick, Bedford, **Bedfordshire**, MK45 1DA, ENG.
(T) 01525 712204
Speciality: Osteopathy.
● **Owner** Ms K Robinson
**P** **S** **T** (**Ref:**HM17486)

**ROBINSON, KAY**

**Kay Robinson**, 134 Broad St, Parkgate, Rotherham, **Yorkshire (South)**, S62 6ES, ENG.
(T) 01709 522334
Speciality: Chiropodists (Podiatrists).
**S** (**Ref:**HM17487)

**ROBINSON, KEITH**

**Keith Robinson**, 23 Waltham Rd, Grimsby, **Humberside (South)**, DN33 2LY, ENG.
Speciality: Chiropody, Cryo Surgery, Nail Surgery. ✓
● **Chiropodist (Podiatrist)**
Mr K Robinson
(T) 01472 752762 Q: DPodM, S.R.Ch. M: S.C.P.
**M** Yrs. Est.: 30 (**Ref:**HM17488)

**ROBINSON, KEITH**

**Keith Robinson**, 131 Eastgate, Louth, **Lincolnshire**, LN11 9QE, ENG.
(T) 01507 608838
Speciality: Chiropodists (Podiatrists).
● **Owner** Mr K Robinson
**S** (**Ref:**HM17489)

**ROBINSON, L K**

**L K Robinson**, Lactodorum, 38 Brackley Rd,
(T) 01924 387394
Speciality: Physiotherapy.
**P** **S** **T** (**Ref:**HM17491)

**ROBINSON, LINDSEY A**

**Lindsey A Robinson**, Linken Natural Health Therapy Centre, 22 Pallister Rd, Clacton-On-Sea, **Essex**, CO15 1PG, ENG.
(T) 01255 221651
Speciality: Osteopathy.
● **Owner** Ms L Robinson Q: DO.
**P** **S** **T** (**Ref:**HM17492)

**ROBINSON, M**

**M Robinson**, 10 McPherson Drive, Gourock, **Inverclyde**, PA19 1LJ, SCO.
(T) 01475 637968
Speciality: Acupuncture.
● **Doctor** Dr M Robinson
**O** (**Ref:**HM17493)

**ROBINSON, M**

**M Robinson**, Bailiffs Cottage, Park Rd, Addington, West Malling, **Kent**, ME19 5BQ, ENG.
(T) 01732 840003
Speciality: Physiotherapy.
**P** **S** **T** (**Ref:**HM17494)

**ROBINSON, MARGARET**

**Margaret Robinson**, 3 Middle Rd, Aylesbury, **Buckinghamshire**, HP21 7AD, ENG.
(T) 01296 425361 (F) 01296 425361
Speciality: Hypnosis.
● **Owner** Mrs M Robinson
**B** (**Ref:**HM17495)

**ROBINSON, MICHAEL**

**Michael Robinson**, Fleet Cottage, Granville Rd, Cowes, **Isle of Wight**, PO31 7JD, ENG.
(T) 01983 292014
Speciality: Osteopathy.
**P** **S** **T** (**Ref:**HM17496)

**ROBINSON, MICHAEL J**

**Michael J Robinson**, 14 Rockland Rd, London, **London (Greater)**, SW15 2LN, ENG.
(T) 020 8788 0723
Speciality: Osteopathy.
**P** **S** **T** (**Ref:**HM17497)

**ROBINSON, MIG**

**Mig Robinson**, Starlight, 1 North End, Pinvin, Pershore, **Worcestershire**, WR10 2LD, ENG.
(T) 01386 561227
Speciality: Clairvoyants & Palmists, Mediumship, Tarot, Past Life Regression.
● **Medium** Mig Robinson
**C** Yrs. Est.: 6 (**Ref:**HM17498)

**ROBINSON, N**

**N Robinson**, Chelsea Lane, Inverurie, **Aberdeenshire**, AB51 3QQ, SCO.
(T) 01467 624888 (F) 01467 624888
Speciality: Osteopathy.
● **Partner** Mrs C Craigmile
**P** **S** **T** (**Ref:**HM17499)

**ROBINSON, R S**

**R S Robinson**, 33 Blacklow Brow, Liverpool, **Merseyside**, L36 5XE, ENG.
(T) 01514 806350
Speciality: Complementary Medicines & Therapy.
**C** **M** (**Ref:**HM17500)

**ROBINSON, RACHEL**

**Rachel Robinson**, Osteopathic Clinic, 216 Marton Rd, Middlesbrough, **Cleveland**, TS4 2ET, ENG.
(T) 01642 253515
Speciality: Osteopathy.
**P** **S** **T** (**Ref:**HM17501)

**ROBINSON, RACHEL**

**Rachel Robinson**, 62 Hardwick Lane, Bury St.
Therapy.
**M** (**Ref:**HM17503)

**ROBINSON, SUSAN**

**Susan Robinson**, Redditch, Worcester, **Worcestershire**, B98, ENG.
(T) 01527 547194
Speciality: Bach Remedies.
**M** (**Ref:**HM17504)

**ROBINSON, T**

**T Robinson**, P O Box 3319, Brentwood, **Essex**, CM14 4YB, ENG.
(T) 07850 357524
Speciality: Chiropodists (Podiatrists).
● **Owner** Mr T Robinson
**S** (**Ref:**HM17505)

**ROBINSON, V**

**V Robinson**, 46 Rushen Drive, Hertford Heath, Hertford, **Hertfordshire**, SG13 7RB, ENG.
(T) 01992 554227
Speciality: Complementary Medicines & Therapy.
● **Owner** Mrs V Robinson
**C** **M** (**Ref:**HM17506)

**ROBINSONS HOLISTIC**

**Robinsons Holistic**, 7a High St, Clare, Sudbury, **Suffolk**, CO10 8NY, ENG.
(T) 01787 277733 (F) 01787 278786
Speciality: Complementary Medicines & Therapy.
● **Partner** Mrs S Marsh
**C** **M** (**Ref:**HM17507)

**ROBINSON-ZEL, B**

**Mrs B Robinson-Zel**, 10 Amhurst Court, Cambridge, **Cambridgeshire**, CB3 9BH, ENG.
(T) 01223 366189
Speciality: Psychotherapy. ✓
● **Owner** Mrs B Robinson-Zel Q: C.Psychol, MA. M: BPS.
**C** Yrs. Est.: 30 (**Ref:**HM17508)

**ROBSHAW, HELEN**

**Helen Robshaw**, Beaself, Kiln, Grayshott, Hindhead, **Surrey**, GU26 6JF, ENG.
(T) 01428 712761 (F) 01428 712761
Speciality: Psychotherapy.
● **Owner** Mrs H Robshaw
**B** (**Ref:**HM17509)

**ROBSON, ELAINE**

**Elaine Robson**, 121 Harley St, London, **London (Greater)**, W1N 1DE, ENG.
(T) 020 7935 3960
Speciality: Chiropodists (Podiatrists).
**S** (**Ref:**HM17510)

**ROBSON, ELAINE**

**Elaine Robson**, 10 Hornby Cl, London, **London (Greater)**, NW3 3JL, ENG.
(T) 020 7722 3980
Speciality: Chiropodists (Podiatrists).
● **Owner** Mrs E Robson
**S** (**Ref:**HM17511)

**ROBSON, MARIA**

**Maria Robson**, Ingledale, 1 Tanhouse Rd, Oxted, **Surrey**, RH8 9PE, ENG.
(T) 01883 717277
Speciality: Aromatherapy.
**M** **O** (**Ref:**HM17512)

**ROBSON, PAUL**

**Paul Robson**, Scott St Complementary Therapy Centre, 58 Scott St, Barrow-in-Furness, **Cumbria**, LA14 1QE, ENG.
(T) 01229 826700
Speciality: Hypnotherapy.
**B** (**Ref:**HM17513)

**ROBSON, VANESSA**

**Vanessa Robson**, 89 Bournemouth Rd, Poole, **Dorset**, BH14 0EB, ENG.

(T) 01925 411400
Speciality: Osteopathy.
P S T (Ref:HM17515)

**ROBYNA, ANNETTE**

**Natural Alternatives**, The Walled Garden, Church Rd, Shepperton, **Surrey**, TW17 9JS, ENG.
(T) 01932 222687
(E) annetteholgatew@hotmail.com
Speciality: Acupressure, Aromatherapy, Colour Therapy, Complementary Therapy, Dietician, Healing Therapy, Massage (Therapeutic), Meditation, Polarity Therapy, Reflexology, Reiki, Yoga. ✓
● **Aromatherapist/Nutritionist**
Ms R Blake
● **Owner/Aromatherapist**
Mrs A Holgate Q: BRCP, ITEC, MIFA. M: BRCP, IFA.
T Yrs. Est.: 8 (Ref:HM17516)

**ROCHE CLINICS IRELAND**

**Roche Clinics Ireland**, 18 Bayview Cl, Kilcoole, **County Wicklow**, IRE.
(T) 01287 7627 (F) 01287 1374
Speciality: Chiropractors.
P S T (Ref:HM17517)

**ROCHE, G M**

**G M Roche**, 18 Priory Cl, Caerleon, Newport, NP18 3SY, WAL.
(T) 01633 421799
Speciality: Acupuncture.
O (Ref:HM17518)

**ROCHESTER CHIRO HEALTH CENTRE**

**Rochester Chiropractic Health Centre**, Sir Thomas Longley Rd, Medway City Estate, Rochester, **Kent**, ME2 4FX, ENG.
(T) 01634 710980
Speciality: Chiropractic.
P S T (Ref:HM17519)

**ROCHESTER PHYSIO & SPORTS**

**Rochester Physiotherapy & Sports Injuries Clinic**, St Marys Medical Centre, Vicarage Rd, Strood, Rochester, **Kent**, ME2 4DG, ENG.
(T) 01634 290370
Speciality: Acupuncture, Physiotherapy. ✓
● **Principal/Physiotherapist**
Mr S Pruce Q: Grad Dip Phys, MCSP, SRP. M: CSP.
S Yrs. Est.: 10 (Ref:HM17520)

**ROCK & ROLL THERAPY**

**Rock & Roll Therapy**, 75 Kingsley Avenue, London, **London (Greater)**, W13 0EH, ENG.
(T) 020 8997 6869 (F) 020 8997 6869
Speciality: Psychotherapy.
● **Owner** Mrs J Gerald
B (Ref:HM17521)

**ROCK CLINIC**

**Rock Clinic (The)**, 270 Eastern Rd, Brighton, **Sussex (East)**, BN2 5TA, ENG.
(T) 01273 621841
Speciality: Complementary Medicines & Therapy.
● **Owner** Mrs M Withers
C M (Ref:HM17522)

**ROCK ROAD PSYCHOTHERAPY CENTRE**

**Rock Road Psychotherapy Centre**, 110 Rock Rd, Booterstown, Dublin, **County Dublin**, IRE.
(T) 01288 2749
Speciality: Psychotherapy.
B (Ref:HM17523)

**ROCK SHOP**

**Rock Shop**, St Brigids Well, Liscannor, **County Clare**, IRE.
(T) 06570 81930
Speciality: Complementary Medicines & Therapy.
M (Ref:HM17524)

**ROCKLEY, A M**

**A M Rockley**, 104A Upper Parliament St, Nottingham, **Nottinghamshire**, NG1 6LF, ENG.
(T) 01159 413085
Speciality: Chiropodists (Podiatrists).
● **Partner** Mrs A Rockley
S (Ref:HM17525)

**RODGERS REFLEXOLOGY**

**Rodgers Reflexology**, 32A Low Coniscliffe, Low Coniscliffe, Darlington, **County Durham**, DL2 2JY, ENG.
(T) 01325 467357
Speciality: Reflexology.
● **Owner** Mr M Rodgers
S T (Ref:HM17526)

**RODGERS, J**

**J Rodgers**, 1 King Edward Rd, Saltash, **Cornwall**, PL12 4EQ, ENG.
(T) 01752 844955 (F) 01752 846880
Speciality: Chiropodists (Podiatrists).
● **Owner** Mrs J Hill
S (Ref:HM17527)

**RODHAM, SANDIE**

**Sandie Rodham**, Alresford, **Hampshire**, SO24, ENG.
(T) 01962 734404
Speciality: Bach Remedies.
M (Ref:HM17528)

**RODNEY FERTILITY CLINIC**

**Rodney Fertility Clinic**, 37 Rodney St, Liverpool, **Merseyside**, L1 9EN, ENG.
(T) 01517 093505
Speciality: Hypnosis.
B (Ref:HM17529)

**RODNEY STREET HYPNOTHERAPY**

**Rodney Street Hypnotherapy**, 12 Rodney St, Liverpool, **Merseyside**, L1 2TE, ENG.
(T) 01517 273448
Speciality: Hypnosis.
● **Partner** Mrs T McClatchey
B (Ref:HM17530)

**RODWAY & ASSOCIATES**

**David J Rodway DO & Associates**, 40 Sketty Rd, Uplands, Swansea, SA2 0LJ, WAL.
(T) 01792 298767
Speciality: Cranial Osteopathy, Osteopathy. ✓
● **Osteopath** Mr D Rodway Q: DO. M: GOsC.
C S Yrs. Est.: 21 (Ref:HM17531)

**RODWAY, D J**

**D J Rodway**, First Floor Brecon Complimentary Centre, Bridge St, Llanfaes, Brecon, **Powys**, LD3 7AP, WAL.
(T) 01874 624000
Speciality: Osteopathy.
P S T (Ref:HM17532)

**RODWAY, LI LING**

**Li Ling Rodway**, 84 Congleton Rd, Sandbach, **Cheshire**, CW11 1HG, ENG.
(T) 01270 763926
Speciality: Acupuncture.
● **Manager** Ms K Jones
O (Ref:HM17533)

**ROE GREEN CLINIC**

**Roe Green Clinic**, 7 Sunny Hill, London, **London (Greater)**, NW4 4LN, ENG.
(T) 020 8908 2604
Speciality: Osteopathy.
● **Therapist** Ms Y Daoust
P S T (Ref:HM17534)

**ROEHAMPTON PHYSIO/SPORTS**

**Roehampton Physiotherapy & Sports Injury Clinic**, 356 Dover House Rd, London, **London (Greater)**, SW15 5BL, ENG.
(T) 020 8788 2471 (F) 020 8780 2447
Speciality: Physiotherapy. ✓
● **Owner/Neuro Physiotherapist**
Mrs S Olds Q: MCSP, SRP. M: CSP.
S (Ref:HM17535)

**ROELLGEN, BETH**

**Beth Roellgen**, 52 Stoke Newington Church St, London, **London (Greater)**, N16 0NB, ENG.
(T) 020 7249 9671
Speciality: Acupuncture.
● **Senior Partner** Mrs J Sheridan
O (Ref:HM17536)

**ROESAAS CHIROPODY**

**Roesaas Chiropody**, 1 King Georges Pl, Maldon, **Essex**, CM9 5BZ, ENG.
(T) 01621 851544 (F) 01621 856231
Speciality: Chiropodists (Podiatrists).
● **Owner** Mrs T Roesaas
S (Ref:HM17537)

**ROFF, A M**

**A M Roff**, Wych Cottage, Langport Rd, Somerton, **Somerset**, TA11 6RT, ENG.
(T) 01458 273660 (F) 01458 273660
Speciality: Chiropodists (Podiatrists).
● **Owner** Mr A Roff
S (Ref:HM17538)

**ROFFE, S L**

**S L Roffe**, 13 Stanley St, Bourne, **Lincolnshire**, PE10 9BJ, ENG.
(T) 01778 393098
Speciality: Chiropodists (Podiatrists).
● **Owner** Mrs S Roffe
S (Ref:HM17539)

**ROGER, ANDREA**

**Andrea Roger**, 10 High St, Glastonbury, **Somerset**, BA6 9DU, ENG.
(T) 01458 834236
Speciality: Homeopathy.
● **Director** Ms J Sanders
M (Ref:HM17540)

**ROGERS, A P**

**A P Rogers**, 17 Lester Cl, Plymouth, **Devon**, PL3 6PX, ENG.
(T) 01752 771706
Speciality: Chiropodists (Podiatrists).
● **Partner** Mrs A Rogers
S (Ref:HM17541)

**ROGERS, ALISON**

**Alison Rogers**, Sheffield Clinic Of Complementary Medicine, 378 Ecclesall Rd, Sheffield, **Yorkshire (South)**, S11 8PJ, ENG.
(T) 01142 680236
Speciality: Hypnotherapy.
B (Ref:HM17542)

**ROGERS, ALISON**

**Alison Rogers**, Ione, Chelmsford Rd, Felsted, Dunmow, **Essex**, CM6 3ES, ENG.
(T) 01371 820039
Speciality: Reflexology.
S T (Ref:HM17543)

**ROGERS, AMY**

**Amy Rogers**, 8 Temair House, Tarves Way, London, **London (Greater)**, SE10 9JX, ENG.
(T) 020 8293 7956
Speciality: Reflexology.
S T (Ref:HM17544)

**ROGERS, ANDREA**

**Andrea Rogers**, 16 Carleton St, Portadown, Craigavon, **County Armagh**, BT62 3EN, NIR.
(T) 028 3839 2220
Speciality: Chiropodists (Podiatrists).
● **Owner** Mrs A Morrow
S (Ref:HM17545)

**ROGERS, DEBORAH**

**Deborah Rogers**, The Doctors House Annexe, Victoria Rd, Marlow, **Buckinghamshire**, SL7 1DN, ENG.
(T) 01628 477466
Speciality: Osteopathy.
P S T (Ref:HM17546)

**ROGERS, HEATHER**

**Heather Rogers**, Polstead, 43 The Avenue, Ingol, Preston, **Lancashire**, PR2 7AY, ENG.
(T) 01772 735477
Speciality: Reflexology.
S T (Ref:HM17547)

**ROGERS, JOHN**

**John Rogers**, 211 Ansley Rd, Nuneaton, **Warwickshire**, CV10 8NG, ENG.
(T) 024 7632 9882
Speciality: Chiropodists (Podiatrists).
● **Owner** Mr J Rogers
S (Ref:HM17548)

**ROGERS, L J**

**Mrs L J Rogers**, 45 Alexandra Rd, Hemel Hempstead, **Hertfordshire**, HP2 4AQ, ENG.
(T) 01442 256506
Speciality: Chiropodists (Podiatrists).
S (Ref:HM17549)



Key: B Mind-Body Medicine C Complementary Medicine H Self Help Treatment M Medicinal Therapy O Oriental Medicine P Postural Therapy S Manipulative Structural Therapy T Touch Therapy

**ROGERS, P D (DR)**
**Dr P D Rogers**, 376 Finchley Rd, London, **London (Greater)**, NW3 7AJ, ENG.
(T) 020 7431 1787 (F) 020 7209 4596
Speciality: Homeopathy.
● **Doctor** Dr P Rogers
M (Ref:HM17550)

**ROGERS, PAMELA**
**Pamela Rogers**, 4 Bow Rd, Harbertonford, Totnes, **Devon**, TQ9 7TQ, ENG.
(T) 01803 732616
Speciality: Herbalists.
● **Owner** Ms P Rogers
M (Ref:HM17551)

**ROGERS, PAMELA**
**Pamela Rogers**, 2 Hernaford Rd, Harbertonford, Totnes, **Devon**, TQ9 7TX, ENG.
(T) 01803 732616
Speciality: Herbal Medicine.
M (Ref:HM17552)

**ROGERS, REBECCA**
**Rebecca Rogers**, 32 Albert St, Milverton, Leamington Spa, **Warwickshire**, CV32 6BB, ENG.
(T) 01926 772873
Speciality: Reflexology.
S T (Ref:HM17553)

**ROGERS, S E**
**S E Rogers**, 17 Lester Cl, Plymouth, **Devon**, PL3 6PX, ENG.
(T) 01752 771706
Speciality: Chiropodists (Podiatrists).
● **Partner** Mrs A Rogers
S (Ref:HM17554)

**ROGERS, SUSAN**
**Susan Rogers**, 401A London Rd, High Wycombe, **Buckinghamshire**, HP11 1EL, ENG.
(T) 01494 531856
Speciality: Reflexology.
S T (Ref:HM17555)

**ROGERS, T**
**T Rogers**, Gill Bank, Copse Lane, Jordans, Beaconsfield, **Buckinghamshire**, HP9 2TA, ENG.
(T) 01494 874171
Speciality: Chiropodists (Podiatrists).
S (Ref:HM17556)

**ROGERSON, GEORGE**
**George Rogerson**, Hendon Natural Health Centre, 12 Golders Rise, London, **London (Greater)**, NW4 2HR, ENG.
(T) 020 8202 9747 (F) 020 8202 3890
Speciality: Chiropractors.
● **Owner** Ms K McCarroll
P S T (Ref:HM17557)

**ROGUSKI, CATHERINE**
**Catherine Roguski**, 5 Monmouth Avenue, Topsham, Exeter, **Devon**, EX3 0AF, ENG.
(T) 01392 873747
Speciality: Herbal Medicine.
● **Owner** Mrs C Roguski
M (Ref:HM17558)

**ROHN, E**
**E Rohn**, 41 Retford Rd, Blyth, Worksop, **Nottinghamshire**, S81 8HB, ENG.
(T) 01909 591246 (F) 01909 591246
Speciality: Complementary Medicines & Therapy.
● **Owner** Mrs E Rohn
C M (Ref:HM17559)

**ROHRIG, A**
**A Rohrig**, 168 Overhill Rd, London, **London (Greater)**, SE22 0PS, ENG.
(T) 020 8299 4587
Speciality: Psychotherapy.
● **Owner** Mrs A Rohrig
B (Ref:HM17560)

**ROKPA HOUSE**
**Rokpa House**, 7 Ashley St, Glasgow, **Glasgow (City of)**, G3 6DR, SCO.
(T) 01413 329950 (F) 01413 329950
Speciality: Complementary Medicines & Therapy.
M (Ref:HM17561)

**ROLFE, BRIAN**
**Brian Rolfe**, West View, Winsford Rd, Cholmondeston, Winsford, **Cheshire**, CW7 4DP, ENG.
(T) 01270 528473
Speciality: Complementary Medicines & Therapy.
● **Owner** Mr B Rolfe
C M (Ref:HM17562)

**ROLLAND, C R**
**C R Rolland**, 297 Allison St, Glasgow, **Glasgow (City of)**, G42 8HH, SCO.
(T) 01414 236876
Speciality: Chiropody, Nail Surgery, Electro Surgery. ✓
● **Chiropodist** Mr C Rolland Q: S.R.Ch.
M Yrs. Est.: 37 (Ref:HM17563)

**ROLLAND, C R**
**C R Rolland**, 16 Hamilton Rd, Motherwell, **Lanarkshire (North)**, ML1 3BB, SCO.
(T) 01698 264276
Speciality: Chiropodists (Podiatrists).
S (Ref:HM17564)

**ROLLAND, STEPHEN N**
**Stephen N Rolland**, 24 Breck Rd, Poulton-le-Fylde, **Lancashire**, FY6 7AA, ENG.
(T) 01253 893010
Speciality: Chiropodists (Podiatrists).
S (Ref:HM17565)

**ROLLESTON-SMITH, C**
**Mrs C Rolleston-Smith**, The Old Bakery, High St, Wadhurst, **Sussex (East)**, TN5 6AA, ENG.
(T) 01892 783707
Speciality: Alexander Technique.
● **Owner** Mrs C Rolleston - Smith Q: BA, MSTAT.
P S (Ref:HM17566)

**ROLLS MILL COMP HEALTH CENTRE**
**Rolls Mill Complementary Health Centre**, 111 Rolls Mill, Sturminster Newton, **Dorset**, DT10 2HP, ENG.
(T) 01258 473109 (F) 01258 473421
(E) info@rollsmill.co.uk
(W) www.rollsmill.co.uk
Speciality: Acupressure, Acupuncture, Allergy Testing, Aromatherapy, Bach Remedies, Chiropractic, Complementary Therapy, Counselling, Dietician, Herbal Medicine, Homeopathy, Hypnotherapy, Kinesiology, Manipulation, Massage (Therapeutic), Meditation, Moxibustion, Naturopathy, Nutritional Therapy, Phytotherapy, Postural Integration, Reflexology, Shiatsu, Spiritual Healing, Stress Therapy, Touch Therapy, Vitamin Therapy, Ying & Yang, McTimoney Chiropractic. ✓
● **Massage Therapist** Ms Z Heritage Q: ITEC.
● **Massage Therapist** Mr N Rabbets Q: ITEC. M: GCP.
● **Nutritionist** Chris D'cruz Q: BSc.
● **Homeopath** Ms A Young Q: RSHom.
● **Chiropractor** Ms T White Q: DC, Dip.Chiro, MMCA. M: MCA.
● **Acupuncturist** Mr R Farrington Q: Cert.Ac, Dip.Ac. M: BRCP.
● **Therapist** Joss Vining Q: MAR.
● **Hypnotherapist** Ms D Doggrell Q: MNCH.
● **Nutritionist** Ms A Wise
● **Reflexologist** Ms A Milburn Q: MAR.
● **Shiatsu Practitioner** Mr S Coburn
● **Spiritual Counsellor** Ms V Coburn Q: MSc, MTI.
S Yrs. Est.: 2 (Ref:HM17567)

**ROMA ROMANI HYPNOTHERAPY**
**Roma Romani Hypnotherapy**, 18A Richmond St, City Centre, Liverpool, **Merseyside**, L1 1EF, ENG.
(T) 01516 510140
Speciality: Clairvoyants & Palmists.
B (Ref:HM17568)

**ROMANDA HEALTH CARE**
**Romanda Health Care**, Ashley Walk, London, **London (Greater)**, NW7 1DU, ENG.
(T) 020 8346 0784
Speciality: Complementary Medicines & Therapy, Trichology.
M (Ref:HM17569)

**ROMANINI, ADRIANO**
**Adriano Romanini**, 28 Rochester Cl, Rochester Gardens, Hove, **Sussex (East)**, BN3 3AX, ENG.
(T) 01273 728801
Speciality: Reflexology.
S T (Ref:HM17570)

**ROMEO, GILLIAN**
**Gillian Romeo**, 165 Gaddesden Cres, Wavendon Gate, **Buckinghamshire**, MK7 7SF, ENG.
(T) 01908 282132
Speciality: Reflexology.
S T (Ref:HM17571)

**ROMEO, GILLIAN**
**Gillian Romeo**, 49A Newport Rd, Woburn Sands, **Buckinghamshire**, MK17 8UQ, ENG.
(T) 01908 282132
Speciality: Reflexology.
S T (Ref:HM17572)

**ROMER, A C**
**A C Romer**, 62 Collywell Bay Rd, Seaton Sluice, Whitley Bay, **Tyne and Wear**, NE26 4RG, ENG.
(T) 01912 371063 (F) 01912 371063
Speciality: Herbal Medicine.
● **Owner** Mrs A Romer
M (Ref:HM17573)

**ROMNEY MARSH OSTEOPATHS**
**Kate Miles**, The Priory, 44 The High St, New Romney, **Kent**, TN28 8BZ, ENG.
(T) 07071 224274
(E) katemiles@supanet.com
Speciality: Cranial Osteopathy, Manipulation, Osteopathy, Osteoporosis Screening is available. ✓
● **Osteopath** Ms K Miles
(T) 01797 361111 Q: BSc, Hons (OST). M: GOsC.
S Yrs. Est.: 3 (Ref:HM17574)

**ROMSEY CHIROPRACTIC CLINIC**
**Romsey Chiropractic Clinic**, Unit 5, Abbey Walk, Church St, Romsey, **Hampshire**, SO51 8JQ, ENG.
(T) 01794 519330
Speciality: Chiropractors.
● **Owner** Dr A Miller
P S T (Ref:HM17575)

**ROMSEY HEALTH CENTRE**
**Romsey Health Centre**, 1st Floor 8 Church St, Romsey, **Hampshire**, SO51 8BU, ENG.
(T) 01794 514879
Speciality: Osteopathy.
P S T (Ref:HM17576)

**ROMSEY PHYSIO & SPORTS**
**Romsey Physiotherapy & Sports Injury Clinic**, Figure Shapers, Newton Lane, Romsey, **Hampshire**, SO51 8GZ, ENG.
(T) 01794 518081
Speciality: Physiotherapy.
● **Owner** Mrs S Mills
P S T (Ref:HM17577)

**ROMSLEY PHYSIOTHERAPY PRACTICE**
**Romsley Physiotherapy Practice**, 332 Bromsgrove Rd, Hunnington, Halesowen, **Midlands (West)**, B62 0JE, ENG.
(T) 01215 508005 (F) 01215 508005
Speciality: Acupuncture, Aromatherapy, Electrotherapy, Hypnotherapy, Manipulation, Massage (Therapeutic), Moxibustion, Reflexology. ✓
● **Physiotherapist** Ms J Reading Q: MCSP, SRP. M: CSP.
S Yrs. Est.: 10 (Ref:HM17578)

**RONCIA INSTITUTE OF HYPNOSIS**
**Roncia Institute Of Hypnosis**, 66 Harpenden Drive, Dunscroft, Doncaster, **Yorkshire (South)**, DN7 4HN, ENG.
(T) 01302 846166 (F) 01302 846166
Speciality: Hypnosis.
● **Owner** Mr R Martin
B (Ref:HM17579)

**ROOK, J**
**J Rook**, Surgery, Cae Glas House, 36 Church St, Oswestry, **Shropshire**, SY11 2SP, ENG.


Key continued: Yrs.Est: Years Established Q: Qualifications M: Professional Membership ✓ Indemnity Insurance Accept Credit Cards

(T) 01691 672909
Speciality: Chiropodists (Podiatrists).
S (Ref:HM17580)

**ROOK, JANE**
**Jane Rook**, 36 Church St, Oswestry, **Shropshire**, SY11 2SP, ENG.
(T) 01691 671413
Speciality: Chiropodists (Podiatrists).
● **Practice Manager** Mrs J Gill
S (Ref:HM17581)

**ROOK, MARY**
**Mary Rook**, Weighton Wold, Beverley Rd, Market Weighton, York, **Yorkshire (North)**, YO43 4NE, ENG.
(T) 01696 873552
Speciality: Physiotherapy.
P S T (Ref:HM17582)

**ROOKER, P A**
**P A Rooker**, 66 Cape Hill, Smethwick, **Midlands (West)**, B66 4PB, ENG.
(T) 01215 581785
Speciality: Chiropodists (Podiatrists).
● **Owner** Miss P Rooker
S (Ref:HM17583)

**ROOM FOR GROWTH**
**Room For Growth**, 85 Fortess Rd, London, **London (Greater)**, NW5 1AG, ENG.
(T) 020 7267 7234 (F) 020 7428 5855
Speciality: Complementary Medicines & Therapy.
● **Owner** Mr M Fisher
M (Ref:HM17584)

**ROOM FOR HEALING**
**Room For Healing**, 4 Walton House, Walton Lane, Bosham, Chichester, **Sussex (West)**, PO18 8QB, ENG.
(T) 01243 574385
Speciality: Reflexology, Reiki. ✔
● **Owner/Reflexologist** Mrs S Petch Q: MAR.
C Yrs. Est.: 8 (Ref:HM17585)

**ROOT, A C**
**A C Root**, 49 Chalk Farm Rd, London, **London (Greater)**, NW1 8AN, ENG.
(T) 020 7916 1298
Speciality: Chiropodists (Podiatrists).
S (Ref:HM17586)

**ROOT, A C**
**A C Root**, 50 Haverstock Hill, London, **London (Greater)**, NW3 2BH, ENG.
(T) 020 7916 1298
Speciality: Chiropodists (Podiatrists).
S (Ref:HM17587)

**ROOTS, HAZEL**
**Hazel Roots**, 35 Hemingford Rd, Sutton, **Surrey**, SM3 8HG, ENG.
(T) 020 8641 5513
Speciality: Homeopathy.
● **Owner** Mrs H Roots
M (Ref:HM17588)

**ROOTS, HAZEL**
**Hazel Roots**, The Limetree Centre, Fitzroy House, Lynwood Drive, Worcester Park, **Surrey**, KT4 7AB, ENG.
(T) 020 8330 0100
Speciality: Homeopathy.
M (Ref:HM17589)

**ROOTS, WENDY**
**Wendy Roots**, 53 Vine Rd, Tiptree, Colchester, **Essex**, CO5 0LR, ENG.
(T) 01621 818380
Speciality: Reflexology.
S T (Ref:HM17590)

**ROPER, J**
**J Roper**, Payden Chemist, 24-26 High St, Snodland, **Kent**, ME6 5DE, ENG.
(T) 01634 240539
Speciality: Chiropodists (Podiatrists).
S (Ref:HM17591)

**ROPER, JANET**
**Janet Roper**, 17 Abingdon St, Burnham-on-Sea, **Somerset**, TA8 1PH, ENG.
(T) 01278 795322
Speciality: Hypnosis.
● **Owner** Mrs J Roper
B (Ref:HM17592)

**ROSAMBEAU, VALERIE**
**Valerie Rosambeau**, 36 Mannock Rd, London, **London (Greater)**, N22 6AA, ENG.
(T) 020 8889 0757
Speciality: Reflexology.
S T (Ref:HM17593)

**ROSAMUND PARKE, JORDAN**
**Rosamund Parke Jordan**, 9 Kings Rd, St. Leonards-On-Sea, **Sussex (East)**, TN37 6EA, ENG.
(T) 01424 714800
Speciality: Complementary Medicines & Therapy.
M (Ref:HM17594)

**ROSBOTHAM, VALERIE**
**Valerie Rosbotham**, Swevenings, 77 Blithemeadow Drive, Sprowston, Norwich, **Norfolk**, NR7 8PZ, ENG.
(T) 01603 423891
Speciality: Reflexology.
S T (Ref:HM17595)

**ROSCOE, JULIA**
**Julia Roscoe**, 20 Coppice Walk, Shirley, Solihull, **Midlands (West)**, B90 4HY, ENG.
(T) 01564 702186
Speciality: Reflexology.
● **Partner** Mrs J Spence
S T (Ref:HM17596)

**ROSE & ASSOCIATES**
**Colin Rose & Associates**, 220 London Rd, Leicester, **Leicestershire**, LE2 1NE, ENG.
(T) 01162 542380 (F) 01162 542746
Speciality: Chiropractic.
● **Owner** Mr C Rose
P S T (Ref:HM17597)

**ROSE & CROWN CLINIC**
**Rose & Crown Clinic**, 6 South St, South Molton, **Devon**, EX36 4AA, ENG.
(T) 01769 572608
Speciality: Acupuncture, Alexander Technique, Aromatherapy, Counselling, Healing Therapy, Herbal Medicine, Homeopathy, Hypnotherapy, Reflexology, Remedial Massage, Spiritual Healing, McTimoney Chiropractic. ✔
● **Aromatherapist/Massage Therapist/Spiritual Healer** Ms S Loftus Q: ISPA, ITEC.
● **McTimoney Chiropractic** Mr F Loftus Q: DC, MMCA.
● **McTimoney Chiropractic** Ms S Loftus Q: DC, MMCA.
● **Teacher of the Alexander Technique** Ms C Parks M: STAT.
● **Counsellor** Ms S Beanland Q: Dip.Couns, MBAcC.
● **Hypnotherapist** Ms A Kirkland Page Q: MNCH, NLP.
● **Holistic Aromatherapist/Massage Therapist** Ms J Braid M: IFA.
● **Bach Foundation Registered Practitioner** Ms L Drummond
● **Homeopath** Ms V Fitzroy Q: BA.
● **Remedial Massage Therapist** Ms A Clark Q: ITEC.
● **Acupuncturist** Mr R Hill
(T) 01392 841022 Q: MA, MBAcC.
● **Medical Herbalist/Reflexologist** Ms H Loder Q: MAR.
C Yrs. Est.: 10 (Ref:HM17598)

**ROSE OAK HEALTH & BEAUTY CLNC**
**Rose Oak Health & Beauty Clinic**, 250 Maidstone Rd, Gillingham, **Kent**, ME8 0HH, ENG.
(T) 01634 234880 (F) 01634 238400
Speciality: Complementary Medicines & Therapy.
● **Owner** Mrs S Evans
M (Ref:HM17599)

**ROSE STREET CLINIC**
**Rose Street Clinic Covent Garden**, 24 Rose St, London, **London (Greater)**, WC2E 9EA, ENG.
(T) 020 7379 9486 (F) 020 7836 7696
Speciality: Chiropodists (Podiatrists).
● **Owner** Mr L Slater
S (Ref:HM17600)

**ROSE, A C**
**A C Rose**, 73 Frinton Rd, Holland-On-Sea, Clacton-On-Sea, **Essex**, CO15 5UH, ENG.
(T) 01255 813673
Speciality: Chiropodists (Podiatrists).
S (Ref:HM17601)

**ROSE, ADELE**
**Adele Rose**, Penfolds Patch, 20 Haig Rd, Grays, **Essex**, RM16 4XL, ENG.
(T) 01375 851338
Speciality: Clairvoyants & Palmists.
● **Owner** Mrs A Rose
B (Ref:HM17602)

**ROSE, AMBER**
**Amber Rose**, 50 Northumberland Rd, Thornaby, Stockton-On-Tees, **Cleveland**, TS17 8BH, ENG.
(T) 01642 616967
Speciality: Clairvoyants & Palmists.
● **Owner** Mrs A Rose
B (Ref:HM17603)

**ROSE, B S**
**B S Rose**, 626 London Rd, Davenham, Northwich, **Cheshire**, CW9 8LG, ENG.
(T) 01606 42662
Speciality: Homeopathy.
M (Ref:HM17604)

**ROSE, CYNTHIA J**
**Cynthia J Rose**, 174 Barnett Wood Lane, Ashtead, **Surrey**, KT21 2LW, ENG.
(T) 01372 274501
Speciality: Reflexology, Reiki. ✔
● **Reflexologist** Ms C Rose M: AoR, BRA.
T Yrs. Est.: 12 (Ref:HM17605)

**ROSE, ELIZABETH**
**Elizabeth Rose**, 8 Wensleydale Cl, Forest Town, Mansfield, **Nottinghamshire**, NG19 0PG, ENG.
(T) 01623 423444
Speciality: Clairvoyants & Palmists.
● **Owner** Ms J Openshaw
B (Ref:HM17606)

**ROSE, F A**
**F A Rose**, 48B Castle Rd, Newport, **Isle of Wight**, PO30 1DP, ENG.
(T) 01983 522087
Speciality: Physiotherapy.
● **Owner** Mr F Rose
P S T (Ref:HM17607)

**ROSE, JILL**
**Jill Rose**, 27 Hall Dene Cl, Guildford, **Surrey**, GU1 2UL, ENG.
(T) 01483 575835
Speciality: Reflexology.
S T (Ref:HM17608)

**ROSE, LESLEY**
**Lesley Rose**, 6 Horace Rd, Ilford, **Essex**, IG6 2BG, ENG.
(T) 020 8551 0816
Speciality: Psychotherapy.
B (Ref:HM17609)

**ROSE, MARCIA**
**Marcia Rose**, 13A Martin Avenue, Leicester Forest East, Leicester, **Leicestershire**, LE3 3JH, ENG.
(T) 01162 394327
Speciality: Reflexology.
S T (Ref:HM17610)

**ROSE, MARTIN J**
**Martin J Rose**, St Hildas Business Centre, The Ropery, Whitby, **Yorkshire (North)**, YO22 4ET, ENG.
(T) 01947 821235
Speciality: Osteopathy.
● **Owner** Mr M Rose
P S T (Ref:HM17611)

**ROSE, NAOMI**
**Naomi Rose**, 80 Thorold Rd, Chatham, **Kent**, ME5 7EB, ENG.
(T) 01634 405605
Speciality: Aromatherapy, Complementary Therapy, Faith Healing, Healer, Healing Therapy, Massage (Therapeutic), Reflexology, Spiritual

Healing, Touch Therapy. ✔
● **Aromatherapist/Reflexologist**
Ms N Rose Q: BSc, MIFA, MIFR, PGCE. M: IFA, IFR.
T Yrs. Est.: 6 (Ref:HM17612)

## ROSE, NICHOLAS
**Osteopath**, 76 Overton Drive, Wanstead, London, **London (Greater)**, E11 2NW, ENG.
(T) 020 8989 9810
(E) njrose@compuserve.com
Speciality: Manipulation, Massage (Therapeutic), Osteopathy, Ultrasonics. ✔
● **Osteopath** Mr N Rose Q: DO. M: GOsC.
S Yrs. Est.: 19 (Ref:HM17613)

## ROSE, S M
**S M Rose**, 55 Trinity Rd, London, **London (Greater)**, N2 8JJ, ENG.
(T) 020 8444 7217
Speciality: Homeopathy.
M (Ref:HM17614)

## ROSEAROMA
**Rosearoma**, 3 Sherwood Avenue, Blidworth, Mansfield, **Nottinghamshire**, NG21 0SX, ENG.
(T) 01623 794933
Speciality: Complementary Medicines & Therapy.
C M (Ref:HM17615)

## ROSEDALE CLINIC
**Rosedale Clinic**, 48 Redlands Rd, Reading, **Berkshire**, RG1 5HR, ENG.
(T) 01189 866635 (F) 01189 874461
Speciality: Acupuncture, Aromatherapy, Homeopathy, Bicom, Bioresonance. ✔
● **Acupuncturist** Mr C Boardman Q: Reg.BP. M: BAcC, HMA, IRAFMRH.
C (Ref:HM17616)

## ROSEFIELD CONSULTANCY
**Rosefield Consultancy (The)**, The Surgery, Old Bridge, Newlyn, Penzance, **Cornwall**, TR18 5PR, ENG.
(T) 01736 330588
Speciality: Complementary Medicines & Therapy.
C M (Ref:HM17617)

## ROSEHILL CENTRE
**Rosehill Centre (The)**, West Hill Lane, Budleigh Salterton, **Devon**, EX9 6BU, ENG.
(T) 01395 443073
Speciality: Complementary Medicines & Therapy.
C M (Ref:HM17618)

## ROSELANDS CLINIC
**Roselands Clinic**, Clayton Rd, Newcastle, **Staffordshire**, ST5 3AH, ENG.
(T) 01782 636469 (F) 01782 636469
Speciality: Acupuncture.
● **Owner** Mr G Lather
O (Ref:HM17619)

## ROSEMARY HILL CLINIC
**Rosemary Hill Clinic (The)**, 15 Rosemary Hill Rd, Sutton Coldfield, **Midlands (West)**, B74 4HL, ENG.
(T) 01213 521611 (F) 01213 521611
Speciality: Osteopathy.
● **Owner** Mrs A Greaves
P S T (Ref:HM17620)

## ROSEMARY, CHRISTIE
**Christie Rosemary**, 107 Poulton Rd, Wallasey, **Merseyside**, CH44 9DE, ENG.
(T) 01516 396464
Speciality: Hypnotherapy.
● **Owner** Ms R Christie
B (Ref:HM17621)

## ROSEMARY, TARGETT
**Targett Rosemary**, 1st Floor, 399 Cowbridge Rd East, Cardiff, **Glamorgan (Vale of)**, CF5 1JG, WAL.
(T) 029 2022 2942
Speciality: Aromatherapy.
M O (Ref:HM17622)

## ROSEMOUNT CENTRE
**Rosemount Centre (The)**, 1c Mount St, Rosemount, Aberdeen, **Aberdeenshire**, AB25 2RA, SCO.
(T) 01224 636378
Speciality: Acupuncture, Aromatherapy, Art Therapy, Bowen Therapy, Chiropractic, Clinical Ecology, Cognitive Therapy, Counselling, Cranio-Sacral Therapy, Dance Movement Therapy, Gestalt Therapy, Healer, Herbal Medicine, Homeopathy, Hypnotherapy, Indian Head Massage, Massage (Therapeutic), Metamorphic Therapy, Nutritional Therapy, Psychotherapy, Reflexology, Reiki, Shiatsu, Colonic Hydrotherapy, Remedial/Sports Massage, On-Site Massage ✔
● **Director/Homeopath** Mr N Spence Q: RGN, RSHom. M: Soc.Hom.
● **Aromatherapist/Reflexologist** Ms M Inch
● **Nutritional Therapist** Ms C Blakey Q: MCSP, SRP.
● **Acupuncturist** Mr N McGuire Q: Lic.Ac. M: BAcC.
● **Cognitive Behavioural Counsellor** Ms B Rennie Q: BSc, SRN.
● **Cranio-Sacral/Healer/Shiatsu Practitioner** Ms L Davison Q: BSc, MRSS, RCST.
● **Homeopath** Ms E Cairney Q: RGN, RSHom.
● **Psychotherapist/Shiatsu Practitioner** Mr M Julich Q: MRSS.
● **Medical Herbalist** Mr D Gordon Q: BSc, MNIMH, MSc.
● **Remedial/Sports Massage Therapist** Vivien Wraae
● **Bowen Therapist/Hypnotherapist** Mr D Smillie M: NCH.
● **Aromatherapist/Reiki Master** Ms E Harley Q: Karuna Master, Reiki Master, RGN. M: ISPA.
● **Chiropractor** Dr D Norton Q: B.App.Sc, BSc.
● **Hypnotherapist/Massage Therapist/Reflexologist** Ms S Cameron Q: GSSR.
● **Colonic Hydrotherapist** Ms K Christie
● **Art Psychotherapist/Counsellor/Hypnotherapist** Ms W Stewart Q: BA (Hons), Dip.Couns.
B H O P S T
Yrs. Est.: 4 (Ref:HM17623)

## ROSEMOUNT CLINIC OF COMP MED
**Rosemount Clinic Of Complementary Medicines**, 61 Old Woking Rd, West Byfleet, **Surrey**, KT14 6LF, ENG.
(T) 01932 354535 (F) 01932 851300
Speciality: Homeopathy.
M (Ref:HM17624)

## ROSEMOUNT OSTEOPATHY
**Rosemount Osteopathy**, 85 Leadside Rd, Aberdeen, **Aberdeenshire**, AB25 1RX, SCO.
(T) 01224 635999
Speciality: Osteopathy.
● **Owner** Ms F Davison
P S T (Ref:HM17625)

## ROSENFELD, M
**M Rosenfeld**, 148 Sydenham Rd, London, **London (Greater)**, SE26 5JZ, ENG.
(T) 020 8244 9536
Speciality: Chiropodists (Podiatrists).
● **Owner** Mr M Rosenfeld
S (Ref:HM17626)

## ROSENGARD, L (DR)
**Dr L Rosengard Homeopathic and Consultant**, 102 Hamilton Rd, Rutherglen, Glasgow, **Glasgow (City of)**, G73 3DS, SCO.
(T) 01416 472800 (F) 01416 472800
Speciality: Homeopathy.
● **Doctor** Mr L Rosengard Q: Ch.B, MB, MFHom, MRCOG. M: FHom, RCOG.
M (Ref:HM17627)

## ROSEWELL NATURAL HEALTH CLINIC
**Rosewell Natural Health Clinic**, 108A Brighton Rd, Coulsdon, **London (Greater)**, CR5 2NB, ENG.
(T) 020 8763 2123
Speciality: Complementary Medicines & Therapy.
● **Owner** Mrs P York
C M (Ref:HM17628)

## ROSEWOOD AROMATHERAPY ROOM
**Rosewood Aromatherapy Room**, 41 Rosewood Avenue, Paisley, **Renfrewshire**, PA2 9NJ, SCO.
(T) 01418 841811
Speciality: Aromatherapy, Bowen Therapy, Japanese Sitted Massage. ✔
● **Holistic Therapist** Mrs I Reid Q: Dip.Holistic Therapy.
C Yrs. Est.: 5 (Ref:HM17629)

## ROSEWOOD HEALTH CLINIC
**Rosewood Health Clinic**, 33 Clontarf Drive, Omagh, **County Tyrone**, BT78 5BD, NIR.
(T) 028 8224 4755
Speciality: Chiropody, Reflexology. ✔
● **Reflexologist** Mrs Campbell M: IRI.
● **Chiropodist** Mr Campbell M: BSY, IRI.
C Yrs. Est.: 6 (Ref:HM17630)

## ROSNEY LEE, JO
**Jo Rosney Lee**, 823 Manchester Rd, Linthwaite, Huddersfield, **Yorkshire (West)**, HD7 5NF, ENG.
(T) 01484 842428
Speciality: Acupuncture.
O (Ref:HM17631)

## ROSS HERBAL & NTRL HLTH CTRE
**Ross Herbal & Natural Health Centre**, 6 Cantilupe Rd, Ross-on-Wye, **Herefordshire**, HR9 7AN, ENG.
(T) 01989 768437
Speciality: Complementary Medicines & Therapy.
C M (Ref:HM17632)

## ROSS, ALICE I
**Alice I Ross**, 10 Muirlees Cres, Milngavie, Glasgow, **Glasgow (City of)**, G62 7JA, SCO.
(T) 01419 564811
Speciality: Chiropodists (Podiatrists).
● **Owner** Mrs A Ross
S (Ref:HM17633)

## ROSS, COLIN R
**Colin R Ross**, 63 Burns Rd, Aberdeen, **Aberdeenshire**, AB15 4NT, SCO.
(T) 01224 310500
Speciality: Osteopathy.
P S T (Ref:HM17634)

## ROSS, J
**J Ross**, 5 The Chestnuts, Charlton, Wantage, **Oxfordshire**, OX12 7HJ, ENG.
(T) 01235 767220
Speciality: Hypnosis.
● **Owner** Mrs J Ross
B (Ref:HM17635)

## ROSS, JULIETTE
**Juliette Ross**, Entry Hill, Bath, **Somerset**, BA2 5LZ, ENG.
(T) 01225 338453
Speciality: Aromatherapy.
● **Owner** Miss J Ross
M O (Ref:HM17636)

## ROSS, L
**L Ross**, 2 Winchester Avenue, Penylan, Cardiff, **Glamorgan (Vale of)**, CF23 9BT, WAL.
(T) 029 2048 9308
Speciality: Psychology.
B (Ref:HM17637)

## ROSS, L
**L Ross**, 68 Ratcliffe Trce, Edinburgh, **Edinburgh (City of)**, EH9 1ST, SCO.
(T) 01316 673001
Speciality: Chiropodists (Podiatrists).
S (Ref:HM17638)

## ROSS, PATRICK
**Patrick Ross**, Beech House, 12 Church St, Cobham, **Surrey**, KT11 3EG, ENG.
(T) 01932 865994
Speciality: Osteopathy.
● **Owner** Mr P Ross
P S T (Ref:HM17639)

## ROSS, PATRICK M
**Patrick M Ross**, 16 Petworth Drive, Horsham, **Sussex (West)**, RH12 5JH, ENG.
(T) 01403 272147


Key continued: Yrs.Est: Years Established Q: Qualifications M: Professional Membership ✔ Indemnity Insurance Accept Credit Cards

Speciality: Osteopathy.
● Owner Mr P Ross
P S T (Ref:HM17640)

## ROSS, PATRICK M
**Patrick M Ross**, 98 Trafalgar Rd, Horsham, **Sussex (West)**, RH12 2QL, ENG.
(T) 01403 272147
Speciality: Osteopathy.
P S T (Ref:HM17641)

## ROSS, SHEENA
**Sheena Ross**, 131 Huntingdon Rd, Thrapston, Kettering, **Northamptonshire**, NN14 4NG, ENG.
(T) 01832 735392
Speciality: Acupuncture.
O (Ref:HM17642)

## ROSS, V
**V Ross**, 56 Bramble Rd, Hatfield, **Hertfordshire**, AL10 9SE, ENG.
(T) 01707 260081
Speciality: Aromatherapy.
M O (Ref:HM17643)

## ROSSBEIGH THERAPIES
**Rossbeigh Therapies**, Woodenbridge, Boyle, **County Roscommon**, IRE.
(T) 07964 935
(E) rtherapies@eircom.net
(W) www.welcome.to/rtherapies
Speciality: Complementary Medicines & Therapy.
M (Ref:HM17644)

## ROSSENDALE NTRL HEALTH CLINIC
**Rossendale Natural Health Clinic**, 227 Bury Rd, Rawtenstall, Rossendale, **Lancashire**, BB4 6DJ, ENG.
(T) 01706 213671
Speciality: Acupuncture.
● Owner Mrs M Ashworth
O (Ref:HM17645)

## ROSSER, JASON
**Jason Rosser**, 71 Leckhampton Rd, Cheltenham, **Gloucestershire**, GL53 0BS, ENG.
(T) 01242 260444 (F) 01242 260444
Speciality: Osteopathy.
● Owner Mr J Rosser
P S T (Ref:HM17646)

## ROSSER, JASON
**Jason Rosser**, Cheltenham Holistic Centre, 66 Suffolk Rd, Cheltenham, **Gloucestershire**, GL50 2ED, ENG.
(T) 01242 584140
Speciality: Osteopathy.
P S T (Ref:HM17647)

## ROSSETTE, J
**J Rossette**, 103A Olive Rd, London, **London (Greater)**, NW2 6UR, ENG.
(T) 020 8208 1442
Speciality: Complementary Medicines & Therapy.
C M (Ref:HM17648)

## ROSSI, JAN
**Jan Rossi**, 15 Brassey Avenue, Eastbourne, **Sussex (East)**, BN22 9NH, ENG.
(T) 01323 768080
Speciality: Hypnosis.
● Owner Ms J Rossi
B (Ref:HM17649)

## ROSSITER, E & GILLEN, M
**Rossiter E Phd & Gillen M**, Rosecliffe Camden Rd, Crosshaven, **County Cork**, IRE.
(T) 021 4831 991
Speciality: Complementary Medicines & Therapy.
M (Ref:HM17650)

## ROSTED, P
**P Rosted**, 200 Abbey Lane, Sheffield, **Yorkshire (South)**, S8 0BU, ENG.
(T) 01142 360077
Speciality: Acupuncture.
● Owner Dr P Rosted
O (Ref:HM17651)

## ROSTRON, ALISON
**Alison Rostron**, 373 Unthank Rd, Norwich, **Norfolk**, NR4 7QG, ENG.
(T) 01603 250595 (F) 01603 454050
Speciality: Complementary Medicines & Therapy.
● Owner Mrs A Rostron
C M (Ref:HM17652)

## ROTHERAY, MERYL J
**Meryl J Rotheray**, Noctorum, Vicarage Lane, North Weald, Epping, **Essex**, CM16 6ET, ENG.
(T) 01992 522571
Speciality: Chiropodists (Podiatrists).
● Owner Ms M Rotheray
S (Ref:HM17653)

## ROTHERHAM HEALTH CHIR DEPT
**Rotherham Priority Health Chiropody Department**, Care Of Doncaster Gate Hospital, Rotherham, **Yorkshire (South)**, S65 1DW, ENG.
(T) 01709 820000
Speciality: Chiropodists (Podiatrists).
S (Ref:HM17654)

## ROTHERHAM HYPNOTHERAPY CLINIC
**Rotherham Hypnotherapy Clinic (The)**, 15 Moorgate Rd, Rotherham, **Yorkshire (South)**, S60 2EN, ENG.
(T) 01709 555529
Speciality: Hypnotherapy.
● Owner Mr B Jarvill
B (Ref:HM17655)

## ROTHERHAM PRIORITY HEALTH
**Chiropody Department-Rotherham Priority Health**, Doncaster Gate Hospital, Doncaster Gate, Rotherham, **Yorkshire (South)**, S65 1DW, ENG.
(T) 01709 304801
Speciality: Chiropodists (Podiatrists).
S (Ref:HM17656)

## ROTHERHAM PRIORITY HEALTH
**Rotherham Priority Health N H S Trust**, Doncaster Gate Hospital, Doncaster Gate, Rotherham, **Yorkshire (South)**, S65 1DW, ENG.
(T) 01709 830678 (F) 01709 824849
Speciality: Chiropodists (Podiatrists).
S (Ref:HM17657)

## ROTHWELL SPORTS CENTRE
**Rothwell Sports Centre**, Rothwell Sports Centre, Wakefield Rd, Oulton, Leeds, **Yorkshire (West)**, LS26 8EL, ENG.
(T) 01132 824110
Speciality: Acupuncture, Mobilsation massage.
● Physiotherapist Mr S Love Q: BA, Grad Dip Phys, MCSP, SRP. M: CSP.
● Nurse Julia Love Q: RGN.
S (Ref:HM17658)

## ROTHWELL, DECLAN
**Rothwell Declan B Sc , Lic Ac**, 15 Grattan Lodge Hole-In-The-W Donaghmede, Dublin, **County Dublin**, IRE.
(T) 01848 5878
Speciality: Complementary Medicines & Therapy.
M (Ref:HM17659)

## ROTHWELL, K
**K Rothwell**, 18 Sheep Hill Lane, New Longton, Preston, **Lancashire**, PR4 4ZN, ENG.
(T) 01772 612165 (F) 01772 612165
Speciality: Hypnosis.
● Owner Mr K Rothwell
B (Ref:HM17660)

## ROUBINI, DAPHNE
**Daphne Roubini**, The Haelan Clinic, 41 The Broadway, Crouch End, London, **London (Greater)**, N8 8DT, ENG.
(T) 020 8340 1518
Speciality: Complementary Medicines & Therapy.
● Manager Mr J Krahn
M (Ref:HM17661)

## ROULSTONE, LILIAS
**Lilias Roulstone**, South Molton, **Devon**, EX36, ENG.
(T) 01769 573142
Speciality: Bach Remedies.
M (Ref:HM17662)

## ROUND ROOM
**Round Room (The)**, Monks Meadow Oast, Appledore Rd, Tenterden, **Kent**, TN30 7DB, ENG.
(T) 01580 766488
Speciality: Indian Head Massage, Massage (Therapeutic), Reflexology. ✔
● Complementary Therapist Ms J Burgess
C Yrs. Est.: 17 (Ref:HM17663)

## ROUND, NOLA M
**Nola M Round**, Restormel 29 Liskey Hill, Perranporth, **Cornwall**, TR6 0EX, ENG.
(T) 01872 572359
Speciality: Physiotherapy.
P S T (Ref:HM17664)

## ROUNDABOUT DRAMA/MOVEMENT
**Roundabout Drama & Movement Therapy**, Cornerstone House, 14 Willis Rd, Croydon, **Surrey**, CR0 2XX, ENG.
(T) 020 8665 0038
Speciality: Drama Therapy, Special needs. ✔
● Drama Therapist/Project Director Ms D Haythorne M: CPSM.
C Yrs. Est.: 15 (Ref:HM17665)

## ROUNDABOUT HEALTH
**RoundAbout Health**, 21 Market Pl, Melksham, **Wiltshire**, SN12 6ES, ENG.
(T) 01225 793939
Speciality: Complementary Medicines & Therapy.
● Owner Mrs P Baker
C M (Ref:HM17666)

## ROUNDHAY CHIROPRACTIC CLINIC
**Roundhay Chiropractic Clinic**, 160 St Lane, Leeds, **Yorkshire (West)**, LS8 2AD, ENG.
(T) 01132 661419 (F) 01132 662806
Speciality: Chiropractic, Manipulation, Massage (Therapeutic). ✔
● Chiropractor Mr C Binks Q: BSc (Chiro), DC. M: BCA, GCC.
● Chiropractor Nicola Morrison Q: BSc (Chiro), DC. M: BCA, GCC.
● Chiropractor Mr M Hoibek Q: BSc (Chiro), DC. M: BCA, GCC.
● Chiropractor Mr N Peacock Q: BSc (Chiro), DC. M: BCA, GCC.
S Yrs. Est.: 65 (Ref:HM17667)

## ROURKE, HELEN
**Helen Rourke**, 6 Primrose Way, Sutton-in-Ashfield, **Nottinghamshire**, NG17 1HX, ENG.
(T) 01623 551968
Speciality: Reflexology.
● Owner Ms H Rourke
S T (Ref:HM17668)

## ROURKE, S
**S Rourke**, 110 Town St, Rodley, Leeds, **Yorkshire (West)**, LS13 1HP, ENG.
(T) 01132 566123
Speciality: Chiropodists (Podiatrists).
S (Ref:HM17669)

## ROUSE, ALAN
**Alan Rouse**, 169 Leigh Rd, Eastleigh, **Hampshire**, SO50 9DW, ENG.
(T) 023 8061 2166
Speciality: Osteopathy.
● Practice Manager Mrs C Pritchard
P S T (Ref:HM17670)

## ROUSE, ALISON
**Alison Rouse**, 185a Torridon Rd, London, **London (Greater)**, SE6 1RG, ENG.
(T) 020 8480 9905
Speciality: Reflexology.
● Owner Ms L Griffin
S T (Ref:HM17671)

## ROUSE, BARBARA
**Barbara Rouse**, 22 Northbourne Rd, Gillingham, **Kent**, ME8 6QN, ENG.
(T) 01634 389764
Speciality: Reflexology.
S T (Ref:HM17672)

## ROUSE, J
**J Rouse**, 169 Leigh Rd, Eastleigh, **Hampshire**, SO50 9DW, ENG.
(T) 023 8062 0332
Speciality: Osteopathy.
● Practice Manager Mrs C Pritchard



Key: B Mind-Body Medicine C Complementary Medicine H Self Help Treatment M Medicinal Therapy O Oriental Medicine P Postural Therapy S Manipulative Structural Therapy T Touch Therapy

P S T (Ref:HM17673)

**ROUSE, JOHN**

**John Rouse**, 185a Torridon Rd, London, **London (Greater)**, SE6 1RG, ENG.
(T) 020 8480 9905
Speciality: Chiropodists (Podiatrists).
● **Owner** Ms L Griffin
S (Ref:HM17674)

**ROUSE, JOHN**

**John Rouse**, 24 Lansdowne Avenue, Bexleyheath, **Kent**, DA7 5ST, ENG.
(T) 020 8301 3009
Speciality: Chiropodists (Podiatrists).
S (Ref:HM17675)

**ROUSSEAU, JAMES**

**James Rousseau**, 131 Edgbaston Rd, Birmingham, **Midlands (West)**, B12 9QA, ENG.
(T) 01214 497766 (F) 01214 424357
Speciality: Chiropractic.
● **Senior Partner** Mr J Rousseau
P S T (Ref:HM17676)

**ROUSSOS, AMANDA**

**Amanda Roussos**, 15 The Thicket, Romsey, **Hampshire**, SO51 5SZ, ENG.
(T) 01794 517831
Speciality: Acupuncture, Aromatherapy, Auricular Therapy, Hopi Ear Candles, Kinesiology, Massage (Therapeutic), Reflexology, Reiki.
O (Ref:HM17677)

**ROUX, ANITA DE**

**Anita De Roux**, 56 Cheylesmore Drive, Frimley, Camberley, **Surrey**, GU16 5BW, ENG.
(T) 01276 61744
Speciality: Reflexology.
S T (Ref:HM17678)

**ROW, PATRICIA**

**Patricia Row**, 37 Lockhurst St, London, **London (Greater)**, E5 0AP, ENG.
(T) 020 8985 2355
Speciality: Osteopathy.
P S T (Ref:HM17679)

**ROWAN CLINIC**

**Rowan Clinic**, 43-44 Bedford Pl, Southampton, **Hampshire**, SO15 2DG, ENG.
(T) 023 8086 6499 (F) 023 8086 6499
Speciality: Complementary Medicines & Therapy.
● **Owner** Miss B Perry
M (Ref:HM17680)

**ROWAN TREE CENTRE**

**Rowan Tree Centre (The)**, Park Pl, Knaresborough, **Yorkshire (North)**, HG5 0ER, ENG.
(T) 01423 867356
Speciality: Complementary Medicines & Therapy.
● **Manageress** Mrs S Partridge
C M (Ref:HM17681)

**ROWAN, G**

**Mrs G Rowan**, Oak Cottage, High St, Hawkhurst, Cranbrook, **Kent**, TN18 4JS, ENG.
(T) 01580 752192
Speciality: Chiropodists (Podiatrists).
● **Owner** Mrs G Rowan
S (Ref:HM17682)

**ROWAN, MAGGIE**

**Maggie Rowan**, 32 West Brook Rd, Wirral, **Merseyside**, CH46 5NN, ENG.
(T) 01516 784122
Speciality: Aromatherapy.
M O (Ref:HM17683)

**ROWBOTHAM, DARCIE**

**Darcie Rowbotham**, 6 Williams Way, Longwick, Princes Risborough, **Buckinghamshire**, HP27 9RP, ENG.
(T) 01844 342437
Speciality: Aromatherapy.
M O (Ref:HM17684)

**ROWE, GEOFF**

**Geoff Rowe**, Pen-Lan, 1a McCarthy Way, Finchampstead, Wokingham, **Berkshire**, RG40 4UA, ENG.
(T) 01189 328126
Speciality: Reflexology.
S T (Ref:HM17685)

**ROWE, HELEN & JEREMY**

**Helen & Jeremy Rowe**, 20 Cintra Avenue, Reading, **Berkshire**, RG2 7AU, ENG.
(T) 01189 863305
Speciality: Complementary Medicines & Therapy.
● **Partner** Mrs H Rowe
C M (Ref:HM17686)

**ROWE, HOLLIE ANN**

**Hollie Ann Rowe**, 10 Bideford Rd, Ruislip, **London (Greater)**, HA4 0UB, ENG.
(T) 020 8845 2549
Speciality: Reflexology.
S T (Ref:HM17687)

**ROWE, M**

**M Rowe**, Limetrees, The Way, Reigate, **Surrey**, RH2 0LB, ENG.
(T) 01737 225948 (F) 01737 240723
Speciality: Psychology.
● **Principal** Mr M Rowe
B (Ref:HM17688)

**ROWE, PENNY**

**Ms Penny Rowe**, Pawprint House, 4 Ropers Lane, Wareham, **Dorset**, BH20 4QT, ENG.
(T) 01929 552616
Speciality: Bach Remedies, Holistic Healing, Homeopathy. ✓
● **Owner** Ms P Rowe Q: L.C.C.H, MHMA, SRN. M: HMA.
C Yrs. Est.: 2 (Ref:HM17689)

**ROWE, PENNY**

**Penny Rowe**, 7 St Martins Lane, Wareham, **Dorset**, BH20 4HF, ENG.
(T) 01929 552616
Speciality: Homeopathy.
M (Ref:HM17690)

**ROWLAND, G A**

**G A Rowland**, 7 Lower Green Rd, Pembury, Tunbridge Wells, **Kent**, TN2 4DZ, ENG.
(T) 01892 825640
Speciality: Hypnosis.
B (Ref:HM17691)

**ROWLAND, JETHRO**

**Jethro Rowland**, 36 Thatchers End, Hitchin, **Hertfordshire**, SG4 0PD, ENG.
(T) 01462 440762
(E) micjeta@aol.com
Speciality: Acupressure, Acupuncture, Herbal Medicine.
● **Owner** Mr J Rowland
O Yrs. Est.: 10 (Ref:HM17692)

**ROWLAND, JETHRO**

**Jethro Rowland**, Aberfoyle House, Stapley Rd, St. Albans, **Hertfordshire**, AL3 5EP, ENG.
(T) 01727 856687
Speciality: Acupuncture.
● **Manager** Mrs S Bassett
O (Ref:HM17693)

**ROWLAND, JETHRO**

**Jethro Rowland**, The Hertford Chiropractic Clinic, 5 Port Hill, Hertford, **Hertfordshire**, SG14 1PJ, ENG.
(T) 01992 501659
Speciality: Acupuncture.
O (Ref:HM17694)

**ROWLAND, S**

**S Rowland**, The Old Golf House, Rectory Rd, Streatley, Reading, **Berkshire**, RG8 9QA, ENG.
(T) 01491 874455
Speciality: Osteopathy.
● **Owner** Ms S Rowland
P S T (Ref:HM17695)

**ROWLAND-CLARK, A**

**A Rowland-Clark**, 28 Cicada Rd, London, **London (Greater)**, SW18 2NW, ENG.
(T) 020 8870 4244 (F) 020 8870 4244
Speciality: Physiotherapy.
● **Owner** Mrs A Rowland-Clark
P S T (Ref:HM17696)

**ROWLANDS, BERNARD**

**Bernard Rowlands**, Newport Clinic Of Holistic Health, 36 Godfrey Rd, Newport, NP20 4PE, **WAL**.
(T) 01633 843333
Speciality: Complementary Medicines & Therapy.
● **Owner** Mr J Francis
M (Ref:HM17697)

**ROWLANDS, CHRISTINE**

**Christine Rowlands**, Newport Clinic Of Holistic Health, 36 Godfrey Rd, Newport, NP20 4PE, **WAL**.
(T) 01633 843333
Speciality: Complementary Medicines & Therapy.
● **Owner** Mr J Francis
M (Ref:HM17698)

**ROWLANDS, MARGARET**

**Margaret Rowlands**, The Weaver House Clinic, 19A Pillory St, Nantwich, **Cheshire**, CW5 5BZ, ENG.
(T) 01270 629933
Speciality: Aromatherapy.
M O (Ref:HM17699)

**ROWLANDSON, CATHY**

**Mrs Cathy Rowlandson**, 89 St. Margarets Rd, Twickenham, **London (Greater)**, TW1 2LJ, ENG.
(T) 020 8892 1380
Speciality: Physiotherapy.
P S T (Ref:HM17700)

**ROWLEY, JULIA**

**Julia Rowley**, Castle Clinic, 5 Castle Hill Rd, Dover, **Kent**, CT16 1QG, ENG.
(T) 01304 202352 (F) 01304 216366
Speciality: Hypnotherapy.
● **Practice Manager** Ms J Lehane
B (Ref:HM17701)

**ROWLEY, M**

**M Rowley**, London Rd, Chesterton, Newcastle, **Staffordshire**, ST5 7DY, ENG.
(T) 01782 566241
Speciality: Chiropodists (Podiatrists).
S (Ref:HM17702)

**ROWLEY, SONIA**

**Sonia Rowley**, 280 Balham High Rd, London, **London (Greater)**, SW17 7AL, ENG.
(T) 020 8682 1800
Speciality: Complementary Medicines & Therapy.
M (Ref:HM17703)

**ROWLINSON, MIKE**

**Mike Rowlinson**, Martindale House, Lombard St, Newark, **Nottinghamshire**, NG24 1XG, ENG.
(T) 01636 611150
Speciality: Homeopathy.
● **Administrator** Mrs S Taylor
M (Ref:HM17704)

**ROWNEY, ERICA**

**Erica Rowney**, Little West Farm, Melford Rd, Lawshall, Bury St. Edmunds, **Suffolk**, IP29 4PX, ENG.
(T) 01284 830629
Speciality: Reflexology.
S T (Ref:HM17705)

**ROWNTREE, D**

**D Rowntree**, 1 St. James Trce, Selby, **Yorkshire (North)**, YO8 4HL, ENG.
(T) 01757 704074
Speciality: Homeopathy.
● **Owner** Ms D Rowntree
M (Ref:HM17706)

**ROWSELL**

**Rowsell**, 1 Zinnia Cl, Wokingham, **Berkshire**, RG41 3ND, ENG.
(T) 01189 794312
Speciality: Chiropodists (Podiatrists).
● **Owner** Mrs J Rowsell
S (Ref:HM17707)

**ROXANNES HOMEOPATHIC PHARMACY**

**Roxannes Homeopathic Pharmacy**, 446 Chiswick High Rd, London, **London (Greater)**, W4 5TT, ENG.
(T) 020 8994 6655 (F) 020 8994 6655
Speciality: Herbal Medicine, Homeopathy.
M (Ref:HM17708)


Key continued: **Yrs.Est:** Years Established **Q:** Qualifications **M:** Professional Membership ✓ Indemnity Insurance Accept Credit Cards

## ROY MORRIS CLINIC

**Roy Morris Clinic (The)**, Blaenau-Dwr, Froncysyllte, Llangollen, **Denbighshire**, LL20 7RY, WAL.
(T) 01691 772992
(E) roy-morris-clinic@supanet.com
Speciality: Acupuncture, Iridology, Reflexology, Shiatsu, Crystal Therapy. ✓
● **Complementary Therapist**
Mr R Morris Q: DO.
● **Complementary Therapist**
Ms Z Williams Q: DO.
C (Ref:HM17709)

## ROY, COLLEEN

**Colleen Roy**, 103 Owls Rd, Verwood, **Dorset**, BH31 6HH, ENG.
(T) 01202 828306
Speciality: Holistic Healing, Homeopathy. ✓
● **Homeopath** Miss C Roy Q: L.C.C.H.
C Yrs. Est.: 5 (Ref:HM17710)

## ROY, GILLIAN

**Gillian Roy**, Crud Yr Awel, Pelcomb Cross, Haverfordwest, **Pembrokeshire**, SA62 6AA, WAL.
(T) 01437 710301
Speciality: Chiropractic.
● **Partner** Mr J Hatwell
P S T (Ref:HM17711)

## ROY, MAGARET

**Magaret Roy**, 39 Clydesdale St, Hamilton, **Lanarkshire (South)**, ML3 0DD, SCO.
(T) 01698 283653
Speciality: Homeopathy.
M (Ref:HM17712)

## ROY, MARGARET

**Margaret Roy**, 11 Lynedoch Pl, Glasgow, **Glasgow (City of)**, G3 6AB, SCO.
(T) 01413 323917
Speciality: Homeopathy.
M (Ref:HM17713)

## ROYAL COLLEGE OF PSYCHIATRISTS

**Royal College of Psychiatrists Scottish Office**, 9 Queen St, Edinburgh, **Edinburgh (City of)**, EH2 1JQ, SCO.
(T) 01312 202910
Speciality: Psychiatry.
B (Ref:HM17714)

## ROYAL DEVON & EXETER HOSPITAL

**Royal Devon & Exeter Hospital**, Chiropody, Gladstone Rd, Exeter, **Devon**, EX1 2ED, ENG.
(T) 01392 405158
Speciality: Chiropodists (Podiatrists).
● **Employee** Mr R Aggett
S (Ref:HM17715)

## ROYAL LONDON HOMOEOPATHIC HOSP

**Royal London Homoeopathic Hospital**, Great Ormond St, London, **London (Greater)**, WC1N 3HR, ENG.
(T) 020 7837 8833
Speciality: Homeopathy.
● **Executive Secretary**
Cathy Sullivan
M (Ref:HM17716)

## ROYCE CLINIC

**Royce Clinic (The)**, 27 Bloomfield Avenue, Bath, **Somerset**, BA2 3AB, ENG.
(T) 01225 444033
Speciality: Physiotherapy.
P S T (Ref:HM17717)

## ROYLANCE, HEATHER

**Heather Roylance**, 26 South St, Newtownards, **County Down**, BT23 4JT, NIR.
(T) 028 9146 9731
Speciality: Reflexology.
S T (Ref:HM17718)

## ROYLANCE, JOHN

**John Roylance**, 5 Southgate Rd, Tenterden, **Kent**, TN30 7BS, ENG.
(T) 01580 765267
Speciality: Psychotherapy.
B (Ref:HM17719)

## ROYSTON COMP HEALTH CENTRE

**Royston Complementary Health Centre**, Halstead Chambers, 31C Market Hill, Royston, **Hertfordshire**, SG8 9JS, ENG.
(T) 01763 247440
Speciality: Complementary Medicines & Therapy.
C M (Ref:HM17720)

## ROYSTON PHYSIOTHERAPY CLINIC

**Royston Physiotherapy Clinic**, Royston Hospital, London Rd, Royston, **Hertfordshire**, SG8 9EN, ENG.
(T) 01763 248337
Speciality: Physiotherapy.
P S T (Ref:HM17721)

## ROZARIO, G

**G Rozario**, 1st Floor 45 Dale St, Ossett, **Yorkshire (West)**, WF5 9HE, ENG.
(T) 01924 277772
Speciality: Complementary Medicines & Therapy.
M (Ref:HM17722)

## RUANE, MARION

**Marion Ruane**, Hair 21, 12 Boston Prde, Boston Rd, London, **London (Greater)**, W7 1DG, ENG.
(T) 020 8567 7126
Speciality: Chiropodists (Podiatrists).
S (Ref:HM17723)

## RUBINSTEIN, ADAM

**Adam Rubinstein**, North Lakes Clinic, 41A Main St, Cockermouth, **Cumbria**, CA13 9JS, ENG.
Speciality: Cranio-Sacral Therapy. ✓
● **Cranio-Sacral Therapist/Homeopath**
Mr A Rubinstein
(T) 01539 824099 Q: RCST. M: CTA.
T Yrs. Est.: 4 (Ref:HM17724)

## RUBINSTEIN, ADAM

**Adam Rubinstein**, 122 Highgate, Kendal, **Cumbria**, LA9, ENG.
(T) 01539 824099
Speciality: Cranio-Sacral Therapy. ✓
● **Cranio-Sacral Therapist**
Mr A Rubinstein Q: RCST. M: CTA.
T Yrs. Est.: 4 (Ref:HM17725)

## RUBY

**Ruby**, 43 Norton Rd, Mumbles, Swansea, SA3 5TQ, WAL.
(T) 01792 403016
Speciality: Clairvoyants & Palmists.
● **Owner** Ms J Llwellyn
B (Ref:HM17726)

## RUDCENKO, H

**H Rudcenko**, The White House, 56 Brighton Rd, 2 Copse Hill, Sutton, **Surrey**, SM2 5BN, ENG.
(T) 020 8642 0121
Speciality: Chiropodists (Podiatrists).
S (Ref:HM17727)

## RUDD, J

**J Rudd**, Oakdale, 15 Kerver Lane, Dunnington, York, **Yorkshire (North)**, YO19 5SH, ENG.
(T) 01904 488953
Speciality: Reflexology.
● **Owner** Mrs J Rudd
S T (Ref:HM17728)

## RUDD, STEVEN (DR)

**Dr Steven Rudd**, 1 Clover Court, Church Rd, Haywards Heath, **Sussex (West)**, RH16 3UF, ENG.
(T) 01444 416911
Speciality: Chiropractic.
● **Owner** Dr S Rudd
P S T (Ref:HM17729)

## RUDD, SUSAN

**Susan Rudd**, 99 Thistleberry Avenue, Newcastle, **Staffordshire**, ST5 2LR, ENG.
(T) 01782 251224
Speciality: Reflexology.
S T (Ref:HM17730)

## RUDDICK, DAVID

**David Ruddick**, 362 Banbury Rd, Oxford, **Oxfordshire**, OX2 7PP, ENG.
(T) 01865 558561
Speciality: Osteopathy.
P S T (Ref:HM17731)

## RUDDOCK, CAROL

**Carol Ruddock**, 40 Spencer Rd, Twickenham, **London (Greater)**, TW2 5TQ, ENG.
(T) 020 8894 7850
Speciality: Homeopathy.
● **Owner** Ms C Ruddock
M (Ref:HM17732)

## RUDDOLPH, FRANK

**Frank Ruddolph**, 3 Valentines Rd, Ilford, **Essex**, IG1 4RZ, ENG.
(T) 020 8518 6878
Speciality: Complementary Medicines & Therapy.
C M (Ref:HM17733)

## RUDENKO, MARIEA

**Mariea Rudenko**, Natural Healing Centre, 25 Belmont Rd, Sutton, **Surrey**, SM2 6DW, ENG.
(T) 020 8770 3765
Speciality: Reflexology.
S T (Ref:HM17734)

## RUDERMAN, HOWARD

**Howard Ruderman**, 24 Rosemary St, Belfast, **County Antrim**, BT1 1QD, NIR.
(T) 028 9033 1717
Speciality: Clairvoyants & Palmists.
B (Ref:HM17735)

## RUDGE, ELAINE

**Elaine Rudge**, 12 Florence Rd, Wingerworth, Chesterfield, **Derbyshire**, S42 6QX, ENG.
(T) 01246 222016
Speciality: Chiropodists (Podiatrists).
S (Ref:HM17736)

## RUDGE, R V

**R V Rudge**, 18 Forest Drive, London, **London (Greater)**, E12 5DF, ENG.
(T) 020 8478 2355
Speciality: Chiropodists (Podiatrists).
● **Owner** Mr R Rudge
S (Ref:HM17737)

## RUDKIN, JULIE

**Julie Rudkin**, Haddon Physiotherapy & Sports Injury Clinic, Covert Farm, East Haddon, Northampton, **Northamptonshire**, NN6 8DU, ENG.
(T) 01604 770089 (F) 01604 771107
Speciality: Physiotherapy.
● **Owner** Ms J Rudkin
P S T (Ref:HM17738)

## RUFFELL, JILLIAN

**Jillian Ruffell**, Linslade Chartered Physiotherapy Clinic, 47A Coniston Rd, Leighton Buzzard, **Bedfordshire**, LU7 7PJ, ENG.
(T) 01525 853462
Speciality: Physiotherapy.
● **Practice Manager** Ms E Jones
P S T (Ref:HM17739)

## RUFFORD PHYSIOTHERAPY CLINIC

**Rufford Physiotherapy Clinic**, 14 Rufford Avenue, Yeadon, Leeds, **Yorkshire (West)**, LS19 7QR, ENG.
(T) 01132 505825
Speciality: Physiotherapy.
● **Owner** Mr S Redmonds
P S T (Ref:HM17740)

## RUGBY PSYCHOLOGY SERVICE

**Rugby Psychology Service**, Orchard Centre, Lower Hillmorton Rd, Rugby, **Warwickshire**, CV21 3SR, ENG.
(T) 01788 555101
Speciality: Psychology.
B (Ref:HM17741)

## RUISLIP CHIROPRACTIC CLINIC

**Ruislip Chiropractic Clinic**, 17 Fairfield Avenue, Ruislip, **London (Greater)**, HA4 7PG, ENG.
(T) 01895 639976
Speciality: Chiropractors.
● **Owner** Dr S Jones
P S T (Ref:HM17742)

## RUIZ-GOLVANO, E

**E Ruiz-Golvano**, 40 Church Lane, Oxted, **Surrey**, RH8 9LB, ENG.
(T) 01883 715127



Key: B Mind-Body Medicine; C Complementary Medicine; H Self Help Treatment; M Medicinal Therapy; O Oriental Medicine; P Postural Therapy; S Manipulative Structural Therapy; T Touch Therapy

Speciality: Osteopathy.
P S T (Ref:HM17743)

**RUIZ-GOLVANO, ELENA**

**Elena Ruiz-Golvano**, 37A Lowfield St, Dartford, **Kent**, DA1 1HP, ENG.
(T) 01322 284898
Speciality: Osteopathy.
P S T (Ref:HM17744)

**RULER, B**

**B Ruler**, 43 Liverpool Rd, Hindley, Wigan, **Lancashire**, WN2 3HQ, ENG.
(T) 01942 255313
Speciality: Chiropodists (Podiatrists).
● **Owner** Mr B Ruler
S (Ref:HM17745)

**RUMBALL, ALMA**

**Alma Rumball**, 35 St Helens Cres, Hastings, **Sussex (East)**, TN34 2EN, ENG.
(T) 01424 715900
Speciality: Psychotherapy.
● **Owner** Mrs A Rumball
B (Ref:HM17746)

**RUMBOLD, C G**

**C G Rumbold**, Spen Physiotherapy Clinic, Hamilton House, 4 Grange Rd, Cleckheaton, **Yorkshire (West)**, BD19 3DY, ENG.
(T) 01274 877839
Speciality: Physiotherapy.
P S T (Ref:HM17747)

**RUMNEY, KATHLEEN**

**Kathleen Rumney**, 13 Hillview Rd, Edinburgh, **Edinburgh (City of)**, EH12 8QN, SCO.
(T) 01313 345413
Speciality: Aromatherapy, Manual Lymph Drainage, Massage (Therapeutic), Reflexology, Reiki, Voder Method, Basic Polarity, Bach Flower Remedies, Metamorphic Technique. ✔
● **Owner/Holistic Therapist**
Mrs K Rumney M: SIR.
C Yrs. Est.: 13 (Ref:HM17748)

**RUMNEY, MICHAEL**

**Michael Rumney**, 53 Charlton Rd, Tetbury, **Gloucestershire**, GL8 8DX, ENG.
(T) 01666 505262
Speciality: Osteopathy.
● **Owner** Mr M Rumney
P S T (Ref:HM17749)

**RUMSEY, S**

**S Rumsey**, 5 Tylers, Sewards End, Saffron Walden, **Essex**, CB10 2LN, ENG.
(T) 01799 527533
Speciality: Osteopathy.
P S T (Ref:HM17750)

**RUNDLE, ANNETTE**

**Annette Rundle**, 1 Welsh Row, Nantwich, **Cheshire**, CW5 5ED, ENG.
(T) 01270 623669
Speciality: Reflexology.
S T (Ref:HM17751)

**RUNDLE, RICHARD**

**Natural Therapy Centre**, 39 Stapleton Cl, Marlow, **Buckinghamshire**, SL7 1TZ, ENG.
(T) 01628 481253
(E) r.rundle@hotmail.com
Speciality: Absent Healing, Acupressure, Acupuncture, Auto Suggestion, Bach Remedies, Cognitive Therapy, Complementary Therapy, Counselling, Cupping, Dietician, Hay Diet, Healer, Healing Therapy, Holistic Healing, Hypnosis, Hypnotherapy, Indian Head Massage, Manipulation, Manual Lymph Drainage, Massage (Therapeutic), Moxibustion, Oriental Diagnosis, Reflexology, Shiatsu, Spiritual Healing, Sports Massage, Stress Therapy, Visualisation Therapy, Vitamin Therapy, Ying & Yang, Equire, Infant Massage, Deep Tissue Massage. ✔
● **Physiotherapist** Mr R Rundle Q: Dip.Ac, Dip.Body Massage, Dip.Reiki, MAR. M: IPTI.
B Yrs. Est.: 10 (Ref:HM17752)

**RUNNING EARTH HOLISTIC CLINIC**

**Running Earth Holistic Clinic**, Fairview, High St, Winchcombe, Cheltenham, **Gloucestershire**, GL54 5LJ, ENG.
(T) 01242 604694
Speciality: Complementary Medicines & Therapy.
● **Director** Ms H Holt
C M (Ref:HM17753)

**RUSH, DENNIS**

**Dennis Rush**, 25 Coris Cl, Marton Manor, Middlesbrough, **Cleveland**, TS7 8SR, ENG.
(T) 01642 300654
Speciality: Auto Suggestion, Autogenic Training, Counselling, Hypnosis, Hypnotherapy, Psychotherapy, Sound Therapy, Stress Therapy, Transactional Analysis, Visualisation Therapy. ✔
● **Hypnotherapist** Mr D Rush M: NCH.
B Yrs. Est.: 20 (Ref:HM17754)

**RUSH, J A**

**J A Rush**, Diss Chiropractors Clinic, 1 Roydon Rd, Diss, **Norfolk**, IP22 4LN, ENG.
(T) 01379 650020
Speciality: Chiropractic.
P S T (Ref:HM17755)

**RUSH, M K**

**M K Rush**, 37 The Boulevard, Lytham St. Annes, **Lancashire**, FY8 1EH, ENG.
(T) 01253 720367
Speciality: Physiotherapy.
P S T (Ref:HM17756)

**RUSHANT, LYNDA**

**Lynda Rushant**, Oakbeam, 30 Hadham Rd, Bishop's Stortford, **Hertfordshire**, CM23 2QS, ENG.
(T) 01279 507888
Speciality: Reflexology.
S T (Ref:HM17757)

**RUSHBROOKE, P**

**P Rushbrooke**, Flat 12 Fresham House, 12 Durham Rd, Bromley, **Kent**, BR2 0SG, ENG.
(T) 020 8460 7044
Speciality: Complementary Medicines & Therapy.
● **Owner** Mrs P Rushbrooke
C M (Ref:HM17758)

**RUSHCLIFFE ED PSYCHOLOGY SV**

**Rushcliffe Educational Psychology Service**, Mundella Centre, Green St, Nottingham, **Nottinghamshire**, NG2 2LA, ENG.
(T) 01159 868968
Speciality: Psychology.
B (Ref:HM17759)

**RUSHTON, AVRIL**

**Avril Rushton**, 8 Fircroft Drive, Chandlers Ford, Eastleigh, **Hampshire**, SO53 2HE, ENG.
(T) 023 8025 3509
Speciality: Reflexology.
S T (Ref:HM17760)

**RUSSELL THERAPEUTIC CENTRE**

**Russell Therapeutic Centre (The)**, Journey's End, Russell Cl, Wells-next-the-Sea, **Norfolk**, NR23 1BX, ENG.
(T) 01328 710862
Speciality: Complementary Medicines & Therapy.
C M (Ref:HM17761)

**RUSSELL, AVRIL**

**Avril Russell**, 5 Hillhouse Rd, Edinburgh, **Edinburgh (City of)**, EH4 3QP, SCO.
(T) 01313 324624
Speciality: Chiropodists (Podiatrists).
● **Owner** Mrs A Russell
S (Ref:HM17762)

**RUSSELL, CAROL**

**Carol Russell**, 2 Blossom Cl, Botley, Southampton, **Hampshire**, SO30 2FR, ENG.
(T) 01489 690488
Speciality: Complementary Medicines & Therapy.
C M (Ref:HM17763)

**RUSSELL, CAROLINE**

**Caroline Russell**, Harrogate, **Yorkshire (North)**, HG2, ENG.
(T) 01423 873165
Speciality: Reflexology.
S T (Ref:HM17764)

**RUSSELL, CHRIS**

**Chris Russell**, 11 Manor Cres, Portsmouth, **Hampshire**, PO6 2HP, ENG.
(T) 023 9220 1366
Speciality: Hypnosis, Psychotherapy.
B (Ref:HM17765)

**RUSSELL, COLIN**

**Colin Russell**, 13 Castle Cl, Henley-In-Arden, Solihull, **Warwickshire**, B95 5LR, ENG.
(T) 01564 792749
Speciality: Biomechanics, Chiropody. ✔
● **Chiropodist (Podiatrist)**
Mr C Russell Q: DPodM, M.S.C.P, S.R.Ch.
M Yrs. Est.: 25 (Ref:HM17766)

**RUSSELL, GILLIAN**

**Gillian Russell**, Smarts, Lofty Green, Pleshey, Chelmsford, **Essex**, CM3 1HU, ENG.
(T) 01245 231397
Speciality: Complementary Medicines & Therapy.
● **Owner** Mrs G Russell
C M (Ref:HM17767)

**RUSSELL, JOHN**

**John Russell**, 40 Old Rd, Barlaston, Stoke-On-Trent, **Staffordshire**, ST12 9EQ, ENG.
(T) 01782 372992
Speciality: Chiropodists (Podiatrists).
● **Owner** Mr J Russell
S (Ref:HM17768)

**RUSSELL, M J**

**M J Russell**, 17 Woodend Rd, Ayr, **Ayrshire (South)**, KA7 4QP, SCO.
(T) 01292 441359
Speciality: Complementary Medicines & Therapy.
C M (Ref:HM17769)

**RUSSELL, SARAH**

**Sarah Russell**, 26 Diamond Ridge, Camberley, **Surrey**, GU15 4LD, ENG.
(T) 01276 685033
Speciality: Physiotherapy.
● **Owner** Ms S Russell
P S T (Ref:HM17770)

**RUSSELL, STEVE**

**Steve Russell**, Natural Therapy Centre, 7 Westgate Rd, Guisborough, **Cleveland**, TS14 6EA, ENG.
(T) 01287 633591
Speciality: Homeopathy.
M (Ref:HM17771)

**RUSSELL, SUSAN**

**Susan Russell**, Smiths Farm, Axminster Rd, Charmouth, **Dorset**, DT6 6BY, ENG.
(T) 01297 560167
Speciality: Complementary Medicines & Therapy.
● **Owner** Susan Russell
M (Ref:HM17772)

**RUSSO, HAZEL**

**Hazel Russo**, 14 Allison Rd, London, **London (Greater)**, N8 0AT, ENG.
(T) 020 8341 3393/07779111563
(W) www.hazelrusso.com
Speciality: Metamorphic Therapy, Reflexology, Reiki.
S T (Ref:HM17773)

**RUSSO, JACQUELINE**

**Jacqueline Russo**, 86 St Pauls Rd, London, **London (Greater)**, N1 2QP, ENG.
(T) 020 7359 8177
Speciality: Reflexology.
S T (Ref:HM17774)

**RUTH SAUNDERS HEALTH CLINIC**

**Ruth Saunders Health Clinic**, 36 Tudor Way, Uxbridge, **London (Greater)**, UB10 0BE, ENG.
(T) 01895 239049
Speciality: Hypnosis.
B (Ref:HM17775)

**RUTH WHITE YOGA CENTRE**

**Ruth White Yoga Centre**, Church Farm House, Springclose Lane, Sutton, **Surrey**, SM3 8PU, ENG.
(T) 020 8644 0309



Key continued: Yrs.Est: Years Established Q: Qualifications M: Professional Membership ✔ Indemnity Insurance Accept Credit Cards

Speciality: Yoga.
M (Ref:HM17776)

**RUTH WOOD CHARTERED PHYSIO**

**Ruth Wood Chartered Physiotherapist**, 14 Ladythorn Rd, Bramhall, Stockport, **Cheshire**, SK7 2ER, ENG.
(T) 01614 394806
Speciality: Physiotherapy.
P S T (Ref:HM17777)

**RUTH, GORDON**

**Gordon Ruth**, 24 First St, Low Moor, Bradford, **Yorkshire (West)**, BD12 0JQ, ENG.
(T) 01274 607854 (F) 01274 607833
Speciality: Aromatherapy.
● **Owner** Ms R Gordon
M O (Ref:HM17778)

**RUTH, MOIRA**

**Moira Ruth**, 366 Croydon Rd, Beckenham, **Kent**, BR3 4EX, ENG.
(T) 020 8663 3878 (F) 020 8663 3878
Speciality: Homeopathy.
● **Doctor** Dr M Chippendale
M (Ref:HM17779)

**RUTHERFORD, BERWYN**

**Berwyn Rutherford**, 43 Nassington Rd, London, **London (Greater)**, NW3 2TY, ENG.
(T) 020 7435 4753
Speciality: Cranial Osteopathy, Life Style Coaching, Manipulation, Massage (Therapeutic), Naturopathy, Osteopathy. ✔
● **Osteopath** Miss B Rutherford Q: BA, DO. M: GOsC.
S Yrs. Est.: 14 (Ref:HM17780)

**RUTHERFORD, JOHN**

**John Rutherford**, 103-105 Harley St, London, **London (Greater)**, W1N 1HD, ENG.
(T) 020 7935 4750
Speciality: Physiotherapy.
P S T (Ref:HM17781)

**RUTHERFORD, W D**

**W D Rutherford**, 3 Cedar Row, King's Lynn, **Norfolk**, PE30 3BA, ENG.
(T) 01553 671814
Speciality: Chiropodists (Podiatrists).
● **Owner** Mr W Rutherford
S (Ref:HM17782)

**RUTH'S REFLEXOLOGY**

**Ruth's Reflexology**, 8 Chadworth Avenue, Dorridge, Solihull, **Midlands (West)**, B93 8SR, ENG.
(T) 01564 779498
Speciality: Reflexology.
● **Owner** Mrs R Billingham
S T (Ref:HM17783)

**RUTLAND HEALTH & BEAUTY CLINIC**

**Rutland Health & Beauty Clinic**, 1a Market St, Oakham, **Leicestershire**, LE15 6DY, ENG.
(T) 01572 756589
Speciality: Electrolysis.
● **Owner** Ms J Davis
T (Ref:HM17784)

**RUTLAND PHYSIOTHERAPY CLINIC**

**Rutland Physiotherapy Clinic (The)**, 3 Westgate, Oakham, **Leicestershire**, LE15 6BH, ENG.
(T) 01572 757795
Speciality: Physiotherapy.
P S T (Ref:HM17785)

**RUXTON, HUGH**

**Hugh Ruxton**, 33 St Marys St, Bridgnorth, **Shropshire**, WV16 4DW, ENG.
(T) 01746 761050
Speciality: Osteopathy.
P S T (Ref:HM17786)

**RUXTON, HUGH**

**Hugh Ruxton**, 194 Penn Rd, Wolverhampton, **Midlands (West)**, WV3 0EQ, ENG.
(T) 01902 620387
Speciality: Osteopathy.
P S T (Ref:HM17787)

**RYAN, ANN**

**Ann Ryan**, 52 Rosebery Avenue, Sidcup, **Kent**, DA15 8HZ, ENG.
(T) 020 8302 8258
Speciality: Reflexology.
S T (Ref:HM17788)

**RYAN, KATHY (DR)**

**Dr Kathy Ryan**, Northgate Avenue, Chester, **Cheshire**, CH2 2DX, ENG.
(T) 01244 390396 (F) 01244 370762
Speciality: Homeopathy.
● **Practice Manager** Mrs B Waugh
M (Ref:HM17789)

**RYAN, MAUREEN**

**Maureen Ryan**, 225 Cirencester Rd, Charlton Kings, Cheltenham, **Gloucestershire**, GL53 8DF, ENG.
(T) 01242 573365
Speciality: Clairvoyants & Palmists, Fortune Teller. ✔
● **Owner/Fortune Teller** Mrs M Ryan
B Yrs. Est.: 12 (Ref:HM17790)

**RYAN, NICOLE**

**Ryan Nicole**, Oakpark Medical Ctre Listowel R, Tralee, **County Kerry**, IRE.
(T) 06671 27708
Speciality: Complementary Medicines & Therapy.
M (Ref:HM17791)

**RYAN, NOEL T (DR)**

**Ryan Dr Noel T**, Rocklands Gracedieu, **County Waterford**, IRE.
(T) 05185 5481
Speciality: Chiropractors.
P S T (Ref:HM17792)

**RYAN, PAT**

**Pat Ryan**, 52 Stoke Newington Church St, London, **London (Greater)**, N16 0NB, ENG.
(T) 020 7249 9671
Speciality: Complementary Medicines & Therapy.
● **Senior Partner** Mrs J Sheridan
M (Ref:HM17793)

**RYAN, ROSEMARY**

**Rosemary Ryan**, 82 Cavendish Rd, London, **London (Greater)**, E4 9NH, ENG.
(T) 020 8527 9478
Speciality: Reflexology.
S T (Ref:HM17794)

**RYAN, VALERIE**

**Ryan Valerie D O M C O**, Celtic Health & Natural Health, Dublin, **County Dublin**, IRE.
(T) 01491 0689
Speciality: Complementary Medicines & Therapy.
M (Ref:HM17795)

**RYAN-O'SHEA, LUCILLE (DR)**

**Ryan-O'Shea Dr Lucille Ph D**, Ballintleva Clogher, Westport, **County Mayo**, IRE.
(T) 09827 730
Speciality: Psychology.
B (Ref:HM17796)

**RYCHMOND, R**

**Mrs R Rychmond**, Harlequin House, 43 Chester Rd, Ilford, **Essex**, IG3 8PT, ENG.
(T) 020 8599 6013
Speciality: Physiotherapy.
P S T (Ref:HM17797)

**RYDE PHYSIOTHERAPY CLINIC**

**Ryde Physiotherapy Clinic**, 10 Lind St, Ryde, **Isle of Wight**, PO33 2NQ, ENG.
(T) 01983 811861 (F) 01983 811861
Speciality: Physiotherapy.
P S T (Ref:HM17798)

**RYDER, FRANK**

**Ryder Frank Counselling**, 4 Alden Pk, Sutton, **County Dublin**, IRE.
(T) 01832 4576
Speciality: Counselling.
B H (Ref:HM17799)

**RYDER, JULIE**

**Julie Ryder**, Over, **Cambridgeshire**, CB4, ENG.
(T) 01954 200762
Speciality: Physiotherapy.
P S T (Ref:HM17800)

**RYE OSTEOPATHIC PRACTICE**

**Rye Osteopathic Practice**, 16 Ferry Rd, Rye, **Sussex (East)**, TN31 7DN, ENG.
(T) 01797 225099
Speciality: Osteopathy.
P S T (Ref:HM17801)

**RYECOTEWOOD COLLEGE**

**Ryecotewood College**, Priest End, Thame, **Oxfordshire**, OX9 2AF, ENG.
(T) 01844 212501
Speciality: Alexander Technique.
● **Teacher** Mr M Cross
P S (Ref:HM17802)

**RYEDALE CLINIC**

**Ryedale Clinic For Physical Therapies**, 18a Market Pl, Malton, **Yorkshire (North)**, YO17 7LX, ENG.
(T) 01653 690808
Speciality: Bowen Therapy, Electrotherapy, Manipulation, Massage (Therapeutic), Reflexology. ✔
● **Practitioner/Owner** Mr E Jowitt M: LCSP.
● **Reflexologist** Ms J Jowitt Q: Dip.Reflex.
S Yrs. Est.: 7 (Ref:HM17803)

**S DERBYSHIRE DEPT-PSYCHO**

**Southern Derbyshire Department Of Psychotherapy**, Temple House, Mill Hill Lane, Derby, **Derbyshire**, DE23 6SA, ENG.
(T) 01332 207283 (F) 01322 293316
Speciality: Psychotherapy.
● **Administrator** Mrs E Godwin
B (Ref:HM17804)

**S E E D INSTITUTE**

**S E E D Institute (The)**, 10 Magnolia Way, Fleet, **Hampshire**, GU13 9JZ, ENG.
(T) 01252 626448
Speciality: Aromatherapy. ✔ CREDIT
● **Owner** Mrs A Perratt
C Yrs. Est.: 15 (Ref:HM17805)

**S H A**

**S H A**, 138 Harrow Rd, West Bridgford, Nottingham, **Nottinghamshire**, NG2 7DX, ENG.
(T) 01159 232104
Speciality: Psychology.
B (Ref:HM17806)

**S H L**

**S H L**, 27-29 Ashley Rd, Altrincham, **Cheshire**, WA14 2DP, ENG.
(T) 01619 298299 (F) 01619 298289
Speciality: Psychology.
● **Director** Ms G Parry
B (Ref:HM17807)

**S HECQUER PRACTICE**

**Susan Hecquer Practice & Sports Injury Clinic**, 4 Hazelwood Upper Park, Loughton, **Essex**, IG10 4ET, ENG.
(T) 020 8508 1510
Speciality: Physiotherapy.
P S T (Ref:HM17808)

**S J DYSON REFLEX-AROMA**

**S J Dyson Reflexologist-Aromatherapist**, Organ Makers Cottage, North Lyminge, Lyminge, Folkestone, **Kent**, CT18 8EE, ENG.
(T) 01303 862595
Speciality: Aromatherapy, Reflexology.
M (Ref:HM17809)

**S K PHYSIOTHERAPY**

**S K Physiotherapy**, 2b Mount Pleasant Rd, Caterham, **Surrey**, CR3 6LP, ENG.
(T) 01883 330077 (F) 01883 330077
Speciality: Physiotherapy.
● **Owner** Mr K Blackburn
P S T (Ref:HM17810)

**S K REFLEXOLOGY**

**S K Reflexology**, 65 Linthorpe Rd, Cockfosters, Barnet, **Hertfordshire**, EN4 9BX, ENG.
(T) 07949 399718 (F) 020 8844 17051
(E) sheltonk@ntlworld.com
(W) www.sktherapy.co.uk
Speciality: Bach Remedies, Counselling, Crystal Healing, Healer, Massage (Therapeutic), Reflexology, Spiritual Healing, Stress Therapy.
✔



Key: B Mind-Body Medicine C Complementary Medicine H Self Help Treatment M Medicinal Therapy O Oriental Medicine P Postural Therapy S Manipulative Structural Therapy T Touch Therapy

● **Owner/Therapist** Mr S Kartun **Q:** BSc (Hons), ITEC.
S Yrs. Est.: 10 (**Ref:**HM17811)

## S K REFLEXOLOGY & AROMATHERAPY

**S K Reflexology & Aromatherapy**, 60 King Edwards Rd, Enfield, **London (Greater)**, EN3 7DB, ENG.
(T) 020 8372 1936
Speciality: Aromatherapy, Reflexology.
S T (**Ref:**HM17812)

## S L R HEALTHCARE

**S L R Healthcare**, 48 Beckfield Lane, Acomb, **Yorkshire (North)**, YO26 5RJ, ENG.
(T) 01904 786623
Speciality: Complementary Medicines & Therapy.
C M (**Ref:**HM17813)

## S LOWNDES SPORTS INJURY

**Steve Lowndes Sports Injury & Physiotherapy Clinic**, 2 Manor Chase, Undy, Caldicot, **Monmouthshire**, NP26 3PA, WAL.
(T) 01633 881874
Speciality: Physiotherapy.
P S T (**Ref:**HM17814)

## S M GORDON ANALYTICAL PSYCH

**S M Gordon Analytical Psychotherapist**, 222 South Norwood Hill, London, **London (Greater)**, SE25 6AS, ENG.
(T) 020 8771 7074
Speciality: Psychotherapy.
B (**Ref:**HM17815)

## S MONTAGU (DR)

**Dr S Montagu**, Glebe Barn, St. Enoder, Summercourt, Newquay, **Cornwall**, TR8 5DF, ENG.
(T) 01726 860706
Speciality: Homeopathy.
● **Owner** Dr S Montegu
M (**Ref:**HM17816)

## S O S PHYSIO & OSTEOPATHY

**S O S Physiotherapy & Osteopathy**, 32 Canbury Pk Rd, Kingston Upon Thames, **Surrey**, KT2 6JX, ENG.
(T) 020 8546 8314
Speciality: Physiotherapy.
P S T (**Ref:**HM17817)

## S T A T BOOKS

**S T A T Books**, 20 London House, 266 Fulham Rd, London, **London (Greater)**, SW10 9EL, ENG.
(T) 020 7352 0666
Speciality: Alexander Technique.
● **Sole Director**
James Noel McDowell
P S (**Ref:**HM17818)

## S.T.A.T.

**Society Of Teachers Of The Alexander Technique (The)**, 20 London House, 266 Fulham Rd, London, **London (Greater)**, SW10 9EL, ENG.
(T) 020 7351 0828
Speciality: Alexander Technique.
P S (**Ref:**HM17819)

## SAAG, INGRID

**Ingrid Saag**, 57 Cobham Rd, Kingston Upon Thames, **Surrey**, KT1 3AE, ENG.
(T) 020 8974 5465
Speciality: Reflexology.
S T (**Ref:**HM17820)

## SABATINI, A

**A Sabatini**, 73 Admirals Walk, West Cliff Rd, Bournemouth, **Dorset**, BH2 5HG, ENG.
(T) 01202 557557
Speciality: Chiropodists (Podiatrists).
● **Owner** Mr A Sabatini
S (**Ref:**HM17821)

## SABBATIC TECHNOLOGY

**Sabbatic Technology**, Woodchurch Rd, London, **London (Greater)**, NW6 3PP, ENG.
(T) 020 7328 4475 (F) 020 7328 4475
Speciality: Psychology.
● **Owner** Mr F Post
B (**Ref:**HM17822)

## SABER, J

**J Saber**, 45 Hatherley Rd, Winchester, **Hampshire**, SO22 6RR, ENG.
(T) 01962 851321 (F) 01962 851321
Speciality: Acupuncture.
● **Owner** Dr J Saber
O (**Ref:**HM17823)

## SABINE, P M

**P M Sabine**, Bardfield, 8a High St, Ingatestone, **Essex**, CM4 9EE, ENG.
(T) 01277 355310
Speciality: Chiropodists (Podiatrists).
S (**Ref:**HM17824)

## SACHDEV, P

**P Sachdev**, 145 Torbay Rd, Harrow, **London (Greater)**, HA2 9QG, ENG.
(T) 020 8422 2202
Speciality: Homeopathy.
● **Owner** Mrs P Sachdev
M (**Ref:**HM17825)

## SACKETT, M B

**M B Sackett**, 28 Bishop Rd, Bournemouth, **Dorset**, BH9 1HB, ENG.
(T) 01202 529364
Speciality: Chiropodists (Podiatrists).
S (**Ref:**HM17826)

## SACKLIN, CECILIA

**Cecilia Sacklin**, 53 Frankfurt Rd, London, **London (Greater)**, SE24 9NX, ENG.
(T) 020 7738 6918
Speciality: Reflexology.
S T (**Ref:**HM17827)

## SACKS, PATRICA

**Patrica Sacks**, 12 Holbrook Lane, Chislehurst, **Kent**, BR7 6PF, ENG.
(T) 020 8467 3361
Speciality: Chiropody, Podiatry. ✔
● **Owner/Chiropodist** Mrs P Sacks **Q:** MSSCh, S.R.Ch, SRN. **M:** B.A.Ch.P.
M Yrs. Est.: 8 (**Ref:**HM17828)

## SACRED EARTH

**Sacred Earth**, 6 Upper Orwell St, Ipswich, **Suffolk**, IP4 1HW, ENG.
(T) 01473 417474
Speciality: Herbal Medicine.
● **Owner** Mr A Moorhouse
M (**Ref:**HM17829)

## SADAR, TONY

**Sadar Tony A A P H**, 37 Woodlands Rd, Johnstown Dun Laoire, Dublin, **County Dublin**, IRE.
(T) 01285 2271
Speciality: Hypnotherapy.
B (**Ref:**HM17830)

## SADDLER, J M

**J M Saddler**, 2 Crown Lane, Littleport, Ely, **Cambridgeshire**, CB6 1PP, ENG.
(T) 01353 863218
Speciality: Complementary Medicines & Therapy.
M (**Ref:**HM17831)

## SADLER, MARY

**Mary Sadler**, Clivia, Windmill Hill, Coleshill, Amersham, **Buckinghamshire**, HP7 0LZ, ENG.
(T) 01494 726277
Speciality: Alexander Technique.
● **Owner** Mrs M Sadler
P S (**Ref:**HM17832)

## SADLER, RUTH

**Ruth Sadler**, Old School House, Belsay, Newcastle Upon Tyne, **Tyne and Wear**, NE20 0EU, ENG.
(T) 01661 881654
Speciality: Homeopathy.
M (**Ref:**HM17833)

## SADOWSKI, J T & L Y

**J T & L Y Sadowski**, 219 Unthank Rd, Norwich, **Norfolk**, NR2 2PH, ENG.
(T) 01603 455273
Speciality: Chiropodists (Podiatrists).
S (**Ref:**HM17834)

## SAFFRON OILS

**Saffron Oils**, Belmont House, Newport, Saffron Walden, **Essex**, CB11 3RF, ENG.
(T) 01799 540622
Speciality: Aromatherapy.
M O (**Ref:**HM17835)

## SAGE, CLARY

**Clary Sage**, 3 Station Rd, Hesketh Bank, Preston, **Lancashire**, PR4 6SN, ENG.
(T) 01772 813811
Speciality: Aromatherapy.
M O (**Ref:**HM17836)

## SAGE, J

**J Sage (Crawford)**, Wyld Meadow Farm, Monkton Wyld, Bridport, **Dorset**, DT6 6DD, ENG.
(T) 01297 678789
Speciality: Chiropractic.
● **Owner** Mrs J Sage
P S T (**Ref:**HM17837)

## SAGGU, S

**Mr S Saggu**, 1827 Leek Rd, Stoke-On-Trent, **Staffordshire**, ST2 7AD, ENG.
(T) 01782 570008
Speciality: Chiropody. ✔
● **Owner/Chiropodist** Mr S Saggu **Q:** M.S.C.P, S.R.Ch. **M:** S.C.P, S.R.Ch.
C Yrs. Est.: 15 (**Ref:**HM17838)

## SAGIR, SHARON

**Sharon Sagir**, 128 Farm Rd, Edgware, **London (Greater)**, HA8 9LW, ENG.
(T) 020 8958 5104
Speciality: Reflexology.
S T (**Ref:**HM17839)

## SAI HOMEOPATHIC CLINIC

**Sai Homeopathic Clinic**, 49 Victoria Avenue, Hounslow, **London (Greater)**, TW3 3SU, ENG.
(T) 020 8570 9177
Speciality: Homeopathy.
● **Doctor** Mrs J Gandhi
M (**Ref:**HM17840)

## SAINI, R P

**R P Saini**, 256-258 Ealing Rd, Wembley, **London (Greater)**, HA0 4QL, ENG.
(T) 020 8902 1166
Speciality: Electrolysis.
● **Dentist** Mr R Saini
T (**Ref:**HM17841)

## SAINSBURY

**Sainsbury**, 10 Rivers Rd, Teynham, Sittingbourne, **Kent**, ME9 9TD, ENG.
(T) 01795 520176 (F) 01795 520176
Speciality: Reflexology.
● **Owner** Ms K Sainsbury
S T (**Ref:**HM17842)

## SAINT CLAIRE, MAGGIE

**Maggie Saint Claire**, 3 Elms St, Derby, **Derbyshire**, DE1 3HN, ENG.
(T) 01332 342149
Speciality: Clairvoyants & Palmists.
● **Owner** Miss M Saintclaire
B (**Ref:**HM17843)

## SAKAL V

**Sakal V**, Tithe Barn, Lake End Rd, Taplow, Maidenhead, **Berkshire**, SL6 0PN, ENG.
(T) 01628 603484
Speciality: Hypnotherapy.
B (**Ref:**HM17844)

## SALAVARY, CHRIS

**Chris Salavary**, 30 The Piazza, Covent Garden, London, **London (Greater)**, WC2E 8BE, ENG.
(T) 020 7836 4835
Speciality: Complementary Medicines & Therapy.
M (**Ref:**HM17845)

## SALES, F P I

**F P I Sales Ltd**, Wilds Lodge, Stamford Rd, Careby, Stamford, **Lincolnshire**, PE9 4EB, ENG.
(T) 01780 482200 (F) 01780 482112
Speciality: Aromatherapy.
● **Managing Director** Mr S Hughes
M O (**Ref:**HM17846)

## SALES, F P I

**F P I Sales Ltd**, Unit 2A Radcliffe Rd, Stamford, **Lincolnshire**, PE9 1EE, ENG.
(T) 01780 482672 (F) 01780 751259
Speciality: Aromatherapy.
● **Manager** Mr B Warner



Key continued: **Yrs.Est:** Years Established **Q:** Qualifications **M:** Professional Membership ✔ Indemnity Insurance ▬ Accept Credit Cards

M O (Ref:HM17847)

## SALIS FANE DE, AMANDA
**Amanda Fane De Salis**, 30A Brook St, Tavistock, **Devon**, PL19 0HE, ENG.
(T) 01822 610020
Speciality: Chiropodists (Podiatrists).
● **Owner** Miss A Fane-De-Salis
S (Ref:HM17848)

## SALISBURY CENTRE
**Salisbury Centre (The)**, 2 Salisbury Rd, Edinburgh, **Edinburgh (City of)**, EH16 5AB, SCO.
(T) 01316 675438 (F) 01316 675438
Speciality: Complementary Medicines & Therapy.
● **Director** Mrs L Morrigan
C M (Ref:HM17849)

## SALISBURY CHIROPODY CLINIC
**Salisbury Chiropody Clinic**, 16 Salt Lane, Salisbury, **Wiltshire**, SP1 1EE, ENG.
(T) 01722 415771
Speciality: Chiropodists (Podiatrists).
● **Owner** Mrs P Piggott
S (Ref:HM17850)

## SALISBURY CHIROPRACTIC CLINIC
**Salisbury Chiropractic Clinic**, 9 New St, Salisbury, **Wiltshire**, SP1 2PH, ENG.
(T) 01722 328606 (F) 01722 330036
Speciality: Chiropractic.
● **Practice Manager** Mrs E Shergold
P S T (Ref:HM17851)

## SALISBURY HOMEOPATHY CENTRE
**Salisbury Homeopathy Centre**, Flat, 24 Catherine St, Salisbury, **Wiltshire**, SP1 2DA, ENG.
(T) 01722 411766
Speciality: Homeopathy.
M (Ref:HM17852)

## SALISBURY, CLAIRE
**Claire Salisbury**, Gestalt Studio, Croftdown Rd, London, **London (Greater)**, NW5 1EN, ENG.
(T) 020 7624 4322
Speciality: Psychotherapy.
● **Owner** Ms C Salisbury
B (Ref:HM17853)

## SALISBURY, D G
**D G Salisbury**, 311 London Rd, Benfleet, **Essex**, SS7 5XP, ENG.
(T) 01268 753208
Speciality: Chiropodists (Podiatrists).
S (Ref:HM17854)

## SALISBURY, ERICA
**Erica Salisbury**, 43 Molyneux St, London, **London (Greater)**, W1H 5HW, ENG.
(T) 020 7262 1490
Speciality: Osteopathy.
● **Owner** Ms E Salisbury
P S T (Ref:HM17855)

## SALMON, JONATHAN
**Jonathan Salmon**, 853 Finchley Rd, London, **London (Greater)**, NW11 8LX, ENG.
(T) 020 8455 5646
Speciality: Osteopathy.
P S T (Ref:HM17856)

## SALMON, LOUISE
**Louise Salmon**, Clissold Park Health Centre, 154 Stoke Newington Church St, London, **London (Greater)**, N16 0JU, ENG.
(T) 020 7249 2990 (F) 020 7249 3977
Speciality: Homeopathy.
● **Owner** Mr D Berg
M (Ref:HM17857)

## SALMON, MARGARET
**Margaret Salmon**, Priory Farm Granary, Halstead Rd, Earls Colne, Colchester, **Essex**, CO6 2LR, ENG.
(T) 01787 224865
Speciality: Aromatherapy, Holistic Healing, Massage (Therapeutic), Reflexology.
S T (Ref:HM17858)

## SALMON, PHILIP
**Philip Salmon**, 52 Primrose Ridge, Godalming, **Surrey**, GU7 2NX, ENG.
(T) 01483 423240
Speciality: Reflexology.
S T (Ref:HM17859)

## SALMON, RUTH V
**Ruth V Salmon**, 6 Whins Lane, Simonstone, Burnley, **Lancashire**, BB12 7QR, ENG.
(T) 01282 778445 (F) 01282 778445
Speciality: Chiropodists (Podiatrists).
● **Owner** Mrs R Salmon
S (Ref:HM17860)

## SALMONS, P
**P Salmons**, 45 Rodney St, Liverpool, **Merseyside**, L1 9EW, ENG.
(T) 01517 080842 (F) 01517 095679
Speciality: Psychiatry.
● **Chief Executive** Miss S Lunt
B (Ref:HM17861)

## SALON VICTORIA
**Salon Victoria**, 23 Bruntsfield Pl, Edinburgh, **Edinburgh (City of)**, EH10 4HN, SCO.
(T) 01312 290020
Speciality: Electrolysis.
T (Ref:HM17862)

## SALON, JANIES
**Janies Salon**, 114 Birchwood Avenue, Lincoln, **Lincolnshire**, LN6 0JD, ENG.
(T) 01522 800485
Speciality: Aromatherapy, Beauty Therapy, Indian Head Massage, Reflexology, Reiki. ✔
● **Holistic Therapist** Mrs J Davies Q: IIHHT. M: IIHHT.
C Yrs. Est.: 2 (Ref:HM17863)

## SALTAIRE COMP HEALTH STUDIO
**Saltaire Complementary Health Studio**, 89 Bingley Rd, Shipley, **Yorkshire (West)**, BD18 4SB, ENG.
(T) 01274 581611
Speciality: Aromatherapy, Massage (Therapeutic), Reflexology, Australian Health Products, Aloe Vera, Skin Care facials, Weight Management. ✔ CREDIT
● **Owner/Holistic Practitioner** Mrs S Weatherall Q: MIFA. M: IFA, IFR.
C Yrs. Est.: 3 (Ref:HM17864)

## SALTASH FOOT CLINIC
**Saltash Foot Clinic**, 166 Fore St, Saltash, **Cornwall**, PL12 6JR, ENG.
(T) 01752 841434
Speciality: Chiropody.
● **Owner** Ms L Hosking
S (Ref:HM17865)

## SALTER, C
**C Salter**, Natural Health York Clinic, Guildford Rd, Woking, **Surrey**, GU22 7QU, ENG.
(T) 01483 720464
Speciality: Homeopathy.
M (Ref:HM17866)

## SALTER, L
**L Salter**, Flat A, 110 Brondesbury Villas, London, **London (Greater)**, NW6 6AD, ENG.
(T) 020 7328 3199
Speciality: Homeopathy.
● **Owner** Ms L Salter
M (Ref:HM17867)

## SALTER, L
**L Salter**, Lambton Pl, Westbourne Gr, London, **London (Greater)**, W11 2SH, ENG.
(T) 020 7229 2291
Speciality: Homeopathy.
M (Ref:HM17868)

## SALTER, LIZ
**Liz Salter BA(Hons) RSHom**, Bushmaster Natural Health Practice, 204 Uxbridge Rd, Shepherds Bush, London, **London (Greater)**, W12 7JD, ENG.
(T) 020 8749 3792
Speciality: Homeopathy, Quantum Xxorroid Health Scan. ✔
● **Joint Director** Peter Lee Chappell
● **Joint Director** Ashley Stafford
● **Homeopath** Ms L Salter Q: BA (Hons), RSHom.
B Yrs. Est.: 7 (Ref:HM17869)

## SALTERGATE SPINAL & SPORTS
**Saltergate Spinal & Sports Clinic**, 124 Saltergate, Chesterfield, **Derbyshire**, S40 1NG, ENG.
(T) 01246 208325
Speciality: Physiotherapy.
● **Owner** Mr E Jones
P S T (Ref:HM17870)

## SALUBRITY
**Salubrity**, 12 Robbery Bottom Lane, Welwyn, **Hertfordshire**, AL6 0UW, ENG.
(T) 01438 840908 (F) 01438 840908
Speciality: Complementary Medicines & Therapy.
● **Director** Mr H O'Brien
C M (Ref:HM17871)

## SALUS NATURAL HEALING
**Salus Natural Healing**, 192 Sandbrook Rd, Southport, **Merseyside**, PR8 3RW, ENG.
(T) 01704 571920
Speciality: Complementary Medicines & Therapy.
● **Owner** Mr P Regan
M (Ref:HM17872)

## SALUTARIS HEALTH
**Salutaris Health**, 21 Zetland Rd, Loftus, Saltburn-by-the-Sea, **Cleveland**, TS13 4PW, ENG.
(T) 01287 644777 (F) 01287 644777
Speciality: Complementary Medicines & Therapy.
● **Owner** Mr M Ogden
M (Ref:HM17873)

## SALUTARIS HEALTH
**Salutaris Health**, 16 St Cuthberts Walk, Liverton, Saltburn-by-the-Sea, **Cleveland**, TS13 4QL, ENG.
(T) 01287 644777
Speciality: Complementary Medicines & Therapy.
C M (Ref:HM17874)

## SAMALIN ORIENTAL
**Samalin Oriental & Holistic Therapies**, 30 Rood Hill, Congleton, **Cheshire**, CW12 1LQ, ENG.
(T) 01260 274085
Speciality: Complementary Medicines & Therapy.
C M (Ref:HM17875)

## SAMANTHA
**Samantha**, 14 Newton Court, Leeds, **Yorkshire (West)**, LS8 2PH, ENG.
(T) 01132 403798 (F) 01132 403798
Speciality: Clairvoyants & Palmists.
● **Owner** Mrs S Davies
B (Ref:HM17876)

## SAMANTHA WHITE AROMATICA
**Samantha White Aromatica**, 27 Princes Avenue, Hull, **Humberside (North)**, HU5 3RX, ENG.
(T) 01482 448679
(E) sw@sip.karoo.co.uk
(W) www.aromatica.co.uk
Speciality: Aromatherapy, Aura Therapy, Complementary Therapy, Healer, Indian Head Massage, Massage (Therapeutic), Polarity Therapy, Reiki, Stress Therapy. ✔
● **Aromatherapist** Ms S White Q: MIFA. M: IFA.
B Yrs. Est.: 11 (Ref:HM17877)

## SAMBIDGE, GORDON
**Gordon Sambidge**, 53 Bramber Rd, London, **London (Greater)**, N12 9ND, ENG.
(T) 020 8445 1641
Speciality: Homeopathy.
● **Owner** Mr G Sambidge
M (Ref:HM17878)

## SAMLER, LYN
**Lyn Samler**, 19 Staplers Reach, Gosport, **Hampshire**, PO13 0EY, ENG.
(T) 01489 574692
Speciality: Osteopathy.
● **Owner** Ms L Samler
P S T (Ref:HM17879)



Key: B Mind-Body Medicine C Complementary Medicine H Self Help Treatment M Medicinal Therapy O Oriental Medicine P Postural Therapy S Manipulative Structural Therapy T Touch Therapy

## SAMLER, LYN
**Lyn Samler**, 43 Albacore Avenue, Warsash, **Hampshire**, SO31 9BP, ENG.
(T) 01489 574692
Speciality: Osteopathy.
P S T (Ref:HM17880)

## SAMMUT & SAMMUT ASSOCIATES
**Sammut & Sammut Associates**, 376 Walton Rd, West Molesey, **Surrey**, KT8 2JE, ENG.
(T) 020 8979 7444
Speciality: Osteopathy.
● **Partner** Mr E Sammut
P S T (Ref:HM17881)

## SAMMY, MARGO
**Margo Sammy**, 113 Hendon Lane, London, **London (Greater)**, N3 3PR, ENG.
(T) 020 8369 3456
Speciality: Physiotherapy.
P S T (Ref:HM17882)

## SAMPLE, JUDY
**Judy Sample**, 11 Manor Rd, Burgess Hill, **Sussex (West)**, RH15 0NP, ENG.
(T) 01444 250591
Speciality: Electrolysis.
● **Owner** Mrs J Sample
T (Ref:HM17883)

## SAM'S EXERCISE FORMULA
**Sam's Exercise Formula**, 3 Church Rd, Stanmore, **London (Greater)**, HA7 4AR, ENG.
(T) 020 8954 0288 (F) 020 8954 0229
Speciality: Complementary Medicines & Therapy.
● **Manager** Mr A Gunasekera
C M (Ref:HM17884)

## SAMUELS, CAROLANN
**Carolann Samuels**, 22 Castle Rd, Hythe, **Kent**, CT21 5HL, ENG.
(T) 01303 266253
Speciality: Reflexology.
S T (Ref:HM17885)

## SAMUELS, L W
**L W Samuels**, Bowood Medical Centre, 3 Wellington Rd, Bournemouth, **Dorset**, BH8 8JQ, ENG.
(T) 01202 295990
Speciality: Chiropodists (Podiatrists).
● **Owner** Mr L Samuels
S (Ref:HM17886)

## SAN LING CHINESE MED CENTRE
**San Ling Chinese Medicine Centre**, 209 Baker St, London, **London (Greater)**, NW1 6UY, ENG.
(T) 020 7486 8715
Speciality: Acupuncture.
● **Owner** Mrs I Wen
O (Ref:HM17887)

## SAN LING CHINESE MED CENTRE
**San Ling Chinese Medicine Centre**, 3 New College Prde, Finchley Rd, London, **London (Greater)**, NW3 5EP, ENG.
(T) 020 7722 9808
Speciality: Acupuncture.
O (Ref:HM17888)

## SANBORN, CATHERINE
**Sanborn Catherine**, 3 Westview Military Rd, Cork, **County Cork**, IRE.
(T) 021 4500 423
Speciality: Complementary Medicines & Therapy.
M (Ref:HM17889)

## SANCTUARY COVE
**Sanctuary Cove**, The Octagon, Brighton Marina Village, Brighton, **Sussex (East)**, BN2 5UU, ENG.
(T) 01273 818898
Speciality: Aromatherapy.
M O (Ref:HM17890)

## SANCTUARY HEALING
**Sanctuary Healing**, 11 Frensham Cl, Hedge End, **Hampshire**, SO30 0JT, ENG.
(T) 01489 780774
Speciality: Reiki, Soul Retrieval Therapy.
B (Ref:HM17891)

## SANCTUARY HOUSE
**Sanctuary House**, 4 Upper Norfolk St, North Shields, **Tyne and Wear**, NE30 1PT, ENG.
(T) 01912 577774
Speciality: Complementary Medicines & Therapy.
C M (Ref:HM17892)

## SANCTUARY NATURAL HEALTH
**Sanctuary Natural Health**, 11 Fairfield Cres, Fairfield, Liverpool, **Merseyside**, L6 8PH, ENG.
(T) 01512 283884 (F) 01512 283884
(E) mariamshh@tinyworld.com
Speciality: Aromatherapy, Reflexology, Reiki, Shiatsu, Touch Therapy. ✓
● **Therapist** Ms M Barrington Q: Dip.Clin.Arom, Dip.Reflex, Dip.Shiatsu, Dip.Sports Injuries, KFRP, Reiki Master. M: AoR, ISPA, Shiatsu Society UK.
B C T Yrs. Est.: 14 (Ref:HM17893)

## SANCTUARY OF HEALING
**Sanctuary Of Healing**, Mills Trce, Chatham, **Kent**, ME4 5NZ, ENG.
(T) 01634 880039
Speciality: Complementary Medicines & Therapy.
C M (Ref:HM17894)

## SANCTUARY ROOM
**Sanctuary Room**, 61 Downlands, Stevenage, **Hertfordshire**, SG2 7BH, ENG.
(T) 01438 723921
Speciality: Complementary Medicines & Therapy.
● **Owner** Mr P Banting
C M (Ref:HM17895)

## SANCTUM HOLISTIC THERAPY CTRE
**Sanctum Holistic Therapy Centre**, 180 Petts Wood Rd, Orpington, **Kent**, BR5 1LG, ENG.
(T) 01689 871515 (F) 01689 871515
Speciality: Acupressure, Aromatherapy, Beauty Therapy, Cranio-Sacral Therapy, Indian Head Massage, Reflexology, Intensive Hand Therapy. ✓
● **Beauty Therapist** Ms D Chapman
● **Owner/Holistic Therapist** Mrs J Yoxall M: IFR.
C Yrs. Est.: 4 (Ref:HM17896)

## SANCTUM NATURAL THERAPY CTRE
**Sanctum Natural Therapy Centre**, 28A High St, Swadlincote, **Derbyshire**, DE11 8HY, ENG.
(T) 01283 221764 (F) 01283 221764
Speciality: Complementary Medicines & Therapy.
● **Owner** Mr K Guy
C M (Ref:HM17897)

## SANDALL, S
**S Sandall**, 10 Eldon Rd, Reading, **Berkshire**, RG1 4DH, ENG.
(T) 01189 502002
Speciality: Biomechanics, Chiropody, Cryo Surgery, Nail Surgery, Podiatry. ✓ [credit card]
● **Physiotherapist** Ms E Carney
(T) 01189 062800 Q: MCSP, SRP. M: CSP, SRP.
● **Physiotherapist** Mr A Knee-Robinson
(T) 01189 062800 Q: MCSP, SRP. M: CSP, SRP.
● **Chiropodist (Podiatrist)** S Sandall
(T) 01189 062800 Q: DPodM. M: S.C.P, S.R.Ch.
C (Ref:HM17898)

## SANDBACH HYPNOSIS CLINIC
**Sandbach Hypnosis Clinic**, 56 Fairfield Avenue, Sandbach, **Cheshire**, CW11 4BP, ENG.
(T) 01270 765941
Speciality: Biofeedback, Hypnosis, Hypnotherapy. ✓
● **Owner** Mr B Perry
B Yrs. Est.: 17 (Ref:HM17899)

## SANDBACH PHYSIO & SPORTS
**Sandbach Physiotherapy & Sports Injuries Clinic**, 7 Davenport Cl, Sandbach, **Cheshire**, CW11 1YP, ENG.
(T) 07970 511835
Speciality: Physiotherapy.
● **Owner** Mrs B Oakes
P S T (Ref:HM17900)

## SANDELLS, DIANNE
**Dianne Sandells**, The Weaver House Clinic, 19A Pillory St, Nantwich, **Cheshire**, CW5 5BZ, ENG.
(T) 01270 629933
Speciality: Reflexology.
S T (Ref:HM17901)

## SANDERLING HYPNOTHERAPY CENTRE
**Sanderling Hypnotherapy Centre**, Sanderling Rise, Kingswinford, **Midlands (West)**, DY6 8XN, ENG.
(T) 01384 296791
Speciality: Hypnosis.
● **Owner** Mr P Evans
B (Ref:HM17902)

## SANDERS ROYLE, A
**A Sanders Royle**, 22 Mount St, Shrewsbury, **Shropshire**, SY3 8QJ, ENG.
(T) 01743 241869
Speciality: Chiropractors.
● **Owner** Ms A Sanders Royle
P S T (Ref:HM17903)

## SANDERS, A W
**A W Sanders**, 6 London Rd, Hinckley, **Leicestershire**, LE10 1HJ, ENG.
(T) 01455 636533
Speciality: Physiotherapy.
● **Owner** Mr A Sanders
P S T (Ref:HM17904)

## SANDERS, BRYON
**Bryon Sanders**, Nottingham Chiropractic Clinic, 3 Hawksworth St, Nottingham, **Nottinghamshire**, NG3 2EG, ENG.
(T) 01159 472131
Speciality: Chiropractors.
● **Owner** Ms E Aldren
P S T (Ref:HM17905)

## SANDERS, CAROLE
**Carole Sanders**, Beverley Clinic, 362 Coombe Lane, London, **London (Greater)**, SW20 0RJ, ENG.
(T) 020 8241 2515
Speciality: Homeopathy.
M (Ref:HM17906)

## SANDERS, CHRISTINE
**Christine Sanders**, 37 High Town Rd, Maidenhead, **Berkshire**, SL6 1PA, ENG.
(T) 01628 638390
Speciality: Homeopathy.
● **Owner** Mrs C Sanders
M (Ref:HM17907)

## SANDERS, CHRISTINE
**Christine Sanders**, Nine Mile Ride, Bracknell, **Berkshire**, RG12 7PB, ENG.
(T) 01344 869066
Speciality: Homeopathy.
● **Owner** Mrs C Sanders
M (Ref:HM17908)

## SANDERS, G
**Mrs G Sanders**, 51 Lampits Hill, Corringham, Stanford-Le-Hope, **Essex**, SS17 9HN, ENG.
(T) 01268 556038
Speciality: Biomechanics, Chiropody, Nail Surgery, Podiatry. ✓
● **Chiropodist (Podiatrist)** Mrs G Sanders Q: BSc (Hons), DPodM, MSc.
C Yrs. Est.: 25 (Ref:HM17909)

## SANDERS, J A
**J A Sanders**, Physiotherapy Clinic, 13 Alexandra Rd, Gloucester, **Gloucestershire**, GL1 3DR, ENG.
(T) 01452 506512
Speciality: Physiotherapy.
P S T (Ref:HM17910)

## SANDERS, JANE
**Jane Sanders**, 10 High St, Glastonbury, **Somerset**, BA6 9DU, ENG.
(T) 01458 834236
Speciality: Psychotherapy.
● **Director** Ms J Sanders
B (Ref:HM17911)

## SANDERS, LOUISE
**Miss Louise Sanders**, Deer Pk View, Odiham, Hook, **Hampshire**, RG29 1JY, ENG.


Key continued: Yrs.Est: Years Established Q: Qualifications M: Professional Membership ✓ Indemnity Insurance [credit card] Accept Credit Cards

(T) 01256 702371
Speciality: Osteopathy.
P S T (Ref:HM17912)

## SANDERS, PEMA

**Pema Sanders**, 23 De Montfort Rd, Brighton, **Sussex (East)**, BN2 3AW, ENG.
(T) 01273 699775
Speciality: Homeopathy.
M (Ref:HM17913)

## SANDERS, PETER

**Peter Sanders**, 258 Chislehurst Rd, Petts Wood, Orpington, **Kent**, BR5 1NT, ENG.
(T) 01689 876582
Speciality: Manipulation, Massage (Therapeutic), Osteopathy. ✔
● **Osteopath** Mr P Sanders Q: DO. M: GOsC.
S T Yrs. Est.: 17 (Ref:HM17914)

## SANDERS, PETER

**Peter Sanders**, Midsummer House, 66 St. Helens Pk Rd, Hastings, **Sussex (East)**, TN34 2JJ, ENG.
(T) 01424 420615 (F) 01424 420615
Speciality: Psychotherapy.
● **Owner** Mr P Sanders
B (Ref:HM17915)

## SANDERS, RACHEL

**Rachel Sanders**, Swiss Cottage, Forster Rd, Salcombe, **Devon**, TQ8 8EB, ENG.
(T) 01548 842078 (F) 01548 842078
Speciality: Chiropody. ✔
● **Owner/Chiropodist** Mrs R Sanders
Q: M.S.C.P. M: S.C.P.
C Yrs. Est.: 3 (Ref:HM17916)

## SANDERS, RAIJA

**Raija Sanders**, Martindale House, Lombard St, Newark, **Nottinghamshire**, NG24 1XG, ENG.
(T) 01636 611150
Speciality: Hypnotherapy.
● **Administrator** Mrs S Taylor
B (Ref:HM17917)

## SANDERS, T E

**T E Sanders**, 41 Christchurch St, Ipswich, **Suffolk**, IP4 2DF, ENG.
(T) 01473 257009
Speciality: Physiotherapy.
● **Owner** Mrs T Sanders
P S T (Ref:HM17918)

## SANDERSON & ELEMENT

**Suzie Sanderson & Chris Element**, 20 Meads, Eastbourne, **Sussex (East)**, ER7 3B1, ENG.
(T) 01273 605226
(W) www.alexandertechnique.org.uk
Speciality: Alexander Technique. ✔
● **Teacher of the Alexander Technique** Mr C Element Q: MSTAT.
● **Teacher of the Alexander Technique** Ms S Sanderson Q: MSTAT.
P Yrs. Est.: 10 (Ref:HM17919)

## SANDERSON & ELEMENT

**Suzie Sanderson & Chris Element**, 7 College Pl, Brighton, **Sussex (East)**, BN2 1HN, ENG.
(T) 01273 605226
(W) www.alexandertechnique.org.uk
Speciality: Alexander Technique. ✔
● **Teacher of the Alexander Technique** Mr C Element Q: MSTAT.
● **Associate** Mrs S Sanderson Q: MSTAT.
P T Yrs. Est.: 10 (Ref:HM17920)

## SANDERSON & ELEMENT

**Suzie Sanderson & Chris Element**, Sunnyglen, London Rd, Crawley, **Sussex (West)**, CR1 4B2, ENG.
(T) 01273 605226
Speciality: Alexander Technique. ✔
● **Teacher of the Alexander Technique** Ms S Sanderson Q: MSTAT.
● **Teacher of the Alexander Technique** Mr C Element Q: MSTAT.
P Yrs. Est.: 10 (Ref:HM17921)

## SANDERSON & ELEMENT

**Suzie Sanderson & Chris Element**, The Star Gallery, Fisher St, Lewes, **Sussex (East)**, BN7 2DG, ENG.
(T) 01273 605226
Speciality: Alexander Technique. ✔
● **Teacher of the Alexander Technique** Ms S Sanderson Q: MSTAT.
● **Teacher of the Alexander Technique** Mr C Element Q: MSTAT.
P Yrs. Est.: 10 (Ref:HM17922)

## SANDERSON, ANN

**Ann Sanderson**, 4 Carr Houses, Far Common, Methley, Leeds, **Yorkshire (West)**, LS26 9AG, ENG.
(T) 01977 518011
Speciality: Homeopathy.
● **Owner** Mrs A Sanderson
M (Ref:HM17923)

## SANDLER & AST

**Stephen E Sandler & Associates**, 26A Station Rd, London, **London (Greater)**, E4 7BE, ENG.
(T) 020 8529 0815
Speciality: Osteopathy.
● **Owner** Mr S Sandler
P S T (Ref:HM17924)

## SANDON, PATER H G (DR)

**Dr Peter H G Sandon**, Doctors Surgery, 263 Goring Rd, Goring-By-Sea, Worthing, **Sussex (West)**, BN12 4PA, ENG.
(T) 01903 241995
Speciality: Homeopathy. ✔
● **Owner** Dr P Sandon Q: BS, MB.
C Yrs. Est.: 16 (Ref:HM17925)

## SANDOWN CLINIC FOR COMP MED

**Sandown Clinic For Complementary Medicine**, 171 Sandown Rd, Deal, **Kent**, CT14 6NX, ENG.
(T) 01304 364879
Speciality: Aromatherapy, Chiropractic, Reflexology, Reiki, Aura Soma Colour Therapy. ✔
● **Practitioner** Mrs S Fairley
C Yrs. Est.: 14 (Ref:HM17926)

## SANDRA DAY SCHOOL OF HEALTH

**Sandra Day School Of Health Related Studies**, Ashley House, Drake St, Rochdale, **Lancashire**, OL11 1EF, ENG.
(T) 01706 750302 (F) 01706 750304
Speciality: Complementary Medicines & Therapy.
● **Owner** Mrs S Day
C M (Ref:HM17927)

## SANDRINGHAM OSTEOPATHY CLINIC

**Sandringham Osteopathy Clinic**, 156 Sandringham Rd, London, **London (Greater)**, E8 2HS, ENG.
(T) 020 7254 2038
Speciality: Osteopathy.
● **Owner** Mrs A Akincioglu
P S T (Ref:HM17928)

## SANDS PHYSIOTHERAPY SERVICES

**Sands Physiotherapy Services**, 106 Montgomery St, Edinburgh, **Edinburgh (City of)**, EH7 5HE, SCO.
(T) 01315 565830
Speciality: Physiotherapy.
P S T (Ref:HM17929)

## SANDS, A J

**A J Sands**, 5 The Mount, Weybridge, **Surrey**, KT13 9LT, ENG.
(T) 01932 226639
Speciality: Chiropodists (Podiatrists).
● **Owner** Mr A Sands
S (Ref:HM17930)

## SANDY HILL PHYSICAL THRPY CTRE

**Sandy Hill Physical Therapy Centre**, 14 Sandy Hill, St. Austell, **Cornwall**, PL25 3AT, ENG.
(T) 01726 67567 (F) 01726 67567
Speciality: Physiotherapy.
● **Manager** Mr G Gilchrist
P S T (Ref:HM17931)

## SANDY, I M & A N

**I M & A N Sandy**, 1 Church Lane, Brighouse, **Yorkshire (West)**, HD6 1AT, ENG.
(T) 01484 715665
Speciality: Chiropodists (Podiatrists).
S (Ref:HM17932)

## SANDY, I M & A N

**I M & A N Sandy**, 84 Birkby Lodge Rd, Huddersfield, **Yorkshire (West)**, HD2 2BL, ENG.
(T) 01484 423796
Speciality: Chiropodists (Podiatrists).
● **Office Manager** Mr B Sandy
S (Ref:HM17933)

## SANGEELEE, BERNADETTE

**Bernadette Sangeelee**, 86 Drake Avenue, Minster On Sea, Sheerness, **Kent**, ME12 3RZ, ENG.
(T) 01795 876967
Speciality: Physiotherapy.
● **Owner** Mrs B Sangeelee
P S T (Ref:HM17934)

## SANGHERA, PARMJIT

**Parmjit Sanghera**, Nottingham, **Nottinghamshire**, NG10, ENG.
(T) 01159 461002
Speciality: Bach Remedies.
M (Ref:HM17935)

## SANGWAY, DIANE

**Diane Sangway**, The McTimoney Chiropractic Clinic, 17 Alexandra Rd, Malvern, **Worcestershire**, WR14 1HA, ENG.
(T) 01684 567480
Speciality: Chiropractors.
● **Owner** Ms D Sangway
P S T (Ref:HM17936)

## SANHAJI, DANA

**Dana Sanhaji**, 24 Byron Avenue, Sutton, **Surrey**, SM1 3RA, ENG.
(T) 020 8715 2821
Speciality: Reflexology.
S T (Ref:HM17937)

## SANZ DE DEAS, HILDA C

**Hilda C Sanz De Deas**, 90 Victoria Rd, Oxford, **Oxfordshire**, OX2 7QE, ENG.
(T) 01865 553939
Speciality: Acupuncture.
O (Ref:HM17938)

## SANZ DE DEAS, HILDA C

**Hilda C Sanz De Deas**, Watchbell House, 8 Lugley St, Newport, **Isle of Wight**, PO30 5HD, ENG.
(T) 01983 522477
Speciality: Acupuncture.
● **Owner** Mr G Creed
O (Ref:HM17939)

## SAPIR, NINETTE

**Ninette Sapir**, Ingledale, 1 Tanhouse Rd, Oxted, **Surrey**, RH8 9PE, ENG.
(T) 01883 717277
Speciality: Acupuncture.
O (Ref:HM17940)

## SARA NADAF TRICHOLOGIST

**Sara Nadaf Trichologist**, 11 Park Avenue, Barking, **Essex**, IG11 8QU, ENG.
(T) 020 8591 2973
Speciality: Complementary Medicines & Therapy, Trichology.
M (Ref:HM17941)

## SARA, HANRAHAN

**Hanrahan Sara MRO**, 21 Church Rd, Dalkey, **County Dublin**, IRE.
(T) 01280 1925
Speciality: Complementary Medicines & Therapy.
M (Ref:HM17942)

## SARAH

**Sarah**, 23 Winetavern St, Belfast, **County Antrim**, BT1 1JQ, NIR.
(T) 028 9023 1912
Speciality: Clairvoyants & Palmists.
● **Owner** Miss S Redmond
B (Ref:HM17943)

## SARAH BOGUE HOMEOPATH

**Sarah Bogue**, The Burrow, Puttenham, Guildford, **Surrey**, GU3 1AT, ENG.
(T) 01483 812070
Speciality: Homeopathy. ✔
● **Classical Homeopath** Ms S Bogue
Q: L.C.C.H, RSHom. M: Soc.Hom.

M Yrs. Est.: 4 (Ref:HM17944)

**SARAH KEY PHYSIOTHERAPY CENTRE**

**Sarah Key Physiotherapy Centre**, 27 Weymouth St, London, **London (Greater)**, W1N 3FJ, ENG.
(T) 020 7636 3433 (F) 020 7255 1522
Speciality: Physiotherapy.
• **Owner** Mr R Brown
P S T (Ref:HM17945)

**SARDAR, AHMAD**

**Ahmad Sardar**, 4 Camborne Rd, London, **London (Greater)**, SW18 4BJ, ENG.
(T) 020 8870 1004
Speciality: Chiropractors.
• **Owner** A Sardar
P S T (Ref:HM17946)

**SARUM PHYSIOTHERAPY CENTRE**

**Sarum Physiotherapy Centre**, 213 Devizes Rd, Salisbury, **Wiltshire**, SP2 9LT, ENG.
(T) 01722 415055 (F) 01722 330413
Speciality: Physiotherapy. ✓ [credit card]
• **Physiotherapist** Heather Waite
• **Practice Manager** Mrs J Rogers Q: Grad Dip Phys, MCSP, SRP M: CSP
• **Physiotherapist** Mrs J Mears Q: Grad Dip Phys, MCSP, SRP M: CSP
S Yrs. Est.: 7 (Ref:HM17947)

**SASHA HEALTH & SAUNA CLUB**

**Sasha Health & Sauna Club**, 387 Alexandra Avenue, Harrow, **London (Greater)**, HA2 9EF, ENG.
(T) 020 8933 0577
Speciality: Complementary Medicines & Therapy.
C M (Ref:HM17948)

**SASSE, LOUISE**

**Louise Sasse**, Parkwood Chiropractic Clinic, 189 Fidlas Rd, Llanishen, Cardiff, **Glamorgan (Vale of)**, CF14 5LZ, WAL.
(T) 029 2076 6777 (F) 029 2076 6777
Speciality: Chiropractors.
• **Senior Partner** Ms L Sasse
P S T (Ref:HM17949)

**SAUMEEL PATEL ACU CLINIC**

**Saumeel Patel Acupuncture Clinic**, 48 High Beeches, Banstead, **Surrey**, SM7 1NB, ENG.
(T) 01737 360996
Speciality: Acupuncture. ✓
• **Acupuncturist/Owner** Mr S Patel Q: Lic.Ac, MBAcC. M: BAcC.
O Yrs. Est.: 3 (Ref:HM17950)

**SAUNDERS, A J**

**A J Saunders**, 18 Wimpole St, London, **London (Greater)**, W1M 7HE, ENG.
(T) 020 7631 0724
Speciality: Chiropodists (Podiatrists).
• **Owner** A Saunders
S (Ref:HM17951)

**SAUNDERS, BEVERLEY**

**Beverley Saunders**, 74 Hogarth Cr, London, **London (Greater)**, SW19 2DW, ENG.
(T) 020 8646 5003
Speciality: Complementary Medicines & Therapy.
• **Owner** Ms B Saunders
M (Ref:HM17952)

**SAUNDERS, ELIZABETH**

**Elizabeth Saunders**, 27A Cephas Avenue, Stepney Green, London, **London (Greater)**, E1 4AS, ENG.
(T) 020 7702 7993
Speciality: Alexander Technique.
• **Owner** Ms E Saunders
P S (Ref:HM17953)

**SAUNDERS, JUDY**

**Judy Saunders**, 65 Chesham Rd, Amersham, **Buckinghamshire**, HP6 5JQ, ENG.
(T) 01494 434500
Speciality: Physiotherapy.
• **Owner** Miss J Saunders
P S T (Ref:HM17954)

**SAUNDERS, K**

**K Saunders**, 4 Beech Tree Drive, Shanklin, **Isle of Wight**, PO37 7DS, ENG.
(T) 01983 866514
Speciality: Chiropractic.
• **Owner** Mr K Saunders
P S T (Ref:HM17955)

**SAUNDERS, K A**

**K A Saunders**, 3 Clevedon Rd, Newport, NP19 8LZ, WAL.
(T) 07932 054926
Speciality: Chiropractors.
• **Owner** Ms K Saunders
P S T (Ref:HM17956)

**SAUNDERS, MARGARET**

**Margaret Saunders**, 4 Elmwood Gr, Uttoxeter, **Staffordshire**, ST14 7HQ, ENG.
(T) 01889 563770
Speciality: Physiotherapy.
P S T (Ref:HM17957)

**SAUNDERS, N**

**N Saunders**, Desford, Glebe Avenue, Ripley, **Derbyshire**, DE5 3GA, ENG.
(T) 01773 570859
Speciality: Osteopathy.
P S T (Ref:HM17958)

**SAUNDERS, NICHOLAS**

**Nicholas Saunders**, The Old Rectory, Rectory Lane, Gatcombe, Newport, **Isle of Wight**, PO30 3EF, ENG.
(T) 01983 721442
Speciality: Osteopathy.
P S T (Ref:HM17959)

**SAUNDERS, P**

**P Saunders**, 7b Annandale Rd, London, **London (Greater)**, W4 2HE, ENG.
(T) 020 8742 0578 (F) 020 8747 9728
Speciality: Osteopathy.
• **Owner** Mr P Saunders
P S T (Ref:HM17960)

**SAUNDERS, STEPHANIE**

**Stephanie Saunders**, 20 Ailsa Rd, Twickenham, **London (Greater)**, TW1 1QW, ENG.
(T) 020 8891 6265 (F) 020 8891 6265
Speciality: Physiotherapy.
• **Owner** Ms S Saunders
P S T (Ref:HM17961)

**SAUNDERS, SUE**

**Sue Saunders**, 64 Bethel St, Norwich, **Norfolk**, NR2 1NR, ENG.
(T) 01603 666546 (F) 01603 666759
Speciality: Homeopathy.
• **Owner** Ms S Saunders
M (Ref:HM17962)

**SAVAGE, E**

**E Savage**, 6 Roseville St, Dartmouth, **Devon**, TQ6 9QH, ENG.
(T) 01803 834755
Speciality: Chiropodists (Podiatrists).
• **Owner** Mrs E Savage
S (Ref:HM17963)

**SAVAGE, EDNA**

**Edna Savage**, 13 Langley Rd, Southampton, **Hampshire**, SO15 8PJ, ENG.
(T) 023 8077 4987
Speciality: Complementary Medicines & Therapy.
• **Owner** Mrs E Savage
C M (Ref:HM17964)

**SAVAGE, GERALD**

**Gerald Savage**, 20 Coppice Walk, Shirley, Solihull, **Midlands (West)**, B90 4HY, ENG.
(T) 01564 702186
Speciality: Hypnotherapy.
• **Partner** Mrs J Spence
B (Ref:HM17965)

**SAVAGE, GERALD**

**Gerald Savage**, Suite 3 Albion House, 13 John St, Stratford-Upon-Avon, **Warwickshire**, CV37 6UB, ENG.
(T) 01789 267080
Speciality: Cognitive Therapy, Counselling, Hypnosis, Hypnotherapy, Neuro-Linguistic Program, Phytotherapy, Stress Therapy, Transactional Analysis, Psychodynamic therapy, Hypno- analysis, Psycho analysis. ✓
• **Hypnotherapist/Hypno-Analyst** Mr G Savage Q: Dip.Hyp, Dip.Psych, MCPS, MHRS, MIAH, MNCH. M: HS, IAH, NCH, NRAH.
B Yrs. Est.: 7 (Ref:HM17966)

**SAVAGE, J**

**J Savage**, 2 Ashmore Trce, Sunderland, **Tyne and Wear**, SR2 7DE, ENG.
(T) 01915 140666
Speciality: Physiotherapy.
P S T (Ref:HM17967)

**SAVAGE, JUDITH**

**Judith Savage**, Brittany Rd, St. Leonards-On-Sea, **Sussex (East)**, TN38 0RB, ENG.
(T) 01424 461066
Speciality: Reflexology.
• **Owner** Mrs J Savage
S T (Ref:HM17968)

**SAVAGE, PAUL**

**Paul Savage**, 9 Western Hill, Sunderland, **Tyne and Wear**, SR2 7PH, ENG.
(T) 01915 673478
Speciality: Chiropodists (Podiatrists).
• **Owner** Mr P Savage
S (Ref:HM17969)

**SAVAGE, R H (DR)**

**Dr R H Savage**, 2 Richmond Rd, Taunton, **Somerset**, TA1 1EW, ENG.
(T) 01823 286251 (F) 01823 327199
Speciality: Homeopathy.
• **Principal** Dr R Savage
M (Ref:HM17970)

**SAVAGE, ROGER**

**Roger Savage**, 29 High St, Harlow, **Essex**, CM17 0DN, ENG.
(T) 01279 438444
Speciality: Homeopathy.
• **Partner** Mr N Bruce
M (Ref:HM17971)

**SAVAGE, ROGER**

**Roger Savage**, 26 Winstanley Rd, Saffron Walden, **Essex**, CB11 3EQ, ENG.
(T) 01799 524442
Speciality: Homeopathy.
• **Owner** Mr R Savage
M (Ref:HM17972)

**SAVANNAH ENTERPRISES**

**Savannah Enterprises**, 49 Druids Lane, Birmingham, **Midlands (West)**, B14 5SR, ENG.
(T) 01214 305524
Speciality: Complementary Medicines & Therapy.
• **Owner** Mrs C McPherson
M (Ref:HM17973)

**SAVILLE & HOLDSWORTH**

**Saville & Holdsworth (UK) Ltd**, 2 Caxton St, London, **London (Greater)**, SW1H 0QE, ENG.
(T) 020 7799 3464 (F) 020 7799 3106
Speciality: Psychology.
• **Managing Director** Ms A Burnip
B (Ref:HM17974)

**SAVILLE & HOLDSWORTH**

**Saville & Holdsworth Ltd**, Management Centre, Woodstock Lane North, Surbiton, **Surrey**, KT6 5HN, ENG.
(T) 020 8398 4141 (F) 020 8335 7000
Speciality: Psychology.
• **Managing Director** Mr A Bernett
B (Ref:HM17975)

**SAVILLE & HOLDSWORTH**

**Saville & Holdsworth Ltd**, 3 A C Court, High St, Thames Ditton, **Surrey**, KT7 0SR, ENG.
(T) 020 8398 4170 (F) 020 8398 9544
Speciality: Psychology.
• **Managing Director** Ms L Cramp
B (Ref:HM17976)

**SAVILLE, ELAINE**

**Elaine Saville**, 69 Princess Rd, Urmston, Manchester, **Manchester (Greater)**, M41 5ST, ENG.
(T) 01617 470697
Speciality: Complementary Medicines & Therapy.



Key continued: **Yrs.Est:** Years Established **Q:** Qualifications **M:** Professional Membership ✓ Indemnity Insurance [credit card] Accept Credit Cards

C M (Ref:HM17977)

**SAVILLE, KATHY**

**Kathy Saville**, 1 Portsea Rd, Sheffield, **Yorkshire (South)**, S6 4QA, ENG.
(T) 01142 347894
Speciality: Aromatherapy.
● **Owner** Ms K Saville
M O (Ref:HM17978)

**SAVLA, N (DR)**

**Dr N Savla**, Roding Hospital, Roding Lane South, Ilford, **Essex**, IG4 5PZ, ENG.
(T) 020 8551 1100
Speciality: Psychiatry.
B (Ref:HM17979)

**SAVORY, BARRIE**

**Barrie Savory**, 27 Bickenhall Mansions, Bickenhall St, London, **London (Greater)**, W1H 3LE, ENG.
(T) 020 7935 0844
Speciality: Osteopathy.
P S T (Ref:HM17980)

**SAVOURE, CHRISTOPHE**

**Christophe Savoure**, 4 Highbury, Newcastle Upon Tyne, **Tyne and Wear**, NE2 3BX, ENG.
(T) 01912 813711
Speciality: Chiropractors.
● **Partner** Dr M Bailey
P S T (Ref:HM17981)

**SAWAYA, ALICIA**

**Alicia Sawaya MHCT**, Marlborough Natural Health Centre, 47 Kingsbury St, Marlborough, **Wiltshire**, SN8 1JE, ENG.
(T) 01672 515057
(E) aliciasawaya@supawomen.com
Speciality: Dowsing, Hay Diet, Healer, Healing Therapy, Herbal Medicine, Holistic Healing, Colonic Therapy, Vortex Healing, Essences. ✓
● **Herbalist/Colonic Therapist** Ms A Sawaya
(T) 01672 871278 M: AMH.
M Yrs. Est.: 5 (Ref:HM17982)

**SAWDAY, CAROLINE**

**Caroline Sawday**, 20 Rhiwlas, Dunvant, Swansea, **Glamorgan (Vale of)**, SA2 7PW, WAL.
(T) 01792 281580
Speciality: Reflexology.
S T (Ref:HM17983)

**SAWYER, E**

**E Sawyer**, 22 Inchmery Rd, London, **London (Greater)**, SE6 2NE, ENG.
(T) 020 8698 1809
Speciality: Homeopathy.
● **Owner** Mrs E Sawyer
M (Ref:HM17984)

**SAWYER, KEN**

**Ken Sawyer**, 31 Cairngrassie Circle, Portlethen, Aberdeen, **Aberdeenshire**, AB12 4TZ, SCO.
(T) 01224 781452
Speciality: Counselling, Hypnosis, Hypnotherapy, Psychotherapy, Thought Field Therapy. ✓
● **Therapist/Counsellor** Mr K Sawyer Q: BA, Dip.Hyp, Dip.Psych, MSc, NLP.
B H Yrs. Est.: 8 (Ref:HM17985)

**SAWYER, PAUL**

**Paul Sawyer**, 20 Dominion Rd, Bristol, BS16 3EW, ENG.
(T) 01179 658464
Speciality: Hypnosis.
B (Ref:HM17986)

**SAXBY, LAURA**

**Laura Saxby**, 17 Ben Garrisdale Pl, Glasgow, **Glasgow (City of)**, G53 7QE, SCO.
(T) 01416 210792
Speciality: Hypnotherapy.
● **Owner** Mrs L Saxby
B (Ref:HM17987)

**SAXBY, SUE**

**Sue Saxby**, 1 Bronsley Villas, Fairmead Rd, Saltash, **Cornwall**, PL12 4JQ, ENG.
(T) 01752 847305
Speciality: Reflexology.
S T (Ref:HM17988)

**SAXBY, W**

**Mrs W Saxby**, 134a High St, Maldon, **Essex**, CM9 5BX, ENG.
(T) 01621 852479
Speciality: Osteopathy.
P S T (Ref:HM17989)

**SAXELBY, M**

**M Saxelby**, 12 Clough Meadow, Woodley, Stockport, **Cheshire**, SK6 1JZ, ENG.
(T) 01614 949229
Speciality: Chiropody. ✓
● **Chiropodist (Podiatrist)** Mrs M Saxelby Q: MBChA. M: B.A.Ch.P.
C Yrs. Est.: 11 (Ref:HM17990)

**SAXON, RONALD**

**Ronald Saxon**, 78 Lynton Mead, London, **London (Greater)**, N20 8DJ, ENG.
(T) 020 8446 0131
Speciality: Chiropodists (Podiatrists).
● **Owner** Mr R Saxon
S (Ref:HM17991)

**SAYER CLINIC**

**Sayer Clinic**, Aldwick House, 74 Croydon Rd, Beddington, Croydon, **Surrey**, CR0 4PB, ENG.
(T) 020 8686 9265 (F) 020 8686 9265
(E) mail@sayerclinic.co.uk
Speciality: Chiropractic. ✓ CREDIT
● **Chiropractor** Dr J Goaly Q: DC. M: GCC.
● **Chiropractor** Dr K Harm Q: DC. M: GCC.
● **Chiropractor** Dr J Napier Q: DC. M: GCC.
● **Chiropractor** Dr J Speed Q: DC. M: GCC.
P Yrs. Est.: 10 (Ref:HM17992)

**SAYER CLINIC**

**Sayer Clinic (The)**, 8 Sunningdale Gardens, Kensington, London, **London (Greater)**, W8 6PX, ENG.
(T) 020 7937 8978 (F) 020 7937 3720
(E) mail@sayerclinics.co.uk
Speciality: Acupuncture, Chiropractic, Manipulation, Massage (Therapeutic), Postural Integration, X-Ray. ✓ CREDIT
● **Chiropractor** Dr C Berlingieri Q: DC. M: GCC.
● **Owner** Dr M Durtnall Q: DC. M: GCC.
● **Chiropractor** Dr J Napier Q: DC. M: GCC.
● **Chiropractor** Dr F Bennett Q: DC. M: GCC.
P S Yrs. Est.: 22 (Ref:HM17993)

**SAYER CLINIC**

**Sayer Clinic (The)**, 22 Seymour St, London, **London (Greater)**, W1H 5WD, ENG.
(T) 020 7723 2725
Speciality: Chiropractic. ✓ CREDIT
● **Chiropractor** Dr J Napier Q: DC. M: GCC.
● **Owner** Dr M Durtnall Q: DC. M: GCC.
● **Chiropractor** Dr F Bennett Q: DC. M: GCC.
● **Chiropractor** Dr C Berlingieri Q: DC. M: GCC.
P Yrs. Est.: 15 (Ref:HM17994)

**SAYER, MARK**

**Mark Sayer**, 85 Fairfield Drive, Dorking, **Surrey**, RH4 1JG, ENG.
(T) 01306 500991
Speciality: Hypnosis.
● **Owner** Mr M Sayer
B (Ref:HM17995)

**SAYER, SANDRA**

**Sandra Sayer**, Home Farm House, North Wootton, Shepton Mallet, **Somerset**, BA4 4HB, ENG.
(T) 01749 890650
Speciality: Hypnosis.
B (Ref:HM17996)

**SAYER, YKKE**

**Ykke Sayer**, Mayfield, **Sussex (East)**, TN20, ENG.
(T) 01435 872154
Speciality: Bach Remedies.
M (Ref:HM17997)

**SAYERS, FIONA**

**Fiona Sayers**, Upper Flat, 57 Woodside, London, **London (Greater)**, SW19 7AF, ENG.
(T) 020 8946 7993
Speciality: Reflexology.
S T (Ref:HM17998)

**SAYERS, MARGARET**

**Margaret Sayers**, 3 Beech Rise, Crowton, Northwich, **Cheshire**, CW8 2SD, ENG.
(T) 01928 787495
Speciality: Reflexology.
S T (Ref:HM17999)

**SAYERS, R B**

**R B Sayers**, Windy Hill, Penffordd, Clynderwen, **Carmarthenshire**, SA66 7HU, WAL.
(T) 01437 563830 (F) 01437 563830
Speciality: Hypnosis.
● **Owner** Mr R Sayers
B (Ref:HM18000)

**SCAMPTON, KATIE**

**Katie Scampton**, 397 Priory Rd, London, **London (Greater)**, NW6 3NL, ENG.
(T) 020 7625 9384
Speciality: Acupuncture.
O (Ref:HM18001)

**SCANDINAVIAN CHIROPRACTIC CTRE**

**Scandinavian Chiropractic Centre**, 3 Elm Court, 27 Old Milton Rd, New Milton, **Hampshire**, BH25 6DY, ENG.
(T) 01425 628844
(W) www.scanchiro.com
Speciality: Chiropractic. ✓
● **Owner** Dr M Westergaard Q: BSc, DC, MSc (Hons). M: BCA.
P Yrs. Est.: 4 (Ref:HM18002)

**SCARBOROUGH, KATE**

**Kate Scarborough**, 19 Newry Park East, Chester, **Cheshire**, CH2 2BF, ENG.
(T) 01244 375483
Speciality: Reflexology.
S T (Ref:HM18003)

**SCARBRO, J M**

**J M Scarbro**, 35C Bear St, Barnstaple, **Devon**, EX32 7BZ, ENG.
(T) 01271 376191
Speciality: Chiropractic.
● **Owner** Mrs M Scarbro
P S T (Ref:HM18004)

**SCARR, G M**

**G M Scarr**, 4 Wellington Circus, Nottingham, **Nottinghamshire**, NG1 5AL, ENG.
(T) 01159 484141 (F) 01159 532727
Speciality: Osteopathy.
● **Owner** Mr N Woodhead
P S T (Ref:HM18005)

**SCARR, G M**

**G M Scarr**, 8 Market St, Buxton, **Derbyshire**, SK17 6JY, ENG.
(T) 01298 78008
Speciality: Osteopathy.
● **Owner** Mr G Scarr
P S T (Ref:HM18006)

**SCARTHO OSTEOPATHIC PRACTICE**

**Scartho Osteopathic Practice**, 23 Waltham Rd, Scartho, Grimsby, **Humberside (South)**, DN33 2LY, ENG.
(T) 01472 877969
Speciality: Beauty Therapy, Chiropody, Massage (Therapeutic), Osteopathy, Reflexology. ✓
● **Osteopath** Mr H De La Hoyde Q: DO. M: GOsC.
S Yrs. Est.: 12 (Ref:HM18007)

**SCENT OF DELIGHT**

**Scent Of Delight**, 5 Bradshawgate, Leigh, **Manchester (Greater)**, WN7 4LX, ENG.
(T) 01942 704185
Speciality: Aromatherapy.
● **Manager** Mr M Hayes
M O (Ref:HM18008)

**SCENT OF DELIGHT**

**Scent Of Delight**, Unit 103G, New Market Hall, Wigan, **Lancashire**, WN1 1PX, ENG.
(T) 01942 704185
Speciality: Aromatherapy.
● **Owner** Mr M Hayes
M O (Ref:HM18009)

**SCENT STATION**

**Scent Station (The)**, Hereward Cross Shopping



Key: B Mind-Body Medicine C Complementary Medicine H Self Help Treatment M Medicinal Therapy O Oriental Medicine P Postural Therapy S Manipulative Structural Therapy T Touch Therapy

Centre, Farcet, Peterborough, **Cambridgeshire**, PE7 3BH, **ENG**.
**(T)** 01733 244343 **(F)** 01733 240678
Speciality: Aromatherapy.
● **Partner** Mrs L McMurray
M O (Ref:HM18010)

**SCENTED GARDENS**

**Scented Gardens (The)**, 14 Godstall Lane, Chester, **Cheshire**, CH1 1LN, **ENG**.
**(T)** 01244 344335 **(F)** 01244 344335
Speciality: Aromatherapy.
● **Aromatherapist** Mrs L Gerrard Q: Dip.Arom. M: ITEC.
C Yrs. Est.: 5 (Ref:HM18011)

**SCENTSUAL**

**Scentsual**, 32 George St, Leeds, **Yorkshire (West)**, LS2 7HY, **ENG**.
**(T)** 01132 443636
Speciality: Aromatherapy.
● **Owner** Mrs J Kelly
M O (Ref:HM18012)

**SCHARSACH, C**

**C Scharsach**, The Laurels, 39 Rickmansworth Rd, Watford, **Hertfordshire**, WD1 7HS, **ENG**.
**(T)** 01923 221303
Speciality: Osteopathy.
● **Owner** Mr M Tunmore
P S T (Ref:HM18013)

**SCHICK, A**

**A Schick**, 58 Stamford Brook Rd, London, **London (Greater)**, W6 0XL, **ENG**.
**(T)** 020 8740 5405
Speciality: Physiotherapy.
● **Owner** A Schick
P S T (Ref:HM18014)

**SCHIFFMAN, A**

**Mr A Schiffman**, 38 Torquay Gardens, Ilford, **Essex**, IG1 1JP, **ENG**.
**(T)** 020 8553 5211
Speciality: Chiropodists (Podiatrists).
S (Ref:HM18015)

**SCHIFFMAN, ALAN**

**Alan Schiffman**, 38 Torquay Gdns, Ilford, **Essex**, IG4 5PT, **ENG**.
**(T)** 020 8551 1190
Speciality: Chiropodists (Podiatrists).
● **Owner** Mr A Schiffman
S (Ref:HM18016)

**SCHLINDWEIN, HELENA**

**Helena Schlindwein**, Derry City, Londonderry, **County Londonderry**, BT48, **NIR**.
**(T)** 028 7126 3439
Speciality: Bach Remedies.
M (Ref:HM18017)

**SCHOFIELD, G A**

**G A Schofield**, 3 Kelvin Gr, On Huddersfield Rd, Millbrook, Stalybridge, **Manchester (Greater)**, SK15 3JW, **ENG**.
**(T)** 01613 383274
Speciality: Biomechanics, Chiropody, Nail Surgery, Podiatry.
● **Chiropodist (Podiatrist)**
Mr G Schofield Q: Inst.CH.P. M: Inst.CH.P.
C Yrs. Est.: 10 (Ref:HM18018)

**SCHOFIELD, I**

**I Schofield**, 23 Quarry Hill Rd, Tonbridge, **Kent**, TN9 2RN, **ENG**.
**(T)** 01732 355634
Speciality: Osteopathy.
P S T (Ref:HM18019)

**SCHOFIELD, IAN**

**Ian Schofield**, 7 Langley St, London, **London (Greater)**, WC2H 9JA, **ENG**.
**(T)** 020 7240 9099
Speciality: Osteopathy.
P S T (Ref:HM18020)

**SCHOFIELD, P B**

**P B Schofield**, 16 Fraser St, Ashton-under-Lyne, **Manchester (Greater)**, OL6 6LL, **ENG**.
**(T)** 01613 302197
Speciality: Physiotherapy.
● **Owner** Mr P Schofield
P S T (Ref:HM18021)

**SCHOFIELD, SHEILA**

**Sheila Schofield**, 10 Lupton Avenue, Coventry, **Midlands (West)**, CV3 5BQ, **ENG**.
**(T)** 024 7641 4249
Speciality: Acupuncture.
O (Ref:HM18022)

**SCHOFIELD, ZENA**

**Zena Scholfield**, The Blackheath Physiotherapy Practice, 6a Lee Rd, London, **London (Greater)**, SE3 9RT, **ENG**.
**(T)** 020 8852 9294
Speciality: Physiotherapy.
P S T (Ref:HM18023)

**SCHOLEY, PAMELA**

**Pamela Scholey**, 22 Pryors Lane, Bognor Regis, **Sussex (West)**, PO21 4LQ, **ENG**.
**(T)** 01243 268672
Speciality: Reflexology.
S T (Ref:HM18024)

**SCHOLL CENTRE**

**Scholl Centre**, 61 Albion St, Leeds, **Yorkshire (West)**, LS1 5AA, **ENG**.
**(T)** 01132 451846
Speciality: Chiropodists (Podiatrists).
● **Manageress** Mrs D Wilson
S (Ref:HM18025)

**SCHOLL CENTRE**

**Scholl Centre**, 20 Guild Hall Arcade, Lancaster Rd, Preston, **Lancashire**, PR1 1HR, **ENG**.
**(T)** 01772 253468
Speciality: Chiropodists (Podiatrists).
● **Manager** Mrs C Woodhead
S (Ref:HM18026)

**SCHOLL CENTRE**

**Scholl Centre**, 22-24 Church St, Lancaster, **Lancashire**, LA1 1NP, **ENG**.
**(T)** 01524 32060
Speciality: Chiropodists (Podiatrists).
S (Ref:HM18027)

**SCHOLL CENTRE**

**Scholl Centre**, 94A Brompton Rd, London, **London (Greater)**, SW3 1ER, **ENG**.
**(T)** 020 7589 1887
Speciality: Chiropodists (Podiatrists).
● **Manageress** Mrs K Guess
S (Ref:HM18028)

**SCHOLL CENTRE**

**Scholl Centre**, 23 Upper Brook St, Ipswich, **Suffolk**, IP4 1ED, **ENG**.
**(T)** 01473 254949
Speciality: Chiropodists (Podiatrists).
● **Manageress** Miss K Roper
S (Ref:HM18029)

**SCHOLL CENTRE**

**Scholl Centre**, 24 Parliament St, York, **Yorkshire (North)**, YO1 8RS, **ENG**.
**(T)** 01904 624469
Speciality: Chiropodists (Podiatrists).
S (Ref:HM18030)

**SCHOLL CENTRE**

**Scholl Centre**, 27 Catherine St, Salisbury, **Wiltshire**, SP1 2DQ, **ENG**.
**(T)** 01722 333071
Speciality: Chiropodists (Podiatrists).
● **Manager** Mrs L Milburn
S (Ref:HM18031)

**SCHOLL CENTRE**

**Scholl Centre**, 32 Arndale Centre, Eastbourne, **Sussex (East)**, BN21 3NW, **ENG**.
**(T)** 01323 722412
Speciality: Chiropody, Podiatry.
● **Manageress** Mrs M Trumble
● **Chiropodist** Hannah Smith Q: BSc, FCPod(s), M.S.C.P, S.R.Ch.
● **Podiatrist** Jane Falkner Q: BSc, FCPod(s), M.S.C.P, S.R.Ch.
M (Ref:HM18032)

**SCHOLL CENTRE**

**Scholl Centre**, 32 The Pallasades, Birmingham, **Midlands (West)**, B2 4XJ, **ENG**.
**(T)** 01216 435254
Speciality: Chiropodists (Podiatrists).
● **Manager** Mrs K Rowe
S (Ref:HM18033)

**SCHOLL CENTRE**

**Scholl Centre**, 33 Lister Gate, Nottingham, **Nottinghamshire**, NG1 7EE, **ENG**.
**(T)** 01159 472618
Speciality: Chiropodists (Podiatrists).
● **Manageress** Miss J Pegg
S (Ref:HM18034)

**SCHOLL CENTRE**

**Scholl Centre**, 35 Princes Walk, Northampton, **Northamptonshire**, NN1 2EL, **ENG**.
**(T)** 01604 638813
Speciality: Chiropodists (Podiatrists).
● **Manageress** Miss T Kramer
S (Ref:HM18035)

**SCHOLL CENTRE**

**Scholl Centre**, 3-5 Queens Rd, Watford, **Hertfordshire**, WD1 2LH, **ENG**.
**(T)** 01923 243410
Speciality: Chiropodists (Podiatrists).
S (Ref:HM18036)

**SCHOLL CENTRE**

**Scholl Centre**, 76 Old Christchurch Rd, Bournemouth, **Dorset**, BH1 1LR, **ENG**.
**(T)** 01202 557944
Speciality: Chiropodists (Podiatrists).
● **Manageress** Mrs T Cockwell
S (Ref:HM18037)

**SCHOLL CENTRE**

**Scholl Centre**, 20 Cornwall St, Plymouth, **Devon**, PL1 1LP, **ENG**.
**(T)** 01752 664433
Speciality: Chiropodists (Podiatrists).
S (Ref:HM18038)

**SCHOLL CENTRE**

**Scholl Centre**, 59-61 Queen St, Glasgow, **Glasgow (City of)**, G1 3EN, **SCO**.
**(T)** 01412 211146
Speciality: Chiropody, Cryo Surgery, Nail Surgery, Podiatry.
● **Chiropodist (Podiatrist)**
Leslie Johnston Q: DPodM, S.R.Ch. M: S.C.P.
● **Chiropodist (Podiatrist)**
Dorothy Donnelly Q: DPodM, S.R.Ch. M: S.C.P.
● **Chiropodist (Podiatrist)**
Nicola Greenwood Q: S.R.Ch. M: S.C.P.
● **Trainee** Cathrine McGowan
● **Branch Manager** Mrs N Tunnah
● **Chiropodist (Podiatrist)**
Norma Lee Q: DPodM, S.R.Ch. M: S.C.P.
S Yrs. Est.: 10 (Ref:HM18039)

**SCHOLL CENTRE**

**Scholl Centre**, 69 Lower Precinct, Coventry, **Midlands (West)**, CV1 1DS, **ENG**.
**(T)** 024 7622 3560
Speciality: Chiropodists (Podiatrists).
● **Manager** Ms P Harvey
S (Ref:HM18040)

**SCHOLL CENTRE**

**Scholl Centre**, 74 High St, Sutton, **Surrey**, SM1 1EZ, **ENG**.
**(T)** 020 8642 1528
Speciality: Chiropodists (Podiatrists).
● **Branch Manager** Miss J Taylor
S (Ref:HM18041)

**SCHOLL CENTRE**

**Scholl Centre**, 8 Alderman Judge Mall, Kingston Upon Thames, **Surrey**, KT1 1BS, **ENG**.
**(T)** 020 8546 1629
Speciality: Chiropodists (Podiatrists).
● **Manageress** Mrs V Wilson
S (Ref:HM18042)

**SCHOLL CENTRE**

**Scholl Centre**, 8-10 Eastgate Row, Chester, **Cheshire**, CH1 1LF, **ENG**.
**(T)** 01244 321884
Speciality: Chiropodists (Podiatrists).
● **Manager** Mrs M Wardroper
S (Ref:HM18043)

**SCHOLL CENTRE**

**Scholl Centre**, 14 Deanery Way, Stockport, **Cheshire**, SK1 1PP, **ENG**.
**(T)** 01614 802543


Key continued: Yrs.Est: Years Established Q: Qualifications M: Professional Membership Indemnity Insurance Accept Credit Cards

Speciality: Chiropodists (Podiatrists).
● **Manageress** Mrs C Marshall
S (Ref:HM18044)

## SCHOLL CENTRE

**Scholl Centre**, 8 The Spot, Osmaston Rd, Derby, **Derbyshire**, DE1 2JA, ENG.
(T) 01332 342216
Speciality: Chiropodists (Podiatrists).
● **Manager** Miss J Pegg
S (Ref:HM18045)

## SCHOLL CENTRE

**Scholl Centre**, 8 Priory Pl, Doncaster, **Yorkshire (South)**, DN1 1BL, ENG.
(T) 01302 342971
Speciality: Biomechanics, Chiropody, Cryo Surgery.
● **Manageress** Mrs E Wordsworth
● **Chiropodist (Podiatrist)**
Louise Smith Q: M.S.C.P. M: S.C.P.
M Yrs. Est.: 9 (Ref:HM18046)

## SCHOLL CENTRE

**Scholl Centre**, 44 London St, Norwich, **Norfolk**, NR2 1LA, ENG.
(T) 01603 626606
Speciality: Chiropodists (Podiatrists).
● **Manager** Mrs M Scannell
S (Ref:HM18047)

## SCHOLL CENTRE

**Scholl Centre**, 4-6 Knowsley St, Bolton, **Lancashire**, BL1 2AH, ENG.
(T) 01204 521688
Speciality: Chiropodists (Podiatrists).
● **Manager** Mrs C Haden
S (Ref:HM18048)

## SCHOLL CENTRE

**Scholl Centre**, 475 Capability Green, Luton, **Bedfordshire**, LU1 3LU, ENG.
(T) 01582 443300 (F) 01582 484940
Speciality: Chiropodists (Podiatrists).
● **Manager** Mr M Courtney
S (Ref:HM18049)

## SCHOLL CENTRE

**Scholl Centre**, 5 New Inn Hall St, Oxford, **Oxfordshire**, OX1 2DH, ENG.
(T) 01865 725957
Speciality: Chiropodists (Podiatrists).
● **Branch Manager** Mrs J Green
S (Ref:HM18050)

## SCHOLL CENTRE

**Scholl Centre**, 505-507 Lord St, Southport, **Merseyside**, PR9 0AY, ENG.
(T) 01704 533366
Speciality: Chiropodists (Podiatrists).
● **Manageress** Mrs A Alcock
S (Ref:HM18051)

## SCHOLL CENTRE

**Scholl Centre**, 57 Darley St, Bradford, **Yorkshire (West)**, BD1 3HN, ENG.
(T) 01274 725474
Speciality: Chiropodists (Podiatrists).
● **Manageress** Miss D Verity
S (Ref:HM18052)

## SCHOLL CENTRE

**Scholl Centre**, 40 Upper St, London, **London (Greater)**, N1 0PN, ENG.
(T) 020 7226 3781
Speciality: Chiropodists (Podiatrists).
● **Manager** Mrs B Bourne
S (Ref:HM18053)

## SCHOLL CENTRE

**Scholl Centre**, Unit 2 15 Market Buildings, Maidstone, **Kent**, ME14 1HP, ENG.
(T) 01622 692694
Speciality: Chiropodists (Podiatrists).
● **Director** Mr A Ward
S (Ref:HM18054)

## SCHOLL CENTRE

**Scholl Centre**, Unit 82 The Exchange Shopping Centre, Ilford, **Essex**, IG1 3RS, ENG.
(T) 020 8514 8736
Speciality: Chiropodists (Podiatrists).
● **Manageress** Mrs C Duke
S (Ref:HM18055)

## SCHOLL CENTRE

**Scholl Centre**, 157 Royal Victoria Place Shopping Centre, Tunbridge Wells, **Kent**, TN1 2SR, ENG.
(T) 01892 525842
Speciality: Chiropodists (Podiatrists).
● **Manageress** Ms S Young
S (Ref:HM18056)

## SCHOLL CENTRE

**Scholl Centre**, Unit 7 Bards Walk, Stratford-Upon-Avon, **Warwickshire**, CV37 6EY, ENG.
(T) 01789 299310
Speciality: Chiropodists (Podiatrists).
● **Manager** Mrs M McAulis
S (Ref:HM18057)

## SCHOLL CENTRE

**Scholl Centre**, 19 Hotel St, Leicester, **Leicestershire**, LE1 5AW, ENG.
(T) 01162 510095
Speciality: Chiropodists (Podiatrists).
● **Branch Manager** Miss K Warner
S (Ref:HM18058)

## SCHOLL CENTRE

**Scholl Centre**, 102-104 Union St, Torquay, **Devon**, TQ2 5PY, ENG.
(T) 01803 292153
Speciality: Chiropodists (Podiatrists).
● **Manager** Mrs B Gayle
S (Ref:HM18059)

## SCHOLL CENTRE

**Scholl Centre**, 115-117 Rose St, Edinburgh, **Edinburgh (City of)**, EH2 3DT, SCO.
(T) 01312 255398
Speciality: Chiropodists (Podiatrists).
● **Branch Manager** Mrs V McDaid
S (Ref:HM18060)

## SCHOLL CENTRE

**Scholl Centre**, 125 Queen St, Cardiff, **Glamorgan (Vale of)**, CF10 2BJ, WAL.
(T) 029 2022 7988
Speciality: Chiropodists (Podiatrists).
S (Ref:HM18061)

## SCHOLL CENTRE

**Scholl Centre**, 13 Lamb St, Stoke-On-Trent, **Staffordshire**, ST1 1PF, ENG.
(T) 01782 262108
Speciality: Chiropodists (Podiatrists).
● **Manager** Mrs S Malville
S (Ref:HM18062)

## SCHOLL CENTRE

**Scholl Centre**, 13-14 Victoria Arcade, Great Yarmouth, **Norfolk**, NR30 2NU, ENG.
(T) 01493 843798
Speciality: Chiropodists (Podiatrists).
● **Manageress** Mrs S Tiller
S (Ref:HM18063)

## SCHOLL CENTRE

**Scholl Centre**, 134-135 Friar St, Reading, **Berkshire**, RG1 1EX, ENG.
(T) 01189 574270
Speciality: Chiropodists (Podiatrists).
S (Ref:HM18064)

## SCHOLL CENTRE

**Scholl Centre**, Foot & Leg Centre, Unit 1 Market St, Winchester, **Hampshire**, SO23 9EP, ENG.
(T) 01962 842723
Speciality: Chiropodists (Podiatrists).
● **Manageress** Mrs D Duncan
S (Ref:HM18065)

## SCHOLL CENTRE

**Scholl Centre**, 14 Mealcheapen St, Worcester, **Worcestershire**, WR1 2DQ, ENG.
(T) 01905 25799
Speciality: Chiropodists (Podiatrists).
● **Manageress** Mrs B Morris-Casey
S (Ref:HM18066)

## SCHOLL CENTRE

**Scholl Centre**, 180 Sidwell St, Exeter, **Devon**, EX4 6RD, ENG.
(T) 01392 274562
Speciality: Chiropodists (Podiatrists).
● **Manager** Mrs S Morgan
S (Ref:HM18067)

## SCHOLL CENTRE

**Scholl Centre**, 18-20 Portland Rd, Worthing, **Sussex (West)**, BN11 1QN, ENG.
(T) 01903 200707
Speciality: Chiropodists (Podiatrists).
● **Manager** Mrs K Knivett
S (Ref:HM18068)

## SCHOLL CENTRE

**Scholl Centre**, 185 Regent St, London, **London (Greater)**, W1R 7FB, ENG.
(T) 020 7437 0850
Speciality: Chiropodists (Podiatrists).
● **Practice Manager** Mrs M Reed
S (Ref:HM18069)

## SCHOLL CENTRE

**Scholl Centre**, 128 Above Bar St, Southampton, **Hampshire**, SO14 7DU, ENG.
(T) 023 8033 3015
Speciality: Chiropodists (Podiatrists).
S (Ref:HM18070)

## SCHOLL CENTRE

**Scholl Centre**, Unit 16 Donegall Arcade, Castle Pl, Belfast, **County Antrim**, BT1 1GA, NIR.
(T) 028 9032 5901
Speciality: Chiropodists (Podiatrists).
● **Manager** Mrs M Haron
S (Ref:HM18071)

## SCHOLL CHIROPODY CLINIC

**Scholl Chiropody Clinic**, 18 Green St, Bath, **Somerset**, BA1 2JZ, ENG.
(T) 01225 481086
Speciality: Chiropodists (Podiatrists).
● **Manager** Ms W Caddogan
S (Ref:HM18072)

## SCHOLL FOOT & LEG CARE CENTRE

**Scholl Foot & Leg Care Centre**, 20 Oxford St, Harrogate, **Yorkshire (North)**, HG1 1PU, ENG.
(T) 01423 504831
Speciality: Chiropodists (Podiatrists).
● **Manageress** Miss L Davies
S (Ref:HM18073)

## SCHOLL FOOTCARE

**Scholl Footcare**, 7 Bold St, Liverpool, **Merseyside**, L1 4DN, ENG.
(T) 01517 093302
Speciality: Chiropodists (Podiatrists).
● **Manageress** Mrs J Breeze
S (Ref:HM18074)

## SCHOLL FOOTCARE CENTRE

**Scholl Footcare Centre**, 49 Deansgate, Manchester, **Manchester (Greater)**, M3 2AY, ENG.
(T) 01618 348570
Speciality: Chiropodists (Podiatrists).
S (Ref:HM18075)

## SCHOLL FOOTCARE CENTRE

**Scholl Footcare Centre**, 31 Priory Walk, Colchester, **Essex**, CO1 1LG, ENG.
(T) 01206 369253
Speciality: Chiropodists (Podiatrists).
● **Manager** Miss P Bray
S (Ref:HM18076)

## SCHOLL FOOTWEAR CENTRE

**Scholl Footwear Centre**, 12 Newgate Shopping Centre, Newcastle Upon Tyne, **Tyne and Wear**, NE1 5RB, ENG.
(T) 01912 329276
Speciality: Biomechanics, Chiropody, Podiatry.
● **Chiropodist (Podiatrist)**
Mr C Burton Q: BSc (Hons), DPodM, M.S.C.P, S.R.Ch. M: S.C.P.
C Yrs. Est.: 30 (Ref:HM18077)

## SCHONBERG, VERA

**Vera Schonberg**, Longhouse Lodge, Ermyn Way, Leatherhead, **Surrey**, KT22 8TN, ENG.
(T) 01372 274920
Speciality: Absent Healing, Aromatherapy, Auto Suggestion, Faith Healing, Healer, Healing Therapy, Holistic Healing, Hypnosis, Hypnotherapy, Kinesiology, Massage (Therapeutic), Meditation, Reflexology, Reiki, Seichem, Spiritual Healing, Vitamin Therapy.



Key: B Mind-Body Medicine C Complementary Medicine H Self Help Treatment M Medicinal Therapy O Oriental Medicine P Postural Therapy S Manipulative Structural Therapy T Touch Therapy

● **Owner/Alternative Therapist**
Mrs V Schonberg Q: MCAH.
B Yrs. Est.: 20 (Ref:HM18078)

## SCHOOL OF CHIROPODY

**School Of Chiropody**, 18-20 Portland Rd, Worthing, **Sussex (West)**, BN11 1QN, ENG.
(T) 01903 200707
Speciality: Chiropodists (Podiatrists).
● **Manager** Mrs K Knivett
S (Ref:HM18079)

## SCHOOL OF COMPLEMENTARY HEALTH

**School Of Complementary Health**, 38 South St, Exeter, **Devon**, EX1 1ED, ENG.
(T) 01392 410954 (F) 01392 410954
Speciality: Complementary Medicines & Therapy.
C M (Ref:HM18080)

## SCHOOL OF CONSCIOUS LIVING

**School Of Conscious Living (The)**, Park Farm, Hambridge, Langport, **Somerset**, TA10 0AE, ENG.
(T) 01458 252082 (F) 01458 252082
Speciality: Complementary Medicines & Therapy.
● **Partner** Mrs S Tatzel
C M (Ref:HM18081)

## SCHOOL OF ICASA

**School Of ICASA (The)**, Top Farm House, Beadlow, Shefford, **Bedfordshire**, SG17 5PL, ENG.
(T) 07000 607080 (F) 01582 451995
(E) enquiries@icasa.co.uk
(W) www.icasa.co.uk
Speciality: Complementary Medicines & Therapy, Sexual Therapy.
● **Sexual Training Director**
Mr D Brown Q: I.C.A.S.A. M: ISPA.
● **Principal** Mrs J Brown Q: I.C.A.S.A. M: ISPA.
T Yrs. Est.: 3 (Ref:HM18082)

## SCHOOL OF INSIGHT & INTUITION

**School Of Insight & Intuition**, Midford, Uxbridge Rd, Hampton Hill, Hampton, **London (Greater)**, TW12 1BD, ENG.
(T) 020 8979 0940 (F) 020 8255 8303
Speciality: Complementary Medicines & Therapy.
● **Managing Director** Mrs J Soskin
C M (Ref:HM18083)

## SCHOOL OF PSYCHO & COUNSELLING

**School Of Psychotherapy & Counselling**, Inner Circle, Regents Pk, London, **London (Greater)**, NW1 4NS, ENG.
(T) 020 7487 7406 (F) 020 7487 7446
Speciality: Psychotherapy.
B (Ref:HM18084)

## SCHOOL OF SPIRITUAL KNOWLEDGE

**School Of Spiritual Knowledge**, The Office, Cross St, Wigston, **Leicestershire**, LE18 2HE, ENG.
(T) 01162 100549
(E) annemilnes11@hotmail.com
Speciality: Spiritual Healing. ✔
● **Healer** Ms V McGready
(T) 01162 929788
● **Healer** Mrs A Milnes
(T) 01162 214033
M Yrs. Est.: 1 (Ref:HM18085)

## SCHOOL OF T'AI-CHI CH'UAN

**School of T'ai-Chi Ch'uan**, 83 St Quintin Avenue, London, **London (Greater)**, W10 6PB, ENG.
(T) 020 8960 2141
Speciality: Relaxation Technique.
● **Teacher** Richard Vebb
H T (Ref:HM18086)

## SCHOOL OF THE LIVING LIGHT

**School Of The Living Light**, Orchard House, 47 Aldreth Rd, Haddenham, Ely, **Cambridgeshire**, CB6 3PW, ENG.
(T) 01353 741760 (F) 01353 741782
Speciality: Complementary Medicines & Therapy.
● **Principal** Mr M Alberti
M (Ref:HM18087)

## SCHOOL OF THE LIVING LIGHT

**School Of The Living Light**, Millslade Hall, Station Rd, Ashcott, Bridgewater, **Somerset**, TA7 9QP, ENG.
(T) 01458 211047
(W) www.schoolofthelivinglight.co.uk
Speciality: Reiki.
M (Ref:HM18088)

## SCHOOL OF YOGA

**G Spence Trading As School Of Yoga**, 22 Old Farleigh Rd, South Croydon, **Surrey**, CR2 8PB, ENG.
(T) 020 8657 3258
(E) tutor@schoolofyoga.co.uk
Speciality: Counselling, Psychotherapy, Yoga, Anti-Natal Yoga. ✔
● **Additional Yoga Tutor** Ms C Simms
Q: BWY.Dip.
● **Additional Yoga Tutor**
Ms R Heaword Q: BWY.Dip.
● **Principal Tutor/Therapist**
Mr G Spence Q: BWY.Dip. M: BACP, BWY.
B Yrs. Est.: 15 (Ref:HM18089)

## SCHOOL PSYCHOLOGICAL CENTRE

**School Psychological Centre**, Nantgwin Centre, Hendrecafn Rd, Tonypandy, **Rhondda Cynon Taff**, CF40 1LW, WAL.
(T) 01443 432067
Speciality: Psychology.
B (Ref:HM18090)

## SCHOOL PSYCHOLOGICAL SERVICE

**School Psychological Service**, Middle Lane, Denbigh, **Denbighshire**, LL16 3UW, WAL.
(T) 01745 816591
Speciality: Psychology.
B (Ref:HM18091)

## SCHOUTEN, ADRIAN

**Adrian Schouten**, Deer Park, Henfield, **Sussex (West)**, BN5 9JQ, ENG.
(T) 01273 495990 (F) 01273 495050
Speciality: Physiotherapy.
● **Manager** Mr A Schouten
P S T (Ref:HM18092)

## SCHREIBER, ANETTE

**Anette Schreiber**, Clissold Park Health Centre, 154 Stoke Newington Church St, London, **London (Greater)**, N16 0JU, ENG.
(T) 020 7249 2990 (F) 020 7249 3977
Speciality: Osteopathy.
● **Director** Mr D Berg
P S T (Ref:HM18093)

## SCHREIBER, ANNE

**Anne Schreiber**, Abbey View Complementary Clinic, Abbey View Medical Centre, Shaftesbury, **Dorset**, SP7 8DH, ENG.
(T) 01747 856719 (F) 01747 856701
Speciality: Complementary Medicines & Therapy.
M (Ref:HM18094)

## SCHUSZLER, RANJA

**Ranja Schuszler**, 37A Lowfield St, Dartford, **Kent**, DA1 1HP, ENG.
(T) 01322 284898
Speciality: Reflexology.
● **Owner** Mrs R Schuszler
S T (Ref:HM18095)

## SCHWARZ, JANE

**Jane Schwarz**, 2 Rodwell Cl, Bournemouth, **Dorset**, BH10 7JH, ENG.
(T) 01202 770356
Speciality: Chiropodists (Podiatrists).
● **Owner** Mrs J Schwarz
S (Ref:HM18096)

## SCIATICA CENTRE

**Sciatica Centre (The)**, 48 High St, Bletchingley, Redhill, **Surrey**, RH1 4PA, ENG.
(T) 01883 743111
Speciality: Osteopathy.
● **Partner** Mr J Horner
P S T (Ref:HM18097)

## SCLAIRE, B L

**B L Sclaire**, 535 Rainham Rd South, Dagenham, **Essex**, RM10 7XJ, ENG.
(T) 020 8595 9751
Speciality: Chiropodists (Podiatrists).
● **Owner** Mrs B Sclaire
S (Ref:HM18098)

## SCOBIE, D C O

**D C O Scobie**, 1st Floor, 10 Coinagehall St, Helston, **Cornwall**, TR13 8EB, ENG.
(T) 01326 563022 (F) 01326 565603
Speciality: Osteopathy.
● **Principal** Mr D Scobie
P S T (Ref:HM18099)

## SCOBLE, ALISON

**Alison Scoble**, 37A Lowfield St, Dartford, **Kent**, DA1 1HP, ENG.
(T) 01322 284898
Speciality: Osteopathy.
● **Owner** Miss S Sedgwick
P S T (Ref:HM18100)

## SCOBLE, ALISON

**Alison Scoble**, 4 Clanricarde Gardens, Tunbridge Wells, **Kent**, TN1 1PE, ENG.
(T) 01892 525065 (F) 01892 618413
Speciality: Osteopathy.
● **Practice Manager** Mrs J Cumymn
P S T (Ref:HM18101)

## SCOFIELD CHIROPRATIC CLINIC

**Scofield Chiropratic Clinic**, 11 Kings Hill, Great Cornard, Sudbury, **Suffolk**, CO10 0EH, ENG.
(T) 01787 372825 (F) 01787 372825
Speciality: Chiropractic.
● **Owner** Dr K Cropp
P S T (Ref:HM18102)

## SCORPIO PHYSIOTHERAPY

**Scorpio Physiotherapy**, Egham Sports Centre, Vicarage Rd, Egham, **Surrey**, TW20 8NL, ENG.
(T) 01784 433973
(E) sophie-dhenin@moontight.co.uk
Speciality: Acupressure, Acupuncture, Cupping, Manipulation, Massage (Therapeutic), Osteopathy, Physiotherapy, Pilates. ✔
● **Physiotherapist/Acupuncturist**
Ms S Gaastra Q: Grad Dip Phys. M: CSP.
● **Osteopath/Physiotherapist**
Mr J Eyres Q: BSc, DO, Grad Dip Phys. M: CSP, GOsC.
● **Osteopath/Physiotherapist**
Ms S Dehnin Q: BA, BSc, DO, Grad Dip Phys. M: CSP, GOsC.
● **Physiotherapist** Mr K Dewsbury Q: Grad Dip Phys. M: CSP.
S Yrs. Est.: 13 (Ref:HM18103)

## SCOTT & THOMPSON

**Scott & Thompson**, Lyttleton House, Abbey Rd, Malvern, **Worcestershire**, WR14 3ES, ENG.
(T) 01684 563660 (F) 01684 563660
Speciality: Chiropodists (Podiatrists).
● **Owner** Mrs R Scott
S (Ref:HM18104)

## SCOTT STREET COMP THERAPY CTRE

**Scott Street Complementary Therapy Centre**, 58 Scott St, Barrow-in-Furness, **Cumbria**, LA14 1QE, ENG.
(T) 01229 826700
Speciality: Complementary Medicines & Therapy.
C M (Ref:HM18105)

## SCOTT, ALISON

**Alison Scott**, 21 Harcourt House, 19 Cavendish Sq, London, **London (Greater)**, W1M 9AB, ENG.
(T) 020 7409 3216
Speciality: Physiotherapy.
P S T (Ref:HM18106)

## SCOTT, ANDREW

**Andrew Scott**, 21 Thurne Way, Liverpool, **Merseyside**, L25 4SQ, ENG.
(T) 01517 227475 (F) 01517 227475
(E) andy@school of shiatsu.co.uk
(W) www.schoolofshiatsu.co.uk
Speciality: Acupuncture, Cupping, Do-In, Moxibustion, Shiatsu. ✔
● **Practitioner** Mr A Scott Q: BSc, Dip.Shiatsu, MRSS.
C O Yrs. Est.: 7 (Ref:HM18107)



Key continued: Yrs.Est: Years Established Q: Qualifications M: Professional Membership ✔ Indemnity Insurance Accept Credit Cards

**SCOTT, ANTONIA**
**Antonia Scott**, Aberfoyle House, Stapley Rd, St. Albans, **Hertfordshire**, AL3 5EP, ENG.
(T) 01727 856687
Speciality: Homeopathy.
● **Manager** Mrs S Bassett
M (Ref:HM18108)

**SCOTT, B W**
**Mr B W Scott**, 28 Peveril Avenue, Rutherglen, Glasgow, **Glasgow (City of)**, G73 4RD, SCO.
(T) 01416 341393
Speciality: Physiotherapy.
P S T (Ref:HM18109)

**SCOTT, BRIDGET**
**Bridget Scott**, 190 Mannamead Rd, Plymouth, **Devon**, PL3 5RE, ENG.
(T) 01752 770041
Speciality: Aromatherapy.
M O (Ref:HM18110)

**SCOTT, CELIA**
**Celia Scott**, 4 Loxley Rd, Stratford-Upon-Avon, **Warwickshire**, CV37 7DP, ENG.
(T) 01789 293766
Speciality: Homeopathy.
● **Owner** Mrs C Scott
M (Ref:HM18111)

**SCOTT, DAVID L (DR)**
**Dr David Scott L**, Ravelstone Manley Rd, Manley, Frodsham, **Cheshire**, WA6 9ED, ENG.
(T) 01928 740376
Speciality: Hypnotherapy.
● **Owner** Dr D Scott
B (Ref:HM18112)

**SCOTT, ELAINE**
**Elaine Scott**, Lawfield House, West End Lane, Henfield, **Sussex (West)**, BN5 9UH, ENG.
(T) 01273 493676
Speciality: Physiotherapy.
P S T (Ref:HM18113)

**SCOTT, ELY JARED**
**Ely Jared Scott**, 3 Park-En-Vine, St. Issey, Wadebridge, **Cornwall**, PL27 7QG, ENG.
(T) 01841 541176
Speciality: Chiropodists (Podiatrists).
S (Ref:HM18114)

**SCOTT, HEATHER**
**Heather Scott**, 30E Catisfield Lane, Fareham, **Hampshire**, PO15 5NN, ENG.
(T) 01329 314151
Speciality: Aromatherapy.
M O (Ref:HM18115)

**SCOTT, JANE**
**Jane Scott**, 1 Moat Walk, Crawley, **Sussex (West)**, RH10 7ED, ENG.
(T) 01293 888706
Speciality: Reflexology.
S T (Ref:HM18116)

**SCOTT, JOHNSTON ROBERT**
**Johnston Robert Scott D O M R O**, Arden House Kenyon St, Nenagh, **County Tipperary**, IRE.
(T) 06732 272
(E) johnston@indigo.ie
Speciality: Osteopathy.
P S T (Ref:HM18117)

**SCOTT, JUDITH**
**Judith Scott**, 60A High St, Boston Spa, Wetherby, **Yorkshire (West)**, LS23 6EA, ENG.
(T) 01937 842471
Speciality: Homeopathy.
M (Ref:HM18118)

**SCOTT, JUDY**
**Judy Scott**, The Old School House, Church St, Croscombe, Wells, **Somerset**, BA5 3QS, ENG.
(T) 01749 343069
Speciality: Psychotherapy.
● **Owner** Mrs J Scott
B (Ref:HM18119)

**SCOTT, K D**
**K D Scott**, 1 Beverley Cres, Gateshead, **Tyne and Wear**, NE9 5UP, ENG.
(T) 01914 879648
Speciality: Chiropodists (Podiatrists).
S (Ref:HM18120)

**SCOTT, KATHY**
**Kathy Scott**, 1 Crosby Rd, Northallerton, **Yorkshire (North)**, DL6 1AA, ENG.
(T) 01609 783600 (F) 01609 783600
Speciality: Homeopathy.
● **Owner** Miss J Waterworth
M (Ref:HM18121)

**SCOTT, LAURA**
**Laura Scott**, 28 Kenton Gardens, St. Albans, **Hertfordshire**, AL1 1JS, ENG.
(T) 01727 832757
Speciality: Reiki.
● **Owner** Miss L Scott
M (Ref:HM18122)

**SCOTT, M**
**M Scott**, 11 Sedum Cl, Huntington, Chester, **Cheshire**, CH3 6BL, ENG.
(T) 01244 320294
Speciality: Aromatherapy.
M O (Ref:HM18123)

**SCOTT, MARY**
**Mary Scott**, 6 Beech Avenue, Brentwood, **Essex**, CM13 2DS, ENG.
(T) 01277 216806
Speciality: Aromatherapy. ✔
● **Owner** Mrs M Scott Q: TIDHA. M: ISPA.
C Yrs. Est.: 2 (Ref:HM18124)

**SCOTT, S J**
**S J Scott**, 48 Roseford Rd, Cambridge, **Cambridgeshire**, CB4 2HD, ENG.
(T) 01223 369618
Speciality: Alexander Technique.
P S (Ref:HM18125)

**SCOTT, SARA**
**Sara Scott**, 6 Archers Lane, Stoke Orchard, Cheltenham, **Gloucestershire**, GL52 4SH, ENG.
(T) 01242 681036
Speciality: Chiropodists (Podiatrists).
● **Owner** Miss S Scott
S (Ref:HM18126)

**SCOTT, STEPHEN**
**Stephen Scott**, 36 East Claremont St, Edinburgh, **Edinburgh (City of)**, EH7 4JR, SCO.
(T) 01315 583535
Speciality: Chiropractic.
P S T (Ref:HM18127)

**SCOTT, SUE**
**Sue Scott**, 110 Sedlescombe Gardens, St. Leonards-On-Sea, **Sussex (East)**, TN38 0YW, ENG.
(T) 01424 713360
Speciality: Homeopathy.
M (Ref:HM18128)

**SCOTT, VIVIENNE**
**Vivienne Scott**, 26 Upton Way, Broadstone, **Dorset**, BH18 9LY, ENG.
(T) 01202 697186
Speciality: Reflexology.
● **Owner** Mrs V Scott
S T (Ref:HM18129)

**SCOTTISH CENTRE**
**Scottish Centre For Eating Disorders**, 3 Sciennes Rd, Edinburgh, **Edinburgh (City of)**, EH9 1LE, SCO.
(T) 01316 683051
Speciality: Psychotherapy.
B (Ref:HM18130)

**SCOTTISH CHIROPRACTIC ASS**
**Scottish Chiropractic Association**, 16 Jenny Moores Rd, St. Boswells, Melrose, **Scottish Borders**, TD6 0AL, SCO.
(T) 01835 824026 (F) 01835 824046
Speciality: Chiropractic.
P S T (Ref:HM18131)

**SCOTTISH HYDROTHERAPY SYSTEMS**
**Scottish Hydrotherapy Systems**, Suite 26a Caledonia House, Longford Avenue, Kilwinning, **Ayrshire (North)**, KA13 6EX, SCO.
(T) 01294 558658 (F) 01294 550077
Speciality: Physiotherapy.
● **Owner** Mr G Kennedy
P S T (Ref:HM18132)

**SCOTTISH INSTITUTE-HUMAN REL**
**Scottish Institute Of Human Relations**, 13 Park Trce, Glasgow, **Glasgow (City of)**, G3 6BY, SCO.
(T) 01413 320011
Speciality: Psychotherapy.
B (Ref:HM18133)

**SCOTTISH KINESIOLOGY CENTRE**
**Scottish Kinesiology Centre**, Bog Park Rd, Musselburgh, **Lothian (Mid)**, EH21 6RT, SCO.
(T) 01316 659599 (F) 01316 659577
Speciality: Kinesiology. ✔
● **Owner/Kinesiologist**
Ms G McKerrow Q: DIBAK. M: BRCP.
C Yrs. Est.: 7 (Ref:HM18134)

**SCOTTISH SCHOOL OF HERBAL MED**
**Scottish School Of Herbal Medicine**, Unit 22 Govan Workspace, 6 Harmony Row, Glasgow, **Glasgow (City of)**, G51 3BA, SCO.
(T) 01414 018889 (F) 01414 018891
(W) www.herbalmedicine.org.uk
Speciality: Aromatherapy, Herbal Medicine, Massage (Therapeutic).
● **Herbal Consultant** Mr K Robertson
M: NIMH.
C Yrs. Est.: 10 (Ref:HM18135)

**SCOTTISH SCHOOL OF REFLEXOLOGY**
**Scottish School Of Reflexology (The)**, 2 Wheatfield Rd, Ayr, **Ayrshire (South)**, KA7 2XB, SCO.
(T) 01292 287142
Speciality: Reflexology.
M (Ref:HM18136)

**SCOTT-MONCRIEFF, C M (DR)**
**Dr C M Scott-Moncrieff**, 36 Gipsy Lane, Warminster, **Wiltshire**, BA12 9LR, ENG.
(T) 01225 421034
Speciality: Homeopathy.
M (Ref:HM18137)

**SCOTT-ROBINSON, JAMES**
**James Scott-Robinson**, 57 Aylsham Rd, Norwich, **Norfolk**, NR3 3EZ, ENG.
(T) 01603 615041 (F) 01603 615041
Speciality: Osteopathy.
● **Owner** Mr J Scott-Robinson
P S T (Ref:HM18138)

**SCOTT-SMITH, CLARE**
**Clare Scott-Smith**, Daphne Cottage, Dacre, Harrogate, **Yorkshire (North)**, HG3 4AE, ENG.
(T) 01423 780762
Speciality: Physiotherapy.
● **Owner** Mrs C Scott-Smith
P S T (Ref:HM18139)

**SCOULAR, F M F**
**Mrs F M F Scoular**, 17 Crab Tree Lane, Atherton, Manchester, **Manchester (Greater)**, M46 0AU, ENG.
(T) 01942 873279
Speciality: Chiropodists (Podiatrists).
● **Owner** Mrs F Scoular
S (Ref:HM18140)

**SCOVELL, MICHAEL**
**Michael Scovell**, 8a St James St, Taunton, **Somerset**, TA1 1JH, ENG.
(T) 01823 323006
Speciality: Psychotherapy.
● **Owner** Mr M Scovell
B (Ref:HM18141)

**SCRABO HEALTH PRODUCTS**
**Scrabo Health Products Ltd**, 20 Thomas St, Ballymena, **County Antrim**, BT43 6AX, NIR.
(T) 028 2564 7692
Speciality: Homeopathy.
● **Sole Director** Ms R McMinn
M (Ref:HM18142)

**SCRABO HEALTH PRODUCTS**
**Scrabo Health Products Ltd**, 337 Ormeau Rd, Belfast, **County Antrim**, BT7 3GL, NIR.
(T) 028 9064 6721 (F) 028 9064 6721
(E) jarmstrong@freenetname.co.uk
(W) www.scrabohealthproducts.co.uk
Speciality: Aromatherapy, Bach Remedies,

Herbal Medicine, Homeopathy, Naturopathy. [CREDIT]
● **Homeopath** Ms J Armstrong **Q:** Dip.Hom.
M: NAHS.
**M** Yrs. Est.: 29 (**Ref:**HM18143)

## SCRABO HEALTH PRODUCTS

**Scrabo Health Products Ltd**, 19 Regent St, Newtownards, **County Down**, BT23 4AB, **NIR**.
**(T)** 028 9181 7775 **(F)** 028 9064 6721
Speciality: Homeopathy.
**M** (**Ref:**HM18144)

## SCRATCHLEY, J H

**J H Scratchley**, 30 Rotten Row, Lichfield, **Staffordshire**, WS13 6JB, **ENG**.
**(T)** 01543 252673
Speciality: Osteopathy.
● **Senior Partner** Ms J Scratchley
**P S T** (**Ref:**HM18145)

## SCREEN, D

**D Screen**, Care Of Debenhams, 48-66 Sandgate Rd, Folkestone, **Kent**, CT20 1DN, **ENG**.
**(T)** 01303 850171
Speciality: Chiropodists (Podiatrists).
**S** (**Ref:**HM18146)

## SCREENE, D

**D Screene**, 25 Castle St, Dover, **Kent**, CT16 1PT, ENG.
**(T)** 01304 202425
Speciality: Chiropodists (Podiatrists).
● **Owner** Mr D Screene
**S** (**Ref:**HM18147)

## SCRIMSHAW, J D

**J D Scrimshaw**, Redland House Clinic, 118 Redland Rd, Bristol, BS6 6QT, **ENG**.
**(T)** 01179 420200
Speciality: Chiropractors.
**P S T** (**Ref:**HM18148)

## SCRIMSHAW, S J

**S J Scrimshaw**, Redland House Clinic, 118 Redland Rd, Bristol, BS6 6QT, **ENG**.
**(T)** 01179 420200
Speciality: Chiropractors.
**P S T** (**Ref:**HM18149)

## SCRIVEN, D

**D Scriven**, 71A High St, Reigate, **Surrey**, RH2 9AE, **ENG**.
**(T)** 01737 243389
Speciality: Homeopathy.
**M** (**Ref:**HM18150)

## SCRIVEN, SARA

**Sara Scriven**, Clockhouse Clinic, Cobblestone Walk, 74 High St, Steyning, **Sussex (West)**, BN44 3RD, **ENG**.
**(T)** 01903 816483
Speciality: Alexander Technique.
● **Owner** Miss S Scriven
**P S** (**Ref:**HM18151)

## SCRIVEN, SARA

**Sara Scriven**, 321 Ditchling Rd, Brighton, **Sussex (East)**, BN1 6JJ, **ENG**.
**(T)** 01273 330127
Speciality: Alexander Technique.
● **Owner** Miss S Scriven
**P S** (**Ref:**HM18152)

## SCRIVENER, BARBARA

**Barbara Scrivener**, Cliffe House, Coldwell End, Youlgrave, Bakewell, **Derbyshire**, DE45 1WB, ENG.
**(T)** 01629 636601
Speciality: Reflexology.
**S T** (**Ref:**HM18153)

## SCRIVENER, JEAN

**Jean Scrivener**, 33 Red Lion Lane, Overton, Basingstoke, **Hampshire**, RG25 3HH, **ENG**.
**(T)** 01256 770896
Speciality: Aromatherapy.
● **Owner** Ms J Scrivener
**M O** (**Ref:**HM18154)

## SCRIVENER, PATRICIA

**Patricia Scrivener**, The Weaver House Clinic, 19A Pillory St, Nantwich, **Cheshire**, CW5 5BZ, ENG.
**(T)** 01270 629933
Speciality: Osteopathy.
**P S T** (**Ref:**HM18155)

## SCULLION, BRENDA

**Brenda Scullion**, **County Antrim**, BT8, **NIR**.
**(T)** 028 9081 3864
Speciality: Bach Remedies.
**M** (**Ref:**HM18156)

## SCUNTHORPE CHIROPRACTIC CLINIC

**Scunthorpe Chiropractic Clinic**, 12 West Common Lane, Scunthorpe, **Humberside**, DN17 1DX, **ENG**.
**(T)** 01724 844453
Speciality: Alexander Technique, Chiropractic, Manipulation, Massage (Therapeutic), Postural Integration, Ultrasonics. ✔
● **Chiropractor** Mr F Usher **Q:** BSc, DC.
M: BCA.
**S** Yrs. Est.: 13 (**Ref:**HM18157)

## SCUNTHORPE CLINIC

**Scunthorpe Clinic Of Chiropody & Podiatric Med (The)**, 95 Mary St, Scunthorpe, **Humberside**, DN15 6LB, **ENG**.
**(T)** 01724 853700
Speciality: Chiropodists (Podiatrists).
**S** (**Ref:**HM18158)

## SCUNTHORPE COMMUNITY HLTH CARE

**Scunthorpe Community Health Care**, Brumby Hospital, East Common Lane, Scunthorpe, **Humberside**, DN16 1QQ, **ENG**.
**(T)** 01724 290072
Speciality: Chiropodists (Podiatrists).
● **Chief Executive** Mr R Powell
**S** (**Ref:**HM18159)

## SCURR, PETER M

**Peter M Scurr**, Groundfloor Rooms, 12A Fore St, Tiverton, **Devon**, EX16 4LH, **ENG**.
**(T)** 01884 254545
Speciality: Biomechanics, Chiropody, Nail Surgery, Podiatry. ✔
● **Chiropodist (Podiatrist)**
Mr P Scurr **Q:** BSc, M.S.C.P, S.R.Ch. **M:** S.R.Ch.
**C M** Yrs. Est.: 6 (**Ref:**HM18160)

## SCUTT, KENNETH I R

**Kenneth I R Scutt**, 26 Nyewood Lane, Bognor Regis, **Sussex (West)**, PO21 2QB, **ENG**.
**(T)** 01243 824824
Speciality: Physiotherapy.
**P S T** (**Ref:**HM18161)

## SEABROOKE, TED

**Ted Seabrooke**, 140 Wigmore St, London, **London (Greater)**, W1H 9FF, **ENG**.
**(T)** 020 7486 7405
Speciality: Chiropodists (Podiatrists).
**S** (**Ref:**HM18162)

## SEAFIELD CLINIC

**Seafield Clinic (The)**, 21 Seafield Rd, Inverness, **Highland**, IV1 1SG, **SCO**.
**(T)** 01463 713757
Speciality: Hypnosis.
**B** (**Ref:**HM18163)

## SEAGER, NATALIE

**Natalie Seager**, The Woodberry Clinic, 351 Muswell Hill Broadway, London, **London (Greater)**, N10 1BX, **ENG**.
**(T)** 020 8883 6079
Speciality: Osteopathy.
● **Owner** Mr D Newman
**P S T** (**Ref:**HM18164)

## SEAL COMMUNITY HEALTH PROJECT

**Seal Community Health Project**, 192 McNeil St, Glasgow, **Glasgow (City of)**, G5 0NZ, **SCO**.
**(T)** 01414 292568 **(F)** 01414 292568
Speciality: Complementary Medicines & Therapy.
● **Manager** Mr J Stewart
**M** (**Ref:**HM18165)

## SEAL, RAYMOND

**Raymond Seal**, 7 Church Rd, Kettleburgh, Woodbridge, **Suffolk**, IP13 7LE, **ENG**.
**(T)** 01728 724745
Speciality: Psychotherapy.
● **Owner** Mr R Seal
**B** (**Ref:**HM18166)

## SEAL, W

**W Seal**, Rainbows, Thurleston Lodge Cottages, Thurleston Lane, Ipswich, **Suffolk**, IP1 6TF, **ENG**.
**(T)** 01473 226650
Speciality: Reflexology.
● **Partner** Ms W Seal
**S T** (**Ref:**HM18167)

## SEALE, DONNA

**Donna Seale**, 25 Woodland Rise, London, **London (Greater)**, N10 3UP, **ENG**.
**(T)** 020 8444 9990
Speciality: Psychology.
● **Owner** Mrs D Seale
**B** (**Ref:**HM18168)

## SEALE, TONY

**Tony Seale**, Mobile Service, 97 Fairway, Chertsey, **Surrey**, KT16 8EE, **ENG**.
**(T)** 01932 565868
Speciality: Complementary Medicines & Therapy.
**M** (**Ref:**HM18169)

## SEAMER, R

**Miss R Seamer**, 40 Church Lane, Oxted, **Surrey**, RH8 9LB, **ENG**.
**(T)** 01883 715127
Speciality: Osteopathy.
**P S T** (**Ref:**HM18170)

## SEAMUS CONNOLLY SHIATSU PRACT

**Seamus Connolly Shiatsu Practitioner**, 67 Wilfield Rd, Ballsbridge, **County Dublin**, **IRE**.
**(T)** 01260 4669
**(E)** enquiries@shiatsuireland.com
**(W)** www.shiatsuireland.com
Speciality: Complementary Medicines & Therapy.
**M** (**Ref:**HM18171)

## SEAN, FARRELL

**Farrell Sean L ADHP MICHP**, Fairview, **County Dublin**, **IRE**.
**(T)** 01857 0541
**(W)** www.hypnosiseire.com
Speciality: Hypnotherapy.
**B** (**Ref:**HM18172)

## SEAR, JULIE

**Julie Sear**, 21 Wickham Way, Haywards Heath, **Sussex (West)**, RH16 1UG, **ENG**.
**(T)** 01444 455242
Speciality: Chiropodists (Podiatrists).
● **Owner** Mrs J Sear
**S** (**Ref:**HM18173)

## SEARBY, JOE

**Joe Searby - Alexander Technique**, 71 Wandsworth Bridge Rd, London, **London (Greater)**, SW6 2TB, **ENG**.
**(T)** 020 7371 7128 **(F)** 020 7371 7128
**(E)** joe@searbyville.demon.co.uk
Speciality: Alexander Technique. ✔
● **Teacher** Joe Searby **M:** STAT.
**B** Yrs. Est.: 6 (**Ref:**HM18174)

## SEARLE, MAUREEN

**Maureen Searle**, Tullymore, 38 Medlicott Way, Swanmore, Southampton, **Hampshire**, SO32 2NE, **ENG**.
**(T)** 01489 894633
Speciality: Aromatherapy.
● **Owner** Mrs M Searle
**M O** (**Ref:**HM18175)

## SEARS, J

**J Sears**, Myrtle Earth Farm, Edge Lane, Rossendale, **Lancashire**, BB4 7SS, **ENG**.
**(T)** 01706 830207
Speciality: Hypnosis.
● **Owner** Ms J Sears
**B** (**Ref:**HM18176)

## SEARY, ANDREW

**Mr Andrew Seary**, 27 Heol, Cardiff, **Glamorgan (Vale of)**, CF14 1JU, **WAL**.
**(T)** 029 2062 8365
Speciality: Physiotherapy.
**P S T** (**Ref:**HM18177)

## SEASONS BEAUTY CENTRE

**Seasons Beauty Centre**, 75 Middlewood Rd, Sheffield, **Yorkshire (South)**, S6 4GX, **ENG**.



Key continued: **Yrs.Est:** Years Established **Q:** Qualifications **M:** Professional Membership ✔ Indemnity Insurance [CREDIT] Accept Credit Cards

(T) 01142 364017
(E) lee.jayne@cablenet.co.uk
Speciality: Aromatherapy, Reflexology, Reiki, Hopi Ear Candles. ✓
● **Complementary Therapist** Ms M Kirby Q: MIIR. M: IIR.
● **Beauty Therapist** Ms C Hackett Q: Reiki 1.
● **Reiki Master** Ms J Wilmot Q: Reiki 1, Reiki 2, Reiki 3, Reiki Master.
C Yrs. Est.: 7 (Ref:HM18178)

## SEBASTIAN, ADELA
**Adela Sebastian**, 11 Montserrat Rd, Putney, London, **London (Greater)**, SW15 2LD, ENG.
(T) 020 8789 2548
Speciality: Physiotherapy.
● **Owner** A Sebastian
P S T (Ref:HM18179)

## SECRET GARDEN
**Secret Garden**, Midhurst Walk, West St, Midhurst, **Sussex (West)**, GU29 9NF, ENG.
(T) 01730 817717
Speciality: Complementary Medicines & Therapy.
● **Owner** Mrs A Crannan
M (Ref:HM18180)

## SECRET REMEDIES
**Secret Remedies**, Unit D2 Horsted Keynes Industrial Estate, Horsted Keynes, Haywards Heath, **Sussex (West)**, RH17 7BE, ENG.
(T) 01342 811266
Speciality: Aromatherapy.
● **Director** Mrs Y Jordon
M O (Ref:HM18181)

## SEDDON, ALECK RICH
**Aleck Rich Seddon**, 2 Washdyke Lane, Hucknall, Nottingham, **Nottinghamshire**, NG15 6QQ, ENG.
(T) 01159 533922 (F) 01159 533922
Speciality: Hypnotherapy.
● **Owner** Mr A Seddon
B (Ref:HM18182)

## SEDDON, J
**Mrs J Seddon**, Wrexham Physiotherapy Clinic, Sports Connection, Tenters Sq, Wrexham, LL13 7AA, WAL.
(T) 01978 291154
Speciality: Physiotherapy.
P S T (Ref:HM18183)

## SEDGE, R
**R Sedge**, Post Office Rd, Hawkhurst, Cranbrook, **Kent**, TN18 4AA, ENG.
(T) 01580 753883
Speciality: Chiropodists (Podiatrists).
● **Owner** Mrs R Sedge
S (Ref:HM18184)

## SEDGEBERROW MCTIMONEY
**Sedgeberrow McTimoney Chiropractic Clinic**, 100 Main St, Sedgeberrow, Evesham, **Worcestershire**, WR11 6UF, ENG.
(T) 01386 881978
Speciality: Chiropractic.
● **Owner** Mr S Dudley
P S T (Ref:HM18185)

## SEDGEWICK, SARAH JANE
**Sarah Jane Sedgewick**, 37A Lowfield St, Dartford, **Kent**, DA1 1HP, ENG.
(T) 01322 284898
Speciality: Osteopathy.
● **Owner** Miss S Sedgwick
P S T (Ref:HM18186)

## SEDGLEY COMP THERAPIES
**Sedgley Complementary Therapies**, Bourne House, 7 High St, Sedgley, Dudley, **Midlands (West)**, DY3 1RL, ENG.
(T) 01902 880122
Speciality: Complementary Medicines & Therapy.
C M (Ref:HM18187)

## SEDGLEY PHYSIO & ACU CENTRE
**Sedgley Physiotherapy & Acupuncture Centre (The)**, Suite 4 October House, 17 Dudley St, Sedgley, Dudley, **Midlands (West)**, DY3 1SA, ENG.
(T) 01902 676026
Speciality: Physiotherapy.
● **Owner** Mr S Tah
P S T (Ref:HM18188)

## SEEAR, MICHAEL (DR)
**Dr Michael Seear**, 86 Harley St, London, **London (Greater)**, W1N 1AE, ENG.
(T) 020 7580 3256
(E) healing@amserve.net
Speciality: Absent Healing, Acupressure, Acupuncture, Faith Healing, Healer, Healing Therapy, Holistic Healing, Homeopathy, Hypnosis, Massage (Therapeutic), Neuro-Linguistic Program, Psionic Therapy, Psychotherapy, Remedial Massage, Touch Therapy, Ying & Yang.
● **Therapist** Dr M Seear Q: MRCGP. M: RSM.
B Yrs. Est.: 12 (Ref:HM18189)

## SEEDS
**Seeds**, 704-708 High Rd, Finchley, London, **London (Greater)**, N12 9QL, ENG.
(T) 020 8446 5657
Speciality: Complementary Medicines & Therapy.
● **Owner** Mrs F Seed
C M (Ref:HM18190)

## SEEDS, COLIN
**Colin Seeds**, 26 Hallfield Rd, Newton, Alfreton, **Derbyshire**, DE55 5UB, ENG.
(T) 01773 590966
Speciality: Hypnosis.
B (Ref:HM18191)

## SEEKERS CENTRES FOR YOGA
**Seekers Centres For Yoga & Natural Therapies**, The Orange House, Church Rd, Windlesham, **Surrey**, GU20 6BT, ENG.
(T) 01276 473371 (F) 01276 473371
Speciality: Complementary Medicines & Therapy.
● **Employee** Ms S Saraswati
C M (Ref:HM18192)

## SEELEY, I D
**I D Seeley**, 1 Grove Avenue, New Costessey, Norwich, **Norfolk**, NR5 0JD, ENG.
(T) 01603 740602
Speciality: Physiotherapy.
● **Owner** Mr I Seeley
P S T (Ref:HM18193)

## SEELEY, JANICE
**Othergates Clinic of Natural Medicine**, 45 Barrington St, Tiverton, **Devon**, EX16 6QP, ENG.
(T) 01884 258143 (F) 01884 258143
Speciality: Allergy Testing, Homeopathy, Naturopathy, Bio Electric Function Diagnostics (Electro Acupuncture).
● **Homeopath/Electro Acupuncturist** Mrs J Seeley M: CH.
M Yrs. Est.: 17 (Ref:HM18194)

## SEELEY, M
**M Seeley**, 40 Elton Rd, Bishopston, Bristol, BS7 8DD, ENG.
(T) 01179 248739
Speciality: Chiropodists (Podiatrists).
S (Ref:HM18195)

## SEELY, SUSAN
**Susan Seely**, 14 Ampthill St, Norwich, **Norfolk**, NR2 2RG, ENG.
(T) 01603 661773
Speciality: Osteopathy.
P S T (Ref:HM18196)

## SEER
**Seer**, Broadbent Avenue, Warrington, **Cheshire**, WA4 1UR, ENG.
(T) 01925 245972
Speciality: Clairvoyants & Palmists.
● **Owner** Ms S Derbyshire
B (Ref:HM18197)

## SEFTON PARK NATURAL THRPY CTRE
**Sefton Park Natural Therapy Centre**, 15 Bentley Rd, Liverpool, **Merseyside**, L8 0SY, ENG.
(T) 01517 274244
Speciality: Acupuncture, Aromatherapy, Bach Remedies, Bowen Therapy, Cognitive Therapy, Counselling, Cranial Osteopathy, Healing Therapy, Homeopathy, Humanistic Psychology, Hypnotherapy, Life Style Coaching, Manipulation, Massage (Therapeutic), Nutritional Therapy, Polarity Therapy, Postural Integration, Psychotherapy, Reichian Therapy. ✓
● **Mind Body Therapist** Mr D Donnelly Q: BA, DO, FLCSP, MA. M: IPN, LCSP.
B C S T Yrs. Est.: 12 (Ref:HM18198)

## SEFTON, PHILIP
**Philip Sefton**, The Acupuncture And Osteopathy Clinic, 10 Christchurch St Wes, Frome, **Somerset**, BA11 1EQ, ENG.
(T) 01373 455993
Speciality: Osteopathy.
P S T (Ref:HM18199)

## SEFTON, PHILIP
**Philip Sefton**, The Centre For Complementary Medicine, 129 Newbridge Hill, Bath, **Somerset**, BA1 3PT, ENG.
(T) 01225 475505
Speciality: Osteopathy.
● **Manager** Mrs G Bridgman
P S T (Ref:HM18200)

## SEH ORTHOTICS
**Seh Orthotics**, 3b Manor Rd, Streetly, Sutton Coldfield, **Midlands (West)**, B74 3NQ, ENG.
(T) 01213 538892
Speciality: Chiropodists (Podiatrists).
● **Owner** Mr S Hatchard
S (Ref:HM18201)

## SEITAI/SHIATSU & MANIPULATION
**Seitai & Shiatsu & Digital Manipulation Clinic**, 2 Ingestre Cl, Walsall, **Midlands (West)**, WS3 3UT, ENG.
(T) 01922 475417
Speciality: Shiatsu, Seitai. ✓
● **Partner** Mrs A Hall
● **Seitai Practitioner** Mr K Hall Q: BCMA. M: Nakamura Foundation.
C Yrs. Est.: 3 (Ref:HM18202)

## SELBY PODIATRY CENTRE
**Selby Podiatry Centre**, 16 Wren Lane, Selby, **Yorkshire (North)**, YO8 4PH, ENG.
(T) 01757 704747
Speciality: Chiropodists (Podiatrists).
● **Owner** Mrs C Barnes
S (Ref:HM18203)

## SELF AWARENESS HEALING
**Self Awareness Healing Practice**, Amber House Natural Healing Centre, 46 Spital Rd, Maldon, **Essex**, CM9 6ED, ENG.
(T) 01621 856410 (F) 01621 856410
(E) christine@selfhealing.icom43.net
(W) www.selfhealing.icom43.net
Speciality: Absent Healing, Counselling, Healer, Healing Therapy, Meditation, Spiritual Healing, Stress Therapy, Spiritual Awareness, Self Development. ✓
● **Healer/Counsellor** Ms C Chinnery Q: Cert.Prog.Couns. M: ISRHA, WFH.
B Yrs. Est.: 10 (Ref:HM18204)

## SELF CENTRE
**Self Centre**, 140 Harley St, London, **London (Greater)**, W1N 1AH, ENG.
(T) 020 7224 2393 (F) 020 7371 4486
Speciality: Complementary Medicines & Therapy.
● **Manageress** Miss J Amerena
C M (Ref:HM18205)

## SELF HEAL TRUST
**Self Heal Trust**, Wellbeing Centre, Old School House, Churchtown, Illogan, Redruth, **Cornwall**, TR16 4SW, ENG.
(T) 01209 842999
Speciality: Complementary Medicines & Therapy.
C M (Ref:HM18206)

## SELF REALISATION MEDITATION
**Self Realisation Meditation Healing Centre**, Self Realisation Healing Centre, Laurel Lane, Queen Camel, Yeovil, **Somerset**, BA22 7NU, ENG.
(T) 01935 850266 (F) 01935 850234
Speciality: Meditation.
● **Employee** Ms T Caira



Key: B Mind-Body Medicine C Complementary Medicine H Self Help Treatment M Medicinal Therapy O Oriental Medicine P Postural Therapy S Manipulative Structural Therapy T Touch Therapy

M (Ref:HM18207)

**SELF REALISATION MEDITATION**

**Self Realisation Meditation Healing Centre**, Treetops, Windmill Hill, Launceston, **Cornwall**, PL15 9TF, ENG.
(T) 01566 779329
Speciality: Complementary Medicines & Therapy.
M (Ref:HM18208)

**SELHI, I K**

**I K Selhi**, 72 Freelands Rd, Bromley, **Kent**, BR1 3HY, ENG.
(T) 020 8464 9119
Speciality: Reflexology.
S T (Ref:HM18209)

**SELIGMAN, PHILIPPA**

**Philippa Seligman**, 22 West Orchard Cres, Cardiff, **Glamorgan (Vale of)**, CF5 1AR, WAL.
(T) 029 2056 1491
Speciality: Psychotherapy.
B (Ref:HM18210)

**SELL, NICOLA**

**Nicola Sell**, 249A Otley Rd, Leeds, **Yorkshire (West)**, LS16 5LQ, ENG.
(T) 01132 745126
Speciality: Osteopathy.
● **Partner** Ms N Sell
P S T (Ref:HM18211)

**SELLAR, W**

**W Sellar**, 75 Tewkesbury Ter, London, **London (Greater)**, N11 2LU, ENG.
(T) 020 8361 8216
Speciality: Aromatherapy.
● **Owner** Mrs W Sellar
M O (Ref:HM18212)

**SELLARS, C**

**C Sellars**, 47 Wills Avenue, Paignton, **Devon**, TQ3 2RG, ENG.
(T) 01803 552483
Speciality: Chiropodists (Podiatrists).
● **Owner** Mrs C Sellars
S (Ref:HM18213)

**SELLARS, SHEILA**

**Sheila Sellars**, 7 Rose Hill, Stalybridge, **Manchester (Greater)**, SK15 1UT, ENG.
(T) 01613 039278
Speciality: Hypnotherapy.
● **Owner** Ms S Sellars
B (Ref:HM18214)

**SELLEN, SUSAN**

**Susan Sellen**, 116 Rouncil Lane, Kenilworth, **Warwickshire**, CV8 1FP, ENG.
(T) 01926 853611
Speciality: Reflexology.
S T (Ref:HM18215)

**SELLENS DRAKE, ANGELA**

**Angela Sellens Drake**, 247 College Rd, Norwich, **Norfolk**, NR2 3JD, ENG.
(T) 01603 503794
Speciality: Reflexology.
S T (Ref:HM18216)

**SELLER OIL**

**Seller Oil (The)**, 10 Clifton Pl, Salcombe, **Devon**, TQ8 8BX, ENG.
(T) 01548 843003 (F) 01548 843003
Speciality: Aromatherapy.
● **Owner** Mrs E Bupmsteed
M O (Ref:HM18217)

**SELLERS, JACQUELINE**

**Jacqueline Sellers**, 102 Harrow Court, Stevenage, **Hertfordshire**, SG1 1JT, ENG.
(T) 01438 225306
Speciality: Chiropodists (Podiatrists).
● **Owner** Mrs J Sellers
S (Ref:HM18218)

**SELLICK, A C**

**A C Sellick**, 41 Jowitt Avenue, Kempston, Bedford, **Bedfordshire**, MK42 8NW, ENG.
(T) 01234 854802
Speciality: Chiropodists (Podiatrists).
● **Owner** Miss A Sellick
S (Ref:HM18219)

**SELSDON COMP/RESP CLINIC**

**Selsdon Complementary & Respiratory Health Clinic**, 6 Sundale Avenue, Selsdon, Croydon, **Surrey**, CR2 8RY, ENG.
(T) 020 8657 1453
(E) croyclinic@aol.com
Speciality: Absent Healing, Acupressure, Acupuncture, Bach Remedies, Complementary Therapy, Counselling, Dietician, Floral Essence Therapy, Gestalt Therapy, Healer, Healing Therapy, Herbal Medicine, Holistic Healing, Homeopathy, Humanistic Psychology, Hypnosis, Hypnotherapy, Iridology, Kinesiology, Meditation, Naturopathy, Nutritional Therapy, Oriental Diagnosis, Orthomolecular Medicine, Psychotherapy, Reiki, Spiritual Healing, Visualisation Therapy, Vitamin Therapy, Buteyko, NLP, Metabolic Typing, Hair Analysis. ✔
● **Natural Health Practitioner** Mr J Bayford
(T) 020 8657 1457 Q: C.Hyp, CMH, IAOBP, ICAK, MFAN, MNGH, NLP, UKGHE. M: BIAET, FAN, UKGHE.
● **Reiki Master/Teacher** Ms L Gosney
(T) 020 8668 3429 Q: Reiki Master.
B C Yrs. Est.: 20 (Ref:HM18220)

**SELSEY TOWN CHIROP/POD PRAC**

**Selsey Town Chiropody & Podiatry Practice**, 1 Constable Drive, Selsey, Chichester, **Sussex (West)**, PO20 0EG, ENG.
(T) 01243 603423
Speciality: Chiropodists (Podiatrists).
● **Owner** Miss L Dunlop
S (Ref:HM18221)

**SELVES, KATIE**

**Katie Selves**, The Herb Garden, 110 Tortoiseshell Way, Braintree, **Essex**, CM7 8WG, ENG.
(T) 01376 339049
(W) www.medicalherbalist.co.uk
Speciality: Herbal Medicine. ✔
● **Medical Herbalist** Mrs K Selves Q: BSc (Hons), MNIMH. M: NIMH.
M Yrs. Est.: 3 (Ref:HM18222)

**SEMLEY**

**Semley**, 376 Fleetwood Rd, Thornton, **Lancashire**, FY5 1SN, ENG.
(T) 01253 867705
Speciality: Osteopathy.
● **Owner** Mrs S Semley
P S T (Ref:HM18223)

**SEMPRE LIBERA**

**Sempre Libera**, Unit 1, 16 Dalziel Workspace, Mason St, Motherwell, **Lanarkshire (North)**, ML1 1YE, SCO.
(T) 01698 269909
Speciality: Aromatherapy, Reflexology. ✔
● **Aromatherapist** Mrs A Dunwoody Q: Dip.Arom, ISPA. M: SIR.
C Yrs. Est.: 6 (Ref:HM18224)

**SEN-GUPTA, (DR)**

**Dr Sen-Gupta**, 11 Grafton Rd, Shirley, Solihull, **Midlands (West)**, B90 1NG, ENG.
(T) 01214 744686 (F) 01214 367407
Speciality: Acupuncture.
● **Owner** Dr D Sen-Gupta
O (Ref:HM18225)

**SENSATIONS**

**Sensations**, 2a Blackboy Rd, Exeter, **Devon**, EX4 6SG, ENG.
(T) 01392 252229
Speciality: Aromatherapy.
● **Owner** Mrs A Wilton
M O (Ref:HM18226)

**SENSATIONS AROMATHERAPY**

**Sensations Aromatherapy**, 68 Carnegie Avenue, Tipton, **Midlands (West)**, DY4 8SX, ENG.
(T) 01215 570983
Speciality: Aromatherapy.
● **Owner** Mrs E Bainbridge
M O (Ref:HM18227)

**SENSIBLE SCENTS**

**Sensible Scents**, Connies House, Rhymney River Bridge Rd, Cardiff, **Glamorgan (Vale of)**, CF23 9AF, WAL.
(T) 029 2048 7282
Speciality: Aromatherapy.
● **Director** Mrs J McCann
M O (Ref:HM18228)

**SENSORAMA**

**Sensorama**, 45 King St, Wrexham, LL11 1HR, WAL.
(T) 01978 357298 (F) 01978 265104
Speciality: Aromatherapy, Reflexology. ✔
● **Owner/Aromatherapist** Mrs J Williams
C Yrs. Est.: 2 (Ref:HM18229)

**SEOW, PENG**

**Peng Seow**, 17 Cleveland Mansions, Widley Rd, London, **London (Greater)**, W9 2LA, ENG.
(T) 020 7266 2399
Speciality: Alexander Technique.
P S (Ref:HM18230)

**SEPHTON, ANN**

**Ann Sephton**, 43 Cissbury Avenue, Peacehaven, **Sussex (East)**, BN10 8TN, ENG.
(T) 01273 582820
Speciality: Reflexology.
S T (Ref:HM18231)

**SERENDIPITY**

**Serendipity**, 28 Marischal St, Aberdeen, **Aberdeenshire**, AB11 5AJ, SCO.
(T) 01224 213808
Speciality: Acupuncture, Aromatherapy, Healer, Homeopathy, Massage (Therapeutic), Reflexology, Reiki.
● **Owner/Complementary Therapist** Mrs H Lee Q: Dip.Swedish Massage. M: SMTO.
● **Beauty Therapist** Jayna Donald
● **Acupuncturist** Mr A Morrison Q: CCA, Dip.TCM.
● **Homeopath** Mr S Gerald Q: MNFSH. M: NSPH.
● **Aromatherapist** Mrs M Grant Q: Dip.Arom. M: ISPA.
● **Reiki Master** Ms J Scott Q: Reiki Master.
B T Yrs. Est.: 2 (Ref:HM18232)

**SERENITY**

**Serenity**, 7 Bedford Row, Barnstaple, **Devon**, EX32 8NR, ENG.
(T) 01271 323331
Speciality: Aromatherapy, Chiropractic, Hopi Ear Candles. ✔
● **Chiropractor** Ms M Stockwin Q: DC. M: BAAC, TAO.
● **Therapist** Mrs J Carter Q: ITEC. M: BABTAC.
● **Therapist** Ms A Bloomfield Q: ITEC. M: BABTAC.
C Yrs. Est.: 1 (Ref:HM18233)

**SERENITY**

**Serenity**, 26 High St, Rothwell, Kettering, **Northamptonshire**, NN14 6BQ, ENG.
(T) 01536 713354
Speciality: Complementary Medicines & Therapy.
● **Owner** Ms M Jerome
C M (Ref:HM18234)

**SERENITY**

**Serenity**, 56 Church Rd, London, **London (Greater)**, SE19 2EZ, ENG.
(T) 020 8768 1121
Speciality: Complementary Medicines & Therapy.
● **Owner** Ms P Quailey
C M (Ref:HM18235)

**SERENITY NATURAL HEALING**

**Serenity Natural Healing Reiki & Aromatherapy**, 4 Pendeen Cl, Gainsborough, **Lincolnshire**, DN21 1YE, ENG.
(T) 01427 616887
Speciality: Complementary Medicines & Therapy.
M (Ref:HM18236)

**SERIOUS MASSAGE**

**Serious Massage Co Ltd (The)**, Churchill House, 29 Mill Hill Rd, Pontefract, **Yorkshire (West)**, WF8 4HY, ENG.
(T) 01977 705080 (F) 01977 690011
Speciality: Complementary Medicines &



Key continued: Yrs.Est: Years Established Q: Qualifications M: Professional Membership ✔ Indemnity Insurance Accept Credit Cards

Therapy.
● **Sole Director** Neil Donald Binder
M (Ref:HM18237)

### SERLIN CLINIC OF HEALING
**Serlin Clinic Of Healing (The)**, Flat 34 Talman Gr, Stanmore, **London (Greater)**, HA7 4UQ, ENG.
(T) 020 8954 1714
Speciality: Complementary Medicines & Therapy.
C M (Ref:HM18238)

### SERMON, C
**C Sermon**, 1 Firs Avenue, Ripon, **Yorkshire (North)**, HG4 1NJ, ENG.
(T) 01765 601375
Speciality: Physiotherapy.
P S T (Ref:HM18239)

### SERVICE, G
**G Service**, 9 Maldon Rd, Danbury, Chelmsford, **Essex**, CM3 4QH, ENG.
(T) 01245 222804
Speciality: Osteopathy.
● **Owner** Mr G Service
P S T (Ref:HM18240)

### SETCHFIELD, WENDY
**Wendy Setchfield**, 22 Scarcroft Hill, York, **Yorkshire (North)**, YO24 1DE, ENG.
(T) 01904 638319
Speciality: Homeopathy.
● **Owner** Mrs W Setchfield
M (Ref:HM18241)

### SETFORD, JAN
**Jan Setford**, 54 Jewel Walk, Crawley, **Sussex (West)**, RH11 8NZ, ENG.
(T) 01293 514344
Speciality: Hypnosis.
B (Ref:HM18242)

### SEVEN HIGH STREET THERAPY CTRE
**Seven High Street Therapy Centre**, 7 High St, Penistone, Sheffield, **Yorkshire (South)**, S36 6BR, ENG.
(T) 01226 763136
Speciality: Physiotherapy.
● **Partner** Miss S Jubb
P S T (Ref:HM18243)

### SEVEN SIGHS
**Seven Sighs**, 4 Hamilton Court, Fernhill Rd, Blackwater, Camberley, **Surrey**, GU17 9HL, ENG.
(T) 01252 687784 (F) 01252 687784
Speciality: Bach Remedies, Crystal Healing, Indian Head Massage, Metamorphic Therapy, Reflexology, Reiki. ✓
● **Therapist** C Carter Q: BFRP, Reiki Master. M: IPTI.
B Yrs. Est.: 6 (Ref:HM18244)

### SEVENOAKS OSTEOPATHIC PRACTICE
**Sevenoaks Osteopathic Practice**, Springbank House, 13 Pembroke Rd, Sevenoaks, **Kent**, TN13 1XR, ENG.
(T) 01732 453956
Speciality: Osteopathy.
● **Partner** Mrs P Pitcairn-Knowles
P S T (Ref:HM18245)

### SEVENTH HEAVEN
**Seventh Heaven**, Chanctonbury, 2 St Johns Rd, Haywards Heath, **Sussex (West)**, RH16 4EH, ENG.
(T) 01444 412191
Speciality: Acupuncture, Reiki.
O (Ref:HM18246)

### SEVENTHMOON NATURAL THRPY CTRE
**Philippa Dean**, 44 Sevenoaks Cres, Bramcote Hills, Nottingham, **Nottinghamshire**, NG9 3FP, ENG.
(T) 01159 251184
(E) phil@seventhmoon.co.uk
(W) www.seventhmoon.co.uk
Speciality: Absent Healing, Acupressure, Acupuncture, Bach Remedies, Cupping, Dowsing, Healing Therapy, Indian Head Massage, Massage (Therapeutic), Reflexology, Reiki, Remedial Massage, Stress Therapy, Telephone advice can be given as well as Reiki/Seichem training courses and Massage, Indian Head, Neck and Shoulder Massage and Reflexology Workshops. Massages are only given to women. ✓
● **Reflexologist/Reiki Healer/Massage Therapist**
Mrs P Dean M: IIR.
T Yrs. Est.: 9 (Ref:HM18247)

### SEVENTREES CHIROPODY CLINIC
**Seventrees Chiropody Clinic**, Baring St, Plymouth, **Devon**, PL4 8NF, ENG.
(T) 01752 255528
Speciality: Chiropodists (Podiatrists).
S (Ref:HM18248)

### SEVERN NHS TRUST CHIROP SV
**Severn NHS Trust Chiropody Service**, Gloucestershire Royal Hospital, Great Western Rd, Gloucester, **Gloucestershire**, GL1 3NN, ENG.
(T) 01452 300190
Speciality: Chiropodists (Podiatrists).
S (Ref:HM18249)

### SEVERNSIDE INSTITUTE
**Severnside Institute For Psychotherapy**, 11 Orchard St, Bristol, BS1 5EH, ENG.
(T) 01275 333266 (F) 01275 333266
Speciality: Psychotherapy.
● **Director** Dr M Brown
B (Ref:HM18250)

### SEVITT, E A
**E A Sevitt**, 461 Harrogate Rd, Leeds, **Yorkshire (West)**, LS17 7AD, ENG.
(T) 01132 691727
Speciality: Chiropody.
● **Owner** Mrs E Servitt
S (Ref:HM18251)

### SEWARD, HAROLD M
**Harold M Seward**, 29 Ide Lane, Exeter, **Devon**, EX2 8UR, ENG.
(T) 01392 431719
Speciality: Chiropodists (Podiatrists).
● **Owner** Mr H Seaward
S (Ref:HM18252)

### SEXTON, MAURICE
**Sexton Maurice**, 24 Park Lane, Denny St, Tralee, **County Kerry**, IRE.
(T) 06671 80231
Speciality: Complementary Medicines & Therapy.
M (Ref:HM18253)

### SEYBOTH, PAT
**Pat Seyboth**, 98 Pringle Rd, Brinsworth, Rotherham, **Yorkshire (South)**, S60 5BE, ENG.
(T) 01709 377863
Speciality: Reflexology.
● **Owner** Mrs P Seyboth
S T (Ref:HM18254)

### SEYDOUX, B (DR)
**Dr B Seydoux**, 366 Croydon Rd, Beckenham, **Kent**, BR3 4EX, ENG.
(T) 020 8663 3878 (F) 020 8663 3878
Speciality: Chiropractors.
● **Doctor** Dr M Chippendale
P S T (Ref:HM18255)

### SEYDOUX, BENIOT (DR)
**Dr Beniot Seydoux**, The Chiswick Chiropractic Clinic, 1 Airedale Avenue, London, **London (Greater)**, W4 2NW, ENG.
(T) 020 8742 7423
Speciality: Chiropractors.
P S T (Ref:HM18256)

### SEYMOUR PRACTICE
**Seymour Practice**, 30 Cumberland Mansions, Seymour Pl, London, **London (Greater)**, W1H 5TF, ENG.
(T) 020 7262 3022 (F) 020 7262 3022
(E) osteopath2000@hotmail.com
(W) www.starosteopath.com
Speciality: Cranial Osteopathy, Manipulation, Osteopathy. ✓
● **Osteopath** Mr R Stubbs Q: DO. M: RoO.
S Yrs. Est.: 21 (Ref:HM18257)

### SEYMOUR, E J
**E J Seymour**, 36 Breach Avenue, Emsworth, **Hampshire**, PO10 8NB, ENG.
(T) 01243 373608
Speciality: Psychotherapy.
B (Ref:HM18258)

### SEYMOUR, LOUISE
**Louise Seymour**, The Brentwood Clinic, 31 Shenfield Rd, Brentwood, **Essex**, CM15 8AG, ENG.
(T) 01277 210664
Speciality: Biomechanics, Chiropody, Cryo Surgery, Nail Surgery, Orthotics. ✓
● **Owner/Chiropodist** Miss L Seymour Q: BSc (Hons), M.S.C.P., S.R.Ch.
M Yrs. Est.: 5 (Ref:HM18259)

### SEYNER, GORDON
**Gordon Seyner**, 140A Chiswick High Rd, London, **London (Greater)**, W4 1PU, ENG.
(T) 020 8994 2587
Speciality: Chiropodists (Podiatrists).
● **Owner** Mr G Seyner
S (Ref:HM18260)

### SHAANAN, A
**A Shaanan**, 178 East Barnet Rd, Barnet, **Hertfordshire**, EN4 8RD, ENG.
(T) 020 8449 7754 (F) 020 8449 0174
Speciality: Osteopathy.
● **Principal** Mr L Hartman
P S T (Ref:HM18261)

### SHACKLADY, EVE
**Eve Shacklady**, Lloyds Bank Chambers, Deansgate, Bolton, **Lancashire**, BL1 1HB, ENG.
(T) 01204 531853
Speciality: Electrolysis.
T (Ref:HM18262)

### SHACKLETON, JOHN A
**John A Shackleton**, 2 Mornington Villas, Bradford, **Yorkshire (West)**, BD8 7HB, ENG.
(T) 01274 546665
Speciality: Chiropody. ✓
● **Chiropodist (Podiatrist)**
Mr J Shackleton Q: LCH, M.S.C.P., MRSS.
M Yrs. Est.: 40 (Ref:HM18263)

### SHACKLETON, MAUREEN
**Maureen Shackleton**, 8 Leadhall View, Harrogate, **Yorkshire (North)**, HG2 9PF, ENG.
(T) 01423 871255
Speciality: Hypnosis, Hypnotherapy, Psychotherapy, NLP. ✓
● **Owner/Hypnotherapist**
Mrs M Shackleton Q: PSHP. M: UKGHE.
B Yrs. Est.: 10 (Ref:HM18264)

### SHAFTOE, MARINA
**Marina Shaftoe**, 46 Clayhill Cres, London, **London (Greater)**, SE9 4JB, ENG.
(T) 020 8851 2513
Speciality: Hypnosis.
● **Owner** Mrs M Shaftoe
B (Ref:HM18265)

### SHAFTSBURY PRACTICE
**Shaftsbury Practice (The)**, Castleton House, Castle St, Mere, Warminster, **Wiltshire**, BA12 6JE, ENG.
(T) 01747 856719
Speciality: Acupuncture, Chiropody, Herbal Medicine, Homeopathy, Hypnotherapy, Massage (Therapeutic), Osteopathy, Podiatry, Reflexology, Manual Lymphatic Drainage. ✓
● **Acupuncturist** Dr R Gribble Q: Dip.Med.Ac.
● **Owner** Mrs Dawson Q: BSc, MCSP.
M Yrs. Est.: 4 (Ref:HM18266)

### SHAH
**Shah**, 12 Madeira Drive, Brighton, **Sussex (East)**, BN2 1TW, ENG.
(T) 01273 606996
Speciality: Clairvoyants & Palmists.
● **Owner** Mr M Imran
B (Ref:HM18267)

### SHAH, ATUL
**Mr Atul Shah**, 31 Scarcroft Hill, York, **Yorkshire (North)**, YO24 1DF, ENG.
(T) 01904 623693
(E) atul@atul-shah.freeserve.co.uk
(W) www.registerednaturopaths.org
Speciality: Dietician, Hay Diet, Holistic Healing, Life Style Coaching, Manipulation, Massage (Therapeutic), Micro Manipulation, Naturopathy,

Nutritional Therapy, Stress Therapy. ✔
● **Owner** Mr A Shah **Q:** RN. **M:** ISRN, RPS.
C H Yrs. Est.: 11 (**Ref:**HM18268)

## SHAH, NUTAN

**Nutan Shah**, Kenton Bridge Medical Centre, 155-175 Kenton Rd, Harrow, **London (Greater)**, HA3 0YX, ENG.
(T) 020 8907 6989
Speciality: Chiropodists (Podiatrists).
S (**Ref:**HM18269)

## SHAH, REKHA

**Rekha Shah**, 52 Dorchester Way, Harrow, **London (Greater)**, HA3 9RE, ENG.
(T) 020 8204 0629
Speciality: Reflexology.
● **Owner** Mrs R Shah
S T (**Ref:**HM18270)

## SHALIMAR HEALING CENTRE

**Shalimar Healing Centre (The)**, 10 Frances Rd, Bournemouth, **Dorset**, BH1 3RZ, ENG.
(T) 01202 553848
Speciality: Complementary Medicines & Therapy.
C M (**Ref:**HM18271)

## SHALOM

**Shalom**, 6 Lindrum Avenue, Lyme Green, Macclesfield, **Cheshire**, SK11 0LG, ENG.
(T) 01260 253245
Speciality: Complementary Medicines & Therapy.
● **Owner** Mrs B Stubbs
C M (**Ref:**HM18272)

## SHAMAL, LYN

**Lyn Shamal**, Scott Street Complementary Therapy Centre, 58 Scott St, Barrow-in-Furness, **Cumbria**, LA14 1QE, ENG.
(T) 01229 826700
Speciality: Complementary Medicines & Therapy.
M (**Ref:**HM18273)

## SHAMBAHALA MEDITATION CENTRE

**Shambahala Meditation Centre**, 27 Belmont Cl, London, **London (Greater)**, SW4 6AY, ENG.
(T) 020 7720 3207
Speciality: Complementary Medicines & Therapy.
C M (**Ref:**HM18274)

## SHAMBHALA

**Shambhala**, Coursing Batch, Glastonbury, **Somerset**, BA6 8BH, ENG.
(T) 01458 831797 (F) 01458 834751
(E) findyourself@shambhala.co.uk
(W) www.shambhala.co.uk
Speciality: Absent Healing, Aromatherapy, Auto Suggestion, Bio-energetics, Bowen Therapy, Complementary Therapy, Cranial Osteopathy, Dietician, Flotation Therapy, Healer, Healing Therapy, Herbal Medicine, Holistic Healing, Indian Head Massage, Iridology, Life Style Coaching, Manipulation, Massage (Therapeutic), Meditation, Nutritional Therapy, Pattern Therapies, Reflexology, Reiki, Spiritual Healing, Vibrational Therapy, Vortex Healing, Rebirthing, Channelling, Tuition, Healing Courses, Sacred Journeys. 
● **Therapist** Isis Livingstone
B C Yrs. Est.: 15 (**Ref:**HM18275)

## SHAMROCK HEALING CLINIC

**Shamrock Healing Clinic**, 12 Birchview Cl, Kilnamanagh, Tallaght, **County Dublin**, IRE.
(T) 01451 0212
Speciality: Complementary Medicines & Therapy.
M (**Ref:**HM18276)

## SHANAHAN, CAROL

**Carol Shanahan**, 65 Ely Way, Thetford, **Norfolk**, IP24 1DR, ENG.
(T) 01842 765588
Speciality: Chiropodists (Podiatrists).
● **Owner** Mrs C Shanahan
S (**Ref:**HM18277)

## SHAND, GRAHAM

**Graham Shand**, 208 Birmingham Rd, Stratford-Upon-Avon, **Warwickshire**, CV37 0AX, ENG.
(T) 01789 415773
(E) grahamshand@virgin.net
Speciality: Massage (Therapeutic), Treatment of muscular sport injuries, sports massage, remedial massage, non intrusive corporate massage and personal training. ✔
● **Partner** Mr G Shand **M:** AST.
S Yrs. Est.: 2 (**Ref:**HM18278)

## SHAND, R J

**R J Shand**, 10A Albert St, Aberdeen, **Aberdeenshire**, AB25 1XQ, SCO.
(T) 01224 643803
Speciality: Chiropodists (Podiatrists).
● **Employee** Mr G Mitchell
S (**Ref:**HM18279)

## SHANGHAI ACUPUNCTURE CLINIC

**Shanghai Acupuncture Clinic**, 74 Portland St, Manchester, **Manchester (Greater)**, M1 4GU, ENG.
(T) 01612 361319
Speciality: Acupuncture, Herbal Medicine. ✔
● **Acupuncturist/Herbalist** Mrs J L **M:** BAcC.
C Yrs. Est.: 17 (**Ref:**HM18280)

## SHANGHAI ACUPUNCTURE CLINIC

**Shanghai Acupuncture Clinic**, 26 Princess St, Manchester, **Manchester (Greater)**, M1 4LB, ENG.
(T) 01612 361319
Speciality: Acupuncture.
O (**Ref:**HM18281)

## SHANGRI-LA ACUPUNCTURE CLINIC

**Shangri-La Acupuncture Clinic**, 117 Birches Barn Rd, Wolverhampton, **Midlands (West)**, WV3 7BJ, ENG.
(T) 01902 336288
Speciality: Acupuncture.
O (**Ref:**HM18282)

## SHANGRI-LA NATURAL THERAPIES

**Shangri-La Natural Therapies**, 5 Ace Prde, Hook Rd, Chessington, **Surrey**, KT9 1DR, ENG.
(T) 020 8974 1611
Speciality: Complementary Medicines & Therapy.
● **Owner** Mr D Anderson
M (**Ref:**HM18283)

## SHANKS, ALAN

**Alan Shanks**, St Helens Chiropractic & Acupuncture Clinic, 1 Victoria Sq, St. Helens, **Merseyside**, WA10 1HQ, ENG.
(T) 01744 22441
Speciality: Acupuncture.
● **Principal** Mr A Shanks
O (**Ref:**HM18284)

## SHANKS, S C

**S C Shanks**, The Old Police House, Main St, Burnsall, Skipton, **Yorkshire (North)**, BD23 6BP, ENG.
(T) 01756 720260
Speciality: Complementary Medicines & Therapy.
● **Owner** Mrs S Shanks
C M (**Ref:**HM18285)

## SHANLEY, P

**P Shanley**, St Etaine, Crellow Lane, Stithians, Truro, **Cornwall**, TR3 7BA, ENG.
(T) 01209 860030
Speciality: Alexander Technique.
● **Owner** Mrs M Deglos
P S (**Ref:**HM18286)

## SHANNAH, A

**A Shannah**, Dorset Mews, London, **London (Greater)**, N3 2BN, ENG.
(T) 020 8346 9159 (F) 020 8882 3745
Speciality: Osteopathy.
● **Owner** Mr A Shannah
P S T (**Ref:**HM18287)

## SHANON, D

**D Shanon**, 31 Highridge, Gillingham, **Kent**, ME7 3EW, ENG.
(T) 01634 305763
Speciality: Hypnosis.
● **Owner** Mrs D Shanon
B (**Ref:**HM18288)

## SHANTI HEALTH HERBAL PRODUCTS

**Shanti Health Herbal Products**, 5 Templar Rd, Temple Ewell, Dover, **Kent**, CT16 3DL, ENG.
(T) 01304 820129
Speciality: Herbal Medicine.
● **Owner** Mr G Pillai
M (**Ref:**HM18289)

## SHAOCK HEALTH CARE

**Shamrock Health Care**, P.O. Box 48, Northampton, **Northamptonshire**, NN4 0ZE, ENG.
(T) 01604 677854
Speciality: Complementary Medicines & Therapy.
C M (**Ref:**HM18290)

## SHAPLAND, ANDREW

**Andrew Shapland**, 16A Duke St, Chelmsford, **Essex**, CM1 1HL, ENG.
(T) 01245 347277
Speciality: Acupuncture.
● **Owner** Mr A Shapland
O (**Ref:**HM18291)

## SHARCO

**Sharco Ltd**, Unit 4 Westlink Ind Est Wilton, **County Cork**, IRE.
(T) 021 4366 111
Speciality: Complementary Medicines & Therapy.
M (**Ref:**HM18292)

## SHARE PSYCHOTHERAPY AGENCY

**Share Psychotherapy Agency**, 176 Crookesmoor Rd, Sheffield, **Yorkshire (South)**, S6 3FS, ENG.
(T) 01142 682883 (F) 01142 682883
Speciality: Psychotherapy.
● **Director** Mr B Daines
B (**Ref:**HM18293)

## SHARE, J L

**J L Share**, 59 High Rd, Buckhurst Hill, **Essex**, IG9 5SR, ENG.
(T) 020 8559 1949 (F) 020 8553 0155
Speciality: Psychology.
● **Owner** Ms J Share
B (**Ref:**HM18294)

## SHARIFI, M

**M Sharifi**, 69 West Green Rd, London, **London (Greater)**, N15 5DA, ENG.
(T) 020 8800 8414
Speciality: Chiropodists (Podiatrists).
S (**Ref:**HM18295)

## SHARIFI-HOSSEINI, M

**M Sharifi-Hosseini**, 69 Bridgemere Rd, Eastbourne, **Sussex (East)**, BN22 8TF, ENG.
(T) 01323 640182
Speciality: Chiropodists (Podiatrists).
● **Owner** Mr M Sharifi-Hosseini
S (**Ref:**HM18296)

## SHARK CARTILAGE PRODUCTS

**Shark Cartilage Products**, 17 Ascot Drive, Mansfield, **Nottinghamshire**, NG18 3BX, ENG.
(T) 01623 421420 (F) 01623 722400
Speciality: Complementary Medicines & Therapy.
● **Owner** Mr J Steeples
M (**Ref:**HM18297)

## SHARKEY, CATHERINE

**Catherine Sharkey**, 9 Tanwood Cl, Solihull, **Midlands (West)**, B91 3JX, ENG.
(T) 01217 058882
Speciality: Hypnosis.
B (**Ref:**HM18298)

## SHARKEY, JANICE

**Janice Sharkey**, 4 Hawthorn Walk, Cambuslang, Glasgow, **Glasgow (City of)**, G72 7AQ, SCO.
(T) 01416 472403
Speciality: Hypnosis.
B (**Ref:**HM18299)

## SHARKEY, TAMSIN

**Tamsin Sharkey**, 82 New Rd, Llanelli, **Carmarthenshire**, SA15 3DT, WAL.
(T) 01554 773484
Speciality: Chiropodists (Podiatrists).
S (**Ref:**HM18300)



Key continued: **Yrs.Est:** Years Established **Q:** Qualifications **M:** Professional Membership ✔ Indemnity Insurance Accept Credit Cards

**SHARMA, (DR)**
**Dr Sharma**, 10 Eldon Rd, Reading, **Berkshire**, RG1 4DH, ENG.
(T) 01189 502002
Speciality: Psychiatry.
B (Ref:HM18301)

**SHARMA, R P**
**R P Sharma**, Castle Hill Clinic, 1c Tilehurst Clinic, Reading, **Berkshire**, RG1 7TW, ENG.
(T) 01189 586766
Speciality: Acupuncture.
O (Ref:HM18302)

**SHARMA, SHASHI MOHAN (DR)**
**Dr Shashi Mohan Sharma**, 399 Goodman Pk, Slough, **Berkshire**, SL2 5NW, ENG.
(T) 01753 821230
Speciality: Homeopathy.
M (Ref:HM18303)

**SHARMA, V K**
**V K Sharma**, The Ealing Clinic, 3 Fielding Trce, Uxbridge Rd, London, **London (Greater)**, W5 3HQ, ENG.
(T) 020 8992 0321
Speciality: Chiropodists (Podiatrists).
S (Ref:HM18304)

**SHARMAN, SARAH**
**Sarah Sharman**, 51 Goldsmith Rd, Birmingham, **Midlands (West)**, B14 7EH, ENG.
(T) 01214 434976
Speciality: Osteopathy.
● **Owner** Mrs S Sharman
P S T (Ref:HM18305)

**SHARP & ASSOCIATES**
**E J Sharp & Associates**, Middlemarsh Clinic, Middlemarsh St, Poundbury, Dorchester, **Dorset**, DT1 3GX, ENG.
(T) 01305 262498
Speciality: Chiropodists (Podiatrists).
● **Owner** Mrs J Sharp
S (Ref:HM18306)

**SHARP, DENISE**
**Denise Sharp**, 17 The Avenue, Sheringham, **Norfolk**, NR26 8DG, ENG.
(T) 01263 823682
Speciality: Magnetic Therapy, Reflexology. ✔
● **Reflexologist** Ms D Sharp M: BSR, GCP.
C Yrs. Est.: 10 (Ref:HM18307)

**SHARP, DOROTHY**
**Dorothy Sharp**, Park Rd Chiropody, 81 Park Rd, Bingley, **Yorkshire (West)**, BD16 4BY, ENG.
(T) 01274 569635
Speciality: Chiropodists (Podiatrists).
S (Ref:HM18308)

**SHARP, ELIZABETH**
**Elizabeth Sharp**, 139 Grove Lane, London, **London (Greater)**, SE5 8BG, ENG.
(T) 020 7274 2621
Speciality: Physiotherapy.
P S T (Ref:HM18309)

**SHARP, G M**
**G M Sharp**, 16 Braithwaite Rd, Keighley, **Yorkshire (West)**, BD22 6PA, ENG.
(T) 01535 602033
Speciality: Physiotherapy.
P S T (Ref:HM18310)

**SHARP, J A**
**J A Sharp**, 3 Manor Rd, Bishopsteignton, Teignmouth, **Devon**, TQ14 9SU, ENG.
(T) 01626 776186
Speciality: Physiotherapy.
● **Owner** Mrs J Sharp
P S T (Ref:HM18311)

**SHARP, JANET**
**Janet Sharp**, 137 Magdalen Rd, Oxford, **Oxfordshire**, OX4 1RJ, ENG.
(T) 01865 396939
Speciality: Reflexology.
● **Owner** Mr M Franklin
S T (Ref:HM18312)

**SHARP, JUSTIN**
**Sharp Justin**, 183a High St, Beckenham, **Kent**, BR3 1AH, ENG.
(T) 020 8658 3308
Speciality: Osteopathy.
P S T (Ref:HM18313)

**SHARP, LINDA A**
**Linda A Sharp**, Dumfries Holistic Health Centre, 98 Loreburn St, Dumfries, **Dumfries and Galloway**, DG1 1HW, SCO.
(T) 01387 267617
Speciality: Acupressure, Acupuncture, Herbal Medicine. ✔
● **Acupuncturist/Traditional Chinese Herbalist**
Ms L Sharp Q: Dip.Ac, Dip.TCHM. M: BAcC, RCHM.
O Yrs. Est.: 7 (Ref:HM18314)

**SHARPE, ISABEL**
**Isabel Sharpe**, 1-3 Wells Rd, Fakenham, **Norfolk**, NR21 9EG, ENG.
(T) 01328 856601
Speciality: Osteopathy.
● **Partner** Miss I Sharpe
P S T (Ref:HM18315)

**SHARPE, ISOBEL**
**Isobel Sharpe**, 13 Meridian Pl, Bristol, BS8 1JG, ENG.
(T) 01179 730160
Speciality: Hypnotherapy.
● **Owner** Mrs I Sharpe
B (Ref:HM18316)

**SHARPE, SALLY**
**Sally Sharpe**, Westrop, Corsham, **Wiltshire**, SN13 9QF, ENG.
(T) 01249 714544
Speciality: Homeopathy.
● **Owner** Mrs S Sharpe
M (Ref:HM18317)

**SHARPLES, ANITA**
**Anita Sharples**, Wispington House, Worster Rd, Cookham, Maidenhead, **Berkshire**, SL6 9JG, ENG.
(T) 01628 520221
Speciality: Psychotherapy.
● **Owner** Ms A Sharples
B (Ref:HM18318)

**SHARPLES, JEAN**
**Jean Sharples**, Ashburner St Markets, Ashburner St, Bolton, **Lancashire**, BL1 1TQ, ENG.
(T) 01204 366606 (F) 01204 366287
Speciality: Complementary Medicines & Therapy.
● **Partner** Mr M Sharples
C M (Ref:HM18319)

**SHARPLES, LINDA**
**Linda Sharples**, 33 Mabel Gr, West Bridgford, Nottingham, **Nottinghamshire**, NG2 5GT, ENG.
(T) 01159 820334 (F) 01159 143782
Speciality: Complementary Medicines & Therapy.
● **Principal** Mrs L Sharple
C M (Ref:HM18320)

**SHARPLES, SARAH**
**Sarah Sharples**, 60 Windmill St, Worminghall, Aylesbury, **Buckinghamshire**, HP18 9LE, ENG.
(T) 01844 238662
Speciality: Aromatherapy.
M O (Ref:HM18321)

**SHARPLEY, ROGER**
**Roger Sharpley**, 20 The Green, Twickenham, **London (Greater)**, TW2 5AB, ENG.
(T) 020 8898 1952
Speciality: Homeopathy.
M (Ref:HM18322)

**SHARROCKS, LYNN**
**Lynn Sharrocks**, 83 Burley Avenue, Killinghall, Harrogate, **Yorkshire (North)**, HG3 2RY, ENG.
(T) 01423 568332
Speciality: Reflexology.
S T (Ref:HM18323)

**SHARRON CHIROPODY CLINIC**
**Sharron Chiropody Clinic**, 10 Wostenholm Rd, Sheffield, **Yorkshire (South)**, S7 1LJ, ENG.
(T) 01142 552205
Speciality: Biomechanics, Chiropody, Orthotics. ✔
● **Chiropodist** Mr S Lambert
C Yrs. Est.: 7 (Ref:HM18324)

**SHAVE, G M**
**G M Shave**, 28 East St, Warminster, **Wiltshire**, BA12 9BN, ENG.
(T) 01985 216141
Speciality: Chiropody. ✔
● **Owner** Mr G Shave Q: DS.Ch.Pod, Inst.CH.P. M: Inst.CH.P.
C Yrs. Est.: 8 (Ref:HM18325)

**SHAVERIN, MICHAEL**
**Michael Shaverin**, 16 Hazel Gardens, Edgware, **London (Greater)**, HA8 8PB, ENG.
(T) 020 8905 4452
Speciality: Chiropodists (Podiatrists).
S (Ref:HM18326)

**SHAW CHIROPRACTIC CLINIC**
**Shaw Chiropractic Clinic**, Unit 5 Ramleaze House, Shaw Village Centre, Ramleaze Drive, Shaw, Swindon, **Wiltshire**, SN5 9PY, ENG.
(T) 01793 887801
Speciality: Chiropractic.
P S T (Ref:HM18327)

**SHAW LANE PHYSIOTHERAPY CLINIC**
**Shaw Lane Physiotherapy Clinic**, 19 Shaw Lane, Leeds, **Yorkshire (West)**, LS6 4DH, ENG.
(T) 01132 249583
Speciality: Physiotherapy.
P S T (Ref:HM18328)

**SHAW, A D**
**A D Shaw**, 21 Highwood Gardens, Ilford, **Essex**, IG5 0AZ, ENG.
(T) 020 8551 5374
Speciality: Chiropodists (Podiatrists).
● **Owner** Mrs A Shaw
S (Ref:HM18329)

**SHAW, ANGELA**
**Shaw Angela D AC**, 23 Church Rd, Dalkey, **County Dublin**, IRE.
(T) 01280 6419
Speciality: Complementary Medicines & Therapy.
M (Ref:HM18330)

**SHAW, B**
**B Shaw**, 47 Primrose Lane, Halton, Leeds, **Yorkshire (West)**, LS15 7RX, ENG.
(T) 01132 326182
Speciality: Chiropodists (Podiatrists).
● **Owner** Mr B Shaw
S (Ref:HM18331)

**SHAW, C**
**C Shaw**, 58 Hartington St, Barrow-in-Furness, **Cumbria**, LA14 5SR, ENG.
(T) 01229 839042
Speciality: Chiropodists (Podiatrists).
S (Ref:HM18332)

**SHAW, CHRISTINE**
**Christine Shaw**, 3 Nathaniel Walk, Tring, **Hertfordshire**, HP23 5DQ, ENG.
(T) 01442 824505
Speciality: Reflexology, Yoga.
● **Reflexologist** Ms C Shaw Q: Reg.Reflex. M: BRA.
T Yrs. Est.: 15 (Ref:HM18333)

**SHAW, EDWINA M**
**Edwina M Shaw**, 6 Byron Rd, Mablethorpe, **Lincolnshire**, LN12 1HZ, ENG.
(T) 01507 472544
Speciality: Chiropodists (Podiatrists).
● **Owner** Mrs E Shaw
S (Ref:HM18334)

**SHAW, FIONA**
**Fiona Shaw**, Lodge Farm House, Clifton Reynes, Olney, **Buckinghamshire**, MK46 5DS, ENG.
(T) 01234 713842
(E) fiona@cliftonreynesfreeserve.net
Speciality: Aromatherapy, Sports Massage, Holistic Massage. ✔
● **Complementary Therapist**
Fiona Shaw Q: IIHHT, ITEC, MICHT, RGN. M: FHT, ITEC.



Key: B Mind-Body Medicine C Complementary Medicine H Self Help Treatment M Medicinal Therapy O Oriental Medicine P Postural Therapy S Manipulative Structural Therapy T Touch Therapy

C Yrs. Est.: 4 (Ref:HM18335)

**SHAW, GAIL**

**Gail Shaw**, 98 West Lane, Hayling Island, **Hampshire**, PO11 0JN, ENG.
(T) 023 9246 2250
Speciality: Complementary Medicines & Therapy.
● **Owner** Mrs G Shaw
C M (Ref:HM18336)

**SHAW, J**

**J Shaw**, 31 Lodge Cl, Stoke D'Abernon, Cobham, **Surrey**, KT11 2SG, ENG.
(T) 01932 863202
Speciality: Chiropodists (Podiatrists).
● **Owner** Mrs J Shaw
S (Ref:HM18337)

**SHAW, J K**

**J K Shaw**, 17 The Dale, Waterlooville, **Hampshire**, PO7 5DB, ENG.
(T) 023 9232 6953
Speciality: Chiropodists (Podiatrists).
S (Ref:HM18338)

**SHAW, JONATHAN**

**Jonathan Shaw**, 1 Lower Rd, Loughton, **Essex**, IG10 2RS, ENG.
(T) 020 8508 7514
Speciality: Osteopathy.
P S T (Ref:HM18339)

**SHAW, JONATHAN**

**Jonathan Shaw**, 1 Lower Rd, Ilford, **Essex**, IG1 3PF, ENG.
(T) 020 8518 5581
Speciality: Osteopathy.
P S T (Ref:HM18340)

**SHAW, L M**

**L M Shaw**, 16 Elms Gardens, Ruddington, Nottingham, **Nottinghamshire**, NG11 6DZ, ENG.
(T) 01159 842221
Speciality: Homeopathy.
M (Ref:HM18341)

**SHAW, L M**

**L M Shaw**, 28 Elmwood St, Sunderland, **Tyne and Wear**, SR2 7JJ, ENG.
(T) 01915 142526
Speciality: Hypnosis.
B (Ref:HM18342)

**SHAW, LENISE**

**Lenise Shaw**, Chichester, **Sussex (West)**, PO20, ENG.
(T) 01243 773755
Speciality: Bach Remedies.
M (Ref:HM18343)

**SHAW, M J**

**M J Shaw**, 9 Brecks Lane, Kippax, Leeds, **Yorkshire (West)**, LS25 7EB, ENG.
(T) 01132 871425
Speciality: Chiropodists (Podiatrists).
S (Ref:HM18344)

**SHAW, NICOLA**

**Nicola Shaw**, 31 Birch Cr, Leeds, **Yorkshire (West)**, LS15 7SU, ENG.
(T) 01132 948484
Speciality: Chiropodists (Podiatrists).
● **Owner** Mrs N Shaw
S (Ref:HM18345)

**SHAW, P R**

**P R Shaw**, 12 Litchfield Rise, Arnold, Nottingham, **Nottinghamshire**, NG5 8HU, ENG.
(T) 01159 263996
Speciality: Chiropodists (Podiatrists).
● **Owner** Mr P Shaw
S (Ref:HM18346)

**SHAW, R G B**

**R G B Shaw**, 41 St. John St, Ashbourne, **Derbyshire**, DE6 1GP, ENG.
(T) 01335 300440
Speciality: Osteopathy.
P S T (Ref:HM18347)

**SHAW, REBECCA**

**Rebecca Shaw**, Wightwick Bank, Wolverhampton, **Midlands (West)**, WV6 8EE, ENG.
(T) 01902 761728
Speciality: Hypnosis.
● **Owner** Mrs R Shaw
B (Ref:HM18348)

**SHAW, ROBERT C**

**Robert C Shaw**, 5 Marchmont Rd, Ayr, **Ayrshire (South)**, KA7 2SB, SCO.
(T) 01292 282201
Speciality: Chiropodists (Podiatrists).
S (Ref:HM18349)

**SHAWCROSS, ROSALIND**

**Rosalind Shawcross**, 19 Blenheim Rd, Deal, **Kent**, CT14 7AJ, ENG.
(T) 01304 374755
Speciality: Reflexology.
S T (Ref:HM18350)

**SHAWE AVENUE OSTEO PRACTICE**

**Shawe Avenue Osteopathic Practice**, 5 Shawe Avenue, Weddington, Nuneaton, **Warwickshire**, CV10 0EL, ENG.
(T) 024 7674 2012
(E) joseph-stapleton@hotmail.co.uk
Speciality: Bonesetting, Counselling, Cranial Osteopathy, Manipulation, Massage (Therapeutic), Micro Manipulation, Osteopathy, Rolfing, Vitamin Therapy. ✔
● **Osteopath/Nurse** Mr J Stapleton Q: BA, BSc, Hons (OST), RGN. M: GNC, GOsC.
S Yrs. Est.: 2 (Ref:HM18351)

**SHAWLANDS HYPNOTHERAPY CLINIC**

**Shawlands Hypnotherapy Clinic**, 69 Deanston Drive, Glasgow, **Glasgow (City of)**, G41 3AQ, SCO.
(T) 01416 328885
(E) hypnoheal@tinyworld.co.uk
Speciality: Hypnosis, Hypnotherapy, Hypno-Analysis. ✔
● **Owner/Hypnotherapist**
Mr J Whitten Q: DABCH, MNGH. M: MCA.
B Yrs. Est.: 3 (Ref:HM18352)

**SHAY-STEPHENSON, KATE**

**Kate Shay-Stephenson**, 70-72 Grange Rd, West Kirby, Wirral, **Merseyside**, CH48 4EG, ENG.
(T) 01516 251395
Speciality: Homeopathy.
● **Owner** Mrs K Shay-Stephenson
M (Ref:HM18353)

**SHEAD, JULIE**

**Julie Shead**, 222 Seafield Rd, Bournemouth, **Dorset**, BH6 5LL, ENG.
(T) 01202 428208
Speciality: Hypnotherapy.
● **Owner** Mrs J Shead
B (Ref:HM18354)

**SHEAF, JACOLIN**

**Jacolin Sheaf**, 3 Castle Walk, Lower St, Stansted, **Essex**, CM24 8LY, ENG.
(T) 01279 815907
Speciality: Osteopathy.
● **Owner** Ms J Sheaf
P S T (Ref:HM18355)

**SHEARER & ASSOCIATES**

**Dr Colin Shearer & Associates**, 9 Eskside West, Musselburgh, **Lothian (Mid)**, EH21 6PL, SCO.
(T) 01316 651234 (F) 01316 651234
Speciality: Chiropractic.
● **Owner** Dr C Shearer
P S T (Ref:HM18356)

**SHEARER, GAYLE**

**Gayle Shearer**, 7-9 Hawley Sq, Margate, **Kent**, CT9 1PF, ENG.
(T) 01843 292056 (F) 01843 299347
Speciality: Cranial Osteopathy, Osteopathy. ✔
● **Owner** Mr Shearer
● **Osteopath** Mrs G Shearer Q: BAAR, DO. M: GOsC.
S Yrs. Est.: 17 (Ref:HM18357)

**SHEARS, D J**

**D J Shears**, 77 Thurleston Avenue, Morden, **Surrey**, SM4 4BN, ENG.
(T) 020 8542 8323
Speciality: Chiropodists (Podiatrists).
● **Owner** Mrs D Shears
S (Ref:HM18358)

**SHEARS, S**

**S Shears**, 99 Morden Rd, Mitcham, **Surrey**, CR4 4DF, ENG.
(T) 020 8648 9395
Speciality: Aromatherapy.
● **Owner** Mrs S Shears
M O (Ref:HM18359)

**SHEASBY, DEBI**

**Debi Sheasby**, 30 Albany Rd, Stratford-Upon-Avon, **Warwickshire**, CV37 6PG, ENG.
(T) 01789 292052
Speciality: Aromatherapy.
M O (Ref:HM18360)

**SHEBORNE CHIROPRACTIC CENTRE**

**Sheborne Chiropractic Centre**, First Floor, House Of Steps, Half Moon St, Sherborne, **Dorset**, DT9 3LN, ENG.
(T) 01935 815660
Speciality: Chiropractic, Kinesiology, Manipulation, Ultrasonics. ✔
● **Principal** Mr M Rufus Q: BSc (Hons), DC. M: BCA, CC.
S Yrs. Est.: 20 (Ref:HM18361)

**SHEEHAN, MIKE**

**Mike Sheehan**, 51 William St, Herne Bay, **Kent**, CT6 5NR, ENG.
(T) 01227 375608
Speciality: Hypnotherapy.
● **Owner** Mr M Sheehan
B (Ref:HM18362)

**SHEEHAN, NICHOLAS**

**Nicholas Sheehan**, 7 East Prde, Heworth, York, **Yorkshire (North)**, YO31 7YB, ENG.
(T) 01904 431335
Speciality: Osteopathy. ✔
● **Osteopath** Mr N Sheehan Q: DO. M: GOsC.
S Yrs. Est.: 11 (Ref:HM18363)

**SHEEHAN, OLIVIA**

**Sheehan Olivia**, 62 Southquay Rd, Wilton, **County Cork**, IRE.
(T) 021 4342 045
Speciality: Reflexology.
S T (Ref:HM18364)

**SHEEHAN, PAMELA**

**Sheehan Pamela BSc (Hons) Ost Med**, The Gables Miltown, **County Kerry**, IRE.
(T) 06697 67304
Speciality: Osteopathy.
P S T (Ref:HM18365)

**SHEEHY, ALAN**

**Sheehy Alan MPRTCM**, Upr Bridge St, Killorglin, **County Kerry**, IRE.
(T) 06697 62344
Speciality: Complementary Medicines & Therapy.
M (Ref:HM18366)

**SHEER PERFECTION**

**Sheer Perfection**, 8 Sybils Way, Houghton Conquest, Bedford, **Bedfordshire**, MK45 3AQ, ENG.
(T) 01234 742618
Speciality: Aromatherapy, Indian Head Massage, Reflexology, Holistic Therapy Facials. ✔
● **Owner/Holistic Therapist**
Mrs E Georgiou Q: IIHHT. M: APS, FHT.
C Yrs. Est.: 4 (Ref:HM18367)

**SHEER TECHNIQUE**

**Sheer Technique**, 52 Rosegarth Walk, Nottingham, **Nottinghamshire**, NG6 0LY, ENG.
(T) 01159 423261 (F) 01159 160305
(E) veronicaowen@breathemail.net
Speciality: Acupressure, Aromatherapy, Aura Therapy, Auto Suggestion, Bio-energetics, Biofeedback, Colour Therapy, Complementary Therapy, Counselling, Crystal Healing, Cupping, Douching, Dowsing, Faith Healing, Family Planning (Natural), Family Therapy, Gem Essence Therapy, Group Therapy, Healer, Healing Therapy, Holistic Healing, Hypnosis, Hypnotherapy, Indian Head Massage, Inhalation Therapy, Iridology, Kinesiology, Life Style Coaching, Manipulation,

Massage (Therapeutic), Meditation, Polarity Therapy, Postural Integration, Reflexology, Reiki, Seichem, Spiritual Healing, Stress Therapy, Touch Therapy, Visualisation Therapy, Magno-Therapy. ✔
● **Holistic Therapist** Ms V Owen M: APS, BSY.
C Yrs. Est.: 10 (Ref:HM18368)

## SHEER, JENNY

**Jenny Sheer**, 6 North Malvern Rd, Malvern, **Worcestershire**, WR14 4LT, ENG.
(T) 01684 565586
Speciality: Acupuncture.
● **Owner** Mrs J Sherr
O (Ref:HM18369)

## SHEERINS, ROZ

**Roz Sheerins**, 12 Brunton Quadrant, Glenrothes, **Fife**, KY7 4EQ, SCO.
(T) 01592 752486
Speciality: Chiropody, Podiatry. ✔
● **Chiropodist** Miss R Sheerin Q: BSc, S.R.Ch. M: S.C.P.
M Yrs. Est.: 4 (Ref:HM18370)

## SHEFFIELD CHIROPRATIC CLINIC

**Sheffield Chiropratic Clinic**, 789 Chesterfield Rd, Sheffield, **Yorkshire (South)**, S8 0SP, ENG.
(T) 01142 745656
Speciality: Chiropractors.
● **Principal** Dr U Sandstorm
P S T (Ref:HM18371)

## SHEFFIELD NATURAL HEALTH CTRE

**Sheffield Natural Health Centre**, 289 Abbeydale Rd, Sheffield, **Yorkshire (South)**, S7 1FJ, ENG.
(T) 01142 509900
Speciality: Acupuncture, Aromatherapy, Chinese Herbal Medicine, Counselling, Homeopathy, Massage (Therapeutic), Osteopathy, Phytotherapy, Reflexology, Shiatsu. ✔
● **Partner** Mr M Mamin
C Yrs. Est.: 14 (Ref:HM18372)

## SHEFFIELD SCHOOL OF BEAUTY

**Sheffield School Of Beauty (The)**, Barkers Pool House, Burgess St, Sheffield, **Yorkshire (South)**, S1 2HF, ENG.
(T) 01142 750201 (F) 01142 750201
Speciality: Complementary Medicines & Therapy.
● **Manageress** Ms C Forrester
M (Ref:HM18373)

## SHEFFORD OSTEOPATHIC CLINIC

**Shefford Osteopathic Clinic**, 14A Clifton Rd, Shefford, **Bedfordshire**, SG17 5AE, ENG.
(T) 01462 811006
Speciality: Osteopathy.
● **Owner** Ms C Robinson
P S T (Ref:HM18374)

## SHEILA

**Sheila**, 34 Heath Drive, Brookwood, Woking, **Surrey**, GU24 0HG, ENG.
(T) 01483 473218
Speciality: Clairvoyants & Palmists.
● **Owner** Mrs S Bedwell
B (Ref:HM18375)

## SHEILA'S BODY CARE

**Sheila's Body Care**, Rockwell End Farm, Hambleden, Henley-on-Thames, **Oxfordshire**, RG9 6NG, ENG.
(T) 01491 579748 (F) 01491 579748
Speciality: Aromatherapy.
● **Owner** Ms S Keene
M O (Ref:HM18376)

## SHEKINAH PLACE PHYSIO

**Shekinah Place Physiotherapy & Sports Injury Clinic**, 106 St Leonards Rd, Leicester, **Leicestershire**, LE2 1WR, ENG.
(T) 01162 745629 (F) 01162 235020
Speciality: Physiotherapy.
● **Owner** Mr F McFarlane
P S T (Ref:HM18377)

## SHELAGH, MATTHEWS

**Matthews Shelagh**, Silverhill Chiropodist Centre, 71 Sedlescombe Rd North, St. Leonards-On-Sea, **Sussex (East)**, TN37 7DS, ENG.
(T) 01424 425025
Speciality: Chiropodists (Podiatrists).
S (Ref:HM18378)

## SHELDON

**Sheldon**, 28 Horse Shoes Lane, Birmingham, **Midlands (West)**, B26 3HY, ENG.
(T) 01217 432672 (F) 01217 439137
Speciality: Chiropodists (Podiatrists).
● **Owner** Mrs L Davies
S (Ref:HM18379)

## SHELDON, PEGGY

**Peggy Sheldon**, 3 Airlie Gardens, Ilford, **Essex**, IG1 4LB, ENG.
(T) 020 8554 1569 (F) 020 8554 1569
(E) peggysheldon@onetel.net.uk
Speciality: Bowen Therapy, Massage (Therapeutic), Reflexology, Reiki, Shiatsu, Nutritional Advice, Chronic Healing. ✔
● **Owner/Complementary Therapist** Peggy Sheldon Q: A.I.P.T.I, BTER. M: BTER.
C Yrs. Est.: 6 (Ref:HM18380)

## SHELFORD PHYSIOTHERAPY

**Shelford Physiotherapy**, 12 Beech Cl, Little Shelford, Cambridge, **Cambridgeshire**, CB2 5EP, ENG.
(T) 01223 844488
Speciality: Physiotherapy.
● **Owner** Mrs S Osborne
P S T (Ref:HM18381)

## SHELLEY MEDIUM & MIRRORLOGY

**Shelley Medium & Mirrorology**, 62 Centre Drive, Epping, **Essex**, CM16 4JE, ENG.
(T) 01992 571589
Speciality: Clairvoyants & Palmists.
B (Ref:HM18382)

## SHELLEY, P A

**P A Shelley**, 510 Nottingham Rd, Giltbrook, Nottingham, **Nottinghamshire**, NG16 2GE, ENG.
(T) 01159 383616
Speciality: Physiotherapy.
● **Owner** Mrs P Shelley
P S T (Ref:HM18383)

## SHELLEY, P A

**P A Shelley**, 11 Regent St, Nottingham, **Nottinghamshire**, NG1 5BS, ENG.
(T) 01159 473772
Speciality: Physiotherapy.
P S T (Ref:HM18384)

## SHELTON, J K

**J K Shelton**, Chapel House, 16 Old St, Ludlow, **Shropshire**, SY8 1NP, ENG.
(T) 01584 876153
Speciality: Chiropodists (Podiatrists).
● **Owner** Mr J Shelton
S (Ref:HM18385)

## SHELTON, J K

**J K Shelton**, 45 High St, Church Stretton, **Shropshire**, SY6 6BX, ENG.
(T) 01694 722750
Speciality: Chiropodists (Podiatrists).
● **Owner** Mr J Shelton
S (Ref:HM18386)

## SHELTON, JANE

**Jane Shelton**, 35 Town Moor Avenue, Doncaster, **Yorkshire (South)**, DN2 6BW, ENG.
(T) 01302 361316
Speciality: Reflexology.
● **Owner** Mrs J Shelton
S T (Ref:HM18387)

## SHELTON, JULIE

**Julie Shelton**, 82 Shakespeare Cres, Dronfield, **Derbyshire**, S18 1ND, ENG.
(T) 01246 416789
Speciality: Chiropodists (Podiatrists).
● **Partner** Mr D Shelton
S (Ref:HM18388)

## SHELTON, MICHAEL

**Michael Shelton**, 38 The Leazes, Sunderland, **Tyne and Wear**, SR1 3SW, ENG.
(T) 01915 145742
Speciality: Chiropodists (Podiatrists).
S (Ref:HM18389)

## SHEN ACUPUNCTURE CLINIC

**Shen Acupuncture Clinic (The)**, 145-149 Cardigan Rd, Leeds, **Yorkshire (West)**, LS6 1LJ, ENG.
(T) 01132 755550
Speciality: Acupuncture.
● **Partner** Mr G Watts
O (Ref:HM18390)

## SHEN CLINIC

**Shen Clinic (The)**, Holyrood Chambers, Holyrood St, Newport, **Isle of Wight**, PO30 5AZ, ENG.
(T) 01983 521811 (F) 01983 521811
Speciality: Acupuncture, Allergy Testing, Hypnotherapy, Moxibustion, Nutritional Therapy, Psychotherapy, Shiatsu, Chinese Herbal Formulae. ✔
● **Health Therapist** Mr M Lambert Q: Dip.Hyp, Dip.Psych.
● **Acupuncturist** Ms R Smith Q: BA (Hons), Dip.Ac, Lic.Ac, MBAcC.
B C T Yrs. Est.: 3 (Ref:HM18391)

## SHEN HOLISTIC THERAPIES

**Shen Holistic Therapies**, 81 High St, Gosforth, Newcastle Upon Tyne, **Tyne and Wear**, NE3 4AA, ENG.
(T) 01912 858989
Speciality: Aromatherapy, Indian Head Massage, Manual Lymph Drainage. ✔
● **Holistic Therapist** Ms J Baynton Q: Dip.Arom, Reiki 1, Reiki 2. M: ISPA.
● **Holistic Therapist** Ms P Carlson Q: Dip.Arom, Reiki 1, Reiki 2. M: AoR, ISPA.
C Yrs. Est.: 1 (Ref:HM18392)

## SHEN NONG CHINESE MED CTRE

**Shen Nong Chinese Medical Centre**, 1b London Rd, St. Albans, **Hertfordshire**, AL1 1LA, ENG.
(T) 01727 847031 (F) 01727 847031
Speciality: Acupuncture.
● **Owner** Mr L Li
O (Ref:HM18393)

## SHEN THERAPY CENTRE

**Shen Therapy Centre**, P O Box 13034, Edinburgh, **Edinburgh (City of)**, EH13 9NU, SCO.
(T) 01314 784780 (F) 01314 784780
Speciality: Complementary Medicines & Therapy.
● **Owner** Mrs C Logan
M (Ref:HM18394)

## SHENANDOAH HEALING

**Shenandoah Healing**, 61 Esmondale, Naas, **County Kildare**, IRE.
(T) 04587 4349
Speciality: Absent Healing, Aura Therapy, Bach Remedies, Complementary Therapy, Dowsing, Healer, Healing Therapy, Holistic Healing, Life Style Coaching, Massage (Therapeutic), Spiritual Healing, Touch Therapy, Vortex Healing.
● **Healer** Mr A Doody
H Yrs. Est.: 5 (Ref:HM18395)

## SHENFIELD ACUPUNCTURE CENTRE

**Shenfield Acupuncture Centre**, 27 Hutton Rd, Shenfield, Brentwood, **Essex**, CM15 8JU, ENG.
(T) 01277 225551
Speciality: Acupuncture.
● **Owner** Mr S Finch
O (Ref:HM18396)

## SHENFIELD HEALTH CLINIC

**Shenfield Health Clinic**, 27 Hutton Rd, Shenfield, Brentwood, **Essex**, CM15 8JU, ENG.
(T) 01277 263760
Speciality: Acupuncture.
M (Ref:HM18397)

## SHENKER, SHARON

**Sharon Shenker**, 53 Arlington Rd, London, **London (Greater)**, N14 5BB, ENG.
(T) 020 8361 5373
Speciality: Homeopathy.
● **Owner** Mrs S Shenker
M (Ref:HM18398)

## SHENLEY CHIROPRACTIC CLINIC

**Shenley Chiropractic Clinic**, 12 Benbow Court, Shenley Church End, Milton Keynes, **Buckinghamshire**, MK5 6JG, ENG.



Key: B Mind-Body Medicine C Complementary Medicine H Self Help Treatment M Medicinal Therapy O Oriental Medicine P Postural Therapy S Manipulative Structural Therapy T Touch Therapy

(T) 01908 506154 (F) 01908 506795
Speciality: Chiropractic, Rehabilition. ✔
● **Chiropractor** Dr J Dennett Q: BCA, DC, MSc. M: GCC.
● **Chiropractor** Dr S Richards Q: BCA, BSc, DC. M: GCC.
● **Chiropractor** Dr J Benepal Q: BCA, DC. M: GCC.
● **Chiropractor** Per Kleberg Q: BCA, BSc, DC. M: GCC.
P Yrs. Est.: 6 (Ref:HM18399)

## SHENSTON, RICHARD

**Richard Shenston**, 23 Whitehouse Avenue, Wednesbury, **Midlands (West)**, WS10 7HT, ENG.
(T) 08707 879109
Speciality: Complementary Medicines & Therapy.
● **Owner** Mr R Shenston
C M (Ref:HM18400)

## SHEN-TI CLINIC

**Shen-Ti Clinic**, 90 Mill Lane, North Hykeham, Lincoln, **Lincolnshire**, LN6 9PD, ENG.
(T) 01522 686577
Speciality: Complementary Medicines & Therapy.
C M (Ref:HM18401)

## SHENTON, DIANNE

**Dianne Shenton**, 46 Bavelaw Rd, Balerno, **Edinburgh (City of)**, EH14 7AE, SCO.
(T) 01314 515026
Speciality: Biomechanics, Chiropody. ✔
● **Chiropodist** Diane Shenton Q: M.S.C.P, S.R.Ch.
M Yrs. Est.: 34 (Ref:HM18402)

## SHENTON, MAXINE

**Maxine Shenton**, Church End Cottage, Great Hormead, Buntingford, **Hertfordshire**, SG9 0NH, ENG.
(T) 01763 289235
Speciality: Alexander Technique.
P S (Ref:HM18403)

## SHEPARD, BARBARA

**Barbara Shepard**, 3 Unity St, Hebden Bridge, **Yorkshire (West)**, HX7 8HQ, ENG.
(T) 01422 842344
Speciality: Osteopathy.
● **Holistic Therapist** Ms B Shepard Q: ITEC, MA, RCST.
P S T (Ref:HM18404)

## SHEPHARD, SALLY

**Mrs Sally Shephard**, Rose Farm, Sway Rd, Pennington, Lymington, **Hampshire**, SO41 8LR, ENG.
(T) 01590 674381
Speciality: Physiotherapy.
P S T (Ref:HM18405)

## SHEPHEARD, P

**P Shepheard**, 36 Wykeham Cr, Oxford, **Oxfordshire**, OX4 3SB, ENG.
(T) 01865 712712
Speciality: Aromatherapy.
M O (Ref:HM18406)

## SHEPHERD, A R

**Mrs A R Shepherd**, 1 Blenheim Cl, Forest Town, Mansfield, **Nottinghamshire**, NG19 0PN, ENG.
(T) 01623 658677
Speciality: Chiropodists (Podiatrists).
S (Ref:HM18407)

## SHEPHERD, B

**B Shepherd**, Suite 1, Churchill House, Queen St, Wellington, Telford, **Shropshire**, TF1 1SN, ENG.
(T) 01952 245518
Speciality: Chiropodists (Podiatrists).
S (Ref:HM18408)

## SHEPHERD, CLARE

**Clare Shepherd**, 286 Ecclesall Rd South, Sheffield, **Yorkshire (South)**, S11 9PS, ENG.
(T) 01142 621187
Speciality: Indian Head Massage, Reflexology.
S T (Ref:HM18409)

## SHEPHERD, DIANNE

**Dianne Shepherd**, The Oak House, Horsell Vale, Woking, **Surrey**, GU21 4QU, ENG.
(T) 01483 768252
Speciality: Osteopathy.
● **Owner** Mrs D Shepherd
P S T (Ref:HM18410)

## SHEPHERD, JAN

**Jan Shepherd**, Flat 19 Mannock House, Military Rd, Canterbury, **Kent**, CT1 1JP, ENG.
(T) 01227 455187
Speciality: Clairvoyants & Palmists.
● **Partner** Ms J Shephard
B (Ref:HM18411)

## SHEPHERD, JEAN

**Jean Shepherd**, 88 Tylney Rd, Forest Gate, London, **London (Greater)**, E7 0LY, ENG.
(T) 020 8555 9655
Speciality: Alexander Technique.
● **Owner** Mrs J Shepherd
P S (Ref:HM18412)

## SHEPHERD, KAREN

**Karen Shepherd**, 13 Fosters Lane, Bradwell, **Buckinghamshire**, MK13 9HD, ENG.
(T) 01908 220870
Speciality: Reflexology.
S T (Ref:HM18413)

## SHEPHERD, P A

**P A Shepherd**, 17 Highfield Lane, Southampton, **Hampshire**, SO17 1QD, ENG.
(T) 01489 574524
Speciality: Acupuncture.
● **Owner** Mrs P Shepherd
O (Ref:HM18414)

## SHEPHERD, RACHEL

**Rachel Shepherd**, Aberfoyle House, Stapley Rd, St. Albans, **Hertfordshire**, AL3 5EP, ENG.
(T) 01727 856687
Speciality: Reflexology.
● **Manager** Mrs S Bassett
S T (Ref:HM18415)

## SHEPHERD, S

**S Shepherd**, 59 Valley Rd, Crewe, **Cheshire**, CW2 8JZ, ENG.
(T) 01270 661593
Speciality: Osteopathy.
● **Owner** Mr M Davies
P S T (Ref:HM18416)

## SHEPHERD, STEVEN

**Steven Shepherd**, 4 Grosvenor Rd, Wrexham, LL11 1BU, WAL.
(T) 01978 262120
Speciality: Osteopathy.
● **Owner** Mr S Shepherd
P S T (Ref:HM18417)

## SHEPHERD, STEVEN

**Steven Shepherd**, Trevenna, South Crescent Rd, Chester, **Cheshire**, CH4 7AU, ENG.
(T) 01244 671919
Speciality: Osteopathy.
P S T (Ref:HM18418)

## SHEPHERDSON, ANTHONY

**Anthony Shepherdson**, Eastfield, Gernon Walk, Letchworth, **Hertfordshire**, SG6 3HW, ENG.
(T) 01462 684358
Speciality: Chiropodists (Podiatrists).
S (Ref:HM18419)

## SHEPPARD & ASSOCIATES

**Sheppard & Associates**, Flat 2, 12 The Ridgeway, London, **London (Greater)**, E4 6PP, ENG.
(T) 020 8524 0608
Speciality: Psychology.
● **Owner** Ms S Sheppard
B (Ref:HM18420)

## SHEPPARD, HELEN

**Helen Sheppard**, The Connifers, Llechfaen, Brecon, **Powys**, LD3 7SP, WAL.
(T) 01874 665461
Speciality: Bach Remedies, Crystal Healing, Dowsing, Floral Essence Therapy, Gem Essence Therapy, Music Therapy, Reflexology. ✔
● **Reflexologist** Ms H Sheppard Q: MAR, MGCP. M: GCP.
B Yrs. Est.: 3 (Ref:HM18421)

## SHEPPARD, PAM

**Pam Sheppard**, Hambrook, **Sussex (West)**, PO18, ENG.
(T) 01243 574456
Speciality: Bach Remedies.
M (Ref:HM18422)

## SHEPPARD, SERENA

**Serena Sheppard**, Larne, Antrim, **County Antrim**, BT40, NIR.
(T) 028 2826 0710
Speciality: Bach Remedies.
M (Ref:HM18423)

## SHEPPERTON CHIROPRACTIC CLINIC

**Shepperton Chiropractic Clinic**, 149 Laleham Rd, Shepperton, **Surrey**, TW17 0AH, ENG.
(T) 01932 429584
Speciality: Chiropractic.
● **Employee** Mr H Murray
P S T (Ref:HM18424)

## SHEPPERTON PHYSIOFIRST CENTRE

**Shepperton PhysioFirst Centre**, 15B Station Rd, Shepperton, **Surrey**, TW17 8AU, ENG.
(T) 01932 230240
Speciality: Acupuncture, Physiotherapy.
● **Physiotherapist** Mrs J Jones Q: MCSP, SRP. M: CSP.
S Yrs. Est.: 3 (Ref:HM18425)

## SHER, CAROLE

**Carole Sher**, 94 Fawe Park Rd, London, **London (Greater)**, SW15 2EA, ENG.
(T) 020 8870 4981
Speciality: Alexander Technique.
P S (Ref:HM18426)

## SHERBOURNE CLINIC

**Sherbourne Clinic Of Acupuncture & Kinesiology**, 2 Sir Thomas Whites Rd, Coventry, **Midlands (West)**, CV5 8DQ, ENG.
(T) 024 7667 0147
Speciality: Acupuncture.
● **Owner** Mr B Deol
O (Ref:HM18427)

## SHERIDAN

**Sheridan**, 45 Rotherey Avenue, London, **London (Greater)**, SW20 8JU, ENG.
(T) 020 8540 4901
Speciality: Reflexology.
S T (Ref:HM18428)

## SHERIDAN & AST

**Adam Sheridan D O & Associates**, 69 Albert St, Rugby, **Warwickshire**, CV21 2SN, ENG.
(T) 01788 560646
Speciality: Osteopathy.
● **Owner** A Sheridan
P S T (Ref:HM18429)

## SHERIDAN, PATRICIA

**Sheridan Patricia**, 62 Maple Dr Castleknock, Dublin, **County Dublin**, IRE.
(T) 01820 6554
Speciality: Aromatherapy.
M O (Ref:HM18430)

## SHERIDAN, SARAH

**Sarah Sheridan**, 7 Cedar Lawn Avenue, Barnet, **Hertfordshire**, EN5 2LW, ENG.
(T) 020 8440 2449
Speciality: Reflexology.
S T (Ref:HM18431)

## SHERIDON, J

**Mrs J Sheridon**, 75 Knutsford Rd, Wilmslow, **Cheshire**, SK9 6JH, ENG.
(T) 01625 521239
Speciality: Chiropodists (Podiatrists).
● **Owner** Mrs J Sherridon
S (Ref:HM18432)

## SHERIF, F (DR)

**Dr F Sherif**, 7 Greenhill Court, 25B Green Lane, Northwood, **London (Greater)**, HA6 2UZ, ENG.
(T) 01923 826305
Speciality: Acupuncture.
● **Owner** Dr F Sherif
O (Ref:HM18433)

## SHERMAN, EDWARD J

**Edward J Sherman**, 1 Grafton Park Rd,


Key continued: Yrs.Est: Years Established Q: Qualifications M: Professional Membership ✔ Indemnity Insurance Accept Credit Cards

Worcester Park, **Surrey**, KT4 7HS, ENG.
**(T)** 020 8337 5296
**Speciality:** Chiropodists (Podiatrists).
S (**Ref:**HM18434)

## SHEROMA THERAPY

**Sheroma Therapy**, 44 Nursery Rd, Great Cornard, Sudbury, **Suffolk**, CO10 0NJ, ENG.
**(T)** 01787 379428
**Speciality:** Acupressure, Aromatherapy, Colour Therapy, Complementary Therapy, Counselling, Herbal Medicine, Holistic Healing, Hypnosis, Hypnotherapy, Indian Head Massage, Massage (Therapeutic), Meditation, Oriental Diagnosis, Reflexology, Reichian Therapy, Reiki, Stress Therapy. ✔
● **Therapist** Ms S Waterson Q: Dip.Arom, Dip.Couns, Dip.Hyp, Dip.Massage, Dip.Orient.Med. M: IPTI, NCH.
C **Yrs. Est.:** 6 (**Ref:**HM18435)

## SHERQIA, DARULSHAFA

**Darulshafa Sherqia**, 108 Lumb Lane, Bradford, **Yorkshire (West)**, BD8 7RS, ENG.
**(T)** 01274 721755 **(F)** 01274 721755
**(E)** hakimrana@darulshafa.co.uk
**(W)** www.darulshafa.co.uk
**Speciality:** Herbal Medicine, Homeopathy, Naturopathy, Pyscho-Synthesis, Eastern Medicine. ✔
● **Medical Herbalist/Homeopath**
Rana Mazhar Q: Dip.Herb.Med, Dip.Hom.
M: BHMA, EMPA.
M **Yrs. Est.:** 34 (**Ref:**HM18436)

## SHERRATT, SUZY

**Suzy Sherratt**, 41 Holly Bank, Ackworth, Pontefract, **Yorkshire (West)**, WF7 7LE, ENG.
**(T)** 01977 612008
**Speciality:** Reflexology.
S T (**Ref:**HM18437)

## SHERRY, M B

**M B Sherry**, Friths Cottage, Bacup Rd, Todmorden, **Yorkshire (West)**, OL14 7PJ, ENG.
**(T)** 01706 818808
**Speciality:** Reflexology.
S T (**Ref:**HM18438)

## SHERRY'S HEALTH FOODS

**Sherry's Health Foods**, 58 High St, Biggleswade, **Bedfordshire**, SG18 0LJ, ENG.
**(T)** 01767 220020 **(F)** 01234 782663
**Speciality:** Complementary Medicines & Therapy, Health Food Store.
C **Yrs. Est.:** 20 (**Ref:**HM18439)

## SHERWOOD CHIROPRACTIC CLINIC

**Sherwood Chiropractic Clinic**, 480A Mansfield Rd, Nottingham, **Nottinghamshire**, NG5 2EL, ENG.
**(T)** 01159 857785 **(F)** 01159 857785
**Speciality:** Chiropractic.
● **Owner** Miss J Pedersen
P S T (**Ref:**HM18440)

## SHERWOOD PSYCHO TRAINING INS

**Sherwood Psychotherapy Training Institute**, 2 St James's Trce, Nottingham, **Nottinghamshire**, NG1 6FW, ENG.
**(T)** 01159 243994 **(F)** 01159 242738
**Speciality:** Art Therapy, Counselling, Gestalt Therapy, Humanistic Psychology, Meditation, Phytotherapy, Psychotherapy, Reiki, Rogerian Therapy, Spiritual Healing, Transactional Analysis. ✔
● **Director** Mr K Evans Q: UKCP (Reg). M: UKCP.
B **Yrs. Est.:** 15 (**Ref:**HM18441)

## SHERWOOD PSYCHO TRAINING INS

**Sherwood Psychotherapy Training Institute**, 89 Marylebone High St, London, **London (Greater)**, W1M 3DE, ENG.
**(T)** 020 7486 2393
**Speciality:** Psychotherapy.
B (**Ref:**HM18442)

## SHERWOOD, L M

**Mrs L M Sherwood**, Willow Green Surgery, Station Rd, East Preston, Littlehampton, **Sussex (West)**, BN16 3AH, ENG.
**(T)** 01903 859159
**Speciality:** Chiropodists (Podiatrists).
● **Owner** Mrs L Sherwood
S (**Ref:**HM18443)

## SHERWOOD, T A

**T A Sherwood**, 14 Mount St, Harrogate, **Yorkshire (North)**, HG2 8DQ, ENG.
**(T)** 01423 870916
**Speciality:** Chiropodists (Podiatrists).
S (**Ref:**HM18444)

## SHEVAK, C

**C Shevak**, Beverley Clinic, 362 Coombe Lane, London, **London (Greater)**, SW20 0RJ, ENG.
**(T)** 020 8241 2515
**Speciality:** Chiropodists (Podiatrists).
S (**Ref:**HM18445)

## SHEVILL, L A

**L A Shevill**, Gullaveis, Long Lane, High St, St. Austell, **Cornwall**, PL26 7SX, ENG.
**(T)** 01726 823141
**Speciality:** Chiropodists (Podiatrists).
S (**Ref:**HM18446)

## SHEVILLS, JERRY

**Jerry Shevills**, 52 Albany Rd, Sheffield, **Yorkshire (South)**, S7 1DP, ENG.
**(T)** 01142 551227
**Speciality:** Complementary Medicines & Therapy.
C M (**Ref:**HM18447)

## SHIATSU

**Shiatsu**, The Manor Farm House, The Green, Beeston, Sandy, **Bedfordshire**, SG19 1PG, ENG.
**(T)** 01767 680214
**Speciality:** Physiotherapy.
● **Owner** Ms S Wale
P S T (**Ref:**HM18448)

## SHIATSU

**Shiatsu**, Bodywise Natural Health Centre, 119 Roman Rd, London, **London (Greater)**, E2 0QN, ENG.
**(T)** 020 8981 6938
**Speciality:** Complementary Medicines & Therapy.
● **Owner** Ms S Lancaster
M (**Ref:**HM18449)

## SHIATSU

**Shiatsu**, 36A Walnut Rd, Torquay, **Devon**, TQ2 6HS, ENG.
**(T)** 01803 605025
**Speciality:** Complementary Medicines & Therapy.
● **Owner** Mr C Ashington-Hall
M (**Ref:**HM18450)

## SHIATSU

**Shiatsu, Physiotherapy and Counselling**, 23 Shalmsford St, Chartham, Canterbury, **Kent**, CT4 7RZ, ENG.
**(T)** 01227 738902
**(E)** lucy.moorhead@virgin.net
**Speciality:** Acupressure, Counselling, Holistic Healing, Massage (Therapeutic), Meditation, Oriental Diagnosis, Shiatsu, Spiritual Healing. ✔
● **Therapist** Ms L Moorhead Q: BA (Hons), Dip.ESS. M: IPTI.
B **Yrs. Est.:** 5 (**Ref:**HM18451)

## SHIATSU

**Shiatsu**, 4 Fernwood Douglas Rd, Cork, **County Cork**, IRE.
**(T)** 021 4965 890
**(E)** idit@eircom.net
**Speciality:** Acupressure, Bach Remedies, Cupping, Do-In, Moxibustion, Oriental Diagnosis, Shiatsu, Sotai - Corrective Movements. ✔
● **Shiatsu Practitioner**
Idit Hourigan M: ISS.
O **Yrs. Est.:** 12 (**Ref:**HM18452)

## SHIATSU CENTRE

**Shiatsu Centre (The)**, 20A Lower Goat Lane, Norwich, **Norfolk**, NR2 1EL, ENG.
**(T)** 01603 632555 **(F)** 01603 663391
**Speciality:** Acupuncture, Shiatsu. ✔
● **Shiatsu Practitioner/Teacher**
Mr C Andrews Q: BA, MRSS. M: RSS.
M **Yrs. Est.:** 15 (**Ref:**HM18453)

## SHIATSU CLINIC

**Shiatsu Clinic (The)**, The Whitehouse Studio, 80 Meadlands Drive, Richmond, **Surrey**, TW10 7EE, ENG.
**(T)** 020 8332 6673
**Speciality:** Complementary Medicines & Therapy.
C M (**Ref:**HM18454)

## SHIATSU COLLEGE HASTINGS

**Shiatsu College Hastings**, 10 St. Helens Cr, Hastings, **Sussex (East)**, TN34 2EW, ENG.
**(T)** 01424 460355
**Speciality:** Complementary Medicines & Therapy.
M (**Ref:**HM18455)

## SHIATSU COLLEGE LONDON

**Shiatsu College London**, Unit 62, 126-128 Barlby Rd, London, **London (Greater)**, W10 6BL, ENG.
**(T)** 020 8987 0208
**Speciality:** Complementary Medicines & Therapy.
C M (**Ref:**HM18456)

## SHIATSU IRELAND

**Shiatsu Ireland**, 67 Wilfield Rd, Ballsbridge, **County Dublin**, IRE.
**(T)** 01260 4669
**(E)** enquiries@shiatsuireland.com
**(W)** www.shiatsuireland.com
**Speciality:** Complementary Medicines & Therapy.
M (**Ref:**HM18457)

## SHIATSU PLACE

**Exstatic Ltd**, 97-99 Severn Sisters Rd, London, **London (Greater)**, N7 7QP, ENG.
**(T)** 020 7281 1412 **(F)** 020 7281 1413
**(E)** shiatsu.do@btinternet.com
**Speciality:** Acupuncture, Bowen Therapy, Cranial Osteopathy, Cranio-Sacral Therapy, Do-In, Homeopathy, Osteopathy, Reiki, Shiatsu, T'ai-Chi Ch'uan, Yoga, Seitai, Time Therapy.
● **Therapist** Ms K Dowell
**(T)** 020 8281 1412
● **Principal** Hiliary Totah Q: MRSS(t).
M: Shiatsu Society UK.
O **Yrs. Est.:** 2 (**Ref:**HM18458)

## SHIATSU PLACE

**Shiatsu Place**, 97-99 Severn Sisters Rd, London, **London (Greater)**, N7 7QP, ENG.
**(T)** 020 7281 1412
**Speciality:** Complementary Medicines & Therapy.
● **Practitioner** Karen Dowell
M (**Ref:**HM18459)

## SHIATSU PRACTICE

**Shiatsu Practice**, 51 Prestbury Rd, Cheltenham, **Gloucestershire**, GL52 2BY, ENG.
**(T)** 01242 233949
**(E)** lidavlcek@lineone.net
**Speciality:** Shiatsu. ✔
● **Shiatsu Practitioner** Lida Vlcek M: RSS.
O **Yrs. Est.:** 9 (**Ref:**HM18460)

## SHIATSU PRACTITIONER

**Shiatsu Practitioner**, 3 Brincliffe Court, Nether Edge Rd, Sheffield, **Yorkshire (South)**, S7 1RX, ENG.
**(T)** 01142 551303
**Speciality:** Complementary Medicines & Therapy.
● **Owner** Ms M Grundy-Wakelin
M (**Ref:**HM18461)

## SHIATSU SCHOOL

**Shiatsu School (The)**, Townsend House, The Shortyard, Wolverley, Kidderminster, **Worcestershire**, DY11 5XF, ENG.
**(T)** 01562 852880
**Speciality:** Shiatsu.
M (**Ref:**HM18462)

## SHIATSU SOCIETY

**Shiatsu Society**, Barber House, Storeys Bar Rd, Peterborough, **Cambridgeshire**, PE1 5YS, ENG.
**(T)** 01733 758341 **(F)** 01733 758342
**Speciality:** Complementary Medicines & Therapy.



Key: B Mind-Body Medicine C Complementary Medicine H Self Help Treatment M Medicinal Therapy O Oriental Medicine P Postural Therapy S Manipulative Structural Therapy T Touch Therapy

M (Ref:HM18463)

## SHIATSU SOCIETY

**Shiatsu Society (UK)**, Eastlands Court, St. Peters Rd, Rugby, **Warwickshire**, CV21 3QP, ENG.
(T) 01788 555051 (F) 01788 555052
(W) www.shiatsu.org
Speciality: Shiatsu. ✔
T Yrs. Est.: 20 (Ref:HM18464)

## SHIATSU STUDIO

**Shiatsu Studio**, 17 Queensberry Mews West, London, **London (Greater)**, SW7 2DY, ENG.
(T) 020 7581 4241 (F) 020 7581 2286
(W) www.shiatsustudio.com
Speciality: Reiki, Seichem, Shiatsu. ✔
● **Shiatsu Practitioner**
Vannessa Jeffcoat M: RSS.
C O Yrs. Est.: 5 (Ref:HM18465)

## SHIATSU THERAPY

**Shiatsu Therapy**, 3 Palmers Way, Hutton, Weston-Super-Mare, **Somerset**, BS24 9QT, ENG.
(T) 01934 815110
Speciality: Shiatsu.
● **Owner** Ms M McFarlene
M (Ref:HM18466)

## SHIATSU TOUCH CENTRE

**Shiatsu Touch Centre**, 68 Fairfield Rd, East Grinstead, **Sussex (West)**, RH19 4HB, ENG.
(T) 01342 328240
Speciality: Complementary Medicines & Therapy.
C M (Ref:HM18467)

## SHIATSU WORKS

**Shiatsu Works**, Royal Star Arcade, High St, Maidstone, **Kent**, ME14 1JL, ENG.
(T) 01622 756090
Speciality: Complementary Medicines & Therapy.
● **Principal** Mr K Oliver
M (Ref:HM18468)

## SHIATSU-DO CLINIC

**Shiatsu-Do Clinic**, 102 Geary Rd, London, **London (Greater)**, NW10 1HR, ENG.
(T) 020 8450 8688
Speciality: Complementary Medicines & Therapy.
M (Ref:HM18469)

## SHIELD CHIROPRACTIC CLINIC

**Shield Chiropractic Clinic**, 15 Princes Rd, Newcastle Upon Tyne, **Tyne and Wear**, NE3 5TT, ENG.
(T) 01912 170387
Speciality: Chiropractic.
● **Owner** Dr A Scott
P S T (Ref:HM18470)

## SHIELDS, CAROL

**Carol Shields**, 64 Broom Park, Teddington, **London (Greater)**, TW11 9RR, ENG.
(T) 020 8977 9341
Speciality: Electrolysis.
● **Owner** Mrs C Shields
T (Ref:HM18471)

## SHIELS, RITA

**Rita Shiels**, Red Lodge, Cryers Hill Lane, Cryers Hill, High Wycombe, **Buckinghamshire**, HP15 6AA, ENG.
(T) 01494 714359
Speciality: Chiropodists (Podiatrists).
● **Owner** Mrs R Shiels
S (Ref:HM18472)

## SHILLING, TARA

**Tara Shilling**, 74 Darland Avenue, Gillingham, **Kent**, ME7 3AP, ENG.
(T) 01634 850964
Speciality: Hypnosis.
B (Ref:HM18473)

## SHILLITO, C

**C Shillito**, 49 Green Lane, Lofthouse, Wakefield, **Yorkshire (West)**, WF3 3QJ, ENG.
(T) 01924 824387
Speciality: Chiropodists (Podiatrists).
● **Owner** Mr C Shillitto
S (Ref:HM18474)

## SHINER, SONIA

**Sonia Shiner**, Farnham, **Surrey**, GU10, ENG.
(T) 01420 478372
Speciality: Bach Remedies.
M (Ref:HM18475)

## SHINH, NATALIE

**Natalie Shinh**, 4 Disraeli Cres, High Wycombe, **Buckinghamshire**, HP13 5EJ, ENG.
(T) 01494 530354
Speciality: Osteopathy.
P S T (Ref:HM18476)

## SHINTON, S

**S Shinton**, Wanstead Village Dental & Health Centre, 24 High St, London, **London (Greater)**, E11 2AQ, ENG.
(T) 020 8530 2126
Speciality: Chiropodists (Podiatrists).
S (Ref:HM18477)

## SHIPBOURNE HOUSE

**Shipbourne House**, Stumble Hill, Shipbourne, Tonbridge, **Kent**, TN11 9PE, ENG.
(T) 01732 810225
Speciality: Complementary Medicines & Therapy.
● **Owner** Mrs G Walker
M (Ref:HM18478)

## SHIPMAN, PAUL

**Mr Paul Shipman**, 340 Whitchurch Rd, Cardiff, **Glamorgan (Vale of)**, CF14 3NG, WAL.
(T) 029 2061 9980
Speciality: Chiropodists (Podiatrists).
S (Ref:HM18479)

## SHIPP, MARION

**Marion Shipp**, 6 Little Gaynes Lane, Upminster, **Essex**, RM14 2JP, ENG.
(T) 01708 227799
Speciality: Chiropodists (Podiatrists).
● **Owner** Mrs M Shipp
S (Ref:HM18480)

## SHIPRA, AMIN

**Mrs Shipra Amin**, 9 Mount Drive, Harrow, **London (Greater)**, HA2 7RW, ENG.
(T) 020 8868 4146
Speciality: Osteopathy.
P S T (Ref:HM18481)

## SHIPSTON NATURAL HEALTH CLINIC

**Shipston Natural Health Clinic**, 14 Market Pl, Shipston on Stour, **Warwickshire**, CV36 4AG, ENG.
(T) 01608 664664 (F) 01608 664289
Speciality: Complementary Medicines & Therapy.
● **Owner** Ms P Harris
C M (Ref:HM18482)

## SHIPTON, NICK

**Nick Shipton**, 39 Tydfil Pl, Cardiff, **Glamorgan (Vale of)**, CF23 5HP, WAL.
(T) 029 2048 4555
Speciality: Chiropractors.
P S T (Ref:HM18483)

## SHIRLEY CHIROPRACTIC CLINIC

**Shirley Chiropractic Clinic**, 26 Kineton Rd, Southampton, **Hampshire**, SO15 7PQ, ENG.
(T) 01703 783942
Speciality: Chiropractic.
● **Manager** N Coulson
P S T (Ref:HM18484)

## SHIRLEY FRANKLIN AROMATHERAPY

**Shirley Franklin Aromatherapy**, 23 Dalby Rd, Melton Mowbray, **Leicestershire**, LE13 0BG, ENG.
(T) 01664 410056
(E) shirleyfranklin@breathemail.net
Speciality: Aromatherapy, Counselling, Indian Head Massage, Massage (Therapeutic). ✔
● **Owner** Mrs S Franklin
B H P T Yrs. Est.: 16 (Ref:HM18485)

## SHIRLEY PRICE AROMATHERAPY

**Shirley Price Aromatherapy Ltd**, Essentia House, Upper Bond St, Hinckley, **Leicestershire**, LE10 1RS, ENG.
(T) 01455 615466 (F) 01455 615054
Speciality: Aromatherapy.
M O (Ref:HM18486)

## SHIRLEY PRICE COLLEGE

**Shirley Price College Of Aromatherapy**, P.O. Box 16, **County Wicklow**, IRE.
(T) 04044 7319
Speciality: Aromatherapy.
M O (Ref:HM18487)

## SHIRLEY, JAMES

**James Shirley**, The Elms, London Rd, Ryarsh, West Malling, **Kent**, ME19 5AS, ENG.
(T) 01732 843532
Speciality: Physiotherapy.
● **Owner** Mr J Shirley
P S T (Ref:HM18488)

## SHIRLEY'S AROMATHERAPY

**Shirley's Aromatherapy**, 76 Middle St, Brixham, **Devon**, TQ5 8EJ, ENG.
(T) 01803 859596
Speciality: Aromatherapy.
M O (Ref:HM18489)

## SHIZHEN TCM UK

**Shizhen TCM UK Ltd**, 50 Sandy Lane, Manchester, **Manchester (Greater)**, M21 8TN, ENG.
(T) 01618 810088
Speciality: Herbal Medicine.
● **Director** Mrs S Tang
M (Ref:HM18490)

## SHOBHA, ARTURI (DR)

**Dr Arturi Shobha**, 46 Hoddersdon Rd, Stanstead Abbotts, Ware, **Hertfordshire**, SG12 8EQ, ENG.
(T) 01920 872107
Speciality: Acupuncture.
O (Ref:HM18491)

## SHOOTER, J

**J Shooter**, 6 Hockley Lane, Wingerworth, Chesterfield, **Derbyshire**, S42 6QG, ENG.
(T) 01246 273531
Speciality: Chiropodists (Podiatrists).
● **Owner** Mrs J Shooter
S (Ref:HM18492)

## SHOOTERS HILL CENTRE

**Shooters Hill Centre**, 5 Cleanthus Rd, London, **London (Greater)**, SE18 3DE, ENG.
(T) 020 8854 5080
Speciality: Alexander Technique.
● **Owner** Ms L Henderson
P S (Ref:HM18493)

## SHORE, JAMES

**James Shore**, 95 Main St, East Leake, Loughborough, **Leicestershire**, LE12 6PF, ENG.
(T) 01509 852532
Speciality: Hypnosis.
● **Owner** Mr J Shore
B (Ref:HM18494)

## SHORE, ROBIN

**Robin Shore**, 8 Well St, Paignton, **Devon**, TQ3 3AW, ENG.
(T) 01803 664243
Speciality: Chiropodists (Podiatrists).
● **Owner** Mr R Shore
S (Ref:HM18495)

## SHOREHAM PHYSIOTHERAPY CLINIC

**Shoreham Physiotherapy Clinic**, 316 Upper Shoreham Rd, Shoreham-by-Sea, **Sussex (West)**, BN43 6BA, ENG.
(T) 01273 440350
Speciality: Physiotherapy.
P S T (Ref:HM18496)

## SHORT, J J

**J J Short**, 37 Curzon St, Maryport, **Cumbria**, CA15 6LW, ENG.
(T) 01900 812061
Speciality: Osteopathy.
P S T (Ref:HM18497)

## SHORT, P

**P Short**, 10 Eldon Rd, Reading, **Berkshire**, RG1 4DH, ENG.
(T) 01189 502002
Speciality: Psychology.
B (Ref:HM18498)



Key continued: Yrs.Est: Years Established Q: Qualifications M: Professional Membership ✔ Indemnity Insurance Accept Credit Cards

**SHORT, S L**

**S L Short**, 5 Glenwood Cl, Swindon, **Wiltshire**, SN1 4EB, ENG.
(T) 01793 641842
Speciality: Osteopathy.
P S T (Ref:HM18499)

**SHORT, STEVEN**

**Steven Short**, Health Hydro, Milton Rd, Swindon, **Wiltshire**, SN1 5JA, ENG.
(T) 01793 465631
Speciality: Osteopathy.
P S T (Ref:HM18500)

**SHORTS, KAREN**

**Karen Shorts**, 41 Woodcroft Avenue, Stanmore, **London (Greater)**, HA7 3PT, ENG.
(T) 07970 077276
Speciality: Chiropodists (Podiatrists).
● **Owner** Miss K Shorts
S (Ref:HM18501)

**SHOULDERS, A**

**A Shoulders**, 32 Panfield Lane, Braintree, **Essex**, CM7 2TH, ENG.
(T) 01376 343891
Speciality: Chiropodists (Podiatrists).
● **Owner** Miss A Shoulders
S (Ref:HM18502)

**SHRAGAI, NAOMI**

**Naomi Shragai**, 36 Loveridge Rd, London, **London (Greater)**, NW6 2DT, ENG.
(T) 020 7328 8073
Speciality: Alexander Technique.
● **Owner** Miss N Shragai
P S (Ref:HM18503)

**SHREE-BERKE, L**

**L Shree-Berke**, 5 Shepherds Cl, London, **London (Greater)**, N6 5AG, ENG.
(T) 020 8348 4681
Speciality: Psychotherapy.
B (Ref:HM18504)

**SHREEVE, RACHEL KATHRYN**

**Rachel Kathryn Shreeve**, 6 Lindens Cl, Emsworth, **Hampshire**, PO10 7PY, ENG.
(T) 01243 373769
Speciality: Reflexology.
S T (Ref:HM18505)

**SHREWSBURY CHIROPODY & BEAUTY**

**Shrewsbury Chiropody & Beauty Clinic**, 1 Swan Hill, Shrewsbury, **Shropshire**, SY1 1NQ, ENG.
(T) 01743 361054
Speciality: Chiropodists (Podiatrists).
● **Owner** Mrs M Morris
S (Ref:HM18506)

**SHREWSBURY SOLE CARE**

**Shrewsbury Sole Care**, 4 St. Marys Water Lane, Shrewsbury, **Shropshire**, SY1 2BX, ENG.
(T) 01743 231611
Speciality: Chiropody. ✓
● **Owner/Chiropodist** Mrs J Youde Q: Inst.CH.P.
S Yrs. Est.: 7 (Ref:HM18507)

**SHREWSBURY, MARTIN J**

**Martin J Shrewsbury**, 21 Walter Rd, Swansea, SA1 5NQ, WAL.
(T) 08081 002110 (F) 01792 475264
Speciality: Psychotherapy.
● **Owner** Mr M Shrewsbury
B (Ref:HM18508)

**SHRIMPLIN, BRIAN**

**Brian Shrimplin**, 194 Bull Lane, Rayleigh, **Essex**, SS6 8NN, ENG.
(T) 01268 742676
Speciality: Physiotherapy.
● **Owner** Mr B Shrimplin
P S T (Ref:HM18509)

**SHRIMPTON, D**

**D Shrimpton**, 78 Wrentham Avenue, London, **London (Greater)**, NW10 3HG, ENG.
(T) 020 8964 8757
Speciality: Alexander Technique.
● **Owner** Mr D Shrimpton
P S (Ref:HM18510)

**SHRIMPTON, K**

**K Shrimpton**, 337 Main Rd, Emsworth, **Hampshire**, PO10 8JH, ENG.
(T) 01243 378101 (F) 01243 378101
Speciality: Physiotherapy.
P S T (Ref:HM18511)

**SHRUBBERIES**

**Shrubberies (The)**, Eastwood Rd, London, **London (Greater)**, E18 1BN, ENG.
(T) 020 8491 7077
Speciality: Hypnosis, Psychotherapy.
B (Ref:HM18512)

**SHUKLA, D K**

**D K Shukla**, 245 Kenton Rd, Harrow, **London (Greater)**, HA3 0HQ, ENG.
(T) 020 8907 4352
Speciality: Osteopathy.
P S T (Ref:HM18513)

**SHULAN CLINIC OF ACUPUNCTURE**

**Shulan Clinic Of Acupuncture & Chinese Herbs**, 66 Mowbray Rd, Cambridge, **Cambridgeshire**, CB1 7SY, ENG.
(T) 01223 566888 (F) 01223 566888
Speciality: Acupuncture.
● **Doctor** Dr J Wang
C (Ref:HM18514)

**SHUN-TEN HYPNOTHERAPY**

**Shun-Ten Hypnotherapy**, 10 Fairlands West, Sunderland, **Tyne and Wear**, SR6 9QY, ENG.
(T) 01915 675556 (F) 01915 675556
Speciality: Hypnosis.
● **Director** Mr E Angel
B (Ref:HM18515)

**SHUTTLEWOOD, JOANNE**

**Joanne Shuttlewood**, 12 Orchard St, Hinckley, **Leicestershire**, LE10 1DZ, ENG.
(T) 01455 636425
Speciality: Chiropodists (Podiatrists).
● **Owner** Mrs J Shuttlewood
S (Ref:HM18516)

**SHUTTLEWORTH, JACK**

**Jack Shuttleworth**, Alda House Natural Therapy Centre, Manor House Drive, Coventry, **Midlands (West)**, CV1 2EY, ENG.
(T) 07930 507337
(E) jaq@dial.pipex.com
(W) www.backfixer.co.uk
Speciality: Chiropractic.
● **McTimoney-Corley Chiropractor** Mr J Shuttleworth Q: Dip.Chiro. M: BAAC.
C (Ref:HM18517)

**SHUTTLEWORTH, R E**

**R E Shuttleworth**, 259 Park West, London, **London (Greater)**, W2 2QZ, ENG.
(T) 020 7402 7532
Speciality: Psychiatry.
● **Partner** Mr R Shuttleworth
B (Ref:HM18518)

**SI SHEN CLINIC**

**Si Shen Clinic**, 8 Eastgate Sq, Pickering, **Yorkshire (North)**, YO18 7DP, ENG.
(T) 01751 477439
Speciality: Chiropody, Reflexology. ✓
● **Reflexologist** Karen Clark Q: ITEC. M: ITEC.
● **Chiropodist** Elizabeth Bertley Q: MBChA.
C Yrs. Est.: 9 (Ref:HM18519)

**SIBBALD, A**

**A Sibbald**, 100B Saughton Rd North, Edinburgh, **Edinburgh (City of)**, EH12 7JB, SCO.
(T) 01314 767272
Speciality: Chiropodists (Podiatrists).
● **Owner** Mrs A Sibbald
S (Ref:HM18520)

**SIBBALD, ANNE**

**Anne Sibbald**, 185 Whitehouse Rd, Edinburgh, **Edinburgh (City of)**, EH4 6BU, SCO.
(T) 01313 392141
Speciality: Chiropodists (Podiatrists).
● **Owner** Mrs A Sibbald
S (Ref:HM18521)

**SIBSON, A**

**A Sibson**, The March Centre, 52 Egerton Avenue, Leicester, **Leicestershire**, LE4 0DN, ENG.
(T) 01162 665239
Speciality: Reflexology.
S T (Ref:HM18522)

**SIBSON, AVRIL**

**Avril Sibson**, 45 Rectory Rd, Wanlip, **Leicestershire**, LE7 4PL, ENG.
(T) 01162 675281
Speciality: Reflexology.
S T (Ref:HM18523)

**SIDCUP CHIROPODY SURGERY**

**Sidcup Chiropody Surgery**, 161 Halfway St, Sidcup, **Kent**, DA15 8DA, ENG.
(T) 020 8300 9142
Speciality: Chiropodists (Podiatrists).
S (Ref:HM18524)

**SIDDALL, MARY**

**Mary Siddall**, 19 Kennel Lane, Brockworth, Gloucester, **Gloucestershire**, GL3 4NP, ENG.
(T) 01452 862959
Speciality: Reflexology.
● **Owner** Ms M Siddall
S T (Ref:HM18525)

**SIDDELL, ANGELA**

**Angela Siddell**, 1 Lime Avenue, Camberley, **Surrey**, GU15 2BS, ENG.
(T) 01276 671677
Speciality: Psychotherapy.
● **Owner** Mrs A Siddell
B (Ref:HM18526)

**SIDEBOTTOM, MARGARET**

**Margaret Sidebottom**, 27 Hayward Rd, Oxford, **Oxfordshire**, OX2 8LN, ENG.
(T) 01865 515700
Speciality: Physiotherapy. ✓
● **Physiotherapist** Mrs J Walker Q: MCSP, SRP. M: CSP.
● **Physiotherapist** Mrs M Sidebottom Q: MCSP, SRP. M: CSP.
S (Ref:HM18527)

**SIDEY, J**

**J Sidey**, 52 Furrow Way, Maidenhead, **Berkshire**, SL6 3NY, ENG.
(T) 01628 418787
Speciality: Reflexology.
● **Owner** Mrs J Sidey
S T (Ref:HM18528)

**SIDHOM, A**

**A Sidhom**, Ladywood Surgery, 35 Morville St, Birmingham, **Midlands (West)**, B16 8BU, ENG.
(T) 01214 543774 (F) 01214 565713
Speciality: Acupuncture, Homeopathy, Hypnotherapy, Osteopathy, Psychotherapy. ✓
● **Owner** Dr A Sidhom
● **Practice Manager** Mrs M Lane
C (Ref:HM18529)

**SIDLEY, SAM**

**Sam Sidley**, 12B Oakengrove Court, Oakengrove Rd, Hazlemere, High Wycombe, **Buckinghamshire**, HP15 7LW, ENG.
(T) 07884 268926
Speciality: Reflexology.
S T (Ref:HM18530)

**SIEW, ALLEN**

**Allen Siew**, Scott St Complementary Therapy Centre, 58 Scott St, Barrow-in-Furness, **Cumbria**, LA14 1QE, ENG.
(T) 01229 826700
Speciality: Acupuncture.
O (Ref:HM18531)

**SIGGERY, MARCINE**

**Marcine Siggery**, 5 Fox Hill, Bath, **Somerset**, BA2 5QN, ENG.
(T) 01225 840088
Speciality: Chiropodists (Podiatrists).
● **Owner** Mrs M Siggery
S (Ref:HM18532)

**SIGNALYSIS**

**Signalysis Ltd**, Silver Birches, Private Rd, Rodborough Common, Stroud, **Gloucestershire**, GL5 5BT, ENG.
(T) 01453 873668
Speciality: Complementary Medicines & Therapy.



Key: B Mind-Body Medicine C Complementary Medicine H Self Help Treatment M Medicinal Therapy O Oriental Medicine P Postural Therapy S Manipulative Structural Therapy T Touch Therapy

M (Ref:HM18533)

## SIGNOL, J A

**J A Signol**, 76 Stockport Rd, Romiley, Stockport, **Cheshire**, SK6 3AN, ENG.
(T) 01614 303697
Speciality: Physiotherapy.
● **Owner** Mrs J Signol
P S T (Ref:HM18534)

## SIGRID DE VRIES

**Sigrid De Vries**, 10 Whitethorn Drive, Brackla, Bridgend, CF31 2PQ, WAL.
(T) 01656 767588
Speciality: Chiropractors.
P S T (Ref:HM18535)

## SILLETT, PAULINE

**Pauline Sillett**, Flat 3, 12 Egremont St, Ely, **Cambridgeshire**, CB6 1AE, ENG.
(T) 01353 663064
Speciality: Complementary Medicines & Therapy.
● **Owner** Mrs P Sillett
C M (Ref:HM18536)

## SILLITOE, CHRISTOPHER

**Christopher Sillitoe**, 7 Albert Rd, St. Mary Cray, Orpington, **Kent**, BR5 4AF, ENG.
(T) 01689 606119
Speciality: Reflexology.
S T (Ref:HM18537)

## SILMON, MARY

**Mary Silmon**, 114 London Rd, Gloucester, **Gloucestershire**, GL2 0RR, ENG.
(T) 01452 414976 (F) 01452 414976
Speciality: Hypnosis, Psychotherapy.
● **Owner** Mrs M Silmon
B (Ref:HM18538)

## SILSDEN CHIROPODY CENTRE

**Silsden Chiropody Centre**, 82 Kirkgate, Silsden, Keighley, **Yorkshire (West)**, BD20 0PA, ENG.
(T) 01535 658980
Speciality: Chiropodists (Podiatrists).
● **Owner** Mrs J Ruthven
S (Ref:HM18539)

## SILVER GREY CLINIC

**Silver Grey Clinic**, Silver Grey, London Rd, East Grinstead, **Sussex (West)**, RH19 1QF, ENG.
(T) 01342 324375
Speciality: Osteopathy.
P S T (Ref:HM18540)

## SILVER WING CENTRE

**Silver Wing Centre**, Hillview, Lidsing Rd, Lidsing, Gillingham, **Kent**, ME7 3NH, ENG.
(T) 01634 389904
Speciality: Complementary Medicines & Therapy.
● **Owner** Mrs S Grose
C M (Ref:HM18541)

## SILVER, EVELYN

**Evelyn Silver**, 12 Chapel St, Belper, **Derbyshire**, DE56 1AR, ENG.
(T) 01773 820220
Speciality: Acupuncture.
O (Ref:HM18542)

## SILVER, J

**Mr J Silver**, The Chigwell Lane Surgery, 16 Chigwell Lane, Loughton, **Essex**, IG10 3RW, ENG.
(T) 020 8508 9223
Speciality: Chiropodists (Podiatrists).
S (Ref:HM18543)

## SILVER, JEANETTE

**Jeanette Silver**, 3 Pepperbox Rise, Whaddon, Salisbury, **Wiltshire**, SP5 3BF, ENG.
(T) 01722 711114
Speciality: Complementary Medicines & Therapy.
● **Owner** Miss J Silver
C M (Ref:HM18544)

## SILVERCREST HOLISTIC CLINIC

**Silvercrest Holistic Clinic**, Perciville St, Kanturk, **County Cork**, IRE.
(T) 029 5133 8
Speciality: Healing.
B (Ref:HM18545)

## SILVERHILL CHIROPODIST CENTRE

**Silverhill Chiropodist Centre**, 71 Sedlescombe Rd North, St. Leonards-On-Sea, **Sussex (East)**, TN37 7DS, ENG.
(T) 01424 425025
Speciality: Chiropodists (Podiatrists).
S (Ref:HM18546)

## SILVER-LEIGH, V

**V Silver-Leigh**, 64B Princes Way, London, **London (Greater)**, SW19 6JF, ENG.
(T) 020 8788 5291 (F) 020 8788 5291
Speciality: Psychotherapy.
● **Owner** Ms V Silver-Leigh
B (Ref:HM18547)

## SILVERMAN, MAURICE

**Maurice Silverman**, 2 Ringley Drive, Whitefield, Manchester, **Manchester (Greater)**, M45 7LF, ENG.
(T) 01617 663576
Speciality: Psychiatry.
● **Owner** Dr M Silverman
B (Ref:HM18548)

## SIMCOE CLINIC

**Simcoe Clinic**, 39 Archers Rd, Southampton, **Hampshire**, SO15 2NB, ENG.
(T) 023 8022 7200 (F) 023 8033 3176
Speciality: Acupressure, Chiropody, Chiropractic, Herbal Medicine, Homeopathy, Manipulation, Naturopathy, Nutritional Therapy, Podiatry, Reflexology, Ultrasonics, Vitamin Therapy, X-Ray. ✓
● **Doctor** Dr E Holme Q: DC, ND. M: BCA, GCC, RN.
S Yrs. Est.: 38 (Ref:HM18549)

## SIMISTER, KAREN

**Karen Simister**, 53 Mallion Court, Waltham Abbey, **Essex**, EN9 3EQ, ENG.
(T) 01992 715745
Speciality: Reflexology.
S T (Ref:HM18550)

## SIMMERLING, LUNIA

**Lunia Simmerling**, 69 Parkland Gr, Ashford, **Surrey**, TW15 2JF, ENG.
(T) 01784 252474
Speciality: Reflexology.
S T (Ref:HM18551)

## SIMMONDS HERBAL SUPPLIES

**Simmonds Herbal Supplies**, Unit 12 Hove Bus Centre, Fonthill Rd, Hove, **Sussex (East)**, BN3 6HA, ENG.
(T) 01273 381937
Speciality: Herbal Medicine.
M (Ref:HM18552)

## SIMMONDS, BRIAN

**Brian Simmonds**, Green Park Rd, Dudley, **Midlands (West)**, DY2 7LZ, ENG.
(T) 01384 254627
Speciality: Chiropodists (Podiatrists).
● **Owner** Mr B Simmonds
S (Ref:HM18553)

## SIMMONDS, J

**J Simmonds**, Stafford Clinic, Crown House, The Boulevard, Weston-Super-Mare, **Somerset**, BS23 1NN, ENG.
(T) 01934 412011
Speciality: Physiotherapy.
P S T (Ref:HM18554)

## SIMMONDS, J

**J Simmonds**, 47 Hewett Rd, Portsmouth, **Hampshire**, PO2 0QS, ENG.
(T) 023 9235 3547
Speciality: Floral Essence Therapy, Metamorphic Therapy, Reflexology. ✓ [credit card]
● **Complementary Therapist**
Ms J Simmonds Q: DHH, Dr.Ac. M: BFVEA, BRA.
C T Yrs. Est.: 17 (Ref:HM18555)

## SIMMONDS, JEAN

**Jean Simmonds**, 3 Chapel St, Chichester, **Sussex (West)**, PO19 1BU, ENG.
(T) 01243 786050
Speciality: Chiropodists (Podiatrists).
S (Ref:HM18556)

## SIMMONDS, JENNI

**Jenni Simmonds**, 11 High St, Greenhithe, **Kent**, DA9 9NL, ENG.
(T) 01322 380110 (F) 01322 383033
Speciality: Aromatherapy.
● **Director** Mrs J Simmonds
M O (Ref:HM18557)

## SIMMONDS, JENNI

**Jenni Simmonds**, Lakeside Shopping Centre, West Thurrock, Grays, **Essex**, RM20 2ZT, ENG.
(T) 01708 862209
Speciality: Aromatherapy.
● **Owner** Mrs J Simmonds
M O (Ref:HM18558)

## SIMMONDS, K M

**K M Simmonds**, Hafodlas, Tregaron, **Ceredigion**, SY25 6UG, WAL.
(T) 01974 298920
Speciality: Acupuncture.
O (Ref:HM18559)

## SIMMONS, BEATRICE

**Beatrice Simmons**, 41 Sylvester Rd, London, **London (Greater)**, N2 8HN, ENG.
(T) 020 8346 3638
Speciality: Alexander Technique.
● **Owner** Mrs B Simmons
P S (Ref:HM18560)

## SIMMONS, J C

**J C Simmons**, 32 Clairview Rd, Furzedown, London, **London (Greater)**, SW19 6LD, ENG.
(T) 020 8677 5329
Speciality: Physiotherapy.
P S T (Ref:HM18561)

## SIMMONS, R

**Mr R Simmons**, 41 Evelyn Cresent, Sunbury-On-Thames, **Surrey**, TW16 6ND, ENG.
(T) 01932 770601
Speciality: Osteopathy.
P S T (Ref:HM18562)

## SIMMONS, ROBIN

**Robin Simmons**, 4 Martys Yard, Hampstead High St, London, **London (Greater)**, NW3 1QW, ENG.
(T) 020 7435 4940 (F) 020 7794 2652
Speciality: Alexander Technique.
● **Owner** Mr R Simmons
P S (Ref:HM18563)

## SIMMS, KATHERINE

**Katherine Simms**, 28 Baring Rd, Croydon, **Surrey**, CR0 7DD, ENG.
(T) 020 8656 3603
Speciality: Absent Healing, Crystal Healing, Meditation, Pilates, Reflexology, Yoga. ✓
● **Owner/Teacher/Healer**
Miss K Simms Q: Dip.Crys.Heal, Dip.Reflex, Dip.Yoga. M: BWY.
B Yrs. Est.: 10 (Ref:HM18564)

## SIMMS, SYLVIA D

**Sylvia D Simms**, 55 Hearsall Lane, Coventry, **Midlands (West)**, CV5 6HF, ENG.
(T) 024 7667 6859
Speciality: Complementary Medicines & Therapy.
C M (Ref:HM18565)

## SIMON LAU CENTRE

**Simon Lau Centre**, 28 Old Brompton Rd, London, **London (Greater)**, SW7 3DL, ENG.
(T) 020 7581 1118 (F) 020 7581 1118
Speciality: Complementary Medicines & Therapy.
● **Owner** Mr S Lau
C M (Ref:HM18566)

## SIMON, CAROLYN

**Carolyn Simon**, 12 Asmun's Hill, Hampstead Garden Suberb, London, **London (Greater)**, NW11 6ET, ENG.
(T) 020 8458 2147
(E) carolyn_simon@tmi.co.uk
(W) www.alexandertechnique.com/londonnw11
Speciality: Alexander Technique. ✓
● **Teacher of the Alexander Technique**
Ms C Simon Q: ATI, MSTAT. M: ATI, STAT.
H Yrs. Est.: 5 (Ref:HM18567)

**SIMON, DAVE**

**Dave Simon**, Ashton House, 4 West St, Ryde, **Isle of Wight**, PO33 2NN, ENG.
(T) 01983 614795
Speciality: Psychotherapy.
B (Ref:HM18568)

**SIMONDS, KATHARINE**

**Katharine Simonds**, 202 Wendover Rd, Weston Turville, Aylesbury, **Buckinghamshire**, HP22 5TG, ENG.
(T) 01296 612585
Speciality: Physiotherapy.
● **Owner** Mrs K Simonds
P S T (Ref:HM18569)

**SIMONE OLDS ASSOCIATES**

**Simone Olds Associates**, 134 Harley St, London, **London (Greater)**, W1N 1AH, ENG.
(T) 020 7486 0669 (F) 020 7486 0669
Speciality: Physiotherapy.
● **Owner** Ms S Olds
P S T (Ref:HM18570)

**SIMONE OLDS ASSOCIATES**

**Simone Olds Associates**, The Southghate Beaumont, 15 Cannon Hill, Old Southgate, London, **London (Greater)**, N14 7JU, ENG.
(T) 07973 498520 (F) 020 8886 5381
Speciality: Physiotherapy.
● **Owner** Ms S Olds
P S T (Ref:HM18571)

**SIMONS, ROBERT ALLEN (DR)**

**Dr Robert Allen Simons**, Breaffy South, Spanish Point, Miltown Malbay, **County Clare**, IRE.
(T) 06570 84728
Speciality: Counselling, Family Therapy, Group Therapy, Humanistic Psychology, Psychotherapy, Rogerian Therapy.
● **Clinical Psychologist**
Dr R Simons Q: BA, PhD.
B Yrs. Est.: 35 (Ref:HM18572)

**SIMPKIN, JOY**

**Joy Simpkin**, 5 Grassington Rd, Eastbourne, **Sussex (East)**, BN20 7BP, ENG.
(T) 01323 452343
Speciality: Complementary Medicines & Therapy.
C M (Ref:HM18573)

**SIMPKINS, JILL**

**Jill Simpkins**, 29 Market Pl, Poulton-le-Fylde, **Lancashire**, FY6 7BS, ENG.
(T) 01253 893738
Speciality: Hypnotherapy.
● **Owner** Mrs J Simpkins
B (Ref:HM18574)

**SIMPLE ESSENTIALS**

**Simple Essentials**, The Garden Room Clinic, Deanhouse Farm, Church Rd, Newdigate, Dorking, **Surrey**, RH5 5DL, ENG.
(T) 01306 631930 (F) 01306 631930
Speciality: Complementary Medicines & Therapy.
● **Owner** Ms K Joslig
M (Ref:HM18575)

**SIMPLY FIT & HEALTHY**

**Simply Fit & Healthy**, 25 Heatherside Rd, Epsom, **Surrey**, KT19 9QS, ENG.
(T) 020 8224 8749 (F) 020 8873 2843
Speciality: Complementary Medicines & Therapy.
● **Owner** Mrs B Dimmock
M (Ref:HM18576)

**SIMPLY HERBAL CLINIC**

**Simply Herbal Clinic**, Highcroft Cottage, Totteridge, London, **London (Greater)**, N20 8NL, ENG.
(T) 020 8446 4031
Speciality: Aromatherapy, Complementary Therapy, Do-In, Herbal Medicine, Massage (Therapeutic), Nutritional Therapy, Stress Therapy.
● **Medical Herbalist** Mrs C Poster Q: ITEC (Hons), MH, Reg.Med.Herb. M: GCP, IRCH.
M (Ref:HM18577)

**SIMPLY HERBAL COLLEGE**

**Simply Herbal College Of Complementary Therapies**, 22A Edgwarebury Lane, Edgware, **London (Greater)**, HA8 8LW, ENG.
(T) 020 8958 8442
Speciality: Complementary Medicines & Therapy.
● **Partner** Mr C Poster
M (Ref:HM18578)

**SIMPLY NATURAL**

**Simply Natural**, 13 Mountain View Cl, Connah's Quay, Deeside, **Flintshire**, CH5 4HH, WAL.
(T) 01244 836615
Speciality: Aromatherapy.
● **Owner** Mrs M Pipkins
M O (Ref:HM18579)

**SIMPLY NATURAL ESSENTIAL OILS**

**Simply Natural Essential Oils**, 5 Dalton Court, Astmoor Industrial Estate, Runcorn, **Cheshire**, WA7 1PU, ENG.
(T) 01928 574777
Speciality: Aromatherapy.
● **Partner** Mrs M Pipkin
M O (Ref:HM18580)

**SIMPLY PERFECT BY JAN**

**Simply Perfect by Jan**, 144 Buccleuch St, Barrow-in-Furness, **Cumbria**, LA14 1BZ, ENG.
(T) 01229 828446
Speciality: Aromatherapy, Beauty Therapy, Relaxation. ✔
● **Beauty Therapist/Aromatherapist**
Ms J Jeffs M: BABTAC.
C Yrs. Est.: 2 (Ref:HM18581)

**SIMPLY QUARTZ**

**Simply Quartz**, Clyde Valley Country Estate, Crossford, Carluke, **Lanarkshire (South)**, ML8 5NJ, SCO.
(T) 01555 860847
Speciality: Complementary Medicines & Therapy.
● **Owner** Mr M Taylor
M (Ref:HM18582)

**SIMPLY SOAPS**

**Simply Soaps**, Unit B, Ronald Rolph Court, Wadloes Rd, Cambridge, **Cambridgeshire**, CB5 8PX, ENG.
(T) 01223 413066
Speciality: Aromatherapy.
● **Owner** Mr L Campion
M O (Ref:HM18583)

**SIMPSON CLINIC**

**Simpson Clinic**, The Simpson Clinic, 106 Higher Lane, Rainford, St. Helens, **Merseyside**, WA11 8AZ, ENG.
(T) 01744 883737
(E) harry-julie@fsmail
Speciality: Acupuncture, Allergy Testing, Aromatherapy, Aura Therapy, Bach Remedies, Bio-energetics, Biofeedback, Chiropractic, Cognitive Therapy, Complementary Therapy, Cranial Osteopathy, Dietician, Dowsing, Electrotherapy, Gem Essence Therapy, Hay Diet, Herbal Medicine, Homeopathy, Iridology, Kinesiology, Life Style Coaching, Macrobiotics, Manipulation, Massage (Therapeutic), Miasm Therapy, Micro Manipulation, Music Therapy, Naturopathy, Nutritional Therapy, Osteopathy, Phytotherapy, Vitamin Therapy, Ying & Yang, Clinical Kinesiololgy, Applied Kinesiology, Life Style Advice, De-Tox Therapy, Health Checks, Total Health Rebalancing, Alternative Medicine, Alternative Medical Therapy. ✔ CREDIT
● **Practitioner** Mr H Simpson Q: Dip.Ac, DO. M: BOrthA, ICAK, MAA.
S Yrs. Est.: 23 (Ref:HM18584)

**SIMPSON, ANNE**

**Anne Simpson**, 94 Parrock St, Gravesend, **Kent**, DA12 1EX, ENG.
(T) 01474 326657
Speciality: Homeopathy.
● **Partner** Ms A Simpson
M (Ref:HM18585)

**SIMPSON, ANNE**

**Anne Simpson**, 240 Maidstone Rd, Chatham, **Kent**, ME4 6JN, ENG.
(T) 01634 842583
Speciality: Homeopathy.
● **Partner** Mrs A Simpson
M (Ref:HM18586)

**SIMPSON, ANNE**

**Anne Simpson**, 26 Station Rd, Meopham, Gravesend, **Kent**, DA13 0LX, ENG.
(T) 01474 815755
Speciality: Homeopathy.
● **Owner** Ms A Simpson
M (Ref:HM18587)

**SIMPSON, HEATHER**

**Heather Simpson**, Mayfield, **Sussex (East)**, TN20, ENG.
(T) 01435 872556
Speciality: Bach Remedies.
M (Ref:HM18588)

**SIMPSON, HEIDI**

**Heidi Simpson**, 2 Garden Court, Aldwick Grange, Bognor Regis, **Sussex (West)**, PO21 4XW, ENG.
(T) 01243 822512 (F) 01243 827216
Speciality: Complementary Medicines & Therapy.
● **Owner** Heidi Simpson
C M (Ref:HM18589)

**SIMPSON, JACQUELINE**

**Jacqueline Simpson**, 49 High St, Steeton, Keighley, **Yorkshire (West)**, BD20 6NT, ENG.
(T) 01535 655371
Speciality: Reflexology.
S T (Ref:HM18590)

**SIMPSON, JANET**

**Janet Simpson**, 33 Limebrest Avenue, Thornton, **Lancashire**, FY5 5AT, ENG.
(T) 01253 825035 (F) 01253 825035
Speciality: Physiotherapy.
● **Owner** Mrs J Simpson
P S T (Ref:HM18591)

**SIMPSON, JUNE**

**June Simpson**, 19 Perryhill Drive, Sandhurst, **Berkshire**, GU47 8HS, ENG.
(T) 01252 878239
Speciality: Reflexology.
S T (Ref:HM18592)

**SIMPSON, K C**

**K C Simpson**, Appledore Cottage, 56 Church St, Boughton Monchelsea, Maidstone, **Kent**, ME17 4HN, ENG.
(T) 01622 743062
Speciality: Chiropodists (Podiatrists).
● **Owner** Mr K Simpson
S (Ref:HM18593)

**SIMPSON, MARGARET**

**Margaret Simpson**, 3 Lindfield Rd, London, **London (Greater)**, W5 1QS, ENG.
(T) 020 8997 3613
Speciality: Reflexology.
S T (Ref:HM18594)

**SIMPSON, NICK**

**Nick Simpson**, 17 Chiltern Cl, Halesowen, **Midlands (West)**, B63 1HS, ENG.
(T) 01215 501751
Speciality: Osteopathy.
P S T (Ref:HM18595)

**SIMPSON, PAT**

**Pat Simpson**, 68 Bond St, Englefield Green, Egham, **Surrey**, TW20 0PX, ENG.
(T) 01784 438340
Speciality: Hypnosis.
● **Owner** Mrs P Simpson
B (Ref:HM18596)

**SIMPSON, S**

**S Simpson**, 337 Main Rd, Emsworth, **Hampshire**, PO10 8JH, ENG.
(T) 01243 378101 (F) 01243 378101
Speciality: Physiotherapy.
P S T (Ref:HM18597)

**SIMPSON, SARAH E**

**Sarah E Simpson**, 8 Vicarage Way, Arksey, Doncaster, **Yorkshire (South)**, DN5 0TG, ENG.
(T) 01302 874630
Speciality: Chiropody. ✔
● **Owner/Chiropodist** Mrs S Simpson Q: MBChA. M: SSCh.
M Yrs. Est.: 20 (Ref:HM18598)



Key: B Mind-Body Medicine; C Complementary Medicine; H Self Help Treatment; M Medicinal Therapy; O Oriental Medicine; P Postural Therapy; S Manipulative Structural Therapy; T Touch Therapy

## SIMPSON, STELLA
**Stella Simpson**, The Craven Clinic, 54 Cambridge Gr, Hammersmith, London, **London (Greater)**, W6 0LA, ENG.
(T) 07973 684908 (F) 08701 249274
(E) stella.simpson@lineone.net
Speciality: Acupuncture, Herbal Medicine, Massage (Therapeutic).
● **Owner** Ms S Simpson
(T) 020 8451 1529
O (Ref:HM18599)

## SIMS, A
**A Sims**, 1 Marine Hill, Clevedon, **Somerset**, BS21 7PW, ENG.
(T) 01275 874832
Speciality: Osteopathy.
● **Director** Mr A Sims
P S T (Ref:HM18600)

## SIMS, MICHAEL
**Michael Sims**, 162 South Norwood Hill, London, **London (Greater)**, SE25 6AJ, ENG.
(T) 020 8771 4344
Speciality: Chiropodists (Podiatrists).
S (Ref:HM18601)

## SIMS, TRACEY
**Tracey Sims**, 14 Churchill Way, Cardiff, **Glamorgan (Vale of)**, CF10 2DW, WAL.
(T) 029 2064 5335
Speciality: Chiropody. ✔
● **Chiropodist** Ms T Sims
M Yrs. Est.: 18 (Ref:HM18602)

## SIN MUI CHONG-MARTIN
**Sin Mui Chong-Martin**, Littlehampton Natural Health Centre, 10C Granville Rd, Littlehampton, **Sussex (West)**, BN17 5JU, ENG.
(T) 01903 734373
Speciality: Acupuncture.
● **Owner** Mrs S Chong-Martin
O (Ref:HM18603)

## SINCLAIR, W J
**W J Sinclair**, 215 Kingsway, Dunmurry, Belfast, **County Antrim**, BT17 9SB, NIR.
(T) 028 9030 1202
Speciality: Osteopathy.
P S T (Ref:HM18604)

## SINDALL, K M J
**K M J Sindall**, Hollytree Cottage, 45 Station Rd, Cogenhoe, Northampton, **Northamptonshire**, NN7 1LU, ENG.
(T) 01604 891588
Speciality: Chiropodists (Podiatrists).
S (Ref:HM18605)

## SINENORE, S
**S Sinenore**, Chesterfield Clinic, Holywell Annexe, Holywell St, Chesterfield, **Derbyshire**, S41 7SH, ENG.
(T) 01246 200311
Speciality: Chiropractic.
P S T (Ref:HM18606)

## SINGER, S
**S Singer**, 80 Peppard Rd, Sonning Common, Reading, **Berkshire**, RG4 9RP, ENG.
(T) 01189 724615
Speciality: Chiropodists (Podiatrists).
S (Ref:HM18607)

## SINGH, A
**A Singh**, 44 Kingsford Avenue, Nottingham, **Nottinghamshire**, NG7 5QR, ENG.
(T) 01159 700504
Speciality: Chiropodists (Podiatrists).
● **Owner** Mr A Singh
S (Ref:HM18608)

## SINGH, GURU
**Guru Singh**, 100a Priory Rd, West Hampstead, London, **London (Greater)**, NW6 3NS, ENG.
(T) 020 7916 9295
Speciality: Osteopathy.
P S T (Ref:HM18609)

## SINGLETON, ANNE
**Anne Singleton**, 33 Field Barn Rd, Hampton Magna, Warwick, **Warwickshire**, CV35 8RX, ENG.
(T) 01926 402206
Speciality: Complementary Medicines & Therapy.
● **Owner** Mrs A Singleton
C M (Ref:HM18610)

## SINGLETON, MARI
**Mari Singleton**, 8 Lyttelton Rd, Droitwich, **Worcestershire**, WR9 7AA, ENG.
(T) 01905 774077
Speciality: Reflexology.
S T (Ref:HM18611)

## SINGLETON, POLLY
**Polly Singleton**, Kendal Physiotherapy And Sports Injury Centre, 96 Stricklandgate, Kendal, **Cumbria**, ENG.
(T) 01539 725220
Speciality: Floral Essence Therapy, Herbal Medicine, Homeopathy, Nutritional Therapy.
● **Homeopath** Ms P Singleton
M Yrs. Est.: 2 (Ref:HM18612)

## SINNOTT, A
**A Sinnott**, 18 Thurstaston Rd, Irby, Wirral, **Merseyside**, CH61 0HE, ENG.
(T) 01516 481759
Speciality: Psychology.
● **Owner** A Sinnott
B (Ref:HM18613)

## SINO HERBS & HEALTH
**Sino Herbs & Health**, 116 The Broadway, London, **London (Greater)**, SW19 1RH, ENG.
(T) 020 8543 0248
Speciality: Herbalists.
● **Owner** Mr P Wu
M (Ref:HM18614)

## SINO-HERBAL CLINIC
**Sino-Herbal Clinic**, 249 Dumbarton Rd, Glasgow, **Glasgow (City of)**, G11 6AB, SCO.
(T) 01413 410888 (F) 01413 410888
Speciality: Acupressure, Acupuncture, Complementary Therapy, Cupping, Herbal Medicine, Massage (Therapeutic). ✔
● **Manager** Dr G Guo M: ATCM UK.
C O Yrs. Est.: 4 (Ref:HM18615)

## SINYARD, CONSTANCE
**Constance Sinyard**, 76 Russell Rd, Lee-On-The-Solent, **Hampshire**, PO13 9HP, ENG.
(T) 023 9255 0726
Speciality: Chiropodists (Podiatrists).
● **Owner** Mrs C Sinyard
S (Ref:HM18616)

## SIOW, YONG CHAI
**Yong Chai Siow**, 139 Preston Rd, Wembley, **London (Greater)**, HA9 8NW, ENG.
(T) 020 8904 9388 (F) 020 8904 8888
Speciality: Acupuncture.
● **Owner** Mr Y Siow
O (Ref:HM18617)

## SIOW, YONG CHAI
**Yong Chai Siow**, 10 Harley St, London, **London (Greater)**, W1N 1AA, ENG.
(T) 020 7467 9300
Speciality: Acupuncture.
O (Ref:HM18618)

## SIRDEFIELD, PAUL
**Paul Sirdefield**, 5 Vimy Rd, Wednesbury, **Midlands (West)**, WS10 9BQ, ENG.
(T) 01215 318645
Speciality: Reflexology.
S T (Ref:HM18619)

## SIRIUS LODGE
**Sirius Lodge Of Natural Therapy & Teaching**, 11 Arundle House, 22 The Drive, Hove, **Sussex (East)**, BN3 3JD, ENG.
(T) 01273 777464
Speciality: Complementary Medicines & Therapy.
C M (Ref:HM18620)

## SITTERS, LATONA
**Latona Sitters**, 192 Sandbrook Rd, Southport, **Merseyside**, PR8 3RW, ENG.
(T) 01704 571920
Speciality: Psychotherapy.
● **Owner** Mrs C Regan
B (Ref:HM18621)

## SITTING ROOMS
**Sitting Rooms**, 6 Sydney Pl, Wellington Rd, **County Cork**, IRE.
(T) 021 4507 033
Speciality: Complementary Medicines & Therapy.
M (Ref:HM18622)

## SITTINGBOURNE OSTEO PRACTICE
**Sittingbourne Osteopathic Practice (The)**, Suit 1 The Old Ct House, Roman Sq, Sittingbourne, **Kent**, ME10 4BJ, ENG.
(T) 01795 420408
Speciality: Osteopathy.
● **Owner** Mr M Smith
P S T (Ref:HM18623)

## SIVANANDA YOGA TEACHER
**Affiliated Sivananda Yoga Teacher**, Parsonage Hall, Bishop's Stortford, **Hertfordshire**, CM23 2DT, ENG.
(T) 01279 834670
Speciality: Relaxation Technique.
● **Owner** Mr N Kerby
H T (Ref:HM18624)

## SIVES, ALEX
**Alex Sives**, 25 The Fairway, Flackwell Heath, High Wycombe, **Buckinghamshire**, HP10 9NF, ENG.
(T) 01628 521689
Speciality: Chiropodists (Podiatrists).
● **Owner** Mr A Sives
S (Ref:HM18625)

## SIVYER, ANNE-MARIE
**Anne-Marie Sivyer**, Back To Health, 2 Charles St, Petersfield, **Hampshire**, GU32 3EH, ENG.
(T) 01730 267423
Speciality: Osteopathy.
P S T (Ref:HM18626)

## SIXTH SCENTS
**Sixth Scents**, 15 Oliver Twist Cl, Rochester, **Kent**, ME1 1RT, ENG.
(T) 01634 408603
Speciality: Complementary Medicines & Therapy.
● **Owner** Mr C Herbert
C M (Ref:HM18627)

## SJY CHINESE MEDICINE
**SJY Chinese Medicine**, 96 Tower Bridge Rd, London, **London (Greater)**, SE1 4TP, ENG.
(T) 020 7252 0698 (F) 020 8801 6618
Speciality: Herbal Medicine.
● **Owner** Mr Y Shi
M (Ref:HM18628)

## SKEDD, L A
**L A Skedd**, 169 Dalkeith Rd, Edinburgh, **Edinburgh (City of)**, EH16 5BY, SCO.
(T) 01316 672676
Speciality: Chiropody. ✔
● **Chiropodist** Mrs L Skedd Q: DPodM, M.S.C.P, S.R.Ch.
● **Owner/Chiropodist** Mrs M Ellis Q: BSc, DPodM, M.S.C.P, S.R.Ch.
B Yrs. Est.: 16 (Ref:HM18629)

## SKEELS, LILIAN
**Lilian Skeels**, 29 Wellingtonians, Warfield Park, Bracknell, **Berkshire**, RG42 3RL, ENG.
(T) 01344 886269
Speciality: Clairvoyants & Palmists.
B (Ref:HM18630)

## SKELCEY, SUE
**Sue Skelcey**, Ingledale, 1 Tanhouse Rd, Oxted, **Surrey**, RH8 9PE, ENG.
(T) 01883 717277
Speciality: Homeopathy.
M (Ref:HM18631)

## SKELIAN CHIROPRACTIC CLINIC
**Skelian Chiropractic Clinic**, St Pauls Medical Centre, 121 Swindon Rd, Cheltenham, **Gloucestershire**, GL50 4DP, ENG.
(T) 01242 254000 (F) 01242 254400
Speciality: Chiropractors.
● **Partner** Mr S Smillie
P S T (Ref:HM18632)



Key continued: **Yrs.Est:** Years Established **Q:** Qualifications **M:** Professional Membership ✔ Indemnity Insurance Accept Credit Cards

## SKELIAN CHIROPRACTIC CLINIC
**Skelian Chiropractic Clinic**, 314A Prestbury Rd, Prestbury, Cheltenham, **Gloucestershire**, GL52 3DD, ENG.
(T) 01242 252222 (F) 01242 254488
Speciality: Chiropractic.
● **Owner** Mr K Walker
P S T (Ref:HM18633)

## SKELLAM, L J
**L J Skellam**, Market Pl, Leek, **Staffordshire**, ST13 5HH, ENG.
(T) 01538 383726
Speciality: Physiotherapy.
● **Owner** Mrs L Skellam
P S T (Ref:HM18634)

## SKELTON, JAN
**Jan Skelton**, 39 Fairlane, Shaftesbury, **Dorset**, SP7 8RT, ENG.
(T) 01747 852604
Speciality: Aromatherapy, Complementary Therapy, Holistic Healing, Massage (Therapeutic), Reflexology, Touch Therapy, Baby Massage Instruction/Workshops. ✔
● **Owner** Mrs J Skelton Q: ITEC. M: AoR, DACP, GCP.
T Yrs. Est.: 6 (Ref:HM18635)

## SKELTON, VAL
**Val Skelton**, 12 Beulah Walk, Woldingham, Caterham, **Surrey**, CR3 7LL, ENG.
(T) 01883 652098 (F) 01883 652890
Speciality: Reflexology.
● **Owner** Mrs V Skelton
S T (Ref:HM18636)

## SKERRIES HEALING CENTRE
**Skerries Healing Centre**, 85 Strand St, Skerries, **County Dublin**, IRE.
(T) 01849 4457
Speciality: Healing.
B (Ref:HM18637)

## SKIDDY, SUSAN
**Susan Skiddy**, 2 Tunbridge Gr, Kents Hill, Milton Keynes, **Buckinghamshire**, MK7 6JD, ENG.
(T) 01908 663032
Speciality: Reflexology.
S T (Ref:HM18638)

## SKIDMORE, JOYCE
**Joyce Skidmore**, Oldham, **Lancashire**, OL8, ENG.
(T) 01616 205183
Speciality: Bach Remedies.
M (Ref:HM18639)

## SKILLING, GRAHAN
**Graham Skilling**, 11 Coburg Rd, Dorchester, **Dorset**, DT1 2HN, ENG.
(T) 01305 260016
Speciality: Homeopathy.
● **Owner** Mr G Skilling
M (Ref:HM18640)

## SKILLING, W
**W Skilling**, 49 John St, Sunderland, **Tyne and Wear**, SR1 1QH, ENG.
(T) 01915 655125
Speciality: Chiropodists (Podiatrists).
● **Owner** Mr W Skilling
S (Ref:HM18641)

## SKILTON, GINA
**Gina Skilton**, 6a Moss Drive, Basildon, **Essex**, SS16 4SA, ENG.
(T) 01268 584869
Speciality: Reflexology.
S T (Ref:HM18642)

## SKIN CLINIC
**Skin Clinic (The)**, 98 The Drive, Hove, **Sussex (East)**, BN3 6GP, ENG.
(T) 01273 776499
Speciality: Complementary Medicines & Therapy.
● **Manager** Mr M Al-Khasaji
C M (Ref:HM18643)

## SKIN DEEP
**Skin Deep**, Holstein Avenue, Rochdale, **Lancashire**, OL12 6DL, ENG.
(T) 01706 522931
Speciality: Complementary Medicines & Therapy.
● **Owner** Miss J Devereux
C M (Ref:HM18644)

## SKIN DEEP BEAUTY SALON
**Skin Deep Beauty Salon**, 345A Copnor Rd, Portsmouth, **Hampshire**, PO3 5EQ, ENG.
(T) 023 9267 0746
Speciality: Electrolysis.
● **Sole Director** Ranjiv Kaur Gill
T (Ref:HM18645)

## SKINGLE, C F
**C F Skingle**, 16 High St, Stony Stratford, Milton Keynes, **Buckinghamshire**, MK11 1AF, ENG.
(T) 01908 562355
Speciality: Chiropodists (Podiatrists).
● **Owner** Mr D Roberts
S (Ref:HM18646)

## SKINGLE, P
**Mr P Skingle**, 20 William Avenue, Folkestone, **Kent**, CT19 5TL, ENG.
(T) 01303 850650 (F) 01303 850650
Speciality: Chiropodists (Podiatrists).
● **Owner** Mr P Skingle
S (Ref:HM18647)

## SKINGLEY, R M
**R M Skingley**, Brynsiriol, St. Clears, Carmarthen, **Carmarthenshire**, SA33 4AH, WAL.
(T) 01994 230289
Speciality: Chiropodists (Podiatrists).
● **Owner** Mrs R Skingley
S (Ref:HM18648)

## SKINNER, A
**A Skinner**, 4 Stansby Pk, The Reddings, Cheltenham, **Gloucestershire**, GL51 6RS, ENG.
(T) 01452 713221
Speciality: Complementary Medicines & Therapy.
● **Owner** Mr A Skinner
M (Ref:HM18649)

## SKINNER, B
**B Skinner**, 26 Poulton Cl, Birmingham, **Midlands (West)**, B13 9SD, ENG.
(T) 01214 491964
Speciality: Chiropodists (Podiatrists).
S (Ref:HM18650)

## SKINNER, C
**C Skinner**, Old Vicarage Court, Chiverton Cross, Blackwater, Truro, **Cornwall**, TR4 8HS, ENG.
(T) 01872 560400
Speciality: Physiotherapy.
● **Owner** Mrs C Skinner
P S T (Ref:HM18651)

## SKINNER, G
**G Skinner**, The Chestnuts, Mounton Rd, Chepstow, **Monmouthshire**, NP16 6AA, WAL.
(T) 01291 624498
Speciality: Osteopathy.
● **Owner** Mr G Skinner
P S T (Ref:HM18652)

## SKINNER, JEAN R
**Skinner Jean R**, 7c Bolton Rd, Eastbourne, **Sussex (East)**, BN21 3JU, ENG.
(T) 01323 643754
Speciality: Chiropodists (Podiatrists).
S (Ref:HM18653)

## SKINNER, JEAN R
**Jean R Skinner**, Vicarage Rd, Hailsham, **Sussex (East)**, BN27 1BN, ENG.
(T) 01323 841500
Speciality: Chiropodists (Podiatrists).
S (Ref:HM18654)

## SKINNER, LORNA
**Lorna Skinner**, 66 Crouch Field, Boxmoor, Hemel Hempstead, **Hertfordshire**, HP1 1PD, ENG.
(T) 01442 215639
Speciality: Acupuncture.
● **Owner** Ms L Skinner Q: MBAcC.
O (Ref:HM18655)

## SKINNER, NICOLA
**Nicola Skinner**, 18 Kelly Cl, **Dorset**, BH17 8QP, ENG.
(T) 01202 381906
Speciality: Indian Head Massage, Reflexology, Remedial Massage.
S T (Ref:HM18656)

## SKIPPINGS & ASSOCIATES
**Skippings & Associates**, Christine House, Sorbonne Cl, Thornaby, Stockton-On-Tees, **Cleveland**, TS17 6DA, ENG.
(T) 01642 633888 (F) 01642 608886
(W) www.chiro.c.uk
Speciality: Chiropractic. ✔
● **Chiropractor** Miss A Laursen Q: BSc, MSc. M: GCC.
● **Chiropractor** Mr R Skippings Q: DC. M: GCC.
P Yrs. Est.: 6 (Ref:HM18657)

## SKIPTON CHIROPODY CENTRE
**Skipton Chiropody Centre**, 10 Sackville St, Skipton, **Yorkshire (North)**, BD23 2PH, ENG.
(T) 01756 793223
Speciality: Chiropody. ✔
● **Chiropodist (Podiatrist)**
Mr B Jones Q: DPodM, M.S.C.P, S.R.Ch. M: S.C.P.
S Yrs. Est.: 38 (Ref:HM18658)

## SKIPTON PHYSIOTHERAPY CLINIC
**Skipton Physiotherapy Clinic**, 10 Sackville St, Skipton, **Yorkshire (North)**, BD23 2PH, ENG.
(T) 01756 790089
Speciality: Physiotherapy.
● **Owner** Mrs A Iveson
P S T (Ref:HM18659)

## SKOLFIELD, PEARL
**Pearl Skolfield**, 118 Tile Kiln Lane, Hemel Hempstead, **Hertfordshire**, HP3 8NX, ENG.
(T) 01442 254243
Speciality: Complementary Medicines & Therapy.
● **Owner** Mrs P Skofield
C M (Ref:HM18660)

## SKULL, MARK
**Mark Skull**, Marlborough Physiotherapy Clinic, 3 New Rd, Marlborough, **Wiltshire**, SN8 1ZZ, ENG.
(T) 01672 516182
Speciality: Physiotherapy.
P S T (Ref:HM18661)

## SKUSE, CLARE
**Clare Skuse**, 4 Forest Rd, Fishponds, Bristol, BS16 3XJ, ENG.
(T) 01179 652667
Speciality: Reflexology.
S T (Ref:HM18662)

## SKY DANCING UK TANTRA
**Sky Dancing UK Tantra**, 47 Maple Rd, Bristol, BS7 8RE, ENG.
(T) 01179 830958
Speciality: Complementary Medicines & Therapy.
● **Owner** Mr D Thompson
C M (Ref:HM18663)

## SKY DANCING UK TANTRA
**Sky Dancing UK Tantra**, 183 Godstow Rd, Oxford, **Oxfordshire**, OX2 8PG, ENG.
(T) 01865 428374
Speciality: Complementary Medicines & Therapy.
● **Organiser** Robert Osborn
M (Ref:HM18664)

## SLACK, ANDREW
**Andrew Slack State Registered Chiropodist**, 681 Edenfield Rd, Rochdale, **Lancashire**, OL11 5SL, ENG.
(T) 01706 657631
Speciality: Chiropodists (Podiatrists).
S (Ref:HM18665)

## SLADDIN, ANGELA J
**Angela J Sladdin**, 5 Heath Gardens, Halifax, **Yorkshire (West)**, HX3 0BD, ENG.
(T) 01422 352926
Speciality: Chiropodists (Podiatrists).
● **Owner** Ms A Sladdin
S (Ref:HM18666)

## SLADE OSTEOPATHIC PRACTICE
**Slade Osteopathic Practice**, 12 The Slade, Plumstead, London, **London (Greater)**, SE18

Key: B Mind-Body Medicine, C Complementary Medicine, H Self Help Treatment, M Medicinal Therapy, O Oriental Medicine, P Postural Therapy, S Manipulative Structural Therapy, T Touch Therapy

2NB, ENG.
(T) 020 8316 5316
Speciality: Cranial Osteopathy, Osteopathy.
✔
● **Osteopath** Miss T Turner Q: BSc, Hons (OST). M: GOsC.
C Yrs. Est.: 3 (Ref:HM18667)

## SLADE, JOHN

**John Slade**, 86 Clifden Rd, London, **London (Greater)**, E5 0LN, ENG.
(T) 020 8533 0022
Speciality: Psychotherapy.
B (Ref:HM18668)

## SLADE, LORNA

**Lorna Slade**, 85 Aylesbury Rd, Aston Clinton, Aylesbury, **Buckinghamshire**, HP22 5AQ, ENG.
(T) 01296 632054
Speciality: Hypnosis.
B (Ref:HM18669)

## SLADE, ZENA

**Zena Slade**, 24 Market St, Staveley, Chesterfield, **Derbyshire**, S43 3UT, ENG.
(T) 01246 477725
Speciality: Chiropodists (Podiatrists).
● **Owner** Mr J Ward
S (Ref:HM18670)

## SLANE, JOHN

**John Slane**, 5 Cambridge Avenue, Consett, **County Durham**, DH8 8DQ, ENG.
(T) 01207 501859
Speciality: Complementary Medicines & Therapy.
● **Owner** Mr J Slane
M (Ref:HM18671)

## SLATER, D C

**D C Slater**, 8 Lapwing Cl, Northway, Tewkesbury, **Gloucestershire**, GL20 8TN, ENG.
(T) 01684 290305
Speciality: Counselling, Hypnosis, Hypnotherapy, Smoking & Weight £45.00 includes 2 sessions and self help support packs.
✔
● **Clinical Hypnotherapist**
Mr D Slater Q: BA, Dip.Couns, Dip.Hyp, DSc, MASC. M: HA.
B Yrs. Est.: 9 (Ref:HM18672)

## SLATER, GISELE

**Gisele Slater**, Timbers, The Spinney, Springfield Lane, Marford, **Wrexham**, LL12 8TG, WAL.
(T) 01244 570259
Speciality: Reflexology.
S T (Ref:HM18673)

## SLATER, HUGH

**Hugh Slater**, 14 Beach Avenue, Leigh-On-Sea, **Essex**, SS9 1HP, ENG.
(T) 01702 473044
Speciality: Reflexology.
S T (Ref:HM18674)

## SLATER, JULIA

**Julia Slater**, South View, Whitegate, Halifax, **Yorkshire (West)**, HX3 9JP, ENG.
(T) 01422 346894
Speciality: Reflexology.
● **Owner** Mrs J Slater
S T (Ref:HM18675)

## SLATER, M

**M Slater**, 53 Vicarage Avenue, Derby, **Derbyshire**, DE23 6TQ, ENG.
(T) 01332 383219
Speciality: Hypnosis.
B (Ref:HM18676)

## SLATTERY, BRIDGET

**Bridget Slattery**, 67 Brighton Rd, Purley, **Surrey**, CR8 4HD, ENG.
(T) 020 8660 3592
Speciality: Counselling. ✔
● **Counsellor/Therapist**
Ms B Slattery M: BACP.
B Yrs. Est.: 3 (Ref:HM18677)

## SLATTERY, DENIS (DR)

**Slattery Dr Denis M R O**, Spine Sport & Limb Clinic Long Longford Rd, Mullingar, **County Westmeath**, IRE.
(T) 04442 993 (F) 04443 046
Speciality: Osteopathy.
P S T (Ref:HM18678)

## SLATTERY, JENNIFER

**Jennifer Slattery**, Downs House, Baydon, Marlborough, **Wiltshire**, SN8 2JS, ENG.
(T) 01488 71055
Speciality: Physiotherapy.
P S T (Ref:HM18679)

## SLATTERY, KAREN

**Slattery Karen**, No1 Stratford Haven Orwell Rd, Rathgar, **County Dublin**, IRE.
(T) 01492 3720
Speciality: Psychotherapy.
B (Ref:HM18680)

## SLATTERY, NOELEEN

**Slattery Noeleen D Ac P Hyp**, Main St, Rathcoole, **County Dublin**, IRE.
(T) 01458 9672 (F) 01458 9705
(E) noleencm@gofree.indigo.ie
Speciality: Complementary Medicines & Therapy.
M (Ref:HM18681)

## SLAUGHTER, J

**J Slaughter**, 6 Chandlers Cl, Wymondham, **Norfolk**, NR18 0BS, ENG.
(T) 01953 603242
Speciality: Chiropodists (Podiatrists).
S (Ref:HM18682)

## SLEE, L R

**Mr L R Slee**, Bickington Rd, Sticklepath, Barnstaple, **Devon**, EX31 2DB, ENG.
(T) 01271 379355
Speciality: Chiropodists (Podiatrists).
S (Ref:HM18683)

## SLEIGHT, C

**C Sleight**, 8 Princess Rd, Seaham, **County Durham**, SR7 7SP, ENG.
(T) 01915 130122
Speciality: Chiropodists (Podiatrists).
● **Owner** Mrs C Sleight
S (Ref:HM18684)

## SLESS, DEBORAH

**Deborah Sless**, 23 Patshull Rd, London, **London (Greater)**, NW5 2JX, ENG.
(T) 020 7485 2664
Speciality: Psychotherapy.
● **Owner** Ms D Sless
B (Ref:HM18685)

## SLIGO CHIROPRACTIC

**Sligo Chiropractic**, 4 Lr Pearse Rd, **County Sligo**, IRE.
(T) 07160 001 (F) 07161 010
(W) www.chiropractic-ireland.com
Speciality: Chiropractic, X-Ray. ✔
● **Chiropractor** Dr H Mc Quaid Q: BSc, DC. M: CAI.
B S Yrs. Est.: 4 (Ref:HM18686)

## SLIGO HYPNOTHERAPY CLINIC

**Sligo Hypnotherapy Clinic**, Weston House, Union St, **County Sligo**, IRE.
(T) 07150 255
Speciality: Hypnotherapy.
B (Ref:HM18687)

## SLIP, ANNE

**Anne Slip**, 44 Heathermount Drive, Crowthorne, **Berkshire**, RG45 6HN, ENG.
(T) 01344 775329
Speciality: Acupuncture.
● **Owner** Mrs A Slip
O (Ref:HM18688)

## SLOPER, P

**P Sloper**, 41 Oak Rd, Stowupland, Stowmarket, **Suffolk**, IP14 4DP, ENG.
(T) 01449 674142
Speciality: Chiropodists (Podiatrists).
● **Owner** Mr P Sloper
S (Ref:HM18689)

## SLOUGH SPORTS INJURIES CLINIC

**Slough Sports Injuries Clinic (The)**, Station Rd, Langley, Slough, **Berkshire**, SL3 8BY, ENG.
(T) 01753 584458 (F) 01753 584458
Speciality: Physiotherapy. ✔
● **Physiotherapist/Owner**
Mrs A Thompson Q: MCSP, SRP. M: CSP.
S Yrs. Est.: 20 (Ref:HM18690)

## SLR HEALTHCARE

**SLR Healthcare**, 6 Main St, Staveley, Knaresborough, **Yorkshire (North)**, HG5 9LD, ENG.
(T) 01423 340791
Speciality: Complementary Medicines & Therapy.
● **Owner** Ms S Richards
M (Ref:HM18691)

## SMALL, JONATHAN

**Jonathan Small**, Health First, Daventry St, Southam, **Warwickshire**, CV47 1PH, ENG.
(T) 01926 811272
Speciality: Chiropodists (Podiatrists).
● **Owner** Mr J Small
S (Ref:HM18692)

## SMALL, LORNA

**Lorna Small**, 17 Hamford Drive, Great Oakley, Harwich, **Essex**, CO12 5AU, ENG.
(T) 01255 886037
Speciality: Reflexology.
S T (Ref:HM18693)

## SMALL, P C

**P C Small**, 73 Oxford St, Burnham-on-Sea, **Somerset**, TA8 1EW, ENG.
(T) 01278 783188
Speciality: Chiropodists (Podiatrists).
S (Ref:HM18694)

## SMALLBROOK CLINIC

**Smallbrook Clinic**, Smallbrook Barn, Thursley, Godalming, **Surrey**, GU8 6QN, ENG.
(T) 01252 703607
Speciality: Osteopathy.
P S T (Ref:HM18695)

## SMALLCORN, KAREN A

**Karen A Smallcorn**, 5 High St, Bognor Regis, **Sussex (West)**, PO21 1RQ, ENG.
(T) 01243 862832 (F) 01243 841849
Speciality: Osteopathy.
● **Owner** Mrs K Smallcorn
P S T (Ref:HM18696)

## SMALLWOOD ELECTRICAL

**Smallwood Electrical**, Unit 23 Ard Business Park, Polo Grounds, New Inn, Pontypool, **Monmouthshire**, NP4 0SW, WAL.
(T) 01495 740074 (F) 01495 740044
Speciality: Electrolysis.
● **Owner** Mr S Smallwood
T (Ref:HM18697)

## SMALLWOOD, P

**P Smallwood**, 64 Clarendon St, Leamington Spa, **Warwickshire**, CV32 4PE, ENG.
(T) 01926 314839
Speciality: Biomechanics, Chiropody, Cryo Surgery, Orthotics, Podiatry. ✔
● **Owner/Chiropodist** Mr P Smallwood Q: B.A.Ch.P, BSc (Hons), M.S.C.P, S.R.Ch.
● **Secretary** Mrs J Rose
M Yrs. Est.: 18 (Ref:HM18698)

## SMALLWOOD, TREVOR

**Trevor Smallwood**, 41 Tilehouse Green Lane, Knowle, Solihull, **Midlands (West)**, B93 9EZ, ENG.
(T) 01564 776488
Speciality: Hypnosis.
● **Owner** Mr A Smallwood
B (Ref:HM18699)

## SMART, DOUGLAS & LOGAN

**Smart, Douglas & Logan**, 15 Victoria Rd, Darlington, **County Durham**, DL1 5SF, ENG.
(T) 01325 486503
Speciality: Chiropodists (Podiatrists).
● **Partner** Mrs K Douglas
S (Ref:HM18700)

## SMART, JULIE

**Julie Smart**, Abbey View Complementary Clinic, Abbey View Medical Centre, Shaftesbury, **Dorset**, SP7 8DH, ENG.
(T) 01747 856719 (F) 01747 856701
Speciality: Chiropodists (Podiatrists).


Key continued: Yrs.Est: Years Established Q: Qualifications M: Professional Membership ✔ Indemnity Insurance Accept Credit Cards

**S** (**Ref:**HM18701)

### SMEED, BEATE

**Beate Smeed**, 110 Salmon St, London, **London (Greater)**, NW9 8NJ, ENG.
**(T)** 020 8200 6149
Speciality: Reflexology.
**S T** (**Ref:**HM18702)

### SMER, IRENE

**Irene Smer**, 6 Northolm, Edgware, **London (Greater)**, HA8 9RL, ENG.
**(T)** 020 8959 2099
Speciality: Reflexology.
● **Owner** Mrs I Smer
**S T** (**Ref:**HM18703)

### SMETHURST, ALISON

**Alison Smethurst-Reflexology & Therapeutic Massage**, First Floor, 15 Friar St, Reading, **Berkshire**, RG1 1DB, ENG.
**(T)** 01189 585551 **(F)** 01189 585551
**(E)** handyfeet@freeserve.co.uk
Speciality: Aromatherapy, Massage (Therapeutic), Reflexology. ✓
● **Reflexologist/Masseuse**
Ms A Smethurst **Q:** HND, ITEC. **M:** IIHHT, IPTI.
**C** Yrs. Est.: 3 (**Ref:**HM18704)

### SMILE CENTRE

**Smile Centre**, Dental Surgery, 5 Victoria Embankment, Nottingham, **Nottinghamshire**, NG2 2JY, ENG.
**(T)** 01159 864745 **(F)** 01159 864741
Speciality: Complementary Medicines & Therapy.
● **Principal** Mr M Mander
**C M** (**Ref:**HM18705)

### SMITH, A

**A Smith**, 16 Beckenham Rd, Beckenham, **Kent**, BR3 4LS, ENG.
**(T)** 020 8650 4313
Speciality: Osteopathy.
● **Owner** A Smith
**P S T** (**Ref:**HM18706)

### SMITH, A C

**A C Smith**, 17 Arran Rd, Troon, **Ayrshire (South)**, KA10 6TD, SCO.
**(T)** 01292 313290
Speciality: Complementary Medicines & Therapy.
● **Owner** A C Smith
**C M** (**Ref:**HM18707)

### SMITH, A C

**A C Smith**, The Rolle Clinic, 6 Rolle Rd, Exmouth, **Devon**, EX8 2AB, ENG.
**(T)** 01395 222666
Speciality: Osteopathy.
● **Owner** Mr A Smith
**P S T** (**Ref:**HM18708)

### SMITH, ALAN

**Alan Smith**, 21 Coleridge Rd, Oldham, **Lancashire**, OL1 4RH, ENG.
**(T)** 01616 337731
Speciality: Hypnotherapy.
● **Owner** Mr A Smith
**B** (**Ref:**HM18709)

### SMITH, ALAN

**Alan Smith**, 44 Wood Lane, Wickersley, Rotherham, **Yorkshire (South)**, S66 1JX, ENG.
**(T)** 01709 544661 **(F)** 01709 533635
Speciality: Physiotherapy.
● **Owner** Mr A Smith
**P S T** (**Ref:**HM18710)

### SMITH, ALAN P

**Alan P Smith**, 38 The Barroon, Castle Donington, Derby, **Derbyshire**, DE74 2PE, ENG.
**(T)** 01332 853777
**(W)** www.healthcounts.co.uk
Speciality: Osteopathy. ✓
● **Osteopath** Alan Smith **Q:** BSc (Hons), DO, MSc. **M:** GOsC.
**S** Yrs. Est.: 8 (**Ref:**HM18711)

### SMITH, ALICIA

**Alicia Smith**, 17 Fotheringham Rd, Ayr, **Ayrshire (South)**, KA8 0EY, SCO.
**(T)** 01292 281793
**(E)** aliciasmith@supanet.com
Speciality: Cognitive Therapy, Complementary Therapy, Counselling, Hypnosis, Hypnotherapy, Psychotherapy, Reflexology, Stress Therapy. ✓
● **Therapist** Ms A Smith **Q:** BA, Dip.Hyp, Dip.Psych, GSSR. **M:** BACP, COSCA, NRHP, SIR, UKCP.
**B** Yrs. Est.: 9 (**Ref:**HM18712)

### SMITH, ALLAN

**Allan Smith**, Gemellus, Coychurch, Bridgend, CF35 5HB, WAL.
**(T)** 01656 863450
Speciality: Osteopathy.
**P S T** (**Ref:**HM18713)

### SMITH, AMANDA

**Amanda Smith**, Willow Lodge, 114 London Rd, Worcester, **Worcestershire**, WR5 2DY, ENG.
**(T)** 01905 763234
Speciality: Reflexology.
**S T** (**Ref:**HM18714)

### SMITH, ANDREW

**Andrew Smith**, 59A Greenside Rd, London, **London (Greater)**, W12 9JQ, ENG.
**(T)** 08456 012572
Speciality: Hypnosis.
● **Owner** Mr A Smith
**B** (**Ref:**HM18715)

### SMITH, ANN

**Ann Smith**, 22 Herbert Rd, Bath, **Somerset**, BA2 3PP, ENG.
**(T)** 01225 336729
Speciality: Reflexology.
**S T** (**Ref:**HM18716)

### SMITH, ANNE C

**Anne C Smith**, 3 High St, Snaith, Goole, **Humberside (North)**, DN14 9HF, ENG.
**(T)** 01405 869196
Speciality: Chiropodists (Podiatrists).
● **Owner** Mrs A Smith
**S** (**Ref:**HM18717)

### SMITH, ANNE C

**Anne C Smith**, 38 New Lane, Selby, **Yorkshire (North)**, YO8 4QB, ENG.
**(T)** 01757 213413
Speciality: Chiropodists (Podiatrists).
● **Partner** Mr D Davies
**S** (**Ref:**HM18718)

### SMITH, B S

**Miss B S Smith**, 17 The Sq, Kenilworth, **Warwickshire**, CV8 1EB, ENG.
**(T)** 01926 856397
Speciality: Chiropodists (Podiatrists).
● **Owner** Miss B Smith
**S** (**Ref:**HM18719)

### SMITH, BARBARA

**Barbara Smith**, 50 Stocks Lane, East Wittering, Chichester, **Sussex (West)**, PO20 8NJ, ENG.
**(T)** 01243 673812
Speciality: Chiropody. ✓
● **Chiropodist (Podiatrist)**
Ms B Smith **Q:** MBChA, MSSCh.
**C** Yrs. Est.: 16 (**Ref:**HM18720)

### SMITH, BERYL

**Beryl Smith**, 50 Nethermead Court, Northampton, **Northamptonshire**, NN3 8NF, ENG.
**(T)** 01604 786284
Speciality: Clairvoyants & Palmists.
● **Owner** Mrs B Smith
**B** (**Ref:**HM18721)

### SMITH, C

**C Smith**, Royal British Legion Club, Lansdown, Bourton-On-The-Water, Cheltenham, **Gloucestershire**, GL54 2AR, ENG.
**(T)** 01451 821840
Speciality: Chiropodists (Podiatrists).
● **Owner** Ms C Smith
**S** (**Ref:**HM18722)

### SMITH, C J

**C J Smith**, Fisher Medical Centre, Millfields, Coach St, Skipton, **Yorkshire (North)**, BD23 1EU, ENG.
**(T)** 01756 797838 **(F)** 01756 796194
Speciality: Chiropractic. ✓
● **Owner/Chiropractor** Dr C Smith **Q:** BCA, DC. **M:** BCA.
**P** Yrs. Est.: 5 (**Ref:**HM18723)

### SMITH, CANDIDA

**Candida Smith**, 7 The Burdwood Centre, Thatcham, **Berkshire**, RG19 4YA, ENG.
**(T)** 01635 871948
Speciality: Osteopathy.
● **Owner** Miss C Smith
**P S T** (**Ref:**HM18724)

### SMITH, CHARLES

**Charles Smith**, 29 Burcott Rd, Purley, **Surrey**, CR8 4AD, ENG.
**(T)** 020 8660 4086
Speciality: Osteopathy.
● **Owner** Mr C Smith
**P S T** (**Ref:**HM18725)

### SMITH, CHERYL

**Cheryl Smith**, 90 Margaret House, Berryfields Rd, Sutton Coldfield, **Midlands (West)**, B76 2UQ, ENG.
**(T)** 01213 784487
Speciality: Reflexology.
**S T** (**Ref:**HM18726)

### SMITH, CHRISTINE R

**Christine R Smith**, 10C West St, Oundle, Peterborough, **Cambridgeshire**, PE8 4EF, ENG.
**(T)** 01832 275050
Speciality: Chiropodists (Podiatrists).
**S** (**Ref:**HM18727)

### SMITH, CHRISTOPHER (DR)

**Dr Christopher Smith**, 24 Warehouse Lane, Foulridge, Colne, **Lancashire**, BB8 7PP, ENG.
**(T)** 01282 866199
Speciality: Aromatherapy, Chiropractic. ✓
● **Chiropractor** Dr C Smith **Q:** BCA, DC.
**P** Yrs. Est.: 3 (**Ref:**HM18728)

### SMITH, CHRISTOPHER R A

**Christopher R A Smith**, Manse Health Centre, 54 East St, Andover, **Hampshire**, SP10 1ES, ENG.
**(T)** 01264 323901
Speciality: Osteopathy.
● **Owner** Mr C Smith
**P S T** (**Ref:**HM18729)

### SMITH, COLIN

**Colin Smith**, 44 Oak Lodge Avenue, Chigwell, **Essex**, IG7 5HZ, ENG.
**(T)** 020 8500 5957
Speciality: Chiropodists (Podiatrists).
● **Owner** Mr C Smith
**S** (**Ref:**HM18730)

### SMITH, D

**D Smith**, 22 Bullsmoor Lane, Enfield, **London (Greater)**, EN3 6TN, ENG.
**(T)** 01992 763119
Speciality: Acupuncture.
● **Owner** Mrs D Smith
**O** (**Ref:**HM18731)

### SMITH, D

**D Smith**, Lynch View, Cheltenham Rd, Bagendon, Cirencester, **Gloucestershire**, GL7 7BH, ENG.
**(T)** 01285 831222
Speciality: Chiropodists (Podiatrists).
● **Owner** Mrs D Smith
**S** (**Ref:**HM18732)

### SMITH, DEBORAH

**Deborah Smith**, Flat 3, 23 Limes Gr, London, **London (Greater)**, SE13 6DD, ENG.
**(T)** 020 8318 0160
Speciality: Psychotherapy.
**B** (**Ref:**HM18733)

### SMITH, DEREK M

**Derek M Smith**, 1 Hone Court, Oldbury Rd, Tewkesbury, **Gloucestershire**, GL20 5NB, ENG.
**(T)** 01684 296277
Speciality: Chiropodists (Podiatrists).
● **Owner** Mr D Smith
**S** (**Ref:**HM18734)

### SMITH, DOUGLAS V

**Douglas V Smith**, Fairport, Beacon Reach, Hope Cove, Kingsbridge, **Devon**, TQ7 3HF, ENG.

(T) 01548 561304
Speciality: Chiropodists (Podiatrists).
S (Ref:HM18735)

### SMITH, E
**E Smith**, 1a Rockfield Drive, Llandudno, **Conwy**, LL30 1PF, WAL.
(T) 01492 583330
Speciality: Physiotherapy.
P S T (Ref:HM18736)

### SMITH, E
**E Smith**, Physiotherapy Clinic, 1 High St, Houghton Regis, Dunstable, **Bedfordshire**, LU5 5BE, ENG.
(T) 01582 867831
Speciality: Physiotherapy.
P S T (Ref:HM18737)

### SMITH, EDWARD J
**Edward J Smith**, 9a Rosebery Rd, Epsom, **Surrey**, KT18 6AF, ENG.
(T) 01372 278597
Speciality: Hypnosis.
B (Ref:HM18738)

### SMITH, EILEEN
**Eileen Smith**, 32A Rockingham Avenue, Hornchurch, **Essex**, RM11 1HH, ENG.
(T) 01708 441317
Speciality: Reflexology.
S T (Ref:HM18739)

### SMITH, ELIZABETH M
**Elizabeth M Smith**, 6 Raikes Prde, Blackpool, **Lancashire**, FY1 4EX, ENG.
(T) 01253 751894
Speciality: Chiropodists (Podiatrists).
● **Owner** Mrs E Smith
S (Ref:HM18740)

### SMITH, EVELYN
**Evelyn Smith**, 5 Stanhope Drive, Wirral, **Merseyside**, CH62 2DF, ENG.
(T) 01513 342579
Speciality: Homeopathy.
M (Ref:HM18741)

### SMITH, G
**G Smith**, 20 Sydenham Villas Rd, Cheltenham, **Gloucestershire**, GL52 6DZ, ENG.
(T) 01242 514347
Speciality: Chiropodists (Podiatrists).
● **Owner** Mr G Smith
S (Ref:HM18742)

### SMITH, G
**G Smith**, 58 High St, Ilfracombe, **Devon**, EX34 9QB, ENG.
(T) 01271 865989
Speciality: Chiropodists (Podiatrists).
● **Owner** Mr G Smith
S (Ref:HM18743)

### SMITH, GILL
**Gill Smith**, 14 Morvale Gardens, Stourbridge, **Midlands (West)**, DY9 8DF, ENG.
(T) 07710 216012
Speciality: Reflexology.
S T (Ref:HM18744)

### SMITH, GILLIAN
**Gillian Smith**, 16 Wetherfield, Stansted, **Essex**, CM24 8JA, ENG.
(T) 01279 815606 (F) 01279 815606
Speciality: Complementary Medicines & Therapy.
● **Owner** Mrs G Smith
C M (Ref:HM18745)

### SMITH, GINA MERRETT
**Gina Merrett Smith**, Backwell, Bristol, BS48, ENG.
(T) 01275 462069
Speciality: Bach Remedies.
M (Ref:HM18746)

### SMITH, GRAHAM
**Graham Smith**, 39 Nutgrove Avenue, Bristol, BS3 4QF, ENG.
(T) 01179 639639
Speciality: Hypnosis.
B (Ref:HM18747)

### SMITH, IRENE B
**Irene B Smith**, 267 Brandon St, Motherwell, **Lanarkshire (North)**, ML2 1RS, SCO.
(T) 01698 253223
Speciality: Bowen Therapy, Massage (Therapeutic), Reiki, Remedial Massage, Sports Massage. ✔
● **Owner** Mrs I Smith Q: Dip.Massage, RGN. M: BRCP.
T Yrs. Est.: 4 (Ref:HM18748)

### SMITH, J
**Mrs J Smith**, 73 Woodchester Rd, Dorridge, Solihull, **Midlands (West)**, B93 8EL, ENG.
(T) 01564 771888
Speciality: Chiropodists (Podiatrists).
● **Owner** Mrs J Smith
S (Ref:HM18749)

### SMITH, J R
**J R Smith**, 16 Beckenham Rd, Beckenham, **Kent**, BR3 4LS, ENG.
(T) 020 8650 4313
Speciality: Osteopathy.
P S T (Ref:HM18750)

### SMITH, JANET
**Janet Smith**, 12 Windermere Rd, Townville, Castleford, **Yorkshire (West)**, WF10 3NQ, ENG.
(T) 01977 511030
Speciality: Bowen Therapy, Kinesiology, Massage (Therapeutic), Reiki, Yoga. ✔
● **Holistic Health Care Practitioner** Ms J Smith Q: BTER, KFRP, LCSP, MASC. M: BSY, BTER, KFRP, LCSP.
S Yrs. Est.: 21 (Ref:HM18751)

### SMITH, JEANETTE
**Jeanette Smith**, 6 Quince Rd, Hardwick, Cambridge, **Cambridgeshire**, CB3 7XJ, ENG.
(T) 01954 211102
Speciality: Reflexology. ✔
● **Reflexologist** Mrs J Smith Q: MCSR, MRxS.
T Yrs. Est.: 9 (Ref:HM18752)

### SMITH, JENNIE
**Jennie Smith**, 17 The Birchwoods, Tilehurst, Reading, **Berkshire**, RG31 5UH, ENG.
(T) 01189 426378
Speciality: Reflexology.
S T (Ref:HM18753)

### SMITH, JEREMY
**Jeremy Smith**, 2a Wrightington St, Wigan, **Lancashire**, WN1 2AZ, ENG.
(T) 01942 244873
Speciality: Chiropodists (Podiatrists).
S (Ref:HM18754)

### SMITH, JODY
**Jody Smith**, 10 Donaldson Cr, Kirkintilloch, Glasgow, **Glasgow (City of)**, G66 1XF, SCO.
(T) 01417 775002
Speciality: Physiotherapy.
P S T (Ref:HM18755)

### SMITH, JOHN
**John Smith**, 5 Radcot Cl, Nine Elms, Swindon, **Wiltshire**, SN5 9UY, ENG.
(T) 01793 878956
Speciality: Complementary Medicines & Therapy.
M (Ref:HM18756)

### SMITH, JUDY
**Judy Smith**, 21 Wheelwrights, Weston Turville, Aylesbury, **Buckinghamshire**, HP22 5QS, ENG.
(T) 01296 612003
Speciality: Reflexology.
S T (Ref:HM18757)

### SMITH, JULIET L
**Juliet L Smith**, Otteley, Oddington, Kidlington, **Oxfordshire**, OX5 2RA, ENG.
(T) 01865 331681
Speciality: Homeopathy.
M (Ref:HM18758)

### SMITH, K B
**K B Smith**, 22 Wellfield Rd, Walsall, **Midlands (West)**, WS9 8JD, ENG.
(T) 01922 451499
Speciality: Aromatherapy.
● **Owner** Mrs K Smith
M O (Ref:HM18759)

### SMITH, K C
**K C Smith**, 48 Church Rd, Malvern, **Worcestershire**, WR14 1NG, ENG.
(T) 01684 568744 (F) 01684 568744
Speciality: Osteopathy.
● **Owner** Mr H Smith
P S T (Ref:HM18760)

### SMITH, K S
**K S Smith**, 68 Gravesend Rd, Rochester, **Kent**, ME2 3PN, ENG.
(T) 01634 724308
Speciality: Chiropodists (Podiatrists).
● **Owner** Mrs K Smith
S (Ref:HM18761)

### SMITH, KATHY
**Kathy Smith**, Rippleside, Portishead, Bristol, BS20 6ND, ENG.
(T) 01275 848117
Speciality: Complementary Medicines & Therapy.
● **Owner** Mrs K Smith
C M (Ref:HM18762)

### SMITH, KENNETH
**Kenneth Smith**, 2 Golf Cottages, Godden Green, Sevenoaks, **Kent**, TN15 0JJ, ENG.
(T) 01732 763848
Speciality: Reflexology.
S T (Ref:HM18763)

### SMITH, LEONIE MARIA
**Smith Leonie Maria**, 182 The Willows Ballincollig, Cork, **County Cork**, IRE.
(T) 021 4871 559
Speciality: Complementary Medicines & Therapy.
M (Ref:HM18764)

### SMITH, LES
**Les Smith**, 118 Westcroft, Honley, Huddersfield, **Yorkshire (West)**, HD7 2JP, ENG.
(T) 01484 661996
Speciality: Hypnosis.
● **Owner** Mr L Smith
B (Ref:HM18765)

### SMITH, LESLEY
**Lesley Smith**, 10 Witchards, Basildon, **Essex**, SS16 5BG, ENG.
(T) 01268 281885
Speciality: Hypnosis.
B (Ref:HM18766)

### SMITH, LORRETTA W
**Lorretta W Smith**, Old Rectory Practice, Duck St, Wendens Ambo, Saffron Walden, **Essex**, CB11 4JU, ENG.
(T) 01799 540980 (F) 01799 525546
Speciality: Physiotherapy.
● **Owner** Ms L Smith
P S T (Ref:HM18767)

### SMITH, LYNDSAY
**Lyndsay Smith**, 2 York Rise, Rayleigh, **Essex**, SS6 8SD, ENG.
(T) 01702 525227
Speciality: Reflexology.
S T (Ref:HM18768)

### SMITH, M
**M Smith**, 6 North Malvern Rd, Malvern, **Worcestershire**, WR14 4LT, ENG.
(T) 01684 562371
Speciality: Homeopathy.
● **Owner** Mr M Smith
M (Ref:HM18769)

### SMITH, M
**M Smith**, 272 Gordon Avenue, Camberley, **Surrey**, GU15 2NU, ENG.
(T) 01276 20411 (F) 01276 20411
Speciality: Osteopathy.
● **Owner** Mr S Green
P S T (Ref:HM18770)

### SMITH, M
**M Smith**, 45 High St, Rochester, **Kent**, ME1 1LP, ENG.
(T) 01634 880202
Speciality: Osteopathy.
● **Owner** Mr M Smith



Key continued: Yrs.Est: Years Established Q: Qualifications M: Professional Membership ✔ Indemnity Insurance Accept Credit Cards

P S T (Ref:HM18771)

**SMITH, M F**

**M F Smith**, 30 Valley Rd, Bromley, **Kent**, BR2 0HD, ENG.
(T) 020 8460 1489
Speciality: Chiropodists (Podiatrists).
S (Ref:HM18772)

**SMITH, MAGGIE**

**Maggie Smith**, 28 Russell Rd, Walton-On-Thames, **Surrey**, KT12 2JZ, ENG.
(T) 01932 225810
Speciality: Complementary Medicines & Therapy.
● **Owner** Miss M Smith
C M (Ref:HM18773)

**SMITH, MARC**

**Marc Smith**, 8 Woodlands Cr, Harrogate, **Yorkshire (North)**, HG2 7BA, ENG.
(T) 01423 886487
Speciality: Hypnotherapy.
● **Owner** Mr M Smith
B (Ref:HM18774)

**SMITH, MARK**

**Mark Smith**, 5 Jacob Cl, Windsor, **Berkshire**, SL4 5PT, ENG.
(T) 01753 854674
Speciality: Chiropodists (Podiatrists).
● **Owner** Mr M Smith
S (Ref:HM18775)

**SMITH, MARK**

**Mark Smith**, 71A Highgate, Kendal, **Cumbria**, LA9 4ED, ENG.
(T) 01539 721796
Speciality: Chiropractors.
P S T (Ref:HM18776)

**SMITH, MARTIN**

**Martin Smith**, 35 St Marks Rd, Windsor, **Berkshire**, SL4 3BD, ENG.
(T) 01753 850613
Speciality: Alexander Technique.
P S (Ref:HM18777)

**SMITH, MATTHEW**

**Matthew Smith**, 23 Eyre Pl, Edinburgh, **Edinburgh (City of)**, EH3 5EX, SCO.
(T) 01315 572211
Speciality: Osteopathy.
P S T (Ref:HM18778)

**SMITH, MATTHEW**

**Matthew Smith**, Edinburgh Osteopatic Surgery, 187 Dalkeith Rd, Edinburgh, **Edinburgh (City of)**, EH16 5BY, SCO.
(T) 01316 671234
Speciality: Osteopathy.
P S T (Ref:HM18779)

**SMITH, MICHAEL**

**Michael Smith**, 8 Wedgewood Rd, Lincoln, **Lincolnshire**, LN6 3LU, ENG.
(T) 01522 883991
Speciality: Hypnosis, Hypnotherapy. ✔
● **Hypnotherapist** Mr M Smith Q: Dip.Hyp. M: HS, NCH.
H Yrs. Est.: 2 (Ref:HM18780)

**SMITH, MING**

**Ming Smith**, 45 Hartwell Rd, Hanslope, Milton Keynes, **Buckinghamshire**, MK19 7BY, ENG.
(T) 01908 510594
Speciality: Chiropodists (Podiatrists).
● **Owner** Mrs M Smith
S (Ref:HM18781)

**SMITH, MOLLY-ANN**

**Molly-Ann Smith**, 40 Shotteswell Rd, Shirley, Solihull, **Midlands (West)**, B90 2RN, ENG.
(T) 01217 446279
Speciality: Hypnosis.
● **Owner** Mrs M Smith
B (Ref:HM18782)

**SMITH, NIGEL (DR)**

**Dr Nigel Smith**, 20A Central Avenue, West Bridgeford, West Bridgford, Nottingham, **Nottinghamshire**, NG2 5GR, ENG.
(T) 01159 143311
Speciality: Hypnotherapy.
B (Ref:HM18783)

**SMITH, P**

**P Smith**, 252 Cheriton Rd, Folkestone, **Kent**, CT19 4DN, ENG.
(T) 01303 278188
Speciality: Osteopathy.
● **Owner** Mr P Smith
P S T (Ref:HM18784)

**SMITH, P (DR)**

**Dr P Smith**, Plas Penrhyn, Penrhyn Bay, Llandudno, **Conwy**, LL30 3EU, WAL.
(T) 01492 549368
Speciality: Chiropractors.
● **Senior Partner** Dr P Edwards
P S T (Ref:HM18785)

**SMITH, P L**

**P L Smith**, 6 Pippin Lane, Little Billing, Northampton, **Northamptonshire**, NN3 9TQ, ENG.
(T) 01604 409406
Speciality: Chiropodists (Podiatrists).
● **Owner** Mrs P Smith
S (Ref:HM18786)

**SMITH, PAM**

**Pam Smith**, Harrogate, **Yorkshire (North)**, HG2, ENG.
(T) 01423 880456
Speciality: Bach Remedies.
M (Ref:HM18787)

**SMITH, PATRICIA**

**Patricia Smith**, Rathkeeland House, 1 Blaney Rd, Crossmaglen, Newry, **County Down**, BT35 9JJ, NIR.
(T) 028 3086 1552
Speciality: Chiropodists (Podiatrists).
● **Owner** Mrs P Smith
S (Ref:HM18788)

**SMITH, PATRICIA A**

**Patricia A Smith**, 6 Emery Cl, Walsall, **Midlands (West)**, WS1 3AL, ENG.
(T) 01922 720948
Speciality: Chiropodists (Podiatrists).
● **Owner** Mrs P Smith
S (Ref:HM18789)

**SMITH, PENNY**

**Penny Smith**, 37 High Town Rd, Maidenhead, **Berkshire**, SL6 1PA, ENG.
(T) 01628 788420
Speciality: Aromatherapy.
● **Owner** Mrs C Sanders
M O (Ref:HM18790)

**SMITH, PETER (DR)**

**Dr Peter Smith**, 108 Wood St, London, **London (Greater)**, E17 3HX, ENG.
(T) 020 8520 4080
Speciality: Chiropractors.
● **Owner** Dr P Smith
P S T (Ref:HM18791)

**SMITH, PETER (DR)**

**Dr Peter Smith**, 43 Albert Avenue, London, **London (Greater)**, E4 8LG, ENG.
(T) 020 8524 0601
Speciality: Chiropractors.
● **Owner** Dr P Smith
P S T (Ref:HM18792)

**SMITH, PHILIP**

**Philip Smith**, 94 Rotton Park Rd, Birmingham, **Midlands (West)**, B16 0LU, ENG.
(T) 01214 296828
Speciality: Physiotherapy.
P S T (Ref:HM18793)

**SMITH, R**

**Mrs R Smith**, 93 Castle St, Luton, **Bedfordshire**, LU1 3AJ, ENG.
(T) 01582 876866
Speciality: Chiropodists (Podiatrists).
S (Ref:HM18794)

**SMITH, R**

**R Smith**, 48 Portsmouth Rd, Southampton, **Hampshire**, SO19 9AF, ENG.
(T) 023 8043 1776
Speciality: Osteopathy.
P S T (Ref:HM18795)

**SMITH, R**

**R Smith**, 7 Norfolk St, Sunderland, **Tyne and Wear**, SR1 1EA, ENG.
(T) 01915 676020
Speciality: Osteopathy.
P S T (Ref:HM18796)

**SMITH, R J**

**R J Smith**, 11 Moor Park Avenue, Preston, **Lancashire**, PR1 6AS, ENG.
(T) 01772 251507 (F) 01772 558761
Speciality: Psychology.
● **Manager** Mr F Iddon
B (Ref:HM18797)

**SMITH, RACHEL E**

**Rachel E Smith**, Woodnuts Cottage, Duver Rd, St. Helens, Ryde, **Isle of Wight**, PO33 1XY, ENG.
(T) 01983 874641
Speciality: Complementary Medicines & Therapy.
M (Ref:HM18798)

**SMITH, RONA**

**Rona Smith**, 20 Cavendish St, Keighley, **Yorkshire (West)**, BD21 3RG, ENG.
(T) 01535 644162
Speciality: Complementary Medicines & Therapy.
● **Owner** Mrs R Smith
M (Ref:HM18799)

**SMITH, ROY**

**Roy Smith**, 3 Rockcliffe Gardens, Whitley Bay, **Tyne and Wear**, NE26 2NL, ENG.
(T) 01912 534389
Speciality: Osteopathy.
● **Owner** Mr R Smith
M (Ref:HM18800)

**SMITH, RUTHIE**

**Ruthie Smith**, 63 Lothair Rd South, London, **London (Greater)**, N4 1EN, ENG.
(T) 020 8341 5438
Speciality: Psychotherapy.
● **Owner** Ms R Smith
B (Ref:HM18801)

**SMITH, S**

**S Smith**, 2 East St, Bromley, **Kent**, BR1 1QU, ENG.
(T) 020 8402 5421
Speciality: Psychotherapy.
B (Ref:HM18802)

**SMITH, S J**

**S J Smith**, 18 Penybont, Penpedairheol, Hengoed, **Caerphilly**, CF82 8HD, WAL.
(T) 01443 821894
Speciality: Chiropodists (Podiatrists).
● **Owner** Mr S Smith
S (Ref:HM18803)

**SMITH, S J**

**S J Smith Registered Osteopath**, Crossways, 42 St Albans Rd, Reigate, **Surrey**, RH2 9LN, ENG.
(T) 01737 244202
Speciality: Osteopathy.
P S T (Ref:HM18804)

**SMITH, S L**

**S L Smith**, 2 Flint Cottages, Church End, Barley, Royston, **Hertfordshire**, SG8 8JR, ENG.
(T) 01763 848561
Speciality: Physiotherapy.
P S T (Ref:HM18805)

**SMITH, SALLY**

**Sally Smith**, Lime Gr, High St, Harby, Newark, **Nottinghamshire**, NG23 7EB, ENG.
(T) 01522 704294
Speciality: Reflexology.
S T (Ref:HM18806)

**SMITH, SANDRA**

**Sandra Smith**, Woodend Reflexology, 14 Hilly Plantation, Norwich, **Norfolk**, NR7 0JN, ENG.
(T) 01603 701705
Speciality: Reflexology.
S T (Ref:HM18807)

**SMITH, SHAN**

**Shan Smith**, 54 Thornbury Rd, Isleworth, **London (Greater)**, TW7 4LN, ENG.



Key: B Mind-Body Medicine, C Complementary Medicine, H Self Help Treatment, M Medicinal Therapy, O Oriental Medicine, P Postural Therapy, S Manipulative Structural Therapy, T Touch Therapy

(T) 020 8847 1284
Speciality: Reflexology.
S T (Ref:HM18808)

**SMITH, SHEILA**

**Mrs Sheila Smith**, 29 Clarendon Rd East, Blackburn, **Lancashire**, BB1 5QA, ENG.
(T) 01254 55935
Speciality: Complementary Medicines & Therapy.
C M (Ref:HM18809)

**SMITH, SHEILA**

**Sheila Smith**, 4 Rowley Cl, Fleckney, **Leicestershire**, LE8 8BU, ENG.
(T) 01162 403384
Speciality: Reflexology.
S T (Ref:HM18810)

**SMITH, SOPHIA**

**Sophia Smith**, 28 Meadow Rd, Berkhamsted, **Hertfordshire**, HP4 1DZ, ENG.
(T) 01442 863915
Speciality: Reflexology.
S T (Ref:HM18811)

**SMITH, SUE**

**Sue Smith**, Wellbrook Clinic, 21 Stafford Rd, Wallington, **Surrey**, SM6 9AN, ENG.
(T) 020 8401 0011
Speciality: Reflexology.
S T (Ref:HM18812)

**SMITH, SUSAN**

**Susan Smith**, 15 Ware Rd, Hertford, **Hertfordshire**, SG13 7DZ, ENG.
(T) 01992 504323
(E) susan-healthline@hotmail.com
Speciality: Aromatherapy, Life Style Coaching, Reflexology. ✔
● **Complementary Practitioner**
Ms S Smith Q: BA (Hons). M: AOC, IFR.
C Yrs. Est.: 5 (Ref:HM18813)

**SMITH, SUSAN M**

**Susan M Smith**, 11 Cross Lane, Faversham, **Kent**, ME13 8PN, ENG.
(T) 01795 537832
Speciality: Osteopathy.
P S T (Ref:HM18814)

**SMITH, SUZANNE**

**Suzanne Smith**, 5 Alamein Cl, Broxbourne, **Hertfordshire**, EN10 7TF, ENG.
(T) 01992 447747
Speciality: Reflexology.
S T (Ref:HM18815)

**SMITH, TRACEY**

**Tracey Smith**, 432 Devon Mansions, Tooley St, London, **London (Greater)**, SE1 2XS, ENG.
(T) 020 7403 1076
Speciality: Reflexology.
● **Owner** Ms T Smith
S T (Ref:HM18816)

**SMITH, V L**

**V L Smith**, Stanwood, Skegness Rd, Partney, Spilsby, **Lincolnshire**, PE23 4PY, ENG.
(T) 01790 754062 (F) 01790 754062
Speciality: Complementary Medicines & Therapy.
● **Owner** Mrs V Smith
C M (Ref:HM18817)

**SMITH, W**

**W Smith**, 6 Segontium Trce, Caernarfon, **Gwynedd**, LL55 2PN, WAL.
(T) 01286 673118
Speciality: Chiropodists (Podiatrists).
● **Owner** Mr W Smith
S (Ref:HM18818)

**SMITH, WALTER**

**Walter Smith**, 45 Kingsbridge Cres, Glasgow, **Glasgow (City of)**, G44 4JX, SCO.
(T) 01416 495075
Speciality: Chiropodists (Podiatrists).
S (Ref:HM18819)

**SMITH, WYN**

**Wyn Smith**, 9 Salem Trce, Criccieth, **Gwynedd**, LL52 0AD, WAL.
(T) 01766 522806 (F) 01766 522806
Speciality: Chiropodists (Podiatrists).
● **Owner** Mr W Smith
S (Ref:HM18820)

**SMITH, YVONNE**

**Yvonne Smith**, **Yorkshire (North)**, YO6, ENG.
(T) 01347 810246
Speciality: Bach Remedies.
M (Ref:HM18821)

**SMITHERS, DENISE**

**Denise Smithers**, Dumfries Holistic Health Centre, 98 Loreburn St, Dumfries, **Dumfries and Galloway**, DG1 1HW, SCO.
(T) 01387 267617
Speciality: Homeopathy.
M (Ref:HM18822)

**SMITH-OLIVER, J M**

**J M Smith-Oliver**, 64 Broadway Market, London, **London (Greater)**, E8 4QJ, ENG.
(T) 020 7275 8434
Speciality: Reflexology.
P S T (Ref:HM18823)

**SMITHSON, J**

**J Smithson**, 19 Cooke St, Bentley, Doncaster, **Yorkshire (South)**, DN5 0BH, ENG.
(T) 01302 874036
Speciality: Chiropodists (Podiatrists).
● **Owner** Mr J Smithson
S (Ref:HM18824)

**SMITHWHITE, AMBER**

**Amber Smithwhite**, 12 Hillside Avenue, Saltash, **Cornwall**, PL12 6HF, ENG.
(T) 01752 848444
Speciality: Aromatherapy.
● **Owner** Mrs A Smithwhite
M O (Ref:HM18825)

**SMOKERS CLINIC**

**Smokers Clinic**, 12 North Gr, London, **London (Greater)**, N6 4SL, ENG.
(T) 020 8348 1440 (F) 020 8372 9426
Speciality: Hypnosis.
● **Owner** Mrs L King
B (Ref:HM18826)

**SMOUT, SARAH L**

**Sarah L Smout**, The Mesnes Centre, 55 Mesnes Rd, Wigan, **Lancashire**, WN1 2DF, ENG.
(T) 01942 245040
Speciality: Chiropodists (Podiatrists).
● **Owner** Mr H Smout
S (Ref:HM18827)

**SMYCZ, LISA**

**Lisa Smycz**, 60 Hill St, Hinckley, **Leicestershire**, LE10 1DT, ENG.
(T) 01455 635488 (F) 01455 635488
Speciality: Chiropractors.
● **Director** Mr A Smycz
P S T (Ref:HM18828)

**SMYTH, CATHERINE**

**Catherine Smyth**, The Mews Clinic, Hitchmans Mews, 4c West St, Chipping Norton, **Oxfordshire**, OX7 5AA, ENG.
(T) 01608 730239
Speciality: Chiropractic.
P S T (Ref:HM18829)

**SMYTH, DAVID**

**David Smyth**, Dean View, Linden Rd, The Pludds, Ruardean, **Gloucestershire**, GL17 9UH, ENG.
(T) 01594 860169
(E) dsmyth9619@aol.com
(W) www.reharmonising.co.uk
Speciality: Absent Healing, Acupressure, Acupuncture, Bach Remedies, Chinese Herbal Medicine, Complementary Therapy, Dowsing, Hay Diet, Healer, Herbal Medicine, Kinesiology, Oriental Diagnosis, Ying & Yang, Traditional Chinese Medicine, Re-Harmonising. ✔
● **Natural Health Practitioner**
Mr D Smyth Q: Cert.Ac, Lic.Ac. M: BAcC.
O Yrs. Est.: 14 (Ref:HM18830)

**SMYTH, J**

**J Smyth**, Petersfield Hospital, Swan St, Petersfield, **Hampshire**, GU32 3LB, ENG.
(T) 01730 263221
Speciality: Chiropodists (Podiatrists).
S (Ref:HM18831)

**SMYTH, SARA**

**Sara Smyth**, 20 Harold Rd, London, **London (Greater)**, N8 7DE, ENG.
(T) 020 8348 8898
Speciality: Homeopathy.
● **Owner** Ms S Smyth
M (Ref:HM18832)

**SMYTHE, CARMEL**

**Carmel Smythe**, Flat 2, 2 Market St, Nailsworth, Stroud, **Gloucestershire**, GL6 0BX, ENG.
(T) 01453 835582
Speciality: Osteopathy.
P S T (Ref:HM18833)

**SNEDDON, GRAHAM**

**Graham Sneddon**, 1 Bartholomew Trce, Exeter, **Devon**, EX4 3BW, ENG.
(T) 01392 499450
Speciality: Chiropodists (Podiatrists).
● **Partner** Mr G Sneddon
S (Ref:HM18834)

**SNELL, J**

**J Snell**, 14 Binswood End, Harbury, Leamington Spa, **Warwickshire**, CV33 9LN, ENG.
(T) 01926 614614
Speciality: Physiotherapy.
● **Owner** Mrs J Snell
P S T (Ref:HM18835)

**SNELSON, KAREN**

**Karen Snelson**, Honeysuckle Cottage, Upper Helmsley, York, **Yorkshire (North)**, YO41 1JY, ENG.
(T) 01759 372491
Speciality: Hypnosis.
● **Owner** Mrs K Snelson
B (Ref:HM18836)

**SNEYD PARK**

**Sneyd Park**, 4 Rockleaze Rd, Bristol, BS9 1NF, ENG.
(T) 01179 685107 (F) 01179 685107
Speciality: Osteopathy.
● **Owner** Ms C Brice
P S T (Ref:HM18837)

**SNOAD, R J**

**R J Snoad**, 29 High St, Bookham, Leatherhead, **Surrey**, KT23 4AA, ENG.
(T) 01372 454583
Speciality: Chiropodists (Podiatrists).
● **Owner** Mr R Snoad
S (Ref:HM18838)

**SNOAD, RICHARD JOHN**

**Richard John Snoad**, 113 Station Rd, West Wickham, **Kent**, BR4 0PX, ENG.
(T) 020 8776 0343
Speciality: Chiropodists (Podiatrists).
● **Owner** Mr R Snoad
S (Ref:HM18839)

**SNOW, DAVID**

**David Snow**, 2 Kenwood Rd, Sheffield, **Yorkshire (South)**, S7 1NP, ENG.
(T) 01142 552048
Speciality: Complementary Medicines & Therapy.
● **Owner** Mr D Wainwright
M (Ref:HM18840)

**SNOW, MARIAN**

**Marian Snow**, 32 Lister St, Falmouth, **Cornwall**, TR11 3BS, ENG.
(T) 01326 318973
Speciality: Hypnosis.
B (Ref:HM18841)

**SNOWBIRD CENTRE**

**Snowbird Centre**, 11 The Sq, Sedgefield, Stockton-On-Tees, **Cleveland**, TS21 2BN, ENG.
(T) 01740 621111
Speciality: Complementary Medicines & Therapy.
● **Partner** Mrs S White
C M (Ref:HM18842)

**SNOWDON, JANET**

**Janet Snowdon**, Stillpoint, Broad St Pl, Bath, **Somerset**, BA1 5LH, ENG.
(T) 01225 460106
Speciality: Holistic Healing, Homeopathy. ✔



Key continued: Yrs.Est: Years Established Q: Qualifications M: Professional Membership ✔ Indemnity Insurance ▬ Accept Credit Cards

● **Physiotherapist** Mrs E Sykes Q: MCSP, SRP. M: CSP, SRP.
S Yrs. Est.: 10 (Ref:HM18909)

**SOUTH LONDON HYPNOTHERAPY CTRE**

**South London Hypnotherapy Centre**, Oaklands House, 29 Oakland Rd, Bromley, **Kent**, BR1 3SJ, ENG.
(T) 020 8460 7578
Speciality: Hypnosis, Hypnotherapy.
● **Hypnotherapist** Mr D Crussell
B Yrs. Est.: 30 (Ref:HM18910)

**SOUTH LONDON NATURAL HLTH CTRE**

**Winsmill Ltd**, 7a Clapham Common South Side, London, **London (Greater)**, SW4 7AA, ENG.
(T) 020 7720 8817 (F) 020 7627 3381
(E) ronkemeny@onetel.net.uk
(W) www.southlondonnaturalhealthcentre.com
Speciality: Acupressure, Acupuncture, Alexander Technique, Aromatherapy, Art Therapy, Ayurvedic Medicine, Bach Remedies, Bowen Therapy, Chiropractic, Complementary Therapy, Counselling, Cranial Osteopathy, Crystal Healing, Dietician, Feldenkrais Methodology, Floral Essence Therapy, Flotation Therapy, Gem Essence Therapy, Hay Diet, Healer, Healing Therapy, Herbal Medicine, Holistic Healing, Homeopathy, Indian Head Massage, Iridology, Kinesiology, Massage (Therapeutic), Meditation, Moxibustion, Naturopathy, Nutritional Therapy, Oriental Diagnosis, Osteopathy, Pilates, Polarity Therapy, Postural Integration, Reflexology, Reiki. ✓
● **Therapist** Mr J Googe
● **Therapist** Pip Waller
● **Therapist** Ms A Watson
● **Therapist** Ms F Spencer
● **Reflexologist** Ms K Broadhead
● **Therapist** Zofia Hockin
● **Kinesiologist** Mr B Shaw
● **Reflexologist** Ms L Sanders
● **Clinical Hypnotherapist** Mr M Cohen
● **McTimoney Chiropractor** Mr R Swaine
● **Nutritional Therapist** Ms M Cesari
● **Therapist** Ms L Staples-White
C Yrs. Est.: 13 (Ref:HM18911)

**SOUTH LONDON PSYCH GROUP**

**South London Psychotherapy Group**, P O Box 111, Richmond, **Surrey**, TW9 2TY, ENG.
(T) 020 8332 7131
Speciality: Psychotherapy.
B (Ref:HM18912)

**SOUTH PETHERTON CHIROPODY**

**South Petherton Chiropody Clinic**, 8 Market Sq, South Petherton, **Somerset**, TA13 5BT, ENG.
(T) 01460 242474
Speciality: Chiropodists (Podiatrists).
S (Ref:HM18913)

**SOUTH WEST CHIROPRACTIC CLINIC**

**South West Chiropractic Clinic**, 253 Gower Rd, Sketty, Swansea, SA2 9JL, WAL.
(T) 01792 281100
Speciality: Chiropractic.
P S T (Ref:HM18914)

**SOUTH WORCESTERSHIRE HYP**

**South Worcestershire Hypnotherapy Centre**, Frontia, 4 Bath Rd, Worcester, **Worcestershire**, WR5 3EJ, ENG.
(T) 01905 640598
(E) john@frontia.eq.uk
Speciality: Allergy Testing, Hypnosis, Hypnotherapy, Stress Therapy.
● **Curative Hypnotherapist** Mr J Freeman-Cartwright Q: BHA. M: GCH.
B Yrs. Est.: 18 (Ref:HM18915)

**SOUTH, JANE**

**Jane South**, Flat 1, 10 Boyne Park, Tunbridge Wells, **Kent**, TN4 8ET, ENG.
(T) 01892 536113
Speciality: Chiropodists (Podiatrists).
S (Ref:HM18916)

**SOUTH, JO**

**Jo South**, 16 Hockerill St, Bishop's Stortford, **Hertfordshire**, CM23 2DW, ENG.
(T) 07976 152726 (F) 07970 631975
(E) info@josouth.co.uk
(W) www.josouth.co.uk
Speciality: Bach Remedies, Homeopathy, Reflexology. ✓
● **Homeopath** Ms J South Q: LCH. M: Soc.Hom.
M Yrs. Est.: 3 (Ref:HM18917)

**SOUTH, JO**

**Jo South**, Sharon Crickitt Complementary Health, 4 Jolliffes Court, 51-57 High St, Wivenhoe, **Essex**, CO7 9AZ, ENG.
(T) 07976 152726 (F) 07970 631975
(E) info@josouth.co.uk
Speciality: Bach Remedies, Homeopathy, Reflexology. ✓
● **Homeopath** Ms J South Q: LCH. M: Soc.Hom.
M Yrs. Est.: 3 (Ref:HM18918)

**SOUTHALL CHINESE MED CENTRE**

**Southall Chinese Medical Centre**, 9 High St, Southall, **London (Greater)**, UB1 3DA, ENG.
(T) 020 8574 7548
Speciality: Herbal Medicine.
M (Ref:HM18919)

**SOUTHAMPTON CTRE OF COMP MED**

**Southampton Centre of Complementary Medicine**, 51 Bedford Pl, Southampton, **Hampshire**, SO15 2DT, ENG.
(T) 023 8033 4752
Speciality: Complementary Medicines & Therapy.
● **Therapist** Mr A Mills
C M (Ref:HM18920)

**SOUTHBOROUGH COMP HLTH PRAC**

**Southborough Complementary Health Practice**, 74 Grange Rd, Chessington, **Surrey**, KT9 1EY, ENG.
(T) 020 8391 1876
Speciality: Hypnosis.
● **Owner** Mr M Ferris
B (Ref:HM18921)

**SOUTHBOURNE & FONTWELL**

**Southbourne & Fontwell Physiotherapy**, The Wolds, Fontwell Avenue, Eastergate, Chichester, **Sussex (West)**, PO20 6RU, ENG.
(T) 01243 544333 (F) 01243 544333
Speciality: Physiotherapy.
● **Manager** Mrs K Shrimpton
P S T (Ref:HM18922)

**SOUTHBOURNE & FONTWELL PHYSIO**

**Southbourne & Fontwell Physiotherapy Clinic**, 337 Main Rd, Emsworth, **Hampshire**, PO10 8JH, ENG.
(T) 01243 378101 (F) 01243 378101
Speciality: Physiotherapy.
P S T (Ref:HM18923)

**SOUTHBOURNE HERBAL CLINIC**

**Southbourne Herbal Clinic**, 149 Seafield Rd, Bournemouth, **Dorset**, BH6 5LH, ENG.
(T) 01202 418567 (F) 01202 418567
(E) andy@southbourneherbalclinic.co.uk
Speciality: Complementary Therapy, Herbal Medicine. ✓
● **Owner/Registered Medical Herbalist** Mr A Cutler M: IRCH.
M Yrs. Est.: 10 (Ref:HM18924)

**SOUTHBOURNE NATURAL HLTH CTRE**

**Southbourne Natural Health Centre**, 102 Southbourne Rd, Bournemouth, **Dorset**, BH6 3QQ, ENG.
(T) 01202 424833
Speciality: Chiropractic, Homeopathy. ✓ CREDIT
● **Chiropractor** Mrs J Duff Q: BSc.
● **Homeopathic Doctor** Dr J Milward
C Yrs. Est.: 7 (Ref:HM18925)

**SOUTHBOURNE SPORTS & MEDICAL**

**Southbourne Sports Medical Clinic**, 231 Main Rd, Emsworth, **Hampshire**, PO10 8JD, ENG.
(T) 01243 377155
Speciality: Physiotherapy.
P S T (Ref:HM18926)

**SOUTHCOTE CHIROPRACTIC CLINIC**

**Southcote Chiropractic Clinic**, The Southcote Chiropractic Clinic, 3 Sittingbourne Rd, Maidstone, **Kent**, ME14 5ES, ENG.
(T) 01622 661883
(E) nikolaj@southcote.com
Speciality: Chiropractic, Sacro-Occipital Technique, Remedial and Rehabilitative Exercises. ✓ CREDIT
● **Chiropractor** Mr J Dahl Q: CCEP, CCSP, DC. M: BCA.
● **Chiropractor** Lene Linnet Feldborg Q: BSc, CCEP, DC. M: BCA.
● **Chiropractor** Nikolaj Krogsgaard Q: BSc, DC. M: BCA.
● **Chiropractor** Ms C With Q: CCEP, CCSP, DC. M: BCA.
S Yrs. Est.: 10 (Ref:HM18927)

**SOUTHCOTT, J**

**J Southcott**, 366 Croydon Rd, Beckenham, **Kent**, BR3 4EX, ENG.
(T) 020 8663 3878 (F) 020 8663 3878
Speciality: Acupuncture.
● **Doctor** Dr M Chippendale
O (Ref:HM18928)

**SOUTHDOWN CHIROPODY PRACTICE**

**Southdown Chiropody Practice**, 136A Southdown Rd, Harpenden, **Hertfordshire**, AL5 1PU, ENG.
(T) 01582 766614
Speciality: Chiropody. ✓ CREDIT
● **Owner/Chiropodist** Miss S McBean Q: MSSCh.
M Yrs. Est.: 7 (Ref:HM18929)

**SOUTHDOWN PHYSIOTHERAPY CLINIC**

**Southdown Physiotherapy Clinic**, 11 Stafford Rd, Seaford, **Sussex (East)**, BN25 1UE, ENG.
(T) 01323 894354 (F) 01323 899744
Speciality: Physiotherapy.
● **Partner** Mrs A Gamble
P S T (Ref:HM18930)

**SOUTHEAST HYPNOTHERAPY CENTRE**

**Southeast Hypnotherapy Centre**, 21 Hill Rd, Eastbourne, **Sussex (East)**, BN20 8SL, ENG.
(T) 01323 734019
Speciality: Hypnosis.
B (Ref:HM18931)

**SOUTHERTON, C S**

**C S Southerton**, 75-77 Broad St, Chipping Sodbury, Bristol, BS37 6AE, ENG.
(T) 01454 320088
Speciality: Chiropractors.
P S T (Ref:HM18932)

**SOUTHERTON, C S**

**C S Southerton**, 75-77 Broad St, Chipping Sodbury, Bristol, BS17 6AE, ENG.
(T) 01454 320088
Speciality: Chiropractic.
P S T (Ref:HM18933)

**SOUTHFIELD PHYSIO CLINIC**

**Southfield Physiotherapy Clinic**, 127 Elsenham St, London, **London (Greater)**, SW18 5NY, ENG.
(T) 020 8870 8421
Speciality: Physiotherapy.
P S T (Ref:HM18934)

**SOUTHFIELDS CLINIC**

**Southfields Clinic (The)**, 41 Southfields Rd, London, **London (Greater)**, SW18 1QW, ENG.
(T) 020 8874 4125
Speciality: Acupuncture. ✓
● **Acupuncturist/Owner** Mr Stoddart Q: B.Ac, BSc, MBAcC.
O Yrs. Est.: 20 (Ref:HM18935)

**SOUTHGATE HOLISTIC HEALTH**

**Southgate Holistic Health Clinic**, 20 Tresillian Avenue, London, **London (Greater)**, N21 1TJ, ENG.
(T) 020 8351 9787
Speciality: Aromatherapy.
M O (Ref:HM18936)

**SOUTHGATE NAT THERAPY CLINIC**

**Southgate Natural Therapy Clinic**, Ground

Floor, 13 Southgate St, Winchester, **Hampshire**, SO23 9DZ, ENG.
(T) 01962 866903 (F) 01962 714041
Speciality: Acupuncture, Aromatherapy, Bowen Therapy, Complementary Therapy, Counselling, Cranial Osteopathy, Hypnosis, Hypnotherapy, Moxibustion, Osteopathy, Psychotherapy, Shiatsu. ✓
● **Acupuncturist/Bowen Therapist** Ms S Woodhead Q: Cert.ECBS, Lic.Ac. M: BAcC, BTER.
C M Yrs. Est.: 18 (Ref:HM18937)

## SOUTHMEAD HOUSE

**Southmead House**, Southmead House, Blackpond Lane, Farnham Common, Slough, **Berkshire**, SL2 3ER, ENG.
(T) 01753 645567 (F) 01753 645567
Speciality: Physiotherapy.
● **Owner** Mr R Tripp
P S T (Ref:HM18938)

## SOUTHORN, VALERIE

**Valerie Southorn**, 35 Avenue Rd, Brentford, **London (Greater)**, TW8 9NS, ENG.
(T) 020 8400 7699
Speciality: Homeopathy.
● **Owner** Ms V Southorn
M (Ref:HM18939)

## SOUTHPORT & TARLETON PHYSIO

**Southport & Tarleton Physiotherapy Services**, 72 Tulketh St, Southport, **Merseyside**, PR8 1BX, ENG.
(T) 01704 500635 (F) 01704 500635
Speciality: Physiotherapy.
● **Director** Mr R Bramford
P S T (Ref:HM18940)

## SOUTHPORT & TARLETON PHYSIO

**Southport & Tarleton Physiotherapy Services**, 93 Church Rd, Tarleton, Preston, **Lancashire**, PR4 6UP, ENG.
(T) 01772 816816 (F) 01772 816816
Speciality: Physiotherapy.
● **Owner** Mr R Bramford
P S T (Ref:HM18941)

## SOUTHPORT OSTEO & ACUPUNCTURE

**Southport Osteopathy & Acupuncture Clinic**, 72 Portland St, Southport, **Merseyside**, PR8 6QX, ENG.
(T) 01704 543532
Speciality: Acupuncture, Osteopathy, Remedial Massage. ✓
● **Osteomyologist** Mr Moore
● **Osteopath** Mr P Howard Q: DO. M: GOsC.
● **Remedial Massage** Mrs Howard
S (Ref:HM18942)

## SOUTHSEA CENTRE FOR COMP MED

**Southsea Centre For Complementary Medicine**, 25 Osborne Rd, Southsea, **Hampshire**, PO5 3ND, ENG.
(T) 023 9287 4748 (F) 023 9229 1076
(E) info@sccm.com
Speciality: Absent Healing, Acupressure, Acupuncture, Aromatherapy, Aversion Therapy, Chiropractic, Complementary Therapy, Cranial Osteopathy, Cupping, Dietician, Dowsing, Healer, Healing Therapy, Herbal Medicine, Holistic Healing, Homeopathy, Hypnosis, Hypnotherapy, Indian Head Massage, Inhalation Therapy, Iridology, Kinesiology, Manipulation, Massage (Therapeutic), Moxibustion, Nutritional Therapy, Oriental Diagnosis, Osteopathy, Postural Integration, Reflexology, Reiki, Shiatsu, Stress Therapy, Vitamin Therapy. ✓
● **Manager** Helen Knight
● **Homeopath** Mr R Cook Q: BSc, MCH, RSHom. M: Soc.Hom.
● **Chiropractor** H Faulkner Q: BA, DC, MMCA. M: CC.
● **Cranial Osteopath** L Heib Q: DO. M: GOsC.
● **Acupuncturist** Wilson Q: Dip.Med.Ac. M: BAcC.
M Yrs. Est.: 10 (Ref:HM18943)

## SOUTHSEA CHIROPRACTIC CLINIC

**Southsea Chiropractic Clinic**, 86 Marmion Rd, Southsea, **Hampshire**, PO5 2BB, ENG.
(T) 023 9286 3099
Speciality: Chiropractic.
● **Partner** Mrs G Blackman
P S T (Ref:HM18944)

## SOUTHSIDE COUNSELLING

**Southside Counselling MNAPCP MSc (Couns)**, Dundrum, **County Dublin**, IRE.
(T) 01298 3535
Speciality: Counselling.
B H (Ref:HM18945)

## SOUTHWARD, G

**G Southward**, 82 Trumpet Rd, Cleator, **Cumbria**, CA23 3EQ, ENG.
(T) 01946 812393
Speciality: Physiotherapy.
P S T (Ref:HM18946)

## SOUTHWARD, P

**P Southward**, 91 Winston Avenue, Poole, **Dorset**, BH12 1PB, ENG.
(T) 01202 743351
Speciality: Chiropodists (Podiatrists).
● **Director** Mr P Southward
S (Ref:HM18947)

## SOUTHWELL ACUPUNCTURE CLINIC

**Southwell Acupuncture Clinic**, Dumble Rise, 38 Ridgeway, Southwell, **Nottinghamshire**, NG25 0DU, ENG.
(T) 01636 816156
(E) hannahgr@onetel.net.uk
Speciality: Acupuncture, Promotes and Sells Non Toxic Personal Care and Health Care Products. ✓
● **Acupunturist** Ms H Townsend Q: EN(g), Lic.Ac, MBAcC.
O Yrs. Est.: 5 (Ref:HM18948)

## SOUTHWELL ACUPUNCTURE CLINIC

**Southwell Acupuncture Clinic**, 7a Church St, Southwell, **Nottinghamshire**, NG25 0HQ, ENG.
(T) 01636 816156
Speciality: Acupuncture.
O (Ref:HM18949)

## SOUTHWORTH, L

**L Southworth**, 6 St Katherines Drive, Blackrod, Bolton, **Lancashire**, BL6 5EJ, ENG.
(T) 01204 691710
Speciality: Osteopathy.
P S T (Ref:HM18950)

## SOUTHWORTH, LINDA

**Linda Southworth**, 52 York St, Clitheroe, **Lancashire**, BB7 2DL, ENG.
(T) 01200 422959
Speciality: Osteopathy.
P S T (Ref:HM18951)

## SOWELU ASSOCIATES

**Sowelu Associates Education Consultancy**, Collywell, Brownston, Ivybridge, **Devon**, PL21 0SQ, ENG.
(T) 01548 821192 (F) 01548 821192
Speciality: Psychotherapy.
● **Partner** Ms L Gerlach
B (Ref:HM18952)

## SOWERBUTTS, G H

**G H Sowerbutts**, Wyngate House, Freckleton Rd, Kirkham, Preston, **Lancashire**, PR4 3RB, ENG.
(T) 01772 683532
Speciality: Osteopathy.
● **Owner** Mr G Sowerbutts
P S T (Ref:HM18953)

## SPALDING OSTEOPATHIC CLINIC

**Spalding Osteopathic Clinic**, 31 The Crescent, Spalding, **Lincolnshire**, PE11 1AF, ENG.
(T) 01775 766966
Speciality: Osteopathy.
P S T (Ref:HM18954)

## SPALDING, JULIE

**Julie Spalding**, 90 Dereham Avenue, Ipswich, **Suffolk**, IP3 0QG, ENG.
(T) 01473 726094
Speciality: Cognitive Therapy, Complementary Therapy, Counselling, Hypnosis, Hypnotherapy, Neuro-Linguistic Program, Polarity Therapy, Psychotherapy, Stress Therapy, Visualisation Therapy.
● **Hypnotherapist/Psychotherapist** Ms J Spalding Q: Dip.Hyp, Dip.Psych. M: BIH.
B Yrs. Est.: 4 (Ref:HM18955)

## SPALDING, PAUL

**Paul Spalding**, 5 Two Acres, Capel St. Mary, Ipswich, **Suffolk**, IP9 2XP, ENG.
(T) 01473 310164
Speciality: Reflexology.
S T (Ref:HM18956)

## SPALL MEDICAL CENTRE

**Spall Medical Centre**, Homoeopathic & Herbal Clinic, 6 Crescent Rd, Eastham, London, **London (Greater)**, E6 1ED, ENG.
(T) 020 8471 8811 (F) 020 8552 7716
Speciality: Acupressure, Acupuncture, Ayurvedic Medicine, Bach Remedies, Bio-energetics, Complementary Therapy, Family Planning (Natural), Herbal Medicine, Homeopathy, Stress Therapy, Vitamin Therapy, Ying & Yang.
● **Practitioner** Dr J Spall M: HMA.
H M O (Ref:HM18957)

## SPANTON, LORRAINE

**Lorraine Spanton**, Elmfield, Fortescue Rd, Sidmouth, **Devon**, EX10 9QB, ENG.
(T) 01395 579742
Speciality: Complementary Medicines & Therapy.
● **Owner** Mrs L Spanton
C M (Ref:HM18958)

## SPARGO, W & CROWE, F D

**William Spargo & Frances D Crowe**, Gincocks, 26a Church Lane, East Peckham, Tonbridge, **Kent**, TN12 5JH, ENG.
(T) 01622 872025
Speciality: Psychology.
B (Ref:HM18959)

## SPARKES, F V

**F V Sparkes**, 1st Floor, 8 Church St, Romsey, **Hampshire**, SO51 8BU, ENG.
(T) 01794 514879
Speciality: Chiropodists (Podiatrists).
● **Owner** Mr F Sparkes Q: BSc (Hons).
S (Ref:HM18960)

## SPARKES, MARTIN J

**Martin J Sparkes**, 11 Catharine Pl, Bath, **Somerset**, BA1 2PR, ENG.
(T) 01225 445888
Speciality: Osteopathy.
P S T (Ref:HM18961)

## SPARKS, MARTIN ANDREW

**Martin Andrew Sparks**, Dorden Cottage, Lidstone, Chipping Norton, **Oxfordshire**, OX7 4HL, ENG.
(T) 01608 677326
Speciality: Reflexology.
S T (Ref:HM18962)

## SPARKS, R

**R Sparks**, 35 Park Drive, London, **London (Greater)**, W3 8ND, ENG.
(T) 020 8993 2871
Speciality: Homeopathy.
M (Ref:HM18963)

## SPARLING & ASSOCIATES

**Keith Sparling & Associates**, Ashwells, Ashwell Rd, Brentwood, **Essex**, CM15 9SE, ENG.
(T) 01277 374848
Speciality: Osteopathy.
P S T (Ref:HM18964)

## SPEAK, PAUL

**Paul Speak**, 34 Claremont Rd, Morecambe, **Lancashire**, LA4 4HL, ENG.
(T) 01524 410541
Speciality: Chiropodists (Podiatrists).
S (Ref:HM18965)

## SPEAR, A E Y

**A E Y Spear**, Linden Lea, 7 New Barn Lane, Alton, **Hampshire**, GU34 2RU, ENG.
(T) 01420 80325
Speciality: Chiropodists (Podiatrists).
● **Owner** A Spear
S (Ref:HM18966)

## SPEAR, F G

**F G Spear**, 326 Ecclesall Rd South, Sheffield, **Yorkshire (South)**, S11 9PU, ENG.
(T) 01142 366766



Key continued: Yrs.Est: Years Established Q: Qualifications M: Professional Membership ✓ Indemnity Insurance Accept Credit Cards

Speciality: Psychiatry.
B (Ref:HM18967)

## SPEARING, SIMON

**Simon Spearing**, 16 Clarence Sq, Cheltenham, **Gloucestershire**, GL50 4JN, ENG.
(T) 01242 241933
Speciality: Chiropractors.
P S T (Ref:HM18968)

## SPEARS, SUSAN

**Susan Spears**, Lasyard House, Underhill St, Bridgnorth, **Shropshire**, WV16 4BB, ENG.
(T) 01746 768370
Speciality: Complementary Medicines & Therapy.
● **Owner** Mrs S Spears
C M (Ref:HM18969)

## SPECIAL ELECTROLYSIS CLINIC

**Special Electrolysis Clinic**, 2nd Floor Lion Chambers, John William St, Huddersfield, **Yorkshire (West)**, HD1 1ES, ENG.
(T) 01484 511891
Speciality: Electrolysis.
T (Ref:HM18970)

## SPECIAL MOMENTS

**Special Moments**, 35 Belmont Trce, Foulridge, Colne, **Lancashire**, BB8 7PF, ENG.
(T) 01282 859574
Speciality: Aromatherapy.
● **Owner** Mrs L Hodgkinson
M O (Ref:HM18971)

## SPECIALIST HEALTH

**Specialist Health**, The Specialist Health And Laser Care Clinic, 144 Harley St, London, **London (Greater)**, W1N 1ED, ENG.
(T) 020 7224 0988 (F) 020 7224 0987
(E) woodsideclinic@talk21.com
Speciality: Acupuncture, Manipulation, Massage (Therapeutic), Osteopathy, Tai massage. ✔
● **Osteopath** Mr J Betser Q: DO. M: GOsC.
S Yrs. Est.: 2 (Ref:HM18972)

## SPECIALIST HERBAL SUPPLIES

**Specialist Herbal Supplies**, Portslade Hall, 18 Station Rd, Portslade, Brighton, **Sussex (East)**, BN41 1GB, ENG.
(T) 01273 424333 (F) 01273 424345
Speciality: Herbalists.
● **Director** Miss S Day
M (Ref:HM18973)

## SPECIALIST PSYCHOLOGICAL SVS

**Specialist Psychological Services**, 8 Loxley Rd, London, **London (Greater)**, SW18 3LJ, ENG.
(T) 020 8874 1569
Speciality: Psychology.
B (Ref:HM18974)

## SPECTRUM CENTRE

**Spectrum Centre Humanistic Psychotherapy**, 7 Endymion Rd, London, **London (Greater)**, N4 1EE, ENG.
(T) 020 8341 2277 (F) 020 8340 0426
Speciality: Psychotherapy.
● **Administrator**
B (Ref:HM18975)

## SPECTRUM HEALTH TRUST

**Spectrum Health Trust**, 10 Bedford Rd, Barton-Le-Clay, Bedford, **Bedfordshire**, MK45 4JU, ENG.
(T) 01582 883800 (F) 01582 883800
Speciality: Absent Healing, Acupressure, Aromatherapy, Aura Therapy, Autogenic Training, Bach Remedies, Cognitive Therapy, Colour Therapy, Complementary Therapy, Counselling, Crystal Healing, Dietician, Dowsing, Faith Healing, Family Therapy, Group Therapy, Healer, Healing Therapy, Herbal Medicine, Holistic Healing, Homeopathy, Hypnotherapy, Indian Head Massage, Kinesiology, Life Style Coaching, Manipulation, Massage (Therapeutic), Meditation, Nutritional Therapy, Phytotherapy, Reflexology, Reiki, Shiatsu, Spiritual Healing, Stress Therapy, T'ai-Chi Ch'uan, Touch Therapy, Vibrational Therapy, Visualisation Therapy, Yoga, Positive Imagery, Baby Massage, Colour Puncture, Holistic Energy Therapy. ✔
● **Administrator** Mr J Offer
(T) 01582 707090 M: BACP.
B Yrs. Est.: 15 (Ref:HM18976)

## SPECTRUM REIKI & SEKHEM

**Spectrum Reiki & Sekhem**, 39 Blenheim Rd, Old Basing, Basingstoke, **Hampshire**, RG24 7HP, ENG.
(T) 01256 326088 (F) 01256 326088
Speciality: Complementary Medicines & Therapy.
● **Owner** Mr M Dowling
M (Ref:HM18977)

## SPEED, J A

**J A Speed**, 23 Westbourne Rd, Wirral, **Merseyside**, CH48 4DG, ENG.
(T) 01516 258479
Speciality: Chiropodists (Podiatrists).
S (Ref:HM18978)

## SPELLER CONSULTANTS

**Speller Consultants Ltd**, 241 Banstead Rd, Banstead, **Surrey**, SM7 1RB, ENG.
(T) 020 8786 8161 (F) 020 8393 3313
Speciality: Psychology.
B (Ref:HM18979)

## SPELLER, BRIDGET

**Bridget Speller**, Glenrock, 7 Highridge, Alton, **Hampshire**, GU34 1QN, ENG.
(T) 01420 87916
Speciality: Reflexology.
S T (Ref:HM18980)

## SPENCE & LYNN

**Spence & Lynn**, 49 Clooney Trce, Londonderry, **County Londonderry**, BT47 6AP, NIR.
(T) 028 7131 1170
Speciality: Physiotherapy.
P S T (Ref:HM18981)

## SPENCE, ALEX

**Alex Spence**, Ely Complementary Health Centre, 29A St Marys St, Ely, **Cambridgeshire**, CB7 4HF, ENG.
(T) 01353 664476
Speciality: Acupuncture, Aromatherapy, Counselling, Homeopathy, Osteopathy, Phytotherapy. ✔
● **Owner/Osteopath** Mr A Spence Q: DO.
S Yrs. Est.: 5 (Ref:HM18982)

## SPENCE, JACQUELINE

**Jacqueline Spence**, 27 Kempton Cl, Chester, **Cheshire**, CH1 4PS, ENG.
(T) 01244 372390
Speciality: Hypnosis.
● **Owner** Mrs J Spence
B (Ref:HM18983)

## SPENCE, M

**M Spence**, 19 Applegarth Drive, Ilford, **Essex**, IG2 7TQ, ENG.
(T) 020 8590 5162
Speciality: Hypnosis.
● **Owner** Ms M Spence
B (Ref:HM18984)

## SPENCE, R

**R Spence**, 22 Rougemont Avenue, Torquay, **Devon**, TQ2 7JP, ENG.
(T) 01803 613647
Speciality: Hypnosis.
● **Owner** Mr R Spence
B (Ref:HM18985)

## SPENCE, SYLVIA

**Sylvia Spence**, Halifax, **Yorkshire (West)**, HX3, ENG.
(T) 01422 353544
Speciality: Reflexology.
S T (Ref:HM18986)

## SPENCE, V

**V Spence**, Relaxation Centre, 4 Grange St, St. Albans, **Hertfordshire**, AL3 5NB, ENG.
(T) 01727 867071
Speciality: Complementary Medicines & Therapy.
C M (Ref:HM18987)

## SPENCELEY, M

**Michael Spenceley Naturopath & Osteopath**, 35 Gudge Heath Lane, Fareham, **Hampshire**, PO15 5AB, ENG.
(T) 01329 822657
Speciality: Osteopathy.
P S T (Ref:HM18988)

## SPENCER & POWELL

**Spencer & Powell**, 4 Stanley St, Colne, **Lancashire**, BB8 9DE, ENG.
(T) 01282 864402
Speciality: Physiotherapy.
● **Partner** Mr A Powell
P S T (Ref:HM18989)

## SPENCER AROMATHERAPY

**Spencer Aromatherapy**, Llwyn Yr Ynn, Llandeilo Rd, Gorslas, Llanelli, **Carmarthenshire**, SA14 7LU, WAL.
(T) 01269 845296 (F) 01269 844335
Speciality: Aromatherapy, Reflexology, Sports Massage. ✔
● **Managing Director/Aromatherapist** Mr D Spencer Q: Dip.Reflex, IIHHT, IVQ. M: AoR, ICHT.
C Yrs. Est.: 5 (Ref:HM18990)

## SPENCER, A

**A Spencer**, Bonser Rd, Twickenham, **London (Greater)**, TW1 4RG, ENG.
(T) 020 8892 8400
Speciality: Complementary Medicines & Therapy.
● **Owner** A Spencer
M (Ref:HM18991)

## SPENCER, BARBARA

**Barbara Spencer**, 8 Hardwicke House, 55 Abbey Rd, Great Malvern, **Worcestershire**, WR14 3HH, ENG.
(T) 01684 572926
Speciality: Reflexology.
S T (Ref:HM18992)

## SPENCER, DIANE

**Diane Spencer**, 5 Sitwell Trce, Bucknell, **Shropshire**, SY7 0DB, ENG.
(T) 01547 530891
Speciality: Reflexology.
S T (Ref:HM18993)

## SPENCER, GILLIAN

**Gillian Spencer**, 30 Three Acre Rd, Newbury, **Berkshire**, RG14 7AW, ENG.
(T) 01635 846745
Speciality: Reflexology.
S T (Ref:HM18994)

## SPENCER, GORDON

**Gordon Spencer**, The Hale Clinic, 7 Park Cresent, London, **London (Greater)**, W1N 3HE, ENG.
(T) 020 7631 0604
Speciality: Hypnotherapy.
B (Ref:HM18995)

## SPENCER, J

**J Spencer**, 64 Springfield Avenue, Horfield, Bristol, BS7 9QT, ENG.
(T) 01179 512504
Speciality: Chiropodists (Podiatrists).
S (Ref:HM18996)

## SPENCER, MARGARET

**Margaret Spencer**, 24 Parsonage Lane, Bishop's Stortford, **Hertfordshire**, CM23 5BG, ENG.
(T) 01279 659662
Speciality: Chiropodists (Podiatrists).
S (Ref:HM18997)

## SPENCER, MARTIN

**Martin Spencer**, Surgery/Elgon Chemists, 312-316 High St, Enfield, **London (Greater)**, EN3 4HF, ENG.
(T) 020 8366 7230
Speciality: Chiropodists (Podiatrists).
● **Owner** Mr M Spencer
S (Ref:HM18998)

## SPENCER, P

**P Spencer**, 7 Bedford Row, Barnstaple, **Devon**, EX32 8NR, ENG.
(T) 01271 373346
Speciality: Osteopathy.
P S T (Ref:HM18999)

Key: B Mind-Body Medicine C Complementary Medicine H Self Help Treatment M Medicinal Therapy O Oriental Medicine P Postural Therapy S Manipulative Structural Therapy T Touch Therapy

## SPENCER, PHILIP

**Philip Spencer**, 102 Wellesley Rd, London, **London (Greater)**, W4 3AP, ENG.
(T) 020 8994 7554
Speciality: Chiropodists (Podiatrists).
S (Ref:HM19000)

## SPENCER, PIERS

**Piers Spencer**, Belgrave Medical Centre, 13 Pimlico Rd, London, **London (Greater)**, SW1W 8NA, ENG.
(T) 020 7730 5771
Speciality: Manipulation, Osteopathy, Ultrasonics. ✓
● **Osteopath** Mr P Spencer Q: DO. M: GOsC.
S Yrs. Est.: 7 (Ref:HM19001)

## SPENCER, S A

**S A Spencer**, 12 Pontey Mount, Huddersfield, **Yorkshire (West)**, HD5 8RE, ENG.
(T) 01484 306767
Speciality: Chiropodists (Podiatrists).
S (Ref:HM19002)

## SPENCER, SUSAN J

**Susan J Spencer**, 45 Wordsworth Drive, Bletchley, Milton Keynes, **Buckinghamshire**, MK3 5HR, ENG.
(T) 01908 643684
Speciality: Chiropodists (Podiatrists).
● **Owner** Mrs S Spencer
S (Ref:HM19003)

## SPENCER, TERESA

**Teresa Spencer**, Harbour Lights, 30 Manor Lane, Selsey, Chichester, **Sussex (West)**, PO20 0NX, ENG.
(T) 01243 602058
Speciality: Hypnosis.
● **Owner** Mrs T Spencer
B (Ref:HM19004)

## SPENCER, VALERIE

**Valerie Spencer**, The Old Convent, Beeches Green, Stroud, **Gloucestershire**, GL5 4AD, ENG.
(T) 01453 825858
Speciality: Hypnosis.
● **Owner** Ms V Spencer
B (Ref:HM19005)

## SPENCER-EDWARDS, K

**K Spencer-Edwards**, Sheerwater Beach Rd, Heybrook Bay, Plymouth, **Devon**, PL9 0BS, ENG.
(T) 01752 863295
Speciality: Aromatherapy.
M O (Ref:HM19006)

## SPERRE-DANSIE, B

**Mrs B Sperre-Dansie**, 15A Codicote Rd, Welwyn, **Hertfordshire**, AL6 9NE, ENG.
(T) 01438 716838
Speciality: Physiotherapy.
P S T (Ref:HM19007)

## SPIBY, L

**L Spiby**, 59 Valley Rd, Crewe, **Cheshire**, CW2 8JZ, ENG.
(T) 01270 661593
Speciality: Osteopathy.
● **Owner** Mr M Davies
P S T (Ref:HM19008)

## SPICE DIRECT

**Spice Direct**, 10 Three Crowns Rd, Colchester, **Essex**, CO4 5AD, ENG.
(T) 01206 751660 (F) 01206 751084
Speciality: Aromatherapy.
● **Owner** Mrs S Cole-Clouth
M O (Ref:HM19009)

## SPICE SHOP

**Spice Shop (The)**, 1 Blenheim Cres, London, **London (Greater)**, W11 2EE, ENG.
(T) 020 7221 4448 (F) 020 7229 1591
Speciality: Herbal Medicine.
● **Owner** Mrs B Erath
M (Ref:HM19010)

## SPICKERNELL, J

**J Spickernell**, 8 Wykeham Rd, Farnham, **Surrey**, GU9 7JR, ENG.
(T) 01252 733294
Speciality: Complementary Medicines & Therapy.
C M (Ref:HM19011)

## SPILLANE, EMMA

**Emma Spillane**, Lanheverne Parc, St. Keverne, Helston, **Cornwall**, TR12 6LX, ENG.
(T) 01326 280515
Speciality: Chiropodists (Podiatrists).
● **Owner** Ms E Spliiane
S (Ref:HM19012)

## SPILLMAN, HOLLY

**Holly Spillman**, 1 Ville Franche, Rue De L'aitte, Torteval, **Guernsey**, GY8 0PD, ENG.
(T) 01481 267117
Speciality: Reflexology.
S T (Ref:HM19013)

## SPILSBURY, FIDELMA

**Fidelma Spilsbury**, 42 Lees Gardens, Maidenhead, **Berkshire**, SL6 4NT, ENG.
(T) 01628 783659
Speciality: Complementary Medicines & Therapy.
C M (Ref:HM19014)

## SPINAL HEALTH CLINIC

**Spinal Health Clinic**, Church Rd, Tunbridge Wells, **Kent**, TN1 1JT, ENG.
(T) 01892 524774 (F) 01892 618522
Speciality: Osteopathy.
● **Owner** Mrs M Horner
P S T (Ref:HM19015)

## SPINES CLINIC

**Spines Clinic**, 45 Planks Lane, Wombourne, Wolverhampton, **Midlands (West)**, WV5 8DX, ENG.
(T) 01902 894613
Speciality: Physiotherapy.
● **Owner** Mr P Evans
P S T (Ref:HM19016)

## SPINK, BERNADETTE

**Clinic of Holistic Natural Therapy**, Clinic Of Holistic Natural Therapy, 5 Longthorpe Cl, Littleover, Derby, **Derbyshire**, DE23 7WE, ENG.
(T) 01332 523181
Speciality: Remedial Massage, Sports Massage, Manipulative Therapy, Clinical Aromatherapy. ✓
● **Owner** Ms B Spink Q: LCSP, MRQA. M: AOC, LCSP, RQA.
B Yrs. Est.: 14 (Ref:HM19017)

## SPINK, F R

**F R Spink**, 17 Nottingham Rd, South Croydon, **Surrey**, CR2 6AR, ENG.
(T) 020 8688 0534
Speciality: Homeopathy.
● **Principal** Dr F Spink
M (Ref:HM19018)

## SPINOZA, DAVID

**David Spinoza**, 48 The Meadway, Cuffley, Potters Bar, **Hertfordshire**, EN6 4ES, ENG.
(T) 01707 876161 (F) 01707 876161
(E) davidspinoza@cs.com
Speciality: Acupressure, Acupuncture, Aura Therapy, Autogenic Training, Bio-energetics, Biofeedback, Complementary Therapy, Cranial Osteopathy, Dowsing, Herbal Medicine, Hypnosis, Hypnotherapy, Iridology, Kinesiology, Kirlian Photography, Naturopathy, Osteopathy, T'ai-Chi Ch'uan, Yoga, Zen Therapy, Trichology, Hair Analysis. ✓
● **Director** Mr D Spinoza Q: DO, ND. M: BOrthA.
B H P S Yrs. Est.: 40 (Ref:HM19019)

## SPIRAC PHYSIOTHERAPY

**Spirac Physiotherapy**, Century House, 417-419 Chatsworth Rd, Chesterfield, **Derbyshire**, S40 3AD, ENG.
(T) 01246 558317
Speciality: Physiotherapy. ✓
● **Physiotherapist** Mr J Flecther Q: MCSP, SRP. M: CSP.
● **Physiotherapist** Mr K Simons Q: MCSP, SRP. M: CSP.
P S T Yrs. Est.: 10 (Ref:HM19020)

## SPIRAL CENTRE

**Spiral Centre**, 2 Shelburne Rd, London, **London (Greater)**, N7 6DL, ENG.
(T) 020 7607 5503
Speciality: Complementary Medicines & Therapy.
● **Director** Ms A Ridge
C M (Ref:HM19021)

## SPIRIT 2000

**Spirit 2000**, 121 Linden Rd, Seaton Delaval, Whitley Bay, **Tyne and Wear**, NE25 0DB, ENG.
(T) 01912 373114
Speciality: Clairvoyants & Palmists.
● **Owner** Mrs J Wheatley
B (Ref:HM19022)

## SPIRIT HEALTH & FITNESS

**Spirit Health & Fitness**, 14 Chapel Rd, Tiptree, Colchester, **Essex**, CO5 0RA, ENG.
(T) 01621 816955
Speciality: Complementary Medicines & Therapy.
● **Owner** Mrs S Caroll
M (Ref:HM19023)

## SPIRIT WITHIN

**Spirit Within**, 182 London Rd West, Bath, **Somerset**, BA1 7DQ, ENG.
(T) 01225 852584 (F) 01225 852584
Speciality: Complementary Medicines & Therapy.
● **Owner** Ms S Cawthorne
C M (Ref:HM19024)

## SPIRITUAL & HEALING CENTRE

**Spiritual & Healing Centre**, 8 Church St, Carlton, Barnsley, **Yorkshire (South)**, S71 3EY, ENG.
(T) 01226 727172
Speciality: Clairvoyants & Palmists.
● **Owner** Mrs R Broadbent
B (Ref:HM19025)

## SPIRITUAL HEALER

**Spiritual Healer**, 5 The New Severalls, Milton Lilbourne, Pewsey, **Wiltshire**, SN9 5LL, ENG.
(T) 01672 564143
Speciality: Spiritual Healing. ✓
● **Owner/Spiritual Healer** Mrs J Puttick
T Yrs. Est.: 4 (Ref:HM19026)

## SPIRITUAL HEALING

**Spiritual Healing**, The Bentley Centre, Isis Trading Estate, Swindon, **Wiltshire**, SN1 2SH, ENG.
(T) 01793 791317
Speciality: Complementary Medicines & Therapy.
● **Owner** Miss I James
C M (Ref:HM19027)

## SPIRITUAL PATHWAYS

**Spiritual Pathways**, 4a Overton Arcade, High St, Wrexham, LL13 8LL, WAL.
(T) 01978 314477 (F) 01978 314477
Speciality: Complementary Medicines & Therapy.
● **Owner** Ms C Thomas
M (Ref:HM19028)

## SPIRITUAL THERAPIST

**Elaine Crook**, 156 Cornelian St, Blackburn, **Lancashire**, BB1 9QN, ENG.
(T) 01254 727521
Speciality: Absent Healing, Aura Therapy, Complementary Therapy, Counselling, Crystal Healing, Faith Healing, Healer, Healing Therapy, Holistic Healing, Meditation, Paranormal Therapies, Reiki, Spiritual Healing, Visualisation Therapy, Past Life Healing/Therapy, Clairvoyant Readings - find life purpose and finding solutions to problems.
● **Therapist/Healer/Clairvoyant** Miss E Crook
H Yrs. Est.: 12 (Ref:HM19029)

## SPIRITUALIST ASS OF GB

**Spiritualist Association Of Great Britain**, 33 Belgrave Sq, London, **London (Greater)**, SW1X 8QB, ENG.
(T) 020 7235 3351
Speciality: Clairvoyants & Palmists.
● **Manager** Mrs C Blight
B (Ref:HM19030)



Key continued: Yrs.Est: Years Established Q: Qualifications M: Professional Membership ✓ Indemnity Insurance Accept Credit Cards

## SPIRITUALIST NAT UNION HEALERS

**Spiritualist National Union Healers**, Molandi, Northwood Lane, Hayling Island, **Hampshire**, PO11 0LR, ENG.
(T) 023 9246 6927
Speciality: Complementary Medicines & Therapy.
● **Chairman** Mr J Weir
C M (Ref:HM19031)

## SPITERI-RUTTER, R

**R Spiteri-Rutter**, 20 Hursley Rd, Havant, **Hampshire**, PO9 4RE, ENG.
(T) 023 9247 7452
Speciality: Clairvoyants & Palmists.
B (Ref:HM19032)

## SPIVACK, A

**A Spivack**, 97 Netley Rd, Ilford, **Essex**, IG2 7NW, ENG.
(T) 020 8554 0999 (F) 020 8518 2045
Speciality: Physiotherapy.
● **Owner** Mr A Spivack
P S T (Ref:HM19033)

## SPLASHDOWN WATER BIRTH SVS

**Splashdown Water Birth Services**, 17 Wellington Trce, Harrow, **London (Greater)**, HA1 3EP, ENG.
(T) 020 8422 9308
Speciality: Complementary Medicines & Therapy.
C M (Ref:HM19034)

## SPONDON CHIROPODY CLINIC

**Spondon Chiropody Clinic**, 2a Chapel St, Spondon, Derby, **Derbyshire**, DE21 7JP, ENG.
(T) 01332 671392
Speciality: Chiropodists (Podiatrists).
● **Owner** Mr K Thompson
S (Ref:HM19035)

## SPOONER, K E

**K E Spooner**, Franklin House, Stanhope Rd, Horncastle, **Lincolnshire**, LN9 5DG, ENG.
(T) 01507 526116
Speciality: Chiropodists (Podiatrists).
● **Owner** Mrs K Spooner
S (Ref:HM19036)

## SPOONER, K M

**K M Spooner**, Granary Farm, Long Dolver Drove, Hasse Rd, Soham, Ely, **Cambridgeshire**, CB7 5UP, ENG.
(T) 01353 721820
Speciality: Chiropractic.
P S T (Ref:HM19037)

## SPOONER, PATRICIA

**Patricia Spooner**, Norold, Northgate, Pinchbeck, Spalding, **Lincolnshire**, PE11 3TB, ENG.
(T) 01775 640321
Speciality: Hypnosis.
● **Owner** Mrs P Horton
B (Ref:HM19038)

## SPOORS, L & D

**L & D Spoors**, 1a Ashfield Trce, Chester Le Street, **County Durham**, DH3 3PD, ENG.
(T) 01913 883059
Speciality: Osteopathy, Surgical Chiropody, Sport Injuries. ✓
● **Osteopath** Mr Spoors Q: DO, DO (Hons), MSSCh. M: B.A.Ch.P.
S Yrs. Est.: 11 (Ref:HM19039)

## SPORT MOTIVATION

**Sport Motivation**, Chantry House, Nuthurst Rd, Monks Gate, Horsham, **Sussex (West)**, RH13 6LG, ENG.
(T) 01403 891728
Speciality: Psychology.
● **Owner** Mr A Jones
B (Ref:HM19040)

## SPORT, ALEXANDER

**Alexander Sport**, 5 Wybridge, Keysoe, Bedford, **Bedfordshire**, MK44 2HL, ENG.
(T) 01234 708777
(E) roymstat@aol.com
Speciality: Alexander Technique. ✓
● **Teacher of the Alexander Technique** Mr R Palmer Q: MSTAT. M: STAT.
P Yrs. Est.: 3 (Ref:HM19041)

## SPORT-MED

**Sport-Med**, Norbury Chambers, Norbury St, Stockport, **Cheshire**, SK1 3SH, ENG.
(T) 01614 804500 (F) 01614 747469
Speciality: Physiotherapy.
● **Owner** Mr T Deykin
P S T (Ref:HM19042)

## SPORTS INJURIES & REHAB CENTRE

**Sports Injuries & Rehabilitation Centre**, Woodhouse Station Enterprise Centre, Mansfield Woodhouse, Mansfield, **Nottinghamshire**, NG19 9NZ, ENG.
(T) 01623 453918
Speciality: Physiotherapy.
● **Owner** Mr I Pearce
P S T (Ref:HM19043)

## SPORTS INJURY CLINIC

**Sports Injury Clinic**, Abbey Sports Centre, Abbey Rd, Durham, **County Durham**, DH1 5DQ, ENG.
(T) 01913 831199
Speciality: Physiotherapy.
P S T (Ref:HM19044)

## SPORTS MASSAGE CENTRE

**Sports Massage Centre**, Kelvin Gr, North Shields, **Tyne and Wear**, NE29 9LE, ENG.
(T) 01912 571043
Speciality: Physiotherapy.
● **Owner** Mr J Addison
P S T (Ref:HM19045)

## SPORTS THERAPY

**Sports Therapy**, 12 Cedar Court, Sheen Lane, London, **London (Greater)**, SW14 8LY, ENG.
(T) 020 8876 2833
Speciality: Physiotherapy.
● **Manager** Mrs A Sweeney
P S T (Ref:HM19046)

## SPRENT, N

**N Sprent**, 145 Iffley Rd, Oxford, **Oxfordshire**, OX4 1EJ, ENG.
(T) 01865 249337
Speciality: Hypnosis.
● **Owner** Mr N Sprent
B (Ref:HM19047)

## SPRENT, N

**N Sprent**, 9 Park End St, Oxford, **Oxfordshire**, OX1 1HH, ENG.
(T) 01865 251055
Speciality: Hypnosis.
● **Principal** Mr N Sprent
B (Ref:HM19048)

## SPREYER, DIANNE

**Dianne Spreyer**, 19A The Oval, Sidcup, **Kent**, DA15 9ER, ENG.
(T) 020 8308 0963
Speciality: Complementary Medicines & Therapy.
C M (Ref:HM19049)

## SPRINGALL, CHERRY

**Cherry Springall**, 28 Richmond Rd, Westerton, Chichester, **Sussex (West)**, PO18 0PQ, ENG.
(T) 01243 786652
Speciality: Hypnotherapy.
● **Owner** Mrs C Springhall
B (Ref:HM19050)

## SPRINGETT, K

**K Springett**, 58 Hill Rd, Eastbourne, **Sussex (East)**, BN20 8SN, ENG.
(T) 01323 412135
Speciality: Chiropodists (Podiatrists).
S (Ref:HM19051)

## SPRINGFIELD LODGE HEALTH CARE

**Springfield Lodge Health Care Centre**, 337-339 Norwich Rd, Ipswich, **Suffolk**, IP1 4BN, ENG.
(T) 01473 464300
Speciality: Acupressure, Acupuncture, Alexander Technique, Aromatherapy, Chiropody, Chiropractic, Counselling, Healing Therapy, Herbal Medicine, Homeopathy, Hypnotherapy, Indian Head Massage, Iridology, Kinesiology, Neuro-Linguistic Program, Nutritional Therapy, Osteopathy, Physiotherapy, Psychotherapy, Reflexology, Reiki, Shiatsu, Yoga, Colonic Hydrotherapy, Empulse Therapy, Holistic Massage, McTimoney Chorley Chiropratic, Osteoporosis Screening, Power Assisted Manipulation and Sports Injury Treatments. ✓
● **Colonic Therapist** Ms G Cooper Q: RCT, RGN. M: CIA.
● **Verruca Treating Chiropodist** Ms J Knowles Q: MBChA, MSSCh.
● **Nutritional Therapist** Ms P Prior M: BANT.
● **Chiropractor** Mr P Parolin Q: DC, RCST. M: BCA.
● **Shiatsu Practitioner** Ms T Dent Q: BSc, Dip.Eass. M: Shiatsu Society UK.
● **Counsellor** Ms M Gayland Q: Dip.Couns. M: BACP.
● **Homeopath** Ms C Putus Q: Cert.Couns, Cert.Couns.Groupwork, Dip.Hom, RMANM. M: ANM.
● **Osteopath** Philippe Gely Q: BSc (Hons), Hons (OST).
● **Hypnotherapist** Mr M Buckley Q: Dip.Hyp, Dip.Psych, DIPC, MABH, UKHR. M: UKHR.
● **Acupuncturist** Shaun Taylor Q: Lic.Ac, MBAcC.
● **Reflexologist** Ms A Barnes
● **Alexander Technique Teacher** Mr S Wainman M: STAT.
● **Swedish/Therapeutic Massage Therapist** Jane Hayman Q: Dip.AP, ITEC.
C Yrs. Est.: 10 (Ref:HM19052)

## SPRINGHILL CENTRE

**Springhill Centre**, Cuddington Rd, Cuddington, Aylesbury, **Buckinghamshire**, HP18 0AD, ENG.
(T) 01296 748278
Speciality: Complementary Medicines & Therapy.
C M (Ref:HM19053)

## SPRINGWELL HEALTH CLINIC

**Springwell Health Clinic**, 10 Agbrigg Rd, Wakefield, **Yorkshire (West)**, WF2 6AF, ENG.
(T) 01924 250969
Speciality: Physiotherapy.
● **Owner** Miss S Slater
P S T (Ref:HM19054)

## SPRINGWOOD COMP HEALTH

**Springwood Complementary Health**, 33 Woodcock Court, Three Mile Cross, Reading, **Berkshire**, RG7 1BZ, ENG.
(T) 01189 888913
Speciality: Indian Head Massage, Reflexology.
S T (Ref:HM19055)

## SPYROS MOUZOURIDES

**Spyros Mouzourides**, 261 Queens Lane, Muswell Hill, London, **London (Greater)**, N10 1DN, ENG.
(T) 020 8886 7546 (F) 020 8883 5760
Speciality: Complementary Therapy, Dietician, Hay Diet, Herbal Medicine, Holistic Healing, Iridology, Miasm Therapy, Naturopathy, Nutritional Therapy, Reflexology. ✓
● **Therapist** Mr S Mouzourides M: BANT.
C Yrs. Est.: 9 (Ref:HM19056)

## SQUAREY, J V D

**J V D Squarey**, The Vicarage, Shaston Rd, Stourpaine, Blandford Forum, **Dorset**, DT11 8TA, ENG.
(T) 01258 480580 (F) 01258 450378
Speciality: Physiotherapy.
P S T (Ref:HM19057)

## SQUIRE, E

**E Squire**, Coombe Lane, London, **London (Greater)**, SW20 0QY, ENG.
(T) 020 8946 1470
Speciality: Reflexology.
● **Owner** Mrs E Squire
S T (Ref:HM19058)

## SQUIRE, ELIZABETH

**Elizabeth Squire**, Marwood House, 15 The Avenue, Haslemere, **Surrey**, GU27 1JT, ENG.
(T) 01428 643943
Speciality: Reflexology.
S T (Ref:HM19059)

## SQUIRES, J

**J Squires**, 17 North Rd, South Ockendon, **Essex**,



Key: B Mind-Body Medicine C Complementary Medicine H Self Help Treatment M Medicinal Therapy O Oriental Medicine P Postural Therapy S Manipulative Structural Therapy T Touch Therapy

RM15 6PT, ENG.
(T) 01708 857912
Speciality: Chiropodists (Podiatrists).
● **Owner** Mrs J Squires
S (Ref:HM19060)

## SREENAN, JOAN

**Sreenan Joan B A Reg Psychol MIA**, Ballyvisteale, Glanmire, **County Cork**, IRE.
(T) 021 4823 210
Speciality: Complementary Medicines & Therapy.
M (Ref:HM19061)

## SRI AMMAN CLINIC

**Sri Amman Clinic**, 1 Keelers Way, Great Horkesley, Colchester, **Essex**, CO6 4EE, ENG.
(T) 01206 272279
Speciality: Osteopathy.
● **Owner** Mr R Murigiah
P S T (Ref:HM19062)

## ST ALBANS CHIROPRACTIC CLINIC

**St Albans Chiropractic Clinic**, Aberfoyle House, Stapley Rd, St. Albans, **Hertfordshire**, AL3 5EP, ENG.
(T) 01727 856687
Speciality: Acupuncture, Chinese Herbal Medicine, Chiropody, Chiropractic, Counselling, Podiatry. ✓
● **Chiropractor** Asaf Ben-Shahar
● **Chiropractor** Mr S Bassett Q: BSc, MSc (Chiro). M: BCA.
● **Chiropractor** Mr J Rowland Q: Dip.Ac, Dip.CHM, MBAcC.
● **Chiropractor** Dr J Baker
● **Chiropractor** Mr S Jones M: BCA.
● **Chiropractor** Dr M Bassett Q: DC.
● **Chiropractor** Kelsie Short
● **Homeopath** Ms V Newton Q: RSHom.
● **Chiropractor** Mr T Hull M: BCMA, ISPA.
● **Relate Counsellor** Mr Walker Q: BSc.
M Yrs. Est.: 30 (Ref:HM19063)

## ST ANDREWS

**St Andrews**, 56 St Andrews Avenue, Wembley, **London (Greater)**, HA0 2QD, ENG.
(T) 020 8908 6452
Speciality: Chiropodists (Podiatrists).
● **Owner** Mr M Kamdar
S (Ref:HM19064)

## ST ANDREWS OSTEOPATHS

**St Andrews Osteopaths**, 2 Lockhart Pl, St. Andrews, **Fife**, KY16 9XB, SCO.
(T) 01334 477000
Speciality: Acupuncture, Cranial Osteopathy, Massage (Therapeutic), Osteopathy. ✓
● **Osteopath** Ms S Tongue Q: BSc, Hons (OST), RGN. M: GOsC.
● **Osteopath** Mr B Babington Q: BSc, Hons (OST). M: GOsC.
S Yrs. Est.: 3 (Ref:HM19065)

## ST ANDREWS PHYSIO PRACTICE

**St Andrews Physiotherapy Practice**, 147 Market St, St. Andrews, **Fife**, KY16 9PE, SCO.
(T) 01334 477398 (F) 01334 477786
Speciality: Physiotherapy.
● **Partner** Mr C Hardisty
P S T (Ref:HM19066)

## ST ANDREWS PRACTICE

**St Andrews Practice**, Ashley Hill, Bristol, BS7 9BE, ENG.
(T) 01179 445542 (F) 01179 445542
Speciality: Homeopathy.
M (Ref:HM19067)

## ST ANNES PHYSIOTHERAPY CLINIC

**St Annes Physiotherapy Clinic**, Dorset House, St Annes Rd, Eastbourne, **Sussex (East)**, BN21 2HR, ENG.
(T) 01323 739666 (F) 01323 739666
Speciality: Physiotherapy.
● **Partner** Mr D Gladwin
P S T (Ref:HM19068)

## ST AUGUSTINES PSYCHOTHRPY CTRE

**St Augustines Psychotherapy Centre**, 26 St Augustines St, Norwich, **Norfolk**, NR3 3BZ, ENG.
(T) 01603 633791
Speciality: Psychotherapy.
● **Partner** Mrs R Wood-Bevan
B (Ref:HM19069)

## ST AUSTELL CHIROPRACTIC CLINIC

**St Austell Chiropractic Clinic**, 87 Alexandra Rd, St. Austell, **Cornwall**, PL25 4QW, ENG.
(T) 01726 66002
Speciality: Acupuncture, Aromatherapy, Chiropractic, Homeopathy, Psychotherapy, Reflexology. ✓
● **Owner** Dr G Perry Q: DC, MAB Phys. M: BAAC, GCC.
● **Chiropractor** Dr D Styles Q: DC. M: BCA, GCC.
P Yrs. Est.: 30 (Ref:HM19070)

## ST AUSTELL NTRL HLTH PRACTICE

**St Austell Natural Health Practice**, 117 Slades Rd, St. Austell, **Cornwall**, PL25 4HE, ENG.
(T) 01726 66060
Speciality: Complementary Medicines & Therapy.
C M (Ref:HM19071)

## ST BOSWELLS CHIRO CLINIC

**Scotia Chiropractic Ltd**, St Boswells Chiropractic Clinic, 16 Jenny Moores Rd, St. Boswells, **Scottish Borders**, TD6 0AL, SCO.
(T) 01835 823645 (F) 01835 823930
(E) carlahow@scottishborders.co.uk
Speciality: Chiropractic, Applied Kinesiology. ✓
● **Director/Chiropractor** Ms C How Q: DC. M: GCC, SCA.
● **Chiropractor** Claude Fournier Q: DC. M: SCA.
● **Chiropractor** Ms A Sharp Q: BSc (Chiro). M: SCA.
S Yrs. Est.: 14 (Ref:HM19072)

## ST CROSS HOMOEOPATHIC CLINIC

**St Cross Homoeopathic Clinic**, 49 St Cross Rd, Winchester, **Hampshire**, SO23 9PS, ENG.
(T) 01962 878040
Speciality: Homeopathy.
M (Ref:HM19073)

## ST DAVIDS OSTEOPATHIC CLINIC

**St Davids Osteopathic Clinic**, 1 Walnut Gardens, Exeter, **Devon**, EX4 4DH, ENG.
(T) 01392 221321
Speciality: Osteopathy.
● **Senior Partner** Mr C Crewdson
P S T (Ref:HM19074)

## ST GEORGES MULTI THERAPY CTRE

**St Georges Multi Therapy Centre**, 50 St. Georges Rd, Bolton, **Lancashire**, BL1 2DD, ENG.
(T) 01204 654662
Speciality: Acupressure, Acupuncture, Allergy Testing, Aromatherapy, Chinese Herbal Medicine, Chiropody, Chiropractic, Cognitive Therapy, Complementary Therapy, Counselling, Family Therapy, Group Therapy, Herbal Medicine, Homeopathy, Hypnosis, Hypnotherapy, Indian Head Massage, Life Style Coaching, Osteopathy, Physiotherapy, Psychotherapy, Reflexology, Stress Therapy, Visualisation Therapy. ✓
● **Counsellor/Psychotherapist** Ms K Gorton Q: Cert.Couns, Cert.Couns.Groupwork, Dip.Couns, Dip.Hyp, Dip.Psych. M: BACP.
B (Ref:HM19075)

## ST GEORGES OSTEOPATHIC CLINIC

**St Georges Osteopathic Clinic**, 25 St. Georges Rd, Worthing, **Sussex (West)**, BN11 2DS, ENG.
(T) 01903 879323
Speciality: Homeopathy.
M (Ref:HM19076)

## ST JAMES CHIROPRACTIC CLINIC

**St James Chiropractic Clinic**, 158 Winchester Rd, Shirley, Southampton, **Hampshire**, SO16 6UE, ENG.
(T) 023 8078 8111
Speciality: Chiropractors.
P S T (Ref:HM19077)

## ST JAMES MEDICAL CENTRE

**St James Medical Centre**, 3 Herbet St, Pontardawe, **Neath Port Talbot**, SA3 3EB, WAL.
Speciality: Counselling, Hypnotherapy, Psychotherapy. ✓
● **Practitioner** Mr Shrewsbury
C Yrs. Est.: 7 (Ref:HM19078)

## ST JAMES'S SURGERY

**Charlotte Wightman**, 8-9 Northampton Buildings, Bath, **Somerset**, BA1 2SR, ENG.
(T) 01225 422911
Speciality: Complementary Therapy, Cranial Osteopathy, Holistic Healing, Osteopathy.
● **Osteopath** Ms C Wightman Q: BSc, Hons (OST). M: GOsC.
S Yrs. Est.: 2 (Ref:HM19079)

## ST JOHN STREET PHYSIO PRACTICE

**St John Street Physiotherapy Practice**, 19 St John St, Manchester, **Manchester (Greater)**, M3 4DS, ENG.
(T) 01618 348997 (F) 01618 345312
Speciality: Electrotherapy, Kinesiology, Manipulation, Massage (Therapeutic), Phytotherapy, Ultrasonics. ✓
● **Owner/Chartered Physiotherapist** Mr P Emm Q: Chartered Physio, SRP. M: CSP.
S Yrs. Est.: 30 (Ref:HM19080)

## ST JOHN, RUTH MOYRA

**Ruth Moyra St John**, 87 Woking Cl, London, **London (Greater)**, SW15 5LB, ENG.
(T) 020 8392 1154
Speciality: Reflexology.
S T (Ref:HM19081)

## ST JOHNS OSTEOPATHIC

**St Johns Osteopathic & Natural Health Care Clinic**, 2 St Johns St, Manchester, **Manchester (Greater)**, M3 4DA, ENG.
(T) 01618 195559
Speciality: Osteopathy.
● **Owner** Mr F Connor
P S T (Ref:HM19082)

## ST JOHN'S PHYSICAL THERAPISTS

**St John's Physical Therapists**, Kingsbury Rd, Worcester, **Worcestershire**, WR2 4JH, ENG.
(T) 01905 426393
Speciality: Complementary Medicines & Therapy.
● **Partner** Mrs J Jones
M (Ref:HM19083)

## ST LAWRENCE HOUSE CHIROPRACTIC

**St Lawrence House Chiropractic Clinic**, St Lawrence House, 2 Barnes Cl, Winchester, **Hampshire**, SO23 9QX, ENG.
(T) 01962 843242
Speciality: Chiropractic.
● **Owner** Mr M Kennedy
P S T (Ref:HM19084)

## ST LUKES MEDICAL & THRPY CTRE

**St Lukes Medical & Therapy Centre**, 57 Cainscross Rd, Stroud, **Gloucestershire**, GL5 4EX, ENG.
(T) 01453 753450
Speciality: Complementary Medicines & Therapy.
C M (Ref:HM19085)

## ST MARTINS LANE PRACTICE

**St Martins Lane Practice**, 8 Hop Gardens, Covent Garden, London, **London (Greater)**, WC2N 4EA, ENG.
(T) 020 7240 4211
Speciality: Osteopathy.
● **Practice Manager** Ms J Ovett
P S T (Ref:HM19086)

## ST MARY'S CLINIC

**St Mary's Clinic**, 14-16 St. Marys Pl, Bury, **Lancashire**, BL9 0DZ, ENG.
(T) 01617 971800 (F) 01617 971800
Speciality: Manipulation, Massage (Therapeutic), Sports Therapy, Exercise Therapy. ✓ CREDIT
● **Therapist** Mr S Pennington M: LCSP.
● **Podiatrist** Ms B O'Fardell Q: S.R.Ch, SRPod.
● **Manipulative Therapist** Mr E Caldwell M: LCSP.
● **Remedial Masseur** Mr C Caldwell M: LCSP.
S Yrs. Est.: 15 (Ref:HM19087)



Key continued: **Yrs.Est:** Years Established **Q:** Qualifications **M:** Professional Membership ✓ Indemnity Insurance CREDIT Accept Credit Cards

## ST MARYS PRACTICE

**St Marys Practice**, Lower Olland St, Bungay, **Suffolk**, NR35 1BY, ENG.
(T) 01986 892846
Speciality: Acupuncture, Chiropody, Herbal Medicine, Nutritional Therapy, Osteopathy. ✓
- **Partner/Osteopath** Ms K McDonald Q: BSc. M: GOsC.
- **Partner/Osteopath** Mr M James Q: DO. M: GOsC.
- **Practice Manager** Ms E Shawe
- **Chiropodist** Mr D Measer

C Yrs. Est.: 3 (Ref:HM19088)

## ST MICHAELS CHIROPRACTIC

**St Michaels Chiropractic Clinic**, St Michaels Surgery, Walwyn Cl, Bath, **Somerset**, BA2 1ER, ENG.
(T) 01225 484800
Speciality: Chiropractic. ✓
- **Chiropractor** Mr W Rhodes Q: DC, NACM.

P Yrs. Est.: 10 (Ref:HM19089)

## ST MICHAEL'S HYPNOTHERAPY

**St Michael's Hypnotherapy**, 4 St Michaels Cl, Stoke St. Michael, Radstock, **Somerset**, BA3 5LF, ENG.
(T) 01749 840838
(E) jpl7534@aol.com
Speciality: Hypnotherapy, Stress Therapy, Curative Hypnotherapy.
- **Hypnotherapist** Ms J Larner Q: Brit.Sch.Cur.Hyp.

B Yrs. Est.: 6 (Ref:HM19090)

## ST MICHAELS REST

**St Michaels Rest**, The Haws, The Green, Millom, **Cumbria**, LA18 5HQ, ENG.
(T) 01229 775775 (F) 01229 772192
Speciality: Complementary Medicines & Therapy.
- **Partner** Mr R Belder

C M (Ref:HM19091)

## ST NEOTS OSTEOPATHIC CLINIC

**St Neots Osteopathic Clinic**, 23A Huntingdon St, St. Neots, **Cambridgeshire**, PE19 1BG, ENG.
(T) 01480 211411 (F) 01480 211411
Speciality: Osteopathy.

P S T (Ref:HM19092)

## ST NICHOLAS SURGERY

**St Nicholas Surgery**, The Health Centre, Canterbury Way, Stevenage, **Hertfordshire**, SG1 4LH, ENG.
(T) 01438 317738
Speciality: Chiropodists (Podiatrists).
- **Owner** Mr G Webb

S (Ref:HM19093)

## ST PAULS OSTEOPATHY PRACTICE

**St Pauls Osteopathy Practice and Complementary Health Clinic**, 50-54 St Pauls Sq, Birmingham, **Midlands (West)**, B3 1QS, ENG.
(T) 01212 362169 (F) 01212 2362169
Speciality: Absent Healing, Acupuncture, Aromatherapy, Bach Remedies, Cranial Osteopathy, Electrotherapy, Healer, Holistic Healing, Homeopathy, Indian Head Massage, Manipulation, Massage (Therapeutic), Naturopathy, Osteopathy, Reiki, Ultrasonics. ✓
- **Therapist** Mr B Hubball Q: LCPH.
- **Therapist** Ms S Jay Q: Dip.AF, MIPTI. M: IPTI.
- **Therapist** Mrs D Bailey Q: DO. M: GOsC.
- **Therapist** Mr B Bodle Q: BSc (Hons), DO, MBA. M: GOsC.

S Yrs. Est.: 6 (Ref:HM19094)

## ST PETERS CLINIC

**St Peters Clinic**, 143 St Peters Rd, Walkinstown, Dublin, **County Dublin**, IRE.
(T) 01460 3474
Speciality: Complementary Medicines & Therapy.

M (Ref:HM19095)

## ST PETERSGATE PRIVATE CLINIC

**St Petersgate Private Clinic**, 39 St Petersgate, Stockport, **Cheshire**, SK1 1DH, ENG.
(T) 01617 482280
Speciality: Physiotherapy.
- **Assistant Manager** Mr M Bennett

P S T (Ref:HM19096)

## ST RUMONS HAIR & NTRL HEALTH

**St Rumons Hair & Natural Health**, 16 Place Lane, Seaford, **Sussex (East)**, BN25 1LA, ENG.
(T) 01323 899563
Speciality: Complementary Medicines & Therapy.

C M (Ref:HM19097)

## ST SAMPSON'S MEDICAL CENTRE

**St Sampson's Medical Centre**, Grandes Maisons Rd, St. Sampson's, Guernsey, **Channel Islands**, GY2 4JS, ENG.
(T) 01481 45915
Speciality: Chiropractic, Manipulation. ✓
- **Chiropractor** Mr R Ions Q: DO. M: GCC, MCA.

S Yrs. Est.: 8 (Ref:HM19098)

## ST STEPHENS PRACTICE

**St Stephens Practice**, 21A St. Stephens Rd, Norwich, **Norfolk**, NR1 3SP, ENG.
(T) 01603 630226
Speciality: Acupressure, Acupuncture, Chiropody, Crystal Healing, Herbal Medicine, Homeopathy, Hypnotherapy, Massage (Therapeutic), Osteopathy, Reiki, Spiritual Healing. ✓
- **Osteopath** Ms A Tonkin Q: BSc. M: GOsC.
- **Reiki Master** Mrs M Cardwell Q: ITEC, Reiki Master.
- **Osteopath** Mr C Lim Q: DO. M: GOsC.
- **Chiropodist** Mrs M Prime Q: S.R.Ch. M: S.C.P.
- **Acupunturist** Mr N Hurn Q: Lic.Ac. M: BAcC.
- **Hypnotherapist** Ms C Hurn

C (Ref:HM19099)

## ST VINCENTS COMMUNITY PHYSIO

**St Vincents Community Physiotherapy Clinic**, Wiltshire Lane, Pinner, **London (Greater)**, HA5 2NB, ENG.
(T) 020 8426 1964
Speciality: Physiotherapy.
- **Manager** Mrs J Farrant

P S T (Ref:HM19100)

## STABLEFORD, JOYCE

**Joyce Stableford**, 18 Alma Cl, Benfleet, **Essex**, SS7 2EG, ENG.
(T) 01702 557649
Speciality: Hypnosis, Meditation, Psychotherapy, T'ai-Chi Ch'uan.
- **Owner** Mrs J Stableford

B (Ref:HM19101)

## STACEY, R A

**R A Stacey**, 29a Lemon St, Truro, **Cornwall**, TR1 2LS, ENG.
(T) 01872 274355
Speciality: Chiropodists (Podiatrists).
- **Owner** Mr R Stacey

S (Ref:HM19102)

## STACEY, R A

**R A Stacey**, 7 City Rd, Truro, **Cornwall**, TR1 2JJ, ENG.
(T) 01872 320030
Speciality: Chiropodists (Podiatrists).
- **Owner** Mr R Stacey

S (Ref:HM19103)

## STACKTHEME

**Stacktheme Ltd**, 59 Bridge St, Dollar, **Clackmannanshire**, FK14 7DQ, SCO.
(T) 01259 743200 (F) 01259 743002
Speciality: Complementary Medicines & Therapy.
- **Owner** Mr N Bowler

C M (Ref:HM19104)

## STADLER, M L

**M L Stadler**, 19 Well Lane, Shaftesbury, **Dorset**, SP7 8LP, ENG.
(T) 01747 855167
Speciality: Homeopathy.

M (Ref:HM19105)

## STAEBLER, F E

**F E Staebler**, 81 St Georges Avenue, London, **London (Greater)**, N7 0AJ, ENG.
(T) 020 7700 7078
Speciality: Acupuncture.
- **Owner** Dr F Staebler

O (Ref:HM19106)

## STAFF, TREVOR J

**Trevor J Staff**, 1 Station Approach, Longford Rd, Bognor Regis, **Sussex (West)**, PO21 1BS, ENG.
(T) 01243 822575
Speciality: Chiropodists (Podiatrists).
- **Owner** Mr T Staff

S (Ref:HM19107)

## STAFFORD CHIROPRACTIC CLINIC

**Stafford Chiropractic Clinic**, 1 The Rise, Walton On The Hill, Stafford, **Staffordshire**, ST17 0LH, ENG.
(T) 01785 614040
Speciality: Chiropractic, Manipulation, Massage (Therapeutic), X-Ray. ✓
- **Sports Massage Therapist** Ms K Dreaves Q: BSc (Hons), Dip.AST, Dip.LSSM, MGCP.
- **Chiropractor** Ms J Hvas Q: DC. M: BCA, CC.
- **Chiropractor** Dr K Jacobsen Q: BSc, DC. M: BCA, CC.
- **Chiropractor** Ms J Martingale Q: BSc, DC. M: BCA.

P S Yrs. Est.: 8 (Ref:HM19108)

## STAFFORD, ASHLEY

**Ashley Stafford**, Bushmaster Natural Health Practice, 204 Uxbridge Rd, London, **London (Greater)**, W12 7JD, ENG.
(T) 020 8749 3792
Speciality: Osteopathy.

P S T (Ref:HM19109)

## STAFFORD, CAROL

**STAFFORD CAROL BSc HDipEd**, Dip Psych Miahm, Sutton, **County Dublin**, IRE.
(T) 01832 6792
Speciality: Complementary Medicines & Therapy.

M (Ref:HM19110)

## STAFFORDSHIRE MCTIMONEY

**Staffordshire McTimoney Chiropractic**, Ishta Centre, 26 Kings Avenue, Stone, **Staffordshire**, ST15 8HD, ENG.
(T) 01785 616010 (F) 01785 616010
(E) sue@ishta.co.uk
(W) www.ishta.co.uk
Speciality: Chiropractic, Cranio-Sacral Therapy, Nutritional Advice, McTimoney Chiropractic, Ishta Spinal Touch. ✓
- **Chiropractor** Ms S Weller Q: BSc, DC. M: ALTT.

S Yrs. Est.: 5 (Ref:HM19111)

## STAGGS, JANE

**Jane Staggs**, 22 Leys Avenue, Cambridge, **Cambridgeshire**, CB4 2AW, ENG.
(T) 01223 312374 (F) 01223 312374
Speciality: Alexander Technique.
- **Owner** Mrs J Staggs

P S (Ref:HM19112)

## STAINER, A

**Miss A Stainer**, The Osteopathic Practice, 56b Collins Rd, Southsea, **Hampshire**, PO4 9NZ, ENG.
(T) 023 9273 4815
Speciality: Osteopathy.
- **Owner** Mrs A Stainer

P S T (Ref:HM19113)

## STAINES FAMILY CHIROPRACTIC

**Staines Family Chiropractic**, 10a Goring Sq, Church St, Staines, **Surrey**, TW18 4EW, ENG.
(T) 08003 283260
Speciality: Chiropractors.
- **Doctor** Dr J Sykes

P S T (Ref:HM19114)

## STAINSBY, TRICIA S

**Tricia S Stainsby**, 44 Otto Trce, Sunderland, **Tyne and Wear**, SR2 7LP, ENG.
(T) 01915 676152
Speciality: Osteopathy.
- **Owner** Ms T Stainsby

P S T (Ref:HM19115)

## STAINTON, USHA

**Miss Usha Stainton**, Lorien Clinic Peachey

Key: B Mind-Body Medicine C Complementary Medicine H Self Help Treatment M Medicinal Therapy O Oriental Medicine P Postural Therapy S Manipulative Structural Therapy T Touch Therapy

House, Midhurst, **Sussex (West)**, GU29 9LU, ENG.
(T) 01730 816861 (F) 01730 812248
Speciality: Acupuncture.
● **Owner** Miss U Stainton
O (Ref:HM19116)

**STAKIM, SHELIA**

**Shelia Stakim**, 15 Oxford Rd, Worthing, **Sussex (West)**, BN11 1XQ, ENG.
(T) 01903 533631
Speciality: Chiropractic.
P S T (Ref:HM19117)

**STALMEISTERS, D V**

**D V Stalmeisters**, The Moorings, Main St, Bleasby, Nottingham, **Nottinghamshire**, NG14 7GH, ENG.
(T) 01636 831062 (F) 01636 831062
Speciality: Psychotherapy.
● **Owner** Ms D Stalmeisters
B (Ref:HM19118)

**STAMFORD CHIROPODY PRACTICE**

**Stamford Chiropody Practice**, 3 St Leonards St, Stamford, **Lincolnshire**, PE9 2HU, ENG.
(T) 01780 482038
Speciality: Chiropodists (Podiatrists).
● **Partner** Mr R Capewell
S (Ref:HM19119)

**STAMP & ASSOCIATES**

**Paul Stamp & Associates**, 19 College Green, Gloucester, **Gloucestershire**, GL1 2LR, ENG.
(T) 01452 301748
Speciality: Osteopathy.
P S T (Ref:HM19120)

**STAMP, G R**

**G R Stamp**, Lark Barrow, Southdown Rd, Woldingham, Caterham, **Surrey**, CR3 7DP, ENG.
(T) 01883 653103
Speciality: Acupuncture.
O (Ref:HM19121)

**STAMP, N**

**N Stamp**, 43 Queen St, Seaton, **Devon**, EX12 2RB, ENG.
(T) 01297 625878
Speciality: Chiropodists (Podiatrists).
● **Owner** Mr N Stamp
S (Ref:HM19122)

**STANCOMBE, H**

**H Stancombe**, Rose House, Lund Lane, Killinghall, Harrogate, **Yorkshire (North)**, HG3 2BQ, ENG.
(T) 01423 506578
Speciality: Physiotherapy.
P S T (Ref:HM19123)

**STANDERING, A**

**A Standering**, 165 Hemper Lane, Sheffield, **Yorkshire (South)**, S8 7FB, ENG.
(T) 01142 378338
Speciality: Chiropodists (Podiatrists).
● **Owner** Mr A Standering
S (Ref:HM19124)

**STANDISH-HAYES, QUENTIN**

**Quentin Standish-Hayes**, Casterbridge Chiropractic Clinic (The), 7 Icen Way, Dorchester, **Dorset**, DT1 1EW, ENG.
(T) 01305 263048 (F) 01305 259449
Speciality: Chiropractic. ✓
● **Owner** Mr Q Standish-Hayes Q: DC. M: GCC.
● **Chiropractor** Dr B Price Q: DC. M: GCC.
● **Chiropractor** Dr S Hill Q: BSc, DC. M: GCC.
P Yrs. Est.: 6 (Ref:HM19125)

**STANHOPE-WILLIAMSON, BARBARA**

**Barbara Stanhope-Williamson**, Flat 5, 60 West End Lane, London, **London (Greater)**, NW6 2NE, ENG.
(T) 020 7625 6925
Speciality: Reflexology.
S T (Ref:HM19126)

**STANLEY COURT SURGERY**

**Stanley Court Surgery**, 55 High St, Midsomer Norton, Bath, **Somerset**, BA3 2DQ, ENG.
(T) 01761 414692 (F) 01373 467753
Speciality: Chiropractic, Homeopathy. ✓
● **Clinic Manager** Mrs H Jones Q: DC.
M: BCA.
● **Chiropractor** Mr R Jones Q: DC. M: BCA.
P Yrs. Est.: 12 (Ref:HM19127)

**STANLEY, H W (DR)**

**Dr H W Stanley**, Plantation House, Bennett Rd, Salcombe, **Devon**, TQ8 8JJ, ENG.
(T) 01548 842538
Speciality: Acupuncture.
● **Owner** Dr H Stanley
O (Ref:HM19128)

**STANLEY, M P**

**M P Stanley**, 115 Tangier Rd, Portsmouth, **Hampshire**, PO3 6PB, ENG.
(T) 023 9266 4295
Speciality: Chiropodists (Podiatrists).
S (Ref:HM19129)

**STANLEY, STUART**

**Stuart Stanley**, The Chiropractic Clinic, Main St, North Newington, Banbury, **Oxfordshire**, OX15 6AJ, ENG.
(T) 01295 738167
Speciality: Chiropractic.
● **Manager** Mrs L Stanley
P S T (Ref:HM19130)

**STANMORE CENTRE**

**Stanmore Centre For Psychotherapy & Hypnotherapy**, 29 Belmont Lane, Stanmore, **London (Greater)**, HA7 2PU, ENG.
(T) 020 8954 8804
Speciality: Hypnosis.
B (Ref:HM19131)

**STANMORE PHYSIO PRACTICE**

**Stanmore Physiotherapy Practice**, Hillbrow, The Common, Stanmore, **London (Greater)**, HA7 3HF, ENG.
(T) 07050 038954
(E) maggi@romer.freeserve.co.uk
Speciality: Acupuncture, Physiotherapy. (Acupuncture is also used but only in conjunction with the Physiotherapy). ✓
● **Chartered Physiotherapist** Margaret Romer Q: MCSP, SRP. M: CSP.
S Yrs. Est.: 9 (Ref:HM19132)

**STANNARD, L**

**L Stannard**, 5 Mitchell St, Wellington, **Somerset**, TA21 8LF, ENG.
(T) 01823 667104 (F) 01823 667104
Speciality: Herbal Medicine.
● **Owner** Mrs L Stannard
M (Ref:HM19133)

**STANNARD, LAURA**

**Laura Stannard**, Natural Path Health Centre, 3 Holyrood St, Chard, **Somerset**, TA20 2AH, ENG.
(T) 01460 62953 (F) 01460 63809
Speciality: Herbalists.
● **Owner** Mr M Newbound
M (Ref:HM19134)

**STANTON, BARRIE**

**Barrie Stanton**, 12 Merryfields, Strood, Rochester, **Kent**, ME2 3ND, ENG.
(T) 01634 715560
Speciality: Chiropodists (Podiatrists).
● **Owner** Mr B Stanton
S (Ref:HM19135)

**STANTON, JACKIE**

**Jackie Stanton**, 16 Sunlaws St, Glossop, **Derbyshire**, SK13 8EQ, ENG.
(T) 01457 861940
Speciality: Homeopathy.
● **Owner** Ms J Stanton
M (Ref:HM19136)

**STANTON, JULIE**

**Julie Stanton**, 34 Canterbury Way, Stevenage, **Hertfordshire**, SG1 4DG, ENG.
(T) 01438 720873
Speciality: Aromatherapy.
M O (Ref:HM19137)

**STANTON, MARTIN (DR)**

**Dr Martin Stanton**, 169 Peckham Rye, London, **London (Greater)**, SE15 3HZ, ENG.
(T) 020 7358 1748
Speciality: Psychotherapy.
B (Ref:HM19138)

**STAPEL, PAUL R**

**Paul R Stapel**, 20 Merkland Rd, Aberdeen, **Aberdeenshire**, AB24 3HR, SCO.
(T) 01224 626677
Speciality: Chiropodists (Podiatrists).
S (Ref:HM19139)

**STAPLES, ELAINE**

**Elaine Staples**, 155 Cromwell Rd, Whitstable, **Kent**, CT5 1NQ, ENG.
(T) 01227 263177
Speciality: Reflexology.
S T (Ref:HM19140)

**STAPLETON, C M**

**C M Stapleton**, 4 Wellington Circus, Nottingham, **Nottinghamshire**, NG1 5AL, ENG.
(T) 01159 484141 (F) 01159 532727
Speciality: Osteopathy.
● **Owner** Mr N Woodhead
P S T (Ref:HM19141)

**STAPLEY, J**

**J Stapley**, 6 Southwood Cl, Walkford, Christchurch, **Dorset**, BH23 5RW, ENG.
(T) 01425 277716 (F) 01425 279022
Speciality: Chiropodists (Podiatrists).
● **Owner** Miss J Stapley
S (Ref:HM19142)

**STAR**

**Star**, Foothold Reflexology, 11 Tregenna Hill, St. Ives, **Cornwall**, TR26 1SE, ENG.
(T) 07808 917683
(W) www.complementary-healthcare.co.uk/info/star
Speciality: Reflexology.
S T (Ref:HM19143)

**STARCHILD**

**Starchild**, 2-4 The Courtyard, High St, Glastonbury, **Somerset**, BA6 9DU, ENG.
(T) 01458 834663 (F) 01458 831109
(W) www.starchild.co.uk
Speciality: Aromatherapy.
● **Owner** Mr G Childs
H (Ref:HM19144)

**STARFIELDS HOLISTIC HLTH CTRE**

**Starfields Holistic Health Centre**, Hale Clinic, 7 Calverley Park Cresent, Tunbridge Wells, **Kent**, TN1 2NB, ENG.
(T) 01892 527680 (F) 01892 527680
(E) starfields@holistic.com
Speciality: Absent Healing, Acupressure, Anthroposohical Medicine, Aura Therapy, Bach Remedies, Chiropractic, Complementary Therapy, Counselling, Cranial Osteopathy, Dietician, Dowsing, Hay Diet, Healer, Healing Therapy, Herbal Medicine, Holistic Healing, Homeopathy, Humanistic Psychology, Kinesiology, Manipulation, Meditation, Naturopathy, Reiki, Spiritual Healing, Vitamin Therapy, Rebirthing/Remothering, Pastlife Therapy, Soul Retrieval. ✓
● **Owner/Facilitator** Mr R McCulloch Q: DC, DIBAK. M: BCA, GCC, ICAK.
B Yrs. Est.: 20 (Ref:HM19145)

**STARK, J**

**J Stark**, 16 Ferry Rd, Rye, **Sussex (East)**, TN31 7DN, ENG.
(T) 01797 225099
Speciality: Osteopathy.
P S T (Ref:HM19146)

**STARKEY, DAVID**

**David Starkey**, 50 Pages Lane, Birmingham, **Midlands (West)**, B43 6LR, ENG.
(T) 01213 573327 (F) 01902 410590
Speciality: Complementary Medicines & Therapy, Remedial Therapy. ✓
● **Remedial Therapist** Mr D Starkey Q: ITEC, LCSP, MBRA. M: BCMA, PMBCA.
C Yrs. Est.: 11 (Ref:HM19147)

**STARKEY, JOHN F**

**John F Starkey**, 210 Penn Rd, Wolverhampton, **Midlands (West)**, WV4 4AA, ENG.
(T) 01902 334224
Speciality: Clairvoyants & Palmists.
B (Ref:HM19148)



Key continued: Yrs.Est: Years Established Q: Qualifications M: Professional Membership ✓ Indemnity Insurance Accept Credit Cards

**STARKIE, A M**

**A M Starkie**, Warner House, 27 Warner St, Accrington, **Lancashire**, BB5 1HN, ENG.
(T) 01254 233803
Speciality: Chiropodists (Podiatrists).
● **Owner** Mr A Starkie
S (Ref:HM19149)

**STARKS, M H**

**M H Starks**, 43 Wortley Rd, Highcliffe, Christchurch, **Dorset**, BH23 5DR, ENG.
(T) 01425 274377
Speciality: Chiropodists (Podiatrists).
● **Owner** Mr M Starks
S (Ref:HM19150)

**STARLIGHT CENTRE**

**Starlight Centre for Natural Health**, Hull, **Humberside (North)**, HU14, ENG.
(T) 01482 633449
(W) www.complementary-healthcare.co.uk/info/starlight
Speciality: Aromatherapy, Cranio-Sacral Therapy, Kinesiology, Reflexology, High Touch Jin Shin.
M O (Ref:HM19151)

**STARLIGHT THERAPY TABLES**

**Starlight Therapy Tables Ltd**, Unit 22-31, The Business Innovation Centre, Innova Business Pk, Enfield, **London (Greater)**, EN3 7XU, ENG.
(T) 020 8350 1344 (F) 020 8350 1351
Speciality: Complementary Medicines & Therapy, Therapy Tables.
● **Managing Director** Mr A Teager
C (Ref:HM19152)

**STARSCOPE INTERNATIONAL**

**Starscope International**, 10 Star Hill, Rochester, **Kent**, ME1 1XB, ENG.
(T) 01634 406082
Speciality: Clairvoyants & Palmists.
● **Owner** Miss M Potter
B (Ref:HM19153)

**STARTIN, A M**

**A M Startin**, 10 Charingworth Rd, Solihull, **Midlands (West)**, B92 8HT, ENG.
(T) 01217 422002
Speciality: Reflexology.
● **Owner** Mrs A Startin
S T (Ref:HM19154)

**STARTUP, SALLY**

**Sally Startup**, 4 New Cottages, Furzedown Lane, Amport, Andover, **Hampshire**, SP11 8BQ, ENG.
(T) 01264 771212
Speciality: Herbal Medicine.
● **Owner** Mrs S Startup
M (Ref:HM19155)

**STARWAYS**

**Starways**, 15 Heathfield Court, Heath Gr, London, **London (Greater)**, SE20 8XE, ENG.
(T) 020 8659 3913
Speciality: Clairvoyants & Palmists.
B (Ref:HM19156)

**STATE REGISTERED CHIROPODISTS**

**State Registered Chiropodists**, 30 Gillinggate, Kendal, **Cumbria**, LA9 4JE, ENG.
(T) 01539 729400
Speciality: Chiropodists (Podiatrists).
● **Partner** Mrs J McCarthy
S (Ref:HM19157)

**STATE REGISTERED CHIROPODISTS**

**State Registered Chiropodists**, 90-92 Warwick Rd South, Manchester, **Manchester (Greater)**, M16 0HU, ENG.
(T) 01613 743545
Speciality: Chiropodists (Podiatrists).
S (Ref:HM19158)

**STATFOLD SEED OILS**

**Statfold Seed Oils Ltd**, Ashby Rd, Tamworth, **Staffordshire**, B79 0BU, ENG.
(T) 01827 830871 (F) 01827 830875
(W) www.statfold-oils.co.uk
Speciality: Aromatherapy.
● **Director** Mr P Sedgbeer
C Yrs. Est.: 5 (Ref:HM19159)

**STATHER, M**

**M Stather**, 21 Mayfield Avenue, Scarborough, **Yorkshire (North)**, YO12 6DF, ENG.
(T) 01723 362615
Speciality: Chiropody. ✔
● **Chiropodist** Mrs M Stather Q: MBChA, MSSCh. M: SSChA.
C Yrs. Est.: 9 (Ref:HM19160)

**STATTON, A**

**A Statton**, 39 Tydfil Pl, Penylan, Cardiff, **Glamorgan (Vale of)**, CF23 5HA, WAL.
(T) 029 2048 4555
Speciality: Chiropractors.
P S T (Ref:HM19161)

**STAUNTON, ANN**

**STAUNTON ANN Ph D Dip Psych**, Clyde Rd, IRE.
(T) 01668 3957
Speciality: Complementary Medicines & Therapy.
M (Ref:HM19162)

**STAYNES, I G**

**I G Staynes**, Vinings Clinic, Clover Court, Church Rd, Haywards Heath, **Sussex (West)**, RH16 3UF, ENG.
(T) 01444 441210
Speciality: Acupuncture.
O (Ref:HM19163)

**STEAD, JULIE ANN**

**Julie Ann Stead**, 32 New Way, Guiseley, Leeds, **Yorkshire (West)**, LS20 8JR, ENG.
(T) 01943 873373
Speciality: Chiropody, Massage (Therapeutic), Reflexology, Reiki. ✔
● **Owner/Chiropodist** Mrs J Stead Q: CIBTAC, ITEC, MBChA, MSSCh.
M Yrs. Est.: 8 (Ref:HM19164)

**STEAD, N W**

**N W Stead**, 2 Lancaster Cl, Lee-On-The-Solent, **Hampshire**, PO13 9AY, ENG.
(T) 023 9255 0913
Speciality: Hypnosis.
● **Owner** Mr N Stead
B (Ref:HM19165)

**STEAD, SIMON**

**Simon Stead**, 10 Old Orchards, Forton, Chard, **Somerset**, TA20 2LX, ENG.
(T) 01460 67175 (F) 01460 63700
Speciality: Reflexology.
● **Owner** Mr S Stead
S T (Ref:HM19166)

**STEAD, SUSAN**

**Susan Stead**, 13 Commercial St, Harrogate, **Yorkshire (North)**, HG1 1UB, ENG.
(T) 01423 531892
Speciality: Reflexology.
● **Owner** Mrs S Stead
S T (Ref:HM19167)

**STEARNE, M**

**M Stearne**, 70 High St, New Sharlston, Wakefield, **Yorkshire (West)**, WF4 1BE, ENG.
(T) 01924 864523
Speciality: Aromatherapy.
M O (Ref:HM19168)

**STEARS, M J (DR)**

**Dr M J Stears**, 42 Grand Drive, London, **London (Greater)**, SW20 9DY, ENG.
(T) 020 8543 1144 (F) 020 8543 1144
Speciality: Chiropractic.
● **Principal** Dr M Stears
P S T (Ref:HM19169)

**STECKLER, LAURA**

**Laura Steckler**, The Park, Findhorn, Forres, **Moray**, IV36 3TZ, SCO.
(T) 01309 690251
Speciality: Psychotherapy.
● **Owner** Ms L Steckler
B (Ref:HM19170)

**STEED, CAROL**

**Carol Steed**, Ingledale, 1 Tanhouse Rd, Oxted, **Surrey**, RH8 9PE, ENG.
(T) 01883 717277
Speciality: Chiropodists (Podiatrists).
S (Ref:HM19171)

**STEELE, A M**

**A M Steele**, Rear Of Dore Chemist, Townhead Rd, Sheffield, **Yorkshire (South)**, S17 3DG, ENG.
(T) 01142 362048
Speciality: Chiropodists (Podiatrists).
S (Ref:HM19172)

**STEELE, A R**

**A R Steele**, 33 Watlands View, Newcastle, **Staffordshire**, ST5 8AB, ENG.
(T) 01782 636600
Speciality: Chiropodists (Podiatrists).
● **Owner** Mr A Steele
S (Ref:HM19173)

**STEELE, ALANNA**

**Alanna Steele**, 190 Bridge Rd, Sarisbury Green, Southampton, **Hampshire**, SO31 7ED, ENG.
(T) 01489 574670
Speciality: Hypnotherapy.
● **Owner** Alanna Steele
B (Ref:HM19174)

**STEELE, AMANDA**

**Amanda Steele**, 43 Blackburn Avenue, Brough, **Humberside (North)**, HU15 1BD, ENG.
(T) 01482 662077
Speciality: Reflexology.
S T (Ref:HM19175)

**STEELE, ASHLEY**

**Ashley Steele**, 7 Tresilian Cl, Llantwit Major, **Glamorgan (Vale of)**, CF61 1QX, WAL.
(T) 01446 796193
Speciality: Reflexology.
S T (Ref:HM19176)

**STEELE, DIANNE**

**Dianne Steele**, The Old Forge, Waldron, Heathfield, **Sussex (East)**, TN21 0QY, ENG.
(T) 01435 813630
Speciality: Chiropodists (Podiatrists).
● **Owner** Mrs D Steele
S (Ref:HM19177)

**STEELE, FRED**

**Fred Steele**, 1 Gainsborough Rise, Bedford, **Bedfordshire**, MK41 7NG, ENG.
(T) 01234 355937
Speciality: Acupuncture.
● **Owner** Mr F Steele
O (Ref:HM19178)

**STEELE, GREG**

**Greg Steele**, Health Hydro, Milton Rd, Swindon, **Wiltshire**, SN1 5JA, ENG.
(T) 01793 465631
Speciality: Chiropodists (Podiatrists).
S (Ref:HM19179)

**STEELE, JULIE**

**Julie Steele**, 301 Victoria Rd, Ruislip, **London (Greater)**, HA4 9DG, ENG.
(T) 01895 632458
Speciality: Reflexology.
S T (Ref:HM19180)

**STEELE, P A**

**P A Steele**, 80 Pitfield Rd, Birmingham, **Midlands (West)**, B33 0NZ, ENG.
(T) 01217 707100
Speciality: Chiropodists (Podiatrists).
S (Ref:HM19181)

**STEELE, PAM**

**Pam Steele**, 154A High St, Slough, **Berkshire**, SL1 1JP, ENG.
(T) 01753 575009
Speciality: Chiropodists (Podiatrists).
● **Owner** Mrs P Steele
S (Ref:HM19182)

**STEELE, T M**

**T M Steele**, 25 Hinchliffe Rd, Poole, **Dorset**, BH15 4ED, ENG.
(T) 01202 674433
Speciality: Osteopathy, Osteomyology. ✔
● **Osteomyologist** Mr T Steele Q: DO. M: TAO.
S Yrs. Est.: 4 (Ref:HM19183)

**STEEPER, P T**

**P T Steeper**, 41 Laneham St, Scunthorpe, **Humberside**, DN15 6PB, ENG.



Key: B Mind-Body Medicine C Complementary Medicine H Self Help Treatment M Medicinal Therapy O Oriental Medicine P Postural Therapy S Manipulative Structural Therapy T Touch Therapy

(T) 01724 854132
Speciality: Osteopathy.
● **Owner** Mr P Steeper
P S T (Ref:HM19184)

**STEFFEN, E**

**E Steffen**, 6 Marwell, Westerham, **Kent**, TN16 1SB, ENG.
(T) 01959 562376
Speciality: Chiropodists (Podiatrists).
● **Owner** Mrs E Steffen
S (Ref:HM19185)

**STEIL, J**

**J Steil**, Abbey Wood Podiatry Clinic, 124 McLeod Rd, London, **London (Greater)**, SE2 0BS, ENG.
(T) 020 8311 1660
Speciality: Chiropodists (Podiatrists).
S (Ref:HM19186)

**STEIL, J**

**J Steil**, Amity Clinic, Amity Gr, London, **London (Greater)**, SW20 0LS, ENG.
(T) 020 8947 3510
Speciality: Chiropodists (Podiatrists).
S (Ref:HM19187)

**STEINA SPORTS & PHYSIOTHERAPY**

**Steina Sports & Physiotherapy Clinic**, 11 Liverpool Rd North, Liverpool, **Merseyside**, L31 2HB, ENG.
(T) 01515 263955
Speciality: Acupuncture, Physiotherapy, Reflexology. ✔
● **Physiotherapist** Ms T Newbold Q: MCSP, SRP. M: CSP.
● **Owner** Mrs C Goodson
S Yrs. Est.: 11 (Ref:HM19188)

**STEINBERG, PAMELA**

**Pamela Steinberg**, 55 Blind Lane, Bourne End, **Buckinghamshire**, SL8 5LF, ENG.
(T) 01628 526806 (F) 01628 532090
Speciality: Alexander Technique, Cranial Therapy. ✔
● **Teacher of the Alexander Technique** Mrs P Steinberg Q: MSTAT, S.C.M, SRN.
H Yrs. Est.: 17 (Ref:HM19189)

**STEINER, LYNDA**

**Lynda Steiner**, The Old Vicarage, Christchurch, Coleford, **Gloucestershire**, GL16 7NS, ENG.
(T) 01594 835330 (F) 01594 837555
Speciality: Chiropractic.
● **Owner** Mrs L Steiner
S (Ref:HM19190)

**STELLA ARDEN ASSOCIATES**

**Stella Arden Associates**, 32 Eastgate, Louth, **Lincolnshire**, LN11 9NG, ENG.
(T) 01507 608166
Speciality: Osteopathy.
P S T (Ref:HM19191)

**STENNING, J**

**J Stenning**, 1 Chelford Rd, Knutsford, **Cheshire**, WA16 8LU, ENG.
(T) 01565 653039
Speciality: Chiropodists (Podiatrists).
● **Owner** Mrs J Stenning
S (Ref:HM19192)

**STENSLAND-SLOANE, BARBARA**

**Barbara Stensland-Sloane**, Llanberis, 7 Brook Rd, Whitchurch, Cardiff, **Glamorgan (Vale of)**, CF14 1DU, WAL.
(T) 029 2061 8295
Speciality: Complementary Medicines & Therapy.
C M (Ref:HM19193)

**STENSON, L**

**L Stenson**, 10 Station Rd, Chatteris, **Cambridgeshire**, PE16 6AG, ENG.
(T) 01354 694703
Speciality: Physiotherapy.
● **Owner** Mrs L Stenson
P S T (Ref:HM19194)

**STEP INTO THE FUTURE**

**Step Into The Future**, 42-44 Grainger St, Newcastle Upon Tyne, **Tyne and Wear**, NE1 5JG, ENG.
(T) 01912 302822 (F) 01912 527942
Speciality: Clairvoyants & Palmists.
● **Owner** Miss S Pemble
B (Ref:HM19195)

**STEP, SUE**

**Sue Step**, 246 Holly Lodge Mansions, Oakeshott Avenue, London, **London (Greater)**, N6 6EA, ENG.
(T) 020 8340 5472
Speciality: Osteopathy.
● **Owner** Ms S Step
P S T (Ref:HM19196)

**STEPHEN GORDON**

**Wei Clinic**, 57A Garland St, Bury St. Edmunds, **Suffolk**, ENG.
(T) 01284 704228
Speciality: Homeopathy. ✔
● **Homeopath** Mr S Gordon Q: RSHom. M: Soc.Hom.
M Yrs. Est.: 20 (Ref:HM19197)

**STEPHENS, BERYL**

**Beryl Stephens**, 2 Bakery Court, Market St, Ashby-de-la-Zouch, **Leicestershire**, LE65 1AN, ENG.
(T) 01530 414576
Speciality: Chiropodists (Podiatrists).
● **Owner** Mrs B Stephens
S (Ref:HM19198)

**STEPHENS, BRENDA**

**Brenda Stephens**, 10 Romsey Drive, Farnham Common, Slough, **Berkshire**, SL2 3RE, ENG.
(T) 01753 647570
Speciality: Hypnosis.
B (Ref:HM19199)

**STEPHENS, DANNY (DR)**

**Dr Danny Stephens**, 126 Clontarf Rd, Clontarf, IRE.
(T) 01853 2011
Speciality: Chiropractors.
P S T (Ref:HM19200)

**STEPHENS, DERRICK G**

**Derrick G Stephens**, 9 Richmond Dale, Bristol, BS8 2UB, ENG.
(T) 01179 732381
Speciality: Chiropodists (Podiatrists).
● **Owner** Mr D Stephens
S (Ref:HM19201)

**STEPHENS, G F**

**G F Stephens**, 99 Mansel St, Swansea, SA1 5UE, WAL.
(T) 01792 462001
Speciality: Osteopathy.
● **Owner** Miss G Stephens
P S T (Ref:HM19202)

**STEPHENS, JANE**

**Jane Stephens**, 66 Gorse Farm, Gorse Farm Estate, Llandrindod Wells, **Powys**, LD1 5SH, WAL.
(T) 01597 829393
Speciality: Reflexology.
S T (Ref:HM19203)

**STEPHENS, LYN**

**Lyn Stephens**, 9 Montpellier Gr, Cheltenham, **Gloucestershire**, GL50 2XB, ENG.
(T) 01242 521945
Speciality: Psychotherapy.
● **Owner** Ms L Stephens
B (Ref:HM19204)

**STEPHENS, SARAH**

**Sarah Stephens**, 102 Chosen Drive, Churchdown, Gloucester, **Gloucestershire**, GL3 2QU, ENG.
(T) 01452 714511 (F) 01452 541369
Speciality: Osteopathy.
● **Partner** Mr C Hayden
P S T (Ref:HM19205)

**STEPHENSON, ANN**

**Ann Stephenson**, 65 Liberty Rd, Glenfield, **Leicestershire**, LE3 8JG, ENG.
(T) 01162 330245
Speciality: Reflexology.
S T (Ref:HM19206)

**STEPHENSON, C**

**C Stephenson**, Courtyard Clinic, 12 Parsonage St, Dursley, **Gloucestershire**, GL11 4EA, ENG.
(T) 01453 548119 (F) 01453 548662
Speciality: Physiotherapy.
● **Owner** Mr C Stephenson
P S T (Ref:HM19207)

**STEPHENSON, L**

**L Stephenson**, 1 High St, Inverurie, **Aberdeenshire**, AB51 3QA, SCO.
(T) 01467 625026
Speciality: Chiropody. ✔
● **Owner/Chiropodist** Lyn Stephenson Q: M.S.C.P, SHEN Therapy.
M Yrs. Est.: 12 (Ref:HM19208)

**STEPHENSON, MALCOLM**

**Malcolm Stephenson**, Middle Red Lumb Farm, Red Lumb, Rochdale, **Lancashire**, OL12 7TX, ENG.
(T) 01706 643257
Speciality: Physiotherapy.
● **Owner** Mr M Stephenson
P S T (Ref:HM19209)

**STEPNEY, EVE**

**Eve Stepney**, Elm House, Station Rd, Crawley Down, Crawley, **Sussex (West)**, RH10 4HZ, ENG.
(T) 01342 716972 (F) 01342 715508
Speciality: Chiropodists (Podiatrists).
● **Dentist** Mr A Whitehead
S (Ref:HM19210)

**STEPNEY, LESLEY**

**Holostic Aromatherapy With Lesley Stepney**, 29A South St, Tarring, Worthing, **Sussex (West)**, BN14 7LG, ENG.
(T) 01903 201808
Speciality: Aromatherapy.
● **Owner** Mrs L Stepney
M O (Ref:HM19211)

**STEPNEY, NICK**

**Nick Stepney**, Flat 15, Davids Heights, Kings Avenue, Eastbourne, **Sussex (East)**, BN21 2PH, ENG.
(T) 01323 417810 (F) 01323 417810
Speciality: Psychotherapy.
● **Owner** Mr N Stepney
B (Ref:HM19212)

**STEPPING STONES**

**Stepping Stones**, Po Box 108, Evesham, **Worcestershire**, WR11 5ZL, ENG.
(T) 01386 833899 (F) 01386 833848
Speciality: Complementary Medicines & Therapy.
● **Owner** Ms J Wakeman
M (Ref:HM19213)

**STEPPING STONES**

**Stepping Stones Mind Body & Soul Centre**, 97 Trafalgar Rd, Greenwich, London, **London (Greater)**, SE10 9TS, ENG.
(T) 020 8853 2733
Speciality: Aromatherapy.
● **Owner** Miss G Renzullo
M O (Ref:HM19214)

**STEREX ELECTROLYSIS**

**Sterex Electrolysis International Ltd**, 6 Broadwell, Dursley, **Gloucestershire**, GL11 4JE, ENG.
(T) 01453 547632 (F) 01453 547431
Speciality: Electrolysis.
● **Sales Manager** Mrs E Moore
T (Ref:HM19215)

**STEREX ELECTROLYSIS INT**

**Sterex Electrolysis International Ltd**, 174 Kings Rd, Tyseley, Birmingham, **Midlands (West)**, B11 2AP, ENG.
(T) 01217 082404
Speciality: Electrolysis.
● **Sales/Marketing Director** Robert Jack Chapman
T (Ref:HM19216)

**STERN, J**

**J Stern**, 18 Landseer Rd, Clarendon Park, Leicester, **Leicestershire**, LE2 3EE, ENG.
(T) 01162 709363
Speciality: Counselling, Psychotherapy.
● **Counsellor** Mr J Stern Q: BA, MA. M: BACP.
H Yrs. Est.: 6 (Ref:HM19217)

**STERNBERG, M P**
**M P Sternberg**, 2 Clifton Park, Bristol, BS8 3BS, ENG.
(T) 01179 737371 (F) 01179 730887
Speciality: Psychiatry.
● **Senior Partner** Dr M Sternberg
B (Ref:HM19218)

**STERRY, MICHAEL**
**Michael Sterry**, 46 Cavendish Avenue, Sidcup, **Kent**, DA15 9EB, ENG.
(T) 020 8302 1506
Speciality: Chiropodists (Podiatrists).
S (Ref:HM19219)

**STEVE THE MEDIUM**
**Steve The Medium**, Dinan Way, Exmouth, **Devon**, EX8 4EZ, ENG.
(T) 01395 270110
Speciality: Clairvoyants & Palmists.
● **Owner** Mr S Watkins
B (Ref:HM19220)

**STEVEN, PATRICIA**
**Patricia Steven**, Abbey View Complementary Clinic, Abbey View Medical Centre, Shaftesbury, **Dorset**, SP7 8DH, ENG.
(T) 01747 856719 (F) 01747 856701
Speciality: Physiotherapy.
P S T (Ref:HM19221)

**STEVEN, PATRICIA**
**Patricia Steven**, Castleton House, Castle St, Mere, Warminster, **Wiltshire**, BA12 6JE, ENG.
(T) 01747 860161
Speciality: Physiotherapy.
P S T (Ref:HM19222)

**STEVEN, PAUL**
**Paul Steven**, Halifax Clinic Of Natural Medicine, 22 Clare Rd, Halifax, **Yorkshire (West)**, HX1 2HX, ENG.
(T) 01422 340919
Speciality: Psychotherapy.
B (Ref:HM19223)

**STEVENS & ASSOCIATES**
**J E Stevens & Associates**, 56 Bank Prde, Burnley, **Lancashire**, BB11 1TS, ENG.
(T) 01282 453110 (F) 01282 453110
Speciality: Physiotherapy.
● **Owner** Mrs J Stevens
P S T (Ref:HM19224)

**STEVENS, BEN**
**Ben Stevens**, 2 South Villas, Kensington Rd, Redland, Bristol, BS6 6NL, ENG.
(T) 01179 420666
Speciality: Acupuncture. ✔
● **Owner** Mr B Stevens M: BAcC.
O (Ref:HM19225)

**STEVENS, BRETT (DR)**
**Dr Brett Stevens**, 126 Clontarf Rd, IRE.
(T) 01833 6198
Speciality: Chiropractors.
P S T (Ref:HM19226)

**STEVENS, BRETT (DR)**
**Stevens Dr Brett**, Unit 1, Church Hill,, Navan, **County Meath**, IRE.
(T) 07767 1066
Speciality: Chiropractors.
P S T (Ref:HM19227)

**STEVENS, CAROLINE**
**Caroline Stevens**, 86 Melbury Rd, Nottingham, **Nottinghamshire**, NG8 4AU, ENG.
(T) 01159 190500
Speciality: Complementary Medicines & Therapy.
M (Ref:HM19228)

**STEVENS, CHARMIAN**
**Charmian Stevens**, 15 Wentworth Rd, Birmingham, **Midlands (West)**, B17 9SH, ENG.
(T) 07778 564967
Speciality: Chiropodists (Podiatrists).
● **Owner** Ms C Stevens
S (Ref:HM19229)

**STEVENS, D J**
**Mr D J Stevens**, 4 Bentinck, Bentinck St, London, **London (Greater)**, W1M 5RJ, ENG.
(T) 020 7486 6865
Speciality: Physiotherapy.
● **Owner** Mr D Stevens
P S T (Ref:HM19230)

**STEVENS, G**
**G Stevens**, 32 Church St, Warsop, Mansfield, **Nottinghamshire**, NG20 0AJ, ENG.
(T) 01623 844332
Speciality: Chiropodists (Podiatrists).
● **Owner** Mrs G Stevens
S (Ref:HM19231)

**STEVENS, HELEN**
**Helen Stevens**, 6 Ness Bank, Inverness, **Highland**, IV2 4SF, SCO.
(T) 01463 250400
Speciality: Physiotherapy.
● **Owner** Miss H Stevens
P S T (Ref:HM19232)

**STEVENS, ITOKO**
**Itoko Stevens**, 12B Montpelier Gr, London, **London (Greater)**, NW5 2XD, ENG.
(T) 020 7267 6620
Speciality: Hypnosis.
B (Ref:HM19233)

**STEVENS, JEAN**
**Jean Stevens**, 48 Clwyd Park, Kinmel Bay, Rhyl, **Denbighshire**, LL18 5EJ, WAL.
(T) 01745 342544 (F) 01745 360329
Speciality: Hypnosis.
● **Owner** Mrs J Stevens
B (Ref:HM19234)

**STEVENS, JOY P**
**Joy P Stevens**, 8 Arlington Rd, Southend-On-Sea, **Essex**, SS2 4UW, ENG.
(T) 01702 601332
Speciality: Chiropodists (Podiatrists).
● **Owner** Mrs J Stevens
S (Ref:HM19235)

**STEVENS, MARGARET**
**Margaret Stevens**, 45 Woodland Way, Burntwood, **Staffordshire**, WS7 8UP, ENG.
(T) 01543 319733 (F) 01543 319733
Speciality: Psychotherapy.
● **Owner** Mrs M Stevens
B (Ref:HM19236)

**STEVENS, NIGEL GATES**
**Nigel Gates Stevens**, 18 Longdown La North, Epsom, **Surrey**, KT17 3JQ, ENG.
(T) 020 8393 9736
Speciality: Osteopathy.
P S T (Ref:HM19237)

**STEVENS, PAT**
**Pat Stevens**, 83 Littlehampton Rd, Worthing, **Sussex (West)**, BN13 1QP, ENG.
(T) 01903 830565
Speciality: Electrolysis, Skenar Therapy. ✔
● **Owner** Mrs P Stevens
B Yrs. Est.: 30 (Ref:HM19238)

**STEVENS, RICHARD**
**Richard Stevens**, Ravenscroft Medical Centre, 166A Golders Green Rd, London, **London (Greater)**, NW11 8BB, ENG.
(T) 020 8209 0922
Speciality: Physiotherapy.
P S T (Ref:HM19239)

**STEVENS, TARA L**
**Tara L Stevens**, 7 Judges St, Loughborough, **Leicestershire**, LE11 1RU, ENG.
(T) 01509 558459
Speciality: Aromatherapy, Massage (Therapeutic), Reflexology.
M O (Ref:HM19240)

**STEVENS, WARD (DR)**
**Dr Ward Stevens**, 1 Lr Rathmines Rd, IRE.
(T) 01491 0448
Speciality: Chiropractors.
P S T (Ref:HM19241)

**STEVENS, WARD (DR)**
**STEVENS WARD DR**, Herbert St, IRE.
(T) 01676 3036
Speciality: Chiropractors.
P S T (Ref:HM19242)

**STEVENSON & ASSOCIATES**
**Joseph Stevenson & Associates**, 33 The Chequers, Hills Rd, Buckhurst Hill, **Essex**, IG9 5RH, ENG.
(T) 020 8559 1927
Speciality: Hypnotherapy.
B (Ref:HM19243)

**STEVENSON, E J**
**E J Stevenson**, Four Oaks Medical Centre, 18 Mere Green Rd, Sutton Coldfield, **Midlands (West)**, B75 5BS, ENG.
(T) 01213 088003
Speciality: Chiropodists (Podiatrists).
S (Ref:HM19244)

**STEVENSON, G**
**G Stevenson**, The Newcastle Clinic, 52 Mitchell Avenue, Newcastle Upon Tyne, **Tyne and Wear**, NE2 3LA, ENG.
(T) 01912 810193
Speciality: Osteopathy.
P S T (Ref:HM19245)

**STEVENSON, IAN W**
**Ian W Stevenson**, 18 Barossa Pl, Perth, **Perth and Kinross**, PH1 1JP, SCO.
(T) 01738 623530 (F) 01728 560460
Speciality: Biomechanics, Chiropody, Homeopathy, Nail Surgery, Podiatry, Homeopathy in relation to Podiatry uses only. ✔
● **Chiropodist (Podiatrist)**
Mr I Stevenson Q: DPodM, M.S.C.P, S.R.Ch.
C Yrs. Est.: 35 (Ref:HM19246)

**STEVENSON, J**
**J Stevenson**, 4 Cadogan Lane, London, **London (Greater)**, SW1X 9EB, ENG.
(T) 020 7631 1209 (F) 020 7235 5942
Speciality: Psychology.
● **Owner** Mr J Stevenson
B (Ref:HM19247)

**STEVENSON, J E**
**J E Stevenson**, 4 Shaw Cl, Cliffe Woods, Rochester, **Kent**, ME3 8JR, ENG.
(T) 01634 220660
Speciality: Chiropodists (Podiatrists).
● **Owner** Mr J Stevenson
S (Ref:HM19248)

**STEVENSON, JACKIE**
**Jackie Stevenson**, 87 Heanor Rd, Ilkeston, **Derbyshire**, DE7 8DY, ENG.
(T) 01159 326152
Speciality: Counselling, Herbal Medicine, Psychotherapy. ✔
● **Partner** Mr B Stevenson Q: BSCH, NLP.
● **Owner** Mrs J Stevenson Q: BSCH, NLP.
C Yrs. Est.: 17 (Ref:HM19249)

**STEVENSON, LEIGH**
**Leigh Stevenson**, 42 Orchard Way, Mill End, Rickmansworth, **Hertfordshire**, WD3 2HZ, ENG.
(T) 01923 444867
Speciality: Reflexology.
S T (Ref:HM19250)

**STEVENSON, SCOTT**
**Scott Stevenson**, 7 Afton Gdns, Troon, **Ayrshire (South)**, KA10 7BW, SCO.
(T) 01292 318785
Speciality: Healing Therapy, Hypnotherapy. ✔
● **Owner/Hypnotherapist**
Mr S Stevenson
B Yrs. Est.: 4 (Ref:HM19251)

**STEWARD, J A**
**J A Steward**, 10 Fonnereau Rd, Ipswich, **Suffolk**, IP1 3JP, ENG.
(T) 01473 252378 (F) 01473 286646
Speciality: Osteopathy.
● **Owner** Mr J Steward
P S T (Ref:HM19252)

**STEWARD, J A**
**J A Steward**, 13 High St, Saxmundham, **Suffolk**, IP17 1DF, ENG.
(T) 01728 602514
Speciality: Manipulation, Osteopathy.
● **Partner** Mr J Steward
C (Ref:HM19253)

Key: B Mind-Body Medicine C Complementary Medicine H Self Help Treatment M Medicinal Therapy O Oriental Medicine P Postural Therapy S Manipulative Structural Therapy T Touch Therapy

**STEWART & JONES**

**Stewart & Jones**, Bridgend Health Care Centre, Sir Georges St, Thurso, **Highland**, KW14 7AW, SCO.
(T) 01847 896363
Speciality: Chiropodists (Podiatrists).
S (Ref:HM19254)

**STEWART PALMER HYPNOTHERAPIST**

**Stewart Palmer Hypnotherapist**, 47 Duncombe Cl, Luton, **Bedfordshire**, LU3 2HR, ENG.
(T) 01582 571762
Speciality: Hypnosis.
B (Ref:HM19255)

**STEWART, A**

**A Stewart**, 5 Irvine Gardens, Milton Of Campsie, Glasgow, **Glasgow (City of)**, G66 8JL, SCO.
(T) 01360 311041 (F) 01600 311041
Speciality: Chiropodists (Podiatrists).
● **Owner** Mr A Stewart
S (Ref:HM19256)

**STEWART, ALAN**

**Alan Stewart**, 8 Aitkenbrae Drive, Prestwick, **Ayrshire (South)**, SCO.
(T) 01292 477965
Speciality: Indian Head Massage, Massage (Therapeutic), Reiki, Swedish Body Massage.
H T (Ref:HM19257)

**STEWART, ANN**

**Ann Stewart**, The Terrace, 35 Staplegrove Rd, Taunton, **Somerset**, TA1 1DG, ENG.
(T) 01823 338968
Speciality: Homeopathy.
● **Owner** Ms J Gotto
M (Ref:HM19258)

**STEWART, ANNIE**

**Annie Stewart**, Little Barn House, 162 Gloucester Rd, Bishopstone, Bristol, BS7 8NT, ENG.
(T) 01275 332482
Speciality: Complementary Medicines & Therapy.
● **Owner** Annie Stewart
M (Ref:HM19259)

**STEWART, BRITTA**

**Stewart Britta**, U 17 Mullingar Enterprise Ctr Mullingar, IRE.
(T) 04443 444
Speciality: Aromatherapy.
M O (Ref:HM19260)

**STEWART, C J**

**C J Stewart**, 10 Portsmouth Rd, Southampton, **Hampshire**, SO19 9AA, ENG.
(T) 023 8044 8134
Speciality: Chiropodists (Podiatrists).
● **Manager** Mr C Stewart
S (Ref:HM19261)

**STEWART, D S**

**D S Stewart**, Ashurst, 17 Duke St, Formby, Liverpool, **Merseyside**, L37 4AN, ENG.
(T) 01704 875122
Speciality: Chiropodists (Podiatrists).
● **Owner** Mr D Stewart
S (Ref:HM19262)

**STEWART, DIANE**

**Diane Stewart**, Church St, St. Germans, Saltash, **Cornwall**, PL12 5LG, ENG.
(T) 01503 230676
Speciality: Reflexology.
● **Owner** Mrs D Stewart
S T (Ref:HM19263)

**STEWART, GILLIAN A**

**Gillian A Stewart**, 19A Westgate, Sleaford, **Lincolnshire**, NG34 7PJ, ENG.
(T) 01529 305066
Speciality: Chiropodists (Podiatrists).
S (Ref:HM19264)

**STEWART, H**

**H Stewart**, 16 Ferncroft Avenue, London, **London (Greater)**, NW3 7PH, ENG.
(T) 020 7435 8696
Speciality: Psychoanalysis.
● **Owner** Dr H Stewart
B (Ref:HM19265)

**STEWART, HILARY A**

**Hilary A Stewart**, The Apothecary, Morthern Rd, Wickersley, Rotherham, **Yorkshire (South)**, S66 1EU, ENG.
(T) 01709 531177 (F) 01709 531302
Speciality: Homeopathy.
● **Managing Director** Mr A Watson
M (Ref:HM19266)

**STEWART, I**

**I Stewart**, 3 Willow Cottage, Godstone Hill, Godstone, **Surrey**, RH9 8AJ, ENG.
(T) 01883 744021
Speciality: Chiropody. ✔
● **Chiropodist** Mr I Stewart Q: MBChA. M: B.A.Ch.P.
C Yrs. Est.: 9 (Ref:HM19267)

**STEWART, IAN (DR)**

**Dr Ian Stewart**, Old School House, Kingston-On-Soar, Nottingham, **Nottinghamshire**, NG11 0DE, ENG.
(T) 01509 673569
Speciality: Psychotherapy.
B (Ref:HM19268)

**STEWART, JAMES HARVEY**

**James Harvey Stewart**, Woodville, Hatton, Peterhead, **Aberdeenshire**, AB42 7QQ, SCO.
(T) 01779 841439
Speciality: Chiropodists (Podiatrists).
S (Ref:HM19269)

**STEWART, JIM (DR)**

**Dr Jim Stewart**, 72 Stamperland Drive, Clarkston, Glasgow, **Glasgow (City of)**, G76 8HF, SCO.
(T) 01416 441333
(E) jim.stewart@ntlworld.com
Speciality: Cognitive Therapy, Counselling, Hypnosis, Hypnotherapy, Meditation, Psychotherapy, Stress Therapy, Visualisation Therapy. ✔
● **Doctor of Hypnosis** Dr J Stewart Q: Dip.Hyp, FIHP, MHA. M: HA.
B Yrs. Est.: 14 (Ref:HM19270)

**STEWART, KAREN**

**Karen Stewart**, 8 Bellesdale Avenue, Largs, **Ayrshire (North)**, KA30 9EE, SCO.
(T) 01475 672508
Speciality: Chiropodists (Podiatrists).
● **Owner** Miss K Stewart
S (Ref:HM19271)

**STEWART, LINDSEY**

**Lindsey Stewart**, 81 Aberdale Rd, Leicester, **Leicestershire**, LE2 6GE, ENG.
(T) 01162 888443
Speciality: Osteopathy.
● **Owner** Ms L Stewart
P S T (Ref:HM19272)

**STEWART, PATRICIA**

**Stewart Patricia M Psych Sc**, 81 Monkstown Rd, Monkstown, Dublin, **County Dublin**, IRE.
(T) 01280 9565
Speciality: Psychotherapy.
B (Ref:HM19273)

**STEWART, PAULA**

**Paula Stewart**, 68 Long Lane, Hindley, Wigan, **Lancashire**, WN2 4QL, ENG.
(T) 01942 519274
Speciality: Chiropodists (Podiatrists).
● **Owner** Mrs P Stewart
S (Ref:HM19274)

**STEWART, RICHARD**

**Richard Stewart**, 48 Newlands Park, London, **London (Greater)**, SE26 5NE, ENG.
(T) 020 8659 5001
Speciality: Osteopathy.
P S T (Ref:HM19275)

**STEWART, S**

**S Stewart**, 25 High St, Belfast, **County Antrim**, BT1 2AA, NIR.
(T) 028 9032 2702
Speciality: Chiropody. ✔
● **Owner/Chiropodist** Mrs S Stewart Q: M.S.C.P. M: S.C.P.
S Yrs. Est.: 18 (Ref:HM19276)

**STEWART, SHEILA**

**Sheila Stewart**, 111 Lower Oldfield Park, Bath, **Somerset**, BA2 3HR, ENG.
(T) 01225 317374
Speciality: Reflexology.
S T (Ref:HM19277)

**STEWART, SUSAN**

**Susan Stewart**, 36 Friars Way, Dover, **Kent**, CT16 2DW, ENG.
(T) 01304 823343
Speciality: Reflexology.
S T (Ref:HM19278)

**STEWART, T A**

**T A Stewart**, 12 Cathcart Rd, Largs, **Ayrshire (North)**, KA30 8JB, SCO.
(T) 01475 689880
Speciality: Chiropodists (Podiatrists).
S (Ref:HM19279)

**STEWART, T M R**

**T M R Stewart**, 264 Glasgow Rd, Clydebank, **Argyll and Bute**, G81 1PG, SCO.
(T) 01419 521013
Speciality: Chiropodists (Podiatrists).
S (Ref:HM19280)

**STEWART, V**

**V Stewart**, 36 Hamilton Rd, Rutherglen, Glasgow, **Glasgow (City of)**, G73 3DG, SCO.
(T) 01416 472639
Speciality: Chiropodists (Podiatrists).
● **Owner** Mr V Stewart
S (Ref:HM19281)

**STEWART, W**

**W Stewart**, 7 Lime Avenue, High Wycombe, **Buckinghamshire**, HP11 1DP, ENG.
(T) 01494 452871
Speciality: Homeopathy.
● **Owner** Mrs W Stewart
M (Ref:HM19282)

**STEYNE HOUSE NTRL THRPY CTRE**

**Steyne House Natural Therapy Centre**, 35 Steyne Rd, Seaford, **Sussex (East)**, BN25 1HT, ENG.
(T) 01323 895088
Speciality: Complementary Medicines & Therapy.
● **Owner** Mrs J Deakin
C M (Ref:HM19283)

**STH WST COLLEGE OF ORIENTL MED**

**South West College Of Oriental Medicine (The)**, 35 North View, Westbury Park, Bristol, BS6 7PY, ENG.
(T) 01179 078891 (F) 01179 078891
Speciality: Complementary Medicines & Therapy.
● **Director** Mr K Ferris
C M (Ref:HM19284)

**STH WST COLLEGE OF ORIENTL MED**

**South West College of Oriental Medicine (The)**, Po Box 795, Bristol, BS99 5WZ, ENG.
(T) 01179 078891
Speciality: Acupuncture, Complementary Therapy, Shiatsu.
O (Ref:HM19285)

**STICK, ALEX W**

**Alex W Stick**, 10 High St, Orpington, **Kent**, BR6 0JG, ENG.
(T) 01689 873130
Speciality: Chiropractors.
● **Owner** Dr M Chippendale
P S T (Ref:HM19286)

**STICKLAND, PAULINE**

**Pauline Stickland**, Bennebroek, 45 St. Johns Rd, Saxmundham, **Suffolk**, IP17 1BD, ENG.
(T) 01728 602193
Speciality: Reflexology.
S T (Ref:HM19287)

**STICKLAND, ROBERTA**

**Roberta Stickland**, The Chiropractic Centre, 8 The Mall Bridge, Andover, **Hampshire**, SP10 1QL, ENG.
(T) 01264 337133
Speciality: Chiropractic.



Key continued: Yrs.Est: Years Established Q: Qualifications M: Professional Membership ✔ Indemnity Insurance Accept Credit Cards

P S T (Ref:HM19288)

## STILES & ASS

**Christine M J Stiles & Associates**, Weybridge Chiropody Surgery, 8 Monument Green, Weybridge, **Surrey**, KT13 8QS, ENG.
(T) 01932 849373 (F) 01932 849373
Speciality: Chiropodists (Podiatrists).
● **Owner** Miss C Stiles
S (Ref:HM19289)

## STILL POINT

**Still Point**, Barrack St, Ennis, **County Clare**, IRE.
(T) 06568 20454
Speciality: Acupuncture.
O (Ref:HM19290)

## STILL, PETER

**Peter Still**, 2 Cromwell Rd, Grays, **Essex**, RM17 5HF, ENG.
(T) 01375 377105 (F) 01375 396402
Speciality: Osteopathy.
● **Owner** Mr P Still
P S T (Ref:HM19291)

## STILL, PETER

**Peter Still**, 8 Coronation Avenue, East Tilbury, Tilbury, **Essex**, RM18 8SJ, ENG.
(T) 01375 858657
Speciality: Osteopathy.
P S T (Ref:HM19292)

## STILLE, SAMANTHA

**Samantha Stille**, 94 St James's St, Brighton, **Sussex (East)**, BN2 1TP, ENG.
(T) 01273 672952
Speciality: Herbalists.
● **Owner** Mr L Moore
M (Ref:HM19293)

## STILLMARK, NADIA

**Nadia Stillmark**, Clissold Park Health Centre, 154 Stoke Newington Church St, London, **London (Greater)**, N16 0JU, ENG.
(T) 020 7249 2990 (F) 020 7249 3977
Speciality: Complementary Medicines & Therapy.
● **Director** Mr D Berg
M (Ref:HM19294)

## STILLPOINT

**Stillpoint**, Broad St Pl, Bath, **Somerset**, BA1 5LH, ENG.
(T) 01225 460106
Speciality: Osteopathy.
● **Owner** Mr Z Bozic
P S T (Ref:HM19295)

## STIMULUS FOR CHANGE

**Stimulus For Change**, 51 St Leonards Rd, Exeter, **Devon**, EX2 4LS, ENG.
(T) 01392 411311
(E) kris.frank@virgin.net
(W) www.stimulusforchange.co.uk
Speciality: Complementary Therapy, Homeopathy. ✔
● **Homeopathic Practitioner**
Mr K Frank Q: BA, L.C.C.H, RSHom.
M: Soc.Hom.
B Yrs. Est.: 15 (Ref:HM19296)

## STIR SPICES

**Stir Spices**, P O Box 361, Cardiff, **Glamorgan (Vale of)**, CF2 3UD, WAL.
(T) 029 2049 6047
Speciality: Herbal Medicine.
M (Ref:HM19297)

## STIRLAND, HAZEL

**Hazel Stirland**, Cornerstones, 1 Highfield Rd, Peasedown St. John, Bath, **Somerset**, BA2 8HF, ENG.
(T) 01761 432097
Speciality: Aromatherapy.
● **Owner** Ms H Stirland
M O (Ref:HM19298)

## STIRLING & BRIDGE

**Stirling & Bridge Of Allan Physiotherapy & Sports** , 20 Westerton Drive, Bridge Of Allan, Stirling, FK9 4QL, SCO.
(T) 01786 471252 (F) 01786 471252
Speciality: Physiotherapy.
● **Owner** Mrs A Fairlie
P S T (Ref:HM19299)

## STIRLING CHIROPRACTIC CLINIC

**Stirling Chiropractic Clinic**, 6 Pitt Trce, Stirling, FK8 2EZ, SCO.
(T) 01786 448820
Speciality: Chiropractors.
P S T (Ref:HM19300)

## STIRLING, DIANNE

**Dianne Stirling**, 46 Algernon St, Eccles, Manchester, **Manchester (Greater)**, M30 9PG, ENG.
(T) 01612 812012
(E) stirlingdianne@hotmail.com
Speciality: Massage (Therapeutic), Reflexology, Reiki. ✔
● **Holistic Therapist** Ms D Stirling Q: BSc, IIHHT. M: FHT.
B C Yrs. Est.: 3 (Ref:HM19301)

## STIRLING, P

**P Stirling**, 11 Argyle Pl, Bristol, BS8 4RH, ENG.
(T) 01179 273205
(E) penelope@tantroweb.co.uk
Speciality: Holistic Healing, Homeopathy. ✔
● **Owner** Ms P Stirling Q: MA, RSHom.
C Yrs. Est.: 12 (Ref:HM19302)

## STIRRAT, ANTONIA

**Antonia Stirrat**, 44 Greenbank Drive, Edinburgh, **Edinburgh (City of)**, EH10 5RF, SCO.
(T) 01314 477791
Speciality: Homeopathy.
● **Owner** Mrs A Stirrat
M (Ref:HM19303)

## STIRRAT, KATRINA

**Katrina Stirrat**, 76 North Rd, Richmond, **Surrey**, TW9 4HQ, ENG.
(T) 020 8785 7482
Speciality: Aromatherapy.
● **Owner** Miss K Stirrat
M O (Ref:HM19304)

## STOBART, A

**A Stobart**, The Clinic, 37 St Peter St, Tiverton, **Devon**, EX16 6NW, ENG.
(T) 01884 255990
Speciality: Herbalists.
M (Ref:HM19305)

## STOBART, ANNE

**Anne Stobart**, 21 Dean St, Crediton, **Devon**, EX17 3EN, ENG.
(T) 01363 777531
Speciality: Herbal Medicine.
M (Ref:HM19306)

## STOBEZKI, YAEL

**Yael Stobezki**, 46E Fairhazel Gdns, London, **London (Greater)**, NW6 3SJ, ENG.
(T) 020 7328 9015
Speciality: Art Therapy, Counselling, Humanistic Psychology, Psychotherapy. ✔
● **Owner** Miss Y Stobezki Q: BA, Dip.Phys, Dip.Supervision, UKCP (Reg).
H Yrs. Est.: 4 (Ref:HM19307)

## STOBIE, JENNY

**Jenny Stobie**, 16 Marionville Rd, Edinburgh, **Edinburgh (City of)**, EH7 5TX, SCO.
(T) 01316 200372
Speciality: Reflexology.
S T (Ref:HM19308)

## STOCKDALE, MEL

**Mel Stockdale**, 13 Mill Rise, Robertsbridge, **Sussex (East)**, TN32 5EF, ENG.
(T) 01580 881857
Speciality: Psychotherapy.
● **Owner** Mr M Stockdale
B (Ref:HM19309)

## STOCKLEY, PHILIP

**Philip Stockley**, 41A High St, Ely, **Cambridgeshire**, CB7 4LF, ENG.
(T) 01353 666384
Speciality: Osteopathy.
● **Owner** Mr P Stockley
P S T (Ref:HM19310)

## STOCKLEY, PHILIP E

**Philip E Stockley**, 249 Queen Edith's Way, Cambridge, **Cambridgeshire**, CB1 8NJ, ENG.
(T) 01223 248233
Speciality: Osteopathy.
P S T (Ref:HM19311)

## STOCKLEY, R

**R Stockley**, The Cottage, Copse Wood Way, Northwood, **London (Greater)**, HA6 2TU, ENG.
(T) 01923 842351 (F) 01923 840470
Speciality: Psychotherapy.
● **Owner** Mrs R Stockely
B (Ref:HM19312)

## STOCKS, CHRIS

**Chris Stocks**, 6 King Cross St, Halifax, **Yorkshire (West)**, HX1 2SH, ENG.
(T) 01422 322236
Speciality: Hypnotherapy.
B (Ref:HM19313)

## STOCKS, JIM

**Jim Stocks**, Homestead Farm, 10 Alfreton Rd, Newton, Alfreton, **Derbyshire**, DE55 5TP, ENG.
(T) 01773 875683
Speciality: Psychology.
● **Owner** Mr J Stocks
B (Ref:HM19314)

## STOCKTON, CAROL LESLEY

**Carol Lesley Stockton**, 48 Hanworth Rd, Feltham, **London (Greater)**, TW13 5AY, ENG.
(T) 020 8890 3789
Speciality: Osteopathy.
● **Owner** Mrs C Stockton
P S T (Ref:HM19315)

## STOCKWELL CENTRE

**Stockwell Centre (The)**, 44 East Stockwell St, Colchester, **Essex**, CO1 1SR, ENG.
(T) 01206 768211
Speciality: Psychotherapy.
● **Therapist** David Tune
B (Ref:HM19316)

## STOCKWELL, J

**J Stockwell**, 62B Minster Rd, London, **London (Greater)**, NW2 3RE, ENG.
(T) 020 7794 2478
Speciality: Homeopathy.
● **Owner** Mrs J Stockwell
M (Ref:HM19317)

## STOCKWELL, J E

**J E Stockwell Homoeopath**, 34-36A Warwick Way, London, **London (Greater)**, SW1V 1RY, ENG.
(T) 020 7834 0861
Speciality: Homeopathy.
● **Owner** Mr M Cozzi
M (Ref:HM19318)

## STOCKWELLS CHIROPODY CLINIC

**Stockwells Chiropody Clinic**, 22 The Green, London, **London (Greater)**, W5 5DA, ENG.
(T) 020 8579 8066
Speciality: Chiropodists (Podiatrists).
S (Ref:HM19319)

## STODDART, H D

**H D Stoddart**, Deramore House, 76 Main St, Moira, Craigavon, **County Armagh**, BT67 0LQ, NIR.
(T) 028 9261 2907
Speciality: Physiotherapy.
P S T (Ref:HM19320)

## STOKE DAMEREL CHIROPODY CLINIC

**Stoke Damerel Chiropody Clinic**, Stoke Damerel Business Centre, 5 Church St, Plymouth, **Devon**, PL3 4DT, ENG.
(T) 01752 605675
Speciality: Chiropodists (Podiatrists).
● **Owner** Mr E Wietscher
S (Ref:HM19321)

## STOKES, J E

**J E Stokes**, Rex Buildings, Alderley Rd, Wilmslow, **Cheshire**, SK9 1HY, ENG.
(T) 01625 530794
Speciality: Physiotherapy.
P S T (Ref:HM19322)

## STOKES, PAM

**Pam Stokes**, 8 Kingsmanor Wharf, Devizes, **Wiltshire**, SN10 2ES, ENG.



Key: B Mind-Body Medicine · C Complementary Medicine · H Self Help Treatment · M Medicinal Therapy · O Oriental Medicine · P Postural Therapy · S Manipulative Structural Therapy · T Touch Therapy

(T) 01380 723425 (F) 01380 723425
Speciality: Reflexology.
● **Owner** Mrs P Stokes
S T (**Ref:**HM19323)

## STOKES, PAM

**Pam Stokes**, 18 Walnut Cl, Cheltenham, **Gloucestershire**, GL52 3AG, ENG.
(T) 01242 250036
Speciality: Reflexology.
S T (**Ref:**HM19324)

## STOKES, TERRY

**Terry Stokes**, Canal Bank Cottage, Tavern Lane, Newnham Bridge, Tenbury Wells, **Worcestershire**, WR15 8LR, ENG.
(T) 01584 781384
(E) rapha@lineone.net
Speciality: Acupuncture, Bach Remedies, Bowen Therapy, Complementary Therapy, Homeopathy, Manipulation, Naturopathy, Osteopathy, Reflexology. ✔
● **Consultant** Mr T Stokes Q: Dip.Ac, Dip.Hom, DO. M: BTER, FHom.
C S Yrs. Est.: 13 (**Ref:**HM19325)

## STOLLARD, R D

**Mrs R D Stollard**, 6 Throstle Nest Drive, Harrogate, **Yorkshire (North)**, HG2 9PB, ENG.
(T) 01423 872249
Speciality: Physiotherapy.
P S T (**Ref:**HM19326)

## STONE CROSS NHS CLINIC

**Stone Cross NHS Clinic**, Jervoise Lane, West Bromwich, **Midlands (West)**, B71 3AR, ENG.
(T) 01215 887665
Speciality: Chiropodists (Podiatrists).
S (**Ref:**HM19327)

## STONE, ANN

**Ann Stone**, Devon View, Bovey Tracey, Newton Abbot, **Devon**, TQ13 9JT, ENG.
(T) 01626 835893
Speciality: Reflexology.
● **Owner** Mrs A Stone
S T (**Ref:**HM19328)

## STONE, ANNE L

**Anne Stone Physiotherapy Practice**, 11 Wye Cl, Droitwich, **Worcestershire**, WR9 8TE, ENG.
(T) 01905 774432 (F) 08701 218563
(E) annestone@droitwich-physio.fsnet.co.uk
(W) www.droitwich-physio.fsnet.co.uk
Speciality: Acupuncture, Electrotherapy, Manipulation, Massage (Therapeutic), Postural Integration, Ultrasonics. ✔
● **Physiotherapist** Ms A Stone Q: MCSP, SRP. M: CSP.
S Yrs. Est.: 9 (**Ref:**HM19329)

## STONE, ANTHONY

**Anthony Stone**, 7 Westholm, London, **London (Greater)**, NW11 6LH, ENG.
(T) 020 8455 0794
Speciality: Psychotherapy.
B (**Ref:**HM19330)

## STONE, ANTHONY

**Anthony Stone**, 7 Endymion Rd, **London**, N4 1EE, ENG.
(T) 020 8348 4400
Speciality: Psychotherapy.
● **Owner** Mr A Stone
B (**Ref:**HM19331)

## STONE, BARRY

**Barry Stone**, Aston Clinic, 26 Kingston Rd, New Malden, **Surrey**, KT3 3LS, ENG.
(T) 020 8942 3148 (F) 020 8949 7050
Speciality: Acupuncture.
O (**Ref:**HM19332)

## STONE, C A

**C A Stone**, 41 Slade Rd, Newton, Swansea, SA3 4UF, WAL.
(T) 01792 360217
Speciality: Physiotherapy.
P S T (**Ref:**HM19333)

## STONE, CHARLES

**Charles Stone**, New Dimensions, 105 High St, Chatham, **Kent**, ME4 4DH, ENG.
(T) 01634 842617
(E) charlesstone@lineone.net
Speciality: Aromatherapy, Bowen Therapy, Colour Therapy, Crystal Healing, Healing Therapy, Hypnosis, Hypnotherapy, Indian Head Massage, Massage (Therapeutic), Meditation, Neuro-Linguistic Program, Osteopathy, Reflexology, Reiki, Spiritual Healing, Stress Therapy, Thought Field Therapy, Chakra and Aura Healing, Regression Therapy, Sports Therapy/Personal Fitness Training. ✔ [credit card]
● **Owner/Therapist** Mr C Stone Q: C.Hyp, Dip.Corp.Stress, NLP, Thought Field Therapy L1, Thought Field Therapy L2. M: HA.
B C Yrs. Est.: 5 (**Ref:**HM19334)

## STONE, I C

**Stone I C**, 1 Tomline Rd, Felixstowe, **Suffolk**, IP11 7QW, ENG.
(T) 01394 282396
Speciality: Chiropodists (Podiatrists).
● **Owner** Mrs P Stone
S (**Ref:**HM19335)

## STONE, JANET

**Janet Stone**, 4 Yew Tree Cottages, Rhoswiel, Weston Rhyn, Oswestry, **Shropshire**, SY10 7TB, ENG.
(T) 01691 773993 (F) 01691 773993
Speciality: Reflexology, Diet & Nutrition, Magnified Healing. ✔
● **Owner/Complementary Therapist** Mrs J Stone Q: MAR.
C Yrs. Est.: 6 (**Ref:**HM19336)

## STONE, JUNE

**June Stone**, 14 Beachmont Cl, Leonard Rd, Greatstone, New Romney, **Kent**, TN28 8UG, ENG.
(T) 01797 361276
Speciality: Reflexology.
S T (**Ref:**HM19337)

## STONE, S

**S Stone**, 11 Woodland Rd, Northfield, Birmingham, **Midlands (West)**, B31 2HU, ENG.
(T) 01214 752560 (F) 01214 779964
Speciality: Physiotherapy.
● **Owner** Mrs S Stone
P S T (**Ref:**HM19338)

## STONEBRIDGE, A H

**A H Stonebridge**, 33 Regent Rd, Brightlingsea, Colchester, **Essex**, CO7 0NL, ENG.
(T) 01206 304525 (F) 01206 304525
Speciality: Chiropodists (Podiatrists).
● **Owner** Mrs A Stonebridge
S (**Ref:**HM19339)

## STONEMAN, SUSAN

**Susan Stoneman**, 22 Hesketh Rd, Yardley Gobion, Towcester, **Northamptonshire**, NN12 7TS, ENG.
(T) 01908 543050
Speciality: Complementary Medicines & Therapy.
C M (**Ref:**HM19340)

## STONES, DAMIEN M

**Stones Damien M**, Hillcrest Gr, Butlerstown, **County Waterford**, IRE.
(T) 05139 2929
Speciality: Complementary Medicines & Therapy.
M (**Ref:**HM19341)

## STONES, DAVE

**Dave Stones**, 3 Little Dockray, Penrith, **Cumbria**, CA11 7HL, ENG.
(T) 01768 867843
Speciality: Complementary Medicines & Therapy.
C M (**Ref:**HM19342)

## STONES, KAREN

**Karen Stones**, East View, Rotherham Rd, Halfway, Sheffield, **Yorkshire (South)**, S20 8GL, ENG.
(T) 01142 482635
Speciality: Indian Head Massage, Reflexology, Reiki, Swedish Masage. ✔
● **Reflexologist** Mrs K Stones Q: MAR, MIIR. M: AoR, IIR.
C Yrs. Est.: 3 (**Ref:**HM19343)

## STOPFORD, H

**H Stopford (Shiatsu)**, 1 Ladysmith Drive, Ashton-under-Lyne, **Manchester (Greater)**, OL6 9DL, ENG.
(T) 01613 390381
Speciality: Complementary Medicines & Therapy.
● **Owner** Miss H Stopford
C M (**Ref:**HM19344)

## STORES, J

**J Stores**, 34 Welch Rd, Hyde, **Cheshire**, SK14 4DJ, ENG.
(T) 01613 669590
Speciality: Reflexology.
C S T (**Ref:**HM19345)

## STOREY ANNE ADHP MICHP RPN

**Storey Anne ADHP MICHP RPN**, 14 The Park Kingswood Heights, IRE.
(T) 01451 2102
(W) www.hypnosiseire.com
Speciality: Hypnotherapy.
B (**Ref:**HM19346)

## STOREY, ADA

**Ada Storey**, Glendyn, Broomhill, Hetton-Le-Hole, Houghton le Spring, **Tyne and Wear**, DH5 9PT, ENG.
(T) 01915 260248
Speciality: Hypnosis.
● **Owner** Mrs A Storey
B (**Ref:**HM19347)

## STOREY, RACHEL

**Rachel Storey**, 16 Delves Wood Rd, Huddersfield, **Yorkshire (West)**, HD4 7AS, ENG.
(T) 01484 311827
Speciality: Reflexology.
S T (**Ref:**HM19348)

## STOREY, SUE

**Sue Storey**, 68 Bailgate, Lincoln, **Lincolnshire**, LN1 3AR, ENG.
(T) 01522 537449 (F) 01522 537449
Speciality: Physiotherapy.
● **Owner** Mrs S Storey
P S T (**Ref:**HM19349)

## STORRS, PAULINE

**Pauline Storrs**, 8 Hitchen Cl, Dukinfield, **Cheshire**, SK16 5HL, ENG.
(T) 01613 385028
Speciality: Aromatherapy.
● **Owner** Mrs P Storrs
M O (**Ref:**HM19350)

## STORT COUNS & PSYCHOTHERAPY

**Stort Counselling & Psychotherapy Practice (The)**, Wilton House, 16B Hockerhill St, Bishop's Stortford, **Hertfordshire**, CM23 2DW, ENG.
(T) 01279 466099
Speciality: Counselling, Gestalt Therapy, Group Therapy, Humanistic Psychology, Psychotherapy, Stress Therapy, Relaxation Tuition, Integrative Humanistic Psychotherapy, Brief (Solution Focused) Therapy. ✔
● **Psychotherapist** Ms K Creasy M: BACP.
B Yrs. Est.: 8 (**Ref:**HM19351)

## STORTFORD GRANGE PHYSIO CENTRE

**Stortford Grange Physiotherapy Centre**, Jenkins Lane, Bishop's Stortford, **Hertfordshire**, CM22 7QL, ENG.
(T) 01279 654020 (F) 01279 655637
Speciality: Acupuncture, Physiotherapy.
✔ [credit card]
● **Consultant Physiotherapist**
Mrs M Emberson Q: Grad Dip Phys, MCSP, SRP. M: CSP.
● **Neuro Physiotherapist**
Ms W Penwill Q: BSc (Hons), MCSP, SRP. M: CSP.
● **Senior Physiotherapist**
Mr Vellerman Q: BSc (Hons), MCSP, SRP. M: CSP.
● **Physiotherapist**
Mrs P Emberton-Brookes Q: Grad Dip Phys, MCSP, SRP. M: CSP.
S Yrs. Est.: 20 (**Ref:**HM19352)

## STORY, MARGARET

**Margaret Story**, 50 Heath Park, Newton Abbot, **Devon**, TQ12 4JQ, ENG.


Key continued: Yrs.Est: Years Established Q: Qualifications M: Professional Membership ✔ Indemnity Insurance [credit card] Accept Credit Cards

(T) 01626 361061
Speciality: Chiropodists (Podiatrists).
● **Owner** Ms M Story
S (Ref:HM19353)

## STOTT, K M

**K M Stott**, 29 St Georges Rd, Winsford, **Cheshire**, CW7 1BY, ENG.
(T) 01606 593966
Speciality: Physiotherapy.
● **Owner** Mrs K Stott
P S T (Ref:HM19354)

## STOTT-DURHAM, ANDREW

**Andrew Stott-Durham**, 12 Hatherleigh Cl, Bognor Regis, **Sussex (West)**, PO21 5JA, ENG.
(T) 01243 821673
Speciality: Acupressure, Cranio-Sacral Therapy, Massage (Therapeutic), Shiatsu, Creiumum.
● **Owner/Holistic Therapist**
Mr A Stott-Durham Q: RCST. M: RCST.
C Yrs. Est.: 13 (Ref:HM19355)

## STOURBRIDGE ACU & OSTEO CTRE

**Stourbridge Acupuncture & Osteopathic Centre**, 15-17 Lawn Avenue, Stourbridge, **Midlands (West)**, DY8 3UR, ENG.
(T) 01384 375271 (F) 01384 375271
Speciality: Osteopathy.
● **Owner/Osteopath** Mr P Rees Q: DO, Lic.Ac. M: GOsC.
S (Ref:HM19356)

## STOURBRIDGE CHIROPRACTIC

**Stourbridge Chiropractic Clinic**, 258 Hagley Rd, Stourbridge, **Midlands (West)**, DY9 0RW, ENG.
(T) 01562 887388
Speciality: Chiropractic.
● **Owner** Mr A Smycz
P S T (Ref:HM19357)

## STOURBRIDGE PHYSIO PRACTICE

**Stourbridge Physiotherapy Practice**, 14 Hagley Rd, Stourbridge, **Midlands (West)**, DY8 1PS, ENG.
(T) 01384 371261 (F) 01384 443378
Speciality: Physiotherapy.
● **Partner** Mrs K York
P S T (Ref:HM19358)

## STOUT, HEATHER

**Heather Stout**, Bamford House, 14 Silver St, Tetbury, **Gloucestershire**, GL8 8DH, ENG.
(T) 01666 502214
(E) jillpeacey@hotmail.com
Speciality: Cranial Osteopathy, Homeopathy, Osteopathy. ✔
● **Homeopath** Ms J Peacey
(T) 01666 503089 Q: LSH, RSHom. M: Soc.Hom.
● **Osteopath** Mrs H Stout Q: DO. M: GOsC.
● **Homeopath** Ms P Howell
(T) 01666 503500 Q: LSH, RSHom. M: Soc.Hom.
● **Osteopath** Mr P Roberts Q: BSc (Hons), DO. M: GOsC.
C Yrs. Est.: 19 (Ref:HM19359)

## STOVELL, J

**J Stovell**, 106 Chessel Cresent, Southampton, **Hampshire**, SO19 4BS, ENG.
(T) 023 8021 1607
Speciality: Chiropodists (Podiatrists).
S (Ref:HM19360)

## STOW PHYSIOTHERAPY SERVICE

**Stow Physiotherapy Service**, Cheltenham House, The Sq, Stow On The Wold, Cheltenham, **Gloucestershire**, GL54 1AB, ENG.
(T) 01451 831370
Speciality: Physiotherapy.
● **Director** Mrs M Greenhill
P S T (Ref:HM19361)

## STOW, A L

**A L Stow**, 7 Roundhay Rd, Bridlington, **Humberside (North)**, YO15 3LA, ENG.
(T) 01262 679647
Speciality: Osteopathy.
● **Owner** Mr A Stow
P S T (Ref:HM19362)

## STOWMARKET OSTEOPATHS

**Stowmarket Osteopaths**, 15-17 Childer Rd, Stowmarket, **Suffolk**, IP14 1PP, ENG.
(T) 01449 613633 (F) 01449 675181
Speciality: Cranial Osteopathy, Osteopathy. ✔
● **Principal Osteopath** Mr T Oxbrow Q: BSc (Hons), DO, FRSH. M: BOrthA, GOsC.
● **Senior Osteopath** Mr N Salway Q: BSc (Hons). M: GOsC.
● **Senior Osteopath** Claire Farleigh Q: BSc, RGN. M: GOsC.
● **Principal Of Childrens Clinic**
Mr S Levien Q: BSc. M: GOsC.
S Yrs. Est.: 19 (Ref:HM19363)

## STRACHAN, JO-ANNE

**Jo-Anne Strachan**, 'Oaklands', Grove Rd, Mollington, Chester, **Cheshire**, CH1 6LG, ENG.
(T) 01244 851455
Speciality: Reflexology.
S T (Ref:HM19364)

## STRACHAN, SUSAN

**Susan Strachan**, Spendlove Centre, Enstone Rd, Charlbury, Chipping Norton, **Oxfordshire**, OX7 3PQ, ENG.
(T) 01608 811185
Speciality: Herbalists.
● **Owner** Mrs S Strachan
M (Ref:HM19365)

## STRAKER, JANE

**Jane Straker**, Physiotherapy & Sports Injury Clinic, Donyngs Recreation Centre, Redhill, **Surrey**, RH1 1DP, ENG.
(T) 01737 763632
Speciality: Physiotherapy.
P S T (Ref:HM19366)

## STRANKS, KATHY

**Genesis**, Trees Farm, Butt Hill, Napton, Southam, **Warwickshire**, CV47 8NE, ENG.
(T) 01926 814375
Speciality: Counselling, Homeopathy, Parapsychology.
● **Homeopath/Counsellor/Parapsychologist**
Ms K Stranks
M (Ref:HM19367)

## STRANKS, KATHY

**Genesis**, Alda House Therapy Centre, Manor House Drive, Coventry, **Midlands (West)**, CV1 2EY, ENG.
(T) 024 7655 3793
Speciality: Counselling, Homeopathy, Parapsychology.
● **Therapist** Ms K Stranks
(T) 01926 814375
C (Ref:HM19368)

## STRATFORD ACU & HOLISTIC HLTH

**Stratford Acupuncture & Holistic Health Centre**, 57 Ely St, Stratford-Upon-Avon, **Warwickshire**, CV37 6LN, ENG.
(T) 01789 299228
Speciality: Acupuncture, Bowen Therapy, Chiropractic, Healer, Herbal Medicine, Homeopathy, Iridology, Manipulation, Massage (Therapeutic), Moxibustion, Nutritional Therapy, Oriental Diagnosis, Reflexology, Reiki. ✔
● **Centre Manager** Ms D Cosby Q: MBAcC, MRCHM. M: BAcC, RCHM.
B Yrs. Est.: 16 (Ref:HM19369)

## STRATFORD PHYSIO CLINIC

**Stratford Physiotherapy Clinic**, 14 West St, Stratford-Upon-Avon, **Warwickshire**, CV37 6DW, ENG.
(T) 01789 294721
Speciality: Physiotherapy, Specialises in Dance Physiotherapy and has worked with the Royal Shakespeare Company. ✔
● **Owner/Physiotherapist**
Mrs C Arnold Q: Grad Dip Phys, MCSP, SRP. M: CSP.
S Yrs. Est.: 16 (Ref:HM19370)

## STRATH NATURAL THERAPIES

**Strath Natural Therapies**, 30 Grahamshill Avenue, Airdrie, **Lanarkshire (North)**, ML6 7EP, SCO.
(T) 01236 767731
(E) strathnt@cableinet.co.uk
(W) www.strathnt.com
Speciality: Hypnotherapy, Reflexology, Stress Therapy, Dream Interpretation, Relaxation. ✔
● **Hypnotherapist** Ms C Orr Q: BA, RGN.
B Yrs. Est.: 2 (Ref:HM19371)

## STRATTON, FIONA

**Fiona Stratton**, 11 Sycamore Trce, Bootham, York, **Yorkshire (North)**, YO30 7DN, ENG.
(T) 01904 638938
Speciality: Absent Healing, Acupressure, Acupuncture, Aromatherapy, Complementary Therapy, Healer, Holistic Healing, Massage (Therapeutic), Reflexology, Spiritual Healing, Gua Sha. ✔
● **Acupuncturist/Health Care Practitioner**
Miss F Stratton Q: Bayley School Cert, Cert.NCA, Dip.OSMA, ITEC. M: IPTI, NFSH.
B C Yrs. Est.: 7 (Ref:HM19372)

## STRATTON, KAREN

**Karen Stratton**, 70 High St, New Sharlston, Wakefield, **Yorkshire (West)**, WF4 1BE, ENG.
(T) 01924 864523
Speciality: Complementary Medicines & Therapy.
C M (Ref:HM19373)

## STRATTON, SUNNY

**Mrs Sunny Stratton**, 259 Newbold Rd, Chesterfield, **Derbyshire**, S41 7AL, ENG.
(T) 01246 550538
Speciality: Osteopathy.
P S T (Ref:HM19374)

## STRAUB, DESMOND

**Desmond Straub**, 46 Lavender Pl, Ilford, **Essex**, IG1 2BE, ENG.
(T) 020 8514 8672
Speciality: Chiropodists (Podiatrists).
● **Owner** Mr D Straub
S (Ref:HM19375)

## STRAW, SANDRA

**Sandra Straw**, London, **London (Greater)**, NW6, ENG.
(T) 020 7624 0363
Speciality: Bach Remedies.
M (Ref:HM19376)

## STRAWBERRY HILL PRACTICE

**Strawberry Hill Practice (The)**, P.O. Box 233 Strawberry Hill, Twickenham, **London (Greater)**, TW1 4XB, ENG.
(T) 020 8607 9013
Speciality: Complementary Medicines & Therapy.
C M (Ref:HM19377)

## STRAWBERRY HOW CLINIC

**Strawberry How Clinic**, Lorton Rd, Cockermouth, **Cumbria**, CA13 9XQ, ENG.
(T) 01900 828810
Speciality: Acupressure, Physiotherapy. ✔ CREDIT
● **Owner/Physiotherapist/Acupuncturist**
Mrs K Evans Q: MCSP. M: BAcC, CSP.
O S Yrs. Est.: 9 (Ref:HM19378)

## STRAWBRIDGE, GAYNOR

**Gaynor Strawbridge**, 11 Wareings Lane, Denton, Northampton, **Northamptonshire**, NN7 1DS, ENG.
(T) 01604 890462
Speciality: Chiropodists (Podiatrists).
● **Owner** Mrs G Strawbridge
S (Ref:HM19379)

## STRAWSON, M R

**M R Strawson**, 94 Stowmarket Rd, Needham Market, Ipswich, **Suffolk**, IP6 8DX, ENG.
(T) 01449 721168
Speciality: Chiropodists (Podiatrists).
● **Principal** Mrs M Strawson
S (Ref:HM19380)

## STREAMS HYPNOTHERAPY

**Streams Hypnotherapy**, First Floor Therapy Suite, Egham Sports Centre, Egham, **Surrey**, TW20 8NL, ENG.
(T) 07977 698728
Speciality: Hypnotherapy.
B (Ref:HM19381)



Key: B Mind-Body Medicine C Complementary Medicine H Self Help Treatment M Medicinal Therapy O Oriental Medicine P Postural Therapy S Manipulative Structural Therapy T Touch Therapy

## STREET CHIROPRACTIC CLINIC

**Dr Diane Brown**, St Chiropractic Clinic, 74A High St, Street, **Somerset**, BA16 0EG, ENG.
(T) 01458 840490
Speciality: Chiropody, Chiropractic. ✓
● **Associate** Dr E Donovan Q: BSc, DC. M: BCA.
● **Owner** Dr D Brown Q: BA, BSc (Chiro), DC. M: BCA.
● **Associate** Dr L Malin Q: BS, DC. M: BCA.
P Yrs. Est.: 8 (**Ref:**HM19382)

## STREET CHIROPRACTIC CLINIC

**Street Chiropractic Clinic**, 74A High St, Street, **Somerset**, BA16 0EN, ENG.
(T) 01458 840490
(E) leroulxt@msn.com
Speciality: Aromatherapy, Chiropractic, Complementary Therapy, Electrotherapy, Manipulation, Massage (Therapeutic), Ultrasonics, X-Ray. ✓
● **Chiropractor** Ms D Le Roux Q: BSc (Chiro), DC, FCC, MSc. M: BCA, CC.
● **Chiropractor** Ms E Donovan M: BCC, CC.
S Yrs. Est.: 9 (**Ref:**HM19383)

## STREET, R E F

**R E F Street**, The Old College, Uttoxeter New Rd, Derby, **Derbyshire**, DE22 3WZ, ENG.
(T) 01332 346601
Speciality: Hypnotherapy.
B (**Ref:**HM19384)

## STRESS BODY MANAGEMENT

**Stress Body Management**, 14 Cedar Drive, Bracknell, **Berkshire**, RG42 2LG, ENG.
(T) 01344 303606 (F) 01344 867451
Speciality: Complementary Medicines & Therapy.
● **Owner** Mrs S Brown
C M (**Ref:**HM19385)

## STRESS CENTRE

**Stress Centre**, 42 East St, Bromley, **Kent**, BR1 1QW, ENG.
(T) 020 8402 5421
Speciality: Herbalists.
M (**Ref:**HM19386)

## STRESS CENTRE

**Stress Centre (The)**, 2 Rossie Pl, Auchterarder, **Perth and Kinross**, PH3 1AJ, SCO.
(T) 01764 661112
Speciality: Aromatherapy.
● **Owner** Mrs J Cherry
M O (**Ref:**HM19387)

## STRESS CLINIC

**Stress Clinic (The)**, 73 New Bold Rd, Chesterfield, **Derbyshire**, S40 1NH, ENG.
(T) 01246 559455
Speciality: Hypnotherapy.
● **Owner** Mr W Wagstaff
B (**Ref:**HM19388)

## STRESS CLINIC & NTRL HLTH CTRE

**Stress Clinic and Natural Health Centre (The)**, 14-15 North Prde, Frome, **Somerset**, BA11 1AU, ENG.
(T) 01373 454595
(W) www.thestressclinic.co.uk
Speciality: Acupressure, Acupuncture, Aromatherapy, Chiropractic, Cognitive Therapy, Complementary Therapy, Counselling, Cranial Osteopathy, Dietician, Family Planning (Natural), Family Therapy, Gestalt Therapy, Group Therapy, Herbal Medicine, Homeopathy, Humanistic Psychology, Hypnotherapy, Indian Head Massage, Kinesiology, Manipulation, Massage (Therapeutic), Meditation, Moxibustion, Oriental Diagnosis, Osteopathy, Psychotherapy, Pyscho-Synthesis, Reflexology, Reiki, Shiatsu, Stress Therapy, Yoga. ✓
● **Director** Ms C Richardson
C Yrs. Est.: 5 (**Ref:**HM19389)

## STRESS COMPANY

**Stress Company (The)**, 50 Robinswood Gardens, Robinswood, Gloucester, **Gloucestershire**, GL4 6TB, ENG.
(T) 01452 521008
Speciality: Complementary Therapy, Hypnosis, Magnetic Therapy, Stress Therapy, Occupational Therapy, Regression Therapy.
B (**Ref:**HM19390)

## STRESS COUNSELLING

**Stress Counselling**, 72 Sherwood Drive, Marske-By-The-Sea, Redcar, **Cleveland**, TS11 6DY, ENG.
(T) 01642 494193
(E) shirley-robson@hotmail.com
(W) www.geocities.com/psychotherapy-counsellinguk
Speciality: Aromatherapy, Cognitive Therapy, Counselling, Gestalt Therapy, Humanistic Psychology, Hypnosis, Hypnotherapy, Life Style Coaching, Meditation, Music Therapy, Psychotherapy, Rogerian Therapy, Stress Therapy, Transactional Analysis, Visualisation Therapy, Oniro Therapy(Image Work), Rational Emotive Therapy, Behavioural Therapy, Cause And Effect Therapy. ✓
● **Psychotherapist/Counsellor** Ms S Robson Q: MIP. M: BACP, IP.
B Yrs. Est.: 9 (**Ref:**HM19391)

## STRESS FREE ZONE

**Stress Free Zone**, 26 Mochrum Drive, Crossford, Dunfermline, **Fife**, KY12 8YH, SCO.
(T) 01383 624544 (F) 01383 624544
Speciality: Reflexology.
● **Owner** Mrs J Hawkins
S T (**Ref:**HM19392)

## STRESS MANAGEMENT

**Stress Management**, 34 Oldborough Rd, Wembley, **London (Greater)**, HA0 3PR, ENG.
(T) 020 8931 7021
Speciality: Hypnosis.
B (**Ref:**HM19393)

## STRESS MANAGEMENT

**Stress Management**, The Haven, 28 Corser St, Stourbridge, **Midlands (West)**, DY8 2DE, ENG.
(T) 01384 444264
Speciality: Hypnosis.
● **Owner** Ms C Jasper
B (**Ref:**HM19394)

## STRESS MANAGEMENT

**Stress Management**, The Priory, Dalton Piercy, Hartlepool, **Cleveland**, TS27 3HS, ENG.
(T) 01429 232948
Speciality: Hypnosis.
B (**Ref:**HM19395)

## STRESS MANAGEMENT

**Stress Management**, 62 Liverpool Rd, Crosby, Liverpool, **Merseyside**, L23 5SJ, ENG.
(T) 01519 320047
Speciality: Hypnosis.
B (**Ref:**HM19396)

## STRESS MANAGEMENT CENTRE

**Stress Management Centre**, 92 Harley St, London, **London (Greater)**, W1N 1AF, ENG.
(T) 020 7486 7734 (F) 020 8689 5877
Speciality: Psychotherapy.
● **Principal** Mr B Hill
B (**Ref:**HM19397)

## STRESS MATTERS

**Stress Matters**, Delphi, Common Rd, West Bilney, King's Lynn, **Norfolk**, PE32 1JX, ENG.
(T) 01553 841462 (F) 01553 841462
Speciality: Complementary Medicines & Therapy.
● **Owner** Mrs P Hill
M (**Ref:**HM19398)

## STRESS PROJECT

**Stress Project (The)**, Shelburne House, 2 Shelburne Rd, London, **London (Greater)**, N7 6DL, ENG.
(T) 020 7700 3938 (F) 020 7607 6961
Speciality: Complementary Medicines & Therapy.
● **Manager** Mr E Keogh
C M (**Ref:**HM19399)

## STRESS RELEASE

**Stress Release**, 11 St Georges Trce, Jesmond, Newcastle Upon Tyne, **Tyne and Wear**, NE2 2SU, ENG.
(T) 01912 812251 (F) 01912 812251
Speciality: Complementary Medicines & Therapy.
● **Owner** Mr D Johnson
C M (**Ref:**HM19400)

## STRESS SENSE

**Stress Sense**, 74 Newlands Rd, Glasgow, **Glasgow (City of)**, G43 2JH, SCO.
(T) 01416 361110 (F) 01416 361110
Speciality: Hypnotherapy.
● **Owner** Mrs A Maguire
B (**Ref:**HM19401)

## STRESSED OUT

**Stressed Out**, 76 Castle Court, Broomburn Drive, Newton Mearns, Glasgow, **Glasgow (City of)**, G77 5JE, SCO.
(T) 01416 397989
Speciality: Aromatherapy.
M O (**Ref:**HM19402)

## STRICK, STUART

**Stuart Strick**, 15 St Michaels Cl, Plymouth, **Devon**, PL1 4RX, ENG.
(T) 01752 607069
Speciality: Chiropodists (Podiatrists).
● **Owner** Mr S Strick
S (**Ref:**HM19403)

## STRICKLAND, IAN

**Ian Strickland**, 6 Silverlow Rd, Nailsea, Bristol, BS48 2AD, ENG.
(T) 01275 858095
Speciality: Chiropodists (Podiatrists).
S (**Ref:**HM19404)

## STRIDE, D

**D Stride**, 196 Wigmore Rd, Gillingham, **Kent**, ME8 0TL, ENG.
(T) 01634 365510
Speciality: Complementary Medicines & Therapy.
M (**Ref:**HM19405)

## STRIKE, SUE

**Sue Strike**, 17 Binstead Drive, Blackwater, Camberley, **Surrey**, GU17 0HJ, ENG.
(T) 01252 655978
Speciality: Indian Head Massage, Reflexology.
S T (**Ref:**HM19406)

## STRINGER, FRANCES

**Frances Stringer**, 4 Prince Consort Cottages, Windsor, **Berkshire**, SL4 1JA, ENG.
(T) 01753 866067
Speciality: Alexander Technique. ✓
● **Practitioner** Ms F Stinger Q: MSTAT.
P Yrs. Est.: 11 (**Ref:**HM19407)

## STRINGER, G D

**G D Stringer**, 339A Ballards Lane, London, **London (Greater)**, N12 8LJ, ENG.
(T) 020 8444 8273
Speciality: Hypnotherapy.
B (**Ref:**HM19408)

## STRINGER, R A (DR)

**Dr R A Stringer**, Chapel St Medical Centre, Ashton-under-Lyne, **Manchester (Greater)**, OL6 6EW, ENG.
(T) 01613 399292
Speciality: Acupuncture.
O (**Ref:**HM19409)

## STRINO, GEORGE

**George Strino**, Aldrens Lane, Lancaster, **Lancashire**, LA1 2DU, ENG.
(T) 01524 69864 (F) 01524 848155
Speciality: Complementary Medicines & Therapy.
M (**Ref:**HM19410)

## STRODE, ALISON

**Alison Strode**, Clissold Park Health Centre, 154 Stoke Newington Church St, London, **London (Greater)**, N16 0JU, ENG.
(T) 020 7249 2990 (F) 020 7249 3977
Speciality: Osteopathy.
● **Director** Mr D Berg
P S T (**Ref:**HM19411)

## STROKE & HEAD INJURY CLINIC

**Stroke & Head Injury Clinic (The)**, 95 Prenton Village Rd, Prenton, **Merseyside**, CH43 0TF, ENG.
(T) 01516 090597
Speciality: Physiotherapy.



Key continued: Yrs.Est: Years Established Q: Qualifications M: Professional Membership ✓ Indemnity Insurance Accept Credit Cards

**• Manageress** Mrs S Williams
P S T (Ref:HM19412)

## STRONACH, LORNA

**Lorna Stronach**, Darroch, Blairingone, Dollar, **Clackmannanshire**, FK14 7NU, SCO.
(T) 01259 742914
Speciality: Chiropodists (Podiatrists).
S (Ref:HM19413)

## STRONG, A C

**A C Strong**, 31 Beulah Rd, Tunbridge Wells, **Kent**, TN1 2NS, ENG.
(T) 01892 520058
Speciality: Chiropodists (Podiatrists).
**• Owner** Mrs A Strong
S (Ref:HM19414)

## STRONG, JENNY

**Jenny Strong**, 16 Clarence Sq, Cheltenham, **Gloucestershire**, GL50 4JN, ENG.
(T) 01242 241933
Speciality: Complementary Medicines & Therapy.
M (Ref:HM19415)

## STRONG, L A E

**L A E Strong**, 31 Beulah Rd, Tunbridge Wells, **Kent**, TN1 2NS, ENG.
(T) 01892 520058
Speciality: Chiropodists (Podiatrists).
**• Owner** Mr L Strong
S (Ref:HM19416)

## STRONG, MRS

**Mrs Strong**, 254 Goodwood Avenue, Hornchurch, **Essex**, RM12 6DH, ENG.
(T) 01708 455126 (F) 01708 455126
Speciality: Chiropodists (Podiatrists).
**• Owner** Mr R Strong
S (Ref:HM19417)

## STRONG, R R M

**R R M Strong**, 13 Baird Trce, Edinburgh, **Edinburgh (City of)**, EH12 5RR, SCO.
(T) 01313 377976
Speciality: Chiropodists (Podiatrists).
**• Owner** Mrs R Strong
S (Ref:HM19418)

## STRONG, STELLA

**Stella Strong Registered Osteopath**, 16 St Paul St, London, **London (Greater)**, N1 7AB, ENG.
(T) 020 7226 8499
Speciality: Counselling, Cranial Osteopathy, Healer, Osteopathy, Transpersonal Psychology Counselling, Shamanic Healing, Therapeutic Massage. ✓
**• Owner/Registered Osteopath**
Ms S Strong Q: DO. M: GOsC.
B Yrs. Est.: 9 (Ref:HM19419)

## STRONG, SUSAN M

**Susan M Strong**, 94 Hurcott Rd, Kidderminster, **Worcestershire**, DY10 2QT, ENG.
(T) 01562 751185
Speciality: Physiotherapy.
P S T (Ref:HM19420)

## STROUD CHIROPRACTIC CLINIC

**Stroud Chiropractic Clinic**, Cotswold House, 37 London Rd, Stroud, **Gloucestershire**, GL5 2AJ, ENG.
(T) 01453 755527
Speciality: Chiropractic.
**• Owner** Mrs L Burbank
P S T (Ref:HM19421)

## STROUD NATURAL HEALTH CLINIC

**Stroud Natural Health Clinic**, Witheys Yard, High St, Stroud, **Gloucestershire**, GL5 1AP, ENG.
(T) 01453 750796
Speciality: Acupuncture, Aromatherapy, Cranio-Sacral Therapy, Homeopathy, Indian Head Massage, Massage (Therapeutic), Osteopathy, Reflexology, Shiatsu, Allergy Therapy, Metamorphic Technique, Lymphatic Drainage. ✓
**• Acupuncturist** Ms K Wells Q: BA, Lic.Ac, MBAcC, MRCHM.
**• Allergy Therapist** Mrs M Kirkman M: BIAT.
**• Therapeutic Massage Therapist**
Mr M Taylor Q: APNT, BSc, RCST.
**• Shiatsu Practitioner** Jo Hofman Q: BA.
**• Therapeutic Massage Therapist**
Ms S Kean Q: APNT, BSc, Cert.Ed, RCST.
**• McTimoney Chiropractor**
Ms H Morris Q: BSc, DC, MMCA.
**• Osteopath** Mr M Rumney Q: BA, DO. M: GOsC.
**• Reflexologist** Lesley Doran Q: ITEC. M: AoR.
**• Practitioner** Ms L Battman Q: APNT, MBRCP.
C Yrs. Est.: 14 (Ref:HM19422)

## STROUD, GRAEME

**Graeme Stroud**, Cornwallis House, Howard Chase, Basildon, **Essex**, SS14 3BB, ENG.
(T) 01268 287733
Speciality: Osteopathy.
P S T (Ref:HM19423)

## STRUCTURE & FUNCTION CLINIC

**Structure & Function Clinic (The)**, 65 Duke St, Darlington, **County Durham**, DL3 7SD, ENG.
(T) 01325 466022 (F) 01325 466022
Speciality: Osteopathy.
P S T (Ref:HM19424)

## STRUDWICK, H J

**H J Strudwick**, 35 Howitt St, Heanor, **Derbyshire**, DE75 7AU, ENG.
(T) 01773 760945
Speciality: Osteopathy.
P S T (Ref:HM19425)

## STRUTT, COLLEEN

**Colleen Strutt**, Wentbrook, 13 Whinney Lane, Streethouse, Pontefract, **Yorkshire (West)**, WF7 6BY, ENG.
(T) 01977 792565
Speciality: Complementary Medicines & Therapy.
**• Owner** Mrs C Strutt
M (Ref:HM19426)

## STRUTT, T

**T Strutt**, Ashdown Osteopathic Centre, The Sq, Lewes Rd, Forest Row, **Sussex (East)**, RH18 5ES, ENG.
(T) 01342 822505 (F) 01342 822505
Speciality: Osteopathy.
**• Owner** Mr T Strutt
P S T (Ref:HM19427)

## STUART, LOUISE

**Louise Stuart**, Victoria House, 43 Chapel St, Leigh, **Manchester (Greater)**, WN7 2PB, ENG.
(T) 01942 683103
Speciality: Chiropodists (Podiatrists).
**• Owner** Mrs L Stewart
S (Ref:HM19428)

## STUART-MENTETH, R A

**R A Stuart-Menteth**, 67 Comiston Rd, Edinburgh, **Edinburgh (City of)**, EH10 6AG, SCO.
(T) 01314 474080
Speciality: Osteopathy.
**• Partner** Mrs R Stuart-Menteth
P S T (Ref:HM19429)

## STUART-MENTETH, W J

**W J Stuart-Menteth**, 67 Comiston Rd, Edinburgh, **Edinburgh (City of)**, EH10 6AG, SCO.
(T) 01314 474080
Speciality: Osteopathy.
**• Partner** Mrs R Stuart-Menteth
P S T (Ref:HM19430)

## STUBBER, MAXINE HAMILTON

**Maxine Hamilton Stubber**, Balance Clinic, 250 Kings Rd, London, **London (Greater)**, SW3 5UE, ENG.
(T) 020 7565 0333
Speciality: Osteopathy.
**• Owner** Ms M Hamiltonstubber
P S T (Ref:HM19431)

## STUBBINGTON NTRL HEALTH CLINIC

**Stubbington Natural Health Clinic**, 3 Stubbington Lane, **Hampshire**, PO14 2PP, ENG.
(T) 01329 665871
Speciality: Alexander Technique.
**• Therapist** Mr T York
P S (Ref:HM19432)

## STUBBS, D A

**Mrs D A Stubbs**, The Osteopathic Health Centre, 99 Cheyney Rd, Chester, **Cheshire**, CH1 4BS, ENG.
(T) 01244 371820
Speciality: Osteopathy.
P S T (Ref:HM19433)

## STUBBS, DAVID

**David Stubbs**, 5 Danyon Cl, Rainham, **Kent**, RM13 9LS, ENG.
(T) 01708 520536
Speciality: Chiropodists (Podiatrists).
S (Ref:HM19434)

## STUBBS, FIONA

**Fiona Stubbs**, 11 Oldbury Prior, Calne, **Wiltshire**, SN11 0AF, ENG.
(T) 01249 821660
Speciality: Chiropodists (Podiatrists).
**• Owner** Ms F Stubbs
S (Ref:HM19435)

## STUBBS, I J

**I J Stubbs**, 9 Victoria Cres, High St, Dover, **Kent**, CT16 1DU, ENG.
(T) 01304 206770
Speciality: Chiropodists (Podiatrists).
**• Owner** Mr I Stubbs
S (Ref:HM19436)

## STUBBS, RICHARD

**Richard Stubbs**, 13 Shaw Rd, Newbury, **Berkshire**, RG14 1HG, ENG.
(T) 01635 34679
Speciality: Osteopathy.
**• Owner** Mr R Stubbs
P S T (Ref:HM19437)

## STUDART, P J

**P J Studart**, 421 Crofton Rd, Orpington, **Kent**, BR6 8NL, ENG.
(T) 01689 852483 (F) 01689 852483
Speciality: Chiropodists (Podiatrists).
**• Owner** Mr P Studart
S (Ref:HM19438)

## STUDENSKI, ELIZABETH

**Studenski Elizabeth**, Doon Corrigeenroe, Roscommon, **County Roscommon**, IRE.
(T) 07966 072
Speciality: Complementary Medicines & Therapy.
M (Ref:HM19439)

## STUDIO 1

**Studio 1**, 40 St Marys St, Eynesbury, St. Neots, **Cambridgeshire**, PE19 2TA, ENG.
(T) 01480 471439
Speciality: Relaxation Technique.
H T (Ref:HM19440)

## STUDIO BEAUTY/NATURAL HEALING

**Studio Beauty & Natural Healing**, 86 Queen St, Great Harwood, Blackburn, **Lancashire**, BB6 7AL, ENG.
(T) 01254 882233
Speciality: Aromatherapy.
**• Owner** Mrs E Aspin
M O (Ref:HM19441)

## STUDLEY PHYSIOTHERAPY CENTRE

**Studley Physiotherapy Centre**, Austrey House, 19 Station Rd, Studley, **Warwickshire**, B80 7HR, ENG.
(T) 01527 852534 (F) 01527 852534
(E) spc.physio@btinternet.com
Speciality: Acupressure, Acupuncture, Biofeedback, Electrotherapy, Manipulation, Massage (Therapeutic), Physiotherapy, Pilates, Postural Integration, Ultrasonics. ✓ CREDIT
**• Practice Principal** Ms R John Q: Grad Dip Phys, MCSP, SRP. M: CSP.
**• Practice Principal** Ms M John Q: Grad Dip Phys, MCSP, SRP. M: CSP.
**• Associate/Physiotherapist**
Ms J Morris Q: Grad Dip Phys, MCSP, ONC, SRP.
**• Associate/Physiotherapist**
Ms S Harris Q: BSc (Hons), MCSP, SRP. M: CSP.
**• Associate/Physiotherapist**
Ms A Harris Q: Grad Dip Phys, MCSP, SRP. M: CSP.
**• Associate/Physiotherapist**



Key: B Mind-Body Medicine C Complementary Medicine H Self Help Treatment M Medicinal Therapy O Oriental Medicine P Postural Therapy S Manipulative Structural Therapy T Touch Therapy

Noel Reeve Q: Grad Dip Phys, MCSP, ONC, SRP. M: CSP.
● **Associate/Physiotherapist** Ms M Betts Q: Grad Dip Phys, MCSP, MMACP, SRP. M: CSP.
S Yrs. Est.: 35 (Ref:HM19442)

## STUDLEY, MARGARET
**Margaret Studley**, 33 Cremer St, Sheringham, **Norfolk**, NR26 8DZ, ENG.
(T) 01263 825406
Speciality: Reflexology.
S T (Ref:HM19443)

## STUMMER, G
**G Stummer**, 7 Langfield Avenue, Manchester, **Manchester (Greater)**, M16 8LH, ENG.
(T) 01612 327692
Speciality: Psychotherapy.
● **Owner** Miss G Stummer
B (Ref:HM19444)

## STURGE, DEBBIE
**Debbie Sturge Nutrition Consultancy**, The Art Of Well-Being Alternative Health Centre, Bank House, 38 St Mildreds Rd, Westgate-on-Sea, **Kent**, CT8 8RF, ENG.
(T) 01843 836653 (F) 01843 230653
(E) debbiesturge@hotmail.com
Speciality: Complementary Therapy, Holistic Healing, Nutritional Therapy, Vitamin Therapy. ✓
● **Clinical Nutritional Consultant** Ms D Sturge Q: Dip.ION. M: BANT.
M Yrs. Est.: 3 (Ref:HM19445)

## STURGE, R F
**R F Sturge**, 2 Crescent Rd, Ramsgate, **Kent**, CT11 9QU, ENG.
(T) 01843 597527
Speciality: Chiropodists (Podiatrists).
● **Owner** Mr R Sturge
S (Ref:HM19446)

## STURGEON, JOHN
**John Sturgeon**, 4 Hardgrove Cottages, Ruthwell, Dumfries, **Dumfries and Galloway**, DG1 4NT, SCO.
(T) 01387 840309
Speciality: Chiropodists (Podiatrists).
● **Owner** Mr J Sturgeon
S (Ref:HM19447)

## STURGESS, ELAINE
**Elaine Sturgess**, Laburnums, Hook Lane, Aldingbourne, Chichester, **Sussex (West)**, PO20 6TE, ENG.
(T) 01243 545200
Speciality: Osteopathy.
P S T (Ref:HM19448)

## STURGESS, PETER
**Peter Sturgess**, 5 Derby Rd, Kingsbridge, **Devon**, TQ7 1JJ, ENG.
(T) 01548 853030
Speciality: Osteopathy.
● **Owner** Mr P Sturgess
P S T (Ref:HM19449)

## STURGESS, PETER
**Peter Sturgess**, 12 Temple Sq, Aylesbury, **Buckinghamshire**, HP20 2QL, ENG.
(T) 01296 423331
Speciality: Osteopathy.
P S T (Ref:HM19450)

## STURMEY, GRAHAME
**Grahame Sturmey**, 32 Handsworth Gardens, Armthorpe, Doncaster, **Yorkshire (South)**, DN3 3SZ, ENG.
(T) 01302 835457
Speciality: Reflexology.
S T (Ref:HM19451)

## STURROCK, T
**T Sturrock**, 67 Front St, Monkseaton, Whitley Bay, **Tyne and Wear**, NE25 8AA, ENG.
(T) 01912 510202
Speciality: Chiropodists (Podiatrists).
● **Owner** Mr T Sturrock
S (Ref:HM19452)

## STURRY'S REFLEXOLOGY PRACTICE
**Sturry's Reflexology Practice**, 26 Meadow Rd, Sturry, Canterbury, **Kent**, CT2 0JF, ENG.
(T) 01227 711455
Speciality: Complementary Medicines & Therapy.
M (Ref:HM19453)

## STURZAKER, NICOLA
**Nicola Sturzaker**, 75 Risbygate St, Bury St. Edmunds, **Suffolk**, IP33 3AQ, ENG.
(T) 01284 769153
Speciality: Osteopathy.
P S T (Ref:HM19454)

## STUTZ, GABRIELE
**Gabriele Stutz**, 37 Peel Rd, Wolverton, Milton Keynes, **Buckinghamshire**, MK12 5AX, ENG.
(T) 01908 225051
Speciality: Acupuncture.
O (Ref:HM19455)

## STYAN, JENNY
**Jenny Styan**, 162 Barrowby Rd, Grantham, **Lincolnshire**, NG31 8AF, ENG.
(T) 01476 573122
Speciality: Reflexology.
S T (Ref:HM19456)

## STYLES, D M
**D M Styles**, 108 Fore St, Kingsbridge, **Devon**, TQ7 1AW, ENG.
(T) 01548 852542
Speciality: Chiropractic.
P S T (Ref:HM19457)

## STYLES, PATRICIA
**Patricia Styles**, 44 Bath Hill, Keynsham, Bristol, BS31 1HG, ENG.
(T) 01179 860455 (F) 01179 860455
Speciality: Biomechanics, Chiropody, Cryo Surgery, Podiatry. ✓
● **Owner/Chiropodist** Mrs P Styles Q: DPodM.
M Yrs. Est.: 12 (Ref:HM19458)

## SUAIMHNEAS AROMATHERAPY
**Suaimhneas Aromatherapy**, 28 Auburn Vlge, Mullingar, **County Westmeath**, IRE.
(T) 04442 591
Speciality: Aromatherapy.
M O (Ref:HM19459)

## SUAN TRA NATURAL THERAPY CTRE
**Suan Tra Natural Therapy Centre**, Manor Village, Tralee, **County Kerry**, IRE.
(T) 06671 28390
Speciality: Complementary Medicines & Therapy.
M (Ref:HM19460)

## SUCCESSWORKS
**Successworks**, Po Box 7093, Birmingham, **Midlands (West)**, B15 2HH, ENG.
(T) 01217 844942 (F) 01217 844942
Speciality: Absent Healing, Complementary Therapy, Counselling, Healer, Holistic Healing, Humanistic Psychology, Life Style Coaching, Meditation, Reiki, Spiritual Healing, Stress Therapy, Visualisation Therapy. ✓
● **Company Director** Ms G Bond Q: Reiki Master. M: BPS.
H Yrs. Est.: 5 (Ref:HM19461)

## SUDBURY CHIROPRACTIC CLINIC
**Sudbury Chiropractic Clinic (The)**, The Old Bakery, King St, Sudbury, **Suffolk**, CO10 2EB, ENG.
(T) 01787 377300 (F) 01787 466749
Speciality: Chiropractic, Manipulation, Physiotherapy, Ultrasonic Treatment. ✓
● **Principal** Dr A Corrigan Q: GCC (Reg). M: BCA.
S Yrs. Est.: 5 (Ref:HM19462)

## SUDWELL, MARIE
**Marie Sudwell**, 9 Connop Way, Frimley, Camberley, **Surrey**, GU16 5RX, ENG.
(T) 01276 64066
Speciality: Chiropodists (Podiatrists).
● **Owner** Mrs M Sudwell
S (Ref:HM19463)

## SUE
**SUE**, Grosvenor Drive, Loughton, **Essex**, IG10 2JX, ENG.
(T) 020 8502 3544
Speciality: Clairvoyants & Palmists.
B (Ref:HM19464)

## SUE ANN
**Sue Ann**, 59 Tudor Avenue, Worcester Park, **Surrey**, KT4 8TX, ENG.
(T) 020 8337 3396
Speciality: Clairvoyants & Palmists.
● **Owner** Mr S Seville
B (Ref:HM19465)

## SUE CHARLES AROMATHERAPY
**Sue Charles Aromatherapy**, Unit 2, Forest Court, Linden Way, Coalville, **Leicestershire**, LE67 3JY, ENG.
(T) 01530 814171
Speciality: Acupressure, Aromatherapy, Complementary Therapy, Indian Head Massage, Massage (Therapeutic), Shiatsu, Stress Therapy, Touch Therapy. ✓
● **Clinical Aromatherapist** Ms S Charles Q: Dip.Clin.Arom. M: ESIPF, IFA, ISPA.
B Yrs. Est.: 18 (Ref:HM19466)

## SUE RICKS COMP THERAPY
**Sue Ricks Complementary Therapy Clinic**, 15 Cropston Avenue, Loughborough, **Leicestershire**, LE11 4PR, ENG.
(T) 01509 214373 (F) 01509 214373
(E) suericksuk@aol.com
Speciality: Absent Healing, Bach Remedies, Complementary Therapy, Healer, Neuro-Linguistic Program, Reflexology, Reiki, Vibrational Therapy, Electro Crystal Therapy. ✓
● **Principal** Mrs S Ricks Q: Cert.Ed, MAR, MGCP, MSDI. M: AoR.
C T Yrs. Est.: 10 (Ref:HM19467)

## SUEN, J
**J Suen**, 46 Chelmsford Trce, Bradford, **Yorkshire (West)**, BD3 8AG, ENG.
(T) 01274 662035
Speciality: Acupuncture.
O (Ref:HM19468)

## SUFI MYSTICAL ORDER
**Sufi Mystical Order**, P O Box 1033, London, **London (Greater)**, SE15 2HF, ENG.
(T) 020 7639 6420 (F) 020 7639 6420
Speciality: Clairvoyants & Palmists.
● **Owner** Dr A Wahib
B (Ref:HM19469)

## SUGARMAN, J
**J Sugarman**, Edgware Clinic For Natural Health, 128 High St, Edgware, **London (Greater)**, HA8 7EL, ENG.
(T) 020 8951 3475
Speciality: Osteopathy.
● **Owner** Mr J Sugarman
P S T (Ref:HM19470)

## SUGDEN, A E
**A E Sugden**, 15 Tuesday Market Pl, King's Lynn, **Norfolk**, PE30 1JN, ENG.
(T) 01553 760044
Speciality: Acupuncture.
● **Practice Manager** Mrs C Zimmer
O (Ref:HM19471)

## SUGDEN, TONY
**Tony Sugden**, 29 High St, Oakington, Cambridge, **Cambridgeshire**, CB4 5AG, ENG.
(T) 01223 237459 (F) 01223 237459
Speciality: Acupuncture.
● **Partner** Mr G Giddings
O (Ref:HM19472)

## SUGG, BARRY
**Barry Sugg**, 9 The Cliff, Brighton, **Sussex (West)**, BN2 5RF, ENG.
(T) 01273 689567
Speciality: Complementary Medicines & Therapy.
C M (Ref:HM19473)

## SULLIVAN, CAROL
**Carol Sullivan**, 22 Rydal Bank, Wirral, **Merseyside**, CH63 7LL, ENG.
(T) 01516 459956
Speciality: Clairvoyants & Palmists.
● **Owner** Mrs C Sullivan
B (Ref:HM19474)


Key continued: Yrs.Est: Years Established Q: Qualifications M: Professional Membership ✓ Indemnity Insurance Accept Credit Cards

## SULLIVAN, CHRISTIAN
**Christian Sullivan**, 6 Market St, Bradford-on-Avon, **Wiltshire**, BA15 1LH, ENG.
(T) 01225 868282
Speciality: Osteopathy.
P S T (**Ref:**HM19475)

## SULLIVAN, CHRISTINE
**Christine Sullivan**, Ingledale, 1 Tanhouse Rd, Oxted, **Surrey**, RH8 9PE, ENG.
(T) 01883 717277
Speciality: Alexander Technique.
P S (**Ref:**HM19476)

## SULLIVAN, DAWN
**Dawn Sullivan**, 90 Cranbourne Avenue, London, **London (Greater)**, E11 2BQ, ENG.
(T) 020 8491 0102
Speciality: Reflexology.
S T (**Ref:**HM19477)

## SULLIVAN, HELEN
**Helen Sullivan**, 17 Randall Rd, Chandler's Ford, Eastleigh, **Hampshire**, SO53 5AJ, ENG.
(T) 023 8026 6845
Speciality: Chiropodists (Podiatrists).
● **Owner** Mrs H Sullivan
S (**Ref:**HM19478)

## SULLIVAN, J L
**J L Sullivan**, 1 Church St, Wombwell, Barnsley, **Yorkshire (South)**, S73 0DQ, ENG.
(T) 01226 755611
Speciality: Chiropodists (Podiatrists).
S (**Ref:**HM19479)

## SULLIVAN, KIM
**Kim Sullivan**, Fantails, Eastbourne Rd, Godstone (South), **Surrey**, RH9 8EY, ENG.
(T) 01342 893516
Speciality: Chiropodists (Podiatrists).
S (**Ref:**HM19480)

## SULLIVAN, MARGARET
**Margaret Sullivan**, The Goodlife Natural Health Centre, 207 High St, Sutton, **Surrey**, SM1 1JU, ENG.
(T) 020 8770 1156
Speciality: Aromatherapy.
M O (**Ref:**HM19481)

## SULLIVAN, MARGARET
**Margaret Sullivan**, Flat Aa, 7 Woodside Rd, Sutton, **Surrey**, SM1 3SU, ENG.
(T) 020 8641 6141
Speciality: Reflexology.
S T (**Ref:**HM19482)

## SULLIVAN, MARY
**Mary Sullivan**, Mycenae House, Mycenae Rd, London, **London (Greater)**, SE3 7SE, ENG.
(T) 020 8858 5960
Speciality: Psychotherapy.
B (**Ref:**HM19483)

## SULLIVAN, SUZANNE
**Suzanne Sullivan**, Shoreham-by-Sea, **Sussex (West)**, BN43, ENG.
(T) 01273 870949
Speciality: Bach Remedies.
M (**Ref:**HM19484)

## SUMMERS, A
**A Summers**, 301 Brandon St, Motherwell, **Lanarkshire (North)**, ML1 1RS, SCO.
(T) 01698 264174
Speciality: Physiotherapy.
● **Owner** Ms A Summers
P S T (**Ref:**HM19485)

## SUMMERS, A A
**A A Summers**, Hillcroft Dental Surgery, Church Rd, Woolton, Liverpool, **Merseyside**, L25 6DD, ENG.
(T) 01514 283173
Speciality: Chiropodists (Podiatrists).
● **Practice Manager** Mrs C Forshaw
S (**Ref:**HM19486)

## SUMMERS, ALFRED A
**Alfred A Summers**, 54 Rodney St, Liverpool, **Merseyside**, L1 9AD, ENG.
(T) 01517 091010
Speciality: Chiropody, Nail Surgery. ✓
● **Owner/Chiropodist** Mr A Summers
Q: B.A.Ch.P, M.S.C.P, S.R.Ch.
M Yrs. Est.: 40 (**Ref:**HM19487)

## SUMMERS, ANGIE
**Angie Summers**, Aston Clinic, 26 Kingston Rd, New Malden, **Surrey**, KT3 3LS, ENG.
(T) 020 8942 3148 (F) 020 8949 7050
Speciality: Hypnotherapy.
B (**Ref:**HM19488)

## SUMMERS, CHRISTINE S
**Christine S Summers**, 33 Parkfield Rd, Northwich, **Cheshire**, CW9 7AR, ENG.
(T) 01606 40334
Speciality: Osteopathy.
P S T (**Ref:**HM19489)

## SUMMERS, DIANE
**Diane Summers**, 63 Honeywood Cl, Portsmouth, **Hampshire**, PO3 5BW, ENG.
(T) 023 9267 1728
Speciality: Acupuncture.
● **Owner** Ms D Summers
O (**Ref:**HM19490)

## SUMMERS, GORDON
**Gordon Summers**, 13 Peverell Park Rd, Plymouth, **Devon**, PL3 4LS, ENG.
(T) 01803 732728
Speciality: Homeopathy.
M (**Ref:**HM19491)

## SUMMERS, GORDON
**Gordon Summers**, Clissold Park Health Centre, 154 Stoke Newington Church St, London, **London (Greater)**, N16 0JU, ENG.
(T) 020 7249 2990 (F) 020 7249 3977
Speciality: Homeopathy.
● **Director** Mr D Berg
M (**Ref:**HM19492)

## SUMMERS, GRAEME
**Graeme Summers**, Aldrens Lane, Lancaster, **Lancashire**, LA1 2DU, ENG.
(T) 01524 69864 (F) 01524 848155
Speciality: Psychotherapy.
B (**Ref:**HM19493)

## SUMMERS, LAURENCE
**Laurence Summers**, 17 Chestnut Court, Middle Lane, London, **London (Greater)**, N8 8NU, ENG.
(T) 020 8341 1205
Speciality: Reflexology.
S T (**Ref:**HM19494)

## SUMMERS, M
**M Summers**, 188 The St, Boughton-Under-Blean, Faversham, **Kent**, ME13 9AL, ENG.
(T) 01227 751886 (F) 01227 751886
Speciality: Homeopathy.
● **Owner** Mrs M Summers
M (**Ref:**HM19495)

## SUMMERS, S J
**Mrs S J Summers**, 292 Ipswich Rd, Colchester, **Essex**, CO4 4ES, ENG.
(T) 01206 854300
Speciality: Chiropodists (Podiatrists).
S (**Ref:**HM19496)

## SUMMERS, VAL
**Val Summers**, Tralee, Middleton Rd, Winterslow, Salisbury, **Wiltshire**, SP5 1PQ, ENG.
(T) 01980 862927
Speciality: Chiropractors.
● **Owner** Miss V Summers
P S T (**Ref:**HM19497)

## SUMMERTON CLINIC
**Medical Herbalist**, Summertown Clinic, 362 Banbury Rd, Oxford, **Oxfordshire**, OX2 7PP, ENG.
(T) 01865 513388
Speciality: Auricular Therapy, Herbal Medicine, Hopi Ear Candles, Phytotherapy.
● **Medical Herbalist** Ms J Scanlon Q: BSc (Hons), MNIMH. M: NIMH.
M (**Ref:**HM19498)

## SUMNER, ALLISON J
**Allison J Sumner**, 2 Endsleigh Gdns, Leigh, **Manchester (Greater)**, WN7 1LR, ENG.
(T) 01942 260714
Speciality: Physiotherapy.
P S T (**Ref:**HM19499)

## SUN ESSENCES
**Sun Essences**, 3a Low Rd, Drayton, Norwich, **Norfolk**, NR8 6AA, ENG.
(T) 01603 865408 (F) 01603 861317
Speciality: Complementary Medicines & Therapy.
● **Owner** Mrs V Williamson
M (**Ref:**HM19500)

## SUN HERB HOUSE
**Sun Herb House**, 52 Charles St, Leicester, **Leicestershire**, LE1 1FB, ENG.
(T) 01162 621300
Speciality: Herbal Medicine.
● **Owner** Mr J Sun
M (**Ref:**HM19501)

## SUN HOUSE HOLISTIC HEALING
**Sun House Holistic Healing**, 125 Union St, Maidstone, **Kent**, ME14 1EE, ENG.
(T) 01622 203220
Speciality: Complementary Medicines & Therapy.
● **Owner** Mr D Howard
M (**Ref:**HM19502)

## SUN, R
**R Sun**, 14 Woodside Rd, Poole, **Dorset**, BH14 9JJ, ENG.
(T) 01202 739730
Speciality: Acupuncture.
O (**Ref:**HM19503)

## SUNBOX DESIGNS
**Sunbox Designs Ltd**, 37 Eastern Rd, London, **London (Greater)**, N2 9LB, ENG.
(T) 020 8444 9218 (F) 020 8292 1613
Speciality: Complementary Medicines & Therapy.
C M (**Ref:**HM19504)

## SUNDERLAND, CYNTHIA
**Cynthia Sunderland**, 25 Glentworth Avenue, Coventry, **Midlands (West)**, CV6 2HU, ENG.
(T) 024 7633 5204 (F) 024 7666 7051
Speciality: Psychotherapy.
● **Owner** Mrs C Sunderland
B (**Ref:**HM19505)

## SUNDIAL HOUSE CHIROPRACTIC
**Sundial House Chiropractic Clinic**, Sundial House, 111 Queens Rd, Brighton, **Sussex (East)**, BN1 3XF, ENG.
(T) 01273 774114 (F) 01273 773059
Speciality: Chiropractic. ✓ CREDIT
● **Chiropractor** Dr M Bennett Q: FCC.
● **Chiropractor** Dr P Jones Q: BSc, DC.
● **Chiropractor** Dr J McTavish Q: MSc.
● **Chiropractor** Dr S Bird Q: BSc, DC.
P Yrs. Est.: 10 (**Ref:**HM19506)

## SUNFLOWER VITAL HEALTH
**Sunflower Vital Health Initiative**, 17 Bristol Rd, Ilkeston, **Derbyshire**, DE7 5HD, ENG.
(T) 01159 323373
Speciality: Herbal Medicine.
M (**Ref:**HM19507)

## SUNLAN HOLISTICS
**Sunlan Holistics**, 1 Earl St, Carlisle, **Cumbria**, CA1 1DP, ENG.
(T) 01228 818891
Speciality: Complementary Medicines & Therapy.
● **Owner** Mr A Newlands
M (**Ref:**HM19508)

## SUNNINGDALE HEALING CENTRE
**Sunningdale Healing Centre**, Village Hall, Church Rd, Sunningdale, Ascot, **Berkshire**, SL5 0NJ, ENG.
(T) 01344 625566
Speciality: Spiritual Healing. ✓
● **Healer** Louise M: NFSH.
● **Healer** Bruce M: NFSH.
● **Treasurer/Practitioner/Healer** Mr T Reed M: NFSH.
● **Healer** Jane M: NFSH.
● **Healer** Steve M: NFSH.
C Yrs. Est.: 2 (**Ref:**HM19509)

## SUNNYSIDE MANSIONS
**Sunnyside Mansions**, Flat 3, 12 Sunnyside Rd,



Key: B Mind-Body Medicine C Complementary Medicine H Self Help Treatment M Medicinal Therapy O Oriental Medicine P Postural Therapy S Manipulative Structural Therapy T Touch Therapy

Clevedon, **Somerset**, BS21 7TA, ENG.
(T) 01275 340360
Speciality: Osteopathy.
● **Owner** Mr M Morgan
P S T (Ref:HM19510)

## SUNRIDER REGENERATIVE FOOD

**Sunrider Regenerative Food Herbs**, 21 Harcourt Rd, Southampton, **Hampshire**, SO18 1GQ, ENG.
(T) 023 8055 9008
Speciality: Herbal Medicine.
M (Ref:HM19511)

## SUNRISE CENTRE

**Sunrise Centre**, 2 West Malvern Rd, Malvern, **Worcestershire**, WR14 4NA, ENG.
(T) 01684 574407
Speciality: Complementary Medicines & Therapy.
● **Owner** Mr A Lewis
C M (Ref:HM19512)

## SUNRISE NATURAL THERAPY CLINIC

**Sunrise Natural Therapy Clinic**, Chapel St, Charleville, **County Cork**, IRE.
(T) 06321 466
Speciality: Complementary Medicines & Therapy.
M (Ref:HM19513)

## SURBITON NATURAL HEALTH CENTRE

**Surbiton Natural Health Centre**, 14 Claremont Rd, Surbiton, **Surrey**, KT6 4QU, ENG.
(T) 020 8390 9362
Speciality: Acupuncture, Alexander Technique, Aromatherapy, Herbal Medicine, Nutritional Therapy, Osteopathy, Reflexology. ✔ CREDIT
● **Manageress** Mrs V Soignot
M Yrs. Est.: 12 (Ref:HM19514)

## SURBITON PHYSIOTHERAPY

**Surbiton Physiotherapy & Sports Injury Clinic**, 35 Herne Rd, Surbiton, **Surrey**, KT6 5BX, ENG.
(T) 020 8397 4745
Speciality: Physiotherapy.
P S T (Ref:HM19515)

## SURE FOOT PODIATRY PRACTICE

**Sure Foot Podiatry Practice**, 114 Blyth Rd, Bromley, **Kent**, BR1 3RT, ENG.
(T) 020 8460 9526
Speciality: Chiropodists (Podiatrists).
S (Ref:HM19516)

## SUREN, CHARLES

**Charles Suren**, 33 Clydesdale Gardens, Richmond, **Surrey**, TW10 5EG, ENG.
(T) 020 8876 2862
Speciality: Complementary Medicines & Therapy.
● **Owner** Mr C Suren
C M (Ref:HM19517)

## SURENDRA, S B

**S B Surendra**, 23 Treforthlan Estate, Paynters Lane End, Redruth, **Cornwall**, TR16 4RN, ENG.
(T) 01209 842662
Speciality: Physiotherapy.
● **Owner** Mrs S Surendra
P S T (Ref:HM19518)

## SURGERY

**Surgery**, 452 Leeds Rd, Dewsbury, **Yorkshire (West)**, WF12 7QE, ENG.
(T) 01924 450183 (F) 01924 450183
(E) dokellphysiochir@faxvin.net
Speciality: Acupressure, Acupuncture, Chiropody, Electrotherapy, Kinesiology, Manipulation, Massage (Therapeutic), Moxibustion, Physiotherapy, Podiatry, Ultrasonics, Vitamin Therapy. ✔
● **Receptionist/Assistant**
Ms J O'Kell
● **Physiotherapist** Mr D O'Kell Q: Dip.Adv.M.Ac, Dip.RG&RT, MCSP. M: AACP, CSP.
S Yrs. Est.: 25 (Ref:HM19519)

## SURGERY

**Surgery (The)**, 5 Batchen St, Forres, **Moray**, IV36 1DA, SCO.
(T) 01309 672695
Speciality: Chiropodists (Podiatrists).
S (Ref:HM19520)

## SURGICAL CHIROPODIST

**Surgical Chiropodist**, Flat 3 Heatherdune, Heatherdune Rd, Bexhill-on-Sea, **Sussex (East)**, TN39 4HB, ENG.
(T) 01424 730980
Speciality: Chiropodists (Podiatrists).
S (Ref:HM19521)

## SURREY HEALING SANCTUARY

**Surrey Healing Sanctuary (The)**, Penduckshaw, Rabies Heath Rd, Bletchingley, Redhill, **Surrey**, RH1 4NB, ENG.
(T) 01883 741800
Speciality: Absent Healing, Complementary Therapy, Faith Healing, Healer, Healing Therapy, Herbal Medicine, Holistic Healing, Phytotherapy, Reflexology, Spiritual Healing, Psychic Surgery, (Spirit Operations). ✔
● **Owner/Medical Herbalist/Reflexologist**
Mrs M Nicolas Q: Dip.Herb.Med, MAR. M: AoR, FNT.
● **Partner/Spirtual Healer**
Mr A Nicolas M: WFH.
B C (Ref:HM19522)

## SURREY PHYSIOTHERAPY CLINIC

**Surrey Physiotherapy Clinic**, Carshalton War Memorial Hospital, The Park, Carshalton, **Surrey**, SM5 3DB, ENG.
(T) 020 8669 8006 (F) 020 8669 8006
Speciality: Physiotherapy.
● **Principal** Mrs A Middleditch
P S T (Ref:HM19523)

## SURREY PHYSIOTHERAPY CLINIC

**Surrey Physiotherapy Clinic**, 180 Brighton Rd, Coulsdon, **London (Greater)**, CR5 2NF, ENG.
(T) 020 8660 8070 (F) 020 8660 8070
Speciality: Physiotherapy.
● **Partner** Mrs A Middleditch
P S T (Ref:HM19524)

## SURTEES, JOANNE

**Joanne Surtees**, 18 Cavalry Fields, Weedon, Northampton, **Northamptonshire**, NN7 4TG, ENG.
(T) 01327 342456
Speciality: Reflexology.
S T (Ref:HM19525)

## SURVIVAL TRUST SURGERY

**Survival Trust Surgery**, The Centre, Codicote Rd, Welwyn, **Hertfordshire**, AL6 9TU, ENG.
(T) 01438 716478 (F) 01438 717538
(W) www.theearth.org
Speciality: Homeopathy, Preventative Medicine. ✔
● **Homeopath** Dr T Moore
C Yrs. Est.: 24 (Ref:HM19526)

## SUSAN JAMES CONSULTANCY

**Susan James Consultancy**, 14 Belfield Avenue, Maybank, Newcastle, **Staffordshire**, ST5 9NH, ENG.
(T) 01782 712145
(E) susanjamesconsultancy@yahoo.com
Speciality: Absent Healing, Aura Therapy, Auto Suggestion, Bach Remedies, Bio-energetics, Cognitive Therapy, Counselling, Dietician, Dowsing, Family Planning (Natural), Healer, Homeopathy, Nutritional Therapy, Psychotherapy, Spiritual Healing, Radionics, Reflexology will be available in 2002.
● **Consultant** Ms S James
B (Ref:HM19527)

## SUSAN JONES HOLISTIC PRACT

**Susan Jones Holistic Practitioner F Inst H T**, 10 Bellmaine Avenue, Corringham, Stanford-Le-Hope, **Essex**, SS17 7TB, ENG.
(T) 01375 678810
Speciality: Hypnotherapy.
B (Ref:HM19528)

## SUSAN, CHINNERY

**Chinnery Susan**, Ravenscroft, Watford, **Hertfordshire**, WD2 4FE, ENG.
(T) 01923 672379
Speciality: Complementary Medicines & Therapy.
M (Ref:HM19529)

## SUSAN, DOYLE

**Doyle Susan**, 42 Belmont Avenue, Ayr, **Ayrshire (South)**, KA7 2JQ, SCO.
(T) 01292 268177
Speciality: Hypnosis.
B (Ref:HM19530)

## SUSANNA, LINDSEY

**Lindsey Susanna**, Gorse Cottage, The Mount, Philpott Lane, Chobham, Woking, **Surrey**, GU24 8AP, ENG.
(T) 01276 858022
Speciality: Chiropodists (Podiatrists).
S (Ref:HM19531)

## SUSSEX PRIVATE CLINIC

**Sussex Private Clinic**, The Green, St. Leonards-On-Sea, **Sussex (East)**, TN38 0SG, ENG.
(T) 01424 446736
Speciality: Physiotherapy.
P S T (Ref:HM19532)

## SUTCLIFFE, T

**T Sutcliffe**, Weston Surgery, 36 Combe Park, Bath, **Somerset**, BA1 3NR, ENG.
(T) 01225 446089
Speciality: Osteopathy.
P S T (Ref:HM19533)

## SUTCLIFFE, T

**T Sutcliffe**, 17 High St, Twerton On Avon, Bath, **Somerset**, BA2 1BZ, ENG.
(T) 01225 351089
Speciality: Osteopathy.
P S T (Ref:HM19534)

## SUTCLIFFE, T

**T Sutcliffe**, 3 Horse St, Chipping Sodbury, Bristol, BS37 6DA, ENG.
(T) 01454 326256
Speciality: Osteopathy.
● **Owner** Mr A Harcourt
P S T (Ref:HM19535)

## SUTER, ROSMANUND

**Rosmanund Suter**, Orchard Cottage, Lower Icknield Way, Chinnor, **Oxfordshire**, OX9 4EB, ENG.
(T) 01844 353037
Speciality: Physiotherapy.
P S T (Ref:HM19536)

## SUTHERLAND, COLIN J

**Colin J Sutherland**, 11 Lambert Rd, Ribbleton, Preston, **Lancashire**, PR2 6YQ, ENG.
(T) 01772 705465
Speciality: Hypnosis.
● **Owner** Mr C Sutherland
B (Ref:HM19537)

## SUTHERLAND, J

**Mr John Sutherland**, Flat 15, Walton Bridge House, Shepperton, **Surrey**, TW17 8LU, ENG.
(T) 01932 254584
Speciality: Osteopathy.
P S T (Ref:HM19538)

## SUTHERLAND, JENNY

**Jenny Sutherland**, 9 Ross Rd, Wallington, **Surrey**, SM6 8QN, ENG.
(T) 020 8773 2308
Speciality: Aromatherapy, Reflexology, Reiki. ✔
● **Reflexologist** Jenny Sutherland Q: ITEC, MIFR. M: ITEC.
C Yrs. Est.: 10 (Ref:HM19539)

## SUTOR, CHRIS

**Chris Sutor**, Oakington Therapy Centre, 12 High St, Oakington, Cambridge, **Cambridgeshire**, CB4 5AG, ENG.
(T) 01223 237459 (F) 01223 237459
Speciality: Osteopathy.
● **Director** Mr R Giddings
P S T (Ref:HM19540)

## SUTTON ALTERNATIVE HEALTH

**Sutton Alternative Health Clinic**, 22 Throwley Way, Sutton, **Surrey**, SM1 4AF, ENG.
(T) 020 8642 2307
Speciality: Acupuncture.
O (Ref:HM19541)


Key continued: Yrs.Est: Years Established Q: Qualifications M: Professional Membership ✔ Indemnity Insurance CREDIT Accept Credit Cards

### SUTTON BRIEF THERAPY CENTRE
**Sutton Brief Therapy Centre**, Sundale House, Fivegate Lane, Sutton Coldfield, **Midlands (West)**, B73 5TR, ENG.
(T) 01213 213277
Speciality: Psychoanalysis.
B (Ref:HM19542)

### SUTTON CHIROPRACTIC CLINIC
**Sutton Chiropractic Clinic**, 137 Brighton Rd, Sutton, **Surrey**, SM2 5SW, ENG.
(T) 020 8661 1614 (F) 020 8770 9517
Speciality: Chiropractic, Osteopathy. ✓
● **Practice Manager** Miss A Harvey
● **Owner** Dr B Hammond Q: DC, DO, PhD. M: BCA, BOA, GCC, GOsC.
P S T Yrs. Est.: 25 (Ref:HM19543)

### SUTTON COLDFIELD HEALTH CLINIC
**Sutton Coldfield Health Clinic**, 5 While Rd, Sutton Coldfield, **Midlands (West)**, B72 1ND, ENG.
(T) 01213 547306
Speciality: Acupuncture, Cupping, T'ai-Chi Ch'uan. ✓
● **Physiotherapist** Mrs A Robinson
● **Chiropodist (Podiatrist)** Ms G Collard
● **Physiotherapist** Ms R Backhouse
● **Chiropodist (Podiatrist)** Mr S Gwynn - Thomas
● **Chiropodist (Podiatrist)** Mr C Wood
● **Acupuncturist** Mr E Garland Q: BSc, Lic.Ac. M: BAcC.
● **Homeopath** Ms J Butcher
● **Physiotherapist** Mr M Maybury
● **Physiotherapist** Mr M Robinson
C O (Ref:HM19544)

### SUTTON COLDFIELD HYPNOTHERAPY
**Sutton Coldfield Hypnotherapy**, 104a Lindridge Rd, Sutton Coldfield, **Midlands (West)**, B75 6HJ, ENG.
(T) 01213 783478
Speciality: Hypnosis.
B (Ref:HM19545)

### SUTTON COURTENAY CHIROPRACTIC
**Sutton Courtenay Chiropractic Clinic**, 19 The Nursery, Sutton Courtenay, Abingdon, **Oxfordshire**, OX14 4UA, ENG.
(T) 01235 848008
Speciality: Chiropractic.
● **Owner** Dr D Hales
P S T (Ref:HM19546)

### SUTTON HOMOEOPATHIC PRACTICE
**Sutton Homoeopathic Practice (The)**, 58 Birmingham Rd, Sutton Coldfield, **Midlands (West)**, B72 1QJ, ENG.
(T) 01213 211044
Speciality: Homeopathy.
M (Ref:HM19547)

### SUTTON HYPNOTHERAPY
**Sutton Hypnotherapy**, 1 Restoration House, Stafford Rd, Wallington, **Surrey**, SM6 9AP, ENG.
(T) 020 8669 5555
Speciality: Hypnosis.
● **Owner** Mr C Flaherty
B (Ref:HM19548)

### SUTTON OSTEOPATHY & NTRL HEALTH
**Sutton Osteopathy & Natural Health Clinic**, Sutton, **Surrey**, SM1 4AF, ENG.
(T) 020 8642 2307
Speciality: Acupuncture.
● **Practitioner** Aideen O'Sullivan
O (Ref:HM19549)

### SUTTON THERAPY CENTRE
**Sutton Therapy Centre**, 129 Kirkby Rd, Sutton-in-Ashfield, **Nottinghamshire**, NG17 1GW, ENG.
(T) 01623 550900
Speciality: Osteopathy.
● **Partner** Mrs R Walker
P S T (Ref:HM19550)

### SUTTON, G M
**G M Sutton**, 4 Bellevue Mansions, Bellevue Rd, Clevedon, **Somerset**, BS21 7NU, ENG.
(T) 01275 879507
Speciality: Physiotherapy.
P S T (Ref:HM19551)

### SUTTON, HELEN
**Helen Sutton**, Rosane, 46 Cheapside, Woking, **Surrey**, GU21 4JL, ENG.
(T) 01483 763258
Speciality: Reflexology.
S T (Ref:HM19552)

### SUTTON, M A C
**M A C Sutton**, Seasons, Lenchwick, Evesham, **Worcestershire**, WR11 4TG, ENG.
(T) 01386 870585
Speciality: Chiropodists (Podiatrists).
S (Ref:HM19553)

### SUTTON, NICOLA
**Nicola Sutton**, 37 Richmond Rd, Twickenham, **London (Greater)**, TW1 3AW, ENG.
(T) 020 8891 6136
Speciality: Aromatherapy.
● **Owner** Ms N Sutton
M O (Ref:HM19554)

### SUTTON, R W
**R W Sutton**, Windermere Health Centre, Goodley Dale, Windermere, **Cumbria**, LA23 2EG, ENG.
(T) 01539 444383
Speciality: Osteopathy.
● **Owner** Mr R Sutton
P S T (Ref:HM19555)

### SUTTON, RUSSELL
**Russell Sutton**, 102 Chosen Drive, Churchdown, Gloucester, **Gloucestershire**, GL3 2QU, ENG.
(T) 01452 714511 (F) 01452 541369
Speciality: Osteopathy.
● **Partner** Mr C Hayden
P S T (Ref:HM19556)

### SUTTON, S
**S Sutton**, 177 Park Rd, Keynsham, Bristol, BS31 1AS, ENG.
(T) 01179 860086
Speciality: Reflexology.
C (Ref:HM19557)

### SUTTON, SUSAN
**Susan Sutton**, Sturdie House, Broom Way, Weybridge, **Surrey**, KT13 9TQ, ENG.
(T) 01932 221268
Speciality: Acupuncture.
O (Ref:HM19558)

### SUTTON, YVONNE V
**Yvonne V Sutton**, 18 Clarence Gr Rd, Weston-Super-Mare, **Somerset**, BS23 4AQ, ENG.
(T) 01934 419136
Speciality: Chiropodists (Podiatrists).
S (Ref:HM19559)

### SUZANNE
**Suzanne**, 44 Common Rise, Hitchin, **Hertfordshire**, SG4 0HN, ENG.
(T) 01462 420160
Speciality: Clairvoyants & Palmists.
● **Owner** Ms S Howe
B (Ref:HM19560)

### SWABY, DINAH
**Dinah Swaby**, 32 Windmill Hill, Alton, **Hampshire**, GU34 2SL, ENG.
(T) 01420 83919
Speciality: Aromatherapy.
● **Owner** Mrs D Swaby
M O (Ref:HM19561)

### SWAIN, HILARY ANNE
**Hilary Anne Swain**, Care Of Bodywise, 119 Roman Rd, London, **London (Greater)**, E2 0QN, ENG.
(T) 020 8981 6938
Speciality: Osteopathy.
P S T (Ref:HM19562)

### SWAIN, P A
**P A Swain**, Kimberley, Noads Way, Dibden Purlieu, Southampton, **Hampshire**, SO45 4PB, ENG.
(T) 023 8084 6639
Speciality: Physiotherapy.
P S T (Ref:HM19563)

### SWAINE, A J
**A J Swaine**, Mayflower Cottage, Stondon Rd, Nine Ashes, Ingatestone, **Essex**, CM4 0JY, ENG.
(T) 01277 822146
Speciality: Physiotherapy.
● **Owner** Mrs A Swaine
P S T (Ref:HM19564)

### SWAINE, PAULA
**Paula Swaine**, 58 Free School Lane, Halifax, **Yorkshire (West)**, HX1 2PW, ENG.
(T) 01422 344325
Speciality: Chiropody, Podiatry. ✓
● **Owner/Chiropodist** Miss P Swaine Q: DPodM, MSSCh. M: B.A.Ch.P.
M Yrs. Est.: 15 (Ref:HM19565)

### SWAINE, R F
**R F Swaine**, 93 Loddon Bridge Rd, Woodley, Reading, **Berkshire**, RG5 4AE, ENG.
(T) 01189 697769
Speciality: Chiropractic.
● **Owner** Mr R Swaine
P S T (Ref:HM19566)

### SWAINE, T
**T Swaine**, 4-10 Pellon Lane, Halifax, **Yorkshire (West)**, HX1 5SP, ENG.
(T) 01422 350179
Speciality: Physiotherapy.
P S T (Ref:HM19567)

### SWALES, CATHERINE
**Catherine Swales**, Towngate Healthcare Clinic, 102 Towngate, Leyland, Preston, **Lancashire**, PR5 1HX, ENG.
(T) 01772 456657
Speciality: Complementary Medicines & Therapy.
● **Practice Manager** Ms S Keady
M (Ref:HM19568)

### SWALES, JANE
**Jane Swales**, 53 Queens Rd, Aldershot, **Hampshire**, GU11 3JE, ENG.
(T) 01252 313881
Speciality: Chiropodists (Podiatrists).
S (Ref:HM19569)

### SWALLOW, FRED
**Fred Swallow**, 14 Rectory Rd, Sible Hedingham, Halstead, **Essex**, CO9 3NU, ENG.
(T) 01787 462843
Speciality: Hypnosis.
● **Owner** Mr F Swallow
B (Ref:HM19570)

### SWALLOW, R M
**R M Swallow**, Porecroft, 342 Stanstead Rd, Hoddesdon, **Hertfordshire**, EN11 0RZ, ENG.
(T) 01992 462151
Speciality: Chiropodists (Podiatrists).
● **Owner** Mrs R Swallow
S (Ref:HM19571)

### SWAN & SWAN
**Swan & Swan**, The Chiropody Clinic, 4 St Stephens Hill, St. Albans, **Hertfordshire**, AL1 2DS, ENG.
(T) 01727 847309
Speciality: Chiropody, Podiatry, Nail Removal. ✓
● **Chiropodist** Ms R Swan Q: M.S.C.P, S.R.Ch. M: S.C.P.
● **Chiropodist** Mr C Swan Q: M.S.C.P, S.R.Ch. M: S.C.P.
M Yrs. Est.: 11 (Ref:HM19572)

### SWAN, ALAN
**Alan Swan**, 1 Ancroft Pl, Ashington, **Northumberland**, NE63 0TP, ENG.
(T) 01670 811601
Speciality: Chiropodists (Podiatrists).
● **Owner** Mr A Swan
S (Ref:HM19573)

### SWAN, LAURIE C
**Laurie C Swan**, 1 Valencia Rd, Worthing, **Sussex (West)**, BN11 4QB, ENG.
(T) 01903 501831
(E) laurieswan@composerve.com
Speciality: Colour Therapy, Kinesiology, Stress Therapy. ✓



Key: B Mind-Body Medicine  C Complementary Medicine  H Self Help Treatment  M Medicinal Therapy  O Oriental Medicine  P Postural Therapy  S Manipulative Structural Therapy  T Touch Therapy

● **Owner/Kinesiologist/Surgical Chiropodist** Mrs L Swan **Q:** MBChA, MSSCh. **M:** B.A.Ch.P.
**B** Yrs. Est.: 17 (**Ref:**HM19574)

## SWAN, VIVA

**Viva Swan (The)**, 35 Bournewood Rd, Orpington, **Kent**, BR5 4JN, **ENG**.
**(T)** 01689 822055
Speciality: Physiotherapy, Yoga, Natural Healing. ✓
● **Physiotherapist/Yoga Teacher/Therapist** Mr B Hateley **Q:** Dip.Yoga. **M:** LCSP.
**C** Yrs. Est.: 22 (**Ref:**HM19575)

## SWANN, PATRICIA

**Patricia Swann**, 19 Mayall Drive, Sutton Coldfield, **Midlands (West)**, B75 5LR, **ENG**.
**(T)** 01213 082245
Speciality: Complementary Medicines & Therapy.
**C M** (**Ref:**HM19576)

## SWANS

**Swans**, Spring Cottage, Delmonden Rd, Hawkhurst, Cranbrook, **Kent**, TN18 4XL, **ENG**.
**(T)** 01580 753658
Speciality: Complementary Medicines & Therapy.
● **Owner** Mrs L McGurk
**C M** (**Ref:**HM19577)

## SWANSEA CLINIC OF NATURAL MED

**Swansea Clinic Of Natural Medicine**, 20 Walter Rd, Swansea, SA1 5NQ, **WAL**.
**(T)** 01792 644362 **(F)** 01792 281041
Speciality: Acupuncture.
● **Doctor** Dr L Zhu
**O** (**Ref:**HM19578)

## SWANSEA VALLEY PHYSIO PRACTICE

**Swansea Valley Physiotherapy Practice**, 11 Lloyd St, Trebanos, Pontardawe, Swansea, **Glamorgan (Vale of)**, SA8 4DR, **WAL**.
**(T)** 01792 830117
Speciality: Biofeedback, Electrotherapy, Manipulation, Massage (Therapeutic), Ultrasonics, Credentialled McKenzie Therapist - For treatment of all spinal and spine related disorders. Exercise Therapy. ✓
● **Physiotherapist** Mr J Hopkins **Q:** MCSP, SRP. **M:** CSP.
**S** Yrs. Est.: 9 (**Ref:**HM19579)

## SWARTHMORE CENTRE

**Swarthmore Centre (The)**, 3-7 Woodhouse Sq, Leeds, **Yorkshire (West)**, LS3 1AD, **ENG**.
**(T)** 01132 445559
Speciality: Alexander Technique.
**P S** (**Ref:**HM19580)

## SWAY HOUSE PUBLICATIONS

**Sway House Publications**, Hazelwood, Broadmead, Sway, **Hampshire**, SO41 6DH, **ENG**.
**(T)** 01590 681088
Speciality: Hypnosis, Neuro-Linguistic Program, Psychotherapy.
**C** (**Ref:**HM19581)

## SWEENEY, MARIE

**Sweeney Marie SRN SCM**, Oakton Farranlea Pk, Model Farm Rd, Cork, **County Cork**, **IRE**.
**(T)** 021 4546 040
Speciality: Complementary Medicines & Therapy.
**M** (**Ref:**HM19582)

## SWEET AROMA'S

**Sweet Aroma's**, 4 Regent Arcade, Grimsby, **Humberside (South)**, DN31 1JP, **ENG**.
**(T)** 01472 362328
Speciality: Complementary Medicines & Therapy.
**M** (**Ref:**HM19583)

## SWEET BREEZE

**Sweet Breeze**, Sweet Breeze House, 1 New Rd - 16 Wing Rd, Linslade, Leighton Buzzard, **Bedfordshire**, LU7 7LS, **ENG**.
**(T)** 01525 381785 **(F)** 01525 381785
**(E)** swee@aol.com
**(W)** www.sweetbreeze.co.uk
Speciality: Aromatherapy, Indian Head Massage, Reflexology. ✓ CREDIT
● **Partner** Mrs L Heinsen
**C** Yrs. Est.: 8 (**Ref:**HM19584)

## SWEET BREEZE

**Sweet Breeze**, 11 Cochran Cl, Crownhill, Milton Keynes, **Buckinghamshire**, MK8 0AJ, **ENG**.
**(T)** 01908 263455 **(F)** 01908 263187
Speciality: Aromatherapy.
● **Partner** Mrs L Heinsen
**M O** (**Ref:**HM19585)

## SWEET EARTH

**Sweet Earth**, U337 Dun Laoire S.C, Dun Laoire, Dublin, **County Dublin**, **IRE**.
**(T)** 01280 9873 **(F)** 01280 2195
Speciality: Healing.
**B** (**Ref:**HM19586)

## SWEET RITA

**Sweet Rita**, The Limit, Low Rd, South Wootton, King's Lynn, **Norfolk**, PE30 3LF, **ENG**.
**(T)** 01553 671462
Speciality: Aromatherapy.
**M O** (**Ref:**HM19587)

## SWEET THYME THERAPY CENTRE

**Sweet Thyme Therapy Centre**, 19 Hawkeys Lane, North Shields, **Tyne and Wear**, NE29 0JF, **ENG**.
**(T)** 01912 900300 **(F)** 01912 900300
Speciality: Complementary Medicines & Therapy.
● **Owner** Ms P Russell
**C M** (**Ref:**HM19588)

## SWIFT THERAPY

**Swift Therapy**, 1 Windsor House, Lenton Town Rd, London, **London (Greater)**, NW5 1DJ, **ENG**.
**(T)** 020 8932 8368
Speciality: Complementary Medicines & Therapy.
**M** (**Ref:**HM19589)

## SWIFT, BRIAN

**Brian Swift**, 82 High St, Canvey Island, **Essex**, SS8 7SQ, **ENG**.
**(T)** 01268 683280
Speciality: Chiropodists (Podiatrists).
● **Owner** Mr B Swift
**S** (**Ref:**HM19590)

## SWIFT, CAROL I

**Carol I Swift**, 10 Bramhope Rd, Cleckheaton, **Yorkshire (West)**, BD19 3DZ, **ENG**.
**(T)** 01274 876003
Speciality: Aromatherapy.
● **Owner** Mrs C Swift
**M O** (**Ref:**HM19591)

## SWIFT, G B

**G B Swift**, 35 The Beeches, Beaminster, **Dorset**, DT8 3SL, **ENG**.
**(T)** 01308 863710
Speciality: Chiropodists (Podiatrists).
● **Owner** Mrs G Swift
**S** (**Ref:**HM19592)

## SWIM GYM

**Swim Gym**, 1-3 Quarry House, Luddenden, Halifax, **Yorkshire (West)**, HX2 6SS, **ENG**.
**(T)** 01422 884770
Speciality: Complementary Medicines & Therapy.
● **Owner** Mrs C Hiller
**C M** (**Ref:**HM19593)

## SWINDALE, TESSA

**Tessa Swindale**, 89 Warwick Rd, Carlisle, **Cumbria**, CA1 1EB, **ENG**.
**(T)** 01228 523182
Speciality: Chiropody. ✓
● **Chiropodist** Mrs T Swindale **Q:** S.R.Ch. **M:** S.C.P.
**M** Yrs. Est.: 30 (**Ref:**HM19594)

## SWINDON CHIROPRACTIC CLINIC

**Swindon Chiropractic Clinic**, 10 Swindon Rd, Stratton St. Margaret, Swindon, **Wiltshire**, SN3 4PZ, **ENG**.
**(T)** 01793 820599
Speciality: Aromatherapy, Chiropractic. ✓ CREDIT
● **Chiropractor** Mr I Blankenstein **Q:** DC, FCC. **M:** BCA, GCC.
**S** Yrs. Est.: 19 (**Ref:**HM19595)

## SWINDON OSTEOPATHIC CENTRE

**Swindon Osteopathic Centre**, 165-166 Victoria Rd, Swindon, **Wiltshire**, SN1 3BU, **ENG**.
**(T)** 01793 484977
Speciality: Osteopathy.
● **Owner** Mr J Hutson
**P S T** (**Ref:**HM19596)

## SWINN, J

**J Swinn**, 40 Gervis Rd, Bournemouth, **Dorset**, BH1 3DH, **ENG**.
**(T)** 01202 296969 **(F)** 01202 296969
Speciality: Physiotherapy.
● **Owner** Mrs J Swinn
**P S T** (**Ref:**HM19597)

## SWINNERTON, SHIELA

**Shiela Swinnerton**, 25 Lower Gungate, Tamworth, **Staffordshire**, B79 7AT, **ENG**.
**(T)** 01827 68374
Speciality: Hypnotherapy.
**B** (**Ref:**HM19598)

## SWINTON HEALTH CENTRE

**Swinton Health Centre**, Charnwood St, Swinton, Mexborough, **Yorkshire (South)**, S64 8LY, **ENG**.
**(T)** 01709 302230 **(F)** 01709 302200
Speciality: Psychiatry.
● **Owner** Dr P McColl
**B** (**Ref:**HM19599)

## SWINTON HEALTH FOODS

**Swinton Health Foods**, 177 Moorside Rd, Swinton, Manchester, **Manchester (Greater)**, M27 9LD, **ENG**.
**(T)** 01617 930091 **(F)** 01617 286087
Speciality: Acupuncture, Alexander Technique, Allergy Testing, Aromatherapy, Counselling, Crystal Healing, Herbal Medicine, Homeopathy, Hypnotherapy, Indian Head Massage, Nutritional Therapy, Phytotherapy, Reflexology, Reiki.
● **Homeopath** Liz Hennel **Q:** RGN, RMN, RSHom.
● **Owner** Catherine Kane
**C** Yrs. Est.: 15 (**Ref:**HM19600)

## SWITALA, F (DR)

**Dr F Switala**, 245 Manningham Lane, Bradford, **Yorkshire (West)**, BD8 7ER, **ENG**.
**(T)** 01274 484514
Speciality: Osteopathy.
● **Doctor** Dr F Switala
**P S T** (**Ref:**HM19601)

## SWOPE, JEFF (DR)

**Dr Jeff Swope D C**, Lucys Lane, Barrett Pl, Macroom Co, **County Cork**, **IRE**.
**(T)** 026 4211 6
Speciality: Chiropractors.
**P S T** (**Ref:**HM19602)

## SWORDS CHIROPRACTIC

**Swords Chiropractic**, 58 Main St, Swords, **County Dublin**, **IRE**.
**(T)** 01840 3305
Speciality: Chiropractors.
**P S T** (**Ref:**HM19603)

## SWORDS HOMEOPATHIC

**Swords Homeopathic & Holistic Clinic (The)**, 10 Howth Junction Cottages, Sutton, **County Dublin**, **IRE**.
**(T)** 01839 1009
Speciality: Homeopathy.
● **Homeopath** Mr P Redman
**M** (**Ref:**HM19604)

## SWORDS HOMOEOPATHIC

**Swords Homoeopathic & Holistic Clinic**, U 3 28 Main St, Swords, **County Dublin**, **IRE**.
**(T)** 01840 7766
Speciality: Homeopathy.
**M** (**Ref:**HM19605)

## SYCAMORE, TONI

**Toni Sycamore**, Willow Cottage, Sheephurst Lane, Marden, Tonbridge, **Kent**, TN12 9NX, **ENG**.
**(T)** 01892 730794 **(F)** 01892 730794
**(E)** toni.sycamore@talk21.com
**(W)** www.nomorerubbish.com
Speciality: Complementary Medicines & Therapy.
● **Owner** Mrs T Sycamore



Key continued: **Yrs.Est:** Years Established **Q:** Qualifications **M:** Professional Membership ✓ Indemnity Insurance CREDIT Accept Credit Cards

M Yrs. Est.: 22 (Ref:HM19606)

## SYDENHAM, ERIC J
**Eric J Sydenham**, 68 Mount Pleasant, Tadley, **Hampshire**, RG26 4BW, ENG.
(T) 01189 813798
Speciality: Chiropodists (Podiatrists).
S (Ref:HM19607)

## SYDENHAM, T
**T Sydenham**, 37 Vernon Trce, Brighton, **Sussex (East)**, BN1 3JH, ENG.
(T) 01273 202221
Speciality: Acupuncture.
O (Ref:HM19608)

## SYKES & ASSOCIATES
**David A Sykes & Associates**, 8 King Cross St, Bull Green, Halifax, **Yorkshire (West)**, HX1 2SH, ENG.
(T) 01422 360759
Speciality: Osteopathy.
P S T (Ref:HM19609)

## SYKES CLINIC
**Dr V C Sykes**, 3 Troy Rd, Morley, Leeds, **Yorkshire (West)**, LS27 8JJ, ENG.
(T) 01132 533494 (F) 01332 533494
Speciality: Hypnosis, Hypnotherapy. ✔
● **Consultant Hypnotherapist**
Mr V Sykes Q: FRSH, M.R.Pharm.S, MCHC, MISMA, MNCH, NCP (Acc), PhD. M: NCH.
B Yrs. Est.: 35 (Ref:HM19610)

## SYKES, DAVID A
**David A Sykes**, 30 Queen St, Huddersfield, **Yorkshire (West)**, HD1 2SP, ENG.
(T) 01484 424329
Speciality: Osteopathy.
P S T (Ref:HM19611)

## SYKES, FRANCES
**Frances Sykes**, 16 Keyberry Park, Newton Abbot, **Devon**, TQ12 1BZ, ENG.
(T) 01626 366840 (F) 01626 533334
Speciality: Chiropractors.
P S T (Ref:HM19612)

## SYKES, JASON
**Jason Sykes**, 83 Harvest Rd, Englefield Green, Egham, **Surrey**, TW20 0QR, ENG.
(T) 01784 454422
Speciality: Chiropractors.
P S T (Ref:HM19613)

## SYKES, KAREN
**Karen Sykes**, 4 Dewsbury Rd, Brighouse, **Yorkshire (West)**, HD6 3QB, ENG.
(T) 01484 717506
Speciality: Chiropodists (Podiatrists).
S (Ref:HM19614)

## SYKES, LIZZIE
**Lizzie Sykes**, 142 Stanpit, Christchurch, **Dorset**, BH23 3NE, ENG.
(T) 07778 423235
Speciality: Reflexology.
S T (Ref:HM19615)

## SYKES, LYNNE
**Lynne Sykes**, 36 Angate St, Wolsingham, Bishop Auckland, **County Durham**, DL13 3EW, ENG.
(T) 01388 526394 (F) 01388 526394
Speciality: Homeopathy.
● **Owner** Mrs L Sykes
M (Ref:HM19616)

## SYKES, PETER W
**Peter W Sykes**, Lulworth, 13 Hadfield Pl, Glossop, **Derbyshire**, SK13 8JE, ENG.
(T) 01457 858255
Speciality: Chiropody. ✔
● **Owner/Chiropodist** Mr P Sykes
C (Ref:HM19617)

## SYLVAN SPIRITUAL HEALING
**Sylvan Spiritual Healing Sanctuary**, 33 The Mall, London, **London (Greater)**, N14 6LR, ENG.
(T) 020 8886 2746
Speciality: Complementary Medicines & Therapy.
C M (Ref:HM19618)

## SYLVIA
**Sylvia**, 77 Oakhill Rd, Old Swan, Liverpool, **Merseyside**, L13 5UF, ENG.
(T) 01514 752688
Speciality: Clairvoyants & Palmists.
B (Ref:HM19619)

## SYLVIA LEWIS CLINIC
**Sylvia Lewis Clinic (The)**, 108 New Bond St, London, **London (Greater)**, W1Y 9AA, ENG.
(T) 020 7491 4919 (F) 020 8206 1888
Speciality: Electrolysis.
● **Director** Mrs S Lewis
T (Ref:HM19620)

## SYLVIA, NAGLE
**Nagle Sylvia**, 3 Ellison St, Castlebar, **County Mayo**, IRE.
(T) 09425 722
(E) smnagle@eircom.net
Speciality: Physiotherapy.
P S T (Ref:HM19621)

## SYMBIOSIS HEALTH CLINIC
**Symbiosis Health Clinic**, Hornsey Rd, London, **London (Greater)**, N7 7NY, ENG.
(T) 020 7607 0382 (F) 020 8211 8042
Speciality: Osteopathy.
P S T (Ref:HM19622)

## SYMBIOSIS OSTEO/NATURAL HEALTH
**Symbiosis Osteopathy & Natural Health**, 390A Seven Sisters Rd, London, **London (Greater)**, N4 2PQ, ENG.
(T) 020 8802 2649
Speciality: Osteopathy.
P S T (Ref:HM19623)

## SYMBIOSIS OSTEOPATHIC
**Symbiosis Osteopathic & Natural Health Clinic**, Hornsey Rd, London, **London (Greater)**, N7 7NY, ENG.
(T) 020 7609 2166 (F) 020 7700 3094
Speciality: Osteopathy.
● **Chief Executive** Mr M Tebett
P S T (Ref:HM19624)

## SYMMONDS, ROSE
**Rose Symmonds**, Creswick House, 9 Small St, Bristol, BS1 1DB, ENG.
(T) 01761 451145 (F) 01761 451155
Speciality: Clairvoyants & Palmists.
● **Partner** Mr A Symmonds
B (Ref:HM19625)

## SYMONDS, G B
**G B Symonds**, 213C Woodhouse Rd, London, **London (Greater)**, N12 9AY, ENG.
(T) 020 8361 2293 (F) 020 8361 2293
Speciality: Osteopathy.
● **Owner** Mr G Symonds
P S T (Ref:HM19626)

## SYMONS, JANE
**Jane Symons**, 17 Northwood Avenue, Purley, **Surrey**, CR8 2ER, ENG.
(T) 020 8668 2980
Speciality: Chiropodists (Podiatrists).
S (Ref:HM19627)

## SYMONS, MARLIESE
**Marliese Symons**, 109 Woodpecker M.T., Pixton Way, Croydon, **Surrey**, CR0 9JB, ENG.
(T) 020 8651 6704
Speciality: Homeopathy.
M (Ref:HM19628)

## SYNERGY HEALTH
**Synergy Health**, 55 Peach St, Wokingham, **Berkshire**, RG40 1XP, ENG.
(T) 01189 782080 (F) 01189 782080
Speciality: Complementary Medicines & Therapy.
● **Owner** Mr R Nolan
M (Ref:HM19629)

## SYNERGY HEALTH
**Synergy Health**, 10 Rose St, Wokingham, **Berkshire**, RG40 1XU, ENG.
(T) 01189 782080
Speciality: Complementary Medicines & Therapy.
C M (Ref:HM19630)

## SYNERGY THERAPIES
**Synergy Therapies**, 6a Cumnor Hill, Oxford, **Oxfordshire**, OX2 9HA, ENG.
(T) 01865 865769
Speciality: Complementary Medicines & Therapy.
C M (Ref:HM19631)

## SYNGE, TERAN
**Synge Teran B A D O**, St Judes Dublin Rd, Arklow, **County Wicklow**, IRE.
(T) 07702 32473
Speciality: Complementary Medicines & Therapy.
M (Ref:HM19632)

## SYSTEMS THERAPY
**Systems Therapy (UK) Ltd**, 26 Wervin Rd, Prenton, **Merseyside**, CH43 0UZ, ENG.
(T) 01516 090068
Speciality: Psychotherapy.
B (Ref:HM19633)

## SZARY, G
**G Szary**, West Villas, Stockton-On-Tees, **Cleveland**, TS18 4HW, ENG.
(T) 01642 678653
Speciality: Hypnotherapy.
B (Ref:HM19634)

## SZAWEJKO, MARGARET
**Margaret Szawejko**, 6 Bigbury Lane, Stourport-on-Severn, **Worcestershire**, DY13 9JG, ENG.
(T) 01299 824911
Speciality: Reflexology.
S T (Ref:HM19635)

## SZMELSKYJ, ALAN
**Alan Szmelskyj**, Godmanchester Osteopathic Practice, 36 St Anns Lane, Godmanchester, Huntingdon, **Cambridgeshire**, PE29 2JE, ENG.
(T) 01480 435554
Speciality: Osteopathy.
P S T (Ref:HM19636)

## T A IN THE THAMES VALLEY
**T A In The Thames Valley**, 131 Norcot Rd, Tilehurst, Reading, **Berkshire**, RG30 6BS, ENG.
(T) 01189 453388 (F) 01189 454477
Speciality: Psychotherapy.
● **Owner** Mr J Parr
B (Ref:HM19637)

## T C CLINIC
**T C Clinic**, 55 Tweedy Rd, Bromley, **Kent**, BR1 3NH, ENG.
(T) 020 8313 1577
Speciality: Osteopathy.
P S T (Ref:HM19638)

## T C M CENTRE
**T C M Centre**, Main St, Rathcoole, Dublin, **County Dublin**, IRE.
(T) 014 589 705
Speciality: Acupressure, Acupuncture, Bio-energetics, Bonesetting, Chiropractic, Complementary Therapy, Counselling, Cupping, Dietician, Healing Therapy, Herbal Medicine, Holistic Healing, Hypnotherapy, Indian Head Massage, Moxibustion, Nutritional Therapy, Oriental Diagnosis, Stress Therapy, Vibrational Therapy, Ying & Yang, Qi Gong - including group sessions weekly. ✔
● **TCM Practitioner** Ms N Slattery
● **Acupuncturist** Ms C McGlinchy
M Yrs. Est.: 15 (Ref:HM19639)

## T C M HEALTHCARE
**T C M Healthcare Ltd**, 101 Bulwer Rd, London, **London (Greater)**, E11 1BU, ENG.
(T) 020 8556 8843 (F) 020 8532 8946
(E) herb@tcm.uk.com
Speciality: Acupressure, Acupuncture, Herbal Medicine.
● **Medical Practitioner** Hong Yang Q: BSc. M: RCHM.
● **Director** Mr S Au Q: MBA.
C O Yrs. Est.: 2 (Ref:HM19640)

## T J'S ELECTRICIAN
**T J's Electrician**, 36 Birchwood Ave, Wallington, **Surrey**, SM6 7EN, ENG.
(T) 020 8647 8672
Speciality: Electrolysis.
T (Ref:HM19641)



Key: B Mind-Body Medicine C Complementary Medicine H Self Help Treatment M Medicinal Therapy O Oriental Medicine P Postural Therapy S Manipulative Structural Therapy T Touch Therapy

**T R GREGORY CHIROPODIST**
**T R Gregory Chiropodist**, 69 King St, Dukinfield, **Cheshire**, SK16 4NN, ENG.
(T) 01613 308220
Speciality: Chiropodists (Podiatrists).
S (Ref:HM19642)

**T SERVICE**
**T Service**, Chelsea Lane, Inverurie, **Aberdeenshire**, AB51 3QQ, SCO.
(T) 01467 624888 (F) 01467 624888
Speciality: Chiropodists (Podiatrists).
● **Partner** Mrs C Craigmile
S (Ref:HM19643)

**TABERNER, JOHN**
**John Taberner**, 24 Beaumont Rd, Plymouth, **Devon**, PL4 9BN, ENG.
(T) 01752 266058
Speciality: Chiropodists (Podiatrists).
● **Owner** Mr J Taberner
S (Ref:HM19644)

**TABOR COUNSELLING & THRPY CTRE**
**Tabor Counselling & Therapy Centre**, 316 The Lawns Belgard Heights, Tallaght, **County Dublin**, IRE.
(T) 01451 8869
(E) taborcounselling@esatclear.ie
Speciality: Psychotherapy.
B (Ref:HM19645)

**TACHAUER, JACQULINE**
**Jacquline Tauchauer**, 2 Henniker Gate, Chelmsford, **Essex**, CM2 6QH, ENG.
(T) 01245 465781
Speciality: Chiropodists (Podiatrists).
● **Owner** Mr J Tachauer
S (Ref:HM19646)

**TADLEIGH FOOT HEALTH**
**Tadleigh Foot Health**, Franklin Avenue, Tadley, **Hampshire**, RG26 4ER, ENG.
(T) 01189 811127
Speciality: Chiropodists (Podiatrists).
● **Owner** Ms E McEleney
S (Ref:HM19647)

**TAFT, FRANCES**
**Frances Taft**, 46 New Rd, Bromsgrove, **Worcestershire**, B60 2JS, ENG.
(T) 01527 875155
Speciality: Physiotherapy.
P S T (Ref:HM19648)

**TAGG, D**
**D Tagg**, Po Box 67, Basingstoke, **Hampshire**, RG24 8YG, ENG.
(T) 01256 351080
Speciality: Complementary Medicines & Therapy.
● **Partner** Mrs L Tagg
M (Ref:HM19649)

**TAGG, D**
**D Tagg**, 52 Ivar Gardens, Lychpit, Basingstoke, **Hampshire**, RG24 8YD, ENG.
(T) 01256 351080
Speciality: Complementary Medicines & Therapy.
C M (Ref:HM19650)

**TAGG, LINDA A**
**Linda A Tagg**, Po Box 67, Basingstoke, **Hampshire**, RG24 8YG, ENG.
(T) 01256 351080
Speciality: Complementary Medicines & Therapy.
● **Partner** Mrs L Tagg
M (Ref:HM19651)

**TAGGART, RUTH**
**Ruth Taggart**, 23 Beaconsfield Pl, Aberdeen, **Aberdeenshire**, AB15 4AB, SCO.
(T) 01224 643751
Speciality: Aromatherapy, Complementary Therapy, Massage (Therapeutic), Remedial Massage, Stress Therapy. ✔
● **Remedial Masseur/Clinical Aromatherapist**
Mrs R Taggatt M: IFA, ISPA, LCSP.
B M S Yrs. Est.: 11 (Ref:HM19652)

**TAGOE, P J**
**P J Tagoe**, 8 Wells Park Rd, London, **London (Greater)**, SE26 6JB, ENG.
(T) 020 8699 5758 (F) 01344 423044
Speciality: Chiropodists (Podiatrists).
● **Owner** Mrs P Tagoe
S (Ref:HM19653)

**TAI CHI CHU'UAN**
**Tai Chi Chu'uan**, 49A St Catherines Rd, Bournemouth, **Dorset**, BH6 4AQ, ENG.
(T) 01202 425542
Speciality: T'ai-Chi Ch'uan.
● **Owner** Mr P Parsons
M (Ref:HM19654)

**TAI CHI UNION FOR GB**
**Tai Chi Union For Great Britain (The)**, 1 Littlemill Drive, Balmoral Gardens, Crookston, Glasgow, **Glasgow (City of)**, G53 7GE, ENG.
(T) 01418 103482 (F) 01418 103741
(E) secretary@taichiunion.com
(W) www.taichiunion.com
Speciality: T'ai-Chi Ch'uan, Ying & Yang, Qi Gong, Chi Kung. ✔
● **Secretary** Mr R Robinson M: TCUGB.
H Yrs. Est.: 10 (Ref:HM19655)

**T'AI CHI, QIGONG & SHIATSU**
**T'ai Chi, Qigong & Shiatsu Treatment Centre**, 12 Windsor Tce, Garden Flat, Dun Laoghaire, **County Dublin**, IRE.
(T) 01284 2662
Speciality: Complementary Medicines & Therapy.
M (Ref:HM19656)

**TAI-CHI CHUAN**
**Tai-Chi Chuan**, 38 Banyard Rd, London, **London (Greater)**, SE16 2YA, ENG.
(T) 020 7237 5140
Speciality: T'ai-Chi Ch'uan, Ying & Yang, Tao Kung, Chi Kung.
● **Teacher** Ms R Harris M: UKTCA.
B Yrs. Est.: 8 (Ref:HM19657)

**TAIT PHYSIOTHERAPY CLINIC**
**Tait Physiotherapy Clinic (The)**, 2 Selborne Rd, London, **London (Greater)**, N14 7DH, ENG.
(T) 020 8886 7503
Speciality: Physiotherapy.
P S T (Ref:HM19658)

**TAKE IT EASY**
**Take It Easy**, 12 Regent St, Pocklington, York, **Yorkshire (North)**, YO42 2QL, ENG.
(T) 01759 303289
Speciality: Complementary Medicines & Therapy.
● **Owner** Mrs M Jackson
M (Ref:HM19659)

**TALBOT, G M**
**G M Talbot**, 63 Malthouse Lane, Kenilworth, **Warwickshire**, CV8 1AD, ENG.
(T) 01926 856451 (F) 01926 863236
Speciality: Hypnosis.
● **Owner** Mrs G Talbot
B (Ref:HM19660)

**TALBOT, MICHAEL**
**Michael Talbot**, 205 Littlemoor Rd, Weymouth, **Dorset**, DT3 6AF, ENG.
(T) 01305 833800
Speciality: Osteopathy.
P S T (Ref:HM19661)

**TALISMAN CANDLE**
**Talisman Candle & Home Fragrance Centre**, Unit 46, New Market Hall, Market St, Swindon, **Wiltshire**, SN1 1RZ, ENG.
(T) 01793 535619
Speciality: Aromatherapy.
M O (Ref:HM19662)

**TALKING SYSTEMS**
**Talking Systems**, 22 Heavitree Rd, Exeter, **Devon**, EX1 2LQ, ENG.
(T) 01392 211184
Speciality: Psychology.
B (Ref:HM19663)

**TALLANT, ANDREA**
**Andrea Tallant**, 3a Manor Lane, Shipley, **Yorkshire (West)**, BD18 3EA, ENG.
(T) 01274 583956
Speciality: Chiropodists (Podiatrists).
● **Owner** Ms A Tallant
S (Ref:HM19664)

**TALLON, ANNETTE**
**Annette Tallon**, Clinic, IRE.
(T) 01288 7328
Speciality: Acupuncture.
O (Ref:HM19665)

**TALLYN, J**
**J Tallyn**, 79 Middle Way, Oxford, **Oxfordshire**, OX2 7LE, ENG.
(T) 01865 559641
Speciality: Complementary Medicines & Therapy.
C M (Ref:HM19666)

**TALWAR, ARUN (DR)**
**Dr Arun Talwar**, 27 Pantbach Rd, Cardiff, **Glamorgan (Vale of)**, CF14 1TU, WAL.
(T) 029 2061 1446
Speciality: Complementary Medicines & Therapy.
● **Owner** Dr A Talwar
C M (Ref:HM19667)

**TAMARA, YVETTE**
**Yvette Tamara**, 1-3 Mill St, Maidstone, **Kent**, ME15 6XW, ENG.
(T) 01622 759372 (F) 01622 685091
Speciality: Clairvoyants & Palmists.
● **Owner** Mr N Harvey
B (Ref:HM19668)

**TAMARA, YVETTE**
**Yvette Tamara**, 2 Golden Sq, Sussex Rd, New Romney, **Kent**, TN28 8DT, ENG.
(T) 01797 366913
Speciality: Clairvoyants & Palmists.
B (Ref:HM19669)

**TAMARA, YVETTE**
**Yvette Tamara**, Rockstow, Somerfield Rd, Maidstone, **Kent**, ME16 8JJ, ENG.
(T) 01622 695977 (F) 01622 695977
Speciality: Clairvoyants & Palmists.
● **Owner** Ms Y Tamara
B (Ref:HM19670)

**TAMBOLY, KERSI**
**Kersi Tamboly**, 3 Cavendish Court, 86 Waldegrave Rd, Teddington, **London (Greater)**, TW11 8LN, ENG.
(T) 020 8943 1975
Speciality: Reflexology.
S T (Ref:HM19671)

**TAME, STEPHEN**
**Stephen Tame**, 11 Lower Collins Rd, Totnes, **Devon**, TQ9 5PS, ENG.
(T) 01803 857070
Speciality: Psychotherapy.
● **Owner** Mr S Tame
B (Ref:HM19672)

**TAME, STEPHEN**
**Stephen Tame**, 2 Holne Cross, Ashburton, Newton Abbot, **Devon**, TQ13 7QU, ENG.
(T) 01803 857070
Speciality: Psychotherapy.
B (Ref:HM19673)

**TAMMAM, B**
**B Tammam**, 57 Buckmaster House, Holloway Rd, London, **London (Greater)**, N7 9SB, ENG.
(T) 020 7609 6305 (F) 020 7609 6305
Speciality: Psychology.
● **Owner** Dr B Tammam
B (Ref:HM19674)

**TAMWORTH PHYSIOTHERAPY CLINIC**
**Tamworth Physiotherapy Clinic**, 5 Albert Rd, Tamworth, **Staffordshire**, B79 7JN, ENG.
(T) 01827 52875
Speciality: Physiotherapy. ✔
● **Owner** Mr S Harris Q: MCSP, SRP. M: CSP.
S (Ref:HM19675)

**TAN & BEAUTY STUDIO**
**Tan & Beauty Studio (The)**, 20 Queen St, Market Drayton, **Shropshire**, TF9 1PS, ENG.
(T) 01630 658888



Key continued: Yrs.Est: Years Established Q: Qualifications M: Professional Membership ✔ Indemnity Insurance Accept Credit Cards

Speciality: Aromatherapy, Reflexology. ✔
● **Owner** Mrs A Fox
● **Reflexologist** Mr R Fox
● **Beauty Therpist** Mrs K Reece
C Yrs. Est.: 1 (**Ref:**HM19676)

## TANDY, E

**E Tandy**, 9a Kings Rd, Sutton Coldfield, **Midlands (West)**, B73 5AB, ENG.
(T) 01213 557214 (F) 01213 212299
Speciality: Chiropodists (Podiatrists).
● **Principal** Mrs E Tandy
S (**Ref:**HM19677)

## TANDY, SUE

**Sue Tandy**, 89 New North Rd, Huddersfield, **Yorkshire (West)**, HD1 5ND, ENG.
(T) 01484 548134
Speciality: Physiotherapy.
● **Owner** Mr P Leary
P S T (**Ref:**HM19678)

## TANG, ALAN

**Alan Tang**, 185A Torridon Rd, London, **London (Greater)**, SE6 1RG, ENG.
(T) 020 8480 9905
Speciality: Hypnotherapy.
● **Owner** Ms L Griffin
B (**Ref:**HM19679)

## TANG, B (DR)

**Dr B Tang**, 39 Crossway, Manchester, **Manchester (Greater)**, M20 6TU, ENG.
(T) 01614 451018
Speciality: Complementary Medicines & Therapy.
M (**Ref:**HM19680)

## TANG, SHULAN

**Shulan Tang**, Aldrens Lane, Lancaster, **Lancashire**, LA1 2DU, ENG.
(T) 01524 69864 (F) 01524 848155
Speciality: Acupuncture.
O (**Ref:**HM19681)

## TANG, SHULAN

**Shulan Tang**, 50 Sandy Lane, Manchester, **Manchester (Greater)**, M21 8TN, ENG.
(T) 01618 810088 (F) 01618 810888
Speciality: Acupuncture.
● **Owner** Dr J Xu
O (**Ref:**HM19682)

## TANG, SIMON

**Simon Tang**, 13 Temple Rd, Epsom, **Surrey**, KT19 8EY, ENG.
(T) 01372 728533
Speciality: Osteopathy.
P S T (**Ref:**HM19683)

## TANNER, MICHELLE

**Michelle Tanner**, 74 Somerset Rd, Doncaster, **Yorkshire (South)**, DN1 2BL, ENG.
(T) 01302 340273 (F) 01302 340273
Speciality: Hypnosis.
● **Owner** Miss M Tanner
B (**Ref:**HM19684)

## TANNER, P T

**P T Tanner**, Oving Clinic, Church Lane, Oving, Chichester, **Sussex (West)**, PO20 6DG, ENG.
(T) 01243 773167 (F) 01243 530567
Speciality: Physiotherapy.
● **Owner** Dr J Tanner
P S T (**Ref:**HM19685)

## TANNER, T L

**T L Tanner**, 21 Greenfield, Christchurch, Newport, NP18 1JN, WAL.
(T) 01633 421817
Speciality: Physiotherapy.
● **Owner** Mrs T Tanner
P S T (**Ref:**HM19686)

## TANSER, THEO

**Theo Tanser**, The Business Centre, 33 Chapel St, Buckfastleigh, **Devon**, TQ11 0AB, ENG.
(T) 01364 642499
Speciality: Homeopathy.
M (**Ref:**HM19687)

## TANSEY, B R

**B R Tansey**, 15 Heatherlaw, Washington, **Tyne and Wear**, NE37 1JX, ENG.
(T) 01914 178870
Speciality: Chiropodists (Podiatrists).
● **Owner** Mr B Tansey
S (**Ref:**HM19688)

## TANSILL, LUCY

**Lucy Tansill**, 64 Penwortham Rd, South Croydon, **Surrey**, CR2 0QS, ENG.
(T) 020 8668 6456
Speciality: Hypnotherapy, Naturopathy, Osteopathy, Nutrition, Manipulation Therapy. ✔
● **Naturopath** Ms L Tansill **Q:** Dip.Hyp, Dip.Med.Ac, ND. **M:** BAcC.
P S T Yrs. Est.: 12 (**Ref:**HM19689)

## TANSLEY, LINDEN

**Linden Tansley**, Seasons, Bridge End, Chester Le Street, **County Durham**, DH3 3RE, ENG.
(T) 01913 734823
Speciality: Aromatherapy.
● **Owner** Mrs L Tansley
M O (**Ref:**HM19690)

## TANSLEY, LINDEN

**Linden Tansley**, Black Health Food Centre, 91 Claypath, Durham, **County Durham**, DH1 1RF, ENG.
(T) 01913 734823
Speciality: Aromatherapy.
M O (**Ref:**HM19691)

## TANSWELL, P

**P Tanswell**, 2 Neal's Yard, Convent Garden, London, **London (Greater)**, WC2H 9DP, ENG.
(T) 020 7379 7662
Speciality: Osteopathy.
P S T (**Ref:**HM19692)

## TANSWELL, PHILLIP J

**Phillip J Tanswell**, 4 Limetree House, Hall St, Long Melford, Sudbury, **Suffolk**, CO10 9JF, ENG.
(T) 01787 378320
Speciality: Osteopathy.
● **Owner** Mr P Tanswell
P S T (**Ref:**HM19693)

## TANT, M

**Mr M Tant**, 141 Luton Rd, Harpenden, **Hertfordshire**, AL5 3BB, ENG.
(T) 01582 622000
Speciality: Osteopathy.
● **Owner** Mr M Tant
P S T (**Ref:**HM19694)

## TANYA ANDREWS

**Tanya Andrews**, 53 Cranbury Rd, London, **London (Greater)**, SW6 2NJ, ENG.
(T) 020 7736 9714
Speciality: Physiotherapy.
P S T (**Ref:**HM19695)

## TAPERELL, AVRIL

**Avril Taperell**, 16 Parkhall Croft, Birmingham, **Midlands (West)**, B34 7BU, ENG.
(T) 01217 476084
Speciality: Reflexology.
S T (**Ref:**HM19696)

## TAPHOUSE, K T

**K T Taphouse**, Woodlands, Highleigh Rd, Highleigh, Chichester, **Sussex (West)**, PO20 7NR, ENG.
(T) 01243 641624
Speciality: Aromatherapy.
● **Owner** Mrs K Taphouse
M O (**Ref:**HM19697)

## TAPSELL, DANIEL

**Daniel Tapsell**, Flat 16, Chater House, Roman Rd, London, **London (Greater)**, E2 0SA, ENG.
(T) 020 8981 4006
Speciality: Acupuncture.
● **Owner** Mr D Tapsell
O (**Ref:**HM19698)

## TARA ROKPA ENDINBURGH

**Tara Rokpa Edinburgh**, 250 Ferry Rd, Edinburgh, **Edinburgh (City of)**, EH5 3AS, SCO.
(T) 01315 521431 (F) 01315 521431
(E) tararokpa@tararokpa.fsnet.co.uk
(W) www.rokpa.org
Speciality: Acupuncture, Counselling, Nutritional Therapy, Psychotherapy, Yoga, Meditation Group, Clinical Massage, Traditional Tibetan Medicine, Medical Herbalists and there is a Cranial Sacrial Worker. ✔
● **Administrator** Mr Antle
C O Yrs. Est.: 15 (**Ref:**HM19699)

## TARA SCHOOL

**Tara School**, Tateetra, Dundalk, **County Louth**, IRE.
(T) 04293 39815
Speciality: Aromatherapy.
M O (**Ref:**HM19700)

## TARA SCHOOL OF HYPNOTHERAPY

**Tara School Of Hypnotherapy**, 104 Rainbow Drive, Halewood, Liverpool, **Merseyside**, L26 7AG, ENG.
(T) 01514 873470
(E) j.mahony@cable1net.co.uk
Speciality: Cognitive Therapy, Hypnosis, Hypnotherapy, Meditation, Visualisation Therapy, Transpersonal Therapy. ✔
● **Hypnotherapist** Ms P Mahony
● **Hypnotherapist** Mr A Mahony **Q:** BSc (Hons). **M:** BPS.
B Yrs. Est.: 14 (**Ref:**HM19701)

## TARA SCHOOL-INTEGRATIVE THRPY

**Tara School of Integrative Therapy**, Tateetra Newtownbalregan, **County Louth**, IRE.
(T) 04293 39815
Speciality: Aromatherapy.
M O (**Ref:**HM19702)

## TARAS PHYSIO SPORTS INJURIES

**Taras Physiotherapy Sports Injuries Clinic**, Grains Rd, Shaw, Oldham, **Lancashire**, OL2 8JB, ENG.
(T) 01706 841460
Speciality: Physiotherapy.
● **Manager** Mrs S Hackwell
P S T (**Ref:**HM19703)

## TARETH CENTRE

**Tareth Centre (The)**, The Old Clinic, 10 St Johns Sq, Glastonbury, **Somerset**, BA6 9LJ, ENG.
(T) 01458 833707
(W) www.tareth.org
Speciality: Aromatherapy, Herbal Medicine, Holistic Healing, Homeopathy, Hypnotherapy, Indian Head Massage, Massage (Therapeutic), Meditation, Spiritual Healing, Teacher of Spiritual Healing, Spiritual Development Workshop.
✔ CREDIT
● **Manager** Mr Tareth
C Yrs. Est.: 25 (**Ref:**HM19704)

## TARETH CENTRE

**Tareth Centre (The)**, 8a Market Pl, Glastonbury, **Somerset**, BA6 9HW, ENG.
(T) 01458 833929
Speciality: Complementary Medicines & Therapy.
● **Office Manager** Mrs A Hannah
C M (**Ref:**HM19705)

## TARKA CLINIC

**Tarka Clinic**, Paiges Lane, Barnstaple, **Devon**, EX31 1EF, ENG.
(T) 01271 373346
Speciality: Chiropodists (Podiatrists).
● **Owner** Mr M Matthews
S (**Ref:**HM19706)

## TARO

**Taro**, 1 Perry Rd, Continuation Of Park Row, Bristol, BS1 5BQ, ENG.
(T) 01179 214869
Speciality: Clairvoyants & Palmists.
● **Owner** Mrs J Clements
B (**Ref:**HM19707)

## TARONA, GAIL HAWKINS

**Gail Tarona Hawkins**, 51 Barr Cres, Whitwick, Coalville, **Leicestershire**, LE67 5FF, ENG.
(T) 01530 811395
Speciality: Clairvoyants & Palmists.
B (**Ref:**HM19708)

## TAROT CONSULTATIONS

**Tarot Consultations**, 303A Westbourne Park Rd, London, **London (Greater)**, W11 1EF, ENG.
(T) 020 7243 1535
Speciality: Complementary Medicines & Therapy.
● **Owner** Mr I Winter



Key: B Mind-Body Medicine C Complementary Medicine H Self Help Treatment M Medicinal Therapy O Oriental Medicine P Postural Therapy S Manipulative Structural Therapy T Touch Therapy

M (Ref:HM19709)

## TAROT READINGS BY PROF

**Tarot Readings By Professionals**, The Plassey Craft Centre, Eyton, Wrexham, LL13 0SP, WAL.
(T) 07711 929216
Speciality: Clairvoyants & Palmists.
B (Ref:HM19710)

## TAROT, JAYS

**Jays Tarot**, The Plassey Centre, Eyton, Wrexham, LL13 0SP, WAL.
(T) 01978 780229
Speciality: Clairvoyants & Palmists.
● **Owner** Mr C Lavender
B (Ref:HM19711)

## TAROTS CARD READING

**Tarots Card Reading With Psychic Support**, 5 Hillingdon Court, Yeovil, **Somerset**, BA21 3TA, ENG.
(T) 01935 476145
Speciality: Complementary Medicines & Therapy.
● **Owner** Mrs S Clensy
M (Ref:HM19712)

## TARPEY, ALISON J

**Alison J Tarpey**, Barnsite, Lycrome Rd, Chesham, **Buckinghamshire**, HP5 3LQ, ENG.
(T) 01494 771115 (F) 01494 771115
Speciality: Chiropodists (Podiatrists).
● **Owner** Mrs A Tarpey
S (Ref:HM19713)

## TARSEY, SANDRA

**Sandra Tarsey**, 94 Marford Rd, Wheathampstead, St. Albans, **Hertfordshire**, AL4 8NQ, ENG.
(T) 01582 831040
Speciality: Chiropodists (Podiatrists).
S (Ref:HM19714)

## TARU, BURSTALL

**Burstall Taru**, 11 North Tce, Inchicore, Dublin, **County Dublin**, IRE.
(T) 01473 3819
Speciality: Complementary Medicines & Therapy.
M (Ref:HM19715)

## TASS, DIANA

**Diana Tass**, Rivers Hospital, Thomas Rivers Medical Centre, High Wych Rd, Sawbridgeworth, **Hertfordshire**, CM21 0HH, ENG.
(T) 01279 600282
Speciality: Physiotherapy.
P S T (Ref:HM19716)

## TATHAM, ALAN

**Alan Tatham**, 11 St John St, Manchester, **Manchester (Greater)**, M3 4DW, ENG.
(T) 01618 344122
Speciality: Psychology.
● **Psychologist** Alan Tatham
B (Ref:HM19717)

## TATHAM, R S

**R S Tatham**, 11 Stanley Gardens, London, **London (Greater)**, NW2 4QH, ENG.
(T) 020 8452 5856
Speciality: Osteopathy.
P S T (Ref:HM19718)

## TATTERSALL, KAREN

**Karen Tattersall**, 26 Carlton Rd, Leyland, Preston, **Lancashire**, PR5 1LP, ENG.
(T) 01772 424048
Speciality: Biomechanics, Chiropody, Nail Surgery. ✔
● **Owner/Chiropodist**
Mrs K Tattersall Q: M.S.C.P. M: S.C.P.
C (Ref:HM19719)

## TATTON, ALISTAIR M

**Alistair M Tatton**, Cleswith, Sea View Rd, Falmouth, **Cornwall**, TR11 4EF, ENG.
(T) 01326 319440
Speciality: Osteopathy.
● **Owner** Mr A Tatton
P S T (Ref:HM19720)

## TATTON, DAVID

**David Tatton**, 65 Vespan Rd, London, **London (Greater)**, W12 9QG, ENG.
(T) 020 8749 0581
Speciality: Osteopathy.
P S T (Ref:HM19721)

## TAUNTON FOOT SURGERY

**Taunton Foot Surgery**, Oakgate Chambers, Bath Pl, Taunton, **Somerset**, TA1 4EP, ENG.
(T) 01823 286287 (F) 01823 286287
Speciality: Biomechanics, Chiropody, Podiatry. ✔
● **Podiatrist** Mr P Scurr Q: BSc, M.S.C.P, S.R.Ch.
● **Owner/Podiatric Surgeon** Mr G May Q: FCPod(s), S.R.Ch.
C Yrs. Est.: 21 (Ref:HM19722)

## TAURINS, ALISON

**Alison Taurins**, 27 George St, Brighton, **Sussex (West)**, BN2 1RH, ENG.
(T) 01273 239977
Speciality: Aromatherapy.
● **Owner** Miss A Taurins
M O (Ref:HM19723)

## TAVAKKOLI, KIAN

**Kian Tavakkoli**, 17 Rudge Cl, Chatham, **Kent**, ME5 8UJ, ENG.
(T) 01634 868232
Speciality: Reflexology.
S T (Ref:HM19724)

## TAVISTOCK CHIROPRACTIC CENTRE

**Tavistock Chiropractic Centre**, 58 West St, Tavistock, **Devon**, PL19 8JZ, ENG.
(T) 01822 616806
Speciality: Chiropractic.
● **Owner** Mr T Wallis
P S T (Ref:HM19725)

## TAVY COVER

**Tavy Cover**, Kimberleigh, Bolt House Cl, Tavistock, **Devon**, PL19 8LN, ENG.
(T) 01822 615434
Speciality: Complementary Medicines & Therapy.
● **Partner** Mrs C Hicks
C M (Ref:HM19726)

## TAWSTOCK MEDICAL CENTRE

**Tawstock Medical Centre**, 7 High St, Chard, **Somerset**, TA20 1QF, ENG.
(T) 01460 67763
Speciality: Alexander Technique.
● **Therapist** Mr D Howlett
P S (Ref:HM19727)

## TAYLOR & ASSOCIATES

**Don Taylor & Associates**, 2 University Rd, Southampton, **Hampshire**, SO17 1TJ, ENG.
(T) 023 8031 5176 (F) 023 8031 5176
Speciality: Psychotherapy.
● **Owner** Mr D Taylor
B (Ref:HM19728)

## TAYLOR, A B

**A B Taylor**, Cloth Hall Chambers, Cloth Hall St, Huddersfield, **Yorkshire (West)**, HD1 2EG, ENG.
(T) 01484 532188
Speciality: Chiropodists (Podiatrists).
● **Owner** Mr A Taylor
S (Ref:HM19729)

## TAYLOR, A C

**A C Taylor**, Riverside, Tansor, Peterborough, **Cambridgeshire**, PE8 5HN, ENG.
(T) 01832 226357
Speciality: Physiotherapy.
● **Owner** Mrs A Taylor
P S T (Ref:HM19730)

## TAYLOR, A J

**A J Taylor**, 7 Jacksons Lane, London, **London (Greater)**, N6 5SR, ENG.
(T) 020 8341 2188
Speciality: Psychotherapy.
● **Owner** A Taylor
B (Ref:HM19731)

## TAYLOR, ALISON

**Alison Taylor**, Innis Free, Elm Lane, Bourne End, **Buckinghamshire**, SL8 5PF, ENG.
(T) 01628 523290
Speciality: Chiropodists (Podiatrists).
● **Owner** Mrs A Taylor
S (Ref:HM19732)

## TAYLOR, ANNA

**Anna Taylor**, Therapy Rooms, St. Andrews Mews, St. Andrews Lane, Lewes, **Sussex (East)**, BN7 1UW, ENG.
(T) 01825 722579
Speciality: Homeopathy.
M (Ref:HM19733)

## TAYLOR, ANTHONY B

**Anthony B Taylor**, 14 Bank St, Castleford, **Yorkshire (West)**, WF10 1HZ, ENG.
(T) 01977 603282
Speciality: Chiropodists (Podiatrists).
● **Owner** Mr A Taylor
S (Ref:HM19734)

## TAYLOR, ANTHONY B

**Anthony B Taylor**, 92 The Avenue, Alwoodley, Leeds, **Yorkshire (West)**, LS17 7PB, ENG.
(T) 01132 671180
Speciality: Chiropodists (Podiatrists).
● **Owner** Mr A Taylor
S (Ref:HM19735)

## TAYLOR, BARBARA

**Barbara Taylor**, 234 Willerby Rd, Hull, **Humberside (North)**, HU5 5JR, ENG.
(T) 01482 353194
Speciality: Physiotherapy.
● **Owner** Mrs B Taylor
P S T (Ref:HM19736)

## TAYLOR, BERYL

**Beryl Taylor**, 24 Sandringham Rd, Doncaster, **Yorkshire (South)**, DN2 5HU, ENG.
(T) 01302 341595
Speciality: Homeopathy.
● **Owner** Mrs B Taylor
M (Ref:HM19737)

## TAYLOR, C

**C Taylor**, 1105 Christchurch Rd, Bournemouth, **Dorset**, BH7 6BQ, ENG.
(T) 01202 424164
Speciality: Chiropodists (Podiatrists).
● **Owner** Mrs C Taylor
S (Ref:HM19738)

## TAYLOR, C E

**C E Taylor**, 10 Coinagehall St, Helston, **Cornwall**, TR13 8EB, ENG.
(T) 01326 564671
Speciality: Chiropodists (Podiatrists).
● **Owner** Mrs C Taylor
S (Ref:HM19739)

## TAYLOR, C L (DR)

**Dr C L Taylor**, 19 St Augustines Rd, Canterbury, **Kent**, CT1 1XP, ENG.
(T) 01227 768884
Speciality: Chiropractors.
● **Owner** Dr F Collingwood
P S T (Ref:HM19740)

## TAYLOR, CAROL

**Carol Taylor**, Bennett House, 14 Horsemarket, Darlington, **County Durham**, DL1 5PT, ENG.
(T) 01642 363542
Speciality: Alexander Technique.
P S (Ref:HM19741)

## TAYLOR, CAROL D

**Carol D Taylor**, 20 Bridge Green, Prestbury, Macclesfield, **Cheshire**, SK10 4HR, ENG.
(T) 01625 829070
Speciality: Physiotherapy.
P S T (Ref:HM19742)

## TAYLOR, CAROLYN

**Carolyn Taylor**, 66 High St, Great Shelford, Cambridge, **Cambridgeshire**, CB2 5EH, ENG.
(T) 01223 842978
Speciality: Osteopathy.
P S T (Ref:HM19743)

## TAYLOR, CHRISTIAN

**Mr Christian Taylor**, New Rd, Brighton, **Sussex (West)**, BN1 1UF, ENG.
(T) 01273 324790
Speciality: Holistic Healing, Homeopathy. ✔
● **Homeopath** Mr C Taylor Q: RSHom. M: Soc.Hom.
C Yrs. Est.: 10 (Ref:HM19744)



Key continued: Yrs.Est: Years Established Q: Qualifications M: Professional Membership ✔ Indemnity Insurance Accept Credit Cards

**TAYLOR, CHRISTINE**

**Christine Taylor**, 102 Altrincham Rd, Wilmslow, **Cheshire**, SK9 5NQ, ENG.
(T) 01625 523693
Speciality: Chiropodists (Podiatrists).
● **Owner** Miss C Taylor
S (Ref:HM19745)

**TAYLOR, CHRISTINE**

**Christine Taylor**, 3 Borough Fields Shopping Centre, Wootton Bassett, Swindon, **Wiltshire**, SN4 7AX, ENG.
(T) 01249 716291
Speciality: Homeopathy.
● **Owner** Mrs C Taylor
M (Ref:HM19746)

**TAYLOR, CLAIRE**

**Claire Taylor**, 28A Rickford Hill, Worplesdon, Guildford, **Surrey**, GU3 3PG, ENG.
(T) 01483 236026
Speciality: Reflexology.
● **Owner** Ms C Taylor
S T (Ref:HM19747)

**TAYLOR, CLARE**

**Clare Taylor**, 42 Lavender Lane, Stourbridge, **Midlands (West)**, DY8 3EF, ENG.
(T) 01384 349191
Speciality: Aromatherapy.
● **Owner** Mrs C Taylor
M O (Ref:HM19748)

**TAYLOR, D**

**D Taylor - Hypnotherapy**, 10 The Maltings, North William St, Perth, **Perth and Kinross**, PH1 5PG, SCO.
(T) 01738 560644 (F) 01738 441100
(E) burrelton@aol.com
(W) www.power2change.co.uk
Speciality: Aversion Therapy, Counselling, Healer, Hypnosis, Hypnotherapy, Psychotherapy. ✓
● **Hypnotherapist** Mr D Taylor Q: Dip.Hyp, Dip.Psych, NLP. M: HA, NCH, NRAH.
B Yrs. Est.: 8 (Ref:HM19749)

**TAYLOR, D**

**D Taylor**, 82c Town Centre, Hatfield, **Hertfordshire**, AL10 0JW, ENG.
(T) 01707 260399
Speciality: Physiotherapy.
● **Owner** Mr D Taylor
P S T (Ref:HM19750)

**TAYLOR, D W**

**D W Taylor**, Gornal Cottage, Main Rd, Woodside, Blairgowrie, **Perth and Kinross**, PH13 9NP, SCO.
(T) 01828 670581
Speciality: Hypnotherapy.
B (Ref:HM19751)

**TAYLOR, DAVID**

**David Taylor**, 22 West Avenue, Crawley, **Sussex (West)**, RH10 1SJ, ENG.
(T) 01293 429660
Speciality: Chiropodists (Podiatrists).
S (Ref:HM19752)

**TAYLOR, DAVID E**

**David E Taylor**, 17 Ray St, Heanor, **Derbyshire**, DE75 7GE, ENG.
(T) 01773 715751
Speciality: Chiropodists (Podiatrists).
● **Owner** Mr D Taylor
S (Ref:HM19753)

**TAYLOR, DESMOND**

**Desmond Taylor**, The Old Malthouse, Bridge Sq, Farnham, **Surrey**, GU9 7QP, ENG.
(T) 01252 714514
Speciality: Osteopathy.
● **Owner** Mr D Taylor
P S T (Ref:HM19754)

**TAYLOR, E**

**E Taylor**, 8 Eurgan Cl, Llantwit Major, **Glamorgan (Vale of)**, CF61 1QY, WAL.
(T) 01446 796255
Speciality: Complementary Medicines & Therapy.
C M (Ref:HM19755)

**TAYLOR, E F**

**E F Taylor**, 41 St. John St, Ashbourne, **Derbyshire**, DE6 1GP, ENG.
(T) 01335 300440
Speciality: Osteopathy, Psychotherapy. ✓
● **Osteopath** Mrs E Taylor Q: DO. M: GOsC.
● **Osteopath** Dr R Shaw Q: DO. M: GOsC.
S Yrs. Est.: 10 (Ref:HM19756)

**TAYLOR, E F**

**E F Taylor**, 32 Friargate, Derby, **Derbyshire**, DE1 1BX, ENG.
(T) 01332 371184
Speciality: Cranial Osteopathy, Osteopathy, Psychotherapy. ✓
● **Osteopath** Dr R Shaw Q: DO. M: GOsC.
● **Osteopath** Mrs E Taylor Q: DO. M: GOsC.
S Yrs. Est.: 10 (Ref:HM19757)

**TAYLOR, ELIZABETH**

**Elizabeth Taylor**, 25 Hickmans Lane, Lindfield, Haywards Heath, **Sussex (West)**, RH16 2BN, ENG.
(T) 01444 414420
Speciality: Reflexology.
S T (Ref:HM19758)

**TAYLOR, EVE**

**Eve Taylor (London) Ltd**, Unit 9 Papyrus Rd, Peterborough, **Cambridgeshire**, PE4 5BH, ENG.
(T) 01733 321101
Speciality: Aromatherapy, Bach Remedies, Complementary Therapy, Massage (Therapeutic), Nutritional Therapy, Oriental Diagnosis, Reflexology, Swedish Body Massage, Natural Skin Care.
● **Production Manager** Raymond Neil Taylor
M O (Ref:HM19759)

**TAYLOR, GILLIAN**

**Gillian Taylor**, 49 St. Pauls Rd, Weston-Super-Mare, **Somerset**, BS23 4AD, ENG.
(T) 01934 620235
Speciality: Chiropody. ✓
● **Owner/Chiropodist** Miss G Taylor Q: MBChA, RN2. M: SSCh.
M Yrs. Est.: 3 (Ref:HM19760)

**TAYLOR, H M**

**H M Taylor**, 154 Gibbins Rd, Birmingham, **Midlands (West)**, B29 6NJ, ENG.
(T) 01214 711023
Speciality: Chiropodists (Podiatrists).
● **Owner** Mrs H Taylor
S (Ref:HM19761)

**TAYLOR, HEATHER**

**Heather Taylor**, 115 Baddow Rd, Chelmsford, **Essex**, CM2 7PY, ENG.
(T) 01621 784700
Speciality: Physiotherapy.
P S T (Ref:HM19762)

**TAYLOR, IAN E**

**Ian E Taylor**, 7 Coggeshall Gr, Wavendon Gate, Milton Keynes, **Buckinghamshire**, MK7 7SN, ENG.
(T) 01908 582933
Speciality: Chiropody, Homeopathy, Reflexology, Magnet Therapy. ✓
● **Chiropodist** Mr I Taylor Q: BSY.Reflex, Inst.CH.P. M: Inst.CH.P.
M Yrs. Est.: 1 (Ref:HM19763)

**TAYLOR, J**

**J Taylor**, 42 Shepherds Lane, Dartford, **Kent**, DA1 2NY, ENG.
(T) 01322 275456
Speciality: Complementary Medicines & Therapy.
M (Ref:HM19764)

**TAYLOR, J**

**J Taylor**, All Hallows House, Idol Lane, London, **London (Greater)**, EC3R 5DD, ENG.
(T) 020 7283 8908
Speciality: Psychotherapy.
B (Ref:HM19765)

**TAYLOR, J D**

**J D Taylor**, Gofer Glas, Maesybont, Llanelli, **Carmarthenshire**, SA14 7HH, WAL.
(T) 01558 668338
Speciality: Physiotherapy.
● **Owner** Mrs J Taylor
P S T (Ref:HM19766)

**TAYLOR, JAMES M**

**James M Taylor**, 104 Fitzalan Rd, Arundel, **Sussex (West)**, BN18 9JY, ENG.
(T) 01903 884089
Speciality: Alexander Technique. ✓
● **Teacher of the Alexander Technique** Mr J Taylor Q: MSTAT. M: STAT.
H P Yrs. Est.: 25 (Ref:HM19767)

**TAYLOR, JAMIE**

**Jamie Taylor**, 10 Bloomfield Rd, Bath, **Somerset**, BA2 2AB, ENG.
(T) 01225 310245 (F) 01225 310245
Speciality: Homeopathy.
● **Owner** Mr J Taylor
M (Ref:HM19768)

**TAYLOR, JANE**

**Jane Taylor**, Blue Houses, Bridgend, **Argyll and Bute**, PA44 7PQ, SCO.
(T) 01496 810900
Speciality: Complementary Medicines & Therapy.
● **Owner** Ms J Taylor
C M (Ref:HM19769)

**TAYLOR, JOANNE**

**Joanne Taylor**, 20 Littleworth, Mansfield, **Nottinghamshire**, NG18 2SH, ENG.
(T) 01623 653151
Speciality: Chiropodists (Podiatrists).
S (Ref:HM19770)

**TAYLOR, JOHN**

**John Taylor**, 585 Prince Avenue, Westcliff-on-Sea, **Essex**, SS0 0JQ, ENG.
(T) 01702 475063
Speciality: Physiotherapy.
● **Owner** Mr J Tayor
P S T (Ref:HM19771)

**TAYLOR, JULIE**

**Julie Taylor**, 9 Pasture Fold, Burley In Wharfedale, Ilkley, **Yorkshire (West)**, LS29 7RP, ENG.
(T) 01943 865850
Speciality: Reflexology.
S T (Ref:HM19772)

**TAYLOR, JUNE**

**June Taylor**, 7 Midmills Rd, Inverness, **Highland**, IV2 3NZ, SCO.
(T) 01463 225732
Speciality: Reflexology, Reiki. ✓
● **Owner/Reflexologist** Mrs J Taylor
T Yrs. Est.: 12 (Ref:HM19773)

**TAYLOR, KAREN**

**Karen Taylor**, Westgate Lodge, Low St, North Wheatley, Retford, **Nottinghamshire**, DN22 9DS, ENG.
(T) 01427 881457
Speciality: Hypnosis.
B (Ref:HM19774)

**TAYLOR, KAREN**

**Karen Taylor**, 437 Frankby Rd, Greasby, Wirral, **Merseyside**, CH49 3PJ, ENG.
(T) 01516 783715
Speciality: Reflexology.
S T (Ref:HM19775)

**TAYLOR, L**

**L Taylor**, 13A Ross Prde, Wallington, **Surrey**, SM6 8QG, ENG.
(T) 020 8288 0391
Speciality: Osteopathy.
P S T (Ref:HM19776)

**TAYLOR, L P A**

**L P A Taylor**, 11A Beetham Rd, Milnthorpe, **Cumbria**, LA7 7QL, ENG.
(T) 01539 562844
Speciality: Osteopathy.
● **Owner** Mrs L Taylor
P S T (Ref:HM19777)

**TAYLOR, L P A**

**L P A Taylor**, 11a Firs Rd, Milnthorpe, **Cumbria**, LA7 7QF, ENG.



Key: B Mind-Body Medicine, C Complementary Medicine, H Self Help Treatment, M Medicinal Therapy, O Oriental Medicine, P Postural Therapy, S Manipulative Structural Therapy, T Touch Therapy

(T) 01539 562844
Speciality: Osteopathy.
P S T (Ref:HM19778)

**TAYLOR, LEON (DR)**
**Chiropractic Association Of Ireland Dr Leon Taylor**, Douglas Chiropractic Clinic, Broadale Maryborough, County Cork, IRE.
(T) 021 4773 617
Speciality: Chiropractors.
P S T (Ref:HM19779)

**TAYLOR, LESLEY**
**Mrs Lesley Taylor**, 60 High St, Wootton Bassett, Swindon, **Wiltshire**, SN4 7AQ, ENG.
(T) 01793 849914
Speciality: Chiropodists (Podiatrists).
● **Owner** Mrs L Taylor
S (Ref:HM19780)

**TAYLOR, LYNETTE**
**Lynette Taylor**, Croy Lodge, 15A Cleveland Rd, Paignton, **Devon**, TQ4 6EL, ENG.
(T) 01803 556789
Speciality: Osteopathy.
P S T (Ref:HM19781)

**TAYLOR, LYNN**
**Lynn Taylor**, 32 Whalley Cl, Timperley, Altrincham, **Cheshire**, WA15 6TP, ENG.
(T) 01619 692115
Speciality: Hypnosis.
B (Ref:HM19782)

**TAYLOR, M**
**M Taylor**, Stillpoint, Whiteway, Stroud, **Gloucestershire**, GL6 7EP, ENG.
(T) 01285 821648 (F) 01285 821648
Speciality: Complementary Medicines & Therapy.
● **Owner** Mr M Taylor
C M (Ref:HM19783)

**TAYLOR, MELANIE**
**Melanie Taylor**, Elmstead, Sandford Rd, Wareham, **Dorset**, BH20 4DH, ENG.
(T) 01929 551513
Speciality: Chiropractic.
● **Owner** Miss M Taylor
P S T (Ref:HM19784)

**TAYLOR, MONICA**
**Monica Taylor**, 202 Pensby Rd, Heswall, Wirral, **Merseyside**, CH60 7RJ, ENG.
(T) 01513 429141
Speciality: Chiropodists (Podiatrists).
S (Ref:HM19785)

**TAYLOR, P**
**P Taylor**, 2 Springfield Rd, Kings Heath, Birmingham, **Midlands (West)**, B14 7DS, ENG.
(T) 01214 413228
Speciality: Chiropodists (Podiatrists).
S (Ref:HM19786)

**TAYLOR, P J**
**P J Taylor**, 76 St. Mary's Rd, London, **London (Greater)**, N9 8NJ, ENG.
(T) 020 8805 4785
Speciality: Chiropodists (Podiatrists).
● **Owner** Mrs P Taylor
S (Ref:HM19787)

**TAYLOR, R C**
**Mr R C Taylor**, 8 Chertion Drive, London, **London (Greater)**, SE18 2RD, ENG.
(T) 020 8854 2315
Speciality: Chiropodists (Podiatrists).
S (Ref:HM19788)

**TAYLOR, RACHEL**
**Rachel Taylor**, Down House, West View Rd, Sparsholt, Winchester, **Hampshire**, SO22 5RB, ENG.
(T) 01962 855931
Speciality: Complementary Medicines & Therapy.
● **Owner** Mrs R Taylor
C M (Ref:HM19789)

**TAYLOR, S**
**S Taylor**, 39 Tydfil Pl, Penylan, Cardiff, **Glamorgan (Vale of)**, CF23 5HA, WAL.
(T) 029 2048 4555
Speciality: Chiropractors.
P S T (Ref:HM19790)

**TAYLOR, S A**
**S A Taylor**, 6 Atherley Cross Rd, Shanklin, **Isle of Wight**, PO37 7AX, ENG.
(T) 01983 865027
Speciality: Chiropody. ✓
● **Chiropodist** Mr S Taylor Q: MBChA, MSSCh. M: B.A.Ch.P, SSCh.
C Yrs. Est.: 13 (Ref:HM19791)

**TAYLOR, S S**
**S S Taylor**, 23 Kingfisher Way, Blyth, **Northumberland**, NE24 3QW, ENG.
(T) 01670 353573
Speciality: Chiropodists (Podiatrists).
● **Owner** Mr S Taylor
S (Ref:HM19792)

**TAYLOR, SHANE**
**Shane Taylor**, Half Acre, East Woodlands, Frome, **Somerset**, BA11 5LY, ENG.
(T) 01373 467187
Speciality: Hypnosis.
● **Owner** Mr S Taylor
B (Ref:HM19793)

**TAYLOR, SIMON**
**Simon Taylor**, Thornton Chambers, 57 The Headrow, Leeds, **Yorkshire (West)**, LS1 6LR, ENG.
(T) 01132 428930
Speciality: Chiropodists (Podiatrists).
● **Owner** Mr S Taylor
S (Ref:HM19794)

**TAYLOR, SIMON**
**Simon Taylor**, 2 Woodhall Court, Leeds, **Yorkshire (West)**, LS15 9BP, ENG.
(T) 01132 600180
Speciality: Chiropodists (Podiatrists).
S (Ref:HM19795)

**TAYLOR, SUE**
**Sue Taylor Mobile**, Woodland Avenue, Hindley, Wigan, **Lancashire**, WN2 4PP, ENG.
(T) 01942 703040
Speciality: Chiropodists (Podiatrists).
S (Ref:HM19796)

**TAYLOR, SUSAN**
**Susan Taylor**, 426 Bradford Rd, Batley, **Yorkshire (West)**, WF17 5LF, ENG.
(T) 01924 446003
Speciality: Chiropodists (Podiatrists).
S (Ref:HM19797)

**TAYLOR, T B**
**T B Taylor**, 12 The Crescent, Spalding, **Lincolnshire**, PE11 1AE, ENG.
(T) 01775 723000
Speciality: Chiropodists (Podiatrists).
● **Owner** Mr T Taylor
S (Ref:HM19798)

**TAYLORSON, JUDITH**
**Ms Judith Taylorson**, 11 Tavistock Rd, Exeter, **Devon**, EX4 4BN, ENG.
(T) 01392 210076
Speciality: Acupuncture.
● **Owner** Ms J Taylorson
O (Ref:HM19799)

**TAYLOR-WEEKES, HELEN**
**Helen Taylor-Weekes**, 88 Great Northern Rd, Dunstable, **Bedfordshire**, LU5 4BT, ENG.
(T) 01582 608400 (F) 01582 471371
Speciality: Acupuncture.
● **Owner** Mr J Betser
O (Ref:HM19800)

**TCHOREK, CATHERINE**
**Catherine Tchorek**, 23 Chisholm Rd, Croydon, **Surrey**, CR0 6UQ, ENG.
(T) 020 8686 7694
Speciality: Physiotherapy.
● **Owner** Mrs C Tchorek
P S T (Ref:HM19801)

**TCS RESEARCH**
**TCS Research**, Unit H7, Montpelier Business Park, Leacon Rd, Ashford, **Kent**, TN23 4FG, ENG.
(T) 01233 646600 (F) 01233 645890
Speciality: Aromatherapy.
● **Owner** Mr T McMullen
M O (Ref:HM19802)

**TE NOSCE**
**Te Nosce**, 6 Berkeley St, Stone, **Staffordshire**, ST15 8LS, ENG.
(T) 01785 616409 (F) 01785 616010
(E) sue@tenosce.com
(W) www.tenosce.com
Speciality: Complementary Medicines & Therapy.
● **Therapist** Ms S Weller
C (Ref:HM19803)

**TE VELDE, JOHANNA**
**Johanna Te Velde**, 6 Beaconsfield St, Leamington Spa, **Warwickshire**, CV31 1DT, ENG.
(T) 01926 311298
Speciality: Psychotherapy.
● **Owner** Mr V Johanna
B (Ref:HM19804)

**TEACHER OF THE ALEXNDR TECH**
**Teacher Of The Alexander Technique**, 123 New Dover Rd, Capel Le Ferne, Folkestone, **Kent**, CT18 7JL, ENG.
(T) 01303 241736
Speciality: Alexander Technique.
P S (Ref:HM19805)

**TEACHERS OF ALEXNDR TECH**
**Teachers Of The Alexander Technique**, Pigdeon Tower Cottage, Green Dragon Lane, Flackwell Heath, High Wycombe, **Buckinghamshire**, HP10 9JU, ENG.
(T) 01628 521147
Speciality: Alexander Technique. ✓
● **Owner/Teacher of the Alexander Technique**
Mrs V Staveley M: STAT.
P Yrs. Est.: 15 (Ref:HM19806)

**TEAHAN, MONICA**
**Monica Teahan**, Rathasker Sq, Kilcullen Rd, Naas, **County Kildare**, IRE.
(T) 04587 6687
Speciality: Acupuncture.
O (Ref:HM19807)

**TEALE, PAT**
**Pat Teale**, 32 Halifax Rd, Batley, **Yorkshire (West)**, WF17 7BH, ENG.
(T) 01924 464507
Speciality: Reflexology.
● **Owner** Mrs P Teale
S T (Ref:HM19808)

**TEALE, PAUL**
**Paul Teale**, Melrose, 24 Downs Rd, Hastings, **Sussex (East)**, TN34 2DX, ENG.
(T) 01424 428754 (F) 01424 427214
Speciality: Cranial Osteopathy, Osteopathy. ✓
● **Osteopath** Mr P Teale Q: DO (Hons), Reg.Osteopath. M: GOsC.
S Yrs. Est.: 16 (Ref:HM19809)

**TEAM FOCUS**
**Team Focus Ltd**, Heritage House, 13 Bridge St, Maidenhead, **Berkshire**, SL6 8LR, ENG.
(T) 01628 637338 (F) 01628 626264
Speciality: Psychology.
● **Managing Director** Mr R Childs
B (Ref:HM19810)

**TEAMWORK**
**Teamwork**, 51 Lothian Rd, Edinburgh, **Edinburgh (City of)**, EH1 2DJ, SCO.
(T) 01312 283841 (F) 01312 283841
Speciality: Psychotherapy.
● **Partner** Mrs G Williams
B (Ref:HM19811)

**TEASDALE & ASSOCIATES**
**J Teasdale & Associates**, 21 Front St, Brampton, **Cumbria**, CA8 1NG, ENG.
(T) 01697 72191
Speciality: Chiropodists (Podiatrists).
S (Ref:HM19812)

**TEASDALE, J**
**J Teasdale**, 25 Burswell Avenue, Hexham, **Northumberland**, NE46 3JL, ENG.
(T) 01434 608612
Speciality: Chiropodists (Podiatrists).


Key continued: Yrs.Est: Years Established Q: Qualifications M: Professional Membership ✓ Indemnity Insurance Accept Credit Cards

● **Owner** Mr J Teasdale
[S] (**Ref:**HM19813)

## TEDDER, CATHRINE

**Cathrine Tedder**, 12 Church St, Ross-on-Wye, **Herefordshire**, HR9 5HN, ENG.
**(T)** 01989 563721
Speciality: Chiropody, Nail Surgery. ✔
● **Chiropodist** Miss C Tedder **Q:** S.R.Ch. **M:** S.C.P.
[M] Yrs. Est.: 18 (**Ref:**HM19814)

## TEDSTONE, ALISON

**Alison Tedstone**, 8 Sovereign Cl, Murdishaw, Runcorn, **Cheshire**, WA7 6JT, ENG.
**(T)** 01928 779916
Speciality: Chiropody. ✔
● **Owner/Chiropodist** Mrs A Tedstone **Q:** Inst.CH.P.
[C] Yrs. Est.: 2 (**Ref:**HM19815)

## TEES, MALCOLM

**Malcolm Tees**, 244 Penns Lane. Sutton Coldfield, **Midlands (West)**, B76 1LQ, ENG.
**(T)** 01213 511409
Speciality: Hypnosis.
[B] (**Ref:**HM19816)

## TEESDALE OSTEOPATHIC CLINIC

**Teesdale Osteopathic Clinic**, 40 Newgate, Barnard Castle, **County Durham**, DL12 8NJ, ENG.
**(T)** 01833 630640
Speciality: Alexander Technique, Homeopathy, Osteopathy, Reflexology, Therapeutic Massage. ✔
● **Owner/Osteopath** Mr P Hairsine **Q:** BSc. **M:** GOsC.
● **Registered Osteopath/Chartered Physiotherapist** Miss Barstra **Q:** BSc. **M:** GOsC.
[S] Yrs. Est.: 7 (**Ref:**HM19817)

## TEFT, REBECCA

**Rebecca Teft**, 13 Tamar Rd, Chivenor, Barnstaple, **Devon**, EX31 4BQ, ENG.
**(T)** 01271 815734
Speciality: Chiropodists (Podiatrists).
[S] (**Ref:**HM19818)

## TEIGNMOUTH CHIROPODY

**Teignmouth Chiropody**, 14 Station Rd, Teignmouth, **Devon**, TQ14 8PE, ENG.
**(T)** 01626 773369
Speciality: Chiropodists (Podiatrists).
● **Owner** Mr L Younger
[S] (**Ref:**HM19819)

## TELFORD, JOHN

**John Telford**, 262 Coombe Lane, London, **London (Greater)**, SW20 0RW, ENG.
**(T)** 020 8947 5827
Speciality: Osteopathy.
[P] [S] [T] (**Ref:**HM19820)

## TELLING, KAREN

**Karen Telling**, 4 Denehurst Gardens, Richmond, **Surrey**, TW10 5DL, ENG.
**(T)** 020 8876 4771
Speciality: Osteopathy.
[P] [S] [T] (**Ref:**HM19821)

## TELLING, MELANIE

**Melanie Telling**, 22 Mayfair, Stourbridge, **Midlands (West)**, DY9 0XE, ENG.
**(T)** 01562 883850
Speciality: Hopi Ear Candles, Indian Head Massage, Reflexology, Reiki, Virtical Reflex Therapy, Synergistic Therapy. ✔
● **Owner** Ms M Telling **Q:** ITEC, MAR, Reiki Master. **M:** AoR, BEST.
[T] Yrs. Est.: 6 (**Ref:**HM19822)

## TELLING, MELANIE

**Melanie Telling**, 52 Hagley Rd, Stourbridge, **Midlands (West)**, DY8 1QD, ENG.
**(T)** 01384 379141
**(W)** www.pathways2health.co.uk
Speciality: Indian Head Massage, Reflexology, Reiki, Hopi Ear Candles, Virtical Reflex Therapy, Synergistic Therapy. ✔
● **Reflexologist** Ms M Telling **Q:** ITEC, MAR, Reiki Master. **M:** AoR.
[T] Yrs. Est.: 6 (**Ref:**HM19823)

## TELLING, PAUL

**Paul Telling**, The Studio, Lower Broad Oak, Elstead Rd, Seale, Farnham, **Surrey**, GU10 1JA, ENG.
**(T)** 01252 781709 **(F)** 01252 781709
**(E)** paul@thestudiofarnham.co.uk
**(W)** www.thestudiofarnham.co.uk
Speciality: Complementary Therapy, Healer, Healing Therapy, Indian Head Massage, Massage (Therapeutic), Reiki, Ayurvedic massage, LaStone "Hot Rocks" massage.
● **Owner** Mr P Telling **M:** IHBC.
[S] Yrs. Est.: 3 (**Ref:**HM19824)

## TELLURIC, CHRISTINE

**Christine Telluric**, 6 Pagham Cl, Emsworth, **Hampshire**, PO10 8JB, ENG.
**(T)** 01243 370608
Speciality: Reflexology.
● **Owner** Miss C Telluric
[S] [T] (**Ref:**HM19825)

## TEMPLE GROUP OF COMPANIES

**Temple Group Of Companies**, 111 Pitshanger Lane, London, **London (Greater)**, W5 1RH, ENG.
**(T)** 020 8991 2199
Speciality: Chiropodists (Podiatrists).
[S] (**Ref:**HM19826)

## TEMPLE, BARRIE G

**Barrie G Temple**, 17 Farringdon Rd, North Shields, **Tyne and Wear**, NE30 3ER, ENG.
**(T)** 01912 528393 **(F)** 01912 666767
Speciality: Chiropodists (Podiatrists).
● **Owner** Mr B Temple
[S] (**Ref:**HM19827)

## TEMPLE, JACK

**Jack Temple Healing & Dowsing Academy**, Lower Pyrford Rd, Woking, **Surrey**, GU22 8UQ, ENG.
**(T)** 01932 342429 **(F)** 01932 400300
Speciality: Complementary Medicines & Therapy.
● **Owner** Mr J Temple
[M] (**Ref:**HM19828)

## TEMPLE, ROSIE

**Rosie Temple**, 39 Welley Rd, Wraysbury, Staines, **Surrey**, TW19 5DW, ENG.
**(T)** 01784 483634
Speciality: Acupuncture.
● **Owner** Ms R Temple
[O] (**Ref:**HM19829)

## TEMPLEMAN, C

**C Templeman**, 13 St Andrews Sq, Surbiton, **Surrey**, KT6 4EA, ENG.
**(T)** 020 8399 0247
Speciality: Hypnosis.
● **Owner** Miss C Templeman
[B] (**Ref:**HM19830)

## TEMPLEMAN, ROWENA

**Rowena Templeman**, Balnakeil, Bryants Bottom Rd, Great Missenden, **Buckinghamshire**, HP16 9RN, ENG.
**(T)** 01494 488430
Speciality: Reflexology.
[S] [T] (**Ref:**HM19831)

## TEMPLETON, ISOBEL

**Isobel Templeton**, 3 Sunny Bank Gr, Mirfield, **Yorkshire (West)**, WF14 0PF, ENG.
**(T)** 01924 494556
Speciality: Chiropodists (Podiatrists).
[S] (**Ref:**HM19832)

## TEMPLEWOOD CLINIC

**Templewood Clinic**, Church Rd, Iver, **Buckinghamshire**, SL0 0RA, ENG.
**(T)** 01753 630871
Speciality: Osteopathy.
● **Owner** Mr S Butcher
[P] [S] [T] (**Ref:**HM19833)

## TENG, X C

**X C Teng**, 43 Rectory Rd, Salisbury, **Wiltshire**, SP2 7SD, ENG.
**(T)** 01722 410980
Speciality: Acupuncture.
[O] (**Ref:**HM19834)

## TENGER, ZOE

**Zoe Tenger**, 24 St. Marys Way, Guildford, **Surrey**, GU2 8JY, ENG.
**(T)** 01483 828326
Speciality: Homeopathy.
● **Owner** Mr Z Tenger
[M] (**Ref:**HM19835)

## TENGER, ZOE

**Zoe Tenger**, 231 Stoughton Rd, Guildford, **Surrey**, GU2 6PG, ENG.
**(T)** 01483 828326
Speciality: Homeopathy.
[M] (**Ref:**HM19836)

## TENNANT, R C

**R C Tennant**, 98 Union St, Oldham, **Lancashire**, OL1 1DU, ENG.
**(T)** 01616 521853
Speciality: Chiropodists (Podiatrists).
● **Owner** Mr R Tennant
[S] (**Ref:**HM19837)

## TENTERDEN HOM PRACTICE

**Tenterden Homoeopathic Practice (The)**, 30 High St, Tenterden, **Kent**, TN30 6AR, ENG.
**(T)** 01580 766141
Speciality: Homeopathy.
● **Senior Partner** Mr C Griffiths
[M] (**Ref:**HM19838)

## TENYWA, S

**S Tenywa**, Unit 33 The Shopping Hall, Myrtle Rd, London, **London (Greater)**, E6 1HY, ENG.
**(T)** 020 8586 9542
Speciality: Chiropodists (Podiatrists).
● **Owner** Miss S Tenywa
[S] (**Ref:**HM19839)

## TERENCE, ANTHONY

**Terence Anthony**, 28 Grayling Drive, Liverpool, **Merseyside**, L12 0AT, ENG.
**(T)** 01512 834616
Speciality: Reflexology.
● **Owner** Mr T Anthony
[S] [T] (**Ref:**HM19840)

## TERESA'S INSPIRING LIVING

**Teresa's Inspiring Living**, 8 Main St, Raheny, **County Dublin**, IRE.
**(T)** 01832 9464
Speciality: Healing.
[B] (**Ref:**HM19841)

## TERRACE OSTEOPATHIC SURGERY

**Terrace Osteopathic Surgery (The)**, 14 St Michaels Trce, London, **London (Greater)**, N22 7SJ, ENG.
**(T)** 020 8889 1610 **(F)** 020 8889 1610
Speciality: Osteopathy.
● **Owner** Mr W McKone
[P] [S] [T] (**Ref:**HM19842)

## TERRACE THRPY PSYCHO/NTRL HLTH

**Terrace Therapy Psycho & Natural Health Centre (The)**, The Terrace, 35 Staplegrove Rd, Taunton, **Somerset**, TA1 1DG, ENG.
**(T)** 01823 338968
Speciality: Acupuncture, Alexander Technique, Aromatherapy, Counselling, Cranio-Sacral Therapy, Herbal Medicine, Homeopathy, Meditation, Nutritional Therapy, Psychotherapy, Reflexology, Spinal Touch Therapy. ✔
● **Aromatherapist** Ms S Abrahams
● **Psychotherapist** Mr J Witt **Q:** UKCP (Reg).
● **Acupuncturist/Chinese Herbalist** Ms A Courtney **Q:** BA (Hons), MBAcC.
● **Counsellor/Psychotherapist/Gestalt Therapist** Mr D Kalisch **M:** AHPP, BACP.
● **Psychotherapist** Ms J Gotto **Q:** UKCP (Reg).
● **Cranio-Sacral Therapist** Ms C Zeal
● **Manager** Ms R Gosling
● **Homeopath/Spinal Touch Therapist** Ms J Lewis **Q:** LCH, RSHom.
● **Allergy Therapist/Herbalist/Nutritional Therapist** Ms A Stobart **Q:** BSc (Hons), Dip.Herb.Med, MA, MNIMH.
● **Teacher of the Alexander Technique** Ms T Hemmingway **Q:** MSTAT.
● **Meditation Therapist** Ms H Trump

● **Family Lawyer and Mediator** Mr J Loram
● **Homeopath** Ms L Furzer **Q:** RSHom.
C Yrs. Est.: 8 (**Ref:**HM19843)

## TERRELL, R G
**R G Terrell**, 10 The Drive, Beckenham, **Kent**, BR3 1EQ, **ENG**.
(T) 020 8650 4737
Speciality: Chiropodists (Podiatrists).
● **Owner** Mr R Terrell
S (**Ref:**HM19844)

## TERRY ANNE
**Teresa Anne Scholes**, 20 Corner Cl, Wigginton, York, **Yorkshire (North)**, YO32 2QB, **ENG**.
(T) 01904 750880
Speciality: Bates Method, Cognitive Therapy, Complementary Therapy, Gestalt Therapy, Group Therapy, Healer, Healing Therapy, Hypnosis, Hypnotherapy, Neuro-Linguistic Program, Psychotherapy, Stress Therapy, Visualisation Therapy, Ming (NLP). ✔
● **Hypnotherapist** Ms T Scholes **Q:** C.Hyp, CMH, NLP. **M:** UKGHE.
H Yrs. Est.: 2 (**Ref:**HM19845)

## TERRY NEWSOME PHYSIOTHERAPIST
**Terry Newsome Physiotherapist**, 162 Cotterells, Hemel Hempstead, **Hertfordshire**, HP1 1JW, **ENG**.
(T) 01442 249429
Speciality: Physiotherapy.
P S T (**Ref:**HM19846)

## TERRY, EVA
**Eva Terry**, 28 Bringhurst, Orton Goldhay, Peterborough, **Cambridgeshire**, PE2 5RS, **ENG**.
(T) 01733 238577
Speciality: Aromatherapy.
● **Owner** Mrs E Terry
M O (**Ref:**HM19847)

## TERRY, FIONA
**Fiona Terry**, Trevaylor, Hightown Hill, Ringwood, **Hampshire**, BH24 3HG, **ENG**.
(T) 01425 476338
Speciality: Osteopathy.
P S T (**Ref:**HM19848)

## TERRY, LESLEY ANN
**Lesley Ann Terry**, 2 St Annes School House, Crown Pl, Woodbridge, **Suffolk**, IP12 1BU, **ENG**.
(T) 01394 386942 (F) 01394 380943
Speciality: Aromatherapy.
● **Owner** Mrs L Terry
M O (**Ref:**HM19849)

## TERYLENA REFLEXOLOGY
**Terylena Reflexology**, 1 Woodville Rd, Warwick, **Warwickshire**, CV34 5BS, **ENG**.
(T) 01926 401438
Speciality: Reflexology.
● **Owner** Miss A Slinn
S T (**Ref:**HM19850)

## TEST AGENCY
**Test Agency Ltd (The)**, Cray House, Harpsden Woods, Harpsden, Henley-on-Thames, **Oxfordshire**, RG9 4AE, **ENG**.
(T) 01491 413413 (F) 01491 572249
Speciality: Psychology.
● **Managing Director** Mr G Morgan
B (**Ref:**HM19851)

## TETLEY, M R M
**M R M Tetley**, 27 Cunningham Hill Rd, St. Albans, **Hertfordshire**, AL1 5BX, **ENG**.
(T) 01727 854924
Speciality: Physiotherapy.
P S T (**Ref:**HM19852)

## TETTENHALL CHIROPODY PRACTICE
**Tettenhall Chiropody Practice**, 77 Mill Lane, Tettenhall Wood, Wolverhampton, **Midlands (West)**, WV6 8HE, **ENG**.
(T) 01902 746642
Speciality: Chiropodists (Podiatrists).
S (**Ref:**HM19853)

## TEWKESBURY OSTEOPATHY
**Tewkesbury Osteopathy & Acupuncture Clinic**, 16 East St, Tewkesbury, **Gloucestershire**, GL20 5NR, **ENG**.
(T) 01684 850145
Speciality: Osteopathy.
P S T (**Ref:**HM19854)

## TEWKESBURY, NIGEL
**Nigel Tewkesbury**, 7 City Business Centre, Hyde St, Winchester, **Hampshire**, SO23 7TA, **ENG**.
(T) 01962 865994
Speciality: Chiropodists (Podiatrists).
● **Owner** Mrs L Green
S (**Ref:**HM19855)

## TEWKESBURY, NIGEL F
**Nigel F Tewkesbury**, The Montagu Clinic, Clay St, London, **London (Greater)**, W1H 3FS, **ENG**.
(T) 020 7935 4315
Speciality: Chiropodists (Podiatrists).
S (**Ref:**HM19856)

## THACKER, VRINDA
**Vrinda Thacker**, 161 Ilford Lane, Ilford, **Essex**, IG1 2RR, **ENG**.
(T) 020 8478 1050
Speciality: Homeopathy.
● **Owner** Dr V Thacker
M (**Ref:**HM19857)

## THACKERAY, A J
**A J Thackeray**, 8 Grassmoor Fold, Honley, Huddersfield, **Yorkshire (West)**, HD7 2DL, **ENG**.
(T) 01484 664159
Speciality: Chiropodists (Podiatrists).
● **Owner** Mr A Thackery
S (**Ref:**HM19858)

## THACKWAY, FRANCES
**Frances Thackway**, 56 Alum Chine Rd, Bournemouth, **Dorset**, BH4 8DZ, **ENG**.
(T) 01202 769976
Speciality: Hypnotherapy.
B (**Ref:**HM19859)

## THAI ROSE
**Thai Rose**, 58 Paddington St, London, **London (Greater)**, W1M 3RR, **ENG**.
(T) 020 7935 2117
Speciality: Complementary Medicines & Therapy.
● **Owner** Mr E King
C M (**Ref:**HM19860)

## THAI SIAM
**Thai Siam**, 40 Kingsley Park Trce, Northampton, **Northamptonshire**, NN2 7HH, **ENG**.
(T) 01604 721306
Speciality: Reflexology.
● **Owner** Mr S Tompkins
S T (**Ref:**HM19861)

## THAILANDIA-FLOATATION ROOM
**Thailandia-Floatation Room**, 222 Munster Rd, London, **London (Greater)**, SW6 7AY, **ENG**.
(T) 020 7610 2003
Speciality: Complementary Medicines & Therapy.
● **Owner** Mr J Reiss
C Yrs. Est.: 6 (**Ref:**HM19862)

## THAKERAR, J N
**J N Thakerar**, Suite 210 Signal House, Lyon Rd, Harrow, **London (Greater)**, HA1 2AG, **ENG**.
(T) 020 8427 0361
Speciality: Psychology.
● **Owner** Dr J Thakerar
B (**Ref:**HM19863)

## THAME THERAPY CLINIC
**Thame Therapy Clinic**, 23 Upper High St, Thame, **Oxfordshire**, OX9 3EX, **ENG**.
(T) 01844 215555
Speciality: Osteopathy.
● **Partner** Mrs L Curwen
P S T (**Ref:**HM19864)

## THAMES VALLEY CLINIC
**Thames Valley Clinic**, 1 Derby Rd, Caversham, Reading, **Berkshire**, RG4 5HE, **ENG**.
(T) 01189 464626
Speciality: Physiotherapy.
P S T (**Ref:**HM19865)

## THAMS, JUNE
**June Thams**, 2 Boyn Valley Rd, Maidenhead, **Berkshire**, SL6 4ED, **ENG**.
(T) 01628 672005
Speciality: Psychotherapy.
● **Owner** Mr F Dashwood-Evans
B (**Ref:**HM19866)

## THATCHAM CHIROPRACTIC CLINIC
**Thatcham Chiropractic Clinic**, Bath Rd, Thatcham, **Berkshire**, RG18 3HD, **ENG**.
(T) 01635 868691
(W) www.thatchamchiropractic.co.uk
Speciality: Chiropractic. ✔
● **Owner** Dr M Holmes **Q:** B.App.Sc, BSc (Chiro), DC. **M:** BCA, GCC.
P Yrs. Est.: 5 (**Ref:**HM19867)

## THE SANDYCOVE CLINIC
**The Sandycove Clinic**, 50 Sandycove Rd, Dun Laoighre Co, Dublin, **County Dublin**, **IRE**.
(T) 01280 3505
Speciality: Acupuncture.
● **Acupuncturist** Nicholas Power
O (**Ref:**HM19868)

## THEAKSTON, G
**G Theakston**, 330 Cottingham Rd, Hull, **Humberside (North)**, HU6 8QE, **ENG**.
(T) 01482 442448
Speciality: Chiropodists (Podiatrists).
● **Owner** Mr G Theakston
S (**Ref:**HM19869)

## THENUWARA, C D
**C D Thenuwara**, 14 Blendon Rd, Bexley, **Kent**, DA5 1BW, **ENG**.
(T) 020 8304 4140 (F) 020 8303 6151
Speciality: Acupuncture.
● **Owner** Dr C Thenuwara
O (**Ref:**HM19870)

## THENUWARA, CLARENCE (DR)
**Dr Clarence Thenuwara**, Greenhaven Surgery, 118 Restons Cres, London, **London (Greater)**, SE9 2JJ, **ENG**.
(T) 020 8859 7941
Speciality: Acupuncture.
O (**Ref:**HM19871)

## THEODORA, M M E
**M M E Theodora**, Flat 153, Ashley Gardens, Thirleby Rd, London, **London (Greater)**, SW1P 1HW, **ENG**.
(T) 020 7701 1660
Speciality: Clairvoyants & Palmists.
B (**Ref:**HM19872)

## THEOPHILUS, L E
**L E Theophilus**, 10 Oakland Rd, Mumbles, Swansea, SA3 4AQ, **WAL**.
(T) 01792 366900
Speciality: Physiotherapy.
P S T (**Ref:**HM19873)

## THERA SPORT
**Thera Sport**, Thornes Park Athletic Stadium, Horbury Rd, Wakefield, **Yorkshire (West)**, WF2 8QE, **ENG**.
(T) 01924 364474 (F) 01924 364474
Speciality: Physiotherapy.
● **Owner** Mr G Slade
P S T (**Ref:**HM19874)

## THERABEUTIC
**Therabeutic**, 165 Burnley Rd, Padiham, Burnley, **Lancashire**, BB12 8BA, **ENG**.
(T) 01282 777997
Speciality: Complementary Medicines & Therapy.
● **Owner** Mrs J Finlayson
M (**Ref:**HM19875)

## THERA-CARE
**Thera-Care Ltd**, Manor Farm, Wadswick, Box, Corsham, **Wiltshire**, SN13 8JB, **ENG**.
(T) 01225 810900 (F) 01225 810307
Speciality: Complementary Medicines & Therapy.
● **Managing Director** Mr B Jackson
C M (**Ref:**HM19876)

## THERA-PAD
**Thera-Pad**, 70 Brunswick St, Stockton-On-Tees, **Cleveland**, TS18 1DW, **ENG**.
(T) 01642 864001
Speciality: Complementary Medicines & Therapy.


Key continued: **Yrs.Est:** Years Established **Q:** Qualifications **M:** Professional Membership ✔ Indemnity Insurance Accept Credit Cards

● **Owner** Mrs D Krumm
[C] [M] (**Ref:**HM19877)

**THERAPEIA HYPNOTHERAPY**

**Therapeia Hypnotherapy**, 120 Avonmead, Swindon, **Wiltshire**, SN2 3PS, ENG.
(T) 01793 706862
Speciality: Complementary Medicines & Therapy.
● **Owner** Mr M Dee
[C] [M] (**Ref:**HM19878)

**THERAPEUTIC ANTIBODIES UK**

**Therapeutic Antibodies UK Ltd**, Blaenwaun, Ffostrasol, Llandysul, **Carmarthenshire**, SA44 5JT, WAL.
(T) 01239 851127 (F) 01239 858800
Speciality: Complementary Medicines & Therapy.
[M] (**Ref:**HM19879)

**THERAPEUTIC MASSAGE**

**Therapeutic Massage**, Great North Rd, Hatfield, **Hertfordshire**, AL9 5LR, ENG.
(T) 01707 269047
Speciality: Complementary Medicines & Therapy.
● **Owner** Mrs J Hentall
[C] [M] (**Ref:**HM19880)

**THERAPEUTIC MASSAGE**

**Therapeutic Massage**, 5 Brunton St, North Shields, **Tyne and Wear**, NE29 6JL, ENG.
(T) 01912 581518
Speciality: Osteopathy.
[P] [S] [T] (**Ref:**HM19881)

**THERAPEUTIC MASSAGE**

**Therapeutic Massage**, 45 St Johns Rd, Clacton-On-Sea, **Essex**, CO15 4BT, ENG.
(T) 01255 474331
Speciality: Massage (Therapeutic).
● **Owner** Mrs T Deaming
[M] (**Ref:**HM19882)

**THERAPEUTIC MASSAGE**

**Therapeutic Massage**, 31 Milton Rd, Ware, **Hertfordshire**, SG12 0QA, ENG.
(T) 01920 485206
Speciality: Complementary Medicines & Therapy.
[C] [M] (**Ref:**HM19883)

**THERAPEUTIC MASSAGE**

**Therapeutic Massage**, 83 Roberts Ride, Hazlemere, High Wycombe, **Buckinghamshire**, HP15 7AN, ENG.
(T) 01494 716959
Speciality: Massage (Therapeutic).
[M] (**Ref:**HM19884)

**THERAPEUTIC SOUND AND MOVEMENT**

**Therapeutic Sound and Movement Workshops**, 14 Denmark Rd, Ealing, London, **London (Greater)**, W13 8RG, ENG.
(T) 020 8579 9664
Speciality: Complementary Medicines & Therapy.
● **Sound Therapist** Mr J D'angelo
[M] (**Ref:**HM19885)

**THERAPEUTICS**

**Therapeutics**, 44 Bromham Rd, Bedford, **Bedfordshire**, MK40 2QD, ENG.
(T) 01234 212788
Speciality: Complementary Medicines & Therapy.
● **Owner** Ms V Manners
[C] [M] (**Ref:**HM19886)

**THERAPEUTICS**

**Therapeutics (Southampton) Ltd**, Trojans Sports Clb Stoneham Lane, Eastleigh, **Hampshire**, SO50 9HT, ENG.
(T) 023 8065 3707
Speciality: Physiotherapy.
● **Sole Director**
Kim Louise Chesterfield
[P] [S] [T] (**Ref:**HM19887)

**THERAPEUTICS**

**Therapeutics Health and Skin Care**, Radisson Sas, St. Helens Hotel, Shillorgan Rd, Dublin, **County Dublin**, IRE.
(T) 00353 12188198
Speciality: Aromatherapy, Massage (Therapeutic), Reflexology. [✔]
● **Owner** Ms S Rooney
● **Senior Therapist** Ms K Doyle
● **Therapist** Ms C Duffy
[T] Yrs. Est.: 2 (**Ref:**HM19888)

**THERAPUTIC MASSAGE**

**Theraputic Massage**, 7c Nicol St, Kirkcaldy, **Fife**, KY1 1NY, SCO.
(T) 01592 640009
Speciality: Aromatherapy.
● **Owner** Mrs D Wigley
[M] [O] (**Ref:**HM19889)

**THERAPY 21**

**Therapy 21**, 120 Greasby Rd, Greasby, **Merseyside**, ENG.
Speciality: Absent Healing, Acupressure, Aromatherapy, Complementary Therapy, Healer, Healing Therapy, Holistic Healing, Massage (Therapeutic), Reiki, Shiatsu, Stress Therapy, Tera-Mai, Touch Therapy, Stress Management, Coping Strategies. [✔]
● **Therapist** Mr D Bell Q: ITEC, Reiki 1, Reiki 2. M: AOC, GCP.
[T] Yrs. Est.: 1 (**Ref:**HM19890)

**THERAPY BREAK**

**Therapy Break**, Sheepfoot Lane, Manchester, **Manchester (Greater)**, M25, ENG.
Speciality: Acupuncture, Alexander Technique, Aromatherapy, Cranio-Sacral Therapy, Healing Therapy, Herbal Medicine, Homeopathy, Hypnosis, Indian Head Massage, Kinesiology, Massage (Therapeutic), McTimoney Chiropractic, Nutritional Therapy, Physiotherapy, Reflexology, Reiki, Remedial Massage, Spiritual Healing, Stress Therapy, Sports Therapy/Personal Fitness Training.
[C] (**Ref:**HM19891)

**THERAPY CENTRE**

**Therapy Centre (The)**, 29 Winnington Lane, Northwich, **Cheshire**, CW8 4DE, ENG.
(T) 01606 75957
Speciality: Complementary Medicines & Therapy.
[C] [M] (**Ref:**HM19892)

**THERAPY CENTRE**

**Therapy Centre (The)**, 2 Brooklyn Rd, Cheadle, **Cheshire**, SK8 1BS, ENG.
(T) 01614 286655
Speciality: Hypnosis.
[B] (**Ref:**HM19893)

**THERAPY CENTRE**

**Therapy Centre (The)**, 362-364 Goldington Rd, Bedford, **Bedfordshire**, MK41 9NT, ENG.
(T) 01234 351411 (F) 01234 273694
Speciality: Alexander Technique, Chiropody, Dietician, Physiotherapy. [✔]
● **Owner** Mrs K Duffell
● **Physiotherapist** Mr P Duffell Q: MCSP, MSc, SRP. M: CSP.
[S] Yrs. Est.: 10 (**Ref:**HM19894)

**THERAPY CENTRE**

**Therapy Centre (The)**, 3 Springfield Rd, Bishopbriggs, Glasgow, **Glasgow (City of)**, G64 1PD, SCO.
(T) 01417 624162
Speciality: Osteopathy.
● **Teacher** Ms M Hall
[P] [S] [T] (**Ref:**HM19895)

**THERAPY CENTRE**

**Therapy Centre (The)**, Northgate, Cleckheaton, **Yorkshire (West)**, BD19 3HZ, ENG.
(T) 01274 851705
Speciality: Complementary Medicines & Therapy.
● **Owner** Mrs P Wood
[M] (**Ref:**HM19896)

**THERAPY CENTRE**

**Therapy Centre (The)**, 312A Antrim Rd, Newtownabbey, **County Antrim**, BT36 5EG, NIR.
(T) 028 9086 5986
Speciality: Complementary Medicines & Therapy.
● **Partner** Mr K Gannon
[C] [M] (**Ref:**HM19897)

**THERAPY CENTRE**

**Natural Therapy Centre (The)**, 190 Warwick Rd, Carlisle, **Cumbria**, CA1 1LH, ENG.
(T) 01228 515078
(E) fcarson@nildram.co.uk
Speciality: Acupressure, Acupuncture, Alexander Technique, Auto Suggestion, Aversion Therapy, Cranial Osteopathy, Holistic Healing, Hypnosis, Hypnotherapy, Manipulation, Osteopathy. [✔]
● **Acupuncturist** Ms J Bischoff Q: Dip.Ac. M: BAcC.
● **Teacher of the Alexander Technique** Mr M Leighton Q: MSTAT. M: STAT.
● **Acupuncturist/Osteopath** Mr F Carson Q: DO, Lic.Ac. M: BAcC, GOsC.
● **Hypnotherapist/Hypno-Analyst** Ms A McAllister Q: Dip.Hyp, Dip.Psych, MHA. M: HA.
[C] Yrs. Est.: 13 (**Ref:**HM19898)

**THERAPY CLINIC**

**Therapy Clinic (The)**, 281 Roundhay Rd, Leeds, **Yorkshire (West)**, LS8 4HS, ENG.
(T) 01132 481633
Speciality: Complementary Medicines & Therapy.
● **Owner** Mrs B Nelson
[M] (**Ref:**HM19899)

**THERAPY CLINIC**

**Therapy Clinic (The)**, 94 Snowsfields, London, **London (Greater)**, SE1 3SS, ENG.
(T) 020 7403 2571 (F) 020 7403 8272
Speciality: Complementary Medicines & Therapy.
● **Owner** Mr K Harris
[C] [M] (**Ref:**HM19900)

**THERAPY CLINIC**

**Therapy Clinic (The)**, 3 Glebe Cl, Uxbridge, **London (Greater)**, UB10 8PJ, ENG.
(T) 01895 639213
Speciality: Hypnotherapy.
● **Employee** Mrs M Harrod
[B] (**Ref:**HM19901)

**THERAPY CLINIC**

**Therapy Clinic**, 67 Cheltenham Rd, Cirencester, **Gloucestershire**, GL7 2JB, ENG.
(T) 01285 659214
Speciality: Complementary Medicines & Therapy.
● **Owner** Mrs F Laxton
[M] (**Ref:**HM19902)

**THERAPY HEALTH/EDUCATION CTRE**

**Therapy Health & Education Centres**, 33 The Parade, Roath, Cardiff, **Glamorgan (Vale of)**, CF24 3AD, WAL.
(T) 029 2048 8121
Speciality: Physiotherapy.
[P] [S] [T] (**Ref:**HM19903)

**THERAPY LIVERPOOL**

**Therapy Liverpool**, 51a Rodney St, Liverpool, **Merseyside**, L1 9ER, ENG.
(T) 01512 801712
Speciality: Hypnotherapy.
[B] (**Ref:**HM19904)

**THERAPY OF LIFE CLINIC**

**The Therapy Of Life Clinic**, 81 Springhill Rd, Garrowhill, Baillieston, Glasgow, **Glasgow (City of)**, G69 6PP, SCO.
(T) 01415 734228
(E) pwilkie@ntlworld.com
Speciality: Acupuncture, Aromatherapy.
● **Aromatherapist/Auricular Acupuncturist** Mr P Wilkie Q: AOC, NADA. M: AOC, HAF, NADA.
[T] (**Ref:**HM19905)

**THERAPY ON HAND**

**Therapy On Hand**, 1040 Uxbridge Rd, Hayes, **London (Greater)**, UB4 0RJ, ENG.
(T) 020 8813 6685 (F) 020 8569 0830
Speciality: Complementary Medicines & Therapy.
● **Partner** Mr Z Sethna
[M] (**Ref:**HM19906)



Key: [B] Mind-Body Medicine [C] Complementary Medicine [H] Self Help Treatment [M] Medicinal Therapy [O] Oriental Medicine [P] Postural Therapy [S] Manipulative Structural Therapy [T] Touch Therapy

**THERAPY PARTNERSHIP**

**Therapy Partnership**, 60 Bloomsbury St, London, **London (Greater)**, WC1B 3QT, ENG.
(T) 020 7222 6800
Speciality: Hypnotherapy.
● **Partner** Mr W Doult
B (Ref:HM19907)

**THERAPY PLACE**

**Therapy Place (The)**, High St, Beckenham, **Kent**, BR3 1AY, ENG.
(T) 020 8658 9958
Speciality: Psychotherapy.
● **Owner** Ms S Stephens
B (Ref:HM19908)

**THERAPY ROOM**

**Therapy Room (The)**, Chelsea Sports Centre, Chelsea Manor St, London, **London (Greater)**, SW3 5PL, ENG.
(T) 020 7731 3876
Speciality: Osteopathy.
C P S T (Ref:HM19909)

**THERAPY ROOMS**

**Therapy Rooms (The)**, 68-70 Chalk Farm Rd, London, **London (Greater)**, NW1 8AN, ENG.
(T) 020 7267 0110 (F) 020 7267 0110
Speciality: Complementary Medicines & Therapy.
● **Director** Miss A Rodriguez
C M (Ref:HM19910)

**THERAPY TRAINING COLLEGE**

**David Lesser T/A Therapy Training College**, 8 & 10 Balaclava Rd, Kingsheath, Birmingham, **Midlands (West)**, B14 7SG, ENG.
(T) 01214 445435
(E) hypnosis@lesserian.co.uk
(W) www.lesserian.co.uk
Speciality: Hypnosis, Hypnotherapy, Stress Therapy. ✔ CREDIT
● **Owner** Mr D Lesser Q: Dip.Hyp. M: AQCH.
B Yrs. Est.: 31 (Ref:HM19911)

**THERAPYCARE**

**Therapycare Ltd**, 16 The Pavilion, Vaughan Rd, Torquay, **Devon**, TQ2 5EQ, ENG.
(T) 01803 215454 (F) 01803 215454
Speciality: Physiotherapy.
● **Joint Director**
Clinton Charles Thrippleton
P S T (Ref:HM19912)

**THERAPYWORKS**

**Therapyworks**, 9a Pound Field, Llantwit Major, **Glamorgan (Vale of)**, CF61 1DL, WAL.
(T) 01446 794166
Speciality: Physiotherapy.
● **Partner** Ms H Hyett
P S T (Ref:HM19913)

**THERESA MAWSON**

**Theresa Mawson**, 4 Winchester Gdns, Canterbury, **Kent**, CT1 3NA, ENG.
(T) 01227 761744
Speciality: Homeopathy.
● **Owner** Mrs T Mawson
M (Ref:HM19914)

**THEW, CAROLYN**

**Carolyn Thew**, 5 Vauxhall Avenue, Herne Bay, **Kent**, CT6 8AQ, ENG.
(T) 01227 369575
Speciality: Aromatherapy.
M O (Ref:HM19915)

**THEW, NIN**

**Nin Thew**, 7 Montpelier Court, Montpelier Hill, Dublin, **County Dublin**, IRE.
(T) 01679 9265
Speciality: Acupuncture, Cupping, Life Style Coaching, Moxibustion.
● **Traditional Practitioner of Chinese Medicine**
Nin Thew
O Yrs. Est.: 4 (Ref:HM19916)

**THICK, DENISE**

**Denise Thick**, 337-339 Norwich Rd, Ipswich, **Suffolk**, IP1 4BN, ENG.
(T) 01473 464300
Speciality: Chiropodists (Podiatrists).
S (Ref:HM19917)

**THIEBAUD, M F**

**M F Thiebaud**, 203 Golders Green Rd, London, **London (Greater)**, NW11 9BY, ENG.
(T) 020 8458 6330
Speciality: Osteopathy.
● **Owner** Mr M Thiebaud
P S T (Ref:HM19918)

**THIEBAUD, M F**

**M F Thiebaud**, 62 Clarence Rd, Stony Stratford, Milton Keynes, **Buckinghamshire**, MK11 1JD, ENG.
(T) 01908 568175
Speciality: Osteopathy.
P S T (Ref:HM19919)

**THINK NATURAL COM**

**Think Natural Com**, 7 Riverpark, Billet Lane, Berkhamsted, **Hertfordshire**, HP4 1HL, ENG.
(T) 01442 299200 (F) 01442 866977
Speciality: Complementary Medicines & Therapy.
● **Office Manager** Ms S West
M (Ref:HM19920)

**THIRSK CHIROPRACTIC CLINIC**

**Thirsk Chiropractic Clinic**, Carlton Rd, Carlton Miniott, Thirsk, **Yorkshire (North)**, YO7 4NJ, ENG.
(T) 01845 522242 (F) 01845 522189
Speciality: Chiropractic.
● **Principal** Mr R Skipping
P S T (Ref:HM19921)

**THOEYE, JAN**

**Jan Thoeye**, Harrow Health Care Centre, 84-88 Pinner Rd, Harrow, **London (Greater)**, HA1 4HZ, ENG.
(T) 020 8861 1221
Speciality: Acupuncture.
O (Ref:HM19922)

**THOMA, ANDREW**

**Andrew Thoma**, 143 Forest Rd, Liss, **Hampshire**, GU33 7BU, ENG.
(T) 01730 893740
Speciality: Chiropractic. ✔
● **Chiropractor** Mr A Thoma Q: DC, RGN, RMN. M: MCA.
S Yrs. Est.: 10 (Ref:HM19923)

**THOMAS COMPLEMENTARY CLINIC**

**Thomas Complementary Clinic (The)**, Rear Of 61 High St, Ashford, **Kent**, TN24 8SG, ENG.
(T) 01233 334025
Speciality: Complementary Medicines & Therapy.
● **Owner** Mr B Thomas
M (Ref:HM19924)

**THOMAS CONLIN**

**Thomas Conlin**, 5 Morland Drive, Rochester, **Kent**, ME2 3LW, ENG.
(T) 01634 296949 (F) 01634 296949
Speciality: Chiropodists (Podiatrists).
● **Owner** Mr T Conlin
S (Ref:HM19925)

**THOMAS COXON ASSOCIATES**

**Coxon - Thomas Associates**, 26 Mere Rd, Wigston Magna, **Leicestershire**, LE18 3RJ, ENG.
(T) 00162 836777
Speciality: Feng Shui.
M (Ref:HM19926)

**THOMAS HEWETSON**

**Thomas Hewetson**, Rowdell Rd, Northolt, **London (Greater)**, UB5 6AG, ENG.
(T) 020 8841 5611
Speciality: Osteopathy.
P S T (Ref:HM19927)

**THOMAS HEWETSON**

**Thomas Hewetson**, Dragons Health Club, Rowdell Rd, Ruislip, **London (Greater)**, HA4 6QW, ENG.
(T) 020 8842 2003
Speciality: Osteopathy.
P S T (Ref:HM19928)

**THOMAS, AHERNE**

**Thomas Aherne ADHP MICHP**, Co, **County Kildare**, IRE.
(T) 04586 8751
(W) www.hypnosiseire.com
Speciality: Counselling.
B H (Ref:HM19929)

**THOMAS, ALAN**

**Alan Thomas**, 32 Cotswold Cl, Uxbridge, **London (Greater)**, UB8 2NA, ENG.
(T) 01895 237881 (F) 01895 237881
Speciality: Osteopathy.
● **Owner** Mr A Thomas
P S T (Ref:HM19930)

**THOMAS, ANGELA**

**Angela Thomas**, Spar Dale, 11 Serocold Avenue, Neath, **Glamorgan (Vale of)**, SA10 6ED, WAL.
(T) 01792 815733
Speciality: Reflexology.
S T (Ref:HM19931)

**THOMAS, ANNE**

**Anne Thomas**, Barn Cottage, Trehunist, Liskeard, **Cornwall**, PL14 3SD, ENG.
(T) 01579 340140
Speciality: Reflexology.
S T (Ref:HM19932)

**THOMAS, BEVERLEY**

**Beverley Thomas**, 16 Adam Avenue, Great Sutton, Ellesmere Port, **Cheshire**, CH66 4LF, ENG.
(T) 01512 017282
Speciality: Chiropody. ✔
● **Chiropodist** Ms B Thomas Q: MBChA. M: SSCh.
M Yrs. Est.: 4 (Ref:HM19933)

**THOMAS, CARL**

**Carl Thomas**, Ruxox House, Maulden Rd, Flitwick, Bedford, **Bedfordshire**, MK45 5BN, ENG.
(T) 01525 715416
Speciality: Hypnosis.
B (Ref:HM19934)

**THOMAS, CHRIS**

**Chris Thomas**, 8 The Lodge, Western Rd, Crediton, **Devon**, EX17 3RD, ENG.
(T) 01363 776300 (F) 01363 776300
Speciality: Hypnosis.
● **Owner** Mr C Thomas
B (Ref:HM19935)

**THOMAS, D**

**D Thomas**, 115 Cromwell Lane, Coventry, **Midlands (West)**, CV4 8AQ, ENG.
(T) 024 7642 1731
Speciality: Physiotherapy.
● **Owner** Mr D Thomas
P S T (Ref:HM19936)

**THOMAS, D E**

**D E Thomas**, Silverdale, Lower Rd, Forest Row, **Sussex (East)**, RH18 5HE, ENG.
(T) 01342 822802 (F) 01342 824039
Speciality: Chiropractic.
● **Owner** Mr D Thomas
P S T (Ref:HM19937)

**THOMAS, D L C**

**D L C Thomas**, 51 Westerfield Rd, Ipswich, **Suffolk**, IP4 2UU, ENG.
(T) 01473 254555
Speciality: Psychiatry.
● **Owner** Dr D Thomas
B (Ref:HM19938)

**THOMAS, DAVID G**

**David G Thomas**, 21 Splott Rd, Cardiff, **Glamorgan (Vale of)**, CF24 2BU, WAL.
(T) 029 2020 4823
Speciality: Chiropodists (Podiatrists).
S (Ref:HM19939)

**THOMAS, EMLYN**

**Emlyn Thomas**, 26 Ancaster Sq, Llanrwst, **Conwy**, LL26 0LD, WAL.
(T) 01492 642555 (F) 01492 642049
Speciality: Homeopathy.
● **Owner** Mr E Thomas
M (Ref:HM19940)

**THOMAS, G**

**G Thomas**, 244 Withington Rd, Chorlton Cum Hardy, Manchester, **Manchester (Greater)**,



Key continued: Yrs.Est: Years Established Q: Qualifications M: Professional Membership ✔ Indemnity Insurance CREDIT Accept Credit Cards

M21 0YB, **ENG**.
**(T)** 01618 813658
**Speciality:** Chiropodists (Podiatrists).
● **Owner** Mr G Thomas
S (**Ref:**HM19941)

**THOMAS, G A**

**Mrs G A Thomas**, Highover, Udimore, Rye, **Sussex (East)**, TN31 6BG, **ENG**.
**(T)** 01424 882347
**Speciality:** Physiotherapy.
● **Owner** Mrs G Thomas
P S T (**Ref:**HM19942)

**THOMAS, GEOFF**

**Geoff Thomas**, Golden Lodge Healing Centre, 51 Hugon Rd, London, **London (Greater)**, SW6 3ER, **ENG**.
**(T)** 020 7610 6867
**Speciality:** Complementary Medicines & Therapy.
C M (**Ref:**HM19943)

**THOMAS, HELEN**

**Helen Thomas**, 27 Culver Rd, St. Albans, **Hertfordshire**, AL1 4EB, **ENG**.
**(T)** 01727 860737
**Speciality:** Herbal Medicine.
M (**Ref:**HM19944)

**THOMAS, J**

**J Thomas**, All Hallows House, Idol Lane, London, **London (Greater)**, EC3R 5DD, **ENG**.
**(T)** 020 7283 8908
**Speciality:** Chiropractors.
P S T (**Ref:**HM19945)

**THOMAS, J R**

**J R Thomas**, 2 St Philips Rd, Leicester, **Leicestershire**, LE5 5TQ, **ENG**.
**(T)** 01162 738256
**Speciality:** Physiotherapy.
● **Owner** Mr J Thomas
P S T (**Ref:**HM19946)

**THOMAS, JANE**

**Jane Thomas**, Clissold Park Health Centre, 154 Stoke Newington Church St, London, **London (Greater)**, N16 0JU, **ENG**.
**(T)** 020 7249 2990 **(F)** 020 7249 3977
**Speciality:** Reflexology.
● **Director** Mr D Berg
S T (**Ref:**HM19947)

**THOMAS, JANET**

**Janet Thomas**, 2 St. Barnabas Trce, Plymouth, **Devon**, PL1 5NN, **ENG**.
**(T)** 01752 556612
**Speciality:** Reflexology.
S T (**Ref:**HM19948)

**THOMAS, JULIET**

**Juliet Thomas**, Cotebank, Ryehills Rd, Skinburness, Wigton, **Cumbria**, CA7 4QT, **ENG**.
**(T)** 01697 331486
**Speciality:** Chiropractic.
● **Owner** Mrs J Thomas
P S T (**Ref:**HM19949)

**THOMAS, K I**

**K I Thomas**, 75 Abbotswood Gardens, Ilford, **Essex**, IG5 0BH, **ENG**.
**(T)** 020 8594 2450 **(F)** 020 8550 4708
**Speciality:** Physiotherapy.
● **Owner** Mr K Thomas
P S T (**Ref:**HM19950)

**THOMAS, LESLEY**

**Lesley Thomas**, 50A High St, Stourbridge, **Midlands (West)**, DY8 1DE, **ENG**.
**(T)** 01384 834839
**Speciality:** Complementary Medicines & Therapy.
● **Owner** Mrs L Thomas
M (**Ref:**HM19951)

**THOMAS, LYNDA**

**Lynda Thomas**, 10 Cleveland Cl, Ramsbottom, Bury, **Lancashire**, BL0 9FH, **ENG**.
**(T)** 01706 827601
**Speciality:** Reflexology.
S T (**Ref:**HM19952)

**THOMAS, N J**

**N J Thomas**, 42 Lowlands Rd, Pontnewydd, Cwmbran, **Torfaen**, NP44 1RA, **WAL**.
**(T)** 01633 874439
**Speciality:** Chiropodists (Podiatrists).
● **Owner** Mr N Thomas
S (**Ref:**HM19953)

**THOMAS, P (DR)**

**Dr P Thomas**, Reading Clinic, 10 Eldon Rd, Reading, **Berkshire**, RG1 4DH, **ENG**.
**(T)** 01189 502002
**Speciality:** Psychotherapy.
B (**Ref:**HM19954)

**THOMAS, P A**

**P A Thomas**, 51 The Village, Old Warden, Biggleswade, **Bedfordshire**, SG18 9HQ, **ENG**.
**(T)** 01767 627600 **(F)** 01767 627600
**Speciality:** Aromatherapy.
● **Owner** Mrs P Thomas
M O (**Ref:**HM19955)

**THOMAS, S**

**S Thomas**, Meadow Lane, Hartley Wintney, Hook, **Hampshire**, RG27 8RF, **ENG**.
**(T)** 01252 842982
**Speciality:** Clairvoyants & Palmists.
● **Owner** Mrs S Thomas
B (**Ref:**HM19956)

**THOMAS, SUZANNE**

**Suzanne Thomas**, 106 Cheyne Walk, London, **London (Greater)**, SW10 0DG, **ENG**.
**(T)** 020 7352 0914
**Speciality:** Hypnotherapy.
● **Owner** Miss S Thomas
B (**Ref:**HM19957)

**THOMAS, TRUDY**

**Mrs Trudy Thomas**, 68 Lyndale Rd, Yate, Bristol, BS37 4DD, **ENG**.
**(T)** 01454 325429
**Speciality:** Chiropody. ✔
● **Chiropodist** Mrs T Thomas **Q:** MBChA, MSSCh. **M:** B.A.Ch.P.
M **Yrs. Est.:** 4 (**Ref:**HM19958)

**THOMAS, V**

**V Thomas**, 4a Canada Rd, Walmer, Deal, **Kent**, CT14 7DZ, **ENG**.
**(T)** 01304 373007
**Speciality:** Chiropodists (Podiatrists).
● **Partner** Mr W Harrison
S (**Ref:**HM19959)

**THOMASON, M L**

**M L Thomason**, 61 Conway Rd, Taplow, Maidenhead, **Berkshire**, SL6 0LB, **ENG**.
**(T)** 01628 603208
**Speciality:** Chiropodists (Podiatrists).
S (**Ref:**HM19960)

**THOMPSON CHIROPRACTIC**

**Thompson Chiropractic**, Stamford Rd, Duddington, Stamford, **Lincolnshire**, PE9 3QE, **ENG**.
**(T)** 01780 444651 **(F)** 01780 444651
**Speciality:** Chiropractic.
● **Owner** Mr C Thompson
P S T (**Ref:**HM19961)

**THOMPSON DUNN**

**Thompson Dunn**, 34 New Cavendish St, London, **London (Greater)**, W1M 7LH, **ENG**.
**(T)** 020 7486 1199 **(F)** 020 7486 1313
**Speciality:** Psychology.
● **Principal** Mrs P Dunn
B (**Ref:**HM19962)

**THOMPSON, A**

**A Thompson**, 65 Norfolk Rd, Seven Kings, Ilford, **Essex**, IG3 8LJ, **ENG**.
**(T)** 020 8220 1630
**Speciality:** Alexander Technique.
● **Owner** Mrs A Thompson
P S (**Ref:**HM19963)

**THOMPSON, A K**

**A K Thompson**, 45 Field Pl, Naish Estate, New Milton, **Hampshire**, BH25 7RD, **ENG**.
**(T)** 01202 486918
**Speciality:** Chiropodists (Podiatrists).
● **Owner** A K Thompson
S (**Ref:**HM19964)

**THOMPSON, A K**

**A K Thompson**, 53 High St, Lymington, **Hampshire**, SO41 9AH, **ENG**.
**(T)** 01590 672443
**Speciality:** Chiropodists (Podiatrists).
S (**Ref:**HM19965)

**THOMPSON, A P**

**A P Thompson**, 14 Sun St, Lancaster, **Lancashire**, LA1 1EW, **ENG**.
**(T)** 01524 66375
**Speciality:** Chiropodists (Podiatrists).
● **Owner** Mr A Thompson
S (**Ref:**HM19966)

**THOMPSON, ANNE**

**Anne Thompson**, 16 Clayhall Rd, Gosport, **Hampshire**, PO12 2ER, **ENG**.
**(T)** 023 9235 2401
**Speciality:** Chiropodists (Podiatrists).
S (**Ref:**HM19967)

**THOMPSON, ANNE H**

**Anne H Thompson**, 83 Lowther Rd, Bournemouth, **Dorset**, BH8 8NP, **ENG**.
**(T)** 01202 557215
**Speciality:** Chiropractic.
● **Owner** Miss A Thompson
P S T (**Ref:**HM19968)

**THOMPSON, C**

**C Thompson**, Old Tracey, Coronation St, Fairford, **Gloucestershire**, GL7 4HP, **ENG**.
**(T)** 01285 712123
**Speciality:** Physiotherapy.
● **Owner** Mr C Thompson
P S T (**Ref:**HM19969)

**THOMPSON, CAROLINE**

**Caroline Thompson**, Ramsdale Buildings, 15 Ramshill Rd, Scarborough, **Yorkshire (North)**, YO11 2LN, **ENG**.
**(T)** 01723 363947
**Speciality:** Osteopathy.
● **Owner** Mrs C Thompson
P S T (**Ref:**HM19970)

**THOMPSON, CYNTHIA**

**Cynthia Thompson**, Westview Clinic, Newcastle Rd, Blakelow, Nantwich, **Cheshire**, CW5 7ET, **ENG**.
**(T)** 01270 668672
**Speciality:** Osteopathy.
● **Owner** Mrs C Thompson
P S T (**Ref:**HM19971)

**THOMPSON, D**

**D Thompson**, 5 Tempest Avenue, Darfield, Barnsley, **Yorkshire (South)**, S73 9BJ, **ENG**.
**(T)** 01226 752562
**Speciality:** Chiropodists (Podiatrists).
● **Owner** Mr D Thompson
S (**Ref:**HM19972)

**THOMPSON, DARRELL**

**Darrell Thompson**, Trescoe, 17 Studley Avenue, London, **London (Greater)**, E4 9PS, **ENG**.
**(T)** 020 8531 5669
**Speciality:** Reflexology.
S T (**Ref:**HM19973)

**THOMPSON, DOROTHY**

**Dorothy Thompson**, 14 Montagu Mansions, London, **London (Greater)**, W1H 1LD, **ENG**.
**(T)** 020 7486 2366
**Speciality:** Reflexology.
S T (**Ref:**HM19974)

**THOMPSON, E**

**E Thompson**, 1 Kenilworth Rd, Lytham St. Annes, **Lancashire**, FY8 1TZ, **ENG**.
**(T)** 01253 723254 **(F)** 01253 723254
**Speciality:** Chiropodists (Podiatrists).
● **Owner** Mr A Kirk
S (**Ref:**HM19975)

**THOMPSON, EDWARD**

**Edward Thompson**, 41 Hills Rd, Cambridge, **Cambridgeshire**, CB2 1NT, **ENG**.
**(T)** 01223 358206
**Speciality:** Complementary Medicines & Therapy.
● **Owner** Mr E Thompson
C M (**Ref:**HM19976)

**THOMPSON, FRANK**
**Frank Thompson**, 7 Westgate Rd, Guisborough, **Cleveland**, TS14 6EA, ENG.
(T) 01642 480102
Speciality: Hypnosis.
● **Owner** Mr F Thompson
B (Ref:HM19977)

**THOMPSON, G W (DR)**
**Dr G W Thompson**, 4 Catharine Pl, Bath, **Somerset**, BA1 2PR, ENG.
(T) 01225 424394
Speciality: Chiropractic. ✓
● **Owner** Dr G Thompson Q: DC. M: BCA.
P S T Yrs. Est.: 37 (Ref:HM19978)

**THOMPSON, GRAHAM**
**Graham Thompson**, The Essex Alexander School, 65 Norfolk Rd, Ilford, **Essex**, IG3 8LJ, ENG.
(T) 020 8220 1630
Speciality: Alexander Technique.
● **Partner** Mr G Thompson
P S (Ref:HM19979)

**THOMPSON, H J**
**H J Thompson**, 2 Beckham Cl, Luton, **Bedfordshire**, LU2 7BX, ENG.
(T) 01582 654942 (F) 01582 654942
Speciality: Chiropodists (Podiatrists).
● **Owner** Mr H Thompson
S (Ref:HM19980)

**THOMPSON, I**
**I Thompson**, 50 Plungington Rd, Preston, **Lancashire**, PR1 7RB, ENG.
(T) 01772 556520
Speciality: Chiropodists (Podiatrists).
● **Partner** Mr I Cuerden
S (Ref:HM19981)

**THOMPSON, J H**
**J H Thompson**, 39 Oldfield Rd, Bristol, BS8 4QQ, ENG.
(T) 01179 272100
Speciality: Osteopathy.
● **Owner** Mr J Thompson
P S T (Ref:HM19982)

**THOMPSON, J L**
**J L Thompson**, 62 Hathaway Rd, Bury, **Lancashire**, BL9 8EG, ENG.
(T) 01617 968288
Speciality: Reflexology.
● **Owner** Ms J Thompson
S T (Ref:HM19983)

**THOMPSON, JANE**
**Jane Thompson**, 41 Church Rd, Poole, **Dorset**, BH14 0NN, ENG.
(T) 01202 749514
Speciality: Physiotherapy.
P S T (Ref:HM19984)

**THOMPSON, JEANETTE**
**Jeanette Thompson**, The Haelan Clinic, 41 The Broadway, London, **London (Greater)**, N8 8DT, ENG.
(T) 020 8340 1518
Speciality: Osteopathy.
● **Manager** Mr J Krahn
P S T (Ref:HM19985)

**THOMPSON, KEN**
**Ken Thompson**, The Essex Alexander School, 65 Norfolk Rd, Ilford, **Essex**, IG3 8LJ, ENG.
(T) 020 8220 1630
Speciality: Alexander Technique.
● **Partner** Mr G Thompson
P S (Ref:HM19986)

**THOMPSON, KIM**
**Kim Thompson**, 2 Kenwood Rd, Sheffield, **Yorkshire (South)**, S7 1NP, ENG.
(T) 01142 552048
Speciality: Osteopathy.
● **Owner** Mr D Wainwright
P S T (Ref:HM19987)

**THOMPSON, M H L**
**M H L Thompson**, 58A Tennyson Rd, Harpenden, **Hertfordshire**, AL5 4BB, ENG.
(T) 01582 766773
Speciality: Chiropodists (Podiatrists).
● **Owner** Mr M Thompson
S (Ref:HM19988)

**THOMPSON, MARK**
**Mark Thompson**, 9 Manor Drive, Scawby, Brigg, **Humberside**, DN20 9AX, ENG.
(T) 01652 655534
Speciality: Hypnosis.
● **Owner** Mr M Thompson
B (Ref:HM19989)

**THOMPSON, MARK**
**Mark Thompson**, Treborough House, Nottingham Pl, London, **London (Greater)**, W1M 3FP, ENG.
(T) 020 7486 4075
Speciality: Family Planning (Natural), Naturopathy, Osteopathy. ✓ CREDIT
● **Osteopath/Naturopath**
Mr M Thompson Q: BSc (Hons), DO, ND.
M: GOsC.
S Yrs. Est.: 37 (Ref:HM19990)

**THOMPSON, MARK**
**Mark Thompson**, 1st Treatment Rooms, 1 Market Pl, St. Albans, **Hertfordshire**, AL3 5DR, ENG.
(T) 01727 838032
Speciality: Family Therapy, Naturopathy, Osteopathy. ✓ CREDIT
● **Osteopath/Naturopath**
Mr M Thompson Q: BSc, DO, Hons (OST), ND.
M: GOsC.
S Yrs. Est.: 37 (Ref:HM19991)

**THOMPSON, MARTIN**
**Martin Thompson**, 570A Dunstable Rd, Luton, **Bedfordshire**, LU4 8RT, ENG.
(T) 01582 575314
Speciality: Chiropody, Nail Surgery, Orthotics. ✓
● **Registered Chiropodist**
Mr M Thompson Q: S.R.Ch. M: S.C.P.
T Yrs. Est.: 50 (Ref:HM19992)

**THOMPSON, MICHAEL**
**Michael Thompson**, 34 East Park Prde, Northampton, **Northamptonshire**, NN1 4LB, ENG.
(T) 01604 628767 (F) 01604 628767
Speciality: Homeopathy.
● **Owner** Mr M Thompson
M (Ref:HM19993)

**THOMPSON, N J**
**N J Thompson**, 30 Sefton Avenue, Newcastle Upon Tyne, **Tyne and Wear**, NE6 5QR, ENG.
(T) 01912 650202
Speciality: Acupuncture.
● **Owner** Mr N Thompson
O (Ref:HM19994)

**THOMPSON, PAT**
**Pat Thompson**, 28 Whittall St, Kings Sutton, Banbury, **Oxfordshire**, OX17 3RD, ENG.
(T) 01295 812232 (F) 01295 812232
Speciality: Psychotherapy.
● **Owner** Mrs P Thompson
B (Ref:HM19995)

**THOMPSON, PATRICIA**
**Patricia Thompson**, 283A Chester Rd, Little Sutton, Ellesmere Port, **Merseyside**, CH66 1QQ, ENG.
(T) 01513 395912
Speciality: Chiropodists (Podiatrists).
● **Owner** Mrs P Thompson
S (Ref:HM19996)

**THOMPSON, PAUL**
**Paul Thompson**, Fewings Cottage, Christow, Exeter, **Devon**, EX6 7LZ, ENG.
(T) 01647 252885
Speciality: Osteopathy.
P S T (Ref:HM19997)

**THOMPSON, R D A**
**R D A Thompson**, 41A The Tything, Worcester, **Worcestershire**, WR1 1JT, ENG.
(T) 01905 22172
Speciality: Chiropodists (Podiatrists).
● **Partner** Mr R Thompson
S (Ref:HM19998)

**THOMPSON, RITA**
**Rita Thompson**, 57 Peel St, Rochdale, **Lancashire**, OL12 6PN, ENG.
(T) 01706 655877
Speciality: Reflexology.
● **Owner** Mrs R Thompson
S T (Ref:HM19999)

**THOMSON, A N**
**A N Thomson**, 12 Beaufort Rd, Wroughton, Swindon, **Wiltshire**, SN4 9HE, ENG.
(T) 01793 812891
Speciality: Chiropodists (Podiatrists).
● **Owner** A Thompson
S (Ref:HM20000)

**THOMSON, B L**
**B L Thomson**, 21 Cornwall Rd, Bexhill-on-Sea, **Sussex (East)**, TN39 3JN, ENG.
(T) 01424 220169
Speciality: Osteopathy.
● **Owner** Mrs B Thomson
P S T (Ref:HM20001)

**THOMSON, D**
**D Thomson**, 4 Fitzroy Pl, Glasgow, **Glasgow (City of)**, G3 7RH, SCO.
(T) 01412 212221
Speciality: Complementary Medicines & Therapy.
● **Owner** Mr D Thomson
C M (Ref:HM20002)

**THOMSON, D**
**D Thomson**, 7 St James Trce, Winchester, **Hampshire**, SO22 4PP, ENG.
(T) 01962 865560
Speciality: Acupuncture.
O (Ref:HM20003)

**THOMSON, HAZEL**
**Hazel Thomson**, 46 Richmond St, Aberdeen, **Aberdeenshire**, AB25 2TR, SCO.
(T) 01224 622600
Speciality: Hypnosis.
● **Owner** Mrs H Thomson
B (Ref:HM20004)

**THOMSON, J**
**J Thomson**, 24 Faskine Avenue, Airdrie, **Lanarkshire (North)**, ML6 9DX, SCO.
(T) 01236 621023
Speciality: Hypnotherapy.
● **Owner** Mr J Thomson
B (Ref:HM20005)

**THOMSON, JANE**
**Jane Thomson**, 191 Boundary Rd, Wooburn Green, High Wycombe, **Buckinghamshire**, HP10 0DL, ENG.
(T) 01628 531797
Speciality: Homeopathy.
● **Owner** Ms J Thomson
M (Ref:HM20006)

**THOMSON, JANET**
**Janet Thomson**, Manor Croft, Church Path, Fareham, **Hampshire**, PO16 7DT, ENG.
(T) 01329 280750
Speciality: Chiropodists (Podiatrists).
S (Ref:HM20007)

**THOMSON, JEAN**
**Jean Thomson**, Small Barn, Capel Rd, Rusper, Horsham, **Sussex (West)**, RH12 4PY, ENG.
(T) 01293 871674
Speciality: Chiropodists (Podiatrists).
S (Ref:HM20008)

**THOMSON, LORNA**
**Lorna Thomson**, 29 Greenacres, Ardrossan, **Ayrshire (North)**, KA22 7PP, SCO.
(T) 01294 468036
Speciality: Chiropodists (Podiatrists).
S (Ref:HM20009)

**THOMSON, P**
**P Thomson**, 16 New Row, Dunfermline, **Fife**, KY12 7EF, SCO.
(T) 01383 724075
Speciality: Chiropodists (Podiatrists).
● **Owner** Mr P Thomson
S (Ref:HM20010)


Key continued: Yrs.Est: Years Established Q: Qualifications M: Professional Membership ✓ Indemnity Insurance CREDIT Accept Credit Cards

## THOMSON, T G
**T G Thomson**, 1 St Augustines Gardens, Ipswich, **Suffolk**, IP3 8NS, ENG.
(T) 01473 726497
Speciality: Chiropodists (Podiatrists).
● **Owner** Mr T Thomson
S (Ref:HM20011)

## THOMSON, TRUDY
**Trudy Thomson**, Reardon St, London, **London (Greater)**, E1W 2QJ, ENG.
(T) 020 7702 9207
Speciality: Hypnotherapy.
● **Owner** Miss T Thomson
B (Ref:HM20012)

## THOMSON, VENETIA
**Venetia Thomson**, 13 Comiston Drive, Edinburgh, **Edinburgh (City of)**, EH10 5QR, SCO.
(T) 01314 474694
Speciality: Physiotherapy.
● **Owner** Mrs V Thomson
P S T (Ref:HM20013)

## THORN, K
**K Thorn**, Hanham Mills, Bristol, BS15 3NU, ENG.
(T) 01179 673185
Speciality: Hypnosis.
B (Ref:HM20014)

## THORNBER, A
**A Thornber**, 55 Ashburnham Rd, Plymouth, **Devon**, PL5 2LS, ENG.
(T) 01752 362709
Speciality: Reflexology.
● **Owner** Mrs A Thornber
S T (Ref:HM20015)

## THORNBER, A A
**A A Thornber**, 13 Ashfield Rd, Cheadle, **Cheshire**, SK8 1BB, ENG.
(T) 01614 285185
Speciality: Chiropody, Nail Surgery, Phytotherapy. ✔
● **Owner** Mr A Thornber **Q:** MCSP, S.R.Ch. M: CSP, S.C.P.
C Yrs. Est.: 40 (Ref:HM20016)

## THORNE ROAD CHIROPRACTIC
**Thorne Road Chiropractic Clinic**, 63 Thorne Rd, Doncaster, **Yorkshire (South)**, DN1 2EX, ENG.
(T) 01302 739063
Speciality: Chiropractic.
P S T (Ref:HM20017)

## THORNE, I J
**Mrs I J Thorne**, Ratley Lodge Clinic, Ratley, Banbury, **Oxfordshire**, OX15 6DT, ENG.
(T) 01295 670536
Speciality: Physiotherapy.
● **Owner** Mrs I Thorne
P S T (Ref:HM20018)

## THORNELEY, KATHLEEN
**Kathleen Thorneley**, 26 Brook Avenue, Uppermill, Oldham, **Lancashire**, OL3 6DR, ENG.
(T) 01457 876429
Speciality: Aromatherapy.
● **Owner** Mrs K Thorneley
M O (Ref:HM20019)

## THORNELOE, KAREN E
**Karen E Thorneloe**, 19 Harbours Cl, Bromsgrove, **Worcestershire**, B61 7HL, ENG.
(T) 01527 870871
Speciality: Reflexology.
● **Owner** Mrs K Thorneloe
S T (Ref:HM20020)

## THORNHILL, LYNDA
**Lynda Thornhill**, 7 Charlestown, Glossop, **Derbyshire**, SK13 8LF, ENG.
(T) 01457 854372
Speciality: Complementary Medicines & Therapy.
● **Owner** Ms L Thornhill
C M (Ref:HM20021)

## THORNHILL, WANDA
**Wanda Thornhill**, 37 Green Lane, Watford, **Hertfordshire**, WD1 4NL, ENG.
(T) 01923 244460
Speciality: Reflexology.
S T (Ref:HM20022)

## THORNLEY, J (DR)
**Dr J Thornley**, 70 Ashby Rd, Loughborough, **Leicestershire**, LE11 3AE, ENG.
(T) 08002 985845
Speciality: Hypnotherapy.
● **Owner** Dr J Thornley
B (Ref:HM20023)

## THORNTON, CHRISTINE
**Christine Thornton**, 19 Queen St, Blackpool, **Lancashire**, FY1 1NL, ENG.
(T) 01253 297207
Speciality: Chiropodists (Podiatrists).
● **Owner** Mrs C Thornton
S (Ref:HM20024)

## THORNTON, G
**G Thornton**, 396 High St, Lincoln, **Lincolnshire**, LN5 7SS, ENG.
(T) 01522 887887
Speciality: Aromatherapy.
M O (Ref:HM20025)

## THORNTON, MICHAEL
**Michael Thornton**, 110 High St, Tring, **Hertfordshire**, HP23 4AF, ENG.
(T) 01442 822990
Speciality: Osteopathy.
● **Owner** Mr M Thornton
P S T (Ref:HM20026)

## THORNTON, MICHAEL
**Michael Thornton**, 5 Stubbs Wood, Amersham, **Buckinghamshire**, HP6 6EY, ENG.
(T) 01494 729318
Speciality: Osteopathy.
● **Owner** Mr D Thornton
P S T (Ref:HM20027)

## THORNTON, MICHAEL
**Michael Thornton**, The Cottage, 2 The Common, Flackwell Heath, High Wycombe, **Buckinghamshire**, HP10 9PJ, ENG.
(T) 01628 527530
Speciality: Osteopathy.
● **Owner** Mr M Thornton
P S T (Ref:HM20028)

## THORNTONS PHARMACY
**Dr Peter H S Sandon**, 78a High St, Poole, **Dorset**, BH15 1BD, ENG.
(T) 01202 677662
Speciality: Holistic Healing, Homeopathy. ✔
● **Owner** Dr P Sandon
C Yrs. Est.: 16 (Ref:HM20029)

## THOROGOOD, S
**S Thorogood**, 100 Kenwood Drive, Beckenham, **Kent**, BR3 6RA, ENG.
(T) 020 8650 2738
Speciality: Chiropodists (Podiatrists).
● **Owner** Mrs S Thorogood
S (Ref:HM20030)

## THORP, TERRY
**Terry Thorp PhD,DHP**, Greystones, **County Wicklow**, IRE.
(T) 08727 30395
Speciality: Hypnotherapy.
B (Ref:HM20031)

## THORPE CHIROPODY
**Thorpe Chiropody**, 3 School Lane, Illingworth, Halifax, **Yorkshire (West)**, HX2 9SG, ENG.
(T) 01422 249794
Speciality: Chiropodists (Podiatrists).
S (Ref:HM20032)

## THORPE CLINIC
**Thorpe Clinic**, 1 St. Matthews Rd, Norwich, **Norfolk**, NR1 1SP, ENG.
(T) 01603 765298
Speciality: Osteopathy.
● **Owner** Mr S Bach
P S T (Ref:HM20033)

## THORPE, A J
**A J Thorpe**, 6 East St, Nottingham, **Nottinghamshire**, NG1 3AY, ENG.
(T) 01159 190607
Speciality: Hypnotherapy.
B (Ref:HM20034)

## THORPE, M G
**M G Thorpe**, 26 Reed Pool Cl, Countesthorpe, Leicester, **Leicestershire**, LE8 5RE, ENG.
(T) 01162 774550
Speciality: Chiropodists (Podiatrists).
S (Ref:HM20035)

## THORPE, T
**T Thorpe (Mobile)**, 4 Inglewhite Rd, Longridge, Preston, **Lancashire**, PR3 3JR, ENG.
(T) 01772 786249
Speciality: Chiropodists (Podiatrists).
● **Owner** Mr T Thorpe
S (Ref:HM20036)

## THORPE-JENNINGS, M
**M Thorpe-Jennings**, 30 The Drive, Hove, **Sussex (East)**, BN3 3JD, ENG.
(T) 01273 778123 (F) 01273 776266
Speciality: Electrolysis.
● **Practice Manager** Mrs M Ward
T (Ref:HM20037)

## THORPE-JENNINGS, MARGARET
**Margaret Thorpe-Jennings**, 6 Climping Cl, Haywards Heath, **Sussex (West)**, RH16 4DY, ENG.
(T) 01444 456869
Speciality: Electrolysis.
● **Owner** Mrs M Thorpe-Jennings
T (Ref:HM20038)

## THRALE ROAD CLINIC
**Thrale Road Clinic (The)**, 13 Thrale Rd, Streatham, London, **London (Greater)**, SW16 1NS, ENG.
(T) 020 8677 3838
Speciality: Chiropodists (Podiatrists).
● **Owner** Mr S Qureshi
S (Ref:HM20039)

## THREE MOONS OILS
**Three Moons Oils**, C/O 70 Chestergate, Macclesfield, **Cheshire**, SK11 6DY, ENG.
Speciality: Aromatherapy.
M O (Ref:HM20040)

## THRELFALL, P R
**P R Threlfall**, 10 Clifford Trce, Wellington, **Somerset**, TA21 8PQ, ENG.
(T) 01823 663287
Speciality: Chiropodists (Podiatrists).
S (Ref:HM20041)

## THRESH, M G S
**M G S Thresh**, 46 Bower Mount Rd, Maidstone, **Kent**, ME16 8AU, ENG.
(T) 01622 752381
Speciality: Physiotherapy.
P S T (Ref:HM20042)

## THROSSELL PHILIPPA
**Throssell Philippa**, 7 Holly Rd, Northampton, **Northamptonshire**, NN1 4QL, ENG.
(T) 01604 231088
Speciality: Chiropractors.
P S T (Ref:HM20043)

## THROSSELL, PHILIPPA
**Philippa Throssell**, 1 Pool St, Woodford Halse, Daventry, **Northamptonshire**, NN11 3TS, ENG.
(T) 01327 261011
Speciality: Chiropractic.
● **Owner** Miss P Throssell
P S T (Ref:HM20044)

## THROWER, MARIANNE
**Marianne Thrower**, 46 Warwick St, Oxford, **Oxfordshire**, OX4 1SX, ENG.
(T) 01865 248559
Speciality: Reflexology.
S T (Ref:HM20045)

## THRUSH, NORA C
**Nora C Thrush**, Orchard House, 7 Northcote Fold, Linton, Wetherby, **Yorkshire (West)**, LS22 4UZ, ENG.
(T) 01937 580100
Speciality: Physiotherapy.
● **Owner** Mrs N Thrush
P S T (Ref:HM20046)

## THURGOOD, SIMON
**Simon Thurgood**, 265 Green Lanes, London,

**London (Greater)**, N13 4XE, ENG.
(T) 020 8886 9977
Speciality: Osteopathy. ✔
● **Owner** Mr S Thurgood Q: BSc, DO. M: GOsC.
S T Yrs. Est.: 9 (Ref:HM20047)

**THURKETTLE, A D**

**A D Thurkettle**, 72 Erskine Rd, South Shields, **Tyne and Wear**, NE33 2SW, ENG.
(T) 01914 542374
Speciality: Chiropodists (Podiatrists).
● **Owner** Mr A Thurkettle
S (Ref:HM20048)

**THURSTON, JENNY**

**Jenny Thurston**, Millom, **Cumbria**, LA19, ENG.
(T) 01229 717629
Speciality: Bach Remedies.
M (Ref:HM20049)

**TIAN TIAN**

**Tian Tian (UK) Ltd**, The Harlequin, Watford, **Hertfordshire**, WD1 2TA, ENG.
(T) 01923 240888
Speciality: Complementary Medicines & Therapy.
● **Manager** Mr J Lee
C M (Ref:HM20050)

**TIAN TIAN UK**

**Tian Tian UK Ltd**, 47 Princes Walk, Northampton, **Northamptonshire**, NN1 2EL, ENG.
(T) 01604 637888
Speciality: Herbal Medicine.
M (Ref:HM20051)

**TICKTIN, S J**

**S J Ticktin**, 29 Church Garth, Pemberton Gardens, London, **London (Greater)**, N19 5RN, ENG.
(T) 020 7272 2474
Speciality: Psychiatry.
B (Ref:HM20052)

**TIDA CHINESE HERBAL CLINIC**

**Tida Chinese Herbal Clinic**, Wing Yip Business Centre, 544 Purley Way, Croydon, **Surrey**, CR0 4RF, ENG.
(T) 020 8681 0833 (F) 020 8681 0833
Speciality: Complementary Medicines & Therapy.
● **Owner** Mr C Tang
C M (Ref:HM20053)

**TIDBALL, GILLIAN**

**Gillian Tidball**, 5 Reading Rd, Chineham, Basingstoke, **Hampshire**, RG24 8LN, ENG.
(T) 01256 812980
Speciality: Reflexology.
S T (Ref:HM20054)

**TIDCOMBE, MICHAEL B**

**Michael B Tidcombe**, Vantage Pharmacy, 69 Gloucester Rd, Patchway, Bristol, BS34 5JH, ENG.
(T) 01179 405223
Speciality: Chiropodists (Podiatrists).
S (Ref:HM20055)

**TIDESWELL HOM PRACTICE**

**Tideswell Homoeopathic Practice**, Brunswick House, Sherwood Rd, Tideswell, Buxton, **Derbyshire**, SK17 8HS, ENG.
(T) 01298 872595
Speciality: Homeopathy.
● **Partner** Mr P Bailey
M (Ref:HM20056)

**TIDEY, S A**

**S A Tidey**, 2 Glencoe Cl, Frimley, Camberley, **Surrey**, GU16 5YS, ENG.
(T) 01252 838357
Speciality: Chiropodists (Podiatrists).
● **Owner** Mrs S Tidey
S (Ref:HM20057)

**TIDSALL, C**

**C Tidsall**, Aldrens Lane, Lancaster, **Lancashire**, LA1 2DU, ENG.
(T) 01524 69864 (F) 01524 848155
Speciality: Osteopathy.
P S T (Ref:HM20058)

**TIDSWELL, SUSAN**

**Susan Tidswell**, The Sycamores, Dacre, Harrogate, **Yorkshire (North)**, HG3 4ES, ENG.
(T) 01423 780940
Speciality: Reflexology.
S T (Ref:HM20059)

**TIEN HONG HERBLAND**

**Tien Hong Herbland**, 70 Clarence Rd, London, **London (Greater)**, E5 8HB, ENG.
(T) 020 8533 7523
Speciality: Complementary Medicines & Therapy.
C M (Ref:HM20060)

**TIERNAN, MANDA**

**Manda Tiernan**, 17 Burnside, Halebarns, Altrincham, **Cheshire**, WA15 0SG, ENG.
(T) 01619 048209
Speciality: Reflexology.
S T (Ref:HM20061)

**TIESDELL-SMITH, DOREEN**

**Doreen Tiesdell-Smith**, 7 Wilson Rd, Chessington, **Surrey**, KT9 2HE, ENG.
(T) 020 8397 4963
Speciality: Reflexology.
S T (Ref:HM20062)

**TIGER CLINIC**

**Tiger Clinic**, The Garden Flat, 1 Palmeira Sq, Hove, **Sussex (East)**, BN3 2JA, ENG.
(T) 01273 777758
Speciality: Acupuncture.
● **Owner** Mr S Wright
O (Ref:HM20063)

**TIJERINA, CARL (DR)**

**Dr Carl Tijerina**, Ballinderry,, Mullingar, **County Westmeath**, IRE.
(T) 04445 004
Speciality: Complementary Medicines & Therapy.
M (Ref:HM20064)

**TILBURY, PAULINE**

**Pauline Tilbury**, Dumfries Holistic Health Centre, 98 Loreburn St, Dumfries, **Dumfries and Galloway**, DG1 1HW, SCO.
(T) 01387 267617
Speciality: Herbalists.
M (Ref:HM20065)

**TILEHURST PHYSIOTHERAPY SVS**

**Tilehurst Physiotherapy Services**, 218 Tilehurst Rd, Reading, **Berkshire**, RG30 2NE, ENG.
(T) 01189 594099
Speciality: Physiotherapy.
P S T (Ref:HM20066)

**TILL, ELIZABETH**

**Elizabeth Till**, Bryn Goleu, Tyn-Y-Gongl, **Isle of Anglesey**, LL74 8NU, WAL.
(T) 01248 853091
Speciality: Chiropractors.
P S T (Ref:HM20067)

**TILLEY, D S**

**D S Tilley**, 6 Haynes Cl, Swindon, **Wiltshire**, SN3 6DZ, ENG.
(T) 01793 612281
Speciality: Osteopathy.
● **Owner** Mr D Tilley
P S T (Ref:HM20068)

**TILLEY, DARREN**

**Darren Tilley**, Health Hydro, Milton Rd, Swindon, **Wiltshire**, SN1 5JA, ENG.
(T) 01793 465631
Speciality: Osteopathy.
P S T (Ref:HM20069)

**TILLSON, LINDA**

**Linda Tillson**, 6 Pettys Brook Rd, Chineham, Basingstoke, **Hampshire**, RG24 8RW, ENG.
(T) 01256 472938
Speciality: Hypnotherapy.
B (Ref:HM20070)

**TILLYER, SUSAN**

**Susan Tillyer**, College Rd, Durrington, Salisbury, **Wiltshire**, SP4 8HP, ENG.
(T) 01980 594964
Speciality: Chiropractors.
● **Owner** Ms S Tillyer
P S T (Ref:HM20071)

**TILNEY, TONY**

**Tony Tilney**, Thanet Lodge, 63 Victoria Rd, Sutton Coldfield, **Midlands (West)**, B72 1SN, ENG.
(T) 01213 544042
Speciality: Psychotherapy.
B (Ref:HM20072)

**TILSLEY, VINCENT**

**Vincent Tilsley**, 18 Rosslyn Rd, Shoreham-by-Sea, **Sussex (West)**, BN43 6WP, ENG.
(T) 01273 463933
Speciality: Hypnotherapy.
● **Principal** Mr V Tilsley
B (Ref:HM20073)

**TILTON, JANE**

**Jane Tilton**, 107 Crystal Palace Rd, London, **London (Greater)**, SE22 9ES, ENG.
(T) 020 8693 5635
Speciality: Aromatherapy.
● **Owner** Ms J Tilton
M O (Ref:HM20074)

**TIM BROWN CLINIC**

**Tim Brown Clinic (The)**, Northwood, London Rd, Wooburn Green, High Wycombe, **Buckinghamshire**, HP10 0NJ, ENG.
(T) 01494 680847
Speciality: Acupuncture.
● **Owner** Miss F King
O (Ref:HM20075)

**TIMBRELL, GAIL**

**Gail Timbrell**, The Cottage, Church Rd, Long Itchington, Southam, **Warwickshire**, CV47 9PW, ENG.
(T) 01926 812680
Speciality: Aromatherapy.
M O (Ref:HM20076)

**TIME OUT TRAINING**

**Time Out Training**, 24 Lissan View, Omagh, **County Tyrone**, BT78 1TR, NIR.
(T) 028 8224 6845
Speciality: Psychology.
● **Principal** Dr M Magee
B (Ref:HM20077)

**TIMELINE SERVICES**

**Timeline Services**, Guardian Medical Centre, Guardian St, Warrington, **Cheshire**, WA5 1UD, ENG.
(T) 01925 658322
Speciality: Hypnosis.
B (Ref:HM20078)

**TINDALE, M**

**M Tindale**, 57 North Bar Within, Beverley, **Humberside (North)**, HU17 8DG, ENG.
(T) 01482 861083
Speciality: Chiropodists (Podiatrists).
S (Ref:HM20079)

**TINDALL, JOHN**

**John Tindall**, 13 Duncombe Rd, London, **London (Greater)**, SE23 1QY, ENG.
(T) 020 8690 9145
Speciality: Acupuncture.
O (Ref:HM20080)

**TINDALL, T**

**T Tindall**, 81 Halesworth Rd, London, **London (Greater)**, SE13 7TL, ENG.
(T) 020 8692 5010
Speciality: Homeopathy.
M (Ref:HM20081)

**TINGLE, SARAH**

**Sarah Tingle**, 25 College Avenue, Slough, **Berkshire**, SL1 2NB, ENG.
(T) 01753 577886
Speciality: Psychotherapy.
B (Ref:HM20082)

**TINKER, D C**

**D C Tinker**, The Surgery, 106 Briercliffe Rd, Burnley, **Lancashire**, BB10 1TZ, ENG.
(T) 01282 413552
Speciality: Chiropody. ✔
● **Chiropodist (Podiatrist)**
Mr D Tinker Q: DPodM, M.S.C.P, S.R.Ch.
M Yrs. Est.: 21 (Ref:HM20083)



Key continued: Yrs.Est: Years Established Q: Qualifications M: Professional Membership ✔ Indemnity Insurance ▬ Accept Credit Cards

### TINNION, D J
**D J Tinnion**, 58 Avenue Prde, Accrington, **Lancashire**, BB5 6PJ, ENG.
(T) 01254 235008
Speciality: Chiropodists (Podiatrists).
● **Partner** Mrs D Tinnion
S (Ref:HM20084)

### TINSLEY, ABIGAIL
**Abigail Tinsley**, 78 Norbreck Rd, Thornton, **Lancashire**, FY5 1RP, ENG.
(T) 01253 353127
Speciality: Chiropodists (Podiatrists).
● **Owner** A Tinsley
S (Ref:HM20085)

### TIP TOES
**Tip Toes**, 104 Dale St, Milnrow, Rochdale, **Lancashire**, OL16 3NJ, ENG.
(T) 01706 759684 (F) 01706 759684
Speciality: Aromatherapy, Indian Head Massage, Reflexology, Reiki, Remedial Massage, Swedish Body Massage, Beauty Treatments. ✔
● **Complementary Therapist**
Mrs H Shepherd Q: MIIR. M: AoR.
C Yrs. Est.: 8 (Ref:HM20086)

### TIPLING, L
**L Tipling**, 35 Duke Rd, Hyde, **Cheshire**, SK14 4JB, ENG.
(T) 01613 680235
Speciality: Chiropody. ✔
● **Owner/Chiropodist** Mrs L Tipling Q: MBChA, MSSCh.
M Yrs. Est.: 21 (Ref:HM20087)

### TIPPLE, DAWN
**Dawn Tipple**, 79 Glebe Lane, Stockcross, Newbury, **Berkshire**, RG20 8LL, ENG.
(T) 01488 608561
Speciality: Chiropodists (Podiatrists).
S (Ref:HM20088)

### TIPTOES
**Tiptoes**, 8 Main St, Bonnybridge, **Falkirk**, FK4 1BT, SCO.
(T) 01324 882520
Speciality: Chiropodists (Podiatrists).
● **Owner** Mrs V Monroe
S (Ref:HM20089)

### TIPTON, G A
**G A Tipton**, Elwy House, 15 King St, Wrexham, LL11 1HF, WAL.
(T) 01978 263410
Speciality: Chiropodists (Podiatrists).
● **Owner** Ms G Tipton
S (Ref:HM20090)

### TIR NA NOG
**Tir Na Nog**, The Sq, Claremorris, **County Mayo**, IRE.
(T) 09462 678
(E) tng@eircom.net
Speciality: Beauty Therapy.
H T (Ref:HM20091)

### TIR NA NOG HOLISTIC CENTRE
**Tir Na Nog Holistic Centre & Hostel**, Ballyea, Cahir, **County Tipperary**, IRE.
(T) 05241 962
Speciality: Healing.
B (Ref:HM20092)

### TIR NA NOG OILS
**Tir Na Nog Oils**, Ennis, **County Clare**, IRE.
(T) 08722 03980
(E) essentialoil@eircom.net
Speciality: Aromatherapy.
M O (Ref:HM20093)

### TISBURY OSTEOPATHIC PRACTICE
**Rhian Watson**, 4 The Old Dairy, Fonthill Bishop, Salisbury, **Wiltshire**, SP3 5SH, ENG.
(T) 01747 820021
Speciality: Cranial Osteopathy, Osteopathy, Myofascial Dry Needling. ✔
● **Osteopath** Tamari De Bardi Q: DO. M: GOsC.
● **Osteopath** Miss R Watson Q: BSc. M: GOsC.
S Yrs. Est.: 9 (Ref:HM20094)

### TISSERAND
**Tisserand**, Newtown Rd, Hove, **Sussex (East)**, BN3 7BA, ENG.
(T) 01273 325666 (F) 01273 208444
(W) www.tisserand.com
Speciality: Aromatherapy. ✔
● **Marketing Director**
Clive Parker Walker
● **Managing Director** Mr A Harris
● **Principal** Mr R Tisserand
C Yrs. Est.: 32 (Ref:HM20095)

### TISSERAND INSTITUTE
**Tisserand Institute**, 23 Beavor Lane, London, **London (Greater)**, W6 9JT, ENG.
(T) 020 8748 1060 (F) 020 8748 1364
Speciality: Aromatherapy.
● **General Manager** Ms J Badger
M O (Ref:HM20096)

### TITCOMBE, R C
**R C Titcombe**, Ronan, Argyle Rd, Reading, **Berkshire**, RG1 7YL, ENG.
(T) 01189 580991
Speciality: Chiropodists (Podiatrists).
S (Ref:HM20097)

### TIVERTON PHYSIO & SPORTS
**Tiverton Physiotherapy & Sports Injuries Clinic**, 36 Castle St, Tiverton, **Devon**, EX16 6RG, ENG.
(T) 01884 253313 (F) 01884 253313
Speciality: Physiotherapy.
● **Manageress** Mrs T Morgan
P S T (Ref:HM20098)

### TIVOLI INSTITUTE
**Tivoli Institute**, 24 Clarinda Pk, Dun Laoghaire, **County Dublin**, IRE.
(T) 01280 9178
Speciality: Counselling.
B H (Ref:HM20099)

### TIZZARD, CHRISTINE M
**Christine M Tizzard**, Blackrock Cottage, 12 Manor Rd, Selsey, Chichester, **Sussex (West)**, PO20 0SD, ENG.
(T) 01243 604932
Speciality: Chiropodists (Podiatrists).
● **Owner** Mrs C Tizzard
S (Ref:HM20100)

### TOASH CLINIC
**Toash Clinic**, 9 High St, Olney, **Buckinghamshire**, MK46 4EB, ENG.
(T) 01234 241200
Speciality: Acupuncture.
O (Ref:HM20101)

### TOBAR PHADRAIC
**Tobar Phadraic Natural Therapies**, Carrownedan, Ballyhaunis, **County Mayo**, IRE.
(T) 09073 0490
(E) brigidlyons@hotmail.com
Speciality: Absent Healing, Aromatherapy, Bio-energetics, Complementary Therapy, Dietician, Do-In, Hay Diet, Healer, Healing Therapy, Indian Head Massage, Massage (Therapeutic), Meditation, Reflexology, Reiki, Yoga.
● **Therapist** Bridle Lyons Q: ITEC. M: IAA, IRA.
H Yrs. Est.: 10 (Ref:HM20102)

### TOBE, VICKI
**Vicki Tobe**, 2 Clarendon Rd, Bournemouth, **Dorset**, BH4 8AH, ENG.
(T) 01202 768638 (F) 01202 751038
Speciality: Physiotherapy.
● **Practice Manager** Mrs D Amar
P S T (Ref:HM20103)

### TOBIAS, J
**J Tobias**, Ravenscroft Medical Centre, 166-168 Golders Green Rd, London, **London (Greater)**, NW11 8BB, ENG.
(T) 020 8209 0922 (F) 020 8201 8298
Speciality: Homeopathy.
● **Principal** Dr B Golden
M (Ref:HM20104)

### TOBIN, ROSALEEN
**Rosaleen Tobin**, 1 Butterfield Cres, Rathfarnham, **County Dublin**, IRE.
(T) 01493 3964
(E) tobin@eircom.net
Speciality: Absent Healing, Colour Therapy, Counselling, Healer, Healing Therapy, Holistic Healing, Reiki, Seichem, Spiritual Healing, Tera-Mai, Aura Soma Colour Therapy, Transpersonal Counselling, Magnified healing, Feng shui & Sacred space, Reiki-Seichim, Spiritual Counselling.
● **Teacher/Healer/Counsellor**
Rosaleen Tobin Q: BA, Dip.H.E.
H Yrs. Est.: 5 (Ref:HM20105)

### TODD, DEBBIE
**Debbie Todd**, 41 Church Rd, Poole, **Dorset**, BH14 0NN, ENG.
(T) 01202 749514 (F) 01202 718906
Speciality: Physiotherapy.
● **Partner** Mrs C Swinhoe
P S T (Ref:HM20106)

### TODD, PAUL
**Mr Paul Todd**, 6 Highway Court, Beaconsfield, **Buckinghamshire**, HP9 1QB, ENG.
(T) 01494 674025
Speciality: Biomechanics, Chiropody, Cryo Surgery, Nail Surgery, Orthotics, Podiatry. ✔
● **Chiropodist** Mr P Todd Q: BSc, DPodM, S.R.Ch. M: S.C.P.
M Yrs. Est.: 11 (Ref:HM20107)

### TODD, S J
**S J Todd**, 14 Chain Lane, Newark, **Nottinghamshire**, NG24 1AU, ENG.
(T) 01636 702376
(E) billtodd1@virgin.net
Speciality: Chiropody.
● **Owner/Chiropodist** Mrs S Todd Q: MBChA.
S (Ref:HM20108)

### TODD, TREVOR
**Trevor Todd**, 124B Fenaghy Rd, Cullybackey, Ballymena, **County Antrim**, BT42 1EA, NIR.
(T) 028 2588 0542
Speciality: Chiropody. ✔
● **Chiropodist** Mr T Todd Q: M.S.C.P, S.R.Ch. M: S.C.P.
M Yrs. Est.: 33 (Ref:HM20109)

### TOE TO HEEL - REFLEXOLOGY
**Toe To Heel - Reflexology**, 31 Arduthie Rd, Stonehaven, **Aberdeenshire**, AB39 2EH, SCO.
(T) 01569 762189
(E) jane.ponsonby@dial.pipex.com
Speciality: Reflexology, Vacuflex. ✔
● **Therapist** Ms J Ponsonby Q: GSSR. M: AoR, SIR.
T Yrs. Est.: 7 (Ref:HM20110)

### TOETAL CARE
**Toetal Care**, 2 Beach Priory Gardens, Southport, **Merseyside**, PR8 1RT, ENG.
(T) 01704 533018
Speciality: Chiropodists (Podiatrists).
● **Owner** Mr B Taylor
S (Ref:HM20111)

### TOE-TLE FOOTCARE
**Toe-Tle Footcare**, 12 Market St, Pontypridd, **Rhondda Cynon Taff**, CF37 2ST, WAL.
(T) 01443 486256
Speciality: Chiropodists (Podiatrists).
● **Partner** Mrs J Flynn
S (Ref:HM20112)

### TOFT, JANE
**Jane Toft**, Eastbourne Clinic Of Natural Medicine, 69 Meads Rd, Eastbourne, **Sussex (East)**, BN20 7QL, ENG.
(T) 01323 734664 (F) 01323 734664
Speciality: Reflexology.
● **Employee** Mr H Boys
S T (Ref:HM20113)

### TOFTS, E
**E Tofts**, 31 Shenfield Rd, Brentwood, **Essex**, CM15 8AG, ENG.
(T) 01277 210664
Speciality: Complementary Medicines & Therapy.
● **Partner** Mrs L Lemmon
M (Ref:HM20114)

### TOGELANG, T
**Mr T Togelang**, Finchley Osteopathic Surgery, 259 Nether St, London, **London (Greater)**, N3 1PD, ENG.
(T) 020 8346 4869



Key: B Mind-Body Medicine C Complementary Medicine H Self Help Treatment M Medicinal Therapy O Oriental Medicine P Postural Therapy S Manipulative Structural Therapy T Touch Therapy

Speciality: Osteopathy.
P S T (Ref:HM20115)

**TOIBIN, EILEEN**

**Eileen Toibin**, 1 Aubrey Rd, London, **London (Greater)**, N8 9HH, ENG.
(T) 020 8374 7045
Speciality: Psychotherapy.
● **Owner** Ms E Toibin
B (Ref:HM20116)

**TOLBOOTH HOUSE**

**Tolbooth House**, Tolbooth House, 13 Tolbooth St, Kirkcaldy, **Fife**, KY1 1RW, SCO.
(T) 01592 264722
(W) www.tolbooth-house.co.uk
Speciality: Acupuncture, Chiropody, Cryo Surgery, Dietician, Herbal Medicine, Homeopathy, Hypnosis, Hypnotherapy, Indian Head Massage, Massage (Therapeutic), Moxibustion, Nail Surgery, Nutritional Therapy, Osteopathy, Podiatry, Reflexology, Reiki. ✔
● **Chiropodist (Podiatrist)**
Mr C Wilson Q: DPodM, M.S.C.P, S.R.Ch.
M: S.C.P.
H M Yrs. Est.: 10 (Ref:HM20117)

**TOLE, J R E**

**J R E Tole**, 1 Bevans Trce, Dully Hill, Doddington, Sittingbourne, **Kent**, ME9 0BY, ENG.
(T) 01795 886359
Speciality: Psychotherapy.
● **Doctor** Dr J Tole
B (Ref:HM20118)

**TOLL HOUSE CHIROPRACTIC**

**Toll House Chiropractic & Physiotherapy Clinic (The)**, 47 Horse St, Chipping Sodbury, Bristol, BS17 6DA, ENG.
(T) 01454 327222
Speciality: Chiropractic, Physiotherapy.
P S T (Ref:HM20119)

**TOLL HOUSE CLINIC**

**Toll House Clinic**, 47 Horse St, Chipping Sodbury, Bristol, BS37 6DA, ENG.
(T) 01454 322232 (F) 01454 324432
(E) tollhouse.clinic@virgin.net
(W) www.ukphysiotherapy.co.uk
Speciality: Acupuncture, Aromatherapy, Chiropractic, Electrotherapy, Indian Head Massage, Manipulation, Massage (Therapeutic), Micro Manipulation, Physiotherapy, Pilates, Reflexology, Ultrasonics. ✔
● **Sports Massage Therapist**
Lesley Wolfe
● **Physiotherapist** Ms D Golton Q: MCSP, SRP. M: CSP.
● **Chiropractor** Craid De Grost Q: DC. M: SCA.
● **Aromatherapist** Frances Jones
● **Chiropractor** Ms P Cronin Q: DC. M: BCA.
● **Physiotherapist** Ms J Lott Q: MCSP, SRP. M: CSP.
● **Physiotherapist** Ms L Carter Q: MCSP, SRP. M: CSP.
● **Physiotherapist** Ms F Harding Q: MCSP, SRP. M: CSP.
● **Reflexologist** Ms J Barter
P S T Yrs. Est.: 6 (Ref:HM20120)

**TOLLADY, B**

**B Tollady**, 18 Lansdowne Rd, London, **London (Greater)**, W11 3LL, ENG.
(T) 020 7727 7222
Speciality: Alexander Technique.
P S (Ref:HM20121)

**TOLLEY, ELAINE**

**Elaine Tolley**, 4 Dovelea, Rolleston-On-Dove, Burton-On-Trent, **Staffordshire**, DE13 9BL, ENG.
(T) 01283 520431 (F) 01283 520431
Speciality: Chiropodists (Podiatrists).
● **Owner** Mrs E Tolley
S (Ref:HM20122)

**TOLLEY, STEVE**

**Steve Tolley**, 54 Rosedale Avenue, Atherton, Manchester, **Manchester (Greater)**, M46 0EA, ENG.
(T) 01942 892289
Speciality: Hypnotherapy.
B (Ref:HM20123)

**TOLMAN, KEITH (DR)**

**Dr Keith Tolman**, 41 Clapham Common North Side, London, **London (Greater)**, SW4 0AA, ENG.
(T) 020 7498 2380
Speciality: Psychotherapy.
B (Ref:HM20124)

**TOLMIE, LINDA**

**Linda Tolmie**, 42 Southern Way, Farnham, **Surrey**, GU9 8DF, ENG.
(T) 01252 727010
Speciality: Hypnosis.
B (Ref:HM20125)

**TOLSON, S**

**S Tolson**, The Sydney Fisher Clinic, 81 Tressillian Rd, London, **London (Greater)**, SE4 1XZ, ENG.
(T) 020 8694 2714 (F) 020 8694 2714
Speciality: Osteopathy.
● **Partner** Mrs J Mitchell
P S T (Ref:HM20126)

**TOMBLIN, MARIE**

**Marie Tomblin**, 13 Nelson Rd, London, **London (Greater)**, SE10 9JB, ENG.
(T) 020 8858 8557 (F) 020 8293 4323
Speciality: Reflexology.
● **Owner** Ms M Tomblin
S T (Ref:HM20127)

**TOME OSTEOPATHIC & SPORTS**

**Tome Osteopathic & Sports Clinic**, 20 North St, Wellington, **Somerset**, TA21 8LT, ENG.
(T) 01823 666944
Speciality: Osteopathy.
● **Owner** Mr M Edwards
P S T (Ref:HM20128)

**TOMEY PHYSIO & SPORTS CLINIC**

**Tomey Physiotherapy & Sports Injury Clinic**, 14-18 Grange Rd, Billericay, **Essex**, CM11 2RE, ENG.
(T) 01277 656005 (F) 01277 824214
Speciality: Physiotherapy.
● **Owner** Mr K Tomey
P S T (Ref:HM20129)

**TOMKIES, J**

**J Tomkies**, Redland House Clinic, 118 Redland Rd, Bristol, BS6 6QT, ENG.
(T) 01179 420200 (F) 01179 241663
Speciality: Chiropractic.
● **Principal** Mr J Cook
P S T (Ref:HM20130)

**TOMLIN, NORMAN**

**Norman Tomlin**, 39 The Avenue, Mansfield, **Nottinghamshire**, NG18 4PD, ENG.
(T) 01623 640758
Speciality: Chiropractic, PAM.
● **Chiropractor** Mr N Tomlin Q: BSc (Hons), DC, FMCA. M: MCA.
● **Chiropractor** Ms D Tomlin Q: DC, FMCA. M: MCA.
C Yrs. Est.: 16 (Ref:HM20131)

**TOMLIN, NORMAN**

**Norman Tomlin**, 68B Leicester Rd, Loughborough, **Leicestershire**, LE11 2AG, ENG.
(T) 01509 234522
Speciality: Chiropractors.
P S T (Ref:HM20132)

**TOMLIN, P H**

**P H Tomlin**, Two Worlds, Tan Lane, Little Clacton, Clacton-On-Sea, **Essex**, CO16 9PS, ENG.
(T) 01255 860626 (F) 01255 860662
Speciality: Physiotherapy.
● **Owner** Mr P Tomlin
P S T (Ref:HM20133)

**TOMLIN, S**

**Mrs S Tomlin**, 2 Plumtree Cottages, High St, Prestwood, Great Missenden, **Buckinghamshire**, HP16 9EE, ENG.
(T) 01494 865997
Speciality: Chiropodists (Podiatrists).
S (Ref:HM20134)

**TOMLIN, S**

**S Tomlin**, 19 Castle St, High Wycombe, **Buckinghamshire**, HP13 6RU, ENG.
(T) 01494 488517
Speciality: Chiropodists (Podiatrists).
● **Owner** Mrs S Tomlin
S (Ref:HM20135)

**TOMLIN, SUSAN M**

**Susan M Tomlin**, 2 Long Yard, Archway, Studridge Lane, Speen, Princes Risborough, **Buckinghamshire**, HP27 0SF, ENG.
(T) 01494 488989
Speciality: Chiropody, Reflexology. ✔
● **Reflexologist** Ms S Tomlin Q: BSR. M: HAR.
T Yrs. Est.: 1 (Ref:HM20136)

**TOMLIN, WILLIAM W**

**William W Tomlin**, Berkhamsted Chiropractic Clinic, 69 High St, Berkhamsted, **Hertfordshire**, HP4 2DE, ENG.
(T) 01442 863800
Speciality: Chiropractors.
P S T (Ref:HM20137)

**TOMLINS, C & CURRIE, J**

**C Tomlins & J Currie**, 78 Victoria Pk Dr South, Glasgow, **Glasgow (City of)**, G14 9NX, SCO.
(T) 01414 012470 (F) 01419 564253
Speciality: Alexander Technique.
P S (Ref:HM20138)

**TOMLINSON ASSOCIATES**

**Tomlinson Associates**, 34 Church Stile, Rochdale, **Lancashire**, OL16 1QE, ENG.
(T) 01706 642390
Speciality: Osteopathy.
● **Owner** Mrs B Dania-Tomlinson
P S T (Ref:HM20139)

**TOMLINSON, DAWN**

**Dawn Tomlinson**, 8 Kedleston Rd, Derby, **Derbyshire**, DE22 1GU, ENG.
(T) 01332 349479
Speciality: Chiropractors.
● **Owner** Mrs D Tomlinson
P S T (Ref:HM20140)

**TOMLINSON, ELIZABETH**

**Elizabeth Tomlinson**, 104 Barrowford Rd, Colne, **Lancashire**, BB8 9QW, ENG.
(T) 01282 866335
Speciality: Electrolysis. ✔
● **Owner/Electrolysist**
Mrs E Tomlinson Q: SRN.
T Yrs. Est.: 30 (Ref:HM20141)

**TOMLINSON, JUDITH**

**Judith Tomlinson**, The Yoga Studio Richmond Chambers, Richmond Trce, Blackburn, **Lancashire**, BB1 7AR, ENG.
(T) 01254 696036
Speciality: Massage (Therapeutic), Reflexology, Yoga, Lyengar. ✔
● **Owner/Yoga Teacher/Therapist**
Mrs J Tomlinson Q: IHBC, IIHHT, ITEC. M: AoR, FHT, YTA.
H Yrs. Est.: 4 (Ref:HM20142)

**TOMLINSON, K**

**K Tomlinson**, 23 Waldemar Avenue, London, **London (Greater)**, W13 9PZ, ENG.
(T) 020 8840 2468
Speciality: Homeopathy.
● **Owner** Mrs K Tomlinson
M (Ref:HM20143)

**TOMLINSON, KATE**

**Kate Tomlinson**, 561 Arleston Lane, Stenson Fields, Derby, **Derbyshire**, DE24 3DA, ENG.
(T) 01332 720678
Speciality: Chiropodists (Podiatrists).
● **Owner** Mrs K Tomlinson
S (Ref:HM20144)

**TOMLINSON, P**

**P Tomlinson**, 57 North Bar Within, Beverley, **Humberside (North)**, HU17 8DG, ENG.
(T) 01482 861083
Speciality: Hypnotherapy.
B (Ref:HM20145)

**TOMLINSON, PETER J**

**Peter J Tomlinson**, 24 Mile Lane, Seddons Farm Estate, Bury, **Lancashire**, BL8 2JE, ENG.
(T) 01617 616436
Speciality: Chiropodists (Podiatrists).
S (Ref:HM20146)


Key continued: Yrs.Est: Years Established Q: Qualifications M: Professional Membership ✔ Indemnity Insurance Accept Credit Cards

### TOMLINSON, S

**S Tomlinson**, 57 North Bar Within, Beverley, **Humberside (North)**, HU17 8DG, ENG.
(T) 01482 861083
Speciality: Reflexology.
S T (Ref:HM20147)

### TOMLINSON, T J

**T J Tomlinson**, 16 Well Trce, Clitheroe, **Lancashire**, BB7 2AD, ENG.
(T) 01200 422573
Speciality: Chiropodists (Podiatrists).
● **Owner** Mr T Tomlinson
S (Ref:HM20148)

### TOMPKINS, P A

**P A Tompkins**, 147 Oundle Rd, Peterborough, **Cambridgeshire**, PE2 9QZ, ENG.
(T) 01733 313439
Speciality: Chiropodists (Podiatrists).
● **Owner** Mr P Tompkins
S (Ref:HM20149)

### TOMS, L S

**L S Toms**, Melsham House, 27 Market Pl, Melksham, **Wiltshire**, SN12 6ES, ENG.
(T) 01225 705100
Speciality: Physiotherapy.
P S T (Ref:HM20150)

### TONBRIDGE CLINIC

**Tonbridge Clinic (The)**, 339 Shipbourne Rd, Tonbridge, **Kent**, TN10 3EU, ENG.
(T) 01732 350255 (F) 01732 362343
(E) chris@tonbridgeclive.co.uk
Speciality: Acupuncture, Aromatherapy, Cognitive Therapy, Counselling, Cranial Osteopathy, Dietician, Herbal Medicine, Homeopathy, Hypnotherapy, Manipulation, Massage (Therapeutic), Naturopathy, Nutritional Therapy, Osteopathy. ✔
● **Nutrition Consultant**
Ms L Sellars
● **Hypnotherapist**
Ms C Alves Da Silva Q: DHP (NC), MNRHP, NLP.
● **Integrated Chinese/Western Medical Practitioner**
Dr M Jones Q: BA, DCM, DipCH.P, MB, MCMIR.
● **Osteopathic Physician**
Dr C Bowman Q: MB. M: GOsC.
C Yrs. Est.: 2 (Ref:HM20151)

### TONBRIDGE HOMOEOPATHIC CLINIC

**Tonbridge Homoeopathic Clinic**, 44 Lyons Cres, Tonbridge, **Kent**, TN9 1EY, ENG.
(T) 01732 368767
Speciality: Homeopathy.
M (Ref:HM20152)

### TONG, E

**E Tong**, 26 Kineton Rd, Hedge End, Southampton, **Hampshire**, SO30 2PQ, ENG.
(T) 023 8077 2511
Speciality: Physiotherapy.
P S T (Ref:HM20153)

### TONG, JENNY

**Jenny Tong**, 15 College Fields, Woodhead Drive, Cambridge, **Cambridgeshire**, CB4 1YZ, ENG.
(T) 01223 425627
Speciality: Indian Head Massage, Reflexology. ✔
● **Reflexologist** Ms J Tong M: AoR.
M Yrs. Est.: 1 (Ref:HM20154)

### TONGE, B

**B Tonge**, 11 Latchmere Cl, Richmond, **Surrey**, TW10 5HQ, ENG.
(T) 020 8940 4289
Speciality: Alexander Technique.
● **Owner** Miss B Tonge
P S (Ref:HM20155)

### TONGE, B

**B Tonge**, 36-37 Castle St, Guildford, **Surrey**, GU1 3UQ, ENG.
(T) 01483 300400 (F) 01483 300411
Speciality: Alexander Technique.
● **Owner** Ms B Tonge
P S (Ref:HM20156)

### TONYPANDY HEALTH CENTRE

**Tonypandy Health Centre**, De Winton Field, Tonypandy, **Rhondda Cynon Taff**, CF40 2LE, WAL.
(T) 01443 433715
Speciality: Chiropodists (Podiatrists).
● **Senior Partner** Mr R Baber
S (Ref:HM20157)

### TONY'S HAIR & HEALTH CENTRE

**Tony's Hair & Health Centre**, 17 Harford Sq, Lampeter, **Carmarthenshire**, SA48 7HE, WAL.
(T) 01570 422133 (F) 01570 422133
Speciality: Osteopathy.
● **Owner** Mrs T Unsworth
P S T (Ref:HM20158)

### TOOGOOD, VIVIENNE

**Vivienne Toogood**, 25 Leicester Rd, Market Harborough, **Leicestershire**, LE16 7AX, ENG.
(T) 01858 433264 (F) 01858 433264
Speciality: Chiropodists (Podiatrists).
● **Owner** Mrs V Toogood
S (Ref:HM20159)

### TOOMPUU, LINDE

**Linde Toompuu**, 30 Parkgate Cottages, Stansted Park, Rowland's Castle, **Hampshire**, PO9 6DY, ENG.
(T) 023 9263 1295
Speciality: Complementary Medicines & Therapy.
C M (Ref:HM20160)

### TOOMS DEBORAH CHIROPODIST

**Tooms Deborah Chiropodist**, 29 Kent Rd, Grays, **Essex**, RM17 6DE, ENG.
(T) 01375 409444
Speciality: Chiropodists (Podiatrists).
S (Ref:HM20161)

### TOOTH, DIANE

**Diane Tooth**, 185a Torridon Rd, London, **London (Greater)**, SE6 1RG, ENG.
(T) 020 8480 9905
Speciality: Homeopathy.
● **Owner** Ms L Griffin
M (Ref:HM20162)

### TOOTHE, DIANE

**Diane Toothe**, 66 Kingshurst Rd, London, **London (Greater)**, SE12 9LB, ENG.
(T) 020 8857 5869
Speciality: Homeopathy.
M (Ref:HM20163)

### TOP CENTRE

**Top Centre**, 52a Carfax, Horsham, **Sussex (West)**, RH12 1EQ, ENG.
(T) 01403 240224
Speciality: Hypnotherapy.
● **Owner** Mr I Aird
B (Ref:HM20164)

### TOP TO TOE

**Top To Toe**, Unit 5 Plassey Craft Centre, Eyton, Wrexham, LL13 0SP, WAL.
(T) 01978 780688
Speciality: Aromatherapy.
M O (Ref:HM20165)

### TOPEL, A M

**A M Topel**, 11 Hafren Cl, Shrewsbury, **Shropshire**, SY3 8NH, ENG.
(T) 01743 368770
Speciality: Physiotherapy.
● **Owner** Ms A Topel
P S T (Ref:HM20166)

### TOPSHAM PHYSIO/COMP HEALTH

**Topsham Physiotherapy & Complementary Health Clinic**, 38 Fore St, Topsham, Exeter, **Devon**, EX3 0HR, ENG.
(T) 01392 876116
Speciality: Physiotherapy.
P S T (Ref:HM20167)

### TOP-TO-TOE HEALTH & BEAUTY

**Top-To-Toe Health & Beauty Clinic**, 75 Dane Avenue, Thorpe Willoughby, Selby, **Yorkshire (North)**, YO8 9NU, ENG.
(T) 01757 213675
Speciality: Complementary Medicines & Therapy.
● **Partner** Mrs P Jones
M (Ref:HM20168)

### TORBAY CHIROPRACTIC CLINIC

**Torbay Chiropractic Clinic**, 62 Hyde Rd, Paignton, **Devon**, TQ4 5DQ, ENG.
(T) 01803 403041 (F) 01803 403039
Speciality: Chiropractors.
● **Owner** Dr I Vasey
P S T (Ref:HM20169)

### TORBAY OCCUPATIONAL THERAPY

**Torbay Occupational Therapy Services**, 5 Clennon Gardens, Paignton, **Devon**, TQ4 5HH, ENG.
(T) 01803 522774
Speciality: Complementary Medicines & Therapy, Occupational Therapy.
M (Ref:HM20170)

### TORLINGTON, GILL

**Gill Torlington**, 1st Floor Woburn Court, 8 Guildhall Hill, Norwich, **Norfolk**, NR2 1JG, ENG.
(T) 01603 219254
Speciality: Complementary Medicines & Therapy.
● **Partner** Mrs G Torlington
M (Ref:HM20171)

### TORNTON, HOWARD

**Howard Thornton**, 257 Upper Woodlands Rd, Bradford, **Yorkshire (West)**, BD8 9JQ, ENG.
(T) 01274 545095
Speciality: Osteopathy. ✔
● **Osteopath** Mr H Thornton Q: DO. M: GOsC.
S Yrs. Est.: 23 (Ref:HM20172)

### TORRIDON COMP THERAPY CLINIC

**Torridon Complementary Therapy Clinic**, 185a Torridon Rd, London, **London (Greater)**, SE6 1RG, ENG.
(T) 020 8480 9905
Speciality: Aromatherapy, Counselling, Hypnotherapy, Massage (Therapeutic), Reflexology, Reiki. ✔
● **Therapist** Ms L Griffin M: GCP.
● **Hypnotherapist** Mr A Tang M: BSCH.
C (Ref:HM20173)

### TORY, E

**E Tory**, Stud Farm, West Leith, Tring, **Hertfordshire**, HP23 6JR, ENG.
(T) 01442 823364
Speciality: Chiropodists (Podiatrists).
● **Owner** Mrs E Tory
S (Ref:HM20174)

### TOSELAND, DOROTHY

**Dorothy Toseland**, 89 Normandy Avenue, Barnet, **Hertfordshire**, EN5 2HT, ENG.
(T) 020 8449 9935
Speciality: Reflexology.
S T (Ref:HM20175)

### TOSH, CAROLINE

**Caroline Tosh**, 32 Lansdown, Stroud, **Gloucestershire**, GL5 1BW, ENG.
(T) 01453 750399
Speciality: Osteopathy.
P S T (Ref:HM20176)

### TOTAL FOOT CARE

**Total Foot Care**, 250 Clement Rise, Livingston, **Lothian (West)**, EH54 6LR, SCO.
(T) 01506 492391
Speciality: Chiropodists (Podiatrists).
● **Owner** Mr G Raeburn
S (Ref:HM20177)

### TOTAL FOOTCARE

**Total Footcare**, 138A Main St, East Calder, Livingston, **Lothian (West)**, EH53 0HD, SCO.
(T) 01506 885885
Speciality: Chiropodists (Podiatrists).
● **Secretary** Mrs I Purdie
S (Ref:HM20178)

### TOTAL HEALTH CARE

**Total Health Care**, Chart Lodge, Nutfield Rd, Redhill, **Surrey**, RH1 4BA, ENG.
(T) 01737 766792
Speciality: Complementary Medicines & Therapy.
C M (Ref:HM20179)

### TOTAL HEALTHCARE IN SAFETY

**Total Healthcare In Safety**, Molesworth St,



Key: B Mind-Body Medicine C Complementary Medicine H Self Help Treatment M Medicinal Therapy O Oriental Medicine P Postural Therapy S Manipulative Structural Therapy T Touch Therapy

Tintagel, **Cornwall**, PL34 0BZ, ENG.
(T) 01840 770023 (F) 01840 770023
Speciality: Complementary Medicines & Therapy.
● **Partner** Mr D Martin
**M** (Ref:HM20180)

## TOTAL WELLBEING
**Total Wellbeing**, 7 Crouch St, Banbury, **Oxfordshire**, OX16 9PP, ENG.
(T) 01295 255550
Speciality: Aromatherapy.
● **Professor** Mrs P Hastie
**M** **O** (Ref:HM20181)

## TOTTENHAM, NIKKI
**Nikki Tottenham**, 55 Wrottesley Rd, Wolverhampton, **Midlands (West)**, WV6 8SG, ENG.
(T) 01902 758863
Speciality: Reflexology.
● **Owner** Miss N Tottenham
**S** **T** (Ref:HM20182)

## TOTTLE, G
**G Tottle**, Golden Springs Farm, Waddock, Dorchester, **Dorset**, DT2 8QY, ENG.
(T) 01929 462636 (F) 01929 462636
Speciality: Chiropodists (Podiatrists).
● **Owner** Mrs G Tottle
**S** (Ref:HM20183)

## TOUCH
**Touch Ltd**, P.O. Box 20113, London, **London (Greater)**, W12 9ZF, ENG.
(T) 020 8740 7742
Speciality: Complementary Medicines & Therapy.
**C** **M** (Ref:HM20184)

## TOUCH & GO
**Touch & Go**, 16 Bolton Avenue, Poulton-le-Fylde, **Lancashire**, FY6 7TW, ENG.
(T) 01253 890443
Speciality: Electrolysis.
● **Owner** Mrs C Shone
**T** (Ref:HM20185)

## TOUCH FOR HEALTH
**Touch For Health**, Roseneath, Madeira Rd, Seaview, **Isle of Wight**, PO34 5BA, ENG.
(T) 01983 615446
Speciality: Massage (Therapeutic), Reflexology. ✔
● **Reflexologist/Masseur** Mr T Kohle Q: BSc, ITEC. M: ITEC.
**C** **T** Yrs. Est.: 10 (Ref:HM20186)

## TOUCH IN LIVE
**Touch In Live (Babies & Infants)**, 10 Uxbridge Rd, Hampton, **London (Greater)**, TW12 3AB, ENG.
(T) 020 8979 6261 (F) 020 8979 9549
Speciality: Reflexology.
● **Owner** Miss C Barnes
**M** (Ref:HM20187)

## TOUCH OF NATURE
**Touch Of Nature**, 46 Campion Hall Drive, Didcot, **Oxfordshire**, OX11 9RN, ENG.
(T) 01235 815870
(E) harry@metsemakers.screaming.net
Speciality: Absent Healing, Aromatherapy, Bach Remedies, Cognitive Therapy, Complementary Therapy, Counselling, Crystal Healing, Dietician, Dowsing, Faith Healing, Healer, Healing Therapy, Herbal Medicine, Holistic Healing, Indian Head Massage, Massage (Therapeutic), Meditation, Naturopathy, Nutritional Therapy, Phytotherapy, Reflexology, Reiki, Spiritual Healing, Stress Therapy, Vitamin Therapy. ✔
● **Owner** Mr H Metsemakers Q: ITEC, MIPTI.
**C** Yrs. Est.: 5 (Ref:HM20188)

## TOUCHARD, HELEN
**Helen Touchard**, Frog Cottage, 11 School Hill, North Marston, Buckingham, **Buckinghamshire**, MK18 3PE, ENG.
(T) 01296 670844
Speciality: Reflexology.
**S** **T** (Ref:HM20189)

## TOUCHLINE THERAPIES
**Touchline Therapies Ltd**, 26 Fen Rd, Metheringham, Lincoln, **Lincolnshire**, LN4 3AA, ENG.
(T) 01526 323200
Speciality: Reflexology, Reiki, Shiatsu.
● **Partner** Mrs J Ford
**M** (Ref:HM20190)

## TOUCHPRO U K
**Touchpro U K Chair Massage School**, 176 Melrose Avenue, London, **London (Greater)**, NW2 4JY, ENG.
(T) 020 8450 3366
Speciality: Complementary Medicines & Therapy.
**C** **M** (Ref:HM20191)

## TOW, DAVID
**David Tow**, 63 Hilltop Rd, Dronfield, **Derbyshire**, S18 1UJ, ENG.
(T) 01246 414603
Speciality: Physiotherapy.
● **Owner** Mr D Tow
**P** **S** **T** (Ref:HM20192)

## TOWARD, K
**K Toward**, 9 Holcroft Cl, Saltash, **Cornwall**, PL12 4PU, ENG.
(T) 01752 845916
Speciality: Physiotherapy.
**P** **S** **T** (Ref:HM20193)

## TOWCESTER CHIROPRACTIC CLINIC
**Towcester Chiropractic Clinic**, 58 Watling St, Towcester, **Northamptonshire**, NN12 6AF, ENG.
(T) 01327 352225
(E) jennifer@dolphinchiro.co.uk
Speciality: Bach Remedies, Chiropractic. ✔
● **Owner** Ms J Leighton Q: BSc (Chiro), DC, ITEC. M: BAAC, GCC.
**S** Yrs. Est.: 7 (Ref:HM20194)

## TOWERS, DIANA
**Diana Towers**, Kerry House, Common Lane, Mappleborough Green, Studley, **Warwickshire**, B80 7DP, ENG.
(T) 01527 854681 (F) 01527 854681
(E) dianatowers@aol.com
Speciality: Counselling, Hypnosis, Hypnotherapy. ✔
● **Counsellor/Curative Hypnotherapy** Ms D Towers Q: BA, Dip.Couns, Dip.Hyp, NLP. M: GCH, NCH.
**H** Yrs. Est.: 15 (Ref:HM20195)

## TOWERS, FILMER
**Filmer Towers**, 156 Park Rd, London, **London (Greater)**, W4 3HP, ENG.
(T) 020 8995 6370 (F) 020 8580 9187
Speciality: Hypnosis.
● **Owner** Mr F Towers
**B** (Ref:HM20196)

## TOWERS, MELISSA
**Melissa Towers**, 205 Collingwood Rd, Sutton, **Surrey**, SM1 2LX, ENG.
(T) 020 8641 8535
Speciality: Reflexology.
● **Owner** Ms M Towers
**S** **T** (Ref:HM20197)

## TOWLI, BARBARA
**Barbara Towli**, 56 Longmead Drive, Sidcup, **Kent**, DA14 4NZ, ENG.
(T) 020 8302 8542
Speciality: Reflexology.
**S** **T** (Ref:HM20198)

## TOWN, BERNICE
**Bernice Town**, 7a High St, Swanley, **Kent**, BR8 8AE, ENG.
(T) 01322 614421
Speciality: Chiropody. ✔
● **Chiropodist** Mrs B Town Q: MBChA, MSSCh.
**M** Yrs. Est.: 12 (Ref:HM20199)

## TOWNER, JOAN
**Joan Towner**, Hop Fields, Homestead Rd, Medstead, Alton, **Hampshire**, GU34 5PW, ENG.
(T) 01420 562649
Speciality: Complementary Medicines & Therapy.
● **Owner** Mrs J Gibbs
**C** **M** (Ref:HM20200)

## TOWNGATE BACKPAIN CLINIC
**Towngate Backpain Clinic**, 102 Towngate, Leyland, Preston, **Lancashire**, PR5 1LQ, ENG.
(T) 01772 456657
Speciality: Osteopathy.
● **Practice Manager** Mr J Parsons
**C** **P** **S** **T** (Ref:HM20201)

## TOWNS, KATE
**Kate Towns NLP, Hypnotherapy**, Millmead, Snowdenham Lane, Bramley, Guildford, **Surrey**, GU5 0AT, ENG.
(T) 01483 893353 (F) 01483 893353
Speciality: Complementary Therapy, Healing Therapy, Hypnosis, Hypnotherapy, Neuro-Linguistic Program, Stress Therapy. ✔
● **NLP Practitioner/Hypnotherapist** Ms K Towns Q: Dip.Hyp, MBHReg, NLP. M: ANLP, HA.
**B** Yrs. Est.: 4 (Ref:HM20202)

## TOWNSEND, MADELAINE
**Madelaine Townsend**, 2 Chapel Fields, St. Austell, **Cornwall**, PL25 3ES, ENG.
(T) 01726 61883
Speciality: Chiropodists (Podiatrists).
**S** (Ref:HM20203)

## TOY, M F
**M F Toy**, 55 Sylvan Rd, Exeter, **Devon**, EX4 6EY, ENG.
(T) 01392 255984
Speciality: Chiropodists (Podiatrists).
**S** (Ref:HM20204)

## TOYNBEE, J
**J Toynbee**, 77 Park Lane, Histon, Cambridge, **Cambridgeshire**, CB4 9JJ, ENG.
(T) 01223 234967
Speciality: Physiotherapy.
**P** **S** **T** (Ref:HM20205)

## TOYNE, JOY K
**Joy K Toyne**, Oast Meadow, Horsmonden Rd, Brenchley, Tonbridge, **Kent**, TN12 7AT, ENG.
(T) 01892 723799
Speciality: Hypnosis.
● **Owner** Mrs J Toyne
**B** (Ref:HM20206)

## TOYO
**Toyo Ltd**, Unit 1, Leyton Ind Village, Argall Avenue, London, **London (Greater)**, E10 7QP, ENG.
(T) 020 8539 0232
Speciality: Herbalists.
● **Partner** Mr A Sharif
**M** (Ref:HM20207)

## TPS OCCUPATIONAL PSYCHOLOGISTS
**TPS Occupational Psychologists**, Easter Cottage, Southrop Rd, Hook Norton, Banbury, **Oxfordshire**, OX15 5PP, ENG.
(T) 01608 730157
Speciality: Psychology.
● **Owner** Mr G Duggan
**B** (Ref:HM20208)

## TRACEY UNA MCTIMONEY
**Tracey Una McTimoney**, The Crescent Practice, Southernhay Lodge, 1a Barnfield Cres, Exeter, **Devon**, EX1 1QT, ENG.
(T) 01392 432635
Speciality: Chiropractors.
● **Owner** Ms U Tracey
**P** **S** **T** (Ref:HM20209)

## TRACEY UNA MCTIMONEY
**Tracey Una McTimoney**, 44 Powderham Cres, Exeter, **Devon**, EX4 6BZ, ENG.
(T) 01392 432635
Speciality: Chiropractic.
**P** **S** **T** (Ref:HM20210)

## TRACEY, J
**J Tracey**, 11 Massey Avenue, Lymm, **Cheshire**, WA13 0PJ, ENG.
(T) 01925 755229
Speciality: Reflexology.
● **Owner** Mrs T Turton
**S** **T** (Ref:HM20211)

## TRACEY, NICOLE
**Tracey Nicole**, 6 Sandycove Ave, East


Key continued: Yrs.Est: Years Established Q: Qualifications M: Professional Membership ✔ Indemnity Insurance Accept Credit Cards

Sandycove, Dublin, **County Dublin**, IRE.
(T) 01230 1841
Speciality: Herbalists.
M (Ref:HM20212)

## TRAD CHINESE HERBS & HLTH CTRE

**Traditional Chinese Herbs & Health Centre**, 32 High St, Chislehurst, **Kent**, BR7 5AQ, ENG.
(T) 020 8467 1204
Speciality: Complementary Medicines & Therapy.
● **Owner** Mr H Wong
C M (Ref:HM20213)

## TRAD CHINESE MASSOTHERAPY

**Traditional Chinese Massotherapy & Training School**, Pheonix House, 2 Upper Teddington Rd, Kingston Upon Thames, **Surrey**, KT1 4DY, ENG.
(T) 020 8977 2605
Speciality: Complementary Medicines & Therapy.
● **Owner** Mr T Wong
C M (Ref:HM20214)

## TRAD CHINESE MASSOTHERAPY

**Traditional Chinese Massotherapy & Training School**, West End Clinic, 1st Floor, 80 Shaftesbury Avenue, London, **London (Greater)**, W1V 7DG, ENG.
(T) 07802 448620
Speciality: Chinese Herbal Medicine, Massage (Therapeutic), Meditation, Remedial Massage, T'ai-Chi Ch'uan, Tui-na, Chi Kung, Chinese Massage.
M (Ref:HM20215)

## TRAD CHINESE MEDICINE/MASSAGE

**Traditional Chinese Medicine/Massage**, 50 Merrion Sq East, Dublin, **County Dublin**, IRE.
(T) 01678 8762
(E) emily.miggin@ireland.com
Speciality: Acupressure, Acupuncture, Aromatherapy, Healing Therapy, Herbal Medicine, Holistic Healing, Manipulation, Massage (Therapeutic), Moxibustion, Nutritional Therapy, Reflexology, Shiatsu, Sports Therapy, Deep Connective Massage. ✔
● **Therapist** Ms E Miggin
O Yrs. Est.: 3 (Ref:HM20216)

## TRADITIONAL ACUPUNCTURE

**Traditional Acupuncture**, 93 Ancrum Rd, Dundee, **Angus**, DD2 2HN, SCO.
(T) 01382 660314
Speciality: Acupuncture.
O (Ref:HM20217)

## TRADITIONAL ACUPUNCTURE CENTRE

**Traditional Acupuncture Centre**, 75 Roupell St, Waterloo, London, **London (Greater)**, SE1 8SS, ENG.
(T) 020 7928 8333
Speciality: Acupuncture. ✔
● **Manageress** Ms L Cooper
C O Yrs. Est.: 18 (Ref:HM20218)

## TRADITIONAL ACUPUNCTURE CLINIC

**Traditional Acupuncture Clinic (The)**, 26 Clarence St, Gloucester, **Gloucestershire**, GL1 1DP, ENG.
(T) 01452 311998
Speciality: Acupuncture.
O (Ref:HM20219)

## TRADITIONAL ACUPUNCTURE CLINIC

**Traditional Acupuncture Clinic**, 259 Wigan Rd, Bolton, **Lancashire**, BL3 5QP, ENG.
(T) 01204 658532
(E) vivien.onslow@euphony.net
Speciality: Acupuncture. ✔
● **Acupuncturist** Ms V Onslow Q: Adv.Lic.Ac. M: BAcC.
O Yrs. Est.: 12 (Ref:HM20220)

## TRADITIONAL ACUPUNCTURE GROUP

**Traditional Acupuncture Group (The)**, Trinity House, 19 Binswood St, Leamington Spa, **Warwickshire**, CV32 5RW, ENG.
(T) 01926 450990 (F) 01926 887846
Speciality: Acupuncture, Aromatherapy, Bio-energetics, Bowen Therapy, Counselling, Herbal Medicine, Hypnotherapy, Massage (Therapeutic), Reflexology. ✔
● **Acupuncturist** Ms H Skellon Q: M.Ac, MBAcC. M: BACP.
● **Manager** Mrs J Watts
M Yrs. Est.: 11 (Ref:HM20221)

## TRADITIONAL ACUPUNCTURIST

**Traditional Acupuncturist**, 14 Burnham St, Sherwood, Nottingham, **Nottinghamshire**, NG5 2FH, ENG.
(T) 01158 411385
(E) beecherry@hotmail.com
Speciality: Acupressure, Acupuncture, Aromatherapy, Bach Remedies, Complementary Therapy, Cupping, Holistic Healing, Massage (Therapeutic), Moxibustion, Oriental Diagnosis, Reiki. ✔
● **Acupuncture Practitioner** Mrs C Chapman Q: BA, Lic.Ac. M: BAcC.
O Yrs. Est.: 14 (Ref:HM20222)

## TRADITIONAL CHINESE MED CTRE

**Traditional Chinese Medicine Centre**, 21 St. Andrews Rd South, St. Annes, **Lancashire**, FY8 1SX, ENG.
(T) 01253 724920
Speciality: Acupuncture, Herbal Medicine, Moxibustion, Oriental Diagnosis. ✔
● **Acupuncturist/Herbalist** Ms J Almond Q: BA (Hons). M: BAcC, RCHM.
O Yrs. Est.: 13 (Ref:HM20223)

## TRADITIONAL CHINESE MED CTRE

**Traditional Chinese Medical Centre**, 315 Camberwell Rd, London, **London (Greater)**, SE5 0HQ, ENG.
(T) 020 7703 8198
Speciality: Acupuncture.
● **Owner** Mr W Waa
O (Ref:HM20224)

## TRADITIONAL CHINESE MEDICINE

**Traditional Chinese Medicine**, Cheam Clinic, 21 Upper Mulgrave Rd, Sutton, **Surrey**, SM2 7AY, ENG.
(T) 020 8770 0018
(W) www.xinglintcm.co.uk
Speciality: Acupuncture, Psychotherapy. ✔
● **Acupuncturist** Ms A Grant M: BAcC.
● **Acupuncturist** Professor B Ma
C Yrs. Est.: 25 (Ref:HM20225)

## TRADITIONAL CHINESE MEDICINE

**Traditional Chinese Medicine**, 37 Crouch St, Colchester, **Essex**, CO3 3EN, ENG.
(T) 01206 500190 (F) 01206 304130
Speciality: Complementary Medicines & Therapy.
● **Owner** Dr S Doran
C M (Ref:HM20226)

## TRADITIONAL CHINESE MEDICINE

**Traditional Chinese Medicine**, 22-23 One Stop Shopping Centre, Walsall Rd, Perry Barr, Birmingham, **Midlands (West)**, B42 1AA, ENG.
(T) 01213 563339 (F) 01213 563339
Speciality: Complementary Medicines & Therapy.
● **Manager** Mr H Hung
C M (Ref:HM20227)

## TRADITIONAL CHINESE MEDICINE

**Traditional Chinese Medicine**, Portarlington Co, **County Laois**, IRE.
(T) 08682 99525
Speciality: Complementary Medicines & Therapy.
M (Ref:HM20228)

## TRADITIONAL CHINESE MEDICINE

**Traditional Chinese Medicine**, Millstreet Co, **County Cork**, IRE.
(T) 029 7049 8
Speciality: Complementary Medicines & Therapy.
M (Ref:HM20229)

## TRADITIONAL CHINESE MEDICINE

**Traditional Chinese Medicine**, 15/16 West End, Mallow, **County Cork**, IRE.
(T) 08626 70068
Speciality: Complementary Medicines & Therapy.
M (Ref:HM20230)

## TRADITIONAL CHINESE MEDICINE

**Traditional Chinese Medicine**, Douglas Vlge, **County Cork**, IRE.
(T) 021 4509 903
Speciality: Complementary Medicines & Therapy.
M (Ref:HM20231)

## TRADITIONAL CHINESE MEDICINE

**Traditional Chinese Medicine**, Donnybrook, **County Dublin**, IRE.
(T) 01624 7300
Speciality: Complementary Medicines & Therapy.
M (Ref:HM20232)

## TRADITIONAL CHINESE MEDICINE

**Traditional Chinese Medicine**, Clane Co, **County Kildare**, IRE.
(T) 04586 1892
Speciality: Complementary Medicines & Therapy.
M (Ref:HM20233)

## TRADITIONAL CHINESE MEDICINE

**Traditional Chinese Medicine**, 13 Town Hall St, **County Cavan**, IRE.
(T) 04324 356
Speciality: Complementary Medicines & Therapy.
M (Ref:HM20234)

## TRADITIONAL CHINESE MEDICINE

**Traditional Chinese Medicine**, Longford, Mullingar, **County Westmeath**, IRE.
(T) 04346 993
Speciality: Complementary Medicines & Therapy.
M (Ref:HM20235)

## TRADITIONAL CHINESE MEDICINE

**Traditional Chinese Medicine**, Drogheda Co, **County Louth**, IRE.
(T) 04168 52133
Speciality: Complementary Medicines & Therapy.
M (Ref:HM20236)

## TRADITIONAL CHINESE MEDICINE

**Traditional Chinese Medicine**, Tipperary Town, **County Tipperary**, IRE.
(T) 05232 414
Speciality: Complementary Medicines & Therapy.
M (Ref:HM20237)

## TRADITIONAL CHINESE MEDICINE

**Traditional Chinese Medicine**, Upr Bridge St, Killorglin, **County Kerry**, IRE.
(T) 06697 62344
Speciality: Complementary Medicines & Therapy.
M (Ref:HM20238)

## TRADITIONAL CHINESE MEDICINE

**Traditional Chinese Medicine**, Edward St, Tralee, **County Kerry**, IRE.
(T) 08724 80723
Speciality: Complementary Medicines & Therapy.
M (Ref:HM20239)

## TRADITIONAL CHINESE MEDICINE

**Traditional Chinese Medicine**, Church St, Athlone, **County Westmeath**, IRE.
(T) 09023 7454
Speciality: Complementary Medicines & Therapy.
M (Ref:HM20240)

## TRADITIONAL CHINESE MEDICINE

**Traditional Chinese Medicine**, The Crescent, **County Galway**, IRE.
(T) 09158 1575
Speciality: Acupuncture.
O (Ref:HM20241)

## TRADITIONAL CHINESE MEDICINE

**Traditional Chinese Medicine**, 436 Howth Rd, Raheny, **County Dublin**, IRE.
(T) 01832 8491
Speciality: Complementary Medicines & Therapy.



Key: B Mind-Body Medicine C Complementary Medicine H Self Help Treatment M Medicinal Therapy O Oriental Medicine P Postural Therapy S Manipulative Structural Therapy T Touch Therapy

M (Ref:HM20242)

**TRADITIONAL CHINESE MEDICINE**

**Traditional Chinese Medicine**, Cork Rd, Waterford City, IRE.
(T) 05135 8128
Speciality: Complementary Medicines & Therapy.
M (Ref:HM20243)

**TRADITIONAL CHINESE MEDICINE**

**Traditional Chinese Medicine**, Waterford City, IRE.
(T) 05130 77678
Speciality: Complementary Medicines & Therapy.
M (Ref:HM20244)

**TRADITIONAL CHINESE MEDICINE**

**Traditional Chinese Medicine**, Upper Bridge St, Killorglin, **County Kerry**, IRE.
(T) 06697 61066
Speciality: Acupuncture.
● **Practitioner** Mrs J Tucker
O (Ref:HM20245)

**TRADITIONAL CHINESE MEDICINES**

**Traditional Chinese Medicines**, 50 Fore St, Chard, **Somerset**, TA20 1QA, ENG.
(T) 01460 61464
Speciality: Complementary Medicines & Therapy.
● **Owner** Mr P Rogers
M (Ref:HM20246)

**TRAFFORD, DEBORAH**

**Deborah Trafford**, Glenavon, Salhouse Rd, Little Plumstead, Norwich, **Norfolk**, NR13 5JJ, ENG.
(T) 01603 720467
Speciality: Acupressure, Massage (Therapeutic), Reflexology.
S T (Ref:HM20247)

**TRAINER, G**

**G Trainer**, 140 Harley St, London, **London (Greater)**, W1N 1AH, ENG.
(T) 020 7224 1750
Speciality: Osteopathy.
● **Owner** Mr G Trainer
P S T (Ref:HM20248)

**TRAINING SCH OF HYPNO & PSYCHO**

**Centre Training School Of Hypnotherapists & Psychotherapists**, 145 Chapel Lane, Longton, Preston, **Lancashire**, PR4 5NA, ENG.
(T) 01772 617663 (F) 01772 614211
Speciality: Hypnosis.
● **Principal** Ms S Washington
B (Ref:HM20249)

**TRANCE - FORMATIONS HEALING**

**Kathy Philp**, 30 Old Torquay Rd, Preston, Paignton, **Devon**, TQ3 2QZ, ENG.
(T) 01803 405990
(E) mioroger@breathemail.net
Speciality: Auto Suggestion, Biofeedback, Counselling, Family Therapy, Healer, Healing Therapy, Hypnosis, Hypnotherapy, Psychotherapy, Reflexology, Stress Therapy, Visualisation Therapy, Magnet Therapy. ✔
● **Hypnotherapist** Ms K Philp
(T) 01803 405841 Q: Dip.(GC), Dip.Hyp, Dip.NLP, NLP.
● **Psychotherapist** Mr R Philp M: AGPC.
● **Reflexologist** Ms S Cresswell
(T) 01803 558479 Q: Dip.Reflex.
B Yrs. Est.: 11 (Ref:HM20250)

**TRANCE-FORMATIONS**

**Trance-Formations**, 2 Whitford Bridge Cottages, Whitford Bridge Rd, Stoke Prior, Bromsgrove, **Worcestershire**, B60 4HE, ENG.
(T) 01527 873405
Speciality: Hypnotherapy.
● **Owner** Mrs K Dix
B (Ref:HM20251)

**TRANCENDENTAL MEDITATION CTRE**

**Trancendental Meditation Centre**, 39 Pembroke La, (near Baggot St, Ballsbridge, **County Dublin**, IRE.
(T) 01668 9773
Speciality: Complementary Medicines & Therapy.
M (Ref:HM20252)

**TRANQUIL AROMATHERAPY & BEAUTY**

**Tranquil Aromatherapy & Beauty Therapy Clinic**, 88 North Boundary Rd, Brixham, **Devon**, TQ5 8JU, ENG.
(T) 01803 859444
Speciality: Complementary Medicines & Therapy.
C M (Ref:HM20253)

**TRANQUIL SPIRITS**

**Tranquil Spirits**, Raymond Rd, Leicester, **Leicestershire**, LE3 2AT, ENG.
(T) 01162 998535
Speciality: Aromatherapy.
M O (Ref:HM20254)

**TRANQUILITY**

**Tranquility**, 13 Walnut Way, Ruislip, **London (Greater)**, HA4 6TA, ENG.
(T) 020 7841 5656
Speciality: Absent Healing, Acupressure, Aromatherapy, Complementary Therapy, Counselling, Drama Therapy, Faith Healing, Healing Therapy, Holistic Healing, Indian Head Massage, Manipulation, Massage (Therapeutic), Music Therapy, Reflexology, Reiki, Spiritual Healing, Stress Therapy, Swedish Body Massage, Touch Therapy, Holistic Facials, Foot Massages and Relaxation. Journey Work One to One and Louise Hay Counselling and Workshops. ✔
● **Holistic Therapist** Ms L Ottewill Q: ITEC, Reiki 1, Reiki 2. M: ITEC.
H Yrs. Est.: 4 (Ref:HM20255)

**TRANQUILITY**

**Tranquility**, Kemble Court, Downhead Park, Milton Keynes, **Buckinghamshire**, MK15 9AX, ENG.
(T) 01908 609555
Speciality: Reflexology.
● **Owner** Mrs M McMahon
S T (Ref:HM20256)

**TRANQUILITY**

**Tranquility**, 69 Walmgate, York, **Yorkshire (North)**, YO1 9TZ, ENG.
(T) 01904 479799
Speciality: Complementary Medicines & Therapy.
● **Owner** Ms T O'Boyle
M (Ref:HM20257)

**TRANQUILITY**

**Tranquility**, 38 Botanic Rd, Southport, **Merseyside**, PR9 7NE, ENG.
(T) 01704 229577
Speciality: Complementary Medicines & Therapy.
● **Manager** Mrs S Sinclair
M (Ref:HM20258)

**TRANQUILITY**

**Tranquility Ltd**, 135 Linnet Rise, Kidderminster, **Worcestershire**, DY10 4TU, ENG.
(T) 01562 862835
Speciality: Hypnosis.
● **Owner** Miss S Downton
B (Ref:HM20259)

**TRANQUILLITY**

**G Andrews Therapies**, 16 Timberlea Cl, Ashington, Pulborough, **Sussex (West)**, RH20 3LD, ENG.
(T) 01903 892519
Speciality: Absent Healing, Aromatherapy, Healer, Hypnosis, Hypnotherapy, Reiki, Seichem, Stress Therapy, Tera-Mai, Visualisation Therapy. ✔
● **Complementary Therapist** Gloria Andrews Q: EEC, NLP. M: AMIH, ASC.
T Yrs. Est.: 3 (Ref:HM20260)

**TRANQUILLITY**

**Tranquillity**, Main St, Celbridge Co, **County Kildare**, IRE.
(T) 01627 6396
(E) info@tranquility.ie
(W) www.tranquillity.ie
Speciality: Beauty Therapy.
H T (Ref:HM20261)

**TRANQUILLITY CENTRE**

**Tranquillity Centre**, Community Centre, 41 Hurworth Rd, Hurworth Pl, Darlington, **County Durham**, DL2 2BN, ENG.
(T) 01325 722237
Speciality: Complementary Medicines & Therapy.
● **Partner** Ms L Henderson
M (Ref:HM20262)

**TRANS PERSONAL PSYCHOTHERAPIST**

**Trans Personal Psychotherapist**, Avelon, Badger Lane, Oxford, **Oxfordshire**, OX1 5BL, ENG.
(T) 01865 730486 (F) 01865 736623
Speciality: Psychotherapy.
● **Owner** Ms H Larive
B (Ref:HM20263)

**TRANSCENDENTAL MED ASS NORTH**

**Transcendental Meditation Association Northeast**, 30 Cavendish Pl, Newcastle Upon Tyne, **Tyne and Wear**, NE2 2NH, ENG.
(T) 01912 813507
Speciality: Relaxation Technique.
H T (Ref:HM20264)

**TRANSCENDENTAL MEDIATION**

**Transcendental Mediation**, 50 Lynch Rd, Farnham, **Surrey**, GU9 8BY, ENG.
(T) 01252 726535
Speciality: Meditation.
M (Ref:HM20265)

**TRANSCENDENTAL MEDITATION**

**Transcendental Meditation London South**, 143 Chadacre Rd, Worcester Park, Ewell, **Surrey**, KT17 2HQ, ENG.
(T) 020 8224 7611
(E) rgurr@lineone.net
(W) www.t-m.org.uk
Speciality: Meditation. ✔
● **Centre Chairman** Mr R Gurr Q: QTTM. M: Maharishi Foundation.
C Yrs. Est.: 2 (Ref:HM20266)

**TRANSCENDENTAL MEDITATION**

**Transcendental Meditation**, Davenport House Cottage, Carr Lane, Alderley Edge, **Cheshire**, SK9 7SL, ENG.
(T) 01625 582096
Speciality: Complementary Medicines & Therapy.
● **Owner** Mrs M Birchenall
C M (Ref:HM20267)

**TRANSCENDENTAL MEDITATION**

**Transcendental Meditation**, 103 University St, Belfast, **County Antrim**, BT7 1HP, NIR.
(T) 028 9031 0032
Speciality: Meditation.
M (Ref:HM20268)

**TRANSCENDENTAL MEDITATION**

**Transcendental Meditation**, 21 Pinions Rd, High Wycombe, **Buckinghamshire**, HP13 7AT, ENG.
(T) 01494 449486
Speciality: Meditation.
M (Ref:HM20269)

**TRANSCENDENTAL MEDITATION**

**Transcendental Meditation**, 24 Linhope St, London, **London (Greater)**, NW1 6HT, ENG.
(T) 020 7402 3451 (F) 020 7402 0949
Speciality: Complementary Medicines & Therapy.
● **Chairman** Mr T Davids
C M (Ref:HM20270)

**TRANSCENDENTAL MEDITATION**

**Transcendental Meditation**, 34 High St, Bideford, **Devon**, EX39 2AN, ENG.
(T) 01237 477702
Speciality: Complementary Medicines & Therapy.
● **Owner** Mr M Lucas
M (Ref:HM20271)

**TRANSCENDENTAL MEDITATION**

**Transcendental Meditation**, 4 West Newington Pl, Edinburgh, **Edinburgh (City of)**, EH9 1QT, SCO.



Key continued: Yrs.Est: Years Established Q: Qualifications M: Professional Membership ✔ Indemnity Insurance Accept Credit Cards

(T) 01316 624996 (F) 01316 624996
Speciality: Complementary Medicines & Therapy.
● **Chairman** Ms M Ross
M (Ref:HM20272)

### TRANSCENDENTAL MEDITATION
**Transcendental Meditation**, 4 Westend Park, Londonderry, **County Londonderry**, BT48 9JF, NIR.
(T) 028 7126 6116
Speciality: Meditation.
M (Ref:HM20273)

### TRANSCENDENTAL MEDITATION
**Transcendental Meditation**, 43 Lenton Rd, Nottingham, **Nottinghamshire**, NG7 1DU, ENG.
(T) 01159 470364
Speciality: Complementary Medicines & Therapy.
● **Partner** Mr A Christou
C M (Ref:HM20274)

### TRANSCENDENTAL MEDITATION
**Transcendental Meditation**, 5 Brownshill Court, Wick St, Stroud, **Gloucestershire**, GL6 7QN, ENG.
(T) 01453 750156
Speciality: Meditation.
M (Ref:HM20275)

### TRANSCENDENTAL MEDITATION
**Transcendental Meditation**, 81 St Aubyns, Hove, **Sussex (East)**, BN3 2TL, ENG.
(T) 01273 771233
Speciality: Meditation.
M (Ref:HM20276)

### TRANSCENDENTAL MEDITATION
**Transcendental Meditation**, 8a Dell Cl, Harpenden, **Hertfordshire**, AL5 4HP, ENG.
(T) 01582 763703
Speciality: Relaxation Technique.
● **Chairman** Mr B Davis
H T (Ref:HM20277)

### TRANSCENDENTAL MEDITATION
**Transcendental Meditation**, 23 Green Rd, Reading, **Berkshire**, RG6 7BS, ENG.
(T) 01189 660259
Speciality: Complementary Medicines & Therapy.
C M (Ref:HM20278)

### TRANSCENDENTAL MEDITATION
**Transcendental Meditation**, Copythorn Rd, Portsmouth, **Hampshire**, PO2 0DZ, ENG.
(T) 023 9265 4638
Speciality: Complementary Medicines & Therapy.
M (Ref:HM20279)

### TRANSCENDENTAL MEDITATION
**Transcendental Meditation**, Gostins Building, 32-34 Hanover St, Liverpool, **Merseyside**, L1 4LN, ENG.
(T) 01517 099504
Speciality: Complementary Medicines & Therapy.
M (Ref:HM20280)

### TRANSCENDENTAL MEDITATION
**Transcendental Meditation**, Haydon Farmhouse, Haydon Hill, Radstock, Bath, **Somerset**, BA3 3QX, ENG.
(T) 01761 433655 (F) 01761 433655
Speciality: Meditation.
● **Owner** Miss L Royse
M (Ref:HM20281)

### TRANSCENDENTAL MEDITATION
**Transcendental Meditation**, Sunnyside, Mount, Bodmin, **Cornwall**, PL30 4EX, ENG.
(T) 01208 821667
Speciality: Complementary Medicines & Therapy.
M (Ref:HM20282)

### TRANSCENDENTAL MEDITATION
**Transcendental Meditation**, Bury St Edmunds Centre, Livermere Lodge, Great Livermere, Bury St. Edmunds, **Suffolk**, IP31 1JR, ENG.
(T) 01359 269376
Speciality: Meditation.
M (Ref:HM20283)

### TRANSCENDENTAL MEDITATION
**Transcendental Meditation Wales**, 4 East Gr, Cardiff, **Glamorgan (Vale of)**, CF24 3AE, WAL.
(T) 029 2047 1665
Speciality: Meditation.
M (Ref:HM20284)

### TRANSCENDENTAL MEDITATION
**Transcendental Meditation**, 39C Morrland Avenue, Leeds, **Yorkshire (West)**, LS6 1AP, ENG.
(T) 01132 446950
Speciality: Meditation, Transcendental Meditation.
● **Teacher** Mr G Fox
C H (Ref:HM20285)

### TRANSCENDENTAL MEDITATION
**Transcendental Meditation**, 85 Holywell Way, Longthorpe, Peterborough, **Cambridgeshire**, PE3 6SS, ENG.
(T) 01733 268853
(E) peterborough@t-m.org.uk
Speciality: Meditation.
● **Owner** Mr C Brettell Q: Reg.TTM.
C H Yrs. Est.: 8 (Ref:HM20286)

### TRANSCENDENTAL MEDITATION
**Transcendental Meditation**, 21 Clouston St, Glasgow, **Glasgow (City of)**, G20 8QR, SCO.
(T) 01419 464663
Speciality: Meditation.
M (Ref:HM20287)

### TRANSCENDENTAL MEDITATION
**Transcendental Meditation**, 3 Dell Cl, St. Leonards-On-Sea, **Sussex (East)**, TN38 0YS, ENG.
(T) 01424 437618
Speciality: Relaxation Technique.
H T (Ref:HM20288)

### TRANSCENDENTAL MEDITATION CTRE
**Transcendental Meditation Centre**, 12 Tavy Pl, Plymouth, **Devon**, PL4 7DJ, ENG.
(T) 01752 262363
Speciality: Complementary Medicines & Therapy.
● **Director** Ms R Allen
C M (Ref:HM20289)

### TRANSENDENTAL MEDITATION
**Transendental Meditation**, 5 Fitzroy Trce, Bristol, BS6 6TF, ENG.
(T) 01179 737651
Speciality: Meditation.
M (Ref:HM20290)

### TRANSFORM HYPNOTHERAPY CLINIC
**Transform Hypnotherapy Clinic**, Janiveer, Carleton Rd, Pontefract, **Yorkshire (West)**, WF8 3RW, ENG.
(T) 01977 790089
Speciality: Hypnosis.
B (Ref:HM20291)

### TRANSFORMATIONS
**Transformations**, 68 Midway Rd, Midway, Swadlincote, **Derbyshire**, DE11 7NX, ENG.
(T) 01283 216141
Speciality: Hypnosis.
B (Ref:HM20292)

### TRANSFORMATIONS
**Transformations**, 16 Burn Cl, Addlestone, **Surrey**, KT15 2PJ, ENG.
(T) 01932 848828
Speciality: Complementary Medicines & Therapy.
● **Owner** Ms L Percival
C M (Ref:HM20293)

### TRAPMAN YOGA
**Trapman Yoga**, 28 Willow Lane, Great Houghton, Northampton, **Northamptonshire**, NN4 7AW, ENG.
(T) 01604 766760 (F) 01604 766780
Speciality: Relaxation Technique.
● **Owner** Mr J Trapman
H T (Ref:HM20294)

### TRASLER, C
**C Trasler**, 81 Monks Pk Rd, Northampton, **Northamptonshire**, NN1 4LU, ENG.
(T) 01604 604593
Speciality: Chiropodists (Podiatrists).
● **Owner** Miss C Trasler
S (Ref:HM20295)

### TRAUMA RECOVERY THERAPIST
**Trauma Recovery Therapist**, 52 The Broadway, London, **London (Greater)**, W5 5JN, ENG.
(T) 020 8930 9549
Speciality: Complementary Medicines & Therapy.
M (Ref:HM20296)

### TRAUMACARE
**Traumacare**, 80 Bouverie Avenue, Salisbury, **Wiltshire**, SP2 8DX, ENG.
(T) 01722 414155 (F) 01722 327216
Speciality: Physiotherapy.
● **Director** Mr E Patel
P S T (Ref:HM20297)

### TRAVERS, C M
**C M Travers**, Widcombe Surgery, 3-4 Widcombe Prde, Bath, **Somerset**, BA2 4JT, ENG.
(T) 01225 310883 (F) 01225 421600
Speciality: Chiropodists (Podiatrists).
● **Practice Manager** Mrs L Newman
S (Ref:HM20298)

### TRAYNOR, SUSAN
**Susan Traynor**, Bricklayers Cottage, Swan Rd, Beaumont, Clacton-On-Sea, **Essex**, CO16 0AN, ENG.
(T) 01255 862304
Speciality: Complementary Medicines & Therapy.
● **Owner** Ms S Traynor
C M (Ref:HM20299)

### TREACHER, KATE
**Kate Treacher**, Gloucester, **Gloucestershire**, GL4, ENG.
(T) 01452 411860
Speciality: Bach Remedies.
M (Ref:HM20300)

### TREAT FEET
**Treat Feet**, 39 Livingstone Rd, Bournemouth, **Dorset**, BH5 2AS, ENG.
(T) 01202 434442
Speciality: Biomechanics, Chiropody, Nail Surgery, Podiatry. ✔
● **Chiropodist (Podiatrist)**
Ms T Cresswell Q: BSc, S.R.Ch. M: S.C.P.
M Yrs. Est.: 2 (Ref:HM20301)

### TREATMENT ROOM
**Darlington Football & Sports Injury Clinic**, The Leisure Club, Blackwell Grange Hotel, Blackwell Grange, Darlington, **County Durham**, DL3 8QH, ENG.
(T) 01325 354050
(E) markriley@treatmentroom.freeserve.co.uk
Speciality: Acupressure, Acupuncture, Alexander Technique, Aromatherapy, Chiropractic, Electrotherapy, Hypnosis, Hypnotherapy, Kinesiology, Manipulation, Massage (Therapeutic), Physiotherapy, Reflexology, Ultrasonics. ✔
● **Physiotherapist** Mr M Riley Q: BSc, MCSP, MSc, SRP. M: CSP.
C Yrs. Est.: 7 (Ref:HM20302)

### TREBUTH RAINER
**Trebuth Rainer**, 5 Elm Ter, Constantine Rd, London, **London (Greater)**, NW3 2LL, ENG.
(T) 020 7267 4222
Speciality: Hypnotherapy.
● **Owner** Mr R Trebuth
B (Ref:HM20303)

### TREE OF LIFE
**Tree Of Life (The)**, Palace Chambers, Silver St, Bedford, **Bedfordshire**, MK40 1SY, ENG.
(T) 01234 211144 (F) 01234 211144
Speciality: Complementary Medicines & Therapy.
● **Director** Ms N Lindeman
C M (Ref:HM20304)

### TREE OF LIFE AROMATHERAPY
**Tree Of Life Aromatherapy**, Po Box 37, Ryde, **Isle of Wight**, PO33 1RH, ENG.

(T) 01983 811241
Speciality: Aromatherapy.
● **Owner** Mrs A Kettner
M O (Ref:HM20305)

## TREE OF LIFE AROMATHERAPY

**Tree Of Life Aromatherapy**, 9 Scarrots Lane, Newport, **Isle of Wight**, PO30 1JD, ENG.
(T) 01983 811241
Speciality: Aromatherapy.
M O (Ref:HM20306)

## TREE OF LIFE CENTRE

**Tree Of Life Centre (The)**, 47 St Georges St, Cheltenham, **Gloucestershire**, GL50 4AF, ENG.
(T) 01242 520510
Speciality: Crystal Healing, Holistic Healing, Homeopathy, Indian Head Massage, Metamorphic Therapy, Reflexology, Spiritual Healing, Laughter and Happiness Therapy, Deep Tissue Massage. ✔
● **Therapist** Mrs P Sterry
● **Reflexologist** Ms J Burke M: RxS.
B C T Yrs. Est.: 4 (Ref:HM20307)

## TREE OF LIFE CLINIC

**Tree Of Life Clinic**, 1 Portsmouth Rd, Southampton, **Hampshire**, SO19 9BA, ENG.
(T) 023 8036 6992
Speciality: Complementary Medicines & Therapy.
● **Owner** Ms R Chapman
M (Ref:HM20308)

## TREE, J

**J Tree**, The Wellbeing Centre, 11 Musters Rd, West Bridgford, Nottingham, **Nottinghamshire**, NG2 7PP, ENG.
(T) 01159 825353
Speciality: Homeopathy.
M (Ref:HM20309)

## TREECE, B B

**B B Treece**, 216A Old Hall Rd, Chesterfield, **Derbyshire**, S40 1HQ, ENG.
(T) 01246 276275
Speciality: Reflexology.
● **Partner** Mr B Treece
S T (Ref:HM20310)

## TREECE, P M

**P M Treece**, 216A Old Hall Rd, Chesterfield, **Derbyshire**, S40 1HQ, ENG.
(T) 01246 276275
Speciality: Reflexology.
● **Partner** Mr B Treece
S T (Ref:HM20311)

## TREEND, NICOLA

**Nicola Treend**, Mon Abri, Dunmow Rd, Takeley, Bishop's Stortford, **Hertfordshire**, CM22 6SP, ENG.
(T) 01279 870987
Speciality: Reflexology.
S T (Ref:HM20312)

## TREEWICKS

**Treewicks**, 2 Old Court House, George St, Buxton, **Derbyshire**, SK17 6AY, ENG.
(T) 01298 72298
Speciality: Reiki. ✔ CREDIT
● **Reiki Therapist** Mrs J Whitby Q: Reiki 2, Reiki Master. M: RCN, RGN.
C Yrs. Est.: 2 (Ref:HM20313)

## TREFSER, SIGFRIED (DR)

**Dr Sigfried Trefser**, 258 Ashburnham Rd, Richmond, **Surrey**, TW10 7RZ, ENG.
(T) 07973 702461
Speciality: Osteopathy.
P S T (Ref:HM20314)

## TREGELLAS, D L

**D L Tregellas**, 60 Surrey Avenue, Shaw, Oldham, **Lancashire**, OL2 7DP, ENG.
(T) 01706 848646
Speciality: Physiotherapy.
● **Owner** Mr D Tregellas
P S T (Ref:HM20315)

## TREGIDGO, P

**P Tregidgo**, 37 Belmont Rd, Maidenhead, **Berkshire**, SL6 6JL, ENG.
(T) 01628 629652
Speciality: Physiotherapy.
● **Owner** Mrs P Tregidgo
P S T (Ref:HM20316)

## TREMAIN, BARBARA

**Barbara Tremain**, Penzance, **Cornwall**, TR18, ENG.
(T) 01736 740547
Speciality: Bach Remedies.
M (Ref:HM20317)

## TREMAIN, S R

**S R Tremain**, 34 Mill St, Bideford, **Devon**, EX39 2JJ, ENG.
(T) 01237 473262
Speciality: Chiropodists (Podiatrists).
● **Owner** Mr S Tremain
S (Ref:HM20318)

## TRENCHARD, ABIGAIL

**Abigail Trenchard**, Flat 4, 45 Ditchling Rise, Brighton, **Sussex (East)**, BN1 4QN, ENG.
(T) 01273 270925 (F) 01273 270925
Speciality: Counselling, Healing Therapy, Paranormal Therapies, Stress Therapy, Jungian Tarot/Archetypal Visualization Work/Spiritual Guidance. ✔
● **Sole Director**
Despina Katsirea-Cheney
● **Owner/Intuitive Creative Therapist**
Ms H Fairchild Q: BSc, Dip.Couns, PGCE.
H Yrs. Est.: 3 (Ref:HM20319)

## TRENTER, A E

**A E Trenter**, 34 Sutherland Avenue, Bexhill-on-Sea, **Sussex (East)**, TN39 3QL, ENG.
(T) 01424 211717
Speciality: Chiropodists (Podiatrists).
● **Owner** Mrs A Trenter
S (Ref:HM20320)

## TREUHERZ, FRANCIS

**Francis Treuherz**, Cory Pharmacy, 166-168 High Rd, London, **London (Greater)**, N2 9AS, ENG.
(T) 020 8444 9966
Speciality: Homeopathy.
● **Owner** Mr F Treuherz
M (Ref:HM20321)

## TREVAN, RICHARD

**Richard Trevan**, 52 Stoke Newington Church St, London, **London (Greater)**, N16 0NB, ENG.
(T) 020 7249 9671
Speciality: Chiropractors.
● **Senior Partner** Mrs J Sheridan
P S T (Ref:HM20322)

## TREVITT, ELAINE

**Elaine Trevitt D O**, The Coach House, 2 Fern Bank, Lancaster, **Lancashire**, LA1 4TT, ENG.
(T) 01524 846303 (F) 01524 846303
Speciality: Osteopathy.
● **Owner** Mrs E Trevitt
P S T (Ref:HM20323)

## TREVOR COOK HOMOEOPATHY

**Trevor Cook Homoeopathy Ltd**, Cygnet House, Market Sq, Staines, **Surrey**, TW18 4RH, ENG.
(T) 01784 466251 (F) 01784 449887
Speciality: Homeopathy.
M (Ref:HM20324)

## TREWHELLA, JOHN

**John Trewhella**, Castle Gayer, Leys Lane, Marazion, **Cornwall**, TR17 0AQ, ENG.
(T) 01736 711548 (F) 01736 711110
Speciality: Psychotherapy.
● **Partner** Mr J Trewhella
B (Ref:HM20325)

## TRIANCE, E R

**E R Triance**, Long Acre, Keyston Rd, Covington, Huntingdon, **Cambridgeshire**, PE18 0RU, ENG.
(T) 01480 860890
Speciality: Osteopathy.
● **Owner** Mr E Triance
P S T (Ref:HM20326)

## TRIANGLE HEALING TRUST

**Triangle Healing Trust**, 27 Chapelfields, Cuckfield, Haywards Heath, **Sussex (West)**, RH17 5JR, ENG.
(T) 01444 417198
Speciality: Complementary Medicines & Therapy.
C M (Ref:HM20327)

## TRIANGLE HOMOEOPATHIC PRACTICE

**Triangle Homoeopathic Practice**, 43 Stile Trce, Sowerby Bridge, **Yorkshire (West)**, HX6 3NT, ENG.
(T) 01422 839044
Speciality: Homeopathy.
M (Ref:HM20328)

## TRIBE, DARRY L

**Darry L Tribe**, Berkhamsted Chiropractic Clinic, 69 High St, Berkhamsted, **Hertfordshire**, HP4 2DE, ENG.
(T) 01442 863800
Speciality: Chiropractors.
P S T (Ref:HM20329)

## TRICHO-CARE

**Tricho-Care Ltd**, 126 Sandridge Rd, St. Albans, **Hertfordshire**, AL1 4AQ, ENG.
(T) 01727 855594
Speciality: Complementary Medicines & Therapy, Trichology.
M (Ref:HM20330)

## TRICHOLOGICAL CLINIC

**Trichological Clinic**, 24A Heath St, London, **London (Greater)**, NW3 6TE, ENG.
(T) 020 7794 2949
Speciality: Complementary Medicines & Therapy, Trichology.
M (Ref:HM20331)

## TRICHOLOGIST

**Trichologist**, Office 32 Kings St, Off Bradford Rd, Cleckheaton, **Yorkshire (West)**, BD19 3JX, ENG.
(T) 01274 851753
Speciality: Complementary Medicines & Therapy, Trichology.
M (Ref:HM20332)

## TRICHOLOGY CENTRE

**Trichology Centre (The)**, 19A Drake St, Rochdale, **Lancashire**, OL16 1RE, ENG.
(T) 01706 710371
Speciality: Complementary Medicines & Therapy, Trichology.
M (Ref:HM20333)

## TRIGG, REBECCA

**Rebecca Trigg**, 181 Burton Rd, Barnsley, **Yorkshire (South)**, S71 2HG, ENG.
(T) 01226 241552
Speciality: Acupuncture. ✔
● **Acupuncturist** Ms R Trigg Q: Dip.Ac.
O (Ref:HM20334)

## TRIMED TREATMENT

**Trimed Treatment**, Unit 2, 6 Albany Villas, Hove, **Sussex (East)**, BN3 2RU, ENG.
(T) 01273 739463 (F) 01273 736161
Speciality: Complementary Medicines & Therapy.
● **Owner** Mrs K Miranda
M (Ref:HM20335)

## TRINDER, CATHY

**Cathy Trinder**, 1 Conegra Rd, High Wycombe, **Buckinghamshire**, HP13 6DY, ENG.
(T) 01494 525746 (F) 01494 521798
Speciality: Reflexology.
● **Owner** Ms C Trinder
S T (Ref:HM20336)

## TRINH H V

**Trinh H V**, 52 Queens Rd, Southend-On-Sea, **Essex**, SS1 1NL, ENG.
(T) 01702 390305
Speciality: Acupuncture.
● **Owner** Mr H Trinh
O (Ref:HM20337)

## TRINITY CENTRE

**Trinity Centre (The)**, The Trinity Centre, 21 Trinity St, Colchester, **Essex**, CO1 1JN, ENG.
(T) 01206 561150 (F) 01206 767197
(W) www.trinityhealing.org
Speciality: Acupuncture, Alexander Technique, Aromatherapy, Chiropractic. ✔
● **Homeopath** Ms G Pinto



Key continued: Yrs.Est: Years Established Q: Qualifications M: Professional Membership ✔ Indemnity Insurance CREDIT Accept Credit Cards

- **Information Officer** Mr R Charpe
- **Information Officer** Ms C Weekes
- **Teacher of the Alexander Technique** Mr G MacDonald
- **Bach Flower Remedy** Ms M Scheffer
- **Hypnotherapist** Mr R Farago
- **Bach Flower Remedies** Ms H Jones
- **Colour Therapist** Ms P Wills
- **Colour Healing Therapist** Ms T Gimbal
- **Teacher of the Alexander Technique** Mr C Stevens M: STAT.
- **Hypnotherapist** Ms S Jeffers
- **Hypnotherapist** Dr J Gibson
- **Homeopath** Mr M Feldman

**C** Yrs. Est.: 16 (**Ref:**HM20338)

## TRINITY HOUSE PRACTICE

**John Honey Physiotherapy**, 150-152 Cumberland St, Macclesfield, **Cheshire**, SK10 1BP, ENG.
(T) 01625 615762 (F) 01625 615761
(E) honey.physio@virgin.net
Speciality: Acupressure, Acupuncture, Alexander Technique, Aromatherapy, Bowen Therapy, Complementary Therapy, Counselling, Dietician, Electrotherapy, Homeopathy, Indian Head Massage, Manipulation, Massage (Therapeutic), Nutritional Therapy, Osteopathy, Reflexology, Reiki, Remedial Massage, Shiatsu, Physiotherapy, Chinese/Sports Psychologist, Pain Clinic, Anaesthesia. ✔

- **Practice Manager** Mrs L Honey
- **Partner** Mr M Honey Q: BSc (Hons), MCSP, SRP. M: CSP.

**H** **S** Yrs. Est.: 4 (**Ref:**HM20339)

## TRINITY HOUSE PRACTICE

**Trinity House Practice**, 150-152 Cumberland St, Macclesfield, **Cheshire**, SK10 1BP, ENG.
(T) 01625 615762
Speciality: Complementary Medicines & Therapy.

- **Practice Manager** Mrs L Honey

**M** (**Ref:**HM20340)

## TRINITY OSTEOPATHIC PRACTICE

**Trinity Osteopathic Practice**, Trinity Centre, Bimport, Shaftesbury, **Dorset**, SP7 8BW, ENG.
(T) 01747 851726
Speciality: Osteopathy.

- **Partner** Mrs E Childs

**P** **S** **T** (**Ref:**HM20341)

## TRIPTREE, V

**V Triptree**, 86 Melton Rd, West Bridgford, Nottingham, **Nottinghamshire**, NG2 7NF, ENG.
(T) 01159 696209 (F) 01159 827313
Speciality: Physiotherapy.

- **Owner** Mrs V Triptree

**P** **S** **T** (**Ref:**HM20342)

## TRISTER, LAURENCE

**Laurence Trister**, 15 Church Prde, Church Rd, Ashford, **Surrey**, TW15 2TX, ENG.
(T) 01784 250781
Speciality: Chiropractic.

- **Owner** Mr L Trister

**P** **S** **T** (**Ref:**HM20343)

## TRIUNE HEALTHCARE STUDIOS

**Triune Healthcare Studios**, 4 Napier Rd, London, **London (Greater)**, W14 8LQ, ENG.
(T) 020 7603 7899
Speciality: Complementary Medicines & Therapy.

- **Owner** Mrs A Moore

**C** **M** (**Ref:**HM20344)

## TROHEAR, PATRICIA

**Clinical Hypnotherapist**, 127 Belsize Rd, London, **London (Greater)**, NW6 4AD, ENG.
(T) 020 7624 0638
Speciality: Hypnosis, Hypnotherapy, Stress Therapy, EMDR- Eye Movement Desensitisation and Reprocessing. ✔

- **Hypnotherapist** Ms P Trohear Q: BA, Dip.Clin.Hyp. M: BSCH.

**B** (**Ref:**HM20345)

## TROTMAN, SALLY

**Sally Trotman**, 215 Raeburn Avenue, Surbiton, **Surrey**, KT5 9DE, ENG.
(T) 020 8339 9880
Speciality: Reflexology.

**S** **T** (**Ref:**HM20346)

## TROTT, MOLLY V

**Molly V Trott**, Fourwinds, Limekiln Bank, St. Georges, Telford, **Shropshire**, TF2 9NU, ENG.
(T) 01952 612856
Speciality: Complementary Medicines & Therapy.

- **Owner** Mrs M Trott

**C** **M** (**Ref:**HM20347)

## TROUSDELL, PETA

**Peta Trousdell**, 35 Ditchling Cres, Brighton, **Sussex (East)**, BN1 8GD, ENG.
(T) 01273 554812
Speciality: Reflexology.

**S** **T** (**Ref:**HM20348)

## TROY, ROSEMARY

**Rosemary Troy**, Ashbrook House, 10 Main St, Raheny, **County Dublin**, IRE.
(T) 01851 1319
Speciality: Counselling, Psychotherapy. ✔

- **Consultant Psychologist** Rosemary Troy Q: Reg.Psychol. M: PSI.

**B** Yrs. Est.: 10 (**Ref:**HM20349)

## TRUEMAN, M

**M Trueman**, Cornwall Buildings, 45 Newhall St, Birmingham, **Midlands (West)**, B3 3QR, ENG.
(T) 01212 369016
Speciality: Chiropodists (Podiatrists).

- **Partner** Miss A Bellenger

**S** (**Ref:**HM20350)

## TRUEMAN, P

**P Trueman**, New Cross Natural Therapy Centre, 394 New Cross Rd, London, **London (Greater)**, SE14 6TY, ENG.
(T) 020 8469 0858
Speciality: Hypnotherapy.

**B** (**Ref:**HM20351)

## TRUJILLO, DR ORLANDO

**Dr Orlando Trujillo**, Burnside Of Birnie, Elgin, **Moray**, IV30 8SB, SCO.
(T) 01343 490860
Speciality: Acupressure, Hypnosis, Psychotherapy.

**B** (**Ref:**HM20352)

## TRUNDELL, C

**C Trundell**, 9 Wildfell Cl, Christchurch, **Dorset**, BH23 2PU, ENG.
(T) 01202 496246
Speciality: Chiropody. ✔

- **Chiropodist** Mr C Trundell Q: MBChA, MSSCh.

**M** Yrs. Est.: 15 (**Ref:**HM20353)

## TRURO CHIROPRACTIC CLINIC

**Truro Chiropractic Clinic**, Truro Chiropractic Clinic, 28 Falmouth Rd, Truro, **Cornwall**, TR1 2HX, ENG.
(T) 01872 272275
Speciality: Acupuncture, Aromatherapy, Chiropractic, Homeopathy, Psychotherapy, Reflexology. ✔

- **Chiropractor** Dr D Styles Q: DC. M: BCA, GCC.
- **Owner** Dr G Perry Q: DC, MAB Phys. M: GCC.

**P** Yrs. Est.: 30 (**Ref:**HM20354)

## TRURO NATURAL HEALTH CENTRE

**Truro Natural Health Centre**, 56 Fairmantle St, Truro, **Cornwall**, TR1 2EG, ENG.
(T) 01872 240321
Speciality: Complementary Medicines & Therapy.

- **Partner** Ms J Harrison

**M** (**Ref:**HM20355)

## TRURO OSTEOPATHIC PRACTICE

**Jonathan Wills**, 21 Coronation Trce, Truro, **Cornwall**, TR1 3HJ, ENG.
(T) 01872 222701
(E) jonwills@wcso.freeserve.co.uk
Speciality: Counselling, Manipulation, Osteopathy. ✔

- **Osteopath** Mr J Wills Q: DO. M: GOsC.

**S** Yrs. Est.: 11 (**Ref:**HM20356)

## TRUSCOTT PHYSIOTHERAPY CLINIC

**Truscott Physiotherapy Clinic**, The Good Health Centre, 116 St Lane, Leeds, **Yorkshire (West)**, LS8 2AL, ENG.
(T) 01132 661440
Speciality: Physiotherapy.

- **Partner** Mrs H Evers

**P** **S** **T** (**Ref:**HM20357)

## TRUSCOTT, B T

**B T Truscott**, 25 High St, Long Eaton, Nottingham, **Nottinghamshire**, NG10 1HY, ENG.
(T) 01159 732047
Speciality: Chiropodists (Podiatrists).

- **Owner** Mr B Truscott

**S** (**Ref:**HM20358)

## TSENG, PATRICIA

**Patricia Tseng**, Cedar House, Bingley Gr, Woodley, Reading, **Berkshire**, RG5 4TT, ENG.
(T) 01189 697886
Speciality: Acupressure, Aromatherapy, Complementary Therapy, Counselling, Healer, Healing Therapy, Holistic Healing, Indian Head Massage, Massage (Therapeutic), Reflexology, Reiki, Shiatsu, Stress Therapy. ✔

- **Owner** Mrs P Tseng Q: RGN. M: IIR, LCSP, LLSA.

**S** Yrs. Est.: 10 (**Ref:**HM20359)

## TUAM ACUPUNCTURE CLINIC

**Tuam Acupuncture Clinic**, 9 Trinity Ct, Tuam, **County Galway**, IRE.
(T) 09328 507
Speciality: Acupuncture.

**O** (**Ref:**HM20360)

## TUBOKU-METZGER, A F

**A F Tuboku-Metzger**, 136 Streatham Rd, Mitcham, **Surrey**, CR4 2AE, ENG.
(T) 020 8648 2011
Speciality: Acupuncture.

- **Owner** Dr A Tuboku-Metzger

**O** (**Ref:**HM20361)

## TUCK, JANICE

**Janice Tuck**, 27 Berkeley Rd, Loughborough, **Leicestershire**, LE11 3SJ, ENG.
(T) 01509 554101
Speciality: Reflexology.

**S** **T** (**Ref:**HM20362)

## TUCKER, C J

**C J Tucker**, 186 Grange Drive, Swindon, **Wiltshire**, SN3 4JZ, ENG.
(T) 01793 824307
Speciality: Chiropodists (Podiatrists).

**S** (**Ref:**HM20363)

## TUCKER, H

**H Tucker**, 2-4 High St, Glastonbury, **Somerset**, BA6 9DU, ENG.
(T) 01458 833317
Speciality: Osteopathy.

**P** **S** **T** (**Ref:**HM20364)

## TUCKER, JOCELYN

**Jocelyn Tucker**, 88 Chart Lane, Reigate, **Surrey**, RH2 7EA, ENG.
(T) 01737 243009
Speciality: Reflexology.

**S** **T** (**Ref:**HM20365)

## TUCKER, KATH

**Kath Tucker**, 4 Charlton Court, Knaresborough, **Yorkshire (North)**, HG5 0BZ, ENG.
(T) 01423 865738
Speciality: Acupuncture.

- **Owner** Mrs K Tucker

**O** (**Ref:**HM20366)

## TUCKER, PAUL

**Paul Tucker**, Clissold Park Health Centre, 154 Stoke Newington Church St, London, **London (Greater)**, N16 0JU, ENG.
(T) 020 7249 2990 (F) 020 7249 3977
Speciality: Complementary Medicines & Therapy.

- **Owner** Mr D Berg

**M** (**Ref:**HM20367)

## TUCKLEY, N

**N Tuckley**, Ashdown Osteopathic Centre, The Sq, Lewes Rd, Forest Row, **Sussex (East)**, RH18 5ES,

Key: **B** Mind-Body Medicine **C** Complementary Medicine **H** Self Help Treatment **M** Medicinal Therapy **O** Oriental Medicine **P** Postural Therapy **S** Manipulative Structural Therapy **T** Touch Therapy

ENG.
**(T)** 01342 822505 **(F)** 01342 822505
**Speciality:** Osteopathy.
● **Owner** Mr T Strutt
P S T (**Ref:**HM20368)

## TUCKLEY, N

**N Tuckley**, The Wilbury Clinic Of Natural Medicine, 64 Wilbury Rd, Hove, **Sussex (East)**, BN3 3PY, ENG.
**(T)** 01273 324420
**Speciality:** Osteopathy.
P S T (**Ref:**HM20369)

## TUCKWELL, ANN

**Ann Tuckwell**, 93 Manton Avenue, London, **London (Greater)**, W7 2DY, ENG.
**(T)** 020 8567 7337
**Speciality:** Reflexology.
S T (**Ref:**HM20370)

## TUDOR HOUSE CLINIC

**Tudor House Clinic**, Tudor House Clinic, 225 Wendover Rd, Aylesbury, **Buckinghamshire**, HP21 9PB, ENG.
**(T)** 01296 484658 **(F)** 01296 398397
**Speciality:** Acupuncture, Physiotherapy, Sports Injuries Rehab Centre. ✔
● **Physiotherapist** Kerry Peak **Q:** MCSP, SRP.
● **Physiotherapist** Mr D Gatherer **Q:** MBAcC, MCSP, SRP.
S (**Ref:**HM20371)

## TUDOR REFLEXOLOGY

**Tudor Reflexology**, 5 Tudor Abbey, Newtownards, **County Down**, BT23 8YS, NIR.
**(T)** 028 9181 4152
**Speciality:** Reflexology.
S T (**Ref:**HM20372)

## TUDOR, EDWARD G

**Edward G Tudor**, 16 Iverley Rd, Halesowen, **Midlands (West)**, B63 3EP, ENG.
**(T)** 01215 509647
**Speciality:** Chiropodists (Podiatrists).
● **Owner** Mr E Tudor
S (**Ref:**HM20373)

## TUEBROOK OSTEOPATHIC CLINIC

**Tuebrook Osteopathic Clinic**, 66 Marlborough Rd, Tuebrook, Liverpool, **Merseyside**, L13 8ED, ENG.
**(T)** 01512 260752
**Speciality:** Osteopathy.
● **Owner** Mr M Furlong
P S T (**Ref:**HM20374)

## TUEBROOK OSTEOPATHIC CLINIC

**Tuebrook Osteopathic Clinic**, 461 West Derby Rd, Liverpool, **Merseyside**, L6 4BL, ENG.
**(T)** 01512 636442
**Speciality:** Osteopathy.
P S T (**Ref:**HM20375)

## TUEL LANE PHYSIOTHERAPY CLINIC

**Tuel Lane Physiotherapy Sports Injuries & Massage Clinic**, 13 Hill Crest, Tuel Lane, Halifax, **Yorkshire (West)**, HX6 2TJ, ENG.
**(T)** 01422 839383
**Speciality:** Physiotherapy, Sports Massage. ✔
● **Owner/Physiotherapist**
Mr N Scratcherd **Q:** ITEC. **M:** ITEC.
S (**Ref:**HM20376)

## TUESDAY MARKET CHIROP PRACTICE

**Tuesday Market Chiropody Practice**, 15 Tuesday Market Pl, King's Lynn, **Norfolk**, PE30 1JN, ENG.
**(T)** 01553 691550
**Speciality:** Chiropodists (Podiatrists).
S (**Ref:**HM20377)

## TUGNUTT, SALLY

**Sally Tugnutt**, 5 Godstalls Lane, Steyning, **Sussex (West)**, BN44 3NE, ENG.
**(T)** 01903 812967
**Speciality:** Aromatherapy, Indian Head Massage, Massage (Therapeutic), Reflexology.
M O (**Ref:**HM20378)

## TUGWELL, LAURA

**Laura Tugwell**, Scott St Complementary Therapy Centre, 58 Scott St, Barrow-in-Furness, **Cumbria**, LA14 1QE, ENG.
**(T)** 01229 826700
**Speciality:** Aromatherapy.
M O (**Ref:**HM20379)

## TUGWELL, SUZANNE

**Suzanne Tugwell**, The College Osteopathic Practice, 60 Highgate Rd, London, **London (Greater)**, NW5 1PA, ENG.
**(T)** 020 7267 6445 **(F)** 020 7267 6445
**Speciality:** Osteopathy.
● **Partner** Miss S Tugwell
P S T (**Ref:**HM20380)

## TUKE CENTRE

**Tuke Centre (The)**, 28 Green Dykes Lane, York, **Yorkshire (North)**, YO10 3HH, ENG.
**(T)** 01904 430370
**Speciality:** Psychotherapy.
B (**Ref:**HM20381)

## TULIP HOLISTIC THERAPIES

**Tulip Holistic Therapies**, 19 Airedale Cl, Great Sankey, Warrington, **Cheshire**, WA5 3DJ, ENG.
**(T)** 01925 712097
**Speciality:** Complementary Medicines & Therapy.
● **Owner** Mrs S James
C M (**Ref:**HM20382)

## TULLETT, ANNY

**Anny Tullett**, 16 Merry Acre, Witley, Godalming, **Surrey**, GU8 5RG, ENG.
**(T)** 01483 418878
**Speciality:** Physiotherapy.
● **Owner** Ms A Durnez
P S T (**Ref:**HM20383)

## TULLEY, B

**B Tulley**, 39 Battisford Drive, Clacton-On-Sea, **Essex**, CO16 7LB, ENG.
**(T)** 01255 430604 **(F)** 01255 430604
**Speciality:** Chiropodists (Podiatrists).
● **Owner** Mrs B Tulley
S (**Ref:**HM20384)

## TULLOCH CLINIC

**Tulloch Clinic**, 31 Sterne St, London, **London (Greater)**, W12 8AB, ENG.
**(T)** 020 8743 9816 **(F)** 020 8743 0440
**Speciality:** Physiotherapy.
● **Manager** Mr C Swallow
P S T (**Ref:**HM20385)

## TULLOCH CLINIC

**Tulloch Clinic**, Roehampton Lane, London, **London (Greater)**, SW15 5LR, ENG.
**(T)** 020 8940 4289
**Speciality:** Alexander Technique.
● **Therapist** Ms B Tonge
P S (**Ref:**HM20386)

## TULLOCH, S

**S Tulloch**, 12 Aviemore Drive, Oakley, Basingstoke, **Hampshire**, RG23 7EN, ENG.
**(T)** 01256 780882
**Speciality:** Chiropodists (Podiatrists).
● **Owner** Mrs S Tullock
S (**Ref:**HM20387)

## TULLY, CHARLES

**Charles Tully - Teacher of the Alexander Technique**, 437 Didsbury Rd, Heaton Mersey, Stockport, **Cheshire**, SK4 3BY, ENG.
**(T)** 01619 479184
**Speciality:** Alexander Technique, Life Coaching. ✔
● **Owner** Mr C Tully **Q:** BA, MSTAT. **M:** STAT.
P **Yrs. Est.:** 9 (**Ref:**HM20388)

## TULLY, COLIN

**Colin Tully**, 40 Lansdown Rd, Redland, Bristol, BS6 6NS, ENG.
**(T)** 01179 731520
**Speciality:** Alexander Technique.
● **Partner** Mr C Tully
P S (**Ref:**HM20389)

## TULLY, M J

**M J Tully**, 631 Wilmslow Rd, Manchester, **Manchester (Greater)**, M20 6DF, ENG.
**(T)** 01614 450036
**Speciality:** Chiropodists (Podiatrists).
● **Owner** Mr M Tully
S (**Ref:**HM20390)

## TULLY, MELISSA

**Tully Melissa**, 6 Stoneview Pl, Dun Laoghaire, **County Dublin**, IRE.
**(T)** 08681 54889
**Speciality:** Complementary Medicines & Therapy.
M (**Ref:**HM20391)

## TUNBRIDGE WELLS CHIROPRACTIC

**Tunbridge Wells Chiropractic Clinic**, 4 Garden Rd, Tunbridge Wells, **Kent**, TN1 2XL, ENG.
**(T)** 01892 520636
**Speciality:** Chiropractic.
● **Owner** Mr S Green
P S T (**Ref:**HM20392)

## TUNBRIDGE WELLS OSTEO PRACTICE

**Tunbridge Wells Osteopathic Practice**, 5 Upper Grosvenor Rd, Tunbridge Wells, **Kent**, TN1 2DU, ENG.
**(T)** 01892 535858
**Speciality:** Osteopathy.
● **Owner** Mr R Lederman
P S T (**Ref:**HM20393)

## TUNE IN

**Tune In**, 14 St Georges Mews, London, **London (Greater)**, NW1 8XE, ENG.
**(T)** 020 7586 5856
**Speciality:** Acupuncture.
O (**Ref:**HM20394)

## TUNE, DAVID

**David Tune**, 23 Rectory Rd, Wivenhoe, Colchester, **Essex**, CO7 9EP, ENG.
**(T)** 01206 827863
**Speciality:** Psychotherapy.
● **Owner** Mr D Tune
B (**Ref:**HM20395)

## TUNE, VICTORIA

**Victoria Tune**, 34 Springwood Avenue, Halifax, **Yorkshire (West)**, HX3 0UT, ENG.
**(T)** 01422 331006
**Speciality:** Reflexology.
S T (**Ref:**HM20396)

## TUNG FUNG HUNG MEDICINE

**Tung Fung Hung Medicine U K PLC**, 9 Wardour St, London, **London (Greater)**, W1V 3HE, ENG.
**(T)** 020 7734 7822
**Speciality:** Herbalists.
M (**Ref:**HM20397)

## TUNMORE, M

**M Tunmore**, The Laurels, 39 Rickmansworth Rd, Watford, **Hertfordshire**, WD1 7HS, ENG.
**(T)** 01923 221303
**Speciality:** Osteopathy.
● **Owner** Mr M Tunmore
P S T (**Ref:**HM20398)

## TUNMORE, M

**M Tunmore**, Elliott Hall Medical Centre, 165-167 Uxbridge Rd, Pinner, **London (Greater)**, HA5 4EA, ENG.
**(T)** 020 8420 2353
**Speciality:** Osteopathy.
● **Owner** Mr M Tunmore
P S T (**Ref:**HM20399)

## TUNNICLIFFE, JEANETTE

**Jeanette Tunnicliffe**, 27 Green Bank Avenue, Birmingham, **Midlands (West)**, B28 8AP, ENG.
**(T)** 01217 778808
**Speciality:** Reflexology.
S T (**Ref:**HM20400)

## TUNSTALL HYPNOTHERAPY CENTRE

**Tunstall Hypnotherapy Centre**, 4a Rathbone St, Tunstall, Stoke-On-Trent, **Staffordshire**, ST6 6DH, ENG.
**(T)** 01782 825692
**Speciality:** Aromatherapy, Hypnosis, Hypnotherapy, Reiki. ✔
● **Hypnotherapist** Mr H Ravenscroft **Q:** HY.pD, PhD. **M:** GHR, NCH, NHR, NRSCT.
M T **Yrs. Est.:** 15 (**Ref:**HM20401)

## TUNSTILL, PAT

**Pat Tunstill**, Ingledale, 1 Tanhouse Rd, Oxted, **Surrey**, RH8 9PE, ENG.



Key continued: **Yrs.Est:** Years Established **Q:** Qualifications **M:** Professional Membership ✔ Indemnity Insurance Accept Credit Cards

(T) 01883 717277
Speciality: Complementary Medicines & Therapy.
M (Ref:HM20402)

### TUPHOLME, MICHELLE
**Michelle Tupholme**, 7 White Hart Mews, Southgate, Sleaford, **Lincolnshire**, NG34 7RY, ENG.
(T) 01529 305176
Speciality: Physiotherapy.
P S T (Ref:HM20403)

### TURBEFIELD, SHELLEY
**Shelley Turbefield**, Chorley Physiotherapy, 126 Preston Rd, Chorley, **Lancashire**, PR6 7AU, ENG.
(T) 01257 265163 (F) 01257 265163
Speciality: Physiotherapy.
● **Owner** Mrs S Turbefield
P S T (Ref:HM20404)

### TURBUTT, I F
**I F Turbutt**, Manor Hospital, Church End, Biddenham, Bedford, **Bedfordshire**, MK40 4AW, ENG.
(T) 01234 825175
Speciality: Chiropodists (Podiatrists).
● **Owner** Mrs I Turbutt
S (Ref:HM20405)

### TUREY, J T
**J T Turey**, Ashfield House, Ashfield Cresent, Ross-on-Wye, **Herefordshire**, HR9 5PH, ENG.
(T) 01989 762220
Speciality: Chiropractic.
P S T (Ref:HM20406)

### TURFAEN CHIROPODY CLINIC
**Turfaen Chiropody Clinic**, 29 Windsor Rd, Griffithstown, Pontypool, **Monmouthshire**, NP4 5HZ, WAL.
(T) 01495 759970
(E) clevpod@aol.co.uk
Speciality: Chiropody, Podiatry. ✓
● **Podiatrist** Mr A Cleverley Q: BSc, DPodM, M.S.C.P, S.R.Ch. M: S.C.P.
M Yrs. Est.: 15 (Ref:HM20407)

### TURK, BARBARA (DR)
**Dr Barbara Turk**, North Cottage, Dovers Green Rd, Reigate, **Surrey**, RH2 8BU, ENG.
(T) 01737 226338 (F) 01737 226338
Speciality: Homeopathy.
● **Owner** Dr B Turk
M (Ref:HM20408)

### TURKINGTON, VIVIENNE
**Vivienne Turkington**, Bexleyheath Natural Health Clinic, 284 Broadway, Bexleyheath, **Kent**, DA6 8AJ, ENG.
(T) 020 8303 6288 (F) 020 8303 6288
Speciality: Aromatherapy.
● **Owner** Mr P Cousins
M O (Ref:HM20409)

### TURMAINE, VICKI
**Vicki Turmaine RSHom**, Edgware Centre For Natural Health, 128 High St, Edgware, **London (Greater)**, HA8 7EL, ENG.
(T) 020 8951 3475
Speciality: Bach Remedies, Counselling, Homeopathy. ✓
● **Homeopath** Ms V Turmaine Q: RSHom. M: Soc.Hom.
M Yrs. Est.: 20 (Ref:HM20410)

### TURNAROUND LIFESTYLE CON
**Turnaround Lifestyle Consultancy**, 13 Dudley Rd, London, **London (Greater)**, SW19 8PN, ENG.
(T) 020 8542 1560
Speciality: Complementary Medicines & Therapy.
C M (Ref:HM20411)

### TURNBULL, CAROL
**Carol Turnbull**, Fieldholme Byron Avenue, Bishop Auckland, **County Durham**, DL14 6AP, ENG.
(T) 01388 602243
Speciality: Complementary Medicines & Therapy.
C M (Ref:HM20412)

### TURNBULL, JO
**Jo Turnbull**, 73 Flaxman Rd, Camberwell, London, **London (Greater)**, SE5 9DN, ENG.
(T) 020 7274 9984
Speciality: Reflexology. ✓
● **Reflexologist** Ms J Turnbull M: IFR, IPTI.
T Yrs. Est.: 6 (Ref:HM20413)

### TURNBULL, PAT
**Pat Turnbull**, 102 Mobberley Rd, Knutsford, **Cheshire**, WA16 8EP, ENG.
(T) 01565 652719 (F) 01565 652719
Speciality: Chiropodists (Podiatrists).
● **Owner** Mrs P Turnbull
S (Ref:HM20414)

### TURNER CLNC OF ALTERNATIVE MED
**Turner Clinic of Alternative Medicine**, Old Dublin Rd, Stillorgan, **County Dublin**, IRE.
(T) 01288 4327
(E) mer@iol.ie
Speciality: Complementary Medicines & Therapy.
M (Ref:HM20415)

### TURNER, A A
**A A Turner**, Fiddlers Cottage, High St, Longborough, Moreton-in-Marsh, **Gloucestershire**, GL56 0QE, ENG.
(T) 01451 831373
Speciality: Homeopathy.
● **Owner** Dr A Turner
M (Ref:HM20416)

### TURNER, ANDREA
**Andrea Turner**, Oastview, Little Meadow, Upper Harbledown, Canterbury, **Kent**, CT2 9BD, ENG.
(T) 01227 450734
(E) andreaturnermiff@aol.com
Speciality: Aromatherapy, Massage (Therapeutic), Reflexology, Treat females only and children. Pregnant mothers and children of 3months plus. ✓
● **Owner/Reflexologist** Mrs A Turner Q: Dip.AP, Dip.Arom, MIFR.
T Yrs. Est.: 4 (Ref:HM20417)

### TURNER, C
**C Turner**, 85B High St, Yeadon, Leeds, **Yorkshire (West)**, LS19 7TA, ENG.
(T) 01132 501122
Speciality: Chiropodists (Podiatrists).
● **Owner** Mrs C Turner
S (Ref:HM20418)

### TURNER, C C
**Mrs C C Turner**, 1486 Warwick Rd, Knowle, Solihull, **Midlands (West)**, B93 9LE, ENG.
(T) 01564 774500
Speciality: Chiropodists (Podiatrists).
S (Ref:HM20419)

### TURNER, CATHY
**Cathy Turner**, 41 Gally Hill Rd, Church Crookham, Fleet, **Hampshire**, GU52 6QE, ENG.
(T) 01252 816786
Speciality: Aromatherapy, Complementary Therapy, Indian Head Massage, Kinesiology, Massage (Therapeutic), Reflexology, Reiki. ✓
● **Reflexologist** Ms C Turner Q: ART(Reg), ITEC, MAR. M: AoR.
T Yrs. Est.: 5 (Ref:HM20420)

### TURNER, CHARLES
**Charles Turner**, 152 Bourne Vale, Bromley, **Kent**, BR2 7LU, ENG.
(T) 020 8462 3103 (F) 020 8462 3102
Speciality: Complementary Medicines & Therapy.
● **Owner** Mr C Turner
C M (Ref:HM20421)

### TURNER, DIANE M
**Diane M Turner**, 45 Shirley Lane, Longton, Preston, **Lancashire**, PR4 5WJ, ENG.
(T) 01772 614905
Speciality: Complementary Medicines & Therapy.
● **Owner** Mrs D Turner
C M (Ref:HM20422)

### TURNER, EVELYN
**Evelyn Turner**, 45 Down Green Rd, Bolton, **Lancashire**, BL2 3QD, ENG.
(T) 01204 418949
Speciality: Complementary Medicines & Therapy.
C M (Ref:HM20423)

### TURNER, GILL
**Gill Turner**, Bramley Complementary Therapy Clinic, Raynville Rd, Leeds, **Yorkshire (West)**, LS13 2PZ, ENG.
(T) 01274 619323
Speciality: Chiropodists (Podiatrists).
● **Owner** Ms G Turner
S (Ref:HM20424)

### TURNER, HAZEL
**Hazel Turner**, Wimborne, **Dorset**, BH21, ENG.
(T) 01202 696468
Speciality: Reflexology.
S T (Ref:HM20425)

### TURNER, IVYLEA
**Ivylea Turner**, 104 Mill Lane, Old Swan, Liverpool, **Merseyside**, L13 4AH, ENG.
(T) 01512 204647
Speciality: Complementary Medicines & Therapy.
C M (Ref:HM20426)

### TURNER, JANET
**Janet Turner**, 1 Duke's Cottage, Yapton Rd, Barnham, Bognor Regis, **Sussex (West)**, PO22 0BQ, ENG.
(T) 01243 552665
Speciality: Reflexology.
S T (Ref:HM20427)

### TURNER, JULIA
**Julia Turner**, Trevone, 52 Copthorne Rd, Felbridge, East Grinstead, **Sussex (West)**, RH19 2NS, ENG.
(T) 01342 321526
Speciality: Osteopathy.
P S T (Ref:HM20428)

### TURNER, KAREN
**Karen Turner**, 5 Longfellow Rd, Banbury, **Oxfordshire**, OX16 9LB, ENG.
(T) 01295 277485
Speciality: Acupuncture.
● **Owner** Mrs K Turner
O (Ref:HM20429)

### TURNER, KEZZIE
**Kezzie Turner**, Aureole House, Market Sq, Church St, Chesham, **Buckinghamshire**, HP5 1HS, ENG.
(T) 01442 878782
Speciality: Homeopathy.
M (Ref:HM20430)

### TURNER, MARGARET
**Margaret Turner**, 10 High St, Glastonbury, **Somerset**, BA6 9DU, ENG.
(T) 01458 834236
Speciality: Herbalists.
● **Director** Ms J Sanders
M (Ref:HM20431)

### TURNER, MARY
**Mary Turner**, 72 Lower Wyche Rd, Malvern, **Worcestershire**, WR14 4ET, ENG.
(T) 01684 891548 (F) 01684 891548
Speciality: Psychotherapy.
● **Owner** Mrs M Turner
B (Ref:HM20432)

### TURNER, PAULA
**Paula Turner**, 34 Denver Rd, Dartford, **Kent**, DA1 3JS, ENG.
(T) 01322 272052
Speciality: Reflexology.
S T (Ref:HM20433)

### TURNER, PENNY
**Penny Turner**, 37 Coomb Field, Edenbridge, **Kent**, TN8 5HZ, ENG.
(T) 01732 863707
Speciality: Aromatherapy. ✓
● **Owner** Ms P Turner Q: ITEC.
C Yrs. Est.: 3 (Ref:HM20434)

### TURNER, R E
**R E Turner**, 7 Balmoral Cres, West Molesey, **Surrey**, KT8 1QA, ENG.

Key: B Mind-Body Medicine, C Complementary Medicine, H Self Help Treatment, M Medicinal Therapy, O Oriental Medicine, P Postural Therapy, S Manipulative Structural Therapy, T Touch Therapy

(T) 020 8979 6343
Speciality: Cranial Osteopathy, Manipulation, Osteopathy, Manipulative Therapy.
● Manipulative Therapist
Mr R Turner Q: LCSP. M: LCSP.
S Yrs. Est.: 20 (Ref:HM20435)

**TURNER, S**
**S Turner**, 41 Leinster Sq, London, **London (Greater)**, W2 4PU, ENG.
(T) 020 7229 8144 (F) 020 7792 8651
Speciality: Osteopathy.
● Owner Miss S Turner
P S T (Ref:HM20436)

**TURNER, S M**
**S M Turner**, Fairway, North St, Hundon, Sudbury, **Suffolk**, CO10 8EE, ENG.
(T) 01440 786361
Speciality: Chiropodists (Podiatrists).
S (Ref:HM20437)

**TURNER, TERI**
**Teri Turner**, 26A Station Rd, London, **London (Greater)**, E4 7BE, ENG.
(T) 020 8529 0815
Speciality: Cranial Osteopathy, Osteopathy. ✓
● Osteopath Miss T Turner Q: BSc, Hons (OST). M: GOsC.
C Yrs. Est.: 3 (Ref:HM20438)

**TURNER, TERI**
**Teri Turner**, East London Homoeopathic Group Practice, 18 Martello St, London, **London (Greater)**, E8 3PE, ENG.
(T) 020 7241 2171
Speciality: Osteopathy.
P S T (Ref:HM20439)

**TURNER, WENDY**
**Wendy Turner**, Managers Flat, Home Lees House, 61/67 Dyke Rd, Brighton, **Sussex (East)**, BN1 3JP, ENG.
(T) 01273 326235
Speciality: Reflexology.
S T (Ref:HM20440)

**TURNPIKE SURGERY**
**Turnpike Surgery**, 18 Bridge St, Frome, Bath, **Somerset**, BA11 1BB, ENG.
(T) 01373 463098
(W) www.chirojones.co.uk
Speciality: Chiropractic, Homeopathy. ✓
● Owner Mrs H Jones Q: DC. M: BCA.
● Partner Mr R Jones Q: DC. M: BCA.
P Yrs. Est.: 19 (Ref:HM20441)

**TURPIE, JULIE**
**Julie Turpie**, Frome, **Somerset**, BA11, ENG.
(T) 01373 472835
Speciality: Bach Remedies.
M (Ref:HM20442)

**TURRIFF CHIROPRACTIC CLINIC**
**Turriff Chiropractic Clinic**, 1 Balmellie St, Turriff, **Aberdeenshire**, AB53 4DW, SCO.
(T) 01888 569123
Speciality: Chiropractic. ✓
● Chiropractor Dr M Jackson Q: B.App.Sc.
H P S Yrs. Est.: 16 (Ref:HM20443)

**TURTON, TRACEY**
**Tracey Turton**, Sinensis, Appleton Hall Gardens, Appleton, Warrington, **Cheshire**, WA4 5NE, ENG.
(T) 01925 210310
Speciality: Reflexology.
S T (Ref:HM20444)

**TURVEY, D L & BROWNHILL, K**
**Lance D Turvey & Kevin Brownhill**, Lausanne Annexe, 272 Wightman Rd, London, **London (Greater)**, N8 0LX, ENG.
(T) 020 8347 9990
Speciality: Osteopathy.
P S T (Ref:HM20445)

**TUSSIE-MUSSIES**
**Tussie-Mussies**, 28 Market Pl, Kegworth, Derby, **Derbyshire**, DE74 2EE, ENG.
(T) 01509 673080 (F) 01509 673080
Speciality: Aromatherapy.
● Partner Mrs K Sewell
M O (Ref:HM20446)

**TWA ACRES HYPNO TRAINING CTRE**
**Twa Acres Hypnotherapy Training Centre**, 81 Victoria St, Dunfermline, **Fife**, KY12 0LP, SCO.
(T) 01383 726411
(E) twaacres@btconnect.com
(W) www.hypnotherapy-twaacres.co.uk
Speciality: Hypnotherapy. ✓
● Director Mr J Syme Q: C.Hyp, M.S.C.P, MNCP, MNSPH, S.R.Ch. M: NSPH.
B Yrs. Est.: 14 (Ref:HM20447)

**TWA ACRES HYPNOTHERAPY CENTRE**
**Twa Acres Hypnotherapy Centre**, Westwood Lodge, Carsie, Blairgowrie, **Perth and Kinross**, PH10 6QW, SCO.
(T) 01250 874384 (F) 01250 873598
Speciality: Hypnosis.
● Owner Mrs V Watson
B (Ref:HM20448)

**TWESLEDOWN PHYSIOTHERAPY**
**Twesledown Physiotherapy & Sports Injury Clinic**, 54 Tweseldown Rd, Church Crookham, Fleet, **Hampshire**, GU13 0DF, ENG.
(T) 01252 815152
Speciality: Physiotherapy. ✓
● Physiotherapist/Owner Mr J Lange Q: MCSP, SRP. M: CSP.
S (Ref:HM20449)

**TWICKENHAM PHYSIO PRACTICE**
**Twickenham Physiotherapy Practice**, 30 Mallard Pl, Twickenham, **London (Greater)**, TW1 4SR, ENG.
(T) 020 8891 1600
Speciality: Physiotherapy.
● Director Mrs E Sturman
P S T (Ref:HM20450)

**TWICKENHAM PHYSIOFIRST CENTRE**
**Twickenham PhysioFirst Centre**, 60 Popes Gr, Twickenham, **London (Greater)**, TW1 4JX, ENG.
(T) 020 8255 6648
Speciality: Acupuncture, Physiotherapy. ✓
● Owner/Physiotherapist
Mrs J Jones Q: MCSP, SRP. M: CSP.
S Yrs. Est.: 3 (Ref:HM20451)

**TWIN LOTUS HEALING ARTS**
**Twin Lotus Healing Arts**, 20 Caerphilly Rd, Cardiff, **Glamorgan (Vale of)**, CF14 4AF, WAL.
(T) 029 2061 6886
Speciality: Acupuncture.
O (Ref:HM20452)

**TWINE, I E**
**I E Twine**, Charnwood, Littleworth, Faringdon, **Oxfordshire**, SN7 8ED, ENG.
(T) 01367 240473
Speciality: Acupuncture, Alexander Technique, Chiropractic, Counselling, Cranial Osteopathy, Homeopathy, McTimoney Chiropractic, Osteopathy, Reflexology, Holistic Massage. ✓
● Owner Mrs I Twine M: GCC.
S Yrs. Est.: 6 (Ref:HM20453)

**TWINE, I E**
**I E Twine**, 77 Conifer Crest, Newbury, **Berkshire**, RG14 6RS, ENG.
(T) 01635 44320
Speciality: Chiropractors.
● Owner Mrs I Bell
P S T (Ref:HM20454)

**TWINE, IMELDA**
**Imelda Twine**, Health Hydro, Milton Rd, Swindon, **Wiltshire**, SN1 5JA, ENG.
(T) 01793 465629
Speciality: Chiropractors.
P S T (Ref:HM20455)

**TWINE, RAY**
**Ray Twine M A Psychologist**, 4 Hardwicke Rd, Reigate, **Surrey**, RH2 9HJ, ENG.
(T) 01737 217555
Speciality: Psychotherapy.
● Owner Mr R Twine
B (Ref:HM20456)

**TWITCHETT, EVE**
**Eve Twitchett**, 138 Broomhill Rd, Strood, Rochester, **Kent**, ME2 3LQ, ENG.
(T) 01634 295511
Speciality: Aromatherapy.
M O (Ref:HM20457)

**TWO STEPS REFLEXOLOGY**
**Two Steps Reflexology**, Mayfield, Ricketts Hill Rd, Tatsfield, **Surrey**, TN16 2NG, ENG.
(T) 01959 571059
Speciality: Reflexology. ✓
● Reflexologist R P McLaren Gibbs M: BRA.
S Yrs. Est.: 10 (Ref:HM20458)

**TYACK, S**
**S Tyack**, 46 Park Rd, Abingdon, **Oxfordshire**, OX14 1DG, ENG.
(T) 01235 522386
Speciality: Acupuncture.
● Owner Dr S Tyack
O (Ref:HM20459)

**TYE, MARIE**
**Marie Tye**, 136 Steyning Rd, Birmingham, **Midlands (West)**, B26 1JD, ENG.
(T) 01216 059589
Speciality: Reflexology.
S T (Ref:HM20460)

**TYLDEN, E**
**E Tylden**, 322 South Lambeth Rd, London, **London (Greater)**, SW8 1UQ, ENG.
(T) 020 7720 6622
Speciality: Psychiatry.
B (Ref:HM20461)

**TYLER, LIZZY**
**Lizzy Tyler**, 71 The Acres, Martock, **Somerset**, TA12 6DD, ENG.
(T) 01935 822938
Speciality: Indian Head Massage, Reflexology.
S T (Ref:HM20462)

**TYLER, PETER**
**Peter Tyler**, Barn Owl, Llanfair Dyffryn Clwyd, Ruthin, **Denbighshire**, LL15 2EG, WAL.
(T) 01824 707507
Speciality: Psychology.
● Owner Mr P Tyler
B (Ref:HM20463)

**TYLER, SHARON**
**Sharon Tyler**, 26A Station Rd, London, **London (Greater)**, E4 7BE, ENG.
(T) 020 8529 0815
Speciality: Osteopathy.
P S T (Ref:HM20464)

**TYLER, SUE**
**Sue Tyler**, 108 Prospect Rd, Southborough, Tunbridge Wells, **Kent**, TN4 0EG, ENG.
(T) 01892 513421
Speciality: Complementary Medicines & Therapy.
● Owner Miss S Tyler
C M (Ref:HM20465)

**TYLER, VALERIE**
**Valerie Tyler**, 20 Tiptree Rd, Ruislip, **London (Greater)**, HA4 0EW, ENG.
(T) 020 8841 8973
Speciality: Complementary Medicines & Therapy.
C M (Ref:HM20466)

**TYLER, VALERIE**
**Valerie Tyler**, 110 East St, Sittingbourne, **Kent**, ME10 4RX, ENG.
(T) 01795 410794
Speciality: Reflexology.
S T (Ref:HM20467)

**TYMEAESSENCE**
**Tymeaessence**, Bon Accord Centre, George St, Aberdeen, **Aberdeenshire**, AB25 1HZ, SCO.
(T) 01224 647109
Speciality: Aromatherapy.
● Owner Mrs J Hunt
M O (Ref:HM20468)

**TYMM, S L**
**S L Tymm**, Baytree Hill, Liskeard, **Cornwall**, PL14 4BE, ENG.
(T) 01579 343837
Speciality: Chiropodists (Podiatrists).
S (Ref:HM20469)


Key continued: Yrs.Est: Years Established Q: Qualifications M: Professional Membership ✓ Indemnity Insurance Accept Credit Cards

**TYNCE, CHRIS**

**Chris Tynce**, 55 Cheap St, Newbury, **Berkshire**, RG14 5DH, **ENG**.
(T) 01635 581032
Speciality: Hypnosis.
B (Ref:HM20470)

**TYNDALE CLINIC**

**Tyndale Clinic**, 6 Manor Pk, Tralee, **County Kerry**, **IRE**.
(T) 06671 26441
Speciality: Homeopathy.
M (Ref:HM20471)

**TYRELL, MARK**

**Mark Tyrell**, 94 St James's St, Brighton, **Sussex (East)**, BN2 1TP, **ENG**.
(T) 01273 672952
Speciality: Hypnotherapy.
● **Owner** Mr L Moore
B (Ref:HM20472)

**TYRER, HELEN R**

**Helen R Tyrer**, 135 Park Lane, Macclesfield, **Cheshire**, SK11 6UB, **ENG**.
(T) 01625 618577
(E) helen@rtyrer.freeserve.co.uk
Speciality: Biomechanics, Chiropody, Gait Analysis, Nail Surgery, Podiatry. ✔
● **Chiropodist (Podiatrist)**
Ms H Tyrer Q: M.S.C.P, S.R.Ch. M: S.C.P, S.R.Ch.
C Yrs. Est.: 8 (Ref:HM20473)

**TYRER, PATRICIA**

**Patricia Tyrer**, Brighton, **Sussex (East)**, BN1, **ENG**.
(T) 01273 555679
Speciality: Bach Remedies.
M (Ref:HM20474)

**TYRIE, M**

**M Tyrie**, 9 Cissbury Rd, Worthing, **Sussex (West)**, BN14 9LD, **ENG**.
(T) 01903 235360
Speciality: Osteopathy.
P S T (Ref:HM20475)

**TYRINGHAM NATUROPATHIC CLINIC**

**Tyringham Naturopathic Clinic**, Tyringham, Newport Pagnell, **Buckinghamshire**, MK16 9ER, **ENG**.
(T) 01908 610450
Speciality: Complementary Medicines & Therapy.
C M (Ref:HM20476)

**TYRRELL, HAZEL**

**Hazel Tyrrell**, 52 St Georges Rd, Felixstowe, **Suffolk**, IP11 9PW, **ENG**.
(T) 01394 286446
Speciality: Chiropodists (Podiatrists).
● **Owner** Mrs H Tyrrell
S (Ref:HM20477)

**TYRRELL, IVAN**

**Ivan Tyrrell**, Old Church Room, Chalvington, Hailsham, **Sussex (East)**, BN27 3TD, **ENG**.
(T) 01323 811690
Speciality: Hypnosis.
B (Ref:HM20478)

**TYSON, ANDREW**

**Andrew Tyson**, 53 Belgrave Rd, London, **London (Greater)**, E17 8QD, **ENG**.
(T) 020 8520 0051
Speciality: Complementary Medicines & Therapy.
● **Owner** Mr A Tyson
C M (Ref:HM20479)

**UBHI, BEL**

**Mrs Bel Ubhi**, 10 Blackthorn Avenue, West Drayton, **London (Greater)**, UB7 9EU, **ENG**.
(T) 01895 851114
Speciality: Chiropodists (Podiatrists).
S (Ref:HM20480)

**UDEN, CHRISTINE**

**Christine Uden**, Ty Gwyn, Pentre Llyn Cymmer, Cerrigydrudion, Corwen, **Denbighshire**, LL21 9TU, **WAL**.
(T) 01490 420639
Speciality: Psychotherapy.
B (Ref:HM20481)

**UI CHONCHUIR, MARY**

**Ui Chonchuir Mary**, Dromanallaigh Ballingeary, **County Cork**, **IRE**.
(T) 026 4720 2
Speciality: Complementary Medicines & Therapy.
M (Ref:HM20482)

**UK CARE PRODUCTS**

**UK Care Products**, 92 Holme Lane, Sheffield, **Yorkshire (South)**, S6 4JW, **ENG**.
(T) 01142 315050 (F) 01142 315990
Speciality: Complementary Medicines & Therapy.
● **Sales Director** Mr S Smith
M (Ref:HM20483)

**UK COLLEGE SEMWORKS**

**UK College Semworks**, Exmoor St, London, **London (Greater)**, W10 6DZ, **ENG**.
(T) 020 8964 1205
Speciality: Complementary Medicines & Therapy.
C M (Ref:HM20484)

**UK CONFEDERATION OF HYP ORG**

**UK Confederation Of Hypnotherapy Organisations (The)**, 189 Uppingham Rd, Leicester, **Leicestershire**, LE5 4BQ, **ENG**.
(T) 01162 120306 (F) 01162 120306
Speciality: Hypnotherapy.
● **Secretary** Mr M Armstrong-Prior
B (Ref:HM20485)

**UK COUNSELLING SERVICE**

**UK Counselling Service**, Queensway Business Centre, Dunlop Way, Queensway Industrial Estate, Scunthorpe, **Humberside**, DN16 3RN, **ENG**.
(T) 01724 289949
Speciality: Psychology.
B (Ref:HM20486)

**UK OSTEOPATHS**

**UK Osteopaths**, 201-207 Kensington High St, London, **London (Greater)**, W8 6BA, **ENG**.
(T) 020 7937 4333
Speciality: Osteopathy.
● **Owner** Ms S Scott
P S T (Ref:HM20487)

**UK POLARITY THERAPY ASS**

**United Kingdom Polarity Therapy Association**, Monomark House, 27 Old Gloucester St, P O Box 12, London, **London (Greater)**, WC1N 3XX, **ENG**.
(T) 01483 417714
Speciality: Complementary Medicines & Therapy.
M (Ref:HM20488)

**UK TAI-CHI ASSOCIATION**

**UK Tai-Chi Association**, Po Box 159, Bromley, **Kent**, BR1 3XX, **ENG**.
(T) 020 8289 5166
Speciality: Relaxation Technique.
● **Chairman** Mr J Hine
H T (Ref:HM20489)

**UKCP**

**United Kingdom Council For Psychotherapy**, 167-169 Great Portland St, London, **London (Greater)**, W1W 5PF, **ENG**.
(T) 020 7436 3002 (F) 020 7436 3013
(W) www.psychotherapy.org.uk
Speciality: Art Therapy, Autogenic Training, Cognitive Therapy, Counselling, Drama Therapy, Family Therapy, Gestalt Therapy, Group Therapy, Humanistic Psychology, Hypnotherapy, Primal Therapy, Psychotherapy, Pscyho-Synthesis, Reichian Therapy, Rogerian Therapy, Stress Therapy, Transactional Analysis.
● **Chief Executive** Ms P Howard
B (Ref:HM20490)

**ULTIMATE FOOT HEALTH CLINIC**

**Ultimate Foot Health Clinic**, 99 Aigburth Rd, Liverpool, **Merseyside**, L17 4JU, **ENG**.
(T) 01517 275000
Speciality: Chiropodists (Podiatrists).
● **Manager** Mrs A McCarten
S (Ref:HM20491)

**ULTIMATE HEALTH CLINIC**

**Ultimate Health Clinic**, 5 Shannonville Ennis Rd, Limerick, **County Limerick**, **IRE**.
(T) 06132 2011 (F) 06182 323
Speciality: Complementary Medicines & Therapy.
M (Ref:HM20492)

**ULTRASON**

**Ultrason**, 23 Morton St, Edinburgh, **Edinburgh (City of)**, EH15 2HN, **SCO**.
(T) 01316 573588
Speciality: Physiotherapy.
P S T (Ref:HM20493)

**ULVERSTON NATURAL HEALTH CTRE**

**Ulverston Natural Health Centre**, 1 The Gill, Ulverston, **Cumbria**, LA12 7BJ, **ENG**.
(T) 01229 586959
Speciality: Complementary Medicines & Therapy.
C M (Ref:HM20494)

**UNDERHILL, HARRY**

**Harry Underhill**, 7 St Michaels Rd, Leeds, **Yorkshire (West)**, LS6 3AW, **ENG**.
(T) 01132 781818
Speciality: Physiotherapy.
P S T (Ref:HM20495)

**UNDERHILL, K**

**K Underhill**, Hale Clinic, 7 Park Cres, London, **London (Greater)**, W1N 3HE, **ENG**.
(T) 020 7402 4430
Speciality: Acupuncture, Cranial Osteopathy, Iridology, Naturopathy, Osteopathy. ✔
● **Osteopath** Mr K Underhill Q: Reg.Osteopath.
C Yrs. Est.: 46 (Ref:HM20496)

**UNDERHILL, MARGARET**

**Margaret Underhill**, 2 Holt Walk, Leeds, **Yorkshire (West)**, LS16 7QB, **ENG**.
(T) 01132 674504 (F) 01132 674504
Speciality: Physiotherapy.
● **Owner** Mrs M Underhill
P S T (Ref:HM20497)

**UNDERWOOD CLINICS CHIROPRACTIC**

**Underwood Clinics Of Chiropractic**, 291 High St, Epping, **Essex**, CM16 4DA, **ENG**.
(T) 01992 570170
Speciality: Chiropractic.
P S T (Ref:HM20498)

**UNDERWOOD, MARIAN**

**Marian Underwood**, Highmead Lodge, 192 Willingdon Rd, Eastbourne, **Sussex (East)**, BN21 1TT, **ENG**.
(T) 01323 737510 (F) 01323 737510
Speciality: Physiotherapy.
● **Owner** Mrs M Underwood
P S T (Ref:HM20499)

**UNDERWOOD, MARTIN**

**Martin Underwood**, 15 Celia Rd, London, **London (Greater)**, N19 5ET, **ENG**.
(T) 020 7607 5265 (F) 020 7607 5265
Speciality: Osteopathy.
● **Owner** Mr M Underwood
P S T (Ref:HM20500)

**UNDERWOOD, PAUL**

**Paul Underwood**, 6 Colwell Rd, London, **London (Greater)**, SE22 8QP, **ENG**.
(T) 020 8299 3954
Speciality: Acupuncture.
O (Ref:HM20501)

**UNDERWOOD, TRISH**

**Trish Underwood**, 34 Heathfield, **Yorkshire (West)**, LS16 6AQ, **ENG**.
(T) 01132 168253
Speciality: Reflexology.
S T (Ref:HM20502)

**UNERMAN, EVE**

**Eve Unerman**, 32 Clifford Rd, Barnet, **Hertfordshire**, EN5 5PG, **ENG**.
(T) 020 8441 7228 (F) 020 8441 7228
Speciality: Reflexology. ✔
● **Reflexologist** Mrs E Unerman Q: MAR. M: AoR.
T Yrs. Est.: 5 (Ref:HM20503)

Key: B Mind-Body Medicine, C Complementary Medicine, H Self Help Treatment, M Medicinal Therapy, O Oriental Medicine, P Postural Therapy, S Manipulative Structural Therapy, T Touch Therapy

### UNGAR, ANN
**Ann Ungar**, 18 Priory Heights, Eastbourne, **Sussex (East)**, BN20 8SR, ENG.
(T) 01323 726322
Speciality: Chiropodists (Podiatrists).
● **Owner** Mrs A Unger
S (Ref:HM20504)

### UNICORN FAYRES
**Unicorn Fayres**, 24 Headswell Cres, Bournemouth, **Dorset**, BH10 6LH, ENG.
(T) 01202 549132 (F) 01202 258138
Speciality: Clairvoyants & Palmists.
● **Senior Partner** Mrs J Seabright
B (Ref:HM20505)

### UNICORN PRODUCTS
**Unicorn Products**, Lr Abbeygate St, **County Galway**, IRE.
(T) 09156 7955
Speciality: Complementary Medicines & Therapy.
M (Ref:HM20506)

### UNIQUE ASIAN MASSAGE CENTRE
**Unique Asian Massage Centre**, Ground Floor, 1a George St, Southall, **London (Greater)**, UB2 5PS, ENG.
(T) 020 8893 6343
Speciality: Complementary Medicines & Therapy.
C M (Ref:HM20507)

### UNIQUE MASSAGE
**Unique Massage**, 9 Frampton Rd, Potters Bar, **Hertfordshire**, EN6 1JF, ENG.
(T) 01707 662525
Speciality: Aromatherapy.
M O (Ref:HM20508)

### UNITED BRISTOL HEALTHCARE
**United Bristol Healthcare NHS Trust**, The Grange, 1 Woodlands Rd, Clifton, Bristol, BS8 1AU, ENG.
(T) 01179 736071
Speciality: Physiotherapy.
P S T (Ref:HM20509)

### UNITY HEALTH CENTRE
**Unity Health Centre**, 31 Market Hill, Sudbury, **Suffolk**, CO10 2EN, ENG.
(T) 01787 881887 (F) 01787 881887
Speciality: Acupuncture, Light Therapy, Nutritional Therapy.
● **Partner** Mr S Guy-Clarke
M (Ref:HM20510)

### UNITY HOUSE
**Unity House**, 175 Outland Rd, Plymouth, **Devon**, PL2 3PY, ENG.
(T) 01752 770048
Speciality: Complementary Medicines & Therapy.
C M (Ref:HM20511)

### UNIVERSAL HEALING NETWORK
**Universal Healing Network**, Po Box 228, Weston-Super-Mare, **Somerset**, BS23 3FH, ENG.
(T) 01934 420102
Speciality: Healing.
● **Owner** D Pettle
B (Ref:HM20512)

### UNIVERSAL PROMOTIONS
**Universal Promotions**, 148 Ashingdon Rd, Rochford, **Essex**, SS4 1TA, ENG.
(T) 01702 547953 (F) 01702 531952
Speciality: Clairvoyants & Palmists.
● **Manager** Mr D Golding
B (Ref:HM20513)

### UNIVERSITY OF CAMBRIDGE
**University Of Cambridge**, Developmental Psychiatry Dept, Douglas House, Trumpington Rd, Cambridge, **Cambridgeshire**, CB2 2AH, ENG.
(T) 01223 336098 (F) 01223 746122
Speciality: Psychiatry.
● **Professor** Mr I Goodyer
B (Ref:HM20514)

### UNIVERSITY OF EDINBURGH
**University Of Edinburgh**, 46 Pleasance, Edinburgh, **Edinburgh (City of)**, EH8 9TJ, SCO.
(T) 01316 502585
Speciality: Physiotherapy.
P S T (Ref:HM20515)

### UNIVERSITY OF LONDON UNION
**University of London Union**, Malet St, London, **London (Greater)**, WC1E 7HY, ENG.
(T) 020 8882 8562
Speciality: Alexander Technique.
● **Practitioner** Ms S Heidelbach
P S (Ref:HM20516)

### UNIVERSITY OF SURREY
**University Of Surrey Chiropractic Clinc**, 27-29 Frederick Sanger Rd, Surrey Research Park, Guildford, **Surrey**, GU2 7YD, ENG.
(T) 01483 306722 (F) 01483 534169
Speciality: Chiropractors.
● **Administrator** Miss L Lever
P S T (Ref:HM20517)

### UNUIS CLINIC
**Unuis Clinic**, 106 Ealing Rd, Wembley, **London (Greater)**, HA0 4TH, ENG.
(T) 020 8902 2820
Speciality: Osteopathy.
● **Owner** Mr A Unuis
P S T (Ref:HM20518)

### UNVALA, ALISON
**Alison Unvala**, 33 Bedford Gardens, London, **London (Greater)**, W8 7EF, ENG.
(T) 020 7221 7300 (F) 020 7727 9091
Speciality: Chiropodists (Podiatrists).
● **Owner** Mrs A Unvala
S (Ref:HM20519)

### UNWIN LAMBERT, B & PEGG, E
**B Unwin Lambert & Miss Elizabeth Pegg**, Fairlead, Chart Lane, Reigate, **Surrey**, RH2 7EG, ENG.
(T) 01737 245041
Speciality: Osteopathy.
P S T (Ref:HM20520)

### UP & AWAY
**Up & Away**, 79 Brookland Rise, London, **London (Greater)**, NW11 6DT, ENG.
(T) 020 8455 1878
Speciality: Alexander Technique.
● **Owner** Mr A Maunder
P S (Ref:HM20521)

### UPHAM, GILL
**Gill Upham**, 463 Chorley Old Rd, Bolton, **Lancashire**, BL1 6AH, ENG.
(T) 01204 495158
(E) g.upham@ukgateway.net
Speciality: Holistic Healing, Homeopathy. ✔
● **Homeopath** Ms G Upham Q: BSc, LNWCH. M: Soc.Hom.
C Yrs. Est.: 1 (Ref:HM20522)

### UPROOTS HOLISTIC TREATMENT
**Uproots Holistic Treatment Centre Herbal & Health Foods**, 440 Whitehorse Rd, Thornton Heath, **Surrey**, CR7 8SB, ENG.
(T) 020 8239 0038
Speciality: Complementary Medicines & Therapy.
C M (Ref:HM20523)

### UPTON & ASSOCIATES
**M A Upton & Associates**, 33 Rosebery Avenue, Eastbourne, **Sussex (East)**, BN22 9QB, ENG.
(T) 01323 521120
Speciality: Chiropodists (Podiatrists).
● **Owner** Mrs M Upton
S (Ref:HM20524)

### UPTON, KEITH
**Keith Upton**, 19 Highway Rd, Thurmaston, Leicester, **Leicestershire**, LE4 8FR, ENG.
(T) 01162 694893
Speciality: Physiotherapy.
P S T (Ref:HM20525)

### UPTON, M A
**M A Upton**, 13 St Georges Pl, Brighton, **Sussex (East)**, BN1 4GB, ENG.
(T) 01273 609417
Speciality: Chiropodists (Podiatrists).
● **Owner** Mrs M Upton
S (Ref:HM20526)

### URE, MARILYN
**Marilyn Ure**, 32 Vaughan Rd, Wallasey, **Merseyside**, CH45 1LL, ENG.
(T) 01516 393010
Speciality: Psychotherapy.
B (Ref:HM20527)

### URQUHART, R J
**R J Urquhart**, 3 Old Coach Rd, East Kilbride, Glasgow, **Glasgow (City of)**, G74 4DR, SCO.
(T) 01355 225995
Speciality: Osteopathy.
P S T (Ref:HM20528)

### URQUHART, RODERICK J
**Roderick J Urquhart**, 87 Barrington Drive, Glasgow, **Glasgow (City of)**, G4 9ES, SCO.
(T) 01413 394164
Speciality: Osteopathy.
P S T (Ref:HM20529)

### URQUHART, W
**Mr W Urquhart**, The Camberley Clinic, 183A London Rd, Camberley, **Surrey**, GU15 3JS, ENG.
(T) 01276 682980
Speciality: Acupuncture.
O (Ref:HM20530)

### URQUHART-PULLEN, M
**M Urquhart-Pullen**, Ashdown Osteopathic Centre, The Sq, Lewes Rd, Forest Row, **Sussex (East)**, RH18 5ES, ENG.
(T) 01342 822505 (F) 01342 822505
Speciality: Osteopathy.
● **Owner** Mr T Strutt
P S T (Ref:HM20531)

### URQUHART-PULLEN, MARINA
**Marina Urquhart-Pullen**, 12 Blackwell Farm Rd, East Grinstead, **Sussex (West)**, RH19 3HX, ENG.
(T) 01342 326708
Speciality: Osteopathy.
P S T (Ref:HM20532)

### URRUTIA, LORETA
**Loreta Urrutia**, 204 Cortis Rd, London, **London (Greater)**, SW15 3AJ, ENG.
(T) 020 8788 2020 (F) 020 8788 2020
Speciality: Hypnosis.
● **Owner** Mrs L Urrutia
B (Ref:HM20533)

### USEFUL THERAPIES
**Useful Therapies**, Bramblewood, Greenway, Tatsfield, Westerham, **Kent**, TN16 2BS, ENG.
(T) 01959 577803
Speciality: Absent Healing, Aromatherapy, Hypnosis, Hypnotherapy, Kinesiology, Reflexology, Reiki, Shiatsu. ✔
● **Complementary Therapist** Ms A Thomas Q: Dip.Arom, S.C.M, SRN.
M Yrs. Est.: 10 (Ref:HM20534)

### USHER, J
**J Usher**, Abbey Wood Podiatry Clinic, 124 McLeod Rd, London, **London (Greater)**, SE2 0BS, ENG.
(T) 020 8311 1660
Speciality: Homeopathy.
M (Ref:HM20535)

### USUI REIKI PRACTICE
**Usui Reiki Practice (The)**, 131 Rectory Rd, Ashton-In-Makerfield, Wigan, **Lancashire**, WN4 0QF, ENG.
(T) 01942 519675
Speciality: Complementary Medicines & Therapy.
● **Owner** Mr R Mitten
M (Ref:HM20536)

### UTTING, MARTINE
**Martine Utting**, 16 West Prde, Norwich, **Norfolk**, NR2 3DW, ENG.
(T) 01603 662018
Speciality: Complementary Medicines & Therapy.
● **Owner** Mrs M Utting
C M (Ref:HM20537)

### UTTLEY, LINDA
**Linda Uttley**, Manlea House, Trevarren, St. Columb, **Cornwall**, TR9 6PH, ENG.



Key continued: Yrs.Est: Years Established Q: Qualifications M: Professional Membership ✔ Indemnity Insurance Accept Credit Cards

(T) 01726 860265
Speciality: Chiropodists (Podiatrists).
● **Owner** Mrs L Uttley
S (Ref:HM20538)

## UXBRIDGE CHIROPRACTIC CLINIC

**Uxbridge Chiropractic Clinic**, 77 Belmont Rd, Uxbridge, **London (Greater)**, UB8 1QU, ENG.
(T) 01895 238938
Speciality: Chiropractic.
● **Director** Mr K Leizer
P S T (Ref:HM20539)

## V EDIC MEDICAL HALL

**V Edic Medical Hall**, 21 Southwick Mews, London, **London (Greater)**, W2 1JG, ENG.
(T) 020 7706 0070 (F) 020 7706 0060
Speciality: Complementary Medicines & Therapy.
● **Owner** Mr S Gargd
C M (Ref:HM20540)

## V K PATEL STATE RGD CHIROP

**V K Patel State Registered Chiropodist**, 176 Harrow Rd, Wembley, **London (Greater)**, HA9 6QQ, ENG.
(T) 020 8902 5143
Speciality: Chiropody.
S (Ref:HM20541)

## VACCHIERI, DANIEL

**Daniel Vacchieri**, 215 Sunnyside, Coulby Newham, Middlesbrough, **Cleveland**, TS8 0RF, ENG.
(T) 01642 595242
Speciality: Chiropodists (Podiatrists).
S (Ref:HM20542)

## VACUFLEX

**Vacuflex**, 10 High St, Banstead, **Surrey**, SM7 2LJ, ENG.
(T) 01737 371007
Speciality: Reflexology.
● **Owner** Ms E Thompson
S T (Ref:HM20543)

## VACUFLEX REFLEXOLOGY SYSTEM

**Vacuflex Reflexology System**, 148 Portland Rd, Weymouth, **Dorset**, DT4 9AD, ENG.
(T) 01305 782376
Speciality: Reflexology.
● **Owner** Mrs M Brown
S T (Ref:HM20544)

## VADRA-EDWARDS, NEENA

**Neena Vadra-Edwards**, The Manse, High St, Creaton, Northampton, **Northamptonshire**, NN6 8NA, ENG.
(T) 01604 505452
Speciality: Reflexology.
S T (Ref:HM20545)

## VAEZZADEH, M

**M Vaezzadeh**, 48 Rodney St, Liverpool, **Merseyside**, L1 9ER, ENG.
(T) 01517 091774 (F) 01517 092727
Speciality: Osteopathy.
● **Owner** Mr M Vaezzadeh
P S T (Ref:HM20546)

## VAHEY, G

**G Vahey**, Bon Secours Hospital, 36 Mansionhouse Rd, Glasgow, **Glasgow (City of)**, G41 3DW, SCO.
(T) 01416 329231
Speciality: Psychotherapy.
B (Ref:HM20547)

## VAINES, EILEEN

**Eileen Vaines**, Bexhill-on-Sea, **Sussex (East)**, TN39, ENG.
(T) 01424 219768
Speciality: Bach Remedies.
M (Ref:HM20548)

## VALE HOME PHYSIOTHERAPY

**Vale Home Physiotherapy**, 82 Greenhill, Evesham, **Worcestershire**, WR11 4NH, ENG.
(T) 01386 49715
Speciality: Physiotherapy.
P S T (Ref:HM20549)

## VALE PHYSIOTHERAPY

**Vale Physiotherapy**, Hafod Y Fro, Sigingstone, Cowbridge, **Glamorgan (Vale of)**, CF71 7LP, WAL.
(T) 01446 775326 (F) 01446 775326
Speciality: Physiotherapy.
● **Owner** Mrs K Williams
P S T (Ref:HM20550)

## VALE PRACTICE

**Vale Practice (The)**, 64 Grove Vale, London, **London (Greater)**, SE22 8DT, ENG.
(T) 020 8299 9798 (F) 020 8299 9942
(E) info@thevalepractice.co.uk
Speciality: Acupuncture, Alexander Technique, Aromatherapy, Art Therapy, Complementary Therapy, Counselling, Cranial Osteopathy, Cupping, Homeopathy, Hypnosis, Hypnotherapy, Indian Head Massage, Life Style Coaching, Manipulation, Massage (Therapeutic), Miasm Therapy, Moxibustion, Nutritional Therapy, Osteopathy, Pilates, Psychotherapy, Reflexology, Reiki, Shiatsu, Stress Therapy, T'ai-Chi Ch'uan, Vitamin Therapy, Yoga, Rejuvanessence.
● **Therapist** Ms A Fur
● **Owner** Mr P Adlam
C Yrs. Est.: 1 (**Ref:**HM20551)

## VALE ROYAL CHIROPRACTIC CLINIC

**Vale Royal Chiropractic Clinic**, 130A Witton St, Northwich, **Cheshire**, CW9 5NP, ENG.
(T) 01606 350840
Speciality: Chiropractic, Massage (Therapeutic), Reflexology. ✓
● **Owner** Mr L Calland Q: DC, MCC.
P Yrs. Est.: 4 (**Ref:**HM20552)

## VALE ROYAL CHIROPRACTIC CLINIC

**Vale Royal Chiropractic Clinic**, 70 Barrington Rd, Altrincham, **Cheshire**, WA14 1JB, ENG.
(T) 01619 294442 (F) 01606 350840
Speciality: Chiropractic, Massage (Therapeutic), Reflexology. ✓
● **Chiropractor** Ms L Westerbeek Q: BSc (Chiro).
● **Owner** Dr L Calland Q: BSc.
P Yrs. Est.: 3 (**Ref:**HM20553)

## VALENCE ROAD OSTEOPATHS

**Valence Road Osteopaths**, 20 Valence Rd, Lewes, **Sussex (East)**, BN7 1PE, ENG.
(T) 01273 476371
Speciality: Cranial Osteopathy, Massage (Therapeutic), Reflexology. ✓
● **Osteopath** Ms L Peters Q: BSc, Hons (OST). M: GOsC.
S (Ref:HM20554)

## VALENCIA, D

**D Valencia**, 20A Central Avenue, West Bridgford, Nottingham, **Nottinghamshire**, NG2 5GR, ENG.
(T) 01159 143311
Speciality: Psychotherapy.
● **Practice Manager** Mrs S Peacoco
B (Ref:HM20555)

## VALENTINE, ROSS

**Ross Valentine**, 17 Highfield Lane, Southampton, **Hampshire**, SO17 1QD, ENG.
(T) 023 8055 4076
Speciality: Osteopathy.
● **Owner** Mr R Valentine
P S T (Ref:HM20556)

## VALERA, A B

**A B Valera**, 13 Hazelwood, Loughton, **Essex**, IG10 4ET, ENG.
(T) 020 8281 0610
Speciality: Homeopathy.
● **Owner** Mrs A Valera
M (Ref:HM20557)

## VALERIE BETTANY CLINIC

**Valerie Bettany Clinic**, 28-30 Stafford St, Stoke-On-Trent, **Staffordshire**, ST1 1JQ, ENG.
(T) 01782 214198
Speciality: Electrolysis, Red Vein Treatment, Mole & Wart Treatment. Skin Tags. ✓
● **Owner** Mrs V Bettany
C Yrs. Est.: 32 (**Ref:**HM20558)

## VALERIE RICKARDS ELECTROLYSIS

**Valerie Rickards Electrolysis Clinic**, Medlar, Huntington Lane, Ashford Carbonel, Ludlow, **Shropshire**, SY8 4DN, ENG.
(T) 01584 831425
Speciality: Electrolysis.
T (Ref:HM20559)

## VALL, KENNETH

**Kenneth Vall**, Torrens, Balmer Lawn Rd, Brockenhurst, **Hampshire**, SO42 7TS, ENG.
(T) 01590 624257
Speciality: Chiropractors.
● **Owner** Mr K Vall
P S T (Ref:HM20560)

## VALLEY HEALTH PRODUCTS

**Valley Health Products**, 7 Bellard Walk, West Kilbride, **Ayrshire (North)**, KA23 9JL, SCO.
(T) 01294 829997 (F) 01294 605555
Speciality: Complementary Medicines & Therapy.
● **Owner** Mr J Welch
M (Ref:HM20561)

## VALLINS, SAMANTHA

**Samantha Vallins**, 30 Litchdon St, Barnstaple, **Devon**, EX32 8ND, ENG.
(T) 01271 325277
Speciality: Chiropodists (Podiatrists).
● **Owner** Miss S Vallins
S (Ref:HM20562)

## VAN DE BRAAK

**Van De Braak**, Hammond House, 75 Burnmill Rd, Market Harborough, **Leicestershire**, LE16 7JG, ENG.
(T) 01858 465005 (F) 01858 410236
Speciality: Physiotherapy.
● **Owner** Mr H Van De Braak
P S T (Ref:HM20563)

## VAN DE WAL, FREDDY

**Van de Wal Freddy**, Doora, Portmagee, **County Kerry**, IRE.
(T) 06694 77243
Speciality: Complementary Medicines & Therapy.
M (Ref:HM20564)

## VAN DER GRINTEN, PETER

**Peter Van Der Grinten**, 10 Willow Gr, Welwyn Garden City, **Hertfordshire**, AL8 7NA, ENG.
(T) 01707 330641 (F) 01707 330641
Speciality: Alexander Technique.
P S (Ref:HM20565)

## VAN EMDEN, SUE

**Sue Van Emden**, Bridge House, Station Approach East, Hassocks, **Sussex (West)**, BN6 8HW, ENG.
(T) 01273 843780
Speciality: Osteopathy.
● **Owner** Ms S Van Emden
P S T (Ref:HM20566)

## VAN EMDEN, SUE

**Sue Van Emden**, Waytefield Clinic, Preston Drove, Brighton, **Sussex (East)**, BN1 6LA, ENG.
(T) 01273 550727
Speciality: Osteopathy.
● **Owner** Ms S Van Emden
P S T (Ref:HM20567)

## VAN GEND, KATHARINA

**Katharina Van Gend**, 152 Old Fort Rd, Shoreham-by-Sea, **Sussex (West)**, BN43 5HL, ENG.
(T) 01273 464521 (F) 01273 464521
Speciality: Hypnosis.
● **Owner** Ms K Van-Gend
B (Ref:HM20568)

## VAN GRIETHUYSEN, CORLA

**Corla Van Griethuysen**, Wolfson Centre, 106 Rottenrow, Glasgow, **Glasgow (City of)**, G4 0NW, SCO.
(T) 01415 534151 (F) 01417 710031
Speciality: Physiotherapy.
● **Owner** Dr C Van Griethuysen
P S T (Ref:HM20569)

## VAN HAEFTEN, A

**A Van Haeften**, Stepaside Cottage, Petworth Rd, Wormley, Godalming, **Surrey**, GU8 5TU, ENG.
(T) 01428 685777
Speciality: Homeopathy.
● **Owner** A Van Haeften
M (Ref:HM20570)



Key: B Mind-Body Medicine C Complementary Medicine H Self Help Treatment M Medicinal Therapy O Oriental Medicine P Postural Therapy S Manipulative Structural Therapy T Touch Therapy

### VAN HEUVELEN, RON
**Ron Van Heuvelen**, 3 Hurst Rd, Eastbourne, **Sussex (East)**, BN21 2PJ, ENG.
(T) 01323 411900
Speciality: Physiotherapy.
● **Owner** Ms A Rambaut
P S T (Ref:HM20571)

### VAN SCHELLENBECK, JONA-MARION
**Mrs Jona-Marion Van Schellenbeck**, 12 The Grange Mews, Beverley Rd, Leamington Spa, **Warwickshire**, CV32 6PX, ENG.
(T) 01926 332490
Speciality: Acupuncture.
O (Ref:HM20572)

### VAN STRATEN CLINIC
**Van Straten Clinic (The)**, Glebe House, Station Rd, Cheddington, Leighton Buzzard, **Bedfordshire**, LU7 0SG, ENG.
(T) 01296 661215 (F) 01296 662450
Speciality: Osteopathy.
● **Owner** Mr M Van Straten
P S T (Ref:HM20573)

### VAN STRATEN CLINIC
**Van Straten Clinic**, Treborough House, Nottingham Pl, London, **London (Greater)**, W1M 3FP, ENG.
(T) 020 7935 8911
Speciality: Complementary Medicines & Therapy.
● **Director** Mr M Van Straten
C M (Ref:HM20574)

### VAN ZYL, MARTIN
**Martin Van Zyl**, 11A Kingsholm Rd, Gloucester, **Gloucestershire**, GL1 3AY, ENG.
(T) 01452 308812 (F) 01452 505550
Speciality: Osteopathy.
● **Manager** Mr M Van-Zyl
P S T (Ref:HM22122)

### VANBRUGH PHYSIOTHERAPY CLINIC
**Vanbrugh Physiotherapy Clinic**, 121 Trafalgar Rd, London, **London (Greater)**, SE10 9TY, ENG.
(T) 020 8293 5484 (F) 020 8305 1808
Speciality: Acupuncture, Indian Head Massage, Massage (Therapeutic), Nutritional Therapy, Physiotherapy, Reflexology, Reiki, Sports Massage. ✔
● **Physiotherapist** Mr D Higgins Q: MCSP, SRP. M: CSP.
C S Yrs. Est.: 11 (Ref:HM20575)

### VANCOPPENOLLE, J
**J Vancoppenolle**, 11 Mill Cl, Carshalton, **Surrey**, SM5 2NE, ENG.
(T) 020 8669 2163
Speciality: Acupuncture.
● **Owner** Miss J Vancoppenolle
O (Ref:HM20576)

### VANDERMEULEN, K
**Mrs K Vandermeulen**, 104 Copse Hill, London, **London (Greater)**, SW20 0NL, ENG.
(T) 020 8286 7047
Speciality: Physiotherapy.
P S T (Ref:HM20577)

### VANGEN, M A
**M A Vangen**, 257 Woolton Rd, Childwall, Liverpool, **Merseyside**, L16 8NA, ENG.
(T) 01517 228730
Speciality: Chiropractic.
P S T (Ref:HM20578)

### VANGO, S
**Ms S Vango**, Physiotherapy Clinic, Rear Of 709 Harrow Rd, Wembley, **London (Greater)**, HA0 2LL, ENG.
(T) 020 8903 3614
Speciality: Physiotherapy.
P S T (Ref:HM20579)

### VANGO, S A
**S A Vango**, 20 Wellgarth, Greenford, **London (Greater)**, UB6 0RR, ENG.
(T) 020 8903 3614
Speciality: Physiotherapy.
P S T (Ref:HM20580)

### VANRENEN, ANDY
**Andy Vanrenen**, 15 Carlton Rd, Oxford, **Oxfordshire**, OX2 7RZ, ENG.
(T) 01865 558014 (F) 01865 316710
Speciality: Osteopathy.
● **Owner** Mrs E Jewell
P S T (Ref:HM20581)

### VAN-ZAELEN, HENRIETTA
**Henrietta Van-Zaelen**, The Clocktower Practice, Crouch End Health Centre, 50 Park Rd, London, **London (Greater)**, N8 8SU, ENG.
(T) 020 7272 4493
Speciality: Aromatherapy.
● **Owner** Mrs H Van-Zaelen
M O (Ref:HM20582)

### VARA, J & ASSOCIATES
**J Vara & Associates**, 23 Sutton Pk Rd, Seaford, **Sussex (East)**, BN25 1RH, ENG.
(T) 01323 892002
Speciality: Osteopathy.
P S T (Ref:HM20583)

### VARD, ANTHONY
**Anthony Vard**, 81 Upr Georges St, Dunlaoghaire, Dublin, **County Dublin**, IRE.
(T) 01280 1844
(E) acupuncture@complaint.net
(W) www.complaint.net/acupuncture
Speciality: Complementary Medicines & Therapy.
M (Ref:HM20584)

### VARLEY, ANNE
**Varley Anne**, 8 Kinvara Pk, Navan Rd, Dublin, **County Dublin**, IRE.
(T) 01838 0088
Speciality: Complementary Medicines & Therapy.
M (Ref:HM20585)

### VARLEY, D
**Mrs D Varley**, 45 Thorneywood Mount, Nottingham, **Nottinghamshire**, NG3 2PY, ENG.
(T) 01159 502251
Speciality: Chiropodists (Podiatrists).
● **Owner** Mrs D Varley
S (Ref:HM20586)

### VARLEY, M A
**M A Varley**, 17 Marlborough Cl, Ramsbottom, Bury, **Lancashire**, BL0 9YU, ENG.
(T) 01706 828450
Speciality: Chiropodists (Podiatrists).
● **Owner** Mrs M Varley
S (Ref:HM20587)

### VARLEY, M A
**M A Varley**, 44 Haymarket St, Bury, **Lancashire**, BL9 0AY, ENG.
(T) 01617 644479
Speciality: Chiropodists (Podiatrists).
● **Owner** Mrs M Varley
S (Ref:HM20588)

### VARNEY PHYSIO & BACK CLINIC
**Varney Physiotherapy & Back Care Clinic (The)**, 6 Cambridge Prde, Great Cambridge Rd, Enfield, **London (Greater)**, EN1 4JU, ENG.
(T) 020 8367 0321
Speciality: Physiotherapy.
● **Partner** Mrs F Varney
P S T (Ref:HM20589)

### VARNEY PRACTICE
**Varney Practice (The)**, 3a The Maltings, Railway Pl, Hertford, **Hertfordshire**, SG13 7BS, ENG.
(T) 01992 550069
Speciality: Physiotherapy.
P S T (Ref:HM20590)

### VARNEY, MONICA
**Monica Varney**, 16 Ridgeway, Edenbridge, **Kent**, TN8 6AR, ENG.
(T) 01732 863826 (F) 01732 863826
(E) monicavarney@hotmail.com
Speciality: Aromatherapy, Metamorphic Therapy, Reflexology, Reiki. ✔
● **Therapist/Practitioner** Ms M Varney Q: Dip.Arom, RGN, RMN. M: IFA, Reiki Fed, UKCC.
T Yrs. Est.: 10 (Ref:HM20591)

### VARNHAM, GERALD
**Gerald Varnham**, 15 Southampton Rd, Fareham, **Hampshire**, PO16 7DZ, ENG.
(T) 01329 234182
Speciality: Physiotherapy.
P S T (Ref:HM20592)

### VASEY, SARAH
**Sarah Vasey**, 53 Waller Drive, Banbury, **Oxfordshire**, OX16 9NS, ENG.
(T) 01295 251426
Speciality: Chiropodists (Podiatrists).
● **Owner** Miss S Vasey
S (Ref:HM20593)

### VASQUEZ-NALDEN, ESTELA
**Estela Vasquez-Nalden**, 6 Hafer Rd, London, **London (Greater)**, SW11 1HF, ENG.
(T) 020 7564 1699
Speciality: Reflexology.
S T (Ref:HM20594)

### VAUGHAN OWEN, JENI
**Jeni Vaughan Owen**, Glyncoli Farm Cottage, Treorchy, **Rhondda Cynon Taff**, CF42 6SF, WAL.
(T) 01443 775647
Speciality: Reflexology.
● **Owner** Mrs J Vaughan-Owen
S T (Ref:HM20595)

### VAUGHAN, D L
**D L Vaughan**, 21 Manor Cottages, Northwood, **London (Greater)**, HA6 1HS, ENG.
(T) 01923 827222
Speciality: Chiropodists (Podiatrists).
● **Owner** Mr D Vaughan
S (Ref:HM20596)

### VAUGHAN, JANET
**Janet Vaughan**, 12 Hawthorne Cres, Skellow, Doncaster, **Yorkshire (South)**, DN6 8HU, ENG.
(T) 01302 724680
Speciality: Clairvoyants & Palmists.
● **Owner** Mrs J Vaughan
B (Ref:HM20597)

### VAUGHAN, JANET
**Janet Vaughan**, 3 Weston Lane, Totnes, **Devon**, TQ9 5UN, ENG.
(T) 01803 867591
Speciality: Reflexology.
● **Owner** Miss J Vaughan
S T (Ref:HM20598)

### VAUGHAN, L
**L Vaughan**, Lauriston, Wych Hill, Woking, **Surrey**, GU22 0HA, ENG.
(T) 01483 761312
Speciality: Reflexology.
● **Owner** Mrs L Vaughan
S T (Ref:HM20599)

### VAUGHN-OWEN, JENI
**Jeni Vaughn-Owen**, Natural Health Clinic, 98 Cathedral Rd, Cardiff, **Glamorgan (Vale of)**, CF11 9LP, WAL.
(T) 029 2022 2221
Speciality: Reflexology.
● **Practice Manager** Mrs L Powell
S T (Ref:HM20600)

### VAUGHTON, NORMAN D
**Norman D Vaughton**, 8 Fairway Drive, Chilwell, Nottingham, **Nottinghamshire**, NG9 4BN, ENG.
(T) 01159 255025 (F) 01159 255025
Speciality: Counselling, Hypnosis, Hypnotherapy, Psychotherapy, Visualisation Therapy. ✔
● **Therapist** Mr N Vaughton Q: AKC, BSc, C.Hyp.Couns(UK), Dip.Ed, Dip.Hyp, Dip.Psych, FACH. M: ACH, APHP.
B Yrs. Est.: 20 (Ref:HM20601)

### VAUX, P A
**P A Vaux**, 1 Medway Wharf Rd, Tonbridge, **Kent**, TN9 1RE, ENG.
(T) 01732 357563
Speciality: Chiropractic.
● **Owner** Mr P Vaux
P S T (Ref:HM20602)

### VAYRO, CHRISTINE
**Christine Vayro**, 109 Montague Cr, Garforth, Leeds, **Yorkshire (West)**, LS25 2EJ, ENG.


Key continued: Yrs.Est: Years Established Q: Qualifications M: Professional Membership ✔ Indemnity Insurance Accept Credit Cards

(T) 01132 867674
Speciality: Physiotherapy.
● **Owner** Ms C Vayro
P S T (**Ref:**HM20603)

### VEALE, LINDA
**Linda Veale**, 16 North Rd, Stevenage, **Hertfordshire**, SG1 4AL, ENG.
(T) 01438 750600
Speciality: Aromatherapy.
M O (**Ref:**HM20604)

### VEARSOMBE, MOIRA
**Moira Vearsombe**, 32 South St, Bridport, **Dorset**, DT6 3NQ, ENG.
(T) 01308 427777 (F) 01308 427777
Speciality: Complementary Medicines & Therapy.
● **Practice Manager** Mrs S Marsh
M (**Ref:**HM20605)

### VEDIC MEDICAL HALL
**Vedic Medical Hall Ltd**, 6 Chiltern St, London, **London (Greater)**, W1M 1PA, ENG.
(T) 020 7935 0028 (F) 020 7935 5055
Speciality: Complementary Medicines & Therapy.
● **Owner** Mr S Garg
C M (**Ref:**HM20606)

### VEDIC, RU
**RU Vedic Ltd**, 123A The Broadway, Southall, **London (Greater)**, UB1 1LW, ENG.
(T) 020 8574 5552 (F) 020 8574 5552
Speciality: Herbal Medicine.
● **Director** Mr A Ali
M (**Ref:**HM20607)

### VEHILL COMMUNICATIONS
**Vehill Communications**, Unit 2B Sherbourne Mill Studios, 127 Morville St, Birmingham, **Midlands (West)**, B16 8DG, ENG.
(T) 01216 933312
Speciality: Clairvoyants & Palmists.
● **Manager** Mrs L Greene
B (**Ref:**HM20608)

### VEITCH, D
**D Veitch**, 80 Baberton Mains Drive, Edinburgh, **Edinburgh (City of)**, EH14 3BT, SCO.
(T) 01314 424941
Speciality: Chiropodists (Podiatrists).
S (**Ref:**HM20609)

### VENABLES, ALISON
**Alison Venables**, 5 Bonnards Rd, Newton Longville, Milton Keynes, **Buckinghamshire**, MK17 0DS, ENG.
(T) 01908 271752
Speciality: Hypnotherapy.
B (**Ref:**HM20610)

### VENABLES, SUSAN
**Susan Venables**, 26 Western Cl, Lancing, **Sussex (West)**, BN15 8RU, ENG.
(T) 01903 754023
Speciality: Chiropodists (Podiatrists).
● **Owner** Mrs S Venables
S (**Ref:**HM20611)

### VENFIELD, C J
**C J Venfield**, 21 Pound Field, Wootton Wawen, Solihull, **Warwickshire**, B95 6AQ, ENG.
(T) 01564 792180
Speciality: Chiropractic.
● **Owner** Mrs C Venfield
P S T (**Ref:**HM20612)

### VENN, ESTHER K
**Esther K Venn**, Maidstone Chiropractic Clinic, 90 London Rd, Maidstone, **Kent**, ME16 0DP, ENG.
(T) 01622 679775
Speciality: Chiropractic.
P S T (**Ref:**HM20613)

### VENN, V
**V Venn**, 2 Wells Rd, Wookey Hole, Wells, **Somerset**, BA5 1DN, ENG.
(T) 01749 672372
Speciality: Physiotherapy.
● **Owner** Ms V Venn
P S T (**Ref:**HM20614)

### VENN-BROWN, HELEN
**Helen Venn-Brown**, 11 Yewfield Rd, Willesden, London, **London (Greater)**, NW10 9TD, ENG.
(T) 07976 361572
Speciality: Chiropody, Reflexology.
S T (**Ref:**HM20615)

### VENNING, C
**C Venning**, Halton Physiotherapy Clinic, 85 High St, Runcorn, **Cheshire**, WA7 1JF, ENG.
(T) 01928 561358
Speciality: Physiotherapy.
● **Owner** Mrs C Venning
P S T (**Ref:**HM20616)

### VENTHAM-FRASER, CAMILLA
**Camilla Ventham-Fraser**, 14 Hill Cres, Surbiton, **Surrey**, KT5 8DP, ENG.
(T) 020 8390 4068
Speciality: Clairvoyants & Palmists.
● **Owner** Mrs C Ventham-Fraser
B (**Ref:**HM20617)

### VERA BOYES ACUPUNCTURE
**Vera Boyes Acupuncture**, Spindlewood, Well Lane, Perran Downs, Penzance, **Cornwall**, TR20 9HQ, ENG.
(T) 01736 710160
Speciality: Acupuncture, Reflexology, Stress Therapy. ✔
● **Acupuncturist/Reflexologist** Ms V Boyes **Q:** Dip.Reflex, Lic.Ac, S.C.M, SRN. **M:** BAWAc.
O Yrs. Est.: 16 (**Ref:**HM20618)

### VERDE AROMATHERAPY
**Verde Aromatheraphy & Natural Skin Care**, 75 Northcote Rd, London, **London (Greater)**, SW11 6PJ, ENG.
(T) 020 7924 4379
Speciality: Aromatherapy.
● **Director** Mr B Wadsley
M O (**Ref:**HM20619)

### VERDE LONDON
**Verde London Ltd**, 15 Flask Walk, London, **London (Greater)**, NW3 1HJ, ENG.
(T) 020 7431 3314
Speciality: Aromatherapy.
● **Joint Director** Ms R Cook
M O (**Ref:**HM20620)

### VERDE LONDON
**Verde London Ltd**, 3 Princes Cl, London, **London (Greater)**, SW4 0LG, ENG.
(T) 020 7720 1100 (F) 020 7720 1155
Speciality: Aromatherapy.
● **Managing Director** Mr B Wadsley
M O (**Ref:**HM20621)

### VERMETTE, N G
**N G Vermette**, 20 Goda Rd, Littlehampton, **Sussex (West)**, BN17 6AS, ENG.
(T) 01903 715865
Speciality: Chiropodists (Podiatrists).
● **Owner** Mr C Kaye
S (**Ref:**HM20622)

### VERNON, CLIVE J
**Clive J Vernon**, 104 Sheering Mill Lane, Sawbridgeworth, **Hertfordshire**, CM21 9ND, ENG.
(T) 01279 723202 (F) 01279 723202
Speciality: Chiropodists (Podiatrists).
● **Owner** Mr C Vernon
S (**Ref:**HM20623)

### VERNON, JOHN
**John Vernon**, 21 Fairway, Nuneaton, **Warwickshire**, CV11 6NP, ENG.
(T) 024 7632 6405
Speciality: Hypnotherapy.
B (**Ref:**HM20624)

### VERNON, M J & J A
**M J & Mrs J A Vernon**, 100 Market St, Cannock, **Staffordshire**, WS12 5AG, ENG.
(T) 01543 879786
Speciality: Chiropodists (Podiatrists).
S (**Ref:**HM20625)

### VERONICA BEAUTY CLINIC
**Veronica Beauty Clinic**, 6a Market Pl, Howden, Goole, **Humberside (North)**, DN14 7BJ, ENG.
(T) 01430 431003
Speciality: Electrolysis.
● **Owner** Mrs V Sheppard
T (**Ref:**HM20626)

### VERRALL, CATHERINE
**Catherine Verrall**, 73 Hill Farm Way, Southwick, Brighton, **Sussex (East)**, BN42 4YG, ENG.
(T) 01273 385318
Speciality: Chiropodists (Podiatrists).
● **Director** Mrs C Verrall
S (**Ref:**HM20627)

### VERWAY, FRANK
**Frank Verway**, 16 Keyberry Park, Newton Abbot, **Devon**, TQ12 1BZ, ENG.
(T) 01626 353334
Speciality: Chiropractors.
● **Partner** Mr F Verway
P S T (**Ref:**HM20628)

### VERWEY, JULIA
**Julia Verwey**, 16 Keyberry Park, Newton Abbot, **Devon**, TQ12 1BZ, ENG.
(T) 01626 366840
Speciality: Chiropractic.
P S T (**Ref:**HM20629)

### VERWEY, SYKES
**Sykes Verwey**, 16 Keyberry Park, Newton Abbot, **Devon**, TQ12 1BZ, ENG.
(T) 01626 366840
Speciality: Chiropractors.
P S T (**Ref:**HM20630)

### VESEY, JOHN M
**John M Vesey**, 42A Richmond Rd, Kingston Upon Thames, **Surrey**, KT2 5EE, ENG.
(T) 020 8255 4927
Speciality: Osteopathy.
● **Owner** Mr J Vesey
P S T (**Ref:**HM20631)

### VETTERLEIN, JOYCE
**Joyce Vetterlein**, 62 Paul St, London, **London (Greater)**, EC2A 4NA, ENG.
(T) 020 7251 4429 (F) 020 7613 4737
Speciality: Complementary Medicines & Therapy.
M (**Ref:**HM20632)

### VEYSEY-SMITH, T H
**T H Veysey-Smith**, Sunnyside, Plough Rd, Epsom, **Surrey**, KT19 9RP, ENG.
(T) 020 8224 5731
Speciality: Chiropodists (Podiatrists).
● **Owner** Mr T Veysey-Smith
S (**Ref:**HM20633)

### VIALS, REBECCA
**Rebecca Vials**, 1 Western Drive, Blaby, **Leicestershire**, LE8 4FR, ENG.
(T) 01162 781089
Speciality: Reflexology.
S T (**Ref:**HM20634)

### VICARAGE LANE CLINIC
**Vicarage Lane Clinic**, Vicarage Lane, Haslemere, **Surrey**, GU27 1LQ, ENG.
(T) 01428 643503
Speciality: Osteopathy.
P S T (**Ref:**HM20635)

### VICARY, E A
**E A Vicary**, 10 Short Hill, Romsey, **Hampshire**, SO51 7UH, ENG.
(T) 01794 512980
Speciality: Complementary Medicines & Therapy.
● **Owner** Miss E Vicary
C M (**Ref:**HM20636)

### VICEROY
**Viceroy**, Green Farm, Lawshall, Bury St. Edmunds, **Suffolk**, IP29 4QH, ENG.
(T) 01284 828088 (F) 01284 828088
Speciality: Complementary Medicines & Therapy.
● **Director** Mr B French
C M (**Ref:**HM20637)

### VICK, C
**C Vick**, 1 Victoria Rd, Wargrave, Reading, **Berkshire**, RG10 8AD, ENG.
(T) 01189 403088
Speciality: Chiropodists (Podiatrists).
S (**Ref:**HM20638)

### VICKERS, CHARLOTTE

**Charlotte Vickers**, Natural Health Clinic, 98 Cathedral Rd, Cardiff, **Glamorgan (Vale of)**, CF11 9LP, WAL.
(T) 029 2022 2221
Speciality: Chiropractors.
● **Practice Manager** Mrs L Powell
P S T (Ref:HM20639)

### VICKERS, CHRISTOPHER (DR)

**Dr Christopher Vickers**, 2 Tetbury Rd, Cirencester, **Gloucestershire**, GL7 6PY, ENG.
(T) 01285 658769 (F) 01285 642524
Speciality: Chiropractic.
● **Owner** Dr C Vickers
P S T (Ref:HM20640)

### VICKERS, DEREK

**Derek Vickers**, 55 North St, Stilton, Peterborough, **Cambridgeshire**, PE7 3RP, ENG.
(T) 01733 240609 (F) 01733 244605
Speciality: Chiropodists (Podiatrists).
● **Owner** Mr D Vickers
S (Ref:HM20641)

### VICKERS, HUGH

**Hugh Vickers**, 32 Stoke Rd, Taunton, **Somerset**, TA1 3EJ, ENG.
(T) 01823 275948
Speciality: Osteopathy.
● **Owner** Mr A Patten
P S T (Ref:HM20642)

### VICKERS, NATALIE

**Natalie Vickers**, 19 Castle St, High Wycombe, **Buckinghamshire**, HP13 6RU, ENG.
(T) 01494 530004
Speciality: Homeopathy.
M (Ref:HM20643)

### VICKERY, A A

**A A Vickery**, 87 Old Park Ridings, London, **London (Greater)**, N21 2ER, ENG.
(T) 020 8360 5140
Speciality: Osteopathy.
● **Owner** Mr A Vickery
P S T (Ref:HM20644)

### VICKI WHELAN ASSOCIATES

**Vicki Whelan Associates**, The Gatehouse, 62 Ashton Lane, Sale, **Cheshire**, M33 6WQ, ENG.
(T) 01619 762716 (F) 01619 762716
Speciality: Hypnosis.
● **Owner** Mrs V Whelan
B (Ref:HM20645)

### VICKY NOBLE - AROMATHERAPIST

**Vicky Noble - Aromatherapist**, 22 Kempton Rd, Ipswich, **Suffolk**, IP1 6QY, ENG.
(T) 01473 744805
Speciality: Complementary Medicines & Therapy.
M (Ref:HM20646)

### VICO CONSULTATION CENTRE

**Vico Consultation Centre**, Dungar Tce, Dun Laoghaire, **County Dublin**, IRE.
(T) 01284 3336
Speciality: Psychotherapy.
B (Ref:HM20647)

### VICTORIA CENTRE

**Victoria Centre (The)**, Pettits Lane, Romford, **Essex**, RM1 4HP, ENG.
(T) 01708 726727
Speciality: Chiropodists (Podiatrists).
● **Manager** Miss V Geiser
S (Ref:HM20648)

### VICTORIA CHIROPRACTIC CLINIC

**Victoria Chiropractic Clinic**, Victoria House, 98 Victoria St, London, **London (Greater)**, SW1E 5JL, ENG.
(T) 020 7915 0054
Speciality: Chiropractic.
P S T (Ref:HM20649)

### VICTORIA CLINIC

**Clyve Power - Remedial Therapist**, 172-174 London Rd, Leicester, **Leicestershire**, LE2 1ND, ENG.
(T) 01162 470880 (F) 01162 471253
(E) powerheal@fsnet.com
Speciality: Absent Healing, Bach Remedies, Chiropractic, Healer, Kinesiology, Manipulation, Massage (Therapeutic), Nutritional Therapy, Reiki, Spiritual Healing, Stress Therapy, Vitamin Therapy, Three in one concepts - one brain therapy for dyslexia, hyperton-x - correction for learning disorders and sports performance enhancement - both of these use kinesiological techniques. ✔
● **Therapist** Mr C Power Q: DC(OCC), LCSP, RNT. M: LCSP.
S Yrs. Est.: 5 (Ref:HM20650)

### VICTORIA CLINIC

**Victoria Clinic (The)**, 172-174 London Rd, Leicester, **Leicestershire**, LE2 1ND, ENG.
(T) 01162 470880
Speciality: Osteopathy.
P S T (Ref:HM20651)

### VICTORIA CLINIC

**Victoria Clinic (The)**, 1 Chapel Cl, Holywell Green, Halifax, **Yorkshire (West)**, HX4 9BF, ENG.
(T) 01422 376114 (F) 01422 377023
Speciality: Complementary Medicines & Therapy.
● **Owner** Mr J Ogden
M (Ref:HM20652)

### VICTORIA CLINIC

**Victoria Clinic**, 67 Victoria Way, Woking, **Surrey**, GU21 1JR, ENG.
(T) 01483 723688
Speciality: Chiropractic.
P S T (Ref:HM20653)

### VICTORIA COUNSELLING SERVICE

**Victoria Counselling Service**, 135 Victoria Avenue, Southend-On-Sea, **Essex**, SS2 6EL, ENG.
(T) 01702 354118
Speciality: Psychotherapy.
B (Ref:HM20654)

### VICTORIA PRIVATE PHYSIO CLINIC

**Victoria Private Physiotherapy Clinic**, Care Of Victoria Hospital, Haywood Rd, Accrington, **Lancashire**, BB5 6AS, ENG.
(T) 01254 294661
Speciality: Physiotherapy.
● **Manager** Mrs A Aspinall
P S T (Ref:HM20655)

### VICTORIA SPECIAL SCHOOL

**Victoria Special School**, Centre For Physiotherapy, Bell Hill, Birmingham, **Midlands (West)**, B31 1LD, ENG.
(T) 01214 756663
Speciality: Physiotherapy.
● **Manager** Mrs P Sole
P S T (Ref:HM20656)

### VICTORIAN COLLECTION

**Victorian Collection (The)**, Unit 11 Littleton Business Park, Cock Sparrow Lane, Cannock, **Staffordshire**, WS12 4PB, ENG.
(T) 01543 462741 (F) 01543 462785
Speciality: Aromatherapy.
● **Owner** Ms L Fox
M O (Ref:HM20657)

### VICTORY, S

**S Victory**, The Wellbeing Centre, 11 Musters Rd, West Bridgford, Nottingham, **Nottinghamshire**, NG2 7PP, ENG.
(T) 01159 825353
Speciality: Psychotherapy.
B (Ref:HM20658)

### VIDAL-HALL, NICK

**Nick Vidal-Hall**, Homecroft, Brownston St, Modbury, Ivybridge, **Devon**, PL21 0RQ, ENG.
(T) 01548 830716
Speciality: Homeopathy.
M (Ref:HM20659)

### VIDGEN, H E

**Mrs H E Vidgen**, 56 Lowlands Rd, Pinner, **London (Greater)**, HA5 1TU, ENG.
(T) 020 8429 0511
Speciality: Chiropodists (Podiatrists).
S (Ref:HM20660)

### VIDION, BARBARA

**Barbara Vidion**, Metfield Cottage, Christmas Lane, Metfield, Harleston, **Norfolk**, IP20 0JY, ENG.
(T) 01379 586362
Speciality: Reflexology.
S T (Ref:HM20661)

### VIGNAUX, PATRICK

**Patrick Vignaux**, 4 The Corner House, 19 Shorncliffe Rd, Folkestone, **Kent**, CT20 2NA, ENG.
(T) 01303 252905
Speciality: Hypnosis.
● **Owner** Mr P Vignaux
B (Ref:HM20662)

### VILE, CAROL

**Mrs Carol Vile**, 47 Waltham Drive, Edgware, **London (Greater)**, HA8 5PF, ENG.
(T) 020 8952 8149
Speciality: Osteopathy.
● **Owner** Mrs C Vile
P S T (Ref:HM20663)

### VILE, CAROL

**Carol Vile**, 8 Sutherland Avenue, London, **London (Greater)**, W13 8LE, ENG.
(T) 020 8991 8141
Speciality: Osteopathy.
P S T (Ref:HM20664)

### VILLAGE CLINIC

**Village Clinic (The)**, Badhams Pharmacy, 23 Church Rd, Bishops Cleeve, Cheltenham, **Gloucestershire**, GL52 8LR, ENG.
(T) 01242 673507
(W) www.villageclinic.co.uk
Speciality: Chiropody, Electrotherapy, Manipulation, Massage (Therapeutic), Insole Prescription and Provision, Excercise Therapy, Pain Management, Relaxation. ✔
● **Physiotherapist** Ms L Cook Q: BSc (Hons). M: C.P.S.M, CSP.
● **Chiropodist (Podiatrist)** Ms S Cook Q: BSc, S.R.Ch. M: C.P.S.M, S.C.P.
S Yrs. Est.: 5 (Ref:HM20665)

### VILLAGE PHYSIO & SPORTS CLINIC

**Village Physiotherapy & Sports Injury Clinic (The)**, 1a School Lane, Manchester, **Manchester (Greater)**, M20 6RD, ENG.
(T) 01614 487844
Speciality: Physiotherapy.
● **Owner** Ms B Hall
P S T (Ref:HM20666)

### VILLAGE PHYSIOTHERAPY PRACTICE

**Village Physiotherapy Practice (The)**, 42 High St, Farnborough, Orpington, **Kent**, BR6 7BA, ENG.
(T) 01689 851143 (F) 01689 861901
Speciality: Physiotherapy. ✔
● **Owner/Physiotherapist** Ms C Adcock Q: BHSc, BSc, MCSP, SRP. M: CSP.
S (Ref:HM20667)

### VINCE, LINDA

**Linda Vince**, 94 Moody Rd, Fareham, **Hampshire**, PO14 2NR, ENG.
(T) 01329 668500
Speciality: Chiropody. ✔
● **Chiropodist** Ms L Vince Q: MBChA, MSSCh. M: B.A.Ch.P.
C Yrs. Est.: 6 (Ref:HM20668)

### VINCENT, A

**A Vincent**, 25 Minster Rd, Bromley, **Kent**, BR1 4DY, ENG.
(T) 020 8402 0438
Speciality: Physiotherapy.
● **Owner** A Vincent
P S T (Ref:HM20669)

### VINCENT, DAVID

**Mr David Vincent**, 37 North Rd, Kirkby Stephen, **Cumbria**, CA17 4RH, ENG.
(T) 01768 372482
Speciality: Complementary Medicines & Therapy.
● **Partner** Miss J Brown
M (Ref:HM20670)

### VINCENT, EUNICE

**Eunice Vincent**, 79 Foxgrove Rd, Beckenham, **Kent**, BR3 5BB, ENG.
(T) 020 8650 4221
Speciality: Massage (Therapeutic). ✔
● **Staff Nurse** Ms E Vincent Q: DM, RGN.



Key continued: Yrs.Est: Years Established Q: Qualifications M: Professional Membership ✔ Indemnity Insurance Accept Credit Cards

M: RGN.
C Yrs. Est.: 3 (Ref:HM20671)

## VINCENT, FRANK

**Frank Vincent**, Bexleyheath Natural Health Clinic, 284 Broadway, Bexleyheath, **Kent**, DA6 8AJ, ENG.
(T) 020 8303 6288 (F) 020 8303 6288
Speciality: Osteopathy.
● **Owner** Mr P Cousins
P S T (Ref:HM20672)

## VINCENT, JOAN

**Joan Vincent**, 1 Longfield Ter, Halifax, **Yorkshire (West)**, HX3 7BW, ENG.
(T) 01422 200479
Speciality: Clairvoyants & Palmists.
● **Owner** Mrs J Vincent
B (Ref:HM20673)

## VINCES, DENISE

**Denise Vinces**, 23 Hawthorn Bank, Seafield, Bathgate, **Lothian (West)**, EH47 7EB, SCO.
(T) 01506 632926
Speciality: Aromatherapy, Massage (Therapeutic), Reflexology, Reiki. ✔
● **Owner/Reflexologist** Mrs D Vines
C Yrs. Est.: 5 (Ref:HM20674)

## VINE CLINIC

**Vine Clinic (The)**, 228 Richmond Rd, Kingston Upon Thames, **Surrey**, KT2 5HG, ENG.
(T) 020 8546 2426
Speciality: Physiotherapy.
● **Practice Manager** Mrs A Monk
P S T (Ref:HM20675)

## VINE COTTAGE CHIROP PRACTICE

**Vine Cottage Chiropody Practice**, Vine Cottage, 53 Oxford St, Burnham-on-Sea, **Somerset**, TA8 1EN, ENG.
(T) 01278 787159 (F) 01278 787159
Speciality: Chiropodists (Podiatrists).
● **Partner** Mr R Burt
S (Ref:HM20676)

## VINE HERBAL PRODUCTS

**Vine Herbal Products For Animals**, The Vine, Stanton, Broadway, **Worcestershire**, WR12 7NE, ENG.
(T) 01386 584385 (F) 01386 584385
Speciality: Complementary Medicines & Therapy.
● **Owner** Mr L Carenza
C Yrs. Est.: 6 (Ref:HM20677)

## VINE MEWS CLINIC

**Vine Mews Clinic**, 10 Vine Mews, Vine St, Evesham, **Worcestershire**, WR11 4RE, ENG.
(T) 01386 48107
Speciality: Osteopathy.
P S T (Ref:HM20678)

## VINE, MARTIN

**Martin Vine**, Lister Health Centre, 130 Colney Hatch Lane, Muswell Hill, London, **London (Greater)**, N10 1ER, ENG.
(T) 020 8245 5834
Speciality: Chiropodists (Podiatrists).
S (Ref:HM20679)

## VINES REIKI HEALING CENTRE

**Vines Reiki Healing Centre**, The Vines, Southsea Avenue, Minster On Sea, Sheerness, **Kent**, ME12 2NH, ENG.
(T) 01795 870859
(W) www.vines-reiki.co.uk
Speciality: Aromatherapy, Manual Lymph Drainage, Meditation, Osteopathy, Reiki, Sports Massage, T'ai-Chi Ch'uan, Cellulite Massage and Hopi Ear Candles. ✔
● **Holistic Therapist** Mr K Daniels M: ITEC.
C Yrs. Est.: 12 (Ref:HM20680)

## VINES, T

**T Vines**, The Ridge, How Lane, Coulsdon, **London (Greater)**, CR5 3LN, ENG.
(T) 01737 555854 (F) 01737 552057
Speciality: Homeopathy.
● **Owner** Mrs T Vines
M (Ref:HM20681)

## VINEY HALL PHYSIOTHERAPY

**Viney Hall Physiotherapy**, The Old School, Viney Hill, Lydney, **Gloucestershire**, GL15 4ND, ENG.
(T) 01594 516810
Speciality: Chiropody, Electrotherapy, Manipulation, Massage (Therapeutic), Podiatry, Reflexology. ✔
● **Physiotherapist** Mrs T Dufty Q: BSc (Hons), MCSP, SRP. M: CSP.
● **Physiotherapist** Mrs P Deave Q: Grad Dip Phys, MCSP, SRP. M: CSP.
● **Chiropodist (Podiatrist)** Mr M Coates Q: DPodM, S.R.Ch.
● **Massage Therapist** Ms F Drummond Q: ITEC, ONC.
● **Physiotherapist** Mrs S Nancollas Q: Grad Dip Phys, MCSP, SRP. M: CSP.
S Yrs. Est.: 8 (Ref:HM20683)

## VINING, E H

**E H Vining**, Puxey Farm, Puxey, Sturminster Newton, **Dorset**, DT10 2HR, ENG.
(T) 01258 472325
Speciality: Complementary Medicines & Therapy.
● **Owner** Mrs J Vining
C M (Ref:HM20684)

## VININGS NATURAL HEALTH CENTRE

**Vinings Natural Health Centre**, Church Rd, Haywards Heath, **Sussex (West)**, RH16 3UF, ENG.
(T) 01444 455922
Speciality: Complementary Medicines & Therapy.
M (Ref:HM20685)

## VINSON, CAROL

**Carol Vinson**, 3 Yew Tree Avenue, Anston, Sheffield, **Yorkshire (South)**, S25 4EW, ENG.
(T) 01909 560747
Speciality: Chiropody, Nail Surgery. ✔
● **Chiropodist** Ms C Vinson M: B.A.Ch.P.
C Yrs. Est.: 1 (Ref:HM20686)

## VINTEN, J E

**J E Vinten**, The Oaks, 52 Fernleigh Drive, Leigh-On-Sea, **Essex**, SS9 1LQ, ENG.
(T) 01702 476355
Speciality: Physiotherapy.
● **Owner** Mrs J Vinten
P S T (Ref:HM20687)

## VIOLET HILL STUDIOS

**Violet Hill Studios**, 6 Violet Hill, London, **London (Greater)**, NW8 9EB, ENG.
(T) 020 7624 6101
Speciality: Complementary Medicines & Therapy.
C M (Ref:HM20688)

## VIRGINIA COTTAGE

**Virginia Cottage**, St. James Rd, Netherbury, Bridport, **Dorset**, DT6 5LP, ENG.
(T) 01308 488225 (F) 01308 488225
Speciality: Complementary Medicines & Therapy.
● **Owner** Mrs E Nicoll
C M (Ref:HM20689)

## VIRGO BODYWORK TABLES

**Virgo Bodywork Tables**, Unit 5 Rowleys Yard, Woodlands Park Rd, London, **London (Greater)**, N15 3RT, ENG.
(T) 020 8802 5008
Speciality: Complementary Medicines & Therapy.
C M (Ref:HM20690)

## VIRIK, MANJIT

**Manjit Virik**, Health Hydro, Milton Rd, Swindon, **Wiltshire**, SN1 5JA, ENG.
(T) 01793 465631
Speciality: Homeopathy.
M (Ref:HM20691)

## VIRINDER SAINI'S BEAUTY CLINIC

**Virinder Saini's Beauty Clinic For Ladies**, 256 Ealing Rd, Wembley, **London (Greater)**, HA0 4QL, ENG.
(T) 020 8903 9626
Speciality: Electrolysis.
● **Owner** Mrs V Saini
T (Ref:HM20692)

## VIRTUE CHINESE MEDICAL CENTRE

**Virtue Chinese Medical Centre Ltd**, 9 Sheaveshill Prde, Sheaveshill Avenue, London, **London (Greater)**, NW9 6RS, ENG.
(T) 020 8200 8118
Speciality: Complementary Medicines & Therapy.
● **Doctor** Mr R Gur
C M (Ref:HM20693)

## VISAGE

**Visage**, Gatehouse, White Cross Industrial Estate, South Rd, Lancaster, **Lancashire**, LA1 4XQ, ENG.
(T) 01524 34532
Speciality: Electrolysis.
T (Ref:HM20694)

## VISION, R E

**R E -Vision**, 97 Brondesbury Rd, London, **London (Greater)**, NW6 6RY, ENG.
(T) 020 8357 8881
Speciality: Psychotherapy.
B (Ref:HM20695)

## VISIONS & DREAMS

**Visions & Dreams**, Station Lane, Hornchurch, **Essex**, RM12 6JF, ENG.
(T) 01708 452592
Speciality: Clairvoyants & Palmists.
● **Partner** Ms D Cracknell
B (Ref:HM20696)

## VISITING CHIROPODIST

**Visiting Chiropodist**, 21 Kestrel Drive, Shrewsbury, **Shropshire**, SY1 4TT, ENG.
(T) 01743 448575 (F) 01743 448575
Speciality: Chiropodists (Podiatrists).
● **Owner** Mrs P Price
S (Ref:HM20697)

## VISITING CHIROPODY SERVICE

**Visiting Chiropody Service**, 11 South Drive, Ruislip, **London (Greater)**, HA4 8EU, ENG.
(T) 01895 470534
Speciality: Chiropodists (Podiatrists).
● **Owner** Mr T Ogorman
S (Ref:HM20698)

## VISITING MASSAGE AROMATHERAPY

**Visiting Massage Aromatherapy**, 1a Marylebone High St, London, **London (Greater)**, W1M 3PA, ENG.
(T) 07091 001217
Speciality: Aromatherapy.
● **Owner** Ms A Glynne
M O (Ref:HM20699)

## VISITING THERAPEUTIC MASSAGE

**Visiting Therapeutic Massage**, 1a Marylebone High St, London, **London (Greater)**, W1M 3PA, ENG.
(T) 020 8785 9145
Speciality: Complementary Medicines & Therapy.
M (Ref:HM20700)

## VITA HEALTH ALLERGY TESTING

**Vita Health Allergy Testing & Treatment Clinic**, 367 Brighton Rd, South Croydon, **Surrey**, CR2 6ES, ENG.
(T) 020 8686 6955
Speciality: Complementary Medicines & Therapy.
C M (Ref:HM20701)

## VITAL ENERGY

**Vital Energy**, 2 Beloe Rd, Bristol, BS7 8RB, ENG.
(T) 01179 441738
Speciality: Complementary Medicines & Therapy.
● **Partner** Miss N Lewis
C M (Ref:HM20702)

## VITAL TOUCH

**Vital Touch Ltd**, P O Box 108, Totnes, **Devon**, TQ9 5PY, ENG.
(T) 01803 840670 (F) 01803 840113
(E) katie@vitaltouch.com
(W) www.vitaltouch.com
Speciality: Aromatherapy, Massage (Therapeutic), Reflexology.
● **Director** Ms K Whitehouse Q: Dip.Arom, Dip.Massage, Dip.Reflex. M: APNT.



Key: B Mind-Body Medicine C Complementary Medicine H Self Help Treatment M Medicinal Therapy O Oriental Medicine P Postural Therapy S Manipulative Structural Therapy T Touch Therapy

M (Ref:HM20703)

## VITAPURE
**Vitapure Ltd**, Unit A, Blois Meadow Business Centre, Blois Rd, Steeple Bumpstead, Haverhill, **Suffolk**, CB9 7BN, ENG.
(T) 01440 731733 (F) 01440 731734
Speciality: Complementary Medicines & Therapy.
● **Managing Director** Mr R Sparrow
M (Ref:HM20704)

## VITASPRAY
**Vitaspray**, Three Gables, Mill Rd, Marlow, **Buckinghamshire**, SL7 1QB, ENG.
(T) 01628 482393
Speciality: Complementary Medicines & Therapy.
C M (Ref:HM20705)

## VITTLE, MARY
**Mary Vittle**, 12 Park View, Sedbury, Chepstow, **Monmouthshire**, NP16 7BE, WAL.
(T) 01291 624458
Speciality: Chiropodists (Podiatrists).
● **Owner** Mrs M Vittle
S (Ref:HM20706)

## VIV HOUSE
**Viv House**, 12 Alexandra Rd, London, **London (Greater)**, SE26 5NL, ENG.
(T) 020 8778 3068
Speciality: Reflexology.
S T (Ref:HM20707)

## VIVIAN, DAWSON
**Dawson Vivian**, 9 Beeches Avenue, Carshalton, **Surrey**, SM5 3LB, ENG.
(T) 020 8773 4508
Speciality: Acupuncture.
O (Ref:HM20708)

## VOICE THERAPY
**Voice Therapy**, 78B Inverine Road- Charlton, London, **London (Greater)**, SE7 7NL, ENG.
(T) 020 8858 8069
Speciality: Voice Therapy.
M (Ref:HM20709)

## VOIGHTS, M F
**M F Voights**, Thorpe Bay Clinic, 169 The Broadway, Southend-On-Sea, **Essex**, SS1 3EX, ENG.
(T) 01702 582485
Speciality: Osteopathy.
P S T (Ref:HM20710)

## VOLK & ASSOCIATES
**Caroline Volk & Associates**, 5 Firs Walk, Northwood, **London (Greater)**, HA6 2BZ, ENG.
(T) 01923 822368
Speciality: Psychotherapy.
● **Owner** Ms C Volk
B (Ref:HM20711)

## VOLLERS, J
**Mrs J Vollers**, Otter House, Harpford, Sidmouth, **Devon**, EX10 0NH, ENG.
(T) 01395 568330
Speciality: Reflexology.
● **Owner** Mrs J Vollers
S T (Ref:HM20712)

## VON ZIECHMANN, ALEXANDRA
**Alexandra Von Ziechmann**, Violet Hill Studios, Violet Hill, London, **London (Greater)**, NW8 9EB, ENG.
(T) 020 7286 9247
Speciality: Homeopathy.
● **Owner** A Von Ziechmann
M (Ref:HM20713)

## VOY, JOAN
**Joan Voy**, 3 Manseview Trce, Eaglesham, Glasgow, **Glasgow (City of)**, G76 0JB, SCO.
(T) 01355 303417
Speciality: Reflexology.
S T (Ref:HM20714)

## VOYSEY, KIM
**Kim Voysey**, St Chiropractic Clinic, 74A High St, Street, **Somerset**, BA16 0EG, ENG.
(T) 01458 840490
Speciality: Chiropractors.
P S T (Ref:HM20715)

## VOYSEY, KIM R
**Kim R Voysey**, 24 Downend Rd, Fishponds, Bristol, BS16 5AP, ENG.
(T) 01179 583043
Speciality: Chiropractic.
● **Owner** Ms K Voysey
P S T (Ref:HM20716)

## VRIES, J DE
**J De Vries**, Hadley Wood Halth Centre, 28 Crescent West, Barnet, **Hertfordshire**, EN4 0EJ, ENG.
(T) 020 8441 8352 (F) 020 8441 9950
Speciality: Osteopathy.
● **Director** Mr M Webb
P S T (Ref:HM20717)

## VUKOVICH, IRENA
**Irena Vukovich**, 37 Abbey Avenue, St. Albans, **Hertfordshire**, AL3 4BH, ENG.
(T) 01727 833698 (F) 01727 844976
Speciality: Osteopathy.
P S T (Ref:HM20718)

## VUKOVICH, NIGEL
**Nigel Vukovich**, 37 Abbey Avenue, St. Albans, **Hertfordshire**, AL3 4BH, ENG.
(T) 01727 833698 (F) 01727 844976
Speciality: Osteopathy.
P S T (Ref:HM20719)

## VULCANS LANE CHIROPODY
**Vulcans Lane Chiropody**, 6 Vulcans Lane, Workington, **Cumbria**, CA14 2NX, ENG.
(T) 01900 870900
Speciality: Aromatherapy, Chiropody, Massage (Therapeutic), Reflexology, Bowel Irrigation. ✔
● **Chiropodist/Reflexologist/Aromatherapist**
Mr R Hommerson Q: IIHHT, S.R.Ch. M: S.C.P, Soc.Comp.Therapy, Soc.Hom.
T Yrs. Est.: 8 (Ref:HM20720)

## W E PARK WINDER
**W E Park Winder**, 32 Baring Rd, Cowes, **Isle of Wight**, PO31 8DE, ENG.
(T) 01983 293103
Speciality: Psychoanalysis.
B (Ref:HM20721)

## W M RYAN AND SON
**W M Ryan And Son**, 215 Kingsway, Dunmurry, Belfast, **County Antrim**, BT17 9SB, NIR.
(T) 028 9030 1202
Speciality: Manipulation, Massage (Therapeutic), Reflexology. ✔
● **Manipulative Therapist** W M Ryan
Q: Dip.Man.Th.
● **Reflexologist/Sports Therapist**
Miss N Crooks Q: Dip.Reflex, Dip.Sports Therapy.
● **Manipulative Therapist**
J W Sinclair Q: Dip.Man.Th.
● **Manipulative Therapist** B Jackson
Q: Dip.Man.Th.
● **Manipulative Therapist** M D Agnew
Q: Dip.Man.Th.
● **Manipulative Therapist** W K Ryan
Q: Dip.Man.Th.
S Yrs. Est.: 15 (Ref:HM20722)

## W P F COUNSELLING
**W P F Counselling Ltd**, 23 Kensington Sq, London, **London (Greater)**, W8 5HN, ENG.
(T) 020 7937 6956 (F) 020 7376 1914
Speciality: Psychotherapy.
● **Office Manager** Ms H Ben-Brown
B (Ref:HM20723)

## WADDELL, J U
**J U Waddell**, 22 Cow Wynd, Falkirk, FK1 1PU, SCO.
(T) 01324 621398
Speciality: Chiropodists (Podiatrists).
● **Owner** Mr J Waddell
S (Ref:HM20724)

## WADDINGTON, P
**P Waddington**, 165-167 Knightlow Rd, Birmingham, **Midlands (West)**, B17 8PY, ENG.
(T) 01214 273592
Speciality: Chiropodists (Podiatrists).
S (Ref:HM20725)

## WADDINGTON, R M
**R M Waddington**, 122 Rectory Gr, Leigh-On-Sea, **Essex**, SS9 2HL, ENG.
(T) 01702 480640
Speciality: Chiropody, Nail Surgery. ✔
● **Owner/Chiropodist**
Mr R Waddington Q: DPodM, M.S.C.P, S.R.Ch, SRN.
C Yrs. Est.: 25 (Ref:HM20726)

## WADEBRIDGE CHIROPODY CLINIC
**Wadebridge Chiropody Clinic**, Bridge House, Bridgend, Wadebridge, **Cornwall**, PL27 6DA, ENG.
(T) 01208 813753 (F) 01208 813753
Speciality: Chiropodists (Podiatrists).
● **Owner** Mr R Berridge
S (Ref:HM20727)

## WADEBRIDGE OSTEOPATHS
**Wadebridge Osteopaths**, 48 Molesworth St, Wadebridge, **Cornwall**, PL27 7DP, ENG.
(T) 01208 812048
Speciality: Osteopathy.
● **Owner** Mr M Retallick
P S T (Ref:HM20728)

## WADHURST PHYSIO/SPORTS CLNC
**Wadhurst Physiotherapy & Sports Injuries Clinic**, The Haven, High St, Wadhurst, **Sussex (East)**, TN5 6AG, ENG.
(T) 01892 785095 (F) 01892 785095
Speciality: Acupuncture, Physiotherapy.
✔ CREDIT
● **Practice Manager** Ms S Black
● **Physiotherapist** Mrs J Sands Q: MCSP, SRP. M: CSP.
● **Physiotherapist** Ms M Tunstall Q: MCSP, SRP. M: CSP.
● **Principal** Mrs C Roche Q: MMACP.
S (Ref:HM20729)

## WADHURST PHYSIO/SPORTS CLNC
**Crowborough Physiotherapy & Sports Injuries Clinic**, The Brook Health Centre, Crowborough Hill, Crowborough, **Sussex (East)**, TN5, ENG.
(T) 01892 668968 (F) 01892 785095
Speciality: Physiotherapy. ✔ CREDIT
● **Physiotherapist** Ms C McCarthy Q: MCSP, SRP. M: CSP.
● **Physiotherapist** Mrs C Roche Q: MCSP, MMACP, SRP. M: CSP.
S (Ref:HM20730)

## WADSWORTH OSTEOPATHS
**Wadsworth Osteopaths**, Holly House Clinic, 199 Hull Rd, Cottingham Rd, Hull, **Humberside (North)**, HU6 8RG, ENG.
(T) 01482 875004 (F) 01482 875004
Speciality: Osteopathy.
● **Owner** Mr R Wadsworth
P S T (Ref:HM20731)

## WADSWORTH, ROBERT
**Robert Wadsworth**, 39 Norwood, Beverley, **Humberside (North)**, HU17 9HN, ENG.
(T) 01482 869678 (F) 01482 886305
Speciality: Osteopathy.
● **Owner** Mr R Wadsworth
P S T (Ref:HM20732)

## WAGLAND, C
**C Wagland**, 14 Cornwallis Avenue, Folkestone, **Kent**, CT19 5JA, ENG.
(T) 01303 246099
Speciality: Chiropodists (Podiatrists).
S (Ref:HM20733)

## WAGNER, A
**A Wagner**, Neal's Yard Remedies, 9 Rotunda Trce, Montpellier St, Cheltenham, **Gloucestershire**, GL50 1SW, ENG.
(T) 01242 524209
Speciality: Homeopathy.
● **Owner** Ms A Wagner
M (Ref:HM20734)

## WAH, G
**G Wah**, Rosebank Cottage, Invergordon, **Highland**, IV18 0LQ, SCO.
(T) 01349 853703
Speciality: Reflexology. ✔


Key continued: Yrs.Est: Years Established Q: Qualifications M: Professional Membership ✔ Indemnity Insurance CREDIT Accept Credit Cards

● **Reflexologist** Mrs G Wah Q: Cert.PLR. M: BRA, FPLR.
T Yrs. Est.: 8 (Ref:HM20735)

**WAINWRIGHT, COLIN**

**Colin Wainwright**, 2 Kenwood Rd, Sheffield, **Yorkshire (South)**, S7 1NP, ENG.
(T) 01142 552048
Speciality: Osteopathy.
● **Owner** Mr D Wainwright
P S T (Ref:HM20736)

**WAINWRIGHT, DAVID**

**David Wainwright**, 2 Kenwood Rd, Sheffield, **Yorkshire (South)**, S7 1NP, ENG.
(T) 01142 552048
Speciality: Osteopathy.
● **Owner** Mr D Wainwright
P S T (Ref:HM20737)

**WAINWRIGHT, MARY**

**Mary Wainwright**, Brynfforest, Llandovery, **Carmarthenshire**, SA20 0UL, WAL.
(T) 01550 720615
Speciality: Homeopathy, Reiki, Seichem, Flower Remedy. ✓
● **Homeopath** Ms M Wainwright Q: LCPH.
C (Ref:HM20738)

**WAINWRIGHT, P**

**P Wainwright**, 5a Hornby St, Heywood, **Manchester (Greater)**, OL10 1AA, ENG.
(T) 01706 369893
Speciality: Chiropody, Complementary Therapy, Podiatry, Reflexology, Reiki. ✓
● **Chiropodist (Podiatrist)**
Mrs P Wainwrght Q: MSSCh, S.R.Ch.
M T Yrs. Est.: 22 (Ref:HM20739)

**WAITE, J**

**J Waite**, 400 Manchester Rd, Stocksbridge, Sheffield, **Yorkshire (South)**, S30 2DS, ENG.
(T) 01142 884200
Speciality: Reflexology.
S T (Ref:HM20740)

**WAITE, J C**

**J C Waite**, 106 Durham Rd, Stockton-On-Tees, **Cleveland**, TS19 0DQ, ENG.
(T) 01642 679538
Speciality: Chiropodists (Podiatrists).
● **Owner** Mr J Waite
S (Ref:HM20741)

**WAKE, J**

**J Wake**, 16 Priors Green, Spennymoor, **County Durham**, DL16 6XL, ENG.
(T) 01388 813220
Speciality: Aromatherapy.
● **Owner** Mrs J Wake
M O (Ref:HM20742)

**WAKEFIELD CHIROPRACTIC CLINIC**

**Wakefield Chiropractic Clinic**, 26 Leeds Rd, Wakefield, **Yorkshire (West)**, WF1 3JL, ENG.
(T) 01924 200805 (F) 01924 201530
Speciality: Chiropractic.
● **Practice Manager** Mrs S Corlet
P S T (Ref:HM20743)

**WAKEFIELD, M**

**M Wakefield**, 6 Hauxwell Drive, Yeadon, Leeds, **Yorkshire (West)**, LS19 7RU, ENG.
(T) 01132 503191
Speciality: Chiropodists (Podiatrists).
S (Ref:HM20744)

**WAKEFIELD, ROBERT**

**Robert Wakefield**, 2 Knolles Rd, Oxford, **Oxfordshire**, OX4 3HS, ENG.
(T) 01865 777747
Speciality: Complementary Medicines & Therapy.
● **Owner** Mr R Wakefield
C M (Ref:HM20745)

**WAKEFIELD, ROBERT**

**Robert Wakefield**, 109 Shirley Avenue, Croydon, **Surrey**, CR0 8SQ, ENG.
(T) 020 8654 3318
Speciality: Chiropodists (Podiatrists).
S (Ref:HM20746)

**WAKELING, ANN**

**Ann Wakeling**, Mead House, School Lane, Chearsley, Aylesbury, **Buckinghamshire**, HP18 0BT, ENG.
(T) 01844 201026
Speciality: Alexander Technique.
● **Owner** Mrs A Wakeling
P S (Ref:HM20747)

**WAKEMAN, BEVERLEY**

**Beverley Wakeman**, 22 Valley View, Greenhithe, **Kent**, DA9 9LU, ENG.
(T) 01322 383488
Speciality: Chiropodists (Podiatrists).
S (Ref:HM20748)

**WAKNELL, PETER**

**Peter Waknell**, 39 Sowerberry Cl, Chelmsford, **Essex**, CM1 4YB, ENG.
(T) 01245 441858
Speciality: Hypnosis.
● **Owner** Mr P Waknell
B (Ref:HM20749)

**WALDBAUM, HANNA**

**Hanna Waldbaum**, Highgate End, Lewes Rd, Forest Row, **Sussex (East)**, RH18 5AN, ENG.
(T) 01342 823714
Speciality: Homeopathy.
● **Owner** Mrs H Waldbaum
M (Ref:HM20750)

**WALDENBERG, HILARY**

**Hilary Waldenberg**, 39 Winding Way, Leeds, **Yorkshire (West)**, LS17 7RG, ENG.
(T) 01132 678193
Speciality: Aromatherapy.
M O (Ref:HM20751)

**WALDER, PATRICIA**

**Patricia Walder**, 1 Polden Rd, Salisbury, **Wiltshire**, SP1 2JU, ENG.
(T) 01722 334923
Speciality: Hypnosis.
● **Owner** Mrs P Walder
B (Ref:HM20752)

**WALDMAN, MERVYN**

**Mervyn Waldman**, 853 Finchley Rd, London, **London (Greater)**, NW11 8LX, ENG.
(T) 020 8455 5646
Speciality: Osteopathy.
P S T (Ref:HM20753)

**WALDRON, BRIAN J**

**Brian J Waldron**, 66 Abbey Rd, Torquay, **Devon**, TQ2 5NH, ENG.
(T) 01803 212070
Speciality: Chiropodists (Podiatrists).
S (Ref:HM20754)

**WALDRON, GABRIELLE**

**Gabrielle Waldron**, 834 Fishponds Rd, Fishponds, Bristol, BS16 3XA, ENG.
(T) 01179 491290
Speciality: Osteopathy.
P S T (Ref:HM20755)

**WALFORD, PENELOPE**

**Penelope Walford**, Rickmansworth Rd, Chorleywood, Rickmansworth, **Hertfordshire**, WD3 5SD, ENG.
(T) 01923 282133
Speciality: Hypnosis.
B (Ref:HM20756)

**WALK CHIROPODIST**

**Walk Chiropodist (The)**, 2 The Walk, High St, Billericay, **Essex**, CM12 9YB, ENG.
(T) 01277 633220
Speciality: Biomechanics, Chiropody, Cyro-Surgery. ✓
● **Chiropodist** Mr D Holmes Q: M.S.C.P. M: S.C.P.
M Yrs. Est.: 2 (Ref:HM20757)

**WALK IN BACK RUB**

**Walk In Back Rub (The)**, 4th Floor Bath And Body, Selfridges, Oxford St, London, **London (Greater)**, W1, ENG.
(T) 020 7436 9876
(W) www.walkinbackrub.co.uk
Speciality: Shiatsu, Chair Massage. ✓ CREDIT
● **Shiatsu Practitioner/Owner**
Mr D Higgins Q: Dip.School Shiatsu, Dip.Shiatsu.
T Yrs. Est.: 4 (Ref:HM20758)

**WALK IN BACKRUB**

**Walk In Back Rub (The)**, 11 Charlotte Pl, London, **London (Greater)**, W1P 1AD, ENG.
(T) 020 7436 9876
(W) www.walkinbackrub.co.uk
Speciality: Shiatsu. ✓ CREDIT
● **Therapist** Ms J Wolf
● **Owner/Shiatsu Practitioner**
Mr D Higgins Q: Dip.School Shiatsu, Dip.Shiatsu.
T Yrs. Est.: 4 (Ref:HM20759)

**WALK IN BACKRUB**

**Walk In Back Rub (The)**, 14 Neals Yard, Covent Garden, London, **London (Greater)**, WC2H 9DP, ENG.
(T) 020 7836 9111
(W) www.walkinbackrub.co.uk
Speciality: Shiatsu. ✓ CREDIT
● **Owner/Shiatsu Practitioner**
Mr D Higgins Q: Dip.School Shiatsu. M: Shiatsu Society UK.
C T Yrs. Est.: 4 (Ref:HM20760)

**WALKER, A**

**A Walker**, 55 Hall End Rd, Wootton, Bedford, **Bedfordshire**, MK43 9HP, ENG.
(T) 01234 766571
Speciality: Chiropodists (Podiatrists).
● **Owner** Mrs A Walker
S (Ref:HM20761)

**WALKER, A M**

**A M Walker**, 23 Shenley Hill Rd, Leighton Buzzard, **Bedfordshire**, LU7 8BY, ENG.
(T) 01525 385151
Speciality: Chiropodists (Podiatrists).
S (Ref:HM20762)

**WALKER, ADELE**

**Adele Walker**, 2 Pownall Rd, Cheadle Hulme, Cheadle, **Cheshire**, SK8 5AZ, ENG.
(T) 01614 851028
Speciality: Chiropodists (Podiatrists).
● **Owner** Miss A Walker
S (Ref:HM20763)

**WALKER, B**

**B Walker**, 140 Church St, Spondon, **Derbyshire**, DE21 7LL, ENG.
(T) 01332 676025
Speciality: Hypnosis.
B (Ref:HM20764)

**WALKER, BARRIE**

**Barrie Walker**, 33 Cyprus Rd, Burgess Hill, **Sussex (West)**, RH15 8DX, ENG.
(T) 01444 232437
Speciality: Chiropodists (Podiatrists).
● **Principal** Mr B Walker
S (Ref:HM20765)

**WALKER, CHARLOTTE**

**Charlotte Walker**, 15 Bridewell St, Devizes, **Wiltshire**, SN10 1NQ, ENG.
(T) 01380 728453
Speciality: Osteopathy.
P S T (Ref:HM20766)

**WALKER, DYLANIE**

**Dylanie Walker**, 19 Leaf Cl, Northwood, **London (Greater)**, HA6 2YY, ENG.
(T) 01923 824140
Speciality: Psychotherapy.
B (Ref:HM20767)

**WALKER, E S**

**E S Walker**, 28 Hardhorn Rd, Poulton-le-Fylde, **Lancashire**, FY6 7SR, ENG.
(T) 01253 882051 (F) 01253 882051
Speciality: Physiotherapy.
● **Principal** Mrs E Walker
P S T (Ref:HM20768)

**WALKER, ELAINE**

**Elaine Walker**, Centre For Whole Health, 12 Victoria Pl, Bristol, BS3 3BP, ENG.
(T) 01179 231138
Speciality: Homeopathy.
M (Ref:HM20769)

**WALKER, ELAINE**

**Elaine Walker**, 2 Potts Farm, Guston, Ash, Canterbury, **Kent**, CT3 2NH, ENG.
(T) 01304 812133

Key: B Mind-Body Medicine C Complementary Medicine H Self Help Treatment M Medicinal Therapy O Oriental Medicine P Postural Therapy S Manipulative Structural Therapy T Touch Therapy

Speciality: Homeopathy.
● Owner Ms E Walker
M (Ref:HM20770)

## WALKER, ELIZABETH

**Elizabeth Walker**, Blackberry Orthopaedic Clinic, Blackberry Court, Walnut Tree, Milton Keynes, **Buckinghamshire**, MK7 7PB, ENG.
(T) 01908 604666
Speciality: Osteopathy.
P S T (Ref:HM20771)

## WALKER, H L

**H L Walker**, 10 Cross St, Nelson, **Lancashire**, BB9 7EN, ENG.
(T) 01282 613056
Speciality: Chiropodists (Podiatrists).
● Owner Mr H Walker
S (Ref:HM20772)

## WALKER, HELEN

**Helen Walker**, 2 The Orchard, Langley, Macclesfield, **Cheshire**, SK11 0DG, ENG.
(T) 01625 503646
Speciality: Aromatherapy.
M O (Ref:HM20773)

## WALKER, IAN

**Ian Walker**, 7 Angel Lane, Penrith, **Cumbria**, CA11 7BP, ENG.
(T) 01768 899600
Speciality: Chiropodists (Podiatrists).
● Owner Mr I Walker
S (Ref:HM20774)

## WALKER, J E

**J E Walker**, 41 Market St, Hemsworth, Pontefract, **Yorkshire (West)**, WF9 4LR, ENG.
(T) 01977 610989
Speciality: Chiropodists (Podiatrists).
● Owner Mr J Walker
S (Ref:HM20775)

## WALKER, J M

**J M Walker**, Georgian House, 81 Carolgate, Retford, **Nottinghamshire**, DN22 6EH, ENG.
(T) 01777 709543
Speciality: Acupuncture, Herbal Medicine, Hypnosis.
M (Ref:HM20776)

## WALKER, J W

**J W Walker**, Kendrick House, 96 Kendrick Rd, Reading, **Berkshire**, RG1 5DW, ENG.
(T) 01189 872191
Speciality: Hypnosis.
B (Ref:HM20777)

## WALKER, JAN

**Jan Walker**, Graham House, Graham Rd, London, **London (Greater)**, SW19 3SR, ENG.
(T) 020 8296 0405
Speciality: Homeopathy.
● Owner Mrs J Walker
M (Ref:HM20778)

## WALKER, K

**K Walker**, 3 Royal Oak Cottages, Old Mills, Paulton, Bristol, BS39 7SS, ENG.
(T) 01761 419630
Speciality: Chiropodists (Podiatrists).
● Owner Mr K Walker
S (Ref:HM20779)

## WALKER, K

**K Walker**, 38 Green Park, Bath, **Somerset**, BA1 1HZ, ENG.
(T) 01225 424784
Speciality: Chiropodists (Podiatrists).
● Owner Mr K Walker
S (Ref:HM20780)

## WALKER, KEITH

**Keith Walker**, 23 Helston Drive, Royton, Oldham, **Lancashire**, OL2 6JS, ENG.
(T) 01706 844400
Speciality: Chiropodists (Podiatrists).
S (Ref:HM20781)

## WALKER, KEVIN C

**Kevin C Walker**, Whitwell Green Lane, Elland, **Yorkshire (West)**, HX5 9EG, ENG.
(T) 01422 371126
Speciality: Clairvoyants & Palmists.
● Employee Mrs S Walker
B (Ref:HM20782)

## WALKER, KRISTINE

**Kristine Walker**, 223 Hartington Rd, Brighton, **Sussex (East)**, BN2 3PA, ENG.
(T) 01273 623577
Speciality: Reflexology.
S T (Ref:HM20783)

## WALKER, L

**L Walker**, Beech House, Farnham Lane, Haslemere, **Surrey**, GU27 1HE, ENG.
(T) 01428 654893
Speciality: Chiropodists (Podiatrists).
S (Ref:HM20784)

## WALKER, LEONIE

**Leonie Walker**, The Natural Therapy Clinic, 17a Northumberland Sq, North Shields, **Tyne and Wear**, NE30 1PX, ENG.
(T) 01912 962160
Speciality: Acupuncture.
O (Ref:HM20785)

## WALKER, LINDA

**Linda Walker**, 11 Oxford Cl, Great Cornard, Sudbury, **Suffolk**, CO10 0HN, ENG.
(T) 01787 881218
Speciality: Reflexology.
S T (Ref:HM20786)

## WALKER, MARGARET

**Margaret Walker**, 28 Anderson Drive, Aberdeen, **Aberdeenshire**, AB15 4TY, SCO.
(T) 01224 312564
Speciality: Complementary Medicines & Therapy.
C M (Ref:HM20787)

## WALKER, MARIAN

**Marian Walker**, The Maple Clinic, 3-5 Horndean Rd, Bracknell, **Berkshire**, RG12 0XQ, ENG.
(T) 01344 862646
Speciality: Homeopathy.
● Owner Dr W Baker
M (Ref:HM20788)

## WALKER, MICHAEL

**Michael Walker**, Jasmine House, Valley Way, Pamber Heath, Tadley, **Hampshire**, RG26 3DJ, ENG.
(T) 01189 700047
Speciality: Chiropodists (Podiatrists).
● Owner Mr M Walker
S (Ref:HM20789)

## WALKER, NATASHA

**Natasha Walker**, 19 Chestnut Springs, Lydiard Millicent, Swindon, **Wiltshire**, SN5 9NA, ENG.
(T) 01793 772434
Speciality: Psychotherapy.
B (Ref:HM20790)

## WALKER, NEL

**Nel Walker**, 56 Melrose Pl, Watford, **Hertfordshire**, WD1 3LX, ENG.
(T) 01923 801720
(E) nw@grovecounselling.co.uk
(W) www.grovecounselling.co.uk
Speciality: Cognitive Therapy, Counselling, Humanistic Psychology, Psychotherapy, Stress Therapy, EMDR- Eye Movement Desensitisation and Reprocessing. ✓
● **Counselling Psychologist** Ms N Walker Q: AACP, BSc, Dip.Couns, EMDR. M: AACP, BPS, EMDR.
B Yrs. Est.: 9 (Ref:HM20791)

## WALKER, O A

**O A Walker**, 117 Great Western Rd, Aberdeen, **Aberdeenshire**, AB10 6PT, SCO.
(T) 01224 586097
Speciality: Chiropodists (Podiatrists).
S (Ref:HM20792)

## WALKER, P

**P Walker**, 2 Soresby St, Chesterfield, **Derbyshire**, S40 1JN, ENG.
(T) 01246 273676
Speciality: Chiropodists (Podiatrists).
● Owner Mr P Walker
S (Ref:HM20793)

## WALKER, PATRICIA

**Patricia Walker**, Bridge End, Chester Le Street, **County Durham**, DH3 3RA, ENG.
(T) 01913 865175
Speciality: Homeopathy.
● Partner Ms P Walker
M (Ref:HM20794)

## WALKER, PENELOPE

**Penelope Walker**, Red Jacket, 68 Cockney Hill, Tilehurst, Reading, **Berkshire**, RG30 4EU, ENG.
(T) 01189 421915
Speciality: Reflexology.
S T (Ref:HM20795)

## WALKER, R

**R Walker**, Kendrick House, 96 Kendrick Rd, Reading, **Berkshire**, RG1 5DW, ENG.
(T) 01189 872191
Speciality: Aromatherapy.
M O (Ref:HM20796)

## WALKER, RICHARD

**Richard Walker**, 50 Kimberley Park Rd, Falmouth, **Cornwall**, TR11 2DB, ENG.
(T) 01326 318539
Speciality: Chiropodists (Podiatrists).
● Owner Mr R Walker
S (Ref:HM20797)

## WALKER, RICHARD

**Richard Walker**, 7 Overtrees, Hollybush Lane, Harpenden, **Hertfordshire**, AL5 4AW, ENG.
(T) 01582 461762
(E) abetterlife@tripod.co.uk
Speciality: Auto Suggestion, Aversion Therapy, Complementary Therapy, Hypnosis, Hypnotherapy, Meditation. ✓
● **Consultant/Therapist** Mr R Walker Q: BSc, DIC, DipCH.P, MSc, PgDCH. M: BSCH.
B Yrs. Est.: 2 (Ref:HM20798)

## WALKER, ROY

**Roy Walker**, 5 High St, Worsley, Manchester, **Manchester (Greater)**, M28 3JH, ENG.
(T) 01617 900097
Speciality: Chiropodists (Podiatrists).
● Owner Mr R Walker
S (Ref:HM20799)

## WALKER, S

**S Walker**, 8 Queens Prde, Bath, **Somerset**, BA1 2NL, ENG.
(T) 01225 424460
Speciality: Complementary Medicines & Therapy.
C M (Ref:HM20800)

## WALKER, S

**S Walker**, The Surgery, 20 Oxford St, Wellingborough, **Northamptonshire**, NN8 4HY, ENG.
(T) 01933 222418
Speciality: Chiropodists (Podiatrists).
S (Ref:HM20801)

## WALKER, SAM

**Sam Walker**, 10 Broadmeadow End, Thatcham, **Berkshire**, RG18 4ED, ENG.
(T) 01635 873686
Speciality: Aromatherapy.
● Owner Mrs S Walker
M O (Ref:HM20802)

## WALKER, SARAH

**Sarah Walker**, Hill Cottage, Glynswood, Camberley, **Surrey**, GU15 1HU, ENG.
(T) 01276 66471
Speciality: Aromatherapy, Chinese Herbal Medicine, Indian Head Massage, Naturopathy, Nutritional Therapy, Traditional Therapeutic Body Work, Herbal Medicine. ✓
● **Owner/Naturopath** Miss S Walker Q: ITHMA, MION, RQA. M: AOC, ION, ITHMA.
C O Yrs. Est.: 9 (Ref:HM20803)

## WALKER, SUE

**Sue Walker**, 44 Christ Church Rd, Doncaster, **Yorkshire (South)**, DN1 2QL, ENG.
(T) 01302 341514
Speciality: Acupuncture.
● Owner Ms S Walker
O (Ref:HM20804)

## WALKER, SUSAN J

**Susan J Walker**, 178 Wigan Rd, Westhoughton,


Key continued: Yrs.Est: Years Established Q: Qualifications M: Professional Membership ✓ Indemnity Insurance Accept Credit Cards

Bolton, **Lancashire**, BL5 2AG, ENG.
(T) 01942 818403
Speciality: Chiropodists (Podiatrists).
● **Owner** Mrs S Walker
S (Ref:HM20805)

**WALKER, VALERIE**

**Valerie Walker**, 137 Magdalen Rd, Oxford, **Oxfordshire**, OX4 1RJ, ENG.
(T) 01865 396939
Speciality: Aromatherapy.
● **Owner** Mr M Franklin
M O (Ref:HM20806)

**WALKER, VICTOR J**

**Victor J Walker**, Wellspring, 29 Trumlands Rd, Torquay, **Devon**, TQ1 4RN, ENG.
(T) 01803 329869
Speciality: Hypnosis.
● **Owner** Mr V Walker
B (Ref:HM20807)

**WALKER-DENDLE, VALERIE**

**Valerie Walker-Dendle**, Haslemere, **Surrey**, GU27, ENG.
(T) 01428 656496
Speciality: Bach Remedies.
M (Ref:HM20808)

**WALK-IN BACK STUDIO**

**Walk-In Back Studio (The)**, 6 Rufus Court, Chester, **Cheshire**, CH1 2JW, ENG.
(T) 01244 321116
Speciality: Complementary Medicines & Therapy.
● **Partner** Ms D Jefford
M (Ref:HM20809)

**WALKINGTON, LORAINE**

**Loraine Walkington**, 6 Oundle Drive, Mansfield, **Nottinghamshire**, NG19 6BZ, ENG.
(T) 01623 635522
Speciality: Reflexology.
S T (Ref:HM20810)

**WALKLETT, B**

**B Walklett**, 40 Church Lane, Oxted, **Surrey**, RH8 9LB, ENG.
(T) 01883 715127
Speciality: Osteopathy.
P S T (Ref:HM20811)

**WALKOM, N E**

**N E Walkom**, 33 Park Rd, Ramsgate, **Kent**, CT11 7QP, ENG.
(T) 01843 592799
Speciality: Chiropodists (Podiatrists).
S (Ref:HM20812)

**WALKRITE CHIROPODY SERVICES**

**Walkrite Chiropody Services**, 10 Eldon Rd, Birmingham, **Midlands (West)**, B16 9DP, ENG.
(T) 01212 461623 (F) 01212 478711
Speciality: Chiropodists (Podiatrists).
● **Owner** Mrs L Stancliffe-Deams
S (Ref:HM20813)

**WALL, (DR)**

**Dr Wall**, 12 Clarinda Pk, Nth D'laoire, Dublin, **County Dublin**, IRE.
(T) 01280 0488
Speciality: Chiropractors.
P S T (Ref:HM20814)

**WALL, HELEN**

**Helen Wall**, 270 Penns Lane, Sutton Coldfield, **Midlands (West)**, B76 1LQ, ENG.
(T) 01213 511381
Speciality: Acupuncture.
● **Owner** Mrs H Wall
O (Ref:HM20815)

**WALL, M**

**M Wall**, 18B Highweek Rd, Newton Abbot, **Devon**, TQ12 1TP, ENG.
(T) 01626 360959
Speciality: Complementary Medicines & Therapy.
● **Owner** Mr M Wall
C M (Ref:HM20816)

**WALL, M W**

**M W Wall**, 23 Broomhill Rd, Bristol, BS4 4SQ, ENG.
(T) 01179 776665
Speciality: Chiropodists (Podiatrists).
● **Owner** Mr M Wall
S (Ref:HM20817)

**WALL, MARIAN**

**Marian Wall**, Holywell Annexe, Holywell St, Chesterfield, **Derbyshire**, S41 7SH, ENG.
(T) 01246 239547
Speciality: Reflexology.
S T (Ref:HM20818)

**WALL, R A**

**R A Wall**, 6 Responso Avenue, Grimsby, **Humberside (South)**, DN32 9RG, ENG.
(T) 01472 357726
Speciality: Absent Healing, Chiropody, Reflexology. ✔
● **Owner/Chiropodist/Reflexologist**
Mr R Wall Q: DPodM, MBChA, MSSCh. M: B.A.Ch.P.
M T Yrs. Est.: 16 (Ref:HM20819)

**WALL, SEAN (DR)**

**Wall Dr Sean**, 12 Clarinda Pk, Nth, Dun Laoghaire, **County Dublin**, IRE.
(T) 01280 0488
Speciality: Chiropractors.
P S T (Ref:HM20820)

**WALLACE, ALICE**

**Alice Wallace**, 139 Killinghall Rd, Bradford, **Yorkshire (West)**, BD3 8AA, ENG.
(T) 01274 669265
Speciality: Homeopathy.
● **Owner** Ms A Wallace
M (Ref:HM20821)

**WALLACE, GENEVIEVE**

**Genevieve Wallace**, Cornborough Farm, Well Lane, Sutton-on-the-Forest, **Yorkshire (North)**, YO61 1EF, ENG.
(T) 01347 878784
Speciality: Reflexology.
S T (Ref:HM20822)

**WALLACE, KEITH**

**Keith Wallace**, 10 East Bridge St, Crook, **County Durham**, DL15 9BJ, ENG.
(T) 01388 767317
Speciality: Chiropodists (Podiatrists).
● **Owner** Mr K Wallace
S (Ref:HM20823)

**WALLACE, LYN**

**Lyn Wallace**, Victoria Health & Leisure Club, The Promenade, Southport, **Merseyside**, PR8 1QY, ENG.
(T) 01704 544464
Speciality: Complementary Medicines & Therapy.
M (Ref:HM20824)

**WALLACE, MARGARET A R**

**Margaret A R Wallace**, Redhurst, Barrmill Rd, Beith, **Ayrshire (North)**, KA15 1EU, SCO.
(T) 01505 502538
Speciality: Chiropodists (Podiatrists).
● **Owner** Mrs M Wallace
S (Ref:HM20825)

**WALLACE, MAUREEN**

**Maureen Wallace**, 57 Church St, Inverness, **Highland**, IV1 1DR, SCO.
(T) 01463 718310
Speciality: Complementary Medicines & Therapy.
C M (Ref:HM20826)

**WALLACE, PATRICIA**

**Wallace Patricia**, 15 Wicklow St, Dublin, **County Dublin**, IRE.
(T) 01677 1021
Speciality: Healing.
B (Ref:HM20827)

**WALLACE, R J**

**R J Wallace**, Church Farm Mews, Church Lane, Yapton, Arundel, **Sussex (West)**, BN18 0ER, ENG.
(T) 01243 551529
Speciality: Physiotherapy.
● **Owner** Mrs R Wallace
P S T (Ref:HM20828)

**WALLACE, RUTH**

**Ruth Wallace**, 8 Cleveden Cr, Glasgow, **Glasgow (City of)**, G12 0PB, SCO.
(T) 01413 396339
Speciality: Physiotherapy.
P S T (Ref:HM20829)

**WALLACE, S**

**S Wallace**, 64 Crondall Lane, Farnham, **Surrey**, GU9 7DD, ENG.
(T) 01252 724510
Speciality: Chiropodists (Podiatrists).
S (Ref:HM20830)

**WALLACE, SARAH S**

**Sarah S Wallace**, 59 Cornwall Rd, Sutton, **Surrey**, SM2 6DU, ENG.
(T) 020 8642 6562
Speciality: Osteopathy.
P S T (Ref:HM20831)

**WALLACE, SUE**

**Sue Wallace**, 2 Caenwood Cl, Weybridge, **Surrey**, KT13 8TY, ENG.
(T) 01932 856027
Speciality: Acupressure, Complementary Therapy, Holistic Healing, Shiatsu, Spiritual Healing. ✔
● **Owner** Ms S Wallace
O Yrs. Est.: 7 (Ref:HM20832)

**WALLACE, VICTORIA**

**Victoria Wallace**, 11 Church Rd, London, **London (Greater)**, N6 4QH, ENG.
(T) 020 8340 9422
Speciality: Physiotherapy.
● **Practice Manager** Mr C Turpin
P S T (Ref:HM20833)

**WALLACE, W K**

**W K Wallace**, 23 Matthews Court, Highbury Grange, London, **London (Greater)**, N5 2PD, ENG.
(T) 020 7354 1927
Speciality: Psychology.
B (Ref:HM20834)

**WALLEN, ANN**

**Ann Wallen**, Elfinsward, Chandler Rd, Stoke Holy Cross, Norwich, **Norfolk**, NR14 8RG, ENG.
(T) 01508 493225
Speciality: Reflexology.
S T (Ref:HM20835)

**WALLEN, R G**

**R G Wallen**, 13 Tythegston Cl, Nottage, Porthcawl, Bridgend, CF36 3HJ, WAL.
(T) 01656 771618
Speciality: Chiropodists (Podiatrists).
S (Ref:HM20836)

**WALLIKER, EMMA**

**Emma Walliker**, The Lodge, East Cranmore, Shepton Mallet, **Somerset**, BA4 4SE, ENG.
(T) 01749 880662
Speciality: Complementary Medicines & Therapy.
● **Owner** Miss E Walliker
C M (Ref:HM20837)

**WALLINGTON, FRANCIS**

**Francis Wallington**, 19B High St, Tarring, Worthing, **Sussex (West)**, BN14 7NN, ENG.
(T) 01903 232981
Speciality: Osteopathy.
● **Owner** Mr F Wallington
P S T (Ref:HM20838)

**WALLIS, C A**

**C A Wallis**, 110 Ladysmith Rd, Enfield, **London (Greater)**, EN1 3AB, ENG.
(T) 020 8366 3205
Speciality: Chiropodists (Podiatrists).
● **Owner** Mrs C Wallis
S (Ref:HM20839)

**WALLIS, J**

**J Wallis**, 68 Middlefield, Horley, **Surrey**, RH6 9XP, ENG.
(T) 01293 452858 (F) 01293 452858
Speciality: Complementary Medicines & Therapy.
● **Owner** Ms J Wallis
M (Ref:HM20840)



Key: B Mind-Body Medicine, C Complementary Medicine, H Self Help Treatment, M Medicinal Therapy, O Oriental Medicine, P Postural Therapy, S Manipulative Structural Therapy, T Touch Therapy

**WALLIS, P A**

**P A Wallis**, The Downs House, Green Lane, Trottiscliffe, West Malling, **Kent**, ME19 5DX, ENG.
(T) 01732 823189
Speciality: Physiotherapy.
● **Owner** Mrs P Wallis
P S T (Ref:HM20841)

**WALLIS, SHEILA**

**Mrs Sheila Wallis**, 5 Woodburn Avenue, Newcastle Upon Tyne, **Tyne and Wear**, NE4 9EL, ENG.
(T) 01912 745925
Speciality: Physiotherapy.
● **Owner** Mrs S Wallis
P S T (Ref:HM20842)

**WALLIS, SHIRLEY**

**Shirley Wallis**, 244 Milby Drive, Nuneaton, **Warwickshire**, CV11 6UH, ENG.
(T) 024 7637 0643
Speciality: Reflexology.
● **Owner** Mrs S Walis
S T (Ref:HM20843)

**WALLS, ANNE**

**Anne Walls**, 3 Dunlin Court, Kelvedon, Colchester, **Essex**, CO5 9LU, ENG.
(T) 01376 572306
Speciality: Reflexology.
S T (Ref:HM20844)

**WALLS, JOHN P**

**Walls John P**, Caherogan, Athenry, **County Galway**, IRE.
(T) 09184 4196
Speciality: Psychotherapy.
B (Ref:HM20845)

**WALLSEND CLINIC**

**Wallsend Clinic (The)**, 58 Station Rd, Wallsend, **Tyne and Wear**, NE28 6TB, ENG.
(T) 01912 624029
Speciality: Osteopathy.
● **Owner** Mr E Hough
P S T (Ref:HM20846)

**WALMER HOLISTIC CENTRE**

**Walmer Holistic Centre**, Tonlegee Hse, Millbrook Gr, D13, IRE.
(T) 01847 5410
(E) walmer@indigo.ie
Speciality: Complementary Medicines & Therapy.
M (Ref:HM20847)

**WALMSLEY, RUTH**

**Ruth Walmsley**, 6 Queen St, Broseley, **Shropshire**, TF12 5NB, ENG.
(T) 01952 883410
(E) markandruth@onetel.net.uk
Speciality: Acupressure, Aromatherapy, Bach Remedies, Complementary Therapy, Cupping, Massage (Therapeutic), Reflexology, Stress Therapy, Touch Therapy. ✔
● **Massage Therapist** Ms R Walmsley Q: Dip.Th.Massage. M: SHP.
C T Yrs. Est.: 11 (Ref:HM20848)

**WALNUT BARN CLINIC**

**Walnut Barn Clinic**, Walnut Barn, The St, Bodham, Holt, **Norfolk**, NR25 6NW, ENG.
(T) 01263 588091
Speciality: Complementary Medicines & Therapy.
● **Owner** Mrs K Gosden
M (Ref:HM20849)

**WALNUT NATURAL THERAPY CLINIC**

**Walnut Natural Therapy Clinic**, 3 Walnut Gr, Redcar, **Cleveland**, TS10 3PQ, ENG.
(T) 01642 480340
Speciality: Complementary Medicines & Therapy.
C M (Ref:HM20850)

**WALSALL CHIROPRACTIC HEALTH**

**Walsall Chiropractic Health Clinic**, 81 Broadway, Walsall, **Midlands (West)**, WS1 2NJ, ENG.
(T) 01922 634959 (F) 01922 634959
Speciality: Chiropractic.
● **Owner** Mr P Malone
P S T (Ref:HM20851)

**WALSALL COMMUNITY HEALTH TRUST**

**Walsall Community Health Trust**, Psychology Department, Greybury House, Bridge St, Walsall, **Midlands (West)**, WS1 1EP, ENG.
(T) 01922 858450 (F) 01922 858453
Speciality: Psychology.
B (Ref:HM20852)

**WALSALL PHYSIOTHERAPY CLINIC**

**Walsall Physiotherapy Clinic**, 10 Vicarage Pl, Walsall, **Midlands (West)**, WS1 3NA, ENG.
(T) 01922 622112 (F) 01922 622112
(E) max.jacklin@amserve.net
Speciality: Acupuncture, Physiotherapy. ✔
● **Physiotherapist** Mr S Jacklin Q: MCSP, SRP. M: CSP.
S Yrs. Est.: 7 (Ref:HM20853)

**WALSBY, L**

**L Walsby**, 35 St Paul St, Chippenham, **Wiltshire**, SN15 1LJ, ENG.
(T) 01249 656400
Speciality: Complementary Medicines & Therapy.
● **Owner** Mrs L Walsby
C M (Ref:HM20854)

**WALSGRAVE CHIROPRACTIC CLINIC**

**Walsgrave Chiropractic Clinic**, 380 Walsgrave Rd, Coventry, **Midlands (West)**, CV2 4AF, ENG.
(T) 024 7645 2357 (F) 024 7645 9924
Speciality: Chiropractic. ✔ 
● **Owner** Mr R Hatfield Q: DC. M: GCC.
● **Chiropractor** Ms D Mazzini Q: DC. M: GCC.
● **Chiropractor** Mrs M Kibklo Q: DC. M: GCC.
P Yrs. Est.: 15 (Ref:HM20855)

**WALSH, ANTHONY (DR)**

**Walsh Dr Anthony**, Robertstown, Carrigaline, **County Cork**, IRE.
(T) 021 4771 551
Speciality: Complementary Medicines & Therapy.
M (Ref:HM20856)

**WALSH, B B**

**B B Walsh**, Denewood, 74 Woodlands Avenue, Rustington, Littlehampton, **Sussex (West)**, BN16 3EY, ENG.
(T) 01903 773074
Speciality: Chiropodists (Podiatrists).
● **Owner** Mr B Walsh
S (Ref:HM20857)

**WALSH, DEAN**

**Dean Walsh**, 711 Chester Rd, Kingshurst, Birmingham, **Midlands (West)**, B36 0LN, ENG.
(T) 01217 709009 (F) 07970 093048
Speciality: Chiropodists (Podiatrists).
● **Owner** Mr D Walsh
S (Ref:HM20858)

**WALSH, J A**

**J A Walsh**, 132 Corporation Rd, Cardiff, **Glamorgan (Vale of)**, CF11 7AX, WAL.
(T) 029 2025 2678
(E) thefoot10@hotmail.com
Speciality: Chiropody. ✔
● **Owner/Chiropodist** Mr J Walsh Q: S.R.Ch. M: S.C.P.
M (Ref:HM20859)

**WALSH, J P**

**J P Walsh**, 6 White Hart St, Mansfield, **Nottinghamshire**, NG18 1DG, ENG.
(T) 01623 627780 (F) 01623 627780
Speciality: Chiropodists (Podiatrists).
● **Owner** Mrs J Walsh
S (Ref:HM20860)

**WALSH, JAMES**

**Walsh James LIC ACU**, 111 Walkinstown Rd, Dublin, **County Dublin**, IRE.
(T) 01450 8232
Speciality: Complementary Medicines & Therapy.
M (Ref:HM20861)

**WALSH, JOHN**

**John Walsh**, 24 Chatburn Rd, Clitheroe, **Lancashire**, BB7 2AP, ENG.
(T) 01200 424901
Speciality: Osteopathy.
P S T (Ref:HM20862)

**WALSH, JOHN**

**John Walsh**, Aldrens Lane, Lancaster, **Lancashire**, LA1 2DU, ENG.
(T) 01524 69864 (F) 01524 848155
Speciality: Osteopathy.
P S T (Ref:HM20863)

**WALSH, LINDA**

**Linda Walsh**, 18 Dunsford Rd, Smethwick, **Midlands (West)**, B66 4EH, ENG.
(T) 01215 503022
Speciality: Chiropodists (Podiatrists).
● **Owner** Mrs L Walsh
S (Ref:HM20864)

**WALSH, M J**

**Mr M J Walsh**, 1 Lushington Rd, Eastbourne, **Sussex (East)**, BN21 4LG, ENG.
(T) 01323 723887
Speciality: Cranial Osteopathy, Osteopathy.
● **Osteopath** Mr D Barron M: GOsC.
● **Osteopath** Mr M Walsh Q: DO. M: GOsC.
● **Osteopath** Ms P Barnett M: GOsC.
S Yrs. Est.: 15 (Ref:HM20865)

**WALSH, MICHAEL**

**Walsh Michael ADHP MICHP**, Southern Cross Rd, Bray Co, **County Wicklow**, IRE.
(T) 08724 21704
(W) www.hypnosiseire.com
Speciality: Complementary Medicines & Therapy.
M (Ref:HM20866)

**WALSH, R M**

**R M Walsh**, 2 Brookhead Drive, Cheadle, **Cheshire**, SK8 2HZ, ENG.
(T) 01614 286269
Speciality: Chiropodists (Podiatrists).
● **Owner** Mr R Walsh
S (Ref:HM20867)

**WALSH, TARA**

**Tara Walsh**, 44 Northgate, Almondbury, Huddersfield, **Yorkshire (West)**, HD5 8RX, ENG.
(T) 01484 323419
Speciality: Reflexology.
● **Owner** Ms T Walsh
S T (Ref:HM20868)

**WALSHE, D (DR)**

**Walshe Dr D**, U 11 South Tce, Ct West, **County Cork**, IRE.
(T) 021 4313 163
Speciality: Psychiatry.
B (Ref:HM20869)

**WALSHE, JOHN (DR)**

**Walshe, Dr John**, Walkinstown,, IRE.
(T) 01456 4804
Speciality: Chiropractors.
P S T (Ref:HM20870)

**WALSHE, JOHN (DR)**

**Walshe, Dr John**, Donnybrook,, IRE.
(T) 01660 9012
Speciality: Chiropractors.
P S T (Ref:HM20871)

**WALSINGHAM CLN CTRE - NTRL MED**

**Walsingham Clinic Centre For Natural Medicine**, 2 Walsingham Pl, Truro, **Cornwall**, TR1 2RP, ENG.
(T) 01872 263163
Speciality: Complementary Medicines & Therapy.
C M (Ref:HM20872)

**WALSINGHAM, CAROLE**

**Carole Walsingham**, Holcutt Cl, Wootton, Northampton, **Northamptonshire**, NN4 6AE, ENG.
(T) 01604 674661
Speciality: Complementary Medicines & Therapy.
● **Owner** Mrs C Walsingham
C M (Ref:HM20873)

**WALTER, MAX**

**Max Walter**, Ibex House, 42-47 Minories, London, **London (Greater)**, EC3N 1DY, ENG.



Key continued: **Yrs.Est:** Years Established **Q:** Qualifications **M:** Professional Membership ✔ Indemnity Insurance Accept Credit Cards

(T) 020 7488 4133
Speciality: Osteopathy.
● **Owner** Mr W Max
P S T (**Ref:**HM20874)

### WALTERS, A B

**A B Walters**, 172E The Broadway, Bexleyheath, **Kent**, DA6 7BN, ENG.
(T) 020 8303 1896
Speciality: Psychotherapy.
B (**Ref:**HM20875)

### WALTERS, CAROLINE BARWICK

**Caroline Barwick Walters**, 56 Abbeygate St, Bury St. Edmunds, **Suffolk**, IP33 1LB, ENG.
(T) 01284 753563
Speciality: Chiropodists (Podiatrists).
● **Owner** Mrs C Walters
S (**Ref:**HM20876)

### WALTERS, MARGARET

**Margaret Walters**, 5 Nunns Court, Featherstone, Pontefract, **Yorkshire (West)**, WF7 5PW, ENG.
(T) 01977 700991 (F) 01977 700991
Speciality: Hypnosis.
● **Owner** Mrs M Walters
B (**Ref:**HM20877)

### WALTERS, MARGARET

**Margaret Walters**, Ulvik, Moor Lane, Sculthorpe, Fakenham, **Norfolk**, NR21 9PY, ENG.
(T) 01328 863170
Speciality: Reflexology.
S T (**Ref:**HM20878)

### WALTERS, MARIE

**Marie Walters**, 104 Conway Drive, Shrewsbury, **Shropshire**, SY2 5UJ, ENG.
(T) 01743 270197
Speciality: Reflexology.
● **Owner** Mrs M Walters
S T (**Ref:**HM20879)

### WALTERS, RICHARD

**Richard Walters**, The Natural Health Practice, 2 Spicer Rd, Exeter, **Devon**, EX1 1SX, ENG.
(T) 01392 499364
Speciality: Acupuncture, Zero Balancing. ✓
● **Owner/Acupuncturist** Mr R Walters Q: BSc, Lic.Ac, MBAcC.
O (**Ref:**HM20880)

### WALTERS, RICHARD

**Richard Walters**, Lyme Community Care Centre, Uplyme Rd, Lyme Regis, **Dorset**, DT7 3LS, ENG.
(T) 01297 445461
Speciality: Acupuncture.
● **Owner/Acupuncturist** Mr R Walters Q: BSc, Lic.Ac.
O (**Ref:**HM20881)

### WALTERS, RICHARD

**Richard Walters**, 4 Brookvale, Metcombe, Ottery St. Mary, **Devon**, EX11 1RS, ENG.
(T) 01404 813784
Speciality: Acupuncture. ✓
● **Owner/Acupuncturist** Mr R Walters Q: BSc, Lic.Ac.
O (**Ref:**HM20882)

### WALTON HOMOEOPATHY

**Walton Homoeopathy**, 3 Bowes Rd, Walton-On-Thames, **Surrey**, KT12 3HS, ENG.
(T) 01932 252899
Speciality: Homeopathy.
M (**Ref:**HM20883)

### WALTON, DEBORAH

**Deborah Walton**, Glenside, Farnham Lane, Farnham Royal, Slough, **Berkshire**, SL2 3RY, ENG.
(T) 01753 648212
Speciality: Chiropodists (Podiatrists).
S (**Ref:**HM20884)

### WALTON, J

**J Walton**, 11 Welbeck Avenue, Littleborough, **Manchester (Greater)Manchester (Greater)**, OL15 9HX, ENG.
(T) 01706 378416
Speciality: Complementary Medicines & Therapy.
● **Owner** Mrs J Walton
C M (**Ref:**HM20885)

### WALTON, S K

**Miss S K Walton**, West Elloe Avenue, Spalding, **Lincolnshire**, PE11 2BY, ENG.
(T) 01775 725530 (F) 01775 766168
Speciality: Osteopathy.
● **Doctor** Dr A Walton
P S T (**Ref:**HM20886)

### WANDSWORTH ASS OF PSYCHO

**Wandsworth Association Of Psychotherapists**, 63 Franciscan Rd, London, **London (Greater)**, SW17 8EA, ENG.
(T) 020 8767 2828
Speciality: Psychotherapy.
● **Director** Mr R Lewis
B (**Ref:**HM20887)

### WANG, JING

**Jing Wang**, 10 West Trce, Eastbourne, **Sussex (East)**, BN21 4QX, ENG.
(T) 01323 641576
Speciality: Acupuncture.
● **Partner** Mrs C Scorzon
O (**Ref:**HM20888)

### WANG, JING

**Jing Wang**, 9 Coton Lane, Birmingham, **Midlands (West)**, B23 6TP, ENG.
(T) 01213 502018
Speciality: Acupuncture.
O (**Ref:**HM20889)

### WANSBOROUGH, CHARLES

**Charles Wansborough**, 1369 High Rd, London, **London (Greater)**, N20 9LN, ENG.
(T) 020 8445 2675
Speciality: Homeopathy.
M (**Ref:**HM20890)

### WANTAGE NATURAL HEALTH CENTRE

**Wantage Natural Health Centre**, 34A Market Pl, Wantage, **Oxfordshire**, OX12 8AH, ENG.
(T) 01235 760079
Speciality: Alexander Technique, Chiropractic, Counselling, Holistic Healing, Homeopathy, Massage (Therapeutic), Osteopathy, Reflexology, Training. ✓
● **Homeopath** Ms M Brock Q: RSHom.
● **Chiropractor** Mrs I Twine Q: DC. M: MCA.
● **Reflexologist** Ms K King
● **Osteopath** Ms C Abrams Q: DO.
S Yrs. Est.: 7 (**Ref:**HM20891)

### WANTAGE OSTEOPATHIC PRACTICE

**Katherine J Harris Wantage Osteopathic Practice**, Wantage Osteopathic Practice, 13-17 Newbury St, Wantage, **Oxfordshire**, OX12 8BU, ENG.
(T) 01235 768748
Speciality: Osteopathy. ✓
● **Osteopath** Miss K Harris Q: BSc. M: GOsC.
S Yrs. Est.: 6 (**Ref:**HM20892)

### WARBOYS, R E

**R E Warboys**, 10 Meadow Cl, Great Bromley, Colchester, **Essex**, CO7 7UG, ENG.
(T) 01206 250940
Speciality: Physiotherapy.
● **Owner** Mrs M Warboys
P S T (**Ref:**HM20893)

### WARBURTON, G L

**G L Warburton**, 96 Broadway, Morecambe, **Lancashire**, LA4 5XY, ENG.
(T) 01524 414082
Speciality: Osteopathy.
● **Owner** Mr G Warburton
P S T (**Ref:**HM20894)

### WARD CHIROPRACTIC

**Ward Chiropractic**, Prospect House, Rawmarsh Hill, Parkgate, Rotherham, **Yorkshire (South)**, S62 6EX, ENG.
(T) 01709 527121
Speciality: Chiropractic.
● **Owner** Dr B Ward
P S T (**Ref:**HM20895)

### WARD SHIATSU

**Ward Shiatsu**, 64 Cornerswell Rd, Penarth, **Glamorgan (Vale of)**, CF64 2WA, WAL.
(T) 029 2070 0135
Speciality: Complementary Medicines & Therapy.
M (**Ref:**HM20896)

### WARD, A

**A Ward**, 41 Frankfield Rise, Tunbridge Wells, **Kent**, TN2 5LF, ENG.
(T) 01892 525799
Speciality: Acupuncture.
● **Owner** A Ward
O (**Ref:**HM20897)

### WARD, A T

**A T Ward**, 1 Crown Court, Woolley St, Bradford-on-Avon, **Wiltshire**, BA15 1BG, ENG.
(T) 01225 862654 (F) 01225 862654
Speciality: Homeopathy.
● **Owner** Mr A Ward
M (**Ref:**HM20898)

### WARD, DIANE

**Diane Ward**, 2 Tower Court, 15 Dean Park Rd, Bournemouth, **Dorset**, BH1 1HU, ENG.
(T) 01202 778675
Speciality: Reflexology.
S T (**Ref:**HM20899)

### WARD, ELIZABETH

**Elizabeth Ward**, 67 Nile Gr, Edinburgh, **Edinburgh (City of)**, EH10 4SN, SCO.
(T) 01314 476513 (F) 01314 476573
Speciality: Holistic Healing, Shen Therapy.
✓
● **Complementary Therapist**
Ms E Ward Q: BTER, SHEN Therapy. M: BTER, SHEN.
C T Yrs. Est.: 8 (**Ref:**HM20900)

### WARD, FRANCES

**Frances Ward**, Davington Manor, Brent Hill, Faversham, **Kent**, ME13 7EF, ENG.
(T) 01795 534901
Speciality: Reflexology.
S T (**Ref:**HM20901)

### WARD, G

**G Ward**, 48 Chapel St, Wath-Upon-Dearne, Rotherham, **Yorkshire (South)**, S63 7RG, ENG.
(T) 01709 877438 (F) 01709 877439
Speciality: Acupuncture.
● **Owner** Mr G Ward
O (**Ref:**HM20902)

### WARD, G C

**G C Ward**, 7 Peterscroft Avenue, Ashurst, Southampton, **Hampshire**, SO40 7AB, ENG.
(T) 023 8029 2194
Speciality: Osteopathy.
P S T (**Ref:**HM20903)

### WARD, GERALD

**Ward Gerald**, Corboy Mostrim, Longford, **County Longford**, IRE.
(T) 04346 993
Speciality: Complementary Medicines & Therapy.
M (**Ref:**HM20904)

### WARD, JAN

**Jan Ward**, 35 Masons Rise, Broadstairs, **Kent**, CT10 1AY, ENG.
(T) 01843 604095
Speciality: Reflexology.
S T (**Ref:**HM20905)

### WARD, JAQUELINE

**Jaqueline Ward**, Hagley Centre Of Complementary Medicine, 137 Worcester Rd, Hagley, Stourbridge, **Midlands (West)**, DY7 6EB, ENG.
(T) 01384 878640
(E) jawardhyp@aol.com
Speciality: Hypnosis, Hypnotherapy.
● **Clinical Hypnotherapist**
Mrs J Ward Q: BSCH, Dip.Hyp, DipCH.P. M: BSCH.
B C Yrs. Est.: 2 (**Ref:**HM20906)

### WARD, KAREN

**WARD KAREN BSc, Dip Psych MIAHM**, The Rhiannon Clinic Smithfield, Dublin, **County Dublin**, IRE.
(T) 01670 4905
Speciality: Complementary Medicines &



Key: B Mind-Body Medicine C Complementary Medicine H Self Help Treatment M Medicinal Therapy O Oriental Medicine P Postural Therapy S Manipulative Structural Therapy T Touch Therapy

Therapy.
M (Ref:HM20907)

**WARD, KATE**

**Kate Ward**, Alexander Suite, Crossbeck Rd, Ilkley, **Yorkshire (West)**, LS29 9JP, ENG.
(T) 01943 816727
Speciality: Complementary Medicines & Therapy.
M (Ref:HM20908)

**WARD, MARY**

**Mary Ward**, Kairos Centre, Mount Angelus Rd, London, **London (Greater)**, SW15 4JA, ENG.
(T) 020 8788 4188
Speciality: Reflexology.
S T (Ref:HM20909)

**WARD, P G**

**P G Ward**, Unit 12 Workspace, 80 Rainey St, Magherafelt, **County Londonderry**, BT45 5AH, NIR.
(T) 028 7930 1312
Speciality: Complementary Medicines & Therapy.
● **Owner** Mrs P Ward
M (Ref:HM20910)

**WARD, R**

**R Ward**, The Helix Centre, Woodbrook House, 27 Bridge St, Loughborough, **Leicestershire**, LE11 1NH, ENG.
(T) 01509 230200
Speciality: Complementary Medicines & Therapy.
M (Ref:HM20911)

**WARD, ROBIN E**

**Robin E Ward**, Woodlands Mews, 2 Dell Cl, Templewood Lane, Farnham Common, Slough, **Berkshire**, SL2 3PZ, ENG.
(T) 01753 646049
Speciality: Chiropodists (Podiatrists).
S (Ref:HM20912)

**WARD, SANDRA**

**Sandra Ward**, 53 East Ham Rd, Littlehampton, **Sussex (West)**, BN17 7BE, ENG.
(T) 01903 722025
Speciality: Reflexology.
S T (Ref:HM20913)

**WARD, SARAH**

**Sarah Ward**, 5 Lincoln Cottages, Brighton, **Sussex (East)**, BN2 2UJ, ENG.
(T) 01273 625108
Speciality: Complementary Medicines & Therapy.
C M (Ref:HM20914)

**WARD, V J**

**V J Ward**, Balls Farm, Balls Farm Rd, Ide, Exeter, **Devon**, EX2 9RA, ENG.
(T) 01392 275696
Speciality: Chiropodists (Podiatrists).
S (Ref:HM20915)

**WARD-DAVIS, J**

**Mrs J Ward-Davis**, The Wynd, Hutton Rudby, Yarm, **Cleveland**, TS15 0ES, ENG.
(T) 01642 700845
Speciality: Acupuncture.
● **Owner** Mrs J Ward-Davis
O (Ref:HM20916)

**WARDELL, A A**

**A A Wardell**, Gorman Castle Farm, Bugthorpe, York, **Yorkshire (North)**, YO41 1QU, ENG.
(T) 01759 368271
Speciality: Reflexology.
● **Owner** Mrs A Wardell
S T (Ref:HM20917)

**WARDELL, L**

**L Wardell**, 46 Dollis Avenue, London, **London (Greater)**, N3 1BU, ENG.
(T) 020 8346 6715
Speciality: Osteopathy.
● **Partner** Mr L Wardell
P S T (Ref:HM20918)

**WARDELL, SUSAN JANE**

**Susan Jane Wardell**, 4 Millers Meadow, Rainow, Macclesfield, **Cheshire**, SK10 5UE, ENG.
(T) 01625 575781
Speciality: Aromatherapy.
● **Owner** Mrs S Wardell
M O (Ref:HM20919)

**WARDEN, J S**

**J S Warden**, 8 Meads Rd, Bexhill-on-Sea, **Sussex (East)**, TN39 4SY, ENG.
(T) 01424 846626 (F) 01424 846626
Speciality: Chiropodists (Podiatrists).
● **Owner** Mrs J Walden
S (Ref:HM20920)

**WARDLAW, MICHAEL**

**Michael Wardlaw**, 12 Benbow Court, Shenley Church End, Milton Keynes, **Buckinghamshire**, MK5 6JG, ENG.
(T) 01908 506154 (F) 01908 506795
(E) wardlowm@hotmail.com
Speciality: Chiropody, Podiatry, Podiatric Surgery.
M Yrs. Est.: 4 (Ref:HM20921)

**WARDLEY, P DEANNE**

**P Deanne Wardley**, 22 Church Rd, Woburn Sands, Milton Keynes, **Buckinghamshire**, MK17 8TA, ENG.
(T) 01908 583448
Speciality: Physiotherapy.
● **Owner** Mrs D Wardley
P S T (Ref:HM20922)

**WARDLEY, SUE**

**Sue Wardley**, 16 West Bar St, Banbury, **Oxfordshire**, OX16 9RR, ENG.
(T) 01295 275660
Speciality: Physiotherapy.
● **Owner** Mrs S Wardley
P S T (Ref:HM20923)

**WARD-SAUNDERS, WENDY**

**Wendy Ward-Saunders**, Barton-Le-Cley, **Bedfordshire**, MK45, ENG.
(T) 01582 883274
Speciality: Bach Remedies.
M (Ref:HM20924)

**WARE, J**

**J Ware**, 9 Hurley Gardens, Guildford, **Surrey**, GU4 7YH, ENG.
(T) 01483 824510
Speciality: Chiropodists (Podiatrists).
● **Owner** Mr S Ware
S (Ref:HM20925)

**WARE, PAUL J**

**Paul J Ware**, 33 Bramhall Lane South, Bramhall, Stockport, **Cheshire**, SK7 2DN, ENG.
(T) 01614 392048
Speciality: Chiropodists (Podiatrists).
S (Ref:HM20926)

**WARING, D**

**D Waring**, 53 Headley Way, Headington, Oxford, **Oxfordshire**, OX3 0LS, ENG.
(T) 01865 767196
Speciality: Chiropractors.
● **Owner** Miss D Waring
P S T (Ref:HM20927)

**WARING, D**

**D Waring**, 40 Lowther Gr, Garforth, **Yorkshire (West)**, LS25 1EN, ENG.
(T) 01132 862346
Speciality: Osteopathy.
P S T (Ref:HM20928)

**WARMINSTER OSTEOPATHIC CLINIC**

**Warminster Osteopathic Clinic**, 4 Station Rd, Warminster, **Wiltshire**, BA12 9BR, ENG.
(T) 01985 213927
Speciality: Acupuncture, Aromatherapy, Counselling, Cranial Osteopathy, Homeopathy, Indian Head Massage, Manipulation, Massage (Therapeutic), Osteopathy, Psychotherapy, Reflexology, Reiki, Ultrasonics. ✓
● **Osteopath** Mr D Lewis Q: BSc (Hons). M: GOsC.
● **Reflexologist** Ms B Such Q: ITEC. M: IPTI.
● **Homeopath** Ms L Peddle Q: LSH.
● **Traditional Acupuncturist** Ms P French Q: Lic.Ac, MBAcC, SRN. M: BAcC.
● **Osteopath** Ms P Crosbie Q: BSc (Hons). M: GOsC.
● **Osteopath** Ms M Monru Q: BSc (Hons). M: GOsC.
● **Osteopath** Mr J Penny Q: DO. M: GOsC.
● **Spa Counselling** Ms S Chamberlain M: BACP, UKRC.
● **Holistic Therapist** Ms J Levy Q: ICHT, IIHHT. M: ICHT.
S Yrs. Est.: 111 (Ref:HM20929)

**WARNE, A J**

**A J Warne**, 63 Cobbold Rd, Woodbridge, **Suffolk**, IP12 1HA, ENG.
(T) 01394 383868
Speciality: Chiropodists (Podiatrists).
S (Ref:HM20930)

**WARNE, JANET**

**Janet Warne**, Kirkby Lonsdale Natural Health Clinic, 1 Jingling Court, Kirkby Lonsdale, Carnforth, **Lancashire**, LA6 2FD, ENG.
(T) 01524 272998
Speciality: Homeopathy.
M (Ref:HM20931)

**WARNE, P F**

**P F Warne**, 26 Manor Cl, Havant, **Hampshire**, PO9 1BD, ENG.
(T) 023 9247 9106
Speciality: Osteopathy.
P S T (Ref:HM20932)

**WARNER, HAZEL**

**Hazel Warner**, 41 Avondale Rd, Lancaster, **Lancashire**, LA1 4BZ, ENG.
(T) 01524 383251
Speciality: Reflexology.
S T (Ref:HM20933)

**WARNER, JEAN**

**Jean Warner**, 16 Robin Hill Drive, Standish, Wigan, **Lancashire**, WN6 0QW, ENG.
(T) 01257 422003
Speciality: Osteopathy.
● **Owner** Mrs J Warner
P S T (Ref:HM20934)

**WARNER, K**

**K Warner**, 74 Ledgers Rd, Slough, **Berkshire**, SL1 2RL, ENG.
(T) 01753 820303
Speciality: Complementary Medicines & Therapy.
C M (Ref:HM20935)

**WARNES, JENNIFER**

**Jennifer Warnes**, Ovington House, Far Lane, Coleby, Lincoln, **Lincolnshire**, LN5 0AH, ENG.
(T) 01522 810911
Speciality: Reflexology.
● **Owner** Ms J Warnes
S T (Ref:HM20936)

**WARNOCK, PETER**

**Peter Warnock**, 337-339 Norwich Rd, Ipswich, **Suffolk**, IP1 4BN, ENG.
(T) 01473 464300
Speciality: Complementary Medicines & Therapy.
M (Ref:HM20937)

**WARNOCK, POLLY**

**Polly Warnock**, 58 Hartington St, Barrow-in-Furness, **Cumbria**, LA14 5SR, ENG.
(T) 01229 832855 (F) 01229 832855
Speciality: Physiotherapy.
● **Partner** Mrs A Frost
P S T (Ref:HM20938)

**WARNOCK, R J**

**R J Warnock**, 37 Albion St, St Georges, Telford, **Shropshire**, TF2 9AX, ENG.
(T) 01952 613795
Speciality: Hypnosis.
B (Ref:HM20939)

**WARR, V W & D L**

**V W & D L Warr**, The Croft, 13 Wynnstay Lane, Marford, Wrexham, LL12 8LF, WAL.
(T) 01978 852407 (F) 01978 856800
Speciality: Osteopathy.
● **Owner** Mr V Warr
P S T (Ref:HM20940)

**WARRELL, PIPPA**

**Pippa Warrell**, 110 Harley St, London, **London (Greater)**, W1N 1AF, ENG.



Key continued: Yrs.Est: Years Established Q: Qualifications M: Professional Membership ✓ Indemnity Insurance Accept Credit Cards

(T) 020 7224 4588 (F) 020 7224 4588
Speciality: Physiotherapy.
P S T (Ref:HM20941)

## WARREN CLINIC

**Warren Clinic (The)**, Panthers Health Fitness Centre, Uxbridge, **London (Greater)**, UB8 2XN, ENG.
(T) 07889 975174 (F) 01895 233200
Speciality: Osteopathy.
● **Owner** Mr S O'Reilly
P S T (Ref:HM20942)

## WARREN HOUSE CHIRO CLNC

**Warren House Chiropractic Clinic Barnsley**, 231 Sheffield Rd, Barnsley, **Yorkshire (South)**, S70 4DE, ENG.
(T) 01226 770908
Speciality: Chiropractic.
P S T (Ref:HM20943)

## WARREN, ANNE

**Anne Warren**, 4 Second Avenue, Havant, **Hampshire**, PO9 2QP, ENG.
(T) 023 9247 6293
Speciality: Chiropodists (Podiatrists).
S (Ref:HM20944)

## WARREN, CAROL

**Carol Warren**, 56 Woodthorpe Drive, Bewdley, **Worcestershire**, DY12 2RH, ENG.
(T) 01299 405033
Speciality: Reflexology.
S T (Ref:HM20945)

## WARREN, DAVID

**David Warren**, 82 Montagu Mansions, London, **London (Greater)**, W1H 1LG, ENG.
(T) 020 7486 2299
Speciality: Osteopathy.
● **Owner** Mr D Warren
P S T (Ref:HM20946)

## WARREN, E W (DR)

**DR E W Warren**, 33 Jersey Gdns, Wickford, **Essex**, SS11 7AG, ENG.
(T) 01268 763589
Speciality: Psychology.
B (Ref:HM20947)

## WARREN, GILLIAN

**Gillian Warren**, 52 Warwick Rd, Bishop's Stortford, **Hertfordshire**, CM23 5NW, ENG.
(T) 01279 651049
Speciality: Physiotherapy.
● **Owner** Mrs G Warren
P S T (Ref:HM20948)

## WARREN, HELEN

**Helen Warren**, 68 Green Lane, Bovingdon, Hemel Hempstead, **Hertfordshire**, HP3 0JZ, ENG.
(T) 01442 833915
Speciality: Homeopathy.
● **Owner** Ms H Warren
M (Ref:HM20949)

## WARREN, M

**M Warren**, 2-4 High St, Glastonbury, **Somerset**, BA6 9DU, ENG.
(T) 01458 833317
Speciality: Reflexology.
S T (Ref:HM20950)

## WARREN, P S

**P S Warren**, 12 South Meadow, South Horrington Village, Wells, **Somerset**, BA5 3DJ, ENG.
(T) 01749 678964
Speciality: Physiotherapy.
P S T (Ref:HM20951)

## WARREN, SUSAN

**Susan Warren**, The Old Smithy, Dudleston Heath, Ellesmere, **Shropshire**, SY12 9JY, ENG.
(T) 01691 690463
Speciality: Reflexology.
S T (Ref:HM20952)

## WARREN, TONY

**Tony Warren**, 16 Noel Green, Burgess Hill, **Sussex (West)**, RH15 8BS, ENG.
(T) 01444 246660
Speciality: Reflexology.
● **Owner** Mr T Warren
S T (Ref:HM20953)

## WARREN-DAVIS, A

**Mrs A Warren-Davis**, Northfields Farm Herbary, Fontwell Avenue, Eastergate, Chichester, **Sussex (West)**, PO20 6RX, ENG.
(T) 01243 542349
Speciality: Herbal Medicine.
M (Ref:HM20954)

## WARRILOW, ALISON

**Alison Warrilow**, 30 Buxton Rd, Leek, **Staffordshire**, ST13 6EE, ENG.
(T) 01538 399636
Speciality: Chiropodists (Podiatrists).
S (Ref:HM20955)

## WARRINGTON ACUPUNCTURE CLINIC

**Warrington Acupuncture Clinic**, 7 Bold St, Warrington, **Cheshire**, WA1 1DN, ENG.
(T) 01925 231200
Speciality: Acupuncture.
O (Ref:HM20956)

## WARRINGTON CHIROPRACTIC CLINIC

**Warrington Chiropractic Clinic**, 491 Winwick Rd, Winwick, Warrington, **Cheshire**, WA2 8QF, ENG.
(T) 01925 417817 (F) 01925 417057
(E) nilssonchiro@hotmail.com
(W) www.chiropractor-warrington.co.uk
Speciality: Chiropractic, Homeopathy, Kinesiology, Manipulation, Massage (Therapeutic), Nutritional Therapy, X-Ray, Food intolerance testing. ✔
● **Chiropractor** Dr M Handa Q: BSc, DC. M: BCA, GCC.
● **Chiropractor** Mr S Nilsson Q: DC, MSc. M: GCC.
P S Yrs. Est.: 12 (Ref:HM20957)

## WARRINGTON, MARY

**Mary Warrington**, 1 Gloucester Trce, Southend-On-Sea, **Essex**, SS1 3AZ, ENG.
(T) 01702 585463
Speciality: Physiotherapy.
● **Partner** Mrs L Palmer
P S T (Ref:HM20958)

## WART, D

**D Wart**, 10 Thurloe St, London, **London (Greater)**, SW7 2ST, ENG.
(T) 020 7591 3847
Speciality: Osteopathy, Physiotherapy. ✔
● **Owner** Mr D Wart
P S T Yrs. Est.: 12 (Ref:HM20959)

## WARTNABY, MARY

**Mary Wartnaby**, 52 Kings Avenue, Poole, **Dorset**, BH14 9QJ, ENG.
(T) 01202 746552
Speciality: Physiotherapy.
● **Owner** Mrs M Wartnaby
P S T (Ref:HM20960)

## WARWICK ALTERNATIVE HEALTH

**Warwick Alternative Health**, 44 Goldsdown Rd, Enfield, **London (Greater)**, EN3 7QZ, ENG.
(T) 020 8443 2005
Speciality: Acupressure, Hypnotherapy, Indian Head Massage, Life Style Coaching, Physiotherapy, Reflexology, Reiki. ✔
● **Reflexologist** Mr M Warwick Q: BHA, MASC.
T Yrs. Est.: 3 (Ref:HM20961)

## WARWICK CHIROPRACTIC CLINIC

**Warwick Chiropractic Clinic**, 54 Saltisford, Warwick, **Warwickshire**, CV34 4TD, ENG.
(T) 01926 419404 (F) 01926 495184
Speciality: Chiropractic.
● **Owner** Mr K Walker
P S T (Ref:HM20962)

## WARWICK CONSULTANTS

**Warwick Consultants Ltd**, 8 Elm Court, Arden St, Stratford-Upon-Avon, **Warwickshire**, CV37 6PA, ENG.
(T) 01789 414828
Speciality: Psychology.
● **Sole Director** Dr T Kellard
B (Ref:HM20963)

## WARWICK FOOT CLINIC

**Warwick Foot Clinic**, 49 Manor Farm Rd, Birmingham, **Midlands (West)**, B11 2HT, ENG.
(T) 01217 078558
Speciality: Chiropodists (Podiatrists).
S (Ref:HM20964)

## WARWICK HOUSE MEDICAL CENTRE

**Warwick House Medical Centre**, Holway Green, Upper Holway Rd, Taunton, **Somerset**, TA1 2YJ, ENG.
(T) 01823 282147
Speciality: Alexander Technique.
● **Therapist** Mr M Brown
P S (Ref:HM20965)

## WARWICK OSTEOPATHIC PRACTICE

**Warwick Osteopathic Practice**, 22a Swan St, Warwick, **Warwickshire**, CV34 4BJ, ENG.
(T) 01926 411497
(E) mail@wholebodies.fsnet.co.uk
Speciality: Complementary Therapy, Cranial Osteopathy, Cupping, Family Planning (Natural), Herbal Medicine, Holistic Healing, Homeopathy, Life Style Coaching, Manipulation, Massage (Therapeutic), Naturopathy, Nutritional Therapy, Osteopathy. ✔
● **Osteopath/Naturopath** Ms A Donley Q: BSc, DO, Hons (OST), ND, RN. M: GCRN, GOsC.
S Yrs. Est.: 10 (Ref:HM20966)

## WARWICK, ANDREA

**A W Natural Therapies**, Hare And Hounds Cottage, 41 Teesway, Neasham, Darlington, **County Durham**, DL2 1QT, ENG.
(T) 01325 721628 (F) 01325 721628
(E) andreawarwick@naturaltherapies.org.uk
Speciality: Acupressure, Allergy Testing, Colour Therapy, Complementary Therapy, Gestalt Therapy, Healer, Holistic Healing, Hypnosis, Hypnotherapy, Indian Head Massage, Kinesiology, Massage (Therapeutic), Metamorphic Therapy, Reflexology, Spiritual Healing, Ear Candling, Colonic Hydrotherapy. ✔
● **Natural Health Practitioner** Miss A Warwick Q: C.Hyp, CMH. M: BCHE, CIA, IFA.
C Yrs. Est.: 18 (Ref:HM20967)

## WARWICK, JULIE

**Julie Warwick**, 146 High St, Banstead, **Surrey**, SM7 2NZ, ENG.
(T) 01737 373684
Speciality: Complementary Medicines & Therapy.
M (Ref:HM20968)

## WARWICK, M

**M Warwick**, 77-81 High St, Waltham Cross, **Hertfordshire**, EN8 7AG, ENG.
(T) 01992 701110
Speciality: Hypnotherapy.
B (Ref:HM20969)

## WARWICK, MAUREEN

**Maureen Warwick**, 78 Kynaston Rd, Bromley, **Kent**, BR1 5AW, ENG.
(T) 020 8851 7867
Speciality: Reflexology.
S T (Ref:HM20970)

## WASHINGTON & ASSOCIATES

**Sue Washington & Associates**, 145 Chapel Lane, Longton, Preston, **Lancashire**, PR4 5NA, ENG.
(T) 01772 617663 (F) 01772 614211
Speciality: Hypnotherapy.
● **Principal** Ms S Washington
B (Ref:HM20971)

## WASHINGTON CHIROPRACTIC CLINIC

**Washington Chiropractic Clinic**, Coniston House, Washington, **Tyne and Wear**, NE38 7RN, ENG.
(T) 01914 159988
Speciality: Chiropractors.
● **Owner** Mr G Lee
P S T (Ref:HM20972)

## WASHINGTON PODIATRY PART

**Washington Podiatry Partnership**, Unit 1H, Mountjoy Research Centre, Durham, **County Durham**, DH1 3SW, ENG.
(T) 01913 864428
Speciality: Chiropodists (Podiatrists).
● **Owner** Mrs M Forster



Key: B Mind-Body Medicine C Complementary Medicine H Self Help Treatment M Medicinal Therapy O Oriental Medicine P Postural Therapy S Manipulative Structural Therapy T Touch Therapy

S (Ref:HM20973)

**WASHINGTON SCH CLIN/ADV HYP**

**Washington School Of Clinical & Advanced Hypnotherapy (The)**, 2-25 Edge Lane, Manchester, **Manchester (Greater)**, M21 9JH, ENG.
(T) 01618 820400
Speciality: Hypnosis.
B (Ref:HM20974)

**WASS, ANNETTE**

**Annette Wass**, 115 High St, Trumpington, Cambridge, **Cambridgeshire**, CB2 2JD, ENG.
(T) 01223 840114
Speciality: Herbal Medicine, Holistic Healing. ✓
● **Medical Herbalist** Ms A Wass Q: BA, MNIMH. M: NIMH.
H M Yrs. Est.: 1 (Ref:HM20975)

**WASSERMAN, D**

**D Wasserman**, Greenaway House, Underlane, Holsworthy, **Devon**, EX22 6BL, ENG.
(T) 01409 254410 (F) 01409 259109
Speciality: Osteopathy.
● **Owner** Mr D Wasserman
P S T (Ref:HM20976)

**WASSERMAN, DAVID**

**David Wasserman**, Hatherleigh Medical Centre, Pipers Meadow, Hatherleigh, Okehampton, **Devon**, EX20 3JT, ENG.
(T) 01837 810283 (F) 01837 810876
Speciality: Osteopathy.
● **Principal** Dr M Downey
P S T (Ref:HM20977)

**WATCHAM, G**

**G Watcham**, The Boot, Upper St, Quainton, Aylesbury, **Buckinghamshire**, HP22 4AY, ENG.
(T) 01296 655229
Speciality: Complementary Medicines & Therapy.
● **Owner** Mrs G Watcham
C M (Ref:HM20978)

**WATCHBELL HSE NTRL THRPY CTRE**

**Watchbell House Natural Therapy Centre**, Watchbell House, 8 Lugley St, Newport, **Isle of Wight**, PO30 5HD, ENG.
(T) 01983 522477
Speciality: Homeopathy.
M (Ref:HM20979)

**WATER MASSAGE**

**Water Massage**, 19 Bloomfield House, Old Montague St, London, **London (Greater)**, E1 5PA, ENG.
(T) 020 7247 4727
Speciality: Aromatherapy.
M O (Ref:HM20980)

**WATERFORD ACUPUNCTURE CLINIC**

**Waterford Acupuncture Clinic**, 13 Gladstone St, **County Waterford**, IRE.
(T) 05253 185
Speciality: Acupuncture.
O (Ref:HM20981)

**WATERFORD ALLERGY TEST CTRE**

**Waterford Allergy Test Ctr**, **County Waterford**, IRE.
(T) 08681 22861
Speciality: Complementary Medicines & Therapy.
M (Ref:HM20982)

**WATERFORD SPORTS INJURY CLINIC**

**Waterford Sports Injury Clinic**, 19 Thomas St, **County Waterford**, IRE.
(T) 05184 1360
Speciality: Complementary Medicines & Therapy.
M (Ref:HM20983)

**WATERHOUSE, C**

**C Waterhouse**, 58 Knights Rd, Oxford, **Oxfordshire**, OX4 6DG, ENG.
(T) 01865 772384
Speciality: Complementary Medicines & Therapy.
● **Owner** Mrs C Waterhouse
M (Ref:HM20984)

**WATERLOOVILLE NTRL HLTH CTRE**

**Waterlooville Natural Health Centre**, 7 Wellington Way, Waterlooville, **Hampshire**, PO7 7ED, ENG.
(T) 023 9226 6822
Speciality: Complementary Medicines & Therapy.
M (Ref:HM20985)

**WATERS & WINTERSTEIN AST**

**Waters & Winterstein Associates**, 49 Sandycoombe Rd, Twickenham, **London (Greater)**, TW1 2LR, ENG.
(T) 020 8891 4047 (F) 020 8891 4047
Speciality: Psychology.
● **Partner** Dr S Waters
B (Ref:HM20986)

**WATERS, CHRISTINA**

**Christina Waters**, The Ridge, St. Leonards-On-Sea, **Sussex (East)**, TN37 7RE, ENG.
(T) 01424 757400 (F) 01424 757424
Speciality: Physiotherapy.
● **Owner** Ms C Waters
P S T (Ref:HM20987)

**WATERS, FRANK**

**Frank Waters**, 19A Station Rd, Opposite Cliffs Pavilion, Westcliff-on-Sea, **Essex**, SS0 7RA, ENG.
(T) 01702 391393
Speciality: Osteopathy.
P S T (Ref:HM20988)

**WATERS, J**

**J Waters**, 21 Northgate St, Bury St. Edmunds, **Suffolk**, IP33 1HP, ENG.
(T) 01284 702796 (F) 01284 724118
Speciality: Chiropodists (Podiatrists).
● **Partner** Mrs P Waters
S (Ref:HM20989)

**WATERS, ROSALIE**

**Rosalie Waters**, 77 Robbery Bottom Lane, Welwyn, **Hertfordshire**, AL6 0UL, ENG.
(T) 01438 716749 (F) 01438 715566
Speciality: Chiropodists (Podiatrists).
● **Owner** Miss R Waters
S (Ref:HM20990)

**WATERS, YVONNE**

**Yvonne Waters**, 45 Ham Green, Pill, Bristol, BS20 0HA, ENG.
(T) 01275 374848
Speciality: Chiropodists (Podiatrists).
● **Owner** Mrs Y Waters
S (Ref:HM20991)

**WATERWORTH, JANE**

**Jane Waterworth**, 9 King St, Ripon, **Yorkshire (North)**, HG4 1PJ, ENG.
(T) 01765 604932
Speciality: Chiropodists (Podiatrists).
S (Ref:HM20992)

**WATHERSTON, M**

**M Watherston**, 25 Murray Rd, Northwood, **London (Greater)**, HA6 2YP, ENG.
(T) 01923 822224
Speciality: Homeopathy.
M (Ref:HM20993)

**WATKINS, DENISE**

**Denise Watkins**, 10 Hillcroft Cres, London, **London (Greater)**, W5 2SQ, ENG.
(T) 020 8997 5907
Speciality: Physiotherapy.
● **Partner** Mrs D Watkins
P S T (Ref:HM20994)

**WATKINS, G**

**Mrs G Watkins**, The Coach House, 66 Northfield End, Henley-on-Thames, **Oxfordshire**, RG9 2JN, ENG.
(T) 01491 577129 (F) 01491 577129
Speciality: Physiotherapy.
P S T (Ref:HM20995)

**WATKINS, JEAN**

**Jean Watkins**, 57 St Chads Drive, Leeds, **Yorkshire (West)**, LS6 3PZ, ENG.
(T) 01132 741463
Speciality: Reflexology. ✓
● **Reflexologist** Mrs J Watkins M: BSR, GCP.
C Yrs. Est.: 7 (Ref:HM20996)

**WATKINS, PHILIPPA**

**Philippa Watkins**, Ty Nant, Cwm Farm Lane, Sketty, Swansea, SA2 9AU, WAL.
(T) 01792 281455 (F) 01792 208661
(E) philippa.watkins@btinternet.com
Speciality: Homeopathy. ✓
● **Homeopath** Ms P Watkins Q: BA. M: Soc.Hom.
B M Yrs. Est.: 5 (Ref:HM20997)

**WATKINS, ROBIN N**

**Robin N Watkins**, 44 Harley Trce, Newcastle Upon Tyne, **Tyne and Wear**, NE3 1UL, ENG.
(T) 01912 843678 (F) 01912 843678
Speciality: Osteopathy.
● **Owner** Mr R Watkins
P S T (Ref:HM20998)

**WATKINSON, BARBARA**

**Barbara Watkinson**, Euxton House Farm, Southport Rd, Euxton, Chorley, **Lancashire**, PR7 6DD, ENG.
(T) 01257 270455
Speciality: Bach Remedies, Indian Head Massage, Massage (Therapeutic), Reflexology, Reiki. ✓
● **Owner/Clinical Reflexologist** Mrs B Watkinson Q: Dip.Indian Head Massage, Dip.Reflex, Dip.Rem.Massage, Reiki 1, Reiki 2. M: AoR, GCP, RCBFR.
T Yrs. Est.: 9 (Ref:HM20999)

**WATKISS, VALERIE**

**Valerie Watkiss**, 170 Station Rd, Pendlebury, Swinton, Manchester, **Manchester (Greater)**, M27 6BY, ENG.
(T) 01617 942066
Speciality: Electrolysis.
T (Ref:HM21000)

**WATLING STREET THERAPY CTRE**

**Watling Street Therapy Centre**, The Old Surgery, 24 Watling St, Canterbury, **Kent**, CT1 2UB, ENG.
(T) 01227 452202 (F) 01795 533133
Speciality: Acupressure, Acupuncture, Alexander Technique, Aromatherapy, Aura Therapy, Bach Remedies, Biofeedback, Bowen Therapy, Chiropractic, Complementary Therapy, Counselling, Cranial Osteopathy, Healer, Herbal Medicine, Holistic Healing, Homeopathy, Hypnosis, Hypnotherapy, Indian Head Massage, Inhalation Therapy, Iridology, Kinesiology, Life Style Coaching, Massage (Therapeutic), Meditation, Naturopathy, Nutritional Therapy, Oriental Diagnosis, Osteopathy, Phytotherapy, Polarity Therapy, Psychotherapy, Reflexology, Reiki, Shiatsu, Stress Therapy, Touch Therapy, Vitamin Therapy, Hopi Ear Candling. ✓
● **Practice Director** Ms J Langbridge Q: Cert.Ed, MIFA, MIFR. M: IFA.
B Yrs. Est.: 5 (Ref:HM21001)

**WATSON, ALEXANDRA**

**Alexandra Watson**, 322 The Parkway, Iver, **Buckinghamshire**, SL0 0RL, ENG.
(T) 01753 651955
Speciality: Reflexology.
S T (Ref:HM21002)

**WATSON, ANGELA**

**Angela Watson**, Fairoak, Portsmouth Rd, Esher, **Surrey**, KT10 9PJ, ENG.
(T) 01372 470542
Speciality: Physiotherapy.
● **Owner** Mrs A Watson
P S T (Ref:HM21003)

**WATSON, ANTHONY**

**Anthony Watson**, 75 Leaford Cres, Watford, **Hertfordshire**, WD2 5JQ, ENG.
(T) 01923 447265
Speciality: Chiropodists (Podiatrists).
S (Ref:HM21004)

**WATSON, BILL**

**Bill Watson**, Penpol Chy, Trewoon Rd, Mullion, Helston, **Cornwall**, TR12 7DL, ENG.
(T) 01326 241284
Speciality: Homeopathy.
M (Ref:HM21005)



Key continued: Yrs.Est: Years Established Q: Qualifications M: Professional Membership ✓ Indemnity Insurance Accept Credit Cards

### WATSON, CARRIE
**Carrie Watson**, 10 Burtree Lane, Darlington, **County Durham**, DL3 0XQ, ENG.
(T) 01325 355388
Speciality: Homeopathy.
M (Ref:HM21006)

### WATSON, CECILY
**Cecily Watson**, 107 Marshalswick Lane, St. Albans, **Hertfordshire**, AL1 4UU, ENG.
(T) 01727 853395
Speciality: Physiotherapy.
● **Owner** Mrs C Watson
P S T (Ref:HM21007)

### WATSON, G T
**G T Watson**, 11B Victoria Rd, Tamworth, **Staffordshire**, B79 7DN, ENG.
(T) 01827 62079
Speciality: Chiropody. ✔
● **Chiropodist** Mr G Watson Q: BSc (Hons), MSSCh. M: SSCh.
M Yrs. Est.: 15 (Ref:HM21008)

### WATSON, GEORGINA
**Georgina Watson**, 16 Grammar School Rd, Lymm, **Cheshire**, WA13 0BQ, ENG.
(T) 01925 752264
Speciality: Chiropodists (Podiatrists).
S (Ref:HM21009)

### WATSON, IAN
**Ian Watson**, 5 Belsize Sq, London, **London (Greater)**, NW3 4HT, ENG.
(T) 020 7431 9102
Speciality: Alexander Technique.
P S (Ref:HM21010)

### WATSON, IRENE
**Irene Watson**, 8 Deepdene, Ingatestone, **Essex**, CM4 0AN, ENG.
(T) 01277 352679
Speciality: Aromatherapy.
M O (Ref:HM21011)

### WATSON, J
**J Watson**, Low Lidmoor, Bransdale, Fadmoor, York, **Yorkshire (North)**, YO62 7JL, ENG.
(T) 01751 432214
Speciality: Reflexology.
M O (Ref:HM21012)

### WATSON, J
**J Watson**, 276 Woodstock Rd, Belfast, **County Antrim**, BT6 9DN, NIR.
(T) 028 9073 1650
Speciality: Chiropodists (Podiatrists).
● **Owner** Miss J Watson
S (Ref:HM21013)

### WATSON, JEAN
**Jean Watson**, Leeds Complementary Therapy Centre, 249A Otley Rd, Leeds, **Yorkshire (West)**, LS16 5LQ, ENG.
(T) 01132 370700
Speciality: Hypnosis.
● **Owner** Mrs J Watson
B (Ref:HM21014)

### WATSON, KATHRYN
**Medical Herbalist Kathryn Watson**, 29 West Way, Rickmansworth, **Hertfordshire**, WD3 2EH, ENG.
(T) 01923 772060
(E) jollyherbalist@lineone.net
Speciality: Herbal Medicine, Nutritional Therapy. ✔
● **Herbalist** Ms K Watson Q: Dip.Herb.Med, MNIMH. M: NIMH.
M Yrs. Est.: 2 (Ref:HM21015)

### WATSON, KEITH
**Keith Watson**, 48 Ellis Rd, Whitstable, **Kent**, CT5 2AX, ENG.
(T) 01227 275826 (F) 01227 275826
Speciality: Chiropodists (Podiatrists).
● **Owner** Mr K Watson
S (Ref:HM21016)

### WATSON, M
**M Watson**, 7 Garfield Rd, London, **London (Greater)**, SW11 5PL, ENG.
(T) 020 7228 8370
Speciality: Chiropractic.
P S T (Ref:HM21017)

### WATSON, MALCOLM
**Malcolm Watson**, 49 Hunslet Rd, Burntwood, **Staffordshire**, WS7 9LA, ENG.
(T) 01543 682715
Speciality: Hypnosis.
● **Owner** Mr M Watson
B (Ref:HM21018)

### WATSON, NEVILLE
**Neville Watson**, 27 Rowsham Dell, Giffard Park, Milton Keynes, **Buckinghamshire**, MK14 5JS, ENG.
(T) 01908 618425 (F) 08700 520546
Speciality: Complementary Medicines & Therapy.
● **Owner** Mr N Watson
M (Ref:HM21019)

### WATSON, NOREEN
**Noreen Watson**, 2 McDonald Drive, Ellon, **Aberdeenshire**, AB41 8BD, SCO.
(T) 01358 721109
Speciality: Reflexology.
● **Owner** Ms N Watson
S T (Ref:HM21020)

### WATSON, R J
**R J Watson**, 36 Walton Rd, Stockton Heath, Warrington, **Cheshire**, WA4 6NL, ENG.
(T) 01925 861061
Speciality: Chiropodists (Podiatrists).
● **Owner** Mr R Watson
S (Ref:HM21021)

### WATSON, RHIAN
**Rhian Watson**, Tisbury Osteopathic Practice, High St, Tisbury, Salisbury, **Wiltshire**, SP3 6HH, ENG.
(T) 01747 871482
Speciality: Osteopathy.
● **Owner** Miss R Watson
P S T (Ref:HM21022)

### WATSON, RHONA
**Rhona Watson**, Physiotherapy & Sports Injury Clinic, 3 Franchise St, Kidderminster, **Worcestershire**, DY11 6RE, ENG.
(T) 01562 67129
Speciality: Physiotherapy.
● **Senior Partner** Mrs R Watson
P S T (Ref:HM21023)

### WATSON, S
**S Watson**, 1 Carron House, Carron Way, Cumbernauld, Glasgow, **Glasgow (City of)**, G67 1ER, SCO.
(T) 01236 781958
Speciality: Chiropractors.
P S T (Ref:HM21024)

### WATSON'S COURT CLINIC
**Watson's Court Clinic**, Watson's Court, High St, Melksham, **Wiltshire**, SN12 6JU, ENG.
(T) 01225 700668 (F) 01225 700668
Speciality: Chiropody, Orthotics, Reflexology, Bio-Mechanical Assessments, Cyro-Surgery. ✔
● **Partner** Ms N Price Q: Dip.Crys, MBChA, MSSCh. M: B.A.Ch.P, SSCh.
● **Partner** Ms J Pickavance Q: MBChA, MSSCh. M: B.A.Ch.P, SSCh.
● **Practitioner** Ms A McAllister Q: BRCP, MIPTI. M: BRCP.
M Yrs. Est.: 4 (Ref:HM21025)

### WATSON-VOKES, LINDA
**Linda Watson-Vokes**, 61 Coniscliffe Rd, Darlington, **County Durham**, DL3 7EH, ENG.
(T) 01325 480265
Speciality: Electrolysis.
● **Owner** Mrs L Watson-Vokes
T (Ref:HM21026)

### WATT, A
**A Watt**, 39 Moor Pk, Ruskington, Sleaford, **Lincolnshire**, NG34 9AJ, ENG.
(T) 01526 834341
Speciality: Physiotherapy.
● **Owner** Mr A Watt
P S T (Ref:HM21027)

### WATT, A S
**A S Watt**, East Rectory, Tweed Brae, Peebles, **Scottish Borders**, EH45 8AX, SCO.
(T) 01721 720803
Speciality: Chiropody. ✔
● **Chiropodist (Podiatrist)/Owner** Mr A Watt Q: M.S.C.P, S.R.Ch. M: S.C.P.
M Yrs. Est.: 43 (Ref:HM21028)

### WATT, J M
**Mrs J M Watt**, Watt Physiotherapy, Devonvale Cr, Tillicoultry, **Clackmannanshire**, FK13 6NR, SCO.
(T) 01259 750960
Speciality: Physiotherapy.
P S T (Ref:HM21029)

### WATT, KEVIN
**Kevin Watt**, 85 High St, Market Deeping, Peterborough, **Cambridgeshire**, PE6 8ED, ENG.
(T) 01778 344618
Speciality: Chiropodists (Podiatrists).
● **Owner** Mr K Watt
S (Ref:HM21030)

### WATT, V
**V Watt**, 53 Tiverton Rd, Loughborough, **Leicestershire**, LE11 2RU, ENG.
(T) 01509 267673
Speciality: Acupuncture.
● **Partner** Mr A Watt
O (Ref:HM21031)

### WATTERSON, GEOFF
**Geoff Watterson**, 206 Bannerdale Rd, Sheffield, **Yorkshire (South)**, S7 2DT, ENG.
(T) 01142 818724
Speciality: Chiropodists (Podiatrists).
S (Ref:HM21032)

### WATTON PHYSIOTHERAPY CLINIC
**Watton Physiotherapy Clinic**, 94 Merton Rd, Watton, Thetford, **Norfolk**, IP25 6AZ, ENG.
(T) 01953 885847
Speciality: Physiotherapy. ✔
● **Owner** Mr M Kay Q: LCSP, MNIM.
S Yrs. Est.: 11 (Ref:HM21033)

### WATTS, I
**I Watts**, 174A Shelbourne Rd, Bournemouth, **Dorset**, BH8 8RA, ENG.
(T) 01202 524685
Speciality: Chiropodists (Podiatrists).
● **Owner** Mrs I Watts
S (Ref:HM21034)

### WATTS, LOUISE
**Louise Watts**, 15 Watermill Lane, North Stainley, Ripon, **Yorkshire (North)**, HG4 3LA, ENG.
(T) 01765 635387
Speciality: Alexander Technique.
P S (Ref:HM21035)

### WATTS, TERENCE
**Terence Watts**, 1164A London Rd, Leigh-On-Sea, **Essex**, SS9 2AH, ENG.
(T) 01702 471646
Speciality: Hypnosis.
B (Ref:HM21036)

### WATTS, W D
**W D Watts**, 9 Russell Avenue, St. Albans, **Hertfordshire**, AL3 5ES, ENG.
(T) 01727 854933
Speciality: Chiropodists (Podiatrists).
● **Owner** Mr W Watts
S (Ref:HM21037)

### WAUGH, G
**G Waugh**, 50 Hook Rd, Epsom, **Surrey**, KT19 8TR, ENG.
(T) 01372 727492
Speciality: Reflexology.
● **Owner** Miss G Waugh
S T (Ref:HM21038)

### WAYMAN, C R
**C R Wayman**, 104 Pennsylvania Rd, Exeter, **Devon**, EX4 6DQ, ENG.
(T) 01392 279761
Speciality: Osteopathy.
P S T (Ref:HM21039)

### WAYMAN, W N
**W N Wayman**, 91 Kingsdown Pk, Whitstable, **Kent**, CT5 2DL, ENG.
(T) 01227 264044 (F) 01227 264044

Speciality: Osteopathy.
● **Owner** Mr W Wayman
P S T (Ref:HM21040)

**WAYMAN, W N**

**W N Wayman**, 17 Church St, Bishop's Stortford, **Hertfordshire**, CM23 2LY, ENG.
(T) 01279 651859
Speciality: Osteopathy.
P S T (Ref:HM21041)

**WAYNE, ANTHONY**

**Anthony Wayne**, 9 The Cottages, Hospital Lane, Mickleover, Derby, **Derbyshire**, DE3 5DR, ENG.
(T) 01332 510578 (F) 01332 510578
Speciality: Clairvoyants & Palmists.
● **Owner** Mr A Wayne
B (Ref:HM21042)

**WAYNE-WRIGHT, M S**

**M S Wayne-Wright**, 41 Broomfield Rd, Chelmsford, **Essex**, CM1 1SY, ENG.
(T) 01245 281150
Speciality: Chiropody. ✔
● **Chiropodist** Mrs S Wayne-Wright Q: M.S.C.P, S.R.Ch. M: S.C.P.
M Yrs. Est.: 32 (Ref:HM21043)

**WAYWELL, PAULINE**

**Pauline Waywell**, Health Hydro, Milton Rd, Swindon, **Wiltshire**, SN1 5JA, ENG.
(T) 01793 465631
Speciality: Homeopathy.
M (Ref:HM21044)

**WEALDEN WHOLEFOODS**

**Wealden Wholefoods Co-operative Ltd**, High St, Wadhurst, **Sussex (East)**, TN5 6AA, ENG.
(T) 01892 783065 (F) 01892 783351
(W) www.wealdenwholefoods.co.uk
Speciality: Complementary Medicines & Therapy.
● **Co-op Member** Mrs B Godsalve
M (Ref:HM21045)

**WEATHERHOGG, D J**

**Miss D J Weatherhogg**, Cwch Gwenyn, 13 Fairfield Rd, Bude, **Cornwall**, EX23 8DH, ENG.
(T) 01288 355692
(E) deborah@weatherhogg.com
Speciality: Osteopathy. ✔
● **Osteopath** Miss D Weatherhogg Q: DO. M: RoO.
S Yrs. Est.: 14 (Ref:HM21046)

**WEATHERILL, CHRISTINE**

**Christine Weatherill**, Coldblow Cottage, Alderstead Heath, Redhill, **Surrey**, RH1 3AG, ENG.
(T) 01737 643567
Speciality: Aromatherapy.
● **Owner** Ms C Weatherill
M O (Ref:HM21047)

**WEATHERSTONE, M**

**M Weatherstone**, 20 Aldreth Gr, Bishopthorpe Rd, York, **Yorkshire (North)**, YO23 1LB, ENG.
(T) 01904 613644
Speciality: Herbalists.
● **Owner** Mrs M Weather
M (Ref:HM21048)

**WEAVER HOUSE CLINIC**

**Weaver House Clinic (The)**, The Weaver House Clinic, 19A Pillory St, Nantwich, **Cheshire**, CW5 5BZ, ENG.
(T) 01270 629933
(W) www.weaverhouse.com
Speciality: Acupuncture, Allergy Testing, Aromatherapy, Counselling, Herbal Medicine, Homeopathy, Hypnotherapy, Indian Head Massage, Massage (Therapeutic), Osteopathy, Psychotherapy, Reflexology, Stress Therapy, Cranial Osteopathy. Equine, Canine and Feline Osteopathy. We have the only qualified Thai body Masseur in Cheshire. ✔ 💳
● **Clinic Manager** Mrs M Nin M: GOsC.
● **Owner/Senior Osteopath** Mr A Tilstone Q: DO. M: GOsC.
C Yrs. Est.: 5 (Ref:HM21049)

**WEAVER, CAROL**

**Carol Weaver**, Sonning, 7 Woodley Rd, Orpington, **Kent**, BR6 9BN, ENG.
(T) 01689 828919
Speciality: Chiropodists (Podiatrists).
S (Ref:HM21050)

**WEAVER, JULIE**

**Julie Weaver**, Aldrens Lane, Lancaster, **Lancashire**, LA1 2DU, ENG.
(T) 01524 69864 (F) 01524 848155
Speciality: Aromatherapy.
M O (Ref:HM21051)

**WEAVER, K N J**

**K N J Weaver**, Happy House, Durham Rd, Sunderland, **Tyne and Wear**, SR3 4BY, ENG.
(T) 01915 201521 (F) 01915 282626
Speciality: Acupuncture.
● **Owner** Mr K Weaver
O (Ref:HM21052)

**WEAVER, ROBIN**

**Robin Weaver**, 2 Kenwood Rd, Sheffield, **Yorkshire (South)**, S7 1NP, ENG.
(T) 01142 552048
Speciality: Chiropodists (Podiatrists).
● **Owner** Mr R Weaver
S (Ref:HM21053)

**WEAVER, SARAH**

**Sarah Weaver**, 11 Merley Park Rd, Ashington, Wimborne, **Dorset**, BH21 3DA, ENG.
(T) 01202 573248
Speciality: Physiotherapy.
● **Owner** Ms S Weaver
P S T (Ref:HM21054)

**WEBB, ALAN**

**Alan D F Webb**, Oxford St Health Clinic, 38 Oxford St, Whitstable, **Kent**, CT5 1DG, ENG.
(T) 01227 264655
Speciality: Osteopathy.
● **Owner** Mr A Webb
P S T (Ref:HM21055)

**WEBB, ANNE**

**Anne Webb**, 18 Culverton Hill, Princes Risborough, **Buckinghamshire**, HP27 9AS, ENG.
(T) 01844 345596
Speciality: Electrolysis.
T (Ref:HM21056)

**WEBB, C M**

**C M Webb**, Harleywood, 10 Weelsby Rd, Grimsby, **Humberside (South)**, DN32 0PP, ENG.
(T) 01472 877649
Speciality: Chiropody, Cryo Surgery, Nail Surgery, Orthotics, Podiatry. ✔
● **Owner/Chiropodist** Mr I Webb Q: DPodM, M.S.C.P, S.R.Ch.
● **Chiropodist (Podiatrist)** Mrs C Webb Q: DPodM, M.S.C.P, S.R.Ch.
M Yrs. Est.: 44 (Ref:HM21057)

**WEBB, CHARLOTTE**

**Charlotte Webb**, 14 Hatcliffe Cl, London, **London (Greater)**, SE3 9UE, ENG.
(T) 020 8318 9123
Speciality: Osteopathy.
P S T (Ref:HM21058)

**WEBB, D F**

**D F Webb**, 15 The Rise, Partridge Green, Horsham, **Sussex (West)**, RH13 8JB, ENG.
(T) 01403 710829
Speciality: Chiropodists (Podiatrists).
● **Owner** Mr D Webb
S (Ref:HM21059)

**WEBB, DEREK**

**Derek Webb**, 74 Lavender Sweep, London, **London (Greater)**, SW11 1HD, ENG.
(T) 020 7228 8368
Speciality: Reflexology.
● **Owner** Mr D Webb
S T (Ref:HM21060)

**WEBB, EDWINA**

**Edwina Webb**, 54 Rosedale Avenue, Atherton, Manchester, **Manchester (Greater)**, M46 0EA, ENG.
(T) 01942 892289
Speciality: Acupuncture.
O (Ref:HM21061)

**WEBB, EDWINA**

**Edwina Webb**, Clarendon Private Clinic, 115 Chorley Rd, Swinton, Manchester, **Manchester (Greater)**, M27 4AA, ENG.
(T) 01617 942950
Speciality: Acupuncture.
O (Ref:HM21062)

**WEBB, FIONA**

**Fiona Webb**, 49 Devon Avenue, Twickenham, **London (Greater)**, TW2 6PN, ENG.
(T) 020 8894 0167
Speciality: Reflexology.
S T (Ref:HM21063)

**WEBB, GILL**

**Gill Webb**, 2 Lechlade Gardens, **Dorset**, BH7 7JD, ENG.
(T) 01202 424991
Speciality: Reflexology.
S T (Ref:HM21064)

**WEBB, I M**

**I M Webb**, Harleywood, 10 Weelsby Rd, Grimsby, **Humberside (South)**, DN32 0PP, ENG.
(T) 01472 877649
Speciality: Chiropodists (Podiatrists).
● **Owner** Mr I Webb
S (Ref:HM21065)

**WEBB, J E**

**J E Webb**, 50B Edwards Avenue, Ruislip, **London (Greater)**, HA4 6UT, ENG.
(T) 020 8841 5508
Speciality: Physiotherapy.
● **Owner** Mrs J Webb
P S T (Ref:HM21066)

**WEBB, JENNIFER**

**Jennifer Webb**, 35b Oxenhill Rd, Kemsing, Sevenoaks, **Kent**, TN15 6RG, ENG.
(T) 01959 524317
Speciality: Reflexology. ✔
● **Owner** Mrs J Webb Q: MIFR. M: IFA.
C Yrs. Est.: 6 (Ref:HM21067)

**WEBB, JOAN**

**Joan Webb**, 23 Henconner Lane, Chapel Allerton, Leeds, **Yorkshire (West)**, LS7 3NX, ENG.
(T) 01132 623766
Speciality: Psychotherapy.
● **Owner** Mrs J Webb
B (Ref:HM21068)

**WEBB, M**

**M Webb**, Flat 91, Gascoyne House, Gascoyne Rd, London, **London (Greater)**, E9 7BL, ENG.
(T) 020 8525 5964
Speciality: Alexander Technique.
● **Owner** Ms M Webb
P S (Ref:HM21069)

**WEBB, M F**

**M F Webb**, 8 Sherwood Rd, Birchington, **Kent**, CT7 0EJ, ENG.
(T) 01843 845259
Speciality: Chiropodists (Podiatrists).
● **Owner** Mrs M Webb
S (Ref:HM21070)

**WEBB, MADELENE**

**Madelene Webb**, 30 Jubilee Market, The Piazza, London, **London (Greater)**, WC2E 8BE, ENG.
(T) 020 7836 4835
Speciality: Alexander Technique.
● **Owner** Ms M Webb
P S (Ref:HM21071)

**WEBB, MADELENE**

**Webb Madelene**, 154 Stoke Newington Church St, London, **London (Greater)**, N16 0JU, ENG.
(T) 020 7249 2990
Speciality: Alexander Technique.
● **Owner** Miss M Webb
P S (Ref:HM21072)

**WEBB, MARCUS**

**Marcus Webb**, Hadley Wood Health Centre, 28 Crescent West, Barnet, **Hertfordshire**, EN4 0EJ, ENG.
(T) 020 8441 8352 (F) 020 8441 9150
Speciality: Osteopathy.
● **Director** Mr M Webb



Key continued: Yrs.Est: Years Established Q: Qualifications M: Professional Membership ✔ Indemnity Insurance 💳 Accept Credit Cards

P S T (Ref:HM21073)

## WEBB, MARY

**Mary Webb**, 144 St Albans Rd, Sandridge, St. Albans, **Hertfordshire**, AL4 9LL, ENG.
(T) 01727 852920
Speciality: Osteopathy.
● **Owner** Mrs M Webb
P S T (Ref:HM21074)

## WEBB, RAYMOND

**Raymond Webb**, 41 North Rd, Shanklin, **Isle of Wight**, P037 6DE, ENG.
(T) 01983 862422
Speciality: Chiropodists (Podiatrists).
S (Ref:HM21075)

## WEBB, ROSEMARY

**Rosemary Webb**, Damask Rose, Harts Boatyard, Portsmouth Rd, Surbiton, **Surrey**, KT6 4HJ, ENG.
(T) 020 8390 5996
Speciality: Aromatherapy.
● **Owner** Ms R Webb
M O (Ref:HM21076)

## WEBB, S

**S Webb**, Joseph Lister Court, Upton Lane, London, **London (Greater)**, E7 9PS, ENG.
(T) 020 8471 8836
Speciality: Chiropodists (Podiatrists).
● **Owner** Ms S Webb
S (Ref:HM21077)

## WEBB, S E

**S E Webb**, Buttery Farm, The Buttery, Kynnersley, Telford, **Shropshire**, TF6 6EG, ENG.
(T) 01952 670237
Speciality: Chiropodists (Podiatrists).
● **Owner** Mrs S Webb
S (Ref:HM21078)

## WEBB-DE SISTO, MARION

**Marion Webb-De Sisto**, Belvedere, **Kent**, DA17, ENG.
(T) 020 8312 2402
Speciality: Bach Remedies.
M (Ref:HM21079)

## WEBBER, IRENE

**Irene Webber**, Old Coach Rd, Playing Pl, Truro, **Cornwall**, TR3 6ER, ENG.
(T) 01872 864620 (F) 01872 864620
Speciality: Aromatherapy.
● **Owner** Mrs I Webber
M O (Ref:HM21080)

## WEBBORN, S H P

**S H P Webborn**, 108 London Rd, Neath, **Glamorgan (Vale of)**, SA11 1HL, WAL.
(T) 01639 633292
Speciality: Osteopathy.
P S T (Ref:HM21081)

## WEBER, MARALYN

**Maralyn Weber**, 10 Stamford Brook Rd, London, **London (Greater)**, W6 0XH, ENG.
(T) 020 8749 1528
Speciality: Reflexology. ✔
● **Reflexologist** Ms M Weber Q: MAR. M: AoR.
C Yrs. Est.: 2 (Ref:HM21082)

## WEBLEY, JOSEPHINE

**Josephine Webley**, Fieldfare, Salisbury Rd, Horsham, **Sussex (West)**, RH13 7AL, ENG.
(T) 01403 218314
Speciality: Chiropodists (Podiatrists).
● **Owner** Mrs J Webley
S (Ref:HM21083)

## WEBSTER, BARBARA

**Barbara Webster**, Chatteris Drive, Derby, **Derbyshire**, DE21 4SF, ENG.
(T) 01332 834775
Speciality: Chiropodists (Podiatrists).
● **Owner** Mrs B Webster
S (Ref:HM21084)

## WEBSTER, G E

**G E Webster**, 114 Cannons Gate, Clevedon, **Somerset**, BS21 5HZ, ENG.
(T) 01275 340231
Speciality: Chiropodists (Podiatrists).
● **Owner** Mrs G Webster
S (Ref:HM21085)

## WEBSTER, GEORGINA

**Georgina Webster**, 117 Sinclair Rd, London, **London (Greater)**, E4 8PP, ENG.
(T) 020 8529 6392
Speciality: Reflexology.
S T (Ref:HM21086)

## WEBSTER, GILES

**Giles Webster**, 103-105 Harley St, London, **London (Greater)**, W1N 1HD, ENG.
(T) 020 7935 4750
Speciality: Physiotherapy.
P S T (Ref:HM21087)

## WEBSTER, I

**I Webster**, The Orchard, Knowle Cl, Ashburton, Newton Abbot, **Devon**, TQ13 7RA, ENG.
(T) 01364 653394
Speciality: Homeopathy.
● **Owner** Mr I Webster
M (Ref:HM21088)

## WEBSTER, J B

**J B Webster**, 20 The Sq, Penicuik, **Lothian (Mid)**, EH26 8LH, SCO.
(T) 01968 673927
Speciality: Chiropodists (Podiatrists).
S (Ref:HM21089)

## WEBSTER, JAMES B

**James B Webster**, 47 High St, Tonbridge, **Kent**, TN9 1SD, ENG.
(T) 01732 353497
Speciality: Chiropodists (Podiatrists).
S (Ref:HM21090)

## WEBSTER, JAYNE

**Jayne Webster**, 27 New Rd, Bromsgrove, **Worcestershire**, B60 2JL, ENG.
(T) 01527 578001
Speciality: Reflexology.
S T (Ref:HM21091)

## WEBSTER, JOANNE

**Joanne Webster**, 43 Springfield Avenue, Chesterfield, **Derbyshire**, S40 1HL, ENG.
(T) 08000 748681
Speciality: Aromatherapy.
M O (Ref:HM21092)

## WEBSTER, KAREN

**Karen Webster**, 10 Pitstone Cl, St. Albans, **Hertfordshire**, AL4 9JS, ENG.
(T) 01727 839435
Speciality: Reflexology.
S T (Ref:HM21093)

## WEBSTER, TINA

**Tina Webster**, Elvenbrook, Water Lane, Thurnham, Maidstone, **Kent**, ME14 3LT, ENG.
(T) 01622 734466 (F) 01622 734466
Speciality: Reflexology.
● **Owner** Miss T Webster
S T (Ref:HM21094)

## WEBSTER-DICKS, J

**Mrs J Webster-Dicks**, 320 Hoylake Rd, Wirral, **Merseyside**, CH46 6DE, ENG.
(T) 01516 770514
Speciality: Chiropodists (Podiatrists).
● **Owner** Mrs J Webster-Dicks
S (Ref:HM21095)

## WECK, LYN

**Lyn Weck**, Willows, Stroudwood, Upham, **Hampshire**, SO32 1HG, ENG.
(T) 01489 860148
Speciality: Reflexology.
S T (Ref:HM21096)

## WEDLAKE-GRIFFITHS, J

**Mr J Wedlake-Griffiths**, Wedlake Clinic, Clackhams Lane, Crowborough, **Sussex (East)**, TN6 3RN, ENG.
(T) 01892 655468 (F) 01892 655468
(E) jwedlakeg@lineone.net
Speciality: Complementary Therapy, Electrotherapy, Hay Diet, Herbal Medicine, Manipulation, Massage (Therapeutic), Nutritional Therapy. ✔
● **Manipulative Therapist**
Mr J Wedlake-Griffiths Q: Dip.NIM, LCSP.
M: LCSP.
H P S Yrs. Est.: 15 (Ref:HM21097)

## WEDLOCK, P

**P Wedlock**, The Clinic, 36 Knockbreda Rd, Belfast, **County Antrim**, BT6 0JB, NIR.
(T) 028 9064 1089
Speciality: Acupuncture.
O (Ref:HM21098)

## WEDMORE

**Wedmore**, 11 The Borough Mall, Wedmore, **Somerset**, BS28 4EB, ENG.
(T) 01934 713122
Speciality: Chiropodists (Podiatrists).
S (Ref:HM21099)

## WEDNESFIELD HOL THRPY CTRE

**Wednesfield Holistic Therapy Centre**, 12 High St, Wednesfield, Wolverhampton, **Midlands (West)**, WV11 1SZ, ENG.
(T) 01902 723527
Speciality: Complementary Medicines & Therapy.
C M (Ref:HM21100)

## WEEDON, BRIAN J

**Brian J Weedon**, Station House, Old Redbridge Rd, Southampton, **Hampshire**, SO15 0NE, ENG.
(T) 023 8087 1761 (F) 023 8087 1761
Speciality: Osteopathy.
● **Owner** Mr B Weedon
P S T (Ref:HM21101)

## WEEDON, HAZEL

**Hazel Weedon**, 33 Chiltern Way, Tring, **Hertfordshire**, HP23 5LD, ENG.
(T) 01442 823285
Speciality: Reflexology.
S T (Ref:HM21102)

## WEEDS, MARK

**Mark Weeds**, Llanelli Physiotherapy Clinic, 134 Station Rd, Llanelli, **Carmarthenshire**, SA15 1YU, WAL.
(T) 01554 749965
Speciality: Physiotherapy.
● **Owner** Mr M Weeds
P S T (Ref:HM21103)

## WEEKES, CHRIS

**Chris Weekes**, 3a Scotia Building, Atlantic Wharf, 5 Jardine Rd, London, **London (Greater)**, E1W 3WA, ENG.
(T) 020 7790 3455
Speciality: Reflexology.
S T (Ref:HM21104)

## WEEKS, J

**Mr J Weeks**, 20 Brittany Rd, St. Leonards-On-Sea, **Sussex (East)**, TN38 0RD, ENG.
(T) 01424 424591
Speciality: Physiotherapy.
P S T (Ref:HM21105)

## WEEKS, MELANIE

**Melanie Weeks**, 3 Steeple Drive, Exeter, **Devon**, EX2 8FL, ENG.
(T) 01392 435904
Speciality: Chiropodists (Podiatrists).
● **Owner** Mrs M Weeks
S (Ref:HM21106)

## WEEKS, MICHAEL

**Michael Weeks**, 37 The Crescent, Southwick, Brighton, **Sussex (East)**, BN42 4LB, ENG.
(T) 01273 870320 (F) 01273 870320
Speciality: Chiropodists (Podiatrists).
● **Owner** Mr M Weeks
S (Ref:HM21107)

## WEERASEKERA, H

**Mr H Weerasekera**, 124 Gleneagle Rd, London, **London (Greater)**, SW16 6BA, ENG.
(T) 020 8677 5822
Speciality: Homeopathy.
● **Owner** Mr H Weerasekra
M (Ref:HM21108)

## WEGUELIN, JESSICA

**Jessica Weguelin**, Unit 6 Riverside Business Park, Gosport St, Lymington, **Hampshire**, SO41 9BB, ENG.
(T) 01590 688788
Speciality: Physiotherapy.
P S T (Ref:HM21109)



Key: B Mind-Body Medicine · C Complementary Medicine · H Self Help Treatment · M Medicinal Therapy · O Oriental Medicine · P Postural Therapy · S Manipulative Structural Therapy · T Touch Therapy

## WEHMEYER, CATHERINE
**Catherine Wehmeyer**, 176 St. Johns Rd, Colchester, **Essex**, CO4 4JQ, ENG.
(T) 01206 502386
Speciality: Reflexology.
S T (Ref:HM21110)

## WEI CLINIC
**Wei Clinic**, 57a Garland St, Bury St. Edmunds, **Suffolk**, IP33 1EZ, ENG.
(T) 01284 704228 (F) 01284 704228
(E) dbaker@weiclinicfreeserve.co.uk
Speciality: Acupuncture, Aromatherapy, Bach Remedies, Homeopathy, Hypnotherapy, Reflexology. ✓
● **Principle** Ms D Baker Q: MBAcC. M: BAcC.
C Yrs. Est.: 21 (Ref:HM21111)

## WEIGHTMAN, BRENDA
**Brenda Weightman**, 27 Heathside Rd, Manchester, **Manchester (Greater)**, M20 4XW, ENG.
(T) 01614 453952
Speciality: Reflexology.
● **Owner** Mrs B Weightman
S T (Ref:HM21112)

## WEIGHTMAN, LAURA
**Laura Weightman**, 12 Fan Court, Longcross Rd, Longcross, Chertsey, **Surrey**, KT16 0DJ, ENG.
(T) 01932 874877
Speciality: Chiropractic.
● **Owner** Mrs L Weightman
P S T (Ref:HM21113)

## WEIGHTMAN, LAURA
**Laura Weightman**, Spectrum Health Care, 4 Church St, Cobham, **Surrey**, KT11 3EG, ENG.
(T) 01932 863104
Speciality: Chiropractors.
P S T (Ref:HM21114)

## WEILAND, CRISTINA
**Cristina Weiland**, 69 Terrace Rd, Walton-On-Thames, **Surrey**, KT12 2SW, ENG.
(T) 01932 247887
Speciality: Complementary Medicines & Therapy.
● **Owner** Mrs C Weiland
M (Ref:HM21115)

## WEILAND, MICHAEL
**Michael Weiland**, 69 Terrace Rd, Walton-On-Thames, **Surrey**, KT12 2SW, ENG.
(T) 01932 247887
Speciality: Complementary Medicines & Therapy.
● **Owner** Mr M Weiland
C M (Ref:HM21116)

## WEIR, ANDREW
**Andrew Weir**, 27 Appletree Lane, Spencers Wood, Reading, **Berkshire**, RG7 1EE, ENG.
(T) 01189 884106 (F) 01189 887189
Speciality: Complementary Medicines & Therapy.
● **Owner** Mr A Weir
M (Ref:HM21117)

## WEIR-MCGOWAN, ANNETTE
**Annette Weir-McGowan**, 117 Main St, Uddingston, Glasgow, **Glasgow (City of)**, G71 7EW, SCO.
(T) 01698 814785
Speciality: Chiropodists (Podiatrists).
● **Owner** Mrs A Weir-McGowan
S (Ref:HM21118)

## WELBAC CLINIC
**Welbac Clinic**, Maylands, 98 Ashley Lane, Hordle, Lymington, **Hampshire**, SO41 0GA, ENG.
(T) 01425 620177
Speciality: Chiropractic.
P S T (Ref:HM21119)

## WELBECK CLINIC
**Welbeck Clinic**, 689B Finchley Rd, London, **London (Greater)**, NW2 2JN, ENG.
(T) 020 7435 0915
Speciality: Complementary Medicines & Therapy.
C M (Ref:HM21120)

## WELBECK PHYSIOTHERAPY CLINIC
**Welbeck Physiotherapy Clinic**, 2 Durkar Court, Durkar, Wakefield, **Yorkshire (West)**, WF4 3QR, ENG.
(T) 01924 250547
Speciality: Physiotherapy.
P S T (Ref:HM21121)

## WELBOURNE, SONIA D
**Sonia D Welbourne**, 43 Denmark Villas, Hove, **Sussex (East)**, BN3 3TD, ENG.
(T) 01273 722518
Speciality: Osteopathy.
● **Owner** Mrs S Welbourne
P S T (Ref:HM21122)

## WELBY, S J
**S J Welby**, Bernard House, Narrow Way, Wenhaston, Halesworth, **Suffolk**, IP19 9EJ, ENG.
(T) 01502 478541
Speciality: Chiropodists (Podiatrists).
● **Owner** Mrs S Welby
S (Ref:HM21123)

## WELCH, J
**J Welch**, 29 Hersham Rd, Walton-On-Thames, **Surrey**, KT12 1LF, ENG.
(T) 01932 227360 (F) 01932 254395
Speciality: Chiropractors.
● **Principal** Mr S Barron
P S T (Ref:HM21124)

## WELCH, MARTIN
**Martin Welch**, 11 Moat Drive, Slough, **Berkshire**, SL2 5TG, ENG.
(T) 01753 675828
Speciality: Hypnotherapy.
● **Owner** Mr M Welsh
B (Ref:HM21125)

## WELCH, RONALD
**Ronald Welch**, 30A Dobbins Lane, Wendover, Aylesbury, **Buckinghamshire**, HP22 6DH, ENG.
(T) 01296 622108
Speciality: Alexander Technique.
P S (Ref:HM21126)

## WELCH, STEPHEN
**Stephen Welch**, 'Hedgerows', 106 Upper Way, Rugeley, **Staffordshire**, WS15 1QD, ENG.
(T) 01543 490851
Speciality: Reflexology.
S T (Ref:HM21127)

## WELEDA
**Weleda (UK) Ltd**, Heanor Rd, Ilkeston, **Derbyshire**, DE7 8TN, ENG.
(T) 01159 448200
Speciality: Complementary Medicines & Therapy.
M (Ref:HM21128)

## WELFORD, MARTIN
**Martin Welford**, 38 Leslie Rd, Rayleigh, **Essex**, SS6 8PB, ENG.
(T) 01268 776078
Speciality: Alexander Technique.
P S (Ref:HM21129)

## WELFORD, ROY
**Roy Welford**, 54 The Avenue, Yeovil, **Somerset**, BA21 4BN, ENG.
(T) 01935 422488
Speciality: Homeopathy.
M (Ref:HM21130)

## WELL BEING
**Well Being**, West London Ymca, 14 Bond St, Ealing, London, **London (Greater)**, W5 5AA, ENG.
(T) 020 8832 1600 (F) 020 8998 1162
(E) helen.wellbeing@talkzi.com
Speciality: Herbal Medicine, Homeopathy, Hopi Ear Candles, Bush Flower Remedies. ✓
● **Homeopathic Practitioner**
Ms H Kimball-Brooke Q: LCPH. M: HMA.
B Yrs. Est.: 3 (Ref:HM21131)

## WELL BEING
**Well Being**, 71 Glaslough St, **County Monaghan**, IRE.
(T) 04784 299
Speciality: Complementary Medicines & Therapy.
M (Ref:HM21132)

## WELL BEING CENTRE
**Well Being Centre For Complementary Therapy**, 225 High Rd, London, **London (Greater)**, E18 2PB, ENG.
(T) 020 8505 6070
Speciality: Complementary Medicines & Therapy.
● **Manager** Miss T Brooks
C M (Ref:HM21133)

## WELL BEING CLINIC
**Well Being Clinic**, 6 Kingston Rd, Oxford, **Oxfordshire**, OX2 6EF, ENG.
(T) 01865 311704
Speciality: Alexander Technique.
● **Therapist** Mr J Carpmael
P S (Ref:HM21134)

## WELL BEING CLINIC
**Well Being Clinic**, 4a George St, Pocklington, York, **Yorkshire (North)**, YO42 2DF, ENG.
(T) 01759 302162
Speciality: Physiotherapy.
● **Owner** Mrs M Rimes
P S T (Ref:HM21135)

## WELL BEING COMP HLTH CARE
**Well Being Complimentary Health Care Practice**, 19 O'Connell St, **County Waterford**, IRE.
(T) 05185 8255
(E) wellbeing@eircom.net
Speciality: Complementary Medicines & Therapy.
M (Ref:HM21136)

## WELL CONNECTED
**Well Connected**, 54-56 Gallowgate St, Largs, **Ayrshire (North)**, KA30 8LX, SCO.
(T) 01475 675533 (F) 01475 675533
Speciality: Physiotherapy.
● **Practice Manager** Mrs G Crawford
P S T (Ref:HM21137)

## WELL HOUSE HOLISTIC HLTH CTRE
**Well House Holistic Health Centre**, 13 St. Thomas St, Winchester, **Hampshire**, SO23 9HE, ENG.
(T) 01962 869789
Speciality: Acupuncture, Aromatherapy, Counselling, Crystal Healing, Holistic Healing, Meditation, Reiki, Shiatsu, Yoga, Rebursing, Holistic Massage, Feldenkrais. ✓
● **Holistic Therapist/Centre Manager**
Mrs R Heeks Q: BA.
C Yrs. Est.: 10 (Ref:HM21138)

## WELL NATURAL HEALTH CENTRE
**Well Natural Health Centre (The)**, 89 Institute Rd, Kings Heath, Birmingham, **Midlands (West)**, B14 7EU, ENG.
(T) 01214 431580
Speciality: Acupuncture, Allergy Testing, Aromatherapy, Auricular Therapy, Bowen Therapy, Chiropody, Chiropractic, Counselling, Cranial Osteopathy, Healing Therapy, Hellerwork, Homeopathy, Hypnotherapy, Indian Head Massage, Massage (Therapeutic), Meditation, Naturopathy, Nutritional Therapy, Podiatry, Psychotherapy, Reflexology, Reiki, Stress Therapy, Swedish Body Massage, McTimoney Chiropractic. ✓
● **Hypnotherapist** Mr B Spour Q: BA.
● **Acupuncturist** Jacky Turner Q: Lic.Ac.
● **Therapist** Mr A Swan
● **Aromatherapist** Ms M Barr M: IPTI.
● **Hypnotherapist** Ms A Smith
● **Teacher of the Alexander Technique**
Ms R Knight M: STAT.
● **Acupuncturist** Ms A Garland Q: BA, Lic.Ac. M: BAcC.
● **Chiropractor** Leslie Smith Q: DC. M: MCA.
● **Chiropractor** Ms K Hooley Q: DC. M: MCA.
● **Aromatherapist** Ms S Ford
● **Counsellor** Pank Hania
● **Homeopath** Roz Lowe Q: DC. M: LCH, MCA.
● **Chiropractor** Ms A Loveday Q: DC. M: MCA.
● **Sports Massage Therapist**
Sandi Pemberton
● **Bowen Therapist** Peta Jackson Q: ITEC.



Key continued: Yrs.Est: Years Established Q: Qualifications M: Professional Membership ✓ Indemnity Insurance Accept Credit Cards

- **Counsellor** Mr M Walker
- **Chiropractor** Ms J Hanstead **Q:** DC, MSc. M: MCA, RCST.
- **Healer** Mr M Blansten
- **Aromatherapist** Ms H Drummond **Q:** ISPA. M: ITEC, TATh.
- **Aromatherapist** Ms K Cooper M: IHBC.
- **Therapist** Geri Harries
- **Chiropodist** Ms L Callam
- **Nutritionist** Ms C Halford **Q:** ND.
- **Homeopath** Pat Collins
- **General Practitioner** Ms B King

P Yrs. Est.: 10 (**Ref:**HM21139)

## WELL NATURAL HEALTH CENTRE

**Well Natural Health Centre (The)**, Keys Counselling & Psychotherapy, 131A Alcester Rd, Birmingham, **Midlands (West)**, B13 8JP, ENG.
(T) 01214 431580
Speciality: Acupuncture, Alexander Technique, Allergy Testing, Aromatherapy, Bowen Therapy, Chiropractic, Complementary Therapy, Counselling, Cranial Osteopathy, Healer, Hellerwork, Herbal Medicine, Holistic Healing, Homeopathy, Hypnotherapy, Indian Head Massage, Massage (Therapeutic), Metamorphic Therapy, Naturopathy, Nutritional Therapy, Phytotherapy, Reflexology, Reiki, Spiritual Healing, Stress Therapy, Visualisation Therapy, Remedial Therapy, McTimoney Chiropractic.
- **Homeopath** Ms R Lowe **Q:** LCH. M: Soc.Hom.
- **Chiropractor/Director** Ms J Hanstead **Q:** DC, FCC, MMCA. M: MCA.
- **Hypnotherapist/Managing Director** Ms A Smith **Q:** C.Hyp, CMH.
- **Acupuncturist** Ms J Turner **Q:** MBAcC. M: BAcC.
- **Counselling** Ms B King

B P S T Yrs. Est.: 10 (**Ref:**HM21140)

## WELL OILED

**Well Oiled**, 156 Keswick Drive, Chesterfield, **Derbyshire**, S41 8HH, ENG.
(T) 01246 202242
Speciality: Aromatherapy.
M O (**Ref:**HM21141)

## WELL OILED

**Well Oiled**, 11 Frankforte Gate, Plymouth, **Devon**, PL1 1QA, ENG.
(T) 01752 229481 (F) 01752 229538
Speciality: Aromatherapy.
- **Owner** Mrs S Privett

M O (**Ref:**HM21142)

## WELL SPRING CLINIC

**Well Spring Clinic**, 90 Islington High St, London, **London (Greater)**, N1 8EG, ENG.
(T) 020 7704 1555 (F) 020 7226 9001
Speciality: Complementary Medicines & Therapy.
- **Director** Mr S Kirby

M (**Ref:**HM21143)

## WELL WITHIN THERAPIES

**Well Within Therapies**, 26 Orchard Rd, Kingston Upon Thames, **Surrey**, KT1 2QW, ENG.
(T) 020 8549 1784
Speciality: Complementary Medicines & Therapy.
- **Partner** Mrs H Hain

C M (**Ref:**HM21144)

## WELLAN, J

**J Wellan**, 22 Northgate St, Warwick, **Warwickshire**, CV34 4SP, ENG.
(T) 01926 412433 (F) 01926 418032
Speciality: Psychology.
- **Principal** Ms J Wellan

B (**Ref:**HM21145)

## WELLBEING

**Wellbeing**, 19A Leopold Pl, Edinburgh, **Edinburgh (City of)**, EH7 5LB, SCO.
(T) 01315 587879
Speciality: Indian Head Massage, Reiki, Aura Cleaning. ✔
- **Owner** Mrs L McGlennon **Q:** Reiki Master. M: IPTI.

B T Yrs. Est.: 4 (**Ref:**HM21146)

## WELLBEING

**Wellbeing**, 25 Hollin Lane, Leeds, **Yorkshire (West)**, LS16 5NB, ENG.
(T) 01132 787132
Speciality: Aromatherapy.
M O (**Ref:**HM21147)

## WELLBEING AT WORK

**Wellbeing At Work**, 11 Musters Rd, West Bridgford, Nottingham, **Nottinghamshire**, NG2 7PP, ENG.
(T) 01159 812939 (F) 01159 812939
Speciality: Psychology.
- **Owner** Ms S Hooper

B (**Ref:**HM21148)

## WELLBEING CENTRE

**Wellbeing Centre (The)**, 11 Musters Rd, Nottingham, **Nottinghamshire**, NG5 3GQ, ENG.
(T) 01159 825353 (F) 01159 812939
Speciality: Complementary Medicines & Therapy, Irrational Emotive Behaviour Therapy. ✔
- **Director/Psychologist** Mrs S Hooper **Q:** BA, Dip.FEM, MSc. M: BPS.

B Yrs. Est.: 20 (**Ref:**HM21149)

## WELLBEING CENTRE-HOMOEOPATHY

**Wellbeing Centre For Homoeopathy (The)**, The Old Convent, Beeches Green, Stroud, **Gloucestershire**, GL5 4AD, ENG.
(T) 01453 885781
Speciality: Homeopathy.
- **Partner** Ms A Sapieha

M (**Ref:**HM21150)

## WELLBEING CLINIC

**Wellbeing Clinic**, Wentworth House, Vernon Gate, Derby, **Derbyshire**, DE1 1UR, ENG.
(T) 01332 224820
Speciality: Chiropractors.
- **Manager** Mrs A Reed

P S T (**Ref:**HM21151)

## WELLBEING NATURALLY

**Wellbeing Naturally**, 78 Dereham Rd, Norwich, **Norfolk**, NR2 4BU, ENG.
(T) 01603 485776
(W) www.hummingbird-one.co.uk
Speciality: Cranio-Sacral Therapy. ✔
- **Cranio-Sacral Therapist** Mr A Cook **Q:** MSc, RCST. M: RCST.

B S T Yrs. Est.: 7 (**Ref:**HM21152)

## WELLBROOK CLINIC

**Wellbrook Clinic (The)**, 21 Stafford Rd, Wallington, **Surrey**, SM6 9AN, ENG.
(T) 020 8401 0011
Speciality: Complementary Medicines & Therapy.
M (**Ref:**HM21153)

## WELLBURN

**Mrs Wellburn**, 24 Bathurst Walk, Iver, **Buckinghamshire**, SL0 9AZ, ENG.
(T) 01753 653383
Speciality: Acupuncture, Massage (Therapeutic), Shiatsu. ✔
- **Shiatsu Therapist** Mrs M Wellburn **Q:** BA (Hons). M: RSS.

B T Yrs. Est.: 15 (**Ref:**HM21154)

## WELLBURN, JOCELYN

**Jocelyn Wellburn (Highgate)**, 38 Westhill Court, Millfield Lane, London, **London (Greater)**, N6 6JJ, ENG.
(T) 020 7209 2464
Speciality: Shiatsu.
M (**Ref:**HM21155)

## WELLER, JACK

**Jack Weller**, 51 Highland Rd, Amersham, **Buckinghamshire**, HP7 9AY, ENG.
(T) 01494 723813 (F) 01494 723813
Speciality: Auto Suggestion, Aversion Therapy, Counselling, Humanistic Psychology, Hypnosis, Hypnotherapy, Life Style Coaching, Meditation, Psychotherapy, Reiki, Stress Therapy, Visualisation Therapy.
- **Hypnotherapist** Mr J Weller M: HS, NCH, NCP.

B (**Ref:**HM21156)

## WELLER, JACK

**Jack Weller**, 2 Plumtree Cottages, High St, Prestwood, Great Missenden, **Buckinghamshire**, HP16 9ER, ENG.
(T) 01494 865997
Speciality: Hypnotherapy.
B (**Ref:**HM21157)

## WELLESBOURNE HAIR RESTORATION

**Wellesbourne Hair Restoration Centre (The)**, Suite 23, Wellesbourne House, Walton Rd, Wellesbourne, Warwick, **Warwickshire**, CV35 9JB, ENG.
(T) 01789 470800
Speciality: Complementary Medicines & Therapy, Trichology.
M (**Ref:**HM21158)

## WELLFOODS

**Wellfoods Ltd**, Unit 6, Mapplewell Business Park, Blacker Rd, Mapplewell, Barnsley, **Yorkshire (South)**, S75 6BP, ENG.
(T) 01226 381712 (F) 01226 381858
Speciality: Nutritional Therapy.
- **Director** Ms J Woodwood **Q:** BA (Hons), MBA.

M Yrs. Est.: 2 (**Ref:**HM21159)

## WELLFORCE

**Wellforce**, 28 Wilkinson St, Sheffield, **Yorkshire (South)**, S10 2GB, ENG.
(T) 01142 769500
(E) clare@wellforce.fsnet.co.uk
Speciality: Acupuncture, Aromatherapy, Bach Remedies, Chiropractic, Counselling, Cranial Osteopathy, Homeopathy, Kinesiology, Osteopathy, Psychotherapy, Reflexology, Shiatsu.
- **Osteopath** Chris Johnson M: GOsC.
- **Director/Homeopath** Dr Strong **Q:** BS, MB, MFHom. M: FHom.
- **Director/Homeopath** Ms C Relton **Q:** BA (Hons), RSHom. M: Soc.Hom.

M (**Ref:**HM21160)

## WELLHURST GOLF & CTRY CLUB

**Wellhurst Golf and Country Club**, North St, Hellingley, **Sussex (East)**, BN27 4EE, ENG.
(T) 01435 813636
Speciality: Physiotherapy.
- **General Manager** Norma Self

P S T (**Ref:**HM21161)

## WELLING CLINIC

**Welling Clinic (The)**, 45A Upper Wickham Lane, Welling, **Kent**, DA16 3AD, ENG.
(T) 020 8303 8439
Speciality: Osteopathy.
- **Partner** Mrs C Hodges

M (**Ref:**HM21162)

## WELLINGBOROUGH PHYSIO CLINIC

**Wellingborough Physiotherapy Clinic**, 19 Bentley Court, Finedon Rd Industrial Estate, Wellingborough, **Northamptonshire**, NN8 4BQ, ENG.
(T) 01933 279815 (F) 01933 279815
Speciality: Physiotherapy.
- **Partner** Mrs J White

P S T (**Ref:**HM21163)

## WELLINGS, CLIVE

**Clive Wellings**, 76 Hamilton Rd, Reading, **Berkshire**, RG1 5RD, ENG.
(T) 01189 264401
Speciality: Complementary Medicines & Therapy.
M (**Ref:**HM21164)

## WELLINGS, INGA

**Inga Wellings**, 4 The Green, Woodford Green, **Essex**, IG8 0NF, ENG.
(T) 020 8504 0407
Speciality: Reflexology.
S T (**Ref:**HM21165)

## WELLS CENTRE

**Wells Centre (The)**, 85 High St, Tunbridge Wells, **Kent**, TN1 1YG, ENG.
(T) 01892 548688
Speciality: Reflexology.
- **Owner** Mrs B Freeman

S T (**Ref:**HM21166)

## WELLS HYPNOTHERAPY CLINIC

**Wells Hypnotherapy Clinic**, Wells Hypnotherapy Clinic, 16a Duke St, Chelmsford, **Essex**, CM1 1HL, ENG.
(T) 01702 353006



Key: B Mind-Body Medicine C Complementary Medicine H Self Help Treatment M Medicinal Therapy O Oriental Medicine P Postural Therapy S Manipulative Structural Therapy T Touch Therapy

Speciality: Hypnotherapy, Smoking £60.00 for 1 session 1hr 30mins. ✓
- **Hypnotherapist** Mr C Jack Q: DipCH.P, DSMH, NLP (Master). M: NCH.

[B] Yrs. Est.: 3 (Ref:HM21167)

## WELLS PHYSIO & SPORTS CLINIC

**Wells Physiotherapy & Sports Clinic (The)**, 4 Clanricarde Gardens, Tunbridge Wells, **Kent**, TN1 1PE, ENG.
(T) 01892 525065 (F) 01892 618413
Speciality: Acupuncture, Manipulation, Physiotherapy. ✓
- **Physiotherapist** Mr P McClean Q: MCSP, SRP. M: CSP.
- **Physiotherapist** Mr B Burke Q: MCSP, SRP. M: CSP.

[S] Yrs. Est.: 9 (Ref:HM21168)

## WELLS PHYSIO PRACTICE

**Wells Physiotherapy Practice & Sports Injury Clinic**, 20 Tor St, Wells, **Somerset**, BA5 2US, ENG.
(T) 01749 675568
Speciality: Physiotherapy.
- **Owner** Mr A Evans

[P] [S] [T] (Ref:HM21169)

## WELLS, C

**C Wells**, 88 Great Northern Rd, Dunstable, **Bedfordshire**, LU5 4BT, ENG.
(T) 01582 608400 (F) 01582 471371
Speciality: Osteopathy.
- **Owner** Mr J Betser

[P] [S] [T] (Ref:HM21170)

## WELLS, C R

**C R Wells**, Fairfields Clinic, Skippetts Lane West, Basingstoke, **Hampshire**, RG21 3HP, ENG.
(T) 01256 326980
Speciality: Chiropodists (Podiatrists).
[S] (Ref:HM21171)

## WELLS, GEORGINA

**Georgina Wells Mobile**, 5 Kingley Rd, Cashes Green, Stroud, **Gloucestershire**, GL5 4LS, ENG.
(T) 01453 757499
Speciality: Aromatherapy, Healing Therapy, Massage (Therapeutic), Polarity Therapy, Reflexology, Prepares mothers for child birth, using massage oils, also prepares dads for the labour room by showing them a simple massage method for mum. ✓
- **Clinical Aromatherapist/Masseur** Ms G Wells Q: Dip.Clin.Arom, Dip.Reflex, ITEC. M: GCP, IFA.

[M] [O] Yrs. Est.: 12 (Ref:HM21172)

## WELLS, H P

**H P Wells**, 5 Lynn Rd, Downham Market, **Norfolk**, PE38 9NN, ENG.
(T) 01366 388401
Speciality: Chiropodists (Podiatrists).
[S] (Ref:HM21173)

## WELLS, HEIDI

**Heidi Wells**, Trimithi, Tower Rd, Hindhead, **Surrey**, GU26 6SL, ENG.
(T) 01428 609590
Speciality: Physiotherapy.
- **Owner** Ms H Wells

[P] [S] [T] (Ref:HM21174)

## WELLS, HENRIETTA

**Henrietta Wells**, Bowehouse, Chitterne, Warminster, **Wiltshire**, BA12 0LG, ENG.
(T) 01985 850551
Speciality: Holistic Healing, Homeopathy. ✓
- **Homeopath** Ms H Wells Q: M.S.C.P, RSHom. M: Soc.Hom.

[C] Yrs. Est.: 25 (Ref:HM21175)

## WELLS, KIM

**Kim Wells**, The Haelan Clinic, 41 The Broadway, Crouch End, London, **London (Greater)**, N8 8DT, ENG.
(T) 020 8340 1518
Speciality: Acupuncture.
- **Manager** Mr J Krahn

[O] (Ref:HM21176)

## WELLS, MADELEINE

**Madeleine Wells**, 30 Walsingham Rd, Woodthorpe, Nottingham, **Nottinghamshire**, NG5 4NW, ENG.
(T) 01159 204417
Speciality: Reflexology.
[S] [T] (Ref:HM21177)

## WELLS, PAMELA

**Pamela Wells**, London, **London (Greater)**, N14, ENG.
(T) 020 8368 3270
Speciality: Bach Remedies.
[M] (Ref:HM21178)

## WELLSPRING

**Wellspring**, 13 Smith's Pl, Edinburgh, **Edinburgh (City of)**, EH6 8NT, SCO.
(T) 01315 536660
Speciality: Psychotherapy.
[B] (Ref:HM21179)

## WELLSPRING

**Wellspring**, Coosehecca Farm, Chacewater, Truro, **Cornwall**, TR4 8QU, ENG.
(T) 01872 561171 (F) 01872 560148
Speciality: Complementary Medicines & Therapy.
- **Owner** Ms V Brammer

[C] [M] (Ref:HM21180)

## WELLSPRING OSTEO/NTRL HEALTH

**Wellspring Osteopathy & Natural Health**, 2 Priory Rd, Wells, **Somerset**, BA5 1SY, ENG.
(T) 01749 673300
Speciality: Acupuncture, Aromatherapy, Counselling, Cranial Osteopathy, Herbal Medicine, Homeopathy, Massage (Therapeutic), Osteopathy, Reflexology. ✓
- **Acupuncturist** Ms A Warner Q: Lic.Ac, MBAcC. M: BAcC.
- **Medical Herbalist** Ms L Crockett Q: BA, MNIMH. M: NIMH.
- **Homeopath** Ms S Kemp Q: BA, DSH. M: Soc.Hom.
- **Osteopath** Mr P Leigh Q: BSc, Hons (OST). M: GOsC.

[C] Yrs. Est.: 3 (Ref:HM21181)

## WELLSTEAD, LINDSAY

**Lindsay Wellstead**, 104a Elm Gr, Brighton, **Sussex (East)**, BN2 3DB, ENG.
(T) 01273 679555
Speciality: Clairvoyants & Palmists.
[B] (Ref:HM21182)

## WELSH CHIROPRACTIC

**Welsh Chiropractic Clinics**, 89 Middle Lane, Rotherham, **Yorkshire (South)**, S65 2TE, ENG.
(T) 01709 720200 (F) 01709 512322
Speciality: Aromatherapy, Chiropractic, Complementary Therapy, Counselling, Group Therapy, Homeopathy, Manipulation, Massage (Therapeutic), Nutritional Therapy, X-Ray, Craniopathy. ✓
- **Chiropractor** Mr P Welsh (T) 01709 720400 Q: BSc, DC. M: BCA, GCC.
- **Homeopath** Elke Rohn (T) 01709 720400 Q: Dip.Hom, RSHom.
- **Aromatherapist/Counsellor** Ms P Rotherham (T) 01709 720400 Q: ITEC, MGCP.
- **Chiropractor** Ms N Lewis (T) 01709 720400 Q: BSc, DC. M: BCA, GCC.

[S] Yrs. Est.: 6 (Ref:HM21183)

## WELSH, A C

**A C Welsh**, 18 Burnside Pl, Irvine, **Ayrshire (North)**, KA12 0UN, SCO.
(T) 01294 271891
Speciality: Hypnotherapy.
- **Owner** Mrs A Welsh

[B] (Ref:HM21184)

## WELSH, ANNE

**Anne Welsh**, Tanglewood, Bridle Rd, Whitchurch Hill, Reading, **Berkshire**, RG8 7PR, ENG.
(T) 01189 844133
Speciality: Reflexology.
[S] [T] (Ref:HM21185)

## WELSH, P A

**P A Welsh**, 4 Newall Mount, Otley, **Yorkshire (West)**, LS21 2DY, ENG.
(T) 01943 461846
Speciality: Chiropractic.
[P] [S] [T] (Ref:HM21186)

## WELSH, R P

**R P Welsh**, 2 Church Cl, Andover, **Hampshire**, SP10 1DP, ENG.
(T) 01264 350062
Speciality: Osteopathy.
- **Owner** Mr R Welsh

[P] [S] [T] (Ref:HM21187)

## WELSH, R P & C J

**R P & C J Welsh**, 15 Tadfield Rd, Romsey, **Hampshire**, SO51 5AL, ENG.
(T) 01794 523371
Speciality: Osteopathy.
[P] [S] [T] (Ref:HM21188)

## WELSH-ROLLINGS, SUSANNE

**Susanne Welsh-Rollings**, 64 Bolton St, Brixham, **Devon**, TQ5 9DH, ENG.
(T) 01803 858297
Speciality: Chiropodists (Podiatrists).
[S] (Ref:HM21189)

## WELSH-ROLLINGS, SUSANNE

**Susanne Welsh-Rollings**, Byron House, 37 The Strand, Dawlish, **Devon**, EX7 9PT, ENG.
(T) 01626 862648
Speciality: Chiropodists (Podiatrists).
[S] (Ref:HM21190)

## WELTON COMMUNITY SERVICES

**Welton Community Services**, 4 Cliff Rd, Welton, Lincoln, **Lincolnshire**, LN2 3JJ, ENG.
(T) 01673 862187
Speciality: Physiotherapy.
[P] [S] [T] (Ref:HM21191)

## WELWYN CHIROPRACTIC CLINIC

**Welwyn Chiropractic Clinic (The)**, Herts Country Club, Chequers Field, Welwyn Garden City, **Hertfordshire**, AL7 4HY, ENG.
(T) 01707 394500 (F) 01707 395151
Speciality: Chiropractic. ✓
- **Owner** Dr K Singh Q: DC.
- **Chiropractor** Dr D Stronagh Q: BCA, DC.

[P] Yrs. Est.: 6 (Ref:HM21192)

## WEMBLEY MEDICAL CENTRE

**Wembley Medical Centre**, 130 Llanover Rd, Wembley, **London (Greater)**, HA9 7LT, ENG.
(T) 08000 180604
Speciality: Hypnotherapy.
[B] (Ref:HM21193)

## WEN, ISABELLE

**Isabelle Wen**, 337-339 Norwich Rd, Ipswich, **Suffolk**, IP1 4BN, ENG.
(T) 01473 464300
Speciality: Acupuncture.
[O] (Ref:HM21194)

## WENDALS HERBS

**Wendals Herbs Ltd**, Westfield House, Sutton Rd, Terrington St. Clement, King's Lynn, **Norfolk**, PE34 4EX, ENG.
(T) 01553 828111 (F) 01553 829400
Speciality: Herbal Medicine.
- **Joint Director** Martin Paul Jennings

[M] (Ref:HM21195)

## WENDT, ANNE E

**Anne E Wendt**, 31 Lancelot Drive, Stretton, Burton-On-Trent, **Staffordshire**, DE13 0GJ, ENG.
(T) 01283 542163
Speciality: Chiropodists (Podiatrists).
[S] (Ref:HM21196)

## WENDY JILLEY - MEDICAL HERB

**Wendy Jilley - Medical Herbalist**, The Natural Therapy Centre, The Granaries, Nelson St, King's Lynn, **Norfolk**, PE30 5DY, ENG.
(T) 01553 777133
Speciality: Herbal Medicine. ✓
- **Medical Herbalist** Ms W Jilley (T) 01485 540332 Q: BA (Hons), MNIMH. M: NIMH.

[M] Yrs. Est.: 11 (Ref:HM21197)

## WENDY PRICE HOLISTIC RIDING

**Wendy Price Holistic Riding**, 11 Churchill Drive, Upper Bruntingthorpe, Lutterworth, **Leicestershire**, LE17 5QX, ENG.
(T) 08007 830292



Key continued: Yrs.Est: Years Established Q: Qualifications M: Professional Membership ✓ Indemnity Insurance [card] Accept Credit Cards

(E) wendy@holisticriding.com
(W) www.holisticriding.com
Speciality: Absent Healing, Bach Remedies, Counselling, Healer, Healing Therapy, Life Style Coaching, Reiki, Spiritual Healing, Stress Therapy, Visualisation Therapy, Holistic Riding Therapy, Metaphysical and Spiritual counselling. ✔
● **Riding Instructor/Therapist/Life Coach** Miss W Price M: BRCP.
H Yrs. Est.: 10 (Ref:HM21198)

**WENDY ROBINSON ACUPUNCTURE**

**Wendy Robinson Acupuncture**, 63 Clifton Pl, Shipley, **Yorkshire (West)**, BD18 2AB, ENG.
(T) 01274 775858
Speciality: Acupuncture.
O (Ref:HM21199)

**WENSLEY, MARTIN**

**Martin Wensley**, 35 Cleland Park North, Bangor, **County Down**, BT20 3EN, NIR.
(T) 028 9127 0032 (F) 028 9127 0032
Speciality: Physiotherapy.
● **Owner** Mr M Wensley
P S T (Ref:HM21200)

**WENTWORTH HEALTH CLINIC**

**Wentworth Health Clinic**, Wentworth House, Bradford St, Braintree, **Essex**, CM7 9AU, ENG.
(T) 01376 325621 (F) 01376 552976
Speciality: Aromatherapy, Counselling, Massage (Therapeutic), Reflexology, Spiritual Healing, Stress Therapy. ✔
● **Reflexologist/Aromatherapist** Miss E Sale M: RQA.
● **Reflexologist/Aromatherapist** Mrs C Sale Q: Cert.Couns, Cert.Couns.Groupwork, Dip.Reflex, RQA.
C T Yrs. Est.: 5 (Ref:HM21201)

**WENTWORTH, MARK**

**Mark Wentworth**, 120 Wellingborough Rd, Rushden, **Northamptonshire**, NN10 9TD, ENG.
(T) 01933 418634 (F) 01933 410883
Speciality: Complementary Medicines & Therapy.
● **Owner** Mr M Wentworth
M (Ref:HM21202)

**WERNINCK, RODNEY**

**Rodney Werninck**, 44 The Mall, London, **London (Greater)**, W5 3TJ, ENG.
(T) 020 8840 9979 (F) 020 8579 2915
Speciality: Psychotherapy.
● **Owner** Mr R Werninck
B (Ref:HM21203)

**WERTS, DOUGLAS**

**Douglas Werts**, 9 Borden Lane, Sittingbourne, **Kent**, ME10 1BU, ENG.
(T) 01795 471394
Speciality: Complementary Medicines & Therapy.
C M (Ref:HM21204)

**WESLEY, D E**

**D E Wesley**, Bronze Barrow, 38 Lone Pine Drive, West Parley, Ferndown, **Dorset**, BH22 8LS, ENG.
(T) 01202 872149
Speciality: Chiropodists (Podiatrists).
● **Owner** Mrs D Wesley
S (Ref:HM21205)

**WESSEL, C A**

**C A Wessel**, Wolds Farm, Narrow Lane, Wymeswold, Loughborough, **Leicestershire**, LE12 6SD, ENG.
(T) 01509 880804
Speciality: Physiotherapy.
P S T (Ref:HM21206)

**WESSEX CENTRE FOR WELLBEING**

**Wessex Centre For Wellbeing**, 6 Hatherley Rd, Winchester, **Hampshire**, SO22 6RT, ENG.
(T) 01962 866302
Speciality: Complementary Medicines & Therapy.
C M (Ref:HM21207)

**WESSEX HEALTHY LIVING FOUND**

**Wessex Healthy Living Foundation**, 6c St Catherines Rd, Southbourne, Bournemouth, **Dorset**, BH6 4AA, ENG.
(T) 01202 422087
Speciality: Acupuncture, Alexander Technique, Allergy Testing, Aromatherapy, Auricular Therapy, Auto Suggestion, Bach Remedies, Beauty Therapy, Bowen Therapy, Chiropody, Chiropractic, Colour Therapy, Complementary Therapy, Counselling, Dietician, Family Planning (Natural), Hay Diet, Healer, Healing Therapy, Herbal Medicine, Holistic Healing, Homeopathy, Hopi Ear Candles, Hypnosis, Hypnotherapy, Indian Head Massage, Kinesiology, Manipulation, Massage (Therapeutic), Moxibustion, Neuro-Linguistic Program, Nutritional Therapy, Osteopathy, Psychotherapy, Reflexology, Reiki, Remedial Massage, Shiatsu, Stress Therapy, Vitamin Therapy. ✔
● **Clinic Manager** Raksha Peters
C M Yrs. Est.: 24 (Ref:HM21208)

**WESSEX KINESIOLOGY CENTRE**

**Wessex Kinesiology Centre**, Suite 3 Floor 3 Newfoundland House, The Quay, **Dorset**, BH15 1HJ, ENG.
(T) 01202 678947
Speciality: Kinesiology.
M (Ref:HM21209)

**WESSEX OSTEOPATHY CLINIC**

**Wessex Osteopathy Clinic**, 28 St Clements Way, Bishopdown, Salisbury, **Wiltshire**, SP1 3FF, ENG.
(T) 01722 416006
Speciality: Osteopathy.
● **Owner** Mr C Gobell
P S T (Ref:HM21210)

**WESSEX OSTEOPATHY CLINIC**

**Wessex Osteopathy Clinic**, 71B High St, Lymington, **Hampshire**, SO41 9AL, ENG.
(T) 01590 670706
Speciality: Osteopathy.
P S T (Ref:HM21211)

**WEST & ASSOCIATES**

**David West & Associates**, 395A Addiscombe Rd, Croydon, **Surrey**, CR0 7LJ, ENG.
(T) 020 8655 4133
Speciality: Physiotherapy.
P S T (Ref:HM21212)

**WEST & ASSOCIATES**

**F J West & Associates**, 106 Water Lane, Wilmslow, **Cheshire**, SK9 5BB, ENG.
(T) 01625 252475
Speciality: Physiotherapy.
● **Owner** Ms F West
P S T (Ref:HM21213)

**WEST BAR CLINIC**

**West Bar Clinic**, West House, 50 West Bar St, Banbury, **Oxfordshire**, OX16 9RZ, ENG.
(T) 01295 279095
Speciality: Psychotherapy.
B (Ref:HM21214)

**WEST BERKSHIRE PSYCHOTHERAPY**

**West Berkshire Psychotherapy Service**, Winterbourne House, 53-55 Argyle Rd, Reading, **Berkshire**, RG1 7YL, ENG.
(T) 01189 561250 (F) 01189 565251
Speciality: Psychotherapy.
● **Doctor** Mr R Haigh
B (Ref:HM21215)

**WEST BYFLEET PHYSIOTHERAPY**

**West Byfleet Physiotherapy & Sports Injuries Clinic**, 22A Station Approach, West Byfleet, **Surrey**, KT14 6NF, ENG.
(T) 01932 341114
Speciality: Physiotherapy.
P S T (Ref:HM21216)

**WEST DIDSBURY HOLISTIC HEALTH**

**West Didsbury Holistic Health Clinic**, 115A Lapwing Lane, Manchester, **Manchester (Greater)**, M20 6UR, ENG.
(T) 01614 487474
Speciality: Aromatherapy.
M O (Ref:HM21217)

**WEST DRAYTON PHYSIO/SPORTS**

**West Drayton Physiotherapy & Sports Injury Clinic (The)**, 147 Station Rd, West Drayton, **London (Greater)**, UB7 7ND, ENG.
(T) 01895 420950
Speciality: Physiotherapy.
● **Owner** Mr J Shotbolt
P S T (Ref:HM21218)

**WEST END PHYSIOTHERAPY**

**West End Physiotherapy & Sport Injury Clinic**, 124 Union Gr, Aberdeen, **Aberdeenshire**, AB10 6SB, SCO.
(T) 01224 585224 (F) 01224 585224
Speciality: Acupuncture, Manipulation, Physiotherapy. ✔
● **Physiotherapist** Mrs G Howarth Q: MCSP, SRP. M: CSP.
S Yrs. Est.: 5 (Ref:HM21219)

**WEST END PHYSIOTHERAPY**

**West End Physiotherapy & Sports Injury Clinic**, The Cedars, 44 Ardgowan St, Greenock, **Inverclyde**, PA16 8EL, SCO.
(T) 01475 729670
Speciality: Physiotherapy.
P S T (Ref:HM21220)

**WEST END THERAPY CENTRE**

**West End Therapy Centre & Homeopathic Clinic**, 143 Whittingehame Drive, Jordanhill, Glasgow, **Glasgow (City of)**, G13 1NW, SCO.
(T) 01419 547350
Speciality: Homeopathy, Reflexology, Reiki. ✔
● **Practitioner** Ms J Ogle Q: GSSR, SCH. M: SIR, Soc.Hom.
C Yrs. Est.: 11 (Ref:HM21221)

**WEST END THERAPY CLINIC**

**West End Therapy Clinic**, 2a Torphichen St, Edinburgh, **Edinburgh (City of)**, EH3 8JQ, SCO.
(T) 01312 292200
Speciality: Chiropractic.
P S T (Ref:HM21222)

**WEST KIRBY PHYSIOTHERAPY**

**West Kirby Physiotherapy**, 26A Hydro Avenue, Wirral, **Merseyside**, CH48 3HR, ENG.
(T) 01516 252431
Speciality: Physiotherapy.
● **Partner** Mrs F Creedon
P S T (Ref:HM21223)

**WEST LANCS MCTIMONEY**

**West Lancashire McTimoney Chiropractic Clinic**, 4 Middlewood, Ashurst, Skelmersdale, **Lancashire**, WN8 6SR, ENG.
(T) 01695 732538
Speciality: Chiropractic. ✔
● **McTimoney Chiropractor** Ms C Corcoran Q: DC, MA, MMCA. M: GCC, MCA.
S Yrs. Est.: 11 (Ref:HM21224)

**WEST LONDON CENTRE**

**West London Centre**, 50 Upham Park Rd, London, **London (Greater)**, W4 1PG, ENG.
(T) 020 8742 7926
Speciality: Hypnosis.
● **Director** Mr D Rosswood
B (Ref:HM21225)

**WEST LONDON HOLISTIC CENTRE**

**Oliver Aida Alexandra**, 26 Priory Cl, Denham, Uxbridge, **London (Greater)**, UB9 5AT, ENG.
(T) 01895 831939 (F) 01895 835742
(E) aa.oliver@zoom.co.uk
Speciality: Auto Suggestion, Bach Remedies, Cognitive Therapy, Colour Therapy, Complementary Therapy, Counselling, Crystal Healing, Drama Therapy, Faith Healing, Floral Essence Therapy, Gestalt Therapy, Group Therapy, Healer, Healing Therapy, Herbal Medicine, Holistic Healing, Homeopathy, Hypnosis, Hypnotherapy, Indian Head Massage, Life Style Coaching, Meditation, Naturopathy, Nutritional Therapy, Oriental Diagnosis, Phytotherapy, Rogerian Therapy, Spiritual Healing, Stress Therapy, Transactional Analysis, Vibrational Therapy, Visualisation Therapy, Ying & Yang.
● **Owner/Therapist** Ms A Oliver Q: DABCH. M: CAH.
B (Ref:HM21226)

**WEST LONDON PSYCHOTHERAPY**

**West London Psychotherapy Clinic**, 120 Church Rd, Hannell, London, **London (Greater)**,



Key: B Mind-Body Medicine C Complementary Medicine H Self Help Treatment M Medicinal Therapy O Oriental Medicine P Postural Therapy S Manipulative Structural Therapy T Touch Therapy

W7 3BE, ENG.
(T) 020 8567 7411
(E) jzpearson71@redroof10.freeserve.co.uk
(W) www.psychotherapyclinic.co.uk
Speciality: Psychotherapy. ✔
● **Psychotherapist** Ms J Pearson Q: BAP. M: BCP.
[B] Yrs. Est.: 5 (Ref:HM21227)

## WEST LONDON YOGA SHALA

**West London Yoga Shala**, 134 Gloucester Trce, London, **London (Greater)**, W2 6HR, ENG.
(T) 020 7402 2217
(E) wly@freent.com
(W) www.yogashala.co.uk
Speciality: Yoga. ✔
● **Hatha Yoga Instructor**
Mr W Robertson Q: RGN.
[P] Yrs. Est.: 6 (Ref:HM21228)

## WEST MIDLAND HYPNOTHERAPY

**West Midland Hypnotherapy**, 85 Priory Rd, Dudley, **Midlands (West)**, DY1 4EY, ENG.
(T) 01384 238178
Speciality: Absent Healing, Auto Suggestion, Bach Remedies, Counselling, Hypnosis, Hypnotherapy, Life Style Coaching, Reiki, Stress Therapy, Past Life Regression, Relaxation, Self Hypnosis for Relaxation.
● **Therapist** Mr D Westwood Q: MNCH. M: NCH.
[B] Yrs. Est.: 18 (Ref:HM21229)

## WEST MOORS CHIROPRACTIC CLINIC

**West Moors Chiropractic Clinic**, Unit 3 Crossways, 175 Station Rd, West Moors, Ferndown, **Dorset**, BH22 0HT, ENG.
(T) 01202 870852
Speciality: Chiropractic. ✔
● **Owner** Dr H Hopkins Q: DC. M: BCA.
[P] Yrs. Est.: 11 (Ref:HM21230)

## WEST OF ENGLAND ALOE VERA CTRE

**West Of England Aloe Vera Centre**, The Piece, Cutwell, Tetbury, **Gloucestershire**, GL8 8EB, ENG.
(T) 01666 504718 (F) 01666 505301
Speciality: Nutritional Therapy, Vitamin Therapy.
● **Owner** Mr J Townsend
[C] (Ref:HM21231)

## WEST OF ENGLAND PSYCHOLOGY SVS

**West Of England Psychology Services**, Honiton Rd, South Molton, **Devon**, EX36 4JA, ENG.
(T) 01769 573775
Speciality: Psychology.
● **Owner** Mrs L Faulkner
[B] (Ref:HM21232)

## WEST PARADE OSTEOPATHS

**West Parade Osteopaths**, 102 West Prde, Lincoln, **Lincolnshire**, LN1 1JZ, ENG.
(T) 01522 537103
Speciality: Osteopathy.
● **Senior Partner** Mr S Tyreman
[P] [S] [T] (Ref:HM21233)

## WEST PARK STRESS MANAGEMENT

**West Park Stress Management**, 23 Kepstorn Rd, Leeds, **Yorkshire (West)**, LS16 5HT, ENG.
(T) 01132 788673
Speciality: Hypnosis.
● **Owner** Mr S Kilner
[B] (Ref:HM21234)

## WEST ROAD CHIROPODY CENTRE

**West Road Chiropody Centre**, 243A Hampstead Rd, Newcastle Upon Tyne, **Tyne and Wear**, NE4 8TP, ENG.
(T) 01912 567464
Speciality: Chiropodists (Podiatrists).
● **Owner** Mr D Sturrock
[S] (Ref:HM21235)

## WEST STREET OSTEO PRACTICE

**West Street Osteopathic Practice**, 8a West St, Blandford Forum, **Dorset**, DT11 7AW, ENG.
(T) 01258 455194
Speciality: Osteopathy.
● **Owner** Mr R Hill
[P] [S] [T] (Ref:HM21236)

## WEST STREET THERAPY CENTRE

**West Street Therapy Centre**, 43 West St, Reading, **Berkshire**, RG1 1TZ, ENG.
(T) 01189 391833
Speciality: Complementary Medicines & Therapy.
[M] (Ref:HM21237)

## WEST THAMES

**West Thames**, 31 Hounslow Rd, Twickenham, **London (Greater)**, TW2 7BZ, ENG.
(T) 020 8893 8676
Speciality: Physiotherapy.
[P] [S] [T] (Ref:HM21238)

## WEST WIRRAL CHIROPRACTIC

**West Wirral Chiropractic Clinic**, 390 Pensby Rd, Heswall, Wirral, **Merseyside**, CH61 9NH, ENG.
(T) 01516 485000
Speciality: Aromatherapy, Chiropractic. ✔
● **Owner/Chiropractor** Mr F McBride Q: BSc (Chiro), DC. M: BCA, GCC.
● **Practice Manager** Ms A Burgess
[P] Yrs. Est.: 5 (Ref:HM21239)

## WEST WYCOMBE CHIRO CLINIC

**Chiroplus**, 53 West Wycombe Rd, High Wycombe, **Buckinghamshire**, HP11 2LR, ENG.
(T) 01494 558061 (F) 01494 448990
Speciality: Chiropractic. ✔
● **Owner** Dr K Cairns Q: BSc, DC(USA). M: CCEP.
● **Chiropractor** Dr A Bamber Q: DC. M: CCEP.
[P] Yrs. Est.: 10 (Ref:HM21240)

## WEST WYCOMBE CHIROPRACTIC

**West Wycombe Chiropractic Clinic**, 53 West Wycombe Rd, High Wycombe, **Buckinghamshire**, HP11 2LR, ENG.
(T) 01494 558061
Speciality: Chiropractic.
[P] [S] [T] (Ref:HM21241)

## WEST YORKSHIRE CLINIC

**West Yorkshire Clinic Of Complementary Medicine**, 2 Walmer Villas, Manningham Lane, Bradford, **Yorkshire (West)**, BD8 7ET, ENG.
(T) 01274 547020 (F) 01274 547020
(E) wyclinic@csi.com
Speciality: Acupressure, Acupuncture, Complementary Therapy, Manipulation, Massage (Therapeutic), Moxibustion, Osteopathy, Shiatsu, Stress Therapy. ✔
● **Osteopath** Mrs J Ashley Q: DO. M: GOsC.
● **Acupuncture Associate** Mr B Nolan M: BAcC, RSS.
● **Clinical Director** Ms Samuel M: BAcC, RCHM.
● **Osteopath** Mr J McEwen Q: DO. M: GOsC.
[C] Yrs. Est.: 14 (Ref:HM21242)

## WEST YORKSHIRE M S THRPY CTRE

**Multiple Sclerosis Therapy Centre (West Yorkshire)**, Airdale, Leeds Rd, Rawdon, Leeds, **Yorkshire (West)**, LS19 6JY, ENG.
(T) 01132 504528 (F) 01132 504528
(W) www.mstherapy.org.uk
Speciality: Complementary Medicines & Therapy.
[C] [H] Yrs. Est.: 16 (Ref:HM21243)

## WEST YORKSHIRE PHYSIO CENTRE

**West Yorkshire Physiotherapy Centre**, The Old School House, Town Gate, Wyke, Bradford, **Yorkshire (West)**, BD12 9PA, ENG.
(T) 01274 693591
Speciality: Acupuncture, Physiotherapy, Sports Massage. ✔
● **Physiotherapist/Owner**
Ms J Midgley Q: Dip.App.Sports, MCSP, SRP. M: CSP.
● **Physiotherapist** Ms K Helliwell Q: MCSP, SRP. M: CSP.
● **Physiotherapist** Ms G Cannon Q: MCSP, SRP. M: CSP.
● **Physiotherapist** Ms K May Q: BSc, MCSP, SRP. M: CSP.
● **Physiotherapist** Ms R Wilson Q: BSc (Hons), MCSP, SRP. M: CSP.
[S] (Ref:HM21244)

## WEST, DAVID

**David West**, Health Hydro, Milton Rd, Swindon, **Wiltshire**, SN1 5JA, ENG.
(T) 01793 465631
Speciality: Alexander Technique.
[P] [S] (Ref:HM21245)

## WEST, DAVID

**David West**, 12 Bennett Hill Cl, Wootton Bassett, **Wiltshire**, SN4 8LR, ENG.
(E) david@pdwest.freeserve.co.uk
Speciality: Alexander Technique, Chiropractic.
● **McTimoney Chiropractor** Mr D West Q: AMC, MMCA. M: MCA.
[S] Yrs. Est.: 2 (Ref:HM21246)

## WEST, DENISE

**Denise West**, 74 High St, Sturminster Marshall, Wimborne, **Dorset**, BH21 4AY, ENG.
(T) 01258 858413
Speciality: Chiropodists (Podiatrists).
[S] (Ref:HM21247)

## WEST, DIANA

**Diana West**, 39 Hazel Rd, Loughborough, **Leicestershire**, LE11 2JQ, ENG.
(T) 01509 827269
Speciality: Reflexology.
[S] [T] (Ref:HM21248)

## WEST, JOHN A

**John A West**, 6a Whitehill Cl, Cambridge, **Cambridgeshire**, CB5 8NE, ENG.
(T) 01223 248018
Speciality: Hypnosis.
● **Owner** Mr J West
[B] (Ref:HM21249)

## WEST, JOY

**Joy West**, 46 Beechwood Avenue, Coventry, **Midlands (West)**, CV5 6QG, ENG.
(T) 024 7667 5775
Speciality: Complementary Medicines & Therapy.
[C] [M] (Ref:HM21250)

## WEST, KATHRYN

**Kathryn West**, 1-3 Berry Rd, Newquay, **Cornwall**, TR7 1SF, ENG.
(T) 01637 878645
Speciality: Osteopathy.
[P] [S] [T] (Ref:HM21251)

## WEST, LAINA

**Laina West**, 30 The Willows, Newington, Sittingbourne, **Kent**, ME9 7LS, ENG.
(T) 01795 844995
Speciality: Reflexology.
[S] [T] (Ref:HM21252)

## WEST, MARCUS

**Marcus West**, High Bank, 45 Cross Lane, Findon, Worthing, **Sussex (West)**, BN14 0UB, ENG.
(T) 01903 877039
Speciality: Psychotherapy.
[B] (Ref:HM21253)

## WEST, MARIE-CLAIRE

**Marie-Claire West**, 1 Knowsley Rd, Hoole, Chester, **Cheshire**, CH2 3RL, ENG.
(T) 01244 320600
Speciality: Reflexology.
[S] [T] (Ref:HM21254)

## WEST, TERENCE

**Terence West**, 76 Northend Rd, Erith, **Kent**, DA8 3QH, ENG.
(T) 01322 349189
Speciality: Complementary Medicines & Therapy.
● **Owner** Mr T West
[C] [M] (Ref:HM21255)

## WESTACOTT, EILEEN

**Eileen Westacott**, Yarrow Cl, Horsham, **Sussex (West)**, RH12 5FP, ENG.
(T) 01403 242494
Speciality: Aromatherapy, Massage (Therapeutic). ✔
● **Aromatherapist** Mrs E Westacott Q: AOC, MGCP. M: AOC, GCP.
[C] Yrs. Est.: 7 (Ref:HM21256)



Key continued: Yrs.Est: Years Established Q: Qualifications M: Professional Membership ✔ Indemnity Insurance [card] Accept Credit Cards

### WESTBANK NATURAL HEALTH CENTRE
**Westbank Natural Health Centre**, Cash Feus, Strathmiglo, Cupar, **Fife**, KY14 7QP, SCO.
(T) 01337 860233
Speciality: Complementary Medicines & Therapy.
C M (**Ref:**HM21257)

### WESTBURY CHIROPRACTIC
**Westbury Chiropractic & Homeopathic Clinic**, Angel Mill, Edward St, Westbury, **Wiltshire**, BA13 3BD, ENG.
(T) 01373 859900
(W) www.chirojones.co.uk
Speciality: Chiropractic, Homeopathy. ✔
● **Owner** Helle Jones Q: DC. M: BCA.
● **Partner** Mr R Jones Q: DC. M: BCA.
P Yrs. Est.: 3 (**Ref:**HM21258)

### WESTBURY CHIROPRACTIC CLINIC
**Westbury Chiropractic Clinic**, 3 Westbury Mews, Bellevue Cottages, Westbury-On-Trym, Bristol, BS9 3QA, ENG.
(T) 01179 623135 (F) 01179 077831
Speciality: Chiropractic.
P S T (**Ref:**HM21259)

### WESTBURY REFLEXOLOGY CLINIC
**Westbury Reflexology Clinic**, Royce Clinic, St Thomas Rd, Trowbridge, **Wiltshire**, BA13 3NZ, ENG.
(T) 01373 822915
Speciality: Reflexology. ✔
● **Reflexologist** Ms A Lewis
M Yrs. Est.: 7 (**Ref:**HM21260)

### WESTCOTT, C N
**C N Westcott**, 22 Larch Cl, New Inn, Pontypool, **Monmouthshire**, NP4 0RT, WAL.
(T) 01495 758860
Speciality: Chiropodists (Podiatrists).
S (**Ref:**HM21261)

### WESTCOTT, CHARLES
**Charles Westcott**, 56 Wellsway, Bath, **Somerset**, BA2 4SA, ENG.
(T) 01225 460480
Speciality: Chiropractic.
● **Owner** Mr C Westcott
P S T (**Ref:**HM21262)

### WESTERN CHIROPRACTIC CLINIC
**Western Chiropractic Clinic**, 15 Combe Pk, Bath, **Somerset**, BA1 3NP, ENG.
(T) 01225 423333 (F) 01225 42345
(E) janecourtis@btinternet.com
Speciality: Acupuncture, Aromatherapy, Chiropractic, Kinesiology, Manipulation, Massage (Therapeutic), Sacro-Occipital Technique (S.O.T.), Chiropractic Craniopathy, Equine Chiropractic. ✔
● **Chiropractor** Dr D Marks Q: BCA, BSc (Chiro), DC, MCC. M: BCA, GCC.
● **Aromatherapist/Massage** Jane Courtis M: BFMT.
● **Chiropractor** Dr G Courtis Q: BCA, DC. M: BCA, CC, GCC.
P S Yrs. Est.: 7 (**Ref:**HM21263)

### WESTERN COLLEGE-ALT THERAPY
**Western College Of Alternative Therapy**, 15 Cedar Cl, Chard, **Somerset**, TA20 1DB, ENG.
(T) 01460 61777
Speciality: Complementary Medicines & Therapy.
C M (**Ref:**HM21264)

### WESTERN, G
**Mr G Western**, 317 Plumstead High St, London, **London (Greater)**, SE18 1JX, ENG.
(T) 020 8310 0031
Speciality: Aromatherapy, Cranial Osteopathy, Osteopathy. ✔
● **Osteopath** Mr G Western M: GOsC.
S Yrs. Est.: 14 (**Ref:**HM21265)

### WESTERN, GRAME
**Grame Western**, The Bexley Osteopathic Clinic, 16A High St, Bexley, **Kent**, DA5 1AD, ENG.
(T) 01322 529326
Speciality: Osteopathy.
P S T (**Ref:**HM21266)

### WESTGATE HOUSE CHIROPODY
**Westgate House Chiropody**, Westgate House, Park Rd, Peterborough, **Cambridgeshire**, PE1 2TA, ENG.
(T) 01733 565622
Speciality: Chiropodists (Podiatrists).
S (**Ref:**HM21267)

### WESTGATE OSTEOPATHIC PRACTICE
**Westgate Osteopathic Practice**, 43 Station Rd, Westgate-on-Sea, **Kent**, CT8 8QY, ENG.
(T) 01843 833055
Speciality: Osteopathy.
● **Owner** Mr H Cole
P S T (**Ref:**HM21268)

### WESTLAKE, D E
**D E Westlake**, 9 Gosditch St, Cirencester, **Gloucestershire**, GL7 2AG, ENG.
(T) 01285 653624
Speciality: Physiotherapy.
P S T (**Ref:**HM21269)

### WESTLAKE, DAVID
**David Westlake**, 16 Keyberry Park, Newton Abbot, **Devon**, TQ12 1BZ, ENG.
(T) 01626 353334 (F) 01626 353334
Speciality: Chiropractors.
● **Senior Partner** Mr F Verwey
P S T (**Ref:**HM21270)

### WESTLAKE, ROSEMARY
**Rosemary Westlake**, Natural Health Clinic, 98 Cathedral Rd, Cardiff, **Glamorgan (Vale of)**, CF11 9LP, WAL.
(T) 029 2022 2221
Speciality: Herbalists.
● **Practice Manager** Mrs L Powell
M (**Ref:**HM21271)

### WESTLAKE-GUY, C
**C Westlake-Guy**, 13 The Spinney, Heswall, Wirral, **Merseyside**, CH60 3SU, ENG.
(T) 01513 424540
Speciality: Acupuncture.
● **Owner** Ms C Westlake-Guy
O (**Ref:**HM21272)

### WESTMINSTER ALEXANDER CENTRE
**Westminster Alexander Centre**, 8 Hop Gardens, London, **London (Greater)**, WC2N 4EH, ENG.
(T) 020 7240 2118
Speciality: Alexander Technique.
● **Practitioner** Mr J Hunter
● **Practitioner** Mrs D Magonet
P S (**Ref:**HM21273)

### WESTMINSTER NTRL HEALTH CLINIC
**Westminster Natural Health Clinic**, 34-36A Warwick Way, London, **London (Greater)**, SW1V 1RY, ENG.
(T) 020 7834 0861
Speciality: Osteopathy.
● **Owner** Mr M Cozzi
P S T (**Ref:**HM21274)

### WESTMINSTER PASTORAL FOUND
**Westminster Pastoral Foundation**, 23 Kensington Sq, London, **London (Greater)**, W8 5HN, ENG.
(T) 020 7937 6224
Speciality: Complementary Medicines & Therapy.
M (**Ref:**HM21275)

### WESTMINSTER PHYSIO CENTRE
**Westminster Physiotherapy Centre**, 34-36A Warwick Way, London, **London (Greater)**, SW1V 1RY, ENG.
(T) 020 7976 6440
Speciality: Physiotherapy.
P S T (**Ref:**HM21276)

### WESTOE PRACTICE
**Westoe Practice**, 106a Westoe Rd, South Shields, **Tyne and Wear**, NE33 3PF, ENG.
(T) 01914 250101
Speciality: Biomechanics, Chiropody, Nail Surgery, Podiatry. ✔
● **Chiropodist (Podiatrist)** Mr D Glozier Q: BSc (Hons), M.S.C.P.
M Yrs. Est.: 6 (**Ref:**HM21277)

### WESTON, JOHN
**John Weston - Osteopath**, The Surgery, 1 Chapel St, Pelsall, Walsall, **Midlands (West)**, WS3 4LN, ENG.
(T) 01922 685278
Speciality: Acupuncture, Bonesetting, Complementary Therapy, Electrotherapy, Manipulation, Massage (Therapeutic), Micro Manipulation, Osteopathy, Postural Integration. ✔
● **Osteopath** Mr J Weston Q: DO. M: BOA.
S Yrs. Est.: 17 (**Ref:**HM21278)

### WESTON, JOHN
**John Weston - Osteopath**, Tim Vanes Opticians, 6 Church St, Shifnal, **Shropshire**, TF11 9AA, ENG.
(T) 01952 463383 (F) 01952 461387
Speciality: Acupressure, Bonesetting, Electrotherapy, Manipulation, Massage (Therapeutic), Micro Manipulation, Osteopathy. ✔
● **Osteopath** Mr J Weston Q: DO. M: BOA.
S Yrs. Est.: 17 (**Ref:**HM21279)

### WESTON, JOHN M
**John M Weston**, 7 Twinney Lane, Ellerdine, Telford, **Shropshire**, TF6 6QQ, ENG.
(T) 01952 541790
Speciality: Osteopathy.
P S T (**Ref:**HM21280)

### WESTON, JULIE
**Julie Weston**, 12 Regent Rd, Wallasey, **Merseyside**, CH45 8JU, ENG.
(T) 01516 389132
Speciality: Acupuncture.
● **Owner** Mr P Lloyd
O (**Ref:**HM21281)

### WESTON, M E
**M E Weston**, 49 Ashfield, Stantonbury, Milton Keynes, **Buckinghamshire**, MK14 6AU, ENG.
(T) 01908 316243 (F) 01908 316243
Speciality: Physiotherapy.
● **Owner** Mrs M Weston
P S T (**Ref:**HM21282)

### WESTON, SOPHIE
**Sophie Weston**, 37 Hemingford Rd, Cambridge, **Cambridgeshire**, CB1 3BY, ENG.
(T) 01223 562667
Speciality: Reflexology.
S T (**Ref:**HM21283)

### WESTPORT AROMATHERAPY
**Westport Aromatherapy**, 41 Templehill, Troon, **Ayrshire (South)**, KA10 6BQ, SCO.
(T) 01292 319412
Speciality: Aromatherapy.
● **Owner** Mrs V Norris
M O (**Ref:**HM21284)

### WESTWOOD, ANGELA
**Angela Westwood**, 6 Kemshead Avenue, Birmingham, **Midlands (West)**, B31 2SQ, ENG.
(T) 01214 755328
Speciality: Metamorphic Therapy, Reflexology, Reiki, VRT- Virtual Reflex Therapy. ✔
● **Reflexologist** Mrs A Westwood Q: TCCAR.
M Yrs. Est.: 14 (**Ref:**HM21285)

### WESTWOOD, CHRISTINE
**Christine Westwood**, 25 Kite House, 50 Meyrick Rd, London, **London (Greater)**, SW11 2NJ, ENG.
(T) 020 7585 3445
Speciality: Complementary Medicines & Therapy.
C M (**Ref:**HM21286)

### WESTWOOD, TERRY
**Terry Westwood**, 1 Linden Gr, Great Linford, Milton Keynes, **Buckinghamshire**, MK14 5HF, ENG.
(T) 01908 674062
Speciality: Counselling, Hypnosis, Hypnotherapy, Stress Therapy. ✔
● **Owner** Mr T Westwood M: HA.
B Yrs. Est.: 10 (**Ref:**HM21287)

### WETHERALL, P
**P Wetherall**, 26 Canford Cliffs Avenue, Poole,

Key: B Mind-Body Medicine C Complementary Medicine H Self Help Treatment M Medicinal Therapy O Oriental Medicine P Postural Therapy S Manipulative Structural Therapy T Touch Therapy

**Dorset**, BH14 9QN, ENG.
(T) 01202 708894
Speciality: Physiotherapy.
● **Owner** Mrs P Wetherall
P S T (Ref:HM21288)

### WETHERALL, STUART

**Stuart Wetherall**, Moulsham Mill, Parkway, Chelmsford, **Essex**, CM2 7PX, ENG.
(T) 01245 600056 (F) 01245 346333
Speciality: Counselling, Hypnosis, Hypnotherapy, Sedona Method. ✔
● **Hypnotherapist** Mr S Weatherall Q: DHP (NC), NLP.
B Yrs. Est.: 17 (Ref:HM21289)

### WETHERBY PHYSIO PRACTICE

**Wetherby Physiotherapy Practice**, The New Medical Centre, Crossley St, Wetherby, **Yorkshire (West)**, LS22 6RT, ENG.
(T) 01937 588329
Speciality: Acupuncture, Physiotherapy. ✔
● **Physiotherapist** Ms N Thrush Q: MCSP, SRP. M: CSP.
● **Practice Manager** Mrs J Ryder
● **Physiotherapist** Ms B Milligan Q: MCSP, SRP. M: CSP.
S Yrs. Est.: 5 (Ref:HM21290)

### WETHERELL, PAULINE

**Pauline Wetherell**, 29 Stanley Buildings, Clarence Passage, London, **London (Greater)**, NW1 2TG, ENG.
(T) 020 7837 6932
Speciality: Alexander Technique.
● **Owner** Ms P Wetherell
P S (Ref:HM21291)

### WETHERELL, PAULINE

**Pauline Wetherell**, Imperial College Health Centre, 14 Princes Gardens, London, **London (Greater)**, SW7 1NA, ENG.
(T) 020 7584 6301
Speciality: Alexander Technique.
P S (Ref:HM21292)

### WEYBRIDGE CHIROPRACTIC CLINIC

**Weybridge Chiropractic Clinic Ltd**, Care Of The Portmore Practice, 4 Balfour Rd, Weybridge, **Surrey**, KT13 8HD, ENG.
(T) 01932 859006
Speciality: Chiropractors. ✔
● **Chiropractor/Clinic Director** Mr A Mazur Q: BSc (Chiro), DC. M: BCA, GCC.
● **Chiropractor/Clinic Director** Mr A Kerrigan Q: BA, BSc (Chiro), DC. M: BCA, GCC.
P S T Yrs. Est.: 5 (Ref:HM21293)

### WEYMOUTH CHIROPRACTIC CLINIC

**Weymouth Chiropractic Clinic**, 425A Chickerall Rd, Weymouth, **Dorset**, DT4 0BN, ENG.
(T) 01305 768393
Speciality: Chiropractic.
P S T (Ref:HM21294)

### WHALEY, IAN

**Ian Whaley**, 14 Kingsland, Newcastle Upon Tyne, **Tyne and Wear**, NE2 3AL, ENG.
(T) 01912 818032
Speciality: Alexander Technique.
P S (Ref:HM21295)

### WHALLEY, J

**J Whalley**, 23 Prospect, Corsham, **Wiltshire**, SN13 9AD, ENG.
(T) 01249 712248
Speciality: Chiropodists (Podiatrists).
● **Owner** Mrs J Whalley
S (Ref:HM21296)

### WHARAM, J

**J Wharam**, Green Shutters, Bullbeggars Lane, Woking, **Surrey**, GU21 4SQ, ENG.
(T) 01483 721355
Speciality: Herbal Medicine.
M (Ref:HM21297)

### WHARMBY, D

**D Wharmby**, 1 The Crescent, Stockport, **Cheshire**, SK3 8SQ, ENG.
(T) 01614 839826
Speciality: Chiropodists (Podiatrists).
● **Owner** Mr D Wharmby
S (Ref:HM21298)

### WHARTON, A R

**A R Wharton**, 146 County Rd, Ormskirk, **Lancashire**, L39 1NN, ENG.
(T) 01695 575103
Speciality: Chiropractors.
● **Owner** A Wharton
P S T (Ref:HM21299)

### WHARTON, ALINE

**Aline Wharton**, 145 St Marys Rd, Market Harborough, **Leicestershire**, LE16 7DT, ENG.
(T) 01858 434314
Speciality: Reflexology.
● **Owner** Ms A Wharton
S T (Ref:HM21300)

### WHARTON, COLIN

**Colin Wharton**, 23 Craig Drive, Hillingdon, Uxbridge, **London (Greater)**, UB8 3HL, ENG.
(T) 01895 420543
Speciality: Chiropodists (Podiatrists).
S (Ref:HM21301)

### WHARTON, SUE

**Sue Wharton**, Main Rd, Radcliffe-On-Trent, Nottingham, **Nottinghamshire**, NG12 2GD, ENG.
(T) 01159 333181
Speciality: Complementary Medicines & Therapy.
● **Owner** Mrs B Bilkhu
M (Ref:HM21302)

### WHATLEY, JUDITH

**Judith Whatley**, Ty-Mari, Heolgerrig Rd, Merthyr Tydfil, **Glamorgan (Vale of)**, CF48 1SB, WAL.
(T) 01685 370096
Speciality: Nutritional Therapy, Reflexology.
S T (Ref:HM21303)

### WHATLING, E P

**E P Whatling**, Blue Cedar, 1 Dorset Drive, Shaftesbury Rd, Woking, **Surrey**, GU22 7DX, ENG.
(T) 01483 765530
Speciality: Physiotherapy.
● **Owner** Mrs E Whatling
P S T (Ref:HM21304)

### WHATLING, M J

**M J Whatling**, Littleover Chiropractic Clinic, 569A Burton Rd, Derby, **Derbyshire**, DE23 6FW, ENG.
(T) 01332 768408
Speciality: Chiropractic.
● **Owner** Mr M Whatling
P S T (Ref:HM21305)

### WHATLING, NICOLA

**Nicola Whatling**, 4 Caling Croft, New Ash Green, Longfield, **Kent**, DA3 8PX, ENG.
(T) 07958 448242
Speciality: Reflexology.
S T (Ref:HM21306)

### WHEADON, LOUISE

**Louise Wheadon**, 137 Magdalen Rd, Oxford, **Oxfordshire**, OX4 1RJ, ENG.
(T) 01865 396939
Speciality: Aromatherapy.
● **Owner** Mr M Franklin
M O (Ref:HM21307)

### WHEATLEY COMP THERAPY

**Wheatley Complementary Therapy Clinic**, 45 High St, Wheatley, Oxford, **Oxfordshire**, OX33 1XX, ENG.
(T) 08009 701559 (F) 01865 556306
(W) www.aromapost.com
Speciality: Aromatherapy, Bach Remedies, Complementary Therapy, Counselling, Holistic Healing, Homeopathy, Hopi Ear Candles, Indian Head Massage, Kinesiology, Massage (Therapeutic), Reflexology, Remedial Massage. ✔ [credit card]
● **Therapist** Ms J Evans Q: ITEC, MAR. M: AoR.
● **Therapist** Ms R Murphy Q: MAR. M: AoR.
● **Therapist** Ms C Donnelly Q: MAR, SRN. M: AoR.
● **Therapist** G Blackburn Q: MAR. M: AoR.
C M Yrs. Est.: 4 (Ref:HM21308)

### WHEATLEY, F

**F Wheatley**, 29 Walters Row, Dunvant, Swansea, SA2 7TB, WAL.
(T) 01792 290458
Speciality: Aromatherapy.
● **Owner** Mrs F Wheatley
M O (Ref:HM21309)

### WHEATLEY, RON

**Ron Wheatley**, 29 Basilon Rd, Bexleyheath, **Kent**, DA7 4RQ, ENG.
(T) 020 8303 6154
Speciality: Clairvoyants & Palmists.
● **Owner** Mr R Wheatley
B (Ref:HM21310)

### WHEATMAN, G H P

**G H P Wheatman**, Pinecopse, Windmill Rd, Bradfield, Manningtree, **Essex**, CO11 2QN, ENG.
(T) 01206 392683
Speciality: Hypnosis.
● **Owner** Mr G Wheatman
B (Ref:HM21311)

### WHEATON, JOHN (DR)

**Reverend Dr John Wheaton**, Brookdale, Quarry Lane, Exeter, **Devon**, EX2 5JR, ENG.
(T) 01392 275878
Speciality: Acupuncture.
● **Owner** Rev J Wheaton
O (Ref:HM21312)

### WHEEL OF LIFE CENTRE

**Wheel Of Life Centre (The)**, 6 North Malvern Rd, Malvern, **Worcestershire**, WR14 4LT, ENG.
(T) 01684 565586
Speciality: Complementary Medicines & Therapy.
● **Owner** Mrs J Sherr
M (Ref:HM21313)

### WHEELER, D

**D Wheeler**, 108 Veronica Gardens, London, **London (Greater)**, SW16 5JS, ENG.
(T) 020 8764 3048
Speciality: Electrolysis.
T (Ref:HM21314)

### WHEELER, J

**J Wheeler**, 2a St James Trce, Selby, **Yorkshire (North)**, YO8 4HL, ENG.
(T) 01757 704152
Speciality: Osteopathy.
● **Owner** Mr J Wheeler
P S T (Ref:HM21315)

### WHEELER, M A

**M A Wheeler**, 22 Hockley Rd, Rayleigh, **Essex**, SS6 8EB, ENG.
(T) 01268 742534 (F) 01268 772142
Speciality: Acupressure, Biomechanics, Chiropody, Nail Surgery, Osteopathy, Podiatry, Bunion Surgery, Hammer Toe Surgery. ✔
● **Podiatrist** Ms J Wade Q: M.S.C.P., S.R.Ch. M: S.C.P., S.R.Ch.
● **Podiatric Surgeon** Miss M Wheeler Q: B.A.Ch.P. M: S.C.P., S.R.Ch.
C Yrs. Est.: 60 (Ref:HM21316)

### WHEELER, M A

**M A Wheeler**, 4 Somerset Avenue, Rochford, **Essex**, SS4 1QA, ENG.
(T) 01702 544336
Speciality: Biomechanics, Chiropody, Nail Surgery, Podiatry, Bunion Surgery, Hammer Toe Surgery. ✔
● **Podiatric Surgeon** Miss M Wheeler Q: B.A.Ch.P. M: S.C.P., S.R.Ch.
C Yrs. Est.: 35 (Ref:HM21317)

### WHEELER, ROBERT

**Robert Wheeler**, 26 Wrafton Rd, Braunton, **Devon**, EX33 2BT, ENG.
(T) 01271 814087
Speciality: Osteopathy.
P S T (Ref:HM21318)

### WHEEN, WILLIAM

**William Wheen**, Preston Park Clinic, 207-209 Ditchling Rd, Brighton, **Sussex (East)**, BN1 6JB, ENG.
(T) 01273 504488
Speciality: Chiropractors.
● **Owner** Mr W Wheen
P S T (Ref:HM21319)


Key continued: Yrs.Est: Years Established Q: Qualifications M: Professional Membership ✔ Indemnity Insurance [credit card] Accept Credit Cards

## WHEEN, WILLIAM
**William Wheen**, 94 St James's St, Brighton, **Sussex (East)**, BN2 1TP, ENG.
(T) 01273 672952
Speciality: Chiropractors.
● **Owner** Mr L Moore
P S T (Ref:HM21320)

## WHEILAND, M
**M Wheiland**, Beverley Clinic, 362 Coombe Lane, London, **London (Greater)**, SW20 0RJ, ENG.
(T) 020 8241 2515
Speciality: Acupuncture.
O (Ref:HM21321)

## WHEILDON, SARAH J
**Sarah J Wheildon**, 75 Victoria Rd East, Thornton, **Lancashire**, FY5 5BU, ENG.
(T) 01253 822948
Speciality: Osteopathy.
● **Owner** Miss S Wheildon
P S T (Ref:HM21322)

## WHELAN, BERNADETTE
**Whelan Bernadette LIC AC M B A C C**, 3 Ballyannon Ct Coolbawn, Midleton, **County Cork**, IRE.
(T) 021 4631 119
Speciality: Physiotherapy.
P S T (Ref:HM21323)

## WHELAN, P
**Mrs P Whelan**, 19 Park Farm Rd, Bromley, **Kent**, BR1 2PE, ENG.
(T) 020 8295 0626
Speciality: Reflexology.
S (Ref:HM21324)

## WHELDON, KATHERINE
**Katherine Wheldon**, **Buckinghamshire**, MK15, ENG.
(T) 01908 675922
Speciality: Bach Remedies.
M (Ref:HM21325)

## WHENT, NICKY
**Aromatherapy & Reflexology By Nicky Whent**, Tudor Briars, St Johns Rd, Farnham, **Surrey**, GU9 8NT, ENG.
(T) 01252 717102
Speciality: Reflexology.
S T (Ref:HM21326)

## WHETSTONE CHIROPRACTIC CLINIC
**Whetstone Chiropractic Clinic**, 88 Oakleigh Rd North, London, **London (Greater)**, N20 9EZ, ENG.
(T) 020 8446 7314
Speciality: Chiropractic.
P S T (Ref:HM21327)

## WHEWELL, ANITA
**Anita Whewell**, 29 Parkside Rd, Lytham St. Annes, **Lancashire**, FY8 3SZ, ENG.
(T) 01253 728601
Speciality: Aromatherapy.
M O (Ref:HM21328)

## WHICKER, EILEEN
**Eileen Whicker**, 14 Weston Park, Thames Ditton, **Surrey**, KT7 0HQ, ENG.
(T) 020 8398 4309
Speciality: Homeopathy.
M (Ref:HM21329)

## WHIPPY, TESSA
**Tessa Whippy**, 19 Mildmay Rd, Lewes, **Sussex (East)**, BN7 1PJ, ENG.
(T) 01273 478688
Speciality: Reflexology.
S T (Ref:HM21330)

## WHISHAW, M G
**M G Whishaw**, 23 Bassett Crescent West, Southampton, **Hampshire**, SO16 7EB, ENG.
(T) 023 8079 1001
Speciality: Physiotherapy.
P S T (Ref:HM21331)

## WHITBY, ALAN R
**Alan R Whitby**, 30 High St, Trelewis, Treharris, **Glamorgan (Vale of)**, CF46 6AB, WAL.
(T) 01443 412245
Speciality: Chiropodists (Podiatrists).
● **Owner** Mr A Whitby
S (Ref:HM21332)

## WHITBY, LORRAINE
**Lorraine Whitby**, 9 Mole Abbey Gardens, West Molesey, **Surrey**, KT8 1QD, ENG.
(T) 020 8979 9837
Speciality: Chiropodists (Podiatrists).
● **Owner** Mrs L Whitby
S (Ref:HM21333)

## WHITBY, S E
**Mrs S E Whitby**, 10 Sargeant Avenue, Stoke-On-Trent, **Staffordshire**, ST6 7LD, ENG.
(T) 01782 834948
Speciality: Acupuncture, Physiotherapy. ✔
● **Owner/Physiotherapist**
Mrs S Whitby Q: MCSP, SRP.
S Yrs. Est.: 26 (Ref:HM21334)

## WHITE CRANE HEALING CENTRE
**White Crane Healing Centre (The)**, 13 St. Georges Mews, London, **London (Greater)**, NW1 8XE, ENG.
(T) 020 7689 0768
Speciality: Herbalists.
● **Owner** Ms A Pavier
C M (Ref:HM21335)

## WHITE EARTH
**White Earth**, 15 The Broadway, Haywards Heath, **Sussex (West)**, RH16 3AQ, ENG.
(T) 01444 414500
Speciality: Complementary Medicines & Therapy.
● **Owner** Mr T Jupp
M (Ref:HM21336)

## WHITE FLOWER CENTRE
**White Flower Centre (The)**, 34 Meadowside, Mosterton, Beaminster, **Dorset**, DT8 3LP, ENG.
(T) 01308 867022
Speciality: Aromatherapy, Bowen Therapy, Electrolipolysis, Indian Head Massage, Massage (Therapeutic), Reflexology. ✔
● **Natural Therapist**
Frances Branchflower Q: ITEC. M: ITEC.
● **Natural Therapist/Tutor**
Mr K Branchflower Q: ITEC. M: ITEC.
C T Yrs. Est.: 8 (Ref:HM21337)

## WHITE HART LANE THERAPY CENTRE
**White Hart Lane Therapy Centre**, 10 White Hart Lane, London, **London (Greater)**, SW13 0PY, ENG.
(T) 020 8876 9897 (F) 020 8392 9393
(E) whltc@cs.com
Speciality: Acupuncture, Chiropody, Counselling, Massage (Therapeutic), Nutritional Therapy, Osteopathy, Physiotherapy, Reflexology.
● **Owner** Mr C Bird
P S T Yrs. Est.: 7 (Ref:HM21338)

## WHITE HOUSE MEDICO-LEGAL
**White House Medico-Legal (The)**, 3 Sandygate Pk, Sheffield, **Yorkshire (South)**, S10 5TZ, ENG.
(T) 01142 630525 (F) 01142 301795
Speciality: Physiotherapy.
● **Director** Mrs P Howard
P S T (Ref:HM21339)

## WHITE HOUSE PHYSIOTHERAPY
**White House Physiotherapy & Sports Injuries Clinic**, 3 Sandygate Park, Sheffield, **Yorkshire (South)**, S10 5TZ, ENG.
(T) 01142 302030
Speciality: Physiotherapy.
P S T (Ref:HM21340)

## WHITE HOUSE PHYSIOTHERAPY
**White House Physiotherapy & Sports Injuries Clinic**, Shelton House, 4 Bennetthorpe, Doncaster, **Yorkshire (South)**, DN2 6AD, ENG.
(T) 01302 323489 (F) 01302 368609
Speciality: Physiotherapy.
● **Owner** Mr J Howard
P S T (Ref:HM21341)

## WHITE LODGE ASSOCIATION
**White Lodge Association Ltd**, Stockland Green Rd, Tunbridge Wells, **Kent**, TN3 0TT, ENG.
(T) 01892 863166 (F) 01892 861330
Speciality: Complementary Medicines & Therapy.
C M (Ref:HM21342)

## WHITE SPACE
**White Space (The)**, 10 Dover Rd, Sheffield, **Yorkshire (South)**, S11 8RH, ENG.
(T) 01142 687255 (F) 01142 687255
Speciality: Complementary Medicines & Therapy.
● **Owner** Mr J Easten
C M (Ref:HM21343)

## WHITE SUE & MARTIN MAUREEN
**Sue White & Maureen Martin**, 6 Malton Trce, Sedgefield, **County Durham**, TS21 3AP, ENG.
(T) 01740 623096
Speciality: Complementary Medicines & Therapy.
C M (Ref:HM21344)

## WHITE WATER HEALING CENTRE
**White Water Healing Centre**, 79 Victoria Rd, Barking, **Essex**, IG11 8PY, ENG.
(T) 020 8514 5769
(W) www.whitewaterhealingcentre.com
Speciality: Absent Healing, Aura Therapy, Complementary Therapy, Dowsing, Healer, Healing Therapy, Holistic Healing, Meditation, Spiritual Healing, Stress Therapy. ✔
● **Healer** Mr P Richardson Q: NFSH. M: NFSH.
B C (Ref:HM21345)

## WHITE, A C (DR)
**Dr A C White**, 17 Portland Rd, Birmingham, **Midlands (West)**, B16 9HN, ENG.
(T) 01214 542217 (F) 01214 542217
Speciality: Psychiatry.
● **Owner** Dr A White
B (Ref:HM21346)

## WHITE, ANN
**Ann White**, 200 Lydgate Lane, Sheffield, **Yorkshire (South)**, S10 5FS, ENG.
(T) 01142 679085
Speciality: Aromatherapy.
● **Owner** Mrs A White
M O (Ref:HM21347)

## WHITE, C
**C White**, Lamington, Biggar, **Lanarkshire (South)**, ML12 6HW, SCO.
(T) 01899 850227
Speciality: Aromatherapy.
M O (Ref:HM21348)

## WHITE, CHARLES
**Charles White**, 42 Huntriss Row, Scarborough, **Yorkshire (North)**, YO11 2EF, ENG.
(T) 01723 372528
Speciality: Chiropodists (Podiatrists).
● **Partner** Mrs C White
S (Ref:HM21349)

## WHITE, CHRISTINE
**Miss Christine White**, 3 Parkhurst Rd, Bexhill-on-Sea, **Sussex (East)**, TN40 1DF, ENG.
(T) 01424 222545
Speciality: Chiropodists (Podiatrists).
S (Ref:HM21350)

## WHITE, D
**Mr D White**, Cashlin 35 Montague Rd, Bournemouth, **Dorset**, BH5 2EW, ENG.
(T) 01202 427442
Speciality: Alexander Technique.
P S (Ref:HM21351)

## WHITE, DARRELL
**Darrell White**, 5 Moss Lane, Maghull, Liverpool, **Merseyside**, L31 9AE, ENG.
(T) 01515 318214
Speciality: Chiropodists (Podiatrists).
● **Principal** Mr D White
S (Ref:HM21352)

## WHITE, EDWARD
**Edward White**, 2 Albany Rd, Sheffield, **Yorkshire (South)**, S7 1DP, ENG.
(T) 01142 551335
Speciality: Physiotherapy.
● **Owner** Mr E White
P S T (Ref:HM21353)

## WHITE, ELIZABETH
**Elizabeth White**, 57 Broad Acres, Hatfield,

Key: B Mind-Body Medicine, C Complementary Medicine, H Self Help Treatment, M Medicinal Therapy, O Oriental Medicine, P Postural Therapy, S Manipulative Structural Therapy, T Touch Therapy

**Hertfordshire**, AL10 9LE, ENG.
(T) 01707 266117
Speciality: Reflexology.
● **Owner** Mrs E White
**S** **T** (Ref:HM21354)

### WHITE, GRAHAM C

**Graham C White**, 77B South St, Bishop's Stortford, **Hertfordshire**, CM23 2AC, ENG.
(T) 01279 305793
(E) gcwhite@ntlworld.com
Speciality: Aromatherapy, Complementary Therapy, Herbal Medicine, Nutritional Therapy, Phytotherapy. ✔
● **Medical Herbalist** Mr G White Q: BSc. M: NIMH.
**M** Yrs. Est.: 2 (Ref:HM21355)

### WHITE, GRAHAM C

**Graham C White**, 3 Mazoe Cl, Bishop's Stortford, **Hertfordshire**, CM23 3JU, ENG.
(T) 01162 661128
Speciality: Herbal Medicine.
**M** (Ref:HM21356)

### WHITE, HEATHER

**Relaxation Therapist**, Callunae, 10 Gorse Rd, Grantham, **Lincolnshire**, NG31 9LQ, ENG.
(T) 01476 419021
Speciality: Complementary Therapy, Counselling, Hypnotherapy, Indian Head Massage, Massage (Therapeutic), Psychotherapy, Stress Therapy, Visualisation Therapy. ✔
● **Relaxation Therapist** Ms H White M: BIH.
**B** Yrs. Est.: 10 (Ref:HM21357)

### WHITE, J

**J White**, 21 Boscastle Rd, London, **London (Greater)**, NW5 1EE, ENG.
(T) 020 7485 0794 (F) 020 7916 8751
Speciality: Acupuncture.
● **Owner** Mr J White
**O** (Ref:HM21358)

### WHITE, JACQUELINE

**Jacqueline White**, 8 Oakwood Garth, **Yorkshire (West)**, LS8 2QX, ENG.
(T) 01132 931955
Speciality: Reflexology.
**S** **T** (Ref:HM21359)

### WHITE, JANET

**Janet White**, 346 Sheffield Rd, Birdwell, Barnsley, **Yorkshire (South)**, S70 5TU, ENG.
(T) 01226 748179 (F) 01226 748179
Speciality: Homeopathy.
● **Owner** Mrs J White
**M** (Ref:HM21360)

### WHITE, JILL

**Jill White**, Main Rd, Radcliffe-On-Trent, Nottingham, **Nottinghamshire**, NG12 2GD, ENG.
(T) 01159 333181
Speciality: Complementary Medicines & Therapy.
● **Owner** Mrs B Bilkhu
**C** **M** (Ref:HM21361)

### WHITE, KAREN

**Karen White**, Cambridge City Football Club, The Long Room, Milton Rd, Cambridge, **Cambridgeshire**, CB4 1UY, ENG.
(T) 01223 368886 (F) 01223 351582
Speciality: Physiotherapy.
● **Owner** Miss K White
**P** **S** **T** (Ref:HM21362)

### WHITE, KIM

**Kim White**, Freathingcott Farm, Holcombe Rogus, Wellington, **Somerset**, TA21 0NG, ENG.
(T) 01823 672925 (F) 01823 672330
Speciality: Osteopathy.
● **Owner** Mrs K White
**P** **S** **T** (Ref:HM21363)

### WHITE, LESLEY

**Lesley White**, 12 Droveside, Cholsey, Wallingford, **Oxfordshire**, OX10 9PU, ENG.
(T) 01491 651103
Speciality: Chiropractic.
● **Owner** Ms L White
**P** **S** **T** (Ref:HM21364)

### WHITE, MADELINE M

**Madeline M White**, 47 Rectory Cres, Middle Barton, Chipping Norton, **Oxfordshire**, OX7 7BP, ENG.
(T) 01869 347282 (F) 01869 347282
Speciality: Alexander Technique.
● **Owner** Ms M White
**P** **S** (Ref:HM21365)

### WHITE, MARGARET

**Margaret White**, Avon House, 29 New Broad St, Stratford-Upon-Avon, **Warwickshire**, CV37 6HW, ENG.
(T) 01789 204803
Speciality: Chiropodists (Podiatrists).
**S** (Ref:HM21366)

### WHITE, MERYL

**Meryl White**, 25 Market Pl, Newark, **Nottinghamshire**, NG24 1EA, ENG.
(T) 01636 701840
Speciality: Hypnotherapy.
● **Owner** Ms M White
**B** (Ref:HM21367)

### WHITE, MR

**Mr White**, 210 Victoria Rd, Ruislip, **London (Greater)**, HA4 0AP, ENG.
(T) 01895 622663
Speciality: Chiropodists (Podiatrists).
**S** (Ref:HM21368)

### WHITE, NICOLAS

**Nicolas White**, Western Rd, Stratford-Upon-Avon, **Warwickshire**, CV37 0AH, ENG.
(T) 01789 263505
Speciality: Chiropractors.
**P** **S** **T** (Ref:HM21369)

### WHITE, NULA

**Nula White**, 10 Alexander Rd, London, **London (Greater)**, N19 3PQ, ENG.
(T) 020 7263 2076
Speciality: Psychotherapy.
**B** (Ref:HM21370)

### WHITE, P

**P White**, 30 Shelley Cres, Oulton, Leeds, **Yorkshire (West)**, LS26 8ER, ENG.
(T) 07798 538270
Speciality: Physiotherapy.
● **Owner** Mrs P White
**P** **S** **T** (Ref:HM21371)

### WHITE, PHILIP (DR)

**Dr Philip White**, 2 Harley St, London, **London (Greater)**, W1N 1AA, ENG.
(T) 020 7467 8470
Speciality: Homeopathy.
● **Doctor** Dr P White
**M** (Ref:HM21372)

### WHITE, R G D (DR)

**Dr R G D White**, 6 Pembury Cl, Worthing, **Sussex (West)**, BN14 7DW, ENG.
(T) 01903 214717 (F) 01903 214717
Speciality: Psychology.
● **Owner** Mr R White
**B** (Ref:HM21373)

### WHITE, R M

**R M White**, Hill House, 21 Spur Rd, Cosham, Portsmouth, **Hampshire**, PO6 3DY, ENG.
(T) 023 9220 0000
Speciality: Osteopathy.
**P** **S** **T** (Ref:HM21374)

### WHITE, RALPH E

**Ralph E White**, 4 Castlemain Avenue, Bournemouth, **Dorset**, BH6 5EQ, ENG.
(T) 01202 423466
Speciality: Osteopathy.
● **Owner** Mr R White
**M** (Ref:HM21375)

### WHITE, SALLY

**Sally White**, The Terrace, 35 Staplegrove Rd, Taunton, **Somerset**, TA1 1DG, ENG.
(T) 01823 338968
Speciality: Chiropractors.
● **Owner** Ms J Gotto
**P** **S** **T** (Ref:HM21376)

### WHITE, SARAH

**Sarah White**, 28 Writtle Rd, Chelmsford, **Essex**, CM1 3BX, ENG.
(T) 01245 609389
Speciality: Reflexology.
**S** **T** (Ref:HM21377)

### WHITE, SHELLEY

**Shelley White**, 50 Stanley Rd, Oldbury, **Midlands (West)**, B68 0EQ, ENG.
(T) 01214 212526
Speciality: Massage (Therapeutic), Reflexology. ✔
● **Owner/Reflexologist** Mrs S White M: BSR.
**M** Yrs. Est.: 8 (Ref:HM21378)

### WHITE, SUSAN

**Susan White**, 1 Gloucester Trce, Southend-On-Sea, **Essex**, SS1 3AZ, ENG.
(T) 01702 585463
Speciality: Physiotherapy.
● **Partner** Mrs L Palmer
**P** **S** **T** (Ref:HM21379)

### WHITE, TRUDY

**Trudy White**, 29 Boulthurst Way, Oxted, **Surrey**, RH8 0HT, ENG.
(T) 01883 723316
Speciality: Complementary Medicines & Therapy.
● **Owner** Ms T White
**C** **M** (Ref:HM21380)

### WHITE, V

**V White**, 17 Belchers Lane, Birmingham, **Midlands (West)**, B8 3ET, ENG.
(T) 01213 270642
Speciality: Chiropodists (Podiatrists).
● **Owner** Mrs V White
**S** (Ref:HM21381)

### WHITE, V L

**V L White**, Ashgates, Walton Lane, Brocton, Stafford, **Staffordshire**, ST17 0TT, ENG.
(T) 01785 660852
Speciality: Chiropodists (Podiatrists).
● **Owner** Miss V White
**S** (Ref:HM21382)

### WHITE, W

**W White**, 7 Clausentum Rd, Winchester, **Hampshire**, SO23 9QE, ENG.
(T) 01962 868315
Speciality: Psychotherapy.
**B** (Ref:HM21383)

### WHITECHAPEL OSTEOPATHS

**Whitechapel Osteopaths**, Wickham House, 10 Cleveland Way, London, **London (Greater)**, E1 4TR, ENG.
(T) 020 7265 8262
Speciality: Osteopathy.
**P** **S** **T** (Ref:HM21384)

### WHITEHALL, CAROL

**Carol Whitehall**, 49 Greenwood Rd, Walsall, **Midlands (West)**, WS9 8XA, ENG.
(T) 01922 455989
Speciality: Chiropody. ✔
● **Owner/Chiropodist**
Mrs C Whitehall Q: MBChA, MSSCh, SMAE.
**C** Yrs. Est.: 13 (Ref:HM21385)

### WHITEHEAD, BRIAN

**Brian Whitehead**, 22 Cedar Mount, Lyndhurst, **Hampshire**, SO43 7ED, ENG.
(T) 023 8028 3422
Speciality: Hypnotherapy.
● **Owner** Mr B Whitehead
**B** (Ref:HM21386)

### WHITEHEAD, T

**T Whitehead**, 14 Petersfield Drive, Rowley Regis, **Midlands (West)**, B65 0SA, ENG.
(T) 01215 611301
Speciality: Homeopathy.
**M** (Ref:HM21387)

### WHITEHOUSE CONSULTANCY

**Whitehouse Consultancy (The)**, 828A Ecclesall Rd, Sheffield, **Yorkshire (South)**, S11 8TD, ENG.
(T) 01142 664883
Speciality: Hypnosis.



Key continued: **Yrs.Est:** Years Established **Q:** Qualifications **M:** Professional Membership ✔ Indemnity Insurance Accept Credit Cards

B (Ref:HM21388)

## WHITEHOUSE, J

**J Whitehouse**, 30 Comyn Rd, London, **London (Greater)**, SW11 1QD, ENG.
(T) 020 7978 7935 (F) 020 7978 7935
Speciality: Herbal Medicine.
● **Owner** Dr J Whitehouse
M (Ref:HM21389)

## WHITEHOUSE, J E

**J E Whitehouse**, 47 Madeline Rd, Petersfield, **Hampshire**, GU31 4AL, ENG.
(T) 01730 261725
Speciality: Chiropodists (Podiatrists).
S (Ref:HM21390)

## WHITEHOUSE, PAMELA

**Pamela Whitehouse**, 414 Station Rd, Dorridge, Solihull, **Midlands (West)**, B93 8EU, ENG.
(T) 01564 770137
Speciality: Reflexology.
● **Owner** Mrs P Whitehouse
S T (Ref:HM21391)

## WHITEING CHIROPODISTS

**Whiteing Chiropodists**, 39 Challands Way, Hasland, Chesterfield, **Derbyshire**, S41 0ER, ENG.
(T) 01246 557173
(E) john@whiteingj.freeserve.co.uk
Speciality: Chiropody, Podiatry. ✔
● **Chiropodist** Mr J Whiteing Q: BSc (Hons), S.R.Ch. M: S.R.Ch.
● **Chiropodist** Mrs A Whiteing Q: DPodM, S.R.Ch. M: S.R.Ch.
M Yrs. Est.: 9 (Ref:HM21392)

## WHITEING, J P

**J P Whiteing**, Osbourne Dental Care, Osbourne House, Moorgate St, Rotherham, **Yorkshire (South)**, S60 2EY, ENG.
(T) 01709 364404
(E) john@whiteingj.freeserve.co.uk
Speciality: Biomechanics, Chiropody, Podiatry. ✔ CREDIT
● **Chiropodist** Mr J Whiteing Q: BSc (Hons), S.R.Ch. M: S.R.Ch.
M Yrs. Est.: 1 (Ref:HM21393)

## WHITEING, J P

**J P Whiteing**, 4 Skeldale Drive, Chesterfield, **Derbyshire**, S40 2UW, ENG.
(T) 01246 557173
Speciality: Chiropodists (Podiatrists).
S (Ref:HM21394)

## WHITEKNIGHTS SPORTS CLINIC

**Whiteknights Sports Injury Clinic**, David Lloyd Sports Centre, 1 Thames Valley Park Drive, Reading, **Berkshire**, RG6 1PT, ENG.
(T) 01189 260440
Speciality: Physiotherapy.
● **Owner** Mrs S Beamish
P S T (Ref:HM21395)

## WHITELEGG, MARGARET

**Margaret Whitelegg**, Aldrens Lane, Lancaster, **Lancashire**, LA1 2DU, ENG.
(T) 01524 69864 (F) 01524 848155
Speciality: Herbalists.
M (Ref:HM21396)

## WHITELEY, BRUCE

**Bruce Whiteley**, 13 St. Marys Gr, London, **London (Greater)**, W4 3LL, ENG.
(T) 020 8995 2643
Speciality: Chiropodists (Podiatrists).
● **Owner** Mr B Whiteley
S (Ref:HM21397)

## WHITELEY, CHRIS

**Chris Whiteley**, 36 Carrfield Avenue, Long Eaton, Nottingham, **Nottinghamshire**, NG10 2BW, ENG.
(T) 01159 469464
Speciality: Psychotherapy.
B (Ref:HM21398)

## WHITELEY, E S

**E S Whiteley**, Heather Cottage, Christchurch Rd, Virginia Water, **Surrey**, GU25 4PT, ENG.
(T) 01344 842359 (F) 01344 845021
Speciality: Physiotherapy.
● **Owner** Mrs E Whiteley
P S T (Ref:HM21399)

## WHITELEY, STEVEN

**Steven Whiteley**, 34 Underdale Rd, Shrewsbury, **Shropshire**, SY2 5DW, ENG.
(T) 01743 366628
Speciality: Aromatherapy, Massage (Therapeutic), Reflexology. ✔
● **Therapeutic Masseur/Owner** Mr S Whiteley M: LCSP.
C Yrs. Est.: 9 (Ref:HM21400)

## WHITELEYS OF BAYSWATER

**Whiteleys Of Bayswater**, Whiteleys Shopping Centre, Queensway, London, **London (Greater)**, W2 4YN, ENG.
(T) 020 7229 6620 (F) 020 7243 2780
Speciality: Complementary Medicines & Therapy.
● **Owner** Mr B Bowers
M (Ref:HM21401)

## WHITESIDE, V

**V Whiteside**, 5 Kestrel Cl, Waterlooville, **Hampshire**, PO8 0LZ, ENG.
(T) 023 9259 6971
Speciality: Chiropodists (Podiatrists).
S (Ref:HM21402)

## WHITFIELD, M

**M Whitfield**, 26 Clarence St, Gloucester, **Gloucestershire**, GL1 1DP, ENG.
(T) 01452 303360
Speciality: Chiropodists (Podiatrists).
● **Owner** Mr M Whitfield
S (Ref:HM21403)

## WHITING, JENNIE

**Jennie Whiting**, 7 The Sq, Ramsbury, Marlborough, **Wiltshire**, SN8 2PE, ENG.
(T) 01672 520523
Speciality: Aromatherapy.
● **Owner** Ms J Whiting
M O (Ref:HM21404)

## WHITING, JOHN C

**John C Whiting**, 138 Godstone Rd, Whyteleafe, **Surrey**, CR3 0EB, ENG.
(T) 020 8668 3656
Speciality: Complementary Medicines & Therapy.
● **Owner** Mr J Whiting
C M (Ref:HM21405)

## WHITLEY BAY CHIROPRACTOR

**Whitley Bay Chiropractor Clinic**, 58 Park Prde, Whitley Bay, **Tyne and Wear**, NE26 1DX, ENG.
(T) 01912 524834
Speciality: Chiropractic. ✔ CREDIT
● **Clinic Manager** Dr V Sharkey Q: BCA, DC. M: GCC.
● **Chiropractor** Mr D Middleton Q: BCA, DC. M: GCC.
● **Owner** Mrs A Middleton
C (Ref:HM21406)

## WHITLEY BAY OSTEOPATHIC CENTRE

**Whitley Bay Osteopathic Centre**, 65 Whitley Rd, Whitley Bay, **Tyne and Wear**, NE26 2EP, ENG.
(T) 01912 521555
Speciality: Osteopathy.
● **Owner** Miss J Dent
P S T (Ref:HM21407)

## WHITLEY CLINIC FOR HEALING

**Whitley Clinic For Healing**, 12 Carfield St, Bradford, **Yorkshire (West)**, BD1 3PY, ENG.
(T) 01274 722335
Speciality: Complementary Medicines & Therapy.
C M (Ref:HM21408)

## WHITLEY, JILL

**Jill Whitley**, 16 Briardale Rd, Bradford, **Yorkshire (West)**, BD9 6PT, ENG.
(T) 01274 822095
Speciality: Reflexology.
● **Owner** Mrs J Whitley
S T (Ref:HM21409)

## WHITLEY, LIS

**Lis Whitley**, 38 Brunswick Sq, Penrith, **Cumbria**, CA11 7LS, ENG.
(T) 01768 899941
Speciality: Psychotherapy.
B (Ref:HM21410)

## WHITLOCK, BARBARA

**Barbara Whitlock**, 52 Stoke Newington Church St, London, **London (Greater)**, N16 0NB, ENG.
(T) 020 7241 5033 (F) 020 7502 1182
Speciality: Hypnotherapy.
● **Senior Partner** Mrs J Sharidan
B (Ref:HM21411)

## WHITMORE, ELIZABETH

**Elizabeth Whitmore**, 8 Makins Rd, Henley-on-Thames, **Oxfordshire**, RG9 1PP, ENG.
(T) 01491 412356
Speciality: Reflexology.
S T (Ref:HM21412)

## WHITMORE, STEVEN

**Steven Whitmore**, 9 Chessher St, Hinckley, **Leicestershire**, LE10 0AH, ENG.
(T) 01455 891224
Speciality: Alexander Technique.
● **Owner** Mr S Whitmore
P S (Ref:HM21413)

## WHITNALL, LINDA

**Linda Whitnall**, 33A Wycombe Rd, Holmer Green, High Wycombe, **Buckinghamshire**, HP15 6RX, ENG.
(T) 01494 714333
Speciality: Kinesiology, Massage (Therapeutic), Reflexology.
S T (Ref:HM21414)

## WHITNEY, GERALDINE

**Geraldine Whitney**, Courtnell, Treadaway Hill, Flackwell Heath, High Wycombe, **Buckinghamshire**, HP10 9PD, ENG.
(T) 01628 521708
Speciality: Clairvoyants & Palmists.
B (Ref:HM21415)

## WHITTAKER, ANNE

**Anne Whittaker**, 19 Haig Rd, Bury, **Lancashire**, BL8 2ND, ENG.
(T) 01617 979096
Speciality: Complementary Medicines & Therapy.
C M (Ref:HM21416)

## WHITTAKER, B

**B Whittaker**, 29 Alexandra Rd, Stafford, **Staffordshire**, ST17 4DE, ENG.
(T) 01785 223491
Speciality: Physiotherapy.
● **Owner** Mr P Whittaker
P S T (Ref:HM21417)

## WHITTAKER, MARGARET C

**Margaret C Whittaker**, 618 Warwick Rd, Solihull, **Midlands (West)**, B91 1AA, ENG.
(T) 01217 117477
Speciality: Physiotherapy.
P S T (Ref:HM21418)

## WHITTAKER, WENDY

**Wendy Whittaker**, 37 Southdown Cr, Cheadle Hulme, Cheadle, **Cheshire**, SK8 6EQ, ENG.
(T) 01614 857200
Speciality: Physiotherapy.
P S T (Ref:HM21419)

## WHITTELL, JOHN

**John Whittell**, 37 Devonshire St, Keighley, **Yorkshire (West)**, BD21 2BH, ENG.
(T) 01535 604928
Speciality: Chiropodists (Podiatrists).
● **Owner** Mr J Whittell
S (Ref:HM21420)

## WHITTEMORE, JANE

**Jane Whittemore**, 32 Heathfield Rd, London, **London (Greater)**, SW18 2ZZ, ENG.
(T) 020 8870 2185
Speciality: Reflexology.
S T (Ref:HM21421)

## WHITTINGTON, LIZ

**Liz Whittington**, 41 Church Rd, Poole, **Dorset**,



Key: B Mind-Body Medicine · C Complementary Medicine · H Self Help Treatment · M Medicinal Therapy · O Oriental Medicine · P Postural Therapy · S Manipulative Structural Therapy · T Touch Therapy

BH14 0NN, ENG.
(T) 01202 749514 (F) 01202 718906
Speciality: Physiotherapy.
● **Partner** Mrs C Swinhoe
P S T (Ref:HM21422)

## WHITTLE, MARK

**Mark Whittle**, Aberfoyle House, Stapley Rd, St. Albans, **Hertfordshire**, AL3 5EP, ENG.
(T) 01727 856687
Speciality: Chiropractors.
● **Manager** Mrs S Bassett
P S T (Ref:HM21423)

## WHITTLE, MARK

**Mark Whittle**, The Hertford Chiropractic Clinic, 5 Port Hill, Hertford, **Hertfordshire**, SG14 1PJ, ENG.
(T) 01992 501659
Speciality: Chiropractic.
P S T (Ref:HM21424)

## WHITTLE, S

**S Whittle**, 90 Market St, New Mills, High Peak, **Derbyshire**, SK22 4AA, ENG.
(T) 01663 745828
Speciality: Biomechanics, Chiropody. ✔
● **Chiropodist (Podiatrist)**
Mr S Whittle Q: S.R.Ch. M: S.C.P.
C Yrs. Est.: 17 (Ref:HM21425)

## WHITTOCK, ANNE

**Anne Whittock**, 10 Waringfield Drive, Moira, Craigavon, **County Armagh**, BT67 0FB, NIR.
(T) 028 9261 3421
Speciality: Reflexology.
S T (Ref:HM21426)

## WHITTON, SHIRLEY

**Shirley Whitton**, 114 Clifton Rd, Kingston Upon Thames, **Surrey**, KT2 6PN, ENG.
(T) 020 8549 1659
Speciality: Aromatherapy.
● **Owner** Ms S Whitton
M O (Ref:HM21427)

## WHITTONBOURNE, J

**J Whittonbourne**, 288 The Ridgeway, St. Albans, **Hertfordshire**, AL4 9RJ, ENG.
(T) 01727 836001 (F) 01727 836002
Speciality: Hypnosis.
● **Owner** Mrs J Whittonbourne
B (Ref:HM21428)

## WHITWELL, D

**D Whitwell**, 2 Clifton Pk, Bristol, BS8 3BS, ENG.
(T) 01179 737371 (F) 01179 730887
Speciality: Psychiatry.
● **Senior Partner** Dr M Sternberg
B (Ref:HM21429)

## WHITWORTH, M T

**M T Whitworth**, Whitegates, Highlands Rd, Farnham, **Surrey**, GU9 0LX, ENG.
(T) 01252 327533
Speciality: Chiropodists (Podiatrists).
● **Owner** Mr M Whitworth
S (Ref:HM21430)

## WHITWORTH, MICHAEL T

**Michael T Whitworth**, 60 Woodbridge Rd, Guildford, **Surrey**, GU1 4RF, ENG.
(T) 01483 562031
Speciality: Biomechanics, Chiropody, Orthotics, Podiatry.
● **Owner/Chiropodist** Mr M Whitworth
Q: M.S.C.P., S.R.Ch.
M (Ref:HM21431)

## WHITWORTH, TARN

**Tarn Whitworth**, 25 Wellcroft, Otley, **Yorkshire (West)**, LS21 1JJ, ENG.
(T) 01943 461457
Speciality: Chiropodists (Podiatrists).
● **Owner** Ms T Whitworth
S (Ref:HM21432)

## WHOLE HEALTH COMP THERAPY CTRE

**Whole Health Complementary Therapy Centre**, 140 High St, Cefn Coed, Merthyr Tydfil, **Glamorgan (Vale of)**, CF48 2PL, WAL.
(T) 01685 382631 (F) 01443 814293
Speciality: Complementary Medicines & Therapy.
● **Secretary** Mr P Sweeney
M (Ref:HM21433)

## WHOLE WORKS

**Whole Works (The)**, Jacksons Cl, 209 High St, Edinburgh, **Edinburgh (City of)**, EH1 1PZ, SCO.
(T) 01312 258092
Speciality: Complementary Medicines & Therapy.
M (Ref:HM21434)

## WHOLE-BEING INTERACTIVE HYP

**Whole-Being Interactive Hypnotherapy**, Chesham House, 5th Floor 150 Regent St, London, **London (Greater)**, NW6 1PN, ENG.
(T) 020 7432 0307 (F) 07031 150396
(W) www.marshall-warren.com
Speciality: Hypnosis, Hypnotherapy. ✔
● **Interactive Hypnotherapist**
Ms D Marshall-Warren Q: Dip.Hyp, PGCE. M: HS.
B Yrs. Est.: 6 (Ref:HM21435)

## WHYKE, LINDA

**Linda Whyke**, 41 Church Rd, Poole, **Dorset**, BH14 0NN, ENG.
(T) 01202 749514
Speciality: Physiotherapy.
P S T (Ref:HM21436)

## WHYMAN, RAYMOND

**Raymond Whyman**, Downing, Smiths Lane, Snitterfield, Stratford-Upon-Avon, **Warwickshire**, CV37 0JZ, ENG.
(T) 01789 731144
Speciality: Chiropodists (Podiatrists).
S (Ref:HM21437)

## WHYTE, AILEEN (DR)

**Whyte Dr Aileen**, Suite 2 South Trce, Medical, **County Cork**, IRE.
(T) 021 4322 566
Speciality: Complementary Medicines & Therapy.
M (Ref:HM21438)

## WHYTE, IAN

**Ian Whyte**, 19 Lichfield St, Stone, **Staffordshire**, ST15 8NA, ENG.
(T) 01785 816481
Speciality: Osteopathy.
P S T (Ref:HM21439)

## WHYTE, IAN

**Ian Whyte**, Castlefields Surgery, Castle Way, Stafford, **Staffordshire**, ST16 1BS, ENG.
(T) 01785 248298
Speciality: Osteopathy.
● **Practice Manager** Mrs W Mellor
P S T (Ref:HM21440)

## WHYTE, M

**Mrs M Whyte**, Heaton Physiotherapy, 40 Lesbury Rd, Newcastle Upon Tyne, **Tyne and Wear**, NE6 5LB, ENG.
(T) 01912 655297
Speciality: Physiotherapy.
● **Owner** Mr C Whyte
P S T (Ref:HM21441)

## WIBERG, J H

**J H Wiberg**, 7 The Cloisters, Belmore Lane, Lymington, **Hampshire**, SO41 3QX, ENG.
(T) 01590 673012
Speciality: Chiropodists (Podiatrists).
● **Owner** Mr J Wiberg
S (Ref:HM21442)

## WIBLIN, CARON

**Caron Wiblin**, 86A Glebe St, Penarth, **Glamorgan (Vale of)**, CF64 1EF, WAL.
(T) 029 2035 0275
Speciality: Reflexology.
● **Owner** Miss C Wiblin
S T (Ref:HM21443)

## WICKER HERBAL STORES

**Wicker Herbal Stores Ltd**, 20 Market St, Meadowhall Centre, Sheffield, **Yorkshire (South)**, S9 1EJ, ENG.
(T) 01142 568408
Speciality: Herbal Medicine.
● **Manageress** Mrs E Holland
M (Ref:HM21444)

## WICKER HERBAL STORES

**Wicker Herbal Stores Ltd**, 12 St. Pauls Prde, Sheffield, **Yorkshire (South)**, S1 2JL, ENG.
(T) 01142 724572 (F) 01142 721608
Speciality: Herbal Medicine.
● **Manager** Mr S Hodgeson
M (Ref:HM21445)

## WICKER, DIANE

**Diane Wicker**, 151 Eglinton Hill, London, **London (Greater)**, SE18 3DU, ENG.
(T) 020 8854 4456
Speciality: Acupuncture.
● **Owner** Miss D Wicker
O (Ref:HM21446)

## WICKER, GEMMA

**Gemma Wicker**, 6 Cunningham Avenue, Guildford, **Surrey**, GU1 2PE, ENG.
(T) 01483 301911
Speciality: Reflexology.
S T (Ref:HM21447)

## WICKFORD PHYSIOTHERAPY CLINIC

**Wickford Physiotherapy Clinic**, 1 Brookside Cottages, Runwell Rd, Runwell, Wickford, **Essex**, SS11 7PN, ENG.
(T) 01268 765883
Speciality: Physiotherapy.
P S T (Ref:HM21448)

## WICKINS, ANN

**Ann Wickins**, 4 The Limes, Galleywood, Chelmsford, **Essex**, CM2 8RA, ENG.
(T) 01245 358423
Speciality: Reflexology.
S T (Ref:HM21449)

## WICKS, ANITA

**Anita Wicks**, Clissold Park Health Centre, 154 Stoke Newington Church St, London, **London (Greater)**, N16 0JU, ENG.
(T) 020 7249 2990 (F) 020 7249 3977
Speciality: Homeopathy.
● **Owner** Mr D Berg
M (Ref:HM21450)

## WICKS, ANITA

**Anita Wicks**, 42 King Edward Rd, London, **London (Greater)**, E17 6HZ, ENG.
(T) 020 8527 5570
Speciality: Homeopathy.
M (Ref:HM21451)

## WICKS, CLIFF

**Cliff Wicks**, 216 Marton Rd, Middlesbrough, **Cleveland**, TS4 2ET, ENG.
(T) 01642 246385
Speciality: Acupuncture.
● **Partner** Mr C Wicks
O (Ref:HM21452)

## WICKS, DIANE

**Diane Wicks**, 1 Alcester Rd, Radford, Worcester, **Worcestershire**, WR7 4LS, ENG.
(T) 01386 792929
Speciality: Reflexology.
S T (Ref:HM21453)

## WIDDOP, JANET

**Janet Widdop**, Roxmoor, Skircoat Moor Rd, Halifax, **Yorkshire (West)**, HX3 0HJ, ENG.
(T) 01422 352075
Speciality: Aromatherapy.
M O (Ref:HM21454)

## WIDDOPP, BRIAN

**Brian Widdopp M S T A T**, Roxmoor, Skircoat Moor Rd, Savile Park, Halifax, **Yorkshire (West)**, HX3 0HJ, ENG.
(T) 01422 352075
Speciality: Alexander Technique. ✔
● **Alexander Technique Teacher**
Mr B Widdopp M: STAT.
P Yrs. Est.: 3 (Ref:HM21455)

## WIDGER, CHRISTINE

**Christine Widger**, Cumery Farm, Aveton Gifford, Kingsbridge, **Devon**, TQ7 4NN, ENG.
(T) 01548 830271
Speciality: Reflexology.
S T (Ref:HM21456)



Key continued: **Yrs.Est:** Years Established **Q:** Qualifications **M:** Professional Membership ✔ Indemnity Insurance Accept Credit Cards

### WIDLAKE, N R

**N R Widlake**, 134 Valley Rd, Clacton-On-Sea, **Essex**, CO15 6LX, ENG.
(T) 01255 424248
Speciality: Chiropodists (Podiatrists).
● **Owner** Mr N Widlake
S (Ref:HM21457)

### WIDNES HOLISTIC CENTRE

**Widnes Holistic Centre**, Market St, Widnes, **Lancashire**, ENG.
(T) 01514 207266
Speciality: Alexander Technique.
● **Therapist** Mrs M Farrand
P S (Ref:HM21458)

### WIDNES OSTEOPATHIC CLINIC

**Widnes Osteopathic Clinic**, 184 Liverpool Rd, Widnes, **Cheshire**, WA8 7JB, ENG.
(T) 01514 203398 (F) 01514 203398
Speciality: Acupressure, Acupuncture, Complementary Therapy, Cranial Osteopathy, Electrotherapy, Herbal Medicine, Homeopathy, Indian Head Massage, Kinesiology, Manipulation, Massage (Therapeutic), Nutritional Therapy, Osteopathy, Phytotherapy, Reflexology. ✔
● **Osteopath** Mr Thomas
(T) 01515 467405
● **Osteopath** Mrs Thomas
(T) 01515 467405
C Yrs. Est.: 11 (Ref:HM21459)

### WIEDERHOLD, KAREN

**Karen Wiederhold**, 8 Linden Cl, Prestbury, Cheltenham, **Gloucestershire**, GL52 3DU, ENG.
(T) 01242 519543
Speciality: Indian Head Massage, Reflexology, Reiki, Spiritual Healing.
S T (Ref:HM21460)

### WIELER, JANNY

**Wieler Janny ITEC**, Coomleigh, Bantry, **County Cork**, IRE.
(T) 027 6617 9
Speciality: Complementary Medicines & Therapy.
M (Ref:HM21461)

### WIENHOLT, VALERIE

**Valerie Wienholt**, 2 Clare Avenue, Handforth, Wilmslow, **Cheshire**, SK9 3EQ, ENG.
(T) 01625 532349
Speciality: Reflexology.
S T (Ref:HM21462)

### WIERSMA, IRIS

**Iris Wiersma**, 48 Newlands Park, London, **London (Greater)**, SE26 5NE, ENG.
(T) 020 8659 5001
Speciality: Aromatherapy.
M O (Ref:HM21463)

### WIGAN FAMILY CHIROPRACTIC

**Wigan Family Chiropractic Clinic**, 27 Bridgeman Trce, Wigan, **Lancashire**, WN1 1TD, ENG.
(T) 01942 498480 (F) 01942 243123
Speciality: Chiropractic.
● **Partner** Mr D Kenny
P S T (Ref:HM21464)

### WIGG, SARA

**Sara Wigg**, 41 Fore St, Plympton, Plymouth, **Devon**, PL7 1LZ, ENG.
(T) 01752 335580
Speciality: Complementary Medicines & Therapy.
C M (Ref:HM21465)

### WIGGIN, SALLY

**Sally Wiggin**, Henley-on-Thames, **Oxfordshire**, RG9, ENG.
(T) 01491 572979
Speciality: Bach Remedies.
M (Ref:HM21466)

### WIGGINTON, P R

**P R Wigginton**, 10 Fitzwilliam Rd, Rotherham, **Yorkshire (South)**, S65 1PT, ENG.
(T) 01709 370480
Speciality: Chiropodists (Podiatrists).
● **Owner** Mr P Wigginton
S (Ref:HM21467)

### WIGHAM, A

**A Wigham**, Elms Rd, Clapham, London, **London (Greater)**, SW4 9ER, ENG.
(T) 020 7622 9114
Speciality: Art Therapy, Cognitive Therapy, Counselling, Humanistic Psychology, Hypnotherapy, Life Style Coaching, Psychotherapy, Pscyho-Synthesis, Stress Therapy, Visualisation Therapy. ✔
● **Therapist** Ms A Wigham Q: BA (Hons), Dip.EH, Dip.NLP, Dip.P.E.T, NLP, RATh. M: BACP, CPSM, UKCP.
B Yrs. Est.: 16 (Ref:HM21468)

### WIGHT CHIROPRACTIC CLINIC

**Wight Chiropractic Clinic**, 28 Leonard St, Perth, **Perth and Kinross**, PH2 8ES, SCO.
(T) 01738 633811 (F) 01738 633811
Speciality: Chiropractic.
● **Manager** Miss J Dow
P S T (Ref:HM21469)

### WIGHT CHIROPRACTIC CLINIC

**Wight Chiropractic Clinic**, West End, High St, Melrose, **Scottish Borders**, TD6 9RU, SCO.
(T) 01896 822712 (F) 01896 822712
Speciality: Chiropractic.
● **Manager** Mrs M Ford
P S T (Ref:HM21470)

### WIGHT CHIROPRACTIC CLINIC

**Wight Chiropractic Clinic**, 1b Melville Trce, Stirling, FK8 2ND, SCO.
(T) 01786 471717 (F) 01786 471717
Speciality: Chiropractic.
P S T (Ref:HM21471)

### WIGHT HOMEOPATHY

**Wight Homeopathy**, Fairlea, Baring Rd, Cowes, **Isle of Wight**, PO31 8DW, ENG.
(T) 01983 289600
Speciality: Homeopathy.
● **Owner** Mrs C La'touche
M (Ref:HM21472)

### WIGHT THERAPY

**Wight Therapy**, 15 Fairlee Rd, Newport, **Isle of Wight**, PO30 2EA, ENG.
(T) 01983 522979
Speciality: Electrolysis.
T (Ref:HM21473)

### WIGHT, STUART

**Stuart Wight**, 2 Torphichen Pl, Edinburgh, **Edinburgh (City of)**, EH3 8DU, SCO.
(T) 01312 282288 (F) 01312 284826
Speciality: Chiropractic.
● **Principal** Dr G Haig
P S T (Ref:HM21474)

### WIGHTMAN, T

**T Wightman**, 43 Newlaithes Rd, Horsforth, Leeds, **Yorkshire (West)**, LS18 4SX, ENG.
(T) 01132 589332
Speciality: Herbal Medicine.
● **Owner** Ms T Wightman
M (Ref:HM21475)

### WIGLEY, CABELLA

**Cabella Wigley**, 18 Clay Hill House, Weyhill, Haslemere, **Surrey**, GU27 1DA, ENG.
(T) 01428 642577
Speciality: Physiotherapy.
P S T (Ref:HM21476)

### WIGRAM, J

**J Wigram**, Exeter Physio & Sports Clinic, 11-15 Dixs Field, Exeter, **Devon**, EX1 1QA, ENG.
(T) 01392 211066
Speciality: Physiotherapy.
P S T (Ref:HM21477)

### WIGRAM, J R

**J R Wigram**, Ashe, Druid Rd, Ashburton, Newton Abbot, **Devon**, TQ13 7HB, ENG.
(T) 01364 652883
Speciality: Physiotherapy.
P S T (Ref:HM21478)

### WIJAY, JUDITH

**Judith Wijay**, 30 Church Trce, Exeter, **Devon**, EX2 5DU, ENG.
(T) 01392 490055
Speciality: Chiropodists (Podiatrists).
● **Owner** Mrs J Wijay
S (Ref:HM21479)

### WILBURY PHYSIOTHERAPY

**Wilbury Physiotherapy**, 40 Wilbury Rd, Hove, **Sussex (East)**, BN3 3JP, ENG.
(T) 01273 206206
Speciality: Chiropody, Counselling, Manipulation, Massage (Therapeutic), Physiotherapy, Podiatry, Shiatsu. ✔
● **Physiotherapist** Miss S Maund Q: Grad Dip Phys, MCSP, SRP. M: CSP.
● **Therapist** Ms B Simons M: FGUK.
● **Chiropodist (Podiatrist)** Ms E Farley Q: BSc (Hons), DPodM, S.R.Ch.
● **Counsellor** Ms C Archer M: BACP.
● **Therapist** Ms S Serale
● **Physiotherapist** Mrs C Popley Q: Grad Dip Phys, MCSP, SRP. M: CSP.
● **Physiotherapist** Mrs S Wykes Q: Grad Dip Phys, MCSP, SRP. M: CSP.
● **Physiotherapist** S Carnaghan Q: Grad Dip Phys, MCSP, SRP. M: CSP.
● **Shiatsu Massage Therapist** Ms H Burrows Q: ITEC, MRSS.
● **Massage Therapist** Ms R Welsh Q: BA, ITEC, PGCE.
S (Ref:HM21480)

### WILBURY SCHOOL-NATURAL THERAPY

**Wilbury School Of Natural Therapy (The)**, 274 Dyke Rd, Brighton, **Sussex (East)**, BN1 5AE, ENG.
(T) 01273 552766
Speciality: Complementary Therapy.
● **Owner** Mrs L Gillam
C (Ref:HM21481)

### WILBY, J

**Mrs J Wilby**, 57 Water Lane, Ashton-On-Ribble, Preston, **Lancashire**, PR2 2NL, ENG.
(T) 01772 768770
Speciality: Herbalists.
● **Owner** Mrs J Wilby
M (Ref:HM21482)

### WILBY, J

**J Wilby**, Natures Way Health & Beauty, Centre, 187 Tulketh Brow, Ashton On Ribble, Preston, **Lancashire**, PR2 2JD, ENG.
(T) 01772 768770
Speciality: Herbal Medicine.
M (Ref:HM21483)

### WILBY, MARY ANN

**Mary Ann Wilby**, 47 Inchbonnie Rd, South Woodham Ferrers, Chelmsford, **Essex**, CM3 5FD, ENG.
(T) 01245 329256
Speciality: Hypnosis.
● **Owner** Mrs M Wilby
B (Ref:HM21484)

### WILCOCKSON, L

**L Wilcockson**, 7 Allendale Avenue, Attenborough, Beeston, Nottingham, **Nottinghamshire**, NG9 6AN, ENG.
(T) 01159 225136
Speciality: Chiropodists (Podiatrists).
S (Ref:HM21485)

### WILCOX & ASSOCIATES

**Mark Wilcox & Associates**, 25-27 Cheapside, Wakefield, **Yorkshire (West)**, WF1 2TF, ENG.
(T) 01924 369077
Speciality: Osteopathy.
● **Owner** Mr M Willcox
P S T (Ref:HM21486)

### WILCOX, MARK

**Mark Wilcox**, 2 Kenwood Rd, Sheffield, **Yorkshire (South)**, S7 1NP, ENG.
(T) 01142 552048
Speciality: Osteopathy.
● **Owner** Mr D Wainwright
P S T (Ref:HM21487)

### WILD ROSE

**Wild Rose (The)**, 20 The Parade, St. Marys Pl, Shrewsbury, **Shropshire**, SY1 1DL, ENG.
(T) 01743 360589
Speciality: Aromatherapy, Massage (Therapeutic). ✔

Key: B Mind-Body Medicine; C Complementary Medicine; H Self Help Treatment; M Medicinal Therapy; O Oriental Medicine; P Postural Therapy; S Manipulative Structural Therapy; T Touch Therapy

● **Owner** Mrs K Ravenscroft **Q:** LLSA(Adv). **M:** IFA, LCSP.
**S** Yrs. Est.: 13 (**Ref:**HM21488)

### WILDE, ELIZABETH A
**Elizabeth A Wilde**, 6 Brookley Rd, Brockenhurst, **Hampshire**, SO42 7RR, ENG.
**(T)** 01590 622661
Speciality: Hypnosis.
● **Owner** Mrs E Wilde
**B** (**Ref:**HM21489)

### WILDEN, J D
**J D Wilden**, Victoria House, Victoria Avenue, Llanidloes, **Powys**, SY18 6AS, WAL.
**(T)** 01686 412230 **(F)** 01686 411058
Speciality: Osteopathy.
**P S T** (**Ref:**HM21490)

### WILDEN, JANE
**Jane Wilden**, 5 Walters Rd, Oldbury, **Midlands (West)**, B68 0QA, ENG.
**(T)** 01214 233176
Speciality: Chiropodists (Podiatrists).
● **Owner** Ms J Wilden
**S** (**Ref:**HM21491)

### WILKEN, ANGEL
**Angel Wilken**, 20 North Silver St, Aberdeen, **Aberdeenshire**, AB10 1RL, SCO.
**(T)** 01224 622409
Speciality: Aromatherapy, Massage (Therapeutic), Reflexology, Stress Therapy, Remedial Massage. ✔
● **Owner/Complementary Practitioner**
Ms A Wilken **Q:** Dip.Reflex, Dip.Swedish Massage, DM. **M:** SMTO.
**B M T** Yrs. Est.: 7 (**Ref:**HM21492)

### WILKES, MARA
**Mara Wilkes**, 101 Southmoor Rd, Oxford, **Oxfordshire**, OX2 6RE, ENG.
**(T)** 01865 316329
Speciality: Chiropractic.
● **Owner** Miss M Wilkes
**P S T** (**Ref:**HM21493)

### WILKEY, A S (DR)
**Dr A S Wilkey**, Hopwood House, Lees Rd, Oldham, **Lancashire**, OL4 1JN, ENG.
**(T)** 01616 287319 **(F)** 01616 286021
Speciality: Chiropractic.
● **Owner** Dr A Wilkey
**P S T** (**Ref:**HM21494)

### WILKIE, J (DR)
**Dr J Wilkie**, 108 Berrybrook Meadow, Exminster, Exeter, **Devon**, EX6 8UA, ENG.
**(T)** 01392 824242
Speciality: Psychiatry.
● **Doctor** Dr J Wilkie
**B** (**Ref:**HM21495)

### WILKIN, KEN
**Ken Wilkin**, 1 Turnpole Cl, Stamford, **Lincolnshire**, PE9 1DT, ENG.
**(T)** 01780 755126
Speciality: Chiropodists (Podiatrists).
● **Owner** Mr K Wilkin
**S** (**Ref:**HM21496)

### WILKIN, P (DR)
**Dr P Wilkin**, 43 Charmouth Court, St. Albans, **Hertfordshire**, AL1 4SJ, ENG.
**(T)** 01727 840278
Speciality: Osteopathy.
● **Owner** Dr P Wilkin
**P S T** (**Ref:**HM21497)

### WILKIN, P (DR)
**Dr P Wilkin**, Buttercups, Hurst, Reading, **Berkshire**, RG10 0DS, ENG.
**(T)** 01189 342774
Speciality: Osteopathy.
● **Owner** Mr P Wilkin
**P S T** (**Ref:**HM21498)

### WILKINS, A
**A Wilkins**, 53 Woodlea Drive, Solihull, **Midlands (West)**, B91 1PQ, ENG.
**(T)** 01217 054969
Speciality: Chiropodists (Podiatrists).
● **Owner** Mrs A Wilkins
**S** (**Ref:**HM21499)

### WILKINS, D
**D Wilkins**, 109 Stanley Rd North, Rainham, **Kent**, RM13 8BA, ENG.
**(T)** 01708 500866
Speciality: Aromatherapy.
● **Owner** Mrs D Wilkins
**M O** (**Ref:**HM21500)

### WILKINS, DAVID
**David Wilkins**, Park House, Burbidge Rd, Shepperton, **Surrey**, TW17 0ED, ENG.
**(T)** 01932 232401
Speciality: Hypnosis.
● **Owner** Mr D Wilkins
**B** (**Ref:**HM21501)

### WILKINS, G R F
**G R F Wilkins**, 47 Park Rd, Banbury, **Oxfordshire**, OX16 0DH, ENG.
**(T)** 01295 264332
Speciality: Chiropractic.
● **Owner** Mr G Wilkins
**P S T** (**Ref:**HM21502)

### WILKINS, MARILYN
**Marilyn Wilkins**, 37 Grange Avenue, Twickenham, **London (Greater)**, TW2 5TW, ENG.
**(T)** 020 8898 0412
Speciality: Reflexology.
**S T** (**Ref:**HM21503)

### WILKINSON, ANNE
**Anne Wilkinson**, 137 The Avenue, Hertford, **Hertfordshire**, SG14 3DX, ENG.
**(T)** 01992 583366
Speciality: Reflexology.
**S T** (**Ref:**HM21504)

### WILKINSON, GILL
**Gill Wilkinson**, 22 Lower Common South, London, **London (Greater)**, SW15 1BP, ENG.
**(T)** 020 8789 1747
**(E)** gill@wilkinson.homechoice.co.uk
Speciality: Alexander Technique, Counselling, Psychotherapy.
● **Pyschotherapist/Counsellor**
Ms G Wilkinson **Q:** Dip.Int.Psych, MA. **M:** BACP.
**B** Yrs. Est.: 4 (**Ref:**HM21505)

### WILKINSON, GLYNNIS
**Glynnis Wilkinson**, 29A St Marys St, Ely, **Cambridgeshire**, CB7 4HF, ENG.
**(T)** 01353 664476
Speciality: Biomechanics, Chiropody. ✔
● **Chiropodist** Glynnis Wilkinson **Q:** DPodM, MSSCh.
**M** Yrs. Est.: 4 (**Ref:**HM21506)

### WILKINSON, GWEN
**Gwen Wilkinson**, 2 Lemontree Lane, Loughborough, **Leicestershire**, LE11 2QS, ENG.
**(T)** 01509 211281
**(E)** g.wilki-spldc@lycos.com
**(W)** www.spldc.org.uk
Speciality: Allergy Testing, Sound Therapy, Neural Development Therapy.
● **Development Consultant Practitioner**
Gwen Wilkinson **Q:** BSc (Hons), PGCE. **M:** DPA.
**C** Yrs. Est.: 10 (**Ref:**HM21507)

### WILKINSON, J
**Miss J Wilkinson**, 193 Tonge Moor Rd, Bolton, **Lancashire**, BL2 2HR, ENG.
**(T)** 01204 387577
Speciality: Chiropodists (Podiatrists).
● **Owner** Miss J Wilkinson
**S** (**Ref:**HM21508)

### WILKINSON, JANICE
**Janice Wilkinson**, 615 Smithdown Rd, Liverpool, **Merseyside**, L15 5AG, ENG.
**(T)** 01517 345909
Speciality: Chiropodists (Podiatrists).
**S** (**Ref:**HM21509)

### WILKINSON, LESLEY
**Lesley Wilkinson**, 6 Brambledown Rd, Sanderstead, Croydon, **Surrey**, CR2 0BL, ENG.
**(T)** 020 8657 8698 **(F)** 020 8657 8698
**(E)** lesley.wilkinson1@virgin.net
Speciality: Bach Remedies, Bio-energetics, Floral Essence Therapy, Holistic Healing, Homeopathy.
● **Homeopath** Ms L Wilkinson **Q:** MCPH. **M:** HMA.
**M** Yrs. Est.: 6 (**Ref:**HM21510)

### WILKINSON, MARY
**Mary Wilkinson - McTimoney Chiropractor**, The Natural Health Centre, Parkfield Surgeries, 13 Parkfield Rd, Taunton, **Somerset**, TA1 4RL, ENG.
**(T)** 01823 271066
Speciality: Complementary Medicines & Therapy, McTimoney Chiropractic for humans and animals. ✔
● **McTimoney Chiropractor**
Mrs M Wilkinson **Q:** AMC, DC. **M:** CC, MCA.
**S** Yrs. Est.: 6 (**Ref:**HM21511)

### WILKINSON, MARY
**Mary Wilkinson - McTimoney Chiropractor**, 6 Sylvan Rd, Exeter, **Devon**, EX4 6EW, ENG.
**(T)** 01643 841660 **(F)** 01643 841660
Speciality: Chiropractic. ✔
● **McTimoney Chiropractor**
Ms M Wilkinson **Q:** AMC, DC. **M:** CC, MCA.
**S** Yrs. Est.: 6 (**Ref:**HM21512)

### WILKINSON, PHILIP
**Philip Wilkinson**, Cheadle, **Cheshire**, SK8, ENG.
**(T)** 01614 856777
Speciality: Bach Remedies.
**M** (**Ref:**HM21513)

### WILKINSON, W P
**W P Wilkinson**, 4 Drill St, Keighley, **Yorkshire (West)**, BD21 3DN, ENG.
**(T)** 01535 669203
Speciality: Chiropodists (Podiatrists).
**S** (**Ref:**HM21514)

### WILKS, JOHN
**John Wilks**, Natural Path Health Centre, 3 Holyrood St, Chard, **Somerset**, TA20 2AH, ENG.
**(T)** 01460 62953 **(F)** 01460 63809
Speciality: Complementary Medicines & Therapy.
● **Owner** Mr M Newbound
**M** (**Ref:**HM21515)

### WILKS, S A
**S A Wilks**, 9 Dendy Rd, Paignton, **Devon**, TQ4 5DB, ENG.
**(T)** 01803 521880
Speciality: Chiropodists (Podiatrists).
● **Owner** Mr S Wilks
**S** (**Ref:**HM21516)

### WILLAIMS, D
**D Willaims**, 126 High St, Lymington, **Hampshire**, SO41 9AQ, ENG.
**(T)** 01590 679560
Speciality: Aromatherapy.
● **Senior Partner** Dr P Hardy
**M O** (**Ref:**HM21517)

### WILLASTON PHYSIOTHERAPY CLINIC
**Willaston Physiotherapy Clinic**, Neston Rd, Willaston, Neston, **Cheshire**, CH64 2TL, ENG.
**(T)** 01513 273361
Speciality: Physiotherapy.
● **Partner** Mrs J Callow
**P S T** (**Ref:**HM21518)

### WILLCOCKS, T & S
**Tim & Sue Willcocks**, 9 Evendine Corner, Colwall Green, **Herefordshire**, WR13 6DX, ENG.
**(T)** 01684 541606
**(E)** sue@bowen-therapy.net
**(W)** www.bowen-therapy.net
Speciality: Aromatherapy, Bowen Therapy, Indian Head Massage, Massage (Therapeutic), Metamorphic Therapy, Reflexology, Reiki, Spiritual Healing, Equine Bowen Therapy. ✔
● **Therapist** Mr T Willcocks **Q:** BTER, ITEC, PGCE.
● **Support Worker/Therapist**
Ms S Willcocks **Q:** BTER, NVQ L3.
**T** Yrs. Est.: 4 (**Ref:**HM21519)

### WILLCOX, JAN
**Jan Willcox**, The Old Maltings, 32 High St, Braunston, Daventry, **Northamptonshire**, NN11 7HR, ENG.
**(T)** 01788 890826
Speciality: Reflexology.



Key continued: **Yrs.Est:** Years Established **Q:** Qualifications **M:** Professional Membership ✔ Indemnity Insurance Accept Credit Cards

S T (Ref:HM21520)

## WILLDER, J
**J Willder**, 29 Brock St, Bath, **Somerset**, BA1 2LN, ENG.
(T) 01225 424601
Speciality: Acupuncture.
● **Dentist** Mr R Talbot
O (Ref:HM21521)

## WILLDER, JAMES
**James Willder**, 29 Brock St, Bath, **Somerset**, BA1 2LN, ENG.
(T) 01225 445164
Speciality: Acupuncture.
O (Ref:HM21522)

## WILLER, A P
**A P Willer**, Merrywaters, Brook Avenue, Bosham, Chichester, **Sussex (West)**, PO18 8LQ, ENG.
(T) 01243 575262
Speciality: Physiotherapy.
● **Owner** Mrs A Willer
P S T (Ref:HM21523)

## WILLER, ANGELA P
**Angela P Willer**, Old Pavillion, 28A Wilton Gr, London, **London (Greater)**, SW19 3QX, ENG.
(T) 020 8542 7788
Speciality: Acupuncture.
● **Owner** Ms A Willer Q: DIC, Grad Dip Phys, MCSP, SRP.
O (Ref:HM21524)

## WILLERTON, A
**A Willerton**, 69 Wykeham St, Scarborough, **Yorkshire (North)**, YO12 7SA, ENG.
(T) 01723 501613
Speciality: Complementary Medicines & Therapy.
C M (Ref:HM21525)

## WILLETT, OLIVIA
**Olivia Willett**, 12 University Rd, London, **London (Greater)**, SW19 2BX, ENG.
(T) 020 8544 1894
Speciality: Reflexology.
S T (Ref:HM21526)

## WILLETT, R
**R Willett**, 84 Merritt Flats, Totnes Rd, Paignton, **Devon**, TQ3 3RP, ENG.
(T) 01803 664625
Speciality: Chiropodists (Podiatrists).
● **Owner** Mrs R Willett
S (Ref:HM21527)

## WILLEY, STEPHEN
**Stephen Willey**, 15 Sunningdale Cl, Swinton, Mexborough, **Yorkshire (South)**, S64 8SS, ENG.
(T) 01709 586396 (F) 01709 586396
Speciality: Chiropodists (Podiatrists).
● **Owner** Mr S Willey
S (Ref:HM21528)

## WILLGOTT, K
**K Willgott**, 7-9 Hawley Sq, Margate, **Kent**, CT9 1PF, ENG.
(T) 01843 292056 (F) 01843 299347
Speciality: Osteopathy.
P S T (Ref:HM21529)

## WILLIAMS CHIROPODY SERVICE
**Williams Chiropody Service**, 40 Grange Rd West, Birkenhead, **Merseyside**, CH41 4DA, ENG.
(T) 01516 478733
Speciality: Chiropody. ✔
● **Chiropodist** Mrs S Johnston Q: L.S.Ch.
M Yrs. Est.: 35 (Ref:HM21530)

## WILLIAMS CLINIC
**Williams Clinic**, 31 St. Marychurch Rd, Torquay, **Devon**, TQ1 3JF, ENG.
(T) 01803 293346 (F) 01803 293346
Speciality: Homeopathy, Bio-Magnetics. ✔
● **Acupuncturist** Mrs R Gardener Q: MBAcC. M: BAcC.
C (Ref:HM21531)

## WILLIAMS OSTEOPATHIC CLINIC
**Williams Osteopathic Clinic**, 64 Marsland Rd, Salt, Sale, **Cheshire**, M33 3HG, ENG.
(T) 01619 696555 (F) 01619 696555
Speciality: Aromatherapy, Chiropody, Counselling, Cranial Osteopathy, Hypnosis, Hypnotherapy, Manipulation, Massage (Therapeutic), Osteopathy, Reflexology, Stress Therapy.
● **Osteopath** Ms A Hewitt Q: DO. M: GOsC.
● **Osteopath** Alex Langdon Q: DO. M: GOsC.
● **Osteopath** Ms C O'Toole Q: DO. M: GOsC.
S Yrs. Est.: 25 (Ref:HM21532)

## WILLIAMS, A
**A Williams**, 854 Wimborne Rd, Bournemouth, **Dorset**, BH9 2DS, ENG.
(T) 01202 519897
Speciality: Chiropodists (Podiatrists).
● **Owner** Mrs A Williams
S (Ref:HM21533)

## WILLIAMS, A
**A Williams**, 96 Harley St, London, **London (Greater)**, W1N 1AF, ENG.
(T) 020 7935 0856
Speciality: Physiotherapy.
● **Owner** Miss A Williams
P S T (Ref:HM21534)

## WILLIAMS, A
**A Williams**, Hafodlas, Tregaron, **Ceredigion**, SY25 6UG, WAL.
(T) 01974 298920
Speciality: Psychotherapy.
B (Ref:HM21535)

## WILLIAMS, ALAN
**Alan Williams**, 67 Rita Rd, London, **London (Greater)**, SW8 1JX, ENG.
(T) 020 7587 1710
Speciality: Herbal Medicine.
● **Owner** Mr A Williams
M (Ref:HM21536)

## WILLIAMS, ANDREA
**Andrea Williams**, 17 Chalvington Cl, Beddau, Pontypridd, **Rhondda Cynon Taff**, CF38 2RR, WAL.
(T) 01443 204500
Speciality: Reflexology.
S T (Ref:HM21537)

## WILLIAMS, ANGELA
**Angela Williams**, Premier House, 29 Lloyd St, Llandudno, **Conwy**, LL30 2UU, WAL.
(T) 01492 877533
Speciality: Complementary Medicines & Therapy.
● **Owner** Mrs A Williams
C M (Ref:HM21538)

## WILLIAMS, ANNIE
**Annie Williams**, Hallamshire Natural Health Centre, 10 Dover Rd, Sheffield, **Yorkshire (South)**, S11 8RH, ENG.
(T) 01142 662321
Speciality: Homeopathy.
M (Ref:HM21539)

## WILLIAMS, B
**B Williams**, 140 Reevy Rd, Bradford, **Yorkshire (West)**, BD6 3PS, ENG.
(T) 01274 677092
Speciality: Chiropodists (Podiatrists).
S (Ref:HM21540)

## WILLIAMS, B A
**B A Williams Chemist (Acupuncture)**, 14 Albany Prde, High St, Brentford, **London (Greater)**, TW8 0JW, ENG.
(T) 020 8560 3834 (F) 020 8568 1200
Speciality: Acupuncture, Chiropody, Counselling, Homeopathy, Reflexology. ✔
● **Pharmacist and Owner** Mr R Savani
O Yrs. Est.: 40 (Ref:HM21541)

## WILLIAMS, BERNADETTE
**Bernadette Williams**, Better Health, Harrow, **London (Greater)**, HA2, ENG.
(T) 020 8248 8441
Speciality: Reflexology.
S T (Ref:HM21542)

## WILLIAMS, BRIAN
**Brian Williams**, Brecon, **Powys**, LD3, WAL.
(T) 01874 624302
Speciality: Bach Remedies.
M (Ref:HM21543)

## WILLIAMS, C
**C Williams**, Greenfields Cres, Shifnal, **Shropshire**, TF11 8ED, ENG.
(T) 01952 461873
Speciality: Chiropodists (Podiatrists).
● **Owner** Mr C Williams
S (Ref:HM21544)

## WILLIAMS, C S
**C S Williams**, The Atman Clinic, 108 St. Johns Rd, Tunbridge Wells, **Kent**, TN4 9PH, ENG.
(T) 01892 544783
Speciality: Chiropodists (Podiatrists).
S (Ref:HM21545)

## WILLIAMS, CATHERINE
**Catherine Williams**, 203 Storeton Rd, Birkenhead, **Merseyside**, CH42 8LY, ENG.
(T) 01516 082146
Speciality: Chiropody. ✔
● **Owner/Chiropodist** Mrs C Williams Q: Inst.CH.P. M: Inst.CH.P.
M Yrs. Est.: 40 (Ref:HM21546)

## WILLIAMS, CATHERINE
**Catherine Williams**, 16 Thingwall Rd, Wirral, **Merseyside**, CH61 3UE, ENG.
(T) 01516 481208
Speciality: Chiropodists (Podiatrists).
S (Ref:HM21547)

## WILLIAMS, CHARLES
**Charles Williams**, 49 Kemshead Avenue, Birmingham, **Midlands (West)**, B31 2SG, ENG.
(T) 01214 760227
Speciality: Hypnosis.
● **Owner** Mr C Williams
B (Ref:HM21548)

## WILLIAMS, CHRIS
**Chris Williams**, Heath House, 14 Worcester Rd, Stourport-on-Severn, **Worcestershire**, DY13 9AR, ENG.
(T) 01299 828591
Speciality: Chiropodists (Podiatrists).
S (Ref:HM21549)

## WILLIAMS, CHRISTINE
**Christine Williams**, 47 Denham Avenue, Llanelli, **Carmarthenshire**, SA15 4DB, WAL.
(T) 01554 776607
Speciality: Reflexology.
● **Owner** Mrs C Williams
S T (Ref:HM21550)

## WILLIAMS, CLIVE
**Clive Williams**, 84 Haven Chase, Leeds, **Yorkshire (West)**, LS16 6SG, ENG.
(T) 01132 301873
Speciality: Hypnosis.
B (Ref:HM21551)

## WILLIAMS, DANNY
**Danny Williams**, 26A Station Rd, London, **London (Greater)**, E4 7BE, ENG.
(T) 020 8529 0815
Speciality: Osteopathy.
P S T (Ref:HM21552)

## WILLIAMS, DAVID
**David Williams**, 124 John St, Porthcawl, Bridgend, CF36 3DT, WAL.
(T) 01656 783590
Speciality: Chiropodists (Podiatrists).
● **Owner** Mr D Williams
S (Ref:HM21553)

## WILLIAMS, DOUGLAS G
**Douglas G Williams**, Heritage House, 48 Chorley New Rd, Bolton, **Lancashire**, BL1 4UL, ENG.
(T) 01204 525400
Speciality: Complementary Medicines & Therapy.
C M (Ref:HM21554)

## WILLIAMS, EMILIE
**Emilie Williams**, Kilsall Farm, Neachley, Shifnal, **Shropshire**, TF11 8PJ, ENG.
(T) 01902 374631
Speciality: Complementary Medicines & Therapy.
● **Owner** Miss E Williams
C M (Ref:HM21555)



Key: B Mind-Body Medicine  C Complementary Medicine  H Self Help Treatment  M Medicinal Therapy  O Oriental Medicine  P Postural Therapy  S Manipulative Structural Therapy  T Touch Therapy

**WILLIAMS, FRANCES**

**Frances Williams**, 6 St. Marks Rd, Bath, **Somerset**, BA2 4PA, ENG.
(T) 01225 460431
Speciality: Reflexology.
S T (Ref:HM21556)

**WILLIAMS, G A**

**G A Williams**, School House, Llangattock Lingoed, Abergavenny, **Monmouthshire**, NP7 8RR, WAL.
(T) 01873 821258
Speciality: Chiropodists (Podiatrists).
S (Ref:HM21557)

**WILLIAMS, GEOFFREY**

**Geoffrey Williams**, 46 Sea Rd, Milford On Sea, Lymington, **Hampshire**, SO41 0PG, ENG.
(T) 01590 643418
Speciality: Chiropractic.
P S T (Ref:HM21558)

**WILLIAMS, GWYN**

**Gwyn Williams**, Friars Rd Chiropody & Therapy Centre, 22 Friars Rd, Coventry, **Midlands (West)**, CV1 2LL, ENG.
(T) 024 7622 8967
Speciality: Chiropodists (Podiatrists).
S (Ref:HM21559)

**WILLIAMS, H**

**H Williams**, Portchester Rd, Bournemouth, **Dorset**, BH8 8JT, ENG.
(T) 01202 780189
Speciality: Chiropodists (Podiatrists).
S (Ref:HM21560)

**WILLIAMS, H M**

**H M Williams**, 9 Mallard Cres, Poynton, Stockport, **Cheshire**, SK12 1XG, ENG.
(T) 01625 871756
Speciality: Hypnosis.
● **Owner** Mrs H Williams
B (Ref:HM21561)

**WILLIAMS, HAZEL**

**Hazel Williams**, 21 Ascot Cl, Bishop's Stortford, **Hertfordshire**, CM23 5BP, ENG.
(T) 01279 504787
Speciality: Osteopathy.
● **Owner** Ms H Williams
P S T (Ref:HM21562)

**WILLIAMS, I**

**Ms I Williams**, 16 Hubert Drive, Middlewich, **Cheshire**, CW10 0AB, ENG.
(T) 01606 832759
Speciality: Chiropodists (Podiatrists).
● **Owner** Ms I Williams
S (Ref:HM21563)

**WILLIAMS, I V**

**I V Williams**, 11 Grange Rd, Bushey, Watford, **Hertfordshire**, WD2 2LF, ENG.
(T) 01923 227172
Speciality: Chiropodists (Podiatrists).
● **Owner** Mr I Williams
S (Ref:HM21564)

**WILLIAMS, IAN**

**Ian Williams**, 456 Green Lanes, Palmers Green, London, **London (Greater)**, N13 5XD, ENG.
(T) 020 8886 5259
Speciality: Chiropody, Nail Surgery. ✓
● **Chiropodist** Mr I Williams Q: BSc, S.R.Ch. M: S.C.P.
M Yrs. Est.: 23 (Ref:HM21565)

**WILLIAMS, J**

**J Williams**, 68 Streatham Hill, London, **London (Greater)**, SW2 4RD, ENG.
(T) 020 8674 3799 (F) 020 8674 3799
Speciality: Complementary Medicines & Therapy.
● **Manager** Mr P Goss
M (Ref:HM21566)

**WILLIAMS, J**

**J Williams**, Sydney House, School Gardens, Castle Gates, Shrewsbury, **Shropshire**, SY1 2AJ, ENG.
(T) 01743 358785
Speciality: Osteopathy.
P S T (Ref:HM21567)

**WILLIAMS, JANE**

**Jane Williams**, 1 Boltons Cl, Brackley, **Northamptonshire**, NN13 6ND, ENG.
(T) 01280 700251
Speciality: Acupuncture.
● **Owner** Jane Williams
O (Ref:HM21568)

**WILLIAMS, JANE**

**Jane Williams**, 45 York St, Heywood, **Manchester (Greater)**, OL10 4NN, ENG.
(T) 01706 622755
Speciality: Psychotherapy.
B (Ref:HM21569)

**WILLIAMS, JOANNA**

**Joanna Williams**, Town Hall Practice, High St, Garstang, Preston, **Lancashire**, PR3 1ZA, ENG.
(T) 01995 600353
Speciality: Chiropodists (Podiatrists).
● **Owner** Mrs J Williams
S (Ref:HM21570)

**WILLIAMS, JOANNE**

**Joanne Williams**, 108 London Rd, Neath, **Glamorgan (Vale of)**, SA11 1HL, WAL.
(T) 01639 633292
Speciality: Aromatherapy.
M O (Ref:HM21571)

**WILLIAMS, JUDITH**

**Judith Williams**, 140 Streatham Hill, London, **London (Greater)**, SW2 4RS, ENG.
(T) 020 8671 9316
Speciality: Complementary Medicines & Therapy.
● **Owner** Ms J Williams
C M (Ref:HM21572)

**WILLIAMS, K**

**K Williams**, 55 Flitwick Rd, Westoning, Bedford, **Bedfordshire**, MK45 5JA, ENG.
(T) 01525 718785
Speciality: Complementary Medicines & Therapy.
C M (Ref:HM21573)

**WILLIAMS, K**

**K Williams**, 6 Wildman Rd, Law, Carluke, **Lanarkshire (South)**, ML8 5ET, SCO.
(T) 01698 375071
Speciality: Chiropodists (Podiatrists).
● **Owner** Mr K Williams
S (Ref:HM21574)

**WILLIAMS, K**

**K Williams**, 6 Linley Wood Rd, Walsall, **Midlands (West)**, WS9 0JY, ENG.
(T) 01922 452933
Speciality: Chiropodists (Podiatrists).
● **Owner** Mr K Williams
S (Ref:HM21575)

**WILLIAMS, KELLY**

**Kelly Williams**, Galloway Villa, 60 Main St, Kirkcowan, Newton Stewart, **Dumfries and Galloway**, DG8 0HG, SCO.
(T) 01671 830329
Speciality: Reflexology.
S T (Ref:HM21576)

**WILLIAMS, L**

**L Williams**, 157 Manchester Rd, Burnley, **Lancashire**, BB11 4HT, ENG.
(T) 01282 426820
Speciality: Hypnosis.
● **Owner** Mr L Williams
B (Ref:HM21577)

**WILLIAMS, LIZ-BETH**

**Liz-Beth Williams**, 12 Trafalgar Pl, Lymington, **Hampshire**, SO41 9BN, ENG.
(T) 01590 677438
Speciality: Reflexology.
S T (Ref:HM21578)

**WILLIAMS, M**

**M Williams**, Bridgend Clinic, Coity Rd, Bridgend, CF31 1RQ, WAL.
(T) 01656 649534 (F) 01656 649534
Speciality: Acupuncture.
● **Manager** Mrs P Blackwell
O (Ref:HM21579)

**WILLIAMS, MARILYN**

**Marilyn Williams**, 98A Chestnut Rise, London, **London (Greater)**, SE18 1RL, ENG.
(T) 020 8855 0360
Speciality: Reflexology.
S T (Ref:HM21580)

**WILLIAMS, MICHAEL (DR)**

**Dr Michael Williams**, Parkway Clinic, 253 Gower Rd, Sketty, Swansea, SA2 9JL, WAL.
(T) 01792 201040
Speciality: Acupuncture.
O (Ref:HM21581)

**WILLIAMS, NEVILLE L**

**Neville L Williams**, 22 Marford Rd, Wheathampstead, St. Albans, **Hertfordshire**, AL4 8AS, ENG.
(T) 01582 833429
Speciality: Herbal Medicine, Massage (Therapeutic), Remedial Massage.
● **Owner** Mr N Williams
M (Ref:HM21582)

**WILLIAMS, R D**

**R D Williams**, 7 Highlands, Taunton, **Somerset**, TA1 4HP, ENG.
(T) 01823 284644
Speciality: Physiotherapy.
● **Owner** Mrs R Williams
P S T (Ref:HM21583)

**WILLIAMS, R J**

**R J Williams**, 12 Coley Avenue, Reading, **Berkshire**, RG1 6LQ, ENG.
(T) 01189 572102
Speciality: Chiropodists (Podiatrists).
S (Ref:HM21584)

**WILLIAMS, R T & S M**

**R T & S M Williams**, 8 Ramsey Rd, Hadleigh, Ipswich, **Suffolk**, IP7 6AN, ENG.
(T) 01473 824110
Speciality: Homeopathy.
● **Partner** Mrs S Williams
M (Ref:HM21585)

**WILLIAMS, RUTH**

**Ruth Williams**, Garden Flat, 33 Croftdown Rd, London, **London (Greater)**, NW5 1EL, ENG.
(T) 020 7515 2012
Speciality: Psychotherapy.
● **Owner** Ms R Williams
B (Ref:HM21586)

**WILLIAMS, RUTH**

**Ruth Williams**, The Centre, Forth Noweth, Redruth, **Cornwall**, TR15 1AU, ENG.
(T) 01209 315500
Speciality: Complementary Medicines & Therapy.
● **Employee** Mrs R Williams
C M (Ref:HM21587)

**WILLIAMS, RUTH**

**Ruth Williams**, Hillside Practice, 1 Hillside, Highgate Rd, London, **London (Greater)**, NW5 1QT, ENG.
(T) 020 7515 2012
(E) ruthwilliams@msn.com
Speciality: Counselling, Gestalt Therapy, Psychotherapy. ✓
● **Psychotherapist/Sole Practitioner** Ms R Williams Q: UKCP (Reg).
B Yrs. Est.: 10 (Ref:HM21588)

**WILLIAMS, S M**

**S M Williams**, 22 Albany Rd, London, **London (Greater)**, W13 8PG, ENG.
(T) 020 8998 3705
Speciality: Chiropodists (Podiatrists).
S (Ref:HM21589)

**WILLIAMS, SAM**

**Sam Williams**, Bridport Clinic Of Complementary Medicines, 32 South St, Bridport, **Dorset**, DT6 3NQ, ENG.
(T) 01308 427777 (F) 01308 427777
Speciality: Complementary Medicines & Therapy.
● **Practice Manager** Mrs S Marsh
M (Ref:HM21590)


Key continued: Yrs.Est: Years Established Q: Qualifications M: Professional Membership ✓ Indemnity Insurance Accept Credit Cards

## WILLIAMS, SONIA
**Sonia Williams**, 19 Blanchmans Rd, Warlingham, **Surrey**, CR6 9DF, ENG.
(T) 01883 624855
Speciality: Hypnosis.
● **Owner** Mrs S Williams
B (Ref:HM21591)

## WILLIAMS, STEPHEN P
**Stephen P Williams**, St James Chiropractic Clinic, 158 Winchester Rd, Southampton, **Hampshire**, SO16 6UE, ENG.
(T) 023 8078 8111 (F) 023 8078 8111
Speciality: Chiropractors.
P S T (Ref:HM21592)

## WILLIAMS, SUSAN
**Susan Williams**, 118 High St, Northwood, **London (Greater)**, HA6 1BJ, ENG.
(T) 01923 828832
Speciality: Reflexology.
S T (Ref:HM21593)

## WILLIAMS, SUSAN
**Susan Williams**, 21B Queens Rd, Uxbridge, **London (Greater)**, UB8 2NN, ENG.
(T) 01895 847957
Speciality: Reflexology.
● **Owner** Miss S Williams
S T (Ref:HM21594)

## WILLIAMS, SUSAN
**Susan Williams**, 72 Shortlands Rd, Bromley, **Kent**, BR2 0JP, ENG.
(T) 020 8460 5026
Speciality: Reflexology.
S T (Ref:HM21595)

## WILLIAMS, T E
**T E Williams**, 43 North Cross Rd, London, **London (Greater)**, SE22 9ET, ENG.
(T) 020 8693 4374
Speciality: Chiropodists (Podiatrists).
● **Owner** Mr T Williams
S (Ref:HM21596)

## WILLIAMS, T H
**T H Williams**, 120 Greasby Rd, Greasby, **Merseyside**, L49 3NG, ENG.
(T) 01513 344031
Speciality: Chiropody, Podiatry. ✔
● **Chiropodist (Podiatrist)**
Mr T Williams Q: DPodM, S.R.Ch. M: S.C.P.
M Yrs. Est.: 24 (Ref:HM21597)

## WILLIAMS, TECWYN H
**Tecwyn H Williams**, 53 Allport Lane, Wirral, **Merseyside**, CH62 7HH, ENG.
(T) 01513 344031
Speciality: Chiropody, Podiatry. ✔
● **Chiropodist (Podiatrist)**
Mr T Williams Q: DPodM, S.R.Ch. M: S.C.P.
M Yrs. Est.: 24 (Ref:HM21598)

## WILLIAMS, TIM
**Tim Williams**, Uplyme Rd, Lyme Regis, **Dorset**, DT7 3LS, ENG.
(T) 01297 445242
Speciality: Osteopathy.
● **Owner** Mr T Williams
P S T (Ref:HM21599)

## WILLIAMS, TIMOTHY
**Timothy Williams**, Richmond House, 69 South St, Bridport, **Dorset**, DT6 3NZ, ENG.
(T) 01308 427033
Speciality: Osteopathy.
● **Owner** Mr T Williams
P S T (Ref:HM21600)

## WILLIAMS, TOM
**Tom Williams**, 3 Tair Onen, Cowbridge, **Glamorgan (Vale of)**, CF71 7UA, WAL.
(T) 01446 781525
Speciality: Herbal Medicine.
● **Owner** Mr T Williams
M (Ref:HM21601)

## WILLIAMS, TONY
**Tony Williams**, 51 Bassett Rd, London, **London (Greater)**, W10 6JR, ENG.
(T) 020 8969 3057
Speciality: Psychotherapy.
B (Ref:HM21602)

## WILLIAMS, VALERIE MOLYNEUX
**Valerie Molyneux Williams**, Hygrove, Whitestone, Hereford, **Herefordshire**, HR1 3SG, ENG.
(T) 01432 850777
Speciality: Reflexology.
S T (Ref:HM21603)

## WILLIAMS, VERONICA
**Veronica Williams**, 3 Spinney Cl, Glossop, **Derbyshire**, SK13 7BR, ENG.
(T) 01457 853563
Speciality: Bach Remedies, Reflexology, Reiki.
S T (Ref:HM21604)

## WILLIAMSON, A
**A Williamson**, 13 Edge Lane, Stretford, Manchester, **Manchester (Greater)**, M32 8HN, ENG.
(T) 01618 658126
Speciality: Chiropodists (Podiatrists).
● **Owner** A Williamson
S (Ref:HM21605)

## WILLIAMSON, DONNA M
**Donna M Williamson**, 50 Denmark Rd, Northampton, **Northamptonshire**, NN1 5QS, ENG.
(T) 01604 635012
Speciality: Chiropodists (Podiatrists).
● **Owner** Mrs D Williamson
S (Ref:HM21606)

## WILLIAMSON, I M
**I M Williamson**, 2 Rosemary Court, 53 Chantrey Rd, Sheffield, **Yorkshire (South)**, S8 8QU, ENG.
(T) 01142 500370
Speciality: Chiropodists (Podiatrists).
S (Ref:HM21607)

## WILLIAMSON, P A
**P A Williamson**, High St, Hawkhurst, Cranbrook, **Kent**, TN18 4ER, ENG.
(T) 01580 753526
Speciality: Osteopathy.
P S T (Ref:HM21608)

## WILLIAMSON, ROSEMARY
**Rosemary Williamson**, 30-32 Albert St, Aylesbury, **Buckinghamshire**, HP20 1LX, ENG.
(T) 01296 425748
Speciality: Aromatherapy.
M O (Ref:HM21609)

## WILLINGALE, M
**M Willingale**, 175 Banstead Rd, Caterham, **Surrey**, CR3 5QN, ENG.
(T) 01883 382804
Speciality: Reflexology.
● **Owner** Ms M Willingale
S T (Ref:HM21610)

## WILLINGSON, TOM
**Tom Willingson**, 37 Bell Lane, Eton Wick, Windsor, **Berkshire**, SL4 6LQ, ENG.
(T) 01753 862819
Speciality: Psychotherapy.
B (Ref:HM21611)

## WILLIS, ALAN
**Alan Willis**, 9 Westfield Rd, Bedford, **Bedfordshire**, MK40 4DQ, ENG.
(T) 01234 217411
Speciality: Chiropodists (Podiatrists).
● **Owner** Alan Willis
S (Ref:HM21612)

## WILLIS, GRAHAM
**Graham Willis**, 76 Bedford Pl, Southampton, **Hampshire**, SO15 2DF, ENG.
(T) 023 8033 0090
Speciality: Chiropodists (Podiatrists).
● **Owner** Mr G Willis
S (Ref:HM21613)

## WILLIS, IAN
**Ian Willis**, 2 Carrick Rd, Portadown, Craigavon, **County Armagh**, BT62 1PR, NIR.
(T) 028 3833 0803
Speciality: Biomechanics, Chiropody, Nail Surgery, Podiatry. ✔
● **Practice Manager** Ms R Willis
● **Chiropodist (Podiatrist)**
Mr I Willis Q: DPodM, M.S.C.P., S.R.Ch. M: S.C.P.
M Yrs. Est.: 18 (Ref:HM21614)

## WILLIS, JANET
**Janet Willis**, 27 Overbrook, **Wiltshire**, SN3 6AW, ENG.
(T) 01793 694919
Speciality: Reflexology.
S T (Ref:HM21615)

## WILLIS, KATHRYN
**Kathryn Willis**, Exmouth Herbal Clinic, 61 Bicton St, Exmouth, **Devon**, EX8 2RU, ENG.
(T) 01395 223307
Speciality: Herbalists.
● **Owner** Mrs K Willis
M (Ref:HM21616)

## WILLIS, M
**M Willis**, Croyde, Braunton, **Devon**, EX33 1QB, ENG.
(T) 01271 891004 (F) 01271 891004
Speciality: Chiropodists (Podiatrists).
● **Owner** Mrs M Willis
S (Ref:HM21617)

## WILLIS, SALLY
**Sally Willis**, 50D Maple Rd, Surbiton, **Surrey**, KT6 4AE, ENG.
(T) 020 8839 3334 (F) 020 8399 8326
(E) sallywillis@themutual.net
(W) www.sally-willis.co.uk
Speciality: Counselling, Group Therapy, Psychotherapy. ✔
● **Psychotherapist/Group Analyst**
Ms S Willis Q: BA (Hons), MIGA. M: IGA.
B Yrs. Est.: 15 (Ref:HM21618)

## WILLMOTT, BERYL
**Beryl Willmott**, 2 Pear St, Oxenhope, Keighley, **Yorkshire (West)**, BD22 9LU, ENG.
(T) 01535 644113
Speciality: Reflexology.
S T (Ref:HM21619)

## WILLMOTT, BRENDA
**Brenda Willmott**, Chard, **Somerset**, TA20, ENG.
(T) 01460 57100
Speciality: Bach Remedies.
M (Ref:HM21620)

## WILLMOTT, ISOBEL
**Isobel Willmott**, 44 Main St, Desford, **Leicestershire**, LE9 9GR, ENG.
(T) 01455 828008
Speciality: Reflexology.
S T (Ref:HM21621)

## WILLMOTT, JENNIFER
**Jennifer Willmott**, 8-10 Regent St, Long Eaton, Nottingham, **Nottinghamshire**, NG10 1JX, ENG.
(T) 01159 730152 (F) 01159 730152
Speciality: Chiropodists (Podiatrists).
S (Ref:HM21622)

## WILLMOTT, SUSAN
**Susan Willmott**, Spectrum, 7 Endymion Rd, London, **London (Greater)**, N4 1EE, ENG.
(T) 020 8341 3413
(E) susan.willmott@virgin.net
Speciality: Auto Suggestion, Counselling, Gestalt Therapy, Group Therapy, Humanistic Psychology, Hypnosis, Hypnotherapy, Psychotherapy, Pyscho-Synthesis, Transactional Analysis, Somatic/Emotional Therapy. ✔
● **Psychotherapist/Hypnotherapist**
Ms S Willmott
(T) 020 8374 8728 M: ACHE, UKCP.
H Yrs. Est.: 9 (Ref:HM21623)

## WILLOCK, LORNA
**Lorna Willock**, Dumfries Holistic Health Centre, 98 Loreburn St, Dumfries, **Dumfries and Galloway**, DG1 1HW, SCO.
(T) 01387 267617
Speciality: Aromatherapy.
M O (Ref:HM21624)

## WILLOW
**Willow**, 2 Nantymynydd, Four Roads, Kidwelly, **Carmarthenshire**, SA17 4SE, WAL.
(T) 01269 861013
Speciality: Aromatherapy.
● **Owner** Mrs M Rees

Key: B Mind-Body Medicine C Complementary Medicine H Self Help Treatment M Medicinal Therapy O Oriental Medicine P Postural Therapy S Manipulative Structural Therapy T Touch Therapy

M O (Ref:HM21625)

## WILLOW THERAPIES

**Willow Therapies**, Suite 3 Newspaper House, Tannery Lane, Penketh, Warrington, **Cheshire**, WA5 2UD, ENG.
(T) 01925 722336
Speciality: Reflexology.
S T (Ref:HM21626)

## WILLOW TREE THERAPEUTIC AGENCY

**Willow Tree Therapeutic Agency Ltd**, 12 Gurnays Mead, West Wellow, Romsey, **Hampshire**, SO51 6GB, ENG.
(T) 01794 324360
Speciality: Psychotherapy.
B (Ref:HM21627)

## WILLOWHERB AROMATHERAPY

**Willowherb Aromatherapy**, P O Box 1429, Rugby, **Warwickshire**, CV21 3ZL, ENG.
(T) 01788 540749
Speciality: Aromatherapy.
● **Owner** Ms S Sarup
M O (Ref:HM21628)

## WILLOWS CLINIC

**Willows Clinic (The)**, 120 Station Rd, Nailsea, Bristol, BS48 1TB, ENG.
(T) 01275 810505
Speciality: Osteopathy.
● **Partner** Ms Z Ford
P S T (Ref:HM21629)

## WILLOWS CLNC COMP HEALTH CTRE

**Mrs I R Thambirajah Tia The Willows Clinic**, 105 Short Heath Rd, Erdington, Birmingham, **Midlands (West)**, B23 6LH, ENG.
(T) 01213 506550 (F) 01213 503303
Speciality: Acupressure, Acupuncture, Aromatherapy, Chiropody, Complementary Therapy, Counselling, Cranial Osteopathy, Cupping, Floral Essence Therapy, Herbal Medicine, Holistic Healing, Homeopathy, Hypnotherapy, Indian Head Massage, Massage (Therapeutic), Naturopathy, Nutritional Therapy, Osteopathy, Phytotherapy, Psychotherapy, Reflexology, Sports Massage, Stress Therapy, Ying & Yang, Hopi Ear Candles. ✔
● **Therapist** Mr W Buchanan Q: BSc (Hons), Dip.CHM, MSc.
● **Therapist** Ms J Freeman-Phillips
● **Therapist/Owner** Dr R Thambirajah Q: MBAcC.
● **Therapist** Ms M Adams Q: UKCP (Reg). M: UKCP.
● **Therapist** Ms S Jackson Q: ITEC (Hons), MAR.
● **Therapist** Mr C Nelson Q: BSc (Hons), M.S.C.P, S.R.Ch.
● **Therapist** Ms P Russell Q: ISPA. M: ISPA.
● **Therapist** Ms J Morton Q: ITEC, MAR. M: ITEC.
T Yrs. Est.: 6 (Ref:HM21630)

## WILLS, ANNE

**Anne Wills**, 3 Bond St, Redruth, **Cornwall**, TR15 2QA, ENG.
(T) 01209 215012
Speciality: Hypnotherapy.
● **Owner** Miss K Triniman
B (Ref:HM21631)

## WILLS, JONATHAN

**Jonathan Wills**, Castle St Practice, 1a Castle St, Launceston, **Cornwall**, PL15 8AZ, ENG.
(T) 01566 775005
Speciality: Acupuncture, Aromatherapy, Beauty Therapy, Chiropody, Cranial Osteopathy, Electrolysis, Homeopathy, Indian Head Massage, Manipulation, Massage (Therapeutic), Moxibustion, Osteopathy, Podiatry, Reflexology, Sugaring. ✔
● **Osteopath** Mr J Wills Q: DO. M: GOsC.
● **Osteopath** Mr D Wells Q: BSc, Hons (OST). M: GOsC.
S Yrs. Est.: 13 (Ref:HM21632)

## WILLSHER, ERNEST R

**Ernest R Willsher**, Old Forge, Lamerton, Tavistock, **Devon**, PL19 8RY, ENG.
(T) 01822 614179
Speciality: Chiropody. ✔
● **Owner/Chiropodist** Mr E Wilsher Q: MBChA, MSSCh. M: B.A.Ch.P, SSCh.
C Yrs. Est.: 10 (Ref:HM21633)

## WILLSHER, SUE

**Sue Willsher**, 60 Carisbrooke Avenue, Fareham, **Hampshire**, PO14 3PR, ENG.
(T) 01329 664220
Speciality: Homeopathy.
● **Owner** Mrs S Willsher
M (Ref:HM21634)

## WILLSON, AUDREY

**Audrey Willson**, 6 Alexa Court, 6 Overton Rd, Sutton, **Surrey**, SM2 6QF, ENG.
(T) 020 8642 0187
Speciality: Reflexology.
S T (Ref:HM21635)

## WILLSON, GILLIAN

**Gillian Willson**, Fernleigh, 16 Woodrolfe Farm Lane, Tollesbury, Maldon, **Essex**, CM9 8SX, ENG.
(T) 01621 868245
Speciality: Reflexology.
S T (Ref:HM21636)

## WILMOT, D

**D Wilmot**, Farthings Drove, Brandon Creek, Downham Market, **Norfolk**, PE38 0PR, ENG.
(T) 01353 676365 (F) 01353 676365
Speciality: Psychotherapy.
● **Owner** Mr D Wilmot
B (Ref:HM21637)

## WILMOT, E

**E Wilmot**, 62 Petworth Rd, Haslemere, **Surrey**, GU27 3AU, ENG.
(T) 01428 643912 (F) 01428 643912
Speciality: Osteopathy.
● **Owner** Mr E Wimot
P S T (Ref:HM21638)

## WILMOT, MARGARET

**Margaret Wilmot**, 98 Popes Lane, London, **London (Greater)**, W5 4NS, ENG.
(T) 020 8840 9449
Speciality: Clairvoyants & Palmists.
B (Ref:HM21639)

## WILMOTT, DELCIA

**Delcia Wilmott**, Allergy Testing, 97 High St, Maidenhead, **Berkshire**, SL6 1JX, ENG.
(T) 01628 788420
Speciality: Complementary Medicines & Therapy.
● **Owner** Mrs D Wilmott
M (Ref:HM21640)

## WILSDON, S

**S Wilsdon**, Garden House, Links Rd, Bramley, Guildford, **Surrey**, GU5 0AL, ENG.
(T) 01483 892811
Speciality: Chiropodists (Podiatrists).
● **Owner** Mrs S Wilsdon
S (Ref:HM21641)

## WILSON, A F J

**A F J Wilson**, 22 Howard Rd, Southampton, **Hampshire**, SO15 5BN, ENG.
(T) 023 8022 3113
Speciality: Chiropodists (Podiatrists).
● **Owner** Mr A Wilson
S (Ref:HM21642)

## WILSON, ALLES

**Alles Wilson**, Wood Green, London, **London (Greater)**, N22, ENG.
(T) 020 8881 5147
Speciality: Bach Remedies.
M (Ref:HM21643)

## WILSON, AMANDA

**Mrs Amanda Wilson**, Hilton Chambers, Roushill, Shrewsbury, **Shropshire**, SY1 1PN, ENG.
(T) 01743 363028
(W) www.thechiropodist.net
Speciality: Biomechanics, Chiropody, Nail Surgery. ✔
● **Owner/Chiropodist** Mrs A Wilson Q: M.S.C.P, S.R.Ch. M: S.C.P, S.R.Ch.
C Yrs. Est.: 1 (Ref:HM21644)

## WILSON, ANGELA

**Angela Wilson**, 294 Mill Rd, Cambridge, **Cambridgeshire**, CB1 3NL, ENG.
(T) 01353 862470
Speciality: Chiropodists (Podiatrists).
S (Ref:HM21645)

## WILSON, AVIS

**Avis Wilson**, The Oaks, Oak Lane, Broadbridge Heath, Horsham, **Sussex (West)**, RH12 3NX, ENG.
(T) 01403 259437
Speciality: Acupressure, Electrolipolysis, Electrotherapy, Massage (Therapeutic), Reflexology, Clinical Aromatherapy. ✔
● **Therapist** Ms M Owen
● **Therapist** Avis Wilson M: LCSP.
C Yrs. Est.: 25 (Ref:HM21646)

## WILSON, C

**C Wilson**, 7 Avery Cl, Lutterworth, **Leicestershire**, LE17 4PX, ENG.
(T) 01455 556595
Speciality: Chiropodists (Podiatrists).
S (Ref:HM21647)

## WILSON, C

**Mrs C Wilson**, 6 Avebury, Bracknell, **Berkshire**, RG12 8SQ, ENG.
(T) 01344 451677
Speciality: Chiropodists (Podiatrists).
● **Owner** Mrs C Wilson
S (Ref:HM21648)

## WILSON, C M

**C M Wilson**, 1 Braid Drive, Glenrothes, **Fife**, KY7 4ES, SCO.
(T) 01592 756723
Speciality: Hypnotherapy.
● **Owner** Mr C Wilson
B (Ref:HM21649)

## WILSON, CHRIS

**Chris Wilson**, 12 Market Sq, Horsham, **Sussex (West)**, RH12 1EU, ENG.
(T) 01403 252228
Speciality: Osteopathy.
P S T (Ref:HM21650)

## WILSON, CHRISTOPHER

**Christopher Wilson**, 225 High Rd, South Woodford, London, **London (Greater)**, E18 2PB, ENG.
(T) 020 8505 0444
(E) cwilson@yahoo.com
Speciality: Counselling, Herbal Medicine, Massage (Therapeutic), Reiki. ✔
● **Massage Therapist** Ms C Tunks
(T) 020 8505 6070 Q: ITEC.
● **Massage Therapist/Reiki Therapist** Ms T Brooks
(T) 020 8505 6070 Q: ELSR, ITEC.
● **Owner/Chiropodist (Podiatrist)** Mr C Wilson Q: DPodM, M.S.C.P. M: S.C.P.
● **Massage Therapist** Ms C O'Donovan
(T) 020 8505 6070 Q: ELSR, ITEC, MAR, MTI.
S Yrs. Est.: 12 (Ref:HM21651)

## WILSON, D J

**D J Wilson**, 124a Fleetwood Rd North, Thornton, **Lancashire**, FY5 4BL, ENG.
(T) 01253 823074
Speciality: Chiropodists (Podiatrists).
● **Owner** Mr D Wilson
S (Ref:HM21652)

## WILSON, DAVID

**David Wilson**, Amerie Court, 100 Newlands, Pershore, **Worcestershire**, WR10 1BP, ENG.
(T) 01386 561488
Speciality: Homeopathy.
M (Ref:HM21653)

## WILSON, DIBALL &

**Diball & Wilson**, 176 Sunderland Rd, South Shields, **Tyne and Wear**, NE34 6AB, ENG.
(T) 01914 556089
Speciality: Chiropodists (Podiatrists).
● **Partner** Mr I Wilson
S (Ref:HM21654)

## WILSON, FIONA

**Fiona Wilson**, 297 Hollyhedge Rd, Gatley, Cheadle, **Cheshire**, SK8 4HH, ENG.
(T) 01614 912372
Speciality: Chiropodists (Podiatrists).
S (Ref:HM21655)



Key continued: Yrs.Est: Years Established Q: Qualifications M: Professional Membership ✔ Indemnity Insurance Accept Credit Cards

## WILSON, G

**G Wilson**, 1 Beetham Pl, Layton, Blackpool, **Lancashire**, FY3 8HL, ENG.
(T) 01253 319466
Speciality: Cognitive Therapy, Counselling, Humanistic Psychology, Hypnosis, Hypnotherapy, Psychotherapy, Stress Therapy, Behavioural Therapy.
● **Owner** Mr G Wilson
(T) 01253 395135 Q: BSc (Hons), CHP, MSc, NRHP (Assoc). M: NRHP.
B Yrs. Est.: 6 (Ref:HM21656)

## WILSON, HELEN

**Helen Wilson**, Burnside, Alterwall, Lyth, Wick, **Caithness**, KW1 4UG, SCO.
(T) 01955 641383 (F) 01955 641383
Speciality: Hypnosis.
● **Owner** Mrs H Wilson
B (Ref:HM21657)

## WILSON, JOHN PAUL

**John Paul Wilson**, 1 Station Rd, Lundwood, Barnsley, **Yorkshire (South)**, S71 5LA, ENG.
(T) 01226 715551
Speciality: Chiropody. ✓
● **Chiropodist** Mr J Wilson Q: Inst.CH.P, MBChA, MSSCh, SMAE. M: SMAE.
C Yrs. Est.: 18 (Ref:HM21658)

## WILSON, JULIE

**Julie Wilson**, 103 Rowheath Rd, Birmingham, **Midlands (West)**, B30 2EU, ENG.
(T) 01214 334640
Speciality: Chiropodists (Podiatrists).
● **Owner** Miss J Wilson
S (Ref:HM21659)

## WILSON, MARGARET R E

**Margaret R E Wilson**, 25 Fairfield Rd, London, **London (Greater)**, E3 2QA, ENG.
(T) 020 8980 2431
Speciality: Aromatherapy.
M O (Ref:HM21660)

## WILSON, MICHAEL F

**Michael F Wilson**, 34 Beech Grove Terrace South, Ryton, **Tyne and Wear**, NE40 4TW, ENG.
(T) 01914 137465
Speciality: Chiropodists (Podiatrists).
S (Ref:HM21661)

## WILSON, N

**N Wilson**, 304 Galley Hill, Hemel Hempstead, **Hertfordshire**, HP1 3LE, ENG.
(T) 01442 252250
Speciality: Osteopathy.
P S T (Ref:HM21662)

## WILSON, NICOLA

**Nicola Wilson**, 28 Hembury Avenue, Manchester, **Manchester (Greater)**, M19 1FH, ENG.
(T) 01612 253043
Speciality: Reflexology.
S T (Ref:HM21663)

## WILSON, P M

**P M Wilson**, 37 Chiswick St, Carlisle, **Cumbria**, CA1 1HJ, ENG.
(T) 01228 526906
Speciality: Chiropody. ✓
● **Chiropodist** P M Wilson Q: BA (Hons), MBChA, MSSCh.
M Yrs. Est.: 8 (Ref:HM21664)

## WILSON, PAUL

**Paul Wilson**, The Southsea Centre For Complementary Medicine, 25 Osborne Rd, Southsea, **Hampshire**, PO5 3ND, ENG.
(T) 023 9287 4748
Speciality: Acupuncture.
● **Practitioner** Mr P Wilson Q: MBAcC.
O (Ref:HM21665)

## WILSON, R

**R Wilson**, 18 Broomhill Rd, Aberdeen, **Aberdeenshire**, AB10 6HS, SCO.
(T) 01224 572727
Speciality: Osteopathy.
● **Principal** Mr R Wilson
P S T (Ref:HM21666)

## WILSON, R A

**R A Wilson**, Mount Stuart, Chalmerston Rd, Drip Bridge, Stirling, FK9 4UF, SCO.
(T) 01786 472988
Speciality: Osteopathy.
● **Owner** Mr R Wilson
P S T (Ref:HM21667)

## WILSON, S

**S Wilson**, The Old Vicarage, Somerset Sq, Nailsea, Bristol, BS48 2EF, ENG.
(T) 01275 857912
Speciality: Osteopathy.
P S T (Ref:HM21668)

## WILSON, S A

**S A Wilson**, 9 Broomgate, Lanark, **Lanarkshire (South)**, ML11 9EE, SCO.
(T) 01555 665866
Speciality: Osteopathy.
● **Owner** Mr S Wilson
P S T (Ref:HM21669)

## WILSON, SALLY

**Sally Wilson**, Harley House, 56 Marylebone Rd, London, **London (Greater)**, NW1 5HL, ENG.
(T) 020 7486 8087 (F) 020 7486 4115
Speciality: Complementary Medicines & Therapy.
● **Owner** Mrs S Wilson
C M (Ref:HM21670)

## WILSON, SALLY-ANNE

**Sally-Anne Wilson**, Still Waters, Mayfield Rd, Weybridge, **Surrey**, KT13 8XD, ENG.
(T) 01932 855730
Speciality: Homeopathy.
● **Owner** Ms S Wilson
M (Ref:HM21671)

## WILSON, SEAN

**Sean Wilson**, Flat 1, 424 Clapham Rd, London, **London (Greater)**, SW9 9DA, ENG.
(T) 020 7720 5852
Speciality: Hypnotherapy.
B (Ref:HM21672)

## WILSON, SHIRLEY

**Shirley Wilson**, 40a Herbert St, Hemel Hempstead, **Hertfordshire**, HP2 5HW, ENG.
(T) 01442 236282
Speciality: Aromatherapy.
M O (Ref:HM21673)

## WILSON, SUE

**Sue Wilson**, 41 West Hill Drive, Mansfield, **Nottinghamshire**, NG18 1PL, ENG.
(T) 01623 659035
Speciality: Complementary Medicines & Therapy.
● **Owner** Miss S Wilson
M (Ref:HM21674)

## WILSON, SUE

**Sue Wilson**, 3 Woodford Cottages, Mansfield, **Nottinghamshire**, NG18 2RS, ENG.
(T) 01623 659035
Speciality: Complementary Medicines & Therapy.
C M (Ref:HM21675)

## WILSON, TONY

**Tony Wilson**, The Medical Centre, 15 Cawley Rd, Chichester, **Sussex (West)**, PO19 1XT, ENG.
(T) 01243 532356 (F) 01243 530042
Speciality: Physiotherapy.
● **Principal** Mr T Wilson
P S T (Ref:HM21676)

## WILSON, VERONICA

**Veronica Wilson**, 2 Rose Green, Colchester Rd, Chappel, Colchester, **Essex**, CO6 2AB, ENG.
(T) 01206 241031
Speciality: Reflexology.
M (Ref:HM21677)

## WILSON, VERONICA

**Veronica Wilson**, 1 Hunts Hill Cottage, Wittersham, Tenterden, **Kent**, TN30 7PR, ENG.
(T) 01797 270621
Speciality: Psychotherapy.
● **Owner** Ms V Wilson
B (Ref:HM21678)

## WILSON, VIRGINIA

**Virginia Wilson**, Ingledale, 1 Tanhouse Rd, Oxted, **Surrey**, RH8 9PE, ENG.
(T) 01883 717277
Speciality: Aromatherapy.
M O (Ref:HM21679)

## WILSON, W

**W Wilson**, 40 Hogarth Drive, Washington, **Tyne and Wear**, NE38 7LT, ENG.
(T) 01914 179971
Speciality: Osteopathy.
● **Owner** Mr W Wilson
P S T (Ref:HM21680)

## WILSON-SMITH, ANDREW

**Andrew Wilson-Smith**, 1-2A Clayhill House, Weyhill, Haslemere, **Surrey**, GU27 1DA, ENG.
(T) 01428 651067
Speciality: Osteopathy.
P S T (Ref:HM21681)

## WILTSHIRE, WENDY

**Wendy Wiltshire**, 7 Hulme St, Sowerby Bridge, **Yorkshire (West)**, HX6 3BD, ENG.
(T) 01422 833424 (F) 01422 833424
Speciality: Aromatherapy.
M O (Ref:HM21682)

## WIMBLEDON CLINIC OF NTRL MED

**Wimbledon Clinic Of Natural Medicine**, 1 Evelyn Rd, Wimbledon, London, **London (Greater)**, SW19 8NU, ENG.
(T) 020 8540 3389 (F) 020 8543 5477
Speciality: Osteopathy.
● **Director** Mr P Manifold
P S T (Ref:HM21683)

## WIMBLEDON HERBAL CENTRE

**Wimbledon Herbal Centre**, 656-658 Garratt Lane, London, **London (Greater)**, SW17 0NP, ENG.
(T) 020 8947 7588 (F) 020 8879 3388
Speciality: Complementary Medicines & Therapy.
● **Manager** Dr Z Tong
M (Ref:HM21684)

## WIMBLEDON OSTEO & SPORTS

**Wimbledon Osteopathic & Sports Injuries Clinic**, 87 Hamilton Rd, London, **London (Greater)**, SW19 1JG, ENG.
(T) 020 8879 3053
Speciality: Osteopathy.
P S T (Ref:HM21685)

## WIMBLEDON, R A

**R A Wimbledon**, Little Garlands, The St, Ewhurst, Cranleigh, **Surrey**, GU6 7QA, ENG.
(T) 01483 277505
Speciality: Chiropodists (Podiatrists).
● **Owner** Mrs R Wimbledon
S (Ref:HM21686)

## WIMBORNE CHIROPODY SURGERY

**Wimborne Chiropody Surgery**, 5 Leigh Rd, Wimborne, **Dorset**, BH21 1AB, ENG.
(T) 01202 841751
Speciality: Chiropody, Podiatry. ✓
● **Chiropodist (Podiatrist)**
Mrs L Dow-Davies Q: M.Ch.A. M: S.C.P.
M Yrs. Est.: 9 (Ref:HM21687)

## WIMBORNE HERBAL CLINIC

**Wimborne Herbal Clinic**, 5 West Borough, Wimborne, **Dorset**, BH21 1LT, ENG.
(T) 01202 888272
Speciality: Herbal Medicine.
● **Owner** Mrs L Harold
M (Ref:HM21688)

## WIMBORNE MINSTER PHYSIO

**Wimborne Minster Physiotherapy Clinic**, 30 West Borough, Wimborne, **Dorset**, BH21 1NF, ENG.
(T) 01202 848474 (F) 01202 848474
Speciality: Physiotherapy.
● **Partner** Mr R Goddard
P S T (Ref:HM21689)

## WINCANTON CHIROPRACTIC CLINIC

**Wincanton Chiropractic Clinic**, 75 High St, Wincanton, **Somerset**, BA9 9JZ, ENG.
(T) 01963 32986

Key: B Mind-Body Medicine · C Complementary Medicine · H Self Help Treatment · M Medicinal Therapy · O Oriental Medicine · P Postural Therapy · S Manipulative Structural Therapy · T Touch Therapy

Speciality: Chiropractic. ✓
● **Chiropractor** Ms M Jacobson Q: MSc (Chiro). M: BCA.
● **Chiropractor** Dr E Rigby Q: DC. M: BCA.
P Yrs. Est.: 6 (Ref:HM21690)

## WINCHESTER CHIROPRACTIC CLINIC

**Winchester Chiropractic Clinic**, 53 Parchment St, Winchester, **Hampshire**, SO23 8BA, ENG.
(T) 01962 853984 (F) 01489 878702
(E) mikehutch@parchmentclinic.co.uk
(W) www.parchmentclinic.co.uk
Speciality: Acupuncture, Chiropractic, Kinesiology, Manipulation, Massage (Therapeutic), Micro Manipulation, Reflexology, Remedial Massage, X-Ray, Medical Herbalist. ✓
● **Chiropractor** Mr M Hutchinson M: ACA, BCA, CC, EChiroU, GCC.
S Yrs. Est.: 22 (Ref:HM21691)

## WINCHESTER HOM PRACTICE

**Winchester Homoeopathic Practice**, 106 Stockbridge Rd, Winchester, **Hampshire**, SO22 6RL, ENG.
(T) 01962 856310 (F) 01962 852014
Speciality: Acupressure, Acupuncture, Aromatherapy, Bach Remedies, Complementary Therapy, Counselling, Cranial Osteopathy, Crystal Healing, Dietician, Healer, Healing Therapy, Herbal Medicine, Holistic Healing, Homeopathy, Hypnosis, Hypnotherapy, Manipulation, Massage (Therapeutic), Nutritional Therapy, Osteopathy, Reflexology, Spiritual Healing. ✓
● **Medical Homeopath** Eril Asher M: FFHom.
● **Chinese Herbalist/Acupuncturist** Ruolin Sun Q: DChH, Lic.Ac. M: BAcC.
● **Medical Homeopath** Mr D Owen M: FFHom.
● **Medical Homeopath** Ms G Pearson M: FHom.
H M O S Yrs. Est.: 15 (Ref:HM21692)

## WINCHESTER PHYSIO/SPORTS

**Winchester Physiotherapy & Sports Injury Clinic**, River Park Leisure Centre, Gordon Rd, Winchester, **Hampshire**, SO23 7DD, ENG.
(T) 01962 864398
Speciality: Physiotherapy.
P S T (Ref:HM21693)

## WINCHMORE CLINIC OF OSTEOPATHY

**M Hunt (Reg Osteopaths) & Associates**, 925 Green Lanes, Winchmore Hill, London, **London (Greater)**, N21 2PB, ENG.
(T) 020 8360 3485 (F) 020 8372 4316
(E) michaelhunt@tinyworld.co.uk
(W) www.winchmore-osteopaths.co.uk
Speciality: Acupuncture, Counselling, Cranial Osteopathy, Electrotherapy, Manipulation, Massage (Therapeutic), Osteopathy, Psychotherapy, Reflexology, Shiatsu, Transactional Analysis, Ultrasonics. ✓
● **Associate Osteopath** Mr J Fudge Q: DO. M: GOsC.
● **Principle Osteopath** Mr M Hunt (T) 020 8360 1024 Q: BSc (Hons), DO. M: GOsC.
P S T Yrs. Est.: 17 (Ref:HM21694)

## WINDMILL HILL CLINIC

**Windmill Hill Clinic**, 74 Bedford Rd, Hitchin, **Hertfordshire**, SG5 2UD, ENG.
(T) 01462 450264
Speciality: Osteopathy.
P S T (Ref:HM21695)

## WINDSOR CTRE - TRAD CHINESE AC

**Windsor Centre of Traditional Chinese Acupuncture**, 5 St Leonards Rd, Windsor, **Berkshire**, SL4 3BN, ENG.
(T) 01753 854429
Speciality: Acupuncture.
O (Ref:HM21696)

## WINE, SUE

**Sue Wine**, 75 Heath Lane, Great Boughton, Chester, **Cheshire**, CH3 5SY, ENG.
(T) 01244 314241
Speciality: Chiropractic.
● **Owner** Mrs S Wine
P S T (Ref:HM21697)

## WINER, J

**J Winer**, 152 Harley St, London, **London (Greater)**, W1N 1HH, ENG.
(T) 020 7935 7335
Speciality: Osteopathy.
P S T (Ref:HM21698)

## WINFALCON HEALING CENTRE

**Winfalcon Healing Centre & Holistic Shop**, 28-29 Ship St, Brighton, **Sussex (East)**, BN1 1AD, ENG.
(T) 01273 728997 (F) 01273 720411
Speciality: Complementary Medicines & Therapy.
M (Ref:HM21699)

## WINFALCON'S AURA CENTRE

**Winfalcon's Aura Centre**, 28 Ship St, Brighton, **Sussex (East)**, BN1 1AD, ENG.
(T) 01273 728997
Speciality: Complementary Medicines & Therapy.
● **Manager** Maria Helsby
M (Ref:HM21700)

## WINFIELD, H & D

**H & D Winfield**, 46 Holliers Hill, Bexhill-on-Sea, **Sussex (East)**, TN40 2DD, ENG.
(T) 01424 221757
Speciality: Chiropodists (Podiatrists).
S (Ref:HM21701)

## WING, A C & T L

**A C & T L Wing**, 127 Park Rd, Peterborough, **Cambridgeshire**, PE1 2UD, ENG.
(T) 01733 568515
Speciality: Chiropodists (Podiatrists).
S (Ref:HM21702)

## WING, BARRY

**Barry Wing**, 43A Market Pl, Thirsk, **Yorkshire (North)**, YO7 1HA, ENG.
(T) 01845 525804
Speciality: Chiropodists (Podiatrists).
● **Owner** Mr B Wing
S (Ref:HM21703)

## WINGROVE, KATHLEEN

**Kathleen Wingrove**, Bearsted Rd, Weavering, Maidstone, **Kent**, ME14 5LD, ENG.
(T) 01622 730133
Speciality: Complementary Medicines & Therapy.
● **Owner** Mr K Wingrove
M (Ref:HM21704)

## WINGROVE, ROSEMARY

**Rosemary Wingrove**, 10 Copping Cl, Croydon, **Surrey**, CR0 5JZ, ENG.
(T) 020 8681 7182
Speciality: Reflexology.
S T (Ref:HM21705)

## WINGROVE-GIBBONS, KENNETH

**Kenneth Wingrove-Gibbons**, 1 Lower Grosvenor Pl, London, **London (Greater)**, SW1W 0EJ, ENG.
(T) 020 7233 5566 (F) 020 7931 8181
Speciality: Psychotherapy.
● **Owner** Ms R Delman
B (Ref:HM21706)

## WINGS AROMATHERAPY

**Wings Aromatherapy**, Lavandin House, 75 Clifton Way, Hinckley, **Leicestershire**, LE10 0UZ, ENG.
(T) 01455 633906
Speciality: Aromatherapy.
M O (Ref:HM21707)

## WINGS NATURAL THERAPIES

**Wings Natural Therapies**, Pulteney Drive, Stafford, **Staffordshire**, ST16 1NU, ENG.
(T) 01785 224922
Speciality: Complementary Medicines & Therapy.
C M (Ref:HM21708)

## WINN, NIGEL

**Nigel Winn**, 296A Ashby High St, Scunthorpe, **Humberside**, DN16 2RY, ENG.
(T) 01724 270165
Speciality: Hypnosis.
B (Ref:HM21709)

## WINN, NIGEL

**Nigel Winn**, 26 Dudley St, Grimsby, **Humberside (South)**, DN31 2AB, ENG.
(T) 01472 210378 (F) 01472 230788
Speciality: Hypnosis.
● **Owner** Mr N Winn
B (Ref:HM21710)

## WINNERSH HYPNOTHERAPY PRACTICE

**Winnersh Hypnotherapy Practice**, 7 Arun Cl, Winnersh, Wokingham, **Berkshire**, RG41 5PG, ENG.
(T) 01189 780134
(E) david.wise@talk21.com
Speciality: Counselling, Hypnosis, Hypnotherapy, Analysis. ✓
● **Hypnotherapist** Mr D Wise M: HA.
B Yrs. Est.: 11 (Ref:HM21711)

## WINNERT, NORMA

**Norma Winnert**, Sunnydown, Hightown Hill, Ringwood, **Hampshire**, BH24 3HG, ENG.
(T) 01425 479360
Speciality: Complementary Medicines & Therapy.
● **Owner** Mrs N Winnert
C M (Ref:HM21712)

## WINSKELL, HEIDI

**Heidi Winskell**, Knelle View, Main St, Beckley, Rye, **Sussex (East)**, TN31 6RG, ENG.
(T) 01797 260360
Speciality: Reflexology.
● **Owner** Ms H Winskell
S T (Ref:HM21713)

## WINSOR, REBECCA

**Rebecca Winsor**, Stillpoint, Broad St Pl, Bath, **Somerset**, BA1 5LH, ENG.
(T) 01225 460106
Speciality: Osteopathy.
P S T (Ref:HM21714)

## WINSTON, LAURIE

**Laurie Winston**, 60 Aldergill, Heelands, **Buckinghamshire**, MK13 7PT, ENG.
(T) 01908 322027
Speciality: Reflexology.
S T (Ref:HM21715)

## WINTER, B

**B Winter**, Westwood Heath Rd, Coventry, **Midlands (West)**, CV4 8AA, ENG.
(T) 024 7647 4847
Speciality: Psychology.
B (Ref:HM21716)

## WINTER, CLAIRE

**Claire Winter**, Derwent, High St, Ramsden, **Oxfordshire**, OX7 3AU, ENG.
(T) 01993 868019
Speciality: Massage (Therapeutic), Reflexology.
S T (Ref:HM21717)

## WINTER, DAVID

**David Winter**, 3 Farnham Park Drive, Farnham, **Surrey**, GU9 0HS, ENG.
(T) 01252 724059 (F) 01252 724059
(W) www.bssf-shiatsu-do.co.uk
Speciality: Shiatsu, Teaches Shiatsu and Runs Courses. ✓
● **Shiatsu Practitioner** Mr D Winter Q: Dip.Shiatsu, PhD. M: RSS.
C Yrs. Est.: 5 (Ref:HM21718)

## WINTER, DOROTHY

**Dorothy Winter**, 33 St John's Avenue, London, **London (Greater)**, SW15 6AL, ENG.
(T) 020 8789 4139
Speciality: Reflexology.
S T (Ref:HM21719)

## WINTER, JENNIFER

**Jennifer Winter**, 46 Alcester Rd, Stratford-Upon-Avon, **Warwickshire**, CV37 9DB, ENG.
(T) 01789 551461
Speciality: Acupuncture.
● **Owner** Mrs J Winter
O (Ref:HM21720)

## WINTER, SALLY

**Sally Winter**, 7 Nevern Gardens, Biddenham, Bedford, **Bedfordshire**, MK40 4RW, ENG.
(T) 01234 359545

Speciality: Chiropody. ✔
● **Joint Owner** Mr B Winter
● **Owner/Chiropodist** Ms S Winter Q: MBChA, MSSCh. M: S.C.P.
[T] Yrs. Est.: 6 (**Ref:**HM21721)

**WINTERBOTTOM, J T**

**J T Winterbottom**, 96A Agbrigg Rd, Wakefield, **Yorkshire (West)**, WF1 5AY, ENG.
(T) 01924 257250
Speciality: Chiropodists (Podiatrists).
[S] (**Ref:**HM21722)

**WINTERMEYER, IRENE**

**Irene Wintermeyer**, Clissold Park Health Centre, 154 Stoke Newington Church St, London, **London (Greater)**, N16 0JU, ENG.
(T) 020 7249 2990 (F) 020 7249 3977
Speciality: Complementary Medicines & Therapy.
● **Director** Mr D Berg
[M] (**Ref:**HM21723)

**WINTERS, J**

**J Winters**, 58 Ferrier Rd, Stevenage, **Hertfordshire**, SG2 0NU, ENG.
(T) 01438 213587
Speciality: Hypnotherapy.
[B] (**Ref:**HM21724)

**WINTERTON, SUZANNE**

**Suzanne Winterton**, 99 Eastbrook Rd, Lincoln, **Lincolnshire**, LN6 7EW, ENG.
(T) 01522 688494
(E) suzanne@merak-healing.org.uk
(W) www.merak-healing.org.uk
Speciality: Spiritual Healing.
● **Spiritual Healer** Ms S Winterton M: SMN.
[C] Yrs. Est.: 1 (**Ref:**HM21725)

**WINTON, BARBARA**

**Barbara Winton**, Brockaly, Broxwood, Leominster, **Herefordshire**, HR6 9JS, ENG.
(T) 01544 388814
Speciality: Homeopathy.
● **Owner** Mrs B Winton
[M] (**Ref:**HM21726)

**WINTON, DIANNA**

**Dianna Winton**, 6 Lasham Walk, Fareham, **Hampshire**, PO14 1SD, ENG.
(T) 01329 282657
Speciality: Hypnosis.
● **Owner** Mrs D Winton
[B] (**Ref:**HM21727)

**WINTOUR, BOBBY**

**Bobby Wintour**, Park Farm House, Clanna Rd, Alvington, Lydney, **Gloucestershire**, GL15 6AF, ENG.
(T) 01594 529234
Speciality: Reflexology.
[S] [T] (**Ref:**HM21728)

**WIRRAL CHIROPODY SERVICE**

**Wirral Chiropody Service & Foot Shop**, 96A Market St, Hoylake, Wirral, **Merseyside**, CH47 3BD, ENG.
(T) 01516 324848 (F) 01516 324848
Speciality: Chiropodists (Podiatrists).
● **Owner** Mrs H Coward
[S] (**Ref:**HM21729)

**WIRRALL CLINIC**

**Wirral Clinic (The)**, 43 The Wiend, Birkenhead, **Merseyside**, CH42 6RY, ENG.
(T) 01516 459073
Speciality: Acupuncture, Sports Therapy. ✔
● **Owner** Mr I Griffiths Q: Dip.Ac, MSc.
[B] Yrs. Est.: 10 (**Ref:**HM21730)

**WISE, ALAN**

**Alan Wise**, 49A High St, Bushey, Watford, **Hertfordshire**, WD2 1BD, ENG.
(T) 07973 744256 (F) 020 8950 0006
Speciality: Psychotherapy.
● **Owner** Mr A Wise
[B] (**Ref:**HM21731)

**WISE, CAROL**

**Carol Wise**, 24 Rose Bank, Burley In Wharfedale, Ilkley, **Yorkshire (West)**, LS29 7PQ, ENG.
(T) 01943 863213 (F) 01943 862549
Speciality: Homeopathy, Metamorphic Therapy, T'ai-Chi Ch'uan. ✔
● **Owner/Registered Homeopath** Ms C Wise Q: BA (Hons), RSHom. M: Soc.Hom.
[M] Yrs. Est.: 25 (**Ref:**HM21732)

**WISEMAN, DEBBIE**

**Debbie Wiseman**, 64 Millais Rd, Southampton, **Hampshire**, SO19 2FW, ENG.
(T) 023 8043 1120
Speciality: Chiropodists (Podiatrists).
● **Partner** Mrs D Wiseman
[S] (**Ref:**HM21733)

**WISEMAN, LOUISE**

**Louise Wiseman**, The Forge, Lamphey, Pembroke, **Pembrokeshire**, SA71 5NS, WAL.
(T) 01646 672238
Speciality: Acupuncture.
[O] (**Ref:**HM21734)

**WISEMAN, SANDRA**

**Sandra Wiseman**, 12 Southwood Gardens, Leigh-On-Sea, **Essex**, SS9 5DP, ENG.
(T) 01702 523951
Speciality: Reflexology.
[S] [T] (**Ref:**HM21735)

**WISHAHI, IRIS**

**Iris Wishahi**, 41 Stuart Rd, Richmond, **Surrey**, TW10 7QU, ENG.
(T) 020 8948 6673
Speciality: Hypnotherapy.
● **Owner** Ms I Wisahi
[B] (**Ref:**HM21736)

**WISHART, M A**

**M A Wishart**, 63 Rowley Rd, Orsett, Grays, **Essex**, RM16 3ET, ENG.
(T) 01375 673671
Speciality: Physiotherapy.
[P] [S] [T] (**Ref:**HM21737)

**WISHING WELL**

**Wishing Well (The)**, 7 - 9 Market Pl, Jedburgh, **Scottish Borders**, TD8 6AP, SCO.
(T) 01835 862685
Speciality: Acupuncture, Aromatherapy, Bach Remedies, Bowen Therapy, Colour Therapy, Complementary Therapy, Counselling, Cranial Osteopathy, Crystal Healing, Family Therapy, Group Therapy, Herbal Medicine, Holistic Healing, Homeopathy, Iridology, Kinesiology, Massage (Therapeutic), Nutritional Therapy, Phytotherapy, Reflexology, Reiki, Stress Therapy. ✔
● **Remedial Practitioner** Ms S Crawshaw Q: CQSW. M: SMTO.
[C] [M] Yrs. Est.: 3 (**Ref:**HM21738)

**WISHING WELL**

**Wishing Well**, Harmony Centre, 19 Greenacres, Oxted, **Surrey**, RH8 0PA, ENG.
(T) 01883 723246
Speciality: Complementary Medicines & Therapy.
[M] (**Ref:**HM21739)

**WISY, CHRISTINE**

**Christine Wisby**, 29 North Way, Bognor Regis, **Sussex (West)**, PO22 7BT, ENG.
(T) 01243 863457
Speciality: Chiropodists (Podiatrists).
[S] (**Ref:**HM21740)

**WISZNIEWSKI, H**

**H Wiszniewski**, 12 Millwood Lane, Todmorden, **Yorkshire (West)**, OL14 5SB, ENG.
(T) 01706 817525
Speciality: Osteopathy.
● **Owner** Miss H Wiszniewski
[M] (**Ref:**HM21741)

**WITCHELL, YVONNE**

**Yvonne Witchell**, 28 Salisbury Avenue, Westcliff-on-Sea, **Essex**, SS0 7AX, ENG.
(T) 01702 303912
Speciality: Homeopathy.
● **Owner** Miss Y Witchell
[M] (**Ref:**HM21742)

**WITCHES WAY**

**Witches Way (The)**, 5-6 Market Pl, Burton-On-Trent, **Staffordshire**, DE14 1HA, ENG.
(T) 01283 541500 (F) 01283 541500
Speciality: Complementary Medicines & Therapy.
● **Owner** Mr D Powell
[C] [M] (**Ref:**HM21743)

**WITCOMB, C**

**C Witcomb**, The Willows Clinic, 105 Short Heath Rd, Birmingham, **Midlands (West)**, B23 6LH, ENG.
(T) 01213 506550
Speciality: Chiropodists (Podiatrists).
[S] (**Ref:**HM21744)

**WITH COMPLEMENTS**

**With Complements**, 60B High St, Burton Latimer, Kettering, **Northamptonshire**, NN15 5LB, ENG.
(T) 01536 724441
Speciality: Reiki.
● **Owner** Mrs A Pinckney
[C] (**Ref:**HM21745)

**WITHERLEY, J E**

**J E Witherley**, 27 Berners St, Ipswich, **Suffolk**, IP1 3LN, ENG.
(T) 01473 253870
Speciality: Chiropodists (Podiatrists).
[S] (**Ref:**HM21746)

**WITHY, M**

**M Withy**, White Friars House, 14 White Friars, Chester, **Cheshire**, CH1 1NZ, ENG.
(T) 01244 322275
Speciality: Physiotherapy.
[P] [S] [T] (**Ref:**HM21747)

**WITHY, M A**

**M A Withy**, 35 Sandfields, Frodsham, **Cheshire**, WA6 6PT, ENG.
(T) 01928 731652
Speciality: Physiotherapy.
[P] [S] [T] (**Ref:**HM21748)

**WITHYMOOR PHYSIOTHERAPY CLINIC**

**Withymoor Physiotherapy Clinic**, Turners Lane, Brierley Hill, **Midlands (West)**, DY5 2PG, ENG.
(T) 01384 70374 (F) 01384 70374
Speciality: Physiotherapy. ✔
● **Owner/Physiotherapist** Mrs L Chell Q: MCSP, SRP. M: CSP.
[S] (**Ref:**HM21749)

**WITNEY CHIROPRACTIC/CHIROPODY**

**Witney Chiropractic And Chiropody Clinic (The)**, Moorland Rd, Witney, **Oxfordshire**, OX8 5PT, ENG.
(T) 01993 776619
Speciality: Chiropody, Chiropractic, X-Ray.
● **Chiropractor** Mr R Bonamy-Price Q: DO. M: BCA.
[C] Yrs. Est.: 15 (**Ref:**HM21750)

**WITNEY NATURAL HEALTH CLINIC**

**Witney Natural Health Clinic**, 41A Corn St, Witney, **Oxfordshire**, OX8 7DQ, ENG.
(T) 01993 708583 (F) 01993 772937
Speciality: Acupressure, Acupuncture, Aromatherapy, Bowen Therapy, Chiropractic, Colour Therapy, Complementary Therapy, Counselling, Crystal Healing, Dance Movement Therapy, Family Therapy, Herbal Medicine, Holistic Healing, Homeopathy, Hypnosis, Hypnotherapy, Indian Head Massage, Kinesiology, Manipulation, Massage (Therapeutic), Neuro-Linguistic Program, Oriental Diagnosis, Pilates, Reflexology, Reiki, Seichem, Shiatsu, Spiritual Healing, Sports Massage, Stress Therapy, T'ai-Chi Ch'uan, Transactional Analysis, Yoga, Manual Lymphatic Drainage, Trichology, Various Massage Therapies. ✔
● **Hypnotherapist** Mr W Fox Q: BCMA, Dip.Hyp, Dip.Psych, MCAH, MIAH. M: CAH, IAH.
● **Chiropractor** Mr M Anderson Q: DC.
[C] Yrs. Est.: 4 (**Ref:**HM21751)

**WITNEY OSTEOPATHIC CLINIC**

**Witney Osteopathic Clinic (The)**, Cogges Surgery, Cogges Hill Rd, Witney, **Oxfordshire**, OX8 6FP, ENG.
(T) 01993 709966
Speciality: Osteopathy.
[P] [S] [T] (**Ref:**HM21752)

Key: [B] Mind-Body Medicine [C] Complementary Medicine [H] Self Help Treatment [M] Medicinal Therapy [O] Oriental Medicine [P] Postural Therapy [S] Manipulative Structural Therapy [T] Touch Therapy

### WITTY, P E J

**P E J Witty**, St Georges House, 56 Billing Rd, Northampton, **Northamptonshire**, NN1 5DB, ENG.
(T) 01604 601641 (F) 01604 601641
Speciality: Physiotherapy.
● **Partner** Mr P Witty
P S T (**Ref:**HM21753)

### WIVENHOE DENTAL PRACTICE

**Wivenhoe Dental Practice**, 94 The Avenue, Wivenhoe, Colchester, **Essex**, CO7 9PP, ENG.
(T) 01206 825950
Speciality: Osteopathy.
● **Manager** Mrs L Lee
P S T (**Ref:**HM21754)

### WOBURN CLINIC

**Woburn Natural Therapy Centre**, 4 Tombland, Norwich, **Norfolk**, NR3 1HE, ENG.
(T) 01603 219254
(E) gretel@woburnhealth.co.uk
(W) www.woburnhealth.co.uk
Speciality: Acupuncture, Aromatherapy, Art Therapy, Bach Remedies, Cognitive Therapy, Colour Therapy, Complementary Therapy, Counselling, Cranial Osteopathy, Cranio-Sacral Therapy, Dance Movement Therapy, Gestalt Therapy, Healer, Herbal Medicine, Holistic Healing, Homeopathy, Hypnotherapy, Indian Head Massage, Iridology, Life Style Coaching, Massage (Therapeutic), Naturopathy, Neuro-Linguistic Program, Nutritional Therapy, Osteopathy, Pilates, Psychotherapy, Reflexology, Reiki, Shiatsu, Spiritual Healing, Stress Therapy, Yoga, Bio-Dynamic Massage, Astrology. ✔
● **Centre Director** Ms G Brice
● **Cranio-Sacral Therapist**
Mr P Malachowski M: RCST.
B Yrs. Est.: 1 (**Ref:**HM21755)

### WOBURN NATURAL HEALING CENTRE

**Woburn Natural Healing Centre**, 1st Floor Woburn Court, 8 Guildhall Hill, Norwich, **Norfolk**, NR2 1JG, ENG.
(T) 01603 219254
Speciality: Complementary Medicines & Therapy.
● **Manager** Mrs D Bunting
C M (**Ref:**HM21756)

### WOHL, M

**M Wohl**, 86 Alexandra Park Rd, London, **London (Greater)**, N10 2AD, ENG.
(T) 020 8883 4800
Speciality: Psychoanalysis.
● **Owner** Dr M Wohl
B (**Ref:**HM21757)

### WOHL, M (DR)

**Dr M Wohl**, 35 St. James Rd, Leicester, **Leicestershire**, LE2 1HR, ENG.
(T) 01162 404243 (F) 01162 404243
(E) miriamwohl@hotmail.com
Speciality: Alexander Technique, Medio legal reports and Medical reports for (DLA and AA) customers of the benefits agency. ✔
● **A.T Teacher/Doctor of Medicine**
Dr M Wohl Q: MSTAT. M: STAT.
B H P S T
Yrs. Est.: 11 (**Ref:**HM21758)

### WOHLER, A

**A Wohler**, Hiltingbury, Chandler's Ford, Eastleigh, **Hampshire**, SO53 5NY, ENG.
(T) 023 8026 7203
Speciality: Complementary Medicines & Therapy.
● **Owner** A Wohler
M (**Ref:**HM21759)

### WOKINGHAM CHIROPRACTIC CENTRE

**Wokingham Chiropractic Centre**, 18 Denton Rd, Wokingham, **Berkshire**, RG40 2DX, ENG.
(T) 01189 787466
Speciality: Chiropractic.
P S T (**Ref:**HM21760)

### WOKINGHAM COMP HEALTH CENTRE

**Wokingham Complementary Health Centre**, 3 Old Row Court, Rose St, Wokingham, **Berkshire**, RG40 1XZ, ENG.
(T) 01189 340035
Speciality: Alexander Technique.
● **Therapist** Ms R Tate
P S (**Ref:**HM21761)

### WOLFE, ROBERT

**Robert Wolfe**, 22 Ravenswood Cres, West Wickham, **Kent**, BR4 0JJ, ENG.
(T) 020 8777 1971
Speciality: Biomechanics, Nail Surgery, Electro Surgery, Lazer Therapy. ✔
● **Chiropodist (Podiatrist)**
Mr R Wolfe Q: DPodM, M.S.C.P, S.R.Ch. M: S.C.P.
M Yrs. Est.: 30 (**Ref:**HM21762)

### WOLSTENCROFT, B

**B Wolstencroft**, 30 Wordsworth Rd, Wallington, **Surrey**, SM6 9RH, ENG.
(T) 020 8669 8631
Speciality: Chiropodists (Podiatrists).
● **Owner** Mrs B Wolstencroft
S (**Ref:**HM21763)

### WOLSTENHOLME, SHEILA

**Sheila Wolstenholme**, Harrogate, **Yorkshire (North)**, HG3, ENG.
(T) 01423 770486
Speciality: Bach Remedies.
M (**Ref:**HM21764)

### WOLVERHAMPTON CHINESE MED CTRE

**Z&H Promo Ltd**, 5a Cleveland St, Wolverhampton, **Midlands (West)**, B73 5DR, ENG.
(T) 01902 428558
Speciality: Acupuncture, Herbal Medicine.
✔ [credit card]
● **Herbalist** Weiying Hu Q: Dip.Ac, Dip.CHM. M: RCHM.
O Yrs. Est.: 7 (**Ref:**HM21765)

### WOLVERHAMPTON HOMOEOPATHY

**Wolverhampton Homoeopathy Clinic**, 194 Penn Rd, Wolverhampton, **Midlands (West)**, WV3 0EQ, ENG.
(T) 01902 620622
Speciality: Homeopathy.
M (**Ref:**HM21766)

### WOLVERHAMPTON NUFFIELD HOSP

**Wolverhampton Nuffield Hospital**, Wood Rd, Wolverhampton, **Midlands (West)**, WV6 8LE, ENG.
(T) 01902 754177
Speciality: Physiotherapy.
P S T (**Ref:**HM21767)

### WOLVERHAMPTON PHYSIO/SPORTS

**Wolverhampton Physiotherapy & Sports Clinic**, Molineux Stadium Waterloo Rd, Wolverhampton, **Midlands (West)**, WV1 4QR, ENG.
(T) 01902 687060
Speciality: Physiotherapy.
P S T (**Ref:**HM21768)

### WOLVERTON COURT

**Wolverton Court**, Alkham Valley Rd, Alkham, Dover, **Kent**, CT15 7DS, ENG.
(T) 01304 825544
Speciality: Psychology.
● **Manager** Mr A Young
B (**Ref:**HM21769)

### WOMBWELL ACUPUNCTURE CLINIC

**Wombwell Acupuncture Clinic**, Wombwell Acupuncture Clinic, 10 Station Rd, Wombwell, Barnsley, **Yorkshire (South)**, S73 0AY, ENG.
(T) 01226 757447
Speciality: Acupuncture, Shiatsu. ✔
● **Owner/Acupuncturist** Mr D Bell Q: Dip.Ac.
C Yrs. Est.: 4 (**Ref:**HM21770)

### WOMEN & HEALTH

**Women & Health**, 4 Carol St, London, **London (Greater)**, NW1 0HU, ENG.
(T) 020 7482 2786
Speciality: Complementary Medicines & Therapy.
● **Manager** Mrs R Armstrong
C M (**Ref:**HM21771)

### WOMEN & MEDICAL PRACTICE

**Women & Medical Practice**, 40 Turnpike Lane, London, **London (Greater)**, N8 0PS, ENG.
(T) 020 8888 2782 (F) 020 8365 8157
Speciality: Psychotherapy.
● **Manager** Mrs C Moeckli
B (**Ref:**HM21772)

### WOMEN THERAPISTS REFERRAL SV

**Women Therapists Referral Service**, 86 Eleanor Rd, London, **London (Greater)**, E8 1DN, ENG.
(T) 020 8340 9016
Speciality: Psychotherapy.
● **Manager** Ms J Abram
B (**Ref:**HM21773)

### WOMENS COUNS & THERAPY SV

**Womens Counselling & Therapy Service**, Oxford Chambers, Oxford Pl, Leeds, **Yorkshire (West)**, LS1 3AX, ENG.
(T) 01132 455725
Speciality: Psychotherapy.
B (**Ref:**HM21774)

### WOMEN'S THERAPY CENTRE

**Women's Therapy Centre (The)**, 10 Manor Gardens, London, **London (Greater)**, N7 6AA, ENG.
(T) 020 7263 6200 (F) 020 7281 7879
Speciality: Psychotherapy.
● **Director** Mrs S Lanigan
B (**Ref:**HM21775)

### WOMENS THERAPY LINK

**Womens Therapy Link**, P O Box 2704, London, **London (Greater)**, NW5 2LW, ENG.
(T) 020 7916 0123 (F) 020 7916 0123
Speciality: Psychotherapy.
B (**Ref:**HM21776)

### WONG, ANGELA

**Angela Wong**, 8a Thurlow St, Bedford, **Bedfordshire**, MK40 1LR, ENG.
(T) 01234 352455
Speciality: Chiropodists (Podiatrists).
● **Owner** Mr B Damiano
S (**Ref:**HM21777)

### WONG, PO-YEE

**Wong Po-Yee**, 2 Harlington Rd East, Feltham, **London (Greater)**, TW14 0AB, ENG.
(T) 020 8890 8008
Speciality: Acupuncture.
● **Owner** Ms W Po-Yee
O (**Ref:**HM21778)

### WONGS ACUPUNCTURE

**Wongs Acupuncture**, 206 Cheltenham Rd, Bristol, BS6 5QU, ENG.
(T) 01179 427467 (F) 01179 427467
Speciality: Acupuncture.
● **Owner** Mr F Banh
O (**Ref:**HM21779)

### WOOD STREET CHIROPRACTIC CLNC

**Annette Dypping**, 133 Wood St, Barnet, **Hertfordshire**, EN5 5RY, ENG.
(T) 020 8441 0231
Speciality: Acupuncture, Alexander Technique, Allergy Testing, Chiropody, Chiropractic, Homeopathy, Hypnotherapy, Osteopathy. ✔
● **Chiropractor** Ms A Dypping Q: DO. M: BCA.
S Yrs. Est.: 10 (**Ref:**HM21780)

### WOOD STREET CLINIC

**Wood Street Clinic**, 133 Wood St, Barnet, **Hertfordshire**, EN5 4BX, ENG.
(T) 020 8441 0231/4497656 (F) 020 8441 0231
(E) woodstreetclinic@madasapish.com
Speciality: Bio-energetics, Clinical Ecology, Complementary Therapy, Homeopathy, Nutritional Therapy, Vibrational Therapy. ✔
● **Clinical Ecologist** Mr M Cole Q: DBRT. M: BPA, GCP.
M Yrs. Est.: 16 (**Ref:**HM21781)

### WOOD, A

**A Wood**, 26 Meadow Rd, Netherfield, Nottingham, **Nottinghamshire**, NG4 2FR, ENG.
(T) 01159 870140
Speciality: Chiropodists (Podiatrists).
● **Owner** Mr A Wood
S (**Ref:**HM21782)


Key continued: **Yrs.Est:** Years Established **Q:** Qualifications **M:** Professional Membership ✔ Indemnity Insurance [credit card] Accept Credit Cards

### WOOD, A R
**Mr A R Wood**, 291 Union Gr, Aberdeen, **Aberdeenshire**, AB10 6TB, **SCO**.
(T) 01224 315000
Speciality: Chiropody. ✔
● **Chiropodist** Mr A Wood Q: BSc, DPodM, M.S.C.P. M: S.C.P.
[M] Yrs. Est.: 5 (Ref:HM21783)

### WOOD, ALISON
**Alison Wood**, 9 Mossland Cl, Heywood, **Manchester (Greater)**, OL10 2PB, ENG.
(T) 01706 364913 (F) 01706 364913
Speciality: Reflexology.
● **Owner** Mrs A Wood
[S] [T] (Ref:HM21784)

### WOOD, ALISON
**Alison Wood**, 849 Burnley Rd, Walmersley, Bury, **Lancashire**, BL9 5JT, ENG.
(T) 01617 617448
Speciality: Massage (Therapeutic), Reflexology.
[S] [T] (Ref:HM21785)

### WOOD, ALLAN R
**Allan R Wood**, 3 Stondon Park, London, **London (Greater)**, SE23 1LB, ENG.
(T) 020 8699 4139
Speciality: Chiropodists (Podiatrists).
[S] (Ref:HM21786)

### WOOD, ANGELA
**Angela Wood**, 15 Copsleigh Cl, Salfords, Redhill, **Surrey**, RH1 5BJ, ENG.
(T) 01737 764485
Speciality: Chiropodists (Podiatrists).
[S] (Ref:HM21787)

### WOOD, ANNE
**Anne Wood**, Dalhousie, Tennis Lane, Winslow, Buckingham, **Buckinghamshire**, MK18 3HR, ENG.
(T) 01296 712041
Speciality: Chiropodists (Podiatrists).
● **Owner** Mrs A Wood
[S] (Ref:HM21788)

### WOOD, ARTHUR
**Arthur Wood**, 138 Westgate, Southwell, **Nottinghamshire**, NG25 0LT, ENG.
(T) 01636 813781
Speciality: Chiropodists (Podiatrists).
● **Owner** Mr A Woods
[S] (Ref:HM21789)

### WOOD, C
**C Wood**, 33 Causewayside, Edinburgh, **Edinburgh (City of)**, EH9 1QF, SCO.
(T) 01316 629686
Speciality: Chiropodists (Podiatrists).
[S] (Ref:HM21790)

### WOOD, CAROLINE
**Caroline Wood**, 193 Church Rd, Harold Wood, Romford, **Essex**, RM3 0SA, ENG.
(T) 01708 377549
Speciality: Chiropodists (Podiatrists).
● **Owner** Miss C Wood
[S] (Ref:HM21791)

### WOOD, COLIN
**Colin Wood**, Ivy House, 20 High St, Sutton Coldfield, **Midlands (West)**, B72 1AA, ENG.
(T) 01213 545551
Speciality: Chiropodists (Podiatrists).
[S] (Ref:HM21792)

### WOOD, DEANA
**Deana Wood M A R**, 91 Algernon Rd, London, **London (Greater)**, SE13 7AP, ENG.
(T) 020 8690 2475
Speciality: Reflexology.
[S] [T] (Ref:HM21793)

### WOOD, ELEANOR
**Eleanor Wood**, 57 Portchester Rd, Portsmouth, **Hampshire**, PO2 7HZ, ENG.
(T) 023 9261 0100
Speciality: Complementary Medicines & Therapy.
[M] (Ref:HM21794)

### WOOD, G W
**G W Wood**, 105 East Main St, Whitburn, Bathgate, **Lothian (West)**, EH47 0RQ, **SCO**.
(T) 01501 740732
Speciality: Physiotherapy.
● **Owner** Mr G Wood
[P] [S] [T] (Ref:HM21795)

### WOOD, GILLIAN
**Gillian Wood**, 19 Midmoor Rd, London, **London (Greater)**, SW19 4JD, ENG.
(T) 020 8946 2474
Speciality: Reflexology.
[S] [T] (Ref:HM21796)

### WOOD, J
**J Wood**, 81 Wilkinson St, Sheffield, **Yorkshire (South)**, S10 2GJ, ENG.
(T) 01142 761770 (F) 01142 761770
Speciality: Acupuncture.
● **Owner** Mr J Wood
[P] [S] [T] (Ref:HM21797)

### WOOD, J G
**Mrs J G Wood**, Rowan Garth, 39 Kingsway, Craigweil, Bognor Regis, **Sussex (West)**, PO21 4DH, ENG.
(T) 01243 262494
Speciality: Acupuncture, Complementary Therapy, Electrotherapy, Manipulation, Massage (Therapeutic), Pilates, Postural Integration, Stress Therapy, Ultrasonics. ✔
● **Physiotherapist** Mrs J Wood Q: Grad Dip Phys, MCSP, SRP. M: CSP, OCPPP.
[S] Yrs. Est.: 17 (Ref:HM21798)

### WOOD, JANE
**Jane Wood**, 28 High St, Standish, Wigan, **Lancashire**, WN6 0HL, ENG.
(T) 01257 421476
Speciality: Chiropodists (Podiatrists).
[S] (Ref:HM21799)

### WOOD, JANET
**Janet Wood**, Mews House, Hassall Rd, Alsager, Stoke-On-Trent, **Staffordshire**, ST7 2SL, ENG.
(T) 01270 878140
Speciality: Herbalists.
[M] (Ref:HM21800)

### WOOD, JEANIE M
**Jeanie M Wood**, South Lodge, Fulmer Grange, Framewood Rd, Wexham, Slough, **Berkshire**, SL2 4QS, ENG.
(T) 01753 662325
(E) jeanie.wood@.ukgateway.net
Speciality: Alexander Technique. ✔
● **Owner** Mrs J Wood Q: MSTAT.
[P] Yrs. Est.: 2 (Ref:HM21801)

### WOOD, JOHN V
**John V Wood**, 74 Cissbury Cr, Saltdean, Brighton, **Sussex (East)**, BN2 8RJ, ENG.
(T) 01273 301892
Speciality: Reflexology.
[S] [T] (Ref:HM21802)

### WOOD, JULIE
**Julie Wood**, Ashnicol, Gabwell Hill, Maidencombe, Torquay, **Devon**, TQ1 4TW, ENG.
(T) 01803 324422
Speciality: Hypnosis.
● **Owner** Mrs J Wood
[B] (Ref:HM21803)

### WOOD, P D
**P D Wood**, 11 Heath Rd, Haywards Heath, **Sussex (West)**, RH16 3AX, ENG.
(T) 01444 450162 (F) 01444 459816
Speciality: Physiotherapy.
● **Practice Manager** Mrs W Langley
[P] [S] [T] (Ref:HM21804)

### WOOD, S B
**S B Wood**, Cogges Hill Surgery, Cogges Hill Rd, Witney, **Oxfordshire**, OX8 6FP, ENG.
(T) 01993 779775
Speciality: Chiropodists (Podiatrists).
[S] (Ref:HM21805)

### WOOD, SAMANTHA
**Samantha Wood**, 15 Radstock Rd, Midsomer Norton, Bath, **Somerset**, BA3 2AJ, ENG.
(T) 01761 411839
Speciality: Chiropodists (Podiatrists).
● **Owner** Ms S Wood
[S] (Ref:HM21806)

### WOOD, SAMANTHA CRAIG
**Samantha Craig Wood**, Cherry Health Care, 53 High St, Cape Pl, Dorking, **Surrey**, RH4 1AW, ENG.
(T) 01306 876400
Speciality: Osteopathy.
[P] [S] [T] (Ref:HM21807)

### WOOD, TINA
**Tina Wood**, 3 Hurst Rd, Eastbourne, **Sussex (East)**, BN21 2PJ, ENG.
(T) 01323 411900
Speciality: Reflexology.
● **Owner** Ms A Rambaut
[S] [T] (Ref:HM21808)

### WOOD, TRACEY
**Tracey Wood**, The Albion Clinic, 4 Albion Pl, Doncaster, **Yorkshire (South)**, DN1 2EG, ENG.
(T) 01302 768638
Speciality: Osteopathy.
[P] [S] [T] (Ref:HM21809)

### WOOD, TRACY
**Tracy Wood**, 1 Bank Bottom Trce, Marsden, Huddersfield, **Yorkshire (West)**, HD7 6LX, ENG.
(T) 01484 845941
Speciality: Reflexology.
[S] [T] (Ref:HM21810)

### WOOD, VALERIE
**Valerie Wood**, 21 Streets Heath, West End, Woking, **Surrey**, GU24 9QY, ENG.
(T) 01276 857243 (F) 01276 857243
Speciality: Aromatherapy. ✔
● **Aromatherapist** Mrs V Wood Q: ITEC. M: ITEC.
[C] Yrs. Est.: 18 (Ref:HM21811)

### WOOD, W H & D
**W H & D Wood**, Nash Rd, Thornborough, Buckingham, **Buckinghamshire**, MK18 2DY, ENG.
(T) 01280 812565 (F) 01280 812019
Speciality: Complementary Medicines & Therapy.
● **Partner** Mr W Woods
[M] (Ref:HM21812)

### WOOD, WIN
**Win Wood**, Cinder Hill Farm, Ashby Rd, Thringstone, Coalville, **Leicestershire**, LE67 8UH, ENG.
(T) 01530 222385
Speciality: Psychotherapy.
● **Owner** Ms W Wood
[B] (Ref:HM21813)

### WOODALL, DOROTHY
**Dorothy Woodall**, 31 Village Rd, Clifton, Nottingham, **Nottinghamshire**, NG11 8NP, ENG.
(T) 01159 211567
Speciality: Reflexology.
[S] [T] (Ref:HM21814)

### WOODBERRY CLINIC
**Woodberry Clinic (The)**, 351 Muswell Hill Broadway, London, **London (Greater)**, N10 1BX, ENG.
(T) 020 8883 6079
Speciality: Osteopathy. ✔
● **Osteopath** Mr D Newman Q: DO. M: GOsC.
● **Osteopath** Ms N Seager Q: BSc. M: GOsC.
[S] Yrs. Est.: 9 (Ref:HM21815)

### WOODBRIDGE COMP HEALTH CENTRE
**Woodbridge Complementary Health Centre**, The Bungalow, Sandy Lane, Martlesham, Woodbridge, **Suffolk**, IP12 4SD, ENG.
(T) 07803 792796
Speciality: Bach Remedies, Indian Head Massage, Reflexology, Reiki, Spiritual Healing, Stress Therapy.
● **Partner** Mr A Luita
[C] (Ref:HM21816)

### WOODBRIDGE COUNS & PSYCHO CTRE
**Woodbridge Counselling & Psychotherapy Centre (The)**, Cumberland House, Cumberland St, Woodbridge, **Suffolk**, IP12 4AH, ENG.
(T) 01394 385915
Speciality: Psychotherapy.

Key: [B] Mind-Body Medicine [C] Complementary Medicine [H] Self Help Treatment [M] Medicinal Therapy [O] Oriental Medicine [P] Postural Therapy [S] Manipulative Structural Therapy [T] Touch Therapy

B (Ref:HM21817)

## WOODBRIDGE HILL CHIROPRACTOR

**Woodbridge Hill Chiropractor Clinic**, 1 Deerbarn Rd, Guildford, **Surrey**, GU2 8AT, ENG.
(T) 01483 454422
Speciality: Chiropractors.
● **Owner** Dr A Pouramini
P S T (Ref:HM21818)

## WOODBRIDGE PHYSIO PRACTICE

**Woodbridge Physiotherapy Practice**, Prentices Lane, Woodbridge, **Suffolk**, IP12 4LF, ENG.
(T) 01394 387916
Speciality: Physiotherapy.
● **Partner** Mrs D Golding
P S T (Ref:HM21819)

## WOODBURY COUNSELLING

**Woodbury Counselling**, Berkley House, 31 Bower Way, Slough, **Berkshire**, SL1 5HW, ENG.
(T) 01753 693630 (F) 01753 693630
Speciality: Hypnosis.
● **Owner** Mr T Sylvester
B (Ref:HM21820)

## WOODCOCK, JAMES

**James Woodcock**, 17 Swinley St, Wigan, **Lancashire**, WN1 2ED, ENG.
(T) 01942 239042
Speciality: Physiotherapy.
P S T (Ref:HM21821)

## WOODEN, SUSAN

**Susan Wooden**, 19 Crab Lane, Bradwell, Great Yarmouth, **Norfolk**, NR31 8DJ, ENG.
(T) 01493 667722
Speciality: Reflexology.
S T (Ref:HM21822)

## WOODFORD HALSE CHIROPRACTIC

**Woodford Halse Chiropractic Clinic (The)**, The Medical Centre, Station Rd, Woodford Halse, Daventry, **Northamptonshire**, NN11 3RB, ENG.
(T) 01327 261869
Speciality: Chiropractic.
● **Owner** Ms M Brzeski
P S T (Ref:HM21823)

## WOODHEAD, C S

**C S Woodhead**, 4 Wellington Circus, Nottingham, **Nottinghamshire**, NG1 5AL, ENG.
(T) 01159 484141 (F) 01159 532727
Speciality: Osteopathy.
● **Owner** Mr N Woodhead
P S T (Ref:HM21824)

## WOODHEAD, N D

**N D Woodhead**, 4 Wellington Circus, Nottingham, **Nottinghamshire**, NG1 5AL, ENG.
(T) 01159 484141 (F) 01159 532727
Speciality: Osteopathy.
● **Owner** Mr N Woodhead
P S T (Ref:HM21825)

## WOODHOUSE CLINIC

**Woodhouse Clinic (The)**, 2 Woodhouse Cliff, Leeds, **Yorkshire (West)**, LS6 2HF, ENG.
(T) 01132 753692 (F) 01132 740269
(E) apling@woodhouseclinic.co.uk
(W) www.woodhouseclinic.co.uk
Speciality: Chiropody, Complementary Therapy, Cranial Osteopathy, Electrotherapy, Homeopathy, Manipulation, Massage (Therapeutic), Micro Manipulation, Osteopathy, Non Surgical Face Lift, Cellulite Treatment, Hair Removal by Laser.
✔ CREDIT
● **Osteopath/Chiropodist**
Mr A Apling Q: BSc, DO, MBChA, MSSCh, PhD. M: BCA, GOsC.
S Yrs. Est.: 12 (Ref:HM21826)

## WOODHOUSE ROAD CHIROPRACTIC

**Woodhouse Road Chiropractic Clinic**, 22 Woodhouse Rd, Mansfield, **Nottinghamshire**, NG18 2AF, ENG.
(T) 01623 421401 (F) 01623 628880
Speciality: Chiropractic.
● **Owner** Mr U Sandstrom
P S T (Ref:HM21827)

## WOODIER, A

**A Woodier**, 2 Parliament St, Harrogate, **Yorkshire (North)**, HG1 2QZ, ENG.
(T) 01423 569158
Speciality: Chiropodists (Podiatrists).
S (Ref:HM21828)

## WOODINGTON, N J

**N J Woodington**, 32 Prince Of Wales Rd, Dorchester, **Dorset**, DT1 1PW, ENG.
(T) 01305 269164
Speciality: Osteopathy.
P S T (Ref:HM21829)

## WOODINGTON, NICHOLAS J

**Nicholas J Woodington**, 18A Madeira Rd, Clevedon, **Somerset**, BS21 7TJ, ENG.
(T) 01275 875464 (F) 01275 349051
Speciality: Osteopathy.
● **Owner** Mr N Woodington
P S T (Ref:HM21830)

## WOODLANDS NATURAL HEALTH CTRE

**Woodlands Natural Health Centre**, Woodland Rd, Derby, **Derbyshire**, DE22 1GR, ENG.
(T) 01332 299133
Speciality: Complementary Medicines & Therapy.
● **Therapist** Mr A Sanderson
M (Ref:HM21831)

## WOODLANDS NATURAL HLTH THERAPY

**Woodlands Natural Health Therapy Practice (The)**, 19 Talbot Cl, Reigate, **Surrey**, RH2 7HY, ENG.
(T) 01737 245586 (F) 01737 245655
(E) angelacooke@activelives.co.uk
Speciality: Aromatherapy, Bach Remedies, Complementary Therapy, Healer, Iridology, Nutritional Therapy, Reflexology. ✔
● **Owner/Therapist** Mrs A Cooke
Q: Dip.Naturecare, ITEC. M: AOC, AoR, GCP.
H T Yrs. Est.: 4 (Ref:HM21832)

## WOODLANDS REFLEXOLOGY

**Woodlands Reflexology**, 48 Woodlands Park Rd, Birmingham, **Midlands (West)**, B30 1HA, ENG.
(T) 01214 586901 (F) 01214 586901
Speciality: Reflexology.
● **Owner** Mrs M Heath
S T (Ref:HM21833)

## WOODLAWN HOLISTIC THERAPY CTRE

**Woodlawn Holistic Therapy Centre**, Woodlawn Rd, Killarney, **County Kerry**, IRE.
(T) 06433 360
Speciality: Acupressure, Aromatherapy, Bach Remedies, Colour Therapy, Homeopathy, Indian Head Massage, Massage (Therapeutic), Osteopathy, Reflexology, Reiki, Stress Therapy, Vibrational Therapy. ✔
● **Osteopath** Jeri A Moore
(T) 06439 764
● **Homeopath** Broadberry
(T) 06697 68945
● **Therapist** Ms M Quinlan M: IFR.
B Yrs. Est.: 12 (Ref:HM21834)

## WOODLEIGH, R M

**R M Woodleigh**, 73 Mundania Rd, London, **London (Greater)**, SE22 0NW, ENG.
(T) 020 8299 0181
Speciality: Osteopathy.
● **Owner** Mr R Woodleigh
P S T (Ref:HM21835)

## WOODLEY HEALING CENTRE

**A C Natural Therapy (Woodley) Ltd**, 5 Headley Rd, Woodley, Reading, **Berkshire**, RG5 4JB, ENG.
(T) 01189 628280 (F) 01189 628281
Speciality: Aromatherapy, Complementary Therapy, Dietician, Herbal Medicine, Holistic Healing, Life Style Coaching, Massage (Therapeutic), Nutritional Therapy, Phytotherapy, Reflexology, Remedial Massage, Vitamin Therapy, Oral Chelation Therapy. ✔
● **Director** Ms A Choules Q: BA, MBChA, MSSCh, RMANM.
M Yrs. Est.: 6 (Ref:HM21836)

## WOODLEY, ANDREW

**Andrew Woodley**, 79 Mallards, Shoeburyness, Southend-On-Sea, **Essex**, SS3 8XE, ENG.
(T) 01702 299417
Speciality: Clairvoyants & Palmists.
● **Owner** Mr A Woodley
B (Ref:HM21837)

## WOODLEY, SIMONE

**Simone Woodley**, 382 Godstone Rd, Kenley, **Surrey**, CR8 5BH, ENG.
(T) 020 8668 4195
Speciality: Clairvoyants & Palmists.
● **Owner** Mrs S Woodley
B (Ref:HM21838)

## WOODMAN, LINDA

**Linda Woodman**, Robins Hill, Townsend, Nympsfield, Stonehouse, **Gloucestershire**, GL10 3UG, ENG.
(T) 01453 861137
Speciality: Reflexology.
S T (Ref:HM21839)

## WOODNUTT, S

**S Woodnutt**, 32 Beaumont Rd, Totton, Southampton, **Hampshire**, SO40 3AN, ENG.
(T) 023 8086 0380
Speciality: Chiropodists (Podiatrists).
● **Owner** Mrs S Woodnutt
S (Ref:HM21840)

## WOODROW, ANNE

**Anne Woodrow**, Wishing Well Cottage, South Gorley, Fordingbridge, **Hampshire**, SP6 2PW, ENG.
(T) 01425 653623
Speciality: Reflexology.
S T (Ref:HM21841)

## WOODROW, IAN

**Ian Woodrow**, 1 Church Rd, Newton Abbot, **Devon**, TQ12 1AL, ENG.
(T) 01626 333382 (F) 01626 333382
Speciality: Hypnosis.
● **Owner** Mr I Woodrow
B (Ref:HM21842)

## WOODROW, IRENE

**Irene Woodrow**, Hazeley Cottage, Nightingale Lane, Mortimer, Reading, **Berkshire**, RG7 3PS, ENG.
(T) 01189 333400 (F) 01189 331130
Speciality: Alexander Technique.
● **Owner** Mrs I Woodrow
P S (Ref:HM21843)

## WOODROW, LORRAINE

**Lorraine Woodrow**, 16 Lavington Gardens, North Baddesley, **Hampshire**, SO52 9NR, ENG.
(T) 023 8073 1717
Speciality: Reflexology.
S T (Ref:HM21844)

## WOODS PLACE FITNESS CENTRE

**Woods Place Fitness Centre**, 1 Woods Pl, Tower Bridge, London, **London (Greater)**, SE1 3BS, ENG.
(T) 07769 696311
Speciality: Complementary Medicines & Therapy.
● **Kinesiologist** Elaine Mills
M (Ref:HM21845)

## WOODS, A

**A Woods**, 2 Cedar Way, Stafford, **Staffordshire**, ST17 0LU, ENG.
(T) 01785 661308
Speciality: Chiropodists (Podiatrists).
● **Owner** Mr A Woods
S (Ref:HM21846)

## WOODS, JILL

**Jill Woods**, 84 Beauly Way, Romford, **Essex**, RM1 4XR, ENG.
(T) 01708 726053
Speciality: Bach Remedies.
● **Owner** Mrs J Woods
C (Ref:HM21847)

## WOODS, JILL

**Jill Woods**, Romford, **Essex**, RM1, ENG.
(T) 01708 726053
Speciality: Bach Remedies.
M (Ref:HM21848)

## WOODS, K M

**K M Woods**, 15 Royal Cres, Glasgow, **Glasgow**



Key continued: Yrs.Est: Years Established Q: Qualifications M: Professional Membership ✔ Indemnity Insurance CREDIT Accept Credit Cards

**(City of)**, G3 7SL, **SCO**.
(T) 01413 530906 (F) 01416 160107
Speciality: Physiotherapy.
● **Owner** Mrs K Woods
**P S T** (**Ref:**HM21849)

### WOODS, K M

**Mrs K M Woods**, Mearns Medical Centre, 3 Eaglesham Rd, Newton Mearns, Glasgow, **Glasgow (City of)**, G77 6TS, **SCO**.
(T) 01416 399143
Speciality: Physiotherapy.
**P S T** (**Ref:**HM21850)

### WOODS, L

**L Woods**, 7 Wellington Avenue, Reading, **Berkshire**, RG2 7BP, **ENG**.
(T) 01189 670139
Speciality: Complementary Medicines & Therapy.
● **Owner** Louise Woods
**M** (**Ref:**HM21851)

### WOODS, LAWRENCE (DR)

**Woods Dr Lawrence**, 42 Baggot St, Lr, Dublin, **County Dublin**, **IRE**.
(T) 01678 7979 (F) 01678 7911
(E) advancedchiropractic@ireland.com
(W) www.chiropractorireland.com
Speciality: Chiropractors.
**P S T** (**Ref:**HM21852)

### WOODS, LAWRENCE (DR)

**Woods Dr Lawrence B Sc D C**, North Mall, Westport, **County Mayo**, **IRE**.
(T) 09828 545
Speciality: Chiropractors.
**P S T** (**Ref:**HM21853)

### WOODS, LEONIE

**Leonie Woods**, Church Cottage, Owston Village, Owston, Doncaster, **Yorkshire (South)**, DN6 9JF, **ENG**.
(T) 01302 330587
Speciality: Aromatherapy.
● **Owner** Mrs L Woods
**M O** (**Ref:**HM21854)

### WOODS, PETER

**Peter Woods**, 6 Dacre Rd, Rochdale, **Lancashire**, OL11 2LH, **ENG**.
(T) 01706 648263
Speciality: Hypnotherapy.
● **Owner** Mr P Woods
**B** (**Ref:**HM21855)

### WOODS, ROBERT

**Robert Woods**, 63A Belsize Lane, London, **London (Greater)**, NW3 5AU, **ENG**.
(T) 020 7435 3479
Speciality: Psychotherapy.
● **Owner** Mr R Woods
**B** (**Ref:**HM21856)

### WOODSIDE CLINIC

**Woodside Clinic**, 88 Great Northern Rd, Dunstable, **Bedfordshire**, LU5 4BT, **ENG**.
(T) 01582 608400 (F) 01582 471371
(E) woodsideclinic@talk21.com
Speciality: Acupressure, Acupuncture, Aromatherapy, Complementary Therapy, Cranial Osteopathy, Cupping, Electrotherapy, Herbal Medicine, Homeopathy, Indian Head Massage, Manipulation, Massage (Therapeutic), Moxibustion, Osteopathy, Phytotherapy, Pilates, Reflexology, Physiotherapy and Neurophysiotherapy.
● **Clinical Director/Osteopath**
Mr J Betser **Q:** DO. **M:** GOsC.
● **Osteopath** Alex Hamilton **M:** GOsC.
● **Senior Receptionist**
Jeanette Ward
● **Osteopath** Natalie Seager **Q:** BSc, Hons (OST). **M:** GOsC.
● **Physiotherapist** Mr A Renwick **M:** CSP, SRP.
**S** Yrs. Est.: 13 (**Ref:**HM21857)

### WOODSIDE COUNSELLING

**Woodside Counselling**, 2 Woodside Mansions, Fortis Green, London, **London (Greater)**, N10 3NY, **ENG**.
(T) 020 8883 2651
Speciality: Psychotherapy.
**B** (**Ref:**HM21858)

### WOODSIDE NATURAL HEALTH

**Woodside Natural Health**, 43 Woodside, Leigh-On-Sea, **Essex**, SS9 4QX, **ENG**.
(T) 01702 525391
(E) frankwaters@connectfree.co.uk
Speciality: Absent Healing, Acupressure, Aromatherapy, Cranial Osteopathy, Healer, Healing Therapy, Kinesiology, Manipulation, Massage (Therapeutic), Nutritional Therapy, Oriental Diagnosis, Osteopathy, Polarity Therapy, Reiki, Shiatsu, Spiritual Healing, Qi Gong Tuina.
● **Nutritionist/Kinesiologist**
Ms J Johnson **Q:** NFSH.
● **Manipulative/Cranial Therapist**
Mr F Waters
(T) 01702 474874 **Q:** DO, LCSP, MAO. **M:** LCSP.
**B C** Yrs. Est.: 17 (**Ref:**HM21859)

### WOODSIDE OSTEOPATHIC CLINIC

**Woodside Osteopathic Clinic**, 47a Bancroft, Hitchin, **Hertfordshire**, SG5 1LA, **ENG**.
(T) 01462 452929
Speciality: Osteopathy.
● **Senior Partner** Mr A El-Sayed
**P S T** (**Ref:**HM21860)

### WOODWARD, A J

**A J Woodward**, 422 Wigan Rd, Bolton, **Lancashire**, BL3 4QH, **ENG**.
(T) 01204 452364 (F) 01204 452364
Speciality: Chiropodists (Podiatrists).
● **Owner** Mr A Woodward
**S** (**Ref:**HM21861)

### WOODWARD, ANITA

**Anita Woodward**, Natural Health Clinic, 177 Moorside Rd, Swinton, Manchester, **Manchester (Greater)**, M27 9LD, **ENG**.
(T) 01617 930091
Speciality: Complementary Medicines & Therapy.
● **Partner** Mr B Jordan
**M** (**Ref:**HM21862)

### WOODWARD, CHRISTINE

**Christine Woodward**, 16 Freeman Avenue, Eastbourne, **Sussex (East)**, BN22 9NT, **ENG**.
(T) 01323 508138
Speciality: Reflexology.
**S T** (**Ref:**HM21863)

### WOODWARD, CLIVE

**Clive Woodward**, 1 Jasmine Cottage, Withyham Rd, Groombridge, Tunbridge Wells, **Kent**, TN3 9QN, **ENG**.
(T) 01892 862308
Speciality: Chiropodists (Podiatrists).
**S** (**Ref:**HM21864)

### WOODWARD, JILL

**Jill Woodward**, 11A Stoneleigh Rd, Coventry, **Midlands (West)**, CV4 7AB, **ENG**.
(T) 024 7641 8272
Speciality: Physiotherapy.
**P S T** (**Ref:**HM21865)

### WOODWARD, MARGARET

**Margaret Woodward**, The Tilt House, 10 Brownswood Rd, Beaconsfield, **Buckinghamshire**, HP9 2NU, **ENG**.
(T) 01494 673903
(E) mw.healthworks@btinternet.com
Speciality: Bach Remedies, Complementary Therapy, Healer, Indian Head Massage, Naturopathy, Reflexology, Reiki, Spiritual Healing.
● **Complementary Therapist**
Ms M Woodward **Q:** BFRP, ITEC, MIFA. **M:** IFR.
**T** Yrs. Est.: 8 (**Ref:**HM21866)

### WOODWARD, MARGARET

**LornMargaret Woodward**, Beaconsfield, **Buckinghamshire**, HP9, **ENG**.
(T) 01494 673903
Speciality: Bach Remedies.
**M** (**Ref:**HM21867)

### WOODWARD, MARGARET

**Margaret Woodward**, Inverurie, **Aberdeenshire**, AB51, **SCO**.
(T) 01651 872325
Speciality: Bach Remedies.
**M** (**Ref:**HM21868)

### WOODWARD, SUZANNE

**Suzanne Woodward**, 23 West St, Reigate, **Surrey**, RH2 9BL, **ENG**.
(T) 01737 226263
Speciality: Herbalists.
● **Owner** Ms S Woodward
**M** (**Ref:**HM21869)

### WOOLCOCK & ASSOCIATES

**M Woolcock & Associates**, 26 Cheriton Gardens, Folkestone, **Kent**, CT20 2AS, **ENG**.
(T) 01303 850077 (F) 01303 226225
Speciality: Osteopathy.
● **Owner** Mr T Drion
**P S T** (**Ref:**HM21870)

### WOOLF, JOY

**Joy Woolf**, 158 Ivory Down, Bromley, **Kent**, BR1 5EF, **ENG**.
(T) 020 8697 7877
Speciality: Shiatsu.
● **Shiatsu Practitioner** Ms J Woolf
**Q:** Dip.Shiatsu.
**C** Yrs. Est.: 3 (**Ref:**HM21871)

### WOOLF, PERRY

**Perry Woolf Podiatrist**, 31 Queen Anne St (Off Harley Street), London, **London (Greater)**, W1M 9FB, **ENG**.
(T) 020 7636 1823 (F) 020 8906 1686
(E) perryfoot@hotmail.com
Speciality: Chiropody, Electrotherapy, Manipulation, Massage (Therapeutic), Phytotherapy, Podiatry, Ultrasonics.
● **Therapist** Mr W Perry **Q:** DPodM, FRSH, M.S.C.P, S.R.Ch. **M:** S.C.P.
**M** Yrs. Est.: 30 (**Ref:**HM21872)

### WOOLFE, MICHAEL & LESLIE

**Michael & Leslie Woolfe**, 77 Windermere Avenue, London, **London (Greater)**, N3 3RD, **ENG**.
(T) 020 8349 2728
Speciality: Reflexology.
● **Owner** Mr M Woolfe
**S T** (**Ref:**HM21873)

### WOOLFSON, GERALD

**Gerald Woolfson**, 97 Harley St, London, **London (Greater)**, W1N 1DF, **ENG**.
(T) 020 7935 3400
Speciality: Psychiatry.
**B** (**Ref:**HM21874)

### WOOLFSON, L J

**L J Woolfson**, 25 Irwin Avenue, York, **Yorkshire (North)**, YO31 7TX, **ENG**.
(T) 01904 422518 (F) 01904 422518
Speciality: Chiropodists (Podiatrists).
● **Owner** Mr L Woolfson
**S** (**Ref:**HM21875)

### WOOLLARD, J

**J Woollard**, 5 Henry St, Keighley, **Yorkshire (West)**, BD21 3DR, **ENG**.
(T) 01535 604164
Speciality: Chiropodists (Podiatrists).
**S** (**Ref:**HM21876)

### WOOLLEY, LESLEY ANN

**Lesley Ann Woolley**, Flat 1, 36 Cissbury Rd, Worthing, **Sussex (West)**, BN14 9LF, **ENG**.
(T) 01903 212349
Speciality: Reflexology.
● **Owner** Mrs L Woolley
**S T** (**Ref:**HM21877)

### WOOLLEY, M E

**M E Woolley**, 73 Wellington Rd, Bollington, Macclesfield, **Cheshire**, SK10 5HT, **ENG**.
(T) 01625 572354
Speciality: Chiropody.
● **Chiropodist (Podiatrist)**
Ms M Woolley **Q:** DPodM, S.R.Ch. **M:** S.R.Ch.
**C** Yrs. Est.: 26 (**Ref:**HM21878)

### WOOLLEY, N

**N Woolley**, The Cottage, Threshers Dean, Headley, Epsom, **Surrey**, KT18 6LJ, **ENG**.
(T) 01372 379270
Speciality: Osteopathy.

Key: **B** Mind-Body Medicine **C** Complementary Medicine **H** Self Help Treatment **M** Medicinal Therapy **O** Oriental Medicine **P** Postural Therapy **S** Manipulative Structural Therapy **T** Touch Therapy

● **Owner** Mr N Woolley
P S T (**Ref:**HM21879)

### WOOLLISCROFT, J
**J Woolliscroft**, 28 Whitehall Gardens, London, **London (Greater)**, E4 6EH, ENG.
**(T)** 020 8559 3568
**Speciality:** Psychotherapy.
● **Owner** Mrs J Woolliscroft
B (**Ref:**HM21880)

### WOOLPITPHYSIO
**WoolpitPhysio**, Church Gate House, Stowmarket Rd, Woolpit, Bury St. Edmunds, **Suffolk**, IP30 9QQ, ENG.
**(T)** 01359 241304 **(F)** 01359 242980
**Speciality:** Physiotherapy.
● **Physiotherapist** Ms S Howard **Q:** Grad Dip Phys, MCSP, SRP. **M:** CSP.
S (**Ref:**HM21881)

### WOOLRICH, R J
**R J Woolrich**, Leek Rd, Stoke-On-Trent, **Staffordshire**, ST2 7AA, ENG.
**(T)** 01782 543113 **(F)** 01782 543113
**Speciality:** Homeopathy.
● **Owner** Mrs R Woolrich
S T (**Ref:**HM21882)

### WOOLSGROVE, F A
**F A Woolsgrove**, 15 Handen Rd, London, **London (Greater)**, SE12 8NP, ENG.
**(T)** 020 8318 3833
**Speciality:** Homeopathy.
● **Owner** Mr F Woolsgrove
M (**Ref:**HM21883)

### WOOLTORTON, S J
**S J Wooltorton**, The Brambles, 11 Oakwood Drive, Wymondham, **Norfolk**, NR18 0UG, ENG.
**(T)** 01953 607540
**Speciality:** Chiropodists (Podiatrists).
S (**Ref:**HM21884)

### WOOTTON BASSETT
**Wootton Bassett Physiotherapy Practice**, 60 High St, Wootton Bassett, Swindon, **Wiltshire**, SN4 7AQ, ENG.
**(T)** 01793 848424 **(F)** 01793 848424
**Speciality:** Acupuncture, Bowen Therapy, Manipulation, Ultrasonics. ✔
● **Practice Owner** Ms L Catling **Q:** MCSP, SRP. **M:** CSP, OCPPP.
S **Yrs. Est.:** 5 (**Ref:**HM21885)

### WORCESTER NATURAL THERAPY CTRE
**Worcester Natural Therapy Centre**, 36A The Tything, Worcester, **Worcestershire**, WR1 1JL, ENG.
**(T)** 01905 612521
**(W)** www.worcesternaturaltherapycentre.co.uk
**Speciality:** Acupuncture, Alexander Technique, Allergy Testing, Aromatherapy, Bowen Therapy, Chiropractic, Crystal Healing, Dietician, Healing Therapy, Homeopathy, Kinesiology, Osteopathy, Reflexology, Reiki, Shiatsu, Emotional Relief, Vibrotherapy. ✔
● **Director/Holistic Therapist** Mrs C Davis **Q:** BEd (Hons), MSc.
● **Psychotherapeutic Counsellor** Ms T Abbott **Q:** BSc (Hons), Dip.Couns.
● **Osteopath** Ms M Olorenshaw **Q:** BSc, Hons (OST). **M:** GOsC.
● **Chiropractor** Ms R Newell
● **Homeopath** Ms R Hermolle **Q:** LCPH, MHMA.
● **Holistic Massage Practitioner** Ms K Don
● **Acupuncturist** Ms J Hillman **Q:** BRCP, BSc (Hons), Cert.Ac, Dip.Ac.
● **Stress Manager/Hypnotherapist/Counsellor** Ms E Shenton **Q:** MNCH.
● **Allergy Therapist** Ms S Hough
● **Smoking Cessation Consultant** Ms J Morris
● **Aromatherapist/Nutritional Therapist** Ms M Dadswell **Q:** BABTAC.
● **Therapist** Ms J Maund **Q:** BTER.
● **Acupuncturist/Shiatsu Practitioner** Altair De Almeida **Q:** Lic.Ac, MBAcC, MRSS.
● **Reflexologist** Ms S Bradley **M:** AoR.
C **Yrs. Est.:** 20 (**Ref:**HM21886)

### WORDEN, JENNY
**Jenny Worden**, 14 Woodside Rd, Poole, **Dorset**, BH14 9JJ, ENG.
**(T)** 01202 739730
**Speciality:** Homeopathy.
M (**Ref:**HM21887)

### WORDEN, W M
**W M Worden**, 175 Heene Rd, Worthing, **Sussex (West)**, BN11 4NN, ENG.
**(T)** 01903 200650 **(F)** 01903 200650
**Speciality:** Chiropodists (Podiatrists).
● **Owner** Mr M Worden
S (**Ref:**HM21888)

### WORDSWOOD PHYSIO PRACTICE
**Wordswood Physiotherapy Practice**, 54 Lordswood Rd, Birmingham, **Midlands (West)**, B17 9DB, ENG.
**(T)** 01214 264300
**Speciality:** Physiotherapy.
● **Owner** Ms J Preston
P S T (**Ref:**HM21889)

### WORDSWORTH, LINDA
**Linda Wordsworth**, 4 Sheriff Way, Garston, Watford, **Hertfordshire**, WD25 7QF, ENG.
**(T)** 01923 662843
**Speciality:** Reflexology, Reiki, The Wordsworth Technique. ✔
● **Owner/Therapist** Ms L Wordsworth **Q:** BSc (Hons), MAR. **M:** AoR.
T **Yrs. Est.:** 8 (**Ref:**HM21890)

### WORDSWORTH, P M
**P M Wordsworth**, St Helens Cottage, St Helens Lane, Leeds, **Yorkshire (West)**, LS16 8BR, ENG.
**(T)** 01132 610992
**Speciality:** Physiotherapy.
● **Owner** Mr P Wordsworth
P S T (**Ref:**HM21891)

### WORK WITH ME
**Work With Me**, 245 Old Heath Rd, Colchester, **Essex**, CO2 8BN, ENG.
**(T)** 01206 797276
**Speciality:** Reflexology.
S T (**Ref:**HM21892)

### WORKER, MALCOLM
**Malcolm Worker**, 111 Cilfynydd Rd, Pontypridd, **Rhondda Cynon Taff**, CF37 4NF, WAL.
**(T)** 01443 405550
**Speciality:** Complementary Medicines & Therapy.
● **Owner** Mr M Worker
C M (**Ref:**HM21893)

### WORKSOP CHIROPRACTIC CLINIC
**Worksop Chiropractic Clinic**, 9 Newcastle St, Worksop, **Nottinghamshire**, S80 2AS, ENG.
**(T)** 01909 531484
**Speciality:** Chiropractors.
● **Principal** Dr P Western
P S T (**Ref:**HM21894)

### WORKSOP HEALTH CENTRE
**Worksop Health Centre**, Newgate St, Worksop, **Nottinghamshire**, S80 1HP, ENG.
**(T)** 01909 500519
**Speciality:** Chiropodists (Podiatrists).
S (**Ref:**HM21895)

### WORLAND, ANN
**Ann Worland**, 20 Blenheim Avenue, Stony Stratford, Milton Keynes, **Buckinghamshire**, MK11 1EX, ENG.
**(T)** 01908 563391
**Speciality:** Aromatherapy.
M O (**Ref:**HM21896)

### WORLD OF HEALTH
**World of Health (The)**, 17 Kitchener St, Wishaw, **Lanarkshire (North)**, ML2 7JQ, SCO.
**(T)** 01698 355138
**Speciality:** Aromatherapy, Vitamin Therapy, Hypericum, Natural Skin Care.
C (**Ref:**HM21897)

### WORLD OF LIGHT
**World Of Light Ltd**, 260 Kilburn Lane, London, **London (Greater)**, W10 4BA, ENG.
**(T)** 020 8964 0809 **(F)** 020 8964 0336
**(E)** yubraj@world-of-light.com
**(W)** www.world-of-light.com
**Speciality:** Acupressure, Acupuncture, Aromatherapy, Bowen Therapy, Chiropractic, Complementary Therapy, Counselling, Crystal Healing, Healer, Herbal Medicine, Homeopathy, Massage (Therapeutic), Meditation, Reflexology, Reiki, Spiritual Healing. ✔
● **Shop Manager** Mr A Wallis
● **Doctor** Yubraj Sharma **Q:** BS, Dip.Ac, MB, MFHom, MRCP. **M:** FHom.
B **Yrs. Est.:** 2 (**Ref:**HM21898)

### WORLD OF SCENTS
**World Of Scents**, 3 Old Foundry Rd, Ipswich, **Suffolk**, IP4 2AS, ENG.
**(T)** 01473 222322 **(F)** 01473 444446
**Speciality:** Aromatherapy.
M O (**Ref:**HM21899)

### WORLD TREE NATURAL CRYSTALS
**World Tree Natural Crystals**, 17 Station Prde, Richmond, **Surrey**, TW9 3PS, ENG.
**(T)** 020 8332 0162
**Speciality:** Complementary Medicines & Therapy.
● **Owner** Mr J Love
C M (**Ref:**HM21900)

### WORLD WIDE HEALTH
**World Wide Health**, Blackbrook Farm House, Ashby Rd, Shepshed, Loughborough, **Leicestershire**, LE12 9BP, ENG.
**(T)** 01509 505600 **(F)** 01509 650286
**Speciality:** Complementary Medicines & Therapy.
● **Owner** Mr S Presbury
M (**Ref:**HM21901)

### WORSFOLD, ALAN R
**Alan R Worsfold**, 12 New Rd, Wonersh, Guildford, **Surrey**, GU5 0SE, ENG.
**(T)** 01483 892362
**Speciality:** Chiropodists (Podiatrists).
● **Owner** Mr A Worsfold
S (**Ref:**HM21902)

### WORSFOLD, CHRISTINE
**Christine Worsfold**, 31 Hazelhurst Cres, Worthing, **Sussex (West)**, BN14 0HW, ENG.
**(T)** 01903 873752
**(E)** worsfold@btinternet.com
**Speciality:** Chiropody. ✔
● **Chiropodist (Podiatrist)** Mrs C Worsfold **Q:** M.S.C.P, S.R.Ch. **M:** S.C.P, S.R.Ch.
M **Yrs. Est.:** 27 (**Ref:**HM21903)

### WORSLEY, JULIA
**Julia Worsley**, Toft Lea, New Rd, Toft Monks, Beccles, **Suffolk**, NR34 0JW, ENG.
**(T)** 01502 677423
**Speciality:** Reflexology.
S T (**Ref:**HM21904)

### WORTH PHYSIO/SPORTS CLINIC
**Worth Physiotherapy & Sports Injury Clinic**, 25 The Canter, Crawley, **Sussex (West)**, RH10 7YX, ENG.
**(T)** 01293 884507
**Speciality:** Physiotherapy.
P S T (**Ref:**HM21905)

### WORTH, PHILIP
**Philip Worth**, The Whitehouse, 282 St. Johns Rd, Hemel Hempstead, **Hertfordshire**, HP1 1QG, ENG.
**(T)** 01442 219808
**Speciality:** Complementary Medicines & Therapy.
M (**Ref:**HM21906)

### WORTHING CHIROPRACTIC CLINIC
**R C Cracknell**, 25 Shakespeare Rd, Worthing, **Sussex (West)**, BN11 4AS, ENG.
**(T)** 01903 210536
**Speciality:** Chiropractic. ✔
● **Chiropractor** Dr R Cracknell **Q:** DC.
P **Yrs. Est.:** 14 (**Ref:**HM21907)

### WORTHING CLINIC OF ACUPUNCTURE
**Worthing Clinic Of Acupuncture**, 27A Goring Rd, Goring-By-Sea, Worthing, **Sussex (West)**, BN12 4AR, ENG.
**(T)** 01903 502048

Speciality: Acupuncture, Psychotherapy. ✔
● **Acupuncturist** Alex Paton Q: Lic.Ac.
M: BAcC.
O Yrs. Est.: 2 (Ref:HM21908)

## WORTHING CLINIC OF ACUPUNCTURE

**Worthing Clinic Of Acupuncture**, 1 Drummond Rd, Goring-By-Sea, Worthing, **Sussex (West)**, BN12 4DX, ENG.
(T) 01903 502048
Speciality: Acupuncture.
O (Ref:HM21909)

## WORTHINGTON EYRE DR GLENN

**Worthington Eyre Dr Glenn**, Loughrea, **County Galway**, IRE.
(T) 09184 1859 (F) 09184 1863
(E) eyre@iol.ie
Speciality: Chiropractors.
P S T (Ref:HM21910)

## WORTHINGTON, MICHAEL

**Michael Worthington**, 37 Mersea Rd, Colchester, **Essex**, CO2 7QS, ENG.
(T) 01206 364636
Speciality: Hypnotherapy.
● **Owner** Mr M Worthington
B (Ref:HM21911)

## WORTLEY, A F

**A F Wortley**, 74 Newport, Lincoln, **Lincolnshire**, LN1 3DT, ENG.
(T) 01522 525986
Speciality: Physiotherapy.
● **Owner** A Wortley
P S T (Ref:HM21912)

## WORTLEY, J

**J Wortley**, 74 Newport, Lincoln, **Lincolnshire**, LN1 3DT, ENG.
(T) 01522 525986
Speciality: Chiropodists (Podiatrists).
S (Ref:HM21913)

## WOTHERSPOON, E

**E Wotherspoon**, The Surgery, 1 Boxwell Rd, Berkhamsted, **Hertfordshire**, HP4 3EU, ENG.
(T) 01442 863119 (F) 01442 879909
Speciality: Physiotherapy.
● **Senior Partner** Dr A Pride
P S T (Ref:HM21914)

## WOZNIAK, HELEN

**Helen Wozniak**, 42 Borden Avenue, Enfield, **London (Greater)**, EN1 2BY, ENG.
(T) 020 8364 3778
Speciality: Hypnosis.
● **Owner** Ms H Wozniak
B (Ref:HM21915)

## WRATHALL, DOROTHY M

**Dorothy M Wrathall**, 5 Kingsdale Cl, Leyland, Preston, **Lancashire**, PR5 2DS, ENG.
(T) 01772 433020
Speciality: Physiotherapy.
● **Owner** Mrs D Wrathall
P S T (Ref:HM21916)

## WRAY, CAROLE

**Carole Wray**, 34 Lucerne Prde, **County Antrim**, BT9 5FT, NIR.
(T) 028 9066 9913
Speciality: Reflexology.
S T (Ref:HM21917)

## WRAY, TANYA

**Tanya Wray**, 19 Lyndon Cl, Bramham, Wetherby, **Yorkshire (West)**, LS23 6SR, ENG.
(T) 01937 541714
Speciality: Aromatherapy.
● **Owner** Mrs T Wray
M O (Ref:HM21918)

## WREN CLINIC

**Wren Clinic (The)**, All Hallows House, Idol Lane, London, **London (Greater)**, EC3R 5DD, ENG.
(T) 020 7283 8908 (F) 020 7626 3800
Speciality: Acupuncture, Alexander Technique, Aromatherapy, Autogenic Training, Bowen Therapy, Counselling, Cranio-Sacral Therapy, Herbal Medicine, Holistic Healing, Kinesiology, Massage (Therapeutic), McTimoney Chiropractic, Meditation, Naturopathy, Nutritional Therapy, Osteopathy, Psychotherapy, Reflexology, Shiatsu.
● **Practitioner** Mr R Kidd
M (Ref:HM21919)

## WREN, ANTHONY

**Anthony Wren**, 1 Chesholm Rd, Stoke Newington, London, **London (Greater)**, N16 0DP, ENG.
(T) 020 7923 4929 (F) 020 7502 0412
Speciality: Cranio-Sacral Therapy, Massage (Therapeutic). ✔
● **Cranio-Sacral Therapist** Mr A Wren M: CTA.
C P Yrs. Est.: 4 (Ref:HM21920)

## WREN, JENNY

**Jenny Wren**, 1 St Georges Cl, Toddington, Dunstable, **Bedfordshire**, LU5 6AT, ENG.
(T) 01525 874753
Speciality: Chiropodists (Podiatrists).
● **Owner** Mrs J Sutton
C S (Ref:HM21921)

## WREN, PAULINE

**Pauline Wren Associates**, 2 Paddox House, 25 Dunsmore, Rugby, **Warwickshire**, CV22 5HD, ENG.
(T) 01788 560793 (F) 01788 540294
(E) pwren@dircon.co.uk
(W) www.paulinewren.com
Speciality: Cognitive Therapy, Counselling, Faith Healing, Healer, Healing Therapy, Holistic Healing, Hypnosis, Hypnotherapy, Life Style Coaching, Meditation, Psychotherapy, Reiki, Rogerian Therapy, Spiritual Healing, Stress Therapy, Visualisation Therapy, Personal Development. ✔
● **Owner** Ms P Wren Q: BA (Hons), DICS, Dip.Hyp, Dip.Psych, Louise Hay Trainer, PGCE.
M: BACP, NRHP, UKCP.
B H Yrs. Est.: 7 (Ref:HM21922)

## WREN, PAULINE

**Pauline Wren**, 13 Hillmorton Rd, Rugby, **Warwickshire**, CV22 5DF, ENG.
(T) 01788 560793
Speciality: Hypnosis.
B (Ref:HM21923)

## WRIGHT FOOT FORWARD

**Wright Foot Forward**, 30 The Headlands, **County Durham**, DL3 8RP, ENG.
(T) 01325 358550
Speciality: Massage (Therapeutic), Reflexology, Reiki, Remedial Massage.
S T (Ref:HM21924)

## WRIGHT, ANDREW

**Andrew Wright**, Marple Physiotherapy Practice, 5 Station Rd, Marple, Stockport, **Cheshire**, SK6 6AJ, ENG.
(T) 01614 260100
Speciality: Physiotherapy.
P S T (Ref:HM21925)

## WRIGHT, ANNE & SEYMOUR, LARA

**Anne V V Wright D O & Lara E G Seymour Bsc (Hons)**, Southcote Clinic, Southcote Rise, Ruislip, **London (Greater)**, HA4 7LW, ENG.
(T) 01895 677179
Speciality: Osteopathy.
P S T (Ref:HM21926)

## WRIGHT, AUDREY

**Audrey Wright**, Puckshill, Heathfield Rd, Burwash, Etchingham, **Sussex (East)**, TN19 7HN, ENG.
(T) 01435 882751
Speciality: Herbal Medicine.
● **Owner** Miss A Wright
M (Ref:HM21927)

## WRIGHT, CLARE

**Clare Wright**, 29 Metcalfe Rd, Cambridge, **Cambridgeshire**, CB4 2DB, ENG.
(T) 01223 319274
Speciality: Reflexology.
S T (Ref:HM21928)

## WRIGHT, CYNTHIA

**Cynthia Wright**, The Cottage, Treneague, St. Stephen, St. Austell, **Cornwall**, PL26 7QB, ENG.
(T) 01726 823414
Speciality: Counselling, Hypnosis, Hypnotherapy, Visualisation Therapy. ✔
● **Hypnotherapist** Ms C Wright Q: MNCH.
M: NCH.
B H Yrs. Est.: 12 (Ref:HM21929)

## WRIGHT, DAVE

**Dave Wright (Mobile)**, 39 Elizabeth Rd, Basingstoke, **Hampshire**, RG22 6BA, ENG.
(T) 01256 461820
Speciality: Reflexology.
S T (Ref:HM21930)

## WRIGHT, DOREEN

**Doreen Wright**, 3 Cottonmill Lane, St. Albans, **Hertfordshire**, AL1 1HL, ENG.
(T) 01727 831110
Speciality: Holistic Healing, Homeopathy. ✔
● **Owner** Mrs D Wright Q: L.C.C.H, MHA.
M Yrs. Est.: 7 (Ref:HM21931)

## WRIGHT, GEORGINA

**Georgina Wright**, 12 Poplar Rise, **Yorkshire (West)**, LS13 4SQ, ENG.
(T) 01132 635677
Speciality: Reflexology.
S T (Ref:HM21932)

## WRIGHT, GWYNETH

**Gwyneth Wright**, 31a Highgate High St, London, **London (Greater)**, N6 5JT, ENG.
(T) 020 8340 2739
Speciality: Complementary Medicines & Therapy.
● **Owner** Ms G Wright
M (Ref:HM21933)

## WRIGHT, J D

**J D Wright**, 1a Chapel Lane, Burscough, Ormskirk, **Lancashire**, L40 7RA, ENG.
(T) 01704 894254
Speciality: Hypnosis.
B (Ref:HM21934)

## WRIGHT, J L

**J L Wright**, 15 Grundisburgh Rd, Woodbridge, **Suffolk**, IP12 4HH, ENG.
(T) 01394 386540 (F) 01394 386540
Speciality: Osteopathy.
● **Owner** Ms J Wright
P S T (Ref:HM21935)

## WRIGHT, JENNY

**Jenny Wright**, 60 Leighton Rd, London, **London (Greater)**, NW5 2QE, ENG.
(T) 020 7485 9433
(E) jcw@dircon.co.uk
Speciality: Auto Suggestion, Biofeedback, Cognitive Therapy, Counselling, Humanistic Psychology, Hypnosis, Hypnotherapy, Life Style Coaching, Meditation, Psychotherapy, Stress Therapy.
● **Hypnotherapist** Ms J Wright Q: BHReg, EH.P, NLP. M: NCH.
B Yrs. Est.: 7 (Ref:HM21936)

## WRIGHT, JENNY

**Jenny Wright**, 5 Sefton Way, Crowborough, **Sussex (East)**, TN6 2TE, ENG.
(T) 01892 652799
Speciality: Homeopathy.
● **Owner** Mrs J Wright
M (Ref:HM21937)

## WRIGHT, JONATHAN

**Jonathan Wright**, Gibb St, Birmingham, **Midlands (West)**, B9 4AA, ENG.
(T) 01216 874448
Speciality: Complementary Medicines & Therapy.
C M (Ref:HM21938)

## WRIGHT, JUDITH

**Judith Wright**, The Grosvenor Centre, 16 Grosvenor Avenue, Birmingham, **Midlands (West)**, B20 3NR, ENG.
(T) 01213 565886
Speciality: Complementary Medicines & Therapy.
C M (Ref:HM21939)

## WRIGHT, KAREN

**Karen Wright**, 161 High St, Barnet, **Hertfordshire**, EN5 5SU, ENG.
(T) 020 8440 8977 (F) 020 8449 3196
Speciality: Biomechanics, Chiropody, Nail

Surgery, Electro Surgery. ✔ CREDIT
● **Chiropodist** Mrs K Wright Q: BSc (Hons), S.R.Ch. M: S.C.P.
M Yrs. Est.: 10 (Ref:HM21940)

**WRIGHT, KAREN**
**Karen Wright**, Cromlech, 101 Victoria Gr, Bridport, **Dorset**, DT6 3AE, ENG.
(T) 01308 456079
Speciality: Reflexology.
S T (Ref:HM21941)

**WRIGHT, L**
**L Wright**, 9 Vicarage Gardens, Mitcham, **Surrey**, CR4 3BL, ENG.
(T) 020 8646 1391
Speciality: Hypnosis.
● **Owner** Ms L Wright
B (Ref:HM21942)

**WRIGHT, LAWRIE**
**Lawrie Wright**, 21 Radstock Rd, Reading, **Berkshire**, RG1 3PS, ENG.
(T) 01189 612127
Speciality: Alexander Technique.
P S (Ref:HM21943)

**WRIGHT, MARTIN**
**Martin Wright**, 59 Hayfield Rd, Salford, **Manchester (Greater)**, M6 8QA, ENG.
(T) 01617 360446
Speciality: Physiotherapy.
P S T (Ref:HM21944)

**WRIGHT, N J (DR)**
**Dr N J Wright**, 76A North St, Wellington, **Somerset**, TA21 8NA, ENG.
(T) 01823 660618
Speciality: Chiropodists (Podiatrists).
● **Owner** Dr N Wright
S (Ref:HM21945)

**WRIGHT, P A**
**P A Wright**, 1 Lushington Rd, Eastbourne, **Sussex (East)**, BN21 4LG, ENG.
(T) 01323 728886
Speciality: Biomechanics, Chiropody, Laser Treatment, Nail Surgery, Podiatry, Ultrasound Therapy, Cryo Therapy. ✔
● **Chiropodist (Podiatrist)**
Mr P Wright Q: DPodM, S.R.Ch. M: S.R.Ch.
● **Chiropodist (Podiatrist)**
Ms E Carman Q: BSc, S.R.Ch. M: S.C.P.
M Yrs. Est.: 22 (Ref:HM21946)

**WRIGHT, R G**
**R G Wright**, 34 Parkstone Rd, Leicester, **Leicestershire**, LE5 1NN, ENG.
(T) 01162 431330
Speciality: Chiropodists (Podiatrists).
S (Ref:HM21947)

**WRIGHT, SAMANTHA**
**Samantha Wright**, Petersfield Hospital, Swan St, Petersfield, **Hampshire**, GU32 3LB, ENG.
(T) 01730 263221
Speciality: Chiropody.
S (Ref:HM21948)

**WRIGHT, SEAN**
**Sean Wright**, 111 Douglas Rd, Hornchurch, **Essex**, RM11 1AW, ENG.
(T) 01708 755415
Speciality: Osteopathy.
● **Owner** Mr S Wright
P S T (Ref:HM21949)

**WRIGHT, STEPHEN**
**Stephen Wright**, 638 Great Thornton St, Hull, **Humberside (North)**, HU3 2LX, ENG.
(T) 01482 216537
Speciality: Reflexology.
S T (Ref:HM21950)

**WRIGHT, STUART**
**Stuart Wright**, 94 St James's St, Brighton, **Sussex (East)**, BN2 1TP, ENG.
(T) 01273 672952
Speciality: Acupuncture.
● **Owner** Mr L Moore
O (Ref:HM21951)

**WRIGHT, T**
**T Wright**, 17 Wentworth Rd, York, **Yorkshire (North)**, YO24 1DG, ENG.
(T) 01904 651411
Speciality: Alexander Technique.
P S (Ref:HM21952)

**WRIGHT, TRACY**
**Tracy Wright**, 19 Hogshill Mead, Beaminster, **Dorset**, DT8 3DA, ENG.
(T) 01308 863334
Speciality: Complementary Medicines & Therapy.
● **Owner** Ms T Wright
M (Ref:HM21953)

**WRIGHT, W J**
**W J Wright**, Southover Medical Practice, Bronshill Rd, Torquay, **Devon**, TQ1 3HD, ENG.
(T) 01803 313057
Speciality: Physiotherapy.
P S T (Ref:HM21954)

**WRIGHTSON, VERONICA**
**Veronica Wrightson**, Woodcote, Barnes Lane, Milford On Sea, Lymington, **Hampshire**, SO41 0RR, ENG.
(T) 01590 642274
Speciality: Electrolysis.
● **Owner** Mrs V Wrightson
T (Ref:HM21955)

**WRIGLEY, BARBARA**
**Barbara Wrigley**, 51 Newnham Rd, Ryde, **Isle of Wight**, PO33 3TE, ENG.
(T) 01983 616416 (F) 01983 616416
Speciality: Massage (Therapeutic), The Sarney Therapy Nutrient. ✔
● **Owner** Mrs B Wrigley M: BANT.
C Yrs. Est.: 15 (Ref:HM21956)

**WRIGLEY, DAVID**
**David Wrigley**, 17 Chester Rd, Poynton, Stockport, **Cheshire**, SK12 1EU, ENG.
(T) 01625 879853 (F) 01625 879853
Speciality: Chiropodists (Podiatrists).
● **Owner** Mr D Wrigley
S (Ref:HM21957)

**WROUGHTON, C J**
**C J Wroughton**, 11 Taddington Rd, Eastbourne, **Sussex (East)**, BN22 7EG, ENG.
(T) 01323 728408
Speciality: Chiropodists (Podiatrists).
● **Owner** Mr C Wroughton
S (Ref:HM21958)

**WST LONDON SCH - THERA MASS**
**West London School Of Therapeutic Massage (The)**, 41 St. Lukes Rd, London, **London (Greater)**, W11 1DD, ENG.
(T) 020 7229 4672
Speciality: Complementary Medicines & Therapy.
● **Administrator** Mr J Collins
C M (Ref:HM21959)

**WSZOLEK, ANNA**
**Anna Wszolek**, 9 Woodcock Way, Ashby-de-la-Zouch, **Leicestershire**, LE65 1AX, ENG.
(T) 01530 563331
Speciality: Acupuncture.
O (Ref:HM21960)

**WSZOLEK, ANNA**
**Anna Wszolek**, Nottingham Natural Health Centre, 354 Mansfield Rd, Nottingham, **Nottinghamshire**, NG5 2EF, ENG.
(T) 01159 608855
Speciality: Acupuncture.
O (Ref:HM21961)

**WUEBBELER, H**
**H Wuebbeler**, 2 Shelburne Rd, London, **London (Greater)**, N7 6DL, ENG.
(T) 020 7326 5324 (F) 020 7326 5324
Speciality: Psychotherapy.
● **Owner** Mr H Wuebbeler
B (Ref:HM21962)

**WUYTS, ANTHONY**
**Anthony Wuyts**, 7 Collingwood Rd, Witham, **Essex**, CM8 2DY, ENG.
(T) 01376 502484 (F) 01376 521650
Speciality: Hypnotherapy.
● **Owner** Mr A Wuyts
B (Ref:HM21963)

**WWW.CHIRO-FIRST.COM**
**www.chiro-first.com**, Unit 2 Church Hill, Navan, **County Meath**, IRE.
(T) 07767 1022
Speciality: Complementary Medicines & Therapy.
M (Ref:HM21964)

**WYATT, JOANNA**
**Joanna Wyatt**, Dorking Osteopathic Clinic, 2 Victoria Trce, Dorking, **Surrey**, RH4 2LD, ENG.
(T) 01306 881249
Speciality: Osteopathy.
P S T (Ref:HM21965)

**WYATT, JULIE**
**Julie Wyatt**, Belvedere, Eastwick Rd, Bookham, Leatherhead, **Surrey**, KT23 4BJ, ENG.
(T) 01372 453537
Speciality: Hypnosis.
B (Ref:HM21966)

**WYE OSTEOPATHIC PRACTICE**
**Wye Osteopathic Practice**, 5a Oxenturn Rd, Wye, Ashford, **Kent**, TN25 5BH, ENG.
(T) 01233 812196 (F) 01233 812018
Speciality: Osteopathy.
P S T (Ref:HM21967)

**WYE VALLEY CHIROPRACTIC CLINIC**
**Wye Valley Chiropractic Clinic**, Stuart House, The Back, Chepstow, **Monmouthshire**, NP16 5HH, WAL.
(T) 01291 627066
Speciality: Chiropractic.
● **Owner** Mr C Oliver
P S T (Ref:HM21968)

**WYE, DEBORAH**
**Deborah Wye**, 56 Stanstead Rd, Hoddesdon, **Hertfordshire**, EN11 0RJ, ENG.
(T) 01992 467394
Speciality: Chiropody. ✔
● **Owner/Chiropodist** Mrs D Wye Q: DPodM, M.S.C.P, S.R.Ch.
M Yrs. Est.: 16 (Ref:HM21969)

**WYKES, MARY**
**Mary Wykes**, 23 Church St, Broughton, Kettering, **Northamptonshire**, NN14 1LU, ENG.
(T) 01536 791033
Speciality: Complementary Medicines & Therapy.
M (Ref:HM21970)

**WYLDBORE, VICTORIA**
**Victoria Wyldbore**, New Roans, Sheriff Hutton, Strensall, York, **Yorkshire (North)**, YO32 5TU, ENG.
(T) 01347 878663
Speciality: Aromatherapy.
M O (Ref:HM21971)

**WYLIE WARREN, FRANCES**
**Wylie Warren Mrs Frances**, Keely Drumcliff, **County Sligo**, IRE.
(T) 07163 694
Speciality: Complementary Medicines & Therapy.
M (Ref:HM21972)

**WYLIE, DIANE**
**Diane Wylie**, 63 St. Albans Avenue, London, **London (Greater)**, W4 5JS, ENG.
(T) 020 8747 9727
Speciality: Reflexology.
S T (Ref:HM21973)

**WYLIE, DORIS**
**Doris Wylie**, 2 West Mill Rd, Lasswade, **Lothian (Mid)**, EH18 1LX, SCO.
(T) 01316 603798
Speciality: Reflexology.
S T (Ref:HM21974)

**WYLLIE, KIM**
**Kim Wyllie**, 9 Woodcroft Trce, Woodcroft, Chepstow, **Monmouthshire**, NP16 7QA, WAL.
(T) 01291 620165
Speciality: Aromatherapy.
● **Owner** Miss K Wyllie
M O (Ref:HM21975)



Key continued: Yrs.Est: Years Established Q: Qualifications M: Professional Membership ✔ Indemnity Insurance CREDIT Accept Credit Cards

## WYNDHAM CENTRE
**Wyndham Centre (The)**, 86 Hatton Garden, London, **London (Greater)**, EC1N 8QN, ENG.
(T) 020 7404 0023
Speciality: Physiotherapy.
P S T (Ref:HM21976)

## WYNDHAM CLINIC
**Wyndham Clinic (The)**, 8 Pinnocks Lane, Baldock, **Hertfordshire**, SG7 6DF, ENG.
(T) 01462 893586 (F) 01462 893596
(E) baldock@wyndham-centre.co.uk
(W) www.wyndham-centre.co.uk
Speciality: Acupuncture, Aromatherapy, Chiropody, Clinical Ecology, Complementary Therapy, Cranio-Sacral Therapy, Herbal Medicine, Homeopathy, Manipulation, Massage (Therapeutic), Meditation, Nutritional Therapy, Physiotherapy, Podiatry, Reflexology.
- **Physiotherapist** Ms A Wyndham Q: Grad Dip Phys, MCSP, SRP. M: CSP.

C S Yrs. Est.: 21 (Ref:HM21977)

## WYNNE-JONES, J
**Mrs J Wynne-Jones**, 6-8 Temple Chambers, Frodsham St, Chester, **Cheshire**, CH1 3LE, ENG.
(T) 01244 322854
Speciality: Chiropody, Nail Surgery, Local Anaestheisa used for nail surgery. ✔
- **Podiatrist** Mrs J Wynne-Jones Q: DPodM, M.S.C.P, S.R.Ch. M: S.C.P.
- **Podiatrist** R A Slater Q: DPodM, M.S.C.P, S.R.Ch. M: S.C.P.
- **Podiatrist** G Cassells Q: DPodM, M.S.C.P, S.R.Ch. M: S.C.P.

S Yrs. Est.: 13 (Ref:HM21978)

## WYNNE-SIMMONS, A (DR)
**Dr A Wynne-Simmons - Homeopathic Practice**, 34 Dartmouth Row, Greenwich, London, **London (Greater)**, SE10 8AW, ENG.
(T) 020 8694 2320
Speciality: Homeopathy.
- **Homeopath** Dr Wynne-Simmons Q: BS, DipCH.P, MB, MFHom, MRCGP. M: FHom.

M (Ref:HM21979)

## WYSMAN, ALAN
**Mr Alan Wysman**, 1 York House, 59 Ridinghouse St, London, **London (Greater)**, W1P 7PP, ENG.
(T) 020 7636 3139 (F) 020 7636 3139
Speciality: Acupuncture.
- **Owner** Mr A Wysman

O (Ref:HM21980)

## XANADU BEAUTY & THERAPY CLINIC
**Xanadu Beauty & Therapy Clinic**, 4-10 Pellon Lane, Halifax, **Yorkshire (West)**, HX1 5SP, ENG.
(T) 01422 350179
Speciality: Physiotherapy.
P S T (Ref:HM21981)

## XENETEK
**Xenetek Ltd**, P O Box 949, Oxford, **Oxfordshire**, OX2 9XT, ENG.
(T) 01865 865049 (F) 01865 860921
Speciality: Complementary Medicines & Therapy.
M (Ref:HM21982)

## XENON CENTRE
**Xenon Centre Ltd**, 83-85 Dunnikier Rd, Kirkcaldy, **Fife**, KY1 2QW, SCO.
(T) 01592 644060 (F) 01592 644040
Speciality: Complementary Medicines & Therapy.
M (Ref:HM21983)

## X-VEE ONE ELEVEN
**X-Vee One Eleven**, 18 Park St, Weymouth, **Dorset**, DT4 7DQ, ENG.
(T) 01305 772707 (F) 01305 784937
Speciality: Complementary Medicines & Therapy.
- **Owner** Mr T Smith

C M (Ref:HM21984)

## YAGHMAIE, MASSIH
**Massih Yaghmaie**, 26 Rydal Gardens, Wembley, **London (Greater)**, HA9 8RZ, ENG.
(T) 020 8908 1236
Speciality: Acupuncture.
O (Ref:HM21985)

## YARDLEY, IAN
**Ian Yardley**, 35 Bedser Drive, Greenford, **London (Greater)**, UB6 0SE, ENG.
(T) 020 8422 9957 (F) 020 8422 9957
Speciality: Hypnosis.
- **Owner** Mr I Yardley

B (Ref:HM21986)

## YARM OSTEOPATHIC CLINIC
**Yarm Osteopathic Clinic**, Yarm Clinic, Worsall Rd, Yarm, **Cleveland**, TS15 9DD, ENG.
(T) 01642 788755
Speciality: Osteopathy.
P S T (Ref:HM21987)

## YARMOUTH CHIROPRACTIC CLINIC
**Yarmouth Chiropractic Clinic**, 1 The Quay, Yarmouth, **Isle of Wight**, PO41 0PG, ENG.
(T) 01983 761100
Speciality: Chiropractic.
- **Owner** Mr G Blomfield

P S T (Ref:HM21988)

## YARNFIELD PARK- HEALTH/SPORTS
**Yarnfield Park Health and Sports Complex**, Yarnfield Park, Stone, **Staffordshire**, ST15 0NL, ENG.
(T) 01785 762749
Speciality: Aromatherapy.
- **Aromatherapist** Ms A Wynn

(T) 01785 859017 Q: Dip.Arom. M: IIHHT.
C (Ref:HM21989)

## YARNTON, C
**C Yarnton**, Dover Barton, Lonesome Lane, Reigate, **Surrey**, RH2 7QT, ENG.
(T) 01737 240821
Speciality: Psychotherapy.
B (Ref:HM21990)

## YARO
**Yaro**, 151A Bloomfield Avenue, Belfast, **County Antrim**, BT5 5AB, NIR.
(T) 028 9045 7717
Speciality: Aromatherapy. ✔
- **Aromatherapist** Ms K Armstrong Q: Dip.SPA. M: BABTAC, ISPA.

C Yrs. Est.: 1 (Ref:HM21991)

## YARROW, B M
**B M Yarrow**, 65 Silverwood Cl, Cambridge, **Cambridgeshire**, CB1 3HA, ENG.
(T) 01223 359196
Speciality: Complementary Medicines & Therapy.
- **Owner** Mrs B Yarrow

C M (Ref:HM21992)

## YATES, MICHAEL
**Michael Yates**, 4 Camp Rd, Weymouth, **Dorset**, DT4 9HE, ENG.
(T) 01305 774685
Speciality: Chiropodists (Podiatrists).
- **Owner** Mr M Yates

S (Ref:HM21993)

## YATTON FAMILY PRACTICE
**Yatton Family Practice**, 155 Mendip Rd, Yatton, Bristol, BS49 4ER, ENG.
(T) 01275 857912
Speciality: Osteopathy.
P S T (Ref:HM21994)

## YAU, K FAN
**Miss K Fan Yau**, 18 Cheyneys Avenue, Edgware, **London (Greater)**, HA8 6SF, ENG.
(T) 020 8952 2715
Speciality: Osteopathy.
P S T (Ref:HM21995)

## YEAMAN, DAVID
**David Yeaman**, 67 Schoolfield, Bamber Bridge, Preston, **Lancashire**, PR5 8BH, ENG.
(T) 01772 620573
Speciality: Biomechanics, Chiropody. ✔
- **Owner/Chiropodist** Mr D Yeaman Q: S.R.Ch.

C Yrs. Est.: 4 (Ref:HM21996)

## YEARBY, CLAIRE
**Claire Yearby**, 479 Wellingborough Rd, Northampton, **Northamptonshire**, NN3 3HN, ENG.
(T) 01604 711456
Speciality: Complementary Medicines & Therapy.
C M (Ref:HM21997)

## YEATES, ANNE
**Anne Yeates**, Laverstock Physiotherapy Practice, Halliwell, Kingswood Rd, Tunbridge Wells, **Kent**, TN2 4UJ, ENG.
(T) 01892 546657
Speciality: Physiotherapy.
P S T (Ref:HM21998)

## YEATES, JANET A
**Janet A Yeates**, 12 Netherhampton Rd, Salisbury, **Wiltshire**, SP2 8HE, ENG.
(T) 01722 339646
Speciality: Chiropodists (Podiatrists).
- **Owner** Mrs J Yeates

S (Ref:HM21999)

## YEHIA, CHRISTINE
**Christine Yehia**, 67 Hebden Rd, Haworth, Keighley, **Yorkshire (West)**, BD22 8RQ, ENG.
(T) 01535 646429
Speciality: Reflexology.
S T (Ref:HM22000)

## YELDHAM, S
**S Yeldham**, 24 Southcote Avenue, West Wittering, Chichester, **Sussex (West)**, PO20 8EY, ENG.
(T) 01243 672248
Speciality: Aromatherapy.
- **Owner** Mrs S Yeldham

M O (Ref:HM22001)

## YELLOW BRICK ROAD
**Yellow Brick Road**, 8 Bachelors Walk, Dublin, **County Dublin**, IRE.
(T) 01873 0177
Speciality: Complementary Medicines & Therapy.
M (Ref:HM22002)

## YELLOW EMPEROR
**Yellow Emperor Co (The)**, 6 New Bridge St, Exeter, **Devon**, EX4 3JW, ENG.
(T) 01392 413888
Speciality: Complementary Medicines & Therapy.
- **Owner** Mrs S Kromer

M (Ref:HM22003)

## YELLOW EMPEROR CORP
**Yellow Emperor Corp Ltd (The)**, 1 Eastgate, Taunton, **Somerset**, TA1 3NB, ENG.
(T) 01823 334888 (F) 01458 251567
Speciality: Acupuncture, Herbal Medicine, Chinese Massage.
- **Acupuncturist** Dr Young
- **Acupuncturist** Dr Tian
- **Manager** Mrs S Edwards

C Yrs. Est.: 4 (Ref:HM22004)

## YELLOW HOUSE
**Yellow House**, 49 Seabourne Rd, Bournemouth, **Dorset**, BH5 2HA, ENG.
(T) 01202 427860 (F) 01202 771248
(W) www.yellowhouse.org.uk
Speciality: Acupuncture, Allergy Testing, Aromatherapy, Counselling, Crystal Healing, Homeopathy, Hypnotherapy, Indian Head Massage, Massage (Therapeutic), Naturopathy, Osteopathy, Reflexology, Reiki, Bach Flower Remedies, Back Energy Alignment, Chakra Balancing, Herbalism, Inversion Therapy, N.L.P, Nutritional/Diet and Lifestyle Therapy, Sports Injury Rehabilitation, Tarot Reading, Thai Massage, Whole System Health Scan. ✔
- **Reiki Master** Mr J Light

B C Yrs. Est.: 4 (Ref:HM22005)

## YEN YANG
**Yen Yang Co**, 1a The Cotswold Court, The Green, Broadway, **Worcestershire**, WR12 7AA, ENG.
(T) 01386 852463
Speciality: Chiropractic.
P S T (Ref:HM22006)

## YEN YANG
**Yen Yang Co**, 10 Marlborough Rd, Chipping Norton, **Oxfordshire**, OX7 5PD, ENG.
(T) 01608 645133 (F) 01608 645546
Speciality: Chiropractic.

Key: B Mind-Body Medicine; C Complementary Medicine; H Self Help Treatment; M Medicinal Therapy; O Oriental Medicine; P Postural Therapy; S Manipulative Structural Therapy; T Touch Therapy

● **Owner** Mr Y Yang Co
P S T (**Ref:**HM22007)

## YEOVIL CHIROPRACTIC CLINIC

**Yeovil Chiropractic Clinic**, Yeovil Chiropractic Clinic, 142 Sherborne Rd, Yeovil, **Somerset**, BA21 4HQ, **ENG**.
**(T)** 01935 423138
**Speciality:** Allergy Testing, Aromatherapy, Chiropractic, Homeopathy, Osteopathy, Osteopathy Scanning. ✔
● **Chiropractor** Ms C Gordon **Q:** DC.
● **Chiropractor** Antoinette Young **Q:** DC, FCC.
● **Chiropractor** Mr M Young **Q:** DC, FCC.
P (**Ref:**HM22008)

## YERBURY, JACQUELINE

**Jacqueline Yerbury**, Ivy Lodge, High St, Purton, Swindon, **Wiltshire**, SN5 9AD, **ENG**.
**(T)** 01793 770552
**Speciality:** Physiotherapy.
● **Owner** Mrs J Yerbury
P S T (**Ref:**HM22009)

## YEWS

**Yews (The)**, Church St, Barkston, Grantham, **Lincolnshire**, NG32 2NB, **ENG**.
**(T)** 01400 250224
**Speciality:** Chiropodists (Podiatrists).
● **Owner** Mrs J Everett
S (**Ref:**HM22010)

## YEZHANG, MISS

**Miss Yezhang**, Chinese Herbal Medicine And Health Care, 369 Eastern Avenue, Ilford, **Essex**, IG2 6NE, **ENG**.
**(T)** 020 8550 8585 **(F)** 020 8530 4352
**Speciality:** Complementary Medicines & Therapy.
● **Partner** Dr W Hu
C M (**Ref:**HM22011)

## YIN YANG CHINESE MEDICAL CTRE

**Yin Yang Chinese Medical Centre**, 14 Goodmayes Rd, Ilford, **Essex**, IG3 9UN, **ENG**.
**(T)** 020 8598 8880
**Speciality:** Complementary Medicines & Therapy.
● **Doctor** Dr C Wu
C M (**Ref:**HM22012)

## YING & YANG COMP CENTRE

**Ying & Yang Complementary Centre**, 1210 London Rd, London, **London (Greater)**, SW16 4DN, **ENG**.
**(T)** 020 8764 1424 **(F)** 020 8679 3126
**Speciality:** Complementary Medicines & Therapy.
● **Manager** Mr M Smith
C M (**Ref:**HM22013)

## YING, FRANK

**Mr Ying T/A Westbourne Grove Osteopathic Practice**, The Basement, 4 Hatherley Gr, Bayswater, London, **London (Greater)**, W2 5RB, **ENG**.
**(T)** 020 7221 7077 **(F)** 020 7229 7933
**Speciality:** Manipulation, Massage (Therapeutic), Osteopathy. ✔
● **Osteopath** Mr F Ying **Q:** DO. **M:** BOA, GOsC.
● **Osteopath** Ms C Kirby **Q:** BSc (Hons), SRN. **M:** GOsC.
S **Yrs. Est.:** 21 (**Ref:**HM22014)

## YIZHEN, JIA (DR)

**Dr Yizhen Jia**, 62 Paul St, London, **London (Greater)**, EC2A 4NA, **ENG**.
**(T)** 020 7251 4429 **(F)** 020 7613 4737
**Speciality:** Complementary Medicines & Therapy.
M (**Ref:**HM22015)

## YMCA HEALTH & FITNESS CLUB

**YMCA Health & Fitness Club**, 4 Shakespeare St, Nottingham, **Nottinghamshire**, NG1 4GH, **ENG**.
**(T)** 01159 528803
**Speciality:** Complementary Medicines & Therapy.
C M (**Ref:**HM22016)

## YNODDFA MARKETING

**Ynoddfa Marketing**, 38 Pentyla Baglan Rd, Port Talbot, **Neath Port Talbot**, SA12 8AA, **WAL**.
**(T)** 01639 871777
**(W)** www.goodbye2cancer.co.uk
**Speciality:** Complementary Medicines & Therapy. [credit card]
● **Owner** Mr J Wright
C **Yrs. Est.:** 2 (**Ref:**HM22017)

## YNYSWEN CLINIC

**Ynyswen Clinic**, Ynyswen Rd, Treorchy, **Rhondda Cynon Taff**, CF42 6ED, **WAL**.
**(T)** 01443 771464
**Speciality:** Chiropodists (Podiatrists).
● **Manager** Mrs L Evans
S (**Ref:**HM22018)

## YOGA & RELAXATION

**Yoga & Relaxation**, Crofters Mead, Court Wood Lane, Croydon, **Surrey**, CR0 9HT, **ENG**.
**(T)** 020 8651 1700
**Speciality:** Relaxation Technique.
● **Owner** Mrs M Thomas
H T (**Ref:**HM22019)

## YOGA & THERAPY CENTRE

**Yoga & Therapy Centre (The)**, 26 Oakwood Lane, Barnton, Northwich, **Cheshire**, CW8 4HE, **ENG**.
**(T)** 01606 781306
**Speciality:** Yoga.
● **Owner** Mr D Bowler
M (**Ref:**HM22020)

## YOGA BIOMEDICAL TRUST

**Yoga Biomedical Trust (The)**, 103 Edenderry Village, Belfast, **County Antrim**, BT8 8LQ, **NIR**.
**(T)** 028 9064 2508 **(F)** 028 9064 2508
**Speciality:** Yoga.
● **Manager** Mrs M Quail
M (**Ref:**HM22021)

## YOGA BIOMEDICAL TRUST

**Yoga Biomedical Trust**, 156 Cockerell Rd, Cambridge, **Cambridgeshire**, CB4 3RZ, **ENG**.
**(T)** 01223 367301
**Speciality:** Complementary Medicines & Therapy.
M (**Ref:**HM22022)

## YOGA CENTRE OF IRELAND

**Yoga Centre Of Ireland (The)**, 10 Clanbrassil Rd, Holywood, **County Down**, BT18 0AR, **NIR**.
**(T)** 028 9042 8370 **(F)** 028 9042 3908
**Speciality:** Yoga. ✔
● **Director** Ms N Duffield
B **Yrs. Est.:** 21 (**Ref:**HM22023)

## YOGA DRUVAM JIVAN YOGA SOCIETY

**Yoga Druvam Jivan Yoga Society**, British School, Slad Rd, Stroud, **Gloucestershire**, GL5 1QW, **ENG**.
**(T)** 01453 759006 **(F)** 01453 759211
**(E)** gsn@st-clarepatel.fsnet.co.uk
**Speciality:** Counselling, Do-In, Indian Head Massage, Meditation, Stress Therapy, Yoga, Relaxation, Self-Discovery, Services, Retreats, Hoildays - Yoga based Workshops. ✔
● **Director** Mrs S Patel **Q:** BA (Hons).
● **Owner** Mr G Patel **Q:** IIHHT. **M:** IHT.
B **Yrs. Est.:** 19 (**Ref:**HM22024)

## YOGA FELLOWSHIP OF N.IRELAND

**Yoga Fellowship Of Northern Ireland**, 19 Elsmere Park, Belfast, **County Antrim**, BT5 7QZ, **NIR**.
**(T)** 028 9070 5913
**Speciality:** Relaxation Technique.
H T (**Ref:**HM22025)

## YOGA FOR ALL

**Yoga For All**, 5 Willow Gr, Elmfield Trce, York, **Yorkshire (North)**, YO31 1EJ, **ENG**.
**(T)** 01904 423340 **(F)** 01904 423340
**(E)** yogaforall@aol.com
**(W)** www.yogaforall.co.uk
**Speciality:** Yoga. ✔
● **Yoga Teacher/Therapist** Mrs J Reed **Q:** BSc, BWY.Teach.Dip, Cert.Ed, Dip.Health.Ed. **M:** BWY.
H **Yrs. Est.:** 10 (**Ref:**HM22026)

## YOGA FOR HEALTH FOUNDATION

**Yoga For Health Foundation**, Ickwell Bury, The Green, Ickwell, Biggleswade, **Bedfordshire**, SG18 9EF, **ENG**.
**(T)** 01767 627271
**Speciality:** Relaxation Technique.
● **Director** Mr H Kent
H T (**Ref:**HM22027)

## YOGA HEALTH STUDIO

**Yoga Health Studio (The)**, Suryaloka, 9 Copp Hill Lane, Budleigh Salterton, **Devon**, EX9 6DT, **ENG**.
**(T)** 01395 442249
**Speciality:** Yoga. ✔
● **Yoga Therapy Practitioner/Teacher** Mrs M Kuyper **Q:** BSc (Hons). **M:** BRCP.
B C **Yrs. Est.:** 19 (**Ref:**HM22028)

## YOGA MEDITATION RELAXATION

**Yoga Meditation Relaxation Classes**, 151 Headstone Lane, Harrow, **London (Greater)**, HA2 6LX, **ENG**.
**(T)** 020 8428 6691
**Speciality:** Relaxation Technique.
● **Owner** Mr K Patel
H T (**Ref:**HM22029)

## YOGA STUDIOS

**Yoga Studios**, 3 Bushey Rd, Sutton, **Surrey**, SM1 1QR, **ENG**.
**(T)** 020 8641 1792
**Speciality:** Complementary Medicines & Therapy.
C M (**Ref:**HM22030)

## YOGA TAI-CHI & CHI-KUNG

**Yoga Tai-Chi & Chi-Kung**, 26 Parkfield Gardens, Harrow, **London (Greater)**, HA2 6JR, **ENG**.
**(T)** 020 8427 6597 **(F)** 020 8427 6597
**Speciality:** Relaxation Technique.
● **Owner** Mr P Griffin
H T (**Ref:**HM22031)

## YOGA THERAPY CENTRE

**Yoga Therapy Centre**, 60 Great Ormond St, London, **London (Greater)**, WC1N 3HR, **ENG**.
**(T)** 020 7419 7199 **(F)** 020 7419 7196
**Speciality:** Yoga.
● **Director** Dr R Munro
C (**Ref:**HM22032)

## YOGA THERAPY CENTRE

**Yoga Biomedical Trust**, 60 Great Ormond St, London, **London (Greater)**, WC1N 3HR, **ENG**.
**(T)** 020 7419 7195 **(F)** 020 7419 7196
**(E)** enquiries.yogatherapy@virgin.net
**(W)** www.yogatherapy.org
**Speciality:** Yoga, Yoga Therapy. ✔ [credit card]
B **Yrs. Est.:** 17 (**Ref:**HM22033)

## YOGA TUITION

**Yoga Tuition**, Station Rd, Harborne, Birmingham, **Midlands (West)**, B17 9JT, **ENG**.
**(T)** 01214 276721
**Speciality:** Yoga.
● **Owner** Mrs J Degraaf
M (**Ref:**HM22034)

## YOGA WITH RENA NICHOLAOU

**Yoga With Rena Nicholaou**, 31a Grantbridge St, London, **London (Greater)**, N1 8JL, **ENG**.
**(T)** 020 7354 2450
**Speciality:** Relaxation Technique.
H T (**Ref:**HM22035)

## YOGA, IYENGAR

**Iyengar Yoga**, 40 Howitt Rd, London, **London (Greater)**, NW3 4LJ, **ENG**.
**(T)** 022 0772 25511
**Speciality:** Relaxation Technique.
● **Owner** Geraldine Ross
H T (**Ref:**HM22036)

## YONGE, V

**V Yonge**, The Homoeopathic Practice, The St, Hartlip, Sittingbourne, **Kent**, ME9 7TL, **ENG**.
**(T)** 01795 844562
**Speciality:** Homeopathy.
M (**Ref:**HM22037)

## YONI INTERNATIONAL

**Yoni International**, Mail Order, 11 Bennett Cl, Northwood, **London (Greater)**, HA6 1EP, **ENG**.
**(T)** 01923 835739 **(F)** 01923 835806
**Speciality:** Complementary Medicines & Therapy.


Key continued: **Yrs.Est:** Years Established **Q:** Qualifications **M:** Professional Membership ✔ Indemnity Insurance [credit card] Accept Credit Cards

● **Owner** Mr J Karmi
**C** **M** (**Ref:**HM22038)

## YORK CHIROPRACTIC CLINIC

**York Chiropractic Clinic**, 312 Stockton Lane, York, **Yorkshire (North)**, YO31 1JW, ENG.
**(T)** 01904 430300
Speciality: Chiropractic, X-Ray. ✓
● **Chiropractor** Mr K Burns **Q:** BSc (Hons). **M:** BCA.
● **Chiropractor** Chris Langtry-Lynas **Q:** BSc (Hons), MSc. **M:** BCA.
**S** Yrs. Est.: 15 (**Ref:**HM22039)

## YORK CLINIC

**York Clinic**, 296 Tadcaster Rd, York, **Yorkshire (North)**, YO24 1ET, ENG.
**(T)** 01904 709688
Speciality: Acupuncture, Allergy Testing, Aromatherapy, Chinese Herbal Medicine, Chiropody, Counselling, Homeopathy, Hypnotherapy, Osteopathy, Podiatry, Reflexology, Holistic Massage, Sports Therapy. ✓
● **Acupuncturist** Mr H Macpherson **Q:** Dip.Ac. **M:** BAcC, RCHM.
**C** Yrs. Est.: 10 (**Ref:**HM22040)

## YORK CLINIC FOR COMP MEDICINE

**York Clinic for Complementary Medicine**, 296 Tadcaster Rd, York, **Yorkshire (North)**, YO24 1ET, ENG.
**(T)** 01904 709688
Speciality: Complementary Medicines & Therapy.
● **Practitioner** E Mills
**M** (**Ref:**HM22041)

## YORK COUNSELLING

**York Counselling & Hypnotherapy Clinic**, Broadway West, York, **Yorkshire (North)**, YO10 4JJ, ENG.
**(T)** 01904 621866
Speciality: Counselling, Hypnosis, Hypnotherapy, Life Style Coaching, Psychotherapy, Rogerian Therapy, Stress Therapy. ✓
● **Counsellor/Hypnotherapist** Ms S Chambier **Q:** BA (Hons), NRHP (Assoc), PGCE. **M:** ICM, UKCP.
**B** Yrs. Est.: 13 (**Ref:**HM22042)

## YORK HEALTH SERVICES NHS TRUST

**York Health Services NHS Trust**, Bootham Pk Hospital, Bootham, York, **Yorkshire (North)**, YO30 7BY, ENG.
**(T)** 01904 645165 **(F)** 01904 454774
Speciality: Psychology.
**B** (**Ref:**HM22043)

## YORK HOUSE CHIROPODY

**York House Chiropody**, Stoke Damerel Business Centre, 5 Church St, Plymouth, **Devon**, PL3 4DT, ENG.
**(T)** 01752 607008 **(F)** 01752 605675
Speciality: Biomechanics, Chiropody, Nail Surgery, Podiatry. ✓
● **Chiropodist** Mr E Wietscher
**C** Yrs. Est.: 9 (**Ref:**HM22044)

## YORK HOUSE CHIROPRACTIC CLINIC

**York House Chiropractic Clinic**, Stoke Damerel Business Centre, 5 Church St, Plymouth, **Devon**, PL3 4DT, ENG.
**(T)** 01752 607008
Speciality: Chiropractic, Massage (Therapeutic). ✓
● **Chiropractor** Mr G Walker **Q:** DC. **M:** BCA.
**C** Yrs. Est.: 30 (**Ref:**HM22045)

## YORK NUTRITIONAL LABORATORY

**York Nutritional Laboratory Ltd**, Murton Way, Osbaldwick, York, **Yorkshire (North)**, YO19 5GS, ENG.
**(T)** 01904 410410 **(F)** 01904 422000
Speciality: Complementary Medicines & Therapy.
● **Partner** Mr J Graham
**C** **M** (**Ref:**HM22046)

## YORK PHYSIOTHERAPY PRACTICE

**York Physiotherapy Practice**, 55 Gale Lane, York, **Yorkshire (North)**, YO24 3AD, ENG.
**(T)** 01904 784055 **(F)** 01904 780445
Speciality: Physiotherapy.
● **Owner** Mr A Blake
**P** **S** **T** (**Ref:**HM22047)

## YORK PLACE HOM PRACTICE

**York Place Homoeopathic Practice (The)**, 39A York Pl, Edinburgh, **Edinburgh (City of)**, EH1 3HP, SCO.
**(T)** 01315 572927 **(F)** 01316 247171
Speciality: Homeopathy.
● **Partner** Ms R Preston
**M** (**Ref:**HM22048)

## YORK PSYCHOTHERAPY CLINIC

**York Psychotherapy Clinic**, 13 Huntington Rd, York, **Yorkshire (North)**, YO31 8RB, ENG.
**(T)** 01904 671104
Speciality: Psychotherapy.
**B** (**Ref:**HM22049)

## YORK SCHOOL OF COMP MEDICINE

**York School Of Complementary Medicine (The)**, Newton On Ouse, Newton On Ouse, York, **Yorkshire (North)**, YO30 2BU, ENG.
**(T)** 01347 848154 **(F)** 01347 848154
Speciality: Aromatherapy, Massage (Therapeutic), Nutritional Therapy, Reflexology.
● **Principal** Mrs P Watt
**C** (**Ref:**HM22050)

## YORK, B D

**B D York**, Cringleford, Five Ash Down, Uckfield, **Sussex (East)**, TN22 3AN, ENG.
**(T)** 01825 733604
Speciality: Chiropractic.
● **Owner** Mr B York
**P** **S** **T** (**Ref:**HM22051)

## YORK, SALLY

**Sally York**, 2 Nestor Court, Malling Rd, Teston, Maidstone, **Kent**, ME18 5AD, ENG.
**(T)** 01622 813181
Speciality: Physiotherapy.
● **Owner** Ms S York
**P** **S** **T** (**Ref:**HM22052)

## YORK, SUSAN

**Susan York**, La Niche, 5d Back St, Clophill, Bedford, **Bedfordshire**, MK45 4BY, ENG.
**(T)** 01525 860711 **(F)** 01525 860711
Speciality: Alexander Technique.
● **Owner** Mrs S York
**P** **S** (**Ref:**HM22053)

## YORK, TIM

**Tim York**, 30 Stirling Rd, Chichester, **Sussex (West)**, PO19 2ES, ENG.
**(T)** 01243 787507
Speciality: Alexander Technique.
● **Teacher of the Alexander Technique** Ms J Brigden **M:** STAT.
● **Teacher of the Alexander Technique** Mr T York **Q:** Cert.Alex.Tech. **M:** STAT.
**B** **C** Yrs. Est.: 11 (**Ref:**HM22054)

## YORKSHIRE ASS - PSYCHO

**Yorkshire Assoc For Psychodynamic Psychotherapy**, 5a Westgate, Otley, **Yorkshire (West)**, LS21 3AT, ENG.
**(T)** 01943 851110
Speciality: Psychotherapy.
**B** (**Ref:**HM22055)

## YORKSHIRE NEUROLOGY CLINIC

**Yorkshire Neurology Clinic (The)**, York House, Bawtry Rd, Wickersley, Rotherham, **Yorkshire (South)**, S66 2BL, ENG.
**(T)** 01709 700530
Speciality: Physiotherapy.
**P** **S** **T** (**Ref:**HM22056)

## YORKSHIRE SCHOOL OF SHIATSU

**Yorkshire School Of Shiatsu**, Cardigan Centre, 145-149 Cardigan Rd, Leeds, **Yorkshire (West)**, LS6 1LJ, ENG.
**(T)** 01422 845507 **(F)** 01422 845507
Speciality: Shiatsu.
● **Principal** Ms J Dixon
**M** (**Ref:**HM22057)

## YORVIK CHIROPRACTIC CLINIC

**Yorvik Chiropractic Clinic**, 22A Fishergate, York, **Yorkshire (North)**, YO10 4AB, ENG.
**(T)** 01904 632408
Speciality: Chiropractic.
**P** **S** **T** (**Ref:**HM22058)

## YOUELL, A (DR)

**Dr A Youell**, 17 Nottingham St, London, **London (Greater)**, W1M 3RD, ENG.
**(T)** 020 7486 8937
Speciality: Psychotherapy.
● **Owner** Dr A Youell
**B** (**Ref:**HM22059)

## YOUNG, A

**A Young**, Steeple Leeze Farm, Steeple, Wareham, **Dorset**, BH20 5NY, ENG.
**(T)** 01929 481325
Speciality: Herbalists.
● **Owner** Mrs A Young
**M** (**Ref:**HM22060)

## YOUNG, ALEX

**Alex Young**, 17 Nuns Moor Rd, Newcastle Upon Tyne, **Tyne and Wear**, NE4 9AU, ENG.
**(T)** 01912 736422
Speciality: Chiropodists (Podiatrists).
● **Owner** Mr A Young
**S** (**Ref:**HM22061)

## YOUNG, ALEX

**Alex Young**, The Basement, 2 Northumberland Pl, North Shields, **Tyne and Wear**, NE30 1QP, ENG.
**(T)** 01912 962160
Speciality: Chiropodists (Podiatrists).
● **Owner** Mr A Young
**S** (**Ref:**HM22062)

## YOUNG, ANGELA

**Angela Young**, Sackmore Lane, Marnhull, Sturminster Newton, **Dorset**, DT10 1PJ, ENG.
**(T)** 01258 821167
Speciality: Homeopathy.
**M** (**Ref:**HM22063)

## YOUNG, ANTOINETTE & MARTIN

**Antoinette Young & Martin Young Chiropractors**, 142 Sherborne Rd, Yeovil, **Somerset**, BA21 3AE, ENG.
**(T)** 01935 423138
Speciality: Chiropractic.
**P** **S** **T** (**Ref:**HM22064)

## YOUNG, B

**B Young**, 25 Lower Church St, Chepstow, **Monmouthshire**, NP16 5HJ, WAL.
**(T)** 01291 623538
Speciality: Chiropodists (Podiatrists).
**S** (**Ref:**HM22065)

## YOUNG, CAROLE

**Carole Young**, 53 Blacksmiths Lane, Rainham, **Kent**, RM13 7AH, ENG.
**(T)** 01708 550087
Speciality: Reflexology.
**S** **T** (**Ref:**HM22066)

## YOUNG, COURTENAY

**Courtenay Young**, The Park, Findhorn, Forres, **Moray**, IV36 3TZ, SCO.
**(T)** 01309 690251 **(F)** 01309 690974
Speciality: Psychotherapy.
● **Owner** Mr C Young
**B** (**Ref:**HM22067)

## YOUNG, D

**D Young**, Portman Lodge, Durweston, Blandford Forum, **Dorset**, DT11 0QA, ENG.
**(T)** 01258 452168 **(F)** 01258 450456
Speciality: Acupuncture.
● **Owner** Ms D Young
**O** (**Ref:**HM22068)

## YOUNG, D

**D Young**, Trinity Centre, Bimport, Shaftesbury, **Dorset**, SP7 8BW, ENG.
**(T)** 01747 851726
Speciality: Acupuncture.
● **Partner** Mrs E Childs
**O** (**Ref:**HM22069)

## YOUNG, D

**D Young**, High Views, Overway, Donhead St. Andrew, Shaftesbury, **Dorset**, SP7 9LH, ENG.
**(T)** 01747 828391
Speciality: Acupuncture.
● **Owner** Mrs D Young
**O** (**Ref:**HM22070)

### YOUNG, DOROTHY
**Dorothy Young**, 40 Roe Lane, Southport, **Merseyside**, PR9 9DZ, ENG.
(T) 01704 548002
Speciality: Electrolysis.
● **Owner** Mrs D Young
T (Ref:HM22071)

### YOUNG, HILARY
**Hilary Young**, 20A Burdon Lane, Sutton, **Surrey**, SM2 7PT, ENG.
(T) 020 8642 3935
Speciality: Acupuncture.
O (Ref:HM22072)

### YOUNG, JANE
**Jane Young**, 5 Lawns Avenue, Eastbourne, **Sussex (East)**, BN21 1PJ, ENG.
(T) 01323 724321
Speciality: Chiropodists (Podiatrists).
● **Owner** Miss J Young
S (Ref:HM22073)

### YOUNG, JOANNA
**Joanna Young**, 102 Chosen Drive, Churchdown, Gloucester, **Gloucestershire**, GL3 2QU, ENG.
(T) 01452 714511 (F) 01452 541369
Speciality: Osteopathy.
● **Partner** Mr C Hayden
P S T (Ref:HM22074)

### YOUNG, JOANNA
**Joanna Young Osteopath**, Ravenshill Farm Clinic, Tibberton, Droitwich, **Worcestershire**, WR9 7NR, ENG.
(T) 01905 345409
Speciality: Cranial Osteopathy, Osteopathy. ✔
● **Osteopath** Miss J Young Q: DO. M: GOsC.
S Yrs. Est.: 4 (Ref:HM22075)

### YOUNG, JUDITH (DR)
**Dr Judith Young D C**, Youghal Co, **County Cork**, IRE.
(T) 021 4505 133
Speciality: Chiropractors.
P S T (Ref:HM22076)

### YOUNG, LINDA
**Linda Young**, 42 Brook Rd, Horsham, **Sussex (West)**, RH12 5FY, ENG.
(T) 01789 400484
Speciality: Aromatherapy, Reflexology.
S T (Ref:HM22077)

### YOUNG, PATRICIA
**Patricia Young**, 131 Wells Green Rd, Solihull, **Midlands (West)**, B92 7PQ, ENG.
(T) 01217 433979
Speciality: Reflexology.
S T (Ref:HM22078)

### YOUNG, ROSEMARY
**Rosemary Young**, 6 Willow Gr, Essington, Wolverhampton, **Midlands (West)**, WV11 2JE, ENG.
(T) 01922 496440
Speciality: Reflexology.
S T (Ref:HM22079)

### YOUNG, SUE
**Sue Young**, 52 Stoke Newington Church St, London, **London (Greater)**, N16 0NB, ENG.
(T) 020 7249 9671
Speciality: Homeopathy.
● **Senior Partner** Mrs J Sheridan
M (Ref:HM22080)

### YOUNG, SUE
**Sue Young**, Waters Reach, Bascombe Rd, Churston Ferrers, Brixham, **Devon**, TQ5 0JJ, ENG.
(T) 01803 842592
Speciality: Aromatherapy.
● **Owner** Miss S Young
M O (Ref:HM22081)

### YOUNG, VEDA
**Veda Young**, 54A Eynham Rd, London, **London (Greater)**, W12 0HA, ENG.
(T) 020 8749 6523
Speciality: Homeopathy.
● **Owner** Ms V Young
M (Ref:HM22082)

### YOUNGER YOU
**Younger You**, Woodcock Hill, Felbridge, East Grinstead, **Sussex (West)**, RH19 2RD, ENG.
(T) 01342 310903 (F) 01342 310909
Speciality: Complementary Medicines & Therapy.
M (Ref:HM22083)

### YOUNGS, BRIAN K
**Brian K Youngs**, 112 Draycott Avenue, Harrow, **London (Greater)**, HA3 0BY, ENG.
(T) 020 8907 1704
Speciality: Osteopathy.
P S T (Ref:HM22084)

### YOUNGS, C
**Mr C Youngs**, 5 Mount Beacon, Bath, **Somerset**, BA1 5QP, ENG.
(T) 01225 312399
Speciality: Physiotherapy.
● **Owner** Mrs J Bardner
P S T (Ref:HM22085)

### YR APOTHECARI
**Yr Apothecari**, 3 Shoppers Gardens, Jacksons Lane, Carmarthen, **Carmarthenshire**, SA31 1QD, WAL.
(T) 01267 223738
Speciality: Complementary Medicines & Therapy.
C M (Ref:HM22086)

### YULE, AILEEN
**Aileen Yule**, 2 Downside, Strawberry Hill, Twickenham, **London (Greater)**, TW1 4QD, ENG.
(T) 020 8892 3025
Speciality: Reflexology.
S T (Ref:HM22087)

### YULE, J
**J Yule**, 21 Reynes Drive, Oakley, Bedford, **Bedfordshire**, MK43 7SD, ENG.
(T) 01234 823976 (F) 01234 823976
Speciality: Reflexology.
● **Owner** Mrs J Yule
S T (Ref:HM22088)

### YUSUPOFF, LAWRENCE
**Lawrence Yusupoff**, 25 St John St, Manchester, **Manchester (Greater)**, M3 4DT, ENG.
(T) 01614 450329
Speciality: Psychology.
● **Owner** Mr L Yusupoff
B (Ref:HM22089)

### YVONNE
**Yvonne**, 33 Oakleigh Cres, Totton, Southampton, **Hampshire**, SO40 9AR, ENG.
(T) 023 8086 3936 (F) 023 8086 3936
Speciality: Clairvoyants & Palmists.
● **Owner** Mrs Y Wickett
B (Ref:HM22090)

### YVONNE HENRY HYPNOTHERAPIST
**Yvonne Henry Hypnotherapist**, 5 Cloondara Ballisodare, **County Sligo**, IRE.
(T) 07130 569
Speciality: Hypnotherapy.
B (Ref:HM22091)

### ZACHARIA, T (DR)
**Dr T Zacharia**, The Chiropractic & Pain Management Centres, 17 Mt Rd, London, **London (Greater)**, NW4 3QA, ENG.
(T) 020 8202 1140
Speciality: Chiropractors.
● **Owner** Dr T Zacharia
P S T (Ref:HM22092)

### ZAHNISER, E
**E Zahniser**, 25 Horsell Rd, London, **London (Greater)**, N5 1XL, ENG.
(T) 020 7700 1308
Speciality: Psychotherapy.
● **Owner** Ms E Zahniser
B (Ref:HM22093)

### ZAHNISER, ESTHER
**Esther Zahniser**, 19 Wilmot Rd, London, **London (Greater)**, N17 6LH, ENG.
(T) 020 7700 1308
Speciality: Psychotherapy.
B (Ref:HM22094)

### ZARA THE CLAIRVOYANT
**Zara The Clairvoyant**, 1 Cannock Wood Rd, Cannock, **Staffordshire**, WS12 5PZ, ENG.
(T) 01543 451921
Speciality: Clairvoyants & Palmists.
● **Owner** Ms Z Evans
B (Ref:HM22095)

### ZARBAFI, A
**A Zarbafi**, 30 Magnolia Rd, London, **London (Greater)**, W4 3QW, ENG.
(T) 020 8747 0408
Speciality: Psychotherapy.
● **Owner** Mr A Zarbafi
B (Ref:HM22096)

### ZARVIS-LONDON
**Zarvis-London**, Unit 4, 281 Portobello Rd, London, **London (Greater)**, W10 5TZ, ENG.
(T) 020 8968 5435
Speciality: Herbal Medicine.
M (Ref:HM22097)

### ZEN AT THE WATERS EDGE
**Zen At The Waters Edge**, Brindleyplace, Birmingham, **Midlands (West)**, B1 2HL, ENG.
(T) 01216 433933
Speciality: Complementary Medicines & Therapy.
C M (Ref:HM22098)

### ZEN HEALTH & BEAUTY
**Zen Health & Beauty**, 3 St. Marys Row, Moseley, Birmingham, **Midlands (West)**, B13 8HW, ENG.
(T) 01214 494995
Speciality: Aromatherapy, Indian Head Massage, Massage (Therapeutic), Reflexology, Reiki. CREDIT
● **Therapist** Ms Goodman
● **Therapist** Ms S Lowe
● **Therapist** Ms S Chandler
B C Yrs. Est.: 7 (Ref:HM22099)

### ZEN HEALTH CENTRE
**Zen Health Centre**, 32 Notting Hill Gate, London, **London (Greater)**, W11 3HX, ENG.
(T) 020 7229 8666 (F) 020 7229 8686
(E) c7pook@yahoo.com
Speciality: Acupressure, Acupuncture, Aromatherapy, Biofeedback, Chiropractic, Colonic Hydrotherapy, Complementary Therapy, Counselling, Cranial Osteopathy, Cupping, Dietician, Electrotherapy, Floral Essence Therapy, Healer, Healing Therapy, Herbal Medicine, Holistic Healing, Homeopathy, Indian Head Massage, Iridology, Manual Lymph Drainage, Massage (Therapeutic), Meditation, Moxibustion, Naturopathy, Nutritional Therapy, Oriental Diagnosis, Osteopathy, Reflexology, Reiki, Shiatsu, Spiritual Healing, Vitamin Therapy, Ying & Yang, Zen Therapy, Karuna Bodywork and Healing, Food Intolerance Testing, Thai Yoga Massage, Full Body Scan, Bio Energetic Stress Test, Heavy Metal Tests, Live Blood Cell Tests, Detox and Weight Control Programmes, Urine and Toxicological Testing, Hair Mineral Analysis, Buteyko Method, Urine Analysis, Hormone and Amino Acid Testing, Glyco Protein Tests, Free Radical Tests, Ultra Sound Organ Scanning, Doppier Sona Tests. ✔ CREDIT
● **Massage Therapist/Bodyworker** Miss C Pulver Q: ITEC. M: ITEC.
● **Bodyworker/Healer** Miss H Ratip
● **Manager** Ms C Liu
● **Chinese Doctor** Dr L Zhang M: WACM.
B C O T Yrs. Est.: 2 (Ref:HM22100)

### ZEN SHIATSU & HEALING TAO
**Zen Shiatsu & Healing Tao**, 3rd Floor, 19-21 Phipp St, London, **London (Greater)**, EC2A 4NP, ENG.
(T) 07000 781195 (F) 020 7739 9916
(E) kris@llearn.shiatsu.co.uk
(W) www.learn-shiatsu.co.uk
Speciality: Absent Healing, Acupressure, Healing Therapy, Meditation, Oriental Diagnosis, Shiatsu, T'ai-Chi Ch'uan, Tantra Therapy, Chi Nei Tsang (Taoist Massage), Qigong Healing ( Taist Colour Healing). ✔ CREDIT
● **Senior Teacher** Mr M Cullingworth
(T) 020 8291 7981 Q: MRSS(t). M: Shiatsu Society UK.


Key continued: Yrs.Est: Years Established Q: Qualifications M: Professional Membership ✔ Indemnity Insurance CREDIT Accept Credit Cards

● **Teacher** Ms B Careise
**(T)** 020 8985 0320 **M:** GCP.
● **Teacher** Beata Kociatyn
**(T)** 020 8488 0616
● **Owner** Mr K Larthe **Q:** MRSS(t). **M:** Shiatsu Society UK.
**B** Yrs. Est.: 7 (**Ref:**HM22101)

## ZENA CLAIRVOYANT & TAROT READ

**Zena Clairvoyant & Tarot Reader**, Viscount Gardens, West Byfleet, **Surrey**, KT14 6HE, **ENG**.
**(T)** 01932 341281
Speciality: Clairvoyants & Palmists.
● **Owner** Ms Z White
**B** (**Ref:**HM22102)

## ZENERGY CITY SHIATSU CLGE

**Zenergy City Shiatsu Collective**, Flat 161, Waxham, Mansfield Rd, London, **London (Greater)**, NW3 2JL, **ENG**.
**(T)** 020 7419 9571
Speciality: Complementary Medicines & Therapy.
**C** **M** (**Ref:**HM22103)

## ZEPHRINA, D'ARCY

**D'Arcy Zephrina L L S A M I R I**, 35 Cecil St, **County Limerick**, **IRE**.
**(T)** 06141 0077
Speciality: Aromatherapy.
**M** **O** (**Ref:**HM22104)

## ZERO BALANCING ASSOCIATION

**Zero Balancing Association (The)**, 10 Victoria Gr, Bridport, **Dorset**, DT6 3AA, **ENG**.
**(T)** 01308 420007
Speciality: Complementary Medicines & Therapy.
● **Owner** Ms Z Heighton
**C** **M** (**Ref:**HM22105)

## ZEST SKIN & BODY CLINIC

**Zest Skin & Body Clinic**, 16 Mill St, Bedford, **Bedfordshire**, MK40 3HD, **ENG**.
**(T)** 01234 346363
Speciality: Complementary Medicines & Therapy.
● **Owner** Ms J Benson
**C** **M** (**Ref:**HM22106)

## ZEUS P M C

**Zeus P M C**, 430 Bury New Rd, Prestwich, Manchester, **Manchester (Greater)**, M25 1BD, **ENG**.
**(T)** 01617 986873 **(F)** 01617 986873
Speciality: Aromatherapy.
● **Owner** Mr M Higson
**M** **O** (**Ref:**HM22107)

## ZHANG (DR)

**Zhang Dr Surgery & Pharmacy**, 1st Floor 18 Upr Georges St, Dun Laoghaire, **County Dublin**, **IRE**.
**(T)** 01284 4268
Speciality: Complementary Medicines & Therapy.
**M** (**Ref:**HM22108)

## ZIA, ROBINA

**Robina Zia**, 106 Roundwood Rd, London, **London (Greater)**, NW10 9UN, **ENG**.
**(T)** 020 8451 7359
Speciality: Reflexology.
**S** **T** (**Ref:**HM22109)

## ZIAD, PATRICIA

**Patricia Ziad**, Surgery, 3 Cornerswell Rd, Penarth, **Glamorgan (Vale of)**, CF64 2UW, **WAL**.
**(T)** 029 2070 3125
Speciality: Chiropodists (Podiatrists).
**S** (**Ref:**HM22110)

## ZIELINSKI, KRYSTYNA

**Krystyna Zielinski**, 18 Daybrook Rd, London, **London (Greater)**, SW19 3DH, **ENG**.
**(T)** 020 8542 8596
Speciality: Osteopathy.
● **Owner** Miss K Zielinski
**P** **S** **T** (**Ref:**HM22111)

## ZINGAS, STELLA

**Stella Zingas**, 49 Jubilee Rd, Knowle, Bristol, BS4 2LR, **ENG**.
**(T)** 01179 711740
Speciality: Hypnosis.
**B** (**Ref:**HM22112)

## ZISMAN, A

**A Zisman**, Beverley Clinic, 362 Coombe Lane, London, **London (Greater)**, SW20 0RJ, **ENG**.
**(T)** 020 8241 2515
Speciality: Aromatherapy.
● **Practice Manager** Mrs P Conway
**M** **O** (**Ref:**HM22113)

## ZODIAC

**Zodiac**, 28 Lord Sq, Blackburn, **Lancashire**, BB1 7JA, **ENG**.
**(T)** 01254 278220 **(F)** 01254 677327
Speciality: Aromatherapy.
● **Owner** Mrs C Scholfield
**H** (**Ref:**HM22114)

## ZOTA

**Zota Ltd**, Units 2 & 3 John St, Ind Est Jo, Ardee, **County Louth**, **IRE**.
**(T)** 04168 57995
Speciality: Herbalists.
**M** (**Ref:**HM22115)

## ZUBAIR, S

**Mrs S Zubair**, 9 Cambridge Drive, Ruislip, **London (Greater)**, HA4 9JS, **ENG**.
**(T)** 020 8868 0493
Speciality: Chiropodists (Podiatrists).
**S** (**Ref:**HM22116)

## ZUIDYK, TOSCA

**Tosca Zuidyk**, The Osteopathy And Complementary Therapy Clinic, Walnuts Leis, Orpington, **Kent**, BR6 0TJ, **ENG**.
**(T)** 020 8467 9001
Speciality: Acupuncture.
● **Owner** Miss T Zuidyk
**O** (**Ref:**HM22117)

## ZUIDYK, TOSCA

**Tosca Zuidyk**, St Lukes Hospital For The Clergy, 14 Fitzroy Sq, London, **London (Greater)**, W1P 6AH, **ENG**.
**(T)** 020 7388 4954
Speciality: Acupuncture.
● **Owner** Miss T Zuidyk
**O** (**Ref:**HM22118)

## ZULEWSKI, STEFAN

**Stefan Zulewski**, Blake Farm, Blake End, Rayne, Braintree, **Essex**, CM7 8SH, **ENG**.
**(T)** 01376 345976
Speciality: Osteopathy.
● **Owner** Mr S Zulewski
**P** **S** **T** (**Ref:**HM22119)

## ZWIERCHOWSKA, ZENNA

**Zenna Zwierchowska**, Clissold Park Health Centre, 154 Stoke Newington Church St, London, **London (Greater)**, N16 0JU, **ENG**.
**(T)** 020 7249 2990 **(F)** 020 7249 2990
Speciality: Osteopathy.
● **Owner** Mr D Berg
**P** **S** **T** (**Ref:**HM22120)

## ZWIERZCHOWSKA, Z

**Z Zwierzchowska**, Sutherland House, 1a Ashbourne Avenue, London, **London (Greater)**, NW11 0DP, **ENG**.
**(T)** 020 8458 7869
Speciality: Osteopathy.
**P** **S** **T** (**Ref:**HM22121)

## ZYS, A & S

**Andreas & Susannah Zys**, Heathend House, Checkendon, Reading, **Berkshire**, RG8 0UR, **ENG**.
**(T)** 01491 680992
Speciality: Homeopathy.
**M** (**Ref:**HM22123)



Key: **B** Mind-Body Medicine **C** Complementary Medicine **H** Self Help Treatment **M** Medicinal Therapy **O** Oriental Medicine **P** Postural Therapy **S** Manipulative Structural Therapy **T** Touch Therapy

HEALTH MYSELF

# SECTION 2

## Locate a Practitioner listed A-Z by County by Town, within Country

# BEDFORDSHIRE

## BARTON-LE-CLEY

- WARD-SAUNDERS, WENDY

## BEDFORD

- ACUPUNCTURE CLINIC
- ALDER, E R
- ALEXANDER TECHNIQUE
- ALLMAN, LESLIE
- ALOE VERA SPECIALISTS
- AMPTHILL & FLITWICK CLINIC
- BEDFORD ACUPUNCTURE CLINIC
- BEDFORD CHIROPRACTIC SURGERY
- BEDFORD PHYSIOTHERAPY CENTRE
- BEDFORD PHYSIOTHERAPY CLINIC
- BEDFORD PSYCHOTHERAPY PRACTICE
- BISHOP, PATRICIA
- BODYTUNE
- BRAMPTON SCIEN FOOD ALLERGY
- BRETHERTON, S M
- BROOKE, JUDITH
- BUMFREY, CAROL
- BURTON, MERILYNN
- CHARTERED PHYSIOTHERAPIST
- CHINESE HERBS & MEDICINE
- COLDWELL, VERONICA
- CREWE, N V
- DISS, KATHRYN
- EVANS, LINDA
- FELCE, S E
- HAVEN AROMATHERAPY CTRE
- HOLISTIC HYPNOTHERAPY
- HYNE, JOANNA E M
- JADE COLLEGE-NATURAL THERAPY
- KEMPSTON CHIROPRACTIC CLINIC
- LAMB CHIROPRATIC CLINIC
- LESSELL, C B
- LIKISMA
- MCELROY, BEVERLY
- MEIGHAN, JUDITH
- MUIR, P M
- MULTIPLE SCLEROSIS THRPY CTRE
- N A P A
- NATURAL HEALTH CLINIC
- NORTH BEDS OSTEOPATHIC CLINIC
- OSBORN, HELEN
- O'SHEA, LESLEY
- OWEN, VICTOR
- PALMER, ROY
- PHYSIO SPORTS & SPINAL CLINIC
- PRICE, SARAH
- REFLEXOLOGY BY DEBORAH
- RISING CRANE CENTRE
- ROBERTSON, IAN R
- ROBINSON, KAREN
- SELLICK, A C
- SHEER PERFECTION
- SPECTRUM HEALTH TRUST
- SPORT, ALEXANDER
- STEELE, FRED
- THERAPEUTICS
- THERAPY CENTRE
- THOMAS, CARL
- TREE OF LIFE
- TURBUTT, I F
- WALKER, A
- WILLIAMS, K
- WILLIS, ALAN
- WINTER, SALLY
- WONG, ANGELA
- YORK, SUSAN
- YULE, J
- ZEST SKIN & BODY CLINIC

## BIGGLESWADE

- DUNTON CTRE-COUN/PSYCHOTHERAPY
- GOODCHILD, ROGER A
- HALE, J N
- MACBRAYNE, KEITH
- MORRIS, A E
- POYNTER, K J
- SHERRY'S HEALTH FOODS
- THOMAS, P A
- YOGA FOR HEALTH FOUNDATION

## CADDINGTON

- JENNIFER K HOUGH - PHYSIO

## DUNSTABLE

- ALTERNATIVE HEALTH & BEAUTY
- AROMAZ HOLISTIC CLINIC
- BELLAMY, R D
- BOYCE, MICHAEL
- D'ARCY, M
- FOX, G A
- GIBBONS, J A
- GORANIA, V D (DR)
- GREEN, DAVID
- JOHNSON, ANNE
- JOY, NICOLA & TOMMY
- JUST IMAGINE
- KEMP, G
- KJAERVIK, SUSANNE
- LEDGER, DIANE
- LINANE, IAN
- LOCKLEY, J
- MCCARTHY, ROSALYN
- NORMAN, I
- O'BRIEN, HELEN
- PHILIPS, J
- SMITH, E
- TAYLOR-WEEKES, HELEN
- WELLS, C
- WOODSIDE CLINIC
- WREN, JENNY

## LEIGHTON BUZZARD

- ARMSTRONG, DEE
- BANFIELD, KEITH
- BETSER, J
- CHIROPRACTIC CONSULTANT SVS
- CLNC OF ACU & CHINESE HERB MED
- COULSTOCK, JUDY
- CRIBB, PAULINE
- DA SILVA, CAROLE
- DAVIES, TRACY A
- GROVE NATURAL THERAPY CLINIC
- HAMILTON, ALEX
- HEALEY, NORMAN
- INWARD BOUND THERAPIES
- JARMAN, JANET
- KJAERVIK, SUSANNE
- LAMB, VICTORIA
- LEIGHTON CHIROPODY PRACTICE
- MAGNETS 4 HEALTH
- NAPLES, EILEEN
- NIGHTINGALE, ROSE
- RADIANT HEALTH CLINIC
- RUFFELL, JILLIAN
- SWEET BREEZE
- VAN STRATEN CLINIC
- WALKER, A M

## LUTON

- ABELA, P
- ACTIVE BALANCE
- ALLSOP, L M
- ALTERNATIVE THERAPY AT WORK
- AMBACARE
- BACK TO BACK CHIRO CLINIC
- BOA
- CHINESE HERB HOUSE
- CHINESE HERBS
- CHIROPRACTIC CONSULTANT SVS
- CHRYSALIS
- CLARIDGE, B M
- DANS CHINESE MEDICINE CLINIC
- DE PRINCE, THESSALONIA
- EASTERN THERAPIES
- FEET FIRST
- GALLEN, ANNE
- GOUGH, E & P T
- HAMILTON-WILSON, JOAN
- HEALES CHIROPRACTIC CLINIC
- HEMMENS, JANE
- HENDEN, CHRIS
- HIGGS, M
- HINKSMAN, DOROTHY
- HUGHES, JEAN
- HUTCHINSON, JANE
- HYPNOSIS HEALTH CLINIC
- JENNY'S
- JOHNSTONS CHIROPODIST
- KATZ, JANICE
- KIRBY, DAVE
- KIRK, DONNA
- LOBO, GLENN P
- LUTON PHYSIO SPORTS INJURY
- MARFLEET, RACHAEL
- MARFLEET, RACHAEL DE VERE
- MCALLISTER, C (DR)
- NEWELL, A J
- PEARCE, G
- PERRET, NICOLE
- PHYSIO & SPORTS CLINIC
- PHYSIO & SPORTS INJURY CLINIC
- PRIEDE, C L
- PYLE, RAYMOND
- RINALDINI, RENATA
- SCHOLL CENTRE
- SMITH, R
- STEWART PALMER HYPNOTHERAPIST
- THOMPSON, H J
- THOMPSON, MARTIN

## SANDY

- CHAPPELL, D
- MACLUSKY, K A
- SHIATSU

## SHEFFORD

- SCHOOL OF ICASA
- SHEFFORD OSTEOPATHIC CLINIC

# BERKSHIRE

## ASCOT

- ASCOT PHYSIOFIRST CENTRE
- BEAUMONT, ANNA
- BODY & SOUL
- CHAPMAN, GILLIAN
- FLYNN, JANE C
- JONES, LYNDA
- LANSMAN, ROBIN J
- MUNCEY, ALAN
- MYSTICAL PATHWAYS
- SUNNINGDALE HEALING CENTRE

## BRACKNELL

- AMBER NATURAL THERAPY
- ATKINSON NEILSON
- BAKER, CAROLINE
- BALDWIN, P D
- BERKSHIRE CHIROPRACTIC
- BIOFEEDBACK
- BRACKNELL CHIROPRACTIC CLINIC
- BRACKNELL PHYSIOTHERAPY CLINIC
- BRUCE, ANN
- CARMEN NATURAL THERAPIES
- CHANDLER, PETER E
- CLASSICAL OSTEOPATH
- DAVIS, LOUISE
- FISHER, HEATHER
- GARDNER, E
- GOLD, HELENA S
- HALFORD, EVELYN
- INNER SENSE
- IRWIN, VICKY
- JONES, PAULA
- NORFOLK, JILL
- NS3UK NUTRITION SERVICES
- OSMAN, ELIZABETH
- ROBERTS, EMMA
- SANDERS, CHRISTINE
- SKEELS, LILIAN
- STRESS BODY MANAGEMENT
- WALKER, MARIAN
- WILSON, C

## COOKHAM DEAN

- PLUMMER, VALERIE

## CROWTHORNE

- CHEUNG, JAMES T (DR)
- CROWTHORNE CHIROPODIST CLINIC
- HALL, GRACE
- HOLLOWAY, JANE
- KING, S
- NATURAL HEALTH CONSULTANCY
- PIM, MICHAEL (DR)
- SLIP, ANNE

## HUNGERFORD

- HAMM, D R
- LILLEY CLINIC
- OSTEOPATHIC & SPORTS CLINIC
- PAMFLETT, E C
- RIVETT, LYNN

## MAIDENHEAD

- A & M KENNEDY
- ALLERGY TESTING
- BASSIL, L
- BLYTH, SIMON
- COOKHAM CHIROPRACTIC CLINIC
- CRESCENT OSTEOPATHIC CENTRE
- DAY, SYLVIA
- DUNCAN, M
- EIGHT WINDS ACUPUNCTURE
- ENHANCED SUCCESS PERFORMANCE
- FERINGA, MARLIES
- GHEORGHIU, E (DR)
- GIBSON, MALCOLM
- GRIFFITH, G D
- HAIR TOMMOROW GROUP
- HARRIS, J
- HAZEL'S HOLISTIC HEALTH CARE
- HERBAL MEDICINE CLINIC
- HODGSON, ANN
- IKIN, SALLY
- JACKYS ALTERNATIVE THERAPIES
- JAMIL, M T (DR)
- KENNEDY, GRAHAM
- LANSMAN, ROBIN J
- LAVENDER, S
- LI, G Q (DR)
- LINDQUIST, I
- MAIDENHEAD CHIROPRACTIC
- MAIDENHEAD PHYSIO & SPORTS
- MANNING, PAMELA
- MATRAVES, SUE
- MEADEN, C A
- MILLER, ADELE
- MOFFAT, C
- NATURAL THERAPY CLINIC
- NATURAL THERAPY CLINIC
- NATURE'S GIFT
- NEWCOME, ROBERT
- PARKER, WILLIAM
- PEGASUS CENTRE
- PENNEFATHER, R J
- PLUMMER, VALERIE
- RAWLINSON, MARGARET
- REIBL, TINA
- RELAX AROMATHERAPY
- SAKAL V
- SANDERS, CHRISTINE
- SHARPLES, ANITA
- SIDEY, J
- SMITH, PENNY
- SPILSBURY, FIDELMA
- TEAM FOCUS
- THAMS, JUNE
- THOMASON, M L
- TREGIDGO, P
- WILMOTT, DELCIA

## NEWBURY

- ABBOTT, LORNA
- ALLISON, V C
- BRZOZOWSKI-MAN, ISABELLA
- BURNETT, KIM
- CRAVEN, INGA
- CUTLER, JENNY
- DAVIS, ANDREW & VICTORIA
- DAVIS, MICHAEL
- DIAMOND HOLISTIC CENTRE
- DIGGENS, SUE
- DOEY, ROSEMARY
- E M S
- EATON, JOHN
- EIGHAN, PENELOPE
- FAIRBOURNE CLINIC
- FEET TREAT
- HAMILTON, MELANIE
- HAMM, D R
- JACKSON & RUDLAND
- KIRKE, STEPHANIE
- LILWALL, EMMA
- LOCKYER, ROSEMARY
- M MAGDALENE HEALING/MEDITATION
- MAY, AMANDA
- MCGREGOR, S
- MCGREGOR, TONY
- MESSOM, C A
- NASEBY ACUPUNCTURE CLINIC
- NATURAL HEALTH CENTRE
- NEWBURY CHIROPRACTIC CENTRE
- NEWBURY PHYSIOTHERAPY
- NEWBURY PRACTICE
- PARIS, LYN
- PHYSIOTHERAPY CLINIC
- PSYCHIC CIRCLE
- SPENCER, GILLIAN
- STUBBS, RICHARD
- TIPPLE, DAWN
- TWINE, I E
- TYNCE, CHRIS

## READING

- 1ST CHIROPRACTIC CLINIC
- 3 WAY PHYSIOTHERAPY
- ACUPUNCTURE/CHINESE HERBAL ASS
- ADASTRAL HEALTH
- ALDER, CHRISTINE
- ALVAREZ, ANDREA
- ANTSCHERL, M
- APPLETREE COUNSELLING
- ATKINSON, N T
- BAREFIELD, SHIRLEY
- BOON, JEAN
- BRADBURY, VALMA
- BRITISH CHIROPRACTIC ASS
- BRYANT, C
- BUPA DUNEDIN HOSPITAL
- BUTTERBUR & SAGE
- CANNEY, E
- CARDY BEAVER PHYSIO CENTRE
- CASTLE HILL CLINIC
- CASTLE TAROT
- CAVERSHAM CHIROPRACTIC CLINC
- CAVERSHAM COUN & PSYCHOTHERAPY
- CAVERSHAM FOOT CLINIC
- CHEFLAND, GERTI
- CHUMBLEY, COLIN
- CHUMBLEY, SYLVIA
- CLARK, J
- CLARK, J
- CLASSICAL OSTEOPATH
- CLEAR, SEAN
- CLEERE, SEAN
- COLLEGE OF INTEG CHINESE MED
- CONNERY, PAUL
- COUZENS, D R
- COZENS, DAVID R
- DE JODE, S
- DEJODE, SONIA
- DEPILLE
- DOBSON, SUE
- EASBY, DAVID N
- EDWARDS, JOHN
- ELLIOTT, KATHI
- EVANS, H
- FARRAND, ELAINE
- FIELDING, ANNA
- FOX, E
- GILL, A
- GORING & STREATLEY OSTEOPATHIC
- GREEN, W
- HALL, BEVERLEY
- HALLAM, JANET
- HART, S
- HASELTON, HOWARD
- HEATH, J
- HERBAL SCHOOL
- HEWISON, F
- HEWITT, ANDREW
- HINTON, LYNN
- HOLDAWAY, MICHELLE
- JACKSON, ANDREW
- JUNA, F
- KEEL, JULIAN
- KEMP-WHEELER, S (DR)
- KENT, JANET
- KILNER, FELICIA
- KINGFISHERS COMP HEALTH CARE
- LANE, CORINNE
- LATCHFORD, A
- LESLIE MAYNERD
- LEWIS, GILL
- LIKISMA
- LISSADELL HOUSE PRACTICE
- LOGUE, JOHN
- LOUISE
- MACRAE, BARBARA
- MAHER, CARRON
- MARCHANT, SUE
- MARIANNE, RALPH
- MCGREADY, NORMA
- MENSANA PSYCHOLOGICAL THRP
- MITTAL, R (DR)
- MORRISS, C
- MORRISS, CHRISTOPHER J
- MYSTICAL PATHWAYS
- NAISH, P
- NATURE SUN SHINE HERBS
- NEVILLE-TOWLE, V
- NEW OXFORD HOUSE CLINICS
- NIJSSEN, M C
- PANGBOURNE CHIROPODY CLINIC
- PAPWORTH, H A
- PARRY-ELLIS, MARGARET
- PETER THERAPEUTIC MASSEUR
- PHILLIPS, J A
- PHYSIOCARE
- PHYSIOCARE
- PHYSIOTHERAPY CONSULTANCY SVS
- PIENAAR, DOROTHY
- PIM CHIROPRACTIC CLINIC
- PIM HEALTH CLINIC
- PIM, R D
- POTTERTON, DAVID
- PRICE, M P
- RADFORD, PAULINE
- RAYNER, BEN
- READING CHIROPRACTIC CLINIC
- RICHARDS, HILARY
- RINTU, BASU
- ROSEDALE CLINIC
- ROWE, HELEN & JEREMY
- ROWLAND, S
- SANDALL, S
- SCHOLL CENTRE
- SHARMA, (DR)
- SHARMA, R P
- SHORT, P
- SINGER, S
- SMETHURST, ALISON
- SMITH, JENNIE
- SPRINGWOOD COMP HEALTH
- SWAINE, R F
- T A IN THE THAMES VALLEY
- THAMES VALLEY CLINIC
- THOMAS, P (DR)
- TILEHURST PHYSIOTHERAPY SVS
- TITCOMBE, R C
- TRANSCENDENTAL MEDITATION
- TSENG, PATRICIA
- VICK, C
- WALKER, J W
- WALKER, PENELOPE
- WALKER, R
- WEIR, ANDREW
- WELLINGS, CLIVE
- WELSH, ANNE
- WEST BERKSHIRE PSYCHOTHERAPY
- WEST STREET THERAPY CENTRE
- WHITEKNIGHTS SPORTS CLINIC
- WILKIN, P (DR)
- WILLIAMS, R J
- WOODLEY HEALING CENTRE
- WOODROW, IRENE
- WOODS, L
- WRIGHT, LAWRIE
- ZYS, A & S

## SANDHURST

- AMBLER, S J
- BROADHEAD, MARILYN
- COPPERTHWAITE, ERIC
- NATURAL PATH TO RADIANT HEALTH
- SIMPSON, JUNE

## SLOUGH

- ACUPUNCTURE CLINIC
- ARCHER, JULIE
- BAJWA, K S & O'DRISCOLL, P
- BURNHAM CHIROPRACTIC CLINIC
- CARROLL, D
- CLARK, D
- CUMMING, LLOYD
- DR LIP ONG CRANIOSACRAL
- GENGE, DAVID
- GREEN, PAULINE
- HERBAL HEALTH CLINIC
- HERBMEDIC

- HILLSIDE OSTEOPATHIC PRACTICE
- JEFFREY, R
- JONES, P R
- JUKES, CLARE
- KANAKAM, JONATHAN
- KEEN, ANDREW R
- KULWINDER, S
- LANES MEDICAL PRACTICE
- LANGLEY CHIROPRACTORS CLINIC
- LIFE GUIDANCE
- LIP ONG
- MANN, H S
- MILLS, MARGARET
- MOMENTA
- MONROE, T
- NATHAN, HARRY
- NORTON, DAVID
- OSBORNE, JO
- PETERS, JEAN
- POOL, NICKY
- PRACTICE
- PREECE, R E
- RATH, MATTHIAS
- RICH, ELIZABETH
- ROBINSON, S
- SHARMA, SHASHI MOHAN (DR)
- SLOUGH SPORTS INJURIES CLINIC
- SOUTH BUCKS PHYSIOTHERAPISTS
- SOUTH LODGE CONSULTING
- SOUTHMEAD HOUSE
- STEELE, PAM
- STEPHENS, BRENDA
- TINGLE, SARAH
- WALTON, DEBORAH
- WARD, ROBIN E
- WARNER, K
- WELCH, MARTIN
- WOOD, JEANIE M
- WOODBURY COUNSELLING

## SUNNINGDALE

- REED, TED

## THATCHAM

- CLERE PHYSIOTHERAPY
- EDMONDS, ANN
- ESSENTIAL ELEMENTS
- JONES, JACQUELINE A
- KHAN, FARIDA
- ORTHOMOL
- PARSONS, G H
- POTTER, J
- SMITH, CANDIDA
- THATCHAM CHIROPRACTIC CLINIC
- WALKER, SAM

## WALTHAM ST LAWRENCE

- MCCARTHY, SUSAN

## WINDSOR

- ANABELLE'S THERAPEUTIC MASSAGE
- BACK TO HEALTH - WINDSOR
- BERESFORD, KATE
- BISHOPS LODGE
- BUNCE THERAPEUTIC MASSAGE
- CAMPBELL, ELSPETH
- CARPENTER, M P
- DEAN RUSSELL & BRYDGES ROBERT
- DICKINSON, E H
- FARAGO CLINIC
- HERBAL INNOVATIONS
- HOLDING, MARTIN
- INNERSANCTUM HOLISTIC HEALTH
- KEEN, STEVE
- PRINCESS MARGARET HOSPITAL
- QURESHI, JOHN
- REDDING-THOMAS, K
- REGUVA-CELL
- SMITH, MARK
- SMITH, MARTIN
- STRINGER, FRANCES
- WILLINGSON, TOM
- WINDSOR CTRE - TRAD CHINESE AC

## WOKINGHAM

- BALDWYN ANIMAL PHYSIOTHERAPY
- BARRELL, L A
- BINGHAM, JULIE
- BURT, JOHN
- CANNING, LORRAINE
- COLLINGS, S
- DAY, R M
- DUCKWORTH, ROGER
- EDNEY, C S
- FLEMING, M K
- FLYNN, GILLIAN
- FORREST, SAMANTHA
- GUILD OF COMP PRACTITIONERS
- HORSBURGH, PENNY
- LIDDELL-SMITH, P J
- NEW SPIRIT NATURALS
- POLAK, CAROL
- RELF, M J
- ROWE, GEOFF
- ROWSELL
- SYNERGY HEALTH
- SYNERGY HEALTH
- WINNERSH HYPNOTHERAPY PRACTICE
- WOKINGHAM CHIROPRACTIC CENTRE
- WOKINGHAM COMP HEALTH CENTRE

## BRISTOL

- ABSOLUTELY YOU
- ACORN PHYSIOTHERAPY CLINIC
- ADAM, G S
- ADLER, DAVID
- ADVANCED HYPNOSIS/HYNOTHERAPY
- ALEXANDER HOUSE PRACTICE
- ALEXANDER TECHNIQUE
- ALEXANDER, KAREN
- ALLISON JOY REFLEXOLOGY
- ALOE VERA CENTRE
- ALOE VERA PRODUCT CENTRE
- AMBER LANE
- AMPHORA AROMATICS
- ANDERSON, KEITH
- APEX HYPNOTHERAPY
- AQUARIUS HEALTH CENTRE
- ARGYLL HERBS DIRECT
- ARMSTRONG, ELIZABETH
- AROMATHERAPY FOR LADIES
- ASS-DANCE MOVEMENT THERAPY
- ATTERTON, P
- AVON COMPLEMENTARY MEDICINE
- AVON COUNSELLING/PSYCHOTHERAPY
- AYLARD, P
- AYUR VED, MAHARISHI
- BABBAGE, SARAH
- BAGGLEY, J M
- BAKER, P H
- BARDSLEY PHYSIOTHERAPY CLINIC
- BARNACLE, MARIAN
- BARNSLEY, C
- BASHALL, L (DR)
- BATH ROAD MASSAGE
- BEAVEN STRESS CLINIC
- BENJAMIN, MAUREEN
- BENTLEY, JANE
- BEVAN, RUSS
- BLACKBERRY HILL HOSPITAL
- BLOOR, HILARY
- BOES, AGNES M
- BOOTH, LYNNE
- BOOTH, PHILLIP
- BRINSON, L
- BRISTOL ALOE CENTRE
- BRISTOL BUDDHIST CENTRE
- BRISTOL HYPNOTHERAPY CLINIC
- BRISTOL NATURAL HEALTH SERVICE
- BRISTOL SCHOOL
- BRISTOL SCHOOL OF SHIATSU
- BROWN, SARAH
- BUCK, IAN
- BURROWS, A
- BUTCHER, PETER
- CAPLE, J
- CARDINAL, PAUL
- CASTLE CHIROPODY CLINIC
- CHARLES CLINIC
- CHAWDHARY, B S
- CHEE KUNG HEALTH CENTRE
- CHERINGTON PRACTICE
- CHIROPODY CLINIC
- CITY CENTRE CHIRO CLINIC
- CLAIRVOYANT PREDICTIONS
- CLARK, LYN
- CLARK, R (DR)
- CLEGHORN, BURNES & HOWNSFIELD
- CLIFTON ACUPUNCTURE CLINIC
- CLIFTON CHIROPRACTIC CLINIC
- CLIFTON COMPLEMENTARY MED CTRE
- CLIFTON PRACTICE
- CLINIC OF NATURAL MEDICINE
- CLOVER HOUSE
- COLLINS, CLARE
- COLLINS, VERNON
- CONSTANTINE, V
- COOK, J C H
- CORONELLI, DANIELLA
- COSSINS, M
- COURT, C A
- COVERDALE, ANNE
- COX, MARTIN
- CRAM, JULIANA
- CRANHAM, NIGEL
- CRIPPS, C
- CROSS HANDS CHIRO CLINIC
- CTRE FOR KINESIOLOGY
- DANCE VOICE THERAPY CENTRE
- DANNE, IVAN
- DAY, BRIAN J
- DEDMAN, PAUL
- DIMASCIO, CAROLINE
- DOBBINS, ALISON
- DODDS, L
- DOWNEND COUNS & PSYCHOTHERAPY
- DOWRY CHIROPRACTIC CLINIC
- DURBAN, PAMELA
- EASY WAY TO STOP SMOKING
- EATOCK, SARAH
- EDENS ESSENTIALS
- EDWARDS, R L
- ENGLISH, J
- EVANS, A R
- EYRES, BELINDA
- FACULTY OF HOMEOPATHY
- FAGG, A P
- FIELDING, HELEN
- FILE, CHRISTINE
- FOOT STUDIO
- FORD, ZARA & ASSOCIATES
- FORTEY, KEVIN
- FOSTER, J D
- FOSTER, JOY
- FOWDEN, M G
- FRANCIS, PATRICIA
- FREEMAN, ANN
- FROME VALLEY PHYSIO CLINIC
- G H M VICKERS
- G P F CONSULTANCY
- GARDNER, PETER (DR)
- GARLAND, C
- GASKIN, T
- GAUNT, DAVID
- GAUNT, DAVID
- GAUNTLETT, E J
- GESTALT SOUTHWEST
- GHAMY, M R
- GIBBONS, RICHARD
- GIDDINGS, JANE
- GIL, JOHN
- GILBERT, EDWARD J
- GINAS AROMATHERAPY
- GLOUCESTER ROAD PRACTITIONER
- GLOVER, J
- GODFREY, BRIAN
- GOLDEN ROSE
- GOLDIE, BRENDA
- GRACE, R C E
- GREEN, JULIA
- GREEN, JULIA
- GROUP ANALYTIC NETWORK WEST
- HAHN, HERBERT
- HANSEN, VIVI
- HARCOURT, A
- HARRIS, PAUL H G
- HART, ELLEN
- HAWKINS, LEONARD S
- HAWKINS, M
- HEALING WITH GABRIELLE TWINE
- HEALTH & FITNESS CLINIC
- HEALTH & HEALING
- HEALTH RELATED TRAINING
- HEALTHWISE
- HICKS, JACKIE

- HITCHINGS, CYNTHIA
- HOBBS, S J
- HOLISTIC HEALING
- HOLST MCQUAIG SYSTEMS
- HOPLEY, DENISE
- HUDSON, JOHN
- HUFTON, MARK
- HUNT, KEITH G
- HURFORD, A J
- IN THE KNOW
- INGRAMS, D (DR)
- INGREY, DAVID
- INSIGHTS THERAPY CLINIC
- INTL INS OF REFLEX-WESTERN
- IRELAND, MARIKA
- J H SPORTS INJURIES CLINIC
- JACKMAN, K
- JAMES, KEITH
- JANQUILLITY
- JARRETT, EMMA
- JOLY, S
- JONES, CHERYL
- KELLY, MARY
- KELSEY, L R
- KEOGH, DAVID
- KEYNSHAM CHIROPRACTIC CLINIC
- KINGHAM, D
- KINGSCOTT, DAVID
- KINGSWOOD CHIROPRACTIC CLINIC
- KNIGHTSWOOD CLINIC
- KRISTENSEN, MARIANNE
- LAM RIM CTRE FOR WHOLE HEALTH
- LANE-WILLAM, AVIS
- LATHAM, R
- LEFEBVRE, COLLETTE
- LOCKHART, A R
- LONG, C
- MACQUIRE-SAMSON, P
- MADHU, ANHES
- MAGNO-PULSE
- MAGUIRE, KEVIN
- MARSHALL & STOCKER
- MARSTON, ZENA
- MATTHEWS, M
- MAYFAIR GROUP
- MCCATTY, RONALD R
- MCCURRICH, J
- MIDDA, JULIAN OST & SPORTS THER
- MILLS, CLARE
- MOORE, TERESA
- MORGAN, MARTYN
- MORGAN, V
- MORLEY, VALERIE
- MUSCATY, J
- NAILSEA CHIROPRACTIC CLINIC
- NANCHOLAS, DAPHNE
- NATURAL HEALTH CLINIC
- NATURECARE
- NATURES WAY
- NAYDLER, NICK
- NEAL'S YARD REMEDIES
- NEW BEGINNINGS
- NICHOLS, JONATHAN
- NUTRITION FOR LIFE
- OBSERVATORY
- ORCHARD MEDICAL CENTRE
- ORCHARD, H
- ORIENTAL MEDICINE PRACTICE
- OSBORNE, D
- OSBORNE, M
- OSBORNE, R
- PARKER CLINIC
- POCOCK, A
- POPLE, S R
- REDDING-THOMAS, K
- REDDING-THOMAS, K
- REDFERN - MEDICAL HERBALIST
- REDLANDS HOUSE CLINIC
- REDMOND, CAROLINE
- RICHARD GIBBONS - ACUPUNCT
- RICHARDSON, DAVID
- RISING DRAGON TAI CHI
- RISING DRAGON TAI CHI SCHOOL
- ROBERTS, CATHERINE
- ROBERTS, FRANK
- ROBINSON, ELLIE
- SAWYER, PAUL
- SCRIMSHAW, J D
- SCRIMSHAW, S J
- SEELEY, M
- SEVERNSIDE INSTITUTE
- SHARPE, ISOBEL
- SKUSE, CLARE
- SKY DANCING UK TANTRA
- SMITH, GINA MERRETT
- SMITH, GRAHAM
- SMITH, KATHY
- SNEYD PARK
- SOUTHERTON, C S
- SOUTHERTON, C S
- SPENCER, J
- ST ANDREWS PRACTICE
- STEPHENS, DERRICK G
- STERNBERG, M P
- STEVENS, BEN
- STEWART, ANNIE
- STH WST COLLEGE OF ORIENTL MED
- STH WST COLLEGE OF ORIENTL MED
- STIRLING, P
- STRICKLAND, IAN
- STYLES, PATRICIA
- SUTCLIFFE, T
- SUTTON, S
- SYMMONDS, ROSE
- TARO
- THOMAS, TRUDY
- THOMPSON, J H
- THORN, K
- TIDCOMBE, MICHAEL B
- TOLL HOUSE CHIROPRACTIC
- TOLL HOUSE CLINIC
- TOMKIES, J
- TRANSENDENTAL MEDITATION
- TULLY, COLIN
- UNITED BRISTOL HEALTHCARE
- VITAL ENERGY
- VOYSEY, KIM R
- WALDRON, GABRIELLE
- WALKER, ELAINE
- WALKER, K
- WALL, M W
- WATERS, YVONNE
- WESTBURY CHIROPRACTIC CLINIC
- WHITWELL, D
- WILLOWS CLINIC
- WILSON, S
- WONGS ACUPUNCTURE
- YATTON FAMILY PRACTICE
- ZINGAS, STELLA

## BUCKINGHAMSHIRE

### AMERSHAM

- AMERSHAM CHIROPRACTIC CLINIC
- AMERSHAM OSTEOPATHIC CLINIC
- BARNES, J
- CAMPBELL, LOUISE
- CANNING, D M
- CHESNEY, SIMON
- CHILTERN CHIROPODY SERVICE
- CHILTERN OSTEOPATHIC PRACTICE
- COATES, SUSAN E
- EDWARDS, EMMA
- GLOVER, JEAN
- HALCYON LIFESTYLE
- HANKINS, SUSAN
- HEATH, SUSAN
- HOLDCOFT, LIA
- LORENZ, BERNICE
- NATURE'S REMEDIES
- ORCHARD CLNC CTRE FOR COMP MED
- RELEASE COUNS & TRAINING SVS
- SADLER, MARY
- SAUNDERS, JUDY
- SOUL TO SOLE NATURAL THERAPY
- THORNTON, MICHAEL
- WELLER, JACK

### AYLESBURY

- A BREATH OF FRESH AIR
- AKERS, DENISE
- AYLESBURY CHIROPRACTIC CLINIC
- AYLESBURY COMPLEMENTARY HEALTH
- AYLESBURY FOOT HEALTH CENTRE
- AYLESBURY VALE THERAPY
- BARHAM, PENNY
- BARRELL, PETER
- BATSON, BARBARA
- BRACEWELL, J
- BREE, SEAN
- BURKE, SHARON
- CASE, BRENDA
- COMPLEMENTARY HEALTH CENTRE
- COX, H J E (DR)
- DATHAN, PENNY
- DURNDELL, CLAIRE
- EDWARDS, SIMON
- FEWSTER, DAMON
- GLYNN, ELIZABETH
- GROVE, NICHOLAS
- GUY, R A
- HASTINGS, THERESA
- HAYTER & OVERY
- HULCOTT END PRACTICE
- JORDAN, PAMELA
- LONG CRENDON OSTEOPATHS
- LORDAN, KATHERINE
- MIDDLE WAY RE-EDUCATION CTRE
- MILLER, SANDRA
- OXFORDSHIRE BOWEN CLINIC
- PARKER, DIANA
- PEPPLER, EILEEN
- POWNALL, JILL
- REFLEXOLOGY
- REIKI HEALTH CENTRE
- RICKETTS, ANNE
- ROBINSON, MARGARET
- SHARPLES, SARAH
- SIMONDS, KATHARINE
- SLADE, LORNA
- SMITH, JUDY
- SPRINGHILL CENTRE
- STURGESS, PETER
- TUDOR HOUSE CLINIC
- WAKELING, ANN
- WATCHAM, G
- WELCH, RONALD
- WILLIAMSON, ROSEMARY

### BEACONSFIELD

- ACU-DIET CENTRE
- ACUPRESSURE MASSAGE
- ASHBERRY PHYSIOTHERAPY CLINIC
- ASHER, PATRICIA
- BEACONSFIELD CHIRO CLINIC
- FIRMAN, BARBARA
- GOUGH, J
- JUKES, M
- KENTISH, LORNE
- KIM PERRY QUALIFIED CHIROP
- PARTON, KAY
- PATON, BARBARA
- PRIVATE CLINIC OF NAT THRPY
- ROGERS, T
- TODD, PAUL
- WOODWARD, MARGARET
- WOODWARD, MARGARET

### BLAKELANDS

- MUMBRAY, LINDA

### BOURNE END

- CHERRY PLUS
- HOLISTIC HEALING
- KEVAN, ROBERT
- LEWIS, JANET
- MORRISSEY, BLANCHE
- MYOGENICS
- RAMAKRISHNA VEDANTA CENTRE
- REDGRAVE CLINIC
- REDGRAVE, ANN
- STEINBERG, PAMELA
- TAYLOR, ALISON

### BRADWELL

- SHEPHERD, KAREN

### BUCKINGHAM

- BARTON HARTSHORN MANOR
- BRIGGS, JO
- BUCKINGHAM CHIROPRACTIC CLINIC
- DEMETRIUS, B
- EAST, R J
- EVANS, JENNY
- HAILSTONE, NEIL
- HOMOEOPATHY IN BUCKINGHAM
- LAWSON, JANET
- LINFORD, ANITA
- MIND AND BODY
- NEAL, JULIE

- OMICRON
- TOUCHARD, HELEN
- WOOD, ANNE
- WOOD, W H & D

## CHALFONT ST. GILES

- BEAVIS, ANN
- HAZELL, PRISCILLA
- HOLLAND, JACQUELINE

## CHESHAM

- ADAMS, PAUL
- BURGESS, SANDY
- CHESHAM HOSPITAL
- DOIG, PAUL
- GREEN, JULIA A
- HOBBS, SALLY
- HYATT, EDWARD B
- MATHEW HUNT CHIROPODIST
- MATTHEWS, JAN
- REHAB
- RICHARDSON, MARTIN
- TARPEY, ALISON J
- TURNER, KEZZIE

## FURZTON

- RICHARDSON, JACQUI

## GERRARDS CROSS

- ALTERNATIVE THERAPIES TRAINING
- BREEZE, T
- CARMA HEALING SANCTUARY
- CHILTERN CHIROPRACTIC CLINIC
- GERRARDS CROSS SPORTS & BACK
- GOLDING, PAULINE
- HUNT, CHARLES
- LAWRENSON, MONICA M
- POLLARD, CYNTHIA

## GREAT HORWOOD

- MCCAFFERTY, SUSANNE

## GREAT LINFORD

- COLLEGE OF AYURVEDA

## GREAT MISSENDEN

- COX, LINDY
- ENFIELD, CLAUDIA
- FEWSTER, HELEN
- FEWSTER, HELEN
- GREEN, STEVE
- KEMP, SHELAGH
- LAWSON, HEATHER
- PRESTWOOD PHYSIOTHERAPY CLINIC
- TEMPLEMAN, ROWENA
- TOMLIN, S
- WELLER, JACK

## HEELANDS

- HAISELDEN, JENNIE
- SOLE CONCERN REFLEXOLOGY
- WINSTON, LAURIE

## HIGH WYCOMBE

- ARMITSTEAD, JOHN
- AROMA SHEET
- AYRES, JUDITH
- BELLMAN, ERICA
- BENHAM, CHARLES
- BIRD, ELAINE
- BRINTON, MEG
- BUTTERFIELD, SUSAN A
- CAMERON, ANNE
- CANDLEWELL CLINIC
- CASTLE STREET CLINIC
- CHALLENER HYPNOTHERAPY
- CHILTERN AROMATHERAPY
- CHILTERN NATURAL THERAPY
- CHILTERNS COMPLEMENTARY CARE
- CHINESE HERBAL MEDICINE CENTRE
- COACHING FOR SUCCESS
- CONRAN, JAN
- DOWLE, C M
- DULLER, R V
- ELMIDORO, JANE
- ENFIELD, CLAUDIA
- GILCHRIST, P
- GLADWIN, G L
- HALL, JOY
- HALL, JOY
- HALLEWELL, LOUISA
- HANSFORD, JANE
- HIGH WYCOMBE CHIRO CLINIC
- HORNER, C
- HUBBARD, LEE
- J J COUNSELLING SERVICES
- JACKSON, F N
- JOHNSON, HELEN JANE
- KEILDSON, HANNAH
- LATHAM, E
- LETHEREN, V A
- LI (PROFESSOR)
- MANNERING, PAM
- METTE MARUP & MIKKELSEN
- O'SULLIVAN, SHEILA
- OUILLON-PALMER, LAURENCE
- PARK, ANGELA
- PENN COUNSELLING/PSYCHOTHERAPY
- PERFECT OILS
- PHYSIO FIRST PRACTICE
- POOL, J M
- PURTON HOUSE HOMEOPATHIC CTRE
- RADFORD, ANDREA
- RANDELL, BELINDA
- ROBERTSON, KENNETH P
- ROBINSON, DENEASE
- ROGERS, SUSAN
- SHIELS, RITA
- SHINH, NATALIE
- SIDLEY, SAM
- SIVES, ALEX
- SOUTER, MIRANDA
- STEWART, W
- TEACHERS OF ALEXNDR TECH
- THERAPEUTIC MASSAGE
- THOMSON, JANE
- THORNTON, MICHAEL
- TIM BROWN CLINIC
- TOMLIN, S
- TRANSCENDENTAL MEDITATION
- TRINDER, CATHY
- VICKERS, NATALIE
- WEST WYCOMBE CHIRO CLINIC
- WEST WYCOMBE CHIROPRACTIC
- WHITNALL, LINDA
- WHITNEY, GERALDINE

## IVER

- JOURNEY SEMINARS
- LYNOSIS
- O'NEIL, PAULA
- PINEWOOD CHIROPODY PRACTICE
- TEMPLEWOOD CLINIC
- WATSON, ALEXANDRA
- WELLBURN

## MARLOW

- ABBEY CLINIC
- BAKER, CAROLINE
- BIGGS, SYLVIA
- CAMPBELL, NIKKI
- CHAMBERS, MICHAEL R C
- COLLINS, STUART
- CONCORDA HEALTH-SPORTS THERAPY
- EDWARDS, MICHAEL
- ELIZABETH HELEN BEAUTY THER
- FOUR ALL SEASONS
- GRICE, ANNIE
- IKIN, SALLY
- JARVIS, MAGGIE
- JOHNSON, HELEN
- LE HUNTE, ASHIKA
- MARLOW HOMOEOPATHIC CLINIC
- MARLOW OSTEOPATHIC CLINIC
- MARLOW PHYSIO & SPORTS INJURY
- NASH, RICHARD
- OASIS NATURAL THERAPY CLINIC
- PEERS-JOHNSON, D R
- REYNOLDS, DAVID
- ROGERS, DEBORAH
- RUNDLE, RICHARD
- VITASPRAY

## MILTON KEYNES

- ABBOT, JENNY
- ALLMAN, JANNINE
- ALTERNATE WAYS
- ANSTEE, M J
- ANTON HOUSE OF AVILON
- BELL, MARTYN
- BELL, PHILIP (DR)
- BELL, Y
- BLACKBERRY ORTHO & SPRTS CLNC
- BODY & SOUL
- BRADFORD, SONIA
- CARTER, YVONNE
- CHINN, HEDLEY
- COCKINGS-MASON, FIONA
- COLDWELL, VERONICA
- CULTRON SERVICES
- CUMMINGS, J S
- DE SILVA, M
- DEVINE, C
- DOBELL, R
- DOWDELL, FIONA K
- EAST, R J
- EDUCATIONAL PSYCHOLOGY
- ELAINE MCCARTHY REFLEXOLOGIST
- ERLICK, STEVEN
- FLEET, BARBARA
- FREESTONE, EILEEN
- GARRATT, J R
- GODAGAMA, SHANTHA
- GREETHAM, ALISTAIR
- GRIFFITHS, JAMES (DR)
- HALES, GERALD (DR)
- HALLIN, ANDREAS (DR)
- HAVEN HYPNOTHERAPY
- HIGHSTEAD, KATE
- HOWE, DENISE G
- ICE & FIRE
- INSTITUTE OF ELECTROLYSIS
- INSTITUTE OF ELECTROLYSIS
- IVY HOUSE CLINIC
- JACKSON, ANDREW
- JACKSON, RYAN
- JONES, SHIRLEY
- KERSEY, M D
- LAMBOURN COURT INTERNATIONAL
- LEACH, P
- M K CLINIC
- MADAM MORGANA & MERLIN
- MAGIC TOUCH
- MARSHALL, CAROLYN
- MASON, DAVID
- MATTHEWS, FRANK
- MCQUILLAN, D
- MILTON KEYNES CHIRO CLINIC
- MILTON KEYNES HOMEOPATHIC
- MILTON KEYNES SPORTS INJURY
- MORNINGSIDE HEALTH CLINIC
- NEWMAN, BARBARA
- ORMSBY, NEIL
- OUSEBANK HYPNOTHERAPY
- REHAB WITHOUT WALLS
- RENJI CHINESE MEDICINE CENTRE
- REYNOLDS, CAROL
- RICHARDSON, JILL
- SHENLEY CHIROPRACTIC CLINIC
- SKIDDY, SUSAN
- SKINGLE, C F
- SMITH, MING
- SOMMERSETH, RICHARD (DR)
- SPENCER, SUSAN J
- STUTZ, GABRIELE
- SWEET BREEZE
- TAYLOR, IAN E
- THIEBAUD, M F
- TRANQUILITY
- VENABLES, ALISON
- WALKER, ELIZABETH
- WARDLAW, MICHAEL
- WARDLEY, P DEANNE
- WATSON, NEVILLE
- WESTON, M E
- WESTWOOD, TERRY
- WHELDON, KATHERINE
- WORLAND, ANN

## NEWPORT PAGNELL

- BALFOUR-LAYDEN, ISABEL
- BHAGWAT-BROWN, GINA
- BOOTH, MARK
- CLIFTON COURT COMP HEALTH CTRE
- DEWERT, ERWIN
- HEAYNS, C H
- HENDERSON, IRENE
- KINGFISHER CHIROP & HYP
- MARKHAM, I

- N P PHYSIOTHERAPY SERVICES
- NEWPORT ACUPUNCTURE CLINIC
- QUICKSTROM, BETH
- TYRINGHAM NATUROPATHIC CLINIC

### OLNEY

- BASHFORD, JANET
- GROVE, D
- MESSENGER, DENISE
- OLNEY OSTEOPATHIC SURGERY
- SHAW, FIONA
- TOASH CLINIC

### PENN

- MIRZOEFF, PETER

### PRINCES RISBOROUGH

- COOPER, MARGARET
- LANGLEY, CHRISTINE
- MARSLAND, MICHELLE
- MORGAN, GILLIAN
- PADDOCKS PHYSIO/SPORT INJ CTRE
- RELAXATION REMEDIAL THERAPIES
- ROWBOTHAM, DARCIE
- TOMLIN, SUSAN M
- WEBB, ANNE

### SALFORD

- ROBERTSON, ANGUS

### STOKE MANDEVILLE

- BANFIELD, KATIE

### WAVENDON GATE

- FISHER, CLAIRE
- ROMEO, GILLIAN

### WHITCHURCH

- COMPLEMENTARY HEALTH

### WINSLOW

- K BANFIELD NATUROPATHY/OSTEO

### WOBURN SANDS

- ROMEO, GILLIAN

## CAMBRIDGESHIRE

### CAMBRIDGE

- ABBEY HOUSE HEALTH AND BEAUTY
- ACHILLES PHYSIOTHERAPY CLINIC
- ADAMS, JULIA
- ANDERSON, M
- ANDERSON, PAUL
- ANDREASEN CENTRE
- ARJUNA NATURAL HEALTH CENTRE
- BACK ON TRACK
- BACK ON TRACK
- BACK ON TRACK
- BATES, SUE
- BEESLEY, RODERICK
- BENSON, HUGH
- BODYLINE HEALTH
- BRATHERTON, W J
- BRITISH ASS-PSYCHOPHARMACOLOGY
- BULL, MARTIN
- CAMBRIDGE BIODYNAMIC PRACTICE
- CAMBRIDGE CHIROPRACTIC CENTRE
- CAMBRIDGE COMP HEALTH PRACTICE
- CAMBRIDGE MEDICAL HERBALIST
- CAMBRIDGE PHYSIOTHERAPY CLINIC
- CAMBRIDGE PSYCHOTHERAPY
- CAMBRIDGE TRAD ACUPUNC CENTRE
- CONWAY, RONALD
- COPCUTT
- COPPING, A G
- CULPEPER
- CULPEPER
- CUTTING, VALERIE
- DAWBER, PAULINE
- DE MENTHON, FRANCOIS
- DIXON, GAYLE
- ENERGY CENTRE
- FAULKNER, CINDY
- FLOOD, RICHARD
- GEE, SUSAN
- GENTRY, V
- GIDDINGS, STARMER-JONES, BEAZL
- GILBERT RD OSTEOPATHIC
- GORDON, JOSEPH
- GREVIS, MICHAEL
- HARMAN, ABIGAIL
- HAYNES, ERIC
- HEAL, CHRISTIANNE
- HUMAN I T
- HYPNOSIS AND HEALTH
- IN TOUCH MOBILE MASSAGE
- INGHAM, NICHOLAS
- JAFFEY, JOEL
- JANET MARTIN BEAUTY SPECIALIST
- JANOWSKI, ANNE
- JEFFERY, HELEN
- JOOP TANIS
- KELLY, ROBERT
- LAMBDA HEALTHCARE
- LANT, JOHN & PARTNERS
- LEVY, DAVID
- LIFE PREGNANCY CARE CENTRE
- LIZ HALE HANDSON HEALTH
- LLOYD, N
- LLOYD-BOTTING, N
- LOW, C J
- LY, THI PHUNG (DR)
- MARSHALL, STEVE
- MATHIESON, M A
- MAYNARD, SUSANNE
- MCDOUALL, VERONICA
- MELIOR
- MONAS, MARIAN
- OAKTREE COMP HEALTH PRACTICE
- OSTEOPATHIC CENTRE
- OUTSIDE IN
- PAIN, JEAN
- PHIL SEAL PSYCHOTHERAPY
- PIKE, ROGER
- PITMAN, SUE
- PRINCE, KAREN
- RADHA, CELIA
- RATHBONE, M J
- READ, GRAHAM
- ROBINSON-ZEL, B
- SCOTT, S J
- SHELFORD PHYSIOTHERAPY
- SHULAN CLINIC OF ACUPUNCTURE
- SIMPLY SOAPS
- SMITH, JEANETTE
- STAGGS, JANE
- STOCKLEY, PHILIP E
- SUGDEN, TONY
- SUTOR, CHRIS
- TAYLOR, CAROLYN
- THOMPSON, EDWARD
- TONG, JENNY
- TOYNBEE, J
- UNIVERSITY OF CAMBRIDGE
- WASS, ANNETTE
- WEST, JOHN A
- WESTON, SOPHIE
- WHITE, KAREN
- WILSON, ANGELA
- WRIGHT, CLARE
- YARROW, B M
- YOGA BIOMEDICAL TRUST

### CHATTERIS

- ALOE IN ACTION
- COMPLEMENTARY HEALTH CLINIC
- STENSON, L

### ELY

- AROMATHERAPY WORLD
- BARRETT BOWEN TREATMENT
- BEAZLEIGH, SALLY
- BILLINGS, A
- BJORK, CARINA
- CHECCHIA, TERESSA
- CROWDER, SUZANNE
- CROWN TREATMENT CENTRE
- ELY COMPLEMENTARY HEALTH CTRE
- ESCOBAR-FRANCO, A
- HAYNES, E
- HEALTH TEAM
- JILLEY, W
- KENT, MATTHEW
- KIRKSOPP, B K
- PHILLIPS, JEAN
- PRING, R
- SADDLER, J M
- SCHOOL OF THE LIVING LIGHT
- SILLETT, PAULINE
- SPENCE, ALEX
- SPOONER, K M
- STOCKLEY, PHILIP
- WILKINSON, GLYNNIS

### HUNTINGDON

- ALDWINCKLE, PAUL
- APACHE
- BRAMPTON CHIROPRACTIC CLINIC
- CLARK, S J
- CLIPSHAM, VANESSA
- COUNTRYSIDE HYPNOTHERAPIST
- CTRE FOR COMPLEMENTARY HEALTH
- DERBYSHIRE, GILL
- FENSTANTON PHYSIOTHERAPY
- HART, OLIVIA
- HOLMES, KYLIE
- HUNTINGDON COMPLEMENTARY
- HUNTS CLINICAL CARE
- JURY, CATHY
- MACKAY, JOHN
- MCMULLAN, J
- MORRIS & ASSOCIATES
- PECK, S K
- SZMELSKYJ, ALAN
- TRIANCE, E R

### LITTLEPORT

- CAMBRIDGE NUTRITIONAL SCIENCES

### MARCH

- HILLIER, L V
- HOOPER, SARAH JANE

### OVER

- RYDER, JULIE

### PETERBOROUGH

- A P HEALEY CHIROPODY SERVICE
- ACUPUNCTURE HERBAL REMEDIES
- ANGLIA BACK CLINIC
- BOWDEN, ANN
- BROADWAY CHIROPRACTIC CLINIC
- BROE, NEIL
- BROOKS, WENDY J
- CHRIS SMITH HYPNOTHERAPY
- CLARE, A E
- COHEN, DAVID
- COXELL REMEDIAL CLINIC
- FAGAN, STEVE
- FRENCH, DAVID
- FRISBY, JOHN
- FULBRIDGE REFLEXOLOGY
- GINN, ALAN
- GREEN, J A
- GRIFFIN, CORRINNE
- HANCOCK, JOHN
- HEALTH CARE
- HUNT, PHILLIP R
- HUSEIN, JIWA (DR)
- JOAN ELIZABETH CLAIRVOYANT
- JOHNSON, ANNE
- LIFELINE
- LOCKE, SUSAN
- LUFF, JIM
- MASON, J W
- MCKIE, IAN
- MCLAUGHLIN, AIMEE
- MENZIES, S J
- MIND MATTERS
- MIND MATTERS
- OLIVER, PETER
- OUNDLE COMMUNITY CARE UNIT
- OVERTONES
- OXBOROUGH, JOY
- PHOENIX ACUPUNCTURE CLINIC
- PRESTONS CHRTRD PHYSIOTHERAPY
- PROBERT, DIANA
- PURE ESSENCE
- SCENT STATION
- SHIATSU SOCIETY
- SMITH, CHRISTINE R
- SNUGGS, D R
- TAYLOR, A C
- TAYLOR, EVE
- TERRY, EVA
- TOMPKINS, P A
- TRANSCENDENTAL MEDITATION
- VICKERS, DEREK

- WATT, KEVIN
- WESTGATE HOUSE CHIROPODY
- WING, A C & T L

### ST. IVES

- DAVIES, G W

### ST. NEOTS

- COLES, BARBARA
- GOODMAN, JEAN
- GOODMAN, WENDY
- MAJOR, ROSEMARY
- ST NEOTS OSTEOPATHIC CLINIC
- STUDIO 1

### WISBECH

- AKINDELE, KOLA
- APPS, JENNY
- BEATTIE, JOHN
- BOORMAN, CATHERINE
- BROWN, CLAIRE
- CHEETHAM, D
- CHIROPRATIC & HOM HEALTH CTRE
- FINLAY, TAMARA
- HALISK ASSOCIATES
- HANEKE CHIROPRACTIC CLINIC
- HATTERSLEY, DAVID
- HAYES, GILL
- JAKINGS, S
- JUNIPA SALES
- NORFOLK ESSENTIAL OILS
- PENNINGTON, BERNARD
- RATNAYAKE, MALINI
- RATNAYAKE, MIKE
- REID, SUSAN
- REIKI

## CHANNEL ISLANDS

### GUERNSEY

- ST SAMPSON'S MEDICAL CENTRE

## CHESHIRE

### ALDERLEY EDGE

- BILLINGTON, JANE
- DAWSON, J P
- GENTLE TOUCH
- HALE, R C
- JACKSON, ANGELA
- LYON, ANDREW
- MEDICINE SHOP
- TRANSCENDENTAL MEDITATION

### ALSAGER

- JONES, MARILYN

### ALTRINCHAM

- ATHERTON, NICOLA
- BATES VISION EDUCATION
- BETTER UNDERSTANDINGS
- BROOK, ELIZABETH
- CHAN, K P
- CRAWFORD, S
- DAINTREE, FREDERICA JEAN
- DICKMAN, KAREN
- DUTTON, N S
- FILSON, SUSAN
- GREENFIELD, T A
- HADFIELD, M D
- HOFTON, EFFIE
- HOLISTIC
- HOLLAND & ROBERTS
- HOWARTH, M
- HYGEIA CENTRE
- JENKINSON, LEILA
- JONES, JOYCE
- KENNEDY, J
- KENYON, JACELYN
- LEIGH, SUSAN
- LOWE, D L
- LYONS, JACQUELINE
- MALLION, CAROLINE E
- MALLION, CHRISTINE
- MANN, PAUL
- MAPLES PHYSIO & REFLEXTHERAPY
- MCCANN, ALEXANDRA
- MORAN, SUSAN
- MORGAN, JANE
- PANK, SARAH
- PHYSICAL THERAPY CLINIC
- PHYSIO PLUS
- REFLECTIONS REFLEXOLOGISTS
- REIKI SCHOOL
- ROBERTS, TRACEY
- S H L
- TAYLOR, LYNN
- TIERNAN, MANDA
- VALE ROYAL CHIROPRACTIC CLINIC

### CHEADLE

- ADVANCED SKIN THERAPY CLINIC
- BACK PAIN CLINIC
- BLANK, JUNE
- BRITISH SOC OF CLINICAL HYPNO
- CHEADLE SPORTS INJURIES CLINIC
- EVANS, CAROL
- FAGAN, B W
- FRANCESCA
- GILLMAN, G J
- HARDY, CHRISTINE
- HOWETT, ROY
- KAYE, JANET
- MEHTA HYPNOTHERAPY
- MISSION, CHAITANYA
- NATURAL HEALTH CLINIC
- NOLAN, J A
- PRICE, H M
- PSYCHOLOGIST NORTH WEST
- THERAPY CENTRE
- THORNBER, A A
- WALKER, ADELE
- WALSH, R M
- WHITTAKER, WENDY
- WILKINSON, PHILIP
- WILSON, FIONA

### CHESTER

- AMBLESIDE CLINIC
- ATHERTON, PAUL
- BACHE CHIROPODY
- BAXTER, GILLIAN
- BETTER HEALTH CLINIC
- BOWEN, KAREN
- BRADLEY, ANDREW
- CARA
- CHESTER ALEXANDER TECH ST
- CHESTER CHIROPODY
- CHESTER CHIROPRACTIC CLINIC
- CHESTER CLINIC
- CHESTER HEALTH
- CHESTER HEALTH & BEAUTY STUDIO
- CHESTER HOMEOPATHIC CLINIC
- CHESTER PODIATRY GROUP
- CHESTER THERAPY CENTRE
- COLHOUN, PETER
- COOPER, GEOFFREY M
- COPELAND, KATIE
- CULPEPER
- CULSHAW, S
- DAVIES, TERESA
- DAVIS, JAMES E
- DEVA OSTEOPATHIC CLINIC
- DICKENSON, A G
- DRASPA, J
- ELSON, MONICA
- EVANS, DI
- FAROOQ AHMED, KHAN
- FEET FIRST
- FORESTRIDGE HLTH & DRUG STORE
- GAMBLE-CLEE, SARA
- GARDEN LANE PHYSIO SERVICE
- GEORGE, DIANA
- GLENDON, NOEL
- GOLDENHEAD HYPNOSIS
- HEAVENLY BODIES
- INDIGO HEALTH CONSULTANCY
- IPHOFEN, RON (DR)
- JEFFERYS, SIMON
- KELSALL, D
- KNOX, DAWN
- LASERTROLYSIS UK
- LEGGE, PAT
- LEWIS, KEN
- LLOYD, H
- MCMILLAN ANIMAL HEALTH
- MEREDITH, DAVID
- MILLER, J
- NEEDHAM, ANGELA
- OASIS COMPLEMENTARY THERAPIES
- ONLY NATURAL TREATMENT CENTRE
- PINE LODGE
- RICHARDS, DAVID
- RYAN, KATHY (DR)
- SCARBOROUGH, KATE
- SCENTED GARDENS
- SCHOLL CENTRE
- SCOTT, M
- SHEPHERD, STEVEN
- SPENCE, JACQUELINE
- STRACHAN, JO-ANNE
- STUBBS, D A
- WALK-IN BACK STUDIO
- WEST, MARIE-CLAIRE
- WINE, SUE
- WITHY, M
- WYNNE-JONES, J

### CONGLETON

- BERESFORD, KATHLEEN
- BODY LANGUAGE
- BOULTON, ERIC C
- BRADLEY, F
- CONGLETON COUNSELLING PRACTICE
- CONGLETON HOMEOPATHIC PRACTICE
- DALE, LYNNE
- ECHO ESSENTIAL OILS
- HORNER, MARGARET
- MAINES, C
- NATURAL THERAPIES
- NORRIS ASSOCIATES
- SAMALIN ORIENTAL

### CREWE

- ASHMOUNT PHYSIOTHERAPY CLINIC
- CRAIG, MAUREEN
- CREWE & NANT PHYSIO CLINIC
- CREWE & NANT PHYSIO CLINIC
- CREWE & NANTWICH HOLISTIC
- DAPAYNE, IMEL
- DAVIES & ASSOCIATES
- DENNING, MICHAEL
- DREAM AIR
- EVANS, SUSAN
- FIELD VIEW SURGERY
- GOOSTREY NATURAL THERAPY CTRE
- HAYES, VAL
- HOLLINSHEAD
- LOCKETT, LEIGH
- LORRAINE DOCHERTY HOL PRACT
- OLD SURGERY
- PATTERSON, J W
- PENNYCOOK, AMANDA
- REECE, EMMA
- REIKI
- SHEPHERD, S
- SPIBY, L

### DUKINFIELD

- A & H PAIN CLINIC
- APPLETON, CARRIE
- FACULTY OF CHIROPODY
- MULHOLLAND, ANDREA
- MYERS, LINDA
- SOUL SYMMETRY
- STORRS, PAULINE
- T R GREGORY CHIROPODIST

### ELLESMERE PORT

- HEALD, M T
- THOMAS, BEVERLEY

### FRODSHAM

- CROSSLEY-JONES, SYLVIA
- DAVIES, C M
- DEAN, BRIAN
- GALLIENNE-SMITH, HELEN
- HALE, STUART
- HALL, J
- HAMBLETT, S P
- SCOTT, DAVID L (DR)
- WITHY, M A

### HYDE

- BOWN, LYNNE
- CLARENDON DENTAL PRACTICE
- FERNLEY, B
- GOTHIC
- HANCOCK, J
- HYDE PHYSIOTHERAPY CENTRE
- KERSHNER, F
- LYONS, STEVEN
- O Z

- RICHMOND HOUSE PHYSIO
- STORES, J
- TIPLING, L

## KNUTSFORD

- ALEXANDER, A (DR)
- BERWITZ, ANDREW
- CARMICHAEL CLINIC
- ELLIS, A C
- ELLIS, E A
- HAMMOND, ANNE
- HEALTHPOINT
- HEWITT, C A
- HOWDEN, ELIZABETH
- JONES, DAVID
- KNUTSFORD CHIROPRACTIC CLINIC
- MCDONALD, MARGARET
- MOBBERLEY COMP HEALTHCARE
- MORTON, J V
- RICHARDS, KERRY
- STENNING, J
- TURNBULL, PAT

## LYMM

- CROSS CLINIC
- DELOOZE, ANNE
- GIBBS, NICOLA
- MCCOLGAN, NEWTON
- PULMAN, SUZETTE
- TRACEY, J
- WATSON, GEORGINA

## MACCLESFIELD

- BILLINGTON, JANE
- BROWN & PARTNERS OSTEO
- CHESTERGATE CLINIC
- CRYSTAL AROMATICS
- DEMOOR, MANON
- DRAPER, J M
- FULLER, HILARY
- GARDINER, JOHN MICHAEL
- GILL, SHEILA
- GRIFFITHS, JOHN E
- HARRISON, DUNCAN
- HONEY, MICHAEL J
- HUGHAN, M J & D J
- NUTRITIONAL THERAPY
- OPTIMUM HEALTH
- PHYSIO & SPORTS INJURY CLINIC
- PRINCE, TANIA A
- QUINTON, R M
- SHALOM
- TAYLOR, CAROL D
- THREE MOONS OILS
- TRINITY HOUSE PRACTICE
- TRINITY HOUSE PRACTICE
- TYRER, HELEN R
- WALKER, HELEN
- WARDELL, SUSAN JANE
- WOOLLEY, M E

## MALPAS

- ARNOLD, SUE
- PATON, W A

## MIDDLEWICH

- COWPER, F M
- WILLIAMS, I

## NANTWICH

- ACTON ACUPUNTURE CLINIC
- BRUCE, ADAM
- BURTON, J S
- CHAPEL COURT CENTRE
- CHEW, J KENDALL
- CHINESE MEDICINE CENTRE
- DAVIES, M K
- FINCH, WENDY
- HYPNOTHERAPY CENTRE
- KEMP, JANET
- KUSIAR, C W
- LEHNERT, MANFRED L
- MACALLAN, STEPHEN
- MACALLAN, STEPHEN
- MACLURE, IAN (DR)
- MANSELL-HOPE, CAROLE
- NANTWICH CHIROPODY CLINIC
- ROWLANDS, MARGARET
- RUNDLE, ANNETTE
- SANDELLS, DIANNE
- SCRIVENER, PATRICIA
- THOMPSON, CYNTHIA
- WEAVER HOUSE CLINIC

## NESTON

- BUSH, ANTONY J
- CENTRE FOR HOLISTIC THERAPIES
- CROPPER, AGNES
- PARKGATE CLINIC
- PROTHERO, PEGGY
- WILLASTON PHYSIOTHERAPY CLINIC

## NORTHWICH

- ALLEN, SANDRA
- BODY ESSENCES
- BUNN, ANDREW
- CHESHIRE FOOT-HEALTH CENTRE
- CONSTANTINE, J C
- HARVISON, K N
- JANE HAMMOND THERAPY
- LYTHGOE, A G
- MID-CHESHIRE HOM GRP
- MORTON, J V
- ORIGINALS
- PAOLA WEINBERG SYLT
- PHYSIO SPORTS INJURY CLINIC
- REDGRAVE, KENNETH
- ROSE, B S
- SAYERS, MARGARET
- SUMMERS, CHRISTINE S
- THERAPY CENTRE
- VALE ROYAL CHIROPRACTIC CLINIC
- YOGA & THERAPY CENTRE

## POYNTON

- EDDIE, DAVID

## RUNCORN

- BODY BALANCE THERAPIES
- CHESTER & HALTON COM
- FISHER, DEIRDRE
- HUSKISSON, EILEEN
- MARTIN, S & N
- MORAN, S M F
- PALOMBELLA, SARAH
- POT POURRI PRETTIES
- PREW, BEVERLEY
- SIMPLY NATURAL ESSENTIAL OILS
- TEDSTONE, ALISON
- VENNING, C

## SALE

- ARMITAGE, D R
- BELLE, M
- BRAEMAR HOMEOPATHIC CENTRE
- CHINESE MEDICAL & SKIN CENTRE
- CHINESE MEDICAL & SKIN CENTRE
- COMPLEMENTARY THERAPIES CON
- CRUICKSHANKS, P
- DEWHURST, PATRICA A
- ENTHEOS HOLISTIC REFLEXOLOGY
- EVERETT, J
- FRANEY, JAMES R
- HIGHLEY, T J
- JOHNSON, ANDREW N
- JONES, S
- LEWIS, REBECCA
- MURPHY, K
- NORRIS ASSOCIATES
- PANK, SARAH
- REIKI HEALING
- VICKI WHELAN ASSOCIATES
- WILLIAMS OSTEOPATHIC CLINIC

## SANDBACH

- BEHAN, J C
- CHESHIRE HEALTH CLINIC
- FORSTER, FIONA
- HYPNOTHERAPY & COUNSELLING
- KEATING, J
- RICHARDS, KERRY L
- RODWAY, LI LING
- SANDBACH HYPNOSIS CLINIC
- SANDBACH PHYSIO & SPORTS

## STOCKPORT

- AINSWORTH, J
- BARTUP, ALISON
- BENEDICT-SMITH, M
- BERNICE
- BODYTONE
- BRAMHALL PARK PHYSIO CLINIC
- BURNES, DAVID T
- BUXTON, JOHN
- CASSIDY, LINDA
- CHAPMAN, M J
- CHEADLE HULME NATURAL HEALTH
- CHEANEY, JOANNA C
- CHIROPODIST SURGERY
- CLINIC OF ACUPUNCTURE
- CLUSKEY, LYNN M
- CRAWFORD, ANDREW
- DAGNALL, J C
- DISLEY PHYSIO SERVICES
- DOWNIE, F W
- DYSON, S M
- EDDIE, DAVID
- FAMILY CLINIC
- FINDLOW, GLENDA
- FIVE WAYS OSTEOPATHIC SURGERY
- FRANCES
- GRAHAM COOMBE - MCTIMONEY
- HARDIE, LYNN
- HAYWARD, SOPHIE
- HAZELDENE, BARBARA
- HEATON, LYNDA
- HILL, DAPHNE
- HINDLEY, DAVID
- HOLISTIC THERAPY CENTRE
- INSIGHT THERAPIES
- JAFARI, CAROLINE
- JENNINGS-BROWN, S
- KARAGIANNI, CHRISTINA
- KNOTT, ELIZABETH
- KNOWLES, BARBARA
- LAFFERTY, C
- LINKS CLINIC
- LOMAS, CLIFFORD
- MCCABE, PAULINE J
- MCQUINN, S
- MEDICINE WHEEL
- MEHREZ, ANITA
- NEW LIFE NATURAL HEALTH CARE
- NORTH AREA COLLEGE STOCKPORT
- NUTRITION AND ALLERGY CLINIC
- OLD HALL CLINIC
- OLDHAM, TERRY
- PHOENIX CENTRE
- PHYSIO SPORT
- POTTS, DEBORAH
- POYNTON CHIROPRACTIC CLINIC
- PREST, C
- RAINS, KEN
- REJUVENATION
- RELAX
- RENSHAW, SARAH J
- RUTH WOOD CHARTERED PHYSIO
- SAXELBY, M
- SCHOLL CENTRE
- SIGNOL, J A
- SPORT-MED
- ST PETERSGATE PRIVATE CLINIC
- TULLY, CHARLES
- WARE, PAUL J
- WHARMBY, D
- WILLIAMS, H M
- WRIGHT, ANDREW
- WRIGLEY, DAVID

## TARPORLEY

- AROMASPHERE
- AROMATHERAPY SHOP
- CARING HANDS
- COTEBROOK NATURAL HEALTH CTRE
- GREEN, J
- KEATING, J
- OLDROYD, P J
- PSYCHOLOGICAL SERVICES

## WARRINGTON

- A CHARTERED PHYSIOTHERAPIST
- ADULT & CHILD FOOT CLINIC
- ALOE VERA DIRECT
- ASHCROFT, D M
- ASS WARRINGTON - REG CHIROP
- ASSOCIATION FOR FAMILY THERAPY
- B SHAW HOLISTIC THERAPIST
- BAXTER, HELEN
- BERGIN, ALICE
- BERRY, K L
- BLENKINSOP, KAREN
- BRETHERTON-CROWE, LINDA
- BRITISH MED ACUPUNCTURE SOC
- CHINESE MEDICAL & SKIN CENTRE

- CHIROPODY CORNER
- CLARKE, DAVID
- CLOUGH, G J
- COMMUNICATE
- CONNOLLY, SANDRA
- CULCHETH REMEDIAL CLINIC
- DUNNING, CAROL
- E TULLY HOMEOPATHIC PRACT
- ENTERPRISE Q
- FEET FIRST MOBILE CHIROPODY SV
- FILLAUDEAU, SARAH-JAYNE
- FINCH, CHRIS
- FINCH, CHRISTOPHER
- FOOTWORKS
- GRACE & ASSOCIATES
- GREAT SANKEY PHYSIOTHERAPY
- H LEICESTER
- HAUGHTON, G W
- KEN, HOWARD
- LIPKIN, F J
- LYTHGOE, J C
- MARCH, JANIS
- MARSH, F W
- MCCORMICK, BRIAN
- MCKAY & ASSOCIATES
- MILES, DOROTHEA
- NEWTON HOUSE
- NEWTON, J C
- NICHOLAS, YVONNE
- NORTH WEST LIFESTYLE MNGMT
- OAKES, JILL
- ORGANISATIONAL HEALING
- P B AROMATHERAPY
- P M ASSOCIATES
- PALMIST & TAROT READING
- PAUL TAYLOR HYPNOTHERAPY
- PHYSIOTHERAPY CLINIC
- POWNALL, C J
- REFLEXOLOGY THERAPY
- ROBY, R
- SEER
- TIMELINE SERVICES
- TULIP HOLISTIC THERAPIES
- TURTON, TRACEY
- WARRINGTON ACUPUNCTURE CLINIC
- WARRINGTON CHIROPRACTIC CLINIC
- WATSON, R J
- WILLOW THERAPIES

### WIDNES

- ALTERNATIVE HEALTH CENTRE
- ALTERNATIVE HEALTH STUDIO
- ANDREWS, KATHRYN
- ESSENCE OF LIFE
- GRIFFITHS, C
- HYPNOS PRACTICE
- JONES, J W
- MARSH, F W
- PEARL AROMATICS
- WIDNES OSTEOPATHIC CLINIC

### WILMSLOW

- ALLEN ASSOCIATES
- AMELAN, RACHEL
- AUBREY, C J
- BLOCH, PETER
- BOYD, M C
- BRADSHAW, DIANNE
- CHADWICK, CAROL
- COMP THERAPIES INFORMATION SVS
- EMM, PHILIP & BERYL
- ESSENTIAL OIL WORKS
- EYRE, JACQUELINE
- GOODWIN, SIMON P
- HANDS ON PHYSIOTHERAPY
- HARDISTY, CHRIS
- HOWE, BARBARA
- HOWE, KENNETH L
- KERR, A N F
- MIDDLETON & ASSOCIATES
- MOORE, ROBERT P
- NUTTALL, A J
- OLIVER ASSOCIATES
- PLANT CHIROPODY
- SHERIDON, J
- STOKES, J E
- TAYLOR, CHRISTINE
- WEST & ASSOCIATES
- WIENHOLT, VALERIE

### WINSFORD

- LALLY, KAREN
- ROLFE, BRIAN
- STOTT, K M

## CLEVELAND

### BILLINGHAM

- AROMA HEALTH NORTH EAST
- HOGAN, KATE
- PRICE, JACKIE

### GUISBOROUGH

- BARNARD, SIMON
- BETTER HEALTH REFLEXOLOGY
- CLEVELAND CHIROPODY/SPORTS INJ
- DOYLE, TERRY
- HANNEY, DOROTHY
- HASTIE, A
- JOHNSON, LINDA
- MAUGHAN, ANNA
- MAXWELL, P S
- NATURAL THERAPY CENTRE
- OLIVIER, JONATHAN
- RUSSELL, STEVE
- THOMPSON, FRANK

### HARTLEPOOL

- ACTIVE BALANCE CLINIC
- ALFORD, M A
- BODY BALANCE
- FOREMAN, R
- HARTLEPOOL CHIROPRACTIC CLINIC
- LIDDELL, D
- MERMAID CHIROPRACTIC PRACTICE
- O'MALLEY, MOIRA
- STRESS MANAGEMENT

### MIDDLESBROUGH

- ALLINSON, IAN
- BARRON, ANGELA L
- BIRKS, W KEITH
- BRENNAN, JULIA
- BRUCE, P L
- CASTLETON, S
- CLEVELAND HOMEOPATHIC CLINIC
- CROSS, ANDREW
- GABLES CLINIC NHS
- GARDINER, C C
- HEAVEN SCENT
- IDESON, S M
- LAWSON, R J
- MITCHESON, D
- MORTON, H
- NEW DIRECTIONS
- NOLAN, BERNADETTE
- NORTON, STEVE
- O'DONNELL, C M
- PAGET P & MORTON H
- PAGET, P
- PARRY, CATHERYN
- PLUMMER, ANNE
- RAINBOW BRIDGE SCHOOL
- ROBINSON, RACHEL
- RUSH, DENNIS
- VACCHIERI, DANIEL
- WICKS, CLIFF

### REDCAR

- CLEVELAND NAT HEALTH CLINIC
- ERSKINE, SUE
- HARTLEY, ELAINE
- JEMSON, SANDRA
- MADAM ZENA
- OLLIVIER, D R
- OLLIVIER, J P
- REDCAR PHYSIO & SPORTS
- STRESS COUNSELLING
- WALNUT NATURAL THERAPY CLINIC

### SALTBURN-BY-THE-SEA

- CAMPBELL-COATES, EVEANN
- HANDS ON THERAPY CLINIC
- SALUTARIS HEALTH
- SALUTARIS HEALTH

### STOCKTON-ON-TEES

- ALEXANDER TECHNIQUE
- AYTON, P E
- BRADLEY, ALAN
- CLARK, LEE
- DUELL, C
- ELLISON, TIM
- FISHER, E
- FUNCTIONAL HEALTH CARE
- GARWOOD, CATHERINE
- GRIFFIN, SANDRA
- HARTBURN PHYSIOTHERAPY
- HEIMER, F
- JACKSON, R M & P M
- JANES, G
- NORTHERN GUILD-PSYCHOTHERAPY
- OLDHAM, P A
- RELAX
- RIDLEY MEWS COMP HEALTH CTRE
- ROSE, AMBER
- SKIPPINGS & ASSOCIATES
- SNOWBIRD CENTRE
- SZARY, G
- THERA-PAD
- WAITE, J C

### YARM

- AMATSU SPINEWORKS CLINIC
- BARWICK & LEVEN SPORTS CLINIC
- HERBALIFE
- INNER HLTH & HEALING PRACTICE
- OGDEN, GEOFF
- OLDHAM, P A
- WARD-DAVIS, J
- YARM OSTEOPATHIC CLINIC

## CORNWALL

### BODMIN

- DUCHY CHIROPRACTIC CLINIC
- LOBB, JUDY
- MCGORRIN, RICHARD
- NATURAL HEALING CENTRE
- ROBINSON, J W
- TRANSCENDENTAL MEDITATION

### BOSCASTLE

- BEECHWOOD CENTRE

### BUDE

- BRUNT, LINDA
- BURCH, E
- C H M SWANPOEL
- MATHESON, B & P
- PENWETHERS HOLISTIC CARE CTRE
- POOLER, ADENEY
- RICHARDSON, J
- WEATHERHOGG, D J

### CALLINGTON

- NATURAL PARTNERS
- REEVES, J

### CALSTOCK

- NERVA, VALERIE

### CAMBORNE

- AROMATICA
- BAKER, A W J
- CAMBORNE COMP HEALTH CENTRE
- FOOTCARE
- HILLIARD, N & R
- IVINS, V J
- MILLSTREAM
- MORRIS, CLIFFORD A

### CAMELFORD

- HILDER, DEBORAH
- MM MOBILE MASSAGE

### FALMOUTH

- BEARE, M E
- BRIERLEY, MATTHEW
- COVENTON, DOROTHY
- FALMOUTH HOMEOPATHIC PRACTICE
- FELSTEAD, PETER
- FOUNDATIONS PSYCHOTHERAPY
- GAVAN, JUDITH
- HENRY, R H S
- LISTER NATURAL HEALTH PRACTICE
- PASCOE, J E
- SNOW, MARIAN
- TATTON, ALISTAIR M
- WALKER, RICHARD

## GUNNISLAKE
- HULME, A

## HELSTON
- CARPENTER, P M
- IVILL, WENDY
- SCOBIE, D C O
- SPILLANE, EMMA
- TAYLOR, C E
- WATSON, BILL

## LAUNCESTON
- CHIROPODY CLINIC
- DANIEL, L G
- MARKET STREET CLINIC
- MASTERS, B
- MATHESON, P A
- ROBBINS, A L
- SELF REALISATION MEDITATION
- WILLS, JONATHAN

## LISKEARD
- BANBURY, A E
- BITS & BOBS
- CARADON CHIROPRACTIC CLINIC
- CHIROPODY SURGERY
- LISKEARD CHIROPRACTIC CLINIC
- PENGELLY, D W
- PLYMOUTH IND COMP PSYCH NURS
- THOMAS, ANNE
- TYMM, S L

## LOOE
- DRANSFIELD, GILL
- FINESSE
- HEALTH AT HOME

## LOSTWITHIEL
- REIKI & SEICHEM
- REIKI SEICHEM

## MARAZION
- IVORY, BRIAN S
- TREWHELLA, JOHN

## NEWQUAY
- BODY & SOUL NAT HLTH AND BTY
- COKER, M
- MEYERS, K L C
- NEWQUAY CHIROPRACTIC CLINIC
- NEWQUAY FOOT CLINIC
- NEWQUAY PHYSIOTHERAPY CENTRE
- S MONTAGU (DR)
- WEST, KATHRYN

## PAR
- DRAGE, STEPHEN

## PENRYN
- FALMOUTH CHIROPRACTIC CLINIC
- HALL, PETER

## PENZANCE
- CONBOYE, M CLARE
- GARDINER, NICKY
- GOUGH, LOUISE
- HALLS, D O
- HALLS, DENNIS
- HAYWARD, MONICA
- HEALING STAR
- LIFE-WORK POTENTIAL
- MORSE, EMMA
- PENZANCE NATURAL HEALTH CENTRE
- PRYCE, JOHN
- ROSEFIELD CONSULTANCY
- TREMAIN, BARBARA
- VERA BOYES ACUPUNCTURE

## PERRANPORTH
- ROUND, NOLA M

## REDRUTH
- BATEMAN, P W
- HUNTERS LODGE CLINIC
- LANNER NATURAL HEALTH CLINIC
- LAWRENCE, M A
- LAWS, F J
- LIFE 'N' LIMB
- NATURES TREASURES
- POOLEY, ALISON
- SELF HEAL TRUST
- SURENDRA, S B
- WILLIAMS, RUTH
- WILLS, ANNE

## SALTASH
- BARNNETT, ANN
- ECOFLOW
- LUCE, PETER J
- MASON, JAY
- RASHBROOKE, K M
- RAY, F
- REEVES, J
- RODGERS, J
- SALTASH FOOT CLINIC
- SAXBY, SUE
- SMITHWHITE, AMBER
- STEWART, DIANE
- TOWARD, K

## ST. AUSTELL
- ALEXANDRA FOOT CLINIC
- ALLEN, CHERYL
- BATEMAN, P W
- BISHOP, HEATHER
- BROWNE, ANNE
- BUCK, SUE
- FORCE, GAYLE
- JONES, MARILYN D
- KEILBART, P A
- NICHOLLS, SUE
- ROBERTS, T J
- SANDY HILL PHYSICAL THRPY CTRE
- SHEVILL, L A
- ST AUSTELL CHIROPRACTIC CLINIC
- ST AUSTELL NTRL HLTH PRACTICE
- TOWNSEND, MADELAINE
- WRIGHT, CYNTHIA

## ST. COLUMB
- UTTLEY, LINDA

## ST. IVES
- AURAVISION
- COMP HEALTH INITIATIVE
- HILLIARD, N
- HOPCROFT, JULIE
- MIDDLETON, CAROLE
- PHYSIOTHERAPY DEPARTMENT
- STAR

## TINTAGEL
- TOTAL HEALTHCARE IN SAFETY

## TORPOINT
- AROMA-WISE
- BARNETT, ANNE
- BROWN, LOUISE
- BURDEN, C
- GRIFFITHS, R J
- LIVINGSTONE, SHIRLEY
- MILLBROOK HEALTH & BEAUTY

## TRURO
- ACUPUNCTURE & PHYSIO CLINIC
- ASPINALL, JEAN
- BIOFLOW
- CELTIC GRAINBAGS
- CHIROPODIST/PODIATRIST
- CORNWALL CHIROPRACTIC SERVICES
- D'SOUZA, R J
- ELEMENT, JOANNE
- ELLIOTT, TIMOTHY
- FEET FIRST
- FLEMING, J
- FLEMING, R D
- GRANNY M'S AROMATHERAPY PRODS
- GREEN, A J
- HARBAGE, RALPH
- HOLZAMER, MARIA
- HYP HEALING & REFLEX CTRE
- LEMON ST NTRL HLTH PRACTICE
- LIFE 'N' LIMB
- MCLEAVY, CANDY
- MERIDIAN RADIONICS
- MONTAGUE-THOMAS, A
- OSTEOPATHIC FAMILY CENTRE
- RENTOUL, J W
- SHANLEY, P
- SKINNER, C
- STACEY, R A
- STACEY, R A
- TRURO CHIROPRACTIC CLINIC
- TRURO NATURAL HEALTH CENTRE
- TRURO OSTEOPATHIC PRACTICE
- WALSINGHAM CLN CTRE - NTRL MED
- WEBBER, IRENE
- WELLSPRING

## WADEBRIDGE
- GILL, SARAH
- HAWKSLAND PHYSIOTHERAPY CENTRE
- JONES, ANN
- MORPHEW, JOHN (DR)
- RAINBOWS AROMATHERAPY CLINIC
- SCOTT, ELY JARED
- WADEBRIDGE CHIROPODY CLINIC
- WADEBRIDGE OSTEOPATHS

# COUNTY DURHAM

## BARNARD CASTLE
- CALLAGHAN, M M
- HAIRSINE, P W
- JOHNSON S & O'BRIEN A
- TEESDALE OSTEOPATHIC CLINIC

## BISHOP AUCKLAND
- AUCKLAND ACUPUNCTURE CLINIC
- BEADLE, TRUDY
- BENNETT, MARGARET
- BISHOP AUCKLAND CHIROPODY
- FIONA OTTEWELL CHRTRD PHYSIO
- LEAKE, DIANE
- MCKEAG, JULIE
- MCLAUGHLIN, K D
- RICHARDSON, T G
- SYKES, LYNNE
- TURNBULL, CAROL

## CHESTER LE STREET
- ABEL, STEFFAN H
- CHESTER LE STREET HEALTH CTRE
- KIRKUP, KEVIN
- MADAM SIAN
- MORRISON, C H
- PALLISTER, TRUDY C
- SPOORS, L & D
- TANSLEY, LINDEN
- WALKER, PATRICIA

## CONSETT
- CONSETT PHYSIOTHERAPY
- CUMBERLEDGE, P J
- SLANE, JOHN

## CROOK
- LAMBERT, KAREN
- WALLACE, KEITH

## DARLINGTON
- ALOE VERA ADVICE CENTRE
- ARMSTRONG, OLWYN
- AROMAS OF JOY
- BARRAS, L
- BROWN, IAN
- CORBY, MICHAEL
- CORNER, CAROLYN
- DARLINGTON CHIROPRACTIC CLINIC
- DARLINGTON CTRE OF ORIENTL MED
- DARLINGTON F C SPORTS CLINIC
- DARLINGTON HOMEOPATHIC CLINIC
- DUKE STREET CHIROPODY
- FOOTEZE
- HALE, FRANCIS R
- HAMBLY, PHILIP
- HARVEST GRAIN
- HOBSON, I K
- JOHN ROBERTS-JAMES CLINIC
- KINGSLEY, V
- LAWTON, HELEN
- LEIGH, NIGEL
- MARSHALL, ANNE
- MUDDLE, SIMON & ASSOCIATES
- NATURAL HEALING CENTRE
- NRTH OF ENGLAND STRESS MNGMT
- O'BYRNE, A
- PARK PLACE HEALTH CLINIC
- R & M TRADING
- REID, K
- RODGERS REFLEXOLOGY
- SMART, DOUGLAS & LOGAN
- STRUCTURE & FUNCTION CLINIC

- TAYLOR, CAROL
- TRANQUILLITY CENTRE
- TREATMENT ROOM
- WARWICK, ANDREA
- WATSON, CARRIE
- WATSON-VOKES, LINDA
- WRIGHT FOOT FORWARD

### DURHAM
- AAAAAI HYPNOTISM & TRAINING
- ANDREADIS, ANTHONIA
- ASHCROFT, E
- BODYWORK HEALTH CLUB & CLINIC
- BOWBURN PHYSICAL THERAPY CLNC
- CENTRE FOR SELF HEALING ART
- CHILDS, HAZEL
- CLAYPATH MEDICAL PRACTICE
- COTTRELL, SANDRA
- DAVIS-JONES, ANN
- DIXON, LYNNE
- DOONAN, A
- DOVE CENTRE
- EASTWEST CLINIC
- EPSTEIN, WENDY
- ESSENTIAL TOUCH
- FOOTPRINTS
- FROST, PATRICIA
- HEDLEY HILL HEALTH SERVICES
- HILDITCH, JUDITH
- HOWARTH, D
- MARCUS, MARY
- MCSHANE, M
- MERIDIAN MASSAGE & REFLEXOLOGY
- NEWCASTLE/NE TRANS MEDITA CTRE
- OLD PIT PRACTICE
- OPTIMUM NUTRITION & ALOE VERA
- PEACOCK, ANGELA
- ROBINSON, H
- SPORTS INJURY CLINIC
- TANSLEY, LINDEN
- WASHINGTON PODIATRY PART

### FERRYHILL
- MOUNTFORD, PAUL

### MIDDLETON ST GEORGE
- RAYMOND, GEOFF

### NEWTON AYCLIFFE
- BALANCE HOLISTIC HEALTHCARE
- ELIZABETH BLAYLOCK REIKI PRACT
- HIND, CAROLE
- MARSHALL, S A
- MIDGLEY, CLARE
- PADGET, CHRIS

### PETERLEE
- ANN

### SEAHAM
- SLEIGHT, C

### SEDGEFIELD
- WHITE SUE & MARTIN MAUREEN

### SHILDON
- EVANS, BRUCE (DR)
- HARVEST GRAIN

### SPENNYMOOR
- CHRISTINE
- HORNER, L
- MAUGHAN, E
- WAKE, J

### STANLEY
- CUMBERLEDGE, PAUL JAMES
- HEALTH MATTERS

## CUMBRIA

### ALSTON
- ALADDIN AROMAS
- BARTSTRA, R

### AMBLESIDE
- ALLONBY, R M
- EVANS, D G
- MARRIS, TIMOTHY

### APPLEBY-IN-WESTMORLAND
- IMPORT, SELINA

### ASKAM-IN-FURNESS
- GARNETT, JANE

### BARROW-IN-FURNESS
- ABBYCARE HYPNOTHERAPY
- BELDER, TAMARA
- CAIN, SUSAN
- FROST, ANDREA
- GOWLDING, P & N
- HALL, MARGARET
- HUSTINGS, LESLEY
- KING, VERONICA
- MACMILLAN, JOHN
- OXFORD CLINIC
- PRESTON, ZINA
- ROBERTS, GARRY
- ROBSON, PAUL
- SCOTT STREET COMP THERAPY CTRE
- SHAMAL, LYN
- SHAW, C
- SIEW, ALLEN
- SIMPLY PERFECT BY JAN
- TUGWELL, LAURA
- WARNOCK, POLLY

### BRAMPTON
- TEASDALE & ASSOCIATES

### CARLISLE
- BIRD, NEIL
- BRETT, T
- CARLISLE PHYSIO & SPORTS CLNC
- CHIROPODIST & REMEDIAL MASSAGE
- DUNLOP, JAMES R W
- FEVAR, R
- FLYNN, T G
- GLAISTER, J E
- GOBLE, L M
- HEALTH FOOD CENTRE
- JOLLY, G M
- LAKELAND AROMATICS
- LLOYD, R N
- MARY'S PALMIST
- MATTHEWS, ERIC
- MATTHEWS, V
- MCGREGOR, SHERRY
- MORRISON, D C
- NORMAN, HILARY
- SUNLAN HOLISTICS
- SWINDALE, TESSA
- THERAPY CENTRE
- WILSON, P M

### CLEATOR
- SOUTHWARD, G

### COCKERMOUTH
- CUMBRIA PHYSIO & SPORTS CLINIC
- DUNCAN, E
- HERBS AND HELPERS
- RHAM, TRICIA
- RUBINSTEIN, ADAM
- STRAWBERRY HOW CLINIC

### EGREMONT
- ALLAN, DIANNE
- BOWNESS, B

### GRANGE-OVER-SANDS
- CLEREY, J D
- DEERING, CHRISTINE
- FLOOKBURGH CLINIC
- HARDWICKE, MICHAEL

### KENDAL
- AIREY, L M
- BLUNT, W W
- BROOME, ALISON
- CHOICE NATURAL HEALTH CENTRE
- COATES, ELIZABETH
- CONWAY, C
- CONWAY, J
- CROSSLEY, C
- HARRISON, DAVID
- JACKSON, D M
- JACKSON, D M
- LAKELAND CHIROPRACTIC CENTRE
- LAKELAND HYPNOTHERAPY CENTRE
- LOWE, JOHN
- MCWATT, LIZ
- PAINSOOTHER HEALTH PRODUCTS
- RUBINSTEIN, ADAM
- SINGLETON, POLLY
- SMITH, MARK
- STATE REGISTERED CHIROPODISTS

### KESWICK
- FOOTWORKS
- GALLOWAY, N

### KIRKBY STEPHEN
- HOLISTIC HEALTH CENTRE
- VINCENT, DAVID

### MARYPORT
- SHORT, J J

### MILLOM
- ST MICHAELS REST
- THURSTON, JENNY

### MILNTHORPE
- CARRINGTON, DORA
- TAYLOR, L P A
- TAYLOR, L P A

### PENRITH
- BILLINGHAM, K
- EDEN PHYSIO & SPORTS
- EDWARDS, D E
- GALLOWAY, NEIL
- KEMP, E A
- O'HARA, CHRISTINE
- STONES, DAVE
- WALKER, IAN
- WHITLEY, LIS

### ULVERSTON
- AINSWORTH, D & C
- COOKSON, N
- MCQUILLAN, JANE
- ULVERSTON NATURAL HEALTH CTRE

### WHITEHAVEN
- BERRY, RUTH
- BOYD, JOHN
- KERR, R
- LIBRA THERAPY CENTRE

### WIGTON
- THOMAS, JULIET

### WINDERMERE
- CRAIG, J
- GUTTERIDGE, A C (DR)
- HUGHGONSON, SUE
- SUTTON, R W

### WORKINGTON
- HYPNOTHERAPY CENTRE
- JACKSON, B
- LYLEE, URWIN
- PETER STREET CLINIC
- VULCANS LANE CHIROPODY

## DERBYSHIRE

### ALFRETON
- BATEMAN, STEPHEN W
- EAREY, C A
- HUMAN RELATIONS SERVICES
- MATTHEWS, A
- NATURAL CHOICE HEALTH FOODS
- NATURAL THERAPY SERVICES
- SEEDS, COLIN
- STOCKS, JIM

### ALLESTREE
- GRANGE, DIANA

### ASHBOURNE
- ASHBOURNE PHYSIOTHERAPY CLINIC
- BAXTER, C
- HALTON, A
- HIGGS, ANN
- SHAW, R G B
- TAYLOR, E F

### ASHOVER
- FARMER, VAL

## BAKEWELL

- BODY & SOUL
- JACKSON-BASS, ALISON
- MONSAL HEAD NATURAL THRPY CTRE
- SCRIVENER, BARBARA

## BELPER

- ALOE VERA INTERNATIONAL
- BELPER BACKPAIN CLINIC
- BELPER HOMEOPATHY
- BELPER NATURAL HEALTH CENTRE
- BELPER PHYSIOTHERAPY CLINIC
- G J D ELECTRICAL SERVICES
- GALLEY, D G
- LANCASHIRE, LINDA
- PEAK PSYCHOLOGY SERVICE
- REDFERN, AMANDA
- SILVER, EVELYN

## BUXTON

- AROMATHERAPY & REFLEX CTRE
- HUTSON, ANNE
- KARDAHJI, F C
- SCARR, G M
- TIDESWELL HOM PRACTICE
- TREEWICKS

## CHESTERFIELD

- ACRE HEALTH
- BANKS, LINDA
- BARNSDALE, K
- BENTON, LINDSEY
- BOWMER, S
- BRILL, PAULINE
- BROWN, HELEN
- BROWN, T
- CARRICK-SMITH, L
- CARRUTHERS, G (DR)
- CHESTERFIELD CHIROP & PODIATRY
- DREW, ADA
- FALCON YARD CHIROPODY
- FOOT CARE CLINIC
- FREESTON-SMITH, M P
- GARRISON-TODD, WENDY
- GARRISON-TODD, WENDY
- GUIDING LIGHTS
- HINCHCLIFFE, AMANDA
- HOLME, CHRISTINE
- HOLYWELL ANNEXE CLINIC
- IN STEP CHIROPODY CLINIC
- JAMES, CHRIS
- MASON, DIANE
- MCFARLANE, BILL
- MCLAUGHLIN, L
- MEAKIN, JACKIE
- MOORE, JACKIE
- NATURAL CHOICE HEALTH FOODS
- NEWBOLD CHIROPODY CENTRE
- NUNN, PAULINE
- PEARCE, YVONNE
- PEDLEY, ANNE
- RICKARD, CLIVE A
- RUDGE, ELAINE
- SALTERGATE SPINAL & SPORTS
- SHOOTER, J
- SINENORE, S
- SLADE, ZENA
- SPIRAC PHYSIOTHERAPY
- STRATTON, SUNNY
- STRESS CLINIC
- TREECE, B B
- TREECE, P M
- WALKER, P
- WALL, MARIAN
- WEBSTER, JOANNE
- WELL OILED
- WHITEING CHIROPODISTS
- WHITEING, J P

## DERBY

- ABBA, TERRI
- ACUPUNCTURE CENTRE
- ACUPUNCTURE CLINIC
- ALLEN, J
- ASHBURNER, P
- AUCOTT, M J
- AVON HYPNOTHERAPY
- BATE, ALAN
- BERNE INSTITUTE
- BEWLEY, COLIN A
- BHOGAL, V R K
- BRADSHAW, P J
- BRAHMA KUMARIS RAJA YOGA CTRE
- BRIDGE CENTRE
- BRONKS, IAN G
- CENTRAL CHARTERED PHYSIO
- CHARTERED PSYCHOLOGISTS
- CLINIC OF NATURAL MEDICINE
- CONTOUR DESIGNS
- CONTOUR THERAPY SCHOOL
- CULLEN, D
- DARBY, ANN
- DERBY ACUPUNCTURE CENTRE
- DERBY HOMEOPATHIC PRACTICE
- DERBYSHIRE SPORTS INJURIES
- DICKINSON, ANN
- DONNA-MARIA FRAHER
- EAST MIDLANDS NUFFIELD HOSP
- ELLIOTT, DAVID W
- ENJOY SPORT
- FACE UP FOR BEAUTY
- FENG SHUI
- GRIFFIN, A D
- HALE, JO
- HALL, A
- HARDING, MANDY
- HARE, CAROL L
- HARTWELL, A E
- HAWKINS & FIELDING
- HILL CREST HEALING
- HODGSON, M
- HORAN, MARTIN
- HOUSE OF AROMATHERAPY
- HUDSON, H
- HUNT, J H
- JEFFERY & ASSOCIATES
- KEMP, G (DR)
- KEMP, G D
- KEMP, GILLIAN
- LENNOX, CHRISTOPHER
- LIKISMA
- LLOYD-DAVIES, T
- LONG TUONG VAN
- MEYER, A
- MOONEEGAN, V
- NATURAL HEALTH CLINIC
- NEWELL, JOHN
- OCCUPATIONAL PSYCHOL SOLUTIONS
- OSTEOPATH CLINIC
- PARK FARM CHIROPODY SERVICES
- PEEBLES, P M
- PERRY, VIC
- PILATES FOUNDATION UK
- PIZER, ISAAC
- PRIESTLEY, E
- PRIESTLEY, E
- QURBAN, AMIR
- REID, BARBARA
- RIGLEY, T
- S DERBYSHIRE DEPT-PSYCHO
- SAINT CLAIRE, MAGGIE
- SCHOLL CENTRE
- SLATER, M
- SMITH, ALAN P
- SOLUNA HOMOEOPATHY CENTRE
- SPINK, BERNADETTE
- SPONDON CHIROPODY CLINIC
- STREET, R E F
- TAYLOR, E F
- TOMLINSON, DAWN
- TOMLINSON, KATE
- TUSSIE-MUSSIES
- WAYNE, ANTHONY
- WEBSTER, BARBARA
- WELLBEING CLINIC
- WHATLING, M J
- WOODLANDS NATURAL HEALTH CTRE

## DRONFIELD

- AROMATIC
- BARROWCLIFFE, GRAHAM (DR)
- BELL, T A
- BIGG, VANESSA
- DRONFIELD NAT HEALTH CLINIC
- DRONFIELD PHYSIOTHERAPY CLINIC
- FLYNN, FRANCESCA
- GOODALL, L G
- HILL, ANGELA
- KAY, P
- KAY, R M
- LIFESOLUTIONS
- MATTHEWS, AMANDA
- MEAKIN, JACKIE
- MOROZ, CAROLYN
- MYERS, WENDY
- PHYSIOTHERAPY CENTRE
- SHELTON, JULIE
- TOW, DAVID

## GLOSSOP

- BATES METHOD VISION EDUCATION
- BUCKLEY, B
- CHIROPODY & PHYSIOTHERAPY
- COMPLEMENTARY MEDICINE CENTRE
- DICKINSON, LYNNE
- LONDON COLLEGE OF CLINICAL HYP
- OZ
- PEAKE, C F
- PHILIP STOCK - PHYSIOTHERAPIST
- PHYSIO ACTIVE
- STANTON, JACKIE
- SYKES, PETER W
- THORNHILL, LYNDA
- WILLIAMS, VERONICA

## HEANOR

- DANIELS, FRANK
- HEANOR CHIROPRACTIC CLINIC
- HEANOR PHYSIO & SPORTS
- STRUDWICK, H J
- TAYLOR, DAVID E

## HIGH PEAK

- ALEXANDER TECHNIQUE
- BACH FLOWER REMEDIES
- COVERLEY PHYSIOTHERAPY CLINIC
- DE MIERRE, MAVIS
- FOX-DAVIES, DAWN
- WHITTLE, S

## HOPE VALLEY

- HATHERSAGE HEALTH & THRPY CTRE
- I P CONSULTANCIES

## ILKESTON

- ALTERNATIVE THERAPIES CENTRE
- BATH STREET CHIROPODIST
- CHARLTON, P
- GENT, B
- HARDWICK, JUDITH
- ILKESTONE OSTEO & MED CTRE
- JOHNSON, MELVYN
- JOYOUS FEET
- LIFECHANGERS
- LOCK, MICHAEL
- MYDDLETON, TRACY
- STEVENSON, JACKIE
- SUNFLOWER VITAL HEALTH
- WELEDA

## MATLOCK

- CLARK, HAZEL
- FLETCHER, S & V M
- GRAY, BARBARA
- INNER PEACE
- MATLOCK CHIROPRACTIC CLINIC
- MATLOCK PHYSIOTHERAPY CENTRE
- PARSONS, IAN H
- PRICE, GRAHAM

## RIPLEY

- FORSYTH, JUSTIN
- GALLEY, D G
- HOUSE OF AROMATHERAPY
- LANCASHIRE, A W
- NATURAL CHOICE HEALTH FOODS
- NICOL, A
- RIPLEY THERAPY CENTRE
- SAUNDERS, N

## SPONDON

- WALKER, B

## SWADLINCOTE

- ALTER-MED
- COPE, C G
- GREYSTONE CHARTERED PHYSIO
- HAYWOOD, T J
- HOLFORD CHIROPODISTS

- JUST 4 U
- KNIGHT, JAYNE
- O'CONNOR, R
- PETER SADLER NATURAL MED CTRE
- PRICE, TRACY
- READ, MATTHEW J
- SANCTUM NATURAL THERAPY CTRE
- TRANSFORMATIONS

# DEVON

## AXMINSTER

- AWARENESS CENTRE
- BINMORE, B J
- BODY FOCUS
- DOUGLAS-MORT, D J & R F
- FEU, DU
- GAYLOR, A A
- HARRIS, LYN
- HIETT, ANNE
- HOWLETT, DAVID
- LOADER, JANE
- MOORE, BEVERLEY

## BARNSTAPLE

- ADAMS, J R
- ALDAN PHYSIOTHERAPY CLINIC
- AURA
- BARNSTAPLE HYPNOTHERAPY
- BIGDEN, ROGER
- BONTEIN, SARA
- CASTLE CHIROPRACTIC CLINIC
- FELIX, S Z
- FELIX, S Z
- FLYNN, LISA
- FOXWELL, CORALIE
- IOKAI CENTRE FOR COMP MEDICINE
- ISIS CENTRE
- JULIE ADAMS REFLEXOLOGIST
- JUSTRICH SWISS HRBL BODY CARE
- KREY, JOHN
- KRYSTYNA, KRZYZAK
- LAWRENCE, J M
- MALCOLM, M J
- NATURAL HEALTH CLINIC
- NELSON, PAUL
- NIGEL DE SALENGRE
- PICKARD, OWEN
- PILTON PHYSIOTHERAPY CENTRE
- REFLEXOLOGY CENTRE
- RIVERSIDE CHIROPRACTIC CLINIC
- SCARBRO, J M
- SERENITY
- SLEE, L R
- SPENCER, P
- TARKA CLINIC
- TEFT, REBECCA
- VALLINS, SAMANTHA

## BIDEFORD

- AYRES, DAVID
- BARTON, VIRGINIA
- BIDEFORD CHIROPRACTIC CLINIC
- COX, MIRANDA
- DE SALENGRE & SPENCER
- FARMER, RON
- GEBALA, K
- JACKSON, G P
- LANGDON, E M
- MACDONALD, R S J
- MOAT, ANTOINETTE
- REYNOLDS, HELEN
- TRANSCENDENTAL MEDITATION
- TREMAIN, S R

## BRAUNTON

- CUMMING, JANE
- FOOTSTEPS
- MILSOM, CAROLINE
- WHEELER, ROBERT
- WILLIS, M

## BRIXHAM

- ANDREWS, R
- AROMAGLOW
- BIRD, JANE
- BRITISH SCHOOL OF HOMOEOPATHY
- BRIXHAM HEALING HANDS CENTRE
- DELTER REFLEXOLOGY
- HATTON, JUNE
- HEALTH CONSULTANCY
- LOCKWOOD, CHARLES M A
- OLIVER, P H
- READ, S R
- SHIRLEY'S AROMATHERAPY
- TRANQUIL AROMATHERAPY & BEAUTY
- WELSH-ROLLINGS, SUSANNE
- YOUNG, SUE

## BUCKFASTLEIGH

- TANSER, THEO

## BUDLEIGH SALTERTON

- COOK, J E
- COOPER, LESLEY
- HODGINS, HELEN
- HOLISTIC HEALTH
- ROSEHILL CENTRE
- YOGA HEALTH STUDIO

## CHULMLEIGH

- ELLIS, SUE
- LODER, H

## COLYTON

- BUTSON, JUDITH
- EAST DEVON CONSULTANCY

## CREDITON

- AROMATHERAPY CENTRE
- BARTLETT, LOUIS
- BLAND, AMANDA
- BURY, CHRIS
- CHALTON, SANDRA
- CREDITON CHIROPRACTIC CLINIC
- DALLAS, JENNIE
- EVERETT HEALTH CARE
- FOSTER, JENNIE
- FRANK, KRIS
- GRACELINGS NATURAL HEALTH
- HAWKINS, JACKIE
- INTAHEALTH UK
- KING, S
- MARSHALL, G
- MASSON, C R
- REDWOOD, DAWN
- STOBART, ANNE
- THOMAS, CHRIS

## CULLOMPTON

- BERRY, A R
- BROWNBILL-LOWE, GAIL
- COTTAGE CLINIC
- CULLOMPTON CHIROPRACTIC CLINIC
- KALLAWAY, KATHLEEN

## DARTMOUTH

- CLARKE, P P
- ELLISON, ANNE
- ENGLAND, ANITA
- SAVAGE, E

## DAWLISH

- CLEGG, D P
- GRAHAM, GEOFF
- HANDS, PETER
- JEFFRIES, BARBARA
- WELSH-ROLLINGS, SUSANNE

## EXETER

- ACUPUNCTURE/CHINESE HERB SHOP
- AROMATHERAPY PLUS
- ASHTON, ANTHONY
- BATTEN, C
- BEACON CENTRE
- BOOBIER, A
- BOODAN, D
- BOUNDY, C
- BREADING, MARGARET
- BROADWAY HOUSE
- BROWN, B T
- BROWN, P A
- BURNING DESIRE
- BURT, JANE
- BURY, CHRIS
- CARSON, BRONWYN
- CHINESE MEDICAL CENTRE
- CHRISTINES MASSAGE THERAPY
- CLAY, ANITA (DR)
- CLEMO, ANNE
- CLINIC OF CHINESE MEDICINE
- CLYDE HOUSE CHIRO CLINIC
- COLLEGE OF NATURAL NUTRITION
- COLOMBI, F
- CONVERGENCE CENTRE
- COPE, ANNE
- CRECY MASSAGE STUDIO
- DEAN, S
- DEPARTMENT OF COMP MEDICINE
- DICKSON, JANE
- DOWNES, W P
- EARDLEY, S
- EVENNETT, P J
- EVOLUTION
- EXETER CHIROPRACTIC CLINIC
- EXETER SKIN CARE CENTRE
- FILLERY, PAUL L
- FIRST HAND PHYSIO PRACTICE
- FISH, ALINA
- GOODALL, PAULINE
- GRANT, L
- HANSELL, A S
- HARRIS, K R
- HEALTH WAVES
- HEAVITREE CHIROPRACTIC CENTRE
- HEMINGWAY, T
- HILL, R B
- HOLLINGSWORTH, ELAINE
- HOOPER, J A
- HOURIGAN, P
- JENKINS, HUGH
- JENKINS, KATHERINE
- JONES, A C
- JUPP, J
- KEOGH, MARTIN
- KOBASHI
- LAMBERT, B
- LAPKA, M S L
- LATHAM, P
- LONGBROOK CENTRE
- MADAM RIO
- MALCOLM, JOYCE
- MARTIN, J H
- MARTINEAU, M
- MORRISH, MO
- NAT INSTITUTE OF MED HERBAL
- NATURAL HEALTH & HEALING
- NIGHTINGALE, J
- NIGHTINGALE, JERRY
- PALMER, JONATHAN C
- PERCIVAL, C
- PHILPOTT, J
- PIPER CHIROPODY
- POTTER, J
- PSYCHOTHERAPY/HYPNOTHERAPY
- PURVES, SHIRLEY A
- REMEDIES ELECTROLYSIS
- RIVERSIDE PRACTICE
- ROBINSON, IRIS E M
- ROGUSKI, CATHERINE
- ROYAL DEVON & EXETER HOSPITAL
- SCHOLL CENTRE
- SCHOOL OF COMPLEMENTARY HEALTH
- SENSATIONS
- SEWARD, HAROLD M
- SNEDDON, GRAHAM
- SOMMERVILLE, R E
- ST DAVIDS OSTEOPATHIC CLINIC
- STIMULUS FOR CHANGE
- TALKING SYSTEMS
- TAYLORSON, JUDITH
- THOMPSON, PAUL
- TOPSHAM PHYSIO/COMP HEALTH
- TOY, M F
- TRACEY UNA MCTIMONEY
- TRACEY UNA MCTIMONEY
- WALTERS, RICHARD
- WARD, V J
- WAYMAN, C R
- WEEKS, MELANIE
- WHEATON, JOHN (DR)
- WIGRAM, J
- WIJAY, JUDITH
- WILKIE, J (DR)
- WILKINSON, MARY
- YELLOW EMPEROR

## EXMOUTH

- EXMOUTH CHIROPODY
- HORTON, R M

- INGRAM, RACHAEL
- JACKSON, ANDREA
- KENDAL, D J
- KETTLE, LESLEY
- MARTINEAU, M (DR)
- MCTIMONEY CHIROPRACTIC CLINIC
- PARKER, RICHARD
- SMITH, A C
- STEVE THE MEDIUM
- WILLIS, KATHRYN

## HOLSWORTHY

- MERIDIAN HEALTH
- WASSERMAN, D

## HONITON

- BADCOCK, ELAINE
- CHANNING, N & A M
- CHIROPRACTIC CARE
- COATES, ALAN
- COPE, ANNE
- DOUGLAS-MORT, D J & R F
- PHIL FOGGITT

## ILFRACOMBE

- EAMES, MARGARET (DR)
- HAINES, C
- LERWILL, SARAH
- NELSON, CHRISTINE
- RIDLER, SHIRLEY
- SMITH, G

## IVYBRIDGE

- ANSELL, S
- BRUCE, CLAIRE
- HARRIS, MICHAEL
- IVYBRIDGE CHIROPRACTIC CENTRE
- MATTHEWS, FIONA
- MOODY, DAVID
- MOODY, DONALD A
- SOWELU ASSOCIATES
- VIDAL-HALL, NICK

## KINGSBRIDGE

- BEWLEY-JONES, ELIZABETH
- GAUNT, THERESA
- GRAHAM, JEAN
- GUILDFORD, DILYS
- KEILLER, S T B
- KINGSBRIDGE COMP HLTH PRACTICE
- KINGSBRIDGE PHYSICAL THERAPY
- SMITH, DOUGLAS V
- STURGESS, PETER
- STYLES, D M
- WIDGER, CHRISTINE

## LYNMOUTH

- IOKAI SHIATSU CLINIC

## NEWTON ABBOT

- ABBOTT HYPNOTHERAPY
- ASSOCIATED CHIROPODY SERVICES
- BILLINGHURST, D M
- BODY WORK
- CHIROPRACTIC CLINIC
- CLINIC OF NATURAL MEDICINE
- DELVE, PHILIP
- ELDON HEALTH CLINIC
- FOOTSTEP CHIROPODY
- FOOTSTEP CHIROPODY
- GETHIN, CHRISTOPHER
- HAMILTON, A
- HEALTHSHARE FOUNDATION
- HODGINS, HELEN
- JOHNSON, MICHAEL
- MARSDEN-RYLE, D
- MCDAID, M S
- MIDDLE EARTH AROMA SUPPLIES
- MOORE, CHRISTINE
- PEARSON, K J
- PETERPAN & TINKERBELL
- SOFFE, N S
- STONE, ANN
- STORY, MARGARET
- SYKES, FRANCES
- TAME, STEPHEN
- VERWAY, FRANK
- VERWEY, JULIA
- VERWEY, SYKES
- WALL, M
- WEBSTER, I
- WESTLAKE, DAVID
- WIGRAM, J R
- WOODROW, IAN

## OKEHAMPTON

- LIGHT TOUCH THERAPY TRAINING
- MARTIN, J R
- MCPHIE, SUSAN
- NEWTON, DON
- PEERLESS, M J
- WASSERMAN, DAVID

## OTTERY ST. MARY

- NATURAL HEALTH CLINIC
- WALTERS, RICHARD

## PAIGNTON

- ACUPUNCTURE CLINIC
- BALL, ADRIAN
- BENNETT, W P
- BINMORE, F
- CALVERT, D R
- CREATON, SUE
- ELMSLEIGH PARK CHIRO CLINIC
- FOOT CLINIC & THERAPY ROOM
- GOULDEN, KATHLEEN
- HACKETT, J
- HARRIS, C
- JEWRY, PATRICIA
- LOCKE, PETER A
- MADAM VERITY
- MANDALAY HOTEL
- MATTHEWS, V
- MICHELL, C
- NETHERWAY, JEAN
- PAIGNTON NATURAL HEALTH CENTRE
- PAIGNTON PHYSIOTHERAPY
- REEVES, MICHAEL
- RICHARDSON, D L
- RIVIERA OSTEOPATHIC CLINIC
- SELLARS, C
- SHORE, ROBIN
- TAYLOR, LYNETTE
- TORBAY CHIROPRACTIC CLINIC
- TORBAY OCCUPATIONAL THERAPY
- TRANCE - FORMATIONS HEALING
- WILKS, S A
- WILLETT, R

## PLYMOUTH

- ACORA'S ZODIAC EMPORIUM
- ALEXANDER, CAROL
- ALISON MORTON PHYSIOTHERAPY
- ALLSOP, M A
- ARNOLD, SHIRLEY
- ARNOLDS, SHIRLEY
- ASCLEPION
- AYERS, K
- BACKS R US
- BANBURY, KAREN
- BARRETT, J
- BENWELL, NATALIE
- BIOTHERAPY
- BLACKLER, G G
- BORTHWICK, C M
- CAMERON, ALISON
- CAMPBELL-BEATTIE, JOHN
- CARPENTER, PAUL
- CHAFER, D W
- CHINESE MEDICAL CENTRE
- CLINIC OF HYP & STRESS MNGMT
- COLLING, K A
- COMPLEMENTARY TREATMENT CENTRE
- CROWNHILL CHIROPODY PRACTICE
- DAVIES, D B
- DE-SILVA & WHITTINGHAM
- DEVENISH MUTTON, SUSAN
- DEVONSHIRE HEALTH & RAQUET
- DOUGLAS-RILEY, PENELOPE
- FELL, HELEN
- FOOTEC MEDICAL
- FULLALOVE, D
- GARDNER, PHILIP
- GENTLEMANS CLUB
- GILLARD, J
- HARRIS, JOANNA P
- HEALTH CARE INTERNATIONAL
- HEARN, LORRAINE
- HOLISTIC THERAPY CENTRE
- HUME, PETER D
- HYDE ACUPUNCTURE & HERBALIST
- IM, KIM LAY
- INSTIT-DEVELOPMENTAL POTENTIAL
- KAY, DAVID
- KELLY, KEVIN
- KERR, J A
- KNOWLE HOUSE
- LLEWELLYN, V J
- LOPES, ROBYN
- MANGLES, DENISE
- MONSHIN, DEBORAH J
- MORTON, A P
- OWEN, DAVID A
- OWEN, DAVID A
- PANNELL, R J
- PEDLER, FAY
- PEERS, C
- PLYMOUTH CHIROPODY PRACTICE
- PLYMOUTH OSTEOPATHS
- PLYMPTON OSTEOPATHIC CLINIC
- PROGRAMME HEALTH/HEALING CTRE
- PSYCHIC SHOP
- RAE, J S (DR)
- RAHMAN, AKHLAQUE
- RENDLE, S
- ROBINSON & PIERCE PODIATISTS
- ROGERS, A P
- ROGERS, S E
- SCHOLL CENTRE
- SCOTT, BRIDGET
- SEVENTREES CHIROPODY CLINIC
- SPENCER-EDWARDS, K
- STOKE DAMEREL CHIROPODY CLINIC
- STRICK, STUART
- SUMMERS, GORDON
- TABERNER, JOHN
- THOMAS, JANET
- THORNBER, A
- TRANSCENDENTAL MEDITATION CTRE
- UNITY HOUSE
- WELL OILED
- WIGG, SARA
- YORK HOUSE CHIROPODY
- YORK HOUSE CHIROPRACTIC CLINIC

## RATTERY

- CHEMIN, CHRISTIAN

## SALCOMBE

- SANDERS, RACHEL
- SELLER OIL
- STANLEY, H W (DR)

## SEATON

- AITCHISON, LYNN
- RICHIE, ELIZABETH
- STAMP, N

## SHALDON

- MALLARDO, RENEE

## SIDMOUTH

- BLYTH, DON
- BLYTH, SALLY
- CHARLES-DAVIS, S
- CLEZY, G M
- COLOMBI, FELICITY
- COMPLEXIONS BEAUTY THERAPY
- COOPER, LESLEY
- GILKERSON, PATRICIA
- JACKSON, ANDREA
- KING, SIMON
- LONERGAN, BARRY
- MILLER, NORMAN
- MYATT, R
- NICOLLE, J
- SPANTON, LORRAINE
- VOLLERS, J

## SOUTH BRENT

- BLADES, S
- CARPENTER, FIONA
- ELLISON, ANNE

## SOUTH MOLTON

- CHURCH HOUSE PRACTICE
- POPPLEWELL, REBECCA
- ROSE & CROWN CLINIC

- ROULSTONE, LILIAS
- WEST OF ENGLAND PSYCHOLOGY SVS

## TAVISTOCK

- ABBEYMEAD NATURAL HEALTH CTRE
- BENNETT, ROGER
- COOKE, ANNIE
- HULME, ALICE
- JANE HYDE CHRTRD PHYSIO
- KRAWCHENKO, LOUISE A V
- PEDEN, JOYCE
- PHYSIOTHERAPY CLINIC
- SALIS FANE DE, AMANDA
- TAVISTOCK CHIROPRACTIC CENTRE
- TAVY COVER
- WILLSHER, ERNEST R

## TEIGNMOUTH

- ALEXANDER TECHNIQUE
- ALLSOPP, EMMA
- ARPINO, MARIA
- BERG, DAVID
- CHANNEL VIEW COMP HEALTH
- DAWE, S
- MEANEY-PRICE, SHELIA
- MISTELY, SONIA
- SHARP, J A
- TEIGNMOUTH CHIROPODY

## TIVERTON

- ANNE RAWLINGS HYPNOTHERAPY
- CARSON, NICHOLAS
- CLINIC-COMP & ALT THERAPY
- DRUCE, Y L
- FIELDS, SHIRLEY
- FUDGE, H
- HARRIS, J
- HARRIS, JEANNE
- HARRIS, K R (DR)
- KELLY, L V
- LINDEMAN, A J
- LION HOUSE SURGERY
- MASSAGE RELAXING THERAPEUTIC
- OLSEN, G J D
- PARIS, ANNA
- PARSONS, JEFF
- PLAYERS, MEGAN
- SCURR, PETER M
- SEELEY, JANICE
- STOBART, A
- TIVERTON PHYSIO & SPORTS

## TORQUAY

- ADAMS, JENNIFER
- AROMAGLOW
- AUTOGENICS
- BABBACOMBE CHIROPODY CLINIC
- BAILLIES STUDIO
- BROPHY, MARTHA
- CASTLEBRIDGE CHIRO & REFLEX
- CHELSTON CHIROPODY PRACTICE
- CHIROPRACTIC AND MYOFACIAL
- CHIROPRACTIC HEALTHCARE CLINIC
- COCKINGTON FRAGRANCES
- COOPER, H J
- CUSS, JEAN
- DAVEY, JOAN
- E B H
- EQUILIBRIUM CLINIC
- FARYNA, WARREN G
- FORE STREET CHIROPODY
- FORREST, E
- GARRETTLEY, U
- GREIG, ANDREW
- HASLAM, ANTHONY
- HEDGE, P
- HORNER, ANN
- HUNT, J
- I Y S KEVALA CENTRE
- J T SERVICES
- JAMES, PETER
- METUS, M L
- PAYNE, I J
- PETULENGRO
- PHYSIOTHERAPY CENTRE
- SCHOLL CENTRE
- SHIATSU
- SPENCE, R
- THERAPYCARE
- WALDRON, BRIAN J
- WALKER, VICTOR J
- WILLIAMS CLINIC
- WOOD, JULIE
- WRIGHT, W J

## TORRINGTON

- FOXWELL, CORALIE
- MATTHEWS, MAX

## TOTNES

- ALYSS, THOMAS
- ARCTURUES CLINIC
- BEATTY, CAROLINE
- BECKER, JACKI
- CASTLEBRIDGE CHIRO & REFLEX
- COOK, TOM
- DAWN AWAKENING MUSIC
- DEL MAR, ANTONIA
- DEVON SCHOOL OF SHIATSU
- GRANTHAM, P M
- HOPWOOD, S (DR)
- IRIDOLOGY/NUTRITIONAL THER
- LATCHEM, V
- MASON, MARCUS
- PARKER, JONATHAN
- POTTER, MICHAEL
- ROGERS, PAMELA
- ROGERS, PAMELA
- TAME, STEPHEN
- VAUGHAN, JANET
- VITAL TOUCH

## WINKLEIGH

- REAY, MARIA

## YELVERTON

- BUTLER, SUZANNE
- GREIG, A D
- HANAM-CHAZ, CHAZ
- HERIOT, LYNDA
- LONDON COLLEGE-HYPNOTHERAPY
- PEDEN, G J

# DORSET

## BEAMINSTER

- SWIFT, G B
- WHITE FLOWER CENTRE
- WRIGHT, TRACY

## BLANDFORD FORUM

- ADELAIDE CLINIC
- BLANDFORD OSTEOPATHY PRACTICE
- BRAY, STEPHEN
- CARMICHAEL, R
- CENTRE FOR COMP HEALTHCARE
- M C COPELAND-GRIFFITHS & AST
- PORTMAN LODGE
- SQUAREY, J V D
- WEST STREET OSTEO PRACTICE
- YOUNG, D

## BOURNEMOUTH

- ADAMS & YOUNG
- ADDRESS THE STRESS
- ALEXANDER TECHNIQUE
- ANGLO-EUROPEAN COLLEGE
- ANNEXE CLINIC
- ART OF REFLEXOLOGY
- AUSTIN HEALTH
- AVALON NATURAL HEALTH
- BAC, NULA L
- BEAUMONT COLLEGE OF NAT MED
- BECKETT, MICHAEL D
- BHMA
- BOSCOMBE MANOR MEDICAL CENTRE
- BOURNEMOUTH CHIRO & NTRL HLTH
- BOURNEMOUTH CTRE FOR COMP MED
- BOURNEMOUTH PHYSIO CLINIC
- BOURNEMOUTH THERAPY CLINIC
- BOWEN CLINIC
- BOWOOD HEALTH & BEAUTY CENTRE
- BUDD, M L
- BWT PHYSIOTHERAPY CENTRE
- CARBERY PRACTICE
- CHARMINSTER CHIRO CLINIC
- CHESHIRE, A R E
- CHINESE MEDICINE CENTRE
- CHINESE MEDICINE CLINIC
- CHIROPODY NHS
- CHIROPODY SERVICES
- CHIROPRACTIC CLINIC
- CHIROPRACTIC TREATMENT CENTRE
- CLARK, LYNN
- CLARKE, SAM
- CLINIC OF CHINESE MEDICINE
- COLLINWOOD, LOUIS
- COOK, S C HUDSON
- CROIX, E C DE SAINTE
- CULLING, ADRIAN
- CULLING, CHARMAINE
- CULPEPER
- CUNLIFFE PHARMACY
- DAMAN, WENDY
- DENGATE, L J
- DEPART-PSYCHOLOGICAL THERAPY
- DLP HYPNOTHERAPY CENTRE
- DREIFUSS, L & S
- EVANS, D A
- EVANS, REBECCA MARY
- EVERETT, PAUL
- FIELDER, R
- FURSDON, S V
- GIBSON, VERONICA
- GRAHAM, N
- HAMBLETT, JOHN E (DR)
- HAMPTON, ANNE
- HARDYMAN, D
- HARLING, MARIANNE (DR)
- HASELDEN, MAXINE
- HEALING CLINIC
- HEATH-RUMINSKA, PAULINE (DR)
- HEAVENLY SPIRIT CENTRE
- HEPWORTH, DAVID
- HOPKINS, H G
- HUISMAN, MARTINE
- I A H
- INSIGHT NATURAL HEALTH CENTRE
- JELFS, MARTIN
- JENKINS, RUSSELL
- KENNEDY, EDWARD
- KERRY, LIZ
- KINGS CLINIC
- LAW, DEREK T
- LEE, VICKY
- LEWIS-FRY, K E
- LOVELADY, B M
- LOWSON, H
- LUMINI POTENTIAL
- MADAM ROSINA
- MAHARISHI AYUR-VEDA HLTH CARE
- MINGUY, CHANTEL
- MOTT, DAVID
- NEIJIA
- NICHOLSON, ROSIE
- ONE STEP
- O'REILLY, A
- PARFITT, ALISTAIR H
- PARKER, RAY
- PARTNERSHIP, BAKER (DR)
- PAYNE, SUZANNE
- PERLMAN, M (DR)
- PESTER, ROSLYN
- PHYSIO, MASSAGE & PR ACU
- RAYNER, J D
- RAYNOR, JOHN
- RELAXAROMA
- SABATINI, A
- SACKETT, M B
- SAMUELS, L W
- SCHOLL CENTRE
- SCHWARZ, JANE
- SHALIMAR HEALING CENTRE
- SHEAD, JULIE
- SOUTHBOURNE HERBAL CLINIC
- SOUTHBOURNE NATURAL HLTH CTRE
- SWINN, J
- TAI CHI CHU'UAN
- TAYLOR, C
- THACKWAY, FRANCES
- THOMPSON, ANNE H
- TOBE, VICKI
- TREAT FEET
- UNICORN FAYRES
- WARD, DIANE
- WATTS, I
- WEBB, GILL
- WESSEX HEALTHY LIVING FOUND

- WHITE, D
- WHITE, RALPH E
- WILLIAMS, A
- WILLIAMS, H
- YELLOW HOUSE

## BRANKSOME

- CHIMES AROMATHERAPY

## BRIDPORT

- BRIDPORT COMP MEDICINE CTRE
- COOPER, ANTHONY
- DORWEST HERBS
- GIBBS, T
- GRIER, PHILIPPA
- ISAAC, EVELYN
- KING, M T
- MARSH, ANDREW
- PRICE, ELIZABETH
- REES, ROSEMARY
- RUSSELL, SUSAN
- SAGE, J
- VEARSOMBE, MOIRA
- VIRGINIA COTTAGE
- WILLIAMS, SAM
- WILLIAMS, TIMOTHY
- WRIGHT, KAREN
- ZERO BALANCING ASSOCIATION

## BROADSTONE

- BLACKBURN, OLIVE
- BROADSTONE CENTRE OF COMP MED
- LINDLEY, E A
- MCLAUGHLIN, SANDRA
- SCOTT, VIVIENNE

## CHRISTCHURCH

- B M R THERAPY
- BARLOW, MADELEINE
- BIDWELL, L H
- BRIGHTER FUTURE
- CHRISTCHURCH CHIROPRACTIC CTRE
- CHRISTCHURCH PHYSIO PRACTICE
- CLARKE, J A
- DIRLIK-MERCY
- DRAPER, DEREK
- EASY WAY TO STOP SMOKING
- GROVES, P A
- GURRY, N J
- HERBALIST, GODSHAER
- HIGHCLIFFE CHIROPRACTIC CLINIC
- HIGHCLIFFE CHIROPRACTIC CLINIC
- HIGHCLIFFE OSTEOPATHIC CLINIC
- HOSGOOD, LYNN
- JOLLIFFEE, PAM
- KEATES, BECKY
- LOFT SUITE
- LOWDE, JANIE
- LYNDEN SCHOOL OF REFLEXOLOGY
- PHILLIPS, L
- STAPLEY, J
- STARKS, M H
- SYKES, LIZZIE
- TRUNDELL, C

## DORCHESTER

- ALEXANDER TECHNIQUE
- BARSKY, S & HAWKINS, R W
- BELTAIN CENTRE
- BELTAIN CENTRE
- CASTERBRIDGE CHIROPRACTIC
- COLLITON WALK PSYCHO SVS
- FLAVELL, MARGARET
- HILL, SUSAN CLAIRE
- JENKINSON, CLIFF
- KARUNA CENTRE
- LOCK, ROBERT
- LOW, LORNA
- MARCH-SMITH, ROSIE
- MIDDLEMARSH CLINIC
- NAPPER, WENDY
- RICHARDSON, ELAINE
- SHARP & ASSOCIATES
- SKILLING, GRAHAN
- STANDISH-HAYES, QUENTIN
- TOTTLE, G
- WOODINGTON, N J

## FERNDOWN

- BROWN, A D
- CHIROPRACTIC CLINIC
- FERNDOWN ACUPUNCTURE CLINIC
- FERNDOWN CHIROPRACTIC CLINIC
- FERNDOWN PHYSIOTHERAPY CLINIC
- FINDLAY, MARIE-ANNE
- FULL SPECTRUM THERAPY CENTRE
- KNIGHT, ANNA
- MACFARLANE, T D
- MENEZES, A
- WESLEY, D E
- WEST MOORS CHIROPRACTIC CLINIC

## GILLINGHAM

- DAVIDSON, MICHAEL S
- GILLIBRAND, M
- GILLINGHAM CHIROPRACTIC CLINIC
- HARGREAVES, ALISON
- PARSONS, JOHN
- PHYSIOTHERAPY CENTRE

## ISLE OF PORTLAND

- FREESPIRIT
- GODFREY, BRIAN

## LYME REGIS

- AVATARA
- GREENWAY, ROSEMARY J
- REYNOLDS, C
- WALTERS, RICHARD
- WILLIAMS, TIM

## POOLE

- ADAMS SMOKERS/SLIMMERS CLINIC
- ARIES OSTEOPATHIC HEALTH CLNC
- ARNDALE CHIROPRACTIC
- ASHBY, CAROLINE
- BACK IN FORM
- BARNES, J
- BARNS, MICHAEL
- BATE, J M
- BAZALGETTE, R A
- BEECH, STEVEN
- BOURNE, VIV
- BOURNEMOUTH & POOLE PRACTICE
- BOYLE, MICHAEL
- BROADSTONE CENTRE COMP MED
- BWT PODIATRY
- CAMPBELL ALLERGY TESTING
- CARR-JONES, MICHAEL
- CHIMES THERAPY CENTRE
- CHINESE MEDICAL CENTRE
- CHIROPODY
- CHIU, ANGELA
- DECHOW, DELAINE
- DONOVAN, J A
- DORSET RACQUETS & HEALTH CLUB
- EDMONDSON, MICHAEL
- EDWARDS, BRIAN
- FEET FIRST
- GALLACHER, J
- GOLDIE, RICHARD
- GRIER, A R
- HARMONY
- HAYWARD, JANET
- HEALING HANDS
- HOMEOPATHY HEALS
- HOPLEY, CHRISTINE
- INSTITUTE OF BIO-ENERGETIC MED
- IRVINE, PHILLIPA
- KENDRICK, DIANE
- KIPPING, NICOLA
- LIVINGSTON, RONALD (DR)
- LOVITT, ANGELA
- LOWDE, JANIE
- LYMINGTON PLATING
- MASON, YVONNE
- NATURAL HEALTH CONSULTANCY
- NOBLE, SUE
- OLIVER, EDWARD
- OWEN, D K
- PAOLUCCI, ANNA
- PHILLIPS, JOAN
- PHYSIC SUPPER CLUB
- RENDELL, MARCIA
- RHYS, BILL
- ROBSON, VANESSA
- SKINNER, NICOLA
- SOUTHWARD, P
- STEELE, T M
- SUN, R
- THOMPSON, JANE
- THORNTONS PHARMACY
- TODD, DEBBIE
- WARTNABY, MARY
- WETHERALL, P
- WHITTINGTON, LIZ
- WHYKE, LINDA
- WORDEN, JENNY

## SHAFTESBURY

- ABBEY VIEW COMP CLINIC
- ACU ASS OF CHRTRD PHYSIO
- AWDRY, ROBERT
- BROOM, DAVID
- DOUGLAS, ERICA
- FROST, LESLEY
- KENNEDY, SARAH
- MILLBANK, SALLY-ANN
- MOTCOMBE PARK PHYSIOTHERAPY
- PORTEOUS, TRISH
- SCHREIBER, ANNE
- SKELTON, JAN
- SMART, JULIE
- STADLER, M L
- STEVEN, PATRICIA
- TRINITY OSTEOPATHIC PRACTICE
- YOUNG, D
- YOUNG, D

## SHERBORNE

- ARCHIBALD, LIZ
- BLACK, G
- BROOKS, ANN
- DAVIES, VIVIEN
- GAELEN
- GLENCAIRE CLINIC
- GLENCAIRN HOUSE
- JEANS, SIMON N
- MIDDLES PICCADILLY CTRE
- PRIDEAUX-BRUNE, COLETTE
- REDFERN, JANE
- REFERRAL CENTRE
- RHODES, GEORGINA
- RHODES, GEORGINA
- SHEBORNE CHIROPRACTIC CENTRE

## STURMINSTER NEWTON

- GREEN, T
- HARRIS, G & J
- ROLLS MILL COMP HEALTH CENTRE
- VINING, E H
- YOUNG, ANGELA

## SWANAGE

- ACUPUNCTURE CLINIC
- BRANDWOOD-CORMACK, HAYLEY
- HEALTH MAIL

## THE QUAY

- WESSEX KINESIOLOGY CENTRE

## VERWOOD

- BLAKE, A
- BLORE, ANNE
- COMMUNITY CHIROPRACTIC CLINIC
- COX, LESLEY
- ELLIS, J
- NATURAL THRPY CLNC/TRNING CTRE
- NELMES CHIROPRACTIC CLINIC
- ROY, COLLEEN

## WAREHAM

- BURT, S
- HOLISTIC HEALTH CENTRE
- JOHARI, ULLA
- LEVER, IAN J
- PEARCE, V
- ROWE, PENNY
- ROWE, PENNY
- TAYLOR, MELANIE
- YOUNG, A

## WEYMOUTH

- AWARENESS CENTRE
- BARSKY, S
- BRADEN, WENDY
- BRANCH, SUE
- CUMMINGS, ALISON
- DAUNCEY, CLARE M
- ELWIN, E J
- HANSSON CHIROPRACTIC CENTRE
- HARRISON, MANUELLA

- HASKETT, CHRISTINE
- HAWKINS, R W
- HILL, P
- HOPKINS, ALAN
- JACKSON, A E
- JUBILEE COMP THERAPY CENTRE
- LEE, MAUREEN
- LEVER, I J
- NEALE, ALISON
- PROSPECT HEALTH
- TALBOT, MICHAEL
- VACUFLEX REFLEXOLOGY SYSTEM
- WEYMOUTH CHIROPRACTIC CLINIC
- X-VEE ONE ELEVEN
- YATES, MICHAEL

### WIMBORNE

- ALTERNATIVE APPROACH
- AROMA TRANQUILITY
- BACK IN BALANCE
- BRANDON, DAVE
- BRIGHTER FUTURE
- BROWN, AMANDA
- HOOPER, HELEN
- HORNE, SUE
- LAWRENCE, MICHAEL W
- MELHUISH, J I
- NATURAL THERAPY CENTRE
- PRIDMORE, JOSEPHINE
- TURNER, HAZEL
- WEAVER, SARAH
- WEST, DENISE
- WIMBORNE CHIROPODY SURGERY
- WIMBORNE HERBAL CLINIC
- WIMBORNE MINSTER PHYSIO

## EALING

- EALING BOWEN CLINIC

## ESSEX

### BARDFIELD SALING

- JAMES, DEE

### BARKING

- BARKING PHYSICAL THERAPY CTRE
- FAIRCROSS COMP MEDICAL CLINIC
- FIELD-COULING, KIM
- FITZ-HENRY, THOMAS J
- HERBMEDIC
- HOWLEY & FIELD
- NATURAL BODY TREATMENTS
- NATURAL REMEDY CENTRE
- SARA NADAF TRICHOLOGIST
- WHITE WATER HEALING CENTRE

### BASILDON

- BASILDON CHIROPRACTIC CLINIC
- BIOTHERAPY
- BLAND, C R
- COKER, EILEEN
- CROFT, LESLEY
- HENRY, JOANNE
- HERBAL INN
- HERBAL INN
- HUBBLE CLINIC OF OSTEO & ACU
- KARADIA, V
- KELLY, L
- LEAHY, TONY
- NATURE CARE CLINIC
- NATURE CARE COLLEGE
- PATEL, SUSHILA
- SKILTON, GINA
- SMITH, LESLEY
- STROUD, GRAEME

### BENFLEET

- AARON HYPNOTHERAPY SERVICES
- BENFLEET PHYSIOTHERAPY
- BENFLEET THERAPIES
- CASTLE POINT PHYSIO CLINIC
- CHASE HYPNOTHERAPY
- DHANABALAN, K
- FROST, JANICE
- HADLEIGH PODIATRY CLINIC
- JAYNE & PAYNE
- JOHN, S U
- KUMARESAN, S
- NATURAL HEALTH THERAPY
- SALISBURY, D G
- STABLEFORD, JOYCE

### BILLERICAY

- ALEXANDER, F & JAYNE, V
- ANN'S MIGRAINE DIETARY PLAN
- BE-WELL CLINIC
- BILLERICAY PHYSIO & SPORTS
- BURVILL, J A
- CUMMING, BETTE
- HOMEOPATH AND NAT THERAPIST
- LIVING HEALTHILY
- MILLS, ANDREW D
- MITCHELL, VICTORIA
- NIKKEN INDEPENDENT DISTRIBUTOR
- TOMEY PHYSIO & SPORTS CLINIC
- WALK CHIROPODIST

### BRAINTREE

- BEARD, HELEN
- BENEDICTA
- BRAINTREE CHIROPRACTIC CENTRE
- BRUMMITT, V A
- CARTER-WEBER, LEE
- CHAKRA ROSE
- COOK, JOE
- CROWN CHIROPRACTIC CLINIC
- D HEALY IND FINANCIAL ADV
- DAVIS, S
- DICKASON, J T
- HARDY, L M
- HUNT, PATRICIA
- INDIGO BAY AROMATHERAPY
- MORTIMER, VICTORIA
- SELVES, KATIE
- SHOULDERS, A
- WENTWORTH HEALTH CLINIC
- ZULEWSKI, STEFAN

### BRENTWOOD

- ARYAEENIA, LINDA M
- ASHBY & ASSOCIATES
- BACKS TO BASIC
- BAILEY, DEREK
- BANKS, DENISE
- BANNISTER, PETER
- BARTLETT, GODFREY
- BRANDLER, H
- BRENTWOOD CHIROPODY SURGERY
- BRENTWOOD CHIROPRACTIC CLINIC
- BRENTWOOD HYPNO/PSYCHOTHERAPY
- BRENTWOOD HYPNOTHERAPY
- BUTEYKO BREATHING CLINIC
- CONYERS, MIKE
- CROWN CHIROPRACTIC CLINIC
- DAVIS, MELANIE
- ENCOMPASS THERAPIES
- ESSENTIALLY GREEN
- ESSEX COUNS/PSYCHOTHERAPY SV
- GRAY, P A
- HARMONY
- HELM, HEATHER
- HERBAL AUTHORITY
- JOYNES, IAN
- JUDD, J R
- KELLY, GILLIAN
- LEMMON, LINDA
- MAYFIELD ACUPUNCTURE CLINIC
- MOONSTONE HEALING CENTRE
- MURRAY, ANN
- PYNE, MICHELE
- RIVENDELL CENTRE
- ROBINSON, T
- SCOTT, MARY
- SEYMOUR, LOUISE
- SHENFIELD ACUPUNCTURE CENTRE
- SHENFIELD HEALTH CLINIC
- SPARLING & ASSOCIATES
- TOFTS, E

### BUCKHURST HILL

- BUCKHURST HILL HEALTH PRACTICE
- CARR, J M
- GILLINGS, SONIA
- HERFT, PATRICIA
- HOWARD, L
- JOHNSON, MARCIA
- R L A
- SHARE, J L
- STEVENSON & ASSOCIATES

### BURNHAM-ON-CROUCH

- BURNHAM PHYSIOTHERAPY CLINIC
- ELPHINSTONE, D C R
- LYNDA CROFT REIKI MASTER

### CANVEY ISLAND

- AROMER
- BROOK NATURAL HEALTH CENTRE
- FULTON, A J
- HARMONY HYPNOTHERAPY CTRE
- MURDOCH, R J
- SWIFT, BRIAN

### CHELMSFORD

- ADAMS, NEIL
- AJW CLEMENS OSTEOPATHIC CLINIC
- BEENEY, CHERYL
- BREINBURG, DERYCK
- BROOKS, BERNARD
- CAIN, SHEILA
- CHELMSFORD CHIROPRACTIC CLINIC
- CHINESE HERBAL & MEDICAL CTRE
- CHINESE MEDICINE CLINIC
- CHRIS MOSLIN HYPNOTHERAPIST
- COMPLETE CHIROPRACTIC
- COOPER, M L
- CROFT, DAVID
- DOOLAN, M F
- DUNCOMBE, MARTIN
- EBRAHIMI, SOROUSH
- EFFLEURAGE
- ELDEN, GAYE
- ESSEX FENG SHUI
- ESSEX NATURAL HEALTH CENTRE
- ESSEX PHYSIO & SPORTS INJ CTRE
- FAIRHEAD, RICHARD
- FEWELL, FRANCES
- FOWKES, SUSIE
- GARLICK, STUART
- GENT, WENDY
- GRAY, P A
- GUNNING, ROSALIND
- HALE, B E C (DR)
- HART, P T
- HAWKRIDGE, FRANCOISE
- HOWIE, MARION
- HUGHES, J HACKER
- HUXTER, CHRISTINE
- HYPNOTHERAPY & PSYCHO CONS
- JONES, JEAN
- JONES, KELLIE
- JONES, KELLIE A
- KANUTIN, A
- KENDRICK, MARGARET
- KNIGHT, E
- LEVY, PAUL
- LOVELL, PETER
- MALONEY, M P
- MAY, SUSAN
- MOORE, SUSAN
- NIEHORSTER, R
- OLIVELLE, JOSEPH
- RIVETT, DOREEN
- RUSSELL, GILLIAN
- SERVICE, G
- SHAPLAND, ANDREW
- TACHAUER, JACQULINE
- TAYLOR, HEATHER
- WAKNELL, PETER
- WAYNE-WRIGHT, M S
- WELLS HYPNOTHERAPY CLINIC
- WETHERALL, STUART
- WHITE, SARAH
- WICKINS, ANN
- WILBY, MARY ANN

### CHIGWELL

- BARNETT, SUE
- CHIGWELL HOLISTIC CLINIC
- COWELL, IAN
- GRANGE HYPNOTHERAPY
- KIRKPATRICK, IAN
- SMITH, COLIN

### CLACTON-ON-SEA

- ABBEY, AMANDA
- ADAMSON, ANGELICA
- ALLAN, A
- ARIORI, A R & B M
- ASH, ANNIE
- AVALON HEALTH & THERAPY CENTRE
- BEDFORD, PAULINE

- BEVIS, STUART
- CLACTON CHIROPRACTIC CLINIC
- CLACTON REFLEX & THERAPY CTRE
- FLOATATION RETREAT
- GOOCH, K W
- GRAHAM, V
- LA-SANTE AROMATHERAPY
- LOCK, M J
- MAGNUS, CHRIS
- MARTIN, LEIGH
- NORRIS, T
- NUNN, BARBARA
- ROBINSON, LINDSEY A
- ROSE, A C
- THERAPEUTIC MASSAGE
- TOMLIN, P H
- TRAYNOR, SUSAN
- TULLEY, B
- WIDLAKE, N R

## COLCHESTER

- ARIORI, A R
- BARRYMORE, MIKE
- BATEMAN, R A (DR)
- BROOKS, HELEN
- BRYSON & ASSOCIATES
- BYRNE, ALISON
- CARVER-HARDY, LOUISE
- CHALKLIN, J
- CHARTERS, EUNICE
- CHESTER, MARTIN
- CLARKE, M R
- CLARKE, ROSALEEN
- CLINICAL PSYCHOLOGY SERVICE
- COACH HOUSE
- COLCHESTER CHIROPRACTIC CENTRE
- COLCHESTER OSTEOPATHIC CENTRE
- COOPER, JEFFREY C
- EGNER, JULIE
- ELLIOTT, N S & ROYFFE, G B
- FARRANT, K E
- FARROW, VICKI
- FLEUROMA
- FLEURY, DENISE
- GAMBLE, ADRIAN P
- GARROD, I T (DR)
- GLADWIN, DENIS
- GOSLING, IMOGEN
- HARMONY HEALING CENTRE
- HEAD, BERYL
- HEAD, BERYL
- HERBAL INN
- HODGSON, PATRICIA
- HOLBEN, JENNY
- HUNT, A M
- HYETT, SUE
- HYPNOTHERAPY CENTRE
- HYPNOTHERAPY CENTRE
- JENKINS, E A
- KEMP, R
- KING, ANDREA
- LAING, RICHARD
- LAING, RICHARD (DR)
- LAST, CHRISTINE
- LINSTEAD, J
- LOVELL, JENNY
- MARKS TEY HEALTH CENTRE
- MCDOWALL, SANDRA
- MCMILLAN, D
- METSON, R K
- MILLER, P J (DR)
- MILLINGTON, P
- MOGENSEN, C
- MOGENSEN, K
- MONK, MICHAEL
- MORGAN, GILLIAN
- MOSS, RACHAEL
- MULLER, GLYNIS
- NAPIERS HERBS
- NATURE CURES
- NEW POSSIBILITIES NHS TRUST
- NUGENT, L C
- O'PRESCO, MARGARET
- OSMAN, BRIAN
- PAIN, SALLY
- PALMIST
- PAYNE, MICHAEL
- PETERS, KAREN
- PHYSIO & SPORTS INJURY CLINIC
- PINEWOOD PHYSIOTHERAPY CLINIC
- POWNALL & ASSOCIATES
- REID, MEG
- ROBINSON, DAVID
- ROOTS, WENDY
- SALMON, MARGARET
- SCHOLL FOOTCARE CENTRE
- SPICE DIRECT
- SPIRIT HEALTH & FITNESS
- SRI AMMAN CLINIC
- STOCKWELL CENTRE
- STONEBRIDGE, A H
- SUMMERS, S J
- TRADITIONAL CHINESE MEDICINE
- TRINITY CENTRE
- TUNE, DAVID
- WALLS, ANNE
- WARBOYS, R E
- WEHMEYER, CATHERINE
- WILSON, VERONICA
- WIVENHOE DENTAL PRACTICE
- WORK WITH ME
- WORTHINGTON, MICHAEL

## DAGENHAM

- ABBOTT, LISA
- ACUPUNCTURE
- BANNISTER, PETER J
- BEACONTREE HYPNOTHERAPY
- BECONTREE NHS THERAPY
- DALY, ROWENA
- ELECTROLYSIS CLINIC
- HOLLANDS, K M
- LUCKOCK, M
- PAT, ELLIOTT
- RAM, J
- SCLAIRE, B L

## DANBURY

- DANBURY CLINIC

## DUNMOW

- CULVERHOUSE, DAVID
- DUNMOW PHYSIOTHERAPY SERVICE
- GIBSON, E M
- GRIFFITHS, JOANNE
- KENTON, JEREMY
- LANG, GLORIA
- LINDY, DAVID
- MALOY, ALISON
- MALOY, ALISON
- ROGERS, ALISON

## EPPING

- BULLER, JEMIMA
- CARLISLE, L
- CARLISLE, L
- CURZON, A
- EPPING OSTEOPATHY AND SPORTS
- EPPING PHYSIOTHERAPY PRACTICE
- HOLISTIC WAY
- LAL, VALERIE
- NEWTON, PAULINE
- ROTHERAY, MERYL J
- SHELLEY MEDIUM & MIRROROLOGY
- UNDERWOOD CLINICS CHIROPRACTIC

## FRINTON-ON-SEA

- ANDERSON, GORDON
- BARBER, TOM
- BARBER, TOM
- BARNES, T V
- COOK, S H W
- FUN, MAE
- MILLINGTON, P

## GRAYS

- ADVANCED HYPNOTHERAPY
- BEAUTY ROOM
- BIRD, DAPHNE
- BLUNDELL, STEPHEN
- CORBY, VERONICA
- GRAYS CHIROPRACTIC CLINIC
- GYASI, A
- HALPIN, P J
- MCMAHON, ROSEMARY
- MEDELY CLINIC
- O'DONNELL, ANGELA
- PRIVATE MEDICAL ACUPUNCTURE
- QUIT SMOKING CENTRE
- ROSE, ADELE
- SIMMONDS, JENNI
- STILL, PETER
- TOOMS DEBORAH CHIROPODIST
- WISHART, M A

## HADLEIGH

- BIDMEAD, MARGARET

## HALSTEAD

- BREUKEL, CORINA
- CARPENTER
- EAST OF EDEN
- GREEN LODGE CENTRE
- HUBBARD, NIK
- SWALLOW, FRED

## HARLOW

- BRIGGS, MARGARETE
- BRITISH SCHOOL OF REFLEXOLOGY
- BRUCE, A
- BRUCE, F N
- CHAIR MASSAGE
- CHINESE HERBAL MEDICAL CENTRE
- CHINESE HERBAL MEDICINE
- CHINESE MEDICINE TECH DEVPT
- COOPER, FELICITY
- CRANE SCHOOL OF REFLEXOLOGY
- CULLETON, L
- DAVIDGE, AMANDA
- DE VERE, SUSAN
- GAWLINSKA, CATHERINE
- HARLOW OSTEOPATHIC PRACTICE
- LESLEY WEIGHT MOBILE THERAPIST
- LOMOND, MARSHA
- MORTIMER, GERALDINE
- PRIDDLE, M
- PRIDDLE, P
- RAINEY, C
- SAVAGE, ROGER

## HARWICH

- JILLINS, BOB
- MACINNES, BERYL
- NEWLIFE, A
- NIGHTINGALE, JOANNA
- PAYNE, MICHAEL
- RAYMER, RUTH
- SMALL, LORNA

## HOCKLEY

- BIRD, D
- EMERY, CHRISTINE
- JUNIPER BERRY
- MILLS, K

## HORNCHURCH

- ACTESON, JENNY
- APPLEBEE THERAPY
- BAGLEY, ELIZABETH
- BAXTER, LISA
- BEBER, SHEILA E
- BENRENE HEALTH INTERNATIONAL
- BURNHAM, EMMA-JANE
- CAROL'S TWILIGHT ZONE
- CHAPMAN, ALAN
- CHINESE & MEDICINE CENTRE
- CLARK, BRIAN
- DIXON, RUTH
- FERRIS, JANET
- FLORASSENTIALS
- FULTON, A J
- GARDNER, MARIE
- GRUMBALL, J D
- HANSFORD & KAY
- HAZELS PSYCHIC ADVISORY CENTRE
- HEALTH SHOP & HOMOEOPATHIC
- NATCARE MEDICINE CENTRE
- REFLEXOLOGY CLINIC
- SMITH, EILEEN
- STRONG, MRS
- VISIONS & DREAMS
- WRIGHT, SEAN

## ILFORD

- ABBOT, LISA
- ACCELERATED LEARNING
- ADAIR, JAYNE
- ADATIA, K H (DR)
- AERON, A
- AROMATHERAPY CLINIC
- BERNSTEIN, S

- BLAKE, D
- BOURNE, STACEY
- BRADLEY, HAZEL
- CATON, PETER
- CHINESE MEDICINE TECH DEVPT
- CLAYTON, DEBRA
- COLE, JULIETTE
- COOMBS & COOMBS
- CROWDER, C H J
- CURTIS, PETER
- CZERKAWSKI, MARK
- EDEN, SHARON
- FELDMAN, L H
- FELDMAN, L H
- FELFELLI, FARA
- FOULKES, GEOFFREY LLOYD
- FREEDMAN, M
- FRIEND, JONATHAN
- FROST, JEREMY
- FRY, MARGARET
- HEALING & HYPNOTHERAPY CENTRE
- HEALTH & HARMONY
- HEATHER, LUCKY
- HENNEM, M E A
- HOLISTIC HEALTH CLINIC
- INDIRA
- INTUITION PSYCHIC CENTRE
- JACOBS, FREDERICK
- JULIEN, M
- KUMAR, NIRDOSH
- LEDDY, GILLIAN
- LING, E
- LOTERY, FRANCOISE
- MALHOTRA, A K
- MOSS, GRAEME
- MUNCEY, J
- MURRAY, KAREN
- NURSE, SUE
- PARVEZ, SHAUKAT
- PEARCE, L
- PEPPER, SUSAN
- PHYSIO & ACUPUNCTURIST CENTRE
- PHYSIO & SPORTS INJURY CENTRE
- PHYSIOTHERAPY CLINIC
- PLATT, JOHN
- PREMAL SHAH
- RAJA YOGA MEDITATION
- RAPHAEL, L G
- REDBRIDGE HEALING CENTRE
- ROSE, LESLEY
- RUDDOLPH, FRANK
- RYCHMOND, R
- SAVLA, N (DR)
- SCHIFFMAN, A
- SCHIFFMAN, ALAN
- SCHOLL CENTRE
- SHAW, A D
- SHAW, JONATHAN
- SHELDON, PEGGY
- SOOD, P (DR)
- SPENCE, M
- SPIVACK, A
- STRAUB, DESMOND
- THACKER, VRINDA
- THOMAS, K I
- THOMPSON, A
- THOMPSON, GRAHAM
- THOMPSON, KEN
- YEZHANG, MISS
- YIN YANG CHINESE MEDICAL CTRE

## INGATESTONE

- POWELL, JEANNE
- REDDEN, REBECCA
- SABINE, P M
- SWAINE, A J
- WATSON, IRENE

## LEIGH-ON-SEA

- A C H COMPLEMENTARY
- ACKLAND, J
- ARC HEALTHCARE
- BERNARD, ELAINE
- BLACK, CATHY
- BRITISH INSTITUTE-HYPNOTHERAPY
- CALMING EFFECTS
- CARNELIAN NTRL TREATMENT CTRE
- CLAYTON, SUSAN
- COUSENS, BRENDA
- DODDS, S C
- FOREST COMPLEMENTARY CLINIC
- GUNGADIN, G
- HAMILTON, CYNTHIA
- HAYES PHYSIOTHERAPY CLINIC
- HERB GARDEN
- HIGH SPIRITS
- HUNT, C
- JOHNSTON, NORA
- KEETCH, KIT
- LEIGH SANCTUARY
- LINN, PAMELA
- LOVETT, PAULINE
- MERRYFIELD, C
- MURDOCH, R J
- NATURA
- OAKLEY, STEVEN
- PALMER, DAVID J
- PSYCHOLOGICAL/THERAPEUTIC CONS
- SLATER, HUGH
- VINTEN, J E
- WADDINGTON, R M
- WATTS, TERENCE
- WISEMAN, SANDRA
- WOODSIDE NATURAL HEALTH

## LOUGHTON

- BELLO, L A
- CADWALLADER, PENNY
- CARLISLE, L
- FOOTSTEPS
- GALE CENTRE
- HEWITT P & RUSHTON J
- PERRY, JEAN
- PHYSIO & MANIPULATION CLINIC
- PHYSIOTHERAPY CENTRE
- PRIEST, ROSIE
- PRIVATE ACUPUNCTURE CLINIC
- PRIVATE HEALTH CENTRE CLINIC
- PRIVATE POLYCLINIC
- S HECQUER PRACTICE
- SHAW, JONATHAN
- SILVER, J
- SUE
- VALERA, A B

## MALDON

- COOK, SUE
- ELDRETT, RACHAEL
- JACALAN ESSENTIAL OILS
- LEALAN, HEATHER
- LEVY, PAUL
- MALDON ACUPUNCTURE & HOM
- MALDON HOMOEOPATHIC CLINIC
- MALDON HYPNOTHERAPY CLINIC
- MALONEY, M
- MELLOR, SARA L
- POWNALL & ASSOCIATES
- REEVE, ANNE
- ROESAAS CHIROPODY
- SAXBY, W
- SELF AWARENESS HEALING
- WILLSON, GILLIAN

## MANNINGTREE

- HAMPTON, E M
- NORMAN, ANNE
- PIPER, MARK W
- WHEATMAN, G H P

## OLD HARLOW

- COOPER, FELICITY

## ONGAR

- GRISHKOV, AMANDA
- HAY, PATRICIA

## PURFLEET

- MOONBEAMS

## RAYLEIGH

- ASSAD RAISSI
- BEVAN, K J
- E A O C
- EDEN, FRANCES
- EDWARDS, G E
- FLIGHT, J
- KENT, JOAN
- KINGSLEIGH CLINIC
- KULKARNI, P S
- OTHEN, FIONA
- REYNOLDS, PAULA
- SHRIMPLIN, BRIAN
- SMITH, LYNDSAY
- WELFORD, MARTIN
- WHEELER, M A

## ROCHFORD

- ATKINSON, PEARL
- BLUE PERSON
- HEALING ROOM
- OWEN, RACHEL
- UNIVERSAL PROMOTIONS
- WHEELER, M A

## ROMFORD

- ABACUS THERAPY CENTRE
- ACCELERATED CHANGE CENTRE
- AEQUILIBRIUM
- APPLEBY LEIGH AROMATHERAPIST
- BALGORES SQUARE THERAPY CTRE
- BARUCH, LEONARD A
- BENRENE HEALTH INTERNATIONAL
- BODY BALANCE
- BODY BALANCE HEALTH SOLUTIONS
- BRANDON, LEON
- BULL, J
- CHIROPRACTIC CLINIC
- DAVID CECIL SURGICAL CHIROPODY
- DOVE, COLIN
- EARTH GARDEN
- FORD, AUDREY
- HADLEY, SUSAN
- HEALTH KINESIOLOGY
- HOLLANDS, P R
- HONEY, S L
- HORMASJI, A & F
- HOWTONE, CHRISTINA
- JOYCE, PHILIP
- K L WRIGHT CHIROPODY SERVICES
- LAMPARD, J L
- LAUDER, STEVE
- LAYLAND, ROSALIND
- LEIGH, MARTIN
- MATTHEWS, DIANE
- MCFADYEN, J
- MILES, C J
- MOORE, DENIS
- NOYS, ALISON
- PARDOE, L
- PATEL, ANITA M
- PISCES NATURAL THERAPY CENTRE
- PREMIER PHYSIOTHERAPY CENTRE
- SNOWLING, WENDY
- VICTORIA CENTRE
- WOOD, CAROLINE
- WOODS, JILL
- WOODS, JILL

## SAFFRON WALDEN

- ANDERSON, LINDA
- AUDLEY END PHYSIO CLINIC
- DIANA'S JOY
- FANE, AMANDA
- FOOT HEALTH CLINIC
- FREE, HUGH
- JOHNSTON, J M
- KESTREL
- KESTREL
- MOUCHET, F
- PHILIP, HELEN
- RUMSEY, S
- SAFFRON OILS
- SAVAGE, ROGER
- SMITH, LORRETTA W

## SOUTH OCKENDON

- RIDER, J
- SQUIRES, J

## SOUTHEND-ON-SEA

- A C T CLINIC
- ANGALEE'S
- ARNETT, J I
- BAKER, ANN
- CENTRAL CHIROPRACTIC CLINIC
- DR & HERBS
- EDWARDS, G E
- ELMER CHIROPODY & PODIATRY SVS
- ENRIGHT, VALERIE
- FEET FIRST
- FYFE, M J
- GADD, K
- GURNEY, SHARON

- HALLIDAY, K J
- HALSTEAD, RITA
- HONEYZ
- HORWOOD, MARIE
- JADE HEALTH & BEAUTY
- KENTES PHYSIOTHERAPY CLINIC
- LARHOLT, A
- LATTIMER SPORTS INJURIES
- LEVENE & ASSOCIATES
- MANOR GROVE CLINIC
- MOORE, LEONARD J
- ORGANISATION-CHARTERED PHYSIO
- PAIN RELIEF THERAPIST
- PALMER, LUCILLE
- PENN, J T
- PITHER, ANNE
- PRIORY PRACTICE
- REID, R H
- REIKI MASTER & HEALER
- STEVENS, JOY P
- TRINH H V
- VICTORIA COUNSELLING SERVICE
- VOIGHTS, M F
- WARRINGTON, MARY
- WHITE, SUSAN
- WOODLEY, ANDREW

### SOUTHMINSTER

- BARNES, M

### STANFORD-LE-HOPE

- BRADY, MAUREEN
- FROSTICK, DAVID
- LINGWOOD CLINIC
- PERRY, JEAN
- PETTIT, M J
- SANDERS, G
- SUSAN JONES HOLISTIC PRACT

### STANSTED

- BONDY, PIPPA
- DICK, K
- NOLAN, CLAIRE
- SHEAF, JACOLIN
- SMITH, GILLIAN

### STEEPLE BUMPSTEAD

- CROFT, JOANNA

### TILBURY

- APPLEDORE CENTRE
- GRAYSTON, SUE
- STILL, PETER

### UPMINSTER

- ALLSHORN, SUSAN
- BARDEN, JOANNE
- BRAND, R
- CARGILL, APRIL
- CHAPMAN, JANE
- ENNEVER, M
- FINN, JANE
- GUTTERIDGE, L
- HARPER, CHERYL
- JONES, BARBARA A
- KOTEN, SUSAN
- MASSEY, JULIA
- MATHARU, M K
- SHIPP, MARION

### WALTHAM ABBEY

- BARRETT, JACQUELINE
- BEAUTY BOX THE BEAUTY SALON
- BRUCE, NEIL
- CONNOR, L K J
- ISIS HOUSE THERAPY CENTRE
- MILLER, SUE
- SIMISTER, KAREN

### WALTON ON THE NAZE

- FRINTON PHYSIOTHERAPY CLINIC

### WESTBOURNE

- GRAY, S

### WESTCLIFF-ON-SEA

- ANCHORAGE ANALYSIS
- ANNANDALE CLINIC
- BIRD, G F
- CHINESE HERBAL MEDICAL CENTRE
- CLAIRVOYANT
- CUTTING, MELANIE
- DI-MARI REFLEXOLOGY CLINIC
- ESSENCE OF NATURE
- FRESH HORIZONS
- GILLETT, PHILIP
- HARDY, DIANE
- HAWKINS, SUZI
- HERB LEE
- JACKSON, CYRIL
- KANUTIN, ANTHONY
- KYRIAKOS, GEORGE
- LAMBOURN COURT INTERNATIONAL
- LANG, GILL
- LEVENE & ASSOCIATES
- MASTERS, LEE
- MASTERS, PAUL
- MOORE, CHRIS
- PHARMACARE
- SOOMRO, ARIF
- TAYLOR, JOHN
- WATERS, FRANK
- WITCHELL, YVONNE

### WICKFORD

- ASHELFORD, J L
- AVART, GILLIAN
- ESSEX OSTEOPATHIC CLINICS
- GULLIFORD, A W R
- JOHNSON, BERNADETTE
- LONDON ROAD PHYSIO PRACTICE
- MICKELBOROUGH, ESTELLE
- MORRIS, J K
- PRICE, G J
- REDWOOD, SARAH
- WARREN, E W (DR)
- WICKFORD PHYSIOTHERAPY CLINIC

### WITHAM

- A M R THERAPIES
- ASS OF NATURAL MEDICINES
- CROSS HANDS CHIRO CLINIC
- CROSS, J D
- GRAHAM, R B
- HUGHES, M A
- HUNTSMAN, NATALIE
- JARVIS, PETER
- NATURAL HEALING CENTRE
- NEWMAN, SOGRA
- QUALITY ANALYSIS
- ROBINSON, K
- WUYTS, ANTHONY

### WIVENHOE

- SOUTH, JO

### WOODFORD GREEN

- AJW CLEMENS OSTEOPATHIC CLINIC
- ASSOCIATION OF OSTEOMYOLOGY
- BRIDGE TO HEALTH
- EDEN DREAM
- ELAINE ATKINS ASSOCIATES
- HEYWOODS
- HINTON, IAN
- INSTITUTE OF PAST LIFE
- KURANCHIE, CLAUDETTE
- MOLLOY, PAULINE
- NASTRUCCI, SUSAN
- OCCUPATION/PERSONALITY TESTING
- O'MAHONY, JERRY
- PALK, RICHARD
- PHYSIOTHERAPY CLINIC
- ROBERTS, R N
- WELLINGS, INGA

## GLASGOW (CITY OF)

### GLASGOW

- TAI CHI UNION FOR GB

## GLOUCESTERSHIRE

### BRADLEY STOKE

- POXON, ANJU

### CHELTENHAM

- ABDAY-WHITE, R J
- ACUHEALTH
- ALDRIDGE, JUDITH
- ARAMINTA
- AROMA THERAPEUTICS
- AROMA THERAPEUTICS
- BARNFIELD, HILARY
- BEARD, ANN CHRISTINE
- BERESFORD, G S
- BERESFORD, G S
- BIOFLOW
- BISHOPS CLEEVE PHYSIO & SPORTS
- BLYTH, DANIEL
- BODYHARMONICS CENTRE
- BODYMATTERS
- BRUCE, A R
- BUNTON, LYNN
- BURKE, JAYNE
- CHARLTON, STEPHANIE
- CHELTENHAM CLINIC & TRAD ACU
- CHELTENHAM HOLISTIC HLTH CTRE
- CHELTENHAM HOMEOPATHIC CLINIC
- CHELTENHAM HYPNOTHERAPY
- CHELTENHAM PHYSIO/SPRTS CLNC
- CHRISTIE, ELIZABETH
- CLAPHAM, EUGENIE
- COOMBES, ALISON
- COOPER, ANGELA
- COTSWOLD PHYSIOTHERAPY CENTRE
- COTSWOLD PODIATRY & CHIROPODY
- CREATIVE LIFE INTERNATIONAL
- CROSS, D J
- CULPEPER
- DARRALL, BETH
- DAVIES, S W
- DEAS, VALERIE JOHNSTON
- ECZEMA THERAPY
- EDUCATIONAL PSYCHOLOGY SERVICE
- ELECTROLYSIS & BEAUTY CLINIC
- FREUND, S M
- GOODFELLOW, NORMAN S
- GOWING, LYNN
- GRAY, MARGARET
- GREENWELL, DAVID
- GUYLL, S
- HANSFORD, LIZ
- HARTLEY, J E
- HARTLEY, J E
- HEMMINGS, RITA
- HENCHER, CAROLINE
- HENCHER, CAROLINE
- HERMANN, CELIA
- HOPSON, A J
- IMPERIAL CHIROPODY SERVICES
- JAMES, DIANNE
- JOHN COOPER ASSOCIATES
- JUDGE, BRENDA
- KOCH, H C H
- KOZUBIK, IVA
- LECKHAMPTON CHIROPRACTIC CLNC
- LEJEUNE, LIZ
- M, JACKSON A
- MACNIVEN, S
- MCLAREN, LESLEY
- MCLAREN, LINDA
- MEISHA SKIN CARE
- MYERS, MERRILYN
- NATURAL THERAPEUTICS
- NATURAL THERAPY CLINIC
- NATURELIEF
- NEALE-BROWN, CLAIRE
- NEASMITH, PAULINE
- NEVIN, ANTHONY R
- PARK VIEW CHIROPRACTIC
- PERCIVAL, ANN
- POCKETT, MARGARET
- RAVENSCROFT, GINNY
- REFLEXIONS
- ROBERTS & LEAHY
- ROBERTS, CLARE
- ROSSER, JASON
- ROSSER, JASON
- RUNNING EARTH HOLISTIC CLINIC
- RYAN, MAUREEN
- SCOTT, SARA
- SHIATSU PRACTICE
- SKELIAN CHIROPRACTIC CLINIC
- SKELIAN CHIROPRACTIC CLINIC
- SKINNER, A
- SMITH, C
- SMITH, G
- SPEARING, SIMON
- STEPHENS, LYN
- STOKES, PAM
- STOW PHYSIOTHERAPY SERVICE

- STRONG, JENNY
- TREE OF LIFE CENTRE
- VILLAGE CLINIC
- WAGNER, A
- WIEDERHOLD, KAREN

### CHIPPING CAMPDEN

- JOANNA SMITH AROMATHERAPY

### CINDERFORD

- ELLIOTT, A T

### CIRENCESTER

- CLIFF, R
- CRANSHAW, D V
- FILLINGHAM, MAGGIE
- GREENWOOD, ELAINE
- HALL, GERRY
- HILL, REBECCA A
- HILLTOUT, S
- KNAPP, SALLY
- LIVINGSTON, J
- MCDONALD, M
- OAKEY, D C
- OLIVE TRUST NATURAL THRPY CTRE
- SMITH, D
- THERAPY CLINIC
- VICKERS, CHRISTOPHER (DR)
- WESTLAKE, D E

### COLEFORD

- BRISTOW, M P
- PRICE, JILL
- STEINER, LYNDA

### DURSLEY

- KNIGHT, C E
- KNIGHT, S R
- NATURAL THERAPY CENTRE
- NEWTON, JULIE
- ROBBINS, JAMES H
- STEPHENSON, C
- STEREX ELECTROLYSIS

### DYMOCK

- NEW ROCK HEALING ARTS CENTRE

### FAIRFORD

- BURTON, F J
- THOMPSON, C

### FALFIELD

- DATE, SUSAN

### GLOUCESTER

- A TIME FOR YOU
- AGASCAR, ROBIN
- CARPANI, HANS
- CHIROPRACTIC WELLNESS CENTRE
- CHRISTOPHER, T
- CHURCHDOWN CHIROPODY CLINIC
- CIRENCESTER NATURAL THERAPIES
- CLINIC FOR PHYSICAL MEDICINE
- CLOVELLY NATURAL THERAPY CTRE
- COOK, ALISON
- EDUCATION PSYCHOLOGY SERVICE
- ESSENTIAL AROMATICS
- FILIPOVIC, S
- FINCH, ANNE
- GLOUCESTER CHIROPRACTIC CLINIC
- GLOUCESTER NAT THERAPIES
- GRIFFITHS, J A
- HAPPY FEET CHIROPODY
- HAPPY FEET CHIROPODY SERVICE
- HAYDEN, C J
- HAYDEN, E C
- HEATHVILLE CLINIC
- HERMANN, C
- JONES, L R
- KENDAL, ELIZABETH J
- MARTIN, P
- PERCEPTION BUSINESS PSYCHOL
- PIRANTY, AVERIL
- PITMAN, CLARE
- PRESTBERRIES FARM
- QUARRY, PHILLIP
- SANDERS, J A
- SEVERN NHS TRUST CHIROP SV
- SIDDALL, MARY
- SILMON, MARY
- STAMP & ASSOCIATES
- STEPHENS, SARAH
- STRESS COMPANY
- SUTTON, RUSSELL
- TRADITIONAL ACUPUNCTURE CLINIC
- TREACHER, KATE
- VAN ZYL, MARTIN
- WHITFIELD, M
- YOUNG, JOANNA

### LECHLADE

- BAYLISS, IRENE
- IRENE BAYLISS MCTIMONEY CHIRO
- PENACHE

### LONGHOPE

- GOODSON, KAREN

### LYDNEY

- FOREVER LIVING PRODUCTS
- VINEY HALL PHYSIOTHERAPY
- WINTOUR, BOBBY

### MITCHELDEAN

- COMPLEMENTARY MEDICINE SERVICE

### MORETON-IN-MARSH

- CARSON, D
- NATURAL THERAPIES CLINIC
- TURNER, A A

### NEWENT

- COMPLEMENTARY TOUCH
- GRATION, CHARLIE
- OSTEOPATH

### NEWNHAM

- BRODIE, JEAN M

### RUARDEAN

- SMYTH, DAVID

### STONEHOUSE

- MARLING CLINIC
- WOODMAN, LINDA

### STROUD

- 5 VALLEYS PHYSIOTHERAPY
- ADAMS, EVE
- ADAMS, PETER
- AMER, ANDREW R
- AQUA OLEUM
- BATES, DILYS
- BHMA
- BODDAM-WHETHAM, C
- BONE, LEMAYAH
- BOYES, LESLEY
- BRAYNE, PAULINE
- BROAD, H M
- BROWNING, KAREN
- COLLINGS-WELLS, ANNA
- COTTAGE CLINIC
- DANESH, MOJDEH
- DE LA HOYDE, JUDY
- DORAN, LESLEY
- EDUCATIONAL PSYCHOLOGY SERVICE
- ESSENTIAL BODYWORKS COMPANY
- GAZE, JENNY
- GRANT, K
- HARMONY MASSAGE CENTRE
- HEALTHY HOUSE
- HORSLEY, MARY E
- HUGHES, JANE CHRISTINE
- HUNTER, PHILIPPA
- IND, A E
- LANSDOWN CLNC OF PHYS MED
- LENNIE, ANNE
- LLOYD-JONES, J
- LLOYD-JONES, M A
- MARNEY, KATE
- MINCHINHAMPTON PHYSIO SVS
- NAILSWORTH NATURAL HLTH CTRE
- NEVIN, ANTHONY
- OLD CONVENT
- PARFETT, G
- PARFITT, STEVE
- PARKER, SARAH
- SIGNALYSIS
- SMYTHE, CARMEL
- SPENCER, VALERIE
- ST LUKES MEDICAL & THRPY CTRE
- STROUD CHIROPRACTIC CLINIC
- STROUD NATURAL HEALTH CLINIC
- TAYLOR, M
- TOSH, CAROLINE
- TRANSCENDENTAL MEDITATION
- WELLBEING CENTRE-HOMOEOPATHY
- WELLS, GEORGINA
- YOGA DRUVAM JIVAN YOGA SOCIETY

### TETBURY

- COOK, JACKIE
- COOPER, ANN
- HYGEIA COLLEGE-COLOUR THERAPY
- LAWLER, R & G
- REFLEXOLOGY
- RUMNEY, MICHAEL
- STOUT, HEATHER
- WEST OF ENGLAND ALOE VERA CTRE

### TEWKESBURY

- ACUPUNCTURE CLINIC
- GRAY, NORMAN R
- LLEWELLYN, MARGARET
- LLOYD-JONES, M A
- MONCK, LORRAINE
- SLATER, D C
- SMITH, DEREK M
- TEWKESBURY OSTEOPATHY

### WESTBURY-ON-SEVERN

- FAIRVIEW NAT THERAPY CLINIC

### WOTTON-UNDER-EDGE

- ARTICHOKE NATURAL HEALTH
- COTSWOLD CHIROPODY
- DAVIES, C G
- DEVERY, D
- FLETCHER, J
- HARLEQUIN
- REEVES, ELAINE

## GUERNSEY

### TORTEVAL

- SPILLMAN, HOLLY

### VALE

- CHRISTOPHER, DEBORAH

## HAMPSHIRE

### ALDERSHOT

- BARTLETT, S G A
- BOND, J
- CLEMENTS, CHRISTINE
- CRANIOSACRAL THERAPY
- HERBARY CHINESE MEDICINE CTRE
- KAY SILVER HYPNOTHERAPY
- LEGGETT, JANET
- MARLOR, J
- SWALES, JANE

### ALRESFORD

- ATTIA, GINA
- CASWELL, KERI
- RODHAM, SANDIE

### ALTON

- ABSOLUTE AROMAS
- ALTERNATIVES
- BACK 2 HEALTH
- BIRRELL, M
- BURCHELL, DIANE SUE
- BURCHFIELD PHYSIO PRACTICE
- CAYNE, J COUN & PSYCHOTHERAPY
- DENNISONS CONSULTANCY
- FAMILY CHIRO & ALT MED CTRE
- FORD-HAMMOND, BARBARA
- GOVE, J J
- JOHNS, DAVID M
- JUNE PLATTS ASSOCIATES
- MATOL
- NATURAL THERAPY CENTRE
- OSMAN, SARA
- PURPLE HAZE AROMATHERAPY
- SPEAR, A E Y
- SPELLER, BRIDGET
- SWABY, DINAH
- TOWNER, JOAN

### ANDOVER

- ANDOVER BACK PAIN & PHYSIO
- ANDOVER FOOT HEALTH
- ANKIN, CHRISTINA
- BARNATT, D J

- BEACHER, D R
- BIOTECH HEALTH & NUTRITION
- BOLDICK, K J
- BOLDICK, KATHLEEN
- CTRE-COMPLEMENTARY THERAPY
- GRIFFITH, C J
- HILLBURY CHIROPRACTIC CLINIC
- INGRAM, C
- LONDON COLLEGE-CLINICAL HYP
- MCTIMONEY CHIROPRACTICE
- MCTIMONEY CHIROPRACTICE
- PAUC, R A
- PHEBY, JACQUELINE
- SMITH, CHRISTOPHER R A
- STARTUP, SALLY
- STICKLAND, ROBERTA
- WELSH, R P

## BASINGSTOKE

- ALLISON, C (DR)
- ALSTON, S R
- ARTEMIS
- BACK TO WORK
- BASINGSTOKE CHIROPRACTIC
- BASINGSTOKE FOOT CLINIC
- BATSTONE, I
- BIRD, LYNN
- BROCK, S
- BROOKS, CAROLE
- BROWN, ANN
- BROWN, S M
- CARMICHAEL, GORDON
- CARTER, LINDA
- CASSANDRA
- CHAMPS
- CHANDLER, PAT
- CHIROPODY CLINIC LODDON
- CLINIC OF NATURAL HEALTH
- DAVIES, B D
- DING, LEE
- FAIRFIELDS LANE WEST
- FOGG, HELEN
- FOULDS, PHILLIP
- GANF, JENNIFER
- GODDARD, E A
- GODWIN, PAUL & JENNY
- GREEN, MEG
- GREGORY, F
- GRIFFITH, ALISON
- HAMMERSON, D
- HANNA, MARY
- HARRISON, IAN M
- JONES, DARCY
- JONES, MARGARET
- KRIR, J
- KYPERS, SARAH
- LAMONT, KEITH
- LAURENT, PIERRE
- LESTER, JOHN
- LESTER, MARK
- MEADWAY, SUE
- MOUNTFORD, CAROLINE
- MURPHY, CYNTHIA
- NATURES GATE
- NORTH HAMPS OSTEOPATHIC CLINIC
- NUNNS, PATRICIA
- OVERTON OSTEOPATHIC CLINIC
- OWEN-JONES, JOY
- PHOENIX FOOT HEALTH
- POTTINGER, MARGARET
- POWER, RICHENDA
- RABESS, ANGELA
- RIDGUARD, YVONNE
- SCRIVENER, JEAN
- SPECTRUM REIKI & SEKHEM
- TAGG, D
- TAGG, D
- TAGG, LINDA A
- TIDBALL, GILLIAN
- TILLSON, LINDA
- TULLOCH, S
- WELLS, C R
- WRIGHT, DAVE

## BORDON

- ADVISORY CENTRE
- AROMATHERAPY BY R SKILTON
- BEDDEN, TONY
- CHIANALINO, M L
- GREG KELLOWAY IND ECO FL DIST
- MARISCOTTI, SHEILA

## BROCKENHURST

- BUDD, M L
- HAYTER, M J
- HILL, JULIE
- MARKBY, S B
- VALL, KENNETH
- WILDE, ELIZABETH A

## DRAYTON

- BUDD, RICHARD

## EASTLEIGH

- ALLEN, CAROL
- AROMATHERAPY BY SHEILA BURWOOD
- ASSOCIATED PSYCHOLOGISTS
- CAMPBELL, EDITHA
- CARTER-REES, A G
- CHANDLERS FORD CHIRO CLINIC
- CHANDLERS FORD PHYSIO
- CLARKE, CHRIS
- CONSTABLE, R N
- DOUGLAS, S
- EASTLEIGH CHIROPRACTIC CENTRE
- EASTLEIGH OSTEOPATHIC CLINIC
- FAY, GLENDA
- FED OF HOLISTIC THERAPISTS
- FEET FOR LIFE
- FRIGHT, ANGELA M
- GLASSPOOL, PATRICIA
- HAYTER, HEATHER A
- HEALING STAR
- HEIB, L G
- LANDON, IAN
- MOORE, SARAH
- MORRIS, JENNIFER
- PARKER, NIESJE
- ROUSE, ALAN
- ROUSE, J
- RUSHTON, AVRIL
- SULLIVAN, HELEN
- THERAPEUTICS
- WOHLER, A

## EMSWORTH

- ABEL, ELAINE
- CARPENTER, G W
- CHIROPODY SURGERY
- EMS CHIROPODY
- HAY LOFT CENTRE
- MEDICINE GARDEN
- MENZIES, AVERIL
- MULCHRONE, SUSANNE
- OSBORN, TERRI
- SEYMOUR, E J
- SHREEVE, RACHEL KATHRYN
- SHRIMPTON, K
- SIMPSON, S
- SOUTHBOURNE & FONTWELL PHYSIO
- SOUTHBOURNE SPORTS & MEDICAL
- TELLURIC, CHRISTINE

## FAREHAM

- AGATE, LYNN
- AITKENHEAD, B P
- ALLAWAY, SANDRA
- ALLDRIDGE, T
- AROMATHERAPY
- AUSTEN, HEATHER
- BONFIELD, D M
- CAIRNS, GUY
- CLARK, A L
- COLEBROOKE, DAVID
- COLEBROOKE, LINDA
- COMPLETE ANGEL HEALING CENTRE
- DAWE, PATRICIA
- DUFFIN, INGRID
- EMANUEL, G J
- EQUILIBRIUM CENTRE
- FAREHAM CHIROPRACTIC CENTRE
- FAREHAM PHYSIOTHERAPHY SVS
- FARRIER, M
- FOSTER, JAMES M ASSOCIATES
- HIGH STREET CLINIC
- HOMEWOOD CHIROPRACTIC CLINIC
- HOWARD, T
- INLPTA
- JONES, ELIZABETH
- KINGSMILL, STEPHEN
- LORETTE PARK
- MADAME MOONA
- MARSH, OLIVE
- MURRAY, ARLENE
- PEAPER, C
- PHILBRICK, G
- REIKI NATURAL HEALING CENTRE
- SCOTT, HEATHER
- SPENCELEY, M
- THOMSON, JANET
- VARNHAM, GERALD
- VINCE, LINDA
- WILLSHER, SUE
- WINTON, DIANNA

## FARNBOROUGH

- ACTIVE SPORTS THERAPY
- BARRETT, LINDA
- BEDFORD, H & B
- BOOTY, STEPHEN
- CARTER, LINDA P
- DAVID TIDSALL REIKI PRAC
- DUCAS, KENNETH
- ELEMENT, SUE
- FORMOSA HOUSE HOMEO CLINIC
- GARSIDE, CATHERINE
- HOLMES, M N & M
- JACQUELINE
- LISLE, THOMAS
- MORLAND-AUSTIN, FIONA
- NATURAL THERAPY CENTRE
- NICOLA @ HOLISTIC HOUSE
- OUTRIDGE, M

## FLEET

- BROWN & ASSOCIATES
- BUCK, PETER
- CHILTERN COTTAGE CLINIC
- CROFTS, TREVOR
- ELDRIDGE, NICOLA
- EVANS
- FLEET & DISTRICT HYP CENTRE
- FLEET PHYSIOTHERAPY
- HEARNE, BRIAN
- HILLYER, ANDREW
- LEIGH, PETER A
- MEHRTENS, HELEN
- NORSWORTHY, CLAIRE
- OLIVER, D
- RICHARDSON, SARAH
- S E E D INSTITUTE
- TURNER, CATHY
- TWESLEDOWN PHYSIOTHERAPY

## FORDINGBRIDGE

- BAILEY, JANE
- COLVILE, RICHARD
- EGERTON, S
- GARLAND, GLENN D
- HORNE, SUE
- LOWINGER, LEAH
- MASON, KEITH
- WOODROW, ANNE

## GOSPORT

- AABLE FEET CHIROPODY
- BURNE, JANET
- CRANE, DAVID S
- DICKS, ALISON
- EDGAR, A
- FOSSEY, LYNETTE
- GREIG, MARIANNE
- HENDERSON, DAVID
- HOLISTIC COUNS & HEALING CON
- JACKSON, J
- PEARCE, P J
- PETLEY, KIRSTIE
- RENNIE, KATHRYN
- RIDLEY, STELLA
- SAMLER, LYN
- THOMPSON, ANNE

## HAVANT

- AQUARIUS HEALING
- AROMATHERAPY STUDIO
- BRIGDEN, JENNIFER
- CHAMBERLAIN, A G
- CHAUDHRY, M D
- COFFEY, AIDAN
- HARDY, JONATHAN
- HIND, SUSAN
- HOMOEOPATHIC CLINIC

- HUNT, M
- KONRAD, GABRIEL
- LOMAX, KATE
- PENNINGTON, ZIGGY
- PERCIVAL, A A
- RICHARDSON, SHEILA
- SPITERI-RUTTER, R
- WARNE, P F
- WARREN, ANNE

## HAYLING ISLAND

- CLARK, A L
- CROWBERRY CHIROPODY
- EVERETT, U
- HAYLING ISLAND CHIRO CLINIC
- LAW, MARY
- SHAW, GAIL
- SPIRITUALIST NAT UNION HEALERS

## HEDGE END

- BELL CLINIC
- SANCTUARY HEALING

## HOOK

- CARNELIAN HEALTH PARTNERSHIP
- FOREVER LIVING PRODUCTS
- GORMAN, JOHN
- HARRISON, DENISE
- HOOD, CHRISTINA
- MAITLAND-TITTERTON, SARAH
- MCKINNA, ANNE
- OSBORN, AMY
- SANDERS, LOUISE
- SOLUTIONS
- THOMAS, S

## LEE-ON-THE-SOLENT

- FIT FEET CHIROPODY
- M SUTTON-COULSON SOLENT PHYSIO
- SINYARD, CONSTANCE
- STEAD, N W

## LIPHOOK

- HAIGH, ALEXANDRA L
- INT FLOWER ESSENCE REPERTOIRE
- KING, G Y
- LOWE, KENNETH
- MCCANN, JACQUI
- O'BRIEN, JILL

## LISS

- ACUPUNTURE TAO CLINIC
- ASHLEY, PHILLIPA
- LAND, D F
- THOMA, ANDREW

## LOCKS HEATH

- ANDERSON, ANGELA
- O'NEILL, REGINA

## LYMINGTON

- AKESTER, JANE
- AROMATICA TREATMENT & PRODUCTS
- AROMATICA TREATMENT & PRODUCTS
- ASHER, V A
- AUSTIN, MIRANDA
- BANNON, C
- BENES, G B
- BOYD, LESLEY
- BUDDEN, O
- CHANCE, G D
- CUMMING, LESLEY
- DICKS, DEBORAH
- FURSEY, STEPHEN
- GENERAL HYPNOTHERAPY REGISTER
- GIRLING, SUSAN
- GOBELL, C G
- HENSTRIDGE, EDWARD
- KENNEDY, E
- LEACH, VANDRA
- LEWIS, D J S
- LEWIS, DAVID
- LYMINGTON CHIROPRACTIC CLINIC
- MAGILL, HEATHER
- MAYNARD, CLIVE
- MEDDINGS, GLORIA
- MEWS PHYSIOTHERAPY CLINIC
- MILLER, MORRIS
- NAT COUNCIL-PSYCHOTHERAPISTS
- NOBLE, CAROLINE
- ORTON, S
- RICHARDS, CLAIRE
- SHEPHARD, SALLY
- THOMPSON, A K
- WEGUELIN, JESSICA
- WELBAC CLINIC
- WESSEX OSTEOPATHY CLINIC
- WIBERG, J H
- WILLAIMS, D
- WILLIAMS, GEOFFREY
- WILLIAMS, LIZ-BETH
- WRIGHTSON, VERONICA

## LYNDHURST

- WHITEHEAD, BRIAN

## NEW MILTON

- BARROWCLOUGH, LISA
- BIDDLESTONE, ANN R
- CARROTT, EMMA
- CLEGHORN, ANNE
- CRAIG, PETER
- DEVERILL, PAMELA
- FOOT SHOP
- FOX, ANTONY D (DR)
- HELEN BENFIELD HEALER & CLAIR
- HYPNOSIS & STRESS COUNSELLING
- LUCY, IRENE
- LUNT, JULIE
- MELHUISH, J I (DR)
- NEW MILTON CHIROPRACTIC CLINIC
- PARRY & MCCAFFERY
- PUNTER, EDWARD
- SCANDINAVIAN CHIROPRACTIC CTRE
- SOLENT CHIROPRACTIC CLINIC
- THOMPSON, A K

## NORTH BADDESLEY

- WOODROW, LORRAINE

## OVERTON

- ARMSTRONG, ANNA

## PETERSFIELD

- ALLDRIDGE, T D
- BENNISON, DIANE
- CASSIDY, D J
- CENTRE FOR COMP MEDICINE
- CHRISTIENSEN, MARK
- COOK, RICHARD
- CORELLO, LOUISE
- DAVE WILLIAMSON COUNS PSYCH
- EVANS, CHRISTINE
- FIELD, JONATHAN
- GREY, CHRISTOPHER
- KYPERS, SARAH
- LATTER, STEVEN
- LUBBOCK, BRIDGET
- MARILINA
- MCCLUNG, KENNETH
- NAOMI, ELIA
- NAUGHTON, G
- OSMAN, SARAH
- PETTER, C
- PHILLIPS, DAWN
- SIVYER, ANNE-MARIE
- SMYTH, J
- WHITEHOUSE, J E
- WRIGHT, SAMANTHA

## PORTSMOUTH

- ADAMS, PETER C
- ALLERGY DETECT & NTRL HEALING
- ALLERGY THERAPY
- BALDACCHINO, PAUL
- BENNETT, ROSS
- BIRCH, R F
- BODYBASIC UK
- BROOKES, J R
- CARRUTHERS, D
- CASSELL, JOHN
- CLEGG, D P
- COPNOR OSTEOPATHICS
- COSHAM OSTEOPATHIC CLINIC
- CRYSTAL CLEAR PSYCHIC READINGS
- DEANE, MICHAEL
- DOLPHIN STUDIOS
- DOWN TO EARTH HOLISTIC HEALTH
- DUFFY, MICHELLE
- GOODALL, DAVID
- GUNNS, C M
- HEAL-ALL HERB AND ACU CTRE
- HUTCHINGS, MARGARET
- HYPNOTHRPY FOR POSITIVE CHANGE
- INNER WHISPERS & THERAPY CTRE
- KD PHYSIOTHERAPY
- KIN HON CLINIC
- LANE, JEFF
- LLOYD, TIM
- LLOYD, TIM
- MATHEWS, F G & M D
- MINDWORKS HYPNOTHERAPY CLINIC
- NEW ROAD NATURAL HEALTH CLINIC
- NORTH END CHIROPRACTIC CLINIC
- PEARSON & MARKLOVE
- PHOENIX HOLISTIC CENTRE
- PORTSMOUTH MEDICAL HERBALIST
- RUSSELL, CHRIS
- SIMMONDS, J
- SKIN DEEP BEAUTY SALON
- STANLEY, M P
- STUBBINGTON NTRL HEALTH CLINIC
- SUMMERS, DIANE
- TRANSCENDENTAL MEDITATION
- WHITE, R M
- WOOD, ELEANOR

## RINGWOOD

- 3 WAYS PHYSIOTHERAPY CLINIC
- ASHLEY HEATH CENTRE
- BAXTER, S M
- CHIPPERFIELD, CAMILLA J
- CLARK, LYNDA
- DRAKE, S G
- GARDNER, S
- HEMSTEAD, JOHN S
- HORNE, SUE
- PARRY, N J
- RINGWOOD CHIROPRACTIC CLINIC
- RINGWOOD FOOT SHOP
- RINGWOOD NATURAL HEALTH CLINIC
- RINGWOOD PHYSIOTHERAPY CENTRE
- TERRY, FIONA
- WINNERT, NORMA

## ROMSEY

- ABBEY CHIROPRACTIC CLINIC
- ART DE VIVRE
- BENNETT, ROSS
- BRADY, KATIE
- BROME & SCHIMMER
- CHURCHILL, VANESSA
- NEL, C A
- PORTER, ANTHONY
- ROMSEY CHIROPRACTIC CLINIC
- ROMSEY HEALTH CENTRE
- ROMSEY PHYSIO & SPORTS
- ROUSSOS, AMANDA
- SPARKES, F V
- VICARY, E A
- WELSH, R P & C J
- WILLOW TREE THERAPEUTIC AGENCY

## ROWLAND'S CASTLE

- TOOMPUU, LINDE

## SOUTHAMPTON

- ACUPUNCTURE & PHYSIO CLINIC
- ADAMS, S
- AGER, R W
- AISHA CENTRE
- ALL - HEAL ACU & HERB CENTRE
- ALTERNATE THERAPY
- ALTERNATIVE THERAPY
- APPLETREE CHIROPODY
- ASSOCIATION OF STRESS MNGMT
- ATTIA, GINA
- AVENUE CLINIC
- BAINBRIDGE, ELLEN
- BAMFORD, G X
- BASSETT PHYSIOTHERAPY CLINIC
- BASSETTS CHIROPRACTIC CLINIC
- BERKLEYS HEALTH STUDIO
- BETTERIDGE, SHIRLEY
- BODY SCENT
- BOURNE CONSULTANCY
- CEDAR LODGE

- CEDAR LODGE
- CHANCE, G D
- CHARLETT, DEBORAH
- CHINESE ACUPUNCTURE CLINIC
- CHIROPRACTIC & CRANIAL CENTRE
- CHIVERS, JAMES
- CITY CHIROPRACTIC CLINIC
- CITY OSTEOPATHIC CLINIC
- CLARK, M
- CLARK, MADELEINE
- COAST CLINIC
- COAST CLINIC
- COLEMAN, G P
- COUGHLAN & COUGHLAN
- COURAGE, VANESSA
- CROSS, ANN-LOUISE
- CTRE FOR THE STUDY OF COMP MED
- DAVID
- ELCOCK, B J
- ELECTROLYSIS 2000
- ELKINS, P A (DR)
- EYLES, C
- FAY, ESTHER
- FOOTMATTERS PODIATRY CLINIC
- FOREST CHIROPODY
- FRANKEISS, PETER
- GALLOWAY, CHRISTOPHER
- GOODCHILD, GARY J
- GROVE NATURAL THERAPY CENTRE
- HAMBLETT, J E
- HANTSCARE
- HAREFIELD CLINIC
- HARMONY INDIAN HEAD MASS
- HEALTHWISE
- HEALTHWISE THERAPIES
- HEDGE END CHIROPRACTIC CLINIC
- HERB MEDIC
- HOLBURY CHIROPRACTIC CLINIC
- HOLISTIC TRADING
- HOWE'S HOLISTICS
- HOWES, GRAHAM
- HUTCHINS, J R
- HYPNOTHERAPY & ANALYSIS CENTRE
- HYPNOTHERAPY CONSULTANCY
- HYTHE CHIROPRACTIC CLINIC
- INGRAM, NEIL
- ISIS NATURAL THERAPIES
- JOHNSON, ROSS
- JONES, RUTH C
- JOYCE, HELEN G M
- LAC, J
- LE BON, JOHATHAN
- LE BROCQ
- LEACH, TRICIA
- LECOINTE, PETER
- LIGHT WAYS
- LILLEY, PENNY
- LOCKHAMS THERAPY CENTRE
- MACLEOD, S R M
- MADSEN, N P C
- MANNING, JONATHAN
- MANSBRIDGE PHYSIO PRACTICE
- MAY, DAISY
- MCKELLAR, ROSE
- MEDICAL SCIENCES TECHNOLOGY
- METCALF, M F
- MORAN, DAVID
- MORLEY, KAREN
- MURRAY, GILLIAN E
- NATURAL HEALTH SERVICE
- NEW HORIZON AROMATICS
- NOMA
- OLIVER, G C
- ORCHARD THERAPIES PORTSWOOD
- OXFORD STREET THERAPY CENTRE
- PADDON-ROW, J
- PARK GATE CHIROPRACTIC CENTRE
- PHYSICAL THERAPY CLINIC
- PILLING, M
- POWER & SERCOMBE PRACTICE
- RABLEY, M
- RADIN, J
- REYNOLDS, A R
- ROWAN CLINIC
- RUSSELL, CAROL
- SAVAGE, EDNA
- SCHOLL CENTRE
- SEARLE, MAUREEN
- SHEPHERD, P A
- SHIRLEY CHIROPRACTIC CLINIC
- SIMCOE CLINIC
- SMITH, R
- SOUTHAMPTON CTRE OF COMP MED
- ST JAMES CHIROPRACTIC CLINIC
- STEELE, ALANNA
- STEWART, C J
- STOVELL, J
- SUNRIDER REGENERATIVE FOOD
- SWAIN, P A
- TAYLOR & ASSOCIATES
- TONG, E
- TREE OF LIFE CLINIC
- VALENTINE, ROSS
- WARD, G C
- WEEDON, BRIAN J
- WHISHAW, M G
- WILLIAMS, STEPHEN P
- WILLIS, GRAHAM
- WILSON, A F J
- WISEMAN, DEBBIE
- WOODNUTT, S
- YVONNE

### SOUTHSEA

- ALTERNATIVE THERAPIES
- ATTRIDGE, BRIAN
- B P AITKENHEAD PHYSIO SERVICES
- BARNARD, S P
- BOTHWICK, JOHN
- BRISCOE, WARREN
- BURGESS, MARGARET
- CHANNON, P M
- CITY PHYSIOTHERAPY CENTRE
- COOK, RICHARD
- COULTER, T H L
- EASTON, MERRETT
- ENERGY EXCHANGE
- ENERGY EXCHANGE HOLISTIC CTRE
- FREDA, ROSE
- GEE, L
- GLEICH, M T
- HAWNT, D W
- HERBERT, STUART
- HOLISTIC TREATMENTS
- HOWICK, E
- JENKINS, RUSSELL
- JOYCE, JAMES
- KAYIZA, M S
- MASON, MARK
- MCCORMICK, FRANCES
- PIKE, R P
- SOUTHSEA CENTRE FOR COMP MED
- SOUTHSEA CHIROPRACTIC CLINIC
- STAINER, A
- WILSON, PAUL

### STOCKBRIDGE

- HIPO-ANALYSIS CENTRE SALISBURY

### SWAY

- SWAY HOUSE PUBLICATIONS

### TADLEY

- ARKLEY, BRENDA
- GERMAIN, SUE
- HOBBS, T J
- SYDENHAM, ERIC J
- TADLEIGH FOOT HEALTH
- WALKER, MICHAEL

### TIDWORTH

- HAMPSHIRE THERAPY CENTRE

### TOTTON

- BIDWELL, KAREN

### UPHAM

- WECK, LYN

### WARSASH

- SAMLER, LYN

### WATERLOOVILLE

- ALFORD, JO
- ATTRIDGE, FAY
- BLAKLEY, PAMELA
- BODY BASIC
- DAVID LIST
- DAY, A C
- DICKER, W
- EDMONDS, SCOTT J
- FINN, G T & S E
- FOSTER, J
- FOSTER, P R
- GARRETT-SIMPSON, E A
- GROSVENOR PHYSIOTHERAPY CLINIC
- HERBERT, S J
- HOLISTIC ARTS STUDIOS
- HOLISTIC PEACE
- LUFF, ROBIN R
- MOON-STONE
- PHYSIOTHERAPY CENTRE
- RICHARD JUDD CHIROPODIST
- SHAW, J K
- WATERLOOVILLE NTRL HLTH CTRE
- WHITESIDE, V

### WHITCHURCH

- ARMSTRONG, ANNA

### WINCHESTER

- ARMSTRONG, SIAN
- AROMATHERAPY DIRECT
- ASS OF CHARTERED PHYSIO
- ATTIA, GINA
- BILES, TINA
- BOUNDY, ELIZABETH
- BRADFORD HOUSE CHIRO CLINIC
- CARSON, C
- CHAPMAN, J D
- CLAY, P A
- COATES, MARY
- DAWKINS, S
- DOHERTY, P C
- EVANS, G
- FAIRDOWN CENTRE
- GWILLYM, ELAINE
- HAMPSHIRE MUSIC SPACE
- HARRISON, A
- HOWE, PAMELA
- JONES, G M E
- LAURIDSEN, H
- LAVERTY, SUSIE
- LAVERTY, SUSIE
- LEIBBRANDT
- LEWIS, SARAH
- MILLS, A
- MITCHELL, EMMA
- MOORE, S
- MORGAN, JOANNA
- NELSON, DANIEL
- NORMAN, J M
- PADDOCK, MADELINE
- PARCHMENT STREET CLINIC
- PINDER CENTRE
- PRINCE, R
- SABER, J
- SCHOLL CENTRE
- SOUTHGATE NAT THERAPY CLINIC
- ST CROSS HOMOEOPATHIC CLINIC
- ST LAWRENCE HOUSE CHIROPRACTIC
- TAYLOR, RACHEL
- TEWKESBURY, NIGEL
- THOMSON, D
- WELL HOUSE HOLISTIC HLTH CTRE
- WESSEX CENTRE FOR WELLBEING
- WHITE, W
- WINCHESTER CHIROPRACTIC CLINIC
- WINCHESTER HOM PRACTICE
- WINCHESTER PHYSIO/SPORTS

### YATELEY

- CAMBRAY, ANDREW
- FLEET N F S H HEALING CENTRE
- KNIGHT, KAY

## HEREFORD & WORCESTER

- HALL, LYNN

## HEREFORDSHIRE

### BROMYARD

- POTTS, J

### BUSHEY

- BEAUTY IS YOURS
- BRYAN, SUE
- PHILLPOT, ANN

### COLWALL GREEN

- MOULE, TERRY G
- WILLCOCKS, T & S

## HEREFORD

- BENNETT, S M
- BLACKBURN, ROBERT W
- BODY PERFECTION
- BURNELL, SUE
- CHARVET, BARBARA
- CHURCHER, L A
- HANDOLL & ASSOCIATES
- HANDY, SUSAN
- HEALING EARTH
- HEALING HERBS
- HEREFORD CENTRE
- HEREFORD CHIROPRACTIC CLINIC
- HEREFORD HERBAL & NATURAL HLTH
- HOLT, TIM
- JONES, KEVIN D G
- LENNICK, JOY
- LOOKERS NATURAL THERAPY CLINIC
- MOODY, C B
- PARFETT, GORDON
- POTTS, J
- POWELL, J
- PSYCHOTHERAPY & HYPNOTHERAPY
- RETREAT
- WILLIAMS, VALERIE MOLYNEUX

## KINGTON

- EVANS, JOANNE
- JANE ANNE'S ELECTROLYSIS
- KINGTON PHYSIOTHERAPY DEPT

## LEDBURY

- DANIELS, PENNY
- DAVIES, J G
- FINCH, ANNE
- HEBBLETHWAITE, PRISCILLA
- LEDBURY NATURAL HEALTH CENTRE
- LEDBURY OSTEOPATHIC PRACTICE
- LEDBURY WHOLEFOODS
- MALDWYN-EVANS, M

## LEOMINSTER

- FOSTER, CHRIS
- HALCYON THERAPIES
- HARVEY, MARTIN
- LEOMINSTER OSTEOPATHS
- NEWTON, A C
- NITTY GRITTY WHOLEFOODS
- NOBLE, SUZANNE
- WINTON, BARBARA

## ROSS-ON-WYE

- BROADVIEW NATURAL HEALTH CTRE
- BROADVIEW NATURAL HEALTH CTRE
- COOPER, A
- GIBSON-FORTY, J
- HANDOLL, NICHOLAS & ASSOCIATES
- OLIVER, JENNY
- ROBBINS, CHRISTOPHER
- ROSS HERBAL & NTRL HLTH CTRE
- TEDDER, CATHRINE
- TUREY, J T

# HERTFORDSHIRE

## ABBOTS LANGLEY

- BATE, AMANDA
- IRVING, MARY
- PEACOCK, P

## BALDOCK

- ALDER, DENNIS
- ASHWELL, MELBOURN & BALDOCK
- HUTSON, JOHN
- MOYNIHAN, T
- PERRY, KAREN
- WYNDHAM CLINIC

## BARNET

- ADL-TABATABAI, CAROL
- ALLEN, JULIE & LEN
- ATTEWELL, GAVIN
- BABLEE, S
- BAGINI, LINDA
- BARNET CHIROPODY SURGERY
- BERNER, ERICH
- CHRISTOU, Z
- DAWES, T
- DRAKES, M
- EVANS, C
- EYRES, M R
- FIELD, PAUL
- FOSTER, SHERRIE
- FREEDMAN, AUSTIN
- GODLEY, C
- GOLDIE, S
- HADLEY WOOD HEALTH CENTRE
- HALLOWELL, K
- HARTMAN, SUSAN
- HEALTH CHECK
- HOLLENBERY, SUSAN
- HOWARD-PRAGER, JANET
- HUTCHESON, SALLY ANN
- JENNIFER SAJIR PAED PHYSIO
- JEOFFROY, ANNA
- KAREN
- KING, DERRELL
- KONDIC, CHRIS
- KRAFT, T
- LEANE, MAURICE
- LEIGHTON, A
- MASON GOODMAN NAT MEDICINE
- MEEK, LISA
- MORRIS, HENRY
- NANDLAL, J A
- NATURAL TOUCH
- OSTEOPATHIC CLINIC
- PAYNE, V A
- PENDRY, BARBARA
- PHYSIO & SPORTS INJURIES CLNC
- PLESHETTE, JANET
- PROFESSIONAL HYP CTRE
- QUYE, KARINA
- S K REFLEXOLOGY
- SHAANAN, A
- SHERIDAN, SARAH
- TOSELAND, DOROTHY
- UNERMAN, EVE
- VRIES, J DE
- WEBB, MARCUS
- WOOD STREET CHIROPRACTIC CLNC
- WOOD STREET CLINIC
- WRIGHT, KAREN

## BERKHAMSTED

- BERKHAMSTED CHIRO CLINIC
- BERKHAMSTED PHYSIO CLINIC
- BLUNDELL, ALISON
- BLUNDELL, WAYNE
- CLNC OF ACU & CHINESE HRBL MED
- CONFEDERATION OF HEALING ORG
- CRAIB, MARGARET
- DECKER ASSOCIATES
- DUDGEON, DELIA
- EVANS, HELEN
- GUBBAY, R
- HANWELL, JULIET
- HANWELL, TIM
- HODGES, RAY
- LOVESEY, R M
- MCCAREY, J
- MILTON HOUSE SURGERY
- O'NEILL, SUSAN
- PAINTER, R F
- SMITH, SOPHIA
- THINK NATURAL COM
- TOMLIN, WILLIAM W
- TRIBE, DARRY L
- WOTHERSPOON, E

## BISHOP'S STORTFORD

- ALDRIDGE, VICKI
- ALDRIDGE, VICKI
- ARTURI, S (DR)
- ASINYA, MARY
- BACK PAIN CLINIC
- BARBER, NICHOLAS J
- BARRETT, CAROL-ANN
- BEARD, JANE
- BISHOPS STORTFORD CHIRO CLINIC
- BISHOP'S STORTFORD HOMEOPATHIC
- BOXALL, KERRY
- BRIGGS-WILSON, A
- CLARK, BARRY J
- CLARKE, MO
- DRYER, DIANA
- ELDON, MARTIN
- GERBER, E
- HANDFORD, RICHARD
- HATHAWAY, ELIZABETH
- HYNOTHERAPY SURGERY
- IZOD, M A
- KEW, DEREK
- KONTOU, F
- LAWLESS, GIULIA
- LEE, W E
- LEWIS, CHRISTIAN
- LINDY, D
- LOVELL, A G
- MILLER, C A
- RANDALL, MARGARET
- ROBERTS, SALLY
- RUSHANT, LYNDA
- SIVANANDA YOGA TEACHER
- SOUTH, JO
- SPENCER, MARGARET
- STORT COUNS & PSYCHOTHERAPY
- STORTFORD GRANGE PHYSIO CENTRE
- TREEND, NICOLA
- WARREN, GILLIAN
- WAYMAN, W N
- WHITE, GRAHAM C
- WHITE, GRAHAM C
- WILLIAMS, HAZEL

## BOREHAMWOOD

- ALLIDINA, PARVIZ
- BOREHAMWOOD CHIRO CLINIC
- CHIROPODY PRACTICE
- COLLEGE OF OSTEOPATHS
- FIELD, P M
- GILLING, LINDA
- HASAN, ZADI
- HUSSEIN, ALLIDINA
- LEWIN, ROCHELLE
- MARCUS, CLAIRE HANNAH
- PAUL, EDWINA
- PSYCHOTHERAPY
- SOOTHING STROKES

## BROXBOURNE

- ALEXANDER TECHNIQUE
- MILLHOUSE
- SMITH, SUZANNE

## BUNTINGFORD

- FOZZARD, JOANNA M
- JOE MILLER SPORTS INJURY
- LOWETH, DEBORAH
- NATURAL HEALTH CLINIC
- ORCHARD SURGERY CHIRO CLINIC
- PRINCE, KAREN
- SHENTON, MAXINE

## HARPENDEN

- ASSOCIATES HEAD & SHORT
- AUBEELUCK, L
- BRADBURY, TANYA
- CHANDLER, LENA
- CRANE, B
- CRANE, B
- GEOFF THIEL, COUNS & PSYCHO
- GREENWOOD, SUSAN L
- HAMILTON-PETERS, R & J A
- HARPENDEM OSTEOPATHIC PRACTICE
- HARPENDEN CHIROPRACTIC CLINIC
- HORWICH, L
- JAMES, SUSAN
- KENNAN, PHILIPPA
- KHEIR, DIANE
- MAPLE TREE PRACTICE
- MARCHANT-JONES, ALISON
- MCTIMONEY CHIROPRACTIC CLINIC
- OPEN MINDS
- PALMER, CHRISTINE
- PARROTT, J M
- SOUTHDOWN CHIROPODY PRACTICE
- TANT, M
- THOMPSON, M H L
- TRANSCENDENTAL MEDITATION
- WALKER, RICHARD

## HATFIELD

- A & L AROMATHERAPY SUPPLIES
- AROMA ROOM
- BIRTHWORKS
- BROOKMANS OSTEOPATHY CLINIC
- CHAMBERS, AINE
- HARRISON, S
- HODSDON, L M
- KERSTIN HEALTH & BEAUTY

- MCLAREN, PETER
- PENN, CAROLINE M
- RICARDO, LINDA
- ROSS, V
- TAYLOR, D
- THERAPEUTIC MASSAGE
- WHITE, ELIZABETH

## HEMEL HEMPSTEAD

- A JS CHIROPODIST
- BETA HEALTH CLINIC
- CANNING, LINDA
- CARTER, J P
- CLAIRVOYANTS & REIKI
- CLARK, MICHELLE
- COWARD, JANICE
- CUSWORTH, BRIAN
- DAVEY, SARAH
- DAVIS-PARRY, CLARISSA J B
- EDUCATIONAL TAPES
- ELFICK, J
- FERRUCCI, LORETTA
- GEMS
- GODAGAMA, SHANTA (DR)
- GOODMAN, HENRY
- GORMAN, J
- GREIG, LISA A
- HALLAM, CHRISTINA
- HEMEL CHIROPRACTIC CLINIC
- HODGSON, SALLY
- HUTTON, W
- JACOB, SIMON
- JOHNSON, PAM
- KING, SANDRA
- LEWIS, BRIAN
- MALLARD, CAROLE
- MCCLELLAND, S M
- MCDONALD, JEANETTE
- MESGER-SCHOFIELD, FIONA
- NELSON, A
- NEWBERRY, JOHN L
- PALMER, LYNDA M A
- PUCZYNSKI, JOHN
- RICKETT, MARION
- ROGERS, L J
- SKINNER, LORNA
- SKOLFIELD, PEARL
- TERRY NEWSOME PHYSIOTHERAPIST
- WARREN, HELEN
- WILSON, N
- WILSON, SHIRLEY
- WORTH, PHILIP

## HERTFORD

- ASSOCIATES HEAD & SHORT
- ASSOCIATES HEAD & SHORT
- ATHERTON, ANN LOUISE
- BASSETT & ASSOCIATES
- BOTTERILL, V C
- CHAPMAN, ANNA
- DOYLE, AUDREY
- EVERITT, ELAINE M
- GENTLE FEET
- GREIG, LISA
- HALFORD, ELIZABETH
- HALFORD, ELIZABETH
- HERTFORD CENTRE
- HERTFORD NATURAL THERAPY CTRE
- HUMPHRY, S B
- JACKSON, BARBARA
- PINTO, RANDAL P
- REIKI ROOM
- ROBINSON, V
- ROWLAND, JETHRO
- SMITH, SUSAN
- VARNEY PRACTICE
- WHITTLE, MARK
- WILKINSON, ANNE

## HITCHIN

- ALDER, DENNIS
- ANDREWS, M
- ARNOLD, PETER & JACKIE
- ASHCROFT, J J
- ASSOCIATION OF STRESS MNGMT
- BETSER, J
- BURYHILL PHYSIOTHERAPY
- CHIROPRACTIC CONSULTANT SVS
- CHIROPRACTORS MCTIMONEY
- COLBECK, R M E
- COLVIN, P C (DR)
- COUGHLIN, V IAN
- COUSINS, MATHEW
- FRANCIS, MARILYN
- GROUNDS, L
- HARVEST MOON CENTRE
- HEALES CHIROPRACTIC CLINIC
- KELLETT, DAVID & ASSOCIATES
- NLF CHIROPODY
- PARKER, PHILIP
- PERSONAL REFLECTIONS
- PREMADASA, L (DR)
- REED, PHILIP
- RICHARDS, J
- RICHARDS, JESSICA
- RICHMOND, CLARE
- ROWLAND, JETHRO
- SUZANNE
- WINDMILL HILL CLINIC
- WOODSIDE OSTEOPATHIC CLINIC

## HODDESDON

- ASHLEY HOUSE
- BLANE, LAURA J
- BUTTREY, BEATRICE M
- CLARK, STEPHEN
- CLARK, STEPHEN
- MCCLEMENT, SHIRLEY
- PATEL, M
- SOLDANO, JOANNE
- SWALLOW, R M
- WYE, DEBORAH

## KINGS LANGLEY

- CHARTERED PHYSIOTHERAPISTS
- CLARE JAMES HEALTH FOODS
- CLINIC OF HYPNOTHERAPY
- CONISTON PHYSIOTHERAPY CLINIC
- GOLDSMITH, ANNE
- GOLTEN, ROGER
- KINGS LANGLEY OSTEO PRACTICE
- KINGS LANGLEY PHYSIO CLINIC
- MAWSON, MARY M
- NATURAL-BALANCE CO UK
- NEWMAN, M A

## KNEBWORTH

- GURNEY, JACQUELINE
- KINESIOLOGY FEDERATION

## LETCHWORTH

- BERTRAM-SMITH, MICHAEL R
- CHOPRA, S
- COLE, EVA
- DUDLEY, J A
- HILTON, KAREN
- HUTHERT, J
- HUTHERT, J
- KENNON, SUSAN
- LETCHWORTH CENTRE
- LETCHWORTH-PHYSIOTHERAPY
- NEWMAN, TURNER R
- OVERINGTON, KEL
- PODICARE CHIROPODY
- PURLYS
- RICHARDS, J
- SHEPHERDSON, ANTHONY

## MUCH HADHAM

- ASSESSMENT SERVICES
- COOPER, FELICITY

## POTTERS BAR

- ASHDOWN CLINIC
- BODELL, TERRI
- CHARLES BARR HYPNOTHERAPIST
- FISH, BARBARA A
- FORLAND, ELAINA
- HILTON, DAVID
- KNIGHT, S L
- MAXWELL, A T
- RAINSFORD, JOSEPHINE
- RICHARDS, KATHY
- SPINOZA, DAVID
- UNIQUE MASSAGE

## RADLETT

- ALTERNATIVE HEALTH INFORMATION
- CHALMERS, RICHARD
- COUSINS, MATHEW
- HAMILTON-PLANT, C A
- HASAN, ZADI
- HEALTHY AND WISE
- JACOBS, B L
- KIRBY, ANNIE
- LITTLE SANCTUARY
- MITTERHUBER, P F
- PINNY, JASON
- RADLETT PRACTICE
- RICHMOND, CLAIRE
- ROBINSON, C Z

## RICKMANSWORTH

- ALLEN, R D
- ANTI SNORING
- BAKER, A W
- BALL, GILL
- BENNETT, CHARLES R
- BRIND, KEVIN
- CASKEY, ANYA
- CRONIN, CLAIRE E
- HUGHES, THERESA
- MONTANARO TRUST
- PALMER, ELEANOR
- PHILIP, AARONS
- QUILTER, ALISON J
- STEVENSON, LEIGH
- WALFORD, PENELOPE
- WATSON, KATHRYN

## ROYSTON

- CANNON, VALERIE
- CLAYDON, L
- DAVIES, JACQUELINE
- GOWING, KAY
- HARRY, K M
- IAN COLLANGE ASSOCIATES
- IAN COLLANGE ASSOCIATES
- MOYNIHAN, T
- ROYSTON COMP HEALTH CENTRE
- ROYSTON PHYSIOTHERAPY CLINIC
- SMITH, S L

## SAWBRIDGEWORTH

- BARRETT, C
- BECERRA, P
- BIGGINS, NICHOLAS
- BURTON, S J
- DRISCOLL & ASSOCIATES
- DULIEU, FIONA
- HALL, JACQUELINE
- MAUREEN PRIDDLE
- MELLERICK, N D
- PRIDDLE, PATRICK
- PSYCHO & HYPNOTHERAPY CLINIC
- TASS, DIANA
- VERNON, CLIVE J

## ST. ALBANS

- ADSHEAD, MARK
- ALBAN HEALTH
- ALBAN THERAPY
- ANGLO-AUSTRALIAN SEED
- ARNOTT, R A B
- AROMATHERAPY BY ANTONIO
- AROMATHERAPY BY JOANNA JONES
- ASHETON, BEVERLEY
- ASHETON, KEVIN
- ASSOCIATES HEAD & SHORT
- AUTOGENIC TRAINING
- BASSETT CLINIC
- BASSETT, MIKE
- BEER, SUSAN
- BLACKDEN, J M
- BOOTH, CLARE
- BROUWER JOOP
- CAMERON, SARAH
- CARLTON SPORTS & PHYSIO CLINIC
- CHALMERS, RICHARD
- CHAUHAN, D K
- CHEEK, SUSAN
- CHRISTINA, HALLAM
- CLARIDGE, PATRICIA
- COE, J NICHOLAS
- COE, J NICHOLAS
- COX, MADDI
- COX, T
- CUMMINS, DECLAN
- DAVID HERBERT REFLEXOLOGY
- DUNNE, ALISON
- DUNNE, CAROL
- EVANS, HELEN
- EXETER, SHARON

- FREEMAN, FRANCES
- FURLONG, CATHIE
- GRAHAM & KERSTIN ELLIOTT
- GREIG, LISA
- HALAHAN, ELISABETH
- HARMER, LESLEY
- HEALTH BARN CLINIC
- HEYMANN, RUSSELL
- HULL, TERRI
- JAMES, CHRISTINE
- LAMORISSE, JEANNE
- LAZARUS, GAIL
- LE BAS, ROSS
- LEVER CLINIC
- LEVER CLINIC-ACU & OSTEOPATHY
- LIFELINES
- MAJOR, EMMA
- MAY, IAN
- MCAVOY, JAMES
- MCMAHON, STEPHANIE
- MIDAS TOUCH
- MOULE, TERRY G
- MUGAN, D R
- OCEAN BREEZE SANCTUARY
- O'DONOGHUE, CHRISTINE
- O'HARA, JOHN
- PAVEY, M F
- PERSPECTIVES CLINIC
- PRITCHARD, MAUREEN
- PSYCHOLOGIST-HYPNOTHERAPIST
- QUIGLEY, CAROLINE
- RELAXATION CENTRE
- RIPPER, JULIE
- ROBB, S J
- ROBINSON, CHARLOTTE
- ROBINSON, JACKIE
- ROWLAND, JETHRO
- SCOTT, ANTONIA
- SCOTT, LAURA
- SHEN NONG CHINESE MED CTRE
- SHEPHERD, RACHEL
- SOPWELL COMP HEALTH CENTRE
- SOPWELL OSTEOPATHIC CLINIC
- SPENCE, V
- ST ALBANS CHIROPRACTIC CLINIC
- SWAN & SWAN
- TARSEY, SANDRA
- TETLEY, M R M
- THOMAS, HELEN
- THOMPSON, MARK
- TRICHO-CARE
- VUKOVICH, IRENA
- VUKOVICH, NIGEL
- WATSON, CECILY
- WATTS, W D
- WEBB, MARY
- WEBSTER, KAREN
- WHITTLE, MARK
- WHITTONBOURNE, J
- WILKIN, P (DR)
- WILLIAMS, NEVILLE L
- WRIGHT, DOREEN

### STANDON

- ABUNDANCE HEALING

### STEVENAGE

- BACK PAIN & SPORTS INJURY CLNC
- BIANCO, MOIRA
- CHOPRA, S
- CRAWLEY, K
- DANESTRETE CENTRE
- FOZZARD, JOANNA M
- HERRINGTON, YVONNE
- HOLISTIC MATTERS
- HOPKINS, CAROL
- JONES, ALAN
- KELLY, EILEEN
- KNEBWORTH PHYSIO CLINIC
- LIKISMA
- MALCOLM SMITH ASSOCIATES
- MASON, L C
- MEAD, KATHY
- POPOVIC, M
- SANCTUARY ROOM
- SELLERS, JACQUELINE
- ST NICHOLAS SURGERY
- STANTON, JULIE
- VEALE, LINDA
- WINTERS, J

### TRING

- BUTTERFIELD, ROBIN
- GORMAN, J
- GOURLAY, B
- HONEY B
- KINLOCH, DEBORAH
- MURRELL, JANE
- ROBERTSON, IAN R
- SHAW, CHRISTINE
- THORNTON, MICHAEL
- TORY, E
- WEEDON, HAZEL

### WALTHAM CROSS

- ABSOLUTE ESSENCE
- BEDFORD, JANET
- CHESHUNT CHIROPRACTIC CLINIC
- CHESHUNT OSTEOPATHIC CLINIC
- DONOVAN, DAVID M
- EVERITT, ELAINE
- HEAVEY, MAEVE
- HYPNOCURE
- LAMBERT, MARGARET
- NATURAL THERAPY PRACTICE
- OVER, C J A
- PAULS, A
- PEEDLE, DAVID R
- PUNNI, R
- READ, SANDRA
- WARWICK, M

### WARE

- BENSON, HAZEL
- BODY MECHANICS THERAPY CLINIC
- BRADSHAW, J
- COOPER, FELICITY
- DOYLE, KATH
- FREEMAN DUCKMANTON & MASON
- GARD, GRAHAM
- JOHNSON, IAN RICHARD
- MARSHALL, JILL
- PEEDLE, DAVID
- SHOBHA, ARTURI (DR)
- THERAPEUTIC MASSAGE

### WATFORD

- ACKERMAN, FIONA
- ACUPUNCTURE CENTRE
- ANGAR, VYAS
- ATKINS, F
- BA FOR COUNSELLING
- BARNES, SHEENA
- BASSETT & ASSOCIATES
- BRITISH HOM DENTAL ASS
- BROCKWELL, BADGER
- BUSHEY HEATH PHYSIO CLINIC
- BUSHEY HYPNOTHERAPY CENTRE
- BUSHEY PRACTICE
- CARTWRIGHT-ADAMS, NATALIE
- CHINESE MEDICAL CENTRE
- CHIROPODY
- CLAYTON-ROBB, WAYNE
- COLLISON, SUSAN
- COOMBS
- COUNS & HYPNOTHERAPY PRACTICE
- CURTIS, P A
- DEERING, C
- DENIM, M F
- DEVINE, MARY
- ENGLISH, JEREMY A
- ERABADDA, ERIC
- FORSTER, M
- FOX, J P
- FROST, P
- GARNER, ANGELA
- GARNER, SOPHIE
- GODAGAMA, S (DR)
- GREEN, K B
- GREGORIADIS, SUE
- GREIG, LISA
- HARRISON, MALCOLM
- HARRISON, S
- HEWITT, P M
- HOLLENBERY, S
- HURLEY, M
- IMPERIAL SCHOOL OF FENG SHUI
- ISABELLE DAVIDSON REFLEXOLOGY
- JOYCE, EDWIN
- KING, J R
- KING, R
- KINGSFIELD CTRE-PHYSIOTHERAPY
- LEACOCK, S D
- LOVERIDGE, KATHY
- MCNICOL, KIRSTY
- MONK, PETER
- MOSHTAEL, O
- MURRAY, TERESA
- OLIVER, J P
- ORACLE HEALING CENTRE & SHOP
- PANDIT, HELEN
- PARK PHYSIOTHERAPY & SPORTS
- RAITHATHA, MAHENDRA
- REI KI SEMINARS
- RICHARDS, JONATHAN
- SCHARSACH, C
- SCHOLL CENTRE
- SUSAN, CHINNERY
- THORNHILL, WANDA
- TIAN TIAN
- TUNMORE, M
- WALKER, NEL
- WATSON, ANTHONY
- WILLIAMS, I V
- WISE, ALAN
- WORDSWORTH, LINDA

### WELWYN

- SALUBRITY
- SPERRE-DANSIE, B
- SURVIVAL TRUST SURGERY
- WATERS, ROSALIE

### WELWYN GARDEN CITY

- ALTERNATIVE CHOICES
- AQUARIAN SCHOOL HERTFORDSHIRE
- AROMATHERAPY IS FLOWER POWER
- AVERY, MANDA
- BAKSH, ANITA
- BEACH, CARYL
- BEAUCHAMP BAGENAL
- BRADSHAW, S R
- BUSOLINI, DON
- DAVIS, GEOFFREY
- FELDMANN, MARGARET
- FORD, SUSAN
- HORSLEY, NICOLA
- KERRISON, KEITH
- MAYOR, DAVID F
- MID-HERTS ALEXANDER CENTRE
- PARTINGTON, NICHOLAS
- PERRY, SJ & GRACE, B
- REFLEXOLOGY BY ROSALEEN
- VAN DER GRINTEN, PETER
- WELWYN CHIROPRACTIC CLINIC

## HUMBERSIDE

### BARROW-UPON-HUMBER

- LIFE NATURAL THERAPY CENTRE

### BARTON-UPON-HUMBER

- ODYSSEY FOUNDATION

### BRIGG

- BRIGG CHIROPRACTIC CLINIC
- BRIGG PHYSIOTHERAPY
- BRIGG SKIN SURGERY
- COMPLEMENTARY CARE CLINIC
- EURO THERAPY PRACTICE
- THOMPSON, MARK

### POCKLINGTON

- RILEY, S

### SCUNTHORPE

- APPLEGARTH
- BANNERMAN CHIROPODY CLINIC
- BATH, ANN
- DICKINSON, A
- INNERVISION HYPNOTHERAPY CTRE
- JENSEN, A J
- LANGLEY, LYNNE
- MESSINGHAM CHIROPODIST SURGERY
- MYERS, R J L
- NATURAL HEALING CENTRE
- NORRIS, A H
- PRIOSE COLES
- RAZZMATAZZ INTERNATIONAL
- SCUNTHORPE CHIROPRACTIC CLINIC

- SCUNTHORPE CLINIC
- SCUNTHORPE COMMUNITY HLTH CARE
- STEEPER, P T
- UK COUNSELLING SERVICE
- WINN, NIGEL

## HUMBERSIDE (NORTH)

### BEVERLEY

- AMORA TRADING
- BEVERLEY CHIROPRACTIC CLINIC
- CARMAN, CAROL
- DAMIAN P JOHNS
- GREGORY, BRIAN
- LEHAIN, DAN
- NORTH BAR CLINIC
- TINDALE, M
- TOMLINSON, P
- TOMLINSON, S
- WADSWORTH, ROBERT

### BRIDLINGTON

- AJMERI
- ATTLESEY, C
- BRIDLINGTON CHIROPODY SURGERY
- BUTLER, D A
- HODGSON, M
- STOW, A L

### BROUGH

- CULPIN, SANDRA
- DALCROFT COUNSELLING SERVICES
- GILBERDYKE SPORTS & INJURY
- STEELE, AMANDA

### COTTINGHAM

- BEAUTY CLINIC
- EAST RIDING COLLEGE

### DRIFFIELD

- ACORN SCHOOL OF REFLEXOLOGY
- BAKER, IRENE
- BRINDLEY, ELAINE
- COOPER, KAY
- COUTTS & SONS
- FRAGRANT RETREAT
- HERBAL CLINIC
- NATURAL THERAPY CLINIC
- NITHSDALE, DIANA

### GOOLE

- ANDERSON, J GAVIN
- LODGE, ANGELA H
- MOLES, SUZSI
- NATURAL HEALING CENTRE
- SMITH, ANNE C
- VERONICA BEAUTY CLINIC

### HESSLE

- HULL CLINIC OF COMP MEDICINE

### HORNSEA

- NATURAL THERAPIES

### HULL

- ACADEMY PHYSIOTHERAPY CLINIC
- ALTERNATIVES
- ASHCROFT, PATSY
- BEACONLINK
- CAMPBELL, KRYSTYNA
- CAULKIN, CHRISTOPHER
- DENTON, D
- DOYLES
- DUNEDIN CHIROPODY CLINIC
- GEOFF & JAYNE PLUMMER
- HADFIELD, T
- HALTEMPRICE CHIRO CLINIC
- HARVEY CLINIC
- HARVEY CLINIC
- HOLDERNESS CHIROPRACTIC CLINIC
- NATURAL THERAPY CENTRE
- NATURAL THERAPY CENTRE
- OSTEO-MEDIC SERVICES
- PALIN, J M
- POLLENDINE, I
- SAMANTHA WHITE AROMATICA
- STARLIGHT CENTRE
- TAYLOR, BARBARA
- THEAKSTON, G
- WADSWORTH OSTEOPATHS
- WRIGHT, STEPHEN

## HUMBERSIDE (SOUTH)

### CLEETHORPES

- HARRISON-WILLIAMS
- HARRISON-WILLIAMS CHIROPODIST
- PICKERDEN, P

### GRIMSBY

- ACHILLES CENTRE
- ADAMS, RAYMONDE D
- ALTERNATIVE MEDICINE
- BECKETT-GEORGE, D
- BEDI, N P S (DR)
- BURGESS, P
- CHAPPELL, J
- DAVIES, MICHAEL
- DE LA HOYDE, HUGH
- GOUDIE, A V
- GRIMSBY CHIROPRACTIC CLINIC
- LOUISE HEALING CENTRE
- PANIGRAHI, P
- PETULENGRO, LEE
- POTTLE, C J
- ROBINSON, KEITH
- SCARTHO OSTEOPATHIC PRACTICE
- SWEET AROMA'S
- WALL, R A
- WEBB, C M
- WEBB, I M
- WINN, NIGEL

## ISLE OF MAN

### PORT ERIN

- BAILEY-CONLON, ELIZABETH

### RAMSEY

- BASS, CATHERINE

## ISLE OF WIGHT

### ASHFORD

- GREENFIELD, BRIAN

### BEMBRIDGE

- BURROWS, MARY
- GREENWOOD, A J
- KAULA, CAROLYN M

### COWES

- CROUTEAR, SARAH
- DIDHAM, JUDI
- FEET FIRST
- MONTROSE NATURAL HEALTH CARE
- NORMAN, NANCY
- ROBINSON, MICHAEL
- W E PARK WINDER
- WIGHT HOMEOPATHY

### FRESHWATER

- FLANDERS, H

### NEWPORT

- BEISLY, N L (DR)
- BENFIELD, R E
- CARISBROOKE HEALTH CENTRE
- CENTREPOINT CLINIC
- COLEMAN, B
- CREED, GLENN
- DHILLON, K
- GOLDSMITH, D
- HACKER, S M
- HOWARTH, R
- ISLE OF WIGHT LAVENDER
- MCCALL, P W
- NOIRET, C J P
- OAK HOUSE THERAPY CENTRE
- PARKER, CAROL
- PSYCHOTHERAPY UNIT
- ROSE, F A
- SANZ DE DEAS, HILDA C
- SAUNDERS, NICHOLAS
- SHEN CLINIC
- TREE OF LIFE AROMATHERAPY
- WATCHBELL HSE NTRL THRPY CTRE
- WIGHT THERAPY

### PORCHFIELD

- PARRY, SHEILA
- PARRY, SHELLA

### RYDE

- BIDDLECOMBE, D L
- FOOTSTEPS THERAPY CENTRE
- FORTUNES
- GODDEN, PATRICIA
- GREENWOOD, A
- HAWORTH, E
- HOPE CLINIC
- KAULA, CAROLYN M
- LAMBERT, M J
- MANSBRIDGE, SANDRA
- RYDE PHYSIOTHERAPY CLINIC
- SIMON, DAVE
- SMITH, RACHEL E
- TREE OF LIFE AROMATHERAPY
- WRIGLEY, BARBARA

### SANDOWN

- ASSOCIATED PHYSIOTHERAPISTS
- CARD, J P
- DENLEY, KAREN L
- LITTLEJOHN CLINIC
- MCTIMONEY, R
- REFLECTED HEALTH

### SEAVIEW

- BAILEY, B M
- P D W PRAGNELL SPINAL THRP
- TOUCH FOR HEALTH

### SHANKLIN

- FOOTSTEPS
- HEALING HANDS NAT THERAPIES
- HYPNOTHERAPY CONSULTANCY
- PERCIVAL, PAMELA
- SAUNDERS, K
- TAYLOR, S A
- WEBB, RAYMOND

### TOTLAND BAY

- BROOKSIDE PHYSIOTHERAPY SVS
- ELIZABETH, WENDY

### VENTNOR

- CHRISTOPHER, JERRY
- F VON - MEHREN
- HOARE, MICHAEL C

### YARMOUTH

- YARMOUTH CHIROPRACTIC CLINIC

## KENT

### ASHFORD

- ABNETT, LINDA
- ASHFORD CHIROPODY CENTRE
- ASHFORD CLINIC
- ASHFORD OSTEOPATHIC CLINIC
- BATT, M
- BERRY, ELIZABETH
- BIOFLOW MAGNOTHERAPY
- BIRCH, DIANA
- BLUE CRYSTAL RELAXATION MUSIC
- BODY GOLD /CLOVERWOOD
- BOWEN, CHRISTINE
- BOWER, JOAN
- CHIROPODY CLINIC
- CHRISTINE CHINNERY COMP THER
- CLIFT, HELEN
- CLOVERWOOD
- COPY CENTRE
- COTTERILL, JENNY
- COURTNEY, JOHN
- EAST, MARY
- EVEGATE CLINIC
- FRENCH, K J
- HARPER, D
- HEDDLE, R
- HUTCHIN, MARK
- JULIE ROSE STADIUM
- L A ROSS - ACUPUNCTURIST
- LAWRENCE, P F
- LEGG, PAM
- LENWORTH DAY THERAPY SERVICE
- LIKISMA
- LOWE, JANET
- LYE, JENNY
- MABBERLEY, KATHIE
- MANN, PATRICIA
- MATHER, SUE
- NASH, MONICA
- NICHOLS, SYLVIA

- PARTINGTON, T
- PETTS, PHILIP
- PICKEN, M
- PICKEN, M
- REEVE, ANNA C
- TCS RESEARCH
- THOMAS COMPLEMENTARY CLINIC
- WYE OSTEOPATHIC PRACTICE

## AYLESFORD

- AYLESFORD MEDICAL CENTRE
- AYLESFORD OSTEOPATHIC PRACTICE
- DAVIS, IRIS
- HANDS ON HEALTH
- LEWIS, CARYN
- LOMAS-HARRIS, ELISABETH

## AYLESHAM

- AYLSHAM OSTEOPATHIC PRACTICE

## BECKENHAM

- ARMSTRONG, M G
- BARNES, VINCENT
- BECKENHAM ACUPUNCTURE CLINIC
- BECKENHAM CHINESE MED CTRE
- BECKENHAM PHYSIOTHERAPY CLINIC
- BOWEN THERAPY
- CAST, BRIAN
- CHIPPENDALE, M
- CLARE, S M
- FRANCIS-JONES, T
- GARDENER, B
- GARRONE, J B
- GIANFAGNA, CARMELA
- GIBBONS, J
- JACCQUELINE ELLISON PRACTICE
- KANANI, ALPESH
- KENT HOUSE CHIROPRACTIC CLINIC
- LEBRET, A F
- PASSCHIER, CORNELIUS
- PASSCHIER, MAREANNE SASSEN
- PATEMAN, A R & H G
- PELE, ANDRI
- RUTH, MOIRA
- SEYDOUX, B (DR)
- SHARP, JUSTIN
- SMITH, A
- SMITH, J R
- SOUTHCOTT, J
- TERRELL, R G
- THERAPY PLACE
- THOROGOOD, S
- VINCENT, EUNICE

## BELVEDERE

- ABBEY CLINIC
- KALTCHEVA-HICKS, DANIELA
- REGENT HEALTH
- ROBERTS, J R
- WEBB-DE SISTO, MARION

## BEXLEY

- ALTERNATIVE APPROACHES
- BEXLEY OSTEOPATHIC CLINIC
- BRIDGET READER ALTERNATIVE
- BYATT, J M
- COMPLEMENTARY CARE
- DEMETER, GLENNA
- GUNN, JASON
- MICALLEF, JANICE
- PARKIN, EVELYN
- THENUWARA, C D
- WESTERN, GRAME

## BEXLEYHEATH

- BEAUTY NOW
- BEXLEY HEATH SURGERY
- BEXLEYHEATH CHIRO CLINIC
- BEXLEYHEATH CHIROPRACTIC
- BEXLEYHEATH NATURAL HEALTH
- BREW, LESLEY
- CHINESE MEDICINE & ACUPUNCTURE
- CLIFTON, NIGEL
- COUSINS, MARILYN
- COX, ANGELA
- CROOK LOG CHIROPODY SURGERY
- CROOK LOG PHYSIO & SPORTS
- DADSON, D G
- FERNANDO, OLIVER
- FIGUREFIRM HOLISTIC CENTRE
- HOWARD, TERRY
- JACKSON, CELIA
- LIVING HARMONY
- LUTHER, R E
- MAINI, Y P
- MANDY BALDWIN - TRICHOLOGIST
- MURRELL, PAULINE
- NUTRITIONIST
- PARKER, BRIAN
- PRICE, GILLIAN
- ROUSE, JOHN
- TURKINGTON, VIVIENNE
- VINCENT, FRANK
- WALTERS, A B
- WHEATLEY, RON

## BIRCHINGTON

- ABSOLUTE SOLUTIONS
- CLARK, ANGELA
- CONNELLY, G M
- EGAN, F
- ENCHANTMENT
- EUROPEAN AYUR-VEDA
- HAYDEN, J T
- WEBB, M F

## BROADSTAIRS

- A1 FOOTCARE
- BARRETT, ROSEMARY
- BEE NATURAL PRODUCTS
- BOWYER, MARGARET
- BRITISH ASS OF CLAIRVOYANT
- BUSH, RON
- COX, R W
- DENTON, B
- ENLIGHTENMENT
- HARVEY, H
- ISIS
- MEISE, LINDA
- WARD, JAN

## BROMLEY

- ASHDOWN, LOUISE
- BECKENHAM & BROMLEY
- BLAKE, ADRIAN
- BOORER, ALISON
- BROMLEY CHIROPRACTIC CLINIC
- BROMLEY OSTEOPATHIC CLINIC
- BROMLEY STRESS MANAGEMENT CTRE
- BROMLEY STRESS MANAGEMENT CTRE
- BULOS, K C
- CARDWELL, MARTIN
- CARSTAIRS, K (DR)
- CHIROPODY & PODIATRY CLINIC
- DEAR, DIANA
- DICKMAN, ANNIE
- EAST STREET CENTRE
- EWINS, DAVID
- FONTANA, YVONNE
- GRIMES-SAMUEL, EDNA A
- GUPTA, S
- HATELY, S
- HEALING AND HERBS
- HEYWARD, SHIRLEY
- HODGE, S E
- HOFFMAN, BRIAN ASSOCIATES
- HOPPER, K M
- IVERSON, B
- JOCHIM, ANDREAS
- KELSH, C M E
- KYRIA, S
- LEBRET, A F
- LIVING WELL CLINIC
- N L P ACADEMY
- NEAL'S YARD REMEDIES
- NEWMAN, TANYA
- PIGOTT, MARJORIE
- PIKE, DAVINA
- PSYCLOPS
- READ, CHARLES REG OSTEOPATH
- RUSHBROOKE, P
- SELHI, I K
- SMITH, M F
- SMITH, S
- SOUTH LONDON HYPNOTHERAPY CTRE
- STRESS CENTRE
- SURE FOOT PODIATRY PRACTICE
- T C CLINIC
- TURNER, CHARLES
- UK TAI-CHI ASSOCIATION
- VINCENT, A
- WARWICK, MAUREEN
- WHELAN, P
- WILLIAMS, SUSAN
- WOOLF, JOY

## CANTERBURY

- ACUPUNCTURE CLINIC
- ASH PHYSIOTHERAPY/SPORTS CLNC
- ATHANASIADOU, KATERINA
- BENNETT, J P
- BENNETT, J P
- BLITHE SPIRIT
- BRIERLEY, V A
- BROWN, N W J
- BURDEN, PHILIPPA
- CANTERBURY OSTEOPATHIC CLINIC
- CARACCIOS NATURAL THERAPY CTRE
- CERAMIC WATERFALLS
- CHINESE HERBAL MEDICINE
- CHIROPRACTIC CLINIC
- COLLINGWOOD, F J G
- COUSANS, W E
- CULPEPER
- DAVIES, P J
- DICKINS CHIROPRACTIC CLINIC
- DRAYSON, SAMANTHA
- ELECTROLYSIS & BEAUTY CLINIC
- ESSER, ROB J
- FEDER, A P
- FRIARS HEALING/SPIRITUAL CTRE
- GINSENG
- HOPE CHIROPRACTIC
- HUSSAIN, M F
- INT COLLEGE OF CRYSTAL HEALING
- JANSEN, W
- JOHNSON, P
- LEBOR, JILL
- LEIGH HOUSE NAT HEALTH CLINIC
- LEIGH, JON
- LEY, ALISON
- LIVESEY, PAULE
- MARY CANNON - CLINICAL NUTRI
- MATHEWS, T
- MCCARTHY, C R
- MEADOWS
- MEADOWS
- MIKE L'S SMOKING CESSATION
- MUIRHEAD, MARGARET
- NICE, P
- ORCHARD, DAVID
- PALMER, T J
- PEARSON, E
- PELHAM, P H
- PLEWS, BARBARA
- RALPH & EVANS
- READING, JENNIE
- RIDLEY, VICKY
- ROBERTS, A J
- SHEPHERD, JAN
- SHIATSU
- STURRY'S REFLEXOLOGY PRACTICE
- TAYLOR, C L (DR)
- THERESA MAWSON
- TURNER, ANDREA
- WALKER, ELAINE
- WATLING STREET THERAPY CTRE

## CHATHAM

- BIOTECHNIQUE
- FLACK, G
- GRAHAM, J
- HEALTH & BEAUTY WISE
- HERBRIDGE
- HOLDA-MARTIN, JACQUELINE
- HOLDING, V T
- KARMERS CLINIQUE
- KRAMER, STUART
- LAMB, W G
- LOUISA-JAYNE HILL M INST CH P
- MARYANNE
- MASON & ASSOCIATES
- NORTH KENT CHIROPRACTIC CLINIC
- PRINCES AVENUE OSTEOPATHIC
- ROSE, NAOMI
- SANCTUARY OF HEALING
- SIMPSON, ANNE

- STONE, CHARLES
- TAVAKKOLI, KIAN

## CHISLEHURST

- CHISLEHURST CHIROPODY PRACTICE
- CHISLEHURST NATURAL HEALTH
- CHISTLEHURST NATURAL HLTH CTRE
- COOMBS, ANNIE S
- KIRK, J
- NATURAL HEALTH CENTRE
- PANTELI, H
- PRETLOVE, ANN
- SACKS, PATRICA
- SOUTH EAST PSYCHOTHERAPY GROUP
- TRAD CHINESE HERBS & HLTH CTRE

## CRANBROOK

- ANDERSON COMPLEMENTARY MED
- BRAY, CAROLINE
- BUTLER, J H C
- CARRUTHERS, P
- DOWLING, R
- GWYN-WILLIAMS, S
- HAWKHURST NATURAL THERAPIES
- HOME FARMHOUSE
- HOOL, MERYL
- HYPNOSIS COUNSELLING CENTRE
- ROWAN, G
- SEDGE, R
- SWANS
- WILLIAMSON, P A

## CRAYFORD

- FEET FIRST

## DARTFORD

- BREARE, SARAH
- CANCER INFORMATION & SUPPORT
- CHINESE MEDICAL CENTRE-HERBFIT
- DARTFORD NATURAL HEALTH CENTRE
- DOREY, STELLA
- DROP-IN CENTRE
- ESSENCES OF AROMA/NTRL THRPY
- FENTON, MICHELLE
- FROST, CAROLINE
- HEALER, ANDY JOHNSON
- HEATHSIDE CENTRE
- HERTERICH, NIGEL
- HILTON HEALTH CENTRE
- HINDE, TERESA
- HORNER, LINDLEY
- HOWARD, TERRY
- IDLE & ALLAN
- J SIMMONDS LIFESTYLE PRODUCTS
- LANE, MARGARET J
- LANGRIDGE, LORRAINE
- MURRIN, P
- O'ROURKE, LESLEY
- PATHWAYS HYPNOTHERAPY
- PERFECT, CATHY
- QUEEN ELIZABETH'S FOUNDATION
- RUIZ-GOLVANO, ELENA
- SCHUSZLER, RANJA
- SCOBLE, ALISON
- SEDGEWICK, SARAH JANE
- TAYLOR, J
- TURNER, PAULA

## DEAL

- COCKERELL, IAN
- COMFORT, STEVEN V
- D, CAIN
- DEAL CHIROPRACTIC CLINIC
- DEAL PHYSIOTHERAPY CLINIC
- DUCROTOY, M
- HARRISON, W L
- HILL, ALISON
- PRO PHYSIO CLINIC
- SANDOWN CLINIC FOR COMP MED
- SHAWCROSS, ROSALIND
- THOMAS, V

## DOVER

- CANTERBURY SCHOOL
- CASTLE CLINIC
- CHIDWICK, SAMUEL
- FANTOM, L
- KEVIN POWER PSYCHOTHERAPY
- PRIORY CENTRE
- RIJSKIJK, CAROLE
- ROWLEY, JULIA
- SCREENE, D
- SHANTI HEALTH HERBAL PRODUCTS
- STEWART, SUSAN
- STUBBS, I J
- WOLVERTON COURT

## EDENBRIDGE

- ASHTON, JOHN H
- ASSOCIATION OF STRESS MNGMT
- CARROLL, S F
- FALCONER, PATRICIA
- HIGH STREET CHIROPODY SURGERY
- HOWARD, G
- MCCOY, ROBERT J
- NEW, G S
- TURNER, PENNY
- VARNEY, MONICA

## ERITH

- BLAKE, SHEILA
- LOBB, BRIAN W
- WEST, TERENCE

## FAVERSHAM

- BURTON & KERR
- COMMON SCENTS
- DATE, M S
- FAVERSHAM CLINIC
- HESELDEN, TERESA E
- JENNER, ROSEMARY
- KENT INSTITUTE OF COMP MED
- MURRAY, LESLEY
- PITT, D
- SMITH, SUSAN M
- SUMMERS, M
- WARD, FRANCES

## FOLKESTONE

- ALEXANDER TECHNIQUE
- BAILEY, GILLIAN
- BARRETT, C J & M
- BLOSSOM AROMATHERAPY CENTRE
- BOWLING, ANDREW
- BUTTERFILL, M T
- CHAMPION, ALISON
- CHINESE MEDICINE CENTRE
- CHIROPRACTIC PLUS
- COMMUNITY HEALTH CARE TRUST
- DEAKIN, T
- DOHERTY, ANN
- DOUGLAS, G
- DRION & ASSOCIATES
- EDWARDS, R, HERNE BAY
- EVANS, PHILIP
- FOLKESTONE PHYSIO CENTRE
- FRIS-LAWRENCE, J
- HARVEY CLINIC
- KINGSTON, PATRICIA
- LACK, J E J
- LAMB, G BRIAN
- LUCAS, JANICE T
- LUDKINS, P
- MACLEAN, JANE FERGUSON
- MURRAY, R H
- NORWOOD & STEPHENSON
- PHILLIPS, CAROL
- PROFESSIONAL HYPNOTHERAPY
- S J DYSON REFLEX-AROMA
- SCREEN, D
- SKINGLE, P
- SMITH, P
- TEACHER OF THE ALEXNDR TECH
- VIGNAUX, PATRICK
- WAGLAND, C
- WOOLCOCK & ASSOCIATES

## GILLINGHAM

- ARNOLD, M S
- BAKER, M A
- BAKER, ROY
- BARNES & ASSOCIATES
- BISHOP, SARAH
- COX, K
- COX, RITA
- CREDO THERAPIES FIRST
- GAMP, C
- GILLINGHAM CLINIC OF COMP MED
- HEALING HANDS
- JUDGE, J P
- KENNEDY, JASMINE
- KENT OSTEOPATHIC CLINIC
- MEDWAY ACUPUNCTURE CLINIC
- MEDWAY ALTERNATIVE HEALTH CTRE
- MILLER, R
- MUGHAL, JAVED
- PIDDUCK, J
- PSYCHIC FRIENDS NETWORK
- RICHARDS, GERALDINE
- ROSE OAK HEALTH & BEAUTY CLNC
- ROUSE, BARBARA
- SHANON, D
- SHILLING, TARA
- SILVER WING CENTRE
- STRIDE, D

## GRAVESEND

- ALLERGY TESTING
- ALVA HOUSE
- BODY BEAUTIFUL
- BRUCE, KATHRYN
- CARD, K
- CHAPMAN, STEPHEN
- CUMMINGS, ELIZABETH
- DAVIES, ANGELA
- DERMALUX
- ELECTROLYSIS & BEAUTY CLINIC
- FOOT CLINIC
- GANNON, P
- GRAVESEND HOMOEOPATHY CLINIC
- GROVE CHIROPODY PRACTICE
- HERBMEDIC
- HOMEOPATHIC MEDICAL ASS
- JENNER, SUE
- JOHN PATTISON CHIROPODIST
- KENNERLEY, MAGGIE
- MASON & ASSOCIATES
- MASON, J R
- MEOPHAM CLINIC
- MILLER, R W
- OSTEOPATHIC CLINIC
- PETERS, MATTHEW
- SIMPSON, ANNE
- SIMPSON, ANNE

## GREENHITHE

- ENNIS, CHRIS
- SIMMONDS, JENNI
- WAKEMAN, BEVERLEY

## HERNE BAY

- AROMA HEALTH
- AROMA HEALTH
- ASTROLOGICAL CONSULTANTS
- BAKOWSKA, D
- EDWARDS, R
- HOPPER, ANN
- KEMP, SANDRA
- KENT CURATIVE HYPNOTHERAPY
- KSC
- LLOYD, A
- MULVANEY, ALISTAIR
- MULVANEY, E J
- NUMBER 11 THERAPY CENTRE
- QUEEN VICTORIA MEMORIAL HOSP
- SHEEHAN, MIKE
- SOUTAR, GILLIAN
- THEW, CAROLYN

## HYTHE

- ANGELS CLAIRVOYANCY
- BURGIS, TESSA
- CARTER, AMANDA
- CENTRE
- FALLSHAW, ELIZABETH
- HIROKO, KELLY
- HYTHE CHIROPODY SERVICES
- HYTHE PHYSIOTHERAPY CENTRE
- ISIS
- LAWLESS, D
- MABBERLEY, KATHIE
- O'DONNELL, ANNEGRET
- OLD RECTORY
- SAMUELS, CAROLANN

## LONGFIELD

- ANNIES NATURAL HEALTH CENTRE
- ASSOCIATION OF STRESS MNGMT
- AXTON, PETER
- KATSIS, HAYLEY
- LAISTER, PAMELA

- WHATLING, NICOLA

## MAIDSTONE

- AMBROSE, YVONNE D
- BAKER, C
- BEARSTED CHIROPODY & PODIATRY
- BOWER MOUNT CLINIC
- BRAITHWAITE FOOT CLINIC
- BRUNGER, ANDREW
- CARLEY, R J
- CHALKLEY, E & S
- CHARTIER, SUSAN
- CHINESE MEDICAL CENTRE
- CLINTON, D H
- COMPLEMENTARY THERAPIES
- DAHL, JESPER
- DAVINSKY, MARZO
- DIMENT, GORDON L
- DUFFY, MELANIE
- ELECTROLYSIS CENTRE
- EUROPEAN SCHOOL OF OSTEOPATHY
- EUROPEAN SCHOOL OF OSTEOPATHY
- FERN & CUTTER
- FIELDING, DEBORAH
- GRAVITT CLINIC
- HARRIS, JEREMY
- HEALTHWORKS
- HEATH ROAD CLINIC
- HEATHSIDE PHYSIOTHERAPY DEPT
- HOLMES, S A
- HOWLAND, ANN
- HUNT, H
- LAVINGOTN, A
- LEIPER, BRUCE M
- LONDON ROAD CHIROPODY CLINIC
- LOVELAND, SYLVIA
- MAIDSTONE ACUPUNCTURE CLINIC
- MAIDSTONE CHIROPODY PRACTICE
- MAIDSTONE COLLEGE-OSTEOPATHY
- MAIDSTONE SCHOOL-MASS/AROMA
- MARCER, NICHOLAS
- MURRELL, CHARLES
- NEILL, BOB
- PAUL CHEDGEY MEDICAL HERBALIST
- PRICE, ELIZABETH
- PSYCHOLOGICAL SERVICE
- PULLEN, AUDREY M
- PYE, MICHAEL
- REEVES, SUSAN
- SCHOLL CENTRE
- SHIATSU WORKS
- SIMPSON, K C
- SOUTHCOTE CHIROPRACTIC CLINIC
- SUN HOUSE HOLISTIC HEALING
- TAMARA, YVETTE
- TAMARA, YVETTE
- THRESH, M G S
- VENN, ESTHER K
- WEBSTER, TINA
- WINGROVE, KATHLEEN
- YORK, SALLY

## MARGATE

- BEAGLEY, D R
- BELLAMY, K J
- BOSWELL, EVA
- COLE, C F
- EARL, A
- FORREST, E A
- GREEN, ELIZABETH
- GREEN, M
- HART, KAREN
- LEESON, D J
- MACARI, SALVINA
- METHANANDA, S P
- SHEARER, GAYLE
- WILLGOTT, K

## NEW ROMNEY

- BAXTER, E
- BLAKE, JANET
- EAGLES, EILEEN
- FIGURE WISE THERAPY CLINIC
- GOOCH, S
- ROMNEY MARSH OSTEOPATHS
- STONE, JUNE
- TAMARA, YVETTE

## ORPINGTON

- ACUPUNCTURE/CHINESE HERBAL
- ADBY, SHEILA
- ALOE VERA ADVISORY SERVICE
- ALOE VERA ADVISORY SERVICE
- AYLING, GILL
- BAKER, SANDRA
- BAXTER, BEVERLEY J
- BOADEN, PAM
- BROMLEY CHIROPODY CENTRE
- CALLAGHAN, DENISE
- CHINESE HERBAL MED ACU CTRE
- CLINIQUE DE SANTE
- COSTIN, A E
- COURT, SUSAN
- DANIELLS, JONATHAN
- ESSENTIAL HEALTH MANAGEMENT
- FIELD, KATIE
- FRANCIS-JONES, T
- FRANCIS-JONES, TREVOR (DR)
- GIBSON, JAN
- HOLMDEN, JO-ANNE
- HOME VISITING CHIROPODY SV
- KENT HOUSE CHIROPRACTIC CLINIC
- KENT HOUSE CHIROPRACTIC CLINIC
- KINGSTON, J H
- ORPINGTON CHIROPRACTIC CLINIC
- PARISH, ANN
- PATERSON, MARGARET
- PETTS WOOD CHIROPODY-PODIATRY
- PUNTER, WENDY
- REIKI HEALING CENTRE
- RICHARD ANDREWS HAIR & BEAUTY
- ROBERTS, KATE
- ROBINSON, DENISE
- SANCTUM HOLISTIC THERAPY CTRE
- SANDERS, PETER
- SILLITOE, CHRISTOPHER
- SOUL SEARCHERS
- STICK, ALEX W
- STUDART, P J
- SWAN, VIVA
- VILLAGE PHYSIOTHERAPY PRACTICE
- WEAVER, CAROL
- ZUIDYK, TOSCA

## RAINHAM

- ABBOTT, LISA
- ABBOTT, LISA
- BATTERSHALL, J E
- ELIZABETH ANNE
- GRAHAM, W A
- NIKKEN INDEPENDENT DISTRIBUTOR
- REVEREND CAROL HADDERSLEY
- STUBBS, DAVID
- WILKINS, D
- YOUNG, CAROLE

## RAMSGATE

- ALTERNATIVE HEALTH & BEAUTY
- BEATTIE, J
- BENSON, MICHAEL
- BOHACZ, KIM
- CARTER, TERRI
- EDWARDS, R
- HEAD TO TOE WELL-BEING
- JANSEN, W
- JEANNE OF KENT
- PARKER, R M
- POULTON, J
- RAMSGATE PHYSIO & SPORTS
- STURGE, R F
- WALKOM, N E

## ROCHESTER

- BIO HEALTH
- BLAKEMAN, S M
- BRYANT, M L
- BURGE, ROBERT A
- CHANGE OF LIFE
- COX, KATHERINE
- CRACKNELL, JANICE
- DARWIN, EDWARD
- DILLON, MICHAEL
- FLACK, G
- FRANELLI
- HARWOOD, COLIN
- HAZLEWOOD OSTEOPATHIC PRACTICE
- HOWE, ROBERT
- KEELER, THELMA
- LANE, DAVID
- LEADER, D G
- LUGG, G
- MASON, T G
- MEDWAY CHIROPRACTIC CLINIC
- MEDWAY OSTEOPATHIC CLINIC
- MIND BODY SOUL DEVELOPMNT ORG
- PEARTON, GILL
- PINE & ASSOCIATES
- RAJENDRAN, D
- ROCHESTER CHIRO HEALTH CENTRE
- ROCHESTER PHYSIO & SPORTS
- SIXTH SCENTS
- SMITH, K S
- SMITH, M
- STANTON, BARRIE
- STARSCOPE INTERNATIONAL
- STEVENSON, J E
- THOMAS CONLIN
- TWITCHETT, EVE

## ROMNEY MARSH

- BAXTER, E
- BLAKE, JANET
- CLIFTON, C

## SANDWICH

- ACUPUNCTURE CLINIC
- BLACKBURN, V
- HEALY, STEPHANIE
- HOLOS COMP THERAPY CLINIC
- O'SULLIVAN, PAM

## SEVENOAKS

- ARCHER, ANNE
- BALLARD, MELISSA
- BEADLE HOUSE CLINIC
- BIRKBECK, C A
- BOTHA, M E
- BREARE, SARAH
- CHINESE HERBAL MED & HLTH CARE
- CLEMENCY
- COLE, JEAN
- DAVID, B
- DAVIES, FIONA
- HAYES, JACQUELINE
- HILL, CHARLOTTE
- HOGGARD, J
- HOLISTIC FENG SHUI
- KENT HOUSE CHIROPRACTIC CLINIC
- LINCOLN, FRED
- LOOK 2 NATURE
- MAUGER, GILLY
- MCLAREN, M
- MEW, JILL
- MORTIMORE & STUDART
- NEWBON, B
- OCCUPATIONAL PSYCHOLOGY SVS
- ORPINGTON CHIROPRACTICE CLINIC
- PAMS HOLISTIC THERAPY CENTRE
- PEACOCK, EMMA
- PITCAIRN-KNOWLES, M
- PITCAIRN-KNOWLES, R
- POSITIVE LIVING
- PSARADELIS, T
- SEVENOAKS OSTEOPATHIC PRACTICE
- SMITH, KENNETH
- SOUTH EAST MASSAGE
- WEBB, JENNIFER

## SHEERNESS

- LEIGH, JON H
- MCDOUGALL, NORRIE
- SANGEELEE, BERNADETTE
- VINES REIKI HEALING CENTRE

## SIDCUP

- ANSELL, H
- BALDWIN, MADELEINE
- BLACKFEN HYPNOTHERAPY
- CARRINGTON, DAVID
- COLEBY CENTRE
- DYER, DAVID
- EVANS, A
- GUTH & ASSOCIATES
- HOMOEOPATHIC HEALTH CENTRE
- JOCHIM, ANDREAS
- JORDAN, S E
- NATURAL THERAPIST
- NEUDEGG, KENNETH

- NEW SILHOUETTE
- RYAN, ANN
- SIDCUP CHIROPODY SURGERY
- SPREYER, DIANNE
- STERRY, MICHAEL
- TOWLI, BARBARA

## SITTINGBOURNE

- BEER, L & M
- BENSTED, LUCINDA
- BLACKWOOD, JANE
- BUCKBERRY, TINA
- CARLE, J
- COGGER, N
- CULLEN, KEVIN
- DELTA MEDI CLINIC
- GEORGIOU, C A
- HILLS & DE SOUSA
- HOLISTIC THERAPIES
- LIKISMA PRESENTATIONS
- LYKISMA
- MAY, CELIA
- MILLENNIUM HEALTHCARE
- MILLER, JENNY
- OWEN, LIBBY
- PHYSIOTHERAPY CENTRE
- RELAX AROMA/REFLEXOLOGY
- SAINSBURY
- SITTINGBOURNE OSTEO PRACTICE
- TOLE, J R E
- TYLER, VALERIE
- WERTS, DOUGLAS
- WEST, LAINA
- YONGE, V

## SNODLAND

- D'ALMEIDA, KAREN
- ELLIS & ASSOCIATES
- PANTALL, A L
- ROPER, J

## SOUTHBOROUGH

- SOLE PURPOSE

## SWANLEY

- BROWN, J E
- COULING, J
- HARRISON, DEBORAH
- HONES, JULIA
- RAGGETT, JANET
- TOWN, BERNICE

## TENTERDEN

- ADAMS, JANET
- BOXALL, RICHARD
- CHIROPODY SERVICES
- COACH HOUSE CLINIC
- FERGUSON, SUSAN
- GAINBOROUGH CHIROPODY CLINIC
- GRANVILLE, MICHELLE
- HAMLIN-BRIGNALL, KATHRYN
- HOAD, A S
- HOAD, STUART
- LAWRENCE, P F
- MICHELLE PEARSON AT HARMONY
- OPTIVAVA
- OSBORNE, JEAN
- OSBORNE, JEAN
- ROUND ROOM
- ROYLANCE, JOHN
- TENTERDEN HOM PRACTICE
- WILSON, VERONICA

## TONBRIDGE

- A B C HYPNOSIS
- ANDERSON-DOBLE, CYNTHIA
- ARRAN YOGA
- BRIAR
- BRITISH AIRWAYS TRAVEL CLINICS
- CHINESE HERBAL MED & HLTH CARE
- CLGE OF CLINICAL REFLEX/HOL MASS
- COURT, SUSAN
- EAST PECKHAM OSTEO PRACTICE
- ELIXAROME
- ELSWORTH, K
- ENNESS, SALLY
- FAWKES, R E
- FOX, E
- GORING-THOMAS, DIANE
- IRONSIDE, YOLANDA
- JONES, MARTIN
- LAWSON, PETER R
- MICHIE, CAROL A
- MORETON, JUNE
- NATURAL THERAPY CENTRE
- NOBLE CLINIC
- PASCOE & ASSOCIATES
- PINDER, F C
- SCHOFIELD, I
- SHIPBOURNE HOUSE
- SPARGO, W & CROWE, F D
- SYCAMORE, TONI
- TONBRIDGE CLINIC
- TONBRIDGE HOMOEOPATHIC CLINIC
- TOYNE, JOY K
- VAUX, P A
- WEBSTER, JAMES B

## TUNBRIDGE WELLS

- ARTHUR, ALICIA
- AUSTRALIAN BODY CARE UK
- BALL, JUNE
- BERGMANN, MARIA (DR)
- BIDBOROUGH CHIROPRACTIC CLINIC
- BLUSH
- BOXALL, R J
- BRIDGES, GLYNIS
- CALVER, AMANDA
- CHENG, MIGGI
- CHIROPRACTIC & HERBAL CENTRE
- CHRISTINE & LINDA
- CLAYDON, JOHN
- COOKE, C Y
- COYSTEN & ASSOCIATES
- CROUCH, JANET
- DADSON, D G
- DAVENPORT-FRY, ELIZABETH
- DUFFY, MELANIE
- FOORD, AUDREY
- FREEMAN, BELINDA
- GAY, E A
- GERMANN, KIRSTEN
- GROVE, M
- HAMMOND, RICHARD
- HANNA, MARK
- HANNA, MARK
- HAWTHORN CLINIC
- HELIOS HOMOEOPATHIC CLINIC
- HEMSLEY, SARAH
- HERBAL COTTAGE
- HERBRIDGE CHINESE HEALTH CTRE
- HILLS, MARGARET
- HILLS, MAURICE J
- HOLISTIX AROMATHERAPY
- HOME CHIROPODY SERVICE
- HORSFIELD, FIONA
- ILLUMINADA
- KENT COUNS PSYCHOTHPY UNION
- KORTH & ASSOCIATES
- LAVERSTOCK PHYSIO PRACTICE
- MARTIN, PAULA
- MATTHEWS, S
- MCDOWELL, S
- MCDOWELL, STEPHEN
- MCGREGOR, CAROLYN
- MONTAGUE-SMITH, G
- MONTAGUE-SMITH, T
- MURAYAMA, YOSHIHIRO
- NATURAL CLINIC
- NEW WEALDEN CLINIC
- NORTH, SARAH
- OSTEOPATHIC PRACTICE
- PALMER, SUSAN
- PECK, GORDON
- PLATINGS, T N
- RANDELL, KAREN & STEPHEN
- ROWLAND, G A
- SCHOLL CENTRE
- SCOBLE, ALISON
- SOUTH, JANE
- SPINAL HEALTH CLINIC
- STARFIELDS HOLISTIC HLTH CTRE
- STRONG, A C
- STRONG, L A E
- TUNBRIDGE WELLS CHIROPRACTIC
- TUNBRIDGE WELLS OSTEO PRACTICE
- TYLER, SUE
- WARD, A
- WELLS CENTRE
- WELLS PHYSIO & SPORTS CLINIC
- WHITE LODGE ASSOCIATION
- WILLIAMS, C S
- WOODWARD, CLIVE
- YEATES, ANNE

## WELLING

- BARKER & BENNELL
- BRADLEY, SUSIE
- CROIX, LINDA LA
- EDEN, PATRICIA
- LOCKINGTON & ASSOCIATES
- NELSON, GAN
- WELLING CLINIC

## WEST KINGSDOWN

- CHANDRA PDS

## WEST MALLING

- HASTIE, A
- IRWIN, A C
- KINGS HILL REFLEXOLOGY
- RALPH, ANITA
- RALPH, ANITA
- ROBINSON, M
- SHIRLEY, JAMES
- WALLIS, P A

## WEST WICKHAM

- ADDINGTON ROAD PRACTICE
- BURNETT, PAUL
- HEADON, CHRISTOPHER
- NAT FED OF SPIRITUAL HEALERS
- NATURAL HEALTH CENTRE
- NATURAL MEDICINE CENTRE
- NEWBERRY, JOYCE
- REIKI ASSOCIATION
- SNOAD, RICHARD JOHN
- WOLFE, ROBERT

## WESTERHAM

- BEARD, ROSE
- BODY STRESS RELEASE
- CAPEL, TERRY
- COURTYARD CLINIC
- EASTWOOD, KAREN
- FURZE CORNER NATURAL THERAPIES
- MORRIS, MARGARET
- NOAD, SARA
- ORME, SUE
- STEFFEN, E
- USEFUL THERAPIES

## WESTGATE-ON-SEA

- ART OF WELL-BEING
- PHYSIO & SPORTS INJURY CLNC
- STURGE, DEBBIE
- WESTGATE OSTEOPATHIC PRACTICE

## WHITSTABLE

- CARBONEL-DEERE, M
- CHIROPODY PRACTICE
- CORRIGAN, PETER
- EVOLUTION HEALTH
- HIRON, D
- PATON-SMITH, ARLEEN
- POWELL, ANNE-MARIE
- STAPLES, ELAINE
- WATSON, KEITH
- WAYMAN, W N
- WEBB, ALAN

# LANCASHIRE

## ACCRINGTON

- BRADLEY & ASSOCIATES
- HYNDBURN PRIVATE CLINIC-OSTEO
- J H W PSYCHOLOGICAL SERVICES
- LYONS, STEVEN
- MASTERS, DAVID
- ONE STOP HEALTH & BEAUTY
- PERSONAL READINGS
- RILEY, LYNN
- SOOTHING HANDS
- STARKIE, A M
- TINNION, D J
- VICTORIA PRIVATE PHYSIO CLINIC

## BACUP

- BACUP HOLISTIC THERAPIES
- BOGART, R S

## BARNOLDSWICK

- ALTERNATIVE HEALTH THERAPIES
- JONES, B A

## BLACKBURN

- ALPHAWAVE
- ALTERNATIVE MEDICINE PRACTICE
- ALTERNATIVE MEDICINE PRACTICE
- BIOS NATURE CLINIC
- BLACKBURN PHYSIOTHERAPY CLINIC
- CHIROPRACTIC ASSOCIATES
- COMPLEMENTARY THERAPY CENTRE
- CROOK, G C
- DUCKWORTH, JEAN
- DUCKWORTH, JEAN
- DUXBURY, HELEN
- EDWARDS, G J
- GREENHALGH, A J T
- GROGAN, DIANA E
- GUTTERIDGE, DAVID
- HARWOOD, KEITH J
- HAYDOCK, CLAIRE
- HOLDEN, JOHN H
- HUNT & ASSOCIATES
- JOHN HOLDEN ASSOCIATES
- KARIM, S
- KAY, SHELIA
- KELSALL, PETER T
- MARSLAND PRIVATE CTRE OF ACU
- MILL HILL
- NELSON, S
- PETTIGREW, MICHAEL
- RATCLIFFE, MARK
- RICHARDSON, P
- SMITH, SHEILA
- SPIRITUAL THERAPIST
- STUDIO BEAUTY/NATURAL HEALING
- TOMLINSON, JUDITH
- ZODIAC

## BLACKPOOL

- ABERNETHY, HILARY
- ACTION ORTHO
- ALDEPHI HOUSE
- AROMAZ
- ASTARRE INT TAROT CONSULTANT
- BLACKPOOL CHIROPRACTIC CLINIC
- BLACKPOOL OSTEOPATHY CLINIC
- BRAMLEY, S
- CLAIRVOYANT, ANDREW
- CLAREMONT
- CRESSWELL, JAN
- DAVIES, JOHNATHON
- DICKINSON, R
- DOWDALL, TONY
- FOREST GATE PHYSIOTHERAPY
- HOUGHTON, CHRISTINE
- HYPNOTHERAPIST CENTRE-FYLDE
- INGLE, M T
- INSPIRED TECHNOLOGY
- KELLY, SUSAN
- LAYNE, SUSAN G
- LOPATO, G E
- MACRAE, V C
- MALKIN, DK, MANIP THERAPY
- MARGARET'S AROMA/HEALING
- MECHEN, M
- MIQUEL, SHEILA
- MUNGUR, K
- NATURAL HEALTH CLINIC
- NATURAL THERAPY CLINIC
- OLSSON, J D
- PARADAEMA, PAULA
- PARZIALE, BARBARA
- PETULENGRO, LEAH
- REGENCY ELECTROLYSIS
- RINDER, TONY
- SMITH, ELIZABETH M
- THORNTON, CHRISTINE
- WILSON, G

## BOLTON

- ALEXANDER, GERRARD
- ALYN, PAUL
- BARNES & WILLCOCK
- BARNES, MICHAEL W
- BOLTON CHINESE MEDICAL CENTRE
- BOLTON CHIROPRATIC CLINIC
- BOLTON CLINIC OF ACUPUNCTURE
- BOLTON PHYSIOTHERAPY CLINIC
- BOLTON THERAPY CENTRE
- BRIDGWATER, K A
- BRIDGWATER, K A
- BROMLEY CROSS THERAPY CLINIC
- CHARTERED PHYSIO & SPORTS
- CLINICAL REFLEXOLOGY
- COLLIER, A
- CORNISH, B A
- CRAWFORD, D C
- DOWLING, SHEILA
- DYSON, VICTORIA
- ENTERPRISE
- FLETCHER, J E
- HASLAM, H
- HEAVENS SCENT AROMATHERAPY
- HEYWORTH, S
- HIGGINS, I
- HORWICH SPORTS INJURY & PHYSIO
- HOWARTH, JUNE
- IBBETSON, JOHN A
- ISHERWOOD, NIGEL
- KENNEDY, CLAIRE
- KNIGHTS, VALERIE
- LAMBOURN COURT STRESS MNGMT
- LANCASHIRE EPILIGHT CLINIC
- LEE GATE REMEDIAL CLINIC
- LYONS, A J
- MARKLAND COMP THERAPY CENTRE
- MATHER, A R
- MATTINSON, LESLEY
- METCALF, JOHN
- MILLER, SUSAN
- MORGAN, P D
- NATURES ENERGY
- NRTH WEST ALLERGY & NUTRITION
- NUTTELL, DAVE
- PARR, JIM
- PORRITT, M
- RADIVAN, BARRY
- RAFFIT, PHILIPPE
- RAINBOW PREGNANCY ADVICE
- RAMSEY, L
- SCHOLL CENTRE
- SHACKLADY, EVE
- SHARPLES, JEAN
- SOUTHWORTH, L
- ST GEORGES MULTI THERAPY CTRE
- TRADITIONAL ACUPUNCTURE CLINIC
- TURNER, EVELYN
- UPHAM, GILL
- WALKER, SUSAN J
- WILKINSON, J
- WILLIAMS, DOUGLAS G
- WOODWARD, A J

## BURNLEY

- ALTERNATIVELY
- BALDWIN, M
- BARLOWS
- BRUNTON, A
- BURNLEY CLINIC OF OSTEOPATHY
- CLARK & ASSOCIATES
- CLARK & ASSOCIATES
- COLLIER, ELAINE M
- DYSON, ELIZABETH
- HOFFMAN, W
- HYPNOTHERAPY CENTRE BURNLEY
- LAUNER, M
- LIKISMA
- NUTTER, D
- PERPETUAL INNOVATIONS
- PHYSIO & SPORTS INJURY CLNC
- RATCLIFFE, MARK
- SALMON, RUTH V
- STEVENS & ASSOCIATES
- THERABEUTIC
- TINKER, D C
- WILLIAMS, L

## BURY

- ALTERNATIVE HEALTH CLINICS
- BAND, GILLIAN
- BEARLEY, CAROL
- EMERSON, MICHAEL
- FEET FIRST
- FEET FIRST
- FOOT HEALTH CLINIC
- GILL, Y
- GOSHENS THERAPIES
- GREENMOUNT HYPNOTHERAPY CENTRE
- HAWKSHAW FOOT CENTRE
- HEATON, S
- JACOBS, MARION
- KEATING, B G
- LOWE, ANDREA
- MCENTYRE, NUALA
- MERIDIAN CLINIC
- NORTHERN ACU & OSTEO MED CTRE
- O'NEILL, RICHARD
- ORMEROD
- PHYSIO AND SPORTS INJURIES
- PHYSIOTHERAPY SERVICES
- PURCELL, AMANDA
- RAMSBOTTOM PHYSIO CLINIC
- REMEDIAL MASSAGE/SPORTS
- RIDSDALE, J S
- ROBERT CRAIG THERAPY
- ST MARY'S CLINIC
- THOMAS, LYNDA
- THOMPSON, J L
- TOMLINSON, PETER J
- VARLEY, M A
- VARLEY, M A
- WHITTAKER, ANNE
- WOOD, ALISON

## CARNFORTH

- CONWAY, CLIFFORD
- CONWAY, JANET
- EVANS, PAT
- LANCASTER, L
- LIBRA HOLISTIC THERAPY
- MCCUTCHEON, IAN
- NATURAL HEALTH CLINIC
- NATURES WORLD
- WARNE, JANET

## CHORLEY

- ACORN HYPNOTHERAPY SERVICES
- ACUPUNCTURE PRIVATE CLINIC
- ADLINGTON CHIROPODY
- BODYWORLD
- BRITISH HYPNOTHERAPY ASS
- CENTRE FOR COMP MEDICINE
- CHORLEY & DISTRICT CLINIC
- CHORLEY CHIROPODY PRACTICE
- DENNEY, ANDREA
- DOUGLAS, CAROLINE
- DOVE, JOHN
- ELHALHULI, OTHMAN
- GARSTANG, LINDA
- HARMONIOUS HEALTHCARE
- HARMONIOUS HEALTHCARE
- LAURANT, PIERRE
- MOON, BARBARA
- O'SHEA, SHEILA & PARTNERS
- TURBEFIELD, SHELLEY
- WATKINSON, BARBARA

## CLITHEROE

- CARR, CATHERINE
- CLITHEROE PHYSIOTHERAPY CENTRE
- CRYSTAL & REIKI
- EDWARDS, G J
- JONES, B A
- KENDEL HOUSE CLINIC
- PARK, D
- PERCIVAL, R W & H A
- PHYSIO & SPORTS INJURY CLINIC
- POTTER, CHRISTINE
- SOUTHWORTH, LINDA
- TOMLINSON, T J
- WALSH, JOHN

## COLNE

- HARDMAN, ALAN
- KELLETT-HARRISON, ELAINE
- LEE-CROWTHER, CATHRYN
- NATURES WAY CLINIC
- PENDLE NATURAL HEALING CENTRE
- SMITH, CHRISTOPHER (DR)
- SPECIAL MOMENTS
- SPENCER & POWELL
- TOMLINSON, ELIZABETH

## DARWEN

- BRIDGE STREET CHIROPODY
- BRIGGS, JOHN C
- DARWEN PHYSIOTHERAPY CLINIC

- GREENHALGH, S
- HAWORTH, JAMES
- HEAVEN SCENT HOLISTIC THERAPY
- I'ANSON, K L
- MOBILE CHIROPODIST
- PARKER, RAYMOND
- PARR, CAROL
- PRESTON, LINDA
- RILEY, SUSAN M

## FLEETWOOD

- DOODY, ANDREW
- DOODY, COLLEEN
- HAMPSOM, JAMES
- MANGNALL, J

## LANCASTER

- BANKS, ALASTAIR
- BASHFUL ALLEY CENTRE
- BLACKWELL, HEATHER
- CATTERALL, KEVIN
- COLE, S
- DACRELANDS CLINIC
- DOLEMAN, P
- DYER, JOHN
- EARLY, KAY
- FISHER, C
- FOREVER LIVING PRODUCTS
- FOSTER, W
- HADDOCK, WENDY
- HAYNES, B P
- HEALTH SERVICES
- MAKRAND, HOWARD
- MCGARVEY, LINDA
- MINNERY, SHEILA
- MOODIE, A
- OWEN ROAD SURGERY
- PEPPER, JOHN
- PERELES, JUDE
- RHODES HOUSE NATURAL HEALTH
- SCHOLL CENTRE
- SOLE TO SOUL
- STRINO, GEORGE
- SUMMERS, GRAEME
- TANG, SHULAN
- THOMPSON, A P
- TIDSALL, C
- TREVITT, ELAINE
- VISAGE
- WALSH, JOHN
- WARNER, HAZEL
- WEAVER, JULIE
- WHITELEGG, MARGARET

## LEYLAND

- LEYLAND PHYSIOTHERAPY CENTRE

## LYTHAM ST. ANNES

- BEHESHT
- BODY WORKSHOP
- BRADLEY & ASSOCIATES
- CHIROPRACTIC ASSOCIATES
- COTTAM, O N
- DUDMAN, E J
- GLOVER, PATRICIA
- GRANT SMITH ASSOCIATES
- GRANT SMITH ASSOCIATES
- HAWORTH, DAVID
- HIRST, B
- K I FED GB PURE HEALTH
- KIRK, A S
- KNIGHT, J M
- NORTHERN INS OF ORIENTAL MED
- PARSONS, PETER
- PATERSON, LINDA
- PENFOLD, LYN
- PURE HEALTH
- RILEY, BERNADETTE
- RITCHIE, DOROTHY
- RUSH, M K
- THOMPSON, E
- WHEWELL, ANITA

## MORECAMBE

- DIXON, M L
- GIBSON, J B
- HARMONY
- HOLISTIC CENTRE
- NEWSHAM, R W
- SPEAK, PAUL
- WARBURTON, G L

## NELSON

- BARROWFORD CLINIC
- COMPLEMENTARY HEALTHCARE
- GREEN, PAULINE
- HOLLANDERS, HENRY (DR)
- HOLT, M
- HOWARTH, K
- NAT COLLEGE-HYPNOSIS/PSYCHO
- WALKER, H L

## OLDHAM

- ALLEN, D
- BEESTON, J
- BENTLEY, M J
- BLACKBURN, MARK
- BROOKS, S J
- BURLINSON, RENEE
- CLARKE, SUSAN AMANDA
- CLOUGHS - CHRTRD PHYSIO CLINIC
- CMG ASS NEURO PHYSIOTHERAPY
- COLLINSON, J
- COLLINSON, J
- COMPLEMENTARY HEALTH SERVICES
- DAVID ROBERTS PHYSIO CLINIC
- DICKINSON, ELIZABETH A
- DURRANS, P J
- E K CURATIVE CENTRE
- ELLISON-PERRIN
- ESSENTIAL OILS DIRECT
- HAMNETT-SADLER, G B
- HAMPSON, M R
- HANCOCK, PHILLIP
- HAPPY SOLES MOBILE
- HARTLEY, P E
- HEAD TO TOE THERAPY OLDHAM
- HENTHORN, L P
- INSCAPE
- JOY, ALAN
- KELLY, S
- KELLY, SHEILA
- MOSELEY, B
- MOSELEY, B
- OLDHAM AROMATICS
- OLDHAM PHYSIO & CHIROP CTRE
- P MATTHEWS STRESS MNGMT
- RAMA
- SKIDMORE, JOYCE
- SMITH, ALAN
- TARAS PHYSIO SPORTS INJURIES
- TENNANT, R C
- THORNELEY, KATHLEEN
- TREGELLAS, D L
- WALKER, KEITH
- WILKEY, A S (DR)

## ORMSKIRK

- AROMA ROOM
- AUGHTON PRIVATE CLINIC
- BURSCOUGH PHYSIOTHERAPY
- CROMPTON, CHRISTINE
- FOGDEN, O
- GAWNE, HEATHER
- GUPTA, P
- JENKINS, JUDITH
- MCCLUSKEY, JEAN E
- MCDERMOTT AROMATHERAPY
- MEREDITH, P R
- ORMSKIRK PHYSIO CENTRE
- PAWLEY, PHILIP
- WHARTON, A R
- WRIGHT, J D

## POULTON-LE-FYLDE

- ANNA
- BARLOW, V
- BEITH, W R
- HILTON, PETER
- HOLISTIC APPROACH
- LONGTON, PATRICIA M
- MUNRO, PAULINE A
- ROLLAND, STEPHEN N
- SIMPKINS, JILL
- TOUCH & GO
- WALKER, E S

## PRESTON

- ALLERGY TESTING
- ALTERNATIVE HEALING CENTRE
- ALTERNATIVE MEDICINE
- AQUARIUS AROMATHERAPY
- BALANCED HEALTH
- BAMBER, KAREN
- BFMP
- BILLINGTON, JILL M
- BODY-FOOT REFLEX
- BOLTON, HAZEL
- BRAYFIELD, A IMRIE
- BRAYFIELD, GLYN C
- BURT, VALERIE
- CALDERBANK, W
- CENTRE ASSOCIATION OF PSYCHO
- CEROSIMO, JOSEPH
- CEROSIMO, JOSEPH
- CHATFIELD, KATE
- CHIROPRACTIC ASSOCIATES
- CLAIRE FRETWELL'S ALLERGY CLNC
- CLAYTON, DEBBIE
- CLINIC OFF THE SQUARE
- CUERDEN, I
- DANBY, J
- DAVIES, ANDREW
- DAWSON, JEAN
- DONNELLY, MARGARET
- ESSENTIALLY YOURS
- FIRST CHIROPRACTIC CLINIC
- GEE, D
- GIBSON, STEPHEN J
- GILES-TODHUNTER THERAPY CLINIC
- GREGSON, D
- GREGSON, MICHAEL
- GRIFFITHS, DOROTHY
- GULATI, R K (DR)
- HARGREAVES, B
- HEALTH MATTERS
- HOLISTIC HEALTH & BTY CLINIC
- HUDDLESTONE, BILL
- HYPNOTHERAPY CENTRE
- JARMAN, C
- KATE CLEGG REMEDIAL CLINIC
- KEADY, SUSAN M
- KINGSLEY, JOSIE
- KIRK, A
- KIRKHAM CHIROPODY PRACTICE
- KIRKHAM PHYSIOTHERAPY CENTRE
- KRYPCZYK, ANNA
- LAMBERT, H M
- MAINEY, V D
- MARIA'S AROMATHERAPY CENTRE
- MARSDEN, S A
- MCKENNA, L
- MEADOWS, LINDSEY
- MILO
- MOGEY, E
- MONTEIRO, B T
- NAGLA, P A
- NATURAL HEALTH CENTRE
- NATURAL HOLISTIC THERAPIES
- NEW PINES PRIVATE NURSING HOME
- NICHOLLS, JOHN
- PARK, MARY T
- PENWORTHAM CHIROPODY SERVICE
- PHYSIO & SPORTS INJURY CENTRE
- PRESTON CLINIC OF HERBAL MED
- PRESTON PHYSIOTHERAPY CENTRE
- PRESTON THERAPY CENTRE
- PRIMARY HOUSE PROMOTION SVS
- PSYCHIC CLAIRVOYANT
- PSYCHIC SOLUTIONS INT
- RALPH SUTTON
- RAMONA
- REMEDIAL MASSAGE
- RICE, LAVINIA
- ROBINSON, B J
- ROGERS, HEATHER
- ROTHWELL, K
- SAGE, CLARY
- SCHOLL CENTRE
- SMITH, R J
- SOUTHPORT & TARLETON PHYSIO
- SOWERBUTTS, G H
- SUTHERLAND, COLIN J
- SWALES, CATHERINE
- TATTERSALL, KAREN
- THOMPSON, I
- THORPE, T
- TOWNGATE BACKPAIN CLINIC
- TRAINING SCH OF HYPNO & PSYCHO
- TURNER, DIANE M
- WASHINGTON & ASSOCIATES
- WILBY, J

- WILBY, J
- WILLIAMS, JOANNA
- WRATHALL, DOROTHY M
- YEAMAN, DAVID

### RAWTENSTALL

- BENTLEY AND ASSOCIATES

### ROCHDALE

- AFFECTIVE THERAPY
- BAXTER WILD, IAN
- BELL, MIDGE
- BRADLEY ASSOCIATES
- BROOKES, MICHAEL
- CAMPBELL, LISA
- CHINESE MEDICAL CENTRE
- DALEMILL ESSENTIAL OILS
- DERRYN THERAPEUTIC
- FERNS, J
- FIDLER, MAL
- GINSBERG, ANNE
- GREENWOOD, LINDA
- JONES, MARGARET
- LINKMAN, BEVERLEY
- NEAL, MARIA
- NEEDFUL THINGS
- O'MALLEY, M J
- OWEN, GEORGE
- POULSEN, P (DR)
- SANDRA DAY SCHOOL OF HEALTH
- SKIN DEEP
- SLACK, ANDREW
- STEPHENSON, MALCOLM
- THOMPSON, RITA
- TIP TOES
- TOMLINSON ASSOCIATES
- TRICHOLOGY CENTRE
- WOODS, PETER

### ROSSENDALE

- CORNWELL, K J
- HERBAL HEALTH
- KELLY CHIROPODY
- MCGRAIL, SARAH
- ROSSENDALE NTRL HEALTH CLINIC
- SEARS, J

### SKELMERSDALE

- BODY THERAPY
- GREEN, BRIAN
- HILLSIDE CHIROPODY SERVICES
- MAHARISHI AYUR-VEDA HLTH CTRE
- MCGIBBON, KAREN
- O'SULLIVAN, KEVIN
- PENDLETON, LINDA
- WEST LANCS MCTIMONEY

### ST. ANNES

- TRADITIONAL CHINESE MED CTRE

### THORNTON

- BARRETT & LIPTROTT
- CLAYTON, P A
- COLES CHIROPODY
- COLES, RONNIE
- DOUGLAS, A H
- DUKES, MARTIN
- GARDNER, J
- GARDNER, K
- HOME HOLISTIC THERAPY
- SEMLEY
- SIMPSON, JANET
- TINSLEY, ABIGAIL
- WHEILDON, SARAH J
- WILSON, D J

### WIDNES

- WIDNES HOLISTIC CENTRE

### WIGAN

- ADSHEAD, S
- AINSWORTH, S R
- ALMOND HOUSE HYPNOTHERAPY
- ARROWSMITH, BARRIE
- ASHTON HYPNOTHERAPY CENTRE
- BACK IN TOUCH
- BACK TO BALANCE SHIATSU
- BARNES, S C
- BIRCHALL, ANNE V
- BOLTON, VANESSA
- BOLTON, VANESSA
- BRADLEY, DAVID & JEAN
- BRIDGEMAN CENTRE
- CHURTON, JAMES E
- DALE, M J
- DE LOWE, V
- DEAN, L
- EAVES, ALLAN
- EDWARDS, E M
- GRAHAM, S E
- HARCOMBE, PATRICIA
- HARVEY, P C
- HARVEY, PETER
- HUGHES, HILARY
- LIBRA AROMATICS
- MAKINSON, MAUREEN ANNE
- MARTLAND, B
- NANCOLLAS, C M
- NATURAL CHOICE AROMATHERAPY
- NATURES GIFT AROMATHERAPY
- NOLAN, DOROTHY J
- NORTH WEST ACUPUNCTURE CLINIC
- OAKES, R & GUL, MARGARET
- ORRELL CHIROPODY PRACTICE
- PADAYACHI, ANASUYA (DR)
- PEN-Y-BRYN HOLISTIC THERAPY
- RULER, B
- SCENT OF DELIGHT
- SMITH, JEREMY
- SMOUT, SARAH L
- SODERSTROM, M
- STEWART, PAULA
- TAYLOR, SUE
- USUI REIKI PRACTICE
- WARNER, JEAN
- WIGAN FAMILY CHIROPRACTIC
- WOOD, JANE
- WOODCOCK, JAMES

## LEICESTERSHIRE

### ASHBY-DE-LA-ZOUCH

- ASHBY CHIROPODY/PODIATRY CLNC
- FEMME BEAUTY CLINIC
- NEWELL, JOHN
- STEPHENS, BERYL
- WSZOLEK, ANNA

### BARWELL

- MOORE, GINA

### BIRSTALL

- BOOTH, JACQUELINE

### BLABY

- VIALS, REBECCA

### COALVILLE

- COOK, I M
- DEAN, JAN
- GILL, G M
- QUINESSENCE
- SUE CHARLES AROMATHERAPY
- TARONA, GAIL HAWKINS
- WOOD, WIN

### DESFORD

- WILLMOTT, ISOBEL

### FLECKNEY

- SMITH, SHEILA

### GLENFIELD

- CHADWICK, ATOSHA
- STEPHENSON, ANN

### GROBY

- PATEL, DIPTI

### HINCKLEY

- ACUPUNCTURE SERVICES
- BEASLEY, CAROL
- GREWCOCK, N
- HIGGINSON, ANN
- HINCKLEY CHIROPRACTIC CLINIC
- INT SOCIETY-AROMATHERAPY
- JONES, ALISON
- LIBRA HEALTH BACK PAIN CENTRE
- MERIDIAN HEALTHCARE
- MORRIS, T J
- ORCHARD RESOURCE CENTRE
- PHYSIOTHERAPY CLINIC
- SANDERS, A W
- SHIRLEY PRICE AROMATHERAPY
- SHUTTLEWOOD, JOANNE
- SMYCZ, LISA
- WHITMORE, STEVEN
- WINGS AROMATHERAPY

### LEICESTER

- ACUHERB
- ALLEN, W A
- ANDREWS, SIMON C
- APOTHECARY
- AROMATHERAPY AT PAULINES
- AROMATHERAPY INTERNATIONAL
- ASHFORD, HAYLEY
- ASHLEIGH PHYSIO & BEAUTY CLNC
- AYURVEDIC HERBAL CLINIC
- BCMA
- BERETTA, P
- BLOXHAM, R J
- BROWN, F H
- BUTEYKO BREATHING CENTRE
- CALM WATERS
- CHERRY GRANGE
- CHINESE HERBAL MED & ACU CTRE
- CHIROPODY DEPARTMENT
- CHIROPRACTIC CENTRE
- CLARKE, R J
- CLEMENT, RITA
- CO-CO'S
- COWLINGS FOOT CLINIC
- CULPIN, J I
- DAVIES, CYNTHIA
- ESSENTIA
- ESSENTIAL SELECTION
- ESSENTIALLY NATURAL
- EVA
- EVINGTON THERAPY CENTRE
- EYRE, E M
- FAGAN, FRANCES M
- FARRER, R H
- FENG SHUI ACADEMY
- FIELDING, S H
- FOX, Z
- GABRIEL, CLARE
- GADSBEY, GORDON
- GARNETT, R J S
- GEESON, MARK
- GLENFIELD PRACTICE
- GRAHAM SPOWAGE OSTEOPATHIC SVS
- GREENCROFT THERAPY CLINIC
- HERBAL APOTHECARY
- HERBAL CLINIC
- HERBAL CLINIC
- HILL, VIVIENNE
- HOLMES, H J
- HOMOEOPATHIC CLINIC
- HOPSON-SUGARS
- HOPWOOD, S E
- HUMBERSTONE COUNSELLING
- HURD, J V
- HYDES HERBAL CLINIC
- IN TOUCH
- INDEPENDENT CHILD PSYCHOL SVS
- ISAAC, SUE
- JACQUI BATES COUNSELLING
- JARVIS, DIANE
- KEMP, VALERIE
- KINESIOLOGY & COMP HEALTH CTRE
- KNIGHT, TOM
- LEICESTER ACUPUNCTURE & HERBAL
- MARCH CENTRE
- MCNULTY, RAAKHEE
- MCVEIGH, R G
- MCVEY, JOHN
- MEADS, A E
- MELLOR, RACHAEL
- MITCHELL, JANE
- MOORHOUSE, R C
- OADBY HOUSE
- OADBY THERAPY CENTRE
- O'NEILL, E
- PARTON, S R
- PICKERING, JO
- PIGHTLING, PATRICIA
- POLLARD, JOY
- PRESTON, GEORGE
- R C G FOOTCARE
- RAJA, AMITA (DR)
- RAJA, AMITA S
- RAJA, AMITA S

- RAMSEY, G D
- ROBINSON, J H
- ROSE & ASSOCIATES
- ROSE, MARCIA
- SCHOLL CENTRE
- SHEKINAH PLACE PHYSIO
- SIBSON, A
- SNUGGS, MICHAEL
- SONAL AYURVEDIC/ALT THRPY CTRE
- STERN, J
- STEWART, LINDSEY
- SUN HERB HOUSE
- THOMAS, J R
- THORPE, M G
- TRANQUIL SPIRITS
- UK CONFEDERATION OF HYP ORG
- UPTON, KEITH
- VICTORIA CLINIC
- VICTORIA CLINIC
- WOHL, M (DR)
- WRIGHT, R G

### LOUGHBOROUGH

- ARTHUR, JOHN
- BLOXSOM, R J
- BOWDEN, KAREN
- BROWN, VAL
- BURNS, RICHARD
- CAROLYN'S BEAUTY
- CHARLESWORTH, L M
- CHARMWOOD CHIROPRACTIC CLINIC
- CHARNWOOD PHYSIOTHERAPY
- DEADMAN, P J
- EAST MIDLANDS PHYSIO CLINIC
- EVANS, WENDY
- FAIRFIELD, MARGARET
- GEERE, HELEN
- GILES, KAY
- GILLATT, A C
- GLEAVE, VAL
- GLOVER, ELEANOR L
- GOLD PURE ESSENTIAL OILS
- HARRIS, LESLEY
- HARTSHORN, J
- HELIX CENTRE
- HOWARTH, LYNNE
- JAYES, CERI
- KENDALL, DINA
- KROPP, I E E
- LORRIMAN, MARGARET
- LOUGHBOROUGH CHIRO CLINIC
- LOUGHBOROUGH OSTEOPATHIC
- MANT, I
- MCLEAN, JIM
- MOONEY, ANN
- MURRAY, DOROTHY
- NATIONAL COUNCIL-HYPNOTHERAPY
- NATURAL WAY HEALTH CENTRE
- PADBURY, STEPHANIE
- SHORE, JAMES
- STEVENS, TARA L
- SUE RICKS COMP THERAPY
- THORNLEY, J (DR)
- TOMLIN, NORMAN
- TUCK, JANICE
- WARD, R
- WATT, V
- WESSEL, C A
- WEST, DIANA
- WILKINSON, GWEN
- WORLD WIDE HEALTH

### LUTTERWORTH

- ATTEWELL, D
- BELLAMY, ELIZABETH
- BROWN, RAY
- LEIRE PHYSIOTHERAPY PRACTICE
- RIBBINS, K J
- WENDY PRICE HOLISTIC RIDING
- WILSON, C

### MARKET HARBOROUGH

- ALBANY HOUSE
- ARCHWAY HSE NATURAL HLTH CTRE
- AROMATHERAPY TRADE COUNCIL
- BIGGIN, ALISON
- BODY PRACTICE
- BOWKETT, STEPHEN
- CARROLL, ALISON
- CHAWTONS
- CHESTER, A
- CROWDEN-NAYLOR ASSOCIATES
- FAIRWEATHER, S & E
- HARBOROUGH OSTEOPATHIC CLINIC
- HOLLAND, R
- JACKSON, AMANDA
- LEWIS, JACQUELINE
- LEWIS, JACQUELINE
- MANOR WALK PHYSIO CENTRE
- TOOGOOD, VIVIENNE
- VAN DE BRAAK
- WHARTON, ALINE

### MARKFIELD

- DUHY, CHRISTINE

### MELTON MOWBRAY

- AROMATHERAPY INTERNATIONAL
- CARNEAL COTTAGE
- HASSETT, CHARLES
- MELTON MOWBRAY PHYSIO CLINIC
- SHIRLEY FRANKLIN AROMATHERAPY

### OADBY

- DEAN, JOSIE

### OAKHAM

- CHENERY, P N
- CONLIFFE, LOUISE
- GREETHAM PHYSIOTHERAPY
- HARRIS, DAPHNE
- MARSLAND, L
- OAKHAM OSTEOPATHIC CLINIC
- OAKHAM PHYSIOTHERAPY CLINIC
- ORR, JOSCELYNE
- PROFIT, GILL
- REN-YI
- RUTLAND HEALTH & BEAUTY CLINIC
- RUTLAND PHYSIOTHERAPY CLINIC

### THURMASTON

- CHARLESWORTH, MARIAN

### WANLIP

- SIBSON, AVRIL

### WIGSTON

- COXON, THOMAS
- ELTON, KATHRYN
- FEEL GOOD FACTOR
- MANSELL
- SCHOOL OF SPIRITUAL KNOWLEDGE

### WIGSTON MAGNA

- THOMAS COXON ASSOCIATES

## LINCOLNSHIRE

### BOSTON

- BOSTON CHIROPRACTIC CLINIC
- BROS, GODFREY
- EQUILIBRUIM HOLISTIC HEALTH
- FOOT & BACK CLINIC
- HARDING, B J
- HEADS & FACES
- HOPEWELL, G F
- JOHNSON, SUSAN
- MASON, W J
- RICHMOND, T J

### BOURNE

- HARRISON, FIONA
- RHODES, B
- ROFFE, S L

### GAINSBOROUGH

- BLAND, L
- BLOGG, G
- BRIDGE ST CLINIC
- MARK RIDDLE HYPNOTHERAPY
- PARKER, JAMES
- SERENITY NATURAL HEALING

### GRANTHAM

- ASSOCIATION OF STRESS MNGMT
- CASTLEGATE OSTEO PRACTICE
- COX, J G
- GOLDEN ARROW LEISURE
- GRANTHAM CHIROPODY PRACTICE
- GRANTHAM CHIROPRACTIC CLINIC
- GRANTHAM PHYSIO PRACTICE
- GRESHAM, CLARE
- JOHNSON, P A
- LIVING HEALTH
- MADDICK, ELAINE
- STYAN, JENNY
- WHITE, HEATHER
- YEWS

### HORNCASTLE

- AURA-SOMA
- BODY & SOLE
- HORNCASTLE REMEDIAL CENTRE
- HORNCASTLE WAR MEMORIAL CENTRE
- REMEDIES
- SPOONER, K E

### KIRTON LINDSEY

- REFLEXOLOGY CLINIC

### LINCOLN

- ACUPUNCTURE CLINIC
- BLACKBURN, JENNIFER M
- BRIERLEY, M
- CABOURNE CHIROPODY
- CHAPMAN, PETE
- CHAPMAN, ROBERT
- CHIEN ACUPUNCTURE CLINIC
- CLAIRE FRETWELL'S ALLERGY CLNC
- CLINIC OF NATURAL MEDICINE
- COMPLEMENTARY THERAPY CENTRE
- COPE, PAUL
- COUNTY PSYCHOLOGY SERVICE
- DEPARTMENT OF PSYCHOTHERAPY
- DORMAN, KARL
- DUNSTER, M
- EDMONDS, SANDRA
- FIRST CLASS FOOT CARE
- FLEETWOOD, REBECCA
- GREEN, GILLIAN
- GREENS HEALTH FOODS
- GRIFFIN, ED
- HALL, ALAN
- HALL, ANNIE
- HAWORTH, ROBERT
- HEART TO HEART
- HOBBS, J M
- HURST, JEAN ANN
- IRIS VON SASS-HYDE ART THRPY
- JENKINS, K J
- KEMATEN
- LIFE
- LINCOLN HERBAL TREATMENT CTRE
- LINCOLN PSYCHOTHERAPY PRACTICE
- MADAN DE MOHAN
- MANDARIN THERAPIES
- MOHAN, M T(DR)
- MORLEY-KIRK, JOHN
- NATURES WAY
- NEWLAND CHIROPRACTIC CLINIC
- RATCLIFFE, P
- REDGROVE, N
- ROBINSON, ANN
- SALON, JANIES
- SHEN-TI CLINIC
- SMITH, MICHAEL
- STOREY, SUE
- THORNTON, G
- TOUCHLINE THERAPIES
- WARNES, JENNIFER
- WELTON COMMUNITY SERVICES
- WEST PARADE OSTEOPATHS
- WINTERTON, SUZANNE
- WORTLEY, A F
- WORTLEY, J

### LOUTH

- CLEOPATRA
- GOOD HEALTHKEEPING
- HALL, ANNIE
- JAMES STREET CLINIC
- LONG, R E
- LOUTH CHIROPRACTIC CLINIC
- QUINN, PHILLIP D R
- ROBINSON, KEITH
- STELLA ARDEN ASSOCIATES

### MABLETHORPE

- BEASLEY, D
- RAINBOW CENTRE
- RAVENSARA THERAPIES
- SHAW, EDWINA M

### MARKET RASEN
- BEVERLEYS
- EASTGATE HYPNOTHERAPY CENTRE
- GRAINGER, RACHEL
- HALL, A M
- KOSMEA

### SKEGNESS
- DOWNES, JOHN
- FLAME HYPNOTHERAPY
- GILLENDER, P L
- GLOVER, ROBERT
- LEE, ADELINE
- PAIN, S R

### SLEAFORD
- BRITISH WHEEL OF YOGA
- BRITISH WHEEL OF YOGA
- KESTEVEN NATURAL HEALTH CENTRE
- MAGNOTHERAPY PRODUCTS
- OSTEOPATHIC CLINIC
- STEWART, GILLIAN A
- TUPHOLME, MICHELLE
- WATT, A

### SPALDING
- BEAUMONT, JOHN M
- BODY 'N' SOLE
- COHEN, DAVID
- COXON CLINIC
- DANKS, K W
- ENZYME PROCESS
- JESSOP, ELAINE
- MCGLADE, CHRIS
- MOURTON, JEAN
- MUMBY-CROFT, HELEN
- SPALDING OSTEOPATHIC CLINIC
- SPOONER, PATRICIA
- TAYLOR, T B
- WALTON, S K

### SPILSBY
- GREENWOLD'S THERAPY CENTRE
- SMITH, V L

### STAMFORD
- BARN HOUSE PHYSIO CLINIC
- BRANSON, H J L
- BROAD STREET PRACTICE
- CAPEWELL, L
- CHIROPODY & REFLEX PRACTICE
- GODDENOUGH, J
- LIVINGSTONE, R K
- NEALE, EDWARD
- NEALE, JOAN E
- SALES, F P I
- SALES, F P I
- STAMFORD CHIROPODY PRACTICE
- THOMPSON CHIROPRACTIC
- WILKIN, KEN

### WOODHALL SPA
- ALEXANDER TECHNIQUE
- BENNISON, A J
- JUST JILLS
- MOUNSEY, L A

## LONDON (GREATER)

### BRENTFORD
- B A WILLIAMS CHIROPODY
- B A WILLIAMS REFLEXOLOGY
- BARKER, JOHN
- BOWYER, MO
- GOGIA, D R (DR)
- JACKSON, ALISON
- PENFOLD, CHRISTINE
- SOUTHORN, VALERIE
- WILLIAMS, B A

### COULSDON
- CHURCH, CAROL & STEVEN
- FOOT HEALTH CENTRE
- GREGSON, NEIL R
- HANDS ON HEALTH
- IRELAND, R B
- LUXTON, PAULINE
- MANN, ALAN
- ORGASMATRON UK
- ROSEWELL NATURAL HEALTH CLINIC
- SOCIETY OF STRESS MANAGERS
- SURREY PHYSIOTHERAPY CLINIC
- VINES, T

### CROYDON
- CRYSTAL GARDEN

### EDGWARE
- AROMACLINIC
- BLACKMAN, G P
- BRITISH SOC OF MED/DENT HYP
- BROADWAY CHIROPRACTIC CLINIC
- BROOK HYP & COUNS PRACTICE
- CHASE NATURAL HEALTH CENTRE
- CHINESE MEDICINE CENTRE
- CLINIC FOR COUNSELLING
- COOKE, A D
- DEXTER, NICOLA
- DR SANDRA RICHER CHIRO SPEC
- EDGWARE CHIROPRACTIC CLINIC
- EDGWARE CLINIC
- EDGWARE MEDICAL ACUPUNCTURE
- EDGWARE NATURAL HEALTH CENTRE
- EDGWARE PRACTICE
- FERNANDEZ, M
- GAUNT, GAYNOR
- GOLDENBERG, ILANA
- GRAHAM, NIGEL
- GRANT, SYLVIA
- HARRIS, DAVID B
- HERBAL INN
- HINDE, M J
- HUBBERS, HILARY
- IRWIN, CARL (DR)
- KEISNER, MICHAEL
- KEISNER, MICHAEL
- MAGNA JEWELLERY
- MIDDLETON, IAN W
- MONTROSE CHIROP & POD PRAC
- MYERS, RHONA
- NATHAN, K
- PHILLIPS, ROSALYN
- RHODES, SIMON
- SAGIR, SHARON
- SHAVERIN, MICHAEL
- SIMPLY HERBAL COLLEGE
- SMER, IRENE
- SUGARMAN, J
- TURMAINE, VICKI
- VILE, CAROL
- YAU, K FAN

### ENFIELD
- ACTIVE BALANCE CLINIC
- ALEXANDER TECHNIQUE
- ARCHER, DEBORAH
- BAINES, JEAN
- BELLISSIMA
- BROOMFIELD, HELEN
- BUCKLEY, JUDY
- BUSH HILL PK SPIRITUAL HEALING
- CATHCART, ALISON
- CLAPP, T
- COLLIER & HARVEY
- COOK, JULIE
- COTTON, PAULA
- ENFIELD CLINIC OF HERBAL MED
- ENFIELD HYP & COUNSELLING
- FENN, SHEILA
- FRY, HOWARD
- HOLISTIC THERAPEUTIC MASSAGE
- HOLMES, DAVID
- HYPNOTHERAPY
- INSPIRATIONS
- JACKSON, JANICE
- LAY, VIVIEN & PARTNERS
- LEVER CLINIC
- LONDON SMOKING CESSATION CTRE
- MARTIN, MARIA
- MIDAS TOUCH
- REFLEXOLOGY
- ROBINSON, GABIE
- S K REFLEXOLOGY & AROMATHERAPY
- SMITH, D
- SPENCER, MARTIN
- STARLIGHT THERAPY TABLES
- VARNEY PHYSIO & BACK CLINIC
- WALLIS, C A
- WARWICK ALTERNATIVE HEALTH
- WOZNIAK, HELEN

### FELTHAM
- ANDERSON, LOUISE
- BODYCENTRE
- KAY'S
- OWEN, M
- PEARCE, R P
- PORDAGE, ELIZABETH
- STOCKTON, CAROL LESLEY
- WONG, PO-YEE

### GREENFORD
- BHAGAT, PRITI
- BOURGARD, FRANCOISE
- BURFORD, DOMINIQUE
- DEPENDABILITY
- GODLIMAN, LINDA
- HEALING ARTS UK
- KIRKPATRICK, W H
- KUNDAIKER, J
- PARVEEN, ASMA
- PERRETT, J R
- VANGO, S A
- YARDLEY, IAN

### HAMPTON
- BAKER, V J
- BEASLEY, URSULA E
- BOUSFIELD, A M
- DALKEITH, MICHAEL
- EVANS, ELIZABETH
- FEET ON THE HILL
- GERMAN, PATRICIA
- HAMPTON CLINIC
- LUTZ, PERRY
- LUTZ, PERRY
- SCHOOL OF INSIGHT & INTUITION
- TOUCH IN LIVE

### HARROW
- A APOSTLE & MACKAY
- A K CHINESE HEALTHCARE CENTRE
- ACUPUNCTURE ENERGY PRACTICE
- ADVANCED THERAPY & TRAINING
- BARRIE, ALEXANDER
- BARROW, J
- BELMONT PHYSIOTHERAPY PRACTICE
- BETTER HEALTH
- BIRD, IAN M
- BRAHMBHATT, H B
- CEDARS OSTEOPATH CLINIC
- CHRYSALIS NATURAL HEALING CTRE
- DUSKYS TREATMENTS
- ELEMIS
- FIRST ACUPUNCTURE CLINIC
- FOOTCARE CENTRE
- FORD, A (DR)
- FOWKES, S R
- GILBERT, CHARLES
- GOWING, JOSIE
- GREEN, B
- HARRIS, M M
- HARRISON, TIMOTHY M
- HARROW CHIROPRACTIC CLINIC
- HARROW HEALTH CARE CENTRE
- HOLMES, A
- JAG, SONEJI
- JIVRAJ, T H
- KAMLASHANTI CHIRO CLINIC
- KELTIE, ANNE
- KENTON BRIDGE PHYSIO PRACTICE
- LEVY, M
- LINDA PULLAN CHIROPODIST
- LOCKER, KAY
- MAYERSBACH, ANN C
- NANDLAL, J A
- NATURAL HEALTH CLINIC
- PACIFIC WAVES PRODUCTIONS
- PATEL, K M
- PATEL, MANESH
- PINNER ROAD PHYSIOTHERAPY
- PRAGNELL, C A
- PSL
- PULLAN, LINDA
- SACHDEV, P
- SASHA HEALTH & SAUNA CLUB
- SHAH, NUTAN
- SHAH, REKHA
- SHIPRA, AMIN

- SHUKLA, D K
- SPLASHDOWN WATER BIRTH SVS
- THAKERAR, J N
- THOEYE, JAN
- WILLIAMS, BERNADETTE
- YOGA MEDITATION RELAXATION
- YOGA TAI-CHI & CHI-KUNG
- YOUNGS, BRIAN K

## HAYES

- AROMA ENTERPRISES
- BEST, JOHN G E
- BROOKS, JANE
- CHOHAN, SUKHI
- FLANAGAN, D
- GILCHRIST, F
- HAYES HYPNOTHERAPY CENTRE
- HEATHROW OSTEOPATHIC CLINIC
- HET UK
- KATHEKE, K
- MCGARRELL, L
- MEENA'S
- NATUROPATHIC HEALTH & BEAUTY
- PATEL, SURENDRAKUMAR
- PENN CLINIC
- PENN, D E
- THERAPY ON HAND

## HEATHROW

- PATEL, LINA

## HESTON

- ANGEL HEART CENTRE

## HILLINGDON

- MILLS DE-WIN STUDIOS

## HOUNSLOW

- AYSA SHOES & CHIROPODY
- BACK TO HEALTH CHIRO CLINIC
- BANSAL, SATPAL
- BUCKLE, SHARON ELIZABETH
- CHINESE MEDI CTRE OF LONDON
- HYPNOTHERAPIST
- KILBRIDE, PETER
- NAARIS BEAUTY PARLOUR
- O'NEILL, M P & S J
- PHYSIOTHERAPY CENTRE
- RELAXING HEALTHY OPTIONS
- SAI HOMEOPATHIC CLINIC

## ISLEWORTH

- ARK CLINIC
- CRACKNELL, F J
- FITZGERALD, D
- FORDHAM, SHARON
- HALLIDAY, BRIAN M
- ISLEWORTH HERBAL & OSTEO CLNC
- LUCAS, P
- PATEL, NEIL
- SMITH, SHAN

## LONDON

- 2 NOW
- 21ST CENTURY HEALTH
- A A R H P
- A G C CONSULTANTS
- A G C CONSULTANTS
- A2Z COUNSELLING
- A7 ACUPUNCTURE CLINIC
- AARON ACUPUNCTURE & OSTEOPATHY
- AARON ACUPUNCTURE & OSTEOPATHY
- ABABS NIGHT & DAY
- ABACADE
- ABACUS THERAPY CENTRE
- ABBEY CENTRE
- ABBEY HYPNOTHERAPY
- ABBEYWOOD CHIROPODY CLINIC
- ABIGAIL'S
- ABNEY, ERIKA R (DR)
- ABRAHAMS & BENNETT
- ABRAHAMS & BENNETT
- ABRAHAMS, LISA
- ABSOLUTE RELAXING
- ACCOMPLISHED ACUPUNCTURE
- ACCREDITED HYPNOTHERAPY
- ACNE ECZEMA PSORIASIS CLINIC
- ACORN THERAPY CENTRE
- ACTIVE BIRTH CENTRE
- ACTIVE POWER ELECTRICAL
- ACTON OSTEOPATHS
- ACTON PRACTICE
- ACUMEDIC
- ACUPOINT CHINESE HERBALIST
- ACUPUNCTURE & HERBAL CLINIC
- ACUPUNCTURE & PAIN CLINIC
- ACUPUNCTURE CLINIC
- ACUPUNCTURE CLINIC
- ACUPUNCTURE PRACTICE
- ACUPUNCTURE SCHOOL
- ACUPUNCTURE/HERBAL MEDICINE
- ACUPUNCTURE/STRESS THERAPY
- ADAMS, MICHAEL
- ADDENBROOKE, KAREN
- ADEGOKE, ROTIMI
- ADL-TABATABAI, C
- ADVANCED HYPNOSIS
- AFFINITY
- AGIUS, ANTHONY J
- AGIUS, ANTHONY JOSEPH
- AIHUN, CHARLES
- AINGE, S W
- AINSWORTH HOMEOPATHIC PHARMACY
- AISHER, CAMILLA
- AJANTA CENTRE
- AJWARD, NONA
- AKIN, K
- AKINS CHIROPRACTIC CLINIC
- ALBANY CLINIC
- ALBROW, B
- ALDERFLEY, YVETTE
- ALEXANDER STUDIO
- ALEXANDER TECHNIQUE
- ALEXANDER TECHNIQUE
- ALEXANDER TECHNIQUE
- ALEXANDER TECHNIQUE
- ALEXANDER TECHNIQUE
- ALEXANDER TECHNIQUE
- ALEXANDER TECHNIQUE
- ALEXANDER TECHNIQUE CENTRE
- ALFORD, B
- ALJOE, J
- ALL WELL & GOOD
- ALLABOUTPHSYCOTHERAPY.CO.UK
- ALLAN, PAUL
- ALLEN, CAROL
- ALLEN, TRICIA
- ALLEN, WENDY
- ALLIANCE OF PSYCHOTHERAPISTS
- ALLSHORN, S
- ALOE PRODUCTS
- ALTERNATIVE HEALTH CENTRE
- ALTERNATIVE MEDICAL CLINIC
- ALTERNATIVE THERAPIES CENTRE
- ALTINA, R J
- ALTMAN, JEN
- AMATO, CHRISTOPHER
- AMEE & ASSOCIATES
- AMIR, M
- AN TAM HEALING CENTRE
- ANANDA HOMOEOPATHIC CLINIC
- ANDERSON, ISOBEL
- ANDERSON, J
- ANDERSON, MARGOT
- ANDREW, CHERYL
- ANERLEY NATURAL HEALING CENTRE
- ANGEL
- ANGELIS, LUCIA
- ANGELIS, LUCIA
- ANNALA HERBAL CLINIC
- ANNE
- ANTHONY, PETER
- AP CHEMIST/HOMOEOPATHIC CTRE
- AP CLINIC OF PHYSICAL MEDICINE
- APL INTERNATIONAL
- AQUAMAID
- ARBOURS ASSOCIATION
- ARBOURS CRISIS CENTRE
- ARCHER, SARAH
- ARCHIBALD, VALERIE
- ARCHWAY CLINIC OF HERBAL MED
- ARCIER, MICHELINE
- ARMITAGE, KATHERINE
- ARMITAGE, PETER
- ARMSTRONG, EVELYN
- ARMSTRONG, JOHN
- AROMACUSHION
- AROMACUSHIONS
- AROMAS OF THE HOMELANDS
- AROMATHERAPY ASSOCIATES
- AROMATHERAPY HEALING CLINIC
- AROMATHERAPY ORG COUNCIL
- AROMATHERAPY THAI MASSAGE
- AROMATICS
- ART OF HEALTH
- ARTEMIS AROMATHERAPY
- ARTHUR, A R
- ARTHUR, J R
- ARTS PSYCHOLOGY CONSULTANTS
- ASCLEPION
- ASHA, VALERA
- ASHLEY, CLIVE
- ASHLIN'S NATURAL HEALTH
- ASHTON, C M
- ASHWIN STREET PRACTICE
- ASKEW, SUSAN
- ASMUNS CHIROPRACTIC CLINIC
- ASS FOR GROUP & IND PSYCHO
- ASS OF HUMANISTIC PSYCHOLOGY
- ASS OF IND PSYCHOTHERAPISTS
- ASS OF WOMEN PSYCHOTHERAPISTS
- ASSOCIATION OF CHILD PSYCHO
- ASSOCIATION OF REFLEXOLOGISTS
- ASTON CLINIC
- ATKINSON, SOPHIE
- ATMOSPHERES
- ATTLEE, THOMAS
- ATTWELL, IDA
- AUDSLEY, ADRIAN
- AUSTERBERRY, HELEN
- AUSTERBERRY, HELEN
- AUSTIN, NEIL
- AVALON CHINESE MEDICINE CLINIC
- AVATAR
- AVENUE PSYCHOTHERAPY SERVICES
- AVINGTON, GEORGIA
- AWARENESS & DEVELOPMENT
- AWDRY, ROBERT
- AYRES, D
- AYURVED HERBELI
- AYURVEDIC CO OF GREAT BRITAIN
- AYURVEDIC MEDICAL ASSOCIATION
- BACA
- BACH FLOWER REMEDIES
- BACK 2 BACK
- BACK IN TUNE
- BACK PAIN & SPORTS INJURIES
- BACK PAIN CENTRE
- BACK PAIN CENTRE
- BACK PAIN CENTRE
- BACK PAIN CLINIC
- BACK TO HEALTH - CHISWICK
- BACK TO HEALTH - KINGSTON
- BACK TO HEALTH - NORTH FINCHLEY
- BACK TO HEALTH CHIRO CLINIC
- BACK TO HEALTH-EALING
- BACK TO NATURE
- BAILEY, E J
- BAILEY, SUE
- BAIN, S
- BAINES, PAUL
- BAIRD, JANET
- BALANCE
- BALDWIN, BERNADETTE
- BALDWIN, G
- BALL, SANDRA
- BANBURY, KATE
- BARAN, G
- BARBER, JULIE
- BARBER, M J
- BARBICAN CENTRE
- BARBICAN PODIATRY PRACTICE
- BARKER, DENNIS
- BARKER, JILL
- BARKER, LINDA
- BARLOW, A
- BARNARD-HADLEY, JEAN
- BARNARD-HADLEY, JEAN
- BARNES CHIROPRACTIC HEALTHCARE
- BARNES HOMOEOPATHY CENTRE
- BARNETT, RUTH
- BARNETT, SAMANTHA
- BARON, MARTA
- BARRETT, CARMEL
- BARRY, JOHN

- BARTHROPP, VICTORIA
- BARTLETT, M J
- BARTLETT, PETER
- BARTLETT, PHILIPPA
- BASCOMBE, K E
- BASE
- BASSEY, DAWN
- BASSEY, DAWN
- BATES METHOD
- BATTERSBY, TANIA
- BATTERSEA & CLAPHAM PHYSIO
- BATTERSEA BACK CLINIC
- BATTERSEA SCALP & HAIR CLINIC
- BATTY, JILL
- BAXTER CLINIC
- BAXTER, ROSEMARIE
- BAXTER, STEPHEN
- BEACH, P J
- BEAUCHAMP COLCLOUGH
- BEAUCHAMP FOOT & BODY CARE
- BEAVER, STEPHEN
- BECKER, AMELY
- BECKETT, DALE (DR)
- BEDINGFELD, ANN
- BEHAVIORAL PSYCHOTHERAPY SVS
- BEHAVIOUR TRANSFORMATION
- BEJING TONG REN TANG
- BELL, LIZ
- BELLO, L A
- BENDER, J
- BENDER, S
- BENJAMIN, K
- BENNETT, A
- BENSON, KAREN
- BERG, DAVID
- BERG, STELLA
- BERG, WENDY
- BERKE, JOSEPH
- BERNSTEIN, R
- BERNSTEIN, SAMUEL
- BEVERLEY CLINIC
- BIBBY, KEITH
- BIO SYNERGY
- BIRCH, MARGARET
- BIRKDALE PAEDI & NEURO CLNC
- BISDÉE, EMMA
- BISHOP, RONALD C
- BISHOP-COMPTON, JENNY
- BLACK, R N
- BLACK, R N
- BLACKHEATH & BROCKLEY
- BLACKHEATH CENTRE
- BLACKHEATH CHIROPRACTIC CLINIC
- BLACKHEATH COMP HEALTH CTRE
- BLACKHEATH COMP THERAPIES CTRE
- BLACKHEATH OSTEO & ACU CLINIC
- BLACKHILL HEALTH CARE
- BLACKSTONE, VICTORIA (DR)
- BLAKE, SHEILA
- BLAKOE
- BLANE, LAURA
- BLISS
- BLOMFIELD, VAL
- BLOOMSBURY ALEXANDER CENTRE
- BLOOMSBURY CLINIC
- BLOOMSBURY THERAPY CENTRE
- BOCOCK, RICHARD
- BODY & BREATH WORK
- BODY & SOLE REFLEXOLOGY
- BODY & SOLE REFLEXOLOGY
- BODY CONTROL STUDIOS
- BODY GARAGE
- BODY MAINTENANCE STUDIO
- BODY MIND & SPIRIT ACUPUNCTURE
- BODYMIND THERAPY
- BODYSPACE
- BODYWISE
- BODYWORKERS
- BOLTON, D A
- BOLTON, STEVEN
- BOND, LESLEY
- BONNER, DAVID
- BOOTH, JAMES
- BOOTH, JUDY
- BOR, ROBERT (DR)
- BORKETT, RALPH
- BORRELLI, SCOTT E (DR)
- BOSTON CHIROPODY CLINIC
- BOSTON, SANDY
- BOURN, M
- BOWEN THERAPY
- BOWEN, SARAH
- BOWEN, SARAH
- BOWLES, LESLEY-ANN
- BOWYER, E
- BRACKENBURY NTRL HEALTH CLNC
- BRADFORD, ANN
- BRANDON, NICHOLAS
- BRATERMAN, ELEANOR
- BREATHWORK & BODYWORK
- BRENNAN, STANLEY
- BRESSEY OSTEOPATHIC CLINIC
- BREW, LESLEY
- BREW, LESLIE
- BREWSTER, CARL A
- BRICK LANE NATURAL HEALTH CTRE
- BRIDGE PSYCHOTHERAPY
- BRIDGMONT, NICHOLAS
- BRISFETT, E T
- BRITISH ACUPUNCTURE COUNCIL
- BRITISH ASS FOR DRAMA THRPY
- BRITISH ASS OF GROUP PSYCHO
- BRITISH ASS OF PSYCHO
- BRITISH AUTOGENIC SOCIETY
- BRITISH COLLEGE-NATURO & OSTEO
- BRITISH CONFEDERATION-PSYCHO
- BRITISH HYPNOTHERAPY ASS
- BRITISH MED ACUPUNCTURE SOC
- BRITISH PSYCHO ANALYTICAL SOC
- BRITISH REG-COMP PRACTITIONERS
- BRITISH SCHOOL OF SHIATSU DO
- BRITISH SOCIETY-CLINICAL HYP
- BRITTON, JADE
- BRIXTON TAI CHI
- BROADGATE CHIROPRACTIC CLINIC
- BROADWAY NAT THERAPY CLINIC
- BROMPTON ELECTROLYSIS
- BROOK GREEN CHIRO CLINIC
- BROOK GREEN OSTEOPATHY
- BROOKES, S
- BROOKS, CATHY
- BROOMFIELD HYPNOTHERAPY CENTRE
- BROWN, ALISON R
- BROWN, J
- BROWN, L R
- BROWN, TOM
- BRUCKNER, R J
- BRUGGEMEYER'S
- BRYDEN & KEER
- BST FOUNDATION
- BUCHANAN, ANGELA
- BUCHANAN, ELIZABETH
- BUCHANAN, JO
- BUCHHOLZ, D
- BUCKLAND, CAROLINE
- BUCKLEY, BILLIE
- BUCKMAN, C M
- BUDD, CHRISTINE
- BUDD, S
- BUDDEN, ANDREW M
- BUDDEN, CLARE
- BUDDHIST SOCIETY
- BUDZYNSKI, LESLIE A
- BUENO, JULIA
- BUILDING FUTURES
- BUQI COLLEGE U K
- BURCH, NIGEL
- BURCHELL & ASSOCIATES
- BURCHELL & ASSOCIATES
- BURGER, SALLY
- BURGESS ROAD NAT THERAPY CTRE
- BURGESS, DAVINA
- BURNS, ALEX
- BURNS, M J
- BURY, D R
- BUSINESS PSYCHOL-WEST ASS
- BUTT, M
- BYNG, MELANIE
- BYRNE, JUDY
- BYRNE, M
- CALMARINE
- CAMDEN PSYCHOTHERAPY UNIT
- CAMPBELL & ASSOCIATES
- CAMPBELL-PARKER, PATRICIA
- CANALS, FRANCESC XAVIER
- CANDICE READING
- CANNING, PATRICIA
- CANONBURY CLINIC OF OSTEOPATHY
- CANONS HEALTH CLUB
- CANTASSIUM
- CARBONNEL, JOEL
- CARLISLE, L
- CARLSEN, CHRISTINA
- CAROLINE, BOBBY
- CARPENDALE, O
- CARRINGTON, A J & C D
- CARRINGTON, W H M
- CARROLL, P
- CARROLL, P
- CARSON, STEPHEN
- CARTER, GERALD R
- CARTLIDGE, S
- CASSIDY MEDICAL CENTRE
- CASTLE ROAD OSTEO PRACTICE
- CATHAY CHINESE HERBS
- CATTO & ASSOCIATES
- CELEBRITY CENTRE LONDON
- CENTRAL HYPNOTHERAPY UNIT
- CENTRAL LONDON PHYSIO CLINIC
- CENTRAL LONDON SCHOOL-REFLEX
- CENTRE FOR HEALTH AND HEALING
- CENTRE FOR RATIONAL EMOTIVE
- CENTRE FOR STRESS MANAGEMENT
- CENTRE FOR TRANSFORMATION
- CHAN, C
- CHANCERY LANE PHYSIOTHERAPY
- CHANDLER, J
- CHANDLER, ROBERT & ELIZABETH
- CHAO, FENG (DR)
- CHAPELL, D (DR)
- CHAPMAN, A G
- CHAPMAN, J
- CHAPMAN, RUPERT
- CHAPPLE, MAUREEN
- CHARLEY, EMMA
- CHARTERHOUSE PHYSIOTHERAPY
- CHARTERHOUSE PHYSIOTHERAPY
- CHASE HOPKINS, MARY
- CHATSWORTH CLINIC
- CHELSEA AROMATHERAPISTS
- CHELSEA COMPLEMENTARY CLINIC
- CHELSEA PRACTICE
- CHEN, LO KUEI
- CHENUBE, ROY
- CHENUBE, ROY ADV HYP
- CHERRY, CHRIS
- CHESSELL, KAREN
- CHESSER, HELEN
- CHESSER, HELEN
- CHESTERMAN, ANNE-MARIE
- CHETSINGH, R
- CHEUNG, DANIEL
- CHEUNG, LILY
- CHEVALLIER, ANDREW
- CHI CTRE FOR TRAD CHINESE MED
- CHI HEALTH CENTRES
- CHINESE CLINIC
- CHINESE HEALTH CARE CENTRE
- CHINESE HEALTH CENTRE
- CHINESE HERB MEDICINE CENTRE
- CHINESE HERBAL HEALING CENTRE
- CHINESE HERBAL MED & ACU
- CHINESE HERBAL MED & HLTH CARE
- CHINESE HERBAL MEDICINE
- CHINESE HERBAL MEDICINE
- CHINESE HERBAL MEDICINE CENTRE
- CHINESE HERBAL REMEDY CENTRE
- CHINESE MEDICAL CENTRE
- CHINESE MEDICAL CENTRE
- CHINESE MEDICAL CENTRE
- CHINESE MEDICAL CTRE OF LONDON
- CHINESE MEDICINE CENTRE
- CHINESE MEDICINE TECH DEVPT
- CHINESE MEDICINE TRADITIONAL
- CHINESE NAT HEALTHY LIVING
- CHINESE NATURAL HEALTH CARE
- CHINESE NATURAL HERBAL CENTRE
- CHINESE SHOP
- CHINGFORD FOOT CLINIC
- CHIRO & OCCU ADVISORY SV
- CHIRON CENTRE
- CHIRON CTRE-BODY PSYCHOTHERAPY
- CHIRONIC ENERGY HEALING CENTRE

- CHIROPODY CLINIC
- CHIROPODY CLINIC
- CHIROPODY SURGERY
- CHIROPRACTIC CENTRE
- CHIROPRACTIC CLINIC
- CHISWICK CHIROPRACTIC CLINIC
- CHISWICK CHIROPRACTIC CLINIC
- CHISWICK HYPNOTHERAPY CENTRE
- CHOUDHRY, MAUREEN
- CHOY, STEPHEN
- CHRISTOFI, KATERINA
- CHURCH OF SCIENTOLOGY
- CHURCH ROAD PHYSIOTHERAPY
- CITY CHIROPRACTIC CENTRE
- CITY CHIROPRACTIC CENTRE
- CITY FOOT HEALTH
- CITY HEALTH CENTRE
- CLAGUE, LAURA
- CLAIRE CHOUDHURY HERBAL PRAC
- CLAIRVOYANT & TAROT
- CLAIRVOYANT VERONICA
- CLAPHAM COMMON CLINIC
- CLAPHAM PHYSIOTHERAPY
- CLARK, C Z
- CLARK, GEOFFREY
- CLARK, SIMON
- CLARKE, NICK
- CLASSICAL OSTEOPATH
- CLAY, M
- CLAYTON, E A
- CLEIN, LEWIS (DR)
- CLEMENTS, MICHAEL
- CLINIC
- CLINIC FOR COUNSELLING
- CLINIC OF TRAD CHINESE MED
- CLISSOLD PK NATURAL HLTH CTRE
- CLISSOLD PK NATURAL HLTH CTRE
- COAKLEY, NOIRIN
- COCKELL, VALERIE
- COCKELL, VALERIE
- COHEN, JANE
- COHEN, P N
- COHN, HANS H
- COKER, MARCIA
- COLDHAM, M
- COLE, JEAN
- COLLEGE MASSAGE
- COLLEGE-PRACTICAL HOMEOPATHY
- COLLEGE-PRACTICAL HOMEOPATHY
- COLLINGE, IAN
- COLLINS, M (DR)
- COLLINS, V
- COLONIC IRRIGATION SERVICES
- COLOUR THERAPY ASSOCIATION
- COMP MEDI ASS
- COMPLETE HEALTH CARE
- CONCANON, ANNABELL
- CONLAN, HEATHER
- CONLIN, TOM
- CONN, RONALD & SHALINI
- CONNAUGHT PRACTICE
- CONNAUGHT SQUARE HYPNOTHERAPY
- CONNEXIONS
- CONSULTANT CLINICAL PSYCH
- CONSULTANT CLINICAL PSYCH
- CONTENT, A J
- CONWAY, JONATHAN
- CONWAY, JONATHON
- CONWAY, PENELOPE L
- COOKE, DIANE
- COOPER TOM & PATERSON STUART
- COOPER, BARRINGTON (DR)
- COOPER, J A
- COOTE, JACKIE
- CORAL CALCIUM
- CORIN, E
- CORKE, TONY
- CORPORATE STRESS MANAGEMENT
- CORTEEN, PAOLA
- CORTHINE, S
- COSMOS HERBS
- COTTON, A
- COUNCIL FOR COMP ALT MEDICINE
- COUNCIL FOR COMP/ALT MEDICINE
- COUNSELLING & PSYCHOTHERAPY
- COUNSELLING & PSYCHOTHERAPY
- COUNSELLING SERVICE
- COVIELLO, LINDA
- CRANIOSACRAL THERAPY
- CRANIOSACRAL THERAPY ED TRUST
- CRAVEN CLINIC
- CREATIVE INSIGHTS
- CRESSWELL, R
- CRILL, J
- CRISTA GALLI OSTEOPATHS
- CROCKETT, P
- CROSSFIELD CLINIC-OSTEOPATHY
- CROSTON, GRAHAM
- CROUCH END NATIONAL HLTH CTRE
- CRYSTAL THERAPY
- CTRE - INTEGRAL PSYCHOANALYSIS
- CTRE FOR COUNS/PSYCHO ED
- CTRE FOR CRANIO-SACRAL THERAPY
- CTRE FOR THE STUDY OF COMP MED
- CTRE-ATTACH BASED PSYCHOAN
- CTRE-PSYCHOANALY PSYCHOTHERAPY
- CULL, KAREN
- CULPEPER
- CULPEPER
- CUMMING, DENISE
- CUMMING, JOHN
- CUMMINGS, M
- CUNNINGHAM, DAVID L
- CURTIS, AIDEEN
- CUTLER, PAULINE
- CYGNET HOSPITAL EALING
- CZERNEK, J
- DA COSTA, SALLY
- DALAL, X R
- DALTON CHIROPODY CENTRE
- DALTON, HELEN
- DANCE MOVEMENT THERAPY
- DARNELL, PATRICIA
- DASHWOOD, ANJA
- DAULTRY, CLIFF
- DAVIES, E R
- DAVIS, JULIA
- DAVYS, MICHAEL
- DAWSON, DAVID (DR)
- DAY, JOSEPHINE (DR)
- DAY, JULIE
- DAY, JULIE C
- DAY, MELINA
- DE A'ECHEVARRIA, MARY-CLARE
- DE BURGH, JULIE
- DE FERE, SUSANNA
- DE GROOT, CHRISTINE
- DE GROOT, CHRISTINE
- DE LOURDES DE SOUSA, MARIA
- DE REYHER, ISABELLE
- DE WOLFF, MAARTJE
- DEACON, MAX (DR)
- DEEP RELAXING MASSAGE
- DELAP & SIMPSON
- DELROY, SANDRA (DR)
- DENIM, M F
- DENIM, M F
- DENNIS MICHAEL PRACTICE
- DENNISON, IAN
- DEPTFORD PSYCHOTHERAPY CENTRE
- DESIDERIO, SONIA
- DEVELOPING
- DEVI, JOSEPHA
- DEWANE, JENNY
- DHANJI, FARRA
- DIANETICS INFORMATION CENTRE
- DIDCOCK, ELLEN
- DIEGAN, M
- DIEHL, D
- DIEHL, DOUGLAS (DR)
- DI-LUZIO, HARRIET
- DISTANT HEALING
- DISTANT HEALING
- DMH
- DOCKLANDS CHIROPODY CENTRE
- DOCKLANDS DENTAL/COMP HLTH
- DOCKLANDS HOMEOPATHY CENTRE
- DOCKLANDS OSTEOPATHIC CLINIC
- DOCTOR BENSONS HEALTH PRACTICE
- DOHERTY, ALISON J
- DON, ANNETTE
- DOREY, JANE
- DOUGLAS, ELAINE
- DOVE, JULIE
- DOWIE, SUSANNA
- DOWLING, E
- DOYLE, J
- DRAKEFIELD HOMEOPATHIC CENTRE
- DRAYTON GREEN CHIRO CLINIC
- DREAM LINE
- DREAM RESEARCH CENTRE
- D'ROSE, NICKY
- DRUMMOND, JOANNE
- D'SOUZA, S A
- DUCIE, SONIA
- DUFF, G
- DULEWICZ & AST
- DULWICH AROMATHERAPY & AST
- DULWICH CHIROPODY SURGERY
- DULWICH CHIROPRACTIC CLINIC
- DULWICH PHYSIOTHERAPY
- DURCAN, CAROLE
- DUTT, G C (DR)
- DYSON, PETER
- DYSON, R
- E LOM COMPLEXIONS COM LTD
- E RU CHU
- E S PHYSICAL-THERAPY
- E.LONDON COMPLEMENTARY HEALTH
- EAGLE'S WING
- EALING ACUP/CHINESE HERBAL MED
- EALING CHIROPODY CENTRE
- EALING CHIROPRACTIC CLINIC
- EALING CLINIC
- EALING COUNS & THERAPY CTRE
- EALING PHYSIOTHERAPY
- EAMES, MAX E
- EAST LONDON ALEXANDER CENTRE
- EAST LONDON HOM GROUP PRACTICE
- EAST WEST HERB SHOP
- EAST WEST THERAPIES
- EASTERN CLINIC
- EASTHAM, D
- EASTON CHINESE MEDICAL CLINIC
- EASTON, BRIAN
- EASY WAY TO STOP SMOKING
- EAVES, HELEN
- EBONY MASSAGE
- EDELMAN, JACQUELINE
- EDELMAN, JACQUELINE
- EDGELL, MARJORY
- EDGERTON, NICK
- EDWARDS, JOHN
- EDWARDS-FOWLER, A
- EDWARDS-FOWLER, A
- EGLINTON, DOMINIC
- EINSIEDEL, H
- EISENHAUER, G
- ELBAHJA, MOHAMMED
- ELBAHJA, MOHAMMED
- ELDRAS, T P
- ELECTROLYSIS & BEAUTY CLINIC
- ELIAS, GEORGE
- ELKAN, MIRIAM
- ELLWOOD, CAROLINE
- ELSON, M
- ELTHAM HEALTH CLINIC
- ELTHAM HYPNOTHERAPY ANALYSIS
- ENFIELD CHIROPRACTIC CLINIC
- ENGEL-WARSHAW
- ENGLISH, AILEEN
- EQUANIMITY
- EQUANIMITY NATURAL THERAPY
- EQUILIBRIUM
- EQUILIBRIUM
- EQUILIBRIUM COUNS/THRPY CTRE
- ESSENTIAL ENERGIES
- ESSENTIAL ENERGIES
- ESSENTIAL THERAPEUTIC
- ESSENTIAL TRANCE
- ESSENTIALS
- EUROPEAN JOURNAL
- EVANS, SUE
- EVANS-FOSTER, YVETTE
- EXQUISITE BEAUTY SALON
- FACIAL REJUVINATION AYURVEDIC
- FACULTY OF HOMEOPATHY
- FAIR, ANNETTE
- FAIRMAN, ROBIN
- FAITH, GORDON
- FAITH, JAVAD
- FAMILY FOOT CARE SERVICES
- FAMILY NATURAL HEALTH CENTRE

- FAR EASTERN MASSAGE
- FARMACIA F2
- FARMACIA URBAN HEALING
- FARQUHAR, KATE
- FARRANT, EMMA
- FARRER, PAMELA PALMER
- FARRER-BROWN HISTOPATHOLOGY
- FARUKI, SHIRLEY
- FARWELL, S E
- FEEL GOOD FACTORY
- FEILDER, JEREMY P
- FELDENKRAIS CENTRE
- FELDENKRAIS GUILD UK
- FELDENKRAIS METHOD
- FELDMAN, LARAINE
- FERTILITY ENTHERAPY GROUP
- FIELD, JULIA
- FIELD, ZOFIA
- FIELDING, J
- FINCH, ALTHEA
- FINCH, MARGARET
- FINCHLEY ALTERNATIVE MED CTRE
- FINCHLEY HYPNOTHERAPY PRACTICE
- FINIMORE-SHERMAN & ASS
- FINLAYTER, LENNOX
- FIRST PATH HYPNOTHERAPY
- FIRST PATH HYPNOTHERAPY
- FISH, DAVID
- FISHER, MIKE
- FITENI, SUZANNE
- FITNESS FIRST
- FITZGERALD, M F
- FITZMAURICE, KIERON
- FIZZIOSTUFF UK
- FLETCHER, CLARE
- FLEUR
- FLEXIBLE HOUR
- FLOAT WORKS
- FLOATER, R
- FLOTATION TANK
- FOOT CLINIC
- FOOT FIRST
- FOOTCARE CENTRE
- FOOTCARE SERVICE
- FOOTLOOSE CHIROPODY CLINIC
- FOOTMARK, G & P
- FOOTPAD
- FORE STREET CTRE OF COMP MED
- FORERO-CASAS, SANDYRA
- FOREST COMPLEMENTARY CLINIC
- FOREST-HYPNOPSYCHOTHERAPY
- FORMOSA CENTRE
- FORSYTH, ELNA
- FORUM FOR INDEPENDENT PSYCHO
- FOSTER, S
- FOUNDATION FOR HOLISTIC CONSC
- FOUNDATION FOR INT SPIR
- FOWLER, B R & V A
- FOWNES, SUZANNE
- FOX, GLYNIS
- FOX, SOPHIE LANE
- FRANCES ST CLAIR
- FRANCIS, BARRY
- FRANCOISE, JORDAN
- FRASER, ELIZABETH
- FRASER, HUGH ROSS
- FREEDMAN & ASSOCIATES
- FREEDMAN, L
- FREEDMAN, M
- FREEDMAN, SIMON
- FREEGARD, CHANTAL
- FREEGROVE CENTRE
- FREEMAN-ATWOOD, R
- FREILICH, ELINOR
- FRENCH, BELINDA
- FRENCH, EILEEN (DR)
- FRESHWATER, WILLIAM T
- FREY, YVES
- FRIEDRICH STAEBLER
- FROST, M J
- FROST, RICHARD L
- FRY, HOWARD
- FRYER-DOUGLAS, PATRICIA
- FRYMORGEN, A
- FUDGE, JOHN
- FULHAM CLINIC
- FULHAM MEDICAL CENTRE
- FULHAM OSTEOPATHIC PRACTICE
- FULHAM PALACE
- FULHAM PHYSIOTHERAPY
- G HAMER NUTRITION
- G T CONSULTANCY
- GABB, ELIZABETH DESMOND
- GABRIEL PROGRAMME
- GAGNON THERAPIES
- GAIER, HARALD C
- GAITERO-ARROYO, CRISTINA
- GAJAHARSINGH, GERRY
- GALGUT, CORDELIA
- GALVIN, LILIAN
- GANDY, R S
- GARDEN CLINIC
- GARTLAND, LINDA
- GASKIN, CAROLINE
- GAW, MARY
- GEE, PHILL
- GEEN, SHERYLE
- GENTLE COLON IRRIGATION
- GENTLE COLON IRRIGATION
- GEOFF PICK PSYCHOTHERAPY
- GEORGE
- GEORGE, ROSALIND
- GERAGHTY, B
- GESTALT CENTRE
- GESTALT CONSORTIUM
- GESTALT STUDIO
- GIANFAGNU, CARMELA
- GILBERT, CHARLES N
- GILBEY, BRIGETTE
- GILCREST, P
- GILES, KAY
- GILHEAD, M A
- GILLY-CRUYSMANS, FABIENNE
- GLADSTONE, A R
- GLASSMAN, DAVID
- GLASSMAN, RUTH
- GLATT, M M (DR)
- GLEDHILL, MAUREEN (DR)
- GLENTHORNE
- GLORIA JEANS FASC FOR LAVENDER
- GODAGAMA, S
- GODLEY, C
- GODLEY, CATHERINE
- GODLIMAN, BEN
- GODLIMAN, LINDA
- GODWIN, ROME
- GOJ, STEPHANIE
- GOLD, LULU
- GOLDEN, JEREMY
- GOLDIE, L (DR)
- GOLDIE, SUSIE
- GOLDING, KATE
- GOLDMAN, ALAN J
- GOLDMAN, T
- GONSTEAD CLINICS UK
- GOODFELLOW, DONNA
- GOODMAN, JOSEPH & LINDA
- GORDON, TIM (DR)
- GOSCHEN, MORIORA
- GOUGH, B
- GOUGH, B
- GOULD, JENNY
- GRAHAM, GILLIAN
- GRAHAM, NIGEL
- GRANT, JANE
- GRANT, SUE
- GRANVILLE, MARION
- GRAY, FRANCESCA
- GREEN MEDIC
- GREEN PARK CLASSICAL OSTEOPATH
- GREEN, TRACEY
- GREENCADES
- GREENWICH HOMEOPATHY CENTRE
- GREENWICH NATURAL HEALTH CTRE
- GREIDINGER, CLIVE
- GRIFFITHS, C J
- GROFSKI, JANE
- GROMADZKA, B
- GROSS, A
- GROUNDS, S J
- GROUP ANALYSIS-ROSENDALE
- GROUP ANALYTIC PRACTICE
- GROVE COMP HEALTH CENTRE
- GROWNEY, SHAUN
- GRUNDBERG, SIBYL
- GUERRINI, HEATHER
- GUEST, GRAHAM
- GUILD OF PSYCHOTHERAPISTS
- GUILDHALL SCHOOL
- GUILD-NATUROPATHIC IRIDOLOGY
- GUNDRY, N
- GUNN, HARRY
- GUNTER, MARIGOLD
- GURNET, CATHERINE
- GUYS & ST THOMAS HOSP TRUST
- H R CHINESE MEDICINE CENTRE
- H R CHINESE MEDICINE CENTRE
- H R CHINESE MEDICINE CENTRE
- HACK, SHAMS Z E
- HACKNEY & ISLINGTON PSYCHO
- HACKNEY FOOT CLINIC
- HACKNEY HYPNOTHERAPY
- HAI TIAN HEALTH CENTRE
- HAIN, PATRICIA
- HAJIOFF, RUTH
- HALE CLINIC
- HALE, MARTINE
- HALE, SHIRLEY
- HALL, C
- HALL, KATHARINE
- HALL, SUSANNE
- HALLER, LYNN
- HALLER, R L
- HAMILTON, FIONA
- HAMILTON-BAILY, ALISON E
- HAMMERSMITH ACUPUNCTURE
- HAMMETT, JANET
- HAMMONDS CHIROPODY
- HAMPSTEAD ACU/CHINESE HBL MED
- HAMPSTEAD ALTERNATIVE HEALTH
- HAMPSTEAD CTRE-PSYCHOTHERAPY
- HAMPSTEAD WELL HEALING CENTRE
- HANCOK, FIONA
- HAND-ON HEALING
- HANDS ON THERAPY
- HAPPY FEET
- HAPPY FEET
- HARBEN, PAM
- HARCOMBE, LYDIA
- HARDING, AMANDA C
- HARDY, THEA
- HARES, GARRY
- HAREWOOD, MARCIA M
- HARLEY ST STRESS MNGMT
- HARLEY STREET ACADEMY
- HARLEY STREET COMP MEDICINE
- HARLEY STREET PHYSIOTHERAPY
- HARLEY STREET TCM FERTILITY
- HARLEY, KI
- HARLING, KATRINA
- HARMON, MIKE
- HARMONY CHINESE MED CTRE
- HARPER, SUZANNE G
- HARPER, SUZANNE G
- HARRINGTON, MATTHEW
- HARRIS ELECTRONICS
- HARRIS, NESLI
- HARRIS, STEVEN
- HART Z HYPNOTHERAPIST
- HARTER, J
- HARVEY-KUMMER DIANNA
- HARVEY-KUMMER, DIANNE
- HARWARD, M
- HARWICH, ANDREW
- HARWOOD, B
- HARWOOD, J
- HASLAM, PENELOPE J
- HAVELL, LINDA
- HAVELOCK-SEARLE, PAULINE
- HAVEN CLINIC
- HAVEN GREEN CLINIC
- HAWKINS, CHARLOTTE
- HAWKINS, JAN
- HAWKINS, TINA
- HAWTIN, JANICE
- HAYASHI, MIKI
- HEAL TRUST
- HEAL, CHRISTIANNE
- HEALERS WORLD
- HEALING CTRE NTRL ALT HLTHCARE
- HEALING HANDS
- HEALING REFERALS
- HEALING TO WHOLENESS
- HEALING TOUCH
- HEALING WORKSHOPS
- HEALING WORKSHOPS
- HEALTH EXPRESS

- HEALTHWISE
- HEALTHWORKS
- HEALTHY LIVING CENTRE
- HEATH HEALTH CARE
- HEATH HEALTH CARE CENTRE
- HEATH HEALTH CARE PHYSIO
- HEATHER, GRANT
- HEATON, J M
- HEAVENS, SUSAN
- HEAVENZ AROMA HOME VISITING
- HEDLEY, J H
- HEHIR, K
- HELEN BERNAT - FITNESS TRAINER
- HELIOS CENTRE
- HEMINGWAY, JENNY
- HENDERSON, DAVID
- HENDERSON, DAVID
- HENDON NATURAL HEALTH CENTRE
- HENDON TRAD CHINESE MED CTRE
- HENDRY, FIONA & COLLEAGUES
- HENRY, JOHN
- HENRY, MARTINE
- HENSHAW, COLIN
- HEPBURN, SUSAN
- HERBAL AUTHORITY
- HERBAL CARE
- HERBAL CARE
- HERBAL GARDEN
- HERBAL INN
- HERBAL INN
- HERBAL MEDICINE & IRIDOLOGY
- HERBAL TINCTURES BY DR VOGEL
- HERBAL TREATMENT CLINIC
- HERBAL WORLD
- HERBALIFE
- HERBALIFE INDEPENDENT DIST
- HERBALIST
- HERBALIST CENTRE
- HERBALIST OF COLUMBIA RD
- HERBARY CHINESE MEDICINE CTRE
- HERBERT, DARYL
- HERBMEDIC
- HERBMEDIC
- HERBMEDIC
- HERBMEDIC WEST TWO
- HERBS KINGDOM
- HERBS KINGDOM
- HERBS SPECIALISTS
- HERDMAN, ALAN
- HERSBORG, TORBEN
- HEWETT, EMMA
- HEWSON, JAN
- HIBBITT, L
- HIGGINSON, G & E
- HIGHAMS PARK NEURO PHYSIO CTRE
- HIGHBURY CENTRE
- HIGHBURY PARK CLINIC
- HIGHGATE & HAMPSTEAD PHYSIO
- HIGHGATE HEALTH CENTRE
- HILDRETH & COCKER
- HILL, PHILIP
- HILLER, STEPHANIE
- HINDMARSH, JULIE
- HINDS, PATRICIA
- HINTON, NIKKI
- HOARE, ELIZABETH
- HODGES, ANDREW
- HODGKINSON, ALISON
- HODGSON, BRIAN
- HODSON, D
- HOFFMAN INSTITUTE
- HOGARTH CLINIC
- HOGARTH CLINIC
- HOLE, NIGEL
- HOLISTIC FEMALE THERAPIST
- HOLLAND PARK OSTEO PRACTICE
- HOLLAND, HELEN
- HOLM, KIRSTI
- HOLOS MASSAGE SCHOOL & CLINIC
- HOME VISIT CHIROPODISTS
- HOME VISITING SERVICES
- HOMOEOPATHIC HEALTH CENTRE
- HOMOEOPATHIC HEALTH CENTRE
- HOMOEOPATHIC TRUST
- HONEYBOURNE, VANESSA
- HONG SOFTWARE & HERBAL CLINIC
- HONG, YUEN
- HONORE, NIKI
- HOOD, E
- HOOKER, J
- HOPE, ANN
- HOPE, JAMES
- HOPE-ALLAN, NICOLE
- HORN, JEFFERY
- HORNE-STANLEY, C
- HORROCKS
- HOSPICE INFORMATION SERVICE
- HOUSE OF MISTRY
- HOUSTON, MOIRA
- HOWARD, L
- HOWARD, LYNNE
- HOWARD, LYNNE
- HOWAT, MARGARET
- HOWELL, JANE
- HOWELLS, R (DR)
- HOWLETT, DAVID
- HOWLETT, DAVID
- HOYLAND, WISTY
- HUA TUO HEALTH CLINIC
- HUGHES, CARRIE
- HUGHES, PAUL
- HUMAN ASSETS
- HUMAN FACTORS UK
- HUMPHREY, A
- HUMPHREYS, J E
- HUMPHRIES, JUDITH
- HUNT, MAGGIE
- HUNTE, H (DR)
- HUNTER, CHRISTOPHER
- HURST, EDWARD ASSOCIATES
- HUSSAIN-FARNSWORTH, R
- HUSSEIN, I A
- HUSSEY, DOMINICK
- HUSSEY, DOMINICK
- HUTCHENS, P W
- HUXLEY, CAROL
- HY (DR)
- HYDE BARKER & ASSOCIATES
- HYMALAYAN INSTITUTE
- HYPNO & PSYCHOTHERAPY PRACTICE
- HYPNOTHERAPY & PSYCHO PRACTICE
- HYPNOTHERAPY & TRAINING CENTRE
- HYPNOTHERAPY ADVICE CENTRE
- HYPNOTHERAPY ADVICE LINE
- HYPNOTHERAPY CENTRE
- IMMUNE DEVELOPMENT TRUST
- IMPERIAL COLLEGE HEALTH CENTRE
- INDEPENDANT MED PSYCH SVS
- INDEPENDENT PSYCHOLOGY SERVICE
- INGHAM, MARIE
- INNER POTENTIAL CENTRE
- INNER SPACE
- INNER VISION
- INNERGY YOGA CENTRE
- INNERSCENTS AROMATHERAPY
- INSIDE STORY
- INSIGHT
- INSIGHT PARTNERSHIP
- INSTITUTE FOR COMP MEDICINE
- INSTITUTE FOR COMP MEDICINE
- INSTITUTE OF CHINESE MEDICINE
- INSTITUTE OF CLINICAL HYPNOSIS
- INSTITUTE OF DREAM ANALYSTS
- INSTITUTE OF PSYCHOTHERAPY
- INSTITUTE OF PSYCHOTHERAPY
- INSTITUTE OF TEAM PSYCHOLOGY
- INSTITUTE-COSMIC/PSYCH STUDIES
- INT FEDERATION OF NEUROTHERAPY
- INTERNATIONAL COLLEGE
- INTERNATIONAL FED OF AROMA
- INTERNATIONAL INSTIT-REFLEX
- INTL PSYCHOANALYTICAL ASS
- IRIDOLOGY & HOLISTIC HLTH CLGE
- IRIDOLOGY & NATURAL HEALTH
- ISLAND HEALTH CENTRE
- ISLINGTON CHIROPRACTIC CLINIC
- ISLINGTON CTRE FOR HOMOEOPATHY
- ISLINGTON PSYCHOTHERAPY
- IVES, R
- IVES, R
- IYENGAR YOGA INSTITUTE
- J BIRD AUTOGENIC TRAINING
- JACKSON, ALISON
- JACKSON, FRANCISCA-IRENE
- JACKSON, P G
- JACOBS, BRIAN M
- JAKUBOWSKI & AST
- JAMES OF ROTHERHITHE
- JAMES, M
- JAMES, MAURICE
- JAMES, OLIVER
- JAMES, R
- JAMIESON, M
- JAPAN NATURAL
- JAQUELINE MASSAGE
- JEANNET, ELIZABETH
- JEENA
- JEFFERSON, CARLTON
- JELFS, MARTIN
- JELFS, MARTIN
- JENKINS, R W
- JERONIMUS & HUGHES
- JEWERS, M S
- JIANG CLINIC HERBAL INN
- JILL HENDRY ASS PHYSIOTHERAPY
- JIMENEZ, HILARY
- JINKS, BARBARA
- JOHANSSON, BERIT
- JOHN, JACQUELINE
- JOHN, PETER
- JOHN, T
- JOHNSON, G
- JOHNSON, JAMES D
- JOHNSON, JOHN R
- JOHNSON, L
- JOHNSON, SUE
- JOHNSON, SUE
- JOHNSON, SUE
- JOHNSTON, SALLY
- JONES, ALISON
- JONES, DAVE
- JONES, EILUNED
- JONES, IAN G
- JONES, KATHY
- JONES, MONICA
- JORDAN & ASSOCIATES
- JORDAN, A I
- JOSEPH CLINIC
- JOSEPH, A
- JOSEPH, BRIAN
- JOSEPH, EMMA
- JOURNAL OF ORIGINAL IDEAS
- JUDAH, ALISON
- JULAILA, A
- JULIEN-LAFERRIER, CHRISTINE
- JULLINGS, ANGELA
- JU-PIERRE, FRANK
- JUST FEET CHIROPODY CLINICS
- KADRI, KALPNA
- KAGYU SAMYE DZONG LONDON
- KALLAS, JEMIMA
- KAM, ADELINE K C
- KANANI, ALPESH
- KANE AND ROSS CLINICS
- KANE, MARK
- KANELLAKIS, P
- KAUFMANN & MCROBBIE
- KEARNEY, JOHN
- KEELING, E F
- KEELING, ERNEST
- KEET CLINIC
- KEET, MICHAEL
- KELLY, PENNY
- KEMBER, J M
- KENDALL, P
- KENDALL, SALLY
- KENNINGTON CHIROPODY SURGERY
- KENSINGTON CLINIC
- KENSINGTON THERAPY CENTRE
- KENT, JOANNE
- KEOGH, JENNY
- KEPPENS, I
- KERN, MICHAEL
- KERR, JAMES
- KERRIDGE, SARAH
- KESHET-ORR, J
- KESSLER, GABRIEL
- KHALED, BEN MOUSSA
- KHAN, D
- KHAN, M A
- KIKAI SHIATSU CENTRE
- KIMIA HEALTH CLINIC
- KING, HILARY
- KING, K M

- KING, LESLEY J
- KINGCROSS PRACTICE
- KINGSBURY PSYCHOTHERAPY PRAC
- KINGSGATE ACUPUNCTURE PRACTICE
- KINGSLEY, NOEL
- KIOTECH
- KIPPAX-CHUI, JANE
- KIRCHER, T
- KIRK, ROBIN
- KIRKEVOLL, SHEY
- KIRSH, MALCOLM (DR)
- KIRSH, MALCOLM (DR)
- KLEIN, JEMMA
- KLUG, H S
- KNIGHT & ASSOCIATES
- KNIGHT, A
- KNIGHT, MICHELLE
- KNIGHTSBRIDGE CHIROPRACTIC
- KNOWLAND, VIVIEN
- KNUDSEN, KIM
- KOLTHAMMER, J
- KONTOS, A
- KORTH, STUART
- KOS, JARMILA
- KRAFT, T
- KRISHNA RAMAMOURTHY MNIMH
- KRISS, STEPHEN
- KUDZI C K Y
- KUPRADZE, NADINE
- KYRIAKI PEROS
- L C M CLINIC
- LAHER, RICHARD JOHN
- LAKHAMI, A
- LAKHANI, B V
- LAKSIMI, T
- LAMBTON PLACE HEALTH CLUB
- LAMKIN, CARLA
- LAMS, M A
- LANDO, AGNETA
- LANG, RICHARD
- LANGE, MAXINE
- LANGLEY, CHRISTINA
- LANKESTER, CHARLES
- LAROUCHE, NADINE
- LAROUCHE, PIERRE
- LASSMAN, J
- LAUNAY, C
- LAUREL'S
- LAURENS HOLVE
- LAUS, ROBERT
- LAVENDER HILL HOMEOPATHIC CTRE
- LAVENDER, PAUL
- LAVERTY, J Y
- LAWRENCE, R E
- LAWRENCE, S
- LAWRIE, CAROLINE
- LAWSON, JOSEPHINE
- LAXTON, R
- LAZARUS NONO
- LE CUC, KIM
- LE, J
- LEADER, S
- LECKIE, STEVEN
- LEDERMAN, E (DR)
- LEE COMPLEMENTARY HEALTH CTRE
- LEE, LAURA
- LEE, NICOLA
- LEE-BARBER, S
- LEFEVER, M E
- LENG, N R C
- LEONARD, CHRIS
- LEOPOLD MULLER REHAB CTRE
- LESADD, JENNY
- LESKIN, RICHARD
- LESKIN, RICHARD
- LESLIE, PAM
- LEVER CLINIC
- LEWIS ANDERSON ASSOCIATES
- LEWIS CLINIC
- LEWIS, BERYL
- LEWIS, CAROL
- LEWIS, ERIC R
- LEWIS, JULIE
- LEWIS, MARK
- LEWIS, RICHARD
- LEWISHAM FOOT CLINIC
- LEWISHAM OSTEOPATHIC PRACTICE
- LIBERTY CLINIC
- LIEBERMAN, JACOB
- LIFE & HEALTH MANAGEMENT
- LIFE BY DESIGN
- LIFE CENTRE
- LIFE CRYSTALS
- LIFESTYLE MANAGEMENT
- LIGHTFOOT, ANNA
- LIKISMA
- LILLIE, FRANCIS J
- LIME STREET OSTEOPATHIC
- LINCOLN CLINIC-PSYCHOTHERAPY
- LINDBERG FITNESS
- LINTONBON, DAVID
- LISTENING CENTRE
- LISTER, CHRISTINE
- LITTERICK, GILLIAN
- LITTLE VENICE CHIROPODY
- LITTLEMORE, JAN
- LIU CLINIC
- LIU, K H (DR)
- LIVESEY, SUSAN
- LIVING CENTRE CLINIC
- LIVINGSTONE, J L
- LIZ DAWSON - PSYCHOTHERAPIST
- LJUBO, JACIC
- LLOYD, SANDRA
- LOBASHER, M
- LOCKE, ANNA
- LODDER, JENNY
- LOEWENTHAL, DEL
- LOGUE, MARTIN
- LONDON ASS OF PRIMAL PSYCHO
- LONDON CENTRE OF TRICHOLOGY
- LONDON CLGE OF AC/ORIENTAL MED
- LONDON CLINIC OF PHYSIOTHERAPY
- LONDON COLLEGE OF CLINICAL HYP
- LONDON COLLEGE OF OSTEO MED
- LONDON COLLEGE OF SHIATSU
- LONDON COLLEGE-CLNC HYPNOSIS
- LONDON COLLEGE-HOMEOPATHY
- LONDON COUNSELLING CENTRE
- LONDON CTRE FOR PSYCHOTHERAPY
- LONDON FLOAT CENTRE
- LONDON FOOT CLINIC
- LONDON INDIAN CHAMPISSAGE CTRE
- LONDON INSTITUTE FOR TRAINING
- LONDON SCHOOL OF OSTEOPATHY
- LONDON SCHOOL OF OSTEOPATHY
- LONDON SHIATSU CENTRE
- LONDON SHYNESS CENTRE
- LONDON SPINE AND JOINT CLINIC
- LONDT, CYPRIAN
- LONGARETTI, ANTHONY
- LONGLEY, JOANNA
- LONGWORTH, WENDY
- LONSDALE, FIONA
- LOTUS CLINIC
- LOUGHRAN, MARGARETA
- LOVEGROVE, SHERINE
- LOW, A
- LOW, JANET (DR)
- LOWIS, PETER
- LUMLEY, S J
- LURIE, DAVID
- LUTZ, GARY
- LYON, JOSEPHINE
- LYONS, VERA
- LYTTLE, DEBBIE
- M & M DELIGHTS
- M CULLINGWORTH SHIATSU
- M L C DISABILITY SERVICES
- M S THERAPY CENTRE
- MACDERMOTT, S
- MACDONALD, R S J
- MACDONALD, RODERIC
- MACDONNELL, MICHELLE
- MACFARLANE, GEORGE R
- MACHA, FREDDY
- MACHOVER, ILANA
- MACKEY, D
- MAGEE, MAUREEN
- MAGIC POTIONS BY POST
- MAGIDOV, MISHA & JUDITH
- MAHER, J HYPNOTHERAPY
- MAHIEU, M L
- MAKIN, HOLY
- MAKURAH, LILY
- MANA MANAGEMENT
- MANKOO, KAREN
- MANLEY CLINIC
- MANN, NEIL
- MANN, SUSAN
- MANNING, FRANCES
- MANOR HOUSE CENTRE
- MANSFIELD, ANGELA
- MANTON, JOSEPHINE
- MARCOULLIDES, A G
- MARGA, ANANDA
- MARGO, SAMMY
- MARIAN ASSOCIATION
- MARIE, SOUTA
- MARIE-FRANCE BEAUTY CLINIC
- MARITAL & COUPLES THERAPY CTRE
- MARKS, DARREN HYPNOTHERAPY
- MARLBOROUGH THERAPY PRACTICE
- MARSH, A
- MARSHALL, ALEXANDER
- MARSHALL, IAN
- MARSHALL, JILL
- MARSHALL-MANIFOLD, T
- MARTIN, ANNE
- MARTIN, ANNE
- MARTIN, RHUNA
- MARTINEAU, RACHEL
- MASON, D
- MASSAGE AROMA THAI ORIENTAL
- MASSAGE AROMATHERAPY ORIENTAL
- MASSAGE MARIORA
- MASSAGE THERAPEUTIC
- MASSAGE THERAPY & REFLEXOLOGY
- MASSAGE TRAINING INSTITUTE
- MASSAGE-AROMATHERAPY
- MATHER, JANINE
- MATHESON, CHRISTINE
- MATOL HERBAL BEVERAGE
- MATTHEWS, ROBERT
- MAUNDER, TRACY
- MAXWELL BRIAR
- MAYWAY UK
- MCATEER, K
- MCCAFFREY, GERARDINE
- MCCARTHY, JOHN
- MCCAUSLAND, C
- MCCLOSKEY, P J
- MCDERMOTT, ADRIAN
- MCDERMOTT, ADRIAN
- MCDERMOTT, CLARA
- MCDONNELL, ANN MARIE
- MCGEE, GABRIELLE
- MCGLOIN, TARJA
- MCGUCKEN, LORNA N
- MCINTOSH, IAIN
- MCKAY, B
- MCLEAN, JOHN
- MCMAHON, GLADEANA
- MCMANUS, E
- MCNEIL, D A
- MCNEIL, R D
- MCROBBIE, DAVINA
- MCTEAGUE, S
- MCTIMONEY CHIROPRACTIC
- MCWHITER, J
- MEDHURST, REBECCA
- MEDICAL ALTERNATIVES
- MEDICAL SCIENCES TECH CORP
- MEDITATION
- MEEK, LISA
- MEGAVITAMIN THERAPY
- MEHMET, SUSAN
- MEHTA, P
- MELROSE, DAVID
- MENDOZA, ALISON
- MEPHISTO
- MERIDIAN COUNS & PSYCHO SVS
- METAMORPHIC ASSOCIATION
- MEULENBROEKS, ROSE
- MEYER, LEO
- MEYERSON, SIMON
- MICHAEL, G
- MICHAEL, J
- MICHAEL, MARIE
- MIJATOVICH, NICOLA
- MIKE, MARY
- MILES, JENNIFER
- MILES, JENNIFER
- MILES, NATALIE

- MILL HILL PHYSIO & SPORT
- MILLENNIUM COMP HEALTH CLINIC
- MILLER & ASSOCIATES
- MILLER, D
- MILLER, D
- MILLER-ROLT, SUE
- MILLICAN, JO
- MILLICAN, JO
- MILLIGAN & HILL
- MILLMAN & ASSOCIATES
- MILLS, SUSAN
- MILLWARD, FRAN
- MILTON, R J
- MIND TRAIN
- MINDA'S BEAUTY PARLOUR
- MINERVA HOMEOPATHIC CENTRE
- MING HERBAL CLINIC
- MING IMPERIAL HERBAL MEDICINE
- MINNS, DANIELE
- MIRZA, ALEEM
- MITCHELL, AMY
- MITCHELL, J
- MITCHELL, JOANNA
- MITCHELL, VIRGINIA
- MOBILE FEEL GOOD
- MOBILE PHYSIO
- MOHAMED, ALNOOR
- MOISHE, LEWIS
- MONAS, MARIAN
- MONTAGU CLINIC
- MONTAGUE, D E
- MONTAGUE-COOK, B
- MONTSERRAT CLINIC
- MONYPENNY, HELEN
- MOORE, ANGELA
- MOORTHY, N S
- MORAN, ANGELA
- MORDIN, MARK
- MORGAN, SANDRA
- MORLEY, JOHN
- MORRIS, C B
- MORRIS, MICHELLE
- MORRIS, PENNY
- MORRIS, S
- MORRIS, TIMOTHY
- MORRISON, R
- MORTON, WILLIAM
- MOSS & ASSOCIATES
- MOSS, PAUL
- MOSS, PAUL W
- MOTHERSOLE, VINETA
- MOTTINGHAM HYPNOTHERAPY CTRE
- MOTTRAM, ANN
- MOUNTFORT, KATRINA
- MOUNTVIEW NTRL HEALTH CLINIC
- MOUZOURIDES, S
- M-POWER
- MUIRHEAD ROBERTS
- MULCAHY, TRICIA
- MULCHINOCK, PENNY
- MULLALLY, K
- MULLEN, ANDREW C D
- MUNDAY S S C
- MURPHY & ASSOCIATES
- MURPHY, ALAN
- MURPHY, MAUREEN
- MURRAY, R
- MURRAY, WILFRID
- MUSTAFA, S
- MUSWELL HILL CHIROPRACTIC
- MYSTIC FRAGRANCE
- NAFSIYAT-INTER CULTURAL THRPY
- NAPIER, WILLIAM J M
- NASH, KATE
- NASH, S
- NATIONAL HOMEOPATHIC SERVICE
- NATURAL BY NATURE OILS
- NATURAL ELEMENTS
- NATURAL HEALTH
- NATURAL HLTH AND HEALING CTRE
- NATURAL REMEDIES
- NATURAL THERAPY CENTRE
- NATURAL WAYS
- NATURE HEALTH CENTRE
- NATURE SECRETS
- NATURE WORKS
- NATUREWORKS
- NAYLOR & ASSOCIATES
- NE LONDON PSYCHO COUNS ASS
- NEAL, KATE
- NEALE, CLIVE & LYNNE
- NEALS YARD NATURAL REMEDIES
- NEAL'S YARD REMEDIES
- NEAL'S YARD REMEDIES
- NEAL'S YARD REMEDIES
- NEAL'S YARD REMEDIES
- NEAL'S YARD THERAPY ROOMS
- NEEDHAM, A
- NEEDHAM, ALIX
- NEEDLEMAN, DAVID
- NEIL, ERIC G
- NEIL-ASHER, S
- NEILL, VICTORIA
- NEILSEN, R
- NELLIS, S
- NELSON, A
- NELSON, LISA
- NELSONS HOM & BACH REMEDIES
- NESS, DIEUDONNEE
- NEURURER, MARIANNA
- NEVIES, ALAN
- NEVILLE-TOWLE, E
- NEW AGE FOUNDATION
- NEW CROSS NATURAL THRPY CTRE
- NEW IMAGE SELF-HEALTH CLINIC
- NEW MAGICK
- NEWLANDS PARK NTRL HEALTHCARE
- NEWMAN, JANE
- NEWSOM-DAVIS, R
- NEWTON CLINIC
- NICHOLSON, V E
- NIEBOER, SARAH
- NIEL-ASHER, S
- NIELSEN, RITA C
- NIXON, MICHAEL
- NIXON, MICHAEL
- NIXON, S
- N'KABU, UCHE
- NOBES, PETER
- NOBLETT, ANN
- NORBURY COMP THERAPY CLINIC
- NORGAARD, IDA
- NORMAN, PETER
- NORRIS, JANINE
- NORTH END PRACTICE
- NORTH END ROAD PSYCHO PRACTICE
- NORTH LONDON BACK PAIN CLNC
- NORTH LONDON CTRE-GROUP THRPY
- NORTH LONDON LINK CONSULTANCY
- NORTH LONDON PHYSIO CENTRE
- NORTH POLE SCH OF T'AI-CHI
- NORTHFIELDS PSYCHOTHERAPY SV
- NORTHWOOD CLINIC
- NOTTING HILL TRAD ACU CTRE
- NOYES, DEIDRE
- NRTH LONDON ALEXANDER PRACTICE
- NRTH LONDON PSYCHO COUNS ASS
- NRTH WST LONDON PSYCHOTHY CTRE
- NUTRAMIST
- NUTRI CENTRE
- NUTRITION FOR LIFE INT
- O & L WOMENS HEALTH PHYSIO
- OAK TREES CLINIC
- OAKES, ROBERT
- OAKLEIGH THERAPY CENTRE
- OAKWOOD OSTEOPATHS
- OASIS CENTRE
- O'BRIEN, ANN
- O'BRIEN, ANN
- OCHANDO, MARI-TRINI
- O'CONNOR, AMANDA
- O'CONNOR, PENNY
- OCTAGON PRIVATE CLINIC
- O'DELL, ANNIE
- O'DRISCOLL, PAULINE
- O'FLAHERTY, CHRISTINE
- O'FLYNN, DERMOT (DR)
- O'FLYNN, DERMOT (DR)
- O'HARA, SIMON
- OHUCHE, MARGARET
- OLDING, R D
- OLIVELLE, J S
- OLIVER, KATE
- OPEN CENTRE
- ORIEL METHUEN
- ORIENTAL MEDICAL CENTRE
- ORIENTAL MEDICINE
- ORMAY, A P
- ORSACKOVA, HELENA
- OSBORNE, HOLLY
- OSMAN, JO
- OSMER PSYCHIC CENTRE
- OSTEOPATH SPORTS CARE ASS
- OSTEOPATHIC & SPORTS CLINIC
- OSTEOPATHIC ASSOCIATION CLINIC
- OSTEOPATHIC CENTRE
- OSTEOPATHIC CTRE FOR CHILDREN
- OSTEOPATHIC EMERGENCY SERVICE
- OSTEOPATHIC PRACTICE
- OSTEOPATHIC PRACTICE
- OSTEOPATHIC PRACTICE
- OSTEOPATHIC PRACTICE
- O'SULLIVAN, A
- O'SULLIVAN, M
- OUTCOMES
- OUTREACH CLUB
- OVESEN, PEER B K
- OWEN, JOE
- PAIN RELIEF CENTRE
- PALACE ROAD OSTEOPATHIC CLINIC
- PALFREYMAN, SUE
- PALMER, CLARE
- PALMER, FIONA
- PALMER, STEPHEN
- PANAYIOTOU, ANTOINETTE
- PANESAR, G
- PAPOUTSIS, MARGARET
- PARADISE, PAM
- PARK PRACTICE
- PARK PRACTICE OSTEOPATH CLINIC
- PARK, JAMES
- PARKER, JENNY
- PARKER, JOHN
- PARKIN, JANE
- PARKINSON, JUDI
- PARR, ANDREW
- PARSIFAL OSTEOPATHIC CLINIC
- PARSONS, ROBERT
- PASHLEY, MAGGIE
- PATEL, J (DR)
- PATEL, J C
- PATEL, K
- PATEL, N
- PATEL, P
- PATEL, RIMA
- PATEL, SHITAL
- PATHAK, J
- PATHAN, A S
- PATHWAYS TRUST CTRE - COMP MED
- PAULO, EMMA
- PAYMENT BY RESULTS
- PEACOCK, K
- PEAK PERFORMANCE CONSULTANCY
- PEARSON, EILEEN
- PEDERSEN, PALLE
- PEER, MARISA
- PEKING HERBAL & ACU CENTRE
- PELE, ANDRI
- PELLIN INSTITUTE
- PELLING, KAREN
- PENDRY, ANNA
- PEOPLE CONSULTING
- PEOPLEWISE
- PERCIVAL, JO
- PERICLEOUS, CHRISTINE
- PERMA-JEUNE
- PERRINA, MARIE
- PERRINS, JOSEPH
- PERRY, DANIEL L
- PERSAD, ROBI
- PERSAD, ROBI
- PETER WANLESS & BETTY HOLTROP
- PETERS, DAVID (DR)
- PFEFFER, JEREMY M
- PHILADELPHIA ASSOCIATION
- PHILIP KINGSLEY TRICHOLOGICAL
- PHILLIPS, HARRY (DR)
- PHILLIPS, HILLARY
- PHILLIPS, SAMANTHA
- PHILPS, A
- PHOENIX HOM/ALLGY TESTING CTRE
- PHOKOU, PERI P
- PHOMBEAH, JULIA
- PHONE A PSYCHIC

- PHYSICAL THERAPY STORE
- PHYSIO ACUPUNCTURE CLINIC
- PHYSIO ONE
- PHYSIO SOLUTIONS
- PHYSIO SPORTS & DANCE INJURY
- PHYSIOFIT
- PHYSIOTHERAPY & REHAB PRACTICE
- PHYSIOTHERAPY CENTRE
- PHYSIOTHERAPY CLINIC
- PHYSIOTHERAPY CLINIC
- PHYSIOTHERAPY PRACTICE
- PHYSIOWORKS
- PICKWOAD, BIRTHE H
- PIDD, MARTIN
- PIERCEY, MICHAEL
- PIERRE, LINDA
- PIKE, BEA
- PILATES STUDIO
- PINDER, M
- PINSENT, MARIA
- PINSKER, SUZANNE
- PIPER, ROBIN
- PIRIE, STEPHEN
- PITAMBER, NADINE
- PITE, J
- PITTAM, C
- PLATT, DEE
- PLAYLE, A
- PODIATRY CLINIC
- POLAND STREET PRACTICE
- POPE, THOMAS
- PORCHESTER SPORTS CLINIC
- PORTAL, MEG
- PORTAL, MEG
- PORTER, A J
- POSTER, C
- POST-TRAUMATIC STRESS CLINIC
- POSTURITEBACK CARE PRODUCTS
- POTTER, MICHAEL
- POWELL, G E
- POWELL, JUDITH
- POWER, ANNE
- PRAFULBALA
- PREMIER HEALTH-SPORTS THERAPY
- PRESTON, MARK
- PRESTON, S F
- PRICE, GILLIAN
- PRICE, GILLIAN
- PRICE, GILLIAN
- PRICE, SANDRA
- PRICE, SANDRA
- PRIEST, NIGEL
- PRIMAL INTEGRATION PROGRAMME
- PRIMROSE HEALING CENTRE
- PRINCE
- PRIVATE HEALTH CLINIC
- PRIVATE PRACTICE
- PROCTER, SHARON
- PROPERT, DAVID
- PROWER, JANET
- PSYCHIC READERS
- PSYCHOLOGICAL CONSULTANCY SVS
- PSYCHOSYNTH AND ED TRUST
- PSYCHOTHERAPY & COUNS PRACTICE
- PSYCHOTHERAPY CENTRE
- PSYCHOTHERAPY CENTRE
- PSYCHOTHERAPY REFERRAL SERVICE
- PSYCHOTHERAPY SERVICES
- PUGH, G
- PUGH, JANE
- PULLEN, JOHN D
- PUSHPA, NANA
- PUTNEY CHIROPRACTIC
- PUTNEY HYPNOTHERAPY CLINIC
- PUTNEY NATURAL THERAPY CLINIC
- QUEEN STREET HERBAL CLINIC
- QUICK, JULIA
- QUINTARELLI, G
- R D C PHYSIOTHERAPY CLINIC
- RABAYA HOMOEOPATHIC CLINIC
- RAFTERY, LUKE
- RAHS, EFFIE
- RAILTON, CAROLE
- RAINBOW TREE CENTRE
- RAITZ, SOPHIE
- RAJGURU, RASIK
- RALLEY, JANE
- RAND, E
- RANDALL, CAROLINE
- RANDALL-WOOD, MELANIE
- RANSOME, JENNIFER
- RAOUX, PHILIPPE
- RATHBONE CHIROPODY CLINIC
- RATIGAN, SARAH
- RATSEY, DAVID
- RAVENSCROFT CENTRE
- RAWLINS, E G
- READ, CHARLES
- READHEAD, DIANA
- REDLER, LEON (DR)
- REDMOND, JO
- REED, JEAN
- REEVE, MALCOLM
- REFLEXOLOGY CLINIC
- REFLEXOLOGY CLINIC
- REGENTS CLINIC
- REIKI
- REIKI CENTRE
- REIKI HEALING & TRAINING CTRE
- REIKI HEALING & TRAINING CTRE
- REIKI LIGHT SELF HEALING CTRE
- REIKI PRACTITIONER
- REIKI PRACTITONER
- RELAX NOW
- RELAXATION PLACE
- RENZO, REINALDO
- REPLINGHAM CLINIC
- RESEK, G
- RESTAN, L
- RESTAN, LEILA
- RHODES, SIMON P
- RICHARDS, JESSICA
- RICHARDSON, R F
- RIDDELL, CAROLINE
- RIES, GIDEON
- RIGBY, JACQUI
- RIVIERE, SUSANNA
- ROBERTS, CATHERINE
- ROBERTS, MATT
- ROBERTS, V
- ROBERTSON, FIONA
- ROBERTSON, K & ROWLAND, D
- ROBINSON, MICHAEL J
- ROBSON, ELAINE
- ROBSON, ELAINE
- ROCK & ROLL THERAPY
- ROE GREEN CLINIC
- ROEHAMPTON PHYSIO/SPORTS
- ROELLGEN, BETH
- ROGERS, AMY
- ROGERS, P D (DR)
- ROGERSON, GEORGE
- ROHRIG, A
- ROMANDA HEALTH CARE
- ROOM FOR GROWTH
- ROOT, A C
- ROOT, A C
- ROSAMBEAU, VALERIE
- ROSE STREET CLINIC
- ROSE, NICHOLAS
- ROSE, S M
- ROSENFELD, M
- ROSSETTE, J
- ROUBINI, DAPHNE
- ROUSE, ALISON
- ROUSE, JOHN
- ROW, PATRICIA
- ROWLAND-CLARK, A
- ROWLEY, SONIA
- ROXANNES HOMEOPATHIC PHARMACY
- ROYAL LONDON HOMOEOPATHIC HOSP
- RUANE, MARION
- RUDGE, R V
- RUSSO, HAZEL
- RUSSO, JACQUELINE
- RUTHERFORD, BERWYN
- RUTHERFORD, JOHN
- RYAN, PAT
- RYAN, ROSEMARY
- S M GORDON ANALYTICAL PSYCH
- S T A T BOOKS
- S.T.A.T.
- SABBATIC TECHNOLOGY
- SACKLIN, CECILIA
- SALAVARY, CHRIS
- SALISBURY, CLAIRE
- SALISBURY, ERICA
- SALMON, JONATHAN
- SALMON, LOUISE
- SALTER, L
- SALTER, L
- SALTER, LIZ
- SAMBIDGE, GORDON
- SAMMY, MARGO
- SAN LING CHINESE MED CENTRE
- SAN LING CHINESE MED CENTRE
- SANDERS, CAROLE
- SANDLER & AST
- SANDRINGHAM OSTEOPATHY CLINIC
- SARAH KEY PHYSIOTHERAPY CENTRE
- SARDAR, AHMAD
- SAUNDERS, A J
- SAUNDERS, BEVERLEY
- SAUNDERS, ELIZABETH
- SAUNDERS, P
- SAVILLE & HOLDSWORTH
- SAVORY, BARRIE
- SAWYER, E
- SAXON, RONALD
- SAYER CLINIC
- SAYER CLINIC
- SAYERS, FIONA
- SCAMPTON, KATIE
- SCHICK, A
- SCHOFIELD, IAN
- SCHOFIELD, ZENA
- SCHOLL CENTRE
- SCHOLL CENTRE
- SCHOLL CENTRE
- SCHOOL OF PSYCHO & COUNSELLING
- SCHOOL OF T'AI-CHI CH'UAN
- SCHREIBER, ANETTE
- SCOTT, ALISON
- SEABROOKE, TED
- SEAGER, NATALIE
- SEALE, DONNA
- SEARBY, JOE
- SEBASTIAN, ADELA
- SEEAR, MICHAEL (DR)
- SEEDS
- SELF CENTRE
- SELLAR, W
- SEOW, PENG
- SERENITY
- SEYDOUX, BENIOT (DR)
- SEYMOUR PRACTICE
- SEYNER, GORDON
- SHAFTOE, MARINA
- SHAMBAHALA MEDITATION CENTRE
- SHANNAH, A
- SHARIFI, M
- SHARMA, V K
- SHARP, ELIZABETH
- SHENKER, SHARON
- SHEPHERD, JEAN
- SHEPPARD & ASSOCIATES
- SHER, CAROLE
- SHERIDAN
- SHERWOOD PSYCHO TRAINING INS
- SHEVAK, C
- SHIATSU
- SHIATSU COLLEGE LONDON
- SHIATSU PLACE
- SHIATSU PLACE
- SHIATSU STUDIO
- SHIATSU-DO CLINIC
- SHINTON, S
- SHOOTERS HILL CENTRE
- SHRAGAI, NAOMI
- SHREE-BERKE, L
- SHRIMPTON, D
- SHRUBBERIES
- SHUTTLEWORTH, R E
- SILVER-LEIGH, V
- SIMMONS, BEATRICE
- SIMMONS, J C
- SIMMONS, ROBIN
- SIMON LAU CENTRE
- SIMON, CAROLYN
- SIMONE OLDS ASSOCIATES
- SIMONE OLDS ASSOCIATES
- SIMPLY HERBAL CLINIC
- SIMPSON, MARGARET

- SIMPSON, STELLA
- SIMS, MICHAEL
- SINGH, GURU
- SINO HERBS & HEALTH
- SIOW, YONG CHAI
- SJY CHINESE MEDICINE
- SLADE OSTEOPATHIC PRACTICE
- SLADE, JOHN
- SLESS, DEBORAH
- SMEED, BEATE
- SMITH, ANDREW
- SMITH, DEBORAH
- SMITH, PETER (DR)
- SMITH, PETER (DR)
- SMITH, RUTHIE
- SMITH, TRACEY
- SMITH-OLIVER, J M
- SMOKERS CLINIC
- SMYTH, SARA
- SOCIETY FOR COMP MEDICINE
- SOCIETY OF CHIROP & POD
- SOCIETY OF STRESS MANAGERS
- SODERSTROM, BETH
- SOHAWON, MARTY
- SOHO HEALTH CENTRE
- SOLANKI, P
- SOLEFUL BUSINESS
- SOLIMENO, MARIE
- SOMPER, J D (DR)
- SOOD, P
- SORENSEN, MONICA
- SOUTH LONDON NATURAL HLTH CTRE
- SOUTHFIELD PHYSIO CLINIC
- SOUTHFIELDS CLINIC
- SOUTHGATE HOLISTIC HEALTH
- SPALL MEDICAL CENTRE
- SPARKS, R
- SPECIALIST HEALTH
- SPECIALIST PSYCHOLOGICAL SVS
- SPECTRUM CENTRE
- SPENCER, GORDON
- SPENCER, PHILIP
- SPENCER, PIERS
- SPICE SHOP
- SPIRAL CENTRE
- SPIRITUALIST ASS OF GB
- SPORTS THERAPY
- SPYROS MOUZOURIDES
- SQUIRE, E
- ST JOHN, RUTH MOYRA
- ST MARTINS LANE PRACTICE
- STAEBLER, F E
- STAFFORD, ASHLEY
- STANHOPE-WILLIAMSON, BARBARA
- STANTON, MARTIN (DR)
- STARWAYS
- STEARS, M J (DR)
- STEIL, J
- STEIL, J
- STEP, SUE
- STEPPING STONES
- STEVENS, D J
- STEVENS, ITOKO
- STEVENS, RICHARD
- STEVENSON, J
- STEWART, H
- STEWART, RICHARD
- STILLMARK, NADIA
- STOBEZKI, YAEL
- STOCKWELL, J
- STOCKWELL, J E
- STOCKWELLS CHIROPODY CLINIC
- STONE, ANTHONY
- STONE, ANTHONY
- STRAW, SANDRA
- STRESS MANAGEMENT CENTRE
- STRESS PROJECT
- STRINGER, G D
- STRODE, ALISON
- STRONG, STELLA
- STUBBER, MAXINE HAMILTON
- SUFI MYSTICAL ORDER
- SULLIVAN, DAWN
- SULLIVAN, MARY
- SUMMERS, GORDON
- SUMMERS, LAURENCE
- SUNBOX DESIGNS
- SWAIN, HILARY ANNE
- SWIFT THERAPY
- SYLVAN SPIRITUAL HEALING
- SYLVIA LEWIS CLINIC
- SYMBIOSIS HEALTH CLINIC
- SYMBIOSIS OSTEO/NATURAL HEALTH
- SYMBIOSIS OSTEOPATHIC
- SYMONDS, G B
- T C M HEALTHCARE
- TAGOE, P J
- TAI-CHI CHUAN
- TAIT PHYSIOTHERAPY CLINIC
- TAMMAM, B
- TANG, ALAN
- TANSWELL, P
- TANYA ANDREWS
- TAPSELL, DANIEL
- TAROT CONSULTATIONS
- TATHAM, R S
- TATTON, DAVID
- TAYLOR, A J
- TAYLOR, J
- TAYLOR, P J
- TAYLOR, R C
- TELFORD, JOHN
- TEMPLE GROUP OF COMPANIES
- TENYWA, S
- TERRACE OSTEOPATHIC SURGERY
- TEWKESBURY, NIGEL F
- THAI ROSE
- THAILANDIA-FLOATATION ROOM
- THENUWARA, CLARENCE (DR)
- THEODORA, M M E
- THERAPEUTIC SOUND AND MOVEMENT
- THERAPY CLINIC
- THERAPY PARTNERSHIP
- THERAPY ROOM
- THERAPY ROOMS
- THIEBAUD, M F
- THOMAS, GEOFF
- THOMAS, J
- THOMAS, JANE
- THOMAS, SUZANNE
- THOMPSON DUNN
- THOMPSON, DARRELL
- THOMPSON, DOROTHY
- THOMPSON, JEANETTE
- THOMPSON, MARK
- THOMSON, TRUDY
- THRALE ROAD CLINIC
- THURGOOD, SIMON
- TICKTIN, S J
- TIEN HONG HERBLAND
- TILTON, JANE
- TINDALL, JOHN
- TINDALL, T
- TISSERAND INSTITUTE
- TOBIAS, J
- TOGELANG, T
- TOIBIN, EILEEN
- TOLLADY, B
- TOLMAN, KEITH (DR)
- TOLSON, S
- TOMBLIN, MARIE
- TOMLINSON, K
- TOOTH, DIANE
- TOOTHE, DIANE
- TORRIDON COMP THERAPY CLINIC
- TOUCH
- TOUCHPRO U K
- TOWERS, FILMER
- TOYO
- TRAD CHINESE MASSOTHERAPY
- TRADITIONAL ACUPUNCTURE CENTRE
- TRADITIONAL CHINESE MED CTRE
- TRAINER, G
- TRANSCENDENTAL MEDITATION
- TRAUMA RECOVERY THERAPIST
- TREBUTH RAINER
- TREUHERZ, FRANCIS
- TREVAN, RICHARD
- TRICHOLOGICAL CLINIC
- TRIUNE HEALTHCARE STUDIOS
- TROHEAR, PATRICIA
- TRUEMAN, P
- TUCKER, PAUL
- TUCKWELL, ANN
- TUGWELL, SUZANNE
- TULLOCH CLINIC
- TULLOCH CLINIC
- TUNE IN
- TUNG FUNG HUNG MEDICINE
- TURNAROUND LIFESTYLE CON
- TURNBULL, JO
- TURNER, S
- TURNER, TERI
- TURNER, TERI
- TURVEY, D L & BROWNHILL, K
- TYLDEN, E
- TYLER, SHARON
- TYSON, ANDREW
- UK COLLEGE SEMWORKS
- UK OSTEOPATHS
- UK POLARITY THERAPY ASS
- UKCP
- UNDERHILL, K
- UNDERWOOD, MARTIN
- UNDERWOOD, PAUL
- UNIVERSITY OF LONDON UNION
- UNVALA, ALISON
- UP & AWAY
- URRUTIA, LORETA
- USHER, J
- V EDIC MEDICAL HALL
- VALE PRACTICE
- VAN STRATEN CLINIC
- VANBRUGH PHYSIOTHERAPY CLINIC
- VANDERMEULEN, K
- VAN-ZAELEN, HENRIETTA
- VASQUEZ-NALDEN, ESTELA
- VEDIC MEDICAL HALL
- VENN-BROWN, HELEN
- VERDE AROMATHERAPY
- VERDE LONDON
- VERDE LONDON
- VETTERLEIN, JOYCE
- VICKERY, A A
- VICTORIA CHIROPRACTIC CLINIC
- VILE, CAROL
- VINE, MARTIN
- VIOLET HILL STUDIOS
- VIRGO BODYWORK TABLES
- VIRTUE CHINESE MEDICAL CENTRE
- VISION, R E
- VISITING MASSAGE AROMATHERAPY
- VISITING THERAPEUTIC MASSAGE
- VIV HOUSE
- VOICE THERAPY
- VON ZIECHMANN, ALEXANDRA
- W P F COUNSELLING
- WALDMAN, MERVYN
- WALK IN BACK RUB
- WALK IN BACKRUB
- WALK IN BACKRUB
- WALKER, JAN
- WALLACE, VICTORIA
- WALLACE, W K
- WALTER, MAX
- WANDSWORTH ASS OF PSYCHO
- WANSBOROUGH, CHARLES
- WARD, MARY
- WARDELL, L
- WARRELL, PIPPA
- WARREN, DAVID
- WART, D
- WATER MASSAGE
- WATKINS, DENISE
- WATSON, IAN
- WATSON, M
- WEBB, CHARLOTTE
- WEBB, DEREK
- WEBB, M
- WEBB, MADELENE
- WEBB, MADELENE
- WEBB, S
- WEBER, MARALYN
- WEBSTER, GEORGINA
- WEBSTER, GILES
- WEEKES, CHRIS
- WEERASEKERA, H
- WELBECK CLINIC
- WELL BEING
- WELL BEING CENTRE
- WELL SPRING CLINIC
- WELLBURN, JOCELYN
- WELLS, KIM
- WELLS, PAMELA
- WERNINCK, RODNEY
- WEST LONDON CENTRE

CLUBBING TONIGHT

Includes 1000 wine bars and 2000 Night Clubs

# The Ultimate Guide to over 3,000 Night Venues in the UK & Ireland

www.clubbingtonight.com

Publishing HCC

An HCC Next Generation Directory

- WEST LONDON PSYCHOTHERAPY
- WEST LONDON YOGA SHALA
- WESTERN, G
- WESTMINSTER ALEXANDER CENTRE
- WESTMINSTER NTRL HEALTH CLINIC
- WESTMINSTER PASTORAL FOUND
- WESTMINSTER PHYSIO CENTRE
- WESTWOOD, CHRISTINE
- WETHERELL, PAULINE
- WETHERELL, PAULINE
- WHEELER, D
- WHEILAND, M
- WHETSTONE CHIROPRACTIC CLINIC
- WHITE CRANE HEALING CENTRE
- WHITE HART LANE THERAPY CENTRE
- WHITE, J
- WHITE, NULA
- WHITE, PHILIP (DR)
- WHITECHAPEL OSTEOPATHS
- WHITEHOUSE, J
- WHITELEY, BRUCE
- WHITELEYS OF BAYSWATER
- WHITLOCK, BARBARA
- WHITTEMORE, JANE
- WHOLE-BEING INTERACTIVE HYP
- WICKER, DIANE
- WICKS, ANITA
- WICKS, ANITA
- WIERSMA, IRIS
- WIGHAM, A
- WILKINSON, GILL
- WILLER, ANGELA P
- WILLETT, OLIVIA
- WILLIAMS, A
- WILLIAMS, ALAN
- WILLIAMS, DANNY
- WILLIAMS, IAN
- WILLIAMS, J
- WILLIAMS, JUDITH
- WILLIAMS, MARILYN
- WILLIAMS, RUTH
- WILLIAMS, RUTH
- WILLIAMS, S M
- WILLIAMS, T E
- WILLIAMS, TONY
- WILLMOTT, SUSAN
- WILMOT, MARGARET
- WILSON, ALLES
- WILSON, CHRISTOPHER
- WILSON, MARGARET R E
- WILSON, SALLY
- WILSON, SEAN
- WIMBLEDON CLINIC OF NTRL MED
- WIMBLEDON HERBAL CENTRE
- WIMBLEDON OSTEO & SPORTS
- WINCHMORE CLINIC OF OSTEOPATHY
- WINER, J
- WINGROVE-GIBBONS, KENNETH
- WINTER, DOROTHY
- WINTERMEYER, IRENE
- WOHL, M
- WOMEN & HEALTH
- WOMEN & MEDICAL PRACTICE
- WOMEN THERAPISTS REFERRAL SV
- WOMEN'S THERAPY CENTRE
- WOMENS THERAPY LINK
- WOOD, ALLAN R
- WOOD, DEANA
- WOOD, GILLIAN
- WOODBERRY CLINIC
- WOODLEIGH, R M
- WOODS PLACE FITNESS CENTRE
- WOODS, ROBERT
- WOODSIDE COUNSELLING
- WOOLF, PERRY
- WOOLFE, MICHAEL & LESLIE
- WOOLFSON, GERALD
- WOOLLISCROFT, J
- WOOLSGROVE, F A
- WORLD OF LIGHT
- WREN CLINIC
- WREN, ANTHONY
- WRIGHT, GWYNETH
- WRIGHT, JENNY
- WST LONDON SCH - THERA MASS
- WUEBBELER, H
- WYLIE, DIANE
- WYNDHAM CENTRE
- WYNNE-SIMMONS, A (DR)
- WYSMAN, ALAN
- YING & YANG COMP CENTRE
- YING, FRANK
- YIZHEN, JIA (DR)
- YOGA THERAPY CENTRE
- YOGA THERAPY CENTRE
- YOGA WITH RENA NICHOLAOU
- YOGA, IYENGAR
- YOUELL, A (DR)
- YOUNG, SUE
- YOUNG, VEDA
- ZACHARIA, T (DR)
- ZAHNISER, E
- ZAHNISER, ESTHER
- ZARBAFI, A
- ZARVIS-LONDON
- ZEN HEALTH CENTRE
- ZEN SHIATSU & HEALING TAO
- ZENERGY CITY SHIATSU CLGE
- ZIA, ROBINA
- ZIELINSKI, KRYSTYNA
- ZISMAN, A
- ZUIDYK, TOSCA
- ZWIERCHOWSKA, ZENNA
- ZWIERZCHOWSKA, Z

## NORTHOLT

- GOKANI, M
- HAMID, ALI
- LOGUE, ROSE
- THOMAS HEWETSON

## NORTHWOOD

- A P S THERAPY
- ACUPUNCTURE SOCIETY
- ALTERNATIVES COMP THERAPY CTRE
- BENATAR, WENDY
- BOULANGER, S
- CLASSIC THERAPIES
- FENN, AILEEN
- GILBEY, J
- HOPKIN, A N L
- KELLETT, DAVID
- LAMB, G
- LEVER, JUDITH
- LEVER, R
- OLDROYD, B K
- OLDROYD, B K
- PATEL, K M
- PATEL, S
- ROBERTSON, FIONA
- SHERIF, F (DR)
- STOCKLEY, R
- VAUGHAN, D L
- VOLK & ASSOCIATES
- WALKER, DYLANIE
- WATHERSTON, M
- WILLIAMS, SUSAN
- YONI INTERNATIONAL

## PINNER

- 1ST ALTERNATIVE HEALTH CENTRE
- ADATIA, K H (DR)
- ALEXANDER, R E
- ALLERGY TESTING SERVICE
- ANDERSON, JANE M
- ASHKEN, JOHN J (DR)
- AUSTIN, P
- BIRMINGHAM, LINDA
- BROEKHOFF, MARIA
- BURNETT, JAMES P
- CASSIN SCOTT ASSOCIATES
- CLIFFORD, S H
- DAVEIGAS, DOUGLAS
- DREAMCATCHER
- EASTCOTE NFSH HEALING CENTRE
- FUDGE, Z
- HOBBS, SALLY
- HONG TAD ACUPUNCTURE & HERBAL
- HOSSAIN, EVA N
- HOSSAIN, NATASHA
- KOPELOWITZ, C A
- LAMB, H (DR)
- MARKANDAY, A
- MOTE, CHRISTOPHER C
- PHILLIPS, K
- PINNER HLTH FOODS & THRPY CTRE
- RACHEL YOUNG - HYPNOTHERAPIST
- RAEBURN, JO
- ST VINCENTS COMMUNITY PHYSIO
- TUNMORE, M
- VIDGEN, H E

## RUISLIP

- ADAM, JAMES
- ANNE WRIGHT & LARA SEYMOUR
- BACK PAIN CLINIC
- BATES, DAVID J
- ERDOS CHINESE MEDICAL CENTRE
- FIELD END COMP HEALTH CLINIC
- GHAFOOR, F (DR)
- HATHERLY, R M
- HOLCOMBE, VAL
- MANOR HLTH FOOD/NUTRITION CTRE
- MARY MARTIN SCHOOL - REFLEX
- MAY, CLAIRE
- NATURAL HEALING CENTRE
- PATERSON, KARETH
- ROWE, HOLLIE ANN
- RUISLIP CHIROPRACTIC CLINIC
- SODHA, LALIT (DR)
- STEELE, JULIE
- THOMAS HEWETSON
- TRANQUILITY
- TYLER, VALERIE
- VISITING CHIROPODY SERVICE
- WEBB, J E
- WHITE, MR
- WRIGHT, ANNE & SEYMOUR, LARA
- ZUBAIR, S

## SOUTHALL

- AVETOOM, CARO
- BAKHSHI, R S
- HOMOEOPATHIC HEALTH CLINIC
- KORYO SOOJI CLINIC
- SOHAL, D S
- SOUTHALL CHINESE MED CENTRE
- UNIQUE ASIAN MASSAGE CENTRE
- VEDIC, RU

## STANMORE

- BIRD, J K
- BOXER, IRVING S
- BUREN, VAN
- BURNS, JOLANDA
- GANDHI, MEERA
- HATHA YOGA/COUNSELLING
- HOMEOPATHIC CLINIC
- KOSEFF, S S
- LAIFER, D
- LEWIS, HELEN
- MIDDLESEX SCHOOL OF COMP MED
- MIRZA, A (DR)
- PATEL, SHILPA
- PERSON TO PERSON
- SAM'S EXERCISE FORMULA
- SERLIN CLINIC OF HEALING
- SHORTS, KAREN
- STANMORE CENTRE
- STANMORE PHYSIO PRACTICE

## TEDDINGTON

- ALLEN, SUSAN
- ARNOLD, MARK
- AVERY, PATRICIA
- AVSEC, FAY
- BEAN, GARY
- CHRISTIE, ANITA
- DAVID WEISS HOMEOPATHY
- DIMPNA CENTRE
- ERICA, GUSTAVSSON
- FERGUSON, WILMA
- HETHERTON, ANNE
- INTEGRATIVE PSYCHOSYNTHESIS
- LANGDALE-KING, ROSIE
- O'NEILL, TESS
- PARSONS, G
- ROBINSON, J L
- SHIELDS, CAROL
- TAMBOLY, KERSI

## TWICKENHAM

- AGAINST ALLERGY
- AUSTIN, DIANA
- BARTOSZEWICZ, PATRICIA
- BEAL, J P
- BONNER, DAVID
- BRIDGE WAY CLINIC
- CHIROPODY CENTRE

- GOODCHILD & ORR ASSOCIATES
- GROCHOLSKI, SABINE
- HURST, S
- JONES, JULIE
- JURIANSZ, ALAN & JENNIFER
- LIFE CHANGES
- MAIR, L L
- MAPLE LEAF CLINIC
- NICKALLS, JILL
- NORTH, L W
- OTREMBA, KATHARINA
- OWEN, D
- PEMBERY, S
- PETER PSYCHIC CLAIRVOYANT
- PRUE BRAND
- PSYCHOTHERAPY REFERRAL SERVICE
- RATCLIFF, SUSAN
- RICHMOND CHIROPRACTIC CLINIC
- ROWLANDSON, CATHY
- RUDDOCK, CAROL
- SAUNDERS, STEPHANIE
- SHARPLEY, ROGER
- SPENCER, A
- STRAWBERRY HILL PRACTICE
- SUTTON, NICOLA
- TWICKENHAM PHYSIO PRACTICE
- TWICKENHAM PHYSIOFIRST CENTRE
- WATERS & WINTERSTEIN AST
- WEBB, FIONA
- WEST THAMES
- WILKINS, MARILYN
- YULE, AILEEN

### UXBRIDGE

- ACTIVE BALANCE CLINIC
- ADAMS, SIOBHAN
- BACK PAIN CLINIC
- BARRETT, P M
- CHIROCARE
- COOPER, LAURA
- DRYSDALE, IAN
- F GHAFOOR (DR)
- KEITH EGLETON HYPNOTHERAPY
- NEWNS, DAVID
- PERKINS, SYBIL
- RANDERIA, JAMSHED (DR)
- REFLEXOLOGY & STRESS CLINIC
- RUTH SAUNDERS HEALTH CLINIC
- THERAPY CLINIC
- THOMAS, ALAN
- UXBRIDGE CHIROPRACTIC CLINIC
- WARREN CLINIC
- WEST LONDON HOLISTIC CENTRE
- WHARTON, COLIN
- WILLIAMS, SUSAN

### WEMBLEY

- ALLTREE COMPLEMENTARY THERAPY
- AMANN OSTEOPATHIC CLINIC
- ANGEL, LESLEY
- ANGEL, LESLEY
- BRAHMA KUMARIS INNER SPACE
- DAOUST, YVETTE
- DUNNE, CONOR W
- HERBAL INN
- IN-THERAPY
- JACOBS, K A
- LEE, H (DR)
- LEE, K (DR)
- MARTIN, D
- MELZACK, D
- MURRAY, T A (DR)
- PATEL, PRAGNA
- PERRY, DANIEL L
- SAINI, R P
- SIOW, YONG CHAI
- ST ANDREWS
- STRESS MANAGEMENT
- UNUIS CLINIC
- V K PATEL STATE RGD CHIROP
- VANGO, S
- VIRINDER SAINI'S BEAUTY CLINIC
- WEMBLEY MEDICAL CENTRE
- YAGHMAIE, MASSIH

### WEST DRAYTON

- MACKIE, CHERYL
- UBHI, BEL
- WEST DRAYTON PHYSIO/SPORTS

## MANCHESTER (GREATER)

### ASHTON-UNDER-LYNE

- A SIR ROBERTS ALT PLACE
- ANCIENT HEALING CRYSTALS
- ASHTON CHIROPRACTIC CENTRE
- ASHTON PRIVATE CLINIC
- BURTON, M
- CHARTERED PHYSIOTHERAPY CLINIC
- GARSIDE, D
- GILL, JUNE
- GUILD OF PRACTITIONERS
- HARROP, S
- MASSAGE & REFLEXOLOGY CENTRE
- PARTLAN, ROBERT
- SCHOFIELD, P B
- STOPFORD, H
- STRINGER, R A (DR)

### BRAMHALL

- BRAMHALL CHIROPRACTIC CLINIC

### HEYWOOD

- ASHWORTH, FREDA
- CUNLIFFE, H B
- O'MALLEY, M J
- WAINWRIGHT, P
- WILLIAMS, JANE
- WOOD, ALISON

### LEIGH

- ABBOTTS OF LEIGH
- ANDREWS CLINIC
- BACK PAIN & COMP MED CENTRE
- CLINIC 2000
- COLBOURNE, C H
- FOOTCARE CENTRE
- HADDES
- HULME, J
- LITTLER, J M
- M J HAYLETT - PHYSIOTHERAPIST
- REFLEXOLOGY & CHIROPODY
- SCENT OF DELIGHT
- STUART, LOUISE
- SUMNER, ALLISON J

### LITTLEBOROUGH

- C CARTLEDGE REFLEXOLOGY
- FARNHILL, SANDRA M
- GIBSON, LINDA
- GREGORY, T R
- IBBOTSON, GEOFF (DR)
- WALTON, J

### MANCHESTER

- A6 CHIROPODY PRACTICE
- ACU-HERB CLINIC
- ACUMEDIC
- ACUPUNCTURE CENTRE
- ADVANCED PHYSIOTHERAPY CLINIC
- ALEXANDER TECHNIQUE
- ALEXANDER TECHNIQUE
- ALL IN THE MIND
- ALUNA HOLISTIC THERAPY CENTRE
- ANGEL HLTHY LIVING INITIATIVE
- ARMITAGE, S
- AROMATHERAPY BY SARA
- ASCOTT, TARA
- ASHTON, J G
- ASPEY, A
- ASSOCIATION OF STRESS MNGMT
- ASTLEY COMPLEMENTARY CENTRE
- AURA PHOTOGRAPHY
- AVA
- AVRIL
- AWAKENING
- BAILEY, JO
- BANN, P
- BARLEY, ANDREW
- BARLING, J
- BEACHAM, SONJA
- BEAUTY THERAPY CENTRE
- BENNETT, M A
- BENNETT, MO
- BINE, NICHOLAS
- BODYWISE
- BOOTH, I G P
- BRODY, S M
- BROMILEY, A P
- BROOKES, N
- BROOKES, N ( DR)
- BROOKHOUSE, S
- BROOMHEAD, S J
- BROWN & ROBINSON
- BROWN, K J
- BURGESS, KAREN
- BURKE, ANDREW
- C D THERAPIES
- CASEY, MAXINE
- CENTRE FOR SHIATSU
- CHINESE HERBAL & ACU CENTRE
- CHINESE MEDICAL CENTRE
- CHINESE TRAD HEALTH CENTRE
- CHORLTON STRESS MANAGEMENT
- CITY PHYSIO
- CLARENDON CLINIC
- CLARKE, H G
- CLEVERLY, MARAGRET
- COLLINGE, J C
- COONEY-SMITH, P M
- COSGROVES PHYSIO-FIT CENTRE
- COUNTY BEAUTY CLINIC
- CRAIG GREGG & RUSSELL
- CRAVEN STREET CHIROPODY CLINIC
- CREST HYPNOTHERAPY
- CROSSWAY CLINIC
- CTRE FOR ADVANCED REFLEXOLOGY
- D VAN-BENTUM CHIROPODIST
- DAVEENA ASSOCIATES
- DAVID ROBERTS PHYSIO CLINIC
- D'CRUZE, INGRID
- DEACH, I
- DIDSBURY CHIROPRACTIC CLINIC
- DR & HERBS
- DTR THERAPEUTICS
- E ROWBOTTOM STATE REG CHIROP
- ECKERSLEY, PETER D
- EDUCATIONAL PSYCHOLOGY SERVICE
- FOOT-EASE CHIROPODIST
- FRANCIS, D
- FRANCIS, D
- GOGIA, D R (DR)
- GOODMAN, K (DR)
- GOODWIN, S P
- GORSE HILL CHIROPODY PRACTICE
- GRAHAM COOMBE - MCTIMONEY
- GRAHAM, CHRISTINE
- GREEN, J
- GREEN, NANCY
- HAMMOND, ANNE
- HAMPDEN HOUSE CENTRE
- HARPER, B
- HAYWARD, PERRIN
- HEALTHCARE INTERNATIONAL
- HEATON PARK PHYSIO & SPORTS
- HENCHY, C L
- HENNEL, LIZ
- HESLOP, C
- HIGH PEAK HOLISTIC CENTRE
- HODKINSON, EDWINA
- HOLMED CLINIC
- HOMOEOPATHIC CLINIC
- HOMOEOPATHY CLINIC
- HOPEWELL, ALAN
- HORRIDGE, S P
- HUGHES, MARGARET
- HUMAN TOUCH CENTRE
- HYPNOTHERAPY & COUNSELLING
- HYPNOTHERAPY CENTRE
- IBBETSON, JOHN A
- IMAGE-STICS
- ISAAC, TONI
- JAKUBOWSKI, ANNE
- JEFFREY, C E
- JONES, S
- KAYE, ANDREW
- KELLY, C
- KYPHI
- KYRIAKOS KAPLANIS
- LEATHERBARROW, G L
- LIFEQUEST
- LOCKETT, EMMA
- LOMAX, JAMES
- MACARTNEY HOUSE PSYCHOTHERAPY
- MADELEY, P A
- MAGNETIC PAIN RELIEF SYSTEMS
- MAGNETIC THERAPY
- MALLON, B

- MANCHESTER GESTALT CENTRE
- MANCHESTER HOMOEOPATHIC CLINIC
- MANCHESTER INSTITUTE-PSYCHO
- MANCHESTER SCHOOL OF MASSAGE
- MANCHESTER THERAPY CENTRE
- MANOGUE, ANNIE
- MARGE THE HAMLET
- MCDONNELL, P
- MCGREGOR, J
- MELLOR, V
- MIDDLETON HOM & NAT THRPY CTRE
- MILWARD, S J
- MINTZ, J
- MINTZ, J
- MOBILE COMPLEMENTARY THERAPIES
- MORRIS, RACHEL T
- MOUNT STREET COMP THERAPIES
- NATHAN, ROBERT D
- NEALS YARD REMEDIES
- NEEPHA
- NELSON, ANDREW
- NEWSHAM ASS URMSTON REMEDIAL
- NICKI HAVES PHYSIO CLINIC
- NIVERN, D
- NORTH WEST COMP THERAPY CTRE
- NW COLLEGE-HOMOEOPATHY
- OBANYE, A I (DR)
- OCEAN SUN
- OLD HALL CLINIC
- OLDHAM, VALERIE
- OLIVER-CARTER, JOAN
- O'NEILL, MARLENE
- O'REILLY, JULIA
- OSGOOD, JANE
- PATTONY HYPNOTHERAPY GROUP
- PERRIN & ASSOCIATES
- PHILLIPS, LORRAINE
- POLLARD, JACQUELINE
- POSTON, JONATHAN
- PREST, CAROLINE
- PRESTWICH PHYSIOTHERAPY CLINIC
- PSYCHIC INT AWARENESS SOCIETY
- PYNE, BERNADETTE
- QUEST THERAPY
- RACLE, P
- RADIVAN, B A
- RADIVAN, B A
- RADONS-HARRIS
- RANKIN, PAM
- REDHOUSE
- REHMAN, S (DR)
- REJUVENATION
- REMEDY BOX
- RICHARDS, B
- RILEY, JANE
- RIMMER, CHRISTINE
- ROBERTS, S (DR)
- ROBERTSON & ASSOCIATES
- ROBERTSON & ASSOCIATES
- SAVILLE, ELAINE
- SCHOLL FOOTCARE CENTRE
- SCOULAR, F M F
- SHANGHAI ACUPUNCTURE CLINIC
- SHANGHAI ACUPUNCTURE CLINIC
- SHIZHEN TCM UK
- SILVERMAN, MAURICE
- ST JOHN STREET PHYSIO PRACTICE
- ST JOHNS OSTEOPATHIC
- STATE REGISTERED CHIROPODISTS
- STIRLING, DIANNE
- STUMMER, G
- SWINTON HEALTH FOODS
- TANG, B (DR)
- TANG, SHULAN
- TATHAM, ALAN
- THERAPY BREAK
- THOMAS, G
- TOLLEY, STEVE
- TULLY, M J
- VILLAGE PHYSIO & SPORTS CLINIC
- WALKER, ROY
- WASHINGTON SCH CLIN/ADV HYP
- WATKISS, VALERIE
- WEBB, EDWINA
- WEBB, EDWINA
- WEIGHTMAN, BRENDA
- WEST DIDSBURY HOLISTIC HEALTH
- WILLIAMSON, A
- WILSON, NICOLA
- WOODWARD, ANITA
- YUSUPOFF, LAWRENCE
- ZEUS P M C

### OLDHAM

- HUNT, MARILYN

### SALFORD

- ANDERSON, LOUISE
- CHINESE TRAD HEALTH CENTRE
- COHEN, D (DR)
- COOPER, R P
- DAVIES, L
- DEACH, I
- GILCHRIST, A
- GOWER, CATHERINE
- GRAHAM, CHRISTINE
- HALLACK, VIVIENNE
- HEIMISCHE CLINIC
- HOLISTICA
- MANCHESTER SPORT INJURIES
- MIDDLETON, SCOTT (DR)
- PHILLIPS, LORRAINE
- WRIGHT, MARTIN

### STALYBRIDGE

- ADVANCED CHIROPODY SURGERY
- AROMATHERAPY LADIES MASSAGE
- BODY & MIND THERAPY CENTRE
- BOURGUIGNON, PASCAL
- BROWN, LAWRIE
- CHADWICK, BRIAN L
- EVANS, DAVID
- FAULKNER, MICHELLE
- KARMA COMMUNICATIONS
- LAMB, D
- MAYERS, AMANDA
- RAE, Y
- SCHOFIELD, G A
- SELLARS, SHEILA

## MERSEYSIDE

### BIRKENHEAD

- ACUPUNCTURE CLINIC
- ACUPUNCTURE CLINIC
- ATKINSON, D W
- BIRKENHEAD CHIROPODY CENTRE
- BIRKENHEAD CHIROPRACTIC CLNC
- BUCKLEY, A S
- DIET CENTRE
- FAMILY SCALP & HAIR CLINIC
- MARKET STREET CHIROPODY CLINIC
- MARTIN, JEAN
- MILLIGAN, RICHARD
- RHIANNON'S CAT
- WILLIAMS CHIROPODY SERVICE
- WILLIAMS, CATHERINE
- WIRRALL CLINIC

### BOOTLE

- CLARKE, M D
- MERTON ACUPUNCTURE & HERBAL

### ELLESMERE PORT

- DAKIN, C M
- EILEEN TAYLOR CHIROPODIST
- JONES, JENNIFER
- KINNEY, CAROL
- MCGOVEN, J
- MORRELL, C
- THOMPSON, PATRICIA

### GREASBY

- THERAPY 21
- WILLIAMS, T H

### LIVERPOOL

- ABBEY FOOT CLINIC
- ABBEY FOOT CLINIC
- ABBEY FOOT CLINIC
- ACORN CHIROPODY SURGERY
- ACTIVE PHYSICAL THERAPY
- ADVANCE COUNSELLING SERVICES
- AIGBURTH MCTIMONEY CLINIC
- AINTREE OSTEOPATHIC
- ALFONSO & PETERSON
- ALLERTON CLINIC
- ALLERTON HEALTH CENTRE
- ALLERTON MOBILE PHYSIOTHERAPY
- ALLERTON MOBILE PHYSIOTHERAPY
- ALLERTON REMEDIAL CLINIC
- ALTERNATIVES NTRL HLTH CTRE
- ANDERSON, KATE
- ARBOUR
- AROMATHERAPY TREATMENT
- ATKINSON, D W
- BATE, CAROLE
- BENNETT, ROSEMARY
- BESTEL & ASSOCIATES
- BOYLE, A M
- BOYLE, ANDREW
- BROOKES, CLIVE
- CAWLEY, TONY
- CEPHAS CONSULTANCY
- CHADWICK, PAUL R
- CHAPPELL, L
- CLIFFORD, CORNELIUS
- CONROY, GILLIAN
- CROSBY PHYSIOTHERAPY
- CULPEPER
- DARE TO CARE
- DEVEY, BRENDA
- DIAL-A-MEDIUM
- DUFFY, P W
- DULDZIN BUDHIST CENTRE
- ECCLES CHIROPODY SERVICES
- ECCLES, H R
- EQUILIBRIUM FLOATATION CENTRE
- FAROOQ AHMED, KHAN
- FORMBY PHYSIOTHERAPY
- FOSTER, SUE
- FRANCE, C J
- FRESHLEA PRIVATE CLINICS
- GHOSH, A
- GIBSON LYNDA & MURRAY ANNE
- GOBIN, JOHN
- GOLDEN SAFFRON
- HAMPEL, HILARY
- HARMONY HOLISTICS
- HARRISON, J C
- HAWLEY, DUNCAN
- HAYES, L
- HERB HELPLINE
- HERBERT, P A
- HILL, LESLEY
- HO, ANNE-MARIE
- HODDES, S H (DR)
- HOPE STREET NATURAL HLTH CTRE
- HYNOTHERAPY BY A J FOOTE
- JACQUI
- JONES, GLENNIS
- KARRAN, MARGARETTE
- KEARNEY, V L
- KENNETH ATHERTON HOMOEOPATH
- KENNY, A
- KUA, R P
- LAFFERTY, FRANCIS
- LAVENDER, M J
- LEVENE, L
- LINFORTH, A E
- LIPKIN, FENELLA
- LIVERPOOL CENTRE FOR HEALTH
- LYNN
- MAGENTA THERAPIES
- MAGHULL PHYSIOTHERAPY CLINIC
- MAGNET THERAPY
- MAHARISHI AYUR VEDA HLTH CTRE
- MARTLAND, ANNE
- MASSAGE & REFLEXOLOGY
- MCCONAGHY, M G
- MERSEYSIDE SCHOOL OF MASSAGE
- MIND MATTERS
- MITCHELL, G D
- NEVITT, NEIL
- NEWTON, J
- O'BRIEN, EAMONN
- ORMROD, KEN
- ORR, WILLIAM A
- PARISH, CHRISTOPHER
- PARSONS, C A
- PAWLEY, PHILIP
- PENNY
- PHYTHIAN, KATHLEEN
- PICKIN, N & R J
- POWRIE, S
- PRUDEN, J F
- RAWLINSON, KATE
- REIKI-4-LIFE
- RILEY, JANE E

- ROBERTS, ANN
- ROBERTSON, P
- ROBINSON, R S
- RODNEY FERTILITY CLINIC
- RODNEY STREET HYPNOTHERAPY
- ROMA ROMANI HYPNOTHERAPY
- SALMONS, P
- SANCTUARY NATURAL HEALTH
- SCHOLL FOOTCARE
- SCOTT, ANDREW
- SEFTON PARK NATURAL THRPY CTRE
- SOUTH LIVERPOOL CHIROPODY SVS
- STEINA SPORTS & PHYSIOTHERAPY
- STEWART, D S
- STRESS MANAGEMENT
- SUMMERS, A A
- SUMMERS, ALFRED A
- SYLVIA
- TARA SCHOOL OF HYPNOTHERAPY
- TERENCE, ANTHONY
- THERAPY LIVERPOOL
- TRANSCENDENTAL MEDITATION
- TUEBROOK OSTEOPATHIC CLINIC
- TUEBROOK OSTEOPATHIC CLINIC
- TURNER, IVYLEA
- ULTIMATE FOOT HEALTH CLINIC
- VAEZZADEH, M
- VANGEN, M A
- WHITE, DARRELL
- WILKINSON, JANICE

### NEWTON-LE-WILLOWS

- HALSALL, JANET
- JONES, CHRISTINE
- KNOWLES, JANICE
- LING

### PRENTON

- CARMICHAEL, KAREN
- DONEGAN, P T
- FARMER, BARBARA
- OWEN, T
- PURE ESSENTIALS DIRECT
- STROKE & HEAD INJURY CLINIC
- SYSTEMS THERAPY

### PRESCOT

- BALDWIN, G J
- CUNLIFFE, IAN
- DAVIES, H A
- HOPKINS, B
- LYON, A
- NATURAL HEALTH CLINIC
- PATHS TO MASTERY

### SOUTHPORT

- ABBOTT & WILKINSON
- AINDOW, M J
- AINSDALE OSTEOPATHIC CLINIC
- AINSDALE PHYSIOTHERAPY
- AITKEN, ANNE
- BARKER, KAY E
- BERRILL, P
- BIMPSON, PETER
- BIRKDALE CHIROPRACTIC CLINIC
- BLANCHE, M
- BOYLE, A
- BRITTAIN, HAL
- BURNETT, BOB
- COLLINS, J
- COUNSELLING CLINIC
- D GELDARD PHYSIOTHERAPIST
- FRANCE, C A
- GIBBON, MALCOLM
- HOLISTIC HEALTH CENTRE
- HOMOEOPATHIC VETERINARY CENTRE
- INSTITUTE OF CHIROPODISTS
- JABBAR, A
- JENKINS, JUDITH
- KARN, M
- LEAN, C
- LEON
- MCKITTRICK, S J
- MEREDITH, P R
- MITTAL, A
- MOON, BARBARA
- NATUROPATHIC HEALTH CENTRE
- POWELL, C R
- PREDICTIONS
- PRICE, ANNE
- PUGH, ANNE W
- ROBE-QUINN, BERNICE
- SALUS NATURAL HEALING
- SCHOLL CENTRE
- SITTERS, LATONA
- SOUTHPORT & TARLETON PHYSIO
- SOUTHPORT OSTEO & ACUPUNCTURE
- TOETAL CARE
- TRANQUILITY
- WALLACE, LYN
- YOUNG, DOROTHY

### ST. HELENS

- A & H CHIROPODY SURGERY
- ALTERNATIVE MEDICAL CENTRE
- APPLEBY, W
- ASHBOURNE KNIGHT
- BAKER, E
- BOND, LYNNE
- D A F CLINIC
- DAVIES, H A
- DAVIS, ROSE
- FACE & FIGURE
- HEAL TO TOE
- MARSH, E C
- PSYCHOLOGICAL CONSULTING SVS
- SHANKS, ALAN
- SIMPSON CLINIC

### WALLASEY

- BIEZANEK, A C
- BOLTON, TOM
- CARTER, G R
- CHINESE MEDICAL CENTRE
- COOKE, D M
- GRAYSON, NEIL W
- GREEN YARDS NATURAL HEALTH
- JACKSONS
- LISTCARD CHIROPODY CENTRE
- LLOYD, PETER R
- MANOR CHIROPODY CLINIC
- MCLOUGHLIN, CLAIRE
- ROSEMARY, CHRISTIE
- URE, MARILYN
- WESTON, JULIE

### WIRRAL

- AROMACARE
- BAKRAN, D M
- BESWICK, MARGARET
- BODY MIND & SOLE
- BRENNAN, M A
- BRIDGE HOUSE CLINIC
- CARTER, G R
- CLARKE, PAUL G
- COLLINS, MARY
- CONCANNON, DEIRDRE
- DUNCAN, SIMON
- EDUCATIONAL PSYCHOLOGY ASS
- FARRELL, DEREK P
- GATEAUD, S
- GAYER, PETER
- GROUNDS, L
- HAZLEHURST, JEAN
- HEBARIUM
- HESWALL HOLISTIC HEALTH CENTRE
- HOMOEOPATHIC MEDICINE
- HUGHES, JEAN
- HUMPHRIS, MANDY
- HYPNOCARE
- JAMES, ANN
- JARVIS, K R
- JOINTS & POINTS
- KEETON, JOE
- LAVENDER, M J
- MACLAVERTY, RUTH
- MAWDSLEY, JEAN
- MORETON CHIROPRACTIC CLINIC
- MORETON REMEDIAL CLINIC
- MORRISON, CAROLE
- NELSON, PATRICIA
- ROWAN, MAGGIE
- SHAY-STEPHENSON, KATE
- SINNOTT, A
- SMITH, EVELYN
- SPEED, J A
- SULLIVAN, CAROL
- TAYLOR, KAREN
- TAYLOR, MONICA
- WEBSTER-DICKS, J
- WEST KIRBY PHYSIOTHERAPY
- WEST WIRRAL CHIROPRACTIC
- WESTLAKE-GUY, C
- WILLIAMS, CATHERINE
- WILLIAMS, TECWYN H
- WIRRAL CHIROPODY SERVICE

## MIDLANDS (WEST)

### BILSTON

- ALTERNATIVE BACK CARE
- CHIOTIS, ANNE
- HOLISTICLY YOURS
- LIFE FOUNDATION SCHOOL
- OWEN, L J

### BIRMINGHAM

- 1ST CHIROPRACTIC UK
- A Q C H
- ABBIE HYPNOTHERAPY CENTRE
- ABBIE HYPNOTHERAPY CENTRE
- ACUPOINT MAGNETO CLINIC
- ADAMS, MARGERET REID
- ALEXANDER TEACHERS ASSOCIATION
- ALTONICS
- ANALYSIS CENTRE
- AROMA HEALTH INTERNATIONAL
- ARROW BANK CHIROPRACTIC CLINIC
- ARTHURS, BEV
- ASSOCIATION OF STRESS MNGMT
- ATKIN, MORRIS
- BADDELEY & BANNISTER
- BAIRD, MICHAEL
- BALANCE & HARMONY
- BARNT GREEN
- BARNT GREEN ACUPUNCTURE CLINIC
- BEAUTIFORM COLLEGE
- BELL, PATRICIA
- BELLINGER, A
- BILLINGHAM, S
- BIRCH, GILLIAN
- BIRLEY, PAUL
- BIRMINGHAM & DISTRICT
- BIRMINGHAM ACU/CHIRO CLNC
- BIRMINGHAM CHINESE MEDICINE
- BIRMINGHAM CTRE-ARTS THERAPIES
- BIRMINGHAM DIATHERMY
- BIRMINGHAM HYPNOTHERAPY
- BIRMINGHAM MOBILE CHIRO CTRE
- BIRMINGHAM PHYSIO CLINIC
- BIRMINGHAM SCHOOL OF PODIATRY
- BIRMINGHAM TRAD ACU CENTRE
- BIRMINGHAM WOMENS COUNS
- BLAKE, D H
- BLEBY, J
- BOSTWICK, A
- BOWEN, MARGARET
- BRODIE, JOANNE
- CADGE, A E H
- CARING HYPNOTHERAPY CENTRE
- CARRS LANE CHURCH CENTRE
- CASTLE VALE CHIROPODY SERVICE
- CENTRE FOR NATURAL THERAPIES
- CHAVDA, ANJNA
- CHEEMA, M
- CHELMSLEY WOOD FOOT CLINIC
- CHINESE HERBAL MED & HLTH CARE
- CHINESE HERBAL WAY
- CHINESE MEDICINE CENTRE
- CHIRO MED
- CHIROPODY CLINIC
- CHIROPODY SURGERY
- CHIROPRACTIC CLINIC
- CITY CHIROPRACTIC CLINIC
- CLARKE, IRENE
- CLINIC OF HERBAL MEDICINE
- COLEMAN, JOHN
- COMMUNITY PSYCHIATRIC NURSING
- COMPLEMENTARY HEALING CENTRE
- COMPLEMENTARY THERAPY CENTRE
- COMPLEMENTARY THERAPY CENTRE
- CONNECT THERAPEUTIC COMMUNITY
- COTTERIDGE CHIROPRACTIC CLINIC
- CREATIVE CHANGES
- CRYSTAL CLEAR PRACTICE
- CTIC
- CTRE-REFLEX & AROMATHERAPY

- CULPEPER
- DAVIES, BERYL
- DEACON, ALISON
- DEARLING, FIONA
- DONNAMARIE
- DRUMMOND, HEATHER
- DUNBAR, MAURICE
- EASTY, JANE C
- EDGBASTON ACUPUNCTURE CLINIC
- EDGBASTON HEALTH CLINIC
- ERDINGTHON NATURAL HEALTH CLNC
- ESSENCE OF ELOAH
- EUSTACE-GREAVES, M
- EVE GRAYWOLF LUNG PSYC CONS
- EZRA REMEDIAL AROMATHERAPY
- FAIRFAX PRIVATE THERAPY
- FALKNER-HEYLINGS, J
- FEWTRELL, SALLY
- FIRST CLASS
- FOOT CLINIC
- FOOT TREATMENT SURGERY
- FORD, MARIA
- FRAZER, C C
- FRENCH, ANNE
- FRESHWINDS CHARITABLE TRUST
- GARDENER, STEFANJA
- GAYNOR BULLER CLINIC
- GHOURI HOMEOPATHIC CLINIC
- GIBSON-FORTY, JOHN
- GRACE, MARIE
- GRAHAM, PATRICIA
- GRANT, SUSAN
- GREAT BARR OSTEO PRACTICE
- GREEN, JESSICA
- HALL GREEN ALTERN PRACTICE
- HARPER, M B
- HARRIS, MICHAEL
- HARTE, ELAINE
- HARVEY, K G
- HAYES, ANN
- HEAVEN SCENT
- HERBAL CLINIC
- HERBAL TREATMENT CENTRE
- HERBAVET
- HIGGS, R W
- HILL, ANTHONY W
- HOGG, DEBBI
- HOMOEOPATHIC CLINIC/PHARMACY
- HOMOEOPATHY CENTRE
- HOT-PAK
- HUSBAND, B
- HUSBANDS, STEVE
- HUSSAIN, S (DR)
- I C S
- ILSELEY, BERNARD
- INDRA RASTOGI
- JAY, D
- JING YING WANG
- JOHNSON, A E
- JONES, MICHAEL A
- JONES, SHEILA
- KEMPSON, STEVE
- KEYS
- KNIGHT, ROWENA
- KRISS, PAULINE
- LANDER, H J
- LAST, ALISON
- LEASK, ANDREW
- LEESON, CHRISTINE
- LOCKHART, CLAIRE
- LYNCH, STEPHEN
- MARTINS, P
- MCCORRIE, LISA
- MCDERMOTT, P
- MCMANUS, MARIE
- MCMANUS, RAYMOND
- MCNEILL, MARGARET
- MIDLAND HYPNOTHERAPY CENTRE
- MIDLAND HYPNOTHERAPY CENTRE
- MIDLAND MEDICAL HOM PRACTICE
- MIDLAND MEDICAL OSTEO PRACTICE
- MIDLAND REFLEXOLOGY
- MILLARD, PETER M J
- MINGS CHINESE HERBALISTS
- MINIHANE, LIZ
- MOLYNEUX, DAVID J
- MORRIS, CLAIRE
- MUNRO, JANE
- NATURAL HEALTH CENTRE
- NAYLOR, ESTER
- NELSON, CHRIS
- NORRIS, A J (DR)
- NORTHCROFT CLINIC
- NORTHWOOD, R S
- O'GRADY, MARGARET
- OSBORNE, P
- PARDOE, IAN S (DR)
- PARKES, J
- PASSEY, F
- PATTON, MICHAEL
- PEARCE, KEITH
- PERRY, ALICIA
- POPPLEWELL, SALLY
- POSITIVE HEALING ROOM
- PRIEST, NIGEL
- PRIMECARE
- PSYCHOTHERAPY ASSOCIATES INT
- RAYNER, MARY M (DR)
- REMEDIAL MASSAGE THERAPY
- RENAISSANCE HOLISTIC THRPY
- RITA
- RIVER-MOON
- ROBERT BIRD REFLEXOLOGIST
- ROUSSEAU, JAMES
- SAVANNAH ENTERPRISES
- SCHOLL CENTRE
- SHARMAN, SARAH
- SHELDON
- SIDHOM, A
- SKINNER, B
- SMITH, PHILIP
- SOMASUNDARA-RAJAH, K
- SOMEWAY HERBAL CLINIC
- SOUTH BIRMINGHAM HYP CENTRE
- ST PAULS OSTEOPATHY PRACTICE
- STARKEY, DAVID
- STEELE, P A
- STEREX ELECTROLYSIS INT
- STEVENS, CHARMIAN
- STONE, S
- SUCCESSWORKS
- TAPERELL, AVRIL
- TAYLOR, H M
- TAYLOR, P
- THERAPY TRAINING COLLEGE
- TRADITIONAL CHINESE MEDICINE
- TRUEMAN, M
- TUNNICLIFFE, JEANETTE
- TYE, MARIE
- VEHILL COMMUNICATIONS
- VICTORIA SPECIAL SCHOOL
- WADDINGTON, P
- WALKRITE CHIROPODY SERVICES
- WALSH, DEAN
- WANG, JING
- WARWICK FOOT CLINIC
- WELL NATURAL HEALTH CENTRE
- WELL NATURAL HEALTH CENTRE
- WESTWOOD, ANGELA
- WHITE, A C (DR)
- WHITE, V
- WILLIAMS, CHARLES
- WILLOWS CLNC COMP HEALTH CTRE
- WILSON, JULIE
- WITCOMB, C
- WOODLANDS REFLEXOLOGY
- WORDSWOOD PHYSIO PRACTICE
- WRIGHT, JONATHAN
- WRIGHT, JUDITH
- YOGA TUITION
- ZEN AT THE WATERS EDGE
- ZEN HEALTH & BEAUTY

## BRIERLEY HILL

- GOWER, MONICA
- HOLLOWAY, P
- ROBINSON, JOHN
- WITHYMOOR PHYSIOTHERAPY CLINIC

## COVENTRY

- ABBEY CLINIC
- AION COUNSELLING/PSYCHOTHERAPY
- ALDA HOUSE
- ALDA HOUSE NATURAL THERAPY
- ALDOUS, JOSIE
- ALEXANDER TECHNIQUE
- ALEXANDER, EMMA
- ALLEN, BARBARA
- ALLEN, ELAINE
- ANNMARIE
- APPEARANCE PLUS
- BANKS, RON
- BAZELEY, J
- BELVEDERE PHYSIO CLINIC
- BRADY, J
- BUTLER, M
- CALLIE INT CLAIRVOYANT
- CHEN, LU
- CHEYLESMORE PHYSIO CLINIC
- CHILD & ADOLESCENT PSYCHIATRY
- COLTMAN, J B
- CORLET, LOUISE
- COVENTRY CTRE OF OSTEO & ACU
- COX, B L
- DEOL, SUE
- DINGWALL, J T
- DUNCOMBE CLNC OF PHYSICAL MED
- EBRAHIM, D W
- EDUCATIONAL PSYCHOLOGY SERVICE
- FAULKNER, SUSAN
- FAWKES, CAROL
- FAWKES, R H
- FIRTH, JOHN
- GALE, M H
- GEE
- GREIG, ELIZABETH
- HANDS OF HEALINGS
- HERBAL TREATMENT CENTRE
- HILLFIELDS HEALTH CENTRE
- HUMPHREY, ALISON
- INSIGHT
- J BENSON CHIROPODIST
- JONES, J
- KARYM
- KING & MCDONALD
- LEDDINGTON-WRIGHT, S
- LEIGH, ANNA
- LEWIS, MYRA
- LONGFORD PHYSIO & SPORTS
- LORD, K H
- MAOUDIS, P G
- MAOUDIS, P G
- MAUREEN
- MAUREEN
- MOONSTONES
- MORRIS, CYNTHIA
- NATURAL HEALTH CENTRE
- NATURES PATH
- OLD HOUSE CLINIC
- OLIVER, BETTY
- ORTON, G
- PARK PRACTICE
- PILGRIM, N M
- PRICE, J A J
- PURPLE FLAME AROMATHERAPY
- RAWLINGS, B T
- ROBINSON, CLARE
- SCHOFIELD, SHEILA
- SCHOLL CENTRE
- SHERBOURNE CLINIC
- SHUTTLEWORTH, JACK
- SIMMS, SYLVIA D
- STRANKS, KATHY
- SUNDERLAND, CYNTHIA
- THOMAS, D
- WALSGRAVE CHIROPRACTIC CLINIC
- WEST, JOY
- WILLIAMS, GWYN
- WINTER, B
- WOODWARD, JILL

## DUDLEY

- ACUPUNCTURE CLINIC
- AQCH
- BLANCK, E H
- BRIARS
- DUDLEY PHYSIOTHERAPY CLINIC
- GRAYBURN-HALE, DAVID
- HOMOEPATHY CENTRE
- HOWELLS & BYTHEWAY
- HUGHES, PAMELA J
- JONES, SARAH
- KATE
- PASSEY, FIONA
- POWER-ASHMAN, LINDA
- SEDGLEY COMP THERAPIES

- SEDGLEY PHYSIO & ACU CENTRE
- SIMMONDS, BRIAN
- WEST MIDLAND HYPNOTHERAPY

## HALESOWEN

- ADSHEAD & WESTWOOD
- ANDREWS, S C W
- CHAN ACUPUNCTURE
- CROFT, ANGELA
- DANDO, PAUL
- HALAS THERAPIES
- HODKINSON, J R
- KITSON OSTEOPATH
- MITCHELL, JOY
- MORGAN, VALERIE
- PANSY POTTERS CLOUD 9
- PHYSIO & SPORTS INJURY
- PRISM THERAPIES
- ROMSLEY PHYSIOTHERAPY PRACTICE
- SIMPSON, NICK
- TUDOR, EDWARD G

## KINGSWINFORD

- BEATTIE, R G
- PHYSIOTHERAPY CLINIC
- SANDERLING HYPNOTHERAPY CENTRE

## OLDBURY

- FANTHOM, J K
- FOOT FLEX
- WHITE, SHELLEY
- WILDEN, JANE

## ROWLEY REGIS

- FLETCHER, VICTOR JOHN
- WHITEHEAD, T

## SMETHWICK

- ABEL HOUSE HYPNOTHERAPY
- ACUHERBS CHINESE MEDICINE CTRE
- ARNAOUT, HUDA
- BREEDON, GARY
- GORMAN, PETER
- HALE, GEOFF
- ROOKER, P A
- WALSH, LINDA

## SOLIHULL

- ACUPUNCTURE HEALTH CLINIC
- ACUTECH ACU & ALLERGY CENTRE
- ALSING, FABIENNE
- AROMA SANTE
- ASS OF CHIROP/PODIATRISTS
- BIOENERGY PARTNERSHIP
- BTAC
- CALLAGHAN, R M & J
- CHIROPRACTORS OF WARWICK ROAD
- CLOUD 10
- COMPLEMENTARY MEDICINE CENTRE
- COOPER, D V
- COX, PETER R
- DAVIES, LORNA
- DRANSFIELD, L J
- DURRANT, M
- ESSENTIAL HEALTH
- GREEN VALLEY THERAPY CENTRE
- HANDS, ANNE
- HARTLEY, JANET
- HELEN, MACAULAY
- HOGAN, A
- LANDER, EILEEN
- LIFE'S OPTION
- MAXWELL-WEIR, CHRISTINE
- MCDERMOTT, J V
- MCNEILL, MARGARET
- MIDLAND MEDICAL HOM PRACTICE
- MIDLAND MEDICAL OSTEO PRACTICE
- MOLE, DEBBIE
- NATURAL HOLISTIC THERAPIES
- NATURES SUNSHINE PRODUCTS
- NEWTONS TRADITIONAL REMEDIES
- OCCUPATIONAL CONSULTANCY SVS
- OULTON FOOT CLINIC
- PIKE, ELIZABETH G & J K
- REED, SUZANNE
- ROBERTS, ADRIAN
- ROSCOE, JULIA
- RUTH'S REFLEXOLOGY
- SAVAGE, GERALD
- SEN-GUPTA, (DR)
- SHARKEY, CATHERINE
- SMALLWOOD, TREVOR
- SMITH, J
- SMITH, MOLLY-ANN
- SOLIHULL CHIROPRACTIC CLINIC
- STARTIN, A M
- TURNER, C C
- WHITEHOUSE, PAMELA
- WHITTAKER, MARGARET C
- WILKINS, A
- YOUNG, PATRICIA

## STOURBRIDGE

- CONDUIT, E
- COURTYARD STOURBRIDGE CENTRE
- CREATIVE HEALTH CENTRE
- DALE, JANET
- DHANA, P N
- DHANA, P N
- GREENFIELD AVE CONSULTING ROOM
- HAGLEY CENTRE OF COMP MED
- HEALTH & BEAUTY CLINIC
- HOLISTIC HEALTH CENTRE
- INGRAM, CLARE
- KITSON, PAUL
- KURIAN, M
- LANE, ANNA
- LEES, J D
- LONG LIFE CHINESE HERBAL MED
- MANION, D
- MURPHY, A M
- NORTON HOMOEOPATHIC PRACTICE
- ORME, RUTH
- PARRETTI, ROSEMARY
- PITT, HARRY
- RADAN, P J
- SMITH, GILL
- STOURBRIDGE ACU & OSTEO CTRE
- STOURBRIDGE CHIROPRACTIC
- STOURBRIDGE PHYSIO PRACTICE
- STRESS MANAGEMENT
- TAYLOR, CLARE
- TELLING, MELANIE
- TELLING, MELANIE
- THOMAS, LESLEY
- WARD, JAQUELINE

## SUTTON COLDFIELD

- 1ST CHIROPRACTIC UK
- BOLDMERE HYPNOTHERAPY
- CARTWRIGHT-RAY, JOY
- CLUSKER, P
- FIT FEET
- FOOT WISE CHIROPODY
- FORREST, LISA M
- FOUR OAKS
- FRANCE-SHELTON FOOT HLTH CTRE
- GROVES, MURIEL
- HAMILTON, W
- HARRIS, GERALD
- HERBAL PHARMACY
- HOLLY COTTAGE CHIRO CLINIC
- JOHNSON FOOTCARE
- LANE, R A
- MAPES, JANET
- MCEVOY, RACHEL ANN
- MIDLAND MEDICAL HOM PRACTICE
- MIDLAND MEDICAL OSTEO PRACTICE
- MIDLAND PHYSIOTHERAPY CLINIC
- MIDLAND PHYSIOTHERAPY CLINICS
- MIDLAND PSYCHOLOGICAL SERVICE
- MOTIVATIONAL RESEARCH & DVPT
- NATURAL CHOICE
- NORTON, CHRIS
- PARKES, VAL
- PILLATH, CHRISTINE
- REVIVAL HOLISTIC THERAPY CTRE
- ROSEMARY HILL CLINIC
- SEH ORTHOTICS
- SMITH, CHERYL
- STEVENSON, E J
- SUTTON BRIEF THERAPY CENTRE
- SUTTON COLDFIELD HEALTH CLINIC
- SUTTON COLDFIELD HYPNOTHERAPY
- SUTTON HOMOEOPATHIC PRACTICE
- SWANN, PATRICIA
- TANDY, E
- TEES, MALCOLM
- TILNEY, TONY
- WALL, HELEN
- WOOD, COLIN

## TIPTON

- NATURAL HARMONY
- NATURAL WAY AROMATHERAPY
- SENSATIONS AROMATHERAPY

## WALSALL

- ACCENT ON BEAUTY
- ALDRIDGE PHYSIOTHERAPY CLINIC
- ALLMAN, ANNE
- ARBORETUM/WALSALL CHIROPRACTIC
- BACKCARE & ACUPUNCTURE CLINIC
- BELSIZE HOUSE
- BIRD, CAROLINE
- BULLOCK, JULIE
- BUSY BODIES
- CARPENTER, DAVID
- COLLINS, N T
- DENISE PALMIST & INT CLAIR
- DEVEREAUX M A CHIROPODIST
- ELECTROLYSIS CLINIC
- HATCHARD, REBECCA
- HILL, R E
- HOMOEOPATHY
- INNERSENSE
- JANE'S, BEVERLEY
- JONES, DAVID
- KINSEY, G C
- LEMM, D M
- MARY
- MILLER, VALERIE
- MORRIS, JOHN
- PAUL MAWER PSYCHOLGICAL SVS
- RICHARDSON, CYRIL
- SEITAI/SHIATSU & MANIPULATION
- SMITH, K B
- SMITH, PATRICIA A
- WALSALL CHIROPRACTIC HEALTH
- WALSALL COMMUNITY HEALTH TRUST
- WALSALL PHYSIOTHERAPY CLINIC
- WESTON, JOHN
- WHITEHALL, CAROL
- WILLIAMS, K

## WEDNESBURY

- FULLWOOD, D
- GOLDEN PALMS
- HALL, SUSAN
- JERRETT, CHRIS
- SHENSTON, RICHARD
- SIRDEFIELD, PAUL

## WEST BROMWICH

- CENTRAL CHIROPODY CLINIC
- CHILD PSYCHOLOGY SERVICE
- FINE FRAGRANCES
- KITSON, PAUL
- LONG LIFE CHINESE HERBAL MED
- MCNICHOL CHIROPODY CLINIC
- METCALF, Y
- STONE CROSS NHS CLINIC

## WILLENHALL

- BEECH, MICHAEL
- CHEER, MARIE
- DAVIS A STARKEY REM THERAP
- DAWINDER, JOHAL
- HAMPTON, ANTHONY
- JOBBER, J V
- LESLEY'S REFLEXOLOGY
- MARTIN, T C

## WOLVERHAMPTON

- ALCOCK, E C
- ATKINS, DENISE
- BARNES, JEREMY
- BELLEW, CHRIS
- BENNETTO, CHRIS
- BLAIR, GRAHAM
- BLAIR, GRAHAM
- BREDON HOUSE SPORTS & PHYSIO
- BROCK, SUSAN
- BROWNHILL, D G

- BURNS, JON
- CASEY-KENNEDY, MARGARET
- CENTRE FOR NATURAL HEALING
- CHIROPRACTIC CLINIC
- CODSALL COMP THERAPIES
- COMP-U-CLIC
- CONYERD, D
- COUNSELLING AT ST PETER'S HSE
- CRANE-GRIFFIN, DIANE
- CYNTHIA MOORES REFLEXOLOGY
- DARLINGTON STREET PRACTICE
- DAVIES, V E
- FOSTER, M
- FOTHERBY, J
- GALLOWAY, BEVERLEY
- GURPAL SINGH AROMA/REFLEX
- HALE ASSOCIATES
- HARRISON, CHRISTINE
- HARTNESS, R
- HEALTH SHOP
- HODDELL, P J
- JONES, NEIL
- KEVIN FISHER CHIROPODY
- KHALSA, S S
- KUAN YING, LIM
- KURIAN, M (DR)
- LAW, MARIE
- MASON, CAROLINE A
- MIDLANDS HOM CONSULTANTS
- MURPHY, J E
- MYATT, ANITA
- NATURAL HARMONY
- NATURAL HEALING
- NEWBRIDGE PHARMACY
- NIXON, LOUISE
- NORMAN, KATHY
- NUTMEG CLINIC
- PALMER, BARBARA J
- PEACH, A
- POTTER, DEREK
- QURESHI, M J H
- RENTOUL, R W
- RIES, JOAN L
- ROBERTSHAW, A
- RUXTON, HUGH
- SHANGRI-LA ACUPUNCTURE CLINIC
- SHAW, REBECCA
- SPINES CLINIC
- STARKEY, JOHN F
- TETTENHALL CHIROPODY PRACTICE
- TOTTENHAM, NIKKI
- WEDNESFIELD HOL THRPY CTRE
- WOLVERHAMPTON CHINESE MED CTRE
- WOLVERHAMPTON HOMOEOPATHY
- WOLVERHAMPTON NUFFIELD HOSP
- WOLVERHAMPTON PHYSIO/SPORTS
- YOUNG, ROSEMARY

## NORFOLK

### ATTLEBOROUGH

- BLANCH, KATE
- HAYNES, AVRIL
- QUEENS SQUARE SURGERY

### CROMER

- COMER OSTEOPATHIC CLINIC
- CROMER PHYSIOTHERAPY
- FLYNN, K
- HOLISTIC HEALTH CENTRE
- MAPPERLEY, B S

### DEREHAM

- ARTHURS WHOLEFOODS
- CHIROPODISTS
- HANNAM, R J
- NICHOLLS, FRANK
- REID, C R

### DISS

- BURRIDGE, C
- COTTAGE CLINIC
- COTTAGE NTRL HEALTH CLINIC
- CROWEST, E
- DISS CHIROPODY CLINIC
- DISS CHIROPRACTIC CLINIC
- DISS NATURAL HEALTH CARE CTRE
- DISS NATURAL HEALTH CLINIC
- GLYNN, CLAIR
- HERBS HANDS HEALING
- LEROY, C
- MUSGRAVE-BROWN, LYLEEN
- PULHAM MARKET THERAPY CLINIC
- RUSH, J A

### DOWNHAM MARKET

- COMPLEMENTARY HEALTH CLINIC
- WELLS, H P
- WILMOT, D

### FAKENHAM

- RIVERS, PATRICIA
- SHARPE, ISABEL
- WALTERS, MARGARET

### GREAT YARMOUTH

- BODY BEAUTIFUL
- CARSON, KAREN
- CASSIDY, M
- CRABTREE, JENNY R
- CRABTREE, P W
- CRANIOSACRAL THERAPY
- DOGGETT, C
- FOSTER CLINIC
- GT YARMOUTH PHYSICAL THERAPY
- HAYWARD, ZENA
- HELLY'S HERBAL PRODUCTS
- JAMES, LINDA
- JESSOP CLINIC
- O'KEEFE, C S
- OVERY, J
- POTTS, M C
- PREMIER AROMATHERAPY
- SCHOLL CENTRE
- WOODEN, SUSAN

### HARLESTON

- ESSENTIAL HARMONY
- HARLESTON CHIROPRACTIC CLINIC
- VIDION, BARBARA

### HOLT

- COUNTY HEALTH
- HOBSON, L A
- MCLEISH, JACQUI
- WALNUT BARN CLINIC

### HUNSTANTON

- CLARE, MONICA G
- DOWNS, TINA
- MATKIN, CHARLES
- READE COLLEGE

### KING'S LYNN

- ACTIVE LIFE
- ADVANCED HYP/PSYCHOTHERAPY
- ALTERNATIVE THERAPIES
- BANE, M
- BETTS, DAVID
- CHASE PARK PRACTICE
- CLASSICAL OSTEOPATH
- ELLIS, H
- GIDDINGS, R
- HORSBURGH, E M
- HORSBURGH, S J
- JAMES, MALCOLM
- JAMES, MALCOLM (DR)
- LYNN REFLEXOLOGY CLINIC
- MASSINGHAM CHIROPRACTIC CLINIC
- MCCAFFREY, J E
- MEDICAL HERBALIST
- NORMAN, A J
- PSYCHOTHERAPY
- RUTHERFORD, W D
- STRESS MATTERS
- SUGDEN, A E
- SWEET RITA
- TUESDAY MARKET CHIROP PRACTICE
- WENDALS HERBS
- WENDY JILLEY - MEDICAL HERB

### NORTH WALSHAM

- CHIROPODIST
- GUYTON HOUSE
- NORTH WALSHAM CHIROPRACTIC

### NORWICH

- A P B ACUPUNCTURE PRACTICE
- ALDERBURY CLINIC
- ALEXANDER TECHNIQUE
- ALLEN-DAVIES, GAIL
- ALTERNATIVE HEALTH CARE
- AMALA CHIROPODY CENTRE
- APPLEGATE AROMATHERAPY
- AQUARONE REMY
- AROMATHERAPY CLINIC
- ARROWSMITH, SUSAN
- ASHFORD, T
- BERNEY, SUSAN
- BIRD, C
- BLACKLEDGE, VIVIAN
- BODY & SOUL
- BRUNSWICK PHYSIO
- BUPA HOSPITAL
- CANFOR, HAZEL
- CHANDLER, ANN
- CHILMAN CLINIC
- CLARKE, RACHEL
- CLIFTON, SARAH
- CLIFTON, SARAH
- COMPLEMENTARY MEDICINE CENTRE
- COOPER, D W
- COOPER, P W
- COULL, JUDY
- CULPEPER
- DAINES, MARY
- DICKINS, BEVERLEY
- DOYLE, JULIA
- DUNCANSON, S
- EAST MEETS WEST
- EGGINTON, KATHRYN
- EKE, L
- ELEMENTS OF HEALTH
- ELLIS, STEPHEN
- FARRANT, A
- FARRANT, A F
- FARRANT, A F
- FINCHAM, JOHNNY
- FIND YOUR RAINBOW
- FIRST STEP FOOTCARE
- FOLKER, N
- GEARY, A G
- GOODYEAR, MARGARET
- GORDON, STEPHEN
- GRANGER, J B
- HALL, G J
- HALL, RICHARD
- HAMPSON, G C
- HARGHAM HALL OSTEO PRACTICE
- HARLEY, D
- HART, S
- HARTHEN, A
- HAUGHTON, CATHERINE
- HERRINGTON, I
- HILL, MARTIN
- HOMEOPATHIC CLINIC
- HUDSON, M A
- HURSELL, BARRY
- JENKINS, G M
- JUSTRICH UK
- KERRIDGE, B W
- KING, S
- KING, SIMON
- LAMBOURN COURT
- LESLIE CLIFF
- MACKELLAR, D
- MALACHOWSKI, P
- MALAK, NAJI
- MARSHALL, C A
- MARTIN, J J
- MARTIN, SANDIE
- MCALLISTER, C
- MCTIMONEY CHIROPRACTIC CLINIC
- MONSON, J L B
- MOORE, CAROL
- MUNTING, E
- NEAL'S YARD REMEDIES
- NEW MARKET RD PHYSIO PRACTICE
- NORFOLK CLINIC
- NORWICH CENTRE
- NORWICH SPINAL/SPORTS INJ PRAC
- OLIVE GROVE BODY SCIENCE
- PARK PHYSIOTHERAPY
- PARTRIDGE, DEIRDRE
- PERRY
- PETHER, ANNE
- PHILPOTT, MONIQUE
- POINTER, TERESA
- POTTERGATE PSYCHOTHRPY PRACTCE

- PRIOR-SANDERSON, SARA
- READ, B
- RICHARDSON, A
- RICHARDSON, ALAN
- RICHARDSON, CAROL
- RICHARDSON, SUSAN
- RIGBY COURT CLINIC
- RIGG, SUSAN
- ROSBOTHAM, VALERIE
- ROSTRON, ALISON
- SADOWSKI, J T & L Y
- SAUNDERS, SUE
- SCHOLL CENTRE
- SCOTT-ROBINSON, JAMES
- SEELEY, I D
- SEELY, SUSAN
- SELLENS DRAKE, ANGELA
- SHIATSU CENTRE
- SMITH, SANDRA
- ST AUGUSTINES PSYCHOTHRPY CTRE
- ST STEPHENS PRACTICE
- SUN ESSENCES
- THORPE CLINIC
- TORLINGTON, GILL
- TRAFFORD, DEBORAH
- UTTING, MARTINE
- WALLEN, ANN
- WELLBEING NATURALLY
- WOBURN CLINIC
- WOBURN NATURAL HEALING CENTRE

### SHERINGHAM

- AVIS, JEAN
- CUMMING, NIGEL A
- CUMMINGS, MAUREEN
- HOMOEOPATHIC SUPPLY
- SHARP, DENISE
- STUDLEY, MARGARET

### THETFORD

- BRECKLAND PROMOTIONS
- COTTAGE CHIROPRACTIC CLINIC
- FORD OSTEOPATHIC CLINIC
- HOSKINS, RAYMOND
- HOUSTOUN, J K
- NORFOLK NATURAL HEALTH SERVICE
- SHANAHAN, CAROL
- WATTON PHYSIOTHERAPY CLINIC

### WELLS-NEXT-THE-SEA

- FISHER, JACK E
- RUSSELL THERAPEUTIC CENTRE

### WYMONDHAM

- HOLDEN, BERNARD
- LUCCHETTI, C A
- SLAUGHTER, J
- WOOLTORTON, S J

## NORTHAMPTONSHIRE

### BRACKLEY

- BATES, SANDIE
- CANONBURY PRODUCTS
- DUNLOP, MARION
- LAWSON, JANET
- PAUL BOIZOT AROMATHERAPY
- WILLIAMS, JANE

### CORBY

- CAMERON, LOUISE E

### DAVENTRY

- DAVENTRY NATUREWORKS
- DAVENTRY NATUREWORKS
- DAVIDSON, NIKKI
- FANNING, DOUGLAS
- GENTLE CARE CLINIC
- HUDSON, ELIZABETH
- JAYCOCK, SUE
- NOTIONS
- ONE TO ONE
- THROSSELL, PHILIPPA
- WILLCOX, JAN
- WOODFORD HALSE CHIROPRACTIC

### KETTERING

- ALBION HOMOEOPATHIC CENTRE
- ARMSTRONG, HEATHER
- BLOCK, GEORGINA
- CHIRO SPORTS INJURY CLINIC
- DRAGE, MARJORIE
- HARRIS, RACHEL
- HOPKINS, JUDY
- KETTERING CHIROPRACTIC CLINIC
- KETTERING OSTEOPATH
- MIRANDA, FRANCES
- PAM'S CHIROPODY SERVICE
- PHYSIOTHERAPY CENTRE
- ROSS, SHEENA
- SERENITY
- WITH COMPLEMENTS
- WYKES, MARY

### KINGSTHORPE

- REFLEXOLOGY CLINIC

### NORTHAMPTON

- ACUPUNCTURE CLINIC
- ALLEN, BRIAN C
- ALLEN, GEOFFREY
- ALTERNATIVE HEALTH CENTRE
- ANDREWS, S C
- ANDREWS, SIMON C
- ARBOURS
- AROMA TRADING
- BACK IN STEP
- BARNES, RICHARD
- BELLINGHAM, JANE
- BEVINGTON, ANN
- BUCKINGHAM, MARK
- C F C M
- CHAWTONS
- CHIROPRACTIC CLINIC
- CHROMASOUND
- CLINTON HOUSE CHIROPODY
- COUNTRY GARDEN HOLISTICS
- CROOK, J L
- DAYDREAMS
- DE-BANKE, MARGARET
- DEVON PARADE CLINIC
- DINNAGE, DAWN
- DON, ANITA
- EASTON, JOSEPHINE
- ELLIS, DAVID S
- ELVIN, CHRISTINA
- EQUINOX ORGANICS
- ESSERY, PATRICIA
- ESSERY, TRICIA
- EVANS, ANDY
- FINKE, MARTYN
- FINKE, WENDY
- FLOWERS, H M
- FORSYTH, J M
- FORSYTH, JILLIAN
- GARVEY-WILLIAMS, RICHARD
- GARVEY-WILLIAMS, RICHARD
- GREEN, DANA
- HALL, MANDY
- HAYES, SUE
- HIGGS, E A C
- HOLISTIC HEALTH CONSULTANTS
- HOLISTIC HYPNOTHERAPY
- HOWARD, JOHN & GAIL
- HUTCHINGS, D
- HYPNO CARE HEALTH CENTRE
- IQBAL, Z
- IRONS, FREDA
- JOHNSON, HETTY
- KEITH LORD TAROT READER
- KILBEY, ALISON
- KIRWAN, A M & S P
- LAKE, D
- LEE, STEPHEN
- LERIGO, SYLVIA
- LITCHFIELD, P
- LOWICK, DELIA
- MACKAY, BILL
- MADDISON-PETTS, CHRISTINE
- MAPLE TREE OSTEO PRACTICE
- MORGAN, A
- MOTLEY, MAUREEN
- MULLAN, JENNIFER
- MURRAY, P
- NAYLOR, JOHN
- NENE VALLEY COMP THERAPIES
- NORTH, JUDITH
- NORTHAMPTON CHIROPRACTIC
- NORTHAMPTON CLINIC
- NORTHAMPTON SCHOOL OF PODIATRY
- PARKER, SUSAN
- PARROTT, LINDA
- PASK, PHIL
- PATERSON, MARGARET
- PATERSON, MARGARET
- PHILLIPSON, B J
- PHYSIO & SPORTS INJURY CLNC
- PHYSIOPLUS
- PHYSIOTHERAPY CLINIC
- PICKFORD, J K
- PITT, KATHLEEN
- PLEXUS BIO ENERGY
- PROFESSIONAL PSYCHO CENTRE
- QUATTRO PARTNERSHIP
- REDMAN, L
- REFLEXOLOGY
- RICHARDS, R
- RICHARDSON, J
- RUDKIN, JULIE
- SCHOLL CENTRE
- SHAOCK HEALTH CARE
- SINDALL, K M J
- SMITH, BERYL
- SMITH, P L
- SOCIETY OF HOMOEOPATHS
- STRAWBRIDGE, GAYNOR
- SURTEES, JOANNE
- THAI SIAM
- THOMPSON, MICHAEL
- THROSSELL PHILIPPA
- TIAN TIAN UK
- TRAPMAN YOGA
- TRASLER, C
- VADRA-EDWARDS, NEENA
- WALSINGHAM, CAROLE
- WILLIAMSON, DONNA M
- WITTY, P E J
- YEARBY, CLAIRE

### RUSHDEN

- ANNELISE
- CLARK, PETER
- COLES, G B
- CURRAN, M J
- MIND & BODY NATURAL THERAPIES
- PHYSIOTHERAPY DEPARTMENT
- WENTWORTH, MARK

### TOWCESTER

- CARPENTER, HEATHER
- COCKELL, J
- GEDDES, PIPPA
- ISHERWOOD, SIMON
- JUST RELAX
- LAWSON, JANET
- PHYSIOFIRST
- PLUMMER, FRANK
- REHABFIRST
- ROBINSON, L K
- STONEMAN, SUSAN
- TOWCESTER CHIROPRACTIC CLINIC

### WELLINGBOROUGH

- ALLEN HINDE - PHYSIOTHERAPIST
- AROMATHEUTICS
- BECKWITH, JONATHAN
- BROWN, F K
- BROWN, RITA
- CALLIS THERAPY FOUNDATION
- CALLIS, CHARLES
- COLESHILL, AMANDA Y
- DOWDING, C J
- HALES, J
- KNOWD, KAREN
- LAWSON, R O L
- LIKISMA
- LIKISMA PRESENTATIONS
- MILBORNE, JOHN
- MORLEY, HAZEL
- PARKER, G
- REDWELL PHYSIO CLINIC
- WALKER, S
- WELLINGBOROUGH PHYSIO CLINIC

## NORTHUMBERLAND

### ALNWICK

- ALNWICK CHIROPODY CLINIC
- DYSON, F T & S J
- EATON, MAX
- GREEN BATT PHYSIOTHERAPY

## ASHINGTON

- MAYHEW, C
- MEAD, BRUCE
- SWAN, ALAN

## BEDLINGTON

- BURN, I
- FORSTER, LINDA
- METCALFF, L

## BLYTH

- ANDERSON CENTRE
- CARR, R
- GRANT, CARL
- TAYLOR, S S

## CHOPPINGTON

- BRUCE, BOB

## CORBRIDGE

- GELSON, C J
- HORROCKS, JULIE

## CRAMLINGTON

- ACUCARE
- CRAMLINGTON CHIRO CLINIC
- FOTHERGILL, MICHAEL

## HEXHAM

- ACHILLESPHYSIO
- BARTSTRA, RINSKE
- BODY WORK CENTRE
- BOWEN TECHNIQUE STUDIO
- COSTAR, MARK
- EVISON, ALEX
- HAGGIE, PATRICIA
- HEXHAM CHIROPRACTIC CLINIC
- KI CLINIC
- LIEGIS-JOHNSTON, S
- PARKIN, A G
- RINSKE, BARTSTRA
- TEASDALE, J

## MORPETH

- AYRES, ELIZABETH
- BEARMAN, PATRICIA
- FOWLER, J A
- GRANT, CARL
- MEDICINE
- PHYSIOTHERAPY & SPORTS CLINIC

## NEWBIGGIN-BY-THE-SEA

- IYE

## PRUDHOE

- ASPEN PHYSIOTHERAPY PRACTICE

## WOOLER

- FAIRNINGTON, A & B

# NOTTINGHAMSHIRE

## MANSFIELD

- ALLFREE, J & M (DR)
- ALVEY, DAVID M
- ARCHER, J
- BAINES, ALAN
- BRAGG, SHARON
- BURTON, KIM
- CHIROPODY
- CHIROPODY ADMINISTRATION
- COOPER, PETER
- CRACKNELL, ANNE
- EDWINSTOWE PHYSIO CLINIC
- FISHER, ANDREW
- HARDY, S A
- LIKISMA
- LOCK, J D
- MALCOLM H BROWN CHIROPODIST
- MANSFIELD CHIROPODY
- MANSFIELD CHIROPRACTIC CLINIC
- MURPHY, MAUREEN
- NATURAL THERAPY CLINIC
- NATURE'S HEALING
- PUGH, CHERYL
- ROSE, ELIZABETH
- ROSEAROMA
- SHARK CARTILAGE PRODUCTS
- SHEPHERD, A R
- SPORTS INJURIES & REHAB CENTRE
- STEVENS, G
- TAYLOR, JOANNE
- TOMLIN, NORMAN
- WALKINGTON, LORAINE
- WALSH, J P
- WILSON, SUE
- WILSON, SUE
- WOODHOUSE ROAD CHIROPRACTIC

## NEWARK

- APPLETREE HEALTHY LIVING CTRE
- BODY MATTERS
- CLARKE, J
- DORMAN, KARL
- HURST, D M
- HYMAN, JOHN
- JACKSON, J M M
- JONES, ERIKA
- LIFESOURCE
- MCCORRIE, JOHN
- MOWBRAY, ALISON
- MUMBY, HELEN
- NATURAL HEALTH
- NATURAL HEALTH
- NATURAL HEALTH NEWARK
- NEWARK CHIROPRACTIC CLINIC
- NEWARK OSTEOPATHIC CLINIC
- NEWARK PHYSIOTHERAPY CLINIC
- NISSIM & ASSOCIATES
- O'CONNOR, BARBARA
- PREBBLE, PETER
- RANDALL, PAUL
- ROWLINSON, MIKE
- SANDERS, RAIJA
- SMITH, SALLY
- TODD, S J
- WHITE, MERYL

## NOTTINGHAM

- ACUPUNCTURE CLINIC
- ADDISON, SYLVIA
- ALDRED, E M
- ALLEN, S
- ANGELS
- ARKSEY, LINDA
- AROMATHERAPY CENTRE
- AZRINA
- BAKER, ANNE
- BAKER, N
- BALL, S A
- BATES, MARGARET
- BATEY, PATRICIA
- BEESTON CHIROPRACTIC CLINIC
- BEESTON NATURAL THERAPY CENTRE
- BEESTON PHYSIO & SPORTS CLNC
- BLACKBOURN, STEPHEN
- BLOOMFIELD, MICHAEL
- BOURNE, DAVID
- BRAHMA KUMARIS WORLD
- BRIGHT, JENNY
- BROADLEY, RICHARD
- BROUGHTON, C
- BROUGHTON, G G
- BROWN, NILI
- BULLEN-SPICER ASSOCIATES
- CAMPBELL, RUTH
- CARING HANDS
- CARITAS NATURAL HEALTH CLINIC
- CAROL
- CASSIDY, TRISH
- CASTLE CLINIC
- CENTRE FOR TRANSFORMATION
- CHALLIS, R T
- CHANNON, CHRISTINA
- CHINESE HERBALIST
- CLAYSON, V
- CLEVERLEY, PAULINE
- CLINIC OF HERBAL MEDICINE
- CLINIC OF REFLEXOLOGY
- COLLINS, D
- COLLINS, N T
- COMPLEMENTARY HEALTH CENTRE
- COMPLEMENTARY HEALTH SUITE
- COOKE, BRENDA
- COOPER, EMILY
- COOPER, VAUGHAN
- CORBETT, D
- CORBETT, DIANE
- CORNER, GLENYS
- COULSON, D W H
- COX, BARBARA
- CREWE, GRAHAM
- CUNNINGHAM, MARJORIE
- CWYNAR, B (DR)
- DANIELS, FRANK
- DARBY HOUSE HEALING & LEARNING
- DAVID THERAPY CLINIC
- DAVIES, JUDITH
- DEAN, MARTIN
- DENGLER, REGINA
- DERBY GESTALT CENTRE
- DEVLIN, JULIE
- DEVLIN, JULIE
- DOLPHIN STAR
- DOUGLAS, W
- DRAGONSWAY ACUPUNCTURE CLINIC
- DREAMS
- DREWITT, N R
- DUNFORD, BRYAN
- DUNN, LLOYD
- EAST BRIDGEFORD PHYSIO NEEDS
- EATON, A M
- EDWARDS, T W
- EPWORTH, STEVEN
- FITZPATRICK, TRISH
- FITZPATRICK, TRISH
- FLINT, J
- FORMAN, LESLEY J
- FOUNDATION NATURAL THRPY CTRE
- FRASER, ANNE
- FROST, SAMANTHIA
- GILBERT, CATHERINE
- GLEESON, KAREN
- GLOVER, ELEANOR L
- GOMAN, J
- GOMAN, JOHN
- GOODLIFE, JOHN
- GOTHAM VILLAGE PHSYO CLINIC
- GRAHAM, HILARY E
- GRAHAM, HILARY E
- GREAVES HERBALIST
- GREAVES, N
- GREEN, S P
- GREENWOOD, JULIA
- GUO, J (DR)
- HACKMAN, MARIE
- HAINES, N
- HALLAM, F E & M G
- HAND, J
- HANDS ON HEALTH
- HARBOUR, ANNE
- HARRINGTON, C V
- HARRINGTON, E
- HARTLEY, H S
- HEMINGWAY, IMOGEN
- HEWITT, MAUREEN
- HICKLING, KENNETH
- HOCKEN, D E
- HUGHES, PAT
- HUMPHRIES, MARK
- HUMPHRIES, MARK
- IAIMI HEALTH STUDIOS
- IMPACT PHYSIO & SPORTS INJURIES
- JACKSON, DEREK
- JANE EVEREST SHIATSU PRACT
- JOHNSON, CAROL
- JONES, IAN
- JOYCE BURTON PHYSIO CLINIC
- JUST MAGNOTHERAPY
- KEELING, SHEILA
- KENNEDY, JOHN M
- KENNETH C HUGGINS HYPNOTHERAPY
- LADY BAY
- LAKE, DORRIE
- LAWLOR, M
- LERA, LOUISA
- LERA, LOUISA
- LIGHT UP YOUR LIFE
- LITTLE LONDON HERBAL STORE
- LUKEHURST, DAVID
- LUKEHURST, LINDSAY
- LYON, JAN
- MAGNOTHERAPY
- MANTLE & WHITE ELECTRICAL
- MARSH, PAMELA J
- MARSH, PAMELA J
- MARSHALL, HENRY
- MARSHALL, MICHAEL
- MAUGHAM, ANNE
- MCCANCE, H M
- MCLUCKIE, ALEXANDER

- MCMAHON MOUGHTIN CONSULTANCY
- MOBILE PHYSIOTHERAPY SERVICE
- MOONEY-DANIEL, G C
- MORTIMER, PHILIP
- MUNDAY, SARA DE LACEY
- NAPTHINE, MARYANNE
- NOTTINGHAM BACK PAIN CLINIC
- NOTTINGHAM M S THERAPY CTRE
- NOTTINGHAM NATURAL HEALTH CTRE
- NOTTINGHAM SPORTS INJURY
- NURTURED BY NATURE
- OPTIMUM HEALTH
- ORRIDGE, T
- OSTEOPATH CLINIC
- OWEN, PAM
- PADBURY, F
- PADBURY, S
- PALFREY, MIKE
- PARKSIDE STRESS MANAGEMENT
- PATTERSON, JUDY
- PEARSON, VIVIENNE
- PHYSIO DIRECT
- PHYSIO PLUS
- PHYSIODIRECT
- PHYSIODIRECT
- PHYSIODIRECT SPORTS INJURY
- PHYSIODIRECT WEST BRIDGFORD
- PHYSIOTHERAPY & FITNESS CENTRE
- PICKANCE, GEOFF S
- PIGGOTT, R S
- PLAINS PHYSIO & BACK PAIN
- POLLARD, ELIZABETH
- POWE, M
- PUGH, CHERYL
- PUMO, AMANDA
- PUMO, AMANDA
- RANDHAWA, PAL
- RELAXATION STUDIO
- RICHARDS, PAUL
- ROCKLEY, A M
- RUSHCLIFFE ED PSYCHOLOGY SV
- S H A
- SANDERS, BRYON
- SANGHERA, PARMJIT
- SCARR, G M
- SCHOLL CENTRE
- SEDDON, ALECK RICH
- SEVENTHMOON NATURAL THRPY CTRE
- SHARPLES, LINDA
- SHAW, L M
- SHAW, P R
- SHEER TECHNIQUE
- SHELLEY, P A
- SHELLEY, P A
- SHERWOOD CHIROPRACTIC CLINIC
- SHERWOOD PSYCHO TRAINING INS
- SINGH, A
- SMILE CENTRE
- SMITH, NIGEL (DR)
- SOMERS STRESS CONSULTANCY SVS
- STALMEISTERS, D V
- STAPLETON, C M
- STEVENS, CAROLINE
- STEWART, IAN (DR)
- THORPE, A J
- TRADITIONAL ACUPUNCTURIST
- TRANSCENDENTAL MEDITATION
- TREE, J
- TRIPTREE, V
- TRUSCOTT, B T
- VALENCIA, D
- VARLEY, D
- VAUGHTON, NORMAN D
- VICTORY, S
- WELLBEING AT WORK
- WELLBEING CENTRE
- WELLS, MADELEINE
- WHARTON, SUE
- WHITE, JILL
- WHITELEY, CHRIS
- WILCOCKSON, L
- WILLMOTT, JENNIFER
- WOOD, A
- WOODALL, DOROTHY
- WOODHEAD, C S
- WOODHEAD, N D
- WSZOLEK, ANNA
- YMCA HEALTH & FITNESS CLUB

### RADCLIFFE-ON-TRENT

- MORLEY-KIRK, JOHN

### RETFORD

- BARTON, C
- CARTER, F J
- I P T I
- JOHNSON, STEVEN R
- MEIRA, A P
- RETFORD CHIROPRACTIC CLINIC
- TAYLOR, KAREN
- WALKER, J M

### SOUTHWELL

- ACUPUNCTURE CLINIC
- BOND, DIANORA
- SOUTHWELL ACUPUNCTURE CLINIC
- SOUTHWELL ACUPUNCTURE CLINIC
- WOOD, ARTHUR

### SUTTON-IN-ASHFIELD

- HEALTH SERVICES
- PROUD, N R
- ROURKE, HELEN
- SUTTON THERAPY CENTRE

### WORKSOP

- BLYTH CHIROPRACTIC CLINIC
- HANFORD CHIROPODISTS
- L A M A S HEALTH THERAPEUTICS
- LARWOOD SURGERY
- REDFERN, D J
- ROHN, E
- WORKSOP CHIROPRACTIC CLINIC
- WORKSOP HEALTH CENTRE

## OXFORDSHIRE

### ABINGDON

- ABBEY CHIROPODY CLINIC
- ABINGDON & DIDCOT CLINIC
- BACH FLOWER REMEDIES
- BAKER, MICHAEL
- BEST, BONITA
- BOVEY, MARK
- GREENFORD, S P
- HANDS ON THERAPY
- INGRAM, S
- MCTIMONEY CHIROPRACTIC COLLEGE
- SUTTON COURTENAY CHIROPRACTIC
- TYACK, S

### BANBURY

- ADDERBURY CHIROPRACTIC CLINIC
- ASHCROFT CLINIC
- BACK PAIN & SPORTS CLINIC
- BANBURY CHIROPRACTIC CLINIC
- COOKE, R M
- COTSWOLD COMP THERAPY CTRE
- DAY, RUKMANI G
- ELWELL, R S
- ELWELL, T M
- GODSWELL NATURAL THRPY CTRE
- HAWES, G M
- HYPNOTHERAPY CENTRE
- MARRIOTT, HUGH
- MCTIMONEY CHIROPRACTIC
- NICHOLLS, PAUL
- O'BRIEN, JOHN C
- OXFORD ALLERGY TESTING SVS
- PARK CLINIC
- PARSONS STREET CLINIC
- PAYNTON, M G
- RADIONIC ASSOCIATION
- RAMSEY, CAROLYN
- RATLEY LODGE CLINIC
- STANLEY, STUART
- THOMPSON, PAT
- THORNE, I J
- TOTAL WELLBEING
- TPS OCCUPATIONAL PSYCHOLOGISTS
- TURNER, KAREN
- VASEY, SARAH
- WARDLEY, SUE
- WEST BAR CLINIC
- WILKINS, G R F

### BICESTER

- BICESTER CHIROPRACTIC CLINIC
- BICESTER CHIROPRACTIC CLINIC
- CARTER, S
- CARTER, T
- ELLISON, JENNY
- GILMORE, E M J
- GREEN, J
- HANDS-ON-FEET
- HARLAND, M
- HUDSON, EMMA
- JONES, PATRICIA JEAN
- LINDLEY, CLAIRE
- MOHAN, BERNADETTE
- P OF SPIRITUAL HEART
- PHYSIO & SPORTS INJURY CLNC

### BURFORD

- BARRINGTON-WARD, H B
- BLISS REMEDIES
- DOWER EQUINE RADIONIC THER
- MCTIMONEY CHIROPRACTIC

### CARTERTON

- DAVIES, M D
- FAULKNER, JAMES
- PITTS, RICHARD

### CHINNOR

- RIMES, S C
- SUTER, ROSMANUND

### CHIPPING NORTON

- BALDWIN, JILLIAN
- BENNETT, JAYNE
- BRADSHAW, C
- CHARLBURY NAT HEALTH CLINIC
- COOPER, A
- CROMWELL CHIROPRACTIC CLINIC
- EAST WEST HERBS
- ESSENTIALLY OILS
- HEALTHPACK
- HICKS, SARA
- MARRIOTT, HUGH
- MIDSUMMER COTTAGE CLINIC
- NATURAL THERAPY CENTRE
- ODOM, S A
- PARE, KAREN
- SMYTH, CATHERINE
- SPARKS, MARTIN ANDREW
- STRACHAN, SUSAN
- WHITE, MADELINE M
- YEN YANG

### DIDCOT

- A TOUCH OF HEALTH
- C TAYLOR BEAUTY THERAPY
- CLARK, ALAN
- CORKE, AMI
- HUART, S C
- KEEVIL, P A
- NUTRITION PLUS
- PHYSIOTHERAPY DEPARTMENT
- TOUCH OF NATURE

### FARINGDON

- BENNETT, SHEILA
- CAREY BOYCE CENTRE-KINESIOLOGY
- COCQUEREL, DENISE
- CORLEY, H V
- TWINE, I E

### HENLEY-ON-THAMES

- BACK IN LINE
- FORDHAM, ANNICK S
- GEGG, SARAH
- HENLEY CHIROPRACTIC & COMP
- HOMOEOPATHIC CONSULTANCY
- HOUSE OF GOOD HEALTH
- HYLTON, PENELOPE J
- KARRENBAUER, MONIKA
- PEHRSON, S
- ROBERTS, S
- SHEILA'S BODY CARE
- TEST AGENCY
- WATKINS, G
- WHITMORE, ELIZABETH
- WIGGIN, SALLY

### KENNINGTON

- BODY CONTROL PILATES OXFORD

## KIDLINGTON

- ACUPUNCTURE CLINIC
- BACK TO NORMAL CHIRO CLINIC
- CORRIE REIKI HEALING
- KIDLINGTON CHIROPRACTIC
- KIDLINGTON HERBAL PRACTICE
- MCKEEVER, L
- MILL ST CHIROPRACTIC
- SMITH, JULIET L

## OXFORD

- A BODY ORIENTED HUMANISTIC
- ABRAMS, CAROLINE
- ACUPUNCTURE CENTRE
- AKERS, D
- ALCANTARA, FATIMA
- ALEXANDER TECHNIQUE
- ALEXANDER, MARGARET
- ALTERNATIVE MEDICINE CENTRE
- APPLE TREE CLINIC
- AROMA HEALTH 2000
- ASWAB
- AVERY, MARK
- BAILEY, GILLIAN
- BARBERY, GAERY
- BEDFORD, TOM
- BIRCH, ROBIN
- BJARNASON, MARGARET
- BOARDMAN, C J
- BOBY, KEITH
- BRAHMA KUMARIS WORLD
- BROOME, RAYMOND T
- BROSNAN, J V
- BROWNING, JOY
- BROWNING, JOY K
- BUTTERWORTH, MARK
- CADE, ANNA
- CAMERON-KIRBY, E
- CENTRAL CHIROPRACTIC CLINIC
- CLINIC OF NATURAL MEDICINE
- COLES, L
- COOPER, STEPHEN
- COOPER, STEPHEN
- COTTAGE CLINIC
- COX, S
- CULPEPER
- CURTIN, D
- CUTCLIFFE, PETER G
- DAO CLINIC OF CHINESE MEDICINE
- DAVIES, L
- DUNLOP, JEAN
- EAU DE VIE
- ELLAM, VALERIE
- ELLIOT-SMITH, A
- ENGLAND, PAMELA
- FERGUSON, D
- FINLAY, BRUCE
- FOCUS 4 HEALTH
- FYSON, MELANIE
- GEGGUS, PAM
- GILES, CHRISTOPHER
- GILMORE, V M
- GLEAVE, V W
- GOSS, TOM
- GREEN, VICTORIA
- GRGIC, IGOR
- HANDS ON CLINIC
- HARDING, S J
- HARRIS, CAROLE
- HEADINGTON ALEXANDER SCHOOL
- HELIX HOUSE
- HILL, ROSIE
- HOCK, GABRIELLE
- HORKEY, PHIL
- HOW, G
- HOWAT, JONATHON
- HUMBLE-THOMAS, ELIZABETH
- HUNT, A F
- IFFLEY CLINIC
- ISIS CENTRE
- IVES, DENNIS
- JONES, ROSALIND
- KANDOLA, PEARN
- KIDLINGTON OSTEO PRACTICE
- LANE, DANIEL P
- LAUGH THERAPY & HAPINESS
- LEWIS, MAGGIE
- LOGUE, MARTIN
- LONGTHORP, S V
- LOW-BEER, F E
- LYON, F A
- MANSTON, N
- MEJLAENDER, KARIN
- MILLER, J F
- MOSSMAN, CELIA
- MOSSO, MARINA
- MURRELL, JOHN
- NAPLES, EILEEN
- NASH, B
- NEAL'S YARD REMEDIES
- O'BRIEN, JOHN
- OLESEN, ANNE-GRETE
- OXFORD CHIROPRACTIC CLINIC
- OXFORD NATURAL HEALTH CENTRE
- OXFORD NUTRITION & ALLRGY CTRE
- OXFORD SCHOOL OF MASSAGE
- OXFORD TRANSCENDTL MEDITA CTRE
- PACKARD, JOY
- PACKARD, JOY
- PARIS, LINDA
- PHILLIPS, C
- PLESTED, JOHN
- POD NHS/PRIVATE FOOT HLTH SVS
- PSYCHIATRIC CONSULT PRACTICE
- PULLMAN, JUDITH
- RAWLINGS, S
- RUDDICK, DAVID
- SANZ DE DEAS, HILDA C
- SCHOLL CENTRE
- SHARP, JANET
- SHEPHEARD, P
- SIDEBOTTOM, MARGARET
- SKY DANCING UK TANTRA
- SPRENT, N
- SPRENT, N
- SUMMERTON CLINIC
- SYNERGY THERAPIES
- TALLYN, J
- THROWER, MARIANNE
- TRANS PERSONAL PSYCHOTHERAPIST
- VANRENEN, ANDY
- WAKEFIELD, ROBERT
- WALKER, VALERIE
- WARING, D
- WATERHOUSE, C
- WELL BEING CLINIC
- WHEADON, LOUISE
- WHEATLEY COMP THERAPY
- WILKES, MARA
- XENETEK

## RAMSDEN

- WINTER, CLAIRE

## THAME

- ALBURY, MAVIS
- BIRD, SUZANNE
- BOWLES, JANICE
- CALCUTT, GILLIAN
- FEET FIRST
- KENT, E
- POLLOCK, SUSAN
- RYECOTEWOOD COLLEGE
- THAME THERAPY CLINIC

## WALLINGFORD

- BACH CENTRE
- CHOLSEY CHIROPODY SURGERY
- COLCLOUGH, CAROL
- DR EDWARD BACH FOUNDATION
- ISWARIAH, ROHAN
- JACK, S A
- JESKINS, J
- KEEVIL, P A
- LEADBETTER, E D J
- LOCK, ALISON
- LOCK, ALISON
- MCCARTHY, J P
- METAGENICS UK
- NICHOLLS, SOPHIA
- PEDERSEN, GITTE
- ROBBINS, C A
- WHITE, LESLEY

## WANTAGE

- BROWN, ANGELA
- HARRIS, JONATHAN
- INVESTIGATIVE SCIENCE
- LAVIS, G J & H M
- MCGREGOR, STUART
- NEW SEASONS
- O'DONNELL, ELSPETH
- ROSS, J
- WANTAGE NATURAL HEALTH CENTRE
- WANTAGE OSTEOPATHIC PRACTICE

## WATCHFIELD

- KERNOHAN, SARA

## WITNEY

- A M M TAYLOR
- ALEXANDER, RUPERT
- BODY-INTEGRATION CO UK
- BRADLEY, M A
- BURDEN, GILLIAN
- CARVALHO, CAROL
- CHURCH, PAULINE
- COMING UP FOR AIR
- DUVALL, V
- EDULJEE, STELLA
- FOX, J
- JONES, JANET
- LEE, ELAINE
- O C G
- O'BRIEN, FRANCES
- PLESTED, NICOLA
- POWER, CLIVE
- WITNEY CHIROPRACTIC/CHIROPODY
- WITNEY NATURAL HEALTH CLINIC
- WITNEY OSTEOPATHIC CLINIC
- WOOD, S B

## WOODSTOCK

- CONNER, CAROL
- MOLLOY, RUPERT
- RADWAN, R
- RAJAGOPALAN, J

# RUTLAND

## OAKHAM

- FINNIS, ELIZABETH

# SHROPSHIRE

## BRIDGNORTH

- A J F LABORATORIES
- BEATTIE, R G
- BRIDGNORTH CHIROPRACTIC CLINIC
- CASTLE CLINIC
- MARRIOTT, F
- PERINGER, EVA
- RUXTON, HUGH
- SPEARS, SUSAN

## BROSELEY

- BODYLIFE CENTRE
- JENKS, B R
- WALMSLEY, RUTH

## BUCKNELL

- SPENCER, DIANE

## CHURCH STRETTON

- MURDOCH, M
- OSTEOPATHIC
- SHELTON, J K

## CRAVEN ARMS

- PERRY, JANET

## ELLESMERE

- EVANS, M I
- REYNOLDS, TESS
- WARREN, SUSAN

## LUDLOW

- ARMSTRONG, CAROLYN
- AYRES, JOHN
- FULLERTON, N P
- LUDLOW OSTEOPATHIC CLINIC
- PERRY, JANET
- SHELTON, J K
- VALERIE RICKARDS ELECTROLYSIS

## MARKET DRAYTON

- ALTERNATIVE REMEDIES
- BODYCHECK
- CHAKRAVERTY, R C (DR)
- FERGUSON, PHIL
- FOOTWORKS
- HALES OSTEOPATHIC PRACTICE
- HARRIS, JOHN A

- MARKET DRAYTON COTTAGE HOSP
- MEDAYD PHYSIOTHERAPY
- QI SHEN NATURAL HEALING CENTRE
- TAN & BEAUTY STUDIO

### MUCH WENLOCK

- CHIROPODY CARE
- CORKE, A J

### NEWPORT

- BOOTH, ROBERT
- EDWARDS, A D
- FEATHERSTONE, ROSIE
- FLETCHER, B C
- LIGHTWOOD, P E
- LILLESHALL SPORTS INJURY CTRE
- MOWLEM, BRENDA

### OSWESTRY

- ALLCOCK, RACHAEL
- ANDERSON, BETTY
- ANNANDALE PHYSIOTHERAPY CLINIC
- BEAUTY & ELECTROLYSIS CLINIC
- BEAUTY SPOT
- GABLECROFT-NATURAL THERAPY
- KUSIAR, BILL
- LOUIS, L
- MOVEMENT CENTRE
- NORTH SHROPSHIRE PHYSIO CENTRE
- RICHARDSON, S M W
- ROBERTS, S
- ROOK, J
- ROOK, JANE
- STONE, JANET

### SHIFNAL

- GIARDINO
- PHILLIPS, ANN
- WESTON, JOHN
- WILLIAMS, C
- WILLIAMS, EMILIE

### SHREWSBURY

- ACUMEDIC
- ADLARD, FIONA
- AITKEN, LYNNE
- ALIGNING BODY & SOUL
- ALLEN, RICHARD
- ALLEN, SUSAN
- ALLOT, ALISON M
- ASHTON-GREEN, SUE
- ASHTON-GREEN, SUE
- BENCH, PAUL
- BENNETT, JANET
- BOOTH, ROBERT
- BRITISH HOLISTIC MEDICAL ASS
- BROCKBANK, BRETT
- CHAKRAVERTY, R C (DR)
- COLERIDGE, JUDY
- DRAGE, RONALD A
- ELYSE, GALE
- FACE AND BODY OPTIONS
- FEATHERSTONE, ROSIE
- GEORGE, CHRISTOPHER
- GOODWILLIE, GILL
- HALL, VALERIE
- HANDS ON
- HEALING FOUNDATION
- JONES, GILL
- KUSIAR, C W
- NATURAL HEALTH CENTRE
- NAYLOR, DIANA
- PEARSON, CHRISTINE
- PONTESBURY PHYSIO PRACTICE
- PROF ASS OF ALEXANDER TEACHERS
- PSYCHOLOGY CONSULTANCY SERVICE
- PULLEN, R W
- ROBERTS, J
- SANDERS ROYLE, A
- SHREWSBURY CHIROPODY & BEAUTY
- SHREWSBURY SOLE CARE
- TOPEL, A M
- VISITING CHIROPODIST
- WALTERS, MARIE
- WHITELEY, STEVEN
- WILD ROSE
- WILLIAMS, J
- WILSON, AMANDA

### TELFORD

- BIO-ENERGY THERAPY
- BIRD, DEBBY
- CENTRE FOR POSITIVE HEALTH
- DAWES, LESLEY
- FALLOWS, R D
- GLOBAL HEALTH SERVICES
- HALE, DAVID
- HEAVE, M & HUMPHREY, V
- HUMPHREY, VAL
- LOWE, IRENE
- MADDOCKS CLINIC
- MEDAYD PHYSIOTHERAPY
- MILES, R W
- MOORE, C A
- NEEDHAM, LYNDA M
- OSTEOPATHIC PRACTICE
- OSTLE, SAMANTHA
- PARSONS, BRONDA
- PEAKE, A C
- RAYBOULD, J
- SHEPHERD, B
- TROTT, MOLLY V
- WARNOCK, R J
- WEBB, S E
- WESTON, JOHN M

### WHITCHURCH

- ALDCROFT, R
- CROPPER, LINDA
- PREES COMPLEMENTARY THERAPIES

## SOMERSET

### AXBRIDGE

- ANDERSON, DAVID

### BATH

- ARCANIA
- BARNES SPORTS CLINIC
- BATH ALEXANDER TECHNIQUE
- BATH BACK CLINIC
- BATH CHIROPODY CLINIC
- BATH NATURAL MEDICAL CENTRE
- BATH PRACTICE
- BATH RUGBY CLINIC
- BERRY, LISA
- BLOOM, MARTINE
- BRIERLEY, D
- BRIGGS, JENNI
- CAMERON, IAN L
- CHINESE MEDICAL CENTRE
- CHURCHLEY, RUBY
- CIRCUS HOUSE
- COCKHILL, PETER
- COMPLEMENTARY THERAPY
- COOK, COLIN
- CULPEPER
- DIGBY, DAVID
- DIXON & ASSOCIATES
- GADHER, SATYEN P
- GILLINGHAM, GLENNA
- GROSVENOR REFLEXOLOGY
- HALE, M A
- HARDING, H
- HARRIS, J
- HEALTH & HOLISTIC CENTRE
- HEALTHCARE INTERNATIONAL
- HUDSON, JOHN
- HUDSON, JOHN
- JACQUES, I M
- JASMINE HOLISTIC HEALTH
- JEFFFEREY, P J
- JENKINSON, TRISHA
- JENTERPRISES
- JIM MARSH & STEPHANIE STOCK
- JOHNSON, PETER
- JONES, RAYMOND
- JOY, M E
- KEENAN RESEARCH
- KENT-PAYNE, J
- KEOGH, DAVID
- KEY CENTRE FOR HOMOEOPATHY
- KHAFAF, TARA
- KNIGHT, ALICE
- KUHN, SUE
- LANSDOWN PHYSIOTHERAPY CLINIC
- LATTY & ASSOCIATES
- LAUREL FARM CLINIC
- LAWRENCE, J M
- LOGAN, DAVID
- LOTUS EMPORIUM
- LUNT, CELIA
- MCLOUGHLIN, BRENDAN
- MIDSOMER NORTON CHIROPRACTIC
- MILLER, HELENE
- MILLSMITH, SELBY
- MILSOM STREET CLINIC
- MOIR, GILL
- NAPPER, RICHARD
- NATURAL SPIRITUAL HEALING
- NATURE'S WAY
- NEWCOMBE-JONES, ELAINE
- NORSO BIOMAGNETICS UK
- O'TOOLE, ALAN
- PARK HOUSE CLINIC
- PARKER, L
- PEARSON, A V A (DR)
- PETER, MARTIN
- REFLEXOLOGY CLINIC
- RIETCHEL, F
- ROBERTSON, JULIET
- ROSS, JULIETTE
- ROYCE CLINIC
- SCHOLL CHIROPODY CLINIC
- SEFTON, PHILIP
- SIGGERY, MARCINE
- SMITH, ANN
- SNOWDON, JANET
- SPARKES, MARTIN J
- SPIRIT WITHIN
- ST JAMES'S SURGERY
- ST MICHAELS CHIROPRACTIC
- STANLEY COURT SURGERY
- STEWART, SHEILA
- STILLPOINT
- STIRLAND, HAZEL
- SUTCLIFFE, T
- SUTCLIFFE, T
- TAYLOR, JAMIE
- THOMPSON, G W (DR)
- TRANSCENDENTAL MEDITATION
- TRAVERS, C M
- TURNPIKE SURGERY
- WALKER, K
- WALKER, S
- WESTCOTT, CHARLES
- WESTERN CHIROPRACTIC CLINIC
- WILLDER, J
- WILLDER, JAMES
- WILLIAMS, FRANCES
- WINSOR, REBECCA
- WOOD, SAMANTHA
- YOUNGS, C

### BRIDGEWATER

- SCHOOL OF THE LIVING LIGHT

### BRIDGWATER

- ADAMS, C A
- AROMAKIDS
- BACK, R A
- BALANCE CARE HEALTH
- BAWDRIP CHIROPRACTIC CLINIC
- BEIGHTON, JOSEPH
- BRIDGWATER HEALING CENTRE
- CASTLE SURGERY
- CAVANAGH, CHERYL
- CHURCHILL, MARION
- COULSON, GERALD
- DAWNS
- FENG SHUI
- FRIENDLY FROG
- GARDINER, S D
- GOODCHILD, ROGER
- GOODCHILD, ROGER
- GREEN MAN (THE)
- HILL, CAROLYN
- LORD, LESLEY
- MILL, DAVID
- POMEGRANATE PRODUCTS
- POW, SUE
- PSYCHOLOGY SERVICES INT
- QUINN, G A W

### BRUTON

- BROWN, JULIET
- MALTINGS NATURAL THERAPIES

## BURNHAM-ON-SEA

- BRABNER, JANNINE
- COUNSULTING ROOMS
- CRENOL, J P
- EVERETT, PETER
- HOLISTIC HEALING CENTRE
- PRICE, D E
- PRICE, S C
- ROPER, JANET
- SMALL, P C
- VINE COTTAGE CHIROP PRACTICE

## CASTLE CARY

- HALES, G J
- KNIGHT, ANDREW M
- PITHER'S YARD CLINIC

## CHARD

- ANSON, BARRIE
- ASHA MANIPULATIONS
- BINMORE & ASSOCIATE
- CHARD ELECTROLYSIS CENTRE
- DUGGAN, JOY
- EVANS, ANNE
- GAWEN & ASSOCIATES
- GONZALEZ, PHYLLIS
- GRIMMINGER, C
- GRIMMINGER, C
- GRIMMINGER, J
- GRIMMINGER, J
- HARVEY, ALAN
- HARVEY, LEE
- HIRST, MARY
- IRWIN, NICKY
- NATURAL THERAPIES
- NORTON, ROSEMARY
- ORCHARD CENTRE
- REED, ANN
- STANNARD, LAURA
- STEAD, SIMON
- TAWSTOCK MEDICAL CENTRE
- TRADITIONAL CHINESE MEDICINES
- WESTERN COLLEGE-ALT THERAPY
- WILKS, JOHN
- WILLMOTT, BRENDA

## CHEDDAR

- ALLERGY & ENVIRONMENTAL MED
- BENNETT, B
- CHEDDAR COMP MEDICINE CTRE
- EDUCATIONAL CTRE FOR COMP MED
- PENNINGTON, PAM V

## CLEVEDON

- BAKER, P J
- BRISTOL HAIR & SCALP CENTRE
- FLETCHER, R C
- LANE-WILLAN, AVIS
- MONCRIEFF, CILLA
- OSBORNE, R
- PASS, MARGARET
- REED, W A
- SIMS, A
- SUNNYSIDE MANSIONS
- SUTTON, G M
- WEBSTER, G E
- WOODINGTON, NICHOLAS J

## CREWKERNE

- CLINIC OF NATURAL MEDICINE
- CREWKERNE CHIROPRACTIC CLINIC
- HEAD, PAUL
- HILTON HERBS
- PEARSON, C

## FROME

- ACUPUNCTURE/OSTEO PRACTICE
- BELMONTE, P
- ENGBERG, ANNELI
- EUROPEAN COLLEGE-BOWEN STUDIES
- FROME PHYSIO & SPORTS CLINIC
- GWILT, ALAN
- GWILT, ANNA
- HAMAR, KLARE
- HOGG, B
- MISTRAL, J
- PLUMB, STEPHEN
- SEFTON, PHILIP
- STRESS CLINIC & NTRL HLTH CTRE
- TAYLOR, SHANE
- TURPIE, JULIE

## GLASTONBURY

- ARCHANGEL MICHAEL SOUL
- AVALON CENTRE
- AYURVEDIC TRADING
- BEAUMONT, ROWENA
- BRIDGET HEALING CENTRE
- CHANEY, JOHN
- CHIPPER, MARY
- GERRARD, K
- GLASTONBURY CHIROPRACTIC
- GLASTONBURY EAST WEST CENTRE
- GLASTONBURY HEALING CENTRE
- HARRIS, CAROLINE
- HAWKINS, SHARON
- HAWTHORN HOUSE AROMATHERAPY
- HENSEY, C
- HUNT, P
- HUNWICK, JOSEPH
- JOHNSON, ANDREW
- MIDNIGHT OIL JOURNEYMAN
- NEW AVALONIA DESIGNS
- NEWTON, C
- PARKER, SUZY
- PARKER, SUZY
- RAJA YOGA BRAMA KUMARIS CENTRE
- RIES, GIDEON S
- ROGER, ANDREA
- SANDERS, JANE
- SHAMBHALA
- STARCHILD
- TARETH CENTRE
- TARETH CENTRE
- TUCKER, H
- TURNER, MARGARET
- WARREN, M

## HIGHBRIDGE

- BAILEY, ALISON
- BRENT CENTRE
- K I FEDERATION OF GB
- KIDDLE, B E

## ILMINSTER

- BEECH HOUSE CLINIC
- DUGGAN, JOY M
- HAMLIN, P W
- MELDGAARD, E
- RAWLINS, JANET

## LANGPORT

- BOW HOUSE PHYSIO PRACTICE
- BOWEN TECHNIQUE EURO REG
- FRENCH, N
- HAMLIN, P W
- SCHOOL OF CONSCIOUS LIVING

## MARTOCK

- MARTIN, J
- MEARE, RACHAEL
- TYLER, LIZZY

## MINEHEAD

- CHICK, MARY
- CHIROPODY SURGERY
- COBB, JOANNA
- COBB, JOANNA
- DOWNS HOUSE EQUINE
- IRNHAM LODGE COMP HEALTH CTRE
- LAURIE, ANGELA
- MARY WILKINSON - MCTIMONEY
- PERKINS, L

## RADSTOCK

- ST MICHAEL'S HYPNOTHERAPY

## SHEPTON MALLET

- HODDINOTT, LAURA
- LYONS, A R & G B
- POTTS, ROY
- SAYER, SANDRA
- WALLIKER, EMMA

## SOMERTON

- KNIGHT, ANDREW
- ROFF, A M

## SOUTH PETHERTON

- CLARKE GAIL & RAWLINSON MIKE
- CLEVERLEY, ALUN
- SOUTH PETHERTON CHIROPODY

## STREET

- ALASKAN BACH FLOWER REMEDIES
- GOSWELL HOUSE CLINIC
- KIRKMEAD CENTRE
- PAGE, B
- PENNINGTON, PAM
- STREET CHIROPRACTIC CLINIC
- STREET CHIROPRACTIC CLINIC
- VOYSEY, KIM

## TAUNTON

- ABRAHAMS, SANDRA
- AUSSENS, MIEKE
- BARNACLE, MARION
- BATHPOOL CHIROPRACTIC CLINIC
- BEYNON, E
- BLAGG, NIGEL
- BUSH & MEADOWS
- CAINES, J A
- CHAMELEON OILS
- CHURCHILL, MARION
- CRESCENT THERAPIES
- DAVIES, JULIA
- DREWITT, JENNIFER
- EDWARDS, MATTHEW
- FURZER, LINDA
- HAMMET STREET PRACTICE
- HEALE, SARA
- HENDRY, ANGELA
- HOPKINS, JILL
- HOWIE & ASSOCIATES
- JAY, TIMOTHY C
- JOHNSTONE, ALLAN
- JOWETT, G M
- KALISCH, DAVID
- KENDAL, S L
- KENNARD, S
- KNAPMAN, D J
- LEWIS, JAN
- MACKEY, D
- MARAR, N Z
- MARY WILKINSON - MCTIMONEY
- MAYHEW, PAMELA
- MO, JOSEPH
- MORTIMER WHITE, E
- NATURAL PATH
- NEW DAY NATURAL THERAPY CTRE
- NORTON, ROSEMARY
- PERRET, NICOLE (DR)
- PRICE, MARTHA
- ROBBINS, CAROLINE
- ROBINIA COMP HEALTH CLINIC
- SAVAGE, R H (DR)
- SCOVELL, MICHAEL
- STEWART, ANN
- TAUNTON FOOT SURGERY
- TERRACE THRPY PSYCHO/NTRL HLTH
- VICKERS, HUGH
- WARWICK HOUSE MEDICAL CENTRE
- WHITE, SALLY
- WILKINSON, MARY
- WILLIAMS, R D
- YELLOW EMPEROR CORP

## TEMPLECOMBE

- PITMAN, VICTORIA

## WALTON-IN-GORDANO

- JONES, BECKY

## WATCHET

- PARRY, J M

## WEDMORE

- CAMPION, RICHARD
- CANDY, TIM
- HAMLIN, P W
- WEDMORE

## WELLINGTON

- ORCHARD CLINIC
- PHYSIOTHERAPY DEPT WELLINGTON
- STANNARD, L
- THRELFALL, P R
- TOME OSTEOPATHIC & SPORTS
- WHITE, KIM
- WRIGHT, N J (DR)

## WELLS

- ALEXANDER TECHNIQUE
- AVALON CLINIC

- CLISBY, JANE
- FRANCES-WHITAKER, J A
- HODGSON, JENNIFER
- JEFFERY, JO
- JEFFS, K A
- LIFESTYLE
- LOVELL, P
- PARNELL, R H
- RICHARDS, M J
- SCOTT, JUDY
- VENN, V
- WARREN, P S
- WELLS PHYSIO PRACTICE
- WELLSPRING OSTEO/NTRL HEALTH

### WESTON-SUPER-MARE

- BAILEY, LINDA R
- BATES, SUSAN M
- BLACKBOROW, R A
- BOULEVARD PHARMACY
- CEDARFIELD
- DAHMS, A
- DEVONSHIRE SURGERY
- DOWNES, STEVEN C
- EDMETT, C
- ELDERGILL, D J
- EURASIA DEVELOPMENT
- HARRIS, JANET
- HEALE, SARAH
- HOWARD-BLOOD, LIBBY
- HUXTABLE, ALISON
- HYPNOSIS WORKS
- HYPNOTHERAPY IN HUTTON
- JACKAMAN, SUSAN
- JEFFERIS, PATRICIA
- KEARNS, ANTHONY P
- LETHERBY, S
- MADAM VALMA
- MADAME VALMA
- MORBEY, PETER
- MOULT, MICHAEL A
- PADWICK, J
- PICKETT, L
- PITT, I T
- POWELL, AUDREY E
- PRESSURE WORKS
- REACH DIRECT
- SHIATSU THERAPY
- SIMMONDS, J
- SUTTON, YVONNE V
- TAYLOR, GILLIAN
- UNIVERSAL HEALING NETWORK

### WINCANTON

- HENSHAW, S A
- MAPERTON TRUST
- WINCANTON CHIROPRACTIC CLINIC

### WINSCOMBE

- HELEN SMITH CHIROPODIST
- LARDER-SMITH, JANE
- LAUREL PLACE
- SOLUTIONS

### WRAXALL

- NEWPORT, JANE

### YEOVIL

- ABBEY CHIROPODY SERVICES
- AVENUE CLINIC
- BROOKMAN, U H
- CAMPION & ASSOCIATES
- CLINIC OF COMP MEDICINE
- DAVIES, SALLY
- HARRIS, ROSE
- HAWORTH, JAN
- HAYMAN-BUDDEN, G
- JARVIS, JUNE
- LEGGOTT, C
- ORME, ELIZABETH
- PITMAN, VICKI
- PORTER, M S
- REITER, NED
- RENTON, ANGELA
- ROBERTS, R J (DR)
- SELF REALISATION MEDITATION
- TAROTS CARD READING
- WELFORD, ROY
- YEOVIL CHIROPRACTIC CLINIC
- YOUNG, ANTOINETTE & MARTIN

## STAFFORDSHIRE

### BURNTWOOD

- ANDREA ALLAN CHIROPODIST
- CRAIG, DIANE
- HUGHES, R T
- LVJ COUNSELLING & HYPNOTHERAPY
- MACARTHUR, JACKIE
- ROBINSON, GRAHAM
- STEVENS, MARGARET
- WATSON, MALCOLM

### BURTON-ON-TRENT

- ANDERSON, G
- ANSON CENTRE
- BAILEY, BARBARA
- BARRATT, JAN
- BODY & SOLE
- BURTON CHIROPRACTIC CLINIC
- E A V
- ESSENTIALLY YOU
- EVANS, RICHARD
- HAILWOOD, ADRIAN
- HINGORANI, S
- HOLLOWAY, MICHAEL & AMANDA
- NATURAL HEALERS
- ORIENTAL MEDICINE PRACTICE
- PEACH, LYN
- PEARCE, BRIAN S
- PILKINGTON, MICHAEL
- PITT, S E
- PLANT, R M
- REES, JACQUELINE
- TOLLEY, ELAINE
- WENDT, ANNE E
- WITCHES WAY

### CANNOCK

- ALTERNATIVES
- BRADBURY, C J
- BURGESS, PAUL
- CHACKETT, LINDA
- CHASE CHIROPODY SERVICES
- CHASE NATURAL THERAPY CENTRE
- EDWARDS, J B
- FOOT SOUL & BODYWORKS
- JEANNE
- MOBILE CHIROPODIST
- POWNER, CLIVE
- VERNON, M J & J A
- VICTORIAN COLLECTION
- ZARA THE CLAIRVOYANT

### HAMMERWICH

- COMPLEMENTARY THERAPIES

### LEEK

- COTTAM, MARILYN
- EDWARDS, P A
- HALLARD, SHARON
- HEALING WAYS
- LEEK HOMOEOPATHIC PRACTICE
- LOMAS, CHRISTINA
- PARSONS, CHRISTINA
- PEACEHAVEN AROMATHERAPY
- POVEY, JILL
- SKELLAM, L J
- WARRILOW, ALISON

### LICHFIELD

- BORE ST POD & CHIROP PRACTICE
- CHIROPODY PRACTICE
- DOWNEY, FRANCES
- DRURY, ANNE
- ESSENTIAL HEALTH
- ESSINGTON CHIROPRACTIC CLINIC
- FORTEY, C J
- HARRISON, GRETA
- JUFFS, C
- L C I STRESS MANAGEMENT
- LICHFIELD ELECTROLYSIS CLINIC
- LOUISE BRITTLE
- NARAYAN, M
- NOTTRET, K
- PELL, KAREN
- PERKS, R
- PITT, S E
- SCRATCHLEY, J H

### NEWCASTLE

- BLANK, CHRISTOPHER
- BRADBURY, SHARON
- BRADBURY, SHARON
- BRAMPTON TREES CLINIC
- COOPER, DAVID
- DALE, SUZANNE
- DUNNINGS & ASSOCIATES
- FEET FIRST
- FOULKES, L
- GASCOIGNE, DOROTHY
- HOLDCROFT, P A
- HOWLE, E
- MENZIES-TRULL, CHRISTOPHER
- NATURAL HLTH & IRIDOLOGY CTRE
- PSYCHO & COUNSELLING CENTRE
- ROBERTS, KATE
- ROSELANDS CLINIC
- ROWLEY, M
- RUDD, SUSAN
- STEELE, A R
- SUSAN JAMES CONSULTANCY

### PENKRIDGE

- PRIORS PODIATRY PRACTICE

### RUGELEY

- ARDUINO, JANE
- ASHURST, R F & S A
- HADFIELD, G T
- JOHNSON, JANICE
- MARSHALL, LYNN
- WELCH, STEPHEN

### STAFFORD

- A TOUCH OF HARMONY
- AUSTIN, H L
- BLUE HAZE
- BREWOOD NATURAL THERAPY CENTRE
- CADDEN, D C
- CASTLEFIELDS SURGERY
- CHASE HEALTH FOODS
- COMPLEMENTS
- COUPLAND, J E
- CRESCENT CLINIC
- CRESCENT CLINIC FOR COMP MED
- ECCLESHALL ACUPUNCTURE CLINIC
- GASCOYNE, P
- GILLBRIDE, S A
- GORDON, KAREN
- HAIR FREE EPILIGHT CLINIC
- HANCHER, LYNNE
- JAMES, SUSAN
- KING, KAREN
- LOCKINGTON, W M
- MAGNAFLOW
- MILL BANK OSTEOPATHIC CLINIC
- NORBURY, SUSAN
- OLDACRE, RAY
- PEACH, F J
- PLANT, R M
- PODO KARE
- RICE, LOUISE
- SOLE SCENTS
- STAFFORD CHIROPRACTIC CLINIC
- WHITE, V L
- WHITTAKER, B
- WHYTE, IAN
- WINGS NATURAL THERAPIES
- WOODS, A

### STOKE-ON-TRENT

- ARMSTRONG HEALTH/HERBAL STORE
- BALANCE THERAPY CENTRE
- BARCROFT, J M
- BASFORD CHIROPRACTIC CLINIC
- BEDFORD HOUSE CLINIC
- BIRKIN, H
- BODYTECH
- BONNEBAIGT, ANDRE
- BOWIE, R
- BRIDGETT, A
- BURKE, E
- CADDY, G
- CHADWICK, JAMES L
- CHILD & ADOLESCENT PSYCH DEPT
- CITY CHIROPRACTIC CLINIC
- COPELAND, M E
- CORKER, E

- CORNERSTONES PRACTICE
- DAVIES, MARTIN K
- DOBIE, CLARE
- EDWARDS, P A
- EQUILIBRIUM
- EXECUTIVE ROOMS
- FOOT GALLERY
- HEATH, DAVID
- HOLDCROFT, R A
- HOLDCROFT, ROSEMARIE A
- HOWLE, E
- HUMPHREYS, R
- HYPNOSIS & PARAPSYCHOLOGY
- HYPNOTHERAPY CENTRE
- IBBS, ROGER
- KILGALLON, P
- LAKESIDE PHYSIO CLINIC
- LAZUREK, DONNA
- LIFESTYLE FOOTCARE
- MARCONI, L R
- MARKHAM, IAN
- MELLOR, J SIMON
- MEMORIES HEALTH CENTRE
- MOFFATT, M H
- PARRY, LIZA
- PAYTON, ANTHONY
- PECK, SUE
- PEDLEY, S & D E
- PLANT, R M
- PRICE, M J
- QUINTON, R M
- REECE, P & BRADSHAW, J
- RUSSELL, JOHN
- SAGGU, S
- SCHOLL CENTRE
- TUNSTALL HYPNOTHERAPY CENTRE
- VALERIE BETTANY CLINIC
- WHITBY, S E
- WOOD, JANET
- WOOLRICH, R J

### STONE

- AROMAFLOAT
- COOPER, DAVID
- EDWARDS, ALLYN
- ISHTA CENTRE
- KENDALL, CHEW
- O'CALLAGHAN, STEVE
- STAFFORDSHIRE MCTIMONEY
- TE NOSCE
- WHYTE, IAN
- YARNFIELD PARK- HEALTH/SPORTS

### TAMWORTH

- ADAMS, MEGAN
- ALTERNATIVE THERAPY CENTRE
- BALL, LORRAINE
- BLADEN, DAVE
- CLAIRVOYANT & MEDIUM
- COLUMN OF LIGHT HEALING CENTRE
- EASTY, JAYNE
- FRASER HOUSE CHIROPRACTIC
- GOHIL, SUMAN
- GRAY, WENDY
- GREEN, A L
- LIDSTER, CAROL
- LING, J
- LING, STEPHEN W
- LUXTON, PAT
- MARTIN, BARBARA
- NARAYAN, MAMTA
- SOUTER, N
- STATFOLD SEED OILS
- SWINNERTON, SHIELA
- TAMWORTH PHYSIOTHERAPY CLINIC
- WATSON, G T

### UTTOXETER

- AROMA CARE
- CLOWES, JOANNE
- PLANT, R M
- SAUNDERS, MARGARET

## SUFFOLK

### ALDEBURGH

- FREASHFIELDS

### BECCLES

- BECCLES ACUPUNCTURE CLINIC
- BECCLES PSYCHO & COUNS CTRE
- CRABTREE, P W
- HOPKINS, C J
- MACDONALD, KATHRYN
- MANOR HOUSE
- MILES, JAMES
- WORSLEY, JULIA

### BUNGAY

- FARLEIGH, CLARE E
- FLOWERDEW, M
- GLASBY, H R
- HAYWARD, LISA
- ST MARYS PRACTICE

### BURES

- COLLINS, JOHN
- HEALING HANDS
- HUGHES, LINDA
- HUGHES, LINDA

### BURY ST. EDMUNDS

- ADEN, ROLL
- BATES, SUSAN
- BURY NATURAL HEALTH CENTRE
- BURY PHYSIO & SPORTS CLINIC
- BURY PRACTICE
- BURY ST EDMUNDS PHYSIO CLINIC
- CHADWICK, ANTHONY
- COMMUNITY PSYCHIATRIC TEAM
- DANIEL-BAYLE, M
- DEORA, MARC
- EAREY, C A
- FROST, JEREMY
- GORDON, STEVEN
- GRIMSEY, ALAN R
- HAYMAN, DOROTHY
- JACOBS, F (DR)
- KETTLE, JONATHAN
- LAW, J REYNOLDS
- MANNING, MATTHEW
- MASSAGE FOR HEALTH
- MOHAN, TERRY
- MORRISON, SUSAN
- MOULDING, ANNE
- PEARL LAMONT
- ROBINSON, RACHEL
- ROWNEY, ERICA
- STEPHEN GORDON
- STURZAKER, NICOLA
- TRANSCENDENTAL MEDITATION
- VICEROY
- WALTERS, CAROLINE BARWICK
- WATERS, J
- WEI CLINIC
- WOOLPITPHYSIO

### EYE

- NOAH'S ARK PSYCHOTHERAPY

### FELIXSTOWE

- BULL, C S
- BURT, P
- CHURCHMAN, B
- CHURCHMAN, BERYL
- CROPPER, JAN
- ELF CRAFT
- FELIXSTOWE CHIROPRACTIC CLINIC
- FELIXSTOWE COUNS & PYSCHO CTRE
- FELIXSTOWE HEALING SANCTUARY
- FELIXSTOWE PHYSIO PRACTICE
- FENN, JASON
- JOHNSON, P
- LADYBIRD HEALTHCARE
- STONE, I C
- TYRRELL, HAZEL

### HALESWORTH

- FLOWERDEW, M
- HAMPTON, KAREN
- WELBY, S J

### HAVERHILL

- HAVERHILL CHIROPRACTIC CENTRE
- VITAPURE

### IPSWICH

- ALEXANDER TECHNIQUE
- AROMATHERAPY TRADE COUNCIL
- ARTHEY, ELAINE
- ATC
- BAXTER, PAUL
- BERWICK, E
- BORTH, H
- BRUCE, K
- BULL, OWEN MORGAN
- CAPEL PHYSIOTHERAPY CLINIC
- CATCHPOLE, J
- CHINESE MEDICAL CENTRE
- CHURCHMAN & ASS REG OST
- CLINIC
- COOK, AUBREY
- COOK, LORNA
- CRESSWELL, C
- CUDDEFORD, C
- DALTON, EMMA
- DAVIDSON, H L
- DUNNETT, PAM
- E M D I
- EVENKEEL
- FRESHFIELDS OF ALDEBURGH
- FRIAR, CARL
- GEESON, D
- GILMOUR, PIPER & ASSOCIATES
- GORDON, MARIA
- HARDY, MICHAEL
- HAYNES, S R
- HEALING CONNECTIONS
- HEALING CONNECTIONS
- HOLMAN, M J
- HURLEY, DOT
- IPRS
- IPSWICH CHIROPRACTIC CLINIC
- IPSWICH PHYSIOTHERAPY PRACTICE
- IPSWICH PSYCHOTHERAPY/COUNS
- JAMESON, BARBARA
- JORDAN, TESSA
- JUBY, P
- JUST ESSENTIALS
- KEMP, N J
- KENSHALL, ABIGAL
- KESGRAVE CHIROPRACTIC CLINIC
- KINNEAR, MARGARET
- KIPPAX, JANET
- KIPPAX, STEPHEN
- LEE, FRANK
- MACFARLANE, CLARE
- MACKAY, SUSIE
- MASKERY, M
- MILLER, PAM
- MILLS, SUE
- PARTRIDGE, VERONICA
- PHYSIOTHERAPY CLINIC
- RAINBOW STAR HEALING
- RAINBOW WORLD HEALING CENTRE
- RELAXATION PHYSICAL
- SACRED EARTH
- SANDERS, T E
- SCHOLL CENTRE
- SEAL, W
- SPALDING, JULIE
- SPALDING, PAUL
- SPRINGFIELD LODGE HEALTH CARE
- STEWARD, J A
- STRAWSON, M R
- THICK, DENISE
- THOMAS, D L C
- THOMSON, T G
- VICKY NOBLE - AROMATHERAPIST
- WARNOCK, PETER
- WEN, ISABELLE
- WILLIAMS, R T & S M
- WITHERLEY, J E
- WORLD OF SCENTS

### LOWESTOFT

- AROMA ROOM
- CHARLTON CLINIC
- CLINICAL HYPNOTHERAPY
- COLEBROOK, G
- DOVES THERAPY CENTRE
- FOTHERBY, ROZ
- FOULGER, SONIA
- GREEN PHARMACY COMP MED
- HEPBURN, D
- HEPBURN, DAVID
- INNER SPACE SUFFOLK
- LITTLEWOOD, JULIE
- LOWESTOFT TRAD ACUPUNTURE CLNC
- MALAROC
- MERIDIAN THERAPY

- PAGE, COLIN J
- QUENTIN-HICKS, M
- REIKI THERAPY CENTRE

## NEWMARKET

- BIDDER, N
- COOPER, A R
- CRICKMERE, S D
- EPONA HOMEOPATHIC
- FITZGERALD, ROSEMARY
- GOLD, STEPHEN
- GROSVENOR PHYSIOTHERAPY CLINIC
- HERBS OF GRACE
- HITCHINS, ROSIE
- HODSON, P A
- IVESON
- NATURAL & HOLISTIC CENTRE
- NEWMARKET CHIROPRACTIC CLINIC
- PERTH, F

## SAXMUNDHAM

- KELSALE PHYSIOTHERAPY CENTRE
- ORWELL COUNSELLING GROUP
- STEWARD, J A
- STICKLAND, PAULINE

## SOUTHWOLD

- MARK CHURCH AROMATHERAPY

## STOWMARKET

- HUGHES, DOREEN
- MARSHALL-RAVEN, L
- PARSONS, CAROL
- SLOPER, P
- STOWMARKET OSTEOPATHS

## SUDBURY

- BRIGHTWELL, TONY
- BROOKS, A P
- BYERS, PAULINE
- CARPENTER, ELAINE
- CLAIRVOYANT SERVICES
- CORRIGAN, A J
- COSMIC CONNECTIONS
- CRISP, D M
- CUDDEFORD, C
- DURRANT, D
- HEALTH MATTERS NATURAL HLTH
- MILLINGTON, P
- MURRAY, S L
- NATURECURES
- ROBINSONS HOLISTIC
- SCOFIELD CHIROPRATIC CLINIC
- SHEROMA THERAPY
- SUDBURY CHIROPRACTIC CLINIC
- TANSWELL, PHILLIP J
- TURNER, S M
- UNITY HEALTH CENTRE
- WALKER, LINDA

## WOODBRIDGE

- AJNA
- BARBER, C J
- BODY MECHANICS THERAPY CLINIC
- BRUCE, KATIE
- BUTTRUMS MILL
- CHURCHMAN, B E
- COPPING, P
- CT & IM LEITH
- FRAMLINGHAM PHYSIO PRACTICE
- GREEN FARM CLINIC
- INSTIT-TRAD HERBAL MED-ACUP
- LAVENDER LODGE CLINIC
- LAWRENCE, JILLIAN
- LINDOS PSYCHOTHERAPY CENTRE
- LOTUS HEALING CENTRE
- MCTIMONEY CHIROPRACTIC CLINIC
- NATURAL HEALING CENTRE
- PAROLIN, PAUL
- PIPER, KARREN
- RAWORTH CENTRE
- SEAL, RAYMOND
- TERRY, LESLEY ANN
- WARNE, A J
- WOODBRIDGE COMP HEALTH CENTRE
- WOODBRIDGE COUNS & PSYCHO CTRE
- WOODBRIDGE PHYSIO PRACTICE
- WRIGHT, J L

# SURREY

## ADDLESTONE

- ADDLESTONE THERAPY CENTRE
- GILL JULIE
- KEHOE, JOANNA
- NATURAL HEALING AND REIKI CTRE
- PEET, SANDRA
- TRANSFORMATIONS

## ASHFORD

- AROMATHERAPY CENTRE
- ASHFORD OSTEOPATHIC CLINIC
- BOLD, PHILIP
- BOULTON, FRANCES
- HYPNOTHERAPY & STRESS CON
- KIMS
- SIMMERLING, LUNIA
- TRISTER, LAURENCE

## ASHTEAD

- ASHTEAD CHARTERED PHYSIO SV
- ASHTEAD CHIROPRACTIC CLINIC
- ASHTEAD CLINIC
- CORNELL, LESLEY
- GAZELEY, HELEN
- HOLDEN NATURAL HEALTH CLINIC
- PALMER, JUNE
- ROSE, CYNTHIA J

## BAGSHOT

- ARUNDELL, LINDA
- BECKETT, L J
- BOWIE, S
- BRIDGE VIEW CHIROPODY CLINIC
- BRIDGEVIEW PHYSIO & SPORTS
- CRASKE, DAVID
- HARVEY, N J
- KING, LIZ
- NORRIS, Q

## BANSTEAD

- ARCHER, JULIE
- BARNSTEAD VILLAGE CLINIC
- BODY-MIND HYPNOTHERAPY
- BOWEN THERAPY
- CROWLEY, HEATHER
- GARDENER, DAPHNE
- GOACHER, J
- MURFIN, PAUL
- PINCHES, CHRISTOPHER
- SAUMEEL PATEL ACU CLINIC
- SPELLER CONSULTANTS
- VACUFLEX
- WARWICK, JULIE

## BETCHWORTH

- CLARK, JOYCE
- PARTRIDGE, JENNY

## CAMBERLEY

- 1ST CHIROPRACTIC CENTRES
- ACTIVE HYPNOSIS
- ACUHERBAL CHINESE MEDICINE
- ARTHURWORREY, J
- AVENUE PHYSIO & SPORTS CLNC
- BARNARD, JUDY
- BARTLETT, CLAIRE
- BOOTH, CORINNE
- CAMBERLEY CHIROPRACTIC CLINIC
- CAMBERLEY NATURAL THERAPY CTRE
- CAMBERLEY OSTEOPATHIC CLINIC
- CAMBERLEY PHYSIO & SPORTS CLNC
- COWIESON, MARY
- CREW, D
- CREW, DAVID A
- CURATIVE HYPNOTHERAPY CENTRE
- EVANS, C
- FARNBOROUGH CHIRO CLINIC
- GREEN, S
- HARRISON, VALERIE
- HARTLEY, GILL
- HUTCHINGS, MICHAEL
- JACKSON, NIGEL
- KING-TURNER, P
- LARCOMBE, J
- MIST, CORINNE
- MURPHY, TERRY
- NATURAL HEALTH CARE
- OCEANFLOOD COMPUTERS
- OSTEOPATHY
- OVENDEN, ANDREW
- RAPHAEL ALT THERAPY PRACTICE
- ROUX, ANITA DE
- RUSSELL, SARAH
- SEVEN SIGHS
- SIDDELL, ANGELA
- SMITH, M
- STRIKE, SUE
- SUDWELL, MARIE
- TIDEY, S A
- URQUHART, W
- WALKER, SARAH

## CARSHALTON

- BAILEY, L J
- BEECHES PHYSICAL THERAPY
- C PHILIP & J FOSTER & A MULA
- CUMMINS, R
- DANIELS, INGRID
- DAWSON, VIVIENNE
- DEACKES, C
- DEARSLEY, GILL
- DONOVAN, BRENDA
- FEATHERSTONE-GRIFFIN, B
- FELTHAM, N
- GRAHAM, P D & M E
- HALLS, R
- JIWA, A
- JOHNSON, LOUISE
- KETTLE, NIGEL
- PEACOCK, R
- SURREY PHYSIOTHERAPY CLINIC
- VANCOPPENOLLE, J
- VIVIAN, DAWSON

## CATERHAM

- AINSWORTH HOMEOPATHIC PHARMACY
- AROMA-ACTIVE
- CATERHAM CHIROPRACTIC CLINIC
- CATERHAM OSTEOPATHIC PRACTICE
- CATERHAM VALLEY CHIROPRACTIC
- D 'ARCY, LARRAINE
- DUNNET, GILLIAN
- EREVNA
- FOOT CENTRE
- KINGSLEY-THOMAS, FERNANDA
- NORTH DOWNS PHYSIOTHERAPY
- PEACOCK, SALLY
- RAGLAN PRECINCT SALON
- S K PHYSIOTHERAPY
- SKELTON, VAL
- STAMP, G R
- WILLINGALE, M

## CHERTSEY

- BODY FACTOR
- CANO, D
- CHERTSEY OSTEOPATHIC CLINIC
- CLEMENTS, CHRISTINE
- DAVIES, ANTHONY J
- LATTER, J E
- OTTERSHAW OSTEOPATHIC PRACTICE
- SEALE, TONY
- WEIGHTMAN, LAURA

## CHESSINGTON

- ASW ALLERGY CONSULTANTS
- BAYLISS, CATHERINE
- BAYLISS, JOHN
- CHESSINGTON OSTEOPATHIC CLINIC
- G NORTHWOOD PSYCHOTHERAPY
- HANFORD, S P
- HOOPER, B
- MITCHELL, JANE
- MUSTARD SEED CLINIC
- OSTEOPATHIC CENTRE
- POWER, DAVID J
- SHANGRI-LA NATURAL THERAPIES
- SOUTHBOROUGH COMP HLTH PRAC
- TIESDELL-SMITH, DOREEN

## COBHAM

- BEAUTY IN HARMONY
- COBHAM COMPLEMENTARY THERAPIES
- MATTHEW DAV & SAMANTHA TAY
- NATIONAL COUNCIL OF PSYCHO
- PHYSIO & SPORTS INJURY CLNC

- POPE, ANGELA
- ROSS, PATRICK
- SHAW, J
- WEIGHTMAN, LAURA

## CRANLEIGH

- AROMATHERAPY/REMEDIAL MASSAGE
- BONIFACE, SANDY J
- CRAIG-WOOD, SAMANTHA
- CRANFOLD PHYSIOTHERAPY CENTRE
- CRANLEIGH CHIROPRACTIC CLINIC
- FANYA, M M
- GAUVAIN, TONY
- JONES, PAULINE
- REYNOLDS, DAVID
- WIMBLEDON, R A

## CROYDON

- AROMATHERAPY
- ASSOCIATION OF STRESS MANAGERS
- BACK TO HEALTH
- BARBER, MAVIS
- BARRETT-BOYCE, PATRICK
- BONE, ELIZABETH
- CAMPBELL & ASSOCIATES
- CARPANINI, REGINALD & PENELOPE
- CEDARWOOD CLINIC
- CHANDLER, M D
- CHIROPRACTIC CENTRE
- COX, JULIET
- CROYDON BUDDHIST CENTRE
- CROYDON HEALING CENTRE
- CROYDON PRACTICE-PSYCHOTHERAPY
- DREHER-BROGAN, S K (DR)
- ELLIOTT, BRIAN
- ESSENTIAL CARE TRAINING
- FREED CLINIC
- GARDNER, J
- GLAISTER, BRIAN (DR)
- HARLAND, D S
- HELIANTHUS PRACTICE
- HERBAL KING
- HILL, CHARLOTTE
- INTERNATIONAL FED OF REFLEX
- JAYASINGHE, MIGEL
- MACE, CHRISTOPHER J
- MARSHALL, ANGELA
- MEENEGHAN, TOM
- MICKLEBURGH, P
- MIND AND BODY
- MORRISSEY, PAUL
- MULA, ANIA
- MURRAY, A G
- N J HARRISON CHIROPODY SERVICE
- NATURAL HEALING CLINIC
- NATURAL ORGANICS
- O'BRIEN, JAMES
- PHOENIX
- POLE, G
- PREECE, MARGARET
- PRICE, SANDRA
- RICHARDSON, C E
- ROUNDABOUT DRAMA/MOVEMENT
- SAYER CLINIC
- SELSDON COMP/RESP CLINIC
- SIMMS, KATHERINE
- SOUND MIND & BODY REFLEXOLOGY
- SYMONS, MARLIESE
- TCHOREK, CATHERINE
- TIDA CHINESE HERBAL CLINIC
- WAKEFIELD, ROBERT
- WEST & ASSOCIATES
- WILKINSON, LESLEY
- WINGROVE, ROSEMARY
- YOGA & RELAXATION

## DORKING

- AHMED, NICHOLA
- ALLEN, GRAHAM M
- ALVES-DA SILVA, CARLA
- BAARTZ, MARIAN
- BASTON, MYRA V
- BAXTER, STEPHEN
- BOURNE, LIZ
- BURNS, E M
- COOPER, A
- DORKING CHIROPRACTIC
- EASON, GUY
- FORD, PETER A
- FRIDAY, SARA
- HANCE, PETER
- HILL, F S & M
- KAREN, PEARSON
- LOTIONS & POTIONS
- MAHBOOBANI, KATHY
- MANN, G C & DAVID, R T
- MURRAY, HEATHER
- NICHOLLS, VERITY
- O'DONAGHUE, SHIRLEY
- RAWORTH CLINIC
- SAYER, MARK
- SIMPLE ESSENTIALS
- WOOD, SAMANTHA CRAIG
- WYATT, JOANNA

## EAST MOLESEY

- CLINIC OF NATURAL THERAPIES
- DR LI
- ESSENTIALS
- HARRIS, JOHN
- HUNT, C
- KENT CLINIC OF NATURAL MED
- MACKENZIE, D, HATFIELD, J
- MCATHEY, CAROLE
- NEUBACHER, SYLVIA

## EGHAM

- BARCLAY, JAMES
- CHRISTINE KEY HYPNOTHERAPIST
- CLAIRVOYANT TAROT READER
- EGHAM HYPNOTHERAPY
- FOX, DIANA
- HAWLEY, KAREN
- HOBSON, N
- MOSS, JANICE
- PERRY, ELAINE
- REIKI HEALING & YOGA
- ROBERTS, GRAHAM
- SCORPIO PHYSIOTHERAPY
- SIMPSON, PAT
- STREAMS HYPNOTHERAPY
- SYKES, JASON

## EPSOM

- ACHES & PAINS
- AMIN, S
- BARBER, JOANNE
- BLAZEY, PHILLIPA
- BUTLER, LAWRENCE
- CANE, PAT
- CARR, PAUL
- CENTRE FOR HYPNOSIS
- CITISPORT
- COLLEDGE, SUSAN
- COLLISON, PETER
- COUGHLAN, EILEEN
- DYNAMIC HEALTH
- EPSOM & EWELL ACUPUNCTURE
- EPSOM CHIROPRACTIC CLINIC
- EPSOM HEALTH CARE NHS TRUST
- EWELL CHIROPRACTIC CENTRE
- GOSS, LEN
- HARRIS, JOHN R C
- HERBMEDIC
- HILL, F S
- HOMOEOPATHIC HEALTH CLINIC
- HOUNSFIELD, BRIAN
- JENKINS, DAVID
- KATESMARK, R
- LOGAN, ROBIN
- MEFFAN, JOHN
- MILTON, S & C
- MOHAMMED, CHARLES
- NIRVANA
- NOBLE, TERRY D
- PATTINSON, C J (DR)
- PAXTON, JACQUELINE
- PAYNE, I J
- PENWARDEN, DAVID
- PHYSIO & SPORTS INJURY CLINIC
- PROCTER, SHARON
- RAO, R S
- SIMPLY FIT & HEALTHY
- SMITH, EDWARD J
- STEVENS, NIGEL GATES
- TANG, SIMON
- VEYSEY-SMITH, T H
- WAUGH, G
- WOOLLEY, N

## ESHER

- ADKIN, JEAN
- BRAY, CAROLINE
- CHRISTIAN SCIENCE PRACTITIONER
- COMPLEMENTARY HEALTH PART
- CONFIDENTIAL COUNSELLING SVS
- EDUCATIONAL COUNSELLING
- FITZHERBERT, TINA
- INT COLLEGE OF CRYSTAL HEALING
- JOY WALTER CHARTERED PHYSIO
- LEARY, MARINA T
- LOW, ROYSTON
- MINIHAN-CRANE, BAIRBRE
- MUIR, BEVERLEY
- OSTEOPATHS FOR INDUSTRY
- PEMBERY, SALLY
- PEMBURY, SALLY
- PRINGLE, AMANDA
- WATSON, ANGELA

## EWELL

- TRANSCENDENTAL MEDITATION

## FARNHAM

- AGNEW, B K
- ALDERSHOT & FARNHAM CLINIC
- BODYMIND
- BOWLER, ANNIE
- BRAY, J M
- BROCK, ROBERT
- BROWN, L
- DYSLEXIA ADVISORY BUREAU
- ELLIS, CHRISTOPHER
- FARNHAM CHIROPRACTIC CLINIC
- HANDS ON HEALTH
- J V ASSOCIATES
- JENNY HOK
- LODGE FARM CHIROPRACTIC CENTRE
- MARDEL, JEREMY
- MARDEL, JEREMY
- MERRYDOWN CENTRE
- NAT FED OF SPIRITUAL HEALERS
- ORIENTAL MEDICAL CENTRE
- PINCHES, CHRISTOPHER
- RHIDIAN & COLLEAGUES
- ROBERTON, JILL
- SHINER, SONIA
- SOUTH FARNHAM PHYSIO PRACTICE
- SPICKERNELL, J
- TAYLOR, DESMOND
- TELLING, PAUL
- TOLMIE, LINDA
- TRANSCENDENTAL MEDIATION
- WALLACE, S
- WHENT, NICKY
- WHITWORTH, M T
- WINTER, DAVID

## FRIMLEY

- GILES, ROSEMARY

## GODALMING

- ALEXANDER, JANE
- ANDREWS, ELIZABETH
- BATTEN, P R
- BEVAN, L
- BOYD-JONES, KERVIN (DR)
- DICE, JOHN
- GLASSBOROW, G W
- GODALMING CHIROPRACTIC CLINIC
- HAMBLEDON HOLISTIC HEALTH
- HARRIS-BEACH, JULIE
- HAWE, R V
- HEALTHY OPTIONS
- HERBALS
- HOLISTIC CENTRE
- HUDSON, ROSEMARY
- JOAN PEARNE CHIROPODY CLINIC
- KYPERS, SARAH
- LEWIS, K
- MASON, SARAH
- MILFORD MASSAGE PRACTICE
- MIST, JULIA
- MOSS PHARMACY PODIATRY
- NOYCE, T J
- OASIS CLINIC
- ORIENTAL MEDICAL CENTRE
- ORTHOTICITY
- PERRIN, M

- PHILP, CHRISTINE
- ROBERTS, FIONA
- SALMON, PHILIP
- SMALLBROOK CLINIC
- TULLETT, ANNY
- VAN HAEFTEN, A

## GODSTONE

- NICHOLDS, PATRICIA
- STEWART, I

## GODSTONE (SOUTH)

- SULLIVAN, KIM

## GUILDFORD

- ALDRIDGE, SUSAN
- ALLEN, J
- BACK TO HEALTH - GUILDFORD
- BARKER, GREG
- BATEMAN, JANE
- BATTLEY, STEVEN
- BAYLEY, EVA
- BENNETT, RUSSELL
- BLAMPIED ST HILL
- BOOTH, N
- BRAMLEY NATURAL HEALTH STUDIO
- CASTLE STREET CLINIC
- CHANCE, SUE
- CLEASSON, HAZEL
- COMPTON HOMOEOPATHY CENTRE
- COOK, ANN
- COOPER, DIANA
- CULPEPER
- DIXON, CLAIRE
- EDWARDS, HARRY
- EKSTS, ANNE
- FRANCIS J H WILSON CHIRO
- FRANKCOM, DAVID J
- GARSON, J E
- GOTHAM, SUE
- GRAVELL, NICOLA
- GUILDFORD CTRE-PSYCHOTHERAPY
- GUILDFORD PHYSIO & SPORTS
- HILLS, RUSSELL
- HOBBS, DIANA C
- HOPPER, C A
- JEWERS, T
- JOHNSON, CELIA
- LA TOUCHE, ROBERT
- LEE, ROBIN
- LEWIS, C
- LOCKIE, A H
- LOXTON, K
- LUKLINSKI, B M (DR)
- MACK, DEREK
- MATTHEWS, ALLEN
- MATTHEWS, E G
- MATTHEWS, J
- MCINTOSH, A
- MELVILL, R H
- METAFORCE
- MICHELOTTI, ALAN
- MILLER, IAN A
- MORRISON, G N
- MOUNT ALVERNIA PHYSIOTHERAPY
- MYLES, JOHN
- NASH, A
- NOCKOLDS, JENNY
- NOCKOLDS, JENNY
- NUTRON FOOD SENSITIVITY
- ONSLOW, H
- O'SULLIVAN, TANYA
- PARKER, ANTHONY
- PAVILION, REVE
- PETERS, A J
- PHILLIPS, C
- POURAMINI, A
- PRETORIUS, C
- ROSE, JILL
- SARAH BOGUE HOMEOPATH
- TAYLOR, CLAIRE
- TENGER, ZOE
- TENGER, ZOE
- TONGE, B
- TOWNS, KATE
- UNIVERSITY OF SURREY
- WARE, J
- WHITWORTH, MICHAEL T
- WICKER, GEMMA
- WILSDON, S
- WOODBRIDGE HILL CHIROPRACTOR
- WORSFOLD, ALAN R

## HASLEMERE

- ALPHA AROMATHERAPY
- ARRINDELL, MARK
- CLINIC OF ACUPUNCTURE
- CONCANON, A
- E & E CAINE-WILMOT
- FULLER, MICHAEL A
- HASLEMERE CHIROPRACTIC CLINIC
- HASLEMERE SPORTS & PHYSIO
- HOUE, DAVID
- JAGER, KURT W
- LUFFINGHAM, D & E
- PRIOR, CYNTHIA
- ROBERTS, C M
- SQUIRE, ELIZABETH
- VICARAGE LANE CLINIC
- WALKER, L
- WALKER-DENDLE, VALERIE
- WIGLEY, CABELLA
- WILMOT, E
- WILSON-SMITH, ANDREW

## HERSHAM

- COPELAND, ELAINE

## HINDHEAD

- CLEVERLY, BARBARA
- GLEICH, M T
- GRAYSHOTT ELECTRO-ACUPUNCTURE
- O'SHEA, A C
- ROBSHAW, HELEN
- WELLS, HEIDI

## HORLEY

- ALVEY, J W D
- BEES CRYSTAL SHOP
- BOULTER, NIGEL
- CARLTON CLINIC
- DAVIES, ROBERT
- ECLIPSE
- GREAR, M D
- LLEWELLYN, MARY
- MCMANUS, EILEEN
- NATURAL HEALTH PRACTICE
- NAYLOR, ANTHEA
- PENFOLD, NICOLA
- WALLIS, J

## KENLEY

- NATURAL & HOLISTIC THRPY CTRE
- RAE, M
- WOODLEY, SIMONE

## KINGSTON UPON THAMES

- ALEXANDER TECHNIQUE
- ARCHER, JOANNE
- AROMA SECRETS
- ASARIEL
- BANTICK, ANGELA
- BODYWORKS
- BORDISS, DEBORAH
- CHINESE MEDICINE CENTRE
- EDWARDS, CHERYL
- FAMILY CHIROPRACTIC CENTRE
- GRIFFITHS, CAROL
- HAM CHIROPRACTIC CLINIC
- HARRIS, FRANCIS
- HOLISTIC HEALTH
- JARROLD, RICHARD
- KINGSTON & RICHMOND HYNO CTRE
- KINGSTON CHIROPRACTIC CLINIC
- KINGSTON HYPNOTHERAPY CENTRE
- KINGSTON NATURAL HEALING CTRE
- KINGSTON NATUROPATHIC CENTRE
- KINGSTON OSTEOPATHS
- MAZUR, ARTUR
- MILLER CONSULTANCY
- NEW VICTORIA HOSPITAL
- ONE STEP FOOTCARE
- PAIN CLINIC
- PERSONAL/RELATIONSHIP THERAPY
- QUINTESSENCE AROMATHERAPY
- S O S PHYSIO & OSTEOPATHY
- SAAG, INGRID
- SCHOLL CENTRE
- TRAD CHINESE MASSOTHERAPY
- VESEY, JOHN M
- VINE CLINIC
- WELL WITHIN THERAPIES
- WHITTON, SHIRLEY

## LEATHERHEAD

- BENNETT, ELIZABETH
- BILLINGTON, PEGGY
- COOPER, HEATHER
- EQUILIBRIUM OSTEOPATHIC
- LEATHERHEAD CHIRO CLINIC
- LIONHEART PHYSIO & SPORTS
- MILTON, RHONA M
- NIGHTINGALE, N C
- O'REILLY, FRANCES
- PAYNE, C
- PETERS, CAROLINE
- SCHONBERG, VERA
- SNOAD, R J
- WYATT, JULIE

## LIGHTWATER

- BRADLEY, DAWN
- JUNE NORMAN BEAUTY CLINIC
- LENNAN, CHRIS

## LINGFIELD

- CLARIDGE HOUSE HEALING CENTRE
- CUMBERLIDGE, CAROL

## MITCHAM

- ABBOTTS ROAD PRACTICE
- CROCKETT, NEVILLE
- HARRIS, MICHELLE J
- HUMAN FOCUS RETURN TO WORK
- JEFFREY & ASSOCIATES
- JONES, ELIZABETH M
- MARRIOTT, D A
- SHEARS, S
- TUBOKU-METZGER, A F
- WRIGHT, L

## MORDEN

- BEIJING ACUPUNCTURE CLINIC
- BRADLEY, JOANNAH
- CAHILL, T
- DYNAMIC DEV STRESS MNGMT
- KOLTHAMMER, JOHN
- LONDON SPINE AND JOINT CLINIC
- MORDEN CLINIC
- MULLEN, ANDREW T W
- OSTEOPATHIC CENTRE
- SHEARS, D J

## NEW MALDEN

- ACORN THERAPY CENTRE
- AMBER THERAPEUTIC CLINIC
- ASTON CLINIC
- BST FOUNDATION
- BYRNE, ANGELA
- COLEY, LESLEY
- EDWARDS HEALTH CLINIC
- HALL, CHRISTINE
- HARRIS, FRANCES E
- HAYNES, HILARY
- HUSSEY, DOMINICK
- LANES, TESSA
- LEMON, RORY
- MANTLE, FIONA
- MANTLE, FIONA
- METCALFE, D (DR)
- MURRAY, VICTORIA
- PERRY, L
- PURRETT-SMITH, DEE
- STONE, BARRY
- SUMMERS, ANGIE

## OXTED

- ACE NUTRITION
- BENNETT, J C
- CAREY-MORGAN, SIMON
- CLARKE, ANNE MARI
- CROSS, R
- DA RIN, MANUELA
- GOPAUL, V
- HENRIKSEN, HELLE
- HUNN, MARGARET
- INGLEDALE NATURAL HEALTH CTRE
- KINGSMEAD PHYSIOTHERAPY CLINIC
- LANE, A
- MOODY, PAUL
- MORTIMORE, P G
- OVENDEN, ANDREW
- PLANT, BELINDA
- ROBSON, MARIA

- RUIZ-GOLVANO, E
- SAPIR, NINETTE
- SEAMER, R
- SKELCEY, SUE
- STEED, CAROL
- SULLIVAN, CHRISTINE
- TUNSTILL, PAT
- WALKLETT, B
- WHITE, TRUDY
- WILSON, VIRGINIA
- WISHING WELL

## PURLEY

- ACUPUNCTURE/CHINESE HERBAL MED
- COMMANDER, J
- COPELAND, LIZ
- DUNBAR, NEIL
- INCE, G A
- INCE, ROBERT J
- KAY, ANDREA
- KEATING, JAMES
- MARKS, DARREN HYPNOTHERAPY
- PURLEY CHIROPODY PRACTICE
- PURLEY CHIROPRACTIC CLINIC
- PURLEY OSTEOPATHIC CLINIC
- SLATTERY, BRIDGET
- SMITH, CHARLES
- SYMONS, JANE

## REDHILL

- BOOTH, HILARY
- BUILDERS, MEJ
- BUSWELL, PRISILLA J
- CHEVINGTON CHIROPRACTIC CLINIC
- CRITTELL, SANDRA
- CRUTCHINGTON, JEAN
- EAST SURREY HOSPITAL PHYSIO
- FIONA BROOKES & MORNA ELLIOTT
- FOOT HEALTH CENTRE
- HENDRY, JUDITH
- HENSE, JOHN
- NICOLA FRY-HEALTH & BEAUTY
- PENN, NICOLA
- PETERS, CAROL
- PIRAINO, MARK
- PITMAN, DIANE
- RAINBOW NATURAL HEALTH CENTRE
- SCIATICA CENTRE
- STRAKER, JANE
- SURREY HEALING SANCTUARY
- TOTAL HEALTH CARE
- WEATHERILL, CHRISTINE
- WOOD, ANGELA

## REIGATE

- BALL, J
- BINNIE, D
- CAMPBELL, SEAN
- CANE, FENELLA
- CHART LANE CLINIC
- CROWTHER, GEORGE
- FIONA BROOKES & MORNA ELLIOTT
- FOOT HEALTH CLINIC
- FORSYTH, CHARLES (DR)
- GOODING, NIGEL (DR)
- GRIGGS, LESLEY
- KRILL, W E
- OLORENSHAW, A J
- PHYSIOTHERAPY, S K
- REIGATE CHIROPRACTIC CLINIC
- REIGATE OSTEOPATHIC
- REIGATE OSTEOPATHIC CLINIC
- ROBERTS, P
- ROWE, M
- SCRIVEN, D
- SMITH, S J
- TUCKER, JOCELYN
- TURK, BARBARA (DR)
- TWINE, RAY
- UNWIN LAMBERT, B & PEGG, E
- WOODLANDS NATURAL HLTH THERAPY
- WOODWARD, SUZANNE
- YARNTON, C

## RICHMOND

- AROMA SECRETS
- AROMA TREATMENTS
- BACK TO HEALTH - RICHMOND
- BATTEN, CHRISTOPHER
- BROWN, KAREN
- BURN, LOIC (DR)
- BURNS, MICHAEL & ASSOCIATES
- CHI-KIN, PO
- DANFORD, P H
- EVANS, CHRISTINE
- FAIRBAIM, SARAH
- FENWICK, J
- HAILWOOD, ADRIAN
- HEHIR, S
- JACKSON, J
- JACKSON, ROBIN
- JORGENSEN, ANNE
- KEW CHIROPRACTIC CLINIC
- KINNEAR, E M L
- LEGGETTER, D
- LELJEVAHL, KARIN
- MALONNE, MARIANNE
- MEEKS, FIONA
- MIDDLETON, VALERIE
- MOTTRAM, ROB
- PERFORMANCE PHYSIOTHERAPY
- POLLARD, M
- PRACTITONERS SCHOOL
- RANDALL, JULIA
- RICHMOND HEALING CENTRE
- RICHMOND OSTEOPATHIC
- RICHMOND PHYSIOTHERAPY
- RICHMOND REFLEXOLOGY
- ROBINSON, JAQUELINE
- SHIATSU CLINIC
- SOUTH LONDON PSYCH GROUP
- STIRRAT, KATRINA
- SUREN, CHARLES
- TELLING, KAREN
- TONGE, B
- TREFSER, SIGFRIED (DR)
- WISHAHI, IRIS
- WORLD TREE NATURAL CRYSTALS

## SEALE

- MALIPHANT, JACKIE

## SHEPPERTON

- BIODYNAMICS
- CHARLES, L M (DR)
- LEWIN, SANDRA
- LEWIS, P J
- PERRY, JUDITH
- RAINBOW GROUP
- ROBYNA, ANNETTE
- SHEPPERTON CHIROPRACTIC CLINIC
- SHEPPERTON PHYSIOFIRST CENTRE
- SUTHERLAND, J
- WILKINS, DAVID

## SOUTH CROYDON

- ACORN HEALTH CLINIC
- ACUPUNCTURE & HERBAL CLINIC
- AMIN, S
- ANNES BEAUTY SALON
- BRIND, S
- BRYANT, I E
- BURCHELL & ASSOCIATES
- CORBYN, SANJEE
- CROYDON HYPNOTHERAPY
- DALE, ROGER
- DANIELS, INGRID
- EDWARDS, ZENA
- EXCALIBUR
- FOOT CARE CENTRE
- FORSYTH, CHARLES (DR)
- GOODWIN, HELEN
- HARDY, JACK E
- HODSON, D
- HOLISTIC HEALTH CENTRE
- LIVE PSYCHIC LINE
- LU, X
- MEDINATURALS
- MEERAN, M
- MOORTHY, N S (DR)
- OLIVIA, S
- OSTEO CLINIC & HEALING CENTRE
- REES, MAUREEN E
- SCHOOL OF YOGA
- SPINK, F R
- TANSILL, LUCY
- VITA HEALTH ALLERGY TESTING

## STAINES

- A V CHIROPODY SERVICES
- ANDERSON, GILLIAN
- ASKEY, LAURIE
- CHRISTIE, S A
- GODDARD, TERRI
- GRIFFITH-WARD, JANE
- GROVES, VALERIE
- HERB & HEALTH
- HOLLAND-AVERY, H
- HYPNOTHERAPY FOR CHANGE
- MICHIE, CATRIONA
- NASH, LARAINE S
- PARSONS, CHRIS
- STAINES FAMILY CHIROPRACTIC
- TEMPLE, ROSIE
- TREVOR COOK HOMOEOPATHY

## SUNBURY-ON-THAMES

- ALPHA CONSULTANCY
- CARE THROUGH HYPNOSIS
- DAVIS, P R
- DAVIS, TIM
- FEWSTER, DAVE
- FOSTER, ROSALYN
- HEALTH & HARMONY HOLISTIC
- NAT FED OF SPIRITUAL HEALERS
- SIMMONS, R

## SUNNINGHILL

- ASCOT HOMEOPATHIC CLINIC

## SURBITON

- BLOWES, K L
- BLYTH, JOSEPHINE
- DORKING, PAUL
- EVANS, JUDITH
- FEET FIRST CHIROPODY CLINIC
- HILARY, MARTIN
- JOSHI, NICK
- KATHERINE'S THERAPIES
- KOHLER, SUE
- LANGHORNE, CAROLINE
- LARKMAN, K
- MILLER, JONATHAN
- MILLS, STEPHANIE
- NORTHALL, ANNE
- ORIGINAL CUTTING EDGE
- QUINN, P
- RICHMOND-SMITH, P
- RIGAL, M
- SAVILLE & HOLDSWORTH
- SURBITON NATURAL HEALTH CENTRE
- SURBITON PHYSIOTHERAPY
- TEMPLEMAN, C
- TROTMAN, SALLY
- VENTHAM-FRASER, CAMILLA
- WEBB, ROSEMARY
- WILLIS, SALLY

## SUTTON

- AMIN, S
- BACK TO HEALTH - SUTTON
- BARKER, JACQUI
- BERRIE, INGE
- BIGGS, MARGARET
- BIGWOOD, SIMON
- BROUGHAM, PENNY (DR)
- CALLAWAY, PETER
- CHI CLINIC
- CHINESE HERBAL MED & HLTH CARE
- COHEN, MICHAEL
- CORBIN, CLARE A
- CRAVEN, CLAIRE
- CUMMINS, ROZ
- DEREK MOSS THERAPEUTIC MASSAGE
- GOODLIFE NATURAL HEALTH CENTRE
- GRAHAM, P D
- HERVE, JOYCE
- LOFTUS, J
- MIDGLEY & ASSOCIATES
- MORRIS, PETER
- NATURAL HEALING CENTRE
- NATURAL SLEEP FOUNDATION
- NUNN, KATIE
- PATEL, S A
- PEARSON, NINA
- PENWARDEN, DAVID

- PENWARDEN, F
- PRIEST, JILLIAN
- RATTI, D
- ROOTS, HAZEL
- RUDCENKO, H
- RUDENKO, MARIEA
- RUTH WHITE YOGA CENTRE
- SANHAJI, DANA
- SCHOLL CENTRE
- SULLIVAN, MARGARET
- SULLIVAN, MARGARET
- SUTTON ALTERNATIVE HEALTH
- SUTTON CHIROPRACTIC CLINIC
- SUTTON OSTEOPATHY & NTRL HEALTH
- TOWERS, MELISSA
- TRADITIONAL CHINESE MEDICINE
- WALLACE, SARAH S
- WILLSON, AUDREY
- YOGA STUDIOS
- YOUNG, HILARY

### TADWORTH

- DAVIES, MERYL
- HEARN, JUNE
- HEAVEN MOUNTAIN TAIJI QUAN
- HOOD, CHRISTINA
- JENKINS, SARA
- LEWIS, F M K
- MEDICAL HYPNOTHERAPY CLINIC

### TATSFIELD

- TWO STEPS REFLEXOLOGY

### THAMES DITTON

- BATCHELOR, C
- BRABANT HOUSE CLINIC
- BURTON, GEOFFREY
- CHIMES, MAXINE
- COX, SUSAN
- DOUGAN, PAT
- FERRELLY, HELEN
- HALL, LISA
- HOOLE, AVERIL
- JAMOOJI, MEHRU
- LANE, T A
- MARCH, THIERRY
- MOON, EDWARD
- O'DWYER, ANNEGRET
- SAVILLE & HOLDSWORTH
- WHICKER, EILEEN

### THORNTON HEATH

- ASH, GRAHAM M
- BONTHRON, SARAH
- GORDON, SARAH
- MARRIOTT, D A
- MURRAY, C O
- RIDLEY, ANDREW
- UPROOTS HOLISTIC TREATMENT

### VIRGINIA WATER

- WHITELEY, E S

### WALLINGTON

- ALTERNATIVE THERAPY CENTRE
- ALTERNATIVES
- AQUA
- BENEFEET
- CAMPBELL, SEAN D
- CASTLETON, DAVID
- CHRISTOPHER J FANTHOME HYP
- COLLINS, M
- DONALDSON, J F
- HELLON-HARRIS, HUGH
- HINES, STELLA
- LEACH, JANINE
- LEMON TREE TREATMENT ROOM
- MANGAN PETER & CRAVEN CLAIRE
- PSYCHOLOGICAL & COUNS SVS
- SMITH, SUE
- SUTHERLAND, JENNY
- SUTTON HYPNOTHERAPY
- T J'S ELECTRICIAN
- TAYLOR, L
- WELLBROOK CLINIC
- WOLSTENCROFT, B

### WALTON-ON-THAMES

- BARRON CHIROPRACTIC CLINICS
- BLAMPIED ST HILL
- BOSSERT, ELAINE HARRISON
- CLAXTON, VICKI
- DOUGAN
- ECONS, A (DR)
- ENOCK-SHORE, ANGELA
- HAMILTON, A R
- HILTON, DOROTHY M
- HORSFORD, HELENA
- KIRTON, CHRISTINE
- LIFE STYLE NATURAL HEALTH CTRE
- LOMAX, T
- LUBBOCK, R W H
- MCGOVERN, RITA
- MORAN, CARMEL
- NATURAL LIFE AROMATHERAPY
- ORRISS, GEOFF
- SMITH, MAGGIE
- WALTON HOMOEOPATHY
- WEILAND, CRISTINA
- WEILAND, MICHAEL
- WELCH, J

### WARLINGHAM

- ALLERGY CARE
- APPLIED PSYCHOLOGY SERVICES
- BARRETT, ROS
- BASSETT, LESLEY
- DAVY, TERRY
- FOWLER, B R & V A
- WILLIAMS, SONIA

### WEST BYFLEET

- BUTLER & ASSOCIATES
- FOOT MECHANIX
- HASTRUP, ULLA
- KINGSLAND, S A
- O'BRIEN, JANE
- ROSEMOUNT CLINIC OF COMP MED
- WEST BYFLEET PHYSIOTHERAPY
- ZENA CLAIRVOYANT & TAROT READ

### WEST MOLESEY

- MARTIN, HILARY
- NATURAL MEDICINE SOCIETY
- SAMMUT & SAMMUT ASSOCIATES
- TURNER, R E
- WHITBY, LORRAINE

### WEYBRIDGE

- BARNES, A K R
- ENGLISH, D A
- GRAINNE, MULLANY
- HALLIDAY, C
- IMORTELLE
- MCALLISTER, LIN
- MENDES DA COSTA, P J
- OATLANDS OSTEOPATHIC CLINIC
- RAE, M S
- REDCROFT CLINIC
- SANDS, A J
- STILES & ASS
- SUTTON, SUSAN
- WALLACE, SUE
- WEYBRIDGE CHIROPRACTIC CLINIC
- WILSON, SALLY-ANNE

### WHYTELEAFE

- D'ARCY, LARRAINE
- WHITING, JOHN C

### WINDLESHAM

- COOPER CLINIC
- CREMONA, ROB
- DAVIES, PETER
- DUMASIA, HELGA
- NIPA DAS
- SEEKERS CENTRES FOR YOGA

### WOKING

- BAIN, J
- BAIN, J M
- BARKHAM, KATHRYN
- BODY & BEAUTY STUDIO
- BODY CALM
- BONIFACE, SANDRA
- BONIFACE, SANDRA
- BOURNE HEALTH
- BREWSTER, DAVID J
- BRIDGE COUNSELLING CENTRE
- CREMONA, R J
- CROFTON HOUSE OSTEO CLINIC
- FEATHER, A J
- FISHER, NIGEL
- FLEMING, P
- FORDHAM, S
- FRANCES, ROBBIE
- GATEWAYS CENTRE
- HADDEN, ROGER
- HALLINAN, DEBORAH
- HAMBLIN, R
- HEAD, J M
- HENFREY, MICHELLE
- HILLVIEW PHYSIO & SPORTS CLNC
- HOLVEY, L I H
- HOUE, DAVID
- HUDSON, ANNA
- INTEGRAL HEALTH
- JONSON, RONALD
- KENNING, GILLIAN
- LANEY, RANDELL
- LEWIS, B
- LINDSAY, LISA F
- LOUGHLIN, N
- MARSON, JOY
- MARTIN, TONY
- MIRZA, ISHRET
- MIRZA, ISHRET
- OLD WOKING GRANGE
- ORIGINAL WHEAT BAG
- PARKER, CAROL J
- RASMUSSEN, A C
- SALTER, C
- SHEILA
- SHEPHERD, DIANNE
- SUSANNA, LINDSEY
- SUTTON, HELEN
- TEMPLE, JACK
- VAUGHAN, L
- VICTORIA CLINIC
- WHARAM, J
- WHATLING, E P
- WOOD, VALERIE

### WORCESTER PARK

- BACKCARE CLINIC
- BOWRY, HEATHER
- CHAPMAN, SHEILA
- CLEMENTS, J
- DAWSON, GILLIAN
- DE LIMA, RENUKA
- DORCHESTER HOUSE OSTEOPATHY
- GRIFFITHS, C
- HAWKE, J R
- HOGBEN, A
- KANANI, ALPESH
- LIMETREE CENTRE
- LISLE, T
- LYNWOOD PHYSIO & SPORTS
- MEFFAN, W
- ROOTS, HAZEL
- SHERMAN, EDWARD J
- SUE ANN

## SUSSEX (EAST)

### ALFRISTON

- REYNOLDS, MARION

### BATTLE

- ABBEY CHIROPODY CLINIC
- AROMAFIRE
- BROOK, SHEILA
- CLARK, MALCOLM
- COMPLEMENTARY MEDICINE CLINIC
- JEMPSON, NICOLA
- LONDON SCHOOL OF SPRTS MASSAGE
- PAVEL VITEK
- POSTLETHWAITE, CAROLINE

### BEXHILL-ON-SEA

- ANDERSON, A J
- BEXHILL CHIROPODY CENTRE
- BEXHILL CHIROPRACTIC
- BEXHILL CHIROPRACTIC CLINIC
- BEXHILL OSTEOPATHIC PRACTICE
- BUTCHER, P O
- CHARLES, J H
- COX, IAN
- FEIST, ANNE
- GILLMAN, C M
- GRAYLING, N P
- HEALTHWISE
- HULBERT, PENNY

- KENNY, D J
- LA BELLE SANTE NATURELLE
- LEBROOY, W
- LELLIOTT, P E
- MANNING, D J
- SURGICAL CHIROPODIST
- THOMSON, B L
- TRENTER, A E
- VAINES, EILEEN
- WARDEN, J S
- WHITE, CHRISTINE
- WINFIELD, H & D

## BRIGHTON

- ABELL-FRANCIS, NICKY
- ALBION CLINIC
- ALEXANDER, LAUREL
- ALPHA HYPNOTHERAPY
- AMOS, REBECCA
- ANDREW JOHNSON HYPNOTHERAPIST
- ANNE, NINA
- ARDERN FOOT & HEALTH CLINIC
- AROMA HAIR
- ASLING, JULIA
- BACK TO PERFECTION
- BARKER, C
- BAY HOUSE AROMATICS
- BELL, DERYN
- BLACKER, JOHN
- BODY CONTROL PILATES STUDIO
- BOURNE, JOHN
- BRIDGE, DANIEL
- BRIGHTON ACUPUNCTURE CLINIC
- BRIGHTON ALEXANDER TRAINING
- BRIGHTON NATURAL CLINIC
- BRIGHTON NATURAL HEALTH CENTRE
- BRIGHTON PHYSIOTHERAPY CLINIC
- BROOKS, M
- BRUNTON, DEIRDRE
- BUTLER, CHERYL
- CANTERLA, MARGARET
- CHINESE MED & ACUPUNCTURE CTRE
- CHIROPODY SERVICE
- CLINIC OF PHYSICAL MEDICINE
- COCKMAN, MICHAEL
- COOK, ELAINE
- COWEN, E
- COX, JULIET
- COXHEAD, ANN
- CRAIG, MARIANNE
- CREATIVITY
- CRESENT CLINIC
- CULL, BEN
- CULLEN, MARGARET
- CULPEPER
- DOLPHIN HOUSE CLINIC
- DOOLEY, ELIZABETH
- DRURY, GILLIAN
- DYKE ROAD NATURAL HEALTH
- ELITA HEALING DIVISION
- FAIRCHILD, HAZEL
- FIVEWAYS OSTEOPATHIC PRACTICE
- FLOYD, MICHELLE
- GARRARD, J
- GEIGES, STEPHANIE
- GIBBONS, ELAINE
- GLENDINNING, CATHERINE
- GONZALEZ, SOHANI
- GOODWIN, SALLY
- GREENWOOD, J
- GRIMSHAW, R
- HAGGARD, CAROLINE
- HAI TIAN TRADING
- HARMONY PRODUCTS
- HARRIS, ANYA
- HART, RONALD
- HAUTHAL-SLEE, LORE
- HEWERDINE, VICTORIA
- HOLDON, P
- HUBBARD DIANETICS FOUNDATION
- HUGHES, CLARE
- HUGHES-BARLOW, PAUL
- HYSLOP, C P
- INDIAN PALMIST RAI
- ISIS HEALING CENTRE
- JAGO, W (DR)
- JEFFERIES, TREVOR
- JURY, YAEL
- KEEFE, VIRGINIA
- KEEFE, VIRGINIA
- KIDSON, J H P
- KNOWLES, BERNARD
- LANES CLINIC
- LOTUS EMPORIUM
- LOWER, P R
- MANSFIELD, PETER
- MARINE CLINIC
- MCGHIE, PETER M
- MCKEOWN & ASSOCIATES
- MCKEOWN, KAY
- MEADOWS, ERIC
- MIRZA, (PROFESSOR)
- MITRE HOUSE CENTRE
- MOSELEY, ANNIE
- NATURES COMFORTS HEATPACKS
- NEALS YARD REMEDIES
- NEAT FEET
- NINA, ANNE
- PACKER, COLIN
- PATEL, AARAS
- PATEL, AKKIK
- PATHWAYS TO HEALTH
- PAUL MURFIN HYPNOTHERAPIST
- PAYNE, VERONICA
- PENNY, NICOLA
- PHYSIOTHERAPY PRACTICE
- POINTON, RICHARD
- PREECE, ELLA
- QURESHI, SABREEN
- RAWLINGS, MAXINE
- REEVES, ALAN
- REEVES, ALAN
- REIKI MASTER
- ROCK CLINIC
- SANCTUARY COVE
- SANDERS, PEMA
- SANDERSON & ELEMENT
- SCRIVEN, SARA
- SHAH
- SOCIETY FOR THE BLIND
- SPECIALIST HERBAL SUPPLIES
- STILLE, SAMANTHA
- SUNDIAL HOUSE CHIROPRACTIC
- SYDENHAM, T
- TRENCHARD, ABIGAIL
- TROUSDELL, PETA
- TURNER, WENDY
- TYRELL, MARK
- TYRER, PATRICIA
- UPTON, M A
- VAN EMDEN, SUE
- VERRALL, CATHERINE
- WALKER, KRISTINE
- WARD, SARAH
- WEEKS, MICHAEL
- WELLSTEAD, LINDSAY
- WHEEN, WILLIAM
- WHEEN, WILLIAM
- WILBURY SCHOOL-NATURAL THERAPY
- WINFALCON HEALING CENTRE
- WINFALCON'S AURA CENTRE
- WOOD, JOHN V
- WRIGHT, STUART

## CROWBOROUGH

- AMOS, CLAIRE
- BRIGNALL, PENELOPE
- CHAPEL HOUSE CLINIC
- CROOK, ALAN
- CROWBOROUGH CHIRO/COMP HLTH
- CROWBOROUGH COMP THERAPISTS
- DUNN, HELEN
- GRIFFITHS, J
- PLUCKROSE, S N
- RANDELL, KAREN & STEPHEN
- WADHURST PHYSIO/SPORTS CLNC
- WEDLAKE-GRIFFITHS, J
- WRIGHT, JENNY

## EAST HOATHLY

- DADSWELL, CLAIRE

## EASTBOURNE

- ALEXANDER TECHNIQUE
- ALLERGY CLINIC-EASTBOURNE CLNC
- AVERY, N R (DR)
- BARKWORTH & ASSOCIATES
- BODY BENEFITS
- BOTTING, MELANIE
- BRUCE, JAN
- BRYANT, JACQUELINE
- CHEDGEY, PAUL
- CHILD, SARAH
- CHIROPODY CLINIC
- CLINIC OF CHINESE MED & ACU
- COMP THERAPY & TRAINING CENTRE
- CONCEPTS PHYSIO & NUTRITION
- CROSSLEY CLINIC
- CUDLIPP, G
- DAVIES, ANITA
- DAVIES, DEBRA
- DEVLIN, MARGARET
- DUPKER, PAUL
- EAST BOURNE CLINIC
- EASTBOURNE CHIROPODY CARE
- EASTBOURNE CHIROPRACTIC CLINIC
- ESSENTIAL ESSENCE
- FAMILY FIRST
- GENTRY'S NATURAL MEDICINE
- GIBBENS, JOAN
- GREEN ROOMS
- HEMMINGWAY CHIROPODIST
- HEWETT, CHARMAIN
- HICKMAN, MARGARET GRACE
- IONS, ROBERT
- JONES, SHARON
- JOSLING, A
- KRISTANA
- MEWS CLINIC HOLISTIC HEALTH
- MITCHER, D A
- NATURAL TOUCH THERAPY
- OLD TOWN CHIROPRACTIC CLINIC
- PARFITT, A J
- PARKS, L A
- PATERSON, E C
- PHILIP D HOLMES
- PINKNEY, J G
- PRIORY HEIGHTS
- RAMBAUT, ANN
- REFLEXOLOGY FOR HEALTH
- ROSSI, JAN
- SANDERSON & ELEMENT
- SCHOLL CENTRE
- SHARIFI-HOSSEINI, M
- SIMPKIN, JOY
- SKINNER, JEAN R
- SOUTHEAST HYPNOTHERAPY CENTRE
- SPRINGETT, K
- ST ANNES PHYSIOTHERAPY CLINIC
- STEPNEY, NICK
- TOFT, JANE
- UNDERWOOD, MARIAN
- UNGAR, ANN
- UPTON & ASSOCIATES
- VAN HEUVELEN, RON
- WALSH, M J
- WANG, JING
- WOOD, TINA
- WOODWARD, CHRISTINE
- WRIGHT, P A
- WROUGHTON, C J
- YOUNG, JANE

## ETCHINGHAM

- COUSSENS, C A
- HAWKINS, E
- ORIENTAL THERAPY INTERNATIONAL
- PETTMAN, JENNIFER
- WRIGHT, AUDREY

## FALMER

- BRIGHTON HEALTH & RACQUET CLUB

## FOREST ROW

- ASHDOWN OSTEOPATHIC CENTRE
- BRENNAN-JESSON, L
- FOREST ROW HOMEOPATHY
- FOREST ROW OSTEOPATHIC CLINIC
- FRISBY, S
- GOSSET, N E
- HOLDEN NATURAL HEALTH CLINIC
- HOLDENS HERBAL HEALTH
- LAFITTE, J L
- LEIPER, B
- LEWORTHY, M

- LONDON ACADEMY OF ORIENTAL MED
- MACALEVEY, MIKE
- MCCALL, N
- MICHAEL INSTITUTE-SPATIAL DYN
- OAKENFOLD, L
- REFLEXOLOGY CLINIC
- RHYTHMIC MASSAGE PRACTICE
- STRUTT, T
- THOMAS, D E
- TUCKLEY, N
- URQUHART-PULLEN, M
- WALDBAUM, HANNA

## GOLDEN CROSS

- ALLCHORN, MAGGIE

## HAILSHAM

- AMBERSTONE PHYSIOTHERAPY
- BRIARS CLINIC
- COLLEGE OF PHYTOTHERAPY
- DYER, A
- DYER, ERIC W
- FOX, JACKY
- HEATON, J
- HELESFAY-EVANS, JO
- HERB HELPLINE
- MANNING, D J (DR)
- MENELAUS, CHERYL T (DR)
- MEREDITH, C A
- MILLER, TRISH
- MILLS, D
- O'DWYER, MARY
- PARSON, SYLVIA A
- SKINNER, JEAN R
- TYRRELL, IVAN
- WELLHURST GOLF & CTRY CLUB

## HARTFIELD

- HAYWARD, HILARY

## HASTINGS

- ACADEMY OF HOLISTIC STUDIES
- ALEXANDER TECHNIQUE
- ALLEN, CARRIE
- ALTIMES, BERYL
- BAILEY, BARBARA
- BAIRD, DAVID
- BARNARD, SUSAN
- BASSETT, N S
- BEGBIE, GARY
- CHINESE HERBAL MEDICAL CENTRE
- COLEMAN, D T H
- COLEMAN, M C
- COLEMAN, R
- EATON, MARION
- HASTINGS HOLISTIC HEALTH
- HEFFERNAN, EILEEN
- HERBAL HEALTH CLINIC
- HIGH STREET CLINIC
- HOBBS, CHRISTHEL
- HOBBS, SIMON
- HOLISTIC AROMATHERAPY
- LEECH, JUNE & EASTAUGH, MIRIAM
- LEIGH, P A
- LINDA'S AQUA-AURA
- MEADOWSWEET
- MOONCIE, BENEDICT
- MURPHY, KEVIN
- NATURE SUNSHINE DISTRIBUTOR
- NEWHAM, DAVID
- NOAKES, STEVE
- PEARCE, JOAN
- RAINBOW PATHWAYS
- RAINBOW PATHWAYS
- RUMBALL, ALMA
- SANDERS, PETER
- SHIATSU COLLEGE HASTINGS
- TEALE, PAUL

## HEATHFIELD

- ANDREWS, M E
- DALE-ROBERTS, PAULETTE
- GEALL, SUSAN
- HEALING HANDS
- HEATHFIELD CHIROPRACTIC CLINIC
- RICHMOND, G R
- RIHAL, PAMELA
- STEELE, DIANNE

## HOVE

- ANDERSON, JUDY
- ANGELA MATTHEWS HOMEOPATH
- ANSELL, JOHN
- BAMBROUGH, J
- BATCHELOR, R V
- BEAUTY CLINIC
- BELVAIN, E
- BIRD, J
- BRIGHTON & HOVE SPORTS CLINIC
- BRIGHTON CHIROPRACTIC CLINIC
- CHARTER MEDICAL CENTRE
- CHARTERS PHYSIO & SPORTS
- CLINICAL CENTRE OF CHINESE MED
- COGGAN, ABBY
- COGGAN, ABBY
- CONWAY, SUSAN
- CRUICKSHANK-ROBB, S
- DALRYMPLE, S D (DR)
- DODGSON, PHILIP (DR)
- DRIVE OSTEO AND SPORTS CLINIC
- FEATURES OF HOVE
- GOLDSTONE CLINIC
- GOLDSTONE CLINIC
- GORE, JONATHAN & ASSOCIATES
- GREEN, JENNY
- HABERFELD, N
- HAMILTON, ANITA
- HARRIS & ASSOCIATES
- HAWKINS, LUKE
- HERBS KINGDOM
- HOMOEOPATHIC HOUSE
- HOVE CHIROPODY CLINIC
- HOVE CHIROPRACTIC CLINIC
- HOVE OSTEOPATHIC CLINIC
- KELLEY, M P
- KILGOUR, ALEXANDRA
- LAVENANT, M
- LORAM, CHARLES
- MAECHLER, R P
- MAISNER CTRE-EATING DISORDERS
- MATHEWS, ANGELA
- MEDI-CALL ASSISTANCE
- MORRIS, STEPHEN
- MORRIS, STEPHEN
- NOLAN, CAROL
- PEARCEY, M
- PRICE, JAMES
- QURESHI, S
- REDFORD, SARAH
- REEVES, BOB
- ROBINSON, JACQUELINE
- ROMANINI, ADRIANO
- SIMMONDS HERBAL SUPPLIES
- SIRIUS LODGE
- SKIN CLINIC
- THORPE-JENNINGS, M
- TIGER CLINIC
- TISSERAND
- TRANSCENDENTAL MEDITATION
- TRIMED TREATMENT
- TUCKLEY, N
- WELBOURNE, SONIA D
- WILBURY PHYSIOTHERAPY

## LEWES

- BIZONY, STELLA
- BRENCHLEY, NICOLA
- CARTS, K P
- CLARK, M D C
- COLE, B
- CRITERION PARTNERSHIP
- HART, RONALD
- HEAD MASTER
- HEALTH FOR ALL
- LEWES CHIROPODY
- LEWES CHIROPRACTIC CLINIC
- LEWES THERAPY ROOMS
- LINTON, CHERRIE
- LISTENING CENTRE
- NEWICK PHYSIOTHERAPY CLINIC
- PITMAN, LOU
- REES, PAULINE
- RETIEF & ASSOCIATES
- SANDERSON & ELEMENT
- TAYLOR, ANNA
- VALENCE ROAD OSTEOPATHS
- WHIPPY, TESSA

## MAYFIELD

- SAYER, YKKE
- SIMPSON, HEATHER

## NEWHAVEN

- BAKER, SARAH
- DEEKS, STUART
- NEWHAVEN OSTEOPATHIC CLINIC

## PEACEHAVEN

- ACKERS, R S
- CLINCH, ADELE
- COKAYNE, FRANK
- COKAYNE, FRANK
- CULL, BEN
- O'MEARA, WILLIAM J
- SEPHTON, ANN

## PEVENSEY

- JOY, JANET
- PETT, DIANA
- PEVENSEY BAY NTRL HEALING

## POLEGATE

- BARTON, CHRISTINE
- LEEPER, SARAH

## ROBERTSBRIDGE

- BODYMIND
- STOCKDALE, MEL

## RYE

- BROADWATER, ANNE
- CARRUTHERS, P
- CHIROPODY CLINIC
- EAST, MARY EDGINTON
- GATEHOUSE THERAPY CENTRE
- GOLDINGHAM, ROMEY
- HALPIN, P J
- LAVENANT, MAURICE
- LAWRANCE, ELIZABETH A
- LEIGH, P
- RYE OSTEOPATHIC PRACTICE
- STARK, J
- THOMAS, G A
- WINSKELL, HEIDI

## SEAFORD

- BAY HOUSE AROMATICS
- BOWER, V
- BUNCE, J
- BUNCE, S
- COOKE, C
- FOUNTAIN OF HEALTH
- LINCOLN LAWSON, B
- MAW, M
- NATURES NECTAR
- O'MEARA, WILLIAM
- SOUTHDOWN PHYSIOTHERAPY CLINIC
- ST RUMONS HAIR & NTRL HEALTH
- STEYNE HOUSE NTRL THRPY CTRE
- VARA, J & ASSOCIATES

## ST. LEONARDS-ON-SEA

- 1066 SHIATSU
- ANNE BERTOLUZZI REFLEXOLOGIST
- BALCOMBE, WILLIAM
- BUTLER, RAYMOND
- COX, CHRISTINE
- CRANHAMS
- DOIG, B
- DRYDEN, B A
- EDWARDS, BEN
- EVERSFIELD HOSPITAL
- FOUNDATION, ANGELGATE
- GEORGE A BOWDLER CHIROPODIST
- GORDON, REBECCA
- HOLMES, PHILIP D
- HOUGH, ALAN
- ILSLEY, MARY
- KENNY, DESMOND
- KING, LESLEY
- KINGS ROAD CLINIC
- LAIDLAW, PAUL
- PETERS, LIN
- PFEIFFER, MARIANNA
- PINEHURST
- PIPER, C
- PIPER, CLAIRE
- REDDY, ANNE
- ROSAMUND PARKE, JORDAN
- SAVAGE, JUDITH
- SCOTT, SUE
- SHELAGH, MATTHEWS
- SILVERHILL CHIROPODIST CENTRE

- SUSSEX PRIVATE CLINIC
- TRANSCENDENTAL MEDITATION
- WATERS, CHRISTINA
- WEEKS, J

### UCKFIELD

- ASHDOWN CHIROPRACTIC CLINIC
- BUXTED OSTEOPATHIC PRACTICE
- CREIGHTMORE, R & D
- FIELDS OF FRAGRANCE
- GABLES NATURAL HEALTH CLINIC
- GOSSET & HALES
- HALES, DIANE
- HARRIS, ANN
- HAWKINS, M E
- HUMPHRIES, CARL
- MONT, K
- PICHLER, JOHN F
- PRESTON, M E
- RANDELL, K M & S P
- YORK, B D

### WADHURST

- DE TUTE, MARY
- DENNING, JOHN V
- HAMBLY'S
- MEAKIN, R J
- NORTH, SARAH
- ROLLESTON-SMITH, C
- WADHURST PHYSIO/SPORTS CLNC
- WEALDEN WHOLEFOODS

## SUSSEX (WEST)

### ARUNDEL

- AUROMA
- AYRES, M E
- BOWLES, D
- FONTWELL PHYSIOTHERAPY CLINIC
- GADD, A
- MYERS, H
- NUNN, SALLY
- TAYLOR, JAMES M
- WALLACE, R J

### BILLINGSHURST

- BILLINGSHURST OSTEO PRACTICE
- ESSENTIAL HARMONY CLINIC
- HUGHES, SALLY-ANNE

### BOGNOR REGIS

- ANGELA
- ANISE-STAR MOBILE AROMATHERAPY
- AYRES, KATHLEEN
- BATES, K A C
- BATTY, PETER
- BODY CLINIC
- BROCKBANK, N
- CASH, G G
- CLAIRVOYANT - MEDIUM - HEALER
- COBB, ADRIAN
- CONNOLLY COUNSELLING
- CRAFT, DEREK A
- CROOK, D E
- DUNLOP, JOAN
- FELPHAM NATURAL HEALTH CLINIC
- GEARING, JOHN
- GIBSON, NEIL
- HICKS, C
- LOVELACE, KIM PAUL
- MERRIEN, A
- MISSELBROOK, JILL
- REG CHIROPRACTIC CLINIC
- SCHOLEY, PAMELA
- SCUTT, KENNETH I R
- SIMPSON, HEIDI
- SMALLCORN, KAREN A
- STAFF, TREVOR J
- STOTT-DURHAM, ANDREW
- TURNER, JANET
- WISY, CHRISTINE
- WOOD, J G

### BRIGHTON

- MCCORMICK, KITTY
- MCCRORIE, MARTIN
- MURPHY, BOB
- SUGG, BARRY
- TAURINS, ALISON
- TAYLOR, CHRISTIAN

### BROADWATER

- MIND WORK SOLUTIONS

### BURGESS HILL

- A G PUSEY & ASSOCIATES
- ACKLAND, MAUREEN
- BODY MATTERS
- CORNWELL, S
- KIMBLE, A H
- MID SUSSEX CHIROPRACTIC CLINIC
- MID SUSSEX HOMEOPATHIC CLINIC
- MID SUSSEX HOMEOPATHIC CLINIC
- MILLENNIUM STRESS MANAGEMENT
- PARK ROAD SURGERY
- SAMPLE, JUDY
- WALKER, BARRIE
- WARREN, TONY

### CHICHESTER

- AVES, TREVOR (DR)
- BEVIS, J P
- BILLINGTON, P J
- BOHNET, CAROLE
- BRACEY, RON
- BRIGDEN, JENNIFER
- BROWN, GEORGINA
- CARTEY, SARAH
- CHALICE CRYSTALS
- CHAPLIN-SMITH, S J
- CHASE, PETER
- CHICHESTER ACUPUNCTURE CLINIC
- CHICHESTER CHIROPRACTORS
- CHICHESTER HOMOEOPATHIC MED
- CHICHESTER NATURAL HEALTH CTRE
- CHICHESTER PHYSIO & SPORTS
- COLLIER, A M
- COOK, RICHARD
- DAY, BRIDGET
- DEACON, MAX
- DORRICOTT, C J
- DRAPER, MARK R
- EASEN & GAMAGE
- GRIFFITHS & ASSOCIATES
- HAMILTON, A
- HILLMAN, M D T
- HORTON, JONATHAN
- HOUGHTON, K E
- JAYAWARDENA, A A
- KENT, PATRICIA
- LACY, MELANIE DE
- MANN, LESLEY
- MILTON, CHRIS
- NEUBERT, CHRISTINA
- OUTEN, PAULINE
- PAIN & PARALYSIS SPECIALIST
- PALMER, GAYLE
- PALMER, GAYLE
- PALMER, SIMON
- PATERSON, J
- PAYNE, MAXINE
- RICHARDSON, BRIAN J
- ROOM FOR HEALING
- SELSEY TOWN CHIROP/POD PRAC
- SHAW, LENISE
- SIMMONDS, JEAN
- SMITH, BARBARA
- SOUTHBOURNE & FONTWELL
- SPENCER, TERESA
- SPRINGALL, CHERRY
- STURGESS, ELAINE
- TANNER, P T
- TAPHOUSE, K T
- TIZZARD, CHRISTINE M
- WARREN-DAVIS, A
- WILLER, A P
- WILSON, TONY
- YELDHAM, S
- YORK, TIM

### CRAWLEY

- 7C'S EXPERIENCE
- ANABELLS
- BUNGAY, SHERILYN
- CHIROPRACTIC CLINIC
- CLARKE, STEVEN
- CRAWLEY CHIROPRACTIC CLINIC
- EAST GRINSTAED OSTEOPATHS
- ELLIOTT, MAUREEN
- EMINATIONS ACUPUNCTURE CLINIC
- FORSTER, M M
- FURNACE GREEN CHIRO CTRE
- GLENCOURT REFLEXOLOGY
- HERB LEE
- IFIELD CENTRE
- MARCHAL, ALISON
- MCCANN, VICTORIA
- MILES, E J
- MILLS, B J
- OASIS CLINICS
- PALMER, STEPHEN R
- PARKER, J M
- PHYSIO & SPORTS INJURY CLINIC
- RAINBOW BRIDGE STUDIO
- RICHARDS OSTEOPATHIC CLINIC
- SANDERSON & ELEMENT
- SCOTT, JANE
- SETFORD, JAN
- STEPNEY, EVE
- TAYLOR, DAVID
- WORTH PHYSIO/SPORTS CLINIC

### EAST GRINSTEAD

- ACORN CENTRE
- ACUPUNCTURE CLINIC
- ALAN SMITH CHIROPRACTOR
- ANDREW BATHIE PRACTICE
- ASHURST WOOD PRACTICE
- BIOMED INTERNATIONAL
- CHANGES
- COBURN CTRE FOR NATURAL HEALTH
- COFFEY, RICHARD
- COPPEN, J
- DIEBSCHLAG, FRANCESCA
- DORON, LORRAINE
- ELLALLAM, AISHA
- G & G FOOD SUPPLIES
- HUMPHRIES, C
- I C O M
- IRIS RESEARCH & NUTRITION CTRE
- MILLEN, CAROL
- NORRIS, MARIA
- PELLING, K
- PORTLAND PHYSIOTHERAPY CLINIC
- ROBERTS, ALISON
- SHIATSU TOUCH CENTRE
- SILVER GREY CLINIC
- TURNER, JULIA
- URQUHART-PULLEN, MARINA
- YOUNGER YOU

### HAMBROOK

- SHEPPARD, PAM

### HASSOCKS

- FERGIE-WOODS, D (DR)
- GILLHAM, ALISON
- HEELER CENTRE
- HOLDEN, ELFRIEDE
- INTERNATIONAL PSYCHOLOGY SVS
- JENNY, FRANCIS
- PICHLER, JOHN
- VAN EMDEN, SUE

### HAYWARDS HEATH

- A G PUSEY & ASSOCIATES
- ALLERGY SHOP
- ARUNDALE, C
- BALOOMBE OSTEOPATHIC & SPORTS
- BARTON, MARGOT
- BODYGUIDE ALTERNATE
- CHEN, AC C
- CORK, STEPHEN
- CORNWELL, SUE
- DALE, K
- DAWSON, TONY
- DIMITRI-COOPER, CHRISSIE
- EDMONDS, PHILIP
- FARBER, AARON
- GOSSIT, N
- GURNEY, CHRISTINE
- HAYWARDS HEATH NATURAL THRPY
- HILL, JANE
- HOWELL, D B
- HOWELL, N B
- HUGHES, J
- JOHNSON, PAUL J
- LARKIN, JILL
- LEROUX
- OATHALL PHYSIOTHERAPY CLINIC

- PHYSIO & SPORTS INJURY CLNC
- RUDD, STEVEN (DR)
- SEAR, JULIE
- SECRET REMEDIES
- SEVENTH HEAVEN
- STAYNES, I G
- TAYLOR, ELIZABETH
- THORPE-JENNINGS, MARGARET
- TRIANGLE HEALING TRUST
- VININGS NATURAL HEALTH CENTRE
- WHITE EARTH
- WOOD, P D

### HENFIELD

- CORNERWEIGHS
- FRENCH, JULIE
- GOLDEN SQUARE
- SCHOUTEN, ADRIAN
- SCOTT, ELAINE

### HORSHAM

- BARTHOLOMEW WAY CLINIC
- BODYCARE CLINIC
- BRADFORD, S H
- BRITCHIRO CLINIC
- BULL, MARGARET
- CENTRE FOR HYPNOSIS
- CHURCHES OSTEOPATHIC PRACTICE
- DALLAS, PETER
- DAYTON-LEWIS, R
- DURRANT, NICOLA
- FILBY, P
- FROST, CHARLES
- GATES & ASSOCIATES
- GRANT, C B T (DR)
- HALL, N S (DR)
- HEALTH IS HAPPINESS REFLEX
- HORSHAM CHIROPRACTIC CENTRE
- HORSHAM OSTEOPATHS
- JORDAN, J P
- JUPP, DAVID M
- LANE, F C
- LEE, HENRY
- LESLIE, CAROL
- MASSEY, JANET
- MASSEY, JANET
- MAYNARD, MARTIN A
- MCCLARNON, S A
- MILNE, ALEXANDER
- MOLESWORTH, ROGER
- NEW BROOK OILS
- OLIVE BRANCH
- PEREIRA, L
- PHOENIX
- PHOENIX THERAPY CENTRE
- PODIATRY SERVICES
- POTHECARY, I C (DR)
- ROSS, PATRICK M
- ROSS, PATRICK M
- SPORT MOTIVATION
- THOMSON, JEAN
- TOP CENTRE
- WEBB, D F
- WEBLEY, JOSEPHINE
- WESTACOTT, EILEEN
- WILSON, AVIS
- WILSON, CHRIS
- YOUNG, LINDA

### LANCING

- COOPER, J
- GREENFIELD, KAREN
- HARDY, ELIZABETH
- LAUNDON, J
- OSTEOPATHY AT ESQUIRE'S
- VENABLES, SUSAN

### LITTLEHAMPTON

- AVALON HEALTH CENTRE
- BACK 2 FITNESS CHIROPRACTIC
- BOWER, PHILIPPA
- BROADBENT, S
- BROADBENT, SUSAN
- BURNS, J G
- BURNS, L C
- COYSTEN, T
- EDWARDS, SIMON
- FELLOWS, DOROTHY
- FORD, G
- GARDINER, SAM
- JEREMY, SARAH
- JONES, NIGEL
- KAYE, M P
- KEYE, C
- KWENORA HERBAL HEALTH
- LINFIELD, P
- LITTLEHAMPTON NAT HLTH CTRE
- MILLENNIUM HOMEOPATHY
- PEARSON, YASMIN
- SHERWOOD, L M
- SIN MUI CHONG-MARTIN
- VERMETTE, N G
- WALSH, B B
- WARD, SANDRA

### MIDHURST

- LORIAN CLINIC FOR COMP MED
- LOWE, K
- LUFFINGHAM, D & E
- MIDHURST CHIROPRACTIC CLINIC
- NUTRITION & HEALTH
- OSMAN, SARA
- RAVEN, JANE M
- SECRET GARDEN
- STAINTON, USHA

### PETWORTH

- GRAVES, CELIA

### PULBOROUGH

- CALVERT, G A
- JUPP, DAVID M
- MACHIN, KAREN
- MASON, JOHN
- MILLSTREAM MEDICAL CENTRE
- RICHARDSON, JANET
- TRANQUILLITY

### RUDGWICK

- CUTLER, AMANDA

### SHOREHAM-BY-SEA

- ADUR CLINIC
- BATES ASS FOR VISION ED
- BELLAMY PARTNERSHIP
- BELLAMY, ANTHO A P
- CECIL, MARGO
- CHAPMAN, MARILYN
- DAVISON, DAVID J
- GIBBS, LOUIS
- GRAHAM, LINDA
- GRAVILLE, CHRIS
- PITT, KATHY
- POLLARD, SALLY
- PREMIER ELECTRICS
- SHOREHAM PHYSIOTHERAPY CLINIC
- SOBODU, KUNLE
- SULLIVAN, SUZANNE
- TILSLEY, VINCENT
- VAN GEND, KATHARINA

### STEYNING

- CARTLAND, ANN
- CLOCKHOUSE CLINIC
- GREEN, GEOFFREY C
- JOBAIRE, MELANIE
- KINGSLEY-HOLT, MIRANDA
- MARTIN, LYN
- SCRIVEN, SARA
- TUGNUTT, SALLY

### WORTHING

- ACUPRESSURE
- ACUPUNCTURE/CHIRO CLINIC
- ALDRED, HELEN
- ALOE VERA NATURAL HEALTHCARE
- ALSMEER CHIROPODY SERVICE
- ALTERNATIVES
- B O P
- BABBAGE-CLARK, SACHA
- BAKER, E
- BERWICK, MARK
- BLACK, G
- BLACK, PAULINE
- CANNEY, J
- CHIROPODY SERVICES
- CHIROPODY SERVICES
- CLARE'S BEAUTY CLINIC
- CLARK, GERALD
- COOKSLEY, L J
- COOMBES, JOY
- COOPER, JOHN M
- COOPER, SARAH E J
- CRIGHTON, TINA
- DIXON, MARY
- DYER & ASSOCIATES
- EKF PHYSIOTHERAPY SERVICES
- FOGGETT, GLENDA
- FORSHAW, ROBYN S
- FRENCH, M
- GOLDEN SQUARE
- GORING PHYSIOTHERAPY & SPORTS
- HAMPER, JULIE
- HARRIS, PAUL A E
- HENRY HOUSE HYDROTHERAPY CTRE
- HILDER, MONICA
- HILTON, S P
- HOLISTIC THERAPIST
- HOMOEOPATHIC ADVISORY CENTRE
- JONES, J A
- JONES, WENDY
- LAWSON, J A
- LOVEDAY, J A
- MARTIN, J V
- MERRIOTT, SUSAN J
- MIRAGE BEAUTY ROOMS
- NORMAN, CATHERINE
- PATEL, PRATIKSHA
- POLLARD, SALLY
- POOLE, P J
- POTTER, MARK
- RICHARDS, P
- SANDON, PATER H G (DR)
- SCHOLL CENTRE
- SCHOOL OF CHIROPODY
- ST GEORGES OSTEOPATHIC CLINIC
- STAKIM, SHELIA
- STEPNEY, LESLEY
- STEVENS, PAT
- SWAN, LAURIE C
- TYRIE, M
- WALLINGTON, FRANCIS
- WEST, MARCUS
- WHITE, R G D (DR)
- WOOLLEY, LESLEY ANN
- WORDEN, W M
- WORSFOLD, CHRISTINE
- WORTHING CHIROPRACTIC CLINIC
- WORTHING CLINIC OF ACUPUNCTURE
- WORTHING CLINIC OF ACUPUNCTURE

## TYNE AND WEAR

### BLAYDON-ON-TYNE

- COLLIGAN, H
- DENTON, A
- HEDGEFIELD HOUSE

### EAST BOLDON

- HANNEY, D
- MILLS, M

### GATESHEAD

- ABILITY FOR YOU
- ACUPUNCTURE HEALTH POINT
- BARWICK, M E
- FALKOUS, R J
- GATESHEAD COMPLEMENTARY HEALTH
- HEWITT, STEPHEN J
- HOUSE OF ZODIAC
- ISIS AROMATHERAPY
- LAW'S
- NEEPHA
- NORTHERN COLLEGE CLINIC
- NORTHERN COLLEGE OF HOM MED
- OSTEOPATHIC CLINIC
- RICHARDSON, DEBORAH
- SCOTT, K D

### HEBBURN

- COOK, M V
- ECOLIBRIUM
- FOSTER, G S

### HOUGHTON LE SPRING

- CHIROPODY CLINIC
- HAIR & BODY CARE CLINIC
- HYPNOTHERAPY AND COUNSELLING
- NATURAL ELEMENTS
- PATTERSON, R
- STOREY, ADA

## JARROW

- LEWIS, RHODA

## NEWCASTLE UPON TYNE

- ACHILLESPHYSIO
- ACUPUNCTURE & NAT MED CLINIC
- ACUPUNCTURE MOXIBUSTION CLINIC
- ALEXANDER TECHNIQUE
- ANDREWS & DOW
- AROMATHERAPY IN PRACTICE
- AROMATIC
- B WIGRAM HEALING & REFLEXOLOGY
- BAILEY, MATTHEW G
- BAL, NORMAN
- BALMORAL PHYSIOTHERAPY
- BANNISTER, M
- BASS, MIKE
- BIANCARDI, J
- BIOPHYSICAL TREATMENT SERVICE
- BODY BALANCE HOLISTIC THERAPY
- BRAHMA KUMARIS WORLD
- BRENNAN, J
- BROTHERTON & STEVENSON
- BUBBLES
- CARR, R
- CHIROPODY CLINIC OFFICE
- CONNECT PHYSICAL HEALTH CTRE
- COOP, JOE
- CREE PHYSIOTHERAPY CLINIC
- CTRE-CLASSICAL HOMEOPATHY
- DANCES WITH UNICORNS
- DIAS, E
- DOWNEY, P A
- DOWNS, GEORGE
- DYER, RICHARD J
- EARDLEY, D & J
- EDMUNDSON & WHITE-COOPER
- EIGENWELT, AMIDA
- ENDER, BECKETT
- FAMILY CHIRO WELLNESS CENTRE
- FENG, W W
- FITZPATRICK, G
- FOGGIN, SYLVIA
- FORDHAM, BOB
- FOWLER, CHRISTINE
- GINA
- GORDON, CHARLES
- GRAHAM, G S
- GUO, B
- HALLIDAY, J
- HANCOCK, S & NESS, A
- HANNEY, D
- HAYHOE, A D
- HEALTH ALLIANCE CENTRE
- HEAVEN & EARTH
- HERBAL GARDEN AROMATHERAPY
- HIGGINSON, S
- HOLISTIC CHIROPRACTOR
- HON, ARTHUR M R
- HOWARTH, C D
- HOWARTH, D
- HOWLETT & DICKINSON
- JACKSON, APRIL H A
- JAGER THERAPY CENTRE
- JAMIESON, TOM
- LILBURN, JESSICA
- LINDISFARNE CENTRE
- LOMAX, PETER J
- LOUGHTON, ANDREA
- LYNCH, A MASSEY
- MACEOIN, BETH
- MACLAREN, ALISON
- MARCUS, M
- MCANELLY, J L
- MCCARTHY, JANE
- MULLINS, MARJORIE
- MURRAY, DORIS
- NEAL'S YARD REMEDIES
- NEELS AROMATHERAPY
- NEWCASTLE CLINIC
- NEWCASTLE SPRTS INJ/THRPY CTRE
- NORTHERN GUILD-PSYCHOTHERAPY
- ONE HEALTH
- ORIENTAL HERBALISTS
- OSBORNE CLINIC
- PATTERSON, L F
- PEARSON, K J
- PETCH, MARIAN
- POWELL & GILCHRIST
- RITZ CHIROPODIST
- SADLER, RUTH
- SAVOURE, CHRISTOPHE
- SCHOLL FOOTWEAR CENTRE
- SHEN HOLISTIC THERAPIES
- SHIELD CHIROPRACTIC CLINIC
- STEP INTO THE FUTURE
- STEVENSON, G
- STRESS RELEASE
- THOMPSON, N J
- TRANSCENDENTAL MED ASS NORTH
- WALLIS, SHEILA
- WATKINS, ROBIN N
- WEST ROAD CHIROPODY CENTRE
- WHALEY, IAN
- WHYTE, M
- YOUNG, ALEX

## NORTH SHIELDS

- ALLINSON, IAN
- FARTHING, ANN
- HOGG, J S
- MOSS, OLGA
- NEW LIFE NATURAL HEALTH CARE
- RAMSAY & ASSOCIATES
- SANCTUARY HOUSE
- SPORTS MASSAGE CENTRE
- SWEET THYME THERAPY CENTRE
- TEMPLE, BARRIE G
- THERAPEUTIC MASSAGE
- WALKER, LEONIE
- YOUNG, ALEX

## RYTON

- EMMETT, S
- MOORE, M J
- WILSON, MICHAEL F

## SOUTH SHIELDS

- BARBARA
- CARLSON, PATRICIA
- HALL & FORSTER
- MILLS, C A
- THURKETTLE, A D
- WESTOE PRACTICE
- WILSON, DIBALL &

## SUNDERLAND

- ACUPUNCTURE/ANTI-SMOKING CLNC
- BAIN, C
- BUXTON, PETER
- COZANS, EDDIE
- DEBRA DARKE CHIROPODY CLINIC
- DERWENT CENTRE
- DIMMOCK, K
- DOONAN & MCSHANE
- EQUILIBRIUM
- FEEL GOOD AROMATHERAPY
- FRANCIS, A
- GRIMES, JUNE
- HEPWORTH, J P
- INSIGHT
- JOHANSON, CAROL
- KENNERLEY, JUNE
- MARY STREET CHIRO CLINIC
- MILLINGTON, EDDIE
- NATURAL SELECTION
- OAKS PHYSIO & ACUPUNTURE
- OUTRAM, ANDREA F
- PARK LANE CLINIC
- PHYSIO & SPORTS INJURIES
- PIKE, STUART
- SAVAGE, J
- SAVAGE, PAUL
- SHAW, L M
- SHELTON, MICHAEL
- SHUN-TEN HYPNOTHERAPY
- SKILLING, W
- SMITH, R
- STAINSBY, TRICIA S
- WEAVER, K N J

## WALLSEND

- J C A PSYCHIC CENTRE
- WALLSEND CLINIC

## WASHINGTON

- ARCHER, C A
- ASHDALE CHIROPODY
- BEAUTY WITH COMFORT
- LLOYD-WILLIAMS, KATHLEEN
- NATURAL HEALTH
- TANSEY, B R
- WASHINGTON CHIROPRACTIC CLINIC
- WILSON, W

## WHITLEY BAY

- ALOE VERA NATURAL HEALTH CTRE
- ANGELIS
- CLAREMONT FOOTCARE SURGERY
- DAND, A
- JEFFERSON, JOHN
- MCCOLE, D
- OWERS, DONALD M
- RAINBOW, RICHARD S
- REILLY, MERVYN
- ROMER, A C
- SMITH, ROY
- SPIRIT 2000
- STURROCK, T
- WHITLEY BAY CHIROPRACTOR
- WHITLEY BAY OSTEOPATHIC CENTRE

# WARWICKSHIRE

## ALCESTER

- JACKSON, MICHAEL
- KINGS PHYSIOTHERAPY CENTRE

## ATHERSTONE

- DENNIS, L

## BEDWORTH

- BEARDMORE, CHRIS
- CARVELL, B R
- HELEN C OTTAWAY-FOSTER
- MARTIN, R J

## BULKINGTON

- DAVID HOPE PERSONAL DEV

## KENILWORTH

- BRIEF COUNS & PSYCHOTHERAPY SV
- GURR, J
- KENILWORTH CHIROPODY SURGERY
- KENILWORTH PHYSIOTHERAPY
- MARGARET HILLS CLINIC
- NATURES SUNSHINE DISTRIBUTOR
- NEWEY, RACHEL
- PARKES, JOHN
- PURPLE FLAME AROMATHERAPY
- SELLEN, SUSAN
- SMITH, B S
- TALBOT, G M

## LEAMINGTON SPA

- ACUPUNCTURE CLINIC
- ADELAIDE ROAD CHIROPODY CENTRE
- AROMATHERAPY MASSAGE/REFLEX
- BOULTON, A
- BROMLEY, DAVID
- BROWN, V C
- BUCKLE, WENDY-ANNE
- CHINESE HERBAL MED & ACU CTRE
- CLARKE, ROSEMARY
- CLOISTERS
- CREATIVE HEALTH CENTRE
- CULPEPER
- DRAPER, J
- EDWARDS, IRENE & PETER
- FRAGRANT ROOM
- GREEN, ANN
- HEARTLANDS
- HERBAL ONE
- HOLDEN, G
- HOLT, S L
- HOUSE OF RAINBOWS
- HUSBANDS, S
- JUST MASSAGE
- KLEINMANN, SHIELA
- LEAMINGTON SPA CHIRO CLINIC
- LEAMINGTON SPA PHYSIOTHERAPY
- MACWHINNIE, IAN
- MCCAULEY, R
- MULLALLY, K
- MYERS, MARION
- O'REILLY, TREENA
- OSTEOPATHIC PRACTICE
- PERSONNEL DECISIONS INT UK
- PETERS, EVERARD

- PREISLER, TONI TYE
- PRICE, J
- REFLECTIVE PRACTICE
- REVITALIZE
- ROGERS, REBECCA
- SMALLWOOD, P
- SNELL, J
- TE VELDE, JOHANNA
- TRADITIONAL ACUPUNCTURE GROUP
- VAN SCHELLENBECK, JONA-MARION

## NUNEATON

- ANKERSIDE CLINIC
- COLLINS & ASSOCIATES
- CORLET, LOUISE
- DAVENPORT, ANNETTE
- DONLEY, ALISON
- GREIG, E
- HARPER, TOM
- HARRIS, S J
- HAWTHORN LODGE PHYSIOTHERAPY
- HEALING HEART
- HOWARTH, M L
- KALDESIC, J A
- LOOMS, DAVID W
- MALIN, C J
- MARKS, S
- MCKENZIE, GEORGE
- MCKENZIE, PENELOPE
- METFORD, TIM
- NATURAL HEALTH CENTRE
- NATURAL THERAPY CENTRE
- NRTH WARWICKSHIRE NHS CHIROP
- NUNEATON CHIROPRACTIC CLINIC
- ROGERS, JOHN
- SHAWE AVENUE OSTEO PRACTICE
- VERNON, JOHN
- WALLIS, SHIRLEY

## RUGBY

- BA FOR COUNSELLING
- BARRATT'S HOMEOPATHY
- BARROW, P W
- CANALE-PAROLA, AUDREY
- CHURCH LAWFORD CHIRO CLINIC
- CLIFTON OSTEOPATHIC PRACTICE
- COLHOUN, P S
- DEWDNEY, JOSEPHINE
- ELLIOTT, J E
- ELLIS, DAVID
- FERRIER, K
- FRANCIS, JAKKI
- HINDMARCH, ANNE
- LAKHANI, B V
- MANNING, PAUL
- MCCREA, SUE
- MCDERMOTT, T P
- MCLEAN, TERRI
- REED, G W
- RUGBY PSYCHOLOGY SERVICE
- SHERIDAN & AST
- SHIATSU SOCIETY
- WILLOWHERB AROMATHERAPY
- WREN, PAULINE
- WREN, PAULINE

## SHIPSTON ON STOUR

- BIRTWELL, ANDREW
- HOLYCOMBE
- M J BRADLEY - KINESIOLOGIST
- SHIPSTON NATURAL HEALTH CLINIC

## SOLIHULL

- ARDEN HYPNOTHERAPY
- PEACOCK, ALISON
- RUSSELL, COLIN
- VENFIELD, C J

## SOUTHAM

- AOK INSPIRATIONAL
- BREADON, ROBBIE & HAAG, JUDY
- HICKS, KEVIN
- JAMES, HELEN
- REDFERN, JOY
- SMALL, JONATHAN
- STRANKS, KATHY
- TIMBRELL, GAIL

## STRATFORD-UPON-AVON

- ABERCROMBIE, CAROLINE
- AMBER CONNECTIONS
- AVON HOUSE NATURAL HEALTH CTRE
- BOWYER, SARAH
- BROTHERTON, MARY
- CLAYTON, EMMA
- DAVIS, R J (DR)
- EDWARDS, CHRISTINA
- ENGLAND, SUSAN
- FIGHT
- HOLMES, STEPHEN
- HOUGHTON, REBECCA
- KIRK, LAURENCE
- KITCHEN, H J (DR)/KITCHEN, J A
- LAVENDER HOUSE
- LIFE-WAYS
- LOWRY, H M
- MATTHEWS, ROGER
- MCFARLANE, JOAN
- MCTIMONEY CHIROPRACTOR
- NOBLE, J D
- ORCHARD HSE SGY-DAVID MANDER
- OVERTON, PETER J
- PAYNE, JULIE
- PHYSICAL THERAPY CLINIC
- PICKARD, ROBIN
- PYLE, G J
- REFLEXOLOGY CLINIC
- ROBBERTS, VIVIEN
- SAVAGE, GERALD
- SCHOLL CENTRE
- SCOTT, CELIA
- SHAND, GRAHAM
- SHEASBY, DEBI
- STRATFORD ACU & HOLISTIC HLTH
- STRATFORD PHYSIO CLINIC
- WARWICK CONSULTANTS
- WHITE, MARGARET
- WHITE, NICOLAS
- WHYMAN, RAYMOND
- WINTER, JENNIFER

## STUDLEY

- STUDLEY PHYSIOTHERAPY CENTRE
- TOWERS, DIANA

## WARWICK

- FRAGRANT ROOM
- FRANCIS, SUE
- HAYES, CAROLE
- HEALTHPOINT
- HEART OF ENGLAND SHIATSU
- JAN LLOYD AROMATHERAPY
- JONES, CHRISTINE
- MIDLAND ALOE VERA CENTRE
- NATURAL HEALTH CLINIC
- PYLE, M W
- RILEY FLETCHER FOUNDATION
- SINGLETON, ANNE
- TERYLENA REFLEXOLOGY
- WARWICK CHIROPRACTIC CLINIC
- WARWICK OSTEOPATHIC PRACTICE
- WELLAN, J
- WELLESBOURNE HAIR RESTORATION

# WILTSHIRE

## BRADFORD-ON-AVON

- BRADFORD ON AVON CHIRO CLINIC
- BRADFORD ON AVON OSTEO CENTRE
- BRIDGE ST CTRE FOR COMP MED
- INT INSTITUTE OF REFLEXOLOGY
- MICHAEL, DAVID
- MOURANT, JENNIFER L
- NEWTON, KAREN
- SULLIVAN, CHRISTIAN
- WARD, A T

## CALNE

- BOTT, JENNY
- COMFORT, EMMA
- INTERNATIONAL MEDITATION CTRE
- NOTMAN, JACKIE
- PETTIFER, JUSTINA
- PRICE, NICOLA
- RAINBOW NATURAL THERAPIES
- STUBBS, FIONA

## CHIPPENHAM

- ARAGON, HOLLY
- AROMATHERAPY PLUS OIL SUPPLIER
- ASSOCIATES, G B
- EMERY HOUSE CLINIC
- ESSENTIALLY YOURS
- GRAY, J F
- HURRY, GEOFF
- LACOCK PHYSIO & SPORTS
- LUCK, MARGARET
- MAGNO PULSE
- MAYS, ELLIE
- PARK LANE COMP HEALTH CENTRE
- PHYSIOTHERAPY CLINIC
- WALSBY, L

## CORSHAM

- BANKS, RONALD
- SHARPE, SALLY
- THERA-CARE
- WHALLEY, J

## DEVIZES

- ALTREE, CHRISTOPHER
- ASTILL-SMITH, A
- BEST FOOT FORWARD
- BISHOP, S
- CARTER, G G
- CHIROPODY CLINIC
- CROSS, PHILIPPA
- DECLERCQ, LAURENCE
- DEVIZES ACUPUNCTURE PRACTICE
- FOSTER, MARGARET
- GODWIN, E
- GRANT, L
- HUDD, ALISON
- LYNDA
- METABOLICS
- OATS, A J
- PETRAMAN, FRANCOISE
- STOKES, PAM
- WALKER, CHARLOTTE

## MALMESBURY

- MADDOCK, L
- MALMESBURY CHIROPRACTIC CLINIC
- PETER & CAROLINE
- RIGBY, T L

## MARLBOROUGH

- AVEBURY HYPNOTHERAPY PRACTICE
- BROMILEY, MARY
- BURNETT, KIM
- DINNAGE, GERARD
- EUROPEAN SHIATSU SCHOOL
- HEALTH POTENTIALS
- HIGH STREET CLINIC MALBOROUGH
- JEANES, P J
- MARLBOROUGH CHIRO CLINIC
- MARLBOROUGH NATURAL HLTH CTRE
- MARLBOROUGH PHYSIO CLINIC
- MCTIMONEY CHIROPRACTIC CLINIC
- MULTI-THERAPY CENTRE
- PRESTON, MARTIN
- RADFORD, CHRISTOPHER
- SAWAYA, ALICIA
- SKULL, MARK
- SLATTERY, JENNIFER
- WHITING, JENNIE

## MELKSHAM

- BELLRINGER INTERNATIONAL
- CARTER, SHEILA
- DIRECT HEALING
- ROUNDABOUT HEALTH
- TOMS, L S
- WATSON'S COURT CLINIC

## PEWSEY

- PRESTON, MARTIN
- PSYCHOLOGY OF VISION
- SPIRITUAL HEALER

## SALISBURY

- ALTERNATIVE THERAPY CENTRE
- AMESBURY ABBEY CLINIC
- ANNA'S
- AVONBOURNE CHIROPRACTIC CLINIC
- BACON, D A
- BARNES, JONATHAN P
- BOND, D

- BRAS, I
- CHARLES, JANICE
- CHIROPODY CLINIC
- CHIROPRACTIC PATIENTS ASS
- CHRISTOPHER, CLARE
- COOMBS, NICOLA
- COWELL, SARAH
- CULPEPER
- DAVIES, (DR)
- DAWKINS, SUSAN
- DREW, MALCOLM
- DUCKWORTH, ROSEMARY
- DUNKLEY, KITTY
- ENGLISH, JOHN M (DR)
- FAMILY PLANNING CLINIC
- FOSTER, C
- GAPPER, MILES
- GONZALEZ, M A
- GUILDER CENTRE
- HARMONY THERAPY & HEALING CTRE
- HILL, ELIZABETH
- HOWCROFT, M
- HUBBARD-FORD, PATRICK
- HUMPHREYS, J E M
- HUTCHINSON, N
- HYPNOTHERAPY CENTRE
- KERLEY, JEAN
- LAWES, JENNIFER
- LIFE-ENERGIES
- LIKISMA PRESENTATIONS
- LYON, P
- MANNING-PHILLIPS, J
- MILFORD STREET CHIROPODY
- NEVER FELT BETTER
- OLD ORCHARD SURGERY
- ORTON, S
- OSTEOPATHS
- PALMER, LORRAINE
- QUIRKE, G
- SALISBURY CHIROPODY CLINIC
- SALISBURY CHIROPRACTIC CLINIC
- SALISBURY HOMEOPATHY CENTRE
- SARUM PHYSIOTHERAPY CENTRE
- SCHOLL CENTRE
- SILVER, JEANETTE
- SUMMERS, VAL
- TENG, X C
- TILLYER, SUSAN
- TISBURY OSTEOPATHIC PRACTICE
- TRAUMACARE
- WALDER, PATRICIA
- WATSON, RHIAN
- WESSEX OSTEOPATHY CLINIC
- YEATES, JANET A

### SWINDON

- ABSOLUTE BLISS
- ACUPUNCTURE
- AEQUO ANIMO
- ALTERED STATES FLOTATION CTRE
- ANDREWS, HAZEL
- ANGELA'S NATURAL HEALING
- ASTBURY, PENNIE
- AYRE-SNOWDEN, MARION
- BAINBRIDGE, DAVID
- BAKER, JULIE
- BARLOW, CHRISTINA
- BEATRICE ST CHIROPODY CLINIC
- BEST OF HEALTH THERAPY CENTRE
- BLUNSDON ABBEY PHYSIOTHERAPY
- BODY & SOUL
- BOOTH, JANICE
- BOOTH, JANICE
- BRATLEY-ATKINS, MARY
- BRUNSKILL, DAVID
- BUCHAN, DAVID (DR)
- BURGESS, KAY
- CAMPBELL, HELEN
- CARLING, ANNA
- COOPER, JACQUELINE
- COWELL, D E (DR)
- CRACKNELL, ANGELA
- CRICKLADE ROAD PRACTICE
- CRYSTAL CLEAR
- DALE, TILLY
- DARGIE ANDERSON, G
- DEACON, ALISON
- DUFFY, CATHERINE
- EASE MANAGEMENT CENTRE
- ELLSON, S E
- FARRAR, JOHN
- FARRAR, JOHN A
- FIELD, MERIEL
- GOODMAN, LESLEY
- GOODMAN, STEVEN
- GREGORY, K M
- HALE, M
- HALE, MIKE
- HARRISON, SUSAN
- HEALTH HYDRO
- HIGHWORTH CLINIC
- HIGHWORTH PHYSIOTHERAPY CLINIC
- JENKINS, RUSSELL S
- JOHNSTONE, CHRISTOPHER
- KENEE, HAZEL
- LEVER, A
- LOWE, CATHIE
- LUKER, RONALD H
- MACDONALD-INGLE, HAZEL
- MAGIC TOUCH
- MATHER, PAULINE
- MAY, HELEN
- MCKAY, GAIL
- MENIER, BEA
- MERCER, HAYLEY
- MULCAHY, SANDIE
- NATURAL BALANCE
- NATURAL HEALTH CLINIC
- NATURAL HOUSE & BEAUTY CLINIC
- NATURAL THERAPY CENTRE
- NATURALLY NUTRITION
- POWELL, MARTIN
- QUINN, LEN
- RADFORD, C
- RICHARDSON, DIANA
- RIDGEWAY CHIROPRACTIC CLINIC
- SHAW CHIROPRACTIC CLINIC
- SHORT, S L
- SHORT, STEVEN
- SMITH, JOHN
- SPIRITUAL HEALING
- STEELE, GREG
- SWINDON CHIROPRACTIC CLINIC
- SWINDON OSTEOPATHIC CENTRE
- TALISMAN CANDLE
- TAYLOR, CHRISTINE
- TAYLOR, LESLEY
- THERAPEIA HYPNOTHERAPY
- THOMSON, A N
- TILLEY, D S
- TILLEY, DARREN
- TUCKER, C J
- TWINE, IMELDA
- VIRIK, MANJIT
- WALKER, NATASHA
- WAYWELL, PAULINE
- WEST, DAVID
- WILLIS, JANET
- WOOTTON BASSETT
- YERBURY, JACQUELINE

### TISBURY

- OSTEOPATHIC PRACTICE

### TROWBRIDGE

- BIRLESON, G
- BOWEN TECHNIQUE
- CAREER SEARCH
- CASTLE STREET CHIRO CLINIC
- CASTLE STREET CLINIC
- CHARLES, SARAH
- COPLAND-GRIFFITHS, M C
- COUNSELLING & HYPNOTHERAPY SV
- CREEK, N
- EQUILIBRIUM
- FAIRFAX, A B (DR)
- GALLAGHER, ARTHUR
- KENT, JOY
- LACEY, K
- MASON, DAVID
- MENEZES, ROYCE
- WESTBURY REFLEXOLOGY CLINIC

### WARMINSTER

- ACU ASS OF CHRTRD PHYSIO
- 'BACK IN LINE'
- BALL, GREGORY
- CAWDRON, TESSA
- JEANS, SIMON
- MARTIN, ALISON
- MAWDITT, ELIZABETH
- MERE PRACTICE
- MILLBANK, SALLY ANN
- MILLETT-DEW, ROBERT
- NICHOLSON, SHEILA
- RICHARDSON, CHRIS
- SCOTT-MONCRIEFF, C M (DR)
- SHAFTSBURY PRACTICE
- SHAVE, G M
- STEVEN, PATRICIA
- WARMINSTER OSTEOPATHIC CLINIC
- WELLS, HENRIETTA

### WESTBURY

- LEIGHTON REFLEXOLOGY CLINIC
- NATURAL HEALTH
- POLLOCK & SIMPSON
- WESTBURY CHIROPRACTIC

### WOOTTON BASSETT

- WEST, DAVID

## WORCESTERSHIRE

### BEWDLEY

- ANTHROPOSOPHICAL MEDICAL ASS
- BEWDLEY CHIROPRACTOR CLINIC
- HALL, ELIZABETH
- NUTRIMED
- PARK ATTWOOD CLINIC
- WARREN, CAROL

### BROADWAY

- VINE HERBAL PRODUCTS
- YEN YANG

### BROMSGROVE

- BROMSGROVE CHIROPRACTIC CLINIC
- BYWATER, FAYE
- COMPLETE CARE CLINICAL AROMA
- HINKS, MAXINE
- IRVING, GORDON R
- JACK, R A F
- JONES, VAL
- KRISS, ADRIAN D
- PARDOE, DIANA T
- PRIDDY, G
- RELAX THERAPY
- TAFT, FRANCES
- THORNELOE, KAREN E
- TRANCE-FORMATIONS
- WEBSTER, JAYNE

### DROITWICH

- CARYL, M D
- DANDO, PAUL
- DAVIES PODIATRY
- DROITWICH CHIROPRACTIC CLINIC
- DROITWICH KNEE CLINIC
- EDWARDS, J E
- GAIA CENTRE FOR HEALTHY LIVING
- HOGG, BRIAN
- HOWEY, ROSEMARY
- IN THE PINK
- LAMBON, MICHELE
- NATURE SUNSHINE PRODUCTS
- PRETTY, RUTH
- SINGLETON, MARI
- STONE, ANNE L
- YOUNG, JOANNA

### EVESHAM

- AVALON NATURAL THERAPY CENTRE
- BERESFORD, GUY S
- BLENHEIM BACK PAIN CENTRE
- BRETFORDTON CLINIC
- DOWSING FOR HEALTH
- DREW, JOCELYN
- EDWARDS, CHRISTINA
- EVESHAM NATURAL HEALTH CENTRE
- HARTLEY, JANE E
- LEWINTON, EVELYN
- PRIVATE PHYSIOTHERAPY CLINIC
- RICHARDS, VERONICA
- SEDGEBERROW MCTIMONEY
- STEPPING STONES
- SUTTON, M A C
- VALE HOME PHYSIOTHERAPY
- VINE MEWS CLINIC

## GREAT MALVERN

- SPENCER, BARBARA

## KIDDERMINSTER

- AINSLEY, S
- DANDO, PAUL
- EATOCK, J A
- HIGGINS, ADRIAN R
- INDIGO
- KAVANAGH, NIGEL
- KITSON, PAUL
- LOWMAN, V
- MORGAN, M
- MORLEY, M E
- MORRISON, ANTHONY
- NATURAL HEALTH CENTRE
- POWELL, GRAHAM
- POWELL, GRAHAM
- REES, MARGARET
- RICHARDSON, NAOMI
- SHIATSU SCHOOL
- STRONG, SUSAN M
- TRANQUILITY
- WATSON, RHONA

## MALVERN

- ABBEY CLINIC
- ANNE JORDAN CLINIC
- ASTRID, KELLY
- AWAKENING HYPNOTHERAPY
- CAWLEY, LOUISE
- CENTRE FOR HEALTH HEALING
- COLLEGE OF HEALING
- DE ALMEDIA, ALTAIR
- DOIDGE, FRAN
- ELIAS, IAN
- GIBBINS, JONATHAN
- HUBBARD & PERKINS
- KING, A
- MALVERN CHIROPODY SURGERY
- MALVERN HILLS HOMOEOPATHIC
- MALVERN HILLS PHYSIO CLINIC
- MALVERN HILLS REMEDIES
- MALVERN NATURAL HEALTH CENTRE
- MALVERN OSTEOPATHIC CLINIC
- MATTHEWS, SUSAN
- MCTIMONEY CHIROPRACTIC CLINIC
- MILLETT, HUGH
- MILLETT, HUGH
- MORTON, ALEX
- NATURAL BACK CARE CLINIC
- OAKFIELD CLINIC
- PARROTT, C J
- PIKE, S
- PRACTICE WORKS
- PRICE, LYDIA
- PRICE, ROGER
- SANGWAY, DIANE
- SCOTT & THOMPSON
- SHEER, JENNY
- SMITH, K C
- SMITH, M
- SUNRISE CENTRE
- TURNER, MARY
- WHEEL OF LIFE CENTRE

## MALVERN LINK

- NURCHIR
- ORCHARD LODGE CLINIC

## PERSHORE

- GILLIGAN, TONI
- GREEN, PETER J
- M THORLOW CHIROPODY
- PAGE, FAYE
- PERSHORE
- PERSHORE NAT THERAPY CLINIC
- PERSHORE PHYSIOTHERAPY CLINIC
- RIDLER, PATRICIA
- ROBINSON, MIG
- WILSON, DAVID

## REDDITCH

- 1ST CHIROPRACTIC UK
- ADVANCED HYPNOTHERAPY
- ALEXANDER, S
- ALTERNATIVE MEDICINE
- ALTERNATIVE MEDICINE
- BENNETT, LOIS
- CADMAN, STEPHEN
- CENTRAL PHYSIOTHERAPY SERVICES
- CRANHAM HOLISTIC THERAPY
- FIELDSEND, SARAH
- HOLDEN, NINA
- HURLSTON, DIANE
- IRVING, GORDON R
- KITSON, P
- LISON, CAROLINE
- MEAKIN, D W
- R C C M
- REDDITCH CHIROPRACTIC CLINIC
- REDDITCH FOOTCARE SURGERY
- REIKI HEALING BY TRICIA

## STOURPORT-ON-SEVERN

- BUTLER, KAREN
- HOLLOWAY, P
- JACKSON, M W
- JONES, P
- KAVANAGH, N
- MARSTON, SUE
- POOLE, R L
- SZAWEJKO, MARGARET
- WILLIAMS, CHRIS

## TENBURY WELLS

- RHIANS BEAUTY & THERAPY CENTRE
- STOKES, TERRY

## WORCESTER

- AROMACARE
- BACK PAIN & SPRTS INJ PRACTICE
- BAYLEY SCHOOL OF REFLEXOLOGY
- BROOKS, KENNETH
- BURTON, JENIFER
- CANTO, HILARY
- CARTER, SUSAN
- CHILD & FAMILY SERVICES
- CROWNGATE PHYSIOTHERAPY CLINIC
- DAVIDSON, SUSAN
- FAY, PAULINE
- FRONTIA
- GILLIARD, J H
- HARRISON, DAVID
- HOWARD, KAREN
- HUGHES, VANESSA
- JONES, ALISON
- LLOYD, D E
- MERRY, EWEN
- MEYER, ANDREA
- NICHOLLS, JONATHAN
- NOTTINGHAM, STUART
- PSYCHOTHERAPY & COUNS SVS
- ROBARK CENTRE
- ROBERTS, GRAHAM J
- ROBINSON, SUSAN
- SCHOLL CENTRE
- SMITH, AMANDA
- SOUTH WORCESTERSHIRE HYP
- ST JOHN'S PHYSICAL THERAPISTS
- THOMPSON, R D A
- WICKS, DIANE
- WORCESTER NATURAL THERAPY CTRE

# YORKSHIRE (NORTH)

## ACOMB

- S L R HEALTHCARE

## EASINGWOLD

- HOLLAND, G H R
- LESZCZUK, PAULA

## FILEY

- CRICK, PAUL
- HACKNEY, DAVID T
- MILLER, P M

## HARROGATE

- A TACTILE BUSINESS
- AMYRIS ESSENTIAL OILS
- ASHTON SCHOOL OF REFLEXOLOGY
- BARKER, JEAN
- BEAUTY & AROMATHERAPY
- BREARLEY, SYLVIA
- BUSWELL, RONA
- CAMPLING, J
- CASA DELL' AROMA
- CHILD, HILARY
- CHIROPRACTIC HEALTH CENTRE
- CHUTER-KIRK, SAMANTHA
- CLARK, S L
- COFFEY, EILEEN
- COMPLEMENTARY CLINIC
- COOPER, G R
- CREE, TOM
- DAVIES, DAVID
- DAVIS, ANN
- DOVE, L
- EDDLESTON, SUE
- ELLAN, JAN
- FIRTH, SUE
- FRASER, EMMA L
- FROBISHER, LYNDA
- FULLING, JACK
- GARNER, MARGARET
- GASKELL, CATHERINE
- GROOM, C
- HAIGH, ANNA-LOUISE
- HARROGATE CHIROPRACTIC CLINIC
- HARROGATE HOLISTIC HEALTH CTRE
- HARROGATE PODIATRY PRACTICE
- HARROGATE SCHOOL-AROMATHERAPY
- HODGSON, DAPHNE
- HOLMS, JOHN
- HYPNOTHERAPY CENTRE
- JOWETT, R S J
- JOWETT, R S J
- KEANE, ISOBEL
- MILTON HEALTH
- MOULTON, JAMES
- REEL, SARAH
- RHODES, P
- ROBERTS, S A
- ROBINSON, ELIZABETH
- RUSSELL, CAROLINE
- SCHOLL FOOT & LEG CARE CENTRE
- SCOTT-SMITH, CLARE
- SHACKLETON, MAUREEN
- SHARROCKS, LYNN
- SHERWOOD, T A
- SMITH, MARC
- SMITH, PAM
- STANCOMBE, H
- STEAD, SUSAN
- STOLLARD, R D
- TIDSWELL, SUSAN
- WOLSTENHOLME, SHEILA
- WOODIER, A

## HAWES

- LARKIN, H

## KNARESBOROUGH

- COPE, KAY
- ELLIOTT, JUDITH
- ELLIOTT, KATHRYN L
- HIGGINS, I
- NATURAL BALANCE
- ROWAN TREE CENTRE
- SLR HEALTHCARE
- TUCKER, KATH

## LEYBURN

- AVISON, RITA
- NAISH, P

## MALTON

- BEVERLEY, SHEILA
- RYEDALE CLINIC

## NORTHALLERTON

- CENTRE FOR NATURAL HEALTH
- CROFT HOUSE CLINIC
- DAVIES, S M
- FORCE CENTRE
- METCALFE, MANDY
- MORTIMER, HANNAH
- MORTON, P J
- MUDDLE & ASSOCIATES
- NEEDHAM, P E
- NORTHALLERTON PHYSIOTHERAPY
- RATHBONE, DONNA
- SCOTT, KATHY

## PICKERING

- FORSHAW, VERONICA
- MINISTER, COLIN
- NETHERCLIFT, CAROLYN
- SI SHEN CLINIC

## RICHMOND

- ACUPUNCTURE CLINIC
- BARLOW, GAIL
- HESCOTT, J D
- HOBSON, I K
- KERNOHAN, SARA
- MUDDLE & ASSOCIATES
- PHYSIOTHERAPY TREATMENT CLINIC

## RIPON

- BARNES, JACQUI
- BURTON, JOAN
- CHINESE THERAPY CLINIC
- CHINESE THERAPY CLINIC
- COOKE, E M
- JONES, J A
- RIPON COMP THERAPY CENTRE
- RIPON NATURAL HEALTH CENTRE
- SERMON, C
- WATERWORTH, JANE
- WATTS, LOUISE

## SCARBOROUGH

- ACUPUNCTURE/NATURAL THERAPY
- BARRASS, K I
- BELL, C M
- BROADHEAD, J N & M
- CHIROPRACTIC CLINIC
- CORDEL, MICHAEL
- CULLEN, T C
- DIXON, HEATHER
- EVETTS-SECKER, JOSEPHINE
- INTEGRATIVE COLLEGE
- MARRIOTT, HELEN
- NATURAL ALTERNATIVES
- NELLIS, RAYMOND
- PEGG, M G
- PROUDFOOT SCHOOL
- PROUDFOOT, WILF
- PSYCHOTHERAPY & COUNSELLING SV
- RADFORD, CAROLE A
- RATCLIFFE & STINSON
- STATHER, M
- THOMPSON, CAROLINE
- WHITE, CHARLES
- WILLERTON, A

## SELBY

- ANGEL THERAPIES
- DEAN, KATHY
- KNIGHT, SYLVIA
- MALTINGS PHYSIO & CHIROPODY
- ROWNTREE, D
- SELBY PODIATRY CENTRE
- SMITH, ANNE C
- TOP-TO-TOE HEALTH & BEAUTY
- WHEELER, J

## SKIPTON

- APOTHECARY 2
- AVENA HERBAL PRODUCTS
- BIRRAN, VERONICA
- BULLOCK, WILLIAM
- CRAVEN CLINIC
- MELLOW MOMENTS
- PERSAUD, PENNEY & PARTNERS
- PRIVATE CTRE-CRISIS PSYCHOLOGY
- SHANKS, S C
- SKIPTON CHIROPODY CENTRE
- SKIPTON PHYSIOTHERAPY CLINIC
- SMITH, C J

## SUTTON-ON-THE-FOREST

- WALLACE, GENEVIEVE

## TADCASTER

- BARLOW, J A
- HELSDON, E S

## THIRSK

- CTRE FOR HEALTH/PASTORAL CARE
- HOLMFIELD
- LEARNIT
- MUDDLE & ASSOCIATES
- PAULA LESZCZUK
- THIRSK CHIROPRACTIC CLINIC
- WING, BARRY

## TORQUAY

- FILEY THERAPIST

## WHITBY

- APOTHECARY
- BLACK, SAUL
- GRIFFIN, TRICIA
- NATURAL ORIGINS
- NATURAL THERAPIES
- PAGE, F T
- PHILLIPS, L
- ROSE, MARTIN J

## YORK

- ACOMB CHIROPRACTIC CLINIC
- BAKER, LINDA
- BARNARD, SIMON
- BLACKWELL, Z
- BOROUGHBRIDGE
- BRONZE DRAGON HOLISTIC CENTRE
- BULINSKI, JAN
- BURNS, K P
- CARE FOR YOUR HEALTH
- CHIROPODIST
- CULPEPER
- DAIRY PSYCHOTHERAPY
- DANBY, CAROL
- DOVE COURT CENTRE
- EASY WAY YORKSHIRE
- ESSENTIAL THERAPY
- FERGUSON, A J
- FIELD, ROWENA
- GOOCH, GILL
- GRAVELLS, M
- GRIFFITHS, SAIDA K
- HAMLYNN HEALTH
- HAXBY & HUNTINGTON ACUPUNCTURE
- HAXBY CHIROPRACTIC CLINIC
- HEALING CLINIC
- HERBGARDEN CHINESE MED CTRE
- HEWORTH CHIROPODIST CLINIC
- HIGHTHORN PHYSIOTHERAPY CLINIC
- HOBBY, B
- HOLLINGWORTH, SUSAN
- HOMOEOPATHIC CLINIC
- HOMOEOPATHIC CLINIC
- HOWELL, SHIRLEY
- HUGILL, JULET
- HUYTON, CHRISTOPHER P
- JONATHANS
- KEEFER, W B
- KNOWLES, J
- LACKFORD, M
- LADY FAYRE
- LAZENBY, D
- LESZCZUK, PAULA
- LIFESUPPORT
- LONG, SUSAN
- MACARTHUR, T
- MACARTHUR, T
- MACHADO, LOUISA
- MCARTHUR, JILL
- MOHAMMED (PROFESSOR)
- MORRISON, L
- MORRISON, L
- MORTON, PETER J
- NANCY METCALFE MOBILE CONSULT
- NATURAL CHOICE
- NATURAL ENERGY HEALTH SERVICES
- NORTHERN COLLEGE OF ACU
- NORTHERN COLLEGE OF ACUP
- PANACEA ACUPUNCTURE CLINIC
- PARSONS, J
- RILEY, S
- RILEY, S
- ROOK, MARY
- RUDD, J
- SCHOLL CENTRE
- SETCHFIELD, WENDY
- SHAH, ATUL
- SHEEHAN, NICHOLAS
- SMITH, YVONNE
- SNELSON, KAREN
- STRATTON, FIONA
- TAKE IT EASY
- TERRY ANNE
- TRANQUILITY
- TUKE CENTRE
- WARDELL, A A
- WATSON, J
- WEATHERSTONE, M
- WELL BEING CLINIC
- WOOLFSON, L J
- WRIGHT, T
- WYLDBORE, VICTORIA
- YOGA FOR ALL
- YORK CHIROPRACTIC CLINIC
- YORK CLINIC
- YORK CLINIC FOR COMP MEDICINE
- YORK COUNSELLING
- YORK HEALTH SERVICES NHS TRUST
- YORK NUTRITIONAL LABORATORY
- YORK PHYSIOTHERAPY PRACTICE
- YORK PSYCHOTHERAPY CLINIC
- YORK SCHOOL OF COMP MEDICINE
- YORVIK CHIROPRACTIC CLINIC

# YORKSHIRE (SOUTH)

## BARNSLEY

- AETHERIUS SOCIETY
- AROMATHERAPY MASSAGE
- AROMATICS
- AZAB, M
- BANERJEE, R K
- BARBER, SMITH & ASSOCIATES
- BARNSLEY CHIROPRACTIC CENTRE
- BEAUMONT, SUSAN LAW
- BRANKIN, K
- BRANKIN, M & K
- BRANKLIN, M & K
- CARTWRIGHT, CECILIA
- CHARLESWORTH, M
- CUSWORTH, L E
- DENTON, KATHRYN
- ECHOS CENTRE
- EWINGS, D V
- EXECUTIVE SUITE
- FIRTH, J
- FOSTER, E H
- GAIA HEALTH
- HOLLAND, GLENYS
- JOHNSON, STUART
- KEITH LINLEY HYPNOTHERAPY
- KING, HEATHER
- MELLOR-FRITH BRIDGET
- QUIESSENSE
- RADFORD, CATHERINE
- SPIRITUAL & HEALING CENTRE
- SULLIVAN, J L
- THOMPSON, D
- TRIGG, REBECCA
- WARREN HOUSE CHIRO CLNC
- WELLFOODS
- WHITE, JANET
- WILSON, JOHN PAUL
- WOMBWELL ACUPUNCTURE CLINIC

## DONCASTER

- A 1 ALOE VERA CENTRE
- AARON ABBEY HYPNOTHERAPY
- ALTERNATIVES
- ALTON, C R
- AROMATHERAPY & MASSOLOGY CLNC
- ASSOCIATION OF STRESS MNGMT
- BANI, SUSAN
- BANI, SUSAN
- BAWTRY PHYSIOTHERAPY PRACTICE
- BEDFORD, SUSAN
- BILBE, MARIANNE
- BONESETTER AND MANIPULATOR
- BOSTWICK, B
- BROADBENT, KARL
- BURTON, MAUREEN
- CLARK, L A
- COMPLEMENTARY THERAPY CLINIC
- CONISBROUGH CENTRE
- COOPER, JAMES
- CORTON, JOHN
- DAVIES, BARBARA
- DONCASTER CHIROPRACTIC CLINIC
- DONCASTER PHYSIO & SPORTS
- DOVESTONES HEALING CENTRE
- DUFFIELD, G
- ECOGENIX BODYCARE
- ESSENCE OF HEALTH THERAPIES
- ESSENTIALLY YOURS
- FIRBANK, KENNETH A
- GAINES, GWEN
- GEORGINA'S

- HAIR, LOUISE
- HALL, KEN
- HALL, SHEILA
- HOLLAND, GLENYS J
- HYPNOTHERAPY CENTRE
- INJURY TREATMENT CLINIC
- J J CREDLAND CHIROPODIST
- JABBAR, ABDUL
- JACKSON, W D & SONS
- JAVIAD, M A
- KELLY'S FOOTCARE
- LLEWELLYN CONSULTANCY
- LLEWELLYN, TAM (DR)
- LOWTHER, MAVIS
- MARSDEN, P
- MASON, A
- MCGUIRE, MICK
- MIDDLETON, AUDREY
- NATURAL HEALTH CLINIC
- NEILL, R
- OADES, JANET
- PARK, N
- PEAT, J
- PORTER, CHRISTINE
- PRENDERGAST, LILY
- RONCIA INSTITUTE OF HYPNOSIS
- SCHOLL CENTRE
- SHELTON, JANE
- SIMPSON, SARAH E
- SMITHSON, J
- STURMEY, GRAHAME
- TANNER, MICHELLE
- TAYLOR, BERYL
- THORNE ROAD CHIROPRACTIC
- VAUGHAN, JANET
- WALKER, SUE
- WHITE HOUSE PHYSIOTHERAPY
- WOOD, TRACEY
- WOODS, LEONIE

## MEXBOROUGH

- CLAYTON'S
- DONNELL, N
- DRIVER, M
- HOLLAND, A G
- HYDE, PHILIP
- SWINTON HEALTH CENTRE
- WILLEY, STEPHEN

## ROTHERHAM

- ANDERTON, NORAH
- BARRIE, S C
- BRITISH SOC OF MED/DENT HYP
- CHIROPRACTIC CLINIC
- COUNTRY PRACTICE
- ELIZABETH BECK CHIROPODY
- GLEADALL, A D
- GRAYSON, C M & R J
- HAIGH, J
- HERBAL HEALTH
- HIMSWORTH, V
- KALM PHYSIOTHERAPY SERVICES
- KILVINGTON & ASSOCIATES
- LAISTER, MARTIN
- LAISTER, MARTIN
- M & B SERVICES
- MOORGATE NATURAL HEALING CTRE
- NIGHTINGALE PHYSIO PRACTICE
- PARK REHABILITATION CENTRE
- RICKARD, CLIVE
- ROBINSON, C
- ROBINSON, KAY
- ROTHERHAM HEALTH CHIR DEPT
- ROTHERHAM HYPNOTHERAPY CLINIC
- ROTHERHAM PRIORITY HEALTH
- ROTHERHAM PRIORITY HEALTH
- SEYBOTH, PAT
- SMITH, ALAN
- STEWART, HILARY A
- WARD CHIROPRACTIC
- WARD, G
- WELSH CHIROPRACTIC
- WHITEING, J P
- WIGGINTON, P R
- YORKSHIRE NEUROLOGY CLINIC

## SHEFFIELD

- ALOE VERA FOREVER LVNG PRDCTS
- ALTON & JAMES MED HERBAL
- ANDERSON, A DUDLEY
- ANGEL HEART CENTRE
- APHRODITE'S
- AROMATHERAPY
- AYERS, WENDY
- BANKS, M H (DR)
- BATTLE, J M
- BELLAMY, YVONNE
- BENDLE CALDER
- BIGG, V
- BIRCH, SONIA Y
- BISHOP, N
- BLUFF, ANN
- BOON, G M
- BOORMAN, JUNE
- BRADWAY COMP THERAPY CENTRE
- BRAHMA KUMARIS MEDITATION CTRE
- BRAMLEY HALL CLINIC
- BROOMHILL CHIROPRACTIC CLINIC
- BROOMHILL MEDICAL CENTRE
- BURKE, PAUL E
- BUXTON, ANNE
- C I M TEST PUBLISHERS
- CALVERT, S M
- CARDEW & ASSOCIATES
- CARING CLINIC
- CENTRAL HEALTH CLINIC
- CHIA, G R
- CHIRON
- CHIROPODY SURGERY
- CLAIRE LOUISE
- CLAIRE LOUISE
- CLARK, KATHRYN
- CLARKE, C
- COOPER, BARBARA
- CORNCROFT
- COX ASSOCIATES
- CRESCENT MOON
- CREWE, G
- CROOKES ACUPUNCTURE CENTRE
- CROWDER, E M
- CULLEN, FRANCESCA
- CULPEPER
- DELFOSSE, PATRICIA
- DICKINSON, KATE
- DONNELLY, LUCY
- DONNELLY, PAUL
- DORE PHYSIOTHERAPY PRACTICE
- DR K P BURNS & ASS
- EATON, T C
- ESSENTIAL HARMONY
- FIELD, RICHARD
- FISHER, CHRISTINE A
- FISHER, PAUL
- FLATT, JUNE
- FLYNN, FRANCESCA
- FOOTHOLD REFLEXOLOGY
- FRANKS, PAUL
- GESTALT PSYCHOTHERAPY
- GIBBONS, JUNE
- GOODWIN, JO
- GORNEY, C
- GRAPEVINE HEALTH
- GRAY, W R
- GREENWAYS NATURAL HEALTH CTRE
- GRENOSIDE PHYSIOTHERAPY
- GYALTSABJE BUDDHIST CENTRE
- HALLAM CHIROPODY CLINIC
- HALLAMSHIRE NATURAL HLTH CTRE
- HALLAMSHIRE PHYSIO/SPORTS CTRE
- HAMMOND, DIANNE
- HANDSWORTH CHIROPRACTIC CLINIC
- HARTLEY, S
- HEALING CENTRE
- HEALTHY FEET
- HERBAFAYRE
- HILLSBOROUGH HEALTH CENTRE
- HINCHLIFFE, JACKIE
- HIRST, FIONA
- HOPE, DAVID
- HOPE, J A
- INGLES
- INSTITUTE OF CHIROP & POD
- IRVINE, ALAN
- JARMAN, RON
- JESSIE
- JOHNSON, A
- JOHNSON, SARAH
- JOWSEY, J E
- JUNE, LUCINDA
- KILLAMARSH OSTEOPATHY PRACTICE
- KINESIOLOGY FEDERATION
- KIRBY, M
- LA CREME HAIR & BEAUTY
- LANGSLEY, T
- LAWS, VICKY
- LEVICK, JENNIFER
- LOTUS CLINIC
- MACNEILL, E M
- MARHSALL, E
- MARK, ELLISON
- MARTIN ST JAMES THERAPY CTRE
- MAULE, A A
- MEDICAL HERBALIST
- MERSH, J M
- MILLINGTON, JANET
- MOORE, C
- MOSBOROUGH PHYSIO & SPORTS
- NATURAL THERAPY CLINIC
- NOBREGA, M J N
- NOLAN, JOHN
- O'NEILL, LIZ
- ORAM & ASSOCIATES
- PACKER, RACHEL
- PALMER, E J
- PAUL BOIZOT AROMATHERAPY
- PAUL BURKE ASSOCIATES
- PAWSEY, SUSAN
- PENISTONE
- PENISTONE PHYSIO/CHIROP CTRE
- PIKE, RALPH
- REANEY, L
- ROBERTS, JILL
- ROGERS, ALISON
- ROSTED, P
- SAVILLE, KATHY
- SEASONS BEAUTY CENTRE
- SEVEN HIGH STREET THERAPY CTRE
- SHARE PSYCHOTHERAPY AGENCY
- SHARRON CHIROPODY CLINIC
- SHEFFIELD CHIROPRATIC CLINIC
- SHEFFIELD NATURAL HEALTH CTRE
- SHEFFIELD SCHOOL OF BEAUTY
- SHEPHERD, CLARE
- SHEVILLS, JERRY
- SHIATSU PRACTITIONER
- SNOW, DAVID
- SPEAR, F G
- STANDERING, A
- STEELE, A M
- STONES, KAREN
- THOMPSON, KIM
- UK CARE PRODUCTS
- VINSON, CAROL
- WAINWRIGHT, COLIN
- WAINWRIGHT, DAVID
- WAITE, J
- WATTERSON, GEOFF
- WEAVER, ROBIN
- WELLFORCE
- WHITE HOUSE MEDICO-LEGAL
- WHITE HOUSE PHYSIOTHERAPY
- WHITE SPACE
- WHITE, ANN
- WHITE, EDWARD
- WHITEHOUSE CONSULTANCY
- WICKER HERBAL STORES
- WICKER HERBAL STORES
- WILCOX, MARK
- WILLIAMS, ANNIE
- WILLIAMSON, I M
- WOOD, J

# YORKSHIRE (WEST)

## BATLEY

- AMETHYST HEALING CENTRE
- BOWEN TECHNIQUE
- ELLIS, G R
- HODGE CHIROPODIST
- HOM/ACU PRACTITIONER
- MOLONEY, KATE
- POPPLEWELL, MARK
- TAYLOR, SUSAN
- TEALE, PAT

## BINGLEY

- AROMA BLISS

- BINGLEY HOMOEOPATHIC PRACTICE
- BRAMIN CLINIC
- CHIROPODY CLINIC
- KNISZ, P
- KUNZ, RICHARD
- LANCELOT, M M
- SHARP, DOROTHY

## BRADFORD

- ABBEY HILL & ROBSON
- AKHTAR, J
- ALLSOP, A
- AROMAHEALTH
- ATKINSON, MAURICE
- ATTIC OFFICES
- AVA-CLAIRVOYANT
- BARKHILL OSTEOPATHIC CLINIC
- BEAUTY SPOT
- BERRY, M E
- BRADFORD CHIROPODY & BIO CLNC
- BRADFORD CHIROPRACTIC CLINIC
- BRADFORD PSYCHOTHERAPY & COUNS
- BRADLEY, JUDITH A
- BRADLEY, MICHELLE
- CHAMPANERIA
- CHAMPANERIA, S K
- CITY CENTRE THERAPISTS
- CLEMIT, MIKE
- CRABTREE, JANET
- DAVIES, J C
- DESIGNING CHANGE
- DIMASCIO, CHRISTINE
- DOUGLAS, O A
- ETHERINGTON, B
- FITZROY PARTNERSHIP
- FLOURA, H S
- HEATH ROYD GARDEN PRACTICE
- HEENAN, M C
- HOBSON, ANNE
- HOLLINGS, KATH
- HOLT, R
- HOMEOPATHIC MEDICAL PRACTICE
- HOMOEOPATHY ONLINE
- HOWDEN, LINDA
- HYPNOTHERAPY CENTRE
- IDLE AROMATHERAPY
- J & J HARROP
- KANG DA CLINIC
- KAYE, COLIN
- KEIGHLEY, S J
- LEECE, M
- LEEMING, C
- MORGAN, J D
- MORNINGTON PHYSIOTHERAPY
- ODSAL HEALTH CENTRE
- PADGETT, NATALIE
- PURPLE HAZE
- QUEENSBURY PHYSIO PRACTICE
- RAINTREE HEALTH
- RENJI CHINESE MEDICINE CENTRE
- ROBINSON & SONS
- RUTH, GORDON
- SCHOLL CENTRE
- SHACKLETON, JOHN A
- SHERQIA, DARULSHAFA
- SUEN, J
- SWITALA, F (DR)
- TORNTON, HOWARD
- WALLACE, ALICE
- WEST YORKSHIRE CLINIC
- WEST YORKSHIRE PHYSIO CENTRE
- WHITLEY CLINIC FOR HEALING
- WHITLEY, JILL
- WILLIAMS, B

## BRIGHOUSE

- BIBBY, JANET
- BROOKS, V L J
- CHOPPEN, M
- FIGURA, CATHERINE MARIA
- HARRISON, R G
- INDULGENCE
- RELATIONAL THERAPY
- SANDY, I M & A N
- SYKES, KAREN

## CASTLEFORD

- BENNETT, GINETTE
- DREWITT, ALAN J
- EARNSHAW, P
- INNER CALM
- JDS
- SMITH, JANET
- TAYLOR, ANTHONY B

## CLECKHEATON

- CHOICE AROMAS
- EVERETT, G W
- GRANGE CONSULTING ROOMS
- KINNAIRD, F M
- RUMBOLD, C G
- SWIFT, CAROL I
- THERAPY CENTRE
- TRICHOLOGIST

## DEWSBURY

- BARRY WEST ASSOCIATES
- BROWN, DEBRA
- FLOWERS AROMATICS
- GRAY, ALAN
- HEMINGWAY, I
- LAVENDER ROOMS
- LAVENDER ROOMS
- MAZURKE, B A
- MEESON, LINDA
- MEGSON, BARBARA
- O'KELL, DAVID S
- SURGERY

## ELLAND

- BUPA HOSPITAL ELLAND
- PARKS, HILARY
- WALKER, KEVIN C

## GARFORTH

- WARING, D

## HALIFAX

- A BARCHAM REFLEXOLOGY
- ACTIVE MINDS
- AMBERGRIS
- APPLEYARD, J
- AROMATIX
- BAXTER, A
- BECKETT, V C
- BEST, S
- BOWCOCK, HELEN
- BOYD HYPNOTHERAPY
- CARRIE, CLARE
- COYLE, DAVID
- CROFT CLINIC
- CROSS, ANDREW
- CUNNINGTON, A
- DOYLE, D R
- DRURY, WENDY
- FORTON, LINDA
- GLEDHILL, RACHEL
- HALIFAX CHIROPODY CENTRE
- HALIFAX CHIROPRACTIC CLINIC
- HALIFAX CLINIC OF NATURAL MED
- HEAL ANN CARE
- HEATH MOUNT PHYSIOTHERAPY
- HEATON, BARBARA
- HINCHCLIFFE, SUSANNE
- HOMEOPATHY FOR CHILDREN
- JACKSON, ROGER D
- JONES, PAT
- JOYNES, IAN
- LEEMING, C
- LIGHTBODY, STEWART
- LUMB, JANE
- NEW ROAD SPORT & REMEDIAL
- OWENS, PAULINE
- PEDIWEAR SHOE CENTRE
- PENNINE INS-PSYCHOTHERAPY
- PENNINE NATURAL HEALING CENTRE
- RAWSON, JUDITH
- RHODES, J D & E M
- SLADDIN, ANGELA J
- SLATER, JULIA
- SPENCE, SYLVIA
- STEVEN, PAUL
- STOCKS, CHRIS
- SWAINE, PAULA
- SWAINE, T
- SWIM GYM
- SYKES & ASSOCIATES
- THORPE CHIROPODY
- TUEL LANE PHYSIOTHERAPY CLINIC
- TUNE, VICTORIA
- VICTORIA CLINIC
- VINCENT, JOAN
- WIDDOP, JANET
- WIDDOPP, BRIAN
- XANADU BEAUTY & THERAPY CLINIC

## HARROGATE

- EQUA-LIBRA

## HEADINGLEY

- LEEDS COUNSELLING & PSYCHO SVS
- LEEDS PSYCHOTHERAPY SERVICES

## HEBDEN BRIDGE

- ALCHEMY FOUNDATION
- BACON, JOELLE
- BLACKBURN, SUSAN
- CLEGG, N A
- GOODWIN, SUSAN
- HAMNETT, SHEILA
- HEBDEN BRIDGE CENTRE
- HEBDEN BRIDGE CHIROPODISTS
- HEBDEN BRIDGE-REG CHIROP
- HOPE HEALING CLINIC
- KINGFISHER HOL HEALING CTRE
- LANDALE, J B (DR)
- LOWE, RACHEL
- MOORE, J
- MOORFIELD FLOATATION
- OAKLEY, IAN
- SHEPARD, BARBARA

## HECKMONDWIKE

- RICHARDSON CLINIC

## HUDDERSFIELD

- ADVANCED FOOT THERAPY
- ALLENS
- AROMATIX
- ASH, STACEY
- ASH, STACEY
- ASPEN CLINIC
- BODY ESSENCE
- BUCKLEY, MAUREEN
- CHINESE MEDICINE RENJI CLINIC
- CLOWES, M
- COMMONSCENTS
- CORLETT, D A (DR )
- COSGROVE, CORRINNE
- CROWE, A
- DEPARTMENT OF FOOT HEALTH
- DODSON, E S P
- ELECTROLYSIS CLINIC
- ELLIS, ELIZABETH
- ESSENTIAL HEALTH
- FEET FIRST CHIROPODY
- FIXBY OSTEOPATHIC PRACTICE
- FORD, SUSAN
- HALL, KATHRYN
- HAMLETT, ANN
- HEART & SOUL
- HILL, PETER J
- HOLLYBANK NATURAL HEALTH CTRE
- HOLME VALLEY CLINIC
- HOLME VALLEY SPORTS CLINIC
- HOLMFIRTH PHYSIO/SPORTS INJURY
- HOLT, PATRICIA
- HUDDERSFIELD PHYSIO UNIT
- HUNTER, REBECCA
- JAMES, STEPHANIE
- JONES, P
- LEARY, PAUL
- LITTLE HERBAL
- LLOYD-OWEN CONSULTANCY
- LOCKWOOD, A
- LOFTUS, N
- MASSAGE BY ISOBEL
- MCALLISTER, G C
- MELIA, KAY
- METCALF, RICHARD
- NATURAL HEALING CLINIC
- NATURAL WHEAT BAG
- NATURES WORKROOM
- OCEAN ALTERNATIVE LIFESTYLE
- PAIN & INJURY CLINIC
- PATHWAYS TO HEALTH
- PENNY'S PEDICURE PARLOUR
- PRESTON, CATHY
- ROSNEY LEE, JO
- SANDY, I M & A N
- SMITH, LES
- SPECIAL ELECTROLYSIS CLINIC

- SPENCER, S A
- STOREY, RACHEL
- SYKES, DAVID A
- TANDY, SUE
- TAYLOR, A B
- THACKERAY, A J
- WALSH, TARA
- WOOD, TRACY

## ILKLEY

- BAGGLEY, HILARY
- BAILEY FLOWER ESSENCES
- BAILEY, ANDREW
- CARR, CHRISTINE
- CHAPMAN, E
- CHAPPELL, D S
- DE VERE, G R & R J
- HALFORD, D
- ILKLEY CHIROPODY CLINIC
- KAREN, CUDWORTH
- LLKLEY HEALING CENTRE
- MORGAN, J D
- NEWBOLD, A G
- PAYNE, AUDREY
- PITCAIRN, TONY
- POLLARD, B
- TAYLOR, JULIE
- WARD, KATE
- WISE, CAROL

## KEIGHLEY

- AIREDALE ALLERGY CENTRE
- ALDRIDGE, ANNETTE
- ATKINSON, R J
- BARRETT, CAROLYN
- BERRY, M E
- BISBY, TIFFANY
- BOOTH, KATHERYN
- BREWSTER, J B
- BREWSTER, JOHN J
- COOPER, S
- COOPER, STUART
- GRAY, F
- HERMITAGE OILS
- KEIGHLEY CHIROPODY CLINIC
- KEIGHLEY CHIROPRACTOR CLINIC
- SHARP, G M
- SILSDEN CHIROPODY CENTRE
- SIMPSON, JACQUELINE
- SMITH, RONA
- WHITTELL, JOHN
- WILKINSON, W P
- WILLMOTT, BERYL
- WOOLLARD, J
- YEHIA, CHRISTINE

## KNOTTINGLEY

- BEAUTY SPA
- BRADLEY, S
- COCKCROFT, SIMON
- PSYCHICS, SAM

## LEEDS

- AA CHIROPRACTIC CLINIC
- ALBION CHIROPODISTS
- ALEX TECH TEACHING CENTRE
- ALEXANDER TECHNIQUE
- ALEXANDER, M S
- ARCHWAYS-EFFIE GARDNER
- ARDENTE CHIROPODY SERVICE
- ATHERTON, H R
- AUSTEN, S
- BALL, VIVIENNE
- BALLARD, CATHERINE
- BARSTOW & CLAY
- BARTIG, ANDREA
- BATLEY, KAREN
- BECK, JAMES
- BEECHWOOD CHIROPODY
- BENNETT, MAUREEN E
- BENTLEY, J H
- BEST, SALLY
- BISH, M A & J
- BODY SUITE
- BRAHMA KUMARIS MEDITATION CTRE
- BRAIME, MARTINA
- BRAMLEY COMP THERAPY CLINIC
- BRAY, D N
- BRENT, GILL
- BRIDGER, ADAM
- BRIGGS, J
- BROADBENT, ELAINE
- BROWN, A M
- BROWN, F R
- BROWN, LYNN
- BROWN, PAT
- BURTON, LESLEY
- CHAPMAN, A
- CHINESE MEDICAL CENTRE
- CITY OSTEOPATHS
- CLAPHAM, J W
- CLARKE, DON
- CLINIC OF HERBAL MEDICINE
- CLUDERAY, DAVID
- COOKSON, LORRAINE
- COPLEY, F
- COYNE, MAUREEN ELLEN
- CULPEPER
- CUNNIFFE, J M & J CHIROPODISTS
- DAVID, HOLMS, & COFFEY
- DE BOER, GILLIAN
- DENHAM, A M
- DICKENSON, R
- DIXON, HANNAH
- DONALD, B
- DUNFORD, LIZ
- DYMOND-HAMMILL, C
- EELES, MEGAN
- ESSENTIAL BEING AROMATHERAPY
- ESSENTIALS
- FARRAR, SHARON
- FEET FIRST
- FENTON, J M
- FENTON, P
- GARFORTH CHIROPODY SURGERY
- GILLETT, LIZ
- GUISELEY CHIROPODY CENTRE
- HALKYARD, STEVEN
- HAMER-BLOOM, S
- HAMID, M A
- HAMILTON, SAMANTHA
- HAMPSHAW, ANNA
- HANDYPERSON SCHEME
- HEADINGLEY CHIROPRACTIC CLINIC
- HEADROW CHIROPODY & PODIATRY
- HEALTHCARE INTERNATIONAL
- HOLTHAM, W
- HOPPERS
- HORSFORTH PHYSIO & SPORTS
- HULLAND, ERIC
- HUYTON, CHRISTOPHER
- HYPNOTHERAPY CENTRE
- IBBETSON, A
- IZZARD, SARA
- J R G THERAPY SERVICES
- JEAVONS, JO
- JONES, EILEEN
- JOWETT, R S J
- KELLY, MAUREEN
- KESAVAN, S K
- KINGSMITH, ANNE-MARIE
- LEARMAN, A B
- LEEDS ACUPUNCTURE CLINIC
- LEEDS CHINESE MEDICAL CENTRE
- LEEDS CHIROPODY CLINIC
- LEEDS CHIROPRACTIC CENTRE
- LEEDS COMP THERAPY CENTRE
- LEEDS PHYSIOTHERAPY CLINIC
- LEEDS RUGBY CLUB REHAB CTRE
- LEEDS SCH OF NATURAL THERAPIES
- LEEDS SPORTS INJURY CLINIC
- LEEDS TRICHOLOGY CONSULTANCY
- LINDSAY, ANNE
- LITHERLAND, C B
- LLOYD, C
- LLOYD, CAROLINE
- LPS TRAINING & CONSULTANCY
- MACINTYRE-THOMSON, MARIE
- MILLER, GAIL
- MORE, JO
- MORGAN, J D (DR)
- MORLEY ACUPUNCTURE CLINIC
- NEURO PHYSIOTHERAPY
- NEWMARK, JOSPEHINE
- NOLAN, SARAH
- NORTH & SOUTH
- NORTHERN REIKI PARTNERSHIP
- NRTH LEEDS PHYSIO/SPRTS INJ
- ORANGE TREE
- O'SULLIVAN, FRANCES
- PALLAS, ANDREW
- PHYSICAL THERAPY CLINIC
- PHYSIO MED
- PRASAD, B
- PROCTOR, LYNDA
- PSYCHOLOGICAL SERVICES
- PSYCHOLOGY IN PRACTICE
- PURVES, DONALD A
- RAMSEYER, GEORGINA
- REYNOLDS, NATHAN
- RICHFIELD, MARISE
- RINGWOOD, JAN
- ROBIN LANE MEDICAL CENTRE
- ROTHWELL SPORTS CENTRE
- ROUNDHAY CHIROPRACTIC CLINIC
- ROURKE, S
- RUFFORD PHYSIOTHERAPY CLINIC
- SAMANTHA
- SANDERSON, ANN
- SCENTSUAL
- SCHOLL CENTRE
- SELL, NICOLA
- SEVITT, E A
- SHAW LANE PHYSIOTHERAPY CLINIC
- SHAW, B
- SHAW, M J
- SHAW, NICOLA
- SHEN ACUPUNCTURE CLINIC
- STEAD, JULIE ANN
- SWARTHMORE CENTRE
- SYKES CLINIC
- TAYLOR, ANTHONY B
- TAYLOR, SIMON
- TAYLOR, SIMON
- THERAPY CLINIC
- TRANSCENDENTAL MEDITATION
- TRUSCOTT PHYSIOTHERAPY CLINIC
- TURNER, C
- TURNER, GILL
- UNDERHILL, HARRY
- UNDERHILL, MARGARET
- UNDERWOOD, TRISH
- VAYRO, CHRISTINE
- WAKEFIELD, M
- WALDENBERG, HILARY
- WATKINS, JEAN
- WATSON, JEAN
- WEBB, JOAN
- WELLBEING
- WEST PARK STRESS MANAGEMENT
- WEST YORKSHIRE M S THRPY CTRE
- WHITE, JACQUELINE
- WHITE, P
- WIGHTMAN, T
- WILLIAMS, CLIVE
- WOMENS COUNS & THERAPY SV
- WOODHOUSE CLINIC
- WORDSWORTH, P M
- WRIGHT, GEORGINA
- YORKSHIRE SCHOOL OF SHIATSU

## LIVERSEDGE

- KHAN, H

## MIRFIELD

- HOBSON, RICHARD
- MIRFIELD NATURAL HEALTH CENTRE
- NEVILLE, PAMELA
- NEVILLE, PAMELA
- NORTHERN SCHOOL-AROMATHERAPY
- TEMPLETON, ISOBEL

## MOORTOWN

- GOLDMAN, ELLEN

## NORMANTON

- FAIRWAY PHYSIOTHERAPY CLINIC
- HALCYON AROMATICS
- HELEN BENTLEY COMP THERAPIST

## OSSETT

- AUDSLEY, T
- BROWN, OLWEN
- CRYSTAL BALL
- DIATHERMY CLINIC
- GENTLE HEALTH & BEAUTY
- GOSNAY, SHIRLEY ANNE
- GRAHAM-ROWE, CHRISTOPHER P
- ROZARIO, G

## OTLEY

- DOUGLAS, ANGELA
- ESSENTIAL THERAPEUTIC MASSAGE
- HANSON, S C
- HANSON, S C
- OTLEY PHYSIOTHERAPISTS CLINIC
- PENNY, BARBARA
- WELSH, P A
- WHITWORTH, TARN
- YORKSHIRE ASS - PSYCHO

## PONTEFRACT

- ADAMS, HEATHER DAWN
- ALTERNATIVE MEDICINE CENTRE
- BINGHAM, JULIA
- DIGNAM, P
- DUFFIELD
- FOOT HEALTH CLINIC
- HALSTEAD, DAVE
- JUDITH CARLYLE HYPNOTHERAPIST
- KINESIOLOGIST
- MARIA
- METRO ELECTROLYSIS CLINIC
- NEEDHAM, ANN
- O'BRIEN, J
- PEATFIELD, K J
- POMFRET HERBALIST
- PONTEFRACT CHIROPODY SERVICES
- PONTEFRACT CHIROPRACTIC CLINIC
- RHODES, E A
- SERIOUS MASSAGE
- SHERRATT, SUZY
- STRUTT, COLLEEN
- TRANSFORM HYPNOTHERAPY CLINIC
- WALKER, J E
- WALTERS, MARGARET

## PUDSEY

- BARNATT, A J
- BREARLEY, JILL
- CALVERLEY ACUPUNCTURE CLINIC
- FOOTCARE CLINIC
- FRANKLAND, JULIE D
- GREER, RITA
- LIKISMA
- MILLER, JULIE A
- NEILL-HIGGINS, CHRISTINA
- PUDSEY CLINIC OF ALT MEDICINE

## SHIPLEY

- ABBEY HILL & ROBSON
- BODY & SOLE
- BRADFORD CLINIC OF ALT MED
- BUSSUNT, M
- COOPER, SAFFRON
- HENWOOD, CATHY
- JEPSON, S L
- JULIA GREAVES NEW IMAGE
- SALTAIRE COMP HEALTH STUDIO
- SOLUTIONS FOR CHANGE
- TALLANT, ANDREA
- WENDY ROBINSON ACUPUNCTURE

## SOWERBY BRIDGE

- BENSON, BRIDGET
- RIPPONDEN THERAPY CENTRE
- TRIANGLE HOMOEOPATHIC PRACTICE
- WILTSHIRE, WENDY

## TODMORDEN

- ACUPUNCTURE CENTRE
- BUGLASS, I G
- KING, STELLA
- LOSANG DRAGPA BUDDHIST CENTRE
- MIDWINTER, L
- SHERRY, M B
- WISZNIEWSKI, H

## WAKEFIELD

- ALLEN, CAROL
- ALOE VERA CENTRE
- BARRACLOUGH, HELEN
- BENNETT, JOHN B
- BIROFLOW INDEPENDENT DIST
- CHINESE MEDICAL CLINIC
- CHIROPODY CARE CENTRE
- CLELLAND, J
- COMPLEMENTARY THERAPY CENTRE
- FAIRCLOUGH, LOUISE
- FOLEY, G B & ASSOCIATES
- FOOT CLINIC
- FORENSIC PSYCHOLOGY AGENCY
- FOREVER LIVING PRODUCTS
- GILLESPIE, B
- GRACE, NIGEL
- HAMBLIN, PAT
- HEALTH CHAMBERS
- HEMINGWAY, JANET
- HEY, M J
- HORBURY HYPNOTHERAPY CENTRE
- HOWARD, ELIZABETH
- JEFFS, PAULINE
- JONES, M
- KERSHAW, ALAN DAVID
- LOMAS, V
- MOBILE PHYSIOTHERAPY ASS
- MR THERAPY
- RHODES, RACHEL MISPA
- ROBINSON, L S
- SHILLITO, C
- SPRINGWELL HEALTH CLINIC
- STEARNE, M
- STRATTON, KAREN
- THERA SPORT
- WAKEFIELD CHIROPRACTIC CLINIC
- WELBECK PHYSIOTHERAPY CLINIC
- WILCOX & ASSOCIATES
- WINTERBOTTOM, J T

## WETHERBY

- BOALER, DAVID M
- BRIDGER, ADAM
- BRIDGER, MARY
- CARLYLE EON
- ESCREET, PENNY
- LANCASTER, PAULA
- P A AROMATHERAPY
- PALMER, S F
- PROFESSIONAL PHYSIO CARE
- SCOTT, JUDITH
- THRUSH, NORA C
- WETHERBY PHYSIO PRACTICE
- WRAY, TANYA

## COUNTY CARLOW

### BAGENALSTOWN
- BIOMAG

## COUNTY CAVAN

### BAILIEBORO
- BIO ENERGY HEALING

### BAILIEBOROUGH
- BI-AURA THERAPY

### CAVAN
- GOOD, JEAN

## COUNTY CLARE

### BALLYKETT
- FENNELL, JOHN

### CLARE
- HARRISON, RITA RGN

### CLARECASTLE
- HOLISTIC THERAPY CENTRE

### ENNIS
- ACUPUNCTURE/CHINESE MEDI ORG
- ACUPUNCTURE/CHINESE MEDI ORG
- CLAIRE'S THERAPEUTIC SPA CTRE
- ENNIS ACUPUNCTURE CLINIC
- HEALY, RICHARD
- IAN, MILNE
- KEANE, NOELETTE R G N
- MACNAMARA, MARY V
- MCDONOUGH, TRAVIS (DR)
- MCNAMARA, MARY
- NEYLON, MARIAN
- PLEXUS BIO ENERGY
- STILL POINT
- TIR NA NOG OILS

### KILRUSH
- CLAIR, EILEEN

### LISCANNOR
- ROCK SHOP

### LISDOONVARNA
- EASE

### MILTOWN MALBAY
- ACUPUNCTURE CLINIC
- SIMONS, ROBERT ALLEN (DR)

### SCARIFF
- GRAINEY

## COUNTY CORK

### BALLINCOLLIG
- CORK SCHOOL OF SHIATSU
- LEE, PATRICK (DR)
- MURPHY, GERARD (DR)
- O'CONNOR, COLM (DR)

### BANDON
- BANDON ACUPUNCTURE CLINIC
- BANDON CHIROPRACTIC CLINIC
- BANDON THERAPY ROOMS
- CHIROPRACTIC ASS OF IRELAND
- ENNISKEANE NATURAL THRPY CTRE

### BANTRY
- COMPLIMENTARY HEALTH CLINIC
- CONNER, MATTHEW (DR)
- WIELER, JANNY

### BISHOPSTOWN
- ASTHMA & ALLERGY CLINIC
- MCSHANE, MCSWEENEY, FRANKLIN

### BLARNEY
- HEALING THERAPIES
- NATURAL HEALTH CENTRE
- PARDOE, CHRISTOPHER

### CARRIGALINE
- CARROLL-PHELAN, BERNICE (DR)
- DALY, JENNIFER (DR)
- WALSH, ANTHONY (DR)

### CASTLETOWNBERE
- BEARA CIRCLE

### CHARLEVILLE
- FOLEY, EILISH
- KEATING, MARY
- SUNRISE NATURAL THERAPY CLINIC

### CLONAKILTY
- GASCOIGNE, S (DR)
- NATURAL HEALING ROOMS

### CORK
- ACTIVE BIRTH CENTRE
- ANNAPURNA NATURAL HEALTHCARE
- BAKER, BARBARA
- BLACKROCK ACUPUNCTURE
- BLARNEY ACU & REFLEXOLOGY CTRE
- BRADLEY, AUDREY (DR)
- BREATNACH, MARY
- BROOKFIELD PHYSIOTHERAPY
- BROWNE, MICHELE
- CHANGES HYPNOTHERAPY
- CHIROPRACTIC ASS OF IRELAND
- COLONIC IRRIGATION
- COUGHLAN, SHEILA & THOMAS
- CRONIN, DECLAN
- DALTON, CARRIE
- DANIEL, EILEEN
- FOLEY, TRISHA
- HATTERSLEY, LAURENCE
- HERBAL DISPENSARY
- HORGAN, MARIE
- IRISH ASS OF HYPNO-ANALYSTS
- KEANE, JERRY
- KELLY & ASSOCIATES
- MARTIN, KIELY
- MOONE, ROSEMARY
- MOORE GROARKE, GILLIAN (DR)
- MOORE-GROACKE, GILLIAN (DR)
- MURPHY, GARY
- NATURAL HEALING CENTRE
- NI NARAIGH, JAYAVATI
- O'CONNELL, RYAN (DR)
- O'MAHONY, REGINA
- O'SULLIVAN, MARY
- PAUL DENNEHY - HYPNOTHERAPIST
- PSYCHO ASS & CONSULTING
- QUINN-COTTER, BONNIE
- RAVEN HILL CHIROPRACTIC CLINIC
- RING, MARY
- SANBORN, CATHERINE
- SHIATSU
- SMITH, LEONIE MARIA
- SWEENEY, MARIE

### CROSSHAVEN
- O'BRIEN, CARMEL
- ROSSITER, E & GILLEN, M

### DONERAILE
- MURRAY, CATHERINE

### DOUGLAS
- DOUGLAS BEAUTY CLINIC
- HEGARTY, TOM
- NATURAL HEALTH THERAPY CENTRE
- TRADITIONAL CHINESE MEDICINE

### ENNISKEANE
- ENNISKEANE NATURAL THRPY CTRE

### FERMOY
- FEEHAN, SEAMAS
- FERMOY NTRL HLTH & CHIRO CTRE
- MORAN, CIARAN

### GLANMIRE
- QUINLAN, ANNE-MARIA
- SREENAN, JOAN

### KANTURK
- LYONS, FERGUS
- SILVERCREST HOLISTIC CLINIC

### KILWORTH
- CHIROPRACTIC ASS OF IRELAND
- CHIROPRACTIC ASS OF IRELAND
- KILWORTH CHIROPRACTIC CLINIC

### KINSALE
- KINSALE CHIROPRACTIC CLINIC

### MACROOM
- KEANE, DANIEL (DR)
- SWOPE, JEFF (DR)

### MALLOW
- BOURKE, JOHN (DR)
- CHIROPRACTIC ASS OF IRELAND
- DOORWAY TO HEALTH
- HEFFERNAN, JOE
- LANE, DANIEL
- NATURAL THERAPY CENTRE
- PRENDERGAST, BREDA
- TRADITIONAL CHINESE MEDICINE

### MARYBOROUGH
- TAYLOR, LEON (DR)

### MIDLETON
- BARRETT, SHEILA
- EAST CORK PHYSIOTHERAPY
- FREEDOM HOLISTIC CENTRE
- HENNESSY, PIERCE
- MUCKLEY, ALBERT
- O'FARRELL, MARY
- WHELAN, BERNADETTE

### MILLSTREET
- TRADITIONAL CHINESE MEDICINE

### MONKSTOWN
- ACUPUNCTURE CLINICS
- ESTEEM COUNSELLING & THERAPY
- IRISH INSTIT-INTEGRATED PSYCHO
- MONKSTOWN AROMA & REFLEX
- PAUL MCCARTHY ACUPUNCTURE

### PENROSE
- CHIROPRACTIC ASS OF IRELAND

### ROSCARBERY
- ALTERNATIVE ANIMAL CARE

### SKIBBEREEN
- CONNER, MATTHEW
- DIDDERIENS, BETSY
- RINEEN NATURAL HEALING CENTRE

### WHITECHURCH
- MADIGAN, CARMEL

### WILTON
- CORK CHIROPRACTIC CLINIC
- GRAVINA, A (DR)
- SHARCO
- SHEEHAN, OLIVIA

### YOUGHAL
- DUNLEA, TONY
- HENNESSY, PIERCE

## COUNTY DONEGAL

### BALLYBOFEY
- REID, BOSCO

### BUNCRANA
- FULLERTON, DERMOT M
- MARY, KELLY

### GLENCOLUMBCILLE
- NEW BEGINNINGS HYPNOTHERAPY

### LETTERKENNY
- BIRMINGHAM, MURROUGH (DR)
- CHIROPRACTIC ASS OF IRELAND
- HUMAN DEVELOPMENT & RELATIONS
- JAMSHID, ZADEH HASHEMI
- LETTERKENNY & CHINESE HERBAL
- LETTERKENNY CHIROPRACTIC
- MOUNT SOUTHWELL CLINIC
- NATURAL THERAPY CLINIC

## COUNTY DUBLIN

### BALBRIGGAN
- FLYNN, GIRON DE
- MONIQUES HOLISTIC CLINIC

### BALLSBRIDGE
- BELSHAW, KAREN
- FLYNN, GERARD
- SEAMUS CONNOLLY SHIATSU PRACT
- SHIATSU IRELAND
- TRANCENDENTAL MEDITATION CTRE

### BLACKROCK
- ACUPUNCTURE & MASSAGE CLINIC

- ARDAGH ACUPUNCTURE CLINIC
- BLACKROCK
- BLACKROCK OSTEOPATHS
- CONNECT ASSOCIATES
- FINLEY CHIROPRACTIC CENTRE
- FINLEY CHIROPRACTIC CENTRE
- INCH BY INCH TONING
- PENMAN, ANNE

## CHAPELIZOD

- HANNAN, TIM

## CLONDALKIN

- HOLISTIC SCHOOL OF REFLEXOLOGY
- NEWLANDS INSTITUTE FOR

## CLONSILLA

- NATURAL THERAPY & BEAUTY
- O'CONNOR, AINE

## CLONSKEAGH

- BOLGER, MAEVE

## CLONTARF

- BOURKE, SEAN M
- CLONTARF HOLISTIC CENTRE
- GLEESON, CATHERINE
- HEALTH COUNSEL
- IRISH SCHOOL OF SHIATSU
- IRISH SCHOOL OF SHIATSU

## DALKEY

- COSTIN, KAREN
- PSYCHOLOGICAL CONSULTANCY
- SARA, HANRAHAN
- SHAW, ANGELA

## DONNYBROOK

- AISLING CONSULTANTS
- AISLING INFORMATION SYSTEMS
- DONNYBROOK MEDICAL CENTRE
- IRISH COLLEGE OF COMP MEDICINE
- MCCREADY, M D (DR)
- MCGILLIGAN, DOLORES
- TRADITIONAL CHINESE MEDICINE
- WALSHE, JOHN (DR)

## DRUMCONDRA

- COLETTE, CUNNINGHAM
- HEALING ROOM - DRUMCONDRA

## DUBLIN

- AAROMA INTRIGUE
- AARON ABBA-IMMA CENTRE
- ACORN CLINIC
- ACTIVE BALANCE CLINIC
- ACU/HOM/ALLERGY TESTING
- ACUHERBS
- ACUMEDIC
- ACUPOINT - IRJA FOLEY L AC
- ACUPUNCTURE & CHINESE MEDICAL
- ACUPUNCTURE & SPORTS INJURY
- ACUPUNCTURE FOUNDATION
- ACUPUNCTURE FOUNDATION
- ACUPUNCTURE FOUNDATION
- ACUPUNCTURE FOUNDATION
- ACUPUNCTURE FOUNDATION
- ACUPUNCTURE FOUNDATION
- ACUPUNCTURE/CHINESE MEDI ORG
- ACUPUNCTURE/CHINESE MEDI ORG
- ACUPUNCTURE/CHINESE MEDI ORG
- ACUPUNCTURE/CHINESE MEDI ORG
- ACUPUNCTURE/CHINESE MEDI ORG
- ACUPUNCTURE/CHINESE MEDI ORG
- ADAM BUX SPORTS CLINIC
- ADVANCED CHIROPRACTIC
- ALBANY AROMATHERAPY CLINIC
- ALBANY CLINIC
- AMBERLEY HYP & COUNSELLING
- ANNE, CORCORAN (DR)
- ARDAGH CLINIC
- ARDUNA COUNS & PSYCHOTHPY CTRE
- AROMATHERAPY & REFLEX CENTRE
- AROMATHERAPY & REFLEX CENTRE
- AROMATHERAPY BEAUTY CLINIC
- AROMATHERAPY CENTRE
- AROMATHERAPY CLINIC
- AROMATHERAPY HEALTHCARE
- ASHROY HYP & COUNSELLING
- ASSOCIATED CHIROPRACTIC CLNC
- ASSOCI-SYSTEMATIC KINESIOLOGY
- BACK & HEADACHE CLINIC
- BAYSIDE HOLISTIC CENTRE
- BIO ENERGY HEALING
- BIO ENERGY HEALING
- BIO ENERGY HEALING
- BIO ENERGY HEALING
- BIO ENERGY THERAPY
- BIODYNAMIC BODY THERAPY
- BODY HARMONY
- BREEN, BRENDAN
- BRESLIN, CATHY
- BRUEN, MARY
- BURKE, EMER
- BUTCHER, GERARD
- BUTEYKO
- BUTLER, ELVERA
- B-WELL HYPNOTHERAPY CLINIC
- CAMPBELL, ROSEMARY
- CAROLAN, PAUL
- CARROLL, VINCENT (DR)
- CASTLEKNOCK PHYSIOTHERAPY
- CAWLEY, MICHAEL
- CELTIC HEALTH CLINIC
- CENTRE FOR CREATIVE CHANGE
- CHADHA, PRADEEP K (DR)
- CHEEK 2 CHEEK BEAUTY SALON
- CHINESE ACUPUNCTURE CLINIC
- CHINESE MEDICINE & ACU CENTRE
- CHINESE NATURAL HERBAL CENTRE
- CHIRO CENTRE
- CLINIC OF HOLISTIC MEDICINE
- CLONDALKIN ACUPUNCTURE CLINIC
- COGHLAN, HELENA
- COLLEGE OF MEDICAL
- COLLINS, MICHAEL
- COMPLEMENTARY HEALING CENTRE
- CONCANNON, MAUREEN (DR)
- CONNOLLY, JOHN (DR)
- CONTINENTAL CRAFTS
- CORCORAN, ANNE
- CRIMMINS, JOHN
- CULLINANE/GARDINER
- DENNIS, CLIVE (DR)
- DOYLE, JAMES
- DR NIELSON'S HEALTH CLINIC
- DRAPER, RHOADA
- DUBLIN CENTRE FOR CHINESE MED
- DUBLIN COUNS & THERAPY CTRE
- DUNDRUM GESTALT CENTRE
- DUNNE, SALLY
- E T C CONSULT
- EASY WAY TO STOP SMOKING
- ENDORPHIN RELEASE CLINICS
- EUROPEAN COLLEGE
- FAGAN, RUTH
- FAIRVIEW THERAPY CENTRE
- FAY, JOHN (DR)
- FEARGAL, TOBIN
- FINISHING TOUCHES
- FINN, PATRICK (DR)
- FITZPATRICK, BRENDAN (DR)
- FITZWILLIAM ACUPUNCTURE
- FITZWILLIAM CHIROPRACTOR
- FORDE, M
- FORDE, MARGARET
- GALLIVAN, NOEL M (DR)
- GERALD, KENNY
- GERETY, PATRICIA
- GERRARD, RITA
- GIRON, DANIEL
- GRENHAM, HELENA
- GRIFFIN ROY HYPNOTHERAPIST
- GROUP & INTERPERSONAL TRAINING
- GROUP ANALYTIC PRACTICE
- HANKEY, DAVID
- HARVEST MOON CENTRE
- HAYES, RORY
- HEALING HOUSE
- HEALING ROOM
- HEALING TOUCH MASSAGE
- HEALTH & HARMONY
- HEALY, DECLAN
- HEDERMAN, LINDA
- HELEN MCCORMACK MED HERB
- HERBAL & ACUPUNCTURE
- HERBAL CLINIC
- HERBAL HEALTH SERVICES
- HOEY JOE NATURAL HEALING CTRE
- HOLISTIC HEALING CENTRE
- HOLISTIC HEALTH CENTRE
- HOLISTIC SCH OF REFLEX/MASSAGE
- HOLISTIC SOURCING CENTRE
- HOMEOPATHIC MEDICINES
- HOUSE OF ASTROLOGY
- I MASTERSON PSYCHOANALYTIC
- INNER CIRCLE HEALING CENTRE
- IRISH COLLEGE-OSTEOPATHY
- IRISH INS-COUNS & HYP
- IRISH SPIRITUAL HEALING CENTRE
- JOSEPHINE, LYNCH
- JUNG CENTRE
- KANDOLA, PEARN
- KELLY, ANGELINA
- LALLOO'S ACUPUNCTURE CLINIC
- LARKIN, CATHERINE (DR)
- LENNON, JOY
- LEONARD, CELINE
- LISA MCDONNELL CHIROPODIST
- LITTLEJOHN CLINIC
- LUSCHER INS-COLOUR PSYCHOL
- MAGOVERN, PATK (DR)
- MAIREAD, RYAN
- MARREN, PAULA
- MCCABE, VINCENT
- MCDEVITT, ANNE
- MCNAMEE, BRIAN
- MEDICINE, JOE
- MELT/TEMPLE BAR NATURAL
- MERLIN ENTERTAINMENT
- MERRION SQUARE OSTEOPATHS
- MIGGIN, EMILY
- MONKSTOWN COUNSELLING SVCE
- MORLEY, C
- MULCAHY, ML (DR)
- MURPHY, BRENDAN
- MURPHY, SHARON
- MUSCLE EFFECT THERAPY
- NATURAL OPTIONS
- NELSONS HOMOEOPATHIC PHARMACY
- NEW AGE HOLISTIC & MASSAGE
- O'BRIEN, BRIDGET
- O'BRIEN, THERESE
- O'HARA, CARMEL
- O'LOUGHLIN, ANNE
- O'NEILL, ELIZABETH
- OPTIMUM HEALTHCARE
- POWER, NICHOLAS
- POWER, RICHARD
- PROFESSIONAL REGISTER
- QUINN-BERGER, JUNE
- RAHENY TCM & ACUPUNCTURE
- REDWOOD-COUNS/ PSYCHOTHERAPY
- REGAN & ASSOCIATES
- RESPIRATORY/ALLERGY DIAGNOSTIC
- ROCK ROAD PSYCHOTHERAPY CENTRE
- ROTHWELL, DECLAN
- RYAN, VALERIE
- SADAR, TONY
- SHERIDAN, PATRICIA
- ST PETERS CLINIC
- STEWART, PATRICIA
- SWEET EARTH
- T C M CENTRE
- TARU, BURSTALL
- THE SANDYCOVE CLINIC
- THERAPEUTICS
- THEW, NIN
- TRACEY, NICOLE
- TRAD CHINESE MEDICINE/MASSAGE
- VARD, ANTHONY
- VARLEY, ANNE
- WALL, (DR)
- WALLACE, PATRICIA
- WALSH, JAMES
- WARD, KAREN
- WOODS, LAWRENCE (DR)
- YELLOW BRICK ROAD

## DUN LAOGHAIRE

- ACUPUNCTURE FOUNDATION
- CHINESE MEDICAL CENTRE
- DAVALA, CHRISTOPHER
- DAVALA, CHRISTOPHER
- DUN LAOGHAIRE CHIROPRACTIC
- DUN LAOIRE HEALING ROOM
- FIERMAN B, & KOHNSTAMM B
- GILMORE, J J (DR)

- GOLDIN PAUL CLINIC
- HODGES, BILL (DR)
- INS-CREATIVE COUNS & PSYCHO
- INSTITUTE OF PSYCHOSOCIAL MED
- MANN, RICHARD
- T'AI CHI, QIGONG & SHIATSU
- TIVOLI INSTITUTE
- TULLY, MELISSA
- VICO CONSULTATION CENTRE
- WALL, SEAN (DR)
- ZHANG (DR)

## DUNDRUM

- EPSTEIN, IAN
- EPSTEIN, IAN
- MALONE, PATRICIA
- O'DEA, CATHERINE
- SOUTHSIDE COUNSELLING

## FAIRVIEW

- CARMEL, BRADLEY
- SEAN, FARRELL

## GLASNEVIN

- ACUPUNCTURE FOUNDATION
- ARTHURS, MARY & HUGH
- LINN, DUBH

## HOWTH

- COCOON REIKI CENTRE
- HOWTH COUNSELLING SERVICE

## KILLINEY

- AMETHYST CENTRE
- ARK COUNSELLING
- ARK HYPNOTHERAPY

## KIMMAGE

- COLBERT, BRIAN

## LUCAN

- ACACIA COUNSELLING CENTRE
- ACUPUNCTURE CLINIC
- BODY ELEGANCE
- CASSIDY, SUSAN
- COYNE, MARTINA
- HENNESSY, MARGARET
- LATTIMORE, GILLIAN
- LUCAN FAMILY CENTRE
- LUCAN NATURAL HEALING CENTRE
- MCHUGH HYPNOSIS & REFLEXOLOGY
- MOFFITT, JOHN
- MONAGHAN, CIARAN
- MORROW, CARYS

## MONKSTOWN

- BELGRAVE ACUPUNCTURE CLINIC
- FITZPATRICK, ROISIN
- IRISH INSTIT-INTEGRATED PSYCHO
- LYNCH, SEAMUS
- MCCARTHY, PAUL
- NOLAN FINBARR

## PERRYSTOWN

- BREE, JOHN

## PORTMARNOCK

- ELLE BEAUTY SALON
- KAVANAGH, TERESA

## RAHENY

- ACUPUNCTURE & ALLERGY TESTING
- ALLERGY TESTING CLINIC
- CLINIC OF NATURAL MEDICINE
- FIGURESHAPERS
- HEALING PLACE
- MARTIN REGINA PSYCHOLOGIST
- TERESA'S INSPIRING LIVING
- TRADITIONAL CHINESE MEDICINE
- TROY, ROSEMARY

## RANELAGH

- ALARA BEAUTY SALON
- AURA HYPNOTHERAPY CLINIC
- CELTIC HEALTH CENTRE
- CONNELLY, CHRISTINA
- DWYER, F A M
- FITZGERALD HYP-PSYCHOTHERAPY
- HEALY, GERARD
- IRISH SCHOOL OF FENG SHUI
- LINDA, FULTON
- MADDEN, BRENDAN
- MCCREADY, KEN

## RATHCOOLE

- ACUPUNCTURE FOUNDATION
- SLATTERY, NOELEEN

## RATHFARNHAM

- ACTIVE HEALTH CLINIC
- ACUPUNCTURE & CHINESE
- ACUPUNCTURE FOUNDATION
- BARRA LANE
- BRENNAN, CAROL
- MEADE, SADIE
- O'BRIEN, DAVID
- O'CALLAGHAN, JOHN
- PARKES, MAURA
- PLEXUS BIO-ENERGY HEALING
- TOBIN, ROSALEEN

## RATHGAR

- GIBBS, ALEXANDER
- SLATTERY, KAREN

## RATHMINES

- BELGRAVE
- BIO ENERGY HEALING
- CONFIDENTIAL COUNSELLING SVS
- DYNAMICS INTER SKILLS TRAINING
- FARIS, MUTAIRI
- IKEBANA SPIRIT MIND BODY CTRE
- KILLORAN-GANNON, SHEILA
- MACLIAM, FIONNULA
- MCGRATH, JOE
- MORRISON, LIBBY (DR)
- NATURAL HEALTH CLINIC
- RATHMINES CHIROPRACTIC CENTRE

## SANDYCOVE

- CLARKE, MARGARET
- CORRY, MICHAEL M (DR)
- NUALA WOULFE BEAUTY SALON

## SANDYFORD

- ACUPUNCTURE FOUNDATION

## SANTRY

- BACK TO HEALTH
- BOWER, BRENDA (DR)

## SHANKILL

- CONFIDENTIAL COUNSELLING

## SKERRIES

- ACUPUNCTURE FOUNDATION
- ACUPUNCTURE/CHINESE MEDI ORG
- SKERRIES HEALING CENTRE

## STILLORGAN

- ABSOLUTE MASSAGE & REFLEXOLOGY
- CAPOT, ARLENE
- FREENEY, JOSEPHINE (DR)
- HUGHES, ANTHONY
- INSTITUTE OF PHYSICAL THERAPY
- MANGAN, ANNE
- PRIORY CLINIC OSTEOPATHS
- TURNER CLNC OF ALTERNATIVE MED

## SUTTON

- ABELIA COUNSELLING
- FRANK RYDER HYPNOTHERAPY
- RYDER, FRANK
- STAFFORD, CAROL
- SWORDS HOMEOPATHIC

## SWORDS

- DENNIS, CLIVE (DR)
- JAMES, RONAN
- MURRAY, DECLAN (DR)
- SWORDS CHIROPRACTIC
- SWORDS HOMOEOPATHIC

## TALLAGHT

- ACUPUNCTURE FOUNDATION
- BACK 2 HEALTH
- DOWDALL, ROBERT
- KILTALOWN HSE HOLISTIC HEALING
- SHAMROCK HEALING CLINIC
- TABOR COUNSELLING & THRPY CTRE

# COUNTY GALWAY

## ATHENRY

- WALLS, JOHN P

## BALLINASLOE

- CHIROPRACTIC ASS OF IRELAND
- CLAYTON, HELEN
- ESSENCE OF BEAUTY
- GLENNON, PATRICK & BERNIE

## BARNA

- MEDICINE ORGANISATION

## CRAUGHWELL

- JENNINGS, DONAL

## GALWAY

- ADVANCED CHIROPRACTIC CLINIC
- BAYNES, COLETTE
- BODY & SOLE CENTRE
- BODYWATCH
- DARINA, JOYCE
- DIARMUID, LAVELLE
- GALWAY CHIROPRACTIC CLINIC
- HORAN, THOMAS
- MEDICINE ORGANISATION
- O'COLMAIN, AIDAN (DR)
- PSYCHOL & FAMILY THRPY PRACT

## LOUGHREA

- MARTIN, AHERNE
- WORTHINGTON EYRE DR GLENN

## MENLO

- MEDICINE ORGANISATION

## MOYCULLEN

- ALEXANDER TECHNIQUE CENTRE
- GALWAY BACKCARE & HEALTH
- MALONEY, MONICA

## NEWCASTLE

- GALWAY PSYCHOLOGICAL SERVICES

## ORANMORE

- ORANMORE ACCUPUNCTURE CLINIC

## SALTHILL

- IRWIN, MARY

## SHANTALLA

- BRANNELLY, ALAN

## TUAM

- BETHESDA
- FLANNERY, GERALDINE
- TUAM ACUPUNCTURE CLINIC

## WILLIAMSTOWN

- CHIROPRACTIC ASS OF IRELAND

## WOODQUAY

- COLLEGE OF INTEGRATIVE
- HEFFERNAN, LINDA

# COUNTY KERRY

## BALLYBUNION

- ACUPUNCTURE/CHINESE MEDI ORG

## CAHIRCIVEEN

- ARTEMIS HEALING CENTRE
- CITRUS NATURAL THERAPY CLINIC

## CASTLEISLAND

- ACUPUNCTURE CLINIC

## DINGLE

- ACUPUNCTURE/CHINESE MEDI ORG
- HANKEY, DAVID
- LAMH IOMLANE TEO

## KILLARNEY

- DOLPHIN & THE UNICORN
- HEALTH & BEAUTY CENTRE
- KEEMAN, MARGOT A
- MARIE, PRENDERGAST
- MAXWELL SMITH, FIONA
- O'CONNELL, KATHRYNE R G N
- O'DONOGHUE, AILEEN
- WOODLAWN HOLISTIC THERAPY CTRE

## KILLORGLIN

- SHEEHY, ALAN
- TRADITIONAL CHINESE MEDICINE
- TRADITIONAL CHINESE MEDICINE

## LISTOWEL

- FRAGRANT HAVEN

## MILTOWN
- SHEEHAN, PAMELA

## PORTMAGEE
- VAN DE WAL, FREDDY

## TRALEE
- BRITISH CHIROPODY & POD ASS
- CANTILLON, REGINA (DR)
- CHIROPRACTIC ASS OF IRELAND
- COISCEIM NATURAL THERAPY CTRE
- DALY, CHARLES
- DUNNE, TRISH
- FINNERTY, ML (DR)
- GREYSTONES ALTERNATIVE MED
- LYNCH, GERALDINE
- MCGINLEY, TONY
- O'NEILL, P J
- RYAN, NICOLE
- SEXTON, MAURICE
- SUAN TRA NATURAL THERAPY CTRE
- TRADITIONAL CHINESE MEDICINE
- TYNDALE CLINIC

# COUNTY KILDARE

## ATHY
- JOE, GRIFFIN
- O'MARA, MARY

## CELBRIDGE
- CELBRIDGE PHYSIOTHERAPY
- TRANQUILLITY

## CLANE
- AHERN, ANNE
- CLANE ACUPUNCTURE
- CLANE COUNSELLING/HYPNOTHERAPY
- PENDERGAST, ANN
- TRADITIONAL CHINESE MEDICINE

## DONADEA
- CUNNINGHAM, CAROL

## KILDARE
- CONBA, THOMAS J
- HURLEY KATE LIC ACUP

## LEIXLIP
- 21ST CENTURY LIVING
- CAMPBELL, ANNE
- DAWED, HELEN
- HOLEN HOLISTICNERGY
- KELLY, KEITH
- O'GRADY, TANYA

## MAYNOOTH
- ACHIEVE BALANCE
- AVISION COUNS & PSYCHO SVS
- CORPORATE COUNSELLING IRELAND
- FINLEY-MCKENNA, LINDA (DR)
- LOTUS LODGE
- MCGUINNESS, MICHEAL

## NAAS
- ACUPUNCTURE FOUNDATION
- COE HELEN ALTERNATIVE MEDICINE
- DENNIS, CLIVE (DR)
- DENNIS, CLIVE (DR)
- DRION, FRANCOISE
- ELIZABETH, KENT
- FAIRGREEN HOLISTIC CLINIC
- GIBSON, J S
- ICHP HEADQUARTERS
- LAMBE, BARRY
- NAAS ACUPUNCTURE
- NAAS CHIROPRACTIC CLINIC
- NOONEY, MICHAEL
- O'REILLY, MARK (DR)
- SHENANDOAH HEALING
- TEAHAN, MONICA

## NEWBRIDGE
- D SEXTON HYPNOTHERAPY NLP
- GRANGE CLINIC
- HEAVEY, BRIDGET
- HOFFMAN, BERNIE
- ICHP HEADQUARTERS

## THE CURRAGH
- GREEN ROAD HEALING CENTRE

# COUNTY KILKENNY

## BENNETTSBRIDGE
- BLUE ROOM

## GRAIGUENAMANAGH
- HOLISTIC HEALING CENTRE

## INISTIOGE
- NAMREE FARM

## KILKENNY
- BIOENERGETIC MEDICINE CLINIC

## THOMASTOWN
- MOLLEREAU, ANNE MARIE

# COUNTY LAOIS

## BALLYROAN
- MCCABE, MARY

## PORTARLINGTON
- BYRNE, STEVE
- TRADITIONAL CHINESE MEDICINE

## PORTLAOISE
- MONTE, KEN (DR)
- PORTLAOISE FAMILY CHIROPRACTIC

# COUNTY LEITRIM

## CARRICK-ON-SHANNON
- HEALTH SENSE
- NEW BEGINNINGS

## LEITRIM
- NATURAL HEALING CENTRE

## MOHILL
- AIDAN WRYNNE HEALING CLINIC

# COUNTY LIMERICK

## BALLYCLOUGH
- O'DOWD, MARY

## BRUFF
- O'CONNOR, CELINE CASEY

## CASTLEMAHON
- HILLVIEW HOUSE HEALING CENTRE

## CLARINA
- HUGHES, MICHAEL

## CORBALLY
- KENNEDY CASEY, BRIDGET

## KILMALLOCK
- DREAMLAND BIO-ENERGY

## LIMERICK
- CHIROPRACTIC ASS OF IRELAND
- DALY, JEAN N
- HOLISTIC HEALING
- HYPNOSIS LEARNING CENTRE
- O'MALLEY, DERRY
- ULTIMATE HEALTH CLINIC

## RAHEEN
- ASSOCIATION OF IRISH ACUP
- LIMERICK HEALTH

# COUNTY LONGFORD

## LONGFORD
- WARD, GERALD

# COUNTY LOUTH

## ARDEE
- ZOTA

## BLACKROCK
- HOLISTIC SOL NTRL HEALING CTRE

## DROGHEDA
- ACORN COUNSELLING
- ACUPUNCTURE CLINIC
- FLANNERY, BARNEY
- FOCUS COUNSELLING AND THERAPY
- KELLY, ALISON
- MARREN, PAULA
- RILEY, CHASE (DR)
- TRADITIONAL CHINESE MEDICINE

## DUNDALK
- BEAUTE PLUS
- BUSINESS PSYCHOLOGY
- CALLAN, KAY
- COMPLEMENTARY HEALTH STUDIO
- HERBALWISE
- MARYGOLD AROMATHERAPY CLINIC
- PROGRESSIVE HYPNOTHERAPY
- REMAS CLINIC
- RILEY CHIROPRACTIC CLINIC
- TARA SCHOOL

# COUNTY MAYO

## BALLINA
- CASEMENT THERAPY CENTRE
- JENKINS, CHARLES (DR)
- NEUFELDT, BEATRICE (DR)

## BALLINROBE
- IMAGES HEALTH & BEAUTY CLINIC

## BALLYCASTLE
- MOYLES, JOHN

## BALLYHAUNIS
- KELLY, ROSALEEN
- TOBAR PHADRAIC

## BELMULLET
- NATURAL HEALING CENTRE

## CASTLEBAR
- AMMAROSE HYPNOTHERAPY CLINIC
- ANNE TOBIN BEAUTY CLINIC
- CANAVAN, JOHN (DR)
- CANAVAN, JOHN (DR)
- CASTLEBAR HEALTHCARE CLINIC
- CHIROPRACTIC ASS OF IRELAND
- KILKENNY, STEPHANIE
- MARGARET, DEFFELY
- MEDICINE ORGANISATION
- SYLVIA, NAGLE

## CLAREMORRIS
- BYRNE, MARTIN
- TIR NA NOG

## CONG
- REGAN, ANNE MARIE

## FOXFORD
- CHIROPRACTIC ASS OF IRELAND

## KILTIMAGH
- DOYLE, CAITRIONA

## WESTPORT
- BRIAN, MCCARTHY (DR)
- MACCARTHY, BRIAN (DR)
- MCNICHOLAS, JOAN
- MEDICINE ORGANISATION
- RYAN-O'SHEA, LUCILLE (DR)
- WOODS, LAWRENCE (DR)

# COUNTY MEATH

## ASHBOURNE
- ASHBOURNE CHIROPRACTIC CLINIC
- MCENTEE, DOLORES

## ATHBOY
- COYNE, ANTHONY

## DUNBOYNE
- BOYLAN, SEAN

## DUNSHAUGHLIN
- BRENDA'S BEAUTY SALON
- PRACTICE OF HYPNOTHERAPY

## ENFIELD
- CONNOR, JEANETTE

## NAVAN
- CHIROPRACTIC FIRST
- FRANCES, LEE
- MARTIN, WHYTE
- MITCHELL, AIDAN (DR)
- NATURAL MEDICINE CENTRE
- NATURAL MEDICINE CENTRE
- STEVENS, BRETT (DR)
- WWW.CHIRO-FIRST.COM

## COUNTY MONAGHAN

### BALLYBAY
- AROMA - ZONE

### CARRICKMACROSS
- MITCHELL, AIDAN (DR)

### CASTLEBLANEY
- HEALTHY CHOICES

### CASTLEBLAYNEY
- MONAGHAN
- MONAGHAN CHIROPRACTIC CLINIC
- NORTHAMBER

## COUNTY OFFALY

### TULLAMORE
- BRETT, HALLIDAY
- CENTRE OF HOLISTIC HEALING
- HALLIDAY, BRETT (DR)
- MOTHER EARTH
- NATURAL STUFF HEALTH SHOP

## COUNTY ROSCOMMON

### BALLAGHADERREEN
- FAMILY INSTITUTE

### BALLINASLOE
- HOLISTIC HEALTH FARM

### BOYLE
- ROSSBEIGH THERAPIES

### CASTLEREA
- MCDERMOTT, MARY

### ELPHIN
- NATURAL HEALTH THERAPIES

### ROSCOMMON
- LENNON, MICHAEL
- STUDENSKI, ELIZABETH

## COUNTY SLIGO

### BALLINCAR
- CHIROPRACTIC ASS OF IRELAND

### BALLINODE
- ANAM CHARA COUNSELLING
- MEEHAN, ANNE

### BALLISODARE
- YVONNE HENRY HYPNOTHERAPIST

### DRUMCLIFF
- WYLIE WARREN, FRANCES

### RIVERSTOWN
- CHIROPRACTIC ASS OF IRELAND

## COUNTY TIPPERARY

### CAHIR
- TIR NA NOG HOLISTIC CENTRE

### CARRICK-ON-SUIR
- DOWNEY, JOHN (DR)

### CLONMEL
- DOYLE, JOSEPHINE
- EMER, PURCELL
- KINSELLA, MARIE
- O'BRIEN FAHEY, ANNETTE

### MULLINAHONE
- KEATING, KEVIN

### NENAGH
- KENNY, MARGARET
- SCOTT, JOHNSTON ROBERT

### THURLES
- CHIROPRACTIC ASS OF IRELAND

### TIPPERARY TOWN
- TRADITIONAL CHINESE MEDICINE

## COUNTY WATERFORD

### BUTLERSTOWN
- STONES, DAMIEN M

### DUNGARVAN
- BATES, EDWARD (DR)
- DUNGARVAN ALTERNATIVE HEALTH
- POWER, PATRICK

### FERRYBANK
- AVERDUNG, DAN

### GRACEDIEU
- CHIROPRACTIC ASS OF IRELAND
- RYAN, NOEL T (DR)

### NEWTOWN
- O'MEARA, MAURA

### RATHGORMATH
- KATI, NINA

### SLIEVERUE
- CHINESE MEDICINE

### TRAMORE
- GRAHAM, D (DR)
- GRAHAM, THERESA
- NATURAL HEALTH STORE

### WATERFORD
- AIRMOUNT CHIROPRACTIC CLINIC
- KILLEEN, OLIVER
- TRADITIONAL CHINESE MEDICINE

## COUNTY WESTMEATH

### ATHLONE
- ATHLONE CHIROPRACTIC CLINIC
- MEEHAN, SIOBHAN
- TRADITIONAL CHINESE MEDICINE

### BALLINEA
- OISIN CENTRE

### MULLINGAR
- AROMAFLEX
- BRADSHAW COMP MEDICINE
- CHIROPRACTIC ASS OF IRELAND
- HOWE, JAN
- MULLINGAR CHIROPRACTORS CLINIC
- MULLINGAR THERAPEUTIC CLINIC
- MURPHY, RORY (DR)
- SLATTERY, DENIS (DR)
- STEWART, BRITTA
- SUAIMHNEAS AROMATHERAPY
- TIJERINA, CARL (DR)
- TRADITIONAL CHINESE MEDICINE

### TYRELLSPASS
- JET FORM IRELAND

## COUNTY WEXFORD

### BANNON
- CARTHY, MARY

### BARNTOWN
- MORAN, MARY

### CROSSABEG
- MORRISSEY TRADITIONAL ACU

### DUNCORMICK
- MURPHY, MARY

### ENNISCORTHY
- AISLING CONSULTANTS
- JEFFARIES, PHILIP
- KELLY HYPNOTHERAPY CLINIC

### FERNS
- KINSELLA, DENIS

### GOREY
- GOREY HOLISTIC THERAPIES CTRE

### WEXFORD
- FOURTH MOUNTAIN HOM AND ACU
- JEFFARIES, PHILIP
- OSTEOPATHIC PRACTICE

## COUNTY WICKLOW

### ARKLOW
- ARKLOW CHIROPRACTIC CLINIC
- ARKLOW NATURAL HEALING CENTRE
- SYNGE, TERAN

### BRAY
- BRAY HOLISTIC HEALTH CLINIC
- CALLANAN NOIRIN HEALER
- CALLANAN, NOIRIN
- CONNAWOOD AROMATHERAPY CENTRE
- COSTELLO, JILL
- D'ARCY, PATRICK
- HOLISTIC OPTIONS
- IRISH ESSENTIAL OIL
- JAMES, JAMESON
- JAMES, JAMESON
- O'BRIEN, MARY KENNEDY
- RANDALL, PATRICK
- WALSH, MICHAEL

### DELGANY
- O'NEILL, KATE

### GLEN OF THE DOWNS
- MARK GOULDING - ACUPUNCTURIST

### GREYSTONES
- ACUPUNCTURE CLINICS
- DENNIS & ASSOCIATES
- GREYSTONES CHIROPRACTIC CLINIC
- LADY GREYSTONES BEAUTY SALON
- THORP, TERRY

### KILBRIDE
- BYRNE ASSUMPTA

### KILCOOLE
- BOMAR AROMA OILS & SUPPLIES
- ROCHE CLINICS IRELAND

### WICKLOW
- HAYES, RORY (DR)
- JAMESON PERSONAL EXCELLENCE
- PLEXUS BIO-ENERGY

# COUNTY ANTRIM

## ANTRIM

- ANTRIM CHIROPRACTIC CLINIC
- CRAIG, C J
- GIVEN, CLIVE
- SHEPPARD, SERENA

## BALLYCASTLE

- DOHERTY, COLIN
- MORGAN, D

## BALLYCLARE

- BALLYCLARE CHIROPRACTIC CLINIC
- BALLYCLARE FOOT CLINIC
- REA, J

## BALLYMENA

- ALOE VERA
- ARNOLD, ANNE
- BALLYMENA CHIROPRACTIC CLINIC
- BLAIR, R C
- ECCLESTON, MERVYN E
- FAMILY CHIRO CLINIC BALLYMENA
- HANNA, J
- HEALING LEAVES
- HEALTH & RELAXATION CENTRE
- MCCRYSTALS NATUROPATHIC CENTRE
- SCRABO HEALTH PRODUCTS
- TODD, TREVOR

## BALLYMONEY

- BALLYMONEY CHIROPRACTIC CLINIC
- EAKIN, LINDA
- KENNEDY, SHIRLEY
- RICHMOND, E A

## BELFAST

- AGNEW, M D
- ALBERTBRIDGE ROAD DAY HOSPITAL
- ARMSTRONG, R F
- BAILIE, EILEEN
- BALLY SILLAN FOOT CLINIC
- BELFAST CHIROPRACTIC CLINIC
- BRADLEY, J H
- BROWN, AVRIL
- CHARTERED PHYSIOTHERAPY
- CHEAH, R F S
- CHINESE & COMPLEMENTARY
- CHINESE MEDICAL CENTRE
- CHIROPODY CLINIC
- COMERTON, LIZ
- COMMUNITY PSYCHIATRIST NURSING
- COMP HEALTH & TREATMENT CLNC
- COMPLEMENTARY MEDICAL CENTRE
- COUNTRY CLINIC
- CRAWFORD, J G
- CREGAGH CHIROPRACTIC CLINIC
- EARLS, JAMES
- FINAGHY CHIROPRACTIC CLINIC
- FLANIGAN, JANICE
- FLORENCE SHARPE CHIROPODIST
- FRAMAR NATURAL HEALTH CLINIC
- GIBSON, A E
- GILCHRIST, A
- GLOBAL CHIROPRACTIC CENTRE
- GLOBAL HEALTHCARE
- GRANT, MARY
- GUNNING, R
- HAO CLINIC
- HAYHURST, GEOFFREY A
- HOSWELL, CHRISTINE
- I D AROMATICS
- JACKSON, B
- JONES, M
- KELLY, O H
- KILLOUGH, D
- LAMBERT, RACHEL
- LIFESPRING PRODUCTS
- LONDON INS OF STRESS MNGMT
- MAXWELL, MARY
- MCCANN, ANGELA
- MCCULLY, JOAN
- MCMULLAN, MARITA
- MEDICINE WHEEL
- MUISE, D W
- N I HOMOEOPATHIC SOCIETY
- NEELY, P
- NEW BEGINNINGS
- NEWRY CHIROPRACTIC CLINIC
- NTH IRELAND MUSIC THER TRUST
- NUTRI-SOL
- O'KANE, C
- O'RAWE, IVY
- PHYSIO
- REAY, H
- RUDERMAN, HOWARD
- SARAH
- SCHOLL CENTRE
- SCRABO HEALTH PRODUCTS
- SCULLION, BRENDA
- SINCLAIR, W J
- STEWART, S
- TRANSCENDENTAL MEDITATION
- W M RYAN AND SON
- WATSON, J
- WEDLOCK, P
- WRAY, CAROLE
- YARO
- YOGA BIOMEDICAL TRUST
- YOGA FELLOWSHIP OF N.IRELAND

## CARRICKFERGUS

- BARNES, CHARMAINE
- CLARKE, LORRAINE
- MCATEER, MARK

## LARNE

- CHIROPODIST
- LEDLIE, C
- MYSTIC SCHEHERAZADE
- NIXON, M

## LISBURN

- ACTIVE BALANCE CLINIC
- BACK SHOP
- FARRELL, BARBARA
- FENTON, D
- HYPNOTHERAPY CENTRE
- LISBURN CHIROPRACTIC CLINIC
- MCCARTNEY, W J
- MCMAHON, K

## NEWTOWNABBEY

- FOOT CARE NORTHERN IRELAND
- FOOTCARE NI
- GLENGORMLEY CHIRO CLINIC
- GLENGORMLEY FOOT CARE
- MUISE, DAVID
- PHYSIOTHERAPY ASSOCIATES
- THERAPY CENTRE

# COUNTY ARMAGH

## ARMAGH

- ARMAGH CHIROPRACTIC CLINIC
- CAMPBELL, FIONA
- CUNNINGHAM, H P
- FOOT & ANKLE CLINIC
- MCCRORY, GERALDINE
- NEWRY CHIROPRACTIC CLINIC

## CRAIGAVON

- ANDERSON, R T
- BLACKSTONE PHYSIO & SPORTS
- CRAIGAVON CHIROPRACTIC CLINIC
- LYON, HARRIETTE
- MALONE, P
- MCLOUGHLIN, F
- MITCHELL, DEIRDRE
- NORITEX
- O'NEILL, MARIA
- O'PREY, M J
- ROGERS, ANDREA
- STODDART, H D
- WHITTOCK, ANNE
- WILLIS, IAN

# COUNTY DOWN

## BALLYNAHINCH

- COCHRANE, NIALL
- MCGUIGGAN, MARY
- O'PREY, M

## BANBRIDGE

- MCCORMAC, LOUISE
- MULLIGAN, JEAN H

## BANGOR

- ABBEY COMPLEMENTARY
- ARCHER, D J B
- BANGOR CHIROPRACTIC CLINIC
- BANGOR OSTEOPATHIC CLINIC
- DELICATE ESSENCE CLINIC
- HAO (DR)
- LAPPIN, MARY
- LYCIUM CENTRE
- MCCLURG, T A
- MCDONALD, D W
- NOBLE, ANDREW (DR)
- PUNDYKE, MARIA
- WENSLEY, MARTIN

## COMBER

- NORTH DOWN CLINIC

## CUMBER

- FAMILY CHIROPRACTIC CLINIC

## DONAGHADEE

- BLENHEIM CHIROPODY PRACTICE
- BODY & SOLE HEALTH & SPORTS
- MCDONALD, D W

## DOWNPATRICK

- DUFF, M H
- QUINN, BARBARA

## DROMORE

- KIRK, DONNA

## HOLYWOOD

- BOWMAN, D
- CHIROPRACTICE
- COWAN, KAREN
- MCCOY, DOLORES
- MCCUTCHEON, R M
- PRINGLE CHIROPRACTIC
- YOGA CENTRE OF IRELAND

## KILLINCHY

- NORTHDOWN CLINIC

## NEWCASTLE

- GIBSON, A E

## NEWRY

- CATHRINA'S CLINIC
- HADDEN, MARLENE
- MCCARTAN, DEBORAH
- NATURAL THERAPY CENTRE
- NEWRY CHIROPRACTIC CLINIC
- REFLEXOLOGY CLINIC
- SMITH, PATRICIA

## NEWTOWNARDS

- ALLEN, S
- ARDS CHIROPRACTIC CLINIC
- GORMLEY, A
- HANLEY, I G
- MCCARTHY, A
- MCCUTCHEON, TINA
- MILLER, J
- ROYLANCE, HEATHER
- SCRABO HEALTH PRODUCTS
- TUDOR REFLEXOLOGY

# COUNTY FERMANAGH

## ENNISKILLEN

- ENNISKILLEN CHIRO CLINIC
- FLANAGAN, DENIS
- KILLYNURE THERAPY CENTRE
- MOORE, M
- MULLIGAN, R

# COUNTY LONDONDERRY

## COLERAINE

- BOWMAN, D
- BOYCE, NIGEL
- CHINESE MEDICAL CENTRE
- COLERAINE CHIROPRACTIC CENTRE
- HUNTER, W
- MCBRINE, HAZEL
- NUTT, N
- O'KANE, B A
- PROUDMAN CHIROPRACTIC CLINIC

## DERRY

- LIFE TREE

## LIMAVADY

- PAYNE, R

### LONDONDERRY

- ANDERSON & CRAIG CLINIC
- BODYCARE INJURY CLINIC
- CLARENDON CHIROPRACTIC CLINIC
- CLAUDY CHIROPRACTIC CLINIC
- CURRAN, MAUREEN
- DISPENSERY
- EQUILIBRIUM HOLISTIC CLINIC
- FEET FIRST
- FOYLE HYPNOTHERAPY CENTRE
- HYNES, NANCY
- MCLAUGHLIN, E
- SCHLINDWEIN, HELENA
- SPENCE & LYNN
- TRANSCENDENTAL MEDITATION

### MAGHERAFELT

- ELECTROLYSIS CLINIC
- MAGHERAFELT CHIRO CLINIC
- WARD, P G

### PORTSTEWART

- MCKINNEY, G H

## COUNTY TYRONE

### COOKSTOWN

- BRADLEY, R M
- COOKSTOWN CHIROPRACTIC CLINIC
- COOKSTOWN HERBAL CLINIC
- COOKSTOWN PHYSIO & SPORTS

### DUNGANNON

- DUNGANNON CHIROPRACTIC CLINIC
- SOLANUS GARDEN

### OMAGH

- O'MAHONY, JOHN & BEATE
- ROSEWOOD HEALTH CLINIC
- TIME OUT TRAINING

## ABERDEENSHIRE

### ABERDEEN

- ABERDEEN CHIROPODY & PODIATRY
- ABERDEEN CHIROPRACTIC CLINIC
- ABERDEEN HEALING CENTRE
- ABERDEEN HYPNOTHERAPY CENTRE
- ABERDEEN PHYSIOTHERAPY
- ABERDEEN PHYSIOTHERAPY CTRE
- ABERDEEN SPIRITUALIST CENTRE
- ABERDEEN THERAPY CENTRE
- ALBERT STREET CLINIC
- ALTERNATIVE PRACTICE
- ANTHONY, JOHN
- AROMATHERAPY CLINIC
- ASHANA
- BARBER, FIONA M
- BEECHGROVE CLINIC
- BON-ACCORD CHIROPODY
- BROMLEY, RIA
- BROOKS, MAGGIE
- CAMPHILL MEDICAL PRACTICE
- CARDEN COMPLEMENTARY CENTRE
- CARTER, NICK
- CITY BEACH
- CURRY, AINE
- DAB HANDS MASSAGE
- DAVISON, FIONA
- DEEVIEW AROMATHERAPY
- EDWARDS, KAREEN
- ELYSIUM
- GARIOCH, J
- GRAMPIAN HOMEOPATHIC PRACTICE
- HANDS ACROSS THE VOID
- HARLEY, LIZ
- HOMOEOPATHY CENTRE
- HOWIE, DAVID D
- JAMES, DANIEL D
- KINCORTH CLINIC
- LEAL, DOUGLAS
- LINCOLN COUTTS
- MAIR, MARGARET
- MCINTOSH, IRENE
- MCPHERSON, MALCOLM
- MITCHELL, GILLIAN M
- MOSS PHARMACY
- NATURAL CARE
- PATTERSON, I D
- PSYCHOLOGY SPECIALIST INPUT
- REFLEXOLOGY CLINIC
- REILLY, DANIEL
- RIVERSIDE CHIROPRACTIC CLINIC
- ROBERTSON, MICHAEL
- ROSEMOUNT CENTRE
- ROSEMOUNT OSTEOPATHY
- ROSS, COLIN R
- SAWYER, KEN
- SERENDIPITY
- SHAND, R J
- STAPEL, PAUL R
- TAGGART, RUTH
- THOMSON, HAZEL
- TYMEAESSENCE
- WALKER, MARGARET
- WALKER, O A
- WEST END PHYSIOTHERAPY
- WILKEN, ANGEL
- WILSON, R
- WOOD, A R

### BANCHORY

- BANCHORY CHIROPODY PRACTICE
- EMPTAGE, MARGARET
- MACLEAN, LAURA
- MILNE, P M
- NICOLL, ANGELA
- PRACTICE

### BANFF

- BIRNIE, KATHLEEN

### ELLON

- BODYWORKS
- CLAIRBAUX CLINIC
- GRAY, SHEILA
- RICHARDSON, ROSEMARY
- WATSON, NOREEN

### FRASERBURGH

- GREEN, C M

### HUNTLY

- HUNTLY CHIROPRACTIC CLINIC

### INSCH

- MAY, S P

### INVERURIE

- BATES, K
- CHELSEA HOUSE CLINIC
- COUTTS, L
- HARLEY, LIZ
- MAULE, V
- MAY, S
- MUNRO, EVELYN
- MURRAY, K
- NICOL, L
- PRICE, G
- REIKI TRAINING CENTRE
- ROBINSON, ELIZABETH
- ROBINSON, N
- STEPHENSON, L
- T SERVICE
- WOODWARD, MARGARET

### PETERCULTER

- CHELSEA HOUSE CLINIC

### PETERHEAD

- CLAIRBAUX CLINIC
- DAY, PHILIP
- PODIATRY CLINIC
- STEWART, JAMES HARVEY

### STONEHAVEN

- A WAY WITH THE FAERIES
- CRAN, LORAINE
- TOE TO HEEL - REFLEXOLOGY

### TURRIFF

- TURRIFF CHIROPRACTIC CLINIC

## ANGUS

### ARBROATH

- MCKINNON, A

### CARNOUSTIE

- RAMSAY, A R

### DUNDEE

- ACARSAID CHIROPODY CLINIC
- ALEXANDER TECHNIQUE CENTRE
- ANDERSON, W B
- BAKER, P T
- BEATTIE, ROBERT
- BROUGHTY FERRY HEALTH CENTRE
- DONNELLY, D
- DRYDEN, PHILIP
- DUNDEE, ROKPA
- EARTHWORKING HEALING CENTRE
- FALCONER, N
- FOGGIE, MARGARET
- GREEN, C M
- HOLISTIC HEALING CENTRE
- HOMOEOPATHY CLINIC
- KANE, T
- KAY, ELIZABETH
- LAWRIE, A
- MIND BODY SOUL & ASSOCIATES
- NATURAL HEALTH & CHIROPODY
- NATURAL HEALTH CARE
- NEILSON, J R
- NEWAYS INDEPENDENT CONSULTANT
- TRADITIONAL ACUPUNCTURE

### FORFAR

- ALEXANDER, JAMES
- GREKIN CHIROPRACTIC CLINIC
- NICOLL, ELAINE

### KIRRIEMUIR

- KIRRIEMUIR PHYSIO CLINIC

### MONTROSE

- FRASER, SANDY
- FRASER, SANDY
- GALLOWAY, TRUDY J
- MONTROSE CHIROPODY CLINIC

## ARGYLL AND BUTE

### ALEXANDRIA

- HOMEOPATHIC PODIATRIST/REFLEX

### BRIDGEND

- TAYLOR, JANE

### CLYDEBANK

- BLACKWOOD, R H W
- DALMUIR CLINIC
- DE-STRESS
- FRAGRANT MOODS
- PSYCHOLOGICAL SERVICE
- STEWART, T M R

### DUMBARTON

- MACONOCHIE, A J
- REIKI LIGHT

### HELENSBURGH

- ACTIVE CHIROPRACTIC
- BUTLER, A
- GIBSON, RONALD J
- M H B ASSOCIATES
- MACONOCHIE, A J
- MARTIN, I F
- MHB ASSOCIATES
- NATURAL THERAPY CENTRE

### LOCHGILPHEAD

- INVERNEILL HEALTH & SKIN CARE

### OBAN

- BRIMELOW, KEITH
- COMPLEMENTARY HEALTH CENTRE
- LINTON, THERESA

### ROTHESAY

- GRAPEVINE

## AYRSHIRE (EAST)

### CUMNOCK

- BROWN, IAN
- LITTLEJOHN, S

### DARVEL

- LYNN BROWN CLINICAL AROM

### GALSTON

- BROWN, ISLA M
- GALSTON CLINIC
- JACKSON, J W
- LENA

### KILMARNOCK

- ALLAN, HUGH
- BROWN, JAMES
- BURTON, VICKI
- CAMPBELL, JOHN D
- CHIROPODY & AROMATHERAPY
- CRUISE, M & M
- HEATHER MIXTURE
- HUNTER, HUGH
- HURLFORD CHIROPODY CLINIC
- ISOBEL, GEMMELL
- LIFESTYLE MEDICINE
- MCCABE, P J
- MCCANCE, A B
- O'CONNOR, LYNDA-ANN
- REID, ELIZABETH
- RHONA INGLIS AROMATHERAPY
- ROBERTSON, JENNIFER

### NEWMILNS

- BOITEUX, FRANK
- MINNERY, PATRICIA

## AYRSHIRE (NORTH)

### ARDROSSAN

- KEYES, SUSAN
- MUIR, MARGARET
- THOMSON, LORNA

### BEITH

- MACDONALD, JANICE
- WALLACE, MARGARET A R

### BRODICK

- MCGOVERN, FIONA

### DALRY
- OBONYO, T J

### IRVINE
- BODY & SOUL
- BODYSCENTS
- COMPLEMENTS HOLISTIC THERAPIES
- HANDS FOR FEET
- MUSTARD SEED HEALTH
- PATON, MARY S
- WELSH, A C

### KILBIRNIE
- BANNON, P

### KILWINNING
- AQUARIUS ESSENTIAL OILS
- BURNS, ALAN STEWART
- FERGUSON, AGNES
- KELLY, ANNETTE M
- SCOTTISH HYDROTHERAPY SYSTEMS

### LARGS
- AULD & BONN
- BONN, JANET
- LARGS NATURAL HEALTH CLINIC
- MACPHERSON, IAN R
- STEWART, KAREN
- STEWART, T A
- WELL CONNECTED

### MILLPORT
- COTTERILL, F
- DIACK, A

### SALTCOATS
- CHIRO HEALTH CARE CLINIC
- COX, M M
- HODGKINSON, JAMES R

### WEST KILBRIDE
- REID, E
- VALLEY HEALTH PRODUCTS

## AYRSHIRE (SOUTH)

### AYR
- BACK TO NATURE CLINIC
- BECKETT, MAURICE
- BELL, DOUGLAS W
- BELL, W DOUGLAS
- CRAM, NORMUND
- CREE, L
- CRUISE, M & M
- CRUISE, M & M
- CUMMING, JOHN D
- EARNSHAW, E (DR)
- ESSENCE OF HEALTH
- HARDIE, ANNE
- HODGE, IAN
- HOLISTIC HARMONY
- JAN DE VRIES HEALTH CARE
- LINDSAY, DAVID
- M C S P
- MACPHERSON, VIVIEN M
- MEDICAL ACUPUNCTURE CENTRE
- ORIENTAL HEALTH CENTRE
- REGISTERED OSTEOPATHS
- RUSSELL, M J
- SCOTTISH SCHOOL OF REFLEXOLOGY
- SHAW, ROBERT C
- SMITH, ALICIA
- SUSAN, DOYLE

### PRESTWICK
- CARRICK CLINIC
- HEALTH STRESS & INJURIES
- PEDEN, ANDREW
- STEWART, ALAN

### TROON
- DE VRIES, JAN
- ELDER, SUSANNA
- HEARTLAKE PHYSIOTHERAPY
- JASMINE ROOM
- REID, A
- SMITH, A C
- STEVENSON, SCOTT
- WESTPORT AROMATHERAPY

## CAITHNESS

### WICK
- WILSON, HELEN

## CLACKMANNANSHIRE

### ALLOA
- ALTERNATIVE MEDICAL CLINIC
- ANNAS STUDIO PRACTICE
- CLINICAL AROMATHERAPY
- MURRAY, A

### ALVA
- CULLENS, IONA

### CLACKMANNAN
- RAE, FRED K

### DOLLAR
- GUILD, M D (DR)
- STACKTHEME
- STRONACH, LORNA

### TILLICOULTRY
- WATT, J M

## DUMFRIES AND GALLOWAY

### ANNAN
- SOLWAY PHYSIOTHERAPY CLINIC

### CASTLE DOUGLAS
- CLARK, LUCY
- CURTIS, MORAG
- HARRINGTON, ELIZABETH
- HEPPEL, V

### DALBEATTIE
- GARDNER, MARION
- JAMIESON, ANGELA C
- N H S TRUST CHIROPODY CLINIC

### DUMFRIES
- BURTON, M
- DRANSFIELD, D M
- DUMFIRES NATURAL HEALTH CLINIC
- DUMFRIES HOLISTIC HEALTH CTRE
- DUMFRIES NATURAL HEALTH CENTRE
- DUNLOP, JAMES R W
- HEALTH STRESS & INJURIES CLNC
- HOLDSWORTH, HILARY
- HYPNOTHERAPY CENTRE
- JACKSON, ALISON
- LILLEY, PENNY
- LINDSAY, MARGARET
- MCCLUNE, LORNA
- MILENKOVIC, S
- MOONFLEET CLINIC
- NATURAL HEALTH CENTRE
- SHARP, LINDA A
- SMITHERS, DENISE
- STURGEON, JOHN
- TILBURY, PAULINE
- WILLOCK, LORNA

### LANGHOLM
- BURTON, VICKY

### MOFFAT
- OSTEOPATHIC & PHYSICAL CLINIC
- RANKINE, VANORA

### NEWTON STEWART
- CHLOE'S HERBS
- HARRINGTON, E
- RAINBOW ALTERNATIVES
- WILLIAMS, KELLY

### SANQUHAR
- BUTEYKO

### STRANRAER
- MCCLYMOUNT, JENNIFER
- NATURAL HEALTH CLINIC

### THORNHILL
- DAVIDSON, MORAG

## EDINBURGH (CITY OF)

### BALERNO
- CASE MANAGEMENT SERVICES
- MUNRO, I J
- SHENTON, DIANNE

### CURRIE
- CURRIEHILL CLINIC

### EDINBURGH
- ACTIVE OSTEOPATHS
- ACUPOWER
- ALEXANDER TECHNIQUE
- ALEXANDER TECHNIQUE
- ANDERSON, K
- ARMSTRONG, PAT
- B WILLIAMS CORPORATE PSYCHOL
- BABY HOLISTIC & MASSAGE
- BANNATYNES HEALTH CLUB
- BATE, ROBIN
- BAXTER, F J
- BILL TAYLOR PHYSIOTHERAPY
- BIORADIANT HEALTH
- BLACKHALL CHIROP & PODIATRY
- BLACKHALL PHYSIOTHERAPY CLINIC
- BLAIR, RICHARD
- BOYD, A
- BROUGHAM CHIROPODY CLINIC
- BRUNTSFIELD CTRE-HYPNOTHERAPY
- BUPA MURRAYFIELD HOSPITAL
- CAIRD, DOUGLAS
- CAIRDEAS REMEDIAL
- CAMERON CLINIC
- CAMPBELL, CAROLINE
- CAPLAN, JOHN S
- CARRS, ALLEN
- CASTELL, JENNIE
- CASTLE CENTRE
- CELTIC AROMATICS
- CHAMBERLAIN CONSULTANTS
- CHINESE MED & HEALTHCARE CTRE
- CHIROPODY CENTRE
- CHRISTIE, ADRIAN
- CLAIVOYANTS SHOP
- CLINICAL HYPNO-THERAPY
- CONSULTANT HYP ANALYST
- COOPER, C J C
- CORLEY, SHIAN
- COUNSELLING CENTRE
- COXAN, PATRICIA
- CRAIGLEITH CHIROPRACTIC CLINIC
- DANCE, M G
- DAVID ALLAN CLINIC
- DAVIES, PETER
- DRUMMOND, IAN
- DRUMMOND, TARA W
- E G H P
- EDINBURGH ALEXANDER CENTRE
- EDINBURGH CLINIC
- EDINBURGH COLLEGE-HOMEOPATHY
- EDINBURGH COLLEGE-HOMEOPATHY
- EDINBURGH EAST PSYCHOLOGIC SV
- EDINBURGH FLOATARIUM
- EDINBURGH HEALTH CARE
- EDINBURGH HOMEOPATHIC CENTRE
- EDINBURGH OSTEOPATHIC CLINIC
- EDINBURGH OSTEOPATHIC SURGERY
- EDINBURGH PHYSIOTHERAPY CENTRE
- EDINBURGH WEST PSYCHOLOGIC SV
- ELEMENTAL
- ELLIS, JUNE
- ELLIS, M J H
- EXCLUSIVE HYPNOTHERAPY
- FARVIS, KEITH
- FEET FIRST
- FOX, GLYNIS
- GARDINER, F
- GEBBIE, JAMES
- GLADWIN, JOHN F C
- GREER, M
- HAIG, GEORGE
- HART, MARY
- HAWKINS, JAMES
- HAZEL, J M
- HEANEY, J
- HERB ON LINE
- HERBAL GARDEN AROMATHERAPY
- HOFMAN, PETRA
- HOLDEN, SHEENA

- HOW, HELEN F
- HUNTER, ALAN
- IN HARMONY AROMATHERAPY
- INCHKEITH HOUSE
- INHEALTH CENTRE
- J W PHYSIOTHERAPY & SPORTS
- J W PHYSIOTHERAPY & SPORTS
- JENAI
- KATERYNA
- KEIL CENTRE
- KELLY, T G
- KELLY, T G
- KEYS, J
- KUMARIS, BRAHMA
- LIFE FOUNDATION SCHOOL
- LIVING MIND
- LOGAN, CAROL
- LOTHIAN HERBS
- LOWES, D N
- M T DANCE
- MACKIE, A A
- MACPHERSON, R G
- MAIN, J
- MARCHMONT PHYSIOTHERAPY CLINIC
- MARIPOSA AROMATHERAPY
- MARSHALL, FIONA S
- MARSHALL, S C
- MARTIN, C M
- MASON, D H
- MCCORMICK PHYSIO & SPORTS
- MCDONALD, DAVID S
- MCLEOD ST PHYSIO CLINIC
- MCNAUGHTON PHYSIO CLINIC
- MCNAUGHTON PHYSIO CLINIC
- MCTIMONEY CHIROPRACTIC CLINIC
- MCVITTIE, D
- MOBILE CHIROPODY SERVICES
- MORNINGSIDE NATURAL HLTH CTRE
- MORNINGSIDE PODIATRY SERVICE
- MORRISON, SANDRA
- MOUNTCASTLE CLINIC
- MUKHERJI, P S
- MUKHERJI, PURNENDU
- MUNRO, LESLEY
- N H S
- NAPIERS CLINIC & DISPENSARY
- NAPIERS DISPENSARY STOCKBRIDGE
- NAPIERS MAIL ORDER
- NATURES REMEDIES
- NEALS YARD REMEDIES
- NEWTOWN CHIROPRACTIC SURGERY
- OLIVER & STODDARD
- O'SOBANDE, RICHARD
- O'SULLIVAN, M
- PARKER, ERIC J
- PARKER, KATHY
- PATTERSON, YVONNE
- PILATES FOUNDATION UK
- PROCESS ORIENTED PSYCHOLOGY
- PSYCHIC AND LIFE SOLUTIONS
- RADIANT HEALTH
- RAE, A D
- RAE, S M
- RICHARDSON, SALLY
- ROARTY, JULIE D
- ROBERT STONE THERAPEUTICS
- ROBERTSON, M
- ROBERTSON, MING CHEN
- ROSS, L
- ROYAL COLLEGE OF PSYCHIATRISTS
- RUMNEY, KATHLEEN
- RUSSELL, AVRIL
- SALISBURY CENTRE
- SALON VICTORIA
- SANDS PHYSIOTHERAPY SERVICES
- SCHOLL CENTRE
- SCOTT, STEPHEN
- SCOTTISH CENTRE
- SHEN THERAPY CENTRE
- SIBBALD, A
- SIBBALD, ANNE
- SKEDD, L A
- SMITH, MATTHEW
- SMITH, MATTHEW
- SOMA THE FIRM
- STIRRAT, ANTONIA
- STOBIE, JENNY
- STRONG, R R M
- STUART-MENTETH, R A
- STUART-MENTETH, W J
- TARA ROKPA ENDINBURGH
- TEAMWORK
- THOMSON, VENETIA
- TRANSCENDENTAL MEDITATION
- ULTRASON
- UNIVERSITY OF EDINBURGH
- VEITCH, D
- WARD, ELIZABETH
- WELLBEING
- WELLSPRING
- WEST END THERAPY CLINIC
- WHOLE WORKS
- WIGHT, STUART
- WOOD, C
- YORK PLACE HOM PRACTICE

### KIRKLISTON

- CHIROPODY CENTRE

### NEWBRIDGE

- LINDEN HOUSE PSYCHOLOGICAL SVS

## FALKIRK

- AESTHETICA TOTAL SKIN & BODY
- ANGUS WILLIAMSON CLINIC
- BAINSFORD FOOT CLINIC
- CAMELON CHIROPODY CENTRE
- FALKIRK CHIROPRACTIC CLINIC
- GRANT, LESLIE AND DAWN
- GRANT, MARION
- HENDERSON, MARGARET
- LEAH CHIROPRACTIC CLINIC
- LEAH CHIROPRACTIC CLINIC
- MULLAN, PETER
- NATURAL HEALING CENTRE
- PSYCHIC THOUGHTS
- WADDELL, J U

### BO'NESS

- GRANT, LESLIE & DAWN

### BONNYBRIDGE

- TIPTOES

### GRANGEMOUTH

- LYON & JOHNSTON
- MORRISON, JOHN D

### LARBERT

- KELIMAR CLINIC
- MCTIMONEY CHIROPRACTIC CLINIC

## FIFE

### ANSTRUTHER

- NORTH EAST FIFE CHIROPODY PRAC
- PERTH & KINROSS N H S TRUST

### BURNTISLAND

- PAGE, BARBARA E

### COWDENBEATH

- FORD, MARGARET

### CUPAR

- BOTANIC CHIROPODY
- CUMMINS, LYNN
- HOLISTIC AROMATHERAPY
- MAIN, ERIC G
- WESTBANK NATURAL HEALTH CENTRE

### DUNFERMLINE

- ANDERSON, J
- BODYWORKS COMPLETE
- BRYCE, EDWARD
- CAROLE'S MOBILE THERAPIST
- CENTRE FOR STRESS RELEASE
- HOLISTIC HEALTHCARE
- O'BRIAN, D
- PAUL'S
- PSYCHOLOGICAL SERVICE
- REMEDIES HEALTH CARE
- STRESS FREE ZONE
- THOMSON, P
- TWA ACRES HYPNO TRAINING CTRE

### GLENROTHES

- BODYNEEDS
- DAVIDSON, ANGELA
- DOIG, M
- FIFE CHIRO & SPORTS INJURY
- FORRESTER, CATHY
- HEALING HANDS
- HENDERSON, I A
- JAMES, RUTH
- KEEP IN STEP
- MCGINTY, J
- SHEERINS, ROZ
- WILSON, C M

### KIRKCALDY

- COMPLEMENTARY THERAPY CLINIC
- HOGARTH, L
- KIRKCALDY CHIROPRACTIC CLINIC
- MOORE, M H
- NATURAL REMEDY CLINIC
- NEAT FEET
- PSYCHOLOGICAL SERVICE
- ROBERTSON, A
- THERAPUTIC MASSAGE
- TOLBOOTH HOUSE
- XENON CENTRE

### LEVEN

- BODYNEEDS
- CAMERON, WILLIAM
- LOCKHART, M D
- MCLEOD, S

### LOCHGELLY

- GERRARD, BARBARA
- PSYCHOLOGICAL SERVICE

### ST. ANDREWS

- BOARDMAN, SARA
- CAMILLA HEY HOLISTIC PRACTICE
- EAST FIFE SPORTS INJURY CLINIC
- FORBES, D LOCKHART
- MATHERS, SHONA
- ST ANDREWS OSTEOPATHS
- ST ANDREWS PHYSIO PRACTICE

### ST. MONANS

- FOUNDATION HEALTH

### TAYPORT

- MALCOLM, HANNE

## GLASGOW (CITY OF)

### GLASGOW

- A A A HYPNOTHERAPY ADVICE
- A WELSH COUTTS
- ABOUT FACE
- ACTIVE CHIROPRACTIC
- ACUPUNCTURE CLINIC
- ALEXANDER TECHNIQUE
- ALEXANDER TECHNIQUE
- ALEXANDER TECHNIQUE
- ALEXANDER, LINDA
- ALTERNATIVE STRESS CENTRE
- ANDERSON DOE PODIATRY CLINIC
- ANNE PENMAN THERAPY
- ASHE, SHIRLEY
- ASSOCIATION OF STRESS MNGMT
- AVEVA HERBAL
- BARR, ISABEL
- BATH STREET THERAPY CENTRE
- BEARSDEN CHIROPRACTIC CLINIC
- BEHIND THE VEIL
- BLACK, JIM
- BOTHWELL PHYSIOTHERAPY
- BOYLE, JACK (DR)
- BRAZENALL, A R
- BRIDGETON PSYCHOLOGICAL SVS
- BRIGGS, AGNES
- BRITISH SOC OF MED/DENT HYP
- BUCHAN, L
- BUCKINGHAM CLINIC
- CADENHEAD, SHEENA
- CARRICK STREET PHYSIO & SPORT
- CHINESE MEDICINE CENTRE
- CHIROPODIST
- CHIROPODY AT MUNRO'S
- CLAREMONT HOMEOPATHIC CLINIC
- CLINIC AT CHARING CROSS
- COIA, GRACE
- COLLEGE OF HOLISTIC MEDICINE
- CONWAY, V A (DR)
- CONWAY, VALERIE (DR)
- CONWAY, VALERIE A (DR)

- COSMIC FLOW
- CRAIG, THOMAS M
- CRAM, ALEXANDER
- CRAM, D
- CRAM, DENNIS
- CREATIVE THERAPIES
- CRYSTAL HARMONY
- CURRIE, A M
- DARNLEY HOUSE
- DENEHOLM THERAPY
- DREW
- DRUMCHAPEL PSYCHOLOGICAL SVS
- D'SOUZA, MARGARET
- EAST KILBRIDE SPORTS CLINIC
- EASTERHOUSE PSYCHOLOGICAL SVS
- EDWARDS, JOHN
- ELLIOTT CHIROPRACTIC CLINIC
- ESSENTIAL BEAUTY
- FAIRBAIRN, KAREN
- FERDA
- FIRESTONE, ELLIS
- FITZPATRICK, J H
- FLETCHER, KATIE
- FLYNN, JOHN K
- FOOT SHOP
- FOOTSURE
- FRASER, DINGWALL & ASSOCIATES
- GARNER, J
- GARNETHILL CENTRE
- GAVIN, H T H
- GIBSON, ANDREW
- GIBSON, R G
- GILLEY, EUNICE
- GLASGOW CHIROPRACTIC CLINIC
- GLASGOW, KY
- GLASSER, E C
- GOURLAY, LINDA
- GOURLAY, STEPHEN
- GOVAN PSYCHOLOGICAL SERVICES
- GRAHAM, JANE
- GREENE, STEFANI
- HARLEY, ANN
- HARVEST CLINIC
- HEALTH & VITALITY
- HERBAL DISPENSARY
- HOLISTIC HEALING & HYP
- HOLISTIC HEALING CENTRE
- HOLISTIC SURGERY
- HOLLAND, IAN
- HOMEOPATHIC CLINIC
- HUI CHUN CHINESE ACUPUNCTURE
- HUICHUN CLINIC OF T C M
- HUMAN PERFORMANCE CLINIC
- HUTTON, WILLIAM
- HYDEPARK SAUNA
- HYNDLAND CLINIC
- INDEPENDENT PSYCHOLOGICAL SVS
- IRVING, MAUREEN V
- JEFFREY, G M
- JUNNER, ROSEMARY
- JUST FOR FEET
- KARAVANSERIA
- KAREN SLATER AROMATHERAPIST
- KEIL CENTRE
- KEITH, GILL
- KIDLINGTON CHIROPRACTIC
- KINSELLA, KARLA
- KIRK, J
- KIRKINTILLOCH FOOT CLINIC
- KNOX, HELEN
- LAMBERT, C W
- LANGSIDE PSYCHOLOGICAL SVS
- LASER THERAPY
- LASER THERAPY
- LASER THERAPY CENTRE
- LAURIE, A
- LAWLER-DOCHERTY, JANIS
- LAWTON, D V
- LEAH CLINIC
- LENZIE CLINIC
- LIFE'S ESSENTIALS
- LOBO, MARIETTE
- LOCHRIE, JANE
- LONG RIVER TAI CHI CIRCLE
- LUSH, AUDREY
- MACLEOD, KENNETH
- MARTIN, CHERIE (DR)
- MARTIN, J
- MARY HERAGHTY AT HEALTHY FEET
- MCCALL, LYNN
- MCDONALD PARTNERSHIP
- MCDONALD, EILEEN
- MCFARLANE, R L
- MCGARAHAN, C
- MCINTOSH, G
- MCKAY, MARIA
- MCKAY, MARIA
- MCKENNA, M
- MCLAREN, CATH RENA
- MCLAUGHLIN, M C
- MCLAY, G
- MCLEAN, A M
- MCQUEEN, DAVID
- MCTIMONEY CHIROPRACTIC CLINIC
- MCTIMONEY CHIROPRACTIC CLINIC
- MILNE, ALEC
- MISRA, P C
- MITCHELL, GRACE
- MOONEY, K
- MUIREND CHIROPRACTIC CLINIC
- NAPIER'S DISPENSARY & CLINIC
- NATURAL HEALTH SERVICE
- NEWALL, K
- O'NEILL, H
- OPTIONS FOR CHANGE
- PATTERSON, VICKY
- PHYSICAL EVALUATION SYSTEMS
- PHYSIO CENTRAL
- PLUIDGE, MARK
- POLLOK PSYCHOLOGICAL SERVICES
- PRIVATE LINES
- PSYCHIC & HEALING CENTRE
- PSYCHIC CONSULTANTS
- PSYCHOLOGICAL SERVICES
- PSYCHOLOGICAL SERVICES
- PSYCHOLOGICAL SERVICES
- QUIN, JENNIFER A
- RAMONA, SUE
- RAWORTH, SUZANNE
- RENFIELD CLINIC-HYPNOTHERAPY
- RHODIE, ANDREA
- RICE, OWEN
- ROBERTSON, KEITH
- ROBERTSON, MAUREEN
- ROBERTSON, MAUREEN & KEITH
- ROKPA HOUSE
- ROLLAND, C R
- ROSENGARD, L (DR)
- ROSS, ALICE I
- ROY, MARGARET
- SAXBY, LAURA
- SCHOLL CENTRE
- SCOTT, B W
- SCOTTISH INSTITUTE-HUMAN REL
- SCOTTISH SCHOOL OF HERBAL MED
- SEAL COMMUNITY HEALTH PROJECT
- SHARKEY, JANICE
- SHAWLANDS HYPNOTHERAPY CLINIC
- SINO-HERBAL CLINIC
- SMITH, JODY
- SMITH, WALTER
- STEWART, A
- STEWART, JIM (DR)
- STEWART, V
- STRESS SENSE
- STRESSED OUT
- THERAPY CENTRE
- THERAPY OF LIFE CLINIC
- THOMSON, D
- TOMLINS, C & CURRIE, J
- TRANSCENDENTAL MEDITATION
- URQUHART, R J
- URQUHART, RODERICK J
- VAHEY, G
- VAN GRIETHUYSEN, CORLA
- VOY, JOAN
- WALLACE, RUTH
- WATSON, S
- WEIR-MCGOWAN, ANNETTE
- WEST END THERAPY CENTRE
- WOODS, K M
- WOODS, K M

### NEWTON MEARNS

- NUTRITION WORLD

## HIGHLAND

### ALNESS

- MATTHEW, MARY

### DINGWALL

- DINGWALL HEALTH CENTRE
- HARMONOLOGY CENTRE
- PUFFIN HYDROTHERAPY POOL

### FORT WILLIAM

- GARRINGTON, N
- HIGHLAND COMM NHS TRUST
- MACKENZIE, J D

### GRANTOWN-ON-SPEY

- BUMBLE - BEE'S PHYSIO
- HEALTH CORNER

### INVERGARRY

- MORNING LIGHT

### INVERGORDON

- WAH, G

### INVERNESS

- AUSTIN, JENNIFER
- CENTRE FOR COMP THERAPIES
- CRAWFORD, J
- ESSENTIAL GAEL
- GENTLE WAYS
- GRANT, K
- GRIFFIN, A H
- HELEN N SERVICE
- HIGHLAND CHIROPRACTIC CLINIC
- HIGHLAND COMMUNITIES
- HILTON CLINIC
- MCILWRAITH, B G
- NATURAL THERAPY CENTRE
- SEAFIELD CLINIC
- STEVENS, HELEN
- TAYLOR, JUNE
- WALLACE, MAUREEN

### KYLE OF LOCHALSH

- MACKENZIE, J D

### NAIRN

- AIRLIE COMPLEMENTARY CLINIC
- BRODIE, JACQUELINE
- CHAMBERS, I M
- HUDSON, MICHAEL B
- NAIRN HYDROTHERAPY POOL

### NEWTONMORE

- HOMEOPATHIC PRACTICE

### PORTREE

- MACKENZIE, J D

### THURSO

- KARIM, M
- LAMB, BRIAN V
- MALLOWS, J
- STEWART & JONES

## INVERCLYDE

### GOUROCK

- PETTIGREW, N
- ROBINSON, M

### GREENOCK

- DAVIES, NOEL
- INVERCLYDE OSTEOPATHIC CLINIC
- MCVEY, S A
- WEST END PHYSIOTHERAPY

### KILMACOLM

- ANDERSON, A J
- KELLERMANS

## LANARKSHIRE (NORTH)

### AIRDRIE

- BETTERWORLD
- BUCHANAN, LEONORA
- MAITLAND, J
- PSYCHOLOGICAL SERVICE
- REGISTERED HOMEOPATH
- STRATH NATURAL THERAPIES
- THOMSON, J

### COATBRIDGE
- ATKIN, M B
- PHYSICARE

### MOTHERWELL
- ANDERSON, DAVID
- MCCROSSAN ASSOCIATES
- PHYSIOTHERAPY CLINIC
- ROLLAND, C R
- SEMPRE LIBERA
- SMITH, IRENE B
- SUMMERS, A

### WISHAW
- CAMERON, W M
- DOUGLAS, JACK
- G H B CHIROPODY SERVICES
- GOLDEN HANDS
- MCKIRDY, GILLIAN
- MORGAN, F C
- PHYSIOTHERAPY CLINIC
- WORLD OF HEALTH

## LANARKSHIRE (SOUTH)

### BIGGAR
- WHITE, C

### CARLUKE
- SIMPLY QUARTZ
- WILLIAMS, K

### EAST KILBRIDE
- ABSOLUTE THERAPY

### HAMILTON
- ALTERNATIVE MEDICINE CENTRE
- COLETTE
- FRANCES, JOAN
- HAMILTON FOOT CLINIC
- HAMILTON PSYCHIC FORUM
- KERR, JAMES
- MCCLUSKEY, J
- MEEK, ROSLYN
- ROY, MAGARET

### LANARK
- BIRCH STREET CLINIC
- HUTCHISON, K C
- PHYSICARE
- PSYCHOLOGICAL SERVICES
- ROBB, A (DR)
- WILSON, S A

### LARKHALL
- DEANS, GRACE
- LEO FORTUNE TELLER

### STRATHAVEN
- EPILATION SUITE
- HARDMAN, CHRISTINE
- LEES, PATRICIA
- MCCLUSKEY, J
- QUINN, JIM

## LOTHIAN (EAST)

### DUNBAR
- AROMA
- DARLING, ANNE
- DUNBAR CHIROPODY CLINIC
- DUNBAR PHYSIOTHERAPY
- KINNAIRD, S H

### HADDINGTON
- EAST LOTHIAN PHYSIO CENTRE
- GASCOYNE, L
- HEALTH & BEAUTY CENTRE

### NORTH BERWICK
- CORRIE, D F
- FRASER, GORDON
- FRASER, GORDON
- LOGAN, K

## LOTHIAN (MID)

### BONNYRIGG
- BONNYRIGG CHIROPODY CENTRE
- MCIVOR, K
- NEW DUNDAS CLINIC

### DALKEITH
- BRACHER, C J
- HAMILTON, JAMES
- NATURAL HEALTH CENTRE

### LASSWADE
- WYLIE, DORIS

### LOANHEAD
- NORDOFF-ROBBINS MUSIC THERAPY

### MUSSELBURGH
- BRACHER, C J
- COMPLEMENTARY MEDICINE CENTRE
- CRYSTAL SANCTUARY
- DICKSON, JOHN J
- EASTERN SCENTS
- SCOTTISH KINESIOLOGY CENTRE
- SHEARER & ASSOCIATES

### PENICUIK
- WEBSTER, J B

### ROSLIN
- PEASTON, S
- RADIANT COLOUR

## LOTHIAN (WEST)

### BATHGATE
- BELL, MAUREEN
- BURTON, GAYLE
- CAMPBELL, HELEN
- CUNNING, I
- DONNA'S AROMATHERAPY & GIFTS
- MACKAY, J M
- PHYSIOTHERAPY SERVICES
- VINCES, DENISE
- WOOD, G W

### BROXBURN
- FLANNERY, ANNE
- GEBAL, ANNE
- LIGHTENED PATHWAYS
- MORRISON, R D

### LINLITHGOW
- CORMACK, SUSAN
- HOWARD AFFILIATES
- LINLITHGOW PHYSIO PRACTICE
- NATURAL BALANCE

### LIVINGSTON
- CEDARBANK CENTRE PSYCHOL SVS
- DUIGNAN, KAREN
- GILL, SHIRLEY
- PALMISTRY BY SARAH
- PSYCHOLOGICAL ADVANTAGE
- TOTAL FOOT CARE
- TOTAL FOOTCARE

## MORAY

### ELGIN
- AROMA REMEDY
- BURNETT, A
- CHRISTY, KERRIE
- ELGIN CHIROPRACTIC CLINIC
- LEACH HEALTH CLINIC
- MACKAY, I
- MORAY CHANONRY CENTRE
- NORTH COLLEGE OSTEO PRACTICE
- TRUJILLO, DR ORLANDO

### FOCHABERS
- BURNETT, AILEEN

### FORRES
- AROMANTIC
- FEATHERSTONE (DR)
- FINDHORN FLOWER ESSENCES
- GRINDLEY, E M
- HEALTH WORKS
- HEALTHWORKS
- HOMOEOPATHIC CLINIC
- ROBINSON, ELIZABETH
- STECKLER, LAURA
- SURGERY
- YOUNG, COURTENAY

## NORTHUMBERLAND

### BERWICK-UPON-TWEED
- ANDERSON, DUNCAN
- BERWICK FOOT CLINIC
- BERWICK PHYSIOTHERAPY CENTRE
- JONES, F J
- SOLAR- PLEXUS

## ORKNEY ISLES

### KIRKWALL
- A D S THOM
- DOLPHIN CONNECTION

## PERTH AND KINROSS

### ALYTH
- BARRON, DEIRDRE

### AUCHTERARDER
- ARMFIELD, L S
- AUCHTERARDER CHIROPODY
- BRIDGE OF ALLAN THERAPY CENTRE
- STRESS CENTRE

### BLAIRGOWRIE
- BALGILLO HOMEOPATHIC PRACTICE
- TAYLOR, D W
- TWA ACRES HYPNOTHERAPY CENTRE

### CALLANDER
- LENDRICK LODGE

### COMRIE
- BACK PAIN & SPORTS CLINIC

### CRIEFF
- GRIEVE, J M

### DUNBLANE
- MCGRAW, LIZZIE
- MCGRAW, LIZZIE

### DUNKELD
- ACUPUNCTURE CLINIC DUNKELD
- MOORE, MAGGIE

### KINROSS
- CROUCH, ROBERTA
- MUIR'S NATURAL HEALTH CENTRE

### PERTH
- ACUPUNCTURE CLINIC
- ALM, DENISE
- BAND, NEIL M
- BLAKELEY, K
- CENTRE FOR NATURAL HEALTH
- CRANIOSACRAL SOCIETY
- HOUSTON, ANNE D
- HOWIE, TOM R
- HOWIE, TOM R
- MACKENZIE, BOYD
- MACKENZIE, R
- MACKINTOSH, SUSAN
- MARSHALL, LESLIE
- NORWELL, M
- PEACOCK, J W
- PERTH BACK PAIN CLINIC
- PERTH CHIRO & OSTEO CENTRE
- STEVENSON, IAN W
- TAYLOR, D
- WIGHT CHIROPRACTIC CLINIC

## RENFREWSHIRE

### BRIDGE OF WEIR
- BRIDGE OF WEIR CHIRO CLINIC
- CRAIG, MARY

### ERSKINE
- RAINEY, MARTHA

### JOHNSTONE
- FANNING, M W

### LOCHWINNOCH
- DOUGLAS, ANNE S

### PAISLEY
- ADERCORN PHYSICAL THERAPY
- ALBA CENTRE
- ALLAUDDIN, ASIF
- APT LASER THERAPY
- BLACKHALL PARK CENTRE
- CHIROPODY CLINIC
- CLERKIN, G
- CUMMINGS, ALEX M L
- DOYLE, JOHN

- HOLISTIC HEALING CLINICS
- IRVINE, MAURICE J
- LINTON, UNNA
- MCINTOSH, GILLIAN
- NEW SNEDDON STREET CLINIC
- PAISLEY CHIROPRACTIC CLINIC
- PAISLEY NATURAL THERAPY CENTRE
- PAISLEY PHYSIOTHERAPY CENTRE
- POLSON, KIRSTEN E
- ROSEWOOD AROMATHERAPY ROOM

### PORT GLASGOW

- GILLON, RACHEL

### RENFREW

- ALLAUDDIN, ASIF
- DRIVER, D
- MCINTOSH, GILLIAN
- MITCHELL, CAROLE

## SCOTTISH BORDERS

### COLDSTREAM

- BAINES, HILARY

### DUNS

- BORDERS HEALTH BOARD
- MAIN, ROBERT J
- MURRELL, R J
- OPUS STOOL

### GALASHIELS

- MAIN, BOB
- MARSHALL, KAREN

### HAWICK

- FISHER, J W
- HOGARTH, JAMES
- L W FOOTCARE
- NATURAL THERAPY CENTRE

### JEDBURGH

- WISHING WELL

### KELSO

- FAIRNINGTON, A & B
- MOROZZO, RUTH
- NATURES WAY

### MELROSE

- FOURNIER, C
- HICKEBOTTON, S
- HOLM, M
- HOW, C I
- MAIN, ROBERT J
- NATURES TOUCH
- SCOTTISH CHIROPRACTIC ASS
- WIGHT CHIROPRACTIC CLINIC

### PEEBLES

- LAMBERT, IAN
- WATT, A S

### SELKIRK

- CASTELL, JENNIE

### ST. BOSWELLS

- ST BOSWELLS CHIRO CLINIC

## SHETLAND ISLANDS

### LERWICK

- COMPLEMENTARY HEALTH CENTRE
- LERWICK CHIROPRACTIC CLINIC

## STIRLING

- AITCHISON, JAMES
- ALLAN, C
- BRIDGE OF ALLAN THERAPY CENTRE
- C R PHYSIOTHERAPY
- CUMMING, S W
- GOLD, P
- HILL, SARAH
- KARMANIE HOLISTIC THERAPIES
- LUMSDEN, D
- PATERSON, NINA S
- PHYSIO FOCUS
- ROBERTSON, K
- STIRLING & BRIDGE
- STIRLING CHIROPRACTIC CLINIC
- WIGHT CHIROPRACTIC CLINIC
- WILSON, R A

### DENNY

- MOODMAKERS

### DOUNE

- BARON, COLIN M (DR)

## WESTERN ISLES

### STORNOWAY

- HIGHLAND CHIROPRACTIC CLINIC
- M M AFRIN JUNIOR

# BLAENAU GWENT

## ABERTILLERY
- ABERTILLERY PHYSIOTHERAPY

## EBBW VALE
- CHEE SOO HOLISTIC CLINIC
- CLASSIC CLINIC

## TREDEGAR
- HAMLYN, EIRWEN
- MOUNTWAY

# BRIDGEND
- ACUPUNCTURE CLINIC
- ADEGOKE, ROTIMI
- ALTERNATIVE HEALING CENTRE
- BACK & NECK CLINIC
- BRIDGEND
- CHALINDER-MORGAN, H
- CORNER SURGERY
- DAVIS, BEVERLEY
- DERWEN ELECTROLYSIS CLINIC
- EDUCATIONAL & PSYCHOL SVS
- EVANS, GARFIELD
- FRAZER, P
- GRIFFITHS, IAN
- HALL, J B
- HARRISON, MONICA
- JENKINS, JOHN
- PARKWOOD CHIROPRACTIC CLINIC
- SIGRID DE VRIES
- SMITH, ALLAN
- WALLEN, R G
- WILLIAMS, DAVID
- WILLIAMS, M

# CAERPHILLY

## BARGOED
- BARGOED CHIROPODY CLINIC
- EDWARDS, TINA
- PRITCHARD, JEAN

## BLACKWOOD
- DAVIES, N G
- PARKWOOD CHIROPRACTIC CLINIC

## HENGOED
- BRAKE, C L
- OAKFIELD NATURAL HEALTH CENTRE
- SMITH, S J

# CARMARTHENSHIRE

## AMMANFORD
- HARCOURT-RAY, JILL
- MORGAN, TINA

## BURRY PORT
- OWENS, SPENCER
- RICHARDS, CARMEL

## CARDIGAN
- BODY MATTERS
- HOWELLS, G E
- JABROO, C

## CARMARTHEN
- ASHTON, HAZEL
- AURICULOTHERAPY UK
- BURROWS, BARBARA
- CARMARTHEN
- CHARLES, L
- JONES, J G
- SKINGLEY, R M
- YR APOTHECARI

## CLYNDERWEN
- SAYERS, R B

## FERRYSIDE
- INSIGHT PSYCHOLOGICAL SERVICES

## KIDWELLY
- HEALING HANDS
- WILLOW

## LAMPETER
- BODY MIND & SOLE
- RAMAYA, K
- TONY'S HAIR & HEALTH CENTRE

## LLANDEILO
- HOLISTIC CLINIC/MYDDFAI HERBS
- JONES, M E
- LLANDEILO ACUPUCTURE CLINIC

## LLANDOVERY
- WAINWRIGHT, MARY

## LLANDYSUL
- EVANS, HELEN
- HALFORD, ELIZABETH
- HALFORD, ROBERT
- HEDGES, CECILY
- HYPNOSIS CENTRE
- MILLICAN, SALLY
- THERAPEUTIC ANTIBODIES UK

## LLANELLI
- ADAMS, CHARMAINE
- GREENWAY CONSULTANCY
- GRIFFITHS, IAN
- KENWARD, SANDRA
- LEWIS, ALUN
- MULROY CHIROPODIST
- PEEL, DENNIS
- PENNANT VALLEY
- PHILLIPS, T G
- SHARKEY, TAMSIN
- SPENCER AROMATHERAPY
- TAYLOR, J D
- WEEDS, MARK
- WILLIAMS, CHRISTINE

## LLANWRDA
- ACUPUNCTURE CENTRE

## NEWCASTLE EMLYN
- HAZELBY, TRACY
- KACHA-STONES.COM

## PENCADER
- ALLEN, C E
- ASKINS, A M

## WHITLAND
- BISHOP, S J
- POWNER, MARGARET

# CEREDIGION

## ABERYSTWYTH
- BAKER STREET HEALING CTRE
- CHERRY TREE CTRE FOR NTRL MED
- ENGELKAMP, JOANNA
- FFYNNONWEN NATURAL THRPY CTRE
- JONES, B E
- LEWIS, D MICHAEL

## LAMPETER
- AMIES, SUSAN

## LLANRHYSTUD
- COCKSEDGE, JOHN M

## TALYBONT
- ENGELKAMP, JOANNA

## TREGARON
- SIMMONDS, K M
- WILLIAMS, A

# CONWY

## ABERGELE
- ABERGELE CHIROPODY SERVICES
- EVANS, GAYLE
- HERBS FOR EVERYONE

## COLWYN BAY
- CHESHIRE FOUNDATION
- EVANS, MARGARET
- GREENHALGH, KEITH
- GREENHALGH, P
- MEWIS, R J
- MIERS, IRENE
- NIMAN, GEORGE
- NORTH WALES YOGA/NAT THRPY
- PENDERGAST, E A
- RAYNER, SALLY

## DEGANWY
- DEGANWY OSTEOPATHIC CLINIC

## LLANDUDNO
- CARR, R N D
- DREW, DAVID
- JONES, D A
- MELA CENTRE OF OSTEOPATHY
- PIDGLEY, S
- SMITH, E
- SMITH, P (DR)
- WILLIAMS, ANGELA

## LLANFAIRFECHAN
- NRTH WALES CLI OF RELAXATION
- PARKHOUSE, R

## LLANRWST
- ANDERSON, I M
- THOMAS, EMLYN

## PENMAENMAWR
- HAGGAS, ERNEST

# DENBIGHSHIRE

## CHIRK
- DEWBERRY, MAY

## CORWEN
- MCGILL, L
- UDEN, CHRISTINE

## DENBIGH
- CELESTIAL DESIGNS AROMATHERAPY
- HARNWELL, J P
- KERFOOT OWEN, RITA
- POWELL, IANTO D
- RETREAT
- SCHOOL PSYCHOLOGICAL SERVICE

## LLANGOLLEN
- CONSTABLE, JOY
- HEALING WAYS
- HURD, JOAN
- JEVON, NICKY & DENIS
- ROBERTS, S
- ROY MORRIS CLINIC

## RHYL
- ALLIED PHYSIOTHERAPY
- COULTER, M
- FOOTCARE
- HENDRE SANCTUARY
- KRAUS, R A
- PITSTOW, S P
- STEVENS, JEAN

## RUTHIN
- CONRAD, H
- KEELY, JANETTE
- PEN Y LON
- TYLER, PETER

## ST. ASAPH
- COUPAR, A M
- MAXIM, L

# FLINTSHIRE

## BAGILLT
- REECE, JULIE

## BROUGHTON
- BOOTS HEALTHCARE SERVICES

## BUCKLEY
- PEARL AROMATHERAPY

## DEESIDE
- CHIROPODISTS SURGERY
- DUGGAN, NORA
- EDUCATIONAL PSYCHOLOGY SERVICE
- GUEST, J F
- HAWARDEN PHYSIO PRACTICE
- LIKISMA AROMATHERAPY
- NORTH WALES PHYSIO & SPORTS
- SIMPLY NATURAL

## FLINT
- HAPPY FEET

## HOLYWELL
- A L J RILEY ASSOCIATES
- DAVIES, JOAN

- KAY, PAUL

### MOLD

- BRITTAIN-DODD, RUTH
- GAFFNEY, ALMA
- HOUGH, TREVOR
- HYPNOTHERAPY CENTRE
- JONES, J M
- MADDERN, WENDY
- OSTEOPATHY & ACUPUNCTURE
- POWELL, IANTO D
- POWELL, IANTO D

## GLAMORGAN (VALE OF)

### ABERDARE

- CARE-TECH AROMATHERAPY
- CHICK, TREVOR J
- CREW, R
- EGAN, P K
- HYPNOTHERAPIST
- MALE, R S
- RIDGE, D
- RIVENDELL NAT THERAPY CLINIC

### BARRY

- ACORN CHIROPODY/PODIATRY
- BARRY OSTEOPATHIC CLINIC
- BROWN, ANNE
- FOUR WINDS HEALING CENTRE
- MOONSTONES NAT THERAPY CLINIC
- MURRIN, P M
- NATURAL HEALTHCARE
- OSBORNE, CHRISTINE
- PHELAN, ALAN

### CAERPHILLY

- MOBILE FOOTWORKS
- OVENS, M
- PALMER, G A PETER
- PHYSIOTHERAPY SERVICES
- POLLEY, JOHN G
- POLLEY, LYNDON

### CARDIFF

- ACORN CHIROPODY SERVICES
- ALEXANDER TECHNIQUE
- ALEXANDER TECHNIQUE
- ANGELO, JAN
- ARCOS, LYNNE
- AROMA
- AROMATHERAPY & REIKI CLINIC
- AROMATHERAPY CLINIC
- AYRE CENTRE OF HYPNOTHERAPY
- BACK & NECK CHIRO CLINIC
- BALANCED HEALTH
- BALL DELYTH
- BAY TRADITIONAL REMEDY
- BEIGHTON, JO
- BIO UNIT
- BIRD, MICHELLE
- BRITISH SCHOOL OF SHIATSU-DO
- BRITTON, JAN
- BROWN, HELEN
- BROWN, VICTORIA
- BUTHE, PETER
- CARDIFF & CWMBRAN CHIROPODY
- CARDIFF CHIROPRACTIC CLINIC
- CARDIFF CLINIC OF TRICHOLOGY
- CARDIFF CONSULTANCY
- CARDIFF ELECTRO & BTY CLNC
- CARDIFF HEALTH PRACTICE
- CARDIFF HOMEOPATHIC CLINIC
- CARRINGTON, MARTIN
- CARTLIDGE, S
- CHINESE ACUPUNCTURE CLINIC
- CHINESE HEALTH CENTRE
- CHIROPODY SERVICES
- CITY CENTRE CHIRO CLINIC
- D T R CLINIC
- DAVIES, LARRY
- DAVIES, LOUISE
- DYMOTT, ANGIE C K
- ELIAS, IAN R
- EVANS, MARI
- EVANS, MARI
- FARMER, F F
- FARRINGTON, C
- FAULKNER, M
- FRANKLYN CHIROPODY
- GARDNER, KATHLEEN A
- GHELICH, S BATMAN (DR)
- GILLETT, E
- GOODE, CAROLINE
- GRIMWADE, S
- GRIMWADE, S
- HARRIS, ANTHONY S A
- HARRIS, CHRIS
- HARRY, L M
- HIPKIN, B J
- HOMOEOPATHIC GROUP
- HOPKINS, NORMAN
- HUMBLE-JACKSON, S L
- HYANDS, TONI
- HYPNOTHERAPY CLINIC
- IAN LAWES ELECTRICAL
- JENKINS, MARY (DR)
- JEREMY, C
- JOHNSON, C
- JONES, MARION
- JONES, MARION
- JONES, STEVE
- JUDY COURIE - REFLEX & AROMA
- KJELDSEN, TIM
- LANCEY, V H
- LAST, MARIANNE
- LAVELETTE, PETER
- LEE, FELICITY
- LIFELINE
- LLANISHEN CHIROPODY CLINIC
- LLANISHEN PHYSIOTHERAPY CLINIC
- LONG, A
- M I G'S NATURAL HEATHCARE CTRE
- MARTIN WILLEY ASS OF ST MNGMT
- MCDONALD, ALASTAIR
- MILES, ANDREW
- MOREL, SUZIE
- MORGAN, C
- MORGAN-AYRES, PAUL (PROF)
- MULLINS, JOHN
- NATURAL HEALTHCARE
- NEALS YARD
- NEW CONTEMPORARY AROMATHERAPY
- NEW LIFE NATURAL HEALTH CENTRE
- NUTE, JANET
- NUTE, JANET
- PALMER, PETER G A
- PAMO, NORDZIN
- PARKWOOD CHIROPRACTIC CLINIC
- PARKWOOD CHIROPRACTIC CLINIC
- PARRY, PHIL
- PAYNE, R A
- PENDER, CHRISTINE
- PENDER, CHRISTINE
- PENYLAN CLINIC
- PENYLAN PODIATRIC CENTRE
- PHELAN, ALAN
- PHYSIO & BACK CARE CLINIC
- PHYSIO FIRST CENTRE
- PLUMMER, HOWARD G
- POLLEY, LYNDON
- POLLEY, LYNDON
- RAJA YOGA MEDITATION
- RENMAN, TONY
- ROSEMARY, TARGETT
- ROSS, L
- SASSE, LOUISE
- SCHOLL CENTRE
- SEARY, ANDREW
- SELIGMAN, PHILIPPA
- SENSIBLE SCENTS
- SHIPMAN, PAUL
- SHIPTON, NICK
- SIMS, TRACEY
- STATTON, A
- STENSLAND-SLOANE, BARBARA
- STIR SPICES
- TALWAR, ARUN (DR)
- TAYLOR, S
- THERAPY HEALTH/EDUCATION CTRE
- THOMAS, DAVID G
- TRANSCENDENTAL MEDITATION
- TWIN LOTUS HEALING ARTS
- VAUGHN-OWEN, JENI
- VICKERS, CHARLOTTE
- WALSH, J A
- WESTLAKE, ROSEMARY

### COWBRIDGE

- AT HOME WITH HOMEOPATHY
- CARRINGTON'S CONSULTANCY GROUP
- COWBRIDGE & VALE CLINIC
- COWBRIDGE CHIRO/SPINAL REHAB
- COWBRIDGE OSTEOPATH CLINIC
- COWBRIDGE PRACTICE
- MERILAHT, R
- RENWICK, SARAH NADINE
- VALE PHYSIOTHERAPY
- WILLIAMS, TOM

### DINAS POWYS

- LEWIS, CATERINA
- LEWIS, PETER
- MASON, P R

### LLANTWIT MAJOR

- AMETHYST HEALING CENTRE
- BIRT, JANET
- JONES, W PRITCHARD
- STEELE, ASHLEY
- TAYLOR, E
- THERAPYWORKS

### MERTHYR TYDFIL

- JONES, D E F
- LEWIS, P M
- MID-GLAMORGAN HEALTH AUTHORITY
- NATURAL HEALTH & BEAUTY SALON
- PRICE-PULMAN
- RIDGE, D
- WHATLEY, JUDITH
- WHOLE HEALTH COMP THERAPY CTRE

### NEATH

- AROMACARE
- DICKSON, STUART
- EMERGENCY LIFE SUPPORT
- EVANS, STEVE
- GLAMORGAN HEALTH & RACQUET
- GRAHAM, KATIE
- GRAY, CHRISTINE
- JOHN, KEITH
- JULIES
- LEYSON, S & I
- NEATH CHIROPODY CLINIC
- NEATH HERBAL CLINIC
- REES, R
- THOMAS, ANGELA
- WEBBORN, S H P
- WILLIAMS, JOANNE

### PENARTH

- BODY ESSENTIALS
- BOYLE, MARY
- GREENWOOD, CLARE
- GRIMWADE, J C
- HANCOCK, C B
- HENDERSON, H M
- LEE, KEN
- MCINTOSH, MAUREEN
- PENARTH CHIROPRACTIC CLINIC
- PENARTH HOMEOPATHY CLINIC
- PHELAN, ALAN
- ROBINSON, JAMES
- WARD SHIATSU
- WIBLIN, CARON
- ZIAD, PATRICIA

### SWANSEA

- ACUPUNTURE CENTRE
- BENNER, LAWRENCE M
- HENRIETTA CTRE FOR COMP THRPY
- HOLBOROW, ROBERT
- MARCO, ALAN
- MARSHALL, E
- MORTON, PHILLIPA
- SAWDAY, CAROLINE
- SWANSEA VALLEY PHYSIO PRACTICE

### TREHARRIS

- CANN, D
- WHITBY, ALAN R

## GWYNEDD

### BALA

- JONES, H A P

### BANGOR

- COOK, GARETH

- NATURAL THERAPY CLINIC
- NORTH DOWN CLINIC
- REFLEXOLOGY CLINIC

### BETWS-Y-COED
- MOSSHILL HOLISTIC CENTRE

### BLAENAU FFESTINIOG
- GWYNEDD COMMUNITY TRUST

### CAERNARFON
- CENTRE FOR WELL BEING
- FARRANT, F L
- HALL, ALISON
- O'NEIL, L
- PROTEC PHYSIO & ACUPUNCTURE
- SMITH, W

### CRICCIETH
- PROTEC PHYSIO & ACUPUNCTURE
- SMITH, WYN

### PENRHYNDEUDRAETH
- NATURAL HEALING CENTRE

### PORTHMADOG
- COLE, HARVEY M
- FOSKETT, SARAH J
- HOWORTH, R
- IPHOFEN, R

### PWLLHELI
- JONES B D L
- MARSHALL, E
- PROTEC PHYSIO & ACUPUNCTURE
- PROTEC PHYSIO & ACUPUNCTURE

## ISLE OF ANGLESEY

### AMLWCH
- NATURAL APPROACH

### BEAUMARIS
- ANGLESEY HEALING CENTRE
- LOTUS HERBS

### BODORGAN
- BERNARD-SMITH, H (DR)
- EPHRAIM, NONA
- HUGHES, R L & J L

### GAERWEN
- MAY, ADAM

### HOLYHEAD
- JONES, BARBARA
- LANGLEY, ALLEN
- MASSEY, RAYMOND

### LLANFAIRPWLLGWYNGYLL
- GIBANI, CAROL

### LLANGEFNI
- CHALMERS, D G
- PRINCE

### MENAI BRIDGE
- LORD, WENDY
- OSTEOPATHIC CENTRE

### PENTRAETH
- ALLENS
- MILLS, A R

### TYN-Y-GONGL
- TILL, ELIZABETH

## MONMOUTHSHIRE

### ABERGAVENNY
- ABERGAVENNY THERAPY CTRE
- DAVIS, J H
- DOWNEY, D R
- GARRATT, L J
- SOLOMON, ROGER
- WILLIAMS, G A

### CALDICOT
- CALDICOT CHIROPRACTOR CENTRE
- JONES-GRIFFITHS, A M
- LEWIS, ANDREW J
- MIND BODY SOUL DEVELOPMENT ORG
- NIELD, HELEN
- PRICE, J
- S LOWNDES SPORTS INJURY

### CHEPSTOW
- BROWN, R
- CORBIN, L
- EARLSWOOD PHYSIOTHERAPY CLINIC
- HEWITT, G
- LEWIS, GERRY
- NICHOLS, JONATHAN
- PARKER, EDMUND
- SKINNER, G
- VITTLE, MARY
- WYE VALLEY CHIROPRACTIC CLINIC
- WYLLIE, KIM
- YOUNG, B

### MONMOUTH
- AGINCOURT OSTEOPATHIC CLINIC
- BROOKSIDE PHYSIO PRACTICE
- BUSH HOUSE OSTEO PRACTICE
- CRAM, F
- CRAM, KATHY
- DEVAUDEN, D
- LOVE, CLAIRE
- MCCONNELL, JULIE
- MCTIMONEY DIRECTORY
- MICHIE, A
- MONMOUTH HERBAL CLINIC
- MONMOUTH NATURAL HEALTH CENTRE
- MSM INFORMATION

### PONTYPOOL
- CARDFF/CWMBRN/PONTYPL CHIROP
- CONSULTANT, NUTRITION
- E M D TRADING
- ELECTROMAGNETIC PRODUCTS
- HARMONY
- JONES, CAROLYN
- NUTRITION CLINIC
- SMALLWOOD ELECTRICAL
- TURFAEN CHIROPODY CLINIC
- WESTCOTT, C N

## NEATH PORT TALBOT

### PONTARDAWE
- DAWSON, KAREN
- ST JAMES MEDICAL CENTRE

### PORT TALBOT
- BILLINGHAMS
- COURTLAND
- YNODDFA MARKETING

## NEWPORT
- ALEXANDER TECHNIQUE
- BAJJADA, JUNE
- BARRY, D J
- BEARD, A
- BEIGHTON, J W
- BOWEN, LINDA
- BOWKETT, LYN
- BUTCHER, PETER
- CHIVERS, JEAN
- CHIVERS, JEAN
- CLINIC OF HOLISTIC HEALTH
- EDWARDS, ANNE
- FRANCIS, JOHN
- FRANKLIN CHIROPODY
- GREENFIELD, J
- GREEVES, JANET
- GWENT CHIROPRACTIC CENTRE
- HEALTH MATTERS WALES
- HEMMERMAN, I A
- HEMMERMAN, J L
- HERBAL TREATMENT CLINIC
- HOLISTIC THERAPY CLINIC
- HOWAR, CHRIS
- HUGH-BASSAM, O J (DR)
- HYPNOTHERAPY & RELAXATION CLNC
- HYPNOTHERAPY CLINIC
- KENSINGTON COURT CLINIC
- LAST, MARIANNE
- MCTIMONEY CHIROPRACTIC
- MEMBERS OF NAT INS OF MED HERB
- MORGAN, CLIVE
- MORGAN, JO
- MOXLEY, SHIRLEY
- NAPPER, RICHARD
- NEWPORT CHIROPRACTIC CLINIC
- NEWPORT POWER & LIGHTING
- NLP THERAPY
- OLIVER, MARION
- PENMAN, TONY
- PLOWMAN, JOHN (DR)
- PLOWMAN, JOHN (DR)
- REDFEARN, C M & D R
- ROCHE, G M
- ROWLANDS, BERNARD
- ROWLANDS, CHRISTINE
- SAUNDERS, K A
- TANNER, T L

## PEMBROKESHIRE

### BONCATH
- JABROO, C

### CRYMYCH
- ROBERTSON-WILLIAMS, M T

### FISHGUARD
- CENTRE OF TRADITIONAL HEALING

### HAVERFORDWEST
- ARK NATURAL HEALING CENTRE
- BLACKLAW-JONES, R
- BRIERLEY, ANTHONY
- BURNS VOYLE PARTNERSHIP
- HICKEY, T J
- ROY, GILLIAN

### MILFORD HAVEN
- ACUPUNCTURE CONSULTANT
- LYNDHURST HOUSE

### NARBERTH
- BENTLEY, JOHN
- LANDSKER CHIROPRACTIC CLINIC

### NEWPORT
- CENTRE OF NATURAL MEDICINE

### PEMBROKE
- CLUTTERBUCK, B
- LOFTUS-BAKER, LYNNE
- WISEMAN, LOUISE

### TENBY
- ACUPUNCTURE CLINIC
- BROMBLEY, E
- COOPER, P G
- DUCKWORTH, NIGEL

## POWYS

### BRECON
- BRECON CLINIC
- BRECON COMPLEMENTARY MED CTRE
- BYFLEET, ROSEMARY
- FLINNING, J
- GROVES, FRAN
- HERBAL HELPLINE
- POWYS HEALTH CARE TRUST
- REFLEXOLOGY & ALLERGY THERAPY
- RODWAY, D J
- SHEPPARD, HELEN
- WILLIAMS, BRIAN

### KNIGHTON
- ORTHOAED

### LLANDINAM
- ASHBROOKE THERAPY
- LLANDINAM COUNSELLING

### LLANDRINDOD WELLS
- CHAMBERS, HANNAH
- DAVIES, E
- LLANDRINDOD WELLS SPA TOWN
- NATURAL SCIENCE COM
- STEPHENS, JANE

### LLANFYLLIN
- JONES, MARION

### LLANGAMMARCH WELLS
- PEACE CLINIC

### LLANIDLOES
- WILDEN, J D

### LLANSANTFFRAID
- ASHBY, F J S

### MACHYNLLETH
- BACK PAIN CENTRE
- CONROY, CHRISTINE
- COVENT HOUSE NTRL HEALTH CTRE
- ENGELKAMP, JOANNA
- FISHER, SUSAN
- HUMPRIES-RILEY, B

### MEIFOD
- BERTH-JONES, D

### MONTGOMERY
- RICARDO, D R

### NEWTOWN
- AURORA HEALING CENTRE
- BACK PAIN CENTRE
- FRANCIS, HELEN
- PRITCHARD, AUDREY

### PRESTEIGNE
- DUNNE, TERESA
- FOREST LODGE PSYCHOTHERAPY
- FULL, D M

### WELSHPOOL
- HEALTH FOCUS
- ROBERTSON, FIONA

## RHONDDA CYNON TAFF

### FERNDALE
- BARKER, A D
- CHIROPODY AT FERNDALE CLINIC
- JENKINS, G & G

### PONTYCLUN
- BUSINESS PSYCHOLOGY WALES
- EVANS, CHRISTINE
- HENSTAFF NATURAL HEALTH CLINIC
- REESE, M M

### PONTYPRIDD
- CAVIL, A J
- FIFTH ELEMENT
- HADFIELD, ELIZABETH
- HUNT, JOHN
- LIFE CARING CENTRE
- POLLEY, LYNDON
- PONTYPRIDD TRAD CHINESE MED
- TOE-TLE FOOTCARE
- WILLIAMS, ANDREA
- WORKER, MALCOLM

### PORTH
- MORRIS, A P

### TONYPANDY
- PEARSON, B J
- SCHOOL PSYCHOLOGICAL CENTRE
- TONYPANDY HEALTH CENTRE

### TREORCHY
- BOUND, A J
- VAUGHAN OWEN, JENI
- YNYSWEN CLINIC

## SWANSEA
- ABERTAWE PHYSIOTHERAPY CLINIC
- ACUPUNCTURE CENTRE
- ACUPUNCTURE CLINIC
- ASHERA THERAPY CENTRE
- BARSELL, R H
- BEYNON, MARTIN
- BLACKLAW-JONES, RICHARD
- BRACEWELL, P J
- BRAMMELL, A L
- BURDEN, RICHARD
- CASTELL, PHILIPPA
- CENTRAL CHIROPODY CLINIC
- CITY & COUNTY CHIROPRACTIC
- CLINIC OF CHINESE MEDICINE
- CONTINENTAL SKIN CLINIC
- DAVIES, ANNE
- DAVIES, JACKIE
- DEVELOPMENTAL HEALTH CONSULT
- DEZELU, B J M
- ELECTROLYSIS CLINIC
- EVANS, F S
- GAYNOR, JOHN
- HALE, SUE
- HAYNES, SIOBHAN
- HERBAL CLINIC
- I R C H
- INDEPENDENT ED PSYCHOL SVS
- JOHNSON, JUDITH
- LEE, ALAN
- LEWIS, S M
- LEYSON, S & I
- MATTHEWS, G
- MCPHERSON, PATRICIA
- NEEDS, S J
- O'MALLEY, JOHN
- P C S
- PEDORTHICS FOOT SGY PRACTICE
- PHILLIPS, DAVID
- PRICE, R
- RATCLIFFE, PAULINE
- REES, L E
- REES, R
- REES, TREVOR
- RODWAY & ASSOCIATES
- RUBY
- SHREWSBURY, MARTIN J
- SOAR, TIMOTHY
- SOUTH WEST CHIROPRACTIC CLINIC
- STEPHENS, G F
- STONE, C A
- SWANSEA CLINIC OF NATURAL MED
- THEOPHILUS, L E
- WATKINS, PHILIPPA
- WHEATLEY, F
- WILLIAMS, MICHAEL (DR)

## TORFAEN

### CWMBRAN
- CLUB INDIGO
- CWMBRAN PHYSIOTHERAPY CENTRE
- PHILLIPS, SANDRA
- PUGH, VIV
- THOMAS, N J

## WREXHAM
- ANALYSIS UNDER HYPNOSIS
- BEGINNERS YOGA VIDEO
- CARING HANDS CLINIC
- CHARLES STREET CHIROPODY
- CHARTERED PHYSIOTHERAPY
- DYKINS, PAUL
- EATON, MARGARET
- G P S
- HARMONY IN HEALTH
- HERBARIUM
- HOWELL, STEPHANIE
- JONES, VALERIE I
- KENDRICK, C A
- LATHAM, PATRICIA
- RHONE, B
- SEDDON, J
- SENSORAMA
- SHEPHERD, STEVEN
- SPIRITUAL PATHWAYS
- TAROT READINGS BY PROF
- TAROT, JAYS
- TIPTON, G A
- TOP TO TOE
- WARR, V W & D L

### BRONWYLFA
- HARMONY IN HEALTH

### BRYNTEG
- PRICE, VICTORIA

### MARFORD
- SLATER, GISELE

### RHOS-DDU
- FREEDOM WITHIN

HEALTH MYSELF

# SECTION 3a

## A-F of Therapies at Practices

# A - F Therapies at Practices/Businesses

Business by County with Reference no.

| Business | Absent Healing | Acupressure | Acupuncture | Alexander Technique | Allergy Testing | Anthroposohical Med | Aromatherapy | Art Therapy | Aura Therapy | Auricular Therapy | Auto Suggestion | Autogenic Training | Aversion Therapy | Ayurvedic Medicine | Baby Massage | Bach Remedies | Bates Method | Beauty Therapy | Bio-energetics | Biofeedback | Biomagnetic Therapy | Biomechanics | Bonesetting | Bowen Therapy | Chinese Herbal Medicine | Chiropody | Chiropractic | Clinical Ecology | Cognitive Therapy | Colonic Hydrotherapy | Colour Therapy | Complementary Therapy | Counselling | Cranial Osteopathy | Cranio-Sacral Therapy | Cryo Surgery | Crystal Healing | Cupping | Cymatics | Dance Movement Thrpy | Dietician | Do-In | Douching | Dowsing | Drama Therapy | Electrolipolysis | Electrolysis | Electrotherapy | Encounter Groups | Faith Healing |
|---|---|---|---|---|---|---|---|---|---|---|---|---|---|---|---|---|---|---|---|---|---|---|---|---|---|---|---|---|---|---|---|---|---|---|---|---|---|---|---|---|---|---|---|---|---|---|---|---|---|---|
| **ENGLAND** | | | | | | | | | | | | | | | | | | | | | | | | | | | | | | | | | | | | | | | | | | | | | | | | | | |
| **BEDFORDSHIRE** | | | | | | | | | | | | | | | | | | | | | | | | | | | | | | | | | | | | | | | | | | | | | | | | | | |
| ACUPUNCTURE CLINIC (HM00269) | | | ● | | | | | | | | | | | | | | | | | | | | | | | | | | | | | | | | | | | | | | | | | | | | | | | |
| ALOE VERA SPECIALISTS (HM00681) | | | | | | | | | | | | | | | | | | | | | | | | | | | | | | | | | ● | | | | | | | | | | | | | | | | | |
| ALTERNATIVE THERAPY AT WORK (HM00732) | | ● | | | | | ● | | | | | | | | | | | | | | | | | | | | | | | | | ● | | | | | | | | | | | | | | | | | | |
| AMPTHILL & FLITWICK CLINIC (HM00795) | | | ● | | | | | | | | | | | | | | | | | | | | | | | | | | | | | | | | | | | | | | | | | | | | | | | |
| ARMSTRONG, DEE (HM01020) | | | | | | | ● | | | | | | | | | | | | | | | | | | | | | | | | | | | | | | | | | | | | | | | | | | | |
| BEDFORD ACUPUNCTURE CLINIC (HM02032) | | | ● | | | | | | | | | | | | | | | | | | | | | | | | | | | | | | | | | | | | | | | | | | | | | | | |
| BEDFORD CHIROPRACTIC SURGERY (HM02033) | | | | | | | | | | | | | | | | | | | | | | | | | | | ● | | | | | | | | | | | | | | | | | | | | | | | |
| BEDFORD PHYSIOTHERAPY CENTRE (HM02035) | | | ● | | | | | | | | | | | | | | | | | | | | | | | | | | | | | | | | | | | | | | | | | | | | | | | |
| BROOKE, JUDITH (HM03160) | | | | | | | | | | | | | | | | ● | | | | | | | | | | | | | | | | | | | | | | | | | | | | | | | | | | |
| BURTON, MERILYNN (HM03444) | | | | | | | ● | | | | | | | | | | | | | | | | | | | ● | | | | | | | | | | | | | | | | | | | | | | | | |
| CHARTERED PHYSIOTHERAPIST (HM04042) | | | | | | | | | | | | | | | | | | | | | | | | | | | ● | | | | | | | | | | | | | | | | | | | | | ● | | |
| CHIROPRACTIC CONSULTANT SVS (HM04397) | | | | | | | | | | | | | | | | | | | | | | | | | | | ● | | | | | | | | | | | | | | | | | | | | | | | |
| CLNC OF ACU & CHINESE HERB MED (HM04726) | | | ● | | | | | | | | | | | | | | | | | | | | | | | | | | | | | ● | | | | | | ● | | | | | | | | | | | | |
| CRIBB, PAULINE (HM05437) | | | | | | | ● | | | | | | | | | | | | | | | | | | | | | | | | | | | | | | | | | | | | | | | | | | | |
| DA SILVA, CAROLE (HM05665) | | | | ● | | | | | | | | | | | | | | | | | | | | | | | | | | | | | | | | | | | | | | | | | | | | | | |
| DANS CHINESE MEDICINE CLINIC (HM05730) | | | ● | | | | | | | | | | | | | | | | | | | | | | | | | | | | | | | | | | | | | | | | | | | | | | | |
| DISS, KATHRYN (HM06122) | | | | ● | | | | | | | | | | | | | | | | | | | | | | | | | | | | | | | | | | | | | | | | | | | | | | |
| DUNTON CTRE-COUN/PSYCHOTHERAPY (HM06428) | | | | | | | | | | | | | | | | | | | | | | | | | | | | | | | | | ● | | | | | | | | | | | | | | | | | |
| GALLEN, ANNE (HM07841) | | | | | | | | | | | | | | | | ● | | | | | | | | | | | | | | | | | | | | | | | | | | | | | | | | | | |
| GOUGH, E & P T (HM08314) | | | | | | | | | | | | | | | | | | | | | | | | | | ● | | | | | | | | | | | | | | | | | | | | | | | | |
| GROVE NATURAL THERAPY CLINIC (HM08610) | | | | | ● | | ● | | | | | | | | | | | | | | | | | | | | ● | | | ● | | | ● | ● | | | | | | | | | | | | | | | | |
| HAVEN AROMATHERAPY CTRE (HM09207) | | | | | | | ● | | | | | | | | | | | | | | | | | | | | | | | | | | | | | | | | | | | | | | | | | | | |
| HEALES CHIROPRACTIC CLINIC (HM09321) | | | | | | | | | | | | | | | | | | | | | | | | | | | ● | | | | | | | | | | | | | | | | | | | | | | | |
| INWARD BOUND THERAPIES (HM10707) | | | | | | | | | | | | | | | | | | | | | | | | | | | | | | | | | ● | | | | | | | | | | | | | | | | | |
| JADE COLLEGE-NATURAL THERAPY (HM10867) | | | | | | | ● | | | | | | | | | | | | | | | | | | | | | | | | | | | | | | | | | | | | | | | | | | | |
| JOHNSON, ANNE (HM11068) | | | | | | | | | | | | | | | | | | | | | | | | | | | | | | | | | | ● | | | | | | | | | | | | | | | | |
| JOHNSTONS CHIROPODIST (HM11107) | | | | | | | | | | | | | | | | | | | | | | | | | | ● | | | | | | | | | | | | | | | | | | | | | | | | |
| KEMPSTON CHIROPRACTIC CLINIC (HM11469) | | | | | | | | | | | | | | | | | | | | | | | | | | | ● | | | | | | | | | | | | | | | | | | | | | | | |
| LAMB CHIROPRATIC CLINIC (HM11884) | | | | | | | | | | | | | | | | | | | | | | | | | | | ● | | | | | | | | | | | | | | | | | | | | | | | |
| LIKISMA (HM12380) | | | | | | | ● | | | | | | | | | | | | | | | | | | | | | | | | | | | | | | | | | | | | | | | | | | | |
| LOBO, GLENN P (HM12530) | | | ● | | | | | | | | | | | | | | | | | | | | | | | | | | | | | | | | | | | | | | | | | | | | | | | |

# A - F Therapies at Practices/Businesses

| Business by County with Reference no. | Absent Healing | Acupressure | Acupuncture | Alexander Technique | Allergy Testing | Anthroposohical Med | Aromatherapy | Art Therapy | Aura Therapy | Auricular Therapy | Auto Suggestion | Autogenic Training | Aversion Therapy | Ayurvedic Medicine | Baby Massage | Bach Remedies | Bates Method | Beauty Therapy | Bio-energetics | Biofeedback | Biomagnetic Therapy | Biomechanics | Bonesetting | Bowen Therapy | Chinese Herbal Medicine |
|---|---|---|---|---|---|---|---|---|---|---|---|---|---|---|---|---|---|---|---|---|---|---|---|---|---|
| MARFLEET, RACHAEL DE VERE (HM13084) | | | ● | | | | | | | | | | | | | | | | | | | | | | |
| MULTIPLE SCLEROSIS THRPY CTRE (HM14351) | | | | | | | ● | | | | | | | | | | | | | | | | | | |
| NAPLES, EILEEN (HM14480) | | | | | | | | | | | | | | | | | | | | | | | | | |
| OSBORN, HELEN (HM15418) | | | | ● | | | | | | | | | | | | | | | | | | | | | |
| PRICE, SARAH (HM16596) | | | | | | | ● | | | | | | | | | | | | | | | | | | |
| RADIANT HEALTH CLINIC (HM16849) | | | ● | | | | | | | | | | | | | | | | | | | | | | |
| RISING CRANE CENTRE (HM17368) | | | ● | | | | | | | | | | | | | | | | | | | | | | |
| SHEER PERFECTION (HM18367) | | | | | | | ● | | | | | | | | | | | | | | | | | | |
| SPECTRUM HEALTH TRUST (HM18976) | ● | ● | | | | | ● | | ● | | | ● | | | | ● | | | | | | | | | |
| SPORT, ALEXANDER (HM19041) | | | | ● | | | | | | | | | | | | | | | | | | | | | |
| STEELE, FRED (HM19178) | | | ● | | | | | | | | | | | | | | | | | | | | | | |
| SWEET BREEZE (HM19584) | | | | | | | ● | | | | | | | | | | | | | | | | | | |
| THERAPY CENTRE (HM19894) | | | | ● | | | | | | | | | | | | | | | | | | | | | |
| THOMAS, P A (HM19955) | | | | | | | ● | | | | | | | | | | | | | | | | | | |
| THOMPSON, MARTIN (HM19992) | | | | | | | | | | | | | | | | | | | | | | | | | |
| WARD-SAUNDERS, WENDY (HM20924) | | | | | | | | | | | | | | | | ● | | | | | | | | | |
| WINTER, SALLY (HM21721) | | | | | | | | | | | | | | | | | | | | | | | | | |
| WOODSIDE CLINIC (HM21857) | | ● | ● | | | | ● | | | | | | | | | | | | | | | | | | |
| YORK, SUSAN (HM22053) | | | | ● | | | | | | | | | | | | | | | | | | | | | |
| **BERKSHIRE** | | | | | | | | | | | | | | | | | | | | | | | | | |
| 1ST CHIROPRACTIC CLINIC (HM00004) | | | | | | | | | | | | | | | | | | | | | | | | | |
| ACUPUNCTURE CLINIC (HM00267) | | | ● | | | | | | | | | | | | | | | | | | | | | | |
| ACUPUNCTURE/CHINESE HERBAL ASS (HM00325) | | | ● | | | | | | | | | | | | | | | | | | | | | | |
| ASCOT PHYSIOFIRST CENTRE (HM01178) | | | | ● | | | | | | | | | | | | | | | | | | | | | |
| BACK TO HEALTH - WINDSOR (HM01516) | | | | | | | | | | | | | | | | | | | | | | | | | |
| BERKSHIRE CHIROPRACTIC (HM02195) | | ● | | | | | ● | | | | | | | | | | | | | | | | | | |
| BLYTH, SIMON (HM02541) | | | ● | | | | | | | | | | | | | | | | | | | | | | |
| BODY & SOUL (HM02561) | | | | | | | | | | | | | | | | | | | | | | | | | |
| BRACKNELL CHIROPRACTIC CLINIC (HM02838) | | | | | | | | | | | | | | | | | | | | | | | | | |
| BURNHAM CHIROPRACTIC CLINIC (HM03404) | | | | | | | | | | | | | | | | | | | | | | | | | |
| BUTTERBUR & SAGE (HM03495) | | | | | | | ● | | | | | | | | | | | | | | | | | | |
| CAMPBELL, ELSPETH (HM03597) | | | | | | | | ● | | | | | | | | | | | | | | | | | |
| CASTLE HILL CLINIC (HM03833) | | | ● | | | | | | | | | | | | | | | | | | | | | | |
| CAVERSHAM CHIROPRACTIC CLINC (HM03864) | | | | | | | | | | | | | | | | | | | | | | | | | |

| Business by County with Reference no. | Chiropody | Chiropractic | Clinical Ecology | Cognitive Therapy | Colonic Hydrotherapy | Colour Therapy | Complementary Therapy | Counselling | Cranial Osteopathy | Cranio-Sacral Therapy | Cryo Surgery | Crystal Healing | Cupping | Cymatics | Dance Movement Thrpy | Dietician | Do-In | Douching | Dowsing | Drama Therapy | Electrolipolysis | Electrolysis | Electrotherapy | Encounter Groups | Faith Healing |
|---|---|---|---|---|---|---|---|---|---|---|---|---|---|---|---|---|---|---|---|---|---|---|---|---|---|
| MARFLEET, RACHAEL DE VERE (HM13084) | | | | | | | | | | | | | | | | | | | | | | | | | |
| MULTIPLE SCLEROSIS THRPY CTRE (HM14351) | ● | | | | | | | ● | | | | | | | | ● | | | | | | | | | |
| NAPLES, EILEEN (HM14480) | | ● | | | | | | | | | | | | | | | | | | | | | | | |
| OSBORN, HELEN (HM15418) | | | | | | | | | | | | | | | | | | | | | | | | | |
| PRICE, SARAH (HM16596) | | | | | | | | | | | | | | | | | | | | | | | | | |
| RADIANT HEALTH CLINIC (HM16849) | | | | | | | | | | | | | | | | | | | | | | | | | |
| RISING CRANE CENTRE (HM17368) | | | | | | | | | | | | | | | | | | | | | | | | | |
| SHEER PERFECTION (HM18367) | | | | | | | | | | | | | | | | | | | | | | | | | |
| SPECTRUM HEALTH TRUST (HM18976) | | | | ● | | ● | ● | ● | | | | ● | | | | ● | | | ● | | | | | | ● |
| SPORT, ALEXANDER (HM19041) | | | | | | | | | | | | | | | | | | | | | | | | | |
| STEELE, FRED (HM19178) | | | | | | | | | | | | | | | | | | | | | | | | | |
| SWEET BREEZE (HM19584) | | | | | | | | | | | | | | | | | | | | | | | | | |
| THERAPY CENTRE (HM19894) | ● | | | | | | | | | | | | | | | ● | | | | | | | | | |
| THOMAS, P A (HM19955) | | | | | | | | | | | | | | | | | | | | | | | | | |
| THOMPSON, MARTIN (HM19992) | ● | | | | | | | | | | | | | | | | | | | | | | | | |
| WARD-SAUNDERS, WENDY (HM20924) | | | | | | | | | | | | | | | | | | | | | | | | | |
| WINTER, SALLY (HM21721) | ● | | | | | | | | | | | | | | | | | | | | | | | | |
| WOODSIDE CLINIC (HM21857) | | | | | | | ● | | ● | | | | ● | | | | | | | | | | ● | | |
| YORK, SUSAN (HM22053) | | | | | | | | | | | | | | | | | | | | | | | | | |
| **BERKSHIRE** | | | | | | | | | | | | | | | | | | | | | | | | | |
| 1ST CHIROPRACTIC CLINIC (HM00004) | | ● | | | | | | | | | | | | | | | | | | | | | | | |
| ACUPUNCTURE CLINIC (HM00267) | | | | | | | | | | | | | | | | | | | | | | | | | |
| ACUPUNCTURE/CHINESE HERBAL ASS (HM00325) | | | | | | | | | | | | | | | | | | | | | | | | | |
| ASCOT PHYSIOFIRST CENTRE (HM01178) | | | | | | | | | | | | | | | | | | | | | | | | | |
| BACK TO HEALTH - WINDSOR (HM01516) | | ● | | | | | | | | | | | | | | | | | | | | | | | |
| BERKSHIRE CHIROPRACTIC (HM02195) | | ● | | | | | ● | | | | | | | | | ● | | | | | | | | | |
| BLYTH, SIMON (HM02541) | | | | | | | | | | | | | | | | | | | | | | | | | |
| BODY & SOUL (HM02561) | | | | | | | ● | | | | | | | | | | | | | | | | | | |
| BRACKNELL CHIROPRACTIC CLINIC (HM02838) | | ● | | | | | | | | | | | | | | | | | | | | | | | |
| BURNHAM CHIROPRACTIC CLINIC (HM03404) | | ● | | | | | | | | | | | | | | | | | | | | | | | |
| BUTTERBUR & SAGE (HM03495) | | | | | | | | | | | | | | | | | | | | | | | | | |
| CAMPBELL, ELSPETH (HM03597) | | | | | | | ● | ● | | | | | | | | | | | | | | | | | |
| CASTLE HILL CLINIC (HM03833) | ● | | | | | | | | | | ● | | | | | | | | | | | | | | |
| CAVERSHAM CHIROPRACTIC CLINC (HM03864) | | ● | | | | | | | | | | | | | | | | | | | | | | | |

# A - F Therapies at Practices/Businesses

| Business by County with Reference no. | Absent Healing | Acupressure | Acupuncture | Alexander Technique | Allergy Testing | Anthroposohical Med | Aromatherapy | Art Therapy | Aura Therapy | Auricular Therapy | Auto Suggestion | Autogenic Training | Aversion Therapy | Ayurvedic Medicine | Baby Massage | Bach Remedies | Bates Method | Beauty Therapy | Bio-energetics | Biofeedback | Biomagnetic Therapy | Biomechanics | Bonesetting | Bowen Therapy | Chinese Herbal Medicine | Chiropody | Chiropractic | Clinical Ecology | Cognitive Therapy | Colonic Hydrotherapy | Colour Therapy | Complementary Therapy | Counselling | Cranial Osteopathy | Cranio-Sacral Therapy | Cryo Surgery | Crystal Healing | Cupping | Cymatics | Dance Movement Thrpy | Dietician | Do-In | Douching | Dowsing | Drama Therapy | Electrolipolysis | Electrolysis | Electrotherapy | Encounter Groups | Faith Healing |
|---|---|---|---|---|---|---|---|---|---|---|---|---|---|---|---|---|---|---|---|---|---|---|---|---|---|---|---|---|---|---|---|---|---|---|---|---|---|---|---|---|---|---|---|---|---|---|---|---|---|---|
| CAVERSHAM FOOT CLINIC (HM03866) |●||||||●||||||||||||||||||●||||||●|●||||●|||||||||||●|
| CHEUNG, JAMES T (DR) (HM04142) |||●||||||||||||||||||||||||||||||||||||||||||||||||
| CLARK, J (HM04560) |||●||||||||||||||||||||||||||||||||||||||||||||||||
| COOKHAM CHIROPRACTIC CLINIC (HM05068) ||||||||||||||||||||||||||||●||||||||●|●|||||||||||||||||
| DE JODE, S (HM05908) ||||●|||||||||||||||||||||||||||||||||||||||||||||||
| DEAN RUSSELL & BRYDGES ROBERT (HM05936) |||||||||||||||||||||||||||●|●||||||||||||||||||||||||||
| DEJODE, SONIA (HM05962) ||||●|||||||||||||||||||||||||||||●|||||||||||||||||||
| DIGGENS, SUE (HM06097) |||||||●||||||||||||||||||||||||||||||||||||||||||||
| DR LIP ONG CRANIOSACRAL (HM06274) |||●|||||||||||||||||||||||||||||||●||||||||||||||||
| EDWARDS, JOHN (HM06659) |||||||||||●|●||||||||●|||||||||●||||||●|||||||||||||||||||
| EIGHAN, PENELOPE (HM06689) ||●|||||●|||||||||||||||||||||||||●|●||●|||●|||||||||||||
| EIGHT WINDS ACUPUNCTURE (HM06690) |||●||||||||||||||||||||||||||||||||||||||||||||||||
| FAIRBOURNE CLINIC (HM07051) |||●||||||||||||||●||||||||||||||||||●|●|●|||||||||||||||||
| FERINGA, MARLIES (HM07233) |||●||||||||||||||●||||||||||||||||||●|||||||||||||||||||
| FIELDING, ANNA (HM07271) |||||||●||||||||||||||||||||||||||||||||||||||||||||
| GARDNER, E (HM07877) |||||||●||||||||||||||||||||||||||||||||||||||||||||
| HALL, BEVERLEY (HM08767) ||||●|||||||||||||||||||||||||||||||||||||||||||||||
| HAMILTON, MELANIE (HM08845) ||||||||||||||||||||||||||||●||||||||||||||||||||||||
| HART, S (HM09132) |||●||||||||||||||||||||||||||||||||||||||||||||||||
| HEWITT, ANDREW (HM09703) |||●||||||||||||||||||||||||●||||||||||||||||||||||||
| HILLSIDE OSTEOPATHIC PRACTICE (HM09806) |||||||||||||||||||||||||||||||||●||●|||||||||||||||||
| HINTON, LYNN (HM09837) |||||||||||||||||●||||||||||||||||||||||||||||||||||
| HODGSON, ANN (HM09883) |||||||●||||||||||||||||||||||||||||||||||||||||||||
| HOLDAWAY, MICHELLE (HM09922) ||||●|||||||||||||||||||||||||||||||||||||||||||||||
| HOLLOWAY, JANE (HM10025) |||||||●||||||||||||||||||||||||||||||||||||||||||||
| JAMIL, M T (DR) (HM10909) |||●||||||||||||||||||||||||||||||||||||||||||||||||
| KHAN, FARIDA (HM11587) |||||||●||||||||||||||||||||||||||||||||||||||||||||
| KILNER, FELICIA (HM11610) ||||||||||||||||||||||||||||●||||||||||||||||||||||||
| KINGFISHERS COMP HEALTH CARE (HM11650) |||||||●|||||||||●||||||||||||||||●|||||||||||||||||||
| LANE, CORINNE (HM11931) ||||||||||||||||||||||||||||||||||●|||||||||||||||||||
| LANGLEY CHIROPRACTORS CLINIC (HM11953) ||||||||||||||||||||||||||||●||||||||||||||||||||||||
| LAVENDER, S (HM12029) |||||||||||||||||||||||||●|||||||||||||||||||||||||||
| LEWIS, GILL (HM12294) ||||||||||||||||||||||||||||●||||||||||||||||||||||||
| LIFE GUIDANCE (HM12344) ||||||||||||||||||||||||||||||●||||●||||||||||||●|||||||

# A - F Therapies at Practices/Businesses

| Business by County with Reference no. | Absent Healing | Acupressure | Acupuncture | Alexander Technique | Allergy Testing | Anthroposohical Med | Aromatherapy | Art Therapy | Aura Therapy | Auricular Therapy | Auto Suggestion | Autogenic Training | Aversion Therapy | Ayurvedic Medicine | Baby Massage | Bach Remedies | Bates Method | Beauty Therapy | Bio-energetics | Biofeedback | Biomagnetic Therapy | Biomechanics | Bonesetting | Bowen Therapy | Chinese Herbal Medicine |
|---|---|---|---|---|---|---|---|---|---|---|---|---|---|---|---|---|---|---|---|---|---|---|---|---|---|
| LISSADELL HOUSE PRACTICE (HM12457) | | | | | | | | | | | | | | | | | | | | | | | | | |
| MAIDENHEAD CHIROPRACTIC (HM12933) | | | | | | | | | | | | | | | | | | | | | | | | | |
| MAIDENHEAD PHYSIO & SPORTS (HM12934) | | | ● | | | | | | | | | | | | | | | | | | | | | | |
| MCCARTHY, SUSAN (HM13400) | | | | | | | | | | | | | | | | ● | | | | | | | | | |
| MCGREGOR, TONY (HM13504) | | | | | | | | | | | | | | | | | | | | | | | | | |
| MOFFAT, C (HM14035) | | | | ● | | | | | | | | | | | | | | | | | | | | | |
| NASEBY ACUPUNCTURE CLINIC (HM14487) | | | ● | | | | | | | | | | | | | | | | | | | | | | |
| NATURAL HEALTH CONSULTANCY (HM14591) | | | ● | ● | ● | | ● | | | ● | | | | | | ● | | | | | | | | ● | |
| NATURAL THERAPY CLINIC (HM14655) | | | ● | ● | | | ● | | | | | | | | | ● | | | | | | | | | |
| NATURAL THERAPY CLINIC (HM14656) | | | ● | ● | | | ● | | | | | | | | | ● | | | | | | | | | ● |
| NEWBURY CHIROPRACTIC CENTRE (HM14851) | | | | | | | | | | | | | | | | | | | | | | | | | |
| NEWBURY PHYSIOTHERAPY (HM14852) | | | ● | | | | | | | | | | | | | | | | | | | | | | |
| NORFOLK, JILL (HM14996) | | | | | | | ● | | | | | | | | | | | | | | | | | | |
| PARIS, LYN (HM15659) | | | ● | | | | | | | | | | | | | | | | | | | | | | |
| PETERS, JEAN (HM16086) | | | | | | | ● | | | | | | | | | | | | | | | | | | |
| PIM CHIROPRACTIC CLINIC (HM16300) | | | | | | | | | | | | | | | | | | | | | | | | | |
| PIM HEALTH CLINIC (HM16301) | | | | | | | | | | | | | | | | | | | | | | | | | |
| PIM, MICHAEL (DR) (HM16302) | | | | | | | | | | | | | | | | | | | | | | | | | |
| PLUMMER, VALERIE (HM16384) | | | | | | | ● | | | | | | | | | ● | | | | | | | | | |
| PLUMMER, VALERIE (HM16385) | | | | | | | ● | | | | | | | | | | | | | | | | | | |
| RAWLINSON, MARGARET (HM16975) | | | ● | | | | | | | | | | | | | | | | | | | | | | |
| RELAX AROMATHERAPY (HM17160) | | | | | | | ● | | | | | | | | | | | | | | | | | | |
| RIVETT, LYNN (HM17382) | | | | | | | ● | | | | | | | | | | | | | | | | | | |
| ROSEDALE CLINIC (HM17616) | | | ● | | | | ● | | | | | | | | | | | | | | | | | | |
| SANDALL, S (HM17898) | | | | | | | | | | | | | | | | | | | | | | ● | | | |
| SHARMA, R P (HM18302) | | | ● | | | | | | | | | | | | | | | | | | | | | | |
| SMETHURST, ALISON (HM18704) | | | | | | | ● | | | | | | | | | | | | | | | | | | |
| SMITH, MARTIN (HM18777) | | | | ● | | | | | | | | | | | | | | | | | | | | | |
| SOUTH LODGE CONSULTING (HM18909) | | ● | ● | | | | | | | | | | | | | | | | | ● | | | | | |
| STRINGER, FRANCES (HM19407) | | | | ● | | | | | | | | | | | | | | | | | | | | | |
| SWAINE, R F (HM19566) | | | | | | | | | | | | | | | | | | | | | | | | | |
| THATCHAM CHIROPRACTIC CLINIC (HM19867) | | | | | | | | | | | | | | | | | | | | | | | | | |
| TSENG, PATRICIA (HM20359) | | ● | | | | | ● | | | | | | | | | | | | | | | | | | |
| WALKER, SAM (HM20802) | | | | | | | ● | | | | | | | | | | | | | | | | | | |

| Business by County with Reference no. | Chiropody | Chiropractic | Clinical Ecology | Cognitive Therapy | Colonic Hydrotherapy | Colour Therapy | Complementary Therapy | Counselling | Cranial Osteopathy | Cranio-Sacral Therapy | Cryo Surgery | Crystal Healing | Cupping | Cymatics | Dance Movement Thrpy | Dietician | Do-In | Douching | Dowsing | Drama Therapy | Electrolipolysis | Electrolysis | Electrotherapy | Encounter Groups | Faith Healing |
|---|---|---|---|---|---|---|---|---|---|---|---|---|---|---|---|---|---|---|---|---|---|---|---|---|---|
| LISSADELL HOUSE PRACTICE (HM12457) | | ● | | | | | | | | | | | | | | | | | | | | | | | |
| MAIDENHEAD CHIROPRACTIC (HM12933) | | ● | | | | | | | | | | | | | | | | | | | | | | | |
| MAIDENHEAD PHYSIO & SPORTS (HM12934) | | | | | | | | | | | | | | | | | | | | | | | | | |
| MCCARTHY, SUSAN (HM13400) | | | | | | | | | | | | | | | | | | | | | | | | | |
| MCGREGOR, TONY (HM13504) | | | | | | | | ● | | | | | | | | | | | | | | | | | |
| MOFFAT, C (HM14035) | | | | | | | | | | | | | | | | | | | | | | | | | |
| NASEBY ACUPUNCTURE CLINIC (HM14487) | | | | | | | | | | | | | | | | | | | | | | | | | |
| NATURAL HEALTH CONSULTANCY (HM14591) | | ● | | | | ● | ● | ● | | ● | | ● | | | ● | | | | | | | | | | |
| NATURAL THERAPY CLINIC (HM14655) | | ● | | | | | | ● | | | | ● | | | | | | | | | | | | | |
| NATURAL THERAPY CLINIC (HM14656) | | ● | | ● | | | ● | ● | | | | | | | | | | | | | | | | | |
| NEWBURY CHIROPRACTIC CENTRE (HM14851) | | ● | | | | | | | | | | | | | | | | | | | | | | | |
| NEWBURY PHYSIOTHERAPY (HM14852) | | | | | | | | | | | | | | | | | | | | | | | | | |
| NORFOLK, JILL (HM14996) | | | | | | | | | | | | | | | | | | | | | | | | | |
| PARIS, LYN (HM15659) | | | | | | | | | | | | | | | | | | | | | | | | | |
| PETERS, JEAN (HM16086) | ● | | | | | | | | | | | | | | | | | | | | | | | | |
| PIM CHIROPRACTIC CLINIC (HM16300) | | ● | | | | | | | | | | | | | | | | | | | | | | | |
| PIM HEALTH CLINIC (HM16301) | | ● | | | | | | | | | | | | | | | | | | | | | | | |
| PIM, MICHAEL (DR) (HM16302) | | ● | | | | | | | | | | | | | | | | | | | | | | | |
| PLUMMER, VALERIE (HM16384) | | | | | | | | | | | | | | | | | | | | | | | | | |
| PLUMMER, VALERIE (HM16385) | | | | | | | | | | | | | | | | | | | | | | | | | |
| RAWLINSON, MARGARET (HM16975) | | | | | | | | | | | | | | | | | | | | | | | | | |
| RELAX AROMATHERAPY (HM17160) | | | | | | | | | | | | | | | | | | | | | | | | | |
| RIVETT, LYNN (HM17382) | | | | | | | | | | | | | | | | | | | | | | | | | |
| ROSEDALE CLINIC (HM17616) | | | | | | | | | | | | | | | | | | | | | | | | | |
| SANDALL, S (HM17898) | ● | | | | | | | | | | ● | | | | | | | | | | | | | | |
| SHARMA, R P (HM18302) | | | | | | | | | | | | | | | | | | | | | | | | | |
| SMETHURST, ALISON (HM18704) | | | | | | | | | | | | | | | | | | | | | | | | | |
| SMITH, MARTIN (HM18777) | | | | | | | | | | | | | | | | | | | | | | | | | |
| SOUTH LODGE CONSULTING (HM18909) | | | | | | | | | | | | | | | | | | | | | | | ● | | |
| STRINGER, FRANCES (HM19407) | | | | | | | | | | | | | | | | | | | | | | | | | |
| SWAINE, R F (HM19566) | | ● | | | | | | | | | | | | | | | | | | | | | | | |
| THATCHAM CHIROPRACTIC CLINIC (HM19867) | | ● | | | | | | | | | | | | | | | | | | | | | | | |
| TSENG, PATRICIA (HM20359) | | | | | | | ● | ● | | | | | | | | | | | | | | | | | |
| WALKER, SAM (HM20802) | | | | | | | | | | | | | | | | | | | | | | | | | |

# A - F Therapies at Practices/Businesses

| Business by County with Reference no. | Absent Healing | Acupressure | Acupuncture | Alexander Technique | Allergy Testing | Anthroposohical Med | Aromatherapy | Art Therapy | Aura Therapy | Auricular Therapy | Auto Suggestion | Autogenic Training | Aversion Therapy | Ayurvedic Medicine | Baby Massage | Bach Remedies | Bates Method |
|---|---|---|---|---|---|---|---|---|---|---|---|---|---|---|---|---|---|
| WINDSOR CTRE - TRAD CHINESE AC (HM21696) |||●|||||||||||||||
| WINNERSH HYPNOTHERAPY PRACTICE (HM21711) ||||||||||||||||||
| WOKINGHAM CHIROPRACTIC CENTRE (HM21760) ||||||||||||||||||
| WOOD, JEANIE M (HM21801) ||||●||||||||||||||
| WOODLEY HEALING CENTRE (HM21836) |||||||●|||||||||||
| WOODROW, IRENE (HM21843) ||||●||||||||||||||
| WRIGHT, LAWRIE (HM21943) ||||●||||||||||||||
| **BRISTOL** ||||||||||||||||||
| ALEXANDER, KAREN (HM00565) |||●|||||||||||||||
| AMPHORA AROMATICS (HM00794) |||||||●|||||||||||
| ANDERSON, KEITH (HM00830) ||||||||||||||||●||
| AQUARIUS HEALTH CENTRE (HM00959) |||●||●||●|||||||||||
| ARMSTRONG, ELIZABETH (HM01021) ||||||||||||||||||
| AROMATHERAPY FOR LADIES (HM01110) |||||||●|||||||||||
| ASS-DANCE MOVEMENT THERAPY (HM01268) ||||||||||||||||||
| AVON COMPLEMENTARY MEDICINE (HM01404) |||●|||||||||||||||
| BAGGLEY, J M (HM01536) ||||||||||||||||||
| BATH ROAD MASSAGE (HM01895) |||||||●|||||||||||
| BEVAN, RUSS (HM02242) ||||||||||||||||||
| BLACKBERRY HILL HOSPITAL (HM02429) |||●|||||||||||||||
| BRISTOL HYPNOTHERAPY CLINIC (HM03063) ||||||||||||||||||
| BRISTOL NATURAL HEALTH SERVICE (HM03064) |||●|●|||●|||||||||||
| BRISTOL SCHOOL (HM03065) |||||||●|||||||||||
| BURROWS, A (HM03422) ||||●||||||||||||||
| CASTLE CHIROPODY CLINIC (HM03828) ||||||||||||||||||
| CHARLES CLINIC (HM04020) ||||||||||||||||||
| CLARK, LYN (HM04566) ||||||||||||||||||
| CLIFTON ACUPUNCTURE CLINIC (HM04665) |||●|||||||||||||||
| CLIFTON CHIROPRACTIC CLINIC (HM04666) ||●|●|||||||||||||||
| CLIFTON PRACTICE (HM04670) |||●|●|||●|||||||||||
| CLINIC OF NATURAL MEDICINE (HM04704) |||||||●|||||||||||
| CLOVER HOUSE (HM04737) |||||||●|||||||||||
| COX, MARTIN (HM05315) ||||●||||||||||||||
| CROSS HANDS CHIRO CLINIC (HM05478) ||||||||||||||||||

| Business by County with Reference no. | Beauty Therapy | Bio-energetics | Biofeedback | Biomagnetic Therapy | Biomechanics | Bonesetting | Bowen Therapy | Chinese Herbal Medicine | Chiropody | Chiropractic | Clinical Ecology | Cognitive Therapy | Colonic Hydrotherapy | Colour Therapy | Complementary Therapy | Counselling | Cranial Osteopathy |
|---|---|---|---|---|---|---|---|---|---|---|---|---|---|---|---|---|---|
| WINDSOR CTRE - TRAD CHINESE AC (HM21696) ||||||||||||||||||
| WINNERSH HYPNOTHERAPY PRACTICE (HM21711) ||||||||||||||||●||
| WOKINGHAM CHIROPRACTIC CENTRE (HM21760) ||||||||||●||||||||
| WOOD, JEANIE M (HM21801) ||||||||||||||||||
| WOODLEY HEALING CENTRE (HM21836) |||||||||||||||●|||
| WOODROW, IRENE (HM21843) ||||||||||||||||||
| WRIGHT, LAWRIE (HM21943) ||||||||||||||||||
| **BRISTOL** ||||||||||||||||||
| ALEXANDER, KAREN (HM00565) ||||||||||||||||||
| AMPHORA AROMATICS (HM00794) ||||||||||||||||||
| ANDERSON, KEITH (HM00830) ||||||||||||||●||||
| AQUARIUS HEALTH CENTRE (HM00959) ||||||||||||||||||
| ARMSTRONG, ELIZABETH (HM01021) ||||||||||●||||||||
| AROMATHERAPY FOR LADIES (HM01110) ||||||||||||||||||
| ASS-DANCE MOVEMENT THERAPY (HM01268) ||||||||||||||||||
| AVON COMPLEMENTARY MEDICINE (HM01404) |||||||||||●|||||||
| BAGGLEY, J M (HM01536) |||||||||●|||||||||
| BATH ROAD MASSAGE (HM01895) ||||||||||||||||||
| BEVAN, RUSS (HM02242) |||●|||||||||||||||
| BLACKBERRY HILL HOSPITAL (HM02429) ||||||||||||||||||
| BRISTOL HYPNOTHERAPY CLINIC (HM03063) ||||||||||||●||||||
| BRISTOL NATURAL HEALTH SERVICE (HM03064) ||||||||||●||||||●||
| BRISTOL SCHOOL (HM03065) ||||||||||||||||||
| BURROWS, A (HM03422) ||||||||||||||||||
| CASTLE CHIROPODY CLINIC (HM03828) |||||●||||●|||||||||
| CHARLES CLINIC (HM04020) |||||||||||||||||●|
| CLARK, LYN (HM04566) ||||||||||||||||●||
| CLIFTON ACUPUNCTURE CLINIC (HM04665) ||||||||||||||||||
| CLIFTON CHIROPRACTIC CLINIC (HM04666) ||||||||●||●||||||||
| CLIFTON PRACTICE (HM04670) ||||||||||●||||||||
| CLINIC OF NATURAL MEDICINE (HM04704) ||||||||||||||||||
| CLOVER HOUSE (HM04737) ||||||||||||||||||
| COX, MARTIN (HM05315) ||||||||||||||||||
| CROSS HANDS CHIRO CLINIC (HM05478) ||||||||||●||||||||

| Business by County with Reference no. | Cranio-Sacral Therapy | Cryo Surgery | Crystal Healing | Cupping | Cymatics | Dance Movement Thrpy | Dietician | Do-In | Douching | Dowsing | Drama Therapy | Electrolipolysis | Electrolysis | Electrotherapy | Encounter Groups | Faith Healing |
|---|---|---|---|---|---|---|---|---|---|---|---|---|---|---|---|---|
| WINDSOR CTRE - TRAD CHINESE AC (HM21696) |||||||||||||||||
| WINNERSH HYPNOTHERAPY PRACTICE (HM21711) |||||||||||||||||
| WOKINGHAM CHIROPRACTIC CENTRE (HM21760) |||||||||||||||||
| WOOD, JEANIE M (HM21801) |||||||||||||||||
| WOODLEY HEALING CENTRE (HM21836) |||||||●||||||||||
| WOODROW, IRENE (HM21843) |||||||||||||||||
| WRIGHT, LAWRIE (HM21943) |||||||||||||||||
| **BRISTOL** |||||||||||||||||
| ALEXANDER, KAREN (HM00565) |||||||||||||||||
| AMPHORA AROMATICS (HM00794) |||||||||||||||||
| ANDERSON, KEITH (HM00830) |||||||●|||●|||||||
| AQUARIUS HEALTH CENTRE (HM00959) |||||||||||||||||
| ARMSTRONG, ELIZABETH (HM01021) |||||||||||||||||
| AROMATHERAPY FOR LADIES (HM01110) |||||||||||||||||
| ASS-DANCE MOVEMENT THERAPY (HM01268) ||||||●|||||||||||
| AVON COMPLEMENTARY MEDICINE (HM01404) |||||||||||||||||
| BAGGLEY, J M (HM01536) |||||||||||||||||
| BATH ROAD MASSAGE (HM01895) |||||||||||||||||
| BEVAN, RUSS (HM02242) |||||||||||||||||
| BLACKBERRY HILL HOSPITAL (HM02429) |||||||||||||||||
| BRISTOL HYPNOTHERAPY CLINIC (HM03063) |||||||||||||||||
| BRISTOL NATURAL HEALTH SERVICE (HM03064) |||||||||||||||||
| BRISTOL SCHOOL (HM03065) |||||||||||||||||
| BURROWS, A (HM03422) |||||||||||||||||
| CASTLE CHIROPODY CLINIC (HM03828) |||||||||||||||||
| CHARLES CLINIC (HM04020) |||||||||||||||||
| CLARK, LYN (HM04566) |||||||||||||||||
| CLIFTON ACUPUNCTURE CLINIC (HM04665) |||||||||||||||||
| CLIFTON CHIROPRACTIC CLINIC (HM04666) |||||||||||||||||
| CLIFTON PRACTICE (HM04670) |||||||||||||||||
| CLINIC OF NATURAL MEDICINE (HM04704) |||||||||||||||||
| CLOVER HOUSE (HM04737) |||||||||||||||||
| COX, MARTIN (HM05315) |||||||||||||||||
| CROSS HANDS CHIRO CLINIC (HM05478) |||||||||||||||||

# A - F Therapies at Practices/Businesses

| Business by County with Reference no. | Absent Healing | Acupressure | Acupuncture | Alexander Technique | Allergy Testing | Anthroposohical Med | Aromatherapy | Art Therapy | Aura Therapy | Auricular Therapy | Auto Suggestion | Autogenic Training | Aversion Therapy | Ayurvedic Medicine | Baby Massage | Bach Remedies | Bates Method | Beauty Therapy | Bio-energetics | Biofeedback | Biomagnetic Therapy | Biomechanics | Bonesetting | Bowen Therapy | Chinese Herbal Medicine | Chiropody | Chiropractic | Clinical Ecology | Cognitive Therapy | Colonic Hydrotherapy | Colour Therapy | Complementary Therapy | Counselling | Cranial Osteopathy | Cranio-Sacral Therapy | Cryo Surgery | Crystal Healing | Cupping | Cymatics | Dance Movement Thrpy | Dietician | Do-In | Douching | Dowsing | Drama Therapy | Electrolipolysis | Electrolysis | Electrotherapy | Encounter Groups | Faith Healing |
|---|---|---|---|---|---|---|---|---|---|---|---|---|---|---|---|---|---|---|---|---|---|---|---|---|---|---|---|---|---|---|---|---|---|---|---|---|---|---|---|---|---|---|---|---|---|---|---|---|---|---|
| CTRE FOR KINESIOLOGY (HM05542) | | | | | | | | | | | | | | | | ● | | | | | | | | | | | | ● | | | | ● | | | | | | | | | | | | | | | | | | |
| DANCE VOICE THERAPY CENTRE (HM05709) | | | | | | | | | | | | | | | | | | | | | | | | | | | | | | | | | | | | | | | | ● | | | | | | | | | | |
| DOWRY CHIROPRACTIC CLINIC (HM06255) | | | | | | | | | | | | | | | | | | | | | | | | | | | ● | | | | | | | | | | | | | | | | | | | | | | | |
| EDWARDS, R L (HM06669) | | | ● | | | | | | | | | | | | | | | | | | | | | | | | | | | | | | | | | | | | | | | | | | | | | | | |
| EVANS, A R (HM06955) | | | ● | | | | | | | | | | | | | | | | | | | | | | | | | | | | | | | | | | | | | | | | | | | | | | | |
| FIELDING, HELEN (HM07273) | | | ● | | | | | | | | | | | | | | | | | | | | | | | | | | | | | | | | | | | | | | | | | | | | | | | |
| FILE, CHRISTINE (HM07288) | | | | | | | ● | | | | | | | | | | | | | | | | | | | | | | | | | | | | | | | | | | | | | | | | | | | |
| FOWDEN, M G (HM07623) | | | | | | | ● | | | | | | | | | | | | | | | | | | | | | | | | | | | | | | | | | | | | | | | | | | | |
| FRANCIS, PATRICIA (HM07675) | | | | | | | ● | | | | | | | | | | | | | | | | | | | | | | | | | | | | | | | | | | | | | | | | | | | |
| FREEMAN, ANN (HM07719) | | | | | ● | | | | | | | | | | | | | | | | | | | | | | | | | | | | | | | | | | | | | | | | | | | | | |
| GARLAND, C (HM07889) | | | | | | | ● | | | | | | | | | | | | | | | | | | | | | | | | | | | | | | | | | | | | | | | | | | | |
| GAUNT, DAVID (HM07929) | | | ● | | | | | | | | | | | | | | | | | | | | | | | | | | | | | | | | | | | | | | | | | | | | | | | |
| GHAMY, M R (HM08012) | | | ● | | | | | | | | | | | | | | | | | | | | | | | | | | | | | | | | | | | | | | | | | | | | | | | |
| GIBBONS, RICHARD (HM08028) | | | ● | | | | | | | | | | | | | | | | | | | | | | | | | | | | | | | | | | | | | | | | | | | | | | | |
| GIL, JOHN (HM08053) | | | | ● | | | | | | | | | | | | | | | | | | | | | | | | | | | | | | | | | | | | | | | | | | | | | | |
| GINAS AROMATHERAPY (HM08109) | | | | | | | ● | | | | | | | | | | | | | | | | | | | | | | | | | | | | | | | | | | | | | | | | | | | |
| GREEN, JULIA (HM08464) | | | | ● | | | | | | | | | | | | | | | | | | | | | | | | | | | | | | | | | | | | | | | | | | | | | | |
| HEALING WITH GABRIELLE TWINE (HM09360) | ● | | | | | | | | | | | | | | | ● | | | | | | | | | | | | | | | | | | | | | | | | | | | | | | | | | | |
| HEALTH & HEALING (HM09371) | | | ● | | ● | | ● | | | | | | | | | | | | | | | | | ● | | | ● | | | | | | ● | | | | ● | | | | | | | | | | | | | |
| HITCHINGS, CYNTHIA (HM09846) | | | ● | | | | | | | | | | | | | | | | | | | | | | | | | | | | | | | | | | | | | | | | | | | | | | | |
| HUFTON, MARK (HM10319) | | | | | | | ● | | | | | | | | | | | | | | | | | | | | | | | | | | | | | | | | | | | | | | | | | | | |
| KEYNSHAM CHIROPRACTIC CLINÍC (HM11580) | | | | | | | | | | | | | | | | | | | | | | | | | | | ● | | | | | | | | | | | | | | | | | | | | | | | |
| KINGSWOOD CHIROPRACTIC CLINIC (HM11682) | | | | | | | | | | | | | | | | | | | | | | | | | | | ● | | | | | | | | | | | | | | | | | | | | | | | |
| LAM RIM CTRE FOR WHOLE HEALTH (HM11883) | | | ● | | | | ● | | | | | | | | | | | | | | | | | | | | | | | | | | ● | | | | | | | ● | | | | | | | | | | |
| LEFEBVRE, COLLETTE (HM12173) | | | ● | | | | | | | | | | | | | | | | | | | | | | | | | | | | | | | | | | | | | | | | | | | | | | | |
| MATTHEWS, M (HM13310) | | | ● | | | | | | | | | | | | | | | | | | | | | | | | | | | | | | | | | | | | | | | | | | | | | | | |
| MAYFAIR GROUP (HM13352) | | | | | | | ● | | | | | | | | | | | | | | | | | | | | | | | | | | | | | | | | | | | | | | | | | | | |
| NAILSEA CHIROPRACTIC CLINIC (HM14460) | | | | | | | ● | | | | | | | | | | | | | | | | | | | | ● | | | | | ● | | | | | | | | | | | | | | | | ● | | |
| NAYDLER, NICK (HM14711) | | | | | | | | | | | | | | | | | | | | | | | | | | | | | | | | | ● | | | | | | | | | | | | | | | | | |
| ORCHARD MEDICAL CENTRE (HM15364) | | | | | | | | | | | | | | | | | | | | | | ● | | | | ● | ● | | | | | | | | | | | | | | | | | | | | | | | |
| ORIENTAL MEDICINE PRACTICE (HM15387) | | | ● | | | | | | | | | | | | | | | | | | | | | | | | | | | | | | | | | | | ● | | | ● | | | | | | | | | |
| PARKER CLINIC (HM15683) | | | | | | | | | | | | | | | | | | | | | | | | | | | ● | | | | | | | | | | | | | | | | | | | | | | | |
| POCOCK, A (HM16391) | | | | | | | | | | | | | | | | | | | | | | | | | | ● | | | | | | | | | | | | | | | | | | | | | | | | |
| REDLANDS HOUSE CLINIC (HM17028) | | | | | | | | | | | | | | | | | | | | | | | | | | | ● | | | | | | | | | | | | | | | | | | | | | | | |

# A - F Therapies at Practices/Businesses

| Business by County with Reference no. | Absent Healing | Acupressure | Acupuncture | Alexander Technique | Allergy Testing | Anthroposohical Med | Aromatherapy | Art Therapy | Aura Therapy | Auricular Therapy | Auto Suggestion | Autogenic Training | Aversion Therapy | Ayurvedic Medicine | Baby Massage | Bach Remedies | Bates Method | Beauty Therapy | Bio-energetics | Biofeedback | Biomagnetic Therapy | Biomechanics | Bonesetting | Bowen Therapy | Chinese Herbal Medicine | Chiropody | Chiropractic | Clinical Ecology | Cognitive Therapy | Colonic Hydrotherapy | Colour Therapy | Complementary Therapy | Counselling | Cranial Osteopathy | Cranio-Sacral Therapy | Cryo Surgery | Crystal Healing | Cupping | Cymatics | Dance Movement Thrpy | Dietician | Do-In | Douching | Dowsing | Drama Therapy | Electrolipolysis | Electrolysis | Electrotherapy | Encounter Groups | Faith Healing |
|---|---|---|---|---|---|---|---|---|---|---|---|---|---|---|---|---|---|---|---|---|---|---|---|---|---|---|---|---|---|---|---|---|---|---|---|---|---|---|---|---|---|---|---|---|---|---|---|---|---|---|
| RICHARD GIBBONS - ACUPUNCT (HM17244) ||●||||||||||||||||||||||||||||||||||||||||||||||||
| ROBERTS, CATHERINE (HM17407) ||●||||||||||||||||||||||||||||||||||||||||||||||||
| SMITH, GINA MERRETT (HM18746) ||||||||||||||||●|||||||||||||||||||||||||||||||||||
| SOUTHERTON, C S (HM18933) ||||||||||||||||||||||||||||●||||||||||||||||||||||||
| STEVENS, BEN (HM19225) ||●||||||||||||||||||||||||||||||||||||||||||||||||
| STH WST COLLEGE OF ORIENTL MED (HM19285) ||●|||||||||||||||||||||||||||||●|||||||||||||||||||
| STYLES, PATRICIA (HM19458) |||||||||||||||||||||●||||●||||||||||●|||||||||||||||
| THOMAS, TRUDY (HM19958) |||||||||||||||||||||||||||●|||||||||||||||||||||||||
| TOLL HOUSE CHIROPRACTIC (HM20119) ||||||||||||||||||||||||||||●||||||||||||||||||||||||
| TOLL HOUSE CLINIC (HM20120) ||●||||●||||||||||||||||||||||●|||||||||||||||||||||●|||
| TOMKIES, J (HM20130) ||||||||||||||||||||||||||||●||||||||||||||||||||||||
| VOYSEY, KIM R (HM20716) ||||||||||||||||||||||||||||●||||||||||||||||||||||||
| WESTBURY CHIROPRACTIC CLINIC (HM21259) ||||||||||||||||||||||||||||●||||||||||||||||||||||||
| WONGS ACUPUNCTURE (HM21779) ||●||||||||||||||||||||||||||||||||||||||||||||||||
| **BUCKINGHAMSHIRE** |||||||||||||||||||||||||||||||||||||||||||||||||||
| ACU-DIET CENTRE (HM00210) ||●||||||||||||||||||||||||||||||||||||||||||||||||
| ACUPRESSURE MASSAGE (HM00156) |●|||||||||||||||||||||||||||||||●|||||||||||||||||||
| ALTERNATIVE THERAPIES TRAINING (HM00730) |●|||||●||||||||||||||||||||||||||||||||||||||||||||
| AMERSHAM CHIROPRACTIC CLINIC (HM00779) |●|●||||||||||||||||||||||||●||||||||||||||●||||||||||
| AMERSHAM OSTEOPATHIC CLINIC (HM00780) ||||||||||||||||●|||||||||||||||||||●|||||||||||||||||
| AYLESBURY CHIROPRACTIC CLINIC (HM01422) ||||||||||||||||||||||||||||●||||||||||||||||||||||||
| AYLESBURY COMPLEMENTARY HEALTH (HM01423) ●||||||●|||||||||||||||||||||||||●|●||||||||||||||||||
| AYLESBURY VALE THERAPY (HM01425) |||||||||||||||||||||||||||||||●|||||||||||||||||||
| BANFIELD, KATIE (HM01657) ||||||●|||||||||||||||||||||||||||●|||||||||||||||||
| BATSON, BARBARA (HM01902) ||||||||||||||||●|||||||||||||||||||||||||||||||||||
| BEACONSFIELD CHIRO CLINIC (HM01954) ||●|||||||||||||||||||||||●|●||||||||||||||||||||||||
| BIGGS, SYLVIA (HM02294) ||||||||||||||||||||||||●|||||||||||||||||||||||||||
| BODY & SOUL (HM02565) ||||||●||||||||||||||||||||||||||||||||||||||||||||
| BRADFORD, SONIA (HM02855) ||||||●||||||||||||||||||||||||||||||||||||||||||||
| BREEZE, T (HM02951) ||||||||||||||||||||||||||||●||||||||||||||||||||||||
| BUCKINGHAM CHIROPRACTIC CLINIC (HM03310) ||||||||||||||||||||||||||||●||||||||●||||||||||||||||
| CAMPBELL, LOUISE (HM03604) ||||||●||||||||||||●|||||||||||||||||||||||||||||||||
| CAMPBELL, NIKKI (HM03605) |||||||||||||||||||||||||||||||||||●|||||●|||||||||||
| CANDLEWELL CLINIC (HM03623) |||||||||||||||||||||||||||||||||||●|||||||||||||||||

# A - F Therapies at Practices/Businesses

| Business by County with Reference no. | Absent Healing | Acupressure | Acupuncture | Alexander Technique | Allergy Testing | Anthroposohical Med | Aromatherapy | Art Therapy | Aura Therapy | Auricular Therapy | Auto Suggestion | Autogenic Training | Aversion Therapy |
|---|---|---|---|---|---|---|---|---|---|---|---|---|---|
| CARMA HEALING SANCTUARY (HM03703) | | | | | | | | | | | | | |
| CASTLE STREET CLINIC (HM03837) | | | ● | ● | | | ● | | | | | | |
| CHILTERN AROMATHERAPY (HM04172) | | | | | | | ● | | | | | | |
| CHILTERN CHIROPODY SERVICE (HM04173) | | | | | | | | | | | | | |
| COACHING FOR SUCCESS (HM04750) | | | | | | | | | | | ● | | |
| COLDWELL, VERONICA (HM04810) | ● | ● | | | | | ● | | | | | | |
| COLLEGE OF AYURVEDA (HM04845) | | | | | | | | | | | | | |
| COMPLEMENTARY HEALTH (HM04921) | ● | | | | | | ● | | | | | | |
| COMPLEMENTARY HEALTH CENTRE (HM04923) | | | | | | | ● | | | | | | |
| COX, LINDY (HM05312) | | | ● | | | | | | | | | | |
| DE SILVA, M (HM05919) | | | ● | | | | | | | | | | |
| DOWDELL, FIONA K (HM06234) | | | | | | | | | | | | | |
| EDWARDS, EMMA (HM06650) | | | | | | | ● | | | | | | |
| ELIZABETH HELEN BEAUTY THER (HM06739) | | | | | | | ● | | | | | | |
| ENFIELD, CLAUDIA (HM06820) | | | | | | | ● | | | | | | |
| FEWSTER, HELEN (HM07254) | | | ● | | | | | | | | | | |
| FIRMAN, BARBARA (HM07332) | ● | | | | | | | | | | | | |
| FLEET, BARBARA (HM07402) | | ● | | | | | ● | | | | | | |
| GERRARDS CROSS SPORTS & BACK (HM08004) | | ● | ● | | | | | | | | | | |
| GODAGAMA, SHANTHA (HM08177) | | | ● | | | | | | | | | | |
| GRICE, ANNIE (HM08545) | | | | | | | ● | | | | | | |
| HAZELL, PRISCILLA (HM09293) | | | | | | | ● | | | | | | |
| HEATH, SUSAN (HM09454) | ● | | | | | | | | | | | | |
| HIGH WYCOMBE CHIRO CLINIC (HM09744) | | | | | | | | | | | | | |
| HOLDCOFT, LIA (HM09923) | | | | | | | ● | | | | | | |
| HOLISTIC HEALING (HM09959) | | | | | | | | | | | | | |
| HOLLAND, JACQUELINE (HM10013) | | | | | | | ● | | | | | | |
| HUBBARD, LEE (HM10301) | | | | | | | ● | | | | | | |
| HULCOTT END PRACTICE (HM10352) | | ● | ● | | | | | | | | | | |
| ICE & FIRE (HM10567) | | | | | | | ● | | | | | | |
| J J COUNSELLING SERVICES (HM10798) | | | | | | | | | | | | | |
| JOHNSON, HELEN (HM11074) | | | | | | | | | | | | | |
| JORDAN, PAMELA (HM11210) | | | | | | | | | | | | | |
| K BANFIELD NATUROPATHY/OSTEO (HM11288) | | | | | | | ● | | | | | | |

| Business by County with Reference no. | Ayurvedic Medicine | Baby Massage | Bach Remedies | Bates Method | Beauty Therapy | Bio-energetics | Biofeedback | Biomagnetic Therapy | Biomechanics | Bonesetting | Bowen Therapy | Chinese Herbal Medicine | Chiropody |
|---|---|---|---|---|---|---|---|---|---|---|---|---|---|
| CARMA HEALING SANCTUARY (HM03703) | | | | | | | | | | | | | |
| CASTLE STREET CLINIC (HM03837) | | | | | | | | | | | | | |
| CHILTERN AROMATHERAPY (HM04172) | | | | | | | | | | | | | |
| CHILTERN CHIROPODY SERVICE (HM04173) | | | | | | | | | | | | | |
| COACHING FOR SUCCESS (HM04750) | | | | | | | | | | | | | |
| COLDWELL, VERONICA (HM04810) | | | | | | | | | | | | | |
| COLLEGE OF AYURVEDA (HM04845) | ● | | | | | | | | | | | | |
| COMPLEMENTARY HEALTH (HM04921) | | | | | | | | | | | | | |
| COMPLEMENTARY HEALTH CENTRE (HM04923) | | | ● | | | | | | | | | | |
| COX, LINDY (HM05312) | | | | | | | | | | | | | |
| DE SILVA, M (HM05919) | | | | | | | | | | | | | |
| DOWDELL, FIONA K (HM06234) | | | | | | | | | | | | | |
| EDWARDS, EMMA (HM06650) | | | | | | | | | | | | | |
| ELIZABETH HELEN BEAUTY THER (HM06739) | | | | | | | | | | | | | |
| ENFIELD, CLAUDIA (HM06820) | | | | | | | | | | | ● | | |
| FEWSTER, HELEN (HM07254) | | | | | | | | | | | | | |
| FIRMAN, BARBARA (HM07332) | | | | | ● | | | | | | | | |
| FLEET, BARBARA (HM07402) | | | | | | | | | | | | | |
| GERRARDS CROSS SPORTS & BACK (HM08004) | | | | | | | | | | | | | |
| GODAGAMA, SHANTHA (HM08177) | | | | | | | | | | | | | |
| GRICE, ANNIE (HM08545) | | | | | | | | | | | | | |
| HAZELL, PRISCILLA (HM09293) | | | | | | | | | | | | | |
| HEATH, SUSAN (HM09454) | | | | | | | | | | | | | |
| HIGH WYCOMBE CHIRO CLINIC (HM09744) | | | | | | | | | | | | | |
| HOLDCOFT, LIA (HM09923) | | | | | | | | | | | | | |
| HOLISTIC HEALING (HM09959) | | | | | | | | | | | | | |
| HOLLAND, JACQUELINE (HM10013) | | | | | | | | | | | | | |
| HUBBARD, LEE (HM10301) | | | | | | | | | | | | | |
| HULCOTT END PRACTICE (HM10352) | | | | | | | | | | | | | |
| ICE & FIRE (HM10567) | | | | | | | | | | | | | |
| J J COUNSELLING SERVICES (HM10798) | | | | | | | | | | | | | |
| JOHNSON, HELEN (HM11074) | | | | | | | | | | | | | |
| JORDAN, PAMELA (HM11210) | | | ● | | | | | | | | | | |
| K BANFIELD NATUROPATHY/OSTEO (HM11288) | | | | | | | | | | | | | |

| Business by County with Reference no. | Chiropractic | Clinical Ecology | Cognitive Therapy | Colonic Hydrotherapy | Colour Therapy | Complementary Therapy | Counselling | Cranial Osteopathy | Cranio-Sacral Therapy | Cryo Surgery | Crystal Healing | Cupping |
|---|---|---|---|---|---|---|---|---|---|---|---|---|
| CARMA HEALING SANCTUARY (HM03703) | | | | | ● | | | | | | ● | |
| CASTLE STREET CLINIC (HM03837) | | | | | | | | ● | | | | |
| CHILTERN AROMATHERAPY (HM04172) | | | | | | | | | | | | |
| CHILTERN CHIROPODY SERVICE (HM04173) | ● | | | | | | | | | | | |
| COACHING FOR SUCCESS (HM04750) | | | ● | | | | | | | | | |
| COLDWELL, VERONICA (HM04810) | | | | | | | | | | | ● | |
| COLLEGE OF AYURVEDA (HM04845) | | | | | | ● | | | | | | |
| COMPLEMENTARY HEALTH (HM04921) | | | | | | ● | ● | | | | | |
| COMPLEMENTARY HEALTH CENTRE (HM04923) | | | | | | ● | | | | | | |
| COX, LINDY (HM05312) | | | | | | | | | | | | |
| DE SILVA, M (HM05919) | | | | | | | | | | | | |
| DOWDELL, FIONA K (HM06234) | ● | | | | | | | | | | | |
| EDWARDS, EMMA (HM06650) | | | | | | | | | | | | |
| ELIZABETH HELEN BEAUTY THER (HM06739) | | | | | | | | | | | | |
| ENFIELD, CLAUDIA (HM06820) | | | | | | | | | | | | |
| FEWSTER, HELEN (HM07254) | | | | | | | | | | | | |
| FIRMAN, BARBARA (HM07332) | | | | | | | | | | | | |
| FLEET, BARBARA (HM07402) | | | | | | | | | | | | |
| GERRARDS CROSS SPORTS & BACK (HM08004) | | | | | | | | | | | | |
| GODAGAMA, SHANTHA (HM08177) | | | | | | | | | | | | |
| GRICE, ANNIE (HM08545) | | | | | | | | | | | | |
| HAZELL, PRISCILLA (HM09293) | | | | | | | | | | | | |
| HEATH, SUSAN (HM09454) | | | | | | ● | | | | | | |
| HIGH WYCOMBE CHIRO CLINIC (HM09744) | ● | | | | | | | | | | | |
| HOLDCOFT, LIA (HM09923) | | | | | | | | | | | | |
| HOLISTIC HEALING (HM09959) | | | | | | | ● | | | | | |
| HOLLAND, JACQUELINE (HM10013) | | | | | | | | | | | | |
| HUBBARD, LEE (HM10301) | | | | | | | | | | | | |
| HULCOTT END PRACTICE (HM10352) | | | | | | | | | | | | |
| ICE & FIRE (HM10567) | | | | | | | | | | | | |
| J J COUNSELLING SERVICES (HM10798) | | | | | | | ● | | | | | |
| JOHNSON, HELEN (HM11074) | | ● | | | | | | ● | | | | |
| JORDAN, PAMELA (HM11210) | | | | | | | | | | | | |
| K BANFIELD NATUROPATHY/OSTEO (HM11288) | | | | | | | | ● | | | | |

| Business by County with Reference no. | Cymatics | Dance Movement Thrpy | Dietician | Do-In | Douching | Dowsing | Drama Therapy | Electrolipolysis | Electrolysis | Electrotherapy | Encounter Groups | Faith Healing |
|---|---|---|---|---|---|---|---|---|---|---|---|---|
| CARMA HEALING SANCTUARY (HM03703) | | | | | | | | | | | | |
| CASTLE STREET CLINIC (HM03837) | | | | | | | | | | | | |
| CHILTERN AROMATHERAPY (HM04172) | | | | | | | | | | | | |
| CHILTERN CHIROPODY SERVICE (HM04173) | | | | | | | | | | | | |
| COACHING FOR SUCCESS (HM04750) | | | ● | | | | | | | | | |
| COLDWELL, VERONICA (HM04810) | | | | | | | | | | | | |
| COLLEGE OF AYURVEDA (HM04845) | | | | | | | | | | | | |
| COMPLEMENTARY HEALTH (HM04921) | | | | | | | | | | | | |
| COMPLEMENTARY HEALTH CENTRE (HM04923) | | | ● | | | | | | | | | |
| COX, LINDY (HM05312) | | | | | | | | | | | | |
| DE SILVA, M (HM05919) | | | | | | | | | | | | |
| DOWDELL, FIONA K (HM06234) | | | | | | | | | | | | |
| EDWARDS, EMMA (HM06650) | | | | | | | | | | | | |
| ELIZABETH HELEN BEAUTY THER (HM06739) | | | | | | | | | | | | |
| ENFIELD, CLAUDIA (HM06820) | | | | | | | | | | | | |
| FEWSTER, HELEN (HM07254) | | | | | | | | | | | | |
| FIRMAN, BARBARA (HM07332) | | | | ● | | ● | | | | | | |
| FLEET, BARBARA (HM07402) | | | | | | | | | | | | |
| GERRARDS CROSS SPORTS & BACK (HM08004) | | | | | | | | | | ● | | |
| GODAGAMA, SHANTHA (HM08177) | | | | | | | | | | | | |
| GRICE, ANNIE (HM08545) | | | | | | | | | | | | |
| HAZELL, PRISCILLA (HM09293) | | | | | | | | | | | | |
| HEATH, SUSAN (HM09454) | | ● | | | | | | | | | | |
| HIGH WYCOMBE CHIRO CLINIC (HM09744) | | | | | | | | | | | | |
| HOLDCOFT, LIA (HM09923) | | | | | | | | | | | | |
| HOLISTIC HEALING (HM09959) | | | | | | | | | | | | |
| HOLLAND, JACQUELINE (HM10013) | | | | | | | | | | | | |
| HUBBARD, LEE (HM10301) | | | | | | | | | | | | |
| HULCOTT END PRACTICE (HM10352) | | | | | | | | | | ● | | |
| ICE & FIRE (HM10567) | | | | | | | | | | | | |
| J J COUNSELLING SERVICES (HM10798) | | | | | | | | | | | | |
| JOHNSON, HELEN (HM11074) | | | | | | | | | | | | |
| JORDAN, PAMELA (HM11210) | | | | | | | | | | | | |
| K BANFIELD NATUROPATHY/OSTEO (HM11288) | | | | | | | | | | | | |

# A - F Therapies at Practices/Businesses

| Business by County with Reference no. | Absent Healing | Acupressure | Acupuncture | Alexander Technique | Allergy Testing | Anthroposohical Med | Aromatherapy | Art Therapy | Aura Therapy | Auricular Therapy |
|---|---|---|---|---|---|---|---|---|---|---|
| KENTISH, LORNE (HM11531) | | | | | | | | | | |
| KINGFISHER CHIROP & HYP (HM11648) | | | | | | | | | | |
| LI (PROFESSOR) (HM12322) | | | ● | | | | | | | |
| MATHEW HUNT CHIROPODIST (HM13286) | | | | | | | | | | |
| METTE MARUP & MIKKELSEN (HM13778) | | | | | | | | | | |
| MIDDLE WAY RE-EDUCATION CTRE (HM13813) | | | | ● | | | | | | |
| MILTON KEYNES CHIRO CLINIC (HM13948) | | | | | | | | | | |
| MIND AND BODY (HM13959) | ● | | | | | | ● | | ● | |
| MORNINGSIDE HEALTH CLINIC (HM14190) | | | | | | | | | | |
| MORRISSEY, BLANCHE (HM14236) | | | | | | | | | | |
| NEWPORT ACUPUNCTURE CLINIC (HM14879) | | | ● | | | | | | | |
| OXFORDSHIRE BOWEN CLINIC (HM15545) | | | | | | | | | | |
| PARTON, KAY (HM15765) | | | | | | | ● | | | |
| PATON, BARBARA (HM15823) | | | | ● | | | | | | |
| PEPPLER, EILEEN (HM16011) | | | | | | | ● | | | |
| PERFECT OILS (HM16021) | | | | | | | ● | | | |
| PHYSIO FIRST PRACTICE (HM16199) | | | | | | | | | | |
| PINEWOOD CHIROPODY PRACTICE (HM16312) | | | | | | | | | | |
| PURTON HOUSE HOMEOPATHIC CTRE (HM16775) | | | | | | | | | | |
| RANDELL, BELINDA (HM16932) | | | | | | | | | | |
| REIKI HEALTH CENTRE (HM17137) | | | | | | | ● | | | |
| ROWBOTHAM, DARCIE (HM17684) | | | | | | | ● | | | |
| RUNDLE, RICHARD (HM17752) | ● | ● | ● | | | | | | | |
| SADLER, MARY (HM17832) | | | | ● | | | | | | |
| SHAW, FIONA (HM18335) | | | | | | | ● | | | |
| SHENLEY CHIROPRACTIC CLINIC (HM18399) | | | | | | | | | | |
| STEINBERG, PAMELA (HM19189) | | | | ● | | | | | | |
| SWEET BREEZE (HM19585) | | | | | | | ● | | | |
| TAYLOR, IAN E (HM19763) | | | | | | | | | | |
| TIM BROWN CLINIC (HM20075) | | | ● | | | | | | | |
| TOASH CLINIC (HM20101) | | | ● | | | | | | | |
| TODD, PAUL (HM20107) | | | | | | | | | | |
| TOMLIN, SUSAN M (HM20136) | | | | | | | | | | |
| TUDOR HOUSE CLINIC (HM20371) | | | ● | | | | | | | |

| Business by County with Reference no. | Auto Suggestion | Autogenic Training | Aversion Therapy | Ayurvedic Medicine | Baby Massage | Bach Remedies | Bates Method | Beauty Therapy | Bio-energetics | Biofeedback |
|---|---|---|---|---|---|---|---|---|---|---|
| KENTISH, LORNE (HM11531) | | | | | | | | | | |
| KINGFISHER CHIROP & HYP (HM11648) | | | | | | | | | | |
| LI (PROFESSOR) (HM12322) | | | | | | | | | | |
| MATHEW HUNT CHIROPODIST (HM13286) | | | | | | | | | | |
| METTE MARUP & MIKKELSEN (HM13778) | | | | | | | | | | |
| MIDDLE WAY RE-EDUCATION CTRE (HM13813) | | | | | | | | | | |
| MILTON KEYNES CHIRO CLINIC (HM13948) | | | | | | | | | | |
| MIND AND BODY (HM13959) | | | | | | | | | | |
| MORNINGSIDE HEALTH CLINIC (HM14190) | | | | | | | | | | |
| MORRISSEY, BLANCHE (HM14236) | | | | | | | | | | |
| NEWPORT ACUPUNCTURE CLINIC (HM14879) | | | | | | | | | | |
| OXFORDSHIRE BOWEN CLINIC (HM15545) | | | | | | | | | | |
| PARTON, KAY (HM15765) | | | | | | | | | | |
| PATON, BARBARA (HM15823) | | | | | | | | | | |
| PEPPLER, EILEEN (HM16011) | | | | | | | | | | |
| PERFECT OILS (HM16021) | | | | | | | | | | |
| PHYSIO FIRST PRACTICE (HM16199) | | | | | | | | | | |
| PINEWOOD CHIROPODY PRACTICE (HM16312) | | | | | | | | | | |
| PURTON HOUSE HOMEOPATHIC CTRE (HM16775) | | | | | | | | | | |
| RANDELL, BELINDA (HM16932) | | | | | | | | | | |
| REIKI HEALTH CENTRE (HM17137) | | | | | | | | | | |
| ROWBOTHAM, DARCIE (HM17684) | | | | | | | | | | |
| RUNDLE, RICHARD (HM17752) | ● | | | | | ● | | | | |
| SADLER, MARY (HM17832) | | | | | | | | | | |
| SHAW, FIONA (HM18335) | | | | | | | | | | |
| SHENLEY CHIROPRACTIC CLINIC (HM18399) | | | | | | | | | | |
| STEINBERG, PAMELA (HM19189) | | | | | | | | | | |
| SWEET BREEZE (HM19585) | | | | | | | | | | |
| TAYLOR, IAN E (HM19763) | | | | | | | | | | |
| TIM BROWN CLINIC (HM20075) | | | | | | | | | | |
| TOASH CLINIC (HM20101) | | | | | | | | | | |
| TODD, PAUL (HM20107) | | | | | | | | | | |
| TOMLIN, SUSAN M (HM20136) | | | | | | | | | | |
| TUDOR HOUSE CLINIC (HM20371) | | | | | | | | | | |

| Business by County with Reference no. | Biomagnetic Therapy | Biomechanics | Bonesetting | Bowen Therapy | Chinese Herbal Medicine | Chiropody | Chiropractic | Clinical Ecology | Cognitive Therapy | Colonic Hydrotherapy |
|---|---|---|---|---|---|---|---|---|---|---|
| KENTISH, LORNE (HM11531) | | | | | | ● | | | | |
| KINGFISHER CHIROP & HYP (HM11648) | | | | | | ● | | | | |
| LI (PROFESSOR) (HM12322) | | | | | | | | | | |
| MATHEW HUNT CHIROPODIST (HM13286) | | | | | | ● | | | | |
| METTE MARUP & MIKKELSEN (HM13778) | | | | | | | ● | | | |
| MIDDLE WAY RE-EDUCATION CTRE (HM13813) | | | | | | | | | | |
| MILTON KEYNES CHIRO CLINIC (HM13948) | | | | | | | ● | | | |
| MIND AND BODY (HM13959) | | | | | | | | | | |
| MORNINGSIDE HEALTH CLINIC (HM14190) | | | | | | | ● | | | |
| MORRISSEY, BLANCHE (HM14236) | | ● | | | | ● | | | | |
| NEWPORT ACUPUNCTURE CLINIC (HM14879) | | | | | | | | | | |
| OXFORDSHIRE BOWEN CLINIC (HM15545) | | | | ● | | | | | | |
| PARTON, KAY (HM15765) | | | | | | | | | | |
| PATON, BARBARA (HM15823) | | | | | | | | | | |
| PEPPLER, EILEEN (HM16011) | | | | | | | | | | |
| PERFECT OILS (HM16021) | | | | | | | | | | |
| PHYSIO FIRST PRACTICE (HM16199) | | | | | | | | | | |
| PINEWOOD CHIROPODY PRACTICE (HM16312) | | ● | | | | ● | | | | |
| PURTON HOUSE HOMEOPATHIC CTRE (HM16775) | | | | | | | | | | |
| RANDELL, BELINDA (HM16932) | | | | | | | ● | | | |
| REIKI HEALTH CENTRE (HM17137) | | | | | | | | | | |
| ROWBOTHAM, DARCIE (HM17684) | | | | | | | | | | |
| RUNDLE, RICHARD (HM17752) | | | | | | | | | ● | |
| SADLER, MARY (HM17832) | | | | | | | | | | |
| SHAW, FIONA (HM18335) | | | | | | | | | | |
| SHENLEY CHIROPRACTIC CLINIC (HM18399) | | | | | | | ● | | | |
| STEINBERG, PAMELA (HM19189) | | | | | | | | | | |
| SWEET BREEZE (HM19585) | | | | | | | | | | |
| TAYLOR, IAN E (HM19763) | | | | | | ● | | | | |
| TIM BROWN CLINIC (HM20075) | | | | | | | | | | |
| TOASH CLINIC (HM20101) | | | | | | | | | | |
| TODD, PAUL (HM20107) | | ● | | | | ● | | | | |
| TOMLIN, SUSAN M (HM20136) | | | | | | ● | | | | |
| TUDOR HOUSE CLINIC (HM20371) | | | | | | | | | | |

| Business by County with Reference no. | Colour Therapy | Complementary Therapy | Counselling | Cranial Osteopathy | Cranio-Sacral Therapy | Cryo Surgery | Crystal Healing | Cupping | Cymatics | Dance Movement Thrpy |
|---|---|---|---|---|---|---|---|---|---|---|
| KENTISH, LORNE (HM11531) | | | | | | | | | | |
| KINGFISHER CHIROP & HYP (HM11648) | | | | | | | | | | |
| LI (PROFESSOR) (HM12322) | | | | | | | | | | |
| MATHEW HUNT CHIROPODIST (HM13286) | | | | | | | | | | |
| METTE MARUP & MIKKELSEN (HM13778) | | | | | | | | | | |
| MIDDLE WAY RE-EDUCATION CTRE (HM13813) | | | | | | | | | | |
| MILTON KEYNES CHIRO CLINIC (HM13948) | | | | | | | | | | |
| MIND AND BODY (HM13959) | | ● | ● | | | | | | | |
| MORNINGSIDE HEALTH CLINIC (HM14190) | | | | | | | | | | |
| MORRISSEY, BLANCHE (HM14236) | | | | | | ● | | | | |
| NEWPORT ACUPUNCTURE CLINIC (HM14879) | | | | | | | | | | |
| OXFORDSHIRE BOWEN CLINIC (HM15545) | | | | | | | | | | |
| PARTON, KAY (HM15765) | | | | | | | | | | |
| PATON, BARBARA (HM15823) | | | | | | | | | | |
| PEPPLER, EILEEN (HM16011) | | | | | | | | | | |
| PERFECT OILS (HM16021) | | | | | | | | | | |
| PHYSIO FIRST PRACTICE (HM16199) | | | | | | | | | | |
| PINEWOOD CHIROPODY PRACTICE (HM16312) | | | | | | | | | | |
| PURTON HOUSE HOMEOPATHIC CTRE (HM16775) | | ● | | | | | | | | |
| RANDELL, BELINDA (HM16932) | | | | | | | | | | |
| REIKI HEALTH CENTRE (HM17137) | | | | | | | | | | |
| ROWBOTHAM, DARCIE (HM17684) | | | | | | | | | | |
| RUNDLE, RICHARD (HM17752) | | ● | ● | | | | | ● | | |
| SADLER, MARY (HM17832) | | | | | | | | | | |
| SHAW, FIONA (HM18335) | | | | | | | | | | |
| SHENLEY CHIROPRACTIC CLINIC (HM18399) | | | | | | | | | | |
| STEINBERG, PAMELA (HM19189) | | | | | | | | | | |
| SWEET BREEZE (HM19585) | | | | | | | | | | |
| TAYLOR, IAN E (HM19763) | | | | | | | | | | |
| TIM BROWN CLINIC (HM20075) | | | | | | | | | | |
| TOASH CLINIC (HM20101) | | | | | | | | | | |
| TODD, PAUL (HM20107) | | | | | | ● | | | | |
| TOMLIN, SUSAN M (HM20136) | | | | | | | | | | |
| TUDOR HOUSE CLINIC (HM20371) | | | | | | | | | | |

| Business by County with Reference no. | Dietician | Do-In | Douching | Dowsing | Drama Therapy | Electrolipolysis | Electrolysis | Electrotherapy | Encounter Groups | Faith Healing |
|---|---|---|---|---|---|---|---|---|---|---|
| KENTISH, LORNE (HM11531) | | | | | | | | | | |
| KINGFISHER CHIROP & HYP (HM11648) | | | | | | | | | | |
| LI (PROFESSOR) (HM12322) | | | | | | | | | | |
| MATHEW HUNT CHIROPODIST (HM13286) | | | | | | | | | | |
| METTE MARUP & MIKKELSEN (HM13778) | | | | | | | | | | |
| MIDDLE WAY RE-EDUCATION CTRE (HM13813) | | | | | | | | | | |
| MILTON KEYNES CHIRO CLINIC (HM13948) | | | | | | | | | | |
| MIND AND BODY (HM13959) | | | | ● | | | | | | |
| MORNINGSIDE HEALTH CLINIC (HM14190) | | | | | | | | | | |
| MORRISSEY, BLANCHE (HM14236) | | | | | | | | | | |
| NEWPORT ACUPUNCTURE CLINIC (HM14879) | | | | | | | | | | |
| OXFORDSHIRE BOWEN CLINIC (HM15545) | | | | | | | | | | |
| PARTON, KAY (HM15765) | | | | | | | | | | |
| PATON, BARBARA (HM15823) | | | | | | | | | | |
| PEPPLER, EILEEN (HM16011) | | | | | | | | | | |
| PERFECT OILS (HM16021) | | | | | | | | | | |
| PHYSIO FIRST PRACTICE (HM16199) | | | | | | | | ● | | |
| PINEWOOD CHIROPODY PRACTICE (HM16312) | | | | | | | | | | |
| PURTON HOUSE HOMEOPATHIC CTRE (HM16775) | | | | | | | | | | |
| RANDELL, BELINDA (HM16932) | | | | | | | | | | |
| REIKI HEALTH CENTRE (HM17137) | | | | | | | | | | |
| ROWBOTHAM, DARCIE (HM17684) | | | | | | | | | | |
| RUNDLE, RICHARD (HM17752) | ● | | | | | | | | | |
| SADLER, MARY (HM17832) | | | | | | | | | | |
| SHAW, FIONA (HM18335) | | | | | | | | | | |
| SHENLEY CHIROPRACTIC CLINIC (HM18399) | | | | | | | | | | |
| STEINBERG, PAMELA (HM19189) | | | | | | | | | | |
| SWEET BREEZE (HM19585) | | | | | | | | | | |
| TAYLOR, IAN E (HM19763) | | | | | | | | | | |
| TIM BROWN CLINIC (HM20075) | | | | | | | | | | |
| TOASH CLINIC (HM20101) | | | | | | | | | | |
| TODD, PAUL (HM20107) | | | | | | | | | | |
| TOMLIN, SUSAN M (HM20136) | | | | | | | | | | |
| TUDOR HOUSE CLINIC (HM20371) | | | | | | | | | | |

# A - F Therapies at Practices/Businesses

| Business by County with Reference no. | Absent Healing | Acupressure | Acupuncture | Alexander Technique | Allergy Testing | Anthroposohical Med | Aromatherapy | Art Therapy | Aura Therapy | Auricular Therapy | Auto Suggestion | Autogenic Training | Aversion Therapy | Ayurvedic Medicine | Baby Massage | Bach Remedies | Bates Method | Beauty Therapy | Bio-energetics | Biofeedback | Biomagnetic Therapy | Biomechanics | Bonesetting | Bowen Therapy | Chinese Herbal Medicine |
|---|---|---|---|---|---|---|---|---|---|---|---|---|---|---|---|---|---|---|---|---|---|---|---|---|---|
| WAKELING, ANN (HM20747) | | | | ● | | | | | | | | | | | | | | | | | | | | | |
| WARDLAW, MICHAEL (HM20921) | | | | | | | | | | | | | | | | | | | | | | | | | |
| WELCH, RONALD (HM21126) | | | | ● | | | | | | | | | | | | | | | | | | | | | |
| WELLBURN (HM21154) | | | ● | | | | | | | | | | | | | | | | | | | | | | |
| WELLER, JACK (HM21156) | | | | | | | | | | | ● | | ● | | | | | | | | | | | | |
| WEST WYCOMBE CHIRO CLINIC (HM21240) | | | | | | | | | | | | | | | | | | | | | | | | | |
| WEST WYCOMBE CHIROPRACTIC (HM21241) | | | | | | | | | | | | | | | | | | | | | | | | | |
| WESTWOOD, TERRY (HM21287) | | | | | | | | | | | | | | | | | | | | | | | | | |
| WHELDON, KATHERINE (HM21325) | | | | | | | | | | | | | | | | ● | | | | | | | | | |
| WILLIAMSON, ROSEMARY (HM21609) | | | | | | | ● | | | | | | | | | | | | | | | | | | |
| WOODWARD, MARGARET (HM21866) | | | | | | | | | | | | | | | | ● | | | | | | | | | |
| WOODWARD, MARGARET (HM21867) | | | | | | | | | | | | | | | | ● | | | | | | | | | |
| WORLAND, ANN (HM21896) | | | | | | | ● | | | | | | | | | | | | | | | | | | |
| **CAMBRIDGESHIRE** | | | | | | | | | | | | | | | | | | | | | | | | | |
| ACUPUNCTURE HERBAL REMEDIES (HM00314) | | | ● | | | | | | | | | | | | | | | | | | | | | | |
| AKINDELE, KOLA (HM00466) | | | | | | | | | | | | | | | | | | | | | | | | | |
| ANDERSON, M (HM00834) | | | | | | | | | | | | | | | | | | | | | | | | | |
| ANDERSON, PAUL (HM00836) | | | | | | | | | | | | | | | | | | | | | | | | | |
| ARJUNA NATURAL HEALTH CENTRE (HM01000) | | | ● | ● | | | ● | | | | | | | | | | | | | | | | | | |
| AROMATHERAPY WORLD (HM01130) | | | | | | | ● | | | | | | | | | | | | | | | | | | |
| BACK ON TRACK (HM01487) | | | ● | | | | | | | | | | | | | | | | | | | | | | |
| BACK ON TRACK (HM01486) | | | ● | | | | | | | | | | | | | | | | | | | | | | |
| BACK ON TRACK (HM01488) | | | ● | | | | | | | | | | | | | | | | | | | | | | |
| BEESLEY, RODERICK (HM02057) | | | | ● | | | | | | | | | | | | | | | | | | | | | |
| BRAMPTON CHIROPRACTIC CLINIC (HM02906) | | | | | | | | | | | | | | | | | | | | | | | | | |
| BROADWAY CHIROPRACTIC CLINIC (HM03122) | | | | | | | | | | | | | | | | | | | | | | | | | |
| BROE, NEIL (HM03136) | | | | | | | | | | | | | | | | | | | | | | | | | |
| CAMBRIDGE CHIROPRACTIC CENTRE (HM03572) | | | | | | | | | | | | | | | | | | | | | | | | | |
| CAMBRIDGE TRAD ACUPUNC CENTRE (HM03578) | | | ● | | | | | | | | | | | | | | | | | | | | | | |
| CHIROPRATIC & HOM HEALTH CTRE (HM04408) | | ● | ● | | | | ● | | | | | | | | | | | | | | | | | | |
| COLES, BARBARA (HM04833) | | | | | | | | | | | | | | | | ● | | | | | | | | | |
| COMPLEMENTARY HEALTH CLINIC (HM04927) | | | ● | | | | ● | | | | | | | | | | | | | | | | | | |
| COXELL REMEDIAL CLINIC (HM05324) | | | | | | | | | | | | | | | | | | | | | | | | | |
| DE MENTHON, FRANCOIS (HM05914) | | | ● | | | | | | | | | | | | | | | | | | | | | | |

| Business by County with Reference no. | Chiropody | Chiropractic | Clinical Ecology | Cognitive Therapy | Colonic Hydrotherapy | Colour Therapy | Complementary Therapy | Counselling | Cranial Osteopathy | Cranio-Sacral Therapy | Cryo Surgery | Crystal Healing | Cupping | Cymatics | Dance Movement Thrpy | Dietician | Do-In | Douching | Dowsing | Drama Therapy | Electrolipolysis | Electrolysis | Electrotherapy | Encounter Groups | Faith Healing |
|---|---|---|---|---|---|---|---|---|---|---|---|---|---|---|---|---|---|---|---|---|---|---|---|---|---|
| WAKELING, ANN (HM20747) | | | | | | | | | | | | | | | | | | | | | | | | | |
| WARDLAW, MICHAEL (HM20921) | ● | | | | | | | | | | | | | | | | | | | | | | | | |
| WELCH, RONALD (HM21126) | | | | | | | | | | | | | | | | | | | | | | | | | |
| WELLBURN (HM21154) | | | | | | | | | | | | | | | | | | | | | | | | | |
| WELLER, JACK (HM21156) | | | | | | | | ● | | | | | | | | | | | | | | | | | |
| WEST WYCOMBE CHIRO CLINIC (HM21240) | | ● | | | | | | | | | | | | | | | | | | | | | | | |
| WEST WYCOMBE CHIROPRACTIC (HM21241) | | ● | | | | | | | | | | | | | | | | | | | | | | | |
| WESTWOOD, TERRY (HM21287) | | | | | | | | ● | | | | | | | | | | | | | | | | | |
| WHELDON, KATHERINE (HM21325) | | | | | | | | | | | | | | | | | | | | | | | | | |
| WILLIAMSON, ROSEMARY (HM21609) | | | | | | | | | | | | | | | | | | | | | | | | | |
| WOODWARD, MARGARET (HM21866) | | | | | | | ● | | | | | | | | | | | | | | | | | | |
| WOODWARD, MARGARET (HM21867) | | | | | | | | | | | | | | | | | | | | | | | | | |
| WORLAND, ANN (HM21896) | | | | | | | | | | | | | | | | | | | | | | | | | |
| **CAMBRIDGESHIRE** | | | | | | | | | | | | | | | | | | | | | | | | | |
| ACUPUNCTURE HERBAL REMEDIES (HM00314) | | | | | | | | | | | | | | | | | | | | | | | | | |
| AKINDELE, KOLA (HM00466) | | ● | | | | | | | | | | | | | | | | | | | | | | | |
| ANDERSON, M (HM00834) | | ● | | | | | | | | | | | | | | | | | | | | | | | |
| ANDERSON, PAUL (HM00836) | ● | | | | | | | | | | | | | | | | | | | | | | | | |
| ARJUNA NATURAL HEALTH CENTRE (HM01000) | | | | | | | | ● | | | | | | | | | | | | | | | | | |
| AROMATHERAPY WORLD (HM01130) | | | | | | | | | | | | | | | | | | | | | | | | | |
| BACK ON TRACK (HM01487) | | | | | | | | | | | | | | | | | | | | | | | | | |
| BACK ON TRACK (HM01486) | | | | | | | | | | | | | | | | | | | | | | | | | |
| BACK ON TRACK (HM01488) | | | | | | | | | | | | | | | | | | | | | | | | | |
| BEESLEY, RODERICK (HM02057) | | | | | | | | | | | | | | | | | | | | | | | | | |
| BRAMPTON CHIROPRACTIC CLINIC (HM02906) | | ● | | | | | | | | | | | | | | | | | | | | | | | |
| BROADWAY CHIROPRACTIC CLINIC (HM03122) | | ● | | | | | | | | | | | | | | | | | | | | | | | |
| BROE, NEIL (HM03136) | | ● | | | | | | | | | | | | | | | | | | | | | | | |
| CAMBRIDGE CHIROPRACTIC CENTRE (HM03572) | | ● | | | | | | | | | | | | | | | | | | | | | | | |
| CAMBRIDGE TRAD ACUPUNC CENTRE (HM03578) | | | | | | | | | | | | | | | | | | | | | | | | | |
| CHIROPRATIC & HOM HEALTH CTRE (HM04408) | | ● | | | | | | | | | | | | | | | | | | | | | | | |
| COLES, BARBARA (HM04833) | | | | | | | | | | | | | | | | | | | | | | | | | |
| COMPLEMENTARY HEALTH CLINIC (HM04927) | | | | | | | | | ● | | | | | | | | | | | | | | | | |
| COXELL REMEDIAL CLINIC (HM05324) | | | | | | | | | | | | | | | | | | | | | | | ● | | |
| DE MENTHON, FRANCOIS (HM05914) | | | | | | | | | | | | | | | | | | | | | | | | | |

# A - F Therapies at Practices/Businesses

Business by County with Reference no.

| Business | Absent Healing | Acupressure | Acupuncture | Alexander Technique | Allergy Testing | Anthroposohical Med | Aromatherapy | Art Therapy | Aura Therapy | Auricular Therapy | Auto Suggestion | Autogenic Training | Aversion Therapy | Ayurvedic Medicine | Baby Massage | Bach Remedies | Bates Method | Beauty Therapy | Bio-energetics | Biofeedback | Biomagnetic Therapy | Biomechanics | Bonesetting | Bowen Therapy | Chinese Herbal Medicine |
|---|---|---|---|---|---|---|---|---|---|---|---|---|---|---|---|---|---|---|---|---|---|---|---|---|---|
| FAULKNER, CINDY (HM07141) | | ● | ● | | | | | | | | | | | | | | | | | | | | | | |
| FLOOD, RICHARD (HM07428) | | | | | | | ● | | | | | | | | | | | | | | | | | | |
| GOODMAN, JEAN (HM08259) | | | | | | | | | | | | | | | | ● | | | | | | | | | |
| HANEKE CHIROPRACTIC CLINIC (HM08923) | | | | | | | | | | | | | | | | | | | | | | | | | |
| HEAL, CHRISTIANNE (HM09313) | ● | | | | | | | | | | | | | | | ● | | | | | | | | | |
| HEALTH TEAM (HM09406) | | | | ● | ● | | ● | | | | ● | | | | | ● | | | ● | | | | | | |
| HYPNOSIS AND HEALTH (HM10495) | | | | | | | | | | | | | | | | | | | | ● | | | | | |
| JEFFERY, HELEN (HM10964) | | | | ● | | | | | | | | | | | | | | | | | | | | | |
| LIFELINE (HM12354) | | | | | | | | | | | | | | | | | | | | | | | | | |
| LIZ HALE HANDSON HEALTH (HM12495) | | | | | | | ● | | | | | | | | | ● | | | | | | | | ● | |
| LOW, C J (HM12685) | | | ● | | | | | | | | | | | | | | | | | | | | | | |
| LY, THI PHUNG (DR) (HM12754) | | | ● | | | | | | | | | | | | | | | | | | | | | | |
| MATHIESON, M A (HM13290) | | | | | | | | | | | | | | | | | | | | | | | | | |
| MENZIES, S J (HM13730) | | | ● | | | | | | | | | | | | | | | | | | | | | | |
| MORRIS & ASSOCIATES (HM14198) | | ● | ● | ● | | | | | | | | | | | | | | | | | | | | | |
| NORFOLK ESSENTIAL OILS (HM14994) | | | | | | | ● | | | | | | | | | | | | | | | | | | |
| PHIL SEAL PSYCHOTHERAPY (HM16115) | | | | | | | | | | | | | | | | | | | | | | | | | |
| PHOENIX ACUPUNCTURE CLINIC (HM16153) | | | ● | | | | | | | | | | | | | | | | | | | | | | |
| RATNAYAKE, MALINI (HM16960) | | | ● | | | | | | | | | | | | | | | | | | | | | | |
| REID, SUSAN (HM17121) | | | | ● | | | | | | | | | | | | | | | | | | | | | |
| REIKI (HM17126) | ● | | | | | | | | | | | | | | | | | | | | | | | | |
| SCOTT, S J (HM18125) | | | | ● | | | | | | | | | | | | | | | | | | | | | |
| SHULAN CLINIC OF ACUPUNCTURE (HM18514) | | | ● | | | | | | | | | | | | | | | | | | | | | | |
| SPENCE, ALEX (HM18982) | | | ● | | | | ● | | | | | | | | | | | | | | | | | | |
| SPOONER, K M (HM19037) | | | | | | | | | | | | | | | | | | | | | | | | | |
| STAGGS, JANE (HM19112) | | | | ● | | | | | | | | | | | | | | | | | | | | | |
| TAYLOR, EVE (HM19759) | | | | | | | ● | | | | | | | | | ● | | | | | | | | | |
| TERRY, EVA (HM19847) | | | | | | | ● | | | | | | | | | | | | | | | | | | |
| WILKINSON, GLYNNIS (HM21506) | | | | | | | | | | | | | | | | | | | | | | ● | | | |
| **CHANNEL ISLANDS** | | | | | | | | | | | | | | | | | | | | | | | | | |
| ST SAMPSON'S MEDICAL CENTRE (HM19098) | | | | | | | | | | | | | | | | | | | | | | | | | |
| **CHESHIRE** | | | | | | | | | | | | | | | | | | | | | | | | | |
| A & H PAIN CLINIC (HM00016) | | ● | ● | | | | ● | | | | | | | | | | | | | | | | | | |
| ACTON ACUPUNTURE CLINIC (HM00204) | | | ● | | | | | | | | | | | | | | | | | | | | | | |

| Business | Chiropody | Chiropractic | Clinical Ecology | Cognitive Therapy | Colonic Hydrotherapy | Colour Therapy | Complementary Therapy | Counselling | Cranial Osteopathy | Cranio-Sacral Therapy | Cryo Surgery | Crystal Healing | Cupping | Cymatics | Dance Movement Thrpy | Dietician | Do-In | Douching | Dowsing | Drama Therapy | Electrolipolysis | Electrolysis | Electrotherapy | Encounter Groups | Faith Healing |
|---|---|---|---|---|---|---|---|---|---|---|---|---|---|---|---|---|---|---|---|---|---|---|---|---|---|
| FAULKNER, CINDY (HM07141) | | | | | | | | | | | | | | | | | | | | | | | | | |
| FLOOD, RICHARD (HM07428) | | | | | | | | | | | | | | | | | | | | | | | | | |
| GOODMAN, JEAN (HM08259) | | | | | | | | | | | | | | | | | | | | | | | | | |
| HANEKE CHIROPRACTIC CLINIC (HM08923) | | ● | | | | | | | | | | | | | | | | | | | | | | | |
| HEAL, CHRISTIANNE (HM09313) | | | | | | | | ● | | | | | | | | | | | | | | | | | |
| HEALTH TEAM (HM09406) | ● | | ● | ● | | | ● | | | | | | | | | | | | ● | | | | ● | | |
| HYPNOSIS AND HEALTH (HM10495) | | | | ● | | | ● | ● | | | | | | | | | | | | | | | | | |
| JEFFERY, HELEN (HM10964) | | | | | | | | | | | | | | | | | | | | | | | | | |
| LIFELINE (HM12354) | | | | ● | | | | ● | | | | | | | | | | | | | | | | | |
| LIZ HALE HANDSON HEALTH (HM12495) | | | | | | | ● | | | | | ● | | | | | | | ● | | | | ● | | |
| LOW, C J (HM12685) | | | | | | | | | | | | | | | | | | | | | | | | | |
| LY, THI PHUNG (DR) (HM12754) | | | | | | | | ● | | | | | | | | | | | | | | | | | |
| MATHIESON, M A (HM13290) | ● | | | | | | | | | | | | | | | | | | | | | | | | |
| MENZIES, S J (HM13730) | | | | | | | | | | | | | | | | | | | | | | | | | |
| MORRIS & ASSOCIATES (HM14198) | | | | | | | | | ● | | | | | | | | | | | | | | | | |
| NORFOLK ESSENTIAL OILS (HM14994) | | | | | | | | | | | | | | | | | | | | | | | | | |
| PHIL SEAL PSYCHOTHERAPY (HM16115) | | | | | | | ● | | | | | | | | | | | | | | | | | | |
| PHOENIX ACUPUNCTURE CLINIC (HM16153) | | | | | | | | | | | | | | | | | | | | | | | | | |
| RATNAYAKE, MALINI (HM16960) | | | | | | | | | | | | | | | | | | | | | | | | | |
| REID, SUSAN (HM17121) | | | | | | | | | | | | | | | | | | | | | | | | | |
| REIKI (HM17126) | | | | | | | ● | | | | | | | | | | | | | | | | | | |
| SCOTT, S J (HM18125) | | | | | | | | | | | | | | | | | | | | | | | | | |
| SHULAN CLINIC OF ACUPUNCTURE (HM18514) | | | | | | | | | | | | | | | | | | | | | | | | | |
| SPENCE, ALEX (HM18982) | | | | | | | | ● | | | | | | | | | | | | | | | | | |
| SPOONER, K M (HM19037) | | ● | | | | | | | | | | | | | | | | | | | | | | | |
| STAGGS, JANE (HM19112) | | | | | | | | | | | | | | | | | | | | | | | | | |
| TAYLOR, EVE (HM19759) | | | | | | | ● | | | | | | | | | | | | | | | | | | |
| TERRY, EVA (HM19847) | | | | | | | | | | | | | | | | | | | | | | | | | |
| WILKINSON, GLYNNIS (HM21506) | ● | | | | | | | | | | | | | | | | | | | | | | | | |
| **CHANNEL ISLANDS** | | | | | | | | | | | | | | | | | | | | | | | | | |
| ST SAMPSON'S MEDICAL CENTRE (HM19098) | | ● | | | | | | | | | | | | | | | | | | | | | | | |
| **CHESHIRE** | | | | | | | | | | | | | | | | | | | | | | | | | |
| A & H PAIN CLINIC (HM00016) | | | | | | | | | | | | | | | | | | | | | | | | | |
| ACTON ACUPUNTURE CLINIC (HM00204) | | | | | | | | | | | | | | | | | | | | | | | | | |

# A - F Therapies at Practices/Businesses

| Business by County with Reference no. | Absent Healing | Acupressure | Acupuncture | Alexander Technique | Allergy Testing | Anthroposohical Med | Aromatherapy | Art Therapy | Aura Therapy | Auricular Therapy | Auto Suggestion | Autogenic Training | Aversion Therapy | Ayurvedic Medicine | Baby Massage | Bach Remedies | Bates Method |
|---|---|---|---|---|---|---|---|---|---|---|---|---|---|---|---|---|---|
| ADULT & CHILD FOOT CLINIC (HM00391) | | | | | | | | | | | | | | | | | |
| AMBLESIDE CLINIC (HM00773) | | | ● | | | | | | | | | | | | | | |
| AROMASPHERE (HM01083) | | | | | | | ● | | | | | | | | | | |
| AROMATHERAPY SHOP (HM01124) | | | | | | | ● | | | | | | | | | | |
| BACHE CHIROPODY (HM01471) | | | | | | | | | | | | | | | | | |
| BACK PAIN CLINIC (HM01500) | | | | | | | | | | | | | | | | | |
| BATES VISION EDUCATION (HM01878) | | | | | | | | | | | | | | | | | ● |
| BAXTER, GILLIAN (HM01927) | | | | | | | | | | | | | | | | | |
| BERESFORD, KATHLEEN (HM02183) | | | | ● | | | | | | | | | | | | ● | |
| BILLINGTON, JANE (HM02307) | | | ● | | | | | | | | | | | | | | |
| BLOCH, PETER (HM02510) | | | | ● | | | | | | | | | | | | | |
| BODY ESSENCES (HM02586) | | | | | | | ● | | | | | | | | | | |
| BODY LANGUAGE (HM02593) | | | | | | | ● | | | | | | | | | | |
| BODYTONE (HM02634) | | | | | | | ● | | | | | | | | | | |
| BOWN, LYNNE (HM02802) | | | | | | | ● | | | | | | | | | | |
| BRETHERTON-CROWE, LINDA (HM02971) | | | | | | | | | | | | | | | | ● | |
| BURTON, J S (HM03436) | | | | | | | | | | | | | | | | | |
| CARING HANDS (HM03683) | | | | | | | ● | | | | | | | | | | |
| CARMICHAEL CLINIC (HM03708) | | | ● | | | | | | | | | | | | | | |
| CHAN, K P (HM03968) | | | ● | | | | | | | | | | | | | | |
| CHEADLE HULME NATURAL HEALTH (HM04070) | | | | | | | ● | | | | | | | | | | |
| CHESHIRE HEALTH CLINIC (HM04115) | | | ● | ● | | | ● | | | | | | | | | | |
| CHESTER ALEXANDER TECH ST (HM04125) | | | | ● | | | | | | | | | | | | | |
| CHESTER CHIROPODY (HM04126) | | | | | | | | | | | | | | | | | |
| CHESTER CHIROPRACTIC CLINIC (HM04127) | | | | | | | | | | | | | | | | | |
| CHESTER CLINIC (HM04128) | | ● | ● | | | | ● | | | | | | | | | | |
| CHESTER HEALTH (HM04129) | | | | | | | ● | | | | | | | | | | |
| CHESTER HEALTH & BEAUTY STUDIO (HM04130) | | | | | | | ● | | | | | | | | | | |
| CHESTER THERAPY CENTRE (HM04134) | | | | | | | | | | | | | | | | | |
| CHINESE MEDICINE CENTRE (HM04257) | | ● | ● | | | | | | | | | | | | | | |
| CHIROPODIST SURGERY (HM04295) | | | | | | | | | | | | | | | | | |
| CHIROPODY CORNER (HM04330) | | | | | | | | | | | | | | | | | |
| CLINIC OF ACUPUNCTURE (HM04684) | | ● | ● | | | | | | | | | | | | | | |
| COLHOUN, PETER (HM04842) | | | | | | | | | | | | | | | | | |

| Business by County with Reference no. | Beauty Therapy | Bio-energetics | Biofeedback | Biomagnetic Therapy | Biomechanics | Bonesetting | Bowen Therapy | Chinese Herbal Medicine | Chiropody | Chiropractic | Clinical Ecology | Cognitive Therapy | Colonic Hydrotherapy | Colour Therapy | Complementary Therapy | Counselling |
|---|---|---|---|---|---|---|---|---|---|---|---|---|---|---|---|---|
| ADULT & CHILD FOOT CLINIC (HM00391) | | | | | | | | | ● | | | | | | ● | |
| AMBLESIDE CLINIC (HM00773) | | | | | | | | | | | | | | | ● | |
| AROMASPHERE (HM01083) | | | | | | | | | | | | | | | | |
| AROMATHERAPY SHOP (HM01124) | | | | | | | | | | | | | | | | |
| BACHE CHIROPODY (HM01471) | | | | | ● | | | | ● | | | | | | | |
| BACK PAIN CLINIC (HM01500) | | | | | | | | | | ● | | | | | | |
| BATES VISION EDUCATION (HM01878) | | | | | | | | | | | | | | | | |
| BAXTER, GILLIAN (HM01927) | | | | | | | | | ● | | | | | | | |
| BERESFORD, KATHLEEN (HM02183) | | | | | | | | | | | | | | ● | | |
| BILLINGTON, JANE (HM02307) | | | | | | | | | | | | | | | | |
| BLOCH, PETER (HM02510) | | | | | | | | | | | | | | | | |
| BODY ESSENCES (HM02586) | ● | | | | | | | | | | | | | | | |
| BODY LANGUAGE (HM02593) | | | | | | | | | | | | | | | | |
| BODYTONE (HM02634) | | | | | | | ● | | | | | | | | | |
| BOWN, LYNNE (HM02802) | | | | | | | | | | | | | | | | |
| BRETHERTON-CROWE, LINDA (HM02971) | | | | | | | | | | | | | | | | |
| BURTON, J S (HM03436) | | | | | ● | | | | ● | | | | | | | |
| CARING HANDS (HM03683) | | | | | | | | | | | | | | | | |
| CARMICHAEL CLINIC (HM03708) | | | | | | | | | | | | | | | | |
| CHAN, K P (HM03968) | | | | | | | | | | | | | | | | |
| CHEADLE HULME NATURAL HEALTH (HM04070) | | | | | | | | | | ● | | | | | | ● |
| CHESHIRE HEALTH CLINIC (HM04115) | | | | | | | ● | | | | | | | | | ● |
| CHESTER ALEXANDER TECH ST (HM04125) | | | | | | | | | | | | | | | | |
| CHESTER CHIROPODY (HM04126) | | | | | ● | | | | ● | | | | | | | |
| CHESTER CHIROPRACTIC CLINIC (HM04127) | | | | | | | | | | ● | | | | | | |
| CHESTER CLINIC (HM04128) | | | | | | | ● | ● | | | ● | | | | | ● |
| CHESTER HEALTH (HM04129) | | | | | | | | | | | | | | | ● | |
| CHESTER HEALTH & BEAUTY STUDIO (HM04130) | | | | | | | | | | | | | | | ● | |
| CHESTER THERAPY CENTRE (HM04134) | | | | | | | | | | | | ● | | | | |
| CHINESE MEDICINE CENTRE (HM04257) | | | | | | | | ● | | | | | | | | |
| CHIROPODIST SURGERY (HM04295) | | | | | | | | | ● | | | | | | ● | |
| CHIROPODY CORNER (HM04330) | | | | | | | | | ● | | | | | | | |
| CLINIC OF ACUPUNCTURE (HM04684) | | | | | | | | | | | | | | | | |
| COLHOUN, PETER (HM04842) | | | | | | | | | ● | | | | | | | |

| Business by County with Reference no. | Cranial Osteopathy | Cranio-Sacral Therapy | Cryo Surgery | Crystal Healing | Cupping | Cymatics | Dance Movement Thrpy | Dietician | Do-In | Douching | Dowsing | Drama Therapy | Electrolipolysis | Electrolysis | Electrotherapy | Encounter Groups | Faith Healing |
|---|---|---|---|---|---|---|---|---|---|---|---|---|---|---|---|---|---|
| ADULT & CHILD FOOT CLINIC (HM00391) | | | | | | | | | | | | | | | | | |
| AMBLESIDE CLINIC (HM00773) | | | | | | | | | | | | | | | | | |
| AROMASPHERE (HM01083) | | | | | | | | | | | | | | | | | |
| AROMATHERAPY SHOP (HM01124) | | | | | | | | | | | | | | | | | |
| BACHE CHIROPODY (HM01471) | | | | | | | | | | | | | | | | | |
| BACK PAIN CLINIC (HM01500) | | | | | | | | | | | | | | | | | |
| BATES VISION EDUCATION (HM01878) | | | | | | | | | | | | | | | | | |
| BAXTER, GILLIAN (HM01927) | | | | | | | | | | | | | | | | | |
| BERESFORD, KATHLEEN (HM02183) | | | | | | | | | | | | | | | | | |
| BILLINGTON, JANE (HM02307) | | | | | | | | | | | | | | | | | |
| BLOCH, PETER (HM02510) | | | | | | | | | | | | | | | | | |
| BODY ESSENCES (HM02586) | | | | | | | | | | | | | | | | | |
| BODY LANGUAGE (HM02593) | | | | | | | | | | | | | | | | | |
| BODYTONE (HM02634) | | | | | | | | | | | | | | | | | |
| BOWN, LYNNE (HM02802) | | | | | | | | | | | | | | | | | |
| BRETHERTON-CROWE, LINDA (HM02971) | | | | | | | | | | | | | | | | | |
| BURTON, J S (HM03436) | | | | | | | | | | | | | | | | | |
| CARING HANDS (HM03683) | | | | | | | | | | | | | | | | | |
| CARMICHAEL CLINIC (HM03708) | | | | | ● | | | | | | | | | | ● | | |
| CHAN, K P (HM03968) | | | | | | | | | | | | | | | | | |
| CHEADLE HULME NATURAL HEALTH (HM04070) | | | | | | | | | | | | | | | | | |
| CHESHIRE HEALTH CLINIC (HM04115) | | | | | | | | | | | | | | | | | |
| CHESTER ALEXANDER TECH ST (HM04125) | | | | | | | | | | | | | | | | | |
| CHESTER CHIROPODY (HM04126) | | | | | | | | | | | | | | | | | |
| CHESTER CHIROPRACTIC CLINIC (HM04127) | | | | | | | | | | | | | | | | | |
| CHESTER CLINIC (HM04128) | | | | | ● | | | | | | | | | | | | |
| CHESTER HEALTH (HM04129) | | | | | | | | | | | | | | | | | |
| CHESTER HEALTH & BEAUTY STUDIO (HM04130) | | | | | | | | | | | | | | | | | |
| CHESTER THERAPY CENTRE (HM04134) | | | | | | | | | | | | | | | | | |
| CHINESE MEDICINE CENTRE (HM04257) | | | | | | | | | | | | | | | | | |
| CHIROPODIST SURGERY (HM04295) | | | | | | | | | | | | | | | | | |
| CHIROPODY CORNER (HM04330) | | | | | | | | | | | | | | | | | |
| CLINIC OF ACUPUNCTURE (HM04684) | | | | | | | | | | | | | | | | | |
| COLHOUN, PETER (HM04842) | | | | | | | | | | | | | | | | | |

# A - F Therapies at Practices/Businesses

| Business by County with Reference no. | Absent Healing | Acupressure | Acupuncture | Alexander Technique | Allergy Testing | Anthroposohical Med | Aromatherapy | Art Therapy | Aura Therapy | Auricular Therapy | Auto Suggestion | Autogenic Training | Aversion Therapy | Ayurvedic Medicine | Baby Massage | Bach Remedies | Bates Method | Beauty Therapy | Bio-energetics | Biofeedback | Biomagnetic Therapy | Biomechanics | Bonesetting | Bowen Therapy | Chinese Herbal Medicine | Chiropody | Chiropractic | Clinical Ecology | Cognitive Therapy | Colonic Hydrotherapy | Colour Therapy | Complementary Therapy | Counselling | Cranial Osteopathy | Cranio-Sacral Therapy | Cryo Surgery | Crystal Healing | Cupping | Cymatics | Dance Movement Thrpy | Dietician | Do-In | Douching | Dowsing | Drama Therapy | Electrolipolysis | Electrolysis | Electrotherapy | Encounter Groups | Faith Healing |
|---|---|---|---|---|---|---|---|---|---|---|---|---|---|---|---|---|---|---|---|---|---|---|---|---|---|---|---|---|---|---|---|---|---|---|---|---|---|---|---|---|---|---|---|---|---|---|---|---|---|---|
| CONGLETON COUNSELLING PRACTICE (HM04977) | | | | | | | | | | | | | | | | | | | | | | | | | | | | | ● | | | | ● | | | | | | | | | | | | | | | | | |
| CONSTANTINE, J C (HM05012) | | | | | | | | | | | | | | | | | | | | | | | | | | | | | | | | | | ● | | | | | | | | | | | | | | | | |
| CREWE & NANT PHYSIO CLINIC (HM05431) | | | ● | | | | | | | | | | | | | | | | | | | | | | | | | | | | | | | | | | | | | | | | | | | | | | | |
| CRYSTAL AROMATICS (HM05525) | | | | | | | ● | | | | | | | | | | | | | | | | | | | | | | | | | | | | | | | | | | | | | | | | | | | |
| CULSHAW, S (HM05591) | | | | | | | ● | | | | | | | | | | | | | | | | | | | | | | | | | | | | | | | | | | | | | | | | | | | |
| DAVIES & ASSOCIATES (HM05791) | | | | | | | | | | | | | | | | | | | | | | | ● | | | | | | | | | ● | | ● | | | | | | | | | | | | | | | | |
| DEWHURST, PATRICA A (HM06049) | | | | | ● | | | | | | | | | | | | | | | | | | | | | | | | | | | | | | | | | | | | | | | | | | | | | |
| DICKENSON, A G (HM06068) | | | ● | | | | | | | | | | | | | | | | | | | | | | | | | | | | | | | | | | | | | | | | | | | | | | | |
| DREAM AIR (HM06295) | | | | | | | ● | | | | | | | | | | | | | | | | | | | | | | | | | | | | | | | | | | | | | | | | | | | |
| ESSENTIAL OIL WORKS (HM06913) | | | | | | | ● | | | | | | | | | | | | | | | | | | | | | | | | | | | | | | | | | | | | | | | | | | | |
| EVANS, DI (HM06968) | | | | | | | | | | | | | | | | | | | | | | | | ● | | | | | | | | | | | | | | | | | | | | | | | | | | |
| EVANS, SUSAN (HM06992) | | | ● | | | | | | | | | | | | | | | | | | | | | | | | | | | | | | | | | | | | | | | | | | | | | | | |
| FAGAN, B W (HM07042) | | | ● | | | | | | | | | | | | | | | | | | | | | | | | | | | | | | | | | | | | | | | | | | | | | | | |
| FEET FIRST MOBILE CHIROPODY SV (HM07183) | | | | | | | | | | | | | | | | | | | | | | | | | | ● | | | | | | | | | | | | | | | | | | | | | | | | |
| FIELD VIEW SURGERY (HM07259) | | | | | | | | | | | | | | | | | | | | | | ● | | | | ● | ● | | | | | | | | | | | | | | | | | | | | | | | |
| GILL, SHEILA (HM08079) | | | | | | | | | | | | | | | | ● | | | | | | | | | | | | | | | | | | | | | | | | | | | | | | | | | | |
| GRACE & ASSOCIATES (HM08331) | | | | | | | | | | | | | | | | | | | | | | ● | | | | ● | | | | | | | | | | | | | | | | | | | | | | | | |
| GRAHAM COOMBE - MCTIMONEY (HM08338) | | | | | | | | | | | | | | | | | | | | | | | | | | | ● | | | | | | | | | | | | | | | | | | | | | | | |
| HANDS ON PHYSIOTHERAPY (HM08913) | | | ● | | | | | | | | | | | | | | | | | | | | | | | | | | | | | | | | | | | | | | | | | | | | | | | |
| HAZELDENE, BARBARA (HM09292) | | | | | | | ● | | | | | | | | | | | | | | | | | | | | | | | | | | | | | | | | | | | | | | | | | | | |
| HEALD, M T (HM09316) | | | | | | | | | | | | | | | | | | | | | | | | | | ● | | | | | | | | | | | | | | | | | | | | | | | | |
| HIGHLEY, T J (HM09757) | | | | | | | | | | | | | | | | | | | | | | | | | | ● | | | | | | | | | | | | | | | | | | | | | | | | |
| HOFTON, EFFIE (HM09903) | | | ● | | | | | | | | | | | | | | | | | | | | | | | | | | | | | | | | | | | | | | | | | | | | | | | |
| HUSKISSON, EILEEN (HM10434) | | | | | | | | | | | | | | | | | | | | | | ● | | | | ● | | | | | | | | | | | | | | | | | | | | | | | | |
| HYPNOS PRACTICE (HM10492) | | | | | | | | | | | ● | | | | | | | | | | | | | | | | | | | | | | | | | | | | | | | | | | | | | | | |
| JANE HAMMOND THERAPY (HM10916) | | | | | | | | | | | | | | | | | | | | | | | | | | | | | ● | | | | ● | | | | | | | | | | | | | | | | | |
| JONES, DAVID (HM11137) | | | ● | | | | | | | | | | | | | | | | | | | | | | | | | | | | | | | | | | | | | | | | | | | | | | | |
| JONES, J W (HM11155) | | | | | | | | | | | | | | | | | | | | | | | | | | ● | | | | | | | | | | | | | | | | | | | | | | | | |
| JONES, MARILYN (HM11173) | | | ● | | | | | | | | | | | | | | | | | | | | | | | | | | | | | | | | | | | | | | | | | | | | | | | |
| KARAGIANNI, CHRISTINA (HM11317) | | | | | | | | | | | | | | | | ● | | | | | | | | | | | | | | | | | | | | | | | | | | | | | | | | | | |
| KEATING, J (HM11375) | | | ● | | | | | | | | | | | | | | | | | | | | | | | | | | | | | | | | | | | | | | | | | | | | | | | |
| KNOTT, ELIZABETH (HM11764) | | | | | | | ● | | | | | | | | | | | | | | | | | | | | | | | | | | | | | | | | | | | | | | | | | | | |
| KNOWLES, BARBARA (HM11768) | | | | | | | ● | | | | | | | | | | | | | | | | | | | | | | | | | | | | | | | | | | | | | | | | | | | |
| KNUTSFORD CHIROPRACTIC CLINIC (HM11775) | ● | | | | | | ● | | | | | | | | | | | | | | | | | | | | ● | | | | | ● | ● | | | | | | | | | | | | | | | | | |

# A - F Therapies at Practices/Businesses

| Business by County with Reference no. | Absent Healing | Acupressure | Acupuncture | Alexander Technique | Allergy Testing | Anthroposohical Med | Aromatherapy | Art Therapy | Aura Therapy | Auricular Therapy | Auto Suggestion | Autogenic Training | Aversion Therapy | Ayurvedic Medicine | Baby Massage | Bach Remedies | Bates Method | Beauty Therapy | Bio-energetics | Biofeedback | Biomagnetic Therapy | Biomechanics | Bonesetting | Bowen Therapy | Chinese Herbal Medicine | Chiropody | Chiropractic | Clinical Ecology | Cognitive Therapy | Colonic Hydrotherapy | Colour Therapy | Complementary Therapy | Counselling | Cranial Osteopathy | Cranio-Sacral Therapy | Cryo Surgery | Crystal Healing | Cupping | Cymatics | Dance Movement Thrpy | Dietician | Do-In | Douching | Dowsing | Drama Therapy | Electrolipolysis | Electrolysis | Electrotherapy | Encounter Groups | Faith Healing |
|---|---|---|---|---|---|---|---|---|---|---|---|---|---|---|---|---|---|---|---|---|---|---|---|---|---|---|---|---|---|---|---|---|---|---|---|---|---|---|---|---|---|---|---|---|---|---|---|---|---|---|
| KUSIAR, C W (HM11829) | | | | | | | | | | | | | | | | | | | | | | | | | | | ● | | | | | | | | | | | | | | | | | | | | | | | |
| LEGGE, PAT (HM12176) | | | | | | | ● | | | | | | | | | | | | | | | | | | | | | | | | | | | | | | | | | | | | | | | | | | | |
| LOMAS, CLIFFORD (HM12574) | | | | | | | | | | | | | | | | | | | | | | | | ● | | | | | | | | | | | | | | | | | | | | | | | | | | |
| MACALLAN, STEPHEN (HM12815) | | | ● | | | | | | | | | | | | | | | | | | | | | | | | | | | | | | | | | | | | | | ● | | | | | | | | | |
| MARSH, F W (HM13147) | | | | | | | | | | | | | | | | | | | | | | | | | | ● | | | | | | | | | | | | | | | | | | | | | | | | |
| MEHTA HYPNOTHERAPY (HM13695) | | | | | | | | | | | ● | | | | | | | | | | | | | | | | | | | | | ● | | | | | | | | | | | | | | | | | | |
| MIDDLETON & ASSOCIATES (HM13817) | | | | | | | | | | | | | | | | | | | | | | | | | | | ● | | | | | | | | | | | | | | | | | | | | | | | |
| MORTON, J V (HM14251) | | | | | | | | | | | | | | | | | | | | | | | | | | ● | | | | | | | | | | | | | | | | | | | | | | | | |
| NEW LIFE NATURAL HEALTH CARE (HM14821) | | | | | | | ● | ● | | | | | | | | ● | | | | | | | | ● | | | ● | ● | | | | ● | ● | | | | | | | | | | | | | | | | | |
| NEWTON, J C (HM14898) | | | | | | | | | | | | | | | | | | | | | | ● | | | | ● | | | | | | | | | | | | | | | | | | | | | | | | |
| NUTRITION AND ALLERGY CLINIC (HM15121) | | | | | | | | | | | | | | | | | | | | | | | | | | | | ● | | | | ● | ● | | | | | | | | | | | ● | | | | | | |
| OAKES, JILL (HM15146) | | | | | | | ● | | | | | | | | | | | | | | | | | | | | | | | | | | | | | | | | | | | | | | | | | | | |
| OLD HALL CLINIC (HM15256) | | | ● | | | | | | | | | | | | | | | | | | | | | | | | | | | | | | ● | | | | | | | | | | | | | | | | | |
| ORIGINALS (HM15392) | | | | | | | ● | | | | | | | | | | | | | | | | | | | | | | | | | | | | | | | | | | | | | | | | | | | |
| P B AROMATHERAPY (HM15548) | | | | | | | ● | | | | | | | | | | | | | | | | | | | | | | | | | | | | | | | | | | | | | | | | | | | |
| PEARL AROMATICS (HM15905) | | | | | | | ● | | | | | | | | | | | | | | | | | | | | | | | | | | | | | | | | | | | | | | | | | | | |
| PENNYCOOK, AMANDA (HM15996) | | | | | | | | | | | | | | | | | | | | | | ● | | | | ● | | | | | | | | | | | | | | | | | | | | | | | | |
| PHOENIX CENTRE (HM16154) | ● | | | | | | | | | | | | | | | | | | | | | | | | | | | | | | | | | | | | | | | | | | | | | | | | | |
| PHYSIO & SPORTS INJURY CLINIC (HM16181) | | ● | | ● | | | | | | | | | | | | ● | | | | | | | | | | | | | | | | | | | | | | | | | | | | | | ● | | | | |
| PHYSIO PLUS (HM16203) | | | | | | | ● | | | | | | | | | | | | | | | ● | | | ● | | | | | | | | | | | | | | | | | | | | | | | | | |
| POT POURRI PRETTIES (HM16462) | | | | | | | ● | | | | | | | | | | | | | | | | | | | | | | | | | | | | | | | | | | | | | | | | | | | |
| POYNTON CHIROPRACTIC CLINIC (HM16519) | | | | | | | | | | | | | | | | | | | | | | | | | | | ● | | | | | | | | | | | | | | | | | | | | | | | |
| PREW, BEVERLEY (HM16566) | | | | | | | | | | | | | | | | | | | | | | | | | | | | | | | | ● | | | | | | | | | | | | | | | | | | |
| PRINCE, TANIA A (HM16622) | | | | | | | | | | | | | | | | | | | | | | | | | | | | | | | | | ● | | | | | | | | | | | | | | | | | |
| REDGRAVE, KENNETH (HM17025) | | | | | | | | | | | | | | | | | | | | | | | | | | | | | ● | | | | ● | | | | | | | | | | | | | | | | | |
| RELAX (HM17157) | | | | | | | ● | | | | | | | | | | | | | | | | | | | | | | | | | | | | | | | | | | | | | | | | | | | |
| RICHARDS, DAVID (HM17250) | | | | | | | | | | | | | | | | | | | | | | | | | | ● | | | | | | | | | | | | | | | | | | | | | | | | |
| RICHARDS, KERRY L (HM17260) | | | | | | | | | | | | | | | | | | | | | | | | | | ● | | | | | | | | | | | | | | | | | | | | | | | | |
| SANDBACH HYPNOSIS CLINIC (HM17899) | | | | | | | | | | | | | | | | | | | | ● | | | | | | | | | | | | | | | | | | | | | | | | | | | | | | |
| SAXELBY, M (HM17990) | | | | | | | | | | | | | | | | | | | | | | | | | | ● | | | | | | | | | | | | | | | | | | | | | | | | |
| SCENTED GARDENS (HM18011) | | | | | | | ● | | | | | | | | | | | | | | | | | | | | | | | | | | | | | | | | | | | | | | | | | | | |
| SCOTT, M (HM18123) | | | | | | | ● | | | | | | | | | | | | | | | | | | | | | | | | | | | | | | | | | | | | | | | | | | | |
| SIMPLY NATURAL ESSENTIAL OILS (HM18580) | | | | | | | ● | | | | | | | | | | | | | | | | | | | | | | | | | | | | | | | | | | | | | | | | | | | |
| STORRS, PAULINE (HM19350) | | | | | | | ● | | | | | | | | | | | | | | | | | | | | | | | | | | | | | | | | | | | | | | | | | | | |

# A - F Therapies at Practices/Businesses

| Business by County with Reference no. | Absent Healing | Acupressure | Acupuncture | Alexander Technique | Allergy Testing | Anthroposohical Med | Aromatherapy | Art Therapy | Aura Therapy | Auricular Therapy | Auto Suggestion | Autogenic Training | Aversion Therapy | Ayurvedic Medicine | Baby Massage | Bach Remedies | Bates Method | Beauty Therapy | Bio-energetics | Biofeedback | Biomagnetic Therapy | Biomechanics | Bonesetting | Bowen Therapy | Chinese Herbal Medicine | Chiropody | Chiropractic | Clinical Ecology | Cognitive Therapy | Colonic Hydrotherapy | Colour Therapy | Complementary Therapy | Counselling | Cranial Osteopathy | Cranio-Sacral Therapy | Cryo Surgery | Crystal Healing | Cupping | Cymatics | Dance Movement Thrpy | Dietician | Do-In | Douching | Dowsing | Drama Therapy | Electrolipolysis | Electrolysis | Electrotherapy | Encounter Groups | Faith Healing |
|---|---|---|---|---|---|---|---|---|---|---|---|---|---|---|---|---|---|---|---|---|---|---|---|---|---|---|---|---|---|---|---|---|---|---|---|---|---|---|---|---|---|---|---|---|---|---|---|---|---|---|
| TEDSTONE, ALISON (HM19815) | | | | | | | | | | | | | | | | | | | | | | | | | | ● | | | | | | | | | | | | | | | | | | | | | | | | |
| THOMAS, BEVERLEY (HM19933) | | | | | | | | | | | | | | | | | | | | | | | | | | ● | | | | | | | | | | | | | | | | | | | | | | | | |
| THORNBER, A A (HM20016) | | | | | | | | | | | | | | | | | | | | | | | | | | ● | | | | | | | | | | | | | | | | | | | | | | | | |
| THREE MOONS OILS (HM20040) | | | | | | | ● | | | | | | | | | | | | | | | | | | | | | | | | | | | | | | | | | | | | | | | | | | | |
| TIPLING, L (HM20087) | | | | | | | | | | | | | | | | | | | | | | | | | | ● | | | | | | | | | | | | | | | | | | | | | | | | |
| TRINITY HOUSE PRACTICE (HM20339) | | ● | ● | ● | | | ● | | | | | | | | | | | | | | | | | ● | | | | | | | | ● | ● | | | | | | | | ● | | | | | | | ● | | |
| TULLY, CHARLES (HM20388) | | | | ● | | | | | | | | | | | | | | | | | | | | | | | | | | | | | | | | | | | | | | | | | | | | | | |
| TYRER, HELEN R (HM20473) | | | | | | | | | | | | | | | | | | | | | | ● | | | | ● | | | | | | | | | | | | | | | | | | | | | | | | |
| VALE ROYAL CHIROPRACTIC CLINIC (HM20552) | | | | | | | | | | | | | | | | | | | | | | | | | | | ● | | | | | | | | | | | | | | | | | | | | | | | |
| VALE ROYAL CHIROPRACTIC CLINIC (HM20553) | | | | | | | | | | | | | | | | | | | | | | | | | | | ● | | | | | | | | | | | | | | | | | | | | | | | |
| WALKER, HELEN (HM20773) | | | | | | | ● | | | | | | | | | | | | | | | | | | | | | | | | | | | | | | | | | | | | | | | | | | | |
| WARRINGTON ACUPUNCTURE CLINIC (HM20956) | | | ● | | | | | | | | | | | | | | | | | | | | | | | | | | | | | | | | | | | | | | | | | | | | | | | |
| WARRINGTON CHIROPRACTIC CLINIC (HM20957) | | | | | | | | | | | | | | | | | | | | | | | | | | | ● | | | | | | | | | | | | | | | | | | | | | | | |
| WEAVER HOUSE CLINIC (HM21049) | | | ● | | ● | | ● | | | | | | | | | | | | | | | | | | | | | | | | | | ● | | | | | | | | | | | | | | | | | |
| WIDNES OSTEOPATHIC CLINIC (HM21459) | | ● | ● | | | | | | | | | | | | | | | | | | | | | | | | | | | | | ● | | ● | | | | | | | | | | | | | | ● | | |
| WILKINSON, PHILIP (HM21513) | | | | | | | | | | | | | | | | ● | | | | | | | | | | | | | | | | | | | | | | | | | | | | | | | | | | |
| WILLIAMS OSTEOPATHIC CLINIC (HM21532) | | | | | | | ● | | | | | | | | | | | | | | | | | | | ● | | | | | | | ● | ● | | | | | | | | | | | | | | | | |
| WINE, SUE (HM21697) | | | | | | | | | | | | | | | | | | | | | | | | | | | ● | | | | | | | | | | | | | | | | | | | | | | | |
| WOOLLEY, M E (HM21878) | | | | | | | | | | | | | | | | | | | | | | | | | | ● | | | | | | | | | | | | | | | | | | | | | | | | |
| WYNNE-JONES, J (HM21978) | | | | | | | | | | | | | | | | | | | | | | | | | | ● | | | | | | | | | | | | | | | | | | | | | | | | |
| **CLEVELAND** | | | | | | | | | | | | | | | | | | | | | | | | | | | | | | | | | | | | | | | | | | | | | | | | | | |
| ALEXANDER TECHNIQUE (HM00548) | | | | ● | | | | | | | | | | | | | | | | | | | | | | | | | | | | | | | | | | | | | | | | | | | | | | |
| AROMA HEALTH NORTH EAST (HM01052) | | | | | | | ● | | | | | | | | | | | | | | | | | | | | | | | | | | | | | | | | | | | | | | | | | | | |
| BARNARD, SIMON (HM01732) | | | | | | | | | | | | | | | | | | | | | | | | | | | | | | | | ● | | ● | | | | | | | | | | | | | | | | |
| HARTLEPOOL CHIROPRACTIC CLINIC (HM09138) | | | | | | | | | | | | | | | | | | | | | | | | | | | ● | | | | | | | | | | | | | | | | | | | | | | | |
| HEAVEN SCENT (HM09473) | | | | | | | ● | | | | | | | | | | | | | | | | | | | | | | | | | | | | | | | | | | | | | | | | | | | |
| MERMAID CHIROPRACTIC PRACTICE (HM13749) | | | | | | | | | | | | | | | | | | | | | | | | | | | ● | | | | | | | | | | | | | | | | | | | | | | | |
| NATURAL THERAPY CENTRE (HM14637) | | | ● | | | | ● | | | | | | | | | | | ● | | | | | | | | ● | | | | | | | | | | | | | | | | | | | | | | | | |
| NORTHERN GUILD-PSYCHOTHERAPY (HM15061) | | | | | | | | | | | | | | | | | | | | | | | | | | | | | ● | | | | ● | | | | | | | | | | | | ● | | | | | |
| RAINBOW BRIDGE SCHOOL (HM16875) | | | | | | | ● | | | | | | | | | | | | | | | | | | | | | | | | | | | | | | | | | | | | | | | | | | | |
| REDCAR PHYSIO & SPORTS (HM17007) | | | ● | | | | | | | | | | | | | | | | | | | | | | | | | | | | | | | | | | | | | | | | | | | | | | | |
| RUSH, DENNIS (HM17754) | | | | | | | | | | | ● | ● | | | | | | | | | | | | | | | | | | | | | ● | | | | | | | | | | | | | | | | | |
| SKIPPINGS & ASSOCIATES (HM18657) | | | | | | | | | | | | | | | | | | | | | | | | | | | ● | | | | | | | | | | | | | | | | | | | | | | | |
| STRESS COUNSELLING (HM19391) | | | | | | | ● | | | | | | | | | | | | | | | | | | | | | | ● | | | | ● | | | | | | | | | | | | | | | | | |

# A - F Therapies at Practices/Businesses

| Business by County with Reference no. | Absent Healing | Acupressure | Acupuncture | Alexander Technique | Allergy Testing | Anthroposohical Med | Aromatherapy | Art Therapy | Aura Therapy | Auricular Therapy | Auto Suggestion | Autogenic Training | Aversion Therapy | Ayurvedic Medicine | Baby Massage | Bach Remedies | Bates Method | Beauty Therapy | Bio-energetics | Biofeedback | Biomagnetic Therapy | Biomechanics | Bonesetting | Bowen Therapy | Chinese Herbal Medicine | Chiropody | Chiropractic | Clinical Ecology | Cognitive Therapy | Colonic Hydrotherapy | Colour Therapy | Complementary Therapy | Counselling | Cranial Osteopathy | Cranio-Sacral Therapy | Cryo Surgery | Crystal Healing | Cupping | Cymatics | Dance Movement Thrpy | Dietician | Do-In | Douching | Dowsing | Drama Therapy | Electrolipolysis | Electrolysis | Electrotherapy | Encounter Groups | Faith Healing |
|---|---|---|---|---|---|---|---|---|---|---|---|---|---|---|---|---|---|---|---|---|---|---|---|---|---|---|---|---|---|---|---|---|---|---|---|---|---|---|---|---|---|---|---|---|---|---|---|---|---|---|
| WARD-DAVIS, J (HM20916) | | | ● | | | | | | | | | | | | | | | | | | | | | | | | | | | | | | | | | | | | | | | | | | | | | | | |
| WICKS, CLIFF (HM21452) | | | ● | | | | | | | | | | | | | | | | | | | | | | | | | | | | | | | | | | | | | | | | | | | | | | | |
| **CORNWALL** | | | | | | | | | | | | | | | | | | | | | | | | | | | | | | | | | | | | | | | | | | | | | | | | | | |
| ACUPUNCTURE & PHYSIO CLINIC (HM00246) | | | ● | | | | | | | | | | | | | | | | | | | | | | | | | | | | | | | | | | | | | | | | | | | | | | | |
| ALEXANDRA FOOT CLINIC (HM00573) | | | | | | | | | | | | | | | | | | | | | | | | | | ● | | | | | | | | | | | | | | | | | | | | | | | | |
| BARNNETT, ANN (HM01763) | | | | | | | | | | | | | | | | | | | | | | | | ● | | | | | | | | | | | | | | | | | | | | | | | | | | |
| BEARE, M E (HM01968) | | | | | | | | | | | | | | | | | | | | | | | | | | ● | | | | | | | | | | | | | | | | | | | | | | | | |
| C H M SWANPOEL (HM03524) | | | ● | | | | | | | | | | | | | | | | | | | | | | | | | | | | | | | | | | | | | | | | | | | | | | | |
| CARADON CHIROPRACTIC CLINIC (HM03656) | | | | | | | | | | | | | | | | | | | | | | | | | | | ● | | | | | | | | | | | | | | | | | | | | | | | |
| CHIROPODIST/PODIATRIST (HM04296) | | | | | | | | | | | | | | | | | | | | | | ● | | | | ● | | | | | | | | | | | | | | | | | | | | | | | | |
| COMP HEALTH INITIATIVE (HM04912) | ● | | ● | | | | ● | | | | | | | | | ● | | | | | | | | | | | ● | | | | | ● | ● | | | | ● | | | | | | | ● | | | | | | |
| DUCHY CHIROPRACTIC CLINIC (HM06345) | | | | | | | | | | | | | | | | | | | | | | | | | | | ● | | | | | | | | | | | | | | | | | | | | | | | |
| FALMOUTH CHIROPRACTIC CLINIC (HM07079) | | | | | | | | | | | | | | | | | | | | | | | | | | | ● | | | | | | | | | | | | | | | | | | | | | | | |
| FOOTCARE (HM07492) | | | | | | | | | | | | | | | | | | | | | | | | | | ● | | | | | | | | | | | | | | | | | | | | | | | | |
| FORCE, GAYLE (HM07520) | ● | | | | | | | | | | | | | | | | | | | | | | | | | | | | | | ● | | ● | | | | ● | | | | | | | ● | | | | | | ● |
| GARDINER, NICKY (HM07874) | | | | | | | ● | | | | | | | | | | | | | | | | | | | | | | | | | | | | | | | | | | | | | | | | | | | |
| GOUGH, LOUISE (HM08316) | | | | | | | | | | | | | | | | | | | | | | | | | | | ● | | | | | | | | | | | | | | | | | | | | | | | |
| GRANNY M'S AROMATHERAPY PRODS (HM08374) | | | | | | | ● | | | | | | | | | | | | | | | | | | | | | | | | | | | | | | | | | | | | | | | | | | | |
| HALL, PETER (HM08787) | | ● | ● | | | | | | | | | | | | | | | | | | | | | | | | | | | | | | | ● | | | | ● | | | ● | ● | | | | | | ● | | |
| HAWKSLAND PHYSIOTHERAPY CENTRE (HM09233) | | | ● | | | | | | | | | | | | | | | | | | | | | | | | | | | | | | | | | | | | | | | | | | | | | ● | | |
| LEMON ST NTRL HLTH PRACTICE (HM12206) | | | ● | | | | ● | | | | | | | | | ● | | | | | | | | | ● | | ● | | | | | ● | | | | | | | | | | | | | | | | | | |
| LIFE 'N' LIMB (HM12345) | | | | | | | ● | | | | | | | | | | | | | | | | | | | | | | | | | | | | | | | | | | | | | | | | | | | |
| LIFE 'N' LIMB (HM12346) | | ● | | | | | ● | | | | | | | | | | | | | | | | | | | | | | | | | ● | | | | | | | | | | | | | | | | | | |
| LISKEARD CHIROPRACTIC CLINIC (HM12453) | | | | | | | | | | | | | | | | | | | | | | | | | | | ● | | | | | | | | | | | | | | | | | | | | | | | |
| LISTER NATURAL HEALTH PRACTICE (HM12461) | ● | ● | ● | | | | ● | | | | ● | | ● | | | ● | | | | | | | | | ● | | ● | | ● | | | ● | ● | ● | ● | | | ● | | | | | | | | | | | ● | |
| MASTERS, B (HM13273) | | | | | | | | | | | | | | | | | | | | | | | | | | | ● | | | | | | | | | | | | | | | | | | | | | | | |
| MATHESON, B & P (HM13283) | | | ● | | | | | | | | | | | | | | | | | | | | | | | | | | | | | | | | | | | | | | | | | | | | | | | |
| MATHESON, P A (HM13285) | | | ● | | | | | | | | | | | | | | | | | | | | | | | | | | | | | | | | | | | | | | | | | | | | | | | |
| MORPHEW, JOHN (DR) (HM14196) | | | ● | | | | | | | | | | | | | | | | | | | | | | | | | | | | | | | | | | | | | | | | | | | | | | | |
| MORSE, EMMA (HM14239) | | | | | | | ● | | | | | | | | | | | | | | | | | | | | | | | | | | | | | | | | | | | | | | | | | | | |
| NATURES TREASURES (HM14699) | | | | | | | ● | | | | | | | | | | | | | | | | | | | | | | | | | | | | | | | | | | | | | | | | | | | |
| NEWQUAY CHIROPRACTIC CLINIC (HM14883) | | | ● | | | | ● | | | | | | | | | | | | | | | | | | | | ● | | | | | ● | | | | | | | | | | | | | | | | | | |
| OSTEOPATHIC FAMILY CENTRE (HM15465) | | | | | | | | | | | | | | | | | | | | | | | | | | | | | | | | | | ● | | | | | | | | | | | | | | | | |
| PENZANCE NATURAL HEALTH CENTRE (HM16006) | | | ● | ● | | | ● | | | | | | | | | ● | | | | | | | | | | | | | | | | | ● | ● | | | | | | | | | | | | | | | | |

# A - F Therapies at Practices/Businesses

Business by County with Reference no.

| Business by County with Reference no. | Absent Healing | Acupressure | Acupuncture | Alexander Technique | Allergy Testing | Anthroposohical Med | Aromatherapy | Art Therapy | Aura Therapy | Auricular Therapy | Auto Suggestion | Autogenic Training | Aversion Therapy | Ayurvedic Medicine | Baby Massage | Bach Remedies | Bates Method | Beauty Therapy | Bio-energetics |
|---|---|---|---|---|---|---|---|---|---|---|---|---|---|---|---|---|---|---|---|
| POOLER, ADENEY (HM16431) | | | | | | | | | | | | | | | | | | | |
| REEVES, J (HM17066) | | | | | | | | | | | | | | | | | | | |
| RENTOUL, J W (HM17190) | | | ● | | | | | | | | | | | | | | | | |
| SALTASH FOOT CLINIC (HM17865) | | | | | | | | | | | | | | | | | | | |
| SMITHWHITE, AMBER (HM18825) | | | | | | | ● | | | | | | | | | | | | |
| ST AUSTELL CHIROPRACTIC CLINIC (HM19070) | | | ● | | | | ● | | | | | | | | | | | | |
| TREMAIN, BARBARA (HM20317) | | | | | | | | | | | | | | | | ● | | | |
| TRURO CHIROPRACTIC CLINIC (HM20354) | | | ● | | | | ● | | | | | | | | | | | | |
| TRURO OSTEOPATHIC PRACTICE (HM20356) | | | | | | | | | | | | | | | | | | | |
| VERA BOYES ACUPUNCTURE (HM20618) | | | ● | | | | | | | | | | | | | | | | |
| WILLS, JONATHAN (HM21632) | | | ● | | | | ● | | | | | | | | | | | ● | |
| WRIGHT, CYNTHIA (HM21929) | | | | | | | | | | | | | | | | | | | |
| **COUNTY DURHAM** | | | | | | | | | | | | | | | | | | | |
| ABEL, STEFFAN H (HM00108) | | | | | | | | | | | | | | | | | | | |
| ANDREADIS, ANTHONIA (HM00844) | | | ● | | | | | | | | | | | | | | | | |
| AROMAS OF JOY (HM01081) | | | | | | | ● | | | | | | | | | | | | |
| AUCKLAND ACUPUNCTURE CLINIC (HM01344) | | | ● | | | | | | | | | | | | | | | | |
| BALANCE HOLISTIC HEALTHCARE (HM01606) | ● | | | | | | | | | | | | | | | ● | | | |
| CALLAGHAN, M M (HM03548) | | | | | | | | | | | | | | | | | | | |
| CLAYPATH MEDICAL PRACTICE (HM04619) | | | ● | | | | | | | | | | | | | | | | |
| DARLINGTON CHIROPRACTIC CLINIC (HM05743) | | | | | | | | | | | | | | | | | | | |
| ELIZABETH BLAYLOCK REIKI PRACT (HM06738) | | | | | | | ● | | | | | | | | | | | | |
| ESSENTIAL TOUCH (HM06919) | | | | | | | ● | | | | | | | | | | | | |
| FIONA OTTEWELL CHRTRD PHYSIO (HM07329) | | | ● | | | | | | | | | | | | | | | | |
| FOOTPRINTS (HM07507) | | | | | | | | | | | | | | | | | | | |
| HOBSON, I K (HM09864) | | | | | | | | | | | | | | | | | | | |
| LAWTON, HELEN (HM12073) | | | | | | | | | | | | | | | | ● | | | |
| MIDGLEY, CLARE (HM13826) | | | | | | | | | | | | | | | | ● | | | |
| NATURAL HEALING CENTRE (HM14536) | ● | | | ● | | | ● | | | | | | | | | ● | | ● | |
| NEWCASTLE/NE TRANS MEDITA CTRE (HM14856) | | | | | | | | | | | | | | ● | | | | | |
| OLD PIT PRACTICE (HM15260) | | | ● | | | | | | | | | | | | | | | | |
| R & M TRADING (HM16828) | | | | | | | ● | | | | | | | | | | | | |
| TANSLEY, LINDEN (HM19691) | | | | | | | ● | | | | | | | | | | | | |
| TAYLOR, CAROL (HM19741) | | | | ● | | | | | | | | | | | | | | | |

| Business by County with Reference no. | Biofeedback | Biomagnetic Therapy | Biomechanics | Bonesetting | Bowen Therapy | Chinese Herbal Medicine | Chiropody | Chiropractic | Clinical Ecology | Cognitive Therapy | Colonic Hydrotherapy | Colour Therapy | Complementary Therapy | Counselling | Cranial Osteopathy | Cranio-Sacral Therapy |
|---|---|---|---|---|---|---|---|---|---|---|---|---|---|---|---|---|
| POOLER, ADENEY (HM16431) | | | | | | | | ● | | | | | | | | |
| REEVES, J (HM17066) | | | | | | | ● | | | | | | | | | |
| RENTOUL, J W (HM17190) | | | | | | | | | | | | | | | | |
| SALTASH FOOT CLINIC (HM17865) | | | | | | | ● | | | | | | | | | |
| SMITHWHITE, AMBER (HM18825) | | | | | | | | | | | | | | | | |
| ST AUSTELL CHIROPRACTIC CLINIC (HM19070) | | | | | | | | ● | | | | | | | | |
| TREMAIN, BARBARA (HM20317) | | | | | | | | | | | | | | | | |
| TRURO CHIROPRACTIC CLINIC (HM20354) | | | | | | | | ● | | | | | | | | |
| TRURO OSTEOPATHIC PRACTICE (HM20356) | | | | | | | | | | | | | | ● | | |
| VERA BOYES ACUPUNCTURE (HM20618) | | | | | | | | | | | | | | | | |
| WILLS, JONATHAN (HM21632) | | | | | | | ● | | | | | | | | ● | |
| WRIGHT, CYNTHIA (HM21929) | | | | | | | | | | | | | | ● | | |
| **COUNTY DURHAM** | | | | | | | | | | | | | | | | |
| ABEL, STEFFAN H (HM00108) | | | | | | | | ● | | | | | | | | |
| ANDREADIS, ANTHONIA (HM00844) | | | | | | | | | | | | | | | | |
| AROMAS OF JOY (HM01081) | | | | | | | | | | | | | | | | |
| AUCKLAND ACUPUNCTURE CLINIC (HM01344) | | | | | | | | | | | | | | | | |
| BALANCE HOLISTIC HEALTHCARE (HM01606) | | | | | | | | | | | | | ● | ● | | |
| CALLAGHAN, M M (HM03548) | | | | | | | ● | | | | | | | | | |
| CLAYPATH MEDICAL PRACTICE (HM04619) | | | | | | | | | | | | | | | | |
| DARLINGTON CHIROPRACTIC CLINIC (HM05743) | | | | | | | | ● | | | | | | | | |
| ELIZABETH BLAYLOCK REIKI PRACT (HM06738) | | | | | | | | | | | | | | | | |
| ESSENTIAL TOUCH (HM06919) | | | | | | | | | | | | | | | | |
| FIONA OTTEWELL CHRTRD PHYSIO (HM07329) | | | | | | | | | | | | | | | | |
| FOOTPRINTS (HM07507) | | | ● | | | | ● | | | | | | | | | |
| HOBSON, I K (HM09864) | | | ● | | | | ● | | | | | | | | | |
| LAWTON, HELEN (HM12073) | | | | | | | | | | | | | | | | |
| MIDGLEY, CLARE (HM13826) | | | | | | | | | | | | | | | | |
| NATURAL HEALING CENTRE (HM14536) | | | | | ● | | | | | | | | ● | ● | ● | |
| NEWCASTLE/NE TRANS MEDITA CTRE (HM14856) | | | | | | | | | | | | | | | | |
| OLD PIT PRACTICE (HM15260) | | | | | | | | | | | | | | | | |
| R & M TRADING (HM16828) | | | | | | | | | | | | | | | | |
| TANSLEY, LINDEN (HM19691) | | | | | | | | | | | | | | | | |
| TAYLOR, CAROL (HM19741) | | | | | | | | | | | | | | | | |

| Business by County with Reference no. | Cryo Surgery | Crystal Healing | Cupping | Cymatics | Dance Movement Thrpy | Dietician | Do-In | Douching | Dowsing | Drama Therapy | Electrolipolysis | Electrolysis | Electrotherapy | Encounter Groups | Faith Healing |
|---|---|---|---|---|---|---|---|---|---|---|---|---|---|---|---|
| POOLER, ADENEY (HM16431) | | | | | | | | | | | | | | | |
| REEVES, J (HM17066) | | | | | | | | | | | | | | | |
| RENTOUL, J W (HM17190) | | | | | | | | | | | | | | | |
| SALTASH FOOT CLINIC (HM17865) | | | | | | | | | | | | | | | |
| SMITHWHITE, AMBER (HM18825) | | | | | | | | | | | | | | | |
| ST AUSTELL CHIROPRACTIC CLINIC (HM19070) | | | | | | | | | | | | | | | |
| TREMAIN, BARBARA (HM20317) | | | | | | | | | | | | | | | |
| TRURO CHIROPRACTIC CLINIC (HM20354) | | | | | | | | | | | | | | | |
| TRURO OSTEOPATHIC PRACTICE (HM20356) | | | | | | | | | | | | | | | |
| VERA BOYES ACUPUNCTURE (HM20618) | | | | | | | | | | | | | | | |
| WILLS, JONATHAN (HM21632) | | | | | | | | | | | | ● | | | |
| WRIGHT, CYNTHIA (HM21929) | | | | | | | | | | | | | | | |
| **COUNTY DURHAM** | | | | | | | | | | | | | | | |
| ABEL, STEFFAN H (HM00108) | | | | | | | | | | | | | | | |
| ANDREADIS, ANTHONIA (HM00844) | | | | | | | | | | | | | | | |
| AROMAS OF JOY (HM01081) | | | | | | | | | | | | | | | |
| AUCKLAND ACUPUNCTURE CLINIC (HM01344) | | | | | | | | | | | | | | | |
| BALANCE HOLISTIC HEALTHCARE (HM01606) | | | | | | | | | | | | | | | |
| CALLAGHAN, M M (HM03548) | | | | | | | | | | | | | | | |
| CLAYPATH MEDICAL PRACTICE (HM04619) | | | | | | | | | | | | | | | |
| DARLINGTON CHIROPRACTIC CLINIC (HM05743) | | | | | | | | | | | | | | | |
| ELIZABETH BLAYLOCK REIKI PRACT (HM06738) | | | | | | | | | | | | | | | |
| ESSENTIAL TOUCH (HM06919) | | | | | | | | | | | | | | | |
| FIONA OTTEWELL CHRTRD PHYSIO (HM07329) | | | | | | | | | | | | | ● | | |
| FOOTPRINTS (HM07507) | | | | | | | | | | | | | | | |
| HOBSON, I K (HM09864) | | | | | | | | | | | | | | | |
| LAWTON, HELEN (HM12073) | | | | | | | | | | | | | | | |
| MIDGLEY, CLARE (HM13826) | | | | | | | | | | | | | | | |
| NATURAL HEALING CENTRE (HM14536) | | | | | | ● | | | ● | | | | | | |
| NEWCASTLE/NE TRANS MEDITA CTRE (HM14856) | | | | | | | | | | | | | | | |
| OLD PIT PRACTICE (HM15260) | | | | | | | | | | | | | | | |
| R & M TRADING (HM16828) | | | | | | | | | | | | | | | |
| TANSLEY, LINDEN (HM19691) | | | | | | | | | | | | | | | |
| TAYLOR, CAROL (HM19741) | | | | | | | | | | | | | | | |

# A - F Therapies at Practices/Businesses

Business by County with Reference no.

| Business | Absent Healing | Acupressure | Acupuncture | Alexander Technique | Allergy Testing | Anthroposohical Med | Aromatherapy | Art Therapy | Aura Therapy | Auricular Therapy | Auto Suggestion | Autogenic Training | Aversion Therapy | Ayurvedic Medicine | Baby Massage | Bach Remedies | Bates Method | Beauty Therapy | Bio-energetics | Biofeedback | Biomagnetic Therapy | Biomechanics | Bonesetting | Bowen Therapy | Chinese Herbal Medicine |
|---|---|---|---|---|---|---|---|---|---|---|---|---|---|---|---|---|---|---|---|---|---|---|---|---|---|
| TEESDALE OSTEOPATHIC CLINIC (HM19817) | | | | ● | | | | | | | | | | | | | | | | | | | | | |
| TREATMENT ROOM (HM20302) | | ● | ● | ● | | | ● | | | | | | | | | | | | | | | | | | |
| WAKE, J (HM20742) | | | | | | | ● | | | | | | | | | | | | | | | | | | |
| WARWICK, ANDREA (HM20967) | | ● | | | ● | | | | | | | | | | | | | | | | | | | | |
| **CUMBRIA** | | | | | | | | | | | | | | | | | | | | | | | | | |
| AIREY, L M (HM00442) | | | | | | | ● | | | | | | | | | | | | | | | | | | |
| ALADDIN AROMAS (HM00468) | | | | | | | ● | | | | | | | | | | | | | | | | | | |
| BOYD, JOHN (HM02818) | | | ● | | | | | | | | | | | | | | | | | | | | | | |
| EDWARDS, D E (HM06648) | | | | | | | | | | | | | | | | | | | | | | | | | |
| FOOTWORKS (HM07515) | | | | | | | | | | | | | | | | | | | | | | ● | | | |
| GARNETT, JANE (HM07897) | | | | | | | ● | | | | | | | | | | | | | | | | | | |
| HARDWICKE, MICHAEL (HM08977) | | | | ● | | | | | | | | | | | | | | | | | | | | | |
| LAKELAND AROMATICS (HM11872) | | | | | | | ● | | | | | | | | | | | | | | | | | | |
| LAKELAND CHIROPRACTIC CENTRE (HM11873) | | | | | | | | | | | | | | | | | | | | | | | | | |
| LIBRA THERAPY CENTRE (HM12328) | | ● | | | | | ● | | | | | | | | | | | | | | | | | | |
| LYLEE, URWIN (HM12758) | | | | | | | | | | | | | | | | | | | | | | | | | |
| MCWATT, LIZ (HM13624) | | | | | | | ● | | | | | | | | | ● | | | | | | | | | |
| PETER STREET CLINIC (HM16075) | | | | | | | | | | | | | | | | | | | | | | | | | |
| RHAM, TRICIA (HM17217) | | | | | | | | | | | | | | | | | | | | | | | | | |
| RUBINSTEIN, ADAM (HM17725) | | | | | | | | | | | | | | | | | | | | | | | | | |
| RUBINSTEIN, ADAM (HM17724) | | | | | | | | | | | | | | | | | | | | | | | | | |
| SIMPLY PERFECT BY JAN (HM18581) | | | | | | | ● | | | | | | | | | | | ● | | | | | | | |
| STRAWBERRY HOW CLINIC (HM19378) | | ● | | | | | | | | | | | | | | | | | | | | | | | |
| SWINDALE, TESSA (HM19594) | | | | | | | | | | | | | | | | | | | | | | | | | |
| THERAPY CENTRE (HM19898) | | ● | ● | ● | | | | | | | ● | | ● | | | | | | | | | | | | |
| THOMAS, JULIET (HM19949) | | | | | | | | | | | | | | | | | | | | | | | | | |
| THURSTON, JENNY (HM20049) | | | | | | | | | | | | | | | | ● | | | | | | | | | |
| VULCANS LANE CHIROPODY (HM20720) | | | | | | | ● | | | | | | | | | | | | | | | | | | |
| WILSON, P M (HM21664) | | | | | | | | | | | | | | | | | | | | | | | | | |
| **DERBYSHIRE** | | | | | | | | | | | | | | | | | | | | | | | | | |
| ACRE HEALTH (HM00183) | | | | | | | ● | | | | | | | | | | | | | | | | | | |
| ACUPUNCTURE CENTRE (HM00249) | | | ● | | | | | | | | | | | | | | | | | | | | | | |
| ACUPUNCTURE CLINIC (HM00270) | | | ● | | | | | | | | | | | | | | | | | | | | | | |
| ALTER-MED (HM00690) | | | | | | | ● | | | | | | | | | | | | | | | | | | |

| Business | Chiropody | Chiropractic | Clinical Ecology | Cognitive Therapy | Colonic Hydrotherapy | Colour Therapy | Complementary Therapy | Counselling | Cranial Osteopathy | Cranio-Sacral Therapy | Cryo Surgery | Crystal Healing | Cupping | Cymatics | Dance Movement Thrpy | Dietician | Do-In | Douching | Dowsing | Drama Therapy | Electrolipolysis | Electrolysis | Electrotherapy | Encounter Groups | Faith Healing |
|---|---|---|---|---|---|---|---|---|---|---|---|---|---|---|---|---|---|---|---|---|---|---|---|---|---|
| TEESDALE OSTEOPATHIC CLINIC (HM19817) | | | | | | | | | | | | | | | | | | | | | | | | | |
| TREATMENT ROOM (HM20302) | | ● | | | | | | | | | | | | | | | | | | | | | ● | | |
| WAKE, J (HM20742) | | | | | | | | | | | | | | | | | | | | | | | | | |
| WARWICK, ANDREA (HM20967) | | | | | | ● | ● | | | | | | | | | | | | | | | | | | |
| **CUMBRIA** | | | | | | | | | | | | | | | | | | | | | | | | | |
| AIREY, L M (HM00442) | | | | | | | | | | | | | | | | | | | | | | | | | |
| ALADDIN AROMAS (HM00468) | | | | | | | | | | | | | | | | | | | | | | | | | |
| BOYD, JOHN (HM02818) | | | | | | | | | | | | | | | | | | | | | | | | | |
| EDWARDS, D E (HM06648) | | | | | | | | ● | | | | | | | | | | | | | | | | | |
| FOOTWORKS (HM07515) | ● | | | | | | | | | | | | | | | | | | | | | | | | |
| GARNETT, JANE (HM07897) | | | | | | | | | | | | | | | | | | | | | | | | | |
| HARDWICKE, MICHAEL (HM08977) | | | | | | | | | | | | | | | | | | | | | | | | | |
| LAKELAND AROMATICS (HM11872) | | | | | | | | | | | | | | | | | | | | | | | | | |
| LAKELAND CHIROPRACTIC CENTRE (HM11873) | | ● | | | | | | | | | | | | | | | | | | | | | | | |
| LIBRA THERAPY CENTRE (HM12328) | | | | | | | | | | | | | | | | | | | | | | | | | |
| LYLEE, URWIN (HM12758) | | ● | | | | | | | | | | | | | | | | | | | | | | | |
| MCWATT, LIZ (HM13624) | | | | | | | ● | | | | | | | | | | | | | | | | | | |
| PETER STREET CLINIC (HM16075) | ● | | | | | | | | | | | | | | | | | | | | | | | | |
| RHAM, TRICIA (HM17217) | | ● | | | | | | ● | | ● | | | | | | | | | | | | | | | |
| RUBINSTEIN, ADAM (HM17725) | | | | | | | | | | ● | | | | | | | | | | | | | | | |
| RUBINSTEIN, ADAM (HM17724) | | | | | | | | | | ● | | | | | | | | | | | | | | | |
| SIMPLY PERFECT BY JAN (HM18581) | | | | | | | | | | | | | | | | | | | | | | | | | |
| STRAWBERRY HOW CLINIC (HM19378) | | | | | | | | | | | | | | | | | | | | | | | | | |
| SWINDALE, TESSA (HM19594) | ● | | | | | | | | | | | | | | | | | | | | | | | | |
| THERAPY CENTRE (HM19898) | | | | | | | | | ● | | | | | | | | | | | | | | | | |
| THOMAS, JULIET (HM19949) | | ● | | | | | | | | | | | | | | | | | | | | | | | |
| THURSTON, JENNY (HM20049) | | | | | | | | | | | | | | | | | | | | | | | | | |
| VULCANS LANE CHIROPODY (HM20720) | ● | | | | | | | | | | | | | | | | | | | | | | | | |
| WILSON, P M (HM21664) | ● | | | | | | | | | | | | | | | | | | | | | | | | |
| **DERBYSHIRE** | | | | | | | | | | | | | | | | | | | | | | | | | |
| ACRE HEALTH (HM00183) | | | | | | | | | | | | | | | | | | | | | | | | | |
| ACUPUNCTURE CENTRE (HM00249) | | | | | | | | | | | | | | | | | | | | | | | | | |
| ACUPUNCTURE CLINIC (HM00270) | | | | | | | | | | | | | | | | | | | | | | | | | |
| ALTER-MED (HM00690) | | | | | | | | | | | | | | | | | | | | | | | | | |

# A - F Therapies at Practices/Businesses

Business by County with Reference no.

| Business | Absent Healing | Acupressure | Acupuncture | Alexander Technique | Allergy Testing | Anthroposohical Med | Aromatherapy | Art Therapy | Aura Therapy | Auricular Therapy | Auto Suggestion | Autogenic Training | Aversion Therapy | Ayurvedic Medicine | Baby Massage | Bach Remedies | Bates Method |
|---|---|---|---|---|---|---|---|---|---|---|---|---|---|---|---|---|---|
| AROMATHERAPY & REFLEX CTRE (HM01090) | | | | | | | ● | | | | | | | | | | |
| AROMATIC (HM01134) | | | | | | | ● | | | | | | | | | | |
| BACH FLOWER REMEDIES (HM01469) | | | | | | | | | | | | | | | | ● | |
| BARROWCLIFFE, GRAHAM (DR) (HM01806) | | | ● | | | | | | | | | ● | | | | | |
| BELPER BACKPAIN CLINIC (HM02110) | ● | | | | | | | | | | | | | | | | |
| BELPER NATURAL HEALTH CENTRE (HM02112) | | | ● | | | | ● | | | | | | | | | | |
| BODY & SOUL (HM02562) | | | | | | | ● | | | | | | | | | | |
| BRADSHAW, P J (HM02878) | | | | | | | | | | | ● | | | | | | |
| CARRICK-SMITH, L (HM03744) | | | | | | | | | | | | | | | | | |
| CLARK, HAZEL (HM04558) | | | | | | | ● | | | | | | | | | | |
| DE MIERRE, MAVIS (HM05915) | | | | | | | | | | | | | | | | ● | |
| DERBY ACUPUNCTURE CENTRE (HM06011) | | | ● | | | | | | | | | | | | | | |
| DERBYSHIRE SPORTS INJURIES (HM06014) | | | ● | | | | | | | | | | | | | | |
| DRONFIELD NAT HEALTH CLINIC (HM06319) | | ● | ● | | | | ● | | | | | | | | | | |
| ENJOY SPORT (HM06836) | | | | | | | ● | | | | | | | | | | |
| FARMER, VAL (HM07110) | | | | | | | | | | | | | | | | ● | |
| GALLEY, D G (HM07843) | | | | | | | | | | | | | | | | | |
| GALLEY, D G (HM07842) | | | | | | | | | | | | | | | | | |
| HARDING, MANDY (HM08971) | | | | | | | | | | | | | | | | | |
| HATHERSAGE HEALTH & THRPY CTRE (HM09198) | | | | | | | ● | | | | | | | | | | |
| HEANOR CHIROPRACTIC CLINIC (HM09436) | | | | | | | | | | | | | | | | | |
| HOUSE OF AROMATHERAPY (HM10216) | | | | | | | ● | | | | | | | | | | |
| HOUSE OF AROMATHERAPY (HM10217) | | | | | | | ● | | | | | | | | | | |
| ILKESTONE OSTEO & MED CTRE (HM10580) | | | | | | | ● | | | | | | | | | | |
| JACKSON-BASS, ALISON (HM10853) | | | ● | | | | | | | | | | | | | | |
| JEFFERY & ASSOCIATES (HM10963) | | | | | | | | | | | | | | | | | |
| KARDAHJI, F C (HM11319) | | | | | | | | | | | | | | | | | |
| KAY, P (HM11353) | | | ● | | | | | | | | | | | | | | |
| KEMP, G D (HM11460) | | | | | | | | | | | | | | | | | |
| KEMP, GILLIAN (HM11461) | | ● | | | | | ● | | | | | | | | | | |
| LANCASHIRE, A W (HM11915) | | | | | | | | | | | | | | | | | |
| LIFESOLUTIONS (HM12359) | | | | | | | | | | | ● | ● | | | | | |
| LONG TUONG VAN (HM12618) | | | ● | | | | | | | | | | | | | | |
| MATTHEWS, A (HM13299) | | | | | | | | | | | | | | | | | |

| Business | Beauty Therapy | Bio-energetics | Biofeedback | Biomagnetic Therapy | Biomechanics | Bonesetting | Bowen Therapy | Chinese Herbal Medicine | Chiropody | Chiropractic | Clinical Ecology | Cognitive Therapy | Colonic Hydrotherapy | Colour Therapy | Complementary Therapy | Counselling | Cranial Osteopathy |
|---|---|---|---|---|---|---|---|---|---|---|---|---|---|---|---|---|---|
| AROMATHERAPY & REFLEX CTRE (HM01090) | | | | | | | | | | | | | | | | | |
| AROMATIC (HM01134) | | | | | | | | | | | | | | | | | |
| BACH FLOWER REMEDIES (HM01469) | | | | | | | | | | | | | | | | | |
| BARROWCLIFFE, GRAHAM (DR) (HM01806) | | | | | | | | | | | | ● | | | | | |
| BELPER BACKPAIN CLINIC (HM02110) | | | | | | | | | | | | | | | | | |
| BELPER NATURAL HEALTH CENTRE (HM02112) | | | | | | | | | | | | | | | | ● | ● |
| BODY & SOUL (HM02562) | | | | | | | | | | | | | | | | | |
| BRADSHAW, P J (HM02878) | | ● | | | | | | | | | | ● | | | | ● | |
| CARRICK-SMITH, L (HM03744) | | | | | | | | | | | | | | | | ● | |
| CLARK, HAZEL (HM04558) | | | | | | | | | | | | | | | | | |
| DE MIERRE, MAVIS (HM05915) | | | | | | | | | | | | | | | | | |
| DERBY ACUPUNCTURE CENTRE (HM06011) | | | | | | | | | | | | | | | | | |
| DERBYSHIRE SPORTS INJURIES (HM06014) | | | | | | | | | | | | | | | | | |
| DRONFIELD NAT HEALTH CLINIC (HM06319) | | | | | | | | | | | | | | | ● | ● | |
| ENJOY SPORT (HM06836) | | | | | | | | | | | | | | | | | |
| FARMER, VAL (HM07110) | | | | | | | | | | | | | | | | | |
| GALLEY, D G (HM07843) | | | | | | | | | | ● | | | | | | | |
| GALLEY, D G (HM07842) | | | | | | | | | | ● | | | | | | | |
| HARDING, MANDY (HM08971) | | | | | | | | | ● | | | | | | | | |
| HATHERSAGE HEALTH & THRPY CTRE (HM09198) | | | | | | | | | | | | | | | | | |
| HEANOR CHIROPRACTIC CLINIC (HM09436) | | | | | | | | | | ● | | | | | | | |
| HOUSE OF AROMATHERAPY (HM10216) | | | | | | | | | | | | | | | | | |
| HOUSE OF AROMATHERAPY (HM10217) | | | | | | | | | | | | | | | | | |
| ILKESTONE OSTEO & MED CTRE (HM10580) | | | | | | | | | | | | | | | | | |
| JACKSON-BASS, ALISON (HM10853) | | | | | | | | | | | | | | | | | |
| JEFFERY & ASSOCIATES (HM10963) | | | | | | | | | | ● | | | | | | | |
| KARDAHJI, F C (HM11319) | | | | | | | | | ● | | | | | | | | |
| KAY, P (HM11353) | | | | | | | | | | | | | | | | | |
| KEMP, G D (HM11460) | | | | | | | | | ● | | | | | | | | |
| KEMP, GILLIAN (HM11461) | | | | | | | | | | | | | | | ● | ● | |
| LANCASHIRE, A W (HM11915) | | | | | | | | | ● | | | | | | | | |
| LIFESOLUTIONS (HM12359) | | | | | | | | | | | | ● | | | ● | ● | |
| LONG TUONG VAN (HM12618) | | | | | | | | | | | | | | | | | |
| MATTHEWS, A (HM13299) | | | | | | | | | ● | | | | | | | | |

| Business | Cranio-Sacral Therapy | Cryo Surgery | Crystal Healing | Cupping | Cymatics | Dance Movement Thrpy | Dietician | Do-In | Douching | Dowsing | Drama Therapy | Electrolipolysis | Electrolysis | Electrotherapy | Encounter Groups | Faith Healing |
|---|---|---|---|---|---|---|---|---|---|---|---|---|---|---|---|---|
| AROMATHERAPY & REFLEX CTRE (HM01090) | | | | | | | | | | | | | | | | |
| AROMATIC (HM01134) | | | | | | | | | | | | | | | | |
| BACH FLOWER REMEDIES (HM01469) | | | | | | | | | | | | | | | | |
| BARROWCLIFFE, GRAHAM (DR) (HM01806) | | | | | | | | | | | | ● | | | | |
| BELPER BACKPAIN CLINIC (HM02110) | | | ● | | | | | | | | | | | ● | | |
| BELPER NATURAL HEALTH CENTRE (HM02112) | | | | | | | | | | | | | | | | ● |
| BODY & SOUL (HM02562) | | | | | | | | | | | | | | | | |
| BRADSHAW, P J (HM02878) | | | | | | | | | | | | | | | | |
| CARRICK-SMITH, L (HM03744) | | | | | | | | | | | | | | | | |
| CLARK, HAZEL (HM04558) | | | | | | | | | | | | | | | | |
| DE MIERRE, MAVIS (HM05915) | | | | | | | | | | | | | | | | |
| DERBY ACUPUNCTURE CENTRE (HM06011) | | | | | | | | | | | | | | | | |
| DERBYSHIRE SPORTS INJURIES (HM06014) | | | | | | | | | | | | | | | | |
| DRONFIELD NAT HEALTH CLINIC (HM06319) | | | | | | | | | | | | | | | | |
| ENJOY SPORT (HM06836) | | | | | | | | | | | | | | ● | | |
| FARMER, VAL (HM07110) | | | | | | | | | | | | | | | | |
| GALLEY, D G (HM07843) | | | | | | | | | | | | | | | | |
| GALLEY, D G (HM07842) | | | | | | | | | | | | | | | | |
| HARDING, MANDY (HM08971) | | | | | | | | | | | | | | | | |
| HATHERSAGE HEALTH & THRPY CTRE (HM09198) | | | | | | | | | | | | | | | | |
| HEANOR CHIROPRACTIC CLINIC (HM09436) | | | | | | | | | | | | | | | | |
| HOUSE OF AROMATHERAPY (HM10216) | | | | | | | | | | | | | | | | |
| HOUSE OF AROMATHERAPY (HM10217) | | | | | | | | | | | | | | | | |
| ILKESTONE OSTEO & MED CTRE (HM10580) | | | | | | | | | | | | | | | | |
| JACKSON-BASS, ALISON (HM10853) | | | | | | | | | | | | | | | | |
| JEFFERY & ASSOCIATES (HM10963) | | | | | | | | | | | | | | | | |
| KARDAHJI, F C (HM11319) | | | | | | | | | | | | | | | | |
| KAY, P (HM11353) | | | | | | | | | | | | | | | | |
| KEMP, G D (HM11460) | | | | | | | | | | | | | | | | |
| KEMP, GILLIAN (HM11461) | | | | | | | ● | | | | | | | | | |
| LANCASHIRE, A W (HM11915) | | | | | | | | | | | | | | | | |
| LIFESOLUTIONS (HM12359) | | | | | | | | | | | | | | | | |
| LONG TUONG VAN (HM12618) | | | | | | | | | | | | | | | | |
| MATTHEWS, A (HM13299) | | | | | | | | | | | | | | | | |

# A - F Therapies at Practices/Businesses

| Business by County with Reference no. | Absent Healing | Acupressure | Acupuncture | Alexander Technique | Allergy Testing | Anthroposohical Med | Aromatherapy | Art Therapy | Aura Therapy | Auricular Therapy | Auto Suggestion | Autogenic Training | Aversion Therapy | Ayurvedic Medicine | Baby Massage | Bach Remedies |
|---|---|---|---|---|---|---|---|---|---|---|---|---|---|---|---|---|
| MATTHEWS, AMANDA (HM13301) | | | | | | | | | | | | | | | | |
| NATURAL HEALTH CLINIC (HM14577) | | ● | ● | | | | ● | | | | ● | | | | | ● |
| PARK FARM CHIROPODY SERVICES (HM15664) | | | | | | | | | | | | | | | | |
| PERRY, VIC (HM16052) | | | | | | | ● | | | | | | | | | |
| PHILIP STOCK - PHYSIOTHERAPIST (HM16120) | | | | | | | | | | | | | | | | |
| PHYSIO ACTIVE (HM16193) | | ● | ● | | | | ● | | | | | | | | | |
| SINENORE, S (HM18606) | | | | | | | | | | | | | | | | |
| STEVENSON, JACKIE (HM19249) | | | | | | | | | | | | | | | | |
| SYKES, PETER W (HM19617) | | | | | | | | | | | | | | | | |
| TAYLOR, E F (HM19757) | | | | | | | | | | | | | | | | |
| WELL OILED (HM21141) | | | | | | | ● | | | | | | | | | |
| WHATLING, M J (HM21305) | | | | | | | | | | | | | | | | |
| WHITEING CHIROPODISTS (HM21392) | | | | | | | | | | | | | | | | |
| WHITTLE, S (HM21425) | | | | | | | | | | | | | | | | |
| WILLIAMS, VERONICA (HM21604) | | | | | | | | | | | | | | | | ● |
| DEVON | | | | | | | | | | | | | | | | |
| ABBEYMEAD NATURAL HEALTH CTRE (HM00090) | | | ● | | | | ● | | | | | | | | | |
| ACUPUNCTURE CLINIC (HM00276) | | ● | ● | | | | | | | | | | | | | |
| ALISON MORTON PHYSIOTHERAPY (HM00579) | | | ● | | | | | | | | | | | | | |
| ANNE RAWLINGS HYPNOTHERAPY (HM00901) | | | | | | | | | | | ● | ● | ● | | | |
| ARCTURUES CLINIC (HM00987) | | | ● | | | | | | | | | | | | | |
| AROMAGLOW (HM01077) | | | | | | | ● | | | | | | | | | |
| AROMAGLOW (HM01076) | | | | | | | ● | | | | | | | | | |
| AROMATHERAPY CENTRE (HM01101) | | | | | | | ● | | | | | | | | | |
| AROMATHERAPY PLUS (HM01122) | | | | | | | ● | | | | | | | | | |
| ASCLEPION (HM01175) | | | | | | | ● | | | | | | | | | |
| ASSOCIATED CHIROPODY SERVICES (HM01270) | | | | | | | | | | | | | | | | |
| AWARENESS CENTRE (HM01415) | ● | ● | ● | ● | | | ● | | | | | | | | | |
| BAILLIES STUDIO (HM01557) | | | | | | | ● | | | | | | | | | |
| BARRETT, J (HM01790) | | | | | | | | | | | | | | | | |
| BIDEFORD CHIROPRACTIC CLINIC (HM02283) | | | | | | | | | | | | | | | | |
| BLACKLER, G G (HM02456) | | | | | | | ● | | | | | | | | | |
| BLADES, S (HM02470) | | | ● | | | | | | | | | | | | | |
| BODY FOCUS (HM02589) | | | | | | | ● | | | | | | | | | |

| Business by County with Reference no. | Bates Method | Beauty Therapy | Bio-energetics | Biofeedback | Biomagnetic Therapy | Biomechanics | Bonesetting | Bowen Therapy | Chinese Herbal Medicine | Chiropody | Chiropractic | Clinical Ecology | Cognitive Therapy | Colonic Hydrotherapy | Colour Therapy | Complementary Therapy | Counselling |
|---|---|---|---|---|---|---|---|---|---|---|---|---|---|---|---|---|---|
| MATTHEWS, AMANDA (HM13301) | | | | | | | | | | ● | | | | | | | |
| NATURAL HEALTH CLINIC (HM14577) | | | | | | | | | | | | | ● | | | | ● |
| PARK FARM CHIROPODY SERVICES (HM15664) | | | | | | | | | | ● | | | | | | | |
| PERRY, VIC (HM16052) | | | | | | | | | | | | | | | | | |
| PHILIP STOCK - PHYSIOTHERAPIST (HM16120) | | | | | | | | | | | ● | | | | | | |
| PHYSIO ACTIVE (HM16193) | | | | | | | | | | | | | | | | | ● |
| SINENORE, S (HM18606) | | | | | | | | | | | ● | | | | | | |
| STEVENSON, JACKIE (HM19249) | | | | | | | | | | | | | | | | | ● |
| SYKES, PETER W (HM19617) | | | | | | | | | | ● | | | | | | | |
| TAYLOR, E F (HM19757) | | | | | | | | | | | | | | | | | |
| WELL OILED (HM21141) | | | | | | | | | | | | | | | | | |
| WHATLING, M J (HM21305) | | | | | | | | | | | ● | | | | | | |
| WHITEING CHIROPODISTS (HM21392) | | | | | | | | | | ● | | | | | | | |
| WHITTLE, S (HM21425) | | | | | | ● | | | | ● | | | | | | | |
| WILLIAMS, VERONICA (HM21604) | | | | | | | | | | | | | | | | | |
| DEVON | | | | | | | | | | | | | | | | | |
| ABBEYMEAD NATURAL HEALTH CTRE (HM00090) | | | | | | | | ● | | | ● | | | | | ● | ● |
| ACUPUNCTURE CLINIC (HM00276) | | | | | | | | | | | | | | | | | |
| ALISON MORTON PHYSIOTHERAPY (HM00579) | | | | | | | | | | | | | | | | | |
| ANNE RAWLINGS HYPNOTHERAPY (HM00901) | | | | | | | | | | | | | ● | | | ● | ● |
| ARCTURUES CLINIC (HM00987) | | | | | | | | ● | | | ● | | | | | | |
| AROMAGLOW (HM01077) | | | | | | | | | | | | | | | | | |
| AROMAGLOW (HM01076) | | | | | | | | | | | | | | | | | |
| AROMATHERAPY CENTRE (HM01101) | | | | | | | | | | | | | | | | | |
| AROMATHERAPY PLUS (HM01122) | | | | | | | | | | | | | | | | | |
| ASCLEPION (HM01175) | | | | | | | | | | | | | | | | | |
| ASSOCIATED CHIROPODY SERVICES (HM01270) | | | | | | | | | | ● | | | | | | | |
| AWARENESS CENTRE (HM01415) | | | | | | | | ● | | | | | | | ● | ● | ● |
| BAILLIES STUDIO (HM01557) | | | | | | | | | | | | | | | | | |
| BARRETT, J (HM01790) | | | | | | | | | | ● | | | | | | | |
| BIDEFORD CHIROPRACTIC CLINIC (HM02283) | | | | | | | | | | | ● | | | | | | |
| BLACKLER, G G (HM02456) | | | | | | | | | | | | | | | | | |
| BLADES, S (HM02470) | | | | | | | | | | | | | | | | | |
| BODY FOCUS (HM02589) | | | | | | | | | | | | | | | | | |

| Business by County with Reference no. | Cranial Osteopathy | Cranio-Sacral Therapy | Cryo Surgery | Crystal Healing | Cupping | Cymatics | Dance Movement Thrpy | Dietician | Do-In | Douching | Dowsing | Drama Therapy | Electrolipolysis | Electrolysis | Electrotherapy | Encounter Groups | Faith Healing |
|---|---|---|---|---|---|---|---|---|---|---|---|---|---|---|---|---|---|
| MATTHEWS, AMANDA (HM13301) | | | | | | | | | | | | | | | | | |
| NATURAL HEALTH CLINIC (HM14577) | | | | | | | | | | | ● | | | | ● | | |
| PARK FARM CHIROPODY SERVICES (HM15664) | | | | | | | | | | | | | | | | | |
| PERRY, VIC (HM16052) | | | | | | | | | | | | | | | | | |
| PHILIP STOCK - PHYSIOTHERAPIST (HM16120) | | | | | | | | | | | | | | | ● | | |
| PHYSIO ACTIVE (HM16193) | | | | | | | | | | | | | | | ● | | |
| SINENORE, S (HM18606) | | | | | | | | | | | | | | | | | |
| STEVENSON, JACKIE (HM19249) | | | | | | | | | | | | | | | | | |
| SYKES, PETER W (HM19617) | | | | | | | | | | | | | | | | | |
| TAYLOR, E F (HM19757) | ● | | | | | | | | | | | | | | | | |
| WELL OILED (HM21141) | | | | | | | | | | | | | | | | | |
| WHATLING, M J (HM21305) | | | | | | | | | | | | | | | | | |
| WHITEING CHIROPODISTS (HM21392) | | | | | | | | | | | | | | | | | |
| WHITTLE, S (HM21425) | | | | | | | | | | | | | | | | | |
| WILLIAMS, VERONICA (HM21604) | | | | | | | | | | | | | | | | | |
| DEVON | | | | | | | | | | | | | | | | | |
| ABBEYMEAD NATURAL HEALTH CTRE (HM00090) | ● | | | | | | | | | | | ● | | | | | |
| ACUPUNCTURE CLINIC (HM00276) | | | | | | | | | | | | | | | | | |
| ALISON MORTON PHYSIOTHERAPY (HM00579) | | | | | | | | | | | | | | | | | |
| ANNE RAWLINGS HYPNOTHERAPY (HM00901) | | | | | | | | | | | | | | | | | |
| ARCTURUES CLINIC (HM00987) | | ● | | | | | | | | | | | | | | | |
| AROMAGLOW (HM01077) | | | | | | | | | | | | | | | | | |
| AROMAGLOW (HM01076) | | | | | | | | | | | | | | | | | |
| AROMATHERAPY CENTRE (HM01101) | | | | | | | | | | | | | | | | | |
| AROMATHERAPY PLUS (HM01122) | | | | | | | | | | | | | | | | | |
| ASCLEPION (HM01175) | | | | | | | | | | | | | | | | | |
| ASSOCIATED CHIROPODY SERVICES (HM01270) | | | | | | | | | | | | | | | | | |
| AWARENESS CENTRE (HM01415) | ● | | | ● | | | | ● | | | ● | | | | | | ● |
| BAILLIES STUDIO (HM01557) | | | | | | | | | | | | | | | | | |
| BARRETT, J (HM01790) | | | | | | | | | | | | | | | | | |
| BIDEFORD CHIROPRACTIC CLINIC (HM02283) | | | | | | | | | | | | | | | | | |
| BLACKLER, G G (HM02456) | | | | | | | | | | | | | | | | | |
| BLADES, S (HM02470) | | | | | | | | | | | | | | | | | |
| BODY FOCUS (HM02589) | | | | | | | | | | | | | | | | | |

# A - F Therapies at Practices/Businesses

| Business by County with Reference no. | Absent Healing | Acupressure | Acupuncture | Alexander Technique | Allergy Testing | Anthroposohical Med | Aromatherapy | Art Therapy | Aura Therapy | Auricular Therapy | Auto Suggestion | Autogenic Training | Aversion Therapy | Ayurvedic Medicine | Baby Massage | Bach Remedies | Bates Method | Beauty Therapy | Bio-energetics | Biofeedback | Biomagnetic Therapy | Biomechanics | Bonesetting | Bowen Therapy | Chinese Herbal Medicine | Chiropody | Chiropractic | Clinical Ecology | Cognitive Therapy | Colonic Hydrotherapy | Colour Therapy | Complementary Therapy | Counselling | Cranial Osteopathy | Cranio-Sacral Therapy | Cryo Surgery | Crystal Healing | Cupping | Cymatics | Dance Movement Thrpy | Dietician | Do-In | Douching | Dowsing | Drama Therapy | Electrolipolysis | Electrolysis | Electrotherapy | Encounter Groups | Faith Healing |
|---|---|---|---|---|---|---|---|---|---|---|---|---|---|---|---|---|---|---|---|---|---|---|---|---|---|---|---|---|---|---|---|---|---|---|---|---|---|---|---|---|---|---|---|---|---|---|---|---|---|---|
| BURNING DESIRE (HM03407) | | | | | | |●| | | | | | | | | | | | | | | | | | | | | | | | | | | | | | | | | | | | | | | | | | | |
| CARPENTER, PAUL (HM03734) | | | | | | | | | | | | | | | | | | | | | | | | | |●| | | | | | | | | | | | | | | | | | | | | | | | |
| CASTLE CHIROPRACTIC CLINIC (HM03829) | | | | | | | | | | | | | | | | | | | | | | | | | | |●| | | | | | | | | | | | | | | | | | | | | | | |
| CASTLEBRIDGE CHIRO & REFLEX (HM03844) | | | | | | | | | | | | | | | | | | | | | | | | | |●| | | | | | | | | | | | | | | | | | | | | | | | |
| CHELSTON CHIROPODY PRACTICE (HM04092) | | | | | | | | | | | | | | | | | | | | | | | | | |●| | | | | | | | | | | | | | | | | | | | | | | | |
| CHEMIN, CHRISTIAN (HM04098) | | | | | | | | | | | | | | | | | | | | | | | | | | | | | | | | |●| | | | | | | | | | | | | | | | | |
| CHIROPRACTIC AND MYOFACIAL (HM04350) | |●|●| | | | | | | | | | | | | | | | | | | | | | | |●| | | | |●| | | | | | | | | | | | | | | | | | |
| CHIROPRACTIC HEALTHCARE CLINIC (HM04400) | | | | | | | | | | | | | | | | | | | | | | | | | | |●| | | | | | | | | | | | | | | | | | | | | | | |
| CLINIC OF CHINESE MEDICINE (HM04687) | | |●| | | | | | | | | | | | | | | | | | | | | | | | | | | | | | | | | | | | | | | | | | | | | | | |
| CLYDE HOUSE CHIRO CLINIC (HM04746) | | | | | | | | | | | | | | | | | | | | | | | | | | |●| | | | | | | | | | | | | | | | | | | | | | | |
| COCKINGTON FRAGRANCES (HM04772) | | | | | | |●| | | | | | | | | | | | | | | | | | | | | | | | | | | | | | | | | | | | | | | | | | | |
| COLLEGE OF NATURAL NUTRITION (HM04851) | | | | | | | | | | | | | | | | | | | | | | | | | | | | | | | |●| | | | | | | | |●| | | | | | | | | |
| COLOMBI, F (HM04888) | | | |●| | | | | | | | | | | | | | | | | | | | | | | | | | | | | | | | | | | | | | | | | | | | | | |
| COMPLEMENTARY TREATMENT CENTRE (HM04951) | | | | | | |●| | | | | | | | | | | | | | | | | | | | | | | | | | | | | | | | | | | | | | | | | | | |
| COOK, TOM (HM05058) | | | |●| | | | | | | | | | | | | | | | | | | | | | | | | | | | | | | | | | | | | | | | | | | | | | |
| COOPER, LESLEY (HM05118) | | | |●| | | | | | | | | | | | | | | | | | | | | | | | | | | | | | | | | | | | | | | | | | | | | | |
| COPE, ANNE (HM05134) | |●| | | | | | | | | | | | | |●| | | | | | | | | | | | | | | | |●| | | | | | | | | | | | | | | | | |
| COX, MIRANDA (HM05316) | | | | | | | | | | | | | | | | | | | | | | | | | | | |●| | | |●| | | | | | | | | | | | | | | | | |
| CREDITON CHIROPRACTIC CLINIC (HM05405) | | | | | | | | | | | | | | | | | | | | | | | | | | |●| | | | | | | | | | | | | | | | | | | | | | | |
| CULLOMPTON CHIROPRACTIC CLINIC (HM05568) | | | | | | | | | | | | | | | | | | | | | | | | | | |●| | | | | | | | | | | | | | | | | | | | | | | |
| CUSS, JEAN (HM05640) | | |●| | | | | | | | | | | | | | | | | | | | | | | | | | | | | | | | | | | | | | | | | | | | | | | |
| DEL MAR, ANTONIA (HM05963) | | | |●| | | | | | | | | | | | | | | | | | | | | | | | | | | | | | | | | | | | | | | | | | | | | | |
| DE-SILVA & WHITTINGHAM (HM06023) | | | | | | | | | | | | | | | | | | | | | | | | | | |●| | | | | | | | | | | | | | | | | | | | | | | |
| ELDON HEALTH CLINIC (HM06705) | |●|●| | | |●| | | | | | | | | | | | |●| | | | | | | |●|●| | | |●| | | | | | | | | | | | | | |●| | |
| ELLIS, SUE (HM06773) | |●| | | | | | | | | | | | | | | | | | | | | | | | |●| | | | |●| | | | | | | | | | | | | | | | | | |
| ELMSLEIGH PARK CHIRO CLINIC (HM06783) | | | | | | | | | | | | | | | | | | | | | | | | | | |●| | | | | | | | | | | | | | | | | | | | | | | |
| FOOT CLINIC & THERAPY ROOM (HM07474) | | |●| | | | | | | | | | | | | | | | | | | | | | |●| | | | | | | | | | | | | | | | | | | | | | | | |
| FOOTEC MEDICAL (HM07500) | | | | | | | | | | | | | | | | | | | | | |●| | | |●| | | | | | | | | |●| | | | | | | | | | | | | | |
| FUDGE, H (HM07777) | | | | | | | | | | | | | | | | | | | | | | | | | | | | | | | |●|●| | | | | | | | | | | | | | | | | |
| GRACELINGS NATURAL HEALTH (HM08335) | | | | | | |●| | | | | | | | | | | | | | | | | | | | | | | | | | | | | | | | | | | | | | | | | | | |
| GREIG, A D (HM08525) | | | | | | | | | | | | | | | | | | | | | | | | | | |●| | | | | | | | | | | | | | | | | | | | | | | |
| HARRIS, K R (HM09075) | | | | | | | | | | | | | | | | | | | | | | | | | | |●| | | | | | | | | | | | | | | | | | | | | | | |
| HASLAM, ANTHONY (HM09182) | | | | | | | | | | | | | | | | | | | | | | | | | | |●| | | | | | | | | | | | | | | | | | | | | | | |
| HEALTH CONSULTANCY (HM09382) | | | | | | | | | | | | | | | | | | | | | | | | | | | | | | | | |●| | | | | | | | | | | | | | | | | |

# A - F Therapies at Practices/Businesses

| Business by County with Reference no. | Absent Healing | Acupressure | Acupuncture | Alexander Technique | Allergy Testing | Anthroposohical Med | Aromatherapy | Art Therapy | Aura Therapy | Auricular Therapy | Auto Suggestion | Autogenic Training | Aversion Therapy | Ayurvedic Medicine |
|---|---|---|---|---|---|---|---|---|---|---|---|---|---|---|
| HEALTH WAVES (HM09408) | | | | ● | | | | | | | | | | |
| HEALTHSHARE FOUNDATION (HM09416) | | | ● | | | | | | | | | | | |
| HEAVITREE CHIROPRACTIC CENTRE (HM09483) | | | | | | | | | | | | | | |
| HEMINGWAY, T (HM09532) | | | | ● | | | | | | | | | | |
| HILL, R B (HM09786) | | | ● | | | | | | | | | | | |
| HOLLINGSWORTH, ELAINE (HM10022) | | | | | | | | | | | | | | |
| HUME, PETER D (HM10370) | | | | | | | | | | | | | | |
| HYDE ACUPUNCTURE & HERBALIST (HM10468) | | | ● | | | | | | | | | | | |
| IM, KIM LAY (HM10585) | | | ● | | | | | | | | | | | |
| IOKAI SHIATSU CLINIC (HM10709) | | | | | | | | | | | | | | |
| IVYBRIDGE CHIROPRACTIC CENTRE (HM10787) | | | | | | | | | | | | | | |
| JEFFRIES, BARBARA (HM10972) | | | | | | | | | | | | | | |
| JOHNSON, MICHAEL (HM11087) | | | ● | | | | | | | | | | | |
| KELLY, KEVIN (HM11434) | | | | | | | | | | | | | | |
| KING, SIMON (HM11643) | | | ● | | | | | | | | | | | |
| KINGSBRIDGE COMP HLTH PRACTICE (HM11658) | ● | ● | ● | | | | | | | | | | | |
| KINGSBRIDGE PHYSICAL THERAPY (HM11659) | | ● | | | | | | | | | | | | |
| KREY, JOHN (HM11799) | | | | | | | | | | | | | | |
| LIGHT TOUCH THERAPY TRAINING (HM12369) | | | | | | | | | | | | | | |
| LION HOUSE SURGERY (HM12446) | | | ● | | | | | | | | | | | |
| LOADER, JANE (HM12526) | | | | | | | ● | | | | | | | |
| LOPES, ROBYN (HM12637) | | | | | | | | | | | | | | |
| MALLARDO, RENEE (HM12977) | ● | | | | | | | | | | ● | | ● | |
| MANGLES, DENISE (HM13012) | | | | | | | ● | | | | | | | |
| MARTINEAU, M (HM13214) | | | | | | | | | | | | | | |
| MARTINEAU, M (DR) (HM13215) | | | | | | | | | | | | | | |
| MASON, MARCUS (HM13248) | | | ● | | | | | | | | | | | |
| MATTHEWS, FIONA (HM13305) | | | ● | | | | | | | | | | | |
| MCTIMONEY CHIROPRACTIC CLINIC (HM13608) | | | | | | | | | | | | | | |
| MIDDLE EARTH AROMA SUPPLIES (HM13812) | | | | | | | ● | | | | | | | |
| MOAT, ANTOINETTE (HM14024) | | | | ● | | | | | | | | | | |
| MONSHIN, DEBORAH J (HM14075) | | | | | | | | | | | ● | | ● | |
| MOORE, BEVERLEY (HM14116) | | | | | | | ● | | | | | | | |
| NELSON, PAUL (HM14781) | | | | | | | | | | | | | | |

| Business by County with Reference no. | Baby Massage | Bach Remedies | Bates Method | Beauty Therapy | Bio-energetics | Biofeedback | Biomagnetic Therapy | Biomechanics | Bonesetting | Bowen Therapy | Chinese Herbal Medicine | Chiropody | Chiropractic | Clinical Ecology |
|---|---|---|---|---|---|---|---|---|---|---|---|---|---|---|
| HEALTH WAVES (HM09408) | | | | | | | | | | | | | | |
| HEALTHSHARE FOUNDATION (HM09416) | | | | | | | | | | | | | | |
| HEAVITREE CHIROPRACTIC CENTRE (HM09483) | | | | | | | | | | | | | ● | |
| HEMINGWAY, T (HM09532) | | | | | | | | | | | | | | |
| HILL, R B (HM09786) | | | | | | | | | | | | | | |
| HOLLINGSWORTH, ELAINE (HM10022) | | ● | | | | | | | | | | | | |
| HUME, PETER D (HM10370) | | | | | | | | | | | | ● | | |
| HYDE ACUPUNCTURE & HERBALIST (HM10468) | | | | | | | | | | | | | | |
| IM, KIM LAY (HM10585) | | | | | | | | | | | | | | |
| IOKAI SHIATSU CLINIC (HM10709) | | | | | | | | | | | ● | | | |
| IVYBRIDGE CHIROPRACTIC CENTRE (HM10787) | | | | | | | | | | | | | ● | |
| JEFFRIES, BARBARA (HM10972) | | | | | | | | | | | | | | |
| JOHNSON, MICHAEL (HM11087) | | ● | | | | | | | | | | | | |
| KELLY, KEVIN (HM11434) | | | | | | | | | | | | | ● | |
| KING, SIMON (HM11643) | | | | | | | | | | | | | | |
| KINGSBRIDGE COMP HLTH PRACTICE (HM11658) | | | | | | | | | | | | | | |
| KINGSBRIDGE PHYSICAL THERAPY (HM11659) | | | | | | | | | | | | | | |
| KREY, JOHN (HM11799) | | | | | | | | | | | | | ● | |
| LIGHT TOUCH THERAPY TRAINING (HM12369) | | | | | | | | | | | | | | |
| LION HOUSE SURGERY (HM12446) | | | | | | | | | | | | | ● | |
| LOADER, JANE (HM12526) | | | | | | | | | | | | | | |
| LOPES, ROBYN (HM12637) | | | | | | | | | | | | | ● | |
| MALLARDO, RENEE (HM12977) | | | | | | | | | | | | | | |
| MANGLES, DENISE (HM13012) | | | | | | | | | | | | | | |
| MARTINEAU, M (HM13214) | | | | | | | | | | | | | ● | |
| MARTINEAU, M (DR) (HM13215) | | | | | | | | | | | | | ● | |
| MASON, MARCUS (HM13248) | | | | | | | | | | | | | | |
| MATTHEWS, FIONA (HM13305) | | | | | | | | | | | | | | |
| MCTIMONEY CHIROPRACTIC CLINIC (HM13608) | | | | | | | | | | | | | ● | |
| MIDDLE EARTH AROMA SUPPLIES (HM13812) | | | | | | | | | | | | | | |
| MOAT, ANTOINETTE (HM14024) | | | | | | | | | | | | | | |
| MONSHIN, DEBORAH J (HM14075) | | ● | | | | | | | | | | | | |
| MOORE, BEVERLEY (HM14116) | | | | | | | | | | | | | | |
| NELSON, PAUL (HM14781) | | | | | | | | | | | | | | |

| Business by County with Reference no. | Cognitive Therapy | Colonic Hydrotherapy | Colour Therapy | Complementary Therapy | Counselling | Cranial Osteopathy | Cranio-Sacral Therapy | Cryo Surgery | Crystal Healing | Cupping | Cymatics |
|---|---|---|---|---|---|---|---|---|---|---|---|
| HEALTH WAVES (HM09408) | | | | ● | | | | | | | |
| HEALTHSHARE FOUNDATION (HM09416) | | | | | | | | | | | |
| HEAVITREE CHIROPRACTIC CENTRE (HM09483) | | | | | | | | | | | |
| HEMINGWAY, T (HM09532) | | | | | | | | | | | |
| HILL, R B (HM09786) | | | | | | | | | | | |
| HOLLINGSWORTH, ELAINE (HM10022) | | | | | | | | | | | |
| HUME, PETER D (HM10370) | | | | | | | | | | | |
| HYDE ACUPUNCTURE & HERBALIST (HM10468) | | | | | | | | | | | |
| IM, KIM LAY (HM10585) | | | | | | | | | | | |
| IOKAI SHIATSU CLINIC (HM10709) | | | | | | | | | | | |
| IVYBRIDGE CHIROPRACTIC CENTRE (HM10787) | | | | | | | | | | | |
| JEFFRIES, BARBARA (HM10972) | | | | | ● | | | | | | |
| JOHNSON, MICHAEL (HM11087) | | | | ● | | | | | | ● | |
| KELLY, KEVIN (HM11434) | | | | | | | | | | | |
| KING, SIMON (HM11643) | | | | | | | | | | | |
| KINGSBRIDGE COMP HLTH PRACTICE (HM11658) | | | | ● | ● | | | | | | |
| KINGSBRIDGE PHYSICAL THERAPY (HM11659) | | | | | | | | | | | |
| KREY, JOHN (HM11799) | | | | | | | | | | | |
| LIGHT TOUCH THERAPY TRAINING (HM12369) | | | | ● | ● | | | | | | |
| LION HOUSE SURGERY (HM12446) | | | | | | | | | | | |
| LOADER, JANE (HM12526) | | | | | | | | | | | |
| LOPES, ROBYN (HM12637) | | | | | | | | | | | |
| MALLARDO, RENEE (HM12977) | ● | | | | ● | | | | | | |
| MANGLES, DENISE (HM13012) | | | | | | | | | | | |
| MARTINEAU, M (HM13214) | | | | | | | | | | | |
| MARTINEAU, M (DR) (HM13215) | | | | | | | | | | | |
| MASON, MARCUS (HM13248) | | | | | | | | | | ● | |
| MATTHEWS, FIONA (HM13305) | | | | | | | | | | | |
| MCTIMONEY CHIROPRACTIC CLINIC (HM13608) | | | | | | | | | | | |
| MIDDLE EARTH AROMA SUPPLIES (HM13812) | | | | | | | | | | | |
| MOAT, ANTOINETTE (HM14024) | | | | | | | | | | | |
| MONSHIN, DEBORAH J (HM14075) | | | | | | | | | | | |
| MOORE, BEVERLEY (HM14116) | | | | | | | | | | | |
| NELSON, PAUL (HM14781) | | | | ● | ● | | | | | | |

| Business by County with Reference no. | Dance Movement Thrpy | Dietician | Do-In | Douching | Dowsing | Drama Therapy | Electrolipolysis | Electrolysis | Electrotherapy | Encounter Groups | Faith Healing |
|---|---|---|---|---|---|---|---|---|---|---|---|
| HEALTH WAVES (HM09408) | ● | | ● | | | | | | | | |
| HEALTHSHARE FOUNDATION (HM09416) | | | | | | | | | | | |
| HEAVITREE CHIROPRACTIC CENTRE (HM09483) | | | | | | | | | | | |
| HEMINGWAY, T (HM09532) | | | | | | | | | | | |
| HILL, R B (HM09786) | | | | | | | | | | | |
| HOLLINGSWORTH, ELAINE (HM10022) | | | | | | | | | | | |
| HUME, PETER D (HM10370) | | | | | | | | | | | |
| HYDE ACUPUNCTURE & HERBALIST (HM10468) | | | | | | | | | | | |
| IM, KIM LAY (HM10585) | | | | | | | | | | | |
| IOKAI SHIATSU CLINIC (HM10709) | | | | | | | | | | | |
| IVYBRIDGE CHIROPRACTIC CENTRE (HM10787) | | | | | | | | | | | |
| JEFFRIES, BARBARA (HM10972) | | | | | | | | | | | |
| JOHNSON, MICHAEL (HM11087) | | | | | ● | | | | | | |
| KELLY, KEVIN (HM11434) | | | | | | | | | | | |
| KING, SIMON (HM11643) | | | | | | | | | | | |
| KINGSBRIDGE COMP HLTH PRACTICE (HM11658) | | | | | | | | | | | |
| KINGSBRIDGE PHYSICAL THERAPY (HM11659) | | | | | | | | | ● | | |
| KREY, JOHN (HM11799) | | | | | | | | | | | |
| LIGHT TOUCH THERAPY TRAINING (HM12369) | | | | | | | | | | | |
| LION HOUSE SURGERY (HM12446) | | | | | | | | | | | |
| LOADER, JANE (HM12526) | | | | | | | | | | | |
| LOPES, ROBYN (HM12637) | | | | | | | | | | | |
| MALLARDO, RENEE (HM12977) | | | | | | | | | | | |
| MANGLES, DENISE (HM13012) | | | | | | | | | | | |
| MARTINEAU, M (HM13214) | | | | | | | | | | | |
| MARTINEAU, M (DR) (HM13215) | | | | | | | | | | | |
| MASON, MARCUS (HM13248) | | | | | | | | | | | |
| MATTHEWS, FIONA (HM13305) | | | | | | | | | | | |
| MCTIMONEY CHIROPRACTIC CLINIC (HM13608) | | | | | | | | | | | |
| MIDDLE EARTH AROMA SUPPLIES (HM13812) | | | | | | | | | | | |
| MOAT, ANTOINETTE (HM14024) | | | | | | | | | | | |
| MONSHIN, DEBORAH J (HM14075) | | | | | | | | | | | |
| MOORE, BEVERLEY (HM14116) | | | | | | | | | | | |
| NELSON, PAUL (HM14781) | | ● | | | | | | | | | |

# A - F Therapies at Practices/Businesses

Business by County with Reference no.

| Business | Absent Healing | Acupressure | Acupuncture | Alexander Technique | Allergy Testing | Anthroposohical Med | Aromatherapy | Art Therapy | Aura Therapy | Auricular Therapy | Auto Suggestion | Autogenic Training | Aversion Therapy | Ayurvedic Medicine | Baby Massage | Bach Remedies | Bates Method | Beauty Therapy | Bio-energetics | Biofeedback | Biomagnetic Therapy | Biomechanics | Bonesetting | Bowen Therapy | Chinese Herbal Medicine |
|---|---|---|---|---|---|---|---|---|---|---|---|---|---|---|---|---|---|---|---|---|---|---|---|---|---|
| OWEN, DAVID A (HM15522) | | | | ● | | | | | | | | | | | | | | | | | | | | | |
| PAIGNTON PHYSIOTHERAPY (HM15576) | | | ● | | | | | | | | | | | | | | | | | | | | | | |
| PANNELL, R J (HM15636) | | | | | | | | | | | | | | | | | | | | | | | | | |
| PARIS, ANNA (HM15657) | | | ● | | | | | | | | | | | | | | | | | | | | | | |
| PAYNE, I J (HM15864) | | | ● | | | | | | | | | | | | | | | | | | | | | | |
| PICKARD, OWEN (HM16265) | | | | | | | | | | | | | | | | | | | | | | | | | |
| PSYCHOTHERAPY/HYPNOTHERAPY (HM16739) | | | | | | | | | | | | | | | | | | | | | | | | | |
| RAHMAN, AKHLAQUE (HM16871) | | | | | | | | | | | | | | | | | | | | | | | | | |
| RENDLE, S (HM17182) | | | | | | | | | | | | | | | | | | | | | | | | | |
| RICHIE, ELIZABETH (HM17296) | | | ● | | | | | | | | | | | | | | | | | | | | | | |
| RIVERSIDE CHIROPRACTIC CLINIC (HM17379) | | | | | | | | | | | | | | | | | | | | | | | | | |
| ROBINSON, IRIS E M (HM17476) | | | ● | | | | | | | | | | | | | | | | | | | | | | |
| ROSE & CROWN CLINIC (HM17598) | | | ● | ● | | | ● | | | | | | | | | | | | | | | | | | |
| ROULSTONE, LILIAS (HM17662) | | | | | | | | | | | | | | | | ● | | | | | | | | | |
| SANDERS, RACHEL (HM17916) | | | | | | | | | | | | | | | | | | | | | | | | | |
| SCARBRO, J M (HM18004) | | | | | | | | | | | | | | | | | | | | | | | | | |
| SCOTT, BRIDGET (HM18110) | | | | | | | ● | | | | | | | | | | | | | | | | | | |
| SCURR, PETER M (HM18160) | | | | | | | | | | | | | | | | | | | | | | ● | | | |
| SEELEY, JANICE (HM18194) | | | | | ● | | | | | | | | | | | | | | | | | | | | |
| SELLER OIL (HM18217) | | | | | | | ● | | | | | | | | | | | | | | | | | | |
| SERENITY (HM18233) | | | | | | | ● | | | | | | | | | | | | | | | | | | |
| SHIRLEY'S AROMATHERAPY (HM18489) | | | | | | | ● | | | | | | | | | | | | | | | | | | |
| SPENCER-EDWARDS, K (HM19006) | | | | | | | ● | | | | | | | | | | | | | | | | | | |
| STANLEY, H W (DR) (HM19128) | | | ● | | | | | | | | | | | | | | | | | | | | | | |
| STIMULUS FOR CHANGE (HM19296) | | | | | | | | | | | | | | | | | | | | | | | | | |
| STYLES, D M (HM19457) | | | | | | | | | | | | | | | | | | | | | | | | | |
| TAVISTOCK CHIROPRACTIC CENTRE (HM19725) | | | | | | | | | | | | | | | | | | | | | | | | | |
| TAYLORSON, JUDITH (HM19799) | | | ● | | | | | | | | | | | | | | | | | | | | | | |
| TRACEY UNA MCTIMONEY (HM20210) | | | | | | | | | | | | | | | | | | | | | | | | | |
| TRANCE - FORMATIONS HEALING (HM20250) | | | | | | | | | | | ● | | | | | | | | | ● | | | | | |
| VERWEY, JULIA (HM20629) | | | | | | | | | | | | | | | | | | | | | | | | | |
| VITAL TOUCH (HM20703) | | | | | | | ● | | | | | | | | | | | | | | | | | | |
| WALTERS, RICHARD (HM20880) | | | ● | | | | | | | | | | | | | | | | | | | | | | |
| WALTERS, RICHARD (HM20882) | | | ● | | | | | | | | | | | | | | | | | | | | | | |

| Business | Chiropody | Chiropractic | Clinical Ecology | Cognitive Therapy | Colonic Hydrotherapy | Colour Therapy | Complementary Therapy | Counselling | Cranial Osteopathy | Cranio-Sacral Therapy | Cryo Surgery | Crystal Healing | Cupping | Cymatics | Dance Movement Thrpy | Dietician | Do-In | Douching | Dowsing | Drama Therapy | Electrolipolysis | Electrolysis | Electrotherapy | Encounter Groups | Faith Healing |
|---|---|---|---|---|---|---|---|---|---|---|---|---|---|---|---|---|---|---|---|---|---|---|---|---|---|
| OWEN, DAVID A (HM15522) | | | | | | | | | | | | | | | | | | | | | | | | | |
| PAIGNTON PHYSIOTHERAPY (HM15576) | | | | | | | | | | | | | | | | | | | | | | | | | |
| PANNELL, R J (HM15636) | ● | | | | | | | | | | | | | | | | | | | | | | | | |
| PARIS, ANNA (HM15657) | | | | | | | | | | | | | | | | | | | | | | | | | |
| PAYNE, I J (HM15864) | | | | | | | | | | | | | | | | | | | | | | | | | |
| PICKARD, OWEN (HM16265) | | ● | | | | | | | | | | | | | | | | | | | | | | | |
| PSYCHOTHERAPY/HYPNOTHERAPY (HM16739) | | | | | | | | ● | | | | | | | | | | | | | | | | | |
| RAHMAN, AKHLAQUE (HM16871) | | ● | | | | | | | | | | | | | | | | | | | | | | | |
| RENDLE, S (HM17182) | ● | | | | | | | | | | | | | | | | | | | | | | | | |
| RICHIE, ELIZABETH (HM17296) | | | | | | | | | | | | | | | | | | | | | | | | | |
| RIVERSIDE CHIROPRACTIC CLINIC (HM17379) | | ● | | | | | | | | | | | | | | | | | | | | | | | |
| ROBINSON, IRIS E M (HM17476) | | | | | | | | | | | | | | | | | | | | | | | | | |
| ROSE & CROWN CLINIC (HM17598) | | | | | | | | ● | | | | | | | | | | | | | | | | | |
| ROULSTONE, LILIAS (HM17662) | | | | | | | | | | | | | | | | | | | | | | | | | |
| SANDERS, RACHEL (HM17916) | ● | | | | | | | | | | | | | | | | | | | | | | | | |
| SCARBRO, J M (HM18004) | | ● | | | | | | | | | | | | | | | | | | | | | | | |
| SCOTT, BRIDGET (HM18110) | | | | | | | | | | | | | | | | | | | | | | | | | |
| SCURR, PETER M (HM18160) | ● | | | | | | | | | | | | | | | | | | | | | | | | |
| SEELEY, JANICE (HM18194) | | | | | | | | | | | | | | | | | | | | | | | | | |
| SELLER OIL (HM18217) | | | | | | | | | | | | | | | | | | | | | | | | | |
| SERENITY (HM18233) | | ● | | | | | | | | | | | | | | | | | | | | | | | |
| SHIRLEY'S AROMATHERAPY (HM18489) | | | | | | | | | | | | | | | | | | | | | | | | | |
| SPENCER-EDWARDS, K (HM19006) | | | | | | | | | | | | | | | | | | | | | | | | | |
| STANLEY, H W (DR) (HM19128) | | | | | | | | | | | | | | | | | | | | | | | | | |
| STIMULUS FOR CHANGE (HM19296) | | | | | | | ● | | | | | | | | | | | | | | | | | | |
| STYLES, D M (HM19457) | | ● | | | | | | | | | | | | | | | | | | | | | | | |
| TAVISTOCK CHIROPRACTIC CENTRE (HM19725) | | ● | | | | | | | | | | | | | | | | | | | | | | | |
| TAYLORSON, JUDITH (HM19799) | | | | | | | | | | | | | | | | | | | | | | | | | |
| TRACEY UNA MCTIMONEY (HM20210) | | ● | | | | | | | | | | | | | | | | | | | | | | | |
| TRANCE - FORMATIONS HEALING (HM20250) | | | | | | | | ● | | | | | | | | | | | | | | | | | |
| VERWEY, JULIA (HM20629) | | ● | | | | | | | | | | | | | | | | | | | | | | | |
| VITAL TOUCH (HM20703) | | | | | | | | | | | | | | | | | | | | | | | | | |
| WALTERS, RICHARD (HM20880) | | | | | | | | | | | | | | | | | | | | | | | | | |
| WALTERS, RICHARD (HM20882) | | | | | | | | | | | | | | | | | | | | | | | | | |

# A - F Therapies at Practices/Businesses

| Business by County with Reference no. | Absent Healing | Acupressure | Acupuncture | Alexander Technique | Allergy Testing | Anthroposohical Med | Aromatherapy | Art Therapy | Aura Therapy | Auricular Therapy | Auto Suggestion | Autogenic Training | Aversion Therapy | Ayurvedic Medicine | Baby Massage | Bach Remedies | Bates Method | Beauty Therapy | Bio-energetics | Biofeedback | Biomagnetic Therapy | Biomechanics | Bonesetting | Bowen Therapy | Chinese Herbal Medicine | Chiropody | Chiropractic | Clinical Ecology | Cognitive Therapy | Colonic Hydrotherapy | Colour Therapy | Complementary Therapy | Counselling | Cranial Osteopathy | Cranio-Sacral Therapy | Cryo Surgery | Crystal Healing | Cupping | Cymatics | Dance Movement Thrpy | Dietician | Do-In | Douching | Dowsing | Drama Therapy | Electrolipolysis | Electrolysis | Electrotherapy | Encounter Groups | Faith Healing |
|---|---|---|---|---|---|---|---|---|---|---|---|---|---|---|---|---|---|---|---|---|---|---|---|---|---|---|---|---|---|---|---|---|---|---|---|---|---|---|---|---|---|---|---|---|---|---|---|---|---|---|
| WHEATON, JOHN (DR) (HM21312) | | | ● | | | | | | | | | | | | | | | | | | | | | | | | | | | | | | | | | | | | | | | | | | | | | | | |
| WILKINSON, MARY (HM21512) | | | | | | | | | | | | | | | | | | | | | | | | | | | ● | | | | | | | | | | | | | | | | | | | | | | | |
| WILLSHER, ERNEST R (HM21633) | | | | | | | | | | | | | | | | | | | | | | | | | | ● | | | | | | | | | | | | | | | | | | | | | | | | |
| YORK HOUSE CHIROPODY (HM22044) | | | | | | | | | | | | | | | | | | | | | | ● | | | | ● | | | | | | | | | | | | | | | | | | | | | | | | |
| YORK HOUSE CHIROPRACTIC CLINIC (HM22045) | | | | | | | | | | | | | | | | | | | | | | | | | | | ● | | | | | | | | | | | | | | | | | | | | | | | |
| YOUNG, SUE (HM22081) | | | | | | | ● | | | | | | | | | | | | | | | | | | | | | | | | | | | | | | | | | | | | | | | | | | | |
| DORSET | | | | | | | | | | | | | | | | | | | | | | | | | | | | | | | | | | | | | | | | | | | | | | | | | | |
| ABBEY VIEW COMP CLINIC (HM00088) | | | ● | ● | | | ● | | | | | | | | | | | | | | | | | | | ● | | | | | | | ● | | | | | | | | | | | | | | | | | |
| ACUPUNCTURE CLINIC (HM00272) | | | ● | | | | | | | | | | | | | | | | | | | | | | | | | | | | | | | | | | | | | | | | | | | | | | | |
| ADDRESS THE STRESS (HM00375) | | | | | | | ● | | | | | | | | | | | | | | | | | | | | | | | | | | | | | | | | | | | | | | | | | | | |
| ADELAIDE CLINIC (HM00378) | | | | ● | | | ● | | | | | | | | | | | | | | | | | | | ● | | | | | | | ● | | | | | | | | | | | | | | | | | |
| ALEXANDER TECHNIQUE (HM00540) | | | | ● | | | | | | | | | | | | | | | | | | | | | | | | | | | | | | | | | | | | | | | | | | | | | | |
| ALEXANDER TECHNIQUE (HM00542) | | | | ● | | | | | | | | | | | | | | | | | | | | | | | | | | | | | | | | | | | | | | | | | | | | | | |
| ALTERNATIVE APPROACH (HM00694) | | | | | | | | | | | | | | | | | | | | | | | | | | | ● | | | | | | | | ● | | | | | | | | | | | | | | | |
| ANGLO-EUROPEAN COLLEGE (HM00884) | | | | | | | | | | | | | | | | | | | | | | | | | | | ● | | | | | | | | | | | | | | | | | | | | | | | |
| ARCHIBALD, LIZ (HM00980) | | | | | | | | | | | | | ● | | | | | | | | | | | | | | | | | | | | | | | | | | | | | | | | | | | | | |
| ARNDALE CHIROPRACTIC (HM01031) | | | | | | | | | | | | | | | | | | | | | | | | | | | ● | | | | | | | | | | | | | | | | | | | | | | | |
| AROMA TRANQUILITY (HM01064) | | | | | | | ● | | | | | | | | | | | | | | | | | | | | | | | | | | | | | | | | | | | | | | | | | | | |
| AWDRY, ROBERT (HM01416) | | | ● | | | | | | | | | | | | | | | | | | | | | ● | | | | | | | | | | | | | | | | | | | | | | | | | | |
| BACK IN BALANCE (HM01479) | | | | | | | | | | | | | | | | | | | | | | | | | | | ● | | | | | | | | | | | | | | | | | | | | | | | |
| BACK IN FORM (HM01480) | | | | | | | | | | | | | | | | | | | | | | | | | | | ● | | | | | | | | | | | | | | | | | | | | | | | |
| BEAUMONT COLLEGE OF NAT MED (HM01986) | | | | | | | ● | | | | | | | | | | | | | | | | | | | | | | | | | | | | | | | | | | | | | | | | | | | |
| BEECH, STEVEN (HM02048) | | | | ● | | | | | | | | | | | | | | | | | | | | | | | | | | | | | | | | | | | | | | | | | | | | | | |
| BELTAIN CENTRE (HM02116) | ● | | | | | | | | | | | | | | | | | | | | | | | | | | | | | | | | ● | | | | | | | | | | | | | | | | | ● |
| BELTAIN CENTRE (HM02117) | | | | | | | | | | | | | | | | | | | | | | | | | | | | | | | | ● | ● | | | | | | | | | | | | | | | | | |
| BLACK, G (HM02422) | | | ● | | | | | | | | | | | | | | | | | | | | | | | | | | | | | | | | | | | | | | | | | | | | | | | |
| BOURNEMOUTH CHIRO & NTRL HLTH (HM02760) | | | | | | | | | | | | | | | | | | | | | | | | | | | ● | | | | | | | | | | | | | | | | | | | | | | | |
| BOURNEMOUTH CTRE FOR COMP MED (HM02761) | | | ● | | | | ● | | | | | | | | | | | | | | | | | | | | | | | | | | | | | | | | | | | | | | | | | | | |
| BOWEN CLINIC (HM02771) | | ● | | | | | | | | | | | | | | | | | | | | | | ● | | | | | | | | | | | | | | | | | | | | | | | | ● | | |
| BOWOOD HEALTH & BEAUTY CENTRE (HM02804) | | | | | | | ● | | | | | | | | | | | | | | | | | | | | | | | | | | | | | | | | | | | | | | | | | | | |
| BRANCH, SUE (HM02909) | | | ● | | | | | | | | | | | | | | | | | | | | | | | | | | | | | | | | | | | | | | | | | | | | | | | |
| BRANDON, DAVE (HM02912) | | | | | | | | | | | | | | | | ● | | | | | | | | | | | | | | | | | | | | | | | | | | | | | | | | | | |
| BRIDPORT COMP MEDICINE CTRE (HM03019) | | | | ● | | | | | | | | | | | | | | | | | | | | | | | | | | | | | ● | | | | | | | | | | | | | | | | | |
| BRIGHTER FUTURE (HM03040) | | | | | | | | | | | | | | | | | | | | | | | | | | | | | ● | | | | | | | | | | | | | | | | | | | | | |

# A - F Therapies at Practices/Businesses

| Business by County with Reference no. | Absent Healing | Acupressure | Acupuncture | Alexander Technique | Allergy Testing | Anthroposohical Med | Aromatherapy | Art Therapy | Aura Therapy | Auricular Therapy | Auto Suggestion | Autogenic Training | Aversion Therapy | Ayurvedic Medicine | Baby Massage | Bach Remedies | Bates Method | Beauty Therapy | Bio-energetics | Biofeedback | Biomagnetic Therapy | Biomechanics | Bonesetting | Bowen Therapy | Chinese Herbal Medicine | Chiropody | Chiropractic | Clinical Ecology | Cognitive Therapy | Colonic Hydrotherapy | Colour Therapy | Complementary Therapy | Counselling | Cranial Osteopathy | Cranio-Sacral Therapy | Cryo Surgery | Crystal Healing | Cupping | Cymatics | Dance Movement Thrpy | Dietician | Do-In | Douching | Dowsing | Drama Therapy | Electrolipolysis | Electrolysis | Electrotherapy | Encounter Groups | Faith Healing |
|---|---|---|---|---|---|---|---|---|---|---|---|---|---|---|---|---|---|---|---|---|---|---|---|---|---|---|---|---|---|---|---|---|---|---|---|---|---|---|---|---|---|---|---|---|---|---|---|---|---|---|
| BRIGHTER FUTURE (HM03039) | | | | | | | | | | | | | | | | | | | | | | | | | | | | |●| | | | | | | | | | | | | | | | | | | | | |
| BROADSTONE CENTRE OF COMP MED (HM03118) | |●|●|●|●| |●| | | | | | | | | | | | | | | | | |●|●| | | | | | |●|●| | | | | | | | | | | | | | | | |
| BROWN, A D (HM03208) | | | | | | | | | | | | | | | | | | | | | | | | |●| | | | | | | | | | | | | | | | | | | | | | | | |
| BROWN, AMANDA (HM03211) | | | | | |●| | | | | | | | | | | | | | | | | | | | | | | | | | | | | | | | | | | | | | | | | | | | |
| BURT, S (HM03429) | | | | | | | | | | | | | | | |●| | | | | | | | | | | | | | | |●|●| | | | | | | | | | | | | | | | | | |
| BWT PODIATRY (HM03508) | | | | | | | | | | | | | | | | | | | | | |●| | | | | | | | | | | | | | | | | | | | | | | | | | | | |
| CARBERY PRACTICE (HM03657) | | | | | | |●| | | | | | | | | |●| | | | | | | | | | | | | | | | | | | | | | | | | | | | | | | | | |
| CHARMINSTER CHIRO CLINIC (HM04036) | | | | | | | | | | | | | | | | | | | | | | | | | | |●| | | | | | | | | | | | | | | | | | | | | | | |
| CHIMES AROMATHERAPY (HM04179) | | | | | | |●| | | | | | | | | | | | | | | | | | | | | | | | | | | | | | | | | | | | | | | | | | | |
| CHINESE MEDICINE CENTRE (HM04254) | | |●| | | | | | | | | | | | | | | | | | | | | | | | | | | | | | | | | | | | | | | | | | | | | | | |
| CHINESE MEDICINE CLINIC (HM04258) | | |●| | | | | | | | | | | | | | | | | | | | | |●| | | | | | | | | | | | | | | | | | | | | | | | | |
| CHIROPODY (HM04301) | | | | | | | | | | | | | | | | | | | | | | | | | |●| | | | | | | | | | | | | | | | | | | | | | | | |
| CHIROPODY SERVICES (HM04338) | | | | | | | | | | | | | | | | | | | | | | | | | |●| | | | | | | | | | | | | | | | | | | | | | | | |
| CHIROPRACTIC CLINIC (HM04390) | | | | | | | | | | | | | | | | | | | | | | | | | | |●| | | | | | | | | | | | | | | | | | | | | | | |
| CHIROPRACTIC TREATMENT CENTRE (HM04403) | | | | | | | | | | | | | | | | | | | | | | | | | | |●| | | | | | | | | | | | | | | | | | | | | | | |
| CHIU, ANGELA (HM04415) | | | | | | |●| | | | | | | | | | | | | | | | | | | | | | | | | | | | | | | | | | | | | | | | | | | |
| CHRISTCHURCH CHIROPRACTIC CTRE (HM04435) | | | | | | | | | | | | | | | |●| | | | | | | | | | |●| | | | | | | | | | | | | | | | | | | | | | | |
| CHRISTCHURCH PHYSIO PRACTICE (HM04436) | | |●| | | | | | | | | | | | | | | | | | | | | | | | | | | | | | | | | | | | | | | | | | | | |●| | |
| CLARK, LYNN (HM04568) | | | | | | | | | | | | | | | | | | | | | | | | | |●| | | | | | | | | | | | | | | | | | | | | | | | |
| COLLINWOOD, LOUIS (HM04884) | | | | | | | | | | | | | | | | | | | | | | | | | | |●| | | | | | | | | | | | | | | | | | | | | | | |
| COMMUNITY CHIROPRACTIC CLINIC (HM04906) | | | | | | | | | | | | | | | | | | | | | | | | | | |●| | | | | | | | | | | | | | | | | | | | | | | |
| DAMAN, WENDY (HM05703) | | |●| | | | | | | | | | | | | | | | | | | | | | | | | | | | | | | | | | | | | | | | | | | | | | | |
| DAVIDSON, MICHAEL S (HM05787) | | | | | | | | | | | | | | | | | | | | | | | | | | |●| | | | | | | | | | | | | | | | | | | | | | | |
| DLP HYPNOTHERAPY CENTRE (HM06134) | | | | | | | | | | |●| |●| | | | | | | | | | | | | | | | | | | |●| | | | | | | | | | | | | | | | | |
| DORSET RACQUETS & HEALTH CLUB (HM06205) | | | |●| | | | | | | | | | | | | | | | | | | | | | | | | | | | | | | | | | | | | | | | | | | | | | |
| DORWEST HERBS (HM06206) | | | | | | | | | | | | | | | | | | | | | | | |●| | | | | | | | | | | | | | | | | | | | | | | | | | |
| EDMONDSON, MICHAEL (HM06623) | | |●| | | | | | | | | | | | | | | | | | | | | | | | | | | | | | | | | | | | | | | | | | | | | | | |
| FEET FIRST (HM07171) | | | | | | | | | | | | | | | | | | | | | | | | | |●| | | | | | | | | | | | | | | | | | | | | | | | |
| FERNDOWN ACUPUNCTURE CLINIC (HM07238) | | |●| | | | | | | | | | | | | | | | | | | | | | | | | | | | | | | | | | | | | | | | | | | | | | | |
| FERNDOWN CHIROPRACTIC CLINIC (HM07239) | | | | | | | | | | | | | | | | | | | | | | | | | | |●| | | | | | | | | | | | | | | | | | | | | | | |
| FREESPIRIT (HM07724) | | | | | | | | | | | | | | | | | | | | | | | | | | | | | | |●|●|●| | | | | | | | | | | | | | | | | |
| GILLINGHAM CHIROPRACTIC CLINIC (HM08096) | | | | | | | | | | | | | | | | | | | | | | | | | | |●| | | | | | | | | | | | | | | | | | | | | | | |
| HAMPTON, ANNE (HM08886) | | | | | | | | | | | | | | | | | | | | | | | | | |●| | | | | | | | | | | | | | | | | | | | | | | | |
| HANSSON CHIROPRACTIC CENTRE (HM08946) | | | | | | | | | | | | | | | | | | | | | | | | | | |●| | | | | | | | | | | | | | | | | | | | | | | |

# A - F Therapies at Practices/Businesses

| Business by County with Reference no. | Absent Healing | Acupressure | Acupuncture | Alexander Technique | Allergy Testing | Anthroposohical Med | Aromatherapy | Art Therapy | Aura Therapy | Auricular Therapy | Auto Suggestion | Autogenic Training | Aversion Therapy | Ayurvedic Medicine | Baby Massage | Bach Remedies | Bates Method | Beauty Therapy | Bio-energetics | Biofeedback | Biomagnetic Therapy | Biomechanics | Bonesetting | Bowen Therapy |
|---|---|---|---|---|---|---|---|---|---|---|---|---|---|---|---|---|---|---|---|---|---|---|---|---|
| HIGHCLIFFE CHIROPRACTIC CLINIC (HM09748) | | | | | | | | | | | | | | | | | | | | | | | | |
| HIGHCLIFFE CHIROPRACTIC CLINIC (HM09749) | | | ● | | | | | | | | | | | | | | | | | | | | | |
| HOLISTIC HEALTH CENTRE (HM09973) | | ● | | | | | | | | | | | | | | | | | | | | | | |
| HOPKINS, H G (HM10149) | | | | | | | | | | | | | | | | | | | | | | | | |
| HORNE, SUE (HM10175) | | | ● | | | | | | | | | | | | | | | | | | | | | |
| JACKSON, A E (HM10817) | | | ● | | ● | | | | | | | | | | | | | | | | | | | |
| JELFS, MARTIN (HM10975) | | | | | | | | | | | | | | | | | | | ● | | | | | |
| JOHARI, ULLA (HM11049) | | | ● | | | | | | | | | | | | | | | | | | | | | |
| KINGS CLINIC (HM11652) | | | | | | | | | | | | | | | | | | | | | | | | |
| LEE, MAUREEN (HM12142) | | | | | | | ● | | | | | | | | | | | | | | | | | |
| LOCK, ROBERT (HM12538) | | | ● | | | | | | | | | | | | | | | | | | | | | |
| M C COPELAND-GRIFFITHS & AST (HM12796) | | | | | | | | | | | | | | | | | | | | | | | | |
| MELHUISH, J I (HM13704) | | | | | | | | | | | | | | | | | | | | | | | | |
| MENEZES, A (HM13725) | | | | | | | | | | | | | | | | | | | | | | | | |
| MIDDLES PICCADILLY CTRE (HM13815) | | ● | | ● | | | ● | | | | | | | | | ● | | | | | | | | |
| MOTCOMBE PARK PHYSIOTHERAPY (HM14273) | | | ● | | | | | | | | | | | | | | | | | | | | | |
| NATURAL HEALTH CONSULTANCY (HM14592) | | | | | | | ● | | | | | | | | | | | | | | | | | |
| NEIJIA (HM14759) | | ● | ● | | | | ● | | | | | | | | | | | | | | | | | |
| NELMES CHIROPRACTIC CLINIC (HM14771) | | | | | | | | | | | | | | | | | | | | | | | | |
| PARTNERSHIP, BAKER (DR) (HM15764) | | | | | | | | | | | | | | | | | | | | | | | | |
| PHYSIO, MASSAGE & PR ACU (HM16210) | | | ● | | | | | ● | | | | | | | | | | | | | | | | |
| PRIDEAUX-BRUNE, COLETTE (HM16604) | | | | | | | ● | | | | | | | | | | | | | | | | | |
| PROSPECT HEALTH (HM16667) | | | | | | | ● | | | | ● | | | | | | | ● | | | | | | ● |
| RICHARDSON, ELAINE (HM17278) | | | | ● | | | | | | | | | | | | | | | | | | | | |
| ROBSON, VANESSA (HM17514) | | | | | | | | | | | | | | | | | | | | | | | | |
| ROLLS MILL COMP HEALTH CENTRE (HM17567) | | ● | ● | | ● | | ● | | | | | | | | | ● | | | | | | | | |
| ROWE, PENNY (HM17689) | | | | | | | | | | | | | | | | ● | | | | | | | | |
| SAGE, J (HM17837) | | | | | | | | | | | | | | | | | | | | | | | | |
| SHEBORNE CHIROPRACTIC CENTRE (HM18361) | | | | | | | | | | | | | | | | | | | | | | | | |
| SKELTON, JAN (HM18635) | | | | | | | ● | | | | | | | | | | | | | | | | | |
| SOUTHBOURNE HERBAL CLINIC (HM18924) | | | | | | | | | | | | | | | | | | | | | | | | |
| SOUTHBOURNE NATURAL HLTH CTRE (HM18925) | | | | | | | | | | | | | | | | | | | | | | | | |
| STANDISH-HAYES, QUENTIN (HM19125) | | | | | | | | | | | | | | | | | | | | | | | | |
| SUN, R (HM19503) | | | ● | | | | | | | | | | | | | | | | | | | | | |

| Business by County with Reference no. | Chinese Herbal Medicine | Chiropody | Chiropractic | Clinical Ecology | Cognitive Therapy | Colonic Hydrotherapy | Colour Therapy | Complementary Therapy | Counselling | Cranial Osteopathy | Cranio-Sacral Therapy | Cryo Surgery | Crystal Healing | Cupping | Cymatics | Dance Movement Thrpy | Dietician | Do-In | Douching | Dowsing | Drama Therapy | Electrolipolysis | Electrolysis | Electrotherapy | Encounter Groups | Faith Healing |
|---|---|---|---|---|---|---|---|---|---|---|---|---|---|---|---|---|---|---|---|---|---|---|---|---|---|---|
| HIGHCLIFFE CHIROPRACTIC CLINIC (HM09748) | | | ● | | | | | | | | | | | | | | | | | | | | | | | |
| HIGHCLIFFE CHIROPRACTIC CLINIC (HM09749) | ● | | ● | | | | | | | | | | | | | | | | | | | | | | | |
| HOLISTIC HEALTH CENTRE (HM09973) | | | | | | | | | | | | | | | | | | | | | | | | | | |
| HOPKINS, H G (HM10149) | | | ● | | | | | | | | | | | | | | | | | | | | | | | |
| HORNE, SUE (HM10175) | | | | | | | | | | | | | | | | | | | | | | | | | | |
| JACKSON, A E (HM10817) | | | | ● | | | | | ● | | | | | | | | | | | | | | | | | |
| JELFS, MARTIN (HM10975) | | | | | | | | | ● | | | | | | | | | | | | | | | | | |
| JOHARI, ULLA (HM11049) | | | | | | | | | | | | | | | | | | | | | | | | | | |
| KINGS CLINIC (HM11652) | | | ● | | | | | | | | | | | | | | | | | | | | | | | |
| LEE, MAUREEN (HM12142) | | | | | | | | | | | | | | | | | | | | | | | | | | |
| LOCK, ROBERT (HM12538) | | | | | | | | ● | | | | | | | | | | | | | | | | | | |
| M C COPELAND-GRIFFITHS & AST (HM12796) | | | ● | | | | | | | | | | | | | | | | | | | | | | | |
| MELHUISH, J I (HM13704) | | | ● | | | | | | | | | | | | | | | | | | | | | | | |
| MENEZES, A (HM13725) | | | ● | | | | | | | | | | | | | | | | | | | | | | | |
| MIDDLES PICCADILLY CTRE (HM13815) | | | | | | | | | | | ● | | | | | | | | | | | | | | | |
| MOTCOMBE PARK PHYSIOTHERAPY (HM14273) | | | | | | | | | | | | | | | | | | | | | | | | | | |
| NATURAL HEALTH CONSULTANCY (HM14592) | | | | | | | | | | | | | | | | | | | | | | | | | | |
| NEIJIA (HM14759) | | | | | | | | | | | | | | ● | | | | | | | | | | | | |
| NELMES CHIROPRACTIC CLINIC (HM14771) | | | ● | | | | | | | | | | | | | | | | | | | | | | | |
| PARTNERSHIP, BAKER (DR) (HM15764) | | | | | ● | | | | ● | | | | | | | | | | | | | | | | | |
| PHYSIO, MASSAGE & PR ACU (HM16210) | | | | | | | ● | ● | ● | | | | | | | | | | | | | | | ● | | |
| PRIDEAUX-BRUNE, COLETTE (HM16604) | | | | | | | | | | | | | | | | | | | | | | | | | | |
| PROSPECT HEALTH (HM16667) | | | ● | | | | | | ● | | | | | | | | | | | | | | | | | ● |
| RICHARDSON, ELAINE (HM17278) | | | | | | | | | | | | | | | | | | | | | | | | | | |
| ROBSON, VANESSA (HM17514) | | ● | | | | | | | | | | | | | | | | | | | | | | | | |
| ROLLS MILL COMP HEALTH CENTRE (HM17567) | | | ● | | | | | ● | ● | | | | | | | | ● | | | | | | | | | |
| ROWE, PENNY (HM17689) | | | | | | | | | | | | | | | | | | | | | | | | | | |
| SAGE, J (HM17837) | | | ● | | | | | | | | | | | | | | | | | | | | | | | |
| SHEBORNE CHIROPRACTIC CENTRE (HM18361) | | | ● | | | | | | | | | | | | | | | | | | | | | | | |
| SKELTON, JAN (HM18635) | | | | | | | | ● | | | | | | | | | | | | | | | | | | |
| SOUTHBOURNE HERBAL CLINIC (HM18924) | | | | | | | | ● | | | | | | | | | | | | | | | | | | |
| SOUTHBOURNE NATURAL HLTH CTRE (HM18925) | | | ● | | | | | | | | | | | | | | | | | | | | | | | |
| STANDISH-HAYES, QUENTIN (HM19125) | | | ● | | | | | | | | | | | | | | | | | | | | | | | |
| SUN, R (HM19503) | | | | | | | | | | | | | | | | | | | | | | | | | | |

# A - F Therapies at Practices/Businesses

| Business by County with Reference no. | Absent Healing | Acupressure | Acupuncture | Alexander Technique | Allergy Testing | Anthroposohical Med | Aromatherapy | Art Therapy | Aura Therapy | Auricular Therapy | Auto Suggestion | Autogenic Training | Aversion Therapy | Ayurvedic Medicine | Baby Massage | Bach Remedies | Bates Method | Beauty Therapy | Bio-energetics | Biofeedback | Biomagnetic Therapy | Biomechanics | Bonesetting | Bowen Therapy | Chinese Herbal Medicine | Chiropody | Chiropractic | Clinical Ecology | Cognitive Therapy | Colonic Hydrotherapy | Colour Therapy | Complementary Therapy | Counselling | Cranial Osteopathy | Cranio-Sacral Therapy | Cryo Surgery | Crystal Healing | Cupping | Cymatics | Dance Movement Thrpy | Dietician | Do-In | Douching | Dowsing | Drama Therapy | Electrolipolysis | Electrolysis | Electrotherapy | Encounter Groups | Faith Healing |
|---|---|---|---|---|---|---|---|---|---|---|---|---|---|---|---|---|---|---|---|---|---|---|---|---|---|---|---|---|---|---|---|---|---|---|---|---|---|---|---|---|---|---|---|---|---|---|---|---|---|---|
| TAYLOR, MELANIE (HM19784) | | | | | | | | | | | | | | | | | | | | | | | | | | ● | | | | | | | | | | | | | | | | | | | | | | | | |
| THOMPSON, ANNE H (HM19968) | | | | | | | | | | | | | | | | | | | | | | | | | | ● | | | | | | | | | | | | | | | | | | | | | | | | |
| TREAT FEET (HM20301) | | | | | | | | | | | | | | | | | | | | | ● | | | | ● | | | | | | | | | | | | | | | | | | | | | | | | | |
| TRUNDELL, C (HM20353) | | | | | | | | | | | | | | | | | | | | | | | | | ● | | | | | | | | | | | | | | | | | | | | | | | | | |
| WALTERS, RICHARD (HM20881) | | | ● | | | | | | | | | | | | | | | | | | | | | | | | | | | | | | | | | | | | | | | | | | | | | | | |
| WESSEX HEALTHY LIVING FOUND (HM21208) | | | ● | ● | ● | | ● | | | ● | ● | | | | | ● | | ● | | | | | | ● | | ● | ● | | | | ● | ● | ● | | | | | | | | ● | | | | | | | | | |
| WEST MOORS CHIROPRACTIC CLINIC (HM21230) | | | | | | | | | | | | | | | | | | | | | | | | | | ● | | | | | | | | | | | | | | | | | | | | | | | | |
| WEYMOUTH CHIROPRACTIC CLINIC (HM21294) | | | | | | | | | | | | | | | | | | | | | | | | | | ● | | | | | | | | | | | | | | | | | | | | | | | | |
| WHITE FLOWER CENTRE (HM21337) | | | | | | | ● | | | | | | | | | | | | | | | | | ● | | | | | | | | | | | | | | | | | | | | | | ● | | | | |
| WIMBORNE CHIROPODY SURGERY (HM21687) | | | | | | | | | | | | | | | | | | | | | | | | | ● | | | | | | | | | | | | | | | | | | | | | | | | | |
| YELLOW HOUSE (HM22005) | | | ● | | ● | | ● | | | | | | | | | | | | | | | | | | | | | | | | | | ● | | | | ● | | | | | | | | | | | | | |
| YOUNG, D (HM22070) | | | ● | | | | | | | | | | | | | | | | | | | | | | | | | | | | | | | | | | | | | | | | | | | | | | | |
| **ESSEX** | | | | | | | | | | | | | | | | | | | | | | | | | | | | | | | | | | | | | | | | | | | | | | | | | | |
| A C T CLINIC (HM00028) | | | ● | | | | | | | | | | | | | | | | | | | | | | | | | | | | | | | | | | | | | | | | | | | | | | | |
| A M R THERAPIES (HM00040) | | | | | | | ● | | | | | | | | | | | | | | | | | | | | | | | | | | | | | | | | | | | | | | | | | | | |
| ACUPUNCTURE (HM00228) | | | ● | | | | | | | | | | | | | | | | | | | | | | | | | | | | | | | | | | | | | | | | | | | | | | | |
| APPLEBY LEIGH AROMATHERAPIST (HM00938) | | | | | | | ● | | | | | | | | | | | | | | | | | | | | | | | | | | | | | | | | | | | | | | | | | | | |
| ARC HEALTHCARE (HM00968) | | | | | | | | | | | | | | | | ● | | | | | | | | | | | | | | | | | ● | | | | | | | | | | | | | | | | | |
| AROMATHERAPY CLINIC (HM01107) | | | | | | | ● | | | | | | | | | | | | | | | | | | | | | | | | | | | | | | | | | | | | | | | | | | | |
| AROMER (HM01145) | | | | | | | ● | | | | | | | | | | | | | | | | | | | | | | | | | | | | | | | | | | | | | | | | | | | |
| ASHBY & ASSOCIATES (HM01194) | | | | | | | | | | | | | | | | | | | | | | ● | | | | ● | | | | | | | | | | ● | | | | | | | | | | | | | | |
| ASSAD RAISSI (HM01267) | | | ● | | | | | | | | | | | | | | | | | | | | | | | | | | | | | | | | | | | | | | | | | | | | | | | |
| ASSOCIATION OF OSTEOMYOLOGY (HM01283) | | | ● | | | | ● | | | | | | | | | | | | | | | | | | | | ● | | | | | | | | ● | | | | | | | | | | | | | | | |
| AVART, GILLIAN (HM01383) | ● | | | | | | ● | | | | | | | | | | | | | | | | | | | | | | | | | | | | | | ● | | | | | | | ● | | | | | | ● |
| BANKS, DENISE (HM01664) | | | | | | | ● | | | | | | | | | | | | | | | | | | | | | | | | | | | | | | | | | | | | | | | | | | | |
| BARKING PHYSICAL THERAPY CTRE (HM01715) | | | ● | | | | | | | | | | | | | | | | | | | | | | | | | | | | | | | | | | | | | | | | | | | | | | | |
| BARNETT, SUE (HM01761) | | | | | | | | | | | | | | | | ● | | | | | | | | | | | | | | | | | | | | | | | | | | | | | | | | | | |
| BARTLETT, GODFREY (HM01822) | | | ● | | | | | | | | | | | | | | | | | | | | | | | | | | | | | | | | | | | | | | | | | | | | | | | |
| BAXTER, LISA (HM01929) | | | | | | | ● | | | | | | | | | | | | | | | | | | | | | | | | | | | | | | | | | | | | | | | | | | | |
| BENEDICTA (HM02125) | | | | | | | ● | | | | | | | | | ● | | | | | | | | | | | | | | | | ● | ● | | | | | | | | | | | | | | | | | |
| BERNARD, ELAINE (HM02196) | | | | ● | | | | | | | | | | | | | | | | | | | | | | | | | | | | | | | | | | | | | | | | | | | | | | |
| BE-WELL CLINIC (HM02251) | | | | | | | | | | | | | | | | | | | ● | | | | | | | | | | | | | | | | | | | | | | | | | | | | | | | |
| BIDMEAD, MARGARET (HM02284) | | | | | | | | | | | | | | | | ● | | | | | | | | | | | | | | | | | | | | | | | | | | | | | | | | | | |
| BODY BALANCE (HM02569) | | | ● | | | | | | | | | | | | | | | | | | | | | | | | | | | | | | | | | | | | | | | | | | | | | | | |

# A - F Therapies at Practices/Businesses

| Business by County with Reference no. | Absent Healing | Acupressure | Acupuncture | Alexander Technique | Allergy Testing | Anthroposohical Med | Aromatherapy | Art Therapy | Aura Therapy | Auricular Therapy | Auto Suggestion | Autogenic Training | Aversion Therapy | Ayurvedic Medicine | Baby Massage | Bach Remedies | Bates Method | Beauty Therapy | Bio-energetics | Biofeedback | Biomagnetic Therapy | Biomechanics | Bonesetting | Bowen Therapy | Chinese Herbal Medicine | Chiropody | Chiropractic | Clinical Ecology | Cognitive Therapy | Colonic Hydrotherapy | Colour Therapy | Complementary Therapy | Counselling | Cranial Osteopathy | Cranio-Sacral Therapy | Cryo Surgery | Crystal Healing | Cupping | Cymatics | Dance Movement Thrpy | Dietician | Do-In | Douching | Dowsing | Drama Therapy | Electrolipolysis | Electrolysis | Electrotherapy | Encounter Groups | Faith Healing |
|---|---|---|---|---|---|---|---|---|---|---|---|---|---|---|---|---|---|---|---|---|---|---|---|---|---|---|---|---|---|---|---|---|---|---|---|---|---|---|---|---|---|---|---|---|---|---|---|---|---|---|
| BODY BALANCE HEALTH SOLUTIONS (HM02571) |||●|||||||||||||||||||●||||●||||||||||||||||||||||||||||
| BONDY, PIPPA (HM02673) ||||●|||||||||||||||||||||||||||||||||||||||||||||||||||
| BRAINTREE CHIROPRACTIC CENTRE (HM02895) |||||||||||||||||||||||||||●|||||||||||||||||||||||||
| BRENTWOOD CHIROPODY SURGERY (HM02963) ||||||||||||||||||||||●||||●||||||||||||||||||||||||||||
| BRENTWOOD CHIROPRACTIC CLINIC (HM02964) |||||||||||||||||||||||||||●|||||||||||||||||||||||||
| BRITISH INSTITUTE-HYPNOTHERAPY (HM03085) |||||||||||●|●|||||||||||||||||||●|||||||||||||||||||||||
| CAIN, SHEILA (HM03538) ||||||||||||||||●||||||||||||||||●||||||||||||||||||||
| CALMING EFFECTS (HM03559) |||||||●|||||||||||||||||||||||||||||||||||||||||||||
| CARNELIAN NTRL TREATMENT CTRE (HM03714) ||||||||||||||||●||||||||||||||||||||||||||||||||||||
| CATON, PETER (HM03859) |||||||||||●|●||||||||●|||||||||●||||●||||||||●||||||||||
| CENTRAL CHIROPRACTIC CLINIC (HM03890) |||||||||||||||||||||||||||●|||||||||||||||||||||||||
| CHAIR MASSAGE (HM03941) |||||||●|||||||||||||||||||||||||||||||||||||||||||||
| CHAKRA ROSE (HM03942) |||||||●|||||||||●|||||||||||||●|||●||||||||||||||||||||
| CHELMSFORD CHIROPRACTIC CLINIC (HM04085) |||||||||||||||||||||||||||●|||||||||||||||||||||||||
| CHINESE HERBAL MEDICAL CENTRE (HM04207) |||●|||||||||||||||||||||||||||||||||||||||||||||||||
| CHINESE MEDICINE CLINIC (HM04259) |||●|||||||||||||||||||||||||||||||||||||||||||||||||
| CHIROPRACTIC CLINIC (HM04387) |||||||||||||||||||||||||||●|||||||||||||||||||||||||
| CLACTON CHIROPRACTIC CLINIC (HM04501) |||||||||||||||||||||||||||●|||||||||||||||||||||||||
| CLARKE, M R (HM04593) ||||||||||||||||||||||||||||||||||●||||||||||||||||||
| COKER, EILEEN (HM04800) |||||||●||||||||||||||||||||||||●||||||||||||||||||||
| COLCHESTER CHIROPRACTIC CENTRE (HM04806) |||||||||||||||||||||||||||●|||||||||||||||||||||||||
| COMPLETE CHIROPRACTIC (HM04957) |||||||||||||||||||||||||||●|||||||||||||||||||||||||
| COOK, JOE (HM05048) ||||||||||||||||||||●|||||||||||||●|||||||||||||||||||
| COOPER, FELICITY (HM05104) ||||||||||||||||||||||●||||●||||||||||●||||||||||||||||
| COUSENS, BRENDA (HM05272) |||||||●|||||||||||||||||||||||||||||||||||||||||||||
| CROFT, JOANNA (HM05455) ||||||||||||||||●||||||||||||||||||||||||||||||||||||
| CROFT, LESLEY (HM05456) |||||||●|||||||||||||||||||||||||||||||||||||||||||||
| CROWN CHIROPRACTIC CLINIC (HM05508) |||||||||||||||||||||||||||●|||||||||||||||||||||||||
| CROWN CHIROPRACTIC CLINIC (HM05507) |||||||||||||||||||||||||||●|||||||||||||||||||||||||
| DALY, ROWENA (HM05702) ||||||||||||||||●||||||||||||||||||||||||||||||||||||
| DHANABALAN, K (HM06054) |||●|||||||||||||||||||||||||||||||||||||||||||||||||
| E A O C (HM06465) ||●|●|||||||||||||||||||||●|||||||||||||||●||||||||||||||
| EDWARDS, G E (HM06651) ||||||||||||||||||||||||||●||||||||||||||||||||||||||
| EDWARDS, G E (HM06652) ||||||||||||||||||||||||||●||||||||||||||||||||||||||

# A - F Therapies at Practices/Businesses

Business by County with Reference no.

| Business | Absent Healing | Acupressure | Acupuncture | Alexander Technique | Allergy Testing | Anthroposophical Med | Aromatherapy | Art Therapy | Aura Therapy | Auricular Therapy | Auto Suggestion | Autogenic Training | Aversion Therapy | Ayurvedic Medicine | Baby Massage | Bach Remedies | Bates Method |
|---|---|---|---|---|---|---|---|---|---|---|---|---|---|---|---|---|---|
| EFFLEURAGE (HM06680) | | | | | | | ● | | | | | | | | | | |
| ELMER CHIROPODY & PODIATRY SVS (HM06781) | | | | | | | | | | | | | | | | | |
| EMERY, CHRISTINE (HM06803) | | | | | | | ● | | | | | | | | | | |
| EPPING PHYSIOTHERAPY PRACTICE (HM06855) | | | ● | | | | | | | | | | | | | | |
| ESSENCE OF NATURE (HM06893) | | | | | | | ● | | | | | | | | | | |
| ESSENTIALLY GREEN (HM06921) | | | | | | | ● | | | | | | | | | | |
| ESSEX PHYSIO & SPORTS INJ CTRE (HM06938) | | | ● | | | | ● | | | | | | | | | | |
| FARROW, VICKI (HM07135) | | | | | | | ● | | | | | | | | | | |
| FLEUROMA (HM07418) | | | | | | | ● | | | | | | | | | | |
| FOOT HEALTH CLINIC (HM07482) | | | | | | | | | | | | | | | | | |
| FORD, AUDREY (HM07523) | | | | | | | | | | | | | | | | | |
| FOULKES, GEOFFREY LLOYD (HM07609) | | | ● | | | | ● | | | | | | | | | ● | |
| FULTON, A J (HM07796) | | | | | | | | | | | | | | | | | |
| FULTON, A J (HM07795) | | | | | | | | | | | | | | | | | |
| FUN, MAE (HM07797) | | | ● | | | | | | | | | | | | | | |
| GRAY, P A (HM08417) | | | | | | | | | | | | | | | | | |
| GRAYS CHIROPRACTIC CLINIC (HM08424) | | | | | | | | | | | | | | | | | |
| HADLEIGH PODIATRY CLINIC (HM08695) | | | | | | | | | | | | | | | | | |
| HALSTEAD, RITA (HM08819) | | | ● | | | | | | | | | | | | | | |
| HARLOW OSTEOPATHIC PRACTICE (HM09011) | | | ● | | | | | | | | | | | | | | |
| HAWKRIDGE, FRANCOISE (HM09231) | | | ● | | | | | | | | | | | | | | |
| HEALING ROOM (HM09349) | ● | | | | | | ● | | | | | | | | | | |
| HENRY, JOANNE (HM09568) | | | | | | | ● | | | | | | | | | | |
| HERB GARDEN (HM09587) | | | ● | | | | | | | | | | | | | | |
| HOLISTIC HEALTH CLINIC (HM09978) | | | | | | | | | | | | | | ● | | | |
| HYPNOTHERAPY CENTRE (HM10530) | | | | | | | | | | | | | | | | | |
| HYPNOTHERAPY CENTRE (HM10532) | | | | | | | | | | | | | | | | | |
| INDIGO BAY AROMATHERAPY (HM10613) | | | | | | | ● | | | | | | | | | | |
| JACALAN ESSENTIAL OILS (HM10810) | | | | | | | ● | | | | | | | | | | |
| JOYNES, IAN (HM11239) | | | | | | | | | | | | | | | | | |
| JUNIPER BERRY (HM11268) | | | | | | | ● | | | | | | | | | | |
| KEETCH, KIT (HM11397) | | | | | | | | | | | | | | | | ● | |
| KELLY, GILLIAN (HM11431) | | | ● | | | | | | | | | | | | | | |
| KULKARNI, P S (HM11817) | | | ● | | | | | | | | | | | | | | |

| Business | Beauty Therapy | Bio-energetics | Biofeedback | Biomagnetic Therapy | Biomechanics | Bonesetting | Bowen Therapy | Chinese Herbal Medicine | Chiropody | Chiropractic | Clinical Ecology | Cognitive Therapy | Colonic Hydrotherapy | Colour Therapy | Complementary Therapy | Counselling | Cranial Osteopathy |
|---|---|---|---|---|---|---|---|---|---|---|---|---|---|---|---|---|---|
| EFFLEURAGE (HM06680) | | | | | | | | | | | | | | | | | |
| ELMER CHIROPODY & PODIATRY SVS (HM06781) | | | | | ● | | | | ● | | | | | | | | |
| EMERY, CHRISTINE (HM06803) | | | | | | | | | | | | | | | | | |
| EPPING PHYSIOTHERAPY PRACTICE (HM06855) | | | | | | | | | | | | | | | | | |
| ESSENCE OF NATURE (HM06893) | | | | | | | | | | | | | | | | | |
| ESSENTIALLY GREEN (HM06921) | | | | | | | | | | | | | | | | | |
| ESSEX PHYSIO & SPORTS INJ CTRE (HM06938) | | | | | | | | | | | | | | | | | |
| FARROW, VICKI (HM07135) | | | | | | | | | | | | | | | ● | | |
| FLEUROMA (HM07418) | | | | | | | | | | | | | | | ● | | |
| FOOT HEALTH CLINIC (HM07482) | | | | | ● | | | | | | | | | | | | |
| FORD, AUDREY (HM07523) | | | | | | | | | | ● | | | | | | | |
| FOULKES, GEOFFREY LLOYD (HM07609) | | | | | | | | | | | | | | | ● | | ● |
| FULTON, A J (HM07796) | | | | | ● | | | | ● | | | | | | | | |
| FULTON, A J (HM07795) | | | | | ● | | | | ● | | | | | | | | |
| FUN, MAE (HM07797) | | | | | | | | | | | | | | | | | |
| GRAY, P A (HM08417) | | | | | ● | | | | ● | | | | | | | | |
| GRAYS CHIROPRACTIC CLINIC (HM08424) | | | | | | | | | | ● | | | | | | | |
| HADLEIGH PODIATRY CLINIC (HM08695) | | | | | ● | | | | ● | | | | | | | | |
| HALSTEAD, RITA (HM08819) | | | | | | | | | | | | | | | | | |
| HARLOW OSTEOPATHIC PRACTICE (HM09011) | | | | | | | | | | | | | | | | | |
| HAWKRIDGE, FRANCOISE (HM09231) | | | | | | | | | | | | | | | | | |
| HEALING ROOM (HM09349) | | | | | | | | | | | | | | | ● | | |
| HENRY, JOANNE (HM09568) | | | | | | | | | | | | | | | | | |
| HERB GARDEN (HM09587) | | | | | | | | | | | | | | | | | |
| HOLISTIC HEALTH CLINIC (HM09978) | | | | | | | | | | | | | | | | | |
| HYPNOTHERAPY CENTRE (HM10530) | | | | | | | | | | | | ● | | | | ● | |
| HYPNOTHERAPY CENTRE (HM10532) | | | | | | | | | | | | ● | | | | ● | |
| INDIGO BAY AROMATHERAPY (HM10613) | | | | | | | | | | | | | | | | | |
| JACALAN ESSENTIAL OILS (HM10810) | | | | | | | | | | | | | | | | | |
| JOYNES, IAN (HM11239) | | | | | ● | | | | ● | | | | | | | | |
| JUNIPER BERRY (HM11268) | | | | | | | | | | | | | | | | | |
| KEETCH, KIT (HM11397) | | | | | | | | | | | | | | | | | |
| KELLY, GILLIAN (HM11431) | | | | | | | | | | | | | | | | | |
| KULKARNI, P S (HM11817) | | | | | | | | | | | | | | | | | |

| Business | Cranio-Sacral Therapy | Cryo Surgery | Crystal Healing | Cupping | Cymatics | Dance Movement Thrpy | Dietician | Do-In | Douching | Dowsing | Drama Therapy | Electrolipolysis | Electrolysis | Electrotherapy | Encounter Groups | Faith Healing |
|---|---|---|---|---|---|---|---|---|---|---|---|---|---|---|---|---|
| EFFLEURAGE (HM06680) | | | | | | | | | | | | | | | | |
| ELMER CHIROPODY & PODIATRY SVS (HM06781) | | | | | | | | | | | | | | | | |
| EMERY, CHRISTINE (HM06803) | | | | | | | | | | | | | | | | |
| EPPING PHYSIOTHERAPY PRACTICE (HM06855) | | | | | | | | | | | | | | | | |
| ESSENCE OF NATURE (HM06893) | | | | | | | | | | | | | | | | |
| ESSENTIALLY GREEN (HM06921) | | | | | | | | | | | | | | | | |
| ESSEX PHYSIO & SPORTS INJ CTRE (HM06938) | | | | | | | | | | | | | | | | |
| FARROW, VICKI (HM07135) | | | ● | | | | | | | | | | | | | |
| FLEUROMA (HM07418) | | | | ● | | | | | | | | | | | | |
| FOOT HEALTH CLINIC (HM07482) | | | | | | | | | | | | | | | | |
| FORD, AUDREY (HM07523) | | | | | | | | | | | | | | | | |
| FOULKES, GEOFFREY LLOYD (HM07609) | | | | ● | | | ● | | | | | | | ● | | |
| FULTON, A J (HM07796) | | | | | | | | | | | | | | | | |
| FULTON, A J (HM07795) | | | | | | | | | | | | | | | | |
| FUN, MAE (HM07797) | | | | | | | | | | | | | | | | |
| GRAY, P A (HM08417) | | | | | | | | | | | | | | | | |
| GRAYS CHIROPRACTIC CLINIC (HM08424) | | | | | | | | | | | | | | | | |
| HADLEIGH PODIATRY CLINIC (HM08695) | | | | | | | | | | | | | | | | |
| HALSTEAD, RITA (HM08819) | | | | | | | | | | | | | | | | |
| HARLOW OSTEOPATHIC PRACTICE (HM09011) | | | | | | | | | | | | | | | | |
| HAWKRIDGE, FRANCOISE (HM09231) | | | | | | | | | | | | | | | | |
| HEALING ROOM (HM09349) | | | | | | | | | | | | | | | | |
| HENRY, JOANNE (HM09568) | | | | | | | | | | | | | | | | |
| HERB GARDEN (HM09587) | | | | | | | | | | | | | | | | |
| HOLISTIC HEALTH CLINIC (HM09978) | | | | | | | | | | | | | | | | |
| HYPNOTHERAPY CENTRE (HM10530) | | | | | | | | | | | | | | | | |
| HYPNOTHERAPY CENTRE (HM10532) | | | | | | | | | | | | | | | | |
| INDIGO BAY AROMATHERAPY (HM10613) | | | | | | | | | | | | | | | | |
| JACALAN ESSENTIAL OILS (HM10810) | | | | | | | | | | | | | | | | |
| JOYNES, IAN (HM11239) | | | | | | | | | | | | | | | | |
| JUNIPER BERRY (HM11268) | | | | | | | | | | | | | | | | |
| KEETCH, KIT (HM11397) | | | | | | | | | | | | | | | | |
| KELLY, GILLIAN (HM11431) | | | | | | | | | | | | | | | | |
| KULKARNI, P S (HM11817) | | | | | | | | | | | | | | | | |

# A - F Therapies at Practices/Businesses

| Business by County with Reference no. | Absent Healing | Acupressure | Acupuncture | Alexander Technique | Allergy Testing | Anthroposohical Med | Aromatherapy | Art Therapy | Aura Therapy | Auricular Therapy | Auto Suggestion | Autogenic Training | Aversion Therapy | Ayurvedic Medicine | Baby Massage | Bach Remedies | Bates Method | Beauty Therapy | Bio-energetics | Biofeedback | Biomagnetic Therapy | Biomechanics | Bonesetting | Bowen Therapy | Chinese Herbal Medicine |
|---|---|---|---|---|---|---|---|---|---|---|---|---|---|---|---|---|---|---|---|---|---|---|---|---|---|
| LAING, RICHARD (DR) (HM11866) | | | | | | | | | | | | | | | | ● | | | | | | | | | |
| LA-SANTE AROMATHERAPY (HM11981) | | | | | | | ● | | | | | | | | | | | | | | | | | | |
| LEIGH, MARTIN (HM12189) | | | | | | | ● | | | | | | | | | | | | | | | | | | |
| LESLEY WEIGHT MOBILE THERAPIST (HM12236) | | | | | | | ● | | | | | | | | | | | | | | | | | | |
| LEVY, PAUL (HM12269) | | | | | | | | | | | | | | | | | | | | | | ● | | | |
| LINGWOOD CLINIC (HM12435) | | | ● | | | | ● | | | | | | | | | | | | | | | | | | |
| LONDON ROAD PHYSIO PRACTICE (HM12603) | | | | | | | | | | | | | | | | | | | | | | | | | |
| LOVELL, JENNY (HM12677) | | | ● | | | | | | | | | | | | | | | | | | | | | | |
| MACINNES, BERYL (HM12841) | | | | | | | | | | | | | | | | ● | | | | | | | | | |
| MARTIN, LEIGH (HM13202) | | | | | | | ● | | | | | | | | | | | | | | | | | | |
| MEDELY CLINIC (HM13647) | | | | | | | ● | | | | | | | | | | | | | | | | | | |
| MILES, C J (HM13855) | | | | | | | | | | | | | | | | | | | | | | ● | | | |
| MOONSTONE HEALING CENTRE (HM14111) | ● | | ● | | | | ● | | ● | | | | | | | ● | | | | | | | | ● | |
| MOORE, SUSAN (HM14134) | | | | | | | | | | | | | | | | | | | | | | | | | |
| MOUCHET, F (HM14282) | | | | | | | | | | | | | | | | | | | | | | | | | |
| NATURAL REMEDY CENTRE (HM14620) | ● | ● | ● | | | | ● | | | | | | | | | ● | | | | | | | | | ● |
| OTHEN, FIONA (HM15493) | | | | | | | | | | | | | | | | | | | | | | | | | |
| PALMER, DAVID J (HM15600) | | | | | | | | | | | | | | | | | | | | | | | | ● | |
| PARVEZ, SHAUKAT (HM15771) | | | ● | | | | | | | | | | | | | | | | | | | | | | |
| PEPPER, SUSAN (HM16010) | | | | ● | | | | | | | | | | | | | | | | | | | | | |
| PHARMACARE (HM16109) | | | | | ● | | ● | | | | | | | | | | | | | | | | | | |
| PHYSIO & SPORTS INJURY CLINIC (HM16186) | | | | | | | | | | | | | | | | | | | | ● | | | | | |
| PINEWOOD PHYSIOTHERAPY CLINIC (HM16313) | | | | | | | | | | | | | | | | | | | | | | | ● | | |
| PISCES NATURAL THERAPY CENTRE (HM16330) | | | | | | | | | | | ● | | ● | | | ● | | | | ● | | | | | |
| PRICE, G J (HM16572) | | | | | | | | | | | | | | | | | | | | | | | | | |
| PRIEST, ROSIE (HM16610) | | | | | | | | | | | | | | | | | | | | | | | | | |
| PRIVATE ACUPUNCTURE CLINIC (HM16640) | | | ● | | | | | | | | | | | | | | | | | | | | | | |
| PRIVATE HEALTH CENTRE CLINIC (HM16643) | | | ● | | | | | | | | | | | | | | | | | | | | | | |
| PRIVATE MEDICAL ACUPUNCTURE (HM16646) | | | ● | | | | | | | | | | | | | | | | | | | | | | |
| QUALITY ANALYSIS (HM16790) | | | | | | | ● | | | | | | | | | | | | | | | | | | |
| REFLEXOLOGY CLINIC (HM17088) | | | | | | | | | | | | | | | | | | | | | | | | | |
| SAFFRON OILS (HM17835) | | | | | | | ● | | | | | | | | | | | | | | | | | | |
| SALMON, MARGARET (HM17858) | | | | | | | ● | | | | | | | | | | | | | | | | | | |
| SANDERS, G (HM17909) | | | | | | | | | | | | | | | | | | | | | | ● | | | |

| Business by County with Reference no. | Chiropody | Chiropractic | Clinical Ecology | Cognitive Therapy | Colonic Hydrotherapy | Colour Therapy | Complementary Therapy | Counselling | Cranial Osteopathy | Cranio-Sacral Therapy | Cryo Surgery | Crystal Healing | Cupping | Cymatics | Dance Movement Thrpy | Dietician | Do-In | Douching | Dowsing | Drama Therapy | Electrolipolysis | Electrolysis | Electrotherapy | Encounter Groups | Faith Healing |
|---|---|---|---|---|---|---|---|---|---|---|---|---|---|---|---|---|---|---|---|---|---|---|---|---|---|
| LAING, RICHARD (DR) (HM11866) | | | | | | | | | | | | | | | | | | | | | | | | | |
| LA-SANTE AROMATHERAPY (HM11981) | | | | | | | | | | | | | | | | | | | | | | | | | |
| LEIGH, MARTIN (HM12189) | | | | | | | | | | ● | | | | | | | | | | | | | | | |
| LESLEY WEIGHT MOBILE THERAPIST (HM12236) | | | | | | | | | | | | | | | | | | | | | | | | | |
| LEVY, PAUL (HM12269) | ● | | | | | | | | | | ● | | | | | | | | | | | | | | |
| LINGWOOD CLINIC (HM12435) | | | | | | | | | | | | | | | | | | | | | | | | | |
| LONDON ROAD PHYSIO PRACTICE (HM12603) | ● | | | | | | | | | | | | | | | | | | | | | | | | |
| LOVELL, JENNY (HM12677) | | | | | | | | | | | | | | | | | | | | | | | | | |
| MACINNES, BERYL (HM12841) | | | | | | | | | | | | | | | | | | | | | | | | | |
| MARTIN, LEIGH (HM13202) | | | | | | | | | | ● | | | | | | | | | | | | | | | |
| MEDELY CLINIC (HM13647) | | | | | | | ● | | | | | | | | | | | | | | | | | | |
| MILES, C J (HM13855) | ● | | | | | | | | | | | | | | | | | | | | | | | | |
| MOONSTONE HEALING CENTRE (HM14111) | | | | ● | | | ● | ● | | | | ● | | | | | | | ● | | | | | | |
| MOORE, SUSAN (HM14134) | ● | | | | | | | | | | | | | | | | | | | | | | | | |
| MOUCHET, F (HM14282) | | | | | | | | ● | | | | | | | | | | | | | | | | | |
| NATURAL REMEDY CENTRE (HM14620) | ● | | | | | | | | | | | | ● | | | | | | | | | | | | |
| OTHEN, FIONA (HM15493) | | ● | | | | | | | | | | | | | | | | | | | | | | | |
| PALMER, DAVID J (HM15600) | | | | | | | | | | | | | | | | | | | | | | | | | |
| PARVEZ, SHAUKAT (HM15771) | | ● | | | | | | | | | | | | | | | | | | | | | | | |
| PEPPER, SUSAN (HM16010) | | | | | | | | | | | | | | | | | | | | | | | | | |
| PHARMACARE (HM16109) | | | | | | | ● | | | | | | | | | | | | | | | | | | |
| PHYSIO & SPORTS INJURY CLINIC (HM16186) | | | | | | | | | | | | | | | | | | | | | | | ● | | |
| PINEWOOD PHYSIOTHERAPY CLINIC (HM16313) | | | | | | | | | | | | | | | | | | | | | | | ● | | |
| PISCES NATURAL THERAPY CENTRE (HM16330) | | | | | | | ● | ● | | | | | | | | | | | | | | | | | |
| PRICE, G J (HM16572) | | ● | | | | | | | | | | | | | | ● | | | | | | | ● | | |
| PRIEST, ROSIE (HM16610) | | ● | | | | | | | | | | | | | | | | | | | | | | | |
| PRIVATE ACUPUNCTURE CLINIC (HM16640) | | | | | | | | | | | | | | | | | | | | | | | | | |
| PRIVATE HEALTH CENTRE CLINIC (HM16643) | | | | | | | | | | | | | | | | | | | | | | | | | |
| PRIVATE MEDICAL ACUPUNCTURE (HM16646) | | | | | | | | | | | | | | | | | | | | | | | | | |
| QUALITY ANALYSIS (HM16790) | | | | | | | | | | | | | | | | | | | | | | | | | |
| REFLEXOLOGY CLINIC (HM17088) | | | | | | | | ● | | | | | | | | | | | | | | | | | |
| SAFFRON OILS (HM17835) | | | | | | | | | | | | | | | | | | | | | | | | | |
| SALMON, MARGARET (HM17858) | | | | | | | | | | | | | | | | | | | | | | | | | |
| SANDERS, G (HM17909) | ● | | | | | | | | | | | | | | | | | | | | | | | | |

# A - F Therapies at Practices/Businesses

| Business by County with Reference no. | Absent Healing | Acupressure | Acupuncture | Alexander Technique | Allergy Testing | Anthroposohical Med | Aromatherapy | Art Therapy | Aura Therapy | Auricular Therapy | Auto Suggestion | Autogenic Training | Aversion Therapy | Ayurvedic Medicine | Baby Massage | Bach Remedies | Bates Method | Beauty Therapy | Bio-energetics | Biofeedback | Biomagnetic Therapy | Biomechanics | Bonesetting | Bowen Therapy | Chinese Herbal Medicine |
|---|---|---|---|---|---|---|---|---|---|---|---|---|---|---|---|---|---|---|---|---|---|---|---|---|---|
| SCOTT, MARY (HM18124) | | | | | | | ● | | | | | | | | | | | | | | | | | | |
| SELF AWARENESS HEALING (HM18204) | ● | | | | | | | | | | | | | | | | | | | | | | | | |
| SEYMOUR, LOUISE (HM18259) | | | | | | | | | | | | | | | | | | | | | | ● | | | |
| SHELDON, PEGGY (HM18380) | | | | | | | | | | | | | | | | | | | | | | | | ● | |
| SHENFIELD HEALTH CLINIC (HM18397) | | | ● | | | | | | | | | | | | | | | | | | | | | | |
| SIMMONDS, JENNI (HM18558) | | | | | | | ● | | | | | | | | | | | | | | | | | | |
| SOUTH, JO (HM18918) | | | | | | | | | | | | | | | | ● | | | | | | | | | |
| THOMPSON, GRAHAM (HM19979) | | | | ● | | | | | | | | | | | | | | | | | | | | | |
| TRINITY CENTRE (HM20338) | | | ● | ● | | | ● | | | | | | | | | | | | | | | | | | |
| UNDERWOOD CLINICS CHIROPRACTIC (HM20498) | | | | | | | | | | | | | | | | | | | | | | | | | |
| WADDINGTON, R M (HM20726) | | | | | | | | | | | | | | | | | | | | | | | | | |
| WALK CHIROPODIST (HM20757) | | | | | | | | | | | | | | | | | | | | | | ● | | | |
| WATSON, IRENE (HM21011) | | | | | | | ● | | | | | | | | | | | | | | | | | | |
| WAYNE-WRIGHT, M S (HM21043) | | | | | | | | | | | | | | | | | | | | | | | | | |
| WELFORD, MARTIN (HM21129) | | | | ● | | | | | | | | | | | | | | | | | | | | | |
| WENTWORTH HEALTH CLINIC (HM21201) | | | | | | | ● | | | | | | | | | | | | | | | | | | |
| WETHERALL, STUART (HM21289) | | | | | | | | | | | | | | | | | | | | | | | | | |
| WHEELER, M A (HM21317) | | | | | | | | | | | | | | | | | | | | | | ● | | | |
| WHEELER, M A (HM21316) | | ● | | | | | | | | | | | | | | | | | | | | ● | | | |
| WHITE WATER HEALING CENTRE (HM21345) | ● | | | | | | | | ● | | | | | | | | | | | | | | | | |
| WOODS, JILL (HM21847) | | | | | | | | | | | | | | | | ● | | | | | | | | | |
| WOODS, JILL (HM21848) | | | | | | | | | | | | | | | | ● | | | | | | | | | |
| WOODSIDE NATURAL HEALTH (HM21859) | ● | ● | | | | | ● | | | | | | | | | | | | | | | | | | |
| GLOUCESTERSHIRE | | | | | | | | | | | | | | | | | | | | | | | | | |
| ACUHEALTH (HM00211) | | | ● | | | | | | | | | | | | | | | | | | | | | | |
| ACUPUNCTURE CLINIC (HM00262) | | | ● | | | | ● | | | | | | | | | | | | | | | | | | |
| ADAMS, PETER (HM00360) | | | | | | | | | | | | | | | | | | | | | | | | | |
| AMER, ANDREW R (HM00777) | | | ● | | | | | | | | | | | | | | | | | | | | | | |
| AQUA OLEUM (HM00953) | | | | | | | ● | | | | | | | | | | | | | | | | | | |
| AROMA THERAPEUTICS (HM01062) | | | | | | | ● | | | | | | | | | | | | | | | | | | |
| ARTICHOKE NATURAL HEALTH (HM01168) | | | ● | ● | | | ● | | | | | | | | ● | | | | | | | | | ● | |
| BODYHARMONICS CENTRE (HM02620) | | | ● | | | | | | | | | | | | | | | | | | | | | | |
| BURKE, JAYNE (HM03388) | | | | | | | ● | | | | | | | | | | | | | | | | | | |
| CHARLTON, STEPHANIE (HM04035) | | | ● | | | | | | | | | | | | | | | | | | | | | | |

| Business by County with Reference no. | Chiropody | Chiropractic | Clinical Ecology | Cognitive Therapy | Colonic Hydrotherapy | Colour Therapy | Complementary Therapy | Counselling | Cranial Osteopathy | Cranio-Sacral Therapy | Cryo Surgery | Crystal Healing | Cupping | Cymatics | Dance Movement Thrpy | Dietician | Do-In | Douching | Dowsing | Drama Therapy | Electrolipolysis | Electrolysis | Electrotherapy | Encounter Groups | Faith Healing |
|---|---|---|---|---|---|---|---|---|---|---|---|---|---|---|---|---|---|---|---|---|---|---|---|---|---|
| SCOTT, MARY (HM18124) | | | | | | | | | | | | | | | | | | | | | | | | | |
| SELF AWARENESS HEALING (HM18204) | | | | | | | | ● | | | | | | | | | | | | | | | | | |
| SEYMOUR, LOUISE (HM18259) | ● | | | | | | | | | | ● | | | | | | | | | | | | | | |
| SHELDON, PEGGY (HM18380) | | | | | | | | | | | | | | | | | | | | | | | | | |
| SHENFIELD HEALTH CLINIC (HM18397) | | | | | | | | | | | | | | | | | | | | | | | | | |
| SIMMONDS, JENNI (HM18558) | | | | | | | | | | | | | | | | | | | | | | | | | |
| SOUTH, JO (HM18918) | | | | | | | | | | | | | | | | | | | | | | | | | |
| THOMPSON, GRAHAM (HM19979) | | | | | | | | | | | | | | | | | | | | | | | | | |
| TRINITY CENTRE (HM20338) | | ● | | | | | | | | | | | | | | | | | | | | | | | |
| UNDERWOOD CLINICS CHIROPRACTIC (HM20498) | | ● | | | | | | | | | | | | | | | | | | | | | | | |
| WADDINGTON, R M (HM20726) | ● | | | | | | | | | | | | | | | | | | | | | | | | |
| WALK CHIROPODIST (HM20757) | ● | | | | | | | | | | | | | | | | | | | | | | | | |
| WATSON, IRENE (HM21011) | | | | | | | | | | | | | | | | | | | | | | | | | |
| WAYNE-WRIGHT, M S (HM21043) | ● | | | | | | | | | | | | | | | | | | | | | | | | |
| WELFORD, MARTIN (HM21129) | | | | | | | | | | | | | | | | | | | | | | | | | |
| WENTWORTH HEALTH CLINIC (HM21201) | | | | | | | | ● | | | | | | | | | | | | | | | | | |
| WETHERALL, STUART (HM21289) | | | | | | | | ● | | | | | | | | | | | | | | | | | |
| WHEELER, M A (HM21317) | ● | | | | | | | | | | | | | | | | | | | | | | | | |
| WHEELER, M A (HM21316) | ● | | | | | | | | | | | | | | | | | | | | | | | | |
| WHITE WATER HEALING CENTRE (HM21345) | | | | | | | ● | | | | | | | | | | | | ● | | | | | | |
| WOODS, JILL (HM21847) | | | | | | | | | | | | | | | | | | | | | | | | | |
| WOODS, JILL (HM21848) | | | | | | | | | | | | | | | | | | | | | | | | | |
| WOODSIDE NATURAL HEALTH (HM21859) | | | | | | | | | ● | | | | | | | | | | | | | | | | |
| GLOUCESTERSHIRE | | | | | | | | | | | | | | | | | | | | | | | | | |
| ACUHEALTH (HM00211) | | | | | | | | | | | | | | | | | | | | | | | | | |
| ACUPUNCTURE CLINIC (HM00262) | | | | | | | | | | | | | | | | | | | | | | | | | |
| ADAMS, PETER (HM00360) | | | | | | | ● | | | | | | | | | | | | | | | | | | |
| AMER, ANDREW R (HM00777) | | | | | | | | | | | | | | | | | | | | | | | | | |
| AQUA OLEUM (HM00953) | | | | | | | | | | | | | | | | | | | | | | | | | |
| AROMA THERAPEUTICS (HM01062) | | | | | | | | | | | | | | | | | | | | | | | | | |
| ARTICHOKE NATURAL HEALTH (HM01168) | ● | | | | | | | | ● | | | | | | | | | | | | | | | | |
| BODYHARMONICS CENTRE (HM02620) | | | | | | | | | | | | | | | | | | | | | | | | | |
| BURKE, JAYNE (HM03388) | | | | | | | | | | | | ● | | | | | | | | | | | | | |
| CHARLTON, STEPHANIE (HM04035) | | | | | | | | | | | | | | | | | | | | | | | | | |

# A - F Therapies at Practices/Businesses

| Business by County with Reference no. | Absent Healing | Acupressure | Acupuncture | Alexander Technique | Allergy Testing | Anthroposohical Med | Aromatherapy | Art Therapy | Aura Therapy | Auricular Therapy | Auto Suggestion | Autogenic Training | Aversion Therapy | Ayurvedic Medicine | Baby Massage | Bach Remedies | Bates Method | Beauty Therapy | Bio-energetics | Biofeedback | Biomagnetic Therapy | Biomechanics | Bonesetting | Bowen Therapy | Chinese Herbal Medicine | Chiropody | Chiropractic | Clinical Ecology | Cognitive Therapy | Colonic Hydrotherapy | Colour Therapy | Complementary Therapy | Counselling | Cranial Osteopathy | Cranio-Sacral Therapy | Cryo Surgery | Crystal Healing | Cupping | Cymatics | Dance Movement Thrpy | Dietician | Do-In | Douching | Dowsing | Drama Therapy | Electrolipolysis | Electrolysis | Electrotherapy | Encounter Groups | Faith Healing |
|---|---|---|---|---|---|---|---|---|---|---|---|---|---|---|---|---|---|---|---|---|---|---|---|---|---|---|---|---|---|---|---|---|---|---|---|---|---|---|---|---|---|---|---|---|---|---|---|---|---|---|
| CHELTENHAM CLINIC & TRAD ACU (HM04093) | | | ● | | | | | | | | | | | | | ● | | | | | | | | | | | ● | | | | | | | ● | | | | | | | | | | | | | | | | |
| CHELTENHAM HOLISTIC HLTH CTRE (HM04094) | | | ● | ● | ● | | ● | | | | | | | | | | | | | | | | | | | | ● | | | | | | | | ● | | | | | | | | | | | | | | | |
| CHELTENHAM HYPNOTHERAPY (HM04096) | | | | | | | | | | | ● | | ● | | | | | | | | | | | | | | | | | | | | | | | | | | | | | | | | | | | | | |
| CHELTENHAM PHYSIO/SPRTS CLNC (HM04097) | | | ● | | | | | | | | | | | | | | | | | | | | | | | | | | | | | | | | | | | | | | | | | | | | | | | |
| CHRISTIE, ELIZABETH (HM04440) | | | ● | | | | | | | | | | | | | | | | | | | | | | | | | | | | | | | | | | | | | | | | | | | | | | | |
| CLAPHAM, EUGENIE (HM04529) | | | | | | | | | | | | | | | | ● | | | | | | | | | | | | | | | | | | | | | | | | | | | | | | | | | | |
| CLIFF, R (HM04661) | | | | | | | | | | | | | | | | | | | | | | | | | | | ● | | | | | | | | | | | | | | | | | | | | | | | |
| COMPLEMENTARY TOUCH (HM04950) | | | ● | | | | | | | | | | | | | | | | | | | | | | | | ● | | | | | | ● | | | | | | | | | | | | | | | | | |
| COOPER, ANGELA (HM05089) | | | | | | | | | | | | | | | | | | | | | | | | | | | | | | | | | ● | | | | | | | | | | | | | | | | | |
| COTSWOLD PHYSIOTHERAPY CENTRE (HM05215) | | | ● | | | | | | | | | | | | | | | | | | | | | | | | | | | | | | | | | | | | | | | | | | | | | ● | | |
| DANESH, MOJDEH (HM05716) | | | ● | | | | | | | | | | | | | | | | | | | | | | | | | | | | | | | | | | | | | | | | | | | | | | | |
| DARRALL, BETH (HM05750) | | | | | | | | | | | | | | | | ● | | | | | | | | | | | | | | | | | | | | | | | | | | | | | | | | | | |
| DEAS, VALERIE JOHNSTON (HM05949) | | | | | | | ● | | | | | | | | | | | | | | | | | | | | | | | | | | | | | | | | | | | | | | | | | | | |
| ESSENTIAL BODYWORKS COMPANY (HM06899) | | | | | | | | | | | | | | | | | | | | | | | | | | | | | | | | ● | | | | | | | | | | | | | | | | | | |
| FILLINGHAM, MAGGIE (HM07293) | | | | | | | ● | | | | | | | | | | | | | | | | | | | | | | | | | | | | | | | | | | | | | | | | | | | |
| GLOUCESTER NAT THERAPIES (HM08160) | | | ● | | | | | | | | | | | | | | | | | | | | | | | | | | | | | | | | | | | | | | | | | | | | | | | |
| GREENWELL, DAVID (HM08498) | | | | | | | | | | | | | | | | | | | | | | | | | | | | | | | | ● | ● | | | | | | | | | | | | | | | | | |
| GREENWOOD, ELAINE (HM08505) | | | | | | | | | | | | | | | | ● | | | | | | | | | | | | | | | | | | | | | | | | | | | | | | | | | | |
| HALL, GERRY (HM08772) | | | ● | | | | | | | | | | | | | | | | | | | | | | | | | | | | | | | | | | | | | | | | | | | | | | | |
| HEMMINGS, RITA (HM09536) | | | | | | | | | | | | | | | | | | | | | | | | | | | ● | | | | | | | | | | | | | | | | | | | | | | | |
| HERMANN, C (HM09682) | | | | | | | | | | | | | | | | | | | | | | | | | | | ● | | | | | | | | | | | | | | | | | | | | | | | |
| HORSLEY, MARY E (HM10193) | | | ● | | | | | | | | | | | | | | | | | | | | | | | | | | | | | | | | | | | | | | | | | | | | | | | |
| HUNTER, PHILIPPA (HM10407) | | | | | | | ● | | | | | | | | | | | | | | | | | | | | | | | | | | | | | | | | | | | | | | | | | | | |
| HYGEIA COLLEGE-COLOUR THERAPY (HM10476) | | | | | | | | | | | | | | | | | | | | | | | | | | | | | | | ● | | | | | | | | | | | | | | | | | | | |
| IRENE BAYLISS MCTIMONEY CHIRO (HM10720) | | | | | | | | | | | | | | | | | | | | | | | | | | | ● | | | | | | | | | | | | | | | | | | | | | | | |
| JAMES, DIANNE (HM10885) | | | | | | | | | | | | | | | | ● | | | | | | | | | | | | | | | | | | | | | | | | | | | | | | | | | | |
| JOANNA SMITH AROMATHERAPY (HM11040) | | | | | | | ● | | | | | | | | | ● | | | | | | | | ● | | | | | | | | | | | | | | | | | | | | | | | | | | |
| LANSDOWN CLNC OF PHYS MED (HM11963) | | | | | | | | | | | | | | | | | | | | | | | | | | | ● | | | | | | | | | | | | | | | | | | | | | | | |
| LAWLER, R & G (HM12041) | | | | | | | | | | | | | | | | | | | | | | | | | | | | | | | | | | | | | ● | | | | | | | | | | | | | |
| LECKHAMPTON CHIROPRACTIC CLNC (HM12119) | | | | | | | | | | | | | | | | | | | | | | | | | | | ● | | | | | | | | | | | | | | | | | | | | | | | |
| LLOYD-JONES, J (HM12521) | | | ● | | | | | | | | | | | | | | | | | | | | | | | | | | | | | | | | | | | | | | | | | | | | | | | |
| MEISHA SKIN CARE (HM13700) | | | | | | | ● | | | | | | | | | | | | | | | | | | | | | | | | | | | | | | | | | | | | | | | | | | | |
| MYERS, MERRILYN (HM14438) | | | | | | | | | | | | | | | | ● | | | | | | | | | | | | | | | | | | | | | | | | | | | | | | | | | | |
| NATURAL THERAPEUTICS (HM14628) | | | | | | | | | | | | | | | | ● | | | | | | | | | | | | | | | | | | | | | | | | | | | | | | | | | | |

# A - F Therapies at Practices/Businesses

| Business by County with Reference no. | Absent Healing | Acupressure | Acupuncture | Alexander Technique | Allergy Testing | Anthroposohical Med | Aromatherapy | Art Therapy | Aura Therapy | Auricular Therapy | Auto Suggestion | Autogenic Training | Aversion Therapy | Ayurvedic Medicine | Baby Massage | Bach Remedies | Bates Method | Beauty Therapy | Bio-energetics | Biofeedback | Biomagnetic Therapy | Biomechanics | Bonesetting | Bowen Therapy | Chinese Herbal Medicine |
|---|---|---|---|---|---|---|---|---|---|---|---|---|---|---|---|---|---|---|---|---|---|---|---|---|---|
| NATURAL THERAPIES CLINIC (HM14633) | | | ● | ● | | | ● | | | | | | | | | | | | | | | | | | |
| NATURAL THERAPY CENTRE (HM14649) | | | ● | | | | ● | | | | | | | | | | | | | | | | | | |
| NEALE-BROWN, CLAIRE (HM14725) | | | | ● | | | | | | | | | | | | | | | | | | | | | |
| OLD CONVENT (HM15255) | ● | | | | | ● | | | | | | | | | | | | | | | | | | | |
| OLIVE TRUST NATURAL THRPY CTRE (HM15282) | | | | | | | | | | | | | | | | | | | | | | | | | |
| PENACHE (HM15960) | | | | | | | ● | | | | | | | | | | | | | | | | | | |
| PERCIVAL, ANN (HM16014) | | | | | | | | | | | | | | | | ● | | | | | | | | | |
| QUARRY, PHILLIP (HM16791) | | | ● | | | | | | | | | | | | | | | | | | | | | | |
| SKELIAN CHIROPRACTIC CLINIC (HM18633) | | | | | | | | | | | | | | | | | | | | | | | | | |
| SLATER, D C (HM18672) | | | | | | | | | | | | | | | | | | | | | | | | | |
| SMYTH, DAVID (HM18830) | ● | ● | ● | | | | | | | | | | | | | ● | | | | | | | | | ● |
| STEINER, LYNDA (HM19190) | | | | | | | | | | | | | | | | | | | | | | | | | |
| STOUT, HEATHER (HM19359) | | | | | | | | | | | | | | | | | | | | | | | | | |
| STRESS COMPANY (HM19390) | | | | | | | | | | | | | | | | | | | | | | | | | |
| STROUD CHIROPRACTIC CLINIC (HM19421) | | | | | | | | | | | | | | | | | | | | | | | | | |
| STROUD NATURAL HEALTH CLINIC (HM19422) | | | ● | | | | ● | | | | | | | | | | | | | | | | | | |
| TREACHER, KATE (HM20300) | | | | | | | | | | | | | | | | ● | | | | | | | | | |
| TREE OF LIFE CENTRE (HM20307) | | | | | | | | | | | | | | | | | | | | | | | | | |
| VICKERS, CHRISTOPHER (DR) (HM20640) | | | | | | | | | | | | | | | | | | | | | | | | | |
| VILLAGE CLINIC (HM20665) | | | | | | | | | | | | | | | | | | | | | | | | | |
| VINEY HALL PHYSIOTHERAPY (HM20683) | | | | | | | | | | | | | | | | | | | | | | | | | |
| WELLS, GEORGINA (HM21172) | | | | | | | ● | | | | | | | | | | | | | | | | | | |
| YOGA DRUVAM JIVAN YOGA SOCIETY (HM22024) | | | | | | | | | | | | | | | | | | | | | | | | | |
| **HAMPSHIRE** | | | | | | | | | | | | | | | | | | | | | | | | | |
| ABBEY CHIROPRACTIC CLINIC (HM00075) | | | | | | | | | | | | | | | | | | | | | | | | | |
| ABEL, ELAINE (HM00107) | | | | | | | | | | | | | | | | ● | | | | | | | | | |
| ABSOLUTE AROMAS (HM00137) | | | | | | | ● | | | | | | | | | | | | | | | | | | |
| ACUPUNCTURE & PHYSIO CLINIC (HM00245) | | ● | ● | | | | ● | | | | | | | | | | | | | | | | | | |
| ACUPUNTURE TAO CLINIC (HM00339) | | | ● | | | | | | | | | | | | | | | | | | | | | | |
| AKESTER, JANE (HM00463) | | | | ● | | | | | | | | | | | | | | | | | | | | | |
| ALL - HEAL ACU & HERB CENTRE (HM00581) | | ● | ● | | | | | | | | | | | | | | | | | | | | | | |
| ALLERGY THERAPY (HM00637) | | | | | | | | | | | | | | | | | | | | | | | | | |
| ANDOVER FOOT HEALTH (HM00842) | | | | | | | | | | | | | | | | | | | | | | | | | |
| AROMATHERAPY BY R SKILTON (HM01097) | | | | | | | ● | | | | | | | | | | | | | | | | | | |

| Business by County with Reference no. | Chiropody | Chiropractic | Clinical Ecology | Cognitive Therapy | Colonic Hydrotherapy | Colour Therapy | Complementary Therapy | Counselling | Cranial Osteopathy | Cranio-Sacral Therapy | Cryo Surgery | Crystal Healing | Cupping | Cymatics | Dance Movement Thrpy | Dietician | Do-In | Douching | Dowsing | Drama Therapy | Electrolipolysis | Electrolysis | Electrotherapy | Encounter Groups | Faith Healing |
|---|---|---|---|---|---|---|---|---|---|---|---|---|---|---|---|---|---|---|---|---|---|---|---|---|---|
| NATURAL THERAPIES CLINIC (HM14633) | | ● | | | | | | | | | | | | | | | | | | | | | | | |
| NATURAL THERAPY CENTRE (HM14649) | | | | | | | | | | ● | | | | | | | | | | | | | | | |
| NEALE-BROWN, CLAIRE (HM14725) | | | | | | | | | | | | | | | | | | | | | | | | | |
| OLD CONVENT (HM15255) | | ● | | | | | | | | | | | | | | | | | | | | | | | ● |
| OLIVE TRUST NATURAL THRPY CTRE (HM15282) | | ● | | | | | | | | | | | | | | | | | | | | | | | |
| PENACHE (HM15960) | | | | | | | | | | | | | | | | | | | | | | | | | |
| PERCIVAL, ANN (HM16014) | | | | | | | | | | | | | | | | | | | | | | | | | |
| QUARRY, PHILLIP (HM16791) | | | | | | | | | | | | | | | | | | | | | | | | | |
| SKELIAN CHIROPRACTIC CLINIC (HM18633) | | ● | | | | | | | | | | | | | | | | | | | | | | | |
| SLATER, D C (HM18672) | | | | | | | | ● | | | | | | | | | | | | | | | | | |
| SMYTH, DAVID (HM18830) | | | | | | | ● | | | | | | | | | | | | ● | | | | | | |
| STEINER, LYNDA (HM19190) | | ● | | | | | | | | | | | | | | | | | | | | | | | |
| STOUT, HEATHER (HM19359) | | | | | | | | | ● | | | | | | | | | | | | | | | | |
| STRESS COMPANY (HM19390) | | | | | | | ● | | | | | | | | | | | | | | | | | | |
| STROUD CHIROPRACTIC CLINIC (HM19421) | | ● | | | | | | | | | | | | | | | | | | | | | | | |
| STROUD NATURAL HEALTH CLINIC (HM19422) | | | | | | | | | | ● | | | | | | | | | | | | | | | |
| TREACHER, KATE (HM20300) | | | | | | | | | | | | | | | | | | | | | | | | | |
| TREE OF LIFE CENTRE (HM20307) | | | | | | | | | | | | ● | | | | | | | | | | | | | |
| VICKERS, CHRISTOPHER (DR) (HM20640) | | ● | | | | | | | | | | | | | | | | | | | | | | | |
| VILLAGE CLINIC (HM20665) | ● | | | | | | | | | | | | | | | | | | | | | | ● | | |
| VINEY HALL PHYSIOTHERAPY (HM20683) | ● | | | | | | | | | | | | | | | | | | | | | | ● | | |
| WELLS, GEORGINA (HM21172) | | | | | | | | | | | | | | | | | | | | | | | | | |
| YOGA DRUVAM JIVAN YOGA SOCIETY (HM22024) | | | | | | | | ● | | | | | | | | | ● | | | | | | | | |
| **HAMPSHIRE** | | | | | | | | | | | | | | | | | | | | | | | | | |
| ABBEY CHIROPRACTIC CLINIC (HM00075) | | ● | | | | | | | | | | | | | | | | | | | | | | | |
| ABEL, ELAINE (HM00107) | | | | | | | | | | | | | | | | | | | | | | | | | |
| ABSOLUTE AROMAS (HM00137) | | | | | | | | | | | | | | | | | | | | | | | | | |
| ACUPUNCTURE & PHYSIO CLINIC (HM00245) | | | | | | | | | ● | | | | ● | | | | | | | | | | ● | | |
| ACUPUNTURE TAO CLINIC (HM00339) | | | | | | | | | | | | | | | | | | | | | | | | | |
| AKESTER, JANE (HM00463) | | | | | | | | | | | | | | | | | | | | | | | | | |
| ALL - HEAL ACU & HERB CENTRE (HM00581) | | | | | | | | | | | | | ● | | | | | | | | | | | | |
| ALLERGY THERAPY (HM00637) | | | | | | | | ● | | | | | | | | | | | | | | | | | |
| ANDOVER FOOT HEALTH (HM00842) | | ● | | | | | | | | | | | | | | | | | | | | | | | |
| AROMATHERAPY BY R SKILTON (HM01097) | | | | | | | | | | | | | | | | | | | | | | | | | |

# A - F Therapies at Practices/Businesses

| Business by County with Reference no. | Absent Healing | Acupressure | Acupuncture | Alexander Technique | Allergy Testing | Anthroposohical Med | Aromatherapy | Art Therapy | Aura Therapy | Auricular Therapy | Auto Suggestion | Autogenic Training | Aversion Therapy | Ayurvedic Medicine | Baby Massage | Bach Remedies | Bates Method | Beauty Therapy | Bio-energetics | Biofeedback | Biomagnetic Therapy | Biomechanics | Bonesetting | Bowen Therapy | Chinese Herbal Medicine | Chiropody | Chiropractic | Clinical Ecology | Cognitive Therapy | Colonic Hydrotherapy | Colour Therapy | Complementary Therapy | Counselling | Cranial Osteopathy | Cranio-Sacral Therapy | Cryo Surgery | Crystal Healing | Cupping | Cymatics | Dance Movement Thrpy | Dietician | Do-In | Douching | Dowsing | Drama Therapy | Electrolipolysis | Electrolysis | Electrotherapy | Encounter Groups | Faith Healing |
|---|---|---|---|---|---|---|---|---|---|---|---|---|---|---|---|---|---|---|---|---|---|---|---|---|---|---|---|---|---|---|---|---|---|---|---|---|---|---|---|---|---|---|---|---|---|---|---|---|---|---|
| AROMATHERAPY BY SHEILA BURWOOD (HM01099) | | | | | | | ● | | | | | | | | | | | | | | | | | | | | | | | | | | | | | | | | | | | | | | | | | | | | |
| AROMATHERAPY DIRECT (HM01109) | | | | | | | ● | | | | | | | | | | | | | | | | | | | | | | | | | | | | | | | | | | | | | | | | | | | | |
| AROMATHERAPY STUDIO (HM01125) | | | | | | | ● | | | | | | | | | | | | | | | | | | | | | | | | | | | | | | | | | | | | | | | | | | | | |
| AROMATICA TREATMENT & PRODUCTS (HM01137) | | | | | | | ● | | | | | | | | | | | | | | | | | | | | | | | | | | | | | | | | | | | | | | | | | | | | |
| ART DE VIVRE (HM01152) | | | | | | | ● | | | | | | | | | | | | | | | | | | | | | | | | | | | | | | | | | | | | | | | | | | | | |
| AVENUE CLINIC (HM01389) | | | | | | | | | | | | | | | | | | | | | | | | | | | ● | | | | | | | | | | | | | | | | | | | | | | | | |
| BACK 2 HEALTH (HM01477) | | | | | | | | | | | | | | | | | | | | | | | | | | | ● | | | | | | | | | | | | | | | | | | | | | | | | |
| BASSETTS CHIROPRACTIC CLINIC (HM01858) | | | | | | | | | | | | | | | | | | | | | | | | | | | ● | | | | | | | | | | | | | | | | | | | | | | | | |
| BELL CLINIC (HM02080) | | | ● | | | | | | | | | | | | | | | | | | | | | | | | | | | | | | | | | | | | | | | | | | | | | | | | |
| BENES, G B (HM02128) | | | | | | | | | | | | | | | | | | | | | | | | | | | ● | | | | | | | | | | | | | | | | | | | | | | | | |
| BERKLEYS HEALTH STUDIO (HM02194) | | | | | | | ● | | | | | | | | | | | | | | | | | | | | | | | | | | | | | | | | | | | | | | | | | | | | |
| BIRD, LYNN (HM02368) | | | ● | | | | | | | | | | | | | | | | | | | | | | | | | | | | | | | | | | | | | | | | | | | | | | | | |
| BODY BASIC (HM02575) | | | | | | | ● | | | | | | | | | | | | | | | | | | | | | | | | | | | | | | | | | | | | | | | | | | | | |
| BODY SCENT (HM02606) | | | | | | | ● | | | | | | | | | | | | | | | | | | | | | | | | | | | | | | | | | | | | | | | | | | | | |
| BOLDICK, KATHLEEN (HM02652) | | | | | | | | | | | | | | | | | | | | | | | | | | | | | | | | | | | ● | | | | | | | | | | | | | | | | |
| BOND, J (HM02670) | | | | ● | | | | | | | | | | | | | | | | | | | | | | | | | | | | | | | | | | | | | | | | | | | | | | | |
| BOOTY, STEPHEN (HM02712) | | | | | | | | | | | | | | | | | | | | | | | | | | | ● | | | | | | | | | | | | | | | | | | | | | | | | |
| BRADFORD HOUSE CHIRO CLINIC (HM02849) | | | ● | | | | | | | | | | | | | | | | | | | | | | | | ● | | | | | ● | | | ● | | | | | | | | | | | | | | | | |
| BROWN & ASSOCIATES (HM03205) | | | | | | | | | | | | | | | | | | | | | | | | | | | ● | | | | | | | | | | | | | | | | | | | | | | | | |
| BUCK, PETER (HM03306) | | | | | | | | | | | | | | | | | | | | | | | | | | ● | | | | | | | | | | | | | | | | | | | | | | | | | |
| CAMBRAY, ANDREW (HM03570) | | | ● | | | | | | | | | | | | | | | | | | | | | | | | | | | | | | | | | | | | | | | | | | | | | | | | |
| CARPENTER, G W (HM03730) | | | ● | | | | | | | | | | | | | | | | | | | | | | | | | | | | | | | | | | | | | | | | | | | | | | | | |
| CASSELL, JOHN (HM03814) | | | | | | | | | | | | | | | | | | | | | | | | | | | | | | | | | | | ● | | | | | | | | | | | | | | | | |
| CEDAR LODGE (HM03875) | | | | | | | ● | | | | | | | | | | | | | | | | | | | | | | | | | | | | | | | | | | | | | | | | | | | | |
| CHANDLER, PAT (HM03977) | | | | | | | ● | | | | | | | | | | | | | | | | | | | | | | | | | | | | | | | | | | | | | | | | | | | | |
| CHINESE ACUPUNCTURE CLINIC (HM04185) | | | ● | | | | | | | | | | | | | | | | | | | | | | | | | | | | | | | | | | | | | | | | | | | | | | | | |
| CHIROPRACTIC & CRANIAL CENTRE (HM04348) | | | | | | | | | | | | | | | | | | | | | | | | | | | ● | | | | | | | | | | | | | | | | | | | | | | | | |
| CITY CHIROPRACTIC CLINIC (HM04494) | | | | | | | | | | | | | | | | | | | | | | | | | | | ● | | | | | | | | | | | | | | | | | | | | | | | | |
| CLARKE, CHRIS (HM04584) | | | | | | | ● | | | | | | | | | | | | | | | | | | | | | | | | | | | | | | | | | | | | | | | | | | | | |
| CLAY, P A (HM04616) | | | ● | | | | | | | | | | | | | | | | | | | | | | | | | | | | | | | | | | | | | | | | | | | | | | | | |
| CLEMENTS, CHRISTINE (HM04642) | | | | | | | ● | | | | | | | | ● | | | | | | | | | | | | | | | | | | | ● | | | | | | | | | | | | | | | | | |
| COAST CLINIC (HM04752) | | | | | | | ● | | | | | | | | | | | | | | | | | | | | | | | | | | ● | | | | | | | | | | | | | | | | | | |
| COLVILE, RICHARD (HM04895) | | | | | | | | | | | | | | | | | | | | | | | | | | | | | | | | | ● | | | | | | | | | | | | | | | | | | |
| COMPLETE ANGEL HEALING CENTRE (HM04955) | | | | | | | ● | | | | | | | | | | | | | | | | | | | | | | | | | | | | | | | | | | | | | | | | | | | | |

# A - F Therapies at Practices/Businesses

| Business by County with Reference no. | Absent Healing | Acupressure | Acupuncture | Alexander Technique | Allergy Testing | Anthroposohical Med | Aromatherapy | Art Therapy | Aura Therapy | Auricular Therapy | Auto Suggestion | Autogenic Training | Aversion Therapy | Ayurvedic Medicine | Baby Massage | Bach Remedies | Bates Method | Beauty Therapy | Bio-energetics | Biofeedback | Biomagnetic Therapy | Biomechanics | Bonesetting | Bowen Therapy | Chinese Herbal Medicine | Chiropody | Chiropractic | Clinical Ecology | Cognitive Therapy | Colonic Hydrotherapy | Colour Therapy | Complementary Therapy | Counselling | Cranial Osteopathy | Cranio-Sacral Therapy | Cryo Surgery | Crystal Healing | Cupping | Cymatics | Dance Movement Thrpy | Dietician | Do-In | Douching | Dowsing | Drama Therapy | Electrolipolysis | Electrolysis | Electrotherapy | Encounter Groups | Faith Healing |
|---|---|---|---|---|---|---|---|---|---|---|---|---|---|---|---|---|---|---|---|---|---|---|---|---|---|---|---|---|---|---|---|---|---|---|---|---|---|---|---|---|---|---|---|---|---|---|---|---|---|---|
| CORELLO, LOUISE (HM05161) | | | ● | | | | | | | | | | | | | | | | | | | | | | | | | | | | | | | | | | | | | | | | | | | | | | | |
| COURAGE, VANESSA (HM05263) | | | | | | | | | | | | | | | | ● | | | | | | | | | | | | | | | | | | | | | | | | | | | | | | | | | | |
| CRAIG, PETER (HM05353) | | | | | | | | | | | | | | | | | | | | | | | | | | ● | | | | | | | | | | | | | | | | | | | | | | | | |
| CRANIOSACRAL THERAPY (HM05377) | | | | | | | | | | | | | | | | | | | | | | | | | | | | | | | | | | | ● | | | | | | | | | | | | | | | |
| CTRE FOR THE STUDY OF COMP MED (HM05543) | | | ● | ● | | | | | | | | ● | | | | ● | | | | | | | | | | | | ● | | | | ● | ● | | | | | | | | ● | | | | | | | | | |
| CTRE-COMPLEMENTARY THERAPY (HM05547) | | | | | | | ● | | | | | | | | | | | | | | | | | | | | ● | | | | | | | | ● | | | | | | | | | | | | | | | |
| DAVIES, B D (HM05799) | | | ● | | | | | | | | | | | | | | | | | | | | | | | | | | | | | | | | | | | | | | | | | | | | | | | |
| DOLPHIN STUDIOS (HM06165) | ● | | | | | | | | | | | | | | | | | | | | | | | | | | | | | | | ● | ● | | | | | | | | | | | | | | | | | |
| EASTLEIGH CHIROPRACTIC CENTRE (HM06543) | | | | | | | | | | | | | | | | | | | | | | | | | | | ● | | | | | | | | | | | | | | | | | | | | | | | |
| EASTLEIGH OSTEOPATHIC CLINIC (HM06544) | | | ● | | | | ● | | | | | | | | | | | | | | | | | | | | ● | | | | | | | ● | | | | | | | | | | | | | | | | |
| EDGAR, A (HM06596) | | | | | | | | | | | | | | | | | | | | | | | | | | ● | | | | | | | | | | | | | | | | | | | | | | | | |
| ELDRIDGE, NICOLA (HM06709) | | | | | | | | | | | | | | | | | | | | | | | | | | | ● | | | | | | | | | | | | | | | | | | | | | | | |
| ELKINS, P A (DR) (HM06743) | | | | | | | | | | | | | | | | | | | | | | | | | | | ● | | | | | | | | | | | | | | | | | | | | | | | |
| ENERGY EXCHANGE HOLISTIC CTRE (HM06816) | ● | | | | | | ● | | ● | | | | | | | | | | | | | | | | | | | | | | ● | | | | | | | | | | | | | | | | | | | |
| EVANS (HM06953) | | | | | | | | | | | | | | | | | | | | | | | | | | ● | | | | | | | | | | ● | | | | | | | | | | | | | | |
| FAIRFIELDS LANE WEST (HM07059) | | ● | ● | ● | ● | | ● | | | | | | | | | ● | | | | | | | | ● | | | | | ● | | | ● | ● | | | | | | | | | | | | | | | | | |
| FAMILY CHIRO & ALT MED CTRE (HM07081) | | ● | ● | ● | | | ● | | | | | | | ● | | ● | | | | | | | | | | | ● | | | | ● | ● | | ● | | | | | | | | | | | | | | | | |
| FAREHAM CHIROPRACTIC CENTRE (HM07102) | | | | | | | | | | | | | | | | | | | | | | | | | | | ● | | | | | | | | | | | | | | | | | | | | | | | |
| FIELD, JONATHAN (HM07260) | | | | | | | | | | | | | | | | | | | | | | | | | | | ● | | | | | | | | | | | | | | | | | | | | | | | |
| FIT FEET CHIROPODY (HM07361) | | | | | | | | | | | | | | | | | | | | | | | | | | ● | | | | | | | | | | | | | | | | | | | | | | | | |
| FOOT SHOP (HM07486) | | | | | | | | | | | | | | | | | | | | | | | | | | ● | | | | | | | | | | | | | | | | | | | | | | | | |
| FOREVER LIVING PRODUCTS (HM07555) | | | | | | | | | | | | | | | | | | | | | | | | | | | | | | | | | ● | | | | | | | | | | | | | | | | | |
| FOSSEY, LYNETTE (HM07585) | | | | | | | ● | | | | | | | | | | | | | | | | | | | | | | | | | | | | | | | | | | | | | | | | | | | |
| FOSTER, JAMES M ASSOCIATES (HM07593) | | | | | | | | | | | | | | | | | | | | | | ● | | | | ● | | | | | | | | | | ● | | | | | | | | | | | | | | |
| FOX, ANTONY D (DR) (HM07631) | | | | | | | | | | | | | | | | ● | | | | | | | | | | | | | | | | | | | | | | | | | | | | | | | | | | |
| FREDA, ROSE (HM07705) | | | | | | | ● | | | | | | | | | | | | | | | | | | | | | | | | | | | | | | | | | | | | | | | | | | | |
| GARLAND, GLENN D (HM07890) | | | | | | | | | | | | | | | | | | | | | | | | | | | ● | | | | | | | | | | | | | | | | | | | | | | | |
| GODWIN, PAUL & JENNY (HM08193) | | | | | | | | | | | | | | | | | | | | | | | | | | | ● | | | | | | | | | | | | | | | | | | | | | | | |
| GORMAN, JOHN (HM08293) | | | | | | | | | | | | | | | | | | | | | | | | | | | ● | | | | | | | | | | | | | | | | | | | | | | | |
| GROVE NATURAL THERAPY CENTRE (HM08609) | | | ● | ● | | | ● | | | | | | | | | ● | | | | | | | | | ● | | ● | | | ● | | | | | ● | | | | | | | | | | | | | | | |
| HANTSCARE (HM08947) | | ● | ● | | | | | | | | | | | | | | | | | ● | | | | | | | ● | | | | | | | | | | | | | | | | | | | | | ● | | |
| HAYLING ISLAND CHIRO CLINIC (HM09268) | | | ● | | | | | | | | | | | | | | | | | | | | | | | | ● | | | | | | | | | | | | | | | | | | | | | | | |
| HEAL-ALL HERB AND ACU CTRE (HM09315) | | ● | ● | | | | | | | | | | | | | | | | | | | | | | | | | | | | | | | | | | | ● | | | | | | | | | | | | |
| HEALTHWISE (HM09419) | | | ● | | | | | | | | | | | | | | | | | | | | | | | | | | | | | | | | | | | | | | | | | | | | | | | |

# A - F Therapies at Practices/Businesses

| Business by County with Reference no. | Absent Healing | Acupressure | Acupuncture | Alexander Technique | Allergy Testing | Anthroposohical Med | Aromatherapy | Art Therapy | Aura Therapy | Auricular Therapy | Auto Suggestion | Autogenic Training | Aversion Therapy | Ayurvedic Medicine | Baby Massage | Bach Remedies | Bates Method | Beauty Therapy | Bio-energetics | Biofeedback | Biomagnetic Therapy | Biomechanics | Bonesetting | Bowen Therapy | Chinese Herbal Medicine | Chiropody | Chiropractic | Clinical Ecology | Cognitive Therapy | Colonic Hydrotherapy | Colour Therapy | Complementary Therapy | Counselling | Cranial Osteopathy | Cranio-Sacral Therapy | Cryo Surgery | Crystal Healing | Cupping | Cymatics | Dance Movement Thrpy | Dietician | Do-In | Douching | Dowsing | Drama Therapy | Electrolipolysis | Electrolysis | Electrotherapy | Encounter Groups | Faith Healing |
|---|---|---|---|---|---|---|---|---|---|---|---|---|---|---|---|---|---|---|---|---|---|---|---|---|---|---|---|---|---|---|---|---|---|---|---|---|---|---|---|---|---|---|---|---|---|---|---|---|---|---|
| HEARNE, BRIAN (HM09440) | | | | | | | | | | | | | | | | | | | | | | | | | ● | | | | | | | | | | | | | | | | | | | | | | | | |
| HEDGE END CHIROPRACTIC CLINIC (HM09492) | | | | | | | | | | | | | | | | | | | | | | | | | | ● | | | | | | | | | | | | | | | | | | | | | | | |
| HERB MEDIC (HM09592) | | | ● | | | | | | | | | | | | | | | | | | | | | | ● | | | | | | | | | | | | | | | | | | | | | | | | | |
| HERBERT, S J (HM09655) | | | | | | | | | | | | | | | | | | | | | | | | | | ● | | | | | | | | | | | | | | | | | | | | | | | |
| HERBERT, STUART (HM09656) | | | | | | | | | | | | | | | | | | | | | | | | | | ● | | | | | | | | | | | | | | | | | | | | | | | |
| HIGH STREET CLINIC (HM09742) | | | ● | | | | ● | | | | | | | | | | | | | | | | | | | ● | ● | | | | | | ● | | | | | | | | | | | | | | | | | |
| HILLYER, ANDREW (HM09810) | | | | | | | | | | | | | | | | ● | | | | | | | | | | | | | | | | | | | | | | | | | | | | | | | | | | |
| HOBBS, T J (HM09860) | | | | | | | ● | | | | | | | | | | | | | | | | | ● | | | | | | | | | | | | | | | | | | | | | | | | | | |
| HOLBURY CHIROPRACTIC CLINIC (HM09919) | | | | | | | | | | | | | | | | | | | | | | | | | | ● | | | | | | | | | | | | | | | | | | | | | | | |
| HOLISTIC ARTS STUDIOS (HM09948) | | | | | | | | | | | | | | | | | | | | | | | | | | | | | | | ● | | | | | | | | | | | | | | | | | | |
| HOLISTIC TREATMENTS (HM10000) | | | | | | | ● | | | | | | | | | | | | | | | | | | | | | | | | | | | | | | | | | | | | | | | | | | | |
| HOMEWOOD CHIROPRACTIC CLINIC (HM10082) | | | | | | | | | | | | | | | | | | | | | | | | | | ● | | | | | | | | | | | | | | | | | | | | | | | |
| HOMOEOPATHIC CLINIC (HM10088) | | ● | | | | | | | | | | | | | | | | | | | | | | | | ● | | | | | | | | | | | | | | | | | | | | | | | |
| HORNE, SUE (HM10174) | | | ● | | | | | | | | | | | | | | | | | | | | | | | | | | | | | | | | | | | | | | | | | | | | | | | |
| HORNE, SUE (HM10173) | | | ● | | | | | | | | | | | | | | | | | | | | | | | | | | | | | | | | | | | | | | | | | | | | | | | |
| HUTCHINGS, MARGARET (HM10448) | | | | | | | ● | | | | | | | | | | | | | | | | | | | | | | | | | | | | | | | | | | | | | | | | | | | |
| HYPNOTHRPY FOR POSITIVE CHANGE (HM10542) | | | | | | | | | | | | | ● | | | | | | | | | | | | | | | | | | | | | | | | | | | | | | | | | | | | |
| HYTHE CHIROPRACTIC CLINIC (HM10545) | | | | | | | | | | | | | | | | | | | | | | | | | | ● | | | | | | | | | | | | | | | | | | | | | | | |
| INLPTA (HM10633) | | | | | | | | | | | ● | | | | | | | | | | | | | | | | | | | | | | ● | | | | | | | | | | | | | | | | | |
| JACKSON, J (HM10840) | | | | | | | | | | | | | | | | | | | | | | | | | ● | | | | | | | | | | | | | | | | | | | | | | | | |
| JENKINS, RUSSELL (HM10994) | | | | | | | ● | | | | | | | | | ● | | | | | | | | | | | | | | | | | ● | ● | | | | | | | | | | | | | | | | |
| KAYIZA, M S (HM11361) | | | | | | | | | | | | | | | | | | | | | | | | | | ● | | | | | | | | | | | | | | | | | | | | | | | |
| KD PHYSIOTHERAPY (HM11363) | | | ● | | | | | | | | | | | | | | | | | | | | | | | | | | | | | | | | | | | | | | | | | | | | | | | |
| KIN HON CLINIC (HM11618) | | | ● | | | | | | | | | | | | | | | | | | | | | | | | | | | | | | | | | | | | | | | | | | | | | | | |
| LAMONT, KEITH (HM11910) | | | ● | | | | | | | | | | | | | | | | | | | | | | | | | | | | | | | | | | | | | | | | | | | | | | | |
| LAURENT, PIERRE (HM12013) | | | | | | | ● | | | | | | | | | | | | | | | | | | | | | | | | | | | | | | | | | | | | | | | | | | | |
| LAURIDSEN, H (HM12014) | | | | | | | | | | | | | | | | | | | | | | | | | | ● | | | | | | | | | | | | | | | | | | | | | | | |
| LAVERTY, SUSIE (HM12033) | | | | | | | | | | | | | | | | ● | | | | | | | | | | | | | | | | | | | | | | | | | | | | | | | | | | |
| LAVERTY, SUSIE (HM12032) | | | | | | | | | | | | | | | | ● | | | | | | | | | | | | | | | | | | | | | ● | | | | | | | | | | | | | |
| LEWIS, D J S (HM12288) | | | | | | | | | | | | | | | | ● | | | | | | | | | | | | | | | | | | | | | | | | | | | | | | | | | | |
| LISLE, THOMAS (HM12455) | | | | | | | | | | | | | | | | | | | | | | ● | | | | ● | | | | | | | | | | ● | | | | | | | | | | | | | | |
| LOCKHAMS THERAPY CENTRE (HM12545) | ● | | | | | | | | | | | | | | | | | | | | | | | | | | | | | | | | | | | | | | | | | | | ● | | | | | | |
| LOWE, KENNETH (HM12699) | | ● | ● | | | | | | | | | | | | | | | | | | | | ● | | | | | ● | | | | ● | | | | | | | | | ● | | | | | | | ● | | |
| LUBBOCK, BRIDGET (HM12715) | | | ● | | | | | | | | | | | | | | | | | | | | | | | | | | | | | | | | | | | | | | | | | | | | | | | |

# A - F Therapies at Practices/Businesses

| Business by County with Reference no. | Absent Healing | Acupressure | Acupuncture | Alexander Technique | Allergy Testing | Anthroposohical Med | Aromatherapy | Art Therapy | Aura Therapy | Auricular Therapy | Auto Suggestion | Autogenic Training | Aversion Therapy | Ayurvedic Medicine | Baby Massage | Bach Remedies | Bates Method |
|---|---|---|---|---|---|---|---|---|---|---|---|---|---|---|---|---|---|
| LUNT, JULIE (HM12742) | | | | | | | ● | | | | | | | | | | |
| LYMINGTON CHIROPRACTIC CLINIC (HM12759) | | | | | | | | | | | | | | | | | |
| MAITLAND-TITTERTON, SARAH (HM12952) | | | | | | | | | | | | | | | | ● | |
| MARLOR, J (HM13127) | | | | | | | | | | | | | | | | | |
| MCCANN, JACQUI (HM13389) | | | ● | | | | | | | | | | | | | | |
| MCTIMONEY CHIROPRACTICE (HM13616) | | | | | | | | | | | | | | | | | |
| MELHUISH, J I (DR) (HM13705) | | | | | | | | | | | | | | | | | |
| MILLS, A (HM13923) | | | | ● | | | | | | | | | | | | | |
| MINDWORKS HYPNOTHERAPY CLINIC (HM13969) | | | | | | | | | | | | | | | | | |
| MORLAND-AUSTIN, FIONA (HM14179) | | | | | | | | | | | | | | | | ● | |
| MORLEY, KAREN (HM14184) | | | | | | | ● | | | | | | | | | | |
| NATURAL HEALTH SERVICE (HM14595) | | | | | | | ● | | | | | | | | | | |
| NEW HORIZON AROMATICS (HM14818) | | | | | | | ● | | | | | | | | | | |
| NEW MILTON CHIROPRACTIC CLINIC (HM14825) | | | ● | | | | | | | | | | | | | | |
| NICOLA @ HOLISTIC HOUSE (HM14926) | | | | | | | ● | | | | | | | | | | |
| NOMA (HM14987) | | | ● | | | | | | | | | | | | | | |
| NORMAN, J M (HM15004) | | | | | | | | | | | | | | | | | |
| NORTH END CHIROPRACTIC CLINIC (HM15027) | | | | | | | | | | | | | | | | | |
| O'NEILL, REGINA (HM15336) | | | | | | | | | | | | | | | | | |
| PADDOCK, MADELINE (HM15562) | | | | | | | ● | | | | | | | | | | |
| PARCHMENT STREET CLINIC (HM15646) | | | ● | | | | ● | | | | | | | | | | |
| PARK GATE CHIROPRACTIC CENTRE (HM15665) | | | | | | | | | | | | | | | | | |
| PAUC, R A (HM15837) | | | | | | | | | | | | | | | | | |
| PEARSON & MARKLOVE (HM15907) | | | ● | | | | | | | | | | | | | | |
| PHOENIX HOLISTIC CENTRE (HM16156) | ● | | ● | | | | ● | ● | | | | | | | | | |
| RABLEY, M (HM16835) | | | | | | | | | | | | | | | | | |
| RADIN, J (HM16850) | | | | | | | | | | | | | | | | | |
| RICHARDS, CLAIRE (HM17249) | | | | | | | | | ● | | | | | | | ● | |
| RINGWOOD CHIROPRACTIC CLINIC (HM17355) | | | | | | | | | | | | | | | | | |
| RINGWOOD NATURAL HEALTH CLINIC (HM17357) | | | ● | ● | | | ● | | | | | | | | | | |
| RINGWOOD PHYSIOTHERAPY CENTRE (HM17358) | | | ● | | | | | | | | | | | | | | |
| RODHAM, SANDIE (HM17528) | | | | | | | | | | | | | | | | ● | |
| ROUSSOS, AMANDA (HM17677) | | | ● | | | | ● | | | ● | | | | | | | |
| S E E D INSTITUTE (HM17805) | | | | | | | ● | | | | | | | | | | |

| Business by County with Reference no. | Beauty Therapy | Bio-energetics | Biofeedback | Biomagnetic Therapy | Biomechanics | Bonesetting | Bowen Therapy | Chinese Herbal Medicine | Chiropody | Chiropractic | Clinical Ecology | Cognitive Therapy | Colonic Hydrotherapy | Colour Therapy | Complementary Therapy | Counselling | Cranial Osteopathy |
|---|---|---|---|---|---|---|---|---|---|---|---|---|---|---|---|---|---|
| LUNT, JULIE (HM12742) | | | | | | | | | | | | | | | | | |
| LYMINGTON CHIROPRACTIC CLINIC (HM12759) | | | | | | | | | ● | ● | | | | | | ● | ● |
| MAITLAND-TITTERTON, SARAH (HM12952) | | | | | | | | | | | | | | | | | |
| MARLOR, J (HM13127) | | | | | ● | | | | ● | | | | | | | | |
| MCCANN, JACQUI (HM13389) | | | | | | | | | | | | | | | | | |
| MCTIMONEY CHIROPRACTICE (HM13616) | | | | | | | | | | ● | | | | | | | |
| MELHUISH, J I (DR) (HM13705) | | | | | | | | | | ● | | | | | | | |
| MILLS, A (HM13923) | | | | | | | | | | | | | | | | | |
| MINDWORKS HYPNOTHERAPY CLINIC (HM13969) | | | | | | | | | | | | ● | | | | ● | |
| MORLAND-AUSTIN, FIONA (HM14179) | | | | | | | | | | | | | | | | | |
| MORLEY, KAREN (HM14184) | | | | | | | | | | | | | | | | | |
| NATURAL HEALTH SERVICE (HM14595) | | | | | | | | | | ● | | | | | | ● | |
| NEW HORIZON AROMATICS (HM14818) | | | | | | | | | | | | | | | | | |
| NEW MILTON CHIROPRACTIC CLINIC (HM14825) | | | | | | | | | | ● | | | | | ● | | |
| NICOLA @ HOLISTIC HOUSE (HM14926) | | | | | | | | | | | | | | | | | |
| NOMA (HM14987) | | | | | | | | | | | | | | | | | |
| NORMAN, J M (HM15004) | | | | | | | | | ● | | | | | | | | |
| NORTH END CHIROPRACTIC CLINIC (HM15027) | | | | | | | | | | ● | | | | | | | |
| O'NEILL, REGINA (HM15336) | | | | | | | | | | ● | | | | | | | |
| PADDOCK, MADELINE (HM15562) | | | | | | | | | | | | | | | | | |
| PARCHMENT STREET CLINIC (HM15646) | | | | | | | | | | ● | | | | | ● | ● | |
| PARK GATE CHIROPRACTIC CENTRE (HM15665) | | | | | | | | | | ● | | | | | | | |
| PAUC, R A (HM15837) | | | | | | | | | | ● | | | | | | | |
| PEARSON & MARKLOVE (HM15907) | | | | | | | | | | | | | | | | | |
| PHOENIX HOLISTIC CENTRE (HM16156) | | | | | | | | | | | | | | | ● | ● | |
| RABLEY, M (HM16835) | | | | | | | | | | ● | | | | | | | |
| RADIN, J (HM16850) | | | | | | | | | | ● | | | | | | | |
| RICHARDS, CLAIRE (HM17249) | | | | | | | | | | | | | | ● | | | |
| RINGWOOD CHIROPRACTIC CLINIC (HM17355) | | | | | | | | | | ● | | | | | | | |
| RINGWOOD NATURAL HEALTH CLINIC (HM17357) | | | | | | | ● | | | ● | | | | | | | ● |
| RINGWOOD PHYSIOTHERAPY CENTRE (HM17358) | | | | | | | | | | | | | | | | | |
| RODHAM, SANDIE (HM17528) | | | | | | | | | | | | | | | | | |
| ROUSSOS, AMANDA (HM17677) | | | | | | | | | | | | | | | | | |
| S E E D INSTITUTE (HM17805) | | | | | | | | | | | | | | | | | |

| Business by County with Reference no. | Cranio-Sacral Therapy | Cryo Surgery | Crystal Healing | Cupping | Cymatics | Dance Movement Thrpy | Dietician | Do-In | Douching | Dowsing | Drama Therapy | Electrolipolysis | Electrolysis | Electrotherapy | Encounter Groups | Faith Healing |
|---|---|---|---|---|---|---|---|---|---|---|---|---|---|---|---|---|
| LUNT, JULIE (HM12742) | | | | | | | | | | | | | | | | |
| LYMINGTON CHIROPRACTIC CLINIC (HM12759) | | | | | | | | | | | | | | ● | | |
| MAITLAND-TITTERTON, SARAH (HM12952) | | | | | | | | | | | | | | | | |
| MARLOR, J (HM13127) | | | | | | | | | | | | | | | | |
| MCCANN, JACQUI (HM13389) | | | | | | | | | | | | | | | | |
| MCTIMONEY CHIROPRACTICE (HM13616) | | | | | | | | | | | | | | | | |
| MELHUISH, J I (DR) (HM13705) | | | | | | | | | | | | | | | | |
| MILLS, A (HM13923) | | | | | | | | | | | | | | | | |
| MINDWORKS HYPNOTHERAPY CLINIC (HM13969) | | | | | | | | | | | | | | | | |
| MORLAND-AUSTIN, FIONA (HM14179) | | | | | | | | | | | | | | | | |
| MORLEY, KAREN (HM14184) | | | | | | | | | | | | | | | | |
| NATURAL HEALTH SERVICE (HM14595) | | | | | | | | | | | | | | | | |
| NEW HORIZON AROMATICS (HM14818) | | | | | | | | | | | | | | | | |
| NEW MILTON CHIROPRACTIC CLINIC (HM14825) | | | | | | | | | | | | | | | | |
| NICOLA @ HOLISTIC HOUSE (HM14926) | | | | | | | | | | | | | | | | |
| NOMA (HM14987) | | | | | | | | | | | | | | | | |
| NORMAN, J M (HM15004) | | | | | | | | | | | | | | | | |
| NORTH END CHIROPRACTIC CLINIC (HM15027) | | | | | | | | | | | | | | | | |
| O'NEILL, REGINA (HM15336) | | | | | | | | | | | | | | | | |
| PADDOCK, MADELINE (HM15562) | | | | | | | | | | | | | | | | |
| PARCHMENT STREET CLINIC (HM15646) | | | | | | | | | | | | | | | | |
| PARK GATE CHIROPRACTIC CENTRE (HM15665) | | | | | | | | | | | | | | | | |
| PAUC, R A (HM15837) | | | | | | | | | | | | | | | | |
| PEARSON & MARKLOVE (HM15907) | | | | | | | | | | | | | | | | |
| PHOENIX HOLISTIC CENTRE (HM16156) | | | ● | | | | | | | | | | | | | |
| RABLEY, M (HM16835) | | | | | | | | | | | | | | | | |
| RADIN, J (HM16850) | | | | | | | | | | | | | | | | |
| RICHARDS, CLAIRE (HM17249) | | | ● | | | | | | | ● | | | | | | ● |
| RINGWOOD CHIROPRACTIC CLINIC (HM17355) | | | | | | | | | | | | | | | | |
| RINGWOOD NATURAL HEALTH CLINIC (HM17357) | | | | | | | | | | | | | | | | |
| RINGWOOD PHYSIOTHERAPY CENTRE (HM17358) | | | | | | | | | | | | | | | | |
| RODHAM, SANDIE (HM17528) | | | | | | | | | | | | | | | | |
| ROUSSOS, AMANDA (HM17677) | | | | | | | | | | | | | | | | |
| S E E D INSTITUTE (HM17805) | | | | | | | | | | | | | | | | |

# A - F Therapies at Practices/Businesses

| Business by County with Reference no. | Absent Healing | Acupressure | Acupuncture | Alexander Technique | Allergy Testing | Anthroposohical Med | Aromatherapy | Art Therapy | Aura Therapy | Auricular Therapy | Auto Suggestion | Autogenic Training | Aversion Therapy | Ayurvedic Medicine | Baby Massage | Bach Remedies | Bates Method | Beauty Therapy | Bio-energetics | Biofeedback | Biomagnetic Therapy | Biomechanics | Bonesetting | Bowen Therapy | Chinese Herbal Medicine | Chiropody | Chiropractic | Clinical Ecology | Cognitive Therapy | Colonic Hydrotherapy | Colour Therapy | Complementary Therapy | Counselling | Cranial Osteopathy | Cranio-Sacral Therapy | Cryo Surgery | Crystal Healing | Cupping | Cymatics | Dance Movement Thrpy | Dietician | Do-In | Douching | Dowsing | Drama Therapy | Electrolipolysis | Electrolysis | Electrotherapy | Encounter Groups | Faith Healing |
|---|---|---|---|---|---|---|---|---|---|---|---|---|---|---|---|---|---|---|---|---|---|---|---|---|---|---|---|---|---|---|---|---|---|---|---|---|---|---|---|---|---|---|---|---|---|---|---|---|---|---|
| SCANDINAVIAN CHIROPRACTIC CTRE (HM18002) | | | | | | | | | | | | | | | | | | | | | | | | | | | ● | | | | | | | | | | | | | | | | | | | | | | | | |
| SCOTT, HEATHER (HM18115) | | | | | | | ● | | | | | | | | | | | | | | | | | | | | | | | | | | | | | | | | | | | | | | | | | | | | |
| SCRIVENER, JEAN (HM18154) | | | | | | | ● | | | | | | | | | | | | | | | | | | | | | | | | | | | | | | | | | | | | | | | | | | | | |
| SEARLE, MAUREEN (HM18175) | | | | | | | ● | | | | | | | | | | | | | | | | | | | | | | | | | | | | | | | | | | | | | | | | | | | | |
| SHEPHERD, P A (HM18414) | | | ● | | | | | | | | | | | | | | | | | | | | | | | | | | | | | | | | | | | | | | | | | | | | | | | | |
| SHIRLEY CHIROPRACTIC CLINIC (HM18484) | | | | | | | | | | | | | | | | | | | | | | | | | | | ● | | | | | | | | | | | | | | | | | | | | | | | | |
| SIMCOE CLINIC (HM18549) | | ● | | | | | | | | | | | | | | | | | | | | | | | | ● | ● | | | | | | | | | | | | | | | | | | | | | | | | |
| SOLENT CHIROPRACTIC CLINIC (HM18871) | | | | | | | | | | | | | | | | | | | | | | | | | | | ● | | | | | | | | | | | | | | | | | | | | | | | | |
| SOUTHGATE NAT THERAPY CLINIC (HM18937) | | | ● | | | | ● | | | | | | | | | | | | | | | | | ● | | | | | | | | ● | ● | ● | | | | | | | | | | | | | | | | | |
| SOUTHSEA CENTRE FOR COMP MED (HM18943) | ● | ● | ● | | | | ● | | | | | | ● | | | | | | | | | | | | | | ● | | | | | ● | | ● | | | | ● | | | ● | | | ● | | | | | | |
| SOUTHSEA CHIROPRACTIC CLINIC (HM18944) | | | | | | | | | | | | | | | | | | | | | | | | | | | ● | | | | | | | | | | | | | | | | | | | | | | | | |
| ST LAWRENCE HOUSE CHIROPRACTIC (HM19084) | | | | | | | | | | | | | | | | | | | | | | | | | | | ● | | | | | | | | | | | | | | | | | | | | | | | | |
| STICKLAND, ROBERTA (HM19288) | | | | | | | | | | | | | | | | | | | | | | | | | | | ● | | | | | | | | | | | | | | | | | | | | | | | | |
| SUMMERS, DIANE (HM19490) | | | ● | | | | | | | | | | | | | | | | | | | | | | | | | | | | | | | | | | | | | | | | | | | | | | | | |
| SWABY, DINAH (HM19561) | | | | | | | ● | | | | | | | | | | | | | | | | | | | | | | | | | | | | | | | | | | | | | | | | | | | | |
| THOMA, ANDREW (HM19923) | | | | | | | | | | | | | | | | | | | | | | | | | | | ● | | | | | | | | | | | | | | | | | | | | | | | | |
| THOMSON, D (HM20003) | | | ● | | | | | | | | | | | | | | | | | | | | | | | | | | | | | | | | | | | | | | | | | | | | | | | | |
| TURNER, CATHY (HM20420) | | | | | | | ● | | | | | | | | | | | | | | | | | | | | | | | | | ● | | | | | | | | | | | | | | | | | | | |
| VINCE, LINDA (HM20668) | | | | | | | | | | | | | | | | | | | | | | | | | | ● | | | | | | | | | | | | | | | | | | | | | | | | | |
| WELBAC CLINIC (HM21119) | | | | | | | | | | | | | | | | | | | | | | | | | | | ● | | | | | | | | | | | | | | | | | | | | | | | | |
| WELL HOUSE HOLISTIC HLTH CTRE (HM21138) | | | ● | | | | ● | | | | | | | | | | | | | | | | | | | | | | | | | | ● | | | | ● | | | | | | | | | | | | | |
| WILLIAMS, GEOFFREY (HM21558) | | | | | | | | | | | | | | | | | | | | | | | | | | | ● | | | | | | | | | | | | | | | | | | | | | | | | |
| WINCHESTER CHIROPRACTIC CLINIC (HM21691) | | | ● | | | | | | | | | | | | | | | | | | | | | | | | ● | | | | | | | | | | | | | | | | | | | | | | | | |
| WINCHESTER HOM PRACTICE (HM21692) | | ● | ● | | | | ● | | | | | | | | | ● | | | | | | | | | | | | | | | | ● | ● | ● | | | ● | | | | ● | | | | | | | | | |
| WRIGHT, SAMANTHA (HM21948) | | | | | | | | | | | | | | | | | | | | | | | | | | ● | | | | | | | | | | | | | | | | | | | | | | | | | |
| **HEREFORD & WORCESTER** | | | | | | | | | | | | | | | | | | | | | | | | | | | | | | | | | | | | | | | | | | | | | | | | | | | |
| HALL, LYNN (HM08783) | | | | | | | | | | | | | | | | ● | | | | | | | | | | | | | | | | | | | | | | | | | | | | | | | | | | | |
| **HEREFORDSHIRE** | | | | | | | | | | | | | | | | | | | | | | | | | | | | | | | | | | | | | | | | | | | | | | | | | | | | |
| BEAUTY IS YOURS (HM01999) | | | | | | | ● | | | | | | | | | | | | | | | | | ● | | | | | | | | ● | | | | | ● | | | | | | | | | | | | | |
| BROADVIEW NATURAL HEALTH CTRE (HM03119) | | | ● | | | | ● | | | | | | | | | | | | | | | | | | | | | | | | | | ● | | | | | | | | | | | | | | | | | |
| BROADVIEW NATURAL HEALTH CTRE (HM03120) | | | ● | | | | | | | | | | | | | | | | | | | | | | | | | | | | | | | | | | | | | | | | | | | | | | | | |
| BURNELL, SUE (HM03395) | | | | | | | | | | | | | | | | ● | | | | | | | | | | | | | | | | | | | | | | | | | | | | | | | | | | | |
| HARVEY, MARTIN (HM09164) | | | ● | | | | | | | | | | | | | | | | | | | | | | | | | | | | | | | | | | | | | | | | | | | | | | | | |
| HEALING HERBS (HM09344) | | | | | | | | | | | | | | | | ● | | | | | | | | | | | | | | | | | | | | | | | | | | | | | | | | | | | |

# A - F Therapies at Practices/Businesses

| Business by County with Reference no. | Absent Healing | Acupressure | Acupuncture | Alexander Technique | Allergy Testing | Anthroposohical Med | Aromatherapy | Art Therapy | Aura Therapy | Auricular Therapy | Auto Suggestion | Autogenic Training | Aversion Therapy | Ayurvedic Medicine | Baby Massage | Bach Remedies | Bates Method | Beauty Therapy | Bio-energetics | Biofeedback | Biomagnetic Therapy | Biomechanics | Bonesetting | Bowen Therapy | Chinese Herbal Medicine | Chiropody | Chiropractic | Clinical Ecology | Cognitive Therapy | Colonic Hydrotherapy | Colour Therapy | Complementary Therapy | Counselling | Cranial Osteopathy | Cranio-Sacral Therapy | Cryo Surgery | Crystal Healing | Cupping | Cymatics | Dance Movement Thrpy | Dietician | Do-In | Douching | Dowsing | Drama Therapy | Electrolipolysis | Electrolysis | Electrotherapy | Encounter Groups | Faith Healing |
|---|---|---|---|---|---|---|---|---|---|---|---|---|---|---|---|---|---|---|---|---|---|---|---|---|---|---|---|---|---|---|---|---|---|---|---|---|---|---|---|---|---|---|---|---|---|---|---|---|---|---|
| HEBBLETHWAITE, PRISCILLA (HM09486) | | | | ● | | | | | | | | | | | | | | | | | | | | | | | | | | | | | | | | | | | | | | | | | | | | | | |
| HEREFORD CENTRE (HM09677) | | | ● | ● | ● | | ● | | | | | | | | | | | | | | | | | | | | ● | | | | | ● | ● | | | | | | | | | | | | | | | | | |
| HEREFORD CHIROPRACTIC CLINIC (HM09678) | | | | | | | | | | | | | | | | | | | | | | | | | | | ● | | | | | | | | | | | | | | | | | | | | | | | |
| LEDBURY NATURAL HEALTH CENTRE (HM12122) | | | | ● | ● | | ● | | | | | | | | | ● | | | | | | | | | | | ● | | | | | | ● | | | | | | | | | | | | | | | | | |
| LEOMINSTER OSTEOPATHS (HM12221) | | | | | | | | | | | | | | | | | | | | | | | | | | | | | | | | | | ● | | | | | | | | | | | | | | | | |
| LOOKERS NATURAL THERAPY CLINIC (HM12634) | | | | | | | ● | | | | | | | | | | | | | | | | | | | | | | | | | | | | | | | | | | | | | | | | | | | |
| NITTY GRITTY WHOLEFOODS (HM14953) | | | | | | | ● | | | | | | | | | ● | | | | | | | | | | | | | | | | | | | | | | | | | | | | | | | | | | |
| PARFETT, GORDON (HM15653) | | | ● | | | | | | | | | | | | | | | | | | | | | | | | | | | | | | | | | | | | | | | | | | | | | | | |
| TEDDER, CATHRINE (HM19814) | | | | | | | | | | | | | | | | | | | | | | | | | | ● | | | | | | | | | | | | | | | | | | | | | | | | |
| TUREY, J T (HM20406) | | | | | | | | | | | | | | | | | | | | | | | | | | | ● | | | | | | | | | | | | | | | | | | | | | | | |
| WILLCOCKS, T & S (HM21519) | | | | | | | ● | | | | | | | | | | | | | | | | | ● | | | | | | | | | | | | | | | | | | | | | | | | | | |
| **HERTFORDSHIRE** | | | | | | | | | | | | | | | | | | | | | | | | | | | | | | | | | | | | | | | | | | | | | | | | | | |
| ABUNDANCE HEALING (HM00145) | | | | | | | | | | | | | | | | | | | | | | | | | | | | | | | | | ● | | | | | | | | | | | | | | | | | |
| ACUPUNCTURE CENTRE (HM00250) | | | ● | | | | | | | | | | | | | | | | | | | | | | | | | | | | | | | | | | | | | | | | | | | | | | | |
| ALDER, DENNIS (HM00497) | | | | | | | | | | | | | | | | | | | | | | ● | | | | ● | | | | | | | | | | ● | | | | | | | | | | | | | | |
| ALEXANDER TECHNIQUE (HM00531) | | | | ● | | | | | | | | | | | | | | | | | | | | | | | | | | | | | | | | | | | | | | | | | | | | | | |
| ALLEN, JULIE & LEN (HM00613) | | | | | | | | | | | | | | | | | | | | | | | | | | | | | ● | | | | ● | | | | | | | | | | | | | | | | | |
| ALTERNATIVE CHOICES (HM00697) | | | ● | | | | | | | | | | | | | | | | | | | | | | ● | | | | | | | | | | | | ● | | | | | | | | | | | | | |
| ARNOLD, PETER & JACKIE (HM01036) | | | ● | | | | | | | | | | | | | | | | | | | | | | | | | | | | | | | | | | | | | | | | | | | | | | | |
| AROMA ROOM (HM01055) | | | | | | | ● | | | | | | | | | | | | | | | | | | | | | | | | | | | | | | | | | | | | | | | | | | | |
| AROMATHERAPY BY ANTONIO (HM01095) | | | | | | | ● | | | | | | | | | | | | | | | | | | | | | | | | | | | | | | | | | | | | | | | | | | | |
| AROMATHERAPY BY JOANNA JONES (HM01096) | | | | | | | ● | | | | | | | | | | | | | | | | | | | | | | | | | | | | | | | | | | | | | | | | | | | |
| AROMATHERAPY IS FLOWER POWER (HM01117) | | | | | | | ● | | | | | | | | | | | | | | | | | | | | | | | | | | | | | | | | | | | | | | | | | | | |
| ASHDOWN CLINIC (HM01205) | | | ● | | ● | | ● | | | | | | | | | | | | | | | ● | | ● | ● | | | | | | | | ● | ● | | | | | | | ● | | | | | | | | | |
| ASHETON, KEVIN (HM01214) | | | | ● | | | | | | | | | | | | | | | | | | | | | | | | | | | | | | | | | | | | | | | | | | | | | | |
| ASSOCIATES HEAD & SHORT (HM01276) | | | | | | | | | | | | | | | | | | | | | | ● | | | | ● | | | | | | | | | | ● | | | | | | | | | | | | | | |
| ASSOCIATES HEAD & SHORT (HM01277) | | | | | | | | | | | | | | | | | | | | | | ● | | | | ● | | | | | | | | | | ● | | | | | | | | | | | | | | |
| ASSOCIATION OF STRESS MNGMT (HM01293) | | | | | | | | | | | | | | | | | | | | | | | | | | | | | | | | | ● | | | | | | | | | | | | | | | | | |
| AUBEELUCK, L (HM01341) | | | ● | | | | | | | | | | | | | | | | | | | | | | | | | | | | | | | | | | | | | | | | | | | | | | | |
| AUTOGENIC TRAINING (HM01372) | | | | | | | | | | | | ● | | | | | | | | | | | | | | | | | | | | | | | | | | | | | | | | | | | | | | |
| BARNES, SHEENA (HM01754) | | | | | | | ● | | | | | | | | | | | | | | | | | | | | | | | | | | | | | | | | | | | | | | | | | | | |
| BARNET CHIROPODY SURGERY (HM01757) | | | | | | | | | | | | | | | | | | | | | | ● | | | | ● | | | | | | | | | | ● | | | | | | | | | | | | | | |
| BASSETT & ASSOCIATES (HM01852) | | | | | | | | | | | | | | | | | | | | | | | | | | | ● | | | | | | | | | | | | | | | | | | | | | | | |
| BASSETT CLINIC (HM01853) | | | ● | | | | ● | | | | | | | | | | | | | | | | | | | | ● | | | | | | ● | | | | | | | | | | | | | | | | | |

# A - F Therapies at Practices/Businesses

| Business by County with Reference no. | Absent Healing | Acupressure | Acupuncture | Alexander Technique | Allergy Testing | Anthroposohical Med | Aromatherapy | Art Therapy | Aura Therapy | Auricular Therapy |
|---|---|---|---|---|---|---|---|---|---|---|
| BEAUCHAMP BAGENAL (HM01983) | | | | ● | | | | | | |
| BETA HEALTH CLINIC (HM02229) | | | ● | | | | | | | |
| BISHOPS STORTFORD CHIRO CLINIC (HM02415) | | | | | | | | | | |
| BISHOP'S STORTFORD HOMEOPATHIC (HM02416) | | | | | ● | | | | | |
| BODY MECHANICS THERAPY CLINIC (HM02598) | | | | | | | | | | |
| BOREHAMWOOD CHIRO CLINIC (HM02717) | | | | | | | | | | |
| BRADBURY, TANYA (HM02843) | | | | | | | ● | | | |
| BRIGGS-WILSON, A (HM03037) | ● | | | | | | ● | | | |
| BRIND, KEVIN (HM03053) | | | ● | | | | | | | |
| BROUWER JOOP (HM03204) | | | ● | | | | | | | |
| BURYHILL PHYSIOTHERAPY (HM03456) | | | ● | | | | | | | |
| BUTTERFIELD, ROBIN (HM03496) | | | | | | | | | | |
| CHANDLER, LENA (HM03975) | | | | | | | ● | | | |
| CHESHUNT CHIROPRACTIC CLINIC (HM04117) | | | | | | | | | | |
| CHINESE MEDICAL CENTRE (HM04230) | | | ● | | | | | | | |
| CHIROPRACTIC CONSULTANT SVS (HM04396) | | | | | | | | | | |
| CHIROPRACTORS MCTIMONEY (HM04406) | | | | | | | | | | |
| CHOPRA, S (HM04426) | | | | | | | | | | |
| CHOPRA, S (HM04427) | | | | | | | | | | |
| CLARE JAMES HEALTH FOODS (HM04532) | | | | | | ● | ● | | | |
| CLNC OF ACU & CHINESE HRBL MED (HM04727) | | | ● | | | | | | | |
| COLE, EVA (HM04814) | | | | | | | | | | |
| CONISTON PHYSIOTHERAPY CLINIC (HM04980) | | | ● | | | | | | ● | |
| COOPER, FELICITY (HM05101) | | | | | | | | | | |
| CRAIB, MARGARET (HM05345) | | | | | | | | | | |
| DAVEY, SARAH (HM05770) | | | | ● | | | | | | |
| DEVINE, MARY (HM06036) | | | | | | | | | | |
| DOYLE, AUDREY (HM06257) | | | | | | | | | | |
| DUDGEON, DELIA (HM06353) | | | | ● | | | | | | |
| ENGLISH, JEREMY A (HM06833) | | | | ● | | | | | | |
| EVANS, HELEN (HM06976) | | | | | | | | | | |
| EVANS, HELEN (HM06975) | | | | | | | | | | |
| GEMS (HM07969) | | | | | | | | | | |
| GEOFF THIEL, COUNS & PSYCHO (HM07986) | | | | | | | | | | |

| Business by County with Reference no. | Auto Suggestion | Autogenic Training | Aversion Therapy | Ayurvedic Medicine | Baby Massage | Bach Remedies | Bates Method | Beauty Therapy | Bio-energetics | Biofeedback |
|---|---|---|---|---|---|---|---|---|---|---|
| BEAUCHAMP BAGENAL (HM01983) | | | | | | | | | | |
| BETA HEALTH CLINIC (HM02229) | | | | | | | | | | |
| BISHOPS STORTFORD CHIRO CLINIC (HM02415) | | | | | | | | | | |
| BISHOP'S STORTFORD HOMEOPATHIC (HM02416) | | | | | | ● | | | | |
| BODY MECHANICS THERAPY CLINIC (HM02598) | | | | | | | | | | |
| BOREHAMWOOD CHIRO CLINIC (HM02717) | | | | | | | | | | |
| BRADBURY, TANYA (HM02843) | | | | | | | | | | |
| BRIGGS-WILSON, A (HM03037) | | | | | | | | | | |
| BRIND, KEVIN (HM03053) | | | | | | | | | | |
| BROUWER JOOP (HM03204) | | | | | | | | | | |
| BURYHILL PHYSIOTHERAPY (HM03456) | | | | | | | | | | |
| BUTTERFIELD, ROBIN (HM03496) | | | | | | | | | | |
| CHANDLER, LENA (HM03975) | | | | | | | | | | |
| CHESHUNT CHIROPRACTIC CLINIC (HM04117) | | | | | | | | | | |
| CHINESE MEDICAL CENTRE (HM04230) | | | | | | | | | | |
| CHIROPRACTIC CONSULTANT SVS (HM04396) | | | | | | | | | | |
| CHIROPRACTORS MCTIMONEY (HM04406) | | | | | | | | | | |
| CHOPRA, S (HM04426) | | | | | | | | | | |
| CHOPRA, S (HM04427) | | | | | | | | | | |
| CLARE JAMES HEALTH FOODS (HM04532) | | | | | | ● | | | | |
| CLNC OF ACU & CHINESE HRBL MED (HM04727) | | | | | | | | | | |
| COLE, EVA (HM04814) | | | | | | ● | | | | |
| CONISTON PHYSIOTHERAPY CLINIC (HM04980) | | | | | | | | | | |
| COOPER, FELICITY (HM05101) | | | | | | | | | | |
| CRAIB, MARGARET (HM05345) | | | | | | | | | | |
| DAVEY, SARAH (HM05770) | | | | | | | | | | |
| DEVINE, MARY (HM06036) | | | | | | | | | | |
| DOYLE, AUDREY (HM06257) | | | | | | | | | | |
| DUDGEON, DELIA (HM06353) | | | | | | ● | | | | |
| ENGLISH, JEREMY A (HM06833) | | | | | | | | | | |
| EVANS, HELEN (HM06976) | | | | | | | | | | |
| EVANS, HELEN (HM06975) | | | | | | | | | | |
| GEMS (HM07969) | | | | | | | | | | |
| GEOFF THIEL, COUNS & PSYCHO (HM07986) | | | | | | | | | | |

| Business by County with Reference no. | Biomagnetic Therapy | Biomechanics | Bonesetting | Bowen Therapy | Chinese Herbal Medicine | Chiropody | Chiropractic | Clinical Ecology | Cognitive Therapy | Colonic Hydrotherapy |
|---|---|---|---|---|---|---|---|---|---|---|
| BEAUCHAMP BAGENAL (HM01983) | | | | | | | | | | |
| BETA HEALTH CLINIC (HM02229) | | | | | | ● | | | | |
| BISHOPS STORTFORD CHIRO CLINIC (HM02415) | | | | | | | ● | | | |
| BISHOP'S STORTFORD HOMEOPATHIC (HM02416) | | | | | | | | | | |
| BODY MECHANICS THERAPY CLINIC (HM02598) | | | | ● | | | | | | |
| BOREHAMWOOD CHIRO CLINIC (HM02717) | | | | | | | ● | | | |
| BRADBURY, TANYA (HM02843) | | | | | | | | | | |
| BRIGGS-WILSON, A (HM03037) | | | | | | | | | | |
| BRIND, KEVIN (HM03053) | | | | | | | | | | |
| BROUWER JOOP (HM03204) | | | | | | | | | | |
| BURYHILL PHYSIOTHERAPY (HM03456) | | | | | | | | | | |
| BUTTERFIELD, ROBIN (HM03496) | | | | | | | | | | |
| CHANDLER, LENA (HM03975) | | | | | | | | | | |
| CHESHUNT CHIROPRACTIC CLINIC (HM04117) | | | | | | | ● | | | |
| CHINESE MEDICAL CENTRE (HM04230) | | | | | | | | | | |
| CHIROPRACTIC CONSULTANT SVS (HM04396) | | | | | | | ● | | | |
| CHIROPRACTORS MCTIMONEY (HM04406) | | | | | | | ● | | | |
| CHOPRA, S (HM04426) | | ● | | | | ● | | | | |
| CHOPRA, S (HM04427) | | ● | | | | ● | | | | |
| CLARE JAMES HEALTH FOODS (HM04532) | | | | | | | | | | |
| CLNC OF ACU & CHINESE HRBL MED (HM04727) | | | | | | | | | | |
| COLE, EVA (HM04814) | | | | | | | | | | |
| CONISTON PHYSIOTHERAPY CLINIC (HM04980) | | | | | | | ● | | | |
| COOPER, FELICITY (HM05101) | | | | | | ● | | | | |
| CRAIB, MARGARET (HM05345) | | | | | | | ● | | | |
| DAVEY, SARAH (HM05770) | | | | | | | | | | |
| DEVINE, MARY (HM06036) | | | | | | ● | | | | |
| DOYLE, AUDREY (HM06257) | | ● | | | | ● | | | | |
| DUDGEON, DELIA (HM06353) | | | | | | | | | | |
| ENGLISH, JEREMY A (HM06833) | | | | | | | | | | |
| EVANS, HELEN (HM06976) | | | | | | ● | | | | |
| EVANS, HELEN (HM06975) | | | | | | ● | | | | |
| GEMS (HM07969) | | | | | | | | | | |
| GEOFF THIEL, COUNS & PSYCHO (HM07986) | | | | | | | | | | |

| Business by County with Reference no. | Colour Therapy | Complementary Therapy | Counselling | Cranial Osteopathy | Cranio-Sacral Therapy | Cryo Surgery | Crystal Healing | Cupping | Cymatics | Dance Movement Thrpy |
|---|---|---|---|---|---|---|---|---|---|---|
| BEAUCHAMP BAGENAL (HM01983) | | ● | | | | | | | | |
| BETA HEALTH CLINIC (HM02229) | | | | | | | | | | |
| BISHOPS STORTFORD CHIRO CLINIC (HM02415) | | | | | | | | | | |
| BISHOP'S STORTFORD HOMEOPATHIC (HM02416) | | | | | | | | | | |
| BODY MECHANICS THERAPY CLINIC (HM02598) | | | | | | | | | | |
| BOREHAMWOOD CHIRO CLINIC (HM02717) | | | | | | | | | | |
| BRADBURY, TANYA (HM02843) | | | | | | | | | | |
| BRIGGS-WILSON, A (HM03037) | | ● | | | | | | | | |
| BRIND, KEVIN (HM03053) | | | | | | | | | | |
| BROUWER JOOP (HM03204) | | | | | | | | | | |
| BURYHILL PHYSIOTHERAPY (HM03456) | | | | | | | | | | |
| BUTTERFIELD, ROBIN (HM03496) | | ● | | ● | | | | | | |
| CHANDLER, LENA (HM03975) | | | | | | | | | | |
| CHESHUNT CHIROPRACTIC CLINIC (HM04117) | | | | | | | | | | |
| CHINESE MEDICAL CENTRE (HM04230) | | | | | | | | | | |
| CHIROPRACTIC CONSULTANT SVS (HM04396) | | | | | | | | | | |
| CHIROPRACTORS MCTIMONEY (HM04406) | | | | | | | | | | |
| CHOPRA, S (HM04426) | | | | | | ● | | | | |
| CHOPRA, S (HM04427) | | | | | | ● | | | | |
| CLARE JAMES HEALTH FOODS (HM04532) | | | | | | | | | | |
| CLNC OF ACU & CHINESE HRBL MED (HM04727) | | ● | | | | | | | | |
| COLE, EVA (HM04814) | | | | | | | | ● | | |
| CONISTON PHYSIOTHERAPY CLINIC (HM04980) | | ● | | ● | | | ● | | | |
| COOPER, FELICITY (HM05101) | | | | | | ● | | | | |
| CRAIB, MARGARET (HM05345) | | | | | | | | | | |
| DAVEY, SARAH (HM05770) | | | | | | | | | | |
| DEVINE, MARY (HM06036) | | | | | | | | | | |
| DOYLE, AUDREY (HM06257) | | | | | | ● | | | | |
| DUDGEON, DELIA (HM06353) | | | ● | | | | | | | |
| ENGLISH, JEREMY A (HM06833) | | | | | | | | | | |
| EVANS, HELEN (HM06976) | | | | | | | | | | |
| EVANS, HELEN (HM06975) | | | | | | | | | | |
| GEMS (HM07969) | | | | | | | ● | | | |
| GEOFF THIEL, COUNS & PSYCHO (HM07986) | | | ● | | | | | | | |

| Business by County with Reference no. | Dietician | Do-In | Douching | Dowsing | Drama Therapy | Electrolipolysis | Electrolysis | Electrotherapy | Encounter Groups | Faith Healing |
|---|---|---|---|---|---|---|---|---|---|---|
| BEAUCHAMP BAGENAL (HM01983) | | | | | | | | | | |
| BETA HEALTH CLINIC (HM02229) | | | | | | | | | | |
| BISHOPS STORTFORD CHIRO CLINIC (HM02415) | | | | | | | | | | |
| BISHOP'S STORTFORD HOMEOPATHIC (HM02416) | | | | ● | | | | | | |
| BODY MECHANICS THERAPY CLINIC (HM02598) | | | | | | | | | | |
| BOREHAMWOOD CHIRO CLINIC (HM02717) | | | | | | | | | | |
| BRADBURY, TANYA (HM02843) | | | | | | | | | | |
| BRIGGS-WILSON, A (HM03037) | | | | | | | | | | |
| BRIND, KEVIN (HM03053) | | | | | | | | | | |
| BROUWER JOOP (HM03204) | | | | | | | | | | |
| BURYHILL PHYSIOTHERAPY (HM03456) | | | | | | | | | | |
| BUTTERFIELD, ROBIN (HM03496) | | | | ● | | | | | | |
| CHANDLER, LENA (HM03975) | | | | | | | | | | |
| CHESHUNT CHIROPRACTIC CLINIC (HM04117) | | | | | | | | | | |
| CHINESE MEDICAL CENTRE (HM04230) | | | | | | | | | | |
| CHIROPRACTIC CONSULTANT SVS (HM04396) | | | | | | | | | | |
| CHIROPRACTORS MCTIMONEY (HM04406) | | | | | | | | | | |
| CHOPRA, S (HM04426) | | | | | | | | | | |
| CHOPRA, S (HM04427) | | | | | | | | | | |
| CLARE JAMES HEALTH FOODS (HM04532) | | | | | | | | | | |
| CLNC OF ACU & CHINESE HRBL MED (HM04727) | | | | | | | | | | |
| COLE, EVA (HM04814) | | | | | | | | | | |
| CONISTON PHYSIOTHERAPY CLINIC (HM04980) | | | | | | | | ● | | |
| COOPER, FELICITY (HM05101) | | | | | | | | | | |
| CRAIB, MARGARET (HM05345) | | | | | | | | | | |
| DAVEY, SARAH (HM05770) | | | | | | | | | | |
| DEVINE, MARY (HM06036) | | | | | | | | | | |
| DOYLE, AUDREY (HM06257) | | | | | | | | | | |
| DUDGEON, DELIA (HM06353) | | | | | | | | | | |
| ENGLISH, JEREMY A (HM06833) | | | | | | | | | | |
| EVANS, HELEN (HM06976) | | | | | | | | | | |
| EVANS, HELEN (HM06975) | | | | | | | | | | |
| GEMS (HM07969) | | | | | | | | | | |
| GEOFF THIEL, COUNS & PSYCHO (HM07986) | | | | | | | | | | |

# A - F Therapies at Practices/Businesses

| Business by County with Reference no. | Absent Healing | Acupressure | Acupuncture | Alexander Technique | Allergy Testing | Anthroposohical Med | Aromatherapy | Art Therapy | Aura Therapy | Auricular Therapy | Auto Suggestion | Autogenic Training | Aversion Therapy | Ayurvedic Medicine | Baby Massage | Bach Remedies | Bates Method | Beauty Therapy | Bio-energetics | Biofeedback | Biomagnetic Therapy | Biomechanics | Bonesetting | Bowen Therapy | Chinese Herbal Medicine | Chiropody | Chiropractic | Clinical Ecology | Cognitive Therapy | Colonic Hydrotherapy | Colour Therapy | Complementary Therapy | Counselling | Cranial Osteopathy | Cranio-Sacral Therapy | Cryo Surgery | Crystal Healing | Cupping | Cymatics | Dance Movement Thrpy | Dietician | Do-In | Douching | Dowsing | Drama Therapy | Electrolipolysis | Electrolysis | Electrotherapy | Encounter Groups | Faith Healing |
|---|---|---|---|---|---|---|---|---|---|---|---|---|---|---|---|---|---|---|---|---|---|---|---|---|---|---|---|---|---|---|---|---|---|---|---|---|---|---|---|---|---|---|---|---|---|---|---|---|---|---|
| GILLING, LINDA (HM08095) | | | | | | | | | | | | | | | | | | | | | | | | | | | | | | | | ● | | | | | | | | | | | | | | | | | | | |
| GODAGAMA, SHANTA (DR) (HM08176) | | | ● | | | | | | | | | | | | | | | | | | | | | | | | | | | | | | | | | | | | | | | | | | | | | | | | |
| GOODMAN, HENRY (HM08258) | | | | | | | | | | | | | | | | | | | | | | | | | | | | | ● | | | | | | | | | | | | | | | | | | | | | | |
| GOWING, KAY (HM08327) | | | | | | | ● | | | | | | | | | | | | | | | | | | | | | | | | | | | | | | | | | | | | | | | | | | | | |
| GRAHAM & KERSTIN ELLIOTT (HM08336) | | | | ● | | | | | | | | | | | | | | | | | | | | | | | | | | | | | | | | | | | | | | | | | | | | | | | |
| GREIG, LISA A (HM08532) | | | | | | | | | | | | | | | | | | | | | | | | | | | ● | | | | | | | | | | | | | | | | | | | | | | | | |
| HAMILTON-PETERS, R & J A (HM08849) | | | | | | | | | | | ● | ● | | | | | | | | | | | | | | | | | | | | ● | ● | | | | | | | | | | | | | | | | | | |
| HARPENDEM OSTEOPATHIC PRACTICE (HM09035) | | | ● | | | | | | | | | | | | | | | | | | | | | | | ● | | | | | | | ● | ● | | | | | | | | | | | | | | | | | |
| HARPENDEN CHIROPRACTIC CLINIC (HM09036) | | | | | | | | | | | | | | | | | | | | | | | | | | | ● | | | | | | | | | | | | | | | | | | | | | | | | |
| HASAN, ZADI (HM09178) | | | ● | | | | | | | | | | | | | | | | | | | | | | | | | | | | | | | | | | | | | | | | | | | | | | | | |
| HATHAWAY, ELIZABETH (HM09196) | | | | ● | | | | | | | | | | | | | | | | | | | | | | | | | | | | | | | | | | | | | | | | | | | | | | | |
| HEALES CHIROPRACTIC CLINIC (HM09322) | | | | | | | | | | | | | | | | | | | | | | | | | | | ● | | | | | | | | | | | | | | | | | | | | | | | | |
| HEMEL CHIROPRACTIC CLINIC (HM09527) | | | | | | | | | | | | | | | | | | | | | | | | | | | ● | | | | | | | | | | | | | | | | | | | | | | | | |
| HERTFORD NATURAL THERAPY CTRE (HM09690) | | | ● | | | | ● | | | | | | | | | | | | | | | | | | ● | | ● | | | | | | ● | | | | | | | | | | | | | ● | | | | | |
| HODSDON, L M (HM09893) | | | | | | | | | | | | | | | | | | | | | | | | | | ● | | | | | | | | | | | | | | | | | | | | | | | | | |
| HUTTON, W (HM10458) | | | | ● | | | | | | | | | | | | | | | | | | | | | | | | | | | | | | | | | | | | | | | | | | | | | | | |
| IRVING, MARY (HM10748) | | | | ● | | | | | | | | | | | | | | | | | | | | | | | | | | | | | | | | | | | | | | | | | | | | | | | |
| JACKSON, BARBARA (HM10830) | | | | | | | | | | | | | | | | | | | | | | | | | | | | | | | | | ● | | | | | | | | | | | | | | | | | | |
| JAMES, CHRISTINE (HM10882) | | | | | | | ● | | | | | | | | | | | | | | | | | | | | | | | | | | | | | | | | | | | | | | | | | | | | |
| JAMES, SUSAN (HM10902) | | | | ● | | | | | | | | | | | | | | | | | | | | | | | | | | | | | | | | | | | | | | | | | | | | | | | |
| JOE MILLER SPORTS INJURY (HM11045) | | | | | | | | | | | | | | | | | | | | | | | | | | | ● | | | | | | | | | | | ● | | | | | | | | | | ● | | | |
| JONES, ALAN (HM11115) | | | | | | | | | | | | | | | | | | | | | | | | | | ● | | | | | | | | | | | | | | | | | | | | | | | | | |
| JOYCE, EDWIN (HM11235) | | | | | | | | | | | | | | | | | | | | | | | | | | | ● | | | | | | | | | | | | | | | | | | | | | | | | |
| KEW, DEREK (HM11576) | | | | | | | | | | | | | | | | | | | | | | | | | | | | | | | | | ● | | | | | | | | | | | | | | | | | | |
| KING, DERRELL (HM11627) | | | | ● | | | | | | | | | | | | | | | | | | | | | | | | | | | | | | | | | | | | | | | | | | | | | | | |
| KING, J R (HM11631) | | | ● | | | | | | | | | | | | | | | | | | | | | | | | | | | | | | | | | | | | | | | | | | | | | | | | |
| KNEBWORTH PHYSIO CLINIC (HM11742) | | | | | | | | | | | | | | | | | | | | | | | | | | | | | | | | | | | | | | | | | | | | | | | | ● | | | |
| KNIGHT, S L (HM11756) | | | | | | | ● | | | | | | | | | | | | | | | | | | | | | | | | | | | | | | | | | | | | | | | | | | | | |
| LAWLESS, GIULIA (HM12044) | | | | | | | ● | | | | | | | | | | | | | | | | | | | | | | | | | | | | | | | | | | | | | | | | | | | | |
| LAZARUS, GAIL (HM12079) | | | ● | | | | | | | | | | | | | | | | | | | | | | | | | | | | | | | | | | | | | | | | | | | | | | | | |
| LEVER CLINIC-ACU & OSTEOPATHY (HM12259) | | | ● | | | | | | | | | | | | | | | | | | | | | | | | | | | | | | | | | | | | | | | | | | | | | | | | |
| LEWIN, ROCHELLE (HM12273) | | | | | | | | ● | | | | | | | | | | | | | | | | | | | | | | | | | ● | | | | | | | ● | | | | | ● | | | | | | |
| LINDY, D (HM12426) | | | | | | | | | | | | | | | | | | | | | | | | | | | | | | | | | | ● | | | | | | | | | | | | | | | | | |
| LOVESEY, R M (HM12681) | | | ● | | | | | | | | | | | | | | | | | | | | | | | | | | | | | | | | | | | | | | | | | | | | | | | | |

www.healthmyself.com

# A - F Therapies at Practices/Businesses

| Business by County with Reference no. | Absent Healing | Acupressure | Acupuncture | Alexander Technique | Allergy Testing | Anthroposohical Med | Aromatherapy | Art Therapy | Aura Therapy | Auricular Therapy | Auto Suggestion | Autogenic Training | Aversion Therapy | Ayurvedic Medicine | Baby Massage | Bach Remedies | Bates Method | Beauty Therapy | Bio-energetics | Biofeedback | Biomagnetic Therapy | Biomechanics | Bonesetting | Bowen Therapy | Chinese Herbal Medicine |
|---|---|---|---|---|---|---|---|---|---|---|---|---|---|---|---|---|---|---|---|---|---|---|---|---|---|
| MAJOR, EMMA (HM12953) | | | | | | | | | | | | | | | | | | | | | | | | | |
| MAUREEN PRIDDLE (HM13328) | | | | | | | ● | | | | | | | | | | | | | | | | | | |
| MAYOR, DAVID F (HM13359) | | ● | ● | | | | | | | | | | | | | | | | | | | | | | |
| MCCAREY, J (HM13391) | | | | | | | | | | | | | | | | | | | | | | | | | |
| MCDONALD, JEANETTE (HM13458) | | | | | | | ● | | | | | | | | | | | | | | | | | | |
| MCTIMONEY CHIROPRACTIC CLINIC (HM13612) | | | | | | | ● | | | | | | | | | | | | | | | | | | |
| MEEK, LISA (HM13680) | | | | | | | | | | | | | | | | | | | | | | | | | |
| MESGER-SCHOFIELD, FIONA (HM13759) | | | | | | | ● | | | | | | | | | | | | | | | | | | |
| MIDAS TOUCH (HM13808) | | ● | | | | | ● | | | | | | | | | | | | | | | | | | |
| MID-HERTS ALEXANDER CENTRE (HM13827) | | | | ● | | | | | | | | | | | | | | | | | | | | | |
| MUGAN, D R (HM14316) | | | | | | | ● | | | | | | | | | | | | | | | | | | |
| NATURAL TOUCH (HM14666) | | | | | | | ● | | | | | | | | | | | | | | | | | | |
| NATURAL-BALANCE CO UK (HM14672) | | | | | | | | | | | | | | | | ● | | | | | | | | | |
| ORCHARD SURGERY CHIRO CLINIC (HM15366) | | | | | | | | | | | | | | | | | | | | | | | | | |
| OSTEOPATHIC CLINIC (HM15459) | | ● | ● | | | | ● | | | | | | | | | ● | | | | | | | | | |
| PEEDLE, DAVID R (HM15938) | | | | | | | | | | | | | | | | | | | | | | | | | |
| PERRY, KAREN (HM16049) | | | | | | | | | | | | | | | | | | | | | | | | | |
| PERSONAL REFLECTIONS (HM16061) | ● | | | | | | ● | | | | | | | | | | | | | | | | | | |
| PHYSIO & SPORTS INJURIES CLNC (HM16177) | | | | | | | | | | | | | | | | | | | | ● | | | | | |
| PURLYS (HM16769) | | | ● | | | | | | | | | | | | | | | | | | | | | | |
| ROSS, V (HM17643) | | | | | | | ● | | | | | | | | | | | | | | | | | | |
| ROWLAND, JETHRO (HM17692) | | ● | ● | | | | | | | | | | | | | | | | | | | | | | |
| S K REFLEXOLOGY (HM17811) | | | | | | | | | | | | | | | | ● | | | | | | | | | |
| SHENTON, MAXINE (HM18403) | | | | ● | | | | | | | | | | | | | | | | | | | | | |
| SKINNER, LORNA (HM18655) | | | ● | | | | | | | | | | | | | | | | | | | | | | |
| SMITH, SUSAN (HM18813) | | | | | | | ● | | | | | | | | | | | | | | | | | | |
| SOPWELL OSTEOPATHIC CLINIC (HM18894) | | ● | ● | | | | | | | | | | | | | | | | | | | | ● | | |
| SOUTH, JO (HM18917) | | | | | | | | | | | | | | | | ● | | | | | | | | | |
| SOUTHDOWN CHIROPODY PRACTICE (HM18929) | | | | | | | | | | | | | | | | | | | | | | | | | |
| SPINOZA, DAVID (HM19019) | | ● | ● | | | | | | ● | | | ● | | | | | | | ● | ● | | | | | |
| ST ALBANS CHIROPRACTIC CLINIC (HM19063) | | | ● | | | | | | | | | | | | | | | | | | | | | | ● |
| STANTON, JULIE (HM19137) | | | | | | | ● | | | | | | | | | | | | | | | | | | |
| STORT COUNS & PSYCHOTHERAPY (HM19351) | | | | | | | | | | | | | | | | | | | | | | | | | |
| STORTFORD GRANGE PHYSIO CENTRE (HM19352) | | | ● | | | | | | | | | | | | | | | | | | | | | | |

| Business by County with Reference no. | Chiropody | Chiropractic | Clinical Ecology | Cognitive Therapy | Colonic Hydrotherapy | Colour Therapy | Complementary Therapy | Counselling | Cranial Osteopathy | Cranio-Sacral Therapy | Cryo Surgery | Crystal Healing | Cupping | Cymatics | Dance Movement Thrpy | Dietician | Do-In | Douching | Dowsing | Drama Therapy | Electrolipolysis | Electrolysis | Electrotherapy | Encounter Groups | Faith Healing |
|---|---|---|---|---|---|---|---|---|---|---|---|---|---|---|---|---|---|---|---|---|---|---|---|---|---|
| MAJOR, EMMA (HM12953) | | ● | | | | | | | | | | | | | | | | | | | | | | | |
| MAUREEN PRIDDLE (HM13328) | | | | | | | | | | | | | | | | | | | | | | | | | |
| MAYOR, DAVID F (HM13359) | | | | | | | | | | | | | ● | | | | | | | | ● | | | | |
| MCCAREY, J (HM13391) | | ● | | | | | | | | | | | | | | | | | | | | | | | |
| MCDONALD, JEANETTE (HM13458) | | | | | | | | | | | | | | | | | | | | | | | | | |
| MCTIMONEY CHIROPRACTIC CLINIC (HM13612) | | ● | | | | | | | | | | | | | | | | | | | | | | | |
| MEEK, LISA (HM13680) | | ● | | | | | | | | | | | | | | | | | | | | | | | |
| MESGER-SCHOFIELD, FIONA (HM13759) | | | | | | | | | | | | | | | | | | | | | | | | | |
| MIDAS TOUCH (HM13808) | | | | | | | | | | | | | | | | | | | | | | | | | |
| MID-HERTS ALEXANDER CENTRE (HM13827) | | | | | | | ● | | | | | | | | | | | | | | | | | | |
| MUGAN, D R (HM14316) | | | | | | | | | | | | | | | | | | | | | | | | | |
| NATURAL TOUCH (HM14666) | | | | | | | | | | | | | | | | | | | | | | | | | |
| NATURAL-BALANCE CO UK (HM14672) | | | | | | | ● | | | | | | | | | | | | | | | | | | |
| ORCHARD SURGERY CHIRO CLINIC (HM15366) | | ● | | | | | | | | | | | | | | | | | | | | | | | |
| OSTEOPATHIC CLINIC (HM15459) | ● | | | | | | ● | ● | ● | | | | | | | | | | | | | | | | |
| PEEDLE, DAVID R (HM15938) | ● | | | | | | | | | | | | | | | | | | | | | | | | |
| PERRY, KAREN (HM16049) | ● | | | | | | | | | | | | | | | | | | | | | | | | |
| PERSONAL REFLECTIONS (HM16061) | | | | | | | ● | ● | | | | ● | | | | | | | ● | | | | | | |
| PHYSIO & SPORTS INJURIES CLNC (HM16177) | | | | | | | | | | | | | | | | | | | | | | | ● | | |
| PURLYS (HM16769) | | | | | | | | | | | | | | | | | | | | | | | | | |
| ROSS, V (HM17643) | | | | | | | | | | | | | | | | | | | | | | | | | |
| ROWLAND, JETHRO (HM17692) | | | | | | | | | | | | | | | | | | | | | | | | | |
| S K REFLEXOLOGY (HM17811) | | | | | | | | ● | | | | ● | | | | | | | | | | | | | |
| SHENTON, MAXINE (HM18403) | | | | | | | | | | | | | | | | | | | | | | | | | |
| SKINNER, LORNA (HM18655) | | | | | | | | | | | | | | | | | | | | | | | | | |
| SMITH, SUSAN (HM18813) | | | | | | | | | | | | | | | | | | | | | | | | | |
| SOPWELL OSTEOPATHIC CLINIC (HM18894) | | | | | | | ● | | ● | | | | | | | | | | | | | | | | |
| SOUTH, JO (HM18917) | | | | | | | | | | | | | | | | | | | | | | | | | |
| SOUTHDOWN CHIROPODY PRACTICE (HM18929) | ● | | | | | | | | | | | | | | | | | | | | | | | | |
| SPINOZA, DAVID (HM19019) | | | | | | | ● | | ● | | | | | | | | | | ● | | | | | | |
| ST ALBANS CHIROPRACTIC CLINIC (HM19063) | ● | ● | | | | | | ● | | | | | | | | | | | | | | | | | |
| STANTON, JULIE (HM19137) | | | | | | | | | | | | | | | | | | | | | | | | | |
| STORT COUNS & PSYCHOTHERAPY (HM19351) | | | | | | | | ● | | | | | | | | | | | | | | | | | |
| STORTFORD GRANGE PHYSIO CENTRE (HM19352) | | | | | | | | | | | | | | | | | | | | | | | | | |

# A - F Therapies at Practices/Businesses

| Business by County with Reference no. | Absent Healing | Acupressure | Acupuncture | Alexander Technique | Allergy Testing | Anthroposohical Med | Aromatherapy | Art Therapy | Aura Therapy | Auricular Therapy | Auto Suggestion | Autogenic Training | Aversion Therapy | Ayurvedic Medicine | Baby Massage | Bach Remedies | Bates Method | Beauty Therapy | Bio-energetics | Biofeedback | Biomagnetic Therapy | Biomechanics | Bonesetting | Bowen Therapy | Chinese Herbal Medicine |
|---|---|---|---|---|---|---|---|---|---|---|---|---|---|---|---|---|---|---|---|---|---|---|---|---|---|
| SWAN & SWAN (HM19572) | | | | | | | | | | | | | | | | | | | | | | | | | |
| UNIQUE MASSAGE (HM20508) | | | | | | | ● | | | | | | | | | | | | | | | | | | |
| VAN DER GRINTEN, PETER (HM20565) | | | | ● | | | | | | | | | | | | | | | | | | | | | |
| VEALE, LINDA (HM20604) | | | | | | | ● | | | | | | | | | | | | | | | | | | |
| WALKER, NEL (HM20791) | | | | | | | | | | | | | | | | | | | | | | | | | |
| WALKER, RICHARD (HM20798) | | | | | | | | | | | ● | | ● | | | | | | | | | | | | |
| WELWYN CHIROPRACTIC CLINIC (HM21192) | | | | | | | | | | | | | | | | | | | | | | | | | |
| WHITE, GRAHAM C (HM21355) | | | | | | | ● | | | | | | | | | | | | | | | | | | |
| WHITTLE, MARK (HM21424) | | | | | | | | | | | | | | | | | | | | | | | | | |
| WILSON, SHIRLEY (HM21673) | | | | | | | ● | | | | | | | | | | | | | | | | | | |
| WOOD STREET CHIROPRACTIC CLNC (HM21780) | | | ● | ● | ● | | | | | | | | | | | | | | | | | | | | |
| WOOD STREET CLINIC (HM21781) | | | | | | | | | | | | | | | | | | | ● | | | | | | |
| WRIGHT, KAREN (HM21940) | | | | | | | | | | | | | | | | | | | | | | ● | | | |
| WYE, DEBORAH (HM21969) | | | | | | | | | | | | | | | | | | | | | | | | | |
| WYNDHAM CLINIC (HM21977) | | | ● | | | | ● | | | | | | | | | | | | | | | | | | |
| **HUMBERSIDE** | | | | | | | | | | | | | | | | | | | | | | | | | |
| BATH, ANN (HM01899) | | | | | | | ● | | | | | | | | | | | | | | | | | | |
| BRIGG CHIROPRACTIC CLINIC (HM03028) | | | | | | | | | | | | | | | | | | | | | | | | | |
| LANGLEY, LYNNE (HM11957) | | | | | | | | | | | | | | | | ● | | | | | | | | | |
| MESSINGHAM CHIROPODIST SURGERY (HM13761) | | | | | | | | | | | | | | | | | | | | | | | | | |
| PRIOSE COLES (HM16635) | | | | | | | ● | | | | | | | | | ● | | | | | | | | | |
| SCUNTHORPE CHIROPRACTIC CLINIC (HM18157) | | | | ● | | | | | | | | | | | | | | | | | | | | | |
| **HUMBERSIDE (NORTH)** | | | | | | | | | | | | | | | | | | | | | | | | | |
| ACADEMY PHYSIOTHERAPY CLINIC (HM00149) | | | ● | | | | | | | | | | | | | | | | | | | | | | |
| BEVERLEY CHIROPRACTIC CLINIC (HM02243) | | | | | | | | | | | | | | | | | | | | | | | | | |
| BRIDLINGTON CHIROPODY SURGERY (HM03018) | | | | | | | | | | | | | | | | | | | | | | ● | | | |
| BUTLER, D A (HM03485) | | | | | | | | | | | | | | | | | | | | | | | | | |
| DAMIAN P JOHNS (HM05704) | | | | | | | | | | | | | | | | | | | | | | ● | | | |
| DOYLES (HM06268) | | | | | | | ● | | | | | | | | | | | | | | | | | | |
| EAST RIDING COLLEGE (HM06524) | | | | | | | ● | | | | | | | | | | | | | | | | | | |
| FRAGRANT RETREAT (HM07651) | | | | | | | ● | | | | | | | | | | | | | | | | | | |
| HALTEMPRICE CHIRO CLINIC (HM08820) | | | | | | | | | | | | | | | | | | | | | | | | | |
| HOLDERNESS CHIROPRACTIC CLINIC (HM09936) | | | | | | | | | | | | | | | | | | | | | | | | | |
| HULL CLINIC OF COMP MEDICINE (HM10353) | | | | | | | | | | | | | | | | | | | | | | | | | |

| Business by County with Reference no. | Chiropody | Chiropractic | Clinical Ecology | Cognitive Therapy | Colonic Hydrotherapy | Colour Therapy | Complementary Therapy | Counselling | Cranial Osteopathy | Cranio-Sacral Therapy | Cryo Surgery | Crystal Healing | Cupping | Cymatics | Dance Movement Thrpy | Dietician | Do-In | Douching | Dowsing | Drama Therapy | Electrolipolysis | Electrolysis | Electrotherapy | Encounter Groups | Faith Healing |
|---|---|---|---|---|---|---|---|---|---|---|---|---|---|---|---|---|---|---|---|---|---|---|---|---|---|
| SWAN & SWAN (HM19572) | ● | | | | | | | | | | | | | | | | | | | | | | | | |
| UNIQUE MASSAGE (HM20508) | | | | | | | | | | | | | | | | | | | | | | | | | |
| VAN DER GRINTEN, PETER (HM20565) | | | | | | | | | | | | | | | | | | | | | | | | | |
| VEALE, LINDA (HM20604) | | | | | | | | | | | | | | | | | | | | | | | | | |
| WALKER, NEL (HM20791) | | | | ● | | | | ● | | | | | | | | | | | | | | | | | |
| WALKER, RICHARD (HM20798) | | | | | | | ● | | | | | | | | | | | | | | | | | | |
| WELWYN CHIROPRACTIC CLINIC (HM21192) | | ● | | | | | | | | | | | | | | | | | | | | | | | |
| WHITE, GRAHAM C (HM21355) | | | | | | | ● | | | | | | | | | | | | | | | | | | |
| WHITTLE, MARK (HM21424) | | ● | | | | | | | | | | | | | | | | | | | | | | | |
| WILSON, SHIRLEY (HM21673) | | | | | | | | | | | | | | | | | | | | | | | | | |
| WOOD STREET CHIROPRACTIC CLNC (HM21780) | ● | ● | | | | | | | | | | | | | | | | | | | | | | | |
| WOOD STREET CLINIC (HM21781) | | | ● | | | | ● | | | | | | | | | | | | | | | | | | |
| WRIGHT, KAREN (HM21940) | ● | | | | | | | | | | | | | | | | | | | | | | | | |
| WYE, DEBORAH (HM21969) | ● | | | | | | | | | | | | | | | | | | | | | | | | |
| WYNDHAM CLINIC (HM21977) | ● | | ● | | | | ● | | | ● | | | | | | | | | | | | | | | |
| **HUMBERSIDE** | | | | | | | | | | | | | | | | | | | | | | | | | |
| BATH, ANN (HM01899) | | | | | | | | | | | | | | | | | | | | | | | | | |
| BRIGG CHIROPRACTIC CLINIC (HM03028) | | ● | | | | | | | | | | | | | | | | | | | | | | | |
| LANGLEY, LYNNE (HM11957) | | | | | | | | | | | | | | | | | | | | | | | | | |
| MESSINGHAM CHIROPODIST SURGERY (HM13761) | ● | | | | | | | | | | | | | | | | | | | | | | | | |
| PRIOSE COLES (HM16635) | | | | | | | | ● | | | | ● | | | | | | | | | | | | | |
| SCUNTHORPE CHIROPRACTIC CLINIC (HM18157) | | ● | | | | | | | | | | | | | | | | | | | | | | | |
| **HUMBERSIDE (NORTH)** | | | | | | | | | | | | | | | | | | | | | | | | | |
| ACADEMY PHYSIOTHERAPY CLINIC (HM00149) | | | | | | | | | | | | | | | | | | | | | | | | | |
| BEVERLEY CHIROPRACTIC CLINIC (HM02243) | | ● | | | | | | | | | | | | | | | | | | | | | | | |
| BRIDLINGTON CHIROPODY SURGERY (HM03018) | ● | | | | | | | | | | | | | | | | | | | | | | | | |
| BUTLER, D A (HM03485) | | ● | | | | | | | | | | | | | | | | | | | | | | | |
| DAMIAN P JOHNS (HM05704) | ● | | | | | | | | | | ● | | | | | | | | | | | | | | |
| DOYLES (HM06268) | | | | | | | | | | | | | | | | | | | | | | | | | |
| EAST RIDING COLLEGE (HM06524) | | | | | | | | | | | | | | | | | | | | | | | | | |
| FRAGRANT RETREAT (HM07651) | | | | | | | | | | | | | | | | | | | | | | | | | |
| HALTEMPRICE CHIRO CLINIC (HM08820) | | ● | | | | | | | | | | | | | | | | | | | | | | | |
| HOLDERNESS CHIROPRACTIC CLINIC (HM09936) | | ● | | | | | | | | | | | | | | | | | | | | | | | |
| HULL CLINIC OF COMP MEDICINE (HM10353) | | ● | | | | | | | | | | | | | | | | | | | | | | | |

# A - F Therapies at Practices/Businesses

| Business by County with Reference no. | Absent Healing | Acupressure | Acupuncture | Alexander Technique | Allergy Testing | Anthroposohical Med | Aromatherapy | Art Therapy | Aura Therapy | Auricular Therapy | Auto Suggestion | Autogenic Training | Aversion Therapy | Ayurvedic Medicine | Baby Massage | Bach Remedies | Bates Method |
|---|---|---|---|---|---|---|---|---|---|---|---|---|---|---|---|---|---|
| NATURAL THERAPIES (HM14629) | | ● | ● | | | | | | | | | | | | | | |
| NATURAL THERAPY CENTRE (HM14653) | | | | | | | | | | | | ● | | | | | |
| SAMANTHA WHITE AROMATICA (HM17877) | | | | | | | ● | | ● | | | | | | | | |
| STARLIGHT CENTRE (HM19151) | | | | | | | ● | | | | | | | | | | |
| HUMBERSIDE (SOUTH) | | | | | | | | | | | | | | | | | |
| BECKETT-GEORGE, D (HM02028) | | | ● | | | | | | | | | | | | | | |
| GRIMSBY CHIROPRACTIC CLINIC (HM08582) | | | | | | | | | | | | | | | | | |
| HARRISON-WILLIAMS (HM09113) | | | | | | | | | | | | | | | | | |
| HARRISON-WILLIAMS CHIROPODIST (HM09114) | | | | | | | | | | | | | | | | | |
| LOUISE HEALING CENTRE (HM12668) | ● | ● | | | | | ● | | | | ● | | | | | | |
| PANIGRAHI, P (HM15633) | | | ● | | | | | | | | | | | | | | |
| ROBINSON, KEITH (HM17488) | | | | | | | | | | | | | | | | | |
| SCARTHO OSTEOPATHIC PRACTICE (HM18007) | | | | | | | | | | | | | | | | | |
| WALL, R A (HM20819) | ● | | | | | | | | | | | | | | | | |
| WEBB, C M (HM21057) | | | | | | | | | | | | | | | | | |
| ISLE OF MAN | | | | | | | | | | | | | | | | | |
| BAILEY-CONLON, ELIZABETH (HM01555) | | | | | | | | | | | | | | | | ● | |
| ISLE OF WIGHT | | | | | | | | | | | | | | | | | |
| BURROWS, MARY (HM03424) | | | | | | | | | | | | | | | | | |
| CARISBROOKE HEALTH CENTRE (HM03687) | | | | ● | | | | | | | | | | | | ● | |
| F VON - MEHREN (HM07034) | | | | | | | | | | | | | | | | | |
| FLANDERS, H (HM07391) | | | | | | | | | | | | | | | | | |
| FOOTSTEPS (HM07510) | | | | | | | | | | | | | | | | | |
| FOOTSTEPS THERAPY CENTRE (HM07513) | | | | | | | | | | | | | | | | | |
| GREENFIELD, BRIAN (HM08484) | | ● | | | | | ● | | | ● | | | | | | | |
| HOPE CLINIC (HM10134) | | | ● | | | | ● | | | | | | | | | | |
| MCTIMONEY, R (HM13619) | | | | | | | | | | | | | | | | | |
| NORMAN, NANCY (HM15006) | | | | | | | ● | | | | | | | | | | |
| PARRY, SHEILA (HM15742) | | | | ● | | | | | | | | | | | | | |
| PARRY, SHELLA (HM15743) | | | | ● | | | | | | | | | | | | | |
| SAUNDERS, K (HM17955) | | | | | | | | | | | | | | | | | |
| SHEN CLINIC (HM18391) | | | ● | | ● | | | | | | | | | | | | |
| TAYLOR, S A (HM19791) | | | | | | | | | | | | | | | | | |
| TREE OF LIFE AROMATHERAPY (HM20305) | | | | | | | ● | | | | | | | | | | |

| Business by County with Reference no. | Beauty Therapy | Bio-energetics | Biofeedback | Biomagnetic Therapy | Biomechanics | Bonesetting | Bowen Therapy | Chinese Herbal Medicine | Chiropody | Chiropractic | Clinical Ecology | Cognitive Therapy | Colonic Hydrotherapy | Colour Therapy | Complementary Therapy | Counselling | Cranial Osteopathy |
|---|---|---|---|---|---|---|---|---|---|---|---|---|---|---|---|---|---|
| NATURAL THERAPIES (HM14629) | | | | | | | | | | | | | | | | | |
| NATURAL THERAPY CENTRE (HM14653) | | | | | | | | | | | | | | | | | |
| SAMANTHA WHITE AROMATICA (HM17877) | | | | | | | | | | | | | | | ● | | |
| STARLIGHT CENTRE (HM19151) | | | | | | | | | | | | | | | | | |
| HUMBERSIDE (SOUTH) | | | | | | | | | | | | | | | | | |
| BECKETT-GEORGE, D (HM02028) | | | | | | | | | | | | | | | | | |
| GRIMSBY CHIROPRACTIC CLINIC (HM08582) | | | | | | | | | | ● | | | | | | | |
| HARRISON-WILLIAMS (HM09113) | | | | | | | | | ● | | | | | | | | |
| HARRISON-WILLIAMS CHIROPODIST (HM09114) | | | | | | | | | ● | | | | | | | | |
| LOUISE HEALING CENTRE (HM12668) | | | | | | | | | | | | | | | ● | ● | |
| PANIGRAHI, P (HM15633) | | | | | | | | | | | | | | | | | |
| ROBINSON, KEITH (HM17488) | | | | | | | | | ● | | | | | | | | |
| SCARTHO OSTEOPATHIC PRACTICE (HM18007) | ● | | | | | | | | ● | | | | | | | | |
| WALL, R A (HM20819) | | | | | | | | | ● | | | | | | | | |
| WEBB, C M (HM21057) | | | | | | | | | ● | | | | | | | | |
| ISLE OF MAN | | | | | | | | | | | | | | | | | |
| BAILEY-CONLON, ELIZABETH (HM01555) | | | | | | | | | | | | | | | | | |
| ISLE OF WIGHT | | | | | | | | | | | | | | | | | |
| BURROWS, MARY (HM03424) | | | | | | | | | ● | | | | | | | | |
| CARISBROOKE HEALTH CENTRE (HM03687) | | | | | ● | | | | ● | | | | | | | | |
| F VON - MEHREN (HM07034) | | | | | | | | | ● | | | | | | | | |
| FLANDERS, H (HM07391) | | | | | | | | | ● | | | | | | | | |
| FOOTSTEPS (HM07510) | | | | | ● | | | | ● | | | | | | | | |
| FOOTSTEPS THERAPY CENTRE (HM07513) | | | | | ● | | | | ● | | | | | | | | |
| GREENFIELD, BRIAN (HM08484) | | | | | | | | | | | | | | ● | ● | | |
| HOPE CLINIC (HM10134) | | | | | | | | | | ● | | | | | ● | ● | ● |
| MCTIMONEY, R (HM13619) | | | | | | | | | | ● | | | | | | | |
| NORMAN, NANCY (HM15006) | | | | | | | | | | | | | | | | | |
| PARRY, SHEILA (HM15742) | | | | | | | | | | | | | | | | | |
| PARRY, SHELLA (HM15743) | | | | | | | | | | | | | | | | | |
| SAUNDERS, K (HM17955) | | | | | | | | | | ● | | | | | | | |
| SHEN CLINIC (HM18391) | | | | | | | | | | | | | | | | | |
| TAYLOR, S A (HM19791) | | | | | | | | | ● | | | | | | | | |
| TREE OF LIFE AROMATHERAPY (HM20305) | | | | | | | | | | | | | | | | | |

| Business by County with Reference no. | Cranio-Sacral Therapy | Cryo Surgery | Crystal Healing | Cupping | Cymatics | Dance Movement Thrpy | Dietician | Do-In | Douching | Dowsing | Drama Therapy | Electrolipolysis | Electrolysis | Electrotherapy | Encounter Groups | Faith Healing |
|---|---|---|---|---|---|---|---|---|---|---|---|---|---|---|---|---|
| NATURAL THERAPIES (HM14629) | | | | | | | | | | | | | | | | |
| NATURAL THERAPY CENTRE (HM14653) | | | | | | | | | | | | | | | | |
| SAMANTHA WHITE AROMATICA (HM17877) | | | | | | | | | | | | | | | | |
| STARLIGHT CENTRE (HM19151) | ● | | | | | | | | | | | | | | | |
| HUMBERSIDE (SOUTH) | | | | | | | | | | | | | | | | |
| BECKETT-GEORGE, D (HM02028) | | | | | | | | | | | | | | | | |
| GRIMSBY CHIROPRACTIC CLINIC (HM08582) | | | | | | | | | | | | | | | | |
| HARRISON-WILLIAMS (HM09113) | | | | | | | | | | | | | | | | |
| HARRISON-WILLIAMS CHIROPODIST (HM09114) | | | | | | | | | | | | | | | | |
| LOUISE HEALING CENTRE (HM12668) | | | | | | | | | | | | | | | | ● |
| PANIGRAHI, P (HM15633) | | | | | | | | | | | | | | | | |
| ROBINSON, KEITH (HM17488) | | ● | | | | | | | | | | | | | | |
| SCARTHO OSTEOPATHIC PRACTICE (HM18007) | | | | | | | | | | | | | | | | |
| WALL, R A (HM20819) | | | | | | | | | | | | | | | | |
| WEBB, C M (HM21057) | | ● | | | | | | | | | | | | | | |
| ISLE OF MAN | | | | | | | | | | | | | | | | |
| BAILEY-CONLON, ELIZABETH (HM01555) | | | | | | | | | | | | | | | | |
| ISLE OF WIGHT | | | | | | | | | | | | | | | | |
| BURROWS, MARY (HM03424) | | | | | | | | | | | | | | | | |
| CARISBROOKE HEALTH CENTRE (HM03687) | | | | | | | | | | | | | | | | |
| F VON - MEHREN (HM07034) | | | | | | | | | | | | | | | | |
| FLANDERS, H (HM07391) | | | | | | | | | | | | | | | | |
| FOOTSTEPS (HM07510) | | | | | | | | | | | | | | | | |
| FOOTSTEPS THERAPY CENTRE (HM07513) | | | | | | | | | | | | | | | | |
| GREENFIELD, BRIAN (HM08484) | | | | | | | | | | | | | | | | |
| HOPE CLINIC (HM10134) | | | | | | | | | | | | | | | | |
| MCTIMONEY, R (HM13619) | | | | | | | | | | | | | | | | |
| NORMAN, NANCY (HM15006) | | | ● | | | | | | | | | | | | | |
| PARRY, SHEILA (HM15742) | | | | | | | | | | | | | | | | |
| PARRY, SHELLA (HM15743) | | | | | | | | | | | | | | | | |
| SAUNDERS, K (HM17955) | | | | | | | | | | | | | | | | |
| SHEN CLINIC (HM18391) | | | | | | | | | | | | | | | | |
| TAYLOR, S A (HM19791) | | | | | | | | | | | | | | | | |
| TREE OF LIFE AROMATHERAPY (HM20305) | | | | | | | | | | | | | | | | |

# A - F Therapies at Practices/Businesses

Business by County with Reference no.

| Business | Absent Healing | Acupressure | Acupuncture | Alexander Technique | Allergy Testing | Anthroposohical Med | Aromatherapy | Art Therapy | Aura Therapy | Auricular Therapy | Auto Suggestion | Autogenic Training | Aversion Therapy | Ayurvedic Medicine | Baby Massage | Bach Remedies | Bates Method | Beauty Therapy | Bio-energetics | Biofeedback | Biomagnetic Therapy | Biomechanics | Bonesetting | Bowen Therapy | Chinese Herbal Medicine |
|---|---|---|---|---|---|---|---|---|---|---|---|---|---|---|---|---|---|---|---|---|---|---|---|---|---|
| YARMOUTH CHIROPRACTIC CLINIC (HM21988) | | | | | | | | | | | | | | | | | | | | | | | | | |
| **KENT** | | | | | | | | | | | | | | | | | | | | | | | | | |
| ABSOLUTE SOLUTIONS (HM00142) | | | | | | | | | | | | | | ● | | | | | | | | | | | |
| ACUPUNCTURE CLINIC (HM00256) | | | ● | | | | | | | | | | | | | | | | | | | | | | |
| ACUPUNCTURE CLINIC (HM00274) | | | ● | | | | | | | | | | | | | | | | | | | | | | |
| ACUPUNCTURE/CHINESE HERBAL (HM00324) | | | ● | | | | | | | | | | | | | | | | | | | | | | |
| ADBY, SHEILA (HM00369) | | | ● | | | | | | | | | | | | | | | | | | | | | | |
| ALEXANDER TECHNIQUE (HM00553) | | | | ● | | | | | | | | | | | | | | | | | | | | | |
| ANDERSON COMPLEMENTARY MED (HM00808) | | | | | | | ● | | | | | | | | | | | | | | | | | | |
| ARCHER, ANNE (HM00971) | | | ● | | | | | | | | | | | | | | | | | | | | | | |
| ASHDOWN, LOUISE (HM01207) | | | | | | | | | | | | | | | | ● | | | | | | | | | |
| AXTON, PETER (HM01418) | | | | | | | | | | | | | | | | | | | | | | | | | |
| AYLSHAM OSTEOPATHIC PRACTICE (HM01429) | | | | | | | | | | | | | | | | | | | | | | | | | |
| BECKENHAM & BROMLEY (HM02017) | | | | | | | | | | | | | | | | | | | | | | | | | |
| BECKENHAM ACUPUNCTURE CLINIC (HM02018) | | | ● | | | | | | | | | | | | | | | | | | | | | | |
| BECKENHAM CHINESE MED CTRE (HM02019) | | | ● | | | | | | | | | | | | | | | | | | | | | | |
| BENNETT, J P (HM02143) | | | | | | | | | | | ● | | | | | | | | | | | | | | |
| BENSON, MICHAEL (HM02170) | | | | | | | ● | | | | | | | | | | | | | | | | | | |
| BEXLEY OSTEOPATHIC CLINIC (HM02259) | | | | | | | ● | | | | | | | | | | | | | | | | | | |
| BEXLEYHEATH CHIROPRACTIC (HM02261) | | | | | | | | | | | | | | | | | | | | | | | | | |
| BEXLEYHEATH NATURAL HEALTH (HM02262) | | | ● | | | | | | | | | | | | | | | | | | | | | ● | |
| BIDBOROUGH CHIROPRACTIC CLINIC (HM02279) | | | | | | | | | | | | | | | | | | | | | | | | | |
| BISHOP, SARAH (HM02411) | | | | | | | ● | | | | | | | | | | | | | | | | | ● | |
| BLACKFEN HYPNOTHERAPY (HM02442) | | | | | | | | | | | | | | | | | | | | | | | | | |
| BLAKE, JANET (HM02481) | | | | | | | | | | | | | | | | ● | | | | | | | | | |
| BLAKEMAN, S M (HM02485) | | | ● | | | | | | | | | | | | | | | | | | | | | | |
| BLOSSOM AROMATHERAPY CENTRE (HM02521) | | | | | | | ● | | | | | | | | | | | | | | | | | | |
| BODY BEAUTIFUL (HM02577) | | | | | | | ● | | | | | | | | | | | | | | | | | | |
| BODY GOLD /CLOVERWOOD (HM02591) | | | | | | | ● | | | | | | | | | | | | | | | | | | |
| BRADLEY, SUSIE (HM02873) | | | | | | | ● | | | | | | | | | | | | | | | | | | |
| BROMLEY CHIROPODY CENTRE (HM03142) | | | | | | | | | | | | | | | | | | | | | | ● | | | |
| BROMLEY CHIROPRACTIC CLINIC (HM03143) | | | ● | | | | | | | | | | | | | | | | | | | | | | ● |
| BROMLEY OSTEOPATHIC CLINIC (HM03145) | | | ● | | | | | | | | | | | | | | | | | | | | | | |
| CALVER, AMANDA (HM03560) | | | | | | | ● | | | | | | | | | | | | | | | | | | |

| Business | Chiropody | Chiropractic | Clinical Ecology | Cognitive Therapy | Colonic Hydrotherapy | Colour Therapy | Complementary Therapy | Counselling | Cranial Osteopathy | Cranio-Sacral Therapy | Cryo Surgery | Crystal Healing | Cupping | Cymatics | Dance Movement Thrpy | Dietician | Do-In | Douching | Dowsing | Drama Therapy | Electrolipolysis | Electrolysis | Electrotherapy | Encounter Groups | Faith Healing |
|---|---|---|---|---|---|---|---|---|---|---|---|---|---|---|---|---|---|---|---|---|---|---|---|---|---|
| YARMOUTH CHIROPRACTIC CLINIC (HM21988) | | ● | | | | | | | | | | | | | | | | | | | | | | | |
| **KENT** | | | | | | | | | | | | | | | | | | | | | | | | | |
| ABSOLUTE SOLUTIONS (HM00142) | | | | | | | | | | | | | | | | | | | | | | | | | |
| ACUPUNCTURE CLINIC (HM00256) | | | | | | | | | | | | | | | | | | | | | | | | | |
| ACUPUNCTURE CLINIC (HM00274) | | | | | | | | | | | | | | | | | | | | | | | | | |
| ACUPUNCTURE/CHINESE HERBAL (HM00324) | | | | | | | | | | | | | | | | | | | | | | | | | |
| ADBY, SHEILA (HM00369) | | | | | | | | | | | | | | | | | | | | | | | | | |
| ALEXANDER TECHNIQUE (HM00553) | | | | | | | | | | | | | | | | | | | | | | | | | |
| ANDERSON COMPLEMENTARY MED (HM00808) | | | | | | | | | | | | | | | | | | | | | | | | | |
| ARCHER, ANNE (HM00971) | | | | | | | | | | | | | | | | | | | | | | | | | |
| ASHDOWN, LOUISE (HM01207) | | | | | | | | | | | | | | | | | | | | | | | | | |
| AXTON, PETER (HM01418) | | ● | | | | | | | | | | | | | | | | | | | | | | | |
| AYLSHAM OSTEOPATHIC PRACTICE (HM01429) | | | | | | | | | ● | | | | | | | | | | | | | | | | |
| BECKENHAM & BROMLEY (HM02017) | | ● | | | | | | | | | | | | | | | | | | | | | | | |
| BECKENHAM ACUPUNCTURE CLINIC (HM02018) | | | | | | | | | | | | | | | | | | | | | | | | | |
| BECKENHAM CHINESE MED CTRE (HM02019) | | | | | | | | | | | | | | | | | | | | | | | | | |
| BENNETT, J P (HM02143) | | | | ● | | | | | | | | | | | | | | | | | | | | | |
| BENSON, MICHAEL (HM02170) | | | | | | | | | | | | | | | | | | | | | | | | | |
| BEXLEY OSTEOPATHIC CLINIC (HM02259) | | | | | | | | | ● | | | | | | | | | | | | | | | | |
| BEXLEYHEATH CHIROPRACTIC (HM02261) | | ● | | | | | | | | | | | | | | | | | | | | | | | |
| BEXLEYHEATH NATURAL HEALTH (HM02262) | ● | | | | | | | | | | | | | | | | | | | | | | | | |
| BIDBOROUGH CHIROPRACTIC CLINIC (HM02279) | | ● | | | | | | | | | | | | | | | | | | | | | | | |
| BISHOP, SARAH (HM02411) | | | | | | | | | | | | | | | | | | | | | | | | | |
| BLACKFEN HYPNOTHERAPY (HM02442) | | | | ● | | | | ● | | | | | | | | | | | | | | | | | |
| BLAKE, JANET (HM02481) | | | | | | | | | | | | | | | | | | | | | | | | | |
| BLAKEMAN, S M (HM02485) | | | | | | | | | | | | | | | | | | | | | | | | | |
| BLOSSOM AROMATHERAPY CENTRE (HM02521) | | | | | | | | | | | | | | | | | | | | | | | | | |
| BODY BEAUTIFUL (HM02577) | | | | | | | | | | | | | | | | | | | | | | | | | |
| BODY GOLD /CLOVERWOOD (HM02591) | | | | | | | | | | | | | | | | | | | | | | | | | |
| BRADLEY, SUSIE (HM02873) | | | | | | | | | | | | | | | | | | | | | | | | | |
| BROMLEY CHIROPODY CENTRE (HM03142) | ● | | | | | | | | | | | | | | | | | | | | | | | | |
| BROMLEY CHIROPRACTIC CLINIC (HM03143) | | ● | | | | | | | | | | | | | | | | | | | | | | | |
| BROMLEY OSTEOPATHIC CLINIC (HM03145) | | | | | | | | | | | | | | | | | | | | | | | | | |
| CALVER, AMANDA (HM03560) | | | | | | | | | | | | | | | | | | | | | | | | | |

# A - F Therapies at Practices/Businesses

| Business by County with Reference no. | Absent Healing | Acupressure | Acupuncture | Alexander Technique | Allergy Testing | Anthroposohical Med | Aromatherapy | Art Therapy | Aura Therapy | Auricular Therapy | Auto Suggestion | Autogenic Training | Aversion Therapy | Ayurvedic Medicine | Baby Massage | Bach Remedies | Bates Method | Beauty Therapy | Bio-energetics | Biofeedback | Biomagnetic Therapy | Biomechanics | Bonesetting | Bowen Therapy | Chinese Herbal Medicine |
|---|---|---|---|---|---|---|---|---|---|---|---|---|---|---|---|---|---|---|---|---|---|---|---|---|---|
| CANTERBURY OSTEOPATHIC CLINIC (HM03641) | ● | | | | | | | | | ● | | | | | | | | | ● | ● | | | | | |
| CAPEL, TERRY (HM03648) | | | ● | | | | | | | | | | | | | | | | | | | | | | |
| CARDWELL, MARTIN (HM03673) | ● | | | | | | | | | | | | | | | | | | | | | | | | |
| CARLE, J (HM03689) | | | | | | | | | | | | | | | | | | | | | | | | | |
| CASTLE CLINIC (HM03830) | | | ● | | | | ● | | | | | | | | | | | | | | | | | | |
| CENTRE (HM03897) | | | ● | | ● | | ● | | | | | | | | | | | | | | | | | | |
| CHANDRA PDS (HM03982) | | ● | ● | | | | | | | | | | | | | | | | | | | | | | |
| CHINESE HERBAL MED & HLTH CARE (HM04200) | | | | | | | | | | | | | | | | | | | | | | | | | ● |
| CHINESE HERBAL MED ACU CTRE (HM04205) | | | ● | | | | | | | | | | | | | | | | | | | | | | ● |
| CHIROPRACTIC & HERBAL CENTRE (HM04349) | | | | | | | | | | | | | | | | | | | | | | | | | |
| CHIROPRACTIC CLINIC (HM04392) | | | | | | | | | | | | | | | | | | | | | | | | | |
| CHIROPRACTIC PLUS (HM04402) | | | | | | | | | | | | | | | | | | | | | | | | | |
| CHISLEHURST NATURAL HEALTH (HM04410) | | | ● | | | | ● | | | | | | | | | | | | | | | | | | |
| CHISTLEHURST NATURAL HLTH CTRE (HM04411) | | | ● | | | | ● | | | | | | | | | | | | | | | | | | |
| CHRISTINE CHINNERY COMP THER (HM04446) | | | | | | | ● | | | | | | | | | | | | | | | | | | |
| COMMON SCENTS (HM04903) | | | | | | | ● | | | | | | | | | | | | | | | | | | |
| COMPLEMENTARY THERAPIES (HM04940) | | | | | | | ● | | | | | | | | | | | | | | | | | | |
| COPY CENTRE (HM05150) | | | | | | | ● | | | | | | | | | | | | | | | | | | |
| COURT, SUSAN (HM05266) | | | | | | | | | | | | | | | | | | | | | | | | | |
| COURT, SUSAN (HM05265) | | | | | | | | | | | | | | | | | | | | | | | | | |
| COYSTEN & ASSOCIATES (HM05332) | | | | | | | | | | | | | | | | | | | | | | | | | |
| CRACKNELL, JANICE (HM05343) | | | | | | | | | | | | | | | | ● | | | | | | | | | |
| CROIX, LINDA LA (HM05460) | | | | | | | ● | | | | | | | | | | | | | | | | | | |
| CULLEN, KEVIN (HM05560) | | | | | | | | | | | | | | | | | | | | | | | | | |
| DAVID, B (HM05782) | | | | | | | ● | | | | | | | | | | | | | | | | | | |
| DAVINSKY, MARZO (HM05845) | | | | | | | ● | | | | | | | | | | | | | | | | | | |
| DEAL CHIROPRACTIC CLINIC (HM05934) | | | | | | | | | | | | | | | | | | | | | | | | | |
| DELTA MEDI CLINIC (HM05969) | | | ● | | | | ● | | | | | | | | | | | | | | | | | | |
| DICKMAN, ANNIE (HM06080) | | | | | | | ● | | | | | | | | | | | | | | | | | | |
| DILLON, MICHAEL (HM06100) | | | | | | | | | | | ● | ● | | | | | | | | | | | | | |
| DIMENT, GORDON L (HM06105) | | | | | | | | | | | | | | | | | | | | | | | | | |
| EDWARDS, R (HM06667) | | | | | | | | | | | | | | | | | | | | | | | | | |
| EDWARDS, R (HM06668) | | | | | | | | | | | | | | | | | | | | | | | | | |
| EDWARDS, R, HERNE BAY (HM06670) | | | | | | | | | | | | | | | | | | | | | | | | | |

| Business by County with Reference no. | Chiropody | Chiropractic | Clinical Ecology | Cognitive Therapy | Colonic Hydrotherapy | Colour Therapy | Complementary Therapy | Counselling | Cranial Osteopathy | Cranio-Sacral Therapy | Cryo Surgery | Crystal Healing | Cupping | Cymatics | Dance Movement Thrpy | Dietician | Do-In | Douching | Dowsing | Drama Therapy | Electrolipolysis | Electrolysis | Electrotherapy | Encounter Groups | Faith Healing |
|---|---|---|---|---|---|---|---|---|---|---|---|---|---|---|---|---|---|---|---|---|---|---|---|---|---|
| CANTERBURY OSTEOPATHIC CLINIC (HM03641) | | | | | | ● | ● | ● | ● | ● | | | | | | ● | | | ● | | | | | | |
| CAPEL, TERRY (HM03648) | | | | | | | | | | | | | | | | | | | | | | | | | |
| CARDWELL, MARTIN (HM03673) | | | | | | | ● | | | | | ● | | | | | | | ● | | | | | | ● |
| CARLE, J (HM03689) | | ● | | | | | | | | | | | | | | | | | | | | | | | |
| CASTLE CLINIC (HM03830) | | | | | | | | ● | | | | | | | | | | | | | | | | | |
| CENTRE (HM03897) | | | | | | | | ● | | | | | | | | | | | | | | | | | |
| CHANDRA PDS (HM03982) | | | | | | | | | | | | | | | | | | | | | | | | | |
| CHINESE HERBAL MED & HLTH CARE (HM04200) | | | | | | | | | | | | | | | | | | | | | | | | | |
| CHINESE HERBAL MED ACU CTRE (HM04205) | | | | | | | | | | | | | | | | | | | | | | | | | |
| CHIROPRACTIC & HERBAL CENTRE (HM04349) | | ● | | | | | | | | | | | | | | | | | | | | | | | |
| CHIROPRACTIC CLINIC (HM04392) | | ● | | | | | | | | | | | | | | | | | | | | | | | |
| CHIROPRACTIC PLUS (HM04402) | | ● | | | | | | | | | | | | | | | | | | | | | | | |
| CHISLEHURST NATURAL HEALTH (HM04410) | ● | | | | | | | | | | | | | | | | | | | | | | | | |
| CHISTLEHURST NATURAL HLTH CTRE (HM04411) | ● | | | | | | | | | | | | | | | | | | | | | | | | |
| CHRISTINE CHINNERY COMP THER (HM04446) | | | | | | | ● | | | | | | | | | | | | | | | | | | |
| COMMON SCENTS (HM04903) | | | | | | | | | | | | | | | | | | | | | | | | | |
| COMPLEMENTARY THERAPIES (HM04940) | | | | | | | | | | | | | | | | | | | | | | | | | |
| COPY CENTRE (HM05150) | | | | | | | | | | | | | | | | | | | | | | | | | |
| COURT, SUSAN (HM05266) | | ● | | | | | | | | | | | | | | | | | | | | | | | |
| COURT, SUSAN (HM05265) | | ● | | | | | | | | | | | | | | | | | | | | | | | |
| COYSTEN & ASSOCIATES (HM05332) | | | | | | | | | ● | | | | | | | | | | | | | | | | |
| CRACKNELL, JANICE (HM05343) | | | | | | | | | | | | | | | | | | | | | | | | | |
| CROIX, LINDA LA (HM05460) | | | | | | | | | | | | | | | | | | | | | | | | | |
| CULLEN, KEVIN (HM05560) | | ● | | | | | | | | | | | | | | | | | | | | | | | |
| DAVID, B (HM05782) | | | | | | | | | | | | | | | | | | | | | | | | | |
| DAVINSKY, MARZO (HM05845) | | | | | | | | | | | | | | | | | | | | | | | | | |
| DEAL CHIROPRACTIC CLINIC (HM05934) | | ● | | | | | | | | | | | | | | | | | | | | | | | |
| DELTA MEDI CLINIC (HM05969) | | | | | | | | | | | | | | | | | | | | | | | ● | | |
| DICKMAN, ANNIE (HM06080) | | | | | | | | | | | | | | | | | | | | | | | | | |
| DILLON, MICHAEL (HM06100) | | | | ● | | | ● | ● | | | | | | | | | | | | | | | | | |
| DIMENT, GORDON L (HM06105) | | | | ● | | | | ● | | | | | | | | | | | | | | | | | |
| EDWARDS, R (HM06667) | | ● | | | | | | | | | | | | | | | | | | | | | | | |
| EDWARDS, R (HM06668) | | ● | | | | | | | | | | | | | | | | | | | | | | | |
| EDWARDS, R, HERNE BAY (HM06670) | | ● | | | | | | | | | | | | | | | | | | | | | | | |

# A - F Therapies at Practices/Businesses

Business by County with Reference no.

| Business | Absent Healing | Acupressure | Acupuncture | Alexander Technique | Allergy Testing | Anthroposohical Med | Aromatherapy | Art Therapy | Aura Therapy | Auricular Therapy | Auto Suggestion | Autogenic Training | Aversion Therapy | Ayurvedic Medicine | Baby Massage | Bach Remedies | Bates Method | Beauty Therapy | Bio-energetics | Biofeedback | Biomagnetic Therapy | Biomechanics | Bonesetting | Bowen Therapy | Chinese Herbal Medicine |
|---|---|---|---|---|---|---|---|---|---|---|---|---|---|---|---|---|---|---|---|---|---|---|---|---|---|
| ESSENCES OF AROMA/NTRL THRPY (HM06894) | | | | | | | ● | | | | | | | | | | | | | | | | | | |
| ESSER, ROB J (HM06931) | | | ● | | | | | | | | | | | | | | | | | | | | | | |
| EUROPEAN AYUR-VEDA (HM06944) | | | | | | | ● | | | | | | | ● | | | | | | | | | | | |
| EVEGATE CLINIC (HM06996) | | | ● | | | | | | | | | | | | | | | | | | | | | | |
| EVOLUTION HEALTH (HM07014) | | | | | | | ● | | | | | | | | | | | | | | | | | | |
| FALCONER, PATRICIA (HM07073) | | | | | | | ● | | | | | | | | | | | | | | | | | | |
| FERN & CUTTER (HM07235) | | | | | | | ● | | | | | | | | | | | | | | | | | | |
| FIELDING, DEBORAH (HM07272) | | | ● | | | | | | | | | | | | | | | | | | | | | | |
| FOORD, AUDREY (HM07463) | | | | | | | | | | | | | | | | | | | | | | | | | |
| FRANCIS-JONES, TREVOR (DR) (HM07679) | | | | | | | | | | | | | | | | | | | | | | | | | |
| FRENCH, K J (HM07733) | | | | ● | | | | | | | | | | | | | | | | | | | | | |
| FROST, CAROLINE (HM07759) | | | ● | | | | | | | | | | | | | | | | | | | | | | |
| GERMANN, KIRSTEN (HM08000) | | | ● | | | | | | | | | | | | | | | | | | | | | | |
| GIANFAGNA, CARMELA (HM08017) | | | ● | | | | | | | | | | | | | | | | | | | | | | |
| GIBSON, JAN (HM08040) | ● | | | | | | | | ● | | ● | | ● | | | ● | | | | | | | | | |
| GILLINGHAM CLINIC OF COMP MED (HM08097) | | ● | ● | | | | | | | | | | | | | | | | | | | | | | |
| GORING-THOMAS, DIANE (HM08290) | | | | | | | ● | | | | | | | | | | | | | | | | | | |
| GUNN, JASON (HM08642) | | | | | | | | | | | | | | | | | | | | | | | | | |
| HANNA, MARK (HM08931) | | | | | | | | | | | | | | | | | | | | | | | | | |
| HAYES, JACQUELINE (HM09260) | | | | | | | | | | | | | | | | | | | | | | | | | |
| HEALING AND HERBS (HM09325) | ● | | | | | | | | | | | | | | | | | | | | | | | | |
| HEALTH & BEAUTY WISE (HM09366) | | | | | | | ● | | | | | | | | | | | | | | | | | | |
| HEATHSIDE CENTRE (HM09461) | | | ● | | | | ● | | | | | | | | | | | | | | | | | | |
| HERBRIDGE (HM09666) | | | ● | | | | | | | | | | | | | | | | | | | | | | |
| HESELDEN, TERESA E (HM09693) | | | | | | | ● | | | | | | | | | | | | | | | | | | |
| HEYWARD, SHIRLEY (HM09714) | | | | | | | ● | | | | | | | | | | | | | | | | | | |
| HIRON, D (HM09842) | | | | | | | ● | | | | | | | | | | | | | | | | | | |
| HOLISTIC THERAPIES (HM09993) | | | | | | | ● | | | | | | | | | | | | | | | | | | |
| HOPE CHIROPRACTIC (HM10133) | | | | | | | | | | | | | | | | | | | | | | | | | |
| INT COLLEGE OF CRYSTAL HEALING (HM10684) | | | | | | | | | | | | | | | | | | | | | | | | | |
| ISIS (HM10763) | ● | | | | | | ● | | ● | | | | | ● | | ● | | | | | | | | | |
| JACCQUELINE ELLISON PRACTICE (HM10811) | | | | | | | | | | | | | | | | | | | | | | | | | |
| JENNER, ROSEMARY (HM11002) | | | | | | | ● | | | | | | | | | | | | | | | | | | |
| KARMERS CLINIQUE (HM11328) | | | | | | | ● | | | ● | | | | | | | | | | | | | | | |

| Business | Chiropody | Chiropractic | Clinical Ecology | Cognitive Therapy | Colonic Hydrotherapy | Colour Therapy | Complementary Therapy | Counselling | Cranial Osteopathy | Cranio-Sacral Therapy | Cryo Surgery | Crystal Healing | Cupping | Cymatics | Dance Movement Thrpy | Dietician | Do-In | Douching | Dowsing | Drama Therapy | Electrolipolysis | Electrolysis | Electrotherapy | Encounter Groups | Faith Healing |
|---|---|---|---|---|---|---|---|---|---|---|---|---|---|---|---|---|---|---|---|---|---|---|---|---|---|
| ESSENCES OF AROMA/NTRL THRPY (HM06894) | | | | | | | | | | | | | | | | | | | | | | | | | |
| ESSER, ROB J (HM06931) | | | | | | | | | | | | | | | | | | | | | | | | | |
| EUROPEAN AYUR-VEDA (HM06944) | | | | | | | | | | | | | | | | | | | | | | | | | |
| EVEGATE CLINIC (HM06996) | | ● | | | | | | | | | | | | | | | | | | | | | | | |
| EVOLUTION HEALTH (HM07014) | | ● | | | | | | ● | | | | | | | | | | | | | | | | | |
| FALCONER, PATRICIA (HM07073) | | | | | | | | | | | | | | | | | | | | | | | | | |
| FERN & CUTTER (HM07235) | | | | | | | | | | | | | | | | | | | | | | | | | |
| FIELDING, DEBORAH (HM07272) | | | | | | | | | | | | | | | | | | | | | | | | | |
| FOORD, AUDREY (HM07463) | ● | | | | | | | | | | | | | | | | | | | | | | | | |
| FRANCIS-JONES, TREVOR (DR) (HM07679) | | ● | | | | | | | | | | | | | | | | | | | | | | | |
| FRENCH, K J (HM07733) | | | | | | | | | | | | | | | | | | | | | | | | | |
| FROST, CAROLINE (HM07759) | | | | | | | | | | | | | | | | | | | | | | | | | |
| GERMANN, KIRSTEN (HM08000) | | | | | | | | | | | | | | | | | | | | | | | | | |
| GIANFAGNA, CARMELA (HM08017) | | | | | | | | | | | | | | | | | | | | | | | | | |
| GIBSON, JAN (HM08040) | | | | ● | | ● | ● | ● | | | | | | | | | | | | | | | | | ● |
| GILLINGHAM CLINIC OF COMP MED (HM08097) | | | | | | | ● | | | | | | | | | ● | | | | | | | | | |
| GORING-THOMAS, DIANE (HM08290) | | | | | | | | | | | | | | | | | | | | | | | | | |
| GUNN, JASON (HM08642) | | | | | | | | | ● | | | | | | | | | | | | | | | | |
| HANNA, MARK (HM08931) | | | | ● | | | | ● | | | | | | | | ● | | | | | | | | | |
| HAYES, JACQUELINE (HM09260) | | | | | | | | | ● | | | | ● | | | | | | | | | | | | |
| HEALING AND HERBS (HM09325) | | | | | | | ● | | | | | ● | | | | | | | ● | | | | | | ● |
| HEALTH & BEAUTY WISE (HM09366) | | | | | | | | | | | | | | | | | | | | | | | | | |
| HEATHSIDE CENTRE (HM09461) | | ● | | | | | | | | | | | | | | | | | | | | | | | |
| HERBRIDGE (HM09666) | | | | | | | | | | | | | | | | | | | | | | | | | |
| HESELDEN, TERESA E (HM09693) | | | | | | | | | | | | | | | | | | | | | | | | | |
| HEYWARD, SHIRLEY (HM09714) | | | | | | | | | | | | | | | | | | | | | | | | | |
| HIRON, D (HM09842) | | | | | | | | | | | | | | | | | | | | | | | | | |
| HOLISTIC THERAPIES (HM09993) | | | | | | | | | | | | | | | | | | | | | | | | | |
| HOPE CHIROPRACTIC (HM10133) | | ● | | | | | | | | | | | | | | | | | | | | | | | |
| INT COLLEGE OF CRYSTAL HEALING (HM10684) | | | | | | | | | | | | ● | | | | | | | | | | | | | |
| ISIS (HM10763) | | | | | | ● | | ● | | | | ● | | | | | | | | | | | | | ● |
| JACCQUELINE ELLISON PRACTICE (HM10811) | | | | | | | | | ● | | | | | | | | | | | | | | | | |
| JENNER, ROSEMARY (HM11002) | | | | | | | | | | | | | | | | | | | | | | | | | |
| KARMERS CLINIQUE (HM11328) | | | | | | | | | | | | | | | | | | | | | | | | | |

# A - F Therapies at Practices/Businesses

| Business by County with Reference no. | Absent Healing | Acupressure | Acupuncture | Alexander Technique | Allergy Testing | Anthroposohical Med | Aromatherapy | Art Therapy | Aura Therapy | Auricular Therapy | Auto Suggestion | Autogenic Training | Aversion Therapy | Ayurvedic Medicine | Baby Massage | Bach Remedies | Bates Method | Beauty Therapy | Bio-energetics | Biofeedback | Biomagnetic Therapy | Biomechanics | Bonesetting | Bowen Therapy | Chinese Herbal Medicine |
|---|---|---|---|---|---|---|---|---|---|---|---|---|---|---|---|---|---|---|---|---|---|---|---|---|---|
| KENT HOUSE CHIROPRACTIC CLINIC (HM11517) | | | | | | | | | | | | | | | | | | | | | | | | | |
| KENT HOUSE CHIROPRACTIC CLINIC (HM11518) | | | | | | | | | | | | | | | | | | | | | | | | | |
| KENT HOUSE CHIROPRACTIC CLINIC (HM11519) | | | | | | | | | | | | | | | | | | | | | | | | | |
| KENT HOUSE CHIROPRACTIC CLINIC (HM11520) | | | | | | | | | | | | | | | | | | | | | | | | | |
| KENT INSTITUTE OF COMP MED (HM11521) | | | | | | | ● | | | | | | | | | | | | | | | | | | |
| KSC (HM11812) | | | | | | | ● | | | | | | | | | | | | | | | | | | |
| LAMB, G BRIAN (HM11888) | | | | ● | | | | | | | | | | | | ● | ● | | | | | | | | |
| LAVINGOTN, A (HM12034) | | | | | | | ● | | | | | | | | | | | | | | | | | | |
| LEBOR, JILL (HM12115) | | | | | | | | | | | | | | | | | | | | | | | | ● | |
| LIKISMA (HM12382) | | | | | | | ● | | | | | | | | | | | | | | | | | | |
| LIKISMA PRESENTATIONS (HM12388) | | | | | | | ● | | | | | | | | | | | | | | | | | | |
| LIVING WELL CLINIC (HM12488) | | | | | | | | | | | | | | | | | | | | | | | | | |
| LOBB, BRIAN W (HM12528) | | | | | | | | | | | | | | | | | | | | | | | | | |
| LUDKINS, P (HM12726) | | | ● | | | | | | | | | | | | | | | | | | | | | | |
| LUGG, G (HM12732) | | | | | | | | | | | | | | | | | | | | | | | | | |
| LYKISMA (HM12757) | | | | | | | ● | | | | | | | | | | | | | | | | | | |
| MABBERLEY, KATHIE (HM12812) | | | | | | | ● | | | | | | | | | | | | | | | | | ● | |
| MAIDSTONE ACUPUNCTURE CLINIC (HM12935) | | | ● | | | | | | | | | | | | | | | | | | | | | | |
| MARTIN, PAULA (HM13206) | | | | | | | ● | | | | | | | | | | | | | | | | | | |
| MARY CANNON - CLINICAL NUTRI (HM13221) | | | | | | | | | | | | | | | | | | | | | | | | | |
| MCDOWELL, S (HM13467) | | | | | | | | | | | | | | | | | | | | | | | | | |
| MCDOWELL, STEPHEN (HM13468) | | | | | | | | | | | | | | | | | | | | | | | | | |
| MCLAREN, M (HM13542) | | | ● | | | | | | | | | | | | | | | | | | | | | | |
| MEADOWS (HM13630) | | | | | | | ● | | | | | | | | | | | | | | | | | | |
| MEADOWS (HM13631) | | | | | | | ● | | | | | | | | | | | | | | | | | | |
| MEDWAY ACUPUNCTURE CLINIC (HM13674) | | | ● | | | | | | | | | | | | | | | | | | | | | | |
| MEOPHAM CLINIC (HM13732) | | | ● | | | | ● | | | ● | | | | | | | | | | | | | | ● | |
| MICHELLE PEARSON AT HARMONY (HM13798) | | | | | | | ● | | | | | | | | | | | | | | | | | | |
| MORETON, JUNE (HM14157) | | | | | | | ● | | | | | | | | | | | | | | | | | | |
| MUIRHEAD, MARGARET (HM14323) | | | | | | | | | | | | | | | | | | | | | | | | | |
| MULVANEY, ALISTAIR (HM14353) | | | | | | | | | | | | | | | | | | | | | | ● | | | |
| MURAYAMA, YOSHIHIRO (HM14369) | | | ● | | | | | | | | | | | | | | | | | | | | | | |
| NATURAL HEALTH CENTRE (HM14562) | | | | | | | | | | | | | | | | | | | | | | | | | |
| NATURAL HEALTH CENTRE (HM14568) | | | ● | ● | | | ● | | | | | | | | | ● | | | | | | | | ● | |

| Business by County with Reference no. | Chiropody | Chiropractic | Clinical Ecology | Cognitive Therapy | Colonic Hydrotherapy | Colour Therapy | Complementary Therapy | Counselling | Cranial Osteopathy | Cranio-Sacral Therapy | Cryo Surgery | Crystal Healing | Cupping | Cymatics | Dance Movement Thrpy | Dietician | Do-In | Douching | Dowsing | Drama Therapy | Electrolipolysis | Electrolysis | Electrotherapy | Encounter Groups | Faith Healing |
|---|---|---|---|---|---|---|---|---|---|---|---|---|---|---|---|---|---|---|---|---|---|---|---|---|---|
| KENT HOUSE CHIROPRACTIC CLINIC (HM11517) | | ● | | | | | | | | | | | | | | | | | | | | | | | |
| KENT HOUSE CHIROPRACTIC CLINIC (HM11518) | | ● | | | | | | | | | | | | | | | | | | | | | | | |
| KENT HOUSE CHIROPRACTIC CLINIC (HM11519) | | ● | | | | | | | | | | | | | | | | | | | | | | | |
| KENT HOUSE CHIROPRACTIC CLINIC (HM11520) | | ● | | | | | | | | | | | | | | | | | | | | | | | |
| KENT INSTITUTE OF COMP MED (HM11521) | | | | | | | | | | | | | | | | | | | | | | | | | |
| KSC (HM11812) | | | | | | | | ● | ● | | | | | | | | | | | | | | | | |
| LAMB, G BRIAN (HM11888) | | | | | | | ● | ● | | | | | ● | | | ● | | | | | | | | | |
| LAVINGOTN, A (HM12034) | | | | | | | | | | | | | | | | | | | | | | | | | |
| LEBOR, JILL (HM12115) | | | | | | | | | | | | | | | | | | | | | | | | | |
| LIKISMA (HM12382) | | | | | | | | | | | | | | | | | | | | | | | | | |
| LIKISMA PRESENTATIONS (HM12388) | | | | | | | | | | | | | | | | | | | | | | | | | |
| LIVING WELL CLINIC (HM12488) | | ● | | | | | | | | | | | | | | | | | | | | | | | |
| LOBB, BRIAN W (HM12528) | | | | ● | | | | ● | | | | | | | | | | | | | | | | | |
| LUDKINS, P (HM12726) | | | | | | | | | | | | | | | | | | | | | | | | | |
| LUGG, G (HM12732) | ● | | | | | | | | | | | | | | | | | | | | | | | | |
| LYKISMA (HM12757) | | | | | | | | | | | | | | | | | | | | | | | | | |
| MABBERLEY, KATHIE (HM12812) | | | | | | | | | | | | | | | | | | | | | | | | | |
| MAIDSTONE ACUPUNCTURE CLINIC (HM12935) | | | | | | | | | | | | | | | | | | | | | | | | | |
| MARTIN, PAULA (HM13206) | | | | | | | | | | | | | | | | | | | | | | | | | |
| MARY CANNON - CLINICAL NUTRI (HM13221) | | | ● | | | | ● | | | | | | | | | ● | | | | | | | | | |
| MCDOWELL, S (HM13467) | | ● | | | | | | | | | | | | | | | | | | | | | | | |
| MCDOWELL, STEPHEN (HM13468) | | ● | | | | | | | | | | | | | | | | | | | | | | | |
| MCLAREN, M (HM13542) | | | | | | | | | | | | | | | | | | | | | | | | | |
| MEADOWS (HM13630) | | | | | | | | | | | | | | | | | | | | | | | | | |
| MEADOWS (HM13631) | | | | | | | | | | | | | | | | | | | | | | | | | |
| MEDWAY ACUPUNCTURE CLINIC (HM13674) | | | | | | | | | | | | | | | | | | | | | | | | | |
| MEOPHAM CLINIC (HM13732) | ● | | | | | | | ● | | | | | | | | | | | | | | | | | |
| MICHELLE PEARSON AT HARMONY (HM13798) | | | | | | | | | | | | | | | | | | | | | | | | | |
| MORETON, JUNE (HM14157) | | | | | | | | | | | | | | | | | | | | | | | | | |
| MUIRHEAD, MARGARET (HM14323) | | | | | | | | ● | | | | | | | | | | | | | | | | | |
| MULVANEY, ALISTAIR (HM14353) | ● | | | | | | | | | | | | | | | | | | | | | | | | |
| MURAYAMA, YOSHIHIRO (HM14369) | | | | | | | | | | | | | | | | | | | | | | | | | |
| NATURAL HEALTH CENTRE (HM14562) | | | | | | | | ● | | | | | | | | | | | | | | | | | |
| NATURAL HEALTH CENTRE (HM14568) | ● | | | | | | ● | ● | | | | | | | | | | | | | | | | | |

# A - F Therapies at Practices/Businesses

| Business by County with Reference no. | Absent Healing | Acupressure | Acupuncture | Alexander Technique | Allergy Testing | Anthroposohical Med | Aromatherapy | Art Therapy | Aura Therapy | Auricular Therapy | Auto Suggestion | Autogenic Training | Aversion Therapy | Ayurvedic Medicine | Baby Massage |
|---|---|---|---|---|---|---|---|---|---|---|---|---|---|---|---|
| NATURAL THERAPIST (HM14635) | | | | | | | ● | | | | | | | | |
| NATURAL THERAPY CENTRE (HM14643) | | | ● | | | | | | | | | | | | |
| NICHOLS, SYLVIA (HM14918) | | | | | | | ● | | | | | | | | |
| NORTH KENT CHIROPRACTIC CLINIC (HM15031) | | | | | | | | | | | | | | | |
| ORPINGTON CHIROPRACTICE CLINIC (HM15403) | | | | | | | | | | | | | | | |
| OSTEOPATHIC PRACTICE (HM15466) | | | | | | | | | | | | | | | |
| PARISH, ANN (HM15660) | | | | | | | ● | | | | | | | | |
| PASSCHIER, MAREANNE SASSEN (HM15779) | | | | | | | | | | | | | | | |
| PATERSON, MARGARET (HM15814) | ● | | | | | | | | | | | | | | |
| PEARTON, GILL (HM15919) | | | | | | | | | | | | | | | |
| PECK, GORDON (HM15923) | | | ● | | | | | | | | | | | | |
| PELE, ANDRI (HM15950) | | | | | | | | | | | | | | | |
| PETTS, PHILIP (HM16101) | | | | | | | | | | | | | | | |
| PHYSIOTHERAPY CENTRE (HM16230) | | | | | | | | | | | | | | | |
| PSARADELIS, T (HM16681) | | | | | | | ● | | | | | | | | |
| READ, CHARLES REG OSTEOPATH (HM16994) | | | | | | | | | | | | | | | |
| ROCHESTER CHIRO HEALTH CENTRE (HM17519) | | | | | | | | | | | | | | | |
| ROCHESTER PHYSIO & SPORTS (HM17520) | | | ● | | | | | | | | | | | | |
| ROMNEY MARSH OSTEOPATHS (HM17574) | | | | | | | | | | | | | | | |
| ROSE, NAOMI (HM17612) | | | | | | | ● | | | | | | | | |
| S J DYSON REFLEX-AROMA (HM17809) | | | | | | | ● | | | | | | | | |
| SACKS, PATRICA (HM17828) | | | | | | | | | | | | | | | |
| SANCTUM HOLISTIC THERAPY CTRE (HM17896) | | ● | | | | | ● | | | | | | | | |
| SANDOWN CLINIC FOR COMP MED (HM17926) | | | | | | | ● | | | | | | | | |
| SHEARER, GAYLE (HM18357) | | | | | | | | | | | | | | | |
| SHIATSU (HM18451) | | ● | | | | | | | | | | | | | |
| SIMMONDS, JENNI (HM18557) | | | | | | | ● | | | | | | | | |
| SOUTHCOTE CHIROPRACTIC CLINIC (HM18927) | | | | | | | | | | | | | | | |
| STARFIELDS HOLISTIC HLTH CTRE (HM19145) | ● | ● | | | | ● | | | ● | | | | | | |
| STONE, CHARLES (HM19334) | | | | | | | ● | | | | | | | | |
| STURGE, DEBBIE (HM19445) | | | | | | | | | | | | | | | |
| TEACHER OF THE ALEXNDR TECH (HM19805) | | | | ● | | | | | | | | | | | |
| THENUWARA, C D (HM19870) | | | ● | | | | | | | | | | | | |
| THEW, CAROLYN (HM19915) | | | | | | | ● | | | | | | | | |

| Business by County with Reference no. | Bach Remedies | Bates Method | Beauty Therapy | Bio-energetics | Biofeedback | Biomagnetic Therapy | Biomechanics | Bonesetting | Bowen Therapy | Chinese Herbal Medicine | Chiropody | Chiropractic | Clinical Ecology | Cognitive Therapy | Colonic Hydrotherapy | Colour Therapy | Complementary Therapy |
|---|---|---|---|---|---|---|---|---|---|---|---|---|---|---|---|---|---|
| NATURAL THERAPIST (HM14635) | | | | | | | | | | | | | | | | | |
| NATURAL THERAPY CENTRE (HM14643) | | | | | | | | | | | | | | | | | |
| NICHOLS, SYLVIA (HM14918) | | | | | | | | | | | | | | | | | |
| NORTH KENT CHIROPRACTIC CLINIC (HM15031) | | | | | | | | | | | | ● | | | | | |
| ORPINGTON CHIROPRACTICE CLINIC (HM15403) | | | | | | | | | | | | ● | | | | | |
| OSTEOPATHIC PRACTICE (HM15466) | | | | | | | | | | | | | | | | | |
| PARISH, ANN (HM15660) | | | | | | | | | | | | | | | | | |
| PASSCHIER, MAREANNE SASSEN (HM15779) | ● | | | | | | | | | | | | | | | | |
| PATERSON, MARGARET (HM15814) | | | | | | | | | | | | | | | | | |
| PEARTON, GILL (HM15919) | | | | | | | | | ● | | | | | | | | |
| PECK, GORDON (HM15923) | | | | | | | | | | | | | | | | | |
| PELE, ANDRI (HM15950) | | | | | | | | | | | | | | | | | |
| PETTS, PHILIP (HM16101) | | | | | | | | | | | | ● | | | | | |
| PHYSIOTHERAPY CENTRE (HM16230) | | | | | | | ● | | | | ● | | | | | | |
| PSARADELIS, T (HM16681) | | | | | | | | | | | | | | | | | |
| READ, CHARLES REG OSTEOPATH (HM16994) | | | | | | | | | | | | | | | | | |
| ROCHESTER CHIRO HEALTH CENTRE (HM17519) | | | | | | | | | | | | ● | | | | | |
| ROCHESTER PHYSIO & SPORTS (HM17520) | | | | | | | | | | | | | | | | | |
| ROMNEY MARSH OSTEOPATHS (HM17574) | | | | | | | | | | | | | | | | | |
| ROSE, NAOMI (HM17612) | | | | | | | | | | | | | | | | | ● |
| S J DYSON REFLEX-AROMA (HM17809) | | | | | | | | | | | | | | | | | |
| SACKS, PATRICA (HM17828) | | | | | | | | | | | ● | | | | | | |
| SANCTUM HOLISTIC THERAPY CTRE (HM17896) | | | ● | | | | | | | | | | | | | | |
| SANDOWN CLINIC FOR COMP MED (HM17926) | | | | | | | | | | | | ● | | | | | |
| SHEARER, GAYLE (HM18357) | | | | | | | | | | | | | | | | | |
| SHIATSU (HM18451) | | | | | | | | | | | | | | | | | |
| SIMMONDS, JENNI (HM18557) | | | | | | | | | | | | | | | | | |
| SOUTHCOTE CHIROPRACTIC CLINIC (HM18927) | | | | | | | | | | | | ● | | | | | |
| STARFIELDS HOLISTIC HLTH CTRE (HM19145) | ● | | | | | | | | | | | ● | | | | | ● |
| STONE, CHARLES (HM19334) | | | | | | | | | ● | | | | | | | ● | |
| STURGE, DEBBIE (HM19445) | | | | | | | | | | | | | | | | | ● |
| TEACHER OF THE ALEXNDR TECH (HM19805) | | | | | | | | | | | | | | | | | |
| THENUWARA, C D (HM19870) | | | | | | | | | | | | | | | | | |
| THEW, CAROLYN (HM19915) | | | | | | | | | | | | | | | | | |

| Business by County with Reference no. | Counselling | Cranial Osteopathy | Cranio-Sacral Therapy | Cryo Surgery | Crystal Healing | Cupping | Cymatics | Dance Movement Thrpy | Dietician | Do-In | Douching | Dowsing | Drama Therapy | Electrolipolysis | Electrolysis | Electrotherapy | Encounter Groups | Faith Healing |
|---|---|---|---|---|---|---|---|---|---|---|---|---|---|---|---|---|---|---|
| NATURAL THERAPIST (HM14635) | | | | | | | | | | | | | | | | | | |
| NATURAL THERAPY CENTRE (HM14643) | | | | | | | | | | | | | | | | | | |
| NICHOLS, SYLVIA (HM14918) | | | | | | | | | | | | | | | | | | |
| NORTH KENT CHIROPRACTIC CLINIC (HM15031) | | | | | | | | | | | | | | | | | | |
| ORPINGTON CHIROPRACTICE CLINIC (HM15403) | | | | | | | | | | | | | | | | | | |
| OSTEOPATHIC PRACTICE (HM15466) | | ● | | | | | | | | | | | | | | | | |
| PARISH, ANN (HM15660) | | | | | | | | | | | | | | | | | | |
| PASSCHIER, MAREANNE SASSEN (HM15779) | ● | | | | | | | | | | | | | | | | | |
| PATERSON, MARGARET (HM15814) | | | | | | | | | | | | | | | | | | |
| PEARTON, GILL (HM15919) | | | | | | | | | | | | | | | | | | |
| PECK, GORDON (HM15923) | | | | | | | | | | | | | | | | | | |
| PELE, ANDRI (HM15950) | ● | | | | | | | | | | | | | | | | | |
| PETTS, PHILIP (HM16101) | | | | | | | | | | | | | | | | | | |
| PHYSIOTHERAPY CENTRE (HM16230) | | | | | | | | | | | | | | | | | | |
| PSARADELIS, T (HM16681) | | | | | | | | | | | | | | | | | | |
| READ, CHARLES REG OSTEOPATH (HM16994) | | ● | | | | | | | | | | | | | | | | |
| ROCHESTER CHIRO HEALTH CENTRE (HM17519) | | | | | | | | | | | | | | | | | | |
| ROCHESTER PHYSIO & SPORTS (HM17520) | | | | | | | | | | | | | | | | | | |
| ROMNEY MARSH OSTEOPATHS (HM17574) | | ● | | | | | | | | | | | | | | | | |
| ROSE, NAOMI (HM17612) | | | | | | | | | | | | | | | | | | ● |
| S J DYSON REFLEX-AROMA (HM17809) | | | | | | | | | | | | | | | | | | |
| SACKS, PATRICA (HM17828) | | | | | | | | | | | | | | | | | | |
| SANCTUM HOLISTIC THERAPY CTRE (HM17896) | | | ● | | | | | | | | | | | | | | | |
| SANDOWN CLINIC FOR COMP MED (HM17926) | | | | | | | | | | | | | | | | | | |
| SHEARER, GAYLE (HM18357) | | ● | | | | | | | | | | | | | | | | |
| SHIATSU (HM18451) | ● | | | | | | | | | | | | | | | | | |
| SIMMONDS, JENNI (HM18557) | | | | | | | | | | | | | | | | | | |
| SOUTHCOTE CHIROPRACTIC CLINIC (HM18927) | | | | | | | | | | | | | | | | | | |
| STARFIELDS HOLISTIC HLTH CTRE (HM19145) | ● | ● | | | | | | | ● | | | ● | | | | | | |
| STONE, CHARLES (HM19334) | | | | | ● | | | | | | | | | | | | | |
| STURGE, DEBBIE (HM19445) | | | | | | | | | | | | | | | | | | |
| TEACHER OF THE ALEXNDR TECH (HM19805) | | | | | | | | | | | | | | | | | | |
| THENUWARA, C D (HM19870) | | | | | | | | | | | | | | | | | | |
| THEW, CAROLYN (HM19915) | | | | | | | | | | | | | | | | | | |

# A - F Therapies at Practices/Businesses

| Business by County with Reference no. | Absent Healing | Acupressure | Acupuncture | Alexander Technique | Allergy Testing | Anthroposohical Med | Aromatherapy | Art Therapy | Aura Therapy | Auricular Therapy | Auto Suggestion | Autogenic Training | Aversion Therapy | Ayurvedic Medicine | Baby Massage | Bach Remedies | Bates Method |
|---|---|---|---|---|---|---|---|---|---|---|---|---|---|---|---|---|---|
| TONBRIDGE CLINIC (HM20151) | | | ● | | | | ● | | | | | | | | | | |
| TOWN, BERNICE (HM20199) | | | | | | | | | | | | | | | | | |
| TUNBRIDGE WELLS CHIROPRACTIC (HM20392) | | | | | | | | | | | | | | | | | |
| TURNER, ANDREA (HM20417) | | | | | | | ● | | | | | | | | | | |
| TURNER, PENNY (HM20434) | | | | | | | ● | | | | | | | | | | |
| TWITCHETT, EVE (HM20457) | | | | | | | ● | | | | | | | | | | |
| USEFUL THERAPIES (HM20534) | ● | | | | | | ● | | | | | | | | | | |
| VARNEY, MONICA (HM20591) | | | | | | | ● | | | | | | | | | | |
| VAUX, P A (HM20602) | | | | | | | | | | | | | | | | | |
| VENN, ESTHER K (HM20613) | | | | | | | | | | | | | | | | | |
| VINES REIKI HEALING CENTRE (HM20680) | | | | | | | ● | | | | | | | | | | |
| WARD, A (HM20897) | | | ● | | | | | | | | | | | | | | |
| WATLING STREET THERAPY CTRE (HM21001) | | ● | ● | ● | | | ● | | ● | | | | | | | ● | |
| WEBB-DE SISTO, MARION (HM21079) | | | | | | | | | | | | | | | | ● | |
| WELLS PHYSIO & SPORTS CLINIC (HM21168) | | | ● | | | | | | | | | | | | | | |
| WILKINS, D (HM21500) | | | | | | | ● | | | | | | | | | | |
| WOLFE, ROBERT (HM21762) | | | | | | | | | | | | | | | | | |
| LANCASHIRE | | | | | | | | | | | | | | | | | |
| ABERNETHY, HILARY (HM00123) | | | | | | | ● | | | | | | | | | | |
| ACUPUNCTURE PRIVATE CLINIC (HM00317) | | | ● | | | | | | | | | | | | | | |
| ALPHAWAVE (HM00685) | | | | | | | | | | | | | | | | | |
| ALTERNATIVE MEDICINE (HM00715) | | | ● | | | | | | | | | | | | | | |
| ALTERNATIVE MEDICINE PRACTICE (HM00721) | | | ● | | | | | | | | | | | | | | |
| AQUARIUS AROMATHERAPY (HM00956) | | | | | | | ● | | | | | | | | | | |
| AROMAZ (HM01143) | | | | | | | ● | | | | | | | | | | |
| ARROWSMITH, BARRIE (HM01150) | | | | | | | | | | | | | | | | | |
| BARRETT & LIPTROTT (HM01783) | | | | | | | | | | | | | | | | | |
| BEESTON, J (HM02061) | | | | | | | | | | | | | | | | | |
| BEHESHT (HM02067) | | | | | | | ● | | | | | | | | | | |
| BENTLEY AND ASSOCIATES (HM02172) | | | ● | | | | | | | | | | | | | | |
| BENTLEY, M J (HM02176) | | | | | | | | | | | | | | | | | |
| BFMP (HM02265) | | | ● | | | | ● | | | | | | | | | ● | |
| BIOS NATURE CLINIC (HM02344) | | | | | | | | | | | | | | | | | |
| BLACKPOOL CHIROPRACTIC CLINIC (HM02458) | | | | | | | | | | | | | | | | | |

| Business by County with Reference no. | Beauty Therapy | Bio-energetics | Biofeedback | Biomagnetic Therapy | Biomechanics | Bonesetting | Bowen Therapy | Chinese Herbal Medicine | Chiropody | Chiropractic | Clinical Ecology | Cognitive Therapy | Colonic Hydrotherapy | Colour Therapy | Complementary Therapy | Counselling | Cranial Osteopathy |
|---|---|---|---|---|---|---|---|---|---|---|---|---|---|---|---|---|---|
| TONBRIDGE CLINIC (HM20151) | | | | | | | | | | | | ● | | | | ● | ● |
| TOWN, BERNICE (HM20199) | | | | | | | | | ● | | | | | | | | |
| TUNBRIDGE WELLS CHIROPRACTIC (HM20392) | | | | | | | | | | ● | | | | | | | |
| TURNER, ANDREA (HM20417) | | | | | | | | | | | | | | | | | |
| TURNER, PENNY (HM20434) | | | | | | | | | | | | | | | | | |
| TWITCHETT, EVE (HM20457) | | | | | | | | | | | | | | | | | |
| USEFUL THERAPIES (HM20534) | | | | | | | | | | | | | | | | | |
| VARNEY, MONICA (HM20591) | | | | | | | | | | | | | | | | | |
| VAUX, P A (HM20602) | | | | | | | | | | ● | | | | | | | |
| VENN, ESTHER K (HM20613) | | | | | | | | | | ● | | | | | | | |
| VINES REIKI HEALING CENTRE (HM20680) | | | | | | | | | | | | | | | | | |
| WARD, A (HM20897) | | | | | | | | | | | | | | | | | |
| WATLING STREET THERAPY CTRE (HM21001) | | | ● | | | | ● | | | ● | | | | | ● | ● | ● |
| WEBB-DE SISTO, MARION (HM21079) | | | | | | | | | | | | | | | | | |
| WELLS PHYSIO & SPORTS CLINIC (HM21168) | | | | | | | | | | | | | | | | | |
| WILKINS, D (HM21500) | | | | | | | | | | | | | | | | | |
| WOLFE, ROBERT (HM21762) | | | | | ● | | | | | | | | | | | | |
| LANCASHIRE | | | | | | | | | | | | | | | | | |
| ABERNETHY, HILARY (HM00123) | | | | | | | | | | | | ● | | | ● | | |
| ACUPUNCTURE PRIVATE CLINIC (HM00317) | | | | | | | | | | | | | | | | | |
| ALPHAWAVE (HM00685) | | | | | | | | | | | | ● | | | | | |
| ALTERNATIVE MEDICINE (HM00715) | | | | | | | | | | | | | | | ● | ● | |
| ALTERNATIVE MEDICINE PRACTICE (HM00721) | | | | | | | | | | | | | | | ● | ● | |
| AQUARIUS AROMATHERAPY (HM00956) | | | | | | | | | | | | | | | | | |
| AROMAZ (HM01143) | | | | | | | | | | | | | | | | | |
| ARROWSMITH, BARRIE (HM01150) | | | | | | | | | ● | | | | | | | | |
| BARRETT & LIPTROTT (HM01783) | | | | | | | | | ● | | | | | | | | |
| BEESTON, J (HM02061) | | | | | | | | | | | | | | | | | |
| BEHESHT (HM02067) | | | | | | | | | | | | | | | | | |
| BENTLEY AND ASSOCIATES (HM02172) | | | | | | | | | ● | | | ● | | | | ● | |
| BENTLEY, M J (HM02176) | | | | | | | | | | ● | | | | | | | |
| BFMP (HM02265) | | | | | | | | | | | | | | | ● | | |
| BIOS NATURE CLINIC (HM02344) | | | ● | | | | | | | | ● | | | | | | |
| BLACKPOOL CHIROPRACTIC CLINIC (HM02458) | | | | | | | | | | ● | | | | | | | |

| Business by County with Reference no. | Cranio-Sacral Therapy | Cryo Surgery | Crystal Healing | Cupping | Cymatics | Dance Movement Thrpy | Dietician | Do-In | Douching | Dowsing | Drama Therapy | Electrolipolysis | Electrolysis | Electrotherapy | Encounter Groups | Faith Healing |
|---|---|---|---|---|---|---|---|---|---|---|---|---|---|---|---|---|
| TONBRIDGE CLINIC (HM20151) | | | | | | | ● | | | | | | | | | |
| TOWN, BERNICE (HM20199) | | | | | | | | | | | | | | | | |
| TUNBRIDGE WELLS CHIROPRACTIC (HM20392) | | | | | | | | | | | | | | | | |
| TURNER, ANDREA (HM20417) | | | | | | | | | | | | | | | | |
| TURNER, PENNY (HM20434) | | | | | | | | | | | | | | | | |
| TWITCHETT, EVE (HM20457) | | | | | | | | | | | | | | | | |
| USEFUL THERAPIES (HM20534) | | | | | | | | | | | | | | | | |
| VARNEY, MONICA (HM20591) | | | | | | | | | | | | | | | | |
| VAUX, P A (HM20602) | | | | | | | | | | | | | | | | |
| VENN, ESTHER K (HM20613) | | | | | | | | | | | | | | | | |
| VINES REIKI HEALING CENTRE (HM20680) | | | | | | | | | | | | | | | | |
| WARD, A (HM20897) | | | | | | | | | | | | | | | | |
| WATLING STREET THERAPY CTRE (HM21001) | | | | | | | | | | | | | | | | |
| WEBB-DE SISTO, MARION (HM21079) | | | | | | | | | | | | | | | | |
| WELLS PHYSIO & SPORTS CLINIC (HM21168) | | | | | | | | | | | | | | | | |
| WILKINS, D (HM21500) | | | | | | | | | | | | | | | | |
| WOLFE, ROBERT (HM21762) | | | | | | | | | | | | | | | | |
| LANCASHIRE | | | | | | | | | | | | | | | | |
| ABERNETHY, HILARY (HM00123) | | | | | | | | | | | | | | | | |
| ACUPUNCTURE PRIVATE CLINIC (HM00317) | | | | | | | | | | | | | | | | |
| ALPHAWAVE (HM00685) | | | | | | | | | | | | | | | | |
| ALTERNATIVE MEDICINE (HM00715) | | | | | | | ● | | ● | | | | | ● | | |
| ALTERNATIVE MEDICINE PRACTICE (HM00721) | | | | | | | ● | | | | | | | ● | | |
| AQUARIUS AROMATHERAPY (HM00956) | | | | | | | | | | | | | | | | |
| AROMAZ (HM01143) | | | | | | | | | | | | | | | | |
| ARROWSMITH, BARRIE (HM01150) | | | | | | | | | | | | | | | | |
| BARRETT & LIPTROTT (HM01783) | | | | | | | | | | | | | | | | |
| BEESTON, J (HM02061) | | | | | | | | | | | | | | ● | | |
| BEHESHT (HM02067) | | | | | | | | | | | | | | | | |
| BENTLEY AND ASSOCIATES (HM02172) | | | | | | | | | | | | | | ● | | |
| BENTLEY, M J (HM02176) | | | | | | | | | | | | | | | | |
| BFMP (HM02265) | | | | | | | | | | | | | | ● | | |
| BIOS NATURE CLINIC (HM02344) | | | | | | | | | | | | | | | | |
| BLACKPOOL CHIROPRACTIC CLINIC (HM02458) | | | | | | | | | | | | | | | | |

# A - F Therapies at Practices/Businesses

| Business by County with Reference no. | Absent Healing | Acupressure | Acupuncture | Alexander Technique | Allergy Testing | Anthroposohical Med | Aromatherapy | Art Therapy | Aura Therapy | Auricular Therapy | Auto Suggestion | Autogenic Training | Aversion Therapy | Ayurvedic Medicine | Baby Massage | Bach Remedies | Bates Method | Beauty Therapy | Bio-energetics | Biofeedback | Biomagnetic Therapy | Biomechanics | Bonesetting | Bowen Therapy | Chinese Herbal Medicine |
|---|---|---|---|---|---|---|---|---|---|---|---|---|---|---|---|---|---|---|---|---|---|---|---|---|---|
| BOLTON CHIROPRACTIC CLINIC (HM02656) | | | | | | | | | | | | | | | | | | | | | | | | | |
| BOLTON CLINIC OF ACUPUNCTURE (HM02657) | | | ● | | | | | | | | | | | | | | | | | | | | | | |
| BOLTON PHYSIOTHERAPY CLINIC (HM02658) | | | ● | | | | | | | | | | | | | | | | | | | | | | |
| BOLTON THERAPY CENTRE (HM02659) | | | ● | ● | | | ● | | | | | | | | | | | | | | | | | | |
| BOLTON, VANESSA (HM02664) | | ● | | | | | | | | | | | | | | | | | | | | | | | |
| BROOKES, MICHAEL (HM03163) | | ● | | | | | | | | | | | | | | | | | | | | | | | |
| CEROSIMO, JOSEPH (HM03930) | | | | | | | | | | | | | | | | | | | | | | | | | |
| CEROSIMO, JOSEPH (HM03931) | | | | | | | | | | | | | | | | | | | | | | | | | |
| CHARTERED PHYSIO & SPORTS (HM04041) | | | ● | | | | | | | | | | | | | | | | | | | | | | |
| CHIROPRACTIC ASSOCIATES (HM04378) | | | | | | | | | | | | | | | | | | | | | | | | | |
| CHIROPRACTIC ASSOCIATES (HM04376) | | | ● | | | | | | | | | | | | | | | | | | | | | | |
| CHIROPRACTIC ASSOCIATES (HM04377) | | | | | | | | | | | | | | | | | | | | | | | | | |
| CLARKE, SUSAN AMANDA (HM04605) | | | | | | | ● | | | | | | | | | | | | | | | | | | |
| CLOUGHS - CHRTRD PHYSIO CLINIC (HM04735) | | | | | | | ● | | | | | | | | | | | | | | | | | | |
| COLES, RONNIE (HM04836) | | | | | | | | | | | | | | | | | | | | | | | | | |
| COLLIER, ELAINE M (HM04859) | | | | | | | ● | | | | | | | | | | | | | | | | | | |
| COLLINSON, J (HM04883) | | | ● | | | | | | | | | | | | | | | | | | | | | | |
| COMPLEMENTARY HEALTH SERVICES (HM04929) | | | | | | | | | | | | | | | | | | | | | | | | | |
| COTTAM, O N (HM05224) | | | | | | | | | | | | | | | | | | | | | | | | | |
| CRESSWELL, JAN (HM05424) | | | | | | | ● | | | | | | | | | | | | | | | | | | |
| CRYSTAL & REIKI (HM05524) | | | | | | | | | | | | | | | | | | | | | | | | | |
| DACRELANDS CLINIC (HM05667) | | | ● | | | | ● | | | | | | | | | | | | | | | | | ● | ● |
| DAVIES, ANDREW (HM05794) | | | | | | | | | | | | | | | | | | | | | | | | | |
| DAVIES, JOHNATHON (HM05819) | | | | | | | | | | | | | | | | | | | | | | | | | |
| DEAN, L (HM05941) | | | ● | | | | | | | | | | | | | | | | | | | | | | |
| DOUGLAS, CAROLINE (HM06213) | | | | | | | | | | | | | | | | | | | | | | | | | |
| ELHALHULI, OTHMAN (HM06730) | | | ● | | | | | | | | | | | | | | | | | | | | | | |
| ESSENTIAL OILS DIRECT (HM06914) | | | | | | | ● | | | | | | | | | | | | | | | | | | |
| FIDLER, MAL (HM07257) | | | | | | | ● | | | | | | | | | | | | | | | | | | |
| FOOT HEALTH CLINIC (HM07483) | | | | | | | | | | | | | | | | | | | | | | | | | |
| GEE, D (HM07957) | | | | | | | | | | | | | | | | | | | | | | | | | |
| GINSBERG, ANNE (HM08111) | ● | | | | | | | | ● | | | | | | | | | | | | | | | | |
| GREENHALGH, A J T (HM08489) | | | | | | | | | | | | | | | | | | | | | | | | | |
| GREENWOOD, LINDA (HM08508) | | | ● | | | | | | | | | | | | | | | | | | | | | | |

| Business by County with Reference no. | Chiropody | Chiropractic | Clinical Ecology | Cognitive Therapy | Colonic Hydrotherapy | Colour Therapy | Complementary Therapy | Counselling | Cranial Osteopathy | Cranio-Sacral Therapy | Cryo Surgery | Crystal Healing | Cupping | Cymatics | Dance Movement Thrpy | Dietician | Do-In | Douching | Dowsing | Drama Therapy | Electrolipolysis | Electrolysis | Electrotherapy | Encounter Groups | Faith Healing |
|---|---|---|---|---|---|---|---|---|---|---|---|---|---|---|---|---|---|---|---|---|---|---|---|---|---|
| BOLTON CHIROPRACTIC CLINIC (HM02656) | | ● | | | | | | | | | | | | | | | | | | | | | | | |
| BOLTON CLINIC OF ACUPUNCTURE (HM02657) | | | | | | | | | | | | | | | | | | | | | | | | | |
| BOLTON PHYSIOTHERAPY CLINIC (HM02658) | | | | | | | | | | | | | | | | | | | | | | | | | |
| BOLTON THERAPY CENTRE (HM02659) | | | | | | | ● | ● | | | | | | | | | | | | | | | ● | | |
| BOLTON, VANESSA (HM02664) | ● | | | | | | | | | | | | | | | | | | | | | | | | |
| BROOKES, MICHAEL (HM03163) | | | | | | | ● | | | | | | | | | ● | | | | | | | | | |
| CEROSIMO, JOSEPH (HM03930) | | ● | | | | | | | | | | | | | | | | | | | | | | | |
| CEROSIMO, JOSEPH (HM03931) | | ● | | | | | | | | | | | | | | | | | | | | | | | |
| CHARTERED PHYSIO & SPORTS (HM04041) | | | | | | | | | | | | | | | | | | | | | | | | | |
| CHIROPRACTIC ASSOCIATES (HM04378) | | ● | | | | | | | | | | | | | | | | | | | | | | | |
| CHIROPRACTIC ASSOCIATES (HM04376) | | | | | | | | | | | | | | | | | | | | | | | | | |
| CHIROPRACTIC ASSOCIATES (HM04377) | | ● | | | | | | | | | | | | | | | | | | | | | | | |
| CLARKE, SUSAN AMANDA (HM04605) | | | | | | | | | | | | | | | | | | | | | | | | | |
| CLOUGHS - CHRTRD PHYSIO CLINIC (HM04735) | | | | | | | | | | | | | | | | | | | | | | | | | |
| COLES, RONNIE (HM04836) | ● | | | | | | | | | | | | | | | | | | | | | | | | |
| COLLIER, ELAINE M (HM04859) | | | | | | | | | | | | | | | | | | | | | | | | | |
| COLLINSON, J (HM04883) | | | | | | | | | | | | | | | | | | | | | | | | | |
| COMPLEMENTARY HEALTH SERVICES (HM04929) | | ● | | | | | | | | | | | | | | | | | | | | | | | |
| COTTAM, O N (HM05224) | ● | | | | | | | | | | | | | | | | | | | | | | | | |
| CRESSWELL, JAN (HM05424) | | | | | | | | | | | | | | | | | | | | | | | | | |
| CRYSTAL & REIKI (HM05524) | | | | | | | | | | | | ● | | | | | | | | | | | | | |
| DACRELANDS CLINIC (HM05667) | ● | | | | | | | | ● | ● | | | | | | | | | | | | | | | |
| DAVIES, ANDREW (HM05794) | ● | | | | | | | | | | | | | | | | | | | | | | | | |
| DAVIES, JOHNATHON (HM05819) | ● | | | | | | | | | | | | | | | | | | | | | | | | |
| DEAN, L (HM05941) | | | | | | | | | | | | | | | | | | | | | | | | | |
| DOUGLAS, CAROLINE (HM06213) | ● | | | | | | | | | | | | | | | | | | | | | | | | |
| ELHALHULI, OTHMAN (HM06730) | | | | | | | | | | | | | | | | | | | | | | | | | |
| ESSENTIAL OILS DIRECT (HM06914) | | | | | | | | | | | | | | | | | | | | | | | | | |
| FIDLER, MAL (HM07257) | | | | | | | | | | | | | | | | | | | | | | | | | |
| FOOT HEALTH CLINIC (HM07483) | ● | | | | | | | | | | | | | | | | | | | | | | | | |
| GEE, D (HM07957) | ● | | | | | | | | | | | | | | | | | | | | | | | | |
| GINSBERG, ANNE (HM08111) | | | | | | ● | | | | | | | | | | | | | | | | | | | |
| GREENHALGH, A J T (HM08489) | ● | | | | | | | | | | | | | | | | | | | | | | | | |
| GREENWOOD, LINDA (HM08508) | | | | | | | | | | | | | | | | | | | | | | | | | |

# A - F Therapies at Practices/Businesses

| Business by County with Reference no. | Absent Healing | Acupressure | Acupuncture | Alexander Technique | Allergy Testing | Anthroposohical Med | Aromatherapy | Art Therapy | Aura Therapy | Auricular Therapy | Auto Suggestion | Autogenic Training | Aversion Therapy | Ayurvedic Medicine | Baby Massage | Bach Remedies | Bates Method |
|---|---|---|---|---|---|---|---|---|---|---|---|---|---|---|---|---|---|
| GROGAN, DIANA E (HM08592) | | | ● | | | | | | | | | | | | | ● | |
| GULATI, R K (DR) (HM08637) | | | ● | | | | | | | | | | | | | | |
| GUPTA, P (HM08649) | | | ● | | | | | | | | | | | | | | |
| HAMPSOM, JAMES (HM08878) | | | ● | | | | | | | | | | | | | | |
| HARDMAN, ALAN (HM08974) | | | | | | | | | | | | | | | | | |
| HARMONIOUS HEALTHCARE (HM09015) | | | | | | | ● | | | | | | | | | | |
| HAYDOCK, CLAIRE (HM09254) | | | | | | | | | | | | | | | | | |
| HEAVENS SCENT AROMATHERAPY (HM09478) | | | | | | | ● | | | | | | | | | | |
| HEYWORTH, S (HM09716) | | | | | | | | | | | | | | | | | |
| HOLDEN, JOHN H (HM09932) | | | | | | | | | | | | | | | | | |
| HOLISTIC APPROACH (HM09945) | | | | | | | ● | | | | | | | | | | |
| HOME HOLISTIC THERAPY (HM10066) | | | | | | | ● | | | | | | | | | | |
| JOHN HOLDEN ASSOCIATES (HM11051) | | | | | | | | | | | | | | | | | |
| KELLY CHIROPODY (HM11424) | | | | | | | | | | | | | | | | | |
| KENDEL HOUSE CLINIC (HM11479) | | | ● | | | | | | | | | | | | | | |
| LAYNE, SUSAN G (HM12077) | | | | | | | | | | | | | | | | ● | |
| LEYLAND PHYSIOTHERAPY CENTRE (HM12319) | | | ● | | | | | | | | | | | | | | |
| MAINEY, V D (HM12945) | | | ● | | | | | | | | | | | | | | |
| MALKIN, DK, MANIP THERAPY (HM12975) | | | | | | | ● | | | | | | | | | | |
| MARIA'S AROMATHERAPY CENTRE (HM13097) | | | | | | | ● | | | | | | | | | | |
| MARSLAND PRIVATE CTRE OF ACU (HM13175) | | | ● | | | | | | | | | | | | | | |
| MCDERMOTT AROMATHERAPY (HM13443) | | | | | | | ● | | | | | | | | | | |
| MECHEN, M (HM13643) | | | | | | | ● | | | | | | | | | | |
| MERIDIAN CLINIC (HM13740) | | | | | | | | | | | | | | | | | |
| MILL HILL (HM13866) | | | | | | | | | | | | | | | | | |
| MINNERY, SHEILA (HM13979) | | | | | | | | | | | | | | | | ● | |
| MOBILE CHIROPODIST (HM14027) | | | | | | | | | | | | | | | | | |
| NATURAL CHOICE AROMATHERAPY (HM14523) | | | | | | | ● | | | | | | | | | | |
| NATURAL HEALTH CENTRE (HM14566) | | | ● | | | | ● | | | | | | | | | | |
| NATURES GIFT AROMATHERAPY (HM14690) | | | | | | | ● | | | | | | | | | | |
| NATURES WORLD (HM14706) | | | | | | | ● | | | | | | | | | | |
| NELSON, S (HM14782) | | | | | | | | | | | | | | | | ● | |
| NORTH WEST ACUPUNCTURE CLINIC (HM15041) | | | ● | | | | | | | | | | | | | | |
| NUTTER, D (HM15134) | | | ● | | | | | | | | | | | | | | |

| Business by County with Reference no. | Beauty Therapy | Bio-energetics | Biofeedback | Biomagnetic Therapy | Biomechanics | Bonesetting | Bowen Therapy | Chinese Herbal Medicine | Chiropody | Chiropractic | Clinical Ecology | Cognitive Therapy | Colonic Hydrotherapy | Colour Therapy | Complementary Therapy | Counselling | Cranial Osteopathy |
|---|---|---|---|---|---|---|---|---|---|---|---|---|---|---|---|---|---|
| GROGAN, DIANA E (HM08592) | | | | | | | | | ● | | | | | | | ● | |
| GULATI, R K (DR) (HM08637) | | | | | | | | | | | | | | | | | |
| GUPTA, P (HM08649) | | | | | | | | | | | | | | | | | |
| HAMPSOM, JAMES (HM08878) | | | | | | | | | | | | | | | | | |
| HARDMAN, ALAN (HM08974) | | | | | | | | | ● | | | | | | | | |
| HARMONIOUS HEALTHCARE (HM09015) | | | | | | | | | | | | | | | | | |
| HAYDOCK, CLAIRE (HM09254) | | | | | | | | | ● | | | | | | | | |
| HEAVENS SCENT AROMATHERAPY (HM09478) | | | | | | | | | | | | | | | | | |
| HEYWORTH, S (HM09716) | | | | | | | | | ● | | | | | | | | |
| HOLDEN, JOHN H (HM09932) | | | | | | | | | ● | | | | | | | | |
| HOLISTIC APPROACH (HM09945) | | | | | | | | | | | | | | | | | |
| HOME HOLISTIC THERAPY (HM10066) | | | | | | | | | | | | | | | | | |
| JOHN HOLDEN ASSOCIATES (HM11051) | | | | | ● | | | | ● | | | | | | | | |
| KELLY CHIROPODY (HM11424) | | | | | ● | | | | ● | | | | | | | | |
| KENDEL HOUSE CLINIC (HM11479) | | | | | | | | | ● | | | | | | | | ● |
| LAYNE, SUSAN G (HM12077) | | | | | | | | | | | | | | | ● | | |
| LEYLAND PHYSIOTHERAPY CENTRE (HM12319) | | | | | | | | | | | | | | | | | |
| MAINEY, V D (HM12945) | | | | | | | | | | | | | | | | | |
| MALKIN, DK, MANIP THERAPY (HM12975) | | | | | | | | | | | | | | | ● | | |
| MARIA'S AROMATHERAPY CENTRE (HM13097) | | | | | | | | | | | | | | | | | |
| MARSLAND PRIVATE CTRE OF ACU (HM13175) | | | | | | | | | | | | | | | | | |
| MCDERMOTT AROMATHERAPY (HM13443) | | | | | | | | | | | | | | | | | |
| MECHEN, M (HM13643) | | | | | | | | | | | | | | | | | |
| MERIDIAN CLINIC (HM13740) | | | | | | | | | | ● | | | | | | | |
| MILL HILL (HM13866) | | | | | | | | | ● | | | | | | | | |
| MINNERY, SHEILA (HM13979) | | | | | | | | | | | | | | | | | |
| MOBILE CHIROPODIST (HM14027) | | | | | | | | | ● | | | | | | | | |
| NATURAL CHOICE AROMATHERAPY (HM14523) | | | | | | | | | | | | | | | | | |
| NATURAL HEALTH CENTRE (HM14566) | | | | | | | | | | | | | | | | | |
| NATURES GIFT AROMATHERAPY (HM14690) | | | | | | | | | | | | | | | | | |
| NATURES WORLD (HM14706) | | | | | | | | | | | | | | | | | |
| NELSON, S (HM14782) | | | | | | | | | | | | | | | | | |
| NORTH WEST ACUPUNCTURE CLINIC (HM15041) | | | | | | | | | | | | | | | | | |
| NUTTER, D (HM15134) | | | | | | | | | | | | | | | | | |

| Business by County with Reference no. | Cranio-Sacral Therapy | Cryo Surgery | Crystal Healing | Cupping | Cymatics | Dance Movement Thrpy | Dietician | Do-In | Douching | Dowsing | Drama Therapy | Electrolipolysis | Electrolysis | Electrotherapy | Encounter Groups | Faith Healing |
|---|---|---|---|---|---|---|---|---|---|---|---|---|---|---|---|---|
| GROGAN, DIANA E (HM08592) | | | | ● | | | | | | | | | | | | |
| GULATI, R K (DR) (HM08637) | | | | | | | | | | | | | | | | |
| GUPTA, P (HM08649) | | | | | | | | | | | | | | | | |
| HAMPSOM, JAMES (HM08878) | | | | | | | | | | | | | | | | |
| HARDMAN, ALAN (HM08974) | | | | | | | | | | | | | | | | |
| HARMONIOUS HEALTHCARE (HM09015) | | | | | | | | | | | | | | | | |
| HAYDOCK, CLAIRE (HM09254) | | | | | | | | | | | | | | | | |
| HEAVENS SCENT AROMATHERAPY (HM09478) | | | | | | | | | | | | | | | | |
| HEYWORTH, S (HM09716) | | | | | | | | | | | | | | | | |
| HOLDEN, JOHN H (HM09932) | | | | | | | | | | | | | | | | |
| HOLISTIC APPROACH (HM09945) | | | | | | | | | | | | | | | | |
| HOME HOLISTIC THERAPY (HM10066) | | | | | | | | | | | | | | | | |
| JOHN HOLDEN ASSOCIATES (HM11051) | | | | | | | | | | | | | | | | |
| KELLY CHIROPODY (HM11424) | | | | | | | | | | | | | | | | |
| KENDEL HOUSE CLINIC (HM11479) | | | | | | | | | | | | | | | | |
| LAYNE, SUSAN G (HM12077) | | | | | | | | | | ● | | | | | | |
| LEYLAND PHYSIOTHERAPY CENTRE (HM12319) | | | | | | | | | | | | | | | | |
| MAINEY, V D (HM12945) | | | | | | | | | | | | | | | | |
| MALKIN, DK, MANIP THERAPY (HM12975) | | | | ● | | | | | | | | | | ● | | |
| MARIA'S AROMATHERAPY CENTRE (HM13097) | | | | | | | | | | | | | | | | |
| MARSLAND PRIVATE CTRE OF ACU (HM13175) | | | | | | | | | | | | | | | | |
| MCDERMOTT AROMATHERAPY (HM13443) | | | | | | | | | | | | | | | | |
| MECHEN, M (HM13643) | | | | | | | | | | | | | | | | |
| MERIDIAN CLINIC (HM13740) | | | | | | | | | | | | | | | | |
| MILL HILL (HM13866) | | | | | | | | | | | | | | | | |
| MINNERY, SHEILA (HM13979) | | | | | | | | | | | | | | | | |
| MOBILE CHIROPODIST (HM14027) | | | | | | | | | | | | | | | | |
| NATURAL CHOICE AROMATHERAPY (HM14523) | | | | | | | | | | | | | | | | |
| NATURAL HEALTH CENTRE (HM14566) | | | | | | | | | | | | | | ● | | |
| NATURES GIFT AROMATHERAPY (HM14690) | | | | | | | | | | | | | | | | |
| NATURES WORLD (HM14706) | | | | | | | | | | | | | | | | |
| NELSON, S (HM14782) | | | | | | | | | | | | | | | | |
| NORTH WEST ACUPUNCTURE CLINIC (HM15041) | | | | | | | | | | | | | | | | |
| NUTTER, D (HM15134) | | | | | | | | | | | | | | | | |

# A - F Therapies at Practices/Businesses

Business by County with Reference no.

| Business by County with Reference no. | Absent Healing | Acupressure | Acupuncture | Alexander Technique | Allergy Testing | Anthroposohical Med | Aromatherapy | Art Therapy | Aura Therapy | Auricular Therapy |
|---|---|---|---|---|---|---|---|---|---|---|
| OLDHAM AROMATICS (HM15266) | | | | | | | ● | | | |
| ONE STOP HEALTH & BEAUTY (HM15323) | ● | ● | | | | | ● | | | |
| PAWLEY, PHILIP (HM15856) | | | | ● | | | | | | |
| PEN-Y-BRYN HOLISTIC THERAPY (HM16003) | | | | | | | ● | | | |
| PEPPER, JOHN (HM16009) | | | | | | | | | | |
| PHYSIO AND SPORTS INJURIES (HM16195) | | | | | | | | | | |
| POULSEN, P (DR) (HM16480) | | | | | | | | | | |
| PURE HEALTH (HM16765) | | | | | | | ● | | | |
| RAINBOW PREGNANCY ADVICE (HM16883) | | | | | | | | | | |
| RAMSBOTTOM PHYSIO CLINIC (HM16919) | | | ● | | | | | | | |
| ROSSENDALE NTRL HEALTH CLINIC (HM17645) | | | ● | | | | | | | |
| SKIDMORE, JOYCE (HM18639) | | | | | | | | | | |
| SMITH, CHRISTOPHER (DR) (HM18728) | | | | | | | ● | | | |
| SODERSTROM, M (HM18856) | | | ● | | | | | | | |
| SPIRITUAL THERAPIST (HM19029) | ● | | | | | | | | ● | |
| ST GEORGES MULTI THERAPY CTRE (HM19075) | | ● | ● | | ● | | ● | | | |
| TATTERSALL, KAREN (HM19719) | | | | | | | | | | |
| THORNELEY, KATHLEEN (HM20019) | | | | | | | ● | | | |
| TINKER, D C (HM20083) | | | | | | | | | | |
| TIP TOES (HM20086) | | | | | | | ● | | | |
| TOMLINSON, ELIZABETH (HM20141) | | | | | | | | | | |
| TRADITIONAL ACUPUNCTURE CLINIC (HM20220) | | | ● | | | | | | | |
| TRADITIONAL CHINESE MED CTRE (HM20223) | | | ● | | | | | | | |
| WATKINSON, BARBARA (HM20999) | | | | | | | | | | |
| WEST LANCS MCTIMONEY (HM21224) | | | | | | | | | | |
| WHEWELL, ANITA (HM21328) | | | | | | | ● | | | |
| WIGAN FAMILY CHIROPRACTIC (HM21464) | | | | | | | | | | |
| WILKEY, A S (DR) (HM21494) | | | | | | | | | | |
| WILSON, G (HM21656) | | | | | | | | | | |
| YEAMAN, DAVID (HM21996) | | | | | | | | | | |
| ZODIAC (HM22114) | | | | | | | ● | | | |
| **LEICESTERSHIRE** | | | | | | | | | | |
| ACUPUNCTURE SERVICES (HM00320) | | ● | ● | | | | | | | |
| ALBANY HOUSE (HM00479) | | | | | | | ● | | | |

| Business by County with Reference no. | Auto Suggestion | Autogenic Training | Aversion Therapy | Ayurvedic Medicine | Baby Massage | Bach Remedies | Bates Method | Beauty Therapy | Bio-energetics | Biofeedback |
|---|---|---|---|---|---|---|---|---|---|---|
| OLDHAM AROMATICS (HM15266) | | | | | | | | | | |
| ONE STOP HEALTH & BEAUTY (HM15323) | | | | | | ● | | | | |
| PAWLEY, PHILIP (HM15856) | | | | | | | | | | |
| PEN-Y-BRYN HOLISTIC THERAPY (HM16003) | | | | | | | | | | |
| PEPPER, JOHN (HM16009) | | | | | | | | | | |
| PHYSIO AND SPORTS INJURIES (HM16195) | | | | | | | | | | |
| POULSEN, P (DR) (HM16480) | | | | | | | | | | |
| PURE HEALTH (HM16765) | | | | | | ● | | | | |
| RAINBOW PREGNANCY ADVICE (HM16883) | | | | | | | | | | |
| RAMSBOTTOM PHYSIO CLINIC (HM16919) | | | | | | | | | | |
| ROSSENDALE NTRL HEALTH CLINIC (HM17645) | | | | | | | | | | |
| SKIDMORE, JOYCE (HM18639) | | | | | | ● | | | | |
| SMITH, CHRISTOPHER (DR) (HM18728) | | | | | | | | | | |
| SODERSTROM, M (HM18856) | | | | | | | | | | |
| SPIRITUAL THERAPIST (HM19029) | | | | | | | | | | |
| ST GEORGES MULTI THERAPY CTRE (HM19075) | | | | | | | | | | |
| TATTERSALL, KAREN (HM19719) | | | | | | | | | | |
| THORNELEY, KATHLEEN (HM20019) | | | | | | | | | | |
| TINKER, D C (HM20083) | | | | | | | | | | |
| TIP TOES (HM20086) | | | | | | | | | | |
| TOMLINSON, ELIZABETH (HM20141) | | | | | | | | | | |
| TRADITIONAL ACUPUNCTURE CLINIC (HM20220) | | | | | | | | | | |
| TRADITIONAL CHINESE MED CTRE (HM20223) | | | | | | | | | | |
| WATKINSON, BARBARA (HM20999) | | | | | | ● | | | | |
| WEST LANCS MCTIMONEY (HM21224) | | | | | | | | | | |
| WHEWELL, ANITA (HM21328) | | | | | | | | | | |
| WIGAN FAMILY CHIROPRACTIC (HM21464) | | | | | | | | | | |
| WILKEY, A S (DR) (HM21494) | | | | | | | | | | |
| WILSON, G (HM21656) | | | | | | | | | | |
| YEAMAN, DAVID (HM21996) | | | | | | | | | | |
| ZODIAC (HM22114) | | | | | | | | | | |
| **LEICESTERSHIRE** | | | | | | | | | | |
| ACUPUNCTURE SERVICES (HM00320) | | | | | | | | | | |
| ALBANY HOUSE (HM00479) | | | | | | | | | | |

| Business by County with Reference no. | Biomagnetic Therapy | Biomechanics | Bonesetting | Bowen Therapy | Chinese Herbal Medicine | Chiropody | Chiropractic | Clinical Ecology | Cognitive Therapy | Colonic Hydrotherapy |
|---|---|---|---|---|---|---|---|---|---|---|
| OLDHAM AROMATICS (HM15266) | | | | | | | | | | |
| ONE STOP HEALTH & BEAUTY (HM15323) | | | | | | | | | | |
| PAWLEY, PHILIP (HM15856) | | | | | | | | | | |
| PEN-Y-BRYN HOLISTIC THERAPY (HM16003) | | | | | | | | | | |
| PEPPER, JOHN (HM16009) | | | | | | | | | | |
| PHYSIO AND SPORTS INJURIES (HM16195) | | | | | | | | | ● | |
| POULSEN, P (DR) (HM16480) | | | | | | | ● | | | |
| PURE HEALTH (HM16765) | | | | | | | | | | |
| RAINBOW PREGNANCY ADVICE (HM16883) | | | | | | | | | | |
| RAMSBOTTOM PHYSIO CLINIC (HM16919) | | | | | | | | | | |
| ROSSENDALE NTRL HEALTH CLINIC (HM17645) | | | | | | | | | | |
| SKIDMORE, JOYCE (HM18639) | | | | | | | | | | |
| SMITH, CHRISTOPHER (DR) (HM18728) | | | | | | | ● | | | |
| SODERSTROM, M (HM18856) | | | | | | | | | | |
| SPIRITUAL THERAPIST (HM19029) | | | | | | | | | | |
| ST GEORGES MULTI THERAPY CTRE (HM19075) | | | | | ● | ● | ● | | ● | |
| TATTERSALL, KAREN (HM19719) | | ● | | | | ● | | | | |
| THORNELEY, KATHLEEN (HM20019) | | | | | | | | | | |
| TINKER, D C (HM20083) | | | | | | ● | | | | |
| TIP TOES (HM20086) | | | | | | | | | | |
| TOMLINSON, ELIZABETH (HM20141) | | | | | | | | | | |
| TRADITIONAL ACUPUNCTURE CLINIC (HM20220) | | | | | | | | | | |
| TRADITIONAL CHINESE MED CTRE (HM20223) | | | | | | | | | | |
| WATKINSON, BARBARA (HM20999) | | | | | | | | | | |
| WEST LANCS MCTIMONEY (HM21224) | | | | | | | ● | | | |
| WHEWELL, ANITA (HM21328) | | | | | | | | | | |
| WIGAN FAMILY CHIROPRACTIC (HM21464) | | | | | | | ● | | | |
| WILKEY, A S (DR) (HM21494) | | | | | | | ● | | | |
| WILSON, G (HM21656) | | | | | | | | | ● | |
| YEAMAN, DAVID (HM21996) | | ● | | | | ● | | | | |
| ZODIAC (HM22114) | | | | | | | | | | |
| **LEICESTERSHIRE** | | | | | | | | | | |
| ACUPUNCTURE SERVICES (HM00320) | | | | | | | | | | |
| ALBANY HOUSE (HM00479) | | | | | | | | | | |

| Business by County with Reference no. | Colour Therapy | Complementary Therapy | Counselling | Cranial Osteopathy | Cranio-Sacral Therapy | Cryo Surgery | Crystal Healing | Cupping | Cymatics | Dance Movement Thrpy |
|---|---|---|---|---|---|---|---|---|---|---|
| OLDHAM AROMATICS (HM15266) | | | | | | | | | | |
| ONE STOP HEALTH & BEAUTY (HM15323) | | ● | | | | | | | | |
| PAWLEY, PHILIP (HM15856) | | | | | | | | | | |
| PEN-Y-BRYN HOLISTIC THERAPY (HM16003) | | | | | | | | | | |
| PEPPER, JOHN (HM16009) | | | ● | | | | | | | |
| PHYSIO AND SPORTS INJURIES (HM16195) | | | | | | | | | | |
| POULSEN, P (DR) (HM16480) | | | | | | | | | | |
| PURE HEALTH (HM16765) | | | | | | | | | | |
| RAINBOW PREGNANCY ADVICE (HM16883) | | | ● | | | | | | | |
| RAMSBOTTOM PHYSIO CLINIC (HM16919) | | | | | | | | | | |
| ROSSENDALE NTRL HEALTH CLINIC (HM17645) | | | | | | | | | | |
| SKIDMORE, JOYCE (HM18639) | | | | | | | | | | |
| SMITH, CHRISTOPHER (DR) (HM18728) | | | | | | | | | | |
| SODERSTROM, M (HM18856) | | | | | | | | | | |
| SPIRITUAL THERAPIST (HM19029) | | ● | ● | | | | ● | | | |
| ST GEORGES MULTI THERAPY CTRE (HM19075) | | ● | ● | | | | | | | |
| TATTERSALL, KAREN (HM19719) | | | | | | | | | | |
| THORNELEY, KATHLEEN (HM20019) | | | | | | | | | | |
| TINKER, D C (HM20083) | | | | | | | | | | |
| TIP TOES (HM20086) | | | | | | | | | | |
| TOMLINSON, ELIZABETH (HM20141) | | | | | | | | | | |
| TRADITIONAL ACUPUNCTURE CLINIC (HM20220) | | | | | | | | | | |
| TRADITIONAL CHINESE MED CTRE (HM20223) | | | | | | | | | | |
| WATKINSON, BARBARA (HM20999) | | | | | | | | | | |
| WEST LANCS MCTIMONEY (HM21224) | | | | | | | | | | |
| WHEWELL, ANITA (HM21328) | | | | | | | | | | |
| WIGAN FAMILY CHIROPRACTIC (HM21464) | | | | | | | | | | |
| WILKEY, A S (DR) (HM21494) | | | | | | | | | | |
| WILSON, G (HM21656) | | | ● | | | | | | | |
| YEAMAN, DAVID (HM21996) | | | | | | | | | | |
| ZODIAC (HM22114) | | | | | | | | | | |
| **LEICESTERSHIRE** | | | | | | | | | | |
| ACUPUNCTURE SERVICES (HM00320) | | | | | | | | | | |
| ALBANY HOUSE (HM00479) | | | | | | | | | | |

| Business by County with Reference no. | Dietician | Do-In | Douching | Dowsing | Drama Therapy | Electrolipolysis | Electrolysis | Electrotherapy | Encounter Groups | Faith Healing |
|---|---|---|---|---|---|---|---|---|---|---|
| OLDHAM AROMATICS (HM15266) | | | | | | | | | | |
| ONE STOP HEALTH & BEAUTY (HM15323) | | | | | | | | | | ● |
| PAWLEY, PHILIP (HM15856) | | | | | | | | | | |
| PEN-Y-BRYN HOLISTIC THERAPY (HM16003) | | | | | | | | | | |
| PEPPER, JOHN (HM16009) | | | | | | | | | | |
| PHYSIO AND SPORTS INJURIES (HM16195) | | | | | | ● | | | | |
| POULSEN, P (DR) (HM16480) | | | | | | | | | | |
| PURE HEALTH (HM16765) | | | | | | | | | | |
| RAINBOW PREGNANCY ADVICE (HM16883) | | | | | | | | | | |
| RAMSBOTTOM PHYSIO CLINIC (HM16919) | | | | | | | | | | |
| ROSSENDALE NTRL HEALTH CLINIC (HM17645) | | | | | | | | | | |
| SKIDMORE, JOYCE (HM18639) | | | | | | | | | | |
| SMITH, CHRISTOPHER (DR) (HM18728) | | | | | | | | | | |
| SODERSTROM, M (HM18856) | | | | | | | | | | |
| SPIRITUAL THERAPIST (HM19029) | | | | | | | | | | ● |
| ST GEORGES MULTI THERAPY CTRE (HM19075) | | | | | | | | | | |
| TATTERSALL, KAREN (HM19719) | | | | | | | | | | |
| THORNELEY, KATHLEEN (HM20019) | | | | | | | | | | |
| TINKER, D C (HM20083) | | | | | | | | | | |
| TIP TOES (HM20086) | | | | | | | | | | |
| TOMLINSON, ELIZABETH (HM20141) | | | | | | | ● | | | |
| TRADITIONAL ACUPUNCTURE CLINIC (HM20220) | | | | | | | | | | |
| TRADITIONAL CHINESE MED CTRE (HM20223) | | | | | | | | | | |
| WATKINSON, BARBARA (HM20999) | | | | | | | | | | |
| WEST LANCS MCTIMONEY (HM21224) | | | | | | | | | | |
| WHEWELL, ANITA (HM21328) | | | | | | | | | | |
| WIGAN FAMILY CHIROPRACTIC (HM21464) | | | | | | | | | | |
| WILKEY, A S (DR) (HM21494) | | | | | | | | | | |
| WILSON, G (HM21656) | | | | | | | | | | |
| YEAMAN, DAVID (HM21996) | | | | | | | | | | |
| ZODIAC (HM22114) | | | | | | | | | | |
| **LEICESTERSHIRE** | | | | | | | | | | |
| ACUPUNCTURE SERVICES (HM00320) | | | | | | | | | | |
| ALBANY HOUSE (HM00479) | | | | | | | | | | |

# A - F Therapies at Practices/Businesses

| Business by County with Reference no. | Absent Healing | Acupressure | Acupuncture | Alexander Technique | Allergy Testing | Anthroposohical Med | Aromatherapy | Art Therapy | Aura Therapy | Auricular Therapy | Auto Suggestion | Autogenic Training | Aversion Therapy | Ayurvedic Medicine | Baby Massage | Bach Remedies | Bates Method | Beauty Therapy | Bio-energetics | Biofeedback | Biomagnetic Therapy | Biomechanics | Bonesetting | Bowen Therapy | Chinese Herbal Medicine |
|---|---|---|---|---|---|---|---|---|---|---|---|---|---|---|---|---|---|---|---|---|---|---|---|---|---|
| ANDREWS, SIMON C (HM00859) | | ● | ● | | | | ● | | | | | | | | | | | | | | | | | ● | |
| ARCHWAY HSE NATURAL HLTH CTRE (HM00983) | | | ● | | | | ● | | | | | | | | | | | | | | | | | | |
| AROMATHERAPY INTERNATIONAL (HM01115) | | | | | | | ● | | | | | | | | | | | | | | | | | | |
| AROMATHERAPY TRADE COUNCIL (HM01127) | | | | | | | ● | | | | | | | | | | | | | | | | | | |
| AYURVEDIC HERBAL CLINIC (HM01444) | | ● | | | | | ● | | | | | | | ● | | | | | | | | | | | |
| CAROLYN'S BEAUTY (HM03721) | | | | | | | ● | | | | | | | | | | | | | | | | | | |
| CHARMWOOD CHIROPRACTIC CLINIC (HM04037) | | | | | | | | | | | | | | | | | | | | | | | | | |
| CHAWTONS (HM04068) | | | | | | | ● | | | | | | | | | | | | | | | | | | |
| CHIROPRACTIC CENTRE (HM04381) | | | | | | | | | | | | | | | | | | | | | | | | | |
| CONLIFFE, LOUISE (HM04982) | | | | | | | ● | | | | | | | | | | | | | | | | | | |
| DAVIES, CYNTHIA (HM05804) | | | ● | | | | | | | | | | | | | | | | | | | | | | |
| ESSENTIA (HM06895) | | | | | | | ● | | | | | | | | | | | | | | | | | | |
| ESSENTIAL SELECTION (HM06915) | | | | | | | ● | | | | | | | | | | | | | | | | | | |
| FAIRWEATHER, S & E (HM07068) | | | | | | | | | | | | | | | | | | | | | | | | | |
| FARRER, R H (HM07131) | | | ● | | | | | | | | | | | | | | | | | | | | | | |
| FIELDING, S H (HM07275) | | | ● | | | | | | | | | | | | | | | | | | | | | | |
| GADSBEY, GORDON (HM07825) | | | ● | | | | | | | | | | | | | | | | | | | | | | |
| GLENFIELD PRACTICE (HM08150) | | | ● | | | | | | | | | | | | | | | | | | | | | | |
| HELIX CENTRE (HM09521) | | | ● | ● | | | ● | | | | | | | | | | | | | | | | | | |
| HINCKLEY CHIROPRACTIC CLINIC (HM09823) | | | | | | | | | | | | | | | | | | | | | | | | | |
| INT SOCIETY-AROMATHERAPY (HM10688) | | | | | | | ● | | | | | | | | | | | | | | | | | | |
| JACQUI BATES COUNSELLING (HM10866) | | | | | | | | | | | | | | | | | | | | | | | | | |
| JARVIS, DIANE (HM10932) | | | | | | | ● | | | | | | | | | | | | | | | | | | |
| LEICESTER ACUPUNCTURE & HERBAL (HM12183) | | | ● | | | | | | | | | | | | | | | | | | | | | | |
| MELTON MOWBRAY PHYSIO CLINIC (HM13717) | | | ● | | | | | | | | | | | | | | | | | | | | | | |
| NATURAL WAY HEALTH CENTRE (HM14669) | | | ● | | | | | | | | | | | | | | | | | | | | | | |
| OADBY HOUSE (HM15140) | | | ● | | | | | | | | | | | | | | | | | | | | | | |
| ORR, JOSCELYNE (HM15404) | | | | | | | ● | | | | | | | | | | | | | | | | | | |
| QUINESSENCE (HM16806) | | | | | | | ● | | | | | | | | | | | | | | | | | | |
| ROSE & ASSOCIATES (HM17597) | | | | | | | | | | | | | | | | | | | | | | | | | |
| SHIRLEY FRANKLIN AROMATHERAPY (HM18485) | | | | | | | ● | | | | | | | | | | | | | | | | | | |
| SHIRLEY PRICE AROMATHERAPY (HM18486) | | | | | | | ● | | | | | | | | | | | | | | | | | | |
| SNUGGS, MICHAEL (HM18846) | | | | | | | | | | | | | | | | ● | | | | | | | | | |
| STERN, J (HM19217) | | | | | | | | | | | | | | | | | | | | | | | | | |

| Business by County with Reference no. | Chiropody | Chiropractic | Clinical Ecology | Cognitive Therapy | Colonic Hydrotherapy | Colour Therapy | Complementary Therapy | Counselling | Cranial Osteopathy | Cranio-Sacral Therapy | Cryo Surgery | Crystal Healing | Cupping | Cymatics | Dance Movement Thrpy | Dietician | Do-In | Douching | Dowsing | Drama Therapy | Electrolipolysis | Electrolysis | Electrotherapy | Encounter Groups | Faith Healing |
|---|---|---|---|---|---|---|---|---|---|---|---|---|---|---|---|---|---|---|---|---|---|---|---|---|---|
| ANDREWS, SIMON C (HM00859) | | ● | | | | | ● | | | | | | | | | | | | | | | | | | |
| ARCHWAY HSE NATURAL HLTH CTRE (HM00983) | | ● | | | | | | | | | | | | | | | | | | | | | | | |
| AROMATHERAPY INTERNATIONAL (HM01115) | | | | | | | | | | | | | | | | | | | | | | | | | |
| AROMATHERAPY TRADE COUNCIL (HM01127) | | | | | | | | | | | | | | | | | | | | | | | | | |
| AYURVEDIC HERBAL CLINIC (HM01444) | | | | | | | ● | | | | | | | | | ● | | | | | | | | | |
| CAROLYN'S BEAUTY (HM03721) | | | | | | | | | | | | | | | | | | | | | | | | | |
| CHARMWOOD CHIROPRACTIC CLINIC (HM04037) | | ● | | | | | | | | | | | | | | | | | | | | | | | |
| CHAWTONS (HM04068) | | | | | | | | | | | | | | | | | | | | | | | | | |
| CHIROPRACTIC CENTRE (HM04381) | | ● | | | | | | | | | | | | | | | | | | | | | | | |
| CONLIFFE, LOUISE (HM04982) | | | | | | | ● | | | | | | | | | | | | | | | | | | |
| DAVIES, CYNTHIA (HM05804) | | | | | | | | | | | | | | | | | | | | | | | | | |
| ESSENTIA (HM06895) | | | | | | | | | | | | | | | | | | | | | | | | | |
| ESSENTIAL SELECTION (HM06915) | | | | | | | | | | | | | | | | | | | | | | | | | |
| FAIRWEATHER, S & E (HM07068) | | | | | | | | ● | | | | | | | | | | | | | | | | | |
| FARRER, R H (HM07131) | | | | | | | | | | | | | | | | | | | | | | | | | |
| FIELDING, S H (HM07275) | | | | | | | | | | | | | | | | | | | | | | | | | |
| GADSBEY, GORDON (HM07825) | | | | | | | | | | | | | | | | | | | | | | | | | |
| GLENFIELD PRACTICE (HM08150) | | | | | | | | | ● | | | | | | | | | | | | | | | | |
| HELIX CENTRE (HM09521) | | | | | | | | | | ● | | | | | | | | | | | | | | | |
| HINCKLEY CHIROPRACTIC CLINIC (HM09823) | | ● | | | | | | | | | | | | | | | | | | | | | | | |
| INT SOCIETY-AROMATHERAPY (HM10688) | | | | | | | | | | | | | | | | | | | | | | | | | |
| JACQUI BATES COUNSELLING (HM10866) | | | | | | | | ● | | | | | | | | | | | | | | | | | |
| JARVIS, DIANE (HM10932) | | | | | | | | | | | | | | | | | | | | | | | | | |
| LEICESTER ACUPUNCTURE & HERBAL (HM12183) | | | | | | | | | | | | | | | | | | | | | | | | | |
| MELTON MOWBRAY PHYSIO CLINIC (HM13717) | | | | | | | | | | | | | | | | | | | | | | | | | |
| NATURAL WAY HEALTH CENTRE (HM14669) | | | | | | | | ● | | | | | | | | | | | | | | | | | |
| OADBY HOUSE (HM15140) | | | | | | | | | | | | | | | | | | | | | | | | | |
| ORR, JOSCELYNE (HM15404) | | | | | | | | | | | | | | | | | | | | | | | | | |
| QUINESSENCE (HM16806) | | | | | | | | | | | | | | | | | | | | | | | | | |
| ROSE & ASSOCIATES (HM17597) | | ● | | | | | | | | | | | | | | | | | | | | | | | |
| SHIRLEY FRANKLIN AROMATHERAPY (HM18485) | | | | | | | | ● | | | | | | | | | | | | | | | | | |
| SHIRLEY PRICE AROMATHERAPY (HM18486) | | | | | | | | | | | | | | | | | | | | | | | | | |
| SNUGGS, MICHAEL (HM18846) | | | | | | | | | | | | | | | | | | | | | | | | | |
| STERN, J (HM19217) | | | | | | | | ● | | | | | | | | | | | | | | | | | |

# A - F Therapies at Practices/Businesses

| Business by County with Reference no. | Absent Healing | Acupressure | Acupuncture | Alexander Technique | Allergy Testing | Anthroposohical Med | Aromatherapy | Art Therapy | Aura Therapy | Auricular Therapy | Auto Suggestion | Autogenic Training | Aversion Therapy | Ayurvedic Medicine | Baby Massage | Bach Remedies | Bates Method |
|---|---|---|---|---|---|---|---|---|---|---|---|---|---|---|---|---|---|
| STEVENS, TARA L (HM19240) | | | | | | | ● | | | | | | | | | | |
| SUE CHARLES AROMATHERAPY (HM19466) | | ● | | | | | ● | | | | | | | | | | |
| SUE RICKS COMP THERAPY (HM19467) | ● | | | | | | | | | | | | | | | ● | |
| VICTORIA CLINIC (HM20650) | ● | | | | | | | | | | | | | | | ● | |
| WENDY PRICE HOLISTIC RIDING (HM21198) | ● | | | | | | | | | | | | | | | ● | |
| WHITMORE, STEVEN (HM21413) | | | | ● | | | | | | | | | | | | | |
| WILKINSON, GWEN (HM21507) | | | | | ● | | | | | | | | | | | | |
| WOHL, M (DR) (HM21758) | | | | ● | | | | | | | | | | | | | |
| WSZOLEK, ANNA (HM21960) | | | ● | | | | | | | | | | | | | | |
| **LINCOLNSHIRE** | | | | | | | | | | | | | | | | | |
| ACUPUNCTURE CLINIC (HM00271) | | | ● | | | | | | | | | | | | | | |
| ALEXANDER TECHNIQUE (HM00550) | | | | ● | | | | | | | | | | | | | |
| BEVERLEYS (HM02246) | | ● | | | | | ● | | | | | | | | | | |
| BODY 'N' SOLE (HM02603) | | | | | | | ● | | | | | | | | | | |
| BOSTON CHIROPRACTIC CLINIC (HM02726) | | | | | | | | | | | | | | | | | |
| BRIDGE ST CLINIC (HM02995) | | | ● | | | | | | | | | | | | | | |
| CHIEN ACUPUNCTURE CLINIC (HM04161) | | | ● | | | | | | | | | | | | | | |
| CLINIC OF NATURAL MEDICINE (HM04703) | | | ● | | | | | | | | | | | | | ● | |
| COMPLEMENTARY THERAPY CENTRE (HM04946) | ● | ● | | | | | | | | | | | | | | | |
| COXON CLINIC (HM05326) | | | | | ● | | | | | | | | | | | ● | |
| DORMAN, KARL (HM06201) | | | | | | | | | | | | | | | | | |
| EQUILIBRUIM HOLISTIC HEALTH (HM06877) | | | | | | | ● | | | | | | | | | | |
| FLEETWOOD, REBECCA (HM07403) | | | | | | | ● | | | | | | | | | | |
| GODDENOUGH, J (HM08182) | | | | | | | | | | | | | | | | | |
| GOLDEN ARROW LEISURE (HM08205) | | | | | | | ● | | | | | | | | | | |
| GOOD HEALTHKEEPING (HM08241) | | | | | | ● | | | | | | | | | | ● | |
| GRANTHAM CHIROPRACTIC CLINIC (HM08393) | | | | | | | | | | | | | | | | | |
| GREENS HEALTH FOODS (HM08494) | | | | | | | ● | | | | | | | | | ● | |
| HARRISON, FIONA (HM09098) | | | | | | | ● | | | | | | | | | | |
| HEART TO HEART (HM09443) | | | | | | | | | | | | | | | | ● | |
| HORNCASTLE WAR MEMORIAL CENTRE (HM10172) | | | | | | | | | | | | | | | | | |
| HURST, JEAN ANN (HM10428) | | | | | | | | | | | | | | | | | |
| JUST JILLS (HM11282) | | | | | | | | | | | | | | | | ● | |
| KESTEVEN NATURAL HEALTH CENTRE (HM11564) | | | | | | | | | | | | | | | | ● | |

| Business by County with Reference no. | Beauty Therapy | Bio-energetics | Biofeedback | Biomagnetic Therapy | Biomechanics | Bonesetting | Bowen Therapy | Chinese Herbal Medicine | Chiropody | Chiropractic | Clinical Ecology | Cognitive Therapy | Colonic Hydrotherapy | Colour Therapy | Complementary Therapy | Counselling | Cranial Osteopathy |
|---|---|---|---|---|---|---|---|---|---|---|---|---|---|---|---|---|---|
| STEVENS, TARA L (HM19240) | | | | | | | | | | | | | | | | | |
| SUE CHARLES AROMATHERAPY (HM19466) | | | | | | | | | | | | | | | ● | | |
| SUE RICKS COMP THERAPY (HM19467) | | | | | | | | | | | | | | | ● | | |
| VICTORIA CLINIC (HM20650) | | | | | | | | | | ● | | | | | | | |
| WENDY PRICE HOLISTIC RIDING (HM21198) | | | | | | | | | | | | | | | | ● | |
| WHITMORE, STEVEN (HM21413) | | | | | | | | | | | | | | | | | |
| WILKINSON, GWEN (HM21507) | | | | | | | | | | | | | | | | | |
| WOHL, M (DR) (HM21758) | | | | | | | | | | | | | | | | | |
| WSZOLEK, ANNA (HM21960) | | | | | | | | | | | | | | | | | |
| **LINCOLNSHIRE** | | | | | | | | | | | | | | | | | |
| ACUPUNCTURE CLINIC (HM00271) | | | | | | | | | | | | | | | | | |
| ALEXANDER TECHNIQUE (HM00550) | | | | | | | | | | | | | | | | | |
| BEVERLEYS (HM02246) | | | | | | | | | | | | | | ● | | | |
| BODY 'N' SOLE (HM02603) | | | | | | | | | | | | | | | | | |
| BOSTON CHIROPRACTIC CLINIC (HM02726) | | | | | | | | | | ● | | | | | | | |
| BRIDGE ST CLINIC (HM02995) | | | | | | | | | | | | | | | | | |
| CHIEN ACUPUNCTURE CLINIC (HM04161) | | | | | | | | | | | | | | | | | |
| CLINIC OF NATURAL MEDICINE (HM04703) | | | | | | | | | | | | | | | | | ● |
| COMPLEMENTARY THERAPY CENTRE (HM04946) | | | | | | | ● | | | | | | | | ● | | |
| COXON CLINIC (HM05326) | | | | | | | | | | | | | | | | | |
| DORMAN, KARL (HM06201) | | | | | | | | | | ● | | | | | | | |
| EQUILIBRUIM HOLISTIC HEALTH (HM06877) | | | | | | | | | | | | | | | | | |
| FLEETWOOD, REBECCA (HM07403) | | | | | | | | | | | | | | | | | |
| GODDENOUGH, J (HM08182) | | | | | | | | | | ● | | | | | | | |
| GOLDEN ARROW LEISURE (HM08205) | | | | | | | | | | | | | | | | | |
| GOOD HEALTHKEEPING (HM08241) | | | | | | | | | ● | | ● | | | ● | | ● | |
| GRANTHAM CHIROPRACTIC CLINIC (HM08393) | | | | | | | | | | ● | | | | | | | |
| GREENS HEALTH FOODS (HM08494) | | | | | | | | | | | | | | | | | |
| HARRISON, FIONA (HM09098) | | | | | | | | | | | | | | | | | |
| HEART TO HEART (HM09443) | | | | | | | | | | | | | | | | | |
| HORNCASTLE WAR MEMORIAL CENTRE (HM10172) | | | | | | | | | | ● | | | | | | | |
| HURST, JEAN ANN (HM10428) | | | | | | | | | | ● | | | | | | | |
| JUST JILLS (HM11282) | | | | | | | | | | | | | | | | ● | |
| KESTEVEN NATURAL HEALTH CENTRE (HM11564) | | ● | | | | | | | | | | | | | | ● | |

| Business by County with Reference no. | Cranio-Sacral Therapy | Cryo Surgery | Crystal Healing | Cupping | Cymatics | Dance Movement Thrpy | Dietician | Do-In | Douching | Dowsing | Drama Therapy | Electrolipolysis | Electrolysis | Electrotherapy | Encounter Groups | Faith Healing |
|---|---|---|---|---|---|---|---|---|---|---|---|---|---|---|---|---|
| STEVENS, TARA L (HM19240) | | | | | | | | | | | | | | | | |
| SUE CHARLES AROMATHERAPY (HM19466) | | | | | | | | | | | | | | | | |
| SUE RICKS COMP THERAPY (HM19467) | | | | | | | | | | | | | | | | |
| VICTORIA CLINIC (HM20650) | | | | | | | | | | | | | | | | |
| WENDY PRICE HOLISTIC RIDING (HM21198) | | | | | | | | | | | | | | | | |
| WHITMORE, STEVEN (HM21413) | | | | | | | | | | | | | | | | |
| WILKINSON, GWEN (HM21507) | | | | | | | | | | | | | | | | |
| WOHL, M (DR) (HM21758) | | | | | | | | | | | | | | | | |
| WSZOLEK, ANNA (HM21960) | | | | | | | | | | | | | | | | |
| **LINCOLNSHIRE** | | | | | | | | | | | | | | | | |
| ACUPUNCTURE CLINIC (HM00271) | | | | | | | | | | | | | | | | |
| ALEXANDER TECHNIQUE (HM00550) | | | | | | | | | | | | | | | | |
| BEVERLEYS (HM02246) | | | | | | | | | | | | | | | | |
| BODY 'N' SOLE (HM02603) | | | | | | | | | | | | | | | | |
| BOSTON CHIROPRACTIC CLINIC (HM02726) | | | | | | | | | | | | | | | | |
| BRIDGE ST CLINIC (HM02995) | | | | | | | | | | | | | | | | |
| CHIEN ACUPUNCTURE CLINIC (HM04161) | | | | | | | | | | | | | | | | |
| CLINIC OF NATURAL MEDICINE (HM04703) | | | | | | | | | | | | | | ● | | |
| COMPLEMENTARY THERAPY CENTRE (HM04946) | | | | | | | | | | | | | | | | |
| COXON CLINIC (HM05326) | | | | | | | | | | | | | | | | |
| DORMAN, KARL (HM06201) | | | | | | | | | | | | | | | | |
| EQUILIBRUIM HOLISTIC HEALTH (HM06877) | | | | | | | | | | | | | | | | |
| FLEETWOOD, REBECCA (HM07403) | | | | | | | | | | | | | | | | |
| GODDENOUGH, J (HM08182) | | | | | | | | | | | | | | | | |
| GOLDEN ARROW LEISURE (HM08205) | | | | | | | | | | | | | | | | |
| GOOD HEALTHKEEPING (HM08241) | | | ● | | | | ● | | | ● | | | | | | |
| GRANTHAM CHIROPRACTIC CLINIC (HM08393) | | | | | | | | | | | | | | | | |
| GREENS HEALTH FOODS (HM08494) | | | | | | | | | | | | | | | | |
| HARRISON, FIONA (HM09098) | | | | | | | | | | | | | | | | |
| HEART TO HEART (HM09443) | | | ● | | | | | | | | | | | | | |
| HORNCASTLE WAR MEMORIAL CENTRE (HM10172) | | | | | | | | | | | | | | | | |
| HURST, JEAN ANN (HM10428) | | | | | | | | | | | | | | | | |
| JUST JILLS (HM11282) | | | | | | | | | | | | | | | | |
| KESTEVEN NATURAL HEALTH CENTRE (HM11564) | | | | | | | | | | | | | | | | |

# A - F Therapies at Practices/Businesses

| Business by County with Reference no. | Absent Healing | Acupressure | Acupuncture | Alexander Technique | Allergy Testing | Anthroposohical Med | Aromatherapy | Art Therapy | Aura Therapy | Auricular Therapy | Auto Suggestion | Autogenic Training | Aversion Therapy | Ayurvedic Medicine | Baby Massage | Bach Remedies | Bates Method |
|---|---|---|---|---|---|---|---|---|---|---|---|---|---|---|---|---|---|
| LIFE (HM12335) | | | | | | | | | | | | | | | | | |
| LINCOLN HERBAL TREATMENT CTRE (HM12407) | | | | | | | | | | | | | | | | ● | |
| LIVING HEALTH (HM12485) | | | | | | | | | | | | | | | | | |
| LIVINGSTONE, R K (HM12492) | | | ● | | | | | | | | | | | | | | |
| LOUTH CHIROPRACTIC CLINIC (HM12669) | | | | | | | | | | | | | | | | | |
| MARK RIDDLE HYPNOTHERAPY (HM13108) | | | | | | | | | | | ● | | ● | | | | |
| MORLEY-KIRK, JOHN (HM14187) | | | | | | | | | | | | | | | | | |
| NEWLAND CHIROPRACTIC CLINIC (HM14866) | | | | | | | | | | | | | | | | | |
| REFLEXOLOGY CLINIC (HM17084) | | | | | | | ● | | | | | | | | | | |
| SALES, F P I (HM17847) | | | | | | | ● | | | | | | | | | | |
| SALON, JANIES (HM17863) | | | | | | | ● | | | | | | | | | | |
| THOMPSON CHIROPRACTIC (HM19961) | | | | | | | | | | | | | | | | | |
| THORNTON, G (HM20025) | | | | | | | ● | | | | | | | | | | |
| WHITE, HEATHER (HM21357) | | | | | | | | | | | | | | | | | |
| **LONDON (GREATER)** | | | | | | | | | | | | | | | | | |
| 1ST ALTERNATIVE HEALTH CENTRE (HM00002) | | | | ● | | | ● | | | | | | | | | | |
| A7 ACUPUNCTURE CLINIC (HM00056) | | | ● | | | | | | | | | | | | | | |
| AARON ACUPUNCTURE & OSTEOPATHY (HM00064) | | | ● | | | | | | | | | | | | | | |
| ABABS NIGHT & DAY (HM00066) | | | | | | | ● | | | | | | | | | | |
| ABBEY CENTRE (HM00071) | | | | | | | | | | | | | | | | | |
| ABBEYWOOD CHIROPODY CLINIC (HM00091) | | | | | | | | | | | | | | | | | |
| ABIGAIL'S (HM00126) | | | | | | | ● | | | | | | | | | | |
| ACUMEDIC (HM00217) | | ● | ● | | | | | | | | | | | | | | |
| ACUPUNCTURE & HERBAL CLINIC (HM00240) | | | ● | | | | | | | | | | | | | | |
| ACUPUNCTURE & PAIN CLINIC (HM00244) | | | ● | | | | | | | | | | | | | | |
| ACUPUNCTURE CLINIC (HM00287) | | ● | ● | | | | | | | | | | | | | ● | |
| ACUPUNCTURE CLINIC (HM00258) | | | ● | | | | | | | | | | | | | | |
| ACUPUNCTURE ENERGY PRACTICE (HM00293) | | | ● | | | | | | | | | | | | | | |
| ACUPUNCTURE SCHOOL (HM00319) | | | ● | | | | | | | | | | | | | | |
| ACUPUNCTURE/STRESS THERAPY (HM00330) | | | ● | | | | | | | | | | | | | | |
| AKINS CHIROPRACTIC CLINIC (HM00467) | | | | | | | | | | | | | | | | | |
| ALEXANDER STUDIO (HM00515) | | | | ● | | | | | | | | | | | | | |
| ALEXANDER TECHNIQUE (HM00545) | | | | ● | | | | | | | | | | | | | |
| ALEXANDER TECHNIQUE (HM00533) | | | | ● | | | | | | | | | | | | | |

| Business by County with Reference no. | Beauty Therapy | Bio-energetics | Biofeedback | Biomagnetic Therapy | Biomechanics | Bonesetting | Bowen Therapy | Chinese Herbal Medicine | Chiropody | Chiropractic | Clinical Ecology | Cognitive Therapy | Colonic Hydrotherapy | Colour Therapy | Complementary Therapy | Counselling | Cranial Osteopathy |
|---|---|---|---|---|---|---|---|---|---|---|---|---|---|---|---|---|---|
| LIFE (HM12335) | | | | | | | | | | | | | | | | ● | |
| LINCOLN HERBAL TREATMENT CTRE (HM12407) | | | | | | | | | | | | | | | | | |
| LIVING HEALTH (HM12485) | | | | | | | | | | ● | | | | | | | |
| LIVINGSTONE, R K (HM12492) | | | | | | | | | | | | | | | | | |
| LOUTH CHIROPRACTIC CLINIC (HM12669) | | | | | | | | | | ● | | | | | | | |
| MARK RIDDLE HYPNOTHERAPY (HM13108) | | | ● | | | | | | | | | | | | ● | ● | |
| MORLEY-KIRK, JOHN (HM14187) | | | | | | | | | | | | | | | ● | | |
| NEWLAND CHIROPRACTIC CLINIC (HM14866) | | | | | | | | | | ● | | | | | | | |
| REFLEXOLOGY CLINIC (HM17084) | | | | | | | | | | | | | | | ● | | |
| SALES, F P I (HM17847) | | | | | | | | | | | | | | | | | |
| SALON, JANIES (HM17863) | ● | | | | | | | | | | | | | | | | |
| THOMPSON CHIROPRACTIC (HM19961) | | | | | | | | | | ● | | | | | | | |
| THORNTON, G (HM20025) | | | | | | | | | | | | | | | | | |
| WHITE, HEATHER (HM21357) | | | | | | | | | | | | | | | ● | ● | |
| **LONDON (GREATER)** | | | | | | | | | | | | | | | | | |
| 1ST ALTERNATIVE HEALTH CENTRE (HM00002) | | | | | | | | | | | | | | | | | ● |
| A7 ACUPUNCTURE CLINIC (HM00056) | | | | | | | | | | | | | | | | | |
| AARON ACUPUNCTURE & OSTEOPATHY (HM00064) | | | | | | | | | | | | | | | | | |
| ABABS NIGHT & DAY (HM00066) | | | | | | | | | | | | | | | | | |
| ABBEY CENTRE (HM00071) | | | | | | | | | | | | | | | | ● | |
| ABBEYWOOD CHIROPODY CLINIC (HM00091) | | | | | ● | | | | ● | | | | | | | | |
| ABIGAIL'S (HM00126) | | | | | | | | | | | | | | | | | |
| ACUMEDIC (HM00217) | | | | | | | | ● | | | | | | | | | |
| ACUPUNCTURE & HERBAL CLINIC (HM00240) | | | | | | | | | | | | | | | | | |
| ACUPUNCTURE & PAIN CLINIC (HM00244) | | | | | | | | | | | | | | | | | |
| ACUPUNCTURE CLINIC (HM00287) | | | | | | | | | | | | | | | | | |
| ACUPUNCTURE CLINIC (HM00258) | | | | | | | | | | | | | | | | | |
| ACUPUNCTURE ENERGY PRACTICE (HM00293) | | | | | | | | | | | | | | | | | |
| ACUPUNCTURE SCHOOL (HM00319) | | | | | | | | | | | | | | | | | |
| ACUPUNCTURE/STRESS THERAPY (HM00330) | | | | | | | | | | | | | | | | | |
| AKINS CHIROPRACTIC CLINIC (HM00467) | | | | | | | | | | ● | | | | | | | |
| ALEXANDER STUDIO (HM00515) | | | | | | | | | | | | | | | | | |
| ALEXANDER TECHNIQUE (HM00545) | | | | | | | | | | | | | | | | | |
| ALEXANDER TECHNIQUE (HM00533) | | | | | | | | | | | | | | | | | |

| Business by County with Reference no. | Cranio-Sacral Therapy | Cryo Surgery | Crystal Healing | Cupping | Cymatics | Dance Movement Thrpy | Dietician | Do-In | Douching | Dowsing | Drama Therapy | Electrolipolysis | Electrolysis | Electrotherapy | Encounter Groups | Faith Healing |
|---|---|---|---|---|---|---|---|---|---|---|---|---|---|---|---|---|
| LIFE (HM12335) | | | | | | | | | | | | | | | | |
| LINCOLN HERBAL TREATMENT CTRE (HM12407) | | | | | | | | | | | | | | | | |
| LIVING HEALTH (HM12485) | | | | | | | | | | | | | | | | |
| LIVINGSTONE, R K (HM12492) | | | | | | | | | | | | | | | | |
| LOUTH CHIROPRACTIC CLINIC (HM12669) | | | | | | | | | | | | | | | | |
| MARK RIDDLE HYPNOTHERAPY (HM13108) | | | | | | | ● | | | | | | | | | |
| MORLEY-KIRK, JOHN (HM14187) | | | | | | | | | | | | | | | | |
| NEWLAND CHIROPRACTIC CLINIC (HM14866) | | | | | | | | | | | | | | | | |
| REFLEXOLOGY CLINIC (HM17084) | | | | | | | | | | | | | | | | |
| SALES, F P I (HM17847) | | | | | | | | | | | | | | | | |
| SALON, JANIES (HM17863) | | | | | | | | | | | | | | | | |
| THOMPSON CHIROPRACTIC (HM19961) | | | | | | | | | | | | | | | | |
| THORNTON, G (HM20025) | | | | | | | | | | | | | | | | |
| WHITE, HEATHER (HM21357) | | | | | | | | | | | | | | | | |
| **LONDON (GREATER)** | | | | | | | | | | | | | | | | |
| 1ST ALTERNATIVE HEALTH CENTRE (HM00002) | ● | | | | | | | | | | | | | | | |
| A7 ACUPUNCTURE CLINIC (HM00056) | | | | | | | | | | | | | | | | |
| AARON ACUPUNCTURE & OSTEOPATHY (HM00064) | | | | | | | | | | | | | | | | |
| ABABS NIGHT & DAY (HM00066) | | | | | | | | | | | | | | | | |
| ABBEY CENTRE (HM00071) | | | | | | | | | | | | | | | | |
| ABBEYWOOD CHIROPODY CLINIC (HM00091) | | | | | | | | | | | | | | | | |
| ABIGAIL'S (HM00126) | | | | | | | | | | | | | | | | |
| ACUMEDIC (HM00217) | | | | | | | | | | | | | | | | |
| ACUPUNCTURE & HERBAL CLINIC (HM00240) | | | | | | | | | | | | | | | | |
| ACUPUNCTURE & PAIN CLINIC (HM00244) | | | | | | | | | | | | | | | | |
| ACUPUNCTURE CLINIC (HM00287) | | | | | | | | | | | | | | | | |
| ACUPUNCTURE CLINIC (HM00258) | | | | | | | | | | | | | | | | |
| ACUPUNCTURE ENERGY PRACTICE (HM00293) | | | | | | | | | | | | | | | | |
| ACUPUNCTURE SCHOOL (HM00319) | | | | | | | | | | | | | | | | |
| ACUPUNCTURE/STRESS THERAPY (HM00330) | | | | | | | | | | | | | | | | |
| AKINS CHIROPRACTIC CLINIC (HM00467) | | | | | | | | | | | | | | | | |
| ALEXANDER STUDIO (HM00515) | | | | | | | | | | | | | | | | |
| ALEXANDER TECHNIQUE (HM00545) | | | | | | | | | | | | | | | | |
| ALEXANDER TECHNIQUE (HM00533) | | | | | | | | | | | | | | | | |

# A - F Therapies at Practices/Businesses

| Business by County with Reference no. | Absent Healing | Acupressure | Acupuncture | Alexander Technique | Allergy Testing | Anthroposohical Med | Aromatherapy | Art Therapy | Aura Therapy | Auricular Therapy | Auto Suggestion | Autogenic Training | Aversion Therapy | Ayurvedic Medicine | Baby Massage | Bach Remedies | Bates Method | Beauty Therapy | Bio-energetics | Biofeedback | Biomagnetic Therapy | Biomechanics | Bonesetting | Bowen Therapy | Chinese Herbal Medicine | Chiropody | Chiropractic | Clinical Ecology | Cognitive Therapy | Colonic Hydrotherapy | Colour Therapy | Complementary Therapy | Counselling | Cranial Osteopathy | Cranio-Sacral Therapy | Cryo Surgery | Crystal Healing | Cupping | Cymatics | Dance Movement Thrpy | Dietician | Do-In | Douching | Dowsing | Drama Therapy | Electrolipolysis | Electrolysis | Electrotherapy | Encounter Groups | Faith Healing |
|---|---|---|---|---|---|---|---|---|---|---|---|---|---|---|---|---|---|---|---|---|---|---|---|---|---|---|---|---|---|---|---|---|---|---|---|---|---|---|---|---|---|---|---|---|---|---|---|---|---|---|
| ALEXANDER TECHNIQUE (HM00538) | | | | ● | | | | | | | | | | | | | | | | | | | | | | | | | | | | | | | | | | | | | | | | | | | | | | |
| ALEXANDER TECHNIQUE (HM00544) | | | | ● | | | | | | | | | | | | | | | | | | | | | | | | | | | | | | | | | | | | | | | | | | | | | | |
| ALEXANDER TECHNIQUE (HM00552) | | | | ● | | | | | | | | | | | | | | | | | | | | | | | | | | | | | | | | | | | | | | | | | | | | | | |
| ALEXANDER TECHNIQUE (HM00554) | | | | ● | | | | | | | | | | | | | | | | | | | | | | | | | | | | | | | | | | | | | | | | | | | | | | |
| ALEXANDER TECHNIQUE (HM00547) | | | | ● | | | | | | | | | | | | | | | | | | | | | | | | | | | | | | | | | | | | | | | | | | | | | | |
| ALEXANDER TECHNIQUE CENTRE (HM00555) | | | | ● | | | | | | | | | | | | | ● | | | | | | | | | | | | | | | | | | | | | | | | | | | | | | | | | |
| ALEXANDER, R E (HM00570) | | | ● | | | | | | | | | | | | | | | | | | | | | | | | | | | | | | | | | | | | | | | | | | | | | | | |
| ALL WELL & GOOD (HM00583) | | | | | | | ● | | | | | | | | | | | | | | | | | | | | | | | | | | | | | | | | | | | | | | | | | | | |
| ALTERNATIVE THERAPIES CENTRE (HM00728) | | ● | ● | ● | | | ● | | | | | | | | | ● | | | | ● | | | | ● | | | | | | | | ● | ● | ● | | | ● | ● | | | | | | | | | | | | |
| ALTERNATIVES COMP THERAPY CTRE (HM00743) | | ● | ● | | | | ● | | | | | | | | | ● | | | | | | | | | | | | | | | | ● | ● | | | | | | | | | | | | | | | | | |
| AMATO, CHRISTOPHER (HM00762) | | | ● | | | | | | | | | | | | | | | | | | | | | | | | | | | | | | | | | | | | | | | | | | | | | | | |
| ANERLEY NATURAL HEALING CENTRE (HM00861) | | | | | | | ● | | | | | | | | | | | | | | | | | | | | | | | | | | | | | | | | | | | | | | | | | | | |
| ANGEL HEART CENTRE (HM00867) | ● | | | | | | | | | | | | | | | | | | | | | | | | | | | | | | | | | | | | | | | | | | | | | | | | | |
| ARCHER, DEBORAH (HM00974) | | | | | | | | | | | | | | | | | | | | | | | | | | | ● | | | | | | | | | | | | | | | | | | | | | | | |
| ARCIER, MICHELINE (HM00985) | | | | | | | ● | | | | | | | | | | | | | | | | | | | | | | | | | | | | | | | | | | | | | | | | | | | |
| ARK CLINIC (HM01001) | | | ● | | | | | | | | | | | | | | | | | | | | | | | | | | | | | | | | | | | | | | | | | | | | | | | |
| AROMA ENTERPRISES (HM01046) | | | | | | | ● | | | | | | | | | | | | | | | | | | | | | | | | | | | | | | | | | | | | | | | | | | | |
| AROMACUSHION (HM01071) | | | | | | | ● | | | | | | | | | | | | | | | | | | | | | | | | | | | | | | | | | | | | | | | | | | | |
| AROMATHERAPY ORG COUNCIL (HM01121) | | | | | | | ● | | | | | | | | | | | | | | | | | | | | | | | | | ● | | | | | | | | | | | | | | | | | | |
| ASMUNS CHIROPRACTIC CLINIC (HM01254) | | | | | | | | | | | | | | | | | | | | | | | | | | | ● | | | | | | | | | | | | | | | | | | | | | | | |
| AUSTIN, NEIL (HM01369) | | | | | | | | | | | | | | | | | | | | | | | | | | | ● | | | | | | | | | | | | | | | | | | | | | | | |
| AVALON CHINESE MEDICINE CLINIC (HM01377) | | ● | ● | | | | | | | | | | | | | | | | | | | | | | | | | | | | | | | | | | | ● | | | | | | | | | | ● | | |
| AVATAR (HM01384) | | | | | | | ● | | | | | | | | | | | | | | | | | | | | | | | | | | | | ● | | | | | | | | | | | | | | | |
| AYURVED HERBELI (HM01442) | | | | | | | | | | | | | | ● | | | | | | | | | | | | | | | | | | | | | | | | | | | | | | | | | | | | |
| BACA (HM01466) | | | ● | | | | | | | | | | | | | | | | | | | | | | | | | | | | | | | | | | | | | | | | | | | | | | | |
| BACK PAIN CENTRE (HM01498) | | | | | | | | | | | | | | | | | | | | | | | | | | | ● | | | | | | | | | | | | | | | | | | | | | | | |
| BACK PAIN CENTRE (HM01497) | | | | | | | | | | | | | | | | | | | | | | | | | | | ● | | | | | | | | | | | | | | | | | | | | | | | |
| BACK PAIN CENTRE (HM01499) | | | | | | | | | | | | | | | | | | | | | | | | | | | ● | | | | | | | | | | | | | | | | | | | | | | | |
| BACK PAIN CLINIC (HM01501) | | | | | | | | | | | | | | | | | | | | | | | | | | | ● | | | | | | | | | | | | | | | | | | | | | | | |
| BACK PAIN CLINIC (HM01502) | | | | | | | | | | | | | | | | | | | | | | | | | | | ● | | | | | | | | | | | | | | | | | | | | | | | |
| BACK TO HEALTH - CHISWICK (HM01510) | | | | | | | | | | | | | | | | | | | | | | | | | | | ● | | | | | | | | | | | | | | | | | | | | | | | |
| BACK TO HEALTH - KINGSTON (HM01512) | | | | | | | | | | | | | | | | | | | | | | | | | | | ● | | | | | | | | | | | | | | | | | | | | | | | |
| BACK TO HEALTH - NORTH FINCHLEY (HM01513) | | | | | | | | | | | | | | | | | | | | | | | | | | | ● | | | | | | | | | | | | | | | | | | | | | | | |
| BACK TO HEALTH CHIRO CLINIC (HM01518) | | | | | | | | | | | | | | | | | | | | | | | | | | | ● | | | | | | | | | | | | | | | | | | | | | | | |

# A - F Therapies at Practices/Businesses

| Business by County with Reference no. | Absent Healing | Acupressure | Acupuncture | Alexander Technique | Allergy Testing | Anthroposohical Med | Aromatherapy | Art Therapy | Aura Therapy | Auricular Therapy | Auto Suggestion | Autogenic Training | Aversion Therapy | Ayurvedic Medicine | Baby Massage | Bach Remedies | Bates Method | Beauty Therapy | Bio-energetics | Biofeedback | Biomagnetic Therapy | Biomechanics | Bonesetting | Bowen Therapy | Chinese Herbal Medicine | Chiropody | Chiropractic | Clinical Ecology | Cognitive Therapy | Colonic Hydrotherapy | Colour Therapy | Complementary Therapy | Counselling | Cranial Osteopathy | Cranio-Sacral Therapy | Cryo Surgery | Crystal Healing | Cupping | Cymatics | Dance Movement Thrpy | Dietician | Do-In | Douching | Dowsing | Drama Therapy | Electrolipolysis | Electrolysis | Electrotherapy | Encounter Groups | Faith Healing |
|---|---|---|---|---|---|---|---|---|---|---|---|---|---|---|---|---|---|---|---|---|---|---|---|---|---|---|---|---|---|---|---|---|---|---|---|---|---|---|---|---|---|---|---|---|---|---|---|---|---|---|
| BACK TO HEALTH-EALING (HM01519) | | | | | | | | | | | | | | | | | | | | | | | | | | | ● | | | | | | | | | | | | | | | | | | | | | | | | |
| BAIRD, JANET (HM01570) | | | | | | | | | | | | | | | | ● | | | | | | | | | | | | | | | | | | | | | | | | | | | | | | | | | | | |
| BARBER, JULIE (HM01685) | | | | ● | | | | | | | | | | | | | | | | | | | | | | | | | | | | | | | | | | | | | | | | | | | | | | | |
| BARBICAN CENTRE (HM01693) | | | | | | | | | | | | | | | | | | | | | | ● | | | | ● | | | | | | | | | | ● | | | | | | | | | | | | | | | |
| BARBICAN PODIATRY PRACTICE (HM01694) | | | | | | | | | | | | | | | | | | | | | | ● | | | | | | | | | | | | | | | | | | | | | | | | | | | | | |
| BARLOW, A (HM01719) | | | | ● | | | | | | | | | | | | | | | | | | | | | | | | | | | | | | | | | | | | | | | | | | | | | | | |
| BARNES CHIROPRACTIC HEALTHCARE (HM01740) | | | | | | | | | | | | | | | | | | | | | | | | | | | ● | | | | | | | | | | | | | | | | | | | | | | | | |
| BARON, MARTA (HM01773) | | | | ● | | | | | | | | | | | | | | | | | | | | | | | | | | | | | | | | | | | | | | | | | | | | | | | |
| BARRIE, ALEXANDER (HM01798) | | | | | | | | | | | | | | | | | | | | | | | | | | | | | | | | ● | ● | ● | ● | | | ● | | | | ● | | | | | | | | | ● |
| BARTLETT, PHILIPPA (HM01826) | | | ● | | | | | | | | | | | | | | | | | | | | | | | | | | | | | | | | | | | | | | | | | | | | | | | | |
| BARTOSZEWICZ, PATRICIA (HM01833) | | | | | | | ● | | | | | | | | | | | | | | | | | | | | | | | | | | | | | | | | | | | | | | | | | | | | |
| BATTERSEA BACK CLINIC (HM01910) | | | | | | | | | | | | | | | | | | | | | | | | | | | ● | | | | | | | | | | | | | | | | | | | | | | | | |
| BAXTER, STEPHEN (HM01934) | | | | ● | | | | | | | | | | | | | | | | | | | | | | | | | | | | | | | | | | | | | | | | | | | | | | | |
| BECKER, AMELY (HM02021) | | | | | | | | | | | | | | | | | | | | | | | | | | | | | | | | | ● | | | | | | | | | | | | | | | | | | |
| BELMONT PHYSIOTHERAPY PRACTICE (HM02108) | | | ● | | | | | | | | | | | | | | | | | | | | | | | | | | | | | | | | | | | | | | | | | | | | | | | | |
| BENATAR, WENDY (HM02120) | | | ● | | | | | | | | | | | | | | | | | | | | | | | | | | | | | | | | | | | | | | | | | | | | | | | | |
| BERNSTEIN, SAMUEL (HM02204) | | | | | | | | | | | | | | | | | | | | | | | | | | | | | | | | ● | ● | | | | | | | | | | | | | | | | | | |
| BEVERLEY CLINIC (HM02244) | | | ● | | | | | | | | | | | | | | | | | | | | | | | ● | ● | | | | | | ● | | | | | | | | | | | | | | | | | | |
| BHAGAT, PRITI (HM02266) | | | | | | | ● | | | | | | | | | | | | | | | | | | | | | | | | | | | | | | | | | | | | | | | | | | | | |
| BIRCH, MARGARET (HM02352) | | | | | | | ● | | | | | | | | | | | | | | | | | | | | | | | | | | | | | | | | | | | | | | | | | | | | |
| BIRMINGHAM, LINDA (HM02392) | | | | ● | | | | | | | | | | | | | | | | | | | | | | | | | | | | | | | | | | | | | | | | | | | | | | | |
| BLACKHEATH CENTRE (HM02447) | | | | ● | | | | | | | | | | | | | | | | | | | | | | | | | | | | | | | | | | | | | | | | | | | | | | | |
| BLACKHEATH CHIROPRACTIC CLINIC (HM02448) | | | | | | | | | | | | | | | | | | | | | | | | | | | ● | | | | | | | | | | | | | | | | | | | | | | | | |
| BLACKHEATH COMP THERAPIES CTRE (HM02450) | | | ● | | | | | | | | | | | | | | | | | | | | | | | | | | | | | | | | | | | | | | | | | | | | | | | | |
| BLOOMSBURY ALEXANDER CENTRE (HM02516) | | | | ● | | | | | | | | | | | | | ● | | | | | | | ● | | | | | | | | | | | | | | | | | | | | | | | | | | | |
| BLOOMSBURY THERAPY CENTRE (HM02518) | | | | ● | | | | | | | | | | | | | ● | | | | | | | ● | | | | | | | | | | | ● | | | | | | | | | | | | | | | | |
| BODYSPACE (HM02632) | | | | | | | | | | | | | | | | | | | ● | | | | | | | | | | | | | | ● | | | | | | | | | | | | | | | | | | |
| BOOTH, JAMES (HM02700) | | | ● | | | | | | | | | | | | | | | | | | | | | | | | | | | | | | | | | | | | | | | | | | | | | | | | |
| BOOTH, JUDY (HM02703) | | | | | | | ● | | | | | | | | | | | | | | | | | | | | | | | | | | | | | | | | | | | | | | | | | | | | |
| BOSTON CHIROPODY CLINIC (HM02725) | | | | | | | | | | | | | | | | | | | | | | ● | | | | ● | | | | | | | | | | | | | | | | | | | | | | | | | |
| BOURGARD, FRANCOISE (HM02747) | | | | | | | ● | | | | | | | | | | | | | | | | | | | | | | | | | | | | | | | | | | | | | | | | | | | | |
| BRACKENBURY NTRL HEALTH CLNC (HM02837) | | | ● | ● | ● | | ● | | | | | | | | | | | | | | | | | | | ● | | | | | | | ● | | | | | | | | | | | | | | | | | | |
| BRAHMBHATT, H B (HM02893) | | | ● | | | | | | | | | | | | | | | | | | | | | | | | | | | | | | | | | | | | | | | | | | | | | | | | |
| BRANDON, NICHOLAS (HM02914) | | | | ● | | | ● | | | | | | | | | | | | | | | | | | | | | | | | | | | | | | | | | | | | | | | | | | | | |

# A - F Therapies at Practices/Businesses

| Business by County with Reference no. | Absent Healing | Acupressure | Acupuncture | Alexander Technique | Allergy Testing | Anthroposohical Med | Aromatherapy | Art Therapy | Aura Therapy | Auricular Therapy | Auto Suggestion | Autogenic Training | Aversion Therapy | Ayurvedic Medicine | Baby Massage | Bach Remedies | Bates Method | Beauty Therapy | Bio-energetics | Biofeedback | Biomagnetic Therapy | Biomechanics | Bonesetting | Bowen Therapy | Chinese Herbal Medicine | Chiropody | Chiropractic | Clinical Ecology | Cognitive Therapy | Colonic Hydrotherapy | Colour Therapy | Complementary Therapy | Counselling | Cranial Osteopathy | Cranio-Sacral Therapy | Cryo Surgery | Crystal Healing | Cupping | Cymatics | Dance Movement Thrpy | Dietician | Do-In | Douching | Dowsing | Drama Therapy | Electrolipolysis | Electrolysis | Electrotherapy | Encounter Groups | Faith Healing |
|---|---|---|---|---|---|---|---|---|---|---|---|---|---|---|---|---|---|---|---|---|---|---|---|---|---|---|---|---|---|---|---|---|---|---|---|---|---|---|---|---|---|---|---|---|---|---|---|---|---|---|
| BRITISH AUTOGENIC SOCIETY (HM03076) | | | | | | | | | | | |●| | | | | | | | | | | | | | | | | | | | | | | | | | | | | | | | | | | | | | |
| BROADGATE CHIROPRACTIC CLINIC (HM03113) | | | | | | | | | | | | | | | | | | | | | | | | | | |●| | | | | | | | | | | | | | | | | | | | | | | |
| BROOKS, JANE (HM03177) | | | | | | | | | | | | |●| | | | | | | | | | | | | | | |●| | | |●| | | | | | | | | | | | | | | | |●|
| BROWN, ALISON R (HM03210) | | | | | | | | | | | | | | | | | | | | | | | | | | | | | | | | | |●| | | | | | | | | | | | | | | | |
| BUCHANAN, ANGELA (HM03300) | | | | | | | | | | | | | | | | | | | | | | | | | | | | | | | | | | | | | | | | | | | | | | | |●| | |
| BUCKLEY, BILLIE (HM03318) | | | | | | | | | | | | | | | | | | | | | | | | | | | | |●| | | |●| | | | | | | | | | | | | | | | | |
| BUDZYNSKI, LESLIE A (HM03331) | | | | | | | | | | | | | | | | | | | | | | | | | | |●| | | | | | | | | | | | | | | | | | | | | | | |
| BURGER, SALLY (HM03374) | | | |●| | | | | | | | | | | | | | | | | | | | | | | | | | | | | | | | | | | | | | | | | | | | | | |
| BYNG, MELANIE (HM03512) | | | |●| | | | | | | | | | | | | | | | | | | | | | | | | | | | | | | | | | | | | | | | | | | | | | |
| BYRNE, JUDY (HM03516) | | | | | | | | | | | | | | | | | | | | | | | | | | | | |●| | | |●| | | | | | | | | | | | | | | | | |
| CAMPBELL-PARKER, PATRICIA (HM03612) | | | | | | | | | | | | | | | |●| | | | | | | | | | | | | | | | | | | | | | | | | | | | | | | | | | |
| CARBONNEL, JOEL (HM03659) | | | |●| | | | | | | | | | | | | | | | | | | | | | | | | | | | | | | | | | | | | | | | | | | | | | |
| CARRINGTON, W H M (HM03750) | | | |●| | | | | | | | | | | | | | | | | | | | | | | | | | | | | | | | | | | | | | | | | | | | | | |
| CENTRE FOR TRANSFORMATION (HM03920) | | | | | | | | | | | | | | | | |●| | | | | | | | | | | | | | | | | | | | | | | | | | | | | | | | | |
| CHANDLER, ROBERT & ELIZABETH (HM03979) | | | |●| | | | | | | | | | | | | | | | | | | | | | | | | | | | | | | | | | | | | | | | | | | | | | |
| CHARTERHOUSE PHYSIOTHERAPY (HM04049) | | |●| | | | | | | | | | | | | | | | | | | | | | | | | | | | | | | | | | | | | | | | | | | | | | | |
| CHATSWORTH CLINIC (HM04063) | |●|●| | | |●| | | | | | | | |●| | | | | | | | | | | | | | | |●|●|●| | | | | | | | | | | | | | | | |
| CHELSEA AROMATHERAPISTS (HM04087) | | | | | | |●| | | | | | | | | | | | | | | | | | | | | | | | | | | | | | | | | | | | | | | | | | | |
| CHEUNG, LILY (HM04143) | | |●| | | | | | | | | | | | | | | | | | | | | | | | | | | | | | | | | | | | | | | | | | | | | | | |
| CHINESE MEDICAL CENTRE (HM04231) | | |●| | | | | | | | | | | | | | | | | | | | | | | | | | | | | | | | | | | | | | | | | | | | | | | |
| CHINESE MEDICAL CTRE OF LONDON (HM04245) | | |●| | | | | | | | | | | | | | | | | | | | | | | | | | | | | | | | | | |●| | | | | | | | | | | | |
| CHINESE SHOP (HM04269) | |●|●| | | | | | | | | | | | | | | | | | | | | | | | | | | | | | | | | | | | | | | | | | | | | | | |
| CHIROPODY CENTRE (HM04311) | | | | | | | | | | | | | | | | | | | | | | | | | |●| | | | | | | | | | | | | | | | | | | | | | | | |
| CHIROPRACTIC CLINIC (HM04393) | | |●| | | | | | | | | | | | | | | | | | | | | | | |●| | | | | | | | | | | | | | | | | | | | | | | |
| CHISWICK CHIROPRACTIC CLINIC (HM04412) | | |●| | | | | | | | | | | | | | | | | | | | | | | |●| | | | | | | | | | | | | | | | | | | | | | | |
| CHISWICK CHIROPRACTIC CLINIC (HM04413) | | | | | | | | | | | | | | | | | | | | | | | | | | |●| | | | | | | | | | | | | | | | | | | | | | | |
| CITY CHIROPRACTIC CENTRE (HM04491) | | | | | | | | | | | | | | | | | | | | | | | | | | |●| | | | | | | | | | | | | | | | | | | | | | | |
| CITY HEALTH CENTRE (HM04496) | | | | | | | | | | | | | | | | | | | | | | | | | | | | | | | |●| |●| | | | | | | | | | | | | | | | |
| CLASSICAL OSTEOPATH (HM04610) |●|●| | | | | | | | | | | | | | | | | | | | | | | | | | | | | |●| |●| | | | | | | | | | | | | | | |●|
| CLEMENTS, MICHAEL (HM04645) | | |●| | | | | | | | | | | | | | | | | | | | | | | | | | | | | | | | | | | | | | | | | | | | | | | |
| CLINIC FOR COUNSELLING (HM04681) | | | | | | | | | | | | | | | | | | | | | | | | | | | | | | | | |●| | | | | | | | | | | | | | | | | |
| CLINIC FOR COUNSELLING (HM04680) | | | | | | | | | | | | | | | | | | | | | | | | | | | | | | | | |●| | | | | | | | | | | | | | | | | |
| CLINIC OF TRAD CHINESE MED (HM04709) | | |●| | | | | | | | | | | | | | | | | | | | | | | | | | | | | | | | | | | | | | | | | | | | | | | |
| COAKLEY, NOIRIN (HM04751) | | | | | | | | | | | | | | | |●| | | | | | | | | | | | | | | | | | | | | | | | | | | | | | | | | | |

# A - F Therapies at Practices/Businesses

| Business by County with Reference no. | Absent Healing | Acupressure | Acupuncture | Alexander Technique | Allergy Testing | Anthroposohical Med | Aromatherapy | Art Therapy | Aura Therapy | Auricular Therapy |
|---|---|---|---|---|---|---|---|---|---|---|
| COHEN, P N (HM04794) | | | | | | | | | | |
| COMP MEDI ASS (HM04913) | | ● | ● | ● | | | ● | | | |
| COMPLETE HEALTH CARE (HM04958) | | ● | ● | ● | | | ● | | | |
| CONTENT, A J (HM05018) | | | | ● | | | | | | |
| COOPER, LAURA (HM05116) | | | | | | | | | | |
| COOTE, JACKIE (HM05132) | | | | ● | | | | | | |
| CORTEEN, PAOLA (HM05197) | | | | ● | | | | | | |
| COTTON, PAULA (HM05229) | | | | | | | ● | | | |
| COUNSELLING & PSYCHOTHERAPY (HM05246) | | | | | | | | | | |
| COUNSELLING SERVICE (HM05252) | | | | | | | | | | |
| COVIELLO, LINDA (HM05285) | | | ● | | | | | | | |
| CRANIOSACRAL THERAPY ED TRUST (HM05380) | | | | | | | | | | |
| CRAVEN CLINIC (HM05385) | | | ● | | ● | | ● | | | |
| CREATIVE INSIGHTS (HM05399) | | | | | | | | | | |
| CRISTA GALLI OSTEOPATHS (HM05446) | | | | | | | | | | |
| CROSTON, GRAHAM (HM05492) | | | | ● | | | | | | |
| CTRE FOR CRANIO-SACRAL THERAPY (HM05540) | | | ● | ● | | | ● | | | |
| CTRE FOR THE STUDY OF COMP MED (HM05544) | | | ● | ● | | | | | | |
| DA COSTA, SALLY (HM05663) | | | | ● | | | | | | |
| DALTON, HELEN (HM05698) | | | | | | | | | | |
| DAOUST, YVETTE (HM05732) | | | | ● | | | | | | |
| DAVID WEISS HOMEOPATHY (HM05781) | | | ● | | | | | | | |
| DAVIS, JULIA (HM05854) | | | ● | | | | | | | |
| DAWSON, DAVID (DR) (HM05880) | | | | | | | | | | |
| DE WOLFF, MAARTJE (HM05924) | | | | ● | | | | | | |
| DELROY, SANDRA (DR) (HM05968) | | | | | | | | | | |
| DENNIS MICHAEL PRACTICE (HM05990) | | | ● | | | | | | | |
| DIEHL, D (HM06093) | | | | | | | | | | |
| DISTANT HEALING (HM06123) | ● | | | | | | | | | |
| DOCKLANDS DENTAL/COMP HLTH (HM06141) | | | | | | | | | | |
| DOWIE, SUSANNA (HM06237) | | | ● | | | | | | | |
| DREAM LINE (HM06296) | | ● | | | | | | ● | | |
| DULWICH CHIROPRACTIC CLINIC (HM06382) | | | | | | | | | | |
| E RU CHU (HM06475) | | | ● | | | | | | | |

| Business by County with Reference no. | Auto Suggestion | Autogenic Training | Aversion Therapy | Ayurvedic Medicine | Baby Massage | Bach Remedies | Bates Method | Beauty Therapy | Bio-energetics | Biofeedback |
|---|---|---|---|---|---|---|---|---|---|---|
| COHEN, P N (HM04794) | | | | | | | | | | |
| COMP MEDI ASS (HM04913) | | | | ● | | ● | | | | |
| COMPLETE HEALTH CARE (HM04958) | | | | | | ● | | | | ● |
| CONTENT, A J (HM05018) | | | | | | | | | | |
| COOPER, LAURA (HM05116) | | | | | | | | | | |
| COOTE, JACKIE (HM05132) | | | | | | | | | | |
| CORTEEN, PAOLA (HM05197) | | | | | | | | | | |
| COTTON, PAULA (HM05229) | | | | | | | | | | |
| COUNSELLING & PSYCHOTHERAPY (HM05246) | | | | | | | | | | |
| COUNSELLING SERVICE (HM05252) | | | | | | | | | | |
| COVIELLO, LINDA (HM05285) | | | | | | | | | | |
| CRANIOSACRAL THERAPY ED TRUST (HM05380) | | | | | | | | | | |
| CRAVEN CLINIC (HM05385) | | | | | | | | | | |
| CREATIVE INSIGHTS (HM05399) | ● | | ● | | | | | | | |
| CRISTA GALLI OSTEOPATHS (HM05446) | | | | | | | | | | |
| CROSTON, GRAHAM (HM05492) | | | | | | | | | | |
| CTRE FOR CRANIO-SACRAL THERAPY (HM05540) | | | | | | | | | | |
| CTRE FOR THE STUDY OF COMP MED (HM05544) | | ● | | | | ● | | | | |
| DA COSTA, SALLY (HM05663) | | | | | | | | | | |
| DALTON, HELEN (HM05698) | | | | | | ● | | | | |
| DAOUST, YVETTE (HM05732) | | | | | | | | | | |
| DAVID WEISS HOMEOPATHY (HM05781) | | | | | | | | | | |
| DAVIS, JULIA (HM05854) | | | | | | | | | | |
| DAWSON, DAVID (DR) (HM05880) | | | | | | | | | | |
| DE WOLFF, MAARTJE (HM05924) | | | | | | | | | | |
| DELROY, SANDRA (DR) (HM05968) | | | | | | | | | | |
| DENNIS MICHAEL PRACTICE (HM05990) | | | | | | | | | | |
| DIEHL, D (HM06093) | | | | | | | | | | |
| DISTANT HEALING (HM06123) | | | | | | | | | | |
| DOCKLANDS DENTAL/COMP HLTH (HM06141) | | | | | | | | | | |
| DOWIE, SUSANNA (HM06237) | | | | | | | | | | |
| DREAM LINE (HM06296) | | | | | | | | | | |
| DULWICH CHIROPRACTIC CLINIC (HM06382) | | | | | | | | | | |
| E RU CHU (HM06475) | | | | | | | | | | |

| Business by County with Reference no. | Biomagnetic Therapy | Biomechanics | Bonesetting | Bowen Therapy | Chinese Herbal Medicine | Chiropody | Chiropractic | Clinical Ecology | Cognitive Therapy | Colonic Hydrotherapy |
|---|---|---|---|---|---|---|---|---|---|---|
| COHEN, P N (HM04794) | | | | | | | ● | | | |
| COMP MEDI ASS (HM04913) | | | | ● | ● | | ● | | | |
| COMPLETE HEALTH CARE (HM04958) | | | | | ● | | | | | |
| CONTENT, A J (HM05018) | | | | | | | | | | |
| COOPER, LAURA (HM05116) | | | | | | | ● | | | |
| COOTE, JACKIE (HM05132) | | | | | | | | | | |
| CORTEEN, PAOLA (HM05197) | | | | | | | | | | |
| COTTON, PAULA (HM05229) | | | | | | | | | | |
| COUNSELLING & PSYCHOTHERAPY (HM05246) | | | | | | | | | | |
| COUNSELLING SERVICE (HM05252) | | | | | | | | | | |
| COVIELLO, LINDA (HM05285) | | | | | | | | | | |
| CRANIOSACRAL THERAPY ED TRUST (HM05380) | | | | | | | | | | |
| CRAVEN CLINIC (HM05385) | | | | | | | | | | |
| CREATIVE INSIGHTS (HM05399) | | | | | | | | | ● | |
| CRISTA GALLI OSTEOPATHS (HM05446) | | | | | | | | | | |
| CROSTON, GRAHAM (HM05492) | | | | | | | | | | |
| CTRE FOR CRANIO-SACRAL THERAPY (HM05540) | | | | ● | | | ● | | | |
| CTRE FOR THE STUDY OF COMP MED (HM05544) | | | | | | | | ● | | |
| DA COSTA, SALLY (HM05663) | | | | | | | | | | |
| DALTON, HELEN (HM05698) | | | | | | | | | | |
| DAOUST, YVETTE (HM05732) | | | | | | | | | | |
| DAVID WEISS HOMEOPATHY (HM05781) | | | | | | | | | | |
| DAVIS, JULIA (HM05854) | | | | | | | | | | |
| DAWSON, DAVID (DR) (HM05880) | | | | | | | | ● | | |
| DE WOLFF, MAARTJE (HM05924) | | | | | | | | | | |
| DELROY, SANDRA (DR) (HM05968) | | | | | | | | | | |
| DENNIS MICHAEL PRACTICE (HM05990) | ● | | | | | | | | | |
| DIEHL, D (HM06093) | | | | | | | ● | | | |
| DISTANT HEALING (HM06123) | | | | | | | | | | |
| DOCKLANDS DENTAL/COMP HLTH (HM06141) | | | | | | ● | | | | |
| DOWIE, SUSANNA (HM06237) | | | | | | | | | | |
| DREAM LINE (HM06296) | | | | | | | | | ● | |
| DULWICH CHIROPRACTIC CLINIC (HM06382) | | | | | | | ● | | | |
| E RU CHU (HM06475) | | | | | | | | | | |

| Business by County with Reference no. | Colour Therapy | Complementary Therapy | Counselling | Cranial Osteopathy | Cranio-Sacral Therapy | Cryo Surgery | Crystal Healing | Cupping | Cymatics | Dance Movement Thrpy |
|---|---|---|---|---|---|---|---|---|---|---|
| COHEN, P N (HM04794) | | | | | | | | | | |
| COMP MEDI ASS (HM04913) | | ● | | ● | ● | | ● | | | |
| COMPLETE HEALTH CARE (HM04958) | | ● | ● | ● | | | | | | |
| CONTENT, A J (HM05018) | | | | | | | | | | |
| COOPER, LAURA (HM05116) | | | | | | | | | | |
| COOTE, JACKIE (HM05132) | | | | | | | | | | |
| CORTEEN, PAOLA (HM05197) | | | | | | | | | | |
| COTTON, PAULA (HM05229) | | | | | | | | | | |
| COUNSELLING & PSYCHOTHERAPY (HM05246) | | | ● | | | | | | | |
| COUNSELLING SERVICE (HM05252) | | | ● | | | | | | | |
| COVIELLO, LINDA (HM05285) | | | | | | | | | | |
| CRANIOSACRAL THERAPY ED TRUST (HM05380) | | ● | | | ● | | | | | |
| CRAVEN CLINIC (HM05385) | | | ● | | | | | | | |
| CREATIVE INSIGHTS (HM05399) | | | ● | | | | | | | |
| CRISTA GALLI OSTEOPATHS (HM05446) | | | | ● | | | | | | |
| CROSTON, GRAHAM (HM05492) | | | | | | | | | | |
| CTRE FOR CRANIO-SACRAL THERAPY (HM05540) | | | ● | ● | ● | | | | | |
| CTRE FOR THE STUDY OF COMP MED (HM05544) | | ● | ● | | | | | | | |
| DA COSTA, SALLY (HM05663) | | | | | | | | | | |
| DALTON, HELEN (HM05698) | | | | | | | | | | |
| DAOUST, YVETTE (HM05732) | | | | | | | | | | |
| DAVID WEISS HOMEOPATHY (HM05781) | | | | | | | | | | |
| DAVIS, JULIA (HM05854) | | | | | | | | | | |
| DAWSON, DAVID (DR) (HM05880) | | | | | | | | | | |
| DE WOLFF, MAARTJE (HM05924) | | | | | | | | | | |
| DELROY, SANDRA (DR) (HM05968) | | | ● | | | | | | | |
| DENNIS MICHAEL PRACTICE (HM05990) | | ● | | ● | | | | | | |
| DIEHL, D (HM06093) | | | | | | | | | | |
| DISTANT HEALING (HM06123) | | | | | | | ● | | | |
| DOCKLANDS DENTAL/COMP HLTH (HM06141) | | | | | | | | | | |
| DOWIE, SUSANNA (HM06237) | | | | | | | | | | |
| DREAM LINE (HM06296) | | ● | ● | | | | | | | |
| DULWICH CHIROPRACTIC CLINIC (HM06382) | | | | | | | | | | |
| E RU CHU (HM06475) | | | | | | | | | | |

| Business by County with Reference no. | Dietician | Do-In | Douching | Dowsing | Drama Therapy | Electrolipolysis | Electrolysis | Electrotherapy | Encounter Groups | Faith Healing |
|---|---|---|---|---|---|---|---|---|---|---|
| COHEN, P N (HM04794) | | | | | | | | | | |
| COMP MEDI ASS (HM04913) | | | | | | | | | | |
| COMPLETE HEALTH CARE (HM04958) | | | | | | | | | | |
| CONTENT, A J (HM05018) | | | | | | | | | | |
| COOPER, LAURA (HM05116) | | | | | | | | | | |
| COOTE, JACKIE (HM05132) | | | | | | | | | | |
| CORTEEN, PAOLA (HM05197) | | | | | | | | | | |
| COTTON, PAULA (HM05229) | | | | | | | | | | |
| COUNSELLING & PSYCHOTHERAPY (HM05246) | | | | | | | | | | |
| COUNSELLING SERVICE (HM05252) | | | | | | | | | | |
| COVIELLO, LINDA (HM05285) | | | | | | | | | | |
| CRANIOSACRAL THERAPY ED TRUST (HM05380) | | | | | | | | | | |
| CRAVEN CLINIC (HM05385) | | | | | | | | | | |
| CREATIVE INSIGHTS (HM05399) | | | | | | | | | | ● |
| CRISTA GALLI OSTEOPATHS (HM05446) | | | | | | | | | | |
| CROSTON, GRAHAM (HM05492) | | | | | | | | | | |
| CTRE FOR CRANIO-SACRAL THERAPY (HM05540) | | | | | | | | | | |
| CTRE FOR THE STUDY OF COMP MED (HM05544) | ● | | | | | | | | | |
| DA COSTA, SALLY (HM05663) | | | | | | | | | | |
| DALTON, HELEN (HM05698) | | | | | | | | | | |
| DAOUST, YVETTE (HM05732) | | | | | | | | | | |
| DAVID WEISS HOMEOPATHY (HM05781) | | | | | | | | | | |
| DAVIS, JULIA (HM05854) | | | | | | | | | | |
| DAWSON, DAVID (DR) (HM05880) | | | | | | | | | | |
| DE WOLFF, MAARTJE (HM05924) | | | | | | | | | | |
| DELROY, SANDRA (DR) (HM05968) | | | | | | | | | | |
| DENNIS MICHAEL PRACTICE (HM05990) | ● | | | | | | | | | |
| DIEHL, D (HM06093) | | | | | | | | | | |
| DISTANT HEALING (HM06123) | | | | | | | | | | ● |
| DOCKLANDS DENTAL/COMP HLTH (HM06141) | | | | | | | | | | |
| DOWIE, SUSANNA (HM06237) | | | | | | | | | | |
| DREAM LINE (HM06296) | | | | | | | | | | |
| DULWICH CHIROPRACTIC CLINIC (HM06382) | | | | | | | | | | |
| E RU CHU (HM06475) | | | | | | | | | | |

# A - F Therapies at Practices/Businesses

| Business by County with Reference no. | Absent Healing | Acupressure | Acupuncture | Alexander Technique | Allergy Testing | Anthroposohical Med | Aromatherapy | Art Therapy | Aura Therapy | Auricular Therapy | Auto Suggestion | Autogenic Training | Aversion Therapy | Ayurvedic Medicine | Baby Massage | Bach Remedies | Bates Method | Beauty Therapy | Bio-energetics | Biofeedback | Biomagnetic Therapy | Biomechanics | Bonesetting | Bowen Therapy | Chinese Herbal Medicine |
|---|---|---|---|---|---|---|---|---|---|---|---|---|---|---|---|---|---|---|---|---|---|---|---|---|---|
| E.LONDON COMPLEMENTARY HEALTH (HM06479) | | | | | | | ● | | | | | | | | | | | | | | | | | | |
| EALING ACUP/CHINESE HERBAL MED (HM06483) | | | ● | | | | | | | | | | | | | | | | | | | | | | |
| EALING CHIROPRACTIC CLINIC (HM06486) | | | | | | | | | | | | | | | | | | | | | | | | | |
| EALING COUNS & THERAPY CTRE (HM06488) | | | | | | | | | | | | | | | | | | | | | | | | | |
| EAST WEST HERB SHOP (HM06527) | | | ● | | | | | | | | | | | | | | | | | | | | | | |
| EAST WEST THERAPIES (HM06529) | ● | ● | | | | | | | | | | | | | | ● | | | | | | | | | |
| EDGELL, MARJORY (HM06599) | | | | | | | | | | | | | | | | | | | | | | | | | |
| EDGWARE CHIROPRACTIC CLINIC (HM06601) | | | | | | | | | | | | | | | | | | | | | | | | | |
| EDGWARE NATURAL HEALTH CENTRE (HM06604) | ● | ● | ● | ● | | | | | | | | | | | | | | | | | | | | | |
| ELLWOOD, CAROLINE (HM06780) | | | | | | | | | | | | | | | | | | | | | | | | | |
| ELTHAM HYPNOTHERAPY ANALYSIS (HM06789) | | | | | | | | | | | ● | | ● | | | | | | | | | | | | |
| ENFIELD HYP & COUNSELLING (HM06819) | | | | | | | | | | | | | | | | | | | | | | | | | |
| ENGEL-WARSHAW (HM06826) | | | ● | | | | | | | | | | | | | | | | | | | | | | |
| EQUILIBRIUM (HM06869) | | | | | | | ● | | | | | | | ● | | | | | | | | | | | |
| EQUILIBRIUM COUNS/THRPY CTRE (HM06873) | | | ● | | | | | | | | | | | | | | | | | | | | | | |
| ESSENTIAL THERAPEUTIC (HM06916) | | | | | | | ● | | | | | | | | | | | | | | | | | | |
| EVANS-FOSTER, YVETTE (HM06994) | | | ● | | | | | | | | | | | | | | | | | | | | | | |
| FAR EASTERN MASSAGE (HM07099) | | | | | | | ● | | | | | | | | | | | | | | | | | | |
| FARMACIA URBAN HEALING (HM07107) | | | ● | | | | ● | | | | | | | | | | | | | | | | | | |
| FIRST ACUPUNCTURE CLINIC (HM07333) | | | ● | | | | | | | | | | | | | | | | | | | | | | |
| FITZGERALD, D (HM07365) | | | | ● | | | | | | | | | | | | | | | | | | | | | |
| FITZMAURICE, KIERON (HM07370) | | | | ● | | | | | | | | | | | | | | | | | | | | | |
| FLETCHER, CLARE (HM07410) | | | ● | | | | | | | | | | | | | | | | | | | | | | |
| FLEXIBLE HOUR (HM07420) | | ● | | | | | | | | | | | | | | | | | | | | | | | |
| FLOAT WORKS (HM07424) | | | ● | | | | | | | | | | | | | | | | | | | | | | |
| FOOTLOOSE CHIROPODY CLINIC (HM07503) | | | | | | | | | | | | | | | | | | | | | | | | | |
| FOOTMARK, G & P (HM07504) | | | | | | | | | | | | | | | | | | | | | | | | | |
| FOOTPAD (HM07506) | | | | | | | | | | | | | | | | | | | | | | | | | |
| FOWNES, SUZANNE (HM07630) | | | | ● | | | | | | | | | | | | | | | | | | | | | |
| FREEMAN-ATWOOD, R (HM07722) | | | | | | | ● | | | | | | | | | | | | | | | | | | |
| FREILICH, ELINOR (HM07727) | | | ● | | | | | | | | | | | | | | | | | | | | | | |
| FRIEDRICH STAEBLER (HM07746) | | | ● | | | | | | | | | | | | | | | | | | | | | | |
| FRY, HOWARD (HM07772) | | | | | | | | | | | | | | | | | | | | | | | | | |
| FULHAM CLINIC (HM07781) | | ● | ● | | | | ● | | | | | | | | | ● | | | | | | | | | |

| Business by County with Reference no. | Chiropody | Chiropractic | Clinical Ecology | Cognitive Therapy | Colonic Hydrotherapy | Colour Therapy | Complementary Therapy | Counselling | Cranial Osteopathy | Cranio-Sacral Therapy | Cryo Surgery | Crystal Healing | Cupping | Cymatics | Dance Movement Thrpy | Dietician | Do-In | Douching | Dowsing | Drama Therapy | Electrolipolysis | Electrolysis | Electrotherapy | Encounter Groups | Faith Healing |
|---|---|---|---|---|---|---|---|---|---|---|---|---|---|---|---|---|---|---|---|---|---|---|---|---|---|
| E.LONDON COMPLEMENTARY HEALTH (HM06479) | | | | | | | ● | | ● | | | | | | | | | | | | | | | | |
| EALING ACUP/CHINESE HERBAL MED (HM06483) | | | | | | | | | | | | | | | | | | | | | | | | | |
| EALING CHIROPRACTIC CLINIC (HM06486) | | ● | | | | | | | | | | | | | | | | | | | | | | | |
| EALING COUNS & THERAPY CTRE (HM06488) | | | | | | ● | ● | ● | | | | | | | | | | | | | | | | | |
| EAST WEST HERB SHOP (HM06527) | | | | | | | | | | | | | | | | | | | | | | | | | |
| EAST WEST THERAPIES (HM06529) | | | | | | | ● | | | | | | | | | | ● | | ● | | | | | | |
| EDGELL, MARJORY (HM06599) | | | | | | | | ● | | | | | | | | | | | | | | | | | |
| EDGWARE CHIROPRACTIC CLINIC (HM06601) | | ● | | | | | | | | | | | | | | | | | | | | | | | |
| EDGWARE NATURAL HEALTH CENTRE (HM06604) | | | | | | | | ● | | | | | | | | | | | | | | | | | |
| ELLWOOD, CAROLINE (HM06780) | | | | | | | | | ● | | | | | | | | | | | | | | | | |
| ELTHAM HYPNOTHERAPY ANALYSIS (HM06789) | | | | ● | | | | ● | | | | | | | | | | | | | | | | | |
| ENFIELD HYP & COUNSELLING (HM06819) | | | | | | | | ● | | | | | | | | | | | | | | | | | |
| ENGEL-WARSHAW (HM06826) | | | | | | | | | | | | | | | | | | | | | | | | | |
| EQUILIBRIUM (HM06869) | | | | | | | ● | ● | | ● | | | | | | | | | | | | | | | |
| EQUILIBRIUM COUNS/THRPY CTRE (HM06873) | | | | | | | | ● | ● | | | | | | | | | | | | | | | | |
| ESSENTIAL THERAPEUTIC (HM06916) | | | | | | | | | | | | | | | | | | | | | | | | | |
| EVANS-FOSTER, YVETTE (HM06994) | | | | | | | | | | | | | | | | | | | | | | | | | |
| FAR EASTERN MASSAGE (HM07099) | | | | | | | | | | | | | | | | | | | | | | | | | |
| FARMACIA URBAN HEALING (HM07107) | | | | | | | | | | ● | | | | | | | | | | | | | | | |
| FIRST ACUPUNCTURE CLINIC (HM07333) | | | | | | | | | | | | | | | | | | | | | | | | | |
| FITZGERALD, D (HM07365) | | | | | | | | | | | | | | | | | | | | | | | | | |
| FITZMAURICE, KIERON (HM07370) | | | | | | | | | | | | | | | | | | | | | | | | | |
| FLETCHER, CLARE (HM07410) | | | | | | | | | | | | | | | | | | | | | | | | | |
| FLEXIBLE HOUR (HM07420) | | | | | | | | | | | | | ● | | | | | | | | | | | | |
| FLOAT WORKS (HM07424) | | | | | | | | | | | | | | | | | | | | | | | | | |
| FOOTLOOSE CHIROPODY CLINIC (HM07503) | ● | | | | | | | | | | | | | | | | | | | | | | | | |
| FOOTMARK, G & P (HM07504) | | ● | | | | | | | | | | | | | | | | | | | | | | | |
| FOOTPAD (HM07506) | ● | | | | | | | | | | | | | | | | | | | | | | | | |
| FOWNES, SUZANNE (HM07630) | | | | | | | | | | | | | | | | | | | | | | | | | |
| FREEMAN-ATWOOD, R (HM07722) | | | | | | | | | | | | | | | | | | | | | | | | | |
| FREILICH, ELINOR (HM07727) | | | | | | | | | | | | | | | | | | | | | | | | | |
| FRIEDRICH STAEBLER (HM07746) | | | | | | | | | | | | | | | | | | | | | | | | | |
| FRY, HOWARD (HM07772) | ● | | | | | | | | | | | | | | | | | | | | | | | | |
| FULHAM CLINIC (HM07781) | | ● | | | | | ● | ● | ● | | | | | | | | | | | | | | | | |

# A - F Therapies at Practices/Businesses

| Business by County with Reference no. | Absent Healing | Acupressure | Acupuncture | Alexander Technique | Allergy Testing | Anthroposohical Med | Aromatherapy | Art Therapy | Aura Therapy | Auricular Therapy | Auto Suggestion | Autogenic Training | Aversion Therapy | Ayurvedic Medicine | Baby Massage | Bach Remedies | Bates Method | Beauty Therapy | Bio-energetics | Biofeedback | Biomagnetic Therapy | Biomechanics | Bonesetting | Bowen Therapy | Chinese Herbal Medicine |
|---|---|---|---|---|---|---|---|---|---|---|---|---|---|---|---|---|---|---|---|---|---|---|---|---|---|
| FULHAM OSTEOPATHIC PRACTICE (HM07783) | | | | | | | | | | | | | | | | | | | | | | | | | |
| FULHAM PALACE (HM07784) | | | | | | | | | | | | | | | | | | | | | | | | | |
| G T CONSULTANCY (HM07815) | | | | | | | | | | | | | | | | | | | | | | | | | |
| GEORGE (HM07987) | | | | | | | | | | | | | | | | | | | | | | ● | | | |
| GESTALT CENTRE (HM08005) | | | | | | | | | | | | | | | | | | | | | | | | | |
| GLASSMAN, DAVID (HM08128) | | | | ● | | | | | | | | | | | | | ● | | | | | | | | |
| GLORIA JEANS FASC FOR LAVENDER (HM08158) | | | | | | | ● | | | | | | | | | | | | | | | | | | |
| GODAGAMA, S (HM08174) | | | ● | | | | | | | | | | | | | | | | | | | | | | |
| GODWIN, ROME (HM08194) | | | | ● | | | | | | | | | | | | | | | | | | | | | |
| GOODFELLOW, DONNA (HM08253) | | | | | | | ● | | | | | | | | | | | | | | | | | | |
| GORDON, TIM (DR) (HM08285) | | | ● | | | | | | | | | | | | | | | | | | | | | | |
| GREENCADES (HM08480) | | | | | | | ● | | | | | | | | | | | | | | | | | | |
| GREENWICH NATURAL HEALTH CTRE (HM08500) | | | ● | ● | ● | | ● | | | | | | | | | ● | | | | | | | | | ● |
| GROUP ANALYTIC PRACTICE (HM08605) | | | | | | | | | | | | | | | | | | | | | | | | | |
| HACKNEY HYPNOTHERAPY (HM08685) | | | | | | | | | | | ● | | | | | | | | | | | | | | |
| HAI TIAN HEALTH CENTRE (HM08703) | | | ● | | | | | | | | | | | | | | | | | | | | | | |
| HAJIOFF, RUTH (HM08721) | | | ● | | | | | | | | | | | | | | | | | | | | | | |
| HALL, SUSANNE (HM08791) | | | | ● | | | | | | | | | | | | | | | | | | | | | |
| HAMILTON, FIONA (HM08843) | | | | | | | | | | | | | | | | | | | | | | | | | |
| HAMPSTEAD ACU/CHINESE HBL MED (HM08881) | | | ● | | | | | | | | | | | | | | | | | | | | | | |
| HANDS ON HEALTH (HM08909) | | | | | | | ● | | | | | | | | | | | | | | | | | | |
| HARCOMBE, LYDIA (HM08962) | | | | | | | ● | | | | | | | | | | | | | | | | | | |
| HAREWOOD, MARCIA M (HM08991) | | | | | | | | | | | | | | | | | | | | | | | | | |
| HARLEY ST STRESS MNGMT (HM08999) | | | | | | | | | | | ● | | | | | | | | | | | | | | |
| HARLEY STREET TCM FERTILITY (HM09003) | | ● | ● | | | | | | | | | | | | | | | | | | | | | | |
| HARLEY, KI (HM09006) | | | | | | | | | | | | | | | | | | | | | | | | | |
| HARPER, SUZANNE G (HM09042) | | | ● | | | | | | | | | | | | | ● | | | | | | | | | |
| HARPER, SUZANNE G (HM09041) | | | ● | | | | | | | | | | | | | ● | | | | | | | | | |
| HARROW CHIROPRACTIC CLINIC (HM09120) | | | | | | | | | | | | | | | | | | | | | | | | | |
| HARROW HEALTH CARE CENTRE (HM09121) | | ● | ● | | | | | | | | | | | | | | | | | | | | | | |
| HARWOOD, J (HM09175) | | | ● | | | | | | | | | | | | | | | | | | | | | | |
| HATHA YOGA/COUNSELLING (HM09195) | | | | | | | | | | | | | | | | | | | | | | | | | |
| HAVELOCK-SEARLE, PAULINE (HM09206) | | | | | | | | | | | | | | | | | | | | | | | | | |
| HAVEN GREEN CLINIC (HM09209) | | | ● | | | | | | | | | | | | | | | | | | | | | | |

| Business by County with Reference no. | Chiropody | Chiropractic | Clinical Ecology | Cognitive Therapy | Colonic Hydrotherapy | Colour Therapy | Complementary Therapy | Counselling | Cranial Osteopathy | Cranio-Sacral Therapy | Cryo Surgery | Crystal Healing | Cupping | Cymatics | Dance Movement Thrpy | Dietician | Do-In | Douching | Dowsing | Drama Therapy | Electrolipolysis | Electrolysis | Electrotherapy | Encounter Groups | Faith Healing |
|---|---|---|---|---|---|---|---|---|---|---|---|---|---|---|---|---|---|---|---|---|---|---|---|---|---|
| FULHAM OSTEOPATHIC PRACTICE (HM07783) | | | | | | | | | ● | | | | | | | | | | | | | | | | |
| FULHAM PALACE (HM07784) | | ● | | | | | | | | | | | | | | | | | | | | | | | |
| G T CONSULTANCY (HM07815) | | | | | | | | ● | | | | | | | | | | | | | | | | | |
| GEORGE (HM07987) | ● | | | | | | | | | | | | | | | | | | | | | | | | |
| GESTALT CENTRE (HM08005) | | | | | | | | ● | | | | | | | | | | | | | | | | | |
| GLASSMAN, DAVID (HM08128) | | | | | | | | | | | | | | | | | | | | | | | | | |
| GLORIA JEANS FASC FOR LAVENDER (HM08158) | | | | | | | | | | | | | | | | | | | | | | | | | |
| GODAGAMA, S (HM08174) | | | | | | | | | | | | | | | | | | | | | | | | | |
| GODWIN, ROME (HM08194) | | | | | | | | | | | | | | | | | | | | | | | | | |
| GOODFELLOW, DONNA (HM08253) | | | | | | | | | | | | | | | | | | | | | | | | | |
| GORDON, TIM (DR) (HM08285) | | | | | | | | | | | | | | | | | | | | | | | | | |
| GREENCADES (HM08480) | | | | | | | | | | | | | | | | | | | | | | | | | |
| GREENWICH NATURAL HEALTH CTRE (HM08500) | ● | | | | | | ● | ● | ● | ● | | | | | | | | | | | | | | | |
| GROUP ANALYTIC PRACTICE (HM08605) | | | | | | | | ● | | | | | | | | | | | | | | | | | |
| HACKNEY HYPNOTHERAPY (HM08685) | | | | ● | | | | ● | | | | | | | | | | | | | | | | | |
| HAI TIAN HEALTH CENTRE (HM08703) | | | | | | | | | | | | | | | | | | | | | | | | | |
| HAJIOFF, RUTH (HM08721) | | | | | | | | | | | | | | | | | | | | | | | | | |
| HALL, SUSANNE (HM08791) | | | | | | | | | | | | | | | | | | | | | | | | | |
| HAMILTON, FIONA (HM08843) | | | | | | | | | ● | | | | | | | | | | | | | | | | |
| HAMPSTEAD ACU/CHINESE HBL MED (HM08881) | | | | | | | | | | | | | | | | | | | | | | | | | |
| HANDS ON HEALTH (HM08909) | | | | | | | | | | | | | | | | | | | | | | | | | |
| HARCOMBE, LYDIA (HM08962) | | | | | | | | | | | | | | | | | | | | | | | | | |
| HAREWOOD, MARCIA M (HM08991) | | | | | | | | | ● | | | | | | | | | | | | | | | | |
| HARLEY ST STRESS MNGMT (HM08999) | | | | ● | | | ● | ● | | | | | | | | | | | | ● | | | | | |
| HARLEY STREET TCM FERTILITY (HM09003) | | | | | | | | | | | | | | | | | | | | | | | | | |
| HARLEY, KI (HM09006) | | | | | | | | ● | | | | | | | | | | | | | | | | | |
| HARPER, SUZANNE G (HM09042) | | | | | | | | ● | ● | | | | | | | | | | | | | | | | |
| HARPER, SUZANNE G (HM09041) | | | | | | | | ● | ● | | | | | | | | | | | | | | | | |
| HARROW CHIROPRACTIC CLINIC (HM09120) | | ● | | | | | | | | | | | | | | | | | | | | | | | |
| HARROW HEALTH CARE CENTRE (HM09121) | | | | | | | | | ● | | | | ● | | | | | | | | | | | | |
| HARWOOD, J (HM09175) | | | | | | | | | | | | | | | | | | | | | | | | | |
| HATHA YOGA/COUNSELLING (HM09195) | | | | | | | | ● | | | | | | | | | | | | | | | | | |
| HAVELOCK-SEARLE, PAULINE (HM09206) | | | | | | | | ● | | | | | | | | | | | | | | | | | |
| HAVEN GREEN CLINIC (HM09209) | | | | | | | | | | | | | | | | | | | | | | | | | |

# A - F Therapies at Practices/Businesses

| Business by County with Reference no. | Absent Healing | Acupressure | Acupuncture | Alexander Technique | Allergy Testing | Anthroposohical Med | Aromatherapy | Art Therapy | Aura Therapy | Auricular Therapy | Auto Suggestion | Autogenic Training | Aversion Therapy | Ayurvedic Medicine | Baby Massage | Bach Remedies | Bates Method | Beauty Therapy | Bio-energetics | Biofeedback | Biomagnetic Therapy | Biomechanics | Bonesetting | Bowen Therapy | Chinese Herbal Medicine | Chiropody | Chiropractic | Clinical Ecology | Cognitive Therapy | Colonic Hydrotherapy | Colour Therapy | Complementary Therapy | Counselling | Cranial Osteopathy | Cranio-Sacral Therapy | Cryo Surgery | Crystal Healing | Cupping | Cymatics | Dance Movement Thrpy | Dietician | Do-In | Douching | Dowsing | Drama Therapy | Electrolipolysis | Electrolysis | Electrotherapy | Encounter Groups | Faith Healing |
|---|---|---|---|---|---|---|---|---|---|---|---|---|---|---|---|---|---|---|---|---|---|---|---|---|---|---|---|---|---|---|---|---|---|---|---|---|---|---|---|---|---|---|---|---|---|---|---|---|---|---|
| HAWKINS, JAN (HM09222) | | | | | | | | | | | | | | | | | | | | | | | | | | | | | | | | | ● | | | | | | | | | | | | | | | | ● | |
| HAYASHI, MIKI (HM09250) | | | | | | | | | | | | | | | | ● | | | | | | | | | | | | | | | | | | | | | | | | | | | | | | | | | | |
| HEAL, CHRISTIANNE (HM09314) | | | | | | | | | | | | | | | | ● | | | | | | | | | | | | | | | | | ● | | | | | | | | | | | | | | | | | |
| HEALERS WORLD (HM09320) | | ● | ● | ● | | | ● | ● | | | | | ● | ● | | ● | ● | | ● | ● | | | | ● | | | ● | | ● | | | ● | ● | ● | | | | ● | | | ● | | | | | | | | | ● |
| HEALING ARTS UK (HM09326) | | ● | | | | | | | | | | | | | | | | | | | | | | | | | | | | | | | | | | | | | | | | | | | | | | | | |
| HEATH HEALTH CARE CENTRE (HM09447) | | | ● | | | | | | | | | | | | | | | | | | | | | | | ● | ● | | | | | ● | | | | | | | | | | | | | | | | | | |
| HEAVENZ AROMA HOME VISITING (HM09480) | | | | | | | ● | | | | | | | | | | | | | | | | | | | | | | | | | | | | | | | | | | | | | | | | | | | |
| HERBAL CARE (HM09600) | | | ● | | | | | | | | | | | | | | | | | | | | | | | | | | | | | | | | | | | | | | | | | | | | | | | |
| HERBAL CARE (HM09601) | | | ● | | | | | | | | | | | | | | | | | | | | | | | | | | | | | | | | | | | | | | | | | | | | | | | |
| HERBMEDIC (HM09663) | | ● | ● | | | | | | | | | | | | | | | | | | | | | | | | | | | | | ● | | | | | | ● | | | | | | | | | | | | |
| HIGGINSON, G & E (HM09732) | | | | ● | | | | | | | | | | | | | | | | | | | | | | | | | | | | | | | | | | | | | | | | | | | | | | |
| HIGHBURY CENTRE (HM09746) | | | | ● | | | | | | | | | | | | | | | | | | | | | | | | | | | | | | | ● | | | | | | | | | | | | | | | |
| HOGARTH CLINIC (HM09907) | | ● | ● | ● | | | | | | | | | | | | | | | | | | | ● | | | | ● | | | | | ● | | ● | | | | ● | | | | | | | | | | | | |
| HOLMES, DAVID (HM10040) | | | | | | | | | | | | | | | | | | | | | | | | | | ● | | | | | | | | | | | | | | | | | | | | | | | | |
| HOME VISITING SERVICES (HM10069) | | ● | ● | | | | | | | | | | | | | | | | | | | | | | | | | | | | | ● | | | | | | | | | | | | | | | | | | |
| HONG TAD ACUPUNCTURE & HERBAL (HM10119) | | | ● | | | | | | | | | | | | | ● | | | | | | | | | | | | | | | | | | | | | ● | ● | | | | | | | | | | | | |
| HONG, YUEN (HM10120) | | | ● | | | | | | | | | | | | | | | | | | | | | | | | | | | | | | | | | | | | | | | | | | | | | | | |
| HOPE, ANN (HM10137) | | | | | | | | | | | | | | | | | | | | | | | | | | ● | | | | | | | | | | | | | | | | | | | | | | | | |
| HOUSE OF MISTRY (HM10220) | | ● | ● | | | | ● | | | | | | | ● | | ● | | | | | | | | | | | ● | | | | | ● | ● | | | | | | | | | | | | | | | | | |
| HOWARD, LYNNE (HM10240) | | | | | | | | | | | | | | | | ● | | | | | | | | | | | | | | | | ● | ● | | | | | | | | | | | | | | | | | |
| HOWLETT, DAVID (HM10289) | | | | ● | | | | | | | | | | | | | | | | | | | | | | | | | | | | | | | | | | | | | | | | | | | | | | |
| HUGHES, PAUL (HM10339) | | | | | | | | | | | | ● | | | | | | | | | | | | | | | | | | | | | | | | | | | | | | | | ● | | | | | | |
| HUXLEY, CAROL (HM10460) | | | | | | | ● | | | | | | | | | | | | | | | | | | | | | | | | | | | | | | | | | | | | | | | | | | | |
| HYDE BARKER & ASSOCIATES (HM10469) | | | | | | | | | | | | | | | | | | | | | | ● | | | | ● | | | | | | | | | | | | | | | | | | | | | | | | |
| INDEPENDENT PSYCHOLOGY SERVICE (HM10610) | | | | | | | | ● | | | | | | | | | | | | ● | | | | | | | | | ● | | | | ● | | | | | | | | | | | | ● | | | | | |
| INNERSCENTS AROMATHERAPY (HM10646) | | | | | | | ● | | | | | | | | | | | | | | | | | | | | | | | | | | | | | | | | | | | | | | | | | | | |
| INT FEDERATION OF NEUROTHERAPY (HM10685) | | | | | | | | | | | | | | ● | | | | | | | | | | | | | | | | | | | | | | | | | | | | | | | | | | | | |
| ISLINGTON CHIROPRACTIC CLINIC (HM10773) | | | ● | | | | | | | | | | | | | | | | | | | | | | | | ● | | | | | | | | | | | | | | | | | | | | | | | |
| JACKSON, ALISON (HM10819) | | | ● | | | | | | | | | | | | | | | | | | | | | | | | | | | | | | | | | | | | | | | | | | | | | | | |
| JAKUBOWSKI & AST (HM10876) | | | | | | | | | | | | | | | | | | | | | | | | | | | ● | | | | | | | | | | | | | | | | | | | | | | | |
| JELFS, MARTIN (HM10976) | | | | | | | | | | | | | | | | | | | ● | | | | | | | | | | | | | | ● | | | | | | | | | | | | | | | | | |
| JELFS, MARTIN (HM10977) | | | | | | | | | | | | | | | | | | | ● | | | | | | | | | | | | | | ● | | | | | | | | | | | | | | | | | |
| JEWERS, M S (HM11025) | | | | | | | | | | | | | | | | | | | | | | ● | | | | ● | | | | | | | | | | | | | | | | | | | | | | | | |
| JIANG CLINIC HERBAL INN (HM11028) | | | ● | | | | | | | | | | | | | | | | | | | | | | | | | | | | | | | | | | | | | | | | | | | | | | | |

# A - F Therapies at Practices/Businesses

| Business by County with Reference no. | Absent Healing | Acupressure | Acupuncture | Alexander Technique | Allergy Testing | Anthroposohical Med | Aromatherapy | Art Therapy | Aura Therapy | Auricular Therapy | Auto Suggestion | Autogenic Training |
|---|---|---|---|---|---|---|---|---|---|---|---|---|
| JOSEPH CLINIC (HM11215) | | | ● | | | | | | | | | |
| JURIANSZ, ALAN & JENNIFER (HM11274) | | | | | | | | | | | | |
| KAMLASHANTI CHIRO CLINIC (HM11302) | | | | | | | | | | | | |
| KANE AND ROSS CLINICS (HM11309) | | | ● | | | | | | | | | |
| KEISNER, MICHAEL (HM11411) | | | ● | | | | | | | | | |
| KERN, MICHAEL (HM11544) | | | | | | | | | | | | |
| KHAN, D (HM11586) | | | | | | | | | | | | |
| KHAN, M A (HM11589) | | | ● | | | | | | | | | |
| KILBRIDE, PETER (HM11600) | | | | | | | | | | | | |
| KING, HILARY (HM11630) | | | | ● | | | | | | | | |
| KINGSBURY PSYCHOTHERAPY PRAC (HM11660) | ● | | | | | | | | | | | |
| KINGSGATE ACUPUNCTURE PRACTICE (HM11663) | | ● | ● | | | | | | | | | |
| KINGSLEY, NOEL (HM11667) | | | | ● | | | | | | | | |
| KLEIN, JEMMA (HM11737) | | | | | | | | | | | | |
| KNIGHTSBRIDGE CHIROPRACTIC (HM11761) | | | | | | | | | | | | |
| LAHER, RICHARD JOHN (HM11862) | | | | ● | | | | | | | | |
| LASSMAN, J (HM11986) | | | ● | | | | | | | | | |
| LAWRIE, CAROLINE (HM12059) | | | | | | | | | | | | |
| LE CUC, KIM (HM12085) | | | ● | | | | | | | | | |
| LEE COMPLEMENTARY HEALTH CTRE (HM12130) | | | ● | ● | | | ● | | | | | |
| LEE-BARBER, S (HM12149) | | | | ● | | | | | | | | |
| LESLIE, PAM (HM12241) | | | | | | | ● | | | | | |
| LEVER CLINIC (HM12256) | | ● | ● | | | | | | | | | |
| LIKISMA (HM12381) | | | | | | | ● | | | | | |
| LITTLE VENICE CHIROPODY (HM12469) | | | ● | | | | | | | | | |
| LITTLEMORE, JAN (HM12474) | | | | | | | ● | | | | | |
| LIU, K H (DR) (HM12478) | | | ● | | | | | | | | | |
| LIVING CENTRE CLINIC (HM12483) | | ● | ● | ● | | | ● | | | | | |
| LIZ DAWSON - PSYCHOTHERAPIST (HM12494) | | | | | | | | ● | | | | |
| LONDON CLGE OF AC/ORIENTAL MED (HM12585) | | | ● | | | | | | | | | |
| LONDON FLOAT CENTRE (HM12597) | | ● | ● | ● | | | ● | | | | | |
| LONDON INDIAN CHAMPISSAGE CTRE (HM12599) | | | | | | | | | | | | |
| LONDON SPINE AND JOINT CLINIC (HM12611) | | ● | ● | | | | ● | | | | | |
| LOW, JANET (DR) (HM12686) | | | | | | | | | | | | |

| Business by County with Reference no. | Aversion Therapy | Ayurvedic Medicine | Baby Massage | Bach Remedies | Bates Method | Beauty Therapy | Bio-energetics | Biofeedback | Biomagnetic Therapy | Biomechanics | Bonesetting | Bowen Therapy |
|---|---|---|---|---|---|---|---|---|---|---|---|---|
| JOSEPH CLINIC (HM11215) | | | | | | | | | | | | |
| JURIANSZ, ALAN & JENNIFER (HM11274) | | | | | | | | | | | | |
| KAMLASHANTI CHIRO CLINIC (HM11302) | | | | | | | | | | | | |
| KANE AND ROSS CLINICS (HM11309) | | | | | | | | | | | | |
| KEISNER, MICHAEL (HM11411) | | | | | | | | | | | | |
| KERN, MICHAEL (HM11544) | | | | | | | | | | | | |
| KHAN, D (HM11586) | | | | | | | | | | | | |
| KHAN, M A (HM11589) | | | | | | | | | | | | |
| KILBRIDE, PETER (HM11600) | ● | | | | | | | | | | | |
| KING, HILARY (HM11630) | | | | | | | | | | | | |
| KINGSBURY PSYCHOTHERAPY PRAC (HM11660) | | | | | | | | | | | | |
| KINGSGATE ACUPUNCTURE PRACTICE (HM11663) | | | | | | | | | | | | |
| KINGSLEY, NOEL (HM11667) | | | | | | | | | | | | |
| KLEIN, JEMMA (HM11737) | | | | | | | | | | | | |
| KNIGHTSBRIDGE CHIROPRACTIC (HM11761) | | | | | | | | | | | | |
| LAHER, RICHARD JOHN (HM11862) | | | | | | | | | | | | |
| LASSMAN, J (HM11986) | | | | | | | | | | | | |
| LAWRIE, CAROLINE (HM12059) | | | | | | | | | | | | |
| LE CUC, KIM (HM12085) | | | | | | | | | | | | |
| LEE COMPLEMENTARY HEALTH CTRE (HM12130) | | | | | | | | | | | | |
| LEE-BARBER, S (HM12149) | | | | | | | | | | | | |
| LESLIE, PAM (HM12241) | | | | | | | | | | | | |
| LEVER CLINIC (HM12256) | | | | | | | | | | | | |
| LIKISMA (HM12381) | | | | | | | | | | | | |
| LITTLE VENICE CHIROPODY (HM12469) | | | | | | | | | | ● | | |
| LITTLEMORE, JAN (HM12474) | | | | | | | | | | | | |
| LIU, K H (DR) (HM12478) | | | | | | | | | | | | |
| LIVING CENTRE CLINIC (HM12483) | | | | ● | | | | | | | | |
| LIZ DAWSON - PSYCHOTHERAPIST (HM12494) | | | | | | | | | | | | |
| LONDON CLGE OF AC/ORIENTAL MED (HM12585) | | | | | | | | | | | | |
| LONDON FLOAT CENTRE (HM12597) | | ● | | ● | | | | | | | | |
| LONDON INDIAN CHAMPISSAGE CTRE (HM12599) | | | | | | | | | | | | ● |
| LONDON SPINE AND JOINT CLINIC (HM12611) | | | | | | | | | | | | |
| LOW, JANET (DR) (HM12686) | | | | | | | | | | | | |

| Business by County with Reference no. | Chinese Herbal Medicine | Chiropody | Chiropractic | Clinical Ecology | Cognitive Therapy | Colonic Hydrotherapy | Colour Therapy | Complementary Therapy | Counselling | Cranial Osteopathy | Cranio-Sacral Therapy | Cryo Surgery |
|---|---|---|---|---|---|---|---|---|---|---|---|---|
| JOSEPH CLINIC (HM11215) | | | | | | | | | | | | |
| JURIANSZ, ALAN & JENNIFER (HM11274) | | | ● | | | | | | | | | |
| KAMLASHANTI CHIRO CLINIC (HM11302) | | | ● | | | | | | | | | |
| KANE AND ROSS CLINICS (HM11309) | | | | | | | | | | ● | | |
| KEISNER, MICHAEL (HM11411) | | | | | | | | | | | | |
| KERN, MICHAEL (HM11544) | | | | | | | | | | ● | ● | |
| KHAN, D (HM11586) | | | ● | | | | | | | | | |
| KHAN, M A (HM11589) | | | | | | | | | | | | |
| KILBRIDE, PETER (HM11600) | | | | | ● | | | ● | ● | | | |
| KING, HILARY (HM11630) | | | | | | | | | | | | |
| KINGSBURY PSYCHOTHERAPY PRAC (HM11660) | | | | | ● | | | | ● | | | |
| KINGSGATE ACUPUNCTURE PRACTICE (HM11663) | | | | | | | | | | | | |
| KINGSLEY, NOEL (HM11667) | | | | | | | | | | | | |
| KLEIN, JEMMA (HM11737) | | ● | | | | | | | | | | |
| KNIGHTSBRIDGE CHIROPRACTIC (HM11761) | | | ● | | | | | | | | | |
| LAHER, RICHARD JOHN (HM11862) | | | | | | | | | | | | |
| LASSMAN, J (HM11986) | | | | | | | | | | | | |
| LAWRIE, CAROLINE (HM12059) | | | | | | | | | | | | |
| LE CUC, KIM (HM12085) | | | | | | | | | | | | |
| LEE COMPLEMENTARY HEALTH CTRE (HM12130) | | | | | ● | | | ● | ● | ● | | |
| LEE-BARBER, S (HM12149) | | | | | | | | | | | | |
| LESLIE, PAM (HM12241) | | | | | | | | | | | | |
| LEVER CLINIC (HM12256) | | | | | | | | | | | | |
| LIKISMA (HM12381) | | | | | | | | | | | | |
| LITTLE VENICE CHIROPODY (HM12469) | | ● | | | | | | | ● | | | |
| LITTLEMORE, JAN (HM12474) | | | | | | | | | | | | |
| LIU, K H (DR) (HM12478) | | | | | | | | | | | | |
| LIVING CENTRE CLINIC (HM12483) | ● | ● | ● | | | | | ● | ● | | | |
| LIZ DAWSON - PSYCHOTHERAPIST (HM12494) | | | | | ● | | | | ● | | | |
| LONDON CLGE OF AC/ORIENTAL MED (HM12585) | ● | | | | | | | ● | | | | |
| LONDON FLOAT CENTRE (HM12597) | ● | | ● | | | ● | | ● | | | ● | |
| LONDON INDIAN CHAMPISSAGE CTRE (HM12599) | | | | | | | | | | | | |
| LONDON SPINE AND JOINT CLINIC (HM12611) | | | ● | | | | | ● | | | | |
| LOW, JANET (DR) (HM12686) | | | | | | | | | ● | | | |

| Business by County with Reference no. | Crystal Healing | Cupping | Cymatics | Dance Movement Thrpy | Dietician | Do-In | Douching | Dowsing | Drama Therapy | Electrolipolysis | Electrolysis | Electrotherapy | Encounter Groups | Faith Healing |
|---|---|---|---|---|---|---|---|---|---|---|---|---|---|---|
| JOSEPH CLINIC (HM11215) | | | | | | | | | | | | | | |
| JURIANSZ, ALAN & JENNIFER (HM11274) | | | | | | | | | | | | | | |
| KAMLASHANTI CHIRO CLINIC (HM11302) | | | | | | | | | | | | | | |
| KANE AND ROSS CLINICS (HM11309) | | | | | | | | | | | | | | |
| KEISNER, MICHAEL (HM11411) | | | | | | | | | | | | | | |
| KERN, MICHAEL (HM11544) | | | | | | | | | | | | | | |
| KHAN, D (HM11586) | | | | | | | | | | | | | | |
| KHAN, M A (HM11589) | | | | | | | | | | | | | | |
| KILBRIDE, PETER (HM11600) | | | | | | | | | | | | | | |
| KING, HILARY (HM11630) | | | | | | | | | | | | | | |
| KINGSBURY PSYCHOTHERAPY PRAC (HM11660) | | | | | | | | | | | | | | |
| KINGSGATE ACUPUNCTURE PRACTICE (HM11663) | | ● | | | | | | | | | | | | |
| KINGSLEY, NOEL (HM11667) | | | | | | | | | | | | | | |
| KLEIN, JEMMA (HM11737) | | | | | | | | | | | | | | |
| KNIGHTSBRIDGE CHIROPRACTIC (HM11761) | | | | | | | | | | | | | | |
| LAHER, RICHARD JOHN (HM11862) | | | | | | | | | | | | | | |
| LASSMAN, J (HM11986) | | | | | | | | | | | | | | |
| LAWRIE, CAROLINE (HM12059) | ● | | | | | | | | | | | | | |
| LE CUC, KIM (HM12085) | | | | | | | | | | | | | | |
| LEE COMPLEMENTARY HEALTH CTRE (HM12130) | | | | | | | | | | | | | | |
| LEE-BARBER, S (HM12149) | | | | | | | | | | | | | | |
| LESLIE, PAM (HM12241) | | | | | | | | | | | | | | |
| LEVER CLINIC (HM12256) | | | | | | | | | | | | ● | | |
| LIKISMA (HM12381) | | | | | | | | | | | | | | |
| LITTLE VENICE CHIROPODY (HM12469) | | | | | | | | | | | | | | |
| LITTLEMORE, JAN (HM12474) | | | | | | | | | | | | | | |
| LIU, K H (DR) (HM12478) | | | | | | | | | | | | | | |
| LIVING CENTRE CLINIC (HM12483) | | | | | | | | | | | | | | |
| LIZ DAWSON - PSYCHOTHERAPIST (HM12494) | | | | | | | | | | | | | | |
| LONDON CLGE OF AC/ORIENTAL MED (HM12585) | | | | | | | | | | | | | | |
| LONDON FLOAT CENTRE (HM12597) | ● | | | | | | | | | | | | | |
| LONDON INDIAN CHAMPISSAGE CTRE (HM12599) | | | | | | | | | | | | | | |
| LONDON SPINE AND JOINT CLINIC (HM12611) | | | | | | | | | | | | ● | | |
| LOW, JANET (DR) (HM12686) | | | | | | | | | | | | | | |

# A - F Therapies at Practices/Businesses

| Business by County with Reference no. | Absent Healing | Acupressure | Acupuncture | Alexander Technique | Allergy Testing | Anthroposohical Med | Aromatherapy | Art Therapy | Aura Therapy | Auricular Therapy | Auto Suggestion | Autogenic Training | Aversion Therapy | Ayurvedic Medicine | Baby Massage | Bach Remedies | Bates Method | Beauty Therapy | Bio-energetics | Biofeedback | Biomagnetic Therapy | Biomechanics | Bonesetting | Bowen Therapy | Chinese Herbal Medicine | Chiropody | Chiropractic | Clinical Ecology | Cognitive Therapy | Colonic Hydrotherapy | Colour Therapy | Complementary Therapy | Counselling | Cranial Osteopathy | Cranio-Sacral Therapy | Cryo Surgery | Crystal Healing | Cupping | Cymatics | Dance Movement Thrpy | Dietician | Do-In | Douching | Dowsing | Drama Therapy | Electrolipolysis | Electrolysis | Electrotherapy | Encounter Groups | Faith Healing |
|---|---|---|---|---|---|---|---|---|---|---|---|---|---|---|---|---|---|---|---|---|---|---|---|---|---|---|---|---|---|---|---|---|---|---|---|---|---|---|---|---|---|---|---|---|---|---|---|---|---|---|
| LUXTON, PAULINE (HM12752) | | | | | | | | | | | | | | | | | | | | | | ● | | | | ● | | | | | | | | | | | | | | | | | | | | | | | | |
| MACDERMOTT, S (HM12824) | | | | ● | | | | | | | | | | | | | | | | | | | | | | | | | | | | | | | | | | | | | | | | | | | | | | |
| MACDONNELL, MICHELLE (HM12831) | | | | ● | | | | | | | | | | | | | | | | | | | | | | | | | | | | | | | | | | | | | | | | | | | | | | |
| MACHOVER, ILANA (HM12840) | | | | ● | | | | | | | | | | | | | | | | | | | | | | | | | | | | | | | | | | | | | | | | | | | | | | |
| MAGIDOV, MISHA & JUDITH (HM12911) | | | | ● | | | | | | | | | | | | | | | | | | | | | | | | | | | | | | | | | | | | | | | | | | | | | | |
| MARIE, SOUTA (HM13099) | | | | | | | | | | | | | | | | | | | | | | | | | | | | | | | | | ● | | | | | | | | | | | | | | | | | |
| MARKANDAY, A (HM13110) | | | ● | | | | | | | | | | | | | | | | | | | | | | | | | | | | | | | | | | | | | | | | | | | | | | | |
| MARLBOROUGH THERAPY PRACTICE (HM13125) | | | | | | | | | | | ● | ● | | | | | | | | | | | | | | | | | ● | | | | ● | | | | | | | | | | | | | | | | | |
| MARSHALL, ALEXANDER (HM13153) | | | | ● | | | | | | | | | | | | | | | | | | | | | | | | | | | | | | | | | | | | | | | | | | | | | | |
| MARTIN, RHUNA (HM13208) | | | | ● | | | | | | | | | | | | | | | | | | | | | | | | | | | | | | | | | | | | | | | | | | | | | | |
| MASSAGE-AROMATHERAPY (HM13266) | | | | | | | ● | | | | | | | | | | | | | | | | | | | | | | | | | | | | | | | | | | | | | | | | | | | |
| MATTHEWS, ROBERT (HM13312) | | | | | | | | | | | | | | | | | | | | | | | | | | | | | | | | ● | ● | | | | | | | | | | | | | | | | | |
| MAXWELL BRIAR (HM13334) | | | | ● | | | | | | | | | | | | | | | | | | | | | | | | | | | | | | | | | | | | | | | | | | | | | | |
| MCCAFFREY, GERARDINE (HM13380) | | | | | | | | | | | | | | | | | | | | | | | | | | ● | | | | | | | | | | | | | | | | | | | | | | | | |
| MCCLOSKEY, P J (HM13409) | | | | | | | | | | | | | | | | | | | | | | | | | | ● | | | | | | | | | | | | | | | | | | | | | | | | |
| MEDICAL SCIENCES TECH CORP (HM13654) | | | | | | | | | | | | | | | | | | | | | | | | | | | | | | | | ● | | | | | | | | | | | | | | | | | | |
| MIDAS TOUCH (HM13809) | | ● | | | | | ● | | | | | | | | | | | | | | | | | | | | | | | | | | | | | | | | | | | | | | | | | | | |
| MIDDLETON, IAN W (HM13821) | | | | | | | | | | | | | | | | | | | | | | | | | | | | | | | | | | | | | | | | | ● | | | | | | | | | |
| MILLENNIUM COMP HEALTH CLINIC (HM13875) | | | | | | | ● | | | | | | | | | | | | | | | | | | | | | | | | | | | | | | | | | | | | | | | | | | | |
| MILLS DE-WIN STUDIOS (HM13922) | | | | | | | ● | | | | | | | | | | | | | | | | | ● | | | | | | | | | | | | | | | | | | | | | | | ● | | | |
| MONTSERRAT CLINIC (HM14090) | | | ● | | | | | | | | | | | | | | | | | | | | | | | | | | | | | | | | | | | | | | | | | | | | | ● | | |
| MOORTHY, N S (HM14140) | | | ● | | | | | | | | | | | | | | | | | | | | | | | | | | | | | | | | | | | | | | | | | | | | | | | |
| MORRIS, S (HM14214) | | | | ● | | | | | | | | | | | | | | | | | | | | | | | | | | | | | | | | | | | | | | | | | | | | | | |
| MORTON, WILLIAM (HM14255) | | | | ● | | | | | | | | | | | | | | | | | | | | | | | | | | | | | | | | | | | | | | | | | | | | | | |
| MOTHERSOLE, VINETA (HM20682) | | | | | | | | | | | | | | | | | | | | | | | | | | ● | | | | | | | | | | | | | | | | | | | | | | | | |
| MOTTINGHAM HYPNOTHERAPY CTRE (HM14279) | | | | | | | | | | | | | | | | | | | | | | | | | | | | | | | | | ● | | | | | | | | | | | | | | | | | |
| MOUNTFORT, KATRINA (HM14295) | | | | | | | | | | | | | | | | ● | | | | | | | | | | | | | | | | | | | | | | | | | | | | | | | | | | |
| M-POWER (HM14308) | | | | | | | | | | | ● | | | | | | | | | | | | | | | | | | ● | | | | ● | | | | | | | | | | | | | | | | | |
| MURPHY, MAUREEN (HM14391) | | | | | | | | | | | | | | | | ● | | | | | | | | | | | | | | | | | | | | | | | | | | | | | | | | | | |
| MURRAY, WILFRID (HM14417) | | | | ● | | | | | | | | | | | | | | | | | | | | | | | | | | | | | | | | | | | | | | | | | | | | | | |
| MUSWELL HILL CHIROPRACTIC (HM14431) | | | | | | | | | | | | | | | | | | | | | | | | | | | ● | | | | | | | | | | | | | | | | | | | | | | | |
| NAPIER, WILLIAM J M (HM14473) | | | | | | | | | | | | | | | | | | | | | | | | | | | ● | | | | | | | | | | | | | | | | | | | | | | | |
| NATURAL BY NATURE OILS (HM14519) | | | | | | | ● | | | | | | | | | | | | | | | | | | | | | | | | | | | | | | | | | | | | | | | | | | | |
| NATURAL HEALTH CLINIC (HM14575) | | ● | | | | | | | | | | ● | | | | | | | | | | | | | | | | | | | | | ● | | | | | | | | | | | | | | | | | |

# A - F Therapies at Practices/Businesses

| Business by County with Reference no. | Absent Healing | Acupressure | Acupuncture | Alexander Technique | Allergy Testing | Anthroposohical Med | Aromatherapy | Art Therapy | Aura Therapy | Auricular Therapy | Auto Suggestion | Autogenic Training | Aversion Therapy | Ayurvedic Medicine | Baby Massage | Bach Remedies | Bates Method | Beauty Therapy | Bio-energetics | Biofeedback | Biomagnetic Therapy | Biomechanics | Bonesetting | Bowen Therapy | Chinese Herbal Medicine |
|---|---|---|---|---|---|---|---|---|---|---|---|---|---|---|---|---|---|---|---|---|---|---|---|---|---|
| NEALE, CLIVE & LYNNE (HM14722) | | | | ● | | | | | | | | | | | | | | | | | | | | | |
| NEILL, VICTORIA (HM14764) | | ● | ● | | | | | | | | | | | | | | | | | | | | | | |
| NEURURER, MARIANNA (HM14795) | | | | ● | | | | | | | | | | | | | | | | | | | | | |
| NEW CROSS NATURAL THRPY CTRE (HM14814) | | | ● | ● | | | ● | | | | | | | | | | | | | | | | | | |
| NIELSEN, RITA C (HM14935) | | | | | | | ● | | | | | | | | | | | | | | | | | | |
| NOBES, PETER (HM14966) | | | | ● | | | | | | | | | | | | | | | | | | | | | |
| NORRIS, JANINE (HM15012) | | | ● | | | | | | | | | | | | | | | | | | | | | | |
| NORTHWOOD CLINIC (HM15067) | | | | | | | | | | | | | | | | | | | | | | ● | | | |
| NOTTING HILL TRAD ACU CTRE (HM15081) | | | ● | | | | | | | | | | | | | | | | | | | | | | |
| NRTH LONDON ALEXANDER PRACTICE (HM15092) | | | | ● | | | | | | | | | | | | | | | | | | | | | |
| O'CONNOR, PENNY (HM15214) | | | | ● | | | | | | | | | | | | | | | | | | | | | |
| O'FLYNN, DERMOT (DR) (HM15240) | | | ● | | | | | | | | | | | | | | | | | | | | | | |
| OLDING, R D (HM15272) | | | ● | | | | | | | | | | | | | | | | | | | | | | |
| ORGASMATRON UK (HM15379) | | | | | | | ● | | | | | | | | | | | | | | | | | | |
| ORIENTAL MEDICINE (HM15386) | | ● | ● | | | | | | | | | | | | | | | | | | | | | | |
| OSTEOPATHIC PRACTICE (HM15470) | | ● | ● | | | | | | | | | | | | | | | | | | | | | | |
| OSTEOPATHIC PRACTICE (HM15467) | | | | | | | | | | | | | | | | | | | | | | | | | |
| OSTEOPATHIC PRACTICE (HM15473) | | | | | | | | | | | | | | | | | | | | | | | | | |
| O'SULLIVAN, A (HM15481) | | | ● | | | | | | | | | | | | | | | | | | | | | | |
| OTREMBA, KATHARINA (HM15496) | | | | | | | | | | | | | ● | | | ● | | | | ● | | | | | |
| OUTCOMES (HM15502) | | | | | | | ● | | | | ● | ● | | | | | | | | | | | | | |
| PACIFIC WAVES PRODUCTIONS (HM15553) | | | | | | | | | | | ● | | | | | | | | | | | | | | |
| PASHLEY, MAGGIE (HM15775) | | | | | | | | | | | | | | | | | | | | | | | | | |
| PATEL, J (DR) (HM15787) | | | | | | | | | | | | | | | | | | | | | | | | | |
| PATEL, J C (HM15788) | | | | | | | | | | | | | | | | | | | | | | ● | | | |
| PATEL, SURENDRAKUMAR (HM15805) | | | ● | | | | | | | | | | | | | | | | | | | | | | |
| PEACOCK, K (HM15885) | | | | ● | | | | | | | | | | | | | | | | | | | | | |
| PHYSIO ONE (HM16202) | | | ● | | | | | | | | | | | | | | | | | | | | | | |
| PHYSIO SOLUTIONS (HM16205) | | | ● | | | | | | | | | | | | | | | | | | | | | | |
| PHYSIOTHERAPY PRACTICE (HM16253) | | | | | | | | | | | | | | | | | | | | | | | | | |
| PINNER ROAD PHYSIOTHERAPY (HM16316) | | | ● | | | | | | | | | | | | | | | | | | | | | | |
| PITE, J (HM16335) | | | | ● | | | | | | | | | | | | | | | | | | | | | |
| PITTAM, C (HM16352) | | | | | | | | | | | | | | | | | | | | | | | | | |
| PODIATRY CLINIC (HM16393) | | | | | | | | | | | | | | | | | | | | | | ● | | | |

| Business by County with Reference no. | Chiropody | Chiropractic | Clinical Ecology | Cognitive Therapy | Colonic Hydrotherapy | Colour Therapy | Complementary Therapy | Counselling | Cranial Osteopathy | Cranio-Sacral Therapy | Cryo Surgery | Crystal Healing | Cupping | Cymatics | Dance Movement Thrpy | Dietician | Do-In | Douching | Dowsing | Drama Therapy | Electrolipolysis | Electrolysis | Electrotherapy | Encounter Groups | Faith Healing |
|---|---|---|---|---|---|---|---|---|---|---|---|---|---|---|---|---|---|---|---|---|---|---|---|---|---|
| NEALE, CLIVE & LYNNE (HM14722) | | | | | | | | | | | | | | | | | | | | | | | | | |
| NEILL, VICTORIA (HM14764) | | | | | | | | | | | | | | | | | | | | | | | ● | | |
| NEURURER, MARIANNA (HM14795) | | | | | | | | | | | | | | | | | | | | | | | | | |
| NEW CROSS NATURAL THRPY CTRE (HM14814) | | ● | | | | | ● | ● | ● | ● | | | | | | | | | | | | | | | |
| NIELSEN, RITA C (HM14935) | | | | | | | | | | | | | | | | | | | | | | | | | |
| NOBES, PETER (HM14966) | | | | | | | | | | | | | | | | | | | | | | | | | |
| NORRIS, JANINE (HM15012) | | | | | | | | | | | | | | | | | | | | | | | | | |
| NORTHWOOD CLINIC (HM15067) | ● | | | | | | | | | | | | | | | | | | | | | | | | |
| NOTTING HILL TRAD ACU CTRE (HM15081) | | | | | | | | | | | | | | | | | | | | | | | | | |
| NRTH LONDON ALEXANDER PRACTICE (HM15092) | | | | | | | | | | | | | | | | | | | | | | | | | |
| O'CONNOR, PENNY (HM15214) | | | | | | | | | | | | | | | | | | | | | | | | | |
| O'FLYNN, DERMOT (DR) (HM15240) | | | | | | | | | | | | | | | | | | | | | | | | | |
| OLDING, R D (HM15272) | | | | | | | | | | | | | | | | | | | | | | | | | |
| ORGASMATRON UK (HM15379) | | | | | | | | | | | | | | | | | | | | | | | | | |
| ORIENTAL MEDICINE (HM15386) | | | | | | | | | | | | | ● | | | | | | | | | | | | |
| OSTEOPATHIC PRACTICE (HM15470) | | | | | | | | | ● | | | | ● | | | | | | | | | | | | |
| OSTEOPATHIC PRACTICE (HM15467) | | | | | | | | | ● | | | | | | | | | | | | | | | | |
| OSTEOPATHIC PRACTICE (HM15473) | | | | | | | | | ● | | | | | | | | | | | | | | | | |
| O'SULLIVAN, A (HM15481) | | | | | | | | | | | | | | | | | | | | | | | | | |
| OTREMBA, KATHARINA (HM15496) | | | | ● | | | ● | ● | | | | | | | | | | | ● | | | | | | |
| OUTCOMES (HM15502) | | | | ● | | | ● | ● | | | | | | | | | | | ● | | | | | | |
| PACIFIC WAVES PRODUCTIONS (HM15553) | | | | ● | | | ● | ● | | | | | | | | | | | | | | | | | |
| PASHLEY, MAGGIE (HM15775) | | | | | | | | | | | | ● | | | | | | | | | | | | | |
| PATEL, J (DR) (HM15787) | | ● | | | | | | | | | | | | | | | | | | | | | | | |
| PATEL, J C (HM15788) | ● | | | | | | | | | | | | | | | | | | | | | | | | |
| PATEL, SURENDRAKUMAR (HM15805) | | | | | | | | | | | | | | | | | | | | | | | | | |
| PEACOCK, K (HM15885) | | | | | | | | | | | | | | | | | | | | | | | | | |
| PHYSIO ONE (HM16202) | | | | | | | | | | | | | | | ● | | | | | | | | | | |
| PHYSIO SOLUTIONS (HM16205) | | | | | | | | | | | | | | | | | | | | | | | | | |
| PHYSIOTHERAPY PRACTICE (HM16253) | | | | | | | ● | | | | | | | | | | | | | | | | ● | | |
| PINNER ROAD PHYSIOTHERAPY (HM16316) | | | | | | | | | | | | | | | | | | | | | | | | | |
| PITE, J (HM16335) | | | | | | | | | | | | | | | | | | | | | | | | | |
| PITTAM, C (HM16352) | | ● | | | | | | | | | | | | | | | | | | | | | | | |
| PODIATRY CLINIC (HM16393) | ● | | | | | | | | | | | | | | | | | | | | | | | | |

# A - F Therapies at Practices/Businesses

| Business by County with Reference no. | Absent Healing | Acupressure | Acupuncture | Alexander Technique | Allergy Testing | Anthroposohical Med | Aromatherapy | Art Therapy | Aura Therapy | Auricular Therapy | Auto Suggestion | Autogenic Training | Aversion Therapy | Ayurvedic Medicine | Baby Massage | Bach Remedies | Bates Method | Beauty Therapy | Bio-energetics | Biofeedback | Biomagnetic Therapy | Biomechanics | Bonesetting | Bowen Therapy | Chinese Herbal Medicine |
|---|---|---|---|---|---|---|---|---|---|---|---|---|---|---|---|---|---|---|---|---|---|---|---|---|---|
| POPE, THOMAS (HM16434) | | | | ● | | | | | | | | | | | | | | | | | | | | | |
| PRESTON, MARK (HM16555) | | | ● | | | | | | | | | | | | | | | | | | | | | | |
| PRICE, GILLIAN (HM16575) | | | ● | | | | | | | | | | | | | | | | | | | | | | |
| PRINCE (HM16618) | | | | | | | | | | | | | | | | | | | | | | | | | |
| PRIVATE HEALTH CLINIC (HM16644) | | | ● | | | | | | | | | | | ● | | | | | | | | | | | |
| PSYCHOTHERAPY SERVICES (HM16737) | | | | | | | | | | | | | | | | | | | | | | | | | |
| PUGH, JANE (HM16748) | | | | ● | | | | | | | | | | | | | | | | | | | | | |
| PUSHPA, NANA (HM16779) | | | ● | | | | | | | | | | | | | | | | | | | | | | |
| PUTNEY CHIROPRACTIC (HM16780) | | | | | | | | | | | | | | | | | | | | | | | | | |
| QUICK, JULIA (HM16800) | | | ● | | | | | | | | | | | | | | | | | | | | | | |
| RACHEL YOUNG - HYPNOTHERAPIST (HM16837) | ● | | | | | | | | | | | | ● | | | | | | | | | | | | |
| RAEBURN, JO (HM16865) | | | | | | | ● | | | | | | | | | | | | | | | | | | |
| RAVENSCROFT CENTRE (HM16967) | | | | | | | ● | | | | | | | | | | | | | | | | | | |
| READ, CHARLES (HM16993) | | | | | | | | | | | | | | | | | | | | | | | | | |
| REEVE, MALCOLM (HM17060) | | | ● | | | | | | | | | | | | | | | | | | | | | | |
| RELAXATION PLACE (HM17166) | | | | | | | ● | | | | | | | | | | | | | | | | | | |
| RELAXING HEALTHY OPTIONS (HM17169) | | ● | | | | | ● | | | | | | | | | | | | | | | | | | |
| RENZO, REINALDO (HM17194) | | | | ● | | | | | | | | | | | | | | | | | | | | | |
| REPLINGHAM CLINIC (HM17195) | | ● | ● | ● | | | ● | | | | | | | | | ● | | | | | | | | | |
| RICHMOND CHIROPRACTIC CLINIC (HM17297) | | | | | | | | | | | | | | | | | | | | | | | | | |
| RIGBY, JACQUI (HM17332) | | | | ● | | | | | | | | | | | | | | | | | | | | | |
| RUTHERFORD, BERWYN (HM17780) | | | | | | | | | | | | | | | | | | | | | | | | | |
| S K REFLEXOLOGY & AROMATHERAPY (HM17812) | | | | | | | ● | | | | | | | | | | | | | | | | | | |
| SAN LING CHINESE MED CENTRE (HM17888) | | | ● | | | | | | | | | | | | | | | | | | | | | | |
| SAN LING CHINESE MED CENTRE (HM17887) | | | ● | | | | | | | | | | | | | | | | | | | | | | |
| SAYER CLINIC (HM17994) | | | | | | | | | | | | | | | | | | | | | | | | | |
| SAYER CLINIC (HM17993) | | | ● | | | | | | | | | | | | | | | | | | | | | | |
| SCAMPTON, KATIE (HM18001) | | | ● | | | | | | | | | | | | | | | | | | | | | | |
| SEARBY, JOE (HM18174) | | | | ● | | | | | | | | | | | | | | | | | | | | | |
| SEEAR, MICHAEL (DR) (HM18189) | ● | ● | ● | | | | | | | | | | | | | | | | | | | | | | |
| SEOW, PENG (HM18230) | | | | ● | | | | | | | | | | | | | | | | | | | | | |
| SEYMOUR PRACTICE (HM18257) | | | | | | | | | | | | | | | | | | | | | | | | | |
| SHIATSU PLACE (HM18458) | | | ● | | | | | | | | | | | | | | | | | | | | | ● | |
| SHOOTERS HILL CENTRE (HM18493) | | | | ● | | | | | | | | | | | | | | | | | | | | | |

| Business by County with Reference no. | Chiropody | Chiropractic | Clinical Ecology | Cognitive Therapy | Colonic Hydrotherapy | Colour Therapy | Complementary Therapy | Counselling | Cranial Osteopathy | Cranio-Sacral Therapy | Cryo Surgery | Crystal Healing | Cupping | Cymatics | Dance Movement Thrpy | Dietician | Do-In | Douching | Dowsing | Drama Therapy | Electrolipolysis | Electrolysis | Electrotherapy | Encounter Groups | Faith Healing |
|---|---|---|---|---|---|---|---|---|---|---|---|---|---|---|---|---|---|---|---|---|---|---|---|---|---|
| POPE, THOMAS (HM16434) | | | | | | | | | | | | | | | | | | | | | | | | | |
| PRESTON, MARK (HM16555) | | | | | | | | | | | | | | | | | | | | | | | | | |
| PRICE, GILLIAN (HM16575) | | | | | | | | | | | | | ● | | | | | | | | | | | | |
| PRINCE (HM16618) | | ● | | | | | | | | | | | | | | | | | | | | | | | |
| PRIVATE HEALTH CLINIC (HM16644) | ● | | | | | | | ● | | | | | | | | | | | | | | | | | |
| PSYCHOTHERAPY SERVICES (HM16737) | | | | | | | | ● | | | | | | | | | | | | | | | | | |
| PUGH, JANE (HM16748) | | | | | | | | | | | | | | | | | | | | | | | | | |
| PUSHPA, NANA (HM16779) | | | | | | | | | | | | | | | | | | | | | | | | | |
| PUTNEY CHIROPRACTIC (HM16780) | | ● | | | | | | | | | | | | | | | | | | | | | | | |
| QUICK, JULIA (HM16800) | | | | | | | | | | | | | | | | | | | | | | | | | |
| RACHEL YOUNG - HYPNOTHERAPIST (HM16837) | | | | | | ● | ● | ● | | | | ● | | | | ● | | | ● | | | | | | ● |
| RAEBURN, JO (HM16865) | | | | | | | | | | | | | | | | | | | | | | | | | |
| RAVENSCROFT CENTRE (HM16967) | | | | | | | ● | ● | | | | | | | | | | | | | | | | | |
| READ, CHARLES (HM16993) | | | | | | | | | ● | | | | | | | | | | | | | | | | |
| REEVE, MALCOLM (HM17060) | | | | | | | | | | ● | | | | | | | | | | | | | | | |
| RELAXATION PLACE (HM17166) | | | | | | | | | | | | | | | | | | | | | | | | | |
| RELAXING HEALTHY OPTIONS (HM17169) | | | | | | | | | | | | | | | | | | | | | | | | | |
| RENZO, REINALDO (HM17194) | | | | | | | | | | | | | | | | | | | | | | | | | |
| REPLINGHAM CLINIC (HM17195) | ● | | | | | | ● | ● | ● | | | | | | | | | | | | | | | | |
| RICHMOND CHIROPRACTIC CLINIC (HM17297) | | ● | | | | | | | | | | | | | | | | | | | | | | | |
| RIGBY, JACQUI (HM17332) | | | | | | | | | | | | | | | | | | | | | | | | | |
| RUTHERFORD, BERWYN (HM17780) | | | | | | | | | ● | | | | | | | | | | | | | | | | |
| S K REFLEXOLOGY & AROMATHERAPY (HM17812) | | | | | | | | | | | | | | | | | | | | | | | | | |
| SAN LING CHINESE MED CENTRE (HM17888) | | | | | | | | | | | | | | | | | | | | | | | | | |
| SAN LING CHINESE MED CENTRE (HM17887) | | | | | | | | | | | | | | | | | | | | | | | | | |
| SAYER CLINIC (HM17994) | | ● | | | | | | | | | | | | | | | | | | | | | | | |
| SAYER CLINIC (HM17993) | | ● | | | | | | | | | | | | | | | | | | | | | | | |
| SCAMPTON, KATIE (HM18001) | | | | | | | | | | | | | | | | | | | | | | | | | |
| SEARBY, JOE (HM18174) | | | | | | | | | | | | | | | | | | | | | | | | | |
| SEEAR, MICHAEL (DR) (HM18189) | | | | | | | | | | | | | | | | | | | | | | | | | ● |
| SEOW, PENG (HM18230) | | | | | | | | | | | | | | | | | | | | | | | | | |
| SEYMOUR PRACTICE (HM18257) | | | | | | | | | ● | | | | | | | | | | | | | | | | |
| SHIATSU PLACE (HM18458) | | | | | | | | | ● | ● | | | | | | | ● | | | | | | | | |
| SHOOTERS HILL CENTRE (HM18493) | | | | | | | | | | | | | | | | | | | | | | | | | |

# A - F Therapies at Practices/Businesses

| Business by County with Reference no. | Absent Healing | Acupressure | Acupuncture | Alexander Technique | Allergy Testing | Anthroposohical Med | Aromatherapy | Art Therapy | Aura Therapy | Auricular Therapy | Auto Suggestion | Autogenic Training | Aversion Therapy | Ayurvedic Medicine | Baby Massage | Bach Remedies | Bates Method | Beauty Therapy | Bio-energetics | Biofeedback | Biomagnetic Therapy | Biomechanics | Bonesetting | Bowen Therapy | Chinese Herbal Medicine | Chiropody | Chiropractic | Clinical Ecology | Cognitive Therapy | Colonic Hydrotherapy | Colour Therapy | Complementary Therapy | Counselling | Cranial Osteopathy | Cranio-Sacral Therapy | Cryo Surgery | Crystal Healing | Cupping | Cymatics | Dance Movement Thrpy | Dietician | Do-In | Douching | Dowsing | Drama Therapy | Electrolipolysis | Electrolysis | Electrotherapy | Encounter Groups | Faith Healing |
|---|---|---|---|---|---|---|---|---|---|---|---|---|---|---|---|---|---|---|---|---|---|---|---|---|---|---|---|---|---|---|---|---|---|---|---|---|---|---|---|---|---|---|---|---|---|---|---|---|---|---|
| SHRAGAI, NAOMI (HM18503) | | | | ● | | | | | | | | | | | | | | | | | | | | | | | | | | | | | | | | | | | | | | | | | | | | | | |
| SHRIMPTON, D (HM18510) | | | | ● | | | | | | | | | | | | | | | | | | | | | | | | | | | | | | | | | | | | | | | | | | | | | | |
| SIMMONS, BEATRICE (HM18560) | | | | ● | | | | | | | | | | | | | | | | | | | | | | | | | | | | | | | | | | | | | | | | | | | | | | |
| SIMMONS, ROBIN (HM18563) | | | | ● | | | | | | | | | | | | | | | | | | | | | | | | | | | | | | | | | | | | | | | | | | | | | | |
| SIMON, CAROLYN (HM18567) | | | | ● | | | | | | | | | | | | | | | | | | | | | | | | | | | | | | | | | | | | | | | | | | | | | | |
| SIMPLY HERBAL CLINIC (HM18577) | | | | | | | ● | | | | | | | | | | | | | | | | | | | | | | | | | ● | | | | | | | | | | ● | | | | | | | | |
| SIMPSON, STELLA (HM18599) | | | ● | | | | | | | | | | | | | | | | | | | | | | | | | | | | | | | | | | | | | | | | | | | | | | | |
| SIOW, YONG CHAI (HM18618) | | | ● | | | | | | | | | | | | | | | | | | | | | | | | | | | | | | | | | | | | | | | | | | | | | | | |
| SIOW, YONG CHAI (HM18617) | | | ● | | | | | | | | | | | | | | | | | | | | | | | | | | | | | | | | | | | | | | | | | | | | | | | |
| SLADE OSTEOPATHIC PRACTICE (HM18667) | | | | | | | | | | | | | | | | | | | | | | | | | | | | | | | | | | ● | | | | | | | | | | | | | | | | |
| SMITH, D (HM18731) | | | ● | | | | | | | | | | | | | | | | | | | | | | | | | | | | | | | | | | | | | | | | | | | | | | | |
| SODERSTROM, BETH (HM18855) | | | ● | | | | | | | | | | | | | | | | | | | | | | | | | | | | | | | | | | | | | | | | | | | | | | | |
| SODHA, LALIT (DR) (HM18857) | | | | | | | | | | | | | | | | | | | | | | | | | | | ● | | | | | | | | | | | | | | | | | | | | | | | |
| SORENSEN, MONICA (HM18895) | | | | | | | ● | | | | | | | | | | | | | | | | | | | | | | | | | | | | | | | | | | | | | | | | | | | |
| SOUTH LONDON NATURAL HLTH CTRE (HM18911) | | ● | ● | ● | | | ● | ● | | | | | | ● | | ● | | | | | | | | ● | | | ● | | | | | ● | ● | ● | | | ● | | | | ● | | | | | | | | | |
| SOUTHFIELDS CLINIC (HM18935) | | | ● | | | | | | | | | | | | | | | | | | | | | | | | | | | | | | | | | | | | | | | | | | | | | | | |
| SOUTHGATE HOLISTIC HEALTH (HM18936) | | | | | | | ● | | | | | | | | | | | | | | | | | | | | | | | | | | | | | | | | | | | | | | | | | | | |
| SPALL MEDICAL CENTRE (HM18957) | | ● | ● | | | | | | | | | | | ● | | ● | | | ● | | | | | | | | | | | | | ● | | | | | | | | | | | | | | | | | | |
| SPECIALIST HEALTH (HM18972) | | | ● | | | | | | | | | | | | | | | | | | | | | | | | | | | | | | | | | | | | | | | | | | | | | | | |
| SPYROS MOUZOURIDES (HM19056) | | | | | | | | | | | | | | | | | | | | | | | | | | | | | | | | ● | | | | | | | | | ● | | | | | | | | | |
| STAEBLER, F E (HM19106) | | | ● | | | | | | | | | | | | | | | | | | | | | | | | | | | | | | | | | | | | | | | | | | | | | | | |
| STANMORE PHYSIO PRACTICE (HM19132) | | | ● | | | | | | | | | | | | | | | | | | | | | | | | | | | | | | | | | | | | | | | | | | | | | | | |
| STEARS, M J (DR) (HM19169) | | | | | | | | | | | | | | | | | | | | | | | | | | | ● | | | | | | | | | | | | | | | | | | | | | | | |
| STEPPING STONES (HM19214) | | | | | | | ● | | | | | | | | | | | | | | | | | | | | | | | | | | | | | | | | | | | | | | | | | | | |
| STOBEZKI, YAEL (HM19307) | | | | | | | | ● | | | | | | | | | | | | | | | | | | | | | | | | | ● | | | | | | | | | | | | | | | | | |
| STRAW, SANDRA (HM19376) | | | | | | | | | | | | | | | | ● | | | | | | | | | | | | | | | | | | | | | | | | | | | | | | | | | | |
| STRONG, STELLA (HM19419) | | | | | | | | | | | | | | | | | | | | | | | | | | | | | | | | | ● | ● | | | | | | | | | | | | | | | | |
| SUTTON, NICOLA (HM19554) | | | | | | | ● | | | | | | | | | | | | | | | | | | | | | | | | | | | | | | | | | | | | | | | | | | | |
| T C M HEALTHCARE (HM19640) | | ● | ● | | | | | | | | | | | | | | | | | | | | | | | | | | | | | | | | | | | | | | | | | | | | | | | |
| THENUWARA, CLARENCE (DR) (HM19871) | | | ● | | | | | | | | | | | | | | | | | | | | | | | | | | | | | | | | | | | | | | | | | | | | | | | |
| THOEYE, JAN (HM19922) | | | ● | | | | | | | | | | | | | | | | | | | | | | | | | | | | | | | | | | | | | | | | | | | | | | | |
| TINDALL, JOHN (HM20080) | | | ● | | | | | | | | | | | | | | | | | | | | | | | | | | | | | | | | | | | | | | | | | | | | | | | |
| TISSERAND INSTITUTE (HM20096) | | | | | | | ● | | | | | | | | | | | | | | | | | | | | | | | | | | | | | | | | | | | | | | | | | | | |
| TORRIDON COMP THERAPY CLINIC (HM20173) | | | | | | | ● | | | | | | | | | | | | | | | | | | | | | | | | | | ● | | | | | | | | | | | | | | | | | |

# A - F Therapies at Practices/Businesses

Business by County with Reference no.

| Business | Absent Healing | Acupressure | Acupuncture | Alexander Technique | Allergy Testing | Anthroposohical Med | Aromatherapy | Art Therapy | Aura Therapy | Auricular Therapy | Auto Suggestion | Autogenic Training | Aversion Therapy | Ayurvedic Medicine | Baby Massage | Bach Remedies | Bates Method | Beauty Therapy | Bio-energetics | Biofeedback | Biomagnetic Therapy | Biomechanics | Bonesetting | Bowen Therapy | Chinese Herbal Medicine |
|---|---|---|---|---|---|---|---|---|---|---|---|---|---|---|---|---|---|---|---|---|---|---|---|---|---|
| TRAD CHINESE MASSOTHERAPY (HM20215) | | | | | | | | | | | | | | | | | | | | | | | | | ● |
| TRADITIONAL ACUPUNCTURE CENTRE (HM20218) | | | ● | | | | | | | | | | | | | | | | | | | | | | |
| TRADITIONAL CHINESE MED CTRE (HM20224) | | | ● | | | | | | | | | | | | | | | | | | | | | | |
| TRANQUILITY (HM20255) | ● | ● | | | | | ● | | | | | | | | | | | | | | | | | | |
| TUNE IN (HM20394) | | | ● | | | | | | | | | | | | | | | | | | | | | | |
| TURMAINE, VICKI (HM20410) | | | | | | | | | | | | | | | | ● | | | | | | | | | |
| TURNER, TERI (HM20438) | | | | | | | | | | | | | | | | | | | | | | | | | |
| TWICKENHAM PHYSIOFIRST CENTRE (HM20451) | | | ● | | | | | | | | | | | | | | | | | | | | | | |
| UKCP (HM20490) | | | | | | | | ● | | | | ● | | | | | | | | | | | | | |
| UNDERHILL, K (HM20496) | | | ● | | | | | | | | | | | | | | | | | | | | | | |
| UNDERWOOD, PAUL (HM20501) | | | ● | | | | | | | | | | | | | | | | | | | | | | |
| UXBRIDGE CHIROPRACTIC CLINIC (HM20539) | | | | | | | | | | | | | | | | | | | | | | | | | |
| V K PATEL STATE RGD CHIROP (HM20541) | | | | | | | | | | | | | | | | | | | | | | | | | |
| VALE PRACTICE (HM20551) | | | ● | ● | | | ● | ● | | | | | | | | | | | | | | | | | |
| VANBRUGH PHYSIOTHERAPY CLINIC (HM20575) | | | ● | | | | | | | | | | | | | | | | | | | | | | |
| VENN-BROWN, HELEN (HM20615) | | | | | | | | | | | | | | | | | | | | | | | | | |
| VERDE AROMATHERAPY (HM20619) | | | | | | | ● | | | | | | | | | | | | | | | | | | |
| VERDE LONDON (HM20620) | | | | | | | ● | | | | | | | | | | | | | | | | | | |
| VICTORIA CHIROPRACTIC CLINIC (HM20649) | | | | | | | | | | | | | | | | | | | | | | | | | |
| VISITING MASSAGE AROMATHERAPY (HM20699) | | | | | | | ● | | | | | | | | | | | | | | | | | | |
| WARWICK ALTERNATIVE HEALTH (HM20961) | | ● | | | | | | | | | | | | | | | | | | | | | | | |
| WATER MASSAGE (HM20980) | | | | | | | ● | | | | | | | | | | | | | | | | | | |
| WATSON, IAN (HM21010) | | | | ● | | | | | | | | | | | | | | | | | | | | | |
| WATSON, M (HM21017) | | | | | | | | | | | | | | | | | | | | | | | | | |
| WELLS, PAMELA (HM21178) | | | | | | | | | | | | | | | | ● | | | | | | | | | |
| WEST LONDON HOLISTIC CENTRE (HM21226) | | | | | | | | | | | ● | | | | | ● | | | | | | | | | |
| WESTERN, G (HM21265) | | | | | | | ● | | | | | | | | | | | | | | | | | | |
| WESTMINSTER ALEXANDER CENTRE (HM21273) | | | | ● | | | | | | | | | | | | | | | | | | | | | |
| WETHERELL, PAULINE (HM21292) | | | | ● | | | | | | | | | | | | | | | | | | | | | |
| WETHERELL, PAULINE (HM21291) | | | | ● | | | | | | | | | | | | | | | | | | | | | |
| WHETSTONE CHIROPRACTIC CLINIC (HM21327) | | | | | | | | | | | | | | | | | | | | | | | | | |
| WHITE HART LANE THERAPY CENTRE (HM21338) | | | ● | | | | | | | | | | | | | | | | | | | | | | |
| WHITE, J (HM21358) | | | ● | | | | | | | | | | | | | | | | | | | | | | |
| WICKER, DIANE (HM21446) | | | ● | | | | | | | | | | | | | | | | | | | | | | |

| Business | Chiropody | Chiropractic | Clinical Ecology | Cognitive Therapy | Colonic Hydrotherapy | Colour Therapy | Complementary Therapy | Counselling | Cranial Osteopathy | Cranio-Sacral Therapy | Cryo Surgery | Crystal Healing | Cupping | Cymatics | Dance Movement Thrpy | Dietician | Do-In | Douching | Dowsing | Drama Therapy | Electrolipolysis | Electrolysis | Electrotherapy | Encounter Groups | Faith Healing |
|---|---|---|---|---|---|---|---|---|---|---|---|---|---|---|---|---|---|---|---|---|---|---|---|---|---|
| TRAD CHINESE MASSOTHERAPY (HM20215) | | | | | | | | | | | | | | | | | | | | | | | | | |
| TRADITIONAL ACUPUNCTURE CENTRE (HM20218) | | | | | | | | | | | | | | | | | | | | | | | | | |
| TRADITIONAL CHINESE MED CTRE (HM20224) | | | | | | | | | | | | | | | | | | | | | | | | | |
| TRANQUILITY (HM20255) | | | | | | | ● | ● | | | | | | | | | | | | ● | | | | | ● |
| TUNE IN (HM20394) | | | | | | | | | | | | | | | | | | | | | | | | | |
| TURMAINE, VICKI (HM20410) | | | | | | | | ● | | | | | | | | | | | | | | | | | |
| TURNER, TERI (HM20438) | | | | | | | | | ● | | | | | | | | | | | | | | | | |
| TWICKENHAM PHYSIOFIRST CENTRE (HM20451) | | | | | | | | | | | | | | | | | | | | | | | | | |
| UKCP (HM20490) | | | | ● | | | | ● | | | | | | | | | | | | ● | | | | | |
| UNDERHILL, K (HM20496) | | | | | | | | | ● | | | | | | | | | | | | | | | | |
| UNDERWOOD, PAUL (HM20501) | | | | | | | | | | | | | | | | | | | | | | | | | |
| UXBRIDGE CHIROPRACTIC CLINIC (HM20539) | | ● | | | | | | | | | | | | | | | | | | | | | | | |
| V K PATEL STATE RGD CHIROP (HM20541) | ● | | | | | | | | | | | | | | | | | | | | | | | | |
| VALE PRACTICE (HM20551) | | | | | | | ● | ● | ● | | | | ● | | | | | | | | | | | | |
| VANBRUGH PHYSIOTHERAPY CLINIC (HM20575) | | | | | | | | | | | | | | | | | | | | | | | | | |
| VENN-BROWN, HELEN (HM20615) | ● | | | | | | | | | | | | | | | | | | | | | | | | |
| VERDE AROMATHERAPY (HM20619) | | | | | | | | | | | | | | | | | | | | | | | | | |
| VERDE LONDON (HM20620) | | | | | | | | | | | | | | | | | | | | | | | | | |
| VICTORIA CHIROPRACTIC CLINIC (HM20649) | | ● | | | | | | | | | | | | | | | | | | | | | | | |
| VISITING MASSAGE AROMATHERAPY (HM20699) | | | | | | | | | | | | | | | | | | | | | | | | | |
| WARWICK ALTERNATIVE HEALTH (HM20961) | | | | | | | | | | | | | | | | | | | | | | | | | |
| WATER MASSAGE (HM20980) | | | | | | | | | | | | | | | | | | | | | | | | | |
| WATSON, IAN (HM21010) | | | | | | | | | | | | | | | | | | | | | | | | | |
| WATSON, M (HM21017) | | ● | | | | | | | | | | | | | | | | | | | | | | | |
| WELLS, PAMELA (HM21178) | | | | | | | | | | | | | | | | | | | | | | | | | |
| WEST LONDON HOLISTIC CENTRE (HM21226) | | | | ● | | ● | ● | ● | | | | ● | | | | | | | | ● | | | | | ● |
| WESTERN, G (HM21265) | | | | | | | | | ● | | | | | | | | | | | | | | | | |
| WESTMINSTER ALEXANDER CENTRE (HM21273) | | | | | | | | | | | | | | | | | | | | | | | | | |
| WETHERELL, PAULINE (HM21292) | | | | | | | | | | | | | | | | | | | | | | | | | |
| WETHERELL, PAULINE (HM21291) | | | | | | | | | | | | | | | | | | | | | | | | | |
| WHETSTONE CHIROPRACTIC CLINIC (HM21327) | | ● | | | | | | | | | | | | | | | | | | | | | | | |
| WHITE HART LANE THERAPY CENTRE (HM21338) | ● | | | | | | | ● | | | | | | | | | | | | | | | | | |
| WHITE, J (HM21358) | | | | | | | | | | | | | | | | | | | | | | | | | |
| WICKER, DIANE (HM21446) | | | | | | | | | | | | | | | | | | | | | | | | | |

# A - F Therapies at Practices/Businesses

| Business by County with Reference no. | Absent Healing | Acupressure | Acupuncture | Alexander Technique | Allergy Testing | Anthroposohical Med | Aromatherapy | Art Therapy | Aura Therapy | Auricular Therapy | Auto Suggestion | Autogenic Training | Aversion Therapy | Ayurvedic Medicine | Baby Massage | Bach Remedies | Bates Method | Beauty Therapy | Bio-energetics | Biofeedback | Biomagnetic Therapy | Biomechanics | Bonesetting | Bowen Therapy | Chinese Herbal Medicine | Chiropody | Chiropractic | Clinical Ecology | Cognitive Therapy | Colonic Hydrotherapy | Colour Therapy | Complementary Therapy | Counselling | Cranial Osteopathy | Cranio-Sacral Therapy | Cryo Surgery | Crystal Healing | Cupping | Cymatics | Dance Movement Thrpy | Dietician | Do-In | Douching | Dowsing | Drama Therapy | Electrolipolysis | Electrolysis | Electrotherapy | Encounter Groups | Faith Healing |
|---|---|---|---|---|---|---|---|---|---|---|---|---|---|---|---|---|---|---|---|---|---|---|---|---|---|---|---|---|---|---|---|---|---|---|---|---|---|---|---|---|---|---|---|---|---|---|---|---|---|---|
| WIGHAM, A (HM21468) | | | | | | | | ● | | | | | | | | | | | | | | | | | | | | | ● | | | | ● | | | | | | | | | | | | | | | | | |
| WILKINSON, GILL (HM21505) | | | | ● | | | | | | | | | | | | | | | | | | | | | | | | | | | | | ● | | | | | | | | | | | | | | | | | |
| WILLER, ANGELA P (HM21524) | | | ● | | | | | | | | | | | | | | | | | | | | | | | | | | | | | | | | | | | | | | | | | | | | | | | |
| WILLIAMS, B A (HM21541) | | | ● | | | | | | | | | | | | | | | | | | | | | | | ● | | | | | | | ● | | | | | | | | | | | | | | | | | |
| WILLIAMS, IAN (HM21565) | | | | | | | | | | | | | | | | | | | | | | | | | | ● | | | | | | | | | | | | | | | | | | | | | | | | |
| WILLIAMS, RUTH (HM21588) | | | | | | | | | | | | | | | | | | | | | | | | | | | | | | | | | ● | | | | | | | | | | | | | | | | | |
| WILLMOTT, SUSAN (HM21623) | | | | | | | | | | | ● | | | | | | | | | | | | | | | | | | | | | | ● | | | | | | | | | | | | | | | | | |
| WILSON, ALLES (HM21643) | | | | | | | | | | | | | | | | ● | | | | | | | | | | | | | | | | | | | | | | | | | | | | | | | | | | |
| WILSON, CHRISTOPHER (HM21651) | | | | | | | | | | | | | | | | | | | | | | | | | | | | | | | | | ● | | | | | | | | | | | | | | | | | |
| WILSON, MARGARET R E (HM21660) | | | | | | | ● | | | | | | | | | | | | | | | | | | | | | | | | | | | | | | | | | | | | | | | | | | | |
| WINCHMORE CLINIC OF OSTEOPATHY (HM21694) | | | ● | | | | | | | | | | | | | | | | | | | | | | | | | | | | | | ● | ● | | | | | | | | | | | | | | ● | | |
| WONG, PO-YEE (HM21778) | | | ● | | | | | | | | | | | | | | | | | | | | | | | | | | | | | | | | | | | | | | | | | | | | | | | |
| WOOLF, PERRY (HM21872) | | | | | | | | | | | | | | | | | | | | | | | | | | ● | | | | | | | | | | | | | | | | | | | | | | ● | | |
| WORLD OF LIGHT (HM21898) | | ● | ● | | | | ● | | | | | | | | | | | | | | | | | ● | | | ● | | | | | ● | ● | | | | ● | | | | | | | | | | | | | |
| WREN CLINIC (HM21919) | | | ● | ● | | | ● | | | | | ● | | | | | | | | | | | | ● | | | | | | | | | ● | | ● | | | | | | | | | | | | | | | |
| WREN, ANTHONY (HM21920) | | | | | | | | | | | | | | | | | | | | | | | | | | | | | | | | | | | ● | | | | | | | | | | | | | | | |
| WRIGHT, JENNY (HM21936) | | | | | | | | | | | ● | | | | | | | | | ● | | | | | | | | | ● | | | | ● | | | | | | | | | | | | | | | | | |
| WYSMAN, ALAN (HM21980) | | | ● | | | | | | | | | | | | | | | | | | | | | | | | | | | | | | | | | | | | | | | | | | | | | | | |
| YAGHMAIE, MASSIH (HM21985) | | | ● | | | | | | | | | | | | | | | | | | | | | | | | | | | | | | | | | | | | | | | | | | | | | | | |
| ZEN HEALTH CENTRE (HM22100) | | ● | ● | | | | ● | | | | | | | | | | | | | ● | | | | | | | ● | | | ● | | ● | ● | ● | | | | ● | | | ● | | | | | | | ● | | |
| ZEN SHIATSU & HEALING TAO (HM22101) | ● | ● | | | | | | | | | | | | | | | | | | | | | | | | | | | | | | | | | | | | | | | | | | | | | | | | |
| **MANCHESTER (GREATER)** | | | | | | | | | | | | | | | | | | | | | | | | | | | | | | | | | | | | | | | | | | | | | | | | | | |
| A SIR ROBERTS ALT PLACE (HM00045) | | ● | ● | | | | ● | | | | ● | | | | | ● | | | | ● | | | ● | | | | ● | | | | | ● | ● | | | | | ● | | | | | | ● | | | | | | ● |
| A6 CHIROPODY PRACTICE (HM00055) | | | | | | | | | | | | | | | | | | | | | | | | | | ● | | | | | | | | | | | | | | | | | | | | | | | | |
| ACUMEDIC (HM00220) | | ● | ● | | | | | | | | | | | | | | | | | | | | | | ● | | | | | | | | | | | | | | | | | | | | | | | | | |
| ACUPUNCTURE CENTRE (HM00252) | | | ● | | | | | | | | | | | | | ● | | | | | | | | | | | | | | | | | | | | | | ● | | | | | | | | | | | | |
| ADVANCED CHIROPODY SURGERY (HM00394) | | | | | | | | | | | | | | | | | | | | | | | | | | ● | | | | | | | | | | | | | | | | | | | | | | | | |
| ADVANCED PHYSIOTHERAPY CLINIC (HM00403) | | | ● | | | | | | | | | | | | | | | | | | | | | | | ● | | | | | | | | | | | | | | | | | | | | | | ● | | |
| ALEXANDER TECHNIQUE (HM00541) | | | | ● | | | | | | | | | | | | | | | | | | | | | | | | | | | | | | | | | | | | | | | | | | | | | | |
| ALL IN THE MIND (HM00582) | | | | | | | | | | | | | | | | | | | | | | | | | | | | | | | | ● | | | | | | | | | | | | | | | | | | |
| AROMATHERAPY BY SARA (HM01098) | | | | | | | ● | | | | | | | | | | | | | | | | | | | | | | | | | | | | | | | | | | | | | | | | | | | |
| AROMATHERAPY LADIES MASSAGE (HM01118) | | | | | | | ● | | | | | | | | | | | | | | | | | | | | | | | | | | | | | | | | | | | | | | | | | | | |
| ASHTON CHIROPRACTIC CENTRE (HM01233) | | | | | | | | | | | | | | | | | | | | | | | | | | | ● | | | | | | | | | | | | | | | | | | | | | | | |
| ASTLEY COMPLEMENTARY CENTRE (HM01300) | | | ● | | ● | | ● | | | | | | | | | ● | | | | | | | | ● | ● | | | | ● | | | ● | ● | ● | | | | | | | | | | | | | | ● | | |

# A - F Therapies at Practices/Businesses

Business by County with Reference no.

| Business by County with Reference no. | Absent Healing | Acupressure | Acupuncture | Alexander Technique | Allergy Testing | Anthroposohical Med | Aromatherapy | Art Therapy | Aura Therapy | Auricular Therapy | Auto Suggestion | Autogenic Training | Aversion Therapy | Ayurvedic Medicine | Baby Massage | Bach Remedies | Bates Method | Beauty Therapy | Bio-energetics | Biofeedback | Biomagnetic Therapy | Biomechanics | Bonesetting | Bowen Therapy | Chinese Herbal Medicine |
|---|---|---|---|---|---|---|---|---|---|---|---|---|---|---|---|---|---|---|---|---|---|---|---|---|---|
| BRAMHALL CHIROPRACTIC CLINIC (HM02898) |  |  |  |  |  |  |  |  |  |  |  |  |  |  |  |  |  |  |  |  |  |  |  |  |  |
| BROMILEY, A P (HM03140) |  |  | ● |  |  |  |  |  |  |  |  |  |  |  |  |  |  |  |  |  |  |  |  |  |  |
| BURGESS, KAREN (HM03377) |  |  |  |  |  |  |  |  |  |  |  |  |  |  |  |  |  |  |  |  |  |  |  |  |  |
| CHARTERED PHYSIOTHERAPY CLINIC (HM04046) |  |  | ● |  |  |  |  |  |  |  |  |  |  |  |  |  |  |  |  |  |  |  |  |  |  |
| CHINESE HERBAL & ACU CENTRE (HM04194) |  |  | ● |  |  |  |  |  |  |  |  |  |  |  |  |  |  |  |  |  |  |  |  |  |  |
| CLARENDON CLINIC (HM04540) |  | ● | ● |  |  |  | ● |  |  |  |  |  |  |  |  |  |  |  |  |  |  |  |  |  |  |
| CLEVERLY, MARAGRET (HM04658) |  |  |  |  |  |  | ● |  |  |  |  |  |  |  |  |  |  |  |  |  |  |  |  |  |  |
| COSGROVES PHYSIO-FIT CENTRE (HM05201) |  | ● | ● |  |  |  |  |  |  |  |  |  |  |  |  |  |  |  |  |  |  |  |  |  |  |
| CROSSWAY CLINIC (HM05491) |  |  | ● | ● |  |  | ● |  |  |  |  |  |  |  |  |  |  |  |  |  |  |  |  |  |  |
| DAVEENA ASSOCIATES (HM05763) |  |  |  |  |  |  |  |  |  |  |  |  |  |  |  |  |  |  |  |  |  |  |  |  |  |
| DIDSBURY CHIROPRACTIC CLINIC (HM06090) |  |  |  |  |  |  |  |  |  |  |  |  |  |  |  |  |  |  |  |  |  |  |  |  |  |
| EVANS, DAVID (HM06967) |  |  |  |  |  |  |  |  |  |  | ● |  |  |  |  |  |  |  |  |  |  |  |  |  |  |
| FOOTCARE CENTRE (HM07493) |  |  |  |  |  |  |  |  |  |  |  |  |  |  |  |  |  |  |  |  |  |  |  |  |  |
| GIBSON, LINDA (HM08041) |  |  |  |  |  |  |  |  |  |  |  |  |  |  |  |  |  |  |  |  |  |  |  |  |  |
| GILL, JUNE (HM08077) |  |  |  | ● |  |  |  |  |  |  |  |  |  |  |  |  |  |  |  |  |  |  |  |  |  |
| GUILD OF PRACTITIONERS (HM08627) |  |  |  |  |  |  |  |  |  |  |  |  |  |  |  |  |  |  |  |  |  |  | ● |  |  |
| HIGH PEAK HOLISTIC CENTRE (HM09738) |  |  |  |  |  |  | ● |  |  |  |  |  |  |  |  |  |  |  |  |  |  |  |  |  |  |
| HORRIDGE, S P (HM10182) |  |  |  |  |  |  |  |  |  |  |  |  |  |  |  |  |  |  |  |  |  |  |  |  |  |
| HUMAN TOUCH CENTRE (HM10366) |  |  |  |  |  |  | ● |  |  |  |  |  |  |  |  |  |  |  |  |  |  |  |  |  |  |
| HUNT, MARILYN (HM10399) |  |  |  |  |  |  |  |  |  |  |  |  |  |  |  | ● |  |  |  |  |  |  |  |  |  |
| IBBOTSON, GEOFF (DR) (HM10565) |  |  |  |  |  |  |  |  |  |  |  |  |  |  |  |  |  |  |  |  |  |  |  |  |  |
| LOMAX, JAMES (HM12577) |  |  |  | ● |  |  |  |  |  |  |  |  |  |  |  |  |  |  |  |  |  |  |  |  |  |
| MANCHESTER SCHOOL OF MASSAGE (HM13004) |  |  |  |  |  |  | ● |  |  |  |  |  |  |  |  |  |  |  |  |  |  |  |  |  |  |
| MIDDLETON, SCOTT (DR) (HM13822) |  |  |  |  |  |  |  |  |  |  |  |  |  |  |  |  |  |  |  |  |  |  |  |  |  |
| MOBILE COMPLEMENTARY THERAPIES (HM14029) |  |  |  |  |  |  | ● |  |  |  |  |  |  |  |  |  |  |  |  |  |  |  |  |  |  |
| MOUNT STREET COMP THERAPIES (HM14291) |  |  | ● |  | ● |  | ● |  |  |  |  |  |  |  |  |  |  |  |  |  |  |  |  |  |  |
| NIVERN, D (HM14954) | ● | ● |  |  |  |  | ● |  |  |  |  |  |  |  |  | ● |  |  |  |  |  |  |  |  |  |
| PHILLIPS, LORRAINE (HM16138) |  |  |  |  |  |  | ● |  |  |  |  |  |  |  |  |  |  |  |  |  |  |  |  |  |  |
| REFLEXOLOGY & CHIROPODY (HM17079) |  |  |  |  |  |  |  |  |  |  |  |  |  |  |  |  |  |  |  |  |  |  |  |  |  |
| ROBERTS, S (DR) (HM17427) |  |  |  |  |  |  |  |  |  |  |  |  |  |  |  |  |  |  |  |  |  |  |  |  |  |
| SCENT OF DELIGHT (HM18008) |  |  |  |  |  |  | ● |  |  |  |  |  |  |  |  |  |  |  |  |  |  |  |  |  |  |
| SCHOFIELD, G A (HM18018) |  |  |  |  |  |  |  |  |  |  |  |  |  |  |  |  |  |  |  |  |  | ● |  |  |  |
| SHANGHAI ACUPUNCTURE CLINIC (HM18281) |  |  | ● |  |  |  |  |  |  |  |  |  |  |  |  |  |  |  |  |  |  |  |  |  |  |
| SHANGHAI ACUPUNCTURE CLINIC (HM18280) |  |  | ● |  |  |  |  |  |  |  |  |  |  |  |  |  |  |  |  |  |  |  |  |  |  |

| Business by County with Reference no. | Chiropody | Chiropractic | Clinical Ecology | Cognitive Therapy | Colonic Hydrotherapy | Colour Therapy | Complementary Therapy | Counselling | Cranial Osteopathy | Cranio-Sacral Therapy | Cryo Surgery | Crystal Healing | Cupping | Cymatics | Dance Movement Thrpy | Dietician | Do-In | Douching | Dowsing | Drama Therapy | Electrolipolysis | Electrolysis | Electrotherapy | Encounter Groups | Faith Healing |
|---|---|---|---|---|---|---|---|---|---|---|---|---|---|---|---|---|---|---|---|---|---|---|---|---|---|
| BRAMHALL CHIROPRACTIC CLINIC (HM02898) |  | ● |  |  |  |  |  |  |  |  |  |  |  |  |  |  |  |  |  |  |  |  |  |  |  |
| BROMILEY, A P (HM03140) |  |  |  |  |  |  |  |  |  |  |  |  |  |  |  |  |  |  |  |  |  |  |  |  |  |
| BURGESS, KAREN (HM03377) | ● |  |  |  |  |  |  |  |  |  |  |  |  |  |  |  |  |  |  |  |  |  |  |  |  |
| CHARTERED PHYSIOTHERAPY CLINIC (HM04046) |  | ● |  |  |  |  |  |  |  |  |  |  |  |  |  |  |  |  |  |  |  |  | ● |  |  |
| CHINESE HERBAL & ACU CENTRE (HM04194) |  |  |  |  |  |  |  |  |  |  |  |  |  |  |  |  |  |  |  |  |  |  |  |  |  |
| CLARENDON CLINIC (HM04540) |  |  |  |  |  |  |  |  |  |  |  |  |  |  |  |  |  |  |  |  |  |  | ● |  |  |
| CLEVERLY, MARAGRET (HM04658) |  |  |  |  |  |  |  |  |  |  |  |  |  |  |  |  |  |  |  |  |  |  |  |  |  |
| COSGROVES PHYSIO-FIT CENTRE (HM05201) |  |  |  |  |  |  |  |  |  |  |  |  |  |  |  | ● |  |  |  |  |  |  | ● |  |  |
| CROSSWAY CLINIC (HM05491) |  |  |  |  |  |  |  | ● | ● |  |  |  |  |  |  |  |  |  |  |  |  |  |  |  |  |
| DAVEENA ASSOCIATES (HM05763) |  |  |  |  |  |  |  | ● |  |  |  |  |  |  |  |  |  |  |  |  |  |  |  |  |  |
| DIDSBURY CHIROPRACTIC CLINIC (HM06090) |  | ● |  |  |  |  |  |  |  |  |  |  |  |  |  |  |  |  |  |  |  |  |  |  |  |
| EVANS, DAVID (HM06967) |  |  |  |  |  |  |  | ● |  |  |  |  |  |  |  |  |  |  |  |  |  |  |  |  |  |
| FOOTCARE CENTRE (HM07493) | ● |  |  |  |  |  |  |  |  |  |  |  |  |  |  |  |  |  |  |  |  |  |  |  |  |
| GIBSON, LINDA (HM08041) |  | ● |  |  |  |  |  |  |  |  |  |  |  |  |  |  |  |  |  |  |  |  |  |  |  |
| GILL, JUNE (HM08077) |  |  |  |  |  |  |  |  |  |  |  |  |  |  |  |  |  |  |  |  |  |  |  |  |  |
| GUILD OF PRACTITIONERS (HM08627) |  | ● |  |  |  |  | ● |  |  |  |  |  | ● |  |  |  |  |  |  |  |  |  |  |  |  |
| HIGH PEAK HOLISTIC CENTRE (HM09738) |  |  |  |  |  |  |  | ● |  |  |  |  |  |  |  |  |  |  |  |  |  |  |  |  |  |
| HORRIDGE, S P (HM10182) | ● |  |  |  |  |  |  |  |  |  |  |  |  |  |  |  |  |  |  |  |  |  |  |  |  |
| HUMAN TOUCH CENTRE (HM10366) |  |  |  |  |  |  |  | ● |  |  |  |  |  |  |  |  |  |  |  |  |  |  |  |  |  |
| HUNT, MARILYN (HM10399) |  |  |  |  |  |  |  |  |  |  |  |  |  |  |  |  |  |  |  |  |  |  |  |  |  |
| IBBOTSON, GEOFF (DR) (HM10565) |  |  |  | ● |  |  |  | ● |  |  |  |  |  |  |  |  |  |  |  |  |  |  |  |  |  |
| LOMAX, JAMES (HM12577) |  |  |  |  |  |  |  |  |  |  |  |  |  |  |  |  |  |  |  |  |  |  |  |  |  |
| MANCHESTER SCHOOL OF MASSAGE (HM13004) |  |  |  |  |  |  |  |  |  |  |  |  |  |  |  |  |  |  |  |  |  |  |  |  |  |
| MIDDLETON, SCOTT (DR) (HM13822) |  | ● |  |  |  |  |  |  |  |  |  |  |  |  |  |  |  |  |  |  |  |  |  |  |  |
| MOBILE COMPLEMENTARY THERAPIES (HM14029) |  |  |  |  |  |  | ● |  |  |  |  |  |  |  |  |  |  |  |  |  |  |  |  |  |  |
| MOUNT STREET COMP THERAPIES (HM14291) |  |  |  |  |  |  |  |  |  |  |  |  |  |  |  |  |  |  |  |  |  |  |  |  |  |
| NIVERN, D (HM14954) |  | ● |  |  |  |  | ● | ● |  |  |  |  |  |  |  |  |  |  | ● |  |  |  |  |  |  |
| PHILLIPS, LORRAINE (HM16138) |  |  |  |  |  |  |  |  |  |  |  |  |  |  |  |  |  |  |  |  |  |  |  |  |  |
| REFLEXOLOGY & CHIROPODY (HM17079) |  |  |  |  |  |  | ● |  |  |  |  |  |  |  |  |  |  |  |  |  |  |  |  |  |  |
| ROBERTS, S (DR) (HM17427) |  | ● |  |  |  |  |  |  |  |  |  |  |  |  |  |  |  |  |  |  |  |  |  |  |  |
| SCENT OF DELIGHT (HM18008) |  |  |  |  |  |  |  |  |  |  |  |  |  |  |  |  |  |  |  |  |  |  |  |  |  |
| SCHOFIELD, G A (HM18018) | ● |  |  |  |  |  |  |  |  |  |  |  |  |  |  |  |  |  |  |  |  |  |  |  |  |
| SHANGHAI ACUPUNCTURE CLINIC (HM18281) |  |  |  |  |  |  |  |  |  |  |  |  |  |  |  |  |  |  |  |  |  |  |  |  |  |
| SHANGHAI ACUPUNCTURE CLINIC (HM18280) |  |  |  |  |  |  |  |  |  |  |  |  |  |  |  |  |  |  |  |  |  |  |  |  |  |

# A - F Therapies at Practices/Businesses

| Business by County with Reference no. | Absent Healing | Acupressure | Acupuncture | Alexander Technique | Allergy Testing | Anthroposohical Med | Aromatherapy | Art Therapy | Aura Therapy | Auricular Therapy | Auto Suggestion | Autogenic Training | Aversion Therapy | Ayurvedic Medicine | Baby Massage | Bach Remedies | Bates Method | Beauty Therapy | Bio-energetics | Biofeedback | Biomagnetic Therapy | Biomechanics | Bonesetting | Bowen Therapy | Chinese Herbal Medicine |
|---|---|---|---|---|---|---|---|---|---|---|---|---|---|---|---|---|---|---|---|---|---|---|---|---|---|
| ST JOHN STREET PHYSIO PRACTICE (HM19080) | | | | | | | | | | | | | | | | | | | | | | | | | |
| STRINGER, R A (DR) (HM19409) | | | ● | | | | | | | | | | | | | | | | | | | | | | |
| SWINTON HEALTH FOODS (HM19600) | | | ● | ● | ● | | ● | | | | | | | | | | | | | | | | | | |
| TANG, SHULAN (HM19682) | | | ● | | | | | | | | | | | | | | | | | | | | | | |
| THERAPY BREAK (HM19891) | | | ● | ● | | | ● | | | | | | | | | | | | | | | | | | |
| WAINWRIGHT, P (HM20739) | | | | | | | | | | | | | | | | | | | | | | | | | |
| WEBB, EDWINA (HM21062) | | | ● | | | | | | | | | | | | | | | | | | | | | | |
| MERSEYSIDE | | | | | | | | | | | | | | | | | | | | | | | | | |
| ABBEY FOOT CLINIC (HM00083) | | | | | | | | | | | | | | | | | | | | | | | | | |
| ACUPUNCTURE CLINIC (HM00263) | | | ● | | | | | | | | | | | | | | | | | | | | | | |
| AIGBURTH MCTIMONEY CLINIC (HM00427) | | | | | | | | | | | | | | | | | | | | | | | | ● | |
| AINTREE OSTEOPATHIC (HM00439) | | | ● | | | | ● | | | | | | | | | | | | | | | | | | |
| ALLERTON CLINIC (HM00638) | | | | | | | | | | | | | | | | | | | | | | | | | |
| ALLERTON HEALTH CENTRE (HM00639) | | | ● | | | | | | | | | | | | | | | | | | | | | | ● |
| ANDERSON, KATE (HM00829) | | | | | | | | | | | | | | | | ● | | | | | | | | | |
| AROMATHERAPY TREATMENT (HM01129) | | | | | | | ● | | | | | | | | | | | | | | | | | | |
| BIRKDALE CHIROPRACTIC CLINIC (HM02373) | | | | | | | | | | | | | | | | | | | | | | | | | |
| BIRKENHEAD CHIROPRACTIC CLNC (HM02376) | | | | | | | | | | | | | | | | | | | | | | | | | |
| BOLTON, TOM (HM02663) | | | | | | | ● | | | | | | | | | | | | | | | | | | |
| BOYLE, ANDREW (HM02826) | | ● | ● | | | | ● | | | | | | | | | | | | | | | ● | | | |
| BRENNAN, M A (HM02958) | | | | | | | | | | | | | | | | | | | | | | ● | | | |
| CARTER, G R (HM03778) | | | | | | | | | | | | | | | | | | | | | | ● | | | |
| CAWLEY, TONY (HM03871) | | | | | | | | | | | | | | | | | | | | | | | | | |
| CONCANNON, DEIRDRE (HM04965) | | | | | | | | | | | | | | | | ● | | | | | | | | | |
| D A F CLINIC (HM05655) | | | | | | | | | | | | | | | | | | | | | | | | | |
| DARE TO CARE (HM05739) | | | | | | | ● | | | | | | | | | | | | | | | | | | |
| ECCLES CHIROPODY SERVICES (HM06572) | | | | | | | | | | | | | | | | | | | | | | | | | |
| FARMER, BARBARA (HM01681) | | | | | | | | | | | | | | | | | | | | | | | | | |
| GATEAUD, S (HM07924) | | | | | | | ● | | | | | | | | | | | | | | | | | | |
| GOLDEN SAFFRON (HM08209) | | | | | | | | | | | | | | | | | | | | | ● | | | | |
| GROUNDS, L (HM08600) | | | | | | | | | | | | | | | | | | | | | | | | | |
| HAYES, L (HM09261) | | | ● | | | | | | | | | | | | | | | | | | | | | | |
| HEAL TO TOE (HM09311) | | | | | | | ● | | | | | | | | | | | | | | | | | | |
| HOLISTIC HEALTH CENTRE (HM09975) | | | ● | | | | | | | | | | | | | | | | | | | | | ● | |

| Business by County with Reference no. | Chiropody | Chiropractic | Clinical Ecology | Cognitive Therapy | Colonic Hydrotherapy | Colour Therapy | Complementary Therapy | Counselling | Cranial Osteopathy | Cranio-Sacral Therapy | Cryo Surgery | Crystal Healing | Cupping | Cymatics | Dance Movement Thrpy | Dietician | Do-In | Douching | Dowsing | Drama Therapy | Electrolipolysis | Electrolysis | Electrotherapy | Encounter Groups | Faith Healing |
|---|---|---|---|---|---|---|---|---|---|---|---|---|---|---|---|---|---|---|---|---|---|---|---|---|---|
| ST JOHN STREET PHYSIO PRACTICE (HM19080) | | | | | | | | | | | | | | | | | | | | | | | ● | | |
| STRINGER, R A (DR) (HM19409) | | | | | | | | | | | | | | | | | | | | | | | | | |
| SWINTON HEALTH FOODS (HM19600) | | | | | | | | ● | | | | ● | | | | | | | | | | | | | |
| TANG, SHULAN (HM19682) | | | | | | | | | | | | | | | | | | | | | | | | | |
| THERAPY BREAK (HM19891) | | | | | | | | | | ● | | | | | | | | | | | | | | | |
| WAINWRIGHT, P (HM20739) | ● | | | | | | ● | | | | | | | | | | | | | | | | | | |
| WEBB, EDWINA (HM21062) | | | | | | | | | | | | | | | | | | | | | | | | | |
| MERSEYSIDE | | | | | | | | | | | | | | | | | | | | | | | | | |
| ABBEY FOOT CLINIC (HM00083) | ● | | | | | | | | | | | | | | | | | | | | | | | | |
| ACUPUNCTURE CLINIC (HM00263) | | | | | | | ● | | | | | | | | | | | | | | | | | | |
| AIGBURTH MCTIMONEY CLINIC (HM00427) | | ● | | | | | | | | ● | | | | | | | | | | | | | | | |
| AINTREE OSTEOPATHIC (HM00439) | ● | | | | | | ● | | ● | | | | | | | | | | | | | | ● | | |
| ALLERTON CLINIC (HM00638) | | ● | | | | | | | | | | | | | | | | | | | | | | | |
| ALLERTON HEALTH CENTRE (HM00639) | | | | | | | | | | | | | | | | | | | | | | | | | |
| ANDERSON, KATE (HM00829) | | | | | | | | | | | | | | | | | | | | | | | | | |
| AROMATHERAPY TREATMENT (HM01129) | | | | | | | | | | | | | | | | | | | | | | | | | |
| BIRKDALE CHIROPRACTIC CLINIC (HM02373) | | ● | | | | | | | | | | | | | | | | | | | | | | | |
| BIRKENHEAD CHIROPRACTIC CLNC (HM02376) | | ● | | | | | | | | | | | | | | | | | | | | | | | |
| BOLTON, TOM (HM02663) | | | | | | | | | | | | | | | | | | | | | | | | | |
| BOYLE, ANDREW (HM02826) | ● | | | | | | ● | | | | | | | | | | | | | | | | ● | | |
| BRENNAN, M A (HM02958) | ● | | | | | | | | | | ● | | | | | | | | | | | | | | |
| CARTER, G R (HM03778) | ● | | | | | | | | | | ● | | | | | | | | | | | | | | |
| CAWLEY, TONY (HM03871) | | | | ● | | | | ● | | | | | | | | | | | | | | | | | |
| CONCANNON, DEIRDRE (HM04965) | | ● | | | | | | | | | | | | | | | | | | | | | | | |
| D A F CLINIC (HM05655) | | | | | | | | ● | | | | | | | | | | | | | | | | | |
| DARE TO CARE (HM05739) | | | | | | | | | | | | | | | | | | | | | | | | | |
| ECCLES CHIROPODY SERVICES (HM06572) | ● | | | | | | | | | | | | | | | | | | | | | | | | |
| FARMER, BARBARA (HM01681) | | | | | | | | | | | | | | | | | | | | | | | ● | | |
| GATEAUD, S (HM07924) | | | | | | | | ● | ● | | | | | | | | | | | | | | | | |
| GOLDEN SAFFRON (HM08209) | | | | | | | | | | | | | | | | | | | | | | | | | |
| GROUNDS, L (HM08600) | ● | | | | | | | | | | | | | | | | | | | | | | | | |
| HAYES, L (HM09261) | | | | | | | | | | | | | | | | | | | | | | | | | |
| HEAL TO TOE (HM09311) | | | | | | | | | | | | | | | | | | | | | | | | | |
| HOLISTIC HEALTH CENTRE (HM09975) | | | | | | | ● | | | | | | | | | | | | | | | | ● | | |

# A - F Therapies at Practices/Businesses

| Business by County with Reference no. | Absent Healing | Acupressure | Acupuncture | Alexander Technique | Allergy Testing | Anthroposohical Med | Aromatherapy | Art Therapy | Aura Therapy | Auricular Therapy | Auto Suggestion | Autogenic Training | Aversion Therapy | Ayurvedic Medicine | Baby Massage | Bach Remedies | Bates Method | Beauty Therapy | Bio-energetics | Biofeedback | Biomagnetic Therapy | Biomechanics | Bonesetting | Bowen Therapy | Chinese Herbal Medicine |
|---|---|---|---|---|---|---|---|---|---|---|---|---|---|---|---|---|---|---|---|---|---|---|---|---|---|
| HOPE STREET NATURAL HLTH CTRE (HM10136) | | | ● | | | | | | | | | | | | | | | | | | | | | | |
| JAMES, ANN (HM10880) | | | | | | | ● | | | | | | | | | | | | | | | ● | | | |
| JARVIS, K R (HM10934) | | | | | | | | | | | | | | | | | | | | | | ● | | | |
| KNOWLES, JANICE (HM11771) | | | | | | | | | | | | | | | | | | | | | | ● | | | |
| KUA, R P (HM11813) | | | ● | | | | | | | | | | | | | | | | | | | | | | |
| MARKET STREET CHIROPODY CLINIC (HM13113) | | | | | | | | | | | | | | | | | | | | | | ● | | | |
| MARSH, E C (HM13146) | | | | | | | | | | | | | | | | | | | | | | | | | |
| MCLOUGHLIN, CLAIRE (HM13560) | | | | | | | | | | | | | | | | | | | | | | ● | | | |
| NATURAL HEALTH CLINIC (HM14576) | | | ● | | | | ● | | | | | | | | | | | | | | | | | | |
| NATUROPATHIC HEALTH CENTRE (HM14709) | | | | | | | | | | | | | | | | | | | | | | | | | |
| NELSON, PATRICIA (HM14780) | | | | | | | | | | | | | | | | | | | | | | | | | |
| ORR, WILLIAM A (HM15405) | | | ● | | | | | | | | | | | | | | | | | | | | | | |
| PAWLEY, PHILIP (HM15857) | | | | ● | | | | | | | | | | | | | | | | | | | | | |
| PURE ESSENTIALS DIRECT (HM16764) | | | | | | | ● | | | | | | | | | | | | | | | | | | |
| REIKI-4-LIFE (HM17150) | | | | | | | | | | | | | | | | | | | | | | | | | |
| RHIANNON'S CAT (HM17218) | | | | | | | ● | | | | | | | | | | | | | | | | | | |
| SANCTUARY NATURAL HEALTH (HM17893) | | | | | | | ● | | | | | | | | | | | | | | | | | | |
| SCOTT, ANDREW (HM18107) | | | ● | | | | | | | | | | | | | | | | | | | | | | |
| SEFTON PARK NATURAL THRPY CTRE (HM18198) | | | ● | | | | ● | | | | | | | | | ● | | | | | | | | ● | |
| SHANKS, ALAN (HM18284) | | | ● | | | | | | | | | | | | | | | | | | | | | | |
| SIMPSON CLINIC (HM18584) | | | ● | | ● | | ● | | ● | | | | | | | ● | | | ● | ● | | | | | |
| SOUTHPORT OSTEO & ACUPUNCTURE (HM18942) | | | ● | | | | | | | | | | | | | | | | | | | | | | |
| STEINA SPORTS & PHYSIOTHERAPY (HM19188) | | | ● | | | | | | | | | | | | | | | | | | | | | | |
| SUMMERS, ALFRED A (HM19487) | | | | | | | | | | | | | | | | | | | | | | | | | |
| TARA SCHOOL OF HYPNOTHERAPY (HM19701) | | | | | | | | | | | | | | | | | | | | | | | | | |
| THERAPY 21 (HM19890) | ● | ● | | | | | ● | | | | | | | | | | | | | | | | | | |
| VANGEN, M A (HM20578) | | | | | | | | | | | | | | | | | | | | | | | | | |
| WEST WIRRAL CHIROPRACTIC (HM21239) | | | | | | | ● | | | | | | | | | | | | | | | | | | |
| WILLIAMS CHIROPODY SERVICE (HM21530) | | | | | | | | | | | | | | | | | | | | | | | | | |
| WILLIAMS, CATHERINE (HM21546) | | | | | | | | | | | | | | | | | | | | | | | | | |
| WILLIAMS, T H (HM21597) | | | | | | | | | | | | | | | | | | | | | | | | | |
| WILLIAMS, TECWYN H (HM21598) | | | | | | | | | | | | | | | | | | | | | | | | | |
| WIRRALL CLINIC (HM21730) | | | ● | | | | | | | | | | | | | | | | | | | | | | |
| **MIDDLESEX** | | | | | | | | | | | | | | | | | | | | | | | | | |

| Business by County with Reference no. | Chiropody | Chiropractic | Clinical Ecology | Cognitive Therapy | Colonic Hydrotherapy | Colour Therapy | Complementary Therapy | Counselling | Cranial Osteopathy | Cranio-Sacral Therapy | Cryo Surgery | Crystal Healing | Cupping | Cymatics | Dance Movement Thrpy | Dietician | Do-In | Douching | Dowsing | Drama Therapy | Electrolipolysis | Electrolysis | Electrotherapy | Encounter Groups | Faith Healing |
|---|---|---|---|---|---|---|---|---|---|---|---|---|---|---|---|---|---|---|---|---|---|---|---|---|---|
| HOPE STREET NATURAL HLTH CTRE (HM10136) | | | | | | | | | | | | | | | | | | | | | | | | | |
| JAMES, ANN (HM10880) | | | | | | | ● | | | | | | | | | | | | | | | | | | |
| JARVIS, K R (HM10934) | ● | | | | | | | | | | ● | | | | | | | | | | | | | | |
| KNOWLES, JANICE (HM11771) | ● | | | | | | | | | | | | | | | | | | | | | | | | |
| KUA, R P (HM11813) | | | | | | | | | | | | | | | | | | | | | | | | | |
| MARKET STREET CHIROPODY CLINIC (HM13113) | ● | | | | | | | | | | | | | | | | | | | | | | | | |
| MARSH, E C (HM13146) | ● | | | | | | | | | | | | | | | | | | | | | | | | |
| MCLOUGHLIN, CLAIRE (HM13560) | ● | | | | | | | | | | | | | | | | | | | | | | | | |
| NATURAL HEALTH CLINIC (HM14576) | | | | | | | | ● | | | | | | | | | | | | | | | | | |
| NATUROPATHIC HEALTH CENTRE (HM14709) | | ● | | | | | | | ● | | | ● | | | | | | | | | | | | | |
| NELSON, PATRICIA (HM14780) | ● | | | | | | | | | | | | | | | | | | | | | | | | |
| ORR, WILLIAM A (HM15405) | | | | | | | | | | | | | | | | | | | | | | | | | |
| PAWLEY, PHILIP (HM15857) | | | | | | | | | | | | | | | | | | | | | | | | | |
| PURE ESSENTIALS DIRECT (HM16764) | | | | | | | | | | | | | | | | | | | | | | | | | |
| REIKI-4-LIFE (HM17150) | | | | | | | | | | | | ● | | | | | | | | | | | | | |
| RHIANNON'S CAT (HM17218) | | | | | | | | | | | | | | | | | | | | | | | | | |
| SANCTUARY NATURAL HEALTH (HM17893) | | | | | | | | | | | | | | | | | | | | | | | | | |
| SCOTT, ANDREW (HM18107) | | | | | | | | | | | | | ● | | | | ● | | | | | | | | |
| SEFTON PARK NATURAL THRPY CTRE (HM18198) | | | | ● | | | | ● | ● | | | | | | | | | | | | | | | | |
| SHANKS, ALAN (HM18284) | | | | | | | | | | | | | | | | | | | | | | | | | |
| SIMPSON CLINIC (HM18584) | | ● | | ● | | | ● | | ● | | | | | | | ● | | | ● | | | | ● | | |
| SOUTHPORT OSTEO & ACUPUNCTURE (HM18942) | | | | | | | | | | | | | | | | | | | | | | | | | |
| STEINA SPORTS & PHYSIOTHERAPY (HM19188) | | | | | | | | | | | | | | | | | | | | | | | | | |
| SUMMERS, ALFRED A (HM19487) | ● | | | | | | | | | | | | | | | | | | | | | | | | |
| TARA SCHOOL OF HYPNOTHERAPY (HM19701) | | | | ● | | | | | | | | | | | | | | | | | | | | | |
| THERAPY 21 (HM19890) | | | | | | | ● | | | | | | | | | | | | | | | | | | |
| VANGEN, M A (HM20578) | | ● | | | | | | | | | | | | | | | | | | | | | | | |
| WEST WIRRAL CHIROPRACTIC (HM21239) | | ● | | | | | | | | | | | | | | | | | | | | | | | |
| WILLIAMS CHIROPODY SERVICE (HM21530) | ● | | | | | | | | | | | | | | | | | | | | | | | | |
| WILLIAMS, CATHERINE (HM21546) | ● | | | | | | | | | | | | | | | | | | | | | | | | |
| WILLIAMS, T H (HM21597) | ● | | | | | | | | | | | | | | | | | | | | | | | | |
| WILLIAMS, TECWYN H (HM21598) | ● | | | | | | | | | | | | | | | | | | | | | | | | |
| WIRRALL CLINIC (HM21730) | | | | | | | | | | | | | | | | | | | | | | | | | |
| **MIDDLESEX** | | | | | | | | | | | | | | | | | | | | | | | | | |

# A - F Therapies at Practices/Businesses

Business by County with Reference no.

| Business by County with Reference no. | Absent Healing | Acupressure | Acupuncture | Alexander Technique | Allergy Testing | Anthroposohical Med | Aromatherapy | Art Therapy | Aura Therapy | Auricular Therapy | Auto Suggestion | Autogenic Training | Aversion Therapy | Ayurvedic Medicine | Baby Massage | Bach Remedies | Bates Method | Beauty Therapy | Bio-energetics | Biofeedback | Biomagnetic Therapy | Biomechanics | Bonesetting | Bowen Therapy | Chinese Herbal Medicine |
|---|---|---|---|---|---|---|---|---|---|---|---|---|---|---|---|---|---|---|---|---|---|---|---|---|---|
| CLANRICARDE CLINIC (HM04526) | | | | | | | | | | | | | | | | | | | | | | ● | | ● | |
| MIDLANDS (WEST) | | | | | | | | | | | | | | | | | | | | | | | | | |
| 1ST CHIROPRACTIC UK (HM00005) | | | | | | | | | | | | | | | | | | | | | | | | | |
| 1ST CHIROPRACTIC UK (HM00006) | | | | | | | | | | | | | | | | | | | | | | | | | |
| ABBEY CLINIC (HM00077) | | ● | ● | | | | ● | | | | | | | | | | | | | | | | ● | ● | |
| ABBIE HYPNOTHERAPY CENTRE (HM00093) | | | | | | | | | | | | | | | | | | | | | | | | | |
| ACUPOINT MAGNETO CLINIC (HM00223) | | | ● | | | | | | | | | | | | | | | | | | | | | | |
| ACUPUNCTURE CLINIC (HM00257) | | | ● | | | | | | | | | | | | | | | | | | | | | | |
| ACUPUNCTURE HEALTH CLINIC (HM00312) | | | ● | | | | | | | | | | | | | | | | | | | | | | |
| ADAMS, MARGERET REID (HM00355) | | | | | | | ● | | | | | | | | | | | | | | | | | | |
| ALCOCK, E C (HM00490) | | | | | | | | | | | | | | | | | | | | | | ● | | | |
| ALDA HOUSE NATURAL THERAPY (HM00492) | | ● | ● | | | | ● | | | ● | | | | | ● | ● | | | | | | | | ● | |
| ALEXANDER TEACHERS ASSOCIATION (HM00516) | | | | ● | | | | | | | | | | | | | | | | | | | | | |
| ALEXANDER TECHNIQUE (HM00522) | | | | ● | | | | | | | | | | | | | | | | | | | | | |
| ALLEN, ELAINE (HM00608) | | | | | | | ● | | | | | | | | | | | | | | | | | | |
| ARBORETUM/WALSALL CHIROPRACTIC (HM00963) | | | | | | | | | | | | | | | | | | | | | | | | | |
| AROMA SANTE (HM01057) | | | | | | | ● | | | | | | | | | | | | | | | | | | |
| ARROW BANK CHIROPRACTIC CLINIC (HM01149) | | | | | | | | | | | | | | | | | | | | | | | | | |
| ASSOCIATION OF STRESS MNGMT (HM01288) | | | | | | | | | | | ● | | ● | | | | | | | | | | | | |
| BACKCARE & ACUPUNCTURE CLINIC (HM01526) | | ● | ● | | | | | | | | | | | | | | | | | | | | | | |
| BAIRD, MICHAEL (HM01571) | | | ● | | | | | | | | | | | | | | | | | | | | | | |
| BARNT GREEN ACUPUNCTURE CLINIC (HM01771) | | | ● | | | | | | | | | | | | | | | | | | | | | | |
| BEAUTIFORM COLLEGE (HM01992) | | | | | | | | | | | | | | | | | | | | | | | | | |
| BILLINGHAM, S (HM02301) | | | | | | | | | | | | | | | | | | | | | | | | | |
| BIRMINGHAM ACU/CHIRO CLNC (HM02382) | | | ● | | | | | | | | | | | | | | | | | | | | | | |
| BIRMINGHAM HYPNOTHERAPY (HM02386) | | | | | | | ● | | | | | | | | | | | | | | | | | | |
| BIRMINGHAM PHYSIO CLINIC (HM02388) | | | ● | | | | | | | | | | | | | | | | | | | | | | |
| BIRMINGHAM TRAD ACU CENTRE (HM02390) | | | ● | | | | | | | | | | | | | | | | | | | | | | |
| BLAKE, D H (HM02479) | | | ● | | | | | | | | | | | | | | | | | | | | | | |
| BOLDMERE HYPNOTHERAPY (HM02653) | | | | | | | | | | | ● | | ● | | | | | | | ● | | | | | |
| BROWNHILL, D G (HM03257) | | | | | | | | | | | ● | | | | | | | | | | | | | | |
| BTAC (HM03296) | ● | ● | ● | | | | | | ● | | | | | | | | | | | | | | | | |
| BULLOCK, JULIE (HM03344) | | | | | | | | | | | | | | | | | | | | | | | | | |
| BUSY BODIES (HM03472) | | | | | | | ● | | | | | | | | | | | | | | | | | | |

| Business by County with Reference no. | Chiropody | Chiropractic | Clinical Ecology | Cognitive Therapy | Colonic Hydrotherapy | Colour Therapy | Complementary Therapy | Counselling | Cranial Osteopathy | Cranio-Sacral Therapy | Cryo Surgery | Crystal Healing | Cupping | Cymatics | Dance Movement Thrpy | Dietician | Do-In | Douching | Dowsing | Drama Therapy | Electrolipolysis | Electrolysis | Electrotherapy | Encounter Groups | Faith Healing |
|---|---|---|---|---|---|---|---|---|---|---|---|---|---|---|---|---|---|---|---|---|---|---|---|---|---|
| CLANRICARDE CLINIC (HM04526) | ● | | | | | | | | ● | | ● | | | | | | | | | | | | ● | | |
| MIDLANDS (WEST) | | | | | | | | | | | | | | | | | | | | | | | | | |
| 1ST CHIROPRACTIC UK (HM00005) | | ● | | | | | | | | | | | | | | | | | | | | | | | |
| 1ST CHIROPRACTIC UK (HM00006) | | ● | | | | | | | | | | | | | | | | | | | | | | | |
| ABBEY CLINIC (HM00077) | | ● | | | | | | ● | ● | | | | | | | | | | | | | | | | |
| ABBIE HYPNOTHERAPY CENTRE (HM00093) | | | | | | | | ● | | | | | | | | | | | | | | | | | |
| ACUPOINT MAGNETO CLINIC (HM00223) | | | | | | | | | | | | | | | | | | | | | | | | | |
| ACUPUNCTURE CLINIC (HM00257) | | | | | | | | | | | | | | | | | | | | | | | | | |
| ACUPUNCTURE HEALTH CLINIC (HM00312) | | | | | | | | | | | | | | | | | | | | | | | | | |
| ADAMS, MARGERET REID (HM00355) | | | | | | | | | | | | | | | | | | | | | | | | | |
| ALCOCK, E C (HM00490) | ● | | | | | | | | | | | | | | | | | | | | | | | | |
| ALDA HOUSE NATURAL THERAPY (HM00492) | | ● | | | | | | | | | | | | | | | | | ● | | | | | | |
| ALEXANDER TEACHERS ASSOCIATION (HM00516) | | | | | | | | | | | | | | | | | | | | | | | | | |
| ALEXANDER TECHNIQUE (HM00522) | | | | | | | | | | | | | | | | | | | | | | | | | |
| ALLEN, ELAINE (HM00608) | | | | | | | | | | | | | | | | | | | | | | | | | |
| ARBORETUM/WALSALL CHIROPRACTIC (HM00963) | | ● | | | | | | | | | | | | | | | | | | | | | | | |
| AROMA SANTE (HM01057) | | | | | | | | | | | | | | | | | | | | | | | | | |
| ARROW BANK CHIROPRACTIC CLINIC (HM01149) | | ● | | | | | | | | | | | | | | | | | | | | | | | |
| ASSOCIATION OF STRESS MNGMT (HM01288) | | | | ● | | | | ● | | | | | | | | | | | | | | | | | |
| BACKCARE & ACUPUNCTURE CLINIC (HM01526) | ● | | | | | | ● | | ● | | | | | | | | | | | | | | | | |
| BAIRD, MICHAEL (HM01571) | | | | | | | | | | | | | | | | | | | | | | | | | |
| BARNT GREEN ACUPUNCTURE CLINIC (HM01771) | | | | | | | | | | | | | | | | | | | | | | | | | |
| BEAUTIFORM COLLEGE (HM01992) | | | | | | | | | | | | | | | | | | | | | | | ● | | |
| BILLINGHAM, S (HM02301) | ● | | | | | | | | | | | | | | | | | | | | | | | | |
| BIRMINGHAM ACU/CHIRO CLNC (HM02382) | | ● | | | | | | ● | | | | | | | | | | | | | | | | | |
| BIRMINGHAM HYPNOTHERAPY (HM02386) | | | | | | ● | ● | ● | | | | ● | | | | | | | | | | | | | |
| BIRMINGHAM PHYSIO CLINIC (HM02388) | | | | | | | | | | | | | | | | | | | | | | | | | |
| BIRMINGHAM TRAD ACU CENTRE (HM02390) | | | | | | | | | | | | | | | | | | | | | | | | | |
| BLAKE, D H (HM02479) | | | | | | | | | | | | | | | | | | | | | | | | | |
| BOLDMERE HYPNOTHERAPY (HM02653) | | | | | | | | ● | | | | | | | | | | | | | | | | | |
| BROWNHILL, D G (HM03257) | | | | | | | | | | | | | | | | | | | | | | | | | |
| BTAC (HM03296) | | | | | | | | | | | | | ● | | | | | | | | | | ● | | ● |
| BULLOCK, JULIE (HM03344) | ● | | | | | | | | | | | | | | | | | | | | | | | | |
| BUSY BODIES (HM03472) | | | | | | | | | | | | | | | | | | | | | | | | | |

# A - F Therapies at Practices/Businesses

| Business by County with Reference no. | Absent Healing | Acupressure | Acupuncture | Alexander Technique | Allergy Testing | Anthroposohical Med | Aromatherapy | Art Therapy | Aura Therapy | Auricular Therapy | Auto Suggestion | Autogenic Training | Aversion Therapy | Ayurvedic Medicine | Baby Massage | Bach Remedies | Bates Method | Beauty Therapy | Bio-energetics | Biofeedback | Biomagnetic Therapy | Biomechanics | Bonesetting | Bowen Therapy | Chinese Herbal Medicine |
|---|---|---|---|---|---|---|---|---|---|---|---|---|---|---|---|---|---|---|---|---|---|---|---|---|---|
| CALLAGHAN, R M & J (HM03549) | | | | | | | | | | | | | | | | | | | | | | ● | | | |
| CARPENTER, DAVID (HM03727) | | | | | | | | | | | | | | | | | | | | | | | | | |
| CENTRAL CHIROPODY CLINIC (HM03888) | | | | | | | | | | | | | | | | | | | | | | | | | |
| CENTRE FOR NATURAL THERAPIES (HM03913) | | | | | | | ● | | | | | | | | | | | | | | | | | ● | |
| CHAN ACUPUNCTURE (HM03966) | | | ● | | | | | | | | | | | | | | | | | | | | | | |
| CHEER, MARIE (HM04082) | | ● | | | | | ● | | | | | | | | | | | | | | | | | | |
| CHELMSLEY WOOD FOOT CLINIC (HM04086) | | | | | | | ● | | | | | | | | | | | | | | | | | | |
| CHEN, LU (HM04101) | | | ● | | | | | | | | | | | | | | | | | | | | | | |
| CHEYLESMORE PHYSIO CLINIC (HM04147) | | | | | | | | | | | | | | | | | | | | | | | | | |
| CHINESE MEDICINE CENTRE (HM04256) | | | ● | | | | | | | | | | | | | | | | | | | | | | |
| CHIRO MED (HM04283) | | ● | ● | | | | ● | | | | | | | | | | | | | | | | | | |
| CHIROPRACTIC CLINIC (HM04384) | | | | | | | | | | | | | | | | | | | | | | | | | |
| CHIROPRACTIC CLINIC (HM04388) | | | | | | | | | | | | | | | | | | | | | | | | | |
| CHIROPRACTORS OF WARWICK ROAD (HM04407) | | | | | | | | | | | | | | | | | | | | | | | | | |
| CODSALL COMP THERAPIES (HM04778) | | | | | | | ● | | | | | | | | | | | ● | | | | | | ● | |
| COMPLEMENTARY HEALING CENTRE (HM04919) | | | | | | | | | | | | | | | | | | | | | | | | | |
| COMPLEMENTARY MEDICINE CENTRE (HM04937) | | | ● | | | | ● | | | | ● | | ● | | | | | | | | | | | | |
| COTTERIDGE CHIROPRACTIC CLINIC (HM05225) | | | | | | | | | | | | | | | | | | | | | | | | | |
| CREATIVE HEALTH CENTRE (HM05398) | | | ● | ● | | | ● | | | | | | | | | | | | | | | | | | |
| CRYSTAL CLEAR PRACTICE (HM05528) | | | | | | | ● | | | | | | | | | | | | | | | | | | |
| CTIC (HM05535) | | | | | | | ● | | | | | | | | | | | | | | | | | | |
| CTRE-REFLEX & AROMATHERAPY (HM05549) | | | | | | | ● | | | | | | | | | ● | | | | | | | | | |
| DAVIES, BERYL (HM05801) | | | | | | | ● | | | | | | | | | | | | | | | | | | |
| DHANA, P N (HM06053) | | | | | | | | | | | | | | | | | | | | | | ● | | | |
| DUDLEY PHYSIOTHERAPY CLINIC (HM06354) | | | ● | | | | | | | | | | | | | | | | | | | | | | |
| EDGBASTON ACUPUNCTURE CLINIC (HM06597) | | | ● | | | | | | | | | | | | | | | | | | | | | | |
| ELECTROLYSIS CLINIC (HM06718) | | | | | | | | | | | | | | | | | | | | | | | | | |
| ERDINGTHON NATURAL HEALTH CLNC (HM06880) | | | ● | | | | ● | | | | | | | | | | | | | | | | | | |
| ESSENTIAL HEALTH (HM06909) | | | | | | | ● | | | ● | | | | | | | | | | | | | | | |
| FAIRFAX PRIVATE THERAPY (HM07056) | | | | | | | ● | | | | | | | | | | | | | | | | | | |
| FAULKNER, SUSAN (HM07145) | | | | | | | | | | | | | | | | | | | | | | | | | |
| FEWTRELL, SALLY (HM07255) | | | | | | | | | | | | | | | | | | | | | | | | | |
| FLETCHER, VICTOR JOHN (HM07416) | | | | | | | | | | | | | | | | | | | | | | | | | |
| FRESHWINDS CHARITABLE TRUST (HM07740) | | | ● | ● | | | ● | | | | | | | | | | | | | | | | | | |

| Business by County with Reference no. | Chiropody | Chiropractic | Clinical Ecology | Cognitive Therapy | Colonic Hydrotherapy | Colour Therapy | Complementary Therapy | Counselling | Cranial Osteopathy | Cranio-Sacral Therapy | Cryo Surgery | Crystal Healing | Cupping | Cymatics | Dance Movement Thrpy | Dietician | Do-In | Douching | Dowsing | Drama Therapy | Electrolipolysis | Electrolysis | Electrotherapy | Encounter Groups | Faith Healing |
|---|---|---|---|---|---|---|---|---|---|---|---|---|---|---|---|---|---|---|---|---|---|---|---|---|---|
| CALLAGHAN, R M & J (HM03549) | ● | | | | | | | | | | | | | | | | | | | | | | | | |
| CARPENTER, DAVID (HM03727) | | | | | | | | ● | | | | | | | | | | | | | | | | | |
| CENTRAL CHIROPODY CLINIC (HM03888) | ● | | | | | | | | | | | | | | | | | | | | | | | | |
| CENTRE FOR NATURAL THERAPIES (HM03913) | ● | | | | | | | | | | | | | | | | | | | | | | | | |
| CHAN ACUPUNCTURE (HM03966) | | | | | | | | | | | | | | | | | | | | | | | | | |
| CHEER, MARIE (HM04082) | | | | | | | | | | | | | | | | | | | | | | | | | |
| CHELMSLEY WOOD FOOT CLINIC (HM04086) | ● | | | | | | | | | | | | | | | | | | | | | | | | |
| CHEN, LU (HM04101) | | | | | | | | | | | | | | | | | | | | | | | | | |
| CHEYLESMORE PHYSIO CLINIC (HM04147) | | | | | | | | | | | | | | | | | | | | | | | ● | | |
| CHINESE MEDICINE CENTRE (HM04256) | | | | | | | | | | | | | | | | | | | | | | | | | |
| CHIRO MED (HM04283) | | ● | | ● | | | ● | ● | | | | | ● | | | | | | | | | | | | |
| CHIROPRACTIC CLINIC (HM04384) | | ● | | | | | | | | | | | | | | | | | | | | | | | |
| CHIROPRACTIC CLINIC (HM04388) | | ● | | | | | | | | | | | | | | | | | | | | | | | |
| CHIROPRACTORS OF WARWICK ROAD (HM04407) | | ● | | | | | | | | | | | | | | | | | | | | | | | |
| CODSALL COMP THERAPIES (HM04778) | ● | | | | | | | | | | | | | | | | | | | | | | | | |
| COMPLEMENTARY HEALING CENTRE (HM04919) | | | | | | | | | | | | ● | | | | | | | | | | | | | |
| COMPLEMENTARY MEDICINE CENTRE (HM04937) | | | | | | | | | | | | | | | | | | | | | | | | | |
| COTTERIDGE CHIROPRACTIC CLINIC (HM05225) | | ● | | | | | | | | | | | | | | | | | | | | | | | |
| CREATIVE HEALTH CENTRE (HM05398) | | | | | | | | ● | | | | | | | | | | | | | | | | | |
| CRYSTAL CLEAR PRACTICE (HM05528) | | | | | | | | | | | | | | | | | | | | | | | | | |
| CTIC (HM05535) | | | | | | | | | | | | | | | | | | | | | | | | | |
| CTRE-REFLEX & AROMATHERAPY (HM05549) | | | | | | | | | | | | | | | | | | | | | | | | | |
| DAVIES, BERYL (HM05801) | | | | | | | | | | | | | | | | | | | | | | | | | |
| DHANA, P N (HM06053) | ● | | | | | | | | | | | | | | | | | | | | | | | | |
| DUDLEY PHYSIOTHERAPY CLINIC (HM06354) | | | | | | | | | | | | | | | | | | | | | | | | | |
| EDGBASTON ACUPUNCTURE CLINIC (HM06597) | | | | | | | | | | | | | | | | | | | | | | | | | |
| ELECTROLYSIS CLINIC (HM06718) | | | | | | | | | | | | | | | | | | | | | | ● | | | |
| ERDINGTHON NATURAL HEALTH CLNC (HM06880) | | | | | | | | | | | | | | | | | | | | | | | | | |
| ESSENTIAL HEALTH (HM06909) | | | | | | | | | | | | | | | | | | | | | | | | | |
| FAIRFAX PRIVATE THERAPY (HM07056) | | | | | | | | | | | | | | | | | | | | | | | | | |
| FAULKNER, SUSAN (HM07145) | | ● | | | | | | | | | | | | | | | | | | | | | | | |
| FEWTRELL, SALLY (HM07255) | ● | | | | | | | | | | | | | | | | | | | | | | | | |
| FLETCHER, VICTOR JOHN (HM07416) | ● | | | | | | | | | | | | | | | | | | | | | | | | |
| FRESHWINDS CHARITABLE TRUST (HM07740) | | ● | | | | | | ● | | | | | | | | | | | | | | | | | |

www.healthmyself.com

# A - F Therapies at Practices/Businesses

| Business by County with Reference no. | Absent Healing | Acupressure | Acupuncture | Alexander Technique | Allergy Testing | Anthroposohical Med | Aromatherapy | Art Therapy | Aura Therapy | Auricular Therapy | Auto Suggestion | Autogenic Training | Aversion Therapy | Ayurvedic Medicine | Baby Massage | Bach Remedies | Bates Method | Beauty Therapy | Bio-enērgetics | Biofeedback | Biomagnetic Therapy | Biomechanics | Bonesetting | Bowen Therapy | Chinese Herbal Medicine |
|---|---|---|---|---|---|---|---|---|---|---|---|---|---|---|---|---|---|---|---|---|---|---|---|---|---|
| GAYNOR BULLER CLINIC (HM07945) | | | ● | | | | | | | | | | | | | | | | | | | | | | |
| GOLDEN PALMS (HM08207) | | ● | | | | | ● | | | | | | | | | | | | | | | | | ● | |
| GREEN VALLEY THERAPY CENTRE (HM08443) | | | ● | | ● | | ● | | | | | | | | | | | | | | | | | ● | |
| GREIG, ELIZABETH (HM08528) | | | | | | | ● | | | | | | | | | | | | | | | | | | |
| GROVES, MURIEL (HM08615) | | | | | | | | | | | | | | | | ● | | | | | | | | | |
| GURPAL SINGH AROMA/REFLEX (HM08655) | | | | | | | ● | | | | | | | | | | | | | | | | | | |
| HAGLEY CENTRE OF COMP MED (HM08701) | | | ● | | | | ● | | | | | | | | | ● | | | | | | | | | |
| HALL GREEN ALTERN PRACTICE (HM08760) | | | | | | | | | | | | | | | | ● | | | | | | | | | |
| HALL, SUSAN (HM08790) | | | | | | | | | | | | | | | | | | | | | | | | | |
| HARTNESS, R (HM09149) | | | | | | | | | | | | | | | | | | | | | | ● | | | |
| HAYES, ANN (HM09257) | | | | | | | ● | | | | | | | | | | | | | | | | | | |
| HEALTH SHOP (HM09402) | | | | | | | ● | | | | | | | | | ● | | | | | | | | | |
| HEAVEN SCENT (HM09474) | | | | | | | ● | | | | | | | | | | | | | | | | | | |
| HIGGS, R W (HM09737) | | | | | | | | | | | | | | | | | | | | | | | | | |
| HILLFIELDS HEALTH CENTRE (HM09795) | | | | | | | | | | | | | | | | | | | | | | | | | |
| HOGG, DEBBI (HM09913) | ● | | | | ● | | | | | | | | | | | | | | | | | | | ● | |
| HOLISTIC HEALTH CENTRE (HM09972) | | | | | | | | | ● | | | | | | | ● | | | | | | | | | |
| HOLISTICLY YOURS (HM10003) | | | | | | | ● | | | | | | | | | | | | | | | | | | |
| HOLLOWAY, P (HM10027) | | | | | | | ● | | | | | | | | | | | | | | | | | | |
| HOLLY COTTAGE CHIRO CLINIC (HM10029) | | | | | | | | | | | | | | | | | | | | | | | | | |
| INGRAM, CLARE (HM10624) | | ● | ● | | | | | | | | | | | | | ● | | | | | | | | | |
| INNERSENSE (HM10647) | | | | | | | ● | | | | | | | | | | | ● | | | | | | | |
| J BENSON CHIROPODIST (HM10793) | | | | | | | | | | | | | | | | | | | | | | | | | |
| JING YING WANG (HM11034) | | | ● | | | | | | | | | | | | | | | | | | | | | | |
| JOHNSON FOOTCARE (HM11061) | | | | | | | | | | | | | | | | | | | | | | | | | |
| KEVIN FISHER CHIROPODY (HM11573) | | | | | | | | | | | | | | | | | | | | | | | | | |
| KUAN YING, LIM (HM11814) | | | ● | | | | | | | | | | | | | | | | | | | | | | |
| LANDER, EILEEN (HM11923) | | | | | | | ● | | | | | | | | | | | | | | | | | | |
| LEESON, CHRISTINE (HM12171) | | | ● | | | | | | | | | | | | | | | | | | | | | | |
| LEWIS, MYRA (HM12305) | | | | | | | ● | | | | | | | | | | | | | | | | | | |
| LIFE'S OPTION (HM12358) | | | | | | | ● | | | | | | | | | | | | | | | | | | |
| LONGFORD PHYSIO & SPORTS (HM12627) | | | ● | | | | | | | | | | | | | | | | | | | | | | |
| MANION, D (HM13014) | | | ● | | | | | | | | | | | | | | | | | | | | | | |
| MAPES, JANET (HM13059) | | | | | | | ● | | | | | | | | | ● | | | | | | | | | |

| Business by County with Reference no. | Chiropody | Chiropractic | Clinical Ecology | Cognitive Therapy | Colonic Hydrotherapy | Colour Therapy | Complementary Therapy | Counselling | Cranial Osteopathy | Cranio-Sacral Therapy | Cryo Surgery | Crystal Healing | Cupping | Cymatics | Dance Movement Thrpy | Dietician | Do-In | Douching | Dowsing | Drama Therapy | Electrolipolysis | Electrolysis | Electrotherapy | Encounter Groups | Faith Healing |
|---|---|---|---|---|---|---|---|---|---|---|---|---|---|---|---|---|---|---|---|---|---|---|---|---|---|
| GAYNOR BULLER CLINIC (HM07945) | | | | | | | | | | | | | | | | | | | | | | | | | |
| GOLDEN PALMS (HM08207) | | | | | | | | | | | | | | | | | | | | | | | | | |
| GREEN VALLEY THERAPY CENTRE (HM08443) | | | | | | | | ● | | | | | | | | | | | | | | | | | |
| GREIG, ELIZABETH (HM08528) | | | | | | | | | | | | | | | | | | | | | | | | | |
| GROVES, MURIEL (HM08615) | | | | | | | | | | | | | | | | | | | | | | | | | |
| GURPAL SINGH AROMA/REFLEX (HM08655) | | | | | | | | | | | | | | | | | | | | | | | | | |
| HAGLEY CENTRE OF COMP MED (HM08701) | | ● | | | | | ● | ● | | | | | | | | | | | | | | | | | |
| HALL GREEN ALTERN PRACTICE (HM08760) | | | | | | | | | | | | | | | | | | | | | | | | | |
| HALL, SUSAN (HM08790) | ● | | | | | | | | | | | | | | | | | | | | | | | | |
| HARTNESS, R (HM09149) | ● | | | | | | | | | | ● | | | | | | | | | | | | | | |
| HAYES, ANN (HM09257) | | | | | | | | | | | | | | | | | | | | | | | | | |
| HEALTH SHOP (HM09402) | | | | | | | | | | | | | | | | | | | | | | | | | |
| HEAVEN SCENT (HM09474) | | | | | | | | | | | | | | | | | | | | | | | | | |
| HIGGS, R W (HM09737) | ● | | | | | | | | | | | | | | | | | | | | | | | | |
| HILLFIELDS HEALTH CENTRE (HM09795) | ● | | | | | | | | | | | | | | | | | | | | | | | | |
| HOGG, DEBBI (HM09913) | | | | | | | ● | | | | | | | | | | | | | | | | | | |
| HOLISTIC HEALTH CENTRE (HM09972) | | | | | | | | ● | | | | | | | | | | | | | | | | | |
| HOLISTICLY YOURS (HM10003) | | | | | | | | | | | | | | | | | | | | | | | | | |
| HOLLOWAY, P (HM10027) | | | | | | | | | | | | | | | | | | | | | | | | | |
| HOLLY COTTAGE CHIRO CLINIC (HM10029) | | ● | | | | | | | | | | | | | | | | | | | | | | | |
| INGRAM, CLARE (HM10624) | | | | | | | | | | | | | | | | | | | ● | | | | | | |
| INNERSENSE (HM10647) | | | | | | | | | | | | ● | | | | | | | | | | | | | |
| J BENSON CHIROPODIST (HM10793) | ● | | | | | | | | | | | | | | | | | | | | | | | | |
| JING YING WANG (HM11034) | | | | | | | | | | | | | | | | | | | | | | | | | |
| JOHNSON FOOTCARE (HM11061) | ● | | | | | | | | | | | | | | | | | | | | | | | | |
| KEVIN FISHER CHIROPODY (HM11573) | ● | | | | | | | | | | | | | | | | | | | | | | | | |
| KUAN YING, LIM (HM11814) | | | | | | | | | | | | | | | | | | | | | | | | | |
| LANDER, EILEEN (HM11923) | | | | | | | | | | | | | | | | | | | | | | | | | |
| LEESON, CHRISTINE (HM12171) | | | | | | | | | | | | | | | | | | | | | | | | | |
| LEWIS, MYRA (HM12305) | | | | | | | | | | | | | | | | | | | | | | | | | |
| LIFE'S OPTION (HM12358) | | | | | | | | | | | | | | | | | | | | | | | | | |
| LONGFORD PHYSIO & SPORTS (HM12627) | | | | | | | | | | | | | | | | | | | | | | | ● | | |
| MANION, D (HM13014) | | | | | | | | | | | | | | | | | | | | | | | | | |
| MAPES, JANET (HM13059) | | | | | | | | | | | | | | | | | | | | | | | | | |

# A - F Therapies at Practices/Businesses

| Business by County with Reference no. | Absent Healing | Acupressure | Acupuncture | Alexander Technique | Allergy Testing | Anthroposohical Med | Aromatherapy | Art Therapy | Aura Therapy | Auricular Therapy | Auto Suggestion | Autogenic Training | Aversion Therapy | Ayurvedic Medicine | Baby Massage | Bach Remedies | Bates Method | Beauty Therapy | Bio-energetics | Biofeedback | Biomagnetic Therapy | Biomechanics | Bonesetting | Bowen Therapy | Chinese Herbal Medicine | Chiropody | Chiropractic | Clinical Ecology | Cognitive Therapy | Colonic Hydrotherapy | Colour Therapy | Complementary Therapy | Counselling | Cranial Osteopathy | Cranio-Sacral Therapy | Cryo Surgery | Crystal Healing | Cupping | Cymatics | Dance Movement Thrpy | Dietician | Do-In | Douching | Dowsing | Drama Therapy | Electrolipolysis | Electrolysis | Electrotherapy | Encounter Groups | Faith Healing |
|---|---|---|---|---|---|---|---|---|---|---|---|---|---|---|---|---|---|---|---|---|---|---|---|---|---|---|---|---|---|---|---|---|---|---|---|---|---|---|---|---|---|---|---|---|---|---|---|---|---|---|
| MARTINS, P (HM13217) | | | | ● | | | | | | | | | | | | | | | | | | | | | | | | | | | | | | | | | | | | | | | | | | | | | | |
| MCNEILL, MARGARET (HM13583) | | | ● | | | | | | | | | | | | | | | | | | | | | | | | | | | | | | | | | | | | | | | | | | | | | | | |
| MCNEILL, MARGARET (HM13584) | | | ● | | | | | | | | | | | | | | | | | | | | | | | | | | | | | | | | | | | | | | | | | | | | | | | |
| MIDLAND HYPNOTHERAPY CENTRE (HM13831) | | | | | | | | | | | ● | ● | | | | | | | | | | | | | | | | | | | | | ● | | | | | | | | | | | | | | | | | |
| MIDLAND MEDICAL OSTEO PRACTICE (HM13836) | | | ● | | | | | | | | | | | | | | | | | | | | | | | | | | | | | | | | | | | | | | | | | | | | | | | |
| MIDLAND MEDICAL OSTEO PRACTICE (HM13835) | | | ● | | | | | | | | | | | | | | | | | | | | | | | | | | | | | | | | | | | | | | | | | | | | | | | |
| MIDLAND MEDICAL OSTEO PRACTICE (HM13837) | | | ● | | | | | | | | | | | | | | | | | | | | | | | | | | | | | | | | | | | | | | | | | | | | | | | |
| MILLER, VALERIE (HM13905) | | | | | | | | | | | | | | | | ● | | | | | | | | | | | | | | | | | | | | | | | | | | | | | | | | | | |
| MORGAN, VALERIE (HM14177) | | | ● | | | | | | | | | | | | | ● | | | | | | | | ● | | | | | | | | | | | | | | | | | | | | | | | | | | |
| MORRIS, CLAIRE (HM14202) | | | | | | | | | | | | | | | | | | | | | | | | | | ● | | | | | | | | | | | | | | | | | | | | | | | | |
| MORRIS, CYNTHIA (HM14204) | | | | | | | ● | | | | | | | | | | | | | | | | | | | | | | | | | | | | | | | | | | | | | | | | | | | |
| MYATT, ANITA (HM14432) | | | | | ● | | ● | | | | | | | | | | | | | | | | | | | | | | | | | | | | | | ● | | | | | | | | | | | | | |
| NATURAL CHOICE (HM14522) | | | | | | | ● | | | | | | | | | | | | | | | | | | | | | | | | | | | | | | | | | | | | | | | | | | | |
| NATURAL HARMONY (HM14531) | | | ● | | | | | | | | | | | | | | | | | | | | | | | | | | | | | | | | | | | | | | | | | | | | | | | |
| NATURAL HEALTH CENTRE (HM14574) | | | ● | | | | | | | | | | | | | | | | | | | | | | | | | | | | | | | | | | | | | | | | | | | | | | | |
| NATURAL WAY AROMATHERAPY (HM14668) | | | | | | | ● | | | | | | | | | | | | | | | | | | | | | | | | | | | | | | | | | | | | | | | | | | | |
| NAYLOR, ESTER (HM14715) | | | | | | | | | | | | | | | | ● | | | | | | | | | | | | | | | | | | | | | | | | | | | | | | | | | | |
| NEWBRIDGE PHARMACY (HM14850) | | | ● | | | ● | ● | | | | | | | | | ● | | | | | | | | ● | | | | | | | | ● | | | | | | | | | | | | | | | | ● | | |
| NUTMEG CLINIC (HM15115) | | | | | | | ● | | | | | | | | | | | | | | | | | | | | | | | | | | | | | | | | | | | | | | | | | | | |
| OLD HOUSE CLINIC (HM15258) | | | ● | | | | | | | | | | | | | | | | | | | | | | | | | | | | | | | | | | | | | | | | | | | | | | | |
| OLIVER, BETTY (HM15287) | | | | | | | ● | | | | | | | | | | | | | | | | | | | | | | | | | | | | | | | | | | | | | | | | | | | |
| OULTON FOOT CLINIC (HM15499) | | | | | | | | | | | | | | | | | | | | | | | | | | ● | | | | | | | | | | | | | | | | | | | | | | | | |
| PARK PRACTICE (HM15672) | | | ● | | | | ● | | | | | | | | | | | | | | | | | | | ● | | | | | | | | | | | | | | | | | | | | | | | | |
| PARKES, J (HM15710) | | | | | | | ● | | | | | | | | | | | | | | | | | | | | | | | | | | | | | | | | | | | | | | | | | | | |
| PHYSIOTHERAPY CLINIC (HM16241) | | | ● | | | | | | | | | | | | | | | | | | | | | | | | | | | | | | | | | | | | | | | | | | | | | | | |
| PIKE, ELIZABETH G & J K (HM16286) | | | | | | | | | | | | | | | | | | | | | | | | | | ● | | | | | | | | | | | | | | | | | | | | | | | | |
| PILLATH, CHRISTINE (HM16297) | | | | ● | | | | | | | | | | | | | | | | | | | | | | | | | | | | | | | | | | | | | | | | | | | | | | |
| PLANT, ALISON () | | | | | | | ● | | | | | | | | | | | | | | | | | | | | | | | | | | | | | | | | | | | | | | | | | | | |
| PRISM THERAPIES (HM16636) | | ● | | | | | | | | | | | | | | | | | | | | | | | | | | | | | | | | | | | | | | | | | | | | | | | | |
| PURPLE FLAME AROMATHERAPY (HM16770) | | | | | | | ● | | | | | | | | | | | | | | | | | | | | | | | | | | | | | | | | | | | | | | | | | | | |
| RENAISSANCE HOLISTIC THRPY (HM17180) | | | | | | | ● | | | | | | | | | | | | | | | | | | | | | | | | | | | | | | | | | | | | | | | | | | | |
| REVIVAL HOLISTIC THERAPY CTRE (HM17206) | | | | | | | ● | | | | | | | | | ● | | | | | | | | | | | | | | | | | | | | | | | | | | | | | | | | | | |
| RICHARDSON, CYRIL (HM17273) | | | | | | | | | | | | | | | | | | | | | | | | | | ● | | | | | | | | | | | | | | | | | | | | | | | | |
| RITA (HM17371) | | | | | | | ● | | | | | | | | | | | | | | | | | | | | | | | | | | | | | | | | | | | | | | | | | | | |

# A - F Therapies at Practices/Businesses

| Business by County with Reference no. | Absent Healing | Acupressure | Acupuncture | Alexander Technique | Allergy Testing | Anthroposohical Med | Aromatherapy | Art Therapy | Aura Therapy | Auricular Therapy | Auto Suggestion | Autogenic Training | Aversion Therapy | Ayurvedic Medicine | Baby Massage | Bach Remedies | Bates Method | Beauty Therapy | Bio-energetics | Biofeedback | Biomagnetic Therapy | Biomechanics | Bonesetting | Bowen Therapy | Chinese Herbal Medicine |
|---|---|---|---|---|---|---|---|---|---|---|---|---|---|---|---|---|---|---|---|---|---|---|---|---|---|
| RIVER-MOON (HM17376) | | | | | | | ● | | | | | | | | | | | | | | | | | | |
| ROBINSON, JOHN (HM17484) | | | | | | | | | | | | | | | | | | | | | | | | | |
| ROMSLEY PHYSIOTHERAPY PRACTICE (HM17578) | | | ● | | | | ● | | | | | | | | | | | | | | | | | | |
| ROUSSEAU, JAMES (HM17676) | | | | | | | | | | | | | | | | | | | | | | | | | |
| SCHOFIELD, SHEILA (HM18022) | | | ● | | | | | | | | | | | | | | | | | | | | | | |
| SEN-GUPTA, (DR) (HM18225) | | | ● | | | | | | | | | | | | | | | | | | | | | | |
| SENSATIONS AROMATHERAPY (HM18227) | | | | | | | ● | | | | | | | | | | | | | | | | | | |
| SHANGRI-LA ACUPUNCTURE CLINIC (HM18282) | | | ● | | | | | | | | | | | | | | | | | | | | | | |
| SHERBOURNE CLINIC (HM18427) | | | ● | | | | | | | | | | | | | | | | | | | | | | |
| SHUTTLEWORTH, JACK (HM18517) | | | | | | | | | | | | | | | | | | | | | | | | | |
| SIDHOM, A (HM18529) | | | ● | | | | | | | | | | | | | | | | | | | | | | |
| SOLIHULL CHIROPRACTIC CLINIC (HM18872) | | | | | | | | | | | | | | | | | | | | | | | | | |
| SOMEWAY HERBAL CLINIC (HM18883) | | | ● | | | | | | | | | | | | | | | | | | | | | | |
| ST PAULS OSTEOPATHY PRACTICE (HM19094) | ● | | ● | | | | ● | | | | | | | | | ● | | | | | | | | | |
| STOURBRIDGE CHIROPRACTIC (HM19357) | | | | | | | | | | | | | | | | | | | | | | | | | |
| STRANKS, KATHY (HM19368) | | | | | | | | | | | | | | | | | | | | | | | | | |
| SUCCESSWORKS (HM19461) | ● | | | | | | | | | | | | | | | | | | | | | | | | |
| SUTTON COLDFIELD HEALTH CLINIC (HM19544) | | | ● | | | | | | | | | | | | | | | | | | | | | | |
| TAYLOR, CLARE (HM19748) | | | | | | | ● | | | | | | | | | | | | | | | | | | |
| WALL, HELEN (HM20815) | | | ● | | | | | | | | | | | | | | | | | | | | | | |
| WALSALL CHIROPRACTIC HEALTH (HM20851) | | | | | | | | | | | | | | | | | | | | | | | | | |
| WALSALL PHYSIOTHERAPY CLINIC (HM20853) | | | ● | | | | | | | | | | | | | | | | | | | | | | |
| WALSGRAVE CHIROPRACTIC CLINIC (HM20855) | | | | | | | | | | | | | | | | | | | | | | | | | |
| WELL NATURAL HEALTH CENTRE (HM21139) | | | ● | | ● | | ● | | | ● | | | | | | | | | | | | | | ● | |
| WELL NATURAL HEALTH CENTRE (HM21140) | | | ● | ● | ● | | ● | | | | | | | | | | | | | | | | | ● | |
| WEST MIDLAND HYPNOTHERAPY (HM21229) | ● | | | | | | | | | | ● | | | | | ● | | | | | | | | | |
| WESTON, JOHN (HM21278) | | | ● | | | | | | | | | | | | | | | | | | | | ● | | |
| WHITEHALL, CAROL (HM21385) | | | | | | | | | | | | | | | | | | | | | | | | | |
| WILLOWS CLNC COMP HEALTH CTRE (HM21630) | | ● | ● | | | | ● | | | | | | | | | | | | | | | | | | |
| WOLVERHAMPTON CHINESE MED CTRE (HM21765) | | | ● | | | | | | | | | | | | | | | | | | | | | | |
| ZEN HEALTH & BEAUTY (HM22099) | | | | | | | ● | | | | | | | | | | | | | | | | | | |
| **NORFOLK** | | | | | | | | | | | | | | | | | | | | | | | | | |
| A P B ACUPUNCTURE PRACTICE (HM00041) | | | ● | | | | | | | | | | | | | | | | | | | | | | |
| ALDERBURY CLINIC (HM00500) | | | ● | | | | | | | | | | | | | | | | | | | | | | |

| Business by County with Reference no. | Chiropody | Chiropractic | Clinical Ecology | Cognitive Therapy | Colonic Hydrotherapy | Colour Therapy | Complementary Therapy | Counselling | Cranial Osteopathy | Cranio-Sacral Therapy | Cryo Surgery | Crystal Healing | Cupping | Cymatics | Dance Movement Thrpy | Dietician | Do-In | Douching | Dowsing | Drama Therapy | Electrolipolysis | Electrolysis | Electrotherapy | Encounter Groups | Faith Healing |
|---|---|---|---|---|---|---|---|---|---|---|---|---|---|---|---|---|---|---|---|---|---|---|---|---|---|
| RIVER-MOON (HM17376) | | | | | | | | | | | | | | | | | | | | | | | | | |
| ROBINSON, JOHN (HM17484) | ● | | | | | | | | | | | | | | | | | | | | | | | | |
| ROMSLEY PHYSIOTHERAPY PRACTICE (HM17578) | | | | | | | | | | | | | | | | | | | | | | | ● | | |
| ROUSSEAU, JAMES (HM17676) | | ● | | | | | | | | | | | | | | | | | | | | | | | |
| SCHOFIELD, SHEILA (HM18022) | | | | | | | | | | | | | | | | | | | | | | | | | |
| SEN-GUPTA, (DR) (HM18225) | | | | | | | | | | | | | | | | | | | | | | | | | |
| SENSATIONS AROMATHERAPY (HM18227) | | | | | | | | | | | | | | | | | | | | | | | | | |
| SHANGRI-LA ACUPUNCTURE CLINIC (HM18282) | | | | | | | | | | | | | | | | | | | | | | | | | |
| SHERBOURNE CLINIC (HM18427) | | | | | | | | | | | | | | | | | | | | | | | | | |
| SHUTTLEWORTH, JACK (HM18517) | | ● | | | | | | | | | | | | | | | | | | | | | | | |
| SIDHOM, A (HM18529) | | | | | | | | | | | | | | | | | | | | | | | | | |
| SOLIHULL CHIROPRACTIC CLINIC (HM18872) | | ● | | | | | | | | | | | | | | | | | | | | | | | |
| SOMEWAY HERBAL CLINIC (HM18883) | | | | | | | | | | | | | | | | | | | | | | | | | |
| ST PAULS OSTEOPATHY PRACTICE (HM19094) | | | | | | | | | ● | | | | | | | | | | | | | | ● | | |
| STOURBRIDGE CHIROPRACTIC (HM19357) | | ● | | | | | | | | | | | | | | | | | | | | | | | |
| STRANKS, KATHY (HM19368) | | | | | | | | ● | | | | | | | | | | | | | | | | | |
| SUCCESSWORKS (HM19461) | | | | | | | ● | ● | | | | | | | | | | | | | | | | | |
| SUTTON COLDFIELD HEALTH CLINIC (HM19544) | | | | | | | | | | | | | ● | | | | | | | | | | | | |
| TAYLOR, CLARE (HM19748) | | | | | | | | | | | | | | | | | | | | | | | | | |
| WALL, HELEN (HM20815) | | | | | | | | | | | | | | | | | | | | | | | | | |
| WALSALL CHIROPRACTIC HEALTH (HM20851) | | ● | | | | | | | | | | | | | | | | | | | | | | | |
| WALSALL PHYSIOTHERAPY CLINIC (HM20853) | | | | | | | | | | | | | | | | | | | | | | | | | |
| WALSGRAVE CHIROPRACTIC CLINIC (HM20855) | | ● | | | | | | | | | | | | | | | | | | | | | | | |
| WELL NATURAL HEALTH CENTRE (HM21139) | ● | ● | | | | | | ● | ● | | | | | | | | | | | | | | | | |
| WELL NATURAL HEALTH CENTRE (HM21140) | | ● | | | | | ● | ● | ● | | | | | | | | | | | | | | | | |
| WEST MIDLAND HYPNOTHERAPY (HM21229) | | | | | | | | ● | | | | | | | | | | | | | | | | | |
| WESTON, JOHN (HM21278) | | | | | | | ● | | | | | | | | | | | | | | | | ● | | |
| WHITEHALL, CAROL (HM21385) | ● | | | | | | | | | | | | | | | | | | | | | | | | |
| WILLOWS CLNC COMP HEALTH CTRE (HM21630) | ● | | | | | | ● | ● | ● | | | | ● | | | | | | | | | | | | |
| WOLVERHAMPTON CHINESE MED CTRE (HM21765) | | | | | | | | | | | | | | | | | | | | | | | | | |
| ZEN HEALTH & BEAUTY (HM22099) | | | | | | | | | | | | | | | | | | | | | | | | | |
| **NORFOLK** | | | | | | | | | | | | | | | | | | | | | | | | | |
| A P B ACUPUNCTURE PRACTICE (HM00041) | | | | | | | | | | | | | | | | | | | | | | | | | |
| ALDERBURY CLINIC (HM00500) | | | | | | | | | | | | | | | | | | | | | | | | | |

# A - F Therapies at Practices/Businesses

| Business by County with Reference no. | Absent Healing | Acupressure | Acupuncture | Alexander Technique | Allergy Testing | Anthroposohical Med | Aromatherapy | Art Therapy | Aura Therapy | Auricular Therapy | Auto Suggestion | Autogenic Training | Aversion Therapy | Ayurvedic Medicine | Baby Massage | Bach Remedies | Bates Method | Beauty Therapy | Bio-energetics | Biofeedback | Biomagnetic Therapy | Biomechanics | Bonesetting | Bowen Therapy | Chinese Herbal Medicine | Chiropody | Chiropractic | Clinical Ecology | Cognitive Therapy | Colonic Hydrotherapy | Colour Therapy | Complementary Therapy | Counselling | Cranial Osteopathy | Cranio-Sacral Therapy | Cryo Surgery | Crystal Healing | Cupping | Cymatics | Dance Movement Thrpy | Dietician | Do-In | Douching | Dowsing | Drama Therapy | Electrolipolysis | Electrolysis | Electrotherapy | Encounter Groups | Faith Healing |
|---|---|---|---|---|---|---|---|---|---|---|---|---|---|---|---|---|---|---|---|---|---|---|---|---|---|---|---|---|---|---|---|---|---|---|---|---|---|---|---|---|---|---|---|---|---|---|---|---|---|---|
| ALEXANDER TECHNIQUE (HM00529) | | | | ● | | | | | | | | | | | | | | | | | | | | | | | | | | | | | | | | | | | | | | | | | | | | | | |
| AMALA CHIROPODY CENTRE (HM00760) | | | | | | | | | | | | | | | | | | | | | | ● | | | | ● | | | | | | | | | | | | | | | | | | | | | | | | |
| BIRD, C (HM02357) | | | | | | | ● | | | | | | | | | | | | | | | | | | | | | | | | | | | | | | | | | | | | | | | | | | | |
| BODY BEAUTIFUL (HM02576) | | | | | | | ● | | | | | | | | | | | | | | | | | | | | | | | | | | | | | | | | | | | | | | | | | | | |
| CARSON, KAREN (HM03770) | | | | | | | | | | | | | | | | | | | | | | | | | | ● | | | | | | | | | | | | | | | | | | | | | | | | |
| CHANDLER, ANN (HM03973) | | | ● | | | | | | | | | | | | | | | | | | | | | | | | | | | | | | | | | | | | | | | | | | | | | | | |
| CHASE PARK PRACTICE (HM04060) | | | | | | | | | | | | | | | | | | | | | | | | | | | | | | | | | ● | | | | | | | | | | | | | | | | | |
| CHIROPODIST (HM04291) | | | | | | | | | | | | | | | | | | | | | | | | | | ● | | | | | | | | | | | | | | | | | | | | | | | | |
| CHIROPODISTS (HM04297) | | | | | | | | | | | | | | | | | | | | | | | | | | ● | | | | | | | | | | | | | | | | | | | | | | | | |
| CLASSICAL OSTEOPATH (HM04611) | ● | ● | | | | | ● | | | | | | | | | | | | | | | | | | | | | | | | | ● | | ● | | | | | | | | | | | | | | | | ● |
| COMPLEMENTARY HEALTH CLINIC (HM04926) | | | ● | | | | ● | | | | | | | | | | | | | | | | | | | | | | | | | | | ● | | | | | | | | | | | | | | | | |
| COTTAGE CHIROPRACTIC CLINIC (HM05217) | | | | | | | | | | | | | | | | | | | | | | | | | | | ● | | | | | | | | | | | | | | | | | | | | | | | |
| DICKINS, BEVERLEY (HM06072) | | | ● | | | | | | | | | | | | | | | | | | | | | | | | | | | | | | | | | | | | | | | | | | | | | | | |
| DISS NATURAL HEALTH CLINIC (HM06121) | | | ● | | | | | | | | | | | | | ● | | | | | | | | | | | | | ● | | | ● | | ● | | | | | | | ● | | | | | | | | | |
| DOWNS, TINA (HM06254) | | | | | | | ● | | | | | | | | | | | | | | | | | | | | | | | | | | | | | | | | | | | | | | | | | | | |
| DUNCANSON, S (HM06397) | | | | ● | | | | | | | | | | | | | | | | | | | | | | | | | | | | | | | | | | | | | | | | | | | | | | |
| ELEMENTS OF HEALTH (HM06725) | | | ● | | | | ● | | | | | | | | | | | | | | | | | | | | | | | | | | ● | | | | | | | | | | | | | | | | | |
| ELLIS, STEPHEN (HM06772) | | | ● | | | | | | | | | | | | | | | | | | | | | | | | | | | | | | | | | | | | | | | | | | | | | | | |
| FARRANT, A (HM07118) | | | ● | | | | | | | | | | | | | | | | | | | | | | | | | | | | | | | | | | | | | | | | | | | | | | | |
| FARRANT, A F (HM07120) | | | ● | | | | | | | | | | | | | | | | | | | | | | | | | | | | | | | | | | | | | | | | | | | | | | | |
| FIRST STEP FOOTCARE (HM07340) | | | | | | | | | | | | | | | | | | | | | | ● | | | | ● | | | | | | | | | | | | | | | | | | | | | | | | |
| FISHER, JACK E (HM07355) | | | | | | | | | | | | | | | | | | | | | | | | | | | | | | | | | | | | | | | | | | | | | | | | ● | | |
| FOLKER, N (HM07459) | | | | | | | | | | | | | | | | | | | | | | | | | | | ● | | | | | | | | | | | | | | | | | | | | | | | |
| GEARY, A G (HM07951) | | | | | | | | | | | | | | | | | | | | | | ● | | | | ● | | | | | | | | | | | | | | | | | | | | | | | | |
| GT YARMOUTH PHYSICAL THERAPY (HM08330) | | | | | | | | | | | | | | | | | | | | | | | | | | | | | | | | | | | | | | | | | | | | | | | | ● | | |
| HARGHAM HALL OSTEO PRACTICE (HM08992) | | | | | | | | | | | | | | | | | | | | | | | | | | | | | | | | | | ● | | | | | | | | | | | | | | | | |
| HARLESTON CHIROPRACTIC CLINIC (HM08998) | | | | | | | | | | | | | | | | | | | | | | | | | | | ● | | | | | | | | | | | | | | | | | | | | | | | |
| HELLY'S HERBAL PRODUCTS (HM09524) | | | | | | | ● | | | | | | | | | | | | | | | | | | | | | | | | | | | | | | | | | | | | | | | | | | | |
| HOBSON, L A (HM09865) | | | | | | | | | | | | | | | | | | | | | | | | | | ● | | | | | | | | | | | | | | | | | | | | | | | | |
| HOMEOPATHIC CLINIC (HM10074) | | | | | | | ● | | | | | | | | | ● | | | | | | | | | | | | | | | | ● | | | | | ● | | | | ● | | | | | | | | | ● |
| JAMES, LINDA (HM10890) | | | | | | | ● | | | | | | | | | | | | | | | | | | | | | | | | | | | | | | | | | | | | | | | | | | | |
| JESSOP CLINIC (HM11021) | | | ● | | | | | | | | | | | | | | | | | | | | | | | | | | | | | | | | | | | | | | | | | | | | | ● | | |
| KING, SIMON (HM11644) | | | | | | | | | | | | | | ● | | ● | | | | | | | | | | | | | | | | | | | | | | | | | | | | | | | | | | |
| LUCCHETTI, C A (HM12721) | | | | | | | | | | | | | | | | | | | | | | | | | | | ● | | | | | | | | | | | | | | | | | | | | | | | |

www.healthmyself.com

# A - F Therapies at Practices/Businesses

Business by County with Reference no.

| Business | Absent Healing | Acupressure | Acupuncture | Alexander Technique | Allergy Testing | Anthroposohical Med | Aromatherapy | Art Therapy | Aura Therapy | Auricular Therapy | Auto Suggestion | Autogenic Training | Aversion Therapy | Ayurvedic Medicine | Baby Massage | Bach Remedies | Bates Method | Beauty Therapy | Bio-energetics | Biofeedback | Biomagnetic Therapy | Biomechanics | Bonesetting | Bowen Therapy | Chinese Herbal Medicine |
|---|---|---|---|---|---|---|---|---|---|---|---|---|---|---|---|---|---|---|---|---|---|---|---|---|---|
| MCTIMONEY CHIROPRACTIC CLINIC (HM13606) | | | | | | | | | | | | | | | | | | | | | | | | | |
| MONSON, J L B (HM14076) | | | | | | | | | | | | | | | | | | | | | | | | | |
| NEW MARKET RD PHYSIO PRACTICE (HM14824) | | | ● | | | | | | | | | | | | | | | | | | | | | | |
| NORFOLK CLINIC (HM14993) | | | ● | ● | | | ● | | | | | | | | | | | | | | | | | | |
| NORFOLK NATURAL HEALTH SERVICE (HM14995) | ● | ● | ● | | | | ● | | | | | | | | | ● | | | | | | | | ● | |
| NORMAN, A J (HM14999) | | | | | | | | | | | | | | | | | | | | | | | | | |
| NORTH WALSHAM CHIROPRACTIC (HM15040) | | | | | | | | | | | | | | | | | | | | | | | | | |
| OLIVE GROVE BODY SCIENCE (HM15281) | | | | | | | | | | | | | | | | | | | | | | ● | | | |
| PARK PHYSIOTHERAPY (HM15669) | | | ● | | | | | | | | | | | | | | | | | | | | | | |
| PREMIER AROMATHERAPY (HM16537) | | | | | | | ● | | | | | | | | | | | | | | | | | | |
| RICHARDSON, ALAN (HM17268) | | | | | | | | | | | | | | | | | | | ● | | | | | | |
| RICHARDSON, CAROL (HM17271) | | | | | | | | | | | | | | | | ● | | | | | | | | | |
| RIGBY COURT CLINIC (HM17331) | | ● | ● | | | | ● | | | | | ● | | | | | | | | ● | | | | | |
| RIGG, SUSAN (HM17334) | | | | | | | | | | | | | | | | ● | | | | | | | | | |
| RIVERS, PATRICIA (HM17377) | | | | | | | ● | | | | | | | | | | | | | | | | | | |
| RUSH, J A (HM17755) | | | | | | | | | | | | | | | | | | | | | | | | | |
| SHIATSU CENTRE (HM18453) | | | ● | | | | | | | | | | | | | | | | | | | | | | |
| ST STEPHENS PRACTICE (HM19099) | | ● | ● | | | | | | | | | | | | | | | | | | | | | | |
| SUGDEN, A E (HM19471) | | | ● | | | | | | | | | | | | | | | | | | | | | | |
| TRAFFORD, DEBORAH (HM20247) | | ● | | | | | | | | | | | | | | | | | | | | | | | |
| WELLBEING NATURALLY (HM21152) | | | | | | | | | | | | | | | | | | | | | | | | | |
| WOBURN CLINIC (HM21755) | | | ● | | | | ● | ● | | | | | | | | ● | | | | | | | | | |
| **NORTHAMPTONSHIRE** | | | | | | | | | | | | | | | | | | | | | | | | | |
| ACUPUNCTURE CLINIC (HM00275) | | | ● | | | | | | | | | | | | | | | | | | | | | | |
| ALLEN HINDE - PHYSIOTHERAPIST (HM00598) | | ● | ● | | | | | | | | | | | | | | | | | | | | | | |
| ALTERNATIVE HEALTH CENTRE (HM00703) | | | | | | | ● | | | | | | | | | | | | | | | | | | |
| ANNELISE (HM00906) | | | | | | | ● | | | ● | | | | | | | | | | | | | | | |
| ARBOURS (HM00965) | | | | | | | | | | | | | | | | | | | | | | ● | | | |
| AROMA TRADING (HM01063) | | | | | | | ● | | | | | | | | | | | | | | | | | | |
| AROMATHEUTICS (HM01132) | | | | | | | ● | | | | | | | | | | | | | | | | | | |
| C F C M (HM03523) | | ● | ● | | | | | | | | | | | | | | | | | | | | | | |
| CALLIS THERAPY FOUNDATION (HM03555) | | | | ● | ● | | ● | | | | | | | | | ● | | ● | | | | | | | |
| CALLIS, CHARLES (HM03556) | | | | | | | | | | | | | | | | ● | | | | | | | | | |
| CARPENTER, HEATHER (HM03731) | | | | | | | | | | | | | | | | | | | | | | | | | |

| Business | Chiropody | Chiropractic | Clinical Ecology | Cognitive Therapy | Colonic Hydrotherapy | Colour Therapy | Complementary Therapy | Counselling | Cranial Osteopathy | Cranio-Sacral Therapy | Cryo Surgery | Crystal Healing | Cupping | Cymatics | Dance Movement Thrpy | Dietician | Do-In | Douching | Dowsing | Drama Therapy | Electrolipolysis | Electrolysis | Electrotherapy | Encounter Groups | Faith Healing |
|---|---|---|---|---|---|---|---|---|---|---|---|---|---|---|---|---|---|---|---|---|---|---|---|---|---|
| MCTIMONEY CHIROPRACTIC CLINIC (HM13606) | | ● | | | | | | | | | | | | | | | | | | | | | | | |
| MONSON, J L B (HM14076) | | | | | | | | ● | | | | | | | | | | | | | | | | | |
| NEW MARKET RD PHYSIO PRACTICE (HM14824) | | | | | | | | | | | | | | | | | | | | | | | | | |
| NORFOLK CLINIC (HM14993) | | | | | | | ● | ● | ● | | | | ● | | | | | | | | | | | | |
| NORFOLK NATURAL HEALTH SERVICE (HM14995) | | | | | | | ● | ● | | | | | | | | | | | | | | | | | |
| NORMAN, A J (HM14999) | | ● | | | | | | | | | | | | | | | | | | | | | | | |
| NORTH WALSHAM CHIROPRACTIC (HM15040) | | ● | | | | | | | | | | | | | | | | | | | | | | | |
| OLIVE GROVE BODY SCIENCE (HM15281) | ● | | | | | | | | | | | | | | | | | | | | | | | | |
| PARK PHYSIOTHERAPY (HM15669) | | | | | | | | | ● | ● | | | | | | | | | | | | | ● | | |
| PREMIER AROMATHERAPY (HM16537) | | | | | | | | | | | | | | | | | | | | | | | | | |
| RICHARDSON, ALAN (HM17268) | | | | | | | ● | ● | | | | | | | | | | | | | | | | | |
| RICHARDSON, CAROL (HM17271) | | | | | | | | | | | | | | | | | | | | | | | | | |
| RIGBY COURT CLINIC (HM17331) | | | | ● | | | ● | ● | | | | | ● | | | | | | | | | | | | |
| RIGG, SUSAN (HM17334) | | | | | | | | | | | | | | | | | | | | | | | | | |
| RIVERS, PATRICIA (HM17377) | | | | | | | | | | | | | | | | | | | | | | | | | |
| RUSH, J A (HM17755) | | ● | | | | | | | | | | | | | | | | | | | | | | | |
| SHIATSU CENTRE (HM18453) | | | | | | | | | | | | | | | | | | | | | | | | | |
| ST STEPHENS PRACTICE (HM19099) | ● | | | | | | | | | | | ● | | | | | | | | | | | | | |
| SUGDEN, A E (HM19471) | | | | | | | | | | | | | | | | | | | | | | | | | |
| TRAFFORD, DEBORAH (HM20247) | | | | | | | | | | | | | | | | | | | | | | | | | |
| WELLBEING NATURALLY (HM21152) | | | | | | | | | | ● | | | | | | | | | | | | | | | |
| WOBURN CLINIC (HM21755) | | | | ● | | ● | ● | ● | ● | ● | | | | | ● | | | | | | | | | | |
| **NORTHAMPTONSHIRE** | | | | | | | | | | | | | | | | | | | | | | | | | |
| ACUPUNCTURE CLINIC (HM00275) | | | | | | | | | | | | | | | | | | | | | | | | | |
| ALLEN HINDE - PHYSIOTHERAPIST (HM00598) | | | | | | | | | | | | | | | | | | | | | | | ● | | |
| ALTERNATIVE HEALTH CENTRE (HM00703) | | | | | | | | | | | | | | | | | | | | | | | | | |
| ANNELISE (HM00906) | | | | | | | ● | | | | | | | | | | | | | | | | | | |
| ARBOURS (HM00965) | ● | | | | | | | | | | | | | | | | | | | | | | | | |
| AROMA TRADING (HM01063) | | | | | | | | | | | | | | | | | | | | | | | | | |
| AROMATHEUTICS (HM01132) | | | | | | | | | | | | | | | | | | | | | | | | | |
| C F C M (HM03523) | | | | | | | | | | | | | | | | | | | | | | | | | |
| CALLIS THERAPY FOUNDATION (HM03555) | | | | | | | | ● | | ● | | ● | | | | | | | | | | | | | |
| CALLIS, CHARLES (HM03556) | | | | | | | | | | | | | | | | | | | | | | | | | |
| CARPENTER, HEATHER (HM03731) | | ● | | | | | | | | | | | | | | | | | | | | | | | |

# A - F Therapies at Practices/Businesses

| Business by County with Reference no. | Absent Healing | Acupressure | Acupuncture | Alexander Technique | Allergy Testing | Anthroposohical Med | Aromatherapy | Art Therapy | Aura Therapy | Auricular Therapy | Auto Suggestion | Autogenic Training | Aversion Therapy | Ayurvedic Medicine | Baby Massage | Bach Remedies | Bates Method | Beauty Therapy | Bio-energetics | Biofeedback | Biomagnetic Therapy | Biomechanics | Bonesetting | Bowen Therapy | Chinese Herbal Medicine | Chiropody | Chiropractic | Clinical Ecology | Cognitive Therapy | Colonic Hydrotherapy | Colour Therapy | Complementary Therapy | Counselling | Cranial Osteopathy | Cranio-Sacral Therapy | Cryo Surgery | Crystal Healing | Cupping | Cymatics | Dance Movement Thrpy | Dietician | Do-In | Douching | Dowsing | Drama Therapy | Electrolipolysis | Electrolysis | Electrotherapy | Encounter Groups | Faith Healing |
|---|---|---|---|---|---|---|---|---|---|---|---|---|---|---|---|---|---|---|---|---|---|---|---|---|---|---|---|---|---|---|---|---|---|---|---|---|---|---|---|---|---|---|---|---|---|---|---|---|---|---|
| CHAWTONS (HM04069) | | | | | | | ● | | | | | | | | | | | | | | | | | | | | | | | | | | | | | | | | | | | | | | | | | | | |
| CHIRO SPORTS INJURY CLINIC (HM04284) | | | | | | | | | | | | | | | | | | | | | | | | | | | ● | | | | | | | | | | | | | | | | | | | | | | | |
| CHIROPRACTIC CLINIC (HM04389) | | | | | | | | | | | | | | | | | | | | | | | | | | | ● | | | | | | | | | | | | | | | | | | | | | | | |
| CLINTON HOUSE CHIROPODY (HM04719) | | | | | | | | | | | | | | | | | | | | | | ● | | | | ● | | | | | | | | | | | | | | | | | | | | | | | | |
| DAVENTRY NATUREWORKS (HM05768) | | | ● | | ● | | ● | | | | | | | | | | | | | | | | | ● | | | ● | | | | | | | | | | | | | | | | | | | | | | | |
| DEVON PARADE CLINIC (HM06041) | | ● | ● | | | | ● | | | | | | | | | | | | | | | ● | | | | | ● | | ● | | | ● | ● | ● | | ● | | | | | | | | | | | | ● | | |
| DON, ANITA (HM06166) | | | | | | | ● | | | | | | | | | | | | | | | | | | | | | | | | | | | | | | | | | | | | | | | | | | | |
| DOWDING, C J (HM06235) | | | | | | | ● | | | | | | | | | | | | | | | | | | | | | | | | | | | | | | | | | | | | | | | | | | | |
| ESSERY, PATRICIA (HM06932) | | | | | | | | | | | | | | | | ● | | | | | | | | | | | | | | | | | | | | | | | | | | | | | | | | | | |
| ESSERY, TRICIA (HM06933) | | | | | | | | | | | | | | | | ● | | | | | | | | | | | | | | | | | | | | | ● | | | | | | | | | | | | | |
| GARVEY-WILLIAMS, RICHARD (HM07914) | | | | | | | | | | | | | | | | | | | | | | | | | | | | | | | | | | ● | | | | | | | | | | | | | | | | |
| GARVEY-WILLIAMS, RICHARD (HM07915) | | | | | | | | | | | | | | | | | | | | | | | | | | | | | | | | | | ● | | | | | | | | | | | | | | | | |
| IQBAL, Z (HM10717) | | | | | | | | | | | | | | | | | | | | | | | | | | | ● | | | | | | | | | | | | | | | | | | | | | | | |
| KETTERING OSTEOPATH (HM11568) | | | | | | | | | | | | | | | | | | | | | | | | | | | ● | | | | | | | | | | | | | | | | | | | | | | | |
| LEE, STEPHEN (HM12146) | | | ● | | | | | | | | | | | | | | | | | | | | | | | | | | | | | | | | | | | | | | | | | | | | | | | |
| LIKISMA (HM12377) | | | | | | | ● | | | | | | | | | | | | | | | | | | | | | | | | | | | | | | | | | | | | | | | | | | | |
| LIKISMA PRESENTATIONS (HM12389) | | | | | | | ● | | | | | | | | | | | | | | | | | | | | | | | | | | | | | | | | | | | | | | | | | | | |
| MORGAN, A (HM14158) | | | ● | | | | | | | | | | | | | | | | | | | | | | | | | | | | | | | | | | | | | | | | | | | | | | | |
| MOTLEY, MAUREEN (HM14277) | | | | | | | ● | | | | | | | | | | | | | | | | | | | | | | | | | | | | | | | | | | | | | | | | | | | |
| NENE VALLEY COMP THERAPIES (HM14785) | | | | | | | ● | | | | | | | | | | | | | | | | | | | | | | | | | | | | | | | | | | | | | | | | | | | |
| NORTH, JUDITH (HM15044) | | | | | | | ● | | | | | | | | | | | | | | | | | | | | | | | | | | | | | | | | | | | | | | | | | | | |
| NORTHAMPTON CHIROPRACTIC (HM15051) | | | | | | | | | | | | | | | | | | | | | | | | | | | ● | | | | | | | | | | | | | | | | | | | | | | | |
| PARROTT, LINDA (HM15735) | | | | | | | ● | | | | | | | | | | | | | | | | | | | | | | | | | | | | | | | | | | | | | | | | | | | |
| PATERSON, MARGARET (HM15813) | | | | | | | | | | | | | | | | ● | | | | | | | | | | | | | | | | | | | | | | | | | | | | | | | | | | |
| REFLEXOLOGY CLINIC (HM17085) | | | | | | | | | | | | | | | | | | | | | | | | | | | | | | | | | | | | | | | | | | | | ● | | | | | | |
| ROSS, SHEENA (HM17642) | | | ● | | | | | | | | | | | | | | | | | | | | | | | | | | | | | | | | | | | | | | | | | | | | | | | |
| THROSSELL, PHILIPPA (HM20044) | | | | | | | | | | | | | | | | | | | | | | | | | | | ● | | | | | | | | | | | | | | | | | | | | | | | |
| TOWCESTER CHIROPRACTIC CLINIC (HM20194) | | | | | | | | | | | | | | | | ● | | | | | | | | | | | ● | | | | | | | | | | | | | | | | | | | | | | | |
| WILLIAMS, JANE (HM21568) | | | ● | | | | | | | | | | | | | | | | | | | | | | | | | | | | | | | | | | | | | | | | | | | | | | | |
| WOODFORD HALSE CHIROPRACTIC (HM21823) | | | | | | | | | | | | | | | | | | | | | | | | | | | ● | | | | | | | | | | | | | | | | | | | | | | | |
| **NORTHUMBERLAND** | | | | | | | | | | | | | | | | | | | | | | | | | | | | | | | | | | | | | | | | | | | | | | | | | | |
| ACUCARE (HM00209) | | | ● | | | | | | | | | | | | | | | | | | | | | | | | | | | | | | | | | | | | | | | | | | | | | | | |
| AYRES, ELIZABETH (HM01433) | | | | | | | | | | | | | | | | | | | | | | ● | | | | ● | | | | | | | | | | | | | | | | | | | | | | | | |
| BOWEN TECHNIQUE STUDIO (HM02775) | | | | | | | | | | | | | | | | | | | | | | | | ● | | | | | | | | | | | | | | | | | | | | | | | | | | |

# A - F Therapies at Practices/Businesses

| Business by County with Reference no. | Absent Healing | Acupressure | Acupuncture | Alexander Technique | Allergy Testing | Anthroposohical Med | Aromatherapy | Art Therapy | Aura Therapy | Auricular Therapy | Auto Suggestion | Autogenic Training | Aversion Therapy | Ayurvedic Medicine | Baby Massage | Bach Remedies | Bates Method | Beauty Therapy | Bio-energetics | Biofeedback | Biomagnetic Therapy | Biomechanics | Bonesetting | Bowen Therapy | Chinese Herbal Medicine | Chiropody | Chiropractic | Clinical Ecology | Cognitive Therapy | Colonic Hydrotherapy | Colour Therapy | Complementary Therapy | Counselling | Cranial Osteopathy | Cranio-Sacral Therapy | Cryo Surgery | Crystal Healing | Cupping | Cymatics | Dance Movement Thrpy | Dietician | Do-In | Douching | Dowsing | Drama Therapy | Electrolipolysis | Electrolysis | Electrotherapy | Encounter Groups | Faith Healing |
|---|---|---|---|---|---|---|---|---|---|---|---|---|---|---|---|---|---|---|---|---|---|---|---|---|---|---|---|---|---|---|---|---|---|---|---|---|---|---|---|---|---|---|---|---|---|---|---|---|---|---|
| CARR, R (HM03740) | | | ● | | | | | | | | | | | | | | | | | | | | | | | | | | | | | | | | | | | | | | | | | | | | | | | |
| COSTAR, MARK (HM05207) | | | | | | | ● | | | | | | | | | | | | | | | | | | | | | | | | | | | | | | | | | | | | | | | | | | | |
| EVISON, ALEX (HM07012) | | | | | | | | | | | | | | | | | | | | | | | | | | | | | | | | | ● | | | | | | | | | | | | | | | | | |
| GREEN BATT PHYSIOTHERAPY (HM08434) | | | | | | | | | | | | | | | | ● | | | | | | | | | | | | | | | | | | | | | | | | | | | | | | | | ● | | |
| HEXHAM CHIROPRACTIC CLINIC (HM09711) | | | | | | | | | | | | | | | | | | | | | | | | | | | ● | | | | | | | | | | | | | | | | | | | | | | | |
| KI CLINIC (HM11591) | | ● | ● | | | | ● | | | | | | | | | ● | | | | | | | | | | | | | | | | ● | ● | | | | | | | | | | | | | | | | | |
| MEAD, BRUCE (HM13626) | | | | | | | | | | | | | | | | | | | | | | | | | | ● | | | | | | | | | | | | | | | | | | | | | | | | |
| METCALFF, L (HM13773) | | | | | | | | | | | | | | | | | | | | | | | | | | ● | | | | | | | | | | | | | | | | | | | | | | | | |
| PHYSIOTHERAPY & SPORTS CLINIC (HM16223) | | | ● | | | | | | | | | | | | | | | | | | | | | | | | | | | | | | | | | | | | | | | | | | | | | | | |
| **NOTTINGHAMSHIRE** | | | | | | | | | | | | | | | | | | | | | | | | | | | | | | | | | | | | | | | | | | | | | | | | | | |
| ACUPUNCTURE CLINIC (HM00268) | | | ● | | | | | | | | | | | | | | | | | | | | | | | | | | | | | | | | | | | | | | | | | | | | | | | |
| ACUPUNCTURE CLINIC (HM00264) | | | ● | | | | | | | | | | | | | | | | | | | | | | | | | | | | | | | | | | | | | | | | | | | | | | | |
| ALDRED, E M (HM00504) | | | | | | | | | | | | | | | | | | | | | | | | | | | ● | | | | | | | | | | | | | | | | | | | | | | | |
| AROMATHERAPY CENTRE (HM01102) | | | | | | | ● | | | | | | | | | | | | | | | | | | | | | | | | | | | | | | | | | | | | | | | | | | | |
| BEESTON CHIROPRACTIC CLINIC (HM02058) | | | | | | | | | | | | | | | | | | | | | | | | | | | ● | | | | | | | | | | | | | | | | | | | | | | | |
| BOND, DIANORA (HM02669) | | | | ● | | | | | | | | | | | | | | | | | | | | | | | | | | | | | | | | | | | | | | | | | | | | ● | | |
| BOURNE, DAVID (HM02754) | | | | | | | | | | | | | | | | | | | | | | | | | | | ● | | | | | | | | | | | | | | | | | | | | | | | |
| BROADLEY, RICHARD (HM03116) | | | | | | | | | | | | | | | | | | | | | | | | | | | | | | | | | ● | | | | | | | | | | | | | | | | | |
| BULLEN-SPICER ASSOCIATES (HM03342) | | | | | | | | | | | | | | | | | | | | | | | | | | | | | | | | | ● | | | | | | | | | | | | | | | | ● | |
| CASSIDY, TRISH (HM03820) | | | | | | | ● | | | | | | | | | | | | | | | | | | | | | | | | | | | | | | | | | | | | | | | | | | | |
| CENTRE FOR TRANSFORMATION (HM03921) | | | | | | | | | | | | | | | | | ● | | | | | | | | | | | | | | | | | | | | | | | | | | | | | | | | | |
| CLARKE, J (HM04589) | | | | | | | | | | | | | | | | | | | | | | | | | | | ● | | | | | | | | | | | | | | | | | | | | | | | |
| CORBETT, DIANE (HM05153) | | | | | | | ● | | | | | | | | | | | | | | | | | | | | | | | | | | | | | | | | | | | | | | | | | | | |
| DEAN, MARTIN (HM05942) | ● | | ● | | | | | | ● | | | | ● | | | ● | | | | | | | | | | | | | | | | ● | | | | | ● | ● | | | | | | ● | | | | | | ● |
| DENGLER, REGINA (HM05978) | | | | | | | ● | | | | | | | | | | | | | | | | | | | | | | | | | | | | | | | | | | | | | | | | | | | |
| DEVLIN, JULIE (HM06039) | | | ● | | | | | | | | | | | | | | | | | | | | | | | | | | | | | | | | | | | | | | | | | | | | | | | |
| DORMAN, KARL (HM06202) | | | | | | | | | | | | | | | | | | | | | | | | | | | ● | | | | | | | | | | | | | | | | | | | | | | | |
| DOUGLAS, W (HM06220) | | | | | | | | | | | | | | | | | | | | | | | | | | | ● | | | | | | | | | | | | | | | | | | | | | | | |
| DRAGONSWAY ACUPUNCTURE CLINIC (HM06280) | | | ● | | | | | | | | | | | | | | | | | | | | | | | | | | | | | | | | | | | | | | | | | | | | | | | |
| FORMAN, LESLEY J (HM07558) | | | | | | | ● | | | | | | | | | | | | | | | | | | | | | | | | | | | | | | | | | | | | | | | | | | | |
| GOMAN, JOHN (HM08233) | | | | | | | | | | | | | | | | | | | | | | | | | | | ● | | | | | | | | | | | | | | | | | | | | | | | |
| GREENWOOD, JULIA (HM08507) | | | | | | | | | | | | | | | | | | | | | | ● | | | | ● | | | | | | | | | | | | | | | | | | | | | | | | |
| HACKMAN, MARIE (HM08682) | | | | | | | ● | | | | | | | | | | | | | | | | | | | | | | | | | | | | | | | | | | | | | | | | | | | |
| IMPACT PHYSIO & SPORTS INJURIES (HM10590) | | | ● | | | | | | | | | | | | | | | | | | | | | | | | | | | | | | | | | | | | | | | | | | | | | | | |

# A - F Therapies at Practices/Businesses

| Business by County with Reference no. | Absent Healing | Acupressure | Acupuncture | Alexander Technique | Allergy Testing | Anthroposohical Med | Aromatherapy | Art Therapy | Aura Therapy | Auricular Therapy | Auto Suggestion | Autogenic Training | Aversion Therapy | Ayurvedic Medicine | Baby Massage | Bach Remedies | Bates Method | Beauty Therapy | Bio-energetics | Biofeedback | Biomagnetic Therapy | Biomechanics | Bonesetting | Bowen Therapy | Chinese Herbal Medicine | Chiropody | Chiropractic | Clinical Ecology | Cognitive Therapy | Colonic Hydrotherapy | Colour Therapy | Complementary Therapy | Counselling | Cranial Osteopathy | Cranio-Sacral Therapy | Cryo Surgery | Crystal Healing | Cupping | Cymatics | Dance Movement Thrpy | Dietician | Do-In | Douching | Dowsing | Drama Therapy | Electrolipolysis | Electrolysis | Electrotherapy | Encounter Groups | Faith Healing |
|---|---|---|---|---|---|---|---|---|---|---|---|---|---|---|---|---|---|---|---|---|---|---|---|---|---|---|---|---|---|---|---|---|---|---|---|---|---|---|---|---|---|---|---|---|---|---|---|---|---|---|
| KENNEDY, JOHN M (HM11495) | | | ● | | | | | | | | | | | | | | | | | | | | | | | | | | | | | | | | | | | | | | | | | | | | | | | |
| LIGHT UP YOUR LIFE (HM12370) | ● | | | | | | | | | | | | | | | | | | | | | | | | | | | | | | | | | | | | ● | | | | | | | | | | | | | |
| LIKISMA (HM12379) | | | | | | | ● | | | | | | | | | | | | | | | | | | | | | | | | | | | | | | | | | | | | | | | | | | | |
| LUKEHURST, LINDSAY (HM12734) | | | ● | | | | | | | | | | | | | | | | | | | | | | | | | | | | | | | | | | | | | | | | | | | | | | | |
| MANSFIELD CHIROPODY (HM13046) | | | | | | | | | | | | | | | | | | | | | | | | | | ● | | | | | | | | | | | | | | | | | | | | | | | | |
| MANSFIELD CHIROPRACTIC CLINIC (HM13047) | | | | | | | | | | | | | | | | | | | | | | | | | | | ● | | | | | | | | | | | | | | | | | | | | | | | |
| MORLEY-KIRK, JOHN (HM14188) | | | | | | | | | | | | | | | | | | | | | | | | | | | | | | | | ● | | | | | | | | | | | | | | | | | | |
| NATURAL HEALTH (HM14554) | ● | | ● | | | | ● | ● | | | | | | | | ● | | | | | | | | ● | | | | | | | ● | ● | ● | | | | ● | | | | ● | | | | | | | | | |
| NATURAL THERAPY CLINIC (HM14654) | | | ● | | | | ● | | | | | | | | | | | | | | | | | | | | | | | | | | | | | | | | | | | | | | | | | | | |
| NATURE'S HEALING (HM14691) | | | | | | | ● | | | | | | | | | | | | | | | | | | | | | | | | | | | | | | | | | | | | | | | | | | | |
| NEWARK CHIROPRACTIC CLINIC (HM14841) | | | | | | | | | | | | | | | | | | | | | | | | | | | ● | | | | | | | | | | | | | | | | | | | | | | | |
| NOTTINGHAM M S THERAPY CTRE (HM15083) | | | | | | | ● | | | | | | | | | | | | | | | | | | | | | | | | | | | | | | | | | | | | | | | | | | | |
| NOTTINGHAM NATURAL HEALTH CTRE (HM15084) | | | ● | ● | | | ● | | | | | | | | | | ● | | | | | | | ● | | | ● | | | | | | ● | | ● | | | | | | | | | | | | | | | |
| OPTIMUM HEALTH (HM15348) | ● | ● | ● | | ● | | ● | | | ● | | | | | | ● | | | | | | | | | | | | | | ● | | ● | ● | ● | | | | | | | | | | | | | | | | |
| PARKSIDE STRESS MANAGEMENT (HM15722) | ● | | | | ● | | ● | | ● | | | | | | | ● | | | | | | | | | | | | | | | ● | ● | ● | | | | ● | | | | ● | | | | | | | | | |
| RETFORD CHIROPRACTIC CLINIC (HM17200) | | | | | | | ● | | | | | | | | | | | | | | | | | | | | ● | | | | | ● | | ● | | | | | | | | | | | | | | | | |
| SANGHERA, PARMJIT (HM17935) | | | | | | | | | | | | | | | | ● | | | | | | | | | | | | | | | | | | | | | | | | | | | | | | | | | | |
| SEVENTHMOON NATURAL THRPY CTRE (HM18247) | ● | ● | ● | | | | | | | | | | | | | ● | | | | | | | | | | | | | | | | | | | | | | ● | | | | | | ● | | | | | | |
| SHEER TECHNIQUE (HM18368) | | ● | | | | | ● | | ● | | ● | | | | | | | | ● | ● | | | | | | | | | | | ● | ● | ● | | | | ● | ● | | | | | ● | ● | | | | | | ● |
| SHERWOOD CHIROPRACTIC CLINIC (HM18440) | | | | | | | | | | | | | | | | | | | | | | | | | | | ● | | | | | | | | | | | | | | | | | | | | | | | |
| SHERWOOD PSYCHO TRAINING INS (HM18441) | | | | | | | | ● | | | | | | | | | | | | | | | | | | | | | | | | | ● | | | | | | | | | | | | | | | | | |
| SKELTON, CATHERINE () | | | | | | | | | | | | | | | | | | | | | | | | ● | | | | | | | | | | | | | | | | | | | | | | | | | | |
| SOUTHWELL ACUPUNCTURE CLINIC (HM18949) | | | ● | | | | | | | | | | | | | | | | | | | | | | | | | | | | | | | | | | | | | | | | | | | | | | | |
| SOUTHWELL ACUPUNCTURE CLINIC (HM18948) | | | ● | | | | | | | | | | | | | | | | | | | | | | | | | | | | | | | | | | | | | | | | | | | | | | | |
| TODD, S J (HM20108) | | | | | | | | | | | | | | | | | | | | | | | | | | ● | | | | | | | | | | | | | | | | | | | | | | | | |
| TOMLIN, NORMAN (HM20131) | | | | | | | | | | | | | | | | | | | | | | | | | | | ● | | | | | | | | | | | | | | | | | | | | | | | |
| TRADITIONAL ACUPUNCTURIST (HM20222) | | ● | ● | | | | ● | | | | | | | | | ● | | | | | | | | | | | | | | | | ● | | | | | | ● | | | | | | | | | | | | |
| VAUGHTON, NORMAN D (HM20601) | | | | | | | | | | | | | | | | | | | | | | | | | | | | | | | | | ● | | | | | | | | | | | | | | | | | |
| WALKER, J M (HM20776) | | | ● | | | | | | | | | | | | | | | | | | | | | | | | | | | | | | | | | | | | | | | | | | | | | | | |
| WOODHOUSE ROAD CHIROPRACTIC (HM21827) | | | | | | | | | | | | | | | | | | | | | | | | | | | ● | | | | | | | | | | | | | | | | | | | | | | | |
| **OXFORDSHIRE** | | | | | | | | | | | | | | | | | | | | | | | | | | | | | | | | | | | | | | | | | | | | | | | | | | |
| ACUPUNCTURE CENTRE (HM00255) | | | ● | | | | | | | | | | | | | | | | | | | | | | | | | | | | | | | | | | | | | | | | | | | | | | | |
| ACUPUNCTURE CLINIC (HM00273) | | | ● | | | | | | | | | | | | | | | | | | | | | | | | | | | | | | | | | | | | | | | | | | | | | | | |
| ALCANTARA, FATIMA (HM00487) | | | | | | | | | | | | | | | | | | | | | | | | | | | ● | | | | | | | | | | | | | | | | | | | | | | | |

# A - F Therapies at Practices/Businesses

| Business by County with Reference no. | Absent Healing | Acupressure | Acupuncture | Alexander Technique | Allergy Testing | Anthroposohical Med | Aromatherapy | Art Therapy | Aura Therapy | Auricular Therapy | Auto Suggestion | Autogenic Training | Aversion Therapy | Ayurvedic Medicine | Baby Massage | Bach Remedies | Bates Method | Beauty Therapy | Bio-energetics | Biofeedback | Biomagnetic Therapy | Biomechanics | Bonesetting | Bowen Therapy | Chinese Herbal Medicine |
|---|---|---|---|---|---|---|---|---|---|---|---|---|---|---|---|---|---|---|---|---|---|---|---|---|---|
| ALEXANDER TECHNIQUE (HM00523) | | | | ● | | | | | | | | | | | | | | | | | | | | | |
| AROMA HEALTH 2000 (HM01050) | | | | | | | ● | | | | | | | | | | | | | | | | | | |
| ASHCROFT CLINIC (HM01198) | | | ● | | | | | | | | | | | | | | | | | | | | | | |
| BACK IN LINE (HM01481) | | | ● | | | | | | | | | | | | | | | | | | | | | | |
| BACK TO NORMAL CHIRO CLINIC (HM01522) | | | | | | | | | | | | | | | | | | | | | | | | | |
| BALDWIN, JILLIAN (HM01615) | | | | | | | | | | | | | | | | | | | | | | | | | |
| BANBURY CHIROPRACTIC CLINIC (HM01645) | | | | | | | | | | | | | | | | | | | | | | | | | |
| BARRINGTON-WARD, H B (HM01800) | | | ● | | | | | | | | | | | | | | | | | | | | | | |
| BICESTER CHIROPRACTIC CLINIC (HM02278) | | | | | | | | | | | | | | | | | | | | | | | | | |
| BICESTER CHIROPRACTIC CLINIC (HM02277) | | | | | | | | | | | | | | | | | | | | | | | | | |
| BIRD, SUZANNE (HM02371) | | | | | | | | | | | | | | | | | | | | | | | | | |
| BJARNASON, MARGARET (HM02419) | | | | | | | ● | | | | | | | | | | | | | | | | | | |
| BOARDMAN, C J (HM02545) | | | ● | | | | | | | | | | | | | | | | | | | | | | |
| CAMERON-KIRBY, E (HM03589) | | | ● | | | | | | | | | | | | | | | | | | | | | | |
| CENTRAL CHIROPRACTIC CLINIC (HM03891) | | | | | | | | | | | | | | | | | | | | | | | | | |
| CHURCH, PAULINE (HM04467) | | | | | | | | | | | | | | | | | | | | | | | | | |
| CONNER, CAROL (HM04993) | | | | | | | | | | | | | | | | | | | | | | | | | |
| COOPER, STEPHEN (HM05128) | | | | ● | | | | | | | | | | | | | | | | | | | | | |
| COTTAGE CLINIC (HM05221) | ● | | | | | | | | | | | | | | | | | | | | | | | | |
| COX, S (HM05320) | | | ● | | | | | | | | | | | | | | | | | | | | | | |
| CROMWELL CHIROPRACTIC CLINIC (HM05463) | | | | | | | | | | | | | | | | | | | | | | | | | |
| DAO CLINIC OF CHINESE MEDICINE (HM05731) | | | ● | | | | | | | | | | | | | | | | | | | | | | |
| EDULJEE, STELLA (HM06638) | | | | | | | ● | | | | | | | | | | | | | | | | | | |
| ELWELL, R S (HM06792) | | | | | | | | | | | | | | | | | | | | | | | | | |
| ESSENTIALLY OILS (HM06923) | | | | | | | ● | | | | | | | | | | | | | | | | | | |
| FEET FIRST (HM07179) | | | | | | | | | | | | | | | | | | | | | | | | | |
| GEGGUS, PAM (HM07966) | | | ● | | | | | | | | | | | | | | | | | | | | | | |
| GILMORE, E M J (HM08104) | | | | | | | | | | | | | | | | | | | | | | | | | |
| GODSWELL NATURAL THRPY CTRE (HM08191) | | | ● | ● | | | ● | ● | | | | | | | | ● | | | | | | | | | |
| HARDING, S J (HM08972) | | | | | | | | | | | | | | | | | | | | | | | | | |
| HAWES, G M (HM09214) | | | | | | | | | | | | | | | | | | | | | | | | | |
| HEADINGTON ALEXANDER SCHOOL (HM09306) | | | | ● | | | | | | | | | | | | | | | | | | | | | |
| HEALTHPACK (HM09413) | | | ● | | | | ● | | | | | | | | | | | | | | | | | | ● |
| HELIX HOUSE (HM09522) | | | | | | | | | | | | | | | | | | | | | | | | | |

| Business by County with Reference no. | Chiropody | Chiropractic | Clinical Ecology | Cognitive Therapy | Colonic Hydrotherapy | Colour Therapy | Complementary Therapy | Counselling | Cranial Osteopathy | Cranio-Sacral Therapy | Cryo Surgery | Crystal Healing | Cupping | Cymatics | Dance Movement Thrpy | Dietician | Do-In | Douching | Dowsing | Drama Therapy | Electrolipolysis | Electrolysis | Electrotherapy | Encounter Groups | Faith Healing |
|---|---|---|---|---|---|---|---|---|---|---|---|---|---|---|---|---|---|---|---|---|---|---|---|---|---|
| ALEXANDER TECHNIQUE (HM00523) | | | | | | | | | | | | | | | | | | | | | | | | | |
| AROMA HEALTH 2000 (HM01050) | | | | | | | | | | | | | | | | | | | | | | | | | |
| ASHCROFT CLINIC (HM01198) | ● | | | | | | ● | ● | | | | | | | | | | | | | | | ● | | |
| BACK IN LINE (HM01481) | | ● | | | | | | | | | | | | | | | | | | | | | | | |
| BACK TO NORMAL CHIRO CLINIC (HM01522) | | ● | | | | | | | | | | | | | | | | | | | | | | | |
| BALDWIN, JILLIAN (HM01615) | | ● | | | | | | | | | | | | | | | | | | | | | | | |
| BANBURY CHIROPRACTIC CLINIC (HM01645) | | ● | | | | | | | | | | | | | | | | | | | | | | | |
| BARRINGTON-WARD, H B (HM01800) | | | | | | | | | | | | | | | | | | | | | | | | | |
| BICESTER CHIROPRACTIC CLINIC (HM02278) | | ● | | | | | | | | | | | | | | | | | | | | | | | |
| BICESTER CHIROPRACTIC CLINIC (HM02277) | | ● | | | | | | | | | | | | | | | | | | | | | | | |
| BIRD, SUZANNE (HM02371) | | ● | | | | | | | | | | | | | | | | | | | | | | | |
| BJARNASON, MARGARET (HM02419) | | | | | | | | | | | | | | | | | | | | | | | | | |
| BOARDMAN, C J (HM02545) | | | | | | | | | | | | | | | | | | | | | | | | | |
| CAMERON-KIRBY, E (HM03589) | | | | | | | | | | | | | | | | | | | | | | | | | |
| CENTRAL CHIROPRACTIC CLINIC (HM03891) | | ● | | | | | | | | | | | | | | | | | | | | | | | |
| CHURCH, PAULINE (HM04467) | | ● | | | | | | | | | | | | | | | | | | | | | | | |
| CONNER, CAROL (HM04993) | | ● | | | | | | | | | | | | | | | | | | | | | | | |
| COOPER, STEPHEN (HM05128) | | | | | | | | | | | | | | | | | | | | | | | | | |
| COTTAGE CLINIC (HM05221) | | | | | | | | | | | | | | | | | | | | | | | | | |
| COX, S (HM05320) | | | | | | | | | | | | | | | | | | | | | | | | | |
| CROMWELL CHIROPRACTIC CLINIC (HM05463) | | ● | | | | | | | | | | | | | | | | | | | | | | | |
| DAO CLINIC OF CHINESE MEDICINE (HM05731) | | | | | | | | | | | | | | | | | | | | | | | | | |
| EDULJEE, STELLA (HM06638) | | | | | | | | | | | | | | | | | | | | | | | | | |
| ELWELL, R S (HM06792) | | ● | | | | | | | | ● | | | | | | | | | | | | | | | |
| ESSENTIALLY OILS (HM06923) | | | | | | | | | | | | | | | | | | | | | | | | | |
| FEET FIRST (HM07179) | ● | | | | | | | | | | | | | | | | | | | | | | | | |
| GEGGUS, PAM (HM07966) | | | | | | | | | | | | | | | | | | | | | | | | | |
| GILMORE, E M J (HM08104) | | ● | | | | | | | | | | | | | | | | | | | | | | | |
| GODSWELL NATURAL THRPY CTRE (HM08191) | ● | ● | | | | | | | | ● | | | | | | | | | | | | | | | |
| HARDING, S J (HM08972) | | ● | | | | | | | | | | | | | | | | | | | | | | | |
| HAWES, G M (HM09214) | | ● | | | | | | | | | | | | | | | | | | | | | | | |
| HEADINGTON ALEXANDER SCHOOL (HM09306) | | | | | | | | | | | | | | | | | | | | | | | | | |
| HEALTHPACK (HM09413) | | | | | | | | | | | | | | | | | | | | | | | | | |
| HELIX HOUSE (HM09522) | | | | | | | | | ● | | | | | | | | | | | | | | | | |

# A - F Therapies at Practices/Businesses

| Business by County with Reference no. | Absent Healing | Acupressure | Acupuncture | Alexander Technique | Allergy Testing | Anthroposohical Med | Aromatherapy | Art Therapy | Aura Therapy | Auricular Therapy | Auto Suggestion | Autogenic Training | Aversion Therapy | Ayurvedic Medicine | Baby Massage | Bach Remedies | Bates Method | Beauty Therapy | Bio-energetics | Biofeedback | Biomagnetic Therapy | Biomechanics | Bonesetting | Bowen Therapy | Chinese Herbal Medicine | Chiropody | Chiropractic | Clinical Ecology | Cognitive Therapy | Colonic Hydrotherapy | Colour Therapy | Complementary Therapy | Counselling | Cranial Osteopathy | Cranio-Sacral Therapy | Cryo Surgery | Crystal Healing | Cupping | Cymatics | Dance Movement Thrpy | Dietician | Do-In | Douching | Dowsing | Drama Therapy | Electrolipolysis | Electrolysis | Electrotherapy | Encounter Groups | Faith Healing |
|---|---|---|---|---|---|---|---|---|---|---|---|---|---|---|---|---|---|---|---|---|---|---|---|---|---|---|---|---|---|---|---|---|---|---|---|---|---|---|---|---|---|---|---|---|---|---|---|---|---|---|
| HENLEY CHIROPRACTIC & COMP (HM09559) |||||||||||||||||||||||||||●|||||||||||||||||||||||
| HICKS, SARA (HM09726) |||●|||||||||||||||||||||||||||||||||||||||||||||||
| HOCK, GABRIELLE (HM09868) |||●|||||||||||||||||||||||||||||||||||||||||||||||
| HORKEY, PHIL (HM10168) ||||●||||||||||||||||||||||||||||||||||||||||||||||
| HOUSE OF GOOD HEALTH (HM10219) |||||||||||||||||||||||||||●|||||||||||||||||||||||
| HUART, S C (HM10298) |||●|||||||||||||||||||||||||||||||||||||||||||||||
| HYPNOTHERAPY CENTRE (HM10516) |●|||||||||||||||||||||||||||||||||||||||||||||||||
| KARRENBAUER, MONIKA (HM11331) ||||||||||||||||●||||||||||||||||||||||||||||||||||
| KERNOHAN, SARA (HM11546) |||||||●|||||||||||||||||||||||||||||||||||||||||||
| KIDLINGTON CHIROPRACTIC (HM11594) |||||||||||||||||||||||||||●|||||||||||||||||||||||
| KIDLINGTON OSTEO PRACTICE (HM11596) ||●|||||●||||||||||||||||||||||||||||||||||||||||●|||
| LEE, ELAINE (HM12134) |||||||||||||||||||||||||||●|||||||||||||||||||||||
| LOCK, ALISON (HM12534) ||||||||||||||||●||||||||||||||||●|||||||||||||||||
| MARRIOTT, HUGH (HM13138) ||||||||||||||||||||||||||||||||||●||||||||||||||||
| MCTIMONEY CHIROPRACTIC (HM13600) |||||||||||||||||||||||||||●|||||||||||||||||||||||
| MCTIMONEY CHIROPRACTIC (HM13601) |||||||||||||||||||||||||||●|||||||||||||||||||||||
| MCTIMONEY CHIROPRACTIC COLLEGE (HM13614) |||||||||||||||||||||||||||●|||||●||||||||||||||||||
| MIDSUMMER COTTAGE CLINIC (HM13845) |||●|||||||||||||||||||||||||||||||||||||||||||||||
| MOLLOY, RUPERT (HM14054) |||||||||||||||||||||||||||●|||||||||||||||||||||||
| NAPLES, EILEEN (HM14479) |||||||||||||||||||||||||||●|||||||||||||||||||||||
| NEW SEASONS (HM14832) |||||||●|||||||||||||||||||||||||||||||||||||||||||
| O'BRIEN, FRANCES (HM15179) |||●|||||||||||||||||||||||||||||||||||||||||||||||
| O'DONNELL, ELSPETH (HM15225) ||●||||||||||||||||||||||||||||||||||||||||||||||||
| OLESEN, ANNE-GRETE (HM15279) ||||||||||||||||●||||||||||||||||||||||||||||||||||
| OXFORD CHIROPRACTIC CLINIC (HM15538) |||||||||||||||||||||||||||●|||||||||||||||||||||||
| OXFORD NUTRITION & ALLRGY CTRE (HM15541) ||||||||||||||||||||||||||||●||||●|||||||||●||||||||||
| OXFORD TRANSCENDTL MEDITA CTRE (HM15544) ||||||||||||||●||||||||||||||||||||||||||||||||||||
| PACKARD, JOY (HM15555) ||||●||||||||||||||||||||||||||||||||||||||||||||||
| PARE, KAREN (HM15651) |||||||●|||||||||||||||||||||||||||||||||||||||||||
| PARSONS STREET CLINIC (HM15747) |||●||||●|||||||||●|||||||||||●|||||●|●|●|||||||||||||||●||
| PEHRSON, S (HM15947) ||||●||||||||||||||||||||||||||||||||||||||||||||||
| PLESTED, NICOLA (HM16369) |||||||||||||||||||||||||||●|||||||||||||||||||||||
| POLLOCK, SUSAN (HM16418) |||||||●|||||||||||||||●||||●||||||||||||||||||||||||
| RAJAGOPALAN, J (HM16902) |||●|||||||||||||||||||||||||||||||||||||||||||||||

www.healthmyself.com

# A - F Therapies at Practices/Businesses

| Business by County with Reference no. | Absent Healing | Acupressure | Acupuncture | Alexander Technique | Allergy Testing | Anthroposohical Med | Aromatherapy | Art Therapy | Aura Therapy | Auricular Therapy | Auto Suggestion | Autogenic Training | Aversion Therapy | Ayurvedic Medicine | Baby Massage | Bach Remedies | Bates Method | Beauty Therapy | Bio-energetics | Biofeedback | Biomagnetic Therapy | Biomechanics | Bonesetting | Bowen Therapy | Chinese Herbal Medicine | Chiropody | Chiropractic | Clinical Ecology | Cognitive Therapy | Colonic Hydrotherapy | Colour Therapy | Complementary Therapy | Counselling | Cranial Osteopathy | Cranio-Sacral Therapy | Cryo Surgery | Crystal Healing | Cupping | Cymatics | Dance Movement Thrpy | Dietician | Do-In | Douching | Dowsing | Drama Therapy | Electrolipolysis | Electrolysis | Electrotherapy | Encounter Groups | Faith Healing |
|---|---|---|---|---|---|---|---|---|---|---|---|---|---|---|---|---|---|---|---|---|---|---|---|---|---|---|---|---|---|---|---|---|---|---|---|---|---|---|---|---|---|---|---|---|---|---|---|---|---|---|
| SANZ DE DEAS, HILDA C (HM17938) | | | ● | | | | | | | | | | | | | | | | | | | | | | | | | | | | | | | | | | | | | | | | | | | | | | | |
| SMYTH, CATHERINE (HM18829) | | | | | | | | | | | | | | | | | | | | | | | | | | | ● | | | | | | | | | | | | | | | | | | | | | | | |
| STANLEY, STUART (HM19130) | | | | | | | | | | | | | | | | | | | | | | | | | | | ● | | | | | | | | | | | | | | | | | | | | | | | |
| SUMMERTON CLINIC (HM19498) | | | | | | | | | | ● | | | | | | | | | | | | | | | | | | | | | | | | | | | | | | | | | | | | | | | | |
| SUTTON COURTENAY CHIROPRACTIC (HM19546) | | | | | | | | | | | | | | | | | | | | | | | | | | | ● | | | | | | | | | | | | | | | | | | | | | | | |
| TOUCH OF NATURE (HM20188) | ● | | | | | | ● | | | | | | | | | ● | | | | | | | | | | | | | ● | | | ● | ● | | | | ● | | | | ● | | | ● | | | | | | ● |
| TWINE, I E (HM20453) | | | ● | ● | | | | | | | | | | | | | | | | | | | | | | | ● | | | | | | ● | ● | | | | | | | | | | | | | | | | |
| WANTAGE NATURAL HEALTH CENTRE (HM20891) | | | | ● | | | | | | | | | | | | | | | | | | | | | | | ● | | | | | | ● | | | | | | | | | | | | | | | | | |
| WHEATLEY COMP THERAPY (HM21308) | | | | | | | ● | | | | | | | | | ● | | | | | | | | | | | | | | | | ● | ● | | | | | | | | | | | | | | | | | |
| WHITE, LESLEY (HM21364) | | | | | | | | | | | | | | | | | | | | | | | | | | | ● | | | | | | | | | | | | | | | | | | | | | | | |
| WHITE, MADELINE M (HM21365) | | | | ● | | | | | | | | | | | | | | | | | | | | | | | | | | | | | | | | | | | | | | | | | | | | | | |
| WIGGIN, SALLY (HM21466) | | | | | | | | | | | | | | | | ● | | | | | | | | | | | | | | | | | | | | | | | | | | | | | | | | | | |
| WILKES, MARA (HM21493) | | | | | | | | | | | | | | | | | | | | | | | | | | | ● | | | | | | | | | | | | | | | | | | | | | | | |
| WILKINS, G R F (HM21502) | | | | | | | | | | | | | | | | | | | | | | | | | | | ● | | | | | | | | | | | | | | | | | | | | | | | |
| WITNEY CHIROPRACTIC/CHIROPODY (HM21750) | | | | | | | | | | | | | | | | | | | | | | | | | | ● | ● | | | | | | | | | | | | | | | | | | | | | | | |
| WITNEY NATURAL HEALTH CLINIC (HM21751) | | ● | ● | | | | ● | | | | | | | | | | | | | | | | | ● | | | ● | | | | ● | ● | ● | | | | ● | | | ● | | | | | | | | | | |
| YEN YANG (HM22007) | | | | | | | | | | | | | | | | | | | | | | | | | | | ● | | | | | | | | | | | | | | | | | | | | | | | |
| SHROPSHIRE | | | | | | | | | | | | | | | | | | | | | | | | | | | | | | | | | | | | | | | | | | | | | | | | | | |
| A J F LABORATORIES (HM00035) | | | | | | | | | | | | | | | | | | | | | | | | | | | ● | | | | | | | | | | | | | | | | | | | | | | | |
| ACUMEDIC (HM00218) | | ● | ● | | | | | | | | | | | | | | | | | | | | | | ● | | | | | | | | | | | | | | | | | | | | | | | | | |
| AYRES, JOHN (HM01434) | | | | | | | | | | | | | ● | | | | | | | | | | | | | | | | ● | | | | ● | | | | | | | | | | | | | | | | | |
| BENCH, PAUL (HM02121) | | | | | | | | | | | | | | | | ● | | | | | | | | | | | | | | | | | | | | | | | | | | | | | | | | | | |
| BODYLIFE CENTRE (HM02622) | | | | | | | | | | | | ● | | | | | | | | | | | | | | | | | | | | | | | | | | | | | | | | | | | | | | |
| BOOTH, ROBERT (HM02709) | | | ● | | | | | | | | | | | | | | | | | | | | | | | | | | | | | | | | | | | | | | | | | | | | | | | |
| BRIDGNORTH CHIROPRACTIC CLINIC (HM03014) | | | | | | | | | | | | | | | | | | | | | | | | | | | ● | | | | | | | | | | | | | | | | | | | | | | | |
| CENTRE FOR POSITIVE HEALTH (HM03914) | | | | | | | ● | | | | | | | | | | | | | | | | | | | | | | | | | | | | | | | | | | | | | | | | | | | |
| COLERIDGE, JUDY (HM04831) | | | | | | | | | | | | | | | | | | | | | | | | | | | | | | | | | ● | | | | | | | | | | | | | | | | | |
| CORKE, A J (HM05167) | | | | | | | | | | | ● | ● | | | | | | | | ● | | | | | | | | | | | | | ● | | | | | | | | | | | | | | | | | |
| EDWARDS, A D (HM06640) | | | ● | | | | | | | | | | | | | | | | | | | | | | | | | | | | | | | | | | | | | | | | | | | | | | | |
| FULLERTON, N P (HM07792) | | | | | | | | | | | | | | | | | | | | | | | | | | | ● | | | | | | | | | | | | | | | | | | | | | | | |
| GEORGE, CHRISTOPHER (HM07989) | | | ● | | | | | | | | | | | | | | | | | | | | | | | | | | | | | | | | | | | | | | | | | | | | | | | |
| GIARDINO (HM08019) | | | | | | | ● | | | | | | | | | | | | | | | | | | | | | | | | | | | | | | | | | | | | | | | | | | | |
| HALE, DAVID (HM08730) | | | ● | | | | | | | | | | | | | | | | | | | | | | | | | | | | | | | | | | | | | | | | | | | | | | | |
| HALES OSTEOPATHIC PRACTICE (HM08743) | | | ● | | | | | | | | | | | | | | | | | | | | | | | | | | | | | | | ● | | | | | | | | | | | | | | | | |

# A - F Therapies at Practices/Businesses

Business by County with Reference no.

| Business | Absent Healing | Acupressure | Acupuncture | Alexander Technique | Allergy Testing | Anthroposophical Med | Aromatherapy | Art Therapy | Aura Therapy | Auricular Therapy | Auto Suggestion | Autogenic Training | Aversion Therapy | Ayurvedic Medicine | Baby Massage | Bach Remedies | Bates Method | Beauty Therapy | Bio-energetics | Biofeedback | Biomagnetic Therapy | Biomechanics | Bonesetting | Bowen Therapy | Chinese Herbal Medicine |
|---|---|---|---|---|---|---|---|---|---|---|---|---|---|---|---|---|---|---|---|---|---|---|---|---|---|
| HEAVE, M & HUMPHREY, V (HM09470) | | | ● | | | | | | | | | | | | | | | | | | | | | | |
| KUSIAR, BILL (HM11828) | | | | | | | | | | | | | | | | | | | | | | | | | |
| KUSIAR, C W (HM11830) | | | | | | | | | | | | | | | | | | | | | | | | | |
| LUDLOW OSTEOPATHIC CLINIC (HM12727) | | | | | ● | | | | | | | | | | | | | | | | | | | | |
| MADDOCKS CLINIC (HM12898) | | | ● | | | | | | | | | | | | | | | | | | | | | | |
| NEEDHAM, LYNDA M (HM14751) | | | ● | | | | | | | | | | | | | | | | | | | | | | |
| OSTEOPATHIC (HM15449) | | | | | | | | | | | | | | | | | | | | | | | | | |
| OSTLE, SAMANTHA (HM15480) | | | | | | | | | | | | | | | | | | | | | | | | | |
| PEARSON, CHRISTINE (HM15911) | | | | | | | | | | | | | | | | | | | | | | | | | |
| PERRY, JANET (HM16045) | | | | ● | | | | | | | | | | | | | | | | | | | | | |
| PERRY, JANET (HM16044) | | | | ● | | | | | | | | | | | | | | | | | | | | | |
| PHILLIPS, ANN (HM16124) | | | | | | | ● | | | | | | | | | | | | | | | | | | |
| PREES COMPLEMENTARY THERAPIES (HM16533) | | | | | | | ● | | | | | | | | | | | | | | | | | | |
| PROF ASS OF ALEXANDER TEACHERS (HM16656) | | | | ● | | | | | | | | | | | | | | | | | | | | | |
| REYNOLDS, TESS (HM17216) | | | ● | | | | | | | | | | | | | | | | | | | | | | |
| ROBERTS, S (HM17426) | | | | | | | | | | | | | | | | | | | | | | | | | |
| SHREWSBURY SOLE CARE (HM18507) | | | | | | | | | | | | | | | | | | | | | | | | | |
| TAN & BEAUTY STUDIO (HM19676) | | | | | | | ● | | | | | | | | | | | | | | | | | | |
| WALMSLEY, RUTH (HM20848) | | ● | | | | | ● | | | | | | | | | ● | | | | | | | | | |
| WESTON, JOHN (HM21279) | | ● | | | | | | | | | | | | | | | | | | | | | ● | | |
| WHITELEY, STEVEN (HM21400) | | | | | | | ● | | | | | | | | | | | | | | | | | | |
| WILD ROSE (HM21488) | | | | | | | ● | | | | | | | | | | | | | | | | | | |
| WILSON, AMANDA (HM21644) | | | | | | | | | | | | | | | | | | | | | | ● | | | |
| **SOMERSET** | | | | | | | | | | | | | | | | | | | | | | | | | |
| ABBEY CHIROPODY SERVICES (HM00074) | | | | | | | | | | | | | | | | | | | | | | | | | |
| ALASKAN BACH FLOWER REMEDIES (HM00472) | | | | | | | ● | | | | | | | | | ● | | | | | | | | | |
| ALEXANDER TECHNIQUE (HM00530) | | | | ● | | | | | | | | | | | | | | | | | | | | | |
| ANDERSON, DAVID (HM00816) | | | | | | | | | | | | | | | | | | | | | | | | | |
| ANSON, BARRIE (HM00916) | ● | | | | | | | | | | | | | | | ● | | | | ● | | | | | |
| AROMAKIDS (HM01079) | | | | | | | ● | | | | | | | | | | | | | | | | | | |
| ASHA MANIPULATIONS (HM01185) | | | | | | | | | | | | | | | | | | | | | | | | | |
| AVALON CLINIC (HM01378) | | | ● | | | | | | | | | | | | | | | | | | | | | | |
| AVENUE CLINIC (HM01388) | | | ● | ● | | | ● | | | | | | | ● | | ● | | | | | | | | | |
| BAILEY, LINDA R (HM01552) | | | | | | | | | | | | | | | | | | | | | | | | | |

| Business | Chiropody | Chiropractic | Clinical Ecology | Cognitive Therapy | Colonic Hydrotherapy | Colour Therapy | Complementary Therapy | Counselling | Cranial Osteopathy | Cranio-Sacral Therapy | Cryo Surgery | Crystal Healing | Cupping | Cymatics | Dance Movement Thrpy | Dietician | Do-In | Douching | Dowsing | Drama Therapy | Electrolipolysis | Electrolysis | Electrotherapy | Encounter Groups | Faith Healing |
|---|---|---|---|---|---|---|---|---|---|---|---|---|---|---|---|---|---|---|---|---|---|---|---|---|---|
| HEAVE, M & HUMPHREY, V (HM09470) | | | | | | | | | | | | | | | | | | | | | | | | | |
| KUSIAR, BILL (HM11828) | | ● | | | | | | | | | | | | | | | | | | | | | | | |
| KUSIAR, C W (HM11830) | | ● | | | | | | | | | | | | | | | | | | | | | | | |
| LUDLOW OSTEOPATHIC CLINIC (HM12727) | | | | | | | | | | | | | | | | | | | | | | | | | |
| MADDOCKS CLINIC (HM12898) | | | | | | | | | | | | | | | | | | | | | | | | | |
| NEEDHAM, LYNDA M (HM14751) | | | | ● | | | | ● | | | | | | | | | | | | | | | | | |
| OSTEOPATHIC (HM15449) | | | | | | | | ● | ● | | | | ● | | | | | | | | | | | | |
| OSTLE, SAMANTHA (HM15480) | | ● | | | | | | | | | | | | | | | | | | | | | | | |
| PEARSON, CHRISTINE (HM15911) | | | | | | | | ● | | | | | | | | | | | | | | | | | |
| PERRY, JANET (HM16045) | | | | | | | | | | | | | | | | | | | | | | | | | |
| PERRY, JANET (HM16044) | | | | | | | | | | | | | | | | | | | | | | | | | |
| PHILLIPS, ANN (HM16124) | | | | | | | | | | | | | | | | | | | | | | | | | |
| PREES COMPLEMENTARY THERAPIES (HM16533) | | | | | | | | | | | | | | | | | | | | | | | | | |
| PROF ASS OF ALEXANDER TEACHERS (HM16656) | | | | | | | | | | | | | | | | | | | | | | | | | |
| REYNOLDS, TESS (HM17216) | | | | | | | | | | | | | | | | | | | | | | | | | |
| ROBERTS, S (HM17426) | | ● | | | | | | | | | | | | | | | | | | | | | | | |
| SHREWSBURY SOLE CARE (HM18507) | ● | | | | | | | | | | | | | | | | | | | | | | | | |
| TAN & BEAUTY STUDIO (HM19676) | | | | | | | | | | | | | | | | | | | | | | | | | |
| WALMSLEY, RUTH (HM20848) | | | | | | | ● | | | | | | ● | | | | | | | | | | | | |
| WESTON, JOHN (HM21279) | | | | | | | | | | | | | | | | | | | | | | | ● | | |
| WHITELEY, STEVEN (HM21400) | | | | | | | | | | | | | | | | | | | | | | | | | |
| WILD ROSE (HM21488) | | | | | | | | | | | | | | | | | | | | | | | | | |
| WILSON, AMANDA (HM21644) | ● | | | | | | | | | | | | | | | | | | | | | | | | |
| **SOMERSET** | | | | | | | | | | | | | | | | | | | | | | | | | |
| ABBEY CHIROPODY SERVICES (HM00074) | ● | | | | | | | | | | | | | | | | | | | | | | | | |
| ALASKAN BACH FLOWER REMEDIES (HM00472) | | | | | | | | | | | | | | | | | | | | | | | | | |
| ALEXANDER TECHNIQUE (HM00530) | | | | | | | | | | | | | | | | | | | | | | | | | |
| ANDERSON, DAVID (HM00816) | ● | | | | | | | | | | | | | | | | | | | | | | | | |
| ANSON, BARRIE (HM00916) | | | | | | | ● | ● | | | | | | | | | | | | | | | | | ● |
| AROMAKIDS (HM01079) | | | | | | | | | | | | | | | | | | | | | | | | | |
| ASHA MANIPULATIONS (HM01185) | | ● | | | | | | | | | | | | | | | | | | | | | | | |
| AVALON CLINIC (HM01378) | | | | | | | | | | | | | | | | | | | | | | | | | |
| AVENUE CLINIC (HM01388) | | | | | | | ● | ● | ● | | | | ● | | | | | | | | | | | | |
| BAILEY, LINDA R (HM01552) | | | | | | | | | | | | | | | | | | | ● | | | | | | |

# A - F Therapies at Practices/Businesses

Business by County with Reference no.

| Business by County with Reference no. | Absent Healing | Acupressure | Acupuncture | Alexander Technique | Allergy Testing | Anthroposohical Med | Aromatherapy | Art Therapy | Aura Therapy | Auricular Therapy |
|---|---|---|---|---|---|---|---|---|---|---|
| BATH ALEXANDER TECHNIQUE (HM01890) | | | | ● | | | | | | |
| BATH BACK CLINIC (HM01891) | | | ● | | | | | | | |
| BATH NATURAL MEDICAL CENTRE (HM01893) | | | ● | | | | | | | |
| BATHPOOL CHIROPRACTIC CLINIC (HM01900) | | | | | | | ● | | | |
| BAWDRIP CHIROPRACTIC CLINIC (HM01917) | | | | | | | | | | |
| BEECH HOUSE CLINIC (HM02046) | | | ● | | | | | | | |
| BOULEVARD PHARMACY (HM02739) | | ● | ● | | | | ● | | | |
| BRIDGET HEALING CENTRE (HM03008) | | | | | | | ● | | | |
| CASTLE SURGERY (HM03840) | | | ● | | | | ● | | | |
| CHAMELEON OILS (HM03961) | | | | | | | ● | | | |
| CHEDDAR COMP MEDICINE CTRE (HM04075) | | | ● | ● | | | ● | | | |
| CHICK, MARY (HM04158) | | | | | | | | | | |
| CHINESE MEDICAL CENTRE (HM04238) | | ● | ● | | | | | | | |
| CHIPPER, MARY (HM04278) | | | | | | | ● | | | |
| CHIROPODY SURGERY (HM04344) | | | | | | | | | | |
| CHURCHILL, MARION (HM04472) | | | | | | | | | | |
| CLARKE GAIL & RAWLINSON MIKE (HM04581) | | | | ● | | | | | | |
| COMPLEMENTARY THERAPY (HM04942) | | | ● | | | | | | | |
| COOK, COLIN (HM05041) | | ● | ● | | | | | | | |
| COUNSULTING ROOMS (HM05253) | | | | | | | | | | |
| DAVIES, SALLY (HM05840) | | | | | | | ● | | | |
| DEVONSHIRE SURGERY (HM06044) | | | | | | | | | | |
| DIGBY, DAVID (HM06096) | | | | ● | | | | | | |
| DIXON & ASSOCIATES (HM06125) | | | | | | | | | | |
| DREWITT, JENNIFER (HM06309) | | | | | | | | | | |
| ENGBERG, ANNELI (HM06822) | | | ● | | | | | | | |
| EUROPEAN COLLEGE-BOWEN STUDIES (HM06946) | | | | | | | | | | |
| FRANCES-WHITAKER, J A (HM07665) | | | | | | | | | | |
| FRIENDLY FROG (HM07748) | | | | | | | ● | | | |
| GILLINGHAM, GLENNA (HM08098) | | | ● | | | | | | | |
| GLASTONBURY CHIROPRACTIC (HM08131) | | | | | | | ● | | | |
| GLASTONBURY EAST WEST CENTRE (HM08132) | | | ● | | | | ● | | | |
| HARVEY, LEE (HM09163) | | | | | | | | | | |
| HAWTHORN HOUSE AROMATHERAPY (HM09243) | | | | | | | ● | | | |

| Business by County with Reference no. | Auto Suggestion | Autogenic Training | Aversion Therapy | Ayurvedic Medicine | Baby Massage | Bach Remedies | Bates Method | Beauty Therapy | Bio-energetics | Biofeedback |
|---|---|---|---|---|---|---|---|---|---|---|
| BATH ALEXANDER TECHNIQUE (HM01890) | | | | | | | | | | |
| BATH BACK CLINIC (HM01891) | | | | | | | | | | |
| BATH NATURAL MEDICAL CENTRE (HM01893) | | | | | | | | | | |
| BATHPOOL CHIROPRACTIC CLINIC (HM01900) | | | | | | | | | | |
| BAWDRIP CHIROPRACTIC CLINIC (HM01917) | | | | | | | | | | |
| BEECH HOUSE CLINIC (HM02046) | | | | | | | | | | |
| BOULEVARD PHARMACY (HM02739) | | | | | | ● | | | | |
| BRIDGET HEALING CENTRE (HM03008) | | | | | | | | | | |
| CASTLE SURGERY (HM03840) | | | | | | | | | | |
| CHAMELEON OILS (HM03961) | | | | | | | | | | |
| CHEDDAR COMP MEDICINE CTRE (HM04075) | | | | | | | | | | |
| CHICK, MARY (HM04158) | | | | | | ● | | | | |
| CHINESE MEDICAL CENTRE (HM04238) | | | | | | | | | | |
| CHIPPER, MARY (HM04278) | | | | | | | | | | |
| CHIROPODY SURGERY (HM04344) | | | | | | | | | | |
| CHURCHILL, MARION (HM04472) | | | | | | | | | | |
| CLARKE GAIL & RAWLINSON MIKE (HM04581) | | | | | | | | | | |
| COMPLEMENTARY THERAPY (HM04942) | | | | | | | | | | |
| COOK, COLIN (HM05041) | | | | | | | | | | |
| COUNSULTING ROOMS (HM05253) | ● | ● | ● | | | | | | | ● |
| DAVIES, SALLY (HM05840) | | | | | | | | | | |
| DEVONSHIRE SURGERY (HM06044) | | | | | | | | | | |
| DIGBY, DAVID (HM06096) | | | | | | | | | | |
| DIXON & ASSOCIATES (HM06125) | | | | | | | | | | |
| DREWITT, JENNIFER (HM06309) | | | | | | ● | | | | |
| ENGBERG, ANNELI (HM06822) | | | | | | | | | | |
| EUROPEAN COLLEGE-BOWEN STUDIES (HM06946) | | | | | | | | | | |
| FRANCES-WHITAKER, J A (HM07665) | | | | | | | | | | |
| FRIENDLY FROG (HM07748) | | | | | | | | | | |
| GILLINGHAM, GLENNA (HM08098) | | | | | | | | | | |
| GLASTONBURY CHIROPRACTIC (HM08131) | | | | | | | | | | |
| GLASTONBURY EAST WEST CENTRE (HM08132) | | | | | | | | | | |
| HARVEY, LEE (HM09163) | | | | | | | | | | |
| HAWTHORN HOUSE AROMATHERAPY (HM09243) | | | | | | | | | | |

| Business by County with Reference no. | Biomagnetic Therapy | Biomechanics | Bonesetting | Bowen Therapy | Chinese Herbal Medicine | Chiropody | Chiropractic | Clinical Ecology | Cognitive Therapy | Colonic Hydrotherapy |
|---|---|---|---|---|---|---|---|---|---|---|
| BATH ALEXANDER TECHNIQUE (HM01890) | | | | | | | | | | |
| BATH BACK CLINIC (HM01891) | | | | | | | ● | | | |
| BATH NATURAL MEDICAL CENTRE (HM01893) | | | | | | | ● | | | |
| BATHPOOL CHIROPRACTIC CLINIC (HM01900) | | | | | | | ● | | | |
| BAWDRIP CHIROPRACTIC CLINIC (HM01917) | | | | | | | ● | | | |
| BEECH HOUSE CLINIC (HM02046) | | | | | ● | | ● | | | |
| BOULEVARD PHARMACY (HM02739) | | | | | ● | ● | | | | |
| BRIDGET HEALING CENTRE (HM03008) | | | | | | | | | | |
| CASTLE SURGERY (HM03840) | | | | | | | ● | | | |
| CHAMELEON OILS (HM03961) | | | | | | | | | | |
| CHEDDAR COMP MEDICINE CTRE (HM04075) | | | | | | ● | | | | |
| CHICK, MARY (HM04158) | | | | | | | | | | |
| CHINESE MEDICAL CENTRE (HM04238) | | | | | ● | | | | | |
| CHIPPER, MARY (HM04278) | | | | | | | | | | |
| CHIROPODY SURGERY (HM04344) | | ● | | | | ● | | | | |
| CHURCHILL, MARION (HM04472) | | | | | | | ● | | | |
| CLARKE GAIL & RAWLINSON MIKE (HM04581) | | | | | | | | | | |
| COMPLEMENTARY THERAPY (HM04942) | | | | | | | | ● | | |
| COOK, COLIN (HM05041) | | | | | | | | | | |
| COUNSULTING ROOMS (HM05253) | | | | | | | | | ● | |
| DAVIES, SALLY (HM05840) | | | | | | | | | | |
| DEVONSHIRE SURGERY (HM06044) | | | | | | | ● | | | |
| DIGBY, DAVID (HM06096) | | | | | | | | | | |
| DIXON & ASSOCIATES (HM06125) | | | | | | | ● | | | |
| DREWITT, JENNIFER (HM06309) | | | | | | | | | | |
| ENGBERG, ANNELI (HM06822) | | | | | | | | | | |
| EUROPEAN COLLEGE-BOWEN STUDIES (HM06946) | | | | ● | | | | | | |
| FRANCES-WHITAKER, J A (HM07665) | | | | | | ● | | | | |
| FRIENDLY FROG (HM07748) | | | | | | | | | | |
| GILLINGHAM, GLENNA (HM08098) | | | | | | | | | | |
| GLASTONBURY CHIROPRACTIC (HM08131) | | | | | | | ● | | | |
| GLASTONBURY EAST WEST CENTRE (HM08132) | | | | | | | | | | |
| HARVEY, LEE (HM09163) | | | | | | | ● | | | |
| HAWTHORN HOUSE AROMATHERAPY (HM09243) | | | | | | | | | | |

| Business by County with Reference no. | Colour Therapy | Complementary Therapy | Counselling | Cranial Osteopathy | Cranio-Sacral Therapy | Cryo Surgery | Crystal Healing | Cupping | Cymatics | Dance Movement Thrpy |
|---|---|---|---|---|---|---|---|---|---|---|
| BATH ALEXANDER TECHNIQUE (HM01890) | | | | | | | | | | |
| BATH BACK CLINIC (HM01891) | | | | | | | | | | |
| BATH NATURAL MEDICAL CENTRE (HM01893) | | | | | | | | | | |
| BATHPOOL CHIROPRACTIC CLINIC (HM01900) | | ● | | | | | | | | |
| BAWDRIP CHIROPRACTIC CLINIC (HM01917) | | | | | | | | | | |
| BEECH HOUSE CLINIC (HM02046) | | | | | | | | | | |
| BOULEVARD PHARMACY (HM02739) | | ● | ● | | | | | | | |
| BRIDGET HEALING CENTRE (HM03008) | | | | | | | | | | |
| CASTLE SURGERY (HM03840) | | | ● | | | | | | | |
| CHAMELEON OILS (HM03961) | | | | | | | | | | |
| CHEDDAR COMP MEDICINE CTRE (HM04075) | | | ● | | | | | | | |
| CHICK, MARY (HM04158) | | | | | | | | | | |
| CHINESE MEDICAL CENTRE (HM04238) | | | | | | | | | | |
| CHIPPER, MARY (HM04278) | | | | | | | | | | |
| CHIROPODY SURGERY (HM04344) | | | | | | | | | | |
| CHURCHILL, MARION (HM04472) | | | | | | | | | | |
| CLARKE GAIL & RAWLINSON MIKE (HM04581) | | | | | ● | | | | | |
| COMPLEMENTARY THERAPY (HM04942) | | | | | | | | | | |
| COOK, COLIN (HM05041) | | ● | | | | | | | | |
| COUNSULTING ROOMS (HM05253) | | ● | ● | | | | | | | |
| DAVIES, SALLY (HM05840) | | | | | | | | | | |
| DEVONSHIRE SURGERY (HM06044) | | | | | | | | | | |
| DIGBY, DAVID (HM06096) | | | | | | | | | | |
| DIXON & ASSOCIATES (HM06125) | | | | | | | | | | |
| DREWITT, JENNIFER (HM06309) | | | | | | | | | | |
| ENGBERG, ANNELI (HM06822) | | | | | | | | | | |
| EUROPEAN COLLEGE-BOWEN STUDIES (HM06946) | | ● | | | | | | | | |
| FRANCES-WHITAKER, J A (HM07665) | | | | | | | | | | |
| FRIENDLY FROG (HM07748) | | | | | | | | | | |
| GILLINGHAM, GLENNA (HM08098) | | | | | | | | | | |
| GLASTONBURY CHIROPRACTIC (HM08131) | | | ● | | | | | | | |
| GLASTONBURY EAST WEST CENTRE (HM08132) | | | ● | | | | | | | |
| HARVEY, LEE (HM09163) | | | | | | | | | | |
| HAWTHORN HOUSE AROMATHERAPY (HM09243) | | | | | | | | | | |

| Business by County with Reference no. | Dietician | Do-In | Douching | Dowsing | Drama Therapy | Electrolipolysis | Electrolysis | Electrotherapy | Encounter Groups | Faith Healing |
|---|---|---|---|---|---|---|---|---|---|---|
| BATH ALEXANDER TECHNIQUE (HM01890) | | | | | | | | | | |
| BATH BACK CLINIC (HM01891) | | | | | | | | | | |
| BATH NATURAL MEDICAL CENTRE (HM01893) | | | | | | | | | | |
| BATHPOOL CHIROPRACTIC CLINIC (HM01900) | | | | | | | | | | |
| BAWDRIP CHIROPRACTIC CLINIC (HM01917) | | | | | | | | | | |
| BEECH HOUSE CLINIC (HM02046) | | | | | | | | | | |
| BOULEVARD PHARMACY (HM02739) | ● | | | | | | | | | |
| BRIDGET HEALING CENTRE (HM03008) | | | | | | | | | | |
| CASTLE SURGERY (HM03840) | | | | | | | | | | |
| CHAMELEON OILS (HM03961) | | | | | | | | | | |
| CHEDDAR COMP MEDICINE CTRE (HM04075) | | | | | | | | | | |
| CHICK, MARY (HM04158) | | | | | | | | | | |
| CHINESE MEDICAL CENTRE (HM04238) | | | | | | | | | | |
| CHIPPER, MARY (HM04278) | | | | | | | | | | |
| CHIROPODY SURGERY (HM04344) | | | | | | | | | | |
| CHURCHILL, MARION (HM04472) | | | | | | | | | | |
| CLARKE GAIL & RAWLINSON MIKE (HM04581) | | | | | | | | | | |
| COMPLEMENTARY THERAPY (HM04942) | | | | | | | | | | |
| COOK, COLIN (HM05041) | | | | | | | | ● | | |
| COUNSULTING ROOMS (HM05253) | | | | | | | | | | |
| DAVIES, SALLY (HM05840) | | | | | | | | | | |
| DEVONSHIRE SURGERY (HM06044) | | | | | | | | | | |
| DIGBY, DAVID (HM06096) | | | | | | | | | | |
| DIXON & ASSOCIATES (HM06125) | | | | | | | | | | |
| DREWITT, JENNIFER (HM06309) | | | | | | | | | | |
| ENGBERG, ANNELI (HM06822) | | | | | | | | | | |
| EUROPEAN COLLEGE-BOWEN STUDIES (HM06946) | | | | | | | | | | |
| FRANCES-WHITAKER, J A (HM07665) | | | | | | | | | | |
| FRIENDLY FROG (HM07748) | | | | | | | | | | |
| GILLINGHAM, GLENNA (HM08098) | | | | | | | | | | |
| GLASTONBURY CHIROPRACTIC (HM08131) | | | | | | | | | | |
| GLASTONBURY EAST WEST CENTRE (HM08132) | | | | | | | | | | |
| HARVEY, LEE (HM09163) | | | | | | | | | | |
| HAWTHORN HOUSE AROMATHERAPY (HM09243) | | | | | | | | | | |

# A - F Therapies at Practices/Businesses

| Business by County with Reference no. | Absent Healing | Acupressure | Acupuncture | Alexander Technique | Allergy Testing | Anthroposohical Med | Aromatherapy | Art Therapy | Aura Therapy | Auricular Therapy | Auto Suggestion | Autogenic Training | Aversion Therapy | Ayurvedic Medicine | Baby Massage | Bach Remedies | Bates Method | Beauty Therapy | Bio-energetics | Biofeedback | Biomagnetic Therapy | Biomechanics | Bonesetting | Bowen Therapy | Chinese Herbal Medicine | Chiropody | Chiropractic | Clinical Ecology | Cognitive Therapy | Colonic Hydrotherapy | Colour Therapy | Complementary Therapy | Counselling | Cranial Osteopathy | Cranio-Sacral Therapy | Cryo Surgery | Crystal Healing | Cupping | Cymatics | Dance Movement Thrpy | Dietician | Do-In | Douching | Dowsing | Drama Therapy | Electrolipolysis | Electrolysis | Electrotherapy | Encounter Groups | Faith Healing |
|---|---|---|---|---|---|---|---|---|---|---|---|---|---|---|---|---|---|---|---|---|---|---|---|---|---|---|---|---|---|---|---|---|---|---|---|---|---|---|---|---|---|---|---|---|---|---|---|---|---|---|
| HELEN SMITH CHIROPODIST (HM09515) | | | | | | | | | | | | | | | | | | | | | | | | | | ● | | | | | | | | | | | | | | | | | | | | | | | | |
| HOLISTIC HEALING CENTRE (HM09962) | | | | | | | ● | | | | | | | | | | | | | | | | | | | | | | | | | | | | | | | | | | | | | | | | | | | |
| JASMINE HOLISTIC HEALTH (HM10937) | | | | | | | ● | | | | | | | | | | | | | | | | | | | | | | | | | | | | | | | | | | | | | | | | | | | |
| JAY, TIMOTHY C (HM10941) | | | | | | | | | | | | | | | | | | | | | | | | | | | ● | | | | | | | | | | | | | | | | | | | | | | | |
| JOHNSTONE, ALLAN (HM11105) | | | ● | | | | | | | | | | | | | | | | | | | | | | | | | | | | | | | | | | | | | | | | | | | | | | | |
| JONES, RAYMOND (HM11190) | | | | | ● | | | | | | | | | | | | | | | | | | | | | | ● | | | | | | | | | | | | | | | | | | | | | | | |
| KENDAL, S L (HM11474) | | | | | | | | | | | | | | | | | | | | | | | | | | | ● | | | | | | | | | | | | | | | | | | | | | | | |
| KIRKMEAD CENTRE (HM11718) | | | | | | | ● | | | | | | | | | | | | | | | | | | | | | | | | | | | | | | | | | | | | | | | | | | | |
| KNIGHT, ALICE (HM11745) | | | | ● | | | | | | | | | | | | | | | | | | | | | | | | | | | | | | | | | | | | | | | | | | | | | | |
| LANE-WILLAN, AVIS (HM11944) | | | ● | | | | | | | | | | | | | | | | | | | | | | | | | | | | | | | | | | | | | | | | | | | | | | | |
| LAUREL PLACE (HM12009) | | | ● | | | | ● | | | | | | | | | | | | | | | | | | | | ● | | | | | | | | | | | | | | | | | | | | | | | |
| LEAVEY, J () | | | | | | | ● | | | | | | | | | | | | | | | | | | | | | | | | | | | | | | | | | | | | | | | | | | | |
| LOGAN, DAVID (HM12566) | | | | | | | | | | | | | | | | | | | | | | | | | | | | | | | | | ● | | | | | | | | | | | | | | | | | |
| LOTUS EMPORIUM (HM12655) | | | | | | | ● | | | | | | | | | | | | | | | | | | | | | | | | | | | | | | | | | | | | | | | | | | | |
| MARY WILKINSON - MCTIMONEY (HM13226) | | | | | | | | | | | | | | | | | | | | | | | | | | | ● | | | | | | | | | | | | | | | | | | | | | | | |
| MCLOUGHLIN, BRENDAN (HM13559) | | | | | | | | | | | | | | | | | | | | | | | | | | | | | | | | | ● | | | | | | | | | | | | | | | | | |
| MIDSOMER NORTON CHIROPRACTIC (HM13844) | | | ● | | | | | | | | | | | | | | | | | | | | | | | | ● | | | | | | | | | | | | | | | | | | | | | | | |
| MILSOM STREET CLINIC (HM13944) | | | ● | ● | | | ● | | | | | | | | | | | | | | | | | | | | | | | | | | ● | | ● | | | | | | | | | | | | | | | |
| MOIR, GILL (HM14047) | | | | | | | ● | | | | | | | | ● | | | | | | | | | | | | | | | | | | | | | | | | | | | | | | | | | | | |
| NATURAL SPIRITUAL HEALING (HM14626) | ● | | | | | | | | | | | | | | | | | | | | | | | | | | | | | | | | | | | | | | | | | | | | | | | | | |
| NATURAL THERAPIES (HM14632) | | | | | | | ● | | | | | | | | | | | | | | | | | | | | | | | | ● | | | | | | ● | | | | | | | | | | | | | |
| NORSO BIOMAGNETICS UK (HM15016) | | | | | | | | | | | | | | | | | | | | | ● | | | | | | | | | | | | | | | | | | | | | | | | | | | | | |
| NUTRITION FOR LIFE (HM15123) | | | | | | | | | | | | | | | | | | | | | | | | | | | | | | | | ● | | | | | | | | | | | | | | | | | | |
| ORCHARD CLINIC (HM15360) | | | ● | | | | | | | | | | | | | | | | | | | | | | | | ● | | | | | | | | | | | | | | | | | | | | | | | |
| PARK HOUSE CLINIC (HM15666) | | | ● | | | | | | | | | | | | | | | | | | | | | | | | | | | | | | | ● | | | | | | | | | | | | | | ● | | |
| PARNELL, R H (HM15727) | | | ● | | | | | | | | | | | | | | | | | | | | | | | | | | | | | | | | | | | | | | | | | | | | | | | |
| PARRY, J M (HM15738) | | | | | | | | | | | | | | | | | | | | | | | | | | ● | | | | | | | | | | | | | | | | | | | | | | | | |
| PENNINGTON, PAM (HM15990) | | | | | | | | | | | | | | | | | | | | | | | | | | ● | | | | | | | | | | | | | | | | | | | | | | | | |
| PENNINGTON, PAM V (HM15991) | | | | | | | | | | | | | | | | | | | | | | | | | | ● | | | | | | | | | | | | | | | | | | | | | | | | |
| PERKINS, L (HM16026) | | | | | | | | | | | | | | | | | | | | | | | | | | ● | | | | | | | | | | | | | | | | | | | | | | | | |
| PITMAN, VICKI (HM16342) | | | | | | | ● | | | | | | | | | | | | | | | | | | | | | | | | | | | | | | | | | | | | | | | | | | | |
| PITT, I T (HM16347) | | | ● | | | | | | | | | | | | | | | | | | | | ● | | | | ● | | | | | | | ● | | | | ● | | | ● | | | | | | | ● | | |
| POMEGRANATE PRODUCTS (HM16421) | | | | | | | ● | | | | | | | | | | | | | | | | | | | | | | | | | | | | | | | | | | | | | | | | | | | |
| PRESSURE WORKS (HM16544) | | ● | | | | | | | | | | | | | | | | | | | | | | | | | | | | | | | | | | | | | | | | | | | | | | | | |

# A - F Therapies at Practices/Businesses

| Business by County with Reference no. | Absent Healing | Acupressure | Acupuncture | Alexander Technique | Allergy Testing | Anthroposohical Med | Aromatherapy | Art Therapy | Aura Therapy | Auricular Therapy | Auto Suggestion | Autogenic Training | Aversion Therapy | Ayurvedic Medicine | Baby Massage | Bach Remedies | Bates Method | Beauty Therapy | Bio-energetics | Biofeedback | Biomagnetic Therapy | Biomechanics | Bonesetting | Bowen Therapy | Chinese Herbal Medicine | Chiropody | Chiropractic | Clinical Ecology | Cognitive Therapy | Colonic Hydrotherapy | Colour Therapy | Complementary Therapy | Counselling | Cranial Osteopathy | Cranio-Sacral Therapy | Cryo Surgery | Crystal Healing | Cupping | Cymatics | Dance Movement Thrpy | Dietician | Do-In | Douching | Dowsing | Drama Therapy | Electrolipolysis | Electrolysis | Electrotherapy | Encounter Groups | Faith Healing |
|---|---|---|---|---|---|---|---|---|---|---|---|---|---|---|---|---|---|---|---|---|---|---|---|---|---|---|---|---|---|---|---|---|---|---|---|---|---|---|---|---|---|---|---|---|---|---|---|---|---|---|
| RAWLINS, JANET (HM16973) | | | | | | |●| | | | | | | | | | | | | | | | | | | | | | | | | | | | | | | | | | | | | | | | | | | |
| REED, W A (HM17046) | | | | | | |●| | | | | | | | | | | | | | | | | | | | | | | | | | | | | | | | | | | | | | | | | | | |
| RICHARDS, M J (HM17261) | | | | | | | | | | | | | | | | | | | | | | | | | |●| | | | | | | | | | | | | | | | | | | | | | | | |
| RIETCHEL, F (HM17329) | | | |●| | | | | | | | | | | | | | | | | | | | | | | | | | | | | | | | | | | | | | | | | | | | | | |
| ROBBINS, CAROLINE (HM17392) | | |●| | | | | | | | | | | | | | | | | | | | | | | | | | | | | | | | | | | | | | | | | | | | | | | |
| ROSS, JULIETTE (HM17636) | | | | | | |●| | | | | | | | | | | | | | | | | | | | | | | | | | | | | | | | | | | | | | | | | | | |
| SHAMBHALA (HM18275) |●| | | | | |●| | | |●| | | | | | | |●| | | | |●| | | | | | | |●| |●| | | | | | |●| | | | | | | | | |
| ST JAMES'S SURGERY (HM19079) | | | | | | | | | | | | | | | | | | | | | | | | | | | | | | | |●| |●| | | | | | | | | | | | | | | | |
| ST MICHAELS CHIROPRACTIC (HM19089) | | | | | | | | | | | | | | | | | | | | | | | | | | |●| | | | | | | | | | | | | | | | | | | | | | | |
| STANLEY COURT SURGERY (HM19127) | | | | | | | | | | | | | | | | | | | | | | | | | | |●| | | | | | | | | | | | | | | | | | | | | | | |
| STARCHILD (HM19144) | | | | | | |●| | | | | | | | | | | | | | | | | | | | | | | | | | | | | | | | | | | | | | | | | | | |
| STIRLAND, HAZEL (HM19298) | | | | | | |●| | | | | | | | | | | | | | | | | | | | | | | | | | | | | | | | | | | | | | | | | | | |
| STREET CHIROPRACTIC CLINIC (HM19382) | | | | | | | | | | | | | | | | | | | | | | | | | |●|●| | | | | | | | | | | | | | | | | | | | | | | |
| STREET CHIROPRACTIC CLINIC (HM19383) | | | | | | |●| | | | | | | | | | | | | | | | | | | |●| | | | |●| | | | | | | | | | | | | | | |●| | |
| STRESS CLINIC & NTRL HLTH CTRE (HM19389) | |●|●| | | |●| | | | | | | | | | | | | | | | | | | |●| |●| | |●|●|●| | | | | | |●| | | | | | | | | |
| TARETH CENTRE (HM19704) | | | | | | |●| | | | | | | | | | | | | | | | | | | | | | | | | | | | | | | | | | | | | | | | | | | |
| TAUNTON FOOT SURGERY (HM19722) | | | | | | | | | | | | | | | | | | | | | |●| | | |●| | | | | | | | | | | | | | | | | | | | | | | | |
| TAYLOR, GILLIAN (HM19760) | | | | | | | | | | | | | | | | | | | | | | | | | |●| | | | | | | | | | | | | | | | | | | | | | | | |
| TERRACE THRPY PSYCHO/NTRL HLTH (HM19843) | | |●|●| | |●| | | | | | | | | | | | | | | | | | | | | | | | | |●| |●| | | | | | | | | | | | | | | |
| THOMPSON, G W (DR) (HM19978) | | | | | | | | | | | | | | | | | | | | | | | | | | |●| | | | | | | | | | | | | | | | | | | | | | | |
| TURNPIKE SURGERY (HM20441) | | | | | | | | | | | | | | | | | | | | | | | | | | |●| | | | | | | | | | | | | | | | | | | | | | | |
| TURPIE, JULIE (HM20442) | | | | | | | | | | | | | | | |●| | | | | | | | | | | | | | | | | | | | | | | | | | | | | | | | | | |
| WELLSPRING OSTEO/NTRL HEALTH (HM21181) | | |●| | | |●| | | | | | | | | | | | | | | | | | | | | | | | | |●|●| | | | | | | | | | | | | | | | |
| WESTCOTT, CHARLES (HM21262) | | | | | | | | | | | | | | | | | | | | | | | | | | |●| | | | | | | | | | | | | | | | | | | | | | | |
| WESTERN CHIROPRACTIC CLINIC (HM21263) | | |●| | | |●| | | | | | | | | | | | | | | | | | | |●| | | | | | | | | | | | | | | | | | | | | | | |
| WILLDER, JAMES (HM21522) | | |●| | | | | | | | | | | | | | | | | | | | | | | | | | | | | | | | | | | | | | | | | | | | | | | |
| WILLMOTT, BRENDA (HM21620) | | | | | | | | | | | | | | | |●| | | | | | | | | | | | | | | | | | | | | | | | | | | | | | | | | | |
| WINCANTON CHIROPRACTIC CLINIC (HM21690) | | | | | | | | | | | | | | | | | | | | | | | | | | |●| | | | | | | | | | | | | | | | | | | | | | | |
| YELLOW EMPEROR CORP (HM22004) | | |●| | | | | | | | | | | | | | | | | | | | | | | | | | | | | | | | | | | | | | | | | | | | | | | |
| YEOVIL CHIROPRACTIC CLINIC (HM22008) | | | | |●| |●| | | | | | | | | | | | | | | | | | | |●| | | | | | | | | | | | | | | | | | | | | | | |
| YOUNG, ANTOINETTE & MARTIN (HM22064) | | | | | | | | | | | | | | | | | | | | | | | | | | |●| | | | | | | | | | | | | | | | | | | | | | | |
| STAFFORDSHIRE | | | | | | | | | | | | | | | | | | | | | | | | | | | | | | | | | | | | | | | | | | | | | | | | | | | |
| A TOUCH OF HARMONY (HM00048) | | | | | | |●| | | | | | | | | | | | | | | | | | | | | | | | | | | | | | | | | | | | | | | | | | | |
| ALTERNATIVE THERAPY CENTRE (HM00735) |●| |●|●| | |●| | | | | | | | |●| | | | | | | | | | | | | | | | |●| | | |●| | | | | | |●| | | | | | |●|

# A - F Therapies at Practices/Businesses

| Business by County with Reference no. | Absent Healing | Acupressure | Acupuncture | Alexander Technique | Allergy Testing | Anthroposohical Med | Aromatherapy | Art Therapy | Aura Therapy | Auricular Therapy | Auto Suggestion | Autogenic Training | Aversion Therapy | Ayurvedic Medicine | Baby Massage | Bach Remedies | Bates Method | Beauty Therapy | Bio-energetics | Biofeedback | Biomagnetic Therapy | Biomechanics | Bonesetting | Bowen Therapy | Chinese Herbal Medicine |
|---|---|---|---|---|---|---|---|---|---|---|---|---|---|---|---|---|---|---|---|---|---|---|---|---|---|
| ALTERNATIVES (HM00741) | | | | | | | ● | | | | | | | | | | | | | | | | | | |
| BARCROFT, J M (HM01696) | | | | | | | | | | | | | | | | | | | | | | ● | | | |
| BASFORD CHIROPRACTIC CLINIC (HM01842) | | | | | | | | | | | | | | | | | | | | | | | | | |
| BLANK, CHRISTOPHER (HM02499) | | | | | | | | | | | | | | | | | | | | | | | | | |
| BORE ST POD & CHIROP PRACTICE (HM02716) | | | | | | | | | | | | | | | | | | | | | | ● | | | |
| BOWIE, R (HM02790) | | | | ● | | | | | | | | | | | | | | | | | | | | | |
| BRIDGETT, A (HM03011) | | ● | | | | | | | | | | | | | | | | | | | | | | | |
| BURKE, E (HM03385) | | | ● | | | | | | | | ● | | | | | | | | | | | | | | |
| BURTON CHIROPRACTIC CLINIC (HM03432) | | | | | | | | | | | | | | | | | | | | | | | | | |
| CHACKETT, LINDA (HM03932) | | | | | | | ● | | | | | | | | | | | | | | | | | | |
| CHASE HEALTH FOODS (HM04055) | | | | | | | ● | | | | | | | | | | | | | | | | | | |
| CHASE NATURAL THERAPY CENTRE (HM04059) | | | ● | | | | ● | | | | | | | | | | | | | | | | | ● | |
| CITY CHIROPRACTIC CLINIC (HM04492) | | | ● | | | | | | | | | | | | | | | | | | | | | | |
| CORNERSTONES PRACTICE (HM05182) | | | | | | | | | | | | | | | | | | | | | | | | | |
| CRESCENT CLINIC (HM05417) | | | ● | | ● | | ● | | | | | | | | | | | | | | | | | | |
| CRESCENT CLINIC FOR COMP MED (HM05418) | | | ● | | ● | | ● | | | | | | | | | | | | | | | | | | |
| ECCLESHALL ACUPUNCTURE CLINIC (HM06574) | | | | | | | ● | | | | | | | | | | | | | | | | | | |
| ESSENTIAL HEALTH (HM06911) | | | | | | | ● | | | ● | | | | | | | | | | | | | | | |
| ESSENTIALLY YOU (HM06924) | | | | | | | ● | | | | | | | | | | | | | | | | | | |
| FEET FIRST (HM07176) | | | | | | | | | | | | | | | | | | | | | | ● | | | |
| FOOT SOUL & BODYWORKS (HM07487) | | ● | | | | | ● | | | | | | | | | ● | | | | | | | | | |
| FRASER HOUSE CHIROPRACTIC (HM07691) | | | | | | | | | | | | | | | | | | | | | | | | | |
| GASCOIGNE, DOROTHY (HM07917) | | | | | | | ● | | | | | | | | | | | | | | | | | | |
| GASCOYNE, P (HM07920) | | | | | | | | | | | | | | | | | | | | | | | | | |
| IBBS, ROGER (HM10566) | | | | | | | | | | | | | | | | | | | | | | | | | |
| ISHTA CENTRE (HM10761) | | | ● | | | | ● | | | | | | | | | | | | | | | | | ● | |
| JOHNSON, JANICE (HM11079) | ● | | | | | | | | | | ● | | | | | | | | | | | | | | |
| KING, KAREN (HM11633) | | | | | | | | | | | | | | | | ● | | | | | | | | | |
| LOCKINGTON, W M (HM12551) | | | ● | | | | | | | | | | | | | | | | | | | | | | |
| LOUISE BRITTLE (HM12667) | | | | | | | | | | | | | | | | | | | | | | ● | | | |
| MARCONI, L R (HM13076) | | | | | | | | | | | | | | | | | | | | | | ● | | | |
| MARTIN, BARBARA (HM13188) | | | | | | | ● | | | | | | | | | | | | | | | | | | |
| MELLOR, J SIMON (HM13709) | | | | | | | | | | | | | | | | | | | | | | ● | | | |
| MILL BANK OSTEOPATHIC CLINIC (HM13865) | | | | | | | | | | | | | | | | | | | | | | | | | |

| Business by County with Reference no. | Chiropody | Chiropractic | Clinical Ecology | Cognitive Therapy | Colonic Hydrotherapy | Colour Therapy | Complementary Therapy | Counselling | Cranial Osteopathy | Cranio-Sacral Therapy | Cryo Surgery | Crystal Healing | Cupping | Cymatics | Dance Movement Thrpy | Dietician | Do-In | Douching | Dowsing | Drama Therapy | Electrolipolysis | Electrolysis | Electrotherapy | Encounter Groups | Faith Healing |
|---|---|---|---|---|---|---|---|---|---|---|---|---|---|---|---|---|---|---|---|---|---|---|---|---|---|
| ALTERNATIVES (HM00741) | | | | | | | | | | | | | | | | | | | | | | | | | |
| BARCROFT, J M (HM01696) | ● | | | | | | | | | | | | | | | | | | | | | | | | |
| BASFORD CHIROPRACTIC CLINIC (HM01842) | | ● | | | | | | | | | | | | | | | | | | | | | | | |
| BLANK, CHRISTOPHER (HM02499) | ● | | | | | | | | | | | | | | | | | | | | | | | | |
| BORE ST POD & CHIROP PRACTICE (HM02716) | ● | | | | | | | | | | | | | | | | | | | | | | | | |
| BOWIE, R (HM02790) | | | | | | | | | | | | | | | | | | | | | | | | | |
| BRIDGETT, A (HM03011) | | | | | | | ● | | | | | | | | | | | | | | | | | | |
| BURKE, E (HM03385) | | | | | | | | ● | | | | | | | | ● | | | | | | | | | |
| BURTON CHIROPRACTIC CLINIC (HM03432) | | ● | | | | | | | | | | | | | | | | | | | | | | | |
| CHACKETT, LINDA (HM03932) | | | | | | | | | | | | | | | | | | | | | | | | | |
| CHASE HEALTH FOODS (HM04055) | | | | | | | | | | | | | | | | | | | | | | | | | |
| CHASE NATURAL THERAPY CENTRE (HM04059) | | | | | | | | | | | | | | | | | | | | | | | | | |
| CITY CHIROPRACTIC CLINIC (HM04492) | | ● | | | | | | | | | | | | | | | | | | | | | | | |
| CORNERSTONES PRACTICE (HM05182) | | | | | | | | ● | | | | | | | | | | | | | | | | | |
| CRESCENT CLINIC (HM05417) | | | | | | | | | | | | | | | | | | | | | | | | | |
| CRESCENT CLINIC FOR COMP MED (HM05418) | | | | | | | | | | | | | | | | | | | | | | | | | |
| ECCLESHALL ACUPUNCTURE CLINIC (HM06574) | | | | | | | | | | | | | | | | | | | | | | | | | |
| ESSENTIAL HEALTH (HM06911) | | | | | | | | | | | | | | | | | | | | | | | | | |
| ESSENTIALLY YOU (HM06924) | | | | | | | | | | | | | | | | | | | | | | | | | |
| FEET FIRST (HM07176) | ● | | | | | | | | | | | | | | | | | | | | | | | | |
| FOOT SOUL & BODYWORKS (HM07487) | | | | | | | ● | | | | | | | | | | | | ● | | | | | | |
| FRASER HOUSE CHIROPRACTIC (HM07691) | | ● | | | | | | | | | | | | | | | | | | | | | | | |
| GASCOIGNE, DOROTHY (HM07917) | | | | | | | | | | | | | | | | | | | | | | | | | |
| GASCOYNE, P (HM07920) | ● | | | | | | | | | | | | | | | | | | | | | | | | |
| IBBS, ROGER (HM10566) | ● | | | | | | | | | | | | | | | | | | | | | | | | |
| ISHTA CENTRE (HM10761) | | ● | | | | | | ● | | ● | | | | | | | | | | | | | | | |
| JOHNSON, JANICE (HM11079) | | | | ● | | | | ● | | | | | | | | | | | | | | | | | |
| KING, KAREN (HM11633) | | | | | | | | | | | | | | | | | | | | | | | | | |
| LOCKINGTON, W M (HM12551) | | | | | | | | | | | | | | | | | | | | | | | | | |
| LOUISE BRITTLE (HM12667) | ● | | | | | | | | | | ● | | | | | | | | | | | | | | |
| MARCONI, L R (HM13076) | ● | | | | | | | | | | | | | | | | | | | | | | | | |
| MARTIN, BARBARA (HM13188) | | | | | | | | | | | | | | | | | | | | | | | | | |
| MELLOR, J SIMON (HM13709) | ● | | | | | | | | | | | | | | | | | | | | | | | | |
| MILL BANK OSTEOPATHIC CLINIC (HM13865) | | | | | | | | | ● | | | | | | | | | | | | | | | | |

# A - F Therapies at Practices/Businesses

Business by County with Reference no.

| Business | Absent Healing | Acupressure | Acupuncture | Alexander Technique | Allergy Testing | Anthroposohical Med | Aromatherapy | Art Therapy | Aura Therapy | Auricular Therapy | Auto Suggestion | Autogenic Training | Aversion Therapy | Ayurvedic Medicine | Baby Massage | Bach Remedies | Bates Method | Beauty Therapy | Bio-energetics | Biofeedback | Biomagnetic Therapy | Biomechanics | Bonesetting | Bowen Therapy | Chinese Herbal Medicine |
|---|---|---|---|---|---|---|---|---|---|---|---|---|---|---|---|---|---|---|---|---|---|---|---|---|---|
|NORBURY, SUSAN (HM14990)|||||||●||||||||||||||||||
|PARRY, LIZA (HM15739)|||●||||||||||||||||||||||
|PAYTON, ANTHONY (HM15875)|||||||||||||||||||||●||||
|PEACEHAVEN AROMATHERAPY (HM15877)|||||||●||||||||||||||||||
|PEACH, F J (HM15879)|||||||||||||||||||||●||||
|PECK, SUE (HM15925)|||||||●||||||||||||||||||
|PERKS, R (HM16028)|||●||||||||||||||||||||||
|PLANT, R M (HM16359)|||||||||||||||||||||●||||
|PRIORS PODIATRY PRACTICE (HM16629)|||●||||||||||||||||||●||||
|QUINTON, R M (HM16819)|||●||||||||||||||||||||||
|REECE, P & BRADSHAW, J (HM17039)|||||||||||||||||||||●||||
|ROBERTS, KATE (HM17418)|||||||||||||||||||||||||
|ROSELANDS CLINIC (HM17619)|||●||||||||||||||||||||||
|SAGGU, S (HM17838)|||||||||||||||||||||||||
|STAFFORD CHIROPRACTIC CLINIC (HM19108)|||||||||||||||||||||||||
|STAFFORDSHIRE MCTIMONEY (HM19111)|||||||||||||||||||||||||
|STATFOLD SEED OILS (HM19159)|||||||●||||||||||||||||||
|SUSAN JAMES CONSULTANCY (HM19527)|●||||||||●||●|||||●|||●|||||||
|TUNSTALL HYPNOTHERAPY CENTRE (HM20401)|||||||●||||||||||||||||||
|VICTORIAN COLLECTION (HM20657)|||||||●||||||||||||||||||
|WATSON, G T (HM21008)|||||||||||||||||||||||||
|WHITBY, S E (HM21334)|||●||||||||||||||||||||||
|YARNFIELD PARK- HEALTH/SPORTS (HM21989)|||||||●||||||||||||||||||
|**SUFFOLK**|||||||||||||||||||||||||
|ALEXANDER TECHNIQUE (HM00519)||||●|||||||||||||||||||||
|AROMA ROOM (HM01054)|||||||●||||||||||||||||||
|ARTHEY, ELAINE (HM01159)||||||||||||||||●||||||||||
|ATC (HM01309)|||||||●||||||||||||||||||
|BECCLES ACUPUNCTURE CLINIC (HM02013)|||●||||||||||||||||||||||
|BODY MECHANICS THERAPY CLINIC (HM02599)||||||||||||||||||||||||●||
|CHARLTON CLINIC (HM04033)|||||||●||||||||||||||||||
|CHURCHMAN & ASS REG OST (HM04475)|||||||||||||||||||||||||
|CHURCHMAN, BERYL (HM04478)|||||||||||||||||||||||||
|CLAIRVOYANT SERVICES (HM04518)|||||||||||||||||||||||||

| Business | Chiropody | Chiropractic | Clinical Ecology | Cognitive Therapy | Colonic Hydrotherapy | Colour Therapy | Complementary Therapy | Counselling | Cranial Osteopathy | Cranio-Sacral Therapy | Cryo Surgery | Crystal Healing | Cupping | Cymatics | Dance Movement Thrpy | Dietician | Do-In | Douching | Dowsing | Drama Therapy | Electrolipolysis | Electrolysis | Electrotherapy | Encounter Groups | Faith Healing |
|---|---|---|---|---|---|---|---|---|---|---|---|---|---|---|---|---|---|---|---|---|---|---|---|---|---|
|NORBURY, SUSAN (HM14990)|||||||||||||||||||||||||
|PARRY, LIZA (HM15739)|||||||||||||||||||||||||
|PAYTON, ANTHONY (HM15875)|●||||||||||||||||||||||||
|PEACEHAVEN AROMATHERAPY (HM15877)|||||||||||||||||||||||||
|PEACH, F J (HM15879)|●||||||||||||||||||||||||
|PECK, SUE (HM15925)|||||||||||||||||||||||||
|PERKS, R (HM16028)|||||||||||||||||||||||||
|PLANT, R M (HM16359)|●||||||||||||||||||||||||
|PRIORS PODIATRY PRACTICE (HM16629)|||||||||||||||||||||||||
|QUINTON, R M (HM16819)|||||||||||||||||||||||||
|REECE, P & BRADSHAW, J (HM17039)|●||||||||||●||||||||||||||
|ROBERTS, KATE (HM17418)||||||||●|||||||||||||||||
|ROSELANDS CLINIC (HM17619)|||||||||||||||||||||||||
|SAGGU, S (HM17838)|●||||||||||||||||||||||||
|STAFFORD CHIROPRACTIC CLINIC (HM19108)||●|||||||||||||||||||||||
|STAFFORDSHIRE MCTIMONEY (HM19111)||●||||||||●|||||||||||||||
|STATFOLD SEED OILS (HM19159)|||||||||||||||||||||||||
|SUSAN JAMES CONSULTANCY (HM19527)||||●||||●||||||||●|||●||||||
|TUNSTALL HYPNOTHERAPY CENTRE (HM20401)|||||||||||||||||||||||||
|VICTORIAN COLLECTION (HM20657)|||||||||||||||||||||||||
|WATSON, G T (HM21008)|●||||||||||||||||||||||||
|WHITBY, S E (HM21334)|||||||||||||||||||||||||
|YARNFIELD PARK- HEALTH/SPORTS (HM21989)|||||||||||||||||||||||||
|**SUFFOLK**|||||||||||||||||||||||||
|ALEXANDER TECHNIQUE (HM00519)|||||||||||||||||||||||||
|AROMA ROOM (HM01054)|||||||||||||||||||||||||
|ARTHEY, ELAINE (HM01159)|||||||||||||||||||||||||
|ATC (HM01309)|||||||||||||||||||||||||
|BECCLES ACUPUNCTURE CLINIC (HM02013)|||||||||||||||||||||||||
|BODY MECHANICS THERAPY CLINIC (HM02599)|||||||||||||||||||||||||
|CHARLTON CLINIC (HM04033)||||||||||||||||||||||●|||
|CHURCHMAN & ASS REG OST (HM04475)|||||||||●||||||||||||||||
|CHURCHMAN, BERYL (HM04478)|||||||||●||||||||||||||||
|CLAIRVOYANT SERVICES (HM04518)||||||||●|||||||||||||||||

# A - F Therapies at Practices/Businesses

Business by County with Reference no.

| Business by County with Reference no. | Absent Healing | Acupressure | Acupuncture | Alexander Technique | Allergy Testing | Anthroposohical Med | Aromatherapy | Art Therapy | Aura Therapy | Auricular Therapy | Auto Suggestion | Autogenic Training | Aversion Therapy | Ayurvedic Medicine | Baby Massage | Bach Remedies | Bates Method |
|---|---|---|---|---|---|---|---|---|---|---|---|---|---|---|---|---|---|
| COOPER, A R (HM05088) | | | | | | | | | | | | | | | | | |
| CORRIGAN, A J (HM05194) | | | | | | | | | | | | | | | | | |
| CT & IM LEITH (HM05534) | | | ● | | | | | | | | | | | | | ● | |
| DENT, TRISH () | | | | | | | | | | | | | | | | | |
| EAREY, C A (HM06495) | | | | | | | | | | | | | | | | | |
| FELIXSTOWE CHIROPRACTIC CLINIC (HM07200) | | | | | | | | | | | | | | | | | |
| FITZGERALD, ROSEMARY (HM07367) | | | ● | | | | | | | | | | | | | | |
| FLOWERDEW, M (HM07435) | | | ● | | | | | | | | | | | | | | |
| FRESHFIELDS OF ALDEBURGH (HM07737) | | | ● | | | | ● | | | | | | | | | | |
| HAVERHILL CHIROPRACTIC CENTRE (HM09211) | | | | | | | | | | | | | | | | | |
| HEALING CONNECTIONS (HM09330) | | | | | | | ● | | | | | | | | | | |
| HEALING HANDS (HM09336) | | | | | | | ● | | | | | | | | | ● | |
| HITCHINS, ROSIE (HM09847) | | | | | | | ● | | | | | | | | | | |
| HODSON, P A (HM09896) | | | ● | | | | | | | | | | | | | | |
| HOPKINS, C J (HM10147) | | | ● | | | | | | | | | | ● | | | | |
| INNER SPACE SUFFOLK (HM10641) | | | ● | | | | | | | | | | | | | | |
| INSTIT-TRAD HERBAL MED-ACUP (HM10665) | | | | | | | ● | | | | | | | | | | |
| IPSWICH CHIROPRACTIC CLINIC (HM10714) | | ● | ● | | | | ● | | | | | | | | | | |
| IPSWICH PHYSIOTHERAPY PRACTICE (HM10715) | | | ● | | | | | | | | | | | | | | |
| IVESON (HM10782) | | | | | | | | | | | | | | | | | |
| JACOBS, F (DR) (HM10859) | | | | | | | | | | | | | | | | | |
| JAMESON, BARBARA (HM10904) | | | ● | | | | | | | | | | | | | | |
| JORDAN, TESSA (HM11212) | | | | | | | | | | | | | | | | ● | |
| JUST ESSENTIALS (HM11278) | | | | | | | ● | | | | | | | | | | |
| KESGRAVE CHIROPRACTIC CLINIC (HM11561) | | | | | | | | | | | | | | | | | |
| LAVENDER LODGE CLINIC (HM12023) | ● | ● | | | | | ● | | | | | | | | | | |
| LITTLEWOOD, JULIE (HM12476) | | | | | | | ● | | | | | | | | | | |
| LOWESTOFT TRAD ACUPUNTURE CLNC (HM12703) | | | ● | | | | | | | | | | | | | | |
| MANOR HOUSE (HM13039) | | | ● | | | | | | | | | | | | | | |
| MARK CHURCH AROMATHERAPY (HM13106) | | | | | | | ● | | | | | | | | | | |
| MASSAGE FOR HEALTH (HM13260) | | | | | | | | | | | | | | | | | |
| MCTIMONEY CHIROPRACTIC CLINIC (HM13607) | | | | | | | | | | | | | | | | | |
| MOHAN, TERRY (HM14046) | | | | | | | | | | | | ● | | | | | |
| MOULDING, ANNE (HM14283) | | | | | | | ● | | | | | | | | | | |

| Business by County with Reference no. | Beauty Therapy | Bio-energetics | Biofeedback | Biomagnetic Therapy | Biomechanics | Bonesetting | Bowen Therapy | Chinese Herbal Medicine | Chiropody | Chiropractic | Clinical Ecology | Cognitive Therapy | Colonic Hydrotherapy | Colour Therapy | Complementary Therapy | Counselling | Cranial Osteopathy |
|---|---|---|---|---|---|---|---|---|---|---|---|---|---|---|---|---|---|
| COOPER, A R (HM05088) | | | | | | | | | ● | | | | | | | | |
| CORRIGAN, A J (HM05194) | | | | | | | | | | ● | | | | | | | |
| CT & IM LEITH (HM05534) | | | | | | | | | | | | | | | | | |
| DENT, TRISH () | | | | | | | | | | | | | | | ● | | |
| EAREY, C A (HM06495) | | | | | | | | | | ● | | | | | | | |
| FELIXSTOWE CHIROPRACTIC CLINIC (HM07200) | | | | | | | | | | ● | | | | | | | |
| FITZGERALD, ROSEMARY (HM07367) | | | | | | | | | | | | | | | | | |
| FLOWERDEW, M (HM07435) | | | | | | | | | | | | | | | | | |
| FRESHFIELDS OF ALDEBURGH (HM07737) | | | | | | | | | ● | | | | | | ● | | |
| HAVERHILL CHIROPRACTIC CENTRE (HM09211) | | | | | | | | | | ● | | | | | | | |
| HEALING CONNECTIONS (HM09330) | | | | | | | | | | | | | | | | | |
| HEALING HANDS (HM09336) | | | | | | | | | | | | | | | ● | | |
| HITCHINS, ROSIE (HM09847) | | | | | | | | | | | | | | | | | |
| HODSON, P A (HM09896) | | | | | | | | | | | | | | | | | |
| HOPKINS, C J (HM10147) | | | | | | | | | | | | | | | ● | | |
| INNER SPACE SUFFOLK (HM10641) | | | | | | | | | | | | | | | | | |
| INSTIT-TRAD HERBAL MED-ACUP (HM10665) | | | | | | | | | | | | | | | | | |
| IPSWICH CHIROPRACTIC CLINIC (HM10714) | | | ● | | | | | | | ● | | | | | ● | | |
| IPSWICH PHYSIOTHERAPY PRACTICE (HM10715) | | | | | | | | | | | | | | | | | |
| IVESON (HM10782) | | | | | | | | | | ● | | | | | | | |
| JACOBS, F (DR) (HM10859) | | | | | | | | | | ● | | | | | | | |
| JAMESON, BARBARA (HM10904) | | | | | | | | | | | | | | | | | |
| JORDAN, TESSA (HM11212) | | | | | | | | | | | | | | | | | |
| JUST ESSENTIALS (HM11278) | | | | | | | | | | | | | | | | | |
| KESGRAVE CHIROPRACTIC CLINIC (HM11561) | | | | | | | | | | ● | | | | | | | |
| LAVENDER LODGE CLINIC (HM12023) | | | | | | | | | | | | | | ● | | ● | |
| LITTLEWOOD, JULIE (HM12476) | | | | | | | | | | | | | | | | | |
| LOWESTOFT TRAD ACUPUNTURE CLNC (HM12703) | | | | | | | | | | | | | | | | | |
| MANOR HOUSE (HM13039) | | | | | | | | | ● | | | | | | | | |
| MARK CHURCH AROMATHERAPY (HM13106) | | | | | | | | | | | | | | | | | |
| MASSAGE FOR HEALTH (HM13260) | | | | | | | | | | | | | | | | | |
| MCTIMONEY CHIROPRACTIC CLINIC (HM13607) | | | | | | | | | | ● | | | | | | | |
| MOHAN, TERRY (HM14046) | | | | | | | | | | | | ● | | | | ● | |
| MOULDING, ANNE (HM14283) | | | | | | | | | | | | | | | | | |

| Business by County with Reference no. | Cranio-Sacral Therapy | Cryo Surgery | Crystal Healing | Cupping | Cymatics | Dance Movement Thrpy | Dietician | Do-In | Douching | Dowsing | Drama Therapy | Electrolipolysis | Electrolysis | Electrotherapy | Encounter Groups | Faith Healing |
|---|---|---|---|---|---|---|---|---|---|---|---|---|---|---|---|---|
| COOPER, A R (HM05088) | | | | | | | | | | | | | | | | |
| CORRIGAN, A J (HM05194) | | | | | | | | | | | | | | | | |
| CT & IM LEITH (HM05534) | | | | | | | | | | | | | | | | |
| DENT, TRISH () | | | | | | | | ● | | | | | | | | |
| EAREY, C A (HM06495) | | | | | | | | | | | | | | | | |
| FELIXSTOWE CHIROPRACTIC CLINIC (HM07200) | | | | | | | | | | | | | | | | |
| FITZGERALD, ROSEMARY (HM07367) | | | | | | | | | | | | | | | | |
| FLOWERDEW, M (HM07435) | | | | | | | | | | | | | | | | |
| FRESHFIELDS OF ALDEBURGH (HM07737) | | | | | | | | | | | | | | | | |
| HAVERHILL CHIROPRACTIC CENTRE (HM09211) | | | | | | | | | | | | | | | | |
| HEALING CONNECTIONS (HM09330) | | | | | | | | | | | | | | | | |
| HEALING HANDS (HM09336) | | | | | | | | | | | | | | | | |
| HITCHINS, ROSIE (HM09847) | | | | | | | | | | | | | | | | |
| HODSON, P A (HM09896) | | | | | | | | | | | | | | | | |
| HOPKINS, C J (HM10147) | | | | | | | | | | | | | | | | |
| INNER SPACE SUFFOLK (HM10641) | | | | | | | | | | | | | | | | |
| INSTIT-TRAD HERBAL MED-ACUP (HM10665) | | | | | | | | | | | | | | | | |
| IPSWICH CHIROPRACTIC CLINIC (HM10714) | | | | | | | ● | | | | | | | | | |
| IPSWICH PHYSIOTHERAPY PRACTICE (HM10715) | | | | | | | | | | | | | | | | |
| IVESON (HM10782) | | | | | | | | | | | | | | | | |
| JACOBS, F (DR) (HM10859) | | | | | | | | | | | | | | | | |
| JAMESON, BARBARA (HM10904) | | | | | | | | | | | | | | | | |
| JORDAN, TESSA (HM11212) | | | | | | | | | | | | | | | | |
| JUST ESSENTIALS (HM11278) | | | | | | | | | | | | | | | | |
| KESGRAVE CHIROPRACTIC CLINIC (HM11561) | | | | | | | | | | | | | | | | |
| LAVENDER LODGE CLINIC (HM12023) | | | ● | | | | | | | | | | | ● | | |
| LITTLEWOOD, JULIE (HM12476) | | | | | | | | | | | | | | | | |
| LOWESTOFT TRAD ACUPUNTURE CLNC (HM12703) | | | | | | | | | | | | | | | | |
| MANOR HOUSE (HM13039) | | | | | | | | | | | | | | | | |
| MARK CHURCH AROMATHERAPY (HM13106) | | | | | | | | | | | | | | | | |
| MASSAGE FOR HEALTH (HM13260) | | | | ● | | | | | | | | | | | | |
| MCTIMONEY CHIROPRACTIC CLINIC (HM13607) | | | | | | | | | | | | | | | | |
| MOHAN, TERRY (HM14046) | | | | | | | | | | | | | | | | |
| MOULDING, ANNE (HM14283) | | | | | | | | | | | | | | | | |

# A - F Therapies at Practices/Businesses

| Business by County with Reference no. | Absent Healing | Acupressure | Acupuncture | Alexander Technique | Allergy Testing | Anthroposohical Med | Aromatherapy | Art Therapy | Aura Therapy | Auricular Therapy | Auto Suggestion | Autogenic Training | Aversion Therapy | Ayurvedic Medicine | Baby Massage | Bach Remedies | Bates Method | Beauty Therapy | Bio-energetics | Biofeedback | Biomagnetic Therapy | Biomechanics | Bonesetting | Bowen Therapy | Chinese Herbal Medicine |
|---|---|---|---|---|---|---|---|---|---|---|---|---|---|---|---|---|---|---|---|---|---|---|---|---|---|
| NATURECURES (HM14684) | | ● | ● | | | | | | | | | | | | | | | | | | | | | | |
| NEWMARKET CHIROPRACTIC CLINIC (HM14877) | | | | | | | | | | | | | | | | | | | | | | | | | |
| NOAH'S ARK PSYCHOTHERAPY (HM14964) | | | | | | | | | | | | | | | | | | | | | | | | | |
| PAROLIN, PAUL (HM15728) | | | | | | | | | | | | | | | | | | | | | | | | | |
| PERTH, F (HM16068) | | | | | | | | | | | | | | | | | | | | | | | | | |
| SCOFIELD CHIROPRATIC CLINIC (HM18102) | | | | | | | | | | | | | | | | | | | | | | | | | |
| SHEROMA THERAPY (HM18435) | | ● | | | | | ● | | | | | | | | | | | | | | | | | | |
| SPALDING, JULIE (HM18955) | | | | | | | | | | | | | | | | | | | | | | | | | |
| SPRINGFIELD LODGE HEALTH CARE (HM19052) | | ● | ● | ● | | | ● | | | | | | | | | | | | | | | | | | |
| ST MARYS PRACTICE (HM19088) | | | ● | | | | | | | | | | | | | | | | | | | | | | |
| STOWMARKET OSTEOPATHS (HM19363) | | | | | | | | | | | | | | | | | | | | | | | | | |
| SUDBURY CHIROPRACTIC CLINIC (HM19462) | | | | | | | | | | | | | | | | | | | | | | | | | |
| TERRY, LESLEY ANN (HM19849) | | | | | | | ● | | | | | | | | | | | | | | | | | | |
| UNITY HEALTH CENTRE (HM20510) | | | ● | | | | | | | | | | | | | | | | | | | | | | |
| WEI CLINIC (HM21111) | | | ● | | | | ● | | | | | | | | | ● | | | | | | | | | |
| WOODBRIDGE COMP HEALTH CENTRE (HM21816) | | | | | | | | | | | | | | | | ● | | | | | | | | | |
| SURREY | | | | | | | | | | | | | | | | | | | | | | | | | |
| 1ST CHIROPRACTIC CENTRES (HM00003) | | | | | | | | | | | | | | | | | | | | | | | | | |
| ACORN HEALTH CLINIC (HM00177) | | | ● | | ● | | | | | | | | | | | | | | | | | | | | |
| ACORN THERAPY CENTRE (HM00181) | ● | | | | | | | | | | | | | | | | | | | | | | | | |
| ACUHERBAL CHINESE MEDICINE (HM00214) | | ● | ● | | | | ● | | | | | | | | | | | | | | | | | | |
| ACUPUNCTURE/CHINESE HERBAL MED (HM00326) | | | ● | | | | | | | | | | | | | | | | | | | | | | |
| ADKIN, JEAN (HM00382) | | | | | | | | | | | | | | | | ● | | | | | | | | | |
| ALEXANDER TECHNIQUE (HM00534) | | | | ● | | | | | | | | | | | | | | | | | | | | | |
| ANNES BEAUTY SALON (HM00907) | | | | | | | ● | | | | | | | | | | | | | | | | | | |
| AROMA SECRETS (HM01059) | | | | | | | ● | | | | | | | | | | | | | | | | | | |
| AROMA SECRETS (HM01058) | | | | | | | ● | | | | | | | | | | | | | | | | | | |
| AROMA-ACTIVE (HM01066) | | | | | | | ● | | | | | | | | | | | | | | | | | | |
| AROMATHERAPY CENTRE (HM01100) | | | | | | | ● | | | | | | | | | | | | | | | | | | |
| AROMATHERAPY/REMEDIAL MASSAGE (HM01131) | | | | | | | ● | | | | | | | | | | | | | | | | | | |
| ARTHURWORREY, J (HM01167) | | | | | | | ● | | | | | | | | | | | | | | | | | | |
| ARUNDELL, LINDA (HM01172) | | | | | | | ● | | | | | | | | | | | | | | | | | | |
| ASHTEAD CHARTERED PHYSIO SV (HM01230) | | | | | | | | | | | | | | | | | | | | | | | | | |
| ASHTEAD CLINIC (HM01232) | | | | | | | | | | | | | | | | | | | | | | | | | |

| Business by County with Reference no. | Chiropody | Chiropractic | Clinical Ecology | Cognitive Therapy | Colonic Hydrotherapy | Colour Therapy | Complementary Therapy | Counselling | Cranial Osteopathy | Cranio-Sacral Therapy | Cryo Surgery | Crystal Healing | Cupping | Cymatics | Dance Movement Thrpy | Dietician | Do-In | Douching | Dowsing | Drama Therapy | Electrolipolysis | Electrolysis | Electrotherapy | Encounter Groups | Faith Healing |
|---|---|---|---|---|---|---|---|---|---|---|---|---|---|---|---|---|---|---|---|---|---|---|---|---|---|
| NATURECURES (HM14684) | | | | | | | | | | | | | | | | | | | | | | | | | |
| NEWMARKET CHIROPRACTIC CLINIC (HM14877) | | ● | | | | | | | | | | | | | | | | | | | | | | | |
| NOAH'S ARK PSYCHOTHERAPY (HM14964) | | | | ● | | | | ● | | | | | | | | | | | | | | | | | |
| PAROLIN, PAUL (HM15728) | | ● | | | | | | | ● | ● | | | | | | | | | | | | | | | |
| PERTH, F (HM16068) | | ● | | | | | | | | | | | | | | | | | | | | | | | |
| SCOFIELD CHIROPRATIC CLINIC (HM18102) | | ● | | | | | | | | | | | | | | | | | | | | | | | |
| SHEROMA THERAPY (HM18435) | | | | | | ● | ● | ● | | | | | | | | | | | | | | | | | |
| SPALDING, JULIE (HM18955) | | | | ● | | | ● | ● | | | | | | | | | | | | | | | | | |
| SPRINGFIELD LODGE HEALTH CARE (HM19052) | ● | ● | | | | | | ● | | | | | | | | | | | | | | | | | |
| ST MARYS PRACTICE (HM19088) | ● | | | | | | | | | | | | | | | | | | | | | | | | |
| STOWMARKET OSTEOPATHS (HM19363) | | | | | | | | | ● | | | | | | | | | | | | | | | | |
| SUDBURY CHIROPRACTIC CLINIC (HM19462) | | ● | | | | | | | | | | | | | | | | | | | | | | | |
| TERRY, LESLEY ANN (HM19849) | | | | | | | | | | | | | | | | | | | | | | | | | |
| UNITY HEALTH CENTRE (HM20510) | | | | | | | | | | | | | | | | | | | | | | | | | |
| WEI CLINIC (HM21111) | | | | | | | | | | | | | | | | | | | | | | | | | |
| WOODBRIDGE COMP HEALTH CENTRE (HM21816) | | | | | | | | | | | | | | | | | | | | | | | | | |
| SURREY | | | | | | | | | | | | | | | | | | | | | | | | | |
| 1ST CHIROPRACTIC CENTRES (HM00003) | | ● | | | | | | | | | | | | | | | | | | | | | | | |
| ACORN HEALTH CLINIC (HM00177) | | | | | | | | | | | | | | | | | | | | | | | | | |
| ACORN THERAPY CENTRE (HM00181) | | | | | | | ● | ● | | | | | | | | | | | | | | | | | |
| ACUHERBAL CHINESE MEDICINE (HM00214) | | | | | | ● | | | | | | | | | | | | | | | | | | | |
| ACUPUNCTURE/CHINESE HERBAL MED (HM00326) | | | | | | | | | | | | | | | | | | | | | | | | | |
| ADKIN, JEAN (HM00382) | | | | | | | | | | | | | | | | | | | | | | | | | |
| ALEXANDER TECHNIQUE (HM00534) | | | | | | | | | | | | | | | | | | | | | | | | | |
| ANNES BEAUTY SALON (HM00907) | | | | | | | | | | | | | | | | | | | | | | | | | |
| AROMA SECRETS (HM01059) | | | | | | | | | | | | | | | | | | | | | | | | | |
| AROMA SECRETS (HM01058) | | | | | | | | | | | | | | | | | | | | | | | | | |
| AROMA-ACTIVE (HM01066) | | | | | | | | | | | | | | | | | | | | | | | | | |
| AROMATHERAPY CENTRE (HM01100) | | | | | | | | | | | | | | | | | | | | | | | | | |
| AROMATHERAPY/REMEDIAL MASSAGE (HM01131) | | | | | | | | | | | | | | | | | | | | | | | | | |
| ARTHURWORREY, J (HM01167) | | | | | | | | | | | | | | | | | | | | | | | | | |
| ARUNDELL, LINDA (HM01172) | | | | | | | | | | | | | | | | | | | | | | | | | |
| ASHTEAD CHARTERED PHYSIO SV (HM01230) | | | | | | | | | | | | | | | | | | | | | | ● | | |
| ASHTEAD CLINIC (HM01232) | | | | | | | | | ● | | | | | | | | | | | | | | | | |

# A - F Therapies at Practices/Businesses

| Business by County with Reference no. | Absent Healing | Acupressure | Acupuncture | Alexander Technique | Allergy Testing | Anthroposophical Med | Aromatherapy | Art Therapy | Aura Therapy | Auricular Therapy | Auto Suggestion | Autogenic Training | Aversion Therapy | Ayurvedic Medicine | Baby Massage | Bach Remedies | Bates Method | Beauty Therapy | Bio-energetics | Biofeedback | Biomagnetic Therapy | Biomechanics | Bonesetting | Bowen Therapy | Chinese Herbal Medicine | Chiropody | Chiropractic | Clinical Ecology | Cognitive Therapy | Colonic Hydrotherapy | Colour Therapy | Complementary Therapy | Counselling | Cranial Osteopathy | Cranio-Sacral Therapy | Cryo Surgery | Crystal Healing | Cupping | Cymatics | Dance Movement Thrpy | Dietician | Do-In | Douching | Dowsing | Drama Therapy | Electrolipolysis | Electrolysis | Electrotherapy | Encounter Groups | Faith Healing |
|---|---|---|---|---|---|---|---|---|---|---|---|---|---|---|---|---|---|---|---|---|---|---|---|---|---|---|---|---|---|---|---|---|---|---|---|---|---|---|---|---|---|---|---|---|---|---|---|---|---|---|
| ASTON CLINIC (HM01301) | | | ● | ● | ● | | | | | | | | | | | | | | | | | | | | | ● | | | | | ● | | | | | | | | | | | | | | | | | | | |
| ASW ALLERGY CONSULTANTS (HM01305) | ● | | | | | | | | | | | | | | | | | | | | | | | | | | | | | | | ● | | | | | | | | | | | | ● | | | | | | |
| BACK TO HEALTH (HM01508) | | | | | | | | | | | | | | | | | | | | | | | | | | | ● | | | | | | | | | | | | | | | | | | | | | | | |
| BACK TO HEALTH - GUILDFORD (HM01511) | | | | | | | | | | | | | | | | | | | | | | | | | | | ● | | | | | | | | | | | | | | | | | | | | | | | |
| BACK TO HEALTH - RICHMOND (HM01514) | | | | | | | | | | | | | | | | | | | | | | | | | | | ● | | | | | | | | | | | | | | | | | | | | | | | |
| BACK TO HEALTH - SUTTON (HM01515) | | | | | | | | | | | | | | | | | | | | | | | | | | | ● | | | | | | | | | | | | | | | | | | | | | | | |
| BACKCARE CLINIC (HM01527) | | | ● | | | | | | | | | | | | | | | | | | | | | | | | | | | | | | | | | | | | | | | | | | | | | | | |
| BARCLAY, JAMES (HM01695) | | | | ● | | | | | | | | | | | | | | | | | | | | | | | | | | | | | | | | | | | | | | | | | | | | | | |
| BARNARD, JUDY (HM01729) | | | | | | | ● | | | | | | | | | | | | | | | | | | | | | | | | | | | | | | | | | | | | | | | | | | | |
| BARNSTEAD VILLAGE CLINIC (HM01769) | | | ● | | | | | | | | | | | | | | | | | | | | | | ● | ● | | | | | | | | | | | | | | | | | | | | | | | | |
| BARRON CHIROPRACTIC CLINICS (HM01801) | | | | | | | | | | | | | | | | | | | | | | | | | | | ● | | | | | | | | | | | | | | | | | | | | | | | |
| BATCHELOR, C (HM01863) | | | | | | | | | | | | | | | | | | | | | | | | | | | | | | | | | ● | | | | | | | | | | | | | | | | | |
| BATTEN, CHRISTOPHER (HM01906) | | | | ● | | | | | | | | | | | | | | | | | | | | | | | | | | | | | | | | | | | | | | | | | | | | | | |
| BAXTER, STEPHEN (HM01933) | | | | ● | | | | | | | | | | | | | | | | | | | | | | | | | | | | | | | | | | | | | | | | | | | | | | |
| BEIJING ACUPUNCTURE CLINIC (HM02071) | | | ● | | | | | | | | | | | | | | | | | | | | | | | | | | | | | | | | | | | | | | | | | | | | | | | |
| BIGWOOD, SIMON (HM02295) | | | ● | | | | | | | | | | | | | | | | | | | | | | | | | | | | | | | | | | | | | | | | | | | | | | | |
| BONIFACE, SANDRA (HM02679) | | | | | | | | | | | | | | | | | | | | | | | | | | | ● | | | | | | | | | | | | | | | | | | | | | | | |
| BOURNE HEALTH (HM02753) | | | | | | | ● | | | | | | | | | | | | | | | | | | | | | | | | | | | | | | | | | | | | | | | | | | | |
| BOURNE, LIZ (HM02756) | | | | | | | ● | | | | | | | | | | | | | | | | | | | | | | | | | | | | | | | | | | | | | | | | | | | |
| BRABANT HOUSE CLINIC (HM02830) | | ● | ● | ● | | | ● | | | | | | | | | ● | | | | | | | | | | ● | ● | | ● | | | | ● | ● | | | ● | | | | | | | ● | | | | | | |
| BREWSTER, DAVID J (HM02980) | | | | | | | | | | | ● | | | | | | | | | | | | | | | | | | ● | | | | ● | | | | | | | | | | | | | | | | | |
| BROCK, ROBERT (HM03126) | | | | | | | | | | | | | | | | | | | | | | | | | | | ● | | | | | | | | | | | | | | | | | | | | | | | |
| BROUGHAM, PENNY (DR) (HM03200) | | | ● | | | | | | | | | | | | | | | | | | | | | | | | | | | | | | | | | | | | | | | | | | | | | | | |
| BURN, LOIC (DR) (HM03393) | | | ● | | | | | | | | | | | | | | | | | | | | | | | | | | | | | | | | | | | | | | | | | | | | | | | |
| CAMBERLEY CHIROPRACTIC CLINIC (HM03565) | | | | | | | | | | | | | | | | | | | | | | | | | | | ● | | | | | | | | | | | | | | | | | | | | | | | |
| CAMBERLEY NATURAL THERAPY CTRE (HM03566) | | | ● | | | | ● | | | | | | | | | | | | | | | | | | | | | | | | ● | | | | | | | | | | | | | | | | | | | |
| CAMPBELL, SEAN (HM03608) | | | ● | | | | | | | | | | | | | | | | | | | | | | | | | | | | | | | | | | | | | | | | | | | | | | | |
| CAMPBELL, SEAN D (HM03609) | | | ● | | | | | | | | | | | | | | | | | | | | | | | | | | | | | | | | | | | | | | | | | | | | | | | |
| CARLTON CLINIC (HM03700) | | ● | ● | ● | | | ● | | | | | | | | | ● | | | | | | | ● | ● | | ● | ● | | | | | ● | ● | ● | | | | ● | | | ● | | | | | ● | | ● | | ● |
| CATERHAM CHIROPRACTIC CLINIC (HM03853) | | | | | | | | | | | | | | | | | | | | | | | | | | | ● | | | | | | | | | | | | | | | | | | | | | | | |
| CHART LANE CLINIC (HM04039) | | | | | | | | | | | | | | | | ● | | | | | | | | | | | | | | | | | ● | | | | | | | | | | | | | | | | | |
| CHEVINGTON CHIROPRACTIC CLINIC (HM04145) | | | | | | | | | | | | | | | | | | | | | | | | | | | ● | | | | | | | | | | | | | | | | | | | | | | | |
| CHI CLINIC (HM04148) | | ● | | | | | | | | | | | | | | | | | | | | | | | | | | | | | | | | | | | ● | | | | | | | | | | | | | |
| CHI-KIN, PO (HM04163) | | | ● | | | | | | | | | | | | | | | | | | | | | | | | | | | | | | | | | | | | | | | | | | | | | | | |

www.healthmyself.com

# A - F Therapies at Practices/Businesses

www.healthmyself.com

Business by County with Reference no.

| Business | Absent Healing | Acupressure | Acupuncture | Alexander Technique | Allergy Testing | Anthroposophical Med | Aromatherapy | Art Therapy | Aura Therapy | Auricular Therapy |
|---|---|---|---|---|---|---|---|---|---|---|
| CHIROPRACTIC CENTRE (HM04382) | | | | | | | | | | |
| CHRISTINE KEY HYPNOTHERAPIST (HM04447) | | | | | | | | | | |
| CITISPORT (HM04483) | | | ● | | | | | | | |
| CLARK, JOYCE (HM04561) | | | | | | | ● | | | |
| CLEASSON, HAZEL (HM04631) | | | | | | | ● | | | |
| CLINIC OF ACUPUNCTURE (HM04683) | | | ● | | | | | | | |
| COBHAM COMPLEMENTARY THERAPIES (HM04762) | | | | | | | ● | | | |
| COHEN, MICHAEL (HM04793) | | | | | | | | | | |
| CONFIDENTIAL COUNSELLING SVS (HM04975) | | | | | | | | | | |
| COOPER, A (HM05087) | | | | ● | | | | | | |
| COPELAND, ELAINE (HM05139) | | | | | | | | | | |
| COX, JULIET (HM05307) | | | | ● | | | | | | |
| CRANLEIGH CHIROPRACTIC CLINIC (HM05381) | | ● | | | | | ● | | | |
| CROSS, R (HM05486) | | | ● | | | | | | | |
| CROYDON HEALING CENTRE (HM05515) | ● | | | | | | | | | |
| CROYDON HYPNOTHERAPY (HM05516) | | | | | | | | | | |
| CUMMINS, ROZ (HM05617) | | | | | | | | | | |
| DANFORD, P H (HM05718) | | | | | | | | | | |
| DAWSON, VIVIENNE (HM05886) | | | ● | | | | | | | |
| DICE, JOHN (HM06065) | | | ● | | | | | | | |
| DORCHESTER HOUSE OSTEOPATHY (HM06195) | | | | | | | ● | | | |
| DORKING CHIROPRACTIC (HM06199) | | | | | | | | | | |
| EDWARDS HEALTH CLINIC (HM06639) | | | | | | | | | | |
| EPSOM & EWELL ACUPUNCTURE (HM06856) | | | ● | | | | | | | |
| EPSOM CHIROPRACTIC CLINIC (HM06857) | | | | | | | | | | |
| EQUILIBRIUM OSTEOPATHIC (HM06876) | | | | | | | | | | |
| EREVNA (HM06882) | | | | | | | ● | | | |
| ESSENTIALS (HM06928) | | | | | | | ● | | | |
| EVANS, CHRISTINE (HM06964) | | | | ● | | | | | | |
| EVANS, JUDITH (HM06980) | | | | | | | ● | | | |
| EWELL CHIROPRACTIC CENTRE (HM07015) | | | | | | | | | | |
| FAMILY CHIROPRACTIC CENTRE (HM07084) | | | | | | | | | | |
| FARNBOROUGH CHIRO CLINIC (HM07111) | | | | | | | | | | |
| FARNHAM CHIROPRACTIC CLINIC (HM07112) | | | | | | | | | | |

| Business | Auto Suggestion | Autogenic Training | Aversion Therapy | Ayurvedic Medicine | Baby Massage | Bach Remedies | Bates Method | Beauty Therapy | Bio-energetics | Biofeedback |
|---|---|---|---|---|---|---|---|---|---|---|
| CHIROPRACTIC CENTRE (HM04382) | | | | | | | | | | |
| CHRISTINE KEY HYPNOTHERAPIST (HM04447) | | | | | | | | | | |
| CITISPORT (HM04483) | | | | | | | | | | |
| CLARK, JOYCE (HM04561) | | | | | | | | | | |
| CLEASSON, HAZEL (HM04631) | | | | | | | | | | |
| CLINIC OF ACUPUNCTURE (HM04683) | | | | | | | | | | |
| COBHAM COMPLEMENTARY THERAPIES (HM04762) | | | | | | | | | | |
| COHEN, MICHAEL (HM04793) | ● | ● | | | | | | | | |
| CONFIDENTIAL COUNSELLING SVS (HM04975) | | | | | | | | | | |
| COOPER, A (HM05087) | | | | | | | | | | |
| COPELAND, ELAINE (HM05139) | | | | | | ● | | | | |
| COX, JULIET (HM05307) | | | | | | | | | | |
| CRANLEIGH CHIROPRACTIC CLINIC (HM05381) | | | | | | | | | | |
| CROSS, R (HM05486) | | | | | | | | | | |
| CROYDON HEALING CENTRE (HM05515) | | | | | | | | | | |
| CROYDON HYPNOTHERAPY (HM05516) | | | | | | | | | | |
| CUMMINS, ROZ (HM05617) | | | | | | ● | | | | |
| DANFORD, P H (HM05718) | | | | | | | | | | |
| DAWSON, VIVIENNE (HM05886) | | | | | | | | | | |
| DICE, JOHN (HM06065) | | | | | | | | | | |
| DORCHESTER HOUSE OSTEOPATHY (HM06195) | | | | | | | | | | |
| DORKING CHIROPRACTIC (HM06199) | | | | | | | | | | |
| EDWARDS HEALTH CLINIC (HM06639) | ● | | | | | | | | | |
| EPSOM & EWELL ACUPUNCTURE (HM06856) | | | | | | | | | | |
| EPSOM CHIROPRACTIC CLINIC (HM06857) | | | | | | | | | | |
| EQUILIBRIUM OSTEOPATHIC (HM06876) | | | | | | | | | | |
| EREVNA (HM06882) | | | | | | ● | | | | |
| ESSENTIALS (HM06928) | | | | | | | | | | |
| EVANS, CHRISTINE (HM06964) | | | | | | | | | | |
| EVANS, JUDITH (HM06980) | | | | | | | | | | |
| EWELL CHIROPRACTIC CENTRE (HM07015) | | | | | | | | | | |
| FAMILY CHIROPRACTIC CENTRE (HM07084) | | | | | | | | | | |
| FARNBOROUGH CHIRO CLINIC (HM07111) | | | | | | | | | | |
| FARNHAM CHIROPRACTIC CLINIC (HM07112) | | | | | | | | | | |

| Business | Biomagnetic Therapy | Biomechanics | Bonesetting | Bowen Therapy | Chinese Herbal Medicine | Chiropody | Chiropractic | Clinical Ecology | Cognitive Therapy | Colonic Hydrotherapy |
|---|---|---|---|---|---|---|---|---|---|---|
| CHIROPRACTIC CENTRE (HM04382) | | | | | | | ● | | | |
| CHRISTINE KEY HYPNOTHERAPIST (HM04447) | | | | | | | | | | |
| CITISPORT (HM04483) | | | | | | | | | | |
| CLARK, JOYCE (HM04561) | | | | | | | | | | |
| CLEASSON, HAZEL (HM04631) | | | | | | | | | | |
| CLINIC OF ACUPUNCTURE (HM04683) | | | | | | | | | | |
| COBHAM COMPLEMENTARY THERAPIES (HM04762) | | | | | | | | | | |
| COHEN, MICHAEL (HM04793) | | | | | | | | | ● | |
| CONFIDENTIAL COUNSELLING SVS (HM04975) | | | | | | | | | | |
| COOPER, A (HM05087) | | | | | | | | | | |
| COPELAND, ELAINE (HM05139) | | | | | | | | | | |
| COX, JULIET (HM05307) | | | | | | | | | | |
| CRANLEIGH CHIROPRACTIC CLINIC (HM05381) | | | | | | | ● | | | |
| CROSS, R (HM05486) | | | | | | | | | | |
| CROYDON HEALING CENTRE (HM05515) | | | | | | | | | | |
| CROYDON HYPNOTHERAPY (HM05516) | | | | | | | | | | |
| CUMMINS, ROZ (HM05617) | | | | | | | | | | |
| DANFORD, P H (HM05718) | | | | | | | ● | | | |
| DAWSON, VIVIENNE (HM05886) | | | | | | | | | | |
| DICE, JOHN (HM06065) | | | | | | | | | | |
| DORCHESTER HOUSE OSTEOPATHY (HM06195) | | | | | | ● | | | | |
| DORKING CHIROPRACTIC (HM06199) | | | | | | | ● | | | |
| EDWARDS HEALTH CLINIC (HM06639) | | | | | | | | | | |
| EPSOM & EWELL ACUPUNCTURE (HM06856) | | | | | | | | | | |
| EPSOM CHIROPRACTIC CLINIC (HM06857) | | | | | | | ● | | | |
| EQUILIBRIUM OSTEOPATHIC (HM06876) | | | | | | | | | | |
| EREVNA (HM06882) | | | | | | | | | | |
| ESSENTIALS (HM06928) | | | | | | | | | | |
| EVANS, CHRISTINE (HM06964) | | | | | | | | | | |
| EVANS, JUDITH (HM06980) | | | | | | | | | | |
| EWELL CHIROPRACTIC CENTRE (HM07015) | | | | | | | ● | | | |
| FAMILY CHIROPRACTIC CENTRE (HM07084) | | | | | | | ● | | | |
| FARNBOROUGH CHIRO CLINIC (HM07111) | | | | | | | ● | | | |
| FARNHAM CHIROPRACTIC CLINIC (HM07112) | | | | | | | ● | | | |

| Business | Colour Therapy | Complementary Therapy | Counselling | Cranial Osteopathy | Cranio-Sacral Therapy | Cryo Surgery | Crystal Healing | Cupping | Cymatics | Dance Movement Thrpy |
|---|---|---|---|---|---|---|---|---|---|---|
| CHIROPRACTIC CENTRE (HM04382) | | | | | | | | | | |
| CHRISTINE KEY HYPNOTHERAPIST (HM04447) | | | ● | | | | | | | |
| CITISPORT (HM04483) | | | | | | | | | | |
| CLARK, JOYCE (HM04561) | | | | | | | | | | |
| CLEASSON, HAZEL (HM04631) | | | | | | | | | | |
| CLINIC OF ACUPUNCTURE (HM04683) | | | | | | | | | | |
| COBHAM COMPLEMENTARY THERAPIES (HM04762) | | | | | | | | | | |
| COHEN, MICHAEL (HM04793) | | | ● | | | | | | | |
| CONFIDENTIAL COUNSELLING SVS (HM04975) | | | ● | | | | | | | |
| COOPER, A (HM05087) | | | | | | | | | | |
| COPELAND, ELAINE (HM05139) | | | | | | | | | | |
| COX, JULIET (HM05307) | | | | | | | | | | |
| CRANLEIGH CHIROPRACTIC CLINIC (HM05381) | | | | | | | | | | |
| CROSS, R (HM05486) | | | | | | | | | | |
| CROYDON HEALING CENTRE (HM05515) | | ● | | | | | | | | |
| CROYDON HYPNOTHERAPY (HM05516) | | | ● | | | | | | | |
| CUMMINS, ROZ (HM05617) | | | | | | | | | | |
| DANFORD, P H (HM05718) | | | | | | | | | | |
| DAWSON, VIVIENNE (HM05886) | | | | | | | | | | |
| DICE, JOHN (HM06065) | | | | | | | | | | |
| DORCHESTER HOUSE OSTEOPATHY (HM06195) | | | | | | | | | | |
| DORKING CHIROPRACTIC (HM06199) | | | | | | | | | | |
| EDWARDS HEALTH CLINIC (HM06639) | | ● | ● | | | | | | | |
| EPSOM & EWELL ACUPUNCTURE (HM06856) | | | | | | | | | | |
| EPSOM CHIROPRACTIC CLINIC (HM06857) | | | | | | | | | | |
| EQUILIBRIUM OSTEOPATHIC (HM06876) | | ● | | ● | | | | | | |
| EREVNA (HM06882) | | | | | | | | | | |
| ESSENTIALS (HM06928) | | | | | | | | | | |
| EVANS, CHRISTINE (HM06964) | | | | | | | | | | |
| EVANS, JUDITH (HM06980) | | | | | | | | | | |
| EWELL CHIROPRACTIC CENTRE (HM07015) | | | | | | | | | | |
| FAMILY CHIROPRACTIC CENTRE (HM07084) | | | | | | | | | | |
| FARNBOROUGH CHIRO CLINIC (HM07111) | | | | | | | | | | |
| FARNHAM CHIROPRACTIC CLINIC (HM07112) | | | | | | | | | | |

| Business | Dietician | Do-In | Douching | Dowsing | Drama Therapy | Electrolipolysis | Electrolysis | Electrotherapy | Encounter Groups | Faith Healing |
|---|---|---|---|---|---|---|---|---|---|---|
| CHIROPRACTIC CENTRE (HM04382) | | | | | | | | | | |
| CHRISTINE KEY HYPNOTHERAPIST (HM04447) | | | | | | | | | | |
| CITISPORT (HM04483) | ● | | | | | | | ● | | |
| CLARK, JOYCE (HM04561) | | | | | | | | | | |
| CLEASSON, HAZEL (HM04631) | | | | | | | | | | |
| CLINIC OF ACUPUNCTURE (HM04683) | | | | | | | | | | |
| COBHAM COMPLEMENTARY THERAPIES (HM04762) | | | | | | | | | | |
| COHEN, MICHAEL (HM04793) | | | | | | | | | | |
| CONFIDENTIAL COUNSELLING SVS (HM04975) | | | | | | | | | | |
| COOPER, A (HM05087) | | | | | | | | | | |
| COPELAND, ELAINE (HM05139) | | | | | | | | | | |
| COX, JULIET (HM05307) | | | | | | | | | | |
| CRANLEIGH CHIROPRACTIC CLINIC (HM05381) | | | | | | | | | | |
| CROSS, R (HM05486) | | | | | | | | | | |
| CROYDON HEALING CENTRE (HM05515) | | | | | | | | | | ● |
| CROYDON HYPNOTHERAPY (HM05516) | | | | | | | | | | |
| CUMMINS, ROZ (HM05617) | | | | | | | | | | |
| DANFORD, P H (HM05718) | | | | | | | | | | |
| DAWSON, VIVIENNE (HM05886) | | | | | | | | | | |
| DICE, JOHN (HM06065) | | | | | | | | | | |
| DORCHESTER HOUSE OSTEOPATHY (HM06195) | | | | | | | | | | |
| DORKING CHIROPRACTIC (HM06199) | | | | | | | | | | |
| EDWARDS HEALTH CLINIC (HM06639) | | | | | | | | | | |
| EPSOM & EWELL ACUPUNCTURE (HM06856) | | | | | | | | | | |
| EPSOM CHIROPRACTIC CLINIC (HM06857) | | | | | | | | | | |
| EQUILIBRIUM OSTEOPATHIC (HM06876) | | | | | | | | | | |
| EREVNA (HM06882) | | | | | | | | | | |
| ESSENTIALS (HM06928) | | | | | | | | | | |
| EVANS, CHRISTINE (HM06964) | | | | | | | | | | |
| EVANS, JUDITH (HM06980) | | | | | | | | | | |
| EWELL CHIROPRACTIC CENTRE (HM07015) | | | | | | | | | | |
| FAMILY CHIROPRACTIC CENTRE (HM07084) | | | | | | | | | | |
| FARNBOROUGH CHIRO CLINIC (HM07111) | | | | | | | | | | |
| FARNHAM CHIROPRACTIC CLINIC (HM07112) | | | | | | | | | | |

# A - F Therapies at Practices/Businesses

| Business by County with Reference no. | Absent Healing | Acupressure | Acupuncture | Alexander Technique | Allergy Testing | Anthroposohical Med | Aromatherapy | Art Therapy | Aura Therapy | Auricular Therapy | Auto Suggestion | Autogenic Training | Aversion Therapy | Ayurvedic Medicine | Baby Massage | Bach Remedies | Bates Method | Beauty Therapy | Bio-energetics | Biofeedback | Biomagnetic Therapy | Biomechanics | Bonesetting | Bowen Therapy | Chinese Herbal Medicine |
|---|---|---|---|---|---|---|---|---|---|---|---|---|---|---|---|---|---|---|---|---|---|---|---|---|---|
| FEATHER, A J (HM07155) | | | | | | | | | | | | | | | | | | | | | | | | | |
| FENWICK, J (HM07224) | | | | ● | | | | | | | | | | | | | | | | | | | | | |
| FOOT CARE CENTRE (HM07466) | | | | | | | | | | | | | | | | | | | | | | | | | |
| FRANCIS J H WILSON CHIRO (HM07666) | | | | | | | | | | | | | | | | | | | | | | | | | |
| FREED CLINIC (HM07707) | | | ● | | | | | | | | | | | | | | | | | | | | | | |
| GAUVAIN, TONY (HM07934) | | | | | | | | | | | | | | | | | | | | | | | | | |
| GILL JULIE (HM08074) | | | | | | | ● | | | | | | | | | | | | | | | | | | |
| GLAISTER, BRIAN (DR) (HM08120) | | | | | | | | | | | | | | | | | | | | | | | | | |
| GODALMING CHIROPRACTIC CLINIC (HM08178) | | | | | | | | | | | | | | | | | | | | | | | | | |
| GODDARD, TERRI (HM08180) | | ● | | | | | | | | | | | | | | | | | | | | | | | |
| GORDON, SARAH (HM08282) | | | | | | | ● | | | | | | | | | | | | | | | | | | |
| GRAYSHOTT ELECTRO-ACUPUNCTURE (HM08425) | | | ● | | | | | | | | | | | | | | | | | | | | | | |
| HALL, LISA (HM08782) | | | | | | | ● | | | | | | | | | | | | | | | | | | |
| HALLIDAY, C (HM08806) | | | | | | | ● | | | | | | | | | | | | | | | | | | |
| HAM CHIROPRACTIC CLINIC (HM08822) | | | | | | | | | | | | | | | | | | | | | | | | | |
| HANDS ON HEALTH (HM08911) | | | | | | | | | | | | | | | | | | | | | | | | | |
| HARTLEY, GILL (HM09140) | | | | | | | | | | | | | | | | | | | | | | | | | |
| HASLEMERE CHIROPRACTIC CLINIC (HM09185) | | | | | | | | | | | | | | | | | | | | | | | | | |
| HEHIR, S (HM09505) | | | | | | | | | | | | | | | | | | | | | | | | | |
| HELIANTHUS PRACTICE (HM09518) | | | | | | | | | | | | | | | | ● | | | | | | | | | |
| HERBAL KING (HM09628) | | | ● | | | | | | | | | | | | | | | | | | | | | | |
| HINES, STELLA (HM09832) | | | | | | | ● | | | | | | | | | | | | | | | | | | |
| HOLISTIC CENTRE (HM09949) | | ● | ● | | | | ● | | | | | | | | | | | | | | | | | | ● |
| HOLISTIC HEALTH (HM09968) | | | ● | | | | | | | | | | | | | | | | | | | | | | |
| HOLISTIC HEALTH CENTRE (HM09971) | | | ● | | ● | | | | | | | | | | | | | | | | | | | | |
| HOLLAND-AVERY, H (HM10015) | | | ● | | | | | | | | | | | | | | | | | | | | | | |
| HOPPER, C A (HM10156) | | | | | | | | | | | | | | | | | | | | | | | | | |
| HUMAN FOCUS RETURN TO WORK (HM10362) | | | | | | | | | | | | | | | | | | | | | | | | | |
| HUTCHINGS, MICHAEL (HM10449) | | | ● | | | | | | | | | | | | | | | | | | | | | | |
| IMORTELLE (HM10589) | | | | | | | ● | | | | | | | | | | | | | | | | | | |
| INTEGRAL HEALTH (HM10690) | | | ● | | | | | | | | | | | | | | | | | | ● | | | | |
| JENKINS, SARA (HM10997) | | | | | | | ● | | | | | | | | | | | | | | | | | | |
| KATHERINE'S THERAPIES (HM11339) | | | | | | | ● | | | | | | | | | | | | | | | | | | |
| KEATING, JAMES (HM11377) | | | | ● | | | | | | | | | | | | | | | | | | | | | |

| Business by County with Reference no. | Chiropody | Chiropractic | Clinical Ecology | Cognitive Therapy | Colonic Hydrotherapy | Colour Therapy | Complementary Therapy | Counselling | Cranial Osteopathy | Cranio-Sacral Therapy | Cryo Surgery | Crystal Healing | Cupping | Cymatics | Dance Movement Thrpy | Dietician | Do-In | Douching | Dowsing | Drama Therapy | Electrolipolysis | Electrolysis | Electrotherapy | Encounter Groups | Faith Healing |
|---|---|---|---|---|---|---|---|---|---|---|---|---|---|---|---|---|---|---|---|---|---|---|---|---|---|
| FEATHER, A J (HM07155) | | | | | | | | | | ● | | | | | | | | | | | | | | | |
| FENWICK, J (HM07224) | | | | | | | | | | | | | | | | | | | | | | | | | |
| FOOT CARE CENTRE (HM07466) | ● | | | | | | | | | | | | | | | | | | | | | | | | |
| FRANCIS J H WILSON CHIRO (HM07666) | | ● | | | | | | | | | | | | | | | | | | | | | | | |
| FREED CLINIC (HM07707) | | | | | | | | | | | | | | | | | | | | | | | | | |
| GAUVAIN, TONY (HM07934) | | | | ● | | | | ● | | | | | | | | | | | | | | | | | |
| GILL JULIE (HM08074) | | | | | | | | | | | | | | | | | | | | | | | | | |
| GLAISTER, BRIAN (DR) (HM08120) | | | | ● | | | | ● | | | | | | | | | | | | | | | | | |
| GODALMING CHIROPRACTIC CLINIC (HM08178) | | ● | | | | | | | | | | | | | | | | | | | | | | | |
| GODDARD, TERRI (HM08180) | | | | | | | ● | | | | | | | | | | ● | | | | | | | | |
| GORDON, SARAH (HM08282) | | | | | | | | | | | | | | | | | | | | | | | | | |
| GRAYSHOTT ELECTRO-ACUPUNCTURE (HM08425) | | | | | | | | | | | | | | | | | | | | | | | | | |
| HALL, LISA (HM08782) | | | | | | | | | | | | | | | | | | | | | | | | | |
| HALLIDAY, C (HM08806) | | | | | | | | | | | | | | | | | | | | | | | | | |
| HAM CHIROPRACTIC CLINIC (HM08822) | | ● | | | | | | | | | | | | | | | | | | | | | | | |
| HANDS ON HEALTH (HM08911) | | ● | | | | | | | | ● | | | | | | | | | | | | | | | |
| HARTLEY, GILL (HM09140) | | | | | | | | | | ● | | | | | | | | | | | | | | | |
| HASLEMERE CHIROPRACTIC CLINIC (HM09185) | | ● | | | | | | | | | | | | | | | | | | | | | | | |
| HEHIR, S (HM09505) | | ● | | | | | | | | | | | | | | | | | | | | | | | |
| HELIANTHUS PRACTICE (HM09518) | | | | | | | | ● | | | | | | | | | | | | | | | | | |
| HERBAL KING (HM09628) | | | | | | | | | | | | | | | | | | | | | | | | | |
| HINES, STELLA (HM09832) | | | | | | | | | | | | | | | | | | | | | | | | | |
| HOLISTIC CENTRE (HM09949) | ● | ● | | | | | | ● | | ● | | | | | | | | | | | | | | | |
| HOLISTIC HEALTH (HM09968) | | | | | | | | | | | | | | | | | | | | | | | | | |
| HOLISTIC HEALTH CENTRE (HM09971) | | | | | | | | | | | | | | | | | | | | | | | | | |
| HOLLAND-AVERY, H (HM10015) | | | | | | | | | | | | | | | | | | | | | | | | | |
| HOPPER, C A (HM10156) | | | | | | | | ● | | | | | | | | | | | | | | | | | |
| HUMAN FOCUS RETURN TO WORK (HM10362) | | ● | | ● | | | | ● | | | | | | | | | | | | | | | | | |
| HUTCHINGS, MICHAEL (HM10449) | | | | | | | | | | | | | | | | | | | | | | | | | |
| IMORTELLE (HM10589) | | | | | | | | | | | | | | | | | | | | | | | | | |
| INTEGRAL HEALTH (HM10690) | | | | | | | | | | | | | | | | | | | | | | | | | |
| JENKINS, SARA (HM10997) | | | | | | | | | | | | | | | | | | | | | | | | | |
| KATHERINE'S THERAPIES (HM11339) | | | | | | | | | | | | | | | | | | | | | | | | | |
| KEATING, JAMES (HM11377) | | | | | | | | | | | | | | | | | | | | | | | | | |

# A - F Therapies at Practices/Businesses

| Business by County with Reference no. | Absent Healing | Acupressure | Acupuncture | Alexander Technique | Allergy Testing | Anthroposohical Med | Aromatherapy | Art Therapy | Aura Therapy | Auricular Therapy | Auto Suggestion | Autogenic Training | Aversion Therapy | Ayurvedic Medicine | Baby Massage | Bach Remedies | Bates Method |
|---|---|---|---|---|---|---|---|---|---|---|---|---|---|---|---|---|---|
| KENT CLINIC OF NATURAL MED (HM11514) | ● | ● | ● | | | | ● | | | | | | ● | | | ● | |
| KEW CHIROPRACTIC CLINIC (HM11575) | | | | | | | | | | | | | | | | | |
| KINGSLEY-THOMAS, FERNANDA (HM11670) | | | | | | | | | | | | | | | | ● | |
| KINGSTON CHIROPRACTIC CLINIC (HM11675) | | | | | | | | | | | | | | | | | |
| KINGSTON NATURAL HEALING CTRE (HM11677) | | ● | ● | ● | | | ● | | | | | | | | | ● | |
| KINGSTON OSTEOPATHS (HM11679) | | | | | | | | | | | | | | | | | |
| KOLTHAMMER, JOHN (HM11780) | | | | | | | | | | | | | | | | | |
| LA TOUCHE, ROBERT (HM11847) | | | | | | | | | | | | | | | | | |
| LEATHERHEAD CHIRO CLINIC (HM12114) | | | | | | | | | | | | | | | | | |
| LIFE STYLE NATURAL HEALTH CTRE (HM12349) | | | | | | | ● | | | | | | | | | | |
| LODGE FARM CHIROPRACTIC CENTRE (HM12558) | | | | | | | | | | | | | | | | | |
| LONDON SPINE AND JOINT CLINIC (HM12610) | | | | | | | ● | | | | | | | | | | |
| LOW, ROYSTON (HM12688) | | | ● | | | | | | | | | | | | | | |
| MANTLE, FIONA (HM13053) | | | | | | | | | | | | | | | | ● | |
| MAZUR, ARTUR (HM13362) | | | | | | | | | | | | | | | | | |
| MCINTOSH, A (HM13511) | | | | | | | ● | | | | | | | | | | |
| MCMANUS, EILEEN (HM13569) | | | ● | | | | | | | | | | | | | | |
| MEEKS, FIONA (HM13683) | | | | | | | | | | | | | | | | | |
| MEERAN, M (HM13686) | | | ● | | | | | | | | | | | | | | |
| MELVILL, R H (HM13718) | | | | | | | | | | | | | | | | | |
| MILLER, IAN A (HM13887) | | | | | | | | | | | | | | | | | |
| MILLS, STEPHANIE (HM13933) | | | ● | | | | | | | | | | | | | | |
| MIND AND BODY (HM13958) | | | | | | | ● | | | | | | | | | ● | |
| MIST, CORINNE (HM13996) | | | | | | | ● | | | | | | | | | | |
| MIST, JULIA (HM13997) | | | | | | | ● | | | | | | | | | | |
| MOORTHY, N S (DR) (HM14141) | | | ● | | | | | | | | | | | | | | |
| MOSS PHARMACY PODIATRY (HM14263) | | | | | | | | | | | | | | | | | |
| MUIR, BEVERLEY (HM14318) | | | | | | | ● | | | | | | | | | | |
| MURPHY, TERRY (HM14395) | | | | | | | | | | | | | | | | | |
| MURRAY, A G (HM14397) | | | | | | | | | | | | | | | | | |
| NATURAL HEALING CENTRE (HM14541) | | | | | | | ● | | | | | | | | | | |
| NATURAL HEALING CLINIC (HM14550) | | | | | | | | | | | | | | | | | |
| NATURAL LIFE AROMATHERAPY (HM14608) | | | ● | | | | ● | | | | | | | | | | |
| NICHOLLS, VERITY (HM14915) | | | | | | | | | | | | | | | | | |

| Business by County with Reference no. | Beauty Therapy | Bio-energetics | Biofeedback | Biomagnetic Therapy | Biomechanics | Bonesetting | Bowen Therapy | Chinese Herbal Medicine | Chiropody | Chiropractic | Clinical Ecology | Cognitive Therapy | Colonic Hydrotherapy | Colour Therapy | Complementary Therapy | Counselling | Cranial Osteopathy |
|---|---|---|---|---|---|---|---|---|---|---|---|---|---|---|---|---|---|
| KENT CLINIC OF NATURAL MED (HM11514) | | | | | | | | | | ● | | | | ● | | ● | ● |
| KEW CHIROPRACTIC CLINIC (HM11575) | | | | | | | | | | ● | | | | | | | |
| KINGSLEY-THOMAS, FERNANDA (HM11670) | | | | | | | | | | | | | | | | | |
| KINGSTON CHIROPRACTIC CLINIC (HM11675) | | | | | | | | | | ● | | | | | | | |
| KINGSTON NATURAL HEALING CTRE (HM11677) | | | | | | | | | | | | | | | | ● | ● |
| KINGSTON OSTEOPATHS (HM11679) | | | | | | | | | | | | | | | | | ● |
| KOLTHAMMER, JOHN (HM11780) | | | | | | | | | | ● | | | | | | | |
| LA TOUCHE, ROBERT (HM11847) | | | | | | | | | | ● | | | | | | | |
| LEATHERHEAD CHIRO CLINIC (HM12114) | | | | | | | | | | ● | | | | | | | |
| LIFE STYLE NATURAL HEALTH CTRE (HM12349) | | | | | | | | | ● | | | | | | | | |
| LODGE FARM CHIROPRACTIC CENTRE (HM12558) | | | | | | | | | | ● | | | | | | | |
| LONDON SPINE AND JOINT CLINIC (HM12610) | | | | | | | | | | ● | | | | | ● | | |
| LOW, ROYSTON (HM12688) | | | | | | | | | | | | | | | | | |
| MANTLE, FIONA (HM13053) | | | | | | | | | | | | | | | | | |
| MAZUR, ARTUR (HM13362) | | | | | | | | | | ● | | | | | | | |
| MCINTOSH, A (HM13511) | | | | | | | | | | | | | | | | | |
| MCMANUS, EILEEN (HM13569) | | | | | | | | | | | | | | | | | |
| MEEKS, FIONA (HM13683) | | | | | | | ● | | | | | | | | | | |
| MEERAN, M (HM13686) | | | | | | | | | | | | | | | | | |
| MELVILL, R H (HM13718) | | | | | | | | | | ● | | | | | | | |
| MILLER, IAN A (HM13887) | | | | | | | | | | ● | | | | | | | |
| MILLS, STEPHANIE (HM13933) | | | | | | | | | | | | | | | | | |
| MIND AND BODY (HM13958) | | | | | | | | | | | | | | | | | |
| MIST, CORINNE (HM13996) | | | | | | | | | | | | | | | | | |
| MIST, JULIA (HM13997) | | | | | | | | | | | | | | | | | |
| MOORTHY, N S (DR) (HM14141) | | | | | | | | | | | | | | | | | |
| MOSS PHARMACY PODIATRY (HM14263) | | | | | | | | | | | | | | | | | |
| MUIR, BEVERLEY (HM14318) | | | | | | | | | | | | | | | | | |
| MURPHY, TERRY (HM14395) | | | | | | | | | | ● | | | | | | | |
| MURRAY, A G (HM14397) | | | | | | | | | ● | | | | | | | | |
| NATURAL HEALING CENTRE (HM14541) | ● | | | | | | | | | | | | | | | | |
| NATURAL HEALING CLINIC (HM14550) | | | | | | | ● | | | | | | | | ● | | |
| NATURAL LIFE AROMATHERAPY (HM14608) | | | | | | | | | ● | | | | | | | | |
| NICHOLLS, VERITY (HM14915) | | | | | | | | | ● | | | | | | | | |

| Business by County with Reference no. | Cranio-Sacral Therapy | Cryo Surgery | Crystal Healing | Cupping | Cymatics | Dance Movement Thrpy | Dietician | Do-In | Douching | Dowsing | Drama Therapy | Electrolipolysis | Electrolysis | Electrotherapy | Encounter Groups | Faith Healing |
|---|---|---|---|---|---|---|---|---|---|---|---|---|---|---|---|---|
| KENT CLINIC OF NATURAL MED (HM11514) | | | | | | | | | | ● | | | | | | ● |
| KEW CHIROPRACTIC CLINIC (HM11575) | | | | | | | | | | | | | | ● | | |
| KINGSLEY-THOMAS, FERNANDA (HM11670) | | | | | | | | | | | | | | | | |
| KINGSTON CHIROPRACTIC CLINIC (HM11675) | | | | | | | | | | | | | | | | |
| KINGSTON NATURAL HEALING CTRE (HM11677) | | | | | | | | | | | | | | | | |
| KINGSTON OSTEOPATHS (HM11679) | | | | | | | | | | | | | | | | |
| KOLTHAMMER, JOHN (HM11780) | | | | | | | | | | | | | | | | |
| LA TOUCHE, ROBERT (HM11847) | | | | | | | | | | | | | | | | |
| LEATHERHEAD CHIRO CLINIC (HM12114) | | | | | | | | | | | | | | | | |
| LIFE STYLE NATURAL HEALTH CTRE (HM12349) | | | | | | | | | | | | | | | | |
| LODGE FARM CHIROPRACTIC CENTRE (HM12558) | | | | | | | | | | | | | | | | |
| LONDON SPINE AND JOINT CLINIC (HM12610) | | | | | | | | | | | | | | | | |
| LOW, ROYSTON (HM12688) | | | | | | | | | | | | | | | | |
| MANTLE, FIONA (HM13053) | | | | | | | | | | | | | | | | |
| MAZUR, ARTUR (HM13362) | | | | | | | | | | | | | | | | |
| MCINTOSH, A (HM13511) | | | | | | | | | | | | | | | | |
| MCMANUS, EILEEN (HM13569) | | | | | | | | | | | | | | | | |
| MEEKS, FIONA (HM13683) | | | | | | | | | | | | | | | | |
| MEERAN, M (HM13686) | | | | | | | | | | | | | | | | |
| MELVILL, R H (HM13718) | | | | | | | | | | | | | | | | |
| MILLER, IAN A (HM13887) | | | | | | | | | | | | | | | | |
| MILLS, STEPHANIE (HM13933) | | | | | | | | | | | | | | | | |
| MIND AND BODY (HM13958) | ● | | | | | | | | | | | | | | | |
| MIST, CORINNE (HM13996) | | | | | | | | | | | | | | | | |
| MIST, JULIA (HM13997) | | | | | | | | | | | | | | | | |
| MOORTHY, N S (DR) (HM14141) | | | | | | | | | | | | | | | | |
| MOSS PHARMACY PODIATRY (HM14263) | | ● | | | | | | | | | | | | | | |
| MUIR, BEVERLEY (HM14318) | | | | | | | | | | | | | | | | |
| MURPHY, TERRY (HM14395) | | | | | | | | | | | | | | | | |
| MURRAY, A G (HM14397) | | | | | | | | | | | | | | | | |
| NATURAL HEALING CENTRE (HM14541) | | | | | | | | | | | | | | | | |
| NATURAL HEALING CLINIC (HM14550) | | | | | | | | | | | | ● | | | | |
| NATURAL LIFE AROMATHERAPY (HM14608) | | | | | | | | | | | | | | | | |
| NICHOLLS, VERITY (HM14915) | | | | | | | | | | | | | | | | |

# A - F Therapies at Practices/Businesses

| Business by County with Reference no. | Absent Healing | Acupressure | Acupuncture | Alexander Technique | Allergy Testing | Anthroposohical Med | Aromatherapy | Art Therapy | Aura Therapy | Auricular Therapy | Auto Suggestion | Autogenic Training | Aversion Therapy | Ayurvedic Medicine | Baby Massage | Bach Remedies | Bates Method | Beauty Therapy | Bio-energetics | Biofeedback | Biomagnetic Therapy | Biomechanics | Bonesetting | Bowen Therapy | Chinese Herbal Medicine | Chiropody | Chiropractic | Clinical Ecology | Cognitive Therapy | Colonic Hydrotherapy | Colour Therapy | Complementary Therapy | Counselling | Cranial Osteopathy | Cranio-Sacral Therapy | Cryo Surgery | Crystal Healing | Cupping | Cymatics | Dance Movement Thrpy | Dietician | Do-In | Douching | Dowsing | Drama Therapy | Electrolipolysis | Electrolysis | Electrotherapy | Encounter Groups | Faith Healing |
|---|---|---|---|---|---|---|---|---|---|---|---|---|---|---|---|---|---|---|---|---|---|---|---|---|---|---|---|---|---|---|---|---|---|---|---|---|---|---|---|---|---|---|---|---|---|---|---|---|---|---|
| NICOLA FRY-HEALTH & BEAUTY (HM14927) | | | | | | | ● | | | | | | | | | | | ● | | | | | | | | | | | | | | ● | | | | | | | | | | | | | | | | ● | | |
| NORRIS, Q (HM15014) | | | | ● | | | | | | | | | | | | | | | | | | | | | | | | | | | | | | | | | | | | | | | | | | | | | | |
| NORTHALL, ANNE (HM15048) | | | ● | | | | | | | | | | | | | | | | | | | | | | | | | | | | | | | | | | | | | | | | | | | | | | | |
| O'BRIEN, JAMES (HM15183) | | | ● | | | | | | | | | | | | | | | | | | | | | | | | | | | | | | | | | | | | | | | | | | | | | | | |
| OLD WOKING GRANGE (HM15264) | | ● | ● | ● | | | ● | ● | | | ● | ● | | | | ● | | | | | | | | ● | | | ● | | ● | | ● | | | ● | | | | | | ● | | | | ● | ● | | | | | |
| OLIVIA, S (HM15298) | | | ● | | | | | | | | | | | | | | | | | | | | | | | | | | | | | | | | | | | | | | | | | | | | | | | |
| OSTEOPATHY (HM15477) | | | ● | | | | | | | | | | | | | | | | | | | | | | | | | | | | | | | ● | | | | | | | | | | | | | | | | |
| PARKER, ANTHONY (HM15684) | | | | | | | | | | | | | | | | | | | | | | | | | | | ● | | | | | | | | | | | | | | | | | | | | | | | |
| PARTRIDGE, JENNY (HM15768) | | | | | | | ● | | | | | | | | | | | | | | | | | | | | | | | | | | | | | | | | | | | | | | | | | | | |
| PHILP, CHRISTINE (HM16147) | | | | | | | ● | | | | | | | | | ● | | | | | | | | | | | | | | | | | | | | | | | | | | | | | | | | | | |
| PHOENIX (HM16152) | | | | | | | | | | | | | | | | | | | | | | | | | | | | | | | | | ● | | | | | | | | | | | | | | | | | |
| POURAMINI, A (HM16482) | | | | | | | | | | | | | | | | | | | | | | | | | | | ● | | | | | | | | | | | | | | | | | | | | | | | |
| POWER, DAVID J (HM16503) | | | | | | | | | | | | | | | | | | | | | | | | | | ● | | | | | | | | | | | | | | | | | | | | | | | | |
| PURLEY CHIROPRACTIC CLINIC (HM16767) | | | | | | | | | | | | | | | | | | | | | | | | | | | ● | | | | | | | | | | | | | | | | | | | | | | | |
| PURRETT-SMITH, DEE (HM16774) | | | | ● | | | | | | | | | | | | | | | | | | | | | | | | | | | | | | | | | | | | | | | | | | | | | | |
| QUINTESSENCE AROMATHERAPY (HM16817) | | | | | | | ● | | | | | | | | | | | | | | | | | | | | | | | | | | | | | | | | | | | | | | | | | | | |
| REIGATE CHIROPRACTIC CLINIC (HM17122) | | | | | | | | | | | | | | | | | | | | | | | | | | | ● | | | | | | | | | | | | | | | | | | | | | | | |
| REYNOLDS, DAVID (HM17211) | | | ● | | | | | | | | | | | | | | | | | | | | | | | | | | | | | | | | | | | | | | | | | | | | | | | |
| RIGAL, M (HM17330) | | | | | | | | | | | | | | | | | | | | | | | | | | ● | | | | | | | | | | | | | | | | | | | | | | | | |
| ROBINSON, JAQUELINE (HM17483) | | | | | | | ● | | | | | | | | | | | | | | | | | | | | | | | | | | | | | | | | | | | | | | | | | | | |
| ROBYNA, ANNETTE (HM17516) | | ● | | | | | ● | | | | | | | | | | | | | | | | | | | | | | | | ● | ● | | | | | | | | | ● | | | | | | | | | |
| ROUNDABOUT DRAMA/MOVEMENT (HM17665) | | | | | | | | | | | | | | | | | | | | | | | | | | | | | | | | | | | | | | | | | | | | | ● | | | | | |
| SAUMEEL PATEL ACU CLINIC (HM17950) | | | ● | | | | | | | | | | | | | | | | | | | | | | | | | | | | | | | | | | | | | | | | | | | | | | | |
| SAYER CLINIC (HM17992) | | | | | | | | | | | | | | | | | | | | | | | | | | | ● | | | | | | | | | | | | | | | | | | | | | | | |
| SCHONBERG, VERA (HM18078) | ● | | | | | | ● | | | | ● | | | | | | | | | | | | | | | | | | | | | | | | | | | | | | | | | | | | | | | ● |
| SCHOOL OF YOGA (HM18089) | | | | | | | | | | | | | | | | | | | | | | | | | | | | | | | | | ● | | | | | | | | | | | | | | | | | |
| SCORPIO PHYSIOTHERAPY (HM18103) | | ● | ● | | | | | | | | | | | | | | | | | | | | | | | | | | | | | | | | | | | ● | | | | | | | | | | | | |
| SELSDON COMP/RESP CLINIC (HM18220) | ● | ● | ● | | | | | | | | | | | | | ● | | | | | | | | | | | | | | | | ● | ● | | | | | | | | ● | | | | | | | | | |
| SEVEN SIGHS (HM18244) | | | | | | | | | | | | | | | | ● | | | | | | | | | | | | | | | | | | | | | ● | | | | | | | | | | | | | |
| SHEARS, S (HM18359) | | | | | | | ● | | | | | | | | | | | | | | | | | | | | | | | | | | | | | | | | | | | | | | | | | | | |
| SHEPPERTON CHIROPRACTIC CLINIC (HM18424) | | | | | | | | | | | | | | | | | | | | | | | | | | | ● | | | | | | | | | | | | | | | | | | | | | | | |
| SHEPPERTON PHYSIOFIRST CENTRE (HM18425) | | | ● | | | | | | | | | | | | | | | | | | | | | | | | | | | | | | | | | | | | | | | | | | | | | | | |
| SHINER, SONIA (HM18475) | | | | | | | | | | | | | | | | ● | | | | | | | | | | | | | | | | | | | | | | | | | | | | | | | | | | |
| SIMMS, KATHERINE (HM18564) | ● | | | | | | | | | | | | | | | | | | | | | | | | | | | | | | | | | | | | ● | | | | | | | | | | | | | |

# A - F Therapies at Practices/Businesses

| Business by County with Reference no. | Absent Healing | Acupressure | Acupuncture | Alexander Technique | Allergy Testing | Anthroposohical Med | Aromatherapy | Art Therapy | Aura Therapy | Auricular Therapy | Auto Suggestion | Autogenic Training | Aversion Therapy | Ayurvedic Medicine | Baby Massage | Bach Remedies | Bates Method | Beauty Therapy | Bio-energetics | Biofeedback | Biomagnetic Therapy | Biomechanics | Bonesetting | Bowen Therapy | Chinese Herbal Medicine | Chiropody | Chiropractic | Clinical Ecology | Cognitive Therapy | Colonic Hydrotherapy | Colour Therapy | Complementary Therapy | Counselling | Cranial Osteopathy | Cranio-Sacral Therapy | Cryo Surgery | Crystal Healing | Cupping | Cymatics | Dance Movement Thrpy | Dietician | Do-In | Douching | Dowsing | Drama Therapy | Electrolipolysis | Electrolysis | Electrotherapy | Encounter Groups | Faith Healing |
|---|---|---|---|---|---|---|---|---|---|---|---|---|---|---|---|---|---|---|---|---|---|---|---|---|---|---|---|---|---|---|---|---|---|---|---|---|---|---|---|---|---|---|---|---|---|---|---|---|---|---|
| SLATTERY, BRIDGET (HM18677) | | | | | | | | | | | | | | | | | | | | | | | | | | | | | | | | | ● | | | | | | | | | | | | | | | | | |
| STAMP, G R (HM19121) | | | ● | | | | | | | | | | | | | | | | | | | | | | | | | | | | | | | | | | | | | | | | | | | | | | | |
| STEWART, I (HM19267) | | | | | | | | | | | | | | | | | | | | | | | | | | ● | | | | | | | | | | | | | | | | | | | | | | | | |
| STIRRAT, KATRINA (HM19304) | | | | | | | ● | | | | | | | | | | | | | | | | | | | | | | | | | | | | | | | | | | | | | | | | | | | |
| SULLIVAN, MARGARET (HM19481) | | | | | | | ● | | | | | | | | | | | | | | | | | | | | | | | | | | | | | | | | | | | | | | | | | | | |
| SURBITON NATURAL HEALTH CENTRE (HM19514) | | | ● | ● | | | ● | | | | | | | | | | | | | | | | | | | | | | | | | | | | | | | | | | | | | | | | | | | |
| SURREY HEALING SANCTUARY (HM19522) | ● | | | | | | | | | | | | | | | | | | | | | | | | | | | | | | | ● | | | | | | | | | | | | | | | | | | ● |
| SUTHERLAND, JENNY (HM19539) | | | | | | | ● | | | | | | | | | | | | | | | | | | | | | | | | | | | | | | | | | | | | | | | | | | | |
| SUTTON ALTERNATIVE HEALTH (HM19541) | | | ● | | | | | | | | | | | | | | | | | | | | | | | | | | | | | | | | | | | | | | | | | | | | | | | |
| SUTTON CHIROPRACTIC CLINIC (HM19543) | | | | | | | | | | | | | | | | | | | | | | | | | | | ● | | | | | | | | | | | | | | | | | | | | | | | |
| SUTTON, SUSAN (HM19558) | | | ● | | | | | | | | | | | | | | | | | | | | | | | | | | | | | | | | | | | | | | | | | | | | | | | |
| TELLING, PAUL (HM19824) | | | | | | | | | | | | | | | | | | | | | | | | | | | | | | | | ● | | | | | | | | | | | | | | | | | | |
| TEMPLE, ROSIE (HM19829) | | | ● | | | | | | | | | | | | | | | | | | | | | | | | | | | | | | | | | | | | | | | | | | | | | | | |
| TOWNS, KATE (HM20202) | | | | | | | | | | | | | | | | | | | | | | | | | | | | | | | | ● | | | | | | | | | | | | | | | | | | |
| TRADITIONAL CHINESE MEDICINE (HM20225) | | | ● | | | | | | | | | | | | | | | | | | | | | | | | | | | | | | | | | | | | | | | | | | | | | | | |
| TRISTER, LAURENCE (HM20343) | | | | | | | | | | | | | | | | | | | | | | | | | | | ● | | | | | | | | | | | | | | | | | | | | | | | |
| TUBOKU-METZGER, A F (HM20361) | | | ● | | | | | | | | | | | | | | | | | | | | | | | | | | | | | | | | | | | | | | | | | | | | | | | |
| TURNER, R E (HM20435) | | | | | | | | | | | | | | | | | | | | | | | | | | | | | | | | | | ● | | | | | | | | | | | | | | | | |
| URQUHART, W (HM20530) | | | ● | | | | | | | | | | | | | | | | | | | | | | | | | | | | | | | | | | | | | | | | | | | | | | | |
| VANCOPPENOLLE, J (HM20576) | | | ● | | | | | | | | | | | | | | | | | | | | | | | | | | | | | | | | | | | | | | | | | | | | | | | |
| VICTORIA CLINIC (HM20653) | | | | | | | | | | | | | | | | | | | | | | | | | | | ● | | | | | | | | | | | | | | | | | | | | | | | |
| VIVIAN, DAWSON (HM20708) | | | ● | | | | | | | | | | | | | | | | | | | | | | | | | | | | | | | | | | | | | | | | | | | | | | | |
| WALKER, SARAH (HM20803) | | | | | | | ● | | | | | | | | | | | | | | | | | | ● | | | | | | | | | | | | | | | | | | | | | | | | | |
| WALKER-DENDLE, VALERIE (HM20808) | | | | | | | | | | | | | | | | ● | | | | | | | | | | | | | | | | | | | | | | | | | | | | | | | | | | |
| WALLACE, SUE (HM20832) | | ● | | | | | | | | | | | | | | | | | | | | | | | | | | | | | | ● | | | | | | | | | | | | | | | | | | |
| WEATHERILL, CHRISTINE (HM21047) | | | | | | | ● | | | | | | | | | | | | | | | | | | | | | | | | | | | | | | | | | | | | | | | | | | | |
| WEBB, ROSEMARY (HM21076) | | | | | | | ● | | | | | | | | | | | | | | | | | | | | | | | | | | | | | | | | | | | | | | | | | | | |
| WEIGHTMAN, LAURA (HM21113) | | | | | | | | | | | | | | | | | | | | | | | | | | | ● | | | | | | | | | | | | | | | | | | | | | | | |
| WHITTON, SHIRLEY (HM21427) | | | | | | | ● | | | | | | | | | | | | | | | | | | | | | | | | | | | | | | | | | | | | | | | | | | | |
| WHITWORTH, MICHAEL T (HM21431) | | | | | | | | | | | | | | | | | | | | | | ● | | | | ● | | | | | | | | | | | | | | | | | | | | | | | | |
| WILKINSON, LESLEY (HM21510) | | | | | | | | | | | | | | | | ● | | | ● | | | | | | | | | | | | | | | | | | | | | | | | | | | | | | | |
| WILLIS, SALLY (HM21618) | | | | | | | | | | | | | | | | | | | | | | | | | | | | | | | | | ● | | | | | | | | | | | | | | | | | |
| WOOD, VALERIE (HM21811) | | | | | | | ● | | | | | | | | | | | | | | | | | | | | | | | | | | | | | | | | | | | | | | | | | | | |
| WOODLANDS NATURAL HLTH THERAPY (HM21832) | | | | | | | ● | | | | | | | | ● | | | | | | | | | | | | | | | | ● | | | | | | | | | | | | | | | | | | |

# A - F Therapies at Practices/Businesses

| Business by County with Reference no. | Absent Healing | Acupressure | Acupuncture | Alexander Technique | Allergy Testing | Anthroposohical Med | Aromatherapy | Art Therapy | Aura Therapy | Auricular Therapy | Auto Suggestion | Autogenic Training | Aversion Therapy | Ayurvedic Medicine | Baby Massage | Bach Remedies | Bates Method | Beauty Therapy | Bio-energetics | Biofeedback | Biomagnetic Therapy | Biomechanics | Bonesetting |
|---|---|---|---|---|---|---|---|---|---|---|---|---|---|---|---|---|---|---|---|---|---|---|---|
| YOUNG, HILARY (HM22072) | | | ● | | | | | | | | | | | | | | | | | | | | |
| **SUSSEX (EAST)** | | | | | | | | | | | | | | | | | | | | | | | |
| ALBION CLINIC (HM00483) | | | ● | | | | ● | | | | | | | | | | | | | | | | |
| ALEXANDER TECHNIQUE (HM00549) | | | | ● | | | | | | | | | | | | | | | | | | | |
| ALEXANDER TECHNIQUE (HM00520) | | | | ● | | | | | | | | | | | | | | | | | | | |
| ALLEN, CARRIE (HM00605) | | | | | | | | | | | | | | | | ● | | | | | | | |
| ARDERN FOOT & HEALTH CLINIC (HM00992) | | | | | | | | | | | | | | | | | | | | | | ● | |
| AROMA HAIR (HM01047) | | | | | | | ● | | | | | | | | | | | | | | | | |
| ASHDOWN OSTEOPATHIC CENTRE (HM01206) | | | ● | | | | | | | | | ● | | | | | | | | | | | |
| BAIRD, DAVID (HM01569) | | ● | ● | ● | | | ● | | | | | | | | | ● | | | | | | | |
| BARNARD, SUSAN (HM01733) | | | | | | | ● | | | | | | | | | | | | | | | | |
| BASSETT, N S (HM01857) | | | ● | ● | | | | | | | | | | | | | | | | | | | |
| BAY HOUSE AROMATICS (HM01936) | | | | | | | ● | | | | | | | | | | | | | | | | |
| BELVAIN, E (HM02118) | | ● | | | | | ● | | | | | | | | | | | | | | | | |
| BEXHILL CHIROPRACTIC (HM02255) | | ● | | | | | ● | | | | | | | | | ● | | | | | | | |
| BEXHILL OSTEOPATHIC PRACTICE (HM02257) | | | ● | ● | | | | | | | | | | | | | | | | | | | |
| BLACKER, JOHN (HM02441) | | | | | | | | | | | | | | | | | | | | | | | |
| BRIGHTON ACUPUNCTURE CLINIC (HM03042) | | | ● | | | | | | | | | | | | | | | | | | | | |
| BRIGHTON ALEXANDER TRAINING (HM03043) | | | | ● | | | | | | | | | | | | | | | | | | | |
| BRIGHTON CHIROPRACTIC CLINIC (HM03044) | | | | | | | | | | | | | | | | | | | | | | | |
| BRIGHTON PHYSIOTHERAPY CLINIC (HM03048) | | | ● | | | | ● | | | | | | | | | | | | | | | | |
| BRIGNALL, PENELOPE (HM03050) | | | | | | | | | | | | | | | | | | | | | | | |
| BROOK, SHEILA (HM03159) | | | | | | | ● | | | | | | | | | | | | | | | | |
| BRUNTON, DEIRDRE (HM03283) | | | ● | | | | | | | | | | | | | | | | | | | | |
| CHINESE MED & ACUPUNCTURE CTRE (HM04220) | | | ● | | | | | | | | | | | | | | | | | | | | |
| CLINCH, ADELE (HM04675) | | | | | | | | | | | | | | | | | | | | | | | |
| CLINIC OF CHINESE MED & ACU (HM04685) | | | ● | | | | | | | | | | | | | | | | | | | | |
| CLINICAL CENTRE OF CHINESE MED (HM04712) | | | ● | | | | | | | | | | | | | | | | | | | | |
| COMP THERAPY & TRAINING CENTRE (HM04915) | | ● | ● | | | | | | | | | | | | | | | | | | | | |
| CONCEPTS PHYSIO & NUTRITION (HM04970) | ● | ● | ● | ● | | ● | ● | ● | | | | | | | | | | | | | | | |
| COOK, ELAINE (HM05042) | | | ● | | | | | | | | | | | | | | | | | | | | |
| COX, JULIET (HM05308) | | | | ● | | | | | | | | | | | | | | | | | | | |
| CRANHAMS (HM05375) | | | | | | | ● | | | | | | | | | | | | | | | | |
| CREATIVITY (HM05402) | | | | | | | ● | | | | | | | | | | | | | | | | |

| Business by County with Reference no. | Bowen Therapy | Chinese Herbal Medicine | Chiropody | Chiropractic | Clinical Ecology | Cognitive Therapy | Colonic Hydrotherapy | Colour Therapy | Complementary Therapy | Counselling | Cranial Osteopathy | Cranio-Sacral Therapy | Cryo Surgery | Crystal Healing | Cupping | Cymatics | Dance Movement Thrpy | Dietician | Do-In | Douching | Dowsing | Drama Therapy | Electrolipolysis | Electrolysis | Electrotherapy | Encounter Groups | Faith Healing |
|---|---|---|---|---|---|---|---|---|---|---|---|---|---|---|---|---|---|---|---|---|---|---|---|---|---|---|---|
| YOUNG, HILARY (HM22072) | | | | | | | | | | | | | | | | | | | | | | | | | | | |
| **SUSSEX (EAST)** | | | | | | | | | | | | | | | | | | | | | | | | | | | |
| ALBION CLINIC (HM00483) | | | | ● | | | | | | ● | | ● | | | | | | | | | | | | | | | |
| ALEXANDER TECHNIQUE (HM00549) | | | | | | | | | | | | | | | | | | | | | | | | | | | |
| ALEXANDER TECHNIQUE (HM00520) | | | | | | | | | | | | | | | | | | | | | | | | | | | |
| ALLEN, CARRIE (HM00605) | | | | | | | | | | | | | | | | | | | | | | | | | | | |
| ARDERN FOOT & HEALTH CLINIC (HM00992) | | | ● | | | | | | | | | | | | | | | | | | | | | | | | |
| AROMA HAIR (HM01047) | | | | | | | | | | | | | | | | | | | | | | | | | | | |
| ASHDOWN OSTEOPATHIC CENTRE (HM01206) | | | | | | | | | ● | ● | ● | | | | | | | | | | | | | | | | |
| BAIRD, DAVID (HM01569) | ● | | | | | | | | | | ● | | | ● | | | | | | | | | | | | | |
| BARNARD, SUSAN (HM01733) | | | | | | | | | | | | | | | | | | | | | | | | | | | |
| BASSETT, N S (HM01857) | | | | | | | | | | | ● | | | | | | | | | | | | | | | | |
| BAY HOUSE AROMATICS (HM01936) | | | | | | | | | | | | | | | | | | | | | | | | | | | |
| BELVAIN, E (HM02118) | | | | | | | | | | | | | | | | | | | | | | | | | | | |
| BEXHILL CHIROPRACTIC (HM02255) | | | | ● | | | | | ● | | | | | | | | | | | | | | | | | | |
| BEXHILL OSTEOPATHIC PRACTICE (HM02257) | | | | | | | | | | | ● | | | | | | | | | | | | | | | | |
| BLACKER, JOHN (HM02441) | | | | | | | | | | ● | | | | | | | | | | | | | | | | | |
| BRIGHTON ACUPUNCTURE CLINIC (HM03042) | | | | | | | | | | | | | | | | | | | | | | | | | | | |
| BRIGHTON ALEXANDER TRAINING (HM03043) | | | | | | | | | | | | | | | | | | | | | | | | | | | |
| BRIGHTON CHIROPRACTIC CLINIC (HM03044) | | | | ● | | | | | | | | | | | | | | | | | | | | | | | |
| BRIGHTON PHYSIOTHERAPY CLINIC (HM03048) | | | | | | | | | | | | | | | | | | | | | | | | | | | |
| BRIGNALL, PENELOPE (HM03050) | | | | ● | | | | | | | | | | | | | | | | | | | | | | | |
| BROOK, SHEILA (HM03159) | | | | | | | | | | | | | | | | | | | | | | | | | | | |
| BRUNTON, DEIRDRE (HM03283) | | | | | | | | | | | | | | | | | | | | | | | | | | | |
| CHINESE MED & ACUPUNCTURE CTRE (HM04220) | | | | | | | | | | | | | | | | | | | | | | | | | | | |
| CLINCH, ADELE (HM04675) | | | ● | | | | | | | | | | | | | | | | | | | | | | | | |
| CLINIC OF CHINESE MED & ACU (HM04685) | | | | | | | | | | | | | | | | | | | | | | | | | | | |
| CLINICAL CENTRE OF CHINESE MED (HM04712) | | ● | | | | | | | | | ● | ● | | | | | | | | | | | | | | | |
| COMP THERAPY & TRAINING CENTRE (HM04915) | ● | | | ● | | | | | | ● | | | | | | | | | | | | | | | | | |
| CONCEPTS PHYSIO & NUTRITION (HM04970) | | | | | | | | | ● | ● | | | | | | | | | | | | | ● | | ● | | |
| COOK, ELAINE (HM05042) | | | | | | | | | | | | | | | | | | | | | | | | | | | |
| COX, JULIET (HM05308) | | | | | | | | | | | | | | | | | | | | | | | | | | | |
| CRANHAMS (HM05375) | | | | | | | | | | | | | | | | | | | | | | | | | | | |
| CREATIVITY (HM05402) | | | | | | | | | | | | | | | | | | | | | | | | | | | |

# A - F Therapies at Practices/Businesses

Business by County with Reference no.

| Business by County with Reference no. | Absent Healing | Acupressure | Acupuncture | Alexander Technique | Allergy Testing | Anthroposohical Med | Aromatherapy | Art Therapy | Aura Therapy | Auricular Therapy | Auto Suggestion | Autogenic Training | Aversion Therapy | Ayurvedic Medicine | Baby Massage | Bach Remedies | Bates Method |
|---|---|---|---|---|---|---|---|---|---|---|---|---|---|---|---|---|---|
| CREIGHTMORE, R & D (HM05413) | | | ● | | | | | | | | | | | | | | |
| CRESENT CLINIC (HM05422) | | | | | | | ● | | | | | | | | | ● | |
| CROWBOROUGH CHIRO/COMP HLTH (HM05498) | | | ● | | | | | | | | | | | | | | |
| CROWBOROUGH COMP THERAPISTS (HM05499) | | | | | | | ● | | | | | | | | | | |
| DADSWELL, CLAIRE (HM05670) | | | | | | | | | | | | | | | | | |
| DRIVE OSTEO AND SPORTS CLINIC (HM06314) | | | | | | | ● | | | | | | | | | | |
| DYKE ROAD NATURAL HEALTH (HM06450) | | | ● | ● | | | ● | | | | | | | | | | |
| EAST BOURNE CLINIC (HM06509) | | | ● | ● | ● | | ● | | | | | | | | | | |
| EASTBOURNE CHIROPRACTIC CLINIC (HM06535) | | | | | | | | | | | | | | | | | |
| EATON, MARION (HM06563) | | | | | | | ● | | | ● | | | | | | | |
| FAIRCHILD, HAZEL (HM07052) | | | | | | | | | | | | | | | | | |
| FAMILY FIRST (HM07087) | | | | | | | | | | | | | | | | | |
| FIELDS OF FRAGRANCE (HM07276) | | | | | | | ● | | | | | | | | | | |
| FLOYD, MICHELLE (HM07438) | | | | | | | | | | | | | | | | | |
| FOUNDATION, ANGELGATE (HM07615) | ● | | | | | | ● | | | | | | | | | ● | |
| GATEHOUSE THERAPY CENTRE (HM07925) | | | | | | | | | | | | | | | | | |
| GEIGES, STEPHANIE (HM07967) | | | | ● | | | | | | | | | | | | | |
| GEORGE A BOWDLER CHIROPODIST (HM07988) | | | | | | | | | | | | | | | | | |
| GIBBONS, ELAINE (HM08024) | | | ● | | | | | | | | | | | | | | |
| GOLDSTONE CLINIC (HM08230) | | | | | | | | | | | | | | | | | |
| GOLDSTONE CLINIC (HM08229) | | | | | | | | | | | | | | | | | |
| GRIFFITHS, J (HM08567) | | | | | | | | | | | | | | | | | |
| HAGGARD, CAROLINE (HM08698) | | | | ● | | | | | | | | | | | | | |
| HART, RONALD (HM09131) | | | | | | | | | | | | | | | | | |
| HART, RONALD (HM09130) | | | | | | | | | | | | | | | | | |
| HASTINGS HOLISTIC HEALTH (HM09190) | | | | | | | | | | | | | | | | ● | |
| HAWKINS, LUKE (HM09224) | | | | | | | | | | | | | | | | | |
| HEALTHWISE (HM09418) | | | | | | | | | | | | | | | | ● | |
| HEATHFIELD CHIROPRACTIC CLINIC (HM09458) | | | | | | | | | | | | | | | | | |
| HEMMINGWAY CHIROPODIST (HM09537) | | | | | | | | | | | | | | | | | |
| HERBAL HEALTH CLINIC (HM09617) | | | | | | | ● | | | | | ● | | | | ● | |
| HOBBS, SIMON (HM09859) | | | | | | | | | | | | | | | | | |
| HOLDEN NATURAL HEALTH CLINIC (HM09927) | | | | | | | | | | | | | | | | | |
| HOLISTIC AROMATHERAPY (HM09947) | | | | | | | ● | | | | | | | | | | |

| Business by County with Reference no. | Beauty Therapy | Bio-energetics | Biofeedback | Biomagnetic Therapy | Biomechanics | Bonesetting | Bowen Therapy | Chinese Herbal Medicine | Chiropody | Chiropractic | Clinical Ecology | Cognitive Therapy | Colonic Hydrotherapy | Colour Therapy | Complementary Therapy | Counselling | Cranial Osteopathy | Cranio-Sacral Therapy |
|---|---|---|---|---|---|---|---|---|---|---|---|---|---|---|---|---|---|---|
| CREIGHTMORE, R & D (HM05413) | | | | | | | | | | | | | | | | | | |
| CRESENT CLINIC (HM05422) | | | | | | | ● | | | ● | | | | | | ● | | |
| CROWBOROUGH CHIRO/COMP HLTH (HM05498) | | | | | | | | | | ● | | | | | ● | ● | | |
| CROWBOROUGH COMP THERAPISTS (HM05499) | | | | | | | ● | | | | | | | | | ● | | |
| DADSWELL, CLAIRE (HM05670) | | | ● | | | | | | | | | | | | | | | |
| DRIVE OSTEO AND SPORTS CLINIC (HM06314) | | | | | | | | | | | | | | | | ● | ● | |
| DYKE ROAD NATURAL HEALTH (HM06450) | | | | | | | | | | | | | | | | | | |
| EAST BOURNE CLINIC (HM06509) | | | | | | | | | ● | ● | | | | | | ● | | ● |
| EASTBOURNE CHIROPRACTIC CLINIC (HM06535) | | | | | | | | | | ● | | | | | | | | |
| EATON, MARION (HM06563) | | | | | | | | | | | | | | | | | | |
| FAIRCHILD, HAZEL (HM07052) | | | | | | | | | | | | | | | | ● | | |
| FAMILY FIRST (HM07087) | | | | | | | ● | | | | | ● | | | | ● | | |
| FIELDS OF FRAGRANCE (HM07276) | | | | | | | | | | | | | | | | | | |
| FLOYD, MICHELLE (HM07438) | | | | | | | | | | | | | | | ● | | | |
| FOUNDATION, ANGELGATE (HM07615) | | | | | | | | | | | | | | | ● | | | |
| GATEHOUSE THERAPY CENTRE (HM07925) | | | | | | | | | | | | | | | | ● | | |
| GEIGES, STEPHANIE (HM07967) | | | | | | | | | | | | | | | | | | |
| GEORGE A BOWDLER CHIROPODIST (HM07988) | | | | | | | | | ● | | | | | | | | | |
| GIBBONS, ELAINE (HM08024) | | | | | | | | | | | | | | | | | | |
| GOLDSTONE CLINIC (HM08230) | | | | | | | | | | ● | | | | | | | | |
| GOLDSTONE CLINIC (HM08229) | | | | | | | | | | ● | | | | | | | | |
| GRIFFITHS, J (HM08567) | | | | | | | | | | | | | | | | | | ● |
| HAGGARD, CAROLINE (HM08698) | | | | | | | | | | | | | | | | | | |
| HART, RONALD (HM09131) | | | | | | | | | ● | | | | | | | | | |
| HART, RONALD (HM09130) | | | | | | | | | ● | | | | | | | | | |
| HASTINGS HOLISTIC HEALTH (HM09190) | | | | | | | | | | | | | | | | | | |
| HAWKINS, LUKE (HM09224) | | | | | ● | | | | ● | | | | | | | | | |
| HEALTHWISE (HM09418) | | | | | | | | | | | | | | | | ● | | |
| HEATHFIELD CHIROPRACTIC CLINIC (HM09458) | | | | | | | | | | ● | | | | | | | | |
| HEMMINGWAY CHIROPODIST (HM09537) | | | | | | | | | ● | | | | | | | | | |
| HERBAL HEALTH CLINIC (HM09617) | | | | | | | | | | | | | | ● | ● | ● | | |
| HOBBS, SIMON (HM09859) | | | | | | | | | | ● | | | | | | | | |
| HOLDEN NATURAL HEALTH CLINIC (HM09927) | | | | | | | | | | | | | ● | | | | | |
| HOLISTIC AROMATHERAPY (HM09947) | | | | | | | | | | | | | | | | | | |

| Business by County with Reference no. | Cryo Surgery | Crystal Healing | Cupping | Cymatics | Dance Movement Thrpy | Dietician | Do-In | Douching | Dowsing | Drama Therapy | Electrolipolysis | Electrolysis | Electrotherapy | Encounter Groups | Faith Healing |
|---|---|---|---|---|---|---|---|---|---|---|---|---|---|---|---|
| CREIGHTMORE, R & D (HM05413) | | | | | | | | | | | | | | | |
| CRESENT CLINIC (HM05422) | | | | | | | | | | | | | | | |
| CROWBOROUGH CHIRO/COMP HLTH (HM05498) | | | | | | ● | | | | | | | | | |
| CROWBOROUGH COMP THERAPISTS (HM05499) | | | | | | | | | | | | | | | |
| DADSWELL, CLAIRE (HM05670) | | | | | | | | | | | | | | | |
| DRIVE OSTEO AND SPORTS CLINIC (HM06314) | | | | | | | | | | | | | | | |
| DYKE ROAD NATURAL HEALTH (HM06450) | | | | | | | | | | ● | | | | | |
| EAST BOURNE CLINIC (HM06509) | | | | | | | | | | | | | | | |
| EASTBOURNE CHIROPRACTIC CLINIC (HM06535) | | | | | | | | | | | | | | | |
| EATON, MARION (HM06563) | | | | | | | | | | | | | | | |
| FAIRCHILD, HAZEL (HM07052) | | | | | | | | | | | | | | | |
| FAMILY FIRST (HM07087) | | | | | | | | | | | | | | | |
| FIELDS OF FRAGRANCE (HM07276) | | | | | | | | | | | | | | | |
| FLOYD, MICHELLE (HM07438) | | | | | | | | | | | | | | | |
| FOUNDATION, ANGELGATE (HM07615) | | | | | | | | | | | | | | | |
| GATEHOUSE THERAPY CENTRE (HM07925) | | | | | | | | | | | | | | | |
| GEIGES, STEPHANIE (HM07967) | | | | | | | | | | | | | | | |
| GEORGE A BOWDLER CHIROPODIST (HM07988) | | | | | | | | | | | | | | | |
| GIBBONS, ELAINE (HM08024) | | | | | | | | | | | | | | | |
| GOLDSTONE CLINIC (HM08230) | | | | | | | | | | | | | | | |
| GOLDSTONE CLINIC (HM08229) | | | | | | | | | | | | | | | |
| GRIFFITHS, J (HM08567) | | | | | | | | | | | | | | | |
| HAGGARD, CAROLINE (HM08698) | | | | | | | | | | | | | | | |
| HART, RONALD (HM09131) | | | | | | | | | | | | | | | |
| HART, RONALD (HM09130) | | | | | | | | | | | | | | | |
| HASTINGS HOLISTIC HEALTH (HM09190) | | | | | | | | | | | | | | | |
| HAWKINS, LUKE (HM09224) | | | | | | | | | | | | | | | |
| HEALTHWISE (HM09418) | | | | | | | | | | | | | | | |
| HEATHFIELD CHIROPRACTIC CLINIC (HM09458) | | | | | | | | | | | | | | | |
| HEMMINGWAY CHIROPODIST (HM09537) | | | | | | | | | | | | | | | |
| HERBAL HEALTH CLINIC (HM09617) | | | | | | | | | | | | | | | |
| HOBBS, SIMON (HM09859) | | | | | | | | | | | | | | | |
| HOLDEN NATURAL HEALTH CLINIC (HM09927) | | | | | | | | | | | | | | | |
| HOLISTIC AROMATHERAPY (HM09947) | | | | | | | | | | | | | | | |

# A - F Therapies at Practices/Businesses

| Business by County with Reference no. | Absent Healing | Acupressure | Acupuncture | Alexander Technique | Allergy Testing | Anthroposohical Med | Aromatherapy | Art Therapy | Aura Therapy | Auricular Therapy | Auto Suggestion | Autogenic Training | Aversion Therapy | Ayurvedic Medicine | Baby Massage | Bach Remedies | Bates Method | Beauty Therapy | Bio-energetics | Biofeedback | Biomagnetic Therapy | Biomechanics | Bonesetting | Bowen Therapy | Chinese Herbal Medicine | Chiropody | Chiropractic | Clinical Ecology | Cognitive Therapy | Colonic Hydrotherapy | Colour Therapy | Complementary Therapy | Counselling | Cranial Osteopathy | Cranio-Sacral Therapy | Cryo Surgery | Crystal Healing | Cupping | Cymatics | Dance Movement Thrpy | Dietician | Do-In | Douching | Dowsing | Drama Therapy | Electrolipolysis | Electrolysis | Electrotherapy | Encounter Groups | Faith Healing |
|---|---|---|---|---|---|---|---|---|---|---|---|---|---|---|---|---|---|---|---|---|---|---|---|---|---|---|---|---|---|---|---|---|---|---|---|---|---|---|---|---|---|---|---|---|---|---|---|---|---|---|
| HOVE CHIROPRACTIC CLINIC (HM10227) | | | | | | | | | | | | | | | | | | | | | | | | | | | ● | | | | | | | | | | | | | | | | | | | | | | | |
| HOVE OSTEOPATHIC CLINIC (HM10228) | | | | | | | | | | | | | | | | | | | | | | | | | | | | | | | | | | ● | | | | | | | | | | | | | | | | |
| HUGHES, CLARE (HM10324) | | | | ● | | | | | | | | | | | | | | | | | | | | | | | | | | | | | | | | | | | | | | | | | | | | | | |
| IONS, ROBERT (HM10710) | | | | | | | | | | | | | | | | | | | | | | | | | | | ● | | | | | | | | | | | | | | | | | | | | | | | |
| JOY, JANET (HM11231) | | | | | | | | | | | | | | | | | | | | | | | | | | | | | ● | | ● | ● | ● | | | | | | | | | | | | | | | | | |
| KRISTANA (HM11806) | ● | | | | | | | | | | | | | | | | | | | | | | | | | | | | | | | | ● | | | | | | | | | | | | | | | | | |
| LAFITTE, J L (HM11861) | | | | | | | | | | | | | | | | | | | | | | | | | | | ● | | | | | | | | | | | | | | | | | | | | | | | |
| LEWES CHIROPRACTIC CLINIC (HM12271) | | | | | | | | | | | | | | | | | | | | | | | | | | | ● | | | | | | | | | | | | | | | | | | | | | | | |
| LOTUS EMPORIUM (HM12654) | | | | | | | ● | | | | | | | | | | | | | | | | | | | | | | | | | | | | | | | | | | | | | | | | | | | |
| MANSFIELD, PETER (HM13049) | | | | ● | | | | | | | | | | | | | | | | | | | | | | | | | | | | | | | | | | | | | | | | | | | | | | |
| MARINE CLINIC (HM13102) | | | ● | | | | | | | | | | | | | | | | | | | | | | | | | | | | | | | | | | | | | | | | | | | | | | | |
| MCKEOWN, KAY (HM13532) | | | | ● | | | | | | | | | | | | | | | | | | | | | | | | | | | | | | | | | | | | | | | | | | | | | | |
| MURPHY, KEVIN (HM14387) | | | | | | | | | | | | | | | | | | | | | | | | | | | ● | | | | | | | ● | | | | | | | | | | | | | | | | |
| NATURES NECTAR (HM14692) | | | | | | | ● | | | | | | | | | | | | | | | | | | | | | | | | | | | | | | | | | | | | | | | | | | | |
| NEAT FEET (HM14742) | | | | | | | | | | | | | | | | | | | | | | ● | | | | ● | | | | | | | | | | | | | | | | | | | | | | | | |
| NEWICK PHYSIOTHERAPY CLINIC (HM14865) | | | ● | | | | | | | | | | | | | | | | | | | | | | | | | | | | | | | | | | | | | | | | | | | | | | | |
| OLD TOWN CHIROPRACTIC CLINIC (HM15263) | | | | | | | | | | | | | | | | | | | | | | | | | | | ● | | | | | | | | | | | | | | | | | | | | | | | |
| PARFITT, A J (HM15654) | | | ● | | | | | | | | | | | | | | | | | | | | | | | | | | | | | | | | | | | | | | | | | | | | | | | |
| PEARCE, JOAN (HM15896) | | | | | | | ● | | | | | | | | | | | | | | | | | | | | | | | | | | | | | | | | | | | | | | | | | | | |
| PEARCEY, M (HM15903) | | | | | | | | | | | | | | | | | | | | | | | | | | | ● | | | | | | | | | | | | | | | | | | | | | | | |
| PEVENSEY BAY NTRL HEALING (HM16105) | | | | | | | ● | | | | | | | | | | | | | | | | | | | | | | | | | | | | | | | | | | | | | | | | | | | |
| PFEIFFER, MARIANNA (HM16107) | | | | | | | ● | | | | | | | | | | | | | | | | | | | | | | | | | | | | | | | | | | | | | | | | | | | |
| PHILIP D HOLMES (HM16118) | | | ● | | | | | | | | | | | | | | | | | | | | | | | | | | | | | | | | | | | | | | | | | | | | | | | |
| PRICE, JAMES (HM16583) | | | | | | | | | | | | | | | | | | | | | | | | | | ● | | | | | | | | | | | | | | | | | | | | | | | | |
| PRIORY HEIGHTS (HM16633) | | | ● | | | | | | | | | | | | | | | | | | | | | | | | | | | | | | | | | | | | | | | | | | | | | | | |
| RAINBOW PATHWAYS (HM16882) | | | | | | | | | | | | | | | | | | | | | | | | | | | | | | | | ● | | | | | ● | | | | | | | | | | | | | |
| REEVES, ALAN (HM17062) | | | | | | | | | | | | | | | | | | | | | | | | | | | | | | | | | ● | | | | | | | | | | | | | | | | | |
| ROLLESTON-SMITH, C (HM17566) | | | | ● | | | | | | | | | | | | | | | | | | | | | | | | | | | | | | | | | | | | | | | | | | | | | | |
| SANDERSON & ELEMENT (HM17922) | | | | ● | | | | | | | | | | | | | | | | | | | | | | | | | | | | | | | | | | | | | | | | | | | | | | |
| SANDERSON & ELEMENT (HM17920) | | | | ● | | | | | | | | | | | | | | | | | | | | | | | | | | | | | | | | | | | | | | | | | | | | | | |
| SANDERSON & ELEMENT (HM17919) | | | | ● | | | | | | | | | | | | | | | | | | | | | | | | | | | | | | | | | | | | | | | | | | | | | | |
| SAYER, YKKE (HM17997) | | | | | | | | | | | | | | | | ● | | | | | | | | | | | | | | | | | | | | | | | | | | | | | | | | | | |
| SCHOLL CENTRE (HM18032) | | | | | | | | | | | | | | | | | | | | | | | | | | ● | | | | | | | | | | | | | | | | | | | | | | | | |
| SCRIVEN, SARA (HM18152) | | | | ● | | | | | | | | | | | | | | | | | | | | | | | | | | | | | | | | | | | | | | | | | | | | | | |

# A - F Therapies at Practices/Businesses

| Business by County with Reference no. | Absent Healing | Acupressure | Acupuncture | Alexander Technique | Allergy Testing | Anthroposophical Med | Aromatherapy | Art Therapy | Aura Therapy | Auricular Therapy | Auto Suggestion | Autogenic Training | Aversion Therapy | Ayurvedic Medicine | Baby Massage | Bach Remedies | Bates Method |
|---|---|---|---|---|---|---|---|---|---|---|---|---|---|---|---|---|---|
| SIMPSON, HEATHER (HM18588) | | | | | | | | | | | | | | | | ● | |
| SUNDIAL HOUSE CHIROPRACTIC (HM19506) | | | | | | | | | | | | | | | | | |
| TEALE, PAUL (HM19809) | | | | | | | | | | | | | | | | | |
| THOMAS, D E (HM19937) | | | | | | | | | | | | | | | | | |
| TIGER CLINIC (HM20063) | | | ● | | | | | | | | | | | | | | |
| TISSERAND (HM20095) | | | | | | | ● | | | | | | | | | | |
| TRENCHARD, ABIGAIL (HM20319) | | | | | | | | | | | | | | | | | |
| TYRER, PATRICIA (HM20474) | | | | | | | | | | | | | | | | ● | |
| VAINES, EILEEN (HM20548) | | | | | | | | | | | | | | | | ● | |
| VALENCE ROAD OSTEOPATHS (HM20554) | | | | | | | | | | | | | | | | | |
| WADHURST PHYSIO/SPORTS CLNC (HM20729) | | | ● | | | | | | | | | | | | | | |
| WALSH, M J (HM20865) | | | | | | | | | | | | | | | | | |
| WANG, JING (HM20888) | | | ● | | | | | | | | | | | | | | |
| WEDLAKE-GRIFFITHS, J (HM21097) | | | | | | | | | | | | | | | | | |
| WILBURY PHYSIOTHERAPY (HM21480) | | | | | | | | | | | | | | | | | |
| WILBURY SCHOOL-NATURAL THERAPY (HM21481) | | | | | | | | | | | | | | | | | |
| WRIGHT, P A (HM21946) | | | | | | | | | | | | | | | | | |
| YORK, B D (HM22051) | | | | | | | | | | | | | | | | | |
| **SUSSEX (WEST)** | | | | | | | | | | | | | | | | | |
| ACORN CENTRE (HM00171) | ● | ● | | | | | ● | | | | | | | | | ● | |
| ACUPRESSURE (HM00225) | | ● | | | | | | | | | | | | | | | |
| ACUPUNCTURE CLINIC (HM00277) | | ● | ● | | | | | | | | | | | | | ● | |
| ACUPUNCTURE/CHIRO CLINIC (HM00248) | | | ● | | | | | | | | | | | | | | |
| ALAN SMITH CHIROPRACTOR (HM00470) | | | | | | | | | | | | | | | | | |
| ANABELLS (HM00799) | | | | | | | ● | | | | | | | | | | |
| ANDREW BATHIE PRACTICE (HM00846) | | | | | | | | | | | ● | ● | ● | | | | |
| ANISE-STAR MOBILE AROMATHERAPY (HM00886) | | | | | | | ● | | | | | | | | | | |
| AUROMA (HM01357) | | | | | | | ● | | | | | | | | | | |
| AVALON HEALTH CENTRE (HM01380) | | | | | | | ● | | | | | | | | | | |
| B O P (HM01452) | | | | | | | ● | | | | | | | | | | |
| BACK 2 FITNESS CHIROPRACTIC (HM01476) | | | | | | | | | | | | | | | | | |
| BARTHOLOMEW WAY CLINIC (HM01818) | | | | | | | | | | | | | | | | | |
| BELLAMY PARTNERSHIP (HM02093) | | | ● | | | | | | | | | | | | | | |
| BODYGUIDE ALTERNATE (HM02619) | | | | | | | ● | | | | | | | | | | |

| Business by County with Reference no. | Beauty Therapy | Bio-energetics | Biofeedback | Biomagnetic Therapy | Biomechanics | Bonesetting | Bowen Therapy | Chinese Herbal Medicine | Chiropody | Chiropractic | Clinical Ecology | Cognitive Therapy | Colonic Hydrotherapy | Colour Therapy | Complementary Therapy | Counselling | Cranial Osteopathy |
|---|---|---|---|---|---|---|---|---|---|---|---|---|---|---|---|---|---|
| SIMPSON, HEATHER (HM18588) | | | | | | | | | | | | | | | | | |
| SUNDIAL HOUSE CHIROPRACTIC (HM19506) | | | | | | | | | | ● | | | | | | | |
| TEALE, PAUL (HM19809) | | | | | | | | | | | | | | | | | ● |
| THOMAS, D E (HM19937) | | | | | | | | | | ● | | | | | | | |
| TIGER CLINIC (HM20063) | | | | | | | | | | | | | | | | | |
| TISSERAND (HM20095) | | | | | | | | | | | | | | | | | |
| TRENCHARD, ABIGAIL (HM20319) | | | | | | | | | | | | | | | | ● | |
| TYRER, PATRICIA (HM20474) | | | | | | | | | | | | | | | | | |
| VAINES, EILEEN (HM20548) | | | | | | | | | | | | | | | | | |
| VALENCE ROAD OSTEOPATHS (HM20554) | | | | | | | | | | | | | | | | | ● |
| WADHURST PHYSIO/SPORTS CLNC (HM20729) | | | | | | | | | | | | | | | | | |
| WALSH, M J (HM20865) | | | | | | | | | | | | | | | | | ● |
| WANG, JING (HM20888) | | | | | | | | | | | | | | | | | |
| WEDLAKE-GRIFFITHS, J (HM21097) | | | | | | | | | | | | | | | ● | | |
| WILBURY PHYSIOTHERAPY (HM21480) | | | | | | | | | ● | | | | | | | ● | |
| WILBURY SCHOOL-NATURAL THERAPY (HM21481) | | | | | | | | | | | | | | | ● | | |
| WRIGHT, P A (HM21946) | | | | | ● | | | | ● | | | | | | | | |
| YORK, B D (HM22051) | | | | | | | | | | ● | | | | | | | |
| **SUSSEX (WEST)** | | | | | | | | | | | | | | | | | |
| ACORN CENTRE (HM00171) | | | | | | | | | | | ● | | | | | ● | |
| ACUPRESSURE (HM00225) | | | | | | | | | | | | | | | | | |
| ACUPUNCTURE CLINIC (HM00277) | | | | | | | | | | | | | | | | | |
| ACUPUNCTURE/CHIRO CLINIC (HM00248) | | | | | | | | | | | | | | | | | |
| ALAN SMITH CHIROPRACTOR (HM00470) | | | | | | ● | | | | ● | | | | | | | ● |
| ANABELLS (HM00799) | | | | | | | | | | | | | | | | | |
| ANDREW BATHIE PRACTICE (HM00846) | | | ● | | | | | | | | | ● | | | ● | ● | |
| ANISE-STAR MOBILE AROMATHERAPY (HM00886) | | | | | | | | | | | | | | | | | |
| AUROMA (HM01357) | | | | | | | | | | | | | | | | | |
| AVALON HEALTH CENTRE (HM01380) | | | | | | | | | ● | | | | | | | ● | |
| B O P (HM01452) | | | | | | | | | | | | | | | | | |
| BACK 2 FITNESS CHIROPRACTIC (HM01476) | | | | | | | | | | ● | | | | | | | |
| BARTHOLOMEW WAY CLINIC (HM01818) | | | | | | | | | ● | | | | | | | | |
| BELLAMY PARTNERSHIP (HM02093) | | | | | | | | | | | | | | | | | |
| BODYGUIDE ALTERNATE (HM02619) | | | | | | | | | | | | | | | | | |

| Business by County with Reference no. | Cranio-Sacral Therapy | Cryo Surgery | Crystal Healing | Cupping | Cymatics | Dance Movement Thrpy | Dietician | Do-In | Douching | Dowsing | Drama Therapy | Electrolipolysis | Electrolysis | Electrotherapy | Encounter Groups | Faith Healing |
|---|---|---|---|---|---|---|---|---|---|---|---|---|---|---|---|---|
| SIMPSON, HEATHER (HM18588) | | | | | | | | | | | | | | | | |
| SUNDIAL HOUSE CHIROPRACTIC (HM19506) | | | | | | | | | | | | | | | | |
| TEALE, PAUL (HM19809) | | | | | | | | | | | | | | | | |
| THOMAS, D E (HM19937) | | | | | | | | | | | | | | | | |
| TIGER CLINIC (HM20063) | | | | | | | | | | | | | | | | |
| TISSERAND (HM20095) | | | | | | | | | | | | | | | | |
| TRENCHARD, ABIGAIL (HM20319) | | | | | | | | | | | | | | | | |
| TYRER, PATRICIA (HM20474) | | | | | | | | | | | | | | | | |
| VAINES, EILEEN (HM20548) | | | | | | | | | | | | | | | | |
| VALENCE ROAD OSTEOPATHS (HM20554) | | | | | | | | | | | | | | | | |
| WADHURST PHYSIO/SPORTS CLNC (HM20729) | | | | | | | | | | | | | | | | |
| WALSH, M J (HM20865) | | | | | | | | | | | | | | | | |
| WANG, JING (HM20888) | | | | | | | | | | | | | | | | |
| WEDLAKE-GRIFFITHS, J (HM21097) | | | | | | | | | | | | | | ● | | |
| WILBURY PHYSIOTHERAPY (HM21480) | | | | | | | | | | | | | | | | |
| WILBURY SCHOOL-NATURAL THERAPY (HM21481) | | | | | | | | | | | | | | | | |
| WRIGHT, P A (HM21946) | | | | | | | | | | | | | | | | |
| YORK, B D (HM22051) | | | | | | | | | | | | | | | | |
| **SUSSEX (WEST)** | | | | | | | | | | | | | | | | |
| ACORN CENTRE (HM00171) | | | | | | | | | | ● | | | | | | |
| ACUPRESSURE (HM00225) | | | | | | | | | | | | | | | | |
| ACUPUNCTURE CLINIC (HM00277) | | | | ● | | | | | | | | | | | | |
| ACUPUNCTURE/CHIRO CLINIC (HM00248) | | | | | | | | | | | | | | | | |
| ALAN SMITH CHIROPRACTOR (HM00470) | | | | | | | | | | | | | | ● | | |
| ANABELLS (HM00799) | | | | | | | | | | | | | | | | |
| ANDREW BATHIE PRACTICE (HM00846) | | | | | | | | | | | | | | | | |
| ANISE-STAR MOBILE AROMATHERAPY (HM00886) | | | | | | | | | | | | | | | | |
| AUROMA (HM01357) | | | | | | | | | | | | | | | | |
| AVALON HEALTH CENTRE (HM01380) | | | | | | | | | | | | | | | | |
| B O P (HM01452) | | | | | | | | | | | | | | ● | | |
| BACK 2 FITNESS CHIROPRACTIC (HM01476) | | | | | | | | | | | | | | | | |
| BARTHOLOMEW WAY CLINIC (HM01818) | | | | | | | | | | | | | | | | |
| BELLAMY PARTNERSHIP (HM02093) | | | | | | | | | | | | | | | | |
| BODYGUIDE ALTERNATE (HM02619) | | | | | | | | | | | | | | | | |

# A - F Therapies at Practices/Businesses

| Business by County with Reference no. | Absent Healing | Acupressure | Acupuncture | Alexander Technique | Allergy Testing | Anthroposophical Med | Aromatherapy | Art Therapy | Aura Therapy | Auricular Therapy | Auto Suggestion | Autogenic Training | Aversion Therapy | Ayurvedic Medicine | Baby Massage | Bach Remedies | Bates Method | Beauty Therapy | Bio-energetics | Biofeedback | Biomagnetic Therapy | Biomechanics | Bonesetting | Bowen Therapy | Chinese Herbal Medicine |
|---|---|---|---|---|---|---|---|---|---|---|---|---|---|---|---|---|---|---|---|---|---|---|---|---|---|
| BOHNET, CAROLE (HM02648) | | | | | | | ● | | | | | | | | | | | | | | | | | | |
| BRIGDEN, JENNIFER (HM03027) | | | | ● | | | | | | | | | | | | | | | | | | | | | |
| BRITCHIRO CLINIC (HM03068) | | | | | | | | | | | | | | | | | | | | | | | | | |
| BROCKBANK, N (HM03130) | | | | ● | | | | | | | | | | | | | | | | | | | | | |
| CARTLAND, ANN (HM03794) | | | | | | | | | | | | | | | | | | | | | | | | | |
| CASH, G G (HM03811) | | | | | | | | | | | | | | | | | | | | | | | | | |
| CHANGES (HM03985) | | | | | | | ● | | | | | | | | | ● | | | | | | | | | |
| CHAPMAN, MARILYN (HM04006) | | | | | | | | | | | | | | | | ● | | | | | | | | | |
| CHASE, PETER (HM04061) | | | | | | | | | | | | | | | | | | | | | | | | | |
| CHEN, AC C (HM04099) | | | ● | | | | | | | | | | | | | | | | | | | | | | |
| CHICHESTER ACUPUNCTURE CLINIC (HM04153) | | | ● | | | | | | | | | | | | | | | | | | | | | | |
| CHICHESTER CHIROPRACTORS (HM04154) | | | | | | | | | | | | | | | | | | | | | | | | | |
| CHIROPODIST () | | | | | | | | | | | | | | | | | | | | | | | | | |
| CHIROPRACTIC CLINIC (HM04385) | | | | | | | | | | | | | | | | | | | | | | | | | |
| CLAIRVOYANT - MEDIUM - HEALER (HM04514) | ● | | | | | | | | | | | | | | | | | | | | | | | | |
| CLARE'S BEAUTY CLINIC (HM04542) | | | | | | | ● | | | | | | | | | | | | | | | | | | |
| CLARKE, STEVEN (HM04604) | | | | | | | | | | | ● | | ● | | | | | | | | | | | | |
| CLOCKHOUSE CLINIC (HM04728) | | | | ● | | | | | | | | | | | | | | | | | | | | | |
| COBB, ADRIAN (HM04758) | | | | | | | | | | | | | | | | | | | | | | | | | |
| CORNERWEIGHS (HM05183) | | | | | | ● | ● | | | | | | | | | ● | | | | | | | | | |
| CRAWLEY CHIROPRACTIC CLINIC (HM05394) | | | | | | | | | | | | | | | | | | | | | | | | | |
| CUTLER, AMANDA (HM05644) | | | | | | | ● | | | | | | | | | | | | | | | | | | |
| DALLAS, PETER (HM05691) | | ● | | | | | | | | | | | | | | | | | | | | | | | |
| DAY, BRIDGET (HM05889) | | | | ● | | | | | | | | | | | | | | | | | | | | | |
| DIEBSCHLAG, FRANCESCA (HM06091) | | | ● | | | | | | | | | | | | | | | | | | | | | | |
| DYER & ASSOCIATES (HM06444) | | | ● | | | | ● | | | | | | | | | | | | | | | | | | |
| EDWARDS, SIMON (HM06671) | | | | | | | | | | | | | | | | | | | | | | | | | |
| EMINATIONS ACUPUNCTURE CLINIC (HM06805) | | ● | ● | | | | | | | | | | | | | ● | | | | | | | | | |
| FARBER, AARON (HM07101) | | | | | | | | | | | | | | | | | | | | | | | | | |
| FELPHAM NATURAL HEALTH CLINIC (HM07206) | | | | | ● | | | | | | | | | | | ● | | | | | | | | | |
| FROST, CHARLES (HM07760) | | | | | ● | | | | | | ● | | ● | | | | | | | | | | | | |
| FURNACE GREEN CHIRO CTRE (HM07800) | | | | | | | | | | | | | | | | | | | | | | | | | |
| GARDINER, SAM (HM07876) | | | | | | | | | | | | | | | | | | | | | | | | | |
| GRANT, C B T (DR) (HM08377) | | | ● | | | | | | | | | | | | | | | | | | | | | | |

| Business by County with Reference no. | Chiropody | Chiropractic | Clinical Ecology | Cognitive Therapy | Colonic Hydrotherapy | Colour Therapy | Complementary Therapy | Counselling | Cranial Osteopathy | Cranio-Sacral Therapy | Cryo Surgery | Crystal Healing | Cupping | Cymatics | Dance Movement Thrpy | Dietician | Do-In | Douching | Dowsing | Drama Therapy | Electrolipolysis | Electrolysis | Electrotherapy | Encounter Groups | Faith Healing |
|---|---|---|---|---|---|---|---|---|---|---|---|---|---|---|---|---|---|---|---|---|---|---|---|---|---|
| BOHNET, CAROLE (HM02648) | | | | | | ● | ● | | | | | | | | | | | | | | | | | | |
| BRIGDEN, JENNIFER (HM03027) | | | | | | | | | | | | | | | | | | | | | | | | | |
| BRITCHIRO CLINIC (HM03068) | | ● | | | | | | | | | | | | | | | | | | | | | | | |
| BROCKBANK, N (HM03130) | | | | | | | | | | | | | | | | | | | | | | | | | |
| CARTLAND, ANN (HM03794) | ● | | | | | | | | | | | | | | | | | | | | | | | | |
| CASH, G G (HM03811) | ● | | | | | | | | | | | | | | | | | | | | | | | | |
| CHANGES (HM03985) | | | | | | | | | | | | | | | | | | | | | | | | | |
| CHAPMAN, MARILYN (HM04006) | | | | | | | | | | | | | | | | | | | | | | | | | |
| CHASE, PETER (HM04061) | ● | | | | | | | | | | | | | | | | | | | | | | | | |
| CHEN, AC C (HM04099) | | | | | | | | | | | | | | | | | | | | | | | | | |
| CHICHESTER ACUPUNCTURE CLINIC (HM04153) | | | | | | | | | | | | | | | | | | | | | | | | | |
| CHICHESTER CHIROPRACTORS (HM04154) | | ● | | | | | | | | | | | | | | | | | | | | | | | |
| CHIROPODIST () | ● | | | | | | | | | | | | | | | | | | | | | | | | |
| CHIROPRACTIC CLINIC (HM04385) | | ● | | | | | | | | | | | | | | | | | | | | | | | |
| CLAIRVOYANT - MEDIUM - HEALER (HM04514) | | | | | | | | ● | | | | | | | | | | | | | | | | | |
| CLARE'S BEAUTY CLINIC (HM04542) | | | | | | | | | | | | | | | | | | | | | | | | | |
| CLARKE, STEVEN (HM04604) | | | | | | | ● | ● | | | | | | | | | | | | | | | | | |
| CLOCKHOUSE CLINIC (HM04728) | | | | | | | | | | | | | | | | | | | | | | | | | |
| COBB, ADRIAN (HM04758) | | ● | | | | | | | | | | | | | | | | | | | | | | | |
| CORNERWEIGHS (HM05183) | | | | | | | | | | | | | | | | | | | | | | | | | |
| CRAWLEY CHIROPRACTIC CLINIC (HM05394) | | ● | | | | | | | | | | | | | | | | | | | | | | | |
| CUTLER, AMANDA (HM05644) | | | | | | | | | | | | | | | | | | | | | | | | | |
| DALLAS, PETER (HM05691) | | | | | | | | | | | | | | | | | | | | | | | | | |
| DAY, BRIDGET (HM05889) | | | | | | | | | | | | | | | | | | | | | | | | | |
| DIEBSCHLAG, FRANCESCA (HM06091) | | | | | | | | | | | | | | | | | | | | | | | | | |
| DYER & ASSOCIATES (HM06444) | | | | | | | | ● | | | | | | | | | | | | | | | | | |
| EDWARDS, SIMON (HM06671) | | ● | | | | | | | | | | | | | | | | | | | | | | | |
| EMINATIONS ACUPUNCTURE CLINIC (HM06805) | | | | | | | | | | | | | ● | | | | | | | | | | | | |
| FARBER, AARON (HM07101) | | ● | | | | | | | | | | | | | | | | | | | | | | | |
| FELPHAM NATURAL HEALTH CLINIC (HM07206) | | | | | | | ● | | | | | | | | | | | | | | | | | | |
| FROST, CHARLES (HM07760) | | | | ● | | | | ● | | | | | | | | | | | | | | | | | |
| FURNACE GREEN CHIRO CTRE (HM07800) | | ● | | | | | ● | | | | | | | | | | | | | | | | | | |
| GARDINER, SAM (HM07876) | | | | | | | | ● | | | | | | | | | | | | | | | | | |
| GRANT, C B T (DR) (HM08377) | | | | | | | | | | | | | | | | | | | | | | | | | |

# A - F Therapies at Practices/Businesses

| Business by County with Reference no. | Absent Healing | Acupressure | Acupuncture | Alexander Technique | Allergy Testing | Anthroposohical Med | Aromatherapy | Art Therapy | Aura Therapy | Auricular Therapy | Auto Suggestion | Autogenic Training | Aversion Therapy | Ayurvedic Medicine | Baby Massage | Bach Remedies | Bates Method | Beauty Therapy | Bio-energetics | Biofeedback | Biomagnetic Therapy | Biomechanics | Bonesetting | Bowen Therapy | Chinese Herbal Medicine |
|---|---|---|---|---|---|---|---|---|---|---|---|---|---|---|---|---|---|---|---|---|---|---|---|---|---|
| GRAVILLE, CHRIS (HM08405) | | | | | | | ● | | | | | | | | | | | | | | | | | | |
| HARRIS, PAUL A E (HM09084) | | | | | | | | | | | | | | | | | | | | | | | | | |
| HEELER CENTRE (HM09498) | | ● | ● | | | | ● | | | | | | | | | ● | | | | | | | | ● | |
| HOLISTIC THERAPIST (HM09994) | | | | | | | ● | | | | | | | | | | | | | | | | | | |
| HORSHAM CHIROPRACTIC CENTRE (HM10191) | | | | | | | | | | | | | | | | | | | | | | | | | |
| I C O M (HM10548) | | | ● | | | | | | | | | | | | | | | | | | | | | | |
| JOBAIRE, MELANIE (HM11041) | | | | | | | | | | | | | | | | | | | | | | | | | |
| JONES, WENDY (HM11203) | | | | | | | | | | | | | | | | | | | | | | | | | |
| LARKIN, JILL (HM11976) | | | | | | | | | | | | | | | | | | | | | | | | | |
| LITTLEHAMPTON NAT HLTH CTRE (HM12470) | ● | | ● | ● | | | ● | ● | | | ● | | | | | ● | | | | | | | | ● | |
| MANN, LESLEY (HM13020) | | | | ● | | | | | | | | | | | | | | | | | | | | | |
| MASON, JOHN (HM13245) | | | | | | | | | | | | | | | | | | | | | | | | | |
| MAYNARD, MARTIN A (HM13357) | | | | | | | | | | | | | | | | | | | | | | | | | |
| MID SUSSEX CHIROPRACTIC CLINIC (HM13805) | | | | | | | | | | | | | | | | | | | | | | | | | |
| MILLEN, CAROL (HM13874) | | | | | | | ● | | | | | | | | | | | | | | | | | | |
| MILTON, CHRIS (HM13951) | | | | | | | ● | | | | | | | | | | | | | | | | | | |
| MOLESWORTH, ROGER (HM14051) | | | | | | | ● | | | | | | | | | | | | | | | | | | |
| NEW BROOK OILS (HM14812) | | | | | | | ● | | | | | | | | | | | | | | | | | | |
| OSTEOPATHY AT ESQUIRE'S (HM15479) | | | | | | | | | | | | | | | | | | | | | | | | | |
| PAIN & PARALYSIS SPECIALIST (HM15578) | ● | | | | | | | | ● | | | | | | | | | | ● | | | | | | |
| PALMER, GAYLE (HM15605) | | | | | | | | | | | | | | | | | | | | | | | | | |
| PALMER, GAYLE (HM15606) | | | | | | | | | | | | | | | | | | | | ● | | | ● | | |
| PARK ROAD SURGERY (HM15676) | | | ● | | | | | | | | | | | | | | | | | | | | | | |
| PATEL, PRATIKSHA (HM15799) | | | | | | | | | | | | | | | | | | | | | | | | | |
| PORTLAND PHYSIOTHERAPY CLINIC (HM16451) | | | ● | | | | | | | | | | | | | | | | | | | | | | |
| RICHARDSON, BRIAN J (HM17269) | | | | | | | | | | | | | | | | | | | | | | ● | | | |
| RICHARDSON, JANET (HM17282) | | | | | | | | | | | | | | | | | | | | | | ● | | | |
| ROBERTS, ALISON (HM17403) | | | | | | | ● | | | | | | | | | | | | | | | | | | |
| RUDD, STEVEN (DR) (HM17729) | | | | | | | | | | | | | | | | | | | | | | | | | |
| SANDERSON & ELEMENT (HM17921) | | | | ● | | | | | | | | | | | | | | | | | | | | | |
| SECRET REMEDIES (HM18181) | | | | | | | ● | | | | | | | | | | | | | | | | | | |
| SEVENTH HEAVEN (HM18246) | | | ● | | | | | | | | | | | | | | | | | | | | | | |
| SHAW, LENISE (HM18343) | | | | | | | | | | | | | | | | ● | | | | | | | | | |
| SHEPPARD, PAM (HM18422) | | | | | | | | | | | | | | | | ● | | | | | | | | | |

| Business by County with Reference no. | Chiropody | Chiropractic | Clinical Ecology | Cognitive Therapy | Colonic Hydrotherapy | Colour Therapy | Complementary Therapy | Counselling | Cranial Osteopathy | Cranio-Sacral Therapy | Cryo Surgery | Crystal Healing | Cupping | Cymatics | Dance Movement Thrpy | Dietician | Do-In | Douching | Dowsing | Drama Therapy | Electrolipolysis | Electrolysis | Electrotherapy | Encounter Groups | Faith Healing |
|---|---|---|---|---|---|---|---|---|---|---|---|---|---|---|---|---|---|---|---|---|---|---|---|---|---|
| GRAVILLE, CHRIS (HM08405) | | | | | | | | | | | | | | | | | | | | | | | | | |
| HARRIS, PAUL A E (HM09084) | | ● | | | | | | | | | | | | | | | | | | | | | | | |
| HEELER CENTRE (HM09498) | ● | | | | | | ● | ● | ● | | | | ● | | | ● | | | | | | | | | |
| HOLISTIC THERAPIST (HM09994) | | | | | | | | | | | | | | | | | | | | | | | | | |
| HORSHAM CHIROPRACTIC CENTRE (HM10191) | | ● | | | | | | | | | | | | | | | | | | | | | | | |
| I C O M (HM10548) | | | | | | | ● | | | | | | | | | | | | | | | | | | |
| JOBAIRE, MELANIE (HM11041) | | ● | | | | | | | | | | | | | | | | | | | | | | | |
| JONES, WENDY (HM11203) | | | | | | | | | | | | | | | | | | | | | | | ● | | |
| LARKIN, JILL (HM11976) | | | | | | | | | | | | ● | | | | | | | | | | | | | |
| LITTLEHAMPTON NAT HLTH CTRE (HM12470) | ● | ● | ● | | | ● | | ● | ● | ● | | | | | | ● | | | | | | | | | ● |
| MANN, LESLEY (HM13020) | | | | | | | | | | | | | | | | | | | | | | | | | |
| MASON, JOHN (HM13245) | | ● | | | | | | | | | | | | | | | | | | | | | | | |
| MAYNARD, MARTIN A (HM13357) | ● | | | | | | | | | | | | | | | | | | | | | | | | |
| MID SUSSEX CHIROPRACTIC CLINIC (HM13805) | | ● | | | | | | | ● | | | | | | | | | | | | | | | | |
| MILLEN, CAROL (HM13874) | | | | | | | | | | | | | | | | | | | | | | | | | |
| MILTON, CHRIS (HM13951) | | | | | | | | | | | | | | | | | | | | | | | | | |
| MOLESWORTH, ROGER (HM14051) | | | | | | | | | | | | | | | | | | | | | | | | | |
| NEW BROOK OILS (HM14812) | | | | | | | | | | | | | | | | | | | | | | | | | |
| OSTEOPATHY AT ESQUIRE'S (HM15479) | | | | | | | ● | | ● | | | | | | | | | | | | | | | | |
| PAIN & PARALYSIS SPECIALIST (HM15578) | | | | | | | ● | | | | | | | | | | | | | | | | | | |
| PALMER, GAYLE (HM15605) | | | | | | | ● | ● | ● | | | | | | | | | | ● | | | | | | |
| PALMER, GAYLE (HM15606) | | | | | | | ● | ● | ● | | | | | | | | | | ● | | | | | | |
| PARK ROAD SURGERY (HM15676) | | | | | | | | | | | | | | | | | | | | | | | | | |
| PATEL, PRATIKSHA (HM15799) | | ● | | | | | | | | | | | | | | | | | | | | | | | |
| PORTLAND PHYSIOTHERAPY CLINIC (HM16451) | | | | | | | | | | | | | | | | | | | | | | | | | |
| RICHARDSON, BRIAN J (HM17269) | | | | | | | | | | | | | | | | | | | | | | | | | |
| RICHARDSON, JANET (HM17282) | ● | | | | | | | | | | | | | | | | | | | | | | | | |
| ROBERTS, ALISON (HM17403) | | | | | | | | | | | | | | | | | | | | | | | | | |
| RUDD, STEVEN (DR) (HM17729) | | ● | | | | | | | | | | | | | | | | | | | | | | | |
| SANDERSON & ELEMENT (HM17921) | | | | | | | | | | | | | | | | | | | | | | | | | |
| SECRET REMEDIES (HM18181) | | | | | | | | | | | | | | | | | | | | | | | | | |
| SEVENTH HEAVEN (HM18246) | | | | | | | | | | | | | | | | | | | | | | | | | |
| SHAW, LENISE (HM18343) | | | | | | | | | | | | | | | | | | | | | | | | | |
| SHEPPARD, PAM (HM18422) | | | | | | | | | | | | | | | | | | | | | | | | | |

# A - F Therapies at Practices/Businesses

| Business by County with Reference no. | Absent Healing | Acupressure | Acupuncture | Alexander Technique | Allergy Testing | Anthroposohical Med | Aromatherapy | Art Therapy | Aura Therapy | Auricular Therapy | Auto Suggestion | Autogenic Training | Aversion Therapy | Ayurvedic Medicine | Baby Massage | Bach Remedies | Bates Method | Beauty Therapy | Bio-energetics | Biofeedback | Biomagnetic Therapy | Biomechanics | Bonesetting | Bowen Therapy | Chinese Herbal Medicine | Chiropody | Chiropractic | Clinical Ecology | Cognitive Therapy | Colonic Hydrotherapy | Colour Therapy | Complementary Therapy | Counselling | Cranial Osteopathy | Cranio-Sacral Therapy | Cryo Surgery | Crystal Healing | Cupping | Cymatics | Dance Movement Thrpy | Dietician | Do-In | Douching | Dowsing | Drama Therapy | Electrolipolysis | Electrolysis | Electrotherapy | Encounter Groups | Faith Healing |
|---|---|---|---|---|---|---|---|---|---|---|---|---|---|---|---|---|---|---|---|---|---|---|---|---|---|---|---|---|---|---|---|---|---|---|---|---|---|---|---|---|---|---|---|---|---|---|---|---|---|---|
| SIN MUI CHONG-MARTIN (HM18603) | | | ● | | | | | | | | | | | | | | | | | | | | | | | | | | | | | | | | | | | | | | | | | | | | | | | |
| SMITH, BARBARA (HM18720) | | | | | | | | | | | | | | | | | | | | | | | | | | ● | | | | | | | | | | | | | | | | | | | | | | | | |
| STAINTON, USHA (HM19116) | | | ● | | | | | | | | | | | | | | | | | | | | | | | | | | | | | | | | | | | | | | | | | | | | | | | |
| STAKIM, SHELIA (HM19117) | | | | | | | | | | | | | | | | | | | | | | | | | | | ● | | | | | | | | | | | | | | | | | | | | | | | |
| STAYNES, I G (HM19163) | | | ● | | | | | | | | | | | | | | | | | | | | | | | | | | | | | | | | | | | | | | | | | | | | | | | |
| STEPNEY, LESLEY (HM19211) | | | | | | | ● | | | | | | | | | | | | | | | | | | | | | | | | | | | | | | | | | | | | | | | | | | | |
| STEVENS, PAT (HM19238) | | | | | | | | | | | | | | | | | | | | | | | | | | | | | | | | | | | | | | | | | | | | | | | ● | | | |
| STOTT-DURHAM, ANDREW (HM19355) | | ● | | | | | | | | | | | | | | | | | | | | | | | | | | | | | | | | | ● | | | | | | | | | | | | | | | |
| SULLIVAN, SUZANNE (HM19484) | | | | | | | | | | | | | | | | ● | | | | | | | | | | | | | | | | | | | | | | | | | | | | | | | | | | |
| SWAN, LAURIE C (HM19574) | | | | | | | | | | | | | | | | | | | | | | | | | | | | | | | ● | | | | | | | | | | | | | | | | | | | |
| TAPHOUSE, K T (HM19697) | | | | | | | ● | | | | | | | | | | | | | | | | | | | | | | | | | | | | | | | | | | | | | | | | | | | |
| TAYLOR, JAMES M (HM19767) | | | | ● | | | | | | | | | | | | | | | | | | | | | | | | | | | | | | | | | | | | | | | | | | | | | | |
| TRANQUILLITY (HM20260) | ● | | | | | | ● | | | | | | | | | | | | | | | | | | | | | | | | | | | | | | | | | | | | | | | | | | | |
| TUGNUTT, SALLY (HM20378) | | | | | | | ● | | | | | | | | | | | | | | | | | | | | | | | | | | | | | | | | | | | | | | | | | | | |
| WESTACOTT, EILEEN (HM21256) | | | | | | | ● | | | | | | | | | | | | | | | | | | | | | | | | | | | | | | | | | | | | | | | | | | | |
| WILSON, AVIS (HM21646) | | ● | | | | | | | | | | | | | | | | | | | | | | | | | | | | | | | | | | | | | | | | | | | | ● | | ● | | |
| WOOD, J G (HM21798) | | | ● | | | | | | | | | | | | | | | | | | | | | | | | | | | | | ● | | | | | | | | | | | | | | | | ● | | |
| WORSFOLD, CHRISTINE (HM21903) | | | | | | | | | | | | | | | | | | | | | | | | | | ● | | | | | | | | | | | | | | | | | | | | | | | | |
| WORTHING CHIROPRACTIC CLINIC (HM21907) | | | | | | | | | | | | | | | | | | | | | | | | | | | ● | | | | | | | | | | | | | | | | | | | | | | | |
| WORTHING CLINIC OF ACUPUNCTURE (HM21909) | | | ● | | | | | | | | | | | | | | | | | | | | | | | | | | | | | | | | | | | | | | | | | | | | | | | |
| WORTHING CLINIC OF ACUPUNCTURE (HM21908) | | | ● | | | | | | | | | | | | | | | | | | | | | | | | | | | | | | | | | | | | | | | | | | | | | | | |
| YORK, TIM (HM22054) | | | | ● | | | | | | | | | | | | | | | | | | | | | | | | | | | | | | | | | | | | | | | | | | | | | | |
| YOUNG, LINDA (HM22077) | | | | | | | ● | | | | | | | | | | | | | | | | | | | | | | | | | | | | | | | | | | | | | | | | | | | |
| **TYNE AND WEAR** | | | | | | | | | | | | | | | | | | | | | | | | | | | | | | | | | | | | | | | | | | | | | | | | | | |
| ACUPUNCTURE & NAT MED CLINIC (HM00243) | | ● | ● | | | | | | | | ● | | | | | | | | | | | | | | | | ● | | | | | ● | | | | | | ● | | | | | | | | | | | | |
| ACUPUNCTURE HEALTH POINT (HM00313) | | | ● | | | | | | | | | | | | | | | | | | | | | | | | | | | | | | | | | | | | | | | | | | | | | | | |
| ACUPUNCTURE MOXIBUSTION CLINIC (HM00315) | | | ● | | | | | | | | | | | | | | | | | | | | | | | | | | | | | | | | | | | | | | | | | | | | | | | |
| ACUPUNCTURE/ANTI-SMOKING CLNC (HM00322) | | | ● | | | | | | | | | | | | | | | | | | | | | | | | | | | | | | | | | | | | | | | | | | | | | | | |
| ALEXANDER TECHNIQUE (HM00518) | | | | ● | | | | | | | | | | | | | | | | | | | | | | | | | | | | | | | | | | | | | | | | | | | | | | |
| AROMATHERAPY IN PRACTICE (HM01114) | | | | | | | ● | | | | | | | | | | | | | | | | | | | | | | | | | | | | | | | | | | | | | | | | | | | |
| AROMATIC (HM01133) | | | | | | | ● | | | | | | | | | | | | | | | | | | | | | | | | | | | | | | | | | | | | | | | | | | | |
| B WIGRAM HEALING & REFLEXOLOGY (HM01455) | ● | | | | | | | | | | | | | | | | | | | | | | | | | | | | | | ● | ● | | | | | | | | | | | | | | | | | | |
| BAILEY, MATTHEW G (HM01553) | | | | | | | | | | | | | | | | | | | | | | | | | | | ● | | | | | | | | | | | | | | | | | | | | | | | |
| BEAUTY WITH COMFORT (HM02007) | | | | | | | ● | | | | | | | | | | | | | | | | | | | | | | | | | | | | | | | | | | | | | | | | | | | |

# A - F Therapies at Practices/Businesses

Business by County with Reference no.

| Business by County with Reference no. | Absent Healing | Acupressure | Acupuncture | Alexander Technique | Allergy Testing | Anthroposohical Med | Aromatherapy | Art Therapy | Aura Therapy | Auricular Therapy | Auto Suggestion | Autogenic Training | Aversion Therapy | Ayurvedic Medicine | Baby Massage | Bach Remedies | Bates Method | Beauty Therapy | Bio-energetics | Biofeedback | Biomagnetic Therapy | Biomechanics | Bonesetting | Bowen Therapy | Chinese Herbal Medicine |
|---|---|---|---|---|---|---|---|---|---|---|---|---|---|---|---|---|---|---|---|---|---|---|---|---|---|
| BIOPHYSICAL TREATMENT SERVICE (HM02342) | | | ● | | | | | | | | | | | | | | | | | | | | | | |
| BODY BALANCE HOLISTIC THERAPY (HM02572) | | | | | | | ● | | | | | | | | | | | | | | | | | | |
| CHIROPODY CLINIC (HM04324) | | | | | | | | | | | | | | | | | | | | | | ● | | | |
| CLAREMONT FOOTCARE SURGERY (HM04537) | | | | | | | | | | | | | | | | | | | | | | | | | |
| CONNECT PHYSICAL HEALTH CTRE (HM04989) | | | ● | | | | ● | | | | | | | | | | | | | ● | | | | | |
| DERWENT CENTRE (HM06020) | | | ● | | | | ● | | ● | | | | | | | | | | | | | | | | |
| EARDLEY, D & J (HM06492) | | | | | | | ● | | | | | | | | | | | | | | | | | | |
| FAMILY CHIRO WELLNESS CENTRE (HM07083) | | | | | | | | | | | | | | | | | | | | | | | | | |
| FEEL GOOD AROMATHERAPY (HM07164) | | | | | | | ● | | | | | | | | | | | | | | | | | | |
| FENG, W W (HM07214) | | | ● | | | | | | | | | | | | | | | | | | | | | | |
| FOWLER, CHRISTINE (HM07628) | | | | | | | | | | | | | | | | | | | | | | | | ● | |
| GATESHEAD COMPLEMENTARY HEALTH (HM07927) | | | ● | | | | ● | | | | | | | | | | | | | | | | | | |
| GUO, B (HM08647) | | | ● | | | | | | | | | | | | | | | | | | | | | | |
| HEALTH ALLIANCE CENTRE (HM09375) | | | | | | | | | | | | | | | | | | | | | | | | | |
| HERBAL GARDEN AROMATHERAPY (HM09612) | | | | | | | ● | | | | | | | | | ● | | | | | | | | | |
| HIGGINSON, S (HM09733) | | | | ● | | | | | | | | | | | | | | | | | | | | | |
| HOLISTIC CHIROPRACTOR (HM09951) | | ● | | | | | | | | | | | | | | | | | | | | | | | |
| HON, ARTHUR M R (HM10111) | | | | | | | | | | | | | | | | | | | | | | | | | |
| HOWARTH, D (HM10248) | | | ● | | | | | | | | | | | | | | | | | | | | | | |
| HYPNOTHERAPY AND COUNSELLING (HM10514) | | | | | | | | | | | | | | | | | | | | | | | | | |
| KENNERLEY, JUNE (HM11498) | | | ● | | | | | | | | | | | | | | | | | | | | | | |
| MARCUS, M (HM13079) | | | | ● | | | | | | | | | | | | | | | | | | | | | |
| MARY STREET CHIRO CLINIC (HM13224) | | | | | | | | | | | | | | | | | | | | | | | | | |
| MCANELLY, J L (HM13368) | | | | | | | | | | | | | | | | | | | | | | | | | |
| NATURAL SELECTION (HM14623) | | | | | | | ● | | | | | | | | | | | | ● | | | | | | |
| NEELS AROMATHERAPY (HM14755) | | | | | | | ● | | | | | | | | | | | | | | | | | | |
| NEW LIFE NATURAL HEALTH CARE (HM14820) | | | | | | | ● | ● | | | | | | | | ● | | | | | | | | ● | |
| NEWCASTLE SPRTS INJ/THRPY CTRE (HM14855) | | | ● | | | | | | | | | | | | | | | | | | | | | | |
| OSBORNE CLINIC (HM15420) | | | ● | | | | ● | | | | | | | | | | | | | ● | | | | | |
| RAINBOW, RICHARD S (HM16887) | | | | | | | | | | | ● | | | | | | | | | | | | | | |
| RAMSAY & ASSOCIATES (HM16917) | | | | | | | | | | | | | | | | | | | | | | | | | |
| RICHARDSON, DEBORAH (HM17276) | | | | | | | | | | | | | | | | | | | | | | | | | |
| SCHOLL FOOTWEAR CENTRE (HM18077) | | | | | | | | | | | | | | | | | | | | | | ● | | | |
| SHEN HOLISTIC THERAPIES (HM18392) | | | | | | | ● | | | | | | | | | | | | | | | | | | |

| Business by County with Reference no. | Chiropody | Chiropractic | Clinical Ecology | Cognitive Therapy | Colonic Hydrotherapy | Colour Therapy | Complementary Therapy | Counselling | Cranial Osteopathy | Cranio-Sacral Therapy | Cryo Surgery | Crystal Healing | Cupping | Cymatics | Dance Movement Thrpy | Dietician | Do-In | Douching | Dowsing | Drama Therapy | Electrolipolysis | Electrolysis | Electrotherapy | Encounter Groups | Faith Healing |
|---|---|---|---|---|---|---|---|---|---|---|---|---|---|---|---|---|---|---|---|---|---|---|---|---|---|
| BIOPHYSICAL TREATMENT SERVICE (HM02342) | | | | | | | | | | | | | | | | | | | | | | | | | |
| BODY BALANCE HOLISTIC THERAPY (HM02572) | | | | | | | | | | | | | | | | | | | | | | | | | |
| CHIROPODY CLINIC (HM04324) | ● | | | | | | | | | | | | | | | | | | | | | | | | |
| CLAREMONT FOOTCARE SURGERY (HM04537) | ● | | | | | | | | | | | | | | | | | | | | | | | | |
| CONNECT PHYSICAL HEALTH CTRE (HM04989) | ● | | | | | | ● | | | | | | | | | ● | | | | | | | ● | | |
| DERWENT CENTRE (HM06020) | | | | | | | | ● | | | | ● | | | | | | | | | | | | | |
| EARDLEY, D & J (HM06492) | ● | | | | | | | | | | | | | | | | | | | | | | | | |
| FAMILY CHIRO WELLNESS CENTRE (HM07083) | | ● | | | | | | | | | | | | | | | | | | | | | | | |
| FEEL GOOD AROMATHERAPY (HM07164) | | | | | | | ● | ● | | | | | | | | ● | | | | | | | | | |
| FENG, W W (HM07214) | | | | | | | | | | | | | | | | | | | | | | | | | |
| FOWLER, CHRISTINE (HM07628) | | | | | | | | | | | | | | | | | | | | | | | | | |
| GATESHEAD COMPLEMENTARY HEALTH (HM07927) | | | | | | | | ● | | | | | | | | | | | | | | | | | |
| GUO, B (HM08647) | | | | | | | | | | | | | | | | | | | | | | | | | |
| HEALTH ALLIANCE CENTRE (HM09375) | | ● | | | | | | | | | | | | | | | | | | | | | | | |
| HERBAL GARDEN AROMATHERAPY (HM09612) | | | | | | | ● | | | | | | | | | | | | | | | | | | |
| HIGGINSON, S (HM09733) | | | | | | | | | | | | | | | | | | | | | | | | | |
| HOLISTIC CHIROPRACTOR (HM09951) | | ● | | | | | | | | | | | | | | | | | | | | | | | |
| HON, ARTHUR M R (HM10111) | | ● | | | | | | | | | | | | | | | | | | | | | | | |
| HOWARTH, D (HM10248) | | | | | | | | | | | | | | | | | | | | | | | | | |
| HYPNOTHERAPY AND COUNSELLING (HM10514) | | | | ● | | | | ● | | | | | | | | | | | | | | | | | |
| KENNERLEY, JUNE (HM11498) | | | | | | | | | | | | | | | | | | | | | | | | | |
| MARCUS, M (HM13079) | | | | | | | | | | | | | | | | | | | | | | | | | |
| MARY STREET CHIRO CLINIC (HM13224) | | ● | | | | | | | | | | | | | | | | | | | | | | | |
| MCANELLY, J L (HM13368) | | | | | | | | ● | | | | | | | | | | | | | | | | | |
| NATURAL SELECTION (HM14623) | | | | | | | ● | | | | | | | | | | | | | | | | | | |
| NEELS AROMATHERAPY (HM14755) | | | | | | | | | | | | | | | | | | | | | | | | | |
| NEW LIFE NATURAL HEALTH CARE (HM14820) | | ● | ● | | | | ● | ● | | | | | | | | | | | | | | | | | |
| NEWCASTLE SPRTS INJ/THRPY CTRE (HM14855) | ● | | | | | | | | | | | | | | | | | | | | | | | | |
| OSBORNE CLINIC (HM15420) | | | | | | | ● | ● | | | | | | | | | | | | | | | ● | | |
| RAINBOW, RICHARD S (HM16887) | | | | ● | | | | | | | | | | | | | | | | | | | | | |
| RAMSAY & ASSOCIATES (HM16917) | | ● | | | | | | | | | | | | | | | | | | | | | | | |
| RICHARDSON, DEBORAH (HM17276) | ● | | | | | | | | | | | | | | | | | | | | | | | | |
| SCHOLL FOOTWEAR CENTRE (HM18077) | ● | | | | | | | | | | | | | | | | | | | | | | | | |
| SHEN HOLISTIC THERAPIES (HM18392) | | | | | | | | | | | | | | | | | | | | | | | | | |

# A - F Therapies at Practices/Businesses

Business by County with Reference no.

| Business by County with Reference no. | Absent Healing | Acupressure | Acupuncture | Alexander Technique | Allergy Testing | Anthroposohical Med | Aromatherapy | Art Therapy | Aura Therapy | Auricular Therapy | Auto Suggestion | Autogenic Training | Aversion Therapy | Ayurvedic Medicine | Baby Massage | Bach Remedies | Bates Method | Beauty Therapy | Bio-energetics | Biofeedback | Biomagnetic Therapy | Biomechanics | Bonesetting | Bowen Therapy | Chinese Herbal Medicine |
|---|---|---|---|---|---|---|---|---|---|---|---|---|---|---|---|---|---|---|---|---|---|---|---|---|---|
| SHIELD CHIROPRACTIC CLINIC (HM18470) | | | | | | | | | | | | | | | | | | | | | | | | | |
| THOMPSON, N J (HM19994) | | | ● | | | | | | | | | | | | | | | | | | | | | | |
| WALKER, LEONIE (HM20785) | | | ● | | | | | | | | | | | | | | | | | | | | | | |
| WEAVER, K N J (HM21052) | | | ● | | | | | | | | | | | | | | | | | | | | | | |
| WESTOE PRACTICE (HM21277) | | | | | | | | | | | | | | | | | | | | | | ● | | | |
| WHITLEY BAY CHIROPRACTOR (HM21406) | | | | | | | | | | | | | | | | | | | | | | | | | |
| **WARWICKSHIRE** | | | | | | | | | | | | | | | | | | | | | | | | | |
| ACUPUNCTURE CLINIC (HM00279) | | | ● | | | | | | | | | | | | | | | | | | | | | | |
| AROMATHERAPY MASSAGE/REFLEX (HM01120) | | | | | | | ● | | | | | | | | | | | | | | | | | | |
| BARRATT'S HOMEOPATHY (HM01780) | | | | | | | | | | | | | | | | | | | | | | | | | |
| BIRTWELL, ANDREW (HM02400) | | | | | | | | | | | | | | | | | | | | | | | | | |
| BRIEF COUNS & PSYCHOTHERAPY SV (HM03020) | | | | | | | | | | | | | | | | | | | | | | | | | |
| BROWN, V C (HM03251) | | | ● | | | | | | | | | | | | | | | | | | | | | | |
| BUCKLE, WENDY-ANNE (HM03315) | | | | | | | ● | | | | | | | | | | | | | | | | | | |
| CANALE-PAROLA, AUDREY (HM03617) | | | ● | | | | | | | | | | | | | | | | | | | | | | |
| CHURCH LAWFORD CHIRO CLINIC (HM04463) | | ● | | | | | | | | | | | | | | ● | | | | | | | | | |
| CLIFTON OSTEOPATHIC PRACTICE (HM04669) | | | | | | | | | | | | | | | | | | | | | | | | | |
| CORLET, LOUISE (HM05171) | | | | | | | | | | | | | | | | | | | | | | | | | |
| CREATIVE HEALTH CENTRE (HM05397) | | | | | | | ● | | | | | | | | | ● | | | | | | | | | |
| FIGHT (HM07282) | | ● | | | | | | | | | | | | | | | | | ● | | | | ● | | |
| FRAGRANT ROOM (HM07653) | | | | | | | ● | | | | | | | | | | | | | | | | | | |
| FRAGRANT ROOM (HM07652) | | | | | | | ● | | | | | | | | | | | | | | | | | | |
| GREIG, E (HM08527) | | | | | | | ● | | | | | | | | | ● | | | | | | | | | |
| HEALING HEART (HM09343) | | | | | | | ● | | | | | | | | | | | | | | | | | | |
| HEALTHPOINT (HM09414) | | | ● | | | | | | | | | | | | | | | | | | | | | | |
| HEART OF ENGLAND SHIATSU (HM09442) | | | | | | | | | | | | | | | | | | | | | | | | | |
| HEARTLANDS (HM09445) | | ● | ● | | | | | | | | | | ● | | | | | | | | | | | | |
| HERBAL ONE (HM09631) | | | ● | | | | | | | | | | | | | | | | | | | | | | |
| HOLYCOMBE (HM10060) | ● | | | | | | | | | | | | | | | | | | | | | | | | |
| JAMES, HELEN (HM10886) | | | | | | | | | | | | | | | | | | | | | | | | | |
| JAN LLOYD AROMATHERAPY (HM10913) | | | | | | | ● | | | | | | | | | | | | | | | | | | |
| LAVENDER HOUSE (HM12022) | | | | | | | ● | | | | | | | | | | | | | | | | | | |
| LEAMINGTON SPA CHIRO CLINIC (HM12104) | | | | | ● | | | | | | | | | | | | | | | | | | | | |
| MARKS, S (HM13121) | | | | | | | ● | | | | | | | | | | | | | | | | | | |

| Business by County with Reference no. | Chiropody | Chiropractic | Clinical Ecology | Cognitive Therapy | Colonic Hydrotherapy | Colour Therapy | Complementary Therapy | Counselling | Cranial Osteopathy | Cranio-Sacral Therapy | Cryo Surgery | Crystal Healing | Cupping | Cymatics | Dance Movement Thrpy | Dietician | Do-In | Douching | Dowsing | Drama Therapy | Electrolipolysis | Electrolysis | Electrotherapy | Encounter Groups | Faith Healing |
|---|---|---|---|---|---|---|---|---|---|---|---|---|---|---|---|---|---|---|---|---|---|---|---|---|---|
| SHIELD CHIROPRACTIC CLINIC (HM18470) | | ● | | | | | | | | | | | | | | | | | | | | | | | |
| THOMPSON, N J (HM19994) | | | | | | | | | | | | | | | | | | | | | | | | | |
| WALKER, LEONIE (HM20785) | | | | | | | | | | | | | | | | | | | | | | | | | |
| WEAVER, K N J (HM21052) | | | | | | | | | | | | | | | | | | | | | | | | | |
| WESTOE PRACTICE (HM21277) | ● | | | | | | | | | | | | | | | | | | | | | | | | |
| WHITLEY BAY CHIROPRACTOR (HM21406) | | ● | | | | | | | | | | | | | | | | | | | | | | | |
| **WARWICKSHIRE** | | | | | | | | | | | | | | | | | | | | | | | | | |
| ACUPUNCTURE CLINIC (HM00279) | | | | | | | ● | | | | | | | | | | | | | | | | | | |
| AROMATHERAPY MASSAGE/REFLEX (HM01120) | | | | | | | | | | | | | | | | | | | | | | | | | |
| BARRATT'S HOMEOPATHY (HM01780) | | | | | | | ● | ● | | | | | | | | | | | | | | | | | |
| BIRTWELL, ANDREW (HM02400) | | | | | | | | ● | | | | | | | | | | | | | | | | | |
| BRIEF COUNS & PSYCHOTHERAPY SV (HM03020) | | | | ● | | | | ● | | | | | | | | | | | | | | | | | |
| BROWN, V C (HM03251) | | | | | | | | | | | | | | | | | | | | | | | | | |
| BUCKLE, WENDY-ANNE (HM03315) | | | | | | | | | | | | | | | | | | | | | | | | | |
| CANALE-PAROLA, AUDREY (HM03617) | | | | | | | | | | | | | | | | | | | | | | | | | |
| CHURCH LAWFORD CHIRO CLINIC (HM04463) | | ● | | | | | | | ● | | | | | | | | | | | | | | ● | | |
| CLIFTON OSTEOPATHIC PRACTICE (HM04669) | | | | | | | ● | | ● | | | | ● | | | | | | | | | | | | |
| CORLET, LOUISE (HM05171) | | ● | | | | | | | | | | | | | | | | | | | | | | | |
| CREATIVE HEALTH CENTRE (HM05397) | | ● | | | ● | | | | | ● | | | | | | | | | | | | | | | |
| FIGHT (HM07282) | ● | | | | | | ● | | | | | | | | | | | | | | | | | | |
| FRAGRANT ROOM (HM07653) | | | | | | | | | | | | | | | | | | | | | | | | | |
| FRAGRANT ROOM (HM07652) | | | | | | | | | | | | | | | | | | | | | | | | | |
| GREIG, E (HM08527) | | | | ● | | | | | | | | | | | | | | | | | | | | | |
| HEALING HEART (HM09343) | | | | | | | | | | | | | | | | | | | | | | | | | |
| HEALTHPOINT (HM09414) | | | | | | | | | | | | | | | | | | | | | | | | | |
| HEART OF ENGLAND SHIATSU (HM09442) | | | | | | | | ● | | | | | | | | | ● | | | | | | | | |
| HEARTLANDS (HM09445) | | | | | | | | ● | | | | | | | | | | | | | | | | | |
| HERBAL ONE (HM09631) | | | | | | | | | | | | | | | | | | | | | | | | | |
| HOLYCOMBE (HM10060) | | | | | | | ● | ● | | | | | | | | | | | | | | | | | |
| JAMES, HELEN (HM10886) | | ● | | | | | | | | | | | | | | | | | | | | | | | |
| JAN LLOYD AROMATHERAPY (HM10913) | | | | | | | | | | | | | | | | | | | | | | | | | |
| LAVENDER HOUSE (HM12022) | | | | | | | | | | | | | | | | | | | | | | | | | |
| LEAMINGTON SPA CHIRO CLINIC (HM12104) | | ● | | | | | | | | | | | | | | | | | | | | | | | |
| MARKS, S (HM13121) | | | | | | | | | | | | | | | | | | | | | | | | | |

# A - F Therapies at Practices/Businesses

| Business by County with Reference no. | Absent Healing | Acupressure | Acupuncture | Alexander Technique | Allergy Testing | Anthroposohical Med | Aromatherapy | Art Therapy | Aura Therapy | Auricular Therapy | Auto Suggestion | Autogenic Training | Aversion Therapy | Ayurvedic Medicine | Baby Massage | Bach Remedies | Bates Method | Beauty Therapy | Bio-energetics | Biofeedback | Biomagnetic Therapy | Biomechanics | Bonesetting | Bowen Therapy | Chinese Herbal Medicine | Chiropody | Chiropractic | Clinical Ecology | Cognitive Therapy | Colonic Hydrotherapy | Colour Therapy | Complementary Therapy | Counselling | Cranial Osteopathy | Cranio-Sacral Therapy | Cryo Surgery | Crystal Healing | Cupping | Cymatics | Dance Movement Thrpy | Dietician | Do-In | Douching | Dowsing | Drama Therapy | Electrolipolysis | Electrolysis | Electrotherapy | Encounter Groups | Faith Healing |
|---|---|---|---|---|---|---|---|---|---|---|---|---|---|---|---|---|---|---|---|---|---|---|---|---|---|---|---|---|---|---|---|---|---|---|---|---|---|---|---|---|---|---|---|---|---|---|---|---|---|---|
| MCTIMONEY CHIROPRACTOR (HM13617) | | | | | | | | | | | | | | | | | | | | | | | | | | | ● | | | | | | | | | | | | | | | | | | | | | | | |
| NATURAL HEALTH CENTRE (HM14567) | | | ● | | | | ● | | | | | | | | | ● | | | | | | | | ● | | | | | | | | ● | | ● | | | ● | | | | | | | | | | | | | |
| NATURAL HEALTH CLINIC (HM14588) | | | ● | | | | | | | | | | | | | | | | | | | | | | | | | | | | | | | | | | | | | | | | | | | | | | | |
| NATURAL THERAPY CENTRE (HM14651) | | | | | | | | | | | | | | | | | | | | | | | | ● | | | | | | | | | | | | | | | | | | | | | | | | | | |
| NEWEY, RACHEL (HM14862) | | | | | | | | | | | | | | | | | | | | | | | | | | | ● | | | | | | | | | | | | | | | | | | | | | | | |
| NUNEATON CHIROPRACTIC CLINIC (HM15104) | | | | | | | | | | | | | | | | | | | | | | | | | | | ● | | | | | | | | | | | | | | | | | | | | | | | |
| ORCHARD HSE SGY-DAVID MANDER (HM15362) | | | | | | | | | | | | | | | | | | | | | | | | | | | ● | | | | | | | | | | | | | | | | | | | | | | | |
| PETERS, EVERARD (HM16085) | | | | ● | | | | | | | | | | | | | | | | | | | | | | | | | | | | | | ● | | | | | | | | | | | | | | | | |
| PURPLE FLAME AROMATHERAPY (HM16771) | | | | | | | ● | | | | | | | | | | | | | | | | | | | | | | | | | | | | | | | | | | | | | | | | | | | |
| REVITALIZE (HM17205) | | | | | | | ● | | | | | | | | | | | | | | | | | | | | | | | | | | | | | | | | | | | | | | | | | | | |
| RUSSELL, COLIN (HM17766) | | | | | | | | | | | | | | | | | | | | | | ● | | | | ● | | | | | | | | | | | | | | | | | | | | | | | | |
| SAVAGE, GERALD (HM17966) | | | | | | | | | | | | | | | | | | | | | | | | | | | | | ● | | | | ● | | | | | | | | | | | | | | | | | |
| SHAWE AVENUE OSTEO PRACTICE (HM18351) | | | | | | | | | | | | | | | | | | | | | | | ● | | | | | | | | | | ● | ● | | | | | | | | | | | | | | | | |
| SMALLWOOD, P (HM18698) | | | | | | | | | | | | | | | | | | | | | | ● | | | | ● | | | | | | | | | | ● | | | | | | | | | | | | | | |
| STRANKS, KATHY (HM19367) | | | | | | | | | | | | | | | | | | | | | | | | | | | | | | | | | ● | | | | | | | | | | | | | | | | | |
| STRATFORD ACU & HOLISTIC HLTH (HM19369) | | | ● | | | | | | | | | | | | | | | | | | | | | ● | | | ● | | | | | | | | | | | | | | | | | | | | | | | |
| STUDLEY PHYSIOTHERAPY CENTRE (HM19442) | | ● | ● | | | | | | | | | | | | | | | | | ● | | | | | | | | | | | | | | | | | | | | | | | | | | | | ● | | |
| TIMBRELL, GAIL (HM20076) | | | | | | | ● | | | | | | | | | | | | | | | | | | | | | | | | | | | | | | | | | | | | | | | | | | | |
| TOWERS, DIANA (HM20195) | | | | | | | | | | | | | | | | | | | | | | | | | | | | | | | | | ● | | | | | | | | | | | | | | | | | |
| TRADITIONAL ACUPUNCTURE GROUP (HM20221) | | | ● | | | | ● | | | | | | | | | | | | ● | | | | | ● | | | | | | | | | ● | | | | | | | | | | | | | | | | | |
| VAN SCHELLENBECK, JONA-MARION (HM20572) | | | ● | | | | | | | | | | | | | | | | | | | | | | | | | | | | | | | | | | | | | | | | | | | | | | | |
| VENFIELD, C J (HM20612) | | | | | | | | | | | | | | | | | | | | | | | | | | | ● | | | | | | | | | | | | | | | | | | | | | | | |
| WARWICK CHIROPRACTIC CLINIC (HM20962) | | | | | | | | | | | | | | | | | | | | | | | | | | | ● | | | | | | | | | | | | | | | | | | | | | | | |
| WARWICK OSTEOPATHIC PRACTICE (HM20966) | | | | | | | | | | | | | | | | | | | | | | | | | | | | | | | | ● | | ● | | | | ● | | | | | | | | | | | | |
| WREN, PAULINE (HM21922) | | | | | | | | | | | | | | | | | | | | | | | | | | | | | ● | | | | ● | | | | | | | | | | | | | | | | | ● |
| **WILTSHIRE** | | | | | | | | | | | | | | | | | | | | | | | | | | | | | | | | | | | | | | | | | | | | | | | | | | |
| ABSOLUTE BLISS (HM00138) | | | | | | | ● | | | | | | | | | | | | | | | | | | | | | | | | | | | | | | | | | | | | | | | | | | | |
| ACUPUNCTURE (HM00227) | | | ● | | | | | | | | | | | | | | | | | | | | | | | | | | | | | | | | | | | | | | | | | | | | | | | |
| AMESBURY ABBEY CLINIC (HM00781) | | | ● | | | | | | | | | | | | | | | | | | | | | | | | | | | | | | | | | | | | | | | | | | | | | | | |
| ANDREWS, HAZEL (HM00852) | | | ● | | | | | | | | | | | | | | | | | | | | | | | | | | | | | | | | | | | ● | | | | | | | | | | | | |
| ANNA'S (HM00895) | | | | | | | ● | | | | | | | | | | | | | | | | | | | | | | | | | | | | | | | | | | | | | | | | | | | |
| ARAGON, HOLLY (HM00961) | | | ● | | | | | | | | | | | | | | | | | | | | | | | | | | | | | | | | | | | | | | | | | | | | | | | |
| AROMATHERAPY PLUS OIL SUPPLIER (HM01123) | | | | | | | ● | | | | | | | | | | | | | | | | | | | | | | | | | | | | | | | | | | | | | | | | | | | |
| AVEBURY HYPNOTHERAPY PRACTICE (HM01386) | | | | | | | | | | | | | | | | | | | | | | | | | | | | | ● | | | | ● | | | | | | | | | | | | | | | | | |

# A - F Therapies at Practices/Businesses

| Business by County with Reference no. | Absent Healing | Acupressure | Acupuncture | Alexander Technique | Allergy Testing | Anthroposohical Med | Aromatherapy | Art Therapy | Aura Therapy | Auricular Therapy | Auto Suggestion | Autogenic Training | Aversion Therapy | Ayurvedic Medicine | Baby Massage | Bach Remedies | Bates Method | Beauty Therapy | Bio-energetics | Biofeedback | Biomagnetic Therapy | Biomechanics | Bonesetting | Bowen Therapy | Chinese Herbal Medicine | Chiropody | Chiropractic | Clinical Ecology | Cognitive Therapy | Colonic Hydrotherapy | Colour Therapy | Complementary Therapy | Counselling | Cranial Osteopathy | Cranio-Sacral Therapy | Cryo Surgery | Crystal Healing | Cupping | Cymatics | Dance Movement Thrpy | Dietician | Do-In | Douching | Dowsing | Drama Therapy | Electrolipolysis | Electrolysis | Electrotherapy | Encounter Groups | Faith Healing |
|---|---|---|---|---|---|---|---|---|---|---|---|---|---|---|---|---|---|---|---|---|---|---|---|---|---|---|---|---|---|---|---|---|---|---|---|---|---|---|---|---|---|---|---|---|---|---|---|---|---|---|
| AVONBOURNE CHIROPRACTIC CLINIC (HM01408) |||||||||||||||||||||||||●|||||||||||||||||||||||||
| 'BACK IN LINE' (HM01482) |||||||●||||||||||||||||||||||||||||||||||||||||||||
| BISHOP, S (HM02409) |||●||||||||||||||||||||||||||||||||||||||||||||||||
| BLUNSDON ABBEY PHYSIOTHERAPY (HM02533) |||●||||●||||||||||||||||||||||||||||||||||||||||||||
| BODY & SOUL (HM02563) |||||||●||||||||||||||||||||||||||||||||||||||||||||
| BRATLEY-ATKINS, MARY (HM02924) |||||||●||||||||||||||||||||||||||||||||||||||||||||
| CASTLE STREET CHIRO CLINIC (HM03836) |||||||||||||||||||||||||||●|||||||||||||||||||||||||
| CASTLE STREET CLINIC (HM03839) |||||||||||||||||||||||||||●|||||||||||||||||||||||||
| CHARLES, SARAH (HM04026) |||||||●||||||||||||||||||||||||||||||||||||||||||||
| CHIROPRACTIC PATIENTS ASS (HM04401) |||||||||||||||||||||||||||●|||||||||||||||||||||||||
| COPLAND-GRIFFITHS, M C (HM05143) |||||||||||||||||||||||||||●|||||||||||||||||||||||||
| CREEK, N (HM05411) ||||●||||||||||||||||||||||||||||||||||||||||||||||
| CRICKLADE ROAD PRACTICE (HM05439) |||●||●||●|||||||||||||||||||||||||||||||||||●|||||||||||
| CROSS, PHILIPPA (HM05485) ||||●||||||||||||||||||||||||||||||||||||||||||||||
| DALE, TILLY (HM05686) |||●||||||||||||||||||||||||||||||||||||||||||||||||
| DAVIES, (DR) (HM05793) |||●||||||||||||||||||||||||||||||||||||||||||||||||
| DEVIZES ACUPUNCTURE PRACTICE (HM06037) |||●||||||||||||||||||||||||||||||||||||||||||||||||
| DUNKLEY, KITTY (HM06407) |||||||●||||||||||||||||||||||||||||||||||||||||||||
| EASE MANAGEMENT CENTRE (HM06506) ||||||||||||||||||||●|||||||||●||||●|||||||||||||||||||||
| EMERY HOUSE CLINIC (HM06802) |||||||||||||||||||||||||||●|||||||||||||||||||||||||
| ENGLISH, JOHN M (DR) (HM06834) |||●||||||||||●||||●||||||||||||●||||●||||||||||||||||||||||||
| EQUILIBRIUM (HM06866) |||||||●||||||||||||||||||||||||||||||||||||||||||||
| ESSENTIALLY YOURS (HM06926) |||||||●||||||||||||||||||||||||||||||||||||||||||||
| FAIRFAX, A B (DR) (HM07057) |||●||||||||||||||||||||||||||||||||||||||||||||||||
| FOSTER, MARGARET (HM07597) ||||||||||||||||●||||||||||||||||||||||||||||||||||||
| HEALTH HYDRO (HM09389) |||●|●|||●||||||||||||||||||||||●||||||●||||||||||||||||||||
| HIGHWORTH PHYSIOTHERAPY CLINIC (HM09761) |||●||||||||||||||||||||||||||||||||||||||||||||●|||
| HUDD, ALISON (HM10306) ||||||||||||||||●||||||||||||||||||||||||||||||||||||
| HUTCHINSON, N (HM10452) |||||||●||||||||||||||||||||||||||||||||||||||||||||
| HYPNOTHERAPY CENTRE (HM10529) |●||||||||||●||||||||||||||||||||●||||●|||||||||||||||||||||
| JENKINS, RUSSELL S (HM10996) ||||||||||||||||||||||||||||||||||||||||||||||||●|||
| LEIGHTON REFLEXOLOGY CLINIC (HM12196) ||||||||||||||||||||||||||||||||●||||||||||||||||||||
| LIFE-ENERGIES (HM12352) |||||||●||||||||||||●|||||||||||||||||||||||||||||||||
| LIKISMA PRESENTATIONS (HM12387) |||||||●||||||||||||||||||||||||||||||||||||||||||||

# A - F Therapies at Practices/Businesses

| Business by County with Reference no. | Absent Healing | Acupressure | Acupuncture | Alexander Technique | Allergy Testing | Anthroposohical Med | Aromatherapy | Art Therapy | Aura Therapy | Auricular Therapy | Auto Suggestion | Autogenic Training | Aversion Therapy | Ayurvedic Medicine | Baby Massage | Bach Remedies | Bates Method | Beauty Therapy | Bio-energetics | Biofeedback | Biomagnetic Therapy | Biomechanics | Bonesetting | Bowen Therapy | Chinese Herbal Medicine | Chiropody | Chiropractic | Clinical Ecology | Cognitive Therapy | Colonic Hydrotherapy | Colour Therapy | Complementary Therapy | Counselling | Cranial Osteopathy | Cranio-Sacral Therapy | Cryo Surgery | Crystal Healing | Cupping | Cymatics | Dance Movement Thrpy | Dietician | Do-In | Douching | Dowsing | Drama Therapy | Electrolipolysis | Electrolysis | Electrotherapy | Encounter Groups | Faith Healing |
|---|---|---|---|---|---|---|---|---|---|---|---|---|---|---|---|---|---|---|---|---|---|---|---|---|---|---|---|---|---|---|---|---|---|---|---|---|---|---|---|---|---|---|---|---|---|---|---|---|---|---|
| LOWE, CATHIE (HM12693) | | | | | | |●| | | | | | | | | | | | | | | | | | | | | | | | | | | | | | | | | | | | | | | | | | | |
| LUCK, MARGARET (HM12723) | | | | | | |●| | | | | | | | | | | | | | | | | | | | | | | | | | | | | | | | | | | | | | | | | | | |
| LYON, P (HM12783) | | | |●| | | | | | | | | | | | | | | | | | | | | | | | | | | | | | | | | | | | | | | | | | | | | | |
| MAGNO PULSE (HM12919) | | | | | | | | | | | | | | | | | | | | | | | | | | | | | | | |●| | | | | | | | | | | | | | | | | | |
| MALMESBURY CHIROPRACTIC CLINIC (HM12982) | | | | | | | | | | | | | | | | | | | | | | | | | | |●| | | | | | | | | | | | | | | | | | | | | | | |
| MARLBOROUGH CHIRO CLINIC (HM13122) | | | | | | | | | | | | | | | | | | | | | | | | | | |●| | | | | | | | | | | | | | | | | | | | | | | |
| MARLBOROUGH NATURAL HLTH CTRE (HM13123) | | |●| | | |●| | | | | | | | |●|●| | | | | | | | | | | | | | | |●| | | |●| | | | | | | | | | | | | |
| MATHER, PAULINE (HM13280) | |●| | | | | | | | | | | | | |●| | | | | | | | | | | | | | | | | |●| | | | | | |●| | | | | | | | | |
| MCTIMONEY CHIROPRACTIC CLINIC (HM13604) | | | | | | | | | | | | | | | | | | | | | | | | | | |●| | | | | | | | | | | | | | | | | | | | | | | |
| MOURANT, JENNIFER L (HM14298) | | | | | | | | | | | | | | | |●| | | | | | | | | | | | | | | | | | | | | | | | | | | | | | | | | | |
| MULTI-THERAPY CENTRE (HM14352) | |●| | | | | | | | | | | | | |●| | | | | | | | | | | | | | | | | | | | | | | | | | | | | | | | | | |
| NATURAL HOUSE & BEAUTY CLINIC (HM14607) | | | | | | |●| | | | | | | | | | | | | | | | | | | | | | | | | | | | | | | | | | | | | | | | | | | |
| NATURAL THERAPY CENTRE (HM14639) |●| | | | | | | | | | | | | | | | | | | | | | | | | | | | | | |●| | | | | | | | | | | | | | | | | | |
| NOTMAN, JACKIE (HM15080) | | | | | | |●| | | | | | | | | | | | | | | | | | | | | | | | | | | | | | | | | | | | | | | | | | | |
| OSTEOPATHS (HM15475) | | | | | | | | | | | | | | | | | | | | | | | | | | | | | | | | | |●| | | | | | | | | | | | | | | | |
| PETER & CAROLINE (HM16071) |●|●| | | | |●|●|●| | | | | | | | | | | | | | | | | | | | | |●|●|●| | | | | | | | | | | | | | | | | |
| PETTIFER, JUSTINA (HM16095) | | | | | | |●| | | | | |●| | | | | | | | | | | | | | | |●| | | |●| | | | | | | | | | | | | | | | | |
| PHYSIOTHERAPY CLINIC (HM16247) | | |●| | | | | | | | | | | | | | | | | | | | | | | | | | | | | | | | | | | | | | | | | | | | | | | |
| QUIRKE, G (HM16820) | | | | | | | | | | |●| |●| | | | | | | | | | | | | | | | | | |●| | | | | | | | | | | | | | | | | | |
| RAINBOW NATURAL THERAPIES (HM16880) | | | | | | | | | | | | | | | | | | | | | | | | | | | | | | | | |●| | | | | | | | | | | | | | | | | |
| RICHARDSON, CHRIS (HM17272) | | | | | | | | | | | | | | | | | | | | | | | | | | |●| | | | | | | | | | | | | | | | | | | | | | | |
| RIDGEWAY CHIROPRACTIC CLINIC (HM17317) | | | | | | | | | | | | | | | | | | | | | | | | | | |●| | | | | | | | | | | | | | | | | | | | | | | |
| SALISBURY CHIROPRACTIC CLINIC (HM17851) | | | | | | | | | | | | | | | | | | | | | | | | | | |●| | | | | | | | | | | | | | | | | | | | | | | |
| SAWAYA, ALICIA (HM17982) | | | | | | | | | | | | | | | | | | | | | | | | | | | | | | | | | | | | | | | | | | | |●| | | | | | |
| SHAFTSBURY PRACTICE (HM18266) | | |●| | | | | | | | | | | | | | | | | | | | | | |●| | | | | | | | | | | | | | | | | | | | | | | | |
| SHAVE, G M (HM18325) | | | | | | | | | | | | | | | | | | | | | | | | | |●| | | | | | | | | | | | | | | | | | | | | | | | |
| SHAW CHIROPRACTIC CLINIC (HM18327) | | | | | | | | | | | | | | | | | | | | | | | | | | |●| | | | | | | | | | | | | | | | | | | | | | | |
| SWINDON CHIROPRACTIC CLINIC (HM19595) | | | | | | |●| | | | | | | | | | | | | | | | | | | |●| | | | | | | | | | | | | | | | | | | | | | | |
| TALISMAN CANDLE (HM19662) | | | | | | |●| | | | | | | | | | | | | | | | | | | | | | | | | | | | | | | | | | | | | | | | | | | |
| TENG, X C (HM19834) | | |●| | | | | | | | | | | | | | | | | | | | | | | | | | | | | | | | | | | | | | | | | | | | | | | |
| TISBURY OSTEOPATHIC PRACTICE (HM20094) | | | | | | | | | | | | | | | | | | | | | | | | | | | | | | | | | |●| | | | | | | | | | | | | | | | |
| WARMINSTER OSTEOPATHIC CLINIC (HM20929) | | |●| | | |●| | | | | | | | | | | | | | | | | | | | | | | | | |●|●| | | | | | | | | | | | | | | | |
| WATSON'S COURT CLINIC (HM21025) | | | | | | | | | | | | | | | | | | | | | | | | | |●| | | | | | | | | | | | | | | | | | | | | | | | |
| WEST, DAVID (HM21246) | | | |●| | | | | | | | | | | | | | | | | | | | | | |●| | | | | | | | | | | | | | | | | | | | | | | |

# A - F Therapies at Practices/Businesses

Business by County with Reference no.

| Business | Absent Healing | Acupressure | Acupuncture | Alexander Technique | Allergy Testing | Anthroposohical Med | Aromatherapy | Art Therapy | Aura Therapy | Auricular Therapy | Auto Suggestion | Autogenic Training | Aversion Therapy | Ayurvedic Medicine | Baby Massage | Bach Remedies | Bates Method | Beauty Therapy | Bio-energetics | Biofeedback | Biomagnetic Therapy | Biomechanics | Bonesetting | Bowen Therapy | Chinese Herbal Medicine |
|---|---|---|---|---|---|---|---|---|---|---|---|---|---|---|---|---|---|---|---|---|---|---|---|---|---|
| WESTBURY CHIROPRACTIC (HM21258) | | | | | | | | | | | | | | | | | | | | | | | | | |
| WHITING, JENNIE (HM21404) | | | | | | | ● | | | | | | | | | | | | | | | | | | |
| WOOTTON BASSETT (HM21885) | | | ● | | | | | | | | | | | | | | | | | | | | | ● | |
| **WORCESTERSHIRE** | | | | | | | | | | | | | | | | | | | | | | | | | |
| 1ST CHIROPRACTIC UK (HM00007) | | | | | | | | | | | | | | | | | | | | | | | | | |
| AINSLEY, S (HM00433) | | | | | | | | | | | | | | | | | | | | | | ● | | | |
| ALTERNATIVE MEDICINE (HM00716) | | | ● | | | | | | | | | | | | | | | | | | | | | | |
| AROMACARE (HM01069) | | | | | | | ● | | | | | | | | | | | | | | | | | | |
| BEWDLEY CHIROPRACTOR CLINIC (HM02250) | | | | | | | | | | | | | | | | | | | | | | | | | |
| BRETFORDTON CLINIC (HM02969) | | ● | ● | | | | ● | | | | | | | | | ● | | | ● | | | | | | |
| BROMSGROVE CHIROPRACTIC CLINIC (HM03151) | | | | | | | | | | | | | | | | | | | | | | | | | |
| BURTON, JENIFER (HM03437) | | | | | | | | | | | | | | | | ● | | | | | | | | | |
| CANTO, HILARY (HM03645) | | | | | | | | | | | | | | | | ● | | | | | | | | | |
| CARYL, M D (HM03804) | | | | | | | | | | | | | | | | | | | | | | | | | |
| COLLEGE OF HEALING (HM04846) | | | | | | | | | | | | | | | | | | | | | | | | | |
| COMPLETE CARE CLINICAL AROMA (HM04956) | | | | | | | ● | | | | | | | | | | | | | | | | | | |
| DAVIES PODIATRY (HM05792) | | | | | | | | | | | | | | | | | | | | | | ● | | | |
| DE ALMEDIA, ALTAIR (HM05902) | | | ● | | | | | | | | | | | | | | | | | | | | | | |
| DOIDGE, FRAN (HM06155) | | | | | | | ● | | | | | | | | | | | | | | | | | | |
| EDWARDS, CHRISTINA (HM06647) | | | ● | | | | | | | | | | | | | | | | | | | | | | |
| EVESHAM NATURAL HEALTH CENTRE (HM07009) | | | ● | ● | | | ● | | | | | | | | | | | | | | | | | | |
| FRONTIA (HM07757) | | | ● | ● | | | ● | | | | | | | | | ● | | | | | | | | | |
| GIBBINS, JONATHAN (HM08022) | | | | | | | | | | | | | | | | | | | | | | | | | |
| HINKS, MAXINE (HM09834) | | | | | | | ● | | | | | | | | | | | | | | | | | | |
| HUGHES, VANESSA (HM10344) | | | | | | | | | | | | | | | | ● | | | | | | | | | |
| IN THE PINK (HM10598) | | | | | | | ● | | | | | | | | | | | | | | | | | | |
| INDIGO (HM10612) | | | | | | | ● | | | | | | | | | | | | | | | | | | |
| JONES, VAL (HM11200) | | | | | | | | | | | | | | | | | | | | | | | | | |
| KITSON, P (HM11730) | | | ● | | | | ● | | | | | | | | | | | | | | | | | | |
| KRISS, ADRIAN D (HM11803) | | | | | | | | | | | | | | | | | | | | | | | | | |
| M THORLOW CHIROPODY (HM12810) | | | | | | | | | | | | | | | | | | | | | | ● | | | |
| MALVERN NATURAL HEALTH CENTRE (HM12998) | | | ● | | | | ● | | | | | | | | | | | | | | | | | ● | |
| MALVERN OSTEOPATHIC CLINIC (HM12999) | | | ● | | | | | | | | | | | | | | | | | | | | | | |
| MARSTON, SUE (HM13179) | | | ● | | | | | | | | | | | | | | | | | | | | | | |

| Business | Chiropody | Chiropractic | Clinical Ecology | Cognitive Therapy | Colonic Hydrotherapy | Colour Therapy | Complementary Therapy | Counselling | Cranial Osteopathy | Cranio-Sacral Therapy | Cryo Surgery | Crystal Healing | Cupping | Cymatics | Dance Movement Thrpy | Dietician | Do-In | Douching | Dowsing | Drama Therapy | Electrolipolysis | Electrolysis | Electrotherapy | Encounter Groups | Faith Healing |
|---|---|---|---|---|---|---|---|---|---|---|---|---|---|---|---|---|---|---|---|---|---|---|---|---|---|
| WESTBURY CHIROPRACTIC (HM21258) | | ● | | | | | | | | | | | | | | | | | | | | | | | |
| WHITING, JENNIE (HM21404) | | | | | | | | | | | | | | | | | | | | | | | | | |
| WOOTTON BASSETT (HM21885) | | | | | | | | | | | | | | | | | | | | | | | | | |
| **WORCESTERSHIRE** | | | | | | | | | | | | | | | | | | | | | | | | | |
| 1ST CHIROPRACTIC UK (HM00007) | | ● | | | | | | ● | | | | | | | | | | | | | | | | | |
| AINSLEY, S (HM00433) | | | | | | | | | | | | | | | | | | | | | | | | | |
| ALTERNATIVE MEDICINE (HM00716) | | | | | | | | | | | | | | | | | | | | | | | | | |
| AROMACARE (HM01069) | | | | | | | | | | | | | | | | | | | | | | | | | |
| BEWDLEY CHIROPRACTOR CLINIC (HM02250) | | ● | | | | | | | | | | | | | | | | | | | | | | | |
| BRETFORDTON CLINIC (HM02969) | | ● | | | | ● | ● | | ● | | | | | ● | | | | | | | | | ● | | |
| BROMSGROVE CHIROPRACTIC CLINIC (HM03151) | | ● | | | | | | | | | | | | | | | | | | | | | | | |
| BURTON, JENIFER (HM03437) | | | | | | | | | | | | | | | | | | | | | | | | | |
| CANTO, HILARY (HM03645) | | | | | | | | | | | | | | | | | | | | | | | | | |
| CARYL, M D (HM03804) | ● | | | | | | | | | | | | | | | | | | | | | | | | |
| COLLEGE OF HEALING (HM04846) | | | | | | | ● | | | | | | | | | | | | | | | | | | |
| COMPLETE CARE CLINICAL AROMA (HM04956) | | | | | | | | | | | | | | | | | | | | | | | | | |
| DAVIES PODIATRY (HM05792) | ● | | | | | | | | | | | | | | | | | | | | | | | | |
| DE ALMEDIA, ALTAIR (HM05902) | | | | | | | | | | | | | | | | | | | | | | | | | |
| DOIDGE, FRAN (HM06155) | | | | | | | | | | | | | | | | | | | | | | | | | |
| EDWARDS, CHRISTINA (HM06647) | | | | | | | | | | | | | | | | | | | | | | | | | |
| EVESHAM NATURAL HEALTH CENTRE (HM07009) | | | | | | | | | ● | | | | | | | | | | | | | | | | |
| FRONTIA (HM07757) | | ● | | | | | ● | ● | ● | | | ● | | | | | | | | | | | | | |
| GIBBINS, JONATHAN (HM08022) | | ● | | | | | | | | | | | | | | | | | | | | | | | |
| HINKS, MAXINE (HM09834) | | | | | | | | | | | | | | | | | | | | | | | | | |
| HUGHES, VANESSA (HM10344) | | | | | | | | | | | | | | | | | | | | | | | | | |
| IN THE PINK (HM10598) | | | | | | | | | | | | | | | | | | | | | | | | | |
| INDIGO (HM10612) | | | | | | | | | | | | | | | | | | | | | | | | | |
| JONES, VAL (HM11200) | ● | | | | | | | | | | | | | | | | | | | | | | | | |
| KITSON, P (HM11730) | | | | | | | | | | | | | | | | | | | | | | | | | |
| KRISS, ADRIAN D (HM11803) | ● | | | | | | | | | | | | | | | | | | | | | | | | |
| M THORLOW CHIROPODY (HM12810) | ● | | | | | | | | | | | | | | | | | | | | | | | | |
| MALVERN NATURAL HEALTH CENTRE (HM12998) | | | | | | | | | | | | ● | | | | | | | | | | | | | |
| MALVERN OSTEOPATHIC CLINIC (HM12999) | | | | | | | | | | | | | | | | | | | | | | | | | |
| MARSTON, SUE (HM13179) | | | | | | | | | | | | | | | | | | | | | | | | | |

# A - F Therapies at Practices/Businesses

| Business by County with Reference no. | Absent Healing | Acupressure | Acupuncture | Alexander Technique | Allergy Testing | Anthroposohical Med | Aromatherapy | Art Therapy | Aura Therapy | Auricular Therapy | Auto Suggestion | Autogenic Training | Aversion Therapy | Ayurvedic Medicine | Baby Massage | Bach Remedies | Bates Method | Beauty Therapy | Bio-energetics | Biofeedback | Biomagnetic Therapy | Biomechanics | Bonesetting | Bowen Therapy | Chinese Herbal Medicine | Chiropody | Chiropractic | Clinical Ecology | Cognitive Therapy | Colonic Hydrotherapy | Colour Therapy | Complementary Therapy | Counselling | Cranial Osteopathy | Cranio-Sacral Therapy | Cryo Surgery | Crystal Healing | Cupping | Cymatics | Dance Movement Thrpy | Dietician | Do-In | Douching | Dowsing | Drama Therapy | Electrolipolysis | Electrolysis | Electrotherapy | Encounter Groups | Faith Healing |
|---|---|---|---|---|---|---|---|---|---|---|---|---|---|---|---|---|---|---|---|---|---|---|---|---|---|---|---|---|---|---|---|---|---|---|---|---|---|---|---|---|---|---|---|---|---|---|---|---|---|---|
| MERRY, EWEN (HM13753) | | | | | | | | | | | | | | | | | | | | | | | | | | | ● | | | | | | | | | | | | | | | | | | | | | | | | |
| NATURAL BACK CARE CLINIC (HM14514) | | | | | | | | | | | | | | | | | | | | | | | | | | | ● | | | | | | | | | | | | | | | | | | | | | | | | |
| NATURAL HEALTH CENTRE (HM14564) | | | ● | | | | | | | | | | | | | | | | | | | | | | | | | | | | | | | | | | | | | | | | | | | | | | | | |
| NOTTINGHAM, STUART (HM15086) | | ● | ● | | | | | | | | | | | | | | | | | | | | | | | | | | | | | | | | | | | | | | | | | | | | | ● | | |
| NURCHIR (HM15110) | | | | | | | | | | | | | | | | | | | | | | ● | | | | ● | | | | | | | | | | | | | | | | | | | | | | ● | | |
| PARDOE, DIANA T (HM15648) | | | | | | | | | | | | | | | | | | | | | | | | | | | | | | | | ● | | | | | | | | | | | | | | | | | | |
| PERSHORE NAT THERAPY CLINIC (HM16057) | | | ● | | | | ● | | | | | | | | | ● | | | | | | | | | | | | | | | | | | | | | | ● | | | | | | | | | | | | |
| PRICE, LYDIA (HM16585) | | | | | | | | | | | | | | | | | | | | | | | | | | | ● | | | | | | | | | | | | | | | | | | | | | | | | |
| R C C M (HM16829) | | | ● | | | | ● | | | | | | | | | | | | | | | | | | | | | | | | | | ● | | | | | | | | | | | | | | | | | |
| REDDITCH CHIROPRACTIC CLINIC (HM17013) | | | | | | | | | | | | | | | | | | | | | | | | | | | ● | | | | | | | | | | | | | | | | | | | | | | | | |
| REDDITCH FOOTCARE SURGERY (HM17014) | | | | | | | | | | | | | | | | | | | | | | ● | | | | ● | | | | | | | | | | | | | | | | | | | | | | | | | |
| RHIANS BEAUTY & THERAPY CENTRE (HM17219) | | | | | | | ● | | | | | | | | | | | | | | | | | | | | | | | | | | | | | | | | | | | | | | | | | | | | |
| RIDLER, PATRICIA (HM17319) | | | | | | | | | | | | | | | | | | | | | | | | | | | ● | | | | | | | | | | | | | | | | | | | | | | | | |
| ROBINSON, SUSAN (HM17504) | | | | | | | | | | | | | | | | ● | | | | | | | | | | | | | | | | | | | | | | | | | | | | | | | | | | | |
| SEDGEBERROW MCTIMONEY (HM18185) | | | | | | | | | | | | | | | | | | | | | | | | | | | ● | | | | | | | | | | | | | | | | | | | | | | | | |
| SHEER, JENNY (HM18369) | | | ● | | | | | | | | | | | | | | | | | | | | | | | | | | | | | | | | | | | | | | | | | | | | | | | | |
| SOUTH WORCESTERSHIRE HYP (HM18915) | | | | | ● | | | | | | | | | | | | | | | | | | | | | | | | | | | | | | | | | | | | | | | | | | | | | | |
| STOKES, TERRY (HM19325) | | | ● | | | | | | | | | | | | | ● | | | | | | | | ● | | | | | | | | ● | | | | | | | | | | | | | | | | | | |
| STONE, ANNE L (HM19329) | | | ● | | | | | | | | | | | | | | | | | | | | | | | | | | | | | | | | | | | | | | | | | | | | | ● | | |
| WORCESTER NATURAL THERAPY CTRE (HM21886) | | | ● | ● | ● | | ● | | | | | | | | | | | | | | | | | ● | | | ● | | | | | | | | | | ● | | | | ● | | | | | | | | | |
| YEN YANG (HM22006) | | | | | | | | | | | | | | | | | | | | | | | | | | | ● | | | | | | | | | | | | | | | | | | | | | | | | |
| YOUNG, JOANNA (HM22075) | | | | | | | | | | | | | | | | | | | | | | | | | | | | | | | | | | ● | | | | | | | | | | | | | | | | |
| **YORKSHIRE (NORTH)** | | | | | | | | | | | | | | | | | | | | | | | | | | | | | | | | | | | | | | | | | | | | | | | | | | |
| A TACTILE BUSINESS (HM00046) | | ● | | | | | | | | | | | | | | | | | | | | | | | | | | | | | | | | | | | | | | | | | | | | | | | | |
| ACUPUNCTURE CLINIC (HM00260) | | | ● | | | | | | | | | | | | | | | | | | | | | | | | | | | | | | | | | | | | | | | | | | | | | | | | |
| ACUPUNCTURE/NATURAL THERAPY (HM00328) | | | ● | | | | | | | | | | | | | | | | | | | | | | | | | | | | | | | | | | | | | | | | | | | | | | | | |
| AMYRIS ESSENTIAL OILS (HM00796) | | | | | | | ● | | | | | | | | | | | | | | | | | | | | | | | | | | | | | | | | | | | | | | | | | | | | |
| ANGEL THERAPIES (HM00869) | | | | | | | ● | | | | | | | | | | | | | | | | | | | | | | | | | | | | | | | | | | | | | | | | | | | | |
| BAKER, LINDA (HM01587) | ● | | | | | | ● | | | | | | | | | | ● | | | | | | | | | | | | | | | | | | | | | | | | | | | | | | | | | |
| BARLOW, GAIL (HM01721) | | | | ● | | | | | | | | | | | | | | | | | | | | | | | | | | | | | | | | | | | | | | | | | | | | | | | |
| BARNES, JACQUI (HM01747) | | | | | | | ● | | | | | | | | | | | | | | | | | | | | | | | | | | | | | | | | | | | | | | | | | | | | |
| BARRASS, K I (HM01778) | | | | | | | | | | | | | | | | | | | | | | | | | | ● | | | | | | | | | | | | | | | | | | | | | | | | | |
| BLACK, SAUL (HM02428) | | | | | | | | | | | | | | | | | | | | | | ● | | | | ● | | | | | | | | | | | | | | | | | | | | | | | | | |
| BROADHEAD, J N & M (HM03114) | | | | | | | | | | | | | | | | | | | | | | ● | | | | ● | | | | | | | | | | | | | | | | | | | | | | | | | |

# A - F Therapies at Practices/Businesses

Business by County with Reference no.

| Business | Absent Healing | Acupressure | Acupuncture | Alexander Technique | Allergy Testing | Anthroposohical Med | Aromatherapy | Art Therapy | Aura Therapy | Auricular Therapy | Auto Suggestion | Autogenic Training | Aversion Therapy | Ayurvedic Medicine | Baby Massage | Bach Remedies | Bates Method |
|---|---|---|---|---|---|---|---|---|---|---|---|---|---|---|---|---|---|
| BURNS, K P (HM03416) | | | | | | | | | | | | | | | | | |
| CASA DELL' AROMA (HM03805) | | | | | | | ● | | | | | | | | | | |
| CHINESE THERAPY CLINIC (HM04270) | | | ● | | | | | | | | | | | | | | |
| CHIROPODIST (HM04292) | | | | | | | | | | | | | | | | | |
| CHIROPRACTIC CLINIC (HM04394) | | | | | | | | | | | | | | | | | |
| CORDEL, MICHAEL (HM05160) | | ● | ● | | | | | | | | | | | | | | |
| CRAVEN CLINIC (HM05384) | | ● | ● | ● | ● | | ● | | | | | | | | | ● | |
| CROFT HOUSE CLINIC (HM05452) | | | ● | | | | | | | | | | | | | | |
| DOVE COURT CENTRE (HM06225) | | ● | ● | | | | | | | | | | | | | | |
| EASY WAY YORKSHIRE (HM06557) | | | | | | | | | | | | | | | | | |
| ELLAN, JAN (HM06746) | | | | ● | | | | | | | | | | | | | |
| ELLIOTT, JUDITH (HM06754) | | | | ● | | | | | | | | | | | | | |
| FIRTH, SUE (HM07343) | | | | ● | | | | | | | | | | | | | |
| FORSHAW, VERONICA (HM07568) | | | | | | | ● | | | | | | | | | | |
| GROOM, C (HM08594) | | | | | | | ● | | | | | | | | | | |
| HARROGATE CHIROPRACTIC CLINIC (HM09115) | | | | | | | | | | | | | | | | | |
| HARROGATE HOLISTIC HEALTH CTRE (HM09116) | | ● | ● | | ● | | ● | | | | | | | | | | |
| HARROGATE SCHOOL-AROMATHERAPY (HM09118) | | | | | | | ● | | | | | | | | | | |
| HEALING CLINIC (HM09328) | ● | ● | ● | ● | | | ● | | | | | | | | | ● | |
| HESCOTT, J D (HM09692) | | | | | | | | | | | | | | | | | |
| HEWORTH CHIROPODIST CLINIC (HM09709) | | | | | | | | | | | | | | | | | |
| HIGHTHORN PHYSIOTHERAPY CLINIC (HM09759) | | | ● | ● | | | | | | | | | | | | | |
| HOBSON, I K (HM09863) | | | | | | | | | | | | | | | | | |
| HOLLAND, G H R (HM10008) | | | | | | | | | | | | | | | | | |
| HOLMFIELD (HM10047) | | | | | | | ● | | | | | | | | | | |
| JONATHANS (HM11112) | | | | | | | ● | | | | | | | | | | |
| KNOWLES, J (HM11770) | | | | | | | | | | | | | | | | | |
| LIFESUPPORT (HM12366) | ● | ● | ● | ● | | | ● | | | | ● | | | | | | |
| MARRIOTT, HELEN (HM13137) | | | | | | | | | | | | | | | | ● | |
| MELLOW MOMENTS (HM13714) | | | | | | | ● | | | | | | | | | | |
| NATURAL BALANCE (HM14515) | | | | | | | ● | | | | | | | | | | |
| NORTHERN COLLEGE OF ACUP (HM15059) | | | ● | | | | | | | | | | | | | | |
| PAGE, F T (HM15571) | | | | | | | | | | | | | | | | | |
| PANACEA ACUPUNCTURE CLINIC (HM15628) | | | ● | | | | | | | | | | | | | | |

| Business | Beauty Therapy | Bio-energetics | Biofeedback | Biomagnetic Therapy | Biomechanics | Bonesetting | Bowen Therapy | Chinese Herbal Medicine | Chiropody | Chiropractic | Clinical Ecology | Cognitive Therapy | Colonic Hydrotherapy | Colour Therapy | Complementary Therapy | Counselling | Cranial Osteopathy |
|---|---|---|---|---|---|---|---|---|---|---|---|---|---|---|---|---|---|
| BURNS, K P (HM03416) | | | | | | | | | | ● | | | | | | | |
| CASA DELL' AROMA (HM03805) | | | | | | | | | | | | | | | | | |
| CHINESE THERAPY CLINIC (HM04270) | | | | | | | | | | | | | | | | | |
| CHIROPODIST (HM04292) | | | | | | | | | ● | | | | | | | | |
| CHIROPRACTIC CLINIC (HM04394) | | | | | | | | | | ● | | | | | | | |
| CORDEL, MICHAEL (HM05160) | | | | | | | | | | | | | | | | | |
| CRAVEN CLINIC (HM05384) | | | | | | | | | | ● | | | | | ● | ● | ● |
| CROFT HOUSE CLINIC (HM05452) | | | | | | | | | | | | | | | | | ● |
| DOVE COURT CENTRE (HM06225) | | | | | | | | | | | | | | | | | |
| EASY WAY YORKSHIRE (HM06557) | | | | | | | | | | | | ● | | | | | |
| ELLAN, JAN (HM06746) | | | | | | | | | | | | | | | | | |
| ELLIOTT, JUDITH (HM06754) | | | | | | | | | | | | | | | | | |
| FIRTH, SUE (HM07343) | | | | | | | | | | | | | | | | | |
| FORSHAW, VERONICA (HM07568) | | | | | | | | | | | | | | | | | |
| GROOM, C (HM08594) | | | | | | | | | | | | | | | | | |
| HARROGATE CHIROPRACTIC CLINIC (HM09115) | | | | | | | | | | ● | | | | | | | |
| HARROGATE HOLISTIC HEALTH CTRE (HM09116) | | | | | | | | | | | | ● | | | ● | ● | ● |
| HARROGATE SCHOOL-AROMATHERAPY (HM09118) | | | | | | | | | | | | | | | | | |
| HEALING CLINIC (HM09328) | | | | | | | ● | ● | | ● | | | | | ● | | |
| HESCOTT, J D (HM09692) | | | | | ● | | | | ● | | | | | | | | |
| HEWORTH CHIROPODIST CLINIC (HM09709) | | | | | | | | | ● | | | | | | | | |
| HIGHTHORN PHYSIOTHERAPY CLINIC (HM09759) | | | | | | | | | | | | | | | | | |
| HOBSON, I K (HM09863) | | | | | ● | | | | ● | | | | | | | | |
| HOLLAND, G H R (HM10008) | | | | | | | | | | ● | | | | | | | |
| HOLMFIELD (HM10047) | | | | | | | | | | | | | | | | | |
| JONATHANS (HM11112) | | | | | | | | | | | | | | | | | |
| KNOWLES, J (HM11770) | | | | | ● | | | | ● | | | | | | | | |
| LIFESUPPORT (HM12366) | | | | | | | | | | ● | | | | | | ● | |
| MARRIOTT, HELEN (HM13137) | | | | | | | | | | | | | | | | | |
| MELLOW MOMENTS (HM13714) | | | | | | | | | | | | | | | | | |
| NATURAL BALANCE (HM14515) | | | | | | | | | | | | | | | | | |
| NORTHERN COLLEGE OF ACUP (HM15059) | | | | | | | | | | | | | | | | | |
| PAGE, F T (HM15571) | | | | | | | | | | ● | | | | | | | |
| PANACEA ACUPUNCTURE CLINIC (HM15628) | | | | | | | | | | | | | | | | | |

| Business | Cranio-Sacral Therapy | Cryo Surgery | Crystal Healing | Cupping | Cymatics | Dance Movement Thrpy | Dietician | Do-In | Douching | Dowsing | Drama Therapy | Electrolipolysis | Electrolysis | Electrotherapy | Encounter Groups | Faith Healing |
|---|---|---|---|---|---|---|---|---|---|---|---|---|---|---|---|---|
| BURNS, K P (HM03416) | | | | | | | | | | | | | | | | |
| CASA DELL' AROMA (HM03805) | | | | | | | | | | | | | | | | |
| CHINESE THERAPY CLINIC (HM04270) | | | | | | | | | | | | | | | | |
| CHIROPODIST (HM04292) | | | | | | | | | | | | | | | | |
| CHIROPRACTIC CLINIC (HM04394) | | | | | | | | | | | | | | | | |
| CORDEL, MICHAEL (HM05160) | | | | ● | | | | | | | | | | | | |
| CRAVEN CLINIC (HM05384) | | | | | | | | | | | | | | | | |
| CROFT HOUSE CLINIC (HM05452) | | | | | | | | | | | | | | | | |
| DOVE COURT CENTRE (HM06225) | | | | | | | | | | | | | | | | |
| EASY WAY YORKSHIRE (HM06557) | | | | | | | | | | | | | | | | |
| ELLAN, JAN (HM06746) | | | | | | | | | | | | | | | | |
| ELLIOTT, JUDITH (HM06754) | | | | | | | | | | | | | | | | |
| FIRTH, SUE (HM07343) | | | | | | | | | | | | | | | | |
| FORSHAW, VERONICA (HM07568) | | | | | | | | | | | | | | | | |
| GROOM, C (HM08594) | | | | | | | | | | | | | | | | |
| HARROGATE CHIROPRACTIC CLINIC (HM09115) | | | | | | | | | | | | | | | | |
| HARROGATE HOLISTIC HEALTH CTRE (HM09116) | | | | | | | | | | | | | | | | |
| HARROGATE SCHOOL-AROMATHERAPY (HM09118) | | | | | | | | | | | | | | | | |
| HEALING CLINIC (HM09328) | ● | | | ● | | | | | | | | | | | | |
| HESCOTT, J D (HM09692) | | | | | | | | | | | | | | | | |
| HEWORTH CHIROPODIST CLINIC (HM09709) | | | | | | | | | | | | | | | | |
| HIGHTHORN PHYSIOTHERAPY CLINIC (HM09759) | | | | | | | | | | | | | | | | |
| HOBSON, I K (HM09863) | | | | | | | | | | | | | | | | |
| HOLLAND, G H R (HM10008) | | | | | | | | | | | | | | | | |
| HOLMFIELD (HM10047) | | | | | | | | | | | | | | | | |
| JONATHANS (HM11112) | | | | | | | | | | | | | | | | |
| KNOWLES, J (HM11770) | | | | | | | | | | | | | | | | |
| LIFESUPPORT (HM12366) | | | ● | | | | | | | | | | | | | |
| MARRIOTT, HELEN (HM13137) | | | | | | | | | | | | | | | | |
| MELLOW MOMENTS (HM13714) | | | | | | | | | | | | | | | | |
| NATURAL BALANCE (HM14515) | | | | | | | | | | | | | | | | |
| NORTHERN COLLEGE OF ACUP (HM15059) | | | | | | | | | | | | | | | | |
| PAGE, F T (HM15571) | | | | | | | | | | | | | | | | |
| PANACEA ACUPUNCTURE CLINIC (HM15628) | | | | | | | | | | | | | | | | |

# A - F Therapies at Practices/Businesses

| Business by County with Reference no. | Absent Healing | Acupressure | Acupuncture | Alexander Technique | Allergy Testing | Anthroposohical Med | Aromatherapy | Art Therapy | Aura Therapy | Auricular Therapy | Auto Suggestion | Autogenic Training | Aversion Therapy | Ayurvedic Medicine | Baby Massage | Bach Remedies | Bates Method | Beauty Therapy | Bio-energetics | Biofeedback | Biomagnetic Therapy | Biomechanics | Bonesetting | Bowen Therapy | Chinese Herbal Medicine |
|---|---|---|---|---|---|---|---|---|---|---|---|---|---|---|---|---|---|---|---|---|---|---|---|---|---|
| RATHBONE, DONNA (HM16955) | | | | | | | | | | | | | | | | | | | | | | | | | |
| RIPON NATURAL HEALTH CENTRE (HM17365) | | ● | ● | | | | ● | | | | | | | ● | | ● | ● | | | | | | | | |
| RYEDALE CLINIC (HM17803) | | | | | | | | | | | | | | | | | | | | | | | | ● | |
| SHAH, ATUL (HM18268) | | | | | | | | | | | | | | | | | | | | | | | | | |
| SI SHEN CLINIC (HM18519) | | | | | | | | | | | | | | | | | | | | | | | | | |
| SKIPTON CHIROPODY CENTRE (HM18658) | | | | | | | | | | | | | | | | | | | | | | | | | |
| SMITH, C J (HM18723) | | | | | | | | | | | | | | | | | | | | | | | | | |
| SMITH, PAM (HM18787) | | | | | | | | | | | | | | | | ● | | | | | | | | | |
| SMITH, YVONNE (HM18821) | | | | | | | | | | | | | | | | ● | | | | | | | | | |
| STATHER, M (HM19160) | | | | | | | | | | | | | | | | | | | | | | | | | |
| STRATTON, FIONA (HM19372) | ● | ● | ● | | | | ● | | | | | | | | | | | | | | | | | | |
| TERRY ANNE (HM19845) | | | | | | | | | | | | | | | | | ● | | | | | | | | |
| THIRSK CHIROPRACTIC CLINIC (HM19921) | | | | | | | | | | | | | | | | | | | | | | | | | |
| TUCKER, KATH (HM20366) | | | ● | | | | | | | | | | | | | | | | | | | | | | |
| WOLSTENHOLME, SHEILA (HM21764) | | | | | | | | | | | | | | | | ● | | | | | | | | | |
| WRIGHT, T (HM21952) | | | | ● | | | | | | | | | | | | | | | | | | | | | |
| WYLDBORE, VICTORIA (HM21971) | | | | | | | ● | | | | | | | | | | | | | | | | | | |
| YORK CHIROPRACTIC CLINIC (HM22039) | | | | | | | | | | | | | | | | | | | | | | | | | |
| YORK CLINIC (HM22040) | | | ● | | ● | | ● | | | | | | | | | | | | | | | | | | ● |
| YORK COUNSELLING (HM22042) | | | | | | | | | | | | | | | | | | | | | | | | | |
| YORK SCHOOL OF COMP MEDICINE (HM22050) | | | | | | | ● | | | | | | | | | | | | | | | | | | |
| YORVIK CHIROPRACTIC CLINIC (HM22058) | | | | | | | | | | | | | | | | | | | | | | | | | |
| **YORKSHIRE (SOUTH)** | | | | | | | | | | | | | | | | | | | | | | | | | |
| ALTON & JAMES MED HERBAL (HM00748) | | | | | ● | | | | | | | | | | | ● | | | | | | | | | |
| ALTON, C R (HM00749) | | | | | | | | | | | | | | | | | | | | | | | | | |
| ANDERSON, A DUDLEY (HM00810) | | | | | | | | | | | | | | | | | | | | | | | | | |
| AROMATHERAPY (HM01085) | | | | | | | ● | | | | | | | | | | | | | | | | | | |
| AROMATHERAPY & MASSOLOGY CLNC (HM01087) | | | | | | | ● | | | | | | | | | | | | | | | | | | |
| AROMATICS (HM01139) | | | | | | | ● | | | | | | | | | | | | | | | | | | |
| BEAUMONT, SUSAN LAW (HM01990) | | | ● | | | | | | | | | | | | | | | | | | | | | | |
| BLUFF, ANN (HM02529) | | | | | | | | | | | | | | | | | | | | | | | | | |
| BOON, G M (HM02690) | | | | | | | | | | | | | | | | | | | | | | ● | | | |
| BRADWAY COMP THERAPY CENTRE (HM02880) | | | | | | | | | | | | | | | | | | | | | | | | | |
| BRAMLEY HALL CLINIC (HM02902) | | | ● | | | | | | | | | | | | | ● | | | | | | | | | |

| Business by County with Reference no. | Chiropody | Chiropractic | Clinical Ecology | Cognitive Therapy | Colonic Hydrotherapy | Colour Therapy | Complementary Therapy | Counselling | Cranial Osteopathy | Cranio-Sacral Therapy | Cryo Surgery | Crystal Healing | Cupping | Cymatics | Dance Movement Thrpy | Dietician | Do-In | Douching | Dowsing | Drama Therapy | Electrolipolysis | Electrolysis | Electrotherapy | Encounter Groups | Faith Healing |
|---|---|---|---|---|---|---|---|---|---|---|---|---|---|---|---|---|---|---|---|---|---|---|---|---|---|
| RATHBONE, DONNA (HM16955) | ● | | | | | | | | | | | | | | | | | | | | | | | | |
| RIPON NATURAL HEALTH CENTRE (HM17365) | | | | | | | ● | | ● | | | | ● | | | | | | | | | | | | |
| RYEDALE CLINIC (HM17803) | | | | | | | | | | | | | | | | | | | | | | | ● | | |
| SHAH, ATUL (HM18268) | | | | | | | | | | | | | | | | ● | | | | | | | | | |
| SI SHEN CLINIC (HM18519) | ● | | | | | | | | | | | | | | | | | | | | | | | | |
| SKIPTON CHIROPODY CENTRE (HM18658) | ● | | | | | | | | | | | | | | | | | | | | | | | | |
| SMITH, C J (HM18723) | | ● | | | | | | | | | | | | | | | | | | | | | | | |
| SMITH, PAM (HM18787) | | | | | | | | | | | | | | | | | | | | | | | | | |
| SMITH, YVONNE (HM18821) | | | | | | | | | | | | | | | | | | | | | | | | | |
| STATHER, M (HM19160) | ● | | | | | | | | | | | | | | | | | | | | | | | | |
| STRATTON, FIONA (HM19372) | | | | | | | ● | | | | | | | | | | | | | | | | | | |
| TERRY ANNE (HM19845) | | | | ● | | | ● | | | | | | | | | | | | | | | | | | |
| THIRSK CHIROPRACTIC CLINIC (HM19921) | | ● | | | | | | | | | | | | | | | | | | | | | | | |
| TUCKER, KATH (HM20366) | | | | | | | | | | | | | | | | | | | | | | | | | |
| WOLSTENHOLME, SHEILA (HM21764) | | | | | | | | | | | | | | | | | | | | | | | | | |
| WRIGHT, T (HM21952) | | | | | | | | | | | | | | | | | | | | | | | | | |
| WYLDBORE, VICTORIA (HM21971) | | | | | | | | | | | | | | | | | | | | | | | | | |
| YORK CHIROPRACTIC CLINIC (HM22039) | | ● | | | | | | | | | | | | | | | | | | | | | | | |
| YORK CLINIC (HM22040) | ● | | | | | | | ● | | | | | | | | | | | | | | | | | |
| YORK COUNSELLING (HM22042) | | | | | | | | ● | | | | | | | | | | | | | | | | | |
| YORK SCHOOL OF COMP MEDICINE (HM22050) | | | | | | | | | | | | | | | | | | | | | | | | | |
| YORVIK CHIROPRACTIC CLINIC (HM22058) | | ● | | | | | | | | | | | | | | | | | | | | | | | |
| **YORKSHIRE (SOUTH)** | | | | | | | | | | | | | | | | | | | | | | | | | |
| ALTON & JAMES MED HERBAL (HM00748) | | | | | | | ● | | | | | | | | | | | | | | | | | | |
| ALTON, C R (HM00749) | | ● | | | | | | | | | | | | | | | | | | | | | | | |
| ANDERSON, A DUDLEY (HM00810) | | | | | | | ● | ● | | | | | | | | | | | | | | | | | |
| AROMATHERAPY (HM01085) | | | | | | | | | | | | | | | | | | | | | | | | | |
| AROMATHERAPY & MASSOLOGY CLNC (HM01087) | | | | | | | | | | | | | | | | | | | | | | | | | |
| AROMATICS (HM01139) | | | | | | | | | | | | | | | | | | | | | | | | | |
| BEAUMONT, SUSAN LAW (HM01990) | | | | | | | | | | | | | | | | | | | | | | | | | |
| BLUFF, ANN (HM02529) | ● | | | | | | | | | | | | | | | | | | | | | | | | |
| BOON, G M (HM02690) | ● | | | | | | | | | | | | | | | | | | | | | | | | |
| BRADWAY COMP THERAPY CENTRE (HM02880) | ● | | | | | | | | | | | | | | | | | | | | | | | | |
| BRAMLEY HALL CLINIC (HM02902) | | | | | | | ● | | ● | | | | | | | ● | | | | | | | | | |

# A - F Therapies at Practices/Businesses

| Business by County with Reference no. | Absent Healing | Acupressure | Acupuncture | Alexander Technique | Allergy Testing | Anthroposohical Med | Aromatherapy | Art Therapy | Aura Therapy | Auricular Therapy | Auto Suggestion | Autogenic Training | Aversion Therapy | Ayurvedic Medicine | Baby Massage | Bach Remedies | Bates Method |
|---|---|---|---|---|---|---|---|---|---|---|---|---|---|---|---|---|---|
| BRANKIN, M & K (HM02917) | | | | | | | | | | | | | | | | | |
| BRANKLIN, M & K (HM02918) | | | | | | | | | | | | | | | | | |
| BROOMHILL CHIROPRACTIC CLINIC (HM03192) | | | | | | | | | | | | | | | | | |
| BROOMHILL MEDICAL CENTRE (HM03193) | | | | | | | ● | | | | | | | | | | |
| CARING CLINIC (HM03682) | | | | | | | ● | | | | | | | | | ● | |
| CHIROPODY SURGERY (HM04342) | | | | | | | | | | | | | | | | | |
| CHIROPRACTIC CLINIC (HM04391) | | | | | | | | | | | | | | | | | |
| CLAIRE LOUISE (HM04510) | | | | | | | | | | | | | | | | | |
| COUNTRY PRACTICE (HM05256) | | | | | | | ● | | | | | | | | | | |
| CREWE, G (HM05433) | | | | ● | | | | | | | | | | | | | |
| CROOKES ACUPUNCTURE CENTRE (HM05472) | | | ● | | | | | | | | | | | | | | |
| DELFOSSE, PATRICIA (HM05965) | | | ● | | | | | | | | | | | | | | |
| DONCASTER CHIROPRACTIC CLINIC (HM06170) | | | | | | | | | | | | | | | | | |
| DORE PHYSIOTHERAPY PRACTICE (HM06196) | | | | | | | | | | | | | | | | | |
| DR K P BURNS & ASS (HM06272) | | | | | | | | | | | | | | | | | |
| DUFFIELD, G (HM06361) | | | | | | | ● | | | | | | | | | | |
| EATON, T C (HM06565) | | | | | | | | | | | | | | | | | |
| ESSENTIAL HARMONY (HM06907) | ● | | | | | | ● | | | | | | | | | | |
| ESSENTIALLY YOURS (HM06925) | | | | | | | ● | | | | | | | | | | |
| EXECUTIVE SUITE (HM07021) | | | | | | | ● | | | | | | | | | | |
| FISHER, CHRISTINE A (HM07349) | | | | | | | | | | | | | | | | | |
| FRANKS, PAUL (HM07690) | | | ● | | | | | | | | | | | | | | |
| GAIA HEALTH (HM07830) | | | | | | | ● | | | | | | | | | | |
| HALLAMSHIRE NATURAL HLTH CTRE (HM08798) | ● | | | ● | | | ● | | | | | | | | | ● | ● |
| HEALTHY FEET (HM09427) | | | | | | | | | | | | | | | | | |
| HINCHLIFFE, JACKIE (HM09822) | ● | | | | | | ● | | | | | | | | | | |
| HYPNOTHERAPY CENTRE (HM10515) | | | | | | | | | | | ● | ● | | | | | |
| IRVINE, ALAN (HM10743) | | | ● | | | | | | | | | | | | | | |
| LAISTER, MARTIN (HM11868) | | | | | | | | | | | | | | | | | |
| LLEWELLYN CONSULTANCY (HM12502) | ● | ● | | | | | ● | ● | | | ● | | | | | ● | |
| M & B SERVICES (HM12794) | | | | | | | | | | | | | | | | | |
| MOORGATE NATURAL HEALING CTRE (HM14138) | ● | | | | | | ● | | | | ● | | ● | | | | |
| NIGHTINGALE PHYSIO PRACTICE (HM14937) | | | ● | | | | | | | | | | | | | | |
| PAUL BOIZOT AROMATHERAPY (HM15839) | | | | | | | ● | | | | | | | | | | |

| Business by County with Reference no. | Beauty Therapy | Bio-energetics | Biofeedback | Biomagnetic Therapy | Biomechanics | Bonesetting | Bowen Therapy | Chinese Herbal Medicine | Chiropody | Chiropractic | Clinical Ecology | Cognitive Therapy | Colonic Hydrotherapy | Colour Therapy | Complementary Therapy | Counselling | Cranial Osteopathy |
|---|---|---|---|---|---|---|---|---|---|---|---|---|---|---|---|---|---|
| BRANKIN, M & K (HM02917) | | | | | ● | | | | ● | | | | | | | | |
| BRANKLIN, M & K (HM02918) | | | | | ● | | | | ● | | | | | | | | |
| BROOMHILL CHIROPRACTIC CLINIC (HM03192) | | | | | | | | | | ● | | | | | | | |
| BROOMHILL MEDICAL CENTRE (HM03193) | | | | | | | | | | | | | | | | | |
| CARING CLINIC (HM03682) | | | | | | | | | | | | | | ● | | ● | |
| CHIROPODY SURGERY (HM04342) | | | | | | | | | ● | | | | | | | | |
| CHIROPRACTIC CLINIC (HM04391) | | | | | | | | | | ● | | | | | | | |
| CLAIRE LOUISE (HM04510) | | | | | | | | | ● | | | | | | | | |
| COUNTRY PRACTICE (HM05256) | | | | | | | | | | | | | | | ● | | |
| CREWE, G (HM05433) | | | | | | | | | | | | | | | | | |
| CROOKES ACUPUNCTURE CENTRE (HM05472) | | | | | | | | | | | | | | | | | |
| DELFOSSE, PATRICIA (HM05965) | | | | | | | | | | | | | | | | | |
| DONCASTER CHIROPRACTIC CLINIC (HM06170) | | | | | | | | | | ● | | | | | | | |
| DORE PHYSIOTHERAPY PRACTICE (HM06196) | | | | | | | | | | | | | | | | | |
| DR K P BURNS & ASS (HM06272) | | | | | | | | | | ● | | | | | | | |
| DUFFIELD, G (HM06361) | | | | | | | | | | | | | | | | | |
| EATON, T C (HM06565) | | | | | ● | | | | ● | | | | | | | | |
| ESSENTIAL HARMONY (HM06907) | | | | | | | | | | | | | | | | | |
| ESSENTIALLY YOURS (HM06925) | | | | | | | | | | | | | | | | | |
| EXECUTIVE SUITE (HM07021) | | | | | | | | | | | | | | | | | |
| FISHER, CHRISTINE A (HM07349) | | | | | | | | | ● | | | | | | | | |
| FRANKS, PAUL (HM07690) | | | | | | | | | | | | | | | | | |
| GAIA HEALTH (HM07830) | | | | | | | | | | | | | | | | | |
| HALLAMSHIRE NATURAL HLTH CTRE (HM08798) | | | | | | | ● | | | ● | | | | | ● | ● | |
| HEALTHY FEET (HM09427) | | | | | | | | | | ● | | | | | ● | | |
| HINCHLIFFE, JACKIE (HM09822) | | | | | | | | | | | | | | | | | |
| HYPNOTHERAPY CENTRE (HM10515) | | | | | | | | | | | | | | | ● | ● | |
| IRVINE, ALAN (HM10743) | | | | | | | | | | | | | | | | | |
| LAISTER, MARTIN (HM11868) | | | | | | | | | ● | | | | | | | | |
| LLEWELLYN CONSULTANCY (HM12502) | | | ● | | | | | | | | | ● | | | ● | ● | |
| M & B SERVICES (HM12794) | | | | | | | | | | | | | | | | ● | |
| MOORGATE NATURAL HEALING CTRE (HM14138) | | | | | | | | | | | | | | | ● | | |
| NIGHTINGALE PHYSIO PRACTICE (HM14937) | | | | | | | | | | | | | | | | | |
| PAUL BOIZOT AROMATHERAPY (HM15839) | | | | | | | | | | | | | | | | | |

| Business by County with Reference no. | Cranio-Sacral Therapy | Cryo Surgery | Crystal Healing | Cupping | Cymatics | Dance Movement Thrpy | Dietician | Do-In | Douching | Dowsing | Drama Therapy | Electrolipolysis | Electrolysis | Electrotherapy | Encounter Groups | Faith Healing |
|---|---|---|---|---|---|---|---|---|---|---|---|---|---|---|---|---|
| BRANKIN, M & K (HM02917) | | | | | | | | | | | | | | | | |
| BRANKLIN, M & K (HM02918) | | | | | | | | | | | | | | | | |
| BROOMHILL CHIROPRACTIC CLINIC (HM03192) | | | | | | | | | | | | | | | | |
| BROOMHILL MEDICAL CENTRE (HM03193) | | | | | | | | | | | | | | | | |
| CARING CLINIC (HM03682) | | | ● | | | | | | | | | | | | | |
| CHIROPODY SURGERY (HM04342) | | ● | | | | | | | | | | | | | | |
| CHIROPRACTIC CLINIC (HM04391) | | | | | | | | | | | | | | | | |
| CLAIRE LOUISE (HM04510) | | | | | | | | | | | | | | | | |
| COUNTRY PRACTICE (HM05256) | | | | | | | | | | | | | | | | |
| CREWE, G (HM05433) | | | | | | | | | | | | | | | | |
| CROOKES ACUPUNCTURE CENTRE (HM05472) | | | | | | | | | | | | | | | | |
| DELFOSSE, PATRICIA (HM05965) | | | | | | | | | | | | | | | | |
| DONCASTER CHIROPRACTIC CLINIC (HM06170) | | | | | | | | | | | | | | | | |
| DORE PHYSIOTHERAPY PRACTICE (HM06196) | | | | | | | | | | | | | | ● | | |
| DR K P BURNS & ASS (HM06272) | | | | | | | | | | | | | | | | |
| DUFFIELD, G (HM06361) | | | | | | | | | | | | | | | | |
| EATON, T C (HM06565) | | | | | | | | | | | | | | | | |
| ESSENTIAL HARMONY (HM06907) | | | | | | | | | | | | | | | | |
| ESSENTIALLY YOURS (HM06925) | | | | | | | | | | | | | | | | |
| EXECUTIVE SUITE (HM07021) | | | | | | | | | | | | | | | | |
| FISHER, CHRISTINE A (HM07349) | | | | | | | | | | | | | | | | |
| FRANKS, PAUL (HM07690) | | | | | | | | | | | | | | | | |
| GAIA HEALTH (HM07830) | | | | | | | | | | | | | | | | |
| HALLAMSHIRE NATURAL HLTH CTRE (HM08798) | | | ● | | | | | | | ● | | | | | | |
| HEALTHY FEET (HM09427) | | | | | | | | | | | | | | | | |
| HINCHLIFFE, JACKIE (HM09822) | | | | | | | | | | | | | | | | |
| HYPNOTHERAPY CENTRE (HM10515) | | | | | | | | | | | | | | | | |
| IRVINE, ALAN (HM10743) | | | | | | | | | | | | | | | | |
| LAISTER, MARTIN (HM11868) | | | | | | | | | | | | | | | | |
| LLEWELLYN CONSULTANCY (HM12502) | | | | | | | ● | | | | | | | | | |
| M & B SERVICES (HM12794) | | | | | | | | | | | | | | | | |
| MOORGATE NATURAL HEALING CTRE (HM14138) | | | | | | | | | | | | | | | | |
| NIGHTINGALE PHYSIO PRACTICE (HM14937) | | | | | | | | | | | | | | | | |
| PAUL BOIZOT AROMATHERAPY (HM15839) | | | | | | | | | | | | | | | | |

# A - F Therapies at Practices/Businesses

Business by County with Reference no.

| Business | Absent Healing | Acupressure | Acupuncture | Alexander Technique | Allergy Testing | Anthroposohical Med | Aromatherapy | Art Therapy | Aura Therapy | Auricular Therapy | Auto Suggestion | Autogenic Training | Aversion Therapy | Ayurvedic Medicine | Baby Massage | Bach Remedies | Bates Method | Beauty Therapy | Bio-energetics | Biofeedback | Biomagnetic Therapy | Biomechanics | Bonesetting | Bowen Therapy | Chinese Herbal Medicine |
|---|---|---|---|---|---|---|---|---|---|---|---|---|---|---|---|---|---|---|---|---|---|---|---|---|---|
| ROSTED, P (HM17651) | | | ● | | | | | | | | | | | | | | | | | | | | | | |
| SAVILLE, KATHY (HM17978) | | | | | | | ● | | | | | | | | | | | | | | | | | | |
| SCHOLL CENTRE (HM18046) | | | | | | | | | | | | | | | | | | | | | | ● | | | |
| SEASONS BEAUTY CENTRE (HM18178) | | | | | | | ● | | | | | | | | | | | | | | | | | | |
| SHARRON CHIROPODY CLINIC (HM18324) | | | | | | | | | | | | | | | | | | | | | | ● | | | |
| SHEFFIELD NATURAL HEALTH CTRE (HM18372) | | | ● | | | | ● | | | | | | | | | | | | | | | | | | ● |
| SIMPSON, SARAH E (HM18598) | | | | | | | | | | | | | | | | | | | | | | | | | |
| THORNE ROAD CHIROPRACTIC (HM20017) | | | | | | | | | | | | | | | | | | | | | | | | | |
| TRIGG, REBECCA (HM20334) | | | ● | | | | | | | | | | | | | | | | | | | | | | |
| VINSON, CAROL (HM20686) | | | | | | | | | | | | | | | | | | | | | | | | | |
| WALKER, SUE (HM20804) | | | ● | | | | | | | | | | | | | | | | | | | | | | |
| WARD CHIROPRACTIC (HM20895) | | | | | | | | | | | | | | | | | | | | | | | | | |
| WARD, G (HM20902) | | | ● | | | | | | | | | | | | | | | | | | | | | | |
| WARREN HOUSE CHIRO CLNC (HM20943) | | | | | | | | | | | | | | | | | | | | | | | | | |
| WELLFORCE (HM21160) | | | ● | | | | ● | | | | | | | | | ● | | | | | | | | | |
| WELSH CHIROPRACTIC (HM21183) | | | | | | | ● | | | | | | | | | | | | | | | | | | |
| WHITE, ANN (HM21347) | | | | | | | ● | | | | | | | | | | | | | | | | | | |
| WHITEING, J P (HM21393) | | | | | | | | | | | | | | | | | | | | | | ● | | | |
| WILSON, JOHN PAUL (HM21658) | | | | | | | | | | | | | | | | | | | | | | | | | |
| WOMBWELL ACUPUNCTURE CLINIC (HM21770) | | | ● | | | | | | | | | | | | | | | | | | | | | | |
| WOOD, J (HM21797) | | | ● | | | | | | | | | | | | | | | | | | | | | | |
| WOODS, LEONIE (HM21854) | | | | | | | ● | | | | | | | | | | | | | | | | | | |
| YORKSHIRE (WEST) | | | | | | | | | | | | | | | | | | | | | | | | | |
| ACUPUNCTURE CENTRE (HM00251) | | | ● | | | | | | | | | | | | | | | | | | | | | | |
| AKHTAR, J (HM00464) | | | | | | | ● | | | | | | | | | | | | | | | | | | |
| ALEX TECH TEACHING CENTRE (HM00513) | | | | ● | | | | | | | | | | | | | | | | | | | | | |
| ALEXANDER TECHNIQUE (HM00537) | | | | ● | | | | | | | | | | | | | | | | | | | | | |
| ALLEN, CAROL (HM00602) | | | | | | | | | | | | | | | | | | | | | | | | | |
| AMETHYST HEALING CENTRE (HM00783) | | | | | | | | | | | | | | | | | | | | | | | | | |
| ARDENTE CHIROPODY SERVICE (HM00991) | | | | | | | | | | | | | | | | | | | | | | | | | |
| AROMA BLISS (HM01044) | | | | | | | ● | | | | | | | | | ● | | | | | | | | | |
| AROMATIX (HM01140) | | | | | | | ● | | | | | | | | | | | | | | | | | | |
| ASH, STACEY (HM01183) | | | ● | | | | | | | | | | | | | | | | | | | | | | ● |
| ASH, STACEY (HM01184) | | | ● | | | | | | | | | | | | | | | | | | | | | | |

| Business | Chiropody | Chiropractic | Clinical Ecology | Cognitive Therapy | Colonic Hydrotherapy | Colour Therapy | Complementary Therapy | Counselling | Cranial Osteopathy | Cranio-Sacral Therapy | Cryo Surgery | Crystal Healing | Cupping | Cymatics | Dance Movement Thrpy | Dietician | Do-In | Douching | Dowsing | Drama Therapy | Electrolipolysis | Electrolysis | Electrotherapy | Encounter Groups | Faith Healing |
|---|---|---|---|---|---|---|---|---|---|---|---|---|---|---|---|---|---|---|---|---|---|---|---|---|---|
| ROSTED, P (HM17651) | | | | | | | | | | | | | | | | | | | | | | | | | |
| SAVILLE, KATHY (HM17978) | | | | | | | | | | | | | | | | | | | | | | | | | |
| SCHOLL CENTRE (HM18046) | ● | | | | | | | | | | ● | | | | | | | | | | | | | | |
| SEASONS BEAUTY CENTRE (HM18178) | | | | | | | | | | | | | | | | | | | | | | | | | |
| SHARRON CHIROPODY CLINIC (HM18324) | ● | | | | | | | | | | | | | | | | | | | | | | | | |
| SHEFFIELD NATURAL HEALTH CTRE (HM18372) | | | | | | | | ● | | | | | | | | | | | | | | | | | |
| SIMPSON, SARAH E (HM18598) | ● | | | | | | | | | | | | | | | | | | | | | | | | |
| THORNE ROAD CHIROPRACTIC (HM20017) | | ● | | | | | | | | | | | | | | | | | | | | | | | |
| TRIGG, REBECCA (HM20334) | | | | | | | | | | | | | | | | | | | | | | | | | |
| VINSON, CAROL (HM20686) | ● | | | | | | | | | | | | | | | | | | | | | | | | |
| WALKER, SUE (HM20804) | | | | | | | | | | | | | | | | | | | | | | | | | |
| WARD CHIROPRACTIC (HM20895) | | ● | | | | | | | | | | | | | | | | | | | | | | | |
| WARD, G (HM20902) | | | | | | | | | | | | | | | | | | | | | | | | | |
| WARREN HOUSE CHIRO CLNC (HM20943) | | ● | | | | | | | | | | | | | | | | | | | | | | | |
| WELLFORCE (HM21160) | | ● | | | | | | ● | ● | | | | | | | | | | | | | | | | |
| WELSH CHIROPRACTIC (HM21183) | | ● | | | | | ● | ● | | | | | | | | | | | | | | | | | |
| WHITE, ANN (HM21347) | | | | | | | | | | | | | | | | | | | | | | | | | |
| WHITEING, J P (HM21393) | ● | | | | | | | | | | | | | | | | | | | | | | | | |
| WILSON, JOHN PAUL (HM21658) | ● | | | | | | | | | | | | | | | | | | | | | | | | |
| WOMBWELL ACUPUNCTURE CLINIC (HM21770) | | | | | | | | | | | | | | | | | | | | | | | | | |
| WOOD, J (HM21797) | | | | | | | | | | | | | | | | | | | | | | | | | |
| WOODS, LEONIE (HM21854) | | | | | | | | | | | | | | | | | | | | | | | | | |
| YORKSHIRE (WEST) | | | | | | | | | | | | | | | | | | | | | | | | | |
| ACUPUNCTURE CENTRE (HM00251) | | | | | | | | | | | | | | | | | | | | | | | | | |
| AKHTAR, J (HM00464) | | | | | | | | | | | | | | | | | | | | | | | | | |
| ALEX TECH TEACHING CENTRE (HM00513) | | | | | | | | | | | | | | | | | | | | | | | | | |
| ALEXANDER TECHNIQUE (HM00537) | | | | | | | | | | | | | | | | | | | | | | | | | |
| ALLEN, CAROL (HM00602) | ● | | | | | | | | | | | | | | | | | | | | | | | | |
| AMETHYST HEALING CENTRE (HM00783) | | | | | | ● | | | | | | ● | | | | | | | | | | | | | |
| ARDENTE CHIROPODY SERVICE (HM00991) | ● | | | | | | | | | | | | | | | | | | | | | | | | |
| AROMA BLISS (HM01044) | | | | | | | | | | | | | | | | | | | | | | | | | |
| AROMATIX (HM01140) | | | | | | | | | | | | | | | | | | | | | | | | | |
| ASH, STACEY (HM01183) | | | | | | | | | | | | | | | | | | | | | | | | | |
| ASH, STACEY (HM01184) | | | | | | | | | | | | | | | | | | | | | | | | | |

# A - F Therapies at Practices/Businesses

| Business by County with Reference no. | Absent Healing | Acupressure | Acupuncture | Alexander Technique | Allergy Testing | Anthroposophical Med | Aromatherapy | Art Therapy | Aura Therapy | Auricular Therapy | Auto Suggestion | Autogenic Training | Aversion Therapy | Ayurvedic Medicine | Baby Massage | Bach Remedies | Bates Method | Beauty Therapy | Bio-energetics | Biofeedback | Biomagnetic Therapy | Biomechanics | Bonesetting | Bowen Therapy | Chinese Herbal Medicine | Chiropody | Chiropractic | Clinical Ecology | Cognitive Therapy | Colonic Hydrotherapy | Colour Therapy | Complementary Therapy | Counselling | Cranial Osteopathy | Cranio-Sacral Therapy | Cryo Surgery | Crystal Healing | Cupping | Cymatics | Dance Movement Thrpy | Dietician | Do-In | Douching | Dowsing | Drama Therapy | Electrolipolysis | Electrolysis | Electrotherapy | Encounter Groups | Faith Healing |
|---|---|---|---|---|---|---|---|---|---|---|---|---|---|---|---|---|---|---|---|---|---|---|---|---|---|---|---|---|---|---|---|---|---|---|---|---|---|---|---|---|---|---|---|---|---|---|---|---|---|---|
| ASPEN CLINIC (HM01255) | | | ● | | | | | | | | | | | | | | | | | | | | | | | | | | | | | | | | | | | | | | | | | | | | | | | |
| BALLARD, CATHERINE (HM01633) | | | ● | | | | | | | | | | | | | | | | | | | | | | | | | | | | | | | | | | | | | | | | | | | | | | | |
| BINGLEY HOMOEOPATHIC PRACTICE (HM02315) | | | ● | | | | ● | | | | | | | | | | | | | | | | | | | | | | | | | | ● | | | | | | | | | | | | | | | | | |
| BODY ESSENCE (HM02585) | | | | | | | ● | | | | | | | | | | | | | | | | | | | | | | | | | | | | | | | | | | | | | | | | | | | |
| BODY SUITE (HM02608) | | | | | | | ● | | | | | | | | | | | | | | | | | | | | | | | | | | | | | | | | | | | | | | | | | | | |
| BOYD HYPNOTHERAPY (HM02816) | | | | | | | | | | | ● | | ● | | | | | | | | | | | | | | | | ● | | | | | | | | | | | | | | | | | | | | | |
| BRADFORD CHIROPODY & BIO CLNC (HM02846) | | | | | | | | | | | | | | | | | | | | | | ● | | | | ● | | | | | | | | | | | | | | | | | | | | | | | | |
| BRADFORD CHIROPRACTIC CLINIC (HM02847) | | | | | | | | | | | | | | | | | | | | | | | | | | | ● | | | | | | | | | | | | | | | | | | | | | | | |
| BRADFORD CLINIC OF ALT MED (HM02848) | | | ● | | | | ● | | | | | ● | | | | | | | | | | | | | ● | | | | | | | | ● | | ● | | | | | | | | | | | | | | | |
| BRAMIN CLINIC (HM02900) | | | | | | | | | | | | | | | | | | | | | | | | | | | ● | | | | | | | | | | | | | | | | | | | | | | | |
| BRAMLEY COMP THERAPY CLINIC (HM02901) | ● | ● | ● | | | | ● | | | | ● | | | ● | | ● | | | | | | | | | | ● | | | ● | | | ● | ● | | | | ● | ● | | | ● | | | ● | | | | ● | | ● |
| BROWN, PAT (HM03243) | | | | ● | | | | | | | | | | | | | | | | | | | | | | | | | | | | | | | | | | | | | | | | | | | | | | |
| CALVERLEY ACUPUNCTURE CLINIC (HM03561) | | ● | ● | | | | | | | | | | | | | | | | | | | | | | | | | | | | | ● | | | | | | ● | | | | | | | | | | ● | | |
| CARRIE, CLARE (HM03745) | | | ● | | | | | | | | | | | | | | | | | | | | | | | | | | | | | | | | | | | | | | | | | | | | | | | |
| CHAMPANERIA, S K (HM03963) | | ● | ● | | | | | | | | | | | | | ● | | | ● | ● | | | | | | | | | | | | ● | | | | | | ● | | | | | | | | | | | | |
| CHAPMAN, E (HM04000) | | | ● | | | | | | | | | | | | | | | | | | | | | | | | | | | | | | | | | | | | | | | | | | | | | | | |
| CHINESE MEDICAL CENTRE (HM04228) | | ● | ● | | | | | | | | | | | | | | | | | | | | | | ● | | | | | | | | | | | | | | | | | | | | | | | | | |
| CHOICE AROMAS (HM04421) | | | | | | | ● | | | | | | | | | | | | | | | | | | | | | | | | | | ● | | | | | | | | | | | | | | | | | |
| CLARKE, DON (HM04586) | | | ● | | | | | | | | | | | | | | | | | | | | | | | | | | | | | | | | | | | | | | | | | | | | | | | |
| CLELLAND, J (HM04639) | | | ● | | | | | | | | | | | | | | | | | | | | | | | | | | | | | | | | | | | | | | | | | | | | | | | |
| COMMONSCENTS (HM04904) | | | | | | | ● | | | | | | | | | | | | | | | | | | | | | | | | | | | | | | | | | | | | | | | | | | | |
| CORLETT, D A (DR ) (HM05173) | | | | | | | | | | | | | | | | | | | | | | | | | | | ● | | | | | | | | | | | | | | | | | | | | | | | |
| CROWE, A (HM05504) | | | | | | | ● | | | | | | | | | | | | | | | | | | | | | | | | | | | | | | | | | | | | | | | | | | | |
| DESIGNING CHANGE (HM06022) | | | | | | | | | | | | | | | | | | | | | | | | | | | | | | | | | ● | | | | | | | | | | | | | | | | | |
| DIATHERMY CLINIC (HM06064) | | | | | | | | | | | | | | | | | | | | | | | | | | | | | | | | | | | | | | | | | | | | | | | ● | | | |
| EQUA-LIBRA (HM06863) | | | | | | | ● | | | | | | | | | | | | | | | | | | | | | | | | | ● | | | | | | | | | | | | | | | | | | |
| FIGURA, CATHERINE MARIA (HM07283) | | | | | | | ● | | | | | | | | | | | | | | | | | | | | | | | | | | | | | | | | | | | | | | | | | | | |
| FLOWERS AROMATICS (HM07436) | | | | | | | ● | | | | | | | | | | | | | | | | | | | | | | | | | | | | | | | | | | | | | | | | | | | |
| GILLESPIE, B (HM08086) | | | | | | | ● | | | | | | | | | | | | | | | | | | | | | | | | | | | | | | | | | | | | | | | | | | | |
| HALCYON AROMATICS (HM08724) | | | | | | | ● | | | | | | | | | | | | | | | | | | | | | | | | | | | | | | | | | | | | | | | | | | | |
| HAMER-BLOOM, S (HM08832) | | | | | | | | | | | | | | | | | | | | | | | | | | ● | | | | | | | | | | | | | | | | | | | | | | | | |
| HAMNETT, SHEILA (HM08870) | | | | ● | | | | | | | | | | | | | | | | | | | | | | | | | | | | | | | ● | | | | | | | | | | | | | | | |
| HANSON, S C (HM08944) | | | | | | | | | | | | | | | | | | | | | | ● | | | | | | | | | | | | | | ● | | | | | | | | | | | | | | |
| HEADINGLEY CHIROPRACTIC CLINIC (HM09305) | | | | | | | | | | | | | | | | | | | | | | | | | | | ● | | | | | | | | | | | | | | | | | | | | | | | |

www.healthmyself.com

# A - F Therapies at Practices/Businesses

| Business by County with Reference no. | Absent Healing | Acupressure | Acupuncture | Alexander Technique | Allergy Testing | Anthroposophical Med | Aromatherapy | Art Therapy | Aura Therapy | Auricular Therapy | Auto Suggestion | Autogenic Training | Aversion Therapy | Ayurvedic Medicine | Baby Massage | Bach Remedies | Bates Method | Beauty Therapy | Bio-energetics | Biofeedback | Biomagnetic Therapy | Biomechanics | Bonesetting | Bowen Therapy | Chinese Herbal Medicine |
|---|---|---|---|---|---|---|---|---|---|---|---|---|---|---|---|---|---|---|---|---|---|---|---|---|---|
| HEALTH CHAMBERS (HM09380) |  |  | ● |  |  |  |  |  |  |  |  |  |  |  |  |  |  |  |  |  |  |  |  |  | ● |
| HEBDEN BRIDGE CENTRE (HM09487) |  |  |  |  |  |  |  |  |  |  |  |  |  |  |  |  |  |  |  |  |  |  |  |  |  |
| HELEN BENTLEY COMP THERAPIST (HM09510) |  |  |  |  |  |  | ● |  |  |  |  |  |  |  |  |  |  |  |  |  |  |  |  |  |  |
| HERMITAGE OILS (HM09684) |  |  |  |  |  |  | ● |  |  |  |  |  |  |  |  |  |  |  |  |  |  |  |  |  |  |
| HILL, PETER J (HM09784) |  |  |  |  |  |  | ● |  |  |  |  |  |  |  |  |  |  |  |  |  |  |  |  |  |  |
| HOBSON, ANNE (HM09862) |  |  |  |  |  |  | ● |  |  |  |  |  |  |  |  |  |  |  |  |  |  |  |  |  |  |
| HOLME VALLEY SPORTS CLINIC (HM10036) |  |  | ● |  |  |  |  |  |  |  |  |  |  |  |  |  |  |  |  |  |  |  |  |  |  |
| HOLMFIRTH PHYSIO/SPORTS INJURY (HM10048) |  |  |  |  |  |  | ● |  |  |  |  |  |  |  |  |  |  |  |  |  |  | ● |  |  |  |
| HOMEOPATHIC MEDICAL PRACTICE (HM10076) |  |  |  |  |  |  |  |  |  |  |  |  |  |  |  |  |  |  |  |  |  |  |  |  |  |
| HOWDEN, LINDA (HM10260) |  |  | ● |  |  |  |  |  |  |  |  |  |  |  |  |  |  |  |  |  |  |  |  |  |  |
| HUNTER, REBECCA (HM10408) |  | ● | ● |  |  |  | ● |  |  |  |  |  |  |  |  |  |  |  |  |  |  |  |  |  |  |
| HUNTER, REBECCA () |  |  | ● |  |  |  |  |  |  |  |  |  |  |  |  |  |  |  |  |  |  |  |  |  |  |
| IDLE AROMATHERAPY (HM10574) |  |  |  |  |  |  | ● |  |  |  |  |  |  |  |  |  |  |  |  |  |  |  |  |  |  |
| J & J HARROP (HM10792) |  |  |  |  |  |  |  |  |  |  |  |  |  |  |  |  |  |  |  |  |  |  |  |  |  |
| JACKSON, ROGER D (HM10850) |  |  |  |  |  |  |  |  |  |  |  |  |  |  |  |  |  |  |  |  |  |  |  |  |  |
| JEAVONS, JO (HM10955) |  |  |  |  |  |  |  |  |  |  |  |  |  |  |  | ● |  |  |  |  |  |  |  |  |  |
| JULIA GREAVES NEW IMAGE (HM11255) |  |  |  |  |  |  | ● |  |  |  |  |  |  |  |  |  |  |  |  |  |  |  |  |  |  |
| KANG DA CLINIC (HM11313) |  | ● | ● |  |  |  |  |  |  |  |  |  |  |  |  | ● |  |  |  |  |  |  |  |  |  |
| KINGSMITH, ANNE-MARIE (HM11673) |  |  |  |  |  |  |  |  |  |  |  |  |  |  |  |  |  |  |  |  |  |  |  |  |  |
| KINNAIRD, F M (HM11686) |  |  |  |  |  |  |  |  |  |  |  |  | ● |  |  |  |  |  |  | ● |  |  |  |  |  |
| LAVENDER ROOMS (HM12025) |  |  |  |  |  |  | ● |  |  |  |  |  |  |  |  |  |  |  |  |  |  |  |  |  |  |
| LEEDS ACUPUNCTURE CLINIC (HM12153) |  |  | ● |  |  |  |  |  |  |  |  |  |  |  |  |  |  |  |  |  |  |  |  |  |  |
| LEEDS CHINESE MEDICAL CENTRE (HM12154) |  | ● | ● |  |  |  |  |  |  |  |  |  |  |  |  |  |  |  |  |  |  |  |  |  |  |
| LEEDS CHIROPRACTIC CENTRE (HM12156) |  |  |  |  |  |  |  |  |  |  |  |  |  |  |  |  |  |  |  |  |  |  |  |  |  |
| LEEDS COUNSELLING & PSYCHO SVS (HM12158) |  |  |  |  |  |  |  |  |  |  |  |  |  |  |  |  |  |  |  |  |  |  |  |  |  |
| LIKISMA (HM12383) |  |  |  |  |  |  | ● |  |  |  |  |  |  |  |  |  |  |  |  |  |  |  |  |  |  |
| MASSAGE BY ISOBEL (HM13259) |  |  |  |  |  |  | ● |  |  |  |  |  |  |  |  |  |  |  |  |  |  |  |  |  |  |
| MILLER, JULIE A (HM13893) |  |  |  |  |  |  | ● |  |  |  |  |  |  |  |  |  |  |  |  |  |  |  |  |  |  |
| MORLEY ACUPUNCTURE CLINIC (HM14180) |  |  | ● |  |  |  |  |  |  |  |  |  |  |  |  |  |  |  |  |  |  |  |  |  |  |
| MORNINGTON PHYSIOTHERAPY (HM14193) |  |  |  | ● |  |  |  |  |  |  |  |  |  |  |  |  |  |  |  |  |  |  |  |  |  |
| MR THERAPY (HM14309) |  |  |  |  |  |  | ● |  |  |  |  |  |  |  |  |  |  |  |  |  |  |  |  |  |  |
| NATURES WORKROOM (HM14705) |  |  |  |  |  |  | ● |  |  |  |  |  |  |  |  |  |  |  |  |  |  |  |  |  |  |
| NEWMARK, JOSPEHINE (HM14876) |  |  |  | ● |  |  |  |  |  |  |  |  |  |  |  |  |  |  |  |  |  |  |  |  |  |
| NOLAN, SARAH (HM14986) |  |  | ● |  |  |  |  |  |  |  |  |  |  |  |  |  |  |  |  |  |  |  |  |  |  |

| Business by County with Reference no. | Chiropody | Chiropractic | Clinical Ecology | Cognitive Therapy | Colonic Hydrotherapy | Colour Therapy | Complementary Therapy | Counselling | Cranial Osteopathy | Cranio-Sacral Therapy | Cryo Surgery | Crystal Healing | Cupping | Cymatics | Dance Movement Thrpy | Dietician | Do-In | Douching | Dowsing | Drama Therapy | Electrolipolysis | Electrolysis | Electrotherapy | Encounter Groups | Faith Healing |
|---|---|---|---|---|---|---|---|---|---|---|---|---|---|---|---|---|---|---|---|---|---|---|---|---|---|
| HEALTH CHAMBERS (HM09380) |  |  |  |  |  |  |  |  |  |  |  |  |  |  |  |  |  |  |  |  |  |  |  |  |  |
| HEBDEN BRIDGE CENTRE (HM09487) |  |  |  | ● |  |  |  | ● |  |  |  |  |  |  |  |  |  |  |  |  |  |  |  |  |  |
| HELEN BENTLEY COMP THERAPIST (HM09510) |  |  |  |  |  |  |  |  |  |  |  |  |  |  |  |  |  |  |  |  |  |  |  |  |  |
| HERMITAGE OILS (HM09684) |  |  |  |  |  |  |  |  |  |  |  |  |  |  |  |  |  |  |  |  |  |  |  |  |  |
| HILL, PETER J (HM09784) |  |  |  |  |  |  |  |  |  |  |  |  |  |  |  |  |  |  |  |  |  |  |  |  |  |
| HOBSON, ANNE (HM09862) |  |  |  |  |  |  |  |  |  |  |  |  |  |  |  |  |  |  |  |  |  |  |  |  |  |
| HOLME VALLEY SPORTS CLINIC (HM10036) |  |  |  |  |  |  |  |  |  |  |  |  |  |  |  |  |  |  |  |  |  |  |  |  |  |
| HOLMFIRTH PHYSIO/SPORTS INJURY (HM10048) | ● |  |  |  |  |  |  |  |  |  |  |  |  |  |  |  |  |  |  |  |  |  |  |  |  |
| HOMEOPATHIC MEDICAL PRACTICE (HM10076) |  |  |  |  |  |  | ● |  |  |  |  |  |  |  |  |  |  |  |  |  |  |  |  |  |  |
| HOWDEN, LINDA (HM10260) |  |  |  |  |  |  |  |  |  |  |  |  |  |  |  |  |  |  |  |  |  |  |  |  |  |
| HUNTER, REBECCA (HM10408) |  |  |  |  |  |  |  |  |  |  |  |  |  |  |  |  |  |  |  |  |  |  |  |  |  |
| HUNTER, REBECCA () |  |  |  |  |  |  |  |  |  |  |  |  |  |  |  |  |  |  |  |  |  |  |  |  |  |
| IDLE AROMATHERAPY (HM10574) |  |  |  |  |  |  |  |  |  |  |  |  |  |  |  |  |  |  |  |  |  |  |  |  |  |
| J & J HARROP (HM10792) | ● |  |  |  |  |  |  |  |  |  |  |  |  |  |  |  |  |  |  |  |  |  |  |  |  |
| JACKSON, ROGER D (HM10850) |  |  |  |  |  |  |  |  |  |  |  |  |  |  |  |  |  |  |  |  |  |  | ● |  |  |
| JEAVONS, JO (HM10955) |  |  |  |  |  |  |  |  |  |  |  |  |  |  |  |  |  |  |  |  |  |  |  |  |  |
| JULIA GREAVES NEW IMAGE (HM11255) |  |  |  |  |  |  |  |  |  |  |  |  |  |  |  |  |  |  |  |  |  |  |  |  |  |
| KANG DA CLINIC (HM11313) |  | ● |  |  |  |  | ● |  | ● |  |  |  | ● |  |  |  |  |  |  |  |  |  |  |  |  |
| KINGSMITH, ANNE-MARIE (HM11673) | ● |  |  |  |  |  |  |  |  |  |  |  |  |  |  |  |  |  |  |  |  |  |  |  |  |
| KINNAIRD, F M (HM11686) |  |  |  | ● |  |  |  | ● |  |  |  |  |  |  |  |  |  |  |  |  |  |  |  |  |  |
| LAVENDER ROOMS (HM12025) |  |  |  |  |  |  |  |  |  |  |  |  |  |  |  |  |  |  |  |  |  |  |  |  |  |
| LEEDS ACUPUNCTURE CLINIC (HM12153) |  |  |  |  |  |  |  |  |  |  |  |  |  |  |  |  |  |  |  |  |  |  |  |  |  |
| LEEDS CHINESE MEDICAL CENTRE (HM12154) |  |  |  |  |  |  |  |  |  |  |  |  |  |  |  |  |  |  |  |  |  |  |  |  |  |
| LEEDS CHIROPRACTIC CENTRE (HM12156) |  | ● |  |  |  |  |  |  |  |  |  |  |  |  |  |  |  |  |  |  |  |  |  |  |  |
| LEEDS COUNSELLING & PSYCHO SVS (HM12158) |  |  |  | ● |  |  |  | ● |  |  |  |  |  |  |  |  |  |  |  |  |  |  |  |  |  |
| LIKISMA (HM12383) |  |  |  |  |  |  |  |  |  |  |  |  |  |  |  |  |  |  |  |  |  |  |  |  |  |
| MASSAGE BY ISOBEL (HM13259) |  |  |  |  |  |  |  |  |  |  |  |  |  |  |  |  |  |  |  |  |  |  |  |  |  |
| MILLER, JULIE A (HM13893) |  |  |  |  |  |  |  |  |  |  |  |  |  |  |  |  |  |  |  |  |  |  |  |  |  |
| MORLEY ACUPUNCTURE CLINIC (HM14180) |  |  |  |  |  |  | ● |  |  |  |  |  | ● |  |  |  |  |  | ● |  |  |  |  |  |  |
| MORNINGTON PHYSIOTHERAPY (HM14193) | ● |  |  |  |  |  |  |  |  |  |  |  |  |  |  |  |  |  |  |  |  |  | ● |  |  |
| MR THERAPY (HM14309) |  |  |  |  |  |  |  |  |  |  |  |  |  |  |  |  |  |  |  |  |  |  |  |  |  |
| NATURES WORKROOM (HM14705) |  |  |  |  |  |  |  |  |  |  |  |  |  |  |  |  |  |  |  |  |  |  |  |  |  |
| NEWMARK, JOSPEHINE (HM14876) |  |  |  |  |  |  |  |  |  |  |  |  |  |  |  |  |  |  |  |  |  |  |  |  |  |
| NOLAN, SARAH (HM14986) |  |  |  |  |  |  |  |  |  |  |  |  |  |  |  |  |  |  |  |  |  |  |  |  |  |

# A - F Therapies at Practices/Businesses

| Business by County with Reference no. | Absent Healing | Acupressure | Acupuncture | Alexander Technique | Allergy Testing | Anthroposohical Med | Aromatherapy | Art Therapy | Aura Therapy | Auricular Therapy | Auto Suggestion | Autogenic Training | Aversion Therapy | Ayurvedic Medicine | Baby Massage | Bach Remedies | Bates Method | Beauty Therapy | Bio-energetics | Biofeedback | Biomagnetic Therapy | Biomechanics | Bonesetting | Bowen Therapy | Chinese Herbal Medicine |
|---|---|---|---|---|---|---|---|---|---|---|---|---|---|---|---|---|---|---|---|---|---|---|---|---|---|
| NORTH & SOUTH (HM15018) | | | | | | | ● | | | | | | | | | | | | | | | | | | |
| NRTH LEEDS PHYSIO/SPRTS INJ (HM15091) | | | ● | | | | | | | | | | | | | | | | | | | | | | |
| ORANGE TREE (HM15356) | | | | | | | ● | | | | | | | | | | | | | | | | | | |
| O'SULLIVAN, FRANCES (HM15482) | | | | | | | | | | | | | | | | ● | | | | | | | | | |
| P A AROMATHERAPY (HM15547) | | | | | | | ● | | | | | | | | | | | | | | | | | | |
| PALLAS, ANDREW (HM15595) | | | | | | | | | | | | | | | | | | | | | | | | | |
| PALMER, S F (HM15614) | | | | | | | | | | | | | | | | | | | | | | | | | |
| PAYNE, AUDREY (HM15861) | | | | | | | | | | | | | | | | | | | | | | | | | |
| PONTEFRACT CHIROPRACTIC CLINIC (HM16424) | | | | | | | | | | | | | | | | | | | | | | | | | |
| POPPLEWELL, MARK (HM16437) | | ● | ● | | | | | | | | | | | | | | | | | | | | | | |
| PRASAD, B (HM16527) | | | ● | | | | | | | | | | | | | | | | | | | | | | |
| PRESTON, CATHY (HM16551) | | | | | | | | | | | ● | | | | | | | | | | | | | | |
| RICHARDSON CLINIC (HM17266) | | | ● | | | | ● | | | | | | | | | | | | | | | | | | |
| ROTHWELL SPORTS CENTRE (HM17658) | | | ● | | | | | | | | | | | | | | | | | | | | | | |
| ROUNDHAY CHIROPRACTIC CLINIC (HM17667) | | | | | | | | | | | | | | | | | | | | | | | | | |
| RUTH, GORDON (HM17778) | | | | | | | ● | | | | | | | | | | | | | | | | | | |
| SALTAIRE COMP HEALTH STUDIO (HM17864) | | | | | | | ● | | | | | | | | | | | | | | | | | | |
| SEVITT, E A (HM18251) | | | | | | | | | | | | | | | | | | | | | | | | | |
| SHACKLETON, JOHN A (HM18263) | | | | | | | | | | | | | | | | | | | | | | | | | |
| SHEN ACUPUNCTURE CLINIC (HM18390) | | | ● | | | | | | | | | | | | | | | | | | | | | | |
| SMITH, JANET (HM18751) | | | | | | | | | | | | | | | | | | | | | | | | ● | |
| STEAD, JULIE ANN (HM19164) | | | | | | | | | | | | | | | | | | | | | | | | | |
| SURGERY (HM19519) | | ● | ● | | | | | | | | | | | | | | | | | | | | | | |
| SWAINE, PAULA (HM19565) | | | | | | | | | | | | | | | | | | | | | | | | | |
| SWIFT, CAROL I (HM19591) | | | | | | | ● | | | | | | | | | | | | | | | | | | |
| WAKEFIELD CHIROPRACTIC CLINIC (HM20743) | | | | | | | | | | | | | | | | | | | | | | | | | |
| WALDENBERG, HILARY (HM20751) | | | | | | | ● | | | | | | | | | | | | | | | | | | |
| WELSH, P A (HM21186) | | | | | | | | | | | | | | | | | | | | | | | | | |
| WENDY ROBINSON ACUPUNCTURE (HM21199) | | | ● | | | | | | | | | | | | | | | | | | | | | | |
| WEST YORKSHIRE CLINIC (HM21242) | | ● | ● | | | | | | | | | | | | | | | | | | | | | | |
| WEST YORKSHIRE PHYSIO CENTRE (HM21244) | | | ● | | | | | | | | | | | | | | | | | | | | | | |
| WETHERBY PHYSIO PRACTICE (HM21290) | | | ● | | | | | | | | | | | | | | | | | | | | | | |
| WIDDOPP, BRIAN (HM21455) | | | | ● | | | | | | | | | | | | | | | | | | | | | |
| WOODHOUSE CLINIC (HM21826) | | | | | | | | | | | | | | | | | | | | | | | | | |

| Business by County with Reference no. | Chiropody | Chiropractic | Clinical Ecology | Cognitive Therapy | Colonic Hydrotherapy | Colour Therapy | Complementary Therapy | Counselling | Cranial Osteopathy | Cranio-Sacral Therapy | Cryo Surgery | Crystal Healing | Cupping | Cymatics | Dance Movement Thrpy | Dietician | Do-In | Douching | Dowsing | Drama Therapy | Electrolipolysis | Electrolysis | Electrotherapy | Encounter Groups | Faith Healing |
|---|---|---|---|---|---|---|---|---|---|---|---|---|---|---|---|---|---|---|---|---|---|---|---|---|---|
| NORTH & SOUTH (HM15018) | | | | | | | | | | | | | | | | | | | | | | | | | |
| NRTH LEEDS PHYSIO/SPRTS INJ (HM15091) | | | | | | | | | | | | | | | | | | | | | | | ● | | |
| ORANGE TREE (HM15356) | | | | | | | | | | | | | | | | | | | | | | | | | |
| O'SULLIVAN, FRANCES (HM15482) | | | | | | | | | | | | | | | | | | | | | | | | | |
| P A AROMATHERAPY (HM15547) | | | | | | | | | | | | | | | | | | | | | | | | | |
| PALLAS, ANDREW (HM15595) | | | | | | | | | ● | | | | | | | | | | | | | | | | |
| PALMER, S F (HM15614) | | ● | | | | | | | | | | | | | | | | | | | | | | | |
| PAYNE, AUDREY (HM15861) | | | | | | | ● | | | | | | | | | | | | | | | | | | |
| PONTEFRACT CHIROPRACTIC CLINIC (HM16424) | | ● | | | | | | | | | | | | | | | | | | | | | | | |
| POPPLEWELL, MARK (HM16437) | | | | | | | | | | | | | ● | | | | | | | | | | | | |
| PRASAD, B (HM16527) | | | | | | | | | | | | | | | | | | | | | | | | | |
| PRESTON, CATHY (HM16551) | | | | | | | ● | ● | | | | | | | | | | | | | | | | | |
| RICHARDSON CLINIC (HM17266) | ● | | | | | | | ● | | | | | | | | | | | | | | | | | |
| ROTHWELL SPORTS CENTRE (HM17658) | | | | | | | | | | | | | | | | | | | | | | | | | |
| ROUNDHAY CHIROPRACTIC CLINIC (HM17667) | | ● | | | | | | | | | | | | | | | | | | | | | | | |
| RUTH, GORDON (HM17778) | | | | | | | | | | | | | | | | | | | | | | | | | |
| SALTAIRE COMP HEALTH STUDIO (HM17864) | | | | | | | | | | | | | | | | | | | | | | | | | |
| SEVITT, E A (HM18251) | ● | | | | | | | | | | | | | | | | | | | | | | | | |
| SHACKLETON, JOHN A (HM18263) | ● | | | | | | | | | | | | | | | | | | | | | | | | |
| SHEN ACUPUNCTURE CLINIC (HM18390) | | | | | | | | | | | | | | | | | | | | | | | | | |
| SMITH, JANET (HM18751) | | | | | | | | | | | | | | | | | | | | | | | | | |
| STEAD, JULIE ANN (HM19164) | ● | | | | | | | | | | | | | | | | | | | | | | | | |
| SURGERY (HM19519) | ● | | | | | | | | | | | | | | | | | | | | | | ● | | |
| SWAINE, PAULA (HM19565) | ● | | | | | | | | | | | | | | | | | | | | | | | | |
| SWIFT, CAROL I (HM19591) | | | | | | | | | | | | | | | | | | | | | | | | | |
| WAKEFIELD CHIROPRACTIC CLINIC (HM20743) | | ● | | | | | | | | | | | | | | | | | | | | | | | |
| WALDENBERG, HILARY (HM20751) | | | | | | | | | | | | | | | | | | | | | | | | | |
| WELSH, P A (HM21186) | | ● | | | | | | | | | | | | | | | | | | | | | | | |
| WENDY ROBINSON ACUPUNCTURE (HM21199) | | | | | | | | | | | | | | | | | | | | | | | | | |
| WEST YORKSHIRE CLINIC (HM21242) | | | | | | | ● | | | | | | | | | | | | | | | | | | |
| WEST YORKSHIRE PHYSIO CENTRE (HM21244) | | | | | | | | | | | | | | | | | | | | | | | | | |
| WETHERBY PHYSIO PRACTICE (HM21290) | | | | | | | | | | | | | | | | | | | | | | | | | |
| WIDDOPP, BRIAN (HM21455) | | | | | | | | | | | | | | | | | | | | | | | | | |
| WOODHOUSE CLINIC (HM21826) | ● | | | | | | ● | | ● | | | | | | | | | | | | | | ● | | |

# A - F Therapies at Practices/Businesses

| Business by County with Reference no. | Absent Healing | Acupressure | Acupuncture | Alexander Technique | Allergy Testing | Anthroposohical Med | Aromatherapy | Art Therapy | Aura Therapy | Auricular Therapy | Auto Suggestion | Autogenic Training | Aversion Therapy | Ayurvedic Medicine | Baby Massage | Bach Remedies | Bates Method | Beauty Therapy | Bio-energetics | Biofeedback | Biomagnetic Therapy | Biomechanics | Bonesetting | Bowen Therapy | Chinese Herbal Medicine | Chiropody | Chiropractic | Clinical Ecology | Cognitive Therapy | Colonic Hydrotherapy | Colour Therapy | Complementary Therapy | Counselling | Cranial Osteopathy | Cranio-Sacral Therapy | Cryo Surgery | Crystal Healing | Cupping | Cymatics | Dance Movement Thrpy | Dietician | Do-In | Douching | Dowsing | Drama Therapy | Electrolipolysis | Electrolysis | Electrotherapy | Encounter Groups | Faith Healing |
|---|---|---|---|---|---|---|---|---|---|---|---|---|---|---|---|---|---|---|---|---|---|---|---|---|---|---|---|---|---|---|---|---|---|---|---|---|---|---|---|---|---|---|---|---|---|---|---|---|---|---|
| IRELAND ||||||||||||||||||||||||||||||||||||||||||||||||||||
| COUNTY CAVAN ||||||||||||||||||||||||||||||||||||||||||||||||||||
| BI-AURA THERAPY (HM02274) |||||||||●||||||||||●|||||||||||||||||||||||||||||||||
| COUNTY CLARE ||||||||||||||||||||||||||||||||||||||||||||||||||||
| SIMONS, ROBERT ALLEN (DR) (HM18572) |||||||||||||||||||||||||||||||||●|||||||||||||||||||
| COUNTY CORK ||||||||||||||||||||||||||||||||||||||||||||||||||||
| ANNAPURNA NATURAL HEALTHCARE (HM00894) ||●|||||●||||||||||||||||||||||||||||||●|||||||||||||||||
| BANDON CHIROPRACTIC CLINIC (HM01653) |||||||||||||||||||||||||||●|||||||||||||||||||||||||
| EAST CORK PHYSIOTHERAPY (HM06511) ||●|●|||||||||||||||||||●||||||||||||●||||||●|||||||||||||||●|||
| HATTERSLEY, LAURENCE (HM09200) |||||||||||||||||●|||||||||||||||||||●||||||||||||||||||||●|||
| HEALING THERAPIES (HM09354) |●||||||||●||||||||||||||||||||||||||||||||||||||||||
| INS-CLINICAL HYP & PSYCHO (HM10661) |||||||||●||●|●|●|||||||●|||||||||||●||●|●|●|||||||||||||||||||●|
| JONES, COLEEN (HM11131) |||||||||||||||||||||||||||||||||●|||||||||||||||||||
| KEATING, MARY (HM11379) |||●||||||||||||||||||||||||||||||||||||●||||||||||||||
| MOORE-GROACKE, GILLIAN (DR) (HM14136) |||||||||||||||||||||||||||||●||||●|||||||||||||||||||
| PAUL DENNEHY - HYPNOTHERAPIST (HM15842) |||||||||||●|●|●||||||||||||||||||||||●|●||||||||||||||||●|||||●|
| RAVEN HILL CHIROPRACTIC CLINIC (HM16964) |||||||||||||||||||||||||||●|||||||||||||||||||||||||
| SHIATSU (HM18452) ||●||||||||||||||●|||||||||||||||||||||||●||||||●|||||||||||
| COUNTY DUBLIN ||||||||||||||||||||||||||||||||||||||||||||||||||||
| ABELIA COUNSELLING (HM00110) |||||||||||||||||||||||||||||||||●|||||||||||||||||||
| ARDAGH ACUPUNCTURE CLINIC (HM00988) |||●||||||||||||||||||||||||||||||●|||||●||||||||||||||
| ARDUNA COUNS & PSYCHOTHPY CTRE (HM00995) |||||||||||||||||||||||||||||●||||●|||||||||||||||||||
| BREE, JOHN (HM02947) |●||||||||||||||||||||||||||||||||●|||||||||||||||||||
| B-WELL HYPNOTHERAPY CLINIC (HM03506) |●|●|||||||●||●||||||||●|||||||||||||||||||||||||||||||||
| CHADHA, PRADEEP K (DR) (HM03933) |||||||||||||||||||||||||||||●||||●|||||||||||||||||||
| FAIRVIEW THERAPY CENTRE (HM07066) ||●|●||||●|||||||||||||●||||||||||||||●|||||||||||||||||||
| FINISHING TOUCHES (HM07313) |||||||●||||||||||||||||||||||||||||||||||||||||||||
| HEALING PLACE (HM09347) |||||||||||||||||||||||||||||||||||●|||||||||||||||||
| HEALING ROOM - DRUMCONDRA (HM09351) |||||||●||||||||||||||||||||||||||||||||||||||||||||
| HEALTH COUNSEL (HM09384) |||||||||||●|●|||||||||||||||||||||||●||||||||||||||||||||
| HERBAL & ACUPUNCTURE (HM09595) |||●|||||||||||||||||||||||||||||||||||||||||||||||||
| HERBAL HEALTH SERVICES (HM09618) |||●|||||||||||||||||||||||||||||||||||||||||||||||||
| HOWTH COUNSELLING SERVICE (HM10294) ||||||||●|||||●|●|||||||||||||||||●|●||●||||||||||||||||||||||

# A - F Therapies at Practices/Businesses

Business by County with Reference no.

| Business | Absent Healing | Acupressure | Acupuncture | Alexander Technique | Allergy Testing | Anthroposohical Med | Aromatherapy | Art Therapy | Aura Therapy | Auricular Therapy | Auto Suggestion | Autogenic Training | Aversion Therapy | Ayurvedic Medicine | Baby Massage | Bach Remedies | Bates Method | Beauty Therapy | Bio-energetics | Biofeedback | Biomagnetic Therapy | Biomechanics | Bonesetting | Bowen Therapy | Chinese Herbal Medicine | Chiropody | Chiropractic | Clinical Ecology | Cognitive Therapy | Colonic Hydrotherapy | Colour Therapy | Complementary Therapy | Counselling | Cranial Osteopathy | Cranio-Sacral Therapy | Cryo Surgery | Crystal Healing | Cupping | Cymatics | Dance Movement Thrpy | Dietician | Do-In | Douching | Dowsing | Drama Therapy | Electrolipolysis | Electrolysis | Electrotherapy | Encounter Groups | Faith Healing |
|---|---|---|---|---|---|---|---|---|---|---|---|---|---|---|---|---|---|---|---|---|---|---|---|---|---|---|---|---|---|---|---|---|---|---|---|---|---|---|---|---|---|---|---|---|---|---|---|---|---|---|
| INNER CIRCLE HEALING CENTRE (HM10635) | ● | | ● | | | | ● | | | | | | | | | | | | | | | | | | | | | | | | | ● | | | | | ● | | | | | | | ● | | | | | | |
| INSTITUTE OF PSYCHOSOCIAL MED (HM10678) | | | ● | | | | | | | | | | | | | | | | | | | | | | | | | | | | | | ● | | | | | | | | | | | | | | | | | ● |
| KELLY, ANGELINA (HM11427) | | | | | | | | | | | | | | | | ● | | | | | | | | | | | | | | | | | | | | | | | | | | | | | | | | | | |
| LALLOO'S ACUPUNCTURE CLINIC (HM11881) | ● | ● | ● | | | | ● | | | | | | | | | ● | | | | | | | | | | | | | | | ● | ● | | | | | | | | | | | | | | | | ● | | |
| LITTLEJOHN CLINIC (HM12472) | | | | | | | | | | | | | | | | | | | | | | | | | | | | | | | | | ● | ● | | | | | | | | | | | | | | | | |
| MACLIAM, FIONNULA (HM12867) | | | | | | | | | | | | | | | | | | | | | | | | | | | | | ● | | | | | | | | | | | | | | | | | | | | | |
| MCHUGH HYPNOSIS & REFLEXOLOGY (HM13509) | | | | | | | | | | | | | | | | | | | | | | | | | | | | | ● | | | | ● | | | | | | | | | | | | | | | | | |
| MELT/TEMPLE BAR NATURAL (HM13716) | | ● | ● | | | | ● | ● | ● | | | | | | | ● | | | | | | | | | | | | | | | ● | | ● | | | | | ● | | ● | | | | | | | | | | |
| NATURAL SOLUTIONS (HM14625) | ● | | | | | | | | | | | | | | | | | | | | | | | | | | | | | | | ● | ● | | | | | | | | ● | | | | | | | | | |
| NUALA WOULFE BEAUTY SALON (HM15101) | | ● | | | | | ● | | | | | | | | | | | | | | | | | | | | | | | | | | | | | | | | | | | | | | | | | ● | | |
| RATHMINES CHIROPRACTIC CENTRE (HM16957) | | | | | | | | | | | | | | | | | | | | | | | | | | | ● | | | | | | | ● | | | | | | | | | | | | | | | | |
| T C M CENTRE (HM19639) | | ● | ● | | | | | | | | | | | | | | | | ● | | | | ● | | | | ● | | | | | ● | ● | | | | | ● | | | ● | | | | | | | | | |
| THERAPEUTICS (HM19888) | | | | | | | ● | | | | | | | | | | | | | | | | | | | | | | | | | | | | | | | | | | | | | | | | | | | |
| THEW, NIN (HM19916) | | | ● | | | | | | | | | | | | | | | | | | | | | | | | | | | | | | | | | | | ● | | | | | | | | | | | | |
| TOBIN, ROSALEEN (HM20105) | ● | | | | | | | | | | | | | | | | | | | | | | | | | | | | | | ● | | ● | | | | | | | | | | | | | | | | | |
| TRAD CHINESE MEDICINE/MASSAGE (HM20216) | | ● | ● | | | | ● | | | | | | | | | | | | | | | | | | | | | | | | | | | | | | | | | | | | | | | | | | | |
| TROY, ROSEMARY (HM20349) | | | | | | | | | | | | | | | | | | | | | | | | | | | | | | | | | ● | | | | | | | | | | | | | | | | | |
| **COUNTY GALWAY** | | | | | | | | | | | | | | | | | | | | | | | | | | | | | | | | | | | | | | | | | | | | | | | | | | |
| ALEXANDER TECHNIQUE CENTRE (HM00557) | | | | ● | | | | | | | | | | | | | | | | | | | | | | | | | | | | | | | | | | | | | | | | | | | | | | |
| BODYWATCH (HM02636) | | | | | | | | | | | | | | | | | | | | | | | | | | | | | | | | ● | ● | | | | | | | | | | | | | | | | | |
| IRWIN, MARY (HM10752) | | | | | | | ● | | | | | | | | | | | | | | | | | | | | | | | | | | | | | | | | | | | | | | | | | | | |
| O'COLMAIN, AIDAN (DR) (HM15203) | | | ● | | | | | | | | | | | | | | | | | | | | | | | | | | | | | | | | | | | | | | | | | | | | | | | |
| PRENDERGAST, KARL (HM16542) | | | | | | | | | | | | | | | | | | | | | | | | | | | | | | | | | | ● | | | | | | | | | | | | | | | | |
| PSYCHOL & FAMILY THRPY PRACT (HM16699) | | | | | | | | | | | | | | | | | | | | | | | | | | | | | | | | | ● | | | | | | | | | | | | | | | | | |
| **COUNTY KERRY** | | | | | | | | | | | | | | | | | | | | | | | | | | | | | | | | | | | | | | | | | | | | | | | | | | |
| ACUPUNCTURE CLINIC (HM00286) | | | ● | | | | | | | | | | | | | | | | | | | | | | | | | | | | | | | | | | | ● | | | | | | | | | | | | |
| WOODLAWN HOLISTIC THERAPY CTRE (HM21834) | | ● | | | | | ● | | | | | | | | | ● | | | | | | | | | | | | | | | ● | | | | | | | | | | | | | | | | | | | |
| **COUNTY KILDARE** | | | | | | | | | | | | | | | | | | | | | | | | | | | | | | | | | | | | | | | | | | | | | | | | | | |
| GREEN ROAD HEALING CENTRE (HM08441) | | | | | | | ● | | | | | | | | | ● | | | | | | | | | | | | | | | | ● | | | | | | | | | | | | | | | | | | |
| SHENANDOAH HEALING (HM18395) | ● | | | | | | | | ● | | | | | | | ● | | | | | | | | | | | | | | | | ● | | | | | | | | | | | | ● | | | | | | |
| **COUNTY KILKENNY** | | | | | | | | | | | | | | | | | | | | | | | | | | | | | | | | | | | | | | | | | | | | | | | | | | |
| BLUE ROOM (HM02528) | ● | | | | | | | ● | | | | | | | | ● | | | ● | | | | | | | | | | | | | ● | ● | | | | | | | ● | | | | | | | | | | ● |
| DULCAMARA (HM06375) | | | | | | ● | | | | | | | | | | | | | | | | | | | | | | | | | | | | | | | | | | | | | | | | | | | | |
| HOLISTIC HEALING CENTRE (HM09965) | | | | | | | ● | | | | ● | | | | | | | | | | | | | | | | | | | | | | ● | | | | | | | | | | | ● | | | | | | |

www.healthmyself.com

# A - F Therapies at Practices/Businesses

| Business by County with Reference no. | Absent Healing | Acupressure | Acupuncture | Alexander Technique | Allergy Testing | Anthroposohical Med | Aromatherapy | Art Therapy | Aura Therapy | Auricular Therapy | Auto Suggestion | Autogenic Training | Aversion Therapy | Ayurvedic Medicine | Baby Massage | Bach Remedies | Bates Method | Beauty Therapy | Bio-energetics | Biofeedback | Biomagnetic Therapy | Biomechanics | Bonesetting | Bowen Therapy | Chinese Herbal Medicine |
|---|---|---|---|---|---|---|---|---|---|---|---|---|---|---|---|---|---|---|---|---|---|---|---|---|---|
| COUNTY LIMERICK | | | | | | | | | | | | | | | | | | | | | | | | | |
| HOLISTIC HEALING (HM09960) | ● | ● | | | | | ● | | | | | | | | | | | | ● | | | | | | |
| COUNTY LONGFORD | | | | | | | | | | | | | | | | | | | | | | | | | |
| LONGFORD BEAUTY CLINIC (HM12626) | | | | | | | ● | | | | | | | | | | | | | | | | | | |
| COUNTY LOUTH | | | | | | | | | | | | | | | | | | | | | | | | | |
| HOLISTIC SOL NTRL HEALING CTRE (HM09989) | | | | | | | | | | | ● | | | | | | | | | | | | | | |
| COUNTY MAYO | | | | | | | | | | | | | | | | | | | | | | | | | |
| NATURAL HEALING CENTRE (HM14547) | ● | ● | | | | | | | ● | | | | | | | ● | ● | | | | | | | | |
| TOBAR PHADRAIC (HM20102) | ● | | | | | | ● | | | | | | | | | | | | ● | | | | | | |
| COUNTY MEATH | | | | | | | | | | | | | | | | | | | | | | | | | |
| NATURAL MEDICINE CENTRE (HM14610) | | ● | ● | | | | | | | | | | | | | ● | | | | | | | | | |
| COUNTY MONAGHAN | | | | | | | | | | | | | | | | | | | | | | | | | |
| AROMA - ZONE (HM01043) | | | | | | | ● | | | | | | | | | | | | | | | | | | |
| HEALTHY CHOICES (HM09426) | | | ● | | | | ● | | | | | | | | | ● | | | | | | | | | |
| NORTHAMBER (HM15050) | | ● | ● | | | | | | | | | | | | | ● | | | | | | | | | |
| COUNTY ROSCOMMON | | | | | | | | | | | | | | | | | | | | | | | | | |
| HOLISTIC HEALTH FARM (HM09980) | | | | | | | ● | | | | | | | ● | | ● | | | | | | | | | |
| COUNTY SLIGO | | | | | | | | | | | | | | | | | | | | | | | | | |
| ANAM CHARA COUNSELLING (HM00802) | | | | | | | | ● | | | | | | | | | | | | | | | | | |
| SLIGO CHIROPRACTIC (HM18686) | | | | | | | | | | | | | | | | | | | | | | | | | |
| COUNTY TIPPERARY | | | | | | | | | | | | | | | | | | | | | | | | | |
| KINSELLA, MARIE (HM11693) | | | | | | | | | | | | | | | | | | | | | | | | | |
| COUNTY WESTMEATH | | | | | | | | | | | | | | | | | | | | | | | | | |
| HOWE, JAN (HM10263) | | ● | | | | | | | | | | | | | | | | | | | | | | | |
| COUNTY WEXFORD | | | | | | | | | | | | | | | | | | | | | | | | | |
| FOURTH MOUNTAIN HOM AND ACU (HM07622) | | | ● | | | | | | | | | | | | | | | | | | | | | | |
| MURPHY, MARY (HM14388) | | | | | | | | | | | | | | | | | | | | | | | | | |
| COUNTY WICKLOW | | | | | | | | | | | | | | | | | | | | | | | | | |
| ARKLOW NATURAL HEALING CENTRE (HM01007) | | | | | | | | | | | | | | | | ● | | | | | | | | | |
| HOLISTIC OPTIONS (HM09985) | | | | | | | ● | | | | | | | | | | | | | | | | | | |
| JAMESON PERSONAL EXCELLENCE (HM10903) | ● | | | | | | | | | | ● | | ● | | | | | | | | | | | | |
| MARK GOULDING - ACUPUNCTURIST (HM13107) | | ● | ● | | | | | | | | | | | | | | | | | | | | | | |

| Business by County with Reference no. | Chiropody | Chiropractic | Clinical Ecology | Cognitive Therapy | Colonic Hydrotherapy | Colour Therapy | Complementary Therapy | Counselling | Cranial Osteopathy | Cranio-Sacral Therapy | Cryo Surgery | Crystal Healing | Cupping | Cymatics | Dance Movement Thrpy | Dietician | Do-In | Douching | Dowsing | Drama Therapy | Electrolipolysis | Electrolysis | Electrotherapy | Encounter Groups | Faith Healing |
|---|---|---|---|---|---|---|---|---|---|---|---|---|---|---|---|---|---|---|---|---|---|---|---|---|---|
| COUNTY LIMERICK | | | | | | | | | | | | | | | | | | | | | | | | | |
| HOLISTIC HEALING (HM09960) | | | | | | | | | | | | | | | | | | | | | | | | | |
| COUNTY LONGFORD | | | | | | | | | | | | | | | | | | | | | | | | | |
| LONGFORD BEAUTY CLINIC (HM12626) | | | | | | | | | | | | | | | | | | | | | | | | | |
| COUNTY LOUTH | | | | | | | | | | | | | | | | | | | | | | | | | |
| HOLISTIC SOL NTRL HEALING CTRE (HM09989) | | | | | | | | | | | | | | | | | | | | | | | | | |
| COUNTY MAYO | | | | | | | | | | | | | | | | | | | | | | | | | |
| NATURAL HEALING CENTRE (HM14547) | | | | | | ● | ● | ● | | | | ● | | | ● | | | | | | | | | | |
| TOBAR PHADRAIC (HM20102) | | | | | | | ● | | | | | | | | | ● | ● | | | | | | | | |
| COUNTY MEATH | | | | | | | | | | | | | | | | | | | | | | | | | |
| NATURAL MEDICINE CENTRE (HM14610) | | | | | | | | | | | | | ● | | | | | | | | | | | | |
| COUNTY MONAGHAN | | | | | | | | | | | | | | | | | | | | | | | | | |
| AROMA - ZONE (HM01043) | | | | | | | | | | | | | | | | | | | | | | | | | |
| HEALTHY CHOICES (HM09426) | | | | | | ● | ● | | | | | ● | | | | | | | | | | | | | |
| NORTHAMBER (HM15050) | | ● | | | | | ● | ● | | | | | ● | | | | | | | | | | | | |
| COUNTY ROSCOMMON | | | | | | | | | | | | | | | | | | | | | | | | | |
| HOLISTIC HEALTH FARM (HM09980) | | | | | | | | ● | | | | ● | | | | | | | | | | | | | |
| COUNTY SLIGO | | | | | | | | | | | | | | | | | | | | | | | | | |
| ANAM CHARA COUNSELLING (HM00802) | | | | ● | | | | ● | | | | | | | | | | | | | | | | | |
| SLIGO CHIROPRACTIC (HM18686) | | ● | | | | | | | | | | | | | | | | | | | | | | | |
| COUNTY TIPPERARY | | | | | | | | | | | | | | | | | | | | | | | | | |
| KINSELLA, MARIE (HM11693) | | | | ● | | | | ● | | | | | | | | | | | | | | | | | |
| COUNTY WESTMEATH | | | | | | | | | | | | | | | | | | | | | | | | | |
| HOWE, JAN (HM10263) | | | | | | | | | | | | | | | | | ● | | | | | | | | |
| COUNTY WEXFORD | | | | | | | | | | | | | | | | | | | | | | | | | |
| FOURTH MOUNTAIN HOM AND ACU (HM07622) | | | | | | | | | | | | | | | | | | | | | | | | | |
| MURPHY, MARY (HM14388) | | | | ● | | | | ● | | | | | | | | | | | | | | | | ● | |
| COUNTY WICKLOW | | | | | | | | | | | | | | | | | | | | | | | | | |
| ARKLOW NATURAL HEALING CENTRE (HM01007) | | | | | | | | | | | | | | | | | | | | | | | | | |
| HOLISTIC OPTIONS (HM09985) | | | | | | | ● | | | | | | | | | | | | | | | | | | |
| JAMESON PERSONAL EXCELLENCE (HM10903) | | | | ● | | | ● | ● | | | | | | | | | | | | | | | | | |
| MARK GOULDING - ACUPUNCTURIST (HM13107) | | | | | | | ● | | | | | | ● | | | | | | | | | | ● | | |

# A - F Therapies at Practices/Businesses

| Business by County with Reference no. | Absent Healing | Acupressure | Acupuncture | Alexander Technique | Allergy Testing | Anthroposohical Med | Aromatherapy | Art Therapy | Aura Therapy | Auricular Therapy | Auto Suggestion | Autogenic Training | Aversion Therapy | Ayurvedic Medicine | Baby Massage | Bach Remedies | Bates Method | Beauty Therapy | Bio-energetics | Biofeedback | Biomagnetic Therapy | Biomechanics | Bonesetting | Bowen Therapy | Chinese Herbal Medicine |
|---|---|---|---|---|---|---|---|---|---|---|---|---|---|---|---|---|---|---|---|---|---|---|---|---|---|
| **NORTHERN IRELAND** | | | | | | | | | | | | | | | | | | | | | | | | | |
| **COUNTY ANTRIM** | | | | | | | | | | | | | | | | | | | | | | | | | |
| ACTIVE BALANCE CLINIC (HM00189) | | | | | | | | | | | | | | | | | | | | | | | | | |
| ANTRIM CHIROPRACTIC CLINIC (HM00923) | | | ● | | | | | | | | | | | | | | | | | | | | | | |
| BALLYCLARE CHIROPRACTIC CLINIC (HM01636) | | | | | | | | | | | | | | | | | | | | | | | | | |
| BALLYMENA CHIROPRACTIC CLINIC (HM01638) | | | | | | | | | | | | | | | | | | | | | | | | | |
| BALLYMONEY CHIROPRACTIC CLINIC (HM01639) | | | | | | | | | | | | | | | | | | | | | | | | | |
| BELFAST CHIROPRACTIC CLINIC (HM02077) | | | | | | | | | | | | | | | | | | | | | | | | | |
| CHEAH, R F S (HM04072) | | | ● | | | | | | | | | | | | | | | | | | | | | | |
| CHIROPODIST (HM04290) | | | | | | | | | | | | | | | | | | | | | | ● | | | |
| COMERTON, LIZ (HM04898) | | | | | | | | | | | | | | | | ● | | | | | | | | | |
| CRAWFORD, J G (HM05392) | | | | | | | | | | | | | | | | | | | | | | | | | |
| CREGAGH CHIROPRACTIC CLINIC (HM05412) | | | | | | | | | | | | | | | | | | | | | | | | | |
| EARLS, JAMES (HM06497) | | | | | | | ● | | | | | | | | | | | | | | | | | | |
| FAMILY CHIRO CLINIC BALLYMENA (HM07082) | | | | | | | | | | | | | | | | | | | | | | | | | |
| FINAGHY CHIROPRACTIC CLINIC (HM07295) | | | | | | | | | | | | | | | | | | | | | | | | | |
| FLORENCE SHARPE CHIROPODIST (HM07431) | | | | | | | | | | | | | | | | | | | | | | ● | | | |
| FRAMAR NATURAL HEALTH CLINIC (HM07654) | | ● | ● | | | | ● | | | | | | | | | ● | | | | | | | | | |
| GLENGORMLEY CHIRO CLINIC (HM08151) | | | | | | | | | | | | | | | | | | | | | | | | | |
| LAMBERT, RACHEL (HM11901) | | | | | | | ● | | | | | | | | | | | | | | | | | | |
| LISBURN CHIROPRACTIC CLINIC (HM12452) | | | | | | | | | | | | | | | | | | | | | | | | | |
| MAXWELL, MARY (HM13337) | | | | | | | | | | | | | | | | | | | | | | | | | |
| MCCARTNEY, W J (HM13401) | | | | | | | | | | | | | | | | | | | | | | ● | | | |
| MCCRYSTALS NATUROPATHIC CENTRE (HM13436) | | ● | | | | ● | ● | | | | | | | | | ● | | | | | | | | | |
| MCCULLY, JOAN (HM13437) | | | | | | | | | | | | | | | | | | | | | | | | | |
| MORGAN, D (HM14161) | | | | | | | | | | | | | | | | | | | | | | | | | |
| MYSTIC SCHEHERAZADE (HM14445) | | | | | | | | | | | | | | | | | | | | | | | | | |
| REAY, H (HM17004) | | | | | | | | | | | | | | | | | | | | | | | | | |
| SCRABO HEALTH PRODUCTS (HM18143) | | | | | | | ● | | | | | | | | | ● | | | | | | | | | |
| SCULLION, BRENDA (HM18156) | | | | | | | | | | | | | | | | ● | | | | | | | | | |
| SHEPPARD, SERENA (HM18423) | | | | | | | | | | | | | | | | ● | | | | | | | | | |
| STEWART, S (HM19276) | | | | | | | | | | | | | | | | | | | | | | | | | |
| TODD, TREVOR (HM20109) | | | | | | | | | | | | | | | | | | | | | | | | | |

| Business by County with Reference no. | Chiropody | Chiropractic | Clinical Ecology | Cognitive Therapy | Colonic Hydrotherapy | Colour Therapy | Complementary Therapy | Counselling | Cranial Osteopathy | Cranio-Sacral Therapy | Cryo Surgery | Crystal Healing | Cupping | Cymatics | Dance Movement Thrpy | Dietician | Do-In | Douching | Dowsing | Drama Therapy | Electrolipolysis | Electrolysis | Electrotherapy | Encounter Groups | Faith Healing |
|---|---|---|---|---|---|---|---|---|---|---|---|---|---|---|---|---|---|---|---|---|---|---|---|---|---|
| **NORTHERN IRELAND** | | | | | | | | | | | | | | | | | | | | | | | | | |
| **COUNTY ANTRIM** | | | | | | | | | | | | | | | | | | | | | | | | | |
| ACTIVE BALANCE CLINIC (HM00189) | | | | | | | | | ● | | | | | | | ● | | | | | | | | | |
| ANTRIM CHIROPRACTIC CLINIC (HM00923) | | ● | | | | | | | | | | | | | | | | | | | | | | | |
| BALLYCLARE CHIROPRACTIC CLINIC (HM01636) | | ● | | | | | | | | | | | | | | | | | | | | | | | |
| BALLYMENA CHIROPRACTIC CLINIC (HM01638) | | ● | | | | | | | | | | | | | | | | | | | | | | | |
| BALLYMONEY CHIROPRACTIC CLINIC (HM01639) | | ● | | | | | | | | | | | | | | | | | | | | | | | |
| BELFAST CHIROPRACTIC CLINIC (HM02077) | | ● | | | | | | | | | | | | | | | | | | | | | | | |
| CHEAH, R F S (HM04072) | | | | | | | | | | | | | | | | | | | | | | | | | |
| CHIROPODIST (HM04290) | ● | | | | | | | | | | | | | | | | | | | | | | | | |
| COMERTON, LIZ (HM04898) | | | | | | | | | | | | | | | | | | | | | | | | | |
| CRAWFORD, J G (HM05392) | ● | | | | | | | | | | | | | | | | | | | | | | | | |
| CREGAGH CHIROPRACTIC CLINIC (HM05412) | | ● | | | | | | | | | | | | | | | | | | | | | | | |
| EARLS, JAMES (HM06497) | | | | | | | | | | | | | | | | | | | | | | | | | |
| FAMILY CHIRO CLINIC BALLYMENA (HM07082) | | ● | | | | | | | | | | | | | | | | | | | | | | | |
| FINAGHY CHIROPRACTIC CLINIC (HM07295) | | ● | | | | | | | | | | | | | | | | | | | | | | | |
| FLORENCE SHARPE CHIROPODIST (HM07431) | ● | | | | | | | | | | | | | | | | | | | | | | | | |
| FRAMAR NATURAL HEALTH CLINIC (HM07654) | | | | | | | ● | ● | | | | | | | | | | | | | | | | | |
| GLENGORMLEY CHIRO CLINIC (HM08151) | | ● | | | | | | | | | | | | | | | | | | | | | | | |
| LAMBERT, RACHEL (HM11901) | | | | | | | | | | | | | | | | | | | | | | | | | |
| LISBURN CHIROPRACTIC CLINIC (HM12452) | | ● | | | | | | | | | | | | | | | | | | | | | | | |
| MAXWELL, MARY (HM13337) | ● | | | | | | | | | | | | | | | | | | | | | | | | |
| MCCARTNEY, W J (HM13401) | ● | | | | | | | | | | | | | | | | | | | | | | | | |
| MCCRYSTALS NATUROPATHIC CENTRE (HM13436) | | | | | | | ● | ● | | | | | | | | | | | | | | | | | |
| MCCULLY, JOAN (HM13437) | ● | | | | | | | | | | | | | | | | | | | | | | | | |
| MORGAN, D (HM14161) | | ● | | | | | | | | | | | | | | | | | | | | | | | |
| MYSTIC SCHEHERAZADE (HM14445) | | | | | | | | ● | | | | | | | | | | | | | | | | | |
| REAY, H (HM17004) | ● | | | | | | | | | | | | | | | | | | | | | | | | |
| SCRABO HEALTH PRODUCTS (HM18143) | | | | | | | | | | | | | | | | | | | | | | | | | |
| SCULLION, BRENDA (HM18156) | | | | | | | | | | | | | | | | | | | | | | | | | |
| SHEPPARD, SERENA (HM18423) | | | | | | | | | | | | | | | | | | | | | | | | | |
| STEWART, S (HM19276) | ● | | | | | | | | | | | | | | | | | | | | | | | | |
| TODD, TREVOR (HM20109) | ● | | | | | | | | | | | | | | | | | | | | | | | | |

# A - F Therapies at Practices/Businesses

| Business by County with Reference no. | Absent Healing | Acupressure | Acupuncture | Alexander Technique | Allergy Testing | Anthroposohical Med | Aromatherapy | Art Therapy | Aura Therapy | Auricular Therapy | Auto Suggestion | Autogenic Training | Aversion Therapy | Ayurvedic Medicine | Baby Massage | Bach Remedies | Bates Method | Beauty Therapy | Bio-energetics | Biofeedback | Biomagnetic Therapy | Biomechanics | Bonesetting | Bowen Therapy | Chinese Herbal Medicine |
|---|---|---|---|---|---|---|---|---|---|---|---|---|---|---|---|---|---|---|---|---|---|---|---|---|---|
| WEDLOCK, P (HM21098) | | | ● | | | | | | | | | | | | | | | | | | | | | | |
| YARO (HM21991) | | | | | | | ● | | | | | | | | | | | | | | | | | | |
| COUNTY ARMAGH | | | | | | | | | | | | | | | | | | | | | | | | | |
| ARMAGH CHIROPRACTIC CLINIC (HM01009) | | | | | | | | | | | | | | | | | | | | | | | | | |
| CAMPBELL, FIONA (HM03598) | | | | | | | | | | | | | | | | | | | | | | | | | |
| CRAIGAVON CHIROPRACTIC CLINIC (HM05355) | | | | | | | | | | | | | | | | | | | | | | | | | |
| LYON, HARRIETTE (HM12780) | | | | | | | | | | | | | | | | | | | | | | | | | |
| WILLIS, IAN (HM21614) | | | | | | | | | | | | | | | | | | | | | | ● | | | |
| COUNTY DOWN | | | | | | | | | | | | | | | | | | | | | | | | | |
| ARDS CHIROPRACTIC CLINIC (HM00993) | | | ● | | | | | | | | | | | | | | | | | | | | | | |
| BANGOR CHIROPRACTIC CLINIC (HM01659) | | | | | | | | | | | | | | | | | | | | | | | | | |
| CHIROPRACTICE (HM04405) | | | | | | | | | | | | | | | | | | | | | | | | | |
| COCHRANE, NIALL (HM04764) | | | | | | | | | | | | | | | | | | | | | | | | | |
| DELICATE ESSENCE CLINIC (HM05966) | | | | | | | ● | | | | | | | | | | | | | | | | | | |
| FAMILY CHIROPRACTIC CLINIC (HM07085) | | | | | | | | | | | | | | | | | | | | | | | | | |
| HADDEN, MARLENE (HM08687) | | ● | | | | | ● | | | | | | | | | ● | | | | | | | | ● | |
| LYCIUM CENTRE (HM12755) | | | ● | | | | ● | | | | | | | | | | | | | | | | | | |
| MCCARTAN, DEBORAH (HM13392) | | | | | | | | | | | | | | | | | | | | | | ● | | | |
| MCCLURG, T A (HM13412) | | ● | | | | | | | | | | | | | | | | | | | | | | | |
| MCCUTCHEON, TINA (HM13441) | | | ● | | | | | | | | | | | | | ● | | | | | | | | | |
| NEWRY CHIROPRACTIC CLINIC (HM14886) | | | | | | | | | | | | | | | | | | | | | | | | | |
| NOBLE, ANDREW (DR) (HM14968) | | | | | | | | | | | | | | | | | | | | | | | | | |
| NORTH DOWN CLINIC (HM15023) | | | | | | | | | | | | | | | | | | | | | | | | | |
| PRINGLE CHIROPRACTIC (HM16626) | | ● | ● | ● | | | | | | | | | | | | | | | | | | | ● | ● | |
| QUINN, BARBARA (HM16808) | | | | | | | | | | | | | | | | | | | | | | | | | |
| REFLEXOLOGY CLINIC (HM17092) | | | | | | | ● | | | | | | | | | | | | | | | | | | |
| COUNTY FERMANAGH | | | | | | | | | | | | | | | | | | | | | | | | | |
| ENNISKILLEN CHIRO CLINIC (HM06844) | | | | | | | | | | | | | | | | | | | | | | | | | |
| COUNTY LONDONDERRY | | | | | | | | | | | | | | | | | | | | | | | | | |
| CLARENDON CHIROPRACTIC CLINIC (HM04539) | | | | | | | | | | | | | | | | | | | | | | | | | |
| CLAUDY CHIROPRACTIC CLINIC (HM04612) | | | | | | | | | | | | | | | | | | | | | | | | | |
| COLERAINE CHIROPRACTIC CENTRE (HM04830) | | | | | | | | | | | | | | | | | | | | | | | | | |
| CURRAN, MAUREEN (HM05630) | | | | | | | ● | | | | | | | | | | | ● | | | | | | | |
| DISPENSERY (HM06117) | | | ● | | | | | | | | | | | | | ● | | | | | | | | | |

| Business by County with Reference no. | Chiropody | Chiropractic | Clinical Ecology | Cognitive Therapy | Colonic Hydrotherapy | Colour Therapy | Complementary Therapy | Counselling | Cranial Osteopathy | Cranio-Sacral Therapy | Cryo Surgery | Crystal Healing | Cupping | Cymatics | Dance Movement Thrpy | Dietician | Do-In | Douching | Dowsing | Drama Therapy | Electrolipolysis | Electrolysis | Electrotherapy | Encounter Groups | Faith Healing |
|---|---|---|---|---|---|---|---|---|---|---|---|---|---|---|---|---|---|---|---|---|---|---|---|---|---|
| WEDLOCK, P (HM21098) | | | | | | | | | | | | | | | | | | | | | | | | | |
| YARO (HM21991) | | | | | | | | | | | | | | | | | | | | | | | | | |
| COUNTY ARMAGH | | | | | | | | | | | | | | | | | | | | | | | | | |
| ARMAGH CHIROPRACTIC CLINIC (HM01009) | | ● | | | | | | | | | | | | | | | | | | | | | | | |
| CAMPBELL, FIONA (HM03598) | ● | | | | | | | | | | | | | | | | | | | | | | | | |
| CRAIGAVON CHIROPRACTIC CLINIC (HM05355) | | ● | | | | | | | | | | | | | | | | | | | | | | | |
| LYON, HARRIETTE (HM12780) | ● | | | | | | | | | | | | | | | | | | | | | | | | |
| WILLIS, IAN (HM21614) | ● | | | | | | | | | | | | | | | | | | | | | | | | |
| COUNTY DOWN | | | | | | | | | | | | | | | | | | | | | | | | | |
| ARDS CHIROPRACTIC CLINIC (HM00993) | | ● | | | | | | | | | | | | | | | | | | | | | | | |
| BANGOR CHIROPRACTIC CLINIC (HM01659) | | ● | | | | | | | | | | | | | | | | | | | | | | | |
| CHIROPRACTICE (HM04405) | ● | ● | | | | | | | | | | | | | | | | | | | | | | | |
| COCHRANE, NIALL (HM04764) | ● | | | | | | | | | | | | | | | | | | | | | | | | |
| DELICATE ESSENCE CLINIC (HM05966) | | | | | | | | | | | | | | | | | | | | | | | | | |
| FAMILY CHIROPRACTIC CLINIC (HM07085) | | ● | | | | | | | | | | | | | | | | | | | | | | | |
| HADDEN, MARLENE (HM08687) | | | | | | ● | | ● | | | | | | | | ● | | | | | | | | | |
| LYCIUM CENTRE (HM12755) | | | | | | | | | | | | | ● | | | | | | | | | | | | |
| MCCARTAN, DEBORAH (HM13392) | ● | | | | | | | | | | | | | | | | | | | | | | | | |
| MCCLURG, T A (HM13412) | | | | | | | | | | | | | | | | | | | | | | | | | |
| MCCUTCHEON, TINA (HM13441) | | | | | | | | | ● | | | | | | | | | | | | | | | | |
| NEWRY CHIROPRACTIC CLINIC (HM14886) | | ● | | | | | | | | | | | | | | | | | | | | | | | |
| NOBLE, ANDREW (DR) (HM14968) | | ● | | | | | | | | | | | | | | | | | | | | | | | |
| NORTH DOWN CLINIC (HM15023) | | | | | | | | | ● | | | | | | | | | | | | | | | | |
| PRINGLE CHIROPRACTIC (HM16626) | | ● | | | | | ● | | | | | | | | | | | | | | | | | | |
| QUINN, BARBARA (HM16808) | | | | | | | | | ● | | | | | | | | | | | | | | | | |
| REFLEXOLOGY CLINIC (HM17092) | | | | | | | | | | | | | | | | | | | | | | | | | |
| COUNTY FERMANAGH | | | | | | | | | | | | | | | | | | | | | | | | | |
| ENNISKILLEN CHIRO CLINIC (HM06844) | | ● | | | | | | | | | | | | | | | | | | | | | | | |
| COUNTY LONDONDERRY | | | | | | | | | | | | | | | | | | | | | | | | | |
| CLARENDON CHIROPRACTIC CLINIC (HM04539) | | ● | | | | | | | | | | | | | | | | | | | | | | | |
| CLAUDY CHIROPRACTIC CLINIC (HM04612) | | ● | | | | | | | | | | | | | | | | | | | | | | | |
| COLERAINE CHIROPRACTIC CENTRE (HM04830) | | ● | | | | | | | | | | | | | | | | | | | | | | | |
| CURRAN, MAUREEN (HM05630) | | | | | | | | | | | | | | | | | | | | | | ● | | | |
| DISPENSERY (HM06117) | | | | | | | | ● | | | | | | | | ● | | | | | | | | | |

# A - F Therapies at Practices/Businesses

Business by County with Reference no.

| Therapy | EQUILIBRIUM HOLISTIC CLINIC (HM06875) | FEET FIRST (HM07174) | FOYLE HYPNOTHERAPY CENTRE (HM07646) | HYNES, NANCY (HM10484) | LIFE TREE (HM12350) | MAGHERAFELT CHIRO CLINIC (HM12906) | SCHLINDWEIN, HELENA (HM18017) | COUNTY TYRONE | BRADLEY, R M (HM02871) | COOKSTOWN CHIROPRACTIC CLINIC (HM05072) | DUNGANNON CHIROPRACTIC CLINIC (HM06405) | O'MAHONY, JOHN & BEATE (HM15308) | ROSEWOOD HEALTH CLINIC (HM17630) |
|---|---|---|---|---|---|---|---|---|---|---|---|---|---|
| Faith Healing | | | | | | | | | | | | | |
| Encounter Groups | | | | | | | | | | | | | |
| Electrotherapy | | | ● | | | | | | | | | | |
| Electrolysis | | | | | | | | | | | | | |
| Electrolipolysis | | | | | | | | | | | | | |
| Drama Therapy | | | | | | | | | | | | | |
| Dowsing | | | | | | | | | | | | | |
| Douching | | | | | | | | | | | | | |
| Do-In | | | | | | | | | | | | | |
| Dietician | | | | | | | | | | | | | |
| Dance Movement Thrpy | | | | | | | | | | | | | |
| Cymatics | | | | | | | | | | | | | |
| Cupping | | | | | | | | | | | | | |
| Crystal Healing | | | | | | | | | | | | | |
| Cryo Surgery | | | | | | | | | | | | | |
| Cranio-Sacral Therapy | | | | | | | | | | | | | |
| Cranial Osteopathy | | | | | | | | | | | | | |
| Counselling | | | ● | | | | | | | | | | |
| Complementary Therapy | | | ● | | | | | | | | | | |
| Colour Therapy | | | ● | | | | | | | | | | |
| Colonic Hydrotherapy | | | | | | | | | | | | | |
| Cognitive Therapy | | | ● | | | | | | | | | | |
| Clinical Ecology | | | | | | | | | | | | | |
| Chiropractic | | | | | | ● | | | | ● | ● | | |
| Chiropody | | ● | | | | | | | ● | | | | ● |
| Chinese Herbal Medicine | | | | | | | | | | | | | |
| Bowen Therapy | | | | | | | | | | | | | |
| Bonesetting | | | | | | | | | | | | | |
| Biomechanics | | ● | | | | | | | | | | | |
| Biomagnetic Therapy | | | | | | | | | | | | | |
| Biofeedback | | | | | | | | | | | | | |
| Bio-energetics | | | | | | | | | | | | | |
| Beauty Therapy | | | | | | | | | | | | | |
| Bates Method | | | | | | | | | | | | | |
| Bach Remedies | ● | | | ● | ● | | ● | | | | | | |
| Baby Massage | | | | | | | | | | | | | |
| Ayurvedic Medicine | | | | | | | | | | | | | |
| Aversion Therapy | | | ● | | | | | | | | | | |
| Autogenic Training | | | | | | | | | | | | | |
| Auto Suggestion | | | ● | | | | | | | | | | |
| Auricular Therapy | | | | | | | | | | | | | |
| Aura Therapy | | | | | | | | | | | | | |
| Art Therapy | | | | | | | | | | | | | |
| Aromatherapy | ● | | | | ● | | | | | | | | |
| Anthroposohical Med | | | | | | | | | | | | | |
| Allergy Testing | | | | | ● | | | | | | | | |
| Alexander Technique | | | | | | | | | | | | | |
| Acupuncture | | | ● | | | | | | | | | ● | |
| Acupressure | | | ● | | | | | | | | | | |
| Absent Healing | | | | | | | | | | | | | |

# A - F Therapies at Practices/Businesses

| Business by County with Reference no. | Absent Healing | Acupressure | Acupuncture | Alexander Technique | Allergy Testing | Anthroposohical Med | Aromatherapy | Art Therapy | Aura Therapy | Auricular Therapy | Auto Suggestion | Autogenic Training | Aversion Therapy | Ayurvedic Medicine | Baby Massage | Bach Remedies | Bates Method | Beauty Therapy | Bio-energetics | Biofeedback | Biomagnetic Therapy | Biomechanics | Bonesetting | Bowen Therapy | Chinese Herbal Medicine | Chiropody | Chiropractic | Clinical Ecology | Cognitive Therapy | Colonic Hydrotherapy | Colour Therapy | Complementary Therapy | Counselling | Cranial Osteopathy | Cranio-Sacral Therapy | Cryo Surgery | Crystal Healing | Cupping | Cymatics | Dance Movement Thrpy | Dietician | Do-In | Douching | Dowsing | Drama Therapy | Electrolipolysis | Electrolysis | Electrotherapy | Encounter Groups | Faith Healing |
|---|---|---|---|---|---|---|---|---|---|---|---|---|---|---|---|---|---|---|---|---|---|---|---|---|---|---|---|---|---|---|---|---|---|---|---|---|---|---|---|---|---|---|---|---|---|---|---|---|---|---|
| SCOTLAND | | | | | | | | | | | | | | | | | | | | | | | | | | | | | | | | | | | | | | | | | | | | | | | | | | |
| ABERDEENSHIRE | | | | | | | | | | | | | | | | | | | | | | | | | | | | | | | | | | | | | | | | | | | | | | | | | | |
| A WAY WITH THE FAERIES (HM00051) | | | | | | | ● | | | | | | | | | | | | | | | | | | | | | | | | | | | | | | ● | | | | | | | | | | | | | |
| ABERDEEN CHIROPRACTIC CLINIC (HM00114) | | | | | | | | | | | | | | | | | | | | | | | | | | | ● | | | | | | | | | | | | | | | | | | | | | | | |
| ALTERNATIVE PRACTICE (HM00723) | | | | | | | ● | | | | | | | | | ● | | | | | | | | | | | | | | | | | | | | | | | | | | | | | | | | | | |
| AROMATHERAPY CLINIC (HM01104) | | | | | | | ● | | | | | | | | | | | | | | | | | | | | | | | | | | | | | | | | | | | | | | | | | | | |
| BANCHORY CHIROPODY PRACTICE (HM01649) | | | | | | | | | | | | | | | | | | | | | | | | | | ● | | | | | | | | | | | | | | | | | | | | | | | | |
| BEECHGROVE CLINIC (HM02050) | | | | | | | | | | | | ● | | | | | | | | ● | | ● | | | | | | | | | | | | ● | | | | | | | | | | | | | | ● | | |
| BON-ACCORD CHIROPODY (HM02667) | | | | | | | | | | | | | | | | | | | | | | | | | | ● | | | | | | | | | | | | | | | | | | | | | | | | |
| BROMLEY, RIA (HM03149) | | | | | | | ● | | | | | | | | | | | | | | | | | | | | | | | | | | | | | | | | | | | | | | | | | | | |
| CHELSEA HOUSE CLINIC (HM04090) | | | ● | | | | ● | | | | | | | | | | | | | | | | | | | ● | | | | | | | | | | | | | | | | | | | | | | | | |
| CITY BEACH (HM04486) | | | | | | | ● | | | | | | | | | | | | | | | | | | | | | | | | | | | | | | | | | | | | | | | | ● | | | |
| CLAIRBAUX CLINIC (HM04506) | | | ● | | | | | | | | | | | | | | | | | | | | | | | | | | | | | | | | | | | | | | | | | | | | | | | |
| CLAIRBAUX CLINIC (HM04505) | | | ● | | | | | | | | | | | | | | | | | | | | | | | | | | | | | | | | | | | | | | | | | | | | | | | |
| DEEVIEW AROMATHERAPY (HM05960) | | | | | | | ● | | | | | | | | | | | | | | | | | | | | | | | | | | | | | | | | | | | | | | | | | | | |
| GRAY, SHEILA (HM08419) | | | | | | | | | | | | | | | | | | | | | | | | ● | | | | | | | | | | | | | | | | | | | | | | | | | | |
| HUNTLY CHIROPRACTIC CLINIC (HM10412) | | | | | | | | | | | | | | | | | | | | | | | | | | | ● | | | | | | | | | | | | | | | | | | | | | | | |
| LEAL, DOUGLAS (HM12102) | | | | | | | | | | | | | | | | | | | | | | | | | | ● | | | | | | | | | | | | | | | | | | | | | | | | |
| MAY, S P (HM13348) | | | ● | | | | | | | | | | | | | | | | | | | | | | | | | | | | | | | | | | | | | | | | | | | | | | | |
| MOSS PHARMACY (HM14262) | | | | | | | | | | | | | | | | | | | | | | | | | | ● | | | | | | | | | | | | | | | | | | | | | | | | |
| MUNRO, EVELYN (HM14363) | | | | | | | | | | | | | | | | ● | | | | | | | | | | | | | | | | | | | | | | | | | | | | | | | | | | |
| REIKI TRAINING CENTRE (HM17149) | ● | | | | | | ● | | | | | | | | | | | | | | | | | | | | | | | | | | | | | | | | | | | | | | | | | | | |
| REILLY, DANIEL (HM17151) | | | | ● | | | | | | | | | | | | | | | | | | | | | | | | | | | | | | | | | | | | | | | | | | | | | | |
| RIVERSIDE CHIROPRACTIC CLINIC (HM17378) | | | | | | | | | | | | | | | | | | | | | | | | | | | ● | | | | | | | | | | | | | | | | | | | | | | | |
| ROSEMOUNT CENTRE (HM17623) | | | ● | | | | ● | ● | | | | | | | | | | | | | | | | ● | | | ● | ● | ● | | | | ● | | ● | | | | | ● | | | | | | | | | | |
| SAWYER, KEN (HM17985) | | | | | | | | | | | | | | | | | | | | | | | | | | | | | | | | | ● | | | | | | | | | | | | | | | | | |
| SERENDIPITY (HM18232) | | | ● | | | | ● | | | | | | | | | | | | | | | | | | | | | | | | | | | | | | | | | | | | | | | | | | | |
| STEPHENSON, L (HM19208) | | | | | | | | | | | | | | | | | | | | | | | | | | ● | | | | | | | | | | | | | | | | | | | | | | | | |
| TAGGART, RUTH (HM19652) | | | | | | | ● | | | | | | | | | | | | | | | | | | | | | | | | | ● | | | | | | | | | | | | | | | | | | |
| TURRIFF CHIROPRACTIC CLINIC (HM20443) | | | | | | | | | | | | | | | | | | | | | | | | | | | ● | | | | | | | | | | | | | | | | | | | | | | | |
| WEST END PHYSIOTHERAPY (HM21219) | | | ● | | | | | | | | | | | | | | | | | | | | | | | | | | | | | | | | | | | | | | | | | | | | | | | |
| WILKEN, ANGEL (HM21492) | | | | | | | ● | | | | | | | | | | | | | | | | | | | | | | | | | | | | | | | | | | | | | | | | | | | |
| WOOD, A R (HM21783) | | | | | | | | | | | | | | | | | | | | | | | | | | ● | | | | | | | | | | | | | | | | | | | | | | | | |

# A - F Therapies at Practices/Businesses

| Business by County with Reference no. | Absent Healing | Acupressure | Acupuncture | Alexander Technique | Allergy Testing | Anthroposohical Med | Aromatherapy | Art Therapy | Aura Therapy | Auricular Therapy | Auto Suggestion | Autogenic Training | Aversion Therapy | Ayurvedic Medicine | Baby Massage | Bach Remedies | Bates Method | Beauty Therapy | Bio-energetics | Biofeedback | Biomagnetic Therapy | Biomechanics | Bonesetting | Bowen Therapy | Chinese Herbal Medicine | Chiropody | Chiropractic | Clinical Ecology | Cognitive Therapy | Colonic Hydrotherapy | Colour Therapy | Complementary Therapy | Counselling | Cranial Osteopathy | Cranio-Sacral Therapy | Cryo Surgery | Crystal Healing | Cupping | Cymatics | Dance Movement Thrpy | Dietician | Do-In | Douching | Dowsing | Drama Therapy | Electrolipolysis | Electrolysis | Electrotherapy | Encounter Groups | Faith Healing |
|---|---|---|---|---|---|---|---|---|---|---|---|---|---|---|---|---|---|---|---|---|---|---|---|---|---|---|---|---|---|---|---|---|---|---|---|---|---|---|---|---|---|---|---|---|---|---|---|---|---|---|
| WOODWARD, MARGARET (HM21868) | | | | | | | | | | | | | | | | ● | | | | | | | | | | | | | | | | | | | | | | | | | | | | | | | | | | |
| ANGUS | | | | | | | | | | | | | | | | | | | | | | | | | | | | | | | | | | | | | | | | | | | | | | | | | | |
| ACARSAID CHIROPODY CLINIC (HM00150) | | | | | | | | | | | | | | | | | | | | | | | | | | ● | | | | | | | | | | | | | | | | | | | | | | | | |
| ALEXANDER TECHNIQUE CENTRE (HM00556) | | | | ● | | | | | | | | | | | | | | | | | | | | | | | | | | | | | | | | | | | | | | | | | | | | | | |
| DRYDEN, PHILIP (HM06333) | | | | | | | | | | | | | | | | | | | | | | | | | | ● | | | | | | | | | | | | | | | | | | | | | | | | |
| FOGGIE, MARGARET (HM07454) | | | | | | | | | | | | | | | | | | | | | | | | | | ● | | | | | | | | | | | | | | | | | | | | | | | | |
| GREKIN CHIROPRACTIC CLINIC (HM08534) | | | | | | | | | | | | | | | | | | | | | | | | | | | ● | | | | | | | | | | | | | | | | | | | | | | | |
| KIRRIEMUIR PHYSIO CLINIC (HM11723) | | | ● | | | | | | | | | | | | | | | | | | | | | | | | | | | | | | | | | | | | | | | | | | | | | | | |
| MIND BODY SOUL & ASSOCIATES (HM13960) | | | ● | ● | | | ● | | | | | | | | | | | | | | | | | | | | | | | | | | | | | | | | | | | | | | | | | | | |
| NICOLL, ELAINE (HM14929) | | | | | | | | | | | | | | | | | | | | | | ● | | | | ● | | | | | | | | | | | | | | | | | | | | | | | | |
| TRADITIONAL ACUPUNCTURE (HM20217) | | | ● | | | | | | | | | | | | | | | | | | | | | | | | | | | | | | | | | | | | | | | | | | | | | | | |
| ARGYLL AND BUTE | | | | | | | | | | | | | | | | | | | | | | | | | | | | | | | | | | | | | | | | | | | | | | | | | | |
| ACTIVE CHIROPRACTIC (HM00195) | | | ● | | | | | | | | | | | | | | | | | | | | | | | | ● | | | | | | | | | | | | | | | | | | | | | | | |
| COMPLEMENTARY HEALTH CENTRE (HM04922) | | | | | | | ● | | | | | | | | | | | | | | | | | | | ● | | | | | | | | | | | | | | | | | | | | | | | | |
| FRAGRANT MOODS (HM07650) | | | | | | | ● | | | | | | | | | | | | | | | | | | | | | | | | | | | | | | | | | | | | | | | | | | | |
| GIBSON, RONALD J (HM08045) | | | | | | | | | | | | | | | | | | | | | | | | | | ● | | | | | | | | | | | | | | | | | | | | | | | | |
| GRAPEVINE (HM08398) | | | | | | | | | | | | | | | | | | | | | | | | | | | | | | | | | | | | | ● | | | | | | | | | | | | | |
| HOMEOPATHIC PODIATRIST/REFLEX (HM10078) | | | | | | | | | | | | | | | | | | | | | | | | | | ● | | | | | | ● | | | | | | | | | | | | | | | | | | |
| NATURAL THERAPY CENTRE (HM14648) | | | | ● | | | ● | | | | | | | | | | | | | | | | | | | | | | | | | | | ● | | | | | | | | | | | | | | | | |
| AYRSHIRE (EAST) | | | | | | | | | | | | | | | | | | | | | | | | | | | | | | | | | | | | | | | | | | | | | | | | | | |
| CRUISE, M & M (HM05520) | | | | | | | | | | | | | | | | | | | | | | ● | | | | ● | | | | | | | | | | ● | | | | | | | | | | | | | | |
| HURLFORD CHIROPODY CLINIC (HM10422) | | | | | | | | | | | | | | | | | | | | | | | | | | ● | | | | | | | | | | | | | | | | | | | | | | | | |
| LYNN BROWN CLINICAL AROM (HM12772) | | | | | | | ● | | | | | | | | | | | | | | | | | | | | | | | | | ● | | | | | | | | | | | | | | | | | | |
| MCCABE, P J (HM13376) | | | | | | | | | | | | | | | | | | | | | | ● | | | | ● | | | | | | | | | | | | | | | | | | | | | | | | |
| MINNERY, PATRICIA (HM13978) | | | | | | | ● | | | | | | | | | | | | | | | | | | | | | | | | | | | | | | | | | | | | | | | | | | | |
| REID, ELIZABETH (HM17117) | ● | | | | | | | | | | | | | | | | | | | | | | | | | | | | | | | ● | | | | | | | | | | | | | | | | | | |
| RHONA INGLIS AROMATHERAPY (HM17232) | | | | | | | ● | | | | | | | | | | | | | | | | | | | | | | | | | | | | | | | | | | | | | | | | | | | |
| ROBERTSON, JENNIFER (HM17443) | | | | | | | ● | | | | | | | | | | | | | | | | | | | | | | | | | | | | | | | | | | | | | | | | | | | |
| AYRSHIRE (NORTH) | | | | | | | | | | | | | | | | | | | | | | | | | | | | | | | | | | | | | | | | | | | | | | | | | | |
| BODY & SOUL (HM02564) | | | | | | | ● | | | | | | | | | | | | | | | | | | | | | | | | | | | | | | | | | | | | | | | | | | | |
| BODYSCENTS (HM02631) | | | | | | | ● | | | | | | | | | | | | | | | | | | | | | | | | | | | | | | | | | | | | | | | | | | | |
| BURNS, ALAN STEWART (HM03410) | | | | | | | | | | | | | | | | | | | | | | | | | | ● | | | | | | | | | | | | | | | | | | | | | | | | |
| CHIRO HEALTH CARE CLINIC (HM04282) | | | | | | | ● | | | | | | | | | | | | | | | | | | | | ● | | | | | | | | | | | | | | | | | | | | | | | |
| HANDS FOR FEET (HM08905) | | | | | | | | | | | | | | | | | | | | | | | | | | ● | | | | | | | | | | | | | | | | | | | | | | | | |

# A - F Therapies at Practices/Businesses

| Business by County with Reference no. | Absent Healing | Acupressure | Acupuncture | Alexander Technique | Allergy Testing | Anthroposohical Med | Aromatherapy | Art Therapy | Aura Therapy | Auricular Therapy | Auto Suggestion | Autogenic Training | Aversion Therapy | Ayurvedic Medicine | Baby Massage | Bach Remedies | Bates Method | Beauty Therapy | Bio-energetics | Biofeedback | Biomagnetic Therapy | Biomechanics | Bonesetting | Bowen Therapy | Chinese Herbal Medicine |
|---|---|---|---|---|---|---|---|---|---|---|---|---|---|---|---|---|---|---|---|---|---|---|---|---|---|
| MCGOVERN, FIONA (HM13492) | | | | | | | | | | | | | | | |●| | | | | | | | | |
| PATON, MARY S (HM15824) | | | | | | | | | | | | | | | | | | | | | | | | | |
| REID, E (HM17116) | | | | | | | | | | | | | | | | | | | | | | | | | |
| **AYRSHIRE (SOUTH)** | | | | | | | | | | | | | | | | | | | | | | | | | |
| BELL, W DOUGLAS (HM02091) | | | | | | | | | | | | | | | | | | | | | | | | | |
| CARRICK CLINIC (HM03742) | |●|●|●| | |●| | | | | | | | | | | | | | | | | | |
| CRUISE, M & M (HM05522) | | | | | | | | | | | | | | | | | | | | | |●| | | |
| ESSENCE OF HEALTH (HM06890) | | | |●| | |●| | | | | | | | |●| |●| | | | | | | |
| HARDIE, ANNE (HM08966) | | | | | | |●| | | | | | | | | | | | | | | | | | |
| HEALTH STRESS & INJURIES (HM09404) | | | | | | |●| | | | | | | | | | | | | | | | |●| |
| HEARTLAKE PHYSIOTHERAPY (HM09444) | | |●| | | | | | | | | | | | | | | | | | | | | | |
| HODGE, IAN (HM09874) |●| | | | | | | | | |●|●| | | | | | | | | | | | | |
| ORIENTAL HEALTH CENTRE (HM15381) | | |●| | | | | | | | | | | | | | | | | | | |●| | |
| REID, A (HM17112) | | | | | | | | | | | | | | | | | | | | | |●| | | |
| SMITH, ALICIA (HM18712) | | | | | | | | | | | | | | | | | | | | | | | | | |
| **CLACKMANNANSHIRE** | | | | | | | | | | | | | | | | | | | | | | | | | |
| CLINICAL AROMATHERAPY (HM04711) | | | | | | |●| | | | | | | | | | | | | | | | | | |
| CULLENS, IONA (HM05563) | | | | | | |●| | | | | | | | | | | | | | | | | | |
| **DUMFRIES AND GALLOWAY** | | | | | | | | | | | | | | | | | | | | | | | | | |
| CHLOE'S HERBS (HM04419) | | | | | | | | | | | | | | | |●| | | | | | | | | |
| CLARK, LUCY (HM04565) | | |●| | | | | | | | | | | | | | | | | | | | | | |
| DAVIDSON, MORAG (HM05788) | | | | | | | | | | | | | | | | | | | | | | | | | |
| DUMFRIES HOLISTIC HEALTH CTRE (HM06386) | |●|●|●| | |●| | | | | | | | | | | | | | | | | | |
| HEALTH STRESS & INJURIES CLNC (HM09405) | | | | | | | | | | | | | | | | | | | | | | | |●| |
| MCCLUNE, LORNA (HM13410) | | | | | | | | | | | | | | | | | | | | | |●| | | |
| MCCLYMOUNT, JENNIFER (HM13416) | | | | | | | | | | | | | | | | | | | | | | | | | |
| RANKINE, VANORA (HM16939) | | | | | | | | | | | | | | | | | | | | | | | | | |
| SHARP, LINDA A (HM18314) | |●|●| | | | | | | | | | | | | | | | | | | | | | |
| **EDINBURGH (CITY OF)** | | | | | | | | | | | | | | | | | | | | | | | | | |
| ALEXANDER TECHNIQUE (HM00517) | | | |●| | | | | | | | | | | | | | | | | | | | | |
| ALEXANDER TECHNIQUE (HM00535) | | | |●| | | | | | | | | | | | | | | | | | | | | |
| BIORADIANT HEALTH (HM02343) | | |●| | | |●| | | | | | | | | | | | | | | | | | |
| CHRISTIE, ADRIAN (HM04438) | | | | | | | | | | | | | | | | | | | | | | | | | |
| COOPER, C J C (HM05094) | | | |●| | | | | | | | | | | | | | | | | | | | | |

| Business by County with Reference no. | Chiropody | Chiropractic | Clinical Ecology | Cognitive Therapy | Colonic Hydrotherapy | Colour Therapy | Complementary Therapy | Counselling | Cranial Osteopathy | Cranio-Sacral Therapy | Cryo Surgery | Crystal Healing | Cupping | Cymatics | Dance Movement Thrpy | Dietician | Do-In | Douching | Dowsing | Drama Therapy | Electrolipolysis | Electrolysis | Electrotherapy | Encounter Groups | Faith Healing |
|---|---|---|---|---|---|---|---|---|---|---|---|---|---|---|---|---|---|---|---|---|---|---|---|---|---|
| MCGOVERN, FIONA (HM13492) | | | | | | | | | | | | | | | | | | | | | | | | | |
| PATON, MARY S (HM15824) |●| | | | | | | | | | | | | | | | | | | | | | | | |
| REID, E (HM17116) |●| | | | | | | | | | | | | | | | | | | | | | | | |
| **AYRSHIRE (SOUTH)** | | | | | | | | | | | | | | | | | | | | | | | | | |
| BELL, W DOUGLAS (HM02091) |●| | | | | | | | | | | | | | | | | | | | | | | | |
| CARRICK CLINIC (HM03742) | | | | | | |●| | | | | | | | | |●| | | | | | |●| | |
| CRUISE, M & M (HM05522) |●| | | | | | | | | | | | | | | | | | | | | | | | |
| ESSENCE OF HEALTH (HM06890) |●| | | | | | | | | | | | | | | | | | | | | | | | |
| HARDIE, ANNE (HM08966) | | | | | | | | | | | | | | | | | | | | | | | | | |
| HEALTH STRESS & INJURIES (HM09404) | |●| | | | | | | | | | | | | | | | | | | | | | | |
| HEARTLAKE PHYSIOTHERAPY (HM09444) | | | | | | | | | | | | | | | | | | | | | | | | | |
| HODGE, IAN (HM09874) | | | |●| | |●|●| | | | | | | | |●| | | | | | | | | |
| ORIENTAL HEALTH CENTRE (HM15381) | | | | | | | | | | | | | | | | | | | | | | | | | |
| REID, A (HM17112) |●| | | | | | | | | | | | | | | | | | | | | | | | |
| SMITH, ALICIA (HM18712) | | | |●| | |●|●| | | | | | | | | | | | | | | | | |
| **CLACKMANNANSHIRE** | | | | | | | | | | | | | | | | | | | | | | | | | |
| CLINICAL AROMATHERAPY (HM04711) | | | | | | | | | | | | | | | | | | | | | | | | | |
| CULLENS, IONA (HM05563) | | | | | | | | | | | | | | | | | | | | | | | | | |
| **DUMFRIES AND GALLOWAY** | | | | | | | | | | | | | | | | | | | | | | | | | |
| CHLOE'S HERBS (HM04419) | | | | | | | | | | | | | | | | | | | | | | | | | |
| CLARK, LUCY (HM04565) | | | | | | | | | | | | | | | | | | | | | | | | | |
| DAVIDSON, MORAG (HM05788) |●| | | | | | | | | | | | | | | | | | | | | | | | |
| DUMFRIES HOLISTIC HEALTH CTRE (HM06386) | | | | | |●| |●| | | |●| | | |●| | | | | | | | | |
| HEALTH STRESS & INJURIES CLNC (HM09405) | | | | | | | | | | | | | | | | | | | | | | | | | |
| MCCLUNE, LORNA (HM13410) |●| | | | | | | | | | | | | | | | | | | | | | | | |
| MCCLYMOUNT, JENNIFER (HM13416) |●| | | | | | | | | | | | | | | | | | | | | | | | |
| RANKINE, VANORA (HM16939) |●| | | | | | | | | | | | | | | | | | | | | | | | |
| SHARP, LINDA A (HM18314) | | | | | | | | | | | | | | | | | | | | | | | | | |
| **EDINBURGH (CITY OF)** | | | | | | | | | | | | | | | | | | | | | | | | | |
| ALEXANDER TECHNIQUE (HM00517) | | | | | | | | | | | | | | | | | | | | | | | | | |
| ALEXANDER TECHNIQUE (HM00535) | | | | | | | | | | | | | | | | | | | | | | | | | |
| BIORADIANT HEALTH (HM02343) | | | | | | | | | | | | | | | | | | | | | | | | | |
| CHRISTIE, ADRIAN (HM04438) | | | | | | | |●| | | | | | | | | | | | | | | | | |
| COOPER, C J C (HM05094) | | | | | | | | | | | | | | | | | | | | | | | | | |

# A - F Therapies at Practices/Businesses

| Business by County with Reference no. | Absent Healing | Acupressure | Acupuncture | Alexander Technique | Allergy Testing | Anthroposohical Med | Aromatherapy | Art Therapy | Aura Therapy | Auricular Therapy | Auto Suggestion | Autogenic Training | Aversion Therapy | Ayurvedic Medicine | Baby Massage | Bach Remedies | Bates Method | Beauty Therapy | Bio-energetics | Biofeedback | Biomagnetic Therapy | Biomechanics | Bonesetting | Bowen Therapy | Chinese Herbal Medicine | Chiropody | Chiropractic | Clinical Ecology | Cognitive Therapy | Colonic Hydrotherapy | Colour Therapy | Complementary Therapy | Counselling | Cranial Osteopathy | Cranio-Sacral Therapy | Cryo Surgery | Crystal Healing | Cupping | Cymatics | Dance Movement Thrpy | Dietician | Do-In | Douching | Dowsing | Drama Therapy | Electrolipolysis | Electrolysis | Electrotherapy | Encounter Groups | Faith Healing |
|---|---|---|---|---|---|---|---|---|---|---|---|---|---|---|---|---|---|---|---|---|---|---|---|---|---|---|---|---|---|---|---|---|---|---|---|---|---|---|---|---|---|---|---|---|---|---|---|---|---|---|
| E G H P (HM06468) | | | | | | | | | | | | | | | | | | | | | | | | | | | | | ● | | | | ● | | | | | | | | | | | | | | | | | |
| EDINBURGH ALEXANDER CENTRE (HM06606) | | | | ● | | | | | | | | | | | | | | | | | | | | | | | | | | | | | | | | | | | | | | | | | | | | | | |
| EDINBURGH FLOATARIUM (HM06611) | | | | ● | | | ● | | | | | | | | | | | ● | | | | | | | | ● | | | | | | ● | | | | | ● | | | | | | | | | | | | | |
| EDINBURGH HOMEOPATHIC CENTRE (HM06613) | | | ● | | | | | | | | | | | | | | | | | | | | | | | | | | | | | | | | | | | | | | | | | | | | | | | |
| EDINBURGH OSTEOPATHIC SURGERY (HM06615) | | | ● | | | | | | | | | | | | | | | | | | | | | | | | | | | | | | | ● | | | | | | | | | | | | | | | | |
| EDINBURGH PHYSIOTHERAPY CENTRE (HM06616) | | | ● | | | | | | | | | | | | | | | ● | | | | | | | | | ● | | | | | | | | | | | | | | | | | | | | | | | |
| EXCLUSIVE HYPNOTHERAPY (HM07019) | | | | | | | | | | | ● | | ● | | | | | | | | | | | | | | | | ● | | | | | | | | | | | | | | | | | | | | | |
| GARDINER, F (HM07872) | | | | | | | ● | | | | | | | | | | | | | | | | | | | | | | | | | | | | | | | | | | | | | | | | | | | |
| GREER, M (HM08510) | | | | ● | | | | | | | | | | | | | | | | | | | | | | | | | | | | | | | | | | | | | | | | | | | | | | |
| HAWKINS, JAMES (HM09221) | | | ● | | | | | | | | | | | | | | | | | | | | | | | | | | | | | | | | | | | | | | | | | | | | | | | |
| HAZEL, J M (HM09290) | | | | | | | | | | | | | | | | | | | | | | ● | | | | ● | | | | | | | | | | | | | | | | | | | | | | | | |
| HOFMAN, PETRA (HM09902) | | | | | | | | | | | | | | | | ● | | | | | | | | | | | | | | | | | | | | | | | | | | | | | | | | | | |
| IN HARMONY AROMATHERAPY (HM10595) | | | | | | | ● | | | | | | | | | | | | | | | | | | | | | | | | | | | | | | | | | | | | | | | | | | | |
| J W PHYSIOTHERAPY & SPORTS (HM10805) | | | ● | | | | | | | | | | | | | | | | | | | | | | | | | | | | | | | | | | | | | | | | | | | | | | | |
| J W PHYSIOTHERAPY & SPORTS (HM10804) | | | ● | | | | | | | | | | | | | | | | | | | | | | | | | | | | | | | | | | | | | | | | | | | | | | | |
| KELLY, T G (HM11447) | | | | | | | | | | | | | | | | | | | | | | ● | | | | ● | | | | | | | | | | | | | | | | | | | | | | | | |
| KELLY, T G (HM11446) | | | | | | | | | | | | | | | | | | | | | | ● | | | | ● | | | | | | | | | | | | | | | | | | | | | | | | |
| LIVING MIND (HM12487) | ● | | | | | | | | | | ● | | ● | | | | | | | | | | | | | | | | | | | ● | | | | | | | | | | | | | | | | | | |
| LOGAN, CAROL (HM12565) | | | | | | | | | | | | | | | | | | | | | | | | | | | | | | | | | ● | | | | | | | | | | | | | | | | | |
| MACPHERSON, R G (HM12877) | | | | | | | | | | | | | | | | | | | | | | ● | | | | ● | | | | | | | | | | | | | | | | | | | | | | | | |
| MARIPOSA AROMATHERAPY (HM13103) | | | | | | | ● | | | | | | | | | | | | | | | | | | | | | | | | | | | | | | | | | | | | | | | | | | | |
| MARSHALL, FIONA S (HM13160) | | | | | | | ● | | | | | | | | | | | | | | | | | | | | | | | | | | | | | | | | | | | | | | | | | | | |
| MARSHALL, S C (HM13171) | | | | | | | | | | | | | | | | | | | | | | | | | | ● | | | | | | | | | | | | | | | | | | | | | | | | |
| MCDONALD, DAVID S (HM13456) | | | | | | | | | | | | | | | | | | | | | | ● | | | | ● | | | | | | | | | | | | | | | | | | | | | | | | |
| MOBILE CHIROPODY SERVICES (HM14028) | | | | | | | | | | | | | | | | | | | | | | ● | | | | ● | | | | | | | | | | | | | | | | | | | | | | | | |
| MORNINGSIDE PODIATRY SERVICE (HM14192) | | | | | | | | | | | | | | | | | | | | | | ● | | | | ● | | | | | | | | | | | | | | | | | | | | | | | | |
| MUKHERJI, P S (HM14327) | | | | | | | | | | | | | | | | ● | | | | | | | | | | | | | | | | | | | | | | | | | | | | | | | | | | |
| MUKHERJI, PURNENDU (HM14328) | | | | | | | | | | | | | | | | ● | | | | | | | | | | | | | | | | | | | | | | | | | | | | | | | | | | |
| N H S (HM14449) | | | | | | | | | | | | | | | | | | | | | | | | | | ● | | | | | | | | | | | | | | | | | | | | | | | | |
| NEWTOWN CHIROPRACTIC SURGERY (HM14903) | | | | | | | | | | | | | | | | | | | | | | | | | | | ● | | | | | | | | | | | | | | | | | | | | | | | |
| PATTERSON, YVONNE (HM15833) | | | | | | | ● | | | | | | | | | | | | | | | | | | | | | | | | | | | | | | | | | | | | | | | | | | | |
| PSYCHIC AND LIFE SOLUTIONS (HM16685) | | | | | | | | | | | | | | | | | | | | | | | | | | | | | | | | | ● | | | | | | | | | | | | ● | | | | ● | |
| ROBERT STONE THERAPEUTICS (HM17398) | | | | | | | ● | | | | | | | | | | | | | | | | | | | | | | | | | | | | | | | | | | | | | | | | | | | |
| ROBERTSON, MING CHEN (HM17453) | | | ● | | | | | | | | | | | | | | | | | | | | | | | | | | | | | | | | | | | | | | | | | | | | | | | |

# A - F Therapies at Practices/Businesses

| Business by County with Reference no. | Absent Healing | Acupressure | Acupuncture | Alexander Technique | Allergy Testing | Anthroposohical Med | Aromatherapy | Art Therapy | Aura Therapy | Auricular Therapy | Auto Suggestion | Autogenic Training | Aversion Therapy | Ayurvedic Medicine | Baby Massage | Bach Remedies | Bates Method | Beauty Therapy | Bio-energetics | Biofeedback | Biomagnetic Therapy | Biomechanics | Bonesetting | Bowen Therapy | Chinese Herbal Medicine |
|---|---|---|---|---|---|---|---|---|---|---|---|---|---|---|---|---|---|---|---|---|---|---|---|---|---|
| RUMNEY, KATHLEEN (HM17748) | | | | | | | ● | | | | | | | | | | | | | | | | | | |
| SCOTT, STEPHEN (HM18127) | | | | | | | | | | | | | | | | | | | | | | | | | |
| SHENTON, DIANNE (HM18402) | | | | | | | | | | | | | | | | | | | | | | ● | | | |
| SKEDD, L A (HM18629) | | | | | | | | | | | | | | | | | | | | | | | | | |
| TARA ROKPA ENDINBURGH (HM19699) | | | ● | | | | | | | | | | | | | | | | | | | | | | |
| WEST END THERAPY CLINIC (HM21222) | | | | | | | | | | | | | | | | | | | | | | | | | |
| WIGHT, STUART (HM21474) | | | | | | | | | | | | | | | | | | | | | | | | | |
| **FALKIRK** | | | | | | | | | | | | | | | | | | | | | | | | | |
| AESTHETICA TOTAL SKIN & BODY (HM00411) | | | | | | | ● | | | | | | | | | | | | | | | | | | |
| ANGUS WILLIAMSON CLINIC (HM00885) | | | | | | | ● | | | | | | | | | | | | | | | | | | |
| FALKIRK CHIROPRACTIC CLINIC (HM07074) | | | | | | | | | | | | | | | | | | | | | | | | | |
| GRANT, LESLIE & DAWN (HM08385) | | | | | | | | | | | | | | | | | | | | | | ● | | | |
| GRANT, LESLIE AND DAWN (HM08386) | | | | | | | | | | | | | | | | | | | | | | ● | | | |
| LEAH CHIROPRACTIC CLINIC (HM12098) | | | | | | | | | | | | | | | | | | | | | | | | | |
| NATURAL HEALING CENTRE (HM14543) | ● | | | | | | ● | | | | | | | | | | | | | | | | | | |
| **FIFE** | | | | | | | | | | | | | | | | | | | | | | | | | |
| BODYNEEDS (HM02630) | | | | | | | ● | | | | | | | | | | | | | | | | | | |
| BODYNEEDS (HM02629) | | | | | | | ● | | | | | | | | | | | | | | | | | | |
| CAMERON, WILLIAM (HM03588) | | | | | | | | | | | | | | | | | | | | | | ● | | | |
| COMPLEMENTARY THERAPY CLINIC (HM04949) | ● | | | | | | ● | | | | | | | | | | | | | | | | | ● | |
| DAVIDSON, ANGELA (HM05785) | | | | | | | | | | | | | | | | | | | | | | | | | |
| FOUNDATION HEALTH (HM07613) | | | | | | | | | | | | | | | | | | | | | | | | | |
| HOLISTIC AROMATHERAPY (HM09946) | | | | | | | ● | | | | | | | | | | | | | | | | | | |
| KEEP IN STEP (HM11394) | | | | | | | | | | | | | | | | | | | | | | | | | |
| NATURAL REMEDY CLINIC (HM14621) | ● | | | | | | ● | | | | | | | | | ● | | | ● | | | | | | |
| NEAT FEET (HM14743) | | | | ● | | | | | | | | | | | | | | | | | | | | | |
| O'BRIAN, D (HM15171) | | | | | | | | | | | | | | | | | | | | | | | | | |
| REMEDIES HEALTH CARE (HM17178) | | | | | | | ● | | | | | | | | | | | | | | | | | | |
| SHEERINS, ROZ (HM18370) | | | | | | | | | | | | | | | | | | | | | | | | | |
| ST ANDREWS OSTEOPATHS (HM19065) | | | ● | | | | | | | | | | | | | | | | | | | | | | |
| THERAPUTIC MASSAGE (HM19889) | | | | | | | ● | | | | | | | | | | | | | | | | | | |
| TOLBOOTH HOUSE (HM20117) | | | ● | | | | | | | | | | | | | | | | | | | | | | |
| **GLASGOW (CITY OF)** | | | | | | | | | | | | | | | | | | | | | | | | | |
| ABOUT FACE (HM00131) | | | | | | | ● | | | | | | | | | | | | | | | | | | |

| Business by County with Reference no. | Chiropody | Chiropractic | Clinical Ecology | Cognitive Therapy | Colonic Hydrotherapy | Colour Therapy | Complementary Therapy | Counselling | Cranial Osteopathy | Cranio-Sacral Therapy | Cryo Surgery | Crystal Healing | Cupping | Cymatics | Dance Movement Thrpy | Dietician | Do-In | Douching | Dowsing | Drama Therapy | Electrolipolysis | Electrolysis | Electrotherapy | Encounter Groups | Faith Healing |
|---|---|---|---|---|---|---|---|---|---|---|---|---|---|---|---|---|---|---|---|---|---|---|---|---|---|
| RUMNEY, KATHLEEN (HM17748) | | | | | | | | | | | | | | | | | | | | | | | | | |
| SCOTT, STEPHEN (HM18127) | | ● | | | | | | | | | | | | | | | | | | | | | | | |
| SHENTON, DIANNE (HM18402) | ● | | | | | | | | | | | | | | | | | | | | | | | | |
| SKEDD, L A (HM18629) | ● | | | | | | | | | | | | | | | | | | | | | | | | |
| TARA ROKPA ENDINBURGH (HM19699) | | | | | | | | ● | | | | | | | | | | | | | | | | | |
| WEST END THERAPY CLINIC (HM21222) | | ● | | | | | | | | | | | | | | | | | | | | | | | |
| WIGHT, STUART (HM21474) | | ● | | | | | | | | | | | | | | | | | | | | | | | |
| **FALKIRK** | | | | | | | | | | | | | | | | | | | | | | | | | |
| AESTHETICA TOTAL SKIN & BODY (HM00411) | | | | | | | | | | | | | | | | | | | | | | | | | |
| ANGUS WILLIAMSON CLINIC (HM00885) | | ● | | | | | | | | | | | | | | | | | | | | | | | |
| FALKIRK CHIROPRACTIC CLINIC (HM07074) | | ● | | | | | | | | | | | | | | | | | | | | | | | |
| GRANT, LESLIE & DAWN (HM08385) | ● | | | | | | | | | | ● | | | | | | | | | | | | | | |
| GRANT, LESLIE AND DAWN (HM08386) | ● | | | | | | | | | | | | | | | | | | | | | | | | |
| LEAH CHIROPRACTIC CLINIC (HM12098) | | ● | | | | | | | | | | | | | | | | | | | | | | | |
| NATURAL HEALING CENTRE (HM14543) | | | | | | | | | | | | | | | | | | | | | | | | | |
| **FIFE** | | | | | | | | | | | | | | | | | | | | | | | | | |
| BODYNEEDS (HM02630) | | | | | | | | | | | | | | | | | | | | | | | | | |
| BODYNEEDS (HM02629) | | | | | | | | | | | | | | | | | | | | | | | | | |
| CAMERON, WILLIAM (HM03588) | ● | | | | | | | | | | | | | | | | | | | | | | | | |
| COMPLEMENTARY THERAPY CLINIC (HM04949) | | | | ● | | | ● | ● | | | | | | | | | | | | | | | ● | | |
| DAVIDSON, ANGELA (HM05785) | ● | | | | | | | | | | | | | | | | | | | | | | | | |
| FOUNDATION HEALTH (HM07613) | | | | | | | | | | ● | | | | | | | | | | | | | | | |
| HOLISTIC AROMATHERAPY (HM09946) | | | | | | | | | | | | | | | | | | | | | | | | | |
| KEEP IN STEP (HM11394) | ● | | | | | | | | | | | | | | | | | | | | | | | | |
| NATURAL REMEDY CLINIC (HM14621) | | | | | | | | | ● | | | | ● | | | | | | | | | | | | ● |
| NEAT FEET (HM14743) | | | | | | | | | | | | | | | | | | | | | | | | | |
| O'BRIAN, D (HM15171) | ● | | | | | | | | | | | | | | | | | | | | | | | | |
| REMEDIES HEALTH CARE (HM17178) | | | | | | | | | | | | | | | | | | | | | | | | | |
| SHEERINS, ROZ (HM18370) | ● | | | | | | | | | | | | | | | | | | | | | | | | |
| ST ANDREWS OSTEOPATHS (HM19065) | | | | | | | | | ● | | | | | | | | | | | | | | | | |
| THERAPUTIC MASSAGE (HM19889) | | | | | | | | | | | | | | | | | | | | | | | | | |
| TOLBOOTH HOUSE (HM20117) | ● | | | | | | | | | | ● | | | | | ● | | | | | | | | | |
| **GLASGOW (CITY OF)** | | | | | | | | | | | | | | | | | | | | | | | | | |
| ABOUT FACE (HM00131) | | | | | | | | | | | | | | | | | | | | | | ● | | | |

# A - F Therapies at Practices/Businesses

| Business by County with Reference no. | Absent Healing | Acupressure | Acupuncture | Alexander Technique | Allergy Testing | Anthroposohical Med | Aromatherapy | Art Therapy | Aura Therapy | Auricular Therapy | Auto Suggestion | Autogenic Training | Aversion Therapy | Ayurvedic Medicine | Baby Massage | Bach Remedies | Bates Method |
|---|---|---|---|---|---|---|---|---|---|---|---|---|---|---|---|---|---|
| ACTIVE CHIROPRACTIC (HM00194) | | | ● | | | | | | | | | | | | | | |
| ALEXANDER TECHNIQUE (HM00543) | | | | ● | | | | | | | | | | | | | |
| ALEXANDER TECHNIQUE (HM00521) | | | | ● | | | | | | | | | | | | | |
| ANDERSON DOE PODIATRY CLINIC (HM00809) | | | | | | | | | | | | | | | | | |
| ANNE PENMAN THERAPY (HM00900) | | | | | | | | | | | | | | | | | |
| BEARSDEN CHIROPRACTIC CLINIC (HM01971) | | | | | | | | | | | | | | | | | |
| BEHIND THE VEIL (HM02068) | ● | | | | | | ● | | ● | | | | | | | | |
| BLACK, JIM (HM02424) | | | | | | | | | | | | | | | | | |
| CLINIC AT CHARING CROSS (HM04679) | | | ● | | | | | | | | | | | | | | |
| ELLIOTT CHIROPRACTIC CLINIC (HM06749) | | | | | | | | | | | | | | | | | |
| ESSENTIAL BEAUTY (HM06897) | | | | | | | ● | | | | | | | | | | |
| FITZPATRICK, J H (HM07374) | | | | | | | | | | | | | | | | | |
| FOOTSURE (HM07514) | | | | | | | | | | | | | | | | | |
| FRASER, DINGWALL & ASSOCIATES (HM07693) | | | | | | | | | | | | | | | | | |
| GLASGOW CHIROPRACTIC CLINIC (HM08124) | | | | | | | | | | | | | | | | | |
| GREENE, STEFANI (HM08482) | | | | | | | ● | | | | | | | | | | |
| HARVEST CLINIC (HM09152) | | ● | ● | | | | ● | | | | | | | | | | |
| HEALTH & VITALITY (HM09374) | | | | | | | ● | | | | | | | | | | |
| HOLISTIC HEALING & HYP (HM09961) | | | | | | | | | | | | | | | | | |
| HUI CHUN CHINESE ACUPUNCTURE (HM10348) | | | ● | | | | | | | | | | | | | | |
| HYDEPARK SAUNA (HM10472) | | | | | | | ● | | | | | | | | | | |
| KAREN SLATER AROMATHERAPIST (HM11321) | | | | | | | ● | | | | | | | | | | |
| LAMBERT, C W (HM11895) | | | | | | | | | | | | | | | | | |
| LASER THERAPY (HM11982) | | | ● | | | | | | | | | | | | | | |
| LAURIE, A (HM12015) | | | | | | | | | | | | | | | | | |
| LIFE'S ESSENTIALS (HM12357) | | | | | | | ● | | | | | | | | | | |
| LUSH, AUDREY (HM12745) | | | | | | | | | | | | | | | | | |
| MARY HERAGHTY AT HEALTHY FEET (HM13222) | | | | | | | ● | | | | | | | | | | |
| MCLAREN, CATH RENA (HM13539) | | ● | | | | | ● | | | | | | | | | | |
| MCTIMONEY CHIROPRACTIC CLINIC (HM13611) | | | | | | | | | | | | | | | | | |
| MOONEY, K (HM14107) | | | | | | | ● | | | | | | | | | | |
| MUIREND CHIROPRACTIC CLINIC (HM14321) | | | | | | | | | | | | | | | | | |
| NUTRITION WORLD (HM15126) | | ● | | | | | ● | | | | | | | | | ● | |
| PLUIDGE, MARK (HM16379) | | | | | | | | | | | | | | | | | |

| Business by County with Reference no. | Beauty Therapy | Bio-energetics | Biofeedback | Biomagnetic Therapy | Biomechanics | Bonesetting | Bowen Therapy | Chinese Herbal Medicine | Chiropody | Chiropractic | Clinical Ecology | Cognitive Therapy | Colonic Hydrotherapy | Colour Therapy | Complementary Therapy | Counselling | Cranial Osteopathy |
|---|---|---|---|---|---|---|---|---|---|---|---|---|---|---|---|---|---|
| ACTIVE CHIROPRACTIC (HM00194) | | | | | | | | | | ● | | | | | | | |
| ALEXANDER TECHNIQUE (HM00543) | | | | | | | | | | | | | | | | | |
| ALEXANDER TECHNIQUE (HM00521) | | | | | | | | | | | | | | | | | |
| ANDERSON DOE PODIATRY CLINIC (HM00809) | | | | | ● | | | | ● | | | | | | | | |
| ANNE PENMAN THERAPY (HM00900) | | | | | | | | | | | | | | | ● | ● | |
| BEARSDEN CHIROPRACTIC CLINIC (HM01971) | | | | | | | | | | ● | | | | | | | |
| BEHIND THE VEIL (HM02068) | | | | | | | | | | | | | | | | | |
| BLACK, JIM (HM02424) | | | | | ● | | | | ● | | | | | | | | |
| CLINIC AT CHARING CROSS (HM04679) | | | | | | | | | | | | | | | | | |
| ELLIOTT CHIROPRACTIC CLINIC (HM06749) | | | | | | | | | | ● | | | | | | | |
| ESSENTIAL BEAUTY (HM06897) | | | | | | | | | | | | | | | | | |
| FITZPATRICK, J H (HM07374) | | | | | | | | | ● | | | | | | | | |
| FOOTSURE (HM07514) | | | | | | | | | ● | | | | | | | | |
| FRASER, DINGWALL & ASSOCIATES (HM07693) | | | | | | | | | | ● | | | | | | | |
| GLASGOW CHIROPRACTIC CLINIC (HM08124) | | | | | | | | | | ● | | | | | | | |
| GREENE, STEFANI (HM08482) | | | | | | | | | | | | | | | | | |
| HARVEST CLINIC (HM09152) | | | | | | | ● | | | | | | | | ● | ● | |
| HEALTH & VITALITY (HM09374) | | | | | | | | | | | | | | | ● | | |
| HOLISTIC HEALING & HYP (HM09961) | | | | | | | ● | | | | | ● | | | ● | | |
| HUI CHUN CHINESE ACUPUNCTURE (HM10348) | | | | | | | | | | | | | | | | | |
| HYDEPARK SAUNA (HM10472) | | | | | | | | | | | | | | | | | |
| KAREN SLATER AROMATHERAPIST (HM11321) | | | | | | | | | | | | | | | | | |
| LAMBERT, C W (HM11895) | | | | | ● | | | | ● | | | | | | | | |
| LASER THERAPY (HM11982) | | | | | | | | | | | | | | | | | |
| LAURIE, A (HM12015) | | | | | | | | | ● | | | | | | | | |
| LIFE'S ESSENTIALS (HM12357) | | | | | | | | | | | | | | | | | |
| LUSH, AUDREY (HM12745) | | | | | | | | | | ● | | | | | | | |
| MARY HERAGHTY AT HEALTHY FEET (HM13222) | | | | | | | | | ● | | | | | | | | |
| MCLAREN, CATH RENA (HM13539) | | | | | | | ● | | | | | | | | | | |
| MCTIMONEY CHIROPRACTIC CLINIC (HM13611) | | | | | | | | | | ● | | | | | | | |
| MOONEY, K (HM14107) | | | | | | | | | | | | | | | | | |
| MUIREND CHIROPRACTIC CLINIC (HM14321) | | | | | | | | | | ● | | | | | | | |
| NUTRITION WORLD (HM15126) | | | | | | | ● | | | | | | | | | | ● |
| PLUIDGE, MARK (HM16379) | | | | | ● | | | | ● | | | | | | | | |

| Business by County with Reference no. | Cranio-Sacral Therapy | Cryo Surgery | Crystal Healing | Cupping | Cymatics | Dance Movement Thrpy | Dietician | Do-In | Douching | Dowsing | Drama Therapy | Electrolipolysis | Electrolysis | Electrotherapy | Encounter Groups | Faith Healing |
|---|---|---|---|---|---|---|---|---|---|---|---|---|---|---|---|---|
| ACTIVE CHIROPRACTIC (HM00194) | | | | | | | | | | | | | | | | |
| ALEXANDER TECHNIQUE (HM00543) | | | | | | | | | | | | | | | | |
| ALEXANDER TECHNIQUE (HM00521) | | | | | | | | | | | | | | | | |
| ANDERSON DOE PODIATRY CLINIC (HM00809) | | | | | | | | | | | | | | | | |
| ANNE PENMAN THERAPY (HM00900) | | | | | | | | | | | | | | | | |
| BEARSDEN CHIROPRACTIC CLINIC (HM01971) | | | | | | | | | | | | | | | | |
| BEHIND THE VEIL (HM02068) | | | ● | | | | | | | ● | | | | | | |
| BLACK, JIM (HM02424) | | | | | | | | | | | | | | | | |
| CLINIC AT CHARING CROSS (HM04679) | | | | | | | | | | | | | | | | |
| ELLIOTT CHIROPRACTIC CLINIC (HM06749) | | | | | | | | | | | | | | | | |
| ESSENTIAL BEAUTY (HM06897) | | | | | | | | | | | | | | | | |
| FITZPATRICK, J H (HM07374) | | ● | | | | | | | | | | | | | | |
| FOOTSURE (HM07514) | | | | | | | | | | | | | | | | |
| FRASER, DINGWALL & ASSOCIATES (HM07693) | | | | | | | | | | | | | | | | |
| GLASGOW CHIROPRACTIC CLINIC (HM08124) | | | | | | | | | | | | | | | | |
| GREENE, STEFANI (HM08482) | | | | | | | | | | | | | | | | |
| HARVEST CLINIC (HM09152) | | | | | | | | | | | | | | | | |
| HEALTH & VITALITY (HM09374) | | | | | | | | | | | | | | | | |
| HOLISTIC HEALING & HYP (HM09961) | | | | | | | | | | | | | | | | |
| HUI CHUN CHINESE ACUPUNCTURE (HM10348) | | | | | | | | | | | | | | | | |
| HYDEPARK SAUNA (HM10472) | | | | | | | | | | | | | | | | |
| KAREN SLATER AROMATHERAPIST (HM11321) | | | | | | | | | | | | | | | | |
| LAMBERT, C W (HM11895) | | | | | | | | | | | | | | | | |
| LASER THERAPY (HM11982) | | | | | | | | | | | | | | | | |
| LAURIE, A (HM12015) | | | | | | | | | | | | | | | | |
| LIFE'S ESSENTIALS (HM12357) | | | | | | | | | | | | | | | | |
| LUSH, AUDREY (HM12745) | | | | | | | | | | | | | | | | |
| MARY HERAGHTY AT HEALTHY FEET (HM13222) | | | | | | | | | | | | | | | | |
| MCLAREN, CATH RENA (HM13539) | | | | | | | | | | | | | | | | |
| MCTIMONEY CHIROPRACTIC CLINIC (HM13611) | ● | | | | | | | | | | | | | | | |
| MOONEY, K (HM14107) | | | | | | | | | | | | | | | | |
| MUIREND CHIROPRACTIC CLINIC (HM14321) | | | | | | | | | | | | | | | | |
| NUTRITION WORLD (HM15126) | | | | | | | | | | | | | | | | |
| PLUIDGE, MARK (HM16379) | | | | | | | | | | | | | | | | |

# A - F Therapies at Practices/Businesses

| Business by County with Reference no. | Absent Healing | Acupressure | Acupuncture | Alexander Technique | Allergy Testing | Anthroposohical Med | Aromatherapy | Art Therapy | Aura Therapy | Auricular Therapy | Auto Suggestion | Autogenic Training | Aversion Therapy | Ayurvedic Medicine | Baby Massage | Bach Remedies | Bates Method | Beauty Therapy | Bio-energetics | Biofeedback | Biomagnetic Therapy | Biomechanics | Bonesetting | Bowen Therapy | Chinese Herbal Medicine | Chiropody | Chiropractic | Clinical Ecology | Cognitive Therapy | Colonic Hydrotherapy | Colour Therapy | Complementary Therapy | Counselling | Cranial Osteopathy | Cranio-Sacral Therapy | Cryo Surgery | Crystal Healing | Cupping | Cymatics | Dance Movement Thrpy | Dietician | Do-In | Douching | Dowsing | Drama Therapy | Electrolipolysis | Electrolysis | Electrotherapy | Encounter Groups | Faith Healing |
|---|---|---|---|---|---|---|---|---|---|---|---|---|---|---|---|---|---|---|---|---|---|---|---|---|---|---|---|---|---|---|---|---|---|---|---|---|---|---|---|---|---|---|---|---|---|---|---|---|---|---|
| RHODIE, ANDREA (HM17231) | | | | | | | ● | | | | | | | | | | | | | | | | | | | | | | | | | | | | | | | | | | | | | | | | | | | |
| ROLLAND, C R (HM17563) | | | | | | | | | | | | | | | | | | | | | | | | | | ● | | | | | | | | | | | | | | | | | | | | | | | | |
| SCHOLL CENTRE (HM18039) | | | | | | | | | | | | | | | | | | | | | | | | | | ● | | | | | | | | | | ● | | | | | | | | | | | | | | |
| SCOTTISH SCHOOL OF HERBAL MED (HM18135) | | | | | | | ● | | | | | | | | | | | | | | | | | | | | | | | | | | | | | | | | | | | | | | | | | | | |
| SINO-HERBAL CLINIC (HM18615) | | ● | ● | | | | | | | | | | | | | | | | | | | | | | | | | | | | | ● | | | | | | ● | | | | | | | | | | | | |
| STEWART, JIM (DR) (HM19270) | | | | | | | | | | | | | | | | | | | | | | | | | | | | | ● | | | | ● | | | | | | | | | | | | | | | | | |
| THERAPY OF LIFE CLINIC (HM19905) | | | ● | | | | ● | | | | | | | | | | | | | | | | | | | | | | | | | | | | | | | | | | | | | | | | | | | |
| HIGHLAND | | | | | | | | | | | | | | | | | | | | | | | | | | | | | | | | | | | | | | | | | | | | | | | | | | |
| AUSTIN, JENNIFER (HM01367) | | | | | | | | | | | | | | | | ● | | | | | | | | | | | | | | | | | | | | | | | | | | | | | | | | | | |
| BRODIE, JACQUELINE (HM03132) | | | | | | | | | | | | | | | | ● | | | | | | | | | | | | | | | | | | | | | | | | | | | | | | | | | | |
| BUMBLE - BEE'S PHYSIO (HM03347) | | | | | | | | | | | | | | | | | | | | | | | | | | | | | | | | | | | | | | | | | | | | | | | | ● | | |
| GENTLE WAYS (HM07980) | ● | | | | | | ● | | | | | | | | | ● | | | | | | | | | | | | | | | | ● | | | | | | | | | | | | | | | | | | |
| HARMONOLOGY CENTRE (HM09017) | | | | | | | | | | | | | | | | | | | | | | | | | | | | | | | | | | | ● | | | | | | | | | | | | | | | |
| HEALTH CORNER (HM09383) | | | ● | | | | | | | | | | | | | | | | | | | | | | | | | | | | | ● | ● | ● | | | | | | | | | | | | | | ● | | |
| KARIM, M (HM11324) | | | ● | | | | | | | | | | | | | | | | | | | | | | | | | | | | | | | | | | | | | | | | | | | | | | | |
| INVERCLYDE | | | | | | | | | | | | | | | | | | | | | | | | | | | | | | | | | | | | | | | | | | | | | | | | | | |
| INVERCLYDE OSTEOPATHIC CLINIC (HM10704) | | | ● | | | | ● | | | | | | | | | | | | | | | | | | | | | | | | | | | ● | | | | | | | | | | | | | | | | |
| KELLERMANS (HM11418) | | | ● | | | | ● | | | | | | | | | | | | | | | | | ● | | ● | | | | | | | ● | | ● | | | | | | | | | | | | | | | |
| LANARKSHIRE (NORTH) | | | | | | | | | | | | | | | | | | | | | | | | | | | | | | | | | | | | | | | | | | | | | | | | | | |
| MCKIRDY, GILLIAN (HM13537) | | | | | | | ● | | | | | | | | | | | | | | | | | | | | | | | | | | | | | | | | | | | | | | | | | | | |
| REGISTERED HOMEOPATH (HM17103) | | | | | | | | | | | | | | | | ● | | | | | | | | | | | | | | | | | | | | | | | | | | | | | | | | | | |
| SEMPRE LIBERA (HM18224) | | | | | | | ● | | | | | | | | | | | | | | | | | | | | | | | | | | | | | | | | | | | | | | | | | | | |
| SMITH, IRENE B (HM18748) | | | | | | | | | | | | | | | | | | | | | | | | ● | | | | | | | | | | | | | | | | | | | | | | | | | | |
| WORLD OF HEALTH (HM21897) | | | | | | | ● | | | | | | | | | | | | | | | | | | | | | | | | | | | | | | | | | | | | | | | | | | | |
| LANARKSHIRE (SOUTH) | | | | | | | | | | | | | | | | | | | | | | | | | | | | | | | | | | | | | | | | | | | | | | | | | | |
| ROBB, A (DR) (HM17387) | | | ● | | | | | | | | | | | | | | | | | | | | | | | | | | | | | | | | | | | | | | | | | | | | | | | |
| LOTHIAN (EAST) | | | | | | | | | | | | | | | | | | | | | | | | | | | | | | | | | | | | | | | | | | | | | | | | | | |
| AROMA (HM01042) | | | | | | | ● | | | | | | | | | | | | | | | | | | | | | | | | | | | | | | | | | | | | | | | | | | | |
| EAST LOTHIAN PHYSIO CENTRE (HM06518) | | | ● | | | | | | | | | | | | | | | | | | | | | | | | | | | | | | | | | | | | | | | | | | | | | ● | | |
| FRASER, GORDON (HM07696) | | | | | | | ● | | | | | | | | | | | | | | | | | | | | | | | | | | | | | | | | | | | | | | | | | | | |
| LOTHIAN (MID) | | | | | | | | | | | | | | | | | | | | | | | | | | | | | | | | | | | | | | | | | | | | | | | | | | |
| CRYSTAL SANCTUARY (HM05532) | | | | | | | ● | | | | | | | | | | | | | | | | | | | | | | | | | | | | | | | | | | | | | | | | | | | |
| HAMILTON, JAMES (HM08844) | | | | | | | | | | | | | | | | | | | | | | | | | | ● | | | | | | | | | | | | | | | | | | | | | | | | |
| NATURAL HEALTH CENTRE (HM14573) | | | | | | | ● | | | | | | | | | | | | | | | | | | | | | | | | | | | | | | | | | | | | | | | | | | | |

# A - F Therapies at Practices/Businesses

| Business by County with Reference no. | Absent Healing | Acupressure | Acupuncture | Alexander Technique | Allergy Testing | Anthroposohical Med | Aromatherapy | Art Therapy | Aura Therapy | Auricular Therapy | Auto Suggestion | Autogenic Training | Aversion Therapy | Ayurvedic Medicine | Baby Massage | Bach Remedies | Bates Method | Beauty Therapy | Bio-energetics | Biofeedback | Biomagnetic Therapy | Biomechanics | Bonesetting | Bowen Therapy | Chinese Herbal Medicine |
|---|---|---|---|---|---|---|---|---|---|---|---|---|---|---|---|---|---|---|---|---|---|---|---|---|---|
| NEW DUNDAS CLINIC (HM14817) | | ● | | | | | | | | | | | | | | | | | | | | | | | |
| RADIANT COLOUR (HM16847) | | | | | | | | | | | | | | | | | | | | | | | | | |
| SHEARER & ASSOCIATES (HM18356) | | | | | | | | | | | | | | | | | | | | | | | | | |
| LOTHIAN (WEST) | | | | | | | | | | | | | | | | | | | | | | | | | |
| LINLITHGOW PHYSIO PRACTICE (HM12438) | | | ● | | | | | | | | | | | | | | | | | | | | | | |
| VINCES, DENISE (HM20674) | | | | | | | ● | | | | | | | | | | | | | | | | | | |
| MORAY | | | | | | | | | | | | | | | | | | | | | | | | | |
| AROMANTIC (HM01080) | | | | | | | ● | | | | | | | | | | | | | | | | | | |
| ELGIN CHIROPRACTIC CLINIC (HM06729) | | | | | | | | | | | | | | | | | | | | | | | | | |
| FINDHORN FLOWER ESSENCES (HM07307) | | | | | | | | | | | | | | | | ● | | | | | | | | | |
| HEALTHWORKS (HM09422) | | ● | ● | ● | | | ● | | | | | | | | | ● | | | | | | | | | |
| TRUJILLO, DR ORLANDO (HM20352) | | ● | | | | | | | | | | | | | | | | | | | | | | | |
| NORTHUMBERLAND | | | | | | | | | | | | | | | | | | | | | | | | | |
| SOLAR- PLEXUS (HM18864) | | | | | | | ● | | | | | | | | | | | | | | | | | | |
| ORKNEY ISLES | | | | | | | | | | | | | | | | | | | | | | | | | |
| A D S THOM (HM00030) | | | | | | | | | | | | | | | | | | | | | | ● | | | |
| PERTH AND KINROSS | | | | | | | | | | | | | | | | | | | | | | | | | |
| ACUPUNCTURE CLINIC (HM00288) | | ● | ● | | | | | | | | | | | | | | | | | | | | | | |
| ACUPUNCTURE CLINIC DUNKELD (HM00289) | | ● | ● | | | | | | | | | | | | | | | | | | | | | | |
| AUCHTERARDER CHIROPODY (HM01343) | | | | | | | | | | | | | | | | | | | | | | ● | | | |
| BACK PAIN & SPORTS CLINIC (HM01491) | | ● | | | | | | | | | | | | | | | | | | | | | | | |
| HOWIE, TOM R (HM10284) | | | | | | | | | | | | | | | | | | | | | | | | | |
| HOWIE, TOM R (HM10283) | | | | | | | | | | | | | | | | | | | | | | | | | |
| LENDRICK LODGE (HM12210) | | | ● | | | | ● | | | | | | | | | | | | | | | | | | |
| MARSHALL, LESLIE (HM13167) | | | | | | | | | | | | | | | | | | | | | | | | | |
| MOORE, MAGGIE (HM14130) | | | ● | | | | | | | | | | | | | | | | | | | | | | |
| PERTH CHIRO & OSTEO CENTRE (HM16067) | | | | | | | | | | | | | | | | | | | | | | | | | |
| STEVENSON, IAN W (HM19246) | | | | | | | | | | | | | | | | | | | | | | ● | | | |
| TAYLOR, D (HM19749) | | | | | | | | | | | | | ● | | | | | | | | | | | | |
| WIGHT CHIROPRACTIC CLINIC (HM21469) | | | | | | | | | | | | | | | | | | | | | | | | | |
| RENFREWSHIRE | | | | | | | | | | | | | | | | | | | | | | | | | |
| ALBA CENTRE (HM00473) | | | | | | ● | ● | | ● | | | | | | | | | | | | | | | | |
| BLACKHALL PARK CENTRE (HM02444) | | | | | ● | | | | | | | | | | | | | | | | | | | ● | |
| LINTON, UNNA (HM12444) | | | | | | | | | | | | | | | | | | | | | | | | | |

| Business by County with Reference no. | Chiropody | Chiropractic | Clinical Ecology | Cognitive Therapy | Colonic Hydrotherapy | Colour Therapy | Complementary Therapy | Counselling | Cranial Osteopathy | Cranio-Sacral Therapy | Cryo Surgery | Crystal Healing | Cupping | Cymatics | Dance Movement Thrpy | Dietician | Do-In | Douching | Dowsing | Drama Therapy | Electrolipolysis | Electrolysis | Electrotherapy | Encounter Groups | Faith Healing |
|---|---|---|---|---|---|---|---|---|---|---|---|---|---|---|---|---|---|---|---|---|---|---|---|---|---|
| NEW DUNDAS CLINIC (HM14817) | | | | | | | | | | | | | ● | | | | | | | | | | ● | | |
| RADIANT COLOUR (HM16847) | | | | | | ● | ● | ● | | | | | | | | | | | | | | | | | |
| SHEARER & ASSOCIATES (HM18356) | | ● | | | | | | | | | | | | | | | | | | | | | | | |
| LOTHIAN (WEST) | | | | | | | | | | | | | | | | | | | | | | | | | |
| LINLITHGOW PHYSIO PRACTICE (HM12438) | | | | | | | | | | | | | | | | | | | | | | | | | |
| VINCES, DENISE (HM20674) | | | | | | | | | | | | | | | | | | | | | | | | | |
| MORAY | | | | | | | | | | | | | | | | | | | | | | | | | |
| AROMANTIC (HM01080) | | | | | | | ● | | | | | | | | | ● | | | | | | | | | |
| ELGIN CHIROPRACTIC CLINIC (HM06729) | | ● | | | | | | | | | | | | | | | | | | | | | | | |
| FINDHORN FLOWER ESSENCES (HM07307) | | | | | | | | | | | | | | | | | | | | | | | | | |
| HEALTHWORKS (HM09422) | | ● | | | | | | ● | ● | | | | | | | | | | | | | | | | |
| TRUJILLO, DR ORLANDO (HM20352) | | | | | | | | | | | | | | | | | | | | | | | | | |
| NORTHUMBERLAND | | | | | | | | | | | | | | | | | | | | | | | | | |
| SOLAR- PLEXUS (HM18864) | | | | | | | | | | | | | | | | | | | | | | | | | |
| ORKNEY ISLES | | | | | | | | | | | | | | | | | | | | | | | | | |
| A D S THOM (HM00030) | ● | | | | | | | | | | | | | | | | | | | | | | | | |
| PERTH AND KINROSS | | | | | | | | | | | | | | | | | | | | | | | | | |
| ACUPUNCTURE CLINIC (HM00288) | | | | | | | | | | | | | | | | | | | | | | | | | |
| ACUPUNCTURE CLINIC DUNKELD (HM00289) | | | | | | | | | | | | | | | | | | | | | | | | | |
| AUCHTERARDER CHIROPODY (HM01343) | ● | | | | | | | | | | | | | | | | | | | | | | | | |
| BACK PAIN & SPORTS CLINIC (HM01491) | | | | | | | | | | | | | | | | | | | | | | | ● | | |
| HOWIE, TOM R (HM10284) | ● | | | | | | | | | | | | | | | | | | | | | | | | |
| HOWIE, TOM R (HM10283) | ● | | | | | | | | | | | | | | | | | | | | | | | | |
| LENDRICK LODGE (HM12210) | | | | | | | | | | | | | | | | | | | | | | | | | |
| MARSHALL, LESLIE (HM13167) | | ● | | | | | | | | | | | | | | | | | | | | | | | |
| MOORE, MAGGIE (HM14130) | | | | | | | | | | | | | | | | | | | | | | | | | |
| PERTH CHIRO & OSTEO CENTRE (HM16067) | | ● | | | | | | | | | | | | | | | | | | | | | | | |
| STEVENSON, IAN W (HM19246) | ● | | | | | | | | | | | | | | | | | | | | | | | | |
| TAYLOR, D (HM19749) | | | | | | | | ● | | | | | | | | | | | | | | | | | |
| WIGHT CHIROPRACTIC CLINIC (HM21469) | | ● | | | | | | | | | | | | | | | | | | | | | | | |
| RENFREWSHIRE | | | | | | | | | | | | | | | | | | | | | | | | | |
| ALBA CENTRE (HM00473) | | | | | | | | ● | | | | | | | | | | | | | | | | | |
| BLACKHALL PARK CENTRE (HM02444) | | | | | | | | | | | | | | | | | | | | | | | | | |
| LINTON, UNNA (HM12444) | ● | | | | | | | | | | | | | | | | | | | | | | | | |

# A - F Therapies at Practices/Businesses

| Business by County with Reference no. | Absent Healing | Acupressure | Acupuncture | Alexander Technique | Allergy Testing | Anthroposohical Med | Aromatherapy | Art Therapy | Aura Therapy | Auricular Therapy | Auto Suggestion | Autogenic Training | Aversion Therapy | Ayurvedic Medicine | Baby Massage | Bach Remedies | Bates Method | Beauty Therapy | Bio-energetics | Biofeedback | Biomagnetic Therapy | Biomechanics | Bonesetting | Bowen Therapy | Chinese Herbal Medicine | Chiropody | Chiropractic | Clinical Ecology | Cognitive Therapy | Colonic Hydrotherapy | Colour Therapy | Complementary Therapy | Counselling | Cranial Osteopathy | Cranio-Sacral Therapy | Cryo Surgery | Crystal Healing | Cupping | Cymatics | Dance Movement Thrpy | Dietician | Do-In | Douching | Dowsing | Drama Therapy | Electrolipolysis | Electrolysis | Electrotherapy | Encounter Groups | Faith Healing |
|---|---|---|---|---|---|---|---|---|---|---|---|---|---|---|---|---|---|---|---|---|---|---|---|---|---|---|---|---|---|---|---|---|---|---|---|---|---|---|---|---|---|---|---|---|---|---|---|---|---|---|
| PAISLEY CHIROPRACTIC CLINIC (HM15587) | | ● | | | | | | | | | | | | | | ● | | | | | | | | | | | ● | ● | | | | ● | | | | | | | | | | | | | | | | | | |
| PAISLEY NATURAL THERAPY CENTRE (HM15588) | | | ● | | | | ● | | | | | | | | | ● | | | | | | | | | | | | | | | | | ● | ● | | | | | | | | | | | | | | | | |
| PAISLEY PHYSIOTHERAPY CENTRE (HM15589) | | | ● | | | | | | | | | | | | | | | | | ● | | | | | | | | | | | | ● | | | | | | | | | | | | | | | | ● | | |
| ROSEWOOD AROMATHERAPY ROOM (HM17629) | | | | | | | ● | | | | | | | | | | | | | | | | | ● | | | | | | | | | | | | | | | | | | | | | | | | | | |
| **SCOTTISH BORDERS** | | | | | | | | | | | | | | | | | | | | | | | | | | | | | | | | | | | | | | | | | | | | | | | | | | |
| BAINES, HILARY (HM01565) | | | | | | | | | | | | | | | | ● | | | | | | | | | | | | | | | | | | | | | | | | | | | | | | | | | | |
| HICKEBOTTON, S (HM09718) | | | | | | | | | | | | | | | | | | | | | | | | | | | ● | | | | | | | | | | | | | | | | | | | | | | | |
| HOGARTH, JAMES (HM09908) | | | | | | | | | | | | | | | | | | | | | | ● | | | | ● | | | | | | | | | | | | | | | | | | | | | | | | |
| L W FOOTCARE (HM11844) | | | | | | | | | | | | | | | | | | | | | | ● | | | | ● | | | | | | | | | | | | | | | | | | | | | | | | |
| MAIN, BOB (HM12939) | | | | | | | | | | | | | | | | | | | | | | | | | | | ● | | | | | | | | | | | | | | | | | | | | | | | |
| NATURES TOUCH (HM14698) | | | | | | | ● | | | | | | | | | | | | | | | | | | | | | | | | | | | | | | | | | | | | | | | | | | | |
| NATURES WAY (HM14702) | | | | | | | ● | | | | | | | | | ● | | | | | | | | | | | | | | | | | | | | | | | | | | | | | | | | | | |
| SCOTTISH CHIROPRACTIC ASS (HM18131) | | | | | | | | | | | | | | | | | | | | | | | | | | | ● | | | | | | | | | | | | | | | | | | | | | | | |
| ST BOSWELLS CHIRO CLINIC (HM19072) | | | | | | | | | | | | | | | | | | | | | | | | | | | ● | | | | | | | | | | | | | | | | | | | | | | | |
| WATT, A S (HM21028) | | | | | | | | | | | | | | | | | | | | | | | | | | ● | | | | | | | | | | | | | | | | | | | | | | | | |
| WIGHT CHIROPRACTIC CLINIC (HM21470) | | | | | | | | | | | | | | | | | | | | | | | | | | | ● | | | | | | | | | | | | | | | | | | | | | | | |
| WISHING WELL (HM21738) | | | ● | | | | ● | | | | | | | | | ● | | | | | | | | ● | | | | | | | ● | ● | ● | ● | | | ● | | | | | | | | | | | | | |
| **SHETLAND ISLANDS** | | | | | | | | | | | | | | | | | | | | | | | | | | | | | | | | | | | | | | | | | | | | | | | | | | |
| LERWICK CHIROPRACTIC CLINIC (HM12231) | | | | | | | | | | | | | | | | | | | | | | | | | | | ● | | | | | | | | | | | | | | | | | | | | | | | |
| **STIRLING** | | | | | | | | | | | | | | | | | | | | | | | | | | | | | | | | | | | | | | | | | | | | | | | | | | |
| HILL, SARAH (HM09790) | | | ● | | | | | | | | | | | | | | | | | | | | | | | | | | | | | | | | | | | | | | | | | | | | | | | |
| WIGHT CHIROPRACTIC CLINIC (HM21471) | | | | | | | | | | | | | | | | | | | | | | | | | | | ● | | | | | | | | | | | | | | | | | | | | | | | |
| **WESTERN ISLES** | | | | | | | | | | | | | | | | | | | | | | | | | | | | | | | | | | | | | | | | | | | | | | | | | | |
| HIGHLAND CHIROPRACTIC CLINIC (HM09753) | | | | | | | | | | | | | | | | | | | | | | | | | | | ● | | | | | | | | | | | | | | | | | | | | | | | |

# A - F Therapies at Practices/Businesses

| Business by County with Reference no. | Absent Healing | Acupressure | Acupuncture | Alexander Technique | Allergy Testing | Anthroposohical Med | Aromatherapy | Art Therapy | Aura Therapy | Auricular Therapy | Auto Suggestion | Autogenic Training | Aversion Therapy | Ayurvedic Medicine | Baby Massage | Bach Remedies | Bates Method | Beauty Therapy | Bio-energetics | Biofeedback | Biomagnetic Therapy | Biomechanics | Bonesetting | Bowen Therapy | Chinese Herbal Medicine | Chiropody | Chiropractic | Clinical Ecology | Cognitive Therapy | Colonic Hydrotherapy | Colour Therapy | Complementary Therapy | Counselling | Cranial Osteopathy | Cranio-Sacral Therapy | Cryo Surgery | Crystal Healing | Cupping | Cymatics | Dance Movement Thrpy | Dietician | Do-In | Douching | Dowsing | Drama Therapy | Electrolipolysis | Electrolysis | Electrotherapy | Encounter Groups | Faith Healing |
|---|---|---|---|---|---|---|---|---|---|---|---|---|---|---|---|---|---|---|---|---|---|---|---|---|---|---|---|---|---|---|---|---|---|---|---|---|---|---|---|---|---|---|---|---|---|---|---|---|---|---|
| **WALES** | | | | | | | | | | | | | | | | | | | | | | | | | | | | | | | | | | | | | | | | | | | | | | | | | | |
| **BLAENAU GWENT** | | | | | | | | | | | | | | | | | | | | | | | | | | | | | | | | | | | | | | | | | | | | | | | | | | |
| ABERTILLERY PHYSIOTHERAPY (HM00125) | | | ● | | | | | | | | | | | | | | | | | | | | | | | | | | | | | | | | | | | | | | | | | | | | | | | |
| CLASSIC CLINIC (HM04606) | | | ● | | | | ● | | | | | | | | | | | | | | | | | | | ● | | | | | | | | | | | | | | | | | | | | | | | | |
| **BRIDGEND** | | | | | | | | | | | | | | | | | | | | | | | | | | | | | | | | | | | | | | | | | | | | | | | | | | |
| ACUPUNCTURE CLINIC (HM00261) | | | ● | | | | | | | | | | | | | | | | | | | | | | | | | | | | | | | | | | | | | | | | | | | | | | | |
| ALTERNATIVE HEALING CENTRE (HM00698) | ● | | | | | | | | | | ● | | ● | | | | | | | | | | | | | | | | | | ● | | | | | | | | | | | | | | | | | | | |
| PARKWOOD CHIROPRACTIC CLINIC (HM15725) | | | | | | | | | | | | | | | | | | | | | | | | | | | ● | | | | | | | | | | | | | | | | | | | | | | | |
| **CAERPHILLY** | | | | | | | | | | | | | | | | | | | | | | | | | | | | | | | | | | | | | | | | | | | | | | | | | | |
| OAKFIELD NATURAL HEALTH CENTRE (HM15151) | | | | | | | ● | | | | | | | | | | | | | | | | | | | ● | | | | | | | ● | | | | | | | | | | | | | | | | | |
| PARKWOOD CHIROPRACTIC CLINIC (HM15723) | | | | | | | | | | | | | | | | | | | | | | | | | | | ● | | | | | | | | | | | | | | | | | | | | | | | |
| **CARMARTHENSHIRE** | | | | | | | | | | | | | | | | | | | | | | | | | | | | | | | | | | | | | | | | | | | | | | | | | | |
| ACUPUNCTURE CENTRE (HM00253) | | | ● | | | | | | | | | | | | | | | | | | | | | | | | | | | | | | | | | | | | | | | | | | | | | | | |
| BISHOP, S J (HM02410) | | | | | | | | | | | | | | | | | | | | | | | | | | | ● | | | | | | | | | | | | | | | | | | | | | | | |
| CHARLES, L (HM04024) | | | | | | | ● | | | | | | | | | | | | | | | | | | | | | | | | | | | | | | | | | | | | | | | | | | | |
| GREENWAY CONSULTANCY (HM08495) | ● | | | | | | ● | | | | ● | | | | | | | | | | | | | | | | | | ● | | | ● | ● | | | | | | | | | | | | | | | | | |
| HARCOURT-RAY, JILL (HM08965) | | | | | | | ● | | | | | | | | | | | | | | | | | | | | | | | | | | | | | | | | | | | | | | | | | | | |
| KACHA-STONES.COM (HM11292) | | | | | | | | | ● | | | | | | | | | | | | | | | | | | | | | | | | | | | | ● | | | | | | | ● | | | | | | |
| PENNANT VALLEY (HM15985) | | | | | | | ● | | | | | | | | | | | | | | | | | | | | | | | | | | | | | | | | | | | | | | | | | | | |
| SPENCER AROMATHERAPY (HM18990) | | | | | | | ● | | | | | | | | | | | | | | | | | | | | | | | | | | | | | | | | | | | | | | | | | | | |
| **CEREDIGION** | | | | | | | | | | | | | | | | | | | | | | | | | | | | | | | | | | | | | | | | | | | | | | | | | | |
| AMIES, SUSAN (HM00785) | | | | | | | | | | | | | | | | | | | | | | | | | | ● | | | | | | | | | | | | | | | | | | | | | | | | |
| CHERRY TREE CTRE FOR NTRL MED (HM04109) | | | ● | | | | | | | | | | | | | | | | | | | | | | | | | | | | | | | | | | | | | | | | | | | | | | | |
| COCKSEDGE, JOHN M (HM04774) | | | | | | | | | | | | | | | | | | | | | | ● | | | | ● | | | | | | | | | | | | | | | | | | | | | | | | |
| ENGELKAMP, JOANNA (HM06824) | | | | ● | | | | | | | | | | | | | | | | | | | | | | | | | | | | | | | | | | | | | | | | | | | | | | |
| FFYNNONWEN NATURAL THRPY CTRE (HM07256) | | | | | ● | | | | | | | | | | | ● | | | | | | | | ● | | | | | | | | | ● | | | | | | | | | | | | | | | | | |
| JONES, B E (HM11122) | | | | | | | | | | | | | | | | | | | | | | | | | | ● | | | | | | | | | | | | | | | | | | | | | | | | |
| LEWIS, D MICHAEL (HM12289) | | | | | | | | | | | | | | | | | | | | | | | | | | ● | | | | | | | | | | | | | | | | | | | | | | | | |
| SIMMONDS, K M (HM18559) | | | ● | | | | | | | | | | | | | | | | | | | | | | | | | | | | | | | | | | | | | | | | | | | | | | | |
| **CONWY** | | | | | | | | | | | | | | | | | | | | | | | | | | | | | | | | | | | | | | | | | | | | | | | | | | |
| DREW, DAVID (HM06305) | ● | | | | | | ● | | | | | | | | | | | | | | | | | | | | | | | | | ● | ● | | | | | | | | | | | | | | | | | ● |
| HERBS FOR EVERYONE (HM09669) | | | ● | | | | ● | | | | | | | | | | | | | | | | | | | | | | | | | ● | ● | | | | | | | | | | | | | | | | | |
| MELA CENTRE OF OSTEOPATHY (HM13702) | | | | | | | | | | | | | | | | | | | | | | | | | | | | | | | | ● | | | | | | | | | | | | | | | ● | | | |

# A - F Therapies at Practices/Businesses

| Business by County with Reference no. | Absent Healing | Acupressure | Acupuncture | Alexander Technique | Allergy Testing | Anthroposohical Med | Aromatherapy | Art Therapy | Aura Therapy | Auricular Therapy | Auto Suggestion | Autogenic Training | Aversion Therapy | Ayurvedic Medicine | Baby Massage | Bach Remedies | Bates Method | Beauty Therapy | Bio-energetics | Biofeedback | Biomagnetic Therapy | Biomechanics | Bonesetting | Bowen Therapy | Chinese Herbal Medicine | Chiropody | Chiropractic | Clinical Ecology | Cognitive Therapy | Colonic Hydrotherapy | Colour Therapy | Complementary Therapy | Counselling | Cranial Osteopathy | Cranio-Sacral Therapy | Cryo Surgery | Crystal Healing | Cupping | Cymatics | Dance Movement Thrpy | Dietician | Do-In | Douching | Dowsing | Drama Therapy | Electrolipolysis | Electrolysis | Electrotherapy | Encounter Groups | Faith Healing |
|---|---|---|---|---|---|---|---|---|---|---|---|---|---|---|---|---|---|---|---|---|---|---|---|---|---|---|---|---|---|---|---|---|---|---|---|---|---|---|---|---|---|---|---|---|---|---|---|---|---|---|
| MEWIS, R J (HM13782) | | | | | | | | | | | | | | | | | | | | | | | | | | | ● | | | | | | | | | | | | | | | | | | | | | | | |
| NIMAN, GEORGE (HM14946) | | | ● | | | | | | | | | | | | | | | | | | | | | | | | | | | | | | | | | | | | | | | | | | | | | | | |
| **DENBIGHSHIRE** | | | | | | | | | | | | | | | | | | | | | | | | | | | | | | | | | | | | | | | | | | | | | | | | | | |
| ALLIED PHYSIOTHERAPY (HM00646) | | ● | | | | | | | | | | | | | | | | | | | | | | | | | | | | | | | | | | | | | | | | | | | | | | | | |
| CELESTIAL DESIGNS AROMATHERAPY (HM03882) | | | | | | | ● | | | | | | | | | | | | | | | | | | | | | | | | | | | | | | | | | | | | | | | | | | | |
| KEELY, JANETTE (HM11388) | | | | | | | | | | | | | | | | | | | | | | | | | | | ● | | | | | | | | | | | | | | | | | | | | | | | |
| KERFOOT OWEN, RITA (HM11542) | | | | | | | | | | | | | | | | ● | | | | | | | | | | | | | | | | | | | | | | | | | | | | | | | | | | |
| MCGILL, L (HM13484) | | | | | | | | | | | | | | | | | | | | | | | | | | | | | | | | | ● | | | | | | | | | | | | | | | | | |
| ROBERTS, S (HM17425) | | | | | | | | | | | | | | | | | | | | | | | | | | | ● | | | | | | | | | | | | | | | | | | | | | | | |
| ROY MORRIS CLINIC (HM17709) | | | ● | | | | | | | | | | | | | | | | | | | | | | | | | | | | | | | | | | | | | | | | | | | | | | | |
| **FLINTSHIRE** | | | | | | | | | | | | | | | | | | | | | | | | | | | | | | | | | | | | | | | | | | | | | | | | | | |
| A L J RILEY ASSOCIATES (HM00038) | | | | | | | | | | | | | | | | | | | | | | | | | | | | | | | | ● | | | | | | | | | | | | | | | | | | |
| BOOTS HEALTHCARE SERVICES (HM02711) | | | | | | | | | | | | | | | | | | | | | | ● | | | | ● | | | | | | | | | | | | | | | | | | | | | | | | |
| BRITTAIN-DODD, RUTH (HM03102) | | | | | | | | | | | | | | | | | | | | | | | | | | | ● | | | | | | | | | | | | | | | | | | | | | | | |
| CHIROPODISTS SURGERY (HM04298) | | | | | | | | | | | | | | | | | | | | | | | | | | ● | | | | | | | | | | | | | | | | | | | | | | | | |
| GAFFNEY, ALMA (HM07827) | | | | | | | | | | | | | | | | | | | | | | ● | | | | ● | | | | | | | | | | ● | | | | | | | | | | | | | | |
| JONES, J M (HM11154) | | | ● | | | | | | | | | | | | | | | | | | | | | | | | | | | | | | | | | | | | | | | | | | | | | | | |
| PEARL AROMATHERAPY (HM15904) | | | | | | | ● | | | | | | | | | | | | | | | | | | | | | | | | | | | | | | | | | | | | | | | | | | | |
| REECE, JULIE (HM17038) | | | | | | | | | | | | | | | | | | | | | | ● | | | | ● | | | | | | | | | | | | | | | | | | | | | | | | |
| SIMPLY NATURAL (HM18579) | | | | | | | ● | | | | | | | | | | | | | | | | | | | | | | | | | | | | | | | | | | | | | | | | | | | |
| **GLAMORGAN (VALE OF)** | | | | | | | | | | | | | | | | | | | | | | | | | | | | | | | | | | | | | | | | | | | | | | | | | | |
| ACUPUNTURE CENTRE (HM00338) | | | ● | | | | | | | | | | | | | | | | | | | | | | | | | | | | | | | | | | | | | | | | | | | | | | | |
| ALEXANDER TECHNIQUE (HM00551) | | | | ● | | | | | | | | | | | | | | | | | | | | | | | | | | | | | | | | | | | | | | | | | | | | | | |
| ALEXANDER TECHNIQUE (HM00546) | | | | ● | | | | | | | | | | | | | | | | | | | | | | | | | | | | | | | | | | | | | | | | | | | | | | |
| AMETHYST HEALING CENTRE (HM00784) | | | | | | | ● | | | | | | | | | | | | | | | | | | | | | | | | | | | | | | | | | | | | | | | | | | | |
| AROMA (HM01041) | | | | | | | ● | | | | | | | | | | | | | | | | | | | | | | | | | | | | | | | | | | | | | | | | | | | |
| AROMACARE (HM01068) | | | | | | | ● | | | | | | | | | | | | | | | | | | | | | | | | | | | | | | | | | | | | | | | | | | | |
| AROMATHERAPY CLINIC (HM01105) | | | | | | | ● | | | | | | | | | ● | | | | | | | | | | | | | | | | | | | | | | | | | | | | | | | | | | |
| BENNER, LAWRENCE M (HM02135) | | | | | | | | | | | | | | | | | | | | | | | | | | | ● | | | | | | | | | | | | | | | | | | | | | | | |
| BIO UNIT (HM02330) | | | | | | | ● | | | | | | | | | | | | | | | | | | | | | | | | | | | | | | | | | | | | | | | | | | | |
| BODY ESSENTIALS (HM02587) | | | | | | | ● | | | | | | | | | | | | | | | | | | | | | | | | | | | | | | | | | | | | | | | | | | | |
| BOYLE, MARY (HM02828) | | | ● | | | | | | | | | | | | | | | | | | | | | | | | | | | | | | | | | | | | | | | | | | | | | | | |
| BROWN, ANNE (HM03214) | | | ● | | | | | | | | | | | | | | | | | | | | | | | | | | | | | | | | | | | | | | | | | | | | | ● | | |
| CARDIFF CHIROPRACTIC CLINIC (HM03666) | | | | | | | | | | | | | | | | | | | | | | | | | | | ● | | | | | | | | | | | | | | | | | | | | | | | |

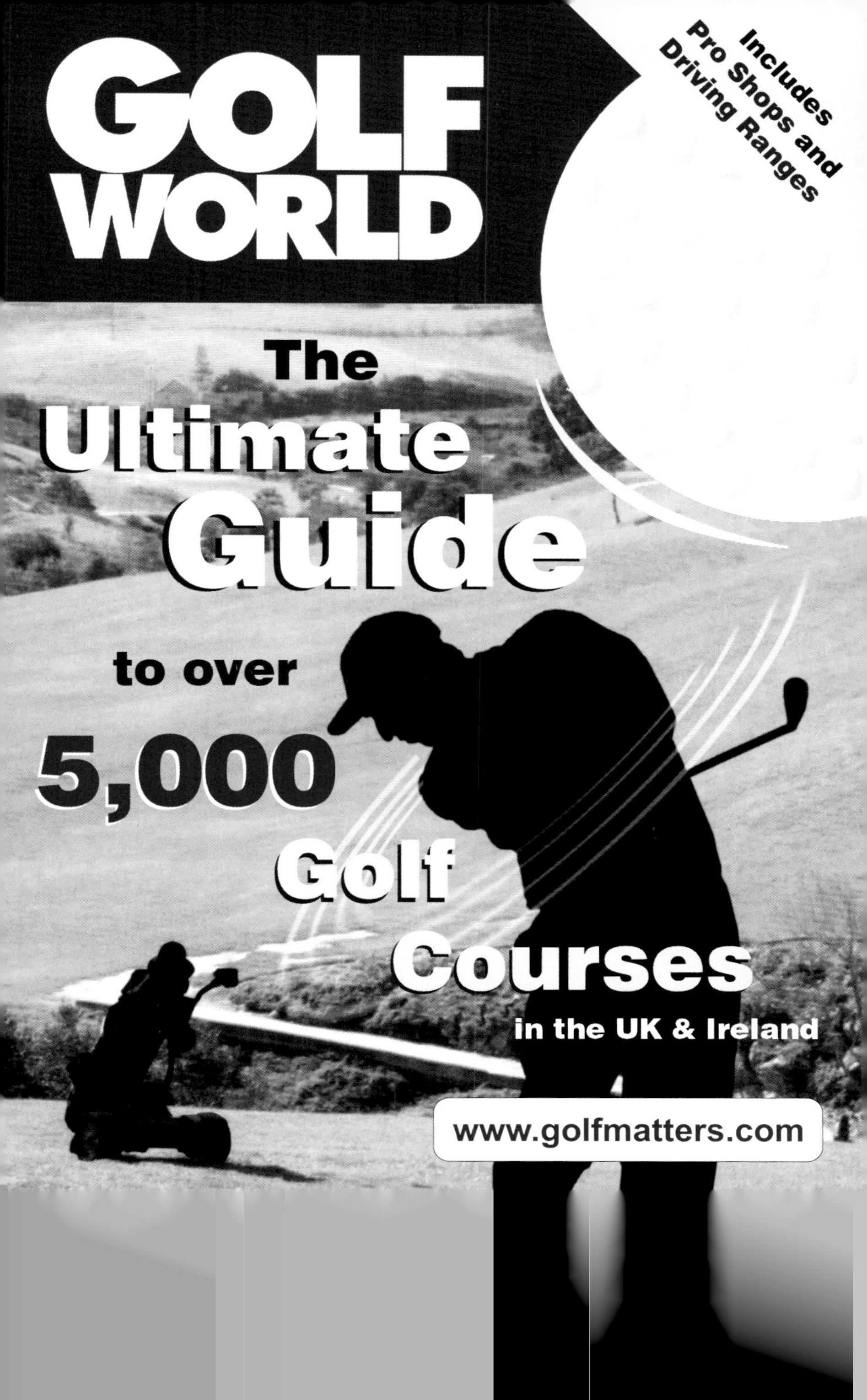
GOLF WORLD
Includes Pro Shops and Driving Ranges
The Ultimate Guide
to over 5,000 Golf Courses
in the UK & Ireland
www.golfmatters.com

# A - F Therapies at Practices/Businesses

Business by County with Reference no.

| Business by County with Reference no. | Absent Healing | Acupressure | Acupuncture | Alexander Technique | Allergy Testing | Anthroposohical Med | Aromatherapy | Art Therapy | Aura Therapy | Auricular Therapy | Auto Suggestion | Autogenic Training | Aversion Therapy | Ayurvedic Medicine | Baby Massage | Bach Remedies | Bates Method | Beauty Therapy | Bio-energetics | Biofeedback | Biomagnetic Therapy | Biomechanics | Bonesetting | Bowen Therapy | Chinese Herbal Medicine |
|---|---|---|---|---|---|---|---|---|---|---|---|---|---|---|---|---|---|---|---|---|---|---|---|---|---|
| **PEMBROKESHIRE** | | | | | | | | | | | | | | | | | | | | | | | | | |
| ACUPUNCTURE CLINIC (HM00266) | | | ● | | | | | | | | | | | | | | | | | | | | | | |
| ACUPUNCTURE CONSULTANT (HM00292) | | | ● | | | | | | | | | | | | | | | | | | | | | | |
| BENTLEY, JOHN (HM02175) | | | | | | | | | | | | | | | | | | | | | | | | | |
| CENTRE OF TRADITIONAL HEALING (HM03926) | | | ● | ● | | | | | | | | | | | | | | | | | | | | | |
| LOFTUS-BAKER, LYNNE (HM12564) | | | | | | | | | | | | | | | | ● | | | | | | | | | |
| LYNDHURST HOUSE (HM12770) | | | | | | | ● | | | | | | | | | | | | | | | | | | |
| ROY, GILLIAN (HM17711) | | | | | | | | | | | | | | | | | | | | | | | | | |
| WISEMAN, LOUISE (HM21734) | | | ● | | | | | | | | | | | | | | | | | | | | | | |
| **POWYS** | | | | | | | | | | | | | | | | | | | | | | | | | |
| BACK PAIN CENTRE (HM01495) | | | | | | | | | | | | | | | | | | | | | | | | | |
| BACK PAIN CENTRE (HM01496) | | | | | | | | | | | | | | | | | | | | | | | | | |
| BRECON CLINIC (HM02944) | | ● | ● | | | | ● | | | | | | | | | | | | | | | | | | |
| BRECON COMPLEMENTARY MED CTRE (HM02945) | | | ● | | ● | | ● | | | | | | | | | | | | | | | | | ● | |
| BYFLEET, ROSEMARY (HM03511) | | | | | | | | | | | | | | | | | | | | | | | | | |
| CONROY, CHRISTINE (HM05007) | ● | | | | | | | | | | | | | | | | | | | | | | | | |
| COVENT HOUSE NTRL HEALTH CTRE (HM05280) | | | ● | ● | | | | | | | | | | | | | | | | | | | | | |
| GROVES, FRAN (HM08614) | | | | | | | | | | | | | | | | | | | | | | | | ● | |
| HEALTH FOCUS (HM09386) | | ● | | | | | ● | | | | | | | | | | | | | | | | | ● | |
| KILGOUR, KATHARINE () | | | ● | | | | | | | | | | | | | | | | | | | | | | |
| LLANDRINDOD WELLS SPA TOWN (HM12499) | | | ● | | ● | | | | | | | | | | | | | | | | | | | | |
| PEACE CLINIC (HM15876) | | | | | | | | | | | | | | | | | | | | | | | | | |
| SHEPPARD, HELEN (HM18421) | | | | | | | | | | | | | | | | ● | | | | | | | | | |
| WILLIAMS, BRIAN (HM21543) | | | | | | | | | | | | | | | | ● | | | | | | | | | |
| **RHONDDA CYNON TAFF** | | | | | | | | | | | | | | | | | | | | | | | | | |
| LIFE CARING CENTRE (HM12338) | | | | | | | | | | | | | | | | | | | | | | | | | |
| POLLEY, LYNDON (HM16416) | | | | | | | | | | | | | | | | | | | | | | ● | | | |
| **SWANSEA** | | | | | | | | | | | | | | | | | | | | | | | | | |
| ABERTAWE PHYSIOTHERAPY CLINIC (HM00124) | | ● | ● | | | | | | | | | | | | | | | | | | | | | | |
| ACUPUNCTURE CENTRE (HM00254) | | | ● | | | | | | | | | | | | | | | | | | | | | | |
| ACUPUNCTURE CLINIC (HM00259) | | | ● | | | | | | | | | | | | | | | | | | | | | | |
| CASTELL, PHILIPPA (HM03825) | | | | ● | | | | | | | | | | | | | | | | | | | | | |
| LEYSON, S & I (HM12321) | | | | | | | | | | | | | | | | | | | | | | | | | |
| PEDORTHICS FOOT SGY PRACTICE (HM15935) | | | | | | | | | | | | | | | | | | | | | | ● | | | |

| Business by County with Reference no. | Chiropody | Chiropractic | Clinical Ecology | Cognitive Therapy | Colonic Hydrotherapy | Colour Therapy | Complementary Therapy | Counselling | Cranial Osteopathy | Cranio-Sacral Therapy | Cryo Surgery | Crystal Healing | Cupping | Cymatics | Dance Movement Thrpy | Dietician | Do-In | Douching | Dowsing | Drama Therapy | Electrolipolysis | Electrolysis | Electrotherapy | Encounter Groups | Faith Healing |
|---|---|---|---|---|---|---|---|---|---|---|---|---|---|---|---|---|---|---|---|---|---|---|---|---|---|
| **PEMBROKESHIRE** | | | | | | | | | | | | | | | | | | | | | | | | | |
| ACUPUNCTURE CLINIC (HM00266) | | | | | | | | | | | | | | | | | | | | | | | | | |
| ACUPUNCTURE CONSULTANT (HM00292) | | | | | | | | | | | | | | | | | | | | | | | | | |
| BENTLEY, JOHN (HM02175) | | ● | | | | | | | | | | | | | | | | | | | | | | | |
| CENTRE OF TRADITIONAL HEALING (HM03926) | | ● | | | | | | | | | | | | | | | | | | | | | | | |
| LOFTUS-BAKER, LYNNE (HM12564) | | | | | | | | | | | | | | | | | | | | | | | | | |
| LYNDHURST HOUSE (HM12770) | | | | | | | | | | | | | | | | | | | | | | | | | |
| ROY, GILLIAN (HM17711) | | ● | | | | | | | | | | | | | | | | | | | | | | | |
| WISEMAN, LOUISE (HM21734) | | | | | | | | | | | | | | | | | | | | | | | | | |
| **POWYS** | | | | | | | | | | | | | | | | | | | | | | | | | |
| BACK PAIN CENTRE (HM01495) | | ● | | | | | | | | | | | | | | | | | | | | | | | |
| BACK PAIN CENTRE (HM01496) | | ● | | | | | | | | | | | | | | | | | | | | | | | |
| BRECON CLINIC (HM02944) | | | | | | | ● | | | | | | | | | | | | | | | | | | |
| BRECON COMPLEMENTARY MED CTRE (HM02945) | ● | | | | | | | ● | | | | | | | | | | | | | | | | | |
| BYFLEET, ROSEMARY (HM03511) | ● | | | | | | | | | | | | | | | | | | | | | | | | |
| CONROY, CHRISTINE (HM05007) | | | | | | | | | ● | | | | | | | | | | | | | | | | |
| COVENT HOUSE NTRL HEALTH CTRE (HM05280) | ● | | | | | | | ● | | ● | | | | | | | | | | | | | | | |
| GROVES, FRAN (HM08614) | | | | | | | | | | | | | | | | | | | | | | | | | |
| HEALTH FOCUS (HM09386) | ● | | | | | | | | | | | | | | | | | | | | | | | | |
| KILGOUR, KATHARINE () | | | | | | | | | | | | | | | | | | | | | | | | | |
| LLANDRINDOD WELLS SPA TOWN (HM12499) | ● | | | | | | | ● | | | | | | | | | | | | | | | | | |
| PEACE CLINIC (HM15876) | | | | | | | | ● | | | | | | | | | | | | | | | | | |
| SHEPPARD, HELEN (HM18421) | | | | | | | | | | | | ● | | | | | | | ● | | | | | | |
| WILLIAMS, BRIAN (HM21543) | | | | | | | | | | | | | | | | | | | | | | | | | |
| **RHONDDA CYNON TAFF** | | | | | | | | | | | | | | | | | | | | | | | | | |
| LIFE CARING CENTRE (HM12338) | | | | | | | | ● | | | | | | | | | | | | | | | | | |
| POLLEY, LYNDON (HM16416) | ● | | | | | | | | | | | | | | | | | | | | | | | | |
| **SWANSEA** | | | | | | | | | | | | | | | | | | | | | | | | | |
| ABERTAWE PHYSIOTHERAPY CLINIC (HM00124) | | | | | | | ● | | | | | | | | | | | | | | | | | | |
| ACUPUNCTURE CENTRE (HM00254) | | | | | | | | | | | | | | | | | | | | | | | | | |
| ACUPUNCTURE CLINIC (HM00259) | | | | | | | | | | | | | | | | | | | | | | | | | |
| CASTELL, PHILIPPA (HM03825) | | | | | | | | | | | | | | | | | | | | | | | | | |
| LEYSON, S & I (HM12321) | | ● | | | | | | | | | | | | | | | | | | | | | | | |
| PEDORTHICS FOOT SGY PRACTICE (HM15935) | | | | | | | | | | | | | | | | | | | | | | | | | |

# A - F Therapies at Practices/Businesses

| Business by County with Reference no. | Absent Healing | Acupressure | Acupuncture | Alexander Technique | Allergy Testing | Anthroposohical Med | Aromatherapy | Art Therapy | Aura Therapy | Auricular Therapy | Auto Suggestion | Autogenic Training | Aversion Therapy | Ayurvedic Medicine | Baby Massage | Bach Remedies | Bates Method | Beauty Therapy | Bio-energetics | Biofeedback | Biomagnetic Therapy | Biomechanics | Bonesetting | Bowen Therapy | Chinese Herbal Medicine |
|---|---|---|---|---|---|---|---|---|---|---|---|---|---|---|---|---|---|---|---|---|---|---|---|---|---|
| PHILLIPS, DAVID (HM16128) | | | | | | | | | | | | | | | | | | | | | | | | | |
| RODWAY & ASSOCIATES (HM17531) | | | | | | | | | | | | | | | | | | | | | | | | | |
| SOAR, TIMOTHY (HM18847) | | | | ● | | | | | | | | | | | | | | | | | | | | | |
| SOUTH WEST CHIROPRACTIC CLINIC (HM18914) | | | | | | | | | | | | | | | | | | | | | | | | | |
| SWANSEA CLINIC OF NATURAL MED (HM19578) | | | ● | | | | | | | | | | | | | | | | | | | | | | |
| WHEATLEY, F (HM21309) | | | | | | | ● | | | | | | | | | | | | | | | | | | |
| **WREXHAM** | | | | | | | | | | | | | | | | | | | | | | | | | |
| FREEDOM WITHIN (HM07715) | | | | | | | ● | | | | | | | | | | | | | | | | | | |
| HOWELL, STEPHANIE (HM10271) | | | | | | | ● | | | | | | | | | | | | | | | | | | |
| SENSORAMA (HM18229) | | | | | | | ● | | | | | | | | | | | | | | | | | | |
| TOP TO TOE (HM20165) | | | | | | | ● | | | | | | | | | | | | | | | | | | |

| Business by County with Reference no. | Chiropody | Chiropractic | Clinical Ecology | Cognitive Therapy | Colonic Hydrotherapy | Colour Therapy | Complementary Therapy | Counselling | Cranial Osteopathy | Cranio-Sacral Therapy | Cryo Surgery | Crystal Healing | Cupping | Cymatics | Dance Movement Thrpy | Dietician | Do-In | Douching | Dowsing | Drama Therapy | Electrolipolysis | Electrolysis | Electrotherapy | Encounter Groups | Faith Healing |
|---|---|---|---|---|---|---|---|---|---|---|---|---|---|---|---|---|---|---|---|---|---|---|---|---|---|
| PHILLIPS, DAVID (HM16128) | | ● | | | | | | | | | | | | | | | | | | | | | | | |
| RODWAY & ASSOCIATES (HM17531) | | | | | | | | | ● | | | | | | | | | | | | | | | | |
| SOAR, TIMOTHY (HM18847) | | | | | | | | | | | | | | | | | | | | | | | | | |
| SOUTH WEST CHIROPRACTIC CLINIC (HM18914) | | ● | | | | | | | | | | | | | | | | | | | | | | | |
| SWANSEA CLINIC OF NATURAL MED (HM19578) | | | | | | | | | | | | | | | | | | | | | | | | | |
| WHEATLEY, F (HM21309) | | | | | | | | | | | | | | | | | | | | | | | | | |
| **WREXHAM** | | | | | | | | | | | | | | | | | | | | | | | | | |
| FREEDOM WITHIN (HM07715) | | | | | | | | | | | | | | | | | | | | | | | | | |
| HOWELL, STEPHANIE (HM10271) | | | | | | | | | | | | | | | | | | | | | | | | | |
| SENSORAMA (HM18229) | | | | | | | | | | | | | | | | | | | | | | | | | |
| TOP TO TOE (HM20165) | | | | | | | | | | | | | | | | | | | | | | | | | |

HEALTH MYSELF

# Practitioner Entry Request Form

If you would like the opportunity to enter your Complementary Medicine Practice **FREE OF CHARGE** into this unique directory then follow any of the easy steps below:

- Fill in the request form below and send it to: **FREEPOST HCC PUBLISHING LTD**
- Fax: **08707 541667**
- Tel: **08707 541676**
- Email: **information@healthmyself.com**
- Visit: **www.healthmyself.com**

Please send a more detailed questionnaire to this Practice, to ensure our details are entered correctly in the Healthmyself Directory.

| | |
|---|---|
| **Your Name** | |
| **Business Name** | |
| **Address** | |
| **County /Postcode** | |
| **Contact Name** | |
| **Job Title** | |
| **Telephone / Fax** | T: F: |
| **Web Address** | www |
| **Email** | |

**Business Type** *(please tick)*

Complementary Medicine ☐ Manipulative Structural Therapy ☐
Mind Body Medicine ☐ Touch Therapy ☐ Self Help Treatment ☐
Medicinal Therapy ☐ Oriental Medicine ☐ Postural Therapy ☐

*Tear here*

HEALTH MYSELF

# SECTION 3b

## F-O of Therapies at Practices

# F - O Therapies at Practices/Businesses

| Business by County with Reference no. | Family Planning (Natural) | Family Therapy | Feldenkrais Methodology | Feng Shui | Floral Essence Therapy | Flotation Therapy | Gait Analysis | Gem Essence Therapy | Gestalt Therapy | Group Therapy | Hay Diet | Healer | Healing Therapy | Hellerwork | Herbal Medicine | Holistic Healing | Homeopathy | Hopi Ear Candles | Humanistic Psychology | Hypnosis | Hypnotherapy | Indian Head Massage | Inhalation Therapy | Iridology | Kinesiology | Kirlian Photography | Laser Treatment | Life Style Coaching | Light Therapy | Macrobiotics | Magnetic Therapy | Manipulation | Manual Lymph Drainage | Massage (Therapeutic) | McTimoney Chiropractic | Meditation | Metamorphic Therapy | Miasm Therapy | Micro Manipulation | Moxibustion | Mud Therapy | Music Therapy | Nail Surgery | Naturopathy | Neuro-Linguistic Program | Neurotherapy | Nutritional Therapy | Orgone Therapy | Oriental Diagnosis | Orthomolecular Medicine |
|---|---|---|---|---|---|---|---|---|---|---|---|---|---|---|---|---|---|---|---|---|---|---|---|---|---|---|---|---|---|---|---|---|---|---|---|---|---|---|---|---|---|---|---|---|---|---|---|---|---|---|
| **ENGLAND** | | | | | | | | | | | | | | | | | | | | | | | | | | | | | | | | | | | | | | | | | | | | | | | | | | |
| **BEDFORDSHIRE** | | | | | | | | | | | | | | | | | | | | | | | | | | | | | | | | | | | | | | | | | | | | | | | | | | |
| ALOE VERA SPECIALISTS (HM00681) | | | | | | | | | | | | | | | ● | | | | | | | | | | | | | | | | | | | | | | | | | | | | | | | | | | | |
| ALTERNATIVE THERAPY AT WORK (HM00732) | | | | | | | | | | | | | | | | | | | | | | ● | | | | | | | | | | | | ● | | | | | | | | | | | | | | | | |
| BANFIELD, KEITH (HM01658) | | | | | | | | | | | | | | | | | | | | ● | | | | | | | | | | | | | | | | | | | | | | | | | | | | | | |
| BOYCE, MICHAEL (HM02814) | | | | | | | | | | | | | | | | | | | | | | | | | ● | | | | | | | | | | | | | | | | | | | | | | | | | |
| BURTON, MERILYNN (HM03444) | | | | | | | | | | | | | | | | | | | | | | | | | | | | | | | | | | ● | | | | | | | | | | | | | | | | |
| CHARTERED PHYSIOTHERAPIST (HM04042) | | | | | | | | | | | | | | | | | | | | | | | | | ● | | | | | | | ● | | ● | | | | | | | | | | | | | | | | |
| CHRYSALIS (HM04458) | | | | | | | | | | | | | | | | | | | | ● | | | | | | | | | | | | | | | | | | | | | | | | | | | | | | |
| CLNC OF ACU & CHINESE HERB MED (HM04726) | | | | | | | | | | | | | | | ● | ● | | | | | | | | | | | | | | | ● | | | | | | | | | ● | | | | | | | | | ● | |
| DE PRINCE, THESSALONIA (HM05916) | | | | | | | | | | | | | | | | | | | | ● | | | | | | | | | | | | | | | | | | | | | | | | | | | | | | |
| DUNTON CTRE-COUN/PSYCHOTHERAPY (HM06428) | | ● | | | | | | | ● | | | | | | | | | | ● | | | | | | | | | | | | | | | | | | | | | | | | | | | | | | | |
| GORANIA, V D (DR) (HM08276) | | | | | | | | | | | | | | | | | ● | | | | | | | | | | | | | | | | | | | | | | | | | | | | | | | | | |
| GROVE NATURAL THERAPY CLINIC (HM08610) | | | | | | | | | | | | | | | | | ● | | | | | | | | | | | | | | | | | ● | ● | | | | | | | | | ● | | | ● | | | |
| HOLISTIC HYPNOTHERAPY (HM09983) | | | | | | | | | | | | ● | ● | | | | | | | ● | ● | | | | | | | | | | | | | | | | | | | | | | | | | | | | | |
| HYPNOSIS HEALTH CLINIC (HM10498) | | | | | | | | | | | | | | | | | | | | ● | | | | | | | | | | | | | | | | | | | | | | | | | | | | | | |
| INWARD BOUND THERAPIES (HM10707) | | | | | | | | | | | | | | | | | | | | | ● | | | | | | | | | | | | | | | | | | | | | | | | | | | | | |
| JADE COLLEGE-NATURAL THERAPY (HM10867) | | | | | | | | | | | | | | | | | | | | | | ● | | | | | | | | | | | | | | | | | | | | | | | | | ● | | | |
| JENNIFER K HOUGH - PHYSIO (HM11004) | | | | | | | | | | | | | | | | | | | | | | | | | | | | | | | | ● | | ● | | | | | | | | | | | | | | | | |
| JOHNSTONS CHIROPODIST (HM11107) | | | | | | | | | | | | | | | | | | | | | | ● | | | | | | | | | | | | | | | | | | | | | | | | | | | | |
| MAGNETS 4 HEALTH (HM12918) | | | | | | | | | | | | | | | | | | | | | | | | | | | | | | | ● | | | | | | | | | | | | | | | | | | | |
| PRICE, SARAH (HM16596) | | | | | | | | | | | | | | | | | | | | | | | | | | | | | | | | | | ● | | | | | | | | | | | | | | | | |
| SHEER PERFECTION (HM18367) | | | | | | | | | | | | | | | | | | | | | | ● | | | | | | | | | | | | | | | | | | | | | | | | | | | | |
| SPECTRUM HEALTH TRUST (HM18976) | | ● | | | | | | | | ● | | ● | ● | | ● | ● | ● | | | | ● | ● | | | ● | | | ● | | | | ● | | ● | | ● | | | | | | | | | | | ● | | | |
| STEWART PALMER HYPNOTHERAPIST (HM19255) | | | | | | | | | | | | | | | | | | | | ● | | | | | | | | | | | | | | | | | | | | | | | | | | | | | | |
| SWEET BREEZE (HM19584) | | | | | | | | | | | | | | | | | | | | | | ● | | | | | | | | | | | | | | | | | | | | | | | | | | | | |
| THOMAS, CARL (HM19934) | | | | | | | | | | | | | | | | | | | | ● | | | | | | | | | | | | | | | | | | | | | | | | | | | | | | |
| THOMPSON, MARTIN (HM19992) | | | | | | | | | | | | | | | | | | | | | | | | | | | | | | | | | | | | | | | | | | | ● | | | | | | | |
| WOODSIDE CLINIC (HM21857) | | | | | | | | | | | | | | | ● | | ● | | | | | ● | | | | | | | | | | ● | | ● | | | | | | ● | | | | | | | | | | |
| **BERKSHIRE** | | | | | | | | | | | | | | | | | | | | | | | | | | | | | | | | | | | | | | | | | | | | | | | | | | |
| ABBOTT, LORNA (HM00101) | | | | | | | | | | | | | | | | | | | | ● | | | | | | | | | | | | | | | | | | | | | | | | | | | | | | |
| ALDER, CHRISTINE (HM00496) | | | | | | | | | | | | | | | ● | | | | | | | | | | | | | | | | | | | | | | | | | | | | | | | | | | | |
| ANABELLE'S THERAPEUTIC MASSAGE (HM00798) | | | | | | | | | | | | | | | | | | | | | | | | | | | | | | | | | | ● | | | | | | | | | | | | | | | | |

# F - O Therapies at Practices/Businesses

| Business by County with Reference no. | Family Planning (Natural) | Family Therapy | Feldenkrais Methodology | Feng Shui | Floral Essence Therapy | Flotation Therapy | Gait Analysis | Gem Essence Therapy | Gestalt Therapy | Group Therapy | Hay Diet | Healer | Healing Therapy | Hellerwork | Herbal Medicine | Holistic Healing | Homeopathy | Hopi Ear Candles | Humanistic Psychology | Hypnosis | Hypnotherapy | Indian Head Massage | Inhalation Therapy | Iridology | Kinesiology | Kirlian Photography | Laser Treatment | Life Style Coaching | Light Therapy | Macrobiotics | Magnetic Therapy | Manipulation | Manual Lymph Drainage | Massage (Therapeutic) | McTimoney Chiropractic | Meditation | Metamorphic Therapy | Miasm Therapy | Micro Manipulation | Moxibustion | Mud Therapy | Music Therapy | Nail Surgery | Naturopathy | Neuro-Linguistic Program | Neurotherapy | Nutritional Therapy | Orgone Therapy | Oriental Diagnosis | Orthomolecular Medicine |
|---|---|---|---|---|---|---|---|---|---|---|---|---|---|---|---|---|---|---|---|---|---|---|---|---|---|---|---|---|---|---|---|---|---|---|---|---|---|---|---|---|---|---|---|---|---|---|---|---|---|---|
| ASCOT PHYSIOFIRST CENTRE (HM01178) |||||||||||||||||||||||||||||||||||●||||||||||||||||||
| BERKSHIRE CHIROPRACTIC (HM02195) |||||||||||||●|||||||||||||||||||●||●||||||||||||●|||||||
| BINGHAM, JULIE (HM02314) |||||||||||||||||||||||||●|||||||||||||||||||||||||||
| BODY & SOUL (HM02561) |||||||||||||●||●|||||||||||||||||||●||||||||||||||||||
| BRUCE, ANN (HM03264) ||||||||||||||||||||●|●|||||||||||||||||||||||||||||||
| BURT, JOHN (HM03427) ||||||||||||||||||||●||||||||||||||||||||||||||||||||
| CAMPBELL, ELSPETH (HM03597) |||||||||||||●|||●||||●|●|||||||||||||||●|||||||||●||||||
| CARROLL, D (HM03754) ||||||||||||||||||||●||||||||||||||||||||||||||||||||
| CASTLE HILL CLINIC (HM03833) |||||||||||||||||●||||●|●||||||||||||||||||||||||||●||||
| CAVERSHAM FOOT CLINIC (HM03866) ||||||||||||●|●|||●|●|||||●||||||●||||||||●|||||||||||●||||
| CHEUNG, JAMES T (DR) (HM04142) |||||||||||||||●|||||||||||||||||||||||||||||||||||
| COOKHAM CHIROPRACTIC CLINIC (HM05068) |||●||||||||||||●|●||||||||●||||||||●||●|●|●|||||||||||●||||
| COPPERTHWAITE, ERIC (HM05147) ||||||||||||||||||||●|●|||||||||||||||||||||||||||||||
| CUTLER, JENNY (HM05645) ||||||||||||||||||||●||||||||||||||||||||||||||||||||
| DEAN RUSSELL & BRYDGES ROBERT (HM05936) |||||||||||||||||||||||||||||||||||●||||||||||||||||||
| EATON, JOHN (HM06561) ||||||||||||||||||||●||||||||||||||||||||||||||||||||
| EDNEY, C S (HM06625) ||||||||||||||||||||||●||||||||||||●||||||||||||||||||
| EDWARDS, JOHN (HM06659) ||||||||||||||||||||●|●|||||||||||||||●||||||||||||||||
| EIGHAN, PENELOPE (HM06689) |||||||||||||●|||||||||●||||||||||||●|||||||||||||||●||
| FAIRBOURNE CLINIC (HM07051) ||||||||||||||||●|●||||●|●||||||||||||●||||||||||||||||||
| FARAGO CLINIC (HM07100) ||||||||||||||||||||●||||||||||||||||||||||||||||||||
| FEET TREAT (HM07186) |||||●|||||||||||||||||●||||||||||||||||||||||||||||||
| FERINGA, MARLIES (HM07233) |||||||||||●|||||||||||||●||||||||||●||||||||||●|||●||||
| FIELDING, ANNA (HM07271) |||||||||||||||||||||||||||||||||||||||||||||||●||||
| GENGE, DAVID (HM07971) ||||||||||||||||||||●||||||||||||||||||||||||||||||||
| HALL, GRACE (HM08773) |||||||||||||||||●|||||||||||||||||||||||||||||●||||
| HASELTON, HOWARD (HM09180) ||||||||||||||||||||●||||||||||||||||||||||||||●||||
| HERBAL HEALTH CLINIC (HM09616) |||||||||||||||●|||||||||||||||||||||||||||||||||||
| HEWITT, ANDREW (HM09703) |||||||||||||||||||||||||||||||||||●||||||||||||||||||
| HILLSIDE OSTEOPATHIC PRACTICE (HM09806) ||||||||||||||||●|||||||||||||||||●||●||||||||||||||||||
| INNER SENSE (HM10639) ||||||||||||||||||||●||||||||||||||||||||||||||||||||
| KINGFISHERS COMP HEALTH CARE (HM11650) ||||||||||||||||||||||●|||●|||||||||||||||||||||||||
| LAVENDER, S (HM12029) ||||||||||||||||||||||||||||||||||||●||||||||||||||||
| LIFE GUIDANCE (HM12344) ||||||||||||||||||||●|●|||||||||||||||||||||||||||||||

# F - O Therapies at Practices/Businesses

| Business by County with Reference no. | Family Planning (Natural) | Family Therapy | Feldenkrais Methodology | Feng Shui | Floral Essence Therapy | Flotation Therapy | Gait Analysis | Gem Essence Therapy | Gestalt Therapy | Group Therapy | Hay Diet | Healer | Healing Therapy | Hellerwork | Herbal Medicine | Holistic Healing | Homeopathy | Hopi Ear Candles | Humanistic Psychology | Hypnosis | Hypnotherapy | Indian Head Massage | Inhalation Therapy | Iridology | Kinesiology |
|---|---|---|---|---|---|---|---|---|---|---|---|---|---|---|---|---|---|---|---|---|---|---|---|---|---|
| LISSADELL HOUSE PRACTICE (HM12457) | | | | | | | | | | | | | | | | | ● | | | | | | | | |
| MAIDENHEAD CHIROPRACTIC (HM12933) | | | | | | | | | | | | | | | | | | | | | | | | | |
| MAIDENHEAD PHYSIO & SPORTS (HM12934) | | | | | | | | | | | | | | | | | | | | | | | | | |
| MARIANNE, RALPH (HM13096) | | | | | | | | | | | | | | | | | ● | | | | | | | | |
| MCGREGOR, TONY (HM13504) | | | | | | | | | | | | | | | | | | | | ● | ● | | | | |
| MILLS, MARGARET (HM13932) | | | | | | | | | | | | | | | | | ● | | | | | | | | |
| MOMENTA (HM14058) | | | | | | | | | | | | | | | | | | | | ● | | | | | |
| NATURAL HEALTH CONSULTANCY (HM14591) | | | | | | | | | | | | ● | | | | ● | ● | | | | ● | ● | | | |
| NATURAL THERAPY CLINIC (HM14656) | | | | | | | | | | | | | ● | | ● | | ● | | | | ● | ● | | ● | ● |
| NATURAL THERAPY CLINIC (HM14655) | | | | | | | | | | | | | | | ● | ● | ● | | | | ● | ● | | ● | ● |
| NEW SPIRIT NATURALS (HM14835) | | | | | | | | | | | | | | | ● | | | | | | | | | | |
| NEWCOME, ROBERT (HM14858) | | | | | | | | | | | | | | | | | | | | ● | | | | | |
| NS3UK NUTRITION SERVICES (HM15099) | | | | | | | | | | | | | | | | | | | | | | | | | |
| PARRY-ELLIS, MARGARET (HM15744) | | | | | | | | | | | | | | | | | | | | ● | | | | | |
| PETERS, JEAN (HM16086) | | | | | | | | | | | | | | | | | | | | | | | | | |
| PIM HEALTH CLINIC (HM16301) | | | | | | | | | | | | | | | ● | | | | | | | | | | |
| POOL, NICKY (HM16428) | | | | | | | | | | | | | | | | | ● | | | | | | | | |
| POTTERTON, DAVID (HM16472) | | | | | | | | | | | | | | | ● | | | | | | | | | | |
| RINTU, BASU (HM17361) | | | | | | | | | | | | | | | | | | | | ● | | | | | |
| ROSEDALE CLINIC (HM17616) | | | | | | | | | | | | | | | | | ● | | | | | | | | |
| SANDALL, S (HM17898) | | | | | | | | | | | | | | | | | | | | | | | | | |
| SHARMA, SHASHI MOHAN (DR) (HM18303) | | | | | | | | | | | | | | | | | ● | | | | | | | | |
| SMETHURST, ALISON (HM18704) | | | | | | | | | | | | | | | | | | | | | | | | | |
| SOUTH LODGE CONSULTING (HM18909) | | | | | | | | | | | | | | | | | | | | | | | | | |
| SPRINGWOOD COMP HEALTH (HM19055) | | | | | | | | | | | | | | | | | | | | | | ● | | | |
| STEPHENS, BRENDA (HM19199) | | | | | | | | | | | | | | | | | | | | ● | | | | | |
| TSENG, PATRICIA (HM20359) | | | | | | | | | | | | ● | ● | | | ● | | | | | | ● | | | |
| TYNCE, CHRIS (HM20470) | | | | | | | | | | | | | | | | | | | | ● | | | | | |
| WALKER, J W (HM20777) | | | | | | | | | | | | | | | | | | | | ● | | | | | |
| WALKER, MARIAN (HM20788) | | | | | | | | | | | | | | | | | ● | | | | | | | | |
| WINNERSH HYPNOTHERAPY PRACTICE (HM21711) | | | | | | | | | | | | | | | | | | | | ● | ● | | | | |
| WOODBURY COUNSELLING (HM21820) | | | | | | | | | | | | | | | | | | | | ● | | | | | |
| WOODLEY HEALING CENTRE (HM21836) | | | | | | | | | | | | | | | ● | ● | | | | | | | | | |
| ZYS, A & S (HM22123) | | | | | | | | | | | | | | | | | ● | | | | | | | | |

| Business by County with Reference no. | Kirlian Photography | Laser Treatment | Life Style Coaching | Light Therapy | Macrobiotics | Magnetic Therapy | Manipulation | Manual Lymph Drainage | Massage (Therapeutic) | McTimoney Chiropractic | Meditation | Metamorphic Therapy | Miasm Therapy | Micro Manipulation | Moxibustion | Mud Therapy | Music Therapy | Nail Surgery | Naturopathy | Neuro-Linguistic Program | Neurotherapy | Nutritional Therapy | Orgone Therapy | Oriental Diagnosis | Orthomolecular Medicine |
|---|---|---|---|---|---|---|---|---|---|---|---|---|---|---|---|---|---|---|---|---|---|---|---|---|---|
| LISSADELL HOUSE PRACTICE (HM12457) | | | | | | | | | ● | | | | | | | | | | | | | ● | | | |
| MAIDENHEAD CHIROPRACTIC (HM12933) | | | | | | | | | ● | | | | | | | | | | | | | | | | |
| MAIDENHEAD PHYSIO & SPORTS (HM12934) | | | | | | | ● | | | | | | | | | | | | | | | | | | |
| MARIANNE, RALPH (HM13096) | | | | | | | | | | | | | | | | | | | | | | | | | |
| MCGREGOR, TONY (HM13504) | | | | | | | | | | | | | | | | | | | | | | | | | |
| MILLS, MARGARET (HM13932) | | | | | | | | | | | | | | | | | | | | | | | | | |
| MOMENTA (HM14058) | | | | | | | | | | | | | | | | | | | | ● | | | | | |
| NATURAL HEALTH CONSULTANCY (HM14591) | | | ● | | | | | | ● | | ● | | ● | | | | | | | | | | | | |
| NATURAL THERAPY CLINIC (HM14656) | | | | | | | ● | | ● | | | | | | ● | | | | | | | | | ● | |
| NATURAL THERAPY CLINIC (HM14655) | | | | | | | ● | | ● | | ● | | | | | | | | | | | ● | | | |
| NEW SPIRIT NATURALS (HM14835) | | | | | | | | | | | | | | | | | | | | | | | | | |
| NEWCOME, ROBERT (HM14858) | | | | | | | | | | | | | | | | | | | | | | | | | |
| NS3UK NUTRITION SERVICES (HM15099) | | | | | | | | | | | | | | | | | | | | | | ● | | | |
| PARRY-ELLIS, MARGARET (HM15744) | | | | | | | | | | | | | | | | | | | | | | | | | |
| PETERS, JEAN (HM16086) | | | | | | | | | ● | | | | | | | | | | | | | | | | |
| PIM HEALTH CLINIC (HM16301) | | | | | | | | | | | | | | | | | | | | | | | | | |
| POOL, NICKY (HM16428) | | | | | | | | | | | | | | | | | | | | | | | | | |
| POTTERTON, DAVID (HM16472) | | | | | | | | | | | | | | | | | | | | | | | | | |
| RINTU, BASU (HM17361) | | | | | | | | | | | | | | | | | | | | | | | | | |
| ROSEDALE CLINIC (HM17616) | | | | | | | | | | | | | | | | | | | | | | | | | |
| SANDALL, S (HM17898) | | | | | | | | | | | | | | | | | | ● | | | | | | | |
| SHARMA, SHASHI MOHAN (DR) (HM18303) | | | | | | | | | | | | | | | | | | | | | | | | | |
| SMETHURST, ALISON (HM18704) | | | | | | | | | ● | | | | | | | | | | | | | | | | |
| SOUTH LODGE CONSULTING (HM18909) | | | | | | | ● | | ● | | | | | | | | | | | | | | | | |
| SPRINGWOOD COMP HEALTH (HM19055) | | | | | | | | | | | | | | | | | | | | | | | | | |
| STEPHENS, BRENDA (HM19199) | | | | | | | | | | | | | | | | | | | | | | | | | |
| TSENG, PATRICIA (HM20359) | | | | | | | | | ● | | | | | | | | | | | | | | | | |
| TYNCE, CHRIS (HM20470) | | | | | | | | | | | | | | | | | | | | | | | | | |
| WALKER, J W (HM20777) | | | | | | | | | | | | | | | | | | | | | | | | | |
| WALKER, MARIAN (HM20788) | | | | | | | | | | | | | | | | | | | | | | | | | |
| WINNERSH HYPNOTHERAPY PRACTICE (HM21711) | | | | | | | | | | | | | | | | | | | | | | | | | |
| WOODBURY COUNSELLING (HM21820) | | | | | | | | | | | | | | | | | | | | | | | | | |
| WOODLEY HEALING CENTRE (HM21836) | | | ● | | | | | | ● | | | | | | | | | | | | | ● | | | |
| ZYS, A & S (HM22123) | | | | | | | | | | | | | | | | | | | | | | | | | |

# F - O Therapies at Practices/Businesses

| Business by County with Reference no. | Family Planning (Natural) | Family Therapy | Feldenkrais Methodology | Feng Shui | Floral Essence Therapy | Flotation Therapy | Gait Analysis | Gem Essence Therapy | Gestalt Therapy | Group Therapy | Hay Diet | Healer | Healing Therapy | Hellerwork | Herbal Medicine | Holistic Healing | Homeopathy | Hopi Ear Candles | Humanistic Psychology | Hypnosis | Hypnotherapy | Indian Head Massage | Inhalation Therapy | Iridology | Kinesiology |
|---|---|---|---|---|---|---|---|---|---|---|---|---|---|---|---|---|---|---|---|---|---|---|---|---|---|
| **BRISTOL** | | | | | | | | | | | | | | | | | | | | | | | | | |
| AQUARIUS HEALTH CENTRE (HM00959) | | | | | | | | | | | | | | | | | ● | | | | | | | | |
| AROMATHERAPY FOR LADIES (HM01110) | | | | | | | | | | | | | | | | | | | | | | | | | |
| AVON COMPLEMENTARY MEDICINE (HM01404) | | | | | | | | | | | | | | | | | ● | | | | | | | | |
| BAGGLEY, J M (HM01536) | | | | | | | | | | | | | | | | | | | | | | | | | |
| BAKER, P H (HM01591) | | | | | | | | | | | | | | | | | | | | ● | | | | | |
| BEVAN, RUSS (HM02242) | | | | | | | | | | | | | | | | | | | | ● | ● | | | | |
| BRISTOL HYPNOTHERAPY CLINIC (HM03063) | | | | | | | | | | | | | | | | | | | | ● | ● | | | | |
| BRISTOL NATURAL HEALTH SERVICE (HM03064) | | | | | | | | | | | | | | | ● | | ● | | | ● | ● | | | | |
| CASTLE CHIROPODY CLINIC (HM03828) | | | | | | | | | | | | | | | | | | | | | | | | | |
| CLARK, LYN (HM04566) | | | | | | | | | | | | | | | | | ● | | | | | | | | |
| CLIFTON CHIROPRACTIC CLINIC (HM04666) | | | | | | | | | | | | | | | | | | | | | | | | | |
| CLIFTON PRACTICE (HM04670) | | | | | | | | | | | | | | | | | ● | | | ● | | ● | | | ● |
| CLINIC OF NATURAL MEDICINE (HM04704) | | | | | | | | | | | | | | | | | | | | | | | | | |
| CLOVER HOUSE (HM04737) | | | | | | | | | | | | | | | | | | | | | | | | | |
| CRANHAM, NIGEL (HM05374) | | | | | | | | | | | | | ● | | | | | | | | | | | | |
| CROSS HANDS CHIRO CLINIC (HM05478) | | | | | | | | | | | | | | | | | | | | | | | | | ● |
| CTRE FOR KINESIOLOGY (HM05542) | | | | | | | | | | | | | | | | ● | | | | | | | | | ● |
| DOWRY CHIROPRACTIC CLINIC (HM06255) | | | | | | | | | | | | | | | | | | | | | | | | | |
| DURBAN, PAMELA (HM06430) | | | | | | | | | | | | | | | | | | | | ● | | | | | |
| FILE, CHRISTINE (HM07288) | | | | | | | | | | | | | | | | | | | | | | | | | |
| FOSTER, JOY (HM07595) | | | | | | | | | | | | | | | | | | | | ● | | | | | |
| FRANCIS, PATRICIA (HM07675) | | | | | | | | | | | | | | | | | | | | | | | | | |
| FREEMAN, ANN (HM07719) | | | | | | | | | | | | | | | ● | | | | | | | | | | |
| GASKIN, T (HM07923) | | | | | | | | | | | | | | | | | ● | | | | | | | | |
| GODFREY, BRIAN (HM08183) | | | | | | | | | | | | | | | | | | | | ● | | | | | |
| GREEN, JULIA (HM08463) | | | | | | | | | | | | | | | ● | | | | | | | | | | |
| HEALING WITH GABRIELLE TWINE (HM09360) | | | | | | | | | | | | ● | ● | | | ● | | | | | | | | | |
| HEALTH & HEALING (HM09371) | | | | | | | | | | | | | | | | | ● | | | | ● | ● | | | |
| HOPLEY, DENISE (HM10154) | | | | | | | | | | | | | | | | | | | | | | | | | |
| HUDSON, JOHN (HM10313) | | | | | | | | | | | | | | | | | | | | ● | ● | | | | |
| LAM RIM CTRE FOR WHOLE HEALTH (HM11883) | | | | | | | | | | | | | | | | | ● | | | | | | | | |
| MAGNO-PULSE (HM12920) | | | | | | | | | | | | | | | | | | | | | | | | | |
| MOORE, TERESA (HM14135) | | | | | | | | | | | | | | | | | ● | | | | | | | | |

| Business by County with Reference no. | Kirlian Photography | Laser Treatment | Life Style Coaching | Light Therapy | Macrobiotics | Magnetic Therapy | Manipulation | Manual Lymph Drainage | Massage (Therapeutic) | McTimoney Chiropractic | Meditation | Metamorphic Therapy | Miasm Therapy | Micro Manipulation | Moxibustion | Mud Therapy | Music Therapy | Nail Surgery | Naturopathy | Neuro-Linguistic Program | Neurotherapy | Nutritional Therapy | Orgone Therapy | Oriental Diagnosis | Orthomolecular Medicine |
|---|---|---|---|---|---|---|---|---|---|---|---|---|---|---|---|---|---|---|---|---|---|---|---|---|---|
| **BRISTOL** | | | | | | | | | | | | | | | | | | | | | | | | | |
| AQUARIUS HEALTH CENTRE (HM00959) | | | | | | | | | | | | | | | | | | | | | | ● | | | |
| AROMATHERAPY FOR LADIES (HM01110) | | | | | | | | | ● | | | | | | | | | | | | | | | | |
| AVON COMPLEMENTARY MEDICINE (HM01404) | | | | | | | | | | | | | | | | | | | | | | | | | |
| BAGGLEY, J M (HM01536) | | | | | | | | | | | | | | | | | | ● | | | | | | | |
| BAKER, P H (HM01591) | | | | | | | | | | | | | | | | | | | | | | | | | |
| BEVAN, RUSS (HM02242) | | | | | | | | | | | | | | | | | | | | | | | | | |
| BRISTOL HYPNOTHERAPY CLINIC (HM03063) | | | | | | | | | | | | | | | | | | | | | | | | | |
| BRISTOL NATURAL HEALTH SERVICE (HM03064) | | | | | | | | | ● | | | | | | ● | | | | ● | | | | | | |
| CASTLE CHIROPODY CLINIC (HM03828) | | | | | | | | | | | | | | | | | | ● | | | | | | | |
| CLARK, LYN (HM04566) | | | | | | | | | | | | | | | | | | | | | | | | | |
| CLIFTON CHIROPRACTIC CLINIC (HM04666) | | | | | ● | | ● | | ● | | | | | | ● | | | | | | | | | ● | |
| CLIFTON PRACTICE (HM04670) | | | | | | | | | ● | | | | | | | | | | | | | | | | |
| CLINIC OF NATURAL MEDICINE (HM04704) | | | | | | | | | ● | | | | | | | | | | | | | | | | |
| CLOVER HOUSE (HM04737) | | | | | | | | | | | | | | | | | | | | | | ● | | | |
| CRANHAM, NIGEL (HM05374) | | | | | | | | | | | | | | | | | | | | | | | | | |
| CROSS HANDS CHIRO CLINIC (HM05478) | | | | | | | | | | | | | | | | | | | | | | | | | |
| CTRE FOR KINESIOLOGY (HM05542) | | | | | | | | | | | | | | | | | | | | | | ● | | | |
| DOWRY CHIROPRACTIC CLINIC (HM06255) | | | | | | | ● | | ● | | | | | | | | | | | | | | | | |
| DURBAN, PAMELA (HM06430) | | | | | | | | | | | | | | | | | | | | | | | | | |
| FILE, CHRISTINE (HM07288) | | | | | | | | | ● | | | | | | | | | | | | | | | | |
| FOSTER, JOY (HM07595) | | | | | | | | | | | | | | | | | | | | | | | | | |
| FRANCIS, PATRICIA (HM07675) | | | | | | | | | ● | | | | | | | | | | | | | | | | |
| FREEMAN, ANN (HM07719) | | | | | | | | | | | | | | | | | | | | | | | | | |
| GASKIN, T (HM07923) | | | | | | | | | | | | | | | | | | | | | | | | | |
| GODFREY, BRIAN (HM08183) | | | | | | | | | | | | | | | | | | | | | | | | | |
| GREEN, JULIA (HM08463) | | | | | | | | | | | | | | | | | | | | | | | | | |
| HEALING WITH GABRIELLE TWINE (HM09360) | | | | | | | | | | | ● | | | | | | | | | | | | | | |
| HEALTH & HEALING (HM09371) | | | | | | | | ● | | | | | | | | | | | | ● | | | | | |
| HOPLEY, DENISE (HM10154) | | | | | | | | | ● | | | | | | | | | | | | | | | | |
| HUDSON, JOHN (HM10313) | | | | | | | | | | | | | | | | | | | | | | | | | |
| LAM RIM CTRE FOR WHOLE HEALTH (HM11883) | | | | | | | | | | | | | | | | | | | | | | | | | |
| MAGNO-PULSE (HM12920) | | | | | | ● | | | | | | | | | | | | | | | | | | | |
| MOORE, TERESA (HM14135) | | | | | | | | | | | | | | | | | | | | | | | | | |

# F - O Therapies at Practices/Businesses

| Business by County with Reference no. | Family Planning (Natural) | Family Therapy | Feldenkrais Methodology | Feng Shui | Floral Essence Therapy | Flotation Therapy | Gait Analysis | Gem Essence Therapy | Gestalt Therapy | Group Therapy | Hay Diet | Healer | Healing Therapy | Hellerwork | Herbal Medicine | Holistic Healing | Homeopathy | Hopi Ear Candles | Humanistic Psychology | Hypnosis | Hypnotherapy | Indian Head Massage | Inhalation Therapy | Iridology | Kinesiology |
|---|---|---|---|---|---|---|---|---|---|---|---|---|---|---|---|---|---|---|---|---|---|---|---|---|---|
| NAILSEA CHIROPRACTIC CLINIC (HM14460) | | | | | | | | | | | | | | | | | | | | | | | | | |
| ORCHARD MEDICAL CENTRE (HM15364) | | | | | | | | | | | | | | | | | | | | | | | | | |
| ORIENTAL MEDICINE PRACTICE (HM15387) | | | | | | | | | | | | | | | ● | | | | | | | | | | |
| PARKER CLINIC (HM15683) | | | | | | | | | | | | | | | | | | | | | | | | | |
| REDFERN - MEDICAL HERBALIST (HM17017) | | | | | | | | | | | | | | | ● | | | | | | | | | | |
| REDMOND, CAROLINE (HM17031) | | | | | | | | | | | | | | | | | ● | | | | | | | | |
| RISING DRAGON TAI CHI (HM17369) | | | | | | | | | | | | | | | | | | | | | | | | | |
| RISING DRAGON TAI CHI SCHOOL (HM17370) | | | | | | | | | | | | | | | | | | | | | | | | | |
| ROBERTS, FRANK (HM17411) | | | | | | | | | | | | | | | ● | | | | | | | | | | |
| SAWYER, PAUL (HM17986) | | | | | | | | | | | | | | | | | | | | ● | | | | | |
| SMITH, GRAHAM (HM18747) | | | | | | | | | | | | | | | | | | | | ● | | | | | |
| STIRLING, P (HM19302) | | | | | | | | | | | | | | | | ● | ● | | | | | | | | |
| THORN, K (HM20014) | | | | | | | | | | | | | | | | | | | | ● | | | | | |
| TOLL HOUSE CLINIC (HM20120) | | | | | | | | | | | | | | | | | | | | | | ● | | | |
| TRANSENDENTAL MEDITATION (HM20290) | | | | | | | | | | | | | | | | | | | | | | | | | |
| ZINGAS, STELLA (HM22112) | | | | | | | | | | | | | | | | | | | | ● | | | | | |
| **BUCKINGHAMSHIRE** | | | | | | | | | | | | | | | | | | | | | | | | | |
| ALTERNATIVE THERAPIES TRAINING (HM00730) | | | | | | | | | | | | | | | | | | | | | | ● | | | |
| AMERSHAM CHIROPRACTIC CLINIC (HM00779) | | | | | | | | | | | | | | | | | | | | | | | | | |
| AMERSHAM OSTEOPATHIC CLINIC (HM00780) | | | | | | | | | | | | | | | | | | | | | | | | | |
| AYLESBURY COMPLEMENTARY HEALTH (HM01423) | | | | | | | | | | | | | ● | | | ● | | | | ● | ● | ● | | | |
| AYLESBURY VALE THERAPY (HM01425) | | | | | | | | | | | | | | | | | | | | | ● | | | | |
| BANFIELD, KATIE (HM01657) | | | | | | | | | | | | | | | | | | | | | | | | | |
| BASHFORD, JANET (HM01844) | | | | | | | | | | | | | | | | | | | | ● | | | | | |
| BRINTON, MEG (HM03057) | | | | | | | | | | | | | | | | | ● | | | | | | | | |
| CANDLEWELL CLINIC (HM03623) | | | | | | | | | | | | ● | | | | | | | | | | | | | |
| CASTLE STREET CLINIC (HM03837) | | | | | | | | | | | | | | | | | ● | | | ● | ● | | | | ● |
| CHALLENER HYPNOTHERAPY (HM03949) | | | | | | | | | | | | | | | | | | | | ● | | | | | |
| CHILTERN NATURAL THERAPY (HM04176) | | | | | | | | | | | | | | | | | | | | ● | | | | | |
| COACHING FOR SUCCESS (HM04750) | | | | | | | | | | | | | | | | | | | | ● | ● | | | | |
| COLDWELL, VERONICA (HM04810) | | | | | | | | | | | | ● | ● | | | ● | ● | | | ● | ● | ● | | | |
| COMPLEMENTARY HEALTH (HM04921) | | | | | | | | | | | | | ● | | | ● | | | | ● | ● | ● | | | |
| COMPLEMENTARY HEALTH CENTRE (HM04923) | | | | | | | | | | | | | | | | | | | | ● | | | | | ● |
| DOIG, PAUL (HM06158) | | | | | | | | | | | | | | | | | ● | | | | | | | | |

| Business by County with Reference no. | Kirlian Photography | Laser Treatment | Life Style Coaching | Light Therapy | Macrobiotics | Magnetic Therapy | Manipulation | Manual Lymph Drainage | Massage (Therapeutic) | McTimoney Chiropractic | Meditation | Metamorphic Therapy | Miasm Therapy | Micro Manipulation | Moxibustion | Mud Therapy | Music Therapy | Nail Surgery | Naturopathy | Neuro-Linguistic Program | Neurotherapy | Nutritional Therapy | Orgone Therapy | Oriental Diagnosis | Orthomolecular Medicine |
|---|---|---|---|---|---|---|---|---|---|---|---|---|---|---|---|---|---|---|---|---|---|---|---|---|---|
| NAILSEA CHIROPRACTIC CLINIC (HM14460) | | | | | | | ● | | ● | | | | | | | | | | | | | | | | |
| ORCHARD MEDICAL CENTRE (HM15364) | | | | | | | | | | | | | | | | | | ● | | | | | | | |
| ORIENTAL MEDICINE PRACTICE (HM15387) | | | ● | | | | | | ● | | | | | | ● | | | | | | | ● | | ● | |
| PARKER CLINIC (HM15683) | | | | | | | | | ● | | | | | | | | | | | | | | | | |
| REDFERN - MEDICAL HERBALIST (HM17017) | | | | | | | | | | | | | | | | | | | | | | | | | |
| REDMOND, CAROLINE (HM17031) | | | | | | | | | | | | | | | | | | | | | | | | | |
| RISING DRAGON TAI CHI (HM17369) | | | | | | | | | | | ● | | | | | | | | | | | | | | |
| RISING DRAGON TAI CHI SCHOOL (HM17370) | | | | | | | | | | | ● | | | | | | | | | | | | | | |
| ROBERTS, FRANK (HM17411) | | | | | | | | | | | | | | | | | | | | | | | | | |
| SAWYER, PAUL (HM17986) | | | | | | | | | | | | | | | | | | | | | | | | | |
| SMITH, GRAHAM (HM18747) | | | | | | | | | | | | | | | | | | | | | | | | | |
| STIRLING, P (HM19302) | | | | | | | | | | | | | | | | | | | | | | | | | |
| THORN, K (HM20014) | | | | | | | | | | | | | | | | | | | | | | | | | |
| TOLL HOUSE CLINIC (HM20120) | | | | | | | ● | | ● | | | | | ● | | | | | | | | | | | |
| TRANSENDENTAL MEDITATION (HM20290) | | | | | | | | | | | ● | | | | | | | | | | | | | | |
| ZINGAS, STELLA (HM22112) | | | | | | | | | | | | | | | | | | | | | | | | | |
| **BUCKINGHAMSHIRE** | | | | | | | | | | | | | | | | | | | | | | | | | |
| ALTERNATIVE THERAPIES TRAINING (HM00730) | | | | | | | | | | | | | | | | | | | | | | | | ● | |
| AMERSHAM CHIROPRACTIC CLINIC (HM00779) | | | | | | | ● | | ● | | | | | | | | | | | | | | | | |
| AMERSHAM OSTEOPATHIC CLINIC (HM00780) | | | | | | | | | ● | | | | | | | | | | ● | | | | | | |
| AYLESBURY COMPLEMENTARY HEALTH (HM01423) | | | | | | | | | ● | | | | | | | | | | | ● | | | | | |
| AYLESBURY VALE THERAPY (HM01425) | | | | | | | | | | | | | | | | | | | | | | | | | |
| BANFIELD, KATIE (HM01657) | | | | | | | ● | | ● | | | | | | | | | | ● | | | ● | | | |
| BASHFORD, JANET (HM01844) | | | | | | | | | | | | | | | | | | | | | | | | | |
| BRINTON, MEG (HM03057) | | | | | | | | | | | | | | | | | | | | | | | | | |
| CANDLEWELL CLINIC (HM03623) | | | | | | | | | | | | | | | | | | | ● | | | | | | |
| CASTLE STREET CLINIC (HM03837) | | | | | | | ● | | | | | | | | | | | | | | | ● | | | |
| CHALLENER HYPNOTHERAPY (HM03949) | | | | | | | | | | | | | | | | | | | | | | | | | |
| CHILTERN NATURAL THERAPY (HM04176) | | | | | | | | | | | | | | | | | | | | | | | | | |
| COACHING FOR SUCCESS (HM04750) | | | ● | | | | | | | | | | | | | | | | | | | | | | |
| COLDWELL, VERONICA (HM04810) | | | | | | | | | ● | | | | | | | | | | | | | | | | |
| COMPLEMENTARY HEALTH (HM04921) | | | | | | | | | ● | | | | | | | | | | | ● | | | | | |
| COMPLEMENTARY HEALTH CENTRE (HM04923) | | | | | | | | | ● | | | | | | | | | | | | | | | | |
| DOIG, PAUL (HM06158) | | | | | | | | | | | | | | | | | | | | | | | | | |

# F - O Therapies at Practices/Businesses

| Business by County with Reference no. | Family Planning (Natural) | Family Therapy | Feldenkrais Methodology | Feng Shui | Floral Essence Therapy | Flotation Therapy | Gait Analysis | Gem Essence Therapy | Gestalt Therapy | Group Therapy | Hay Diet | Healer | Healing Therapy | Hellerwork | Herbal Medicine | Holistic Healing | Homeopathy |
|---|---|---|---|---|---|---|---|---|---|---|---|---|---|---|---|---|---|
| DOWDELL, FIONA K (HM06234) | | | | | | | | | | | | | | | | | |
| EDWARDS, EMMA (HM06650) | | | | | | | | | | | | | | | | | |
| ENFIELD, CLAUDIA (HM06820) | | | | | | | | | | | | | | | | | |
| ERLICK, STEVEN (HM06884) | | | | | | | | | | | | | | | | | ● |
| FIRMAN, BARBARA (HM07332) | | | | | | | | | | | | | ● | | | | |
| FLEET, BARBARA (HM07402) | | | | | | | | | | | | | | | | | |
| GERRARDS CROSS SPORTS & BACK (HM08004) | | | | | | | | | | | | | | | | | |
| GOLDING, PAULINE (HM08222) | | | | | | | | | | | | | | | | | |
| HALL, JOY (HM08778) | | | | | | | | | | | | | | | | | ● |
| HAVEN HYPNOTHERAPY (HM09210) | | | | | | | | | | | | | | | | | |
| HEATH, SUSAN (HM09454) | | | | | | | | | | | | | ● | | | | |
| HOBBS, SALLY (HM09857) | | | | | | | | | | | | | | | | | |
| HOLISTIC HEALING (HM09959) | | | | | | | | | | | | | | | | | |
| HULCOTT END PRACTICE (HM10352) | | | | | | | | | | | | | | | | | |
| J J COUNSELLING SERVICES (HM10798) | | ● | | | | | | | | | | | | | | | |
| JOHNSON, HELEN (HM11074) | | | | | ● | | | ● | | | | | | | | | ● |
| JOHNSON, HELEN JANE (HM11075) | | | | | | | | | | | | | | | | | ● |
| K BANFIELD NATUROPATHY/OSTEO (HM11288) | | | | | | | | | | | | | | | | | |
| KINGFISHER CHIROP & HYP (HM11648) | | | | | | | | | | | | | | | | | |
| LAMBOURN COURT INTERNATIONAL (HM11904) | | | | | | | | | | | | | | | | | |
| LONG CRENDON OSTEOPATHS (HM12614) | | | | | | | | | | | | | | | | | |
| LORDAN, KATHERINE (HM12642) | | | | | | | | | | | | | | | | | |
| MARLOW HOMOEOPATHIC CLINIC (HM13128) | | | | | | | | | | | | | | | | | ● |
| MASON, DAVID (HM13239) | | | | | | | | | | | | | | | | | |
| MATTHEWS, FRANK (HM13306) | | | | | | | | | | | | | | | | | |
| MATTHEWS, JAN (HM13309) | | | | | | | | | | | | | | | | | |
| MESSENGER, DENISE (HM13760) | | | | | | | | | | | | | | | | | |
| MIDDLE WAY RE-EDUCATION CTRE (HM13813) | | | | | | | | | | | | | | | | | |
| MIND AND BODY (HM13959) | | | | | | | | | | | | ● | ● | | | ● | |
| MIRZOEFF, PETER (HM13992) | | | | | | | | | | | | | | | | | |
| OUSEBANK HYPNOTHERAPY (HM15501) | | | | | | | | | | | | | | | | | |
| OXFORDSHIRE BOWEN CLINIC (HM15545) | | | | | | | | | | | | | | | | | |
| PHYSIO FIRST PRACTICE (HM16199) | | | | | | | | | | | | | | | | | |
| PURTON HOUSE HOMEOPATHIC CTRE (HM16775) | | | | | | | | | | | | | | | | | ● |

| Business by County with Reference no. | Hopi Ear Candles | Humanistic Psychology | Hypnosis | Hypnotherapy | Indian Head Massage | Inhalation Therapy | Iridology | Kinesiology | Kirlian Photography | Laser Treatment | Life Style Coaching | Light Therapy | Macrobiotics | Magnetic Therapy | Manipulation | Manual Lymph Drainage | Massage (Therapeutic) |
|---|---|---|---|---|---|---|---|---|---|---|---|---|---|---|---|---|---|
| DOWDELL, FIONA K (HM06234) | | | | | | | | | | | | | | | | | |
| EDWARDS, EMMA (HM06650) | | | | | ● | | | | | | | | | | | | |
| ENFIELD, CLAUDIA (HM06820) | | | | | ● | | | | | | | | | | | ● | |
| ERLICK, STEVEN (HM06884) | | | | | | | | | | | | | | | | | |
| FIRMAN, BARBARA (HM07332) | ● | | | | ● | | | | | | | | | | | | ● |
| FLEET, BARBARA (HM07402) | | | | | | | | | | | | | | | | | ● |
| GERRARDS CROSS SPORTS & BACK (HM08004) | | | | | | | | | | | | | | | ● | | ● |
| GOLDING, PAULINE (HM08222) | | | ● | | | | | | | | | | | | | | |
| HALL, JOY (HM08778) | | | | | | | | | | | | | | | | | |
| HAVEN HYPNOTHERAPY (HM09210) | | | ● | | | | | | | | | | | | | | |
| HEATH, SUSAN (HM09454) | | | | | ● | | | | | | ● | | | | | | |
| HOBBS, SALLY (HM09857) | | | | | | | | | | | | | | | | | |
| HOLISTIC HEALING (HM09959) | | | | | ● | | | | | | | | | | | | |
| HULCOTT END PRACTICE (HM10352) | | | | | | | | | | | | | | | | | ● |
| J J COUNSELLING SERVICES (HM10798) | | | | | | | | | | | | | | | | | |
| JOHNSON, HELEN (HM11074) | | | | | | | | | | | | | | | | | |
| JOHNSON, HELEN JANE (HM11075) | | | | | | | | | | | | | | | | | |
| K BANFIELD NATUROPATHY/OSTEO (HM11288) | | | | | | | | | | | | | | | ● | | ● |
| KINGFISHER CHIROP & HYP (HM11648) | | | | ● | | | | | | | | | | | | | |
| LAMBOURN COURT INTERNATIONAL (HM11904) | | | ● | | | | | | | | | | | | | | |
| LONG CRENDON OSTEOPATHS (HM12614) | | | | | | | | | | | | | | | ● | | ● |
| LORDAN, KATHERINE (HM12642) | | | ● | | | | | | | | | | | | | | |
| MARLOW HOMOEOPATHIC CLINIC (HM13128) | | | | | | | | | | | | | | | | | |
| MASON, DAVID (HM13239) | | | ● | | | | | | | | | | | | | | |
| MATTHEWS, FRANK (HM13306) | | | ● | ● | | | | | | | | | | | | | |
| MATTHEWS, JAN (HM13309) | | | ● | | | | | | | | | | | | | | |
| MESSENGER, DENISE (HM13760) | | | ● | | | | | | | | | | | | | | |
| MIDDLE WAY RE-EDUCATION CTRE (HM13813) | | | | | | | | | | | | | | | | | |
| MIND AND BODY (HM13959) | | | | | ● | | | | | | | | | | | | |
| MIRZOEFF, PETER (HM13992) | | | ● | ● | | | | | | | | | | | | | |
| OUSEBANK HYPNOTHERAPY (HM15501) | | | ● | | | | | | | | | | | | | | |
| OXFORDSHIRE BOWEN CLINIC (HM15545) | | | | | | | | | | | | | | | | | ● |
| PHYSIO FIRST PRACTICE (HM16199) | | | | | | | | | | | | | | | ● | | ● |
| PURTON HOUSE HOMEOPATHIC CTRE (HM16775) | | | | | | | | | | | | | | | | | |

| Business by County with Reference no. | McTimoney Chiropractic | Meditation | Metamorphic Therapy | Miasm Therapy | Micro Manipulation | Moxibustion | Mud Therapy | Music Therapy | Nail Surgery | Naturopathy | Neuro-Linguistic Program | Neurotherapy | Nutritional Therapy | Orgone Therapy | Oriental Diagnosis | Orthomolecular Medicine |
|---|---|---|---|---|---|---|---|---|---|---|---|---|---|---|---|---|
| DOWDELL, FIONA K (HM06234) | ● | | | | | | | | | | | | | | | |
| EDWARDS, EMMA (HM06650) | | | | | | | | | | | | | | | | |
| ENFIELD, CLAUDIA (HM06820) | | | | | | | | | | | | | | | | |
| ERLICK, STEVEN (HM06884) | | | | | | | | | | | | | | | | |
| FIRMAN, BARBARA (HM07332) | | | | | | | | | | | | | | | | |
| FLEET, BARBARA (HM07402) | | | | | | | | | | | | | | | | |
| GERRARDS CROSS SPORTS & BACK (HM08004) | | | | | | | | | | | | | | | | |
| GOLDING, PAULINE (HM08222) | | | | | | | | | | | | | | | | |
| HALL, JOY (HM08778) | | | | | | | | | | | | | | | | |
| HAVEN HYPNOTHERAPY (HM09210) | | | | | | | | | | | | | | | | |
| HEATH, SUSAN (HM09454) | | ● | | | | | | ● | | | | | | | | |
| HOBBS, SALLY (HM09857) | | | | | | | | | | ● | | | | | | |
| HOLISTIC HEALING (HM09959) | | | | | | | | | | | | | | | | |
| HULCOTT END PRACTICE (HM10352) | | | | | | | | | | | | | | | | |
| J J COUNSELLING SERVICES (HM10798) | | | | | | | | | | | | | | | | |
| JOHNSON, HELEN (HM11074) | | | | | | | | | | ● | | | | | | |
| JOHNSON, HELEN JANE (HM11075) | | | | | | | | | | | | | | | | |
| K BANFIELD NATUROPATHY/OSTEO (HM11288) | | | | | | | | | | ● | | | ● | | | |
| KINGFISHER CHIROP & HYP (HM11648) | | | | | | | | | | | | | | | | |
| LAMBOURN COURT INTERNATIONAL (HM11904) | | | | | | | | | | | ● | | | | | |
| LONG CRENDON OSTEOPATHS (HM12614) | | | | | | | | | | | | | | | | |
| LORDAN, KATHERINE (HM12642) | | | | | | | | | | | | | | | | |
| MARLOW HOMOEOPATHIC CLINIC (HM13128) | | | | | | | | | | | | | | | | |
| MASON, DAVID (HM13239) | | | | | | | | | | | | | | | | |
| MATTHEWS, FRANK (HM13306) | | | | | | | | | | | | | | | | |
| MATTHEWS, JAN (HM13309) | | | | | | | | | | | | | | | | |
| MESSENGER, DENISE (HM13760) | | | | | | | | | | | | | | | | |
| MIDDLE WAY RE-EDUCATION CTRE (HM13813) | | ● | | | | | | | | | | | | | | |
| MIND AND BODY (HM13959) | | ● | | | | | | | | | | | | | | |
| MIRZOEFF, PETER (HM13992) | | | | | | | | | | | ● | | | | | |
| OUSEBANK HYPNOTHERAPY (HM15501) | | | | | | | | | | | | | | | | |
| OXFORDSHIRE BOWEN CLINIC (HM15545) | | | | | | | | | | | | | | | | |
| PHYSIO FIRST PRACTICE (HM16199) | | | | | | | | | | | | | | | | |
| PURTON HOUSE HOMEOPATHIC CTRE (HM16775) | | | | | | | | | | | | | | | | |

# F - O Therapies at Practices/Businesses

| Business by County with Reference no. | Family Planning (Natural) | Family Therapy | Feldenkrais Methodology | Feng Shui | Floral Essence Therapy | Flotation Therapy | Gait Analysis | Gem Essence Therapy | Gestalt Therapy | Group Therapy | Hay Diet | Healer | Healing Therapy | Hellerwork | Herbal Medicine | Holistic Healing | Homeopathy | Hopi Ear Candles | Humanistic Psychology | Hypnosis | Hypnotherapy | Indian Head Massage | Inhalation Therapy | Iridology | Kinesiology | Kirlian Photography | Laser Treatment | Life Style Coaching | Light Therapy | Macrobiotics | Magnetic Therapy | Manipulation | Manual Lymph Drainage | Massage (Therapeutic) | McTimoney Chiropractic | Meditation | Metamorphic Therapy | Miasm Therapy | Micro Manipulation | Moxibustion | Mud Therapy | Music Therapy | Nail Surgery | Naturopathy | Neurotherapy | Neuro-Linguistic Program | Nutritional Therapy | Orgone Therapy | Oriental Diagnosis | Orthomolecular Medicine |
|---|---|---|---|---|---|---|---|---|---|---|---|---|---|---|---|---|---|---|---|---|---|---|---|---|---|---|---|---|---|---|---|---|---|---|---|---|---|---|---|---|---|---|---|---|---|---|---|---|---|---|
| REIKI HEALTH CENTRE (HM17137) |  |  |  |  |  |  |  |  |  |  |  |  | ● |  |  |  |  |  |  |  |  |  |  |  |  |  |  |  |  |  |  |  |  |  |  |  |  |  |  |  |  |  |  |  |  |  |  |  |  |  |
| ROBINSON, MARGARET (HM17495) |  |  |  |  |  |  |  |  |  |  |  |  |  |  |  |  |  |  |  | ● |  |  |  |  |  |  |  |  |  |  |  |  |  |  |  |  |  |  |  |  |  |  |  |  |  |  |  |  |  |  |
| RUNDLE, RICHARD (HM17752) |  |  |  |  |  |  |  |  |  |  | ● | ● | ● |  |  | ● |  |  |  | ● | ● | ● |  |  |  |  |  |  |  |  |  | ● | ● | ● |  |  |  |  |  | ● |  |  |  |  |  |  |  |  | ● |  |
| SLADE, LORNA (HM18669) |  |  |  |  |  |  |  |  |  |  |  |  |  |  |  |  |  |  |  | ● |  |  |  |  |  |  |  |  |  |  |  |  |  |  |  |  |  |  |  |  |  |  |  |  |  |  |  |  |  |  |
| STEWART, W (HM19282) |  |  |  |  |  |  |  |  |  |  |  |  |  |  |  |  | ● |  |  |  |  |  |  |  |  |  |  |  |  |  |  |  |  |  |  |  |  |  |  |  |  |  |  |  |  |  |  |  |  |  |
| TAYLOR, IAN E (HM19763) |  |  |  |  |  |  |  |  |  |  |  |  |  |  |  |  | ● |  |  |  |  |  |  |  |  |  |  |  |  |  |  |  |  |  |  |  |  |  |  |  |  |  |  |  |  |  |  |  |  |  |
| THERAPEUTIC MASSAGE (HM19884) |  |  |  |  |  |  |  |  |  |  |  |  |  |  |  |  |  |  |  |  |  |  |  |  |  |  |  |  |  |  |  |  |  | ● |  |  |  |  |  |  |  |  |  |  |  |  |  |  |  |  |
| THOMSON, JANE (HM20006) |  |  |  |  |  |  |  |  |  |  |  |  |  |  |  |  | ● |  |  |  |  |  |  |  |  |  |  |  |  |  |  |  |  |  |  |  |  |  |  |  |  |  |  |  |  |  |  |  |  |  |
| TODD, PAUL (HM20107) |  |  |  |  |  |  |  |  |  |  |  |  |  |  |  |  |  |  |  |  |  |  |  |  |  |  |  |  |  |  |  |  |  |  |  |  |  |  |  |  |  |  | ● |  |  |  |  |  |  |  |
| TRANSCENDENTAL MEDITATION (HM20269) |  |  |  |  |  |  |  |  |  |  |  |  |  |  |  |  |  |  |  |  |  |  |  |  |  |  |  |  |  |  |  |  |  |  |  | ● |  |  |  |  |  |  |  |  |  |  |  |  |  |  |
| TURNER, KEZZIE (HM20430) |  |  |  |  |  |  |  |  |  |  |  |  |  |  |  |  | ● |  |  |  |  |  |  |  |  |  |  |  |  |  |  |  |  |  |  |  |  |  |  |  |  |  |  |  |  |  |  |  |  |  |
| WELLBURN (HM21154) |  |  |  |  |  |  |  |  |  |  |  |  |  |  |  |  |  |  |  |  |  |  |  |  |  |  |  |  |  |  |  |  |  | ● |  |  |  |  |  |  |  |  |  |  |  |  |  |  |  |  |
| WELLER, JACK (HM21156) |  |  |  |  |  |  |  |  |  |  |  |  |  |  |  |  |  |  | ● | ● | ● |  |  |  |  |  |  | ● |  |  |  |  |  |  |  | ● |  |  |  |  |  |  |  |  |  |  |  |  |  |  |
| WESTWOOD, TERRY (HM21287) |  |  |  |  |  |  |  |  |  |  |  |  |  |  |  |  |  |  |  | ● | ● |  |  |  |  |  |  |  |  |  |  |  |  |  |  |  |  |  |  |  |  |  |  |  |  |  |  |  |  |  |
| WHITNALL, LINDA (HM21414) |  |  |  |  |  |  |  |  |  |  |  |  |  |  |  |  |  |  |  |  |  |  |  |  | ● |  |  |  |  |  |  |  |  | ● |  |  |  |  |  |  |  |  |  |  |  |  |  |  |  |  |
| WOODWARD, MARGARET (HM21866) |  |  |  |  |  |  |  |  |  |  |  | ● |  |  |  |  |  |  |  |  |  | ● |  |  |  |  |  |  |  |  |  |  |  |  |  |  |  |  |  |  |  |  |  | ● |  |  |  |  |  |  |
| CAMBRIDGESHIRE |  |  |  |  |  |  |  |  |  |  |  |  |  |  |  |  |  |  |  |  |  |  |  |  |  |  |  |  |  |  |  |  |  |  |  |  |  |  |  |  |  |  |  |  |  |  |  |  |  |  |
| ARJUNA NATURAL HEALTH CENTRE (HM01000) |  |  |  |  |  |  |  |  |  |  |  |  |  |  |  |  | ● |  |  |  | ● | ● |  | ● |  |  |  |  |  |  |  |  |  |  |  |  |  |  |  |  |  |  |  |  |  |  | ● |  |  |  |
| BENSON, HUGH (HM02168) |  |  |  |  |  |  |  |  |  |  |  |  |  |  |  | ● | ● |  |  |  |  |  |  |  |  |  |  |  |  |  |  |  |  |  |  |  |  |  |  |  |  |  |  |  |  |  |  |  |  |  |
| CAMBRIDGE CHIROPRACTIC CENTRE (HM03572) |  |  |  |  |  |  |  |  |  |  |  |  |  |  |  |  | ● |  |  |  |  |  |  |  |  |  |  |  |  |  |  |  |  |  |  |  |  |  |  |  |  |  |  |  |  |  |  |  |  |  |
| CAMBRIDGE MEDICAL HERBALIST (HM03574) |  |  |  |  |  |  |  |  |  |  |  |  |  |  | ● |  |  |  |  |  |  |  |  |  |  |  |  |  |  |  |  |  |  |  |  |  |  |  |  |  |  |  |  |  |  |  |  |  |  |  |
| CHIROPRATIC & HOM HEALTH CTRE (HM04408) |  |  |  |  |  |  |  |  |  |  |  |  |  |  |  |  |  |  |  |  |  |  |  |  |  |  |  |  |  |  |  |  |  | ● |  |  |  |  |  |  |  |  |  |  |  |  | ● |  |  |  |
| CHRIS SMITH HYPNOTHERAPY (HM04434) |  |  |  |  |  |  |  |  |  |  |  |  |  |  |  |  |  |  |  | ● |  |  |  |  |  |  |  |  |  |  |  |  |  |  |  |  |  |  |  |  |  |  |  |  |  |  |  |  |  |  |
| CLARK, S J (HM04576) |  |  |  |  |  |  |  |  |  |  |  |  |  |  |  |  |  |  |  | ● |  |  |  |  |  |  |  |  |  |  |  |  |  |  |  |  |  |  |  |  |  |  |  |  |  |  |  |  |  |  |
| COMPLEMENTARY HEALTH CLINIC (HM04927) |  |  |  |  |  |  |  |  |  |  |  |  |  |  |  |  |  |  |  |  | ● |  |  |  |  |  |  |  |  |  |  |  |  | ● |  |  |  |  |  |  |  |  |  |  |  |  |  |  |  |  |
| CONWAY, RONALD (HM05031) |  |  |  |  |  |  |  |  |  |  |  |  |  |  |  |  |  |  |  | ● |  |  |  |  |  |  |  |  |  |  |  |  |  |  |  |  |  |  |  |  |  |  |  |  |  |  |  |  |  |  |
| COXELL REMEDIAL CLINIC (HM05324) |  |  |  |  |  |  |  |  |  |  |  |  |  |  |  |  |  |  |  |  |  |  |  |  |  |  |  |  |  |  |  | ● |  | ● |  |  |  |  | ● |  |  |  |  |  |  |  |  |  |  |  |
| CULPEPER (HM05588) |  |  |  |  |  |  |  |  |  |  |  |  |  |  | ● |  |  |  |  |  |  |  |  |  |  |  |  |  |  |  |  |  |  |  |  |  |  |  |  |  |  |  |  |  |  |  |  |  |  |  |
| FAULKNER, CINDY (HM07141) |  |  |  |  |  |  |  |  |  |  |  |  |  |  |  |  |  |  |  |  |  |  |  |  |  |  |  |  |  |  |  |  |  | ● |  |  |  |  |  |  |  |  |  |  |  |  |  |  |  |  |
| GILBERT RD OSTEOPATHIC (HM08055) |  |  |  |  |  |  |  |  |  |  |  |  |  |  |  |  |  |  |  |  |  |  |  |  |  |  |  |  |  |  |  | ● |  |  |  |  |  |  |  |  |  |  |  |  |  |  |  |  |  |  |
| HAYNES, ERIC (HM09274) |  |  |  |  |  |  |  |  |  |  |  |  |  |  |  |  |  |  |  | ● |  |  |  |  |  |  |  |  |  |  |  |  |  |  |  |  |  |  |  |  |  |  |  |  |  |  |  |  |  |  |
| HEAL, CHRISTIANNE (HM09313) |  |  |  |  |  |  |  |  |  |  |  | ● | ● |  |  |  |  |  |  |  |  |  |  |  |  |  |  |  |  |  |  |  |  |  |  |  |  |  |  |  |  |  |  |  |  |  |  |  |  |  |
| HEALTH TEAM (HM09406) |  |  |  |  | ● |  | ● |  | ● |  |  |  |  |  |  | ● | ● |  | ● | ● | ● | ● |  |  |  |  |  |  |  | ● |  | ● |  | ● |  | ● |  |  | ● |  |  |  |  | ● |  |  | ● |  |  |  |
| HYPNOSIS AND HEALTH (HM10495) |  |  |  |  |  |  |  |  |  |  |  |  |  |  |  |  |  |  | ● | ● | ● |  |  |  |  |  |  |  |  |  |  |  |  |  |  |  |  |  |  |  |  |  |  |  |  |  |  |  |  |  |

www.healthmyself.com

# F - O Therapies at Practices/Businesses

| Business by County with Reference no. | Family Planning (Natural) | Family Therapy | Feldenkrais Methodology | Feng Shui | Floral Essence Therapy | Flotation Therapy | Gait Analysis | Gem Essence Therapy | Gestalt Therapy | Group Therapy | Hay Diet | Healer | Healing Therapy | Hellerwork | Herbal Medicine | Holistic Healing | Homeopathy | Hopi Ear Candles | Humanistic Psychology | Hypnosis | Hypnotherapy | Indian Head Massage | Inhalation Therapy | Iridology | Kinesiology | Kirlian Photography | Laser Treatment | Life Style Coaching | Light Therapy | Macrobiotics | Magnetic Therapy | Manipulation | Manual Lymph Drainage | Massage (Therapeutic) | McTimoney Chiropractic | Meditation | Metamorphic Therapy | Miasm Therapy | Micro Manipulation | Moxibustion | Mud Therapy | Music Therapy | Nail Surgery | Naturopathy | Neuro-Linguistic Program | Neurotherapy | Nutritional Therapy | Orgone Therapy | Oriental Diagnosis | Orthomolecular Medicine |
|---|---|---|---|---|---|---|---|---|---|---|---|---|---|---|---|---|---|---|---|---|---|---|---|---|---|---|---|---|---|---|---|---|---|---|---|---|---|---|---|---|---|---|---|---|---|---|---|---|---|---|
| JAFFEY, JOEL (HM10870) | | | | | | | | | | | | | | | | | ● | | | | | | | | | | | | | | | | | | | | | | | | | | | | | | | | | |
| KELLY, ROBERT (HM11441) | | | | | | | | | | | | | | | | | | | | ● | | | | | | | | | | | | | | | | | | | | | | | | | | | | | | |
| LIFELINE (HM12354) | | | | | | | | | ● | ● | | | | | | | | | | | | | | | | | | ● | | | | | | | | | | | | | | ● | | | | | | | | |
| LIZ HALE HANDSON HEALTH (HM12495) | | | | | | | | | | | | ● | | | | ● | | | | | | ● | | | | | | | | | | | | ● | | | | | | | | | | | | | | | | |
| LY, THI PHUNG (DR) (HM12754) | | | | | | | | | | | | | | | | | | | | | | | | | | | | | | | | | | | | ● | | | | ● | | | | | | | | | | |
| MAGUIRE, J () | | | | | | | | | | | | | | | | | | | | ● | ● | | | | | | | | | | | | | | | | | | | | | | | | | | | | | |
| MARSHALL, STEVE (HM13172) | | | | | | | | | | | | | | | | | | | | ● | | | | | | | | | | | | | | | | | | | | | | | | | | | | | | |
| MIND MATTERS (HM13965) | | | | | | | | | | | | | | | | | | | | ● | | | | | | | | | | | | | | | | | | | | | | | | | | | | | | |
| MORRIS & ASSOCIATES (HM14198) | | | | | | | | | | | | | | | | | ● | | | | | | | | | | | | | | | | | | | | | | | | | | | | | | | | | |
| OUTSIDE IN (HM15507) | | | | | | | | | | | | | | | | | | | | | | | | | | | | | ● | | | | | | | | | | | | | | | | | | | | | |
| OXBOROUGH, JOY (HM15536) | | | | | | | | | | | | | | | ● | | | | | | | ● | | | | | | | | | | | | ● | | | | | | | | | | | | | ● | | | |
| PHIL SEAL PSYCHOTHERAPY (HM16115) | | | | | | | | | | | | | | | | | | | | ● | ● | | | | | | | | | | | | | | | | | | | | | | | | ● | | | | | |
| REIKI (HM17126) | | | | | | | | | | | | ● | ● | | | | | | | | | | | | | | | | | | | | | | | | | | | | | | | | | | | | | |
| SPENCE, ALEX (HM18982) | | | | | | | | | | | | | | | | | ● | | | | | | | | | | | | | | | | | | | | | | | | | | | | | | | | | |
| TAYLOR, EVE (HM19759) | | | | | | | | | | | | | | | | | | | | | | | | | | | | | | | | | | ● | | | | | | | | | | | | | ● | | ● | |
| TONG, JENNY (HM20154) | | | | | | | | | | | | | | | | | | | | | | ● | | | | | | | | | | | | | | | | | | | | | | | | | | | | |
| TRANSCENDENTAL MEDITATION (HM20286) | | | | | | | | | | | | | | | | | | | | | | | | | | | | | | | | | | | | ● | | | | | | | | | | | | | | |
| WASS, ANNETTE (HM20975) | | | | | | | | | | | | | | | ● | ● | | | | | | | | | | | | | | | | | | | | | | | | | | | | | | | | | | |
| WEST, JOHN A (HM21249) | | | | | | | | | | | | | | | | | | | | ● | | | | | | | | | | | | | | | | | | | | | | | | | | | | | | |
| CHANNEL ISLANDS | | | | | | | | | | | | | | | | | | | | | | | | | | | | | | | | | | | | | | | | | | | | | | | | | | |
| ST SAMPSON'S MEDICAL CENTRE (HM19098) | | | | | | | | | | | | | | | | | | | | | | | | | | | | | | | | ● | | | | | | | | | | | | | | | | | | |
| CHESHIRE | | | | | | | | | | | | | | | | | | | | | | | | | | | | | | | | | | | | | | | | | | | | | | | | | | |
| A & H PAIN CLINIC (HM00016) | | | | | | | | | | | | | | | | | | | | | | | | | | | | | | | | ● | | | | | | | | | | | | | | | | | | |
| ADULT & CHILD FOOT CLINIC (HM00391) | | | | | | | | | | | | | | | | | | | | | | | | | | | | | | | | | | | | | | | | | | | ● | | | | | | | |
| AMBLESIDE CLINIC (HM00773) | | | | | | | | | | | | | | | | | ● | | | | | | | | | | | | | | | | | ● | | | | | | | | | | | | | | | | |
| BACHE CHIROPODY (HM01471) | | | | | | | | | | | | | | | | | | | | | | | | | | | | | | | | | | | | | | | | | | | ● | | | | | | | |
| BERESFORD, KATHLEEN (HM02183) | | | | | | | | | | | | | | | | | ● | | | | | | | | | | | | | | | | | | | | | | | | | | | | | | ● | | | |
| BODYTONE (HM02634) | | | | | | | | | | | | | | | | | | ● | | | | ● | | | | | | | | | | | | | | | | | | | | | | | | | | | | |
| BOULTON, ERIC C (HM02742) | | | | | | | | | | | | | | | | | | | | ● | | | | | | | | | | | | | | | | | | | | | | | | | | | | | | |
| BRADLEY, F (HM02864) | | | | | | | | | | | | | | | | | | | | ● | | | | | | | | | | | | | | | | | | | | | | | | | | | | | | |
| BRITISH SOC OF CLINICAL HYPNO (HM03094) | | | | | | | | | | | | | | | | | | | | ● | | | | | | | | | | | | | | | | | | | | | | | | | | | | | | |
| BURNES, DAVID T (HM03396) | | | | | | | | | | | | | | | | | | | | ● | | | | | | | | | | | | | | | | | | | | | | | | | | | | | | |
| BURTON, J S (HM03436) | | | | | | | | | | | | | | | | | | | | | | | | | | | | | | | | | | | | | | | | | | | ● | | | | | | | |
| CARMICHAEL CLINIC (HM03708) | | | | | | | | | | | | | | | | | | | | | | | | | | | | | | | | ● | | ● | | | | | | | | | | | | | | | | |

# F - O Therapies at Practices/Businesses

Business by County with Reference no.

| Therapy | CHEADLE HULME NATURAL HEALTH (HM04070) | CHESHIRE HEALTH CLINIC (HM04115) | CHESTER CLINIC (HM04128) | CHESTER HEALTH (HM04129) | CHESTER HEALTH & BEAUTY STUDIO (HM04130) | CHESTER HOMEOPATHIC CLINIC (HM04131) | CHIROPODIST SURGERY (HM04295) | CLINIC OF ACUPUNCTURE (HM04684) | COLHOUN, PETER (HM04842) | COMMUNICATE (HM04905) | CONGLETON COUNSELLING PRACTICE (HM04977) | CRUICKSHANKS, P (HM05519) | CULCHETH REMEDIAL CLINIC (HM05554) | CULPEPER (HM05587) | DAVIES & ASSOCIATES (HM05791) | DEWHURST, PATRICA A (HM06049) | EDDIE, DAVID (HM06585) | FAGAN, B W (HM07042) | FAMILY CLINIC (HM07086) | GAMBLE-CLEE, SARA (HM07858) | H LEICESTER (HM08674) | HALL, J (HM08774) | HANDS ON PHYSIOTHERAPY (HM08913) | HARDISTY, CHRIS (HM08973) | HAUGHTON, G W (HM09203) | HAZELDENE, BARBARA (HM09292) | HOWE, BARBARA (HM10261) | HOWETT, ROY (HM10277) | HYPNOS PRACTICE (HM10492) | HYPNOTHERAPY & COUNSELLING (HM10507) | HYPNOTHERAPY CENTRE (HM10523) | IPHOFEN, RON (DR) (HM10712) | JEFFERYS, SIMON (HM10966) | KERSHNER, F (HM11558) |
|---|---|---|---|---|---|---|---|---|---|---|---|---|---|---|---|---|---|---|---|---|---|---|---|---|---|---|---|---|---|---|---|---|---|---|
| Orthomolecular Medicine | | | | | | | | | | | | | | | | | | | | | | | | | | | | | | | | | | |
| Oriental Diagnosis | | | ● | | | | | ● | | | | | | | | | | | | | | | | | | | | | | | | | | |
| Orgone Therapy | | | | | | | | | | | | | | | | | | | | | | | | | | | | | | | | | | |
| Nutritional Therapy | ● | | ● | ● | ● | | | | | | | | | | | | | | | | | | | | | | | | | | | | | |
| Neurotherapy | | | | | | | | | | | | | | | | | | | | | | | | | | | | | | | | | | |
| Neuro-Linguistic Program | | | | | | | | | | | | | | | | | | | | | | | | | | | | | | | | | | |
| Naturopathy | | | | | | | | | | | | | | | ● | | ● | | | | | | | | | | ● | | | | | | | |
| Nail Surgery | | ● | | | | | | | | | | | | | | | | | | | | | | | | | | | | | | | | |
| Music Therapy | | | | | | | | | | | | | | | | | | | | | | | | | | | | | | | | | | |
| Mud Therapy | | | | | | | | | | | | | | | | | | | | | | | | | | | | | | | | | | |
| Moxibustion | | | ● | | | | | ● | | | | | | | | | | | | | | | | | | | | | | | | | | |
| Micro Manipulation | | | | | | | | | | | | | | | | | | | | | | | | | | | | | | | | | | |
| Miasm Therapy | | | | | | ● | | | | | | | | | | | | | | | | | | | | | | | | | | | | |
| Metamorphic Therapy | | | | | | | | | | | | | | | | | | | | | | | | | | | | | | | | | | |
| Meditation | ● | | | | | | | | | | | | | | | | | | | | | | | | | | | | | | | | | |
| McTimoney Chiropractic | | | | | | | | | | | | | | | | | | | | | | | | | | | | | | | | | | |
| Massage (Therapeutic) | ● | | ● | ● | ● | | ● | | | | | | | | ● | | | ● | | | | | ● | | | ● | | | | | | | | |
| Manual Lymph Drainage | | | | | | | | | | | | | | | | | | | | | | | | | | | | | | | | | | |
| Manipulation | | | ● | | | | | | | | | | | | ● | | | ● | | | | | ● | | | | | | | | | | | |
| Magnetic Therapy | | | | | | | | | | | | | | | | | | | | | | | | | | | | | | | | | | |
| Macrobiotics | | | | | | | | | | | | | | | | | | | | | | | | | | | | | | | | | | |
| Light Therapy | | | | | | | | | | | | | | | | | | | | | | | | | | | | | | | | | | |
| Life Style Coaching | | | | | | | | | | | ● | | | | ● | | | | | | | | | | | | | | ● | | | | | |
| Laser Treatment | | | | | | | | | | | | | | | | | | | | | | | | | | | | | | | | | | |
| Kirlian Photography | | | | | | | | | | | | | | | | | | | | | | | | | | | | | | | | | | |
| Kinesiology | | | ● | | | | | | | | | | | | | | | | | | | | | | | | | | | | | | | |
| Iridology | | | | | | | | | | | | | | | | | | | | | | | | | | | | | | | | | | |
| Inhalation Therapy | | | | | | | | | | | | | | | | | | | | | | | | | | | | | | | | | | |
| Indian Head Massage | | | ● | ● | ● | | | | | | | | | | | | | | | | | | | | | | | | | | | | | |
| Hypnotherapy | ● | ● | ● | | | | | | | | | | | | | | | | | | | | | | | | | | ● | | | ● | | |
| Hypnosis | | | | | | | | | | ● | | ● | ● | | | | | | | ● | ● | ● | | ● | | | | ● | ● | ● | ● | ● | ● | |
| Humanistic Psychology | | | | | | | | | | | | | | | | | | | | | | | | | | | | | | | | | | |
| Hopi Ear Candles | | | | | | | | | | | | | | | | | | | | | | | | | | | | | | | | | | |
| Homeopathy | ● | ● | ● | | | ● | | | ● | | | | | | | | | | ● | | | | | | | | | | | | | | | |
| Holistic Healing | | | | ● | ● | | | | | | | | | | | | | | | | | | | | | | | | | | | | | |
| Herbal Medicine | | | ● | | | | | | ● | | | | | ● | | ● | | | | | | | | | ● | | ● | | | | | | | ● |
| Hellerwork | | | | | | | | | | | | | | | | | | | | | | | | | | | | | | | | | | |
| Healing Therapy | | | | ● | ● | | | | | | | | | | | | | | | | | | | | | | | | | | | | | |
| Healer | | | | | | | | | | | | | | | | | | | | | | | | | | | | | | | | | | |
| Hay Diet | | | | | | | | | | | | | | | | | | | | | | | | | | | | | | | | | | |
| Group Therapy | | | | | | | | | | | | | | | | | | | | | | | | | | | | | | | | | | |
| Gestalt Therapy | | | | | | | | | | | | | | | | | | | | | | | | | | | | | | | | | | |
| Gem Essence Therapy | | | | | | | | | | | | | | | | | | | | | | | | | | | | | | | | | | |
| Gait Analysis | | | | | | | | | | | | | | | | | | | | | | | | | | | | | | | | | | |
| Flotation Therapy | | | | | | | | | | | | | | | | | | | | | | | | | | | | | | | | | | |
| Floral Essence Therapy | | | | | | | | | | | | | | | | | | | | | | | | | | | | | | | | | | |
| Feng Shui | | | | | | | | | | | | | | | | | | | | | | | | | | | | | | | | | | |
| Feldenkrais Methodology | | | | | | | | | | | | | | | | | | | | | | | | | | | | | | | | | | |
| Family Therapy | | | | | | | | | | | | | | | | | | | | | | | | | | | | | | | | | | |
| Family Planning (Natural) | | | | | | | | | | | | | | | | | | | | | | | | | | | | | | | | | | |

# F - O Therapies at Practices/Businesses

| Business by County with Reference no. | Family Planning (Natural) | Family Therapy | Feldenkrais Methodology | Feng Shui | Floral Essence Therapy | Flotation Therapy | Gait Analysis | Gem Essence Therapy | Gestalt Therapy | Group Therapy | Hay Diet | Healer | Healing Therapy | Hellerwork | Herbal Medicine | Holistic Healing | Homeopathy | Hopi Ear Candles | Humanistic Psychology | Hypnosis | Hypnotherapy | Indian Head Massage | Inhalation Therapy | Iridology | Kinesiology |
|---|---|---|---|---|---|---|---|---|---|---|---|---|---|---|---|---|---|---|---|---|---|---|---|---|---|
| KNUTSFORD CHIROPRACTIC CLINIC (HM11775) | | | | | | | | | | | | ● | ● | | | ● | | | | ● | | ● | | | |
| LALLY, KAREN (HM11882) | | | | | | | | | | | | | | | | | | | | ● | | | | | |
| LEIGH, SUSAN (HM12194) | | | | | | | | | | | | | | | | | | | | ● | | | | | |
| LOMAS, CLIFFORD (HM12574) | | | | | | | | | | | | | | | | | | | | | | | | | |
| MACALLAN, STEPHEN (HM12815) | | | | | | | | | | | | | | | ● | ● | | | | | | | | | |
| MANN, PAUL (HM13023) | | | | | | | | | | | | | | | | | | | | ● | | | | | |
| MCMILLAN ANIMAL HEALTH (HM13572) | | | | | | | | | | | | | | | | | ● | | | | | | | | |
| MEDICINE WHEEL (HM13670) | | | | | | | | | | | | | ● | | | ● | | | | | | | | | |
| MEHTA HYPNOTHERAPY (HM13695) | | | | | | | | | | | | | | | | | | | | ● | ● | | | | |
| MID-CHESHIRE HOM GRP (HM13810) | | | | | | | | | | | | | | | | | ● | | | | | | | | |
| MIDDLETON & ASSOCIATES (HM13817) | | | | | | | | | | | | | | | | | ● | | | | | | | | |
| MILLER, J (HM13889) | | | | | | | | | | | | | | | ● | | | | | | | | | | |
| MISSION, CHAITANYA (HM13995) | | | | | | | | | | | | | | | | | | | | | | | | | |
| NEEDHAM, ANGELA (HM14749) | | | | | | | | | | | | | | | | ● | ● | | | | | | | | |
| NEW LIFE NATURAL HEALTH CARE (HM14821) | | | | | | | | | | | | | | | ● | ● | ● | | | | | ● | | | ● |
| NEWTON, J C (HM14898) | | | | | | | | | | | | | | | | | | | | | | | | | |
| NORTH WEST LIFESTYLE MNGMT (HM15043) | | | | | | | | | | | | | | | | | | | | | | | | | |
| NUTRITION AND ALLERGY CLINIC (HM15121) | | | | | | | | | | | | ● | ● | | ● | ● | | | | | | | | | |
| OLD HALL CLINIC (HM15256) | | | | | | | | | | | | | | | | | ● | | | | | | | | |
| PAUL TAYLOR HYPNOTHERAPY (HM15846) | | | | | | | | | | | | | | | | | | | | ● | | | | | |
| PHOENIX CENTRE (HM16154) | | | | | | | | | | | | ● | | | | | | | | ● | ● | | | | |
| PHYSIO & SPORTS INJURY CLINIC (HM16181) | | | | | | | | | | | | | | | | | | | | | | | | | |
| PHYSIO PLUS (HM16203) | | | | | | | | | | | | | | | | | | | | | | | | | |
| POYNTON CHIROPRACTIC CLINIC (HM16519) | | | | | | | | | | | | | | | | | | | | | | | | | |
| PREW, BEVERLEY (HM16566) | | | | | | | | | | | | | | | | | | | | | | ● | | | |
| PRINCE, TANIA A (HM16622) | | | | | | | | | | | | | | | | | | | | ● | ● | | | | |
| REDGRAVE, KENNETH (HM17025) | | | | | | | | | | | | | | | | | | | | | ● | | | | |
| REIKI (HM17127) | | | | | | | | | | | | | | | | | | | | ● | | | | | |
| SANDBACH HYPNOSIS CLINIC (HM17899) | | | | | | | | | | | | | | | | | | | | ● | ● | | | | |
| SPENCE, JACQUELINE (HM18983) | | | | | | | | | | | | | | | | | | | | ● | | | | | |
| TAYLOR, LYNN (HM19782) | | | | | | | | | | | | | | | | | | | | ● | | | | | |
| THERAPY CENTRE (HM19893) | | | | | | | | | | | | | | | | | | | | ● | | | | | |
| THORNBER, A A (HM20016) | | | | | | | | | | | | | | | | | | | | | | | | | |
| TIMELINE SERVICES (HM20078) | | | | | | | | | | | | | | | | | | | | ● | | | | | |

| Business by County with Reference no. | Kirlian Photography | Laser Treatment | Life Style Coaching | Light Therapy | Macrobiotics | Magnetic Therapy | Manipulation | Manual Lymph Drainage | Massage (Therapeutic) | McTimoney Chiropractic | Meditation | Metamorphic Therapy | Miasm Therapy | Micro Manipulation | Moxibustion | Mud Therapy | Music Therapy | Nail Surgery | Naturopathy | Neuro-Linguistic Program | Neurotherapy | Nutritional Therapy | Orgone Therapy | Oriental Diagnosis | Orthomolecular Medicine |
|---|---|---|---|---|---|---|---|---|---|---|---|---|---|---|---|---|---|---|---|---|---|---|---|---|---|
| KNUTSFORD CHIROPRACTIC CLINIC (HM11775) | | | | | | | ● | | ● | | ● | | | | | | | | | | | | | | |
| LALLY, KAREN (HM11882) | | | | | | | | | | | | | | | | | | | | | | | | | |
| LEIGH, SUSAN (HM12194) | | | | | | | | | | | | | | | | | | | | | | | | | |
| LOMAS, CLIFFORD (HM12574) | | | | | | | ● | | ● | | | | | | | | | | ● | | | | | | |
| MACALLAN, STEPHEN (HM12815) | | | | | | | | | | | | | | | ● | | | | ● | | | ● | | ● | |
| MANN, PAUL (HM13023) | | | | | | | | | | | | | | | | | | | | | | | | | |
| MCMILLAN ANIMAL HEALTH (HM13572) | | | | | | | | | | | | | | | | | | | | | | | | | |
| MEDICINE WHEEL (HM13670) | | | | | | | | | | | | | | | | | | | | | | | | | |
| MEHTA HYPNOTHERAPY (HM13695) | | | | | | | | | | | | | | | | | | | | ● | | | | | |
| MID-CHESHIRE HOM GRP (HM13810) | | | | | | | | | | | | | | | | | | | | | | | | | |
| MIDDLETON & ASSOCIATES (HM13817) | | | | | | | | | | | | | | | | | | | | | | | | | |
| MILLER, J (HM13889) | | | | | | | | | | | | | | | | | | | | | | | | | |
| MISSION, CHAITANYA (HM13995) | | | | | | | | | | | ● | | | | | | | | | | | | | | |
| NEEDHAM, ANGELA (HM14749) | | | | | | | | | | | | | | | | | | | | | | | | | |
| NEW LIFE NATURAL HEALTH CARE (HM14821) | | | | | | | ● | | ● | | | | ● | | | | | | ● | | | ● | | | |
| NEWTON, J C (HM14898) | | | | | | | | | | | | | | | | | | ● | | | | | | | |
| NORTH WEST LIFESTYLE MNGMT (HM15043) | | | ● | | | | | | ● | | | | | | | | | | | | | ● | | | |
| NUTRITION AND ALLERGY CLINIC (HM15121) | | | | | | | | | | | | | | | | | | | | | | ● | | | ● |
| OLD HALL CLINIC (HM15256) | | | | | | | | | | | | | | | | | | | | | | | | | |
| PAUL TAYLOR HYPNOTHERAPY (HM15846) | | | | | | | | | | | | | | | | | | | | | | | | | |
| PHOENIX CENTRE (HM16154) | | | | | | | | | | | | | | | | | | | | | | | | | |
| PHYSIO & SPORTS INJURY CLINIC (HM16181) | | | | | | | ● | | ● | | | | | | | | | | | | | | | | |
| PHYSIO PLUS (HM16203) | | | | | | | | | | | | | | | | | | | | | | ● | | | |
| POYNTON CHIROPRACTIC CLINIC (HM16519) | | | | | | | ● | | ● | | | | | | | | | | | | | | | | |
| PREW, BEVERLEY (HM16566) | | | | | | | | | ● | | | | | | | | | | | | | | | | |
| PRINCE, TANIA A (HM16622) | | | | | | | | | | | | | | | | | | | | ● | | | | | |
| REDGRAVE, KENNETH (HM17025) | | | | | | | | | | | | | | | | | | | | | | | | | |
| REIKI (HM17127) | | | | | | | | | | | | | | | | | | | | ● | | | | | |
| SANDBACH HYPNOSIS CLINIC (HM17899) | | | | | | | | | | | | | | | | | | | | | | | | | |
| SPENCE, JACQUELINE (HM18983) | | | | | | | | | | | | | | | | | | | | | | | | | |
| TAYLOR, LYNN (HM19782) | | | | | | | | | | | | | | | | | | | | | | | | | |
| THERAPY CENTRE (HM19893) | | | | | | | | | | | | | | | | | | | | | | | | | |
| THORNBER, A A (HM20016) | | | | | | | | | | | | | | | | | | ● | | | | | | | |
| TIMELINE SERVICES (HM20078) | | | | | | | | | | | | | | | | | | | | | | | | | |

# F - O Therapies at Practices/Businesses

| Business by County with Reference no. | Family Planning (Natural) | Family Therapy | Feldenkrais Methodology | Feng Shui | Floral Essence Therapy | Flotation Therapy | Gait Analysis | Gem Essence Therapy | Gestalt Therapy | Group Therapy | Hay Diet | Healer | Healing Therapy | Hellerwork | Herbal Medicine | Holistic Healing | Homeopathy | Hopi Ear Candles | Humanistic Psychology | Hypnosis | Hypnotherapy | Indian Head Massage | Inhalation Therapy | Iridology | Kinesiology |
|---|---|---|---|---|---|---|---|---|---|---|---|---|---|---|---|---|---|---|---|---|---|---|---|---|---|
| TRINITY HOUSE PRACTICE (HM20339) | | | | | | | | | | | | | | | | |●| | | | |●| | | |
| TYRER, HELEN R (HM20473) | | | | | | |●| | | | | | | | | | | | | | | | | | |
| VALE ROYAL CHIROPRACTIC CLINIC (HM20552) | | | | | | | | | | | | | | | | | | | | | | | | | |
| VALE ROYAL CHIROPRACTIC CLINIC (HM20553) | | | | | | | | | | | | | | | | | | | | | | | | | |
| VICKI WHELAN ASSOCIATES (HM20645) | | | | | | | | | | | | | | | | | | | |●| | | | | |
| WARRINGTON CHIROPRACTIC CLINIC (HM20957) | | | | | | | | | | | | | | | | |●| | | | | | | |●|
| WEAVER HOUSE CLINIC (HM21049) | | | | | | | | | | | | | | |●| |●| | | |●|●| | | |
| WIDNES OSTEOPATHIC CLINIC (HM21459) | | | | | | | | | | | | | | |●| |●| | | | |●| | |●|
| WILLIAMS OSTEOPATHIC CLINIC (HM21532) | | | | | | | | | | | | | | | | | | | |●|●| | | | |
| WILLIAMS, H M (HM21561) | | | | | | | | | | | | | | | | | | | |●| | | | | |
| WYNNE-JONES, J (HM21978) | | | | | | | | | | | | | | | | | | | | | | | | | |
| CLEVELAND | | | | | | | | | | | | | | | | | | | | | | | | | |
| BARNARD, SIMON (HM01732) | | | | | | | | | | | | | | | |●| | | | | | | | | |
| BODY BALANCE (HM02570) | | | | | | | | | | | | | | | | | | | | | | | | | |
| FOREMAN, R (HM07541) | | | | | | | | | | | | | | | | | | | |●| | | | | |
| NATURAL THERAPY CENTRE (HM14637) | | | | | | | | | | | | | | | | |●| | | |●| | | | |
| NORTHERN GUILD-PSYCHOTHERAPY (HM15061) | |●| | | | | | |●|●| | | | | | | | | | | | | | | |
| NORTON, STEVE (HM15074) | | | | | | | | | | | | | | | | | | | |●| | | | | |
| REDCAR PHYSIO & SPORTS (HM17007) | | | | | | | | | | | | | | | | | | | | | | | | | |
| RIDLEY MEWS COMP HEALTH CTRE (HM17321) | | | | | | | | | | | | | | | | |●| | | | | | | | |
| RUSH, DENNIS (HM17754) | | | | | | | | | | | | | | | | | | | |●|●| | | | |
| STRESS COUNSELLING (HM19391) | | | | | | | | |●| | | | | | | | | |●|●|●| | | | |
| STRESS MANAGEMENT (HM19395) | | | | | | | | | | | | | | | | | | | |●| | | | | |
| THOMPSON, FRANK (HM19977) | | | | | | | | | | | | | | | | | | | |●| | | | | |
| CORNWALL | | | | | | | | | | | | | | | | | | | | | | | | | |
| AROMATICA (HM01135) | | | | | | | | | | | | | | | | | | | | | |●| | | |
| BEARE, M E (HM01968) | | | | | | | | | | | | | | | | | | | | | | | | | |
| COMP HEALTH INITIATIVE (HM04912) |●|●| | | | | | | | | |●| | |●|●|●| |●| |●|●| | |●|
| DANIEL, L G (HM05720) | | | | | | | | | | | | | | | | | | | |●| | | | | |
| DRAGE, STEPHEN (HM06279) | | | | | | | | | | | | | | |●| | | | |●|●| | | | |
| FEET FIRST (HM07180) | | | | | | | | | | | | | | | | | | | | | | | | | |
| FLEMING, R D (HM07408) | | | | | | | | | | | | | | | | | | | |●| | | | | |
| FORCE, GAYLE (HM07520) | | | | | | | | | | | | | | | | | | | | | | | | | |
| HALL, PETER (HM08787) | | | | | | | | | | | | | | | | | | | | | | | | | |

| Business by County with Reference no. | Kirlian Photography | Laser Treatment | Life Style Coaching | Light Therapy | Macrobiotics | Magnetic Therapy | Manipulation | Manual Lymph Drainage | Massage (Therapeutic) | McTimoney Chiropractic | Meditation | Metamorphic Therapy | Miasm Therapy | Micro Manipulation | Moxibustion | Mud Therapy | Music Therapy | Nail Surgery | Naturopathy | Neuro-Linguistic Program | Neurotherapy | Nutritional Therapy | Orgone Therapy | Oriental Diagnosis | Orthomolecular Medicine |
|---|---|---|---|---|---|---|---|---|---|---|---|---|---|---|---|---|---|---|---|---|---|---|---|---|---|
| TRINITY HOUSE PRACTICE (HM20339) | | | | | | |●| |●| | | | | | | | | | | | |●| | | |
| TYRER, HELEN R (HM20473) | | | | | | | | | | | | | | | | | |●| | | | | | | |
| VALE ROYAL CHIROPRACTIC CLINIC (HM20552) | | | | | | | | |●| | | | | | | | | | | | | | | | |
| VALE ROYAL CHIROPRACTIC CLINIC (HM20553) | | | | | | | | |●| | | | | | | | | | | | | | | | |
| VICKI WHELAN ASSOCIATES (HM20645) | | | | | | | | | | | | | | | | | | | | | | | | | |
| WARRINGTON CHIROPRACTIC CLINIC (HM20957) | | | | | | |●| |●| | | | | | | | | | | | |●| | | |
| WEAVER HOUSE CLINIC (HM21049) | | | | | | | | |●| | | | | | | | | | | | | | | | |
| WIDNES OSTEOPATHIC CLINIC (HM21459) | | | | | | |●| |●| | | | | | | | | | | | |●| | | |
| WILLIAMS OSTEOPATHIC CLINIC (HM21532) | | | | | | |●| |●| | | | | | | | | | | | | | | | |
| WILLIAMS, H M (HM21561) | | | | | | | | | | | | | | | | | | | | | | | | | |
| WYNNE-JONES, J (HM21978) | | | | | | | | | | | | | | | | | |●| | | | | | | |
| CLEVELAND | | | | | | | | | | | | | | | | | | | | | | | | | |
| BARNARD, SIMON (HM01732) | | | | | | |●| |●| | | | | | | | | | | | | | | | |
| BODY BALANCE (HM02570) | | | | | | | | |●| | | | | | | | | | | | | | | | |
| FOREMAN, R (HM07541) | | | | | | | | | | | | | | | | | | | | | | | | | |
| NATURAL THERAPY CENTRE (HM14637) | | | | | | | | | | | | | | | | | | | | | | | | | |
| NORTHERN GUILD-PSYCHOTHERAPY (HM15061) | | | | | | | | | | | | | | | | | | | | | |●| | | |
| NORTON, STEVE (HM15074) | | | | | | | | | | | | | | | | | | | | | | | | | |
| REDCAR PHYSIO & SPORTS (HM17007) | | | | | | |●| |●| | | | | | | | | | | | | | | | |
| RIDLEY MEWS COMP HEALTH CTRE (HM17321) | | | | | | | | | | | | | | | | | | | | | | | | | |
| RUSH, DENNIS (HM17754) | | | | | | | | | | | | | | | | | | | | | | | | | |
| STRESS COUNSELLING (HM19391) | | |●| | | | | | | |●| | | | | |●| | | | | | | | |
| STRESS MANAGEMENT (HM19395) | | | | | | | | | | | | | | | | | | | | | | | | | |
| THOMPSON, FRANK (HM19977) | | | | | | | | | | | | | | | | | | | | | | | | | |
| CORNWALL | | | | | | | | | | | | | | | | | | | | | | | | | |
| AROMATICA (HM01135) | | | | | | | | | | | | | | | | | | | | | | | | | |
| BEARE, M E (HM01968) | | | | | | | | | | | | | | | | | |●| | | | | | | |
| COMP HEALTH INITIATIVE (HM04912) | | |●| | | | | |●| |●|●| | | | | | | | | |●| | | |
| DANIEL, L G (HM05720) | | | | | | | | | | | | | | | | | | | | | | | | | |
| DRAGE, STEPHEN (HM06279) | | | | | | | | | | | | | | | | | | | | | | | | | |
| FEET FIRST (HM07180) | | | | | | | | | | | | | | | | | | |●| | | | | | |
| FLEMING, R D (HM07408) | | | | | | | | | | | | | | | | | | | | | | | | | |
| FORCE, GAYLE (HM07520) | | | | | | | | | | |●| | | | | | | | | | | | | | |
| HALL, PETER (HM08787) | | | | |●| | | | | |●| | | |●| | | | | | | | |●| |

# F - O Therapies at Practices/Businesses

| Business by County with Reference no. | Family Planning (Natural) | Family Therapy | Feldenkrais Methodology | Feng Shui | Floral Essence Therapy | Flotation Therapy | Gait Analysis | Gem Essence Therapy | Gestalt Therapy | Group Therapy | Hay Diet | Healer | Healing Therapy | Hellerwork | Herbal Medicine | Holistic Healing | Homeopathy | Hopi Ear Candles | Humanistic Psychology | Hypnosis | Hypnotherapy | Indian Head Massage | Inhalation Therapy | Iridology | Kinesiology |
|---|---|---|---|---|---|---|---|---|---|---|---|---|---|---|---|---|---|---|---|---|---|---|---|---|---|
| HAWKSLAND PHYSIOTHERAPY CENTRE (HM09233) | | | | | | | | | | | | ● | | | | | | | | | | ● | | | |
| JONES, MARILYN D (HM11174) | | | | | | | | | | | | | | | | | | | | ● | | | | | |
| LAWS, F J (HM12061) | | | | | | | | | | | | | | | | | | | | ● | | | | | |
| LEMON ST NTRL HLTH PRACTICE (HM12206) | | | | | | | | | | | | | | | ● | ● | ● | | | ● | | | | | ● |
| LIFE 'N' LIMB (HM12346) | | | | | | | | | | | | | | | | ● | | | | | | | ● | | |
| LIFE 'N' LIMB (HM12345) | | | | | | | | | | | | | | | | | | | | | | | | | |
| LIFE-WORK POTENTIAL (HM12368) | | | | | | | | | | | | | | | | | | | | | | | | | ● |
| LISTER NATURAL HEALTH PRACTICE (HM12461) | | ● | | | | | | | ● | ● | ● | ● | ● | | ● | ● | ● | | ● | ● | ● | ● | | | |
| LOBB, JUDY (HM12529) | | | | | | | | | | | | | | | | | ● | | | | | | | | |
| LUCE, PETER J (HM12722) | | | | | | | | | | | | | | | | | | | | ● | | | | | |
| MIDDLETON, CAROLE (HM13820) | | | | | | | | | | | | | | | | | ● | | | | | | | | |
| MONTAGUE-THOMAS, A (HM14083) | | | | | | | | | | | | | | | ● | | | | | | | | | | |
| NATURAL PARTNERS (HM14616) | | | | | | | | | | | | | | | ● | | | | | | | | | | |
| NERVA, VALERIE (HM14786) | | | | | | | | | | | | | | | | | | | | ● | | | | | |
| NEWQUAY CHIROPRACTIC CLINIC (HM14883) | | | | | | | | | | | | | | | ● | | ● | | | | | ● | | | ● |
| OSTEOPATHIC FAMILY CENTRE (HM15465) | | | | | | | | | | | | | | | | | | | | | | | | | |
| PENZANCE NATURAL HEALTH CENTRE (HM16006) | | | | | | | | | | | | ● | | | ● | | ● | | | ● | | ● | | | |
| SNOW, MARIAN (HM18841) | | | | | | | | | | | | | | | | | | | | ● | | | | | |
| ST AUSTELL CHIROPRACTIC CLINIC (HM19070) | | | | | | | | | | | | | | | | | ● | | | | | | | | |
| TRURO CHIROPRACTIC CLINIC (HM20354) | | | | | | | | | | | | | | | | | ● | | | | | | | | |
| TRURO OSTEOPATHIC PRACTICE (HM20356) | | | | | | | | | | | | | | | | | | | | | | | | | |
| WILLS, JONATHAN (HM21632) | | | | | | | | | | | | | | | | | ● | | | | | ● | | | |
| WRIGHT, CYNTHIA (HM21929) | | | | | | | | | | | | | | | | | | | | ● | ● | | | | |
| **COUNTY DURHAM** | | | | | | | | | | | | | | | | | | | | | | | | | |
| BALANCE HOLISTIC HEALTHCARE (HM01606) | | | | | | | | | | | | ● | ● | | | ● | | | | | | | | | |
| BODYWORK HEALTH CLUB & CLINIC (HM02639) | | | | | | | | | | | | | | | | | ● | | | | | | | | |
| CORBY, MICHAEL (HM05156) | | | | | | | | | | | | | | | | | | | | ● | | | | | |
| EVANS, BRUCE (DR) (HM06958) | | | | | | | | | | | | | | | | | | | | | | | | | |
| FIONA OTTEWELL CHRTRD PHYSIO (HM07329) | | | | | | | | | | | | | | | | | | | | | | | | | |
| FOOTPRINTS (HM07507) | | | | | | | | | | | | | | | | | | | | | | | | | |
| FROST, PATRICIA (HM07767) | | | | | | | | | | | | | | | | | ● | | | | | | | | |
| HIND, CAROLE (HM09824) | | | | | | | | | | | | | | | | | | | | | | ● | | | |
| HOBSON, I K (HM09864) | | | | | | | ● | | | | | | | | | | | | | | | | | | |
| MERIDIAN MASSAGE & REFLEXOLOGY (HM13744) | | | | | | | | | | | | | | | | | | | | | | | | | |

| Business by County with Reference no. | Kirlian Photography | Laser Treatment | Life Style Coaching | Light Therapy | Macrobiotics | Magnetic Therapy | Manipulation | Manual Lymph Drainage | Massage (Therapeutic) | McTimoney Chiropractic | Meditation | Metamorphic Therapy | Miasm Therapy | Micro Manipulation | Moxibustion | Mud Therapy | Music Therapy | Nail Surgery | Naturopathy | Neuro-Linguistic Program | Neurotherapy | Nutritional Therapy | Orgone Therapy | Oriental Diagnosis | Orthomolecular Medicine |
|---|---|---|---|---|---|---|---|---|---|---|---|---|---|---|---|---|---|---|---|---|---|---|---|---|---|
| HAWKSLAND PHYSIOTHERAPY CENTRE (HM09233) | | | | | | | ● | | ● | | | | | ● | | | | | | | | | | | |
| JONES, MARILYN D (HM11174) | | | | | | | | | | | | | | | | | | | | | | | | | |
| LAWS, F J (HM12061) | | | | | | | | | | | | | | | | | | | | | | | | | |
| LEMON ST NTRL HLTH PRACTICE (HM12206) | | | | | | | | | ● | | | ● | | | | | | | | | | | | | |
| LIFE 'N' LIMB (HM12346) | | | | | | | ● | | ● | | | | | | | | | | | | | | | | |
| LIFE 'N' LIMB (HM12345) | | | | | | | | | ● | | | | | | | | | | | | | | | | |
| LIFE-WORK POTENTIAL (HM12368) | | | | | | | | | | | | | | | | | | | | | | | | | |
| LISTER NATURAL HEALTH PRACTICE (HM12461) | | | ● | | | | | | ● | | ● | | | | ● | | | | | | | ● | | ● | |
| LOBB, JUDY (HM12529) | | | | | | | | | | | | | | | | | | | | | | | | | |
| LUCE, PETER J (HM12722) | | | | | | | | | | | | | | | | | | | | | | | | | |
| MIDDLETON, CAROLE (HM13820) | | | | | | | | | | | | | | | | | | | | | | | | | |
| MONTAGUE-THOMAS, A (HM14083) | | | | | | | | | | | | | | | | | | | | | | | | | |
| NATURAL PARTNERS (HM14616) | | | | | | | | | | | | | | | | | | | | | | | | | |
| NERVA, VALERIE (HM14786) | | | | | | | | | | | | | | | | | | | | | | | | | |
| NEWQUAY CHIROPRACTIC CLINIC (HM14883) | | | | | | | ● | | ● | | | | | | ● | | | | | | | ● | | | |
| OSTEOPATHIC FAMILY CENTRE (HM15465) | | | | | | | ● | | | | | | | | | | | | | | | | | | |
| PENZANCE NATURAL HEALTH CENTRE (HM16006) | | | | | | | | | ● | | ● | | | | | | | | | | | | | | |
| SNOW, MARIAN (HM18841) | | | | | | | | | | | | | | | | | | | | | | | | | |
| ST AUSTELL CHIROPRACTIC CLINIC (HM19070) | | | | | | | | | | | | | | | | | | | | | | | | | |
| TRURO CHIROPRACTIC CLINIC (HM20354) | | | | | | | | | | | | | | | | | | | | | | | | | |
| TRURO OSTEOPATHIC PRACTICE (HM20356) | | | | | | | ● | | | | | | | | | | | | | | | | | | |
| WILLS, JONATHAN (HM21632) | | | | | | | ● | | ● | | | | | | ● | | | | | | | | | | |
| WRIGHT, CYNTHIA (HM21929) | | | | | | | | | | | | | | | | | | | | | | | | | |
| **COUNTY DURHAM** | | | | | | | | | | | | | | | | | | | | | | | | | |
| BALANCE HOLISTIC HEALTHCARE (HM01606) | | | | | | | | | | | | | | | | | | | | | | | | | |
| BODYWORK HEALTH CLUB & CLINIC (HM02639) | | | | | | | | | | | | | | | | | | | | | | | | | |
| CORBY, MICHAEL (HM05156) | | | | | | | | | | | | | | | | | | | | | | | | | |
| EVANS, BRUCE (DR) (HM06958) | | | | | | | ● | | | | | | | ● | | | | | | | | | | | |
| FIONA OTTEWELL CHRTRD PHYSIO (HM07329) | | | | | | | ● | | ● | | | | | | | | | | | | | | | | |
| FOOTPRINTS (HM07507) | | | | | | | | | | | | | | | | | | ● | | | | | | | |
| FROST, PATRICIA (HM07767) | | | | | | | | | | | | | | | | | | | | | | | | | |
| HIND, CAROLE (HM09824) | | | | | | | | | | | | | | | | | | | | | | | | | |
| HOBSON, I K (HM09864) | | | | | | | | | | | | | | | | | | | | | | | | | |
| MERIDIAN MASSAGE & REFLEXOLOGY (HM13744) | | | | | | | | | ● | | | | | | | | | | | | | | | | |

# F - O Therapies at Practices/Businesses

| Business by County with Reference no. | Family Planning (Natural) | Family Therapy | Feldenkrais Methodology | Feng Shui | Floral Essence Therapy | Flotation Therapy | Gait Analysis | Gem Essence Therapy | Gestalt Therapy | Group Therapy | Hay Diet | Healer | Healing Therapy | Hellerwork | Herbal Medicine | Holistic Healing | Homeopathy | Hopi Ear Candles | Humanistic Psychology | Hypnosis | Hypnotherapy | Indian Head Massage | Inhalation Therapy | Iridology | Kinesiology | Kirlian Photography | Laser Treatment | Life Style Coaching | Light Therapy | Macrobiotics | Magnetic Therapy | Manipulation | Manual Lymph Drainage | Massage (Therapeutic) | McTimoney Chiropractic | Meditation | Metamorphic Therapy | Miasm Therapy | Micro Manipulation | Moxibustion | Mud Therapy | Music Therapy | Nail Surgery | Naturopathy | Neuro-Linguistic Program | Neurotherapy | Nutritional Therapy | Orgone Therapy | Oriental Diagnosis | Orthomolecular Medicine |
|---|---|---|---|---|---|---|---|---|---|---|---|---|---|---|---|---|---|---|---|---|---|---|---|---|---|---|---|---|---|---|---|---|---|---|---|---|---|---|---|---|---|---|---|---|---|---|---|---|---|---|
| NATURAL HEALING CENTRE (HM14536) | | | | | | | | | | | | ● | ● | | | ● | ● | | | | ● | ● | | | ● | | | | | | | | | ● | | ● | | | | | | | | | | | ● | | | |
| NEWCASTLE/NE TRANS MEDITA CTRE (HM14856) | | | | | | | | | | | | | | | ● | | | | | | | | | | | | | | | | | | | | | ● | | | | | | | | | | | | | | |
| RICHARDSON, T G (HM17294) | | | | | | | | | | | | | | | | | | | | ● | | | | | | | | | | | | | | | | | | | | | | | | | | | | | | |
| SYKES, LYNNE (HM19616) | | | | | | | | | | | | | | | | | ● | | | | | | | | | | | | | | | | | | | | | | | | | | | | | | | | | |
| TEESDALE OSTEOPATHIC CLINIC (HM19817) | | | | | | | | | | | | | | | | | ● | | | | | | | | | | | | | | | | | | | | | | | | | | | | | | | | | |
| TREATMENT ROOM (HM20302) | | | | | | | | | | | | | | | | | | | | ● | ● | | | | ● | | | | | | | ● | | ● | | | | | | | | | | | | | | | | |
| WARWICK, ANDREA (HM20967) | | | | | | | | | ● | | | ● | | | | ● | | | | ● | ● | ● | | | ● | | | | | | | | | ● | | | ● | | | | | | | | | | | | | |
| WRIGHT FOOT FORWARD (HM21924) | | | | | | | | | | | | | | | | | | | | | | | | | | | | | | | | | | ● | | | | | | | | | | | | | | | | |
| **CUMBRIA** | | | | | | | | | | | | | | | | | | | | | | | | | | | | | | | | | | | | | | | | | | | | | | | | | | |
| FEVAR, R (HM07249) | | | | | | | | | | | | | | | | | ● | | | | | | | | | | | | | | | | | | | | | | | | | | | | | | | | | |
| FOOTWORKS (HM07515) | | | | | | | | | | | | | | | | | | | | | | | | | | | | | | | | | | | | | | | | | | | ● | | | | | | | |
| GARNETT, JANE (HM07897) | | | | | | | | | | | | | | | | | | | | | ● | | | | | | | | | | | | | | | | | | | | | | | | | | | | | |
| HERBS AND HELPERS (HM09668) | | | | | | | | | | | | | | | ● | | | | | | | | | ● | | | | | | | | | | | | | | | | | | | | | | | | | | |
| HUGHGONSON, SUE (HM10346) | | | | | | | | | | | | | | | | | | | | ● | | | | | | | | | | | | | | | | | | | | | | | | | | | | | | |
| HYPNOTHERAPY CENTRE (HM10525) | | | | | | | | | | | | | | | | | | | | ● | ● | | | | | | | | | | | | | | | | | | | | | | | | | | | | | |
| JOLLY, G M (HM11110) | | | | | | | | | | | | | | | | | | | | ● | | | | | | | | | | | | | | | | | | | | | | | | | | | | | | |
| LAKELAND HYPNOTHERAPY CENTRE (HM11874) | | | | | | | | | | | | | | | | | | | | ● | | | | | | | | | | | | | | | | | | | | | | | | | | | | | | |
| MCWATT, LIZ (HM13624) | | | | | ● | | | | | | | | | | | ● | | | | | | | | | | | | | | | | | | ● | | ● | | | | | | | | | | | ● | | | |
| RHAM, TRICIA (HM17217) | | | | | | | | | | | | | | | | | | | | | | | | | | | | | | | | | | | ● | | ● | | | | | | | | | | | | | |
| SINGLETON, POLLY (HM18612) | | | | | ● | | | | | | | | | | ● | | ● | | | | | | | | | | | | | | | | | | | | | | | | | | | | | | ● | | | |
| THERAPY CENTRE (HM19898) | | | | | | | | | | | | | | | | ● | | | | ● | ● | | | | | | | | | | | ● | | | | | | | | | | | | | | | | | | |
| VULCANS LANE CHIROPODY (HM20720) | | | | | | | | | | | | | | | | | | | | | | | | | | | | | | | | | | ● | | | | | | | | | | | | | | | | |
| **DERBYSHIRE** | | | | | | | | | | | | | | | | | | | | | | | | | | | | | | | | | | | | | | | | | | | | | | | | | | |
| ALTER-MED (HM00690) | | | | | | | | | | | | | | | | | | | | | | | | | | | | | | | | | | ● | | | | | | | | | | | | | | | | |
| BANKS, LINDA (HM01665) | | | | | | | | | | | | | | | | | | | | | | ● | | | | | | | | | | | | | | | | | | | | | | | | | | | | |
| BARROWCLIFFE, GRAHAM (DR) (HM01806) | | | | | | | | | | | | | | | | | | | | ● | ● | | | | | | | ● | | | | ● | ● | | | | | | | | | | | | | | | | | |
| BELPER BACKPAIN CLINIC (HM02110) | | | | | | | | | | | | | | | | | | | | | | | | ● | ● | | | | | | | ● | | ● | | | | | | | | | | | | | | | | |
| BELPER HOMEOPATHY (HM02111) | | | | | | | | | | | | | | | | | ● | | | | | | | | | | | | | | | | | | | | | | | | | | | | | | | | | |
| BELPER NATURAL HEALTH CENTRE (HM02112) | | | | | | | | | | | | ● | | | ● | | ● | | | | | ● | | | ● | | | | | | | ● | | ● | | | | | | ● | | | | ● | | | ● | | ● | |
| BRADSHAW, P J (HM02878) | | | | | | | | | ● | | | | | | | | | | | ● | ● | | | | | | | | | | | | | | | ● | | | | | | | | | | | | | | |
| CARRICK-SMITH, L (HM03744) | | | | | | | | | | | | | | | | | | | ● | | | | | | | | | | | | | | | | | | | | | | | | | | | | | | | |
| CONTOUR DESIGNS (HM05021) | | | | | | | | | | | | | | | | | | | | ● | ● | | | | | | | | | | | | | | | | | | | | | | | | | | | | | |
| COVERLEY PHYSIOTHERAPY CLINIC (HM05284) | | | | | | | | | | | | | | | | | | | | | | | | | | | | | | | | ● | | | | | | | | | | | | | | | | | | |
| DANIELS, FRANK (HM05723) | | | | | | | | | | | | | | | | | | | | ● | | | | | | | | | | | | | | | | | | | | | | | | | | | | | | |

# F - O Therapies at Practices/Businesses

| Business by County with Reference no. | Family Planning (Natural) | Family Therapy | Feldenkrais Methodology | Feng Shui | Floral Essence Therapy | Flotation Therapy | Gait Analysis | Gem Essence Therapy | Gestalt Therapy | Group Therapy | Hay Diet | Healer | Healing Therapy | Hellerwork | Herbal Medicine | Holistic Healing | Homeopathy | Hopi Ear Candles | Humanistic Psychology | Hypnosis | Hypnotherapy | Indian Head Massage | Inhalation Therapy | Iridology | Kinesiology |
|---|---|---|---|---|---|---|---|---|---|---|---|---|---|---|---|---|---|---|---|---|---|---|---|---|---|
| DERBY HOMEOPATHIC PRACTICE (HM06013) | | | | | | | | | | | | | | | | | ● | | | | | | | | |
| DRONFIELD NAT HEALTH CLINIC (HM06319) | | | | | | | | | | | | | | | | | ● | | | | ● | ● | | | |
| ENJOY SPORT (HM06836) | | | | | | | | | | | | | | | | | | | | | | | | | |
| FENG SHUI (HM07210) | | | | ● | | | | | | | | | | | | | | | | | | | | | |
| FOX-DAVIES, DAWN (HM07643) | | | | | | | | | | | | | | | | | | | | ● | | | | | |
| HATHERSAGE HEALTH & THRPY CTRE (HM09198) | | | | | | | | | | | | | | | | | | | | | | | | | |
| HAYWOOD, T J (HM09289) | | | | | | | | | | | | | | | | | | | | ● | | | | | |
| HORAN, MARTIN (HM10163) | | | | | | | | | | | | | | | | | | | | ● | | | | | |
| ILKESTONE OSTEO & MED CTRE (HM10580) | | | | | | | | | | | | | | | ● | | | | | | | | | | |
| KARDAHJI, F C (HM11319) | | | | | | | ● | | | | | | | | | | | | | | | | | | |
| KAY, P (HM11353) | | | | | | | | | | | | | | | ● | | | | | | | | | | |
| KEMP, G D (HM11460) | | | | | | | | | | | | | | | | | | | | | | | | | |
| KEMP, GILLIAN (HM11461) | | | | | | | | | | | | | | | | | | | | ● | ● | | | | |
| LIFESOLUTIONS (HM12359) | | | | | | | | | | | | | | | | | | | | ● | ● | | | | |
| MATLOCK PHYSIOTHERAPY CENTRE (HM13293) | | | | | ● | | | | | | | | | | ● | | ● | | | | | | | | |
| MCFARLANE, BILL (HM13475) | | | | | | | | | | | | | | | | | | | | ● | | | | | |
| MEAKIN, JACKIE (HM13639) | | | | | | | | | | | | | | | ● | | | | | | | | | | |
| NATURAL CHOICE HEALTH FOODS (HM14526) | | | | | | | | | | | | | | | ● | | | | | | | | | | |
| NATURAL CHOICE HEALTH FOODS (HM14524) | | | | | | | | | | | | | | | ● | | | | | | | | | | |
| NATURAL CHOICE HEALTH FOODS (HM14525) | | | | | | | | | | | | | | | ● | | | | | | | | | | |
| NATURAL HEALTH CLINIC (HM14577) | | | | | | | | | | | | ● | | | | ● | | | | ● | ● | | | | |
| PHILIP STOCK - PHYSIOTHERAPIST (HM16120) | | | | | | | | | | | | | | | | ● | | | | | | | | | ● |
| PHYSIO ACTIVE (HM16193) | | | | | | | | | | | | | | | | | ● | | | | | ● | | | ● |
| SEEDS, COLIN (HM18191) | | | | | | | | | | | | | | | | | | | | ● | | | | | |
| SLATER, M (HM18676) | | | | | | | | | | | | | | | | | | | | ● | | | | | |
| STEVENSON, JACKIE (HM19249) | | | | | | | | | | | | | | | ● | | | | | | | | | | |
| SUNFLOWER VITAL HEALTH (HM19507) | | | | | | | | | | | | | | | ● | | | | | | | | | | |
| TIDESWELL HOM PRACTICE (HM20056) | | | | | | | | | | | | | | | | | ● | | | | | | | | |
| TRANSFORMATIONS (HM20292) | | | | | | | | | | | | | | | | | | | | ● | | | | | |
| WALKER, B (HM20764) | | | | | | | | | | | | | | | | | | | | ● | | | | | |
| DEVON | | | | | | | | | | | | | | | | | | | | | | | | | |
| ABBEYMEAD NATURAL HEALTH CTRE (HM00090) | | | | | | | | | | | | | | | ● | | ● | | | | ● | ● | | ● | |
| ACUPUNCTURE CLINIC (HM00276) | | | | | | | | | | | | | | | ● | | | | | | | | | | |
| ANNE RAWLINGS HYPNOTHERAPY (HM00901) | | ● | | | | | | | | ● | | ● | ● | | | ● | | | ● | ● | ● | | | | |

| Business by County with Reference no. | Kirlian Photography | Laser Treatment | Life Style Coaching | Light Therapy | Macrobiotics | Magnetic Therapy | Manipulation | Manual Lymph Drainage | Massage (Therapeutic) | McTimoney Chiropractic | Meditation | Metamorphic Therapy | Miasm Therapy | Micro Manipulation | Moxibustion | Mud Therapy | Music Therapy | Nail Surgery | Naturopathy | Neuro-Linguistic Program | Neurotherapy | Nutritional Therapy | Orgone Therapy | Oriental Diagnosis | Orthomolecular Medicine |
|---|---|---|---|---|---|---|---|---|---|---|---|---|---|---|---|---|---|---|---|---|---|---|---|---|---|
| DERBY HOMEOPATHIC PRACTICE (HM06013) | | | | | | | | | | | | | | | | | | | | | | | | | |
| DRONFIELD NAT HEALTH CLINIC (HM06319) | | | | | | | ● | | ● | | | | ● | | | | | | | | | ● | | | |
| ENJOY SPORT (HM06836) | | | | | | | ● | | ● | | | | | | | | | | | | | | | | |
| FENG SHUI (HM07210) | | | | | | | | | | | | | | | | | | | | | | | | | |
| FOX-DAVIES, DAWN (HM07643) | | | | | | | | | | | | | | | | | | | | | | | | | |
| HATHERSAGE HEALTH & THRPY CTRE (HM09198) | | | | | | | | | ● | | | | | | | | | | | | | | | | |
| HAYWOOD, T J (HM09289) | | | | | | | | | | | | | | | | | | | | | | | | | |
| HORAN, MARTIN (HM10163) | | | | | | | | | | | | | | | | | | | | | | | | | |
| ILKESTONE OSTEO & MED CTRE (HM10580) | | | | | | | | | | | | | | | | | | | ● | | | | | | |
| KARDAHJI, F C (HM11319) | | | | | | | | | | | | | | | | | | | | | | | | | |
| KAY, P (HM11353) | | | | | | | | | | | | | | | | | | | | | | | | | |
| KEMP, G D (HM11460) | | | | | | | | | | | | | | | | | | | | | | ● | | | |
| KEMP, GILLIAN (HM11461) | | | | | | | ● | | ● | | | | | | | | | | | | | ● | | | |
| LIFESOLUTIONS (HM12359) | | | ● | | | | | | | | | | | | | | | | | ● | | | | | |
| MATLOCK PHYSIOTHERAPY CENTRE (HM13293) | | | | | | | | | | | | | | | | | | | | | | | | | |
| MCFARLANE, BILL (HM13475) | | | | | | | | | | | | | | | | | | | | | | | | | |
| MEAKIN, JACKIE (HM13639) | | | | | | | | | | | | | | | | | | | | | | | | | |
| NATURAL CHOICE HEALTH FOODS (HM14526) | | | | | | | | | | | | | | | | | | | | | | | | | |
| NATURAL CHOICE HEALTH FOODS (HM14524) | | | | | | | | | | | | | | | | | | | | | | | | | |
| NATURAL CHOICE HEALTH FOODS (HM14525) | | | | | | | | | | | | | | | | | | | | | | | | | |
| NATURAL HEALTH CLINIC (HM14577) | | | | | | | ● | | ● | | | | | | | | | | | | | | | | |
| PHILIP STOCK - PHYSIOTHERAPIST (HM16120) | | | | | | | ● | | ● | | | | | | | | | | | | | | | | |
| PHYSIO ACTIVE (HM16193) | | | | | | | ● | | ● | | | | | | | | | | | | | | | ● | |
| SEEDS, COLIN (HM18191) | | | | | | | | | | | | | | | | | | | | | | | | | |
| SLATER, M (HM18676) | | | | | | | | | | | | | | | | | | | | | | | | | |
| STEVENSON, JACKIE (HM19249) | | | | | | | | | | | | | | | | | | | | | | | | | |
| SUNFLOWER VITAL HEALTH (HM19507) | | | | | | | | | | | | | | | | | | | | | | | | | |
| TIDESWELL HOM PRACTICE (HM20056) | | | | | | | | | | | | | | | | | | | | | | | | | |
| TRANSFORMATIONS (HM20292) | | | | | | | | | | | | | | | | | | | | | | | | | |
| WALKER, B (HM20764) | | | | | | | | | | | | | | | | | | | | | | | | | |
| DEVON | | | | | | | | | | | | | | | | | | | | | | | | | |
| ABBEYMEAD NATURAL HEALTH CTRE (HM00090) | | | | | | | ● | | ● | | ● | | | | | | | | ● | | | ● | | | |
| ACUPUNCTURE CLINIC (HM00276) | | | | | | | | | ● | | ● | | | | | | | | | | | | | ● | |
| ANNE RAWLINGS HYPNOTHERAPY (HM00901) | | | ● | | | | | | | | ● | | | | | | | | | | | | | | |

# F - O Therapies at Practices/Businesses

| Business by County with Reference no. | ARCTURUES CLINIC (HM00987) | AWARENESS CENTRE (HM01415) | BALL, ADRIAN (HM01624) | BEATTY, CAROLINE (HM01982) | BENNETT, W P (HM02160) | BIDEFORD CHIROPRACTIC CLINIC (HM02283) | BIGDEN, ROGER (HM02288) | BINMORE, F (HM02318) | BIRD, JANE (HM02367) | CASTLE CHIROPRACTIC CLINIC (HM03829) | CHALTON, SANDRA (HM03954) | CHIROPRACTIC AND MYOFACIAL (HM04350) | CLINIC OF CHINESE MEDICINE (HM04687) | CLINIC OF HYP & STRESS MNGMT (HM04696) | COLLEGE OF NATURAL NUTRITION (HM04851) | COPE, ANNE (HM05134) | COX, MIRANDA (HM05316) | CRECY MASSAGE STUDIO (HM05404) | EAST DEVON CONSULTANCY (HM06512) | ELDON HEALTH CLINIC (HM06705) | ELLIS, SUE (HM06773) | FARMER, RON (HM07109) | FOOT CLINIC & THERAPY ROOM (HM07474) | FOOTEC MEDICAL (HM07500) | FUDGE, H (HM07777) | GILLARD, J (HM08082) | GRACELINGS NATURAL HEALTH (HM08335) | GRAHAM, GEOFF (HM08345) | HANAM-CHAZ, CHAZ (HM08890) | HARRIS, J (HM09066) | HARRIS, JEANNE (HM09068) | HARRIS, LYN (HM09078) | HEALTH CARE INTERNATIONAL (HM09379) | HEALTH CONSULTANCY (HM09382) |
|---|---|---|---|---|---|---|---|---|---|---|---|---|---|---|---|---|---|---|---|---|---|---|---|---|---|---|---|---|---|---|---|---|---|---|
| Orthomolecular Medicine | | | | | | | | | | | | | | | | | | | | ● | | | | | | | | | | | | | | |
| Oriental Diagnosis | | | | | | | | | | | | | | | | | | | | | | | | | | | | | | | | | | |
| Orgone Therapy | | | | | | | | | | | | | | | | | | | | | | | | | | | | | | | | | | |
| Nutritional Therapy | | ● | | | | | | | | | | | | | ● | ● | | | ● | ● | | | | | | | ● | | | | | | | |
| Neurotherapy | | | | | | | | | | | | | | | | | | | | | | | | | | | | | | | | | | |
| Neuro-Linguistic Program | | | | | | | | | | | | | | | | | | | | | | | | | | | | | | | | | | |
| Naturopathy | | | | | | ● | | | | | | | | | ● | ● | | | ● | ● | | | | | | | | | | | | | | |
| Nail Surgery | | | | | | | | | | | | | | | | | | | | | | | | ● | | | | | | | | | | |
| Music Therapy | | | | | | | | | | | | | | | | | | | | | | | | | | | | | | | | | | |
| Mud Therapy | | | | | | | | | | | | | | | | | | | | | | | | | | | | | | | | | | |
| Moxibustion | | | | | | | | | | | | | | | | | | | | ● | | | | | | | | | | | | | | |
| Micro Manipulation | | | | | | | | | | | | | | | | | | | | | | | | | | | | | | | | | | |
| Miasm Therapy | | | | | | | | | | | | | | | | | | | | | | | | | | | | | | | | | | ● |
| Metamorphic Therapy | | | | | | | | | | | | | | | | | | | | | | | | | | | | | | | | | | |
| Meditation | | ● | | | | | | | | | | | | | | | ● | | | | | | | | | | | | | | | | | |
| McTimoney Chiropractic | | | | | | | | | | | | | | | | | | | | | | | | | | | | | | | | | | |
| Massage (Therapeutic) | ● | | ● | | | | | | | | | | | | | ● | | ● | | ● | ● | | ● | | ● | | ● | | | | | | | ● |
| Manual Lymph Drainage | | | | | | | | | | | | | | | | | | | | | | | | | | | | | | | | | | |
| Manipulation | | | ● | | | | | | | ● | | ● | | | | ● | | | | ● | ● | | | | ● | | | | | | | | | ● |
| Magnetic Therapy | | | | | | | | | | | | | | | | | | | | | | | | | | | ● | | | | | | | |
| Macrobiotics | | ● | | | | | | | | | | | | | | | | | | | | | | | | | | | | | | | | |
| Light Therapy | | | | | | | | | | | | | | | | | | | | | | | | | | | | | | | | | | |
| Life Style Coaching | | | | | | | | | | | | | | | | | | | | | | | | | | | | | | | | | | |
| Laser Treatment | | | | | | | | | | | | | | | | | | | | | | | | | | | | | | | | | | |
| Kirlian Photography | | | | | | | | | | | | | | | | | | | | | | | | | | | | | | | | | | |
| Kinesiology | | | | | | | | ● | | | | | | | | | | | ● | | | | | | ● | | | | | | | | | |
| Iridology | | | | | | | | | | | | | | | | | | | | ● | | | | | | | | | | | | | | |
| Inhalation Therapy | | | | | | | | | | | | | | | | | ● | | | | | | | | | | | | | | | | | |
| Indian Head Massage | | ● | | | | | | | | | | | | | | | | | | | | | ● | | | | ● | | | | | | | |
| Hypnotherapy | | ● | | | | | | | | | | | | | | | | | | ● | | | | | | | | | | | | | | |
| Hypnosis | | ● | | | | | | | ● | | | | | ● | | | | | | | | ● | | | | | | ● | ● | | | | | |
| Humanistic Psychology | | | | | | | | | | | | | | | | | ● | | | | | | | | | | | | | | | | | |
| Hopi Ear Candles | | | | | | | | | | | | | | | | | | | | | | | | | | | | | | | | | | |
| Homeopathy | ● | ● | | | | | ● | | | | | | | | | | | | | ● | | | | | | ● | | | | ● | ● | ● | | ● |
| Holistic Healing | | ● | | | | | | | | | | | | | ● | | | | | | ● | | | | | | | | | | | | | |
| Herbal Medicine | | | | ● | ● | | | | | | ● | | ● | | | ● | | | | | | | | | | | | | | | | | ● | |
| Hellerwork | | | | | | | | | | | | | | | | | | | | | | | | | | | | | | | | | | |
| Healing Therapy | | ● | | | | | | | | | | | | | | | | | | | | | | | | | ● | | | | | | | |
| Healer | | ● | | | | | | | | | | | | | | | | | | | | | | | | | | | | | | | | |
| Hay Diet | | ● | | | | | | | | | | | | | | ● | | | ● | | | | | | | | | | | | | | | |
| Group Therapy | | | | | | | | | | | | | | | | | ● | | | | | | | | | | | | | | | | | |
| Gestalt Therapy | | | | | | | | | | | | | | | | | ● | | | | | | | | | | | | | | | | | |
| Gem Essence Therapy | | | | | | | | | | | | | | | | | | | | | | | | | | | | | | | | | | |
| Gait Analysis | | | | | | | | | | | | | | | | | | | | | | | | ● | | | | | | | | | | |
| Flotation Therapy | | | | | | | | | | | | | | | | | | | | | | | | | | | | | | | | | | |
| Floral Essence Therapy | | | | | | | | | | | | | | | | | | | | | | | | | | | | | | | | | | |
| Feng Shui | | | | | | | | | | | | | | | | | | | | | | | | | | | | | | | | | | |
| Feldenkrais Methodology | | | | | | | | | | | | | | | | | | | | | | | | | | | | | | | | | | |
| Family Therapy | | | | | | | | | | | | | | | | | | | | | | | | | | | | | | | | | | |
| Family Planning (Natural) | | | | | | | | | | | | | | | | | | | | | | | | | | | | | | | | | | |

# F - O Therapies at Practices/Businesses

| Business by County with Reference no. | Family Planning (Natural) | Family Therapy | Feldenkrais Methodology | Feng Shui | Floral Essence Therapy | Flotation Therapy | Gait Analysis | Gem Essence Therapy | Gestalt Therapy | Group Therapy | Hay Diet | Healer | Healing Therapy | Hellerwork | Herbal Medicine | Holistic Healing | Homeopathy | Hopi Ear Candles | Humanistic Psychology | Hypnosis | Hypnotherapy | Indian Head Massage | Inhalation Therapy | Iridology | Kinesiology |
|---|---|---|---|---|---|---|---|---|---|---|---|---|---|---|---|---|---|---|---|---|---|---|---|---|---|
| HEALTH WAVES (HM09408) | | | | | | | | | | | | | ● | | | | | | | | | | | | |
| INSTIT-DEVELOPMENTAL POTENTIAL (HM10664) | | | | | | | | | | | | | | | | | | | | ● | | | | | |
| INTAHEALTH UK (HM10689) | | | | | | | | | | | | | | | | ● | ● | | | | | | | | |
| IRIDOLOGY/NUTRITIONAL THER (HM10723) | | | | | | | | | | | | | | | | | | | | | | | | ● | |
| JANE HYDE CHRTRD PHYSIO (HM10917) | | | | | | | | | | | | | | | | | | | | | | | | | |
| JENKINS, KATHERINE (HM10991) | | | | | | | | | | | | | | | | | | | | ● | | | | | |
| JOHNSON, MICHAEL (HM11087) | | | | | | | | | | | | | | | | | ● | | | | | ● | | | |
| KELLY, L V (HM11436) | | | | | | | | | | | | | | | | | | | | ● | | | | | |
| KERR, J A (HM11548) | | | | | | | | | | | | | | | | | ● | | | | | | | | |
| KINGSBRIDGE COMP HLTH PRACTICE (HM11658) | | | | | | | | | | | | ● | ● | | ● | ● | ● | | | | ● | | | | |
| KINGSBRIDGE PHYSICAL THERAPY (HM11659) | | | | | | | | | | | | | | | | | | | | | | | | | |
| LIGHT TOUCH THERAPY TRAINING (HM12369) | | | | | | | | | | | | | | | | | ● | | | | | | | | |
| LINDEMAN, A J (HM12415) | | | | | | | | | | | | | | | | | ● | | | | | | | ● | |
| LODER, H (HM12557) | | | | | | | | | | | | | | | ● | | | | | | | | | | |
| LONDON COLLEGE-HYPNOTHERAPY (HM12594) | | | | | | | | | | | | | | | | | | | | ● | | | | | |
| MALLARDO, RENEE (HM12977) | | ● | | | | | | | | ● | | | | | | | | | | ● | ● | | | | |
| MASON, MARCUS (HM13248) | | | | | | | | | | | | | ● | | | | | | | | | | | | |
| MASSAGE RELAXING THERAPEUTIC (HM13262) | | | | | | | | | | | | | | | | | | | | | | | | | |
| MONSHIN, DEBORAH J (HM14075) | | | | | | | | | | | | | | | | | | | | ● | ● | | | | |
| MORRISH, MO (HM14219) | | | | | | | | | | | | | | | | | ● | | | | | | | | |
| NAT INSTITUTE OF MED HERBAL (HM14501) | | | | | | | | | | | | | | | ● | | | | | | | | | | |
| NELSON, PAUL (HM14781) | | | | | | | | | | | ● | | | | | ● | ● | | | | | | | | |
| PETERPAN & TINKERBELL (HM16080) | | | | | | | | | | | | | | | | | | | | ● | | | | | |
| PLYMOUTH OSTEOPATHS (HM16388) | | | | | | | | | | | | | | | | | | | | | | | | | ● |
| PSYCHOTHERAPY/HYPNOTHERAPY (HM16739) | | | | | | | | | ● | ● | | | | | | | | | | | | | | | |
| RENDLE, S (HM17182) | | | | | | | | | | | | | | | | | | | | | | | | | |
| RIVERSIDE CHIROPRACTIC CLINIC (HM17379) | | | | | | | | | | | | | | | | | | | | | | | | | |
| ROGERS, PAMELA (HM17552) | | | | | | | | | | | | | | | ● | | | | | | | | | | |
| ROGUSKI, CATHERINE (HM17558) | | | | | | | | | | | | | | | ● | | | | | | | | | | |
| ROSE & CROWN CLINIC (HM17598) | | | | | | | | | | | | | ● | | ● | | ● | | | | ● | | | | |
| SCURR, PETER M (HM18160) | | | | | | | | | | | | | | | | | | | | | | | | | |
| SEELEY, JANICE (HM18194) | | | | | | | | | | | | | | | | | ● | | | | | | | | |
| SERENITY (HM18233) | | | | | | | | | | | | | | | | | | ● | | | | | | | |
| SOFFE, N S (HM18858) | | | | | | | | | | | | | | | | | ● | | | | | | | | |

| Business by County with Reference no. | Kirlian Photography | Laser Treatment | Life Style Coaching | Light Therapy | Macrobiotics | Magnetic Therapy | Manipulation | Manual Lymph Drainage | Massage (Therapeutic) | McTimoney Chiropractic | Meditation | Metamorphic Therapy | Miasm Therapy | Micro Manipulation | Moxibustion | Mud Therapy | Music Therapy | Nail Surgery | Naturopathy | Neuro-Linguistic Program | Neurotherapy | Nutritional Therapy | Orgone Therapy | Oriental Diagnosis | Orthomolecular Medicine |
|---|---|---|---|---|---|---|---|---|---|---|---|---|---|---|---|---|---|---|---|---|---|---|---|---|---|
| HEALTH WAVES (HM09408) | | | | | | | | | ● | | ● | | | | | | | | | | | ● | | | |
| INSTIT-DEVELOPMENTAL POTENTIAL (HM10664) | | | | | | | | | | | | | | | | | | | | | | | | | |
| INTAHEALTH UK (HM10689) | | | | | | | | | | | | | ● | | | | | | | | | ● | | | |
| IRIDOLOGY/NUTRITIONAL THER (HM10723) | | | | | | | | | | | | | | | | | | | | | | ● | | | |
| JANE HYDE CHRTRD PHYSIO (HM10917) | | | | | | | ● | | | | | | | | | | | | | | | | | | |
| JENKINS, KATHERINE (HM10991) | | | | | | | | | | | | | | | | | | | | | | | | | |
| JOHNSON, MICHAEL (HM11087) | | | | | | | | | ● | | | | | | ● | | | | | | | | | ● | |
| KELLY, L V (HM11436) | | | | | | | | | | | | | | | | | | | | | | | | | |
| KERR, J A (HM11548) | | | | | | | | | | | | | | | | | | | | | | | | | |
| KINGSBRIDGE COMP HLTH PRACTICE (HM11658) | | | | | | | ● | | ● | | ● | | ● | | | | | | | | | ● | | ● | |
| KINGSBRIDGE PHYSICAL THERAPY (HM11659) | | | | | | | ● | | ● | | | | | | | | | | | | | | | | |
| LIGHT TOUCH THERAPY TRAINING (HM12369) | | | | | | | | | | | | | | | | | | | | | | | | | |
| LINDEMAN, A J (HM12415) | | | | | | | | | | | | | ● | | | | | | ● | | | | | | |
| LODER, H (HM12557) | | | | | | | | | | | | | | | | | | | | | | | | | |
| LONDON COLLEGE-HYPNOTHERAPY (HM12594) | | | | | | | | | | | | | | | | | | | | | | | | | |
| MALLARDO, RENEE (HM12977) | | | | | | | | | | | | | | | | | | | | | | | | | |
| MASON, MARCUS (HM13248) | | | | | | | | | | | | | | | ● | | | | | | | | | ● | |
| MASSAGE RELAXING THERAPEUTIC (HM13262) | | | | | | | | | ● | | | | | | | | | | | | | | | | |
| MONSHIN, DEBORAH J (HM14075) | | | | | | | | | | | ● | | | | | | | | | | | | | | |
| MORRISH, MO (HM14219) | | | | | | | | | | | | | | | | | | | | | | | | | |
| NAT INSTITUTE OF MED HERBAL (HM14501) | | | | | | | | | | | | | | | | | | | | | | | | | |
| NELSON, PAUL (HM14781) | | | | | | | | | | | | | | | | | | | | | | ● | | | |
| PETERPAN & TINKERBELL (HM16080) | | | | | | | | | | | | | | | | | | | | | | | | | |
| PLYMOUTH OSTEOPATHS (HM16388) | | | | | | | | | | | | | | | | | | | | | | | | | |
| PSYCHOTHERAPY/HYPNOTHERAPY (HM16739) | | | | | | | | | | | | | | | | | | | | | | | | | |
| RENDLE, S (HM17182) | | | | | | | | | | | | | | | | | | ● | | | | | | | |
| RIVERSIDE CHIROPRACTIC CLINIC (HM17379) | | | | | | | ● | | ● | | | | | | | | | | | | | | | | |
| ROGERS, PAMELA (HM17552) | | | | | | | | | | | | | | | | | | | | | | | | | |
| ROGUSKI, CATHERINE (HM17558) | | | | | | | | | | | | | | | | | | | | | | | | | |
| ROSE & CROWN CLINIC (HM17598) | | | | | | | | | | | | | | | | | | | | | | | | | |
| SCURR, PETER M (HM18160) | | | | | | | | | | | | | | | | | | ● | | | | | | | |
| SEELEY, JANICE (HM18194) | | | | | | | | | | | | | | | | | | | ● | | | | | | |
| SERENITY (HM18233) | | | | | | | | | | | | | | | | | | | | | | | | | |
| SOFFE, N S (HM18858) | | | | | | | | | | | | | | | | | | | | | | | | | |

# F - O Therapies at Practices/Businesses

| Business by County with Reference no. | Family Planning (Natural) | Family Therapy | Feldenkrais Methodology | Feng Shui | Floral Essence Therapy | Flotation Therapy | Gait Analysis | Gem Essence Therapy | Gestalt Therapy | Group Therapy | Hay Diet | Healer | Healing Therapy | Hellerwork | Herbal Medicine | Holistic Healing | Homeopathy | Hopi Ear Candles | Humanistic Psychology | Hypnosis | Hypnotherapy | Indian Head Massage | Inhalation Therapy | Iridology | Kinesiology |
|---|---|---|---|---|---|---|---|---|---|---|---|---|---|---|---|---|---|---|---|---|---|---|---|---|---|
| SPENCE, R (HM18985) | | | | | | | | | | | | | | | | | | | | ● | | | | | |
| STIMULUS FOR CHANGE (HM19296) | | | | | | | | | | | | | | | | | ● | | | | | | | | |
| STOBART, ANNE (HM19306) | | | | | | | | | | | | | | | ● | | | | | | | | | | |
| TANSER, THEO (HM19687) | | | | | | | | | | | | | | | | | ● | | | | | | | | |
| THOMAS, CHRIS (HM19935) | | | | | | | | | | | | | | | | | | | | ● | | | | | |
| TRANCE - FORMATIONS HEALING (HM20250) | | ● | | | | | | | | | | ● | ● | | | | | | | ● | ● | | | | |
| VIDAL-HALL, NICK (HM20659) | | | | | | | | | | | | | | | | | ● | | | | | | | | |
| VITAL TOUCH (HM20703) | | | | | | | | | | | | | | | | | | | | | | | | | |
| WALKER, VICTOR J (HM20807) | | | | | | | | | | | | | | | | | | | | ● | | | | | |
| WILLIAMS CLINIC (HM21531) | | | | | | | | | | | | | | | | | ● | | | | | | | | |
| WOOD, JULIE (HM21803) | | | | | | | | | | | | | | | | | | | | ● | | | | | |
| WOODROW, IAN (HM21842) | | | | | | | | | | | | | | | | | | | | ● | | | | | |
| YORK HOUSE CHIROPODY (HM22044) | | | | | | | | | | | | | | | | | | | | | | | | | |
| YORK HOUSE CHIROPRACTIC CLINIC (HM22045) | | | | | | | | | | | | | | | | | | | | | | | | | |
| **DORSET** | | | | | | | | | | | | | | | | | | | | | | | | | |
| ABBEY VIEW COMP CLINIC (HM00088) | | | | | | | | | | | | | | | ● | | ● | | | | ● | | | | |
| ADELAIDE CLINIC (HM00378) | | | | | | | | | | | | | | | | | | | ● | | | | | | |
| ALTERNATIVE APPROACH (HM00694) | | | | | | | | | | | | | | | | | ● | | | | | | | | |
| ARCHIBALD, LIZ (HM00980) | | | | | | | | | | | | | | | | | | | | ● | ● | | | | |
| AROMA TRANQUILITY (HM01064) | | | | | | | | | | | | | | | | | | | | | | | | | |
| AWDRY, ROBERT (HM01416) | | | | | | | | | | | | | | | | | ● | | | | | | | | |
| BEAUMONT COLLEGE OF NAT MED (HM01986) | | | | | | | | | | | | | | | | | | | | | | ● | | | |
| BELTAIN CENTRE (HM02116) | | | | | | | | | | | | ● | ● | | | | | | | | | | | | |
| BELTAIN CENTRE (HM02117) | | | | | | | | | | | | | ● | | | ● | | | | ● | ● | | | | |
| BOURNEMOUTH CTRE FOR COMP MED (HM02761) | | | | | | | | | | | | | | | | | ● | | | ● | | ● | | | |
| BOWEN CLINIC (HM02771) | | | | | | | | | | | | ● | | | | | | | | | | | | | |
| BRANDON, DAVE (HM02912) | | | | | | | | | | | | | | | | ● | ● | | | | | | | | |
| BRIDPORT COMP MEDICINE CTRE (HM03019) | | | | | | | | | | | | | | | | | ● | | | | | | | | |
| BRIGHTER FUTURE (HM03039) | | | | | | | | | | | | | | | | ● | | | | ● | ● | | | | |
| BRIGHTER FUTURE (HM03040) | | | | | | | | | | | | | | | | ● | | | | ● | ● | | | | |
| BROADSTONE CENTRE OF COMP MED (HM03118) | | | | | | | | | | | | | | | ● | | ● | | | | ● | ● | | | |
| BURT, S (HM03429) | | | | | ● | | | | | | | | | | ● | ● | ● | | | | | | | ● | |
| BWT PODIATRY (HM03508) | | | | | | | ● | | | | | | | | | | | | | | | | | | |
| CARBERY PRACTICE (HM03657) | | | | | | | | | | | | | | | | | | | | | ● | ● | | | |

| Business by County with Reference no. | Kirlian Photography | Laser Treatment | Life Style Coaching | Light Therapy | Macrobiotics | Magnetic Therapy | Manipulation | Manual Lymph Drainage | Massage (Therapeutic) | McTimoney Chiropractic | Meditation | Metamorphic Therapy | Miasm Therapy | Micro Manipulation | Moxibustion | Mud Therapy | Music Therapy | Nail Surgery | Naturopathy | Neuro-Linguistic Program | Neurotherapy | Nutritional Therapy | Orgone Therapy | Oriental Diagnosis | Orthomolecular Medicine |
|---|---|---|---|---|---|---|---|---|---|---|---|---|---|---|---|---|---|---|---|---|---|---|---|---|---|
| SPENCE, R (HM18985) | | | | | | | | | | | | | | | | | | | | | | | | | |
| STIMULUS FOR CHANGE (HM19296) | | | | | | | | | | | | | | | | | | | | | | | | | |
| STOBART, ANNE (HM19306) | | | | | | | | | | | | | | | | | | | | | | | | | |
| TANSER, THEO (HM19687) | | | | | | | | | | | | | | | | | | | | | | | | | |
| THOMAS, CHRIS (HM19935) | | | | | | | | | | | | | | | | | | | | | | | | | |
| TRANCE - FORMATIONS HEALING (HM20250) | | | | | | | | | | | | | | | | | | | | | | | | | |
| VIDAL-HALL, NICK (HM20659) | | | | | | | | | | | | | | | | | | | | | | | | | |
| VITAL TOUCH (HM20703) | | | | | | | | | ● | | | | | | | | | | | | | | | | |
| WALKER, VICTOR J (HM20807) | | | | | | | | | | | | | | | | | | | | | | | | | |
| WILLIAMS CLINIC (HM21531) | | | | | | | | | | | | | | | | | | | | | | | | | |
| WOOD, JULIE (HM21803) | | | | | | | | | | | | | | | | | | | | | | | | | |
| WOODROW, IAN (HM21842) | | | | | | | | | | | | | | | | | | | | | | | | | |
| YORK HOUSE CHIROPODY (HM22044) | | | | | | | | | | | | | | | | | | ● | | | | | | | |
| YORK HOUSE CHIROPRACTIC CLINIC (HM22045) | | | | | | | | | ● | | | | | | | | | | | | | | | | |
| **DORSET** | | | | | | | | | | | | | | | | | | | | | | | | | |
| ABBEY VIEW COMP CLINIC (HM00088) | | | | | | | | | | | | | | | | | | | | | | ● | | | |
| ADELAIDE CLINIC (HM00378) | | | | | | | | | ● | | | | | | | | | | | | | | | | |
| ALTERNATIVE APPROACH (HM00694) | | | | | | | | | | | | | | | | | | | | | | | | | |
| ARCHIBALD, LIZ (HM00980) | | | | | | | | | | | | | | | | | | | | | | | | | |
| AROMA TRANQUILITY (HM01064) | | | | | | | | | ● | | | | | | | | | | | | | | | | |
| AWDRY, ROBERT (HM01416) | | | | | | | | | | | | | | | | | | | | | | ● | | | |
| BEAUMONT COLLEGE OF NAT MED (HM01986) | | | | | | | | | ● | | | | | | | | | | | | | | | | |
| BELTAIN CENTRE (HM02116) | | | | | | | | | | | ● | | | | | | | | | | | | | | |
| BELTAIN CENTRE (HM02117) | | | | | | | | | | | ● | | | | | | | | | | | | | | |
| BOURNEMOUTH CTRE FOR COMP MED (HM02761) | | | | | | | | | ● | | | | | | | | | | | | | | | | |
| BOWEN CLINIC (HM02771) | | | | | | | | | ● | | | | | | | | | | | | | | | | |
| BRANDON, DAVE (HM02912) | | | | | | | | | | | | | | | | | | | | | | ● | | | |
| BRIDPORT COMP MEDICINE CTRE (HM03019) | | | | | | | | | ● | | | | | | | | | | | | | ● | | | |
| BRIGHTER FUTURE (HM03039) | | | | | | | | | | | | | | | | | | | | | | | | | |
| BRIGHTER FUTURE (HM03040) | | | | | | | | | | | | | | | | | | | | | | | | | |
| BROADSTONE CENTRE OF COMP MED (HM03118) | | | | | | | | ● | ● | | | | | | | | | | | | | ● | | | |
| BURT, S (HM03429) | | | ● | | | | | | | | | | | | | | | | ● | | | ● | | | |
| BWT PODIATRY (HM03508) | | | | | | | | | | | | | | | | | | ● | | | | | | | |
| CARBERY PRACTICE (HM03657) | | | | | | | ● | | ● | | | | | | | | | | ● | | | | | | |

# F - O Therapies at Practices/Businesses

| Business by County with Reference no. | Family Planning (Natural) | Family Therapy | Feldenkrais Methodology | Feng Shui | Floral Essence Therapy | Flotation Therapy | Gait Analysis | Gem Essence Therapy | Gestalt Therapy | Group Therapy | Hay Diet | Healer | Healing Therapy | Hellerwork | Herbal Medicine | Holistic Healing | Homeopathy | Hopi Ear Candles | Humanistic Psychology | Hypnosis | Hypnotherapy | Indian Head Massage | Inhalation Therapy | Iridology | Kinesiology |
|---|---|---|---|---|---|---|---|---|---|---|---|---|---|---|---|---|---|---|---|---|---|---|---|---|---|
| CARR-JONES, MICHAEL (HM03752) | | | | | | | | | | | | | | | | | | | | ● | | | | | |
| CHINESE MEDICINE CENTRE (HM04254) | | | | | | | | | | | | | | | ● | | | | | | | | | | |
| CHRISTCHURCH CHIROPRACTIC CTRE (HM04435) | | | | | | | | | | | | | | | | | | | | | | | | | |
| CHRISTCHURCH PHYSIO PRACTICE (HM04436) | | | | | | | | | | | | | | | | | | | | | | | | | |
| CLARK, LYNN (HM04568) | | | | | | | | | | | | | | | | | | | | | | | | | |
| CULPEPER (HM05578) | | | | | | | | | | | | | | | ● | | | | | | | | | | |
| DLP HYPNOTHERAPY CENTRE (HM06134) | | | | | | | | | | | | | | | | | | | | ● | ● | | | | |
| DORSET RACQUETS & HEALTH CLUB (HM06205) | | | | | | | | | | | | | | | | | | | | | | ● | | | |
| DORWEST HERBS (HM06206) | | | | | | | | | | | | | | | ● | | | | | | | | | | |
| DRAPER, DEREK (HM06287) | | | | | | | | | | | | | | | | | | | | | | | | | |
| EASY WAY TO STOP SMOKING (HM06555) | | | | | | | | | | | | | | | | | | | | ● | | | | | |
| FLAVELL, MARGARET (HM07398) | | | | | | | | | | | | ● | | | | | | | | | | | | | |
| FREESPIRIT (HM07724) | | | | | | | | | | | | | ● | | | | | | | | | | | | |
| FULL SPECTRUM THERAPY CENTRE (HM07786) | | | | | | | | | | | | | | | | | | | | | ● | | | | |
| GODFREY, BRIAN (HM08184) | | | | | | | | | | | | ● | | | | | | | | | ● | | | | |
| HARLING, MARIANNE (DR) (HM09010) | | | | | | | | | | | | | | | | | ● | | | | | | | | |
| HARMONY (HM09021) | | | | | | | | | | | | | | | | | | | | ● | | | | | |
| HERBALIST, GODSHAER (HM09646) | | | | | | | | | | | | | | | ● | | | | | | | | | | |
| HIGHCLIFFE CHIROPRACTIC CLINIC (HM09749) | | | | | | | | | | | | | | | | | | | | | | | | | ● |
| HOLISTIC HEALTH CENTRE (HM09973) | | | | | | | | | | | | | | | ● | | ● | | | | ● | | | | ● |
| HOMEOPATHY HEALS (HM10081) | | | | | | | | | | | | | | | | | ● | | | | | | | | |
| HORNE, SUE (HM10175) | | | | | | | | | | | | | | | | | | | | | | | | | |
| INSTITUTE OF BIO-ENERGETIC MED (HM10668) | | | | | | | | | | | | | | | | | ● | | | | | | | | |
| JACKSON, A E (HM10817) | | | | | | | | | | | | | | | | | ● | | | | | | | ● | |
| JELFS, MARTIN (HM10975) | | | | | | | | | ● | | | | | | | | | | ● | | | | | | |
| LOCK, ROBERT (HM12538) | | | | | | | | | | | | | | | | | | | | ● | ● | | | | |
| MIDDLES PICCADILLY CTRE (HM13815) | | | | | | | | | | | | | | | | | ● | | | | | ● | | | ● |
| NATURAL HEALTH CONSULTANCY (HM14592) | | | ● | | | | | | | | | | | | ● | ● | ● | | | | | ● | | | |
| NEIJIA (HM14759) | | | | | | | | | | | | | | | | | | | | | | | | | |
| PHYSIO, MASSAGE & PR ACU (HM16210) | | | | | | | | | | | | | ● | | | | | | | | | | | | |
| PROSPECT HEALTH (HM16667) | | | | | | | | | | | | | ● | | | | ● | | | ● | ● | | | | |
| ROLLS MILL COMP HEALTH CENTRE (HM17567) | | | | | | | | | | | | | | | ● | | ● | | | | ● | | | | ● |
| ROWE, PENNY (HM17689) | | | | | | | | | | | | | | | | ● | ● | | | | | | | | |
| ROWE, PENNY (HM17690) | | | | | | | | | | | | | | | | | ● | | | | | | | | |

| Business by County with Reference no. | Kirlian Photography | Laser Treatment | Life Style Coaching | Light Therapy | Macrobiotics | Magnetic Therapy | Manipulation | Manual Lymph Drainage | Massage (Therapeutic) | McTimoney Chiropractic | Meditation | Metamorphic Therapy | Miasm Therapy | Micro Manipulation | Moxibustion | Mud Therapy | Music Therapy | Nail Surgery | Naturopathy | Neuro-Linguistic Program | Neurotherapy | Nutritional Therapy | Orgone Therapy | Oriental Diagnosis | Orthomolecular Medicine |
|---|---|---|---|---|---|---|---|---|---|---|---|---|---|---|---|---|---|---|---|---|---|---|---|---|---|
| CARR-JONES, MICHAEL (HM03752) | | | | | | | | | | | | | | | | | | | | | | | | | |
| CHINESE MEDICINE CENTRE (HM04254) | | | | | | | | | | | | | | | | | | | | | | | | | |
| CHRISTCHURCH CHIROPRACTIC CTRE (HM04435) | | | | | | | ● | | | | | | | | | | | | | | | | | | |
| CHRISTCHURCH PHYSIO PRACTICE (HM04436) | | | | | | | ● | | ● | | | | | | | | | | | | | | | | |
| CLARK, LYNN (HM04568) | | | | | | | | | | | | | | | | | | ● | | | | | | | |
| CULPEPER (HM05578) | | | | | | | | | | | | | | | | | | | | | | | | | |
| DLP HYPNOTHERAPY CENTRE (HM06134) | | | | | | | | | | | | | | | | | | | | | | | | | |
| DORSET RACQUETS & HEALTH CLUB (HM06205) | | | | | | | | | | | | | | | | | | | | | | | | | |
| DORWEST HERBS (HM06206) | | | | | | | | | | | | | | | | | | | | | | | | | |
| DRAPER, DEREK (HM06287) | | | | | | ● | | | | | | | | | | | | | | | | | | | |
| EASY WAY TO STOP SMOKING (HM06555) | | | | | | | | | | | | | | | | | | | | | | | | | |
| FLAVELL, MARGARET (HM07398) | | | | | | | | | | | | | | | | | | | | | | | | | |
| FREESPIRIT (HM07724) | | | | | | | | | | | ● | | | | | | | | | | | | | | |
| FULL SPECTRUM THERAPY CENTRE (HM07786) | | | | | | | | | | | | | | | | | | | | | | | | | |
| GODFREY, BRIAN (HM08184) | | | | | | | | | | | | | | | | | | | | | | | | | |
| HARLING, MARIANNE (DR) (HM09010) | | | | | | | | | | | | | | | | | | | | | | | | | |
| HARMONY (HM09021) | | | | | | | | | | | | | | | | | | | | | | | | | |
| HERBALIST, GODSHAER (HM09646) | | | | | | | | | | | | | | | | | | | | | | | | | |
| HIGHCLIFFE CHIROPRACTIC CLINIC (HM09749) | | | | | | | ● | | ● | | | | | | | | | | | | | ● | | | |
| HOLISTIC HEALTH CENTRE (HM09973) | | | | | | | | | | | | | | | | | | | ● | | | | | | |
| HOMEOPATHY HEALS (HM10081) | | | | | | | | | | | | | | | | | | | | | | ● | | | |
| HORNE, SUE (HM10175) | | | | | | | | | ● | | | | | | | | | | | | | | | | |
| INSTITUTE OF BIO-ENERGETIC MED (HM10668) | | | | | | | | | | | | | | | | | | | | | | | | | |
| JACKSON, A E (HM10817) | | | | | | | | | | | | | | | | | | | | | | | | | |
| JELFS, MARTIN (HM10975) | | | | | | | | | ● | | | | | | | | | | | | | | | | |
| LOCK, ROBERT (HM12538) | | | | | | ● | | | | | | | | | ● | | | | | | | | | ● | |
| MIDDLES PICCADILLY CTRE (HM13815) | | | | | | | | | | | | | | | | | | | | | | | | | |
| NATURAL HEALTH CONSULTANCY (HM14592) | | | | | | | | | ● | | | ● | | | | | | | | | | ● | | | |
| NEIJIA (HM14759) | | | | | | | | | ● | | | | | | ● | | | | | | | | | ● | |
| PHYSIO, MASSAGE & PR ACU (HM16210) | | | | | | | | | ● | | | | | | | | | | | | | | | | |
| PROSPECT HEALTH (HM16667) | | | | | | | ● | | ● | | | | | | | | | | | | | ● | | | |
| ROLLS MILL COMP HEALTH CENTRE (HM17567) | | | | | | | ● | | ● | | ● | | | | ● | | | | ● | | | ● | | | |
| ROWE, PENNY (HM17689) | | | | | | | | | | | | | | | | | | | | | | | | | |
| ROWE, PENNY (HM17690) | | | | | | | | | | | | | | | | | | | | | | | | | |

# F - O Therapies at Practices/Businesses

| Business by County with Reference no. | Family Planning (Natural) | Family Therapy | Feldenkrais Methodology | Feng Shui | Floral Essence Therapy | Flotation Therapy | Gait Analysis | Gem Essence Therapy | Gestalt Therapy | Group Therapy | Hay Diet | Healer | Healing Therapy | Hellerwork | Herbal Medicine | Holistic Healing | Homeopathy | Hopi Ear Candles | Humanistic Psychology | Hypnosis | Hypnotherapy | Indian Head Massage | Inhalation Therapy | Iridology | Kinesiology | Kirlian Photography | Laser Treatment | Life Style Coaching | Light Therapy | Macrobiotics | Magnetic Therapy | Manipulation | Manual Lymph Drainage | Massage (Therapeutic) | McTimoney Chiropractic | Meditation | Metamorphic Therapy | Miasm Therapy | Micro Manipulation | Moxibustion | Mud Therapy | Music Therapy | Nail Surgery | Naturopathy | Neuro-Linguistic Program | Neurotherapy | Nutritional Therapy | Orgone Therapy | Oriental Diagnosis | Orthomolecular Medicine |
|---|---|---|---|---|---|---|---|---|---|---|---|---|---|---|---|---|---|---|---|---|---|---|---|---|---|---|---|---|---|---|---|---|---|---|---|---|---|---|---|---|---|---|---|---|---|---|---|---|---|---|
| ROY, COLLEEN (HM17710) | | | | | | | | | | | | | | | | ● | ● | | | | | | | | | | | | | | | | | | | | | | | | | | | | | | | | | |
| SHEAD, JULIE (HM18354) | | | | | | | | | | | | | | | | | | | | | ● | | | | | | | | | | | | | | | | | | | | | | | | | | | | | |
| SHEBORNE CHIROPRACTIC CENTRE (HM18361) | | | | | | | | | | | | | | | | | | | | | | | | | ● | | | | | | | ● | | | | | | | | | | | | | | | | | | |
| SKELTON, JAN (HM18635) | | | | | | | | | | | | | | | | ● | | | | | | | | | | | | | | | | | | ● | | | | | | | | | | | | | | | | |
| SKINNER, NICOLA (HM18656) | | | | | | | | | | | | | | | | | | | | | | ● | | | | | | | | | | | | | | | | | | | | | | | | | | | | |
| SOUTHBOURNE HERBAL CLINIC (HM18924) | | | | | | | | | | | | | | | ● | | | | | | | | | | | | | | | | | | | | | | | | | | | | | | | | | | | |
| SOUTHBOURNE NATURAL HLTH CTRE (HM18925) | | | | | | | | | | | | | | | | | ● | | | | | | | | | | | | | | | | | | | | | | | | | | | | | | | | | |
| STADLER, M L (HM19105) | | | | | | | | | | | | | | | | | ● | | | | | | | | | | | | | | | | | | | | | | | | | | | | | | | | | |
| THORNTONS PHARMACY (HM20029) | | | | | | | | | | | | | | | | ● | ● | | | | | | | | | | | | | | | | | | | | | | | | | | | | | | | | | |
| TREAT FEET (HM20301) | | | | | | | | | | | | | | | | | | | | | | | | | | | | | | | | | | | | | | | | | | | ● | | | | | | | |
| WESSEX HEALTHY LIVING FOUND (HM21208) | ● | | | | | | | | | | ● | ● | ● | | ● | ● | ● | ● | | ● | ● | ● | | | ● | | | | | | | ● | | ● | | | | | | ● | | | | | ● | | ● | | | |
| WESSEX KINESIOLOGY CENTRE (HM21209) | | | | | | | | | | | | | | | | | | | | | | | | | ● | | | | | | | | | | | | | | | | | | | | | | | | | |
| WHITE FLOWER CENTRE (HM21337) | | | | | | | | | | | | | | | | | | | | | | ● | | | | | | | | | | | | ● | | | | | | | | | | | | | | | | |
| WIMBORNE HERBAL CLINIC (HM21688) | | | | | | | | | | | | | | | ● | | | | | | | | | | | | | | | | | | | | | | | | | | | | | | | | | | | |
| YELLOW HOUSE (HM22005) | | | | | | | | | | | | | | | | | ● | | | | ● | ● | | | | | | | | | | | | ● | | | | | | | | | | ● | | | | | | |
| EALING | | | | | | | | | | | | | | | | | | | | | | | | | | | | | | | | | | | | | | | | | | | | | | | | | | |
| EALING BOWEN CLINIC (HM06484) | | | | | | | | | | | | | | | | | | | | | | | | | | | | | | | | | | ● | | | | | | | | | | | | | | | | |
| ESSEX | | | | | | | | | | | | | | | | | | | | | | | | | | | | | | | | | | | | | | | | | | | | | | | | | | |
| A M R THERAPIES (HM00040) | | | | | | | | | | | | | | | | | | | | | | | | | | | | | | | | | | ● | | | | | | | | | | | | | | | | |
| ADAMS, NEIL (HM00358) | | | | | | | | | | | | | | | | | | | | ● | | | | | | | | | | | | | | | | | | | | | | | | | | | | | | |
| ALLSHORN, SUSAN (HM00658) | | | | | | | | | | | | | | | ● | | | | | | | | | | | | | | | | | | | | | | | | | | | | | | | | | | | |
| ARC HEALTHCARE (HM00968) | | | | | | | | | | | | | | | | | ● | | | | | | | | ● | | | | | | | | | | | | | | | | | | | ● | | | ● | | | |
| AROMATHERAPY CLINIC (HM01107) | | | | | | | | | | | | | | | | | | | | | | | | | | | | | | | | | | ● | | | | | | | | | | | | | | | | |
| ASHBY & ASSOCIATES (HM01194) | | | | | | | | | | | | | | | | | | | | | | | | | | | | | | | | | | | | | | | | | | | ● | | | | | | | |
| ASSOCIATION OF OSTEOMYOLOGY (HM01283) | | | | | | | | | | | | | | | | | ● | | | | | | | | ● | | | | | | | | | ● | ● | | | | | | | | | ● | ● | | | | | |
| AVART, GILLIAN (HM01383) | | | | | | | | | | | | ● | | | | ● | | | | | | ● | | | | | | | | | | | | ● | | | | | | | | | | | | | | | | |
| BARBER, TOM (HM01691) | | | | | | | | | | | | | | | | | | | | ● | | | | | | | | | | | | | | | | | | | | | | | | | | | | | | |
| BARKING PHYSICAL THERAPY CTRE (HM01715) | | | | | | | | | | | | | | | | | | | | | | | | | | | | | | | | | | ● | | | | | | | | | | | | | | | | |
| BAXTER, LISA (HM01929) | | | | | | | | | | | | | | | | | | | | | | ● | | | | | | | | | | | | ● | | | | | | | | | | | | | | | | |
| BEACONTREE HYPNOTHERAPY (HM01955) | | | | | | | | | | | | | | | | | | | | ● | | | | | | | | | | | | | | | | | | | | | | | | | | | | | | |
| BENEDICTA (HM02125) | | | | | | | | | | | | | | | | ● | | | | | | ● | | | | | | | | | | | | ● | | | ● | | | | | | | | | | | | | |
| BENRENE HEALTH INTERNATIONAL (HM02165) | | | | | | | | | | | | | | | ● | | | | | | | | | | | | | | | | | | | | | | | | | | | | | | | | | | | |
| BERNSTEIN, S (HM02203) | | | | | | | | | | | | | | | | | | | | ● | | | | | | | | | | | | | | | | | | | | | | | | | | | | | | |
| BE-WELL CLINIC (HM02251) | | | | | | | | | | | | | | | | | ● | | | | | | | ● | | | | | | | | | | | | | | | | | | | | | | | | | | |

# F - O Therapies at Practices/Businesses

| Business by County with Reference no. | Family Planning (Natural) | Family Therapy | Feldenkrais Methodology | Feng Shui | Floral Essence Therapy | Flotation Therapy | Gait Analysis | Gem Essence Therapy | Gestalt Therapy | Group Therapy | Hay Diet | Healer | Healing Therapy | Hellerwork | Herbal Medicine | Holistic Healing | Homeopathy | Hopi Ear Candles | Humanistic Psychology | Hypnosis | Hypnotherapy | Indian Head Massage | Inhalation Therapy | Iridology | Kinesiology |
|---|---|---|---|---|---|---|---|---|---|---|---|---|---|---|---|---|---|---|---|---|---|---|---|---|---|
| BLUE PERSON (HM02527) |||||||||||||||||||||||||||
| BODY BALANCE HEALTH SOLUTIONS (HM02571) |||||||||||||||||●|||||||||
| BRENTWOOD CHIROPODY SURGERY (HM02963) |||||||||||||||||||||||||||
| BRENTWOOD HYPNO/PSYCHOTHERAPY (HM02965) ||||||||||||||||||||●||||||
| BRITISH INSTITUTE-HYPNOTHERAPY (HM03085) ||||||||||||||||||||●|●|||||
| BRYSON & ASSOCIATES (HM03292) ||||||||||||||||||||●||||||
| CAIN, SHEILA (HM03538) |||||||||||||||||●||||||●||||
| CARLISLE, L (HM03696) |||||||||||||||||●|||||||||
| CARNELIAN NTRL TREATMENT CTRE (HM03714) ||||||||||||||||||||||●||||
| CATON, PETER (HM03859) ||●|||||||||||||●|||||●||||||
| CHAKRA ROSE (HM03942) |||||||||||●|●|||||||||●|●|●|||||
| CHASE HYPNOTHERAPY (HM04057) ||||||||||||||||||||●||||||
| CHRIS MOSLIN HYPNOTHERAPIST (HM04433) |||||||||||||||||●||||●|●|||||
| CLARKE, M R (HM04593) |||||||||||||||||||||||||||
| COKER, EILEEN (HM04800) ||||||||||||||||||||||●||||
| COOK, JOE (HM05048) ||||||||||||||||||||●|●|||||
| COOPER, FELICITY (HM05104) |||||||●|||||||||||||||||||
| DAVIS, MELANIE (HM05856) ||||||||||||||||||||●||||||
| DAVIS, S (HM05861) ||||||||||||||||||||●||||||
| DUNCOMBE, MARTIN (HM06399) |||||||||||||||||●|||||||||
| E A O C (HM06465) |||||||||||||||||||||||||||
| ELMER CHIROPODY & PODIATRY SVS (HM06781) |||||||||||||||||||||||||||
| ESSEX FENG SHUI (HM06935) ||||●|||||||||||||||||||||||
| ESSEX PHYSIO & SPORTS INJ CTRE (HM06938) ||||||||||||||||||||||●||||
| FAIRCROSS COMP MEDICAL CLINIC (HM07054) |||||||||||||||||●|||||||||
| FARROW, VICKI (HM07135) |||||||||||||●|||||||||●||||
| FELDMAN, L H (HM07194) |||||||||||||||||●|||||||||
| FERRIS, JANET (HM07245) ||||||||||||||||||||●||||||
| FLEUROMA (HM07418) ||||||||||||||||●||||||●||||
| FOULKES, GEOFFREY LLOYD (HM07609) |||||||||||●||||●|●|●||||||||●|
| FULTON, A J (HM07795) |||||||||||||||||||||||||||
| FULTON, A J (HM07796) |||||||||||||||||||||||||||
| GENT, WENDY (HM07973) |||||||||||||||||||||||||||
| GILLETT, PHILIP (HM08089) |||||||||||||||●|||||||||||

| Business by County with Reference no. | Kirlian Photography | Laser Treatment | Life Style Coaching | Light Therapy | Macrobiotics | Magnetic Therapy | Manipulation | Manual Lymph Drainage | Massage (Therapeutic) | McTimoney Chiropractic | Meditation | Metamorphic Therapy | Miasm Therapy | Micro Manipulation | Moxibustion | Mud Therapy | Music Therapy | Nail Surgery | Naturopathy | Neuro-Linguistic Program | Neurotherapy | Nutritional Therapy | Orgone Therapy | Oriental Diagnosis | Orthomolecular Medicine |
|---|---|---|---|---|---|---|---|---|---|---|---|---|---|---|---|---|---|---|---|---|---|---|---|---|---|
| BLUE PERSON (HM02527) |||||||||||●|||||||||||||||
| BODY BALANCE HEALTH SOLUTIONS (HM02571) |||||||||||||||||||||||||||
| BRENTWOOD CHIROPODY SURGERY (HM02963) ||||||||||||||||||●||||||||
| BRENTWOOD HYPNO/PSYCHOTHERAPY (HM02965) |||||||||||||||||||||||||||
| BRITISH INSTITUTE-HYPNOTHERAPY (HM03085) |||||||||||||||||||||||||||
| BRYSON & ASSOCIATES (HM03292) |||||||||||||||||||||||||||
| CAIN, SHEILA (HM03538) |||||||||||||||||||||||||||
| CARLISLE, L (HM03696) |||||||||||||||||||||||||||
| CARNELIAN NTRL TREATMENT CTRE (HM03714) |||||||||||||||||||||||||||
| CATON, PETER (HM03859) |||||||||||●||||||||||●||||
| CHAKRA ROSE (HM03942) |||||||||●|||||||||||||●||||
| CHASE HYPNOTHERAPY (HM04057) |||||||||||||||||||||||||||
| CHRIS MOSLIN HYPNOTHERAPIST (HM04433) |||||||||||||||||||||||||||
| CLARKE, M R (HM04593) |||||||●||●||||||||||||||||||
| COKER, EILEEN (HM04800) |||||||||●||||||||||||||||||
| COOK, JOE (HM05048) |||||||||||||||||||||||||||
| COOPER, FELICITY (HM05104) ||||||||||||||||||●||||||||
| DAVIS, MELANIE (HM05856) |||||||||||||||||||||||||||
| DAVIS, S (HM05861) |||||||||||||||||||||||||||
| DUNCOMBE, MARTIN (HM06399) |||||||||||||||||||||||||||
| E A O C (HM06465) |||||||●||●||||||●|||||||||●||
| ELMER CHIROPODY & PODIATRY SVS (HM06781) ||||||||||||||||||●||||||||
| ESSEX FENG SHUI (HM06935) |||||||||||||||||||||||||||
| ESSEX PHYSIO & SPORTS INJ CTRE (HM06938) |||||||||||||||||||||||||||
| FAIRCROSS COMP MEDICAL CLINIC (HM07054) |||||||||||||||||||||||||||
| FARROW, VICKI (HM07135) |||||||||||||||||||||||||||
| FELDMAN, L H (HM07194) |||||||||||||||||||||||||||
| FERRIS, JANET (HM07245) |||||||||||||||||||||||||||
| FLEUROMA (HM07418) |||||||●||●||||||||||||||||||
| FOULKES, GEOFFREY LLOYD (HM07609) |||||||●||●||●||||●||||●|||●||●||
| FULTON, A J (HM07795) ||||||||||||||||||●||||||||
| FULTON, A J (HM07796) ||||||||||||||||||●||||||||
| GENT, WENDY (HM07973) |||||||||●||||||||||||||||||
| GILLETT, PHILIP (HM08089) |||||||||||||||||||||||||||

# F - O Therapies at Practices/Businesses

| Business by County with Reference no. | Family Planning (Natural) | Family Therapy | Feldenkrais Methodology | Feng Shui | Floral Essence Therapy | Flotation Therapy | Gait Analysis | Gem Essence Therapy | Gestalt Therapy | Group Therapy | Hay Diet | Healer | Healing Therapy | Hellerwork | Herbal Medicine | Holistic Healing | Homeopathy | Hopi Ear Candles | Humanistic Psychology | Hypnosis | Hypnotherapy | Indian Head Massage | Inhalation Therapy | Iridology | Kinesiology | Kirlian Photography | Laser Treatment | Life Style Coaching | Light Therapy | Macrobiotics | Magnetic Therapy | Manipulation | Manual Lymph Drainage | Massage (Therapeutic) | McTimoney Chiropractic | Meditation | Metamorphic Therapy | Miasm Therapy | Micro Manipulation | Moxibustion | Mud Therapy | Music Therapy | Nail Surgery | Naturopathy | Neuro-Linguistic Program | Neurotherapy | Nutritional Therapy | Orgone Therapy | Oriental Diagnosis | Orthomolecular Medicine |
|---|---|---|---|---|---|---|---|---|---|---|---|---|---|---|---|---|---|---|---|---|---|---|---|---|---|---|---|---|---|---|---|---|---|---|---|---|---|---|---|---|---|---|---|---|---|---|---|---|---|---|
| GOSLING, IMOGEN (HM08300) | | | | | | | | | | | | | | | | | ● | | | | | | | | | | | | | | | | | | | | | | | | | | | | | | | | | |
| GRANGE HYPNOTHERAPY (HM08371) | | | | | | | | | | | | | | | | | | | | ● | | | | | | | | | | | | | | | | | | | | | | | | | | | | | | |
| GRAY, P A (HM08417) | | | | | | | | | | | | | | | | | | | | | | | | | | | | | | | | | | | | | | | | | | | ● | | | | | | | |
| GRIFFITHS, JOANNE (HM08570) | | | | | | | | | | | | | | | | | ● | | | | | | | | | | | | | | | | | | | | | | | | | | | | | | | | | |
| HADLEIGH PODIATRY CLINIC (HM08695) | | | | | | | | | | | | | | | | | | | | | | | | | | | | | | | | | | | | | | | | | | | ● | | | | | | | |
| HARMONY HYPNOTHERAPY CTRE (HM09027) | | | | | | | | | | | | | | | | | | | | ● | | | | | | | | | | | | | | | | | | | | | | | | | | | | | | |
| HAWKINS, SUZI (HM09229) | | | | | | | | | | | | | | | | | ● | | | | | | | | | | | | | | | | | | | | | | | | | | | | | | | | | |
| HEAD, BERYL (HM09301) | | | | | | | | | | | | | | | | | | | | ● | | | | | | | | | | | | | | | | | | | | | | | | | | | | | | |
| HEALING & HYPNOTHERAPY CENTRE (HM09324) | | | | | | | | | | | | | | | | | | | | ● | | | | | | | | | | | | | | | | | | | | | | | | | | | | | | |
| HEALING ROOM (HM09349) | | | | | | | | | | | | | ● | | | ● | | | | | | ● | | | | | | | | | | | | ● | | | | | | | | | | | | | | | | |
| HEALTH KINESIOLOGY (HM09391) | | | | | | | | | | | | | | | | | | | | | | | | | ● | | | | | | | | | | | | | | | | | | | | | | | | | |
| HEALTH SHOP & HOMOEOPATHIC (HM09403) | | | | | | | | | | | | | | | | | ● | | | | | | | | | | | | | | | | | | | | | | | | | | | | | | | | | |
| HODGSON, PATRICIA (HM09889) | | | | | | | | | | | | | | | | | | | | ● | | | | | | | | | | | | | | | | | | | | | | | | | | | | | | |
| HOLISTIC HEALTH CLINIC (HM09978) | | | | | | | | | | | | | | | | | | | | | | | | | | | | | | | | | | | | | | | | | | | | | | | ● | | | |
| HOLLANDS, K M (HM10017) | | | | | | | | | | | | | | | | | | | | ● | | | | | | | | | | | | | | | | | | | | | | | | | | | | | | |
| HOWIE, MARION (HM10282) | | | | | | | | | | | | | | | | | ● | | | | | | | | | | | | | | | | | | | | | | | | | | | | | | | | | |
| HUGHES, M A (HM10334) | | | | | | | | | | | | | | | | | | | | ● | | | | | | | | | | | | | | | | | | | | | | | | | | | | | | |
| HYETT, SUE (HM10474) | | | | | | | | | | | | | | | | | ● | | | | | | | | | | | | | | | | | | | | | | | | | | | | | | | | | |
| HYPNOTHERAPY & PSYCHO CONS (HM10508) | | | | | | | | | | | | | | | | | | | | ● | ● | | | | | | | | | | | | | | | | | | | | | | | | | | | | | |
| HYPNOTHERAPY CENTRE (HM10530) | | | | | | | | | | | | | | | | | | | | ● | ● | | | | | | | | | | | | | | | | | | | | | | | | | | | | | |
| HYPNOTHERAPY CENTRE (HM10532) | | | | | | | | | | | | | | | | | | | | ● | ● | | | | | | | | | | | | | | | | | | | | | | | | | | | | | |
| INSTITUTE OF PAST LIFE (HM10676) | | | | | | | | | | | | | | | | | | | | ● | | | | | | | | | | | | | | | | | | | | | | | | | | | | | | |
| ISIS HOUSE THERAPY CENTRE (HM10768) | | | | | | | | | | | | | | | | | | | | | | | | | | | | | | | ● | | | | | | | | | | | | | | | | | | | |
| JACKSON, CYRIL (HM10832) | | | | | | | | | | | | | | | | | | | | ● | ● | | | | | | | | | | | | | | | | | | | | | | | | | | | | | |
| JOYNES, IAN (HM11239) | | | | | | | | | | | | | | | | | | | | | | | | | | | | | | | | | | | | | | | | | | | ● | | | | | | | |
| KENDRICK, MARGARET (HM11482) | | | | | | | | | | | | | | | | | | | | ● | | | | | | | | | | | | | | | | | | | | | | | | | | | | | | |
| KOTEN, SUSAN (HM11792) | | | | | | | | | | | | | | | ● | | | | | | | | | | | | | | | | | | | | | | | | | | | | | | | | | | | |
| KUMAR, NIRDOSH (HM11819) | | | | | | | | | | | | | | | | | | | | ● | | | | | | | | | | | | | | | | | | | | | | | | | | | | | | |
| KYRIAKOS, GEORGE (HM11839) | | | | | | | | | | | | | | | | | | | | ● | | | | | | | | | | | | | | | | | | | | | | | | | | | | | | |
| LAING, RICHARD (HM11865) | | | | | | | | | | | | | | | | | ● | | | | | | | | | | | | | | | | | | | | | | | | | | | | | | | | | |
| LAING, RICHARD (DR) (HM11866) | | | | | | | | | | | | | | | | | ● | | | | | | | | | | | | | | | | | | | | | | | | | | | | | | | | | |
| LAMBOURN COURT INTERNATIONAL (HM11905) | | | | | | | | | | | | | | | | | | | | ● | | | | | | | | | | | | | | | | | | | | | | | | | | | | | | |
| LEDDY, GILLIAN (HM12126) | | | | | | | | | | | | | | | ● | | | | | | | | | | | | | | | | | | | | | | | | | | | | | | | | | | | |
| LEIGH, MARTIN (HM12189) | | | | | | | | | | | | | ● | | | | | | | | | | | | | | | | | | | ● | | ● | | | | | | | | | | | | | | | | |

# F - O Therapies at Practices/Businesses

Business by County with Reference no.

| Business by County with Reference no. | Family Planning (Natural) | Family Therapy | Feldenkrais Methodology | Feng Shui | Floral Essence Therapy | Flotation Therapy | Gait Analysis | Gem Essence Therapy | Gestalt Therapy | Group Therapy | Hay Diet | Healer | Healing Therapy | Hellerwork | Herbal Medicine | Holistic Healing | Homeopathy | Hopi Ear Candles | Humanistic Psychology | Hypnosis | Hypnotherapy | Indian Head Massage | Inhalation Therapy | Iridology | Kinesiology |
|---|---|---|---|---|---|---|---|---|---|---|---|---|---|---|---|---|---|---|---|---|---|---|---|---|---|
| LEMMON, LINDA (HM12205) |  |  |  |  |  |  |  |  |  |  |  |  |  |  |  |  | ● |  |  |  |  |  |  |  |  |
| LEVY, PAUL (HM12269) |  |  |  |  |  |  |  |  |  |  |  |  |  |  |  |  | ● |  |  |  |  |  |  |  |  |
| LINGWOOD CLINIC (HM12435) |  |  |  |  |  |  |  |  |  |  |  |  |  |  |  |  | ● |  |  |  |  |  |  |  | ● |
| LOTERY, FRANCOISE (HM12649) |  |  |  |  |  |  |  |  |  |  |  |  |  |  |  |  |  |  |  | ● |  |  |  |  |  |
| MALDON HOMOEOPATHIC CLINIC (HM12968) |  |  |  |  |  |  |  |  |  |  |  |  |  |  |  |  | ● |  |  |  |  |  |  |  |  |
| MALDON HYPNOTHERAPY CLINIC (HM12969) |  |  |  |  |  |  |  |  |  |  |  |  |  |  |  |  |  |  |  | ● |  |  |  |  |  |
| MARTIN, LEIGH (HM13202) |  |  |  |  |  |  |  |  |  |  |  |  | ● |  |  |  |  |  |  |  |  |  |  |  |  |
| MCMAHON, ROSEMARY (HM13566) |  |  |  |  |  |  |  |  |  |  |  |  |  |  |  |  | ● |  |  |  |  |  |  |  |  |
| MEDELY CLINIC (HM13647) |  |  |  |  |  |  |  |  |  |  |  |  |  |  |  |  |  |  |  |  |  | ● |  |  |  |
| MICKELBOROUGH, ESTELLE (HM13803) |  |  |  |  |  |  |  |  |  |  |  |  |  |  |  |  |  |  |  | ● |  |  |  |  |  |
| MILES, C J (HM13855) |  |  |  |  |  |  |  |  |  |  |  |  |  |  |  |  |  |  |  |  |  |  |  |  |  |
| MOONSTONE HEALING CENTRE (HM14111) |  |  |  |  |  |  |  |  |  |  |  | ● | ● |  |  | ● |  |  |  | ● | ● | ● |  |  |  |
| MORRIS, J K (HM14206) |  |  |  |  |  |  |  |  |  |  |  |  |  |  |  |  |  |  |  | ● |  |  |  |  |  |
| NATURAL REMEDY CENTRE (HM14620) |  |  |  |  |  |  |  |  |  |  |  |  |  |  | ● |  | ● |  |  |  | ● | ● |  |  |  |
| NIEHORSTER, R (HM14932) |  |  |  |  |  |  |  |  |  |  |  |  |  |  |  |  | ● |  |  |  |  |  |  |  |  |
| NIGHTINGALE, JOANNA (HM14940) |  |  |  |  |  |  |  |  |  |  |  |  |  |  |  |  |  |  |  | ● |  |  |  |  |  |
| O'PRESCO, MARGARET (HM15344) |  |  |  |  |  |  |  |  |  |  |  |  |  |  |  |  | ● |  |  |  |  |  |  |  |  |
| PALK, RICHARD (HM15594) |  |  |  |  |  |  |  |  |  |  |  |  |  |  |  |  | ● |  |  |  |  |  |  |  |  |
| PALMER, DAVID J (HM15600) |  |  |  |  |  |  |  |  |  |  |  |  |  |  |  |  |  |  |  |  |  |  |  |  |  |
| PENN, J T (HM15983) |  |  |  |  |  |  |  |  |  |  |  |  |  |  |  |  |  |  |  | ● |  |  |  |  |  |
| PERRY, JEAN (HM16046) |  |  |  |  |  |  |  |  |  |  |  |  |  |  |  |  |  |  |  | ● |  |  |  |  |  |
| PHARMACARE (HM16109) |  |  |  |  |  |  |  |  |  |  |  |  |  |  | ● |  | ● |  |  |  |  |  |  |  |  |
| PHYSIO & SPORTS INJURY CLINIC (HM16186) |  |  |  |  |  |  |  |  |  |  |  |  |  |  |  |  |  |  |  |  |  |  |  |  |  |
| PINEWOOD PHYSIOTHERAPY CLINIC (HM16313) |  |  |  |  |  |  |  |  |  |  |  |  |  |  |  |  |  |  |  |  |  |  |  |  |  |
| PISCES NATURAL THERAPY CENTRE (HM16330) |  |  |  |  |  |  |  |  |  |  |  |  |  |  |  |  |  |  |  | ● | ● |  |  |  |  |
| PRICE, G J (HM16572) |  |  |  |  |  |  |  |  |  |  |  |  |  |  | ● |  |  |  |  |  |  |  |  |  |  |
| PRIORY PRACTICE (HM16634) |  |  |  |  |  |  |  |  |  |  |  |  |  |  |  |  |  |  |  | ● |  |  |  |  |  |
| PRIVATE HEALTH CENTRE CLINIC (HM16643) |  |  |  |  |  |  |  |  |  |  |  |  |  |  | ● |  | ● |  |  |  |  |  |  |  |  |
| QUIT SMOKING CENTRE (HM16821) |  |  |  |  |  |  |  |  |  |  |  |  |  |  |  |  |  |  |  | ● | ● |  |  |  |  |
| RAJA YOGA MEDITATION (HM16898) |  |  |  |  |  |  |  |  |  |  |  |  |  |  |  |  |  |  |  |  |  |  |  |  |  |
| REDDEN, REBECCA (HM17009) |  |  |  |  |  |  |  |  |  |  |  |  |  |  |  |  |  |  |  | ● |  |  |  |  |  |
| REFLEXOLOGY CLINIC (HM17088) |  |  |  |  |  |  |  |  |  |  |  |  |  |  |  |  |  |  |  |  | ● | ● |  |  |  |
| ROBINSON, DAVID (HM17466) |  |  |  |  |  |  |  |  |  |  |  |  |  |  |  |  |  |  |  | ● | ● |  |  |  |  |
| SALMON, MARGARET (HM17858) |  |  |  |  |  |  |  |  |  |  |  |  |  |  |  | ● |  |  |  |  |  |  |  |  |  |

| Business by County with Reference no. | Kirlian Photography | Laser Treatment | Life Style Coaching | Light Therapy | Macrobiotics | Magnetic Therapy | Manipulation | Manual Lymph Drainage | Massage (Therapeutic) | McTimoney Chiropractic | Meditation | Metamorphic Therapy | Miasm Therapy | Micro Manipulation | Moxibustion | Mud Therapy | Music Therapy | Nail Surgery | Naturopathy | Neuro-Linguistic Program | Neurotherapy | Nutritional Therapy | Orgone Therapy | Oriental Diagnosis | Orthomolecular Medicine |
|---|---|---|---|---|---|---|---|---|---|---|---|---|---|---|---|---|---|---|---|---|---|---|---|---|---|
| LEMMON, LINDA (HM12205) |  |  |  |  |  |  |  |  |  |  |  |  |  |  |  |  |  |  |  |  |  |  |  |  |  |
| LEVY, PAUL (HM12269) |  |  |  |  |  |  |  |  |  |  |  |  |  |  |  |  |  | ● |  |  |  |  |  |  |  |
| LINGWOOD CLINIC (HM12435) |  |  |  |  |  |  |  |  |  |  |  |  |  |  |  |  |  |  |  |  |  |  |  |  |  |
| LOTERY, FRANCOISE (HM12649) |  |  |  |  |  |  |  |  |  |  |  |  |  |  |  |  |  |  |  |  |  |  |  |  |  |
| MALDON HOMOEOPATHIC CLINIC (HM12968) |  |  |  |  |  |  |  |  |  |  |  |  |  |  |  |  |  |  |  |  |  |  |  |  |  |
| MALDON HYPNOTHERAPY CLINIC (HM12969) |  |  |  |  |  |  |  |  |  |  |  |  |  |  |  |  |  |  |  |  |  |  |  |  |  |
| MARTIN, LEIGH (HM13202) |  |  |  |  |  |  | ● |  | ● |  |  |  |  |  |  |  |  |  |  |  |  |  |  |  |  |
| MCMAHON, ROSEMARY (HM13566) |  |  |  |  |  |  |  |  |  |  |  |  |  |  |  |  |  |  |  |  |  |  |  |  |  |
| MEDELY CLINIC (HM13647) |  |  |  |  |  |  |  |  | ● |  |  |  |  |  |  |  |  |  |  |  |  |  |  |  |  |
| MICKELBOROUGH, ESTELLE (HM13803) |  |  |  |  |  |  |  |  |  |  |  |  |  |  |  |  |  |  |  |  |  |  |  |  |  |
| MILES, C J (HM13855) |  |  |  |  |  |  |  |  |  |  |  |  |  |  |  |  |  | ● |  |  |  |  |  |  |  |
| MOONSTONE HEALING CENTRE (HM14111) | ● |  |  |  |  |  | ● |  | ● |  | ● |  |  |  |  |  |  |  |  |  |  |  |  |  |  |
| MORRIS, J K (HM14206) |  |  |  |  |  |  |  |  |  |  |  |  |  |  |  |  |  |  |  |  |  |  |  |  |  |
| NATURAL REMEDY CENTRE (HM14620) |  |  |  |  |  |  |  |  | ● |  |  |  |  |  | ● |  |  |  |  |  |  |  |  | ● |  |
| NIEHORSTER, R (HM14932) |  |  |  |  |  |  |  |  |  |  |  |  |  |  |  |  |  |  |  |  |  |  |  |  |  |
| NIGHTINGALE, JOANNA (HM14940) |  |  |  |  |  |  |  |  |  |  |  |  |  |  |  |  |  |  |  |  |  |  |  |  |  |
| O'PRESCO, MARGARET (HM15344) |  |  |  |  |  |  |  |  |  |  |  |  |  |  |  |  |  |  |  |  |  |  |  |  |  |
| PALK, RICHARD (HM15594) |  |  |  |  |  |  |  |  |  |  |  |  |  |  |  |  |  |  |  |  |  |  |  |  |  |
| PALMER, DAVID J (HM15600) |  |  |  |  |  |  |  |  | ● |  |  |  |  |  |  |  |  |  |  |  |  |  |  |  |  |
| PENN, J T (HM15983) |  |  |  |  |  |  |  |  |  |  |  |  |  |  |  |  |  |  |  |  |  |  |  |  |  |
| PERRY, JEAN (HM16046) |  |  |  |  |  |  |  |  |  |  |  |  |  |  |  |  |  |  |  |  |  |  |  |  |  |
| PHARMACARE (HM16109) |  |  |  |  |  |  |  |  | ● |  |  |  |  |  |  |  |  |  |  |  |  |  |  |  |  |
| PHYSIO & SPORTS INJURY CLINIC (HM16186) |  |  |  |  |  |  | ● |  | ● |  |  |  |  | ● |  |  |  |  |  |  |  |  |  |  |  |
| PINEWOOD PHYSIOTHERAPY CLINIC (HM16313) |  |  |  |  |  |  | ● |  | ● |  |  |  |  |  |  |  |  |  |  |  |  |  |  |  |  |
| PISCES NATURAL THERAPY CENTRE (HM16330) |  |  |  |  |  |  |  |  |  |  |  |  |  |  |  |  |  |  | ● |  |  |  |  |  |  |
| PRICE, G J (HM16572) |  |  | ● |  |  |  | ● |  |  |  |  |  |  |  |  |  |  |  |  |  |  |  |  |  |  |
| PRIORY PRACTICE (HM16634) |  |  |  |  |  |  |  |  |  |  |  |  |  |  |  |  |  |  |  |  |  |  |  |  |  |
| PRIVATE HEALTH CENTRE CLINIC (HM16643) |  |  |  |  |  |  |  |  |  |  |  |  |  |  |  |  |  |  |  |  |  |  |  |  |  |
| QUIT SMOKING CENTRE (HM16821) |  |  |  |  |  |  |  |  |  |  |  |  |  |  |  |  |  |  |  |  |  |  |  |  |  |
| RAJA YOGA MEDITATION (HM16898) |  |  |  |  |  |  |  |  |  |  | ● |  |  |  |  |  |  |  |  |  |  |  |  |  |  |
| REDDEN, REBECCA (HM17009) |  |  |  |  |  |  |  |  |  |  |  |  |  |  |  |  |  |  |  |  |  |  |  |  |  |
| REFLEXOLOGY CLINIC (HM17088) |  |  |  |  |  |  |  |  | ● |  |  |  |  |  |  |  |  |  |  |  |  | ● |  |  |  |
| ROBINSON, DAVID (HM17466) |  |  |  |  |  |  |  |  |  |  |  |  |  |  |  |  |  |  |  |  |  |  |  |  |  |
| SALMON, MARGARET (HM17858) |  |  |  |  |  |  |  |  | ● |  |  |  |  |  |  |  |  |  |  |  |  |  |  |  |  |

# F - O Therapies at Practices/Businesses

| Business by County with Reference no. | Family Planning (Natural) | Family Therapy | Feldenkrais Methodology | Feng Shui | Floral Essence Therapy | Flotation Therapy | Gait Analysis | Gem Essence Therapy | Gestalt Therapy | Group Therapy | Hay Diet | Healer | Healing Therapy | Hellerwork | Herbal Medicine | Holistic Healing | Homeopathy | Hopi Ear Candles | Humanistic Psychology | Hypnosis | Hypnotherapy | Indian Head Massage | Inhalation Therapy | Iridology | Kinesiology | Kirlian Photography | Laser Treatment | Life Style Coaching | Light Therapy | Macrobiotics | Magnetic Therapy | Manipulation | Manual Lymph Drainage | Massage (Therapeutic) | McTimoney Chiropractic | Meditation | Metamorphic Therapy | Miasm Therapy | Micro Manipulation | Moxibustion | Mud Therapy | Music Therapy | Nail Surgery | Naturopathy | Neuro-Linguistic Program | Neurotherapy | Nutritional Therapy | Orgone Therapy | Oriental Diagnosis | Orthomolecular Medicine |
|---|---|---|---|---|---|---|---|---|---|---|---|---|---|---|---|---|---|---|---|---|---|---|---|---|---|---|---|---|---|---|---|---|---|---|---|---|---|---|---|---|---|---|---|---|---|---|---|---|---|---|
| SANDERS, G (HM17909) | | | | | | | | | | | | | | | | | | | | | | | | | | | | | | | | | | | | | | | | | | | ● | | | | | | | |
| SAVAGE, ROGER (HM17972) | | | | | | | | | | | | | | | | | ● | | | | | | | | | | | | | | | | | | | | | | | | | | | | | | | | | |
| SELF AWARENESS HEALING (HM18204) | | | | | | | | | | | | ● | ● | | | | | | | | | | | | | | | | | | | | | | | ● | | | | | | | | | | | | | | |
| SELVES, KATIE (HM18222) | | | | | | | | | | | | | | | ● | | | | | | | | | | | | | | | | | | | | | | | | | | | | | | | | | | | |
| SEYMOUR, LOUISE (HM18259) | | | | | | | | | | | | | | | | | | | | | | | | | | | | | | | | | | | | | | | | | | | ● | | | | | | | |
| SHELDON, PEGGY (HM18380) | | | | | | | | | | | | | | | | | | | | | | | | | | | | | | | | | | ● | | | | | | | | | | | | | | | | |
| SMITH, LESLEY (HM18766) | | | | | | | | | | | | | | | | | | | | ● | | | | | | | | | | | | | | | | | | | | | | | | | | | | | | |
| SOOD, P (DR) (HM18889) | | | | | | | | | | | | | | | | | ● | | | | | | | | | | | | | | | | | | | | | | | | | | | | | | | | | |
| SOUTH, JO (HM18918) | | | | | | | | | | | | | | | | | ● | | | | | | | | | | | | | | | | | | | | | | | | | | | | | | | | | |
| SPENCE, M (HM18984) | | | | | | | | | | | | | | | | | | | | ● | | | | | | | | | | | | | | | | | | | | | | | | | | | | | | |
| STABLEFORD, JOYCE (HM19101) | | | | | | | | | | | | | | | | | | | | ● | | | | | | | | | | | | | | | | ● | | | | | | | | | | | | | | |
| SWALLOW, FRED (HM19570) | | | | | | | | | | | | | | | | | | | | ● | | | | | | | | | | | | | | | | | | | | | | | | | | | | | | |
| THACKER, VRINDA (HM19857) | | | | | | | | | | | | | | | | | ● | | | | | | | | | | | | | | | | | | | | | | | | | | | | | | | | | |
| THERAPEUTIC MASSAGE (HM19882) | | | | | | | | | | | | | | | | | | | | | | | | | | | | | | | | | | ● | | | | | | | | | | | | | | | | |
| WADDINGTON, R M (HM20726) | | | | | | | | | | | | | | | | | | | | | | | | | | | | | | | | | | | | | | | | | | | ● | | | | | | | |
| WAKNELL, PETER (HM20749) | | | | | | | | | | | | | | | | | | | | ● | | | | | | | | | | | | | | | | | | | | | | | | | | | | | | |
| WATTS, TERENCE (HM21036) | | | | | | | | | | | | | | | | | | | | ● | | | | | | | | | | | | | | | | | | | | | | | | | | | | | | |
| WELLS HYPNOTHERAPY CLINIC (HM21167) | | | | | | | | | | | | | | | | | | | | | ● | | | | | | | | | | | | | | | | | | | | | | | | | | | | | |
| WENTWORTH HEALTH CLINIC (HM21201) | | | | | | | | | | | | | | | | | | | | | | | | | | | | | | | | | | ● | | | | | | | | | | | | | | | | |
| WETHERALL, STUART (HM21289) | | | | | | | | | | | | | | | | | | | | ● | ● | | | | | | | | | | | | | | | | | | | | | | | | | | | | | |
| WHEATMAN, G H P (HM21311) | | | | | | | | | | | | | | | | | | | | ● | | | | | | | | | | | | | | | | | | | | | | | | | | | | | | |
| WHEELER, M A (HM21316) | | | | | | | | | | | | | | | | | | | | | | | | | | | | | | | | | | | | | | | | | | | ● | | | | | | | |
| WHEELER, M A (HM21317) | | | | | | | | | | | | | | | | | | | | | | | | | | | | | | | | | | | | | | | | | | | ● | | | | | | | |
| WHITE WATER HEALING CENTRE (HM21345) | | | | | | | | | | | | ● | ● | | | ● | | | | | | | | | | | | | | | | | | | | ● | | | | | | | | | | | | | | |
| WILBY, MARY ANN (HM21484) | | | | | | | | | | | | | | | | | | | | ● | | | | | | | | | | | | | | | | | | | | | | | | | | | | | | |
| WITCHELL, YVONNE (HM21742) | | | | | | | | | | | | | | | | | ● | | | | | | | | | | | | | | | | | | | | | | | | | | | | | | | | | |
| WOODSIDE NATURAL HEALTH (HM21859) | | | | | | | | | | | | ● | ● | | | | | | | | | | | | ● | | | | | | | ● | | ● | | | | | | | | | | | | | ● | | ● | |
| **GLOUCESTERSHIRE** | | | | | | | | | | | | | | | | | | | | | | | | | | | | | | | | | | | | | | | | | | | | | | | | | | |
| ACUPUNCTURE CLINIC (HM00262) | | | | | | | | | | | | | | | | | | | | | | | | | | | | | | | | | | | | | | | | ● | | | | | | | | | | |
| ADAMS, PETER (HM00360) | | | | | | | | | | | | | | | | ● | ● | | | | | | | | | | | | | | | | | | | | | | | | | | | | | | | | | |
| AGASCAR, ROBIN (HM00416) | | | | | | | | | | | | | | | | | | | | ● | ● | | | | | | | | | | | | | | | | | | | | | | | | | | | | | |
| ARTICHOKE NATURAL HEALTH (HM01168) | | | | | | | | | | | | | | | ● | | | | | | ● | | | | | | | | | | | | | ● | | | | | | | | | | | | | | | | |
| BHMA (HM02269) | | | | | | | | | | | | | | | ● | | | | | | | | | | | | | | | | | | | | | | | | | | | | | | | | | | | |
| BUNTON, LYNN (HM03354) | | | | | | | | | | | | | | | | | | | | | | | | | | | | | | | | | | ● | | | | | | | | | | | | | | | | |

# F - O Therapies at Practices/Businesses

| Business by County with Reference no. | Family Planning (Natural) | Family Therapy | Feldenkrais Methodology | Feng Shui | Floral Essence Therapy | Flotation Therapy | Gait Analysis | Gem Essence Therapy | Gestalt Therapy | Group Therapy | Hay Diet | Healer | Healing Therapy | Hellerwork | Herbal Medicine | Holistic Healing | Homeopathy | Hopi Ear Candles | Humanistic Psychology | Hypnosis | Hypnotherapy | Indian Head Massage | Inhalation Therapy | Iridology | Kinesiology | Kirlian Photography | Laser Treatment | Life Style Coaching | Light Therapy | Macrobiotics | Magnetic Therapy | Manipulation | Manual Lymph Drainage | Massage (Therapeutic) | McTimoney Chiropractic | Meditation | Metamorphic Therapy | Miasm Therapy | Micro Manipulation | Moxibustion | Mud Therapy | Music Therapy | Nail Surgery | Naturopathy | Neuro-Linguistic Program | Neurotherapy | Nutritional Therapy | Orgone Therapy | Oriental Diagnosis | Orthomolecular Medicine |
|---|---|---|---|---|---|---|---|---|---|---|---|---|---|---|---|---|---|---|---|---|---|---|---|---|---|---|---|---|---|---|---|---|---|---|---|---|---|---|---|---|---|---|---|---|---|---|---|---|---|---|
| BURKE, JAYNE (HM03388) | | | | | | | | | | | | | | | | ● | | | | | | | | | | | | | | | | | | | | | ● | | | | | | | | | | | | | |
| CHELTENHAM CLINIC & TRAD ACU (HM04093) | | | | | | | | | | | | | | | ● | | | | | | | | | | | | | | | | | | | | | | ● | | | | | | | | | | | | | |
| CHELTENHAM HOLISTIC HLTH CTRE (HM04094) | | | | | | | | | | | | | | | | | ● | | | | ● | ● | | | ● | | | | | | | | | ● | | ● | | | | | | | | | | | ● | | | |
| CHELTENHAM HYPNOTHERAPY (HM04096) | | | | | | | | | | | | | | | | | | | | ● | ● | | | | | | | | | | | | | | | | | | | | | | | | | | | | | |
| COMPLEMENTARY TOUCH (HM04950) | | | | | | | | | | | | | | | | ● | ● | | | | | | | | | | | | | | | | | | ● | | | | | | | | | | | | | | | |
| COOPER, ANGELA (HM05089) | | | | | | | | | | | | | | | | | | | | | ● | | | | | | | | | | | | | | | | | | | | | | | | | | | | | |
| COTSWOLD PHYSIOTHERAPY CENTRE (HM05215) | | | | | | | | | | | | | | | | | | | | | | | | | | | | | | | | | | ● | | | | | | | | | | | | | | | | |
| CULPEPER (HM05585) | | | | | | | | | | | | | | | ● | | | | | | | | | | | | | | | | | | | | | | | | | | | | | | | | | | | |
| DATE, SUSAN (HM05756) | | | | | | | | | | | | | | | | ● | | ● | | | | | | | | | | ● | | | | | | | | | | | | | | | | | | | ● | | | |
| ESSENTIAL BODYWORKS COMPANY (HM06899) | | | | | | | | | | | | | | | | | | | | | | ● | | | | | | | | | | | | ● | | | | | | | | | | | | | | | | |
| FILIPOVIC, S (HM07290) | | | | | | | | | | | | | | | | | | | | ● | | | | | | | | | | | | | | | | | | | | | | | | | | | | | | |
| GOODSON, KAREN (HM08265) | | | | | | | | | | | | | | | | | | | | ● | | | | | | | | | | | | | | | | | | | | | | | | | | | | | | |
| GRANT, K (HM08382) | | | | | | | | | | | | | | | | | | | | ● | | | | | | | | | | | | | | | | | | | | | | | | | | | | | | |
| GREENWELL, DAVID (HM08498) | | | | | | | | | | | | | | | | | | | | | ● | | | | | | | | | | | | | | | | | | | | | | | | | | | | | |
| HARMONY MASSAGE CENTRE (HM09031) | | | | | | | | | | | | | | | | | | | | | | | | | | | | | | | | | | ● | | | | | | | | | | | | | | | | |
| KNAPP, SALLY (HM11741) | | | | | | | | | | | | | | | | | | | | ● | | | | | | | | | | | | | | | | | | | | | | | | | | | | | | |
| LAWLER, R & G (HM12041) | | | | | ● | | | | | | | | | | | | | | | | | | | | | | | | | | | | | ● | | | | | | | | | | | | | | | | |
| LECKHAMPTON CHIROPRACTIC CLNC (HM12119) | | | | | | | | | | | | | | | | | | | | | | | | | | | | | | | | ● | | ● | | | | | | | | | | | | | | | | |
| MARNEY, KATE (HM13131) | | | | | | | | | | | | | | | | | ● | | | | | | | | | | | | | | | | | | | | | | | | | | | | | | | | | |
| NATURAL THERAPIES CLINIC (HM14633) | | | | | | | | | | | | | | | | | ● | | | | | | | | | | | | | | | | | | | | | | | | | | | ● | | | ● | | | |
| NATURAL THERAPY CENTRE (HM14649) | | | | | | | | | | | | | | | | | ● | | | | | ● | | | | | | | | | | | | ● | | | | | | | | | | | | | ● | | | |
| OLD CONVENT (HM15255) | | | | | | | | | | | | ● | ● | | | | | | | | | | | | | | | | | | | ● | | | | | | | | | | | | | | | | | | |
| OSTEOPATH (HM15445) | | | | | | | | | | | | | | | | | | | | | | | | | | | | | | | | ● | | ● | | | | | | | | | | ● | | | | | | |
| ROBBINS, JAMES H (HM17394) | | | | | | | | | | | | | | | | | | | | ● | | | | | | | | | | | | | | | | | | | | | | | | | | | | | | |
| SILMON, MARY (HM18538) | | | | | | | | | | | | | | | | | | | | ● | | | | | | | | | | | | | | | | | | | | | | | | | | | | | | |
| SLATER, D C (HM18672) | | | | | | | | | | | | | | | | | | | | ● | ● | | | | | | | | | | | | | | | | | | | | | | | | | | | | | |
| SMYTH, DAVID (HM18830) | | | | | | | | | | | ● | ● | | | ● | | | | | | | | | | ● | | | | | | | | | | | | | | | | | | | | | | | | ● | |
| SPENCER, VALERIE (HM19005) | | | | | | | | | | | | | | | | | | | | ● | | | | | | | | | | | | | | | | | | | | | | | | | | | | | | |
| STOUT, HEATHER (HM19359) | | | | | | | | | | | | | | | | | ● | | | | | | | | | | | | | | | | | | | | | | | | | | | | | | | | | |
| STRESS COMPANY (HM19390) | | | | | | | | | | | | | | | | | | | | ● | | | | | | | | | | | ● | | | | | | | | | | | | | | | | | | | |
| STROUD NATURAL HEALTH CLINIC (HM19422) | | | | | | | | | | | | | | | | | ● | | | | | ● | | | | | | | | | | | | ● | | | | | | | | | | | | | | | | |
| TRANSCENDENTAL MEDITATION (HM20275) | | | | | | | | | | | | | | | | | | | | | | | | | | | | | | | | | | | | ● | | | | | | | | | | | | | | |
| TREE OF LIFE CENTRE (HM20307) | | | | | | | | | | | | | | | | ● | ● | | | | | ● | | | | | | | | | | | | | | | ● | | | | | | | | | | | | | |
| VILLAGE CLINIC (HM20665) | | | | | | | | | | | | | | | | | | | | | | | | | | | | | | | | ● | | ● | | | | | | | | | | | | | | | | |

# F - O Therapies at Practices/Businesses

| Business by County with Reference no. | Family Planning (Natural) | Family Therapy | Feldenkrais Methodology | Feng Shui | Floral Essence Therapy | Flotation Therapy | Gait Analysis | Gem Essence Therapy | Gestalt Therapy | Group Therapy | Hay Diet | Healer | Healing Therapy | Hellerwork | Herbal Medicine | Holistic Healing | Homeopathy | Hopi Ear Candles | Humanistic Psychology | Hypnosis | Hypnotherapy | Indian Head Massage | Inhalation Therapy | Iridology | Kinesiology |
|---|---|---|---|---|---|---|---|---|---|---|---|---|---|---|---|---|---|---|---|---|---|---|---|---|---|
| VINEY HALL PHYSIOTHERAPY (HM20683) | | | | | | | | | | | | | | | | | | | | | | | | | |
| WELLBEING CENTRE-HOMOEOPATHY (HM21150) | | | | | | | | | | | | | | | | | ● | | | | | | | | |
| WELLS, GEORGINA (HM21172) | | | | | | | | | | | | | ● | | | | | | | | | | | | |
| WEST OF ENGLAND ALOE VERA CTRE (HM21231) | | | | | | | | | | | | | | | | | | | | | | | | | |
| WIEDERHOLD, KAREN (HM21460) | | | | | | | | | | | | | | | | | | | | | | ● | | | |
| YOGA DRUVAM JIVAN YOGA SOCIETY (HM22024) | | | | | | | | | | | | | | | | | | | | | | ● | | | |
| HAMPSHIRE | | | | | | | | | | | | | | | | | | | | | | | | | |
| ACUPUNCTURE & PHYSIO CLINIC (HM00245) | | | | | | | | | | | | | | | | | | | | | | | | | |
| ALL - HEAL ACU & HERB CENTRE (HM00581) | | | | | | | | | | | | | | | ● | | | | | | | | | | |
| ALLERGY THERAPY (HM00637) | | | | | | | | | | | | | ● | | | | ● | | | | | ● | | | |
| ARMSTRONG, ANNA (HM01017) | | | | | | | | | | | | | | | ● | | | | | | | | | | |
| ARMSTRONG, ANNA (HM01018) | | | | | | | | | | | | | | | ● | | | | | | | | | | |
| ARTEMIS (HM01156) | | | | | | | | | | | | | | | | | | | | ● | ● | | | | |
| AVENUE CLINIC (HM01389) | | | | | | | | | | | | | | | | | | | | | | | | | |
| BALDACCHINO, PAUL (HM01611) | | | | | | | | | | | | | | | | | | | | ● | | | | | |
| BARTLETT, S G A (HM01827) | | | | | | | | | | | | | | | | | | | | ● | | | | | |
| BAXTER, S M (HM01932) | | | | | | | | | | | | | | | | | | | | ● | | | | | |
| BENNISON, DIANE (HM02163) | | | | | | | | | | | | | | | | | | | | ● | | | | | |
| BETTERIDGE, SHIRLEY (HM02237) | | | | | | | | | | | | | | | | | | | | ● | | | | | |
| BIRRELL, M (HM02397) | | | | | | | | | | | | | | | | | | | | ● | | | | | |
| BOTHWICK, JOHN (HM02734) | | | | | | | | | | | | | | | | | | | | | | | | | |
| BOURNE CONSULTANCY (HM02752) | | | | | | | | | | | | | | | | | | | | ● | | | | | |
| BRADFORD HOUSE CHIRO CLINIC (HM02849) | | | | | | | | | | | | | | | | | | | | | | | | | |
| BRISCOE, WARREN (HM03058) | | | | | | | | | | | | | | | | | | | | ● | | | | | |
| CARMICHAEL, GORDON (HM03709) | | | | | | | | | | | | | | | | | | | | | | | | | |
| CENTRE FOR COMP MEDICINE (HM03901) | | | | | | | | | | | | | | | | | ● | | | | | | | | |
| CHAMPS (HM03965) | | | | | | | | | | | | | | | | | | | | ● | | | | | |
| CHILTERN COTTAGE CLINIC (HM04175) | | | | | | | | | | | | | | | | | ● | | | | | | | | |
| CLARK, MADELEINE (HM04571) | | | | | | | | | | | | | | | | | | | | ● | | | | | |
| CLEMENTS, CHRISTINE (HM04642) | | | | | | | | | | | | | | | | | | | | | | | | | |
| COATES, MARY (HM04756) | | | | | | | | | | | | | | | | | | | | ● | | | | | |
| COLVILE, RICHARD (HM04895) | | | | | | | | | | | | | | | ● | | | | | | | | | | |
| COMPLETE ANGEL HEALING CENTRE (HM04955) | | | | | | | | | | | | | | | | | | | | | | ● | | | |
| COOK, RICHARD (HM05054) | | | | | | | | | | | | | | | | | ● | | | | | | | | |

| Business by County with Reference no. | Kirlian Photography | Laser Treatment | Life Style Coaching | Light Therapy | Macrobiotics | Magnetic Therapy | Manipulation | Manual Lymph Drainage | Massage (Therapeutic) | McTimoney Chiropractic | Meditation | Metamorphic Therapy | Miasm Therapy | Micro Manipulation | Moxibustion | Mud Therapy | Music Therapy | Nail Surgery | Naturopathy | Neuro-Linguistic Program | Neurotherapy | Nutritional Therapy | Orgone Therapy | Oriental Diagnosis | Orthomolecular Medicine |
|---|---|---|---|---|---|---|---|---|---|---|---|---|---|---|---|---|---|---|---|---|---|---|---|---|---|
| VINEY HALL PHYSIOTHERAPY (HM20683) | | | | | | | ● | | ● | | | | | | | | | | | | | | | | |
| WELLBEING CENTRE-HOMOEOPATHY (HM21150) | | | | | | | | | | | | | | | | | | | | | | | | | |
| WELLS, GEORGINA (HM21172) | | | | | | | | | ● | | | | | | | | | | | | | | | | |
| WEST OF ENGLAND ALOE VERA CTRE (HM21231) | | | | | | | | | | | | | | | | | | | | | | ● | | | |
| WIEDERHOLD, KAREN (HM21460) | | | | | | | | | | | | | | | | | | | | | | | | | |
| YOGA DRUVAM JIVAN YOGA SOCIETY (HM22024) | | | | | | | | | | | ● | | | | | | | | | | | | | | |
| HAMPSHIRE | | | | | | | | | | | | | | | | | | | | | | | | | |
| ACUPUNCTURE & PHYSIO CLINIC (HM00245) | | | | | | | | | | | | | | | ● | | | | | | | | | | |
| ALL - HEAL ACU & HERB CENTRE (HM00581) | | | | | | | | | | | | | | | ● | | | | | | | | | | |
| ALLERGY THERAPY (HM00637) | | | | | | | | | | | | | | | | | | | | | | | | | |
| ARMSTRONG, ANNA (HM01017) | | | | | | | | | | | | | | | | | | | | | | | | | |
| ARMSTRONG, ANNA (HM01018) | | | | | | | | | | | | | | | | | | | | | | | | | |
| ARTEMIS (HM01156) | | | | | | | | | | | | | | | | | | | | | | | | | |
| AVENUE CLINIC (HM01389) | | | | | | | ● | | | | | | | | | | | | | | | | | | |
| BALDACCHINO, PAUL (HM01611) | | | | | | | | | | | | | | | | | | | | | | | | | |
| BARTLETT, S G A (HM01827) | | | | | | | | | | | | | | | | | | | | | | | | | |
| BAXTER, S M (HM01932) | | | | | | | | | | | | | | | | | | | | | | | | | |
| BENNISON, DIANE (HM02163) | | | | | | | | | | | | | | | | | | | | | | | | | |
| BETTERIDGE, SHIRLEY (HM02237) | | | | | | | | | | | | | | | | | | | | | | | | | |
| BIRRELL, M (HM02397) | | | | | | | | | | | | | | | | | | | | | | | | | |
| BOTHWICK, JOHN (HM02734) | | | | | | | | | ● | | | | | | | | | | | | | | | | |
| BOURNE CONSULTANCY (HM02752) | | | | | | | | | | | | | | | | | | | | | | | | | |
| BRADFORD HOUSE CHIRO CLINIC (HM02849) | | | | | | | ● | | ● | | | | | | | | | | | | | | | | |
| BRISCOE, WARREN (HM03058) | | | | | | | | | | | | | | | | | | | | | | | | | |
| CARMICHAEL, GORDON (HM03709) | | | | | | | | | ● | | | | | | | | | | | | | | | | |
| CENTRE FOR COMP MEDICINE (HM03901) | | | | | | | | | | | | | | | | | | | | | | | | | |
| CHAMPS (HM03965) | | | | | | | | | | | | | | | | | | | | | | | | | |
| CHILTERN COTTAGE CLINIC (HM04175) | | | | | | | | | | | | | | | | | | | | | | | | | |
| CLARK, MADELEINE (HM04571) | | | | | | | | | | | | | | | | | | | | | | | | | |
| CLEMENTS, CHRISTINE (HM04642) | | | | | | | ● | | ● | | | | | | | | | | | | | | | | |
| COATES, MARY (HM04756) | | | | | | | | | | | | | | | | | | | | | | | | | |
| COLVILE, RICHARD (HM04895) | | | | | | | | | | | | | | | | | | | | | | ● | | | |
| COMPLETE ANGEL HEALING CENTRE (HM04955) | | | | | | | | | | | | | | | | | | | | | | | | | |
| COOK, RICHARD (HM05054) | | | | | | | | | | | | | | | | | | | | | | | | | |

# F - O Therapies at Practices/Businesses

| Business by County with Reference no. | Family Planning (Natural) | Family Therapy | Feldenkrais Methodology | Feng Shui | Floral Essence Therapy | Flotation Therapy | Gait Analysis | Gem Essence Therapy | Gestalt Therapy | Group Therapy | Hay Diet | Healer | Healing Therapy | Hellerwork | Herbal Medicine | Holistic Healing | Homeopathy | Hopi Ear Candles | Humanistic Psychology | Hypnosis | Hypnotherapy | Indian Head Massage | Inhalation Therapy | Iridology | Kinesiology | Kirlian Photography | Laser Treatment | Life Style Coaching | Light Therapy | Macrobiotics | Magnetic Therapy | Manipulation | Manual Lymph Drainage | Massage (Therapeutic) | McTimoney Chiropractic | Meditation | Metamorphic Therapy | Miasm Therapy | Micro Manipulation | Moxibustion | Mud Therapy | Music Therapy | Nail Surgery | Naturopathy | Neurotherapy | Neuro-Linguistic Program | Nutritional Therapy | Orgone Therapy | Oriental Diagnosis | Orthomolecular Medicine |
|---|---|---|---|---|---|---|---|---|---|---|---|---|---|---|---|---|---|---|---|---|---|---|---|---|---|---|---|---|---|---|---|---|---|---|---|---|---|---|---|---|---|---|---|---|---|---|---|---|---|---|
| CRANIOSACRAL THERAPY (HM05377) | | | | | ● | | | | | | | | | | | | | | | | | | | | | | | | | | | | | ● | | | | | | | | | | | | | | | | |
| CTRE FOR THE STUDY OF COMP MED (HM05543) | | | | | | | | | | | | | | | ● | | ● | | | ● | | | | | | | | | | ● | | | | | | ● | | | | | | | | | | | ● | | | |
| CTRE-COMPLEMENTARY THERAPY (HM05547) | | | | | | | | | | | | | | | | | ● | | | ● | | ● | | | | | | | | | | | | ● | ● | | | | | | | | | ● | | | | | | |
| DOLPHIN STUDIOS (HM06165) | | | | | | | | | | | | | | | | | | | | ● | ● | | | | | | | | | | | | | | | ● | | | | | | | | | | | | | ● | |
| DUFFY, MICHELLE (HM06366) | | | | | | | | | | | | | | | | | | | | ● | | | | | | | | | | | | | | | | | | | | | | | | | | | | | | |
| EASTLEIGH OSTEOPATHIC CLINIC (HM06544) | | | | | | | | | | | | | | | | | | | | | | | | | | | | | | | | | | | | | | | | ● | | | | ● | | | | | | |
| ENERGY EXCHANGE HOLISTIC CTRE (HM06816) | | | | | | | | | | | | ● | | | | ● | | | | | ● | ● | | | | | | | | | | | | ● | | ● | | | | | | | | | | | | | | |
| FAIRDOWN CENTRE (HM07055) | | | | | | | | | | | | | | | | | | | | ● | | | | | | | | | | | | | | | | | | | | | | | | | | | | | | |
| FAIRFIELDS LANE WEST (HM07059) | | ● | | | | | | | | | | | ● | ● | ● | | ● | | | | ● | ● | | | | ● | | | | | | | | ● | | | | | | | | | | | | | ● | | | |
| FAMILY CHIRO & ALT MED CTRE (HM07081) | | | | | | | | | | | | ● | | | ● | | ● | | | ● | ● | ● | | | ● | | | | | | | ● | | ● | | ● | | | | | | | | | | | ● | | | |
| FARRIER, M (HM07133) | | | | | | | | | | | | | | | | | | | | ● | | | | | | | | | | | | | | | | | | | | | | | | | | | | | | |
| FLEET & DISTRICT HYP CENTRE (HM07399) | | | | | | | | | | | | | | | | | | | | ● | | | | | | | | | | | | | | | | | | | | | | | | | | | | | | |
| FOGG, HELEN (HM07452) | | | | | | | | | | | | | | | | ● | | | | ● | | | | | ● | | | | | | | | | | | | | | | | | | | | | | | | | |
| FORD-HAMMOND, BARBARA (HM07538) | | | | | | | | | | | | | | | | | | | | ● | | | | | | | | | | | | | | | | | | | | | | | | | | | | | | |
| FOSSEY, LYNETTE (HM07585) | | | | | | | | | | | | | | | | | | | | | | | | | | | | | | | | | | ● | | | | | | | | | | | | | | | | |
| FOSTER, JAMES M ASSOCIATES (HM07593) | | | | | | | ● | | | | | | | | | | | | | | | | | | | | | | | | | | | | | | | | | | | | | | | | | | | |
| FOX, ANTONY D (DR) (HM07631) | | | | | | | | | | | | | | | | | ● | | | | | | | | | | | | | | | | | | | | | | | | | | | | | | ● | | | |
| FURSEY, STEPHEN (HM07802) | | | | | | | | | | | | | | | ● | | | | | | | | | | | | | | | | | | | | | | | | | | | | | | | | | | | |
| GENERAL HYPNOTHERAPY REGISTER (HM07970) | | | | | | | | | | | | | | | | | | | | ● | | | | | | | | | | | | | | | | | | | | | | | | | | | | | | |
| GLASSPOOL, PATRICIA (HM08130) | | | | | | | | | | | | | | | | | | | | ● | | | | | | | | | | | | | | | | | | | | | | | | | | | | | | |
| GROVE NATURAL THERAPY CENTRE (HM08609) | | | | | | | | | | | | | ● | | | | ● | | | | | ● | | | | | | | | | | ● | | ● | ● | ● | ● | | | | | | | ● | | | ● | | | |
| HANTSCARE (HM08947) | | | | | | | | | | | | | | | | | | | | | | | | | | | | | | | | ● | | ● | | | | | | | | | | | | | | | | |
| HAYLING ISLAND CHIRO CLINIC (HM09268) | | | ● | | | | | | | | | | | | | | | | | | | | | | | | | | | | | ● | | ● | | | | | | | | | | | | | | | | |
| HEAL-ALL HERB AND ACU CTRE (HM09315) | | | | | | | | | | | | | | | ● | | | | | | | | | | | | | | | | | | | | | | | | | ● | | | | | | | | | | |
| HEMSTEAD, JOHN S (HM09539) | | | | | | | | | | | | | | | | | | | | ● | | | | | | | | | | | | | | | | | | | | | | | | | | | | | | |
| HENDERSON, DAVID (HM09545) | | | | | | | | | | | | | | | | | | | | ● | | | | | | | | | | | | | | | | | | | | | | | | | | | | | | |
| HIGH STREET CLINIC (HM09742) | | | | | | | | | | | | | | | | | ● | | | | | | | | | | | | | | | | | | | | | | | | | | | | | | | | | |
| HIPO-ANALYSIS CENTRE SALISBURY (HM09840) | | | | | | | | | | | | | | | | | | | | ● | | | | | | | | | | | | | | | | | | | | | | | | | | | | | | |
| HOLISTIC ARTS STUDIOS (HM09948) | | | | | | | | | | | | ● | ● | | | ● | | | | | | ● | | | | | | | | | | | | ● | | | | | | | | | | | | | | | | |
| HOMOEOPATHIC CLINIC (HM10088) | | | | | | | | | | | | | | | | | ● | | | | | | | | | | | | | | | ● | | ● | | | | | | | | | | | | | | | | |
| HUTCHINGS, MARGARET (HM10448) | | | | | | | | | | | | | | | | | | | | | | | | | | | | | | | | | | ● | | | | | | | | | | | | | | | | |
| HYPNOSIS & STRESS COUNSELLING (HM10494) | | | | | | | | | | | | | | | | | | | | ● | ● | | | | | | | | | | | | | | | | | | | | | | | | | | | | | |
| HYPNOTHERAPY & ANALYSIS CENTRE (HM10505) | | | | | | | | | | | | | | | | | | | | ● | | | | | | | | | | | | | | | | | | | | | | | | | | | | | | |
| HYPNOTHERAPY CONSULTANCY (HM10538) | | | | | | | | | | | | | | | | | | | | ● | | | | | | | | | | | | | | | | | | | | | | | | | | | | | | |

# F - O Therapies at Practices/Businesses

| Business by County with Reference no. | Family Planning (Natural) | Family Therapy | Feldenkrais Methodology | Feng Shui | Floral Essence Therapy | Flotation Therapy | Gait Analysis | Gem Essence Therapy | Gestalt Therapy | Group Therapy | Hay Diet | Healer | Healing Therapy | Hellerwork | Herbal Medicine | Holistic Healing | Homeopathy | Hopi Ear Candles | Humanistic Psychology | Hypnosis | Hypnotherapy | Indian Head Massage | Inhalation Therapy | Iridology | Kinesiology |
|---|---|---|---|---|---|---|---|---|---|---|---|---|---|---|---|---|---|---|---|---|---|---|---|---|---|
| HYPNOTHRPY FOR POSITIVE CHANGE (HM10542) | | | | | | | | | | | | | | | | | | | | ● | ● | | | | |
| INLPTA (HM10633) | | | | | | | | | | | | | | | | | | | | ● | ● | | | | |
| INNER WHISPERS & THERAPY CTRE (HM10643) | | | | | | | | | | | | | | | | | | | | | | ● | | | |
| JENKINS, RUSSELL (HM10994) | | | | | | | | | | | | | | | | | | | | | | ● | | | ● |
| KAY SILVER HYPNOTHERAPY (HM11349) | | | | | | | | | | | | | | | | | | | | ● | ● | | | | |
| KD PHYSIOTHERAPY (HM11363) | | | | | | | | | | | | | | | | | | | | | | | | | |
| KYPERS, SARAH (HM11834) | | | | | | | | | | | | | | | ● | | ● | | | | | | | | |
| KYPERS, SARAH (HM11833) | | | | | | | | | | | | | | | | | ● | | | ● | | | | | |
| LAVERTY, SUSIE (HM12032) | | | | | | | | | | | | | ● | | | | | | | | | | | | |
| LEIBBRANDT (HM12182) | | | | | | | | | | | | | | | ● | | | | | | | | | | |
| LEWIS, D J S (HM12288) | | | | | | | | | | | | | | | | | ● | | | | | | | | ● |
| LEWIS, DAVID (HM12290) | | | | | | | | | | | | | | | | | ● | | | | | | | | |
| LOCKHAMS THERAPY CENTRE (HM12545) | | | | | | | | | | | | | | | | | | | | | | ● | | | |
| LONDON COLLEGE-CLINICAL HYP (HM12592) | | | | | | | | | | | | | | | | | | | | ● | | | | | |
| LOWE, KENNETH (HM12699) | | | | | | | | | | | ● | | | | | | ● | | | | | | | | ● |
| LYMINGTON CHIROPRACTIC CLINIC (HM12759) | | | | | | | | | | | | | | | ● | | | | | | | | | | |
| MANNING, JONATHAN (HM13030) | | | | | | | | | | | | | | | | | | | | ● | | | | | |
| MARISCOTTI, SHEILA (HM13104) | | | | | | | | | | | | | | | ● | | | | | | | | | | |
| MASON, KEITH (HM13246) | | | | | | | | | | | | | | | | | ● | | | | | | | | |
| MILLER, MORRIS (HM13894) | | | | | | | | | | | | | | | | | | | | ● | | | | | |
| MINDWORKS HYPNOTHERAPY CLINIC (HM13969) | | | | | | | | | | | | | | | | | | | | ● | ● | | | | |
| MORAN, DAVID (HM14145) | | | | | | | | | | | | | | | | | | | | ● | | | | | |
| NAT COUNCIL-PSYCHOTHERAPISTS (HM14497) | | | | | | | | | | | | | | | | | | | | ● | | | | | |
| NATURAL HEALTH SERVICE (HM14595) | | | | | | | | | | | | | | | | | ● | | | | | ● | | | |
| NATURAL THERAPY CENTRE (HM14650) | | | | | | | | | | | | | | | | | | | | ● | | | | | |
| NEW MILTON CHIROPRACTIC CLINIC (HM14825) | | | | | | | | | | | ● | | | | | | | | | | | | | | |
| NICOLA @ HOLISTIC HOUSE (HM14926) | | | | | | | | | | | | | | | | | | | | | | ● | | | |
| NOMA (HM14987) | | | | | | | | | | | | | | | ● | | ● | | | | | | | | |
| OLIVER, D (HM15288) | | | | | | | | | | | | | | | ● | | | | | | | | | | |
| OXFORD STREET THERAPY CENTRE (HM15543) | | | | | | | | | | | | | | | | | | | | ● | | | | | |
| PARCHMENT STREET CLINIC (HM15646) | | | | | | | | | | | | | | | ● | | | | | | | | | | |
| PHOENIX HOLISTIC CENTRE (HM16156) | | | | | | ● | | | | ● | | ● | ● | | ● | ● | | | | | ● | ● | | | |
| PORTSMOUTH MEDICAL HERBALIST (HM16454) | | | | | | | | | | | | | | | ● | | | | | | | | | | |
| RICHARDS, CLAIRE (HM17249) | | | | | | | | | | | | ● | ● | | | ● | | | | | | ● | | | |

| Business by County with Reference no. | Kirlian Photography | Laser Treatment | Life Style Coaching | Light Therapy | Macrobiotics | Magnetic Therapy | Manipulation | Manual Lymph Drainage | Massage (Therapeutic) | McTimoney Chiropractic | Meditation | Metamorphic Therapy | Miasm Therapy | Micro Manipulation | Moxibustion | Mud Therapy | Music Therapy | Nail Surgery | Naturopathy | Neuro-Linguistic Program | Neurotherapy | Nutritional Therapy | Orgone Therapy | Oriental Diagnosis | Orthomolecular Medicine |
|---|---|---|---|---|---|---|---|---|---|---|---|---|---|---|---|---|---|---|---|---|---|---|---|---|---|
| HYPNOTHRPY FOR POSITIVE CHANGE (HM10542) | | | | | | | | | | | | | | | | | | | | | | | | | |
| INLPTA (HM10633) | | | | | | | | | | | | | | | | | | | | ● | | | | | |
| INNER WHISPERS & THERAPY CTRE (HM10643) | | | | | | | | | | | | | | | | | | | | | | | | | |
| JENKINS, RUSSELL (HM10994) | | | | | | | | ● | | | | ● | | | | | | | | | | | | | |
| KAY SILVER HYPNOTHERAPY (HM11349) | | | | | | | | | | | | | | | | | | | | | | | | | |
| KD PHYSIOTHERAPY (HM11363) | | | | | | | ● | | | | | | | | | | | | | | | | | | |
| KYPERS, SARAH (HM11834) | | | | | | | | | | | | | | | | | | | | | | | | | |
| KYPERS, SARAH (HM11833) | | | ● | | | | | | | | | | | | | | | | | | | | | | |
| LAVERTY, SUSIE (HM12032) | | | | | | | | | | | ● | | | | | | | | | | | | | | |
| LEIBBRANDT (HM12182) | | | | | | | | | | | | | | | | | | | | | | | | | |
| LEWIS, D J S (HM12288) | | | | | | | | | | | | | | | | | | | | | | | | | |
| LEWIS, DAVID (HM12290) | | | | | | | | | | | | | | | | | | | | | | | | | |
| LOCKHAMS THERAPY CENTRE (HM12545) | | | | | | | | | ● | | | | | | | | | | | | | | | | |
| LONDON COLLEGE-CLINICAL HYP (HM12592) | | | | | | | | | | | | | | | | | | | | | | | | | |
| LOWE, KENNETH (HM12699) | | | | | | | ● | | ● | | | | | | | | | | ● | | | ● | | | |
| LYMINGTON CHIROPRACTIC CLINIC (HM12759) | | | | | | | ● | | ● | | | | | | | | | | | | | ● | | | |
| MANNING, JONATHAN (HM13030) | | | | | | | | | | | | | | | | | | | | | | | | | |
| MARISCOTTI, SHEILA (HM13104) | | | | | | | | | | | | | | | | | | | | | | | | | |
| MASON, KEITH (HM13246) | | | | | | | | | | | | | | | | | | | | | | | | | |
| MILLER, MORRIS (HM13894) | | | | | | | | | | | | | | | | | | | | | | | | | |
| MINDWORKS HYPNOTHERAPY CLINIC (HM13969) | | | ● | | | | | | | | | | | | | | | | | | | | | | |
| MORAN, DAVID (HM14145) | | | | | | | | | | | | | | | | | | | | | | | | | |
| NAT COUNCIL-PSYCHOTHERAPISTS (HM14497) | | | | | | | | | | | | | | | | | | | | | | | | | |
| NATURAL HEALTH SERVICE (HM14595) | | | | | | | | | | | | | | | | | | | | | | | | | |
| NATURAL THERAPY CENTRE (HM14650) | | | | | | | | | | | | | | | | | | | | | | | | | |
| NEW MILTON CHIROPRACTIC CLINIC (HM14825) | | | | | | | ● | | ● | | | | | ● | | | | | | | | ● | | | |
| NICOLA @ HOLISTIC HOUSE (HM14926) | | | | | | | | | ● | | | | | | | | | | | | | | | | |
| NOMA (HM14987) | | | | | | | | | | | | | | | | | | | | | | | | | |
| OLIVER, D (HM15288) | | | | | | | | | | | | | | | | | | | | | | | | | |
| OXFORD STREET THERAPY CENTRE (HM15543) | | | | | | | | | | | | | | | | | | | | | | | | | |
| PARCHMENT STREET CLINIC (HM15646) | | | | | | | ● | | ● | | | | | | | | | | | | | | | ● | |
| PHOENIX HOLISTIC CENTRE (HM16156) | | | | | | | | | ● | | ● | | | | | | | | | | | ● | | | |
| PORTSMOUTH MEDICAL HERBALIST (HM16454) | | | | | | | | | | | | | | | | | | | | | | | | | |
| RICHARDS, CLAIRE (HM17249) | | | | | | | | | ● | | | | | | | | | | | | | | | | |

# F - O Therapies at Practices/Businesses

| Business by County with Reference no. | Family Planning (Natural) | Family Therapy | Feldenkrais Methodology | Feng Shui | Floral Essence Therapy | Flotation Therapy | Gait Analysis | Gem Essence Therapy | Gestalt Therapy | Group Therapy | Hay Diet | Healer | Healing Therapy | Hellerwork | Herbal Medicine | Holistic Healing | Homeopathy |
|---|---|---|---|---|---|---|---|---|---|---|---|---|---|---|---|---|---|
| RINGWOOD NATURAL HEALTH CLINIC (HM17357) | | | | | | | | | ● | | | | | | | | ● |
| ROUSSOS, AMANDA (HM17677) | | | | | | | | | | | | | | | | | |
| RUSSELL, CHRIS (HM17765) | | | | | | | | | | | | | | | | | |
| SIMCOE CLINIC (HM18549) | | | | | | | | | | | | | | | ● | | ● |
| SIMMONDS, J (HM18555) | | | | | ● | | | | | | | | | | | | |
| SOLUTIONS (HM18876) | | | | | | | | | | | | | | | | | |
| SOUTHGATE NAT THERAPY CLINIC (HM18937) | | | | | | | | | | | | | | | | | |
| SOUTHSEA CENTRE FOR COMP MED (HM18943) | | | | | | | | | | | | ● | ● | | ● | ● | ● |
| ST CROSS HOMOEOPATHIC CLINIC (HM19073) | | | | | | | | | | | | | | | | | ● |
| STARTUP, SALLY (HM19155) | | | | | | | | | | | | | | | ● | | |
| STEAD, N W (HM19165) | | | | | | | | | | | | | | | | | |
| SUNRIDER REGENERATIVE FOOD (HM19511) | | | | | | | | | | | | | | | ● | | |
| SWAY HOUSE PUBLICATIONS (HM19581) | | | | | | | | | | | | | | | | | |
| TURNER, CATHY (HM20420) | | | | | | | | | | | | | | | | | |
| WELL HOUSE HOLISTIC HLTH CTRE (HM21138) | | | | | | | | | | | | | | | | ● | |
| WILDE, ELIZABETH A (HM21489) | | | | | | | | | | | | | | | | | |
| WILLSHER, SUE (HM21634) | | | | | | | | | | | | | | | | | ● |
| WINCHESTER CHIROPRACTIC CLINIC (HM21691) | | | | | | | | | | | | | | | | | |
| WINCHESTER HOM PRACTICE (HM21692) | | | | | | | | | | | | ● | ● | | ● | ● | ● |
| WINTON, DIANNA (HM21727) | | | | | | | | | | | | | | | | | |
| HEREFORDSHIRE | | | | | | | | | | | | | | | | | |
| BEAUTY IS YOURS (HM01999) | | | | | | | | | | | | | | | | | |
| BODY PERFECTION (HM02604) | | | | | | | | | | | | | | | | | |
| BROADVIEW NATURAL HEALTH CTRE (HM03119) | | | | | | | | | | | | | | | | | |
| CHURCHER, L A (HM04469) | | | | | | | | | | | | | | | | | |
| DANIELS, PENNY (HM05727) | | | | | | | | | | | | | | | | | |
| HEALING HERBS (HM09344) | | | | | ● | | | | | | | | | | | | |
| HEREFORD CENTRE (HM09677) | | | | | | | | | | | | | | | ● | | ● |
| LEDBURY NATURAL HEALTH CENTRE (HM12122) | | | | | | | | | | | | | ● | | ● | | ● |
| LEOMINSTER OSTEOPATHS (HM12221) | | | | | | | | | | | | | | | | | |
| MOULE, TERRY G (HM14285) | | | | | | | | | | | | | | | | | |
| NITTY GRITTY WHOLEFOODS (HM14953) | | | | | | | | | | | | | | | ● | | ● |
| NOBLE, SUZANNE (HM14972) | | | | | | | | | | | | | | | | | ● |
| TEDDER, CATHRINE (HM19814) | | | | | | | | | | | | | | | | | |

| Business by County with Reference no. | Hopi Ear Candles | Humanistic Psychology | Hypnosis | Hypnotherapy | Indian Head Massage | Inhalation Therapy | Iridology | Kinesiology | Kirlian Photography | Laser Treatment | Life Style Coaching | Light Therapy | Macrobiotics | Magnetic Therapy | Manipulation | Manual Lymph Drainage | Massage (Therapeutic) |
|---|---|---|---|---|---|---|---|---|---|---|---|---|---|---|---|---|---|
| RINGWOOD NATURAL HEALTH CLINIC (HM17357) | | | | ● | ● | | | ● | | | | | | | | | ● |
| ROUSSOS, AMANDA (HM17677) | ● | | | | | | | ● | | | | | | | | | ● |
| RUSSELL, CHRIS (HM17765) | | | ● | | | | | | | | | | | | | | |
| SIMCOE CLINIC (HM18549) | | | | | | | | | | | | | | | ● | | |
| SIMMONDS, J (HM18555) | | | | | | | | | | | | | | | | | |
| SOLUTIONS (HM18876) | | | ● | | | | | | | | | | | | | | |
| SOUTHGATE NAT THERAPY CLINIC (HM18937) | | | ● | ● | | | | | | | | | | | | | |
| SOUTHSEA CENTRE FOR COMP MED (HM18943) | | | ● | ● | ● | ● | ● | ● | | | | | | | ● | | ● |
| ST CROSS HOMOEOPATHIC CLINIC (HM19073) | | | | | | | | | | | | | | | | | |
| STARTUP, SALLY (HM19155) | | | | | | | | | | | | | | | | | |
| STEAD, N W (HM19165) | | | ● | | | | | | | | | | | | | | |
| SUNRIDER REGENERATIVE FOOD (HM19511) | | | | | | | | | | | | | | | | | |
| SWAY HOUSE PUBLICATIONS (HM19581) | | | ● | | | | | | | | | | | | | | |
| TURNER, CATHY (HM20420) | | | | | ● | | | ● | | | | | | | | | ● |
| WELL HOUSE HOLISTIC HLTH CTRE (HM21138) | | | | | | | | | | | | | | | | | |
| WILDE, ELIZABETH A (HM21489) | | | ● | | | | | | | | | | | | | | |
| WILLSHER, SUE (HM21634) | | | | | | | | | | | | | | | | | |
| WINCHESTER CHIROPRACTIC CLINIC (HM21691) | | | | | | | | ● | | | | | | | ● | | ● |
| WINCHESTER HOM PRACTICE (HM21692) | | | ● | ● | | | | | | | | | | | ● | | ● |
| WINTON, DIANNA (HM21727) | | | ● | | | | | | | | | | | | | | |
| HEREFORDSHIRE | | | | | | | | | | | | | | | | | |
| BEAUTY IS YOURS (HM01999) | | | | | ● | | | | | | | | | | | | ● |
| BODY PERFECTION (HM02604) | | | | | | | | | | | | | | | | | |
| BROADVIEW NATURAL HEALTH CTRE (HM03119) | | | | | | | | | | | | | | | | | ● |
| CHURCHER, L A (HM04469) | | | ● | | | | | | | | | | | | | | |
| DANIELS, PENNY (HM05727) | | | ● | | | | | | | | | | | | | | |
| HEALING HERBS (HM09344) | | | | | | | | | | | | | | | | | |
| HEREFORD CENTRE (HM09677) | | | | ● | | | | ● | | | | | | | ● | | ● |
| LEDBURY NATURAL HEALTH CENTRE (HM12122) | | | | ● | ● | | | | | | | | | | | | ● |
| LEOMINSTER OSTEOPATHS (HM12221) | | | | | | | | | | | | | ● | | | | |
| MOULE, TERRY G (HM14285) | | | | | | | | | | | | | | | | | |
| NITTY GRITTY WHOLEFOODS (HM14953) | | | | | | | | | | | | | | | | | |
| NOBLE, SUZANNE (HM14972) | | | | | | | | | | | | | | | | | |
| TEDDER, CATHRINE (HM19814) | | | | | | | | | | | | | | | | | |

| Business by County with Reference no. | McTimoney Chiropractic | Meditation | Metamorphic Therapy | Miasm Therapy | Micro Manipulation | Moxibustion | Mud Therapy | Music Therapy | Nail Surgery | Naturopathy | Neuro-Linguistic Program | Neurotherapy | Nutritional Therapy | Orgone Therapy | Oriental Diagnosis | Orthomolecular Medicine |
|---|---|---|---|---|---|---|---|---|---|---|---|---|---|---|---|---|
| RINGWOOD NATURAL HEALTH CLINIC (HM17357) | | | ● | | | ● | | | | | | | | | | |
| ROUSSOS, AMANDA (HM17677) | | | | | | | | | | | | | | | | |
| RUSSELL, CHRIS (HM17765) | | | | | | | | | | | | | | | | |
| SIMCOE CLINIC (HM18549) | | | | | | | | | | ● | | | ● | | | |
| SIMMONDS, J (HM18555) | | | ● | | | | | | | | | | | | | |
| SOLUTIONS (HM18876) | | | | | | | | | | | | | | | | |
| SOUTHGATE NAT THERAPY CLINIC (HM18937) | | | | | | ● | | | | | | | | | | |
| SOUTHSEA CENTRE FOR COMP MED (HM18943) | | | | | | ● | | | | | | | ● | | ● | |
| ST CROSS HOMOEOPATHIC CLINIC (HM19073) | | | | | | | | | | | | | | | | |
| STARTUP, SALLY (HM19155) | | | | | | | | | | | | | | | | |
| STEAD, N W (HM19165) | | | | | | | | | | | | | | | | |
| SUNRIDER REGENERATIVE FOOD (HM19511) | | | | | | | | | | | | | | | | |
| SWAY HOUSE PUBLICATIONS (HM19581) | | | | | | | | | | | ● | | | | | |
| TURNER, CATHY (HM20420) | | | | | | | | | | | | | | | | |
| WELL HOUSE HOLISTIC HLTH CTRE (HM21138) | | ● | | | | | | | | | | | | | | |
| WILDE, ELIZABETH A (HM21489) | | | | | | | | | | | | | | | | |
| WILLSHER, SUE (HM21634) | | | | | | | | | | | | | | | | |
| WINCHESTER CHIROPRACTIC CLINIC (HM21691) | | | | | ● | | | | | | | | | | | |
| WINCHESTER HOM PRACTICE (HM21692) | | | | | | | | | | | | | ● | | | |
| WINTON, DIANNA (HM21727) | | | | | | | | | | | | | | | | |
| HEREFORDSHIRE | | | | | | | | | | | | | | | | |
| BEAUTY IS YOURS (HM01999) | | | | | | | | | | | | | ● | | | |
| BODY PERFECTION (HM02604) | | | | | | | | | | ● | | | ● | | | |
| BROADVIEW NATURAL HEALTH CTRE (HM03119) | | | | | | | | | | | | | | | | |
| CHURCHER, L A (HM04469) | | | | | | | | | | | | | | | | |
| DANIELS, PENNY (HM05727) | | | | | | | | | | | | | | | | |
| HEALING HERBS (HM09344) | | | | | | | | | | | | | | | | |
| HEREFORD CENTRE (HM09677) | | | | | | | | | | ● | | | ● | | | |
| LEDBURY NATURAL HEALTH CENTRE (HM12122) | | | | | | | | | | | | | | | | |
| LEOMINSTER OSTEOPATHS (HM12221) | | | | | | | | | | ● | | | | | | |
| MOULE, TERRY G (HM14285) | | | | | | | | | | ● | | | | | | |
| NITTY GRITTY WHOLEFOODS (HM14953) | | | | | | | | | | | | | | | | |
| NOBLE, SUZANNE (HM14972) | | | | | | | | | | | | | | | | |
| TEDDER, CATHRINE (HM19814) | | | | | | | | | ● | | | | | | | |

# F - O Therapies at Practices/Businesses

| Business by County with Reference no. | Family Planning (Natural) | Family Therapy | Feldenkrais Methodology | Feng Shui | Floral Essence Therapy | Flotation Therapy | Gait Analysis | Gem Essence Therapy | Gestalt Therapy | Group Therapy | Hay Diet | Healer | Healing Therapy | Hellerwork | Herbal Medicine | Holistic Healing | Homeopathy | Hopi Ear Candles | Humanistic Psychology | Hypnosis | Hypnotherapy | Indian Head Massage | Inhalation Therapy | Iridology | Kinesiology | Kirlian Photography | Laser Treatment | Life Style Coaching | Light Therapy | Macrobiotics | Magnetic Therapy | Manipulation | Manual Lymph Drainage | Massage (Therapeutic) | McTimoney Chiropractic | Meditation | Metamorphic Therapy | Miasm Therapy | Micro Manipulation | Moxibustion | Mud Therapy | Music Therapy | Nail Surgery | Naturopathy | Neuro-Linguistic Program | Neurotherapy | Nutritional Therapy | Orgone Therapy | Oriental Diagnosis | Orthomolecular Medicine |
|---|---|---|---|---|---|---|---|---|---|---|---|---|---|---|---|---|---|---|---|---|---|---|---|---|---|---|---|---|---|---|---|---|---|---|---|---|---|---|---|---|---|---|---|---|---|---|---|---|---|---|
| WILLCOCKS, T & S (HM21519) | | | | | | | | | | | | | | | | | | | | | | ● | | | | | | | | | | | | ● | | | ● | | | | | | | | | | | | | |
| HERTFORDSHIRE | | | | | | | | | | | | | | | | | | | | | | | | | | | | | | | | | | | | | | | | | | | | | | | | | | |
| ALDER, DENNIS (HM00497) | | | | | | | | | | | | | | | | | | | | | | | | | | | | | | | | | | | | | | | | | | | ● | | | | | | | |
| ALLEN, JULIE & LEN (HM00613) | | | | | | | | | | | | | | | | | ● | | | ● | ● | | | | | | | | | | | | | | | | | | | | | | | | | | | | | |
| ALTERNATIVE CHOICES (HM00697) | | | | | | | | | | | | | | | ● | | | | | | | | | | | | | | | | | | | | | | | | | | | | | | | | | | | |
| ANGLO-AUSTRALIAN SEED (HM00883) | | | | | | | | | | | | | | | ● | | | | | | | | | | | | | | | | | | | | | | | | | | | | | | | | | | | |
| ARNOLD, PETER & JACKIE (HM01036) | | | | | | | | | | | | | | | ● | | | | | | | | | | | | | | | | | | | | | | | | | | | | | | | | | | | |
| AROMA ROOM (HM01055) | | | | | | | | | | | | | | | | | | | | | | | | | | | | | | | | | | ● | | | | | | | | | | | | | | | | |
| AROMATHERAPY BY ANTONIO (HM01095) | | | | | | | | | | | | | | | | | | | | | | | | | | | | | | | | | | ● | | | | | | | | | | | | | | | | |
| ASHDOWN CLINIC (HM01205) | | | | | | | | | | | | | | | | | ● | | | | ● | ● | | | | | | | | | | ● | | ● | | | | | | | | | | ● | | | ● | | | |
| ASHWELL, MELBOURN & BALDOCK (HM01246) | | | | | | | | | | | | | | | | | | | | | | | | | | | | | | | | ● | | ● | | | | | | | | | | | | | | | | |
| ASSOCIATES HEAD & SHORT (HM01277) | | | | | | | ● | | | | | | | | | | | | | | | | | | | | | | | | | | | | | | | | | | | | | | | | | | | |
| ASSOCIATES HEAD & SHORT (HM01276) | | | | | | | ● | | | | | | | | | | | | | | | | | | | | | | | | | | | | | | | | | | | | | | | | | | | |
| ASSOCIATION OF STRESS MNGMT (HM01293) | | | | | | | | | | | | | | | | | | | | | ● | | | | | | | | | | | | | | | | | | | | | | | | | | | | | |
| BASSETT CLINIC (HM01853) | | | | | | | | | | | | | | | | | ● | | | | ● | ● | | | | | | | | | | ● | | ● | | | | | | | | | | | | | | | | |
| BEAUCHAMP BAGENAL (HM01983) | | | | | | | | | | | | | | | | | | | | | | | | | | | | ● | | | | | | | | | | | | | | | | | | | | | | |
| BECERRA, P (HM02015) | | | | | | | | | | | | | | | | | | | | ● | | | | | | | | | | | | | | | | | | | | | | | | | | | | | | |
| BETA HEALTH CLINIC (HM02229) | | | | | | | | | | | | | | | | | ● | | | | ● | | | | | | | | | | | | | ● | | | | | | | | | | | | | | | | |
| BIGGINS, NICHOLAS (HM02292) | | | | | | | | | | | | | | | | | ● | | | | | | | | | | | | | | | | | | | | | | | | | | | | | | | | | |
| BIRTHWORKS (HM02399) | | | | | | | | | | | | | | | | | | | | | | | | | | | | | | | | | | | | | ● | | | | | | | | | | | | | |
| BISHOP'S STORTFORD HOMEOPATHIC (HM02416) | | | | | | | | | | | | | | | | | ● | | | | | | | | ● | | | | | | | | | | | | | | | | | | | ● | | | | | | |
| BLACKDEN, J M (HM02440) | | | | | | | | | | | | | | | | | | | | ● | | | | | | | | | | | | | | | | | | | | | | | | | | | | | | |
| BODELL, TERRI (HM02550) | | | | | | | | | | | | | | | | | | | | ● | | | | | | | | | | | | | | | | | | | | | | | | | | | | | | |
| BOREHAMWOOD CHIRO CLINIC (HM02717) | | | | | | | | | | | | | | | | | | | | | | | | | | | | | | | | ● | | ● | | | | | | | | | | | | | | | | |
| BRIGGS-WILSON, A (HM03037) | | | | | | | | | | | | | ● | | | ● | | | | | | ● | | | | | | | | | | | | ● | | | | | | | | | | | | | | | | |
| BURYHILL PHYSIOTHERAPY (HM03456) | | | | | | | | | | | | | | | | | | | | | | | | | | | | | | | | ● | | | | | | | | | | | | | | | | | | |
| BUSHEY HYPNOTHERAPY CENTRE (HM03463) | | | | | | | | | | | | | | | | | | | | ● | | | | | | | | | | | | | | | | | | | | | | | | | | | | | | |
| BUSOLINI, DON (HM03468) | | | | | | | | | | | | | | | | | | | | ● | | | | | | | | | | | | | | | | | | | | | | | | | | | | | | |
| BUTTERFIELD, ROBIN (HM03496) | | | | | | | | | | | | | ● | | | ● | | | | | | ● | | | ● | | | | | | | ● | ● | ● | | | | | | | | | | ● | | | | | | |
| CARTER, J P (HM03780) | | | | | | | | | | | | | | | | | ● | | | | | | | | | | | | | | | | | | | | | | | | | | | | | | | | | |
| CHALMERS, RICHARD (HM03953) | | | | | | | | | | | | | | | | | | | | ● | | | | | | | | | | | | | | | | | | | | | | | | | | | | | | |
| CHALMERS, RICHARD (HM03952) | | | | | | | | | | | | | | | | | | | | ● | | | | | | | | | | | | | | | | | | | | | | | | | | | | | | |
| CHOPRA, S (HM04426) | | | | | | | ● | | | | | | | | | | | | | | | | | | | | | | | | | | | | | | | | | | | | | | | | | | | |
| CHOPRA, S (HM04427) | | | | | | | ● | | | | | | | | | | | | | | | | | | | | | | | | | | | | | | | | | | | | ● | | | | | | | |

# F - O Therapies at Practices/Businesses

| Business by County with Reference no. | Family Planning (Natural) | Family Therapy | Feldenkrais Methodology | Feng Shui | Floral Essence Therapy | Flotation Therapy | Gait Analysis | Gem Essence Therapy | Gestalt Therapy | Group Therapy | Hay Diet | Healer | Healing Therapy | Hellerwork | Herbal Medicine | Holistic Healing | Homeopathy | Hopi Ear Candles | Humanistic Psychology | Hypnosis | Hypnotherapy | Indian Head Massage | Inhalation Therapy | Iridology | Kinesiology |
|---|---|---|---|---|---|---|---|---|---|---|---|---|---|---|---|---|---|---|---|---|---|---|---|---|---|
| CHRISTOU, Z (HM04455) | | | | | | | | | | | | | | | | | | | | ● | | | | | |
| CLARE JAMES HEALTH FOODS (HM04532) | | | | | | | | | | | ● | | | | ● | | ● | | | | | | | | |
| CLAYTON-ROBB, WAYNE (HM04628) | | | | | | | | | | | | | | | | | | | | ● | | | | | |
| CLINIC OF HYPNOTHERAPY (HM04697) | | | | | | | | | | | | | | | | | | | | ● | | | | | |
| CLNC OF ACU & CHINESE HRBL MED (HM04727) | | | | | | | | | | | | | | | ● | ● | | | | | | | | | |
| CONISTON PHYSIOTHERAPY CLINIC (HM04980) | | | | | | | | | | | | | | | | ● | | | | | | | | | |
| COOPER, FELICITY (HM05101) | | | | | | | ● | | | | | | | | | | | | | | | | | | |
| COUGHLIN, V IAN (HM05234) | | | | | | | | | | | | | | | ● | | | | | | | | | | |
| COUNS & HYPNOTHERAPY PRACTICE (HM05244) | | | | | | | | | | | | | | | | | | | | ● | | | | | |
| DAVID HERBERT REFLEXOLOGY (HM05774) | | | | | | | | | | | | | ● | | | ● | | | | | | ● | | | |
| DOYLE, AUDREY (HM06257) | | | | | | | | | | | | | | | | | | | | | | ● | | | |
| DRISCOLL & ASSOCIATES (HM06313) | | | | | | | | | | | | | | | | | | | | ● | | | | | |
| DUDGEON, DELIA (HM06353) | | | | | | | | | | | | | | | | | | | | | | | | | |
| ELDON, MARTIN (HM06706) | | | | | | | | | | | | | | | | | | | | ● | | | | | |
| EVANS, HELEN (HM06976) | | | | | | | | | | | | | | | | | | | | | | | | | |
| FORLAND, ELAINA (HM07557) | | | | | | | | | | | | | | | | | | | | ● | | | | | |
| FREEMAN, FRANCES (HM07721) | | | | | | | | | | | | | | | | | ● | | | | | | | | |
| GENTLE FEET (HM07977) | | | | | | | | | | | | | | | | | | | | | | ● | | | |
| GILLING, LINDA (HM08095) | | | | | | | | | | | | | | | | | | | | | | ● | | | |
| GOLTEN, ROGER (HM08231) | | | | | | | | | | | | | | ● | | | | | | | | | | | |
| GOODMAN, HENRY (HM08258) | | | | | | | | | | | | | | | | | | | | ● | ● | | | | |
| GRAHAM & KERSTIN ELLIOTT (HM08336) | | | | | | | | | | | | | | | | | | | | | | | | | ● |
| HALAHAN, ELISABETH (HM08722) | | | | | | | | | | | | | | | | | ● | | | | | | | | |
| HAMILTON-PETERS, R & J A (HM08849) | | | | | | | | | | | | | ● | | | ● | | | | ● | ● | | | | |
| HARPENDEM OSTEOPATHIC PRACTICE (HM09035) | | | | | | | | | | | | | | | | | ● | | | | | | | | |
| HARPENDEN CHIROPRACTIC CLINIC (HM09036) | | | | | | | | | | | | | | | ● | | | | | | | | | | |
| HEALTHY AND WISE (HM09425) | | | | | | | | | | | | | | | | | ● | | | | | | | | |
| HERRINGTON, YVONNE (HM09686) | | | | | | | | | | | | | | | | | | | | ● | | | | | |
| HERTFORD NATURAL THERAPY CTRE (HM09690) | | | | | | | | | | | | | | | | | ● | | | | ● | ● | | | |
| HEYMANN, RUSSELL (HM09713) | | | | | | | | | | | | | | | | | | | | ● | | | | | |
| HILTON, DAVID (HM09814) | | | | | | | | | | | | | | | | | | | | ● | | | | | |
| HUTCHESON, SALLY ANN (HM10445) | | | | | | | | | | | | | | | | | ● | | | | | | | | |
| HUTHERT, J (HM10455) | | | | | | | | | | | | | | | | | | | | ● | | | | | |
| HYNOTHERAPY SURGERY (HM10486) | | | | | | | | | | | | | | | | | | | | ● | | | | | |

| Business by County with Reference no. | Kirlian Photography | Laser Treatment | Life Style Coaching | Light Therapy | Macrobiotics | Magnetic Therapy | Manipulation | Manual Lymph Drainage | Massage (Therapeutic) | McTimoney Chiropractic | Meditation | Metamorphic Therapy | Miasm Therapy | Micro Manipulation | Moxibustion | Mud Therapy | Music Therapy | Nail Surgery | Naturopathy | Neuro-Linguistic Program | Neurotherapy | Nutritional Therapy | Orgone Therapy | Oriental Diagnosis | Orthomolecular Medicine |
|---|---|---|---|---|---|---|---|---|---|---|---|---|---|---|---|---|---|---|---|---|---|---|---|---|---|
| CHRISTOU, Z (HM04455) | | | | | | | | | | | | | | | | | | | | | | | | | |
| CLARE JAMES HEALTH FOODS (HM04532) | | | | | | | | | | | | | | | | | | | | | | | | | |
| CLAYTON-ROBB, WAYNE (HM04628) | | | | | | | | | | | | | | | | | | | | | | | | | |
| CLINIC OF HYPNOTHERAPY (HM04697) | | | | | | | | | | | | | | | | | | | | | | | | | |
| CLNC OF ACU & CHINESE HRBL MED (HM04727) | | | | | | ● | | | | | | | | | ● | | | | | | | | | ● | |
| CONISTON PHYSIOTHERAPY CLINIC (HM04980) | | | ● | | | | ● | | | | | | | | | | | | | | | | | | |
| COOPER, FELICITY (HM05101) | | | | | | | | | | | | | | | | | | ● | | | | | | | |
| COUGHLIN, V IAN (HM05234) | | | | | | | | | | | | | | | | | | | | | | | | | |
| COUNS & HYPNOTHERAPY PRACTICE (HM05244) | | | | | | | | | | | | | | | | | | | | | | | | | |
| DAVID HERBERT REFLEXOLOGY (HM05774) | | | | | | | | | | | | | | | | | | | | | | | | | |
| DOYLE, AUDREY (HM06257) | | | | | | | | | | | | | | | | | | ● | | | | | | | |
| DRISCOLL & ASSOCIATES (HM06313) | | | | | | | | | | | | | | | | | | | | | | | | | |
| DUDGEON, DELIA (HM06353) | | | | | | | | | | | | ● | | | | | | | | | | | | | |
| ELDON, MARTIN (HM06706) | | | | | | | | | | | | | | | | | | | | | | | | | |
| EVANS, HELEN (HM06976) | | | | | | | | | | | | | | | | | | ● | | | | | | | |
| FORLAND, ELAINA (HM07557) | | | | | | | | | | | | | | | | | | | | | | | | | |
| FREEMAN, FRANCES (HM07721) | | | | | | | | | | | | | | | | | | | | | | | | | |
| GENTLE FEET (HM07977) | | | | | | | | | | | | | | | | | | | | | | | | | |
| GILLING, LINDA (HM08095) | | | | | | | | | | | | | | | | | | | | | | | | | |
| GOLTEN, ROGER (HM08231) | | | | | | | | | | | | | | | | | | | | | | | | | |
| GOODMAN, HENRY (HM08258) | | | | | | | | | | | | | | | | | | | | | | | | | |
| GRAHAM & KERSTIN ELLIOTT (HM08336) | | | | | | | | | | | | | | | | | | | | | | | | | |
| HALAHAN, ELISABETH (HM08722) | | | | | | | | | | | | | | | | | | | | | | | | | |
| HAMILTON-PETERS, R & J A (HM08849) | | | | | | | | | | | | | | | | | | | | | | | | | |
| HARPENDEM OSTEOPATHIC PRACTICE (HM09035) | | | | | | | ● | | | | | | | | | | | | | | | | | | |
| HARPENDEN CHIROPRACTIC CLINIC (HM09036) | | | | | | | ● | | | | | ● | | | | | | | | | | | | | |
| HEALTHY AND WISE (HM09425) | | | | | | | | | | | | | | | | | | | | | | | | | |
| HERRINGTON, YVONNE (HM09686) | | | | | | | | | | | | | | | | | | | | | | | | | |
| HERTFORD NATURAL THERAPY CTRE (HM09690) | | | | | | | | | ● | | | | | | | | | | | | | ● | | | |
| HEYMANN, RUSSELL (HM09713) | | | | | | | | | | | | | | | | | | | | | | | | | |
| HILTON, DAVID (HM09814) | | | | | | | | | | | | | | | | | | | | | | | | | |
| HUTCHESON, SALLY ANN (HM10445) | | | | | | | | | | | | | | | | | | | | | | | | | |
| HUTHERT, J (HM10455) | | | | | | | | | | | | | | | | | | | | | | | | | |
| HYNOTHERAPY SURGERY (HM10486) | | | | | | | | | | | | | | | | | | | | | | | | | |

# F - O Therapies at Practices/Businesses

Business by County with Reference no.

| Business | Family Planning (Natural) | Family Therapy | Feldenkrais Methodology | Feng Shui | Floral Essence Therapy | Flotation Therapy | Gait Analysis | Gem Essence Therapy | Gestalt Therapy | Group Therapy | Hay Diet | Healer | Healing Therapy | Hellerwork | Herbal Medicine | Holistic Healing | Homeopathy | Hopi Ear Candles | Humanistic Psychology | Hypnosis | Hypnotherapy | Indian Head Massage | Inhalation Therapy | Iridology | Kinesiology |
|---|---|---|---|---|---|---|---|---|---|---|---|---|---|---|---|---|---|---|---|---|---|---|---|---|---|
| HYPNOCURE (HM10491) | | | | | | | | | | | | | | | | | | | | ● | | | | | |
| JOE MILLER SPORTS INJURY (HM11045) | | | | | | | | | | | | | | | | | | | | | | | | | ● |
| JONES, ALAN (HM11115) | | | | | | | | | | | | | | | | | | | | | | | | | |
| KEW, DEREK (HM11576) | | | | | | | | | | | | | | | | | | | | ● | ● | | | | |
| KNEBWORTH PHYSIO CLINIC (HM11742) | | | | | | | | | | | | | | | | | | | | | | | | | |
| LAMBERT, MARGARET (HM11900) | | | | | | | | | | | | | | | | | ● | | | | | | | | |
| LEWIN, ROCHELLE (HM12273) | | | | | | | | | | ● | | | | | | | | | | | | | | | |
| MASON, L C (HM13247) | | | | | | | | | | | | | | | | | | | | ● | ● | | | | |
| MAWSON, MARY M (HM13332) | | | | | | | | | | | | | | | | | ● | | | | | | | | |
| MAYOR, DAVID F (HM13359) | | | | | | | | | | | | | | | | | | | | | | | | | |
| MCLAREN, PETER (HM13543) | | | | | | | | | | | | | | | | | | | | ● | | | | | |
| MIDAS TOUCH (HM13808) | | | | | | | | | | | | | | | | | | | | | | | | | |
| MID-HERTS ALEXANDER CENTRE (HM13827) | | | | | | | | | | | | | | | | | | | | | | | | | |
| MONK, PETER (HM14068) | | | | | | | | | | | | | | | | | | | | ● | | | | | |
| NATURAL HEALTH CLINIC (HM14589) | | | | | | | | | | | | | | | ● | | ● | | | | | | | | |
| NATURAL-BALANCE CO UK (HM14672) | | | | | | | | | | | | | | | | | ● | | | | | | | | |
| OLIVER, J P (HM15291) | | | | | | | | | | | | | | | | | | | | ● | | | | | |
| OPEN MINDS (HM15343) | | | | | | | | | | | | ● | ● | | | | | | | | | | | | |
| OSTEOPATHIC CLINIC (HM15459) | | | | | | | | | | | | | | | ● | | | | | | | ● | | | |
| PENDRY, BARBARA (HM15970) | | | | | | | | | | | | | | | ● | | | | | | | | | | |
| PERSONAL REFLECTIONS (HM16061) | | | | | | | | | | | | ● | ● | | | ● | | | | | | ● | | | |
| PHYSIO & SPORTS INJURIES CLNC (HM16177) | | | | | | | | | | | | | | | | | | | | | | | | | |
| PRIDDLE, PATRICK (HM16602) | | | | | | | | | | | | | | | | | | | | ● | ● | | | | |
| PROFESSIONAL HYP CTRE (HM16658) | | | | | | | | | | | | | | | | | | | | ● | | | | | |
| PSYCHOLOGIST-HYPNOTHERAPIST (HM16719) | | | | | | | | | | | | | | | | | | | | ● | | | | | |
| PURLYS (HM16769) | | | | | | | | | | | | | | | | | ● | | | ● | | | | | |
| RAINSFORD, JOSEPHINE (HM16892) | | | | | | | | | | | | | | | | | ● | | | | | | | | |
| REED, PHILIP (HM17043) | | | | | | | | | | | | | | | | | | | | ● | | | | | |
| RICHARDS, JESSICA (HM17255) | | | | | | | | | | | | | | | | | | | | ● | | | | | |
| RIPPER, JULIE (HM17366) | | | | | | | | | | | | | | | | | | | | ● | | | | | |
| ROWLAND, JETHRO (HM17692) | | | | | | | | | | | | | | | ● | | | | | | | | | | |
| S K REFLEXOLOGY (HM17811) | | | | | | | | | | | | ● | | | | | | | | | | | | | |
| SCOTT, ANTONIA (HM18108) | | | | | | | | | | | | | | | | | ● | | | | | | | | |
| SMITH, SUSAN (HM18813) | | | | | | | | | | | | | | | | | | | | | | | | | |

| Business | Kirlian Photography | Laser Treatment | Life Style Coaching | Light Therapy | Macrobiotics | Magnetic Therapy | Manipulation | Manual Lymph Drainage | Massage (Therapeutic) | McTimoney Chiropractic | Meditation | Metamorphic Therapy | Miasm Therapy | Micro Manipulation | Moxibustion | Mud Therapy | Music Therapy | Nail Surgery | Naturopathy | Neuro-Linguistic Program | Neurotherapy | Nutritional Therapy | Orgone Therapy | Oriental Diagnosis | Orthomolecular Medicine |
|---|---|---|---|---|---|---|---|---|---|---|---|---|---|---|---|---|---|---|---|---|---|---|---|---|---|
| HYPNOCURE (HM10491) | | | | | | | | | | | | | | | | | | | | | | | | | |
| JOE MILLER SPORTS INJURY (HM11045) | | | | | | | ● | | | | | | | | | | | | | | | | | | |
| JONES, ALAN (HM11115) | | | | | | | | | | | | | | | | | | ● | | | | | | | |
| KEW, DEREK (HM11576) | | | | | | | | | | | | | | | | | | | | | | | | | |
| KNEBWORTH PHYSIO CLINIC (HM11742) | | | | | | | ● | | ● | | | | | | | | | | | | | | | | |
| LAMBERT, MARGARET (HM11900) | | | | | | | | | | | | | | | | | | | | | | | | | |
| LEWIN, ROCHELLE (HM12273) | | | ● | | | | | | | | | | | | | | | | | | | | | | |
| MASON, L C (HM13247) | | | | | | | | | | | | | | | | | | | | | | | | | |
| MAWSON, MARY M (HM13332) | | | | | | | | | | | | | | | | | | | | | | | | | |
| MAYOR, DAVID F (HM13359) | | | | | | | | | ● | | | | | | ● | | | | | | | ● | | | |
| MCLAREN, PETER (HM13543) | | | | | | | | | | | | | | | | | | | | | | | | | |
| MIDAS TOUCH (HM13808) | | | | | | | | | ● | | | | | | | | | | | | | | | | |
| MID-HERTS ALEXANDER CENTRE (HM13827) | | | ● | | | | | | | | | | | | | | | | | | | | | | |
| MONK, PETER (HM14068) | | | | | | | | | | | | | | | | | | | | | | | | | |
| NATURAL HEALTH CLINIC (HM14589) | | | | | | | | | | | | | | | | | | | | | | | | | |
| NATURAL-BALANCE CO UK (HM14672) | | | | | | | | | | | | | | | | | | | | | | | | | |
| OLIVER, J P (HM15291) | | | | | | | | | | | | | | | | | | | | | | | | | |
| OPEN MINDS (HM15343) | | | | | | | | | | | | | | | | | | | | | | | | | |
| OSTEOPATHIC CLINIC (HM15459) | | | | | | | ● | | ● | | | | | | | | | | | | | | | | |
| PENDRY, BARBARA (HM15970) | | | | | | | | | | | | | | | | | | | | | | | | | |
| PERSONAL REFLECTIONS (HM16061) | | | | | | | | | | | ● | | | | | | | | | | | | | | |
| PHYSIO & SPORTS INJURIES CLNC (HM16177) | | | | | | | ● | | ● | | | | | | | | | | | | | | | | |
| PRIDDLE, PATRICK (HM16602) | | | | | | | | | | | | | | | | | | | | | | | | | |
| PROFESSIONAL HYP CTRE (HM16658) | | | | | | | | | | | | | | | | | | | | | | | | | |
| PSYCHOLOGIST-HYPNOTHERAPIST (HM16719) | | | | | | | | | | | | | | | | | | | | | | | | | |
| PURLYS (HM16769) | | | | | | | | | | | | | | | | | | | | | | | | | |
| RAINSFORD, JOSEPHINE (HM16892) | | | | | | | | | | | | | | | | | | | | | | | | | |
| REED, PHILIP (HM17043) | | | | | | | | | | | | | | | | | | | | | | | | | |
| RICHARDS, JESSICA (HM17255) | | | | | | | | | | | | | | | | | | | | | | | | | |
| RIPPER, JULIE (HM17366) | | | | | | | | | | | | | | | | | | | | | | | | | |
| ROWLAND, JETHRO (HM17692) | | | | | | | | | | | | | | | | | | | | | | | | | |
| S K REFLEXOLOGY (HM17811) | | | | | | | | | ● | | | | | | | | | | | | | | | | |
| SCOTT, ANTONIA (HM18108) | | | | | | | | | | | | | | | | | | | | | | | | | |
| SMITH, SUSAN (HM18813) | | | ● | | | | | | | | | | | | | | | | | | | | | | |

# F - O Therapies at Practices/Businesses

| Business by County with Reference no. | Family Planning (Natural) | Family Therapy | Feldenkrais Methodology | Feng Shui | Floral Essence Therapy | Flotation Therapy | Gait Analysis | Gem Essence Therapy | Gestalt Therapy | Group Therapy | Hay Diet | Healer | Healing Therapy | Hellerwork | Herbal Medicine | Holistic Healing | Homeopathy | Hopi Ear Candles | Humanistic Psychology | Hypnosis | Hypnotherapy | Indian Head Massage | Inhalation Therapy | Iridology | Kinesiology |
|---|---|---|---|---|---|---|---|---|---|---|---|---|---|---|---|---|---|---|---|---|---|---|---|---|---|
| SOPWELL OSTEOPATHIC CLINIC (HM18894) | | | | | | | | | | | ● | ● | | | | | | | | | | ● | | | |
| SOUTH, JO (HM18917) | | | | | | | | | | | | | | | | | ● | | | | | | | | |
| SPINOZA, DAVID (HM19019) | | | | | | | | | | | | | | | ● | | | | | ● | ● | | | ● | ● |
| STORT COUNS & PSYCHOTHERAPY (HM19351) | | | | | | | | | ● | ● | | | | | | | | | ● | | | | | | |
| SURVIVAL TRUST SURGERY (HM19526) | | | | | | | | | | | | | | | | | ● | | | | | | | | |
| THOMAS, HELEN (HM19944) | | | | | | | | | | | | | | | ● | | | | | | | | | | |
| THOMPSON, MARK (HM19991) | | ● | | | | | | | | | | | | | | | | | | | | | | | |
| THOMPSON, MARK () | ● | | | | | | | | | | | | | | | | | | | | | | | | |
| WALFORD, PENELOPE (HM20756) | | | | | | | | | | | | | | | | | | | | ● | | | | | |
| WALKER, NEL (HM20791) | | | | | | | | | | | | | | | | | | | ● | | | | | | |
| WALKER, RICHARD (HM20798) | | | | | | | | | | | | | | | | | | | | ● | ● | | | | |
| WARREN, HELEN (HM20949) | | | | | | | | | | | | | | | | | ● | | | | | | | | |
| WATSON, KATHRYN (HM21015) | | | | | | | | | | | | | | | ● | | | | | | | | | | |
| WHITE, GRAHAM C (HM21355) | | | | | | | | | | | | | | | ● | | | | | | | | | | |
| WHITE, GRAHAM C (HM21356) | | | | | | | | | | | | | | | ● | | | | | | | | | | |
| WHITTONBOURNE, J (HM21428) | | | | | | | | | | | | | | | | | | | | ● | | | | | |
| WILLIAMS, NEVILLE L (HM21582) | | | | | | | | | | | | | | | ● | | | | | | | | | | |
| WOOD STREET CHIROPRACTIC CLNC (HM21780) | | | | | | | | | | | | | | | | | ● | | | | ● | | | | |
| WOOD STREET CLINIC (HM21781) | | | | | | | | | | | | | | | | | ● | | | | | | | | |
| WRIGHT, DOREEN (HM21931) | | | | | | | | | | | | | | | | ● | ● | | | | | | | | |
| WRIGHT, KAREN (HM21940) | | | | | | | | | | | | | | | | | | | | | | | | | |
| WYNDHAM CLINIC (HM21977) | | | | | | | | | | | | | | | ● | | ● | | | | | | | | |
| **HUMBERSIDE** | | | | | | | | | | | | | | | | | | | | | | | | | |
| EURO THERAPY PRACTICE (HM06943) | | | | | | | | | | | | | | | | | | | | ● | | | | | |
| INNERVISION HYPNOTHERAPY CTRE (HM10648) | | | | | | | | | | | | | | | | | | | | ● | | | | | |
| PRIOSE COLES (HM16635) | | | | | | | | | | | | | ● | | ● | ● | ● | | | | | | | | ● |
| RILEY, S (HM17347) | | | | | | | | | | | | | | | | | ● | | | | | | | | |
| SCUNTHORPE CHIROPRACTIC CLINIC (HM18157) | | | | | | | | | | | | | | | | | | | | | | | | | |
| THOMPSON, MARK (HM19989) | | | | | | | | | | | | | | | | | | | | ● | | | | | |
| WINN, NIGEL (HM21709) | | | | | | | | | | | | | | | | | | | | ● | | | | | |
| **HUMBERSIDE (NORTH)** | | | | | | | | | | | | | | | | | | | | | | | | | |
| BRIDLINGTON CHIROPODY SURGERY (HM03018) | | | | | | | | | | | | | | | | | | | | | | | | | |
| CARMAN, CAROL (HM03704) | | | | | | | | | | | | | | | | | | | | ● | | | | | |
| DAMIAN P JOHNS (HM05704) | | | | | | | | | | | | | | | | | | | | | | | | | |

| Business by County with Reference no. | Kirlian Photography | Laser Treatment | Life Style Coaching | Light Therapy | Macrobiotics | Magnetic Therapy | Manipulation | Manual Lymph Drainage | Massage (Therapeutic) | McTimoney Chiropractic | Meditation | Metamorphic Therapy | Miasm Therapy | Micro Manipulation | Moxibustion | Mud Therapy | Music Therapy | Nail Surgery | Naturopathy | Neuro-Linguistic Program | Neurotherapy | Nutritional Therapy | Orgone Therapy | Oriental Diagnosis | Orthomolecular Medicine |
|---|---|---|---|---|---|---|---|---|---|---|---|---|---|---|---|---|---|---|---|---|---|---|---|---|---|
| SOPWELL OSTEOPATHIC CLINIC (HM18894) | | | | | | | ● | | ● | | ● | | | | | | | | | | | | | | |
| SOUTH, JO (HM18917) | | | | | | | | | | | | | | | | | | | | | | | | | |
| SPINOZA, DAVID (HM19019) | ● | | | | | | | | | | | | | | | | | | ● | | | | | | |
| STORT COUNS & PSYCHOTHERAPY (HM19351) | | | | | | | | | | | | | | | | | | | | | | | | | |
| SURVIVAL TRUST SURGERY (HM19526) | | | | | | | | | | | | | | | | | | | | | | | | | |
| THOMAS, HELEN (HM19944) | | | | | | | | | | | | | | | | | | | | | | | | | |
| THOMPSON, MARK (HM19991) | | | | | | | | | | | | | | | | | | | ● | | | | | | |
| THOMPSON, MARK () | | | | | | | | | | | | | | | | | | | ● | | | | | | |
| WALFORD, PENELOPE (HM20756) | | | | | | | | | | | | | | | | | | | | | | | | | |
| WALKER, NEL (HM20791) | | | | | | | | | | | | | | | | | | | | | | | | | |
| WALKER, RICHARD (HM20798) | | | | | | | | | | | ● | | | | | | | | | | | | | | |
| WARREN, HELEN (HM20949) | | | | | | | | | | | | | | | | | | | | | | | | | |
| WATSON, KATHRYN (HM21015) | | | | | | | | | | | | | | | | | | | | | | ● | | | |
| WHITE, GRAHAM C (HM21355) | | | | | | | | | | | | | | | | | | | | | | ● | | | |
| WHITE, GRAHAM C (HM21356) | | | | | | | | | | | | | | | | | | | | | | | | | |
| WHITTONBOURNE, J (HM21428) | | | | | | | | | | | | | | | | | | | | | | | | | |
| WILLIAMS, NEVILLE L (HM21582) | | | | | | | | | ● | | | | | | | | | | | | | | | | |
| WOOD STREET CHIROPRACTIC CLNC (HM21780) | | | | | | | | | | | | | | | | | | | | | | | | | |
| WOOD STREET CLINIC (HM21781) | | | | | | | | | | | | | | | | | | | | | | ● | | | |
| WRIGHT, DOREEN (HM21931) | | | | | | | | | | | | | | | | | | | | | | | | | |
| WRIGHT, KAREN (HM21940) | | | | | | | | | | | | | | | | | | ● | | | | | | | |
| WYNDHAM CLINIC (HM21977) | | | | | | | ● | | ● | | ● | | | | | | | | | | | ● | | | |
| **HUMBERSIDE** | | | | | | | | | | | | | | | | | | | | | | | | | |
| EURO THERAPY PRACTICE (HM06943) | | | | | | | | | | | | | | | | | | | | | | | | | |
| INNERVISION HYPNOTHERAPY CTRE (HM10648) | | | | | | | | | | | | | | | | | | | | | | | | | |
| PRIOSE COLES (HM16635) | | | | | | | | | ● | | | | | | | | | | ● | | | ● | | | |
| RILEY, S (HM17347) | | | | | | | | | | | | | | | | | | | | | | | | | |
| SCUNTHORPE CHIROPRACTIC CLINIC (HM18157) | | | | | | | ● | | ● | | | | | | | | | | | | | | | | |
| THOMPSON, MARK (HM19989) | | | | | | | | | | | | | | | | | | | | | | | | | |
| WINN, NIGEL (HM21709) | | | | | | | | | | | | | | | | | | | | | | | | | |
| **HUMBERSIDE (NORTH)** | | | | | | | | | | | | | | | | | | | | | | | | | |
| BRIDLINGTON CHIROPODY SURGERY (HM03018) | | | | | | | | | ● | | | | | | | | | | | | | | | | |
| CARMAN, CAROL (HM03704) | | | | | | | | | | | | | | | | | | | | ● | | | | | |
| DAMIAN P JOHNS (HM05704) | | | | | | | | | | | | | | | | | | ● | | | | | | | |

# F - O Therapies at Practices/Businesses

| Business by County with Reference no. | Family Planning (Natural) | Family Therapy | Feldenkrais Methodology | Feng Shui | Floral Essence Therapy | Flotation Therapy | Gait Analysis | Gem Essence Therapy | Gestalt Therapy | Group Therapy | Hay Diet | Healer | Healing Therapy | Hellerwork | Herbal Medicine | Holistic Healing | Homeopathy | Hopi Ear Candles | Humanistic Psychology | Hypnosis | Hypnotherapy | Indian Head Massage | Inhalation Therapy | Iridology | Kinesiology | Kirlian Photography | Laser Treatment | Life Style Coaching | Light Therapy | Macrobiotics | Magnetic Therapy | Manipulation | Manual Lymph Drainage | Massage (Therapeutic) | McTimoney Chiropractic | Meditation | Metamorphic Therapy | Miasm Therapy | Micro Manipulation | Moxibustion | Mud Therapy | Music Therapy | Nail Surgery | Naturopathy | Neuro-Linguistic Program | Neurotherapy | Nutritional Therapy | Orgone Therapy | Oriental Diagnosis | Orthomolecular Medicine |
|---|---|---|---|---|---|---|---|---|---|---|---|---|---|---|---|---|---|---|---|---|---|---|---|---|---|---|---|---|---|---|---|---|---|---|---|---|---|---|---|---|---|---|---|---|---|---|---|---|---|---|
| EAST RIDING COLLEGE (HM06524) |||||||||||||●||||||||||||||||||||||||||||||||||||
| GREGORY, BRIAN (HM08517) |||||||||||||||||||●||||||||||||||||||||||||||||||
| NATURAL THERAPIES (HM14629) |●|||||||||||||||||||●|||||||||||||●||||||●||●||||||||
| NATURAL THERAPY CENTRE (HM14653) ||||||||||||||||||||●|||||||||||||||||||||||||||||||
| NATURAL THERAPY CENTRE (HM14638) |||||||||||||||||||●||||||||||||||||||||||||||||||
| SAMANTHA WHITE AROMATICA (HM17877) ||||||||||||●||||||||||●|||||||||||||●||||||||||||||||
| STARLIGHT CENTRE (HM19151) ||||||||||||||||||||||||●||||||||||||||||||||||||||
| HUMBERSIDE (SOUTH) ||||||||||||||||||||||||||||||||||||||||||||||||||
| LOUISE HEALING CENTRE (HM12668) ||||||||||||●|●||●|●|●||||●|●|||||||||||||●||●||||||||||||||||
| ROBINSON, KEITH (HM17488) ||||||||||||||||||||||||||||||||||||||||||●||||||||
| SCARTHO OSTEOPATHIC PRACTICE (HM18007) |||||||||||||||||||||||||||||||||●||||||||||||||||
| WEBB, C M (HM21057) ||||||||||||||||||||||||||||||||||||||||||●||||||||
| WINN, NIGEL (HM21710) |||||||||||||||||||●||||||||||||||||||||||||||||||
| ISLE OF WIGHT ||||||||||||||||||||||||||||||||||||||||||||||||||
| BAILEY, B M (HM01542) |||||||||||||||||||●|●|||||||||||||||||||||||||||||
| CARISBROOKE HEALTH CENTRE (HM03687) ||||||||||||||||||||||||||||||||||||||||||●||||||||
| CHRISTOPHER, JERRY (HM04453) ||||||||||||||||●||||||||||||||||||||||||||||||||||
| F VON - MEHREN (HM07034) ||||||||||||||||||||||||||||||||||||||||||●||||||||
| FOOTSTEPS (HM07510) ||||||||||||||||||||||||||||||||||||||||||●||||||||
| FOOTSTEPS THERAPY CENTRE (HM07513) ||||||||||||||||||||||||||||||||||||||||||●||||||||
| GREENFIELD, BRIAN (HM08484) ||||||||||||●|●|||●||||||●|||||||||||||●||●||||||||||||||||
| HOARE, MICHAEL C (HM09852) ||||||||||||||||●||||||||||||||||||||||||||||||||||
| HOPE CLINIC (HM10134) ||||||||||||||||●||||●|●|||●|||||||●||●|||||||||||||||||●||
| HYPNOTHERAPY CONSULTANCY (HM10537) ||||||||||||||||||||●|||||||||||||||||||||||||||||
| NORMAN, NANCY (HM15006) |||||||||||||||||||||||||||||||||||●||||||||||||||
| PERCIVAL, PAMELA (HM16017) |||||||||||||||||||●||||||||||||||||||||||||||||||
| SHEN CLINIC (HM18391) ||||||||||||||||||||●||||||||||||||||||●||||||●||||
| TOUCH FOR HEALTH (HM20186) |||||||||||||||||||||||||||||||||●||||||||||||||||
| WATCHBELL HSE NTRL THRPY CTRE (HM20979) ||||||||||||||||●||||||||||||||||||||||||||||||||||
| WRIGLEY, BARBARA (HM21956) |||||||||||||||||||||||||||||||||●||||||||||||||||
| KENT ||||||||||||||||||||||||||||||||||||||||||||||||||
| ABSOLUTE SOLUTIONS (HM00142) |||||||||||||||●|||||||||||||||||||||●||||||||||||||
| ARNOLD, M S (HM01034) ||||||||||||||||●||||||||||||||||||||||||||||||||||
| ASHFORD CLINIC (HM01216) ||||||||||||||||●||||||||||||||||||||||||||||||||||

# F - O Therapies at Practices/Businesses

Business by County with Reference no.

| Business | Family Planning (Natural) | Family Therapy | Feldenkrais Methodology | Feng Shui | Floral Essence Therapy | Flotation Therapy | Gait Analysis | Gem Essence Therapy | Gestalt Therapy | Group Therapy | Hay Diet | Healer | Healing Therapy | Hellerwork | Herbal Medicine | Holistic Healing | Homeopathy | Hopi Ear Candles | Humanistic Psychology | Hypnosis | Hypnotherapy | Indian Head Massage | Inhalation Therapy | Iridology | Kinesiology |
|---|---|---|---|---|---|---|---|---|---|---|---|---|---|---|---|---|---|---|---|---|---|---|---|---|---|
| AYLSHAM OSTEOPATHIC PRACTICE (HM01429) | | | | | | | | | | | | | | | | | | | | | | | | | |
| BAKER, ROY (HM01594) | | | | | | | | | | | | | | | | | | | | ● | | | | | |
| BEARD, ROSE (HM01966) | | | | | | | | | | | | | | | | | | | | ● | | | | | |
| BECKENHAM CHINESE MED CTRE (HM02019) | | | | | | | | | | | | | | | ● | | | | | | | | | | |
| BENNETT, J P (HM02142) | | | | | | | | | | | | | | | | | | | | ● | | | | | |
| BENNETT, J P (HM02143) | | | | | | | | | | ● | | | | | | | | | | | ● | | | | |
| BERGMANN, MARIA (DR) (HM02190) | | | | | | | | | | | | | | | ● | | | | | | | | | | |
| BEXLEYHEATH NATURAL HEALTH (HM02262) | | | | | | | | | | | | | | | | | ● | | | | ● | | | | |
| BISHOP, SARAH (HM02411) | | | | | | | | | | | | | | | | | | | | | | | | | |
| BLACKFEN HYPNOTHERAPY (HM02442) | | | | | | | | | ● | | | | | | | | | | | ● | ● | | | | |
| BRIAR (HM02984) | | | | | | | | | | | | | | | | | | | | ● | | | | | |
| BROMLEY CHIROPODY CENTRE (HM03142) | | | | | | | | | | | | | | | | | | | | | | | | | |
| BROMLEY CHIROPRACTIC CLINIC (HM03143) | | | | | | | | | | | | | | | | | | | | | | | | | ● |
| BRUCE, KATHRYN (HM03270) | | | | | | | | | | | | | | | | | ● | | | | | | | | |
| BURNETT, PAUL (HM03403) | | | | | | | | | | | | | | | | | ● | | | | | | | | |
| CANTERBURY OSTEOPATHIC CLINIC (HM03641) | ● | | | | | | | | | | ● | | ● | | | | | | | ● | | | | | |
| CARDWELL, MARTIN (HM03673) | | | | | | | | | | | | ● | ● | | ● | | | | | | | ● | | | |
| CASTLE CLINIC (HM03830) | | | | | | | | | | | | | | | | | | | | ● | ● | | | | |
| CENTRE (HM03897) | | | | | | | | | | | | | | | | | ● | | | | ● | | | | |
| CHANDRA PDS (HM03982) | | | | | | | | | | | | | | | | | | | | | | | | | ● |
| CHANGE OF LIFE (HM03984) | | | | | | | | | | | | | | | | | | | | | | | | | |
| CHIDWICK, SAMUEL (HM04160) | | | | | | | | | | | | | ● | | | | | | | | | | | | |
| CHINESE HERBAL MED & HLTH CARE (HM04202) | | | | | | | | | | | | | | | ● | | | | | | | | | | |
| CHIROPRACTIC PLUS (HM04402) | | | | | | | | | | | | | | | | | | | | | | | | ● | |
| CHISLEHURST NATURAL HEALTH (HM04410) | | | | | | | | | | | | | | | | | | | | | ● | | | | |
| CHISTLEHURST NATURAL HLTH CTRE (HM04411) | | | | | | | | | | | | | | | | ● | ● | | | | ● | ● | | | |
| CHRISTINE CHINNERY COMP THER (HM04446) | | | | | | | | | | | | | | | | | | | | | | | | | |
| CLARE, S M (HM04535) | | | | | | | | | | | | | | | | | | | | ● | | | | | |
| CLIFTON, NIGEL (HM04672) | | | | | | | | | | | | | | | | | | | | ● | | | | | |
| COLE, JEAN (HM04816) | | | | | | | | | | | | | | | | | ● | | | | | | | | |
| CORRIGAN, PETER (HM05195) | | | | | | | | | | | | | | | | | | | | ● | ● | | | | |
| COURT, SUSAN (HM05266) | | | | | | | | | | | | | | | | | | | | | | | | | |
| COURT, SUSAN (HM05265) | | | | | | | | | | | | | | | | | | | | | | | | | |
| COYSTEN & ASSOCIATES (HM05332) | | | | | | | | | | | | | | | | | | | | | | | | | |

| Business | Kirlian Photography | Laser Treatment | Life Style Coaching | Light Therapy | Macrobiotics | Magnetic Therapy | Manipulation | Manual Lymph Drainage | Massage (Therapeutic) | McTimoney Chiropractic | Meditation | Metamorphic Therapy | Miasm Therapy | Micro Manipulation | Moxibustion | Mud Therapy | Music Therapy | Nail Surgery | Naturopathy | Neuro-Linguistic Program | Neurotherapy | Nutritional Therapy | Orgone Therapy | Oriental Diagnosis | Orthomolecular Medicine |
|---|---|---|---|---|---|---|---|---|---|---|---|---|---|---|---|---|---|---|---|---|---|---|---|---|---|
| AYLSHAM OSTEOPATHIC PRACTICE (HM01429) | | | | | | | ● | | | | | | | | | | | | ● | | | | | | |
| BAKER, ROY (HM01594) | | | | | | | | | | | | | | | | | | | | | | | | | |
| BEARD, ROSE (HM01966) | | | | | | | | | | | | | | | | | | | | | | | | | |
| BECKENHAM CHINESE MED CTRE (HM02019) | | | | | | | | | | | | | | | | | | | | | | | | | |
| BENNETT, J P (HM02142) | | | | | | | | | | | | | | | | | | | | | | | | | |
| BENNETT, J P (HM02143) | | | | | | | | | | | | | | | | | | | | | | | | | |
| BERGMANN, MARIA (DR) (HM02190) | | | | | | | | | | | | | | | | | | | | | | | | | |
| BEXLEYHEATH NATURAL HEALTH (HM02262) | | | | | | | | | | | | | | | | | | | | | | | | | |
| BISHOP, SARAH (HM02411) | | | | | | | | | ● | | | | | | | | | | | | | | | | |
| BLACKFEN HYPNOTHERAPY (HM02442) | | | | | | | | | | | | | | | | | | | | | | | | | |
| BRIAR (HM02984) | | | | | | | | | | | | | | | | | | | | | | | | | |
| BROMLEY CHIROPODY CENTRE (HM03142) | | | | | | | | | | | | | | | | | | ● | | | | | | | |
| BROMLEY CHIROPRACTIC CLINIC (HM03143) | | | | | | | | | | | | | | | | | | | | | | | | | |
| BRUCE, KATHRYN (HM03270) | | | | | | | | | | | | | | | | | | | | | | | | | |
| BURNETT, PAUL (HM03403) | | | | | | | | | | | | | | | | | | | | | | | | | |
| CANTERBURY OSTEOPATHIC CLINIC (HM03641) | | | | | | | ● | | ● | | | | | | | | | | ● | | | ● | | | |
| CARDWELL, MARTIN (HM03673) | | | | | | | | | ● | | ● | | | | | | | | | | | | | | |
| CASTLE CLINIC (HM03830) | | | | | | | | | ● | | | | | | | | | | | | | | | | |
| CENTRE (HM03897) | | | | | | | | | | | ● | | | | | | | | | | | ● | | | |
| CHANDRA PDS (HM03982) | | | | | | | | | | | | | | | | | | | | | | | | | |
| CHANGE OF LIFE (HM03984) | | | | | | | | | | | | | | | | | | | | | | ● | | | |
| CHIDWICK, SAMUEL (HM04160) | | | | | | | | | | | | | | | | | | | | | | | | | |
| CHINESE HERBAL MED & HLTH CARE (HM04202) | | | | | | | | | | | | | | | | | | | | | | | | | |
| CHIROPRACTIC PLUS (HM04402) | | | | | | | | | | | | | | | | | | | | | | ● | | | |
| CHISLEHURST NATURAL HEALTH (HM04410) | | | | | | | | | | | | | | | | | | | | | | | | | |
| CHISTLEHURST NATURAL HLTH CTRE (HM04411) | | | | | | | | | ● | | | | | | | | | | | | | | | | |
| CHRISTINE CHINNERY COMP THER (HM04446) | | | | | | | | | ● | | | | | | | | | | | | | | | | |
| CLARE, S M (HM04535) | | | | | | | | | | | | | | | | | | | | | | | | | |
| CLIFTON, NIGEL (HM04672) | | | | | | | | | | | | | | | | | | | | | | | | | |
| COLE, JEAN (HM04816) | | | | | | | | | | | | | | | | | | | | | | | | | |
| CORRIGAN, PETER (HM05195) | | | | | | | | | | | | | | | | | | | | ● | | | | | |
| COURT, SUSAN (HM05266) | | | | | | | ● | | ● | | | | | | | | | | | | | | | | |
| COURT, SUSAN (HM05265) | | | | | | | ● | | ● | | | | | | | | | | | | | | | | |
| COYSTEN & ASSOCIATES (HM05332) | | | | | | | ● | | ● | | | | | | | | | | | | | | | | |

# F - O Therapies at Practices/Businesses

| Business by County with Reference no. | Family Planning (Natural) | Family Therapy | Feldenkrais Methodology | Feng Shui | Floral Essence Therapy | Flotation Therapy | Gait Analysis | Gem Essence Therapy | Gestalt Therapy | Group Therapy | Hay Diet | Healer | Healing Therapy | Hellerwork | Herbal Medicine | Holistic Healing | Homeopathy | Hopi Ear Candles | Humanistic Psychology | Hypnosis | Hypnotherapy | Indian Head Massage | Inhalation Therapy | Iridology | Kinesiology | Kirlian Photography | Laser Treatment | Life Style Coaching | Light Therapy | Macrobiotics | Magnetic Therapy | Manipulation | Manual Lymph Drainage | Massage (Therapeutic) | McTimoney Chiropractic | Meditation | Metamorphic Therapy | Miasm Therapy | Micro Manipulation | Moxibustion | Mud Therapy | Music Therapy | Nail Surgery | Naturopathy | Neuro-Linguistic Program | Neurotherapy | Nutritional Therapy | Orgone Therapy | Oriental Diagnosis | Orthomolecular Medicine |
|---|---|---|---|---|---|---|---|---|---|---|---|---|---|---|---|---|---|---|---|---|---|---|---|---|---|---|---|---|---|---|---|---|---|---|---|---|---|---|---|---|---|---|---|---|---|---|---|---|---|---|
| CULPEPER (HM05583) | | | | | | | | | | | | | | | ● | | | | | | | | | | | | | | | | | | | | | | | | | | | | | | | | | | | |
| DARWIN, EDWARD (HM05753) | | | | | | | | | | | | | | | | | | | | ● | | | | | | | | | | | | | | | | | | | | | | | | | | | | | | |
| DELTA MEDI CLINIC (HM05969) | | | | | | | | | | | | | | | | | | | | | | | | | | | | | | | | ● | | ● | | | | | | | | | | | | | | | | |
| DICKMAN, ANNIE (HM06080) | | | | | | | | | | | | | | | | | | | | | | | | | | | | | | | | | | ● | | | | | | | | | | | | | | | | |
| DILLON, MICHAEL (HM06100) | | | | | | | | | | ● | | | | | | | | | | ● | ● | | | | | | | | | | | | | | | | | | | | | | | | | | | | | |
| DIMENT, GORDON L (HM06105) | | | | | | | | | | | | | | | | | | | | ● | ● | | | | | | | | | | | | | | | | | | | | | | | | | | | | | |
| EARL, A (HM06496) | | | | | | | | | | | | | | | | | | | | | ● | | | | | | | | | | | | | | | | | | | | | | | | | | | | | |
| EAST, MARY (HM06530) | | | | | | | | | | | | | | | | | ● | | | | | | | | | | | | | | | | | | | | | | | | | | | | | | | | | |
| ELIZABETH ANNE (HM06736) | | | | | | | | | | | | | | | | | | | | ● | ● | | | | | | | | | | | | | | | | | | | | | | | | | | | | | |
| EUROPEAN AYUR-VEDA (HM06944) | | | | | | | | | | | | | | | | | | | | | | ● | | | | | | ● | | | | | | | | ● | | | | | | | | | | | | | | |
| EVANS, PHILIP (HM06987) | | | | | | | | | | | | | | | ● | | | | | | | | | | | | | | | | | | | | | | | | | | | | | | | | | | | |
| EVEGATE CLINIC (HM06996) | | | | | | | | | | | | | | | | | ● | | | | ● | | | | | | | | | | | | | | | | | | | | | | | | | | | | | |
| EVOLUTION HEALTH (HM07014) | | | | | | | | | | | | | | | ● | | | | | | | | | | | | | | | | | | | ● | | | | | | | | | | | | | ● | | | |
| FOORD, AUDREY (HM07463) | | | | | | | | | | | | | | | | | | | | | | ● | | | | | | | | | | | | | | | | | | | | | | | | | | | | |
| GIBSON, JAN (HM08040) | | ● | | | | | | | | ● | | ● | ● | | | ● | | | ● | ● | ● | ● | | | | | | ● | | | | | | | | ● | | | | | | | | | | | | | | |
| GILLINGHAM CLINIC OF COMP MED (HM08097) | | | | | | | | | | | | | | | | ● | ● | | | | | | | | | | | | | | | | | | | | | | | | | | | ● | | | | | | |
| GINSENG (HM08112) | | | | | | | | | | | | | | | ● | | | | | | | | | | | | | | | | | | | | | | | | | | | | | | | | | | | |
| GORING-THOMAS, DIANE (HM08290) | | | | | | | | | | | | | | | | | | | | | | | | | | | | | | | | | | ● | | | | | | | | | | | | | | | | |
| GRAHAM, W A (HM08363) | | | | | | | | | | | | | | | | | | | | ● | | | | | | | | | | | | | | | | | | | | | | | | | | | | | | |
| GRAVESEND HOMOEOPATHY CLINIC (HM08404) | | | | | | | | | | | | | | | | | ● | | | | | | | | | | | | | | | | | | | | | | | | | | | | | | | | | |
| GROVE, M (HM08612) | | | | | | | | | | | | | | | | | ● | | | | | | | | | | | | | | | | | | | | | | | | | | | | | | | | | |
| GUNN, JASON (HM08642) | | | | | | | | | | | | | | | | | ● | | | | | | | | | | | | | | | | | | | | | | | | | | | | | | | | | |
| HAMLIN-BRIGNALL, KATHRYN (HM08856) | | | | | | | | | | | | | | | | | | | | ● | | | | | | | | | | | | | | | | | | | | | | | | | | | | | | |
| HANNA, MARK (HM08932) | | | | | | | | | | | | | | | | | | | | ● | | | | | | | | | | | | | | | | | | | | | | | | | | | | | | |
| HANNA, MARK (HM08931) | | | | | | | | | | | ● | | | | | ● | | | | ● | ● | | | | | | | | | | | | | | | | | | | | | | | | | | | | | |
| HARWOOD, COLIN (HM09174) | | | | | | | | | | | | | | | | | | | | ● | | | | | | | | | | | | | | | | | | | | | | | | | | | | | | |
| HAWKHURST NATURAL THERAPIES (HM09216) | | | | | | | | | | | | | | | | | | | | | | | | | | | | | | | | | | ● | | | | | | | | | | | | | | | | |
| HEAD TO TOE WELL-BEING (HM09300) | | | | | | | | | | | | | | | | | | | | | | ● | | | | | | | | | | | | | | | | | | | | | | | | | | | | |
| HEALING AND HERBS (HM09325) | | | | | | | | | | | | ● | ● | | ● | | | | | | | ● | | | | | | | | | | | | ● | | ● | | | | | | | | | | | | | | |
| HEATHSIDE CENTRE (HM09461) | | | | | | | | | | | | | | | | | | ● | | | | ● | | | | | | | | | | | ● | ● | | | | | | | | | | | | | | | | |
| HOLDA-MARTIN, JACQUELINE (HM09921) | | | | | | | | | | | | | | | | | | | | ● | | | | | | | | | | | | | | | | | | | | | | | | | | | | | | |
| HOLISTIC THERAPIES (HM09993) | | | | | | | | | | | | | | | | | | | | | | ● | | | | | | | | | | | | | | | | | | | | | | | | | | | | |
| HOLMES, S A (HM10045) | | | | | | | | | | | | | | | | | | | | | | | | | | | | | | | | | | ● | | | | | | | | | | | | | | | | |
| HOOL, MERYL (HM10126) | | | | | | | | | | | | | | | | | ● | | | | | | | | | | | | | | | | | | | | | | | | | | | | | | | | | |

# F - O Therapies at Practices/Businesses

| Business by County with Reference no. | Family Planning (Natural) | Family Therapy | Feldenkrais Methodology | Feng Shui | Floral Essence Therapy | Flotation Therapy | Gait Analysis | Gem Essence Therapy | Gestalt Therapy | Group Therapy | Hay Diet | Healer | Healing Therapy | Hellerwork | Herbal Medicine | Holistic Healing | Homeopathy | Hopi Ear Candles | Humanistic Psychology | Hypnosis | Hypnotherapy | Indian Head Massage | Inhalation Therapy | Iridology | Kinesiology |
|---|---|---|---|---|---|---|---|---|---|---|---|---|---|---|---|---|---|---|---|---|---|---|---|---|---|
| HOWARD, TERRY (HM10244) | | | | | | | | | | | | | | | | | ● | | | | | | | | |
| HOWARD, TERRY (HM10243) | | | | | | | | | | | | | | | | | ● | | | | | | | | |
| HYPNOSIS COUNSELLING CENTRE (HM10497) | | | | | | | | | | | | | | | | | | | | ● | | | | | |
| ISIS (HM10763) | | | | | ● | | | ● | | | | ● | ● | | ● | | ● | | | | ● | ● | | ● | ● |
| JACCQUELINE ELLISON PRACTICE (HM10811) | | | | | | | | | | | | | | | | | | | | | | | | | |
| JACKSON, CELIA (HM10831) | | | | | | | | | | | | | | | | | | | | ● | | | | | |
| KARMERS CLINIQUE (HM11328) | | | | | | | | | | | | | | | | | | | | | | | | | |
| KENT CURATIVE HYPNOTHERAPY (HM11516) | | | | | | | | | | | | | | | | | | | | ● | | | | | |
| KSC (HM11812) | | | | | | | | | | | | | | | | | | | | | | | | | |
| LAMB, G BRIAN (HM11888) | | | | | | | | | | | ● | | ● | | ● | ● | | | | | | | | | |
| LANE, DAVID (HM11934) | | | | | | | | | | | | | | | | | | | | ● | | | | | |
| LOBB, BRIAN W (HM12528) | | ● | | | | | | | ● | | | | | | | | | | ● | ● | ● | | | | |
| MABBERLEY, KATHIE (HM12812) | | | | | | | | | | | | | | | | | | | | | | ● | | | |
| MARY CANNON - CLINICAL NUTRI (HM13221) | | | | | | | | | | | ● | | | | ● | ● | | | | | | | | | |
| MASON, T G (HM13252) | | | | | | | | | | | | | | | | | | | | ● | | | | | |
| MATHER, SUE (HM13281) | | | | | | | | | | | | | | | | | ● | | | | | | | | |
| MAY, CELIA (HM13342) | | | | | | | | | | | | | | | | | | | | ● | | | | | |
| MEISE, LINDA (HM13699) | | | | | | | | | | | | | | | | | | | | ● | | | | | |
| MEOPHAM CLINIC (HM13732) | | | | | | | | | | | | | | | ● | | ● | | | | | | | | |
| MICALLEF, JANICE (HM13791) | | | | | | | | | | | | | | | | | ● | | | | | | | | |
| MUIRHEAD, MARGARET (HM14323) | | | | | | | | | | | | | | | ● | | | | | | | | | | |
| MURRAY, R H (HM14412) | | | | | | | | | | | | | | | | | | | | ● | | | | | |
| NATURAL HEALTH CENTRE (HM14568) | | | | | | | | | | | | | ● | | ● | ● | ● | | | | | ● | | | |
| NATURAL THERAPIST (HM14635) | | | | | | | | | | | | | | | | ● | | | | | | | | | |
| NATURAL THERAPY CENTRE (HM14643) | | | | | | | | | | | | | | | ● | | | | | | | | | | |
| NEILL, BOB (HM14762) | | | | | | | | | | | | | | | | | | | | ● | | | | | |
| NORTH, SARAH (HM15047) | | | | | | | | | | | | | | | | | ● | | | | | | | | |
| OLD RECTORY (HM15261) | | | | | | | | | | | | | | | | | ● | | | | | | | | |
| OSBORNE, JEAN (HM15425) | | | | | | | | | | | | | | | | | ● | | | | | | | | |
| OSBORNE, JEAN (HM15424) | | | | | | | | | | | | | | | | | ● | | | | | | | | |
| PALMER, SUSAN (HM15618) | | | | | | | | | | | | | | | | | ● | | | | | | | | |
| PALMER, T J (HM15619) | | | | | | | | | | | | | | | | | | | | ● | | | | | |
| PARTINGTON, T (HM15762) | | | | | | | | | | | | | | | | | ● | | | | | | | | |
| PASSCHIER, CORNELIUS (HM15778) | | | | | | | | | | | | | | | | | ● | | | | | | | | |

| Business by County with Reference no. | Kirlian Photography | Laser Treatment | Life Style Coaching | Light Therapy | Macrobiotics | Magnetic Therapy | Manipulation | Manual Lymph Drainage | Massage (Therapeutic) | McTimoney Chiropractic | Meditation | Metamorphic Therapy | Miasm Therapy | Micro Manipulation | Moxibustion | Mud Therapy | Music Therapy | Nail Surgery | Naturopathy | Neuro-Linguistic Program | Neurotherapy | Nutritional Therapy | Orgone Therapy | Oriental Diagnosis | Orthomolecular Medicine |
|---|---|---|---|---|---|---|---|---|---|---|---|---|---|---|---|---|---|---|---|---|---|---|---|---|---|
| HOWARD, TERRY (HM10244) | | | | | | | | | | | | | | | | | | | | | | | | | |
| HOWARD, TERRY (HM10243) | | | | | | | | | | | | | | | | | | | | | | | | | |
| HYPNOSIS COUNSELLING CENTRE (HM10497) | | | | | | | | | | | | | | | | | | | | | | | | | |
| ISIS (HM10763) | | | ● | | | | | | | | ● | | | | | | | | ● | | | | | | |
| JACCQUELINE ELLISON PRACTICE (HM10811) | | | | | | | ● | | ● | | | | | | | | | | | | | | | | |
| JACKSON, CELIA (HM10831) | | | | | | | | | | | | | | | | | | | | | | | | | |
| KARMERS CLINIQUE (HM11328) | | | | | | | | ● | | | | | | | | | | | | | | | | | |
| KENT CURATIVE HYPNOTHERAPY (HM11516) | | | | | | | | | | | | | | | | | | | | | | | | | |
| KSC (HM11812) | | | | | | | | | ● | | | | | | | | | | | | | ● | | | |
| LAMB, G BRIAN (HM11888) | | | | | | | ● | | ● | | | | | | | | ● | | ● | | | ● | | | |
| LANE, DAVID (HM11934) | | | | | | | | | | | | | | | | | | | | | | | | | |
| LOBB, BRIAN W (HM12528) | | | | | | | | | | | | | | | | | | | | | | | | | |
| MABBERLEY, KATHIE (HM12812) | | | | | | | | | | | | | | | | | | | | | | | | | |
| MARY CANNON - CLINICAL NUTRI (HM13221) | | | | | ● | | | | | | | | | | | | | | | | | ● | | | ● |
| MASON, T G (HM13252) | | | | | | | | | | | | | | | | | | | | | | | | | |
| MATHER, SUE (HM13281) | | | | | | | | | | | | | | | | | | | | | | | | | |
| MAY, CELIA (HM13342) | | | | | | | | | | | | | | | | | | | | | | | | | |
| MEISE, LINDA (HM13699) | | | | | | | | | | | | | | | | | | | | | | | | | |
| MEOPHAM CLINIC (HM13732) | | | | | | | | | ● | | | | | | | | | | | | | | | | |
| MICALLEF, JANICE (HM13791) | | | | | | | | | | | | | | | | | | | | | | | | | |
| MUIRHEAD, MARGARET (HM14323) | | | | | | | | | | | | | | | | | | | | | | ● | | | |
| MURRAY, R H (HM14412) | | | | | | | | | | | | | | | | | | | | | | | | | |
| NATURAL HEALTH CENTRE (HM14568) | | | | | | | | | ● | | ● | | | | | | | | | | | ● | | | |
| NATURAL THERAPIST (HM14635) | | | | | | | ● | | ● | | | | | | | | | | | | | | | | |
| NATURAL THERAPY CENTRE (HM14643) | | | | | | | | | | | | | | | | | | | | | | | | | |
| NEILL, BOB (HM14762) | | | | | | | | | | | | | | | | | | | | | | | | | |
| NORTH, SARAH (HM15047) | | | | | | | | | | | | | | | | | | | | | | | | | |
| OLD RECTORY (HM15261) | | | | | | | | | | | | | | | | | | | | | | | | | |
| OSBORNE, JEAN (HM15425) | | | | | | | | | | | | | | | | | | | | | | | | | |
| OSBORNE, JEAN (HM15424) | | | | | | | | | | | | | | | | | | | | | | | | | |
| PALMER, SUSAN (HM15618) | | | | | | | | | | | | | | | | | | | | | | | | | |
| PALMER, T J (HM15619) | | | | | | | | | | | | | | | | | | | | | | | | | |
| PARTINGTON, T (HM15762) | | | | | | | | | | | | | | | | | | | | | | | | | |
| PASSCHIER, CORNELIUS (HM15778) | | | | | | | | | | | | | | | | | | | | | | | | | |

# F - O Therapies at Practices/Businesses

| Business by County with Reference no. | Family Planning (Natural) | Family Therapy | Feldenkrais Methodology | Feng Shui | Floral Essence Therapy | Flotation Therapy | Gait Analysis | Gem Essence Therapy | Gestalt Therapy | Group Therapy | Hay Diet | Healer | Healing Therapy | Hellerwork | Herbal Medicine | Holistic Healing | Homeopathy | Hopi Ear Candles | Humanistic Psychology | Hypnosis | Hypnotherapy | Indian Head Massage | Inhalation Therapy | Iridology | Kinesiology | Kirlian Photography | Laser Treatment | Life Style Coaching | Light Therapy | Macrobiotics | Magnetic Therapy | Manipulation | Manual Lymph Drainage | Massage (Therapeutic) | McTimoney Chiropractic | Meditation | Metamorphic Therapy | Miasm Therapy | Micro Manipulation | Moxibustion | Mud Therapy | Music Therapy | Nail Surgery | Naturopathy | Neuro-Linguistic Program | Neurotherapy | Nutritional Therapy | Orgone Therapy | Oriental Diagnosis | Orthomolecular Medicine |
|---|---|---|---|---|---|---|---|---|---|---|---|---|---|---|---|---|---|---|---|---|---|---|---|---|---|---|---|---|---|---|---|---|---|---|---|---|---|---|---|---|---|---|---|---|---|---|---|---|---|---|
| PASSCHIER, MAREANNE SASSEN (HM15779) | | | | | | | | | | | | ● | | | | ● | ● | | | | | | | | | | | | | | | | | | | ● | | | | | | | | | | | | | | |
| PATERSON, MARGARET (HM15814) | | | | | | | | | | | | | | | | | | | | | | ● | | | | | | | | | | | | | | | | | | | | | | | | | | | | |
| PELE, ANDRI (HM15950) | | | | | | | | | | | | | | | | | | | | | ● | | | | | | | | | | | | | | | | | | | | | | | | | | | | | |
| PHYSIOTHERAPY CENTRE (HM16230) | | | | | | | | | | | | | | | | | | | | | | | | | | | | | | | | | | | | | | | | | | | ● | | | | | | | |
| PINDER, F C (HM16307) | | | | | | | | | | | | | | | | | | | | ● | | | | | | | | | | | | | | | | | | | | | | | | | | | | | | |
| PROFESSIONAL HYPNOTHERAPY (HM16659) | | | | | | | | | | | | | | | | | | | | ● | | | | | | | | | | | | | | | | | | | | | | | | | | | | | | |
| PUNTER, WENDY (HM16761) | | | | | | | | | | | | | | | | | ● | | | | | | | | | | | | | | | | | | | | | | | | | | | | | | | | | |
| RALPH & EVANS (HM16906) | | | | | | | | | | | | | | | ● | | | | | | | | | | | | | | | | | | | | | | | | | | | | | | | | | | | |
| RALPH, ANITA (HM16909) | | | | | | | | | | | | | | | ● | | | | | | | | | | | | | | | | | | | | | | | | | | | | | | | | | | | |
| READ, CHARLES REG OSTEOPATH (HM16994) | | | | | | | | | | | | | | | | | | | | | | | | | | | | | | | | ● | | | | | | | | | | | | | | | | | | |
| REVEREND CAROL HADDERSLEY (HM17204) | | | | | | | | | | | | ● | | | | | | | | | | | | | | | | | | | | | | | | | | | | | | | | | | | | | | |
| RIDLEY, VICKY (HM17324) | | | | | | | | | | | | | | | ● | | | | | | | | | | | | | | | | | | | | | | | | | | | | | | | | | | | |
| ROMNEY MARSH OSTEOPATHS (HM17574) | | | | | | | | | | | | | | | | | | | | | | | | | | | | | | | | ● | | | | | | | | | | | | | | | | | | |
| ROSE, NAOMI (HM17612) | | | | | | | | | | | | ● | ● | | | | | | | | | | | | | | | | | | | | | ● | | | | | | | | | | | | | | | | |
| ROUND ROOM (HM17663) | | | | | | | | | | | | | | | | | | | | | | ● | | | | | | | | | | | | ● | | | | | | | | | | | | | | | | |
| ROWLAND, G A (HM17691) | | | | | | | | | | | | | | | | | | | | ● | | | | | | | | | | | | | | | | | | | | | | | | | | | | | | |
| RUTH, MOIRA (HM17779) | | | | | | | | | | | | | | | | | ● | | | | | | | | | | | | | | | | | | | | | | | | | | | | | | | | | |
| SANCTUM HOLISTIC THERAPY CTRE (HM17896) | | | | | | | | | | | | | | | | | | | | | | ● | | | | | | | | | | | | | | | | | | | | | | | | | | | | |
| SANDERS, PETER (HM17914) | | | | | | | | | | | | | | | | | | | | | | | | | | | | | | | | ● | | ● | | | | | | | | | | | | | | | | |
| SHANON, D (HM18288) | | | | | | | | | | | | | | | | | | | | ● | | | | | | | | | | | | | | | | | | | | | | | | | | | | | | |
| SHANTI HEALTH HERBAL PRODUCTS (HM18289) | | | | | | | | | | | | | | | ● | | | | | | | | | | | | | | | | | | | | | | | | | | | | | | | | | | | |
| SHIATSU (HM18451) | | | | | | | | | | | | | | | | ● | | | | | | | | | | | | | | | | | | ● | | ● | | | | | | | | | | | | | ● | |
| SHILLING, TARA (HM18473) | | | | | | | | | | | | | | | | | | | | ● | | | | | | | | | | | | | | | | | | | | | | | | | | | | | | |
| SOUTH EAST MASSAGE (HM18905) | | | | | | | | | | | | | ● | | | | | | | | | ● | | | | | | | | | | | | ● | | | | | | | | | | | | | | | | |
| SOUTH LONDON HYPNOTHERAPY CTRE (HM18910) | | | | | | | | | | | | | | | | | | | | ● | ● | | | | | | | | | | | | | | | | | | | | | | | | | | | | | |
| STARFIELDS HOLISTIC HLTH CTRE (HM19145) | | | | | | | | | | | ● | ● | ● | | ● | ● | ● | | ● | | | | | | ● | | | | | | | ● | | | | ● | | | | | | | | ● | | | | | | |
| STONE, CHARLES (HM19334) | | | | | | | | | | | | | ● | | | | | | | ● | ● | ● | | | | | | | | | | | | ● | | ● | | | | | | | | | ● | | | | | |
| STURGE, DEBBIE (HM19445) | | | | | | | | | | | | | | | | ● | | | | | | | | | | | | | | | | | | | | | | | | | | | | | | | ● | | | |
| TENTERDEN HOM PRACTICE (HM19838) | | | | | | | | | | | | | | | | | ● | | | | | | | | | | | | | | | | | | | | | | | | | | | | | | | | | |
| THERESA MAWSON (HM19914) | | | | | | | | | | | | | | | | | ● | | | | | | | | | | | | | | | | | | | | | | | | | | | | | | | | | |
| TONBRIDGE CLINIC (HM20151) | | | | | | | | | | | | | | | ● | | ● | | | | ● | | | | | | | | | | | ● | | ● | | | | | | | | | | ● | | | ● | | | |
| TONBRIDGE HOMOEOPATHIC CLINIC (HM20152) | | | | | | | | | | | | | | | | | ● | | | | | | | | | | | | | | | | | | | | | | | | | | | | | | | | | |
| TOYNE, JOY K (HM20206) | | | | | | | | | | | | | | | | | | | | ● | | | | | | | | | | | | | | | | | | | | | | | | | | | | | | |
| TURNER, ANDREA (HM20417) | | | | | | | | | | | | | | | | | | | | | | | | | | | | | | | | | | ● | | | | | | | | | | | | | | | | |

# F - O Therapies at Practices/Businesses

| Business by County with Reference no. | Family Planning (Natural) | Family Therapy | Feldenkrais Methodology | Feng Shui | Floral Essence Therapy | Flotation Therapy | Gait Analysis | Gem Essence Therapy | Gestalt Therapy | Group Therapy | Hay Diet | Healer | Healing Therapy | Hellerwork | Herbal Medicine | Holistic Healing | Homeopathy |
|---|---|---|---|---|---|---|---|---|---|---|---|---|---|---|---|---|---|
| USEFUL THERAPIES (HM20534) | | | | | | | | | | | | | | | | | |
| VARNEY, MONICA (HM20591) | | | | | | | | | | | | | | | | | |
| VIGNAUX, PATRICK (HM20662) | | | | | | | | | | | | | | | | | |
| VINCENT, EUNICE (HM20671) | | | | | | | | | | | | | | | | | |
| VINES REIKI HEALING CENTRE (HM20680) | | | | | | | | | | | | | | | | | |
| WATLING STREET THERAPY CTRE (HM21001) | | | | | | | | | | | | ● | | | ● | ● | ● |
| WELLS PHYSIO & SPORTS CLINIC (HM21168) | | | | | | | | | | | | | | | | | |
| WOLFE, ROBERT (HM21762) | | | | | | | | | | | | | | | | | |
| **LANCASHIRE** | | | | | | | | | | | | | | | | | |
| ABERNETHY, HILARY (HM00123) | | | | | | | | | | ● | | | | | | ● | |
| ACORN HYPNOTHERAPY SERVICES (HM00178) | | | | | | | | | | | | | | | | | |
| ACUPUNCTURE PRIVATE CLINIC (HM00317) | | | | | | | | | | | | | | | | | ● |
| ALEXANDER, GERRARD (HM00562) | | | | | | | | | | | | | | | ● | | |
| ALPHAWAVE (HM00685) | | | | | | | | | | | | | | | | | |
| ALTERNATIVE MEDICINE (HM00715) | | | | | | | | | | | ● | | | | | ● | ● |
| ALTERNATIVE MEDICINE PRACTICE (HM00721) | | | | | | | | | | | ● | | | | | ● | ● |
| BARLOWS (HM01725) | | | | | | | | | | | | | | | ● | | |
| BARNES, S C (HM01753) | | | | | | | | | | | | | | | | | |
| BARRETT & LIPTROTT (HM01783) | | | | | | | | | | | | | | | | | |
| BEESTON, J (HM02061) | | | | | | | | | | | | | | | ● | | |
| BENTLEY AND ASSOCIATES (HM02172) | | ● | | | | | | | | | | | | | | | |
| BFMP (HM02265) | | | | | | | | | | | | | | | | ● | ● |
| BIOS NATURE CLINIC (HM02344) | | | | | | | | | | | | | | | ● | | ● |
| BOLTON CLINIC OF ACUPUNCTURE (HM02657) | | | | | | | | | | | | | | | | | |
| BOLTON THERAPY CENTRE (HM02659) | | | | | | | | | | | | | | | | | ● |
| BRIDGWATER, K A (HM03016) | | | | | | | | | | | | | | | | | ● |
| BRIDGWATER, K A (HM03017) | | | | | | | | | | | | | | | | | ● |
| BRIGGS, JOHN C (HM03035) | | | | | | | | | | | | | | | | | |
| BRITISH HYPNOTHERAPY ASS (HM03083) | | | | | | | | | | | | | | | | | |
| BROOKES, MICHAEL (HM03163) | | | | | | | | | | | | | | | | | |
| BURLINSON, RENEE (HM03391) | | | | | | | | | | | | | | | | | |
| BURSCOUGH PHYSIOTHERAPY (HM03425) | | | | | | | | | | | | | | | | | |
| CENTRE FOR COMP MEDICINE (HM03900) | | | | | | | | | | | | | | | | | ● |
| CHARTERED PHYSIO & SPORTS (HM04041) | | | | | | | | | | | | | | | | | |

| Business by County with Reference no. | Hopi Ear Candles | Humanistic Psychology | Hypnosis | Hypnotherapy | Indian Head Massage | Inhalation Therapy | Iridology | Kinesiology | Kirlian Photography | Laser Treatment | Life Style Coaching | Light Therapy | Macrobiotics | Magnetic Therapy | Manipulation | Manual Lymph Drainage | Massage (Therapeutic) |
|---|---|---|---|---|---|---|---|---|---|---|---|---|---|---|---|---|---|
| USEFUL THERAPIES (HM20534) | | | ● | ● | | | | ● | | | | | | | | | |
| VARNEY, MONICA (HM20591) | | | | | | | | | | | | | | | | | |
| VIGNAUX, PATRICK (HM20662) | | | ● | | | | | | | | | | | | | | |
| VINCENT, EUNICE (HM20671) | | | | | | | | | | | | | | | | | ● |
| VINES REIKI HEALING CENTRE (HM20680) | | | | | | | | | | | | | | | | ● | |
| WATLING STREET THERAPY CTRE (HM21001) | | | ● | ● | ● | ● | ● | ● | | | ● | | | | | | ● |
| WELLS PHYSIO & SPORTS CLINIC (HM21168) | | | | | | | | | | | | | | | ● | | |
| WOLFE, ROBERT (HM21762) | | | | | | | | | | | | | | | | | |
| **LANCASHIRE** | | | | | | | | | | | | | | | | | |
| ABERNETHY, HILARY (HM00123) | | | | | | | | | | | ● | | | | | | ● |
| ACORN HYPNOTHERAPY SERVICES (HM00178) | | | | | | | | | | | | | | | | | |
| ACUPUNCTURE PRIVATE CLINIC (HM00317) | | | | | | | | | | | | | | | | | |
| ALEXANDER, GERRARD (HM00562) | | | | | | | | | | | | | | | | | |
| ALPHAWAVE (HM00685) | | | | ● | | | | | | | | | | | | | |
| ALTERNATIVE MEDICINE (HM00715) | | | | ● | | | | | | | | | | | ● | | |
| ALTERNATIVE MEDICINE PRACTICE (HM00721) | | | | ● | | | | | | | | | | | ● | | |
| BARLOWS (HM01725) | | | | | | | | | | | | | | | | | |
| BARNES, S C (HM01753) | | | ● | | | | | | | | | | | | | | |
| BARRETT & LIPTROTT (HM01783) | | | | | | | | | | | | | | | | | |
| BEESTON, J (HM02061) | | | | | | | | | | | | | | | ● | | ● |
| BENTLEY AND ASSOCIATES (HM02172) | | | | | | | | | | | | | | | ● | | ● |
| BFMP (HM02265) | | | | | ● | | | | | | | | | | | | ● |
| BIOS NATURE CLINIC (HM02344) | | | | | | | | | | | | | | | | | |
| BOLTON CLINIC OF ACUPUNCTURE (HM02657) | | | | ● | | | | | | | | | | | | | |
| BOLTON THERAPY CENTRE (HM02659) | | | | ● | | | | | | | | | | | ● | | ● |
| BRIDGWATER, K A (HM03016) | | | | | | | | | | | | | | | | | |
| BRIDGWATER, K A (HM03017) | | | | | | | | | | | | | | | | | |
| BRIGGS, JOHN C (HM03035) | | | ● | | | | | | | | | | | | | | |
| BRITISH HYPNOTHERAPY ASS (HM03083) | | | ● | | | | | | | | | | | | | | |
| BROOKES, MICHAEL (HM03163) | | | | | | | | | | | | | | | | | |
| BURLINSON, RENEE (HM03391) | | | ● | | | | | | | | | | | | | | |
| BURSCOUGH PHYSIOTHERAPY (HM03425) | | | | | | | | | | | | | | | ● | | |
| CENTRE FOR COMP MEDICINE (HM03900) | | | | | | | | | | | | | | | | | |
| CHARTERED PHYSIO & SPORTS (HM04041) | | | | | | | | | | | | | | | ● | | |

| Business by County with Reference no. | McTimoney Chiropractic | Meditation | Metamorphic Therapy | Miasm Therapy | Micro Manipulation | Moxibustion | Mud Therapy | Music Therapy | Nail Surgery | Naturopathy | Neuro-Linguistic Program | Neurotherapy | Nutritional Therapy | Orgone Therapy | Oriental Diagnosis | Orthomolecular Medicine |
|---|---|---|---|---|---|---|---|---|---|---|---|---|---|---|---|---|
| USEFUL THERAPIES (HM20534) | | | | | | | | | | | | | | | | |
| VARNEY, MONICA (HM20591) | | | ● | | | | | | | | | | | | | |
| VIGNAUX, PATRICK (HM20662) | | | | | | | | | | | | | | | | |
| VINCENT, EUNICE (HM20671) | | | | | | | | | | | | | | | | |
| VINES REIKI HEALING CENTRE (HM20680) | | ● | | | | | | | | | | | | | | |
| WATLING STREET THERAPY CTRE (HM21001) | | ● | | | | | | | | ● | | | ● | | ● | |
| WELLS PHYSIO & SPORTS CLINIC (HM21168) | | | | | | | | | | | | | | | | |
| WOLFE, ROBERT (HM21762) | | | | | | | | | ● | | | | | | | |
| **LANCASHIRE** | | | | | | | | | | | | | | | | |
| ABERNETHY, HILARY (HM00123) | | ● | | | | | | | | | | | | | | |
| ACORN HYPNOTHERAPY SERVICES (HM00178) | | | | | | | | | | | ● | | | | | |
| ACUPUNCTURE PRIVATE CLINIC (HM00317) | | | | | | | | | | | | | | | | |
| ALEXANDER, GERRARD (HM00562) | | | | | | | | | | | | | | | | |
| ALPHAWAVE (HM00685) | | | | | | | | | | | | | | | | |
| ALTERNATIVE MEDICINE (HM00715) | | | | | | | | | | ● | | | ● | | | ● |
| ALTERNATIVE MEDICINE PRACTICE (HM00721) | | | | | | | | | | ● | | | ● | | | ● |
| BARLOWS (HM01725) | | | | | | | | | | | | | | | | |
| BARNES, S C (HM01753) | | | | | | | | | | | | | | | | |
| BARRETT & LIPTROTT (HM01783) | | | | | | | | | ● | | | | | | | |
| BEESTON, J (HM02061) | | | | | | | | | | | | | | | | |
| BENTLEY AND ASSOCIATES (HM02172) | | | | | | | | | | | | | | | | |
| BFMP (HM02265) | | | | | | | | | | | | | | | | |
| BIOS NATURE CLINIC (HM02344) | | | | | | | | | | ● | | | | | | |
| BOLTON CLINIC OF ACUPUNCTURE (HM02657) | | | | | | | | | | | | | | | | |
| BOLTON THERAPY CENTRE (HM02659) | | | | | ● | ● | | | | | | | | | | |
| BRIDGWATER, K A (HM03016) | | | | | | | | | | | | | | | | |
| BRIDGWATER, K A (HM03017) | | | | | | | | | | | | | | | | |
| BRIGGS, JOHN C (HM03035) | | | | | | | | | | | | | | | | |
| BRITISH HYPNOTHERAPY ASS (HM03083) | | | | | | | | | | | | | | | | |
| BROOKES, MICHAEL (HM03163) | | | | | | | | | | ● | | | ● | | | |
| BURLINSON, RENEE (HM03391) | | | | | | | | | | | | | | | | |
| BURSCOUGH PHYSIOTHERAPY (HM03425) | | | | | | | | | | | | | | | | |
| CENTRE FOR COMP MEDICINE (HM03900) | | | | | | | | | | | | | | | | |
| CHARTERED PHYSIO & SPORTS (HM04041) | | | | | | | | | | | | | | | | |

# F - O Therapies at Practices/Businesses

| Business by County with Reference no. | Family Planning (Natural) | Family Therapy | Feldenkrais Methodology | Feng Shui | Floral Essence Therapy | Flotation Therapy | Gait Analysis | Gem Essence Therapy | Gestalt Therapy | Group Therapy | Hay Diet | Healer | Healing Therapy | Hellerwork | Herbal Medicine | Holistic Healing | Homeopathy | Hopi Ear Candles | Humanistic Psychology | Hypnosis | Hypnotherapy | Indian Head Massage | Inhalation Therapy | Iridology | Kinesiology | Kirlian Photography | Laser Treatment | Life Style Coaching | Light Therapy | Macrobiotics | Magnetic Therapy | Manipulation | Manual Lymph Drainage | Massage (Therapeutic) | McTimoney Chiropractic | Meditation | Metamorphic Therapy | Miasm Therapy | Micro Manipulation | Moxibustion | Mud Therapy | Music Therapy | Nail Surgery | Naturopathy | Neuro-Linguistic Program | Neurotherapy | Nutritional Therapy | Orgone Therapy | Oriental Diagnosis | Orthomolecular Medicine |
|---|---|---|---|---|---|---|---|---|---|---|---|---|---|---|---|---|---|---|---|---|---|---|---|---|---|---|---|---|---|---|---|---|---|---|---|---|---|---|---|---|---|---|---|---|---|---|---|---|---|---|
| CHATFIELD, KATE (HM04062) | | | | | | | | | | | | | | | | ● | | | | | | | | | | | | | | | | | | | | | | | | | | | | | | | | | | |
| COLES, RONNIE (HM04836) | | | | | | | | | | | | | | | | | | | | | | | | | | | | | | | | | | | | | | | | | | ● | | | | | | | | |
| COMPLEMENTARY HEALTH SERVICES (HM04929) | | | | | | | | | | | | | | | | ● | | | | | | | | | | | | | | | ● | | ● | | | | | | | | | | | | | | | | | |
| COMPLEMENTARY THERAPY CENTRE (HM04944) | | | | | | | | | | | | | | | | | | | ● | | | | | | | | | | | | | | | | | | | | | | | | | | | | | | | |
| DACRELANDS CLINIC (HM05667) | | | | | | | | | | | | ● | | ● | | | | | ● | | | | | | | | | | | | | | | | | | | | | | | | | | | | | | | |
| DAVIES, JOHNATHON (HM05819) | | | | | | | | | | | | | | | | | | | | | | | | | | | | | | | | | | | | | | | | | | ● | | | | | | | | |
| DENNEY, ANDREA (HM05985) | | | | | | | | | | | | | | ● | | | | | | | | | | | | | | | | | | | | | | | | | | | | | | | | | | | | |
| DOVE, JOHN (HM06227) | | | | | | | | | | | | | | | | | | | ● | | | | | | | | | | | | | | | | | | | | | | | | | | | | | | | |
| DOWDALL, TONY (HM06233) | | | | | | | | | | | | | | | | ● | | | | | | | | | | | | | | | | | | | | | | | | | | | | | | | | | | |
| DUCKWORTH, JEAN (HM06348) | | | | | | | | | | | | | | | | ● | | | | | | | | | | | | | | | | | | | | | | | | | | | | | | | | | | |
| DUCKWORTH, JEAN (HM06347) | | | | | | | | | | | | | | | | ● | | | | | | | | | | | | | | | | | | | | | | | | | | | | | | | | | | |
| DUKES, MARTIN (HM06374) | | | | | | | | | | | | | | | | | | | ● | | | | | | | | | | | | | | | | | | | | | | | | | | | | | | | |
| GIBSON, STEPHEN J (HM08046) | | | | | | | | | | | | | | | | | | | ● | | | | | | | | | | | | | | | | | | | | | | | | | | | | | | | |
| GINSBERG, ANNE (HM08111) | | | | | | | | | | | ● | ● | | | ● | | | | | | | | | | | | ● | | | | | | | | ● | | | | | | | | | | | | | | | |
| GREENHALGH, A J T (HM08489) | | | | | | | | | | | | | | | | | | | | | | | | | | | | | | | | | | | | | | | | | | ● | | | | | | | | |
| GREENMOUNT HYPNOTHERAPY CENTRE (HM08493) | | | | | | | | | | | | | | | | | | | ● | | | | | | | | | | | | | | | | | | | | | | | | | | | | | | | |
| GROGAN, DIANA E (HM08592) | | | | | | | | | | | | | | | | ● | | | | ● | | | | | | | | | | | ● | | ● | | | | | | ● | | | | | | | | | | | |
| HARMONIOUS HEALTHCARE (HM09015) | | | | | | | | | | | | | | | | | ● | | | | ● | | | | | | | | | | | | ● | | | | | | | | | | | | | | | | | |
| HAWORTH, DAVID (HM09237) | | | | | | | | | | | | | | | | | | | ● | | | | | | | | | | | | | | | | | | | | | | | | | | | | | | | |
| HEAVENS SCENT AROMATHERAPY (HM09478) | | | | | | | | | | | | | | | | | | | | | | | | | | | | | | | | | ● | | | | | | | | | | | | | | | | | |
| HERBAL HEALTH (HM09615) | | | | | | | | | | | | | | ● | | | | | | | | | | | | | | | | | | | | | | | | | | | | | | | | | | | | |
| HYPNOTHERAPIST CENTRE-FYLDE (HM10503) | | | | | | | | | | | | | | | | | | | ● | | | | | | | | | | | | | | | | | | | | | | | | | | | | | | | |
| HYPNOTHERAPY CENTRE (HM10520) | | | | | | | | | | | | | | | | | | | ● | | | | | | | | | | | | | | | | | | | | | | | | | | | | | | | |
| HYPNOTHERAPY CENTRE BURNLEY (HM10533) | | | | | | | | | | | | | | | | | | | ● | | | | | | | | | | | | | | | | | | | | | | | | | | | | | | | |
| INSPIRED TECHNOLOGY (HM10660) | | | | | | | | | | | | | | | | | | | | | | | | | | | | | | ● | | | | | | | | | | | | | | | | | | | | |
| ISHERWOOD, NIGEL (HM10759) | | | | | | | | | | | | | | | | | | | ● | | | | | | | | | | | | | | | | | | | | | | | | | | | | | | | |
| J H W PSYCHOLOGICAL SERVICES (HM10797) | | | | | | | | | | | | | | | | | | | ● | | | | | | | | | | | | | | | | | | | | | | | | | | | | | | | |
| JOHN HOLDEN ASSOCIATES (HM11051) | | | | | | | | | | | | | | | | | | | | | | | | | | | | | | | | | | | | | | | | | | ● | | | | | | | | |
| KARIM, S (HM11325) | | | | | | | | | | | | | | | | | | | ● | | | | | | | | | | | | | | | | | | | | | | | | | | | | | | | |
| KELLY CHIROPODY (HM11424) | | | | | | | | | | | | | | | | | | | | | ● | | | | | | | | | | | | | | | | | | | | | | | | | | | | | |
| KENDEL HOUSE CLINIC (HM11479) | | | | | | | | | | | | | | | | ● | | | | ● | | | | | | | | | | | | | | | | | | | | | | | | | | | | | | |
| LAMBOURN COURT STRESS MNGMT (HM11906) | | | | | | | | | | | | | | | | | | | ● | | | | | | | | | | | | | | | | | | | | | | | | | | | | | | | |
| LANCASTER, L (HM11917) | | | | | | | | | | | | | | | | | | | ● | | | | | | | | | | | | | | | | | | | | | | | | | | | | | | | |
| LAYNE, SUSAN G (HM12077) | | | | | | | | | | | | | | | | | | | | | | | | | | | | | | | | | ● | | ● | ● | | | | | | | | | | | | | | |

www.healthmyself.com

F-0 THERAPIES AVAILABLE England (by County)

# F - O Therapies at Practices/Businesses

| Business by County with Reference no. | Family Planning (Natural) | Family Therapy | Feldenkrais Methodology | Feng Shui | Floral Essence Therapy | Flotation Therapy | Gait Analysis | Gem Essence Therapy | Gestalt Therapy | Group Therapy | Hay Diet | Healer | Healing Therapy | Hellerwork | Herbal Medicine | Holistic Healing | Homeopathy | Hopi Ear Candles | Humanistic Psychology | Hypnosis | Hypnotherapy | Indian Head Massage | Inhalation Therapy | Iridology | Kinesiology |
|---|---|---|---|---|---|---|---|---|---|---|---|---|---|---|---|---|---|---|---|---|---|---|---|---|---|
| MAKRAND, HOWARD (HM12957) | | | | | | | | | | | | | | | ● | | | | | | | | | | |
| MALKIN, DK, MANIP THERAPY (HM12975) | | | | | | | | | | | | | | | | | | | | | | | | | |
| MASTERS, DAVID (HM13274) | | | | | | | | | | | | | | | | | | | | ● | | | | | |
| NAT COLLEGE-HYPNOSIS/PSYCHO (HM14496) | | | | | | | | | | | | | | | | | | | | ● | | | | | |
| NATURAL HEALTH CENTRE (HM14566) | | | | | | | | | | | | | | | | | ● | | | | | ● | | | |
| NELSON, S (HM14782) | | | | | | | | | | | | | | | | ● | | | | | | | | | |
| NUTTELL, DAVE (HM15133) | | | | | | | | | | | | | | | | | | | | ● | | | | | |
| ONE STOP HEALTH & BEAUTY (HM15323) | | | | | ● | | | | | | | ● | | | | ● | ● | | | | | ● | | | |
| O'NEILL, RICHARD (HM15337) | | | | | | | | | | | | | | | | | | | | ● | | | | | |
| P MATTHEWS STRESS MNGMT (HM16072) | | | | | | | | | | | | | | | | | | | | ● | | | | | |
| PEN-Y-BRYN HOLISTIC THERAPY (HM16003) | | | | | | | | | | | | | ● | | | | | ● | | | | ● | | | ● |
| PEPPER, JOHN (HM16009) | | | | | | | | | | | | ● | | | | | | | | | | | | | |
| PHYSIO AND SPORTS INJURIES (HM16195) | | | | | | | | | | | | | | | | | | | | | | | | | ● |
| POTTER, CHRISTINE (HM16464) | | | | | | | | | | | | | | | ● | | | | | | | | | | |
| PRESTON CLINIC OF HERBAL MED (HM16548) | | | | | | | | | | | | | | | ● | | | | | | | | | | |
| PURE HEALTH (HM16765) | | | | | | | | | | | | | | | ● | | ● | | | | | | | | |
| RAMSBOTTOM PHYSIO CLINIC (HM16919) | | | | | | | | | | | | | | | | | | | | | | | | | |
| RATCLIFFE, MARK (HM16949) | | | | | | | | | | | | | | | | | | | | | | | | | |
| RILEY, SUSAN M (HM17348) | | | | | | | | | | | | | | | | | ● | | | | | | | | |
| ROTHWELL, K (HM17660) | | | | | | | | | | | | | | | | | | | | ● | | | | | |
| SEARS, J (HM18176) | | | | | | | | | | | | | | | | | | | | ● | | | | | |
| SPIRITUAL THERAPIST (HM19029) | | | | | | | | | | | | ● | ● | | | ● | | | | | | | | | |
| ST GEORGES MULTI THERAPY CTRE (HM19075) | | ● | | | | | | | | ● | | | | | ● | | ● | | | ● | ● | ● | | | |
| ST MARY'S CLINIC (HM19087) | | | | | | | | | | | | | | | | | | | | | | | | | |
| SUTHERLAND, COLIN J (HM19537) | | | | | | | | | | | | | | | | | | | | ● | | | | | |
| TATTERSALL, KAREN (HM19719) | | | | | | | | | | | | | | | | | | | | | | | | | |
| TIP TOES (HM20086) | | | | | | | | | | | | | | | | | | | | | | ● | | | |
| TOMLINSON, JUDITH (HM20142) | | | | | | | | | | | | | | | | | | | | | | | | | |
| TRADITIONAL CHINESE MED CTRE (HM20223) | | | | | | | | | | | | | | | ● | | | | | | | | | | |
| TRAINING SCH OF HYPNO & PSYCHO (HM20249) | | | | | | | | | | | | | | | | | | | | ● | | | | | |
| UPHAM, GILL (HM20522) | | | | | | | | | | | | | | | | ● | ● | | | | | | | | |
| WATKINSON, BARBARA (HM20999) | | | | | | | | | | | | | | | | | | | | | | ● | | | |
| WILBY, J (HM21483) | | | | | | | | | | | | | | | ● | | | | | | | | | | |
| WILLIAMS, L (HM21577) | | | | | | | | | | | | | | | | | | | | ● | | | | | |

| Business by County with Reference no. | Kirlian Photography | Laser Treatment | Life Style Coaching | Light Therapy | Macrobiotics | Magnetic Therapy | Manipulation | Manual Lymph Drainage | Massage (Therapeutic) | McTimoney Chiropractic | Meditation | Metamorphic Therapy | Miasm Therapy | Micro Manipulation | Moxibustion | Mud Therapy | Music Therapy | Nail Surgery | Naturopathy | Neuro-Linguistic Program | Neurotherapy | Nutritional Therapy | Orgone Therapy | Oriental Diagnosis | Orthomolecular Medicine |
|---|---|---|---|---|---|---|---|---|---|---|---|---|---|---|---|---|---|---|---|---|---|---|---|---|---|
| MAKRAND, HOWARD (HM12957) | | | | | | | | | | | | | | | | | | | | | | | | | |
| MALKIN, DK, MANIP THERAPY (HM12975) | | | | | | | ● | | ● | | | | | | | | | | | | | | | | |
| MASTERS, DAVID (HM13274) | | | | | | | | | | | | | | | | | | | | | | | | | |
| NAT COLLEGE-HYPNOSIS/PSYCHO (HM14496) | | | | | | | | | | | | | | | | | | | | | | | | | |
| NATURAL HEALTH CENTRE (HM14566) | | | | | | | | | ● | | | | | | | | | | | | | ● | | | |
| NELSON, S (HM14782) | | | | | | | | | | | | | | | | | | | | | | | | | |
| NUTTELL, DAVE (HM15133) | | | | | | | | | | | | | | | | | | | | | | | | | |
| ONE STOP HEALTH & BEAUTY (HM15323) | | | ● | | | | ● | | ● | | ● | | | | | | | | | | | | | | |
| O'NEILL, RICHARD (HM15337) | | | | | | | | | | | | | | | | | | | | | | | | | |
| P MATTHEWS STRESS MNGMT (HM16072) | | | | | | | | | | | | | | | | | | | | | | | | | |
| PEN-Y-BRYN HOLISTIC THERAPY (HM16003) | | | | | | | | | ● | | | | | | | | | | | | | | | | |
| PEPPER, JOHN (HM16009) | | | ● | | | | | | | | ● | | | | | | | | | | | | | | |
| PHYSIO AND SPORTS INJURIES (HM16195) | | | | | | | ● | | ● | | | | | ● | | | | | | | | | | | |
| POTTER, CHRISTINE (HM16464) | | | | | | | | | | | | | | | | | | | | | | | | | |
| PRESTON CLINIC OF HERBAL MED (HM16548) | | | | | | | | | | | | | | | | | | | | | | | | | |
| PURE HEALTH (HM16765) | | | ● | | | | ● | | ● | | | | | | | | | | ● | | | ● | | | |
| RAMSBOTTOM PHYSIO CLINIC (HM16919) | | | | | | | ● | | ● | | | | | | | | | | | | | | | | |
| RATCLIFFE, MARK (HM16949) | | | | | | | ● | | | | | | | | | | | | ● | | | | | | |
| RILEY, SUSAN M (HM17348) | | | | | | | | | | | | | | | | | | | | | | | | | |
| ROTHWELL, K (HM17660) | | | | | | | | | | | | | | | | | | | | | | | | | |
| SEARS, J (HM18176) | | | | | | | | | | | | | | | | | | | | | | | | | |
| SPIRITUAL THERAPIST (HM19029) | | | | | | | | | | | ● | | | | | | | | | | | | | | |
| ST GEORGES MULTI THERAPY CTRE (HM19075) | | | ● | | | | | | | | | | | | | | | | | | | | | | |
| ST MARY'S CLINIC (HM19087) | | | | | | | ● | | ● | | | | | | | | | | | | | | | | |
| SUTHERLAND, COLIN J (HM19537) | | | | | | | | | | | | | | | | | | | | | | | | | |
| TATTERSALL, KAREN (HM19719) | | | | | | | | | | | | | | | | | | ● | | | | | | | |
| TIP TOES (HM20086) | | | | | | | | | | | | | | | | | | | | | | | | | |
| TOMLINSON, JUDITH (HM20142) | | | | | | | | | ● | | | | | | | | | | | | | | | | |
| TRADITIONAL CHINESE MED CTRE (HM20223) | | | | | | | | | | | | | | | ● | | | | | | | | | ● | |
| TRAINING SCH OF HYPNO & PSYCHO (HM20249) | | | | | | | | | | | | | | | | | | | | | | | | | |
| UPHAM, GILL (HM20522) | | | | | | | | | | | | | | | | | | | | | | | | | |
| WATKINSON, BARBARA (HM20999) | | | | | | | | | ● | | | | | | | | | | | | | | | | |
| WILBY, J (HM21483) | | | | | | | | | | | | | | | | | | | | | | | | | |
| WILLIAMS, L (HM21577) | | | | | | | | | | | | | | | | | | | | | | | | | |

# F - O Therapies at Practices/Businesses

| Business by County with Reference no. | Family Planning (Natural) | Family Therapy | Feldenkrais Methodology | Feng Shui | Floral Essence Therapy | Flotation Therapy | Gait Analysis | Gem Essence Therapy | Gestalt Therapy | Group Therapy | Hay Diet | Healer | Healing Therapy | Hellerwork | Herbal Medicine | Holistic Healing | Homeopathy | Hopi Ear Candles | Humanistic Psychology | Hypnosis | Hypnotherapy | Indian Head Massage | Inhalation Therapy | Iridology | Kinesiology | Kirlian Photography | Laser Treatment | Life Style Coaching | Light Therapy | Macrobiotics | Magnetic Therapy | Manipulation | Manual Lymph Drainage | Massage (Therapeutic) | McTimoney Chiropractic | Meditation | Metamorphic Therapy | Miasm Therapy | Micro Manipulation | Moxibustion | Mud Therapy | Music Therapy | Nail Surgery | Naturopathy | Neuro-Linguistic Program | Neurotherapy | Nutritional Therapy | Orgone Therapy | Oriental Diagnosis | Orthomolecular Medicine |
|---|---|---|---|---|---|---|---|---|---|---|---|---|---|---|---|---|---|---|---|---|---|---|---|---|---|---|---|---|---|---|---|---|---|---|---|---|---|---|---|---|---|---|---|---|---|---|---|---|---|---|
| WILSON, G (HM21656) | | | | | | | | | | | | | | | | | | | ● | ● | ● | | | | | | | | | | | | | | | | | | | | | | | | | | | | | |
| WOOD, ALISON (HM21785) | | | | | | | | | | | | | | | | | | | | | | | | | | | | | | | | | | ● | | | | | | | | | | | | | | | | |
| WRIGHT, J D (HM21934) | | | | | | | | | | | | | | | | | | | | ● | | | | | | | | | | | | | | | | | | | | | | | | | | | | | | |
| **LEICESTERSHIRE** | | | | | | | | | | | | | | | | | | | | | | | | | | | | | | | | | | | | | | | | | | | | | | | | | | |
| ACUHERB (HM00212) | | | | | | | | | | | | | | | ● | | | | | | | | | | | | | | | | | | | | | | | | | | | | | | | | | | | |
| ACUPUNCTURE SERVICES (HM00320) | | | | | | | | | | | | | | | | | | | | | | | | | | | | | | | | | | ● | | | | | | ● | | | | | | | | | | |
| ANDREWS, SIMON C (HM00859) | | | | | | | | | ● | | | | | | | | ● | | | | ● | | | ● | ● | | | | | | | ● | | ● | | | | | | | | | | | | | | | | |
| APOTHECARY (HM00932) | | | | | | | | | | | | | | | ● | | | | | | | | | | | | | | | | | | | | | | | | | | | | | | | | | | | |
| AYURVEDIC HERBAL CLINIC (HM01444) | | | | | | | | | | | | | | | ● | | | | | | | ● | | | | | | ● | | | | | | ● | | | | | | | | | | ● | | | ● | | | |
| BEASLEY, CAROL (HM01973) | | | | | | | | | | | | | | | | | | | | ● | | | | | | | | | | | | | | | | | | | | | | | | | | | | | | |
| BOWKETT, STEPHEN (HM02793) | | | | | | | | | | | | | | | | | | | | ● | | | | | | | | | | | | | | | | | | | | | | | | | | | | | | |
| CHARLESWORTH, L M (HM04028) | | | | | | | | | | | | | | | | | | | | ● | | | | | | | | | | | | | | | | | | | | | | | | | | | | | | |
| CHERRY GRANGE (HM04107) | | | | | | | | | | | | | | | ● | | | | | | | | | | | | | | | | | | | | | | | | | | | | | | | | | | | |
| CHESTER, A (HM04135) | | | | | | | | | | | | | | | ● | | | | | | | | | | | | | | | | | | | | | | | | | | | | | | | | | | | |
| CONLIFFE, LOUISE (HM04982) | | | | | | | | | | | | | | | | | ● | | | | | | | | | | | | | | | | | ● | | | | ● | | | | | | | | | | | | |
| DEAN, JAN (HM05938) | | | | | | | | | | | | | | | | | | | | ● | | | | | | | | | | | | | | | | | | | | | | | | | | | | | | |
| FAIRWEATHER, S & E (HM07068) | | | | | | | | | | | | | | | | | | | | | ● | | | | | | | | | | | | | ● | | | | | | | | | | | | | | | | |
| FENG SHUI ACADEMY (HM07213) | | | | ● | | | | | | | | | | | | | | | | | | | | | | | | | | | | | | | | | | | | | | | | | | | | | | |
| GLENFIELD PRACTICE (HM08150) | | | | | | | | | | | | | | | | | | | | ● | | | | | | | | | | | | ● | | | | | | | | | | | | | | | | | | |
| HARRIS, LESLEY (HM09077) | | | | | | | | | | | | | | | ● | | | | | | | | | | | | | | | | | | | | | | | | | | | | | | | | | | | |
| HELIX CENTRE (HM09521) | | | | | | | | | | | | | ● | | ● | | ● | | | ● | | ● | | ● | ● | | | | | | | | | ● | ● | | | | | | | | | | | | | | | |
| HILL, VIVIENNE (HM09792) | | | | | | | | | | | | | | | | | ● | | | | | | | | | | | | | | | | | | | | | | | | | | | | | | | | | |
| HUMBERSTONE COUNSELLING (HM10367) | | | | | | | | | | | | | | | | | | | | ● | | | | | | | | | | | | | | | | | | | | | | | | | | | | | | |
| HYDES HERBAL CLINIC (HM10473) | | | | | | | | | | | | | | | ● | | | | | | | | | | | | | | | | | | | | | | | | | | | | | | | | | | | |
| JACKSON, AMANDA (HM10821) | | | | | | | | | | | | | | | | | ● | | | | | | | | | | | | | | | | | | | | | | | | | | | | | | | | | |
| JACQUI BATES COUNSELLING (HM10866) | | | | | | | | | | | | | | | | | | | | ● | ● | | | | | | | | | | | | | | | | | | | | | | | | | | | | | |
| KINESIOLOGY & COMP HEALTH CTRE (HM11621) | | | | | | | | | | | | | | | | | | | | | | | | | ● | | | | | | | | | | | | | | | | | | | | | | | | | |
| LEWIS, JACQUELINE (HM12296) | | | | | | | | | | | | | | | | | | | | | | | | | | | | | | | | | | ● | | | | | | | | | | | | | | | | |
| OADBY THERAPY CENTRE (HM15141) | | | | | | | | | | | | | | | | | | | | ● | | | | | | | | | | | | | | | | | | | | | | | | | | | | | | |
| PICKERING, JO (HM16270) | | | | | | | | | | | | | | | | | ● | | | | | | | | | | | | | | | | | | | | | | | | | | | | | | | | | |
| POLLARD, JOY (HM16407) | | | | | | | | | | | | | | | | | | | | ● | | | | | | | | | | | | | | | | | | | | | | | | | | | | | | |
| RAJA, AMITA (DR) (HM16899) | | | | | | | | | | | | | | | | | ● | | | | | | | | | | | | | | | | | | | | | | | | | | | | | | | | | |
| SHIRLEY FRANKLIN AROMATHERAPY (HM18485) | | | | | | | | | | | | | | | | | | | | | | ● | | | | | | | | | | | | ● | | | | | | | | | | | | | | | | |
| SHORE, JAMES (HM18494) | | | | | | | | | | | | | | | | | | | | ● | | | | | | | | | | | | | | | | | | | | | | | | | | | | | | |

# F - O Therapies at Practices/Businesses

| Business by County with Reference no. | Family Planning (Natural) | Family Therapy | Feldenkrais Methodology | Feng Shui | Floral Essence Therapy | Flotation Therapy | Gait Analysis | Gem Essence Therapy | Gestalt Therapy | Group Therapy | Hay Diet | Healer | Healing Therapy | Hellerwork | Herbal Medicine | Holistic Healing | Homeopathy | Hopi Ear Candles | Humanistic Psychology | Hypnosis | Hypnotherapy | Indian Head Massage | Inhalation Therapy | Iridology | Kinesiology |
|---|---|---|---|---|---|---|---|---|---|---|---|---|---|---|---|---|---|---|---|---|---|---|---|---|---|
| STEVENS, TARA L (HM19240) |  |  |  |  |  |  |  |  |  |  |  |  |  |  |  |  |  |  |  |  |  |  |  |  |  |
| SUE CHARLES AROMATHERAPY (HM19466) |  |  |  |  |  |  |  |  |  |  |  |  |  |  |  |  |  |  |  |  |  | ● |  |  |  |
| SUE RICKS COMP THERAPY (HM19467) |  |  |  |  |  |  |  |  |  |  |  | ● |  |  |  |  |  |  |  |  |  |  |  |  |  |
| SUN HERB HOUSE (HM19501) |  |  |  |  |  |  |  |  |  |  |  |  |  |  | ● |  |  |  |  |  |  |  |  |  |  |
| THOMAS COXON ASSOCIATES (HM19926) |  |  |  | ● |  |  |  |  |  |  |  |  |  |  |  |  |  |  |  |  |  |  |  |  |  |
| VICTORIA CLINIC (HM20650) |  |  |  |  |  |  |  |  |  |  |  | ● |  |  |  |  |  |  |  |  |  |  |  |  | ● |
| WENDY PRICE HOLISTIC RIDING (HM21198) |  |  |  |  |  |  |  |  |  |  |  | ● | ● |  |  |  |  |  |  |  |  |  |  |  |  |
| **LINCOLNSHIRE** |  |  |  |  |  |  |  |  |  |  |  |  |  |  |  |  |  |  |  |  |  |  |  |  |  |
| BEVERLEYS (HM02246) |  |  |  |  |  |  |  |  |  |  |  |  |  |  |  |  |  |  |  |  | ● | ● |  |  |  |
| BROS, GODFREY (HM03195) |  |  |  |  |  |  |  |  |  |  |  |  |  |  | ● |  |  |  |  |  |  |  |  |  |  |
| CHIEN ACUPUNCTURE CLINIC (HM04161) |  |  |  |  |  |  |  |  |  |  |  |  |  |  |  |  | ● |  |  |  |  |  |  |  |  |
| CLINIC OF NATURAL MEDICINE (HM04703) |  |  |  |  |  |  |  |  |  |  |  |  |  |  |  |  |  |  |  |  |  |  |  |  | ● |
| COMPLEMENTARY THERAPY CENTRE (HM04946) |  |  |  |  |  |  |  |  |  |  |  |  |  |  |  |  |  |  |  | ● | ● | ● |  |  |  |
| COPE, PAUL (HM05138) |  |  |  |  |  |  |  |  |  |  |  |  |  |  |  |  |  |  |  | ● |  |  |  |  |  |
| EASTGATE HYPNOTHERAPY CENTRE (HM06541) |  |  |  |  |  |  |  |  |  |  |  |  |  |  |  |  |  |  |  |  | ● |  |  |  |  |
| FLAME HYPNOTHERAPY (HM07387) |  |  |  |  |  |  |  |  |  |  |  |  |  |  |  |  |  |  |  | ● |  |  |  |  |  |
| GOOD HEALTHKEEPING (HM08241) | ● |  |  |  | ● |  |  | ● |  |  | ● |  |  |  | ● | ● | ● |  |  | ● |  |  |  |  |  |
| GREENS HEALTH FOODS (HM08494) |  |  |  |  |  |  |  |  |  |  |  |  |  |  | ● |  | ● |  |  |  |  |  |  |  |  |
| HEART TO HEART (HM09443) |  |  |  |  |  |  |  |  |  |  |  | ● |  |  |  | ● | ● |  |  |  | ● |  |  |  |  |
| JENKINS, K J (HM10990) |  |  |  |  |  |  |  |  |  |  |  |  |  |  |  |  | ● |  |  |  |  |  |  |  |  |
| JUST JILLS (HM11282) |  |  |  |  |  |  |  |  |  |  |  |  |  |  |  |  | ● |  |  |  |  |  |  |  |  |
| LINCOLN HERBAL TREATMENT CTRE (HM12407) |  |  |  |  |  |  |  |  |  |  |  |  |  |  | ● |  |  |  |  |  |  |  |  |  |  |
| LIVING HEALTH (HM12485) |  |  |  |  |  |  |  |  |  |  |  |  |  |  |  |  |  |  |  |  |  |  |  |  | ● |
| MARK RIDDLE HYPNOTHERAPY (HM13108) |  | ● |  |  |  |  |  |  |  |  |  |  |  |  |  | ● |  |  | ● | ● | ● |  |  |  |  |
| MORLEY-KIRK, JOHN (HM14187) |  |  |  |  |  |  |  |  |  |  |  |  |  |  |  |  |  |  |  |  | ● |  |  |  |  |
| NEWLAND CHIROPRACTIC CLINIC (HM14866) |  |  |  |  |  |  |  |  |  |  |  |  |  |  |  |  |  |  |  |  |  |  |  |  |  |
| QUINN, PHILLIP D R (HM16813) |  |  |  |  |  |  |  |  |  |  |  |  |  |  |  |  |  |  |  | ● |  |  |  |  |  |
| REFLEXOLOGY CLINIC (HM17084) |  |  |  |  |  |  |  |  |  |  |  |  |  |  |  |  |  |  |  |  |  | ● |  |  |  |
| SALON, JANIES (HM17863) |  |  |  |  |  |  |  |  |  |  |  |  |  |  |  |  |  |  |  |  |  | ● |  |  |  |
| SMITH, MICHAEL (HM18780) |  |  |  |  |  |  |  |  |  |  |  |  |  |  |  |  |  |  |  | ● | ● |  |  |  |  |
| SPOONER, PATRICIA (HM19038) |  |  |  |  |  |  |  |  |  |  |  |  |  |  |  |  |  |  |  | ● |  |  |  |  |  |
| WHITE, HEATHER (HM21357) |  |  |  |  |  |  |  |  |  |  |  |  |  |  |  |  |  |  |  |  | ● | ● |  |  |  |
| **LONDON** |  |  |  |  |  |  |  |  |  |  |  |  |  |  |  |  |  |  |  |  |  |  |  |  |  |
| FIRST PATH HYPNOTHERAPY (HM07338) |  |  |  |  |  |  |  |  |  |  |  |  |  |  |  |  |  |  |  |  | ● |  |  |  |  |

| Business by County with Reference no. | Kirlian Photography | Laser Treatment | Life Style Coaching | Light Therapy | Macrobiotics | Magnetic Therapy | Manipulation | Manual Lymph Drainage | Massage (Therapeutic) | McTimoney Chiropractic | Meditation | Metamorphic Therapy | Miasm Therapy | Micro Manipulation | Moxibustion | Mud Therapy | Music Therapy | Nail Surgery | Naturopathy | Neuro-Linguistic Program | Neurotherapy | Nutritional Therapy | Orgone Therapy | Oriental Diagnosis | Orthomolecular Medicine |
|---|---|---|---|---|---|---|---|---|---|---|---|---|---|---|---|---|---|---|---|---|---|---|---|---|---|
| STEVENS, TARA L (HM19240) |  |  |  |  |  |  |  |  | ● |  |  |  |  |  |  |  |  |  |  |  |  |  |  |  |  |
| SUE CHARLES AROMATHERAPY (HM19466) |  |  |  |  |  |  |  |  | ● |  |  |  |  |  |  |  |  |  |  |  |  |  |  |  |  |
| SUE RICKS COMP THERAPY (HM19467) |  |  |  |  |  |  |  |  |  |  |  |  |  |  |  |  |  |  |  | ● |  |  |  |  |  |
| SUN HERB HOUSE (HM19501) |  |  |  |  |  |  |  |  |  |  |  |  |  |  |  |  |  |  |  |  |  |  |  |  |  |
| THOMAS COXON ASSOCIATES (HM19926) |  |  |  |  |  |  |  |  |  |  |  |  |  |  |  |  |  |  |  |  |  |  |  |  |  |
| VICTORIA CLINIC (HM20650) |  |  |  |  |  |  | ● |  | ● |  |  |  |  |  |  |  |  |  |  |  |  | ● |  |  |  |
| WENDY PRICE HOLISTIC RIDING (HM21198) |  |  | ● |  |  |  |  |  |  |  |  |  |  |  |  |  |  |  |  |  |  |  |  |  |  |
| **LINCOLNSHIRE** |  |  |  |  |  |  |  |  |  |  |  |  |  |  |  |  |  |  |  |  |  |  |  |  |  |
| BEVERLEYS (HM02246) |  |  |  |  |  |  |  |  |  |  |  |  |  |  |  |  |  |  |  |  |  |  |  |  |  |
| BROS, GODFREY (HM03195) |  |  |  |  |  |  |  |  |  |  |  |  |  |  |  |  |  |  |  |  |  |  |  |  |  |
| CHIEN ACUPUNCTURE CLINIC (HM04161) |  |  |  |  |  |  |  |  | ● |  |  |  |  |  |  |  |  |  |  |  |  |  |  |  |  |
| CLINIC OF NATURAL MEDICINE (HM04703) |  |  |  |  |  |  | ● |  |  |  |  |  |  |  |  |  |  |  |  |  |  |  |  |  |  |
| COMPLEMENTARY THERAPY CENTRE (HM04946) |  |  |  |  |  |  |  |  |  |  | ● |  |  |  |  |  | ● |  |  |  |  |  |  |  |  |
| COPE, PAUL (HM05138) |  |  |  |  |  |  |  |  |  |  |  |  |  |  |  |  |  |  |  |  |  |  |  |  |  |
| EASTGATE HYPNOTHERAPY CENTRE (HM06541) |  |  |  |  |  |  |  |  |  |  |  |  |  |  |  |  |  |  |  |  |  |  |  |  |  |
| FLAME HYPNOTHERAPY (HM07387) |  |  |  |  |  |  |  |  |  |  |  |  |  |  |  |  |  |  |  |  |  |  |  |  |  |
| GOOD HEALTHKEEPING (HM08241) |  |  | ● |  |  |  |  |  |  |  |  |  | ● |  |  |  |  |  | ● |  |  | ● |  |  | ● |
| GREENS HEALTH FOODS (HM08494) |  |  |  |  |  |  |  |  |  |  |  |  |  |  |  |  |  |  |  |  |  |  |  |  |  |
| HEART TO HEART (HM09443) |  |  |  |  |  |  |  |  |  |  |  |  |  |  |  |  |  |  |  |  |  |  |  |  |  |
| JENKINS, K J (HM10990) |  |  |  |  |  |  |  |  |  |  |  |  |  |  |  |  |  |  |  |  |  |  |  |  |  |
| JUST JILLS (HM11282) |  |  |  |  |  |  |  |  |  |  |  |  |  |  |  |  |  |  |  |  |  |  |  |  |  |
| LINCOLN HERBAL TREATMENT CTRE (HM12407) |  |  |  |  |  |  |  |  |  |  |  |  |  |  |  |  |  |  |  |  |  |  |  |  |  |
| LIVING HEALTH (HM12485) |  |  |  |  |  |  |  |  |  |  |  |  |  |  |  |  |  |  |  |  |  |  |  |  |  |
| MARK RIDDLE HYPNOTHERAPY (HM13108) |  |  | ● |  |  |  |  |  |  |  | ● |  |  |  |  |  |  |  |  |  |  |  |  |  |  |
| MORLEY-KIRK, JOHN (HM14187) |  |  |  |  |  |  |  |  |  |  |  |  |  |  |  |  |  |  |  |  |  |  |  |  |  |
| NEWLAND CHIROPRACTIC CLINIC (HM14866) |  |  |  |  |  |  | ● |  | ● |  |  |  |  |  |  |  |  |  |  |  |  |  |  |  |  |
| QUINN, PHILLIP D R (HM16813) |  |  |  |  |  |  |  |  |  |  |  |  |  |  |  |  |  |  |  |  |  |  |  |  |  |
| REFLEXOLOGY CLINIC (HM17084) |  |  |  |  |  |  |  |  |  |  |  |  |  |  |  |  |  |  |  |  |  |  |  |  |  |
| SALON, JANIES (HM17863) |  |  |  |  |  |  |  |  |  |  |  |  |  |  |  |  |  |  |  |  |  |  |  |  |  |
| SMITH, MICHAEL (HM18780) |  |  |  |  |  |  |  |  |  |  |  |  |  |  |  |  |  |  |  |  |  |  |  |  |  |
| SPOONER, PATRICIA (HM19038) |  |  |  |  |  |  |  |  |  |  |  |  |  |  |  |  |  |  |  |  |  |  |  |  |  |
| WHITE, HEATHER (HM21357) |  |  |  |  |  |  |  |  | ● |  |  |  |  |  |  |  |  |  |  |  |  |  |  |  |  |
| **LONDON** |  |  |  |  |  |  |  |  |  |  |  |  |  |  |  |  |  |  |  |  |  |  |  |  |  |
| FIRST PATH HYPNOTHERAPY (HM07338) |  |  |  |  |  |  |  |  |  |  |  |  |  |  |  |  |  |  |  |  |  |  |  |  |  |

# F - O Therapies at Practices/Businesses

Business by County with Reference no.

| Business | Family Planning (Natural) | Family Therapy | Feldenkrais Methodology | Feng Shui | Floral Essence Therapy | Flotation Therapy | Gait Analysis | Gem Essence Therapy | Gestalt Therapy | Group Therapy | Hay Diet | Healer | Healing Therapy | Hellerwork | Herbal Medicine | Holistic Healing | Homeopathy | Hopi Ear Candles | Humanistic Psychology | Hypnosis | Hypnotherapy | Indian Head Massage | Inhalation Therapy | Iridology | Kinesiology |
|---|---|---|---|---|---|---|---|---|---|---|---|---|---|---|---|---|---|---|---|---|---|---|---|---|---|
| HARLEY STREET COMP MEDICINE (HM09001) | | | | | | | | | | | | | | | | | ● | | | | | ● | | | |
| HERBS KINGDOM (HM09671) | | | | | | | | | | | | | | | ● | | | | | | | | | | |
| **LONDON (GREATER)** | | | | | | | | | | | | | | | | | | | | | | | | | |
| 1ST ALTERNATIVE HEALTH CENTRE (HM00002) | | | | | | | | | | | | | | | | | ● | | | | | | | | |
| A K CHINESE HEALTHCARE CENTRE (HM00037) | | | | | | | | | | | | | | | ● | | | | | | | | | | |
| ABBEY CENTRE (HM00071) | | | | | | | | | | | | | | | | | | | | ● | ● | | | | |
| ACORN THERAPY CENTRE (HM00182) | | | | | | | | | | | | | | | | | | | | ● | ● | | | | |
| ACUMEDIC (HM00217) | | | | | | | | | | | | | | | | | | | | | | | | | |
| ACUPUNCTURE CLINIC (HM00287) | | | | | | | | | | | | | | | | | | | | | | | | | ● |
| ALEXANDER TECHNIQUE CENTRE (HM00555) | | | | | | | | | | | | | | | | | | | | | | | | | |
| ALL WELL & GOOD (HM00583) | | | | | | | | | | | | | | | | | | | | | | | | | |
| ALLEN, CAROL (HM00603) | | | | | | | | | | | | | | | | | | | | | ● | | | | |
| ALLEN, TRICIA (HM00621) | | | | | | | | | | | | | | | | | ● | | | | | | | | |
| ALTERNATIVE THERAPIES CENTRE (HM00728) | | | | | ● | | | | | | | ● | ● | | ● | ● | ● | | ● | ● | ● | ● | | | |
| ALTERNATIVES COMP THERAPY CTRE (HM00743) | | | | | | | | | | | | | | | ● | | ● | | | ● | ● | | | | |
| ANDERSON, JANE M (HM00826) | | | | | | | | | | | | | | | | | ● | | | | | | | | |
| ANGEL HEART CENTRE (HM00867) | | | | | | | | | | ● | | ● | | | | | | | | | ● | | | | |
| AROMATHERAPY ORG COUNCIL (HM01121) | | | | | | | | | | | | | | | | | | | | | | | | | |
| AUSTERBERRY, HELEN (HM01363) | | | | | | | | | | | | | | | | | ● | | | | | | | | |
| AUSTERBERRY, HELEN (HM01362) | | | | | | | | | | | | | | | | | ● | | | | | | | | |
| AUSTIN, DIANA (HM01365) | | | | | | | | | | | | | | | ● | | | | | | | | | | |
| AVALON CHINESE MEDICINE CLINIC (HM01377) | | | | | | | | | | | | | | | ● | | | | | | | | | | |
| AVATAR (HM01384) | | | | | | | | | | | | | | | | | | | | | | | | | |
| AWDRY, ROBERT (HM01417) | | | | | | | | | | | | | | | | | ● | | | | | | | | |
| AYURVED HERBELI (HM01442) | | | | | | | | | | | | | | | ● | | | | | | | | | | |
| BACK PAIN CLINIC (HM01503) | | | | | | | | | | | | | | | | | ● | | | | | | | | |
| BAKHSHI, R S (HM01598) | | | | | | | | | | | | | | | | | ● | | | | | | | | |
| BARBICAN CENTRE (HM01693) | | | | | | | ● | | | | | | | | | | | | | | | | | | |
| BARBICAN PODIATRY PRACTICE (HM01694) | | | | | | | ● | | | | | | | | | | | | | | | | | | |
| BARNES CHIROPRACTIC HEALTHCARE (HM01740) | | | | | | | | | | | | | | | | | | | | | | | | | |
| BARRIE, ALEXANDER (HM01798) | | | | | | | | | | | | ● | | | | | | | | | | | | | |
| BEAN, GARY (HM01960) | | | | | | | | | | | | | | | | | | | | ● | | | | | |
| BECKER, AMELY (HM02021) | | | | | | | | | ● | ● | | | | | | | | | ● | | | | | | |
| BECKETT, DALE (DR) (HM02023) | | | | | | | | | | | | | | | | | | | | ● | | | | | |

| Business | Kirlian Photography | Laser Treatment | Life Style Coaching | Light Therapy | Macrobiotics | Magnetic Therapy | Manipulation | Manual Lymph Drainage | Massage (Therapeutic) | McTimoney Chiropractic | Meditation | Metamorphic Therapy | Miasm Therapy | Micro Manipulation | Moxibustion | Mud Therapy | Music Therapy | Nail Surgery | Naturopathy | Neurotherapy | Neuro-Linguistic Program | Nutritional Therapy | Orgone Therapy | Oriental Diagnosis | Orthomolecular Medicine |
|---|---|---|---|---|---|---|---|---|---|---|---|---|---|---|---|---|---|---|---|---|---|---|---|---|---|
| HARLEY STREET COMP MEDICINE (HM09001) | | | | | | | | | | | | | | | | | | | | | | ● | | | |
| HERBS KINGDOM (HM09671) | | | | | | | | | | | | | | | | | | | | | | | | | |
| **LONDON (GREATER)** | | | | | | | | | | | | | | | | | | | | | | | | | |
| 1ST ALTERNATIVE HEALTH CENTRE (HM00002) | | | | | | | ● | | ● | | | | | | | | | | ● | | | | | | |
| A K CHINESE HEALTHCARE CENTRE (HM00037) | | | | | | | | | | | | | | | | | | | | | | | | | |
| ABBEY CENTRE (HM00071) | | | | | | | | | | | | | | | | | | | | | | | | | |
| ACORN THERAPY CENTRE (HM00182) | | | | | | | | | | | | | | | | | | | | | | | | | |
| ACUMEDIC (HM00217) | | | | | | | | | | | | | | | | | | | | | | | | ● | |
| ACUPUNCTURE CLINIC (HM00287) | | | | | | | | | | | ● | | | | ● | | | | | | | | | | |
| ALEXANDER TECHNIQUE CENTRE (HM00555) | | | | | | | | | | | | | | | | | | | | | ● | | | | |
| ALL WELL & GOOD (HM00583) | | | | | | | | | ● | | | | | | | | | | | | | | | | |
| ALLEN, CAROL (HM00603) | | | ● | | | | | | | | | | | | | | | | | | | | | | |
| ALLEN, TRICIA (HM00621) | | | | | | | | | | | | | | | | | | | | | | | | | |
| ALTERNATIVE THERAPIES CENTRE (HM00728) | | | | | | | ● | | ● | | ● | | | | ● | | | | ● | | | ● | | ● | |
| ALTERNATIVES COMP THERAPY CTRE (HM00743) | | | | | | | | | ● | | ● | | | | ● | | | | ● | | | ● | | | |
| ANDERSON, JANE M (HM00826) | | | | | | | | | | | | | | | | | | | | | | | | | |
| ANGEL HEART CENTRE (HM00867) | | | | | | | | | | | | | | | | | | | | | | | | | |
| AROMATHERAPY ORG COUNCIL (HM01121) | | | | | | | | | ● | | | | | | | | | | | | | | | | |
| AUSTERBERRY, HELEN (HM01363) | | | | | | | | | | | | | | | | | | | | | | | | | |
| AUSTERBERRY, HELEN (HM01362) | | | | | | | | | | | | | | | | | | | | | | | | | |
| AUSTIN, DIANA (HM01365) | | | | | | | | | | | | | | | | | | | | | | | | | |
| AVALON CHINESE MEDICINE CLINIC (HM01377) | | | | | | | | | ● | | | | | | ● | | | | | | | | | ● | |
| AVATAR (HM01384) | | | | | | | | | ● | | | | | | | | | | | | | | | | |
| AWDRY, ROBERT (HM01417) | | | | | | | | | | | | | | | | | | | | | | | | | |
| AYURVED HERBELI (HM01442) | | | | | | | | | | | | | | | | | | | | | | | | | |
| BACK PAIN CLINIC (HM01503) | | | | | | | | | | | | | | | | | | | | | | | | | |
| BAKHSHI, R S (HM01598) | | | | | | | | | | | | | | | | | | | | | | | | | |
| BARBICAN CENTRE (HM01693) | | | | | | | | | | | | | | | | | | ● | | | | | | | |
| BARBICAN PODIATRY PRACTICE (HM01694) | | | | | | | | | | | | | | | | | | | | | | | | | |
| BARNES CHIROPRACTIC HEALTHCARE (HM01740) | | | | | | | ● | | ● | | | | | | | | | | | | | | | | |
| BARRIE, ALEXANDER (HM01798) | | | | | | | ● | | | | ● | | | | ● | | | | | | | | | ● | |
| BEAN, GARY (HM01960) | | | | | | | | | | | | | | | | | | | | | | | | | |
| BECKER, AMELY (HM02021) | | | | | | | | | | | ● | | | | | | | | | | | | | | |
| BECKETT, DALE (DR) (HM02023) | | | | | | | | | | | | | | | | | | | | | | | | | |

# F - O Therapies at Practices/Businesses

| Business by County with Reference no. | Family Planning (Natural) | Family Therapy | Feldenkrais Methodology | Feng Shui | Floral Essence Therapy | Flotation Therapy | Gait Analysis | Gem Essence Therapy | Gestalt Therapy | Group Therapy | Hay Diet | Healer | Healing Therapy | Hellerwork | Herbal Medicine | Holistic Healing | Homeopathy |
|---|---|---|---|---|---|---|---|---|---|---|---|---|---|---|---|---|---|
| BEJING TONG REN TANG (HM02075) | | | | | | | | | | | | | | |●| | |
| BERNSTEIN, SAMUEL (HM02204) | | | | | | | | | | | | |●| | | | |
| BEVERLEY CLINIC (HM02244) | | | | | | | | | | | | | | | | |●|
| BIBBY, KEITH (HM02276) | | | | | | | | | | | | | | | | | |
| BIRCH, MARGARET (HM02352) | | | | | | | | | | | | | | | | | |
| BISHOP-COMPTON, JENNY (HM02412) | | | | | | | | | | | | | | | | | |
| BLISS (HM02507) | | | | | | | | | | | | |●| | | | |
| BLOOMSBURY ALEXANDER CENTRE (HM02516) | | | | | | | | | | | | | | | |●|●|
| BOCOCK, RICHARD (HM02548) | | | | | | | | | | | | | | | | |●|
| BODYSPACE (HM02632) | | | | | | | | | |●| | | | | | | |
| BODYWISE (HM02637) | | | | | | | | | | | | | | |●| | |
| BOLTON, STEVEN (HM02662) | | | | | | | | | | | | | | | | | |
| BONNER, DAVID (HM02684) | | | | | | | | | | | | | | | | | |
| BOSTON CHIROPODY CLINIC (HM02725) | | | | | | | | | | | | | | | | | |
| BRACKENBURY NTRL HEALTH CLNC (HM02837) | | | | | | | | | | | | | | | | |●|
| BRAHMA KUMARIS INNER SPACE (HM02886) | | | | | | | | | | | | | | | | | |
| BRATERMAN, ELEANOR (HM02922) | | | | | | | | | | | | | | | | | |
| BRITISH AUTOGENIC SOCIETY (HM03076) | | | | | | | | | |●| | | | | | | |
| BRITISH HYPNOTHERAPY ASS (HM03084) | | | | | | | | | | | | | | | | | |
| BRITISH SOC OF MED/DENT HYP (HM03097) | | | | | | | | | | | | | | | | | |
| BRITISH SOCIETY-CLINICAL HYP (HM03098) | | | | | | | | | | | | | | | | | |
| BROOKS, CATHY (HM03175) | | | | | | | | | | | | | | | | |●|
| BROOKS, JANE (HM03177) | |●| | | | | | |●| |●|●| | | | | |
| BST FOUNDATION (HM03295) | | | | | | | | | | | | | | | | | |
| BUCHANAN, ANGELA (HM03300) | | | | | | | | | | | | | | | | | |
| BUCHANAN, JO (HM03302) | | | | | | | | | | | | | | | | |●|
| BUCKLEY, BILLIE (HM03318) | |●| | | | | | | | | | | | | | | |
| BUREN, VAN (HM03371) | | | | | | | | | | | | | | | | | |
| BURNS, JOLANDA (HM03414) | | | | | | | | | | | | | | | | |●|
| BYRNE, JUDY (HM03516) | | | | | | | | | | | | | | | | | |
| BYRNE, M (HM03517) | | | | | | | | | | | | | | | | |●|
| CASSIDY MEDICAL CENTRE (HM03815) | | | | | | | | | | | | | | | | | |
| CENTRAL HYPNOTHERAPY UNIT (HM03893) | | | | | | | | | | | | | | | | | |
| CENTRE FOR TRANSFORMATION (HM03920) |●| | | | | | | | | | | | | | | |●|

| Business by County with Reference no. | Hopi Ear Candles | Humanistic Psychology | Hypnosis | Hypnotherapy | Indian Head Massage | Inhalation Therapy | Iridology | Kinesiology | Kirlian Photography | Laser Treatment | Life Style Coaching | Light Therapy | Macrobiotics | Magnetic Therapy | Manipulation | Manual Lymph Drainage | Massage (Therapeutic) |
|---|---|---|---|---|---|---|---|---|---|---|---|---|---|---|---|---|---|
| BEJING TONG REN TANG (HM02075) | | | | | | | | | | | | | | | | | |
| BERNSTEIN, SAMUEL (HM02204) | | | |●| | | | | | | | | | | | | |
| BEVERLEY CLINIC (HM02244) | | | |●| | | | | | | | | | | | | |
| BIBBY, KEITH (HM02276) | | |●| | | | | | | | | | | | | | |
| BIRCH, MARGARET (HM02352) | | | | | | | | | | | | | | | | |●|
| BISHOP-COMPTON, JENNY (HM02412) | | |●| | | | | | | | | | | | | | |
| BLISS (HM02507) | | |●| | | | | | | | | | | | | |●|
| BLOOMSBURY ALEXANDER CENTRE (HM02516) | |●| | | | | | | | | | | | | | |●|
| BOCOCK, RICHARD (HM02548) | | | | | | | | | | | | | | | | | |
| BODYSPACE (HM02632) | |●| | | | | | | | | | | | | | | |
| BODYWISE (HM02637) | | | | | | | | | | | | | | | | |●|
| BOLTON, STEVEN (HM02662) | | |●| | | | | | | | | | | | | | |
| BONNER, DAVID (HM02684) | | |●| | | | | | | | | | | | | | |
| BOSTON CHIROPODY CLINIC (HM02725) | | | | | | | | | | | | | | |●| | |
| BRACKENBURY NTRL HEALTH CLNC (HM02837) | | | | |●| | | | | | | | | | | |●|
| BRAHMA KUMARIS INNER SPACE (HM02886) | | | | | | | | | | | | | | | | | |
| BRATERMAN, ELEANOR (HM02922) | | |●| | | | | | | | | | | | | | |
| BRITISH AUTOGENIC SOCIETY (HM03076) | |●| | | | | | | | | | | | | | | |
| BRITISH HYPNOTHERAPY ASS (HM03084) | | | |●| | | | | | | | | | | | | |
| BRITISH SOC OF MED/DENT HYP (HM03097) | | |●| | | | | | | | | | | | | | |
| BRITISH SOCIETY-CLINICAL HYP (HM03098) | | |●| | | | | | | | | | | | | | |
| BROOKS, CATHY (HM03175) | | | | | | | | | | | | | | | | | |
| BROOKS, JANE (HM03177) | |●| | | | | | | | | | | | | | | |
| BST FOUNDATION (HM03295) | | |●|●| | | | | | | | | | | | | |
| BUCHANAN, ANGELA (HM03300) | | | | | | | |●| | | | | | |●| | |
| BUCHANAN, JO (HM03302) | | | | | | | | | | | | | | | | | |
| BUCKLEY, BILLIE (HM03318) | | | | | | | | | | | | | | | | | |
| BUREN, VAN (HM03371) | | | |●| | | | | | | | | | | | | |
| BURNS, JOLANDA (HM03414) | | | | | | | | | | | | | | | | | |
| BYRNE, JUDY (HM03516) | | |●|●| | | | | | | | | | | | | |
| BYRNE, M (HM03517) | | | | | | | | | | | | | | | | | |
| CASSIDY MEDICAL CENTRE (HM03815) | | | | | | | | | | | | | | |●| |●|
| CENTRAL HYPNOTHERAPY UNIT (HM03893) | | |●| | | | | | | | | | | | | | |
| CENTRE FOR TRANSFORMATION (HM03920) | | | | | | | | | | | | | | | | | |

| Business by County with Reference no. | McTimoney Chiropractic | Meditation | Metamorphic Therapy | Miasm Therapy | Micro Manipulation | Moxibustion | Mud Therapy | Music Therapy | Nail Surgery | Naturopathy | Neuro-Linguistic Program | Neurotherapy | Nutritional Therapy | Orgone Therapy | Oriental Diagnosis | Orthomolecular Medicine |
|---|---|---|---|---|---|---|---|---|---|---|---|---|---|---|---|---|
| BEJING TONG REN TANG (HM02075) | | | | | | | | | | | | | | | | |
| BERNSTEIN, SAMUEL (HM02204) | | | | | | | | | | | | | | | | |
| BEVERLEY CLINIC (HM02244) | | | | | | | | | | | | | | | | |
| BIBBY, KEITH (HM02276) | | | | | | | | | | | | | | | | |
| BIRCH, MARGARET (HM02352) | | | | | | | | | | | | | | | | |
| BISHOP-COMPTON, JENNY (HM02412) | | | | | | | | | | | | | | | | |
| BLISS (HM02507) | | | | | | | | | | | | | | | | |
| BLOOMSBURY ALEXANDER CENTRE (HM02516) | | | | | | | | | | | | | | | | |
| BOCOCK, RICHARD (HM02548) | | | | | | | | | | | | | | | | |
| BODYSPACE (HM02632) | | | | | | | | | | | | | | | | |
| BODYWISE (HM02637) | | | | | | | | | | | | | | | | |
| BOLTON, STEVEN (HM02662) | | | | | | | | | | | | | | | | |
| BONNER, DAVID (HM02684) | | | | | | | | | | | | | | | | |
| BOSTON CHIROPODY CLINIC (HM02725) | | | | | | | | | | | | | | | | |
| BRACKENBURY NTRL HEALTH CLNC (HM02837) | | | | | | | | | |●| | | | | | |
| BRAHMA KUMARIS INNER SPACE (HM02886) | |●| | | | | | | | | | | | | | |
| BRATERMAN, ELEANOR (HM02922) | | | | | | | | | | | | | | | | |
| BRITISH AUTOGENIC SOCIETY (HM03076) | | | | | | | | | | | | | | | | |
| BRITISH HYPNOTHERAPY ASS (HM03084) | | | | | | | | | | | | | | | | |
| BRITISH SOC OF MED/DENT HYP (HM03097) | | | | | | | | | | | | | | | | |
| BRITISH SOCIETY-CLINICAL HYP (HM03098) | | | | | | | | | | | | | | | | |
| BROOKS, CATHY (HM03175) | | | | | | | | | | | | | | | | |
| BROOKS, JANE (HM03177) | |●| | | | | | | | | | | | | | |
| BST FOUNDATION (HM03295) | | | | | | | | | | | | | | | | |
| BUCHANAN, ANGELA (HM03300) | | | | | | | | | | | | | | | | |
| BUCHANAN, JO (HM03302) | | | | | | | | | | | | | | | | |
| BUCKLEY, BILLIE (HM03318) | | | | | | | | | | | | | | | | |
| BUREN, VAN (HM03371) | | | | | | | | | | | | | | | | |
| BURNS, JOLANDA (HM03414) | | | | | | | | | | | | | | | | |
| BYRNE, JUDY (HM03516) | | | | | | | | | | | | | | | | |
| BYRNE, M (HM03517) | | | | | | | | | | | | | | | | |
| CASSIDY MEDICAL CENTRE (HM03815) | | | | | | | | | | | | | | | | |
| CENTRAL HYPNOTHERAPY UNIT (HM03893) | | | | | | | | | | | | | | | | |
| CENTRE FOR TRANSFORMATION (HM03920) | | | | | | | | | | | | |●| | | |

# F - O Therapies at Practices/Businesses

Business by County with Reference no.

| Business | Family Planning (Natural) | Family Therapy | Feldenkrais Methodology | Feng Shui | Floral Essence Therapy | Flotation Therapy | Gait Analysis | Gem Essence Therapy | Gestalt Therapy | Group Therapy | Hay Diet | Healer | Healing Therapy | Hellerwork | Herbal Medicine | Holistic Healing | Homeopathy | Hopi Ear Candles | Humanistic Psychology | Hypnosis | Hypnotherapy | Indian Head Massage | Inhalation Therapy | Iridology | Kinesiology |
|---|---|---|---|---|---|---|---|---|---|---|---|---|---|---|---|---|---|---|---|---|---|---|---|---|---|
| CHAPPLE, MAUREEN (HM04016) | | | | | | | | | | | | | | | | | ● | | | | | | | | |
| CHATSWORTH CLINIC (HM04063) | | | | | ● | | | | | | | | ● | | | ● | ● | | | | | ● | | | |
| CHENUBE, ROY (HM04105) | | | | | | | | | | | | | | | | | | | | ● | | | | | |
| CHINESE CLINIC (HM04188) | | | | | | | | | | | | | | | ● | | | | | | | | | | |
| CHINESE HERBAL HEALING CENTRE (HM04196) | | | | | | | | | | | | | | | ● | | | | | | | | | | |
| CHINESE HERBAL MED & ACU (HM04199) | | | | | | | | | | | | | | | ● | | | | | | | | | | |
| CHINESE HERBAL MEDICINE (HM04210) | | | | | | | | | | | | | | | ● | | | | | | | | | | |
| CHINESE HERBAL MEDICINE CENTRE (HM04213) | | | | | | | | | | | | | | | ● | | | | | | | | | | |
| CHINESE MEDICAL CTRE OF LONDON (HM04245) | | | | | | | | | | | | | | | ● | | | | | | | | | | |
| CHINESE MEDICINE TECH DEVPT (HM04263) | | | | | | | | | | | | | | | ● | | | | | | | | | | |
| CHINESE NATURAL HERBAL CENTRE (HM04267) | | | | | | | | | | | | | | | ● | | | | | | | | | | |
| CHINESE SHOP (HM04269) | | | | | | | | | | | | | | | ● | | | | | | | | | | |
| CHISWICK CHIROPRACTIC CLINIC (HM04412) | | | | | | | | | | | | | | | | | | | | | | | | | |
| CHISWICK HYPNOTHERAPY CENTRE (HM04414) | | | | | | | | | | | | | | | | | | | | ● | | | | | |
| CHURCH, CAROL & STEVEN (HM04466) | | | | | | | | | | | | | | | ● | | | | | | | | | | |
| CITY HEALTH CENTRE (HM04496) | | | | | | | | | | | | | | | ● | | ● | | | | | | | | |
| CLAIRE CHOUDHURY HERBAL PRAC (HM04507) | | | | | | | | | | | | | | | ● | | | | | | | | | | |
| CLASSICAL OSTEOPATH (HM04610) | | | | | | | | | | | | ● | ● | | | | | | | | | | | | |
| CLINIC FOR COUNSELLING (HM04680) | | ● | | | | | | | | | | | | | | | | | | | | | | | |
| CLINIC FOR COUNSELLING (HM04681) | | ● | | | | | | | | | | | | | | | | | | | | | | | |
| COCKELL, VALERIE (HM04767) | | | | | | | | | | | | | | | | | ● | | | | | | | | |
| COLLEGE-PRACTICAL HOMEOPATHY (HM04855) | | | | | | | | | | | | | | | | | ● | | | | | | | | |
| COLLINS, V (HM04880) | | | | | | | | | | | | | | | | | | | | ● | | | | | |
| COMP MEDI ASS (HM04913) | | | | ● | | | | | | | | | | | ● | ● | | | | ● | | ● | | ● | ● |
| COMPLETE HEALTH CARE (HM04958) | | | | | | | | | | | | ● | ● | | | ● | ● | | | | ● | | | | |
| CONN, RONALD & SHALINI (HM04984) | | | | | | | | | | | | | | | | | | | | ● | | | | | |
| CONNAUGHT PRACTICE (HM04985) | | | | | | | | | | | | | | | | | | | | ● | | | | | |
| CONNAUGHT SQUARE HYPNOTHERAPY (HM04986) | | | | | | | | | | | | | | | | | | | | | ● | | | | |
| CONWAY, JONATHAN (HM05028) | | | | | | | | | | | | | | | | | | | | ● | ● | | | | |
| CONWAY, JONATHON (HM05029) | | | | | | | | | | | | | | | | | | | | ● | ● | | | | |
| COSMOS HERBS (HM05205) | | | | | | | | | | | | | | | ● | | | | | | | | | | |
| COUNSELLING & PSYCHOTHERAPY (HM05246) | | ● | | | | | | | | ● | | | | | | | | | ● | | | | | | |
| COUNSELLING SERVICE (HM05252) | | ● | | | | | | | | | | | | | | | | | | | | | | | |
| CRAVEN CLINIC (HM05385) | | | | | | | | | | | | | | | | | ● | | | | ● | | | ● | |

| Business | Kirlian Photography | Laser Treatment | Life Style Coaching | Light Therapy | Macrobiotics | Magnetic Therapy | Manipulation | Manual Lymph Drainage | Massage (Therapeutic) | McTimoney Chiropractic | Meditation | Metamorphic Therapy | Miasm Therapy | Micro Manipulation | Moxibustion | Mud Therapy | Music Therapy | Nail Surgery | Naturopathy | Neuro-Linguistic Program | Neurotherapy | Nutritional Therapy | Orgone Therapy | Oriental Diagnosis | Orthomolecular Medicine |
|---|---|---|---|---|---|---|---|---|---|---|---|---|---|---|---|---|---|---|---|---|---|---|---|---|---|
| CHAPPLE, MAUREEN (HM04016) | | | | | | | | | | | | | | | | | | | | | | | | | |
| CHATSWORTH CLINIC (HM04063) | | | | | | | ● | | ● | | ● | | | | ● | | | | | | | ● | | ● | |
| CHENUBE, ROY (HM04105) | | | | | | | | | | | | | | | | | | | | | | | | | |
| CHINESE CLINIC (HM04188) | | | | | | | | | | | | | | | | | | | | | | | | | |
| CHINESE HERBAL HEALING CENTRE (HM04196) | | | | | | | | | | | | | | | | | | | | | | | | | |
| CHINESE HERBAL MED & ACU (HM04199) | | | | | | | | | | | | | | | | | | | | | | | | | |
| CHINESE HERBAL MEDICINE (HM04210) | | | | | | | | | | | | | | | | | | | | | | | | | |
| CHINESE HERBAL MEDICINE CENTRE (HM04213) | | | | | | | | | | | | | | | | | | | | | | | | | |
| CHINESE MEDICAL CTRE OF LONDON (HM04245) | | | | | | | | | | | | | | | ● | | | | | | | | | | |
| CHINESE MEDICINE TECH DEVPT (HM04263) | | | | | | | | | | | | | | | | | | | | | | | | | |
| CHINESE NATURAL HERBAL CENTRE (HM04267) | | | | | | | | | | | | | | | | | | | | | | | | | |
| CHINESE SHOP (HM04269) | | | | | | | | | | | | | | | | | | | | | | | | ● | |
| CHISWICK CHIROPRACTIC CLINIC (HM04412) | | | | | | | ● | | | | | | | | | | | | | | | | | | |
| CHISWICK HYPNOTHERAPY CENTRE (HM04414) | | | | | | | | | | | | | | | | | | | | | | | | | |
| CHURCH, CAROL & STEVEN (HM04466) | | | | | | | | | | | | | | | | | | | | | | | | | |
| CITY HEALTH CENTRE (HM04496) | | | | | | | ● | | | | | | | | ● | | | | | | | | | ● | |
| CLAIRE CHOUDHURY HERBAL PRAC (HM04507) | | | | | | | | | | | | | | | | | | | | | | | | | |
| CLASSICAL OSTEOPATH (HM04610) | | | | | | | ● | | ● | | | | | ● | | | | | | | | | | | |
| CLINIC FOR COUNSELLING (HM04680) | | | | | | | | | | | | | | | | | | | | | | | | | |
| CLINIC FOR COUNSELLING (HM04681) | | | | | | | | | | | | | | | | | | | | | | | | | |
| COCKELL, VALERIE (HM04767) | | | | | | | | | | | | | | | | | | | | | | | | | |
| COLLEGE-PRACTICAL HOMEOPATHY (HM04855) | | | | | | | | | | | | | | | | | | | | | | | | | |
| COLLINS, V (HM04880) | | | | | | | | | | | | | | | | | | | | | | | | | |
| COMP MEDI ASS (HM04913) | | | | ● | | ● | | | ● | | ● | | | | | | | | ● | ● | | ● | | | |
| COMPLETE HEALTH CARE (HM04958) | | | | | | | ● | ● | ● | | | ● | | | | | | | | | | ● | | | |
| CONN, RONALD & SHALINI (HM04984) | | | | | | | | | | | | | | | | | | | | | | | | | |
| CONNAUGHT PRACTICE (HM04985) | | | | | | | | | | | | | | | | | | | | | | | | | |
| CONNAUGHT SQUARE HYPNOTHERAPY (HM04986) | | | ● | | | | | | | | | | | | | | | | | | | | | | |
| CONWAY, JONATHAN (HM05028) | | | | | | | | | | | | | | | | | | | | | | | | | |
| CONWAY, JONATHON (HM05029) | | | | | | | | | | | | | | | | | | | | | | | | | |
| COSMOS HERBS (HM05205) | | | | | | | | | | | | | | | | | | | | | | | | | |
| COUNSELLING & PSYCHOTHERAPY (HM05246) | | | | | | | | | | | | | | | | | | | | | | | | | |
| COUNSELLING SERVICE (HM05252) | | | | | | | | | | | | | | | | | | | | | | | | | |
| CRAVEN CLINIC (HM05385) | | | | | | | | | | | | | | | | | | | ● | | | | | | |

# F - O Therapies at Practices/Businesses

| Business by County with Reference no. | Family Planning (Natural) | Family Therapy | Feldenkrais Methodology | Feng Shui | Floral Essence Therapy | Flotation Therapy | Gait Analysis | Gem Essence Therapy | Gestalt Therapy | Group Therapy | Hay Diet | Healer | Healing Therapy | Hellerwork | Herbal Medicine | Holistic Healing | Homeopathy | Hopi Ear Candles | Humanistic Psychology | Hypnosis | Hypnotherapy | Indian Head Massage | Inhalation Therapy | Iridology | Kinesiology | Kirlian Photography | Laser Treatment | Life Style Coaching | Light Therapy | Macrobiotics | Magnetic Therapy | Manipulation | Manual Lymph Drainage | Massage (Therapeutic) | McTimoney Chiropractic | Meditation | Metamorphic Therapy | Miasm Therapy | Micro Manipulation | Moxibustion | Mud Therapy | Music Therapy | Nail Surgery | Naturopathy | Neuro-Linguistic Program | Neurotherapy | Nutritional Therapy | Orgone Therapy | Oriental Diagnosis | Orthomolecular Medicine |
|---|---|---|---|---|---|---|---|---|---|---|---|---|---|---|---|---|---|---|---|---|---|---|---|---|---|---|---|---|---|---|---|---|---|---|---|---|---|---|---|---|---|---|---|---|---|---|---|---|---|---|
| CREATIVE INSIGHTS (HM05399) | | | | | | | | | | | | | | | | | | | | ● | ● | ● | | | | | | ● | | | | | | | | | | | | | | | | | ● | | | | | |
| CTRE FOR CRANIO-SACRAL THERAPY (HM05540) | | | | | | | | | | | | | | | ● | | ● | | | ● | ● | | | | | | | | | | | ● | | ● | | | ● | | | | | | | | | | | | | |
| CTRE FOR THE STUDY OF COMP MED (HM05544) | | | | | | | | | | | | | | | ● | | ● | | | ● | | | | | | | | | | ● | | | | | | ● | | | | | | | | | | | ● | | | |
| CULL, KAREN (HM05557) | | | | | | | | | | | | | | | | | | | | ● | | | | | | | | | | | | | | | | | | | | | | | | | | | | | | |
| CULPEPER (HM05586) | | | | | | | | | | | | | | | ● | | | | | | | | | | | | | | | | | | | | | | | | | | | | | | | | | | | |
| CULPEPER (HM05573) | | | | | | | | | | | | | | | ● | | | | | | | | | | | | | | | | | | | | | | | | | | | | | | | | | | | |
| CUMMING, JOHN (HM05602) | | | | | | | | | | | | | | | | | ● | | | | | | | | | | | | | | | | | | | | | | | | | | | | | | | | | |
| CUTLER, PAULINE (HM05646) | | | | | | | | | | | | | | | | | ● | | | | | | | | | | | | | | | | | | | | | | | | | | | | | | | | | |
| DALTON, HELEN (HM05698) | | | | | ● | | | | | | | | | | | | ● | | | | | | | | | | | | | | | | | | | | | | | | | | | | | | | | | |
| DARNELL, PATRICIA (HM05748) | | | | | | | | | | | | | | | | | ● | | | | | | | | | | | | | | | | | | | | | | | | | | | | | | | | | |
| DAVEIGAS, DOUGLAS (HM05764) | | | | | | | | | | | | | | | | | | | | ● | | | | | | | | | | | | | | | | | | | | | | | | | | | | | | |
| DAVID WEISS HOMEOPATHY (HM05781) | | | | | | | | | | | | | | | | | ● | | | | | | | | | | | | | | | | | | | | | | | ● | | | | | | | | | | |
| DAVIES, E R (HM05809) | | | | | | | | | | | | | | | | | | | | ● | | | | | | | | | | | | | | | | | | | | | | | | | | | | | | |
| DAWSON, DAVID (DR) (HM05880) | | | | | | | | | | | | | | | | | ● | | | | | | | | | | | | | | | | | | | | | | | | | | | | | | | | | |
| DE BURGH, JULIE (HM05904) | | | | | | | | | | | | | | | | | | | | ● | ● | | | | | | | | | | | | | | | | | | | | | | | | | | | | | |
| DE FERE, SUSANNA (HM05905) | | | | | | | | | | | | | | | | | | | | ● | | | | | | | | | | | | | | | | | | | | | | | | | | | | | | |
| DELROY, SANDRA (DR) (HM05968) | | ● | | | | | | | | ● | | | | | | | | | | | | | | | | | | | | | | | | | | | | | | | | | | | | | | | | |
| DENNIS MICHAEL PRACTICE (HM05990) | | | | | | | | | | | | | | | | | | | | | | | | | | | | | | | | ● | | ● | | | | | | ● | | | | ● | | | ● | | | |
| DEWANE, JENNY (HM06045) | | | | | | | | | | | | | | | | | | | | ● | | | | | | | | | | | | | | | | | | | | | | | | | | | | | | |
| DEXTER, NICOLA (HM06050) | | | | | | | | | | | | | | | | | | | | ● | | | | | | | | | | | | | | | | | | | | | | | | | | | | | | |
| DISTANT HEALING (HM06123) | | | | | | | | | | | | ● | ● | | | | | | | | | | | | | | | | | | | | | | | | | | | | | | | | | | | | | |
| DOVE, JULIE (HM06228) | | | | | | | | | | | | | | | | | | | | ● | | | | | | | | | | | | | | | | | | | | | | | | | | | | | | |
| DOWLING, E (HM06239) | | | | | | | | | | | | | | | | | | | | ● | | | | | | | | | | | | | | | | | | | | | | | | | | | | | | |
| DREAM LINE (HM06296) | | | | | | | | | ● | | | | | | | | | | ● | | | | | | | | | | | | | | | | | | | | | | | | | | | | | | | |
| DYSON, R (HM06461) | | | | | | | | | | | | | | | | | ● | | | | | | | | | | | | | | | | | | | | | | | | | | | | | | | | | |
| E.LONDON COMPLEMENTARY HEALTH (HM06479) | | | | | | | | | | | | | | | | | ● | | | | | ● | | | | | | | | | | | | | | | | | | | | | | | | | | | | |
| EALING COUNS & THERAPY CTRE (HM06488) | | ● | | | | | | | | | | | | | | ● | | | | | | | | ● | | | | | | | | | | | | | | | | | | | | | | | | | | |
| EAST LONDON HOM GROUP PRACTICE (HM06517) | | | | | | | | | | | | | | | | | ● | | | | | | | | | | | | | | | | | | | | | | | | | | | | | | | | | |
| EAST WEST HERB SHOP (HM06527) | | | | | | | | | | | | | | | ● | | | | | | | | | | | | | | | | | | | | | | | | | | | | | | | | | | ● | |
| EAST WEST THERAPIES (HM06529) | | | | | | | | | | | | ● | ● | | | ● | | | | | | ● | | | | | | | | | | ● | | ● | | ● | | | | | | | | | | | | | | |
| EDGELL, MARJORY (HM06599) | | | | | | | | | | | | | | | | | | | | ● | ● | | | | | | | | | | | | | | | | | | | | | | | | | | | | | |
| EDGWARE NATURAL HEALTH CENTRE (HM06604) | | | | | | | | | | | | | | | | | ● | | | | ● | ● | | | | | | | | | | | | | | | | | | | | | | | | | ● | | | |
| ELBAHJA, MOHAMMED (HM06700) | | | | | | | | | | | | | | | | | | | | ● | | | | | | | | | | | | | | | | | | | | | | | | | | | | | | |
| ELLWOOD, CAROLINE (HM06780) | | | | | | | | | | | | | | | | | ● | | | | | | | | | | | | | | | | | | | | | | | | | | | ● | | | | | | |

# F - O Therapies at Practices/Businesses

| Business by County with Reference no. | Family Planning (Natural) | Family Therapy | Feldenkrais Methodology | Feng Shui | Floral Essence Therapy | Flotation Therapy | Gait Analysis | Gem Essence Therapy | Gestalt Therapy | Group Therapy | Hay Diet | Healer | Healing Therapy | Hellerwork | Herbal Medicine | Holistic Healing | Homeopathy | Hopi Ear Candles | Humanistic Psychology | Hypnosis | Hypnotherapy | Indian Head Massage | Inhalation Therapy | Iridology | Kinesiology | Kirlian Photography | Laser Treatment | Life Style Coaching | Light Therapy | Macrobiotics | Magnetic Therapy | Manipulation | Manual Lymph Drainage | Massage (Therapeutic) | McTimoney Chiropractic | Meditation | Metamorphic Therapy | Miasm Therapy | Micro Manipulation | Moxibustion | Mud Therapy | Music Therapy | Nail Surgery | Naturopathy | Neuro-Linguistic Program | Neurotherapy | Nutritional Therapy | Orgone Therapy | Oriental Diagnosis | Orthomolecular Medicine |
|---|---|---|---|---|---|---|---|---|---|---|---|---|---|---|---|---|---|---|---|---|---|---|---|---|---|---|---|---|---|---|---|---|---|---|---|---|---|---|---|---|---|---|---|---|---|---|---|---|---|---|
| ELTHAM HYPNOTHERAPY ANALYSIS (HM06789) | | ● | | | | | | | | | | | | | | | | | ● | ● | ● | | | | | | | | | | | | | | | | | | | | | | | | | | | | | |
| ENFIELD CLINIC OF HERBAL MED (HM06818) | | | | | | | | | | | | | | | ● | | | | | | | | | | | | | | | | | | | | | | | | | | | | | | | | | | | |
| ENFIELD HYP & COUNSELLING (HM06819) | | | | | | | | | | | | | | | | | | | | ● | ● | | | | | | | | | | | | | | | | | | | | | | | | | | | | | |
| EQUILIBRIUM (HM06869) | | | | | | | | | | | | | | | | ● | ● | | | | ● | ● | | | | | | | | | | | | ● | ● | | | | | | | | | ● | | | | | | |
| EQUILIBRIUM COUNS/THRPY CTRE (HM06873) | | | | | | | | | ● | | | | | | | | ● | | ● | ● | ● | | | | | | | | | | | | | ● | | | | | | | | | | ● | | | | | | |
| FACULTY OF HOMEOPATHY (HM07040) | | | | | | | | | | | | | | | | | ● | | | | | | | | | | | | | | | | | | | | | | | | | | | | | | | | | |
| FAITH, GORDON (HM07069) | | | | | | | | | | | | | | | | | | | | ● | | | | | | | | | | | | | | | | | | | | | | | | | | | | | | |
| FARMACIA URBAN HEALING (HM07107) | | | | | | | | | | | | | | | ● | | | | | ● | | ● | | | | | | | | | | | | ● | | | | | | | | | | ● | ● | | ● | | | |
| FARUKI, SHIRLEY (HM07137) | | | | | | | | | | | | | | | | | | | | ● | | | | | | | | | | | | | | | | | | | | | | | | | | | | | | |
| FELDENKRAIS CENTRE (HM07190) | | | ● | | | | | | | | | | | | | | | | | | | | | | | | | | | | | | | | | | | | | | | | | | | | | | | |
| FERGUSON, WILMA (HM07232) | | | | | | | | | | | | | | | | | ● | | | | | | | | | | | | | | | | | | | | | | | | | | | | | | | | | |
| FIRST PATH HYPNOTHERAPY (HM07339) | | | | | | | | | | | | | | | | | | | | ● | | | | | | | | | | | | | | | | | | | | | | | | | | | | | | |
| FITENI, SUZANNE (HM07362) | | | | | | | | | | | | | | | | | ● | | | | | | | | | | | | | | | | | | | | | | | | | | | | | | | | | |
| FLEXIBLE HOUR (HM07420) | | | | | | | | | | | | | | | | | | | | | | | | | | | | | | | | | | ● | | | | | | | | | | | | | | | | |
| FLOAT WORKS (HM07424) | | | | | | | | | | | | | | | | | | | | | | ● | | | | | | | | | | | | | | | | | | | | | | | | | | | | |
| FORDHAM, SHARON (HM07537) | | | | | | | | | | | | | | | | | | | | ● | | | | | | | | | | | | | | | | | | | | | | | | | | | | | | |
| FORERO-CASAS, SANDYRA (HM07543) | | | | | | | | | | | | | | | | | | | | ● | | | | | | | | | | | | | | | | | | | | | | | | | | | | | | |
| FOREST-HYPNOPSYCHOTHERAPY (HM07551) | | | | | | | | | | | | | | | | | | | | ● | | | | | | | | | | | | | | | | | | | | | | | | | | | | | | |
| FRY, HOWARD (HM07772) | | | | | | | | | | | | | | | | | | | | | | | | | | | | | | | | | | | | | | | | | | | ● | | | | | | | |
| FULHAM CLINIC (HM07781) | | | | | | | | | | | | | | | ● | ● | ● | | | | ● | ● | | | | | | | | | | | | ● | | | | | | | | | | | | | | | | |
| G T CONSULTANCY (HM07815) | | | | | | | | | | | | | ● | | | | | | | ● | ● | | | | | | | | | | | | | | | | | | | | | | | | | | | | | |
| GARTLAND, LINDA (HM07913) | | | | | | | | | | | | | | | | | ● | | | | | | | | | | | | | | | | | | | | | | | | | | | | | | | | | |
| GEORGE (HM07987) | | | | | | | | | | | | | | | | | | | | | | | | | | | | | | | | | | | | | | | | | | | ● | | | | | | | |
| GEORGE, ROSALIND (HM07991) | | | | | | | | | | | | | | | | | ● | | | | | | | | | | | | | | | | | | | | | | | | | | | | | | | | | |
| GERMAN, PATRICIA (HM07999) | | | | | | | | | | | | | | | ● | | | | | | | | | | | | | | | | | | | | | | | | | | | | | | | | | | | |
| GESTALT CENTRE (HM08005) | | | | | | | | | ● | ● | | | | | | | | | | | | | | | | | | | | | | | | | | | | | | | | | | | | | | | | |
| GLASSMAN, DAVID (HM08128) | | | | | | | | | | | | | | | | | | | | | | | | | | | | | | | | | | | | | | | | | | | | | ● | | | | | |
| GOLDING, KATE (HM08221) | | | | | | | | | | | | | | | | | ● | | | | | | | | | | | | | | | | | | | | | | | | | | | | | | | | | |
| GOODCHILD & ORR ASSOCIATES (HM08247) | | | | | | | | | | | | | | | | | | | | ● | | | | | | | | | | | | | | | | | | | | | | | | | | | | | | |
| GRANT, SYLVIA (HM08391) | | | | | | | | | | | | | | | | | | | | ● | | | | | | | | | | | | | | | | | | | | | | | | | | | | | | |
| GREENWICH NATURAL HEALTH CTRE (HM08500) | | | | | | | | | | | | | | | ● | | ● | | | | ● | ● | | | | | | | | | | | | ● | | | | | | | | | | | | | | | | |
| GREIDINGER, CLIVE (HM08524) | | | | | | | | | | | | | ● | | | | | | | ● | ● | | | | | | | | | | | | | | | | | | | | | | | | | | | | | |
| GROCHOLSKI, SABINE (HM08590) | | | | | | | | | | | | | | | | | ● | | | | | | | | | | | | | | | | | | | | | | | | | | | | | | | | | |
| GROUP ANALYTIC PRACTICE (HM08605) | | | | | | | | | | ● | | | | | | | | | | | | | | | | | | | | | | | | | | | | | | | | | | | | | | | | |

# F - O Therapies at Practices/Businesses

| Business by County with Reference no. | Family Planning (Natural) | Family Therapy | Feldenkrais Methodology | Feng Shui | Floral Essence Therapy | Flotation Therapy | Gait Analysis | Gem Essence Therapy | Gestalt Therapy | Group Therapy | Hay Diet | Healer | Healing Therapy | Hellerwork | Herbal Medicine | Holistic Healing | Homeopathy | Hopi Ear Candles | Humanistic Psychology | Hypnosis | Hypnotherapy | Indian Head Massage | Inhalation Therapy | Iridology | Kinesiology | Kirlian Photography | Laser Treatment | Life Style Coaching | Light Therapy | Macrobiotics | Magnetic Therapy | Manipulation | Manual Lymph Drainage | Massage (Therapeutic) | McTimoney Chiropractic | Meditation | Metamorphic Therapy | Miasm Therapy | Micro Manipulation | Moxibustion | Mud Therapy | Music Therapy | Nail Surgery | Naturopathy | Neuro-Linguistic Program | Neurotherapy | Nutritional Therapy | Orgone Therapy | Oriental Diagnosis | Orthomolecular Medicine |
|---|---|---|---|---|---|---|---|---|---|---|---|---|---|---|---|---|---|---|---|---|---|---|---|---|---|---|---|---|---|---|---|---|---|---|---|---|---|---|---|---|---|---|---|---|---|---|---|---|---|---|
| GUEST, GRAHAM (HM08623) | | | | | | | | | | | | | ● | | | | | | | | | | | | | | | | | | | | | | | | | | | | | | | | | | | | | |
| GUILD-NATUROPATHIC IRIDOLOGY (HM08635) | | | | | | | | | | | | | | | | | | | | | | | | ● | | | | | | | | | | | | | | | | | | | | | | | | | | |
| HACK, SHAMS Z E (HM08679) | | | | | | | | | | | | | | | | | ● | | | | | | | | | | | | | | | | | | | | | | | | | | | | | | | | | |
| HACKNEY HYPNOTHERAPY (HM08685) | | | | | | | | | | | | | | | | | | | ● | ● | ● | | | | | | | ● | | | | | | | | | | | | | | | | | | | | | | |
| HAIN, PATRICIA (HM08712) | | | | | | | | | | | | | | | | | | | | | | | | | | | | | | | | | | | | | | | | | | | | | | | ● | | | |
| HAREWOOD, MARCIA M (HM08991) | | | | | | | | | | | | | | | ● | | | | | | | | | ● | | | | | | | | ● | | ● | | | | | | | | | | ● | | | ● | | | |
| HARLEY ST STRESS MNGMT (HM08999) | | ● | | | | | | | | ● | | | | | | | | | | ● | ● | | | | ● | | | ● | | | | | | | | | | | | | | | | | ● | | | | | |
| HARLEY STREET TCM FERTILITY (HM09003) | | | | | | | | | | | | | | | ● | | | | | | | | | | | | | | | | | | | | | | | | | | | | | | | | | | ● | |
| HARPER, SUZANNE G (HM09041) | | | | | | | | | | | | | | | | | | | | ● | ● | | | | | | | ● | | | | ● | | | | | | | | ● | | | | ● | | | ● | | ● | |
| HARPER, SUZANNE G (HM09042) | | | | | | | | | | | | | | | | | | | | ● | ● | | | | | | | ● | | | | ● | | | | | | | | ● | | | | ● | | | ● | | ● | |
| HARROW HEALTH CARE CENTRE (HM09121) | | | | | | | | | | | | | | | | | | | | | | | | | | | | | | | | ● | | ● | | | | | | | | | | ● | | | | | | |
| HART Z HYPNOTHERAPIST (HM09124) | | | | | | | | | | | | | | | | | | | | ● | | | | | | | | | | | | | | | | | | | | | | | | | | | | | | |
| HARTER, J (HM09136) | | | | | | | | | | | | | | | | | ● | | | | | | | | | | | | | | | | | | | | | | | | | | | | | | | | | |
| HAVELOCK-SEARLE, PAULINE (HM09206) | | | | | | | | | | | | | | | | | | | | ● | ● | | | | | | | | | | | | | | | ● | | | | | | | | | | | | | | |
| HAWKINS, JAN (HM09222) | | | | | | | | | | ● | | | | | | | | | ● | | | | | | | | | | | | | | | ● | | | | | | | | | | | | | | | | |
| HAWKINS, TINA (HM09230) | | | | | | | | | | | | | | | | | | | | ● | | | | | | | | | | | | | | | | | | | | | | | | | | | | | | |
| HAYES HYPNOTHERAPY CENTRE (HM09255) | | | | | | | | | | | | | | | | | | | | ● | | | | | | | | | | | | | | | | | | | | | | | | | | | | | | |
| HEAL, CHRISTIANNE (HM09314) | | | | | | | | | | | | ● | | | | | | | | | | | | | | | | | | | | | | | | | | | | | | | | | | | | | | |
| HEALERS WORLD (HM09320) | ● | ● | | | | | | | | ● | ● | ● | ● | | ● | | ● | | | ● | ● | ● | | | ● | ● | | | | | | ● | | ● | | ● | | | | ● | ● | | | ● | | | ● | | ● | |
| HEALING ARTS UK (HM09326) | | | | | | | | | | | | | | | | | | | | | | ● | | | | | | | | | | | | ● | | | | | | | | | | | | | | | | |
| HEALTHY LIVING CENTRE (HM09429) | | | | | ● | | | | | | | | | | | | ● | | | | | | | | | | | | | | | | | | | | | | | | | | | | | | ● | | | |
| HELEN BERNAT - FITNESS TRAINER (HM09511) | | | | | | | | | | | | | | | | | | | | | | | | | | | | | | | | | | ● | | | | | | | | | | | | | | | | |
| HEPBURN, SUSAN (HM09582) | | | | | | | | | | | | | | | | | | | | ● | | | | | | | | | | | | | | | | | | | | | | | | | | | | | | |
| HERBAL AUTHORITY (HM09599) | | | | | | | | | | | | | | | ● | | | | | | | | | | | | | | | | | | | | | | | | | | | | | | | | | | | |
| HERBAL CARE (HM09601) | | | | | | | | | | | | | | | ● | | | | | | | | | | | | | | | | | | | | | | | | | | | | | | | | | | | |
| HERBAL CARE (HM09600) | | | | | | | | | | | | | | | ● | | | | | | | | | | | | | | | | | | | | | | | | | | | | | | | | | | | |
| HERBAL GARDEN (HM09611) | | | | | | | | | | | | | | | ● | | | | | | | | | | | | | | | | | | | | | | | | | | | | | | | | | | | |
| HERBAL INN (HM09623) | | | | | | | | | | | | | | | ● | | | | | | | | | | | | | | | | | | | | | | | | | | | | | | | | | | | |
| HERBAL INN (HM09622) | | | | | | | | | | | | | | | ● | | | | | | | | | | | | | | | | | | | | | | | | | | | | | | | | | | | |
| HERBAL TREATMENT CLINIC (HM09638) | | | | | | | | | | | | | | | ● | | | | | | | | | | | | | | | | | | | | | | | | | | | | | | | | ● | | | |
| HERBALIFE (HM09641) | | | | | | | | | | | | | | | ● | | | | | | | | | | | | | | | | | | | | | | | | | | | | | | | | | | | |
| HERBALIFE INDEPENDENT DIST (HM09642) | | | | | | | | | | | | | | | ● | | | | | | | | | | | | | | | | | | | | | | | | | | | | | | | | | | | |
| HERBALIST (HM09643) | | | | | | | | | | | | | | | ● | | | | | | | | | | | | | | | | | | | | | | | | | | | | | | | | | | | |
| HERBALIST CENTRE (HM09644) | | | | | | | | | | | | | | | ● | | | | | | | | | | | | | | | | | | | | | | | | | | | | | | | | | | | |

# F - O Therapies at Practices/Businesses

Business by County with Reference no.

| Business | Family Planning (Natural) | Family Therapy | Feldenkrais Methodology | Feng Shui | Floral Essence Therapy | Flotation Therapy | Gait Analysis | Gem Essence Therapy | Gestalt Therapy | Group Therapy | Hay Diet | Healer | Healing Therapy |
|---|---|---|---|---|---|---|---|---|---|---|---|---|---|
| HERBMEDIC (HM09663) | | | | | | | | | | | | | |
| HERBS SPECIALISTS (HM09675) | | | | | | | | | | | | | |
| HETHERTON, ANNE (HM09697) | | | | | | | | | | | | | |
| HILDRETH & COCKER (HM09767) | | | | | | | | | | | | | |
| HOBBS, SALLY (HM09858) | | | | | | | | | | | | | |
| HODSON, D (HM09895) | | | | | | | | | | | | | |
| HOGARTH CLINIC (HM09907) | | | | | | | | | | | | | |
| HOLISTIC THERAPEUTIC MASSAGE (HM09992) | | | | | | | | | | | | | |
| HOLM, KIRSTI (HM10031) | | | | | | | | | | | | | |
| HOLMES, DAVID (HM10040) | | | | | | | | | | | | | |
| HOMOEOPATHIC HEALTH CENTRE (HM10095) | | | | | | | | | | | | | |
| HONEYBOURNE, VANESSA (HM10116) | | | | | | | | | | | | | |
| HONG SOFTWARE & HERBAL CLINIC (HM10118) | | | | | | | | | | | | | |
| HONG TAD ACUPUNCTURE & HERBAL (HM10119) | | | | | | | | | | | | | |
| HOPE, JAMES (HM10140) | | | | | | | | | | | | | |
| HORNE-STANLEY, C (HM10181) | | | | | | | | | | | | | |
| HOUSE OF MISTRY (HM10220) | | | | | | | | | | | | | |
| HOWARD, L (HM10239) | | | | | | | | | | | | | |
| HOWARD, LYNNE (HM10241) | | | | | | | | | | | | | |
| HOWARD, LYNNE (HM10240) | | | | | ● | | | | | | | | |
| HUGHES, PAUL (HM10339) | | | | | | | | | | | | | |
| HUSSAIN-FARNSWORTH, R (HM10437) | | | | | | | | | | | | | |
| HYPNOTHERAPY & PSYCHO PRACTICE (HM10509) | | | | | | | | | | | | | |
| HYPNOTHERAPY ADVICE LINE (HM10513) | | | | | | | | | | | | | |
| HYPNOTHERAPY CENTRE (HM10527) | | | | | | | | | | | | | |
| INDEPENDENT PSYCHOLOGY SERVICE (HM10610) | | ● | | | | | | | ● | | | | |
| INSTITUTE OF CLINICAL HYPNOSIS (HM10672) | | | | | | | | | | | | | |
| INT FEDERATION OF NEUROTHERAPY (HM10685) | | | | | | | | | | | | | |
| INTERNATIONAL COLLEGE (HM10693) | | | | | | | | | | | | | |
| IN-THERAPY (HM10699) | | | | | | | | | | | | | |
| IRIDOLOGY & HOLISTIC HLTH CLGE (HM10721) | | | | | | | | | | | | | |
| ISLAND HEALTH CENTRE (HM10770) | | | | | | | | | | | | | |
| ISLINGTON CHIROPRACTIC CLINIC (HM10773) | | | | | | | | | | | | | |
| ISLINGTON CTRE FOR HOMOEOPATHY (HM10774) | | | | | | | | | | | | | |

| Business | Hellerwork | Herbal Medicine | Holistic Healing | Homeopathy | Hopi Ear Candles | Humanistic Psychology | Hypnosis | Hypnotherapy | Indian Head Massage | Inhalation Therapy | Iridology | Kinesiology |
|---|---|---|---|---|---|---|---|---|---|---|---|---|
| HERBMEDIC (HM09663) | | ● | ● | | | | | | | | | |
| HERBS SPECIALISTS (HM09675) | | ● | | | | | | | | | | |
| HETHERTON, ANNE (HM09697) | | | | ● | | | | | | | | |
| HILDRETH & COCKER (HM09767) | | ● | | | | | | | | | | |
| HOBBS, SALLY (HM09858) | | | | | | | | | | | | |
| HODSON, D (HM09895) | | | | | | | ● | | | | | |
| HOGARTH CLINIC (HM09907) | | | | | | | | | | | | ● |
| HOLISTIC THERAPEUTIC MASSAGE (HM09992) | | | | | | | | | | | | |
| HOLM, KIRSTI (HM10031) | | | | | | | ● | | | | | |
| HOLMES, DAVID (HM10040) | | | | | | | | | | | | |
| HOMOEOPATHIC HEALTH CENTRE (HM10095) | | | | ● | | | | | | | | |
| HONEYBOURNE, VANESSA (HM10116) | | | | ● | | | | | | | | |
| HONG SOFTWARE & HERBAL CLINIC (HM10118) | | ● | | | | | | | | | | |
| HONG TAD ACUPUNCTURE & HERBAL (HM10119) | | ● | ● | | | | | | | | | |
| HOPE, JAMES (HM10140) | | | | | | | ● | | | | | |
| HORNE-STANLEY, C (HM10181) | | | | | | | ● | | | | | |
| HOUSE OF MISTRY (HM10220) | | ● | | ● | | | | | ● | | | |
| HOWARD, L (HM10239) | | | | ● | | | | | | | | |
| HOWARD, LYNNE (HM10241) | | | | ● | | | | | | | | |
| HOWARD, LYNNE (HM10240) | | ● | | ● | | | | | | | | ● |
| HUGHES, PAUL (HM10339) | | | | ● | | | | | | | | |
| HUSSAIN-FARNSWORTH, R (HM10437) | | | | ● | | | | | | | | |
| HYPNOTHERAPY & PSYCHO PRACTICE (HM10509) | | | | | | | ● | | | | | |
| HYPNOTHERAPY ADVICE LINE (HM10513) | | | | | | | ● | | | | | |
| HYPNOTHERAPY CENTRE (HM10527) | | | | | | | ● | | | | | |
| INDEPENDENT PSYCHOLOGY SERVICE (HM10610) | | | | | | | | | | | | |
| INSTITUTE OF CLINICAL HYPNOSIS (HM10672) | | | | | | | ● | | | | | |
| INT FEDERATION OF NEUROTHERAPY (HM10685) | | | | | | | | | | | | |
| INTERNATIONAL COLLEGE (HM10693) | | | | | | | ● | | | | | |
| IN-THERAPY (HM10699) | | | | | | | ● | | | | | |
| IRIDOLOGY & HOLISTIC HLTH CLGE (HM10721) | | ● | | | | | | | | | ● | |
| ISLAND HEALTH CENTRE (HM10770) | | | | | | | ● | | | | | |
| ISLINGTON CHIROPRACTIC CLINIC (HM10773) | | | | | | | | | | | | |
| ISLINGTON CTRE FOR HOMOEOPATHY (HM10774) | | | | ● | | | | | | | | |

| Business | Kirlian Photography | Laser Treatment | Life Style Coaching | Light Therapy | Macrobiotics | Magnetic Therapy | Manipulation | Manual Lymph Drainage | Massage (Therapeutic) | McTimoney Chiropractic | Meditation | Metamorphic Therapy | Miasm Therapy |
|---|---|---|---|---|---|---|---|---|---|---|---|---|---|
| HERBMEDIC (HM09663) | | | | | | | | | | | | | |
| HERBS SPECIALISTS (HM09675) | | | | | | | | | | | | | |
| HETHERTON, ANNE (HM09697) | | | | | | | | | | | | | |
| HILDRETH & COCKER (HM09767) | | | | | | | | | | | | | |
| HOBBS, SALLY (HM09858) | | | | | | | | | | | | | |
| HODSON, D (HM09895) | | | | | | | | | | | | | |
| HOGARTH CLINIC (HM09907) | | | | | | | ● | | ● | | | | |
| HOLISTIC THERAPEUTIC MASSAGE (HM09992) | | | | | | | | | ● | | | | |
| HOLM, KIRSTI (HM10031) | | | | | | | | | | | | | |
| HOLMES, DAVID (HM10040) | | | | | | | | | | | | | |
| HOMOEOPATHIC HEALTH CENTRE (HM10095) | | | | | | | | | | | | | |
| HONEYBOURNE, VANESSA (HM10116) | | | | | | | | | | | | | |
| HONG SOFTWARE & HERBAL CLINIC (HM10118) | | | | | | | | | | | | | |
| HONG TAD ACUPUNCTURE & HERBAL (HM10119) | | | | | | | | | ● | | ● | | |
| HOPE, JAMES (HM10140) | | | | | | | | | | | | | |
| HORNE-STANLEY, C (HM10181) | | | | | | | | | | | | | |
| HOUSE OF MISTRY (HM10220) | | | | | | | | | ● | | | | |
| HOWARD, L (HM10239) | | | | | | | | | | | | | |
| HOWARD, LYNNE (HM10241) | | | | | | | | | | | | | |
| HOWARD, LYNNE (HM10240) | | | | | | | | | | | | | |
| HUGHES, PAUL (HM10339) | | | | | | | | | | | | | |
| HUSSAIN-FARNSWORTH, R (HM10437) | | | | | | | | | | | | | |
| HYPNOTHERAPY & PSYCHO PRACTICE (HM10509) | | | | | | | | | | | | | |
| HYPNOTHERAPY ADVICE LINE (HM10513) | | | | | | | | | | | | | |
| HYPNOTHERAPY CENTRE (HM10527) | | | | | | | | | | | | | |
| INDEPENDENT PSYCHOLOGY SERVICE (HM10610) | | | | | | | | | | | | | |
| INSTITUTE OF CLINICAL HYPNOSIS (HM10672) | | | | | | | | | | | | | |
| INT FEDERATION OF NEUROTHERAPY (HM10685) | | | | | | | | | | | | | |
| INTERNATIONAL COLLEGE (HM10693) | | | | | | | | | | | | | |
| IN-THERAPY (HM10699) | | | | | | | | | | | | | |
| IRIDOLOGY & HOLISTIC HLTH CLGE (HM10721) | | | | | | | | | | | | | |
| ISLAND HEALTH CENTRE (HM10770) | | | | | | | | | | | | | |
| ISLINGTON CHIROPRACTIC CLINIC (HM10773) | | | | | | | | | ● | | | | |
| ISLINGTON CTRE FOR HOMOEOPATHY (HM10774) | | | | | | | | | | | | | |

| Business | Micro Manipulation | Moxibustion | Mud Therapy | Music Therapy | Nail Surgery | Naturopathy | Neuro-Linguistic Program | Neurotherapy | Nutritional Therapy | Orgone Therapy | Oriental Diagnosis | Orthomolecular Medicine |
|---|---|---|---|---|---|---|---|---|---|---|---|---|
| HERBMEDIC (HM09663) | | ● | | | | | | | | | ● | |
| HERBS SPECIALISTS (HM09675) | | | | | | | | | | | | |
| HETHERTON, ANNE (HM09697) | | | | | | | | | | | | |
| HILDRETH & COCKER (HM09767) | | | | | | ● | | | ● | | | |
| HOBBS, SALLY (HM09858) | | | | | | ● | | | | | | |
| HODSON, D (HM09895) | | | | | | | | | | | | |
| HOGARTH CLINIC (HM09907) | | ● | | | | ● | | | | | | |
| HOLISTIC THERAPEUTIC MASSAGE (HM09992) | | | | | | | | | | | | |
| HOLM, KIRSTI (HM10031) | | | | | | | | | | | | |
| HOLMES, DAVID (HM10040) | | | | | ● | | | | | | | |
| HOMOEOPATHIC HEALTH CENTRE (HM10095) | | | | | | | | | | | | |
| HONEYBOURNE, VANESSA (HM10116) | | | | | | | | | | | | |
| HONG SOFTWARE & HERBAL CLINIC (HM10118) | | | | | | | | | | | | |
| HONG TAD ACUPUNCTURE & HERBAL (HM10119) | | ● | | | | | | | | | | |
| HOPE, JAMES (HM10140) | | | | | | | | | | | | |
| HORNE-STANLEY, C (HM10181) | | | | | | | | | | | | |
| HOUSE OF MISTRY (HM10220) | | | | | | ● | | | | | | |
| HOWARD, L (HM10239) | | | | | | | | | | | | |
| HOWARD, LYNNE (HM10241) | | | | | | | | | | | | |
| HOWARD, LYNNE (HM10240) | | | | | | | | | | | | |
| HUGHES, PAUL (HM10339) | | | | | | | | | | | | |
| HUSSAIN-FARNSWORTH, R (HM10437) | | | | | | | | | | | | |
| HYPNOTHERAPY & PSYCHO PRACTICE (HM10509) | | | | | | | | | | | | |
| HYPNOTHERAPY ADVICE LINE (HM10513) | | | | | | | | | | | | |
| HYPNOTHERAPY CENTRE (HM10527) | | | | | | | | | | | | |
| INDEPENDENT PSYCHOLOGY SERVICE (HM10610) | | | | | | | | | | | | |
| INSTITUTE OF CLINICAL HYPNOSIS (HM10672) | | | | | | | | | | | | |
| INT FEDERATION OF NEUROTHERAPY (HM10685) | | | | | | | | ● | | | | |
| INTERNATIONAL COLLEGE (HM10693) | | | | | | | | | | | | |
| IN-THERAPY (HM10699) | | | | | | | | | | | | |
| IRIDOLOGY & HOLISTIC HLTH CLGE (HM10721) | | | | | | ● | | | | | | |
| ISLAND HEALTH CENTRE (HM10770) | | | | | | | | | | | | |
| ISLINGTON CHIROPRACTIC CLINIC (HM10773) | | | | | | | | | | | | |
| ISLINGTON CTRE FOR HOMOEOPATHY (HM10774) | | | | | | | | | | | | |

# F - O Therapies at Practices/Businesses

| Business by County with Reference no. | Family Planning (Natural) | Family Therapy | Feldenkrais Methodology | Feng Shui | Floral Essence Therapy | Flotation Therapy | Gait Analysis | Gem Essence Therapy | Gestalt Therapy | Group Therapy | Hay Diet | Healer | Healing Therapy | Hellerwork | Herbal Medicine | Holistic Healing | Homeopathy | Hopi Ear Candles | Humanistic Psychology | Hypnosis | Hypnotherapy | Indian Head Massage | Inhalation Therapy | Iridology | Kinesiology | Kirlian Photography | Laser Treatment | Life Style Coaching | Light Therapy | Macrobiotics | Magnetic Therapy | Manipulation | Manual Lymph Drainage | Massage (Therapeutic) | McTimoney Chiropractic | Meditation | Metamorphic Therapy | Miasm Therapy | Micro Manipulation | Moxibustion | Mud Therapy | Music Therapy | Nail Surgery | Naturopathy | Neuro-Linguistic Program | Neurotherapy | Nutritional Therapy | Orgone Therapy | Oriental Diagnosis | Orthomolecular Medicine |
|---|---|---|---|---|---|---|---|---|---|---|---|---|---|---|---|---|---|---|---|---|---|---|---|---|---|---|---|---|---|---|---|---|---|---|---|---|---|---|---|---|---|---|---|---|---|---|---|---|---|---|
| ISLINGTON PSYCHOTHERAPY (HM10775) | | | | | | | | | | | | | | | | | | | | ● | | | | | | | | | | | | | | | | | | | | | | | | | | | | | | |
| JACOBS, BRIAN M (HM10858) | | | | | | | | | | | | | | | | | | | | | ● | | | | | | | | | | | | | | | | | | | | | | | | | | | | | |
| JAG, SONEJI (HM10871) | | | | | | | | | | | | | | | | | ● | | | | | | | | | | | | | | | | | | | | | | | | | | | | | | | | | |
| JELFS, MARTIN (HM10977) | | | | | | | | | ● | | | | | | | | | | ● | | | | | | | | | | | | | | | ● | | | | | | | | | | | | | | | | |
| JELFS, MARTIN (HM10976) | | | | | | | | | ● | | | | | | | | | | ● | | | | | | | | | | | | | | | ● | | | | | | | | | | | | | | | | |
| JEWERS, M S (HM11025) | | | | | | | | | | | | | | | | | | | | | | | | | | | | | | | | | | | | | | | | | | | ● | | | | | | | |
| JONES, MONICA (HM11180) | | | | | | | | | | | | | | | | | | | | ● | | | | | | | | | | | | | | | | | | | | | | | | | | | | | | |
| KADRI, KALPNA (HM11293) | | | | | | | | | | | | | | | | | ● | | | | | | | | | | | | | | | | | | | | | | | | | | | | | | | | | |
| KAGYU SAMYE DZONG LONDON (HM11294) | | | | | | | | | | | | | | | ● | | | | | | | | | | | | | | | | | | | | | | | | | | | | | | | | | | ● | |
| KALLAS, JEMIMA (HM11297) | | | | | | | | | | | | | | | | | ● | | | | | | | | | | | | | | | | | | | | | | | | | | | | | | | | | |
| KANE AND ROSS CLINICS (HM11309) | | | | | | | | | | | | | | | ● | | | | | | | | | | | | | | | | | ● | | | | | | | | | | | | ● | | | | | | |
| KEITH EGLETON HYPNOTHERAPY (HM11412) | | | | | | | | | | | | | | | | | | | | ● | ● | | | | | | | | | | | | | | | | | | | | | | | | | | | | | |
| KERN, MICHAEL (HM11544) | | | | | | | | | | | | | | | | | | | | | | | | | | | | | | | | | | | | | | | | | | | | ● | | | | | | |
| KESSLER, GABRIEL (HM11563) | | | | | | | | | | | | | | | | | ● | | | | | | | | | | | | | | | | | | | | | | | | | | | | | | | | | |
| KIKAI SHIATSU CENTRE (HM11598) | | | | | | | | | | | | | | | | | | | | | | | | | | | | | | | | | | | | | | | | ● | | | | | | | | | ● | |
| KILBRIDE, PETER (HM11600) | | | | | | | | | | | | | | | | | | | | ● | ● | | | | | | | | | | | | | | | | | | | | | | | | | | | | | |
| KINGSBURY PSYCHOTHERAPY PRAC (HM11660) | | | | | | | | | | ● | | ● | ● | | | | | | | ● | ● | | | | | | | | | | | | | | | | | | | | | | | | | | | | | |
| KINGSGATE ACUPUNCTURE PRACTICE (HM11663) | | | | | | | | | | | | | | | | | | | | | | | | | | | | | | | | | | | | | | | | ● | | | | | | | | | ● | |
| KIRSH, MALCOLM (DR) (HM11724) | | | | | | | | | | | | | | | | | | | | ● | ● | | | | | | | | | | | | | | | | | | | | | | | | | | | | | |
| KIRSH, MALCOLM (DR) (HM11725) | | | | | | | | | | | | | | | | | | | | ● | ● | | | | | | | | | | | | | | | | | | | | | | | | | | | | | |
| KRISHNA RAMAMOURTHY MNIMH (HM11802) | | | | | | | | | | | | | | | ● | | | | | | | | | | | | | | | | | | | | | | | | | | | | | | | | | | | |
| LAVENDER HILL HOMEOPATHIC CTRE (HM12021) | | | | | | | | | | | | | | | | | ● | | | | | | | | | | | | | | | | | | | | | | | | | | | | | | | | | |
| LEE COMPLEMENTARY HEALTH CTRE (HM12130) | | | | | | | | | | | | | | | ● | | ● | | | | | | | | | | | | | | | ● | | ● | | | | | | ● | | | | ● | | | ● | | ● | |
| LEVER CLINIC (HM12256) | | | | | | | | | | | | | | | | | | | | | | | | | | | | | | | | ● | | ● | | | | | ● | | | | | | | | ● | | | |
| LIFE CHANGES (HM12340) | | | | | | | | | | | | | | | | | | | | ● | | | | | | | | | | | | | | | | | | | | | | | | | | | | | | |
| LIFESTYLE MANAGEMENT (HM12364) | | | | | | | | | | | | | | | | | | | | ● | | | | | | | | | | | | | | | | | | | | | | | | | | | | | | |
| LIVING CENTRE CLINIC (HM12483) | | | | | | | | | | | | | | | ● | ● | ● | | | ● | ● | ● | | ● | ● | | | | | | ● | | | ● | ● | ● | | | | ● | | | | | | | ● | | | |
| LIZ DAWSON - PSYCHOTHERAPIST (HM12494) | | ● | | | | | | | | ● | | | | | | | | | ● | | | | | | | | | | | | | | | | | | | | | | | | | | | | | | | |
| LJUBO, JACIC (HM12496) | | | | | | | | | | | | | | | | | | | | | | ● | | | | | | | | | | | | ● | | | | | | | | | | | | | | | | |
| LOCKE, ANNA (HM12539) | | | | | | | | | | | | | | | | | | | | | | ● | | | | | | | | | | | | | | | | | | | | | | | | | | | | |
| LOCKER, KAY (HM12542) | | | | | | | | | | | | | | | | | | | | ● | | | | | | | | | | | | | | | | | | | | | | | | | | | | | | |
| LONDON CLINIC OF PHYSIOTHERAPY (HM12586) | | | | | | | | | | | | | | | ● | | | | | | | | | | | | | | | | | | | | | | | | | | | | | | | | | | | |
| LONDON COLLEGE-CLNC HYPNOSIS (HM12591) | | | | | | | | | | | | | | | | | | | | ● | | | | | | | | | | | | | | | | | | | | | | | | | | | | | | |
| LONDON FLOAT CENTRE (HM12597) | | | | | | | | | | | | | | | ● | | ● | ● | | ● | | ● | | ● | ● | | | | | | | | | ● | ● | ● | ● | | | | | | | ● | | | ● | | | |

# F - O Therapies at Practices/Businesses

| Business by County with Reference no. | Family Planning (Natural) | Family Therapy | Feldenkrais Methodology | Feng Shui | Floral Essence Therapy | Flotation Therapy | Gait Analysis | Gem Essence Therapy | Gestalt Therapy | Group Therapy | Hay Diet | Healer | Healing Therapy | Hellerwork | Herbal Medicine | Holistic Healing | Homeopathy | Hopi Ear Candles | Humanistic Psychology | Hypnosis | Hypnotherapy | Indian Head Massage | Inhalation Therapy | Iridology | Kinesiology | Kirlian Photography | Laser Treatment | Life Style Coaching | Light Therapy | Macrobiotics | Magnetic Therapy | Manipulation | Manual Lymph Drainage | Massage (Therapeutic) | McTimoney Chiropractic | Meditation | Metamorphic Therapy | Miasm Therapy | Micro Manipulation | Moxibustion | Mud Therapy | Music Therapy | Nail Surgery | Naturopathy | Neuro-Linguistic Program | Neurotherapy | Nutritional Therapy | Orgone Therapy | Oriental Diagnosis | Orthomolecular Medicine |
|---|---|---|---|---|---|---|---|---|---|---|---|---|---|---|---|---|---|---|---|---|---|---|---|---|---|---|---|---|---|---|---|---|---|---|---|---|---|---|---|---|---|---|---|---|---|---|---|---|---|---|
| LONDON INDIAN CHAMPISSAGE CTRE (HM12599) | | | | | | | | | | | | | | | | | | | | | | ● | | | | | | | | | | ● | | ● | | | | | | | | | | | | | | | | |
| LONDON SHYNESS CENTRE (HM12608) | | | | | | | | | | | | | | | | | ● | | | | | | | | | | | | | | | | | | | | | | | | | | | | | | | | | |
| LONDON SPINE AND JOINT CLINIC (HM12611) | | | | | | | | | | | | | | | | | | | | | | ● | | | | | | ● | | | | ● | | ● | | | | | | | | | | | | | | | | |
| LONGLEY, JOANNA (HM12628) | | | | | | | | | | | | | | | | | | | | ● | | | | | | | | | | | | | | | | | | | | | | | | | | | | | | |
| LOTUS CLINIC (HM12653) | | | | | | | | | | | | | | | | | ● | | | | | | | | | | | | | | | | | | | | | | | | | | | | | | | | | |
| LURIE, DAVID (HM12743) | | | | | | | | | | | | | | | ● | | | | | | | | | | | | | | | | | | | | | | | | | | | | | | | | | | | |
| MACDONALD, R S J (HM12828) | | | | | | | | | | | | | | | ● | | | | | | | | | | | | | | | | | | | | | | | | | | | | | | | | | | | |
| MAGNA JEWELLERY (HM12913) | | | | | | | | | | | | | | | | | | | | | | | | | | | | | | | ● | | | | | | | | | | | | | | | | | | | |
| MAHER, J HYPNOTHERAPY (HM12931) | | | | | | | | | | | | | | | | | | | | ● | | | | | | | | | | | | | | | | | | | | | | | | | | | | | | |
| MANLEY CLINIC (HM13016) | | | | | | | | | | | | | | | | | ● | | | | | | | | | | | | | | | | | | | | | | | | | | | | | | | | | |
| MARKS, DARREN HYPNOTHERAPY (HM13119) | | | | | | | | | | | | | | | | | | | | ● | ● | | | | | | | | | | | | | | | | | | | | | | | | | | | | | |
| MARLBOROUGH THERAPY PRACTICE (HM13125) | | | | | | | | | | | | | | | | | | | | ● | ● | | | | | | | | | | | | | | | | | | | | | | | | | | | | | |
| MARSHALL, IAN (HM13163) | | | | | | | | | | | | | | | | | | | | ● | | | | | | | | | | | | | | | | | | | | | | | | | | | | | | |
| MARSHALL, JILL (HM13165) | | | | | | | | | | | | | | | | | | | | ● | | | | | | | | | | | | | | | | | | | | | | | | | | | | | | |
| MARSHALL-MANIFOLD, T (HM13173) | | | | | | | | | | | | | | | | | ● | | | | | | | | | | | | | | | | | | | | | | | | | | | | | | | | | |
| MARTIN, ANNE (HM13187) | | | | | | | | | | | | | | | | | | | | | | ● | | | | | | | | | | | | ● | | | | | | | | | | | | | | | | |
| MATTHEWS, ROBERT (HM13312) | | | | | | | | | | | | ● | | | | | | | | ● | ● | | | | | | | | | | | | | | | | | | | | | | | | | | | | | |
| MAYWAY UK (HM13361) | | | | | | | | | | | | | | | ● | | | | | | | | | | | | | | | | | | | | | | | | | | | | | | | | | | | |
| MCCAFFREY, GERARDINE (HM13380) | | | | | | | | | | | | | | | | | | | | | | | | | | | | | | | | | | ● | | | | | | | | | | | | | | | | |
| MCDERMOTT, ADRIAN (HM13445) | | | | | | | | | | | | | | | ● | | | | | | | | | | | | | | | | | | | | | | | | | | | | | | | | | | | |
| MCDERMOTT, ADRIAN (HM13444) | | | | | | | | | | | | | | | ● | | | | | | | | | | | | | | | | | | | | | | | | | | | | | | | | | | | |
| MCINTOSH, IAIN (HM13515) | | | | | | | | | | | | | | | | | | | | ● | | | | | | | | | | | | | | | | | | | | | | | | | | | | | | |
| MEDICAL SCIENCES TECH CORP (HM13654) | | | | | | | | | | | | | | | ● | ● | | | | | | | | | | | | | | | | | | | | | | | | | | | | | | | ● | | | |
| MICHAEL, MARIE (HM13796) | | | | | | | | | | | | | | | | | | | | ● | | | | | | | | | | | | | | | | | | | | | | | | | | | | | | |
| MIDAS TOUCH (HM13809) | | | | | | | | | | | | | | | | | | | | | | ● | | | | | | | | | | | | | | | | | | | | | | | | | | | | |
| MIDDLETON, IAN W (HM13821) | | | | | | | | | | | | | | | ● | | | | | | | | | | | | | | | | | | | ● | | | | | | | | | | | | | | | | |
| MILLMAN & ASSOCIATES (HM13921) | | | | | | | | | | | | | | | | | | | | ● | | | | | | | | | | | | | | | | | | | | | | | | | | | | | | |
| MILLS DE-WIN STUDIOS (HM13922) | | | | | | | | | | | | | | | | | | | | | | | | | | | | | | | | | | ● | | | | | | | | | | | | | | | | |
| MILLS, SUSAN (HM13935) | | | | | | | | | | | | | | | | | | | | ● | | | | | | | | | | | | | | | | | | | | | | | | | | | | | | |
| MINERVA HOMEOPATHIC CENTRE (HM13970) | | | | | | | | | | | | | | | | | ● | | | | | | | | | | | | | | | | | | | | | | | | | | | | | | | | | |
| MONTSERRAT CLINIC (HM14090) | | | | | | | | | | | | | | | | | ● | | | | | | | | | | | | | | | ● | | ● | | | | | | | | | | | | | | | | |
| MOTTINGHAM HYPNOTHERAPY CTRE (HM14279) | | | | | | | | | | | | | | | | | | | | ● | ● | | | | | | | | | | | | | | | | | | | | | | | | | | | | | |
| M-POWER (HM14308) | | | | | | | | | | | | | | | | | | | ● | | ● | | | | | | | ● | | | | | | | | | | | | | | | | | | | | | | |
| MYERS, RHONA (HM14440) | | | | | | | | | | | | | | | | | ● | | | | | | | | | | | | | | | | | | | | | | | | | | | | | | | | | |

# F - O Therapies at Practices/Businesses

| Business by County with Reference no. | Family Planning (Natural) | Family Therapy | Feldenkrais Methodology | Feng Shui | Floral Essence Therapy | Flotation Therapy | Gait Analysis | Gem Essence Therapy | Gestalt Therapy | Group Therapy | Hay Diet | Healer | Healing Therapy | Hellerwork | Herbal Medicine | Holistic Healing | Homeopathy | Hopi Ear Candles | Humanistic Psychology | Hypnosis | Hypnotherapy | Indian Head Massage | Inhalation Therapy | Iridology | Kinesiology |
|---|---|---|---|---|---|---|---|---|---|---|---|---|---|---|---|---|---|---|---|---|---|---|---|---|---|
| NATURAL HEALTH CLINIC (HM14575) | | | | | | | | | | | | | ● | | | | ● | | | | | | | | ● |
| NEEDLEMAN, DAVID (HM14753) | | | | | | | | | | | | | | | | | ● | | | | | | | | |
| NEIL-ASHER, S (HM14761) | | | | | | | | | | | | | | | | | | | | | | | | | |
| NEILL, VICTORIA (HM14764) | | | | | | | | | | | | | | | | | | | | | | | | | ● |
| NELSONS HOM & BACH REMEDIES (HM14783) | | | | | | | | | | | | | | | | | ● | | | | | | | | |
| NEW CROSS NATURAL THRPY CTRE (HM14814) | | | ● | | | | | | ● | ● | | ● | | | | | ● | | | | | | | | ● |
| NEWTON CLINIC (HM14892) | | | | | | | | | | | | | | | | | | | | ● | | | | | |
| NIELSEN, RITA C (HM14935) | | | | | | | | | | | | | | | | | | | | | | | | | |
| NOTTING HILL TRAD ACU CTRE (HM15081) | | | | | | | | | | | | | | | | | ● | | | | | | | | |
| NUTRITION FOR LIFE INT (HM15124) | ● | | | | | | | | | | | | | | ● | | | | | | | | | | |
| O'DRISCOLL, PAULINE (HM15230) | | | | | | | | | | | | | | | | | ● | | | | | | | | |
| OLIVER, KATE (HM15293) | | | | | | | | | | | | | | | | | | | | ● | | | | | |
| ORIENTAL MEDICINE (HM15386) | | | | | | | | | | | | | | | ● | | | | | | | | | | |
| OSMAN, JO (HM15437) | | | | | | | | | | | | | | | | | | | | ● | | | | | |
| OSTEOPATHIC ASSOCIATION CLINIC (HM15453) | | | | | | | | | | | | | | | | | | | | | | | | | |
| OSTEOPATHIC PRACTICE (HM15470) | | | | | | | | | | | | | ● | | | | ● | | | | | | | | |
| OSTEOPATHIC PRACTICE (HM15471) | | | | | | | | | | | | | | | | | | | | | | | | | |
| OTREMBA, KATHARINA (HM15496) | | | | | ● | | | ● | | | | | | | | ● | | | | ● | ● | | | | ● |
| OUTCOMES (HM15502) | | ● | | | | | | | ● | ● | | ● | ● | | | ● | | | ● | ● | ● | ● | | | ● |
| PACIFIC WAVES PRODUCTIONS (HM15553) | | ● | | | | | | | ● | ● | | | | | | | | | | ● | ● | | | | |
| PALFREYMAN, SUE (HM15592) | | | | | | | | | | | | | | | | | | | | | | | | | |
| PARADISE, PAM (HM15645) | | | | | | | | | | | | | | | | | | | | ● | | | | | |
| PARK PRACTICE (HM15673) | | | | | | | | | | | | | | | | | ● | | | | | | | | |
| PASHLEY, MAGGIE (HM15775) | | | | | | | | | | | | | | | | | | | | | | ● | | | |
| PATEL, J C (HM15788) | | | | | | | | | | | | | | | | | | | | | | | | | |
| PATEL, LINA (HM15792) | | | | | | | | | | | | | ● | | | | | | | | | ● | | | |
| PATEL, RIMA (HM15800) | | | | | | | | | | | | | | | | | ● | | | | | | | | |
| PATERSON, KARETH (HM15810) | | | | | | | | | | | | | | | | | | | | | | ● | | | |
| PEER, MARISA (HM15940) | | | | | | | | | | | | | | | | | | | | ● | | | | | |
| PERCIVAL, JO (HM16016) | | | | | | | | | | | | | | | | | ● | | | | | | | | |
| PERRINS, JOSEPH (HM16038) | | | | | | | | | | | | | | | | | | | | ● | | | | | |
| PHOENIX HOM/ALLGY TESTING CTRE (HM16157) | | | | | | | | | | | | | | | | | ● | | | | | | | | |
| PHYSIO ONE (HM16202) | | | | | | | | | | | | | | | | | | | | | | | | | |
| PHYSIOTHERAPY PRACTICE (HM16253) | | | | | | | | | | | | | | | | | | | | | | | | | |

| Business by County with Reference no. | Kirlian Photography | Laser Treatment | Life Style Coaching | Light Therapy | Macrobiotics | Magnetic Therapy | Manipulation | Manual Lymph Drainage | Massage (Therapeutic) | McTimoney Chiropractic | Meditation | Metamorphic Therapy | Miasm Therapy | Micro Manipulation | Moxibustion | Mud Therapy | Music Therapy | Nail Surgery | Naturopathy | Neuro-Linguistic Program | Neurotherapy | Nutritional Therapy | Orgone Therapy | Oriental Diagnosis | Orthomolecular Medicine |
|---|---|---|---|---|---|---|---|---|---|---|---|---|---|---|---|---|---|---|---|---|---|---|---|---|---|
| NATURAL HEALTH CLINIC (HM14575) | | | | | | | | | | | | | | | | | | | | | | ● | | | |
| NEEDLEMAN, DAVID (HM14753) | | | | | | | | | | | | | | | | | | | | | | | | | |
| NEIL-ASHER, S (HM14761) | | | | | | | | | | | | | | | | | | | ● | | | | | | |
| NEILL, VICTORIA (HM14764) | | | | | | | ● | | ● | | | | | ● | | | | | | | | | | | |
| NELSONS HOM & BACH REMEDIES (HM14783) | | | | | | | | | | | | | | | | | | | | | | | | | |
| NEW CROSS NATURAL THRPY CTRE (HM14814) | | | | | | | | | ● | | | | | | | | | | | | | ● | | | |
| NEWTON CLINIC (HM14892) | | | | | | | | | | | | | | | | | | | | | | | | | |
| NIELSEN, RITA C (HM14935) | | | | | | | | | | | | | | | | | | | | | | ● | | | |
| NOTTING HILL TRAD ACU CTRE (HM15081) | | | | | | | | | | | | | | | | | | | | | | | | | |
| NUTRITION FOR LIFE INT (HM15124) | | | | | | | | | | | | | | | | | | | | | | ● | | | |
| O'DRISCOLL, PAULINE (HM15230) | | | | | | | | | | | | | | | | | | | | | | | | | |
| OLIVER, KATE (HM15293) | | | | | | | | | | | | | | | | | | | | | | | | | |
| ORIENTAL MEDICINE (HM15386) | | | | | | | | | ● | | | | | | ● | | | | | | | | | ● | |
| OSMAN, JO (HM15437) | | | | | | | | | | | | | | | | | | | | | | | | | |
| OSTEOPATHIC ASSOCIATION CLINIC (HM15453) | | | | | | | ● | | | | | | | | | | | | | | | | | | |
| OSTEOPATHIC PRACTICE (HM15470) | | | | | | | ● | | ● | | | | | | | | | | | | | | | | |
| OSTEOPATHIC PRACTICE (HM15471) | | | | | | | ● | | ● | | | | | | | | | | ● | | | | | | |
| OTREMBA, KATHARINA (HM15496) | | | | | | | | | | | | | | | | | | | | | | ● | | | |
| OUTCOMES (HM15502) | | | ● | | | | | | ● | | ● | | | | | | | | | | | | | | |
| PACIFIC WAVES PRODUCTIONS (HM15553) | | | | | | | | | | | | | | | | | | | | | | | | | |
| PALFREYMAN, SUE (HM15592) | | | | | | | ● | | | | | | | | | | | | | | | | | | |
| PARADISE, PAM (HM15645) | | | | | | | | | | | | | | | | | | | | | | | | | |
| PARK PRACTICE (HM15673) | | | | | | | | | | | | | | | | | | | | | | | | | |
| PASHLEY, MAGGIE (HM15775) | | | | | | ● | | | | | | | | | | | | | | | | | | | |
| PATEL, J C (HM15788) | | | | | | | | | | | | | | | | | | ● | | | | | | | |
| PATEL, LINA (HM15792) | | | | | | | | | | | | | | | | | | | | | | | | | |
| PATEL, RIMA (HM15800) | | | | | | | | | | | | | | | | | | | | | | | | | |
| PATERSON, KARETH (HM15810) | | | | | | | | | | | | | | | | | | | | | | | | | |
| PEER, MARISA (HM15940) | | | | | | | | | | | | | | | | | | | | | | | | | |
| PERCIVAL, JO (HM16016) | | | | | | | | | | | | | | | | | | | | | | | | | |
| PERRINS, JOSEPH (HM16038) | | | | | | | | | | | | | | | | | | | | | | | | | |
| PHOENIX HOM/ALLGY TESTING CTRE (HM16157) | | | | | | | | | | | | | | | | | | | | | | | | | |
| PHYSIO ONE (HM16202) | | | | | | | ● | | ● | | | | | | | | | | | | | | | | |
| PHYSIOTHERAPY PRACTICE (HM16253) | | | | | | | ● | | ● | | | | | | | | | | | | | ● | | | |

# F - O Therapies at Practices/Businesses

Business by County with Reference no.

| Business by County with Reference no. | Family Planning (Natural) | Family Therapy | Feldenkrais Methodology | Feng Shui | Floral Essence Therapy | Flotation Therapy | Gait Analysis | Gem Essence Therapy | Gestalt Therapy | Group Therapy | Hay Diet | Healer | Healing Therapy | Hellerwork | Herbal Medicine | Holistic Healing | Homeopathy |
|---|---|---|---|---|---|---|---|---|---|---|---|---|---|---|---|---|---|
| PINDER, M (HM16308) | | | | | | | | | | | | | | | | | ● |
| PLATT, DEE (HM16363) | | | | | | | | | | | | | | | | | |
| PORTAL, MEG (HM16443) | | | | | | | | | | | | | | | | | ● |
| PRICE, GILLIAN (HM16575) | | | | | | | | | | | | | | | | | |
| PRIEST, NIGEL (HM16609) | | | | | | | | | | | | | | | | | |
| PRIMROSE HEALING CENTRE (HM16616) | | | | | | | | | | | | | | | | | |
| PRIVATE HEALTH CLINIC (HM16644) | | | | | | | | | | | | | | | ● | | ● |
| PSYCHOTHERAPY CENTRE (HM16734) | | | | | | | | | | | | | | | | | |
| PSYCHOTHERAPY SERVICES (HM16737) | | | | | | | | | | | | | | | | | |
| PUTNEY HYPNOTHERAPY CLINIC (HM16781) | | | | | | | | | | | | | | | | | |
| RABAYA HOMOEOPATHIC CLINIC (HM16833) | | | | | | | | | | | | | | | | | ● |
| RACHEL YOUNG - HYPNOTHERAPIST (HM16837) | | | | | | | | | ● | | | ● | ● | | | ● | |
| RAEBURN, JO (HM16865) | | | | | | | | | | | | | | | | | |
| RANDALL, CAROLINE (HM16926) | | | | | | | | | | | | | | | | ● | |
| RANDERIA, JAMSHED (DR) (HM16936) | | | | | | | | | | | | | | | | | ● |
| RATCLIFF, SUSAN (HM16947) | | | | | | | | | | | | | | | | | |
| RAVENSCROFT CENTRE (HM16967) | | | | | | | | | | | | | ● | | | ● | |
| READ, CHARLES (HM16993) | | | | | | | | | | | | | | | | | |
| REFLEXOLOGY CLINIC (HM17089) | | | | | | | | | | | | | | | | | |
| REIKI HEALING & TRAINING CTRE (HM17133) | | | | | | | | | | | | | | | | | |
| RELAXING HEALTHY OPTIONS (HM17169) | | | | | | | | | | | | | | | | | |
| REPLINGHAM CLINIC (HM17195) | | | | | | | | | | | | | | | ● | | ● |
| RICHARDS, JESSICA (HM17256) | | | | | | | | | | | | | | | | | |
| RIDDELL, CAROLINE (HM17313) | | | | | | | | | | | | | | | | | |
| ROBERTS, CATHERINE (HM17406) | | | | | | | | | | | | | | | | | |
| ROBERTS, MATT (HM17420) | | | | | | | | | | | | | | | | | |
| ROBERTSON, FIONA (HM17440) | | | | | | | | | | | | | | | | | |
| ROBINSON, GABIE (HM17473) | | | | | | | | | | | | | | | ● | | |
| ROSE, NICHOLAS (HM17613) | | | | | | | | | | | | | | | | | |
| ROSE, S M (HM17614) | | | | | | | | | | | | | | | | | ● |
| ROXANNES HOMEOPATHIC PHARMACY (HM17708) | | | | | | | | | | | | | | | ● | | ● |
| RUSSO, HAZEL (HM17773) | | | | | | | | | | | | | | | | | |
| RUTH SAUNDERS HEALTH CLINIC (HM17775) | | | | | | | | | | | | | | | | | |
| RUTHERFORD, BERWYN (HM17780) | | | | | | | | | | | | | | | | | |

| Business by County with Reference no. | Hopi Ear Candles | Humanistic Psychology | Hypnosis | Hypnotherapy | Indian Head Massage | Inhalation Therapy | Iridology | Kinesiology | Kirlian Photography | Laser Treatment | Life Style Coaching | Light Therapy | Macrobiotics | Magnetic Therapy | Manipulation | Manual Lymph Drainage | Massage (Therapeutic) |
|---|---|---|---|---|---|---|---|---|---|---|---|---|---|---|---|---|---|
| PINDER, M (HM16308) | | | | | | | | | | | | | | | | | |
| PLATT, DEE (HM16363) | | | | | | | | ● | | | | | | | | | |
| PORTAL, MEG (HM16443) | | | | | | | | | | | | | | | | | |
| PRICE, GILLIAN (HM16575) | | | | | | | | | | | | | | | | | |
| PRIEST, NIGEL (HM16609) | | | ● | | | | | | | | | | | | | | |
| PRIMROSE HEALING CENTRE (HM16616) | | | | ● | | | | | | | | | | | | | |
| PRIVATE HEALTH CLINIC (HM16644) | | | ● | | | | | | | | | | | | | | |
| PSYCHOTHERAPY CENTRE (HM16734) | | | | ● | | | | | | | | | | | | | |
| PSYCHOTHERAPY SERVICES (HM16737) | | | | ● | | | | | | | | | | | | | |
| PUTNEY HYPNOTHERAPY CLINIC (HM16781) | | | ● | | | | | | | | | | | | | | |
| RABAYA HOMOEOPATHIC CLINIC (HM16833) | | | | | | | | | | | | | | | | | |
| RACHEL YOUNG - HYPNOTHERAPIST (HM16837) | | ● | ● | ● | | | | | | | ● | | | | | | |
| RAEBURN, JO (HM16865) | | | | | ● | | | | | | | | | | | | |
| RANDALL, CAROLINE (HM16926) | | | | | | | | | | | | | | | | | ● |
| RANDERIA, JAMSHED (DR) (HM16936) | | | | | | | | | | | | | | | | | |
| RATCLIFF, SUSAN (HM16947) | | | ● | | | | | | | | | | | | | | |
| RAVENSCROFT CENTRE (HM16967) | | | | | | | | | | | ● | | | | | | ● |
| READ, CHARLES (HM16993) | | | | | | | | | | | | | | | ● | | |
| REFLEXOLOGY CLINIC (HM17089) | | | | | | | | | | | | | | | | | ● |
| REIKI HEALING & TRAINING CTRE (HM17133) | | | | | ● | | | | | | | | | | | | |
| RELAXING HEALTHY OPTIONS (HM17169) | | | | | ● | | | | | | | | | | | | ● |
| REPLINGHAM CLINIC (HM17195) | | | ● | ● | ● | | | | | | | | | | | | ● |
| RICHARDS, JESSICA (HM17256) | | | ● | | | | | | | | | | | | | | |
| RIDDELL, CAROLINE (HM17313) | | | ● | | | | | | | | | | | | | | |
| ROBERTS, CATHERINE (HM17406) | | | ● | | | | | | | | | | | | | | |
| ROBERTS, MATT (HM17420) | | | | ● | | | | | | | | | | | | | |
| ROBERTSON, FIONA (HM17440) | | | | | | | | | | | | | | | | | |
| ROBINSON, GABIE (HM17473) | | | | | | | | | | | | | | | | | |
| ROSE, NICHOLAS (HM17613) | | | | | | | | | | | | | | | ● | | ● |
| ROSE, S M (HM17614) | | | | | | | | | | | | | | | | | |
| ROXANNES HOMEOPATHIC PHARMACY (HM17708) | | | | | | | | | | | | | | | | | |
| RUSSO, HAZEL (HM17773) | | | | | | | | | | | | | | | | | |
| RUTH SAUNDERS HEALTH CLINIC (HM17775) | | | ● | | | | | | | | | | | | | | |
| RUTHERFORD, BERWYN (HM17780) | | | | | | | | | | | ● | | | | ● | | ● |

| Business by County with Reference no. | McTimoney Chiropractic | Meditation | Metamorphic Therapy | Miasm Therapy | Micro Manipulation | Moxibustion | Mud Therapy | Music Therapy | Nail Surgery | Naturopathy | Neuro-Linguistic Program | Neurotherapy | Nutritional Therapy | Orgone Therapy | Oriental Diagnosis | Orthomolecular Medicine |
|---|---|---|---|---|---|---|---|---|---|---|---|---|---|---|---|---|
| PINDER, M (HM16308) | | | | | | | | | | | | | | | | |
| PLATT, DEE (HM16363) | | | | | | | | | | | | | | | | |
| PORTAL, MEG (HM16443) | | | | | | | | | | | | | | | | |
| PRICE, GILLIAN (HM16575) | | | | | | ● | | | | | | | | | | |
| PRIEST, NIGEL (HM16609) | | | | | | | | | | | | | | | | |
| PRIMROSE HEALING CENTRE (HM16616) | | | | | | | | | | | | | | | | |
| PRIVATE HEALTH CLINIC (HM16644) | | | | | | | | | | | | | | | | |
| PSYCHOTHERAPY CENTRE (HM16734) | | | | | | | | | | | | | | | | |
| PSYCHOTHERAPY SERVICES (HM16737) | | | | | | | | | | | | | | | | |
| PUTNEY HYPNOTHERAPY CLINIC (HM16781) | | | | | | | | | | | | | | | | |
| RABAYA HOMOEOPATHIC CLINIC (HM16833) | | | | | | | | | | | | | | | | |
| RACHEL YOUNG - HYPNOTHERAPIST (HM16837) | | ● | | | | | | | | | | | | | | |
| RAEBURN, JO (HM16865) | | | | | | | | | | | | | | | | |
| RANDALL, CAROLINE (HM16926) | | | | | | | | | | | | | | | | |
| RANDERIA, JAMSHED (DR) (HM16936) | | | | | | | | | | | | | | | | |
| RATCLIFF, SUSAN (HM16947) | | | | | | | | | | | | | | | | |
| RAVENSCROFT CENTRE (HM16967) | | | | | | | | | | | | | | | | |
| READ, CHARLES (HM16993) | | | | | | | | | | | | | | | | |
| REFLEXOLOGY CLINIC (HM17089) | | | | | | | | | | | | | | | | |
| REIKI HEALING & TRAINING CTRE (HM17133) | | ● | | | | | | | | | | | | | | |
| RELAXING HEALTHY OPTIONS (HM17169) | | | | | | | | | | | | | | | | |
| REPLINGHAM CLINIC (HM17195) | | | | | | | | | | ● | | | | | | |
| RICHARDS, JESSICA (HM17256) | | | | | | | | | | | | | | | | |
| RIDDELL, CAROLINE (HM17313) | | | | | | | | | | | | | | | | |
| ROBERTS, CATHERINE (HM17406) | | | | | | | | | | | | | | | | |
| ROBERTS, MATT (HM17420) | | | | | | | | | | | | | | | | |
| ROBERTSON, FIONA (HM17440) | | | | | | | | | | ● | | | | | | |
| ROBINSON, GABIE (HM17473) | | | | | | | | | | | | | | | | |
| ROSE, NICHOLAS (HM17613) | | | | | | | | | | | | | | | | |
| ROSE, S M (HM17614) | | | | | | | | | | | | | | | | |
| ROXANNES HOMEOPATHIC PHARMACY (HM17708) | | | | | | | | | | | | | | | | |
| RUSSO, HAZEL (HM17773) | | | ● | | | | | | | | | | | | | |
| RUTH SAUNDERS HEALTH CLINIC (HM17775) | | | | | | | | | | | | | | | | |
| RUTHERFORD, BERWYN (HM17780) | | | | | | | | | | ● | | | | | | |

# F - O Therapies at Practices/Businesses

| Business by County with Reference no. | Family Planning (Natural) | Family Therapy | Feldenkrais Methodology | Feng Shui | Floral Essence Therapy | Flotation Therapy | Gait Analysis | Gem Essence Therapy | Gestalt Therapy | Group Therapy | Hay Diet | Healer | Healing Therapy | Hellerwork | Herbal Medicine | Holistic Healing | Homeopathy |
|---|---|---|---|---|---|---|---|---|---|---|---|---|---|---|---|---|---|
| SACHDEV, P (HM17825) | | | | | | | | | | | | | | | | | ● |
| SAI HOMEOPATHIC CLINIC (HM17840) | | | | | | | | | | | | | | | | | ● |
| SALTER, L (HM17867) | | | | | | | | | | | | | | | | | ● |
| SALTER, LIZ (HM17869) | | | | | | | | | | | | | | | | | ● |
| SANDERS, CAROLE (HM17906) | | | | | | | | | | | | | | | | | ● |
| SAWYER, E (HM17984) | | | | | | | | | | | | | | | | | ● |
| SAYER CLINIC (HM17993) | | | | | | | | | | | | | | | | | |
| SEEAR, MICHAEL (DR) (HM18189) | | | | | | | | | | | | ● | ● | | | ● | ● |
| SEYMOUR PRACTICE (HM18257) | | | | | | | | | | | | | | | | | |
| SHAFTOE, MARINA (HM18265) | | | | | | | | | | | | | | | | | |
| SHENKER, SHARON (HM18398) | | | | | | | | | | | | | | | | | ● |
| SHIATSU PLACE (HM18458) | | | | | | | | | | | | | | | | | ● |
| SHRUBBERIES (HM18512) | | | | | | | | | | | | | | | | | |
| SIMPLY HERBAL CLINIC (HM18577) | | | | | | | | | | | | | | | ● | | |
| SIMPSON, STELLA (HM18599) | | | | | | | | | | | | | | | ● | | |
| SJY CHINESE MEDICINE (HM18628) | | | | | | | | | | | | | | | ● | | |
| SMITH, ANDREW (HM18715) | | | | | | | | | | | | | | | | | |
| SMOKERS CLINIC (HM18826) | | | | | | | | | | | | | | | | | |
| SOHAWON, MARTY (HM18860) | | | | | | | | | | | | | | | | | ● |
| SOMPER, J D (DR) (HM18886) | | | | | | | | | | | | | | | | | ● |
| SOOD, P (HM18888) | | | | | | | | | | | | | | | | | ● |
| SOUTH LONDON NATURAL HLTH CTRE (HM18911) | | | ● | | ● | ● | | ● | | | ● | ● | ● | | ● | ● | ● |
| SOUTHALL CHINESE MED CENTRE (HM18919) | | | | | | | | | | | | | | | ● | | |
| SOUTHORN, VALERIE (HM18939) | | | | | | | | | | | | | | | | | ● |
| SPALL MEDICAL CENTRE (HM18957) | ● | | | | | | | | | | | | | | ● | | ● |
| SPARKS, R (HM18963) | | | | | | | | | | | | | | | | | ● |
| SPECIALIST HEALTH (HM18972) | | | | | | | | | | | | | | | | | |
| SPENCER, PIERS (HM19001) | | | | | | | | | | | | | | | | | |
| SPICE SHOP (HM19010) | | | | | | | | | | | | | | | ● | | |
| SPYROS MOUZOURIDES (HM19056) | | | | | | | | | | | ● | | | | ● | ● | |
| STANMORE CENTRE (HM19131) | | | | | | | | | | | | | | | | | |
| STEVENS, ITOKO (HM19233) | | | | | | | | | | | | | | | | | |
| STOBEZKI, YAEL (HM19307) | | | | | | | | | | | | | | | | | |
| STOCKWELL, J (HM19317) | | | | | | | | | | | | | | | | | ● |

| Business by County with Reference no. | Hopi Ear Candles | Humanistic Psychology | Hypnosis | Hypnotherapy | Indian Head Massage | Inhalation Therapy | Iridology | Kinesiology | Kirlian Photography | Laser Treatment | Life Style Coaching | Light Therapy | Macrobiotics | Magnetic Therapy | Manipulation | Manual Lymph Drainage | Massage (Therapeutic) | McTimoney Chiropractic |
|---|---|---|---|---|---|---|---|---|---|---|---|---|---|---|---|---|---|---|
| SACHDEV, P (HM17825) | | | | | | | | | | | | | | | | | | |
| SAI HOMEOPATHIC CLINIC (HM17840) | | | | | | | | | | | | | | | | | | |
| SALTER, L (HM17867) | | | | | | | | | | | | | | | | | | |
| SALTER, LIZ (HM17869) | | | | | | | | | | | | | | | | | | |
| SANDERS, CAROLE (HM17906) | | | | | | | | | | | | | | | | | | |
| SAWYER, E (HM17984) | | | | | | | | | | | | | | | | | | |
| SAYER CLINIC (HM17993) | | | | | | | | | | | | | | | ● | | ● | |
| SEEAR, MICHAEL (DR) (HM18189) | | | ● | | | | | | | | | | | | | | ● | |
| SEYMOUR PRACTICE (HM18257) | | | | | | | | | | | | | | | ● | | | |
| SHAFTOE, MARINA (HM18265) | | | ● | | | | | | | | | | | | | | | |
| SHENKER, SHARON (HM18398) | | | | | | | | | | | | | | | | | | |
| SHIATSU PLACE (HM18458) | | | | | | | | | | | | | | | | | | |
| SHRUBBERIES (HM18512) | | | ● | | | | | | | | | | | | | | | |
| SIMPLY HERBAL CLINIC (HM18577) | | | | | | | | | | | | | | | | | ● | |
| SIMPSON, STELLA (HM18599) | | | | | | | | | | | | | | | | | ● | |
| SJY CHINESE MEDICINE (HM18628) | | | | | | | | | | | | | | | | | | |
| SMITH, ANDREW (HM18715) | | | ● | | | | | | | | | | | | | | | |
| SMOKERS CLINIC (HM18826) | | | ● | | | | | | | | | | | | | | | |
| SOHAWON, MARTY (HM18860) | | | | | | | | | | | | | | | | | | |
| SOMPER, J D (DR) (HM18886) | | | | | | | | | | | | | | | | | | |
| SOOD, P (HM18888) | | | | | | | | | | | | | | | | | | |
| SOUTH LONDON NATURAL HLTH CTRE (HM18911) | | | | | ● | | ● | ● | | | | | | | | | ● | |
| SOUTHALL CHINESE MED CENTRE (HM18919) | | | | | | | | | | | | | | | | | | |
| SOUTHORN, VALERIE (HM18939) | | | | | | | | | | | | | | | | | | |
| SPALL MEDICAL CENTRE (HM18957) | | | | | | | | | | | | | | | | | | |
| SPARKS, R (HM18963) | | | | | | | | | | | | | | | | | | |
| SPECIALIST HEALTH (HM18972) | | | | | | | | | | | | | | | ● | | ● | |
| SPENCER, PIERS (HM19001) | | | | | | | | | | | | | | | ● | | | |
| SPICE SHOP (HM19010) | | | | | | | | | | | | | | | | | | |
| SPYROS MOUZOURIDES (HM19056) | | | | | | | ● | | | | | | | | | | | |
| STANMORE CENTRE (HM19131) | | | ● | | | | | | | | | | | | | | | |
| STEVENS, ITOKO (HM19233) | | | ● | | | | | | | | | | | | | | | |
| STOBEZKI, YAEL (HM19307) | | ● | | | | | | | | | | | | | | | | |
| STOCKWELL, J (HM19317) | | | | | | | | | | | | | | | | | | |

| Business by County with Reference no. | Meditation | Metamorphic Therapy | Miasm Therapy | Micro Manipulation | Moxibustion | Mud Therapy | Music Therapy | Nail Surgery | Naturopathy | Neuro-Linguistic Program | Neurotherapy | Nutritional Therapy | Orgone Therapy | Oriental Diagnosis | Orthomolecular Medicine |
|---|---|---|---|---|---|---|---|---|---|---|---|---|---|---|---|
| SACHDEV, P (HM17825) | | | | | | | | | | | | | | | |
| SAI HOMEOPATHIC CLINIC (HM17840) | | | | | | | | | | | | | | | |
| SALTER, L (HM17867) | | | | | | | | | | | | | | | |
| SALTER, LIZ (HM17869) | | | | | | | | | | | | | | | |
| SANDERS, CAROLE (HM17906) | | | | | | | | | | | | | | | |
| SAWYER, E (HM17984) | | | | | | | | | | | | | | | |
| SAYER CLINIC (HM17993) | | | | | | | | | | | | | | | |
| SEEAR, MICHAEL (DR) (HM18189) | | | | | | | | | | ● | | | | | |
| SEYMOUR PRACTICE (HM18257) | | | | | | | | | | | | | | | |
| SHAFTOE, MARINA (HM18265) | | | | | | | | | | | | | | | |
| SHENKER, SHARON (HM18398) | | | | | | | | | | | | | | | |
| SHIATSU PLACE (HM18458) | | | | | | | | | | | | | | | |
| SHRUBBERIES (HM18512) | | | | | | | | | | | | | | | |
| SIMPLY HERBAL CLINIC (HM18577) | | | | | | | | | | | | ● | | | |
| SIMPSON, STELLA (HM18599) | | | | | | | | | | | | | | | |
| SJY CHINESE MEDICINE (HM18628) | | | | | | | | | | | | | | | |
| SMITH, ANDREW (HM18715) | | | | | | | | | | | | | | | |
| SMOKERS CLINIC (HM18826) | | | | | | | | | | | | | | | |
| SOHAWON, MARTY (HM18860) | | | | | | | | | | | | | | | |
| SOMPER, J D (DR) (HM18886) | | | | | | | | | | | | | | | |
| SOOD, P (HM18888) | | | | | | | | | | | | | | | |
| SOUTH LONDON NATURAL HLTH CTRE (HM18911) | ● | | | | ● | | | | ● | | | ● | | ● | |
| SOUTHALL CHINESE MED CENTRE (HM18919) | | | | | | | | | | | | | | | |
| SOUTHORN, VALERIE (HM18939) | | | | | | | | | | | | | | | |
| SPALL MEDICAL CENTRE (HM18957) | | | | | | | | | | | | | | | |
| SPARKS, R (HM18963) | | | | | | | | | | | | | | | |
| SPECIALIST HEALTH (HM18972) | | | | | | | | | | | | | | | |
| SPENCER, PIERS (HM19001) | | | | | | | | | | | | | | | |
| SPICE SHOP (HM19010) | | | | | | | | | | | | | | | |
| SPYROS MOUZOURIDES (HM19056) | | | ● | | | | | | ● | | | ● | | | |
| STANMORE CENTRE (HM19131) | | | | | | | | | | | | | | | |
| STEVENS, ITOKO (HM19233) | | | | | | | | | | | | | | | |
| STOBEZKI, YAEL (HM19307) | | | | | | | | | | | | | | | |
| STOCKWELL, J (HM19317) | | | | | | | | | | | | | | | |

# F - O Therapies at Practices/Businesses

Business by County with Reference no.

| Business by County with Reference no. | Family Planning (Natural) | Family Therapy | Feldenkrais Methodology | Feng Shui | Floral Essence Therapy | Flotation Therapy | Gait Analysis | Gem Essence Therapy | Gestalt Therapy | Group Therapy | Hay Diet | Healer | Healing Therapy | Hellerwork | Herbal Medicine | Holistic Healing | Homeopathy | Hopi Ear Candles | Humanistic Psychology | Hypnosis | Hypnotherapy | Indian Head Massage | Inhalation Therapy | Iridology | Kinesiology |
|---|---|---|---|---|---|---|---|---|---|---|---|---|---|---|---|---|---|---|---|---|---|---|---|---|---|
| STRESS MANAGEMENT (HM19393) | | | | | | | | | | | | | | | | | | | | ● | | | | | |
| STRONG, STELLA (HM19419) | | | | | | | | | | | | ● | | | | | | | | | | | | | |
| T C M HEALTHCARE (HM19640) | | | | | | | | | | | | | | | ● | | | | | | | | | | |
| THOMPSON, MARK (HM19990) | ● | | | | | | | | | | | | | | | | | | | | | | | | |
| TINDALL, T (HM20081) | | | | | | | | | | | | | | | | | ● | | | | | | | | |
| TOOTHE, DIANE (HM20163) | | | | | | | | | | | | | | | | | ● | | | | | | | | |
| TORRIDON COMP THERAPY CLINIC (HM20173) | | | | | | | | | | | | | | | | | | | | | ● | | | | |
| TOWERS, FILMER (HM20196) | | | | | | | | | | | | | | | | | | | | ● | | | | | |
| TRAD CHINESE MASSOTHERAPY (HM20215) | | | | | | | | | | | | | | | | | | | | | | | | | |
| TRANQUILITY (HM20255) | | | | | | | | | | | | | ● | | | ● | | | | | | ● | | | |
| TROHEAR, PATRICIA (HM20345) | | | | | | | | | | | | | | | | | | | | ● | ● | | | | |
| TURMAINE, VICKI (HM20410) | | | | | | | | | | | | | | | | | ● | | | | | | | | |
| UKCP (HM20490) | | ● | | | | | | | ● | ● | | | | | | | | | ● | | ● | | | | |
| UNDERHILL, K (HM20496) | | | | | | | | | | | | | | | | | | | | | | | | ● | |
| URRUTIA, LORETA (HM20533) | | | | | | | | | | | | | | | | | | | | ● | | | | | |
| USHER, J (HM20535) | | | | | | | | | | | | | | | | | ● | | | | | | | | |
| VALE PRACTICE (HM20551) | | | | | | | | | | | | | | | | | ● | | | ● | ● | ● | | | |
| VANBRUGH PHYSIOTHERAPY CLINIC (HM20575) | | | | | | | | | | | | | | | | | | | | | | ● | | | |
| VEDIC, RU (HM20607) | | | | | | | | | | | | | | | ● | | | | | | | | | | |
| VINES, T (HM20681) | | | | | | | | | | | | | | | | | ● | | | | | | | | |
| WARWICK ALTERNATIVE HEALTH (HM20961) | | | | | | | | | | | | | | | | | | | | | ● | ● | | | |
| WEERASEKERA, H (HM21108) | | | | | | | | | | | | | | | | | ● | | | | | | | | |
| WELL BEING (HM21131) | | | | | | | | | | | | | | | ● | | ● | ● | | | | | | | |
| WEST LONDON CENTRE (HM21225) | | | | | | | | | | | | | | | | | | | | ● | | | | | |
| WEST LONDON HOLISTIC CENTRE (HM21226) | | | | | ● | | | | ● | ● | | ● | ● | | ● | ● | ● | | | ● | ● | ● | | | |
| WHITE HART LANE THERAPY CENTRE (HM21338) | | | | | | | | | | | | | | | | | | | | | | | | | |
| WHITEHOUSE, J (HM21389) | | | | | | | | | | | | | | | ● | | | | | | | | | | |
| WHOLE-BEING INTERACTIVE HYP (HM21435) | | | | | | | | | | | | | | | | | | | | ● | ● | | | | |
| WIGHAM, A (HM21468) | | | | | | | | | | | | | | | | | | | ● | | ● | | | | |
| WILLIAMS, ALAN (HM21536) | | | | | | | | | | | | | | | ● | | | | | | | | | | |
| WILLIAMS, B A (HM21541) | | | | | | | | | | | | | | | | | ● | | | | | | | | |
| WILLIAMS, IAN (HM21565) | | | | | | | | | | | | | | | | | | | | | | | | | |
| WILLIAMS, RUTH (HM21588) | | | | | | | | | ● | | | | | | | | | | | | | | | | |
| WILLMOTT, SUSAN (HM21623) | | | | | | | | | ● | ● | | | | | | | | | ● | ● | ● | | | | |

| Business by County with Reference no. | Kirlian Photography | Laser Treatment | Life Style Coaching | Light Therapy | Macrobiotics | Magnetic Therapy | Manipulation | Manual Lymph Drainage | Massage (Therapeutic) | McTimoney Chiropractic | Meditation | Metamorphic Therapy | Miasm Therapy | Micro Manipulation | Moxibustion | Mud Therapy | Music Therapy | Nail Surgery | Naturopathy | Neuro-Linguistic Program | Neurotherapy | Nutritional Therapy | Orgone Therapy | Oriental Diagnosis | Orthomolecular Medicine |
|---|---|---|---|---|---|---|---|---|---|---|---|---|---|---|---|---|---|---|---|---|---|---|---|---|---|
| STRESS MANAGEMENT (HM19393) | | | | | | | | | | | | | | | | | | | | | | | | | |
| STRONG, STELLA (HM19419) | | | | | | | | | | | | | | | | | | | | | | | | | |
| T C M HEALTHCARE (HM19640) | | | | | | | | | | | | | | | | | | | | | | | | | |
| THOMPSON, MARK (HM19990) | | | | | | | | | | | | | | | | | | | ● | | | | | | |
| TINDALL, T (HM20081) | | | | | | | | | | | | | | | | | | | | | | | | | |
| TOOTHE, DIANE (HM20163) | | | | | | | | | | | | | | | | | | | | | | | | | |
| TORRIDON COMP THERAPY CLINIC (HM20173) | | | | | | | | | ● | | | | | | | | | | | | | | | | |
| TOWERS, FILMER (HM20196) | | | | | | | | | | | | | | | | | | | | | | | | | |
| TRAD CHINESE MASSOTHERAPY (HM20215) | | | | | | | | | ● | | ● | | | | | | | | | | | | | | |
| TRANQUILITY (HM20255) | | | | | | | ● | | ● | | | | | | | | ● | | | | | | | | |
| TROHEAR, PATRICIA (HM20345) | | | | | | | | | | | | | | | | | | | | | | | | | |
| TURMAINE, VICKI (HM20410) | | | | | | | | | | | | | | | | | | | | | | | | | |
| UKCP (HM20490) | | | | | | | | | | | | | | | | | | | | | | | | | |
| UNDERHILL, K (HM20496) | | | | | | | | | | | | | | | | | | | ● | | | | | | |
| URRUTIA, LORETA (HM20533) | | | | | | | | | | | | | | | | | | | | | | | | | |
| USHER, J (HM20535) | | | | | | | | | | | | | | | | | | | | | | | | | |
| VALE PRACTICE (HM20551) | | | ● | | | | ● | | ● | | | | ● | | ● | | | | | | | ● | | | |
| VANBRUGH PHYSIOTHERAPY CLINIC (HM20575) | | | | | | | | | ● | | | | | | | | | | | | | ● | | | |
| VEDIC, RU (HM20607) | | | | | | | | | | | | | | | | | | | | | | | | | |
| VINES, T (HM20681) | | | | | | | | | | | | | | | | | | | | | | | | | |
| WARWICK ALTERNATIVE HEALTH (HM20961) | | | ● | | | | | | | | | | | | | | | | | | | | | | |
| WEERASEKERA, H (HM21108) | | | | | | | | | | | | | | | | | | | | | | | | | |
| WELL BEING (HM21131) | | | | | | | | | | | | | | | | | | | | | | | | | |
| WEST LONDON CENTRE (HM21225) | | | | | | | | | | | | | | | | | | | | | | | | | |
| WEST LONDON HOLISTIC CENTRE (HM21226) | | | ● | | | | | | | | ● | | | | | | | | ● | | | ● | | ● | |
| WHITE HART LANE THERAPY CENTRE (HM21338) | | | | | | | | | ● | | | | | | | | | | | | | ● | | | |
| WHITEHOUSE, J (HM21389) | | | | | | | | | | | | | | | | | | | | | | | | | |
| WHOLE-BEING INTERACTIVE HYP (HM21435) | | | | | | | | | | | | | | | | | | | | | | | | | |
| WIGHAM, A (HM21468) | | | ● | | | | | | | | | | | | | | | | | | | | | | |
| WILLIAMS, ALAN (HM21536) | | | | | | | | | | | | | | | | | | | | | | | | | |
| WILLIAMS, B A (HM21541) | | | | | | | | | | | | | | | | | | | | | | | | | |
| WILLIAMS, IAN (HM21565) | | | | | | | | | | | | | | | | | | ● | | | | | | | |
| WILLIAMS, RUTH (HM21588) | | | | | | | | | | | | | | | | | | | | | | | | | |
| WILLMOTT, SUSAN (HM21623) | | | | | | | | | | | | | | | | | | | | | | | | | |

# F - O Therapies at Practices/Businesses

| Business by County with Reference no. | Family Planning (Natural) | Family Therapy | Feldenkrais Methodology | Feng Shui | Floral Essence Therapy | Flotation Therapy | Gait Analysis | Gem Essence Therapy | Gestalt Therapy | Group Therapy | Hay Diet | Healer | Healing Therapy | Hellerwork | Herbal Medicine | Holistic Healing | Homeopathy | Hopi Ear Candles | Humanistic Psychology | Hypnosis | Hypnotherapy | Indian Head Massage | Inhalation Therapy | Iridology | Kinesiology | Kirlian Photography | Laser Treatment | Life Style Coaching | Light Therapy | Macrobiotics | Magnetic Therapy | Manipulation | Manual Lymph Drainage | Massage (Therapeutic) | McTimoney Chiropractic | Meditation | Metamorphic Therapy | Miasm Therapy | Micro Manipulation | Moxibustion | Mud Therapy | Music Therapy | Nail Surgery | Naturopathy | Neuro-Linguistic Program | Neurotherapy | Nutritional Therapy | Orgone Therapy | Oriental Diagnosis | Orthomolecular Medicine |
|---|---|---|---|---|---|---|---|---|---|---|---|---|---|---|---|---|---|---|---|---|---|---|---|---|---|---|---|---|---|---|---|---|---|---|---|---|---|---|---|---|---|---|---|---|---|---|---|---|---|---|
| WILSON, CHRISTOPHER (HM21651) | | | | | | | | | | | | | | | ● | | | | | | | | | | | | | | | | | | | ● | | | | | | | | | | | | | | | | |
| WINCHMORE CLINIC OF OSTEOPATHY (HM21694) | | | | | | | | | | | | | | | | | | | | | | | | | | | | | | | | ● | | ● | | | | | | | | | | | | | | | | |
| WOOLF, PERRY (HM21872) | | | | | | | | | | | | | | | | | | | | | | | | | | | | | | | | ● | | ● | | | | | | | | | | | | | | | | |
| WORLD OF LIGHT (HM21898) | | | | | | | | | | | | ● | | | ● | | ● | | | | | | | | | | | | | | | | | ● | | ● | | | | | | | | | | | | | | |
| WOZNIAK, HELEN (HM21915) | | | | | | | | | | | | | | | | | | | | ● | | | | | | | | | | | | | | | | | | | | | | | | | | | | | | |
| WREN CLINIC (HM21919) | | | | | | | | | | | | | | | ● | ● | | | | | | | | | ● | | | | | | | | | ● | ● | ● | | | | | | | | ● | | | ● | | | |
| WREN, ANTHONY (HM21920) | | | | | | | | | | | | | | | | | | | | | | | | | | | | | | | | | | ● | | | | | | | | | | | | | | | | |
| WRIGHT, JENNY (HM21936) | | | | | | | | | | | | | | | | | | | ● | ● | ● | | | | | | | ● | | | | | | | | ● | | | | | | | | | | | | | | |
| WYNNE-SIMMONS, A (DR) (HM21979) | | | | | | | | | | | | | | | | | ● | | | | | | | | | | | | | | | | | | | | | | | | | | | | | | | | | |
| YARDLEY, IAN (HM21986) | | | | | | | | | | | | | | | | | | | | ● | | | | | | | | | | | | | | | | | | | | | | | | | | | | | | |
| YING, FRANK (HM22014) | | | | | | | | | | | | | | | | | | | | | | | | | | | | | | | | ● | | ● | | | | | | | | | | | | | | | | |
| YOUNG, VEDA (HM22082) | | | | | | | | | | | | | | | | | ● | | | | | | | | | | | | | | | | | | | | | | | | | | | | | | | | | |
| ZARVIS-LONDON (HM22097) | | | | | | | | | | | | | | | ● | | | | | | | | | | | | | | | | | | | | | | | | | | | | | | | | | | | |
| ZEN HEALTH CENTRE (HM22100) | | | | | ● | | | | | | | ● | ● | | ● | ● | ● | | | | | ● | | ● | | | | | | | | | ● | ● | | ● | | | | ● | | | | ● | | | ● | | ● | |
| ZEN SHIATSU & HEALING TAO (HM22101) | | | | | | | | | | | | | ● | | | | | | | | | | | | | | | | | | | | | | | ● | | | | | | | | | | | | | ● | |
| **MANCHESTER (GREATER)** | | | | | | | | | | | | | | | | | | | | | | | | | | | | | | | | | | | | | | | | | | | | | | | | | | |
| A SIR ROBERTS ALT PLACE (HM00045) | | | | | | | | | | | | ● | ● | | ● | ● | ● | | | ● | ● | | | | | | | ● | | | | ● | | ● | | ● | | | | | | | | ● | | | | | | |
| ACUMEDIC (HM00220) | | | | | | | | | | | | | | | | | | | | | | | | | | | | | | | | | | | | | | | | | | | | | | | | | ● | |
| ACUPUNCTURE CENTRE (HM00252) | | | | | | | | | | | | | | | | | | | | | | | | | | | | | | | | | | | | | | | | ● | | | | | | | | | | |
| ADVANCED PHYSIOTHERAPY CLINIC (HM00403) | | | | | | | | | | | | | | | | | | | | | | | | | | | | | | | | ● | | ● | | | | | | | | | | | | | | | | |
| ALL IN THE MIND (HM00582) | | | | | | | | | | | | | | | | | | | | ● | ● | | | | | | | | | | | | | | | | | | | | | | | | | | | | | |
| AROMATHERAPY LADIES MASSAGE (HM01118) | | | | | | | | | | | | | | | | | | | | | | ● | | | | | | | | | | | | | | | | | | | | | | | | | | | | |
| ASHTON, J G (HM01240) | | | | | | | | | | | | | | | | | | | | ● | | | | | | | | | | | | | | | | | | | | | | | | | | | | | | |
| ASHWORTH, FREDA (HM01248) | | | | | | | | | | | | | | | | | | | | ● | | | | | | | | | | | | | | | | | | | | | | | | | | | | | | |
| ASTLEY COMPLEMENTARY CENTRE (HM01300) | | | | | | | | | | | | | | | | | ● | | | | ● | ● | | | | | | | | | | | | | | | | | | ● | | | | | | | | | ● | |
| BOURGUIGNON, PASCAL (HM02748) | | | | | | | | | | | | | | | | | | | | ● | | | | | | | | | | | | | | | | | | | | | | | | | | | | | | |
| BRAMHALL CHIROPRACTIC CLINIC (HM02898) | | | | | | | | | | | | | | | | | | | | | | | | | | | | | | | | ● | | ● | | | | | | | | | | | | | | | | |
| BROOKES, N (HM03164) | | | | | | | | | | | | | | | | | ● | | | | | | | | | | | | | | | | | | | | | | | | | | | | | | | | | |
| C CARTLEDGE REFLEXOLOGY (HM03521) | | | | | | | | | | | | | | | | | | | | | | ● | | | | | | | | | | | | | | | | | | | | | | | | | | | | |
| CHARTERED PHYSIOTHERAPY CLINIC (HM04046) | | | | | | | | | | | | | | | | | | | | | | | | | | | | | | | | ● | | ● | | | | | | ● | | | | | | | | | | |
| CHORLTON STRESS MANAGEMENT (HM04430) | | | | | | | | | | | | ● | | | | | | | | | ● | | | | | | | | | | | | | | | | | | | | | | | | | | | | | |
| CLARENDON CLINIC (HM04540) | | | | | | | | | | | | | | | | | | | | | | | | ● | ● | | | | | | | ● | | ● | | | | | | | | | | ● | | | | | | |
| CLEVERLY, MARAGRET (HM04658) | | | | | | | | | | | | | | | | | | | | ● | | | | | | | | | | | | | | | | | | | | | | | | | | | | | | |
| COHEN, D (DR) (HM04789) | | | | | | | | | | | | | | | | | ● | | | | | | | | | | | | | | | | | | | | | | | | | | | | | | | | | |

# F - O Therapies at Practices/Businesses

| Business by County with Reference no. | Family Planning (Natural) | Family Therapy | Feldenkrais Methodology | Feng Shui | Floral Essence Therapy | Flotation Therapy | Gait Analysis | Gem Essence Therapy | Gestalt Therapy | Group Therapy | Hay Diet | Healer | Healing Therapy | Hellerwork | Herbal Medicine | Holistic Healing | Homeopathy | Hopi Ear Candles | Humanistic Psychology | Hypnosis | Hypnotherapy | Indian Head Massage | Inhalation Therapy | Iridology | Kinesiology | Kirlian Photography | Laser Treatment | Life Style Coaching | Light Therapy | Macrobiotics | Magnetic Therapy | Manipulation | Manual Lymph Drainage | Massage (Therapeutic) | McTimoney Chiropractic | Meditation | Metamorphic Therapy | Miasm Therapy | Micro Manipulation | Moxibustion | Mud Therapy | Music Therapy | Nail Surgery | Naturopathy | Neuro-Linguistic Program | Neurotherapy | Nutritional Therapy | Orgone Therapy | Oriental Diagnosis | Orthomolecular Medicine |
|---|---|---|---|---|---|---|---|---|---|---|---|---|---|---|---|---|---|---|---|---|---|---|---|---|---|---|---|---|---|---|---|---|---|---|---|---|---|---|---|---|---|---|---|---|---|---|---|---|---|---|
| COSGROVES PHYSIO-FIT CENTRE (HM05201) | | | | | | | | | | | | | | | | | | | | | | | | | | | | | | | | ● | | ● | | | | | | | | | | | | | | | | |
| CREST HYPNOTHERAPY (HM05426) | | | | | | | | | | | | | | | | | | | | ● | | | | | | | | | | | | | | | | | | | | | | | | | | | | | | |
| CROSSWAY CLINIC (HM05491) | | | | | | | | | | | | | | | | | | | | | ● | | | ● | | | | | | | | ● | | ● | | | | | | | | | | | | | | | | |
| DAVIES, L (HM05823) | | | | | | | | | | | | | | | | | | | | ● | | | | | | | | | | | | | | | | | | | | | | | | | | | | | | |
| DIDSBURY CHIROPRACTIC CLINIC (HM06090) | | | | | | | | | | | | | | | | | | | | | | | | | | | | | | | | ● | | ● | | | | | | | | | | | | | | | | |
| EVANS, DAVID (HM06967) | | | | | | | | | | | | ● | ● | | | | | | | ● | ● | | | | | | | | | | | | | | | | | | | | | | | | | | | | | |
| GRAHAM COOMBE - MCTIMONEY (HM08337) | | | | | | | | | | | | | | | | | | | | | | | | | | | | | | | | | | | ● | | | | | | | | | | | | | | | |
| GREEN, NANCY (HM08469) | | | | | | | | | | | | | | | | | ● | | | | | | | | | | | | | | | | | | | | | | | | | | | | | | | | | |
| HARROP, S (HM09119) | | | | | | | | | | | | | | | ● | | | | | | | | | | | | | | | | | | | | | | | | | | | | | | | | | | | |
| HIGH PEAK HOLISTIC CENTRE (HM09738) | | | | | | | | | | | | | | | | | | | | | | ● | | | | | | | | | | | | ● | | | | | | | | | | | | | | | | |
| HUMAN TOUCH CENTRE (HM10366) | | | | | | | | | | | | | | | | ● | | | | | | | | | | | | | | | | | | | | | | | | | | | | | | | ● | | | |
| HYPNOTHERAPY CENTRE (HM10524) | | | | | | | | | | | | | | | | | | | | ● | | | | | | | | | | | | | | | | | | | | | | | | | | | | | | |
| IBBOTSON, GEOFF (DR) (HM10565) | | | | | | | | | | | | | | | | | | | | ● | ● | | | | | | | | | | | | | | | | | | | | | | | | | | | | | |
| ISAAC, TONI (HM10757) | | | | | | | | | | | | | | | | | | | | ● | | | | | | | | | | | | | | | | | | | | | | | | | | | | | | |
| M J HAYLETT - PHYSIOTHERAPIST (HM12802) | | | | | | | | | | | | | | | | | | | | | | | | | | | | | | | | ● | | ● | | | | | | | | | | | | | | | | |
| MAGNETIC THERAPY (HM12917) | | | | | | | | | | | | | | | | | | | | | | | | | | | | | | | ● | | | | | | | | | | | | | | | | | | | |
| MANCHESTER HOMOEOPATHIC CLINIC (HM13002) | | | | | | | | | | | | | | | | | ● | | | | | | | | | | | | | | | | | | | | | | | | | | | | | | | | | |
| MANCHESTER SCHOOL OF MASSAGE (HM13004) | | | | | | | | | | | | | | | | | | | | | | ● | | | | | | | | | | | | ● | | | | | | | | | | | | | | | | |
| MOBILE COMPLEMENTARY THERAPIES (HM14029) | | | | | | | | | | | | | | | | | | | | | | ● | | | | | | | | | | ● | | ● | | | | | | | | | | | | | ● | | | |
| MORRIS, RACHEL T (HM14213) | | | | | | | | | | | | | | | | | | | | ● | | | | | | | | | | | | | | | | | | | | | | | | | | | | | | |
| MOUNT STREET COMP THERAPIES (HM14291) | | | | | | | | | | | | | | | | | ● | | | | | | | | | | | | | | | | | ● | | | | | | | | | | | | | | | | |
| NIVERN, D (HM14954) | | | | | ● | | | | | | | ● | ● | | | ● | | | | | | ● | ● | | | | | | | | | ● | | ● | | ● | | | | | ● | | | | | | | | | |
| NW COLLEGE-HOMOEOPATHY (HM15135) | | | | | | | | | | | | | | | | | ● | | | | | | | | | | | | | | | | | | | | | | | | | | | | | | | | | |
| OLIVER-CARTER, JOAN (HM15297) | | | | | | | | | | | | | | | | | | | | ● | | | | | | | | | | | | | | | | | | | | | | | | | | | | | | |
| PARTLAN, ROBERT (HM15763) | | | | | | | | | | | | | | | | | | | | ● | | | | | | | | | | | | | | | | | | | | | | | | | | | | | | |
| QUEST THERAPY (HM16799) | | | | | | | | | | | | | | | | | | | | ● | | | | | | | | | | | | | | | | | | | | | | | | | | | | | | |
| REFLEXOLOGY & CHIROPODY (HM17079) | | | | | | | | | | | | | | | | | ● | | | | | | | | | | | | | | | | | | | | | | | | | | | | | | | | | |
| REJUVENATION (HM17154) | | | | | | | | | | | | | | | | ● | | | | | | | | | | | | | | | | | | | | | | | | | | | | | | | | | | |
| SCHOFIELD, G A (HM18018) | | | | | | | | | | | | | | | | | | | | | | | | | | | | | | | | | | | | | | | | | | | ● | | | | | | | |
| SHANGHAI ACUPUNCTURE CLINIC (HM18280) | | | | | | | | | | | | | | | ● | | | | | | | | | | | | | | | | | | | | | | | | | | | | | | | | | | | |
| SHIZHEN TCM UK (HM18490) | | | | | | | | | | | | | | | ● | | | | | | | | | | | | | | | | | | | | | | | | | | | | | | | | | | | |
| ST JOHN STREET PHYSIO PRACTICE (HM19080) | | | | | | | | | | | | | | | | | | | | | | | | | ● | | | | | | | ● | | ● | | | | | | | | | | | | | | | | |
| STIRLING, DIANNE (HM19301) | | | | | | | | | | | | | | | | | | | | | | | | | | | | | | | | | | ● | | | | | | | | | | | | | | | | |
| SWINTON HEALTH FOODS (HM19600) | | | | | | | | | | | | | | | ● | | ● | | | | ● | ● | | | | | | | | | | | | | | | | | | | | | | | | | ● | | | |

www.healthmyself.com

# F - O Therapies at Practices/Businesses

| Business by County with Reference no. | Family Planning (Natural) | Family Therapy | Feldenkrais Methodology | Feng Shui | Floral Essence Therapy | Flotation Therapy | Gait Analysis | Gem Essence Therapy | Gestalt Therapy | Group Therapy | Hay Diet | Healer | Healing Therapy | Hellerwork | Herbal Medicine | Holistic Healing | Homeopathy | Hopi Ear Candles | Humanistic Psychology | Hypnosis | Hypnotherapy | Indian Head Massage | Inhalation Therapy | Iridology | Kinesiology | Kirlian Photography | Laser Treatment | Life Style Coaching | Light Therapy | Macrobiotics | Magnetic Therapy | Manipulation | Manual Lymph Drainage | Massage (Therapeutic) | McTimoney Chiropractic | Meditation | Metamorphic Therapy | Miasm Therapy | Micro Manipulation | Moxibustion | Mud Therapy | Music Therapy | Nail Surgery | Naturopathy | Neuro-Linguistic Program | Neurotherapy | Nutritional Therapy | Orgone Therapy | Oriental Diagnosis | Orthomolecular Medicine |
|---|---|---|---|---|---|---|---|---|---|---|---|---|---|---|---|---|---|---|---|---|---|---|---|---|---|---|---|---|---|---|---|---|---|---|---|---|---|---|---|---|---|---|---|---|---|---|---|---|---|---|
| THERAPY BREAK (HM19891) | | | | | | | | | | | | | ● | | ● | | ● | | | ● | | ● | | | ● | | | | | | | | | ● | ● | | | | | | | | | | | | ● | | | |
| WASHINGTON SCH CLIN/ADV HYP (HM20974) | | | | | | | | | | | | | | | | | | | | ● | | | | | | | | | | | | | | | | | | | | | | | | | | | | | | |
| MERSEYSIDE | | | | | | | | | | | | | | | | | | | | | | | | | | | | | | | | | | | | | | | | | | | | | | | | | | |
| ACUPUNCTURE CLINIC (HM00263) | | | | | | | | | | | | | | | | | | | | | | | | | | | | | | | | | | | | | | | | ● | | | | | | | | | | |
| AIGBURTH MCTIMONEY CLINIC (HM00427) | | | | | | | | | | | | | | | | | | | | | | | | | | | | | | | | | | | ● | | | | | | | | | | | | | | | |
| AINTREE OSTEOPATHIC (HM00439) | | | | | | | | | | | | | | | | | | | | | | ● | | | ● | | | | | | | ● | | ● | | | | | | | | | | | | | ● | | | |
| BIMPSON, PETER (HM02311) | | | | | | | | | | | | | | | | | | | | | | | | | | | | | | | | | | ● | | | | | | | | | | | | | | | | |
| BOLTON, TOM (HM02663) | | | | | | | | | | | | | | | | ● | | | | | ● | | | | | | | | | | | | | ● | | | | | | | | | | | | | ● | | | |
| BOYLE, ANDREW (HM02826) | | | | | | | | | | | | | | | | | | | | | | ● | | | | | | | | | | ● | | ● | | | | | | ● | | | ● | | | | | | | |
| BRENNAN, M A (HM02958) | | | | | | | | | | | | | | | | | | | | | | | | | | | | | | | | | | | | | | | | | | | ● | | | | | | | |
| CARTER, G R (HM03778) | | | | | | | | | | | | | | | | | | | | | | | | | | | | | | | | | | | | | | | | | | | ● | | | | | | | |
| CAWLEY, TONY (HM03871) | | | | | | | | | | | | | | | | | | | ● | ● | ● | | | | | | | | | | | | | | | ● | | | | | | | | | | | | | | |
| CLIFFORD, CORNELIUS (HM04662) | | | | | | | | | | | | | | | | | | | | | ● | | | | | | | | | | | | | | | | | | | | | | | | | | | | | |
| CONCANNON, DEIRDRE (HM04965) | | | | | | | | | | | | | | | ● | | | | | | | | | | | | | | | | | | | | | | | | | | | | | | | | | | | |
| CULPEPER (HM05580) | | | | | | | | | | | | | | | ● | | | | | | | | | | | | | | | | | | | | | | | | | | | | | | | | | | | |
| D A F CLINIC (HM05655) | | | | | | | | | | | | | | | | ● | | | | | | | | | | | | | | | | | | ● | | | | | | ● | | | | | | | ● | | | |
| DARE TO CARE (HM05739) | | | | | | | | | | | | | | | | | | | | | | ● | | | | | | | | | | | | | | | | | | | | | | | | | | | | |
| DAVIES, H A (HM05812) | | | | | | | | | | | | | | | ● | | | | | | | | | | | | | | | | | | | | | | | | | | | | | | | | | | | |
| DAVIES, H A (HM05813) | | | | | | | | | | | | | | | ● | | | | | | | | | | | | | | | | | | | | | | | | | | | | | | | | | | | |
| DAVIS, ROSE (HM05860) | | | | | | | | | | | | | | | | | ● | | | | | | | | | | | | | | | | | | | | | | | | | | | | | | | | | |
| FRANCE, C A (HM07656) | | | | | | | | | | | | | | | | | | | | ● | | | | | | | | | | | | | | | | | | | | | | | | | | | | | | |
| GATEAUD, S (HM07924) | | | | | | | | | | | | | | | | | ● | | | | | | | | | | | | | | | | | | | | | | | | | | | | | | ● | | | |
| GIBBON, MALCOLM (HM08023) | | | | | | | | | | | | | | | | | | | | ● | | | | | | | | | | | | | | | | | | | | | | | | | | | | | | |
| HODDES, S H (DR) (HM09871) | | | | | | | | | | | | | | | | | | | | ● | | | | | | | | | | | | | | | | | | | | | | | | | | | | | | |
| HOLISTIC HEALTH CENTRE (HM09975) | | | | | | | | | | | | | | | | | ● | | | | | | | | | | | | | | | | | | | | | | | | | | | | | | | | | |
| HYNOTHERAPY BY A J FOOTE (HM10485) | | | | | | | | | | | | | | | | | | | | ● | | | | | | | | | | | | | | | | | | | | | | | | | | | | | | |
| HYPNOCARE (HM10490) | | | | | | | | | | | | | | | | | | | | | | | | | | | | | | | | | | | | | | | | | | | | | ● | | | | | |
| JACKSONS (HM10854) | | | | | | | | | | | | | | | | | | | | ● | ● | | | | | | | | | | | | | | | | | | | | | | | | | | | | | |
| JAMES, ANN (HM10880) | | | | | | | | | | | | | | | | | | | | | | | | | | | | | | | | | | ● | | | | | | | | | ● | | | | | | | |
| KNOWLES, JANICE (HM11771) | | | | | | | | | | | | | | | | | | | | | | | | | | | | | | | | | | | | | | | | | | | ● | | | | | | | |
| LEVENE, L (HM12255) | | | | | | | | | | | | | | | | | | | | ● | | | | | | | | | | | | | | | | | | | | | | | | | | | | | | |
| MARKET STREET CHIROPODY CLINIC (HM13113) | | | | | | | | | | | | | | | | | | | | | | | | | | | | | | | | | | | | | | | | | | | ● | | | | | | | |
| MASSAGE & REFLEXOLOGY (HM13255) | | | | | | | | | | | | | | | | | | | | | | | | | | | | | | | | | | ● | | | | | | | | | | | | | | | | |
| MCLOUGHLIN, CLAIRE (HM13560) | | | | | | | | | | | | | | | | | | | | | | | | | | | | | | | | | | | | | | | | | | | ● | | | | | | | |

# F - O Therapies at Practices/Businesses

| Business by County with Reference no. | Family Planning (Natural) | Family Therapy | Feldenkrais Methodology | Feng Shui | Floral Essence Therapy | Flotation Therapy | Gait Analysis | Gem Essence Therapy | Gestalt Therapy | Group Therapy | Hay Diet | Healer | Healing Therapy | Hellerwork | Herbal Medicine | Holistic Healing | Homeopathy | Hopi Ear Candles | Humanistic Psychology | Hypnosis | Hypnotherapy | Indian Head Massage | Inhalation Therapy | Iridology | Kinesiology |
|---|---|---|---|---|---|---|---|---|---|---|---|---|---|---|---|---|---|---|---|---|---|---|---|---|---|
| MIND MATTERS (HM13963) | | | | | | | | | | | | | | | | | | | | ● | | | | | |
| NATURAL HEALTH CLINIC (HM14576) | | | | | | | | | | | | | | | | | ● | | | ● | ● | | | | |
| NATUROPATHIC HEALTH CENTRE (HM14709) | | | | | | | | | | | ● | | | | ● | ● | ● | | | | | | | | |
| O'BRIEN, EAMONN (HM15178) | | | | | | | | | | | | | | | | | | | | ● | | | | | |
| ORR, WILLIAM A (HM15405) | | | | | | | | | | | | | | | | | | | | | | | | | |
| PHYTHIAN, KATHLEEN (HM16261) | | | | | | | | | | | | | | | | | | | | ● | | | | | |
| RAWLINSON, KATE (HM16974) | | | | | | | | | | | | | | | | | | | | ● | | | | | |
| REIKI-4-LIFE (HM17150) | | | | | | | | | | | | | ● | | | | | | | | | | | | |
| RILEY, JANE E (HM17343) | | | | | | | | | | | | | | | ● | | | | | | | | | | |
| RODNEY FERTILITY CLINIC (HM17529) | | | | | | | | | | | | | | | | | | | | ● | | | | | |
| RODNEY STREET HYPNOTHERAPY (HM17530) | | | | | | | | | | | | | | | | | | | | ● | | | | | |
| SCOTT, ANDREW (HM18107) | | | | | | | | | | | | | | | | | | | | | | | | | |
| SEFTON PARK NATURAL THRPY CTRE (HM18198) | | | | | | | | | | | | | ● | | | | ● | | ● | | ● | | | | |
| SIMPSON CLINIC (HM18584) | | | | | | | | ● | | | ● | | | | ● | | ● | | | | | | | ● | ● |
| STRESS MANAGEMENT (HM19396) | | | | | | | | | | | | | | | | | | | | ● | | | | | |
| SUMMERS, ALFRED A (HM19487) | | | | | | | | | | | | | | | | | | | | | | | | | |
| TARA SCHOOL OF HYPNOTHERAPY (HM19701) | | | | | | | | | | | | | | | | | | | | ● | ● | | | | |
| THERAPY 21 (HM19890) | | | | | | | | | | | | ● | ● | | | ● | | | | | | | | | |
| **MIDDLESEX** | | | | | | | | | | | | | | | | | | | | | | | | | |
| CLANRICARDE CLINIC (HM04526) | | | | | | | | | | | | | | | | | | | | | | | | | |
| **MIDLANDS (WEST)** | | | | | | | | | | | | | | | | | | | | | | | | | |
| A Q C H (HM00044) | | | | | | | | | | | | | | | | | | | | ● | ● | | | | |
| ABBEY CLINIC (HM00077) | | | | | | | | | | | | | | | ● | | ● | | | ● | | ● | | | |
| ABBIE HYPNOTHERAPY CENTRE (HM00093) | | | | | | | | | | | | | | | | | | | | ● | ● | | | | |
| ALCOCK, E C (HM00490) | | | | | | | ● | | | | | | | | | | | | | | | | | | |
| ALDA HOUSE NATURAL THERAPY (HM00492) | | | | | ● | | | | | | | | | | | | ● | ● | | | | ● | | | ● |
| ALDOUS, JOSIE (HM00503) | | | | | | | | | | | | | | | | | | ● | | | | | | | |
| AROMA SANTE (HM01057) | | | | | | | | | | | | | | | | | | | | | | ● | | | |
| ASSOCIATION OF STRESS MNGMT (HM01288) | | | | | | | | | | | | | | | | | | | | ● | ● | | | | |
| ATKINS, DENISE (HM01318) | | | | | | | | | | | | | | | | | | | | ● | | | | | |
| BACKCARE & ACUPUNCTURE CLINIC (HM01526) | | | | | | | | | | | | | | | | | | | | ● | ● | | | | |
| BEAUTIFORM COLLEGE (HM01992) | | | | | | | | | | | | | | | | | | | | | | | | | |
| BELL, PATRICIA (HM02088) | | | | | | | | | | | | | | | | | | | | ● | | | | | |
| BIOENERGY PARTNERSHIP (HM02334) | | | | | | | | | | | | | | | | ● | | | | | | | | | |

| Business by County with Reference no. | Kirlian Photography | Laser Treatment | Life Style Coaching | Light Therapy | Macrobiotics | Magnetic Therapy | Manipulation | Manual Lymph Drainage | Massage (Therapeutic) | McTimoney Chiropractic | Meditation | Metamorphic Therapy | Miasm Therapy | Micro Manipulation | Moxibustion | Mud Therapy | Music Therapy | Nail Surgery | Naturopathy | Neuro-Linguistic Program | Neurotherapy | Nutritional Therapy | Orgone Therapy | Oriental Diagnosis | Orthomolecular Medicine |
|---|---|---|---|---|---|---|---|---|---|---|---|---|---|---|---|---|---|---|---|---|---|---|---|---|---|
| MIND MATTERS (HM13963) | | | | | | | | | | | | | | | | | | | | | | | | | |
| NATURAL HEALTH CLINIC (HM14576) | | | | | | | | | | | | | | | | | | | | | | | | | |
| NATUROPATHIC HEALTH CENTRE (HM14709) | | | | | | | ● | | ● | | | | | | | | | | ● | | | ● | | | |
| O'BRIEN, EAMONN (HM15178) | | | | | | | | | | | | | | | | | | | | | | | | | |
| ORR, WILLIAM A (HM15405) | | | | | | | ● | | | | | | | | | | | | | | | | | | |
| PHYTHIAN, KATHLEEN (HM16261) | | | | | | | | | | | | | | | | | | | | | | | | | |
| RAWLINSON, KATE (HM16974) | | | | | | | | | | | | | | | | | | | | | | | | | |
| REIKI-4-LIFE (HM17150) | | | | | | | | | ● | | | | | | | | | | | | | | | | |
| RILEY, JANE E (HM17343) | | | | | | | | | | | | | | | | | | | | | | | | | |
| RODNEY FERTILITY CLINIC (HM17529) | | | | | | | | | | | | | | | | | | | | | | | | | |
| RODNEY STREET HYPNOTHERAPY (HM17530) | | | | | | | | | | | | | | | | | | | | | | | | | |
| SCOTT, ANDREW (HM18107) | | | | | | | | | | | | | | | ● | | | | | | | | | | |
| SEFTON PARK NATURAL THRPY CTRE (HM18198) | | | ● | | | | ● | | ● | | | | | | | | | | | | | ● | | | |
| SIMPSON CLINIC (HM18584) | | | ● | | ● | | ● | | ● | | | | ● | ● | | | ● | | ● | | | ● | | | |
| STRESS MANAGEMENT (HM19396) | | | | | | | | | | | | | | | | | | | | | | | | | |
| SUMMERS, ALFRED A (HM19487) | | | | | | | | | | | | | | | | | | ● | | | | | | | |
| TARA SCHOOL OF HYPNOTHERAPY (HM19701) | | | | | | | | | | | ● | | | | | | | | | | | | | | |
| THERAPY 21 (HM19890) | | | | | | | | | ● | | | | | | | | | | | | | | | | |
| **MIDDLESEX** | | | | | | | | | | | | | | | | | | | | | | | | | |
| CLANRICARDE CLINIC (HM04526) | | | | | | | ● | | ● | | | | | | | | | | | | | | | | |
| **MIDLANDS (WEST)** | | | | | | | | | | | | | | | | | | | | | | | | | |
| A Q C H (HM00044) | | | | | | | | | | | | | | | | | | | | | | | | | |
| ABBEY CLINIC (HM00077) | | | | | | | ● | | ● | | | | | ● | | | | | | | | | | | |
| ABBIE HYPNOTHERAPY CENTRE (HM00093) | | | | | | | | | | | | | | | | | | | | | | | | | |
| ALCOCK, E C (HM00490) | | | | | | | | | | | | | | | | | | ● | | | | | | | |
| ALDA HOUSE NATURAL THERAPY (HM00492) | | | | | | | ● | | ● | | | | ● | | ● | | | | | | | | | | |
| ALDOUS, JOSIE (HM00503) | | | | | | | | | | | | | | | | | | | | | | | | | |
| AROMA SANTE (HM01057) | | | | | | | | | | | | | | | | | | | | | | | | | |
| ASSOCIATION OF STRESS MNGMT (HM01288) | | | | | | | | | | | | | | | | | | | | | | | | | |
| ATKINS, DENISE (HM01318) | | | | | | | | | | | | | | | | | | | | | | | | | |
| BACKCARE & ACUPUNCTURE CLINIC (HM01526) | | | ● | | | | ● | | ● | | | | | | ● | | | | | ● | | ● | | ● | |
| BEAUTIFORM COLLEGE (HM01992) | | | | | | | | | ● | | | | | | | | | | | | | | | | |
| BELL, PATRICIA (HM02088) | | | | | | | | | | | | | | | | | | | | | | | | | |
| BIOENERGY PARTNERSHIP (HM02334) | | | | | | | | | | | | | | | | | | | | | | | | | |

# F - O Therapies at Practices/Businesses

| Business by County with Reference no. | Family Planning (Natural) | Family Therapy | Feldenkrais Methodology | Feng Shui | Floral Essence Therapy | Flotation Therapy | Gait Analysis | Gem Essence Therapy | Gestalt Therapy | Group Therapy | Hay Diet | Healer | Healing Therapy | Hellerwork | Herbal Medicine | Holistic Healing | Homeopathy | Hopi Ear Candles | Humanistic Psychology | Hypnosis | Hypnotherapy | Indian Head Massage | Inhalation Therapy | Iridology | Kinesiology |
|---|---|---|---|---|---|---|---|---|---|---|---|---|---|---|---|---|---|---|---|---|---|---|---|---|---|
| BIRMINGHAM ACU/CHIRO CLNC (HM02382) | | | | | | | | | | | | | | | | | | | | | | | | | |
| BIRMINGHAM HYPNOTHERAPY (HM02386) | | | | | | | | | | | | |●| | | | | | |●| |●| | | |
| BIRMINGHAM PHYSIO CLINIC (HM02388) | | | | | | | | | | | | | | | | | | | | | | | | | |
| BLAIR, GRAHAM (HM02473) | | | | | | | | | | | | | | | | | | | |●| | | | | |
| BOLDMERE HYPNOTHERAPY (HM02653) | | | | | | | | | | | | | | | | | | | |●|●| | | | |
| BROWNHILL, D G (HM03257) | | | | | | | | | | | | | | | | | | | | |●| | | | |
| BTAC (HM03296) | | | | | | | | | | | |●|●| | |●| | | | | | | | | |
| CARING HYPNOTHERAPY CENTRE (HM03686) | | | | | | | | | | | | | | | | | | | |●| | | | | |
| CARPENTER, DAVID (HM03727) | | | | | | | | | | | | | | | | | | | |●|●| | | | |
| CARTWRIGHT-RAY, JOY (HM03800) | | | | | | | | | | | | | | | | | | | |●| | | | | |
| CENTRE FOR NATURAL THERAPIES (HM03913) | | | | | | | | | | | | | | | | |●| | | |●| | | | |
| CHEER, MARIE (HM04082) | | | | | | | | | | | | | | |●| | | | | | |●| | | |
| CHELMSLEY WOOD FOOT CLINIC (HM04086) | | | | | | | | | | | | | | | | | | | | | |●| | | |
| CHINESE HERBAL MED & HLTH CARE (HM04201) | | | | | | | | | | | | | | |●| | | | | | | | | | |
| CHIRO MED (HM04283) | |●| | | | | | |●| | | |●| | |●| | | | |●| | | | |
| CLINIC OF HERBAL MEDICINE (HM04692) | | | | | | | | | | | | | | |●| | | | | | | | | | |
| CODSALL COMP THERAPIES (HM04778) | | | | | | | | | | | | | | | | | | | | | |●| | | |
| COMPLEMENTARY HEALING CENTRE (HM04919) | | | | | | | | | | | | | | | | | |●| | | |●| | | |
| COMPLEMENTARY MEDICINE CENTRE (HM04937) | | | | | | | | | | | |●| | |●| |●| | | | | | | | |
| CREATIVE CHANGES (HM05396) | | | | | | | | | | | | | | | | | | | |●| | | | | |
| CREATIVE HEALTH CENTRE (HM05398) | | | | | | | | | | | | | | | | |●|●| | |●|●| | |●|
| CTIC (HM05535) | | | | | | | | | | | | | | | | | | | | |●|●| | | |
| CTRE-REFLEX & AROMATHERAPY (HM05549) | | | | | | | | | | | |●| | | | | |●| | | |●| | | |
| CULPEPER (HM05576) | | | | | | | | | | | | | | |●| | | | | | | | | | |
| DONNAMARIE (HM06175) | | | | | | | | | | | | | | | | | | | |●| | | | | |
| ERDINGTHON NATURAL HEALTH CLNC (HM06880) | | | | | | | | | | | | | | | | |●| | | | |●| | | |
| FAIRFAX PRIVATE THERAPY (HM07056) | | | | | | | | | | | | | | | | | | | | |●| | | | |
| FIRTH, JOHN (HM07342) | | | | | | | | | | | | | | | | |●| | | | | | | | |
| FORD, MARIA (HM07526) | | | | |●| | | | | | | | | | | |●| | | | | | | | |
| FRENCH, ANNE (HM07728) | | | | | | | | | | | | | | | | | | | |●| | | | | |
| FRESHWINDS CHARITABLE TRUST (HM07740) | | | | | | | | | | | |●|●| | | |●| | |●|●|●| | | |
| GOLDEN PALMS (HM08207) | | | | | | | | | | | | | | | |●| | | | | |●| | | |
| GOWER, MONICA (HM08325) | | | | | | | | | | | | | | | | |●| | | | | | | | |
| GRAHAM, PATRICIA (HM08358) | | | | | | | | | | | | | | | | | | | |●| | | | | |

| Business by County with Reference no. | Kirlian Photography | Laser Treatment | Life Style Coaching | Light Therapy | Macrobiotics | Magnetic Therapy | Manipulation | Manual Lymph Drainage | Massage (Therapeutic) | McTimoney Chiropractic | Meditation | Metamorphic Therapy | Miasm Therapy | Micro Manipulation | Moxibustion | Mud Therapy | Music Therapy | Nail Surgery | Naturopathy | Neuro-Linguistic Program | Neurotherapy | Nutritional Therapy | Orgone Therapy | Oriental Diagnosis | Orthomolecular Medicine |
|---|---|---|---|---|---|---|---|---|---|---|---|---|---|---|---|---|---|---|---|---|---|---|---|---|---|
| BIRMINGHAM ACU/CHIRO CLNC (HM02382) | | | | | | | | |●| | | | | | | | | | | | | | | | |
| BIRMINGHAM HYPNOTHERAPY (HM02386) | | |●| | | | | | | | | | | | | | | | |●| | | | | |
| BIRMINGHAM PHYSIO CLINIC (HM02388) | | | | | | |●| | | | | | | | | | | | | | | | | | |
| BLAIR, GRAHAM (HM02473) | | | | | | | | | | | | | | | | | | | | | | | | | |
| BOLDMERE HYPNOTHERAPY (HM02653) | | |●| | | | | | | | | | | | | | | | | | | | | | |
| BROWNHILL, D G (HM03257) | | | | | | | | | | | | | | | | | | | | | | | | | |
| BTAC (HM03296) | | |●| | | | | | | |●| | | |●| | | |●| | |●| |●| |
| CARING HYPNOTHERAPY CENTRE (HM03686) | | | | | | | | | | | | | | | | | | | | | | | | | |
| CARPENTER, DAVID (HM03727) | | | | | | | | | | | | | | | | | | | |●| | | | | |
| CARTWRIGHT-RAY, JOY (HM03800) | | | | | | | | | | | | | | | | | | | | | | | | | |
| CENTRE FOR NATURAL THERAPIES (HM03913) | | | | | | | | | | | | | | | | | | | | | | | | | |
| CHEER, MARIE (HM04082) | | | | | | | | | | | | | | | | | | | | | | | | | |
| CHELMSLEY WOOD FOOT CLINIC (HM04086) | | | | | | | | | | | | | | | | | | | | | | | | | |
| CHINESE HERBAL MED & HLTH CARE (HM04201) | | | | | | | | | | | | | | | | | | | | | | | | | |
| CHIRO MED (HM04283) | | | | | | |●| |●| | | | | | | | | | | | | | | | |
| CLINIC OF HERBAL MEDICINE (HM04692) | | | | | | | | | | | | | | | | | | | | | | | | | |
| CODSALL COMP THERAPIES (HM04778) | | | | | | | | | | | | | | | | | | | | | | | | | |
| COMPLEMENTARY HEALING CENTRE (HM04919) | | | | | | | | |●| | | | | | | | | | | | | | | | |
| COMPLEMENTARY MEDICINE CENTRE (HM04937) | | | | | | | | | | | | | | | | | | | | | | | | | |
| CREATIVE CHANGES (HM05396) | | | | | | | | | | | | | | | | | | | | | | | | | |
| CREATIVE HEALTH CENTRE (HM05398) | | | | | | | | |●| | | | | | | | | | | | | | | | |
| CTIC (HM05535) | | | | | | | | | | | | | | | | | | | | | |●| | | |
| CTRE-REFLEX & AROMATHERAPY (HM05549) | | | | | | | | | | | | | | | | | | | | | | | | | |
| CULPEPER (HM05576) | | | | | | | | | | | | | | | | | | | | | | | | | |
| DONNAMARIE (HM06175) | | | | | | | | | | | | | | | | | | | | | | | | | |
| ERDINGTHON NATURAL HEALTH CLNC (HM06880) | | | | | | | | | | | | | | | | | | | | | | | | | |
| FAIRFAX PRIVATE THERAPY (HM07056) | | | | | | | | | | | | | | | | | | | | | | | | | |
| FIRTH, JOHN (HM07342) | | | | | | | | | | | | | | | | | | | | | | | | | |
| FORD, MARIA (HM07526) | | | | | | | | | | | | | | | | | | | | | | | | | |
| FRENCH, ANNE (HM07728) | | | | | | | | | | | | | | | | | | | | | | | | | |
| FRESHWINDS CHARITABLE TRUST (HM07740) | | | | | | | | | | |●| | | |●| | | | | | | | | | |
| GOLDEN PALMS (HM08207) | | | | | | |●| |●| | | | | | | | | | | | | | | | |
| GOWER, MONICA (HM08325) | | | | | | | | | | | | | | | | | | | | | | | | | |
| GRAHAM, PATRICIA (HM08358) | | | | | | | | | | | | | | | | | | | | | | | | | |

# F - O Therapies at Practices/Businesses

Business by County with Reference no.

| | GRAYBURN-HALE, DAVID (HM08422) | GREEN VALLEY THERAPY CENTRE (HM08443) | HAGLEY CENTRE OF COMP MED (HM08701) | HALL GREEN ALTERN PRACTICE (HM08760) | HALL, SUSAN (HM08790) | HAMPTON, ANTHONY (HM08887) | HARRIS, GERALD (HM09063) | HARRIS, MICHAEL (HM09081) | HARTNESS, R (HM09149) | HEALTH SHOP (HM09402) | HERBAL PHARMACY (HM09632) | HERBAL TREATMENT CENTRE (HM09636) | HERBAVET (HM09652) | HOGG, DEBBI (HM09913) | HOLISTIC HEALTH CENTRE (HM09972) | HOLLOWAY, P (HM10027) | HOMOEOPATHIC CLINIC/PHARMACY (HM10090) | HOMOEOPATHY (HM10103) | HUSBANDS, STEVE (HM10432) | INGRAM, CLARE (HM10624) | INNERSENSE (HM10647) | JONES, J (HM11150) | KEMPSON, STEVE (HM11468) | KHALSA, S S (HM11585) | LEMM, D M (HM12204) | LONGFORD PHYSIO & SPORTS (HM12627) | LYNCH, STEPHEN (HM12765) | MCMANUS, RAYMOND (HM13571) | MIDLAND HYPNOTHERAPY CENTRE (HM13830) | MIDLAND HYPNOTHERAPY CENTRE (HM13831) | MIDLAND MEDICAL HOM PRACTICE (HM13832) | MIDLAND MEDICAL HOM PRACTICE (HM13833) | MIDLAND MEDICAL HOM PRACTICE (HM13834) | MIDLAND MEDICAL OSTEO PRACTICE (HM13837) |
|---|---|---|---|---|---|---|---|---|---|---|---|---|---|---|---|---|---|---|---|---|---|---|---|---|---|---|---|---|---|---|---|---|---|---|
| Orthomolecular Medicine | | | | | | | | | | | | | | | | | | | | | | | | | | | | | | | | | | |
| Oriental Diagnosis | | | | | | | | | | | | | | | | | | | | | | | | | | | | | | | | | | |
| Orgone Therapy | | | | | | | | | | | | | | | | | | | | | | | | | | | | | | | | | | |
| Nutritional Therapy | | ● | | | | | | | | | | | | | | | | | | | | | | | | | | | | | | | | |
| Neurotherapy | | | | | | | | | | | | | | | | | | | | | | | | | | | | | | | | | | |
| Neuro-Linguistic Program | | | | | | | | | | | | | | | | | | | | | | | | | | | | | | | | | | |
| Naturopathy | | | | | | | | | | | | | | | | | | | | | | | | | | | | | | | | | | |
| Nail Surgery | | | | | | | | | ● | | | | | | | | | | | | | | | | | | | | | | | | | |
| Music Therapy | | | | | | | | | | | | | | | | | | | | | | | | | | | | | | | | | | |
| Mud Therapy | | | | | | | | | | | | | | | | | | | | | | | | | | | | | | | | | | |
| Moxibustion | | | | | | | | | | | | | | | | | | | | | | | | | | | | | | | | | | |
| Micro Manipulation | | | | | | | | | | | | | | | | | | | | | | | | | | | | | | | | | | |
| Miasm Therapy | | | | | | | | | | | | | | | | | | | | | | | | | | | | | | | | | | |
| Metamorphic Therapy | | | | | | | | | | | | | | | | | | | | | | | | | | | | | | | | | | |
| Meditation | | | | | | | | | | | | | | | | | | | | | | | | | | | | | | | | | | |
| McTimoney Chiropractic | | | | | | | | | | | | | | | | | | | | | | | | | | | | | | | | | | |
| Massage (Therapeutic) | | ● | ● | | | | | | | | | | | | | | | | | | | | | | | ● | | | | | | | | ● |
| Manual Lymph Drainage | | | | | | | | | | | | | | | | | | | | | | | | | | | | | | | | | | |
| Manipulation | | | | | | | | | | | | | | | | | | | | | | | | | | | | | | | | | | ● |
| Magnetic Therapy | | | | | | | | | | | | | | | | | | | | | | | | | | | | | | | | | | |
| Macrobiotics | | | | | | | | | | | | | | | | | | | | | | | | | | | | | | | | | | |
| Light Therapy | | | | | | | | | | | | | | | | | | | | | | | | | | | | | | | | | | |
| Life Style Coaching | | | | | | | | | | | | | | | | | | | | | | | | | | | | | | | | | | |
| Laser Treatment | | | | | | | | | | | | | | | | | | | | | | | | | | | | | | | | | | |
| Kirlian Photography | | | | | | | | | | | | | | | | | | | | | | | | | | | | | | | | | | |
| Kinesiology | | ● | | ● | | | | | | | | | | | | | | | | ● | | | ● | | | | | | | | | | | |
| Iridology | | | | | | | | | | | | | | | | | | | | | | | | | | | | | | | | | | |
| Inhalation Therapy | | | | | | | | | | | | | | | | | | | | | | | | | | | | | | | | | | |
| Indian Head Massage | | ● | ● | | ● | | | | | | | | | | | | | | | | | | | | | | | | | | | | | |
| Hypnotherapy | | ● | ● | | | | | | | | | | | | | ● | | | | | | | | | | | | | | ● | | | | |
| Hypnosis | ● | | ● | | | | ● | ● | | | | | | | | | | | | | | | | | ● | | ● | ● | ● | ● | | | | |
| Humanistic Psychology | | | | | | | | | | | | | | | | | | | | | | | | | | | | | | | | | | |
| Hopi Ear Candles | | | | | | ● | | | | | | | | | | | | | | | ● | | | | | | | | | | | | | |
| Homeopathy | | ● | ● | ● | | | | | | ● | | | | | ● | | ● | ● | ● | | | | | ● | | | | | | | ● | ● | ● | ● |
| Holistic Healing | | ● | ● | ● | | | | | | | | | | ● | ● | | | | ● | | | | | | | | | | | | | | | |
| Herbal Medicine | | | | | | | | | | | ● | ● | ● | | | | | | | | | ● | | | | | | | | | | | | |
| Hellerwork | | | | | | | | | | | | | | | | | | | | | | | | | | | | | | | | | | |
| Healing Therapy | | | | | | | | | | | | | | | | | | | | | | | | | | | | | | | | | | |
| Healer | | | ● | | | | | | | | | | | | ● | | | | | | | | | | | | | | | | | | | |
| Hay Diet | | | | | | | | | | | | | | | | | | | | | | | | | | | | | | | | | | |
| Group Therapy | | | | | | | | | | | | | | | | | | | | | | | | | | | | | | | | | | |
| Gestalt Therapy | | | | | | | | | | | | | | | | | | | | | | | | | | | | | | | | | | |
| Gem Essence Therapy | | | | | | | | | | | | | | | | | | | | | | | | | | | | | | | | | | |
| Gait Analysis | | | | | | | | | | | | | | | | | | | | | | | | | | | | | | | | | | |
| Flotation Therapy | | | ● | | | | | | | | | | | | | | | | | | | | | | | | | | | | | | | |
| Floral Essence Therapy | | | | | | | | | | | | | | | ● | | | | | | | | | | | | | | | | | | | |
| Feng Shui | | | | | | | | | | | | | | | | | | | | | | | | | | | | | | | | | | |
| Feldenkrais Methodology | | | | | | | | | | | | | | | | | | | | | | | | | | | | | | | | | | |
| Family Therapy | | | | | | | | | | | | | | | | | | | | | | | | | | | | | | | | | | |
| Family Planning (Natural) | | | | | | | | | | | | | | | | | | | | | | | | | | | | | | | | | | |

# F - O Therapies at Practices/Businesses

| Business by County with Reference no. | Family Planning (Natural) | Family Therapy | Feldenkrais Methodology | Feng Shui | Floral Essence Therapy | Flotation Therapy | Gait Analysis | Gem Essence Therapy | Gestalt Therapy | Group Therapy | Hay Diet | Healer | Healing Therapy | Hellerwork | Herbal Medicine | Holistic Healing | Homeopathy | Hopi Ear Candles | Humanistic Psychology | Hypnosis | Hypnotherapy | Indian Head Massage | Inhalation Therapy | Iridology | Kinesiology | Kirlian Photography | Laser Treatment | Life Style Coaching | Light Therapy | Macrobiotics | Magnetic Therapy | Manipulation | Manual Lymph Drainage | Massage (Therapeutic) | McTimoney Chiropractic | Meditation | Metamorphic Therapy | Miasm Therapy | Micro Manipulation | Moxibustion | Mud Therapy | Music Therapy | Nail Surgery | Naturopathy | Neuro-Linguistic Program | Neurotherapy | Nutritional Therapy | Orgone Therapy | Oriental Diagnosis | Orthomolecular Medicine |
|---|---|---|---|---|---|---|---|---|---|---|---|---|---|---|---|---|---|---|---|---|---|---|---|---|---|---|---|---|---|---|---|---|---|---|---|---|---|---|---|---|---|---|---|---|---|---|---|---|---|---|
| MIDLAND MEDICAL OSTEO PRACTICE (HM13836) | | | | | | | | | | | | | | | | | ● | | | | | | | | | | | | | | | ● | | ● | | | | | | | | | | | | | | | | |
| MIDLAND MEDICAL OSTEO PRACTICE (HM13835) | | | | | | | | | | | | | | | | | ● | | | | | | | | | | | | | | | ● | | ● | | | | | | | | | | | | | | | | |
| MIDLANDS HOM CONSULTANTS (HM13842) | | | | | | | | | | | | | | | | | ● | | | | | | | | | | | | | | | | | | | | | | | | | | | | | | | | | |
| MINIHANE, LIZ (HM13976) | | | | | | | | | | | | | | | | | ● | | | | | | | | | | | | | | | | | | | | | | | | | | | | | | | | | |
| MORGAN, VALERIE (HM14177) | | | | | | | | | | | | | | | | | ● | | | | | | | | | | | | | | | | | | | | | | | | | | | ● | | | | | | |
| MOTIVATIONAL RESEARCH & DVPT (HM14276) | | | | | | | | | | | | | | | | | | | | ● | | | | | | | | | | | | | | | | | | | | | | | | | | | | | | |
| MYATT, ANITA (HM14432) | | | | | | | | | | | | | | | ● | | | ● | | | | | | | | | | | | | | | | | | | | | | | | | | | | | ● | | | |
| NEWBRIDGE PHARMACY (HM14850) | | | | | | | | | | | | | | | ● | | ● | | | | | ● | | | | | | | | | | | | | | | | | | | | | | | | | ● | | | |
| NEWTONS TRADITIONAL REMEDIES (HM14902) | | | | | | | | | | | | | | | ● | | | | | | | | | | | | | | | | | | | | | | | | | | | | | | | | | | | |
| NORMAN, KATHY (HM15005) | | | | | | | | | | | | | | | | | | ● | | | | ● | | | | | | | | | | | | | | | | | | | | | | | | | | | | |
| PARK PRACTICE (HM15672) | | | | | | | | | | | | | | | | | ● | | | | ● | | | | | | | | | | | | | | | | | | | | | | | | | | | | | |
| PARRETTI, ROSEMARY (HM15732) | | | | | | | | | | | | | | | | | ● | | | | | | | | | | | | | | | | | | | | | | | | | | | | | | | | | |
| PRIMECARE (HM16615) | | | | | | | | | | | | | | | | | | | | ● | | | | | | | | | | | | | | | | | | | | | | | | | | | | | | |
| PRISM THERAPIES (HM16636) | | | | | | | | | | | | | | | | | | | | ● | ● | | | | | | | | | | | | | | | | | | | | | | | | | | | | | |
| REMEDIAL MASSAGE THERAPY (HM17174) | | | | | | | | | | | | | | | | | | | | | | | | | | | | | | | | ● | | ● | | | | | | | | | | | | | | | | |
| ROMSLEY PHYSIOTHERAPY PRACTICE (HM17578) | | | | | | | | | | | | | | | | | | | | | ● | | | | | | | | | | | ● | | ● | | | | | | ● | | | | | | | | | | |
| SANDERLING HYPNOTHERAPY CENTRE (HM17902) | | | | | | | | | | | | | | | | | | | | ● | | | | | | | | | | | | | | | | | | | | | | | | | | | | | | |
| SHARKEY, CATHERINE (HM18298) | | | | | | | | | | | | | | | | | | | | ● | | | | | | | | | | | | | | | | | | | | | | | | | | | | | | |
| SHAW, REBECCA (HM18348) | | | | | | | | | | | | | | | | | | | | ● | | | | | | | | | | | | | | | | | | | | | | | | | | | | | | |
| SIDHOM, A (HM18529) | | | | | | | | | | | | | | | | | ● | | | | ● | | | | | | | | | | | | | | | | | | | | | | | | | | | | | |
| SMALLWOOD, TREVOR (HM18699) | | | | | | | | | | | | | | | | | | | | ● | | | | | | | | | | | | | | | | | | | | | | | | | | | | | | |
| SMITH, MOLLY-ANN (HM18782) | | | | | | | | | | | | | | | | | | | | ● | | | | | | | | | | | | | | | | | | | | | | | | | | | | | | |
| SOMEWAY HERBAL CLINIC (HM18883) | | | | | | | | | | | | | | | ● | | | | | | | | | | | | | | | | | | | | | | | | | | | | | | | | | | | |
| SOUTH BIRMINGHAM HYP CENTRE (HM18903) | | | | | | | | | | | | | | | | | | | | ● | | | | | | | | | | | | | | | | | | | | | | | | | | | | | | |
| ST PAULS OSTEOPATHY PRACTICE (HM19094) | | | | | | | | | | | | ● | | | | ● | ● | | | | | ● | | | | | | | | | | ● | | ● | | | | | | | | | | ● | | | | | | |
| STRANKS, KATHY (HM19368) | | | | | | | | | | | | | | | | | ● | | | | | | | | | | | | | | | | | | | | | | | | | | | | | | | | | |
| STRESS MANAGEMENT (HM19394) | | | | | | | | | | | | | | | | | | | | ● | | | | | | | | | | | | | | | | | | | | | | | | | | | | | | |
| SUCCESSWORKS (HM19461) | | | | | | | | | | | | ● | | | | ● | | | ● | | | | | | | | | ● | | | | | | | | ● | | | | | | | | | | | | | | |
| SUTTON COLDFIELD HYPNOTHERAPY (HM19545) | | | | | | | | | | | | | | | | | | | | ● | | | | | | | | | | | | | | | | | | | | | | | | | | | | | | |
| SUTTON HOMOEOPATHIC PRACTICE (HM19547) | | | | | | | | | | | | | | | | | ● | | | | | | | | | | | | | | | | | | | | | | | | | | | | | | | | | |
| TEES, MALCOLM (HM19816) | | | | | | | | | | | | | | | | | | | | ● | | | | | | | | | | | | | | | | | | | | | | | | | | | | | | |
| TELLING, MELANIE (HM19823) | | | | | | | | | | | | | | | | | | | | | | ● | | | | | | | | | | | | | | | | | | | | | | | | | | | | |
| TELLING, MELANIE (HM19822) | | | | | | | | | | | | | | | | | | ● | | | | ● | | | | | | | | | | | | | | | | | | | | | | | | | | | | |
| THERAPY TRAINING COLLEGE (HM19911) | | | | | | | | | | | | | | | | | | | | ● | ● | | | | | | | | | | | | | | | | | | | | | | | | | | | | | |

# F - O Therapies at Practices/Businesses

| Business by County with Reference no. | Family Planning (Natural) | Family Therapy | Feldenkrais Methodology | Feng Shui | Floral Essence Therapy | Flotation Therapy | Gait Analysis | Gem Essence Therapy | Gestalt Therapy | Group Therapy | Hay Diet | Healer | Healing Therapy | Hellerwork | Herbal Medicine | Holistic Healing | Homeopathy | Hopi Ear Candles | Humanistic Psychology | Hypnosis | Hypnotherapy | Indian Head Massage | Inhalation Therapy | Iridology | Kinesiology | Kirlian Photography | Laser Treatment | Life Style Coaching | Light Therapy | Macrobiotics | Magnetic Therapy | Manipulation | Manual Lymph Drainage | Massage (Therapeutic) | McTimoney Chiropractic | Meditation | Metamorphic Therapy | Miasm Therapy | Micro Manipulation | Moxibustion | Mud Therapy | Music Therapy | Nail Surgery | Naturopathy | Neuro-Linguistic Program | Neurotherapy | Nutritional Therapy | Orgone Therapy | Oriental Diagnosis | Orthomolecular Medicine |
|---|---|---|---|---|---|---|---|---|---|---|---|---|---|---|---|---|---|---|---|---|---|---|---|---|---|---|---|---|---|---|---|---|---|---|---|---|---|---|---|---|---|---|---|---|---|---|---|---|---|---|
| WARD, JAQUELINE (HM20906) | | | | | | | | | | | | | | | | | | | | ● | ● | | | | | | | | | | | | | | | | | | | | | | | | | | | | | |
| WELL NATURAL HEALTH CENTRE (HM21140) | | | | | | | | | | | | ● | | ● | ● | ● | ● | | | | ● | ● | | | | | | | | | | | | ● | | | ● | | | | | | | ● | | | ● | | | |
| WELL NATURAL HEALTH CENTRE (HM21139) | | | | | | | | | | | | | ● | ● | | | ● | | | | ● | ● | | | | | | | | | | | | ● | | ● | | | | | | | | ● | | | ● | | | |
| WEST MIDLAND HYPNOTHERAPY (HM21229) | | | | | | | | | | | | | | | | | | | | ● | ● | | | | | | | ● | | | | | | | | | | | | | | | | | | | | | | |
| WESTON, JOHN (HM21278) | | | | | | | | | | | | | | | | | | | | | | | | | | | | | | | | ● | | ● | | | | | ● | | | | | | | | | | | |
| WESTWOOD, ANGELA (HM21285) | | | | | | | | | | | | | | | | | | | | | | | | | | | | | | | | | | | | | ● | | | | | | | | | | | | | |
| WHITE, SHELLEY (HM21378) | | | | | | | | | | | | | | | | | | | | | | | | | | | | | | | | | | ● | | | | | | | | | | | | | | | | |
| WHITEHEAD, T (HM21387) | | | | | | | | | | | | | | | | | ● | | | | | | | | | | | | | | | | | | | | | | | | | | | | | | | | | |
| WILLIAMS, CHARLES (HM21548) | | | | | | | | | | | | | | | | | | | | ● | | | | | | | | | | | | | | | | | | | | | | | | | | | | | | |
| WILLOWS CLNC COMP HEALTH CTRE (HM21630) | | | | | ● | | | | | | | | | | ● | ● | ● | | | | ● | ● | | | | | | | | | | | | ● | | | | | | | | | | ● | | | ● | | | |
| WOLVERHAMPTON CHINESE MED CTRE (HM21765) | | | | | | | | | | | | | | | ● | | | | | | | | | | | | | | | | | | | | | | | | | | | | | | | | | | | |
| WOLVERHAMPTON HOMOEOPATHY (HM21766) | | | | | | | | | | | | | | | | | ● | | | | | | | | | | | | | | | | | | | | | | | | | | | | | | | | | |
| ZEN HEALTH & BEAUTY (HM22099) | | | | | | | | | | | | | | | | | | | | | | ● | | | | | | | | | | | | ● | | | | | | | | | | | | | | | | |
| **NORFOLK** | | | | | | | | | | | | | | | | | | | | | | | | | | | | | | | | | | | | | | | | | | | | | | | | | | |
| ADVANCED HYP/PSYCHOTHERAPY (HM00398) | | | | | | | | | | | | | | | | | | | | ● | | | | | | | | | | | | | | | | | | | | | | | | | | | | | | |
| ALTERNATIVE HEALTH CARE (HM00702) | | | | | | | | | | | | | | | | | | | | | | | | ● | | | | | | | | | | | | | | | | | | | | | | | ● | | | |
| ARROWSMITH, SUSAN (HM01151) | | | | | | | | | | | | | | | | | | | | ● | | | | | | | | | | | | | | | | | | | | | | | | | | | | | | |
| BODY BEAUTIFUL (HM02576) | | | | | | | | | | | | | | | | | | | | | | | | | | | | | | | | | | ● | | | | | | | | | | | | | | | | |
| CHASE PARK PRACTICE (HM04060) | | | | | | | | | ● | | | | | | | | | | | | | | | | | | | | | | | | | | | | | | | | | | | | | | | | | |
| CHIROPODIST (HM04291) | | | | | | | | | | | | | | | | | | | | | | | | | | | | | | | | | | | | | | | | | | | ● | | | | | | | |
| CLASSICAL OSTEOPATH (HM04611) | | | | | | | | | | | | ● | ● | | | | | | | | | | | | | | | | | | | ● | | ● | | | | | ● | | | | | | | | | | | |
| COMER OSTEOPATHIC CLINIC (HM04897) | | | | | | | | | | | | | | | | | | | | | | | | | | | | | | | | ● | | | | | | | | | | | | ● | | | | | | |
| COMPLEMENTARY HEALTH CLINIC (HM04926) | | | | | | | | | | | | | | | | | | | | | ● | | | | | | | | | | | | | ● | | | | | | | | | | | | | | | | |
| COTTAGE CLINIC (HM05220) | | | | | | | | | | | | | | | ● | | | | | | | | | | | | | | | | | | | | | | | | | | | | | | | | | | | |
| COULL, JUDY (HM05236) | | | | | | | | | | | | | | | | | ● | | | | | | | | | | | | | | | | | | | | | | | | | | | | | | | | | |
| COUNTY HEALTH (HM05259) | | | | | | | | | | | | | | | | | ● | | | | | | | | | | | | | | | | | | | | | | | | | | | | | | | | | |
| CULPEPER (HM05579) | | | | | | | | | | | | | | | ● | | | | | | | | | | | | | | | | | | | | | | | | | | | | | | | | | | | |
| DISS NATURAL HEALTH CLINIC (HM06121) | | | | | | | | | | | | ● | | | ● | | ● | | | | ● | | | ● | | | | | | | | ● | | ● | | | | | | | | | | | | | ● | | | |
| EAST MEETS WEST (HM06519) | | | | | | | | | | | | | | | ● | | | | | | | | | | | | | | | | | | | | | | | | | | | | | | | | | | | |
| ELEMENTS OF HEALTH (HM06725) | | | | | | | | | | | | | | | ● | | ● | | | ● | ● | ● | | | | | | | | | | | | ● | | | | | | | | | | | | | ● | | | |
| FIRST STEP FOOTCARE (HM07340) | | | | | | | | | | | | | | | | | | | | | | | | | | | | | | | | | | | | | | | | | | | ● | | | | | | | |
| FISHER, JACK E (HM07355) | | | | | | | | | | | | | | | | | | | | ● | ● | | | | | | | | | | | ● | | ● | | | | | | | | | | | | | | | | |
| GORDON, STEPHEN (HM08283) | | | | | | | | | | | | | | | | | ● | | | | | | | | | | | | | | | | | | | | | | | | | | | | | | | | | |
| GT YARMOUTH PHYSICAL THERAPY (HM08330) | | | | | | | | | | | | | | | | | | | | | | | | | | | | | | | | ● | | ● | | | | | | | | | | | | | | | | |

# F - O Therapies at Practices/Businesses

Business by County with Reference no.

| Business by County with Reference no. | Family Planning (Natural) | Family Therapy | Feldenkrais Methodology | Feng Shui | Floral Essence Therapy | Flotation Therapy | Gait Analysis | Gem Essence Therapy | Gestalt Therapy | Group Therapy | Hay Diet | Healer | Healing Therapy | Hellerwork | Herbal Medicine | Holistic Healing | Homeopathy | Hopi Ear Candles | Humanistic Psychology | Hypnosis | Hypnotherapy | Indian Head Massage | Inhalation Therapy | Iridology | Kinesiology |
|---|---|---|---|---|---|---|---|---|---|---|---|---|---|---|---|---|---|---|---|---|---|---|---|---|---|
| HARGHAM HALL OSTEO PRACTICE (HM08992) | | | | | | | | | | | | | | | | | | | | | | | | | |
| HERBS HANDS HEALING (HM09670) | | | | | | | | | | | | | | | ● | | | | | | | | | | |
| HOBSON, L A (HM09865) | | | | | | | | | | | | | | | | | | | | | | | | | |
| HOMEOPATHIC CLINIC (HM10074) | | | | | | | | | | | | ● | | | ● | | ● | | | | | | | | |
| HOSKINS, RAYMOND (HM10201) | | | | | | | | | | | | | | | | | | | | ● | | | | | |
| HURSELL, BARRY (HM10425) | | | | | | | | | | | | | | | | | | | | ● | | | | | |
| JESSOP CLINIC (HM11021) | | | | | | | | | | | | | | | | | | | | | | | | | |
| KING, SIMON (HM11644) | | ● | | | ● | | | ● | | | ● | | ● | | ● | ● | ● | | | | | | | | |
| LAMBOURN COURT (HM11903) | | | | | | | | | | | | | | | | | | | | ● | | | | | |
| LESLIE CLIFF (HM12238) | | | | | | | | | | | | | | | | | | | | ● | | | | | |
| MARSHALL, C A (HM13156) | | | | | | | | | | | | | | | | | | | | ● | | | | | |
| MEDICAL HERBALIST (HM13651) | | | | | | | | | | | | | | | ● | | | | | | | | | | |
| MONSON, J L B (HM14076) | | | | | | | | | | | | | | | | | | | | | ● | | | | |
| NORFOLK CLINIC (HM14993) | | | | | | | | | | | | ● | | | ● | | ● | | | | ● | | | | |
| NORFOLK NATURAL HEALTH SERVICE (HM14995) | | | | | | | | | | | | | ● | | ● | | ● | | | | ● | ● | | ● | |
| NORMAN, A J (HM14999) | | | | | | | | | | | | | | | | | ● | | | | | | | | |
| PARK PHYSIOTHERAPY (HM15669) | | | | | | | | | | | | | | | | | | | | | | | | | |
| PERRY (HM16039) | | | | | | | | | | | | | | | | | | | | ● | | | | | |
| QUEENS SQUARE SURGERY (HM16796) | | | | | | | | | | | | | | | | | ● | | | | | | | | |
| RICHARDSON, ALAN (HM17268) | | | | | | | | | | | | | | | | | | | | | ● | | | | ● |
| RICHARDSON, SUSAN (HM17293) | | | | | | | | | | | | | | | | | | | | ● | | | | | |
| RIGBY COURT CLINIC (HM17331) | | | | | ● | | | | | | | | | | ● | | ● | | | | ● | ● | | | ● |
| SHARP, DENISE (HM18307) | | | | | | | | | | | | | | | | | | | | | | | | | |
| ST STEPHENS PRACTICE (HM19099) | | | | | | | | | | | | | | | ● | | ● | | | | ● | | | | |
| TRAFFORD, DEBORAH (HM20247) | | | | | | | | | | | | | | | | | | | | | | | | | |
| WENDALS HERBS (HM21195) | | | | | | | | | | | | | | | ● | | | | | | | | | | |
| WENDY JILLEY - MEDICAL HERB (HM21197) | | | | | | | | | | | | | | | ● | | | | | | | | | | |
| WOBURN CLINIC (HM21755) | | | | | | | | | ● | | | ● | | | ● | ● | ● | | | | ● | ● | | ● | |
| NORTHAMPTONSHIRE | | | | | | | | | | | | | | | | | | | | | | | | | |
| ALLEN HINDE - PHYSIOTHERAPIST (HM00598) | | | | | | | | | | | | | | | | | | | | | | | | | ● |
| ALLEN, BRIAN C (HM00600) | | | | | | | | | | | | | | | | | | | | ● | | | | | |
| ALLEN, GEOFFREY (HM00609) | | | | | | | | | | | | | | | | | | | | ● | | | | | |
| ANDREWS, S C (HM00857) | | | | | | | | | | | | | | | | | ● | | | | | | | | |
| ANDREWS, SIMON C (HM00860) | | | | | | | | | | | | | | | | | ● | | | | | | | | |

| Business by County with Reference no. | Kirlian Photography | Laser Treatment | Life Style Coaching | Light Therapy | Macrobiotics | Magnetic Therapy | Manipulation | Manual Lymph Drainage | Massage (Therapeutic) | McTimoney Chiropractic | Meditation | Metamorphic Therapy | Miasm Therapy | Micro Manipulation | Moxibustion | Mud Therapy | Music Therapy | Nail Surgery | Naturopathy | Neuro-Linguistic Program | Neurotherapy | Nutritional Therapy | Orgone Therapy | Oriental Diagnosis | Orthomolecular Medicine |
|---|---|---|---|---|---|---|---|---|---|---|---|---|---|---|---|---|---|---|---|---|---|---|---|---|---|
| HARGHAM HALL OSTEO PRACTICE (HM08992) | | | | | | | ● | | | | | | | | | | | | ● | | | | | | |
| HERBS HANDS HEALING (HM09670) | | | | | | | | | | | | | | | | | | | | | | | | | |
| HOBSON, L A (HM09865) | | | | | | | | | | | | | | | | | | ● | | | | | | | |
| HOMEOPATHIC CLINIC (HM10074) | | | | | | | | | ● | | | | | | | | | | | | | | | | |
| HOSKINS, RAYMOND (HM10201) | | | | | | | | | | | | | | | | | | | | | | | | | |
| HURSELL, BARRY (HM10425) | | | | | | | | | | | | | | | | | | | | | | | | | |
| JESSOP CLINIC (HM11021) | | | | | | | ● | | ● | | | | | | | | | | | | | | | | |
| KING, SIMON (HM11644) | | | | | ● | | | | | | | | | | | | | | ● | | | ● | | | |
| LAMBOURN COURT (HM11903) | | | | | | | | | | | | | | | | | | | | | | | | | |
| LESLIE CLIFF (HM12238) | | | | | | | | | | | | | | | | | | | | | | | | | |
| MARSHALL, C A (HM13156) | | | | | | | | | | | | | | | | | | | | | | | | | |
| MEDICAL HERBALIST (HM13651) | | | | | | | | | | | | | | | | | | | | | | | | | |
| MONSON, J L B (HM14076) | | | | | | | | | | | | | | | | | | | | | | | | | |
| NORFOLK CLINIC (HM14993) | | | | | | | | | ● | | | | | | | | | | | | | ● | | | |
| NORFOLK NATURAL HEALTH SERVICE (HM14995) | | | ● | | | | | | ● | | ● | | | | ● | | | | | | | ● | | | |
| NORMAN, A J (HM14999) | | | | | | | | | ● | | | | | | | | | | | | | | | | |
| PARK PHYSIOTHERAPY (HM15669) | | | | | | | ● | | ● | | | | | | | | | | | | | | | | |
| PERRY (HM16039) | | | | | | | | | | | | | | | | | | | | | | | | | |
| QUEENS SQUARE SURGERY (HM16796) | | | | | | | | | | | | | | | | | | | | | | | | | |
| RICHARDSON, ALAN (HM17268) | | | | | | | | | ● | | | | | | | | | | | | | ● | | | |
| RICHARDSON, SUSAN (HM17293) | | | | | | | | | | | | | | | | | | | | | | | | | |
| RIGBY COURT CLINIC (HM17331) | | | ● | | | | | | ● | | | | | | ● | | | | | | | ● | | ● | |
| SHARP, DENISE (HM18307) | | | | | | ● | | | | | | | | | | | | | | | | | | | |
| ST STEPHENS PRACTICE (HM19099) | | | | | | | | | ● | | | | | | | | | | | | | | | | |
| TRAFFORD, DEBORAH (HM20247) | | | | | | | | | ● | | | | | | | | | | | | | | | | |
| WENDALS HERBS (HM21195) | | | | | | | | | | | | | | | | | | | | | | | | | |
| WENDY JILLEY - MEDICAL HERB (HM21197) | | | | | | | | | | | | | | | | | | | | | | | | | |
| WOBURN CLINIC (HM21755) | | | ● | | | | | | ● | | | | | | | | | | ● | ● | | ● | | | |
| NORTHAMPTONSHIRE | | | | | | | | | | | | | | | | | | | | | | | | | |
| ALLEN HINDE - PHYSIOTHERAPIST (HM00598) | | | | | | | ● | | ● | | | | | | | | | | | | | | | | |
| ALLEN, BRIAN C (HM00600) | | | | | | | | | | | | | | | | | | | | | | | | | |
| ALLEN, GEOFFREY (HM00609) | | | | | | | | | | | | | | | | | | | | | | | | | |
| ANDREWS, S C (HM00857) | | | | | | | | | | | | | | | | | | | | | | | | | |
| ANDREWS, SIMON C (HM00860) | | | | | | | | | | | | | | | | | | | | | | | | | |

# F - O Therapies at Practices/Businesses

| Business by County with Reference no. | Family Planning (Natural) | Family Therapy | Feldenkrais Methodology | Feng Shui | Floral Essence Therapy | Flotation Therapy | Gait Analysis | Gem Essence Therapy | Gestalt Therapy | Group Therapy | Hay Diet | Healer | Healing Therapy | Hellerwork | Herbal Medicine | Holistic Healing | Homeopathy | Hopi Ear Candles | Humanistic Psychology | Hypnosis | Hypnotherapy | Indian Head Massage | Inhalation Therapy | Iridology | Kinesiology | Kirlian Photography | Laser Treatment | Life Style Coaching | Light Therapy | Macrobiotics | Magnetic Therapy | Manipulation | Manual Lymph Drainage | Massage (Therapeutic) | McTimoney Chiropractic | Meditation | Metamorphic Therapy | Miasm Therapy | Micro Manipulation | Moxibustion | Mud Therapy | Music Therapy | Nail Surgery | Naturopathy | Neuro-Linguistic Program | Neurotherapy | Nutritional Therapy | Orgone Therapy | Oriental Diagnosis | Orthomolecular Medicine |
|---|---|---|---|---|---|---|---|---|---|---|---|---|---|---|---|---|---|---|---|---|---|---|---|---|---|---|---|---|---|---|---|---|---|---|---|---|---|---|---|---|---|---|---|---|---|---|---|---|---|---|
| NORTHUMBERLAND | | | | | | | | | | | | | | | | | | | | | | | | | | | | | | | | | | | | | | | | | | | | | | | | | | |
| ACUCARE (HM00209) | | | | | | | | | | | | | | | | | | | | | ● | | | | | | | | | | | | | | | | | | | | | | | | | | | | | |
| AYRES, ELIZABETH (HM01433) | | | | | | | | | | | | | | | | | | | | | | | | | | | | | | | | | | | | | | | | | | | ● | | | | | | | |
| BEARMAN, PATRICIA (HM01970) | | | | | | | | | | | | | | | | | | | | ● | | | | | | | | | | | | | | | | | | | | | | | | | | | | | | |
| EVISON, ALEX (HM07012) | | | | | | | | | | | | | | | | | | | | ● | ● | | | | | | | | | | | | | | | | | | | | | | | | | | | | | |
| FORSTER, LINDA (HM07570) | | | | | | | | | | | | | | | | | | | | | | | | | | | | | | | | | | | | | | | | | | | | | | | ● | | | |
| FOWLER, J A (HM07629) | | | | | | | | | | | | | | | | | ● | | | | | | | | | | | | | | | | | | | | | | | | | | | | | | | | | |
| GREEN BATT PHYSIOTHERAPY (HM08434) | | | | | | | | | | | | | | | | | | | | | | | | | | | | | | | | ● | | ● | | | | | | | | | | | | | | | | |
| HAGGIE, PATRICIA (HM08700) | | | | | | | | | | | | | | | | | ● | | | | | | | | | | | | | | | | | | | | | | | | | | | | | | | | | |
| HORROCKS, JULIE (HM10184) | | | | | | | | | | | | | | | | | ● | | | | | | | | | | | | | | | | | | | | | | | | | | | | | | | | | |
| KI CLINIC (HM11591) | | | | | | | | | | | ● | | | | ● | | | | | | | ● | | ● | ● | | | | | | | | | ● | | | | | | ● | | | | | | | ● | | | |
| PHYSIOTHERAPY & SPORTS CLINIC (HM16223) | | | | | | | | | | | | | | | | | | | | | | | | | | | | | | | | ● | | | | | | | | | | | | | | | | | | |
| NOTTINGHAMSHIRE | | | | | | | | | | | | | | | | | | | | | | | | | | | | | | | | | | | | | | | | | | | | | | | | | | |
| BOND, DIANORA (HM02669) | | | | | | | | | | | | | | | | | | | | | | | | | | | | | | | | ● | | ● | | | | | | | | | | | | | | | | |
| BRAHMA KUMARIS WORLD (HM02891) | | | | | | | | | | | | | | | | | | | | | | | | | | | | | | | | | | | | ● | | | | | | | | | | | | | | |
| BULLEN-SPICER ASSOCIATES (HM03342) | | ● | | | | | | | ● | ● | | | | | | | | | ● | | | | | | | | | ● | | | | | | | | ● | | | | | | | | | | | | | | |
| CARITAS NATURAL HEALTH CLINIC (HM03688) | | | | | | | | | | | | | | | | | | | | | | | | | | | | | | | | | | ● | | | | | | | | | | | | | | | | |
| CENTRE FOR TRANSFORMATION (HM03921) | ● | | | | | | | | | | | | | | | | ● | | | | | | | | | | | | | | | | | | | | | | | | | | | | | | ● | | | |
| CHALLIS, R T (HM03950) | | | | | | | | | | | | | | | | | | | | ● | | | | | | | | | | | | | | | | | | | | | | | | | | | | | | |
| CHINESE HERBALIST (HM04217) | | | | | | | | | | | | | | | ● | | | | | | | | | | | | | | | | | | | | | | | | | | | | | | | | | | | |
| COOPER, PETER (HM05123) | | | | | | | | | | | | | | | | | ● | | | | | | | | | | | | | | | | | | | | | | | | | | | | | | | | | |
| DEAN, MARTIN (HM05942) | | | | | | | | | | | | ● | ● | | | ● | | | | | | ● | | | | | | | | | | | | ● | | | | | | ● | | | | | | | | | ● | |
| FITZPATRICK, TRISH (HM07377) | | | | | | | | | | | | | | | | | ● | | | | | | | | | | | | | | | | | | | | | | | | | | | | | | | | | |
| GLEESON, KAREN (HM08141) | | | | | | | | | | | | | | | | | | | | ● | | | | | | | | | | | | | | | | | | | | | | | | | | | | | | |
| GRAHAM, HILARY E (HM08347) | | | | | | | | | | | | | | | | | | | | ● | | | | | | | | | | | | | | | | | | | | | | | | | | | | | | |
| GRAHAM, HILARY E (HM09762) | | | | | | | | | | | | | | | | | | | | ● | | | | | | | | | | | | | | | | | | | | | | | | | | | | | | |
| GREAVES HERBALIST (HM08432) | | | | | | | | | | | | | | | ● | | | | | | | | | | | | | | | | | | | | | | | | | | | | | | | | | | | |
| HANDS ON HEALTH (HM08912) | | | | | | | | | | | | | | | | | | | | | | | | | | | | | | | | | | ● | | | | | | | | | | | | | | | | |
| HICKLING, KENNETH (HM09721) | | | | | | | | | | | | | | | | | | | | ● | | | | | | | | | | | | | | | | | | | | | | | | | | | | | | |
| JACKSON, DEREK (HM10835) | | | | | | | | | | | | | | | | | | | | ● | | | | | | | | | | | | | | | | | | | | | | | | | | | | | | |
| JUST MAGNOTHERAPY (HM11283) | | | | | | | | | | | | | | | | | | | | | | | | | | | | | | | ● | | | | | | | | | | | | | | | | | | | |
| KENNETH C HUGGINS HYPNOTHERAPY (HM11501) | | | | | | | | | | | | | | | | | | | | ● | ● | | | | | | | | | | | | | | | | | | | | | | | | | | | | | |
| LERA, LOUISA (HM12227) | | | | | | | | | | | | | | | | | ● | | | | | | | | | | | | | | | | | | | | | | | | | | | | | | | | | |
| LIGHT UP YOUR LIFE (HM12370) | | | | | | | | | | | | | ● | | | ● | | | | | | | | | | | | | | | | | | | | ● | | | | | | | | | | | | | | |

# F - O Therapies at Practices/Businesses

| Business by County with Reference no. | Family Planning (Natural) | Family Therapy | Feldenkrais Methodology | Feng Shui | Floral Essence Therapy | Flotation Therapy | Gait Analysis | Gem Essence Therapy | Gestalt Therapy | Group Therapy | Hay Diet | Healer | Healing Therapy | Hellerwork | Herbal Medicine | Holistic Healing | Homeopathy |
|---|---|---|---|---|---|---|---|---|---|---|---|---|---|---|---|---|---|
| ANNELISE (HM00906) |  |  |  |  |  |  |  |  |  | ● |  |  |  |  |  | ● |  |
| ARBOURS (HM00965) |  |  |  |  |  |  |  |  |  |  |  |  |  |  |  |  |  |
| BARNES, RICHARD (HM01752) |  |  |  |  |  |  |  |  |  |  |  |  |  |  | ● |  |  |
| BLOCK, GEORGINA (HM02511) |  |  |  |  |  |  |  |  |  |  |  |  |  |  |  |  |  |
| C F C M (HM03523) |  |  |  |  |  |  |  |  |  |  |  |  |  |  | ● |  | ● |
| CALLIS THERAPY FOUNDATION (HM03555) |  |  |  |  |  |  |  |  |  |  |  |  |  |  |  |  | ● |
| CLARK, PETER (HM04574) |  |  |  |  |  |  |  |  |  |  |  |  |  |  |  |  |  |
| DAVENTRY NATUREWORKS (HM05768) |  |  |  |  |  |  |  |  |  |  |  |  |  |  |  |  | ● |
| DE-BANKE, MARGARET (HM05950) |  |  |  |  |  |  |  |  |  |  |  |  |  |  |  |  |  |
| DEVON PARADE CLINIC (HM06041) |  |  |  |  |  |  | ● |  |  |  |  |  |  |  |  |  | ● |
| DON, ANITA (HM06166) |  |  |  |  |  |  |  |  |  |  |  |  |  |  |  |  |  |
| DUNLOP, MARION (HM06413) |  |  |  |  |  |  |  |  |  |  |  |  |  |  |  |  |  |
| ELLIS, DAVID S (HM06764) |  |  |  |  |  |  |  |  |  |  |  |  |  |  |  |  |  |
| ELVIN, CHRISTINA (HM06791) |  |  |  |  |  |  |  |  |  |  |  |  |  |  |  |  |  |
| ESSERY, TRICIA (HM06933) |  |  |  |  |  |  |  |  |  |  |  |  |  |  |  | ● |  |
| GARVEY-WILLIAMS, RICHARD (HM07915) |  |  |  |  |  |  |  |  |  |  |  |  |  |  |  |  | ● |
| GARVEY-WILLIAMS, RICHARD (HM07914) |  |  |  |  |  |  |  |  |  |  |  |  |  |  |  |  | ● |
| HOPKINS, JUDY (HM10151) |  |  |  |  |  |  |  |  |  |  |  |  |  |  |  |  |  |
| HOWARD, JOHN & GAIL (HM10236) |  |  |  |  |  |  |  |  |  |  |  |  |  |  |  |  |  |
| JOHNSON, HETTY (HM11076) |  |  |  |  |  |  |  |  |  |  |  |  |  |  |  |  |  |
| JUST RELAX (HM11285) |  |  |  |  |  |  |  |  |  |  |  |  |  |  |  |  |  |
| LERIGO, SYLVIA (HM12228) |  |  |  |  |  |  |  |  |  |  |  |  |  |  |  |  |  |
| MAPLE TREE OSTEO PRACTICE (HM13061) |  |  |  |  |  |  |  |  |  |  |  | ● |  |  |  |  |  |
| NENE VALLEY COMP THERAPIES (HM14785) |  |  |  |  |  |  |  |  |  |  |  |  |  |  |  |  |  |
| NORTHAMPTON CLINIC (HM15052) |  |  |  |  |  |  |  |  |  |  |  |  |  |  |  |  |  |
| PARKER, SUSAN (HM15706) |  |  |  |  |  |  |  |  |  |  |  |  |  |  |  |  |  |
| PARROTT, LINDA (HM15735) |  |  |  |  |  |  |  |  |  |  |  |  |  |  |  |  |  |
| PHILLIPSON, B J (HM16145) |  |  |  |  |  |  |  |  |  |  |  |  |  |  | ● |  |  |
| REDMAN, L (HM17030) |  |  |  |  |  |  |  |  |  |  |  |  |  |  |  |  | ● |
| REFLEXOLOGY CLINIC (HM17085) |  |  |  |  |  |  |  |  |  |  |  |  |  |  |  |  |  |
| SOCIETY OF HOMOEOPATHS (HM18852) |  |  |  |  |  |  |  |  |  |  |  |  |  |  |  |  | ● |
| THOMPSON, MICHAEL (HM19993) |  |  |  |  |  |  |  |  |  |  |  |  |  |  |  |  | ● |
| TIAN TIAN UK (HM20051) |  |  |  |  |  |  |  |  |  |  |  |  |  |  | ● |  |  |

| Business by County with Reference no. | Hopi Ear Candles | Humanistic Psychology | Hypnosis | Hypnotherapy | Indian Head Massage | Inhalation Therapy | Iridology | Kinesiology | Kirlian Photography | Laser Treatment | Life Style Coaching | Light Therapy | Macrobiotics | Magnetic Therapy | Manipulation | Manual Lymph Drainage | Massage (Therapeutic) |
|---|---|---|---|---|---|---|---|---|---|---|---|---|---|---|---|---|---|
| ANNELISE (HM00906) | ● |  |  |  | ● |  |  |  |  |  | ● |  |  |  |  |  | ● |
| ARBOURS (HM00965) |  |  |  |  |  |  |  |  |  |  |  |  |  |  |  |  |  |
| BARNES, RICHARD (HM01752) |  |  |  |  |  |  |  |  |  |  |  |  |  |  |  |  |  |
| BLOCK, GEORGINA (HM02511) |  |  | ● |  |  |  |  |  |  |  |  |  |  |  |  |  |  |
| C F C M (HM03523) |  |  | ● | ● |  |  |  |  |  |  |  |  |  |  | ● |  |  |
| CALLIS THERAPY FOUNDATION (HM03555) |  |  |  | ● |  |  |  | ● |  |  |  |  |  |  |  |  |  |
| CLARK, PETER (HM04574) |  |  | ● |  |  |  |  |  |  |  |  |  |  |  |  |  |  |
| DAVENTRY NATUREWORKS (HM05768) |  |  |  | ● |  |  |  |  |  |  |  |  |  |  |  |  |  |
| DE-BANKE, MARGARET (HM05950) |  |  | ● |  |  |  |  |  |  |  |  |  |  |  |  |  |  |
| DEVON PARADE CLINIC (HM06041) |  | ● |  |  | ● |  |  |  |  |  |  |  |  |  | ● |  | ● |
| DON, ANITA (HM06166) |  |  |  |  | ● |  |  |  |  |  |  |  |  |  |  |  |  |
| DUNLOP, MARION (HM06413) |  |  | ● |  |  |  |  |  |  |  |  |  |  |  |  |  |  |
| ELLIS, DAVID S (HM06764) |  |  | ● |  |  |  |  |  |  |  |  |  |  |  |  |  |  |
| ELVIN, CHRISTINA (HM06791) |  |  | ● |  |  |  |  |  |  |  |  |  |  |  |  |  |  |
| ESSERY, TRICIA (HM06933) |  |  |  |  |  |  |  |  |  |  |  |  |  |  |  |  |  |
| GARVEY-WILLIAMS, RICHARD (HM07915) |  |  |  |  |  |  |  |  |  |  |  |  |  |  | ● |  |  |
| GARVEY-WILLIAMS, RICHARD (HM07914) |  |  |  |  |  |  |  |  |  |  |  |  |  |  | ● |  |  |
| HOPKINS, JUDY (HM10151) |  |  | ● |  |  |  |  |  |  |  |  |  |  |  |  |  |  |
| HOWARD, JOHN & GAIL (HM10236) |  |  | ● |  |  |  |  |  |  |  |  |  |  |  |  |  |  |
| JOHNSON, HETTY (HM11076) |  |  | ● |  |  |  |  |  |  |  |  |  |  |  |  |  |  |
| JUST RELAX (HM11285) |  |  |  |  | ● |  |  |  |  |  |  |  |  |  |  |  |  |
| LERIGO, SYLVIA (HM12228) |  |  | ● |  |  |  |  |  |  |  |  |  |  |  |  |  |  |
| MAPLE TREE OSTEO PRACTICE (HM13061) |  |  |  |  |  |  |  |  |  |  |  |  |  |  |  |  |  |
| NENE VALLEY COMP THERAPIES (HM14785) |  |  |  |  | ● |  |  |  |  |  |  |  |  |  |  |  |  |
| NORTHAMPTON CLINIC (HM15052) |  |  |  |  |  |  |  | ● |  |  |  |  |  |  |  |  |  |
| PARKER, SUSAN (HM15706) |  |  | ● |  |  |  |  |  |  |  |  |  |  |  |  |  |  |
| PARROTT, LINDA (HM15735) |  |  |  |  | ● |  |  |  |  |  |  |  |  |  |  |  | ● |
| PHILLIPSON, B J (HM16145) |  |  |  |  |  |  |  |  |  |  |  |  |  |  |  |  |  |
| REDMAN, L (HM17030) |  |  |  |  |  |  |  |  |  |  |  |  |  |  |  |  |  |
| REFLEXOLOGY CLINIC (HM17085) |  |  |  |  | ● |  |  |  |  |  |  |  |  |  |  |  |  |
| SOCIETY OF HOMOEOPATHS (HM18852) |  |  |  |  |  |  |  |  |  |  |  |  |  |  |  |  |  |
| THOMPSON, MICHAEL (HM19993) |  |  |  |  |  |  |  |  |  |  |  |  |  |  |  |  |  |
| TIAN TIAN UK (HM20051) |  |  |  |  |  |  |  |  |  |  |  |  |  |  |  |  |  |

| Business by County with Reference no. | McTimoney Chiropractic | Meditation | Metamorphic Therapy | Miasm Therapy | Micro Manipulation | Moxibustion | Mud Therapy | Music Therapy | Nail Surgery | Naturopathy | Neuro-Linguistic Program | Neurotherapy | Nutritional Therapy | Orgone Therapy | Oriental Diagnosis | Orthomolecular Medicine |
|---|---|---|---|---|---|---|---|---|---|---|---|---|---|---|---|---|
| ANNELISE (HM00906) |  |  |  |  |  |  |  |  |  |  |  |  |  |  |  |  |
| ARBOURS (HM00965) |  |  |  |  |  |  |  |  | ● |  |  |  |  |  |  |  |
| BARNES, RICHARD (HM01752) |  |  |  |  |  |  |  |  |  |  |  |  |  |  |  |  |
| BLOCK, GEORGINA (HM02511) |  |  |  |  |  |  |  |  |  |  |  |  |  |  |  |  |
| C F C M (HM03523) |  |  |  |  |  | ● |  |  |  |  |  |  |  |  |  |  |
| CALLIS THERAPY FOUNDATION (HM03555) |  |  | ● |  |  |  |  |  |  |  |  |  | ● |  |  |  |
| CLARK, PETER (HM04574) |  |  |  |  |  |  |  |  |  |  |  |  |  |  |  |  |
| DAVENTRY NATUREWORKS (HM05768) |  |  |  |  |  |  |  |  |  |  |  |  | ● |  |  |  |
| DE-BANKE, MARGARET (HM05950) |  |  |  |  |  |  |  |  |  |  |  |  |  |  |  |  |
| DEVON PARADE CLINIC (HM06041) |  |  |  |  |  |  |  |  | ● |  |  |  |  |  |  |  |
| DON, ANITA (HM06166) |  |  |  |  |  |  |  |  |  |  |  |  |  |  |  |  |
| DUNLOP, MARION (HM06413) |  |  |  |  |  |  |  |  |  |  |  |  |  |  |  |  |
| ELLIS, DAVID S (HM06764) |  |  |  |  |  |  |  |  |  |  |  |  |  |  |  |  |
| ELVIN, CHRISTINA (HM06791) |  |  |  |  |  |  |  |  |  |  |  |  |  |  |  |  |
| ESSERY, TRICIA (HM06933) |  |  |  |  |  |  |  |  |  |  |  |  |  |  |  |  |
| GARVEY-WILLIAMS, RICHARD (HM07915) |  |  |  |  |  |  |  |  |  | ● |  |  |  |  |  |  |
| GARVEY-WILLIAMS, RICHARD (HM07914) |  |  |  |  |  |  |  |  |  | ● |  |  |  |  |  |  |
| HOPKINS, JUDY (HM10151) |  |  |  |  |  |  |  |  |  |  |  |  |  |  |  |  |
| HOWARD, JOHN & GAIL (HM10236) |  |  |  |  |  |  |  |  |  |  |  |  |  |  |  |  |
| JOHNSON, HETTY (HM11076) |  |  |  |  |  |  |  |  |  |  |  |  |  |  |  |  |
| JUST RELAX (HM11285) |  |  |  |  |  |  |  |  |  |  |  |  |  |  |  |  |
| LERIGO, SYLVIA (HM12228) |  |  |  |  |  |  |  |  |  |  |  |  |  |  |  |  |
| MAPLE TREE OSTEO PRACTICE (HM13061) |  |  |  |  |  |  |  |  |  |  |  |  |  |  |  |  |
| NENE VALLEY COMP THERAPIES (HM14785) |  |  |  |  |  |  |  |  |  |  |  |  |  |  |  |  |
| NORTHAMPTON CLINIC (HM15052) |  |  |  |  |  |  |  |  |  |  |  |  | ● |  |  |  |
| PARKER, SUSAN (HM15706) |  |  |  |  |  |  |  |  |  |  |  |  |  |  |  |  |
| PARROTT, LINDA (HM15735) |  |  |  |  |  |  |  |  |  |  |  |  |  |  |  |  |
| PHILLIPSON, B J (HM16145) |  |  |  |  |  |  |  |  |  |  |  |  |  |  |  |  |
| REDMAN, L (HM17030) |  |  |  |  |  |  |  |  |  |  |  |  |  |  |  |  |
| REFLEXOLOGY CLINIC (HM17085) |  |  |  |  |  |  |  |  |  |  |  |  |  |  |  |  |
| SOCIETY OF HOMOEOPATHS (HM18852) |  |  |  |  |  |  |  |  |  |  |  |  |  |  |  |  |
| THOMPSON, MICHAEL (HM19993) |  |  |  |  |  |  |  |  |  |  |  |  |  |  |  |  |
| TIAN TIAN UK (HM20051) |  |  |  |  |  |  |  |  |  |  |  |  |  |  |  |  |

# F - O Therapies at Practices/Businesses

Business by County with Reference no.

| Business | Family Planning (Natural) | Family Therapy | Feldenkrais Methodology | Feng Shui | Floral Essence Therapy | Flotation Therapy | Gait Analysis | Gem Essence Therapy | Gestalt Therapy | Group Therapy |
|---|---|---|---|---|---|---|---|---|---|---|
| LITTLE LONDON HERBAL STORE (HM12467) | | | | | | | | | | |
| MORLEY-KIRK, JOHN (HM14188) | | | | | | | | | | |
| MURPHY, MAUREEN (HM14390) | | | | | | | | | | |
| NATURAL HEALTH (HM14554) | | | | | | | | | ● | |
| NATURAL THERAPY CLINIC (HM14654) | | | | | | | | | | |
| NOTTINGHAM NATURAL HEALTH CTRE (HM15084) | | | | | | | | | | |
| OPTIMUM HEALTH (HM15348) | | | | | ● | | | | ● | ● |
| PARKSIDE STRESS MANAGEMENT (HM15722) | | | | | | | | | | |
| PATTERSON, JUDY (HM15829) | | | | | | | | | | |
| PUGH, CHERYL (HM16745) | | | | | | | | | | |
| PUMO, AMANDA (HM16756) | | | | | | | | | | |
| RETFORD CHIROPRACTIC CLINIC (HM17200) | | | | | | | | | | |
| SEVENTHMOON NATURAL THRPY CTRE (HM18247) | | | | | | | | | | |
| SHAW, L M (HM18341) | | | | | | | | | | |
| SHEER TECHNIQUE (HM18368) | ● | ● | | | | | | ● | | ● |
| SHERWOOD PSYCHO TRAINING INS (HM18441) | | | | | | | | | ● | |
| SKELTON, CATHERINE () | | | | | | | | | | |
| SOMERS STRESS CONSULTANCY SVS (HM18882) | | | | | | | | | | |
| TAYLOR, KAREN (HM19774) | | | | | | | | | | |
| TRADITIONAL ACUPUNCTURIST (HM20222) | | | | | | | | | | |
| VAUGHTON, NORMAN D (HM20601) | | | | | | | | | | |
| WALKER, J M (HM20776) | | | | | | | | | | |
| OXFORDSHIRE | | | | | | | | | | |
| ASHCROFT CLINIC (HM01198) | | | | | | | | | | |
| AVERY, MARK (HM01394) | | | | | | | | | | |
| BACK IN LINE (HM01481) | | | | | | | | | | |
| BOWLES, JANICE (HM02796) | | | | | | | | | | |
| BROWN, ANGELA (HM03212) | | | | | | | | | | |
| CLINIC OF NATURAL MEDICINE (HM04701) | | | | | | | | | | |
| COLCLOUGH, CAROL (HM04808) | | | | | | | | | | |
| COTTAGE CLINIC (HM05221) | | | | | | | | | | |
| CULPEPER (HM05574) | | | | | | | | | | |
| DR EDWARD BACH FOUNDATION (HM06271) | | | | | | | | | | |
| EAST WEST HERBS (HM06528) | | | | | | | | | | |

| Business | Hay Diet | Healer | Healing Therapy | Hellerwork | Herbal Medicine | Holistic Healing | Homeopathy | Hopi Ear Candles | Humanistic Psychology | Hypnosis |
|---|---|---|---|---|---|---|---|---|---|---|
| LITTLE LONDON HERBAL STORE (HM12467) | | | | | ● | | | | | |
| MORLEY-KIRK, JOHN (HM14188) | | | | | | | | | | |
| MURPHY, MAUREEN (HM14390) | | | | | ● | | | | | |
| NATURAL HEALTH (HM14554) | | ● | ● | | ● | ● | ● | | | |
| NATURAL THERAPY CLINIC (HM14654) | | | | | ● | | | | | |
| NOTTINGHAM NATURAL HEALTH CTRE (HM15084) | | | | | ● | | ● | | | |
| OPTIMUM HEALTH (HM15348) | | ● | | | | | ● | ● | | ● |
| PARKSIDE STRESS MANAGEMENT (HM15722) | | ● | ● | | | ● | | | | |
| PATTERSON, JUDY (HM15829) | | | | | ● | | | | | |
| PUGH, CHERYL (HM16745) | | | | | | | | | | ● |
| PUMO, AMANDA (HM16756) | | | | | | | | | | ● |
| RETFORD CHIROPRACTIC CLINIC (HM17200) | | | | | | | | | | |
| SEVENTHMOON NATURAL THRPY CTRE (HM18247) | | | ● | | | | | | | |
| SHAW, L M (HM18341) | | | | | | | ● | | | |
| SHEER TECHNIQUE (HM18368) | | ● | ● | | | ● | | | | ● |
| SHERWOOD PSYCHO TRAINING INS (HM18441) | | | | | | | | | ● | |
| SKELTON, CATHERINE () | | | | | | | | | | |
| SOMERS STRESS CONSULTANCY SVS (HM18882) | | | | | | | | | | ● |
| TAYLOR, KAREN (HM19774) | | | | | | | | | | ● |
| TRADITIONAL ACUPUNCTURIST (HM20222) | | | | | | ● | | | | |
| VAUGHTON, NORMAN D (HM20601) | | | | | | | | | | ● |
| WALKER, J M (HM20776) | | | | | ● | | | | | ● |
| OXFORDSHIRE | | | | | | | | | | |
| ASHCROFT CLINIC (HM01198) | | | | | ● | | | | | |
| AVERY, MARK (HM01394) | | | | | | | ● | | | |
| BACK IN LINE (HM01481) | | | | | | | | | | |
| BOWLES, JANICE (HM02796) | | | | | | | | | | ● |
| BROWN, ANGELA (HM03212) | | | | | | | | | | ● |
| CLINIC OF NATURAL MEDICINE (HM04701) | | | | | ● | | | | | |
| COLCLOUGH, CAROL (HM04808) | | | | | | | | | | ● |
| COTTAGE CLINIC (HM05221) | | | | | | | | | | |
| CULPEPER (HM05574) | | | | | ● | | | | | |
| DR EDWARD BACH FOUNDATION (HM06271) | | | | | | | ● | | | |
| EAST WEST HERBS (HM06528) | | | | | ● | | | | | |

| Business | Hypnotherapy | Indian Head Massage | Inhalation Therapy | Iridology | Kinesiology | Kirlian Photography | Laser Treatment | Life Style Coaching | Light Therapy | Macrobiotics |
|---|---|---|---|---|---|---|---|---|---|---|
| LITTLE LONDON HERBAL STORE (HM12467) | | | | | | | | | | |
| MORLEY-KIRK, JOHN (HM14188) | ● | | | | | | | | | |
| MURPHY, MAUREEN (HM14390) | | | | | | | | | | |
| NATURAL HEALTH (HM14554) | ● | ● | | ● | ● | | | | | |
| NATURAL THERAPY CLINIC (HM14654) | | | | | | | | | | |
| NOTTINGHAM NATURAL HEALTH CTRE (HM15084) | ● | | | ● | ● | | | | | |
| OPTIMUM HEALTH (HM15348) | ● | ● | | | ● | | | | | |
| PARKSIDE STRESS MANAGEMENT (HM15722) | | ● | ● | | ● | | | | | |
| PATTERSON, JUDY (HM15829) | | | | | | | | | | |
| PUGH, CHERYL (HM16745) | | | | | | | | | | |
| PUMO, AMANDA (HM16756) | | | | | | | | | | |
| RETFORD CHIROPRACTIC CLINIC (HM17200) | | ● | | | ● | | | | | |
| SEVENTHMOON NATURAL THRPY CTRE (HM18247) | | ● | | | | | | | | |
| SHAW, L M (HM18341) | | | | | | | | | | |
| SHEER TECHNIQUE (HM18368) | ● | ● | ● | ● | ● | | | ● | | |
| SHERWOOD PSYCHO TRAINING INS (HM18441) | | | | | | | | | | |
| SKELTON, CATHERINE () | | | | | ● | | | | | |
| SOMERS STRESS CONSULTANCY SVS (HM18882) | | | | | | | | | | |
| TAYLOR, KAREN (HM19774) | | | | | | | | | | |
| TRADITIONAL ACUPUNCTURIST (HM20222) | | | | | | | | | | |
| VAUGHTON, NORMAN D (HM20601) | ● | | | | | | | | | |
| WALKER, J M (HM20776) | | | | | | | | | | |
| OXFORDSHIRE | | | | | | | | | | |
| ASHCROFT CLINIC (HM01198) | | | | | | | | | | |
| AVERY, MARK (HM01394) | | | | | | | | | | |
| BACK IN LINE (HM01481) | | | | | | | | | | |
| BOWLES, JANICE (HM02796) | | | | | | | | | | |
| BROWN, ANGELA (HM03212) | | | | | | | | | | |
| CLINIC OF NATURAL MEDICINE (HM04701) | | | | | | | | | | |
| COLCLOUGH, CAROL (HM04808) | | | | | | | | | | |
| COTTAGE CLINIC (HM05221) | | | | | | | | | | |
| CULPEPER (HM05574) | | | | | | | | | | |
| DR EDWARD BACH FOUNDATION (HM06271) | | | | | | | | | | |
| EAST WEST HERBS (HM06528) | | | | | | | | | | |

| Business | Magnetic Therapy | Manipulation | Manual Lymph Drainage | Massage (Therapeutic) | McTimoney Chiropractic | Meditation | Metamorphic Therapy | Miasm Therapy | Micro Manipulation | Moxibustion |
|---|---|---|---|---|---|---|---|---|---|---|
| LITTLE LONDON HERBAL STORE (HM12467) | | | | | | | | | | |
| MORLEY-KIRK, JOHN (HM14188) | | | | | | | | | | |
| MURPHY, MAUREEN (HM14390) | | | | | | | | | | |
| NATURAL HEALTH (HM14554) | | ● | | ● | | | | ● | | |
| NATURAL THERAPY CLINIC (HM14654) | | | | | | | | | | |
| NOTTINGHAM NATURAL HEALTH CTRE (HM15084) | | | | ● | | | | | | |
| OPTIMUM HEALTH (HM15348) | | | | ● | | | | | | |
| PARKSIDE STRESS MANAGEMENT (HM15722) | | | | | | ● | | | | |
| PATTERSON, JUDY (HM15829) | | | | | | | | | | |
| PUGH, CHERYL (HM16745) | | | | | | | | | | |
| PUMO, AMANDA (HM16756) | | | | | | | | | | |
| RETFORD CHIROPRACTIC CLINIC (HM17200) | | ● | | | | | | | | |
| SEVENTHMOON NATURAL THRPY CTRE (HM18247) | | | | ● | | | | | | |
| SHAW, L M (HM18341) | | | | | | | | | | |
| SHEER TECHNIQUE (HM18368) | | ● | | ● | | ● | | | | |
| SHERWOOD PSYCHO TRAINING INS (HM18441) | | | | | | ● | | | | |
| SKELTON, CATHERINE () | | | | | | | | | | |
| SOMERS STRESS CONSULTANCY SVS (HM18882) | | | | | | | | | | |
| TAYLOR, KAREN (HM19774) | | | | | | | | | | |
| TRADITIONAL ACUPUNCTURIST (HM20222) | | | | ● | | | | | | ● |
| VAUGHTON, NORMAN D (HM20601) | | | | | | | | | | |
| WALKER, J M (HM20776) | | | | | | | | | | |
| OXFORDSHIRE | | | | | | | | | | |
| ASHCROFT CLINIC (HM01198) | | ● | | ● | | | | | | ● |
| AVERY, MARK (HM01394) | | | | | | | | | | |
| BACK IN LINE (HM01481) | | | | ● | | | | | | |
| BOWLES, JANICE (HM02796) | | | | | | | | | | |
| BROWN, ANGELA (HM03212) | | | | | | | | | | |
| CLINIC OF NATURAL MEDICINE (HM04701) | | | | | | | | | | |
| COLCLOUGH, CAROL (HM04808) | | | | | | | | | | |
| COTTAGE CLINIC (HM05221) | | | | | | | | | | ● |
| CULPEPER (HM05574) | | | | | | | | | | |
| DR EDWARD BACH FOUNDATION (HM06271) | | | | | | | | | | |
| EAST WEST HERBS (HM06528) | | | | | | | | | | |

| Business | Mud Therapy | Music Therapy | Nail Surgery | Naturopathy | Neuro-Linguistic Program | Neurotherapy | Nutritional Therapy | Orgone Therapy | Oriental Diagnosis | Orthomolecular Medicine |
|---|---|---|---|---|---|---|---|---|---|---|
| LITTLE LONDON HERBAL STORE (HM12467) | | | | | | | | | | |
| MORLEY-KIRK, JOHN (HM14188) | | | | | | | | | | |
| MURPHY, MAUREEN (HM14390) | | | | | | | | | | |
| NATURAL HEALTH (HM14554) | | | | | | | ● | | | |
| NATURAL THERAPY CLINIC (HM14654) | | | | | | | | | | |
| NOTTINGHAM NATURAL HEALTH CTRE (HM15084) | | | | ● | | | ● | | | |
| OPTIMUM HEALTH (HM15348) | | | | | ● | | ● | | | |
| PARKSIDE STRESS MANAGEMENT (HM15722) | | | | | | | ● | | | |
| PATTERSON, JUDY (HM15829) | | | | | | | | | | |
| PUGH, CHERYL (HM16745) | | | | | | | | | | |
| PUMO, AMANDA (HM16756) | | | | | | | | | | |
| RETFORD CHIROPRACTIC CLINIC (HM17200) | | | | | | | ● | | | |
| SEVENTHMOON NATURAL THRPY CTRE (HM18247) | | | | | | | | | | |
| SHAW, L M (HM18341) | | | | | | | | | | |
| SHEER TECHNIQUE (HM18368) | | | | | | | | | | |
| SHERWOOD PSYCHO TRAINING INS (HM18441) | | | | | | | | | | |
| SKELTON, CATHERINE () | | | | | | | | | | |
| SOMERS STRESS CONSULTANCY SVS (HM18882) | | | | | | | | | | |
| TAYLOR, KAREN (HM19774) | | | | | | | | | | |
| TRADITIONAL ACUPUNCTURIST (HM20222) | | | | | | | | | ● | |
| VAUGHTON, NORMAN D (HM20601) | | | | | | | | | | |
| WALKER, J M (HM20776) | | | | | | | | | | |
| OXFORDSHIRE | | | | | | | | | | |
| ASHCROFT CLINIC (HM01198) | | | | | | | ● | | | |
| AVERY, MARK (HM01394) | | | | | | | | | | |
| BACK IN LINE (HM01481) | | | | | | | | | | |
| BOWLES, JANICE (HM02796) | | | | | | | | | | |
| BROWN, ANGELA (HM03212) | | | | | | | | | | |
| CLINIC OF NATURAL MEDICINE (HM04701) | | | | | | | | | | |
| COLCLOUGH, CAROL (HM04808) | | | | | | | | | | |
| COTTAGE CLINIC (HM05221) | | | | | | | | | | |
| CULPEPER (HM05574) | | | | | | | | | | |
| DR EDWARD BACH FOUNDATION (HM06271) | | | | | | | | | | |
| EAST WEST HERBS (HM06528) | | | | | | | | | | |

# F - O Therapies at Practices/Businesses

| Business by County with Reference no. | Family Planning (Natural) | Family Therapy | Feldenkrais Methodology | Feng Shui | Floral Essence Therapy | Flotation Therapy | Gait Analysis | Gem Essence Therapy | Gestalt Therapy | Group Therapy | Hay Diet | Healer | Healing Therapy | Hellerwork | Herbal Medicine | Holistic Healing | Homeopathy | Hopi Ear Candles | Humanistic Psychology | Hypnosis | Hypnotherapy | Indian Head Massage | Inhalation Therapy | Iridology | Kinesiology |
|---|---|---|---|---|---|---|---|---|---|---|---|---|---|---|---|---|---|---|---|---|---|---|---|---|---|
| ELWELL, R S (HM06792) |  |  |  |  |  |  |  |  |  |  |  |  |  |  |  |  |  |  |  |  |  |  |  |  |  |
| FAULKNER, JAMES (HM07142) |  |  |  |  |  |  |  |  |  |  |  |  |  |  |  |  |  |  |  | ● |  |  |  |  |  |
| FYSON, MELANIE (HM07806) |  |  |  |  |  |  |  |  |  |  |  |  |  |  |  |  | ● |  |  |  |  |  |  |  |  |
| GODSWELL NATURAL THRPY CTRE (HM08191) |  |  |  |  |  |  |  |  |  |  |  |  |  |  | ● |  |  |  |  | ● |  |  |  |  |  |
| HANDS ON THERAPY (HM08915) |  |  |  |  |  |  |  |  |  |  |  |  |  |  |  |  |  |  |  |  |  |  |  |  |  |
| HELIX HOUSE (HM09522) |  |  |  |  |  |  |  |  |  |  |  |  | ● |  |  | ● |  |  |  |  |  |  |  |  | ● |
| HOMOEOPATHIC CONSULTANCY (HM10091) |  |  |  |  |  |  |  |  |  |  |  |  |  |  |  |  | ● |  |  |  |  |  |  |  |  |
| HUDSON, EMMA (HM10311) |  |  |  |  |  |  |  |  |  |  |  |  |  |  |  |  |  |  |  |  |  |  |  |  |  |
| HYPNOTHERAPY CENTRE (HM10516) |  |  |  |  |  |  |  |  |  |  |  | ● |  |  |  |  |  |  |  | ● | ● |  |  |  |  |
| IVES, DENNIS (HM10779) |  |  |  |  |  |  |  |  |  |  |  |  |  |  |  |  |  |  |  | ● |  |  |  |  |  |
| KIDLINGTON HERBAL PRACTICE (HM11595) |  |  |  |  |  |  |  |  |  |  |  |  |  |  | ● |  |  |  |  |  |  |  |  |  |  |
| KIDLINGTON OSTEO PRACTICE (HM11596) |  |  |  |  |  |  |  |  |  |  |  |  |  |  |  |  |  |  |  |  |  |  |  |  |  |
| MCTIMONEY CHIROPRACTIC COLLEGE (HM13614) |  |  |  |  |  |  |  |  |  |  |  |  |  |  |  |  |  |  |  |  |  |  |  |  |  |
| MIDSUMMER COTTAGE CLINIC (HM13845) |  |  |  |  |  |  |  |  |  |  |  |  |  |  | ● |  |  |  |  |  |  |  |  |  |  |
| NEAL'S YARD REMEDIES (HM14734) |  |  |  |  |  |  |  |  |  |  |  |  |  |  | ● |  |  |  |  |  |  |  |  |  |  |
| O'DONNELL, ELSPETH (HM15225) |  |  |  |  |  |  |  |  |  |  |  |  |  |  |  |  |  |  |  |  |  |  |  |  |  |
| OXFORD NUTRITION & ALLRGY CTRE (HM15541) |  |  |  |  |  |  |  |  |  |  | ● |  |  |  | ● | ● |  |  |  |  |  |  |  |  |  |
| OXFORD TRANSCENDTL MEDITA CTRE (HM15544) |  |  |  |  |  |  |  |  |  |  |  |  |  |  | ● |  |  |  |  |  |  |  |  |  |  |
| PARSONS STREET CLINIC (HM15747) |  |  |  |  |  |  |  |  |  | ● |  |  |  |  | ● |  | ● |  |  |  |  |  |  |  |  |
| POLLOCK, SUSAN (HM16418) |  |  |  |  |  |  |  |  |  |  |  |  |  |  |  | ● |  |  |  |  |  |  |  |  |  |
| PULLMAN, JUDITH (HM11249) |  |  |  |  |  |  |  |  |  |  |  |  |  |  |  |  |  |  |  | ● |  |  |  |  |  |
| ROSS, J (HM17635) |  |  |  |  |  |  |  |  |  |  |  |  |  |  |  |  |  |  |  | ● |  |  |  |  |  |
| SMITH, JULIET L (HM18758) |  |  |  |  |  |  |  |  |  |  |  |  |  |  |  |  | ● |  |  |  |  |  |  |  |  |
| SPRENT, N (HM19048) |  |  |  |  |  |  |  |  |  |  |  |  |  |  |  |  |  |  |  | ● |  |  |  |  |  |
| SPRENT, N (HM19047) |  |  |  |  |  |  |  |  |  |  |  |  |  |  |  |  |  |  |  | ● |  |  |  |  |  |
| SUMMERTON CLINIC (HM19498) |  |  |  |  |  |  |  |  |  |  |  |  |  |  | ● |  |  | ● |  |  |  |  |  |  |  |
| TOUCH OF NATURE (HM20188) |  |  |  |  |  |  |  |  |  |  |  | ● | ● |  | ● | ● |  |  |  |  |  | ● |  |  |  |
| TWINE, I E (HM20453) |  |  |  |  |  |  |  |  |  |  |  |  |  |  |  |  | ● |  |  |  |  |  |  |  |  |
| WANTAGE NATURAL HEALTH CENTRE (HM20891) |  |  |  |  |  |  |  |  |  |  |  |  |  |  |  | ● | ● |  |  |  |  |  |  |  |  |
| WHEATLEY COMP THERAPY (HM21308) |  |  |  |  |  |  |  |  |  |  |  |  |  |  |  | ● | ● | ● |  |  |  | ● |  |  | ● |
| WINTER, CLAIRE (HM21717) |  |  |  |  |  |  |  |  |  |  |  |  |  |  |  |  |  |  |  |  |  |  |  |  |  |
| WITNEY NATURAL HEALTH CLINIC (HM21751) |  | ● |  |  |  |  |  |  |  |  |  |  |  |  | ● | ● | ● |  |  | ● | ● | ● |  |  | ● |
| SHROPSHIRE |  |  |  |  |  |  |  |  |  |  |  |  |  |  |  |  |  |  |  |  |  |  |  |  |  |
| ACUMEDIC (HM00218) |  |  |  |  |  |  |  |  |  |  |  |  |  |  |  |  |  |  |  |  |  |  |  |  |  |

| Business by County with Reference no. | Kirlian Photography | Laser Treatment | Life Style Coaching | Light Therapy | Macrobiotics | Magnetic Therapy | Manipulation | Manual Lymph Drainage | Massage (Therapeutic) | McTimoney Chiropractic | Meditation | Metamorphic Therapy | Miasm Therapy | Micro Manipulation | Moxibustion | Mud Therapy | Music Therapy | Nail Surgery | Naturopathy | Neuro-Linguistic Program | Neurotherapy | Nutritional Therapy | Orgone Therapy | Oriental Diagnosis | Orthomolecular Medicine |
|---|---|---|---|---|---|---|---|---|---|---|---|---|---|---|---|---|---|---|---|---|---|---|---|---|---|
| ELWELL, R S (HM06792) |  |  |  |  |  |  |  |  |  | ● |  |  |  |  |  |  |  |  |  |  |  |  |  |  |  |
| FAULKNER, JAMES (HM07142) |  |  |  |  |  |  |  |  |  |  |  |  |  |  |  |  |  |  |  |  |  |  |  |  |  |
| FYSON, MELANIE (HM07806) |  |  |  |  |  |  |  |  |  |  |  |  |  |  |  |  |  |  |  |  |  |  |  |  |  |
| GODSWELL NATURAL THRPY CTRE (HM08191) |  |  |  |  |  |  |  |  | ● | ● |  |  |  |  |  |  |  |  |  | ● |  | ● |  |  |  |
| HANDS ON THERAPY (HM08915) |  |  |  |  |  |  |  |  | ● |  |  |  |  |  |  |  |  |  |  |  |  |  |  |  |  |
| HELIX HOUSE (HM09522) |  |  |  |  |  |  |  |  |  |  |  |  |  |  |  |  |  |  |  | ● |  | ● |  |  |  |
| HOMOEOPATHIC CONSULTANCY (HM10091) |  |  |  |  |  |  |  |  |  |  |  |  |  |  |  |  |  |  |  |  |  |  |  |  |  |
| HUDSON, EMMA (HM10311) |  |  |  |  |  |  | ● |  |  |  |  |  |  |  |  |  |  |  |  |  |  |  |  |  |  |
| HYPNOTHERAPY CENTRE (HM10516) |  |  |  |  |  |  |  |  |  |  |  |  |  |  |  |  |  |  |  |  |  |  |  |  |  |
| IVES, DENNIS (HM10779) |  |  |  |  |  |  |  |  |  |  |  |  |  |  |  |  |  |  |  |  |  |  |  |  |  |
| KIDLINGTON HERBAL PRACTICE (HM11595) |  |  |  |  |  |  |  |  |  |  |  |  |  |  |  |  |  |  | ● |  |  |  |  |  |  |
| KIDLINGTON OSTEO PRACTICE (HM11596) |  |  |  |  |  |  |  |  | ● |  |  |  |  |  |  |  |  |  |  |  |  |  |  |  |  |
| MCTIMONEY CHIROPRACTIC COLLEGE (HM13614) |  |  |  |  |  |  |  |  |  | ● |  |  |  |  |  |  |  |  |  |  |  |  |  |  |  |
| MIDSUMMER COTTAGE CLINIC (HM13845) |  |  |  |  |  |  |  |  |  |  |  |  |  |  |  |  |  |  |  |  |  |  |  |  |  |
| NEAL'S YARD REMEDIES (HM14734) |  |  |  |  |  |  |  |  |  |  |  |  |  |  |  |  |  |  |  |  |  |  |  |  |  |
| O'DONNELL, ELSPETH (HM15225) |  |  |  |  |  |  |  |  | ● |  |  |  |  |  |  |  |  |  |  |  |  |  |  |  |  |
| OXFORD NUTRITION & ALLRGY CTRE (HM15541) |  |  |  |  |  |  |  |  |  |  |  |  |  |  |  |  |  |  | ● |  |  | ● |  |  |  |
| OXFORD TRANSCENDTL MEDITA CTRE (HM15544) |  |  |  |  |  |  |  |  |  |  | ● |  |  |  |  |  |  |  |  |  |  |  |  |  |  |
| PARSONS STREET CLINIC (HM15747) |  |  |  |  |  |  | ● |  | ● |  |  |  |  |  | ● |  |  |  |  |  |  |  |  |  |  |
| POLLOCK, SUSAN (HM16418) |  | ● |  |  |  |  |  |  | ● |  |  |  |  |  |  |  |  |  |  |  |  |  |  |  |  |
| PULLMAN, JUDITH (HM11249) |  |  |  |  |  |  |  |  |  |  |  |  |  |  |  |  |  |  |  |  |  |  |  |  |  |
| ROSS, J (HM17635) |  |  |  |  |  |  |  |  |  |  |  |  |  |  |  |  |  |  |  |  |  |  |  |  |  |
| SMITH, JULIET L (HM18758) |  |  |  |  |  |  |  |  |  |  |  |  |  |  |  |  |  |  |  |  |  |  |  |  |  |
| SPRENT, N (HM19048) |  |  |  |  |  |  |  |  |  |  |  |  |  |  |  |  |  |  |  |  |  |  |  |  |  |
| SPRENT, N (HM19047) |  |  |  |  |  |  |  |  |  |  |  |  |  |  |  |  |  |  |  |  |  |  |  |  |  |
| SUMMERTON CLINIC (HM19498) |  |  |  |  |  |  |  |  |  |  |  |  |  |  |  |  |  |  |  |  |  |  |  |  |  |
| TOUCH OF NATURE (HM20188) |  |  |  |  |  |  |  |  | ● |  | ● |  |  |  |  |  |  |  | ● |  |  | ● |  |  |  |
| TWINE, I E (HM20453) |  |  |  |  |  |  |  |  |  | ● |  |  |  |  |  |  |  |  |  |  |  |  |  |  |  |
| WANTAGE NATURAL HEALTH CENTRE (HM20891) |  |  |  |  |  |  |  |  | ● |  |  |  |  |  |  |  |  |  |  |  |  |  |  |  |  |
| WHEATLEY COMP THERAPY (HM21308) |  |  |  |  |  |  |  |  | ● |  |  |  |  |  |  |  |  |  |  |  |  |  |  |  |  |
| WINTER, CLAIRE (HM21717) |  |  |  |  |  |  |  |  | ● |  |  |  |  |  |  |  |  |  |  |  |  |  |  |  |  |
| WITNEY NATURAL HEALTH CLINIC (HM21751) |  |  |  |  |  |  | ● |  | ● |  |  |  |  |  |  |  |  |  |  | ● |  |  |  | ● |  |
| SHROPSHIRE |  |  |  |  |  |  |  |  |  |  |  |  |  |  |  |  |  |  |  |  |  |  |  |  |  |
| ACUMEDIC (HM00218) |  |  |  |  |  |  |  |  |  |  |  |  |  |  |  |  |  |  |  |  |  |  |  | ● |  |

# F - O Therapies at Practices/Businesses

Business by County with Reference no.

| Business | Family Planning (Natural) | Family Therapy | Feldenkrais Methodology | Feng Shui | Floral Essence Therapy | Flotation Therapy | Gait Analysis | Gem Essence Therapy | Gestalt Therapy | Group Therapy | Hay Diet | Healer | Healing Therapy | Hellerwork | Herbal Medicine | Holistic Healing | Homeopathy | Hopi Ear Candles | Humanistic Psychology | Hypnosis | Hypnotherapy | Indian Head Massage | Inhalation Therapy | Iridology | Kinesiology |
|---|---|---|---|---|---|---|---|---|---|---|---|---|---|---|---|---|---|---|---|---|---|---|---|---|---|
| AYRES, JOHN (HM01434) | | ● | | | | | | | ● | ● | | | | | | | | | ● | ● | ● | | | | |
| BEATTIE, R G (HM01979) | | | | | | | | | | | | | | | | | | | | | | | | | |
| BODYLIFE CENTRE (HM02622) | | | | | | | | | | | | | | | | | | | | | | ● | | | |
| COLERIDGE, JUDY (HM04831) | | | | | | | | | | | | | | | | | | | | | | | | | |
| CORKE, A J (HM05167) | | | | | | | | | | | | | | | | | | | | ● | ● | | | | |
| FEATHERSTONE, ROSIE (HM07157) | | | | | | | | | | | | | | | | | ● | | | | | | | | |
| FULLERTON, N P (HM07792) | | | | | | | | | | | | | | | | | | | | | | | | | ● |
| HALES OSTEOPATHIC PRACTICE (HM08743) | ● | | | | | | | | | | ● | | | | | | | | | | | | | | |
| HALL, VALERIE (HM08792) | | | | | | | | | | | | | | | | | | | | ● | | | | | |
| JENKS, B R (HM11001) | | | | | | | | | | | | | | | | | | | | ● | | | | | |
| LUDLOW OSTEOPATHIC CLINIC (HM12727) | | | | | | | | | | | | | | | | | | | | | | | | | |
| MADDOCKS CLINIC (HM12898) | | | | | | | | | | | | | ● | | | | ● | | | | | | | | ● |
| NEEDHAM, LYNDA M (HM14751) | | | | | | | | | | | | | | | | | | | ● | ● | ● | | | | |
| OSTEOPATHIC (HM15449) | | | | | | | | | | | | | | | | | | | | | | | | | |
| PREES COMPLEMENTARY THERAPIES (HM16533) | | | | | | | | | | | | | | | | | | | | ● | ● | | | | |
| RICHARDSON, S M W (HM17289) | | | | | | | | | | | | | | | | | ● | | | | | | | | |
| WALMSLEY, RUTH (HM20848) | | | | | | | | | | | | | | | | | | | | | | | | | |
| WARNOCK, R J (HM20939) | | | | | | | | | | | | | | | | | | | | ● | | | | | |
| WESTON, JOHN (HM21279) | | | | | | | | | | | | | | | | | | | | | | | | | |
| WHITELEY, STEVEN (HM21400) | | | | | | | | | | | | | | | | | | | | | | | | | |
| WILD ROSE (HM21488) | | | | | | | | | | | | | | | | | | | | | | | | | |
| WILSON, AMANDA (HM21644) | | | | | | | | | | | | | | | | | | | | | | | | | |
| **SOMERSET** | | | | | | | | | | | | | | | | | | | | | | | | | |
| ALASKAN BACH FLOWER REMEDIES (HM00472) | | | | | | | | | | | | | | | | | | | | | | | | | |
| ANDERSON, DAVID (HM00816) | | | | | | | | | | | | | | | | | | | | | | | | | |
| ANSON, BARRIE (HM00916) | | | | | ● | | | | | | | ● | ● | | ● | ● | ● | | | ● | ● | | | | |
| AVENUE CLINIC (HM01388) | | | | | | | | | | | | | | | ● | | ● | | | ● | ● | ● | | | |
| BAILEY, LINDA R (HM01552) | | | | | | | | | | | | | | | | | | | | | | | | ● | |
| BATH BACK CLINIC (HM01891) | | | | | | | | | | | | | | | | | | | | | | | | | |
| BATH NATURAL MEDICAL CENTRE (HM01893) | | | | | | | | | | | | | | | | | ● | | | | | ● | | | |
| BATHPOOL CHIROPRACTIC CLINIC (HM01900) | | | | | | | | | | | | | | | | | | | | | | ● | | | |
| BEIGHTON, JOSEPH (HM02070) | | | | | | | | | | | | | | | | | ● | | | | | | | | |
| BOULEVARD PHARMACY (HM02739) | | | | | | | | | | | | | | | ● | | ● | | | ● | ● | ● | | | |
| BRIDGET HEALING CENTRE (HM03008) | | | | | | | | | | | | | | | | | | | | | | ● | | | |

| Business | Kirlian Photography | Laser Treatment | Life Style Coaching | Light Therapy | Macrobiotics | Magnetic Therapy | Manipulation | Manual Lymph Drainage | Massage (Therapeutic) | McTimoney Chiropractic | Meditation | Metamorphic Therapy | Miasm Therapy | Micro Manipulation | Moxibustion | Mud Therapy | Music Therapy | Nail Surgery | Naturopathy | Neuro-Linguistic Program | Neurotherapy | Nutritional Therapy | Orgone Therapy | Oriental Diagnosis | Orthomolecular Medicine |
|---|---|---|---|---|---|---|---|---|---|---|---|---|---|---|---|---|---|---|---|---|---|---|---|---|---|
| AYRES, JOHN (HM01434) | | | | | | | | | | | | | | | | | | | | | | | | | |
| BEATTIE, R G (HM01979) | | | | | | | | | | | | | | | | | | ● | | | | | | | |
| BODYLIFE CENTRE (HM02622) | | | ● | | | | | | ● | | ● | | | | | | | | | | | | | | |
| COLERIDGE, JUDY (HM04831) | | | | | | | | | ● | | | | | | | | | | | | | | | | |
| CORKE, A J (HM05167) | | | | | | | | | | | | | | | | | | | | | | | | | |
| FEATHERSTONE, ROSIE (HM07157) | | | | | | | | | | | | | | | | | | | | | | | | | |
| FULLERTON, N P (HM07792) | | | | | | | ● | | ● | | | | | | | | | | | | | ● | | | |
| HALES OSTEOPATHIC PRACTICE (HM08743) | | | | | | | ● | | | | | | | | | | | | | | | ● | | | |
| HALL, VALERIE (HM08792) | | | | | | | | | | | | | | | | | | | | | | | | | |
| JENKS, B R (HM11001) | | | | | | | | | | | | | | | | | | | | | | | | | |
| LUDLOW OSTEOPATHIC CLINIC (HM12727) | | | | | | | | | | | | | | | | | | | ● | | | | | | |
| MADDOCKS CLINIC (HM12898) | | | | | | | | | | | | | | | | | | | | | | | | | |
| NEEDHAM, LYNDA M (HM14751) | | | ● | | | | | | | | | | | | | | | | | | | | | | |
| OSTEOPATHIC (HM15449) | | | | | | | | | ● | | | | | | | | | | | | | | | | |
| PREES COMPLEMENTARY THERAPIES (HM16533) | | | | | | | | | | | | | | | | | | | | | | | | | |
| RICHARDSON, S M W (HM17289) | | | | | | | | | | | | | | | | | | | | | | | | | |
| WALMSLEY, RUTH (HM20848) | | | | | | | | | ● | | | | | | | | | | | | | | | | |
| WARNOCK, R J (HM20939) | | | | | | | | | | | | | | | | | | | | | | | | | |
| WESTON, JOHN (HM21279) | | | | | | | ● | | ● | | | | | ● | | | | | | | | | | | |
| WHITELEY, STEVEN (HM21400) | | | | | | | | | ● | | | | | | | | | | | | | | | | |
| WILD ROSE (HM21488) | | | | | | | | | ● | | | | | | | | | | | | | | | | |
| WILSON, AMANDA (HM21644) | | | | | | | | | | | | | | | | | | ● | | | | | | | |
| **SOMERSET** | | | | | | | | | | | | | | | | | | | | | | | | | |
| ALASKAN BACH FLOWER REMEDIES (HM00472) | | | | | | | | | ● | | | | | | | | | | | | | | | | |
| ANDERSON, DAVID (HM00816) | | | | | | | | | | | | | | | | | | ● | | | | | | | |
| ANSON, BARRIE (HM00916) | | | | | | | | | | | ● | | | | | | | | | | | ● | | | |
| AVENUE CLINIC (HM01388) | | | | | | | | | ● | | | | | | | | | | | | | ● | | | |
| BAILEY, LINDA R (HM01552) | | | | | | | | | | | | | | | | | | | | | | ● | | | |
| BATH BACK CLINIC (HM01891) | | | | | | | | | | | | | | | | | | | | | | ● | | | |
| BATH NATURAL MEDICAL CENTRE (HM01893) | | | | | | | | | | | | | | | | | | | | | | ● | | | |
| BATHPOOL CHIROPRACTIC CLINIC (HM01900) | | | | | | | | | ● | | | | | | | | | | | | | | | | |
| BEIGHTON, JOSEPH (HM02070) | | | | | | | | | | | | | | | | | | | | | | | | | |
| BOULEVARD PHARMACY (HM02739) | | | | | | | | | ● | | ● | | | | | | | | | | | | | | |
| BRIDGET HEALING CENTRE (HM03008) | | | | | | | | | | | | | | | | | | | | | | | | | |

# F - O Therapies at Practices/Businesses

| Business by County with Reference no. | Family Planning (Natural) | Family Therapy | Feldenkrais Methodology | Feng Shui | Floral Essence Therapy | Flotation Therapy | Gait Analysis | Gem Essence Therapy | Gestalt Therapy | Group Therapy | Hay Diet | Healer | Healing Therapy | Hellerwork | Herbal Medicine | Holistic Healing | Homeopathy | Hopi Ear Candles | Humanistic Psychology | Hypnosis | Hypnotherapy | Indian Head Massage | Inhalation Therapy | Iridology | Kinesiology | Kirlian Photography | Laser Treatment | Life Style Coaching | Light Therapy | Macrobiotics | Magnetic Therapy | Manipulation | Manual Lymph Drainage | Massage (Therapeutic) | McTimoney Chiropractic | Meditation | Metamorphic Therapy | Miasm Therapy | Micro Manipulation | Moxibustion | Mud Therapy | Music Therapy | Nail Surgery | Naturopathy | Neurotherapy | Neuro-Linguistic Program | Nutritional Therapy | Orgone Therapy | Oriental Diagnosis | Orthomolecular Medicine |
|---|---|---|---|---|---|---|---|---|---|---|---|---|---|---|---|---|---|---|---|---|---|---|---|---|---|---|---|---|---|---|---|---|---|---|---|---|---|---|---|---|---|---|---|---|---|---|---|---|---|---|
| CASTLE SURGERY (HM03840) | | | | | | | | | | | | | | | | | ● | | | | | | | | | | | | | | | | | | | | | | | | | | | | | | | | | |
| CHEDDAR COMP MEDICINE CTRE (HM04075) | | | | | | | | | | | | | ● | | ● | | ● | | | | ● | | | | | | | | | | | | | ● | | | | | | | | | | ● | | | | | | |
| CHINESE MEDICAL CENTRE (HM04238) | | | | | | | | | | | | | | | | | | | | | | | | | | | | | | | | | | | | | | | | | | | | | | | | | ● | |
| CHIPPER, MARY (HM04278) | | | | | | | | | | | | | | | | | | | | | | ● | | | | | | | | | | | ● | ● | | | | | | | | | | | | | | | | |
| CHIROPODY SURGERY (HM04344) | | | | | | | | | | | | | | | | | | | | | | | | | | | | | | | | | | | | | | | | | | | ● | | | | | | | |
| CHURCHLEY, RUBY (HM04474) | | | | | | | | | | | | | | | | | | | | ● | | | | | | | | | | | | | | | | | | | | | | | | | | | | | | |
| CLINIC OF COMP MEDICINE (HM04689) | | | | | | | | | | | | | | | | | ● | | | | | | | | | | | | | | | | | | | | | | | | | | | | | | | | | |
| COMPLEMENTARY THERAPY (HM04942) | | | | | | | | | | | | | | | | | ● | | | | | | | | | | | | | | | | | | | | | | | | | | | | | | | | | |
| COOK, COLIN (HM05041) | | | | | | | | | | | | | | | | | | | | | | | | | | | | | | | | ● | | ● | | | | | | | | | | | | | | | | |
| COUNSULTING ROOMS (HM05253) | | | | | | | | | | ● | | | | | | | | | | ● | ● | | | | | | | ● | | | | | | | | | | | | | | | | | | | | | | |
| CULPEPER (HM05577) | | | | | | | | | | | | | | | ● | | | | | | | | | | | | | | | | | | | | | | | | | | | | | | | | | | | |
| DUGGAN, JOY (HM06368) | | | | | | | | | | | | | | | | | | | | ● | | | | | | | | | | | | | | | | | | | | | | | | | | | | | | |
| DUGGAN, JOY M (HM06369) | | | | | | | | | | | | | | | | | | | | ● | | | | | | | | | | | | | | | | | | | | | | | | | | | | | | |
| FRENCH, N (HM07735) | | | | | | | | | | | | | | | | | ● | | | | | | | | | | | | | | | | | | | | | | | | | | | | | | | | | |
| GLASTONBURY CHIROPRACTIC (HM08131) | | | | | | | | | | | | | | | | | | | | | | | | | ● | | | | | | | ● | | | | | | | | | | | | | | | ● | | | |
| GLASTONBURY EAST WEST CENTRE (HM08132) | | | | | ● | | | | | | | | | | ● | | | | | | | | | ● | ● | | | | | | | | | ● | | | | | | | | | | | | | ● | | | |
| HAMMET STREET PRACTICE (HM08863) | | | | | | | | | | | | | | | | | | | | | | | | | ● | | | | | | | | | | | | | | | | | | | | | | | | | |
| HEALE, SARA (HM09317) | | | | | | | | | | | | | | | | | ● | | | | | | | | | | | | | | | | | | | | | | | | | | | | | | | | | |
| HEALE, SARAH (HM09318) | | | | | | | | | | | | | | | | | ● | | | | | | | | | | | | | | | | | | | | | | | | | | | | | | | | | |
| HUDSON, JOHN (HM10314) | | | | | | | | | | | | | | | | | | | | ● | | | | | | | | | | | | | | | | | | | | | | | | | | | | | | |
| HUDSON, JOHN (HM10315) | | | | | | | | | | | | | | | | | | | | | ● | | | | | | | | | | | | | | | | | | | | | | | | | | | | | |
| HYPNOSIS WORKS (HM10500) | | | | | | | | | | | | | | | | | | | | ● | | | | | | | | | | | | | | | | | | | | | | | | | | | | | | |
| HYPNOTHERAPY IN HUTTON (HM10540) | | | | | | | | | | | | | | | | | | | | ● | ● | | | | | | | | | | | | | | | | | | | | | | | | | | | | | |
| JASMINE HOLISTIC HEALTH (HM10937) | | | | | | | | | | | | | | | | | | | | | | ● | | | | | | | | | | | | | | | | | | | | | | | | | | | | |
| JEFFS, K A (HM10973) | | | | | | | | | | | | | | | ● | | | | | | | | | | | | | | | | | | | | | | | | | | | | | | | | | | | |
| JOHNSON, ANDREW (HM11065) | | | | | | | | | | | | | | | ● | | | | | | | | | | | | | | | | | | | | | | | | | | | | | | | | | | | |
| JONES, BECKY (HM11125) | | | | | | | | | | | | | | | | | | | | ● | ● | | | | | | | | | | | | | | | | | | | | | | | | | | | | | |
| KEOGH, DAVID (HM11538) | | | | | | | | | | | | | | | ● | | | | | | | | | | | | | | | | | | | | | | | | | | | | | | | | | | | |
| KEY CENTRE FOR HOMOEOPATHY (HM11577) | | | | | | | | | | | | | | | | | ● | | | | | | | | | | | | | | | | | | | | | | | | | | | | | | | | | |
| LANSDOWN PHYSIOTHERAPY CLINIC (HM11964) | | | | | | | | | | | | | | | | | | | | | | | | | | | | | | | | ● | | | | | | | | | | | | | | | | | | |
| LAUREL PLACE (HM12009) | | | | | | | | | | | | | ● | | | | ● | | | ● | | | | | ● | | | ● | | | | | | | ● | ● | | | | | | | | | | ● | ● | | | |
| LEWIS, JAN (HM12298) | | | | | | | | | | | | | | | | | ● | | | | | | | | | | | | | | | | | | | | | | | | | | | | | | | | | |
| LOGAN, DAVID (HM12566) | | | | | | | | | | | | | | | | | | | | ● | ● | | | | | | | | | | | | | | | | | | | | | | | | | | | | | |
| MACKEY, D (HM12856) | | | | | | | | | | | | | | | | | | | | ● | | | | | | | | | | | | | | | | | | | | | | | | | | | | | | |

# F - O Therapies at Practices/Businesses

| Business by County with Reference no. | Family Planning (Natural) | Family Therapy | Feldenkrais Methodology | Feng Shui | Floral Essence Therapy | Flotation Therapy | Gait Analysis | Gem Essence Therapy | Gestalt Therapy | Group Therapy | Hay Diet | Healer | Healing Therapy | Hellerwork | Herbal Medicine | Holistic Healing | Homeopathy | Hopi Ear Candles | Humanistic Psychology | Hypnosis | Hypnotherapy | Indian Head Massage | Inhalation Therapy | Iridology | Kinesiology |
|---|---|---|---|---|---|---|---|---|---|---|---|---|---|---|---|---|---|---|---|---|---|---|---|---|---|
| MAPERTON TRUST (HM13058) | | | | | | | | | | | | | | | | ● | | | | | | | | | |
| MARAR, N Z (HM13065) | | | | | | | | | | | | | | | | | ● | | | | | | | | |
| MILSOM STREET CLINIC (HM13944) | | | | | | | | | | | | | | | | | | | | | | ● | | | |
| MISTRAL, J (HM13999) | | | | | | | | | | | | | | | | | ● | | | | | | | | |
| MOIR, GILL (HM14047) | | | | | | | | | | | | | | | | | | | | | | ● | | | |
| NATURAL SPIRITUAL HEALING (HM14626) | | | | | | | | | | | | ● | ● | | | | | | | | | | | | |
| NATURAL THERAPIES (HM14632) | | | | | ● | | | ● | | | | | | | | | | | | | | ● | | | |
| NORSO BIOMAGNETICS UK (HM15016) | | | | | | | | | | | | | | | | | | | | | | | | | |
| NUTRITION FOR LIFE (HM15123) | | | | | | | | | | | | | | | | | | | | | | | | | |
| PARKER, SUZY (HM15708) | | | | | | | | | | | | | | | | | ● | | | | | | | | |
| PITT, I T (HM16347) | | | | | | | | | | | | | | | | | ● | | | | | | | | |
| PRESSURE WORKS (HM16544) | | | | | | | | | | | | | | | | | | | | | | | | | |
| PRICE, S C (HM16592) | | | | | | | | | | | | | | | | | ● | | | | | | | | |
| QUINN, G A W (HM16809) | | | | | | | | | | | | | | | | | | | | ● | | | | | |
| ROPER, JANET (HM17592) | | | | | | | | | | | | | | | | | | | | ● | | | | | |
| SAYER, SANDRA (HM17996) | | | | | | | | | | | | | | | | | | | | ● | | | | | |
| SELF REALISATION MEDITATION (HM18207) | | | | | | | | | | | | | | | | | | | | | | | | | |
| SHAMBHALA (HM18275) | | | | | | ● | | | | | | ● | ● | | ● | ● | | | | | | ● | | ● | |
| SNOWDON, JANET (HM18843) | | | | | | | | | | | | | | | | ● | ● | | | | | | | | |
| ST JAMES'S SURGERY (HM19079) | | | | | | | | | | | | | | | | ● | | | | | | | | | |
| ST MICHAEL'S HYPNOTHERAPY (HM19090) | | | | | | | | | | | | | | | | | | | | | ● | | | | |
| STANLEY COURT SURGERY (HM19127) | | | | | | | | | | | | | | | | | ● | | | | | | | | |
| STANNARD, L (HM19133) | | | | | | | | | | | | | | | ● | | | | | | | | | | |
| STREET CHIROPRACTIC CLINIC (HM19383) | | | | | | | | | | | | | | | | | | | | | | | | | |
| STRESS CLINIC & NTRL HLTH CTRE (HM19389) | ● | ● | | | | | | | ● | ● | | | | | ● | | ● | | ● | | ● | ● | | | ● |
| TARETH CENTRE (HM19704) | | | | | | | | | | | | | | | ● | ● | ● | | | | ● | ● | | | |
| TAYLOR, JAMIE (HM19768) | | | | | | | | | | | | | | | | | ● | | | | | | | | |
| TAYLOR, SHANE (HM19793) | | | | | | | | | | | | | | | | | | | | ● | | | | | |
| TERRACE THRPY PSYCHO/NTRL HLTH (HM19843) | | | | | | | | | | | | | | | ● | | ● | | | | | | | | |
| TRANSCENDENTAL MEDITATION (HM20281) | | | | | | | | | | | | | | | | | | | | | | | | | |
| TURNPIKE SURGERY (HM20441) | | | | | | | | | | | | | | | | | ● | | | | | | | | |
| TYLER, LIZZY (HM20462) | | | | | | | | | | | | | | | | | | | | | | ● | | | |
| WELLSPRING OSTEO/NTRL HEALTH (HM21181) | | | | | | | | | | | | | | | ● | | ● | | | | | | | | |
| WESTERN CHIROPRACTIC CLINIC (HM21263) | | | | | | | | | | | | | | | | | | | | | | | | | ● |

| Business by County with Reference no. | Kirlian Photography | Laser Treatment | Life Style Coaching | Light Therapy | Macrobiotics | Magnetic Therapy | Manipulation | Manual Lymph Drainage | Massage (Therapeutic) | McTimoney Chiropractic | Meditation | Metamorphic Therapy | Miasm Therapy | Micro Manipulation | Moxibustion | Mud Therapy | Music Therapy | Nail Surgery | Naturopathy | Neuro-Linguistic Program | Neurotherapy | Nutritional Therapy | Orgone Therapy | Oriental Diagnosis | Orthomolecular Medicine |
|---|---|---|---|---|---|---|---|---|---|---|---|---|---|---|---|---|---|---|---|---|---|---|---|---|---|
| MAPERTON TRUST (HM13058) | | | | | | | | | | | | | | | | | | | | | | | | | |
| MARAR, N Z (HM13065) | | | | | | | | | | | | | | | | | | | | | | | | | |
| MILSOM STREET CLINIC (HM13944) | | | | | | | | | | | | | | | | | | | | | | | | | |
| MISTRAL, J (HM13999) | | | | | | | | | | | | | | | | | | | | | | | | | |
| MOIR, GILL (HM14047) | | | | | | | | | ● | | | | | | | | | | | | | | | | |
| NATURAL SPIRITUAL HEALING (HM14626) | | | | | | | | | | | | | | | | | | | | | | | | | |
| NATURAL THERAPIES (HM14632) | | | | | | | | | ● | | | ● | | | | | | | | | | | | | |
| NORSO BIOMAGNETICS UK (HM15016) | | | | | | ● | | | | | | | | | | | | | | | | | | | |
| NUTRITION FOR LIFE (HM15123) | | | | | | | | | | | | | | | | | | | | | | ● | | | |
| PARKER, SUZY (HM15708) | | | | | | | | | | | | | | | | | | | | | | | | | |
| PITT, I T (HM16347) | | | | | | | ● | | ● | | | | | ● | ● | | | | | | | ● | | | |
| PRESSURE WORKS (HM16544) | | | | | | | | | ● | | | | | | | | | | | | | | | | |
| PRICE, S C (HM16592) | | | | | | | | | | | | | | | | | | | | | | | | | |
| QUINN, G A W (HM16809) | | | | | | | | | | | | | | | | | | | | | | | | | |
| ROPER, JANET (HM17592) | | | | | | | | | | | | | | | | | | | | | | | | | |
| SAYER, SANDRA (HM17996) | | | | | | | | | | | | | | | | | | | | | | | | | |
| SELF REALISATION MEDITATION (HM18207) | | | | | | | | | | | ● | | | | | | | | | | | | | | |
| SHAMBHALA (HM18275) | | | ● | | | | ● | | ● | | ● | | | | | | | | | | | ● | | | |
| SNOWDON, JANET (HM18843) | | | | | | | | | | | | | | | | | | | | | | | | | |
| ST JAMES'S SURGERY (HM19079) | | | | | | | | | | | | | | | | | | | | | | | | | |
| ST MICHAEL'S HYPNOTHERAPY (HM19090) | | | | | | | | | | | | | | | | | | | | | | | | | |
| STANLEY COURT SURGERY (HM19127) | | | | | | | | | | | | | | | | | | | | | | | | | |
| STANNARD, L (HM19133) | | | | | | | | | | | | | | | | | | | | | | | | | |
| STREET CHIROPRACTIC CLINIC (HM19383) | | | | | | | ● | | ● | | | | | | | | | | | | | | | | |
| STRESS CLINIC & NTRL HLTH CTRE (HM19389) | | | | | | | ● | | ● | | ● | | | | ● | | | | | | | | | ● | |
| TARETH CENTRE (HM19704) | | | | | | | | | ● | | ● | | | | | | | | | | | | | | |
| TAYLOR, JAMIE (HM19768) | | | | | | | | | | | | | | | | | | | | | | | | | |
| TAYLOR, SHANE (HM19793) | | | | | | | | | | | | | | | | | | | | | | | | | |
| TERRACE THRPY PSYCHO/NTRL HLTH (HM19843) | | | | | | | | | | | ● | | | | | | | | | | | ● | | | |
| TRANSCENDENTAL MEDITATION (HM20281) | | | | | | | | | | | ● | | | | | | | | | | | | | | |
| TURNPIKE SURGERY (HM20441) | | | | | | | | | | | | | | | | | | | | | | | | | |
| TYLER, LIZZY (HM20462) | | | | | | | | | | | | | | | | | | | | | | | | | |
| WELLSPRING OSTEO/NTRL HEALTH (HM21181) | | | | | | | | | ● | | | | | | | | | | | | | | | | |
| WESTERN CHIROPRACTIC CLINIC (HM21263) | | | | | | | ● | | ● | | | | | | | | | | | | | | | | |

# F - O Therapies at Practices/Businesses

| Business by County with Reference no. | Family Planning (Natural) | Family Therapy | Feldenkrais Methodology | Feng Shui | Floral Essence Therapy | Flotation Therapy | Gait Analysis | Gem Essence Therapy | Gestalt Therapy | Group Therapy | Hay Diet | Healer | Healing Therapy | Hellerwork | Herbal Medicine | Holistic Healing | Homeopathy | Hopi Ear Candles | Humanistic Psychology | Hypnosis | Hypnotherapy | Indian Head Massage | Inhalation Therapy | Iridology | Kinesiology | Kirlian Photography | Laser Treatment | Life Style Coaching | Light Therapy | Macrobiotics | Magnetic Therapy | Manipulation | Manual Lymph Drainage | Massage (Therapeutic) | McTimoney Chiropractic | Meditation | Metamorphic Therapy | Miasm Therapy | Micro Manipulation | Moxibustion | Mud Therapy | Music Therapy | Nail Surgery | Naturopathy | Neuro-Linguistic Program | Neurotherapy | Nutritional Therapy | Orgone Therapy | Oriental Diagnosis | Orthomolecular Medicine |
|---|---|---|---|---|---|---|---|---|---|---|---|---|---|---|---|---|---|---|---|---|---|---|---|---|---|---|---|---|---|---|---|---|---|---|---|---|---|---|---|---|---|---|---|---|---|---|---|---|---|---|
| YELLOW EMPEROR CORP (HM22004) | | | | | | | | | | | | | | | ● | | | | | | | | | | | | | | | | | | | | | | | | | | | | | | | | | | | |
| YEOVIL CHIROPRACTIC CLINIC (HM22008) | | | | | | | | | | | | | | | | | ● | | | | | | | | | | | | | | | | | | | | | | | | | | | | | | | | | |
| **STAFFORDSHIRE** | | | | | | | | | | | | | | | | | | | | | | | | | | | | | | | | | | | | | | | | | | | | | | | | | | |
| ADAMS, MEGAN (HM00356) | | | | | | | | | | | | | | | | | | | | ● | | | | | | | | | | | | | | | | | | | | | | | | | | | | | | |
| ALTERNATIVE THERAPY CENTRE (HM00735) | | | | | | | | | | | | ● | ● | | ● | ● | ● | | | ● | ● | ● | | ● | | | | ● | | | | | | ● | | | | | | | | | | | | | ● | | | |
| ALTERNATIVES (HM00741) | | | | | | | | | | | | | | | | | | | | | | ● | | | | | | | | | | | | ● | | | | | | | | | | | | | | | | |
| ANDERSON, G (HM00818) | | | | | | | | | | | | | | | | | | | | | ● | | | | | | | | | | | | | | | | | | | | | | | | | | | | | |
| ARMSTRONG HEALTH/HERBAL STORE (HM01016) | | | | | | | | | | | | | | | ● | | | | | | | | | | | | | | | | | | | | | | | | | | | | | | | | | | | |
| BARCROFT, J M (HM01696) | | | | | | | | | | | | | | | | | | | | | | | | | | | | | | | | | | | | | | | | | | | ● | | | | | | | |
| BONNEBAIGT, ANDRE (HM02682) | | | | | | | | | | | | | | | | | | | | | ● | | | | | | | | | | | | | | | | | | | | | | | | | | | | | |
| BORE ST POD & CHIROP PRACTICE (HM02716) | | | | | | | | | | | | | | | | | | | | | | | | | | | | | | | | | | | | | | | | | | | ● | | | | | | | |
| BRIDGETT, A (HM03011) | | | | | | | | | | | | | | | | | | | | | | | | | | | | | | | | ● | | ● | | | | | | | | | | | | | | | | |
| BURKE, E (HM03385) | | | | | | | | | | | | | | | | | | | | ● | ● | | | | | | | | | | | | | | | | | | | | | | | | | | | | | |
| CADDEN, D C (HM03530) | | | | | | | | | | | | | | | | | | | | ● | | | | | | | | | | | | | | | | | | | | | | | | | | | | | | |
| CHASE HEALTH FOODS (HM04055) | | | | | | | | | | | | | | | | | ● | | | | | ● | | | | | | | | | | | | | | | | | | | | | | | | | | | | |
| CHASE NATURAL THERAPY CENTRE (HM04059) | | | | | | | | | | | | | | | | | ● | | | | ● | ● | | | | | | | | | | | | ● | | | | | | | | | | | | | | | | |
| CITY CHIROPRACTIC CLINIC (HM04492) | | | | | | | | | | | | | | | | | | | | | | | | | | | | | | | | | | | | | | | | | | | | | | | ● | | | |
| COMPLEMENTARY THERAPIES (HM04941) | | | | | | | | | | | | | | | | | | ● | | | | ● | | | | | | | | | | | | | | | | | | | | | | | | | | | | |
| CORNERSTONES PRACTICE (HM05182) | | | | | | | | | | | | | | | | | ● | | | | | | | | | | | | | | | | | | | | | | | | | | | | | | | | | |
| CRESCENT CLINIC (HM05417) | | | | | | | | | | | | | | | ● | | ● | | | | | | | | ● | | | | | | | ● | | | | | | | | | | | | | | | | | | |
| CRESCENT CLINIC FOR COMP MED (HM05418) | | | | | | | | | | | | | | | ● | | ● | | | | | | | | ● | | | | | | | ● | | | | | | | | | | | | | | | | | | |
| DALE, SUZANNE (HM05685) | | | | | | | | | | | | | | | | | | | | ● | | | | | | | | | | | | | | | | | | | | | | | | | | | | | | |
| FEET FIRST (HM07176) | | | | | | | | | | | | | | | | | | | | | | | | | | | | | | | | | | | | | | | | | | | ● | | | | | | | |
| FOOT SOUL & BODYWORKS (HM07487) | | | | | | | | | | | | ● | | | | ● | | | | | | ● | | | | | | | | | | | | | | ● | ● | | | | | | | | | | ● | | | |
| FOULKES, L (HM07610) | | | | | | | | | | | | | | | | | ● | | | | | | | | | | | | | | | | | | | | | | | | | | | | | | | | | |
| GASCOYNE, P (HM07920) | | | | | | | | | | | | | | | | | | | | | | | | | | | | | | | | | | | | | | | | | | | ● | | | | | | | |
| HADFIELD, G T (HM08692) | | | | | | | | | | | | | | | | | | | | ● | | | | | | | | | | | | | | | | | | | | | | | | | | | | | | |
| HYPNOSIS & PARAPSYCHOLOGY (HM10493) | | | | | | | | | | | | | | | | | | | | ● | | | | | | | | | | | | | | | | | | | | | | | | | | | | | | |
| ISHTA CENTRE (HM10761) | | | | | | | | | | | | | | | | | ● | | | | | | | | ● | | | | | | | ● | | ● | | ● | | | ● | ● | | | | | | | ● | | | |
| JOHNSON, JANICE (HM11079) | | | | | | | | | | | | ● | ● | | | | | | | ● | ● | | | | | | | ● | | | | | | | | ● | | | | | | | | | | | | | | |
| KILGALLON, P (HM11601) | | | | | | | | | | | | | | | | | ● | | | | | | | | | | | | | | | | | | | | | | | | | | | | | | | | | |
| L C I STRESS MANAGEMENT (HM11842) | | | | | | | | | | | | | | | | | | | | ● | | | | | | | | | | | | | | | | | | | | | | | | | | | | | | |
| LOUISE BRITTLE (HM12667) | | | | | | | ● | | | | | | | | | | | | | | | | | | | | | | | | | | | | | | | | | | | | ● | | | | | | | |
| MELLOR, J SIMON (HM13709) | | | | | | | | | | | | | | | | | | | | | | | | | | | | | | | | | | | | | | | | | | | ● | | | | | | | |

# F - O Therapies at Practices/Businesses

| Business by County with Reference no. | Family Planning (Natural) | Family Therapy | Feldenkrais Methodology | Feng Shui | Floral Essence Therapy | Flotation Therapy | Gait Analysis | Gem Essence Therapy | Gestalt Therapy | Group Therapy | Hay Diet | Healer | Healing Therapy | Hellerwork | Herbal Medicine | Holistic Healing | Homeopathy | Hopi Ear Candles | Humanistic Psychology | Hypnosis | Hypnotherapy | Indian Head Massage | Inhalation Therapy | Iridology | Kinesiology | Kirlian Photography | Laser Treatment | Life Style Coaching | Light Therapy | Macrobiotics | Magnetic Therapy | Manipulation | Manual Lymph Drainage | Massage (Therapeutic) | McTimoney Chiropractic | Meditation | Metamorphic Therapy | Miasm Therapy | Micro Manipulation | Moxibustion | Mud Therapy | Music Therapy | Nail Surgery | Naturopathy | Neurotherapy | Neuro-Linguistic Program | Nutritional Therapy | Orgone Therapy | Oriental Diagnosis | Orthomolecular Medicine |
|---|---|---|---|---|---|---|---|---|---|---|---|---|---|---|---|---|---|---|---|---|---|---|---|---|---|---|---|---|---|---|---|---|---|---|---|---|---|---|---|---|---|---|---|---|---|---|---|---|---|---|
| MENZIES-TRULL, CHRISTOPHER (HM13731) | | | | | | | | | | | | | | | ● | | | | | | | | | | | | | | | | | | | | | | | | | | | | | | | | | | | |
| O'CALLAGHAN, STEVE (HM15193) | | | | | | | | | | | | | | | | | | | | | | ● | | | | | | | | | | | | ● | | | | | | | | | | | | | | | | |
| OLDACRE, RAY (HM15265) | | | | | | | | | | | | | | | | | | | | ● | | | | | | | | | | | | | | | | | | | | | | | | | | | | | | |
| PAYTON, ANTHONY (HM15875) | | | | | | | | | | | | | | | | | | | | | | | | | | | | | | | | | | | | | | | | | | | ● | | | | | | | |
| PEACH, F J (HM15879) | | | | | | | | | | | | | | | | | | | | | | | | | | | | | | | | | | | | | | | | | | | ● | | | | | | | |
| PLANT, R M (HM16359) | | | | | | | | | | | | | | | | | | | | | | | | | | | | | | | | | | | | | | | | | | | ● | | | | | | | |
| POVEY, JILL (HM16483) | | | | | | | | | | | | | | | | | ● | | | | | | | | | | | | | | | | | | | | | | | | | | | | | | | | | |
| PRICE, M J (HM16586) | | | | | | | | | | | | | | | | | | | | ● | | | | | | | | | | | | | | | | | | | | | | | | | | | | | | |
| PRIORS PODIATRY PRACTICE (HM16629) | | | | | | | | | | | | | | | | | | | | ● | | | | | | | | | | | | | | | | | | | | | | | | | | | | | | |
| REECE, P & BRADSHAW, J (HM17039) | | | | | | | ● | | | | | | | | | | | | | | | | | | | | | | | | | | | | | | | | | | | | ● | | | | | | | |
| ROBERTS, KATE (HM17418) | | | | | | | | | | | | | | | | | | | ● | | | | | | | | | | | | | | | | | ● | | | | | | | | | | | | | | |
| STAFFORD CHIROPRACTIC CLINIC (HM19108) | | | | | | | | | | | | | | | | | | | | | | | | | | | | | | | | ● | | ● | | | | | | | | | | | | | | | | |
| SUSAN JAMES CONSULTANCY (HM19527) | ● | | | | | | | | | | | ● | | | | | ● | | | | | | | | | | | | | | | | | | | | | | | | | | | | | | ● | | | |
| TUNSTALL HYPNOTHERAPY CENTRE (HM20401) | | | | | | | | | | | | | | | | | | | | ● | ● | | | | | | | | | | | | | | | | | | | | | | | | | | | | | |
| WATSON, MALCOLM (HM21018) | | | | | | | | | | | | | | | | | | | | ● | | | | | | | | | | | | | | | | | | | | | | | | | | | | | | |
| WOOLRICH, R J (HM21882) | | | | | | | | | | | | | | | | | ● | | | | | | | | | | | | | | | | | | | | | | | | | | | | | | | | | |
| **SUFFOLK** | | | | | | | | | | | | | | | | | | | | | | | | | | | | | | | | | | | | | | | | | | | | | | | | | | |
| AJNA (HM00457) | | | | | | | | | | | | | ● | | | | | | | | | | | | | | | | | | | | | | | | | | | | | | | | | | | | | |
| BULL, OWEN MORGAN (HM03341) | | | | | | | | | | | | | | | | | | | | ● | | | | | | | | | | | | | | | | | | | | | | | | | | | | | | |
| CARPENTER, ELAINE (HM03728) | | | | | | | | | | | | | | | | | | | | ● | | | | | | | | | | | | | | | | | | | | | | | | | | | | | | |
| CHARLTON CLINIC (HM04033) | | | | | | | | | | | | | | | | | | | | | | | | | | | | | | | | | | | | | | | | | | | | | | | ● | | | |
| CHURCHMAN & ASS REG OST (HM04475) | | | | | | | | | | | | | | | | | | | | | | | | | | | | | | | | ● | | | | | | | | | | | | | | | | | | |
| CHURCHMAN, BERYL (HM04478) | | | | | | | | | | | | | | | | | | | | | | | | | | | | | | | | ● | | | | | | | | | | | | | | | | | | |
| CLINICAL HYPNOTHERAPY (HM04713) | | | | | | | | | | | | | | | | | | | | ● | | | | | | | | | | | | | | | | | | | | | | | | | | | | | | |
| COLLINS, JOHN (HM04871) | | | | | | | | | | | | | | | | | | | | | | | | | | | | | | | | | | ● | | | ● | | | | | | | | | | | | | |
| COOK, LORNA (HM05050) | | | | | | | | | | | | | | | | | | | | ● | | | | | | | | | | | | | | | | | | | | | | | | | | | | | | |
| COOPER, A R (HM05088) | | | | | | | | | | | | | | | | | | | | | | | | | | | | | | | | | | | | | | | | | | | ● | | | | | | | |
| CT & IM LEITH (HM05534) | | | | | | | | | | | | | | | | | ● | | | | | | | | | | | | | | ● | ● | | | | | | | | | | | | | | | ● | | | |
| DAVIDSON, H L (HM05786) | | | | | | | | | | | | | | | ● | | | | | | | | | | | | | | | | | | | | | | | | | | | | | | | | | | | |
| DENT, TRISH () | | | | | | | | | | | | | | | | | | | | | | ● | | | | | | | | ● | | | | | | | | | | | | | | | | | | | | |
| E M D I (HM06471) | | | | | | | | | | | | | | | | | | | | | | | | | | | | | | | ● | | | | | | | | | | | | | | | | | | | |
| EVENKEEL (HM06997) | | | | | | ● | | | | | | | ● | | | ● | | | | | | ● | | | | | | | | | | | | ● | | | | | | | | | | | | | | | | |
| FOTHERBY, ROZ (HM07605) | | | | | | | | | | | | | | | | | | | | ● | | | | | | | | | | | | | | | | | | | | | | | | | | | | | | |
| FRESHFIELDS OF ALDEBURGH (HM07737) | | | | | | | | | | | | | | | | | ● | | | | | ● | | | | | | | | | | | | | | | | | | | | | | | | | ● | | | |

# F - O Therapies at Practices/Businesses

Business by County with Reference no.

| Business | Family Planning (Natural) | Family Therapy | Feldenkrais Methodology | Feng Shui | Floral Essence Therapy | Flotation Therapy | Gait Analysis | Gem Essence Therapy | Gestalt Therapy | Group Therapy | Hay Diet | Healer | Healing Therapy | Hellerwork | Herbal Medicine | Holistic Healing | Homeopathy |
|---|---|---|---|---|---|---|---|---|---|---|---|---|---|---|---|---|---|
| GREEN FARM CLINIC (HM08435) | | | | | | | | | | | | | | | | | |
| HEALING CONNECTIONS (HM09330) | | | | | | | | | | | | | | | | | |
| HEALING HANDS (HM09336) | | ● | | | | | | | | | | ● | ● | | | ● | |
| HERBS OF GRACE (HM09674) | | | | | | | | | | | | | | | ● | | |
| HOPKINS, C J (HM10147) | | | | | | | | | | | | | | | | | |
| HUGHES, DOREEN (HM10325) | | | | | | | | | | | | | | | | | |
| INNER SPACE SUFFOLK (HM10641) | | | | | | ● | | | | | | | | | | | |
| IPSWICH CHIROPRACTIC CLINIC (HM10714) | | | | | | | | | | | | | | | | ● | |
| KIPPAX, STEPHEN (HM11697) | | | | | | | | | | | | | | | ● | | |
| LAVENDER LODGE CLINIC (HM12023) | | | | | | | | | | | | | ● | | | ● | ● |
| LAWRENCE, JILLIAN (HM12050) | | | | | | | | | | | | | | | | | |
| MALAROC (HM12961) | | | | | | | | | | | | | | | | | |
| MANOR HOUSE (HM13039) | | | | | | | | | | | | | | | ● | | |
| MASSAGE FOR HEALTH (HM13260) | | | | | | | | | | | | ● | ● | | | ● | |
| MCTIMONEY CHIROPRACTIC CLINIC (HM13607) | | | | | | | | | | | | | | | | | |
| MOHAN, TERRY (HM14046) | | | | | | | | | | | | | | | | | |
| NATURECURES (HM14684) | | | | | | | | | | | | | | | | | |
| NOAH'S ARK PSYCHOTHERAPY (HM14964) | | ● | | | | | | | | | | | | | | | |
| PAGE, COLIN J (HM15570) | | | | | | | | | | | | | | | | | |
| PEARL LAMONT (HM15906) | | | | | | | | | | | | | | | | | |
| SACRED EARTH (HM17829) | | | | | | | | | | | | | | | ● | | |
| SHEROMA THERAPY (HM18435) | | | | | | | | | | | | | | | ● | ● | |
| SPALDING, JULIE (HM18955) | | | | | | | | | | | | | | | | | |
| SPRINGFIELD LODGE HEALTH CARE (HM19052) | | | | | | | | | | | | | ● | | ● | | ● |
| ST MARYS PRACTICE (HM19088) | | | | | | | | | | | | | | | ● | | |
| STEPHEN GORDON (HM19197) | | | | | | | | | | | | | | | | | ● |
| STEWARD, J A (HM19253) | | | | | | | | | | | | | | | | | |
| SUDBURY CHIROPRACTIC CLINIC (HM19462) | | | | | | | | | | | | | | | | | |
| TRANSCENDENTAL MEDITATION (HM20283) | | | | | | | | | | | | | | | | | |
| UNITY HEALTH CENTRE (HM20510) | | | | | | | | | | | | | | | | | |
| WEI CLINIC (HM21111) | | | | | | | | | | | | | | | | | ● |
| WILLIAMS, R T & S M (HM21585) | | | | | | | | | | | | | | | | | ● |
| WOODBRIDGE COMP HEALTH CENTRE (HM21816) | | | | | | | | | | | | | | | | | |

| Business | Hopi Ear Candles | Humanistic Psychology | Hypnosis | Hypnotherapy | Indian Head Massage | Inhalation Therapy | Iridology | Kinesiology | Kirlian Photography | Laser Treatment | Life Style Coaching | Light Therapy | Macrobiotics | Magnetic Therapy | Manipulation | Manual Lymph Drainage | Massage (Therapeutic) |
|---|---|---|---|---|---|---|---|---|---|---|---|---|---|---|---|---|---|
| GREEN FARM CLINIC (HM08435) | | | | | | | | | | | | | | | ● | | |
| HEALING CONNECTIONS (HM09330) | | | | | ● | | | | | | | | | | | | ● |
| HEALING HANDS (HM09336) | | | ● | ● | ● | ● | | | | | | | | | | | ● |
| HERBS OF GRACE (HM09674) | | | | | | | | | | | | | | | | | |
| HOPKINS, C J (HM10147) | | | ● | ● | | | | | | | | | | | | | |
| HUGHES, DOREEN (HM10325) | | | | | ● | | | | | | | | | | | | |
| INNER SPACE SUFFOLK (HM10641) | | | ● | | | | | | | | | | | | | | |
| IPSWICH CHIROPRACTIC CLINIC (HM10714) | ● | | | | ● | | | | | | | | | | ● | | ● |
| KIPPAX, STEPHEN (HM11697) | | | | | | | | | | | | | | | | | |
| LAVENDER LODGE CLINIC (HM12023) | | | | | | | | | | | | | | | ● | | ● |
| LAWRENCE, JILLIAN (HM12050) | | | | ● | | | | | | | | | | | | | |
| MALAROC (HM12961) | | | | | | | | | | | | | | | ● | | ● |
| MANOR HOUSE (HM13039) | | | | | | | | | | | | | | | | | |
| MASSAGE FOR HEALTH (HM13260) | | | | | | | | | | | | | | | | | ● |
| MCTIMONEY CHIROPRACTIC CLINIC (HM13607) | | | | | | | | | | | | | | | ● | | ● |
| MOHAN, TERRY (HM14046) | | | ● | ● | | | | | | | | | | | | | |
| NATURECURES (HM14684) | | | | | | | | | | | | | | | ● | | ● |
| NOAH'S ARK PSYCHOTHERAPY (HM14964) | | ● | | ● | | | | | | | | | | | | | |
| PAGE, COLIN J (HM15570) | | | ● | ● | | | | | | | | | | | | | |
| PEARL LAMONT (HM15906) | | | ● | | | | | | | | | | | | | | |
| SACRED EARTH (HM17829) | | | | | | | | | | | | | | | | | |
| SHEROMA THERAPY (HM18435) | | | ● | ● | ● | | | | | | | | | | | | ● |
| SPALDING, JULIE (HM18955) | | | ● | ● | | | | | | | | | | | | | |
| SPRINGFIELD LODGE HEALTH CARE (HM19052) | | | | ● | ● | | ● | ● | | | | | | | | | |
| ST MARYS PRACTICE (HM19088) | | | | | | | | | | | | | | | | | |
| STEPHEN GORDON (HM19197) | | | | | | | | | | | | | | | | | |
| STEWARD, J A (HM19253) | | | | | | | | | | | | | | | ● | | |
| SUDBURY CHIROPRACTIC CLINIC (HM19462) | | | | | | | | | | | | | | | ● | | |
| TRANSCENDENTAL MEDITATION (HM20283) | | | | | | | | | | | | | | | | | |
| UNITY HEALTH CENTRE (HM20510) | | | | | | | | | | | | ● | | | | | |
| WEI CLINIC (HM21111) | | | | ● | | | | | | | | | | | | | |
| WILLIAMS, R T & S M (HM21585) | | | | | | | | | | | | | | | | | |
| WOODBRIDGE COMP HEALTH CENTRE (HM21816) | | | | | ● | | | | | | | | | | | | |

| Business | McTimoney Chiropractic | Meditation | Metamorphic Therapy | Miasm Therapy | Micro Manipulation | Moxibustion | Mud Therapy | Music Therapy | Nail Surgery | Naturopathy | Neuro-Linguistic Program | Neurotherapy | Nutritional Therapy | Orgone Therapy | Oriental Diagnosis | Orthomolecular Medicine |
|---|---|---|---|---|---|---|---|---|---|---|---|---|---|---|---|---|
| GREEN FARM CLINIC (HM08435) | | | | | | | | | | | | | | | | |
| HEALING CONNECTIONS (HM09330) | | | | | | | | | | | | | | | | |
| HEALING HANDS (HM09336) | | | | | | | | | | | | | | | | |
| HERBS OF GRACE (HM09674) | | | | | | | | | | | | | | | | |
| HOPKINS, C J (HM10147) | | | | | | | | | | | | | | | | |
| HUGHES, DOREEN (HM10325) | | | | | | | | | | | | | | | | |
| INNER SPACE SUFFOLK (HM10641) | | | | | | | | | | | | | | | | |
| IPSWICH CHIROPRACTIC CLINIC (HM10714) | | | | | | | | | | | | | ● | | | |
| KIPPAX, STEPHEN (HM11697) | | | | | | | | | | | | | | | | |
| LAVENDER LODGE CLINIC (HM12023) | | ● | | | | | | | | | | | | | | |
| LAWRENCE, JILLIAN (HM12050) | | | | | | | | | | | | | | | | |
| MALAROC (HM12961) | | | | | | | | | | | | | | | | |
| MANOR HOUSE (HM13039) | | | | | | | | | | | | | ● | | | |
| MASSAGE FOR HEALTH (HM13260) | | | | | | | | | | | | | | | | |
| MCTIMONEY CHIROPRACTIC CLINIC (HM13607) | | | | | | | | | | | | | | | | |
| MOHAN, TERRY (HM14046) | | | | | | | | | | | | | | | | |
| NATURECURES (HM14684) | | | | | | ● | | | | | | | ● | | ● | |
| NOAH'S ARK PSYCHOTHERAPY (HM14964) | | | | | | | | | | | | | | | | |
| PAGE, COLIN J (HM15570) | | | | | | | | | | | | | | | | |
| PEARL LAMONT (HM15906) | | | | | | | | | | | | | | | | |
| SACRED EARTH (HM17829) | | | | | | | | | | | | | | | | |
| SHEROMA THERAPY (HM18435) | | ● | | | | | | | | | | | | | ● | |
| SPALDING, JULIE (HM18955) | | | | | | | | | | | ● | | | | | |
| SPRINGFIELD LODGE HEALTH CARE (HM19052) | | | | | | | | | | | ● | | ● | | | |
| ST MARYS PRACTICE (HM19088) | | | | | | | | | | | | | ● | | | |
| STEPHEN GORDON (HM19197) | | | | | | | | | | | | | | | | |
| STEWARD, J A (HM19253) | | | | | | | | | | | | | | | | |
| SUDBURY CHIROPRACTIC CLINIC (HM19462) | | | | | | | | | | | | | | | | |
| TRANSCENDENTAL MEDITATION (HM20283) | | ● | | | | | | | | | | | | | | |
| UNITY HEALTH CENTRE (HM20510) | | | | | | | | | | | | | ● | | | |
| WEI CLINIC (HM21111) | | | | | | | | | | | | | | | | |
| WILLIAMS, R T & S M (HM21585) | | | | | | | | | | | | | | | | |
| WOODBRIDGE COMP HEALTH CENTRE (HM21816) | | | | | | | | | | | | | | | | |

# F - O Therapies at Practices/Businesses

| Business by County with Reference no. | Family Planning (Natural) | Family Therapy | Feldenkrais Methodology | Feng Shui | Floral Essence Therapy | Flotation Therapy | Gait Analysis | Gem Essence Therapy | Gestalt Therapy | Group Therapy | Hay Diet | Healer | Healing Therapy | Hellerwork | Herbal Medicine | Holistic Healing | Homeopathy | Hopi Ear Candles | Humanistic Psychology | Hypnosis | Hypnotherapy | Indian Head Massage | Inhalation Therapy | Iridology | Kinesiology | Kirlian Photography | Laser Treatment | Life Style Coaching | Light Therapy | Macrobiotics | Magnetic Therapy | Manipulation | Manual Lymph Drainage | Massage (Therapeutic) | McTimoney Chiropractic | Meditation | Metamorphic Therapy | Miasm Therapy | Micro Manipulation | Moxibustion | Mud Therapy | Music Therapy | Nail Surgery | Naturopathy | Neuro-Linguistic Program | Neurotherapy | Nutritional Therapy | Orgone Therapy | Oriental Diagnosis | Orthomolecular Medicine |
|---|---|---|---|---|---|---|---|---|---|---|---|---|---|---|---|---|---|---|---|---|---|---|---|---|---|---|---|---|---|---|---|---|---|---|---|---|---|---|---|---|---|---|---|---|---|---|---|---|---|---|
| **SURREY** ||||||||||||||||||||||||||||||||||||||||||||||||||
| ACE NUTRITION (HM00157) |||||||||||||||||||||||||||||||||||||||||||||||●||||
| ACORN HEALTH CLINIC (HM00177) |||||||||||||||||●|||||||||||||||||||||||||||||||||
| ACORN THERAPY CENTRE (HM00181) ||||||||||||●|●|||||||●|●|||||||||||||||●||||||||||||||||
| ACUHERBAL CHINESE MEDICINE (HM00214) |||||||||||||||●|||||||||||||||||||||||||||||||||||
| ALEXANDER, JANE (HM00564) |||||||||||||||||●|||||||||||||||||||||||||||||||||
| AMBER THERAPEUTIC CLINIC (HM00768) ||||||||||||||||||||||||||||||||●||||||||||||||||||
| AROMATHERAPY/REMEDIAL MASSAGE (HM01131) ||||||||||||||||||||||||||||||||||●||||||||||||||||
| ASCOT HOMEOPATHIC CLINIC (HM01177) |||||||||||●|●|||||●|||||||||||||●|||||||||||||||||||||||
| ASH, GRAHAM M (HM01182) ||||||||||||||||||||●||||||||||||||||||||||||||||||
| ASHTEAD CHARTERED PHYSIO SV (HM01230) |||||||||||||||||||||||||||●|||||●||●||||||||||||||||
| ASHTEAD CLINIC (HM01232) |||||||||||||||||●||||||||||||||||||||||||||●||||||
| ASKEY, LAURIE (HM01251) ||||||||||||||||||||●||||||||||||||||||||||||||||||
| ASTON CLINIC (HM01301) |||||||||||||||●||||||●||||●||||||||||●||||||||||||||||
| ASW ALLERGY CONSULTANTS (HM01305) ||||||||||||●|●||●|●|●|||||||||●|||||||||||||||||||||||||
| BACK TO HEALTH (HM01508) |||||||||||||||||●|||||||||||||||||||||||||||||||||
| BAIN, J M (HM01560) |||||||||||||||||●|||||||||||||||||||||||||||||||||
| BARNSTEAD VILLAGE CLINIC (HM01769) |||||||||||||||||●|||||||||||||||||||||||||||||||||
| BATEMAN, JANE (HM01870) ||||||||||||||||||||●||||||||||||||||||||||||||||||
| BAYLISS, CATHERINE (HM01940) ||||||||||||||||||||●||||||||||||||||||||||||||||||
| BENNETT, J C (HM02141) ||||||||||||||||||||●||||||||||||||||||||||||||||||
| BIGGS, MARGARET (HM02293) |||||||||||||||||●|||||||||||||||||||||||||||||||||
| BIODYNAMICS (HM02332) |||||||||||||||●|||||||||||||||||||||||||||||●|||●||||
| BLAZEY, PHILLIPA (HM02502) |||||||||||||||||●|||||||||||||||||||||||||||||||||
| BLYTH, JOSEPHINE (HM02539) ||||||||||||||||||||●||||||||||||||||||||||||||||||
| BOLD, PHILIP (HM02650) |||||||||||||||||●|||||||||||||||||||||||||||||||||
| BOOTH, N (HM02707) |||||||||||||||||●|||||||||||||||||||||||||||||||||
| BOURNE HEALTH (HM02753) |||||||||||||||||●|||||||||||||||||●||||||||||||||||
| BRABANT HOUSE CLINIC (HM02830) |||||||||||●|●|||●||●|||●|●|●|||●|||●||||●||●||●||||●||||●||||||
| BREWSTER, DAVID J (HM02980) ||||||||||||||||||||●|●||||||||||||||||||||||||||||||
| BST FOUNDATION (HM03294) ||||||||||||||||||||●|●||||||||||||||||||||||||||||||
| BURTON, GEOFFREY (HM03435) ||||||||||||||||||||●||||||||||||||||||||||||||||||
| CALLAWAY, PETER (HM03553) ||||||||||||||||||||●||||||||||||||||||||||||||||||
| CAMBERLEY NATURAL THERAPY CTRE (HM03566) |||||||||||||●|||||||||||||||||||||●||●||||||||||||||||

www.healthmyself.com

# F - O Therapies at Practices/Businesses

| Business by County with Reference no. | Family Planning (Natural) | Family Therapy | Feldenkrais Methodology | Feng Shui | Floral Essence Therapy | Flotation Therapy | Gait Analysis | Gem Essence Therapy | Gestalt Therapy | Group Therapy | Hay Diet | Healer | Healing Therapy | Hellerwork | Herbal Medicine | Holistic Healing | Homeopathy | Hopi Ear Candles | Humanistic Psychology | Hypnosis | Hypnotherapy | Indian Head Massage | Inhalation Therapy | Iridology | Kinesiology |
|---|---|---|---|---|---|---|---|---|---|---|---|---|---|---|---|---|---|---|---|---|---|---|---|---|---|
| CANE, PAT (HM03626) | | | | | | | | | | | | | | | | | | | | | | ● | | | |
| CARLTON CLINIC (HM03700) | | | | | ● | | | | | | ● | ● | ● | | ● | ● | ● | | ● | ● | ● | ● | ● | | ● |
| CHART LANE CLINIC (HM04039) | | | | | | | | | | | | | | | | | ● | | | | | | | | |
| CHI CLINIC (HM04148) | | | | | | | | | | | | | | | | | | | | | | | | | |
| CHINESE HERBAL MED & HLTH CARE (HM04204) | | | | | | | | | | | | | | | ● | | | | | | | | | | |
| CHRISTINE KEY HYPNOTHERAPIST (HM04447) | | | | | | | | | | | | | | | | | | | | ● | ● | | | | |
| CITISPORT (HM04483) | | | | | | | | | | | | | | | ● | | | | | | | | | | |
| CLEMENTS, J (HM04644) | | | | | | | | | | | | | | | | | | | | | | | | | |
| COHEN, MICHAEL (HM04793) | | | | | | | | | | | | | | | | | | | | ● | ● | | | | |
| COMPTON HOMOEOPATHY CENTRE (HM04961) | | | | | | | | | | | | | | | | | ● | | | | | | | | |
| COPELAND, ELAINE (HM05139) | | | | | | | | | | | | | | | | | | | | | | | | | ● |
| COPELAND, LIZ (HM05141) | | | | | | | | | | | | | | | ● | | | | | | | | | | |
| CORBYN, SANJEE (HM05158) | | | | | | | | | | | | | | | ● | | | | | | | | | | |
| CRANLEIGH CHIROPRACTIC CLINIC (HM05381) | | | | | | | | | | | | | | | | | ● | | | | | | | | |
| CROYDON HEALING CENTRE (HM05515) | | | | | | | | | | | | ● | ● | | | | | | | | | | | | |
| CROYDON HYPNOTHERAPY (HM05516) | | | | | | | | | | | | | | | | | | | | ● | ● | | | | |
| CULPEPER (HM05582) | | | | | | | | | | | | | | | ● | | | | | | | | | | |
| CUMMINS, ROZ (HM05617) | | | | | | | | | | | | | | | | | | | | | | | | | |
| CURATIVE HYPNOTHERAPY CENTRE (HM05628) | | | | | | | | | | | | | | | | | | | | ● | | | | | |
| D 'ARCY, LARRAINE (HM05656) | | | | | | | | | | | | | | | | | | | | ● | | | | | |
| DANIELS, INGRID (HM05726) | | | | | | | | | | | | | | | | | ● | | | | | | | | |
| DAVIS, TIM (HM05862) | | | | | | | | | | | | | | | | | | | | ● | | | | | |
| DORKING, PAUL (HM06200) | | | | | | | | | | | | | | | | | | | | ● | ● | | | | |
| EASON, GUY (HM06508) | | | | | | | | | | | | | | | | | | | | ● | | | | | |
| ECONS, A (DR) (HM06583) | | | | | | | | | | | | | | | | | | | | | | | | | |
| EDWARDS HEALTH CLINIC (HM06639) | | | | | | | | | | | | | | | | | | | ● | ● | ● | | | | |
| ENOCK-SHORE, ANGELA (HM06845) | | | | | | | | | | | | | | | | | | | | ● | ● | | | | ● |
| EQUILIBRIUM OSTEOPATHIC (HM06876) | | | | | | | | | | | | | | | | ● | | | | | | | | | |
| EREVNA (HM06882) | | | | | | | | | | | | | | | ● | | | | | | | | | | |
| G NORTHWOOD PSYCHOTHERAPY (HM07812) | | | | | | | | | | | | | | | | | | | | ● | | | | | |
| GAUVAIN, TONY (HM07934) | | | | | | | | | | | | | | | | | | | | ● | ● | | | | |
| GLASSBOROW, G W (HM08126) | | | | | | | | | | | | | | | | | | | | ● | | | | | |
| GODDARD, TERRI (HM08180) | | | | | | | | | | | | | ● | | | ● | | | | | | | | | |
| GRAVELL, NICOLA (HM08401) | | | | | | | | | | | | | | | | | | | | ● | ● | | | | |

| Business by County with Reference no. | Kirlian Photography | Laser Treatment | Life Style Coaching | Light Therapy | Macrobiotics | Magnetic Therapy | Manipulation | Manual Lymph Drainage | Massage (Therapeutic) | McTimoney Chiropractic | Meditation | Metamorphic Therapy | Miasm Therapy | Micro Manipulation | Moxibustion | Mud Therapy | Music Therapy | Nail Surgery | Naturopathy | Neuro-Linguistic Program | Neurotherapy | Nutritional Therapy | Orgone Therapy | Oriental Diagnosis | Orthomolecular Medicine |
|---|---|---|---|---|---|---|---|---|---|---|---|---|---|---|---|---|---|---|---|---|---|---|---|---|---|
| CANE, PAT (HM03626) | | | | | | | | | | | | | | | | | | | | | | | | | |
| CARLTON CLINIC (HM03700) | | | ● | | | | ● | | ● | | | | | ● | ● | | | | ● | | | ● | | ● | |
| CHART LANE CLINIC (HM04039) | | | | | | | | | | | | | | | | | | | | | | | | | |
| CHI CLINIC (HM04148) | | | | | | | | | ● | | | | | | | | | | | | | | | | |
| CHINESE HERBAL MED & HLTH CARE (HM04204) | | | | | | | | | | | | | | | | | | | | | | | | | |
| CHRISTINE KEY HYPNOTHERAPIST (HM04447) | | | | | | | | | | | | | | | | | | | | ● | | | | | |
| CITISPORT (HM04483) | | | ● | | | | ● | | ● | | | | | | | | | | ● | | | ● | | | |
| CLEMENTS, J (HM04644) | | | | | | | | | | | | | | | | | | | | | | ● | | | |
| COHEN, MICHAEL (HM04793) | | | ● | | | | | | | | | | | | | | | | | | | | | | |
| COMPTON HOMOEOPATHY CENTRE (HM04961) | | | | | | | | | | | | | | | | | | | | | | | | | |
| COPELAND, ELAINE (HM05139) | | | | | | | | | | | | | | | | | | | | | | | | | |
| COPELAND, LIZ (HM05141) | | | | | | | | | | | | | | | | | | | | | | | | | |
| CORBYN, SANJEE (HM05158) | | | | | | | | | | | | | | | | | | | | | | | | | |
| CRANLEIGH CHIROPRACTIC CLINIC (HM05381) | | | | | | | | | ● | | | | | | | | | | | | | | | | |
| CROYDON HEALING CENTRE (HM05515) | | | | | | | | | | | | | | | | | | | | | | | | | |
| CROYDON HYPNOTHERAPY (HM05516) | | | | | | | | | | | | | | | | | | | | | | | | | |
| CULPEPER (HM05582) | | | | | | | | | | | | | | | | | | | | | | | | | |
| CUMMINS, ROZ (HM05617) | | | | | | | | | | | | | | | | | | | | | | ● | | | |
| CURATIVE HYPNOTHERAPY CENTRE (HM05628) | | | | | | | | | | | | | | | | | | | | | | | | | |
| D 'ARCY, LARRAINE (HM05656) | | | | | | | | | | | | | | | | | | | | | | | | | |
| DANIELS, INGRID (HM05726) | | | | | | | | | | | | | | | | | | | | | | | | | |
| DAVIS, TIM (HM05862) | | | | | | | | | | | | | | | | | | | | | | | | | |
| DORKING, PAUL (HM06200) | | | | | | | | | | | | | | | | | | | | | | | | | |
| EASON, GUY (HM06508) | | | | | | | | | | | | | | | | | | | | | | | | | |
| ECONS, A (DR) (HM06583) | | | | | | | | | | | | | | | | | | | | | | ● | | | |
| EDWARDS HEALTH CLINIC (HM06639) | | | ● | | | | | | | | | | | | | | | | | | | | | | |
| ENOCK-SHORE, ANGELA (HM06845) | | | ● | | | | | | | | | | | | | | | | | | | | | | |
| EQUILIBRIUM OSTEOPATHIC (HM06876) | | | ● | | | | ● | | ● | | | | | | | | | | ● | | | ● | | | |
| EREVNA (HM06882) | | | | | | | | | | | | | | | | | | | | | | | | | |
| G NORTHWOOD PSYCHOTHERAPY (HM07812) | | | | | | | | | | | | | | | | | | | | | | | | | |
| GAUVAIN, TONY (HM07934) | | | ● | | | | | | | | | | | | | | | | | ● | | | | | |
| GLASSBOROW, G W (HM08126) | | | | | | | | | | | | | | | | | | | | | | | | | |
| GODDARD, TERRI (HM08180) | | | | | | | | | | | | | | | | | | | | | | | | ● | |
| GRAVELL, NICOLA (HM08401) | | | | | | | | | | | | | | | | | | | | | | | | | |

# F - O Therapies at Practices/Businesses

Business by County with Reference no.

| Business by County with Reference no. | Family Planning (Natural) | Family Therapy | Feldenkrais Methodology | Feng Shui | Floral Essence Therapy | Flotation Therapy | Gait Analysis | Gem Essence Therapy | Gestalt Therapy | Group Therapy | Hay Diet | Healer | Healing Therapy | Hellerwork | Herbal Medicine | Holistic Healing | Homeopathy | Hopi Ear Candles | Humanistic Psychology | Hypnosis | Hypnotherapy | Indian Head Massage | Inhalation Therapy | Iridology | Kinesiology |
|---|---|---|---|---|---|---|---|---|---|---|---|---|---|---|---|---|---|---|---|---|---|---|---|---|---|
| HADDEN, ROGER (HM08688) | | | | | | | | | | | | | | | | | ● | | | | | | | | |
| HANFORD, S P (HM08925) | | | | | | | | | | | | | | | | | | | | | | | | ● | |
| HARDY, JACK E (HM08981) | | | | | | | | | | | | | | | | | | | | ● | ● | | | | |
| HARRIS, MICHELLE J (HM09082) | | | | | | | | | | | | | | | | | | | | ● | | | | | |
| HARRIS-BEACH, JULIE (HM09090) | | | | | | | | | | | | | | | | | | | | ● | | | | | |
| HELIANTHUS PRACTICE (HM09518) | | | | | | | | | | | | | | | ● | ● | ● | | | | | | | | |
| HERBAL KING (HM09628) | | | | | | | | | | | | | | | ● | | | | | | | | | | |
| HERBALS (HM09647) | | | | | | | | | | | | | | | ● | | | | | | | | | | |
| HOBBS, DIANA C (HM09854) | | | | | | | | | | | | | | | | | | | | ● | | | | | |
| HODSON, D (HM09894) | | | | | | | | | | | | | | | | | | | | ● | | | | | |
| HOLISTIC CENTRE (HM09949) | | | | | | | | | | | | | | | ● | | ● | | | | | ● | | | |
| HOLISTIC HEALTH CENTRE (HM09971) | | | | | | | | | | | | | | | | | ● | | | | | | | | |
| HOPPER, C A (HM10156) | | | | | | | | | ● | | | | | | | | | | | | | | | | |
| HYPNOTHERAPY & STRESS CON (HM10541) | | | | | | | | | | | | | | | | | | | | ● | | | | | |
| HYPNOTHERAPY FOR CHANGE (HM10539) | | | | | | | | | | | | | | | | | | | | ● | | | | | |
| INCE, ROBERT J (HM10602) | | | | | | | | | | | | | | | | | ● | | | | | | | | |
| INTEGRAL HEALTH (HM10690) | | | | | | | | | | | | | | | | | | | | | | | | | ● |
| KATHERINE'S THERAPIES (HM11339) | | | | | | | | | | | | | | | | | | | | | | | | | |
| KAY, ANDREA (HM11350) | | | | | | | | | | | | | | | | | | | | ● | | | | | |
| KENNING, GILLIAN (HM11502) | | | | | | | | | | | | | | | | | | | | ● | | | | | |
| KENT CLINIC OF NATURAL MED (HM11514) | | ● | | | | | | | | | ● | ● | ● | | ● | ● | ● | | ● | ● | ● | | | | ● |
| KEW CHIROPRACTIC CLINIC (HM11575) | | | | | | | | | | | | | | | | | | | | | | | | | ● |
| KINGSTON & RICHMOND HYNO CTRE (HM11674) | | | | | | | | | | | | | | | | | | | | ● | | | | | |
| KINGSTON NATURAL HEALING CTRE (HM11677) | | ● | | | | | | | | | | ● | | | | | ● | | | | ● | | | | ● |
| KINGSTON OSTEOPATHS (HM11679) | | | | | | | | | | | | | | | | | | | | | | | | | |
| KOHLER, SUE (HM11778) | | | | | | | | | | | | | | | | | | | | | | ● | | | |
| KOLTHAMMER, JOHN (HM11780) | | | | | | | | | | | | | | | | | | | | | | | | | |
| LARKMAN, K (HM11977) | | | | | | | | | | | | | | | | | ● | | | | | | | | |
| LEE, ROBIN (HM12145) | | | | | | | | | | | | | | | | | | | | ● | | | | | |
| LEGGETTER, D (HM12178) | | | | | | | | | | | | | | | | | | | | ● | | | | | |
| LEMON, RORY (HM12208) | | | | | | | | | | | | | | | | | | | | | | ● | | | |
| LIFE STYLE NATURAL HEALTH CTRE (HM12349) | | | | | | | | | | | | | | | ● | | ● | | | | | | | ● | |
| LOGAN, ROBIN (HM12568) | | | | | | | | | | | | | | | | | ● | | | | | | | | |
| LONDON SPINE AND JOINT CLINIC (HM12610) | | | | | | | | | | | | | | | | | ● | | | | | ● | | | |

| Business by County with Reference no. | Kirlian Photography | Laser Treatment | Life Style Coaching | Light Therapy | Macrobiotics | Magnetic Therapy | Manipulation | Manual Lymph Drainage | Massage (Therapeutic) | McTimoney Chiropractic | Meditation | Metamorphic Therapy | Miasm Therapy | Micro Manipulation | Moxibustion | Mud Therapy | Music Therapy | Nail Surgery | Naturopathy | Neuro-Linguistic Program | Neurotherapy | Nutritional Therapy | Orgone Therapy | Oriental Diagnosis | Orthomolecular Medicine |
|---|---|---|---|---|---|---|---|---|---|---|---|---|---|---|---|---|---|---|---|---|---|---|---|---|---|
| HADDEN, ROGER (HM08688) | | | | | | | | | | | | | | | | | | | | | | | | | |
| HANFORD, S P (HM08925) | | | | | | | | | | | | | | | | | | | | | | | | | |
| HARDY, JACK E (HM08981) | | | | | | | | | | | | | | | | | | | | | | | | | |
| HARRIS, MICHELLE J (HM09082) | | | | | | | | | | | | | | | | | | | | | | | | | |
| HARRIS-BEACH, JULIE (HM09090) | | | | | | | | | | | | | | | | | | | | | | | | | |
| HELIANTHUS PRACTICE (HM09518) | | | | | | | | | | | | | | | | | | | | | | ● | | | |
| HERBAL KING (HM09628) | | | | | | | | | ● | | | | | | | | | | | | | | | | |
| HERBALS (HM09647) | | | | | | | | | | | | | | | | | | | | | | ● | | | |
| HOBBS, DIANA C (HM09854) | | | | | | | | | | | | | | | | | | | | | | | | | |
| HODSON, D (HM09894) | | | | | | | | | | | | | | | | | | | | | | | | | |
| HOLISTIC CENTRE (HM09949) | | | | | | | | | ● | | | | | | | | | | ● | | | | | | |
| HOLISTIC HEALTH CENTRE (HM09971) | | | | | | | | | | | | | | | | | | | | | | | | | |
| HOPPER, C A (HM10156) | | | | | | | | | | | | | | | | | | | | | | | | | |
| HYPNOTHERAPY & STRESS CON (HM10541) | | | | | | | | | | | | | | | | | | | | | | | | | |
| HYPNOTHERAPY FOR CHANGE (HM10539) | | | | | | | | | | | | | | | | | | | | | | | | | |
| INCE, ROBERT J (HM10602) | | | | | | | | | | | | | | | | | | | | | | | | | |
| INTEGRAL HEALTH (HM10690) | | | | | | | | | | | | | | | | | | | | | | ● | | | |
| KATHERINE'S THERAPIES (HM11339) | | | | | | | | | ● | | | | | | | | | | | | | | | | |
| KAY, ANDREA (HM11350) | | | | | | | | | | | | | | | | | | | | | | | | | |
| KENNING, GILLIAN (HM11502) | | | | | | | | | | | | | | | | | | | | | | | | | |
| KENT CLINIC OF NATURAL MED (HM11514) | | | ● | | | | ● | | ● | | ● | | ● | | | | | | | | | ● | | | |
| KEW CHIROPRACTIC CLINIC (HM11575) | | | | | | | ● | | ● | | | | | | | | | | | | | | | | |
| KINGSTON & RICHMOND HYNO CTRE (HM11674) | | | | | | | | | | | | | | | | | | | | | | | | | |
| KINGSTON NATURAL HEALING CTRE (HM11677) | | | | | | | | | ● | | | | | | | | | | | | | | | | |
| KINGSTON OSTEOPATHS (HM11679) | | | | | | | ● | | ● | | | | | | | | | | | | | | | | |
| KOHLER, SUE (HM11778) | | | | | | | | | | | | | | | | | | | | | | | | | |
| KOLTHAMMER, JOHN (HM11780) | | | | | | | ● | | | | | | | | | | | | | | | | | | |
| LARKMAN, K (HM11977) | | | | | | | | | | | | | | | | | | | | | | | | | |
| LEE, ROBIN (HM12145) | | | | | | | | | | | | | | | | | | | | | | | | | |
| LEGGETTER, D (HM12178) | | | | | | | | | | | | | | | | | | | | | | | | | |
| LEMON, RORY (HM12208) | | | | | | | | | ● | | | | | | | | | | | | | | | | |
| LIFE STYLE NATURAL HEALTH CTRE (HM12349) | | | | | | | | | ● | | | | | | | | | | | | | ● | | | |
| LOGAN, ROBIN (HM12568) | | | | | | | | | | | | | | | | | | | | | | | | | |
| LONDON SPINE AND JOINT CLINIC (HM12610) | | | | | | | ● | | ● | | | | | | | | | | | | | | | | |

# F - O Therapies at Practices/Businesses

| Business by County with Reference no. | Family Planning (Natural) | Family Therapy | Feldenkrais Methodology | Feng Shui | Floral Essence Therapy | Flotation Therapy | Gait Analysis | Gem Essence Therapy | Gestalt Therapy | Group Therapy | Hay Diet | Healer | Healing Therapy | Hellerwork | Herbal Medicine | Holistic Healing | Homeopathy | Hopi Ear Candles | Humanistic Psychology | Hypnosis | Hypnotherapy | Indian Head Massage | Inhalation Therapy | Iridology | Kinesiology |
|---|---|---|---|---|---|---|---|---|---|---|---|---|---|---|---|---|---|---|---|---|---|---|---|---|---|
| MANTLE, FIONA (HM13054) | | | | | | | | | | | | | | | | | | | | | ● | | | | |
| MANTLE, FIONA (HM13053) | | | | | | | | | | | | | | | | | | | | ● | | | | | |
| MARCH, THIERRY (HM13069) | | | | | | | | | | | | | | | ● | | | | | | | | | | |
| MARDEL, JEREMY (HM13081) | | | | | | | | | | | | | | | | | ● | | | | | | | | |
| MARDEL, JEREMY (HM13082) | | | | | | | | | | | | | | | | | ● | | | | | | | | |
| MARKS, DARREN HYPNOTHERAPY (HM13120) | | | | | | | | | | | | | | | | | | | | ● | ● | | | | |
| MARSON, JOY (HM13178) | | | | | | | | | | | | | | | | | | | | | | | | ● | |
| MCALLISTER, LIN (HM13367) | | | | | | | | | | | | | | | | | | | | ● | | | | | |
| MEDICAL HYPNOTHERAPY CLINIC (HM13653) | | | | | | | | | | | | | | | | | | | | ● | | | | | |
| MEENEGHAN, TOM (HM13685) | | | | | | | | | | | | | | | ● | | ● | | | | | | | | |
| METAFORCE (HM13764) | | | | | | | | | | | | | | | | | | | | ● | | | | | |
| MILFORD MASSAGE PRACTICE (HM13863) | | | | | | | | | | | | | | | | | | | | | | | | | |
| MILLER CONSULTANCY (HM13880) | | | | | | | | | | | | | ● | | | | | | | ● | ● | | | | |
| MIND AND BODY (HM13958) | | | | | | | | | | | | | | | | | ● | | | | ● | ● | | ● | ● |
| MIRZA, ISHRET (HM13990) | | | | | | | | | | | | | | | ● | | | | | | | | | | |
| MIST, CORINNE (HM13996) | | | | | | | | | | | | | | | | | | | | | | ● | | | |
| MITCHELL, JANE (HM14011) | | | | | | | | | | | | | | | ● | | | | | | | | | | |
| MYLES, JOHN (HM14442) | | | | | | | | | | | | | | | | | | | | ● | | | | | |
| NATURAL HEALING CENTRE (HM14541) | | | | | | | | | | | | | | | | | | ● | | | | ● | | | |
| NATURAL HEALING CLINIC (HM14550) | | | | | | | | | | | | | | | | | | | | | | | | | |
| NATURAL HEALTH PRACTICE (HM14594) | | | | | | | | | | | | | | | | | | | | | | | | | |
| NATURAL LIFE AROMATHERAPY (HM14608) | | | | | | | | | | | | | | | ● | | ● | | | | | | | ● | |
| NICOLA FRY-HEALTH & BEAUTY (HM14927) | | | | | | | | | | | | | | | | | | | | | | ● | | | |
| NOCKOLDS, JENNY (HM14976) | | | | | | | | | | | | | | | | | ● | | | | | | | | |
| NOCKOLDS, JENNY (HM14977) | | | | | | | | | | | | | | | | | ● | | | | | | | | |
| O'BRIEN, JANE (HM15184) | | | | | | | | | | | | | | | | | ● | | | | | | | | |
| OLD WOKING GRANGE (HM15264) | | | ● | | ● | | | | | | | ● | ● | | | ● | ● | | | ● | ● | ● | | ● | ● |
| ORRISS, GEOFF (HM15408) | | | | | | | | | | | | | | | | | | | | ● | | | | | |
| OSTEOPATHY (HM15477) | | | | | | | | | | | | | | | | | | | | | | | | | |
| PALMER, JUNE (HM15608) | | | | | | | | | | | | | | | | | | | | ● | | | | | |
| PENWARDEN, F (HM16000) | | | | | | | | | | | | | | | | | ● | | | | | | | | |
| PERRY, JUDITH (HM16048) | | | | | | | | | | | | | | | | | ● | | | | | | | | |
| PETERS, CAROL (HM16082) | | | | | | | | | | | | | | | | | | | | ● | | | | | |
| PHILP, CHRISTINE (HM16147) | | | | | | | | | | | | | | | | | | | | | | | | | |

| Business by County with Reference no. | Kirlian Photography | Laser Treatment | Life Style Coaching | Light Therapy | Macrobiotics | Magnetic Therapy | Manipulation | Manual Lymph Drainage | Massage (Therapeutic) | McTimoney Chiropractic | Meditation | Metamorphic Therapy | Miasm Therapy | Micro Manipulation | Moxibustion | Mud Therapy | Music Therapy | Nail Surgery | Naturopathy | Neuro-Linguistic Program | Neurotherapy | Nutritional Therapy | Orgone Therapy | Oriental Diagnosis | Orthomolecular Medicine |
|---|---|---|---|---|---|---|---|---|---|---|---|---|---|---|---|---|---|---|---|---|---|---|---|---|---|
| MANTLE, FIONA (HM13054) | | | | | | | | | | | | | | | | | | | | | | | | | |
| MANTLE, FIONA (HM13053) | | | | | | | | | | | | | | | | | | | | | | | | | |
| MARCH, THIERRY (HM13069) | | | | | | | | | | | | | | | | | | | | | | | | | |
| MARDEL, JEREMY (HM13081) | | | | | | | | | | | | | | | | | | | | | | | | | |
| MARDEL, JEREMY (HM13082) | | | | | | | | | | | | | | | | | | | | | | | | | |
| MARKS, DARREN HYPNOTHERAPY (HM13120) | | | | | | | | | | | | | | | | | | | | | | | | | |
| MARSON, JOY (HM13178) | | | | | | | | | | | | | | | | | | | | | | ● | | | |
| MCALLISTER, LIN (HM13367) | | | | | | | | | | | | | | | | | | | | | | | | | |
| MEDICAL HYPNOTHERAPY CLINIC (HM13653) | | | | | | | | | | | | | | | | | | | | | | | | | |
| MEENEGHAN, TOM (HM13685) | | | | | | | | | | | | | ● | | | | | | | | | | | | |
| METAFORCE (HM13764) | | | | | | | | | | | | | | | | | | | | | | | | | |
| MILFORD MASSAGE PRACTICE (HM13863) | | | | | | | ● | | | | | | | | | | | | | | | | | | |
| MILLER CONSULTANCY (HM13880) | | | | | | ● | | | | | | | | | | | | | | | | | | | |
| MIND AND BODY (HM13958) | | | | | | | | | ● | | | | | | | | | | | | | | | | |
| MIRZA, ISHRET (HM13990) | | | | | | | | | | | | | | | | | | | | | | | | | |
| MIST, CORINNE (HM13996) | | | | | | | | | ● | | | | | | | | | | | | | | | | |
| MITCHELL, JANE (HM14011) | | | | | | | | | | | | | | | | | | | | | | | | | |
| MYLES, JOHN (HM14442) | | | | | | | | | | | | | | | | | | | | | | | | | |
| NATURAL HEALING CENTRE (HM14541) | | | | | | | | | | | | | | | | | | | | | | | | | |
| NATURAL HEALING CLINIC (HM14550) | | | | | | | | | ● | | | | | | | | | | | | | | | | |
| NATURAL HEALTH PRACTICE (HM14594) | | | | | | | | | ● | | | | | | | | | | ● | | | | | | |
| NATURAL LIFE AROMATHERAPY (HM14608) | | | | | | | | | ● | | | | | | | | | | | | | ● | | | |
| NICOLA FRY-HEALTH & BEAUTY (HM14927) | | | | | | | | ● | ● | | | | | | | | | | | | | | | | |
| NOCKOLDS, JENNY (HM14976) | | | | | | | | | | | | | | | | | | | | | | | | | |
| NOCKOLDS, JENNY (HM14977) | | | | | | | | | | | | | | | | | | | | | | | | | |
| O'BRIEN, JANE (HM15184) | | | | | | | | | | | | | | | | | | | | | | | | | |
| OLD WOKING GRANGE (HM15264) | | | ● | | ● | | | | ● | | ● | ● | | | | | ● | | ● | | | ● | | | |
| ORRISS, GEOFF (HM15408) | | | | | | | | | | | | | | | | | | | | | | | | | |
| OSTEOPATHY (HM15477) | | | | | | | ● | | | | | | | | | | | | | | | | | | |
| PALMER, JUNE (HM15608) | | | | | | | | | | | | | | | | | | | | | | | | | |
| PENWARDEN, F (HM16000) | | | | | | | | | | | | | | | | | | | | | | | | | |
| PERRY, JUDITH (HM16048) | | | | | | | | | | | | | | | | | | | | | | | | | |
| PETERS, CAROL (HM16082) | | | | | | | | | | | | | | | | | | | | | | | | | |
| PHILP, CHRISTINE (HM16147) | | | | | | | | | ● | | | | | | | | | | | | | | | | |

# F - O Therapies at Practices/Businesses

| Business by County with Reference no. | Family Planning (Natural) | Family Therapy | Feldenkrais Methodology | Feng Shui | Floral Essence Therapy | Flotation Therapy | Gait Analysis | Gem Essence Therapy | Gestalt Therapy | Group Therapy | Hay Diet | Healer | Healing Therapy | Hellerwork | Herbal Medicine | Holistic Healing | Homeopathy | Hopi Ear Candles | Humanistic Psychology | Hypnosis | Hypnotherapy | Indian Head Massage | Inhalation Therapy | Iridology | Kinesiology |
|---|---|---|---|---|---|---|---|---|---|---|---|---|---|---|---|---|---|---|---|---|---|---|---|---|---|
| PRIEST, JILLIAN (HM16607) | | | | | | | | | | | | | | | | | ● | | | | | | | | |
| RICHMOND PHYSIOTHERAPY (HM17301) | | | | | | | | | | | | | | | | | | | | | | | | | |
| ROBYNA, ANNETTE (HM17516) | | | | | | | | | | | | | ● | | | | | | | | | | | | |
| ROSEMOUNT CLINIC OF COMP MED (HM17624) | | | | | | | | | | | | | | | | | ● | | | | | | | | |
| SARAH BOGUE HOMEOPATH (HM17944) | | | | | | | | | | | | | | | | | ● | | | | | | | | |
| SAYER, MARK (HM17995) | | | | | | | | | | | | | | | | | | | | ● | | | | | |
| SCHONBERG, VERA (HM18078) | | | | | | | | | | | | ● | ● | | | ● | | | | ● | ● | | | | ● |
| SCORPIO PHYSIOTHERAPY (HM18103) | | | | | | | | | | | | | | | | | | | | | | | | | |
| SELSDON COMP/RESP CLINIC (HM18220) | | | | | ● | | | | ● | | | ● | ● | | ● | ● | ● | | ● | ● | ● | | | ● | ● |
| SEVEN SIGHS (HM18244) | | | | | | | | | | | | | | | | | | | | | | ● | | | |
| SIMMS, KATHERINE (HM18564) | | | | | | | | | | | | | | | | | | | | | | | | | |
| SIMPSON, PAT (HM18596) | | | | | | | | | | | | | | | | | | | | ● | | | | | |
| SMITH, EDWARD J (HM18738) | | | | | | | | | | | | | | | | | | | | ● | | | | | |
| SOUTHBOROUGH COMP HLTH PRAC (HM18921) | | | | | | | | | | | | | | | | | | | | ● | | | | | |
| STRIKE, SUE (HM19406) | | | | | | | | | | | | | | | | | | | | | | ● | | | |
| SURBITON NATURAL HEALTH CENTRE (HM19514) | | | | | | | | | | | | | | | ● | | | | | | | | | | |
| SURREY HEALING SANCTUARY (HM19522) | | | | | | | | | | | | ● | ● | | ● | ● | | | | | | | | | |
| SUTTON HYPNOTHERAPY (HM19548) | | | | | | | | | | | | | | | | | | | | ● | | | | | |
| SYMONS, MARLIESE (HM19628) | | | | | | | | | | | | | | | | | ● | | | | | | | | |
| TANSILL, LUCY (HM19689) | | | | | | | | | | | | | | | | | | | | | ● | | | | |
| TELLING, PAUL (HM19824) | | | | | | | | | | | | ● | ● | | | | | | | | | ● | | | |
| TEMPLEMAN, C (HM19830) | | | | | | | | | | | | | | | | | | | | ● | | | | | |
| TENGER, ZOE (HM19836) | | | | | | | | | | | | | | | | | ● | | | | | | | | |
| TOLMIE, LINDA (HM20125) | | | | | | | | | | | | | | | | | | | | ● | | | | | |
| TOWNS, KATE (HM20202) | | | | | | | | | | | | | ● | | | | | | | ● | ● | | | | |
| TRANSCENDENTAL MEDIATION (HM20265) | | | | | | | | | | | | | | | | | | | | | | | | | |
| TRANSCENDENTAL MEDITATION (HM20266) | | | | | | | | | | | | | | | | | | | | | | | | | |
| TURNER, R E (HM20435) | | | | | | | | | | | | | | | | | | | | | | | | | |
| WALKER, SARAH (HM20803) | | | | | | | | | | | | | | | | | | | | | | ● | | | |
| WALLACE, SUE (HM20832) | | | | | | | | | | | | | | | | ● | | | | | | | | | |
| WALTON HOMOEOPATHY (HM20883) | | | | | | | | | | | | | | | | | ● | | | | | | | | |
| WHARAM, J (HM21297) | | | | | | | | | | | | | | | ● | | | | | | | | | | |
| WILKINS, DAVID (HM21501) | | | | | | | | | | | | | | | | | | | | ● | | | | | |
| WILKINSON, LESLEY (HM21510) | | | | | ● | | | | | | | | | | | ● | ● | | | | | | | | |

| Business by County with Reference no. | Kirlian Photography | Laser Treatment | Life Style Coaching | Light Therapy | Macrobiotics | Magnetic Therapy | Manipulation | Manual Lymph Drainage | Massage (Therapeutic) | McTimoney Chiropractic | Meditation | Metamorphic Therapy | Miasm Therapy | Micro Manipulation | Moxibustion | Mud Therapy | Music Therapy | Nail Surgery | Naturopathy | Neuro-Linguistic Program | Neurotherapy | Nutritional Therapy | Orgone Therapy | Oriental Diagnosis | Orthomolecular Medicine |
|---|---|---|---|---|---|---|---|---|---|---|---|---|---|---|---|---|---|---|---|---|---|---|---|---|---|
| PRIEST, JILLIAN (HM16607) | | | | | | | | | | | | | | | | | | | | | | | | | |
| RICHMOND PHYSIOTHERAPY (HM17301) | | | | | | | | | ● | | | | | | | | | | | | | | | | |
| ROBYNA, ANNETTE (HM17516) | | | | | | | | | ● | | ● | | | | | | | | | | | | | | |
| ROSEMOUNT CLINIC OF COMP MED (HM17624) | | | | | | | | | | | | | | | | | | | | | | | | | |
| SARAH BOGUE HOMEOPATH (HM17944) | | | | | | | | | | | | | | | | | | | | | | | | | |
| SAYER, MARK (HM17995) | | | | | | | | | | | | | | | | | | | | | | | | | |
| SCHONBERG, VERA (HM18078) | | | | | | | | | ● | | ● | | | | | | | | | | | | | | |
| SCORPIO PHYSIOTHERAPY (HM18103) | | | | | | | ● | | ● | | | | | | | | | | | | | | | | |
| SELSDON COMP/RESP CLINIC (HM18220) | | | | | | | | | | | ● | | | | | | | | ● | | | ● | | ● | ● |
| SEVEN SIGHS (HM18244) | | | | | | | | | | | | ● | | | | | | | | | | | | | |
| SIMMS, KATHERINE (HM18564) | | | | | | | | | | | ● | | | | | | | | | | | | | | |
| SIMPSON, PAT (HM18596) | | | | | | | | | | | | | | | | | | | | | | | | | |
| SMITH, EDWARD J (HM18738) | | | | | | | | | | | | | | | | | | | | | | | | | |
| SOUTHBOROUGH COMP HLTH PRAC (HM18921) | | | | | | | | | | | | | | | | | | | | | | | | | |
| STRIKE, SUE (HM19406) | | | | | | | | | | | | | | | | | | | | | | | | | |
| SURBITON NATURAL HEALTH CENTRE (HM19514) | | | | | | | | | | | | | | | | | | | | | | ● | | | |
| SURREY HEALING SANCTUARY (HM19522) | | | | | | | | | | | | | | | | | | | | | | | | | |
| SUTTON HYPNOTHERAPY (HM19548) | | | | | | | | | | | | | | | | | | | | | | | | | |
| SYMONS, MARLIESE (HM19628) | | | | | | | | | | | | | | | | | | | | | | | | | |
| TANSILL, LUCY (HM19689) | | | | | | | | | | | | | | | | | | | ● | | | | | | |
| TELLING, PAUL (HM19824) | | | | | | | | | ● | | | | | | | | | | | | | | | | |
| TEMPLEMAN, C (HM19830) | | | | | | | | | | | | | | | | | | | | | | | | | |
| TENGER, ZOE (HM19836) | | | | | | | | | | | | | | | | | | | | | | | | | |
| TOLMIE, LINDA (HM20125) | | | | | | | | | | | | | | | | | | | | | | | | | |
| TOWNS, KATE (HM20202) | | | | | | | | | | | | | | | | | | | | ● | | | | | |
| TRANSCENDENTAL MEDIATION (HM20265) | | | | | | | | | | | ● | | | | | | | | | | | | | | |
| TRANSCENDENTAL MEDITATION (HM20266) | | | | | | | | | | | ● | | | | | | | | | | | | | | |
| TURNER, R E (HM20435) | | | | | | | ● | | | | | | | | | | | | | | | | | | |
| WALKER, SARAH (HM20803) | | | | | | | | | | | | | | | | | | | ● | | | ● | | | |
| WALLACE, SUE (HM20832) | | | | | | | | | | | | | | | | | | | | | | | | | |
| WALTON HOMOEOPATHY (HM20883) | | | | | | | | | | | | | | | | | | | | | | | | | |
| WHARAM, J (HM21297) | | | | | | | | | | | | | | | | | | | | | | | | | |
| WILKINS, DAVID (HM21501) | | | | | | | | | | | | | | | | | | | | | | | | | |
| WILKINSON, LESLEY (HM21510) | | | | | | | | | | | | | | | | | | | | | | | | | |

# F - O Therapies at Practices/Businesses

| Business by County with Reference no. | Family Planning (Natural) | Family Therapy | Feldenkrais Methodology | Feng Shui | Floral Essence Therapy | Flotation Therapy | Gait Analysis | Gem Essence Therapy | Gestalt Therapy | Group Therapy | Hay Diet | Healer | Healing Therapy | Hellerwork | Herbal Medicine | Holistic Healing | Homeopathy | Hopi Ear Candles | Humanistic Psychology | Hypnosis | Hypnotherapy | Indian Head Massage | Inhalation Therapy | Iridology | Kinesiology | Kirlian Photography | Laser Treatment | Life Style Coaching | Light Therapy | Macrobiotics | Magnetic Therapy | Manipulation | Manual Lymph Drainage | Massage (Therapeutic) | McTimoney Chiropractic | Meditation | Metamorphic Therapy | Miasm Therapy | Micro Manipulation | Moxibustion | Mud Therapy | Music Therapy | Nail Surgery | Naturopathy | Neuro-Linguistic Program | Neurotherapy | Nutritional Therapy | Orgone Therapy | Oriental Diagnosis | Orthomolecular Medicine |
|---|---|---|---|---|---|---|---|---|---|---|---|---|---|---|---|---|---|---|---|---|---|---|---|---|---|---|---|---|---|---|---|---|---|---|---|---|---|---|---|---|---|---|---|---|---|---|---|---|---|---|
| WILLIAMS, SONIA (HM21591) |||||||||||||||||||●|||||||||||||||||||||||||||||||
| WILLIS, SALLY (HM21618) |||||||||●||||||||||||||||||||||||||||||||||||||||||
| WILSON, SALLY-ANNE (HM21671) ||||||||||||||||●|||||||||||||||||||||||||||||||||
| WOODLANDS NATURAL HLTH THERAPY (HM21832) |||||||||||●|||||||||||●||||||||||||||||||||||●||||
| WRIGHT, L (HM21942) |||||||||||||||||||●|||||||||||||||||||||||||||||||
| WYATT, JULIE (HM21966) |||||||||||||||||||●|||||||||||||||||||||||||||||||
| SUSSEX (EAST) ||||||||||||||||||||||||||||||||||||||||||||||||||||
| ALBION CLINIC (HM00483) ||||||||||||||●||●||||||||||||||||●|||||||||||||||||
| ALPHA HYPNOTHERAPY (HM00684) |||||||||||||||||||●|●||||||||||||||||||||||||||||||
| ANGELA MATTHEWS HOMEOPATH (HM00873) |||||||||||||||●|●||||||||||||||||||||||||||||||||||
| ARDERN FOOT & HEALTH CLINIC (HM00992) |||||||||||||||||||||●|||||||||||||||||||||||||●||||
| AROMA HAIR (HM01047) ||||||||||||||||||||●|●|||||||||||||||||||||||||||||
| ASHDOWN OSTEOPATHIC CENTRE (HM01206) ||||||||||||||||●|||||●|||●|||||||●||●||||||||||●|||||||
| BAIRD, DAVID (HM01569) |||||||||||||||||||●||●|||●|||||||||●|●|●||||||||●|||●||||
| BALCOMBE, WILLIAM (HM01610) ||||||||||||||||●|||||||||||||||||||||||||||||||||||
| BARKER, C (HM01704) |||||||||||||||||||●|||||||||||||||||||||||||||||||
| BASSETT, N S (HM01857) ||||||||||||||||●|||||||||||||||||||||||||||||||||||
| BELVAIN, E (HM02118) |||||||||||||||||||||||||||||||||●|||||||||||||||||
| BEXHILL CHIROPRACTIC (HM02255) |||||||||||||||||||||||||||||||●||●|||||||||||||||||
| BEXHILL OSTEOPATHIC PRACTICE (HM02257) ||||||||||||||||●|||||||||||||||||||||||||||||||||||
| BLACKER, JOHN (HM02441) |||||||||||||||||||●|●||||||||||||||||||||||||||||||
| BOURNE, JOHN (HM02755) |||||||||||||||||||||●||||||||||||●|||||||||||||||||
| BRIARS CLINIC (HM02986) ||||||||||||||●||||||||||||||||||||||||||||||||||||
| BRIGHTON CHIROPRACTIC CLINIC (HM03044) |||||||||||||||||||||||||||||||||●|||||||||||||||||
| CANTERLA, MARGARET (HM03643) |||||||||||||||●|●||||||||||||||||||||||||||||||||||
| CHEDGEY, PAUL (HM04076) ||||||||||||||●||||||||||||||||||||||||||||||||||||
| CLINIC OF CHINESE MED & ACU (HM04685) ||||||||||||||●||||||||||||||||||||||||||||||||||||
| CLINICAL CENTRE OF CHINESE MED (HM04712) ||||||||||||||●||||||||||||||||||||||||||||||||||||
| COKAYNE, FRANK (HM04799) |||||||||||||||||||●|||||||||||||||||||||||||||||||
| COMP THERAPY & TRAINING CENTRE (HM04915) |||||||||||||||●|●||||●|●|||||||||||||||||||||||||||||
| CONCEPTS PHYSIO & NUTRITION (HM04970) ||||||||||●||||||●||||||||●|||●||||●||●||||||||||●|||●||||
| CONWAY, SUSAN (HM05032) |||||||||||||||||||●|||||||||||||||||||||||||||||||
| COOK, ELAINE (HM05042) |||||||||||||||||||||||||||||||||||||||●|||||||||||
| CRESENT CLINIC (HM05422) ||||||||||||||●|●|●||||●||||●|||||||●||●||||||||||●|||●||||

# F - O Therapies at Practices/Businesses

| Business by County with Reference no. | Family Planning (Natural) | Family Therapy | Feldenkrais Methodology | Feng Shui | Floral Essence Therapy | Flotation Therapy | Gait Analysis | Gem Essence Therapy | Gestalt Therapy | Group Therapy | Hay Diet | Healer | Healing Therapy | Hellerwork | Herbal Medicine | Holistic Healing | Homeopathy | Hopi Ear Candles | Humanistic Psychology | Hypnosis | Hypnotherapy | Indian Head Massage | Inhalation Therapy | Iridology | Kinesiology | Kirlian Photography | Laser Treatment | Life Style Coaching | Light Therapy | Macrobiotics | Magnetic Therapy | Manipulation | Manual Lymph Drainage | Massage (Therapeutic) | McTimoney Chiropractic | Meditation | Metamorphic Therapy | Miasm Therapy | Micro Manipulation | Moxibustion | Mud Therapy | Music Therapy | Nail Surgery | Naturopathy | Neuro-Linguistic Program | Neurotherapy | Nutritional Therapy | Orgone Therapy | Oriental Diagnosis | Orthomolecular Medicine |
|---|---|---|---|---|---|---|---|---|---|---|---|---|---|---|---|---|---|---|---|---|---|---|---|---|---|---|---|---|---|---|---|---|---|---|---|---|---|---|---|---|---|---|---|---|---|---|---|---|---|---|
| CROWBOROUGH CHIRO/COMP HLTH (HM05498) |  |  |  |  |  |  |  |  |  |  |  |  | ● |  |  |  | ● |  |  |  |  |  |  |  |  |  |  |  |  |  |  | ● |  | ● |  | ● |  |  |  |  |  |  |  |  |  |  | ● |  |  |  |
| CROWBOROUGH COMP THERAPISTS (HM05499) |  |  |  |  |  |  |  |  |  |  |  |  |  |  |  |  | ● |  |  |  |  | ● |  |  | ● |  |  |  |  |  |  |  |  | ● |  |  |  |  |  |  |  |  |  |  |  |  |  |  |  |  |
| CULL, BEN (HM05556) |  |  |  |  |  |  |  |  |  |  |  |  |  |  |  |  |  |  |  | ● |  |  |  |  |  |  |  |  |  |  |  |  |  |  |  |  |  |  |  |  |  |  |  |  |  |  |  |  |  |  |
| CULPEPER (HM05584) |  |  |  |  |  |  |  |  |  |  |  |  |  |  | ● |  |  |  |  |  |  |  |  |  |  |  |  |  |  |  |  |  |  |  |  |  |  |  |  |  |  |  |  |  |  |  |  |  |  |  |
| DADSWELL, CLAIRE (HM05670) |  |  |  |  |  |  |  |  |  |  |  |  |  |  |  |  | ● |  |  |  |  |  |  |  |  |  |  |  |  |  |  |  |  |  |  |  |  |  |  |  |  |  |  |  |  |  |  |  |  |  |
| DEEKS, STUART (HM05956) |  |  |  |  |  |  |  |  |  |  |  |  |  |  |  |  | ● |  |  |  |  |  |  |  |  |  |  |  |  |  |  |  |  |  |  |  |  |  |  |  |  |  |  |  |  |  |  |  |  |  |
| DRIVE OSTEO AND SPORTS CLINIC (HM06314) |  |  |  |  |  |  |  |  |  |  |  |  |  |  |  |  | ● |  |  |  |  |  |  |  |  |  |  |  |  |  |  | ● |  | ● |  |  |  |  |  |  |  |  |  |  |  |  |  |  |  |  |
| DRURY, GILLIAN (HM06330) |  |  |  |  |  |  |  |  |  |  |  |  |  |  |  |  |  |  |  | ● |  |  |  |  |  |  |  |  |  |  |  |  |  |  |  |  |  |  |  |  |  |  |  |  |  |  |  |  |  |  |
| DRYDEN, B A (HM06332) |  |  |  |  |  |  |  |  |  |  |  |  |  |  |  |  |  |  |  | ● | ● |  |  |  |  |  |  |  |  |  |  |  |  |  |  |  |  |  |  |  |  |  |  |  |  |  |  |  |  |  |
| DYKE ROAD NATURAL HEALTH (HM06450) |  |  |  |  |  |  |  |  |  |  |  |  |  |  |  |  | ● |  |  |  |  |  |  |  |  |  |  |  |  |  |  |  |  | ● |  |  |  |  |  |  |  |  |  |  |  |  | ● |  |  |  |
| EAST BOURNE CLINIC (HM06509) |  |  |  |  |  |  |  |  |  |  |  |  |  |  | ● |  | ● |  |  |  |  |  |  | ● | ● |  |  |  |  |  |  |  |  |  |  |  |  |  |  |  |  |  |  |  |  |  | ● |  |  |  |
| EAST, MARY EDGINTON (HM06531) |  |  |  |  |  |  |  |  |  |  |  |  |  |  |  |  | ● |  |  |  |  |  |  |  |  |  |  |  |  |  |  |  |  |  |  |  |  |  |  |  |  |  |  |  |  |  |  |  |  |  |
| EATON, MARION (HM06563) |  |  |  |  |  |  |  |  |  |  |  |  |  |  |  |  |  | ● |  |  |  |  |  |  |  |  |  |  |  |  |  |  |  |  |  |  |  |  |  |  |  |  |  |  |  |  |  |  |  |  |
| FAIRCHILD, HAZEL (HM07052) |  |  |  |  |  |  |  |  | ● | ● |  |  |  |  |  |  |  |  |  |  |  |  |  |  |  |  |  |  |  |  |  |  |  |  |  |  |  |  |  |  |  |  |  |  |  |  |  |  |  |  |
| FAMILY FIRST (HM07087) |  |  |  |  |  |  |  |  |  |  |  |  |  |  |  | ● |  |  |  |  | ● |  |  |  |  |  |  | ● |  |  |  |  |  |  |  |  |  |  |  |  |  |  |  |  | ● |  | ● |  |  |  |
| FIVEWAYS OSTEOPATHIC PRACTICE (HM07382) |  |  |  |  |  |  |  |  |  |  |  |  |  |  |  |  |  |  |  |  |  |  |  |  |  |  |  |  |  |  |  | ● |  | ● |  |  |  |  |  |  |  |  |  |  |  |  |  |  |  |  |
| FLOYD, MICHELLE (HM07438) |  |  |  |  |  |  |  |  |  |  |  |  |  |  |  |  | ● |  |  |  |  |  |  |  |  |  |  |  |  |  |  |  |  |  |  | ● |  |  |  |  |  |  |  |  |  |  |  |  |  |  |
| FOUNDATION, ANGELGATE (HM07615) |  |  |  |  |  |  |  |  |  |  |  |  | ● |  |  | ● |  |  |  |  |  | ● |  |  |  |  |  | ● |  |  |  |  |  | ● |  |  | ● |  |  |  |  |  |  |  |  |  | ● |  |  |  |
| GATEHOUSE THERAPY CENTRE (HM07925) |  |  |  |  |  |  |  |  |  | ● |  |  |  |  |  |  |  |  |  |  |  |  |  |  |  |  |  |  |  |  |  |  |  |  |  |  |  |  |  |  |  |  |  |  |  |  |  |  |  |  |
| GEALL, SUSAN (HM07949) |  |  |  |  |  |  |  |  |  |  |  |  |  |  | ● |  |  |  |  |  |  |  |  |  |  |  |  |  |  |  |  |  |  |  |  |  |  |  |  |  |  |  |  |  |  |  |  |  |  |  |
| GIBBENS, JOAN (HM08021) |  |  |  |  |  |  |  |  |  |  |  |  |  |  |  |  |  |  |  | ● |  |  |  |  |  |  |  |  |  |  |  |  |  |  |  |  |  |  |  |  |  |  |  |  |  |  |  |  |  |  |
| GOLDSTONE CLINIC (HM08230) |  |  |  |  |  |  |  |  |  |  |  |  |  |  |  |  |  |  |  |  |  |  |  |  |  |  |  |  |  |  |  |  |  | ● |  |  |  |  |  |  |  |  |  |  |  |  |  |  |  |  |
| GOLDSTONE CLINIC (HM08229) |  |  |  |  |  |  |  |  |  |  |  |  |  |  |  |  |  |  |  |  | ● |  |  |  |  |  |  |  |  |  |  |  |  |  |  |  |  |  |  |  |  |  |  |  |  |  |  |  |  |  |
| GONZALEZ, SOHANI (HM08237) |  |  |  |  |  |  |  |  |  |  |  |  |  |  |  | ● | ● |  |  |  |  |  |  |  |  |  |  |  |  |  |  |  |  |  |  |  |  |  |  |  |  |  |  | ● |  |  | ● |  |  |  |
| GOODWIN, SALLY (HM08270) |  |  |  |  |  |  |  |  |  |  |  |  |  |  |  |  |  |  |  |  |  |  |  |  |  |  |  | ● |  |  |  |  |  |  |  |  |  |  |  |  |  |  |  |  |  |  |  |  |  |  |
| GREEN, JENNY (HM08461) |  |  |  |  |  |  |  |  |  |  |  |  |  |  |  |  |  |  |  | ● |  |  |  |  |  |  |  |  |  |  |  |  |  |  |  |  |  |  |  |  |  |  |  |  |  |  |  |  |  |  |
| GRIFFITHS, J (HM08567) |  |  |  |  |  |  |  |  |  |  |  |  |  |  |  |  |  |  |  |  |  |  |  |  |  |  |  |  |  |  |  |  |  | ● |  |  |  |  |  |  |  |  |  |  |  |  |  |  |  |  |
| HART, RONALD (HM09131) |  |  |  |  |  |  |  |  |  |  |  |  |  |  |  |  |  |  |  |  |  |  |  |  |  |  |  |  |  |  |  |  |  |  |  |  |  |  |  |  |  |  | ● |  |  |  |  |  |  |  |
| HART, RONALD (HM09130) |  |  |  |  |  |  |  |  |  |  |  |  |  |  |  |  |  |  |  |  |  |  |  |  |  |  |  |  |  |  |  |  |  |  |  |  |  |  |  |  |  |  | ● |  |  |  |  |  |  |  |
| HAWKINS, LUKE (HM09224) |  |  |  |  |  |  |  |  |  |  |  |  |  |  |  |  |  |  |  |  |  |  |  |  |  |  |  |  |  |  |  |  |  |  |  |  |  |  |  |  |  |  | ● |  |  |  |  |  |  |  |
| HERBAL HEALTH CLINIC (HM09617) |  |  |  |  | ● |  |  |  |  |  |  | ● | ● |  | ● |  |  |  |  |  |  |  |  |  |  |  |  |  |  |  |  |  |  |  |  |  |  |  |  |  |  |  |  |  |  |  | ● |  |  |  |
| HOLDEN NATURAL HEALTH CLINIC (HM09927) |  |  |  |  |  |  |  |  |  |  |  |  |  |  | ● |  |  |  |  |  |  |  |  | ● |  |  |  |  |  |  |  |  |  |  |  |  |  |  |  |  |  |  |  | ● |  |  |  |  |  |  |
| HOMOEOPATHIC HOUSE (HM10098) |  |  |  |  |  |  |  |  |  |  |  |  |  |  |  |  | ● |  |  |  |  |  |  |  |  |  |  |  |  |  |  |  |  |  |  |  |  |  |  |  |  |  |  |  |  |  |  |  |  |  |
| HOVE CHIROPRACTIC CLINIC (HM10227) |  |  |  |  |  |  |  |  |  |  |  |  |  |  |  |  |  |  |  |  |  |  |  |  |  |  |  |  |  |  |  |  |  | ● | ● |  |  |  |  |  |  |  |  |  |  |  |  |  |  |  |

# F - O Therapies at Practices/Businesses

| Business by County with Reference no. | Family Planning (Natural) | Family Therapy | Feldenkrais Methodology | Feng Shui | Floral Essence Therapy | Flotation Therapy | Gait Analysis | Gem Essence Therapy | Gestalt Therapy | Group Therapy | Hay Diet | Healer | Healing Therapy | Hellerwork | Herbal Medicine | Holistic Healing | Homeopathy | Hopi Ear Candles | Humanistic Psychology | Hypnosis | Hypnotherapy | Indian Head Massage | Inhalation Therapy | Iridology | Kinesiology | Kirlian Photography | Laser Treatment | Life Style Coaching | Light Therapy | Macrobiotics | Magnetic Therapy | Manipulation | Manual Lymph Drainage | Massage (Therapeutic) | McTimoney Chiropractic | Meditation | Metamorphic Therapy | Miasm Therapy | Micro Manipulation | Moxibustion | Mud Therapy | Music Therapy | Nail Surgery | Naturopathy | Neuro-Linguistic Program | Neurotherapy | Nutritional Therapy | Orgone Therapy | Oriental Diagnosis | Orthomolecular Medicine |
|---|---|---|---|---|---|---|---|---|---|---|---|---|---|---|---|---|---|---|---|---|---|---|---|---|---|---|---|---|---|---|---|---|---|---|---|---|---|---|---|---|---|---|---|---|---|---|---|---|---|---|
| HOVE OSTEOPATHIC CLINIC (HM10228) | | | | | | | | | | | | | | | | | | | | | | | | | | | | | | | | ● | | ● | | | | | | | | | | | | | | | | |
| HYSLOP, C P (HM10543) | | | | | | | | | | | | | | | ● | ● | ● | | | | | | | | | | | | | | | | | | | | | | | | | | | | ● | | | | | |
| JOSLING, A (HM11221) | | | | | | | | | | | | | | | | | ● | | | | | | | | | | | | | | | | | | | | | | | | | | | | | | | | | |
| JOY, JANET (HM11231) | | | | | | | | | | | | | ● | | | | | | ● | ● | ● | | | | | | | | | | | | | | | | | | | | | | | | ● | | | | | |
| KENNY, D J (HM11506) | | | | | | | | | | | | | | | | | | | | ● | | | | | | | | | | | | | | | | | | | | | | | | | | | | | | |
| KIDSON, J H P (HM11597) | | | | | | | | | | | | | | | | | ● | | | | | | | | | | | | | | | | | | | | | | | | | | | | | | | | | |
| LA BELLE SANTE NATURELLE (HM11845) | | | | | | | | | | | | | | | | | | | | ● | | | | | | | | | | | | | | | | | | | | | | | | | | | | | | |
| LAVENANT, M (HM12019) | | | | | | | | | | | | | | | ● | | | | | | | | | | | | | | | | | | | | | | | | | | | | | | | | | | | |
| LEWES CHIROPRACTIC CLINIC (HM12271) | | | | | | | | | | | | | | | | | | | | | | | | | | | | | | | | ● | | | | | | | | | | | | | | | | | | |
| MANNING, D J (DR) (HM13028) | | | | | | | | | | | | | | | | | | | | ● | | | | | | | | | | | | | | | | | | | | | | | | | | | | | | |
| MCGHIE, PETER M (HM13482) | | | | | | | | | | | | | | | | | | | | ● | | | | | | | | | | | | | | | | | | | | | | | | | | | | | | |
| MEADOWSWEET (HM13634) | | | | | | | | | | | | | | | | | | | | | | | | | | | | | | | | | | ● | | | | | | | | | | | | | | | | |
| MONT, K (HM14077) | | | | | | | | | | | | | | | | | ● | | | | | | | | | | | | | | | | | | | | | | | | | | | | | | | | | |
| MURPHY, KEVIN (HM14387) | | | | | | | | | | | | ● | | | | | | | | | | | | | ● | | | | | | | | | ● | | | | | | | | | | | | | | | | |
| NEAT FEET (HM14742) | | | | | | | | | | | | | | | | | | | | | | | | | | | ● | | | | | | | | | | | | | | | | ● | | | | | | | |
| NOAKES, STEVE (HM14965) | | | | | | | | | | | | | | | ● | | | | | | | | | | | | | | | | | | | | | | | | | | | | | | | | | | | |
| NORTH, SARAH (HM15046) | | | | | | | | | | | | | | | | | ● | | | | | | | | | | | | | | | | | | | | | | | | | | | | | | | | | |
| OLD TOWN CHIROPRACTIC CLINIC (HM15263) | | | | | | | | | | | | | | | | | | | | | | | | | | | | | | | | ● | | | | | | | | | | | | | | | | | | |
| O'MEARA, WILLIAM J (HM15318) | | | | | | | | | | | | | | | | | ● | | | | | | | | | | | | | | | | | | | | | | | | | | | | | | | | | |
| PAUL MURFIN HYPNOTHERAPIST (HM15845) | | | | | | | | | | | | | | | | | | | | ● | | | | | | | | | | | | | | | | | | | | | | | | | | | | | | |
| PEVENSEY BAY NTRL HEALING (HM16105) | | | | | | | | | | | | | ● | | | | | | | | | | | | | | | | | | | | | | | | | | | | | | | | | | | | | |
| PHILIP D HOLMES (HM16118) | | | | | | | | | | | | | | | ● | | | | | | | | | | | | | | | | | | | | | | | | | ● | | | | | | | | | ● | |
| ROSSI, JAN (HM17649) | | | | | | | | | | | | | | | | | | | | ● | | | | | | | | | | | | | | | | | | | | | | | | | | | | | | |
| SCOTT, SUE (HM18128) | | | | | | | | | | | | | | | | | ● | | | | | | | | | | | | | | | | | | | | | | | | | | | | | | | | | |
| SIMMONDS HERBAL SUPPLIES (HM18552) | | | | | | | | | | | | | | | ● | | | | | | | | | | | | | | | | | | | | | | | | | | | | | | | | | | | |
| SOUTHEAST HYPNOTHERAPY CENTRE (HM18931) | | | | | | | | | | | | | | | | | | | | ● | | | | | | | | | | | | | | | | | | | | | | | | | | | | | | |
| TRANSCENDENTAL MEDITATION (HM20276) | | | | | | | | | | | | | | | | | | | | | | | | | | | | | | | | | | | | ● | | | | | | | | | | | | | | |
| TRENCHARD, ABIGAIL (HM20319) | | | | | | | | | | | | | ● | | | | | | | | | | | | | | | | | | | | | | | | | | | | | | | | | | | | | |
| TYRRELL, IVAN (HM20478) | | | | | | | | | | | | | | | | | | | | ● | | | | | | | | | | | | | | | | | | | | | | | | | | | | | | |
| VALENCE ROAD OSTEOPATHS (HM20554) | | | | | | | | | | | | | | | | | | | | | | | | | | | | | | | | | | ● | | | | | | | | | | | | | | | | |
| WEDLAKE-GRIFFITHS, J (HM21097) | | | | | | | | | | | ● | | | | ● | | | | | | | | | | | | | | | | | ● | | ● | | | | | | | | | | | | | ● | | | |
| WILBURY PHYSIOTHERAPY (HM21480) | | | | | | | | | | | | | | | | | | | | | | | | | | | | | | | | ● | | ● | | | | | | | | | | | | | | | | |
| WRIGHT, AUDREY (HM21927) | | | | | | | | | | | | | | | ● | | | | | | | | | | | | | | | | | | | | | | | | | | | | | | | | | | | |
| WRIGHT, JENNY (HM21937) | | | | | | | | | | | | | | | | | ● | | | | | | | | | | | | | | | | | | | | | | | | | | | | | | | | | |

# F - O Therapies at Practices/Businesses

| Business by County with Reference no. | Family Planning (Natural) | Family Therapy | Feldenkrais Methodology | Feng Shui | Floral Essence Therapy | Flotation Therapy | Gait Analysis | Gem Essence Therapy | Gestalt Therapy | Group Therapy | Hay Diet | Healer | Healing Therapy | Hellerwork | Herbal Medicine | Holistic Healing | Homeopathy | Hopi Ear Candles | Humanistic Psychology | Hypnosis | Hypnotherapy | Indian Head Massage | Inhalation Therapy | Iridology | Kinesiology | Kirlian Photography | Laser Treatment | Life Style Coaching | Light Therapy | Macrobiotics | Magnetic Therapy | Manipulation | Manual Lymph Drainage | Massage (Therapeutic) | McTimoney Chiropractic | Meditation | Metamorphic Therapy | Miasm Therapy | Micro Manipulation | Moxibustion | Mud Therapy | Music Therapy | Nail Surgery | Naturopathy | Neuro-Linguistic Program | Neurotherapy | Nutritional Therapy | Orgone Therapy | Oriental Diagnosis | Orthomolecular Medicine |
|---|---|---|---|---|---|---|---|---|---|---|---|---|---|---|---|---|---|---|---|---|---|---|---|---|---|---|---|---|---|---|---|---|---|---|---|---|---|---|---|---|---|---|---|---|---|---|---|---|---|---|
| WRIGHT, P A (HM21946) | | | | | | | | | | | | | | | | | | | | | | | | | | ● | | | | | | | | | | | | | | | | ● | | | | | | | | |
| **SUSSEX (WEST)** | | | | | | | | | | | | | | | | | | | | | | | | | | | | | | | | | | | | | | | | | | | | | | | | | | |
| ACORN CENTRE (HM00171) | | | | | | | | | | | ● | | | | | ● | | | | ● | | | | | | | | | | | | | ● | | | | | | | | | | | | | | | | | |
| ACUPUNCTURE CLINIC (HM00277) | | | | | | | | | | | | | | | | | | | | | | | | | | | | | | | | | ● | | | | | | ● | | | | | | | | | | | |
| ALAN SMITH CHIROPRACTOR (HM00470) | | | | | | | | | | | ● | | | | | | | | | | | | | | | | | | | | ● | | | | | | | | | | | | | | | | | | | |
| ANDREW BATHIE PRACTICE (HM00846) | | | | | | | | ● | | | | | | | | | | ● | ● | ● | | | | | | | ● | | | | | | | | ● | | | | | | | | | ● | | | | | | |
| AVALON HEALTH CENTRE (HM01380) | | | | | | | | | | | | | | ● | | ● | | | | | | | | | | | | | | | | | ● | | | | | | | | | | | | | ● | | | | |
| AYRES, KATHLEEN (HM01436) | | | | | | | | | | | | | | | | | | | ● | | | | | | | | | | | | | | | | | | | | | | | | | | | | | | | |
| B O P (HM01452) | | | | | | | | | | | | | | | | | | | | | | | | | | | | | | | ● | | ● | | | | | | | | | | | | | | | | | |
| BARTHOLOMEW WAY CLINIC (HM01818) | | | | | | ● | | | | | | | | | | | | | | | | | | ● | | | | | | | ● | | ● | | | | | | | | | | | | | | | | | |
| BARTON, MARGOT (HM01831) | | | | | | | | | | | | | | | | ● | | | | | | | | | | | | | | | | | | | | | | | | | | | | | | | | | | |
| BLACK, PAULINE (HM02425) | | | | | | | | | | | | | | | | ● | | | | | | | | | | | | | | | | | | | | | | | | | | | | | | | | | | |
| BOHNET, CAROLE (HM02648) | | | | | | | | | | | | ● | | | ● | | | | | | ● | | | | | | | | | | | | ● | | | | | | | | | | | | | | | | | |
| CHANGES (HM03985) | | | | ● | | | ● | | | ● | ● | | | | | ● | | | | | | | ● | ● | | | | | | | | | | | | | | | | | | | | | | | | | | |
| CHICHESTER NATURAL HEALTH CTRE (HM04156) | | | | | | | | | | | | | | | | ● | | | | | | | | | | | | | | | | | | | | | | | | | | | | | | | | | | |
| CLAIRVOYANT - MEDIUM - HEALER (HM04514) | | | | | | | | | | | ● | ● | | | | | | | | | | | | | | | | | | | | | | | | | | | | | | | | | | | | | | |
| CLARKE, STEVEN (HM04604) | | | | | | | | | | | | | | | ● | | | | ● | ● | | | | | | | | | | | | | | | | | | | | | | | | | | | | | | |
| COBURN CTRE FOR NATURAL HEALTH (HM04763) | | | | | | | | | | | | | | ● | | | | | | | | | | | | | | | | | | | | | | | | | | | | | | | | | | | | |
| COOK, RICHARD (HM05052) | | | | | | | | | | | | | | | | ● | | | | | | | | | | | | | | | | | | | | | | | | | | | | | | | | | | |
| COOKSLEY, L J (HM05069) | | | | | | | | | | | | | | | | ● | | | | | | | | | | | | | | | | | | | | | | | | | | | | | | | | | | |
| COOMBES, JOY (HM05076) | | | | | | | | | | | | | | | | | | | ● | | | | | | | | | | | | | | | | | | | | | | | | | | | | | | | |
| CORK, STEPHEN (HM05166) | | | | | | | | | | | | | | | | | | | ● | | | | | | | | | | | | | | | | | | | | | | | | | | | | | | | |
| CORNERWEIGHS (HM05183) | | | | | | | | | | | | | | | | | | | | | | | | | | | | | | | | | | | | | | | | | | | ● | | | | | | | |
| CUTLER, AMANDA (HM05644) | | | | | | | | | | | | | | | | | | | | | | | | | | | | | | | | | ● | | | | | | | | | | | | | | | | | |
| DEACON, MAX (HM05930) | | | | | | | | | | | | | | | | ● | | | | | | | | | | | | | | | | | | | | | | | | | | | | | | | | | | |
| DIEBSCHLAG, FRANCESCA (HM06091) | | | | | | | | | | | | | | ● | | | | | | | | | | | | | | | | | | | | | | | | | | | | | | | | | | | | |
| DYER & ASSOCIATES (HM06444) | | | | | | | | | | | | | | | | ● | | | | ● | | | | | | | | | | | | | | | | | | | | | | | | | | | | | | |
| EDMONDS, PHILIP (HM06620) | | | | | | | | | | | | | | | | ● | | | | | | | | | | | | | | | | | | | | | | | | | | | | | | | | | | |
| EMINATIONS ACUPUNCTURE CLINIC (HM06805) | | | | | | | | | | | | | | | | | | | | | | | | | | | | | | | | | ● | | | | | | ● | | | | | | | | | ● | |
| FELPHAM NATURAL HEALTH CLINIC (HM07206) | | | | | | | | | | | ● | ● | | | | | | | | | ● | | | | | | | | | | ● | | ● | | | | | | | | | | | | | | | | | |
| FROST, CHARLES (HM07760) | | | | | | | | | | | | | | | | | | ● | ● | ● | | | | | | | | | | | | | | | | | | | | | | | | | | | | | | |
| FURNACE GREEN CHIRO CTRE (HM07800) | | | | | | | | | | | | | | | | | | | | | | | | | | | | | | | ● | | ● | | | | | | | | | | | | | | | | | |
| G & G FOOD SUPPLIES (HM07807) | | | | | | | | | | | | | | ● | | | | | | | | | | | | | | | | | | | | | | | | | | | | | | | | | | | | |
| GARDINER, SAM (HM07876) | | | | | | | | | | | | | | | | | | | ● | ● | | | | | | | | | | | | | | | | | | | | | | | | | | | | | | |

# F - O Therapies at Practices/Businesses

| Business by County with Reference no. | Family Planning (Natural) | Family Therapy | Feldenkrais Methodology | Feng Shui | Floral Essence Therapy | Flotation Therapy | Gait Analysis | Gem Essence Therapy | Gestalt Therapy | Group Therapy | Hay Diet | Healer | Healing Therapy | Hellerwork | Herbal Medicine | Holistic Healing | Homeopathy | Hopi Ear Candles | Humanistic Psychology | Hypnosis | Hypnotherapy | Indian Head Massage | Inhalation Therapy | Iridology | Kinesiology |
|---|---|---|---|---|---|---|---|---|---|---|---|---|---|---|---|---|---|---|---|---|---|---|---|---|---|
| GIBBS, LOUIS (HM08030) | | | | | | | | | | | | | | | | | | | | ● | | | | | |
| GIBSON, NEIL (HM08043) | | | | | | | | | | | | | | | | | | | | ● | | | | | |
| HALL, N S (DR) (HM08786) | | | | | | | | | | | | | | | | | | | | ● | | | | | |
| HEELER CENTRE (HM09498) | | | | | | | | | | | | | | | | | ● | | | ● | ● | ● | | | |
| I C O M (HM10548) | | | | | | | | | | | | | | | | | | | | | | | | | |
| JONES, NIGEL (HM11182) | | | | | | | | | | | | | | | | | | | | | | | | | |
| JONES, WENDY (HM11203) | | | | | | | | | | | | | | | | | | | | | | | | | |
| KINGSLEY-HOLT, MIRANDA (HM11669) | | | | | | | | | | | | | | | | | ● | | | | | | | | |
| KWENORA HERBAL HEALTH (HM11831) | | | | | | | | | | | | | | | ● | | | | | | | | | | |
| LITTLEHAMPTON NAT HLTH CTRE (HM12470) | | | | | | | | | | | | ● | ● | | ● | ● | ● | | | ● | ● | ● | | ● | ● |
| MASSEY, JANET (HM13268) | | | | | | | | | | | | | | | | | | | | ● | | | | | |
| MERRIOTT, SUSAN J (HM13752) | | | | | | | | | | | | | | | | | ● | | | | | | | | |
| MID SUSSEX CHIROPRACTIC CLINIC (HM13805) | | | | | | | | | | | | | | | | | | | | | ● | | | | ● |
| MID SUSSEX HOMEOPATHIC CLINIC (HM13807) | | | | | | | | | | | | | | | | | ● | | | | | | | | |
| MID SUSSEX HOMEOPATHIC CLINIC (HM13806) | | | | | | | | | | | | | | | | | ● | | | | | | | | |
| MILLENNIUM HOMEOPATHY (HM13877) | | | | | | | | | | | | | | | | | ● | | | | | | | | |
| MILLENNIUM STRESS MANAGEMENT (HM13878) | | | | | | | | | | | | | | | | | | | | ● | | | | | |
| MIND WORK SOLUTIONS (HM13967) | | | | | | | | | | | | | | | | ● | | | | | ● | | | | |
| NUNN, SALLY (HM15108) | | | | | | | | | | | | | | | | | ● | | | | | | | | |
| OSTEOPATHY AT ESQUIRE'S (HM15479) | | | | | | | | | | | | | | | | | | | | | | | | | |
| PAIN & PARALYSIS SPECIALIST (HM15578) | | | | | | | | | | | | ● | | | | ● | | | | | | | | | |
| PALMER, GAYLE (HM15606) | | | | | | | | | | | | | ● | | | | ● | | | | | | | | ● |
| PALMER, GAYLE (HM15605) | | | | | | | | | | | | ● | ● | | | | | | | | | | | | |
| PITT, KATHY (HM16349) | | | | | | | | | | | | | | | | ● | ● | | | | | | | | |
| RICHARDSON, BRIAN J (HM17269) | | | | | | | ● | | | | | | | | | | | | | | | | | | |
| SANDON, PATER H G (DR) (HM17925) | | | | | | | | | | | | | | | | | ● | | | | | | | | |
| SETFORD, JAN (HM18242) | | | | | | | | | | | | | | | | | | | | ● | | | | | |
| SPENCER, TERESA (HM19004) | | | | | | | | | | | | | | | | | | | | ● | | | | | |
| STOTT-DURHAM, ANDREW (HM19355) | | | | | | | | | | | | | | | | | | | | | | | | | |
| SWAN, LAURIE C (HM19574) | | | | | | | | | | | | | | | | | | | | | | | | | ● |
| TAYLOR, CHRISTIAN (HM19744) | | | | | | | | | | | | | | | | ● | ● | | | | | | | | |
| TRANQUILLITY (HM20260) | | | | | | | | | | | | ● | | | | | | | | ● | ● | | | | |
| TUGNUTT, SALLY (HM20378) | | | | | | | | | | | | | | | | | | | | | | ● | | | |
| VAN GEND, KATHARINA (HM20568) | | | | | | | | | | | | | | | | | | | | ● | | | | | |

| Business by County with Reference no. | Kirlian Photography | Laser Treatment | Life Style Coaching | Light Therapy | Macrobiotics | Magnetic Therapy | Manipulation | Manual Lymph Drainage | Massage (Therapeutic) | McTimoney Chiropractic | Meditation | Metamorphic Therapy | Miasm Therapy | Micro Manipulation | Moxibustion | Mud Therapy | Music Therapy | Nail Surgery | Naturopathy | Neuro-Linguistic Program | Neurotherapy | Nutritional Therapy | Orgone Therapy | Oriental Diagnosis | Orthomolecular Medicine |
|---|---|---|---|---|---|---|---|---|---|---|---|---|---|---|---|---|---|---|---|---|---|---|---|---|---|
| GIBBS, LOUIS (HM08030) | | | | | | | | | | | | | | | | | | | | | | | | | |
| GIBSON, NEIL (HM08043) | | | | | | | | | | | | | | | | | | | | | | | | | |
| HALL, N S (DR) (HM08786) | | | | | | | | | | | | | | | | | | | | | | | | | |
| HEELER CENTRE (HM09498) | | | | | | | ● | | ● | | | | | | | | | | ● | | | ● | | | |
| I C O M (HM10548) | | | | | | | | | ● | | | | | | | | | | | | | | | | |
| JONES, NIGEL (HM11182) | | | | | | | ● | | | | | | | | | | | | | | | | | | |
| JONES, WENDY (HM11203) | | | | | | | | | ● | | | | | | | | | | | | | | | | |
| KINGSLEY-HOLT, MIRANDA (HM11669) | | | | | | | | | | | | | | | | | | | | | | | | | |
| KWENORA HERBAL HEALTH (HM11831) | | | | | | | | | | | | | | | | | | | | | | | | | |
| LITTLEHAMPTON NAT HLTH CTRE (HM12470) | | | | | | | ● | | ● | ● | ● | ● | ● | ● | ● | | ● | | ● | | | ● | | ● | |
| MASSEY, JANET (HM13268) | | | | | | | | | | | | | | | | | | | | | | | | | |
| MERRIOTT, SUSAN J (HM13752) | | | | | | | | | | | | | | | | | | | | | | | | | |
| MID SUSSEX CHIROPRACTIC CLINIC (HM13805) | | | ● | | | | ● | | | | ● | | | | | | | | | | | ● | | | |
| MID SUSSEX HOMEOPATHIC CLINIC (HM13807) | | | | | | | | | | | | | | | | | | | | | | | | | |
| MID SUSSEX HOMEOPATHIC CLINIC (HM13806) | | | | | | | | | | | | | | | | | | | | | | | | | |
| MILLENNIUM HOMEOPATHY (HM13877) | | | | | | | | | | | | | | | | | | | | | | | | | |
| MILLENNIUM STRESS MANAGEMENT (HM13878) | | | | | | | | | | | | | | | | | | | | | | | | | |
| MIND WORK SOLUTIONS (HM13967) | | | | | | | | | | | | | | | | | | | | | | | | | |
| NUNN, SALLY (HM15108) | | | | | | | | | | | | | | | | | | | | | | | | | |
| OSTEOPATHY AT ESQUIRE'S (HM15479) | | | | | | | ● | | ● | | | | | | | | | | | | | | | | |
| PAIN & PARALYSIS SPECIALIST (HM15578) | | | | | | | ● | | ● | | | | | | | | | | | | | ● | | | |
| PALMER, GAYLE (HM15606) | | | | | | | ● | | ● | | | | | | | | | | | | | | | | |
| PALMER, GAYLE (HM15605) | | | | | | | | | | | | | | | | | | | | | | | | | |
| PITT, KATHY (HM16349) | | | | | | | | | | | | | | | | | | | | | | | | | |
| RICHARDSON, BRIAN J (HM17269) | | | | | | | | | | | | | | | | | | | | | | | | | |
| SANDON, PATER H G (DR) (HM17925) | | | | | | | | | | | | | | | | | | | | | | | | | |
| SETFORD, JAN (HM18242) | | | | | | | | | | | | | | | | | | | | | | | | | |
| SPENCER, TERESA (HM19004) | | | | | | | | | | | | | | | | | | | | | | | | | |
| STOTT-DURHAM, ANDREW (HM19355) | | | | | | | | | ● | | | | | | | | | | | | | | | | |
| SWAN, LAURIE C (HM19574) | | | | | | | | | | | | | | | | | | | | | | | | | |
| TAYLOR, CHRISTIAN (HM19744) | | | | | | | | | | | | | | | | | | | | | | | | | |
| TRANQUILLITY (HM20260) | | | | | | | | | | | | | | | | | | | | | | | | | |
| TUGNUTT, SALLY (HM20378) | | | | | | | | | ● | | | | | | | | | | | | | | | | |
| VAN GEND, KATHARINA (HM20568) | | | | | | | | | | | | | | | | | | | | | | | | | |

# F - O Therapies at Practices/Businesses

| Business by County with Reference no. | Family Planning (Natural) | Family Therapy | Feldenkrais Methodology | Feng Shui | Floral Essence Therapy | Flotation Therapy | Gait Analysis | Gem Essence Therapy | Gestalt Therapy | Group Therapy | Hay Diet | Healer | Healing Therapy | Hellerwork | Herbal Medicine | Holistic Healing | Homeopathy | Hopi Ear Candles | Humanistic Psychology | Hypnosis | Hypnotherapy | Indian Head Massage | Inhalation Therapy | Iridology | Kinesiology |
|---|---|---|---|---|---|---|---|---|---|---|---|---|---|---|---|---|---|---|---|---|---|---|---|---|---|
| WARREN-DAVIS, A (HM20954) | | | | | | | | | | | | | | | ● | | | | | | | | | | |
| WESTACOTT, EILEEN (HM21256) | | | | | | | | | | | | | | | | | | | | | | | | | |
| WILSON, AVIS (HM21646) | | | | | | | | | | | | | | | | | | | | | | | | | |
| WOOD, J G (HM21798) | | | | | | | | | | | | | | | | | | | | | | | | | |
| **TYNE AND WEAR** | | | | | | | | | | | | | | | | | | | | | | | | | |
| ACUPUNCTURE & NAT MED CLINIC (HM00243) | | | | | | | | | | | | | | | ● | ● | | | | | | | | | |
| AROMATHERAPY IN PRACTICE (HM01114) | | | | | | | | | | | | | | | | | | | | | | | | | |
| B WIGRAM HEALING & REFLEXOLOGY (HM01455) | | | | | | | | | | | | ● | ● | | | | | | | | | | | | |
| BAL, NORMAN (HM01602) | | | | | | | | | | | | | | | | | ● | | | | | | | | |
| BRAHMA KUMARIS WORLD (HM02890) | | | | | | | | | | | | | | | | | | | | | | | | | |
| CHIROPODY CLINIC (HM04324) | | | | | | | | | | | | | | | | | | | | | | | | | |
| CONNECT PHYSICAL HEALTH CTRE (HM04989) | | | | | | | | | | | | | | | | | ● | | | | | ● | | | |
| COOP, JOE (HM05082) | | | | | | | | | | | | | | | | | | | | ● | ● | | | | |
| DENTON, A (HM05998) | | | | | | | | | | | | | | | | | | | | | | | | | ● |
| DERWENT CENTRE (HM06020) | | | | | | | | | | | | | ● | | | | | | | | | ● | | | |
| EQUILIBRIUM (HM06867) | | | | | | | | | | | | | | | | | | | | | | | | | |
| FEEL GOOD AROMATHERAPY (HM07164) | | | | | | | | | | | | ● | | | ● | | | | | | | | | | |
| FOWLER, CHRISTINE (HM07628) | | | | | | | | | | | | | | | | | | | | | | | | | ● |
| GATESHEAD COMPLEMENTARY HEALTH (HM07927) | | | | | | | | | | | | | | | | | | | | ● | ● | | | | |
| HEALTH ALLIANCE CENTRE (HM09375) | | | | | | | | | | | | | | | | | | | | | | | | | |
| HERBAL GARDEN AROMATHERAPY (HM09612) | | | | | ● | | | | | | | | | | ● | ● | ● | | | | | | ● | | |
| HOLISTIC CHIROPRACTOR (HM09951) | | | | | | | | | | | | ● | | | | | | | | | | | | | |
| HYPNOTHERAPY AND COUNSELLING (HM10514) | | | | | | | | | | | | | | | | | | | | | ● | | | | |
| JAGER THERAPY CENTRE (HM10872) | | | | | | | | | | | | | | | | | | | | ● | | | | | |
| JAMIESON, TOM (HM10908) | | | | | | | | | | | | | | | | | ● | | | | | | | | |
| LAW'S (HM12060) | | | | | | | | | | | | | | | ● | | | | | | | | | | |
| LINDISFARNE CENTRE (HM12417) | | | | | | | | | | | | | | | | | ● | | | | | | | | |
| MCANELLY, J L (HM13368) | | | | | | | | | | | | | | | | | | | | ● | ● | | | | |
| MILLS, M (HM13931) | | | | | | | | | | | | | | | | | ● | | | | | | | | |
| NATURAL SELECTION (HM14623) | | | | | | | | | | | | | | | | ● | | | | | | ● | | | |
| NEW LIFE NATURAL HEALTH CARE (HM14820) | | | | | | | | | | | | | | | ● | ● | ● | | | | | ● | | | ● |
| NORTHERN COLLEGE CLINIC (HM15057) | | | | | | | | | | | | | | | | | ● | | | | | | | | |
| OSBORNE CLINIC (HM15420) | | | | | | | | | | | | | | | | | | | | | | | | | |
| PARK LANE CLINIC (HM15667) | | | | | | | | | | | | | | | | | | | | ● | | | | | |

| Business by County with Reference no. | Kirlian Photography | Laser Treatment | Life Style Coaching | Light Therapy | Macrobiotics | Magnetic Therapy | Manipulation | Manual Lymph Drainage | Massage (Therapeutic) | McTimoney Chiropractic | Meditation | Metamorphic Therapy | Miasm Therapy | Micro Manipulation | Moxibustion | Mud Therapy | Music Therapy | Nail Surgery | Naturopathy | Neuro-Linguistic Program | Neurotherapy | Nutritional Therapy | Orgone Therapy | Oriental Diagnosis | Orthomolecular Medicine |
|---|---|---|---|---|---|---|---|---|---|---|---|---|---|---|---|---|---|---|---|---|---|---|---|---|---|
| WARREN-DAVIS, A (HM20954) | | | | | | | | | | | | | | | | | | | | | | | | | |
| WESTACOTT, EILEEN (HM21256) | | | | | | | | | ● | | | | | | | | | | | | | | | | |
| WILSON, AVIS (HM21646) | | | | | | | | | ● | | | | | | | | | | | | | | | | |
| WOOD, J G (HM21798) | | | | | | | ● | | ● | | | | | | | | | | | | | | | | |
| **TYNE AND WEAR** | | | | | | | | | | | | | | | | | | | | | | | | | |
| ACUPUNCTURE & NAT MED CLINIC (HM00243) | | | | | | | ● | | ● | | | | | | | | | | ● | | | ● | | ● | |
| AROMATHERAPY IN PRACTICE (HM01114) | | | | | | | | ● | | | | | | | | | | | | | | | | | |
| B WIGRAM HEALING & REFLEXOLOGY (HM01455) | | | | | | | | | | | ● | | | | | | | | | | | | | | |
| BAL, NORMAN (HM01602) | | | | | | | | | | | | | | | | | | | | | | | | | |
| BRAHMA KUMARIS WORLD (HM02890) | | | | | | | | | | | ● | | | | | | | | | | | | | | |
| CHIROPODY CLINIC (HM04324) | | | | | | | | | | | | | | | | | | ● | | | | | | | |
| CONNECT PHYSICAL HEALTH CTRE (HM04989) | | | | | | | ● | | ● | | | | | | | | | | | | | ● | | | |
| COOP, JOE (HM05082) | | | | | | | | | | | | | | | | | | | | | | | | | |
| DENTON, A (HM05998) | | | | | | | | | | | | | | | | | | | | | | | | | |
| DERWENT CENTRE (HM06020) | | | | | | | | | | | | | | | | | | | | | | | | | |
| EQUILIBRIUM (HM06867) | | | | | | | | | | | | | | | | | | | | | | ● | | | |
| FEEL GOOD AROMATHERAPY (HM07164) | | | ● | | | | | | | | | | | | | | | | ● | | | | | | |
| FOWLER, CHRISTINE (HM07628) | | | | | | | | | | | | | | | | | | | | | | | | | |
| GATESHEAD COMPLEMENTARY HEALTH (HM07927) | | | | | | | | | ● | | | | | | | | | | | | | | | | |
| HEALTH ALLIANCE CENTRE (HM09375) | | | | | | | ● | | ● | | | | | | | | | | | | | | | | |
| HERBAL GARDEN AROMATHERAPY (HM09612) | | | | | | | | | | | | | | | | | ● | | | | | | | | |
| HOLISTIC CHIROPRACTOR (HM09951) | | | | | | | ● | | | | | | | | ● | | | | | | | | | | |
| HYPNOTHERAPY AND COUNSELLING (HM10514) | | | | | | | | | | | | | | | | | | | | | | | | | |
| JAGER THERAPY CENTRE (HM10872) | | | | | | | | | | | | | | | | | | | | | | | | | |
| JAMIESON, TOM (HM10908) | | | | | | | | | | | | | | | | | | | | | | | | | |
| LAW'S (HM12060) | | | | | | | | | | | | | | | | | | | | | | | | | |
| LINDISFARNE CENTRE (HM12417) | | | | | | | | | | | | | | | | | | | | | | | | | |
| MCANELLY, J L (HM13368) | | | | | | | | | | | | | | | | | | | | | | | | | |
| MILLS, M (HM13931) | | | | | | | | | | | | | | | | | | | | | | | | | |
| NATURAL SELECTION (HM14623) | | | | | | | | | ● | | | | | | | | | | | | | | | | |
| NEW LIFE NATURAL HEALTH CARE (HM14820) | | | | | | | ● | | ● | | | | ● | | | | | | ● | | | ● | | | |
| NORTHERN COLLEGE CLINIC (HM15057) | | | | | | | | | | | | | | | | | | | | | | | | | |
| OSBORNE CLINIC (HM15420) | | | | | | | ● | | ● | | | | | | | | | | | | | | | | |
| PARK LANE CLINIC (HM15667) | | | | | | | | | | | | | | | | | | | | | | | | | |

# F - O Therapies at Practices/Businesses

| Business by County with Reference no. | Family Planning (Natural) | Family Therapy | Feldenkrais Methodology | Feng Shui | Floral Essence Therapy | Flotation Therapy | Gait Analysis | Gem Essence Therapy | Gestalt Therapy | Group Therapy | Hay Diet | Healer | Healing Therapy | Hellerwork | Herbal Medicine | Holistic Healing | Homeopathy | Hopi Ear Candles | Humanistic Psychology | Hypnosis | Hypnotherapy | Indian Head Massage | Inhalation Therapy | Iridology | Kinesiology | Kirlian Photography | Laser Treatment | Life Style Coaching | Light Therapy | Macrobiotics | Magnetic Therapy | Manipulation | Manual Lymph Drainage | Massage (Therapeutic) | McTimoney Chiropractic | Meditation | Metamorphic Therapy | Miasm Therapy | Micro Manipulation | Moxibustion | Mud Therapy | Music Therapy | Nail Surgery | Naturopathy | Neuro-Linguistic Program | Neurotherapy | Nutritional Therapy | Orgone Therapy | Oriental Diagnosis | Orthomolecular Medicine |
|---|---|---|---|---|---|---|---|---|---|---|---|---|---|---|---|---|---|---|---|---|---|---|---|---|---|---|---|---|---|---|---|---|---|---|---|---|---|---|---|---|---|---|---|---|---|---|---|---|---|---|
| PIKE, STUART (HM16291) | | | | | | | | | | | | | | | | | | | | ● | | | | | | | | | | | | | | | | | | | | | | | | | | | | | | |
| RAINBOW, RICHARD S (HM16887) | | | | | | | | | | | | | | | | | | | | ● | ● | | | | | | | | | | | | | | | | | | | | | | | | | | | | | |
| REILLY, MERVYN (HM17152) | | | | | | | | | | | | | | | | | | | | ● | | | | | | | | | | | | | | | | | | | | | | | | | | | | | | |
| ROMER, A C (HM17573) | | | | | | | | | | | | | | | ● | | | | | | | | | | | | | | | | | | | | | | | | | | | | | | | | | | | |
| SADLER, RUTH (HM17833) | | | | | | | | | | | | | | | | | ● | | | | | | | | | | | | | | | | | | | | | | | | | | | | | | | | | |
| SHAW, L M (HM18342) | | | | | | | | | | | | | | | | | | | | ● | | | | | | | | | | | | | | | | | | | | | | | | | | | | | | |
| SHEN HOLISTIC THERAPIES (HM18392) | | | | | | | | | | | | | | | | | | | | | | ● | | | | | | | | | | | ● | | | | | | | | | | | | | | | | | |
| SHUN-TEN HYPNOTHERAPY (HM18515) | | | | | | | | | | | | | | | | | | | | ● | | | | | | | | | | | | | | | | | | | | | | | | | | | | | | |
| STOREY, ADA (HM19347) | | | | | | | | | | | | | | | | | | | | ● | | | | | | | | | | | | | | | | | | | | | | | | | | | | | | |
| WESTOE PRACTICE (HM21277) | | | | | | | | | | | | | | | | | | | | | | | | | | | | | | | | | | | | | | | | | | | ● | | | | | | | |
| **WARWICKSHIRE** | | | | | | | | | | | | | | | | | | | | | | | | | | | | | | | | | | | | | | | | | | | | | | | | | | |
| AOK INSPIRATIONAL (HM00925) | | | | | | | | | | | | | | | | | | | | ● | | | | | | | | | | | | | | | | | | | | | | | | | | | | | | |
| ARDEN HYPNOTHERAPY (HM00990) | | | | | | | | | | | | | | | | | | | | | | | | | | | | | | | | | | | | | | | | | | | | | ● | | | | | |
| AROMATHERAPY MASSAGE/REFLEX (HM01120) | | | | | | | | | | | | | | | | | | | | | | | | | | | | | | | | | | ● | | | | | | | | | | | | | | | | |
| BARRATT'S HOMEOPATHY (HM01780) | | | | | | | | | | | | | | | ● | ● | ● | | | | | | | ● | | | | | | | | | | | | | | | | | | | | ● | | | | | | |
| BEARDMORE, CHRIS (HM01967) | | | | | | | | | | | | | | | | | | | | ● | | | | | | | | | | | | | | | | | | | | | | | | | | | | | | |
| BIRTWELL, ANDREW (HM02400) | | ● | | | | | | | ● | ● | | | | | | | | | | | | | | | | | | | | | | | | | | | | | | | | | | | | | | | | |
| BRIEF COUNS & PSYCHOTHERAPY SV (HM03020) | | | | | | | | | | | | | | | | | | | ● | | | | | | | | | | | | | | | | | | | | | | | | | | | | | | | |
| BROMLEY, DAVID (HM03148) | | | | | | | | | | | | | | | | | | | | ● | | | | | | | | | | | | | | | | | | | | | | | | | | | | | | |
| BUCKLE, WENDY-ANNE (HM03315) | | | | | | | | | | | | | | | | | | | | | | | | | | | | | | | | | | ● | | | | | | | | | | | | | | | | |
| CHURCH LAWFORD CHIRO CLINIC (HM04463) | | | | | | | | | | | | | | | | ● | | | | | | | | | | | | | | | | ● | | ● | | | | | | | | | | | | | | | | |
| CLIFTON OSTEOPATHIC PRACTICE (HM04669) | ● | | | | | | | | | | | | | | ● | ● | ● | | | | | | | | | | | ● | | | | ● | | ● | | | | | | | | | | ● | | | ● | | | |
| CREATIVE HEALTH CENTRE (HM05397) | | | | | | | | | | | | | | | ● | | | | | | | | | | | | | | | | | | | ● | ● | ● | | | | | | | | | | | | | | |
| CULPEPER (HM05570) | | | | | | | | | | | | | | | ● | | | | | | | | | | | | | | | | | | | | | | | | | | | | | | | | | | | |
| EDWARDS, IRENE & PETER (HM06656) | | | | | | | | | | | | | | | | | | | | ● | ● | | | | | | | | | | | | | | | | | | | | | | | | | | | | | |
| ELLIS, DAVID (HM06763) | | | | | | | | | | | | | | | | | | | | ● | | | | | | | | | | | | | | | | | | | | | | | | | | | | | | |
| FIGHT (HM07282) | | | | | | | | | | | | | | | | | | | | | | | | | | | | | | | | ● | | ● | | | | | ● | | | | | | | | | | | |
| FRANCIS, SUE (HM07676) | | | | | | | | | | | | | | | | | ● | | | | | | | | | | | | | | | | | | | | | | | | | | | | | | | | | |
| GREIG, E (HM08527) | | | | | | | | | | | ● | | | | | | | | | | ● | | | | | | | | | | | | | | | | | | | | | | | | ● | | ● | | | |
| HEART OF ENGLAND SHIATSU (HM09442) | | | | | | | | | | | | | | | | | | | | | | | | | | | | | | ● | | | | | | | | | | | | | | | | | ● | | ● | |
| HEARTLANDS (HM09445) | | | | | | | | | | | | | | | ● | | | | | | | | | | | | | | | | | | | | | ● | | | | ● | | ● | | | ● | | ● | | ● | |
| HELEN C OTTAWAY-FOSTER (HM09512) | | | | | | | | | | | | | | | | | | | | ● | | | | | | | | | | | | | | | | | | | | | | | | | | | | | | |
| HERBAL ONE (HM09631) | | | | | | | | | | | | | | | | | ● | | | | | | | ● | | | | | | | | | | | | | | | | | | | | | | | | | | |
| HOLYCOMBE (HM10060) | | | | | | | | | ● | | | ● | ● | | | ● | | | | | | | | | | | | | | | | | | | | | | | | | | | | | | | | | | |

# F - O Therapies at Practices/Businesses

Business by County with Reference no.

| Therapy | HUSBANDS, S (HM10431) | JACKSON, MICHAEL (HM10845) | JAN LLOYD AROMATHERAPY (HM10913) | JUST MASSAGE (HM11284) | LEAMINGTON SPA CHIRO CLINIC (HM12104) | LIFE-WAYS (HM12367) | NATURAL HEALTH CENTRE (HM14567) | NATURAL THERAPY CENTRE (HM14651) | PAYNE, JULIE (HM15865) | SAVAGE, GERALD (HM17966) | SHAND, GRAHAM (HM18278) | SHAWE AVENUE OSTEO PRACTICE (HM18351) | STRANKS, KATHY (HM19367) | STRATFORD ACU & HOLISTIC HLTH (HM19369) | STUDLEY PHYSIOTHERAPY CENTRE (HM19442) | TALBOT, G M (HM19660) | TOWERS, DIANA (HM20195) | TRADITIONAL ACUPUNCTURE GROUP (HM20221) | WARWICK OSTEOPATHIC PRACTICE (HM20966) | WREN, PAULINE (HM21922) | WREN, PAULINE (HM21923) | WILTSHIRE | ALTREE, CHRISTOPHER (HM00751) | ANDREWS, HAZEL (HM00852) | AVEBURY HYPNOTHERAPY PRACTICE (HM01386) | 'BACK IN LINE' (HM01482) | BUCHAN, DAVID (DR) (HM03298) | CAMPBELL, HELEN (HM03600) | CRICKLADE ROAD PRACTICE (HM05439) | CULPEPER (HM05581) | DINNAGE, GERARD (HM06113) | EASE MANAGEMENT CENTRE (HM06506) | ENGLISH, JOHN M (DR) (HM06834) | GAPPER, MILES (HM07864) |
|---|---|---|---|---|---|---|---|---|---|---|---|---|---|---|---|---|---|---|---|---|---|---|---|---|---|---|---|---|---|---|---|---|---|---|
| Orthomolecular Medicine | | | | | | | | | | | | | | | | | | | | | | | | | | | | | | | | | | |
| Oriental Diagnosis | | | | | | | ● | | | | | | | ● | | | | | | | | | | | | | | | | | | | | |
| Orgone Therapy | | | | | | | | | | | | | | | | | | | | | | | | | | | | | | | | | | |
| Nutritional Therapy | | | | | ● | | | | | | | | | ● | | | | | ● | | | | | | | | | | | | | | | |
| Neurotherapy | | | | | | | | | | | | | | | | | | | | | | | | | | | | | | | | | | |
| Neuro-Linguistic Program | | | | | | | | | | ● | | | | | | | | | | | | | | | | | | | | | | | | |
| Naturopathy | | | | | | | ● | | | | | | | | | | | | ● | | | | | | | | | | | | | | | |
| Nail Surgery | | | | | | | | | | | | | | | | | | | | | | | | | | | | | | | | | | |
| Music Therapy | | | | | | | | | | | | | | | | | | | | | | | | | | | | | | | | | | |
| Mud Therapy | | | | | | | | | | | | | | | | | | | | | | | | | | | | | | | | | | |
| Moxibustion | | | | | | | | | | | | | | ● | | | | | | | | | | ● | | | | | | | | | | |
| Micro Manipulation | | | | | | | | | | | | ● | | | | | | | | | | | | | | | | | | | | | | |
| Miasm Therapy | | | | | | | | | | | | | | | | | | | | | | | | | | | | | | | | | | |
| Metamorphic Therapy | | | | | | | | | | | | | | | | | | | | | | | | | | | | | | | | | | |
| Meditation | | | ● | | | | | | | | | | | | | | | | | ● | | | | | | | | | | | | | | |
| McTimoney Chiropractic | | | | | | | | | | | | | | | | | | | | | | | | | | | | | | | | | | |
| Massage (Therapeutic) | | | ● | ● | | | ● | | | | ● | ● | | ● | ● | | | ● | ● | | | | | | | ● | | | ● | | | | | |
| Manual Lymph Drainage | | | | | | | | | | | | | | | | | | | | | | | | | | | | | | | | | | |
| Manipulation | | | | | | | | ● | | | | ● | | ● | ● | | | | ● | | | | | | | | | | ● | | | | | |
| Magnetic Therapy | | | | | | | | | | | | | | | | | | | | | | | | | | | | | | | | | | |
| Macrobiotics | | | | | | | | | | | | | | | | | | | | | | | | | | | | | | | | | | |
| Light Therapy | | | | | | | | | | | | | | | | | | | | | | | | | | | | | | | | | | |
| Life Style Coaching | | | | | | | | | | | | | | | | | | | ● | ● | | | | | | | | | | | | ● | | |
| Laser Treatment | | | | | | | | | | | | | | | | | | | | | | | | | | | | | | | | | | |
| Kirlian Photography | | | | | | | | | | | | | | | | | | | | | | | | | | | | | | | | | | |
| Kinesiology | | | | | | | | | | | | | | | | | | | | | | | | | | | | | | | | | ● | |
| Iridology | | | | | | | | | | | | | | ● | | | | | | | | | | | | | | | | | | | | |
| Inhalation Therapy | | | | | | | | | | | | | | | | | | | | | | | | | | | | | | | | | | |
| Indian Head Massage | | | | | | | | | | | | | | | | | | | | | | | | | | ● | | | | | | | | |
| Hypnotherapy | | | | | | | ● | | | ● | | | | | | | ● | ● | | ● | | | | | ● | | | | | | | | | |
| Hypnosis | | ● | | | | | | | | ● | | | | | | ● | ● | | | ● | ● | | ● | | ● | | ● | ● | | | ● | | | ● |
| Humanistic Psychology | | | | | | | | | | | | | | | | | | | | | | | | | | | | | | | | ● | ● | |
| Hopi Ear Candles | | | | | | | | | | | | | | | | | | | | | | | | | | | | | | | | | | |
| Homeopathy | ● | | | | ● | ● | ● | ● | ● | | | | ● | ● | | | | | ● | | | | | | | | | | ● | | | | ● | |
| Holistic Healing | | | | | | | | | | | | | | | | | | | ● | ● | | | | | | | | | | | | | ● | |
| Herbal Medicine | | | | | | | ● | | | | | | | ● | | | | ● | ● | | | | | | | | | | | ● | | | | |
| Hellerwork | | | | | | | | | | | | | | | | | | | | | | | | | | | | | | | | | | |
| Healing Therapy | | | | | | | | | | | | | | | | | | | | ● | | | | | | | | | | | | | | |
| Healer | | | | | | | | | | | | | | ● | | | | | | ● | | | | | | | | | | | | | | |
| Hay Diet | | | | | | | | | | | | | | | | | | | | | | | | | | | | | | | | | ● | |
| Group Therapy | | | | | | | | | | | | | | | | | | | | | | | | | | | | | | | | | | |
| Gestalt Therapy | | | | | | | | | | | | | | | | | | | | | | | | | | | | | | | | | | |
| Gem Essence Therapy | | | | | | | | | | | | | | | | | | | | | | | | | | | | | | | | | | |
| Gait Analysis | | | | | | | | | | | | | | | | | | | | | | | | | | | | | | | | | | |
| Flotation Therapy | | | | | | | | | | | | | | | | | | | | | | | | | | | | | | | | | | |
| Floral Essence Therapy | | | | | | | | ● | | | | | | | | | | | | | | | | | | | | | | | | | | |
| Feng Shui | | | | | | | | | | | | | | | | | | | | | | | | | | | | | | | | | | |
| Feldenkrais Methodology | | | | | | | | | | | | | | | | | | | | | | | | | | | | | | | | | | |
| Family Therapy | | | | | | | | | | | | | | | | | | | | | | | | | | | | | | | | ● | | |
| Family Planning (Natural) | | | | | | | | | | | | | | | | | | | ● | | | | | | | | | | | | | | | |

# F - O Therapies at Practices/Businesses

| Business by County with Reference no. | Family Planning (Natural) | Family Therapy | Feldenkrais Methodology | Feng Shui | Floral Essence Therapy | Flotation Therapy | Gait Analysis | Gem Essence Therapy | Gestalt Therapy | Group Therapy | Hay Diet | Healer | Healing Therapy | Hellerwork | Herbal Medicine | Holistic Healing | Homeopathy | Hopi Ear Candles | Humanistic Psychology | Hypnosis | Hypnotherapy | Indian Head Massage | Inhalation Therapy | Iridology | Kinesiology |
|---|---|---|---|---|---|---|---|---|---|---|---|---|---|---|---|---|---|---|---|---|---|---|---|---|---|
| GRAY, J F (HM08413) | | | | | | | | | | | | | | | | | ● | | | | | | | | |
| HEALTH HYDRO (HM09389) | | | | | | | | | | | | | | | | | ● | | | | | | | | |
| HIGHWORTH PHYSIOTHERAPY CLINIC (HM09761) | | | | | | | | | | | | | | | | | | | | | | | | | |
| HURRY, GEOFF (HM10424) | | | | | | | | | | | | | | | | | | | | ● | | | | | |
| HYPNOTHERAPY CENTRE (HM10529) | | | | | | | | | | | | | | | | ● | | | | ● | ● | | | | |
| JENKINS, RUSSELL S (HM10996) | | | | | | | | | | | | | | | | | | | | | | | | | ● |
| LEIGHTON REFLEXOLOGY CLINIC (HM12196) | | | | | | | | | | | | | ● | | | ● | | | | | | ● | | | |
| LIFE-ENERGIES (HM12352) | | | | | | | | | | | | | | | | ● | | | | | | ● | | | ● |
| MAGNO PULSE (HM12919) | | | | | | | | | | | | | | | | | | | | | | | | | |
| MARLBOROUGH CHIRO CLINIC (HM13122) | | | | | | | | | | | | | | | | | | | | | | | | | |
| MARLBOROUGH NATURAL HLTH CTRE (HM13123) | | | | | | | | | | | | | | | | | | | | | ● | ● | | | ● |
| MATHER, PAULINE (HM13280) | | | | | | | | | | | ● | | | | ● | | | | | | | | | | ● |
| METABOLICS (HM13763) | | | | | | | | | | | | | | | | | | | | | | | | | |
| MILLETT-DEW, ROBERT (HM13909) | | | | | | | | | | | | | | | | | | | | ● | | | | | |
| MOURANT, JENNIFER L (HM14298) | | | | | | | | | | | | | | | | | | | | | | ● | | | |
| MULTI-THERAPY CENTRE (HM14352) | | | | | | | | | | | | | | | | | | | | | | | | | ● |
| NATURAL THERAPY CENTRE (HM14639) | | | | | | | | | | | | | | | ● | | | | | ● | ● | | | | |
| NATURALLY NUTRITION (HM14673) | | | | | | | | | | | | | | | | | | | | | | | | | |
| PETER & CAROLINE (HM16071) | | | | | | | | | | | | ● | ● | | | ● | | | | | | | | | |
| PETTIFER, JUSTINA (HM16095) | | | | | | | | | ● | | | | | | | | | | ● | ● | ● | | | | |
| POLLOCK & SIMPSON (HM16417) | | | | | | | | | | | | | | | | | | | | ● | | | | | |
| QUIRKE, G (HM16820) | | | | | | | | | | | | | | | | | | | | ● | ● | | | | |
| RAINBOW NATURAL THERAPIES (HM16880) | | | | | | | | | | | | | | | | | | | | | | | | | |
| SALISBURY HOMEOPATHY CENTRE (HM17852) | | | | | | | | | | | | | | | | | ● | | | | | | | | |
| SAWAYA, ALICIA (HM17982) | | | | | | | | | | | ● | ● | ● | | ● | ● | | | | | | | | | |
| SHAFTSBURY PRACTICE (HM18266) | | | | | | | | | | | | | | | ● | | ● | | | | ● | | | | |
| SHARPE, SALLY (HM18317) | | | | | | | | | | | | | | | | | ● | | | | | | | | |
| WALDER, PATRICIA (HM20752) | | | | | | | | | | | | | | | | | | | | ● | | | | | |
| WARMINSTER OSTEOPATHIC CLINIC (HM20929) | | | | | | | | | | | | | | | | | ● | | | | | ● | | | |
| WELLS, HENRIETTA (HM21175) | | | | | | | | | | | | | | | | ● | ● | | | | | | | | |
| WESTBURY CHIROPRACTIC (HM21258) | | | | | | | | | | | | | | | | | ● | | | | | | | | |
| WOOTTON BASSETT (HM21885) | | | | | | | | | | | | | | | | | | | | | | | | | |
| **WORCESTERSHIRE** | | | | | | | | | | | | | | | | | | | | | | | | | |
| BRETFORDTON CLINIC (HM02969) | | | | | | | | | | | | ● | ● | | ● | ● | ● | | | | | | | | ● |

| Business by County with Reference no. | Kirlian Photography | Laser Treatment | Life Style Coaching | Light Therapy | Macrobiotics | Magnetic Therapy | Manipulation | Manual Lymph Drainage | Massage (Therapeutic) | McTimoney Chiropractic | Meditation | Metamorphic Therapy | Miasm Therapy | Micro Manipulation | Moxibustion | Mud Therapy | Music Therapy | Nail Surgery | Naturopathy | Neuro-Linguistic Program | Neurotherapy | Nutritional Therapy | Orgone Therapy | Oriental Diagnosis | Orthomolecular Medicine |
|---|---|---|---|---|---|---|---|---|---|---|---|---|---|---|---|---|---|---|---|---|---|---|---|---|---|
| GRAY, J F (HM08413) | | | | | | | | | | | | | | | | | | | | | | | | | |
| HEALTH HYDRO (HM09389) | | | | | | | | | | | | | | | | | | | | | | ● | | | |
| HIGHWORTH PHYSIOTHERAPY CLINIC (HM09761) | | | | | | | ● | | ● | | | | | | | | | | | | | | | | |
| HURRY, GEOFF (HM10424) | | | | | | | | | | | | | | | | | | | | | | | | | |
| HYPNOTHERAPY CENTRE (HM10529) | | | | | | | | | | | | | | | | | | | | | | | | | |
| JENKINS, RUSSELL S (HM10996) | | | | | | | ● | | ● | | | | | | | | | | | | | | | | |
| LEIGHTON REFLEXOLOGY CLINIC (HM12196) | | | | | | | | | ● | | | | | | | | | | | | | | | | |
| LIFE-ENERGIES (HM12352) | | | | | | | | | ● | | | | | | | | | | | | | ● | ● | | |
| MAGNO PULSE (HM12919) | | | | | | ● | | | | | | | | | | | | | | | | | | | |
| MARLBOROUGH CHIRO CLINIC (HM13122) | | | | | | | ● | | ● | | | | | | | | | | | | | | | | |
| MARLBOROUGH NATURAL HLTH CTRE (HM13123) | | | | | | | | | | | | | | | | | | | | | | | | | |
| MATHER, PAULINE (HM13280) | | | | | | | ● | | ● | | | | | | ● | | | | | | | ● | | | |
| METABOLICS (HM13763) | | | | | | | | | | | | | | | | | | | | | | ● | | | |
| MILLETT-DEW, ROBERT (HM13909) | | | | | | | | | | | | | | | | | | | | | | | | | |
| MOURANT, JENNIFER L (HM14298) | | | | | | | | | ● | | | | | | | | | | | | | | | | |
| MULTI-THERAPY CENTRE (HM14352) | | | | | | | | | ● | | | | | | | | | | | | | | | ● | |
| NATURAL THERAPY CENTRE (HM14639) | | | ● | | | | | | ● | | | | | | | | | | | ● | | ● | | | |
| NATURALLY NUTRITION (HM14673) | | | | | | | | | | | | | | | | | | | | | | ● | | | |
| PETER & CAROLINE (HM16071) | | | | | | | | | ● | | ● | | | | | | ● | | | | | ● | | | |
| PETTIFER, JUSTINA (HM16095) | | | ● | | | | | | | | | | | | | | | | | | | | | | |
| POLLOCK & SIMPSON (HM16417) | | | | | | | | | | | | | | | | | | | | | | | | | |
| QUIRKE, G (HM16820) | | | | | | | | | | | | | | | | | | | | | | | | | |
| RAINBOW NATURAL THERAPIES (HM16880) | | | | | | | | | ● | | | | | | | | | | | | | | | | |
| SALISBURY HOMEOPATHY CENTRE (HM17852) | | | | | | | | | | | | | | | | | | | | | | | | | |
| SAWAYA, ALICIA (HM17982) | | | | | | | | | | | | | | | | | | | | | | | | | |
| SHAFTSBURY PRACTICE (HM18266) | | | | | | | | | ● | | | | | | | | | | | | | | | | |
| SHARPE, SALLY (HM18317) | | | | | | | | | | | | | | | | | | | | | | | | | |
| WALDER, PATRICIA (HM20752) | | | | | | | | | | | | | | | | | | | | | | | | | |
| WARMINSTER OSTEOPATHIC CLINIC (HM20929) | | | | | | | ● | | ● | | | | | | | | | | | | | | | | |
| WELLS, HENRIETTA (HM21175) | | | | | | | | | | | | | | | | | | | | | | | | | |
| WESTBURY CHIROPRACTIC (HM21258) | | | | | | | | | | | | | | | | | | | | | | | | | |
| WOOTTON BASSETT (HM21885) | | | | | | | ● | | | | | | | | | | | | | | | | | | |
| **WORCESTERSHIRE** | | | | | | | | | | | | | | | | | | | | | | | | | |
| BRETFORDTON CLINIC (HM02969) | | | | | | | ● | | ● | | | | | | | | ● | | ● | | | | | | |

# F - O Therapies at Practices/Businesses

Business by County with Reference no.

| Business by County with Reference no. | Family Planning (Natural) | Family Therapy | Feldenkrais Methodology | Feng Shui | Floral Essence Therapy | Flotation Therapy | Gait Analysis | Gem Essence Therapy | Gestalt Therapy | Group Therapy | Hay Diet | Healer | Healing Therapy | Hellerwork | Herbal Medicine | Holistic Healing | Homeopathy | Hopi Ear Candles | Humanistic Psychology | Hypnosis | Hypnotherapy | Indian Head Massage | Inhalation Therapy | Iridology | Kinesiology |
|---|---|---|---|---|---|---|---|---|---|---|---|---|---|---|---|---|---|---|---|---|---|---|---|---|---|
| COLLEGE OF HEALING (HM04846) | | | | | | | | | | | | | ● | | | | | | | | | | | | |
| DAVIES PODIATRY (HM05792) | | | | | | | | | | | | | | | | | | | | | | | | | |
| EVESHAM NATURAL HEALTH CENTRE (HM07009) | | | | | | | | | | | | | | | | | | | | | ● | | | | |
| FRONTIA (HM07757) | | | | | | | | | | | | ● | | | | | ● | | | | ● | ● | | | ● |
| IN THE PINK (HM10598) | | | | | | | | | | | | | | | | | | | | | | ● | | | |
| MALVERN HILLS HOMOEOPATHIC (HM12995) | | | | | | | | | | | | | | | | | ● | | | | | | | | |
| MALVERN NATURAL HEALTH CENTRE (HM12998) | | | | | | | | | | | | | | | ● | | ● | | | | ● | | | | |
| MALVERN OSTEOPATHIC CLINIC (HM12999) | | | | | | | | | | | | | | | | | | | | | | | | | |
| MARSTON, SUE (HM13179) | | | | | | | | | | | | | | | | | | | | | ● | | | | |
| MEAKIN, D W (HM13637) | | | | | | | | | | | | | | | | | | | | | | | | | |
| NOTTINGHAM, STUART (HM15086) | | | | | | | | | | | | | | | | | | | | | | | | | |
| NURCHIR (HM15110) | | | | | | | | | | | | | | | | | | | | | | | | | |
| NUTRIMED (HM15118) | | | | | | | | | | | | | | | ● | | | | | | | | | | |
| PARDOE, DIANA T (HM15648) | | | | | | | | | | | | | | | | ● | | | | ● | ● | ● | | | |
| PARROTT, C J (HM15733) | | | | | | | | | | | | | | | | | | | | ● | | | | | |
| PERSHORE (HM16056) | | | | | | | | | | | | | | | | | ● | | | | | | | | |
| PERSHORE NAT THERAPY CLINIC (HM16057) | | | | | | | | | | | | | | | ● | | ● | | | | ● | ● | | | ● |
| REDDITCH FOOTCARE SURGERY (HM17014) | | | | | | | | | | | | | | | | | | | | | | | | | |
| RICHARDS, VERONICA (HM17265) | | | | | | | | | | | | | | | | | ● | | | | | | | | |
| ROBARK CENTRE (HM17386) | | | | | | | | | | | | | | | | | | | | ● | | | | | |
| SOUTH WORCESTERSHIRE HYP (HM18915) | | | | | | | | | | | | | | | | | | | | ● | ● | | | | |
| STOKES, TERRY (HM19325) | | | | | | | | | | | | | | | | | ● | | | | | | | | |
| STONE, ANNE L (HM19329) | | | | | | | | | | | | | | | | | | | | | | | | | |
| TRANQUILITY (HM20259) | | | | | | | | | | | | | | | | | | | | ● | | | | | |
| WORCESTER NATURAL THERAPY CTRE (HM21886) | | | | | | | | | | | | | ● | | | | ● | | | | | | | | ● |
| **YORKSHIRE (NORTH)** | | | | | | | | | | | | | | | | | | | | | | | | | |
| A TACTILE BUSINESS (HM00046) | | | | | | | | | | | | ● | | | | | | | | | | ● | | | |
| APOTHECARY (HM00933) | | | | | | | | | | | | | | | ● | | | | | | | | | | |
| AVENA HERBAL PRODUCTS (HM01387) | | | | | | | | | | | | | | | ● | | | | | | | | | | |
| BAKER, LINDA (HM01587) | | | | | | | | | | | | | | | | ● | | | | | | ● | | | |
| BARRASS, K I (HM01778) | | | | | | | | | | | | | | | | | | | | | | | | | |
| BLACK, SAUL (HM02428) | | | | | | | | | | | | | | | | | | | | | | | | | |
| BROADHEAD, J N & M (HM03114) | | | | | | | ● | | | | | | | | | | | | | | | | | | |
| BUSWELL, RONA (HM03471) | | | | | | | | | | | | ● | | | | | | | | | | | | | |

| Business by County with Reference no. | Kirlian Photography | Laser Treatment | Life Style Coaching | Light Therapy | Macrobiotics | Magnetic Therapy | Manipulation | Manual Lymph Drainage | Massage (Therapeutic) | McTimoney Chiropractic | Meditation | Metamorphic Therapy | Miasm Therapy | Micro Manipulation | Moxibustion | Mud Therapy | Music Therapy | Nail Surgery | Naturopathy | Neuro-Linguistic Program | Neurotherapy | Nutritional Therapy | Orgone Therapy | Oriental Diagnosis | Orthomolecular Medicine |
|---|---|---|---|---|---|---|---|---|---|---|---|---|---|---|---|---|---|---|---|---|---|---|---|---|---|
| COLLEGE OF HEALING (HM04846) | | | | | | | | | | | | | | | | | | | | | | | | | |
| DAVIES PODIATRY (HM05792) | | | | | | | | | | | | | | | | | | ● | | | | | | | |
| EVESHAM NATURAL HEALTH CENTRE (HM07009) | | | | | | | ● | | | | | | | | | | | | | | | | | | |
| FRONTIA (HM07757) | | | | | | | | | ● | | | | | | | | | | | | | ● | | | |
| IN THE PINK (HM10598) | | | | | | | | | | | | | | | | | | | | | | | | | |
| MALVERN HILLS HOMOEOPATHIC (HM12995) | | | | | | | | | | | | | | | | | | | | | | | | | |
| MALVERN NATURAL HEALTH CENTRE (HM12998) | | | | | | | | | | | | | | | | | | | | | | | | | |
| MALVERN OSTEOPATHIC CLINIC (HM12999) | | | | | | | ● | | ● | | | | | | | | | | | | | | | | |
| MARSTON, SUE (HM13179) | | | | | | | | | | | | | | | | | | | | | | | | | |
| MEAKIN, D W (HM13637) | | | | | | | | | | | | | | | | | | | ● | | | | | | |
| NOTTINGHAM, STUART (HM15086) | | | | | | | ● | | ● | | | | | | | | | | | | | | | | |
| NURCHIR (HM15110) | | | | | | | ● | | ● | | | | | | | | | | | | | | | | |
| NUTRIMED (HM15118) | | | | | | | | | | | | | | | | | | | | | | ● | | | |
| PARDOE, DIANA T (HM15648) | | | | | | | | | | | | | | | | | | | | | | | | | |
| PARROTT, C J (HM15733) | | | | | | | | | | | | | | | | | | | | | | | | | |
| PERSHORE (HM16056) | | | | | | | | | | | | | | | | | | | | | | | | | |
| PERSHORE NAT THERAPY CLINIC (HM16057) | | | | | | | | | | | | | | | ● | | | | | | | | | | |
| REDDITCH FOOTCARE SURGERY (HM17014) | | | | | | | | | | | | | | | | | | ● | | | | | | | |
| RICHARDS, VERONICA (HM17265) | | | | | | | | | | | | | | | | | | | | | | | | | |
| ROBARK CENTRE (HM17386) | | | | | | | | | | | | | | | | | | | | | | | | | |
| SOUTH WORCESTERSHIRE HYP (HM18915) | | | | | | | | | | | | | | | | | | | | | | | | | |
| STOKES, TERRY (HM19325) | | | | | | | ● | | | | | | | | | | | | ● | | | | | | |
| STONE, ANNE L (HM19329) | | | | | | | ● | | ● | | | | | | | | | | | | | | | | |
| TRANQUILITY (HM20259) | | | | | | | | | | | | | | | | | | | | | | | | | |
| WORCESTER NATURAL THERAPY CTRE (HM21886) | | | | | | | | | | | | | | | | | | | | | | | | | |
| **YORKSHIRE (NORTH)** | | | | | | | | | | | | | | | | | | | | | | | | | |
| A TACTILE BUSINESS (HM00046) | | | | | | | | | | | | | | | | | | | | | | | | | |
| APOTHECARY (HM00933) | | | | | | | | | | | | | | | | | | | | | | | | | |
| AVENA HERBAL PRODUCTS (HM01387) | | | | | | | | | | | | | | | | | | | | | | | | | |
| BAKER, LINDA (HM01587) | | | | | | | | | ● | | | | | | | | | | | | | | | | |
| BARRASS, K I (HM01778) | | | | | | | | | | | | | | | | | | ● | | | | | | | |
| BLACK, SAUL (HM02428) | | | | | | | | | | | | | | | | | | ● | | | | | | | |
| BROADHEAD, J N & M (HM03114) | | | | | | | | | | | | | | | | | | | | | | | | | |
| BUSWELL, RONA (HM03471) | | | | | | | | | | | | | | | | | | | | | | | | | |

# F - O Therapies at Practices/Businesses

| Business by County with Reference no. | Family Planning (Natural) | Family Therapy | Feldenkrais Methodology | Feng Shui | Floral Essence Therapy | Flotation Therapy | Gait Analysis | Gem Essence Therapy | Gestalt Therapy | Group Therapy | Hay Diet | Healer | Healing Therapy | Hellerwork | Herbal Medicine | Holistic Healing | Homeopathy | Hopi Ear Candles | Humanistic Psychology | Hypnosis | Hypnotherapy | Indian Head Massage | Inhalation Therapy | Iridology | Kinesiology |
|---|---|---|---|---|---|---|---|---|---|---|---|---|---|---|---|---|---|---|---|---|---|---|---|---|---|
| CORDEL, MICHAEL (HM05160) | | | | | | | | | | | | | | | | | | | | | | | | | |
| CRAVEN CLINIC (HM05384) | | | | | | | | | | | | ● | ● | | | ● | ● | | | | ● | ● | | | |
| CRICK, PAUL (HM05438) | | | | | | | | | | | | | | | | | | | | | | | | | |
| CROFT HOUSE CLINIC (HM05452) | | | | | | | | | | | | | | | ● | | ● | | | | | | | | |
| CULPEPER (HM05575) | | | | | | | | | | | | | | | ● | | | | | | | | | | |
| DOVE, L (HM06229) | | | | | | | | | | | | | | | | | | | | ● | | | | | |
| FIELD, ROWENA (HM07267) | | | | | | | | | | | | | | | | | ● | | | | | | | | |
| FILEY THERAPIST (HM07289) | | | | | | | | | | | | | | | | | | | | | | | | | |
| GARNER, MARGARET (HM07894) | | | | | | | | | | | | | | | | | | | | ● | | | | | |
| GRAVELLS, M (HM08402) | | | | | | | | | | | | | | | | | ● | | | | | | | | |
| GRIFFIN, TRICIA (HM08555) | | | | | | | | | | | | | | | | | ● | | | | | | | | |
| HARROGATE HOLISTIC HEALTH CTRE (HM09116) | | | | | | | | | | | | | | | | | ● | | | ● | ● | | | ● | ● |
| HEALING CLINIC (HM09328) | ● | | | | | | | | | | | | | | ● | | ● | | | | | | | | ● |
| HIGHTHORN PHYSIOTHERAPY CLINIC (HM09759) | | | | | | | | | | | | | | | | | ● | | | | | | | | |
| HOBSON, I K (HM09863) | | | | | | | ● | | | | | | | | | | | | | | | | | | |
| HYPNOTHERAPY CENTRE (HM10518) | | | | | | | | | | | | | | | | | | | | ● | | | | | |
| JOWETT, R S J (HM11227) | | | | | | | | | | | | | | | | | | | | ● | | | | | |
| KERNOHAN, SARA (HM11545) | | | | | | | | | | | | | ● | | | | | | | | | | | | |
| KNOWLES, J (HM11770) | | | | | | | | | | | | | | | | | | | | | | | | | |
| LESZCZUK, PAULA (HM12246) | | | | | | | | | | | | | | | | | ● | | | | | | | | |
| LESZCZUK, PAULA (HM12245) | | | | | | | | | | | | | | | | | ● | | | | | | | | |
| LIFESUPPORT (HM12366) | | | | | | | | | | | | ● | | | | | | | | | ● | ● | | | ● |
| NANCY METCALFE MOBILE CONSULT (HM14468) | | | | | | | | | | | | | | | | | | | | | | | | | |
| NATURAL BALANCE (HM14515) | | | | | | | | | | | | | | | | | | | | | | | | | |
| NEEDHAM, P E (HM14752) | | | | | | | | | | | | | | | | | | | | ● | | | | | |
| PAULA LESZCZUK (HM15849) | | | | | | | | | | | | | | | | | ● | | | | | | | | |
| PROUDFOOT SCHOOL (HM16674) | | | | | | | | | | | | | | | | | | | | ● | | | | | |
| PROUDFOOT, WILF (HM16675) | | | | | | | | | | | | | | | | | | | | | ● | | | | |
| RILEY, S (HM17346) | | | | | | | | | | | | | | | | | ● | | | | | | | | |
| RIPON NATURAL HEALTH CENTRE (HM17365) | | ● | | | | | | | | | | ● | ● | | ● | ● | ● | | | | | ● | | | |
| RYEDALE CLINIC (HM17803) | | | | | | | | | | | | | | | | | | | | | | | | | |
| SETCHFIELD, WENDY (HM18241) | | | | | | | | | | | | | | | | | ● | | | | | | | | |
| SHACKLETON, MAUREEN (HM18264) | | | | | | | | | | | | | | | | | | | | ● | ● | | | | |
| SHAH, ATUL (HM18268) | | | | | | | | | | | ● | | | | | ● | | | | | | | | | |

| Business by County with Reference no. | Kirlian Photography | Laser Treatment | Life Style Coaching | Light Therapy | Macrobiotics | Magnetic Therapy | Manipulation | Manual Lymph Drainage | Massage (Therapeutic) | McTimoney Chiropractic | Meditation | Metamorphic Therapy | Miasm Therapy | Micro Manipulation | Moxibustion | Mud Therapy | Music Therapy | Nail Surgery | Naturopathy | Neuro-Linguistic Program | Neurotherapy | Nutritional Therapy | Orgone Therapy | Oriental Diagnosis | Orthomolecular Medicine |
|---|---|---|---|---|---|---|---|---|---|---|---|---|---|---|---|---|---|---|---|---|---|---|---|---|---|
| CORDEL, MICHAEL (HM05160) | | | | | | | | | ● | | | | | | ● | | | | | | | | | | |
| CRAVEN CLINIC (HM05384) | | | | | | | ● | | ● | | ● | ● | | | ● | | | | | | | | | | |
| CRICK, PAUL (HM05438) | | | | | | | | | ● | | | | | | | | | | | | | | | | |
| CROFT HOUSE CLINIC (HM05452) | | | | | | | | | | | | | | | | | | | | | | | | | |
| CULPEPER (HM05575) | | | | | | | | | | | | | | | | | | | | | | | | | |
| DOVE, L (HM06229) | | | | | | | | | | | | | | | | | | | | | | | | | |
| FIELD, ROWENA (HM07267) | | | | | | | | | | | | | | | | | | | | | | | | | |
| FILEY THERAPIST (HM07289) | | | | | | | | | ● | | | | | | | | | | | | | | | | |
| GARNER, MARGARET (HM07894) | | | | | | | | | | | | | | | | | | | | | | | | | |
| GRAVELLS, M (HM08402) | | | | | | | | | | | | | | | | | | | | | | | | | |
| GRIFFIN, TRICIA (HM08555) | | | | | | | | | | | | | | | | | | | | | | | | | |
| HARROGATE HOLISTIC HEALTH CTRE (HM09116) | | | | | | | | | | | | | | | | | | | | | | ● | | | |
| HEALING CLINIC (HM09328) | | | | | | | | | | | | | | | ● | | | | | | | ● | | ● | |
| HIGHTHORN PHYSIOTHERAPY CLINIC (HM09759) | | | | | | | | | | | | | | | | | | | | | | | | | |
| HOBSON, I K (HM09863) | | | | | | | | | | | | | | | | | | | | | | | | | |
| HYPNOTHERAPY CENTRE (HM10518) | | | | | | | | | | | | | | | | | | | | | | | | | |
| JOWETT, R S J (HM11227) | | | | | | | | | | | | | | | | | | | | | | | | | |
| KERNOHAN, SARA (HM11545) | | | | | | | | | | | | | | | | | | | | | | | | | |
| KNOWLES, J (HM11770) | | | | | | | | | | | | | | | | | | ● | | | | | | | |
| LESZCZUK, PAULA (HM12246) | | | | | | | | | | | | | | | | | | | | | | | | | |
| LESZCZUK, PAULA (HM12245) | | | | | | | | | | | | | | | | | | | | | | | | | |
| LIFESUPPORT (HM12366) | | | | | ● | | | | ● | | | ● | | | ● | | | | | | | ● | | ● | |
| NANCY METCALFE MOBILE CONSULT (HM14468) | | | | | | | | | ● | | | | | | | | ● | | | | | | | | |
| NATURAL BALANCE (HM14515) | | | | | | | | | ● | | | | | | | | | | | | | | | | |
| NEEDHAM, P E (HM14752) | | | | | | | | | | | | | | | | | | | | | | | | | |
| PAULA LESZCZUK (HM15849) | | | | | | | | | | | | | | | | | | | | | | | | | |
| PROUDFOOT SCHOOL (HM16674) | | | | | | | | | | | | | | | | | | | | | | | | | |
| PROUDFOOT, WILF (HM16675) | | | | | | | | | | | | | | | | | | | | | | | | | |
| RILEY, S (HM17346) | | | | | | | | | | | | | | | | | | | | | | | | | |
| RIPON NATURAL HEALTH CENTRE (HM17365) | | | | | | | ● | | ● | | ● | | ● | | ● | | | | | | | ● | | | |
| RYEDALE CLINIC (HM17803) | | | | | | | ● | | ● | | | | | | | | | | | | | | | | |
| SETCHFIELD, WENDY (HM18241) | | | | | | | | | | | | | | | | | | | | | | | | | |
| SHACKLETON, MAUREEN (HM18264) | | | | | | | | | | | | | | | | | | | | | | | | | |
| SHAH, ATUL (HM18268) | | | ● | | | | ● | | ● | | | | | ● | | | | | ● | | | ● | | | |

# F - O Therapies at Practices/Businesses

Business by County with Reference no.

| Business | Family Planning (Natural) | Family Therapy | Feldenkrais Methodology | Feng Shui | Floral Essence Therapy | Flotation Therapy | Gait Analysis | Gem Essence Therapy | Gestalt Therapy | Group Therapy | Hay Diet | Healer | Healing Therapy | Hellerwork | Herbal Medicine | Holistic Healing | Homeopathy | Hopi Ear Candles | Humanistic Psychology | Hypnosis | Hypnotherapy | Indian Head Massage | Inhalation Therapy | Iridology | Kinesiology |
|---|---|---|---|---|---|---|---|---|---|---|---|---|---|---|---|---|---|---|---|---|---|---|---|---|---|
| SNELSON, KAREN (HM18836) | | | | | | | | | | | | | | | | | | | | ● | | | | | |
| STRATTON, FIONA (HM19372) | | | | | | | | | | | | ● | | | | ● | | | | | | | | | |
| TERRY ANNE (HM19845) | | | | | | | | | ● | ● | | ● | ● | | | | | | | ● | ● | | | | |
| YORK CLINIC (HM22040) | | | | | | | | | | | | | | | | | ● | | | | ● | | | | |
| YORK COUNSELLING (HM22042) | | | | | | | | | | | | | | | | | | | | ● | ● | | | | |
| YORK SCHOOL OF COMP MEDICINE (HM22050) | | | | | | | | | | | | | | | | | | | | | | | | | |
| **YORKSHIRE (SOUTH)** | | | | | | | | | | | | | | | | | | | | | | | | | |
| ALTERNATIVES (HM00742) | | | | | | | | | | | | | | | | | | | | ● | | | | | |
| ALTON & JAMES MED HERBAL (HM00748) | | | | | | | | | | | | | | | ● | ● | | | | | | | | | |
| ANDERSON, A DUDLEY (HM00810) | | | | | | | | | | | | | | | | | | | | ● | ● | | | | |
| BEDFORD, SUSAN (HM02041) | | | | | | | | | | | | | | | | | ● | | | | | | | | |
| BIRCH, SONIA Y (HM02355) | | | | | | | | | | | | | | | | | | | | ● | | | | | |
| BONESETTER AND MANIPULATOR (HM02676) | | | | | | | | | | | | | | | | | | | | | | | | | |
| BOON, G M (HM02690) | | | | | | | | | | | | | | | | | | | | | | | | | |
| BOORMAN, JUNE (HM02694) | | | | | | | | | | | | | | | | | | | | ● | | | | | |
| BRADWAY COMP THERAPY CENTRE (HM02880) | | | | | | | | | | | | | | | | | | | | | | | | | |
| BRAMLEY HALL CLINIC (HM02902) | | | | | | | | | | | ● | | | | ● | | | | | | | | | | ● |
| BRANKIN, M & K (HM02917) | | | | | | | | | | | | | | | | | | | | | | | | | |
| BRANKLIN, M & K (HM02918) | | | | | | | | | | | | | | | | | | | | | | | | | |
| BRITISH SOC OF MED/DENT HYP (HM03095) | | | | | | | | | | | | | | | | | | | | ● | | | | | |
| CARING CLINIC (HM03682) | | | | | | | | | | | | ● | ● | | | | | | | | ● | ● | | | |
| CHIROPODY SURGERY (HM04342) | | | | | | | ● | | | | | | | | | | | | | | | | | | |
| COUNTRY PRACTICE (HM05256) | | | | | | | | | | | | | | | | | | | | | | | ● | | |
| CULPEPER (HM05571) | | | | | | | | | | | | | | | ● | | | | | | | | | | |
| DORE PHYSIOTHERAPY PRACTICE (HM06196) | | | | | | | | | | | | | | | | | | | | | | | | | |
| EATON, T C (HM06565) | | | | | | | | | | | | | | | | | | | | | | | | | |
| ESSENTIAL HARMONY (HM06907) | | | | | | | | | | | | | | | | | | | | | | ● | | | |
| FISHER, CHRISTINE A (HM07349) | | | | | | | | | | | | | | | | | | | | | | | | | |
| GRAPEVINE HEALTH (HM08399) | | | | | | | | | | | | | | | | | | | | | | | | | |
| GYALTSABJE BUDDHIST CENTRE (HM08672) | | | | | | | | | | | | | | | | | | | | | | | | | |
| HALLAMSHIRE NATURAL HLTH CTRE (HM08798) | | | | | | | | | | | | ● | ● | | ● | ● | ● | | | | | ● | | ● | |
| HARTLEY, S (HM09147) | | | | | | | | | | | | | | | | | ● | | | | | | | | |
| HEALTHY FEET (HM09427) | | | | | | | | | | | | | | | | | | | | | | | | | |
| HINCHLIFFE, JACKIE (HM09822) | | | | | | | | | | | | | | | | | | | | | | ● | | | |

| Business | Kirlian Photography | Laser Treatment | Life Style Coaching | Light Therapy | Macrobiotics | Magnetic Therapy | Manipulation | Manual Lymph Drainage | Massage (Therapeutic) | McTimoney Chiropractic | Meditation | Metamorphic Therapy | Miasm Therapy | Micro Manipulation | Moxibustion | Mud Therapy | Music Therapy | Nail Surgery | Naturopathy | Neuro-Linguistic Program | Neurotherapy | Nutritional Therapy | Orgone Therapy | Oriental Diagnosis | Orthomolecular Medicine |
|---|---|---|---|---|---|---|---|---|---|---|---|---|---|---|---|---|---|---|---|---|---|---|---|---|---|
| SNELSON, KAREN (HM18836) | | | | | | | | | | | | | | | | | | | | | | | | | |
| STRATTON, FIONA (HM19372) | | | | | | | | | ● | | | | | | | | | | | | | | | | |
| TERRY ANNE (HM19845) | | | | | | | | | | | | | | | | | | | | ● | | | | | |
| YORK CLINIC (HM22040) | | | | | | | | | | | | | | | | | | | | | | | | | |
| YORK COUNSELLING (HM22042) | | | ● | | | | | | | | | | | | | | | | | | | | | | |
| YORK SCHOOL OF COMP MEDICINE (HM22050) | | | | | | | | | ● | | | | | | | | | | | | | ● | | | |
| **YORKSHIRE (SOUTH)** | | | | | | | | | | | | | | | | | | | | | | | | | |
| ALTERNATIVES (HM00742) | | | | | | | | | | | | | | | | | | | | | | | | | |
| ALTON & JAMES MED HERBAL (HM00748) | | | | | | | | | | | | | | | | | | | | | | | | | |
| ANDERSON, A DUDLEY (HM00810) | | | | | | | | | ● | | | | | | | | | | | | | | | | |
| BEDFORD, SUSAN (HM02041) | | | | | | | | | | | | | | | | | | | | | | | | | |
| BIRCH, SONIA Y (HM02355) | | | | | | | | | | | | | | | | | | | | | | | | | |
| BONESETTER AND MANIPULATOR (HM02676) | | | | | | | ● | | | | | | | | | | | | | | | | | | |
| BOON, G M (HM02690) | | | | | | | | | | | | | | | | | | ● | | | | | | | |
| BOORMAN, JUNE (HM02694) | | | | | | | | | | | | | | | | | | | | | | | | | |
| BRADWAY COMP THERAPY CENTRE (HM02880) | | | | | | | | | ● | | | | | | | | | | | | | | | | |
| BRAMLEY HALL CLINIC (HM02902) | | | | | | | ● | | ● | | | | | | | | | | ● | | | | | | |
| BRANKIN, M & K (HM02917) | | | | | | | | | | | | | | | | | | ● | | | | | | | |
| BRANKLIN, M & K (HM02918) | | | | | | | | | | | | | | | | | | ● | | | | | | | |
| BRITISH SOC OF MED/DENT HYP (HM03095) | | | | | | | | | | | | | | | | | | | | | | | | | |
| CARING CLINIC (HM03682) | | | | | | | | | | | ● | ● | | | | | | | | | | ● | | | |
| CHIROPODY SURGERY (HM04342) | | | | | | | | | | | | | | | | | | ● | | | | | | | |
| COUNTRY PRACTICE (HM05256) | | | | | | | | | ● | | | | | | | | | ● | | | | | | | |
| CULPEPER (HM05571) | | | | | | | | | | | | | | | | | | | | | | | | | |
| DORE PHYSIOTHERAPY PRACTICE (HM06196) | | | | | | | ● | | ● | | | | | | | | | | | | | | | | |
| EATON, T C (HM06565) | | | | | | | | | | | | | | | | | | ● | | | | | | | |
| ESSENTIAL HARMONY (HM06907) | | | | | | | | | | | | | | | | | | | | | | | | | |
| FISHER, CHRISTINE A (HM07349) | | | | | | | | | | | | | | | | | | ● | | | | | | | |
| GRAPEVINE HEALTH (HM08399) | | | | | | | | | | | | | | | | | | | | | | ● | | | |
| GYALTSABJE BUDDHIST CENTRE (HM08672) | | | | | | | | | | | ● | | | | | | | | | | | | | | |
| HALLAMSHIRE NATURAL HLTH CTRE (HM08798) | | | | | | | ● | | ● | | ● | | | | | | | | | | | ● | | | |
| HARTLEY, S (HM09147) | | | | | | | | | | | | | | | | | | | | | | | | | |
| HEALTHY FEET (HM09427) | | | | | | | ● | | | | | | | | | | | | | | | | | | |
| HINCHLIFFE, JACKIE (HM09822) | | | | | | | | | ● | | | | | | | | | | | | | | | | |

www.healthmyself.com

# F - O Therapies at Practices/Businesses

| Business by County with Reference no. | Family Planning (Natural) | Family Therapy | Feldenkrais Methodology | Feng Shui | Floral Essence Therapy | Flotation Therapy | Gait Analysis | Gem Essence Therapy | Gestalt Therapy | Group Therapy | Hay Diet | Healer | Healing Therapy | Hellerwork | Herbal Medicine | Holistic Healing | Homeopathy | Hopi Ear Candles | Humanistic Psychology | Hypnosis | Hypnotherapy | Indian Head Massage | Inhalation Therapy | Iridology | Kinesiology |
|---|---|---|---|---|---|---|---|---|---|---|---|---|---|---|---|---|---|---|---|---|---|---|---|---|---|
| HYPNOTHERAPY CENTRE (HM10515) | | | | | | | | | | | | | | | | | | | | ● | ● | | | | |
| JACKSON, W D & SONS (HM10852) | | | | | | | | | | | | | | | ● | | | | | | | | | | |
| JOHNSON, STUART (HM11097) | | | | | | | | | | | | | | | | | | | | ● | | | | | |
| KEITH LINLEY HYPNOTHERAPY (HM11413) | | | | | | | | | | | | | | | | | | | | ● | | | | | |
| KILVINGTON & ASSOCIATES (HM11612) | | | | | | | | | | | | | | | | | | | | ● | | | | | |
| LLEWELLYN CONSULTANCY (HM12502) | | ● | | | | | | | ● | ● | | ● | ● | | | ● | ● | | | ● | ● | | | | ● |
| MEDICAL HERBALIST (HM13652) | | | | | | | | | | | | | | | ● | | | | | | | | | | |
| MILLINGTON, JANET (HM13917) | | | | | | | | | | | | | | | | | | | | ● | ● | | | | |
| MOORGATE NATURAL HEALING CTRE (HM14138) | | | | | | | | | ● | | | | | | | | | | ● | ● | ● | | | | |
| NIGHTINGALE PHYSIO PRACTICE (HM14937) | | | | | | | | | | | | | | | | | | | | | | | | | |
| PACKER, RACHEL (HM15557) | | | | | | | | | | | | | | | | | ● | | | | | | | | |
| ROBINSON, C (HM17462) | | | | | | | | | | | | | | | | | | | | ● | | | | | |
| RONCIA INSTITUTE OF HYPNOSIS (HM17579) | | | | | | | | | | | | | | | | | | | | ● | | | | | |
| SHEFFIELD NATURAL HEALTH CTRE (HM18372) | | | | | | | | | | | | | | | | | ● | | | | | | | | |
| SHEPHERD, CLARE (HM18409) | | | | | | | | | | | | | | | | | | | | | | ● | | | |
| STONES, KAREN (HM19343) | | | | | | | | | | | | | | | | | | | | | | ● | | | |
| TANNER, MICHELLE (HM19684) | | | | | | | | | | | | | | | | | | | | ● | | | | | |
| VINSON, CAROL (HM20686) | | | | | | | | | | | | | | | | | | | | | | | | | |
| WELLFOODS (HM21159) | | | | | | | | | | | | | | | | | | | | | | | | | |
| WELLFORCE (HM21160) | | | | | | | | | | | | | | | | | ● | | | | | | | | ● |
| WELSH CHIROPRACTIC (HM21183) | | | | | | | | | | ● | | | | | | | ● | | | | | | | | |
| WHITE, JANET (HM21360) | | | | | | | | | | | | | | | | | ● | | | | | | | | |
| WHITEHOUSE CONSULTANCY (HM21388) | | | | | | | | | | | | | | | | | | | | ● | | | | | |
| WICKER HERBAL STORES (HM21444) | | | | | | | | | | | | | | | ● | | | | | | | | | | |
| WICKER HERBAL STORES (HM21445) | | | | | | | | | | | | | | | ● | | | | | | | | | | |
| **YORKSHIRE (WEST)** | | | | | | | | | | | | | | | | | | | | | | | | | |
| ACTIVE MINDS (HM00199) | | | | | | | | | | ● | | | | | | | | | | | | | | | |
| AIREDALE ALLERGY CENTRE (HM00441) | | | | | | | | | | | | | | | | | | | | | | | | | |
| AMETHYST HEALING CENTRE (HM00783) | | | | | | | | | | | | | | | | | | | | | ● | | | | |
| AUSTEN, S (HM01361) | | | | | | | | | | | | | | | | | | | | ● | | | | | |
| BAGGLEY, HILARY (HM01535) | | | | | | | | | | | | | | | | | | | | ● | | | | | |
| BATLEY, KAREN (HM01901) | | | | | | | | | | | | | | | | | | | | ● | | | | | |
| BENNETT, JOHN B (HM02146) | | | | | | | | | | | | | | | | | | | | ● | | | | | |
| BENTLEY, J H (HM02173) | | | | | | | | | | | | | | | | | | | | | | | | | |

| Business by County with Reference no. | Kirlian Photography | Laser Treatment | Life Style Coaching | Light Therapy | Macrobiotics | Magnetic Therapy | Manipulation | Manual Lymph Drainage | Massage (Therapeutic) | McTimoney Chiropractic | Meditation | Metamorphic Therapy | Miasm Therapy | Micro Manipulation | Moxibustion | Mud Therapy | Music Therapy | Nail Surgery | Naturopathy | Neuro-Linguistic Program | Neurotherapy | Nutritional Therapy | Orgone Therapy | Oriental Diagnosis | Orthomolecular Medicine |
|---|---|---|---|---|---|---|---|---|---|---|---|---|---|---|---|---|---|---|---|---|---|---|---|---|---|
| HYPNOTHERAPY CENTRE (HM10515) | | | | | | | | | | | | | | | | | | | | | | | | | |
| JACKSON, W D & SONS (HM10852) | | | | | | | | | | | | | | | | | | | | | | | | | |
| JOHNSON, STUART (HM11097) | | | | | | | | | | | | | | | | | | | | | | | | | |
| KEITH LINLEY HYPNOTHERAPY (HM11413) | | | | | | | | | | | | | | | | | | | | | | | | | |
| KILVINGTON & ASSOCIATES (HM11612) | | | | | | | | | | | | | | | | | | | | | | | | | |
| LLEWELLYN CONSULTANCY (HM12502) | | | | | | | | | | | | | | | | | | | | | | | | | |
| MEDICAL HERBALIST (HM13652) | | | | | | | | | | | | | | | | | | | | | | | | | |
| MILLINGTON, JANET (HM13917) | | | | | | | | | | | | | | | | | | | | | | | | | |
| MOORGATE NATURAL HEALING CTRE (HM14138) | | | | | | | | | ● | | ● | | | | | | | | | | | | | | |
| NIGHTINGALE PHYSIO PRACTICE (HM14937) | | | | | | | ● | | | | | | | | | | | | | | | | | | |
| PACKER, RACHEL (HM15557) | | | | | | | | | | | | | | | | | | | | | | | | | |
| ROBINSON, C (HM17462) | | | | | | | | | | | | | | | | | | | | | | | | | |
| RONCIA INSTITUTE OF HYPNOSIS (HM17579) | | | | | | | | | | | | | | | | | | | | | | | | | |
| SHEFFIELD NATURAL HEALTH CTRE (HM18372) | | | | | | | | | ● | | | | | | | | | | | | | | | | |
| SHEPHERD, CLARE (HM18409) | | | | | | | | | | | | | | | | | | | | | | | | | |
| STONES, KAREN (HM19343) | | | | | | | | | | | | | | | | | | | | | | | | | |
| TANNER, MICHELLE (HM19684) | | | | | | | | | | | | | | | | | | | | | | | | | |
| VINSON, CAROL (HM20686) | | | | | | | | | | | | | | | | | | ● | | | | | | | |
| WELLFOODS (HM21159) | | | | | | | | | | | | | | | | | | | | | | ● | | | |
| WELLFORCE (HM21160) | | | | | | | | | | | | | | | | | | | | | | | | | |
| WELSH CHIROPRACTIC (HM21183) | | | | | | | ● | | ● | | | | | | | | | | | | | ● | | | |
| WHITE, JANET (HM21360) | | | | | | | | | | | | | | | | | | | | | | | | | |
| WHITEHOUSE CONSULTANCY (HM21388) | | | | | | | | | | | | | | | | | | | | | | | | | |
| WICKER HERBAL STORES (HM21444) | | | | | | | | | | | | | | | | | | | | | | | | | |
| WICKER HERBAL STORES (HM21445) | | | | | | | | | | | | | | | | | | | | | | | | | |
| **YORKSHIRE (WEST)** | | | | | | | | | | | | | | | | | | | | | | | | | |
| ACTIVE MINDS (HM00199) | | | | | | | | | | | | | | | | | | | | | | | | | |
| AIREDALE ALLERGY CENTRE (HM00441) | | | | | | | | | | | | | | | | | | | | | | ● | | | |
| AMETHYST HEALING CENTRE (HM00783) | | | | | | | | | | | | | | | | | | | | | | | | | |
| AUSTEN, S (HM01361) | | | | | | | | | | | | | | | | | | | | | | | | | |
| BAGGLEY, HILARY (HM01535) | | | | | | | | | | | | | | | | | | | | | | | | | |
| BATLEY, KAREN (HM01901) | | | | | | | | | | | | | | | | | | | | | | | | | |
| BENNETT, JOHN B (HM02146) | | | | | | | | | | | | | | | | | | | | | | | | | |
| BENTLEY, J H (HM02173) | | | | | | | | ● | | | | | | | | | | | | | | | | | |

# F - O Therapies at Practices/Businesses

Business by County with Reference no.

| Therapy | BINGLEY HOMOEOPATHIC PRACTICE (HM02315) | BISBY, TIFFANY (HM02401) | BODY ESSENCE (HM02585) | BOYD HYPNOTHERAPY (HM02816) | BRADFORD CLINIC OF ALT MED (HM02848) | BRAMIN CLINIC (HM02900) | BRAMLEY COMP THERAPY CLINIC (HM02901) | BRAY, D N (HM02928) | BROOKS, V L J (HM03182) | BUCKLEY, MAUREEN (HM03320) | BURTON, LESLEY (HM03440) | BUSSUNT, M (HM03469) | CALVERLEY ACUPUNCTURE CLINIC (HM03561) | CHAMPANERIA, S K (HM03963) | CHINESE MEDICAL CENTRE (HM04228) | CHOICE AROMAS (HM04421) | CLAPHAM, J W (HM04530) |
|---|---|---|---|---|---|---|---|---|---|---|---|---|---|---|---|---|---|
| Orthomolecular Medicine | | | | | | | | | | | | | | ● | | | |
| Oriental Diagnosis | | | | | | | ● | | | | | | | ● | | | |
| Orgone Therapy | | | | | | | | | | | | | | | | | |
| Nutritional Therapy | | | | | | | ● | | | | | | | ● | | | |
| Neurotherapy | | | | | | | | | | | | | | | | | |
| Neuro-Linguistic Program | | | | | ● | | | | | | | | | | | | |
| Naturopathy | | | | | | | ● | | | | | | | ● | | | |
| Nail Surgery | | | | | | | | | | | | | | | | | |
| Music Therapy | | | | | | | | | | | | | | | | | |
| Mud Therapy | | | | | | | | | | | | | | | | | |
| Moxibustion | | | | | | | ● | | | | | | ● | | | | |
| Micro Manipulation | | | | | | | ● | | | | | | | | | | |
| Miasm Therapy | | | | | | | | | | | | | | | | | |
| Metamorphic Therapy | | | | | | | ● | | | | | | | | | | |
| Meditation | | | | | | | | | | | | | | | | | |
| McTimoney Chiropractic | | | | | | | | | | | | | | | | | |
| Massage (Therapeutic) | ● | | ● | | ● | | ● | | | | | | ● | ● | | ● | |
| Manual Lymph Drainage | | | | | | | | | | | | | | | | | |
| Manipulation | | | | | | | ● | ● | | | | | | | | | |
| Magnetic Therapy | | | | | | | | | | | | | | | | | |
| Macrobiotics | | | | | | | ● | | | | | | | | | | |
| Light Therapy | | | | | | | | | | | | | | | | | |
| Life Style Coaching | | | | | | | ● | | | | | | | | | | |
| Laser Treatment | | | | | | | | | | | | | | | | | |
| Kirlian Photography | | | | | | | | | | | | | | | | | |
| Kinesiology | | | | | | | | | | | | | | | | | |
| Iridology | | | | | | | ● | | | | | | | | | | |
| Inhalation Therapy | | | | | | | | | | | | | | | | | |
| Indian Head Massage | | | ● | | | | ● | | | | | | | ● | | ● | |
| Hypnotherapy | ● | | | ● | | | ● | | | | | | | | | | |
| Hypnosis | | | | ● | | | ● | | ● | ● | | ● | | | | | |
| Humanistic Psychology | | | | ● | | | | | | | | | | | | | |
| Hopi Ear Candles | | | | | | | | | | | | | | | | | |
| Homeopathy | ● | ● | | | ● | ● | ● | | | | ● | | | | | | |
| Holistic Healing | ● | | | | | | ● | | | | | | | ● | | | |
| Herbal Medicine | | | | | ● | | ● | | | | | | | ● | ● | | ● |
| Hellerwork | | | | | | | | | | | | | | | | | |
| Healing Therapy | | | | | | | ● | | | | | | | | | | |
| Healer | | | | | | | ● | | | | | | | | | | |
| Hay Diet | | | | | | | ● | | | | | | | | | | |
| Group Therapy | | | | | | | ● | | | | | | | | | | |
| Gestalt Therapy | | | | | | | ● | | | | | | | | | | |
| Gem Essence Therapy | | | | | | | ● | | | | | | | | | | |
| Gait Analysis | | | | | | | | | | | | | | | | | |
| Flotation Therapy | | | | | | | | | | | | | | | | | |
| Floral Essence Therapy | | | | | | | ● | | | | | | | ● | | | |
| Feng Shui | | | | | | | | | | | | | | | | | |
| Feldenkrais Methodology | | | | | | | | | | | | | | | | | |
| Family Therapy | | | | | | | | | | | | | | | | | |
| Family Planning (Natural) | | | | | | | | | | | | | | | | | |

| Therapy | CLEMIT, MIKE (HM04646) | CLINIC OF HERBAL MEDICINE (HM04690) | COOPER, SAFFRON (HM05126) | COPLEY, F (HM05144) | CROWE, A (HM05504) | DENHAM, A M (HM05979) | DESIGNING CHANGE (HM06022) | DIGNAM, P (HM06098) | EQUA-LIBRA (HM06863) | GILLETT, LIZ (HM08088) | GOLDMAN, ELLEN (HM08225) | GOODWIN, SUSAN (HM08272) | GRACE, NIGEL (HM08333) | GREER, RITA (HM08511) | HAMID, M A (HM08834) | HANSON, S C (HM08944) | HEAL ANN CARE (HM09310) |
|---|---|---|---|---|---|---|---|---|---|---|---|---|---|---|---|---|---|
| Orthomolecular Medicine | | | | | | | | | | | | | | | | | |
| Oriental Diagnosis | | | | | | | | | | | | | | | | | |
| Orgone Therapy | | | | | | | | | | | | | | | | | |
| Nutritional Therapy | | | | | | | | | | ● | | | | | | | |
| Neurotherapy | | | | | | | | | | | | | | | | | |
| Neuro-Linguistic Program | | | | | | | ● | | | | | | | | | | |
| Naturopathy | | | | | | | | | | | | | | | | | |
| Nail Surgery | | | | | | | | | | | | | | | | ● | |
| Music Therapy | | | | | | | | | | | | | | | | | |
| Mud Therapy | | | | | | | | | | | | | | | | | |
| Moxibustion | | | | | | | | | | | | | | | | | |
| Micro Manipulation | | | | | | | | | | | | | | | | | |
| Miasm Therapy | | | | | | | | | | | | | | | | | |
| Metamorphic Therapy | | | | | | | | | | | | | | | | | |
| Meditation | | | | | | | | | | | | | | | | | |
| McTimoney Chiropractic | | | | | | | | | | | | | | | | | |
| Massage (Therapeutic) | | | | | ● | | | | ● | | | | ● | | | | |
| Manual Lymph Drainage | | | | | | | | | | | | | | | | | |
| Manipulation | | | | | | | | | | | | | | | | | |
| Magnetic Therapy | | | | | | | | | | | | | | | | | |
| Macrobiotics | | | | | | | | | | | | | | | | | |
| Light Therapy | | | | | | | | | | | | | | | | | |
| Life Style Coaching | | | | | | | | | | | | | | | | | |
| Laser Treatment | | | | | | | | | | | | | | | | | |
| Kirlian Photography | | | | | | | | | | | | | | | | | |
| Kinesiology | | | | | | | | | | | | | | | | | |
| Iridology | | | | | | | | | | | | | | | | | |
| Inhalation Therapy | | | | | | | | | | | | | | | | | |
| Indian Head Massage | | | | | | | | | ● | | | | ● | | | | |
| Hypnotherapy | | | | | | | ● | | | | | | | | | | |
| Hypnosis | ● | | | ● | | | ● | ● | | | ● | | | ● | ● | | ● |
| Humanistic Psychology | | | | | | | | | | | | | | | | | |
| Hopi Ear Candles | | | | | | | | | | | | | | | | | |
| Homeopathy | | | ● | | | | | | | | | | | | | | |
| Holistic Healing | | | | | | | | | | | | | | | | | |
| Herbal Medicine | | ● | | | | ● | | | | | | ● | | | | | |
| Hellerwork | | | | | | | | | | | | | | | | | |
| Healing Therapy | | | | | | | | | | | | | | | | | |
| Healer | | | | | | | | | | | | | | | | | |
| Hay Diet | | | | | | | | | | | | | | | | | |
| Group Therapy | | | | | | | | | | | | | | | | | |
| Gestalt Therapy | | | | | | | | | | | | | | | | | |
| Gem Essence Therapy | | | | | | | | | | | | | | | | | |
| Gait Analysis | | | | | | | | | | | | | | | | ● | |
| Flotation Therapy | | | | | | | | | | | | | | | | | |
| Floral Essence Therapy | | | | | | | | | | | | | | | | | |
| Feng Shui | | | | | | | | | | | | | | | | | |
| Feldenkrais Methodology | | | | | | | | | | | | | | | | | |
| Family Therapy | | | | | | | | | | | | | | | | | |
| Family Planning (Natural) | | | | | | | | | | | | | | | | | |

# F - O Therapies at Practices/Businesses

| Business by County with Reference no. | Family Planning (Natural) | Family Therapy | Feldenkrais Methodology | Feng Shui | Floral Essence Therapy | Flotation Therapy | Gait Analysis | Gem Essence Therapy | Gestalt Therapy | Group Therapy | Hay Diet | Healer | Healing Therapy | Hellerwork | Herbal Medicine | Holistic Healing | Homeopathy | Hopi Ear Candles | Humanistic Psychology | Hypnosis | Hypnotherapy | Indian Head Massage | Inhalation Therapy | Iridology | Kinesiology | Kirlian Photography | Laser Treatment | Life Style Coaching | Light Therapy | Macrobiotics | Magnetic Therapy | Manipulation | Manual Lymph Drainage | Massage (Therapeutic) | McTimoney Chiropractic | Meditation | Metamorphic Therapy | Miasm Therapy | Micro Manipulation | Moxibustion | Mud Therapy | Music Therapy | Nail Surgery | Naturopathy | Neuro-Linguistic Program | Neurotherapy | Nutritional Therapy | Orgone Therapy | Oriental Diagnosis | Orthomolecular Medicine |
|---|---|---|---|---|---|---|---|---|---|---|---|---|---|---|---|---|---|---|---|---|---|---|---|---|---|---|---|---|---|---|---|---|---|---|---|---|---|---|---|---|---|---|---|---|---|---|---|---|---|---|
| HEALTH CHAMBERS (HM09380) | | | | | | | | | | | | | | | ● | | ● | | | | | ● | | | | | | | ● | | | | | ● | | | ● | | | | | | | | | | | | | |
| HEBDEN BRIDGE CENTRE (HM09487) | | | | | | | | | ● | ● | | | | | | | | | ● | | | | | | | | | | | | | | | | | | | | | | | | | | | | | | | |
| HELEN BENTLEY COMP THERAPIST (HM09510) | | | | | | | | | | | | | | | | | | | | | | ● | | | | | | | | | | | | ● | | | | | | | | | | | | | | | | |
| HOBSON, RICHARD (HM09867) | | | | | | | | | | | | | | | | | | | | ● | ● | | | | | | | | | | | | | | | | | | | | | | | | | | | | | |
| HOMEOPATHIC MEDICAL PRACTICE (HM10076) | | | | | | | | | | | | | | | | ● | ● | | | | | | | | | | | | | | | | | | | | | | | | | | | | | | | | | |
| HOMEOPATHY FOR CHILDREN (HM10080) | | | | | | | | | | | | | | | | | ● | | | | | | | | | | | | | | | | | | | | | | | | | | | | | | | | | |
| HORBURY HYPNOTHERAPY CENTRE (HM10165) | | | | | | | | | | | | | | | | | | | | ● | | | | | | | | | | | | | | | | | | | | | | | | | | | | | | |
| HULLAND, ERIC (HM10355) | | | | | | | | | | | | | | | | | | | | ● | | | | | | | | | | | | | | | | | | | | | | | | | | | | | | |
| HUNTER, REBECCA (HM10408) | | | | | | | | | | | | | | | ● | | | | | | | | | | | | | | | | | | | ● | | | | | | | | | | | | | ● | | | |
| HYPNOTHERAPY CENTRE (HM10522) | | | | | | | | | | | | | | | | | | | | ● | | | | | | | | | | | | | | | | | | | | | | | | | | | | | | |
| HYPNOTHERAPY CENTRE (HM10519) | | | | | | | | | | | | | | | | | | | | ● | | | | | | | | | | | | | | | | | | | | | | | | | | | | | | |
| JACKSON, ROGER D (HM10850) | | | | | | | | | | | | | | | | | | | | | | | | | | | | | | | | ● | | ● | | | | | | | | | | | | | | | | |
| JONES, P (HM11184) | | | | | | | | | | | | | | | ● | | | | | | | | | | | | | | | | | | | | | | | | | | | | | | | | | | | |
| JOWETT, R S J (HM11225) | | | | | | | | | | | | | | | | | | | | ● | | | | | | | | | | | | | | | | | | | | | | | | | | | | | | |
| KANG DA CLINIC (HM11313) | | | | | | | | | | | | | | | ● | | | | | | | | | | ● | | | | | | | | | ● | | | | | | ● | | | | | | | | | | |
| KESAVAN, S K (HM11560) | | | | | | | | | | | | | | | | | ● | | | | | | | | | | | | | | | | | | | | | | | | | | | | | | | | | |
| KINNAIRD, F M (HM11686) | | | | | | | | | ● | | | | | | | | | | ● | ● | ● | | | | | | | ● | | | | | | | | ● | | | | | | | | | | | | | | |
| LEEDS CHINESE MEDICAL CENTRE (HM12154) | | | | | | | | | | | | | | | ● | ● | | | | | | | | | | | | | | | | | | | | | | | | ● | | | | | | | | | | |
| LEEDS COUNSELLING & PSYCHO SVS (HM12158) | | | | | | | | | | ● | | | | | | | | | ● | | | | | | | | | | | | | | | | | | | | | | | | | | | | | | | |
| LLOYD-OWEN CONSULTANCY (HM12524) | | | | | | | | | | | | | | | | | | | | ● | | | | | | | | | | | | | | | | | | | | | | | | | | | | | | |
| LOWE, RACHEL (HM12700) | | | | | | | | | | | | | | | | | ● | | | | | | | | | | | | | | | | | | | | | | | | | | | | | | | | | |
| LPS TRAINING & CONSULTANCY (HM12713) | | | | | | | | | | | | | | | | | | | | | | | | | | | | | | | | ● | | | | | | | | | | | | | | | | | | |
| MACINTYRE-THOMSON, MARIE (HM12842) | | | | | | | | | | | | | | | | | | | | ● | | | | | | | | | | | | | | | | | | | | | | | | | | | | | | |
| MELIA, KAY (HM13706) | | | | | | | | | | | | | | | | | | | | ● | | | | | | | | | | | | | | | | | | | | | | | | | | | | | | |
| MILLER, GAIL (HM13885) | | | | | | | | | | | | | | | | | | | | | | ● | | | | | | | | | | | | | | | | | | | | | | | | | | | | |
| MOLONEY, KATE (HM14055) | | | | | | | | | | | | | | | | | | | | ● | | | | | | | | | | | | | | | | | | | | | | | | | | | | | | |
| MOORFIELD FLOATATION (HM14137) | | | | | | ● | | | | | | | | | | | | | | | | | | | | | | | | | | | | ● | | | | | | | | | | | | | | | | |
| MORE, JO (HM14153) | | | | | | | | | | | | | | | | | ● | | | | | | | | | | | | | | | | | | | | | | | | | | | | | | | | | |
| MORGAN, J D (HM14165) | | | | | | | | | | | | | | | | | | | | ● | | | | | | | | | | | | | | | | | | | | | | | | | | | | | | |
| MORGAN, J D (HM14166) | | | | | | | | | | | | | | | | | | | | ● | | | | | | | | | | | | | | | | | | | | | | | | | | | | | | |
| MORGAN, J D (DR) (HM14167) | | | | | | | | | | | | | | | | | | | ● | ● | ● | | | | | | | | | | | | | | | | | | | | | | | | | | | | | |
| MORLEY ACUPUNCTURE CLINIC (HM14180) | | | | | | | | | | | ● | | ● | | ● | | | | | | | | | | | | | | | | | | | | | | | | | ● | | | | ● | | | ● | | ● | |
| MORNINGTON PHYSIOTHERAPY (HM14193) | | | | | | | | | | | | | | | | | | | | | | | | | | | | | | | | ● | | ● | | | | | ● | | | | | | | | | | | |
| NATURES WORKROOM (HM14705) | | | | | | | | | | | | | | | | | | | | | | ● | | | | | | | | | | | | ● | | | | | | | | | | | | | | | | |

# F - O Therapies at Practices/Businesses

| Business by County with Reference no. | Family Planning (Natural) | Family Therapy | Feldenkrais Methodology | Feng Shui | Floral Essence Therapy | Flotation Therapy | Gait Analysis | Gem Essence Therapy | Gestalt Therapy | Group Therapy | Hay Diet | Healer | Healing Therapy | Hellerwork | Herbal Medicine | Holistic Healing | Homeopathy | Hopi Ear Candles | Humanistic Psychology | Hypnosis | Hypnotherapy | Indian Head Massage | Inhalation Therapy | Iridology | Kinesiology | Kirlian Photography | Laser Treatment | Life Style Coaching | Light Therapy | Macrobiotics | Magnetic Therapy | Manipulation | Manual Lymph Drainage | Massage (Therapeutic) | McTimoney Chiropractic | Meditation | Metamorphic Therapy | Miasm Therapy | Micro Manipulation | Moxibustion | Mud Therapy | Music Therapy | Nail Surgery | Naturopathy | Neuro-Linguistic Program | Neurotherapy | Nutritional Therapy | Orgone Therapy | Oriental Diagnosis | Orthomolecular Medicine |
|---|---|---|---|---|---|---|---|---|---|---|---|---|---|---|---|---|---|---|---|---|---|---|---|---|---|---|---|---|---|---|---|---|---|---|---|---|---|---|---|---|---|---|---|---|---|---|---|---|---|---|
| NEILL-HIGGINS, CHRISTINA (HM14765) | | | | | | | | | | | | | | | | | ● | | | | | | | | | | | | | | | | | | | | | | | | | | | | | | | | | |
| NEVILLE, PAMELA (HM14799) | | | | | | | | | | | | | | | | | | | | ● | | | | | | | | | | | | | | | | | | | | | | | | | | | | | | |
| NRTH LEEDS PHYSIO/SPRTS INJ (HM15091) | | | | | | | | | | | | | | | | | | | | | | | | | | | | | | | | ● | | ● | | | | | | | | | | | | | | | | |
| PALLAS, ANDREW (HM15595) | | | | | | | | | | | | | | | | | | | | | | | | | | | | | | | | | | | | | | | | | | | | ● | ● | | | | | |
| PARKS, HILARY (HM15720) | | | | | | | | | | | | | | | | | | | | | | ● | | | | | | | | | | | | | | | | | | | | | | | | | | | | |
| PITCAIRN, TONY (HM16332) | | | | | | | | | | | | | | | | | | | | ● | | | | | | | | | | | | | | | | | | | | | | | | | | | | | | |
| POMFRET HERBALIST (HM16422) | | | | | | | | | | | | | | | ● | | | | | | | | | | | | | | | | | | | | | | | | | | | | | | | | | | | |
| POPPLEWELL, MARK (HM16437) | | | | | | | | | | | | | | | | | | | | | | | | | | | | | | | | | | ● | | | | | | ● | | | | | | | | | ● | |
| PRESTON, CATHY (HM16551) | | | | | | | | | | | | | | | | | | | | ● | ● | | | | | | | | | | | | | | | | | | | | | | | | | | | | | |
| PURVES, DONALD A (HM16776) | | | | | | | | | | | | | | | ● | | | | | | | | | | | | | | | | | | | | | | | | | | | | | | | | | | | |
| RAINTREE HEALTH (HM16893) | | | | | | | | | | | | | | | ● | | | | | | | | | | | | | | | | | | | | | | | | | | | | | | | | | | | |
| RICHARDSON CLINIC (HM17266) | | | | | | | | | | | | | | | | | ● | | | ● | | | | | | | | | | | | | | ● | | | | | | | | | | | | | | | | |
| RINGWOOD, JAN (HM17359) | | | | | | | | | | | | | | | | | ● | | | | | | | | | | | | | | | | | | | | | | | | | | | | | | | | | |
| ROBINSON & SONS (HM17459) | | | | | | | | | | | | | | | ● | | | | | | | | | | | | | | | | | | | | | | | | | | | | | | | | | | | |
| ROUNDHAY CHIROPRACTIC CLINIC (HM17667) | | | | | | | | | | | | | | | | | | | | | | | | | | | | | | | | ● | | ● | | | | | | | | | | | | | | | | |
| SALTAIRE COMP HEALTH STUDIO (HM17864) | | | | | | | | | | | | | | | | | | | | | | | | | | | | | | | | | | ● | | | | | | | | | | | | | | | | |
| SCOTT, JUDITH (HM18118) | | | | | | | | | | | | | | | | | ● | | | | | | | | | | | | | | | | | | | | | | | | | | | | | | | | | |
| SHERQIA, DARULSHAFA (HM18436) | | | | | | | | | | | | | | | ● | | ● | | | | | | | | | | | | | | | | | | | | | | | | | | | ● | | | | | | |
| SMITH, JANET (HM18751) | | | | | | | | | | | | | | | | | | | | | | | | | ● | | | | | | | | | ● | | | | | | | | | | | | | | | | |
| SMITH, LES (HM18765) | | | | | | | | | | | | | | | | | | | | ● | | | | | | | | | | | | | | | | | | | | | | | | | | | | | | |
| STEAD, JULIE ANN (HM19164) | | | | | | | | | | | | | | | | | | | | | | | | | | | | | | | | | | ● | | | | | | | | | | | | | | | | |
| SURGERY (HM19519) | | | | | | | | | | | | | | | | | | | | | | | | | ● | | | | | | | ● | | ● | | | | | | ● | | | | | | | | | | |
| SYKES CLINIC (HM19610) | | | | | | | | | | | | | | | | | | | | ● | ● | | | | | | | | | | | | | | | | | | | | | | | | | | | | | |
| TRANSCENDENTAL MEDITATION (HM20285) | | | | | | | | | | | | | | | | | | | | | | | | | | | | | | | | | | | | ● | | | | | | | | | | | | | | |
| TRANSFORM HYPNOTHERAPY CLINIC (HM20291) | | | | | | | | | | | | | | | | | | | | ● | | | | | | | | | | | | | | | | | | | | | | | | | | | | | | |
| TRIANGLE HOMOEOPATHIC PRACTICE (HM20328) | | | | | | | | | | | | | | | | | ● | | | | | | | | | | | | | | | | | | | | | | | | | | | | | | | | | |
| WALTERS, MARGARET (HM20877) | | | | | | | | | | | | | | | | | | | | ● | | | | | | | | | | | | | | | | | | | | | | | | | | | | | | |
| WATSON, JEAN (HM21014) | | | | | | | | | | | | | | | | | | | | ● | | | | | | | | | | | | | | | | | | | | | | | | | | | | | | |
| WEST PARK STRESS MANAGEMENT (HM21234) | | | | | | | | | | | | | | | | | | | | ● | | | | | | | | | | | | | | | | | | | | | | | | | | | | | | |
| WEST YORKSHIRE CLINIC (HM21242) | | | | | | | | | | | | | | | | | | | | | | | | | | | | | | | | ● | | ● | | | | | | ● | | | | | | | | | | |
| WIGHTMAN, T (HM21475) | | | | | | | | | | | | | | | ● | | | | | | | | | | | | | | | | | | | | | | | | | | | | | | | | | | | |
| WILLIAMS, CLIVE (HM21551) | | | | | | | | | | | | | | | | | | | | ● | | | | | | | | | | | | | | | | | | | | | | | | | | | | | | |
| WISE, CAROL (HM21732) | | | | | | | | | | | | | | | | | ● | | | | | | | | | | | | | | | | | | | | ● | | | | | | | | | | | | | |
| WOODHOUSE CLINIC (HM21826) | | | | | | | | | | | | | | | | | ● | | | | | | | | | | | | | | | ● | | ● | | | | | ● | | | | | | | | | | | |

# F - O Therapies at Practices/Businesses

| Business by County with Reference no. | Family Planning (Natural) | Family Therapy | Feldenkrais Methodology | Feng Shui | Floral Essence Therapy | Flotation Therapy | Gait Analysis | Gem Essence Therapy | Gestalt Therapy | Group Therapy | Hay Diet | Healer | Healing Therapy | Hellerwork | Herbal Medicine | Holistic Healing | Homeopathy | Hopi Ear Candles | Humanistic Psychology | Hypnosis | Hypnotherapy | Indian Head Massage | Inhalation Therapy | Iridology | Kinesiology | Kirlian Photography | Laser Treatment | Life Style Coaching | Light Therapy | Macrobiotics | Magnetic Therapy | Manipulation | Manual Lymph Drainage | Massage (Therapeutic) | McTimoney Chiropractic | Meditation | Metamorphic Therapy | Miasm Therapy | Micro Manipulation | Moxibustion | Mud Therapy | Music Therapy | Nail Surgery | Naturopathy | Neuro-Linguistic Program | Neurotherapy | Nutritional Therapy | Orgone Therapy | Oriental Diagnosis | Orthomolecular Medicine |
|---|---|---|---|---|---|---|---|---|---|---|---|---|---|---|---|---|---|---|---|---|---|---|---|---|---|---|---|---|---|---|---|---|---|---|---|---|---|---|---|---|---|---|---|---|---|---|---|---|---|---|
| IRELAND |  |  |  |  |  |  |  |  |  |  |  |  |  |  |  |  |  |  |  |  |  |  |  |  |  |  |  |  |  |  |  |  |  |  |  |  |  |  |  |  |  |  |  |  |  |  |  |  |  |  |
| COUNTY CLARE |  |  |  |  |  |  |  |  |  |  |  |  |  |  |  |  |  |  |  |  |  |  |  |  |  |  |  |  |  |  |  |  |  |  |  |  |  |  |  |  |  |  |  |  |  |  |  |  |  |  |
| SIMONS, ROBERT ALLEN (DR) (HM18572) |  | ● |  |  |  |  |  |  |  | ● |  |  |  |  |  |  |  |  | ● |  |  |  |  |  |  |  |  |  |  |  |  |  |  |  |  |  |  |  |  |  |  |  |  |  |  |  |  |  |  |  |
| COUNTY CORK |  |  |  |  |  |  |  |  |  |  |  |  |  |  |  |  |  |  |  |  |  |  |  |  |  |  |  |  |  |  |  |  |  |  |  |  |  |  |  |  |  |  |  |  |  |  |  |  |  |  |
| ANNAPURNA NATURAL HEALTHCARE (HM00894) |  |  |  |  |  |  |  |  |  |  |  |  |  |  |  |  |  |  |  |  |  |  |  |  |  |  |  |  |  |  |  |  |  | ● |  |  |  |  |  |  |  |  |  |  |  |  |  |  |  |  |
| BANDON CHIROPRACTIC CLINIC (HM01653) |  |  |  |  |  |  |  |  |  |  |  |  |  |  |  |  |  |  |  |  |  |  |  |  |  |  |  |  |  |  |  | ● |  | ● |  |  |  |  |  |  |  |  |  |  |  |  |  |  |  |  |
| EAST CORK PHYSIOTHERAPY (HM06511) |  |  |  |  |  |  |  |  |  |  |  |  |  |  |  |  |  |  |  |  |  |  |  |  |  |  |  |  |  |  |  | ● |  | ● |  |  |  |  |  | ● |  |  |  |  |  |  |  |  | ● |  |
| HATTERSLEY, LAURENCE (HM09200) |  |  |  |  |  |  |  |  |  |  |  |  |  |  |  |  |  |  |  |  |  |  |  |  |  |  |  |  |  |  |  | ● |  |  |  |  |  |  |  |  |  |  |  |  |  |  |  |  |  |  |
| HEALING THERAPIES (HM09354) |  |  |  |  |  |  |  |  |  |  |  | ● | ● |  |  |  |  |  |  |  |  |  |  |  |  |  |  |  |  |  |  |  |  |  |  | ● |  |  |  |  |  |  |  |  |  |  |  |  |  |  |
| HERBAL DISPENSARY (HM09610) |  |  |  |  |  |  |  |  |  |  |  |  |  |  | ● |  |  |  |  |  |  |  |  |  |  |  |  |  |  |  |  |  |  |  |  |  |  |  |  |  |  |  |  |  |  |  |  |  |  |  |
| INS-CLINICAL HYP & PSYCHO (HM10661) |  |  |  |  |  |  |  |  |  |  |  | ● | ● |  |  |  |  |  |  | ● | ● |  |  |  |  |  |  | ● |  |  |  |  |  |  |  | ● |  |  |  |  |  |  |  |  |  |  |  |  |  |  |
| JONES, COLEEN (HM11131) |  | ● |  |  |  |  |  |  | ● | ● |  |  |  |  |  |  |  |  | ● |  |  |  |  |  |  |  |  |  |  |  |  |  |  |  |  |  |  |  |  |  |  |  |  |  |  |  |  |  |  |  |
| KEATING, MARY (HM11379) |  |  |  |  |  |  |  |  |  |  |  |  |  |  |  | ● |  |  |  |  |  |  |  |  |  |  |  |  |  |  |  |  |  |  |  |  |  |  |  | ● |  |  |  |  |  |  |  |  |  |  |
| MOORE-GROACKE, GILLIAN (DR) (HM14136) |  | ● | ● |  |  |  |  |  | ● |  |  |  |  |  |  |  |  |  |  | ● | ● |  |  |  |  |  |  |  |  |  |  |  |  |  |  |  |  |  |  |  |  |  |  |  |  |  |  |  |  |  |
| PAUL DENNEHY - HYPNOTHERAPIST (HM15842) |  |  |  |  |  |  |  |  | ● | ● |  | ● | ● |  |  | ● |  |  |  | ● | ● |  | ● |  | ● |  |  |  |  |  |  |  |  |  |  | ● |  |  |  |  |  | ● |  |  |  |  |  |  |  |  |
| RAVEN HILL CHIROPRACTIC CLINIC (HM16964) |  |  |  |  |  |  |  |  |  |  |  |  |  |  |  |  | ● |  |  |  |  |  |  |  |  |  |  |  |  |  |  |  |  | ● |  |  |  |  |  |  |  |  |  |  |  |  | ● |  |  |  |
| SHIATSU (HM18452) |  |  |  |  |  |  |  |  |  |  |  |  |  |  |  |  |  |  |  |  |  |  |  |  |  |  |  |  |  |  |  |  |  |  |  |  |  |  |  | ● |  |  |  |  |  |  |  |  | ● |  |
| COUNTY DUBLIN |  |  |  |  |  |  |  |  |  |  |  |  |  |  |  |  |  |  |  |  |  |  |  |  |  |  |  |  |  |  |  |  |  |  |  |  |  |  |  |  |  |  |  |  |  |  |  |  |  |  |
| ABELIA COUNSELLING (HM00110) |  |  |  |  |  |  |  |  |  |  |  |  |  |  |  |  |  |  |  | ● | ● |  |  |  |  |  |  |  |  |  |  |  |  |  |  |  |  |  |  |  |  |  |  |  | ● |  |  |  |  |  |
| ARDAGH ACUPUNCTURE CLINIC (HM00988) |  |  |  |  |  |  |  |  |  |  |  |  |  |  |  |  |  |  |  |  |  |  |  |  |  |  |  |  |  |  |  |  |  |  |  |  |  |  |  | ● |  |  |  |  |  |  | ● |  | ● |  |
| ARDUNA COUNS & PSYCHOTHPY CTRE (HM00995) |  | ● |  |  |  |  |  |  |  | ● |  |  |  |  |  |  |  |  |  |  |  |  |  |  |  |  |  |  |  |  |  |  |  |  |  |  |  |  |  |  |  |  |  |  |  |  |  |  |  |  |
| BREE, JOHN (HM02947) |  |  |  |  |  |  |  |  |  |  |  |  | ● |  |  |  |  |  |  |  | ● |  |  |  |  |  |  |  |  |  |  |  |  |  |  |  |  |  |  |  |  |  |  |  |  |  |  |  |  |  |
| B-WELL HYPNOTHERAPY CLINIC (HM03506) |  |  |  |  |  |  |  |  |  |  |  |  |  |  |  |  |  |  |  | ● | ● |  |  |  |  |  |  |  |  |  |  |  |  |  |  | ● |  |  |  |  |  |  |  |  |  |  |  |  |  |  |
| CHADHA, PRADEEP K (DR) (HM03933) |  |  |  |  |  |  |  |  |  |  |  |  |  |  |  |  |  |  |  | ● | ● |  |  |  |  |  |  |  |  |  |  |  |  |  |  | ● |  |  |  |  |  |  |  |  |  |  |  |  |  |  |
| COLBERT, BRIAN (HM04804) |  |  |  |  |  |  |  |  |  |  |  |  |  |  |  |  |  |  |  |  |  |  |  |  |  |  |  | ● |  |  |  |  |  |  |  |  |  |  |  |  |  |  |  |  | ● |  |  |  |  |  |
| FAIRVIEW THERAPY CENTRE (HM07066) |  | ● |  |  |  |  |  |  | ● |  |  |  |  |  |  |  | ● |  | ● |  |  | ● |  |  |  |  |  | ● |  |  |  |  |  | ● |  |  |  |  |  | ● |  |  |  |  |  |  |  |  |  |  |
| FINISHING TOUCHES (HM07313) |  |  |  |  |  |  |  |  |  |  |  | ● |  |  |  |  |  |  |  |  |  |  |  |  |  |  |  |  |  |  |  |  |  | ● |  |  |  |  |  |  |  |  |  |  |  |  | ● |  |  |  |
| FITZGERALD HYP-PSYCHOTHERAPY (HM07364) |  |  |  |  |  |  |  |  |  |  |  |  |  |  |  | ● |  |  |  | ● | ● |  |  |  |  |  |  |  |  |  |  |  |  |  |  | ● |  |  |  |  |  |  |  |  |  |  |  |  |  |  |
| HEALING ROOM - DRUMCONDRA (HM09351) |  |  |  |  |  |  |  |  |  |  |  |  | ● |  |  | ● |  |  |  |  |  | ● |  |  |  |  |  |  |  |  |  |  |  | ● |  |  |  |  |  |  |  |  |  |  |  |  |  |  |  |  |
| HEALTH COUNSEL (HM09384) |  |  |  |  |  |  |  |  | ● |  |  | ● | ● |  |  |  |  |  |  | ● | ● |  |  |  |  |  |  |  |  |  |  |  |  | ● |  | ● |  |  |  |  |  |  |  |  |  |  |  |  |  |  |
| HERBAL & ACUPUNCTURE (HM09595) |  |  |  |  |  |  |  |  |  |  |  |  |  |  | ● |  |  |  |  |  |  |  |  |  |  |  |  |  |  |  |  |  |  |  |  |  |  |  |  |  |  |  |  |  |  |  |  |  |  |  |
| HERBAL HEALTH SERVICES (HM09618) |  |  |  |  |  |  |  |  |  |  |  |  |  |  | ● |  |  |  |  |  |  |  |  |  |  |  |  |  |  |  |  |  |  |  |  |  |  |  |  |  |  |  |  |  |  |  |  |  | ● |  |
| HOWTH COUNSELLING SERVICE (HM10294) |  |  |  |  |  |  |  |  |  |  |  |  |  |  |  |  |  |  | ● |  |  |  |  |  |  |  |  |  |  |  |  |  |  |  |  | ● |  |  |  |  |  |  |  |  |  |  |  |  |  |  |

# F - O Therapies at Practices/Businesses

Business by County with Reference no.

| Business by County with Reference no. | Family Planning (Natural) | Family Therapy | Feldenkrais Methodology | Feng Shui | Floral Essence Therapy | Flotation Therapy | Gait Analysis | Gem Essence Therapy | Gestalt Therapy | Group Therapy | Hay Diet | Healer | Healing Therapy | Hellerwork | Herbal Medicine | Holistic Healing | Homeopathy | Hopi Ear Candles | Humanistic Psychology | Hypnosis | Hypnotherapy | Indian Head Massage | Inhalation Therapy | Iridology | Kinesiology |
|---|---|---|---|---|---|---|---|---|---|---|---|---|---|---|---|---|---|---|---|---|---|---|---|---|---|
| INNER CIRCLE HEALING CENTRE (HM10635) | | | | | | | | | | | | | ● | | | ● | | | | ● | ● | ● | | | |
| INSTITUTE OF PSYCHOSOCIAL MED (HM10678) | | | | | | | | | | | | | | | | | | | | | | | | | |
| LALLOO'S ACUPUNCTURE CLINIC (HM11881) | | | | | | | | | | | | ● | ● | | ● | ● | ● | | | | | ● | | | ● |
| MCHUGH HYPNOSIS & REFLEXOLOGY (HM13509) | | | | | | | | | | | | | | | | | | | | ● | ● | | | | |
| MELT/TEMPLE BAR NATURAL (HM13716) | | | | | | | | | | | | ● | ● | | ● | ● | ● | | | | | ● | | | ● |
| NATURAL SOLUTIONS (HM14625) | | | | | | | | | | | | ● | ● | | | | | | | ● | ● | | | | ● |
| NUALA WOULFE BEAUTY SALON (HM15101) | | | | | | | | | | | | | | | | ● | | | | | | | | | |
| RATHMINES CHIROPRACTIC CENTRE (HM16957) | | | | | | | | | | | | | | | | | | | | | | | | | |
| T C M CENTRE (HM19639) | | | | | | | | | | | | | ● | | ● | ● | | | | | ● | ● | | | |
| THERAPEUTICS (HM19888) | | | | | | | | | | | | | | | | | | | | | | | | | |
| THEW, NIN (HM19916) | | | | | | | | | | | | | | | | | | | | | | | | | |
| TOBIN, ROSALEEN (HM20105) | | | | | | | | | | | | ● | ● | | | ● | | | | | | | | | |
| TRAD CHINESE MEDICINE/MASSAGE (HM20216) | | | | | | | | | | | | | ● | | ● | ● | | | | | | | | | |
| COUNTY GALWAY | | | | | | | | | | | | | | | | | | | | | | | | | |
| PRENDERGAST, KARL (HM16542) | | | | | | | | | | | | | | | | | | | | | | | | | |
| PSYCHOL & FAMILY THRPY PRACT (HM16699) | | ● | | | | | | | | | | | | | | | | | | | | | | | |
| COUNTY KERRY | | | | | | | | | | | | | | | | | | | | | | | | | |
| ACUPUNCTURE CLINIC (HM00286) | | | | | | | | | | | | | | | ● | | | | | | | | | | |
| WOODLAWN HOLISTIC THERAPY CTRE (HM21834) | | | | | | | | | | | | | | | | | ● | | | | | ● | | | |
| COUNTY KILDARE | | | | | | | | | | | | | | | | | | | | | | | | | |
| GREEN ROAD HEALING CENTRE (HM08441) | | | | | | | | | | | | | | | | ● | | | | | | ● | | | |
| SHENANDOAH HEALING (HM18395) | | | | | | | | | | | | ● | ● | | | ● | | | | | | | | | |
| COUNTY KILKENNY | | | | | | | | | | | | | | | | | | | | | | | | | |
| BLUE ROOM (HM02528) | | | | | ● | | | | | ● | | ● | | | | ● | | | ● | | | | | | ● |
| DULCAMARA (HM06375) | | | | | | | | | | | | | | | ● | | ● | | | | | | | | |
| HOLISTIC HEALING CENTRE (HM09965) | | | | | | | | | | | | | | | | ● | ● | | | ● | | ● | | | |
| COUNTY LIMERICK | | | | | | | | | | | | | | | | | | | | | | | | | |
| HOLISTIC HEALING (HM09960) | | | | | | | | | | | | ● | ● | | | ● | | | | | | ● | | | |
| COUNTY LOUTH | | | | | | | | | | | | | | | | | | | | | | | | | |
| HOLISTIC SOL NTRL HEALING CTRE (HM09989) | | | | | | | | | | | | | ● | | | | | | | ● | ● | | | | |
| COUNTY MAYO | | | | | | | | | | | | | | | | | | | | | | | | | |
| NATURAL HEALING CENTRE (HM14547) | | ● | | | ● | | | | | ● | | ● | ● | | ● | ● | | | | | | ● | | | ● |
| TOBAR PHADRAIC (HM20102) | | | | | | | | | | | ● | ● | ● | | | | | | | | | ● | | | |

| Business by County with Reference no. | Kirlian Photography | Laser Treatment | Life Style Coaching | Light Therapy | Macrobiotics | Magnetic Therapy | Manipulation | Manual Lymph Drainage | Massage (Therapeutic) | McTimoney Chiropractic | Meditation | Metamorphic Therapy | Miasm Therapy | Micro Manipulation | Moxibustion | Mud Therapy | Music Therapy | Nail Surgery | Naturopathy | Neuro-Linguistic Program | Neurotherapy | Nutritional Therapy | Orgone Therapy | Oriental Diagnosis | Orthomolecular Medicine |
|---|---|---|---|---|---|---|---|---|---|---|---|---|---|---|---|---|---|---|---|---|---|---|---|---|---|
| INNER CIRCLE HEALING CENTRE (HM10635) | | | ● | | | | | | ● | | ● | | | | | | | | | | | | | | |
| INSTITUTE OF PSYCHOSOCIAL MED (HM10678) | | | | | | | | | ● | | | | | | | | | | | | | ● | | | |
| LALLOO'S ACUPUNCTURE CLINIC (HM11881) | | | | | | | | | | | | | | | ● | | | | ● | | | | | | |
| MCHUGH HYPNOSIS & REFLEXOLOGY (HM13509) | | | | | | | | | | | | | | | | | | | | | | | | | |
| MELT/TEMPLE BAR NATURAL (HM13716) | | | | | ● | | | | ● | | ● | | | | ● | | | | | | | | | ● | |
| NATURAL SOLUTIONS (HM14625) | | | ● | | | | | | | | | | | | | | | | ● | | | ● | | | |
| NUALA WOULFE BEAUTY SALON (HM15101) | | | | | | ● | | | ● | | | | | | | ● | | | | | | | | | |
| RATHMINES CHIROPRACTIC CENTRE (HM16957) | | | | | | | ● | | | | | | | | | | | | | | | | | | |
| T C M CENTRE (HM19639) | | | | | | | | | | | | | | | ● | | | | | | | ● | | ● | |
| THERAPEUTICS (HM19888) | | | | | | | | | ● | | | | | | | | | | | | | | | | |
| THEW, NIN (HM19916) | | | ● | | | | | | | | | | | | ● | | | | | | | | | | |
| TOBIN, ROSALEEN (HM20105) | | | | | | | | | | | | | | | | | | | | | | | | | |
| TRAD CHINESE MEDICINE/MASSAGE (HM20216) | | | | | | | ● | | ● | | | | | | ● | | | | | | | ● | | | |
| COUNTY GALWAY | | | | | | | | | | | | | | | | | | | | | | | | | |
| PRENDERGAST, KARL (HM16542) | | | | | | | ● | | | | | | | | | | | | | | | | | | |
| PSYCHOL & FAMILY THRPY PRACT (HM16699) | | | | | | | | | | | | | | | | | | | | | | | | | |
| COUNTY KERRY | | | | | | | | | | | | | | | | | | | | | | | | | |
| ACUPUNCTURE CLINIC (HM00286) | | | | | | | | | | | | | | | ● | | | | | | | | | ● | |
| WOODLAWN HOLISTIC THERAPY CTRE (HM21834) | | | | | | | | | ● | | | | | | | | | | | | | | | | |
| COUNTY KILDARE | | | | | | | | | | | | | | | | | | | | | | | | | |
| GREEN ROAD HEALING CENTRE (HM08441) | | | | | | | | | ● | | | | | | | | | | | | | | | | |
| SHENANDOAH HEALING (HM18395) | | | ● | | | | | | ● | | | | | | | | | | | | | | | | |
| COUNTY KILKENNY | | | | | | | | | | | | | | | | | | | | | | | | | |
| BLUE ROOM (HM02528) | | | | | | | | | ● | | ● | | | | | | ● | | | | | ● | | | |
| DULCAMARA (HM06375) | | | | | | | | | | | | | | | | | | | | | | | | | |
| HOLISTIC HEALING CENTRE (HM09965) | | | | | | | | | ● | | | ● | | | | | | | | | | | | | |
| COUNTY LIMERICK | | | | | | | | | | | | | | | | | | | | | | | | | |
| HOLISTIC HEALING (HM09960) | | | | | | | | | | | | | | | | | | | | | | | | | |
| COUNTY LOUTH | | | | | | | | | | | | | | | | | | | | | | | | | |
| HOLISTIC SOL NTRL HEALING CTRE (HM09989) | | | | | | | | | | | | | | | | | | | | | | | | | |
| COUNTY MAYO | | | | | | | | | | | | | | | | | | | | | | | | | |
| NATURAL HEALING CENTRE (HM14547) | | | ● | | | | | | ● | | ● | | | | | | | | | | | | | | |
| TOBAR PHADRAIC (HM20102) | | | | | | | | | ● | | ● | | | | | | | | | | | | | | |

# F - O Therapies at Practices/Businesses

| Business by County with Reference no. | Family Planning (Natural) | Family Therapy | Feldenkrais Methodology | Feng Shui | Floral Essence Therapy | Flotation Therapy | Gait Analysis | Gem Essence Therapy | Gestalt Therapy | Group Therapy | Hay Diet | Healer | Healing Therapy | Hellerwork | Herbal Medicine | Holistic Healing | Homeopathy | Hopi Ear Candles | Humanistic Psychology | Hypnosis | Hypnotherapy | Indian Head Massage | Inhalation Therapy | Iridology | Kinesiology | Kirlian Photography | Laser Treatment | Life Style Coaching | Light Therapy | Macrobiotics | Magnetic Therapy | Manipulation | Manual Lymph Drainage | Massage (Therapeutic) | McTimoney Chiropractic | Meditation | Metamorphic Therapy | Miasm Therapy | Micro Manipulation | Moxibustion | Mud Therapy | Music Therapy | Nail Surgery | Naturopathy | Neuro-Linguistic Program | Neurotherapy | Nutritional Therapy | Orgone Therapy | Oriental Diagnosis | Orthomolecular Medicine |
|---|---|---|---|---|---|---|---|---|---|---|---|---|---|---|---|---|---|---|---|---|---|---|---|---|---|---|---|---|---|---|---|---|---|---|---|---|---|---|---|---|---|---|---|---|---|---|---|---|---|---|
| COUNTY MEATH | | | | | | | | | | | | | | | | | | | | | | | | | | | | | | | | | | | | | | | | | | | | | | | | | | |
| NATURAL MEDICINE CENTRE (HM14610) | | | | | | | | | | | | | | | ● | | ● | | | | | | | | | | | | | | | | | | | | | | | ● | | | | | | | | | | |
| COUNTY MONAGHAN | | | | | | | | | | | | | | | | | | | | | | | | | | | | | | | | | | | | | | | | | | | | | | | | | | |
| AROMA - ZONE (HM01043) | | | | | | | | | | | | | | | | | | | | | | ● | | | | | | | | | | | | ● | | | | | | | | | | | | | | | | |
| HEALTHY CHOICES (HM09426) | | | | | | | | | | | | | | | ● | ● | | | | | ● | ● | | | | | | | | | | | | ● | | ● | | | | | | | | | | | ● | | | |
| NORTHAMBER (HM15050) | | | | | | | | | | | | | | | ● | ● | ● | | | ● | ● | | | | | | | | | | | ● | | ● | | ● | | | | | | | | ● | | | ● | | | |
| COUNTY ROSCOMMON | | | | | | | | | | | | | | | | | | | | | | | | | | | | | | | | | | | | | | | | | | | | | | | | | | |
| HOLISTIC HEALTH FARM (HM09980) | | | | | | | | | | | | ● | | | ● | ● | | | | | | ● | | ● | ● | | | ● | | | | | | ● | | ● | | | | | | | | | | | ● | | | |
| COUNTY SLIGO | | | | | | | | | | | | | | | | | | | | | | | | | | | | | | | | | | | | | | | | | | | | | | | | | | |
| ANAM CHARA COUNSELLING (HM00802) | | | | | | | | | ● | ● | | | | | | | | | ● | | | | | | | | | | | | | | | | | | | | | | | | | | | | | | | |
| COUNTY TIPPERARY | | | | | | | | | | | | | | | | | | | | | | | | | | | | | | | | | | | | | | | | | | | | | | | | | | |
| KINSELLA, MARIE (HM11693) | | | | | | | | | ● | ● | | | | | | | | | ● | | | | | | | | | | | | | | | | | | | | | | | | | | | | | | | |
| COUNTY WESTMEATH | | | | | | | | | | | | | | | | | | | | | | | | | | | | | | | | | | | | | | | | | | | | | | | | | | |
| HOWE, JAN (HM10263) | | | | | | | | | | | | | | | | | | | | | | | | | | | | | | ● | | | | ● | | | | | | ● | | | | | | | | | ● | |
| COUNTY WEXFORD | | | | | | | | | | | | | | | | | | | | | | | | | | | | | | | | | | | | | | | | | | | | | | | | | | |
| FOURTH MOUNTAIN HOM AND ACU (HM07622) | | | | | | | | | | | | | | | | | ● | | | | | | | | | | | | | | | | | | | | | | | | | | | | | | | | | |
| MURPHY, MARY (HM14388) | | | | | | | | | ● | ● | | | | | | | | | ● | ● | ● | | | | | | | ● | | | | | | | | | | | | | | | | | | | | | | |
| OSTEOPATHIC PRACTICE (HM15474) | | | | | | | | | | | | | | | | | | | | | | | | | | | | | | | | ● | | ● | | | | | | | | | | | | | | | | |
| COUNTY WICKLOW | | | | | | | | | | | | | | | | | | | | | | | | | | | | | | | | | | | | | | | | | | | | | | | | | | |
| ARKLOW NATURAL HEALING CENTRE (HM01007) | | | | | ● | | | | | | | | | | | | ● | | | | | ● | | | | | | | | ● | | | | | | ● | | | | | | | | | | | | | | |
| HOLISTIC OPTIONS (HM09985) | | | | | | | | | | | | | | | | ● | | | | | | ● | | | | | | | | | | | | ● | | | | | | | | | | | | | | | | |
| JAMESON PERSONAL EXCELLENCE (HM10903) | | | | | | | | | ● | | | ● | ● | | | | | | ● | ● | ● | | | | | | | | | | | | | | | | | | | | | | | | | | | | | |
| MARK GOULDING - ACUPUNCTURIST (HM13107) | | | | | | | | | | | | | | | ● | ● | ● | | | | | | | | | | | | | | | | | | | | | | | ● | | | | ● | | | | | ● | |

# F - O Therapies at Practices/Businesses

Business by County with Reference no.

## NORTHERN IRELAND

### COUNTY ANTRIM

| Business by County with Reference no. | Family Planning (Natural) | Family Therapy | Feldenkrais Methodology | Feng Shui | Floral Essence Therapy | Flotation Therapy | Gait Analysis | Gem Essence Therapy | Gestalt Therapy | Group Therapy | Hay Diet | Healer | Healing Therapy | Hellerwork | Herbal Medicine | Holistic Healing | Homeopathy | Hopi Ear Candles | Humanistic Psychology | Hypnosis | Hypnotherapy | Indian Head Massage | Inhalation Therapy | Iridology |
|---|---|---|---|---|---|---|---|---|---|---|---|---|---|---|---|---|---|---|---|---|---|---|---|---|
| ACTIVE BALANCE CLINIC (HM00189) | | | | | | | | | | | | | | | | | | | | | | | | |
| ANTRIM CHIROPRACTIC CLINIC (HM00923) | | | ● | | | | | | | | | | | | | | | | | | | | | |
| BALLYCLARE CHIROPRACTIC CLINIC (HM01636) | | | | | | | | | | | | | | | | | | | | | | | | |
| BALLYMENA CHIROPRACTIC CLINIC (HM01638) | | | | | | | | | | | | | | | | | | | | | | | | |
| BALLYMONEY CHIROPRACTIC CLINIC (HM01639) | | | | | | | | | | | | | | | | | | | | | | | | |
| BELFAST CHIROPRACTIC CLINIC (HM02077) | | | | | | | | | | | | | | | | | | | | | | | | |
| CHEAH, R F S (HM04072) | | | ● | | | | | | | | | | | | | | | | | | | | | |
| CHIROPODIST (HM04290) | | | | | | | | | | | | | | | | | | | | | | ● | | |
| COMERTON, LIZ (HM04898) | | | | | | | | | | | | | | | | ● | | | | | | | | |
| CRAWFORD, J G (HM05392) | | | | | | | | | | | | | | | | | | | | | | | | |
| CREGAGH CHIROPRACTIC CLINIC (HM05412) | | | | | | | | | | | | | | | | | | | | | | | | |
| EARLS, JAMES (HM06497) | | | | | | | ● | | | | | | | | | | | | | | | | | |
| FAMILY CHIRO CLINIC BALLYMENA (HM07082) | | | | | | | | | | | | | | | | | | | | | | | | |
| FINAGHY CHIROPRACTIC CLINIC (HM07295) | | | | | | | | | | | | | | | | | | | | | | | | |
| FLORENCE SHARPE CHIROPODIST (HM07431) | | | | | | | | | | | | | | | | | | | | | | ● | | |
| FRAMAR NATURAL HEALTH CLINIC (HM07654) | | ● | ● | | | | ● | | | | | | | | | ● | | | | | | | | |
| GLENGORMLEY CHIRO CLINIC (HM08151) | | | | | | | | | | | | | | | | | | | | | | | | |
| LAMBERT, RACHEL (HM11901) | | | | | | | ● | | | | | | | | | | | | | | | | | |
| LISBURN CHIROPRACTIC CLINIC (HM12452) | | | | | | | | | | | | | | | | | | | | | | | | |
| MAXWELL, MARY (HM13337) | | | | | | | | | | | | | | | | | | | | | | | | |
| MCCARTNEY, W J (HM13401) | | | | | | | | | | | | | | | | | | | | | | ● | | |
| MCCRYSTALS NATUROPATHIC CENTRE (HM13436) | | ● | | | | ● | ● | | | | | | | | | ● | | | | | | | | |
| MCCULLY, JOAN (HM13437) | | | | | | | | | | | | | | | | | | | | | | | | |
| MORGAN, D (HM14161) | | | | | | | | | | | | | | | | | | | | | | | | |
| MYSTIC SCHEHERAZADE (HM14445) | | | | | | | | | | | | | | | | | | | | | | | | |
| REAY, H (HM17004) | | | | | | | | | | | | | | | | | | | | | | | | |
| SCRABO HEALTH PRODUCTS (HM18143) | | | | | | | ● | | | | | | | | | ● | | | | | | | | |
| SCULLION, BRENDA (HM18156) | | | | | | | | | | | | | | | | ● | | | | | | | | |
| SHEPPARD, SERENA (HM18423) | | | | | | | | | | | | | | | | ● | | | | | | | | |
| STEWART, S (HM19276) | | | | | | | | | | | | | | | | | | | | | | | | |
| TODD, TREVOR (HM20109) | | | | | | | | | | | | | | | | | | | | | | | | |

| Business by County with Reference no. | Kinesiology | Kirlian Photography | Laser Treatment | Life Style Coaching | Light Therapy | Macrobiotics | Magnetic Therapy | Manipulation | Manual Lymph Drainage | Massage (Therapeutic) | McTimoney Chiropractic | Meditation | Metamorphic Therapy | Miasm Therapy | Micro Manipulation | Moxibustion | Mud Therapy | Music Therapy | Nail Surgery | Naturopathy | Neuro-Linguistic Program | Neurotherapy | Nutritional Therapy | Orgone Therapy | Oriental Diagnosis | Orthomolecular Medicine |
|---|---|---|---|---|---|---|---|---|---|---|---|---|---|---|---|---|---|---|---|---|---|---|---|---|---|---|
| ACTIVE BALANCE CLINIC (HM00189) | | | | | | | | | | ● | | | | | | | ● | | | | | | | | | |
| ANTRIM CHIROPRACTIC CLINIC (HM00923) | | | ● | | | | | | | | | | | | | | | | | | | | | | | |
| BALLYCLARE CHIROPRACTIC CLINIC (HM01636) | | | ● | | | | | | | | | | | | | | | | | | | | | | | |
| BALLYMENA CHIROPRACTIC CLINIC (HM01638) | | | ● | | | | | | | | | | | | | | | | | | | | | | | |
| BALLYMONEY CHIROPRACTIC CLINIC (HM01639) | | | ● | | | | | | | | | | | | | | | | | | | | | | | |
| BELFAST CHIROPRACTIC CLINIC (HM02077) | | | ● | | | | | | | | | | | | | | | | | | | | | | | |
| CHEAH, R F S (HM04072) | | | | | | | | | | | | | | | | | | | | | | | | | | |
| CHIROPODIST (HM04290) | | ● | | | | | | | | | | | | | | | | | | | | | | | | |
| COMERTON, LIZ (HM04898) | | | | | | | | | | | | | | | | | | | | | | | | | | |
| CRAWFORD, J G (HM05392) | | ● | | | | | | | | | | | | | | | | | | | | | | | | |
| CREGAGH CHIROPRACTIC CLINIC (HM05412) | | | ● | | | | | | | | | | | | | | | | | | | | | | | |
| EARLS, JAMES (HM06497) | | | | | | | | | | | | | | | | | | | | | | | | | | |
| FAMILY CHIRO CLINIC BALLYMENA (HM07082) | | | ● | | | | | | | | | | | | | | | | | | | | | | | |
| FINAGHY CHIROPRACTIC CLINIC (HM07295) | | | ● | | | | | | | | | | | | | | | | | | | | | | | |
| FLORENCE SHARPE CHIROPODIST (HM07431) | | ● | | | | | | | | | | | | | | | | | | | | | | | | |
| FRAMAR NATURAL HEALTH CLINIC (HM07654) | | | | | | | | ● | ● | | | | | | | | | | | | | | | | | |
| GLENGORMLEY CHIRO CLINIC (HM08151) | | | ● | | | | | | | | | | | | | | | | | | | | | | | |
| LAMBERT, RACHEL (HM11901) | | | | | | | | | | | | | | | | | | | | | | | | | | |
| LISBURN CHIROPRACTIC CLINIC (HM12452) | | | ● | | | | | | | | | | | | | | | | | | | | | | | |
| MAXWELL, MARY (HM13337) | | ● | | | | | | | | | | | | | | | | | | | | | | | | |
| MCCARTNEY, W J (HM13401) | | ● | | | | | | | | | | | | | | | | | | | | | | | | |
| MCCRYSTALS NATUROPATHIC CENTRE (HM13436) | | | | | | | | ● | ● | | | | | | | | | | | | | | | | | |
| MCCULLY, JOAN (HM13437) | | ● | | | | | | | | | | | | | | | | | | | | | | | | |
| MORGAN, D (HM14161) | | | ● | | | | | | | | | | | | | | | | | | | | | | | |
| MYSTIC SCHEHERAZADE (HM14445) | | | | | | | | | ● | | | | | | | | | | | | | | | | | |
| REAY, H (HM17004) | | ● | | | | | | | | | | | | | | | | | | | | | | | | |
| SCRABO HEALTH PRODUCTS (HM18143) | | | | | | | | | | | | | | | | | | | | | | | | | | |
| SCULLION, BRENDA (HM18156) | | | | | | | | | | | | | | | | | | | | | | | | | | |
| SHEPPARD, SERENA (HM18423) | | | | | | | | | | | | | | | | | | | | | | | | | | |
| STEWART, S (HM19276) | | ● | | | | | | | | | | | | | | | | | | | | | | | | |
| TODD, TREVOR (HM20109) | | ● | | | | | | | | | | | | | | | | | | | | | | | | |

# F - O Therapies at Practices/Businesses

| Business by County with Reference no. | Family Planning (Natural) | Family Therapy | Feldenkrais Methodology | Feng Shui | Floral Essence Therapy | Flotation Therapy | Gait Analysis | Gem Essence Therapy | Gestalt Therapy | Group Therapy | Hay Diet | Healer | Healing Therapy | Hellerwork | Herbal Medicine | Holistic Healing | Homeopathy | Hopi Ear Candles | Humanistic Psychology | Hypnosis | Hypnotherapy | Indian Head Massage | Inhalation Therapy | Iridology | Kinesiology | Kirlian Photography | Laser Treatment | Life Style Coaching | Light Therapy | Macrobiotics | Magnetic Therapy | Manipulation | Manual Lymph Drainage | Massage (Therapeutic) | McTimoney Chiropractic | Meditation | Metamorphic Therapy | Miasm Therapy | Micro Manipulation | Moxibustion | Mud Therapy | Music Therapy | Nail Surgery | Naturopathy | Neuro-Linguistic Program | Neurotherapy | Nutritional Therapy | Orgone Therapy | Oriental Diagnosis | Orthomolecular Medicine |
|---|---|---|---|---|---|---|---|---|---|---|---|---|---|---|---|---|---|---|---|---|---|---|---|---|---|---|---|---|---|---|---|---|---|---|---|---|---|---|---|---|---|---|---|---|---|---|---|---|---|---|
| WEDLOCK, P (HM21098) | | | ● | | | | | | | | | | | | | | | | | | | | | | | | | | | | | | | | | | | | | | | | | | | | | | | |
| YARO (HM21991) | | | | | | | ● | | | | | | | | | | | | | | | | | | | | | | | | | | | | | | | | | | | | | | | | | | | |
| COUNTY ARMAGH | | | | | | | | | | | | | | | | | | | | | | | | | | | | | | | | | | | | | | | | | | | | | | | | | | |
| ARMAGH CHIROPRACTIC CLINIC (HM01009) | | | | | | | | | | | | | | | | | | | | | | | | | | | ● | | | | | | | | | | | | | | | | | | | | | | | |
| CAMPBELL, FIONA (HM03598) | | | | | | | | | | | | | | | | | | | | | | | | | | ● | | | | | | | | | | | | | | | | | | | | | | | | |
| CRAIGAVON CHIROPRACTIC CLINIC (HM05355) | | | | | | | | | | | | | | | | | | | | | | | | | | | ● | | | | | | | | | | | | | | | | | | | | | | | |
| LYON, HARRIETTE (HM12780) | | | | | | | | | | | | | | | | | | | | | | | | | | ● | | | | | | | | | | | | | | | | | | | | | | | | |
| WILLIS, IAN (HM21614) | | | | | | | | | | | | | | | | | | | | | | ● | | | | ● | | | | | | | | | | | | | | | | | | | | | | | | |
| COUNTY DOWN | | | | | | | | | | | | | | | | | | | | | | | | | | | | | | | | | | | | | | | | | | | | | | | | | | |
| ARDS CHIROPRACTIC CLINIC (HM00993) | | | ● | | | | | | | | | | | | | | | | | | | | | | | | ● | | | | | | | | | | | | | | | | | | | | | | | |
| BANGOR CHIROPRACTIC CLINIC (HM01659) | | | | | | | | | | | | | | | | | | | | | | | | | | | ● | | | | | | | | | | | | | | | | | | | | | | | |
| CHIROPRACTICE (HM04405) | | | | | | | | | | | | | | | | | | | | | | | | | | ● | ● | | | | | | | | | | | | | | | | | | | | | | | |
| COCHRANE, NIALL (HM04764) | | | | | | | | | | | | | | | | | | | | | | | | | | ● | | | | | | | | | | | | | | | | | | | | | | | | |
| DELICATE ESSENCE CLINIC (HM05966) | | | | | | | ● | | | | | | | | | | | | | | | | | | | | | | | | | | | | | | | | | | | | | | | | | | | |
| FAMILY CHIROPRACTIC CLINIC (HM07085) | | | | | | | | | | | | | | | | | | | | | | | | | | | ● | | | | | | | | | | | | | | | | | | | | | | | |
| HADDEN, MARLENE (HM08687) | | ● | | | | | ● | | | | | | | | | ● | | | | | | | | ● | | | | | | | ● | | ● | | | | | | | | ● | | | | | | | | | |
| LYCIUM CENTRE (HM12755) | | | ● | | | | ● | | | | | | | | | | | | | | | | | | | | | | | | | | | | | | | ● | | | | | | | | | | | | |
| MCCARTAN, DEBORAH (HM13392) | | | | | | | | | | | | | | | | | | | | | | ● | | | | ● | | | | | | | | | | | | | | | | | | | | | | | | |
| MCCLURG, T A (HM13412) | | ● | | | | | | | | | | | | | | | | | | | | | | | | | | | | | | | | | | | | | | | | | | | | | | | | |
| MCCUTCHEON, TINA (HM13441) | | | ● | | | | | | | | | | | | | ● | | | | | | | | | | | | | | | | | | ● | | | | | | | | | | | | | | | | |
| NEWRY CHIROPRACTIC CLINIC (HM14886) | | | | | | | | | | | | | | | | | | | | | | | | | | | ● | | | | | | | | | | | | | | | | | | | | | | | |
| NOBLE, ANDREW (DR) (HM14968) | | | | | | | | | | | | | | | | | | | | | | | | | | | ● | | | | | | | | | | | | | | | | | | | | | | | |
| NORTH DOWN CLINIC (HM15023) | | | | | | | | | | | | | | | | | | | | | | | | | | | | | | | | | | ● | | | | | | | | | | | | | | | | |
| PRINGLE CHIROPRACTIC (HM16626) | | ● | ● | ● | | | | | | | | | | | | | | | | | | | ● | ● | | | ● | | | | | ● | | | | | | | | | | | | | | | | | | |
| QUINN, BARBARA (HM16808) | | | | | | | | | | | | | | | | | | | | | | | | | | | | | | | | | | ● | | | | | | | | | | | | | | | | |
| REFLEXOLOGY CLINIC (HM17092) | | | | | | | ● | | | | | | | | | | | | | | | | | | | | | | | | | | | | | | | | | | | | | | | | | | | |
| COUNTY FERMANAGH | | | | | | | | | | | | | | | | | | | | | | | | | | | | | | | | | | | | | | | | | | | | | | | | | | |
| ENNISKILLEN CHIRO CLINIC (HM06844) | | | | | | | | | | | | | | | | | | | | | | | | | | | ● | | | | | | | | | | | | | | | | | | | | | | | |
| COUNTY LONDONDERRY | | | | | | | | | | | | | | | | | | | | | | | | | | | | | | | | | | | | | | | | | | | | | | | | | | |
| CLARENDON CHIROPRACTIC CLINIC (HM04539) | | | | | | | | | | | | | | | | | | | | | | | | | | | ● | | | | | | | | | | | | | | | | | | | | | | | |
| CLAUDY CHIROPRACTIC CLINIC (HM04612) | | | | | | | | | | | | | | | | | | | | | | | | | | | ● | | | | | | | | | | | | | | | | | | | | | | | |
| COLERAINE CHIROPRACTIC CENTRE (HM04830) | | | | | | | | | | | | | | | | | | | | | | | | | | | ● | | | | | | | | | | | | | | | | | | | | | | | |
| CURRAN, MAUREEN (HM05630) | | | | | | | ● | | | | | | | | | | | ● | | | | | | | | | | | | | | | | | | | | | | | | | | | | | ● | | | |
| DISPENSERY (HM06117) | | | ● | | | | | | | | | | | | | ● | | | | | | | | | | | | | | | | | ● | | | | | | | | ● | | | | | | | | | |

# F - O Therapies at Practices/Businesses

| Business by County with Reference no. | Family Planning (Natural) | Family Therapy | Feldenkrais Methodology | Feng Shui | Floral Essence Therapy | Flotation Therapy | Gait Analysis | Gem Essence Therapy | Gestalt Therapy | Group Therapy | Hay Diet | Healer | Healing Therapy | Hellerwork | Herbal Medicine | Holistic Healing | Homeopathy | Hopi Ear Candles | Humanistic Psychology | Hypnosis | Hypnotherapy | Indian Head Massage | Inhalation Therapy | Iridology | Kinesiology |
|---|---|---|---|---|---|---|---|---|---|---|---|---|---|---|---|---|---|---|---|---|---|---|---|---|---|
| EQUILIBRIUM HOLISTIC CLINIC (HM06875) | | | | | | | ● | | | | | | | | | ● | | | | | | | | | |
| FEET FIRST (HM07174) | | | | | | | | | | | | | | | | | | | | | | ● | | | |
| FOYLE HYPNOTHERAPY CENTRE (HM07646) | | ● | ● | | | | | | | | ● | | ● | | | | | | | | | | | | |
| HYNES, NANCY (HM10484) | | | | | | | | | | | | | | | | ● | | | | | | | | | |
| LIFE TREE (HM12350) | | | | | ● | | ● | | | | | | | | | ● | | | | | | | | | |
| MAGHERAFELT CHIRO CLINIC (HM12906) | | | | | | | | | | | | | | | | | | | | | | | | | |
| SCHLINDWEIN, HELENA (HM18017) | | | | | | | | | | | | | | | | ● | | | | | | | | | |
| **COUNTY TYRONE** | | | | | | | | | | | | | | | | | | | | | | | | | |
| BRADLEY, R M (HM02871) | | | | | | | | | | | | | | | | | | | | | | | | | |
| COOKSTOWN CHIROPRACTIC CLINIC (HM05072) | | | | | | | | | | | | | | | | | | | | | | | | | |
| DUNGANNON CHIROPRACTIC CLINIC (HM06405) | | | | | | | | | | | | | | | | | | | | | | | | | |
| O'MAHONY, JOHN & BEATE (HM15308) | | | ● | | | | | | | | | | | | | | | | | | | | | | |
| ROSEWOOD HEALTH CLINIC (HM17630) | | | | | | | | | | | | | | | | | | | | | | | | | |

| Business by County with Reference no. | Kirlian Photography | Laser Treatment | Life Style Coaching | Light Therapy | Macrobiotics | Magnetic Therapy | Manipulation | Manual Lymph Drainage | Massage (Therapeutic) | McTimoney Chiropractic | Meditation | Metamorphic Therapy | Miasm Therapy | Micro Manipulation | Moxibustion | Mud Therapy | Music Therapy | Nail Surgery | Naturopathy | Neuro-Linguistic Program | Neurotherapy | Nutritional Therapy | Orgone Therapy | Oriental Diagnosis | Orthomolecular Medicine |
|---|---|---|---|---|---|---|---|---|---|---|---|---|---|---|---|---|---|---|---|---|---|---|---|---|---|
| EQUILIBRIUM HOLISTIC CLINIC (HM06875) | | | | | | | | | | | | | | | | | | | | | | | | | |
| FEET FIRST (HM07174) | ● | | | | | | | | | | | | | | | | | | | | | | | | |
| FOYLE HYPNOTHERAPY CENTRE (HM07646) | | | | ● | | ● | ● | ● | | | | | | | | | | | | | | | ● | | |
| HYNES, NANCY (HM10484) | | | | | | | | | | | | | | | | | | | | | | | | | |
| LIFE TREE (HM12350) | | | | | | | | | | | | | | | | | | | | | | | | | |
| MAGHERAFELT CHIRO CLINIC (HM12906) | | ● | | | | | | | | | | | | | | | | | | | | | | | |
| SCHLINDWEIN, HELENA (HM18017) | | | | | | | | | | | | | | | | | | | | | | | | | |
| **COUNTY TYRONE** | | | | | | | | | | | | | | | | | | | | | | | | | |
| BRADLEY, R M (HM02871) | ● | | | | | | | | | | | | | | | | | | | | | | | | |
| COOKSTOWN CHIROPRACTIC CLINIC (HM05072) | | ● | | | | | | | | | | | | | | | | | | | | | | | |
| DUNGANNON CHIROPRACTIC CLINIC (HM06405) | | ● | | | | | | | | | | | | | | | | | | | | | | | |
| O'MAHONY, JOHN & BEATE (HM15308) | | | | | | | | | | | | | | | | | | | | | | | | | |
| ROSEWOOD HEALTH CLINIC (HM17630) | ● | | | | | | | | | | | | | | | | | | | | | | | | |

# F - O Therapies at Practices/Businesses

| Business by County with Reference no. | Family Planning (Natural) | Family Therapy | Feldenkrais Methodology | Feng Shui | Floral Essence Therapy | Flotation Therapy | Gait Analysis | Gem Essence Therapy | Gestalt Therapy | Group Therapy | Hay Diet | Healer | Healing Therapy | Hellerwork |
|---|---|---|---|---|---|---|---|---|---|---|---|---|---|---|
| **SCOTLAND** | | | | | | | | | | | | | | |
| **ABERDEENSHIRE** | | | | | | | | | | | | | | |
| ABERDEEN CHIROPRACTIC CLINIC (HM00114) | | | | | | | | | | | | | | |
| ALTERNATIVE PRACTICE (HM00723) | | | | | | | | | | | | | | |
| BEECHGROVE CLINIC (HM02050) | | | | | | | | | | | | | | |
| CHELSEA HOUSE CLINIC (HM04090) | | | | | | | | | | | | | | |
| CLAIRBAUX CLINIC (HM04505) | | | | | | | | | | | | | | |
| CLAIRBAUX CLINIC (HM04506) | | | | | | | | | | | | | | |
| DAB HANDS MASSAGE (HM05666) | | | | | | | | | | | | | | |
| DEEVIEW AROMATHERAPY (HM05960) | | | | | | | | | | | | | | |
| EMPTAGE, MARGARET (HM06808) | | | | | | | | | | | | | | |
| HOMOEOPATHY CENTRE (HM10105) | | | | | | | | | | | | | | |
| HOWIE, DAVID D (HM10281) | | | | | | | | | | | | | | |
| JAMES, DANIEL D (HM10883) | | | | | | | | | | | | | | |
| MCINTOSH, IRENE (HM13516) | | | | | | | | | | | | | | |
| REIKI TRAINING CENTRE (HM17149) | | | | | | | | | | | | | | |
| RIVERSIDE CHIROPRACTIC CLINIC (HM17378) | | | | | | | | | | | | | ● | |
| ROSEMOUNT CENTRE (HM17623) | | | | | | | | | ● | | | ● | | |
| SAWYER, KEN (HM17985) | | | | | | | | | | | | | | |
| SERENDIPITY (HM18232) | | | | | | | | | | | | ● | | |
| TAGGART, RUTH (HM19652) | | | | | | | | | | | | | | |
| THOMSON, HAZEL (HM20004) | | | | | | | | | | | | | | |
| WEST END PHYSIOTHERAPY (HM21219) | | | | | | | | | | | | | | |
| WILKEN, ANGEL (HM21492) | | | | | | | | | | | | | | |
| **ANGUS** | | | | | | | | | | | | | | |
| BAKER, P T (HM01593) | | | | | | | | | | | | | | |
| DRYDEN, PHILIP (HM06333) | | | | | | | | | | | | | | |
| FOGGIE, MARGARET (HM07454) | | | | | | | | | | | | | | |
| MIND BODY SOUL & ASSOCIATES (HM13960) | | | | | | | | | | | | | | |
| NATURAL HEALTH & CHIROPODY (HM14558) | | | | | | | | | | | | | | |
| NATURAL HEALTH CARE (HM14560) | | | | | | | | | | | | | | |
| NEWAYS INDEPENDENT CONSULTANT (HM14844) | | | | | | | | | | | | | | |
| NICOLL, ELAINE (HM14929) | | | | | | | | | | | | | | |

| Business by County with Reference no. | Herbal Medicine | Holistic Healing | Homeopathy | Hopi Ear Candles | Humanistic Psychology | Hypnosis | Hypnotherapy | Indian Head Massage | Inhalation Therapy | Iridology | Kinesiology | Kirlian Photography | Laser Treatment | Life Style Coaching | Light Therapy | Macrobiotics | Magnetic Therapy |
|---|---|---|---|---|---|---|---|---|---|---|---|---|---|---|---|---|---|
| **SCOTLAND** | | | | | | | | | | | | | | | | | |
| **ABERDEENSHIRE** | | | | | | | | | | | | | | | | | |
| ABERDEEN CHIROPRACTIC CLINIC (HM00114) | | | | | | | | | | | ● | | | | | | |
| ALTERNATIVE PRACTICE (HM00723) | | | | | | | | ● | | | ● | | | | | | |
| BEECHGROVE CLINIC (HM02050) | | | | | | | | | | | | | | | | | |
| CHELSEA HOUSE CLINIC (HM04090) | | | ● | | | | | | | | | | | | | | |
| CLAIRBAUX CLINIC (HM04505) | | | | | | | | | | | | | | | | | |
| CLAIRBAUX CLINIC (HM04506) | | | | | | | | | | | | | | | | | |
| DAB HANDS MASSAGE (HM05666) | | | | | | | | | | | | | | | | | |
| DEEVIEW AROMATHERAPY (HM05960) | | | | | | | | | | | | | | | | | |
| EMPTAGE, MARGARET (HM06808) | | | | | | ● | | | | | | | | | | | |
| HOMOEOPATHY CENTRE (HM10105) | | | ● | | | | | | | | | | | | | | |
| HOWIE, DAVID D (HM10281) | | | | | | ● | | | | | | | | | | | |
| JAMES, DANIEL D (HM10883) | | | | | | ● | | | | | | | | | | | |
| MCINTOSH, IRENE (HM13516) | | | | | | ● | | | | | | | | | | | |
| REIKI TRAINING CENTRE (HM17149) | | | | | | | | | | | | | | | | | |
| RIVERSIDE CHIROPRACTIC CLINIC (HM17378) | ● | | | | | | | | | | | | | | | | |
| ROSEMOUNT CENTRE (HM17623) | ● | | ● | | | | ● | ● | | | | | | | | | |
| SAWYER, KEN (HM17985) | | | | | | ● | ● | | | | | | | | | | |
| SERENDIPITY (HM18232) | | | ● | | | | | | | | | | | | | | |
| TAGGART, RUTH (HM19652) | | | | | | | | | | | | | | | | | |
| THOMSON, HAZEL (HM20004) | | | | | | ● | | | | | | | | | | | |
| WEST END PHYSIOTHERAPY (HM21219) | | | | | | | | | | | | | | | | | |
| WILKEN, ANGEL (HM21492) | | | | | | | | | | | | | | | | | |
| **ANGUS** | | | | | | | | | | | | | | | | | |
| BAKER, P T (HM01593) | | | | | | | | | | | | | | | | | |
| DRYDEN, PHILIP (HM06333) | | | | | | | | | | | | | | | | | |
| FOGGIE, MARGARET (HM07454) | | | | | | | | ● | | | | | | | | | |
| MIND BODY SOUL & ASSOCIATES (HM13960) | | ● | ● | ● | | | | ● | | | ● | | | | | | |
| NATURAL HEALTH & CHIROPODY (HM14558) | | | | | | | | ● | | | | | | | | | |
| NATURAL HEALTH CARE (HM14560) | | | | | | ● | | | | | | | | | | | |
| NEWAYS INDEPENDENT CONSULTANT (HM14844) | | ● | | | | | | | | | | | | | | | |
| NICOLL, ELAINE (HM14929) | | | | | | | | | | | | | | | | | |

| Business by County with Reference no. | Manipulation | Manual Lymph Drainage | Massage (Therapeutic) | McTimoney Chiropractic | Meditation | Metamorphic Therapy | Miasm Therapy | Micro Manipulation | Moxibustion | Mud Therapy | Music Therapy | Nail Surgery | Naturopathy | Neuro-Linguistic Program | Neurotherapy | Nutritional Therapy | Orgone Therapy | Oriental Diagnosis | Orthomolecular Medicine |
|---|---|---|---|---|---|---|---|---|---|---|---|---|---|---|---|---|---|---|---|
| **SCOTLAND** | | | | | | | | | | | | | | | | | | | |
| **ABERDEENSHIRE** | | | | | | | | | | | | | | | | | | | |
| ABERDEEN CHIROPRACTIC CLINIC (HM00114) | | | | | | | | | | | | | | | | | | | |
| ALTERNATIVE PRACTICE (HM00723) | | | | | | | | | | | | | | | | | | | |
| BEECHGROVE CLINIC (HM02050) | ● | | ● | | | | | | | | | | | | | | | | |
| CHELSEA HOUSE CLINIC (HM04090) | | | | | | | | | | | | | | | | | | | |
| CLAIRBAUX CLINIC (HM04505) | | | | | | | | | | | | | | | | ● | | | |
| CLAIRBAUX CLINIC (HM04506) | | | | | | | | | | | | | | | | ● | | | |
| DAB HANDS MASSAGE (HM05666) | | | ● | | | | | | | | | | | | | | | | |
| DEEVIEW AROMATHERAPY (HM05960) | | | ● | | | | | | | | ● | | | | | | | | |
| EMPTAGE, MARGARET (HM06808) | | | | | | | | | | | | | | | | | | | |
| HOMOEOPATHY CENTRE (HM10105) | | | | | | | | | | | | | | | | | | | |
| HOWIE, DAVID D (HM10281) | | | | | | | | | | | | | | | | | | | |
| JAMES, DANIEL D (HM10883) | | | | | | | | | | | | | | | | | | | |
| MCINTOSH, IRENE (HM13516) | | | | | | | | | | | | | | | | | | | |
| REIKI TRAINING CENTRE (HM17149) | | | | | | ● | | | | | | | | | | | | | |
| RIVERSIDE CHIROPRACTIC CLINIC (HM17378) | | | | | | | | | | | | | | | | | | | |
| ROSEMOUNT CENTRE (HM17623) | | | ● | | | ● | | | | | | | | | | ● | | | |
| SAWYER, KEN (HM17985) | | | | | | | | | | | | | | | | | | | |
| SERENDIPITY (HM18232) | | | ● | | | | | | | | | | | | | | | | |
| TAGGART, RUTH (HM19652) | | | ● | | | | | | | | | | | | | | | | |
| THOMSON, HAZEL (HM20004) | | | | | | | | | | | | | | | | | | | |
| WEST END PHYSIOTHERAPY (HM21219) | ● | | | | | | | | | | | | | | | | | | |
| WILKEN, ANGEL (HM21492) | | | ● | | | | | | | | | | | | | | | | |
| **ANGUS** | | | | | | | | | | | | | | | | | | | |
| BAKER, P T (HM01593) | | | | | | | | | | | | | ● | | | | | | |
| DRYDEN, PHILIP (HM06333) | | | | | | | | | | | | ● | | | | | | | |
| FOGGIE, MARGARET (HM07454) | | | | | | | | | | | | | | | | | | | |
| MIND BODY SOUL & ASSOCIATES (HM13960) | | | ● | | ● | | | | | | | | ● | | | ● | | | |
| NATURAL HEALTH & CHIROPODY (HM14558) | | | | | | | | | | | | | | | | | | | |
| NATURAL HEALTH CARE (HM14560) | | | | | | | | | | | | | | | | | | | |
| NEWAYS INDEPENDENT CONSULTANT (HM14844) | | | | | | | | | | | | | | | | | | | |
| NICOLL, ELAINE (HM14929) | | | | | | | | | | | | ● | | | | | | | |

# F - O Therapies at Practices/Businesses

Business by County with Reference no.

| Business by County with Reference no. | Family Planning (Natural) | Family Therapy | Feldenkrais Methodology | Feng Shui | Floral Essence Therapy | Flotation Therapy | Gait Analysis | Gem Essence Therapy | Gestalt Therapy | Group Therapy | Hay Diet | Healer | Healing Therapy | Hellerwork | Herbal Medicine | Holistic Healing | Homeopathy | Hopi Ear Candles | Humanistic Psychology | Hypnosis | Hypnotherapy | Indian Head Massage | Inhalation Therapy | Iridology | Kinesiology |
|---|---|---|---|---|---|---|---|---|---|---|---|---|---|---|---|---|---|---|---|---|---|---|---|---|---|
| **ARGYLL AND BUTE** | | | | | | | | | | | | | | | | | | | | | | | | | |
| COMPLEMENTARY HEALTH CENTRE (HM04922) | | | | | | | | | | | | | | | ● | | | | | ● | ● | | | | |
| HOMEOPATHIC PODIATRIST/REFLEX (HM10078) | | | | | | | | | | | | | | | | | ● | | | | | | | | |
| M H B ASSOCIATES (HM12799) | | | | | | | | | | | | | | | | | | | | ● | | | | | |
| NATURAL THERAPY CENTRE (HM14648) | | | | | | | | | | | | | | | | | | | | | | | | | |
| **AYRSHIRE (EAST)** | | | | | | | | | | | | | | | | | | | | | | | | | |
| BOITEUX, FRANK (HM02649) | | | | | | | | | | | | | | | | | | | | ● | | | | | |
| CRUISE, M & M (HM05520) | | | | | | | | | | | | | | | | | | | | | | | | | |
| LITTLEJOHN, S (HM12473) | | | | | | | | | | | | | | | | | | | | | | | | | |
| LYNN BROWN CLINICAL AROM (HM12772) | | | | | | | | | | | | | | | | ● | | | | | | | | | |
| MCCABE, P J (HM13376) | | | | | | | | | | | | | | | | | | | | | | | | | |
| REID, ELIZABETH (HM17117) | | | | | | | | | | | | | ● | | | | | | | | | ● | | | |
| **AYRSHIRE (NORTH)** | | | | | | | | | | | | | | | | | | | | | | | | | |
| BURNS, ALAN STEWART (HM03410) | | | | | | | | | | | | | | | | | | | | | | | | | |
| CHIRO HEALTH CARE CLINIC (HM04282) | | | | | | | | | | | | | | | | | | | | | | | | | |
| LARGS NATURAL HEALTH CLINIC (HM11972) | | | | | | | | | | | | | | | | | ● | | | | | | | | |
| **AYRSHIRE (SOUTH)** | | | | | | | | | | | | | | | | | | | | | | | | | |
| BECKETT, MAURICE (HM02025) | | | | | | | | | | | | | | | | | | | | ● | | | | | |
| BELL, W DOUGLAS (HM02091) | | | | | | | | | | | | | | | | | | | | | | | | | |
| CARRICK CLINIC (HM03742) | | | | | | | | | | | | | | | ● | | ● | | | | | | | ● | ● |
| CRUISE, M & M (HM05522) | | | | | | | | | | | | | | | | | | | | | | | | | |
| ESSENCE OF HEALTH (HM06890) | | | | | | | | | | | | | | | ● | ● | ● | | | | | | | | |
| HEALTH STRESS & INJURIES (HM09404) | | | | | | | | | | | | | | | | | | | | | | | | | ● |
| HODGE, IAN (HM09874) | | | | | | | | | ● | | | | | | | | | | ● | ● | ● | | | | |
| ORIENTAL HEALTH CENTRE (HM15381) | | | | | | | | | | | | | | | ● | | | | | | | | | | |
| REID, A (HM17112) | | | | | | | | | | | | | | | | | | | | | | | | | |
| SMITH, ALICIA (HM18712) | | | | | | | | | | | | | | | | | | | | ● | ● | | | | |
| STEVENSON, SCOTT (HM19251) | | | | | | | | | | | | | ● | | | | | | | | ● | | | | |
| STEWART, ALAN (HM19257) | | | | | | | | | | | | | | | | | | | | | | ● | | | |
| SUSAN, DOYLE (HM19530) | | | | | | | | | | | | | | | | | | | | ● | | | | | |
| **CAITHNESS** | | | | | | | | | | | | | | | | | | | | | | | | | |
| WILSON, HELEN (HM21657) | | | | | | | | | | | | | | | | | | | | ● | | | | | |
| **CLACKMANNANSHIRE** | | | | | | | | | | | | | | | | | | | | | | | | | |
| ALTERNATIVE MEDICAL CLINIC (HM00711) | | | | | | | | | | | | | | | | | | | | ● | | | | | |

| Business by County with Reference no. | Kirlian Photography | Laser Treatment | Life Style Coaching | Light Therapy | Macrobiotics | Magnetic Therapy | Manipulation | Manual Lymph Drainage | Massage (Therapeutic) | McTimoney Chiropractic | Meditation | Metamorphic Therapy | Miasm Therapy | Micro Manipulation | Moxibustion | Mud Therapy | Music Therapy | Nail Surgery | Naturopathy | Neuro-Linguistic Program | Neurotherapy | Nutritional Therapy | Orgone Therapy | Oriental Diagnosis | Orthomolecular Medicine |
|---|---|---|---|---|---|---|---|---|---|---|---|---|---|---|---|---|---|---|---|---|---|---|---|---|---|
| **ARGYLL AND BUTE** | | | | | | | | | | | | | | | | | | | | | | | | | |
| COMPLEMENTARY HEALTH CENTRE (HM04922) | | | | | | | | | ● | | | | | | | | | | | | | | | | |
| HOMEOPATHIC PODIATRIST/REFLEX (HM10078) | | | | | | | | | | | | | | | | | | | | | | | | | |
| M H B ASSOCIATES (HM12799) | | | | | | | | | | | | | | | | | | | | | | | | | |
| NATURAL THERAPY CENTRE (HM14648) | | | | | | | | | | | | | | | | | | | ● | | | | | | |
| **AYRSHIRE (EAST)** | | | | | | | | | | | | | | | | | | | | | | | | | |
| BOITEUX, FRANK (HM02649) | | | | | | | | | | | | | | | | | | | | | | | | | |
| CRUISE, M & M (HM05520) | | | | | | | | | | | | | | | | | | ● | | | | | | | |
| LITTLEJOHN, S (HM12473) | | | | | | | | | | | | | | | | | | ● | | | | | | | |
| LYNN BROWN CLINICAL AROM (HM12772) | | | | | | | | | ● | | | | | | | | | | | | | | | | |
| MCCABE, P J (HM13376) | | | | | | | | | | | | | | | | | | ● | | | | | | | |
| REID, ELIZABETH (HM17117) | | | | | | | | | | | | | | | | | | | | | | | | | |
| **AYRSHIRE (NORTH)** | | | | | | | | | | | | | | | | | | | | | | | | | |
| BURNS, ALAN STEWART (HM03410) | | | | | | | | | | | | | | | | | | ● | | | | | | | |
| CHIRO HEALTH CARE CLINIC (HM04282) | | | | | | | | | | | | | | | | | | | | | | ● | | | |
| LARGS NATURAL HEALTH CLINIC (HM11972) | | | | | | | | | | | | | | | | | | | | | | | | | |
| **AYRSHIRE (SOUTH)** | | | | | | | | | | | | | | | | | | | | | | | | | |
| BECKETT, MAURICE (HM02025) | | | | | | | | | | | | | | | | | | | | | | | | | |
| BELL, W DOUGLAS (HM02091) | | | | | | ● | | | | | | | | | | | | | | | | | | | |
| CARRICK CLINIC (HM03742) | | | | | | | ● | | ● | | | | | | | | | | ● | | | | | | |
| CRUISE, M & M (HM05522) | | | | | | | | | | | | | | | | | | ● | | | | | | | |
| ESSENCE OF HEALTH (HM06890) | | | | | | | | | ● | | | | | | | | | | | | | | | | |
| HEALTH STRESS & INJURIES (HM09404) | | | | | | | | | | | | | | | | | | | | | | | | | |
| HODGE, IAN (HM09874) | | | | | | | | | | | ● | | | | | | | | | | | | | | |
| ORIENTAL HEALTH CENTRE (HM15381) | | | | | | | | | | | | | | | | | | | | | | | | | |
| REID, A (HM17112) | | | | | | | | | | | | | | | | | | ● | | | | | | | |
| SMITH, ALICIA (HM18712) | | | | | | | | | | | | | | | | | | | | | | | | | |
| STEVENSON, SCOTT (HM19251) | | | | | | | | | | | | | | | | | | | | | | | | | |
| STEWART, ALAN (HM19257) | | | | | | | | | ● | | | | | | | | | | | | | | | | |
| SUSAN, DOYLE (HM19530) | | | | | | | | | | | | | | | | | | | | | | | | | |
| **CAITHNESS** | | | | | | | | | | | | | | | | | | | | | | | | | |
| WILSON, HELEN (HM21657) | | | | | | | | | | | | | | | | | | | | | | | | | |
| **CLACKMANNANSHIRE** | | | | | | | | | | | | | | | | | | | | | | | | | |
| ALTERNATIVE MEDICAL CLINIC (HM00711) | | | | | | ● | | | | | | | | | | | | | | | | | | | |

# F - O Therapies at Practices/Businesses

| Business by County with Reference no. | Family Planning (Natural) | Family Therapy | Feldenkrais Methodology | Feng Shui | Floral Essence Therapy | Flotation Therapy | Gait Analysis | Gem Essence Therapy | Gestalt Therapy | Group Therapy | Hay Diet | Healer | Healing Therapy | Hellerwork | Herbal Medicine | Holistic Healing | Homeopathy | Hopi Ear Candles | Humanistic Psychology | Hypnosis | Hypnotherapy | Indian Head Massage | Inhalation Therapy | Iridology | Kinesiology |
|---|---|---|---|---|---|---|---|---|---|---|---|---|---|---|---|---|---|---|---|---|---|---|---|---|---|
| **DUMFRIES AND GALLOWAY** | | | | | | | | | | | | | | | | | | | | | | | | | |
| CHLOE'S HERBS (HM04419) | | | | | | | | | | | | | | | ● | | | | | | | | | ● | |
| DUMFRIES HOLISTIC HEALTH CTRE (HM06386) | | | | | | | | | | | | | | | | | ● | | | | | | | | |
| DUMFRIES NATURAL HEALTH CENTRE (HM06387) | | | | | | | | | | | | | | | | | | | | ● | | | | | |
| GARDNER, MARION (HM07883) | | | | | | | | | | | | | | | | | ● | | | | | | | | |
| HEALTH STRESS & INJURIES CLNC (HM09405) | | | | | | | | | | | | | | | | | | | | | ● | | | | |
| HYPNOTHERAPY CENTRE (HM10526) | | | | | | | | | | | | | | | | | | | | ● | | | | | |
| MCCLUNE, LORNA (HM13410) | | | | | | | | | | | | | | | | | | | | | | | | | |
| SHARP, LINDA A (HM18314) | | | | | | | | | | | | | | | ● | | | | | | | | | | |
| **EDINBURGH (CITY OF)** | | | | | | | | | | | | | | | | | | | | | | | | | |
| BATE, ROBIN (HM01869) | | | | | | | | | | | | | | | | | ● | | | | | | | | |
| BIORADIANT HEALTH (HM02343) | | | | | | | | | | | | | | | | | | | | | | | | | |
| BRUNTSFIELD CTRE-HYPNOTHERAPY (HM03284) | | | | | | | | | | | | | | | | | | | | ● | | | | | |
| CASTELL, JENNIE (HM03823) | | | | | | | | | | | | | | | | | ● | | | | | | | | |
| CHRISTIE, ADRIAN (HM04438) | | | | | | | | | | | | | | | | | | | | ● | ● | | | | |
| CONSULTANT HYP ANALYST (HM05016) | | | | | | | | | | | | | | | | | | | | ● | | | | | |
| COUNSELLING CENTRE (HM05249) | | | | | | | | | | | | | | | | | | | | ● | | | | | |
| DRUMMOND, IAN (HM06326) | | | | | | | | | | | | | | | | | | | | ● | ● | | | | |
| E G H P (HM06468) | | | | | | | | | | | | | | | | | | | | ● | ● | | | | |
| EDINBURGH FLOATARIUM (HM06611) | | | | | | ● | | | | | | | | | | | | | | | | | | | |
| EDINBURGH HOMEOPATHIC CENTRE (HM06613) | | | | | | | | | | | | | | | ● | | ● | | | | | | | | |
| EDINBURGH OSTEOPATHIC SURGERY (HM06615) | | | | | | | | | | | | | | | | | | | | | | | | | |
| EDINBURGH PHYSIOTHERAPY CENTRE (HM06616) | | | | | | | | | | | | | | | | | | | | | | | | | |
| EXCLUSIVE HYPNOTHERAPY (HM07019) | | | | | | | | | | | | | | | | | | | | ● | ● | | | | |
| GARDINER, F (HM07872) | | | | | | | | | | | | | | | | | | | | | | ● | | | |
| HART, MARY (HM09127) | | | | | | | | | | | | | | | | | | | | ● | | | | | |
| HAZEL, J M (HM09290) | | | | | | | | | | | | | | | | | | | | | | | | | |
| J W PHYSIOTHERAPY & SPORTS (HM10804) | | | | | | | | | | | | | | | | | | | | | | | | | |
| J W PHYSIOTHERAPY & SPORTS (HM10805) | | | | | | | | | | | | | | | | | | | | | | | | | |
| KELLY, T G (HM11447) | | | | | | | | | | | | | | | | | | | | | | | | | |
| KELLY, T G (HM11446) | | | | | | | | | | | | | | | | | | | | | | | | | |
| LIVING MIND (HM12487) | | | | | | | | | | | | ● | | | | ● | | | | ● | ● | | | | |
| LOGAN, CAROL (HM12565) | | | | | | | | | | | | | | | | | | | | | | | | | |
| MACPHERSON, R G (HM12877) | | | | | | | | | | | | | | | | | | | | | | | | | |

| Business by County with Reference no. | Kirlian Photography | Laser Treatment | Life Style Coaching | Light Therapy | Macrobiotics | Magnetic Therapy | Manipulation | Manual Lymph Drainage | Massage (Therapeutic) | McTimoney Chiropractic | Meditation | Metamorphic Therapy | Miasm Therapy | Micro Manipulation | Moxibustion | Mud Therapy | Music Therapy | Nail Surgery | Naturopathy | Neuro-Linguistic Program | Neurotherapy | Nutritional Therapy | Orgone Therapy | Oriental Diagnosis | Orthomolecular Medicine |
|---|---|---|---|---|---|---|---|---|---|---|---|---|---|---|---|---|---|---|---|---|---|---|---|---|---|
| **DUMFRIES AND GALLOWAY** | | | | | | | | | | | | | | | | | | | | | | | | | |
| CHLOE'S HERBS (HM04419) | | | | | | | | | | | | | | | | | | | ● | | | ● | | | |
| DUMFRIES HOLISTIC HEALTH CTRE (HM06386) | | | | | | | | | ● | | | | | | | | | | | | | | | | |
| DUMFRIES NATURAL HEALTH CENTRE (HM06387) | | | | | | | | | | | | | | | | | | | | | | | | | |
| GARDNER, MARION (HM07883) | | | | | | | | | | | | | | | | | | | | | | | | | |
| HEALTH STRESS & INJURIES CLNC (HM09405) | | | | | | | | | | | | | | | | | | | | | | | | | |
| HYPNOTHERAPY CENTRE (HM10526) | | | | | | | | | | | | | | | | | | | | | | | | | |
| MCCLUNE, LORNA (HM13410) | | | | | | | | | | | | | | | | | | ● | | | | | | | |
| SHARP, LINDA A (HM18314) | | | | | | | | | | | | | | | | | | | | | | | | | |
| **EDINBURGH (CITY OF)** | | | | | | | | | | | | | | | | | | | | | | | | | |
| BATE, ROBIN (HM01869) | | | | | | | | | | | | | | | | | | | | | | | | | |
| BIORADIANT HEALTH (HM02343) | | | | | | | | | ● | | | | | | | | | | | | | | | | |
| BRUNTSFIELD CTRE-HYPNOTHERAPY (HM03284) | | | | | | | | | | | | | | | | | | | | | | | | | |
| CASTELL, JENNIE (HM03823) | | | | | | | | | | | | | | | | | | | | | | | | | |
| CHRISTIE, ADRIAN (HM04438) | | | | | | | | | | | | | | | | | | | | | | | | | |
| CONSULTANT HYP ANALYST (HM05016) | | | | | | | | | | | | | | | | | | | | | | | | | |
| COUNSELLING CENTRE (HM05249) | | | | | | | | | | | | | | | | | | | | | | | | | |
| DRUMMOND, IAN (HM06326) | | | | | | | | | | | | | | | | | | | | | | | | | |
| E G H P (HM06468) | | | | | | | | | | | | | | | | | | | | | | | | | |
| EDINBURGH FLOATARIUM (HM06611) | | | | | | | | | ● | | | | | | | | | | | | | | | | |
| EDINBURGH HOMEOPATHIC CENTRE (HM06613) | | | | | | | | | | | | | | | | | | | | | | | | | |
| EDINBURGH OSTEOPATHIC SURGERY (HM06615) | | | | | | | ● | | | | | | | | | | | | | | | | | | |
| EDINBURGH PHYSIOTHERAPY CENTRE (HM06616) | | | | | | | | | ● | | | | | | | | | | | | | | | | |
| EXCLUSIVE HYPNOTHERAPY (HM07019) | | | | | | | | | | | | | | | | | | | | | | | | | |
| GARDINER, F (HM07872) | | | | | | | | | | | | | | | | | | | | | | | | | |
| HART, MARY (HM09127) | | | | | | | | | | | | | | | | | | | | | | | | | |
| HAZEL, J M (HM09290) | | | | | | | | | | | | | | | | | | ● | | | | | | | |
| J W PHYSIOTHERAPY & SPORTS (HM10804) | | | | | | | ● | | ● | | | | | | | | | | | | | | | | |
| J W PHYSIOTHERAPY & SPORTS (HM10805) | | | | | | | ● | | ● | | | | | | | | | | | | | | | | |
| KELLY, T G (HM11447) | | | | | | | | | | | | | | | | | | ● | | | | | | | |
| KELLY, T G (HM11446) | | | | | | | | | | | | | | | | | | ● | | | | | | | |
| LIVING MIND (HM12487) | | | | | | | | | | | | | | | | | | | | | | | | | |
| LOGAN, CAROL (HM12565) | | | | | | | | | | | | | | | | | | | | | | ● | | | |
| MACPHERSON, R G (HM12877) | | | | | | | | | | | | | | | | | | ● | | | | | | | |

# F - O Therapies at Practices/Businesses

| Business by County with Reference no. | Family Planning (Natural) | Family Therapy | Feldenkrais Methodology | Feng Shui | Floral Essence Therapy | Flotation Therapy | Gait Analysis | Gem Essence Therapy | Gestalt Therapy | Group Therapy | Hay Diet | Healer | Healing Therapy | Hellerwork | Herbal Medicine | Holistic Healing | Homeopathy | Hopi Ear Candles | Humanistic Psychology | Hypnosis | Hypnotherapy | Indian Head Massage | Inhalation Therapy | Iridology | Kinesiology | Kirlian Photography | Laser Treatment | Life Style Coaching | Light Therapy | Macrobiotics | Magnetic Therapy | Manipulation | Manual Lymph Drainage | Massage (Therapeutic) | McTimoney Chiropractic | Meditation | Metamorphic Therapy | Miasm Therapy | Micro Manipulation | Moxibustion | Mud Therapy | Music Therapy | Nail Surgery | Naturopathy | Neuro-Linguistic Program | Neurotherapy | Nutritional Therapy | Orgone Therapy | Oriental Diagnosis | Orthomolecular Medicine |
|---|---|---|---|---|---|---|---|---|---|---|---|---|---|---|---|---|---|---|---|---|---|---|---|---|---|---|---|---|---|---|---|---|---|---|---|---|---|---|---|---|---|---|---|---|---|---|---|---|---|---|
| MARIPOSA AROMATHERAPY (HM13103) | | | | | | | | | | | | | | | | | | | | | | | | | | | | | | | | | | ● | | | | | | | | | | | | | | | | |
| MCDONALD, DAVID S (HM13456) | | | | | | | | | | | | | | | | | | | | | | | | | | | | | | | | | | | | | | | | | | | ● | | | | | | | |
| MORNINGSIDE PODIATRY SERVICE (HM14192) | | | | | | | | | | | | | | | | | | | | | | | | | | | | | | | | | | | | | | | | | | | ● | | | | | | | |
| MUKHERJI, P S (HM14327) | | | | | | | | | | | | | | | | | ● | | | | | | | | | | | | | | | | | | | | | | | | | | | | | | | | | |
| MUNRO, LESLEY (HM14366) | | | | | | | | | | | | | | | | | ● | | | | | | | | | | | | | | | | | | | | | | | | | | | | | | | | | |
| NAPIERS CLINIC & DISPENSARY (HM14474) | | | | | | | | | | | | | | | ● | | | | | | | | | | | | | | | | | | | | | | | | | | | | | | | | | | | |
| NAPIERS DISPENSARY STOCKBRIDGE (HM14476) | | | | | | | | | | | | | | | ● | | | | | | | | | | | | | | | | | | | | | | | | | | | | | | | | | | | |
| NATURES REMEDIES (HM14694) | | | | | | | | | | | | | | | ● | | | | | | | | | | | | | | | | | | | | | | | | | | | | | | | | | | | |
| OLIVER & STODDARD (HM15285) | | | | | | | | | | | | | | | | | | | | | | | | | | | | | | | | | | | | | | | | | | | | | | | ● | | | |
| PARKER, KATHY (HM15697) | | | | | | | | | | | | | | | | | ● | | | | | | | | | | | | | | | | | | | | | | | | | | | | | | | | | |
| PSYCHIC AND LIFE SOLUTIONS (HM16685) | | | | | | | | | | ● | | | | | | | | | ● | | | | | | | | | | | | | | | | | | | | | | | | | | | | | | | |
| ROBERT STONE THERAPEUTICS (HM17398) | | | | | | | | | | | | | | | | | ● | | | | | ● | | | | | | | | | | | | ● | | ● | | | | | | | | | | | | | | |
| RUMNEY, KATHLEEN (HM17748) | | | | | | | | | | | | | | | | | | | | | | | | | | | | | | | | | ● | ● | | | | | | | | | | | | | | | | |
| TARA ROKPA ENDINBURGH (HM19699) | | | | | | | | | | | | | | | | | | | | | | | | | | | | | | | | | | | | | | | | | | | | | | | ● | | | |
| WARD, ELIZABETH (HM20900) | | | | | | | | | | | | | | | | ● | | | | | | | | | | | | | | | | | | | | | | | | | | | | | | | | | | |
| WELLBEING (HM21146) | | | | | | | | | | | | | | | | | | | | | | ● | | | | | | | | | | | | | | | | | | | | | | | | | | | | |
| YORK PLACE HOM PRACTICE (HM22048) | | | | | | | | | | | | | | | | | ● | | | | | | | | | | | | | | | | | | | | | | | | | | | | | | | | | |
| **FALKIRK** | | | | | | | | | | | | | | | | | | | | | | | | | | | | | | | | | | | | | | | | | | | | | | | | | | |
| ANGUS WILLIAMSON CLINIC (HM00885) | | | | | | | | | | | | | | | | | | | | | | | | | | | | | | | | | | ● | | | | | | | | | | | | | | | | |
| GRANT, LESLIE & DAWN (HM08385) | | | | | | | | | | | | | | | | | | | | | | | | | | | | | | | | | | | | | | | | | | | ● | | | | | | | |
| GRANT, LESLIE AND DAWN (HM08386) | | | | | | | | | | | | | | | | | | | | | | | | | | | | | | | | | | | | | | | | | | | ● | | | | | | | |
| **FIFE** | | | | | | | | | | | | | | | | | | | | | | | | | | | | | | | | | | | | | | | | | | | | | | | | | | |
| BODYNEEDS (HM02629) | | | | | | | | | | | | | | | | | | | | | | ● | | | | | | | | | | | | ● | | | | | | | | | | | | | | | | |
| CAMERON, WILLIAM (HM03588) | | | | | | | | | | | | | | | | | | | | | | | | | | | | | | | | | | | | | | | | | | | ● | | | | | | | |
| CAROLE'S MOBILE THERAPIST (HM03718) | | | | | | | | | | | | | | | | | | | | | | | | | | | | | | | | | | ● | | | | | | | | | | | | | | | | |
| COMPLEMENTARY THERAPY CLINIC (HM04949) | | | | | | | | | | ● | | | | | | | | | | | | | | | | | | | | | | | | | | | | | | | | | | | | | | | | |
| FOUNDATION HEALTH (HM07613) | | | | | | | | | | | | | | | | | | | | | | | | | ● | | | | | | | | | ● | | | | | | | | | | | | | ● | | | |
| HEALING HANDS (HM09337) | | | | | | | | | | | | | | | | | | | | | | | | | | | | | | | | | | ● | | | | | | | | | | | | | | | | |
| MALCOLM, HANNE (HM12964) | | | | | | | | | | | | | | | | | | | | ● | | | | | | | | | | | | | | | | | | | | | | | | | | | | | | |
| MATHERS, SHONA (HM13282) | | | | | | | | | | | | | | | | | | | | ● | | | | | | | | | | | | | | | | | | | | | | | | | | | | | | |
| NATURAL REMEDY CLINIC (HM14621) | | | | | | | | | | | | ● | ● | | | | | | | | | | | | | | | | | | | ● | | | | | | | | | | | | | | | | | | |
| NEAT FEET (HM14743) | | | | | | | | | | | | | | | | | | | | | | ● | | | ● | | | | | | | | | ● | | | | | | | | | | | | | | | | |
| ST ANDREWS OSTEOPATHS (HM19065) | | | | | | | | | | | | | | | | | | | | | | | | | | | | | | | | | | ● | | | | | | | | | | | | | | | | |
| TOLBOOTH HOUSE (HM20117) | | | | | | | | | | | | | | | ● | | ● | | | ● | ● | ● | | | | | | | | | | | | ● | | | | | | ● | | | ● | | | | ● | | | |

# F - O Therapies at Practices/Businesses

| Business by County with Reference no. | Family Planning (Natural) | Family Therapy | Feldenkrais Methodology | Feng Shui | Floral Essence Therapy | Flotation Therapy | Gait Analysis | Gem Essence Therapy | Gestalt Therapy | Group Therapy | Hay Diet | Healer | Healing Therapy | Hellerwork | Herbal Medicine | Holistic Healing | Homeopathy | Hopi Ear Candles | Humanistic Psychology | Hypnosis | Hypnotherapy | Indian Head Massage | Inhalation Therapy | Iridology | Kinesiology | Kirlian Photography | Laser Treatment | Life Style Coaching | Light Therapy | Macrobiotics | Magnetic Therapy | Manipulation | Manual Lymph Drainage | Massage (Therapeutic) | McTimoney Chiropractic | Meditation | Metamorphic Therapy | Miasm Therapy | Micro Manipulation | Moxibustion | Mud Therapy | Music Therapy | Nail Surgery | Naturopathy | Neuro-Linguistic Program | Neurotherapy | Nutritional Therapy | Orgone Therapy | Oriental Diagnosis | Orthomolecular Medicine |
|---|---|---|---|---|---|---|---|---|---|---|---|---|---|---|---|---|---|---|---|---|---|---|---|---|---|---|---|---|---|---|---|---|---|---|---|---|---|---|---|---|---|---|---|---|---|---|---|---|---|---|
| TWA ACRES HYPNO TRAINING CTRE (HM20447) | | | | | | | | | | | | | | | | | | | | | ● | | | | | | | | | | | | | | | | | | | | | | | | | | | | | |
| **GLASGOW (CITY OF)** | | | | | | | | | | | | | | | | | | | | | | | | | | | | | | | | | | | | | | | | | | | | | | | | | | |
| ABOUT FACE (HM00131) | | | | | | | | | | | | | | | | | | | | | | | | | | | | | | | | | | ● | | | | | | | | | | | | | | | | |
| ALEXANDER, LINDA (HM00567) | | | | | | | | | | | | | | | | | | | | ● | | | | | | | | | | | | | | | | | | | | | | | | | | | | | | |
| ANDERSON DOE PODIATRY CLINIC (HM00809) | | | | | | | | | | | | | | | | | | | | | | | | | | | | | | | | | | | | | | | | | | | ● | | | | | | | |
| BEHIND THE VEIL (HM02068) | | | | | | | | | | | | ● | ● | | | ● | | | | | | ● | | | | | | | | | | | | ● | | | | | | | | | | | | | | | | |
| BLACK, JIM (HM02424) | | | | | | | | | | | | | | | | | | | | | | | | | | | | | | | | | | | | | | | | | | | ● | | | | | | | |
| BRAZENALL, A R (HM02934) | | | | | | | | | | | | | | | | | | | | | | | | | | | | | | | | ● | | | | | | | | | | | | | | | | | | |
| BRITISH SOC OF MED/DENT HYP (HM03096) | | | | | | | | | | | | | | | | | | | | ● | | | | | | | | | | | | | | | | | | | | | | | | | | | | | | |
| CLINIC AT CHARING CROSS (HM04679) | | | | | | | | | | | | | | | | | | | | ● | ● | | | | | | | | | | | | | | | | | | | | | | | | | | | | | |
| COIA, GRACE (HM04796) | | | | | | | | | | | | | | | | | | | | ● | | | | | | | | | | | | | | | | | | | | | | | | | | | | | | |
| CONWAY, VALERIE (DR) (HM05034) | | | | | | | | | | | | | | | | | ● | | | | | | | | | | | | | | | | | | | | | | | | | | | | | | | | | |
| CONWAY, VALERIE A (DR) (HM05035) | | | | | | | | | | | | | | | | | ● | | | | | | | | | | | | | | | | | | | | | | | | | | | | | | | | | |
| DARNLEY HOUSE (HM05749) | | | | | | | | | | | | | | | | | | | | ● | | | | | | | | | | | | | | | | | | | | | | | | | | | | | | |
| DENEHOLM THERAPY (HM05975) | | | | | | | | | | | | | | | | | | | | ● | | | | | | | | | | | | | | | | | | | | | | | | | | | | | | |
| ESSENTIAL BEAUTY (HM06897) | | | | | | | | | | | | | | | | | | | | | | | | | | | | | | | | | | ● | | | | | | | | | | | | | | | | |
| FITZPATRICK, J H (HM07374) | | | | | | | | | | | | | | | | | | | | | | | | | | | | | | | | | | | | | | | | | | | ● | | | | | | | |
| GIBSON, R G (HM08044) | | | | | | | | | | | | | | | | | ● | | | | | | | | | | | | | | | | | | | | | | | | | | | | | | | | | |
| HARVEST CLINIC (HM09152) | | | | | | | | | | | | ● | ● | | | ● | ● | | | ● | ● | ● | ● | | | | | ● | | | | | | ● | | ● | | | | | | | | | | | | | | |
| HOLISTIC HEALING & HYP (HM09961) | | | | | | | | | | | | ● | ● | | ● | ● | ● | | ● | ● | ● | ● | | | | | | | | | | | | | | ● | | | | | | | | | | | | | | |
| HUMAN PERFORMANCE CLINIC (HM10364) | | | | | | | | | | | | | | | | | | | | ● | ● | | | | | | | | | | | | | | | | | | | | | | | | ● | | | | | |
| LAMBERT, C W (HM11895) | | | | | | | | | | | | | | | | | | | | | | | | | | | | | | | | | | | | | | | | | | | ● | | | | | | | |
| MCKAY, MARIA (HM13523) | | | | | | | | | | | | | | | | | ● | | | | | | | | | | | | | | | | | | | | | | | | | | | | | | | | | |
| MCLEAN, A M (HM13551) | | | | | | | | | | | | | | | ● | | ● | | | | | | | | | | | | | | ● | | | | | | | | | | | | | | | | | | | |
| MCQUEEN, DAVID (HM13592) | | | | | | | | | | | | | | | | | | | | ● | | | | | | | | | | | | | | | | | | | | | | | | | | | | | | |
| MISRA, P C (HM13993) | | | | | | | | | | | | | | | | | | | | ● | | | | | | | | | | | | | | | | | | | | | | | | | | | | | | |
| NUTRITION WORLD (HM15126) | | | | | | | | | | | ● | | | | ● | | | | | | | ● | | | ● | | | | | | | ● | | ● | | | | | | | | | | | | | | | | |
| OPTIONS FOR CHANGE (HM15351) | | | | | | | | | | | | | | | | | | | | ● | | | | | | | | | | | | | | | | | | | | | | | | | ● | | | | | |
| PATTERSON, VICKY (HM15832) | | | | | | | | | | | | | | | | | | | | ● | | | | | | | | | | | | | | | | | | | | | | | | | | | | | | |
| PLUIDGE, MARK (HM16379) | | | | | | | | | | | | | | | | | | | | | | | | | | | | | | | | | | | | | | | | | | | ● | | | | | | | |
| PRIVATE LINES (HM16645) | | | | | | | | | | | | | | | ● | | | | | | | | | | | | | | | | | | | | | | | | | | | | | | | | | | | |
| ROBERTSON, KEITH (HM17447) | | | | | | | | | | | | | | | ● | | | | | | | | | | | | | | | | | | | | | | | | | | | | | | | | | | | |
| ROBERTSON, MAUREEN & KEITH (HM17451) | | | | | | | | | | | | | | | ● | | | | | | | | | | | | | | | | | | | | | | | | | | | | | | | | | | | |
| ROLLAND, C R (HM17563) | | | | | | | | | | | | | | | | | | | | | | | | | | | | | | | | | | | | | | | | | | | ● | | | | | | | |

# F - O Therapies at Practices/Businesses

Business by County with Reference no.

| Business | Family Planning (Natural) | Family Therapy | Feldenkrais Methodology | Feng Shui | Floral Essence Therapy | Flotation Therapy | Gait Analysis | Gem Essence Therapy | Gestalt Therapy | Group Therapy | Hay Diet | Healer | Healing Therapy | Hellerwork | Herbal Medicine | Holistic Healing | Homeopathy | Hopi Ear Candles | Humanistic Psychology | Hypnosis | Hypnotherapy | Indian Head Massage | Inhalation Therapy | Iridology | Kinesiology |
|---|---|---|---|---|---|---|---|---|---|---|---|---|---|---|---|---|---|---|---|---|---|---|---|---|---|
| ROSENGARD, L (DR) (HM17627) | | | | | | | | | | | | | | | | | ● | | | | | | | | |
| SCHOLL CENTRE (HM18039) | | | | | | | | | | | | | | | | | | | | | | | | | |
| SCOTTISH SCHOOL OF HERBAL MED (HM18135) | | | | | | | | | | | | | | | ● | | | | | | | | | | |
| SHARKEY, JANICE (HM18299) | | | | | | | | | | | | | | | | | | | | ● | | | | | |
| SHAWLANDS HYPNOTHERAPY CLINIC (HM18352) | | | | | | | | | | | | | | | | | | | | ● | ● | | | | |
| SINO-HERBAL CLINIC (HM18615) | | | | | | | | | | | | | | | ● | | | | | | | | | | |
| STEWART, JIM (DR) (HM19270) | | | | | | | | | | | | | | | | | | | | ● | ● | | | | |
| TRANSCENDENTAL MEDITATION (HM20287) | | | | | | | | | | | | | | | | | | | | | | | | | |
| WEST END THERAPY CENTRE (HM21221) | | | | | | | | | | | | | | | | | ● | | | | | | | | |
| HIGHLAND | | | | | | | | | | | | | | | | | | | | | | | | | |
| BUMBLE - BEE'S PHYSIO (HM03347) | | | | | | | | | | | | | | | | | | | | | | ● | | | |
| GENTLE WAYS (HM07980) | | | | | | | | | | | | ● | ● | | | | | | | | | | | | |
| HEALTH CORNER (HM09383) | | | | | | | | | | | | | | | | | | | | | | ● | | | |
| HOMEOPATHIC PRACTICE (HM10079) | | | | | | | | | | | | | | | | | ● | | | | | | | | |
| SEAFIELD CLINIC (HM18163) | | | | | | | | | | | | | | | | | | | | ● | | | | | |
| INVERCLYDE | | | | | | | | | | | | | | | | | | | | | | | | | |
| INVERCLYDE OSTEOPATHIC CLINIC (HM10704) | | | | | | | | | | | | | | | | | ● | | | | ● | ● | | | |
| KELLERMANS (HM11418) | | | | | | | | | | | | | ● | | | | ● | | | | ● | ● | | | |
| PETTIGREW, N (HM16097) | | | | | | | | | | | | | | | | | ● | | | | | | | | |
| LANARKSHIRE (NORTH) | | | | | | | | | | | | | | | | | | | | | | | | | |
| REGISTERED HOMEOPATH (HM17103) | | | | | | | | | | | | | | | | | ● | | | | | | | | |
| SMITH, IRENE B (HM18748) | | | | | | | | | | | | | | | | | | | | | | | | | |
| STRATH NATURAL THERAPIES (HM19371) | | | | | | | | | | | | | | | | | | | | | ● | | | | |
| LANARKSHIRE (SOUTH) | | | | | | | | | | | | | | | | | | | | | | | | | |
| LEES, PATRICIA (HM12170) | | | | | | | | | | | | | | | | | | | | ● | | | | | |
| QUINN, JIM (HM16810) | | | | | | | | | | | | | | | | | ● | | | | | | | | |
| ROBB, A (DR) (HM17387) | | | | | | | | | | | | | | | | | ● | | | | | | | | |
| ROY, MAGARET (HM17712) | | | | | | | | | | | | | | | | | ● | | | | | | | | |
| LOTHIAN (EAST) | | | | | | | | | | | | | | | | | | | | | | | | | |
| EAST LOTHIAN PHYSIO CENTRE (HM06518) | | | | | | | | | | | | | | | | | | | | | | | | | |
| FRASER, GORDON (HM07696) | | | | | | | | | | | | | | | | ● | ● | | | | ● | | | ● | |
| LOTHIAN (MID) | | | | | | | | | | | | | | | | | | | | | | | | | |
| CRYSTAL SANCTUARY (HM05532) | | | | | | | | | | | | | | | | ● | ● | | | | | | | | |
| NATURAL HEALTH CENTRE (HM14573) | | | | | | | | | | | | | | | | ● | ● | | | | ● | | | ● | |

| Business | Kirlian Photography | Laser Treatment | Life Style Coaching | Light Therapy | Macrobiotics | Magnetic Therapy | Manipulation | Manual Lymph Drainage | Massage (Therapeutic) | McTimoney Chiropractic | Meditation | Metamorphic Therapy | Miasm Therapy | Micro Manipulation | Moxibustion | Mud Therapy | Music Therapy | Nail Surgery | Naturopathy | Neuro-Linguistic Program | Neurotherapy | Nutritional Therapy | Orgone Therapy | Oriental Diagnosis | Orthomolecular Medicine |
|---|---|---|---|---|---|---|---|---|---|---|---|---|---|---|---|---|---|---|---|---|---|---|---|---|---|
| ROSENGARD, L (DR) (HM17627) | | | | | | | | | | | | | | | | | | | | | | | | | |
| SCHOLL CENTRE (HM18039) | | | | | | | | | | | | | | | | | | ● | | | | | | | |
| SCOTTISH SCHOOL OF HERBAL MED (HM18135) | | | | | | | | | ● | | | | | | | | | | | | | | | | |
| SHARKEY, JANICE (HM18299) | | | | | | | | | | | | | | | | | | | | | | | | | |
| SHAWLANDS HYPNOTHERAPY CLINIC (HM18352) | | | | | | | | | | | | | | | | | | | | | | | | | |
| SINO-HERBAL CLINIC (HM18615) | | | | | | | | | ● | | | | | | | | | | | | | | | | |
| STEWART, JIM (DR) (HM19270) | | | | | | | | | | | ● | | | | | | | | | | | | | | |
| TRANSCENDENTAL MEDITATION (HM20287) | | | | | | | | | | | ● | | | | | | | | | | | | | | |
| WEST END THERAPY CENTRE (HM21221) | | | | | | | | | | | | | | | | | | | | | | | | | |
| HIGHLAND | | | | | | | | | | | | | | | | | | | | | | | | | |
| BUMBLE - BEE'S PHYSIO (HM03347) | | | | | | | ● | | ● | | | ● | | | | | | | | | | | | | |
| GENTLE WAYS (HM07980) | | | | | | | | | | | ● | | | | | | | | | | | | | | |
| HEALTH CORNER (HM09383) | | | | | | | ● | | ● | | | | | | ● | | | | | | | | | | |
| HOMEOPATHIC PRACTICE (HM10079) | | | | | | | | | | | | | | | | | | | | | | | | | |
| SEAFIELD CLINIC (HM18163) | | | | | | | | | | | | | | | | | | | | | | | | | |
| INVERCLYDE | | | | | | | | | | | | | | | | | | | | | | | | | |
| INVERCLYDE OSTEOPATHIC CLINIC (HM10704) | | | | | | | ● | | ● | | | | | | | | | | | | | | | | |
| KELLERMANS (HM11418) | | | ● | | | | | | ● | | | | | | | | | | | ● | | | | | |
| PETTIGREW, N (HM16097) | | | | | | | | | | | | | | | | | | | | | | | | | |
| LANARKSHIRE (NORTH) | | | | | | | | | | | | | | | | | | | | | | | | | |
| REGISTERED HOMEOPATH (HM17103) | | | | | | | | | | | | | | | | | | | | | | | | | |
| SMITH, IRENE B (HM18748) | | | | | | | | | ● | | | | | | | | | | | | | | | | |
| STRATH NATURAL THERAPIES (HM19371) | | | | | | | | | | | | | | | | | | | | | | | | | |
| LANARKSHIRE (SOUTH) | | | | | | | | | | | | | | | | | | | | | | | | | |
| LEES, PATRICIA (HM12170) | | | | | | | | | | | | | | | | | | | | | | | | | |
| QUINN, JIM (HM16810) | | | | | | | | | | | | | | | | | | | | | | | | | |
| ROBB, A (DR) (HM17387) | | | | | | | | | | | | | | | | | | | | | | | | | |
| ROY, MAGARET (HM17712) | | | | | | | | | | | | | | | | | | | | | | | | | |
| LOTHIAN (EAST) | | | | | | | | | | | | | | | | | | | | | | | | | |
| EAST LOTHIAN PHYSIO CENTRE (HM06518) | | | | | | | ● | | ● | | | | | | | | | | | | | | | | |
| FRASER, GORDON (HM07696) | | | | | | | | | | | | | | | | | | | | | | | | | |
| LOTHIAN (MID) | | | | | | | | | | | | | | | | | | | | | | | | | |
| CRYSTAL SANCTUARY (HM05532) | | | | | | | | | ● | | | | | | | | | | | | | | | | |
| NATURAL HEALTH CENTRE (HM14573) | | | | | | | | | | | | | | | | | | | | | | | | | |

# F - O Therapies at Practices/Businesses

Business by County with Reference no.

| Business | Family Planning (Natural) | Family Therapy | Feldenkrais Methodology | Feng Shui | Floral Essence Therapy | Flotation Therapy | Gait Analysis | Gem Essence Therapy | Gestalt Therapy | Group Therapy | Hay Diet | Healer | Healing Therapy | Hellerwork | Herbal Medicine | Holistic Healing | Homeopathy | Hopi Ear Candles | Humanistic Psychology | Hypnosis | Hypnotherapy |
|---|---|---|---|---|---|---|---|---|---|---|---|---|---|---|---|---|---|---|---|---|---|
| NEW DUNDAS CLINIC (HM14817) | | | | | | | | | | | | | | | | | | | | | |
| SCOTTISH KINESIOLOGY CENTRE (HM18134) | | | | | | | | | | | | | | | | | | | | | |
| **LOTHIAN (WEST)** | | | | | | | | | | | | | | | | | | | | | |
| DUIGNAN, KAREN (HM06372) | | | | | | | | | | | | | | | | | | | | ● | ● |
| VINCES, DENISE (HM20674) | | | | | | | | | | | | | | | | | | | | | |
| **MORAY** | | | | | | | | | | | | | | | | | | | | | |
| AROMANTIC (HM01080) | | | | | | | | | | | | | | | | | | | | | |
| FINDHORN FLOWER ESSENCES (HM07307) | | | | | | | | | | | | | | | | | ● | | | | |
| HEALTHWORKS (HM09422) | ● | | | | | | | | | | | | ● | | ● | ● | ● | | | | ● |
| MACKAY, I (HM12845) | | | | | | | | | | | | | | | | | | | | ● | |
| TRUJILLO, DR ORLANDO (HM20352) | | | | | | | | | | | | | | | | | | | | ● | |
| **NORTHUMBERLAND** | | | | | | | | | | | | | | | | | | | | | |
| SOLAR- PLEXUS (HM18864) | | | | | | | | | | | | | | | | | | | | | |
| **PERTH AND KINROSS** | | | | | | | | | | | | | | | | | | | | | |
| AUCHTERARDER CHIROPODY (HM01343) | | | | | | | | | | | | | | | | | | | | | |
| BACK PAIN & SPORTS CLINIC (HM01491) | | | | | | | | | | | | | | | | ● | | | | | |
| BRIDGE OF ALLAN THERAPY CENTRE (HM02992) | | | | | | | | | | | | | | | | | | | | ● | |
| LENDRICK LODGE (HM12210) | | | | | | | | | | | | | | | | | | | | | |
| STEVENSON, IAN W (HM19246) | | | | | | | | | | | | | | | | | ● | | | | |
| TAYLOR, D (HM19749) | | | | | | | | | | | | ● | | | | | | | | ● | ● |
| TWA ACRES HYPNOTHERAPY CENTRE (HM20448) | | | | | | | | | | | | | | | | | | | | ● | |
| **RENFREWSHIRE** | | | | | | | | | | | | | | | | | | | | | |
| ALBA CENTRE (HM00473) | | | | | | | | | | | | | | | | | | | | | |
| APT LASER THERAPY (HM00950) | | | | | | | | | | | | | | | | | | | | | |
| BLACKHALL PARK CENTRE (HM02444) | | | | | | | | | | | | | | | | | | | | | |
| FANNING, M W (HM07095) | | | | | | | | | | | | | | | ● | | | | | | |
| PAISLEY CHIROPRACTIC CLINIC (HM15587) | ● | | | | | | | | | | | | | | | ● | | | | | |
| PAISLEY NATURAL THERAPY CENTRE (HM15588) | | | | | | | | | | | | | | | ● | | ● | | | | ● |
| PAISLEY PHYSIOTHERAPY CENTRE (HM15589) | | | | | | | | | | | | | | | | | | | | | |
| **SCOTTISH BORDERS** | | | | | | | | | | | | | | | | | | | | | |
| WISHING WELL (HM21738) | | ● | | | | | | | | ● | | | | | ● | ● | ● | | | | |
| **SHETLAND ISLANDS** | | | | | | | | | | | | | | | | | | | | | |
| LERWICK CHIROPRACTIC CLINIC (HM12231) | | | | | | | | | | | | | ● | | ● | | | | | | |

| Business | Indian Head Massage | Inhalation Therapy | Iridology | Kinesiology | Kirlian Photography | Laser Treatment | Life Style Coaching | Light Therapy | Macrobiotics | Magnetic Therapy | Manipulation | Manual Lymph Drainage | Massage (Therapeutic) | McTimoney Chiropractic | Meditation | Metamorphic Therapy | Miasm Therapy | Micro Manipulation | Moxibustion | Mud Therapy | Music Therapy | Nail Surgery | Naturopathy | Neuro-Linguistic Program | Neurotherapy | Nutritional Therapy | Orgone Therapy | Oriental Diagnosis | Orthomolecular Medicine |
|---|---|---|---|---|---|---|---|---|---|---|---|---|---|---|---|---|---|---|---|---|---|---|---|---|---|---|---|---|---|
| NEW DUNDAS CLINIC (HM14817) | | | | | | | | | | ● | ● | | ● | | | | | | | | | | | | | | | | |
| SCOTTISH KINESIOLOGY CENTRE (HM18134) | | | | ● | | | | | | | | | | | | | | | | | | | | | | | | | |
| **LOTHIAN (WEST)** | | | | | | | | | | | | | | | | | | | | | | | | | | | | | |
| DUIGNAN, KAREN (HM06372) | | | | | | | | | | | | | | | | | | | | | | | | ● | | | | | |
| VINCES, DENISE (HM20674) | | | | | | | | | | | | | ● | | | | | | | | | | | | | | | | |
| **MORAY** | | | | | | | | | | | | | | | | | | | | | | | | | | | | | |
| AROMANTIC (HM01080) | | | | | | | | | | | | | | | | | | | | | | | ● | | | | | | |
| FINDHORN FLOWER ESSENCES (HM07307) | | | | | | | | | | | | | | | | | | | | | | | | | | | | | |
| HEALTHWORKS (HM09422) | | | | | | | | | | | | | | | | | | | ● | | | | ● | | | | | | |
| MACKAY, I (HM12845) | | | | | | | | | | | | | | | | | | | | | | | | | | | | | |
| TRUJILLO, DR ORLANDO (HM20352) | | | | | | | | | | | | | | | | | | | | | | | | | | | | | |
| **NORTHUMBERLAND** | | | | | | | | | | | | | | | | | | | | | | | | | | | | | |
| SOLAR- PLEXUS (HM18864) | | | | | | | | | | | | | ● | | | | | | | | | | | | | | | | |
| **PERTH AND KINROSS** | | | | | | | | | | | | | | | | | | | | | | | | | | | | | |
| AUCHTERARDER CHIROPODY (HM01343) | | | | | | | | | | | | | | | | | | | | | | ● | | | | | | | |
| BACK PAIN & SPORTS CLINIC (HM01491) | | | | | | | | | | | ● | | ● | | | | | | | | | | | | | | | | |
| BRIDGE OF ALLAN THERAPY CENTRE (HM02992) | | | | | | | | | | | | | | | | | | | | | | | | | | | | | |
| LENDRICK LODGE (HM12210) | | | | | | | | | | | | | ● | | ● | | | | | | | | | | | | | | |
| STEVENSON, IAN W (HM19246) | | | | | | | | | | | | | | | | | | | | | | ● | | | | | | | |
| TAYLOR, D (HM19749) | | | | | | | | | | | | | | | | | | | | | | | | | | | | | |
| TWA ACRES HYPNOTHERAPY CENTRE (HM20448) | | | | | | | | | | | | | | | | | | | | | | | | | | | | | |
| **RENFREWSHIRE** | | | | | | | | | | | | | | | | | | | | | | | | | | | | | |
| ALBA CENTRE (HM00473) | | | | | | | | | | | | | | | ● | | | | | | | | | | | | | | |
| APT LASER THERAPY (HM00950) | | | | | | ● | | | | | | | | | | | | | | | | | | | | | | | |
| BLACKHALL PARK CENTRE (HM02444) | | | | ● | | | | | | | | | ● | | | | | | | | | | | | | | | | |
| FANNING, M W (HM07095) | | | | | | | | | | | | | | | | | | | | | | | | | | | | | |
| PAISLEY CHIROPRACTIC CLINIC (HM15587) | | | | ● | | | | | | ● | | | | | | | | | | | | | | | | ● | | | |
| PAISLEY NATURAL THERAPY CENTRE (HM15588) | ● | | | | | | | | | ● | | | ● | | | | | | | | | | | | | | | | |
| PAISLEY PHYSIOTHERAPY CENTRE (HM15589) | | | | | | | | | | ● | | | ● | | | | | ● | | | | | | | | | | | |
| **SCOTTISH BORDERS** | | | | | | | | | | | | | | | | | | | | | | | | | | | | | |
| WISHING WELL (HM21738) | | | ● | ● | | | | | | | | | ● | | | | | | | | | | | | | ● | | | |
| **SHETLAND ISLANDS** | | | | | | | | | | | | | | | | | | | | | | | | | | | | | |
| LERWICK CHIROPRACTIC CLINIC (HM12231) | | | | | | | | | | | | | | | | | | | | | | | | | | | | | |

# F - O Therapies at Practices/Businesses

| Business by County with Reference no. | Family Planning (Natural) | Family Therapy | Feldenkrais Methodology | Feng Shui | Floral Essence Therapy | Flotation Therapy | Gait Analysis | Gem Essence Therapy | Gestalt Therapy | Group Therapy | Hay Diet | Healer | Healing Therapy | Hellerwork | Herbal Medicine | Holistic Healing | Homeopathy | Hopi Ear Candles | Humanistic Psychology | Hypnosis | Hypnotherapy | Indian Head Massage | Inhalation Therapy | Iridology | Kinesiology | Kirlian Photography | Laser Treatment | Life Style Coaching | Light Therapy | Macrobiotics | Magnetic Therapy | Manipulation | Manual Lymph Drainage | Massage (Therapeutic) | McTimoney Chiropractic | Meditation | Metamorphic Therapy | Miasm Therapy | Micro Manipulation | Moxibustion | Mud Therapy | Music Therapy | Nail Surgery | Naturopathy | Neuro-Linguistic Program | Neurotherapy | Nutritional Therapy | Orgone Therapy | Oriental Diagnosis | Orthomolecular Medicine |
|---|---|---|---|---|---|---|---|---|---|---|---|---|---|---|---|---|---|---|---|---|---|---|---|---|---|---|---|---|---|---|---|---|---|---|---|---|---|---|---|---|---|---|---|---|---|---|---|---|---|---|
| **STIRLING** | | | | | | | | | | | | | | | | | | | | | | | | | | | | | | | | | | | | | | | | | | | | | | | | | | |
| GOLD, P (HM08203) | | | | | | | | | | | | | | | | | ● | | | | | | | | | | | | | | | | | | | | | | | | | | | | | | | | | |

# F - O Therapies at Practices/Businesses

| Business by County with Reference no. | Family Planning (Natural) | Family Therapy | Feldenkrais Methodology | Feng Shui | Floral Essence Therapy | Flotation Therapy | Gait Analysis | Gem Essence Therapy | Gestalt Therapy | Group Therapy | Hay Diet | Healer | Healing Therapy | Hellerwork | Herbal Medicine | Holistic Healing | Homeopathy | Hopi Ear Candles | Humanistic Psychology | Hypnosis | Hypnotherapy | Indian Head Massage | Inhalation Therapy | Iridology | Kinesiology | Kirlian Photography | Laser Treatment | Life Style Coaching | Light Therapy | Macrobiotics | Magnetic Therapy | Manipulation | Manual Lymph Drainage | Massage (Therapeutic) | McTimoney Chiropractic | Meditation | Metamorphic Therapy | Miasm Therapy | Micro Manipulation | Moxibustion | Mud Therapy | Music Therapy | Nail Surgery | Naturopathy | Neuro-Linguistic Program | Neurotherapy | Nutritional Therapy | Orgone Therapy | Oriental Diagnosis | Orthomolecular Medicine |
|---|---|---|---|---|---|---|---|---|---|---|---|---|---|---|---|---|---|---|---|---|---|---|---|---|---|---|---|---|---|---|---|---|---|---|---|---|---|---|---|---|---|---|---|---|---|---|---|---|---|---|
| **WALES** | | | | | | | | | | | | | | | | | | | | | | | | | | | | | | | | | | | | | | | | | | | | | | | | | | |
| **BLAENAU GWENT** | | | | | | | | | | | | | | | | | | | | | | | | | | | | | | | | | | | | | | | | | | | | | | | | | | |
| CLASSIC CLINIC (HM04606) | | | | | | | | | | | | | | | | | | | | | | | | | | | | | | | | | | | | | | | | | | | | | | | ● | | | |
| **BRIDGEND** | | | | | | | | | | | | | | | | | | | | | | | | | | | | | | | | | | | | | | | | | | | | | | | | | | |
| ALTERNATIVE HEALING CENTRE (HM00698) | | ● | | | | | | | | ● | | ● | ● | | | ● | | | | ● | ● | ● | | | | | | | | | | | | | | | ● | | | | | | | | | | | | | |
| JENKINS, JOHN (HM10987) | | | | | | | | | | | | | | | | | | | | | ● | | | | | | | | | | | | | | | | | | | | | | | | | | | | | |
| **CAERPHILLY** | | | | | | | | | | | | | | | | | | | | | | | | | | | | | | | | | | | | | | | | | | | | | | | | | | |
| OAKFIELD NATURAL HEALTH CENTRE (HM15151) | | | | | | | | | | | | | | | | | ● | | | | ● | | | | | | | | | | | | | | | | | | | | | | | | | | | | | |
| **CARMARTHENSHIRE** | | | | | | | | | | | | | | | | | | | | | | | | | | | | | | | | | | | | | | | | | | | | | | | | | | |
| GREENWAY CONSULTANCY (HM08495) | | | | | | | | | | | | ● | | | | ● | ● | | | ● | ● | | | | | | | | | | | | | ● | | ● | | | | | | | | | | | | | | |
| HEALING HANDS (HM09339) | | | | | | | | | | | | | | | | | | | | | | | | | | | | | | | | | | ● | | | | | | | | | | | | | | | | |
| HYPNOSIS CENTRE (HM10496) | | | | | | | | | | | | | | | | | | | | ● | | | | | | | | | | | | | | | | | | | | | | | | | | | | | | |
| JABROO, C (HM10808) | | | | | | | | | | | | | | | ● | | | | | | | | | | | | | | | | | | | | | | | | | | | | | | | | | | | |
| KACHA-STONES.COM (HM11292) | | | | | ● | | | ● | | | | | | | | ● | | | | | | | | | | | | | | | | | | | | | | | | | | | | ● | | | | | | |
| MILLICAN, SALLY (HM13913) | | | | | | | | | | | | | | | ● | | | | | | | | | | | | | | | | | | | | | | | | | | | | | | | | | | | |
| SAYERS, R B (HM18000) | | | | | | | | | | | | | | | | | | | | ● | | | | | | | | | | | | | | | | | | | | | | | | | | | | | | |
| WAINWRIGHT, MARY (HM20738) | | | | | | | | | | | | | | | | | ● | | | | | | | | | | | | | | | | | | | | | | | | | | | | | | | | | |
| **CEREDIGION** | | | | | | | | | | | | | | | | | | | | | | | | | | | | | | | | | | | | | | | | | | | | | | | | | | |
| FFYNNONWEN NATURAL THRPY CTRE (HM07256) | | | | | | | | | | | | | | | ● | | ● | | | | ● | | | | ● | | | | | | | ● | | ● | | | | | | | | | | | | | | | | |
| **CONWY** | | | | | | | | | | | | | | | | | | | | | | | | | | | | | | | | | | | | | | | | | | | | | | | | | | |
| DREW, DAVID (HM06305) | | | | | | | | | | | | ● | ● | | | ● | | | | | | | | | | | | | | | | | | ● | | ● | | | | | | | | | | | | | | |
| HERBS FOR EVERYONE (HM09669) | | | | | | | | | | | | ● | | | ● | | | | | | | | | ● | | | | | | | | | | ● | | | | | | | | | | | | | ● | | | |
| MELA CENTRE OF OSTEOPATHY (HM13702) | | | | | | | | | | | | | | | | | | | | | | | | | | | | | | | | ● | | ● | | | | | | | | | | | | | | | | |
| PIDGLEY, S (HM16277) | | | | | | | | | | | | | | | | | | | | ● | | | | | | | | | | | | | | | | | | | | | | | | | | | | | | |
| **DENBIGHSHIRE** | | | | | | | | | | | | | | | | | | | | | | | | | | | | | | | | | | | | | | | | | | | | | | | | | | |
| ALLIED PHYSIOTHERAPY (HM00646) | | | | | | | | | | | | | | | | | | | | | | | | | | | | | | | | ● | | ● | | | | | | | | | | | | | | | | |
| HARNWELL, J P (HM09034) | | | | | | | | | | | | | | | ● | | | | | | | | | | | | | | | | | | | | | | | | | | | | | | | | ● | | | |
| HEALING WAYS (HM09359) | | | | | | | | | | | | | | | | | | | | | | ● | | | | | | | | | | | ● | | | | | | | | | | | | | | | | | |
| JEVON, NICKY & DENIS (HM11024) | | | | | | | | | | | | | | | ● | | | | | | | | | | | | | | | | | | | | | | | | | | | | | | | | | | | |
| MCGILL, L (HM13484) | | | | | | | | | | | | | | | | | ● | | | | | | | | ● | | | | | | | | | | | | | | | | | | | | | | | | | |
| ROY MORRIS CLINIC (HM17709) | | | | | | | | | | | | | | | | | | | | | | | | ● | | | | | | | | | | | | | | | | | | | | | | | | | | |
| STEVENS, JEAN (HM19234) | | | | | | | | | | | | | | | | | | | | ● | | | | | | | | | | | | | | | | | | | | | | | | | | | | | | |

# F - O Therapies at Practices/Businesses

| Business by County with Reference no. | Family Planning (Natural) | Family Therapy | Feldenkrais Methodology | Feng Shui | Floral Essence Therapy | Flotation Therapy | Gait Analysis | Gem Essence Therapy | Gestalt Therapy | Group Therapy | Hay Diet | Healer | Healing Therapy | Hellerwork | Herbal Medicine | Holistic Healing | Homeopathy | Hopi Ear Candles | Humanistic Psychology | Hypnosis | Hypnotherapy | Indian Head Massage | Inhalation Therapy | Iridology | Kinesiology | Kirlian Photography | Laser Treatment | Life Style Coaching | Light Therapy | Macrobiotics | Magnetic Therapy | Manipulation | Manual Lymph Drainage | Massage (Therapeutic) | McTimoney Chiropractic | Meditation | Metamorphic Therapy | Miasm Therapy | Micro Manipulation | Moxibustion | Mud Therapy | Music Therapy | Nail Surgery | Naturopathy | Neuro-Linguistic Program | Neurotherapy | Nutritional Therapy | Orgone Therapy | Oriental Diagnosis | Orthomolecular Medicine |
|---|---|---|---|---|---|---|---|---|---|---|---|---|---|---|---|---|---|---|---|---|---|---|---|---|---|---|---|---|---|---|---|---|---|---|---|---|---|---|---|---|---|---|---|---|---|---|---|---|---|---|
| **FLINTSHIRE** | | | | | | | | | | | | | | | | | | | | | | | | | | | | | | | | | | | | | | | | | | | | | | | | | | |
| A L J RILEY ASSOCIATES (HM00038) | | | | | | | | | | | | | | | ● | | | | | | | | | | | | | | | | | | | | | | | | | | | | | | | | | | | |
| GAFFNEY, ALMA (HM07827) | | | | | | | | | | | | | | | | | | | | | | | | | | | | | | | | | | | | | | | | | | | ● | | | | | | | |
| HYPNOTHERAPY CENTRE (HM10528) | | | | | | | | | | | | | | | | | | | | ● | ● | | | | | | | | | | | | | | | | | | | | | | | | | | | | | |
| MADDERN, WENDY (HM12894) | | | | | | | | | | | | | | | | | ● | | | | | | | | | | | | | | | | | | | | | | | | | | | | | | | | | |
| **GLAMORGAN (VALE OF)** | | | | | | | | | | | | | | | | | | | | | | | | | | | | | | | | | | | | | | | | | | | | | | | | | | |
| AMETHYST HEALING CENTRE (HM00784) | | | | | | | | | | | | | | | | | | | | | | | | | ● | | | | | | | | | | | | | | | | | | | | | | | | | |
| AYRE CENTRE OF HYPNOTHERAPY (HM01430) | | | | | | | | | | | | | | | | | | | | | ● | | | | | | | | | | | | | | | | | | | | | | | | | | | | | |
| BROWN, ANNE (HM03214) | | | | | | | | | | | | | | | | | | | | | | | | | | | | | | | | | | ● | | | | | | | | | | | | | | | | |
| CARDIFF HOMEOPATHIC CLINIC (HM03671) | | | | | | | | | | | | | | | | ● | ● | | | | | | | | | | | | | | | | | | | | | | | | | | | | | | | | | |
| COWBRIDGE CHIRO/SPINAL REHAB (HM05289) | | | | | | | | | | | | | | | | | ● | | | | | | | | | | | | | | | | | | | | | | | | | | | | | | | | | |
| COWBRIDGE OSTEOPATH CLINIC (HM05290) | | | | | | | | | | | | | | | | | | | | | | | | | | | | | | | | ● | | ● | | | | | | | | | | | | | | | | |
| GRIMWADE, S (HM08586) | | | | | | | | | | | | | | | | | | | | | | | | | | | | | | | | ● | | ● | | | | | | | | | | | | | | | | |
| HENDERSON, H M (HM09547) | | | | | | | | | | | | | | | ● | | | | | | | | | | | | | | | | | | | | | | | | | | | | | | | | | | | |
| HENRIETTA CTRE FOR COMP THRPY (HM09565) | | | | | | | | | | | | | | | | | ● | | | | ● | | | | | | | | | | | | | | | ● | | | | | | | | | | | | | | |
| HOMOEOPATHIC GROUP (HM10092) | | | | | | | | | | | | | | | | | ● | | | | | | | | | | | | | | | | | | | | | | | | | | | | | | | | | |
| HYPNOTHERAPIST (HM10501) | | | | | | | | | | | | | | | | | | | | ● | | | | | | | | | | | | | | | | | | | | | | | | | | | | | | |
| HYPNOTHERAPY CLINIC (HM10534) | | | | | | | | | | | | | | | | | | | | ● | | | | | | | | | | | | | | | | | | | | | | | | | | | | | | |
| JENKINS, MARY (DR) (HM10992) | | | | | | | | | | | | | | | | | | | | ● | | | | | | | | | | | | | | | | | | | | | | | | | | | | | | |
| LEE, KEN (HM12140) | | | | | | | | | | | | | | | | | | | | ● | | | | | | | | | | | | | | | | | | | | | | | | | | | | | | |
| MARTIN WILLEY ASS OF ST MNGMT (HM13183) | | | | | | | | | | | | | | | | | | | | ● | | | | | | | | | | | | | | | | | | | | | | | | | | | | | | |
| MILES, ANDREW (HM13854) | | | | | | | | | | | | | | | | | | | | | | | | | ● | | | | | | | | | | | | | | | | | | | | | | | | | |
| MOBILE FOOTWORKS (HM14031) | | | | | | | | | | | | | | | | ● | | | | | | | | | | | | | | | | | | ● | | | | | | | | | | | | | | | | |
| MORGAN-AYRES, PAUL (PROF) (HM14178) | | | | | | | | | | ● | | ● | ● | | | ● | | | | ● | ● | | | | | | | ● | | | | | | | | ● | | | | | | | | | | | | | | |
| MULLINS, JOHN (HM14348) | | | | | | | | | | | ● | | | | | | | | | | ● | | | | | | | | | | | | | | | | | | | | | | | | | | | | | |
| NATURAL HEALTHCARE (HM14601) | | | | | | | | | | | | | | | | | | | | | | ● | | | | | | | | | | | | ● | | ● | | | | | | | | | | | | | | |
| NATURAL HEALTHCARE (HM14602) | | | | | | | | | | | | | | | ● | | | | | | | | | | | | | | | | | | | | | | | | | | | | | | | | | | | |
| PAMO, NORDZIN (HM15625) | | | | | | | | | | | | | | | | | ● | | | | | | | | | | | | | | | | | | | | | | | | | | | | | | | | | |
| PENARTH CHIROPRACTIC CLINIC (HM15961) | | | | | | | | | | | | | | | | | | | | | | | | | | | | | | | | ● | | ● | | | | | | | | | | | | | | | | |
| PENARTH HOMEOPATHY CLINIC (HM15962) | | | | | | | | | | | | | | | | | ● | | | | | | | | | | | | | | | | | | | | | | | | | | | | | | | | | |
| PENDER, CHRISTINE (HM15963) | | | | | | | | | | | | | | | ● | | | | | | | | | | | | | | | | | | | | | | | | | | | | | | | | | | | |
| PENYLAN PODIATRIC CENTRE (HM16005) | | | | | | | | | | | | | | | | | | | | | | | | | | | | | | | | | | | | | | | | | | | ● | | | | | | | |
| POLLEY, LYNDON (HM16414) | | | | | | | | | | | | | | | | | | | | | | | | | | | | | | | | | | | | | | | | | | | ● | | | | | | | |
| POLLEY, LYNDON (HM16415) | | | | | | | | | | | | | | | | | | | | | | | | | | | | | | | | | | | | | | | | | | | ● | | | | | | | |

# F - O Therapies at Practices/Businesses

| Business by County with Reference no. | Family Planning (Natural) | Family Therapy | Feldenkrais Methodology | Feng Shui | Floral Essence Therapy | Flotation Therapy | Gait Analysis | Gem Essence Therapy | Gestalt Therapy | Group Therapy | Hay Diet | Healer | Healing Therapy | Hellerwork | Herbal Medicine | Holistic Healing | Homeopathy | Hopi Ear Candles | Humanistic Psychology | Hypnosis | Hypnotherapy | Indian Head Massage | Inhalation Therapy | Iridology | Kinesiology |
|---|---|---|---|---|---|---|---|---|---|---|---|---|---|---|---|---|---|---|---|---|---|---|---|---|---|
| POLLEY, LYNDON (HM16413) | | | | | | | | | | | | | | | | | | | | | | | | | |
| RAJA YOGA MEDITATION (HM16897) | | | | | | | | | | | | | | | | | | | | | | | | | |
| RENWICK, SARAH NADINE (HM17192) | ● | ● | ● | | ● | | | ● | ● | | ● | ● | ● | | ● | ● | | | | | | ● | | | |
| RIDGE, D (HM17316) | | | | | | | | | | | | | | | | | | | | | | | | | |
| RIDGE, D (HM17315) | | | | | | | | | | | | | | | | | | | | | | | | | |
| STIR SPICES (HM19297) | | | | | | | | | | | | | | | ● | | | | | | | | | | |
| SWANSEA VALLEY PHYSIO PRACTICE (HM19579) | | | | | | | | | | | | | | | | | | | | | | | | | |
| TRANSCENDENTAL MEDITATION (HM20284) | | | | | | | | | | | | | | | | | | | | | | | | | |
| WHATLEY, JUDITH (HM21303) | | | | | | | | | | | | | | | | | | | | | | | | | |
| WILLIAMS, TOM (HM21601) | | | | | | | | | | | | | | | ● | | | | | | | | | | |
| GWYNEDD | | | | | | | | | | | | | | | | | | | | | | | | | |
| MOSSHILL HOLISTIC CENTRE (HM14270) | | | | | | | | | | | | | | | | | | | | | | | | | |
| NATURAL THERAPY CLINIC (HM14660) | | | | | | | | | | | | | | | | | | | | | ● | ● | | | ● |
| O'NEIL, L (HM15325) | | | | | | | | | | | | | | | | | | | | | ● | | | | |
| ISLE OF ANGLESEY | | | | | | | | | | | | | | | | | | | | | | | | | |
| BERNARD-SMITH, H (DR) (HM02197) | | | | | | | | | | | | | | | | | | | | ● | | | | | |
| CHALMERS, D G (HM03951) | | | | | | | | | | | | | | | | | | | | | | | | | ● |
| MONMOUTHSHIRE | | | | | | | | | | | | | | | | | | | | | | | | | |
| ABERGAVENNY THERAPY CTRE (HM00121) | | | | | | | | | | | | | | | | | | | | | ● | | | | |
| AGINCOURT OSTEOPATHIC CLINIC (HM00419) | | | | | | | | | | | | | | | | | | | | | | | | | |
| BROOKSIDE PHYSIO PRACTICE (HM03184) | | | | | | | | | | | | | | | | | | | | | | | | | |
| MCTIMONEY DIRECTORY (HM13618) | | | | | | | | | | | | | | | | | | | | | | | | | |
| MSM INFORMATION (HM14310) | | | | | | | | | | | | | | | | | | | | | | | | | |
| NUTRITION CLINIC (HM15122) | | | | | | | | | | | | | | | | | | | | | | | | | |
| NEATH PORT TALBOT | | | | | | | | | | | | | | | | | | | | | | | | | |
| ST JAMES MEDICAL CENTRE (HM19078) | | | | | | | | | | | | | | | | | | | | | ● | | | | |
| NEWPORT | | | | | | | | | | | | | | | | | | | | | | | | | |
| BAJJADA, JUNE (HM01572) | | | | | | | | | | | | | | | | | | | | | | | | | |
| BARRY, D J (HM01811) | | | | | | | | | | | | | | | | | | | | ● | | | | | |
| BEIGHTON, J W (HM02069) | | | | | | | | | | | | | | | | | ● | | | | | | | | |
| BOWKETT, LYN (HM02792) | | | | | | | | | | | | | | | | | | | | | | | | | ● |
| CLINIC OF HOLISTIC HEALTH (HM04693) | | | | | | | | | | | | | | | ● | ● | ● | | | | ● | | | | |
| HEMMERMAN, I A (HM09534) | | | | | | | | | | | | | | | | | ● | | | | | | | | |
| HYPNOTHERAPY & RELAXATION CLNC (HM10510) | | | | | | | | | | | | | | | | | | | | ● | | | | | |

| Business by County with Reference no. | Kirlian Photography | Laser Treatment | Life Style Coaching | Light Therapy | Macrobiotics | Magnetic Therapy | Manipulation | Manual Lymph Drainage | Massage (Therapeutic) | McTimoney Chiropractic | Meditation | Metamorphic Therapy | Miasm Therapy | Micro Manipulation | Moxibustion | Mud Therapy | Music Therapy | Nail Surgery | Naturopathy | Neuro-Linguistic Program | Neurotherapy | Nutritional Therapy | Orgone Therapy | Oriental Diagnosis | Orthomolecular Medicine |
|---|---|---|---|---|---|---|---|---|---|---|---|---|---|---|---|---|---|---|---|---|---|---|---|---|---|
| POLLEY, LYNDON (HM16413) | | | | | | | | | | | | | | | | | | ● | | | | | | | |
| RAJA YOGA MEDITATION (HM16897) | | | | | | | | | | | ● | | | | | | | | | | | | | | |
| RENWICK, SARAH NADINE (HM17192) | | | ● | | ● | | ● | | ● | | ● | | | | ● | ● | ● | | | | | ● | | ● | |
| RIDGE, D (HM17316) | | | | | | | ● | | ● | | | | | | | | | | | | | | | | |
| RIDGE, D (HM17315) | | | | | | | ● | | ● | | | | | | | | | | | | | | | | |
| STIR SPICES (HM19297) | | | | | | | | | | | | | | | | | | | | | | | | | |
| SWANSEA VALLEY PHYSIO PRACTICE (HM19579) | | | | | | | ● | | ● | | | | | | | | | | | | | | | | |
| TRANSCENDENTAL MEDITATION (HM20284) | | | | | | | | | | | ● | | | | | | | | | | | | | | |
| WHATLEY, JUDITH (HM21303) | | | | | | | | | | | | | | | | | | | | | | ● | | | |
| WILLIAMS, TOM (HM21601) | | | | | | | | | | | | | | | | | | | | | | | | | |
| GWYNEDD | | | | | | | | | | | | | | | | | | | | | | | | | |
| MOSSHILL HOLISTIC CENTRE (HM14270) | | | | | | | | | | | ● | | | | | | | | | | | | | | |
| NATURAL THERAPY CLINIC (HM14660) | | | | | | | | | | | | | | | | | | | | | | | | | |
| O'NEIL, L (HM15325) | | | | | | | | | | | | | | | | | | | | | | | | | |
| ISLE OF ANGLESEY | | | | | | | | | | | | | | | | | | | | | | | | | |
| BERNARD-SMITH, H (DR) (HM02197) | | | | | | | | | | | | | | | | | | | | | | | | | |
| CHALMERS, D G (HM03951) | | | | | | | ● | | ● | | | | | | | | | | | | | | | | |
| MONMOUTHSHIRE | | | | | | | | | | | | | | | | | | | | | | | | | |
| ABERGAVENNY THERAPY CTRE (HM00121) | | | | | | | | | | | | | | | | | | | | | | | | | |
| AGINCOURT OSTEOPATHIC CLINIC (HM00419) | | | | | | | | | | | | | | | | | | | ● | | | | | | |
| BROOKSIDE PHYSIO PRACTICE (HM03184) | | | | | | | ● | | ● | | | | | | ● | | | | | | | | | | |
| MCTIMONEY DIRECTORY (HM13618) | | | | | | | | | | ● | | | | | | | | | | | | | | | |
| MSM INFORMATION (HM14310) | | | | | | | | | | | | | | | | | | | | | | ● | | | |
| NUTRITION CLINIC (HM15122) | | | | | | | | | | | | | | | | | | | | | | ● | | | |
| NEATH PORT TALBOT | | | | | | | | | | | | | | | | | | | | | | | | | |
| ST JAMES MEDICAL CENTRE (HM19078) | | | | | | | | | | | | | | | | | | | | | | | | | |
| NEWPORT | | | | | | | | | | | | | | | | | | | | | | | | | |
| BAJJADA, JUNE (HM01572) | | | | | | | | | | | ● | | | | ● | | | | | | | | | | |
| BARRY, D J (HM01811) | | | | | | | | | | | | | | | | | | | | | | | | | |
| BEIGHTON, J W (HM02069) | | | | | | | | | | | | | | | | | | | | | | | | | |
| BOWKETT, LYN (HM02792) | | | | | | | | | ● | | | | | | | | | | | | | | | | |
| CLINIC OF HOLISTIC HEALTH (HM04693) | | | | | | | | | ● | | | | | | | | | | | | | | | | |
| HEMMERMAN, I A (HM09534) | | | | | | | | | | | | | | | | | | | | | | | | | |
| HYPNOTHERAPY & RELAXATION CLNC (HM10510) | | | | | | | | | | | | | | | | | | | | | | | | | |

# F - O Therapies at Practices/Businesses

| Business by County with Reference no. | Family Planning (Natural) | Family Therapy | Feldenkrais Methodology | Feng Shui | Floral Essence Therapy | Flotation Therapy | Gait Analysis | Gem Essence Therapy | Gestalt Therapy | Group Therapy | Hay Diet | Healer | Healing Therapy | Hellerwork | Herbal Medicine | Holistic Healing | Homeopathy | Hopi Ear Candles | Humanistic Psychology | Hypnosis | Hypnotherapy | Indian Head Massage | Inhalation Therapy | Iridology | Kinesiology |
|---|---|---|---|---|---|---|---|---|---|---|---|---|---|---|---|---|---|---|---|---|---|---|---|---|---|
| MEMBERS OF NAT INS OF MED HERB (HM13720) | | | | | | | | | | | | | | | ● | | | | | | | | | | |
| NLP THERAPY (HM14962) | | | | | | | | | | | | | | | | | | | | ● | | | | | |
| PLOWMAN, JOHN (DR) (HM16377) | | | | | | | | | | | | | | | | | | | | ● | | | | | |
| **PEMBROKESHIRE** | | | | | | | | | | | | | | | | | | | | | | | | | |
| CENTRE OF TRADITIONAL HEALING (HM03926) | | | | | | | | | | | | | | | | | ● | | | | | | | | |
| JABROO, C (HM10809) | | | | | | | | | | | | | | | ● | | | | | | | | | | |
| **POWYS** | | | | | | | | | | | | | | | | | | | | | | | | | |
| BRECON CLINIC (HM02944) | | | | | | | | | | | | ● | | | ● | | | | | | | | | | |
| BRECON COMPLEMENTARY MED CTRE (HM02945) | | | | | | | | | | | | | | | | | | | | | ● | | | | |
| CONROY, CHRISTINE (HM05007) | | | | | | | | | | | | ● | | | | | | | | | | | | | |
| COVENT HOUSE NTRL HEALTH CTRE (HM05280) | | | | | | | | | | | | | | | | | ● | | | | | | | | |
| FOREST LODGE PSYCHOTHERAPY (HM07548) | | | | | | | | | | | | | | | | | | | | ● | | | | | |
| HEALTH FOCUS (HM09386) | | | | | | | | | | | | | | | | | ● | | | | | ● | | | |
| HERBAL HELPLINE (HM09619) | | | | | | | | | | | | | | | ● | | | | | | | | | | |
| KILGOUR, KATHARINE () | | | | | | | | | | | | | | | | | | | | | | | | | |
| LLANDRINDOD WELLS SPA TOWN (HM12499) | | | | | | | | | | | | | | | | | ● | | | | ● | | | | ● |
| PEACE CLINIC (HM15876) | | | | | | | | | | | | | | | | | | | ● | ● | ● | | | | |
| SHEPPARD, HELEN (HM18421) | | | | | ● | | | ● | | | | | | | | | | | | | | | | | |
| **RHONDDA CYNON TAFF** | | | | | | | | | | | | | | | | | | | | | | | | | |
| MORRIS, A P (HM14200) | | | | | | | | | | | | | | | ● | | | | | | | | | | |
| POLLEY, LYNDON (HM16416) | | | | | | | | | | | | | | | | | | | | | | | | | |
| **SWANSEA** | | | | | | | | | | | | | | | | | | | | | | | | | |
| ABERTAWE PHYSIOTHERAPY CLINIC (HM00124) | | | | | | | | | | | | | | | | | | | | | | | | | |
| BRACEWELL, P J (HM02833) | | | | | | | | | | | | | | | | | ● | | | | | | | | |
| BURDEN, RICHARD (HM03370) | | | | | | | | | | | | | | | | | | | | | | | | | |
| CONTINENTAL SKIN CLINIC (HM05020) | | | | | | | | | | | | | | | | ● | | | | | | | | | |
| HERBAL CLINIC (HM09604) | | | | | | | | | | | | | | | ● | | | | | | | | | | |
| I R C H (HM10554) | | | | | | | | | | | | | | | ● | | ● | | | | | | | | |
| JOHNSON, JUDITH (HM11081) | | | | | | | | | | | | | | | | | ● | | | | | | | | |
| PEDORTHICS FOOT SGY PRACTICE (HM15935) | | | | | | | ● | | | | | | | | | | | | | | | | | | |
| RATCLIFFE, PAULINE (HM16952) | | | | | | | | | | | | | | | | | ● | | | | | | | | |
| REES, L E (HM17049) | | | | | | | | | | | | | | | | | | | | ● | | | | | |
| WATKINS, PHILIPPA (HM20997) | | | | | | | | | | | | | | | | | ● | | | | | | | | |

| Business by County with Reference no. | Kirlian Photography | Laser Treatment | Life Style Coaching | Light Therapy | Macrobiotics | Magnetic Therapy | Manipulation | Manual Lymph Drainage | Massage (Therapeutic) | McTimoney Chiropractic | Meditation | Metamorphic Therapy | Miasm Therapy | Micro Manipulation | Moxibustion | Mud Therapy | Music Therapy | Nail Surgery | Naturopathy | Neuro-Linguistic Program | Neurotherapy | Nutritional Therapy | Orgone Therapy | Oriental Diagnosis | Orthomolecular Medicine |
|---|---|---|---|---|---|---|---|---|---|---|---|---|---|---|---|---|---|---|---|---|---|---|---|---|---|
| MEMBERS OF NAT INS OF MED HERB (HM13720) | | | | | | | | | | | | | | | | | | | | | | | | | |
| NLP THERAPY (HM14962) | | | | | | | | | | | | | | | | | | | | | | | | | |
| PLOWMAN, JOHN (DR) (HM16377) | | | | | | | | | | | | | | | | | | | | | | | | | |
| **PEMBROKESHIRE** | | | | | | | | | | | | | | | | | | | | | | | | | |
| CENTRE OF TRADITIONAL HEALING (HM03926) | | | | | | | | | | ● | | | | | | | | | | | | | | | |
| JABROO, C (HM10809) | | | | | | | | | | | | | | | | | | | | | | | | | |
| **POWYS** | | | | | | | | | | | | | | | | | | | | | | | | | |
| BRECON CLINIC (HM02944) | | | | | | | | | ● | | | | | | ● | | | | | | | | | ● | |
| BRECON COMPLEMENTARY MED CTRE (HM02945) | | | | | | | | | ● | | | | | | | | | | | | | | | | |
| CONROY, CHRISTINE (HM05007) | | | | | | | | | | | | | | | | | | | | | | | | | |
| COVENT HOUSE NTRL HEALTH CTRE (HM05280) | | | | | | | | | ● | | | | | | | | | | | | | | | | |
| FOREST LODGE PSYCHOTHERAPY (HM07548) | | | | | | | | | | | | | | | | | | | | | | | | | |
| HEALTH FOCUS (HM09386) | | | | | | | | | ● | | | | | | | | | | | | | | | | |
| HERBAL HELPLINE (HM09619) | | | | | | | | | | | | | | | | | | | | | | | | | |
| KILGOUR, KATHARINE () | | | | | | | ● | | | | | | | | | | | | | | | | | | |
| LLANDRINDOD WELLS SPA TOWN (HM12499) | | | | | | | | | | | | | | | | | | | | | | | | | |
| PEACE CLINIC (HM15876) | | | | | | | | | | | | | | | | | | | | | | | | | |
| SHEPPARD, HELEN (HM18421) | | | | | | | | | | | | | | | | | ● | | | | | | | | |
| **RHONDDA CYNON TAFF** | | | | | | | | | | | | | | | | | | | | | | | | | |
| MORRIS, A P (HM14200) | | | | | | | | | | | | | | | | | | | | | | | | | |
| POLLEY, LYNDON (HM16416) | | | | | | | | | | | | | | | | | | ● | | | | | | | |
| **SWANSEA** | | | | | | | | | | | | | | | | | | | | | | | | | |
| ABERTAWE PHYSIOTHERAPY CLINIC (HM00124) | | | | | | | ● | | ● | | ● | | | | | | | | | | | | | | |
| BRACEWELL, P J (HM02833) | | | | | | | | | | | | | | | | | | | | | | | | | |
| BURDEN, RICHARD (HM03370) | | | | | | | | | | | | | | | | | | | ● | | | | | | |
| CONTINENTAL SKIN CLINIC (HM05020) | | | | | | | | | | | | | | | | | | | | | | | | | |
| HERBAL CLINIC (HM09604) | | | | | | | | | | | | | | | | | | | | | | | | | |
| I R C H (HM10554) | | | | | | | | | | | | | | | | | | | | | | | | | |
| JOHNSON, JUDITH (HM11081) | | | | | | | | | | | | | | | | | | | | | | | | | |
| PEDORTHICS FOOT SGY PRACTICE (HM15935) | | | | | | | | | | | | | | | | | | | | | | | | | |
| RATCLIFFE, PAULINE (HM16952) | | | | | | | | | | | | | | | | | | | | | | | | | |
| REES, L E (HM17049) | | | | | | | | | | | | | | | | | | | | | | | | | |
| WATKINS, PHILIPPA (HM20997) | | | | | | | | | | | | | | | | | | | | | | | | | |

# F - O Therapies at Practices/Businesses

Business by County with Reference no.

| Therapy | TORFAEN: PHILLIPS, SANDRA (HM16142) | WREXHAM: FREEDOM WITHIN (HM07715) | WREXHAM: HARMONY IN HEALTH (HM09028) | WREXHAM: HERBARIUM (HM09649) |
|---|---|---|---|---|
| Orthomolecular Medicine | | | | |
| Oriental Diagnosis | | | | |
| Orgone Therapy | | | | |
| Nutritional Therapy | | | ● | |
| Neurotherapy | | | | |
| Neuro-Linguistic Program | | | | |
| Naturopathy | | | ● | |
| Nail Surgery | | | | |
| Music Therapy | | | | |
| Mud Therapy | | | | |
| Moxibustion | | | | |
| Micro Manipulation | | | | |
| Miasm Therapy | | | | |
| Metamorphic Therapy | | | | |
| Meditation | | | | |
| McTimoney Chiropractic | | | | |
| Massage (Therapeutic) | | ● | | |
| Manual Lymph Drainage | | | | |
| Manipulation | | | | |
| Magnetic Therapy | | | | |
| Macrobiotics | | | | |
| Light Therapy | | | | |
| Life Style Coaching | | | | |
| Laser Treatment | | | | |
| Kirlian Photography | | | | |
| Kinesiology | | | | |
| Iridology | | | ● | |
| Inhalation Therapy | | | | |
| Indian Head Massage | | | | |
| Hypnotherapy | | | | |
| Hypnosis | ● | | | |
| Humanistic Psychology | | | | |
| Hopi Ear Candles | | | | |
| Homeopathy | | | | |
| Holistic Healing | | | ● | |
| Herbal Medicine | | | | ● |
| Hellerwork | | | | |
| Healing Therapy | | | | |
| Healer | | | ● | |
| Hay Diet | | | | |
| Group Therapy | | | | |
| Gestalt Therapy | | | | |
| Gem Essence Therapy | | | | |
| Gait Analysis | | | | |
| Flotation Therapy | | | | |
| Floral Essence Therapy | | | | |
| Feng Shui | | | | |
| Feldenkrais Methodology | | | | |
| Family Therapy | | | | |
| Family Planning (Natural) | | | | |

HEALTH MYSELF

# SECTION 3c

## O-Z of Therapies at Practices

# O - Z Therapies at Practices/Businesses

Business by County with Reference no.

| Business | Orthotics | Osteomyology | Osteopathy | PAM | Paranormal Therapies | Pattern Therapies | Physiotherapy | Phytotherapy | Pilates | Podiatry | Polarity Therapy | Postural Integration | Primal Therapy | Psionic Therapy | Psychotherapy | Pyramid Power | Pyscho-Synthesis | Reflexology | Reichian Therapy | Reiki | Remedial Massage | Rogerian Therapy | Rolfing | Seichem | Sensitivity Training | Shiatsu | Silva Method | Sound Therapy | Spiritual Healing | Sports Massage | Stress Therapy | Swedish Body Massage | T'ai-Chi Ch'uan | Tantra Therapy | Tera-Mai | Thought Field Therapy | Touch Therapy | Transactional Analysis | Tui-na | Ultrasonics | Vibrational Therapy | Visualisation Therapy | Vitamin Therapy | Voice Therapy | X-Ray | Ying & Yang | Yoga | Zen Therapy | Zero Balancing |
|---|---|---|---|---|---|---|---|---|---|---|---|---|---|---|---|---|---|---|---|---|---|---|---|---|---|---|---|---|---|---|---|---|---|---|---|---|---|---|---|---|---|---|---|---|---|---|---|---|---|
| **ENGLAND** | | | | | | | | | | | | | | | | | | | | | | | | | | | | | | | | | | | | | | | | | | | | | | | | | |
| **BEDFORDSHIRE** | | | | | | | | | | | | | | | | | | | | | | | | | | | | | | | | | | | | | | | | | | | | | | | | | |
| ALOE VERA SPECIALISTS (HM00681) | | | | | | | | | | | | | | | | | | | | | | | | | | | | | | | | | | | | | | | | | | | ● | | | | | | |
| ALTERNATIVE THERAPY AT WORK (HM00732) | | | | | | | | | | | | | | | | | | ● | | | | | ● | | | ● | | | | | ● | | | | | | ● | | | | | | | | | | | | |
| AMBACARE (HM00764) | | | ● | | | | | | | | | | | | | | | | | | | | | | | | | | | | | | | | | | | | | | | | | | | | | | |
| AMPTHILL & FLITWICK CLINIC (HM00795) | | | | | | | ● | | | | | | | | | | | | | | | | | | | | | | | | | | | | | | | | | | | | | | | | | | |
| BEDFORD PHYSIOTHERAPY CENTRE (HM02035) | | | | | | | ● | | | | | | | | | | | | | | | | | | | | | | | | | | | | | | | | | | | | | | | | | | |
| BEDFORD PSYCHOTHERAPY PRACTICE (HM02037) | | | | | | | | | | | | | | | ● | | | | | | | | | | | | | | | | | | | | | | | | | | | | | | | | | | |
| BELLAMY, R D (HM02097) | | | ● | | | | | | | | | | | | | | | | | | | | | | | | | | | | | | | | | | | | | | | | | | | | | | |
| BISHOP, PATRICIA (HM02407) | | | ● | | | | | | | | | | | | | | | | | | | | | | | | | | | | | | | | | | | | | | | | | | | | | | |
| BOA (HM02542) | | | ● | | | | | | | | | | | | | | | | | | | | | | | | | | | | | | | | | | | | | | | | | | | | | | |
| BURTON, MERILYNN (HM03444) | | | | | | | | | | ● | | | | | | | | | | | | | | | | | | | | | | | | | | | | | | | | | | | | | | | |
| CHARTERED PHYSIOTHERAPIST (HM04042) | | | ● | | | | ● | | | | | ● | | | | | | | | | | | | | | | | | | | ● | | | | | | | | | ● | | | | | | | | | |
| COULSTOCK, JUDY (HM05239) | | | | | | | | | | | | | | | | | | ● | | ● | | | | | | | | | | | | | | | | | | | | | | | | | | | | | |
| DUNTON CTRE-COUN/PSYCHOTHERAPY (HM06428) | | | | | | | | | | | | | ● | | ● | | | | | | | | | | | | | | | | ● | | | | | | | | | | | | | | | | | | |
| FOX, G A (HM07635) | | | | | | | | | | | | | | | ● | | | | | | | | | | | | | | | | | | | | | | | | | | | | | | | | | | |
| GOODCHILD, ROGER A (HM08251) | | | ● | | | | | | | | | | | | | | | | | | | | | | | | | | | | | | | | | | | | | | | | | | | | | | |
| GROVE NATURAL THERAPY CLINIC (HM08610) | | | ● | | | | | | | | | | | | ● | | | ● | | ● | | | | | | ● | | | | | | | | | | | | | | | | | | | | | ● | | |
| HEALEY, NORMAN (HM09323) | | | ● | | | | | | | | | | | | | | | | | | | | | | | | | | | | | | | | | | | | | | | | | | | | | | |
| HEMMENS, JANE (HM09533) | | | | | | | | | | | | | | | | | | ● | | | | | | | | | | | | | | | | | | | | | | | | | | | | | | | |
| HENDEN, CHRIS (HM09543) | | | | | | | | | | | | | | | ● | | | | | | | | | | | | | | | | | | | | | | | | | | | | | | | | | | |
| HOLISTIC HYPNOTHERAPY (HM09983) | | | | | | | | | | | | | | | ● | | | | | ● | | | | | | | | | | | ● | | | | | | | | | | | ● | | | | | | | |
| HUTCHINSON, JANE (HM10451) | | | | | | | | | | | | | | | | | | ● | | | | | | | | | | | | | | | | | | | | | | | | | | | | | | | |
| HYNE, JOANNA E M (HM10483) | | | ● | | | | | | | | | | | | | | | | | | | | | | | | | | | | | | | | | | | | | | | | | | | | | | |
| INWARD BOUND THERAPIES (HM10707) | | | | | | | | | | | | | | | ● | | | | | | | | | | | | | | | | ● | | | | | | | | | | | | | | | | | | |
| JADE COLLEGE-NATURAL THERAPY (HM10867) | | | | | | | ● | | | | | | | | | | | ● | | | | | | | | | | | | ● | | | | | | | | | | | | | | | | | | | |
| JARMAN, JANET (HM10928) | | | | | | | | | | | | | | | | | | ● | | | | | | | | | | | | | | | | | | | | | | | | | | | | | | | |
| JENNIFER K HOUGH - PHYSIO (HM11004) | | | | | | | ● | | | | | | | | | | | | | | | | | | | | | | | | | | | | | | | | | | | | | | | | | | |
| JOHNSON, ANNE (HM11068) | | | ● | | | | | | | | | | | | | | | | | | | | | | | | | | | | | | | | | | | | | | | | | | | | | | |
| JOHNSTONS CHIROPODIST (HM11107) | | | | | | | | | | | | | | | | | | ● | | ● | | | | | | | | | | | | | | | | | | | | | | | | | | | | | |
| KATZ, JANICE (HM11342) | | | | | | | | | | | | | | | ● | | | | | | | | | | | | | | | | | | | | | | | | | | | | | | | | | | |
| KIRK, DONNA (HM11707) | | | | | | | | | | | | | | | | | | ● | | | | | | | | | | | | | | | | | | | | | | | | | | | | | | | |
| LEDGER, DIANE (HM12128) | | | | | | | | | | | | | | | | | | ● | | | | | | | | | | | | | | | | | | | | | | | | | | | | | | | |

# O - Z Therapies at Practices/Businesses

| Business by County with Reference no. | Orthotics | Osteomyology | Osteopathy | PAM | Paranormal Therapies | Pattern Therapies | Physiotherapy | Phytotherapy | Pilates | Podiatry | Polarity Therapy | Postural Integration | Primal Therapy | Psionic Therapy | Psychotherapy | Pyramid Power | Pyscho-Synthesis | Reflexology | Reichian Therapy | Reiki | Remedial Massage | Rogerian Therapy | Rolfing | Seichem | Sensitivity Training | Shiatsu | Silva Method | Sound Therapy | Spiritual Healing | Sports Massage | Stress Therapy | Swedish Body Massage | T'ai-Chi Ch'uan | Tantra Therapy | Tera-Mai | Thought Field Therapy | Touch Therapy | Transactional Analysis | Tui-na | Ultrasonics | Vibrational Therapy | Visualisation Therapy | Vitamin Therapy | Voice Therapy | X-Ray | Ying & Yang | Yoga | Zen Therapy | Zero Balancing |
|---|---|---|---|---|---|---|---|---|---|---|---|---|---|---|---|---|---|---|---|---|---|---|---|---|---|---|---|---|---|---|---|---|---|---|---|---|---|---|---|---|---|---|---|---|---|---|---|---|---|
| MCALLISTER, C (DR) (HM13365) | | | | | | | | | | | | | | | ● | | | | | | | | | | | | | | | | | | | | | | | | | | | | | | | | | | |
| MULTIPLE SCLEROSIS THRPY CTRE (HM14351) | | | | | | | | | | | | | | | | | | ● | | | | | | | | ● | | | | | | | | | | | | | | | | | | | | | | | |
| NORTH BEDS OSTEOPATHIC CLINIC (HM15021) | | | ● | | | | | | | | | | | | | | | | | | | | | | | | | | | | | | | | | | | | | | | | | | | | | | |
| O'SHEA, LESLEY (HM15433) | | | | | | | | | | | | | | | | | | ● | | | | | | | | | | | | | | | | | | | | | | | | | | | | | | | |
| PEARCE, G (HM15895) | | | | | | | | | | | | | | | ● | | | | | | | | | | | | | | | | | | | | | | | | | | | | | | | | | | |
| PERRET, NICOLE (HM16032) | | | ● | | | | | | | | | | | | | | | | | | | | | | | | | | | | | | | | | | | | | | | | | | | | | | |
| POYNTER, K J (HM16518) | | | ● | | | | | | | | | | | | | | | | | | | | | | | | | | | | | | | | | | | | | | | | | | | | | | |
| PYLE, RAYMOND (HM16786) | | | ● | | | | | | | | | | | | | | | | | | | | | | | | | | | | | | | | | | | | | | | | | | | | | | |
| SHEER PERFECTION (HM18367) | | | | | | | | | | | | | | | | | | ● | | | | | | | | | | | | | | | | | | | | | | | | | | | | | | | |
| SPECTRUM HEALTH TRUST (HM18976) | | | | | | | | ● | | | | | | | | | | ● | | ● | | | | | | ● | | | ● | | ● | | ● | | | | ● | | | | ● | ● | | | | | ● | | |
| SWEET BREEZE (HM19584) | | | | | | | | | | | | | | | | | | ● | | | | | | | | | | | | | | | | | | | | | | | | | | | | | | | |
| THERAPY CENTRE (HM19894) | | | | | | | ● | | | | | | | | | | | | | | | | | | | | | | | | | | | | | | | | | | | | | | | | | | |
| THOMPSON, MARTIN (HM19992) | ● | | | | | | | | | | | | | | | | | | | | | | | | | | | | | | | | | | | | | | | | | | | | | | | | |
| WOODSIDE CLINIC (HM21857) | | | ● | | | | | ● | ● | | | | | | | | | ● | | | | | | | | | | | | | | | | | | | | | | | | | | | | | | | |
| **BERKSHIRE** | | | | | | | | | | | | | | | | | | | | | | | | | | | | | | | | | | | | | | | | | | | | | | | | | |
| ALVAREZ, ANDREA (HM00754) | | | | | | | | | | | | | | | | | | ● | | | | | | | | | | | | | | | | | | | | | | | | | | | | | | | |
| APPLETREE COUNSELLING (HM00945) | | | | | | | | | | | | | | | ● | | | | | | | | | | | | | | | | | | | | | | | | | | | | | | | | | | |
| ARCHER, JULIE (HM00978) | | | ● | | | | | | | | | | | | | | | | | | | | | | | | | | | | | | | | | | | | | | | | | | | | | | |
| ASCOT PHYSIOFIRST CENTRE (HM01178) | | | | | | | ● | | | | | | | | | | | | | | | | | | | | | | | | | | | | | | | | | | | | | | | | | | |
| ATKINSON, N T (HM01324) | | | ● | | | | | | | | | | | | | | | | | | | | | | | | | | | | | | | | | | | | | | | | | | | | | | |
| BAREFIELD, SHIRLEY (HM01699) | | | | | | | | | | | | | | | | | | ● | | | | | | | | | | | | | | | | | | | | | | | | | | | | | | | |
| BERKSHIRE CHIROPRACTIC (HM02195) | | | | | | | | | | | | | | | | | | | | | | | | | | | | | | | | | | | | | | | | ● | | | | | | | | | |
| BRACKNELL CHIROPRACTIC CLINIC (HM02838) | | | | | | | | ● | | | | | | | | | | | | | | | | | | | | | | | | | | | | | | | | | | | | | | | | | |
| BRADBURY, VALMA (HM02844) | | | | | | | | | | | | | | | | | | ● | | | | | | | | | | | | | | | | | | | | | | | | | | | | | | | |
| BURNETT, KIM (HM03401) | | | ● | | | | | | | | | | | | | | | | | | | | | | | | | | | | | | | | | | | | | | | | | | | | | | |
| CAMPBELL, ELSPETH (HM03597) | | | | | | | | | | | | | | | ● | | | | | | | | | | | | | | ● | | ● | | | | | | | | | | | ● | | | | ● | | | |
| CANNING, LORRAINE (HM03633) | | | | | | | | | | | | | | | | | | ● | | | | | | | | | | | | | | | | | | | | | | | | | | | | | | | |
| CAVERSHAM FOOT CLINIC (HM03866) | | | | | | | | | | | | | | | ● | | | ● | | ● | | | | ● | | | | | | | ● | | | | ● | | | | | | | ● | | | | | | | |
| CHANDLER, PETER E (HM03978) | | | ● | | | | | | | | | | | | | | | | | | | | | | | | | | | | | | | | | | | | | | | | | | | | | | |
| CHEFLAND, GERTI (HM04084) | | | | | | | | | | | | | | | | | | ● | | | | | | | | | | | | | | | | | | | | | | | | | | | | | | | |
| CLASSICAL OSTEOPATH (HM04608) | | | ● | | | | | | | | | | | | | | | | | | | | | | | | | | | | | | | | | | | | | | | | | | | | | | |
| CLASSICAL OSTEOPATH (HM04609) | | | ● | | | | | | | | | | | | | | | | | | | | | | | | | | | | | | | | | | | | | | | | | | | | | | |
| COLLINGS, S (HM04864) | | | ● | | | | | | | | | | | | | | | | | | | | | | | | | | | | | | | | | | | | | | | | | | | | | | |
| COOKHAM CHIROPRACTIC CLINIC (HM05068) | | | | | | | ● | | | | | | | | | | | | | | ● | | | | | | | | ● | | ● | | | | | | | | | | | ● | | | | | ● | | |

# O - Z Therapies at Practices/Businesses

| Business by County with Reference no. | Orthotics | Osteomyology | Osteopathy | PAM | Paranormal Therapies | Pattern Therapies | Physiotherapy | Phytotherapy | Pilates | Podiatry | Polarity Therapy | Postural Integration | Primal Therapy | Psionic Therapy | Psychotherapy | Pyramid Power | Pyscho-Synthesis | Reflexology | Reichian Therapy | Reiki | Remedial Massage | Rogerian Therapy | Rolfing | Seichem | Sensitivity Training | Shiatsu | Silva Method | Sound Therapy | Spiritual Healing | Sports Massage | Stress Therapy | Swedish Body Massage | T'ai-Chi Ch'uan | Tantra Therapy | Tera-Mai | Thought Field Therapy | Touch Therapy | Transactional Analysis | Tui-na | Ultrasonics | Vibrational Therapy | Visualisation Therapy | Vitamin Therapy | Voice Therapy | X-Ray | Ying & Yang | Yoga | Zen Therapy | Zero Balancing |
|---|---|---|---|---|---|---|---|---|---|---|---|---|---|---|---|---|---|---|---|---|---|---|---|---|---|---|---|---|---|---|---|---|---|---|---|---|---|---|---|---|---|---|---|---|---|---|---|---|---|
| COPPERTHWAITE, ERIC (HM05147) | | | | | | | | | | | | | | |● | | | | | | | | | | | | | | | | | | | | | | | | | | | | | | | | | | |
| CRESCENT OSTEOPATHIC CENTRE (HM05420) | | |● | | | | | | | | | | | | | | | | | | | | | | | | | | | | | | | | | | | | | | | | | | | | | | |
| DAY, R M (HM05895) | | |● | | | | | | | | | | | | | | | | | | | | | | | | | | | | | | | | | | | | | | | | | | | | | | |
| DAY, SYLVIA (HM05897) | | | | | | | | | | | | | | | | | |● | | | | | | | | | | | | | | | | | | | | | | | | | | | | | | | |
| DEAN RUSSELL & BRYDGES ROBERT (HM05936) | | | | | | | | |● | | | | | | | | |● | | | | | | | | | | | | | | | | | | | | | | | | | | | | | | | |
| DEJODE, SONIA (HM05962) | | | | | | | | | | | |● | | | | | | | | | | | | | | | | | | | | | | | | | | | | | | | | | | | | | |
| DR LIP ONG CRANIOSACRAL (HM06274) | | | | | | | | | | | | | | | | | | | | | | | | | |● | | | | | | | | | | | | | | | | | | | | | | | |
| EASBY, DAVID N (HM06504) | | | | | | | | | | | | | | |● | | | | | | | | | | | | | | | | | | | | | | | | | | | | | | | | | | |
| EDMONDS, ANN (HM06619) | | | | | | | | | | | | | | | | | |● | | | | | | | | | | | | | | | | | | | | | | | | | | | | | | | |
| EDNEY, C S (HM06625) | | | | | | | | | | | | | | | | | | | | | | | | | |● | | | | | | | | | | | | | | | | | | | | | | | |
| EDWARDS, JOHN (HM06659) | | | | | | | | | | | | | | |● | | | | | | | | | | | | | | | |● | | | | | | |● | | | |● | | | | | | | |
| EIGHAN, PENELOPE (HM06689) | | | | | | | | | | | | | | | | | |● | | | | | | | |● | | | | | | | | | | | | | | | | | | | | | | | |
| EIGHT WINDS ACUPUNCTURE (HM06690) | | | | | | | | | | | | | | | | | | | | | | | | | |● | | | | | | | | | | | | | | | | | | | | | | | |
| ENHANCED SUCCESS PERFORMANCE (HM06835) | | | | | | | | | | | | | | |● | | | | | | | | | | | | | | | | | | | | | | | | | | | | | | | | | | |
| FAIRBOURNE CLINIC (HM07051) | | |● | | | | | | |● | | | | |● | | |● | |● | | | | | | | | | | | | | | | | | | | | | | | | | | | | | |
| FEET TREAT (HM07186) | | | | | | | | | | | | | | | | | |● | | | | | | | | | | | | | | | | | | | | | | | | | | | | | | | |
| FERINGA, MARLIES (HM07233) | | | | | | | | | | | | | | | | | | | | | | | | | | | | | | |● | | | | | | | | | | | |● | | | | | | |
| FIELDING, ANNA (HM07271) | | | | | | | | | | | | | | | | | |● | | |● | | | | | | | | | | | | | | | | | | | | | | | | | | | | |
| FORREST, SAMANTHA (HM07565) | | | | | | | | | | | | | | | | | |● | |● | | | | | | | | | | | | | | | | | | | | | | | | | | | | | |
| GORING & STREATLEY OSTEOPATHIC (HM08288) | | |● | | | | | | | | | | | | | | | | | | | | | | | | | | | | | | | | | | | | | | | | | | | | | | |
| HAMM, D R (HM08860) | | |● | | | | | | | | | | | | | | | | | | | | | | | | | | | | | | | | | | | | | | | | | | | | | | |
| HAMM, D R (HM08859) | | |● | | | | | | | | | | | | | | | | | | | | | | | | | | | | | | | | | | | | | | | | | | | | | | |
| HASELTON, HOWARD (HM09180) | | | | | | | | | | | | | | | | | |● | | | | | | | | | | | | | | | | | | | | | | | | | | | | |● | | |
| HAZEL'S HOLISTIC HEALTH CARE (HM09294) | | | | | | | | | | | | | | | | | |● | | | | | | | |● | | | | | | | | | | | | | | | | | | | | | | | |
| HEWITT, ANDREW (HM09703) | | | | | | | | |● | | | | | | | | | | | | | | | | | | | | | | | | | | | | | | | | | | | | | | | | |
| HILLSIDE OSTEOPATHIC PRACTICE (HM09806) | | |● | | | | | | | | | | | | | | | | | | | | | | | | | | | | | | | | | |● | | | | | | | | | | | | |
| HOLDING, MARTIN (HM09937) | | |● | | | | | | | | | | | | | | | | | | | | | | | | | | | | | | | | | | | | | | | | | | | | | | |
| JACKSON, ANDREW (HM10825) | | |● | | | | | | | | | | | | | | | | | | | | | | | | | | | | | | | | | | | | | | | | | | | | | | |
| JUKES, CLARE (HM11252) | | | | | | | | | | | | | | | | | |● | | | | | | | | | | | | | | | | | | | | | | | | | | | | | | | |
| KANAKAM, JONATHAN (HM11303) | | |● | | | | | | | | | | | | | | | | | | | | | | | | | | | | | | | | | | | | | | | | | | | | | | |
| KENT, JANET (HM11524) | | | | | | | | | | | | | | |● | | | | | | | | | | | | | | | | | | | | | | | | | | | | | | | | | | |
| KINGFISHERS COMP HEALTH CARE (HM11650) | | | | | | | | | | | | | | | | | |● | |● | | | | | |● | | | | | | | | | | | | | | | | | | | | | | | |
| KIRKE, STEPHANIE (HM11713) | | | | | | | | | | | | | | |● | | | | | | | | | | | | | | | | | | | | | | | | | | | | | | | | | | |
| LANE, CORINNE (HM11931) | | | | | | | | | | | | | | |● | | | | | | | | | | | | | | | | | | | | | | | | | | | | | | | | | | |

# O - Z Therapies at Practices/Businesses

| Business by County with Reference no. | Orthotics | Osteomyology | Osteopathy | PAM | Paranormal Therapies | Pattern Therapies | Physiotherapy | Phytotherapy | Pilates | Podiatry | Polarity Therapy | Postural Integration | Primal Therapy | Psionic Therapy | Psychotherapy | Pyramid Power | Pyscho-Synthesis | Reflexology | Reichian Therapy | Reiki | Remedial Massage | Rogerian Therapy | Rolfing | Seichem | Sensitivity Training | Shiatsu | Silva Method | Sound Therapy | Spiritual Healing | Sports Massage | Stress Therapy | Swedish Body Massage | T'ai-Chi Ch'uan | Tantra Therapy | Tera-Mai | Thought Field Therapy | Touch Therapy | Transactional Analysis | Tui-na | Ultrasonics | Vibrational Therapy | Visualisation Therapy | Vitamin Therapy | Voice Therapy | X-Ray | Ying & Yang | Yoga | Zen Therapy | Zero Balancing |
|---|---|---|---|---|---|---|---|---|---|---|---|---|---|---|---|---|---|---|---|---|---|---|---|---|---|---|---|---|---|---|---|---|---|---|---|---|---|---|---|---|---|---|---|---|---|---|---|---|---|
| LANSMAN, ROBIN J (HM11965) | | | ● | | | | | | | | | | | | | | | | | | | | | | | | | | | | | | | | | | | | | | | | | | | | | | |
| LANSMAN, ROBIN J (HM11966) | | | ● | | | | | | | | | | | | | | | | | | | | | | | | | | | | | | | | | | | | | | | | | | | | | | |
| LAVENDER, S (HM12029) | | | | | | | | | | | | | | | | | | | | ● | | | | | | | | | ● | | | | | | | | | | | | | | | | | | | | |
| LIFE GUIDANCE (HM12344) | | | | | | | | | | | | | | | ● | | | | | ● | | | | | | | | | | | ● | | | | | | | | | | | ● | | | | | | | |
| MAIDENHEAD PHYSIO & SPORTS (HM12934) | | | | | | | ● | | | | | | | | | | | | | | | | | | | | | | | | | | | | | | | | | | | | | | | | | | |
| MANN, H S (HM13019) | | | ● | | | | | | | | | | | | | | | | | | | | | | | | | | | | | | | | | | | | | | | | | | | | | | |
| MCGREGOR, S (HM13501) | | | ● | | | | | | | | | | | | | | | | | | | | | | | | | | | | | | | | | | | | | | | | | | | | | | |
| MCGREGOR, TONY (HM13504) | | | | | | | | | | | | | | | ● | | | | | | | | | | | | | | | | ● | | | | | | | | | | | | | | | | | | |
| MENSANA PSYCHOLOGICAL THRP (HM13728) | | | | | | | | | | | | | | | ● | | | | | | | | | | | | | | | | | | | | | | | | | | | | | | | | | | |
| MOMENTA (HM14058) | | | | | | | | | | | | | | | ● | | | | | | | | | | | | | | | | ● | | | | | | | | | | | | | | | | | | |
| MONROE, T (HM14073) | | | ● | | | | | | | | | | | | | | | | | | | | | | | | | | | | | | | | | | | | | | | | | | | | | | |
| NATURAL HEALTH CONSULTANCY (HM14591) | | | ● | | | | | | ● | | | | | | ● | | | ● | | ● | | | | | | ● | | | | | ● | | | ● | | | | | | | | | | | | | ● | | |
| NATURAL THERAPY CLINIC (HM14656) | | | ● | | | | | | | | | | | | ● | | | ● | | | | | | ● | | | | | | | | | | | | | | | | | | | | | | | | | |
| NATURAL THERAPY CLINIC (HM14655) | | | | | | | | | | | ● | | | | | | | ● | | ● | | | | ● | | | | | | | ● | | | | | | ● | | | | | | ● | | | | | | |
| NEVILLE-TOWLE, V (HM14801) | | | ● | | | | | | | | | | | | | | | | | | | | | | | | | | | | | | | | | | | | | | | | | | | | | | |
| NEW OXFORD HOUSE CLINICS (HM14826) | | | ● | | | | | | | | | | | | | | | | | | | | | | | | | | | | | | | | | | | | | | | | | | | | | | |
| NEWBURY PHYSIOTHERAPY (HM14852) | | | | | | | ● | | | | | | | | | | | | | | | | | | | | | | | | | | | | | | | | | | | | | | | | | | |
| OSTEOPATHIC & SPORTS CLINIC (HM15452) | | | ● | | | | | | | | | | | | | | | | | | | | | | | | | | | | | | | | | | | | | | | | | | | | | | |
| PEGASUS CENTRE (HM15945) | | | | | | | | | | | | | | | ● | | | | | | | | | | | | | | | | | | | | | | | | | | | | | | | | | | |
| PENNEFATHER, R J (HM15986) | | | ● | | | | | | | | | | | | | | | | | | | | | | | | | | | | | | | | | | | | | | | | | | | | | | |
| PETERS, JEAN (HM16086) | | | | | | | | | | ● | | | | | | | | ● | | ● | | | | | | ● | | | | | | | | | | | | | | | | | | | | | | | |
| PIENAAR, DOROTHY (HM16278) | | | ● | | | | | | | | | | | | | | | | | | | | | | | | | | | | | | | | | | | | | | | | | | | | | | |
| PIM HEALTH CLINIC (HM16301) | | | ● | | | | | | | | | | | | | | | | | | | | | | | | | | | | ● | | | | | | | | | | | | | | | | | | |
| POLAK, CAROL (HM16400) | | | | | | | | | | | | | | | | | | ● | | | | | | | | | | | | | | | | | | | | | | | | | | | | | | | |
| PRACTICE (HM16520) | | | | | | | | | | | | | | | ● | | | | | | | | | | | | | | | | | | | | | | | | | | | | | | | | | | |
| QURESHI, JOHN (HM16823) | | | ● | | | | | | | | | | | | | | | | | | | | | | | | | | | | | | | | | | | | | | | | | | | | | | |
| RAWLINSON, MARGARET (HM16975) | | | | | | | | | | | | | | | | | | | | | | | | | | ● | | | | | | | | | | | | | | | | | | | | | ● | | |
| REED, TED (HM17045) | | | | | | | | | | | | | | | | | | | | | | | | | | | | | | | | | ● | | | | | | | | | | | | | | | | |
| RELF, M J (HM17171) | | | ● | | | | | | | | | | | | | | | | | | | | | | | | | | | | | | | | | | | | | | | | | | | | | | |
| ROWE, GEOFF (HM17685) | | | | | | | | | | | | | | | | | | ● | | | | | | | | | | | | | | | | | | | | | | | | | | | | | | | |
| ROWLAND, S (HM17695) | | | ● | | | | | | | | | | | | | | | | | | | | | | | | | | | | | | | | | | | | | | | | | | | | | | |
| SANDALL, S (HM17898) | | | | | | | | | | ● | | | | | | | | | | | | | | | | | | | | | | | | | | | | | | | | | | | | | | | |
| SHARPLES, ANITA (HM18318) | | | | | | | | | | | | | | | ● | | | | | | | | | | | | | | | | | | | | | | | | | | | | | | | | | | |
| SIMPSON, JUNE (HM18592) | | | | | | | | | | | | | | | | | | ● | | | | | | | | | | | | | | | | | | | | | | | | | | | | | | | |

# O - Z Therapies at Practices/Businesses

| Business by County with Reference no. | Orthotics | Osteomyology | Osteopathy | PAM | Paranormal Therapies | Pattern Therapies | Physiotherapy | Phytotherapy | Pilates | Podiatry | Polarity Therapy | Postural Integration | Primal Therapy | Psionic Therapy | Psychotherapy | Pyramid Power | Pyscho-Synthesis | Reflexology | Reichian Therapy | Reiki | Remedial Massage | Rogerian Therapy | Rolfing | Seichem | Sensitivity Training |
|---|---|---|---|---|---|---|---|---|---|---|---|---|---|---|---|---|---|---|---|---|---|---|---|---|---|
| SLOUGH SPORTS INJURIES CLINIC (HM18690) | | | | | | | ● | | | | | | | | | | | | | | | | | | |
| SMETHURST, ALISON (HM18704) | | | | | | | | | | | | | | | | | | ● | | | | | | | |
| SMITH, CANDIDA (HM18724) | | | ● | | | | | | | | | | | | | | | | | | | | | | |
| SMITH, JENNIE (HM18753) | | | | | | | | | | | | | | | | | | ● | | | | | | | |
| SOUTH LODGE CONSULTING (HM18909) | | | | | | | | | | | | ● | | | | | | | | | | | | | |
| SPENCER, GILLIAN (HM18994) | | | | | | | | | | | | | | | | | | ● | | | | | | | |
| SPRINGWOOD COMP HEALTH (HM19055) | | | | | | | | | | | | | | | | | | ● | | | | | | | |
| STUBBS, RICHARD (HM19437) | | | ● | | | | | | | | | | | | | | | | | | | | | | |
| SUNNINGDALE HEALING CENTRE (HM19509) | | | | | | | | | | | | | | | | | | | | | | | | | |
| T A IN THE THAMES VALLEY (HM19637) | | | | | | | | | | | | | | | ● | | | | | | | | | | |
| THAMS, JUNE (HM19866) | | | | | | | | | | | | | | | ● | | | | | | | | | | |
| TINGLE, SARAH (HM20082) | | | | | | | | | | | | | | | ● | | | | | | | | | | |
| TSENG, PATRICIA (HM20359) | | | | | | | | | | | | | | | | | | ● | | ● | | | | | |
| WALKER, PENELOPE (HM20795) | | | | | | | | | | | | | | | | | | ● | | | | | | | |
| WEST BERKSHIRE PSYCHOTHERAPY (HM21215) | | | | | | | | | | | | | | | ● | | | | | | | | | | |
| WILKIN, P (DR) (HM21498) | | | ● | | | | | | | | | | | | | | | | | | | | | | |
| WILLINGSON, TOM (HM21611) | | | | | | | | | | | | | | | ● | | | | | | | | | | |
| WOODLEY HEALING CENTRE (HM21836) | | | | | | | | ● | | | | | | | | | | ● | | | ● | | | | |
| **BRISTOL** | | | | | | | | | | | | | | | | | | | | | | | | | |
| ALLISON JOY REFLEXOLOGY (HM00649) | | | | | | | | | | | | | | | | | | ● | | | | | | | |
| ANDERSON, KEITH (HM00830) | | | | | ● | | | | | | | | | | | | | | | | | | | | |
| AQUARIUS HEALTH CENTRE (HM00959) | | | | | | | | | | | | | | | | | | ● | | | | | | | |
| AVON COUNSELLING/PSYCHOTHERAPY (HM01405) | | | | | | | | | | | | | | | ● | | | | | | | | | | |
| BEVAN, RUSS (HM02242) | | | | | | | | | | | | | | | | | | | | | | | | | |
| BOOTH, LYNNE (HM02705) | | | | | | | | | | | | | | | | | | ● | | | | | | | |
| BOOTH, PHILLIP (HM02708) | | | | | | | | | | | | | | | ● | | | | | | | | | | |
| BRISTOL HYPNOTHERAPY CLINIC (HM03063) | | | | | | | | | | | | | | | ● | | | | | | | | | | |
| BRISTOL NATURAL HEALTH SERVICE (HM03064) | | | | | | | | | | | | | | | | | | ● | | ● | | | | | |
| BRISTOL SCHOOL OF SHIATSU (HM03066) | | | | | | | | | | | | | | | | | | | | | | | | | |
| BROWN, SARAH (HM03248) | | | | | | | | | | | | | | | | | | ● | | | | | | | |
| CHARLES CLINIC (HM04020) | | | ● | | | | | | | | | | | | | | | | | | | | | | |
| CHAWDHARY, B S (HM04067) | | | | | | | | | | | | | | | ● | | | | | | | | | | |
| CHERINGTON PRACTICE (HM04106) | | | | | | | ● | | | | | | | | | | | | | | | | | | |
| CLEGHORN, BURNES & HOWNSFIELD (HM04637) | | | ● | | | | | | | | | | | | | | | | | | | | | | |

| Business by County with Reference no. | Shiatsu | Silva Method | Sound Therapy | Spiritual Healing | Sports Massage | Stress Therapy | Swedish Body Massage | T'ai-Chi Ch'uan | Tantra Therapy | Tera-Mai | Thought Field Therapy | Touch Therapy | Transactional Analysis | Tui-na | Ultrasonics | Vibrational Therapy | Visualisation Therapy | Vitamin Therapy | Voice Therapy | X-Ray | Ying & Yang | Yoga | Zen Therapy | Zero Balancing |
|---|---|---|---|---|---|---|---|---|---|---|---|---|---|---|---|---|---|---|---|---|---|---|---|---|
| SLOUGH SPORTS INJURIES CLINIC (HM18690) | | | | | | | | | | | | | | | | | | | | | | | | |
| SMETHURST, ALISON (HM18704) | | | | | | | | | | | | | | | | | | | | | | | | |
| SMITH, CANDIDA (HM18724) | | | | | | | | | | | | | | | | | | | | | | | | |
| SMITH, JENNIE (HM18753) | | | | | | | | | | | | | | | | | | | | | | | | |
| SOUTH LODGE CONSULTING (HM18909) | | | | | | | | | | | | | | | ● | | | | | | | | | |
| SPENCER, GILLIAN (HM18994) | | | | | | | | | | | | | | | | | | | | | | | | |
| SPRINGWOOD COMP HEALTH (HM19055) | | | | | | | | | | | | | | | | | | | | | | | | |
| STUBBS, RICHARD (HM19437) | | | | | | | | | | | | | | | | | | | | | | | | |
| SUNNINGDALE HEALING CENTRE (HM19509) | | | | ● | | | | | | | | | | | | | | | | | | | | |
| T A IN THE THAMES VALLEY (HM19637) | | | | | | | | | | | | | | | | | | | | | | | | |
| THAMS, JUNE (HM19866) | | | | | | | | | | | | | | | | | | | | | | | | |
| TINGLE, SARAH (HM20082) | | | | | | | | | | | | | | | | | | | | | | | | |
| TSENG, PATRICIA (HM20359) | ● | | | | | ● | | | | | | | | | | | | | | | | | | |
| WALKER, PENELOPE (HM20795) | | | | | | | | | | | | | | | | | | | | | | | | |
| WEST BERKSHIRE PSYCHOTHERAPY (HM21215) | | | | | | | | | | | | | | | | | | | | | | | | |
| WILKIN, P (DR) (HM21498) | | | | | | | | | | | | | | | | | | | | | | | | |
| WILLINGSON, TOM (HM21611) | | | | | | | | | | | | | | | | | | | | | | | | |
| WOODLEY HEALING CENTRE (HM21836) | | | | | | | | | | | | | | | | | | ● | | | | | | |
| **BRISTOL** | | | | | | | | | | | | | | | | | | | | | | | | |
| ALLISON JOY REFLEXOLOGY (HM00649) | | | | | | | | | | | | | | | | | | | | | | | | |
| ANDERSON, KEITH (HM00830) | | | | | | | | | | | | | | | | | | | | | | | | |
| AQUARIUS HEALTH CENTRE (HM00959) | ● | | | | | ● | | | | | | | | | | | | | | | | | | |
| AVON COUNSELLING/PSYCHOTHERAPY (HM01405) | | | | | | | | | | | | | | | | | | | | | | | | |
| BEVAN, RUSS (HM02242) | | | | | | ● | | | | | | | | | | | | | | | | | | |
| BOOTH, LYNNE (HM02705) | | | | | | | | | | | | | | | | | | | | | | | | |
| BOOTH, PHILLIP (HM02708) | | | | | | | | | | | | | | | | | | | | | | | | |
| BRISTOL HYPNOTHERAPY CLINIC (HM03063) | | | | | | | | | | | | | | | | | | | | | | | | |
| BRISTOL NATURAL HEALTH SERVICE (HM03064) | ● | | | | | | | | | | | | | | | | | | | | | | | |
| BRISTOL SCHOOL OF SHIATSU (HM03066) | ● | | | | | | | | | | | | | | | | | | | | | | | |
| BROWN, SARAH (HM03248) | | | | | | | | | | | | | | | | | | | | | | | | |
| CHARLES CLINIC (HM04020) | | | | | | | | | | | | | | | | | | | | | | | | |
| CHAWDHARY, B S (HM04067) | | | | | | | | | | | | | | | | | | | | | | | | |
| CHERINGTON PRACTICE (HM04106) | | | | | | | | | | | | | | | | | | | | | | | | |
| CLEGHORN, BURNES & HOWNSFIELD (HM04637) | | | | | | | | | | | | | | | | | | | | | | | | |

# O - Z Therapies at Practices/Businesses

| Business by County with Reference no. | Orthotics | Osteomyology | Osteopathy | PAM | Paranormal Therapies | Pattern Therapies | Physiotherapy | Phytotherapy | Pilates | Podiatry | Polarity Therapy | Postural Integration | Primal Therapy | Psionic Therapy | Psychotherapy | Pyramid Power | Pyscho-Synthesis | Reflexology | Reichian Therapy | Reiki | Remedial Massage | Rogerian Therapy | Rolfing | Seichem | Sensitivity Training |
| --- | --- | --- | --- | --- | --- | --- | --- | --- | --- | --- | --- | --- | --- | --- | --- | --- | --- | --- | --- | --- | --- | --- | --- | --- | --- |
| CLIFTON CHIROPRACTIC CLINIC (HM04666) | | | | | | | | | ● | | | | | | | | | | | | | | | | |
| CLIFTON PRACTICE (HM04670) | | | ● | | | | | | | | | | | | | | | ● | | ● | | | | | |
| CLINIC OF NATURAL MEDICINE (HM04704) | | | | | | | | | | | | | | | | | | ● | | | | | | | |
| CRAM, JULIANA (HM05362) | | | ● | | | | | | | | | | | | | | | | | | | | | | |
| CRANHAM, NIGEL (HM05374) | | | | | | | | | | | | | | | | | | ● | | | | | | | |
| CTRE FOR KINESIOLOGY (HM05542) | | | | | | | | | | | | | | | | | | | | ● | | | | ● | |
| DIMASCIO, CAROLINE (HM06103) | | | | | | | | | | | | | | | | | | ● | | | | | | | |
| DOBBINS, ALISON (HM06136) | | | | | | | | | | | | | | | | | | ● | | | | | | | |
| EYRES, BELINDA (HM07030) | | | ● | | | | | | | | | | | | | | | | | | | | | | |
| FILE, CHRISTINE (HM07288) | | | | | | | | | | | | | | | | | | ● | | | | | | | |
| FREEMAN, ANN (HM07719) | | | | | | | | | | | | | | | | | | | | | | | | | |
| GARLAND, C (HM07889) | | | | | | | | | | | | | | | | | | ● | | | | | | | |
| GIDDINGS, JANE (HM08050) | | | | | | | | | | | | | | | | | | ● | | | | | | | |
| GILBERT, EDWARD J (HM08059) | | | ● | | | | | | | | | | | | | | | | | | | | | | |
| GROUP ANALYTIC NETWORK WEST (HM08604) | | | | | | | | | | | | | | | ● | | | | | | | | | | |
| HARCOURT, A (HM08964) | | | ● | | | | | | | | | | | | | | | | | | | | | | |
| HART, ELLEN (HM09125) | | | ● | | | | | | | | | | | | | | | | | | | | | | |
| HAWKINS, LEONARD S (HM09223) | | | | | | | | | | | | | | | ● | | | | | | | | | | |
| HEALING WITH GABRIELLE TWINE (HM09360) | | | | | | | | | | | | | | | | | | | | | | | | | |
| HEALTH & HEALING (HM09371) | | | | | | | | | | | | | | | | | | ● | | ● | | | | | |
| HEALTHWISE (HM09420) | | | | | | | | | | | | | | | | | | | | | | | | | |
| HOBBS, S J (HM09856) | | | | | | | | | | | | | | | ● | | | | | | | | | | |
| HOPLEY, DENISE (HM10154) | | | | | | | | | | | | | | | | | | | | | ● | | | | |
| HUDSON, JOHN (HM10313) | | | | | | | | | | | | | | | ● | | | | | | | | | | |
| HUNT, KEITH G (HM10396) | | | ● | | | | | | | | | | | | | | | | | | | | | | |
| INGREY, DAVID (HM10629) | | | | | | | | | | | | | | | | | | ● | | | | | | | |
| INSIGHTS THERAPY CLINIC (HM10658) | | | | | | | | | | | | | | | ● | | | | | | | | | | |
| INTL INS OF REFLEX-WESTERN (HM10700) | | | | | | | | | | | | | | | | | | ● | | | | | | | |
| JOLY, S (HM11111) | | | ● | | | | | | | | | | | | | | | | | | | | | | |
| KNIGHTSWOOD CLINIC (HM11762) | | | | | | | ● | | | | | | | | | | | | | | | | | | |
| LAM RIM CTRE FOR WHOLE HEALTH (HM11883) | | | ● | | | | | | | | | | | | | | | ● | | | | | | | |
| MCCATTY, RONALD R (HM13402) | | | ● | | | | | | | | | | | | | | | | | | | | | | |
| MIDDA, JULIAN OST & SPORTS THER (HM13811) | | | ● | | | | | | | | | | | | | | | | | | | | | | |
| MILLS, CLARE (HM13928) | | | | | | | | | | | | | | | | | | ● | | | | | | | |

| Business by County with Reference no. | Shiatsu | Silva Method | Sound Therapy | Spiritual Healing | Sports Massage | Stress Therapy | Swedish Body Massage | T'ai-Chi Ch'uan | Tantra Therapy | Tera-Mai | Thought Field Therapy | Touch Therapy | Transactional Analysis | Tui-na | Ultrasonics | Vibrational Therapy | Visualisation Therapy | Vitamin Therapy | Voice Therapy | X-Ray | Ying & Yang | Yoga | Zen Therapy | Zero Balancing |
| --- | --- | --- | --- | --- | --- | --- | --- | --- | --- | --- | --- | --- | --- | --- | --- | --- | --- | --- | --- | --- | --- | --- | --- | --- |
| CLIFTON CHIROPRACTIC CLINIC (HM04666) | | | | | | | | | | | | | | | | | | ● | | ● | | | | |
| CLIFTON PRACTICE (HM04670) | ● | | | | | | | | | | | | | | | | | | | | | | | |
| CLINIC OF NATURAL MEDICINE (HM04704) | | | | | | | | | | | | | | | | | | | | | | | | |
| CRAM, JULIANA (HM05362) | | | | | | | | | | | | | | | | | | | | | | | | |
| CRANHAM, NIGEL (HM05374) | | | | | | | | | | | | | | | | | | | | | | | | |
| CTRE FOR KINESIOLOGY (HM05542) | | | | | | | | | | | | | | | | ● | | | | | | | | |
| DIMASCIO, CAROLINE (HM06103) | | | | | | | | | | | | | | | | | | | | | | | | |
| DOBBINS, ALISON (HM06136) | | | | | | | | | | | | | | | | | | | | | | | | |
| EYRES, BELINDA (HM07030) | | | | | | | | | | | | | | | | | | | | | | | | |
| FILE, CHRISTINE (HM07288) | | | | | | | | | | | | | | | | | | | | | | | | |
| FREEMAN, ANN (HM07719) | | | | ● | | | | | | | | | | | | | | | | | | | | |
| GARLAND, C (HM07889) | | | | | | | | | | | | | | | | | | | | | | | | |
| GIDDINGS, JANE (HM08050) | | | | | | | | | | | | | | | | | | | | | | | | |
| GILBERT, EDWARD J (HM08059) | | | | | | | | | | | | | | | | | | | | | | | | |
| GROUP ANALYTIC NETWORK WEST (HM08604) | | | | | | | | | | | | | | | | | | | | | | | | |
| HARCOURT, A (HM08964) | | | | | | | | | | | | | | | | | | | | | | | | |
| HART, ELLEN (HM09125) | | | | | | | | | | | | | | | | | | | | | | | | |
| HAWKINS, LEONARD S (HM09223) | | | | | | | | | | | | | | | | | | | | | | | | |
| HEALING WITH GABRIELLE TWINE (HM09360) | | | | ● | | | | | | | | ● | | | | | ● | | | | | | | |
| HEALTH & HEALING (HM09371) | ● | | | | | | | | | | | | | | | | | | | | | | | |
| HEALTHWISE (HM09420) | | | | | | | | | | | | | | | | | | ● | | | | | | |
| HOBBS, S J (HM09856) | | | | | | | | | | | | | | | | | | | | | | | | |
| HOPLEY, DENISE (HM10154) | | | | | | | | | | | | | | | | | | | | | | | | |
| HUDSON, JOHN (HM10313) | | | | | | ● | | | | | | | | | | | | | | | | | | |
| HUNT, KEITH G (HM10396) | | | | | | | | | | | | | | | | | | | | | | | | |
| INGREY, DAVID (HM10629) | | | | | | | | | | | | | | | | | | | | | | | | |
| INSIGHTS THERAPY CLINIC (HM10658) | | | | | | | | | | | | | | | | | | | | | | | | |
| INTL INS OF REFLEX-WESTERN (HM10700) | | | | | | | | | | | | | | | | | | | | | | | | |
| JOLY, S (HM11111) | | | | | | | | | | | | | | | | | | | | | | | | |
| KNIGHTSWOOD CLINIC (HM11762) | | | | | | | | | | | | | | | | | | | | | | | | |
| LAM RIM CTRE FOR WHOLE HEALTH (HM11883) | ● | | | | | | | | | | | | | | | | | | | | | | | |
| MCCATTY, RONALD R (HM13402) | | | | | | | | | | | | | | | | | | | | | | | | |
| MIDDA, JULIAN OST & SPORTS THER (HM13811) | | | | | | | | | | | | | | | | | | | | | | | | |
| MILLS, CLARE (HM13928) | | | | | | | | | | | | | | | | | | | | | | | | |

# O - Z Therapies at Practices/Businesses

| Business by County with Reference no. | Orthotics | Osteomyology | Osteopathy | PAM | Paranormal Therapies | Pattern Therapies | Physiotherapy | Phytotherapy | Pilates | Podiatry | Polarity Therapy | Postural Integration | Primal Therapy | Psionic Therapy | Psychotherapy | Pyramid Power | Pyscho-Synthesis | Reflexology | Reichian Therapy | Reiki | Remedial Massage | Rogerian Therapy | Rolfing | Seichem | Sensitivity Training | Shiatsu | Silva Method | Sound Therapy | Spiritual Healing | Sports Massage | Stress Therapy | Swedish Body Massage | T'ai-Chi Ch'uan | Tantra Therapy | Tera-Mai | Thought Field Therapy | Touch Therapy | Transactional Analysis | Tui-na | Ultrasonics | Vibrational Therapy | Visualisation Therapy | Vitamin Therapy | Voice Therapy | X-Ray | Ying & Yang | Yoga | Zen Therapy | Zero Balancing |
|---|---|---|---|---|---|---|---|---|---|---|---|---|---|---|---|---|---|---|---|---|---|---|---|---|---|---|---|---|---|---|---|---|---|---|---|---|---|---|---|---|---|---|---|---|---|---|---|---|---|
| MUSCATY, J (HM14425) | | | ● | | | | | | | | | | | | | | | | | | | | | | | | | | | | | | | | | | | | | | | | | | | | | | |
| NAILSEA CHIROPRACTIC CLINIC (HM14460) | | | | | | | | | | | | | | | | | | | | | | | | | | | | | | | | | | | | | | | | ● | | | | | ● | | | | |
| NAYDLER, NICK (HM14711) | | | | | | | | | | | | | | | ● | | | | | | | | | | | | | | | | | | | | | | | | | | | | | | | | | | |
| NICHOLS, JONATHAN (HM14916) | | | ● | | | | | | | | | | | | | | | | | | | | | | | | | | | | | | | | | | | | | | | | | | | | | | |
| ORCHARD MEDICAL CENTRE (HM15364) | | | | | | | | | | | | | | | | | | ● | | | | | | | | | | | | | | | | | | | | | | | | | | | | | | | |
| ORIENTAL MEDICINE PRACTICE (HM15387) | | | | | | | | | | | | | | | | | | | | | | | | | | ● | | | | | | | | | | | | | | | | | ● | | | | | | |
| PARKER CLINIC (HM15683) | | | | | | | ● | | | | | | | | | | | | | | | | | | | | | | | | | | | | | | | | | | | | | | | | | | |
| REDLANDS HOUSE CLINIC (HM17028) | | | | | | | ● | | | | | | | | | | | | | | | | | | | | | | | | | | | | | | | | | | | | | | | | | | |
| RICHARDSON, DAVID (HM17275) | | | ● | | | | | | | | | | | | | | | | | | | | | | | | | | | | | | | | | | | | | | | | | | | | | | |
| RISING DRAGON TAI CHI (HM17369) | | | | | | | | | | | | | | | | | | | | | | | | | | | | | | | | | ● | | | | | | | | | | | | | | | | |
| RISING DRAGON TAI CHI SCHOOL (HM17370) | | | | | | | | | | | | | | | | | | | | | | | | | | | | | | | | | ● | | | | | | | | | | | | | | | | |
| SKUSE, CLARE (HM18662) | | | | | | | | | | | | | | | | | | ● | | | | | | | | | | | | | | | | | | | | | | | | | | | | | | | |
| SNEYD PARK (HM18837) | | | ● | | | | | | | | | | | | | | | | | | | | | | | | | | | | | | | | | | | | | | | | | | | | | | |
| STH WST COLLEGE OF ORIENTL MED (HM19285) | | | | | | | | | | | | | | | | | | | | | | | | | | ● | | | | | | | | | | | | | | | | | | | | | | | |
| STYLES, PATRICIA (HM19458) | | | | | | | | | | ● | | | | | | | | | | | | | | | | | | | | | | | | | | | | | | | | | | | | | | | |
| SUTTON, S (HM19557) | | | | | | | | | | | | | | | | | | ● | | | | | | | | | | | | | | | | | | | | | | | | | | | | | | | |
| THOMPSON, J H (HM19982) | | | ● | | | | | | | | | | | | | | | | | | | | | | | | | | | | | | | | | | | | | | | | | | | | | | |
| TOLL HOUSE CHIROPRACTIC (HM20119) | | | | | | | ● | | | | | | | | | | | | | | | | | | | | | | | | | | | | | | | | | | | | | | | | | | |
| TOLL HOUSE CLINIC (HM20120) | | | | | | | ● | | ● | | | | | | | | | ● | | | | | | | | | | | | | | | | | | | | | | ● | | | | | | | | | |
| WILLOWS CLINIC (HM21629) | | | ● | | | | | | | | | | | | | | | | | | | | | | | | | | | | | | | | | | | | | | | | | | | | | | |
| **BUCKINGHAMSHIRE** | | | | | | | | | | | | | | | | | | | | | | | | | | | | | | | | | | | | | | | | | | | | | | | | | |
| AKERS, DENISE (HM00462) | | | | | | | | | | | | | | | | | | ● | | | | | | | | | | | | | | | | | | | | | | | | | | | | | | | |
| ALTERNATIVE THERAPIES TRAINING (HM00730) | | | | | | | | | | | | | | | | | | ● | | ● | | | | | | ● | | | | | | | | | | | | | | | | | | | | | | | |
| AMERSHAM CHIROPRACTIC CLINIC (HM00779) | ● | | | | | | | ● | | | | | | | | | | | | | | | | | | | | | | | | | | | | | | | | | | | | | ● | | | | |
| AMERSHAM OSTEOPATHIC CLINIC (HM00780) | | | ● | | | | | | | | | | | | | | | ● | | ● | | | | | | | | | | | | | | | | | | | | | | | | | | | | | |
| ARMITSTEAD, JOHN (HM01015) | | | ● | | | | | | | | | | | | | | | | | | | | | | | | | | | | | | | | | | | | | | | | | | | | | | |
| ASHBERRY PHYSIOTHERAPY CLINIC (HM01188) | | | | | | | ● | | | | | | | | | | | | | | | | | | | | | | | | | | | | | | | | | | | | | | | | | | |
| AYLESBURY COMPLEMENTARY HEALTH (HM01423) | | | | | | | | | | | | | | | ● | | | | | ● | | | | | | | | | | | ● | | | | | | | | | | | | | | | | | | |
| AYLESBURY VALE THERAPY (HM01425) | | | | | | | | | | | | | | | ● | | | | | | | | | | | | | | | | ● | | | | | | | | | | | ● | | | | | | | |
| AYRES, JUDITH (HM01435) | | | | | | | | | | | | | | | | | | ● | | | | | | | | | | | | | | | | | | | | | | | | | | | | | | | |
| BANFIELD, KATIE (HM01657) | | | ● | | | | | | | | | | | | | | | | | | | | | | | | | | | | | | | | | | | | | | | | ● | | | | | | |
| BODY & SOUL (HM02565) | | | | | | | | | | | | | | | | | | ● | | | | | | | | | | | | | | | | | | | | | | | | | | | | | | | |
| BOOTH, MARK (HM02706) | | | ● | | | | | | | | | | | | | | | | | | | | | | | | | | | | | | | | | | | | | | | | | | | | | | |
| CAMERON, ANNE (HM03583) | | | | | | | | | | | | | | | | | | ● | | | | | | | | | | | | | | | | | | | | | | | | | | | | | | | |

# O - Z Therapies at Practices/Businesses

| Business by County with Reference no. | Orthotics | Osteomyology | Osteopathy | PAM | Paranormal Therapies | Pattern Therapies | Physiotherapy | Phytotherapy | Pilates | Podiatry | Polarity Therapy | Postural Integration | Primal Therapy | Psionic Therapy | Psychotherapy | Pyramid Power | Pyscho-Synthesis | Reflexology | Reichian Therapy | Reiki | Remedial Massage | Rogerian Therapy | Rolfing | Seichem | Sensitivity Training | Shiatsu | Silva Method | Sound Therapy | Spiritual Healing | Sports Massage | Stress Therapy | Swedish Body Massage | T'ai-Chi Ch'uan | Tantra Therapy | Tera-Mai | Thought Field Therapy | Touch Therapy | Transactional Analysis | Tui-na | Ultrasonics | Vibrational Therapy | Visualisation Therapy | Vitamin Therapy | Voice Therapy | X-Ray | Ying & Yang | Yoga | Zen Therapy | Zero Balancing |
|---|---|---|---|---|---|---|---|---|---|---|---|---|---|---|---|---|---|---|---|---|---|---|---|---|---|---|---|---|---|---|---|---|---|---|---|---|---|---|---|---|---|---|---|---|---|---|---|---|---|
| CAMPBELL, LOUISE (HM03604) | | | | | | | | | | | | | | | | | | ● | | | | | | | | | | | | | | | | | | | | | | | | | | | | | | | |
| CAMPBELL, NIKKI (HM03605) | | | | | | | | | | | | | | | | | | ● | | | | | | | | | | | | | | | | | | | | | | | | | | | | | | | |
| CANDLEWELL CLINIC (HM03623) | | | ● | | | | | | | | | | | | | | | | | | | | | | | | | | | | | | | | | | | | | | | | | | | | | | |
| CARTER, YVONNE (HM03789) | | | | | | | | | | | | | | | | | | ● | | | | | | | | | | | | | | | | | | | | | | | | | | | | | | | |
| CASE, BRENDA (HM03807) | | | ● | | | | | | | | | | | | | | | | | | | | | | | | | | | | | | | | | | | | | | | | | | | | | | |
| CASTLE STREET CLINIC (HM03837) | | | ● | | | | | | ● | | | | | | ● | | | ● | | | | | | | | | | | | | | | | | | | | | | | | | | | | | | | |
| CHESNEY, SIMON (HM04119) | | | ● | | | | | | | | | | | | | | | | | | | | | | | | | | | | | | | | | | | | | | | | | | | | | | |
| CHILTERN OSTEOPATHIC PRACTICE (HM04177) | | | ● | | | | | | | | | | | | | | | | | | | | | | | | | | | | | | | | | | | | | | | | | | | | | | |
| COACHING FOR SUCCESS (HM04750) | | | | | | | | | | | | | | | ● | | | | | | | | | | | | | | | | ● | | | | | | | | | | | ● | ● | | | | | | |
| COLDWELL, VERONICA (HM04810) | | | | | ● | | | | | | | | | | | | | ● | | ● | | | | | | | | | | | ● | | | | | | | | | | | | | | | | | | |
| COLLINS, STUART (HM04879) | | | ● | | | | | | | | | | | | | | | | | | | | | | | | | | | | | | | | | | | | | | | | | | | | | | |
| COMPLEMENTARY HEALTH (HM04921) | | | | | | | | | | | | | | | ● | | | | | ● | | | | | | | | | | | ● | | | | | | | | | | | | | | | | | | |
| COMPLEMENTARY HEALTH CENTRE (HM04923) | | | | | | | | | | | | | | | | | | ● | | ● | | | | | | | | | | | ● | | | | | | | | | | | | | | | | | | |
| CONRAN, JAN (HM05006) | | | | | | | | | | | | | | | | | | ● | | | | | | | | | | | | | | | | | | | | | | | | | | | | | | | |
| DATHAN, PENNY (HM05757) | | | ● | | | | | | | | | | | | | | | | | | | | | | | | | | | | | | | | | | | | | | | | | | | | | | |
| EDWARDS, EMMA (HM06650) | | | | | | | | | | | | | | | | | | ● | | ● | | | | | | | | | | | | | | | | | | | | | | | | | | | | | |
| EDWARDS, MICHAEL (HM06664) | | | | | | | | | | | | | | | | | | ● | | | | | | | | | | | | | | | | | | | | | | | | | | | | | | | |
| ELAINE MCCARTHY REFLEXOLOGIST (HM06698) | | | | | | | | | | | | | | | | | | ● | | | | | | | | | | | | | | | | | | | | | | | | | | | | | | | |
| ELMIDORO, JANE (HM06782) | | | | | | | | | | | | | | | | | | ● | | | | | | | | | | | | | | | | | | | | | | | | | | | | | | | |
| FIRMAN, BARBARA (HM07332) | | | | | | | | | | | | | | | | | | ● | | ● | | | | | | | | | | | | | ● | | | | | | | | | | | | | | | | |
| FISHER, CLAIRE (HM07350) | | | | | | | | | | | | | | | | | | ● | | | | | | | | | | | | | | | | | | | | | | | | | | | | | | | |
| GARRATT, J R (HM07900) | | | ● | | | | | | | | | | | | | | | | | | | | | | | | | | | | | | | | | | | | | | | | | | | | | | |
| GERRARDS CROSS SPORTS & BACK (HM08004) | | | | | | | | | | | | ● | | | | | | | | | | | | | | | | | | | | | | | | | | | | ● | | | | | | | | | |
| GLYNN, ELIZABETH (HM08169) | | | | | | | | | | | | | | | | | | ● | | | | | | | | | | | | | | | | | | | | | | | | | | | | | | | |
| GREEN, JULIA A (HM08465) | | | ● | | | | | | | | | | | | | | | | | | | | | | | | | | | | | | | | | | | | | | | | | | | | | | |
| HAISELDEN, JENNIE (HM08720) | | | | | | | | | | | | | | | | | | ● | | | | | | | | | | | | | | | | | | | | | | | | | | | | | | | |
| HEATH, SUSAN (HM09454) | | | | | | | | | | | | | | | | | | | | ● | | | | | | | | | | | | | | | | | | | | | | | | | | | | | |
| HOLISTIC HEALING (HM09959) | | | | | | | | | | | | | | | | | | ● | | ● | | | | | | | | | | | | | | | | | | | | | | | | | | | | | |
| HULCOTT END PRACTICE (HM10352) | | | | | | | ● | | | | | | | | | | | ● | | | | | | | | | | | | | | | | | | | | | | | | | | | | | | | |
| HUNT, CHARLES (HM10391) | | | ● | | | | | | | | | | | | | | | | | | | | | | | | | | | | | | | | | | | | | | | | | | | | | | |
| J J COUNSELLING SERVICES (HM10798) | | | | | | | | | | | | | | | ● | | | | | | | | | | | | | | | | ● | | | | | | | | | | | | | | | | | | |
| JOHNSON, HELEN (HM11074) | | | ● | | | | | | | | | | | | | | | | | | | | | | | | | | | | | | | | | | | | | | | | | | | | | | |
| K BANFIELD NATUROPATHY/OSTEO (HM11288) | | | ● | | | | | | | | | | | | | | | | | | | | | | | | | | | | | | | | | | | | | | | | ● | | | | | | |
| KEILDSON, HANNAH (HM11408) | | | | | | | | | | | | | | | | | | ● | | | | | | | | | | | | | | | | | | | | | | | | | | | | | | | |

# O - Z Therapies at Practices/Businesses

| Business by County with Reference no. | Orthotics | Osteomyology | Osteopathy | PAM | Paranormal Therapies | Pattern Therapies | Physiotherapy | Phytotherapy | Pilates | Podiatry | Polarity Therapy | Postural Integration | Primal Therapy | Psionic Therapy | Psychotherapy | Pyramid Power | Pyscho-Synthesis | Reflexology | Reichian Therapy | Reiki | Remedial Massage | Rogerian Therapy | Rolfing | Seichem | Sensitivity Training | Shiatsu | Silva Method | Sound Therapy | Spiritual Healing | Sports Massage | Stress Therapy | Swedish Body Massage | T'ai-Chi Ch'uan | Tantra Therapy | Tera-Mai | Thought Field Therapy | Touch Therapy | Transactional Analysis | Tui-na | Ultrasonics | Vibrational Therapy | Visualisation Therapy | Vitamin Therapy | Voice Therapy | X-Ray | Ying & Yang | Yoga | Zen Therapy | Zero Balancing |
|---|---|---|---|---|---|---|---|---|---|---|---|---|---|---|---|---|---|---|---|---|---|---|---|---|---|---|---|---|---|---|---|---|---|---|---|---|---|---|---|---|---|---|---|---|---|---|---|---|---|
| LAWSON, HEATHER (HM12063) |||||||||||||||||●|||||||||||||||||||||||||||||||
| LAWSON, JANET (HM12066) ||●||||||||||||||||||||||||||||||||||||||||||||||
| LE HUNTE, ASHIKA (HM12086) |||||||||||||||||●|||||||||||||||||||||||||||||||
| LEACH, P (HM12090) ||●||||||||||||||||||||||||||||||||||||||||||||||
| LONG CRENDON OSTEOPATHS (HM12614) ||●||||||||||||||||||||||||||||||||||||||||||||||
| MARLOW OSTEOPATHIC CLINIC (HM13129) ||●||||||||||||||||||||||||||||||||||||||||||||||
| MARSHALL, CAROLYN (HM13157) |||||||||||||||||●|||||||||||||||||||||||||||||||
| MCCAFFERTY, SUSANNE (HM13379) |||||||||||||||||●|||||||||||||||||||||||||||||||
| MIDDLE WAY RE-EDUCATION CTRE (HM13813) |||||||||||||||||||||||||||●|||||||||||||||||||●||
| MIND AND BODY (HM13959) |||||||||||||||||||●||||||||●||●||||||●|||||●||||||||
| MIRZOEFF, PETER (HM13992) ||||||||||||||●||||||||||||||||||||||||||||||||||
| MORRISSEY, BLANCHE (HM14236) |●|||||||||●|||||||||||||||||||||||||||||||||||||||
| MUMBRAY, LINDA (HM14355) |||||||||||||||||●|||||||||||||||||||||||||||||||
| NEWMAN, BARBARA (HM14870) |||||||||||||||||●||●|||||||||||||||||||||||||||||
| OLNEY OSTEOPATHIC SURGERY (HM15302) ||●||||||||||||||||||||||||||||||||||||||||||||||
| O'NEIL, PAULA (HM15326) |||||||||||||||||●|||||||||||||||||||||||||||||||
| ORCHARD CLNC CTRE FOR COMP MED (HM15361) ||●||||||||||||||||||||||||||||||||||||||||||||||
| ORMSBY, NEIL (HM15399) ||||||||||||||||||||||||||||●||||||||||||||||||||
| OUILLON-PALMER, LAURENCE (HM15498) |||||||||||||||||●|||||||||||||||||||||||||||||||
| PATON, BARBARA (HM15823) |||||||●|||||||||||||||||||||||||||||||||||||||||
| PEERS-JOHNSON, D R (HM15943) ||●||||||||||||||||||||||||||||||||||||||||||||||
| PENN COUNSELLING/PSYCHOTHERAPY (HM15980) ||||||||||||||●||||||||||||||||||||||||||||||||||
| PHYSIO FIRST PRACTICE (HM16199) ||||||●||||||||||||||||||||||||||||||||||||||||||
| PINEWOOD CHIROPODY PRACTICE (HM16312) |||||||||●|||||||||||||||||||||||||||||||||||||||
| PRESTWOOD PHYSIOTHERAPY CLINIC (HM16562) ||||||●||||||||||||||||||||||||||||||||||||||||||
| PRIVATE CLINIC OF NAT THRPY (HM16641) ||●||||||||||||||||||||||||||||||||||||||||||||||
| PURTON HOUSE HOMEOPATHIC CTRE (HM16775) ||||||||||||||●||||||||||||||||||||||||||||||||||
| REDGRAVE, ANN (HM17024) ||●||||||||||||||||||||||||||||||||||||||||||||||
| REIKI HEALTH CENTRE (HM17137) |||||||||||||||||||●|||||||||||||||||||||||||||||
| REYNOLDS, DAVID (HM17210) ||●||||||||||||||||||||||||||||||||||||||||||||||
| RICHARDSON, JACQUI (HM17281) |||||||||||||||||●|||||||||||||||||||||||||||||||
| ROBERTSON, ANGUS (HM17437) |||||||||||||||||●|||||||||||||||||||||||||||||||
| ROBINSON, DENEASE (HM17467) |||||||||||||||||●|||||||||||||||||||||||||||||||
| ROGERS, SUSAN (HM17555) |||||||||||||||||●|||||||||||||||||||||||||||||||

# O - Z Therapies at Practices/Businesses

| Business by County with Reference no. | Orthotics | Osteomyology | Osteopathy | PAM | Paranormal Therapies | Pattern Therapies | Physiotherapy | Phytotherapy | Pilates | Podiatry | Polarity Therapy | Postural Integration | Primal Therapy | Psionic Therapy | Psychotherapy | Pyramid Power | Pyscho-Synthesis |
|---|---|---|---|---|---|---|---|---|---|---|---|---|---|---|---|---|---|
| ROMEO, GILLIAN (HM17571) | | | | | | | | | | | | | | | | | |
| ROMEO, GILLIAN (HM17572) | | | | | | | | | | | | | | | | | |
| RUNDLE, RICHARD (HM17752) | | | | | | | | | | | | | | | | | |
| SHAW, FIONA (HM18335) | | | | | | | | | | | | | | | | | |
| SHEPHERD, KAREN (HM18413) | | | | | | | | | | | | | | | | | |
| SHINH, NATALIE (HM18476) | | | ● | | | | | | | | | | | | | | |
| SIDLEY, SAM (HM18530) | | | | | | | | | | | | | | | | | |
| SKIDDY, SUSAN (HM18638) | | | | | | | | | | | | | | | | | |
| SMITH, JUDY (HM18757) | | | | | | | | | | | | | | | | | |
| SOLE CONCERN REFLEXOLOGY (HM18866) | | | | | | | | | | | | | | | | | |
| SOUL TO SOLE NATURAL THERAPY (HM18898) | | | | | | | | | | | | | | | | | |
| SOUTER, MIRANDA (HM18901) | | | ● | | | | | | | | | | | | | | |
| STURGESS, PETER (HM19450) | | | ● | | | | | | | | | | | | | | |
| TAYLOR, IAN E (HM19763) | | | | | | | | | | | | | | | | | |
| TEMPLEMAN, ROWENA (HM19831) | | | | | | | | | | | | | | | | | |
| TEMPLEWOOD CLINIC (HM19833) | | | ● | | | | | | | | | | | | | | |
| THIEBAUD, M F (HM19919) | | | ● | | | | | | | | | | | | | | |
| THORNTON, MICHAEL (HM20028) | | | ● | | | | | | | | | | | | | | |
| THORNTON, MICHAEL (HM20027) | | | ● | | | | | | | | | | | | | | |
| TODD, PAUL (HM20107) | ● | | | | | | | | | ● | | | | | | | |
| TOMLIN, SUSAN M (HM20136) | | | | | | | | | | | | | | | | | |
| TOUCHARD, HELEN (HM20189) | | | | | | | | | | | | | | | | | |
| TUDOR HOUSE CLINIC (HM20371) | | | | | | | ● | | | | | | | | | | |
| WARDLAW, MICHAEL (HM20921) | | | | | | | | | | ● | | | | | | | |
| WATSON, ALEXANDRA (HM21002) | | | | | | | | | | | | | | | | | |
| WELLBURN (HM21154) | | | | | | | | | | | | | | | | | |
| WELLER, JACK (HM21156) | | | | | | | | | | | | | | | ● | | |
| WESTWOOD, TERRY (HM21287) | | | | | | | | | | | | | | | | | |
| WHITNALL, LINDA (HM21414) | | | | | | | | | | | | | | | | | |
| WINSTON, LAURIE (HM21715) | | | | | | | | | | | | | | | | | |
| WOODWARD, MARGARET (HM21866) | | | | | | | | | | | | | | | | | |
| **CAMBRIDGESHIRE** | | | | | | | | | | | | | | | | | |
| ACHILLES PHYSIOTHERAPY CLINIC (HM00161) | | | | | | | ● | | | | | | | | | | |
| ANGLIA BACK CLINIC (HM00882) | | | ● | | | | | | | | | | | | | | |

| Business by County with Reference no. | Reflexology | Reichian Therapy | Reiki | Remedial Massage | Rogerian Therapy | Rolfing | Seichem | Sensitivity Training | Shiatsu | Silva Method | Sound Therapy | Spiritual Healing | Sports Massage | Stress Therapy | Swedish Body Massage | T'ai-Chi Ch'uan |
|---|---|---|---|---|---|---|---|---|---|---|---|---|---|---|---|---|
| ROMEO, GILLIAN (HM17571) | ● | | | | | | | | | | | | | | | |
| ROMEO, GILLIAN (HM17572) | ● | | | | | | | | | | | | | | | |
| RUNDLE, RICHARD (HM17752) | ● | | | | | | | | ● | | | ● | ● | ● | | |
| SHAW, FIONA (HM18335) | | | | | | | | | | | | | ● | | | |
| SHEPHERD, KAREN (HM18413) | ● | | | | | | | | | | | | | | | |
| SHINH, NATALIE (HM18476) | | | | | | | | | | | | | | | | |
| SIDLEY, SAM (HM18530) | ● | | | | | | | | | | | | | | | |
| SKIDDY, SUSAN (HM18638) | ● | | | | | | | | | | | | | | | |
| SMITH, JUDY (HM18757) | ● | | | | | | | | | | | | | | | |
| SOLE CONCERN REFLEXOLOGY (HM18866) | ● | | | | | | | | | | | | | | | |
| SOUL TO SOLE NATURAL THERAPY (HM18898) | | | ● | | | | | | | | | | | | | |
| SOUTER, MIRANDA (HM18901) | | | | | | | | | | | | | | | | |
| STURGESS, PETER (HM19450) | | | | | | | | | | | | | | | | |
| TAYLOR, IAN E (HM19763) | ● | | | | | | | | | | | | | | | |
| TEMPLEMAN, ROWENA (HM19831) | ● | | | | | | | | | | | | | | | |
| TEMPLEWOOD CLINIC (HM19833) | | | | | | | | | | | | | | | | |
| THIEBAUD, M F (HM19919) | | | | | | | | | | | | | | | | |
| THORNTON, MICHAEL (HM20028) | | | | | | | | | | | | | | | | |
| THORNTON, MICHAEL (HM20027) | | | | | | | | | | | | | | | | |
| TODD, PAUL (HM20107) | | | | | | | | | | | | | | | | |
| TOMLIN, SUSAN M (HM20136) | ● | | | | | | | | | | | | | | | |
| TOUCHARD, HELEN (HM20189) | ● | | | | | | | | | | | | | | | |
| TUDOR HOUSE CLINIC (HM20371) | | | | | | | | | | | | | | | | |
| WARDLAW, MICHAEL (HM20921) | | | | | | | | | | | | | | | | |
| WATSON, ALEXANDRA (HM21002) | ● | | | | | | | | | | | | | | | |
| WELLBURN (HM21154) | | | | | | | | | ● | | | | | | | |
| WELLER, JACK (HM21156) | | | ● | | | | | | | | | | | ● | | |
| WESTWOOD, TERRY (HM21287) | | | | | | | | | | | | | | ● | | |
| WHITNALL, LINDA (HM21414) | ● | | | | | | | | | | | | | | | |
| WINSTON, LAURIE (HM21715) | ● | | | | | | | | | | | | | | | |
| WOODWARD, MARGARET (HM21866) | ● | | ● | | | | | | | | | ● | | | | |
| **CAMBRIDGESHIRE** | | | | | | | | | | | | | | | | |
| ACHILLES PHYSIOTHERAPY CLINIC (HM00161) | | | | | | | | | | | | | | | | |
| ANGLIA BACK CLINIC (HM00882) | | | | | | | | | | | | | | | | |

| Business by County with Reference no. | Tantra Therapy | Tera-Mai | Thought Field Therapy | Touch Therapy | Transactional Analysis | Tui-na | Ultrasonics | Vibrational Therapy | Visualisation Therapy | Vitamin Therapy | Voice Therapy | X-Ray | Ying & Yang | Yoga | Zen Therapy | Zero Balancing |
|---|---|---|---|---|---|---|---|---|---|---|---|---|---|---|---|---|
| ROMEO, GILLIAN (HM17571) | | | | | | | | | | | | | | | | |
| ROMEO, GILLIAN (HM17572) | | | | | | | | | | | | | | | | |
| RUNDLE, RICHARD (HM17752) | | | | | | | | | ● | ● | | | ● | | | |
| SHAW, FIONA (HM18335) | | | | | | | | | | | | | | | | |
| SHEPHERD, KAREN (HM18413) | | | | | | | | | | | | | | | | |
| SHINH, NATALIE (HM18476) | | | | | | | | | | | | | | | | |
| SIDLEY, SAM (HM18530) | | | | | | | | | | | | | | | | |
| SKIDDY, SUSAN (HM18638) | | | | | | | | | | | | | | | | |
| SMITH, JUDY (HM18757) | | | | | | | | | | | | | | | | |
| SOLE CONCERN REFLEXOLOGY (HM18866) | | | | | | | | | | | | | | | | |
| SOUL TO SOLE NATURAL THERAPY (HM18898) | | | | | | | | | | | | | | | | |
| SOUTER, MIRANDA (HM18901) | | | | | | | | | | | | | | | | |
| STURGESS, PETER (HM19450) | | | | | | | | | | | | | | | | |
| TAYLOR, IAN E (HM19763) | | | | | | | | | | | | | | | | |
| TEMPLEMAN, ROWENA (HM19831) | | | | | | | | | | | | | | | | |
| TEMPLEWOOD CLINIC (HM19833) | | | | | | | | | | | | | | | | |
| THIEBAUD, M F (HM19919) | | | | | | | | | | | | | | | | |
| THORNTON, MICHAEL (HM20028) | | | | | | | | | | | | | | | | |
| THORNTON, MICHAEL (HM20027) | | | | | | | | | | | | | | | | |
| TODD, PAUL (HM20107) | | | | | | | | | | | | | | | | |
| TOMLIN, SUSAN M (HM20136) | | | | | | | | | | | | | | | | |
| TOUCHARD, HELEN (HM20189) | | | | | | | | | | | | | | | | |
| TUDOR HOUSE CLINIC (HM20371) | | | | | | | | | | | | | | | | |
| WARDLAW, MICHAEL (HM20921) | | | | | | | | | | | | | | | | |
| WATSON, ALEXANDRA (HM21002) | | | | | | | | | | | | | | | | |
| WELLBURN (HM21154) | | | | | | | | | | | | | | | | |
| WELLER, JACK (HM21156) | | | | | | | | | ● | | | | | | | |
| WESTWOOD, TERRY (HM21287) | | | | | | | | | | | | | | | | |
| WHITNALL, LINDA (HM21414) | | | | | | | | | | | | | | | | |
| WINSTON, LAURIE (HM21715) | | | | | | | | | | | | | | | | |
| WOODWARD, MARGARET (HM21866) | | | | | | | | | | | | | | | | |
| **CAMBRIDGESHIRE** | | | | | | | | | | | | | | | | |
| ACHILLES PHYSIOTHERAPY CLINIC (HM00161) | | | | | | | | | | | | | | | | |
| ANGLIA BACK CLINIC (HM00882) | | | | | | | | | | | | | | | | |

# O - Z Therapies at Practices/Businesses

Business by County with Reference no.

| Business by County with Reference no. | Orthotics | Osteomyology | Osteopathy | PAM | Paranormal Therapies | Pattern Therapies | Physiotherapy | Phytotherapy | Pilates | Podiatry | Polarity Therapy | Postural Integration | Primal Therapy | Psionic Therapy | Psychotherapy | Pyramid Power | Pyscho-Synthesis | Reflexology | Reichian Therapy | Reiki | Remedial Massage | Rogerian Therapy | Rolfing | Seichem | Sensitivity Training | Shiatsu | Silva Method | Sound Therapy | Spiritual Healing | Sports Massage | Stress Therapy | Swedish Body Massage | T'ai-Chi Ch'uan | Tantra Therapy | Tera-Mai | Thought Field Therapy | Touch Therapy | Transactional Analysis | Tui-na | Ultrasonics | Vibrational Therapy | Visualisation Therapy | Vitamin Therapy | Voice Therapy | X-Ray | Ying & Yang | Yoga | Zen Therapy | Zero Balancing |
|---|---|---|---|---|---|---|---|---|---|---|---|---|---|---|---|---|---|---|---|---|---|---|---|---|---|---|---|---|---|---|---|---|---|---|---|---|---|---|---|---|---|---|---|---|---|---|---|---|---|
| ARJUNA NATURAL HEALTH CENTRE (HM01000) |  |  | ● |  |  |  |  |  |  |  |  |  |  |  |  |  |  | ● |  | ● |  |  |  |  |  | ● |  |  |  |  |  |  |  |  |  |  |  |  |  |  |  |  |  |  |  |  |  |  |  |
| BACK ON TRACK (HM01488) |  |  |  |  |  |  | ● |  |  |  |  |  |  |  |  |  |  |  |  |  |  |  |  |  |  |  |  |  |  |  |  |  |  |  |  |  |  |  |  |  |  |  |  |  |  |  |  |  |  |
| BACK ON TRACK (HM01487) |  |  |  |  |  |  | ● |  |  |  |  |  |  |  |  |  |  |  |  |  |  |  |  |  |  |  |  |  |  |  |  |  |  |  |  |  |  |  |  |  |  |  |  |  |  |  |  |  |  |
| BRATHERTON, W J (HM02923) |  |  |  |  |  |  |  |  |  |  |  |  |  |  | ● |  |  |  |  |  |  |  |  |  |  |  |  |  |  |  |  |  |  |  |  |  |  |  |  |  |  |  |  |  |  |  |  |  |  |
| CAMBRIDGE PSYCHOTHERAPY (HM03577) |  |  |  |  |  |  |  |  |  |  |  |  |  |  | ● |  |  |  |  |  |  |  |  |  |  |  |  |  |  |  |  |  |  |  |  |  |  |  |  |  |  |  |  |  |  |  |  |  |  |
| CAMBRIDGE TRAD ACUPUNC CENTRE (HM03578) |  |  |  |  |  |  |  |  |  |  |  |  |  |  |  |  |  |  |  |  |  |  |  |  |  |  |  |  |  |  |  |  |  |  |  |  |  |  |  |  |  |  |  |  |  |  |  |  | ● |
| CHIROPRATIC & HOM HEALTH CTRE (HM04408) |  |  |  |  |  |  |  |  |  |  |  |  |  |  |  |  |  |  |  |  |  |  |  |  |  |  |  |  |  |  | ● |  |  |  |  |  |  |  |  |  |  |  |  |  |  |  |  |  |  |
| CLIPSHAM, VANESSA (HM04721) |  |  |  |  |  |  |  |  |  |  |  |  |  |  |  |  |  | ● |  |  |  |  |  |  |  |  |  |  |  |  |  |  |  |  |  |  |  |  |  |  |  |  |  |  |  |  |  |  |  |
| COHEN, DAVID (HM04791) |  |  | ● |  |  |  |  |  |  |  |  |  |  |  |  |  |  |  |  |  |  |  |  |  |  |  |  |  |  |  |  |  |  |  |  |  |  |  |  |  |  |  |  |  |  |  |  |  |  |
| COMPLEMENTARY HEALTH CLINIC (HM04927) |  |  | ● |  |  |  |  |  |  |  |  |  |  |  |  |  |  | ● |  |  |  |  |  |  |  |  |  |  |  |  |  |  |  |  |  |  |  |  |  |  |  |  |  |  |  |  |  |  |  |
| CUTTING, VALERIE (HM05648) |  |  |  |  |  |  |  |  |  |  |  |  |  |  |  |  |  | ● |  |  |  |  |  |  |  |  |  |  |  |  |  |  |  |  |  |  |  |  |  |  |  |  |  |  |  |  |  |  |  |
| DIXON, GAYLE (HM06127) |  |  | ● |  |  |  |  |  |  |  |  |  |  |  |  |  |  |  |  |  |  |  |  |  |  |  |  |  |  |  |  |  |  |  |  |  |  |  |  |  |  |  |  |  |  |  |  |  |  |
| FAULKNER, CINDY (HM07141) |  |  |  |  |  |  |  |  |  |  |  |  |  |  |  |  |  |  |  |  |  |  |  |  |  | ● |  |  |  |  |  |  |  |  |  |  |  |  |  |  |  |  |  |  |  |  |  |  |  |
| GENTRY, V (HM07982) |  |  |  |  |  |  |  |  |  |  |  |  |  |  | ● |  |  |  |  |  |  |  |  |  |  |  |  |  |  |  |  |  |  |  |  |  |  |  |  |  |  |  |  |  |  |  |  |  |  |
| GILBERT RD OSTEOPATHIC (HM08055) |  |  | ● |  |  |  |  |  |  |  |  |  |  |  |  |  |  |  |  |  |  |  |  |  |  |  |  |  |  |  |  |  |  |  |  |  |  |  |  |  |  |  |  |  |  |  |  |  |  |
| GORDON, JOSEPH (HM08278) |  |  |  |  |  |  |  |  |  |  |  |  |  |  |  |  |  | ● |  |  |  |  |  |  |  |  |  |  |  |  |  |  |  |  |  |  |  |  |  |  |  |  |  |  |  |  |  |  |  |
| HARMAN, ABIGAIL (HM09012) |  |  |  |  |  |  |  |  |  |  |  |  |  |  |  |  |  | ● |  |  |  |  |  |  |  |  |  |  |  |  |  |  |  |  |  |  |  |  |  |  |  |  |  |  |  |  |  |  |  |
| HATTERSLEY, DAVID (HM09199) |  |  | ● |  |  |  |  |  |  |  |  |  |  |  |  |  |  |  |  |  |  |  |  |  |  |  |  |  |  |  |  |  |  |  |  |  |  |  |  |  |  |  |  |  |  |  |  |  |  |
| HEAL, CHRISTIANNE (HM09313) |  |  |  |  |  |  |  |  |  |  |  |  |  |  | ● |  |  | ● |  |  |  |  |  |  |  |  |  |  |  |  |  |  |  |  |  |  |  |  |  |  |  |  |  |  |  |  |  |  |  |
| HEALTH TEAM (HM09406) |  |  |  |  |  |  | ● |  |  | ● |  |  |  |  | ● |  |  | ● | ● | ● |  |  |  |  |  |  |  | ● |  |  | ● |  |  |  |  |  |  |  |  | ● | ● | ● | ● |  |  |  |  |  |  |
| HUNT, PHILLIP R (HM10402) |  |  | ● |  |  |  |  |  |  |  |  |  |  |  |  |  |  |  |  |  |  |  |  |  |  |  |  |  |  |  |  |  |  |  |  |  |  |  |  |  |  |  |  |  |  |  |  |  |  |
| HUNTINGDON COMPLEMENTARY (HM10411) |  |  | ● |  |  |  |  |  |  |  |  |  |  |  |  |  |  |  |  |  |  |  |  |  |  |  |  |  |  |  |  |  |  |  |  |  |  |  |  |  |  |  |  |  |  |  |  |  |  |
| HUSEIN, JIWA (DR) (HM10433) |  |  | ● |  |  |  |  |  |  |  |  |  |  |  |  |  |  |  |  |  |  |  |  |  |  |  |  |  |  |  |  |  |  |  |  |  |  |  |  |  |  |  |  |  |  |  |  |  |  |
| HYPNOSIS AND HEALTH (HM10495) |  |  |  |  |  |  |  |  |  |  |  |  |  |  | ● |  |  |  |  |  |  |  |  |  |  |  |  |  |  |  | ● |  |  |  |  |  |  |  |  |  |  |  |  |  |  |  |  |  |  |
| INGHAM, NICHOLAS (HM10619) |  |  |  |  |  |  |  |  |  |  |  |  |  |  | ● |  |  |  |  |  |  |  |  |  |  |  |  |  |  |  |  |  |  |  |  |  |  |  |  |  |  |  |  |  |  |  |  |  |  |
| JOHNSON, ANNE (HM11067) |  |  | ● |  |  |  |  |  |  |  |  |  |  |  |  |  |  |  |  |  |  |  |  |  |  |  |  |  |  |  |  |  |  |  |  |  |  |  |  |  |  |  |  |  |  |  |  |  |  |
| JURY, CATHY (HM11275) |  |  |  |  |  |  |  |  |  |  |  |  |  |  |  |  |  | ● |  |  |  |  |  |  |  |  |  |  |  |  |  |  |  |  |  |  |  |  |  |  |  |  |  |  |  |  |  |  |  |
| LANT, JOHN & PARTNERS (HM11967) |  |  | ● |  |  |  |  |  |  |  |  |  |  |  |  |  |  |  |  |  |  |  |  |  |  |  |  |  |  |  |  |  |  |  |  |  |  |  |  |  |  |  |  |  |  |  |  |  |  |
| LIFELINE (HM12354) |  |  |  |  |  |  |  |  |  |  |  |  |  |  | ● |  |  |  |  |  |  |  |  |  |  |  |  |  | ● |  | ● |  |  |  |  |  |  |  |  |  |  |  |  |  |  |  |  |  |  |
| LIZ HALE HANDSON HEALTH (HM12495) |  |  |  |  |  |  |  |  |  |  |  |  |  |  |  |  |  | ● |  | ● |  |  |  | ● |  |  |  |  |  |  |  |  |  |  |  |  |  |  |  |  | ● |  |  |  |  |  |  |  |  |
| MAJOR, ROSEMARY (HM12954) |  |  |  |  |  |  |  |  |  |  |  |  |  |  |  |  |  | ● |  |  |  |  |  |  |  |  |  |  |  |  |  |  |  |  |  |  |  |  |  |  |  |  |  |  |  |  |  |  |  |
| MASON, J W (HM13243) |  |  | ● |  |  |  |  |  |  |  |  |  |  |  |  |  |  |  |  |  |  |  |  |  |  |  |  |  |  |  |  |  |  |  |  |  |  |  |  |  |  |  |  |  |  |  |  |  |  |
| MATHIESON, M A (HM13290) |  |  |  |  |  |  |  |  |  | ● |  |  |  |  |  |  |  |  |  |  |  |  |  |  |  |  |  |  |  |  |  |  |  |  |  |  |  |  |  |  |  |  |  |  |  |  |  |  |  |
| MAYNARD, SUSANNE (HM13358) |  |  |  |  |  |  | ● |  |  |  |  |  |  |  |  |  |  |  |  |  |  |  |  |  |  |  |  |  |  |  |  |  |  |  |  |  |  |  |  |  |  |  |  |  |  |  |  |  |  |

# O - Z Therapies at Practices/Businesses

| Business by County with Reference no. | Orthotics | Osteomyology | Osteopathy | PAM | Paranormal Therapies | Pattern Therapies | Physiotherapy | Phytotherapy | Pilates | Podiatry | Polarity Therapy | Postural Integration | Primal Therapy | Psionic Therapy | Psychotherapy | Pyramid Power | Pyscho-Synthesis | Reflexology | Reichian Therapy | Reiki | Remedial Massage | Rogerian Therapy | Rolfing | Seichem | Sensitivity Training | Shiatsu | Silva Method | Sound Therapy | Spiritual Healing | Sports Massage | Stress Therapy | Swedish Body Massage | T'ai-Chi Ch'uan | Tantra Therapy | Tera-Mai | Thought Field Therapy | Touch Therapy | Transactional Analysis | Tui-na | Ultrasonics | Vibrational Therapy | Visualisation Therapy | Vitamin Therapy | Voice Therapy | X-Ray | Ying & Yang | Yoga | Zen Therapy | Zero Balancing |
|---|---|---|---|---|---|---|---|---|---|---|---|---|---|---|---|---|---|---|---|---|---|---|---|---|---|---|---|---|---|---|---|---|---|---|---|---|---|---|---|---|---|---|---|---|---|---|---|---|---|
| MCDOUALL, VERONICA (HM13464) | | | | | | | | | | | | | | | ● | | | | | | | | | | | | | | | | | | | | | | | | | | | | | | | | | | |
| MORRIS & ASSOCIATES (HM14198) | | | ● | | | | ● | ● | ● | | | | | | ● | | | ● | | | | | | | | | | | | | | | | | | | | | | | | | | | | | | | |
| OXBOROUGH, JOY (HM15536) | | | | | | | | | | | | | | | | | | ● | | | | | | | | | | | | | | | | | | | | | | | | | | | | | | | |
| PAIN, JEAN (HM15582) | | | | | | | | | | | | | | | ● | | | | | | | | | | | | | | | | | | | | | | | | | | | | | | | | | | |
| PHIL SEAL PSYCHOTHERAPY (HM16115) | | | | | | | | | | | | | | | ● | | | | | | | | | | | | | | | | ● | | | | | | | | | | | ● | | | | | | | |
| PIKE, ROGER (HM16289) | | | ● | | | | | | | | | | | | | | | | | | | | | | | | | | | | | | | | | | | | | | | | | | | | | | |
| PRESTONS CHRTRD PHYSIOTHERAPY (HM16560) | | | | | | | ● | | | | | | | | | | | | | | | | | | | | | | | | | | | | | | | | | | | | | | | | | | |
| PROBERT, DIANA (HM16651) | | | | | | | | | | | | | | | | | | | | ● | | | | | | | | | | | | | | | | | | | | | | | | | | | | | |
| RATHBONE, M J (HM16956) | | | ● | | | | | | | | | | | | | | | | | | | | | | | | | | | | | | | | | | | | | | | | | | | | | | |
| REID, SUSAN (HM17121) | | | | | | | | | | | | | | | | | | | | | | | | | | | | | | | ● | | | | | | ● | | | | | | | | | | | | |
| REIKI (HM17126) | | | | | | | | | | | | | | | | | | | | ● | | | | | | | | | | | | | | | | | | | | | | | | | | | | | |
| ROBINSON-ZEL, B (HM17508) | | | | | | | | | | | | | | | ● | | | | | | | | | | | | | | | | | | | | | | | | | | | | | | | | | | |
| RYDER, JULIE (HM17800) | | | | | | | ● | | | | | | | | | | | | | | | | | | | | | | | | | | | | | | | | | | | | | | | | | | |
| SMITH, JEANETTE (HM18752) | | | | | | | | | | | | | | | | | | ● | | | | | | | | | | | | | | | | | | | | | | | | | | | | | | | |
| SPENCE, ALEX (HM18982) | | | ● | | | | | ● | | | | | | | | | | | | | | | | | | | | | | | | | | | | | | | | | | | | | | | | | |
| ST NEOTS OSTEOPATHIC CLINIC (HM19092) | | | ● | | | | | | | | | | | | | | | | | | | | | | | | | | | | | | | | | | | | | | | | | | | | | | |
| STOCKLEY, PHILIP (HM19310) | | | ● | | | | | | | | | | | | | | | | | | | | | | | | | | | | | | | | | | | | | | | | | | | | | | |
| STOCKLEY, PHILIP E (HM19311) | | | ● | | | | | | | | | | | | | | | | | | | | | | | | | | | | | | | | | | | | | | | | | | | | | | |
| SZMELSKYJ, ALAN (HM19636) | | | ● | | | | | | | | | | | | | | | | | | | | | | | | | | | | | | | | | | | | | | | | | | | | | | |
| TAYLOR, CAROLYN (HM19743) | | | ● | | | | | | | | | | | | | | | | | | | | | | | | | | | | | | | | | | | | | | | | | | | | | | |
| TAYLOR, EVE (HM19759) | | | | | | | | | | | | | | | | | | ● | | | | | | | | | | | | | | ● | | | | | | | | | | | | | | | | | |
| TONG, JENNY (HM20154) | | | | | | | | | | | | | | | | | | ● | | | | | | | | | | | | | | | | | | | | | | | | | | | | | | | |
| TRIANCE, E R (HM20326) | | | ● | | | | | | | | | | | | | | | | | | | | | | | | | | | | | | | | | | | | | | | | | | | | | | |
| WESTON, SOPHIE (HM21283) | | | | | | | | | | | | | | | | | | ● | | | | | | | | | | | | | | | | | | | | | | | | | | | | | | | |
| WRIGHT, CLARE (HM21928) | | | | | | | | | | | | | | | | | | ● | | | | | | | | | | | | | | | | | | | | | | | | | | | | | | | |
| **CHESHIRE** | | | | | | | | | | | | | | | | | | | | | | | | | | | | | | | | | | | | | | | | | | | | | | | | | |
| A & H PAIN CLINIC (HM00016) | | | | | | | | | | | | | | | | | | ● | | | | | | | | | | | | | | | | | | | | | | | | | | | | | | | |
| ADULT & CHILD FOOT CLINIC (HM00391) | | | | | | | | | | ● | | | | | | | | | | | | | | | | | | | | | | | | | | | | | | | | | | | | | | | |
| ALEXANDER, A (DR) (HM00558) | | | ● | | | | | | | | | | | | | | | | | | | | | | | | | | | | | | | | | | | | | | | | | | | | | | |
| ALTERNATIVE HEALTH CENTRE (HM00704) | | | ● | | | | | | | | | | | | | | | | | | | | | | | | | | | | | | | | | | | | | | | | | | | | | | |
| AMBLESIDE CLINIC (HM00773) | | | | | | | | | | | | | | | | | | ● | | | | | | | | | | | | | | | | | | | | | | | | | | | | | | | |
| AMELAN, RACHEL (HM00776) | | | | | | | | | | | | | | | | | | ● | | | | | | | | | | | | | | | | | | | | | | | | | | | | | | | |
| ANDREWS, KATHRYN (HM00853) | | | | | | | | | | | | | | | | | | ● | | | | | | | | | | | | | | | | | | | | | | | | | | | | | | | |
| ARNOLD, SUE (HM01038) | | | | | | | | | | | | | | | ● | | | | | | | | | | | | | | | | | | | | | | | | | | | | | | | | | | |

# O - Z Therapies at Practices/Businesses

Business by County with Reference no.

| Business | Orthotics | Osteomyology | Osteopathy | PAM | Paranormal Therapies | Pattern Therapies | Physiotherapy | Phytotherapy | Pilates | Podiatry | Polarity Therapy | Postural Integration | Primal Therapy | Psionic Therapy | Psychotherapy | Pyramid Power |
|---|---|---|---|---|---|---|---|---|---|---|---|---|---|---|---|---|
| AROMASPHERE (HM01083) | | | | | | | | | | | | | | | | |
| ASSOCIATION FOR FAMILY THERAPY (HM01280) | | | | | | | | | | | | | | | ● | |
| ATHERTON, PAUL (HM01314) | | | ● | | | | | | | | | | | | | |
| BACHE CHIROPODY (HM01471) | | | | | | | ● | | | | | | | | | |
| BERESFORD, KATHLEEN (HM02183) | | | | | | | | | | | | | | | | |
| BODYTONE (HM02634) | | | | | | | | | | | | | | | | |
| BOWEN, KAREN (HM02780) | | | | | | | | | | | | | | | | |
| BRAMHALL PARK PHYSIO CLINIC (HM02899) | | | | | | | ● | | | | | | | | | |
| BROWN & PARTNERS OSTEO (HM03206) | | | ● | | | | | | | | | | | | | |
| BURTON, J S (HM03436) | ● | | | | | | | | | | | | | | | |
| BUSH, ANTONY J (HM03460) | | | ● | | | | | | | | | | | | | |
| CARING HANDS (HM03683) | | | | | | | | | | | | | | | | |
| CARMICHAEL CLINIC (HM03708) | | | | | | | ● | | | | | | | | | |
| CHAPEL COURT CENTRE (HM03992) | | | | | | | | | | | | | | | ● | |
| CHEADLE HULME NATURAL HEALTH (HM04070) | | | | | | | | | | | | | | | | |
| CHEANEY, JOANNA C (HM04073) | | | ● | | | | | | | | | | | | | |
| CHESHIRE HEALTH CLINIC (HM04115) | | | ● | | | | | | | | | | | | ● | |
| CHESTER CLINIC (HM04128) | | | | | | | | | | | | | | | ● | |
| CHESTER HEALTH (HM04129) | | | | | | | | | | | | | | | | |
| CHESTER HEALTH & BEAUTY STUDIO (HM04130) | | | | | | | | | | | | | | | | |
| CHESTER THERAPY CENTRE (HM04134) | | | | | | | | | | | | | | | ● | |
| CHIROPODIST SURGERY (HM04295) | ● | | | | | | | | | | | | | | | |
| CLINIC OF ACUPUNCTURE (HM04684) | | | | | | | | | | | | | | | | |
| CONGLETON COUNSELLING PRACTICE (HM04977) | | | | | | | | | | | | | | | ● | |
| CONNOLLY, SANDRA (HM05002) | | | | | | | | | | | | | | | | |
| CONSTANTINE, J C (HM05012) | | | ● | | | | | | | | | | | | | |
| COOPER, GEOFFREY M (HM05106) | | | | | | | | | | | | | | | | |
| CREWE & NANT PHYSIO CLINIC (HM05431) | | | | | | | ● | | | | | | | | | |
| CROPPER, AGNES (HM05473) | | | | | | | | | | | | | | | | |
| CROSSLEY-JONES, SYLVIA (HM05490) | | | | | | | | | | | | | | | ● | |
| DAINTREE, FREDERICA JEAN (HM05675) | | | | | | | | | | | | | | | ● | |
| DAVIES & ASSOCIATES (HM05791) | | | ● | | | | | | | | | | | | | |
| DAVIES, M K (HM05828) | | | ● | | | | | | | | | | | | | |
| DENNING, MICHAEL (HM05987) | | | | | | | | | | | | | | | ● | |

| Business | Pyscho-Synthesis | Reflexology | Reichian Therapy | Reiki | Remedial Massage | Rogerian Therapy | Rolfing | Seichem | Sensitivity Training | Shiatsu | Silva Method | Sound Therapy | Spiritual Healing | Sports Massage | Stress Therapy | Swedish Body Massage |
|---|---|---|---|---|---|---|---|---|---|---|---|---|---|---|---|---|
| AROMASPHERE (HM01083) | | ● | | | | | | | | | | | | | | |
| ASSOCIATION FOR FAMILY THERAPY (HM01280) | | | | | | | | | | | | | | | | |
| ATHERTON, PAUL (HM01314) | | | | | | | | | | | | | | | | |
| BACHE CHIROPODY (HM01471) | | | | | | | | | | | | | | | | |
| BERESFORD, KATHLEEN (HM02183) | | ● | | | | | | | | | | | | | | |
| BODYTONE (HM02634) | | ● | | ● | | | | | | | | | | | | |
| BOWEN, KAREN (HM02780) | | ● | | | | | | | | | | | | | | |
| BRAMHALL PARK PHYSIO CLINIC (HM02899) | | | | | | | | | | | | | | | | |
| BROWN & PARTNERS OSTEO (HM03206) | | | | | | | | | | | | | | | | |
| BURTON, J S (HM03436) | | | | | | | | | | | | | | | | |
| BUSH, ANTONY J (HM03460) | | | | | | | | | | | | | | | | |
| CARING HANDS (HM03683) | | ● | | | ● | | | | | | | | | | | |
| CARMICHAEL CLINIC (HM03708) | | | | | | | | | | | | | | | | |
| CHAPEL COURT CENTRE (HM03992) | | | | | | | | | | | | | | | | |
| CHEADLE HULME NATURAL HEALTH (HM04070) | | ● | | ● | | | | | | | | | | | ● | |
| CHEANEY, JOANNA C (HM04073) | | | | | | | | | | | | | | | | |
| CHESHIRE HEALTH CLINIC (HM04115) | | | | | | | | | | | | | | | | |
| CHESTER CLINIC (HM04128) | | ● | | ● | | | | | | ● | | | | | | |
| CHESTER HEALTH (HM04129) | | ● | | ● | | | | | | | | | | | | |
| CHESTER HEALTH & BEAUTY STUDIO (HM04130) | | ● | | ● | | | | | | | | | | | | |
| CHESTER THERAPY CENTRE (HM04134) | | | | | | | | | | | | | | | | |
| CHIROPODIST SURGERY (HM04295) | | | | | | | | | | | | | | | | |
| CLINIC OF ACUPUNCTURE (HM04684) | | | | | | | | | | | | | | | | |
| CONGLETON COUNSELLING PRACTICE (HM04977) | | | | | | ● | | | | | | | | | ● | |
| CONNOLLY, SANDRA (HM05002) | | ● | | | | | | | | | | | | | | |
| CONSTANTINE, J C (HM05012) | | | | | | | | | | | | | | | | |
| COOPER, GEOFFREY M (HM05106) | | ● | | | | | | | | | | | | | | |
| CREWE & NANT PHYSIO CLINIC (HM05431) | | | | | | | | | | | | | | | | |
| CROPPER, AGNES (HM05473) | | ● | | | | | | | | | | | | | | |
| CROSSLEY-JONES, SYLVIA (HM05490) | | | | | | | | | | | | | | | | |
| DAINTREE, FREDERICA JEAN (HM05675) | | | | | | | | | | | | | | | | |
| DAVIES & ASSOCIATES (HM05791) | | | | | | | ● | | | | | | | | | |
| DAVIES, M K (HM05828) | | | | | | | | | | | | | | | | |
| DENNING, MICHAEL (HM05987) | | | | | | | | | | | | | | | | |

| Business | T'ai-Chi Ch'uan | Tantra Therapy | Tera-Mai | Thought Field Therapy | Touch Therapy | Transactional Analysis | Tui-na | Ultrasonics | Vibrational Therapy | Visualisation Therapy | Vitamin Therapy | Voice Therapy | X-Ray | Ying & Yang | Yoga | Zen Therapy | Zero Balancing |
|---|---|---|---|---|---|---|---|---|---|---|---|---|---|---|---|---|---|
| AROMASPHERE (HM01083) | | | | | | | | | | | | | | | | | |
| ASSOCIATION FOR FAMILY THERAPY (HM01280) | | | | | | | | | | | | | | | | | |
| ATHERTON, PAUL (HM01314) | | | | | | | | | | | | | | | | | |
| BACHE CHIROPODY (HM01471) | | | | | | | | | | | | | | | | | |
| BERESFORD, KATHLEEN (HM02183) | | | | | | | | | | | | | | | | | |
| BODYTONE (HM02634) | | | | | | | | | | | | | | | | | |
| BOWEN, KAREN (HM02780) | | | | | | | | | | | | | | | | | |
| BRAMHALL PARK PHYSIO CLINIC (HM02899) | | | | | | | | | | | | | | | | | |
| BROWN & PARTNERS OSTEO (HM03206) | | | | | | | | | | | | | | | | | |
| BURTON, J S (HM03436) | | | | | | | | | | | | | | | | | |
| BUSH, ANTONY J (HM03460) | | | | | | | | | | | | | | | | | |
| CARING HANDS (HM03683) | | | | | | | | | | | | | | | | | |
| CARMICHAEL CLINIC (HM03708) | | | | | | | | ● | | | | | | | | | |
| CHAPEL COURT CENTRE (HM03992) | | | | | | | | | | | | | | | | | |
| CHEADLE HULME NATURAL HEALTH (HM04070) | | | | | | | | | | | | | | | | | |
| CHEANEY, JOANNA C (HM04073) | | | | | | | | | | | | | | | | | |
| CHESHIRE HEALTH CLINIC (HM04115) | | | | | | | | | | | | | | | | | |
| CHESTER CLINIC (HM04128) | | | | | | | | | | | ● | | | | | | |
| CHESTER HEALTH (HM04129) | | | | | ● | | | | | | ● | | | | | | |
| CHESTER HEALTH & BEAUTY STUDIO (HM04130) | | | | | ● | | | | | | ● | | | | | | |
| CHESTER THERAPY CENTRE (HM04134) | | | | | | | | | | | | | | | | | |
| CHIROPODIST SURGERY (HM04295) | | | | | | | | | | | | | | | | | |
| CLINIC OF ACUPUNCTURE (HM04684) | | | | | | | | | | | | | | ● | | | |
| CONGLETON COUNSELLING PRACTICE (HM04977) | | | | | | | | | | | | | | | | | |
| CONNOLLY, SANDRA (HM05002) | | | | | | | | | | | | | | | | | |
| CONSTANTINE, J C (HM05012) | | | | | | | | | | | | | | | | | |
| COOPER, GEOFFREY M (HM05106) | | | | | | | | | | | | | | | | | |
| CREWE & NANT PHYSIO CLINIC (HM05431) | | | | | | | | | | | | | | | | | |
| CROPPER, AGNES (HM05473) | | | | | | | | | | | | | | | | | |
| CROSSLEY-JONES, SYLVIA (HM05490) | | | | | | | | | | | | | | | | | |
| DAINTREE, FREDERICA JEAN (HM05675) | | | | | | | | | | | | | | | | | |
| DAVIES & ASSOCIATES (HM05791) | | | | | | | | | | | | | | | | | |
| DAVIES, M K (HM05828) | | | | | | | | | | | | | | | | | |
| DENNING, MICHAEL (HM05987) | | | | | | | | | | | | | | | | | |

# O - Z Therapies at Practices/Businesses

| Business by County with Reference no. | Orthotics | Osteomyology | Osteopathy | PAM | Paranormal Therapies | Pattern Therapies | Physiotherapy | Phytotherapy | Pilates | Podiatry | Polarity Therapy | Postural Integration | Primal Therapy | Psionic Therapy | Psychotherapy | Pyramid Power | Pyscho-Synthesis |
|---|---|---|---|---|---|---|---|---|---|---|---|---|---|---|---|---|---|
| DICKMAN, KAREN (HM06081) | | | | | | | | | | | | | | | | | |
| EDDIE, DAVID (HM06586) | | | ● | | | | | | | | | | | | | | |
| EDDIE, DAVID (HM06585) | | | ● | | | | | | | | | | | | | | |
| ELSON, MONICA (HM06786) | | | | | | | | | | | | | | | ● | | |
| EVANS, DI (HM06968) | | | | | | | | | | | | | | | | | |
| EYRE, JACQUELINE (HM07029) | | | | | | | | | | | | | | | | | |
| FAGAN, B W (HM07042) | | | | | | | ● | | | | | | | | | | |
| FAROOQ AHMED, KHAN (HM07114) | | | ● | | | | | | | | | | | | | | |
| FIELD VIEW SURGERY (HM07259) | ● | | | | | | | | | | | | | | | | |
| FILLAUDEAU, SARAH-JAYNE (HM07291) | | | | | | | | | | | | | | | | | |
| FIVE WAYS OSTEOPATHIC SURGERY (HM07381) | | | ● | | | | | | | | | | | | | | |
| FULLER, HILARY (HM07789) | | | | | | | | | | | | | | | | | |
| GARDINER, JOHN MICHAEL (HM07873) | | | ● | | | | | | | | | | | | | | |
| GEORGE, DIANA (HM07990) | | | | | | | | | | | | | | | | | |
| GIBBS, NICOLA (HM08031) | | | | | | | | | | | | | | | | | |
| GLENDON, NOEL (HM08149) | | | | | | | | | | | | | | | ● | | |
| GRACE & ASSOCIATES (HM08331) | | | | | | | | | | ● | | | | | | | |
| GRAHAM COOMBE - MCTIMONEY (HM08338) | | | | | | | | | | | | | | | | | |
| HALE, STUART (HM08741) | | | ● | | | | | | | | | | | | | | |
| HAMMOND, ANNE (HM08866) | | | | | | | | | | | | | | | | | |
| HANDS ON PHYSIOTHERAPY (HM08913) | | | | | | | ● | | | | | | | | | | |
| HARDIE, LYNN (HM08967) | | | | | | | | | | | | | | | | | |
| HAYWARD, SOPHIE (HM09286) | | | | | | | | | | | | | | | | | |
| HAZELDENE, BARBARA (HM09292) | | | | | | | | | | | | | | | | | |
| HEWITT, C A (HM09704) | | | ● | | | | | | | | | | | | | | |
| HORNER, MARGARET (HM10180) | | | ● | | | | | | | | | | | | | | |
| HOWDEN, ELIZABETH (HM10259) | | | | | | | | | | | | | | | | | |
| HOWE, BARBARA (HM10261) | | | | | | | | | | | | | | | ● | | |
| HYPNOS PRACTICE (HM10492) | | | | | | | | | | | | | | | | | |
| JANE HAMMOND THERAPY (HM10916) | | | | | | | | | | | | | | | ● | | |
| JENKINSON, LEILA (HM10999) | | | | | | | | | | | | | | | | | |
| JOHNSON, ANDREW N (HM11066) | | | ● | | | | | | | | | | | | | | |
| JONES, J W (HM11155) | | | | | | | | | | ● | | | | | | | |
| JONES, JOYCE (HM11160) | | | | | | | | | | | | | | | | | |

| Business by County with Reference no. | Reflexology | Reichian Therapy | Reiki | Remedial Massage | Rogerian Therapy | Rolfing | Seichem | Sensitivity Training | Shiatsu | Silva Method | Sound Therapy | Spiritual Healing | Sports Massage | Stress Therapy | Swedish Body Massage | T'ai-Chi Ch'uan |
|---|---|---|---|---|---|---|---|---|---|---|---|---|---|---|---|---|
| DICKMAN, KAREN (HM06081) | ● | | | | | | | | | | | | | | | |
| EDDIE, DAVID (HM06586) | | | | | | | | | | | | | | | | |
| EDDIE, DAVID (HM06585) | | | | | | | | | | | | | | | | |
| ELSON, MONICA (HM06786) | | | | | | | | | | | | | | | | |
| EVANS, DI (HM06968) | ● | | ● | | | | | | | | | | | | | |
| EYRE, JACQUELINE (HM07029) | ● | | | | | | | | | | | | | | | |
| FAGAN, B W (HM07042) | | | | | | | | | | | | | | | | |
| FAROOQ AHMED, KHAN (HM07114) | | | | | | | | | | | | | | | | |
| FIELD VIEW SURGERY (HM07259) | ● | | | | | | | | | | | | | | | |
| FILLAUDEAU, SARAH-JAYNE (HM07291) | ● | | | | | | | | | | | | | | | |
| FIVE WAYS OSTEOPATHIC SURGERY (HM07381) | | | | | | | | | | | | | | | | |
| FULLER, HILARY (HM07789) | ● | | | | | | | | | | | | | | | |
| GARDINER, JOHN MICHAEL (HM07873) | | | | | | | | | | | | | | | | |
| GEORGE, DIANA (HM07990) | ● | | | | | | | | | | | | | | | |
| GIBBS, NICOLA (HM08031) | ● | | | | | | | | | | | | | | | |
| GLENDON, NOEL (HM08149) | | | | | | | | | | | | | | | | |
| GRACE & ASSOCIATES (HM08331) | | | | | | | | | | | | | | | | |
| GRAHAM COOMBE - MCTIMONEY (HM08338) | | | ● | | | | | | | | | | | | | |
| HALE, STUART (HM08741) | | | | | | | | | | | | | | | | |
| HAMMOND, ANNE (HM08866) | ● | | | | | | | | | | | | | | | |
| HANDS ON PHYSIOTHERAPY (HM08913) | | | | | | | | | | | | | | | | |
| HARDIE, LYNN (HM08967) | ● | | | | | | | | | | | | | | | |
| HAYWARD, SOPHIE (HM09286) | ● | | | | | | | | | | | | | | | |
| HAZELDENE, BARBARA (HM09292) | ● | | | | | | | | | | | | | | | |
| HEWITT, C A (HM09704) | | | | | | | | | | | | | | | | |
| HORNER, MARGARET (HM10180) | | | | | | | | | | | | | | | | |
| HOWDEN, ELIZABETH (HM10259) | ● | | | | | | | | | | | | | | | |
| HOWE, BARBARA (HM10261) | ● | | | | | | | | | | | | | | | |
| HYPNOS PRACTICE (HM10492) | | | | | | | | | | | | | | ● | | |
| JANE HAMMOND THERAPY (HM10916) | | | | | ● | | | | | | | | | | | |
| JENKINSON, LEILA (HM10999) | ● | | | | | | | | | | | | | | | |
| JOHNSON, ANDREW N (HM11066) | | | | | | | | | | | | | | | | |
| JONES, J W (HM11155) | | | | | | | | | | | | | | | | |
| JONES, JOYCE (HM11160) | ● | | | | | | | | | | | | | | | |

| Business by County with Reference no. | Tantra Therapy | Tera-Mai | Thought Field Therapy | Touch Therapy | Transactional Analysis | Tui-na | Ultrasonics | Vibrational Therapy | Visualisation Therapy | Vitamin Therapy | Voice Therapy | X-Ray | Ying & Yang | Yoga | Zen Therapy | Zero Balancing |
|---|---|---|---|---|---|---|---|---|---|---|---|---|---|---|---|---|
| DICKMAN, KAREN (HM06081) | | | | | | | | | | | | | | | | |
| EDDIE, DAVID (HM06586) | | | | | | | | | | | | | | | | |
| EDDIE, DAVID (HM06585) | | | | | | | | | | | | | | | | |
| ELSON, MONICA (HM06786) | | | | | | | | | | | | | | | | |
| EVANS, DI (HM06968) | | | | | | | | | | | | | | | | |
| EYRE, JACQUELINE (HM07029) | | | | | | | | | | | | | | | | |
| FAGAN, B W (HM07042) | | | | | | | ● | | | | | | | | | |
| FAROOQ AHMED, KHAN (HM07114) | | | | | | | | | | | | | | | | |
| FIELD VIEW SURGERY (HM07259) | | | | | | | | | | | | | | | | |
| FILLAUDEAU, SARAH-JAYNE (HM07291) | | | | | | | | | | | | | | | | |
| FIVE WAYS OSTEOPATHIC SURGERY (HM07381) | | | | | | | | | | | | | | | | |
| FULLER, HILARY (HM07789) | | | | | | | | | | | | | | | | |
| GARDINER, JOHN MICHAEL (HM07873) | | | | | | | | | | | | | | | | |
| GEORGE, DIANA (HM07990) | | | | | | | | | | | | | | | | |
| GIBBS, NICOLA (HM08031) | | | | | | | | | | | | | | | | |
| GLENDON, NOEL (HM08149) | | | | | | | | | | | | | | | | |
| GRACE & ASSOCIATES (HM08331) | | | | | | | | | | | | | | | | |
| GRAHAM COOMBE - MCTIMONEY (HM08338) | | | | | | | | | | | | | | | | |
| HALE, STUART (HM08741) | | | | | | | | | | | | | | | | |
| HAMMOND, ANNE (HM08866) | | | | | | | | | | | | | | | | |
| HANDS ON PHYSIOTHERAPY (HM08913) | | | | | | | | | | | | | | | | |
| HARDIE, LYNN (HM08967) | | | | | | | | | | | | | | | | |
| HAYWARD, SOPHIE (HM09286) | | | | | | | | | | | | | | | | |
| HAZELDENE, BARBARA (HM09292) | | | | | | | | | | | | | | | | |
| HEWITT, C A (HM09704) | | | | | | | | | | | | | | | | |
| HORNER, MARGARET (HM10180) | | | | | | | | | | | | | | | | |
| HOWDEN, ELIZABETH (HM10259) | | | | | | | | | | | | | | | | |
| HOWE, BARBARA (HM10261) | | | | | | | | | | | | | | | | |
| HYPNOS PRACTICE (HM10492) | | | | | | | | | ● | | | | | | | |
| JANE HAMMOND THERAPY (HM10916) | | | | | ● | | | | | | | | | | | |
| JENKINSON, LEILA (HM10999) | | | | | | | | | | | | | | | | |
| JOHNSON, ANDREW N (HM11066) | | | | | | | | | | | | | | | | |
| JONES, J W (HM11155) | | | | | | | | | | | | | | | | |
| JONES, JOYCE (HM11160) | | | | | | | | | | | | | | | | |

# O - Z Therapies at Practices/Businesses

| Business by County with Reference no. | Orthotics | Osteomyology | Osteopathy | PAM | Paranormal Therapies | Pattern Therapies | Physiotherapy | Phytotherapy | Pilates | Podiatry | Polarity Therapy | Postural Integration | Primal Therapy | Psionic Therapy | Psychotherapy | Pyramid Power |
|---|---|---|---|---|---|---|---|---|---|---|---|---|---|---|---|---|
| KAYE, JANET (HM11359) | | | | | | | | | | | | | | | | |
| KENYON, JACELYN (HM11536) | | | | | | | | | | | | | | | | |
| KERR, A N F (HM11547) | | | ● | | | | | | | | | | | | | |
| KNUTSFORD CHIROPRACTIC CLINIC (HM11775) | | | | | | | | | | | | | | | | |
| LINKS CLINIC (HM12437) | | | ● | | | | | | | | | | | | | |
| LOMAS, CLIFFORD (HM12574) | | | ● | | | | | | | | | | | | | |
| LYON, ANDREW (HM12778) | | | ● | | | | | | | | | | | | | |
| MARCH, JANIS (HM13068) | | | | | | | | | | | | | | | | |
| MCCORMICK, BRIAN (HM13423) | | | ● | | | | | | | | | | | | | |
| MCDONALD, MARGARET (HM13460) | | | | | | | | | | | | | | | | |
| MEHREZ, ANITA (HM13693) | | | | | | | | | | | | | | | | |
| MEREDITH, DAVID (HM13737) | | | ● | | | | | | | | | | | | | |
| MIDDLETON & ASSOCIATES (HM13817) | | | | | | | ● | | | | | | | | | |
| MORTON, J V (HM14251) | | | | | | | | | | ● | | | | | | |
| NATURAL HEALTH CLINIC (HM14584) | | | ● | | | | | | | | | | | | | |
| NEW LIFE NATURAL HEALTH CARE (HM14821) | | | | | | | | | ● | | | | | | | |
| NEWTON, J C (HM14898) | | | | | | | | | | ● | | | | | | |
| NORTH WEST LIFESTYLE MNGMT (HM15043) | | | | | | | | | | | | | | | | |
| NUTRITION AND ALLERGY CLINIC (HM15121) | | | | | | | | | | | | | | | | |
| OLD HALL CLINIC (HM15256) | | | ● | | | | | | | | | | | | ● | |
| OLDHAM, TERRY (HM15270) | | | | | | | | | | | | | | | | |
| PALOMBELLA, SARAH (HM15623) | | | | | | | | | | | | | | | | |
| PANK, SARAH (HM15635) | | | ● | | | | | | | | | | | | | |
| PAOLA WEINBERG SYLT (HM15640) | | | | | | | | | | | | | | | | |
| PATON, W A (HM15825) | | | | | | | ● | | | | | | | | | |
| PHOENIX CENTRE (HM16154) | | | | | | | | | | | | | | | | |
| PHYSIO & SPORTS INJURY CLINIC (HM16181) | | | | | | | | | | | | | | | | |
| PHYSIO PLUS (HM16203) | | | | | | | ● | | | ● | | | | | | |
| PHYSIO SPORTS INJURY CLINIC (HM16209) | | | | | | | ● | | | | | | | | | |
| PREW, BEVERLEY (HM16566) | | | | | | | | | | | | | | | | |
| PROTHERO, PEGGY (HM16672) | | | | | | | | | | | | | | | ● | |
| PULMAN, SUZETTE (HM16755) | | | ● | | | | | | | | | | | | | |
| QUINTON, R M (HM16818) | | | ● | | | | | | | | | | | | | |
| REDGRAVE, KENNETH (HM17025) | | | | | | | | | | | | | | | ● | |

| Business by County with Reference no. | Pyscho-Synthesis | Reflexology | Reichian Therapy | Reiki | Remedial Massage | Rogerian Therapy | Rolfing | Seichem | Sensitivity Training | Shiatsu | Silva Method | Sound Therapy | Spiritual Healing | Sports Massage | Stress Therapy | Swedish Body Massage |
|---|---|---|---|---|---|---|---|---|---|---|---|---|---|---|---|---|
| KAYE, JANET (HM11359) | | ● | | | | | | | | | | | | | | |
| KENYON, JACELYN (HM11536) | | ● | | | | | | | | | | | | | | |
| KERR, A N F (HM11547) | | | | | | | | | | | | | | | | |
| KNUTSFORD CHIROPRACTIC CLINIC (HM11775) | | ● | | ● | | | | | | | | | ● | | | |
| LINKS CLINIC (HM12437) | | | | | | | | | | | | | | | | |
| LOMAS, CLIFFORD (HM12574) | | | | | | | | | | | | | | | | |
| LYON, ANDREW (HM12778) | | | | | | | | | | | | | | | | |
| MARCH, JANIS (HM13068) | | ● | | | | | | | | | | | | | | |
| MCCORMICK, BRIAN (HM13423) | | | | | | | | | | | | | | | | |
| MCDONALD, MARGARET (HM13460) | | ● | | | | | | | | | | | | | | |
| MEHREZ, ANITA (HM13693) | | ● | | | | | | | | | | | | | | |
| MEREDITH, DAVID (HM13737) | | | | | | | | | | | | | | | | |
| MIDDLETON & ASSOCIATES (HM13817) | | | | | | | | | | | | | | | | |
| MORTON, J V (HM14251) | | | | | | | | | | | | | | | | |
| NATURAL HEALTH CLINIC (HM14584) | | | | | | | | | | | | | | | | |
| NEW LIFE NATURAL HEALTH CARE (HM14821) | | ● | | | | | | | | | | | | | | |
| NEWTON, J C (HM14898) | | | | | | | | | | | | | | | | |
| NORTH WEST LIFESTYLE MNGMT (HM15043) | | | | | | | | | | | | | | | ● | |
| NUTRITION AND ALLERGY CLINIC (HM15121) | | | | | | | | | | | | | | | | |
| OLD HALL CLINIC (HM15256) | | | | | | | | | | | | | | | | |
| OLDHAM, TERRY (HM15270) | | ● | | | | | | | | | | | | | | |
| PALOMBELLA, SARAH (HM15623) | | ● | | | | | | | | | | | | | | |
| PANK, SARAH (HM15635) | | | | | | | | | | | | | | | | |
| PAOLA WEINBERG SYLT (HM15640) | | ● | | | | | | | | | | | | | | |
| PATON, W A (HM15825) | | | | | | | | | | | | | | | | |
| PHOENIX CENTRE (HM16154) | | | | | | | | | | | | | ● | | | |
| PHYSIO & SPORTS INJURY CLINIC (HM16181) | | | | | | | | | | | | | | | | |
| PHYSIO PLUS (HM16203) | | | | | | | | | | | | | | | | |
| PHYSIO SPORTS INJURY CLINIC (HM16209) | | | | | | | | | | | | | | | | |
| PREW, BEVERLEY (HM16566) | | | | ● | ● | | | | | | | | | | | |
| PROTHERO, PEGGY (HM16672) | | | | | | | | | | | | | | | | |
| PULMAN, SUZETTE (HM16755) | | | | | | | | | | | | | | | | |
| QUINTON, R M (HM16818) | | | | | | | | | | | | | | | | |
| REDGRAVE, KENNETH (HM17025) | | | | | | | | | | | | | | | | |

| Business by County with Reference no. | T'ai-Chi Ch'uan | Tantra Therapy | Tera-Mai | Thought Field Therapy | Touch Therapy | Transactional Analysis | Tui-na | Ultrasonics | Vibrational Therapy | Visualisation Therapy | Vitamin Therapy | Voice Therapy | X-Ray | Ying & Yang | Yoga | Zen Therapy | Zero Balancing |
|---|---|---|---|---|---|---|---|---|---|---|---|---|---|---|---|---|---|
| KAYE, JANET (HM11359) | | | | | | | | | | | | | | | | | |
| KENYON, JACELYN (HM11536) | | | | | | | | | | | | | | | | | |
| KERR, A N F (HM11547) | | | | | | | | | | | | | | | | | |
| KNUTSFORD CHIROPRACTIC CLINIC (HM11775) | | | | | | | | | | ● | | | ● | | ● | | ● |
| LINKS CLINIC (HM12437) | | | | | | | | | | | | | | | | | |
| LOMAS, CLIFFORD (HM12574) | | | | | | | | | | | | | | | | | |
| LYON, ANDREW (HM12778) | | | | | | | | | | | | | | | | | |
| MARCH, JANIS (HM13068) | | | | | | | | | | | | | | | | | |
| MCCORMICK, BRIAN (HM13423) | | | | | | | | | | | | | | | | | |
| MCDONALD, MARGARET (HM13460) | | | | | | | | | | | | | | | | | |
| MEHREZ, ANITA (HM13693) | | | | | | | | | | | | | | | | | |
| MEREDITH, DAVID (HM13737) | | | | | | | | | | | | | | | | | |
| MIDDLETON & ASSOCIATES (HM13817) | | | | | | | | | | | | | | | | | |
| MORTON, J V (HM14251) | | | | | | | | | | | | | | | | | |
| NATURAL HEALTH CLINIC (HM14584) | | | | | | | | | | | | | | | | | |
| NEW LIFE NATURAL HEALTH CARE (HM14821) | | | | | | | | | | | | | | | | | |
| NEWTON, J C (HM14898) | | | | | | | | | | | | | | | | | |
| NORTH WEST LIFESTYLE MNGMT (HM15043) | | | | | | | | | | | | | | | | | |
| NUTRITION AND ALLERGY CLINIC (HM15121) | | | | | | | | | | | ● | | | | | | |
| OLD HALL CLINIC (HM15256) | | | | | | | | | | | | | | | | | |
| OLDHAM, TERRY (HM15270) | | | | | | | | | | | | | | | | | |
| PALOMBELLA, SARAH (HM15623) | | | | | | | | | | | | | | | | | |
| PANK, SARAH (HM15635) | | | | | | | | | | | | | | | | | |
| PAOLA WEINBERG SYLT (HM15640) | | | | | | | | | | | | | | | | | |
| PATON, W A (HM15825) | | | | | | | | | | | | | | | | | |
| PHOENIX CENTRE (HM16154) | | | | | | | | | | | | | | | | | |
| PHYSIO & SPORTS INJURY CLINIC (HM16181) | | | | | | | | ● | | | | | | | | | |
| PHYSIO PLUS (HM16203) | | | | | | | | | | | | | | | | | |
| PHYSIO SPORTS INJURY CLINIC (HM16209) | | | | | | | | | | | | | | | | | |
| PREW, BEVERLEY (HM16566) | | | | | | | | | | | | | | | | | |
| PROTHERO, PEGGY (HM16672) | | | | | | | | | | | | | | | | | |
| PULMAN, SUZETTE (HM16755) | | | | | | | | | | | | | | | | | |
| QUINTON, R M (HM16818) | | | | | | | | | | | | | | | | | |
| REDGRAVE, KENNETH (HM17025) | | | | | | | | | | | | | | | | | |

# O - Z Therapies at Practices/Businesses

| Business by County with Reference no. | Orthotics | Osteomyology | Osteopathy | PAM | Paranormal Therapies | Pattern Therapies | Physiotherapy | Phytotherapy | Pilates | Podiatry | Polarity Therapy | Postural Integration | Primal Therapy | Psionic Therapy | Psychotherapy | Pyramid Power | Pyscho-Synthesis | Reflexology | Reichian Therapy | Reiki | Remedial Massage | Rogerian Therapy | Rolfing | Seichem | Sensitivity Training | Shiatsu | Silva Method | Sound Therapy | Spiritual Healing | Sports Massage | Stress Therapy | Swedish Body Massage | T'ai-Chi Ch'uan | Tantra Therapy | Tera-Mai | Thought Field Therapy | Touch Therapy | Transactional Analysis | Tui-na | Ultrasonics | Vibrational Therapy | Visualisation Therapy | Vitamin Therapy | Voice Therapy | X-Ray | Ying & Yang | Yoga | Zen Therapy | Zero Balancing |
|---|---|---|---|---|---|---|---|---|---|---|---|---|---|---|---|---|---|---|---|---|---|---|---|---|---|---|---|---|---|---|---|---|---|---|---|---|---|---|---|---|---|---|---|---|---|---|---|---|---|
| REIKI (HM17127) |||||||||||||||||||●|||||||||||||||||||||||||||||
| RICHARDS, KERRY L (HM17260) |||||||||●|||||||||||||||||||||||||||||||||||||||
| ROBERTS, TRACEY (HM17431) |||||||||||||||||●|||||||||||||||||||||||||||||||
| SAYERS, MARGARET (HM17999) |||||||||||||||||●|||||||||||||||||||||||||||||||
| SCARBOROUGH, KATE (HM18003) |||||||||||||||||●|||||||||||||||||||||||||||||||
| SHEPHERD, STEVEN (HM18418) ||●||||||||||||||||||||||||||||||||||||||||||||||
| STRACHAN, JO-ANNE (HM19364) |||||||||||||||||●|||||||||||||||||||||||||||||||
| STUBBS, D A (HM19433) ||●||||||||||||||||||||||||||||||||||||||||||||||
| SUMMERS, CHRISTINE S (HM19489) ||●||||||||||||||||||||||||||||||||||||||||||||||
| THOMPSON, CYNTHIA (HM19971) ||●||||||||||||||||||||||||||||||||||||||||||||||
| THORNBER, A A (HM20016) |||||||●|||||||||||||||||||||||||||||||||||||||||
| TIERNAN, MANDA (HM20061) |||||||||||||||||●|||||||||||||||||||||||||||||||
| TRINITY HOUSE PRACTICE (HM20339) ||●||||||||||||||●||●|●|||||●|||||||||||||||||||||||
| TURTON, TRACEY (HM20444) |||||||||||||||||●|||||||||||||||||||||||||||||||
| TYRER, HELEN R (HM20473) |||||||||●|||||||||||||||||||||||||||||||||||||||
| VALE ROYAL CHIROPRACTIC CLINIC (HM20553) |||||||||||||||||●|||||||||||||||||||||||||||||||
| VALE ROYAL CHIROPRACTIC CLINIC (HM20552) |||||||||||||||||●|||||||||||||||||||||||||||||||
| WARRINGTON CHIROPRACTIC CLINIC (HM20957) ||||||||||||||||||||||||||||||||||||||||||||●||||
| WEAVER HOUSE CLINIC (HM21049) ||●|||||||||||●|||●|||||||||||||●||||||||||||||||||
| WEST, MARIE-CLAIRE (HM21254) |||||||||||||||||●|||||||||||||||||||||||||||||||
| WIDNES OSTEOPATHIC CLINIC (HM21459) ||●|||||●|||||||||●|||||||||||||||||||||||||||||||
| WIENHOLT, VALERIE (HM21462) |||||||||||||||||●|||||||||||||||||||||||||||||||
| WILLIAMS OSTEOPATHIC CLINIC (HM21532) ||●||||||||||||||●|||||||||||||●||||||||||||||||||
| YOGA & THERAPY CENTRE (HM22020) ||||||||||||||||||||||||||||||||||||||||||||||●||
| **CLEVELAND** |||||||||||||||||||||||||||||||||||||||||||||||||
| ACTIVE BALANCE CLINIC (HM00187) ||●||||||||||||||||||||||||||||||||||||||||||||||
| ALFORD, M A (HM00577) ||●||||||||||||||||||||||||||||||||||||||||||||||
| AYTON, P E (HM01440) ||●||||||||||||||||||||||||||||||||||||||||||||||
| BARNARD, SIMON (HM01732) ||●||||||||●|||||||||||||||||||||||||||||||||||||
| BIRKS, W KEITH (HM02378) ||●||||||||||||||||||||||||||||||||||||||||||||||
| CROSS, ANDREW (HM05481) ||●||||||||||||||||||||||||||||||||||||||||||||||
| HASTIE, A (HM09188) ||●||||||||||||||||||||||||||||||||||||||||||||||
| HEIMER, F (HM09507) ||●||||||||||||||||||||||||||||||||||||||||||||||
| IDESON, S M (HM10572) ||●||||||||||||||||||||||||||||||||||||||||||||||

# O - Z Therapies at Practices/Businesses

| Business by County with Reference no. | Orthotics | Osteomyology | Osteopathy | PAM | Paranormal Therapies | Pattern Therapies | Physiotherapy | Phytotherapy | Pilates | Podiatry | Polarity Therapy | Postural Integration | Primal Therapy | Psionic Therapy | Psychotherapy | Pyramid Power | Pyscho-Synthesis | Reflexology | Reichian Therapy | Reiki | Remedial Massage | Rogerian Therapy | Rolfing | Seichem | Sensitivity Training | Shiatsu | Silva Method | Sound Therapy | Spiritual Healing | Sports Massage | Stress Therapy | Swedish Body Massage | T'ai-Chi Ch'uan | Tantra Therapy | Tera-Mai | Thought Field Therapy | Touch Therapy | Transactional Analysis | Tui-na | Ultrasonics | Vibrational Therapy | Visualisation Therapy | Vitamin Therapy | Voice Therapy | X-Ray | Ying & Yang | Yoga | Zen Therapy | Zero Balancing |
|---|---|---|---|---|---|---|---|---|---|---|---|---|---|---|---|---|---|---|---|---|---|---|---|---|---|---|---|---|---|---|---|---|---|---|---|---|---|---|---|---|---|---|---|---|---|---|---|---|---|
| JANES, G (HM10919) | | | | | | | | | | | | | | | | | | ● | | | | | | | | | | | | | | | | | | | | | | | | | | | | | | | |
| NATURAL THERAPY CENTRE (HM14637) | | | ● | | | | | | | | | | | | | | | ● | | | | | | | | | | | | | | | | | | | | | | | | | | | | | | | |
| NEW DIRECTIONS (HM14816) | | | | | | | | | | | | | | | ● | | | | | | | | | | | | | | | | | | | | | | | | | | | | | | | | | | |
| NORTHERN GUILD-PSYCHOTHERAPY (HM15061) | | | | | | | | | | | | | | | ● | | | | | | | | | | | | | | | | ● | | | | | | | ● | | | | | | | | | | | |
| RAINBOW BRIDGE SCHOOL (HM16875) | | | | | | | | | | | | | | | | | | ● | | | | | | | | | | | | | | | | | | | | | | | | | | | | | | | |
| REDCAR PHYSIO & SPORTS (HM17007) | | | | | | | ● | | | | | | | | | | | | | | | | | | | | | | | | | | | | | | | | | | | | | | | | | | |
| RUSH, DENNIS (HM17754) | | | | | | | | | | | | | | | ● | | | | | | | | | | | | | ● | | | ● | | | | | | | ● | | | | ● | | | | | | | |
| STRESS COUNSELLING (HM19391) | | | | | | | | | | | | | | | ● | | | | | | | ● | | | | | | | | | ● | | | | | | | ● | | | | ● | | | | | | | |
| YARM OSTEOPATHIC CLINIC (HM21987) | | | ● | | | | | | | | | | | | | | | | | | | | | | | | | | | | | | | | | | | | | | | | | | | | | | |
| **CORNWALL** | | | | | | | | | | | | | | | | | | | | | | | | | | | | | | | | | | | | | | | | | | | | | | | | | |
| ALLEN, CHERYL (HM00606) | | | | | | | | | | | | | | | ● | | | | | | | | | | | | | | | | | | | | | | | | | | | | | | | | | | |
| AROMATICA (HM01135) | | | | | | | | | | | | | | | | | | ● | | | | | | | | | | | | | | | | | | | | | | | | | | | | | | | |
| BANBURY, A E (HM01646) | | | ● | | | | | | | | | | | | | | | | | | | | | | | | | | | | | | | | | | | | | | | | | | | | | | |
| BEARE, M E (HM01968) | | | | | | | | | | ● | | | | | | | | | | | | | | | | | | | | | | | | | | | | | | | | | | | | | | | |
| BRIERLEY, MATTHEW (HM03024) | | | ● | | | | | | | | | | | | | | | | | | | | | | | | | | | | | | | | | | | | | | | | | | | | | | |
| BROWNE, ANNE (HM03255) | | | | | | | | | | | | | | | | | | ● | | | | | | | | | | | | | | | | | | | | | | | | | | | | | | | |
| BRUNT, LINDA (HM03281) | | | | | | | | | | | | | | | | | | ● | | | | | | | | | | | | | | | | | | | | | | | | | | | | | | | |
| CHIROPODIST/PODIATRIST (HM04296) | | | | | | | | | | ● | | | | | | | | | | | | | | | | | | | | | | | | | | | | | | | | | | | | | | | |
| COMP HEALTH INITIATIVE (HM04912) | | | | | | | | | | | ● | | | | ● | | | ● | | ● | | | | | | ● | | | ● | | | | | | | | | | | | | | | | | | | | |
| CONBOYE, M CLARE (HM04964) | | | ● | | | | | | | | | | | | | | | | | | | | | | | | | | | | | | | | | | | | | | | | | | | | | | |
| COVENTON, DOROTHY (HM05281) | | | | | | | | | | | | | | | | | | ● | | | | | | | | | | | | | | | | | | | | | | | | | | | | | | | |
| DRAGE, STEPHEN (HM06279) | | | | | | | | | | | | | | | | | | | | | | | | | | | | | | | | | | | | | | | | | | | ● | | | | | | |
| FEET FIRST (HM07180) | | | | | | | | | | | | | | | | | | ● | | | | | | | | | | | | | | | | | | | | | | | | | | | | | | | |
| FELSTEAD, PETER (HM07207) | | | | | | | | | | | | | | | | | | ● | | | | | | | | | | | | | | | | | | | | | | | | | | | | | | | |
| FOOTCARE (HM07492) | | | | | | | | | | ● | | | | | | | | | | | | | | | | | | | | | | | | | | | | | | | | | | | | | | | |
| FORCE, GAYLE (HM07520) | | | | | ● | | | | | | | | | | | | | | | | | | | | | | | ● | | | | | | | | | | | | | | ● | | ● | | | | | |
| GAVAN, JUDITH (HM07935) | | | | | | | | | | | | | | | | | | ● | | | | | | | | | | | | | | | | | | | | | | | | | | | | | | | |
| HALL, PETER (HM08787) | | | | | | | | | | | | | | | | | | | | | | | | | | ● | | | | | | | ● | | | | | | | | | | | | | | | | |
| HARBAGE, RALPH (HM08958) | | | ● | | | | | | | | | | | | | | | | | | | | | | | | | | | | | | | | | | | | | | | | | | | | | | |
| HAWKSLAND PHYSIOTHERAPY CENTRE (HM09233) | | | | | | | | | | | | | | | | | | | | | | | | | | | | | | | | | | | | | | | | ● | | | | | | | | | |
| HILDER, DEBORAH (HM09764) | | | | | | | | | | | | | | | | | | ● | | | | | | | | | | | | | | | | | | | | | | | | | | | | | | | |
| HILLIARD, N (HM09796) | | | ● | | | | | | | | | | | | | | | | | | | | | | | | | | | | | | | | | | | | | | | | | | | | | | |
| HILLIARD, N & R (HM09797) | | | ● | | | | | | | | | | | | | | | | | | | | | | | | | | | | | | | | | | | | | | | | | | | | | | |
| HOPCROFT, JULIE (HM10132) | | | | | | | | | | | | | | | | | | ● | | | | | | | | | | | | | | | | | | | | | | | | | | | | | | | |

# O - Z Therapies at Practices/Businesses

| Business by County with Reference no. | Orthotics | Osteomyology | Osteopathy | PAM | Paranormal Therapies | Pattern Therapies | Physiotherapy | Phytotherapy | Pilates | Podiatry | Polarity Therapy | Postural Integration | Primal Therapy | Psionic Therapy | Psychotherapy | Pyramid Power | Pyscho-Synthesis | Reflexology | Reichian Therapy | Reiki | Remedial Massage | Rogerian Therapy | Rolfing | Seichem | Sensitivity Training | Shiatsu | Silva Method | Sound Therapy | Spiritual Healing | Sports Massage | Stress Therapy | Swedish Body Massage | T'ai-Chi Ch'uan | Tantra Therapy | Tera-Mai | Thought Field Therapy | Touch Therapy | Transactional Analysis | Tui-na | Ultrasonics | Vibrational Therapy | Visualisation Therapy | Vitamin Therapy | Voice Therapy | X-Ray | Ying & Yang | Yoga | Zen Therapy | Zero Balancing |
|---|---|---|---|---|---|---|---|---|---|---|---|---|---|---|---|---|---|---|---|---|---|---|---|---|---|---|---|---|---|---|---|---|---|---|---|---|---|---|---|---|---|---|---|---|---|---|---|---|---|
| HUNTERS LODGE CLINIC (HM10410) | | | ● | | | | | | | | | | | | | | | | | | | | | | | | | | | | | | | | | | | | | | | | | | | | | | |
| KEILBART, P A (HM11407) | | | ● | | | | | | | | | | | | | | | | | | | | | | | | | | | | | | | | | | | | | | | | | | | | | | |
| LEMON ST NTRL HLTH PRACTICE (HM12206) | | | | | | | | | | | | | | | ● | | | ● | | ● | | | | | | ● | | | | | | | | | | | | | | | | | ● | | | | | | |
| LIFE 'N' LIMB (HM12346) | | | | | | | | | | | | | | | | | | | | | | | | | | | | | | | ● | | | | | | ● | | | | | | | | | | | | |
| LISTER NATURAL HEALTH PRACTICE (HM12461) | | | | | ● | | | | | | | ● | ● | | ● | | | ● | | ● | | | | ● | | | | | | | ● | | ● | | | | | ● | | | | ● | ● | | ● | ● | | | |
| MASON, JAY (HM13244) | | | | | | | | | | | | | | | ● | | | | | | | | | | | | | | | | | | | | | | | | | | | | | | | | | | |
| MEYERS, K L C (HM13788) | | | ● | | | | | | | | | | | | | | | | | | | | | | | | | | | | | | | | | | | | | | | | | | | | | | |
| NERVA, VALERIE (HM14786) | | | | | | | | | | | | | | | ● | | | | | | | | | | | | | | | | | | | | | | | | | | | | | | | | | | |
| NEWQUAY CHIROPRACTIC CLINIC (HM14883) | | | | | | | | | | | | | | | | | | ● | | | | | | | | ● | | | | | | | | | | | | | | | | | | | | | | | |
| OSTEOPATHIC FAMILY CENTRE (HM15465) | | | ● | | | | | | | | | | | | | | | | | | | | | | | | | | | | | | | | | | | | | | | | | | | | | | |
| PENZANCE NATURAL HEALTH CENTRE (HM16006) | | | | | | | | | | | | | | | ● | | | ● | | ● | | | | | | ● | | | ● | | | | | | | | | | | | | | | | | | | | |
| POOLEY, ALISON (HM16432) | | | | | | | | | | | | | | | | | | ● | | | | | | | | | | | | | | | | | | | | | | | | | | | | | | | |
| SAXBY, SUE (HM17988) | | | | | | | | | | | | | | | | | | ● | | | | | | | | | | | | | | | | | | | | | | | | | | | | | | | |
| SCOBIE, D C O (HM18099) | | | ● | | | | | | | | | | | | | | | | | | | | | | | | | | | | | | | | | | | | | | | | | | | | | | |
| ST AUSTELL CHIROPRACTIC CLINIC (HM19070) | | | | | | | | | | | | | | | ● | | | ● | | | | | | | | | | | | | | | | | | | | | | | | | | | | | | | |
| STAR (HM19143) | | | | | | | | | | | | | | | | | | ● | | | | | | | | | | | | | | | | | | | | | | | | | | | | | | | |
| TATTON, ALISTAIR M (HM19720) | | | ● | | | | | | | | | | | | | | | | | | | | | | | | | | | | | | | | | | | | | | | | | | | | | | |
| THOMAS, ANNE (HM19932) | | | | | | | | | | | | | | | | | | ● | | | | | | | | | | | | | | | | | | | | | | | | | | | | | | | |
| TREWHELLA, JOHN (HM20325) | | | | | | | | | | | | | | | ● | | | | | | | | | | | | | | | | | | | | | | | | | | | | | | | | | | |
| TRURO CHIROPRACTIC CLINIC (HM20354) | | | | | | | | | | | | | | | ● | | | ● | | | | | | | | | | | | | | | | | | | | | | | | | | | | | | | |
| TRURO OSTEOPATHIC PRACTICE (HM20356) | | | ● | | | | | | | | | | | | | | | | | | | | | | | | | | | | | | | | | | | | | | | | | | | | | | |
| VERA BOYES ACUPUNCTURE (HM20618) | | | | | | | | | | | | | | | | | | ● | | | | | | | | | | | | | ● | | | | | | | | | | | | | | | | | | |
| WEATHERHOGG, D J (HM21046) | | | ● | | | | | | | | | | | | | | | | | | | | | | | | | | | | | | | | | | | | | | | | | | | | | | |
| WEST, KATHRYN (HM21251) | | | ● | | | | | | | | | | | | | | | | | | | | | | | | | | | | | | | | | | | | | | | | | | | | | | |
| WILLS, JONATHAN (HM21632) | | | ● | | | | | | | ● | | | | | | | | ● | | | | | | | | | | | | | | | | | | | | | | | | | | | | | | | |
| WRIGHT, CYNTHIA (HM21929) | | | | | | | | | | | | | | | | | | | | | | | | | | | | | | | | | | | | | | | | | | ● | | | | | | | |
| **COUNTY DURHAM** | | | | | | | | | | | | | | | | | | | | | | | | | | | | | | | | | | | | | | | | | | | | | | | | | |
| BALANCE HOLISTIC HEALTHCARE (HM01606) | | | | | | | | | | | | | | | | | | ● | | ● | | | | | | | | | | | | | | | | | | | | | | | | | | | | | |
| BENNETT, MARGARET (HM02150) | | | | | | | | | | | | | | | | | | ● | | | | | | | | | | | | | | | | | | | | | | | | | | | | | | | |
| BODYWORK HEALTH CLUB & CLINIC (HM02639) | | | | | | | | | | | | | | | | | | ● | | ● | | | | | | | | | | | | | | | | | | | | | | | | | | | | | |
| EVANS, BRUCE (DR) (HM06958) | | | ● | | | | | | | | | | | | | | | | | | | | | | | | | | | | | | | | | | | | | | | | | | | | | | |
| FIONA OTTEWELL CHRTRD PHYSIO (HM07329) | | | | | | | | | ● | | | | | | | | | | | | | | | | | | | | | | | | | | | | | | | | | | | | | | | | |
| FOOTPRINTS (HM07507) | | | | | | | | | | ● | | | | | | | | | | | | | | | | | | | | | | | | | | | | | | | | | | | | | | | |
| HAIRSINE, P W (HM08719) | | | ● | | | | | | | | | | | | | | | | | | | | | | | | | | | | | | | | | | | | | | | | | | | | | | |

# O - Z Therapies at Practices/Businesses

| Business by County with Reference no. | Orthotics | Osteomyology | Osteopathy | PAM | Paranormal Therapies | Pattern Therapies | Physiotherapy | Phytotherapy | Pilates | Podiatry | Polarity Therapy | Postural Integration | Primal Therapy | Psionic Therapy | Psychotherapy | Pyramid Power | Pyscho-Synthesis | Reflexology | Reichian Therapy | Reiki | Remedial Massage | Rogerian Therapy | Rolfing | Seichem | Sensitivity Training | Shiatsu | Silva Method | Sound Therapy | Spiritual Healing | Sports Massage | Stress Therapy | Swedish Body Massage | T'ai-Chi Ch'uan | Tantra Therapy | Tera-Mai | Thought Field Therapy | Touch Therapy | Transactional Analysis | Tui-na | Ultrasonics | Vibrational Therapy | Visualisation Therapy | Vitamin Therapy | Voice Therapy | X-Ray | Ying & Yang | Yoga | Zen Therapy | Zero Balancing |
|---|---|---|---|---|---|---|---|---|---|---|---|---|---|---|---|---|---|---|---|---|---|---|---|---|---|---|---|---|---|---|---|---|---|---|---|---|---|---|---|---|---|---|---|---|---|---|---|---|---|
| HAMBLY, PHILIP (HM08830) | | | ● | | | | | | | | | | | | | | | | | | | | | | | | | | | | | | | | | | | | | | | | | | | | | | |
| HEDLEY HILL HEALTH SERVICES (HM09496) | | | ● | | | | | | | | | | | | | | | | | | | | | | | | | | | | | | | | | | | | | | | | | | | | | | |
| HIND, CAROLE (HM09824) | | | | | | | | | | | | | | | | | | ● | | ● | | | | | | | | | | | | | | | | | | | | | | | | | | | | | |
| HOBSON, I K (HM09864) | | | | | | | | | | ● | | | | | | | | | | | | | | | | | | | | | | | | | | | | | | | | | | | | | | | |
| KIRKUP, KEVIN (HM11722) | | | ● | | | | | | | | | | | | | | | | | | | | | | | | | | | | | | | | | | | | | | | | | | | | | | |
| MERIDIAN MASSAGE & REFLEXOLOGY (HM13744) | | | | | | | | | | | | | | | | | | ● | | | | | | | | | | | | | | | | | | | | | | | | | | | | | | | |
| NATURAL HEALING CENTRE (HM14536) | | | | | | | | | | | | | | | | | | ● | | ● | | | | | | ● | | | ● | | ● | | | | | | | | | | | | | | | | | | |
| NEWCASTLE/NE TRANS MEDITA CTRE (HM14856) | | | | | | | | | | | | | | | | | | | | | | | | | | | | | | | ● | | | | | | | | | | | | | | | | | | |
| OLD PIT PRACTICE (HM15260) | | | | | | | ● | | | ● | | | | | ● | | | ● | | | | | | | | | | | | ● | | | | | | | | | | | | | | | | | | | |
| PEACOCK, ANGELA (HM15882) | | | | | | | | | | | | | | | | | | ● | | | | | | | | | | | | | | | | | | | | | | | | | | | | | | | |
| SPOORS, L & D (HM19039) | | | ● | | | | | | | | | | | | | | | | | | | | | | | | | | | | | | | | | | | | | | | | | | | | | | |
| TEESDALE OSTEOPATHIC CLINIC (HM19817) | | | ● | | | | | | | | | | | | | | | ● | | | | | | | | | | | | | | | | | | | | | | | | | | | | | | | |
| TREATMENT ROOM (HM20302) | | | | | | | ● | | | | | | | | | | | ● | | | | | | | | | | | | | | | | | | | | | | ● | | | | | | | | | |
| WARWICK, ANDREA (HM20967) | | | | | | | | | | | | | | | | | | ● | | | | | | | | | | | ● | | | | | | | | | | | | | | | | | | | | |
| WRIGHT FOOT FORWARD (HM21924) | | | | | | | | | | | | | | | | | | ● | | ● | ● | | | | | | | | | | | | | | | | | | | | | | | | | | | | |
| **CUMBRIA** | | | | | | | | | | | | | | | | | | | | | | | | | | | | | | | | | | | | | | | | | | | | | | | | | |
| BIRD, NEIL (HM02370) | | | ● | | | | | | | | | | | | | | | | | | | | | | | | | | | | | | | | | | | | | | | | | | | | | | |
| BRETT, T (HM02973) | | | ● | | | | | | | | | | | | | | | | | | | | | | | | | | | | | | | | | | | | | | | | | | | | | | |
| BROOME, ALISON (HM03187) | | | | | | | | | | | | | | | | | | ● | | | | | | | | | | | | | | | | | | | | | | | | | | | | | | | |
| CAIN, SUSAN (HM03539) | | | | | | | | | | | | | | | | | | ● | | | | | | | | | | | | | | | | | | | | | | | | | | | | | | | |
| CARRINGTON, DORA (HM03748) | | | | | | | | | | | | | | | | | | ● | | | | | | | | | | | | | | | | | | | | | | | | | | | | | | | |
| COATES, ELIZABETH (HM04755) | | | | | | | | | | | | | | | | | | ● | | | | | | | | | | | | | | | | | | | | | | | | | | | | | | | |
| CUMBRIA PHYSIO & SPORTS CLINIC (HM05598) | | | | | | | ● | | | | | | | | | | | | | | | | | | | | | | | | | | | | | | | | | | | | | | | | | | |
| DEERING, CHRISTINE (HM05959) | | | | | | | | | | | | | | | ● | | | | | | | | | | | | | | | | | | | | | | | | | | | | | | | | | | |
| DUNCAN, E (HM06394) | | | ● | | | | | | | | | | | | | | | | | | | | | | | | | | | | | | | | | | | | | | | | | | | | | | |
| DUNLOP, JAMES R W (HM06409) | | | ● | | | | | | | | | | | | | | | | | | | | | | | | | | | | | | | | | | | | | | | | | | | | | | |
| EDWARDS, D E (HM06648) | | | | | | | | | | | | | | | ● | | | | | | | | | | | | | | | | | | | | | | | | | | | | | | | | | | |
| FOOTWORKS (HM07515) | | | | | | | | | | ● | | | | | | | | | | | | | | | | | | | | | | | | | | | | | | | | | | | | | | | |
| GARNETT, JANE (HM07897) | | | | | | | | | | | | | | | | | | ● | | | | | | | | | | | | | | | | | | | | | | | | | | | | | | | |
| GUTTERIDGE, A C (DR) (HM08659) | | | ● | | | | | | | | | | | | | | | | | | | | | | | | | | | | | | | | | | | | | | | | | | | | | | |
| HARRISON, DAVID (HM09093) | | | ● | | | | | | | | | | | | | | | | | | | | | | | | | | | | | | | | | | | | | | | | | | | | | | |
| JACKSON, B (HM10828) | | | ● | | | | | | | | | | | | | | | | | | | | | | | | | | | | | | | | | | | | | | | | | | | | | | |
| JACKSON, D M (HM10834) | | | ● | | | | | | | | | | | | | | | | | | | | | | | | | | | | | | | | | | | | | | | | | | | | | | |
| LIBRA THERAPY CENTRE (HM12328) | | | ● | | | | | | | | | | | | | | | ● | | | | | | | | | | | | | | | | | | | | | | | | | | | | | | | |

# O - Z Therapies at Practices/Businesses

| Business by County with Reference no. | Orthotics | Osteomyology | Osteopathy | PAM | Paranormal Therapies | Pattern Therapies | Physiotherapy | Phytotherapy | Pilates | Podiatry | Polarity Therapy | Postural Integration | Primal Therapy | Psionic Therapy | Psychotherapy | Pyramid Power | Pyscho-Synthesis | Reflexology | Reichian Therapy | Reiki | Remedial Massage | Rogerian Therapy | Rolfing | Seichem | Sensitivity Training | Shiatsu | Silva Method | Sound Therapy | Spiritual Healing | Sports Massage | Stress Therapy | Swedish Body Massage | T'ai-Chi Ch'uan | Tantra Therapy | Tera-Mai | Thought Field Therapy | Touch Therapy | Transactional Analysis | Tui-na | Ultrasonics | Vibrational Therapy | Visualisation Therapy | Vitamin Therapy | Voice Therapy | X-Ray | Ying & Yang | Yoga | Zen Therapy | Zero Balancing |
|---|---|---|---|---|---|---|---|---|---|---|---|---|---|---|---|---|---|---|---|---|---|---|---|---|---|---|---|---|---|---|---|---|---|---|---|---|---|---|---|---|---|---|---|---|---|---|---|---|---|
| LLOYD, R N (HM12515) | | | ● | | | | | | | | | | | | | | | | | | | | | | | | | | | | | | | | | | | | | | | | | | | | | | |
| MARRIS, TIMOTHY (HM13140) | | | ● | | | | | | | | | | | | | | | | | | | | | | | | | | | | | | | | | | | | | | | | | | | | | | |
| MATTHEWS, V (HM13316) | | | ● | | | | | | | | | | | | | | | | | | | | | | | | | | | | | | | | | | | | | | | | | | | | | | |
| MCQUILLAN, JANE (HM13594) | | | | | | | | | | | | | | | ● | | | | | | | | | | | | | | | | | | | | | | | | | | | | | | | | | | |
| SHORT, J J (HM18497) | | | ● | | | | | | | | | | | | | | | | | | | | | | | | | | | | | | | | | | | | | | | | | | | | | | |
| STRAWBERRY HOW CLINIC (HM19378) | | | | | | | ● | | | | | | | | | | | | | | | | | | | | | | | | | | | | | | | | | | | | | | | | | | |
| SUTTON, R W (HM19555) | | | ● | | | | | | | | | | | | | | | | | | | | | | | | | | | | | | | | | | | | | | | | | | | | | | |
| TAYLOR, L P A (HM19778) | | | ● | | | | | | | | | | | | | | | | | | | | | | | | | | | | | | | | | | | | | | | | | | | | | | |
| THERAPY CENTRE (HM19898) | | | ● | | | | | | | | | | | | | | | | | | | | | | | | | | | | | | | | | | | | | | | | | | | | | | |
| VULCANS LANE CHIROPODY (HM20720) | | | | | | | | | | | | | | | | | | ● | | | | | | | | | | | | | | | | | | | | | | | | | | | | | | | |
| WHITLEY, LIS (HM21410) | | | | | | | | | | | | | | | ● | | | | | | | | | | | | | | | | | | | | | | | | | | | | | | | | | | |
| **DERBYSHIRE** | | | | | | | | | | | | | | | | | | | | | | | | | | | | | | | | | | | | | | | | | | | | | | | | | |
| ALTER-MED (HM00690) | | | | | | | | | | | | | | | | | | ● | | | | | | | | | | | | | | | | | | | | | | | | | | | | | | | |
| AROMATHERAPY & REFLEX CTRE (HM01090) | | | | | | | | | | | | | | | | | | ● | | | | | | | | | | | | | | | | | | | | | | | | | | | | | | | |
| ASHBURNER, P (HM01193) | | | ● | | | | | | | | | | | | | | | | | | | | | | | | | | | | | | | | | | | | | | | | | | | | | | |
| BANKS, LINDA (HM01665) | | | | | | | | | | | | | | | | | | ● | | ● | | | | | | | | | | | | | | | | | | | | | | | | | | | | | |
| BARROWCLIFFE, GRAHAM (DR) (HM01806) | | | | | | | | | | | | | | | ● | | | | | | | | | | | | | | | | ● | | | | | | | | | | | ● | | | | | | | |
| BELPER BACKPAIN CLINIC (HM02110) | | | | | | | | | | | | | | | | | | | | ● | ● | | | | | | | | | | | | | | | | | | | ● | | | | | | | | | |
| BELPER NATURAL HEALTH CENTRE (HM02112) | | | ● | | | | | | | | | | | | | | | ● | | ● | | | | | | | | | ● | | ● | | | | | | | | | | | | ● | | | | | | |
| BERNE INSTITUTE (HM02198) | | | | | | | | | | | | | | | ● | | | | | | | | | | | | | | | | | | | | | | | | | | | | | | | | | | |
| BRADSHAW, P J (HM02878) | | | | | | | | | | | | | | | ● | | ● | | | | | ● | | | | | ● | | | | | | | | | | | ● | | | | | | | | | | | |
| BRAHMA KUMARIS RAJA YOGA CTRE (HM02889) | | | | | | | | | | | | | | | | | | | | | | | | | | | | | | | | | | | | | | | | | | | | | | | ● | | |
| BRILL, PAULINE (HM03051) | | | | | | | | | | | | | | | | | | ● | | | | | | | | | | | | | | | | | | | | | | | | | | | | | | | |
| CARRICK-SMITH, L (HM03744) | | | | | | | | | | | | | | | ● | | | | | | | ● | | | | | | | | | | | | | | | | | | | | | | | | | | | |
| CHIROPODY & PHYSIOTHERAPY (HM04303) | | | | | | | | | | | | | | | | | | ● | | | | | | | | | | | | | | | | | | | | | | | | | | | | | | | |
| COVERLEY PHYSIOTHERAPY CLINIC (HM05284) | | | | | | | ● | | | | | | | | | | | | | | | | | | | | | | | | | | | | | | | | | | | | | | | | | | |
| DARBY, ANN (HM05735) | | | | | | | | | | | | | | | | | | | | ● | | | | | | | | | | | | | | | | | | | | | | | | | | | | | |
| DERBYSHIRE SPORTS INJURIES (HM06014) | | | | | | | ● | | | | | | | | | | | | | | | | | | | | | | | | | | | | | | | | | | | | | | | | | | |
| DICKINSON, ANN (HM06074) | | | ● | | | | | | | | | | | | | | | | | | | | | | | | | | | | | | | | | | | | | | | | | | | | | | |
| DRONFIELD NAT HEALTH CLINIC (HM06319) | | | ● | | | | | | | | | | | | ● | | | ● | | ● | | | | | | ● | | | | | | | | | | | | | | | | | ● | | | | ● | | |
| DRONFIELD PHYSIOTHERAPY CLINIC (HM06320) | | | | | | | ● | | | | | | | | | | | | | | | | | | | | | | | | | | | | | | | | | | | | | | | | | | |
| ENJOY SPORT (HM06836) | | | ● | | | | | | | | | | | | | | | | | | | | | | | | | | | | | | | | | | | | | | | | | | | | | | |
| GARRISON-TODD, WENDY (HM07905) | | | | | | | | | | | | | | | | | | ● | | ● | | | | | | | | | | | | | | | | | | | | | | | | | | | | | |
| GRANGE, DIANA (HM08372) | | | | | | | | | | | | | | | | | | ● | | | | | | | | | | | | | | | | | | | | | | | | | | | | | | | |

# O - Z Therapies at Practices/Businesses

Business by County with Reference no.

| Business | Orthotics | Osteomyology | Osteopathy | PAM | Paranormal Therapies | Pattern Therapies | Physiotherapy | Phytotherapy | Pilates | Podiatry | Polarity Therapy | Postural Integration | Primal Therapy | Psionic Therapy | Psychotherapy | Pyramid Power |
|---|---|---|---|---|---|---|---|---|---|---|---|---|---|---|---|---|
| HALTON, A (HM08821) | | | ● | | | | | | | | | | | | | |
| HARDWICK, JUDITH (HM08976) | | | | | | | | | | | | | | | | |
| HARTWELL, A E (HM09151) | | | | | | | | | | | | | | | ● | |
| HAWKINS & FIELDING (HM09217) | | | ● | | | | | | | | | | | | | |
| HIGGS, ANN (HM09734) | | | | | | | | | | | | | | | | |
| HUMAN RELATIONS SERVICES (HM10365) | | | | | | | | | | | | | | | ● | |
| ILKESTONE OSTEO & MED CTRE (HM10580) | | | ● | | | | | | | | | | | | | |
| JOHNSON, MELVYN (HM11086) | | | ● | | | | | | | | | | | | | |
| KARDAHJI, F C (HM11319) | | | | | | | | | | ● | | | | | | |
| KEMP, GILLIAN (HM11461) | | | | | | | | | | | | | | | ● | |
| KNIGHT, JAYNE (HM11752) | | | | | | | | | | | | | | | | |
| LANCASHIRE, A W (HM11915) | | | ● | | | | | | | | | | | | | |
| LIFECHANGERS (HM12351) | | | | | | | | | | | | | | | ● | |
| LIFESOLUTIONS (HM12359) | | | | | | | | | | | | | | | ● | |
| MATTHEWS, A (HM13299) | | | | | | | | | | | | | | | | |
| MATTHEWS, AMANDA (HM13301) | | | | | | | | | | | | | | | | |
| NATURAL HEALTH CLINIC (HM14577) | | | | | | | | | | | | | | | ● | |
| OSTEOPATH CLINIC (HM15447) | | | ● | | | | | | | | | | | | | |
| PEARCE, YVONNE (HM15902) | | | | | | | | | | | | | | | | |
| PEDLEY, ANNE (HM15933) | | | ● | | | | | | | | | | | | | |
| PETER SADLER NATURAL MED CTRE (HM16074) | | | ● | | | | | | | | | | | | | |
| PHILIP STOCK - PHYSIOTHERAPIST (HM16120) | | | ● | | | | | ● | | | | | | | | |
| PHYSIO ACTIVE (HM16193) | | | ● | | | | ● | | | | | ● | | | ● | |
| PRICE, GRAHAM (HM16577) | | | ● | | | | | | | | | | | | | |
| PRICE, TRACY (HM16597) | | | | | | | | | | | | | | | | |
| REDFERN, AMANDA (HM17018) | | | | | | | | | | | | | | | | |
| REID, BARBARA (HM17113) | | | | | | | | | | | | | | | | |
| RICKARD, CLIVE A (HM17310) | | | ● | | | | | | | | | | | | | |
| RIPLEY THERAPY CENTRE (HM17363) | | | ● | | | | | | | | | | | | | |
| S DERBYSHIRE DEPT-PSYCHO (HM17804) | | | | | | | | | | | | | | | ● | |
| SAUNDERS, N (HM17958) | | | ● | | | | | | | | | | | | | |
| SCARR, G M (HM18006) | | | ● | | | | | | | | | | | | | |
| SCRIVENER, BARBARA (HM18153) | | | | | | | | | | | | | | | | |
| SHAW, R G B (HM18347) | | | ● | | | | | | | | | | | | | |

| Business | Pyscho-Synthesis | Reflexology | Reichian Therapy | Reiki | Remedial Massage | Rogerian Therapy | Rolfing | Seichem | Sensitivity Training | Shiatsu | Silva Method | Sound Therapy | Spiritual Healing | Sports Massage | Stress Therapy | Swedish Body Massage | T'ai-Chi Ch'uan |
|---|---|---|---|---|---|---|---|---|---|---|---|---|---|---|---|---|---|
| HALTON, A (HM08821) | | | | | | | | | | | | | | | | | |
| HARDWICK, JUDITH (HM08976) | | ● | | | | | | | | | | | | | | | |
| HARTWELL, A E (HM09151) | | | | | | | | | | | | | | | | | |
| HAWKINS & FIELDING (HM09217) | | | | | | | | | | | | | | | | | |
| HIGGS, ANN (HM09734) | | ● | | | | | | | | | | | | | | | |
| HUMAN RELATIONS SERVICES (HM10365) | | | | | | | | | | | | | | | | | |
| ILKESTONE OSTEO & MED CTRE (HM10580) | | | | | | | | | | | | | | ● | | | |
| JOHNSON, MELVYN (HM11086) | | | | | | | | | | | | | | | | | |
| KARDAHJI, F C (HM11319) | | | | | | | | | | | | | | | | | |
| KEMP, GILLIAN (HM11461) | | ● | | | | | | | | | | | | | ● | ● | |
| KNIGHT, JAYNE (HM11752) | | ● | | | | | | | | | | | | | | | |
| LANCASHIRE, A W (HM11915) | | | | | | | | | | | | | | | | | |
| LIFECHANGERS (HM12351) | | | | | | | | | | | | | | | | | |
| LIFESOLUTIONS (HM12359) | | | | | | | | | | | | | | | ● | | |
| MATTHEWS, A (HM13299) | | ● | | | | | | | | | | | | | | | |
| MATTHEWS, AMANDA (HM13301) | | ● | | | | | | | | | | | | | | | |
| NATURAL HEALTH CLINIC (HM14577) | | | | | | | | | | | | | | | ● | | |
| OSTEOPATH CLINIC (HM15447) | | | | | | | | | | | | | | | | | |
| PEARCE, YVONNE (HM15902) | | ● | | | | | | | | | | | | | | | |
| PEDLEY, ANNE (HM15933) | | | | | | | | | | | | | | | | | |
| PETER SADLER NATURAL MED CTRE (HM16074) | | | | | | | | | | | | | | | | | |
| PHILIP STOCK - PHYSIOTHERAPIST (HM16120) | | | | | | | | | | | | | | | | | |
| PHYSIO ACTIVE (HM16193) | | ● | | ● | | | | | | ● | | | | | | | |
| PRICE, GRAHAM (HM16577) | | | | | | | | | | | | | | | | | |
| PRICE, TRACY (HM16597) | | ● | | | | | | | | | | | | | | | |
| REDFERN, AMANDA (HM17018) | | ● | | | | | | | | | | | | | | | |
| REID, BARBARA (HM17113) | | ● | | | | | | | | | | | | | | | |
| RICKARD, CLIVE A (HM17310) | | | | | | | | | | | | | | | | | |
| RIPLEY THERAPY CENTRE (HM17363) | | | | | | | | | | | | | | | | | |
| S DERBYSHIRE DEPT-PSYCHO (HM17804) | | | | | | | | | | | | | | | | | |
| SAUNDERS, N (HM17958) | | | | | | | | | | | | | | | | | |
| SCARR, G M (HM18006) | | | | | | | | | | | | | | | | | |
| SCRIVENER, BARBARA (HM18153) | | ● | | | | | | | | | | | | | | | |
| SHAW, R G B (HM18347) | | | | | | | | | | | | | | | | | |

| Business | Tantra Therapy | Tera-Mai | Thought Field Therapy | Touch Therapy | Transactional Analysis | Tui-na | Ultrasonics | Vibrational Therapy | Visualisation Therapy | Vitamin Therapy | Voice Therapy | X-Ray | Ying & Yang | Yoga | Zen Therapy | Zero Balancing |
|---|---|---|---|---|---|---|---|---|---|---|---|---|---|---|---|---|
| HALTON, A (HM08821) | | | | | | | | | | | | | | | | |
| HARDWICK, JUDITH (HM08976) | | | | | | | | | | | | | | | | |
| HARTWELL, A E (HM09151) | | | | | | | | | | | | | | | | |
| HAWKINS & FIELDING (HM09217) | | | | | | | | | | | | | | | | |
| HIGGS, ANN (HM09734) | | | | | | | | | | | | | | | | |
| HUMAN RELATIONS SERVICES (HM10365) | | | | | | | | | | | | | | | | |
| ILKESTONE OSTEO & MED CTRE (HM10580) | | | | | | | | | | | | | | | | |
| JOHNSON, MELVYN (HM11086) | | | | | | | | | | | | | | | | |
| KARDAHJI, F C (HM11319) | | | | | | | | | | | | | | | | |
| KEMP, GILLIAN (HM11461) | | | | | | | | | | | | | | | | |
| KNIGHT, JAYNE (HM11752) | | | | | | | | | | | | | | | | |
| LANCASHIRE, A W (HM11915) | | | | | | | | | | | | | | | | |
| LIFECHANGERS (HM12351) | | | | | | | | | | | | | | | | |
| LIFESOLUTIONS (HM12359) | | | | | | | | | ● | | | | | | | |
| MATTHEWS, A (HM13299) | | | | | | | | | | | | | | | | |
| MATTHEWS, AMANDA (HM13301) | | | | | | | | | | | | | | | | |
| NATURAL HEALTH CLINIC (HM14577) | | | | | | | | | | | | | | ● | | |
| OSTEOPATH CLINIC (HM15447) | | | | | | | | | | | | | | | | |
| PEARCE, YVONNE (HM15902) | | | | | | | | | | | | | | | | |
| PEDLEY, ANNE (HM15933) | | | | | | | | | | | | | | | | |
| PETER SADLER NATURAL MED CTRE (HM16074) | | | | | | | | | | | | | | | | |
| PHILIP STOCK - PHYSIOTHERAPIST (HM16120) | | | | | | | ● | | | | | | | | | |
| PHYSIO ACTIVE (HM16193) | | | | | | | ● | | | | | | | | | |
| PRICE, GRAHAM (HM16577) | | | | | | | | | | | | | | | | |
| PRICE, TRACY (HM16597) | | | | | | | | | | | | | | | | |
| REDFERN, AMANDA (HM17018) | | | | | | | | | | | | | | | | |
| REID, BARBARA (HM17113) | | | | | | | | | | | | | | | | |
| RICKARD, CLIVE A (HM17310) | | | | | | | | | | | | | | | | |
| RIPLEY THERAPY CENTRE (HM17363) | | | | | | | | | | | | | | | | |
| S DERBYSHIRE DEPT-PSYCHO (HM17804) | | | | | | | | | | | | | | | | |
| SAUNDERS, N (HM17958) | | | | | | | | | | | | | | | | |
| SCARR, G M (HM18006) | | | | | | | | | | | | | | | | |
| SCRIVENER, BARBARA (HM18153) | | | | | | | | | | | | | | | | |
| SHAW, R G B (HM18347) | | | | | | | | | | | | | | | | |

# O - Z Therapies at Practices/Businesses

| Business by County with Reference no. | Orthotics | Osteomyology | Osteopathy | PAM | Paranormal Therapies | Pattern Therapies | Physiotherapy | Phytotherapy | Pilates | Podiatry | Polarity Therapy | Postural Integration | Primal Therapy | Psionic Therapy | Psychotherapy | Pyramid Power | Pyscho-Synthesis | Reflexology | Reichian Therapy | Reiki | Remedial Massage | Rogerian Therapy | Rolfing | Seichem | Sensitivity Training | Shiatsu | Silva Method | Sound Therapy | Spiritual Healing | Sports Massage | Stress Therapy | Swedish Body Massage | T'ai-Chi Ch'uan | Tantra Therapy | Tera-Mai | Thought Field Therapy | Touch Therapy | Transactional Analysis | Tui-na | Ultrasonics | Vibrational Therapy | Visualisation Therapy | Vitamin Therapy | Voice Therapy | X-Ray | Ying & Yang | Yoga | Zen Therapy | Zero Balancing |
|---|---|---|---|---|---|---|---|---|---|---|---|---|---|---|---|---|---|---|---|---|---|---|---|---|---|---|---|---|---|---|---|---|---|---|---|---|---|---|---|---|---|---|---|---|---|---|---|---|---|
| SMITH, ALAN P (HM18711) | | | ● | | | | | | | | | | | | | | | | | | | | | | | | | | | | | | | | | | | | | | | | | | | | | | |
| SPINK, BERNADETTE (HM19017) | | | | | | | | | | | | | | | | | | | | | ● | | | | | | | | | ● | | | | | | | | | | | | | | | | | | | |
| SPIRAC PHYSIOTHERAPY (HM19020) | | | | | | | ● | | | | | | | | | | | | | | | | | | | | | | | | | | | | | | | | | | | | | | | | | | |
| STEVENSON, JACKIE (HM19249) | | | | | | | | | | | | | | | ● | | | | | | | | | | | | | | | | | | | | | | | | | | | | | | | | | | |
| STRATTON, SUNNY (HM19374) | | | ● | | | | | | | | | | | | | | | | | | | | | | | | | | | | | | | | | | | | | | | | | | | | | | |
| STRUDWICK, H J (HM19425) | | | ● | | | | | | | | | | | | | | | | | | | | | | | | | | | | | | | | | | | | | | | | | | | | | | |
| TAYLOR, E F (HM19757) | | | ● | | | | | | | | | | | | ● | | | | | | | | | | | | | | | | | | | | | | | | | | | | | | | | | | |
| TAYLOR, E F (HM19756) | | | ● | | | | | | | | | | | | | | | | | | | | | | | | | | | | | | | | | | | | | | | | | | | | | | |
| TREEWICKS (HM20313) | | | | | | | | | | | | | | | | | | | | ● | | | | | | | | | | | | | | | | | | | | | | | | | | | | | |
| WHITEING CHIROPODISTS (HM21392) | | | | | | | | | | ● | | | | | | | | | | | | | | | | | | | | | | | | | | | | | | | | | | | | | | | |
| WILLIAMS, VERONICA (HM21604) | | | | | | | | | | | | | | | | | | ● | | ● | | | | | | | | | | | | | | | | | | | | | | | | | | | | | |
| **DEVON** | | | | | | | | | | | | | | | | | | | | | | | | | | | | | | | | | | | | | | | | | | | | | | | | | |
| ABBEYMEAD NATURAL HEALTH CTRE (HM00090) | | | ● | | | | | | | | | | | | ● | | | ● | | | | | | | | | | | | | ● | | | | | | | | | | | | | | | | | | |
| ACUPUNCTURE CLINIC (HM00276) | | | | | | | | | | | | | | | | | | | | | | | | | | | | | | | | | | | | | | | | | | | | | | ● | | | |
| ADAMS, JENNIFER (HM00353) | | | | | | | | | | | | | | | | | | ● | | | | | | | | | | | | | | | | | | | | | | | | | | | | | | | |
| ALISON MORTON PHYSIOTHERAPY (HM00579) | | | | | | | ● | | | | | | | | | | | | | | | | | | | | | | | | | | | | | | | | | | | | | | | | | | |
| ALLSOPP, EMMA (HM00662) | | | | | | | | | | | | | | | | | | ● | | | | | | | | | | | | | | | | | | | | | | | | | | | | | | | |
| ANNE RAWLINGS HYPNOTHERAPY (HM00901) | | | | | | | | | | | | | ● | | ● | | ● | | | | | ● | | | | | | | | | ● | | | | | | | ● | | | | ● | | | | | | | |
| ARCTURUES CLINIC (HM00987) | | | ● | | | | | | | | | | | | ● | | | ● | | | | | | | | | | | | | | | | | | | | | | | | | | | | | | | |
| ARPINO, MARIA (HM01146) | | | | | | | | | | | | | | | | | | ● | | | | | | | | | | | | | | | | | | | | | | | | | | | | | | | |
| AWARENESS CENTRE (HM01415) | | | ● | | | | | | | | | | | | ● | | | | | ● | | | | ● | | ● | | | ● | | | | ● | | | | | | | | | ● | ● | | | | ● | | |
| BACKS R US (HM01528) | | | ● | | | | | | | | | | | | | | | | | | | | | | | | | | | | | | | | | | | | | | | | | | | | | | |
| BALL, ADRIAN (HM01624) | | | ● | | | | | | | | | | | | | | | | | | | | | | | | | | | | | | | | | | | | | | | | | | | | | | |
| BENNETT, ROGER (HM02153) | | | | | | | | | | | | | | | ● | | | | | | | | | | | | | | | | | | | | | | | | | | | | | | | | | | |
| BLYTH, DON (HM02538) | | | ● | | | | | | | | | | | | | | | | | | | | | | | | | | | | | | | | | | | | | | | | | | | | | | |
| BONTEIN, SARA (HM02686) | | | | | | | | | | | | | | | | | | ● | | | | | | | | | | | | | | | | | | | | | | | | | | | | | | | |
| BREADING, MARGARET (HM02935) | | | | | | | | | | | | | | | | | | ● | | | | | | | | | | | | | | | | | | | | | | | | | | | | | | | |
| BRIXHAM HEALING HANDS CENTRE (HM03105) | | | | | | | | | | | | | | | | | | | | | | | | | | | | | ● | | | | | | | | | | | | | | | | | | | | |
| BROPHY, MARTHA (HM03194) | | | | | | | | | | | | | | | | | | ● | | | | | | | | | | | | | | | | | | | | | | | | | | | | | | | |
| BURY, CHRIS (HM03454) | | | ● | | | | | | | | | | | | | | | | | | | | | | | | | | | | | | | | | | | | | | | | | | | | | | |
| BUTSON, JUDITH (HM03493) | | | | | | | | | | | | | | | | | | ● | | | | | | | | | | | | | | | | | | | | | | | | | | | | | | | |
| CAMERON, ALISON (HM03582) | | | ● | | | | | | | | | | | | | | | | | | | | | | | | | | | | | | | | | | | | | | | | | | | | | | |
| CARPENTER, PAUL (HM03734) | | | | | | | | | | | | | | | | | | ● | | | | | | | | | | | | | | | | | | | | | | | | | | | | | | | |
| CARSON, BRONWYN (HM03767) | | | ● | | | | | | | | | | | | | | | | | | | | | | | | | | | | | | | | | | | | | | | | | | | | | | |

# O - Z Therapies at Practices/Businesses

| Business by County with Reference no. | Orthotics | Osteomyology | Osteopathy | PAM | Paranormal Therapies | Pattern Therapies | Physiotherapy | Phytotherapy | Pilates | Podiatry | Polarity Therapy | Postural Integration | Primal Therapy | Psionic Therapy | Psychotherapy | Pyramid Power | Pyscho-Synthesis | Reflexology | Reichian Therapy | Reiki | Remedial Massage | Rogerian Therapy | Rolfing | Seichem | Sensitivity Training |
|---|---|---|---|---|---|---|---|---|---|---|---|---|---|---|---|---|---|---|---|---|---|---|---|---|---|
| CARSON, NICHOLAS (HM03771) | | | ● | | | | | | | | | | | | | | | | | | | | | | |
| CASTLE CHIROPRACTIC CLINIC (HM03829) | | | | | | | | | | | | | | | | | | | | | | | | | |
| CASTLEBRIDGE CHIRO & REFLEX (HM03844) | | | | | | | | | | | | | | | | | | ● | | | | | | | |
| CHARLES-DAVIS, S (HM04027) | | | ● | | | | | | | | | | | | | | | | | | | | | | |
| CHEMIN, CHRISTIAN (HM04098) | | | ● | | | | | | | | | | | | | | | | | | | | | | |
| CHIROPRACTIC AND MYOFACIAL (HM04350) | | | | | | | ● | | | | | | | | | | | | | | | | | | |
| CLEMO, ANNE (HM04647) | | | | | | | | | | | | | | | | | | ● | | | | | | | |
| CLINIC OF HYP & STRESS MNGMT (HM04696) | | | | | | | | | | | | | | | | | | | | | | | | | |
| COOKE, ANNIE (HM05060) | | | | | | | | | | | | | | | | | | ● | | | | | | | |
| COOPER, H J (HM05107) | | | ● | | | | | | | | | | | | | | | | | | | | | | |
| COPE, ANNE (HM05134) | | | ● | | | | | | | | | ● | | | | | | ● | | | | | | | |
| COX, MIRANDA (HM05316) | | | | | | | | | | | | | | | ● | | | | | | | ● | | | |
| DELVE, PHILIP (HM05971) | | | ● | | | | | | | | | | | | | | | | | | | | | | |
| DEVONSHIRE HEALTH & RAQUET (HM06043) | | | | | | | ● | | | | | | | | | | | | | | | | | | |
| DICKSON, JANE (HM06084) | | | ● | | | | | | | | | | | | | | | | | | | | | | |
| DOUGLAS-MORT, D J & R F (HM06221) | | | ● | | | | | | | | | | | | | | | | | | | | | | |
| DOUGLAS-RILEY, PENELOPE (HM06223) | | | | | | | | | | | | | | | | | | ● | | | | | | | |
| DOWNES, W P (HM06246) | | | ● | | | | | | | | | | | | | | | | | | | | | | |
| ELDON HEALTH CLINIC (HM06705) | | | ● | | | | ● | | ● | | | | | | | | | ● | | | | | | | |
| ELLISON, ANNE (HM06774) | | | ● | | | | | | | | | | | | | | | | | | | | | | |
| ELLISON, ANNE (HM06775) | | | ● | | | | | | | | | | | | | | | | | | | | | | |
| ENGLAND, ANITA (HM06827) | | | | | | | | | | | | | | | | | | ● | | | | | | | |
| FELL, HELEN (HM07204) | | | | | | | | | | | | | | | | | | ● | | | | | | | |
| FOOT CLINIC & THERAPY ROOM (HM07474) | | | | | | | | | | ● | | | | | | | | | | | | | | | |
| FOOTEC MEDICAL (HM07500) | | | | | | | | | | ● | | | | | | | | | | | | | | | |
| FOXWELL, CORALIE (HM07644) | | | ● | | | | | | | | | | | | | | | | | | | | | | |
| FOXWELL, CORALIE (HM07645) | | | ● | | | | | | | | | | | | | | | | | | | | | | |
| FUDGE, H (HM07777) | | | ● | | | | | | | | | | | | | | | | | | | | | | |
| GARRETTLEY, U (HM07902) | | | | | | | | | | | | | | | | | | ● | | | | | | | |
| GILKERSON, PATRICIA (HM08073) | | | | | | | | | | | | | | | | | | ● | | | | | | | |
| GOODALL, PAULINE (HM08245) | | | ● | | | | | | | | | | | | | | | | | | | | | | |
| GOULDEN, KATHLEEN (HM08318) | | | | | | | | | | | | | | | | | | ● | | | | | | | |
| GRACELINGS NATURAL HEALTH (HM08335) | | | | | | | | | | | | | | | | | | ● | | | ● | | | | |
| HANDS, PETER (HM08918) | | | ● | | | | | | | | | | | | | | | | | | | | | | |

| Business by County with Reference no. | Shiatsu | Silva Method | Sound Therapy | Spiritual Healing | Sports Massage | Stress Therapy | Swedish Body Massage | T'ai-Chi Ch'uan | Tantra Therapy | Tera-Mai | Thought Field Therapy | Touch Therapy | Transactional Analysis | Tui-na | Ultrasonics | Vibrational Therapy | Visualisation Therapy | Vitamin Therapy | Voice Therapy | X-Ray | Ying & Yang | Yoga | Zen Therapy | Zero Balancing |
|---|---|---|---|---|---|---|---|---|---|---|---|---|---|---|---|---|---|---|---|---|---|---|---|---|
| CARSON, NICHOLAS (HM03771) | | | | | | | | | | | | | | | | | | | | | | | | |
| CASTLE CHIROPRACTIC CLINIC (HM03829) | | | | | | | | | | | | | | | | | | ● | | ● | | | | |
| CASTLEBRIDGE CHIRO & REFLEX (HM03844) | | | | | | | | | | | | | | | | | | | | | | | | |
| CHARLES-DAVIS, S (HM04027) | | | | | | | | | | | | | | | | | | | | | | | | |
| CHEMIN, CHRISTIAN (HM04098) | | | | | | | | | | | | | | | | | | | | | | | | |
| CHIROPRACTIC AND MYOFACIAL (HM04350) | | | | | | | | | | | | | | | | | | | | | | | | |
| CLEMO, ANNE (HM04647) | | | | | | | | | | | | | | | | | | | | | | | | |
| CLINIC OF HYP & STRESS MNGMT (HM04696) | | | | | | ● | | | | | | | | | | | | | | | | | | |
| COOKE, ANNIE (HM05060) | | | | | | | | | | | | | | | | | | | | | | | | |
| COOPER, H J (HM05107) | | | | | | | | | | | | | | | | | | | | | | | | |
| COPE, ANNE (HM05134) | | | | | | | | | | | | | | | | | | | | | | | | |
| COX, MIRANDA (HM05316) | | | | | | ● | | | | | | | ● | | | | | | | | | | | |
| DELVE, PHILIP (HM05971) | | | | | | | | | | | | | | | | | | | | | | | | |
| DEVONSHIRE HEALTH & RAQUET (HM06043) | | | | | | | | | | | | | | | | | | | | | | | | |
| DICKSON, JANE (HM06084) | | | | | | | | | | | | | | | | | | | | | | | | |
| DOUGLAS-MORT, D J & R F (HM06221) | | | | | | | | | | | | | | | | | | | | | | | | |
| DOUGLAS-RILEY, PENELOPE (HM06223) | | | | | | | | | | | | | | | | | | | | | | | | |
| DOWNES, W P (HM06246) | | | | | | | | | | | | | | | | | | | | | | | | |
| ELDON HEALTH CLINIC (HM06705) | ● | | | | | | | | | | | | | | | | | ● | | ● | | | | |
| ELLISON, ANNE (HM06774) | | | | | | | | | | | | | | | | | | | | | | | | |
| ELLISON, ANNE (HM06775) | | | | | | | | | | | | | | | | | | | | | | | | |
| ENGLAND, ANITA (HM06827) | | | | | | | | | | | | | | | | | | | | | | | | |
| FELL, HELEN (HM07204) | | | | | | | | | | | | | | | | | | | | | | | | |
| FOOT CLINIC & THERAPY ROOM (HM07474) | | | | | | | | | | | | | | | | | | | | | | | | |
| FOOTEC MEDICAL (HM07500) | | | | | | | | | | | | | | | | | | | | | | | | |
| FOXWELL, CORALIE (HM07644) | | | | | | | | | | | | | | | | | | | | | | | | |
| FOXWELL, CORALIE (HM07645) | | | | | | | | | | | | | | | | | | | | | | | | |
| FUDGE, H (HM07777) | | | | | | | | | | | | | | | | | | | | | | | | |
| GARRETTLEY, U (HM07902) | | | | | | | | | | | | | | | | | | | | | | | | |
| GILKERSON, PATRICIA (HM08073) | | | | | | | | | | | | | | | | | | | | | | | | |
| GOODALL, PAULINE (HM08245) | | | | | | | | | | | | | | | | | | | | | | | | |
| GOULDEN, KATHLEEN (HM08318) | | | | | | | | | | | | | | | | | | | | | | | | |
| GRACELINGS NATURAL HEALTH (HM08335) | | | | | | ● | ● | | | | | | | | | | | | | | | | | |
| HANDS, PETER (HM08918) | | | | | | | | | | | | | | | | | | | | | | | | |

# O - Z Therapies at Practices/Businesses

| Business by County with Reference no. | Orthotics | Osteomyology | Osteopathy | PAM | Paranormal Therapies | Pattern Therapies | Physiotherapy | Phytotherapy | Pilates | Podiatry | Polarity Therapy | Postural Integration | Primal Therapy | Psionic Therapy | Psychotherapy | Pyramid Power | Pyscho-Synthesis |
|---|---|---|---|---|---|---|---|---|---|---|---|---|---|---|---|---|---|
| HARRIS, C (HM09054) | | | ● | | | | | | | | | | | | | | |
| HARRIS, MICHAEL (HM09080) | | | ● | | | | | | | | | | | | | | |
| HEALTH CONSULTANCY (HM09382) | | | | | | | | | | | | | | | ● | | |
| HEALTH WAVES (HM09408) | | | | | | | | | | | | | | | | | |
| HERIOT, LYNDA (HM09681) | | | | | | | | | | | | | | | | | |
| HIETT, ANNE (HM09727) | | | | | | | | | | | | | | | | | |
| HORNER, ANN (HM10176) | | | | | | | | | | | | | | | | | |
| INTAHEALTH UK (HM10689) | | | | | | | | | | | | | | | | | |
| IOKAI SHIATSU CLINIC (HM10709) | | | | | | | | | | | | | | | | | |
| JACKSON, ANDREA (HM10822) | | | ● | | | | | | | | | | | | | | |
| JANE HYDE CHRTRD PHYSIO (HM10917) | | | | | | | | ● | ● | | | | | | | | |
| JEFFRIES, BARBARA (HM10972) | | | | | | | | | | | | | | | ● | | |
| JOHNSON, MICHAEL (HM11087) | | | | | | | | | | | | | | | | | |
| JULIE ADAMS REFLEXOLOGIST (HM11256) | | | | | | | | | | | | | | | | | |
| KEOGH, MARTIN (HM11540) | | | ● | | | | | | | | | | | | | | |
| KINGSBRIDGE COMP HLTH PRACTICE (HM11658) | | | | | | | | | | | | | | | ● | | |
| KINGSBRIDGE PHYSICAL THERAPY (HM11659) | | | ● | | | | | | | | | | | | | | |
| KRAWCHENKO, LOUISE A V (HM11798) | | | ● | | | | | | | | | | | | | | |
| LATCHEM, V (HM11991) | | | ● | | | | | | | | | | | | | | |
| LAWRENCE, J M (HM12048) | | | ● | | | | | | | | | | | | | | |
| LIGHT TOUCH THERAPY TRAINING (HM12369) | | | | | | | | | | | | | | | | | |
| LINDEMAN, A J (HM12415) | | | | | | | | ● | | | | | | | | | |
| LION HOUSE SURGERY (HM12446) | | | | | | | | | | | | | | | | | |
| MALLARDO, RENEE (HM12977) | | | | | | | | | | | | | | | ● | | |
| MANGLES, DENISE (HM13012) | | | | | | | | | | | | | | | | | |
| MCDAID, M S (HM13442) | | | ● | | | | | | | | | | | | | | |
| MONSHIN, DEBORAH J (HM14075) | | | | | | | | | | | | | | | ● | | |
| MOODY, DAVID (HM14095) | | | ● | | | | | | | | | | | | | | |
| MOODY, DONALD A (HM14096) | | | ● | | | | | | | | | | | | | | |
| MOORE, CHRISTINE (HM14121) | | | | | | | | | | | | | | | | | |
| NELSON, CHRISTINE (HM14776) | | | | | | | | | | | | | | | | | |
| NELSON, PAUL (HM14781) | | | | | | | | | | | | | | | ● | | |
| NETHERWAY, JEAN (HM14789) | | | | | | | | | | | | | | | | | |
| NEWTON, DON (HM14896) | | | ● | | | | | | | | | | | | | | |

| Business by County with Reference no. | Reflexology | Reichian Therapy | Reiki | Remedial Massage | Rogerian Therapy | Rolfing | Seichem | Sensitivity Training | Shiatsu | Silva Method | Sound Therapy | Spiritual Healing | Sports Massage | Stress Therapy | Swedish Body Massage | T'ai-Chi Ch'uan | Tantra Therapy |
|---|---|---|---|---|---|---|---|---|---|---|---|---|---|---|---|---|---|
| HARRIS, C (HM09054) | | | | | | | | | | | | | | | | | |
| HARRIS, MICHAEL (HM09080) | | | | | | | | | | | | | | | | | |
| HEALTH CONSULTANCY (HM09382) | ● | | | | | | | | | | | | | ● | | | |
| HEALTH WAVES (HM09408) | ● | | | | | | | | | | ● | | | ● | | | |
| HERIOT, LYNDA (HM09681) | ● | | | | | | | | | | | | | | | | |
| HIETT, ANNE (HM09727) | ● | | | | | | | | | | | | | | | | |
| HORNER, ANN (HM10176) | ● | | | | | | | | | | | | | | | | |
| INTAHEALTH UK (HM10689) | | | | | | | | | | | | | | | | | |
| IOKAI SHIATSU CLINIC (HM10709) | | | | | | | | | ● | | | | | | | | |
| JACKSON, ANDREA (HM10822) | | | | | | | | | | | | | | | | | |
| JANE HYDE CHRTRD PHYSIO (HM10917) | | | | | | | | | | | | | | | | | |
| JEFFRIES, BARBARA (HM10972) | | | | | | | | | | | | | | | | | |
| JOHNSON, MICHAEL (HM11087) | ● | | | | | | | | | | | | | | | | |
| JULIE ADAMS REFLEXOLOGIST (HM11256) | ● | | | | | | | | | | | | | | | | |
| KEOGH, MARTIN (HM11540) | | | | | | | | | | | | | | | | | |
| KINGSBRIDGE COMP HLTH PRACTICE (HM11658) | ● | | ● | | | | | | ● | | | ● | | ● | | | |
| KINGSBRIDGE PHYSICAL THERAPY (HM11659) | | | | | | | | | | | | | | | | | |
| KRAWCHENKO, LOUISE A V (HM11798) | | | | | | | | | | | | | | | | | |
| LATCHEM, V (HM11991) | | | | | | | | | | | | | | | | | |
| LAWRENCE, J M (HM12048) | | | | | | | | | | | | | | | | | |
| LIGHT TOUCH THERAPY TRAINING (HM12369) | | | | | ● | | | | | | | | | ● | | | |
| LINDEMAN, A J (HM12415) | | | | | | | | | | | | | | | | | |
| LION HOUSE SURGERY (HM12446) | | | | ● | | | | | | | | | | | | | |
| MALLARDO, RENEE (HM12977) | | | ● | | ● | | | | | | | | | ● | | | |
| MANGLES, DENISE (HM13012) | ● | | | | | | | | | | | | | | ● | | |
| MCDAID, M S (HM13442) | | | | | | | | | | | | | | | | | |
| MONSHIN, DEBORAH J (HM14075) | | | | | | | | | | | | | | ● | | | |
| MOODY, DAVID (HM14095) | | | | | | | | | | | | | | | | | |
| MOODY, DONALD A (HM14096) | | | | | | | | | | | | | | | | | |
| MOORE, CHRISTINE (HM14121) | ● | | | | | | | | | | | | | | | | |
| NELSON, CHRISTINE (HM14776) | ● | | | | | | | | | | | | | | | | |
| NELSON, PAUL (HM14781) | | | | | ● | | | | | | | | | ● | | | |
| NETHERWAY, JEAN (HM14789) | | | | | | | | | ● | | | | | | | | |
| NEWTON, DON (HM14896) | | | | | | | | | | | | | | | | | |

| Business by County with Reference no. | Tera-Mai | Thought Field Therapy | Touch Therapy | Transactional Analysis | Tui-na | Ultrasonics | Vibrational Therapy | Visualisation Therapy | Vitamin Therapy | Voice Therapy | X-Ray | Ying & Yang | Yoga | Zen Therapy | Zero Balancing |
|---|---|---|---|---|---|---|---|---|---|---|---|---|---|---|---|
| HARRIS, C (HM09054) | | | | | | | | | | | | | | | |
| HARRIS, MICHAEL (HM09080) | | | | | | | | | | | | | | | |
| HEALTH CONSULTANCY (HM09382) | | | | | | | | | | | | | | | |
| HEALTH WAVES (HM09408) | | | | | | | | | | | | | | | |
| HERIOT, LYNDA (HM09681) | | | | | | | | | | | | | | | |
| HIETT, ANNE (HM09727) | | | | | | | | | | | | | | | |
| HORNER, ANN (HM10176) | | | | | | | | | | | | | | | |
| INTAHEALTH UK (HM10689) | | | | | | | | | ● | | | | | | |
| IOKAI SHIATSU CLINIC (HM10709) | | | | | | | | | | | | | | | |
| JACKSON, ANDREA (HM10822) | | | | | | | | | | | | | | | |
| JANE HYDE CHRTRD PHYSIO (HM10917) | | | | | | ● | | | | | | | | | |
| JEFFRIES, BARBARA (HM10972) | | | | | | | | | | | | | | | |
| JOHNSON, MICHAEL (HM11087) | | | | | | | | | | | | ● | | | |
| JULIE ADAMS REFLEXOLOGIST (HM11256) | | | | | | | | | | | | | | | |
| KEOGH, MARTIN (HM11540) | | | | | | | | | | | | | | | |
| KINGSBRIDGE COMP HLTH PRACTICE (HM11658) | | | ● | | | | | | ● | | | | ● | | |
| KINGSBRIDGE PHYSICAL THERAPY (HM11659) | | | | | | | | | | | | | | | |
| KRAWCHENKO, LOUISE A V (HM11798) | | | | | | | | | | | | | | | |
| LATCHEM, V (HM11991) | | | | | | | | | | | | | | | |
| LAWRENCE, J M (HM12048) | | | | | | | | | | | | | | | |
| LIGHT TOUCH THERAPY TRAINING (HM12369) | | | ● | | | | | | ● | | | | | | ● |
| LINDEMAN, A J (HM12415) | | | | | | | | | | | | | | | |
| LION HOUSE SURGERY (HM12446) | | | | | | | | | | | | | | | |
| MALLARDO, RENEE (HM12977) | | | | | | | | | | | | | | | |
| MANGLES, DENISE (HM13012) | | | | | | | | | | | | | | | |
| MCDAID, M S (HM13442) | | | | | | | | | | | | | | | |
| MONSHIN, DEBORAH J (HM14075) | | | | | | | | ● | | | | | | | |
| MOODY, DAVID (HM14095) | | | | | | | | | | | | | | | |
| MOODY, DONALD A (HM14096) | | | | | | | | | | | | | | | |
| MOORE, CHRISTINE (HM14121) | | | | | | | | | | | | | | | |
| NELSON, CHRISTINE (HM14776) | | | | | | | | | | | | | | | |
| NELSON, PAUL (HM14781) | | | | | | | | | ● | | | | | | |
| NETHERWAY, JEAN (HM14789) | | | | | | | | | | | | | | | |
| NEWTON, DON (HM14896) | | | | | | | | | | | | | | | |

# O - Z Therapies at Practices/Businesses

| Business by County with Reference no. | Orthotics | Osteomyology | Osteopathy | PAM | Paranormal Therapies | Pattern Therapies | Physiotherapy | Phytotherapy | Pilates | Podiatry | Polarity Therapy | Postural Integration | Primal Therapy | Psionic Therapy | Psychotherapy | Pyramid Power | Pyscho-Synthesis | Reflexology | Reichian Therapy | Reiki | Remedial Massage | Rogerian Therapy | Rolfing | Seichem | Sensitivity Training | Shiatsu | Silva Method | Sound Therapy | Spiritual Healing | Sports Massage | Stress Therapy | Swedish Body Massage | T'ai-Chi Ch'uan | Tantra Therapy | Tera-Mai | Thought Field Therapy | Touch Therapy | Transactional Analysis | Tui-na | Ultrasonics | Vibrational Therapy | Visualisation Therapy | Vitamin Therapy | Voice Therapy | X-Ray | Ying & Yang | Yoga | Zen Therapy | Zero Balancing |
|---|---|---|---|---|---|---|---|---|---|---|---|---|---|---|---|---|---|---|---|---|---|---|---|---|---|---|---|---|---|---|---|---|---|---|---|---|---|---|---|---|---|---|---|---|---|---|---|---|---|
| NIGEL DE SALENGRE (HM14936) | | | ● | | | | | | | | | | | | | | | | | | | | | | | | | | | | | | | | | | | | | | | | | | | | | | |
| PAIGNTON PHYSIOTHERAPY (HM15576) | | | | | | | ● | | | | | | | | | | | | | | | | | | | | | | | | | | | | | | | | | | | | | | | | | | |
| PANNELL, R J (HM15636) | | | | | | | | | | ● | | | | | | | | | | | | | ● | | | | | | | | | | | | | | | | | | | | | | | | | | |
| PARKER, JONATHAN (HM15696) | | | ● | | | | | | | | | | | | | | | | | | | | | | | | | | | | | | | | | | | | | | | | | | | | | | |
| PEERS, C (HM15942) | | | ● | | | | | | | | | | | | | | | | | | | | | | | | | | | | | | | | | | | | | | | | | | | | | | |
| PLAYERS, MEGAN (HM16365) | | | | | | | | | | | | | | | | | | | | | | | | | | ● | | | | | | | | | | | | | | | | | | | | | | | |
| PLYMOUTH OSTEOPATHS (HM16388) | | | ● | | | | | | | | | | | | | | | | | | | | | | | | | | | | | | | | | | | | | | | | | | | | | | |
| POPPLEWELL, REBECCA (HM16438) | | | ● | | | | | | | | | | | | | | | | | | | | | | | | | | | | | | | | | | | | | | | | | | | | | | |
| PSYCHOTHERAPY/HYPNOTHERAPY (HM16739) | | | | | | | | | | | | | | | ● | | | | | | | | | | | | | | | | | | | | | | | | | | | | | | | | | | |
| REDWOOD, DAWN (HM17034) | | | | | | | | | | | | | | | | | | ● | | | | | | | | | | | | | | | | | | | | | | | | | | | | | | | |
| REFLEXOLOGY CENTRE (HM17083) | | | | | | | | | | | | | | | | | | ● | | | | | | | | | | | | | | | | | | | | | | | | | | | | | | | |
| RIVERSIDE CHIROPRACTIC CLINIC (HM17379) | | | | | | | | | | | | | | | | | | | | | | | | | | | | | | | | | | | | | | | | ● | | | | | ● | | | | |
| ROSE & CROWN CLINIC (HM17598) | | | | | | | | | | | | | | | | | | ● | | | ● | | | | | | | | ● | | | | | | | | | | | | | | | | | | | | |
| SCURR, PETER M (HM18160) | | | | | | | | | | ● | | | | | | | | | | | | | | | | | | | | | | | | | | | | | | | | | | | | | | | |
| SMITH, A C (HM18708) | | | ● | | | | | | | | | | | | | | | | | | | | | | | | | | | | | | | | | | | | | | | | | | | | | | |
| ST DAVIDS OSTEOPATHIC CLINIC (HM19074) | | | ● | | | | | | | | | | | | | | | | | | | | | | | | | | | | | | | | | | | | | | | | | | | | | | |
| STURGESS, PETER (HM19449) | | | ● | | | | | | | | | | | | | | | | | | | | | | | | | | | | | | | | | | | | | | | | | | | | | | |
| TAME, STEPHEN (HM19673) | | | | | | | | | | | | | | | ● | | | | | | | | | | | | | | | | | | | | | | | | | | | | | | | | | | |
| TAYLOR, LYNETTE (HM19781) | | | ● | | | | | | | | | | | | | | | | | | | | | | | | | | | | | | | | | | | | | | | | | | | | | | |
| THOMAS, JANET (HM19948) | | | | | | | | | | | | | | | | | | ● | | | | | | | | | | | | | | | | | | | | | | | | | | | | | | | |
| THOMPSON, PAUL (HM19997) | | | ● | | | | | | | | | | | | | | | | | | | | | | | | | | | | | | | | | | | | | | | | | | | | | | |
| TRANCE - FORMATIONS HEALING (HM20250) | | | | | | | | | | | | | | | ● | | | ● | | | | | | | | | | | | | ● | | | | | | | | | | | ● | | | | | | | |
| VITAL TOUCH (HM20703) | | | | | | | | | | | | | | | | | | ● | | | | | | | | | | | | | | | | | | | | | | | | | | | | | | | |
| WALTERS, RICHARD (HM20880) | | | | | | | | | | | | | | | | | | | | | | | | | | | | | | | | | | | | | | | | | | | | | | | | | ● |
| WASSERMAN, D (HM20976) | | | ● | | | | | | | | | | | | | | | | | | | | | | | | | | | | | | | | | | | | | | | | | | | | | | |
| WASSERMAN, DAVID (HM20977) | | | ● | | | | | | | | | | | | | | | | | | | | | | | | | | | | | | | | | | | | | | | | | | | | | | |
| WHEELER, ROBERT (HM21318) | | | ● | | | | | | | | | | | | | | | | | | | | | | | | | | | | | | | | | | | | | | | | | | | | | | |
| WIDGER, CHRISTINE (HM21456) | | | | | | | | | | | | | | | | | | ● | | | | | | | | | | | | | | | | | | | | | | | | | | | | | | | |
| YOGA HEALTH STUDIO (HM22028) | | | | | | | | | | | | | | | | | | | | | | | | | | | | | | | | | | | | | | | | | | | | | | | ● | | |
| YORK HOUSE CHIROPODY (HM22044) | | | | | | | | | | ● | | | | | | | | | | | | | | | | | | | | | | | | | | | | | | | | | | | | | | | |
| DORSET | | | | | | | | | | | | | | | | | | | | | | | | | | | | | | | | | | | | | | | | | | | | | | | | | |
| ABBEY VIEW COMP CLINIC (HM00088) | | | | | | | | | | | | | | | | | | ● | | | ● | | | | | ● | | | | | | | | | | | | | | | | | | | | | | | |
| ADELAIDE CLINIC (HM00378) | | | | | | | | | | | | | | | | | | ● | | | | | | | | | | | | | | | | | | | | | | | | | | | | | | | |
| ARCHIBALD, LIZ (HM00980) | | | | | | | | ● | | | | | | | | | | | | | | | | | | | | | | | ● | | | | | | | | | | | | | | | | | | |

# O - Z Therapies at Practices/Businesses

| Business by County with Reference no. | Orthotics | Osteomyology | Osteopathy | PAM | Paranormal Therapies | Pattern Therapies | Physiotherapy | Phytotherapy | Pilates | Podiatry | Polarity Therapy | Postural Integration | Primal Therapy | Psionic Therapy | Psychotherapy | Pyramid Power | Pyscho-Synthesis | Reflexology | Reichian Therapy | Reiki | Remedial Massage | Rogerian Therapy | Rolfing | Seichem | Sensitivity Training | Shiatsu | Silva Method | Sound Therapy | Spiritual Healing | Sports Massage | Stress Therapy | Swedish Body Massage | T'ai-Chi Ch'uan | Tantra Therapy | Tera-Mai | Thought Field Therapy | Touch Therapy | Transactional Analysis | Tui-na | Ultrasonics | Vibrational Therapy | Visualisation Therapy | Vitamin Therapy | Voice Therapy | X-Ray | Ying & Yang | Yoga | Zen Therapy | Zero Balancing |
|---|---|---|---|---|---|---|---|---|---|---|---|---|---|---|---|---|---|---|---|---|---|---|---|---|---|---|---|---|---|---|---|---|---|---|---|---|---|---|---|---|---|---|---|---|---|---|---|---|---|
| ARIES OSTEOPATHIC HEALTH CLNC (HM00997) |  |  | ● |  |  |  |  |  |  |  |  |  |  |  |  |  |  |  |  |  |  |  |  |  |  |  |  |  |  |  |  |  |  |  |  |  |  |  |  |  |  |  |  |  |  |  |  |  |  |
| AROMA TRANQUILITY (HM01064) |  |  |  |  |  |  |  |  |  |  |  |  |  |  |  |  |  |  |  |  |  |  |  |  |  |  |  |  |  |  | ● |  |  |  |  |  |  |  |  |  |  |  |  |  |  |  |  |  |  |
| ART OF REFLEXOLOGY (HM01154) |  |  |  |  |  |  |  |  |  |  |  |  |  |  |  |  |  | ● |  |  |  |  |  |  |  |  |  |  |  |  |  |  |  |  |  |  |  |  |  |  |  |  |  |  |  |  |  |  |  |
| ASHBY, CAROLINE (HM01196) |  |  |  |  |  |  |  |  |  |  |  |  |  |  |  |  |  | ● |  |  |  |  |  |  |  |  |  |  |  |  |  |  |  |  |  |  |  |  |  |  |  |  |  |  |  |  |  |  |  |
| BAC, NULA L (HM01465) |  |  |  |  |  |  |  |  |  |  |  |  |  |  | ● |  |  |  |  |  |  |  |  |  |  |  |  |  |  |  |  |  |  |  |  |  |  |  |  |  |  |  |  |  |  |  |  |  |  |
| BARNS, MICHAEL (HM01764) |  |  |  |  |  |  |  |  |  |  |  |  |  |  | ● |  |  |  |  |  |  |  |  |  |  |  |  |  |  |  |  |  |  |  |  |  |  |  |  |  |  |  |  |  |  |  |  |  |  |
| BAZALGETTE, R A (HM01945) |  |  | ● |  |  |  |  |  |  |  |  |  |  |  |  |  |  |  |  |  |  |  |  |  |  |  |  |  |  |  |  |  |  |  |  |  |  |  |  |  |  |  |  |  |  |  |  |  |  |
| BEAUMONT COLLEGE OF NAT MED (HM01986) |  |  |  |  |  |  |  |  |  |  |  |  |  |  |  |  |  | ● |  |  |  |  |  |  |  |  |  |  |  | ● |  |  |  |  |  |  |  |  |  |  |  |  |  |  |  |  |  |  |  |
| BELTAIN CENTRE (HM02117) |  |  |  |  |  |  |  |  |  |  |  |  |  |  | ● |  |  |  |  |  |  |  |  |  |  |  |  |  |  |  | ● |  |  |  |  |  |  |  |  |  |  | ● |  |  |  |  |  |  |  |
| BELTAIN CENTRE (HM02116) |  |  |  |  |  |  |  |  |  |  |  |  |  |  |  |  |  |  |  | ● |  |  |  |  |  |  |  |  |  |  |  |  |  |  |  |  |  |  |  |  |  |  |  |  |  |  |  |  |  |
| BLORE, ANNE (HM02520) |  |  |  |  |  |  |  |  |  |  |  |  |  |  |  |  |  | ● |  |  |  |  |  |  |  |  |  |  |  |  |  |  |  |  |  |  |  |  |  |  |  |  |  |  |  |  |  |  |  |
| BOURNEMOUTH CTRE FOR COMP MED (HM02761) |  |  | ● |  |  |  |  |  |  |  |  |  |  |  |  |  |  | ● |  | ● |  |  |  |  |  |  |  |  |  |  |  | ● |  |  |  |  |  |  |  |  |  |  |  |  |  |  |  |  |  |
| BOURNEMOUTH PHYSIO CLINIC (HM02762) |  |  |  |  |  |  | ● |  |  |  |  |  |  |  |  |  |  |  |  |  |  |  |  |  |  |  |  |  |  |  |  |  |  |  |  |  |  |  |  |  |  |  |  |  |  |  |  |  |  |
| BOWEN CLINIC (HM02771) |  |  |  |  |  |  |  |  |  |  |  |  |  |  |  |  |  |  |  | ● |  |  |  |  |  |  |  |  | ● |  |  |  |  |  |  |  |  |  |  |  |  |  |  |  |  |  |  |  |  |
| BOYLE, MICHAEL (HM02829) |  |  |  |  |  |  |  |  |  |  |  |  |  |  | ● |  |  |  |  |  |  |  |  |  |  |  |  |  |  |  |  |  |  |  |  |  |  |  |  |  |  |  |  |  |  |  |  |  |  |
| BRANDWOOD-CORMACK, HAYLEY (HM02915) |  |  |  |  |  |  |  |  |  |  |  |  |  |  |  |  |  | ● |  |  |  |  |  |  |  |  |  |  |  |  |  |  |  |  |  |  |  |  |  |  |  |  |  |  |  |  |  |  |  |
| BRIDPORT COMP MEDICINE CTRE (HM03019) |  |  | ● |  |  |  |  |  |  |  |  |  |  |  |  |  |  | ● |  |  |  |  |  |  |  | ● |  |  |  |  |  |  |  |  |  |  |  |  |  |  |  |  |  |  |  |  |  |  |  |
| BRIGHTER FUTURE (HM03040) |  |  |  |  |  |  |  |  |  |  |  |  |  |  | ● |  |  |  |  |  |  |  |  |  |  |  |  |  | ● |  |  |  |  |  |  |  |  |  |  |  |  |  |  |  |  |  |  |  |  |
| BRIGHTER FUTURE (HM03039) |  |  |  |  |  |  |  |  |  |  |  |  |  |  | ● |  |  |  |  |  |  |  |  |  |  |  |  |  | ● |  |  |  |  |  |  |  |  |  |  |  |  |  |  |  |  |  |  |  |  |
| BROADSTONE CENTRE COMP MED (HM03117) |  |  |  |  |  |  |  |  |  |  |  |  |  |  |  |  |  |  |  |  |  |  |  |  |  | ● |  |  |  |  |  |  |  |  |  |  |  |  |  |  |  |  |  |  |  |  |  |  |  |
| BROADSTONE CENTRE OF COMP MED (HM03118) |  |  |  |  |  |  |  |  |  | ● |  |  |  |  | ● |  |  | ● |  |  | ● |  |  |  |  | ● |  |  |  |  | ● |  |  |  |  |  |  |  |  |  |  |  |  |  |  |  |  |  |  |
| BURT, S (HM03429) |  |  |  |  |  |  |  |  |  |  |  |  |  |  |  |  |  |  |  |  |  |  |  |  |  |  |  |  |  |  |  |  |  |  |  |  |  |  |  |  |  |  | ● |  |  |  |  |  |  |
| BWT PODIATRY (HM03508) |  |  |  |  |  |  |  |  |  | ● |  |  |  |  |  |  |  |  |  |  |  |  |  |  |  |  |  |  |  |  |  |  |  |  |  |  |  |  |  |  |  |  |  |  |  |  |  |  |  |
| CARBERY PRACTICE (HM03657) |  |  | ● |  |  |  |  |  |  |  |  |  |  |  | ● |  |  |  |  |  |  |  |  |  |  |  |  |  |  |  | ● |  |  |  |  |  |  |  |  |  |  |  |  |  | ● |  |  |  |  |
| CHRISTCHURCH CHIROPRACTIC CTRE (HM04435) |  |  |  |  |  |  |  |  |  |  |  |  |  |  |  |  |  | ● |  |  |  |  |  |  |  |  |  |  |  |  |  |  |  |  |  |  |  |  |  |  |  |  |  |  | ● |  |  |  |  |
| CHRISTCHURCH PHYSIO PRACTICE (HM04436) |  |  |  |  |  |  | ● |  |  |  |  |  |  |  |  |  |  |  |  |  |  |  |  |  |  |  |  |  |  |  |  |  |  |  |  |  |  |  |  |  |  |  |  |  |  |  |  |  |  |
| CLARK, LYNN (HM04568) | ● |  |  |  |  |  |  |  |  |  |  |  |  |  |  |  |  |  |  |  |  |  |  |  |  |  |  |  |  |  |  |  |  |  |  |  |  |  |  |  |  |  |  |  |  |  |  |  |  |
| COX, LESLEY (HM05311) |  |  |  |  |  |  |  |  |  |  |  |  |  |  |  |  |  | ● |  |  |  |  |  |  |  |  |  |  |  |  |  |  |  |  |  |  |  |  |  |  |  |  |  |  |  |  |  |  |  |
| CULLING, ADRIAN (HM05566) |  |  | ● |  |  |  |  |  |  |  |  |  |  |  |  |  |  |  |  |  |  |  |  |  |  |  |  |  |  |  |  |  |  |  |  |  |  |  |  |  |  |  |  |  |  |  |  |  |  |
| DAVIES, VIVIEN (HM05844) |  |  |  |  |  |  |  |  |  |  |  |  |  |  |  |  |  | ● |  |  |  |  |  |  |  |  |  |  |  |  |  |  |  |  |  |  |  |  |  |  |  |  |  |  |  |  |  |  |  |
| DLP HYPNOTHERAPY CENTRE (HM06134) |  |  |  |  |  |  |  |  |  |  |  |  |  |  |  |  |  |  |  |  |  |  |  |  |  |  |  |  |  |  |  |  |  |  |  |  |  |  |  |  |  | ● |  |  |  |  |  |  |  |
| DORSET RACQUETS & HEALTH CLUB (HM06205) |  |  |  |  |  |  |  |  |  |  |  |  |  |  |  |  |  | ● |  | ● |  |  |  |  |  |  |  |  |  |  |  |  |  |  |  |  |  |  |  |  |  |  |  |  |  |  |  |  |  |
| EVANS, REBECCA MARY (HM06988) |  |  | ● |  |  |  |  |  |  |  |  |  |  |  |  |  |  |  |  |  |  |  |  |  |  |  |  |  |  |  |  |  |  |  |  |  |  |  |  |  |  |  |  |  |  |  |  |  |  |
| EVERETT, PAUL (HM07002) |  |  |  |  |  |  |  |  |  |  |  |  |  |  |  |  |  | ● |  |  |  |  |  |  |  |  |  |  |  |  |  |  |  |  |  |  |  |  |  |  |  |  |  |  |  |  |  |  |  |

# O - Z Therapies at Practices/Businesses

| Business by County with Reference no. | Orthotics | Osteomyology | Osteopathy | PAM | Paranormal Therapies | Pattern Therapies | Physiotherapy | Phytotherapy | Pilates | Podiatry | Polarity Therapy | Postural Integration | Primal Therapy | Psionic Therapy | Psychotherapy | Pyramid Power | Pyscho-Synthesis | Reflexology | Reichian Therapy | Reiki | Remedial Massage | Rogerian Therapy | Rolfing | Seichem | Sensitivity Training |
|---|---|---|---|---|---|---|---|---|---|---|---|---|---|---|---|---|---|---|---|---|---|---|---|---|---|
| FREESPIRIT (HM07724) | | | | | | | | | | | | | | | | | | | | | | | | | |
| FROST, LESLEY (HM07764) | | | | | | | | | | | | | | | | | | ● | | | | | | | |
| GIBSON, VERONICA (HM08047) | | | | | | | | | | | | | | | | | | ● | | | | | | | |
| GLENCAIRE CLINIC (HM08145) | | | ● | | | | | | | | | | | | | | | | | | | | | | |
| GRAHAM, N (HM08353) | | | ● | | | | | | | | | | | | | | | | | | | | | | |
| GRIER, PHILIPPA (HM08547) | | | | | | | | | | | | | | | | | | ● | | | | | | | |
| HAMBLETT, JOHN E (DR) (HM08826) | | | ● | | | | | | | | | | | | | | | | | | | | | | |
| HASELDEN, MAXINE (HM09179) | | | | | | | | | | | | | | | | | | ● | | | | | | | |
| HAYWARD, JANET (HM09282) | | | | | | | | | | | | | | | | | | ● | | | | | | | |
| HIGHCLIFFE CHIROPRACTIC CLINIC (HM09749) | | | | | | | | | | | | | | | | | | | | | | | | | |
| HIGHCLIFFE OSTEOPATHIC CLINIC (HM09750) | | | ● | | | | | | | | | | | | | | | | | | | | | | |
| HOLISTIC HEALTH CENTRE (HM09973) | | | | | | | | | | | | | | | | | | | | | | | | | |
| JACKSON, A E (HM10817) | | | ● | | | | | | | | | | | | | | | ● | | | | | | | |
| JELFS, MARTIN (HM10975) | | | | | | | | | | | | | | | ● | | | | ● | | | ● | | | |
| KENDRICK, DIANE (HM11481) | | | | | | | | | | | | | | | | | | ● | | | | | | | |
| KENNEDY, EDWARD (HM11491) | | | ● | | | | | | | | | | | | | | | | | | | | | | |
| LAW, DEREK T (HM12036) | | | ● | | | | | | | | | | | | | | | | | | | | | | |
| LEVER, I J (HM12261) | | | ● | | | | | | | | | | | | | | | | | | | | | | |
| LEVER, IAN J (HM12262) | | | ● | | | | | | | | | | | | | | | | | | | | | | |
| LOW, LORNA (HM12687) | | | ● | | | | | | | | | | | | | | | | | | | | | | |
| LOWSON, H (HM12710) | | | | | | | | | | | | | | | ● | | | | | | | | | | |
| MARCH-SMITH, ROSIE (HM13074) | | | | | | | | | | | | | | | ● | | | | | | | | | | |
| MCLAUGHLIN, SANDRA (HM13549) | | | | | | | | | | | | | | | | | | ● | | | | | | | |
| MIDDLES PICCADILLY CTRE (HM13815) | | | | | | | | | | | | | | | | | | ● | | ● | | | | | |
| MOTCOMBE PARK PHYSIOTHERAPY (HM14273) | | | | | | | ● | | | | | | | | | | | | | | | | | | |
| NATURAL HEALTH CONSULTANCY (HM14592) | | | | | | | | | | | | | | | | | | | | ● | | | | | |
| NEIJIA (HM14759) | | | | | | | | | | | | | | | | | | | | | | | | | |
| PAOLUCCI, ANNA (HM15641) | | | | | | | | | | | | | | | | | | ● | | | | | | | |
| PARKER, RAY (HM15702) | | | | | | | | | | | | | | | | | | ● | | | | | | | |
| PARTNERSHIP, BAKER (DR) (HM15764) | | | | | | | | | | | | | | | ● | | | | | | | ● | | | |
| PHILLIPS, JOAN (HM16134) | | | | | | | | | | | | | | | | | | ● | | | | | | | |
| PHILLIPS, L (HM16136) | | | | | | | | | | | | | | | ● | | | | | | | | | | |
| PHYSIO, MASSAGE & PR ACU (HM16210) | | | | | | | | | | | | | | | | | | | | | | | | | |
| PORTEOUS, TRISH (HM16445) | | | | | | | | | | | | | | | ● | | | | | | | | | | |

| Business by County with Reference no. | Shiatsu | Silva Method | Sound Therapy | Spiritual Healing | Sports Massage | Stress Therapy | Swedish Body Massage | T'ai-Chi Ch'uan | Tantra Therapy | Tera-Mai | Thought Field Therapy | Touch Therapy | Transactional Analysis | Tui-na | Ultrasonics | Vibrational Therapy | Visualisation Therapy | Vitamin Therapy | Voice Therapy | X-Ray | Ying & Yang | Yoga | Zen Therapy | Zero Balancing |
|---|---|---|---|---|---|---|---|---|---|---|---|---|---|---|---|---|---|---|---|---|---|---|---|---|
| FREESPIRIT (HM07724) | | | | | | ● | | | | | | | | | | | | | | | | | | |
| FROST, LESLEY (HM07764) | | | | | | | | | | | | | | | | | | | | | | | | |
| GIBSON, VERONICA (HM08047) | | | | | | | | | | | | | | | | | | | | | | | | |
| GLENCAIRE CLINIC (HM08145) | | | | | | | | | | | | | | | | | | | | | | | | |
| GRAHAM, N (HM08353) | | | | | | | | | | | | | | | | | | | | | | | | |
| GRIER, PHILIPPA (HM08547) | | | | | | | | | | | | | | | | | | | | | | | | |
| HAMBLETT, JOHN E (DR) (HM08826) | | | | | | | | | | | | | | | | | | | | | | | | |
| HASELDEN, MAXINE (HM09179) | | | | | | | | | | | | | | | | | | | | | | | | |
| HAYWARD, JANET (HM09282) | | | | | | | | | | | | | | | | | | | | | | | | |
| HIGHCLIFFE CHIROPRACTIC CLINIC (HM09749) | | | | | | | | | | | | | | | | | | ● | | | | | | |
| HIGHCLIFFE OSTEOPATHIC CLINIC (HM09750) | | | | | | | | | | | | | | | | | | | | | | | | |
| HOLISTIC HEALTH CENTRE (HM09973) | ● | | | | | | | | | | | | | | | | | | | | | | | |
| JACKSON, A E (HM10817) | | | | | | | | | | | | | | | | | | | | | | | | |
| JELFS, MARTIN (HM10975) | | | | | | ● | | | ● | | | | | | | | | | | | | | | |
| KENDRICK, DIANE (HM11481) | | | | | | | | | | | | | | | | | | | | | | | | |
| KENNEDY, EDWARD (HM11491) | | | | | | | | | | | | | | | | | | | | | | | | |
| LAW, DEREK T (HM12036) | | | | | | | | | | | | | | | | | | | | | | | | |
| LEVER, I J (HM12261) | | | | | | | | | | | | | | | | | | | | | | | | |
| LEVER, IAN J (HM12262) | | | | | | | | | | | | | | | | | | | | | | | | |
| LOW, LORNA (HM12687) | | | | | | | | | | | | | | | | | | | | | | | | |
| LOWSON, H (HM12710) | | | | | | | | | | | | | | | | | | | | | | | | |
| MARCH-SMITH, ROSIE (HM13074) | | | | | | | | | | | | | | | | | | | | | | | | |
| MCLAUGHLIN, SANDRA (HM13549) | | | | | | | | | | | | | | | | | | | | | | | | |
| MIDDLES PICCADILLY CTRE (HM13815) | ● | | | | | | | | | | | | | | | | | | | | | | | |
| MOTCOMBE PARK PHYSIOTHERAPY (HM14273) | | | | | | | | | | | | | | | | | | | | | | | | |
| NATURAL HEALTH CONSULTANCY (HM14592) | | | | | | | | | | | | | | | | | | | | | | | | |
| NEIJIA (HM14759) | | | | | | | | ● | | | | | | | | | | | | | | | | |
| PAOLUCCI, ANNA (HM15641) | | | | | | | | | | | | | | | | | | | | | | | | |
| PARKER, RAY (HM15702) | | | | | | | | | | | | | | | | | | | | | | | | |
| PARTNERSHIP, BAKER (DR) (HM15764) | | | | | | ● | | | | | | | | | | | | | | | | | | |
| PHILLIPS, JOAN (HM16134) | | | | | | | | | | | | | | | | | | | | | | | | |
| PHILLIPS, L (HM16136) | | | | | | | | | | | | | | | | | | | | | | | | |
| PHYSIO, MASSAGE & PR ACU (HM16210) | | | | | | ● | | | | | | ● | | | ● | | | | | | | | | |
| PORTEOUS, TRISH (HM16445) | | | | | | | | | | | | | | | | | | | | | | | | |

# O - Z Therapies at Practices/Businesses

| Business by County with Reference no. | Orthotics | Osteomyology | Osteopathy | PAM | Paranormal Therapies | Pattern Therapies | Physiotherapy | Phytotherapy | Pilates | Podiatry | Polarity Therapy | Postural Integration | Primal Therapy | Psionic Therapy | Psychotherapy | Pyramid Power | Pyscho-Synthesis | Reflexology | Reichian Therapy | Reiki | Remedial Massage | Rogerian Therapy | Rolfing | Seichem | Sensitivity Training | Shiatsu | Silva Method | Sound Therapy | Spiritual Healing | Sports Massage | Stress Therapy | Swedish Body Massage | T'ai-Chi Ch'uan | Tantra Therapy | Tera-Mai | Thought Field Therapy | Touch Therapy | Transactional Analysis | Tui-na | Ultrasonics | Vibrational Therapy | Visualisation Therapy | Vitamin Therapy | Voice Therapy | X-Ray | Ying & Yang | Yoga | Zen Therapy | Zero Balancing |
|---|---|---|---|---|---|---|---|---|---|---|---|---|---|---|---|---|---|---|---|---|---|---|---|---|---|---|---|---|---|---|---|---|---|---|---|---|---|---|---|---|---|---|---|---|---|---|---|---|
| PRIDEAUX-BRUNE, COLETTE (HM16604) | | | | | | | | | | | | | | | | | | ● | | | | | | | | | | | | | | | | | | | | | | | | | | | | | | | |
| PRIDMORE, JOSEPHINE (HM16605) | | | | | | | | | | | | | | | | | | | | | | | | | | ● | | | | | | | | | | | | | | | | | | | | | ● | | |
| PROSPECT HEALTH (HM16667) | | | | | | | | | | | | | | | | | | ● | | | | | | | | | | | | | | | | | | | | | | | ● | | | | | | | | |
| ROBSON, VANESSA (HM17514) | | | | | | | | | | ● | | | | | | | | | | | | | | | | | | | | | | | | | | | | | | | | | | | | | | | |
| ROLLS MILL COMP HEALTH CENTRE (HM17567) | | | | | | | | ● | | | | ● | | | | | | ● | | | | | | | | ● | | | ● | | ● | | | | | | ● | | | | | | ● | | | ● | | | |
| SHEBORNE CHIROPRACTIC CENTRE (HM18361) | | | | | | | | | | | | | | | | | | | | | | | | | | | | | | | | | | | | | | | | ● | | | | | | | | | |
| SKELTON, JAN (HM18635) | | | | | | | | | | | | | | | | | | ● | | | | | | | | | | | | | | | | | | | ● | | | | | | | | | | | | |
| SKINNER, NICOLA (HM18656) | | | | | | | | | | | | | | | | | | ● | | | ● | | | | | | | | | | | | | | | | | | | | | | | | | | | | |
| STEELE, T M (HM19183) | | | ● | | | | | | | | | | | | | | | | | | | | | | | | | | | | | | | | | | | | | | | | | | | | | | |
| SYKES, LIZZIE (HM19615) | | | | | | | | | | | | | | | | | | ● | | | | | | | | | | | | | | | | | | | | | | | | | | | | | | | |
| TAI CHI CHU'UAN (HM19654) | | | | | | | | | | | | | | | | | | | | | | | | | | | | | | | | | ● | | | | | | | | | | | | | | | | |
| TALBOT, MICHAEL (HM19661) | | | ● | | | | | | | | | | | | | | | | | | | | | | | | | | | | | | | | | | | | | | | | | | | | | | |
| TREAT FEET (HM20301) | | | | | | | | | | ● | | | | | | | | | | | | | | | | | | | | | | | | | | | | | | | | | | | | | | | |
| TRINITY OSTEOPATHIC PRACTICE (HM20341) | | | ● | | | | | | | | | | | | | | | | | | | | | | | | | | | | | | | | | | | | | | | | | | | | | | |
| TURNER, HAZEL (HM20425) | | | | | | | | | | | | | | | | | | ● | | | | | | | | | | | | | | | | | | | | | | | | | | | | | | | |
| WARD, DIANE (HM20899) | | | | | | | | | | | | | | | | | | ● | | | | | | | | | | | | | | | | | | | | | | | | | | | | | | | |
| WEBB, GILL (HM21064) | | | | | | | | | | | | | | | | | | ● | | | | | | | | | | | | | | | | | | | | | | | | | | | | | | | |
| WESSEX HEALTHY LIVING FOUND (HM21208) | | | ● | | | | | | | | | | | | ● | | | ● | | ● | ● | | | | | ● | | | | | ● | | | | | | | | | | | | ● | | | | | | |
| WHITE FLOWER CENTRE (HM21337) | | | | | | | | | | | | | | | | | | ● | | | | | | | | | | | | | | | | | | | | | | | | | | | | | | | |
| WHITE, RALPH E (HM21375) | | | ● | | | | | | | | | | | | | | | | | | | | | | | | | | | | | | | | | | | | | | | | | | | | | | |
| WILLIAMS, TIM (HM21599) | | | ● | | | | | | | | | | | | | | | | | | | | | | | | | | | | | | | | | | | | | | | | | | | | | | |
| WILLIAMS, TIMOTHY (HM21600) | | | ● | | | | | | | | | | | | | | | | | | | | | | | | | | | | | | | | | | | | | | | | | | | | | | |
| WIMBORNE CHIROPODY SURGERY (HM21687) | | | | | | | | | | ● | | | | | | | | | | | | | | | | | | | | | | | | | | | | | | | | | | | | | | | |
| WOODINGTON, N J (HM21829) | | | ● | | | | | | | | | | | | | | | | | | | | | | | | | | | | | | | | | | | | | | | | | | | | | | |
| WRIGHT, KAREN (HM21941) | | | | | | | | | | | | | | | | | | ● | | | | | | | | | | | | | | | | | | | | | | | | | | | | | | | |
| YELLOW HOUSE (HM22005) | | | ● | | | | | | | | | | | | | | | ● | | ● | | | | | | | | | | | | | | | | | | | | | | | | | | | | | |
| **EALING** | | | | | | | | | | | | | | | | | | | | | | | | | | | | | | | | | | | | | | | | | | | | | | | | | |
| EALING BOWEN CLINIC (HM06484) | | | | | | | ● | | | | | | | | | | | | | | ● | | | | | | | | | | ● | | | | | | | | | | | | | | | | | | |
| **ESSEX** | | | | | | | | | | | | | | | | | | | | | | | | | | | | | | | | | | | | | | | | | | | | | | | | | |
| A M R THERAPIES (HM00040) | | | | | | | | | | | | | | | | | | ● | | | | | | | | | | | | | | | | | | | | | | | | | | | | | | | |
| ABBOT, LISA (HM00095) | | | | | | | | | | | | | | | | | | ● | | ● | | | | | | ● | | | | | | | | | | | | | | | | | | | | | | | |
| ABBOTT, LISA (HM00099) | | | | | | | | | | | | | | | | | | ● | | ● | | | | | | ● | | | | | | | | | | | | | | | | | | | | | | | |
| AEQUILIBRIUM (HM00407) | | | | | | | | | | | | | | | | | | ● | | | | | | | | | | | | | | | | | | | | | | | | | | | | | | | |
| AJW CLEMENS OSTEOPATHIC CLINIC (HM00459) | | | ● | | | | | | | | | | | | | | | | | | | | | | | | | | | | | | | | | | | | | | | | | | | | | | |

# O - Z Therapies at Practices/Businesses

Business by County with Reference no.

| Business by County with Reference no. | Orthotics | Osteomyology | Osteopathy | PAM | Paranormal Therapies | Pattern Therapies | Physiotherapy | Phytotherapy | Pilates | Podiatry | Polarity Therapy | Postural Integration | Primal Therapy | Psionic Therapy | Psychotherapy | Pyramid Power | Pyscho-Synthesis | Reflexology | Reichian Therapy | Reiki | Remedial Massage | Rogerian Therapy | Rolfing | Seichem | Sensitivity Training |
|---|---|---|---|---|---|---|---|---|---|---|---|---|---|---|---|---|---|---|---|---|---|---|---|---|---|
| AJW CLEMENS OSTEOPATHIC CLINIC (HM00458) | | | ● | | | | | | | | | | | | | | | | | | | | | | |
| AROMATHERAPY CLINIC (HM01107) | | | | | | | | | | | | | | | | | | | | ● | | | | | |
| ASHBY & ASSOCIATES (HM01194) | ● | | | | | | | | | ● | | | | | | | | | | | | | | | |
| ASSOCIATION OF OSTEOMYOLOGY (HM01283) | | ● | ● | | | | ● | | | | | | | | | | | | | | ● | | | | |
| AVART, GILLIAN (HM01383) | | | | | ● | | | | | | | | | | | | | ● | | ● | | | | | |
| BAGLEY, ELIZABETH (HM01538) | | | ● | | | | | | | | | | | | | | | | | | | | | | |
| BALGORES SQUARE THERAPY CTRE (HM01622) | | | ● | | | | | | | | | | | | | | | | | | | | | | |
| BARKING PHYSICAL THERAPY CTRE (HM01715) | | | | | | | | | | | | | | | ● | | | | | | | | | | |
| BARNES, M (HM01750) | | | | | | | | | | | | | | | ● | | | | | | | | | | |
| BARRETT, JACQUELINE (HM01791) | | | | | | | | | | | | | | | | | | ● | | | | | | | |
| BAXTER, LISA (HM01929) | | | | | | | | | | | | | | | | | | ● | | | | | | | |
| BEARD, HELEN (HM01964) | | | | | | | | | | | | | | | | | | ● | | | | | | | |
| BECONTREE NHS THERAPY (HM02030) | | | | | | | | | | | | | | | ● | | | | | | | | | | |
| BENEDICTA (HM02125) | | | | | | | | | | | | | | | | | | ● | | ● | | | | | |
| BIRD, DAPHNE (HM02360) | | | ● | | | | | | | | | | | | | | | | | | | | | | |
| BLACK, CATHY (HM02421) | | | | | | | | | | | | | | | | | | ● | | | | | | | |
| BODY BALANCE (HM02569) | | | | | | | | | | | | | | | ● | | | | | | | | | | |
| BODY BALANCE HEALTH SOLUTIONS (HM02571) | | | ● | | | | | | | | | | | | | | | | | | | | | | |
| BOURNE, STACEY (HM02757) | | | ● | | | | | | | | | | | | | | | | | | | | | | |
| BRADLEY, HAZEL (HM02865) | | | ● | | | | | | | | | | | | | | | | | | | | | | |
| BREINBURG, DERYCK (HM02952) | | | ● | | | | | | | | | | | | | | | | | | | | | | |
| BRENTWOOD CHIROPODY SURGERY (HM02963) | ● | | | | | | | | | ● | | | | | | | | | | | | | | | |
| BREUKEL, CORINA (HM02974) | | | ● | | | | | | | | | | | | | | | | | | | | | | |
| BRIGGS, MARGARETE (HM03036) | | | | | | | | | | | | | | | ● | | | | | | | | | | |
| BRITISH INSTITUTE-HYPNOTHERAPY (HM03085) | | | | | | | | | | | | | | | ● | | | | | | | | | | |
| BRITISH SCHOOL OF REFLEXOLOGY (HM03091) | | | | | | | | | | | | | | | | | | ● | | | | | | | |
| BRUCE, NEIL (HM03272) | | | ● | | | | | | | | | | | | | | | | | | | | | | |
| BULLER, JEMIMA (HM03343) | | | | | | | | | | | | | | | ● | | | | | | | | | | |
| BURNHAM PHYSIOTHERAPY CLINIC (HM03405) | | | | | | | ● | | | | | | | | | | | | | | | | | | |
| BURNHAM, EMMA-JANE (HM03406) | | | | | | | | | | | | | | | | | | ● | | | | | | | |
| BYRNE, ALISON (HM03514) | | | | | | | | | | | | | | | | | | ● | | | | | | | |
| CADWALLADER, PENNY (HM03536) | | | ● | | | | | | | | | | | | | | | | | | | | | | |
| CAIN, SHEILA (HM03538) | | | | | | | | | | | | | | | | | | ● | | | | | | | |
| CARNELIAN NTRL TREATMENT CTRE (HM03714) | | | | | | | | | | | | | | | | | | ● | | ● | | | | | |

| Business by County with Reference no. | Shiatsu | Silva Method | Sound Therapy | Spiritual Healing | Sports Massage | Stress Therapy | Swedish Body Massage | T'ai-Chi Ch'uan | Tantra Therapy | Tera-Mai | Thought Field Therapy | Touch Therapy | Transactional Analysis | Tui-na | Ultrasonics | Vibrational Therapy | Visualisation Therapy | Vitamin Therapy | Voice Therapy | X-Ray | Ying & Yang | Yoga | Zen Therapy | Zero Balancing |
|---|---|---|---|---|---|---|---|---|---|---|---|---|---|---|---|---|---|---|---|---|---|---|---|---|
| AJW CLEMENS OSTEOPATHIC CLINIC (HM00458) | | | | | | | | | | | | | | | | | | | | | | | | |
| AROMATHERAPY CLINIC (HM01107) | | | | | | | | | | | | | | | | | | | | | | | | |
| ASHBY & ASSOCIATES (HM01194) | | | | | | | | | | | | | | | | | | | | | | | | |
| ASSOCIATION OF OSTEOMYOLOGY (HM01283) | | | | | | ● | | | | | | | | | | | | | | | | | | |
| AVART, GILLIAN (HM01383) | | | | ● | | | | | | | | | | | | | | | | | | | | |
| BAGLEY, ELIZABETH (HM01538) | | | | | | | | | | | | | | | | | | | | | | | | |
| BALGORES SQUARE THERAPY CTRE (HM01622) | | | | | | | | | | | | | | | | | | | | | | | | |
| BARKING PHYSICAL THERAPY CTRE (HM01715) | | | | | | | | | | | | | | | | | | | | | | | | |
| BARNES, M (HM01750) | | | | | | | | | | | | | | | | | | | | | | | | |
| BARRETT, JACQUELINE (HM01791) | | | | | | | | | | | | | | | | | | | | | | | | |
| BAXTER, LISA (HM01929) | | | | | | | | | | | | | | | | | | | | | | | | |
| BEARD, HELEN (HM01964) | ● | | | | | | | | | | | | | | | | | | | | | | | |
| BECONTREE NHS THERAPY (HM02030) | | | | | | | | | | | | | | | | | | | | | | | | |
| BENEDICTA (HM02125) | | | | | | ● | | | | | | | | | | | | | | | | | | |
| BIRD, DAPHNE (HM02360) | | | | | | | | | | | | | | | | | | | | | | | | |
| BLACK, CATHY (HM02421) | | | | | | | | | | | | | | | | | | | | | | | | |
| BODY BALANCE (HM02569) | | | | | | | | | | | | | | | | | | | | | | | | |
| BODY BALANCE HEALTH SOLUTIONS (HM02571) | | | | | | | | | | | | | | | | | | | | | | | | |
| BOURNE, STACEY (HM02757) | | | | | | | | | | | | | | | | | | | | | | | | |
| BRADLEY, HAZEL (HM02865) | | | | | | | | | | | | | | | | | | | | | | | | |
| BREINBURG, DERYCK (HM02952) | | | | | | | | | | | | | | | | | | | | | | | | |
| BRENTWOOD CHIROPODY SURGERY (HM02963) | | | | | | | | | | | | | | | | | | | | | | | | |
| BREUKEL, CORINA (HM02974) | | | | | | | | | | | | | | | | | | | | | | | | |
| BRIGGS, MARGARETE (HM03036) | | | | | | | | | | | | | | | | | | | | | | | | |
| BRITISH INSTITUTE-HYPNOTHERAPY (HM03085) | | | | | | ● | | | | | | | | | | | ● | | | | | | | |
| BRITISH SCHOOL OF REFLEXOLOGY (HM03091) | | | | | | | | | | | | | | | | | | | | | | | | |
| BRUCE, NEIL (HM03272) | | | | | | | | | | | | | | | | | | | | | | | | |
| BULLER, JEMIMA (HM03343) | | | | | | | | | | | | | | | | | | | | | | | | |
| BURNHAM PHYSIOTHERAPY CLINIC (HM03405) | | | | | | | | | | | | | | | | | | | | | | | | |
| BURNHAM, EMMA-JANE (HM03406) | | | | | | | | | | | | | | | | | | | | | | | | |
| BYRNE, ALISON (HM03514) | | | | | | | | | | | | | | | | | | | | | | | | |
| CADWALLADER, PENNY (HM03536) | | | | | | | | | | | | | | | | | | | | | | | | |
| CAIN, SHEILA (HM03538) | | | | | | | | | | | | | | | | | | | | | | | | |
| CARNELIAN NTRL TREATMENT CTRE (HM03714) | | | | | | | | | | | | | | | | | | | | | | | | |

# O - Z Therapies at Practices/Businesses

| Business by County with Reference no. | Orthotics | Osteomyology | Osteopathy | PAM | Paranormal Therapies | Pattern Therapies | Physiotherapy | Phytotherapy | Pilates | Podiatry | Polarity Therapy | Postural Integration | Primal Therapy | Psionic Therapy | Psychotherapy | Pyramid Power | Pyscho-Synthesis | Reflexology | Reichian Therapy | Reiki | Remedial Massage | Rogerian Therapy | Rolfing | Seichem | Sensitivity Training |
|---|---|---|---|---|---|---|---|---|---|---|---|---|---|---|---|---|---|---|---|---|---|---|---|---|---|
| CARTER-WEBER, LEE (HM03791) | | | | | | | | | | | | | | | | | ● | | | | | | | |
| CATON, PETER (HM03859) | | | | | | | | | | | | | | ● | | | | | | | | | | |
| CHAKRA ROSE (HM03942) | | | | | | | | | | | | | | ● | | | ● | | | | | | | |
| CHAPMAN, ALAN (HM03998) | | | ● | | | | | | | | | | | | | | | | | | | | | | |
| CHRIS MOSLIN HYPNOTHERAPIST (HM04433) | | | | | | | | | | | | | | ● | | | | | | | | | | |
| CLACTON REFLEX & THERAPY CTRE (HM04502) | | | | | | | | | | | | | | | | | ● | | | | | | | |
| CLARKE, M R (HM04593) | | | ● | | | | | | | | | | | | | | | | | | | | | | |
| CLARKE, ROSALEEN (HM04601) | | | | | | | | | | | | | | | | | ● | | | | | | | |
| CLAYTON, DEBRA (HM04622) | | | | | | | | | | | | | | | | | ● | | | | | | | |
| CLAYTON, SUSAN (HM04627) | | | | | | | | | | | | | | | | | ● | | | | | | | |
| COKER, EILEEN (HM04800) | | | | | | | | | | | | | | | | | ● | | | | | | | |
| COLCHESTER OSTEOPATHIC CENTRE (HM04807) | | | ● | | | | | | | | | | | | | | | | | | | | | | |
| COOK, JOE (HM05048) | | | | | | | | | | | | | | ● | | | | | | | | | | |
| COOPER, FELICITY (HM05104) | | | | | | | | | ● | | | | | | | | | | | | | | | |
| COOPER, JEFFREY C (HM05113) | | | ● | | | | | | | | | | | | | | | | | | | | | | |
| CORBY, VERONICA (HM05157) | | | | | | | | | | | | | | | | | ● | | | | | | | |
| CRANE SCHOOL OF REFLEXOLOGY (HM05367) | | | | | | | | | | | | | | | | | ● | | | | | | | |
| CROSS HANDS CHIRO CLINIC (HM05479) | | | | | | ● | | | | | | | | | | | | | | | | | | |
| CROWDER, C H J (HM05501) | | | ● | | | | | | | | | | | | | | | | | | | | | | |
| CURTIS, PETER (HM05638) | | | | | | | | | | | | | | ● | | | | | | | | | | |
| DAVIDGE, AMANDA (HM05784) | | | | | | | | | | | | | | | | | ● | | | | | | | |
| DICKASON, J T (HM06067) | | | ● | | | | | | | | | | | | | | | | | | | | | | |
| DIXON, RUTH (HM06133) | | | | | | | | | | | | | | | | | ● | | | | | | | |
| DOVE, COLIN (HM06226) | | | ● | | | | | | | | | | | | | | | | | | | | | | |
| E A O C (HM06465) | | | ● | | | | | | | | | ● | | | | | | | | | | | | | |
| EDEN, SHARON (HM06594) | | | | | | | | | | | | | | ● | | | | | | | | | | |
| EGNER, JULIE (HM06687) | | | | | | | | | | | | | | | | | ● | | | | | | | |
| ELDRETT, RACHAEL (HM06708) | | | | | | | | | | | | | | | | | ● | | | | | | | |
| ELMER CHIROPODY & PODIATRY SVS (HM06781) | | | | | | | | | ● | | | | | | | | | | | | | | | |
| ENRIGHT, VALERIE (HM06846) | | | | | | | | | | | | | | | | | ● | | | | | | | |
| EPPING OSTEOPATHY AND SPORTS (HM06854) | | | ● | | | | | | | | | | | | | | | | | | | | | | |
| EPPING PHYSIOTHERAPY PRACTICE (HM06855) | | | | | | ● | | | | | | | | | | | | | | | | | | |
| ESSEX COUNS/PSYCHOTHERAPY SV (HM06934) | | | | | | | | | | | | | | ● | | | | | | | | | | |
| ESSEX PHYSIO & SPORTS INJ CTRE (HM06938) | | | | | | ● | | | | | | | | | | | | ● | | | | | |

| Business by County with Reference no. | Shiatsu | Silva Method | Sound Therapy | Spiritual Healing | Sports Massage | Stress Therapy | Swedish Body Massage | T'ai-Chi Ch'uan | Tantra Therapy | Tera-Mai | Thought Field Therapy | Touch Therapy | Transactional Analysis | Tui-na | Ultrasonics | Vibrational Therapy | Visualisation Therapy | Vitamin Therapy | Voice Therapy | X-Ray | Ying & Yang | Yoga | Zen Therapy | Zero Balancing |
|---|---|---|---|---|---|---|---|---|---|---|---|---|---|---|---|---|---|---|---|---|---|---|---|---|
| CARTER-WEBER, LEE (HM03791) | | | | | | | | | | | | | | | | | | | | | | | | |
| CATON, PETER (HM03859) | | | | | | ● | | | | | | | | | | | ● | ● | ● | | | | | |
| CHAKRA ROSE (HM03942) | | | | | | ● | | | | | | | | | | | ● | | | | | | | |
| CHAPMAN, ALAN (HM03998) | | | | | | | | | | | | | | | | | | | | | | | | |
| CHRIS MOSLIN HYPNOTHERAPIST (HM04433) | | | | | | ● | | | | | | | | | | | | | | | | | | |
| CLACTON REFLEX & THERAPY CTRE (HM04502) | | | | | | | | | | | | | | | | | | | | | | | | |
| CLARKE, M R (HM04593) | | | | | | | | | | | | | | | | | | | | | | | | |
| CLARKE, ROSALEEN (HM04601) | | | | | | | | | | | | | | | | | | | | | | | | |
| CLAYTON, DEBRA (HM04622) | | | | | | | | | | | | | | | | | | | | | | | | |
| CLAYTON, SUSAN (HM04627) | | | | | | | | | | | | | | | | | | | | | | | | |
| COKER, EILEEN (HM04800) | | | | | | | ● | | | | | | | | | | | | | | | | | |
| COLCHESTER OSTEOPATHIC CENTRE (HM04807) | | | | | | | | | | | | | | | | | | | | | | | | |
| COOK, JOE (HM05048) | | | | | | ● | | | | | | | | | | | ● | | | | | | | |
| COOPER, FELICITY (HM05104) | | | | | | | | | | | | | | | | | | | | | | | | |
| COOPER, JEFFREY C (HM05113) | | | | | | | | | | | | | | | | | | | | | | | | |
| CORBY, VERONICA (HM05157) | | | | | | | | | | | | | | | | | | | | | | | | |
| CRANE SCHOOL OF REFLEXOLOGY (HM05367) | | | | | | | | | | | | | | | | | | | | | | | | |
| CROSS HANDS CHIRO CLINIC (HM05479) | | | | | | | | | | | | | | | | | | | | | | | | |
| CROWDER, C H J (HM05501) | | | | | | | | | | | | | | | | | | | | | | | | |
| CURTIS, PETER (HM05638) | | | | | | | | | | | | | | | | | | | | | | | | |
| DAVIDGE, AMANDA (HM05784) | | | | | | | | | | | | | | | | | | | | | | | | |
| DICKASON, J T (HM06067) | | | | | | | | | | | | | | | | | | | | | | | | |
| DIXON, RUTH (HM06133) | | | | | | | | | | | | | | | | | | | | | | | | |
| DOVE, COLIN (HM06226) | | | | | | | | | | | | | | | | | | | | | | | | |
| E A O C (HM06465) | | | | | | | | | | | | | | | | | | | | | ● | | | |
| EDEN, SHARON (HM06594) | | | | | | | | | | | | | | | | | | | | | | | | |
| EGNER, JULIE (HM06687) | | | | | | | | | | | | | | | | | | | | | | | | |
| ELDRETT, RACHAEL (HM06708) | | | | | | | | | | | | | | | | | | | | | | | | |
| ELMER CHIROPODY & PODIATRY SVS (HM06781) | | | | | | | | | | | | | | | | | | | | | | | | |
| ENRIGHT, VALERIE (HM06846) | | | | | | | | | | | | | | | | | | | | | | | | |
| EPPING OSTEOPATHY AND SPORTS (HM06854) | | | | | | | | | | | | | | | | | | | | | | | | |
| EPPING PHYSIOTHERAPY PRACTICE (HM06855) | | | | | | | | | | | | | | | | | | | | | | | | |
| ESSEX COUNS/PSYCHOTHERAPY SV (HM06934) | | | | | | | | | | | | | | | | | | | | | | | | |
| ESSEX PHYSIO & SPORTS INJ CTRE (HM06938) | | | | | | | | | | | | | | | | | | | | | | | | |

# O - Z Therapies at Practices/Businesses

| Business by County with Reference no. | Orthotics | Osteomyology | Osteopathy | PAM | Paranormal Therapies | Pattern Therapies | Physiotherapy | Phytotherapy | Pilates | Podiatry | Polarity Therapy | Postural Integration | Primal Therapy | Psionic Therapy | Psychotherapy | Pyramid Power | Pyscho-Synthesis |
|---|---|---|---|---|---|---|---|---|---|---|---|---|---|---|---|---|---|
| FANE, AMANDA (HM07093) | | | | | | | | | | | | | | | | | |
| FARRANT, K E (HM07123) | | | ● | | | | | | | | | | | | | | |
| FARROW, VICKI (HM07135) | | | | | | | | | | | | | | | | | |
| FIELD-COULING, KIM (HM07269) | | | | | | | | | | | | | | | | | |
| FINN, JANE (HM07323) | | | | | | | | | | | | | | | | | |
| FLEUROMA (HM07418) | | | | | | | | | | | | | | | | | |
| FLEURY, DENISE (HM07419) | | | | | | | | | | | | | | | | | |
| FOOT HEALTH CLINIC (HM07482) | | | | | | | | | | ● | | | | | | | |
| FOREST COMPLEMENTARY CLINIC (HM07546) | | | ● | | | | | | | | | | | | | | |
| FOULKES, GEOFFREY LLOYD (HM07609) | | | ● | | | | | | | | | | | | | | |
| FREE, HUGH (HM07706) | | | | | | | | | | | | | | | | | |
| FRIEND, JONATHAN (HM07747) | | | ● | | | | | | | | | | | | | | |
| FROST, JANICE (HM07761) | | | | | | | | | | | | | | | | | |
| FULTON, A J (HM07796) | | | | | | | | | | ● | | | | | | | |
| FULTON, A J (HM07795) | | | | | | | | | | ● | | | | | | | |
| GARLICK, STUART (HM07891) | | | ● | | | | | | | | | | | | | | |
| GENT, WENDY (HM07973) | | | | | | | | | | | | | | | | | |
| GLADWIN, DENIS (HM08117) | | | | | | | | | | | | | | | | | |
| GRAY, P A (HM08417) | ● | | | | | | | | | | | | | | | | |
| GRUMBALL, J D (HM08619) | | | ● | | | | | | | | | | | | | | |
| GURNEY, SHARON (HM08654) | | | | | | | | | | | | | | | | | |
| GUTTERIDGE, L (HM08661) | | | ● | | | | | | | | | | | | | | |
| HADLEY, SUSAN (HM08697) | | | | | | | | | | | | | | | | | |
| HARLOW OSTEOPATHIC PRACTICE (HM09011) | | | ● | | | | | | | | | | | | | | |
| HARPER, CHERYL (HM09038) | | | | | | | | | | | | | | | | | |
| HAY, PATRICIA (HM09249) | | | | | | | | | | | | | | | | | |
| HEALING ROOM (HM09349) | | | | | | | | | | | | | | | | | |
| HERFT, PATRICIA (HM09680) | | | | | | | | | | | | | | | | | |
| HOLBEN, JENNY (HM09917) | | | | | | | | | | | | | | | | | |
| HOWTONE, CHRISTINA (HM10295) | | | | | | | | | | | | | | | ● | | |
| HUBBARD, NIK (HM10302) | | | | | | | | | | | | | | | | | |
| HUBBLE CLINIC OF OSTEO & ACU (HM10305) | | | ● | | | | | | | | | | | | | | |
| HUGHES, J HACKER (HM10328) | | | | | | | | | | | | | | | ● | | |
| HUNT, PATRICIA (HM10401) | | | | | | | | | | | | | | | | | |

| Business by County with Reference no. | Reflexology | Reichian Therapy | Reiki | Remedial Massage | Rogerian Therapy | Rolfing | Seichem | Sensitivity Training | Shiatsu | Silva Method | Sound Therapy | Spiritual Healing | Sports Massage | Stress Therapy | Swedish Body Massage | T'ai-Chi Ch'uan |
|---|---|---|---|---|---|---|---|---|---|---|---|---|---|---|---|---|
| FANE, AMANDA (HM07093) | ● | | | | | | | | | | | | | | | |
| FARRANT, K E (HM07123) | | | | | | | | | | | | | | | | |
| FARROW, VICKI (HM07135) | ● | | ● | | | | | | | | | | | | | |
| FIELD-COULING, KIM (HM07269) | ● | | | | | | | | | | | | | | | |
| FINN, JANE (HM07323) | ● | | | | | | | | | | | | | | | |
| FLEUROMA (HM07418) | ● | | | | | | | | | | | | | | ● | |
| FLEURY, DENISE (HM07419) | ● | | | | | | | | | | | | | | | |
| FOOT HEALTH CLINIC (HM07482) | | | | | | | | | | | | | | | | |
| FOREST COMPLEMENTARY CLINIC (HM07546) | | | | | | | | | | | | | | | | |
| FOULKES, GEOFFREY LLOYD (HM07609) | | | ● | | | | | | | | | | | ● | | |
| FREE, HUGH (HM07706) | ● | | | | | | | | | | | | | | | |
| FRIEND, JONATHAN (HM07747) | | | | | | | | | | | | | | | | |
| FROST, JANICE (HM07761) | ● | | | | | | | | | | | | | | | |
| FULTON, A J (HM07796) | | | | | | | | | | | | | | | | |
| FULTON, A J (HM07795) | | | | | | | | | | | | | | | | |
| GARLICK, STUART (HM07891) | | | | | | | | | | | | | | | | |
| GENT, WENDY (HM07973) | | | ● | ● | | | | | | | | | | | | |
| GLADWIN, DENIS (HM08117) | ● | | | | | | | | | | | | | | | |
| GRAY, P A (HM08417) | | | | | | | | | | | | | | | | |
| GRUMBALL, J D (HM08619) | | | | | | | | | | | | | | | | |
| GURNEY, SHARON (HM08654) | ● | | | | | | | | | | | | | | | |
| GUTTERIDGE, L (HM08661) | | | | | | | | | | | | | | | | |
| HADLEY, SUSAN (HM08697) | ● | | | | | | | | | | | | | | | |
| HARLOW OSTEOPATHIC PRACTICE (HM09011) | | | | | | | | | | | | | | | | |
| HARPER, CHERYL (HM09038) | ● | | | | | | | | | | | | | | | |
| HAY, PATRICIA (HM09249) | ● | | | | | | | | | | | | | | | |
| HEALING ROOM (HM09349) | ● | | ● | | | | | | | | | | | ● | | |
| HERFT, PATRICIA (HM09680) | ● | | | | | | | | | | | | | | | |
| HOLBEN, JENNY (HM09917) | ● | | | | | | | | | | | | | | | |
| HOWTONE, CHRISTINA (HM10295) | | | | | | | | | | | | | | | | |
| HUBBARD, NIK (HM10302) | ● | | | | | | | | | | | | | | | |
| HUBBLE CLINIC OF OSTEO & ACU (HM10305) | | | | | | | | | | | | | | | | |
| HUGHES, J HACKER (HM10328) | | | | | | | | | | | | | | | | |
| HUNT, PATRICIA (HM10401) | ● | | | | | | | | | | | | | | | |

| Business by County with Reference no. | Tantra Therapy | Tera-Mai | Thought Field Therapy | Touch Therapy | Transactional Analysis | Tui-na | Ultrasonics | Vibrational Therapy | Visualisation Therapy | Vitamin Therapy | Voice Therapy | X-Ray | Ying & Yang | Yoga | Zen Therapy | Zero Balancing |
|---|---|---|---|---|---|---|---|---|---|---|---|---|---|---|---|---|
| FANE, AMANDA (HM07093) | | | | | | | | | | | | | | | | |
| FARRANT, K E (HM07123) | | | | | | | | | | | | | | | | |
| FARROW, VICKI (HM07135) | | | | | | | | | | | | | | | | |
| FIELD-COULING, KIM (HM07269) | | | | | | | | | | | | | | | | |
| FINN, JANE (HM07323) | | | | | | | | | | | | | | | | |
| FLEUROMA (HM07418) | | | | | | | | | | | | | | | | |
| FLEURY, DENISE (HM07419) | | | | | | | | | | | | | | | | |
| FOOT HEALTH CLINIC (HM07482) | | | | | | | | | | | | | | | | |
| FOREST COMPLEMENTARY CLINIC (HM07546) | | | | | | | | | | | | | | | | |
| FOULKES, GEOFFREY LLOYD (HM07609) | | | | | | | ● | | | ● | | ● | ● | | | |
| FREE, HUGH (HM07706) | | | | | | | | | | | | | | | | |
| FRIEND, JONATHAN (HM07747) | | | | | | | | | | | | | | | | |
| FROST, JANICE (HM07761) | | | | | | | | | | | | | | | | |
| FULTON, A J (HM07796) | | | | | | | | | | | | | | | | |
| FULTON, A J (HM07795) | | | | | | | | | | | | | | | | |
| GARLICK, STUART (HM07891) | | | | | | | | | | | | | | | | |
| GENT, WENDY (HM07973) | | | | | | | | | | | | | | | | |
| GLADWIN, DENIS (HM08117) | | | | | | | | | | | | | | | | |
| GRAY, P A (HM08417) | | | | | | | | | | | | | | | | |
| GRUMBALL, J D (HM08619) | | | | | | | | | | | | | | | | |
| GURNEY, SHARON (HM08654) | | | | | | | | | | | | | | | | |
| GUTTERIDGE, L (HM08661) | | | | | | | | | | | | | | | | |
| HADLEY, SUSAN (HM08697) | | | | | | | | | | | | | | | | |
| HARLOW OSTEOPATHIC PRACTICE (HM09011) | | | | | | | | | | | | | | | | |
| HARPER, CHERYL (HM09038) | | | | | | | | | | | | | | | | |
| HAY, PATRICIA (HM09249) | | | | | | | | | | | | | | | | |
| HEALING ROOM (HM09349) | | | | | | | | | | | | | | | | |
| HERFT, PATRICIA (HM09680) | | | | | | | | | | | | | | | | |
| HOLBEN, JENNY (HM09917) | | | | | | | | | | | | | | | | |
| HOWTONE, CHRISTINA (HM10295) | | | | | | | | | | | | | | | | |
| HUBBARD, NIK (HM10302) | | | | | | | | | | | | | | | | |
| HUBBLE CLINIC OF OSTEO & ACU (HM10305) | | | | | | | | | | | | | | | | |
| HUGHES, J HACKER (HM10328) | | | | | | | | | | | | | | | | |
| HUNT, PATRICIA (HM10401) | | | | | | | | | | | | | | | | |

# O - Z Therapies at Practices/Businesses

Business by County with Reference no.

| Business | Orthotics | Osteomyology | Osteopathy | PAM | Paranormal Therapies | Pattern Therapies | Physiotherapy | Phytotherapy | Pilates | Podiatry | Polarity Therapy | Postural Integration | Primal Therapy | Psionic Therapy | Psychotherapy | Pyramid Power | Pyscho-Synthesis | Reflexology | Reichian Therapy | Reiki | Remedial Massage | Rogerian Therapy | Rolfing | Seichem | Sensitivity Training | Shiatsu | Silva Method | Sound Therapy | Spiritual Healing | Sports Massage | Stress Therapy | Swedish Body Massage | T'ai-Chi Ch'uan | Tantra Therapy | Tera-Mai | Thought Field Therapy | Touch Therapy | Transactional Analysis | Tui-na | Ultrasonics | Vibrational Therapy | Visualisation Therapy | Vitamin Therapy | Voice Therapy | X-Ray | Ying & Yang | Yoga | Zen Therapy | Zero Balancing |
|---|---|---|---|---|---|---|---|---|---|---|---|---|---|---|---|---|---|---|---|---|---|---|---|---|---|---|---|---|---|---|---|---|---|---|---|---|---|---|---|---|---|---|---|---|---|---|---|---|---|
| HYPNOTHERAPY & PSYCHO CONS (HM10508) | | | | | | | | | | | | | | | ● | | | | | | | | | | | | | | | | | | | | | | | | | | | | | | | | | | |
| HYPNOTHERAPY CENTRE (HM10530) | | | | | | | | | | | | | | | ● | | | | | | | | | | | | | | | | | | | | | | | | | | | | | | | | | | |
| HYPNOTHERAPY CENTRE (HM10532) | | | | | | | | | | | | | | | ● | | | | | | | | | | | | | | | | | | | | | | | | | | | | | | | | | | |
| ISIS HOUSE THERAPY CENTRE (HM10768) | | | | | | | | | | | | | | | | | | ● | | ● | | | | | | | | | | | | | | | | | | | | | | | | | | | | | |
| JARVIS, PETER (HM10936) | | | ● | | | | | | | | | | | | | | | | | | | | | | | | | | | | | | | | | | | | | | | | | | | | | | |
| JILLINS, BOB (HM11031) | | | | | | | | | | | | | | | | | | ● | | | | | | | | | | | | | | | | | | | | | | | | | | | | | | | |
| JOHN, S U (HM11058) | | | ● | | | | | | | | | | | | | | | | | | | | | | | | | | | | | | | | | | | | | | | | | | | | | | |
| JONES, JEAN (HM11158) | | | | | | | | | | | | | | | | | | ● | | | | | | | | | | | | | | | | | | | | | | | | | | | | | | | |
| JONES, KELLIE (HM11163) | | | | | | | | | | | | | | | | | | ● | | | | | | | | | | | | | | | | | | | | | | | | | | | | | | | |
| JOYCE, PHILIP (HM11238) | | | | | | | | | | | | | | | | | | ● | | | | | | | | | | | | | | | | | | | | | | | | | | | | | | | |
| JOYNES, IAN (HM11239) | ● | | | | | | | | | ● | | | | | | | | | | | | | | | | | | | | | | | | | | | | | | | | | | | | | | | |
| JULIEN, M (HM11258) | | | | | | | | | | | | | | | ● | | | | | | | | | | | | | | | | | | | | | | | | | | | | | | | | | | |
| KANUTIN, A (HM11314) | | | ● | | | | | | | | | | | | | | | | | | | | | | | | | | | | | | | | | | | | | | | | | | | | | | |
| KARADIA, V (HM11316) | | | ● | | | | | | | | | | | | | | | | | | | | | | | | | | | | | | | | | | | | | | | | | | | | | | |
| KEMP, R (HM11464) | | | ● | | | | | | | | | | | | | | | | | | | | | | | | | | | | | | | | | | | | | | | | | | | | | | |
| KENT, JOAN (HM11525) | | | | | | | | | | | | | | | | | | ● | | | | | | | | | | | | | | | | | | | | | | | | | | | | | | | |
| KENTON, JEREMY (HM11533) | | | ● | | | | | | | | | | | | | | | | | | | | | | | | | | | | | | | | | | | | | | | | | | | | | | |
| KING, ANDREA (HM11626) | | | | | | | | | | | | | | | | | | ● | | | | | | | | | | | | | | | | | | | | | | | | | | | | | | | |
| KIRKPATRICK, IAN (HM11719) | | | | | | | | | | | | | | | | | | ● | | | | | | | | | | | | | | | | | | | | | | | | | | | | | | | |
| KURANCHIE, CLAUDETTE (HM11825) | | | | | | | | | | | | | | | | | | ● | | | | | | | | | | | | | | | | | | | | | | | | | | | | | | | |
| LANG, GILL (HM11946) | | | | | | | | | | | | | | | | | | ● | | | | | | | | | | | | | | | | | | | | | | | | | | | | | | | |
| LANG, GLORIA (HM11947) | | | | | | | | | | | | | | | | | | ● | | | | | | | | | | | | | | | | | | | | | | | | | | | | | | | |
| LARHOLT, A (HM11973) | | | ● | | | | | | | | | | | | | | | | | | | | | | | | | | | | | | | | | | | | | | | | | | | | | | |
| LAST, CHRISTINE (HM11988) | | | | | | | | | | | | | | | | | | ● | | | | | | | | | | | | | | | | | | | | | | | | | | | | | | | |
| LAYLAND, ROSALIND (HM12076) | | | | | | | | | | | | | | | | | | ● | | | | | | | | | | | | | | | | | | | | | | | | | | | | | | | |
| LEIGH, MARTIN (HM12189) | | | ● | | | | | | | | | | | | | | | | | | | | | | | | | | | | | | | | | | | | | | | | | | | | | | |
| LEVY, PAUL (HM12269) | ● | | | | | | | | | ● | | | | | | | | | | | | | | | | | | | | | | | | | | | | | | | | | | | | | | | |
| LINDY, DAVID (HM12427) | | | ● | | | | | | | | | | | | | | | | | | | | | | | | | | | | | | | | | | | | | | | | | | | | | | |
| LING, E (HM12432) | | | | | | | | | | | | | | | ● | | | | | | | | | | | | | | | | | | | | | | | | | | | | | | | | | | |
| LINGWOOD CLINIC (HM12435) | | | ● | | | | | | | | | | | | | | | | | | | | | | | ● | | | | | | | | | | | | | | | | | | | | | | | |
| LOMOND, MARSHA (HM12581) | | | | | | | | | | | | | | | ● | | | | | | | | | | | | | | | | | | | | | | | | | | | | | | | | | | |
| LONDON ROAD PHYSIO PRACTICE (HM12603) | | | | | | | ● | | | | | | | | | | | | | | | | | | | | | | | | | | | | | | | | | | | | | | | | | | |
| LYNDA CROFT REIKI MASTER (HM12768) | | | | | | | | | | | | | | | | | | | | ● | | | | | | | | | | | | | | | | | | | | | | | | | | | | | |
| MALONEY, M (HM12985) | | | ● | | | | | | | | | | | | | | | | | | | | | | | | | | | | | | | | | | | | | | | | | | | | | | |

# O - Z Therapies at Practices/Businesses

Business by County with Reference no.

| Business | Orthotics | Osteomyology | Osteopathy | PAM | Paranormal Therapies | Pattern Therapies | Physiotherapy | Phytotherapy | Pilates | Podiatry | Polarity Therapy | Postural Integration | Primal Therapy | Psionic Therapy | Psychotherapy | Pyramid Power | Pyscho-Synthesis |
|---|---|---|---|---|---|---|---|---|---|---|---|---|---|---|---|---|---|
| MALONEY, M P (HM12986) | | | ● | | | | | | | | | | | | | | |
| MALOY, ALISON (HM12991) | | | ● | | | | | | | | | | | | | | |
| MASSEY, JULIA (HM13269) | | | | | | | | | | | | | | | | | |
| MASTERS, PAUL (HM13276) | | | ● | | | | | | | | | | | | | | |
| MAY, SUSAN (HM13349) | | | | | | | | | | | | | | | | | |
| MEDELY CLINIC (HM13647) | | | | | | | | | | | | | | | | | |
| MELLOR, SARA L (HM13711) | | | ● | | | | | | | | | | | | | | |
| MILES, C J (HM13855) | | | | | | | | | | ● | | | | | | | |
| MILLER, SUE (HM13902) | | | | | | | | | | | | | | | | | |
| MILLS, ANDREW D (HM13925) | | | ● | | | | | | | | | | | | | | |
| MOLLOY, PAULINE (HM14053) | | | | | | | | | | | | | | | | | |
| MONK, MICHAEL (HM14067) | | | ● | | | | | | | | | | | | | | |
| MOONSTONE HEALING CENTRE (HM14111) | | | | | | | | | | | | | | | ● | | |
| MOORE, SUSAN (HM14134) | | | | | | | | | | ● | | | | | | | |
| MORTIMER, GERALDINE (HM14241) | | | | | | | | | | | | | | | | | |
| MORTIMER, VICTORIA (HM14244) | | | | | | | | | | | | | | | | | |
| MOSS, GRAEME (HM14264) | | | | | | | | | | | | | | | | | |
| MOSS, RACHAEL (HM14269) | | | | | | | | | | | | | | | | | |
| MOUCHET, F (HM14282) | | | | | | | | | | | | | | | ● | | |
| MULLER, GLYNIS (HM14343) | | | | | | | | | | | | | | | | | |
| MURRAY, ANN (HM14398) | | | | | | | | | | | | | | | | | |
| NASTRUCCI, SUSAN (HM14495) | | | ● | | | | | | | | | | | | | | |
| NATURAL REMEDY CENTRE (HM14620) | | | | | | | | | | | | | | | | | |
| NEWMAN, SOGRA (HM14873) | | | ● | | | | | | | | | | | | | | |
| NOLAN, CLAIRE (HM14982) | | | | | | | | | | | | | | | | | |
| NORMAN, ANNE (HM15000) | | | | | | | | | | | | | | | ● | | |
| NOYS, ALISON (HM15090) | | | | | | | | | | | | | | | | | |
| NUGENT, L C (HM15102) | | | ● | | | | | | | | | | | | | | |
| OWEN, RACHEL (HM15529) | | | | | | | | | | | | | | | | | |
| PARVEZ, SHAUKAT (HM15771) | | | ● | | | | | | | | | | | | | | |
| PAT, ELLIOTT (HM15782) | | | | | | | | | | | | | | | | | |
| PERRY, JEAN (HM16047) | | | | | | | | | | | | | | | | | |
| PHARMACARE (HM16109) | | | | | | | | ● | | | | | | | | | |
| PHYSIO & SPORTS INJURY CLINIC (HM16186) | | | | | | | ● | | | | | | | | | | |

| Business | Reflexology | Reichian Therapy | Reiki | Remedial Massage | Rogerian Therapy | Rolfing | Seichem | Sensitivity Training | Shiatsu | Silva Method | Sound Therapy | Spiritual Healing | Sports Massage | Stress Therapy | Swedish Body Massage | T'ai-Chi Ch'uan |
|---|---|---|---|---|---|---|---|---|---|---|---|---|---|---|---|---|
| MALONEY, M P (HM12986) | | | | | | | | | | | | | | | | |
| MALOY, ALISON (HM12991) | | | | | | | | | | | | | | | | |
| MASSEY, JULIA (HM13269) | ● | | | | | | | | | | | | | | | |
| MASTERS, PAUL (HM13276) | | | | | | | | | | | | | | | | |
| MAY, SUSAN (HM13349) | ● | | | | | | | | | | | | | | | |
| MEDELY CLINIC (HM13647) | ● | | | | | | | | | | | | | | | |
| MELLOR, SARA L (HM13711) | | | | | | | | | | | | | | | | |
| MILES, C J (HM13855) | | | | | | | | | | | | | | | | |
| MILLER, SUE (HM13902) | ● | | | | | | | | | | | | | | | |
| MILLS, ANDREW D (HM13925) | | | | | | | | | | | | | | | | |
| MOLLOY, PAULINE (HM14053) | ● | | | | | | | | | | | | | | | |
| MONK, MICHAEL (HM14067) | | | | | | | | | | | | | | | | |
| MOONSTONE HEALING CENTRE (HM14111) | ● | | ● | | | | | | ● | | | ● | ● | ● | | |
| MOORE, SUSAN (HM14134) | ● | | ● | | | | | | | | | | | | | |
| MORTIMER, GERALDINE (HM14241) | ● | | | | | | | | | | | | | | | |
| MORTIMER, VICTORIA (HM14244) | ● | | | | | | | | | | | | | | | |
| MOSS, GRAEME (HM14264) | | | | ● | | | | | | | | | | | | |
| MOSS, RACHAEL (HM14269) | ● | | | | | | | | | | | | | | | |
| MOUCHET, F (HM14282) | | | | | | | | | | | | | | | | |
| MULLER, GLYNIS (HM14343) | ● | | | | | | | | | | | | | | | |
| MURRAY, ANN (HM14398) | ● | | | | | | | | | | | | | | | |
| NASTRUCCI, SUSAN (HM14495) | | | | | | | | | | | | | | | | |
| NATURAL REMEDY CENTRE (HM14620) | ● | | ● | | | | | | | | | | | | | |
| NEWMAN, SOGRA (HM14873) | | | | | | | | | | | | | | | | |
| NOLAN, CLAIRE (HM14982) | ● | | | | | | | | | | | | | | | |
| NORMAN, ANNE (HM15000) | | | | | | | | | | | | | | | | |
| NOYS, ALISON (HM15090) | ● | | | | | | | | | | | | | | | |
| NUGENT, L C (HM15102) | | | | | | | | | | | | | | | | |
| OWEN, RACHEL (HM15529) | ● | | | | | | | | | | | | | | | |
| PARVEZ, SHAUKAT (HM15771) | | | | | | | | | | | | | | | | |
| PAT, ELLIOTT (HM15782) | ● | | | | | | | | | | | | | | | |
| PERRY, JEAN (HM16047) | ● | | | | | | | | | | | | | | | |
| PHARMACARE (HM16109) | | | | | | | | | | | | | | | | |
| PHYSIO & SPORTS INJURY CLINIC (HM16186) | | | | | | | | | | | | | | | | |

| Business | Tantra Therapy | Tera-Mai | Thought Field Therapy | Touch Therapy | Transactional Analysis | Tui-na | Ultrasonics | Vibrational Therapy | Visualisation Therapy | Vitamin Therapy | Voice Therapy | X-Ray | Ying & Yang | Yoga | Zen Therapy | Zero Balancing |
|---|---|---|---|---|---|---|---|---|---|---|---|---|---|---|---|---|
| MALONEY, M P (HM12986) | | | | | | | | | | | | | | | | |
| MALOY, ALISON (HM12991) | | | | | | | | | | | | | | | | |
| MASSEY, JULIA (HM13269) | | | | | | | | | | | | | | | | |
| MASTERS, PAUL (HM13276) | | | | | | | | | | | | | | | | |
| MAY, SUSAN (HM13349) | | | | | | | | | | | | | | | | |
| MEDELY CLINIC (HM13647) | | | | | | | | | | | | | | | | |
| MELLOR, SARA L (HM13711) | | | | | | | | | | | | | | | | |
| MILES, C J (HM13855) | | | | | | | | | | | | | | | | |
| MILLER, SUE (HM13902) | | | | | | | | | | | | | | | | |
| MILLS, ANDREW D (HM13925) | | | | | | | | | | | | | | | | |
| MOLLOY, PAULINE (HM14053) | | | | | | | | | | | | | | | | |
| MONK, MICHAEL (HM14067) | | | | | | | | | | | | | | | | |
| MOONSTONE HEALING CENTRE (HM14111) | | | | | ● | | | | ● | | | | | | | |
| MOORE, SUSAN (HM14134) | | | | | | | | | | | | | | | | |
| MORTIMER, GERALDINE (HM14241) | | | | | | | | | | | | | | | | |
| MORTIMER, VICTORIA (HM14244) | | | | | | | | | | | | | | | | |
| MOSS, GRAEME (HM14264) | | | | | | | | | | | | | | | | |
| MOSS, RACHAEL (HM14269) | | | | | | | | | | | | | | | | |
| MOUCHET, F (HM14282) | | | | | | | | | | | | | | | | |
| MULLER, GLYNIS (HM14343) | | | | | | | | | | | | | | | | |
| MURRAY, ANN (HM14398) | | | | | | | | | | | | | | | | |
| NASTRUCCI, SUSAN (HM14495) | | | | | | | | | | | | | | | | |
| NATURAL REMEDY CENTRE (HM14620) | | | | | | | | | | | | | | | | |
| NEWMAN, SOGRA (HM14873) | | | | | | | | | | | | | | | | |
| NOLAN, CLAIRE (HM14982) | | | | | | | | | | | | | | | | |
| NORMAN, ANNE (HM15000) | | | | | | | | | | | | | | | | |
| NOYS, ALISON (HM15090) | | | | | | | | | | | | | | | | |
| NUGENT, L C (HM15102) | | | | | | | | | | | | | | | | |
| OWEN, RACHEL (HM15529) | | | | | | | | | | | | | | | | |
| PARVEZ, SHAUKAT (HM15771) | | | | | | | | | | | | | | | | |
| PAT, ELLIOTT (HM15782) | | | | | | | | | | | | | | | | |
| PERRY, JEAN (HM16047) | | | | | | | | | | | | | | | | |
| PHARMACARE (HM16109) | | | | | | | | | | ● | | | | | | |
| PHYSIO & SPORTS INJURY CLINIC (HM16186) | | | | | | | ● | | | | | | | | | |

# O - Z Therapies at Practices/Businesses

| Business by County with Reference no. | Orthotics | Osteomyology | Osteopathy | PAM | Paranormal Therapies | Pattern Therapies | Physiotherapy | Phytotherapy | Pilates | Podiatry | Polarity Therapy | Postural Integration | Primal Therapy | Psionic Therapy | Psychotherapy | Pyramid Power | Pyscho-Synthesis | Reflexology | Reichian Therapy | Reiki |
|---|---|---|---|---|---|---|---|---|---|---|---|---|---|---|---|---|---|---|---|---|
| PINEWOOD PHYSIOTHERAPY CLINIC (HM16313) | | | ● | | | | | ● | | | | | | | | | | | | |
| PIPER, MARK W (HM16325) | | | ● | | | | | | | | | | | | | | | | | |
| PISCES NATURAL THERAPY CENTRE (HM16330) | | | | | | | | | | | | | | | ● | | | ● | | |
| PRICE, G J (HM16572) | | | ● | | | | | | | | | | | | | | | | | |
| QUIT SMOKING CENTRE (HM16821) | | | | | | | | | | | | | | | ● | | | | | |
| RAJA YOGA MEDITATION (HM16898) | | | | | | | | | | | | | | | | | | | | |
| REDWOOD, SARAH (HM17035) | | | | | | | | | | | | | | | | | | ● | | |
| REEVE, ANNE (HM17059) | | | | | | | | | | | | | | | | | | ● | | |
| REFLEXOLOGY CLINIC (HM17088) | | | | | | | | | | | | | | | | | | ● | | ● |
| ROGERS, ALISON (HM17543) | | | | | | | | | | | | | | | | | | ● | | |
| ROOTS, WENDY (HM17590) | | | | | | | | | | | | | | | | | | ● | | |
| ROSE, LESLEY (HM17609) | | | | | | | | | | | | | | | ● | | | | | |
| RUMSEY, S (HM17750) | | | ● | | | | | | | | | | | | | | | | | |
| SALMON, MARGARET (HM17858) | | | | | | | | | | | | | | | | | | ● | | |
| SANDERS, G (HM17909) | | | | | | | | | | ● | | | | | | | | | | |
| SAXBY, W (HM17989) | | | ● | | | | | | | | | | | | | | | | | |
| SELF AWARENESS HEALING (HM18204) | | | | | | | | | | | | | | | | | | | | |
| SERVICE, G (HM18240) | | | ● | | | | | | | | | | | | | | | | | |
| SEYMOUR, LOUISE (HM18259) | ● | | | | | | | | | | | | | | | | | | | |
| SHAW, JONATHAN (HM18340) | | | ● | | | | | | | | | | | | | | | | | |
| SHAW, JONATHAN (HM18339) | | | ● | | | | | | | | | | | | | | | | | |
| SHEAF, JACOLIN (HM18355) | | | ● | | | | | | | | | | | | | | | | | |
| SHELDON, PEGGY (HM18380) | | | | | | | | | | | | | | | | | | ● | | ● |
| SIMISTER, KAREN (HM18550) | | | | | | | | | | | | | | | | | | ● | | |
| SKILTON, GINA (HM18642) | | | | | | | | | | | | | | | | | | ● | | |
| SLATER, HUGH (HM18674) | | | | | | | | | | | | | | | | | | ● | | |
| SMALL, LORNA (HM18693) | | | | | | | | | | | | | | | | | | ● | | |
| SMITH, EILEEN (HM18739) | | | | | | | | | | | | | | | | | | ● | | |
| SMITH, LYNDSAY (HM18768) | | | | | | | | | | | | | | | | | | ● | | |
| SOUTH, JO (HM18918) | | | | | | | | | | | | | | | | | | ● | | |
| SPARLING & ASSOCIATES (HM18964) | | | ● | | | | | | | | | | | | | | | | | |
| SRI AMMAN CLINIC (HM19062) | | | ● | | | | | | | | | | | | | | | | | |
| STABLEFORD, JOYCE (HM19101) | | | | | | | | | | | | | | | ● | | | | | |
| STOCKWELL CENTRE (HM19316) | | | | | | | | | | | | | | | ● | | | | | |

| Business by County with Reference no. | Remedial Massage | Rogerian Therapy | Rolfing | Seichem | Sensitivity Training | Shiatsu | Silva Method | Sound Therapy | Spiritual Healing | Sports Massage | Stress Therapy | Swedish Body Massage | T'ai-Chi Ch'uan | Tantra Therapy | Tera-Mai | Thought Field Therapy | Touch Therapy | Transactional Analysis | Tui-na | Ultrasonics | Vibrational Therapy | Visualisation Therapy | Vitamin Therapy | Voice Therapy | X-Ray | Ying & Yang | Yoga | Zen Therapy | Zero Balancing |
|---|---|---|---|---|---|---|---|---|---|---|---|---|---|---|---|---|---|---|---|---|---|---|---|---|---|---|---|---|---|
| PINEWOOD PHYSIOTHERAPY CLINIC (HM16313) | | | | | | | | | | | ● | | | | | | | | | ● | | | | | | | | | |
| PIPER, MARK W (HM16325) | | | | | | | | | | | | | | | | | | | | | | | | | | | | | |
| PISCES NATURAL THERAPY CENTRE (HM16330) | | | | | | | | | | | ● | | | | | | | | | | | | | | | | | | |
| PRICE, G J (HM16572) | | | | | | | | | | | | | | | | | | | | ● | | | ● | | | | | | |
| QUIT SMOKING CENTRE (HM16821) | | | | | | | | | | | | | | | | | | | | | | | | | | | | | |
| RAJA YOGA MEDITATION (HM16898) | | | | | | | | | | | | | | | | | | | | | | | | | | | ● | | |
| REDWOOD, SARAH (HM17035) | | | | | | | | | | | | | | | | | | | | | | | | | | | | | |
| REEVE, ANNE (HM17059) | | | | | | | | | | | | | | | | | | | | | | | | | | | | | |
| REFLEXOLOGY CLINIC (HM17088) | | | | | | | | | | | | | | | | | | | | | | | | | | | | | |
| ROGERS, ALISON (HM17543) | | | | | | | | | | | | | | | | | | | | | | | | | | | | | |
| ROOTS, WENDY (HM17590) | | | | | | | | | | | | | | | | | | | | | | | | | | | | | |
| ROSE, LESLEY (HM17609) | | | | | | | | | | | | | | | | | | | | | | | | | | | | | |
| RUMSEY, S (HM17750) | | | | | | | | | | | | | | | | | | | | | | | | | | | | | |
| SALMON, MARGARET (HM17858) | | | | | | | | | | | | | | | | | | | | | | | | | | | | | |
| SANDERS, G (HM17909) | | | | | | | | | | | | | | | | | | | | | | | | | | | | | |
| SAXBY, W (HM17989) | | | | | | | | | | | | | | | | | | | | | | | | | | | | | |
| SELF AWARENESS HEALING (HM18204) | | | | | | | | | ● | | ● | | | | | | | | | | | | | | | | | | |
| SERVICE, G (HM18240) | | | | | | | | | | | | | | | | | | | | | | | | | | | | | |
| SEYMOUR, LOUISE (HM18259) | | | | | | | | | | | | | | | | | | | | | | | | | | | | | |
| SHAW, JONATHAN (HM18340) | | | | | | | | | | | | | | | | | | | | | | | | | | | | | |
| SHAW, JONATHAN (HM18339) | | | | | | | | | | | | | | | | | | | | | | | | | | | | | |
| SHEAF, JACOLIN (HM18355) | | | | | | | | | | | | | | | | | | | | | | | | | | | | | |
| SHELDON, PEGGY (HM18380) | | | | | | ● | | | | | | | | | | | | | | | | | | | | | | | |
| SIMISTER, KAREN (HM18550) | | | | | | | | | | | | | | | | | | | | | | | | | | | | | |
| SKILTON, GINA (HM18642) | | | | | | | | | | | | | | | | | | | | | | | | | | | | | |
| SLATER, HUGH (HM18674) | | | | | | | | | | | | | | | | | | | | | | | | | | | | | |
| SMALL, LORNA (HM18693) | | | | | | | | | | | | | | | | | | | | | | | | | | | | | |
| SMITH, EILEEN (HM18739) | | | | | | | | | | | | | | | | | | | | | | | | | | | | | |
| SMITH, LYNDSAY (HM18768) | | | | | | | | | | | | | | | | | | | | | | | | | | | | | |
| SOUTH, JO (HM18918) | | | | | | | | | | | | | | | | | | | | | | | | | | | | | |
| SPARLING & ASSOCIATES (HM18964) | | | | | | | | | | | | | | | | | | | | | | | | | | | | | |
| SRI AMMAN CLINIC (HM19062) | | | | | | | | | | | | | | | | | | | | | | | | | | | | | |
| STABLEFORD, JOYCE (HM19101) | | | | | | | | | | | | | ● | | | | | | | | | | | | | | | | |
| STOCKWELL CENTRE (HM19316) | | | | | | | | | | | | | | | | | | | | | | | | | | | | | |

# O - Z Therapies at Practices/Businesses

| Business by County with Reference no. | Orthotics | Osteomyology | Osteopathy | PAM | Paranormal Therapies | Pattern Therapies | Physiotherapy | Phytotherapy | Pilates | Podiatry | Polarity Therapy | Postural Integration | Primal Therapy | Psionic Therapy | Psychotherapy | Pyramid Power | Pyscho-Synthesis | Reflexology | Reichian Therapy | Reiki | Remedial Massage | Rogerian Therapy | Rolfing | Seichem | Sensitivity Training | Shiatsu | Silva Method | Sound Therapy | Spiritual Healing | Sports Massage | Stress Therapy | Swedish Body Massage | T'ai-Chi Ch'uan | Tantra Therapy | Tera-Mai | Thought Field Therapy | Touch Therapy | Transactional Analysis | Tui-na | Ultrasonics | Vibrational Therapy | Visualisation Therapy | Vitamin Therapy | Voice Therapy | X-Ray | Ying & Yang | Yoga | Zen Therapy | Zero Balancing |
|---|---|---|---|---|---|---|---|---|---|---|---|---|---|---|---|---|---|---|---|---|---|---|---|---|---|---|---|---|---|---|---|---|---|---|---|---|---|---|---|---|---|---|---|---|---|---|---|---|---|
| STROUD, GRAEME (HM19423) | | | ● | | | | | | | | | | | | | | | | | | | | | | | | | | | | | | | | | | | | | | | | | | | | | | |
| TUNE, DAVID (HM20395) | | | | | | | | | | | | | | | ● | | | | | | | | | | | | | | | | | | | | | | | | | | | | | | | | | | |
| VICTORIA COUNSELLING SERVICE (HM20654) | | | | | | | | | | | | | | | ● | | | | | | | | | | | | | | | | | | | | | | | | | | | | | | | | | | |
| VOIGHTS, M F (HM20710) | | | ● | | | | | | | | | | | | | | | | | | | | | | | | | | | | | | | | | | | | | | | | | | | | | | |
| WALLS, ANNE (HM20844) | | | | | | | | | | | | | | | | | | ● | | | | | | | | | | | | | | | | | | | | | | | | | | | | | | | |
| WATERS, FRANK (HM20988) | | | ● | | | | | | | | | | | | | | | | | | | | | | | | | | | | | | | | | | | | | | | | | | | | | | |
| WEHMEYER, CATHERINE (HM21110) | | | | | | | | | | | | | | | | | | ● | | | | | | | | | | | | | | | | | | | | | | | | | | | | | | | |
| WELLINGS, INGA (HM21165) | | | | | | | | | | | | | | | | | | ● | | | | | | | | | | | | | | | | | | | | | | | | | | | | | | | |
| WENTWORTH HEALTH CLINIC (HM21201) | | | | | | | | | | | | | | | | | | ● | | | | | | | | | | | | ● | | ● | | | | | | | | | | | | | | | | | |
| WHEELER, M A (HM21316) | | | ● | | | | | | | ● | | | | | | | | | | | | | | | | | | | | | | | | | | | | | | | | | | | | | | | |
| WHEELER, M A (HM21317) | | | | | | | | | | ● | | | | | | | | | | | | | | | | | | | | | | | | | | | | | | | | | | | | | | | |
| WHITE WATER HEALING CENTRE (HM21345) | | | | | | | | | | | | | | | | | | | | | | | | | | | | | | ● | | ● | | | | | | | | | | | | | | | | | |
| WHITE, SARAH (HM21377) | | | | | | | | | | | | | | | | | | ● | | | | | | | | | | | | | | | | | | | | | | | | | | | | | | | |
| WICKINS, ANN (HM21449) | | | | | | | | | | | | | | | | | | ● | | | | | | | | | | | | | | | | | | | | | | | | | | | | | | | |
| WILLSON, GILLIAN (HM21636) | | | | | | | | | | | | | | | | | | ● | | | | | | | | | | | | | | | | | | | | | | | | | | | | | | | |
| WILSON, VERONICA (HM21677) | | | | | | | | | | | | | | | | | | ● | | | | | | | | | | | | | | | | | | | | | | | | | | | | | | | |
| WISEMAN, SANDRA (HM21735) | | | | | | | | | | | | | | | | | | ● | | | | | | | | | | | | | | | | | | | | | | | | | | | | | | | |
| WIVENHOE DENTAL PRACTICE (HM21754) | | | ● | | | | | | | | | | | | | | | | | | | | | | | | | | | | | | | | | | | | | | | | | | | | | | |
| WOODSIDE NATURAL HEALTH (HM21859) | | | ● | | | | | | | | ● | | | | | | | | | ● | | | | | | ● | | | ● | | | | | | | | | | | | | | | | | | | | |
| WRIGHT, SEAN (HM21949) | | | ● | | | | | | | | | | | | | | | | | | | | | | | | | | | | | | | | | | | | | | | | | | | | | | |
| **GLASGOW (CITY OF)** | | | | | | | | | | | | | | | | | | | | | | | | | | | | | | | | | | | | | | | | | | | | | | | | | |
| TAI CHI UNION FOR GB (HM19655) | | | | | | | | | | | | | | | | | | | | | | | | | | | | | | | | | ● | | | | | | | | | | | | | ● | | | |
| **GLOUCESTERSHIRE** | | | | | | | | | | | | | | | | | | | | | | | | | | | | | | | | | | | | | | | | | | | | | | | | | |
| ACUPUNCTURE CLINIC (HM00262) | | | | | | | | | | | | | | | | | | ● | | | | | | | | ● | | | | | | | | | | | | | | | | | | | | | | | |
| ADAMS, EVE (HM00349) | | | | | | | | | | | | | | | ● | | | | | | | | | | | | | | | | | | | | | | | | | | | | | | | | | | |
| ARTICHOKE NATURAL HEALTH (HM01168) | | | ● | | | | | | | | | | | | | | | ● | | | | | | | | ● | | | | | | | | | | | | | | | | | | | | | | | |
| BARNFIELD, HILARY (HM01762) | | | | | | | | | | | | | | | | | | ● | | | | | | | | | | | | | | | | | | | | | | | | | | | | | | | |
| BERESFORD, G S (HM02179) | | | ● | | | | | | | | | | | | | | | | | | | | | | | | | | | | | | | | | | | | | | | | | | | | | | |
| BERESFORD, G S (HM02180) | | | ● | | | | | | | | | | | | | | | | | | | | | | | | | | | | | | | | | | | | | | | | | | | | | | |
| BISHOPS CLEEVE PHYSIO & SPORTS (HM02413) | | | | | | | ● | | | | | | | | | | | | | | | | | | | | | | | | | | | | | | | | | | | | | | | | | | |
| BOYES, LESLEY (HM02822) | | | ● | | | | | | | | | | | | | | | | | | | | | | | | | | | | | | | | | | | | | | | | | | | | | | |
| BROWNING, KAREN (HM03260) | | | | | | | | | | | | | | | | | | ● | | | | | | | | | | | | | | | | | | | | | | | | | | | | | | | |
| BUNTON, LYNN (HM03354) | | | | | | | | | | | | | | | | | | ● | | | | | | | | | | | | | | | | | | | | | | | | | | | | | | | |
| BURKE, JAYNE (HM03388) | | | | | | | | | | | | | | | | | | ● | | | | | | | | | | | ● | | | | | | | | | | | | | | | | | | | | |

# O - Z Therapies at Practices/Businesses

| Business by County with Reference no. | Orthotics | Osteomyology | Osteopathy | PAM | Paranormal Therapies | Pattern Therapies | Physiotherapy | Phytotherapy | Pilates | Podiatry | Polarity Therapy | Postural Integration | Primal Therapy | Psionic Therapy | Psychotherapy | Pyramid Power | Pyscho-Synthesis | Reflexology | Reichian Therapy | Reiki | Remedial Massage | Rogerian Therapy | Rolfing | Seichem | Sensitivity Training | Shiatsu | Silva Method | Sound Therapy | Spiritual Healing | Sports Massage | Stress Therapy | Swedish Body Massage | T'ai-Chi Ch'uan | Tantra Therapy | Tera-Mai | Thought Field Therapy | Touch Therapy | Transactional Analysis | Tui-na | Ultrasonics | Vibrational Therapy | Visualisation Therapy | Vitamin Therapy | Voice Therapy | X-Ray | Ying & Yang | Yoga | Zen Therapy | Zero Balancing |
|---|---|---|---|---|---|---|---|---|---|---|---|---|---|---|---|---|---|---|---|---|---|---|---|---|---|---|---|---|---|---|---|---|---|---|---|---|---|---|---|---|---|---|---|---|---|---|---|---|---|
| CHELTENHAM CLINIC & TRAD ACU (HM04093) | | | | | | | | | | | | | | | | | | ● | | | | | | | | | | | | | | | ● | | | | | | | | | | | | | | | | | |
| CHELTENHAM HOLISTIC HLTH CTRE (HM04094) | | | ● | | | | | | | | | | | | ● | | | ● | | | ● | | | | | ● | | | ● | | | | | | | | | | | | | | | | | | ● | | |
| CHELTENHAM HYPNOTHERAPY (HM04096) | | | | | | | | | | | | | | | ● | | | | | | | | | | | | | | | | | | | | | | | | | | | | | | | | | | |
| CHELTENHAM PHYSIO/SPRTS CLNC (HM04097) | | | | | | | ● | | | | | | | | | | | | | | | | | | | | | | | | | | | | | | | | | | | | | | | | | | |
| CLINIC FOR PHYSICAL MEDICINE (HM04682) | | | ● | | | | | | | | | | | | | | | | | | | | | | | | | | | | | | | | | | | | | | | | | | | | | | |
| COMPLEMENTARY MEDICINE SERVICE (HM04939) | | | ● | | | | | | | | | | | | | | | | | | | | | | | | | | | | | | | | | | | | | | | | | | | | | | |
| COMPLEMENTARY TOUCH (HM04950) | | | | | | | | | | | | | | | | | | ● | | | | | | | | | | | | | | | | | | | | | | | | | | | | | | | |
| COOK, JACKIE (HM05047) | | | | | | | | | | | | | | | | | | ● | | | | | | | | | | | | | | | | | | | | | | | | | | | | | | | |
| COOMBES, ALISON (HM05075) | | | | | | | | | | | | | | | | | | ● | | | | | | | | | | | | | | | | | | | | | | | | | | | | | | | |
| COOPER, ANGELA (HM05089) | | | | | | | | | | | | | | | ● | | | | | | | | | | | | | | | | | | | | | | | | | | | | | | | | | | |
| COOPER, ANN (HM05090) | | | | | | | | | | | | | | | | | | ● | | | | | | | | | | | | | | | | | | | | | | | | | | | | | | | |
| COTSWOLD PHYSIOTHERAPY CENTRE (HM05215) | | | | | | | ● | | ● | | | | | | | | | | | | | | | | | | | | | ● | | | | | | | | | | | | | | | | | | | |
| DATE, SUSAN (HM05756) | | | | | | | | | | | | | | | | | | ● | | ● | | | | | | | | | | | | | | | | | | | | | | | | | | | | | |
| DAVIES, S W (HM05839) | | | ● | | | | | | | | | | | | | | | | | | | | | | | | | | | | | | | | | | | | | | | | | | | | | | |
| DORAN, LESLEY (HM06194) | | | | | | | | | | | | | | | | | | ● | | | | | | | | | | | | | | | | | | | | | | | | | | | | | | | |
| ESSENTIAL BODYWORKS COMPANY (HM06899) | | | | | | | | | | | | | | | | | | | | | | | | | | | | | | ● | | | | | | | ● | | | | | | | | | | | | |
| GOODSON, KAREN (HM08265) | | | | | | | | | | | | | | | ● | | | | | | | | | | | | | | | | | | | | | | | | | | | | | | | | | | |
| GOWING, LYNN (HM08328) | | | | | | | | | | | | | | | | | | ● | | | | | | | | | | | | | | | | | | | | | | | | | | | | | | | |
| GRAY, MARGARET (HM08414) | | | | | | | | | | | | | | | | | | ● | | | | | | | | | | | | | | | | | | | | | | | | | | | | | | | |
| GREENWELL, DAVID (HM08498) | | | | | | | | | | | | | | | ● | | | | | | | | | | | | | | | | ● | | | | | | | | | | | | | | | | | | |
| HANSFORD, LIZ (HM08943) | | | | | | | | | | | | | | | | | | ● | | | | | | | | | | | | | | | | | | | | | | | | | | | | | | | |
| HAYDEN, C J (HM09251) | | | ● | | | | | | | | | | | | | | | | | | | | | | | | | | | | | | | | | | | | | | | | | | | | | | |
| HILL, REBECCA A (HM09788) | | | ● | | | | | | | | | | | | | | | | | | | | | | | | | | | | | | | | | | | | | | | | | | | | | | |
| HUGHES, JANE CHRISTINE (HM10329) | | | | | | | | | | | | | | | | | | ● | | | | | | | | | | | | | | | | | | | | | | | | | | | | | | | |
| JOANNA SMITH AROMATHERAPY (HM11040) | | | | | | | | | | | | | | | | | | ● | | | | | | | | | | | | | | | | | | | | | | | | | | | | | | | |
| LAWLER, R & G (HM12041) | | | | | | | | | | | | | | | | | | ● | | | | | | | | | | | | | | | | | | | | | | | | | | | | | | | |
| LIVINGSTON, J (HM12489) | | | ● | | | | | | | | | | | | | | | | | | | | | | | | | | | | | | | | | | | | | | | | | | | | | | |
| LLEWELLYN, MARGARET (HM12503) | | | | | | | | | | | | | | | | | | ● | | | | | | | | | | | | | | | | | | | | | | | | | | | | | | | |
| LLOYD-JONES, M A (HM12522) | | | ● | | | | | | | | | | | | | | | | | | | | | | | | | | | | | | | | | | | | | | | | | | | | | | |
| MCLAREN, LESLEY (HM13540) | | | | | | | | | | | | | | | | | | ● | | | | | | | | | | | | | | | | | | | | | | | | | | | | | | | |
| NATURAL THERAPIES CLINIC (HM14633) | | | | | | | | | | | | | | | | | | ● | | | ● | | | | | | | ● | | | | | | | | | | | | | | | | | | | | | |
| NATURAL THERAPY CENTRE (HM14649) | | | | | | | | | | | | | | | | | | ● | | ● | | | | | | ● | | | | | | | | | | | | | | | | | | | | | | | |
| NEVIN, ANTHONY (HM14802) | | | ● | | | | | | | | | | | | | | | | | | | | | | | | | | | | | | | | | | | | | | | | | | | | | | |
| NEVIN, ANTHONY R (HM14803) | | | ● | | | | | | | | | | | | | | | | | | | | | | | | | | | | | | | | | | | | | | | | | | | | | | |

# O - Z Therapies at Practices/Businesses

| Business by County with Reference no. | Orthotics | Osteomyology | Osteopathy | PAM | Paranormal Therapies | Pattern Therapies | Physiotherapy | Phytotherapy | Pilates | Podiatry | Polarity Therapy | Postural Integration | Primal Therapy | Psionic Therapy | Psychotherapy | Pyramid Power | Pyscho-Synthesis | Reflexology | Reichian Therapy | Reiki | Remedial Massage | Rogerian Therapy | Rolfing | Seichem | Sensitivity Training | Shiatsu | Silva Method | Sound Therapy | Spiritual Healing | Sports Massage | Stress Therapy | Swedish Body Massage | T'ai-Chi Ch'uan | Tantra Therapy | Tera-Mai | Thought Field Therapy | Touch Therapy | Transactional Analysis | Tui-na | Ultrasonics | Vibrational Therapy | Visualisation Therapy | Vitamin Therapy | Voice Therapy | X-Ray | Ying & Yang | Yoga | Zen Therapy | Zero Balancing |
|---|---|---|---|---|---|---|---|---|---|---|---|---|---|---|---|---|---|---|---|---|---|---|---|---|---|---|---|---|---|---|---|---|---|---|---|---|---|---|---|---|---|---|---|---|---|---|---|---|---|
| OLD CONVENT (HM15255) | | | | | | | | | | | | | | | | | | | | | | | | | | | | | ● | | ● | | | | | | | | | | | | | | | | | | |
| OSTEOPATH (HM15445) | | | ● | | | | | | | | | | | | | | | | | | | | | | | | | | | | | | | | | | | | | | | | | | | | | | |
| POXON, ANJU (HM16517) | | | | | | | | | | | | | | | | | | ● | | | | | | | | | | | | | | | | | | | | | | | | | | | | | | | |
| RAVENSCROFT, GINNY (HM16968) | | | | | | | | | | | | | | | | | | ● | | | | | | | | | | | | | | | | | | | | | | | | | | | | | | | |
| ROSSER, JASON (HM17646) | | | ● | | | | | | | | | | | | | | | | | | | | | | | | | | | | | | | | | | | | | | | | | | | | | | |
| RUMNEY, MICHAEL (HM17749) | | | ● | | | | | | | | | | | | | | | | | | | | | | | | | | | | | | | | | | | | | | | | | | | | | | |
| SHIATSU PRACTICE (HM18460) | | | | | | | | | | | | | | | | | | | | | | | | | | ● | | | | | | | | | | | | | | | | | | | | | | | |
| SILMON, MARY (HM18538) | | | | | | | | | | | | | | | ● | | | | | | | | | | | | | | | | | | | | | | | | | | | | | | | | | | |
| SMYTH, DAVID (HM18830) | | | | | | | | | | | | | | | | | | | | | | | | | | | | | | | | | | | | | | | | | | | | | | ● | | | |
| STAMP & ASSOCIATES (HM19120) | | | ● | | | | | | | | | | | | | | | | | | | | | | | | | | | | | | | | | | | | | | | | | | | | | | |
| STEPHENS, LYN (HM19204) | | | | | | | | | | | | | | | ● | | | | | | | | | | | | | | | | | | | | | | | | | | | | | | | | | | |
| STOKES, PAM (HM19324) | | | | | | | | | | | | | | | | | | ● | | | | | | | | | | | | | | | | | | | | | | | | | | | | | | | |
| STOUT, HEATHER (HM19359) | | | ● | | | | | | | | | | | | | | | | | | | | | | | | | | | | | | | | | | | | | | | | | | | | | | |
| STRESS COMPANY (HM19390) | | | | | | | | | | | | | | | | | | | | | | | | | | | | | | | ● | | | | | | | | | | | | | | | | | | |
| STROUD NATURAL HEALTH CLINIC (HM19422) | | | ● | | | | | | | | | | | | | | | ● | | | | | | | | ● | | | | | | | | | | | | | | | | | | | | | | | |
| TEWKESBURY OSTEOPATHY (HM19854) | | | ● | | | | | | | | | | | | | | | | | | | | | | | | | | | | | | | | | | | | | | | | | | | | | | |
| TOSH, CAROLINE (HM20176) | | | ● | | | | | | | | | | | | | | | | | | | | | | | | | | | | | | | | | | | | | | | | | | | | | | |
| TREE OF LIFE CENTRE (HM20307) | | | | | | | | | | | | | | | | | | ● | | | | | | | | | | | ● | | | | | | | | | | | | | | | | | | | | |
| VINEY HALL PHYSIOTHERAPY (HM20683) | | | | | | | | | | ● | | | | | | | | ● | | | | | | | | | | | | | | | | | | | | | | | | | | | | | | | |
| WELLS, GEORGINA (HM21172) | | | | | | | | | | | ● | | | | | | | ● | | | | | | | | | | | | | | | | | | | | | | | | | | | | | | | |
| WEST OF ENGLAND ALOE VERA CTRE (HM21231) | | | | | | | | | | | | | | | | | | | | | | | | | | | | | | | | | | | | | | | | | | | ● | | | | | | |
| WIEDERHOLD, KAREN (HM21460) | | | | | | | | | | | | | | | | | | ● | | ● | | | | | | | | | ● | | | | | | | | | | | | | | | | | | | | |
| WINTOUR, BOBBY (HM21728) | | | | | | | | | | | | | | | | | | ● | | | | | | | | | | | | | | | | | | | | | | | | | | | | | | | |
| WOODMAN, LINDA (HM21839) | | | | | | | | | | | | | | | | | | ● | | | | | | | | | | | | | | | | | | | | | | | | | | | | | | | |
| YOGA DRUVAM JIVAN YOGA SOCIETY (HM22024) | | | | | | | | | | | | | | | | | | | | | | | | | | | | | | | ● | | | | | | | | | | | | | | | | ● | | |
| ZYL, MARTIN VAN (HM22122) | | | ● | | | | | | | | | | | | | | | | | | | | | | | | | | | | | | | | | | | | | | | | | | | | | | |
| **GUERNSEY** | | | | | | | | | | | | | | | | | | | | | | | | | | | | | | | | | | | | | | | | | | | | | | | | | |
| CHRISTOPHER, DEBORAH (HM04452) | | | | | | | | | | | | | | | | | | ● | | | | | | | | | | | | | | | | | | | | | | | | | | | | | | | |
| SPILLMAN, HOLLY (HM19013) | | | | | | | | | | | | | | | | | | ● | | | | | | | | | | | | | | | | | | | | | | | | | | | | | | | |
| **HAMPSHIRE** | | | | | | | | | | | | | | | | | | | | | | | | | | | | | | | | | | | | | | | | | | | | | | | | | |
| ACUPUNCTURE & PHYSIO CLINIC (HM00245) | | | | | | | | | | | | | | | | | | | | | | | | | | | | | | | | | | | | | | | | ● | | | | | | ● | | | |
| AGER, R W (HM00418) | | | ● | | | | | | | | | | | | | | | | | | | | | | | | | | | | | | | | | | | | | | | | | | | | | | |
| ALLAWAY, SANDRA (HM00592) | | | | | | | | | | | | | | | | | | ● | | | | | | | | | | | | | | | | | | | | | | | | | | | | | | | |
| ALLDRIDGE, T (HM00595) | | | ● | | | | | | | | | | | | | | | | | | | | | | | | | | | | | | | | | | | | | | | | | | | | | | |

# O - Z Therapies at Practices/Businesses

| Business by County with Reference no. | Orthotics | Osteomyology | Osteopathy | PAM | Paranormal Therapies | Pattern Therapies | Physiotherapy | Phytotherapy | Pilates | Podiatry | Polarity Therapy | Postural Integration | Primal Therapy | Psionic Therapy | Psychotherapy | Pyramid Power | Pyscho-Synthesis |
|---|---|---|---|---|---|---|---|---|---|---|---|---|---|---|---|---|---|
| ALLDRIDGE, T D (HM00596) | | | ● | | | | | | | | | | | | | | |
| ALLERGY THERAPY (HM00637) | | | | | | | | | | | | | | | | | |
| ALLISON, C (DR) (HM00650) | | | | | | | | | | | | | | | ● | | |
| ANDERSON, ANGELA (HM00813) | | | | | | | | | | | | | | | | | |
| ANDOVER BACK PAIN & PHYSIO (HM00841) | | | ● | | | | | | | | | | | | | | |
| ANKIN, CHRISTINA (HM00888) | | | | | | | | | | | | | | | | | |
| ARMSTRONG, ANNA (HM01017) | | | | | | | | ● | | | | | | | | | |
| ARMSTRONG, ANNA (HM01018) | | | | | | | | ● | | | | | | | | | |
| ARTEMIS (HM01156) | | | | | | | | | | | | | | | ● | | |
| ATTRIDGE, BRIAN (HM01338) | | | | | | | | | | | | | | | ● | | |
| AVENUE CLINIC (HM01389) | | | | | | | | | | | | | | | | | |
| BAILEY, JANE (HM01549) | | | | | | | | | | | | | | | | | |
| BENNETT, ROSS (HM02155) | | | | | | | | | | | | | | | ● | | |
| BIDWELL, KAREN (HM02285) | | | | | | | | | | | | | | | | | |
| BLAKLEY, PAMELA (HM02486) | | | | | | | | | | | | | | | | | |
| BOLDICK, KATHLEEN (HM02652) | | | | | | | | | | | | | | | | | |
| BRADFORD HOUSE CHIRO CLINIC (HM02849) | | | | | | | | | | | | ● | | | | | |
| BROOKS, CAROLE (HM03174) | | | | | | | | | | | | | | | | | |
| BROWN, ANN (HM03213) | | | | | | | | | | | | | | | | | |
| BUDD, RICHARD (HM03325) | | | | | | | | | | | | | | | | | |
| BURCHELL, DIANE SUE (HM03365) | | | | | | | | | | | | | | | | | |
| BURNE, JANET (HM03394) | | | | | | | | | | | | | | | | | |
| CARMICHAEL, GORDON (HM03709) | | | | | | | | | | | | | | | | | |
| CASWELL, KERI (HM03851) | | | | | | | | | | | | | | | | | |
| CAYNE, J COUN & PSYCHOTHERAPY (HM03872) | | | | | | | | | | | | | | | ● | | |
| CHAPMAN, J D (HM04003) | | | ● | | | | | | | | | | | | | | |
| CHARLETT, DEBORAH (HM04031) | | | | | | | | | | | | | | | | | |
| CITY OSTEOPATHIC CLINIC (HM04497) | | | ● | | | | | | | | | | | | | | |
| CLEMENTS, CHRISTINE (HM04642) | | | ● | | | | | | | | | | | | | | |
| COAST CLINIC (HM04752) | | | | | | | | | | | | | | | | | |
| COLEBROOKE, DAVID (HM04821) | | | ● | | | | | | | | | | | | | | |
| COLEMAN, G P (HM04826) | | | ● | | | | | | | | | | | | | | |
| COMPLETE ANGEL HEALING CENTRE (HM04955) | | | | | | | | | | | | | | | | | |
| COPNOR OSTEOPATHICS (HM05145) | | | ● | | | | | | | | | | | | | | |

| Business by County with Reference no. | Reflexology | Reichian Therapy | Reiki | Remedial Massage | Rogerian Therapy | Rolfing | Seichem | Sensitivity Training | Shiatsu | Silva Method | Sound Therapy | Spiritual Healing | Sports Massage | Stress Therapy | Swedish Body Massage | T'ai-Chi Ch'uan |
|---|---|---|---|---|---|---|---|---|---|---|---|---|---|---|---|---|
| ALLDRIDGE, T D (HM00596) | | | | | | | | | | | | | | | | |
| ALLERGY THERAPY (HM00637) | ● | | ● | | | | | | ● | | | | | | | |
| ALLISON, C (DR) (HM00650) | | | | | | | | | | | | | | | | |
| ANDERSON, ANGELA (HM00813) | ● | | | | | | | | | | | | | | | |
| ANDOVER BACK PAIN & PHYSIO (HM00841) | | | | | | | | | | | | | | | | |
| ANKIN, CHRISTINA (HM00888) | ● | | | | | | | | | | | | | | | |
| ARMSTRONG, ANNA (HM01017) | | | | | | | | | | | | | | | | |
| ARMSTRONG, ANNA (HM01018) | | | | | | | | | | | | | | | | |
| ARTEMIS (HM01156) | | | | | | | | | | | | | | ● | | |
| ATTRIDGE, BRIAN (HM01338) | | | | | | | | | | | | | | | | |
| AVENUE CLINIC (HM01389) | | | | | | | | | | | ● | | | | | |
| BAILEY, JANE (HM01549) | ● | | | | | | | | | | | | | | | |
| BENNETT, ROSS (HM02155) | | | | | | | | | | | | | | | | |
| BIDWELL, KAREN (HM02285) | ● | | | | | | | | | | | | | | | |
| BLAKLEY, PAMELA (HM02486) | ● | | | | | | | | | | | | | | | |
| BOLDICK, KATHLEEN (HM02652) | ● | | | | | | | | | | | | | | | |
| BRADFORD HOUSE CHIRO CLINIC (HM02849) | | | | | | | | | | | | | | | | |
| BROOKS, CAROLE (HM03174) | ● | | | | | | | | | | | | | | | |
| BROWN, ANN (HM03213) | ● | | | | | | | | | | | | | | | |
| BUDD, RICHARD (HM03325) | ● | | | | | | | | | | | | | | | |
| BURCHELL, DIANE SUE (HM03365) | ● | | | | | | | | | | | | | | | |
| BURNE, JANET (HM03394) | ● | | | | | | | | | | | | | | | |
| CARMICHAEL, GORDON (HM03709) | | | | | | | | | | | | | ● | ● | | |
| CASWELL, KERI (HM03851) | ● | | | | | | | | | | | | | | | |
| CAYNE, J COUN & PSYCHOTHERAPY (HM03872) | | | | | | | | | | | | | | | | |
| CHAPMAN, J D (HM04003) | | | | | | | | | | | | | | | | |
| CHARLETT, DEBORAH (HM04031) | ● | | | | | | | | | | | | | | | |
| CITY OSTEOPATHIC CLINIC (HM04497) | | | | | | | | | | | | | | | | |
| CLEMENTS, CHRISTINE (HM04642) | | | | | | | | | | | | | | | | |
| COAST CLINIC (HM04752) | | | ● | | | | | | | | | | ● | | | |
| COLEBROOKE, DAVID (HM04821) | | | | | | | | | | | | | | | | |
| COLEMAN, G P (HM04826) | | | | | | | | | | | | | | | | |
| COMPLETE ANGEL HEALING CENTRE (HM04955) | ● | | ● | | | | | | | | | | | | | |
| COPNOR OSTEOPATHICS (HM05145) | | | | | | | | | | | | | | | | |

| Business by County with Reference no. | Tantra Therapy | Tera-Mai | Thought Field Therapy | Touch Therapy | Transactional Analysis | Tui-na | Ultrasonics | Vibrational Therapy | Visualisation Therapy | Vitamin Therapy | Voice Therapy | X-Ray | Ying & Yang | Yoga | Zen Therapy | Zero Balancing |
|---|---|---|---|---|---|---|---|---|---|---|---|---|---|---|---|---|
| ALLDRIDGE, T D (HM00596) | | | | | | | | | | | | | | | | |
| ALLERGY THERAPY (HM00637) | | | | | | | | | | | | | | | | |
| ALLISON, C (DR) (HM00650) | | | | | | | | | | | | | | | | |
| ANDERSON, ANGELA (HM00813) | | | | | | | | | | | | | | | | |
| ANDOVER BACK PAIN & PHYSIO (HM00841) | | | | | | | | | | | | | | | | |
| ANKIN, CHRISTINA (HM00888) | | | | | | | | | | | | | | | | |
| ARMSTRONG, ANNA (HM01017) | | | | | | | | | | | | | | | | |
| ARMSTRONG, ANNA (HM01018) | | | | | | | | | | | | | | | | |
| ARTEMIS (HM01156) | | | | | | | | | | | | | | | | |
| ATTRIDGE, BRIAN (HM01338) | | | | | | | | | | | | | | | | |
| AVENUE CLINIC (HM01389) | | | | | | | ● | | ● | | | ● | | | | |
| BAILEY, JANE (HM01549) | | | | | | | | | | | | | | | | |
| BENNETT, ROSS (HM02155) | | | | | | | | | | | | | | | | |
| BIDWELL, KAREN (HM02285) | | | | | | | | | | | | | | | | |
| BLAKLEY, PAMELA (HM02486) | | | | | | | | | | | | | | | | |
| BOLDICK, KATHLEEN (HM02652) | | | | | | | | | | | | | | | | |
| BRADFORD HOUSE CHIRO CLINIC (HM02849) | | | | | | | ● | | | | | ● | | | | |
| BROOKS, CAROLE (HM03174) | | | | | | | | | | | | | | | | |
| BROWN, ANN (HM03213) | | | | | | | | | | | | | | | | |
| BUDD, RICHARD (HM03325) | | | | | | | | | | | | | | | | |
| BURCHELL, DIANE SUE (HM03365) | | | | | | | | | | | | | | | | |
| BURNE, JANET (HM03394) | | | | | | | | | | | | | | | | |
| CARMICHAEL, GORDON (HM03709) | | | | | | | | | | | | | | | | |
| CASWELL, KERI (HM03851) | | | | | | | | | | | | | | | | |
| CAYNE, J COUN & PSYCHOTHERAPY (HM03872) | | | | | | | | | | | | | | | | |
| CHAPMAN, J D (HM04003) | | | | | | | | | | | | | | | | |
| CHARLETT, DEBORAH (HM04031) | | | | | | | | | | | | | | | | |
| CITY OSTEOPATHIC CLINIC (HM04497) | | | | | | | | | | | | | | | | |
| CLEMENTS, CHRISTINE (HM04642) | | | | | | | | | | | | | | | | |
| COAST CLINIC (HM04752) | | | | | | | | | | | | | | | | |
| COLEBROOKE, DAVID (HM04821) | | | | | | | | | | | | | | | | |
| COLEMAN, G P (HM04826) | | | | | | | | | | | | | | | | |
| COMPLETE ANGEL HEALING CENTRE (HM04955) | | | | | | | | | | | | | | | | |
| COPNOR OSTEOPATHICS (HM05145) | | | | | | | | | | | | | | | | |

# O - Z Therapies at Practices/Businesses

| Business by County with Reference no. | Orthotics | Osteomyology | Osteopathy | PAM | Paranormal Therapies | Pattern Therapies | Physiotherapy | Phytotherapy | Pilates | Podiatry | Polarity Therapy | Postural Integration | Primal Therapy | Psionic Therapy | Psychotherapy | Pyramid Power | Pyscho-Synthesis | Reflexology | Reichian Therapy | Reiki | Remedial Massage | Rogerian Therapy | Rolfing | Seichem | Sensitivity Training | Shiatsu | Silva Method | Sound Therapy | Spiritual Healing | Sports Massage | Stress Therapy | Swedish Body Massage | T'ai-Chi Ch'uan | Tantra Therapy | Tera-Mai | Thought Field Therapy | Touch Therapy | Transactional Analysis | Tui-na | Ultrasonics | Vibrational Therapy | Visualisation Therapy | Vitamin Therapy | Voice Therapy | X-Ray | Ying & Yang | Yoga | Zen Therapy | Zero Balancing |
|---|---|---|---|---|---|---|---|---|---|---|---|---|---|---|---|---|---|---|---|---|---|---|---|---|---|---|---|---|---|---|---|---|---|---|---|---|---|---|---|---|---|---|---|---|---|---|---|---|---|
| CORELLO, LOUISE (HM05161) | | | | | | | | | | | | | | | | | | | | | | | | | | | | | | | | | | | | | | | | | | | | | | | | | ● |
| COSHAM OSTEOPATHIC CLINIC (HM05202) | | | ● | | | | | | | | | | | | | | | | | | | | | | | | | | | | | | | | | | | | | | | | | | | | | | |
| CTRE-COMPLEMENTARY THERAPY (HM05547) | | | | | | | ● | | | | | | | | | | | ● | | ● | | | | | | | | | | | | | | | | | | | | | | | | | | | ● | | |
| DAVID TIDSALL REIKI PRAC (HM05780) | | | | | | | | | | | | | | | | | | | | ● | | | | | | | | | | | | | | | | | | | | | | | | | | | | | |
| DOLPHIN STUDIOS (HM06165) | | | | | | | | | | | | | | | ● | | | | | ● | | | | | | ● | | | ● | | | | | | | | | | | | | ● | | | | | | | |
| EASTLEIGH OSTEOPATHIC CLINIC (HM06544) | | | ● | | | | | | | | | | | | | | | | | ● | | | | | | | | | | | | | | | | | | | | | | | | | | | | | |
| ELEMENT, SUE (HM06723) | | | | | | | | | | | | | | | | | | ● | | | | | | | | | | | | | | | | | | | | | | | | | | | | | | | |
| ENERGY EXCHANGE HOLISTIC CTRE (HM06816) | | | | | | | | | | | | | | | | | | ● | | ● | | | | | | ● | | | | | | | | | | | | | | | | | | | | | | | |
| FAIRFIELDS LANE WEST (HM07059) | | | ● | | | | | | | | | | | | ● | | | ● | | ● | | | | | | ● | | | ● | | ● | | | | | | | | | | | | | | | | ● | | |
| FAMILY CHIRO & ALT MED CTRE (HM07081) | | | | | | | | | | | ● | ● | | | | | | ● | | ● | | | | ● | | | ● | | | | ● | | | | ● | | | | | | | | ● | | ● | | | | |
| FAY, ESTHER (HM07150) | | | | | | | | | | | | | | | | | | ● | | | | | | | | | | | | | | | | | | | | | | | | | | | | | | | |
| FIT FEET CHIROPODY (HM07361) | | | | | | | | | | | | | | | | | | ● | | | | | | | | | | | | | | | | | | | | | | | | | | | | | | | |
| FLEET & DISTRICT HYP CENTRE (HM07399) | | | | | | | | | | | | | | | | | | | | | | | | | | | | | | | ● | | | | | | | | | | ● | | | | | | | | |
| FOGG, HELEN (HM07452) | | | | | | | | | | | | | | | | | | | | ● | | | | | | | | | | | | | | | | | | | | | | | | | | | | | |
| FOSSEY, LYNETTE (HM07585) | | | | | | | | | | | | | | | | | | ● | | | | | | | | | | | | | | | | | | | | | | | | | | | | | | | |
| FOX, ANTONY D (DR) (HM07631) | | | | | | | | | | | | | | | | | | | | | | | | | | | | | | | | | | | | | | | | | | | ● | | | | | | |
| FRANKEISS, PETER (HM07686) | | | ● | | | | | | | | | | | | | | | | | | | | | | | | | | | | | | | | | | | | | | | | | | | | | | |
| GARSIDE, CATHERINE (HM07909) | | | ● | | | | | | | | | | | | | | | | | | | | | | | | | | | | | | | | | | | | | | | | | | | | | | |
| GLEICH, M T (HM08144) | | | ● | | | | | | | | | | | | | | | | | | | | | | | | | | | | | | | | | | | | | | | | | | | | | | |
| GOVE, J J (HM08323) | | | ● | | | | | | | | | | | | | | | | | | | | | | | | | | | | | | | | | | | | | | | | | | | | | | |
| GREY, CHRISTOPHER (HM08540) | | | ● | | | | | | | | | | | | | | | | | | | | | | | | | | | | | | | | | | | | | | | | | | | | | | |
| GROVE NATURAL THERAPY CENTRE (HM08609) | | | ● | | | | | | | | | | | | ● | | | ● | | ● | | | | | | ● | | | ● | | ● | | | | | | | | | | | | ● | | | | ● | | |
| HAMBLETT, J E (HM08825) | | | ● | | | | | | | | | | | | | | | | | | | | | | | | | | | | | | | | | | | | | | | | | | | | | | |
| HAMMERSON, D (HM08862) | | | ● | | | | | | | | | | | | | | | | | | | | | | | | | | | | | | | | | | | | | | | | | | | | | | |
| HANTSCARE (HM08947) | | | ● | | | | ● | | | ● | | | | | | | | | | | | | | | | | | | | | | | | | | | | | | | | | | | | | | | |
| HAREFIELD CLINIC (HM08989) | | | ● | | | | | | | | | | | | | | | | | | | | | | | | | | | | | | | | | | | | | | | | | | | | | | |
| HARRISON, DENISE (HM09096) | | | | | | | | | | | | | | | | | | ● | | | | | | | | | | | | | | | | | | | | | | | | | | | | | | | |
| HARRISON, IAN M (HM09100) | | | ● | | | | | | | | | | | | | | | | | | | | | | | | | | | | | | | | | | | | | | | | | | | | | | |
| HAYLING ISLAND CHIRO CLINIC (HM09268) | | | | | | | | | | | | ● | | | | | | | | | | | | | | | | | | | | | | | | | | | | ● | | | | | | | | | |
| HEIB, L G (HM09506) | | | ● | | | | | | | | | | | | | | | | | | | | | | | | | | | | | | | | | | | | | | | | | | | | | | |
| HIGH STREET CLINIC (HM09742) | | | | | | | | | | | | | | | | | | ● | | | | | | | | | | | ● | | | | | | | | | | | | | | | | | | | | |
| HIND, SUSAN (HM09825) | | | | | | | | | | | | | | | | | | ● | | | | | | | | | | | | | | | | | | | | | | | | | | | | | | | |
| HOBBS, T J (HM09860) | | | | | | | | | | | | | | | | | | ● | | | | | | | | | | | | | | | | | | | | | | | | | | | | | | | |
| HOLISTIC ARTS STUDIOS (HM09948) | | | | | | | | | | | | | | | | | | ● | | ● | | | | | | | | | ● | | | | | | | | | | | | | | | | | | | | |

# O - Z Therapies at Practices/Businesses

| Business by County with Reference no. | Orthotics | Osteomyology | Osteopathy | PAM | Paranormal Therapies | Pattern Therapies | Physiotherapy | Phytotherapy | Pilates | Podiatry | Polarity Therapy | Postural Integration | Primal Therapy | Psionic Therapy | Psychotherapy | Pyramid Power | Pyscho-Synthesis | Reflexology | Reichian Therapy | Reiki | Remedial Massage | Rogerian Therapy | Rolfing | Seichem | Sensitivity Training | Shiatsu | Silva Method | Sound Therapy | Spiritual Healing | Sports Massage | Stress Therapy | Swedish Body Massage | T'ai-Chi Ch'uan | Tantra Therapy | Tera-Mai | Thought Field Therapy | Touch Therapy | Transactional Analysis | Tui-na | Ultrasonics | Vibrational Therapy | Visualisation Therapy | Vitamin Therapy | Voice Therapy | X-Ray | Ying & Yang | Yoga | Zen Therapy | Zero Balancing |
|---|---|---|---|---|---|---|---|---|---|---|---|---|---|---|---|---|---|---|---|---|---|---|---|---|---|---|---|---|---|---|---|---|---|---|---|---|---|---|---|---|---|---|---|---|---|---|---|---|---|
| HOMOEOPATHIC CLINIC (HM10088) | | | | | | | | | | | | ● | | | | | | | | | | | | | | | | | | | | | | | | | | | | | | | | | | | | | |
| HOOD, CHRISTINA (HM10122) | | | ● | | | | | | | | | | | | | | | | | | | | | | | | | | | | | | | | | | | | | | | | | | | | | | |
| HUTCHINGS, MARGARET (HM10448) | | | | | | | | | | | | | | | | | | ● | | | | | | | | | | | | | | | | | | | | | | | | | | | | | | | |
| HYPNOSIS & STRESS COUNSELLING (HM10494) | | | | | | | | | | | | | | | | | | | | | | | | | | | | | | | ● | | | | | | | | | | | | | | | | | | |
| HYPNOTHRPY FOR POSITIVE CHANGE (HM10542) | | | | | | | | | | | | | | | | | | | | | | | | | | | | | | | ● | | | | | | | | | | | | | | | | | | |
| INLPTA (HM10633) | | | | | | | | | | | | | | | ● | | | | | | | | | | | | | | | | | | | | | | | | | | | ● | | | | | | | |
| INNER WHISPERS & THERAPY CTRE (HM10643) | | | | | | | | | | | | | | | | | | | | ● | | | | | | | | | | | | | | | | | | | | | | | | | | | | | |
| JENKINS, RUSSELL (HM10994) | | | | | | | | | | | ● | | | | | | | ● | | | | | | | | | | | | | | | | | | | | | | | | | | | | | | | |
| JONES, DARCY (HM11134) | | | ● | | | | | | | | | | | | | | | | | | | | | | | | | | | | | | | | | | | | | | | | | | | | | | |
| JOYCE, HELEN G M (HM11236) | | | ● | | | | | | | | | | | | | | | | | | | | | | | | | | | | | | | | | | | | | | | | | | | | | | |
| JUNE PLATTS ASSOCIATES (HM11264) | | | | | | | | | | | | | | | ● | | | | | | | | | | | | | | | | | | | | | | | | | | | | | | | | | | |
| KAY SILVER HYPNOTHERAPY (HM11349) | | | | | | | | | | | | | | | | | | | | | | | | | | | | | | | | | | | | | | | | | | ● | | | | | | | |
| KD PHYSIOTHERAPY (HM11363) | | | | | | | ● | | | | | | | | | | | | | | | | | | | | | | | | | | | | | | | | | | | | | | | | | | |
| KONRAD, GABRIEL (HM11782) | | | ● | | | | | | | | | | | | | | | | | | | | | | | | | | | | | | | | | | | | | | | | | | | | | | |
| LAVERTY, SUSIE (HM12032) | | | | | | | | | | | | | | | | | | | | ● | | | | | | | | | ● | | | | | | | | | | | | | | | | | | | | |
| LE BON, JOHATHAN (HM12083) | | | ● | | | | | | | | | | | | | | | | | | | | | | | | | | | | | | | | | | | | | | | | | | | | | | |
| LEACH, TRICIA (HM12091) | | | | | | | | | | | | | | | | | | | | ● | | | | | | | | | | | | | | | | | | | | | | | | | | | | | |
| LEIGH, PETER A (HM12193) | | | ● | | | | | | | | | | | | | | | | | | | | | | | | | | | | | | | | | | | | | | | | | | | | | | |
| LESTER, MARK (HM12244) | | | ● | | | | | | | | | | | | | | | | | | | | | | | | | | | | | | | | | | | | | | | | | | | | | | |
| LEWIS, D J S (HM12288) | | | | | | | | | | | | | | | | | | | | ● | | | | | | | | | | | | | | | | | | | | | | | | | | | | | |
| LEWIS, SARAH (HM12313) | | | | | | | | | | | | | | | | | | ● | | | | | | | | | | | | | | | | | | | | | | | | | | | | | | | |
| LISLE, THOMAS (HM12455) | ● | | | | | | | | | ● | | | | | | | | | | | | | | | | | | | | | | | | | | | | | | | | | | | | | | | |
| LOCKHAMS THERAPY CENTRE (HM12545) | | | | | | | | | | | | | | | | | | ● | | ● | | | | | | | | | | | | | | | | | | | | | | | | | | | | | |
| LORETTE PARK (HM12644) | | | | | | | | | | | | | | | | | | ● | | | | | | | | | | | | | | | | | | | | | | | | | | | | | | | |
| LOWE, KENNETH (HM12699) | | | | | | | | | | | | ● | | | | | | | | | | | | | | ● | | | | | | | | | | | | | | | | | ● | | | | | | |
| LYMINGTON CHIROPRACTIC CLINIC (HM12759) | | | ● | | | | | | | | | ● | | | ● | | | | | | | | | | | | | | | | | | | | | | | | | ● | | | | | ● | | | | |
| MADSEN, N P C (HM12902) | | | ● | | | | | | | | | | | | | | | | | | | | | | | | | | | | | | | | | | | | | | | | | | | | | | |
| MCCORMICK, FRANCES (HM13424) | | | | | | | | | | | | | | | | | | ● | | | | | | | | | | | | | | | | | | | | | | | | | | | | | | | |
| MELHUISH, J I (DR) (HM13705) | | | | | | | | | | | | | | | | | | ● | | | ● | | | | | | | | | | | | | | | | | | | | | | | | | | | | |
| MINDWORKS HYPNOTHERAPY CLINIC (HM13969) | | | | | | | | | | | | | | | ● | | | | | | | | | | | | | | | | ● | | | | | | | | | | | | | ● | | | | | |
| MITCHELL, EMMA (HM14005) | | | | | | | | | | | | | | | | | | ● | | | | | | | | | | | | | | | | | | | | | | | | | | | | | | | |
| MOORE, S (HM14132) | | | ● | | | | | | | | | | | | | | | | | | | | | | | | | | | | | | | | | | | | | | | | | | | | | | |
| MOORE, SARAH (HM14133) | | | ● | | | | | | | | | | | | | | | | | | | | | | | | | | | | | | | | | | | | | | | | | | | | | | |
| NAT COUNCIL-PSYCHOTHERAPISTS (HM14497) | | | | | | | | | | | | | | | ● | | | | | | | | | | | | | | | | | | | | | | | | | | | | | | | | | | |

# O - Z Therapies at Practices/Businesses

Business by County with Reference no.

| Business | Orthotics | Osteomyology | Osteopathy | PAM | Paranormal Therapies | Pattern Therapies | Physiotherapy | Phytotherapy | Pilates | Podiatry | Polarity Therapy | Postural Integration | Primal Therapy | Psionic Therapy | Psychotherapy | Pyramid Power |
|---|---|---|---|---|---|---|---|---|---|---|---|---|---|---|---|---|
| NATURAL HEALTH SERVICE (HM14595) | | | | | | | | | | | | | | | | |
| NAUGHTON, G (HM14710) | | | | | | | | | | | | | | | ● | |
| NELSON, DANIEL (HM14777) | | | ● | | | | | | | | | | | | | |
| NEW MILTON CHIROPRACTIC CLINIC (HM14825) | | | | | | | | | | | | | | | | |
| NICOLA @ HOLISTIC HOUSE (HM14926) | | | | | | | | | | | | | | | | |
| NORMAN, J M (HM15004) | | | | | | | | | | | | | | | | |
| NORSWORTHY, CLAIRE (HM15017) | | | | | | | | | | | | | | | | |
| O'BRIEN, JILL (HM15185) | | | | | | | | | | | | | | | | |
| ORTON, S (HM15414) | | | ● | | | | | | | | | | | | | |
| OSBORN, TERRI (HM15419) | | | | | | | | | | | | | | | | |
| PARCHMENT STREET CLINIC (HM15646) | | | | | | | | ● | | | | | | | | |
| PARKER, NIESJE (HM15699) | | | | | | | | | | | | | | | ● | |
| PARRY & MCCAFFERY (HM15736) | | | ● | | | | | | | | | | | | | |
| PARRY, N J (HM15740) | | | ● | | | | | | | | | | | | | |
| PHOENIX HOLISTIC CENTRE (HM16156) | | | | | ● | | | | | | | | | | | |
| PHYSIOTHERAPY CENTRE (HM16233) | | | | | | | ● | | | ● | | | | | | |
| POWER & SERCOMBE PRACTICE (HM16500) | | | ● | | | | | | | | | | | | | |
| REIKI NATURAL HEALING CENTRE (HM17142) | | | | | | | | | | | | | | | | |
| RICHARDS, CLAIRE (HM17249) | | | | | | | | | | | | | | | | |
| RICHARDSON, SARAH (HM17291) | | | | | | | | | | | | | | | | |
| RINGWOOD NATURAL HEALTH CLINIC (HM17357) | | | | | | | | | | | | | | | | |
| RINGWOOD PHYSIOTHERAPY CENTRE (HM17358) | | | | | | | ● | | | | | | | | | |
| ROMSEY HEALTH CENTRE (HM17576) | | | ● | | | | | | | | | | | | | |
| ROUSE, J (HM17673) | | | ● | | | | | | | | | | | | | |
| ROUSSOS, AMANDA (HM17677) | | | | | | | | | | | | | | | | |
| RUSHTON, AVRIL (HM17760) | | | | | | | | | | | | | | | | |
| RUSSELL, CHRIS (HM17765) | | | | | | | | | | | | | | | ● | |
| SAMLER, LYN (HM17880) | | | ● | | | | | | | | | | | | | |
| SANCTUARY HEALING (HM17891) | | | | | | | | | | | | | | | | |
| SANDERS, LOUISE (HM17912) | | | ● | | | | | | | | | | | | | |
| SEYMOUR, E J (HM18258) | | | | | | | | | | | | | | | ● | |
| SHREEVE, RACHEL KATHRYN (HM18505) | | | | | | | | | | | | | | | | |
| SIMCOE CLINIC (HM18549) | | | | | | | | | | ● | | | | | | |
| SIMMONDS, J (HM18555) | | | | | | | | | | | | | | | | |

| Business | Pyscho-Synthesis | Reflexology | Reichian Therapy | Reiki | Remedial Massage | Rogerian Therapy | Rolfing | Seichem | Sensitivity Training | Shiatsu | Silva Method | Sound Therapy | Spiritual Healing | Sports Massage | Stress Therapy | Swedish Body Massage |
|---|---|---|---|---|---|---|---|---|---|---|---|---|---|---|---|---|
| NATURAL HEALTH SERVICE (HM14595) | | ● | | ● | | | | | | | | | | ● | | |
| NAUGHTON, G (HM14710) | | | | | | | | | | | | | | | | |
| NELSON, DANIEL (HM14777) | | | | | | | | | | | | | | | | |
| NEW MILTON CHIROPRACTIC CLINIC (HM14825) | | ● | | | | | | | | | | | | | | |
| NICOLA @ HOLISTIC HOUSE (HM14926) | | ● | | | | | | | | | | | | | ● | ● |
| NORMAN, J M (HM15004) | | ● | | | | | | | | | | | | | | |
| NORSWORTHY, CLAIRE (HM15017) | | ● | | ● | | | | | | | | | | | | |
| O'BRIEN, JILL (HM15185) | | ● | | | | | | | | | | | | | | |
| ORTON, S (HM15414) | | | | | | | | | | | | | | | | |
| OSBORN, TERRI (HM15419) | | ● | | | | | | | | | | | | | | |
| PARCHMENT STREET CLINIC (HM15646) | | ● | | | | | | | | | | | | | | |
| PARKER, NIESJE (HM15699) | | | | | | | | | | | | | | | | |
| PARRY & MCCAFFERY (HM15736) | | | | | | | | | | | | | | | | |
| PARRY, N J (HM15740) | | | | | | | | | | | | | | | | |
| PHOENIX HOLISTIC CENTRE (HM16156) | | ● | | ● | | | | | | | | | ● | | | |
| PHYSIOTHERAPY CENTRE (HM16233) | | | | | | | | | | | | | | | | |
| POWER & SERCOMBE PRACTICE (HM16500) | | | | | | | | | | | | | | | | |
| REIKI NATURAL HEALING CENTRE (HM17142) | | | | ● | | | | | | | | | | | | |
| RICHARDS, CLAIRE (HM17249) | | ● | | ● | | | | | | | | | ● | | | |
| RICHARDSON, SARAH (HM17291) | | ● | | | | | | | | | | | | | | |
| RINGWOOD NATURAL HEALTH CLINIC (HM17357) | | ● | | ● | | | | | | ● | | | | | | |
| RINGWOOD PHYSIOTHERAPY CENTRE (HM17358) | | | | | | | | | | | | | | | | |
| ROMSEY HEALTH CENTRE (HM17576) | | | | | | | | | | | | | | | | |
| ROUSE, J (HM17673) | | | | | | | | | | | | | | | | |
| ROUSSOS, AMANDA (HM17677) | | ● | | ● | | | | | | | | | | | | |
| RUSHTON, AVRIL (HM17760) | | ● | | | | | | | | | | | | | | |
| RUSSELL, CHRIS (HM17765) | | | | | | | | | | | | | | | | |
| SAMLER, LYN (HM17880) | | | | | | | | | | | | | | | | |
| SANCTUARY HEALING (HM17891) | | | | ● | | | | | | | | | | | | |
| SANDERS, LOUISE (HM17912) | | | | | | | | | | | | | | | | |
| SEYMOUR, E J (HM18258) | | | | | | | | | | | | | | | | |
| SHREEVE, RACHEL KATHRYN (HM18505) | | ● | | | | | | | | | | | | | | |
| SIMCOE CLINIC (HM18549) | | ● | | | | | | | | | | | | | | |
| SIMMONDS, J (HM18555) | | ● | | | | | | | | | | | | | | |

| Business | T'ai-Chi Ch'uan | Tantra Therapy | Tera-Mai | Thought Field Therapy | Touch Therapy | Transactional Analysis | Tui-na | Ultrasonics | Vibrational Therapy | Visualisation Therapy | Vitamin Therapy | Voice Therapy | X-Ray | Ying & Yang | Yoga | Zen Therapy | Zero Balancing |
|---|---|---|---|---|---|---|---|---|---|---|---|---|---|---|---|---|---|
| NATURAL HEALTH SERVICE (HM14595) | | | | | | | | | | | | | | | | | |
| NAUGHTON, G (HM14710) | | | | | | | | | | | | | | | | | |
| NELSON, DANIEL (HM14777) | | | | | | | | | | | | | | | | | |
| NEW MILTON CHIROPRACTIC CLINIC (HM14825) | | | | | | | | | | | ● | | ● | | | | |
| NICOLA @ HOLISTIC HOUSE (HM14926) | | | | | | | | | | | | | | | | | |
| NORMAN, J M (HM15004) | | | | | | | | | | | | | | | | | |
| NORSWORTHY, CLAIRE (HM15017) | | | | | | | | | | | | | | | | | |
| O'BRIEN, JILL (HM15185) | | | | | | | | | | | | | | | | | |
| ORTON, S (HM15414) | | | | | | | | | | | | | | | | | |
| OSBORN, TERRI (HM15419) | | | | | | | | | | | | | | | | | |
| PARCHMENT STREET CLINIC (HM15646) | | | | | | | | | | | | | ● | | | | |
| PARKER, NIESJE (HM15699) | | | | | | | | | | | | | | | | | |
| PARRY & MCCAFFERY (HM15736) | | | | | | | | | | | | | | | | | |
| PARRY, N J (HM15740) | | | | | | | | | | | | | | | | | |
| PHOENIX HOLISTIC CENTRE (HM16156) | | | | | | | | | | | | | | | | | |
| PHYSIOTHERAPY CENTRE (HM16233) | | | | | | | | | | | | | | | | | |
| POWER & SERCOMBE PRACTICE (HM16500) | | | | | | | | | | | | | | | | | |
| REIKI NATURAL HEALING CENTRE (HM17142) | | | | | | | | | | | | | | | | | |
| RICHARDS, CLAIRE (HM17249) | | | | | | | | | | | | | | | | | |
| RICHARDSON, SARAH (HM17291) | | | | | | | | | | | | | | | | | |
| RINGWOOD NATURAL HEALTH CLINIC (HM17357) | | | | | | | | | | | | | | | | | |
| RINGWOOD PHYSIOTHERAPY CENTRE (HM17358) | | | | | | | | | | | | | | | | | |
| ROMSEY HEALTH CENTRE (HM17576) | | | | | | | | | | | | | | | | | |
| ROUSE, J (HM17673) | | | | | | | | | | | | | | | | | |
| ROUSSOS, AMANDA (HM17677) | | | | | | | | | | | | | | | | | |
| RUSHTON, AVRIL (HM17760) | | | | | | | | | | | | | | | | | |
| RUSSELL, CHRIS (HM17765) | | | | | | | | | | | | | | | | | |
| SAMLER, LYN (HM17880) | | | | | | | | | | | | | | | | | |
| SANCTUARY HEALING (HM17891) | | | | | | | | | | | | | | | | | |
| SANDERS, LOUISE (HM17912) | | | | | | | | | | | | | | | | | |
| SEYMOUR, E J (HM18258) | | | | | | | | | | | | | | | | | |
| SHREEVE, RACHEL KATHRYN (HM18505) | | | | | | | | | | | | | | | | | |
| SIMCOE CLINIC (HM18549) | | | | | | | | ● | | | ● | | ● | | | | |
| SIMMONDS, J (HM18555) | | | | | | | | | | | | | | | | | |

# O - Z Therapies at Practices/Businesses

| Business by County with Reference no. | Orthotics | Osteomyology | Osteopathy | PAM | Paranormal Therapies | Pattern Therapies | Physiotherapy | Phytotherapy | Pilates | Podiatry | Polarity Therapy | Postural Integration | Primal Therapy | Psionic Therapy | Psychotherapy | Pyramid Power | Pyscho-Synthesis | Reflexology | Reichian Therapy | Reiki | Remedial Massage | Rogerian Therapy | Rolfing | Seichem | Sensitivity Training |
|---|---|---|---|---|---|---|---|---|---|---|---|---|---|---|---|---|---|---|---|---|---|---|---|---|---|
| SMITH, CHRISTOPHER R A (HM18729) | | | ● | | | | | | | | | | | | | | | | | | | | | | |
| SMITH, R (HM18795) | | | ● | | | | | | | | | | | | | | | | | | | | | | |
| SOUTHGATE NAT THERAPY CLINIC (HM18937) | | | ● | | | | | | | | | | | | ● | | | | | | | | | | |
| SOUTHSEA CENTRE FOR COMP MED (HM18943) | | | ● | | | | | | | | | ● | | | | | | ● | | ● | | | | | |
| SPELLER, BRIDGET (HM18980) | | | | | | | | | | | | | | | | | | ● | | | | | | | |
| STAINER, A (HM19113) | | | ● | | | | | | | | | | | | | | | | | | | | | | |
| SWAY HOUSE PUBLICATIONS (HM19581) | | | | | | | | | | | | | | | ● | | | | | | | | | | |
| TAYLOR & ASSOCIATES (HM19728) | | | | | | | | | | | | | | | ● | | | | | | | | | | |
| TELLURIC, CHRISTINE (HM19825) | | | | | | | | | | | | | | | | | | ● | | | | | | | |
| TERRY, FIONA (HM19848) | | | ● | | | | | | | | | | | | | | | | | | | | | | |
| TIDBALL, GILLIAN (HM20054) | | | | | | | | | | | | | | | | | | ● | | | | | | | |
| TURNER, CATHY (HM20420) | | | | | | | | | | | | | | | | | | ● | | ● | | | | | |
| TWESLEDOWN PHYSIOTHERAPY (HM20449) | | | | | | | ● | | | | | | | | | | | | | | | | | | |
| VALENTINE, ROSS (HM20556) | | | ● | | | | | | | | | | | | | | | | | | | | | | |
| WARD, G C (HM20903) | | | ● | | | | | | | | | | | | | | | | | | | | | | |
| WARNE, P F (HM20932) | | | ● | | | | | | | | | | | | | | | | | | | | | | |
| WECK, LYN (HM21096) | | | | | | | | | | | | | | | | | | ● | | | | | | | |
| WEEDON, BRIAN J (HM21101) | | | ● | | | | | | | | | | | | | | | | | | | | | | |
| WELL HOUSE HOLISTIC HLTH CTRE (HM21138) | | | | | | | | | | | | | | | | | | | | ● | | | | | |
| WELSH, R P (HM21187) | | | ● | | | | | | | | | | | | | | | | | | | | | | |
| WELSH, R P & C J (HM21188) | | | ● | | | | | | | | | | | | | | | | | | | | | | |
| WESSEX OSTEOPATHY CLINIC (HM21211) | | | ● | | | | | | | | | | | | | | | | | | | | | | |
| WHITE, W (HM21383) | | | | | | | | | | | | | | | ● | | | | | | | | | | |
| WILLIAMS, LIZ-BETH (HM21578) | | | | | | | | | | | | | | | | | | ● | | | | | | | |
| WILLOW TREE THERAPEUTIC AGENCY (HM21627) | | | | | | | | | | | | | | | ● | | | | | | | | | | |
| WINCHESTER CHIROPRACTIC CLINIC (HM21691) | | | | | | | | | | | | | | | | | | ● | | | ● | | | | |
| WINCHESTER HOM PRACTICE (HM21692) | | | ● | | | | | | | | | | | | | | | ● | | | | | | | |
| WOODROW, LORRAINE (HM21844) | | | | | | | | | | | | | | | | | | ● | | | | | | | |
| **HEREFORDSHIRE** | | | | | | | | | | | | | | | | | | | | | | | | | |
| BEAUTY IS YOURS (HM01999) | | | | | | | | | | | | | | | | | | | | ● | | | | | |
| BLACKBURN, ROBERT W (HM02437) | | | ● | | | | | | | | | | | | | | | | | | | | | | |
| BODY PERFECTION (HM02604) | | | | | | | | | | | | | | | | | | | | | | | | | |
| BROADVIEW NATURAL HEALTH CTRE (HM03119) | | | | | | | | | | | | | | | ● | | | | | | | | | | |
| CHARVET, BARBARA (HM04053) | | | | | | | | | | | | | | | | | | ● | | | | | | | |

| Business by County with Reference no. | Shiatsu | Silva Method | Sound Therapy | Spiritual Healing | Sports Massage | Stress Therapy | Swedish Body Massage | T'ai-Chi Ch'uan | Tantra Therapy | Tera-Mai | Thought Field Therapy | Touch Therapy | Transactional Analysis | Tui-na | Ultrasonics | Vibrational Therapy | Visualisation Therapy | Vitamin Therapy | Voice Therapy | X-Ray | Ying & Yang | Yoga | Zen Therapy | Zero Balancing |
|---|---|---|---|---|---|---|---|---|---|---|---|---|---|---|---|---|---|---|---|---|---|---|---|---|
| SMITH, CHRISTOPHER R A (HM18729) | | | | | | | | | | | | | | | | | | | | | | | | |
| SMITH, R (HM18795) | | | | | | | | | | | | | | | | | | | | | | | | |
| SOUTHGATE NAT THERAPY CLINIC (HM18937) | ● | | | | | | | | | | | | | | | | | | | | | | | |
| SOUTHSEA CENTRE FOR COMP MED (HM18943) | ● | | | | | ● | | | | | | | | | | | | ● | | | | | | |
| SPELLER, BRIDGET (HM18980) | | | | | | | | | | | | | | | | | | | | | | | | |
| STAINER, A (HM19113) | | | | | | | | | | | | | | | | | | | | | | | | |
| SWAY HOUSE PUBLICATIONS (HM19581) | | | | | | | | | | | | | | | | | | | | | | | | |
| TAYLOR & ASSOCIATES (HM19728) | | | | | | | | | | | | | | | | | | | | | | | | |
| TELLURIC, CHRISTINE (HM19825) | | | | | | | | | | | | | | | | | | | | | | | | |
| TERRY, FIONA (HM19848) | | | | | | | | | | | | | | | | | | | | | | | | |
| TIDBALL, GILLIAN (HM20054) | | | | | | | | | | | | | | | | | | | | | | | | |
| TURNER, CATHY (HM20420) | | | | | | | | | | | | | | | | | | | | | | | | |
| TWESLEDOWN PHYSIOTHERAPY (HM20449) | | | | | | | | | | | | | | | | | | | | | | | | |
| VALENTINE, ROSS (HM20556) | | | | | | | | | | | | | | | | | | | | | | | | |
| WARD, G C (HM20903) | | | | | | | | | | | | | | | | | | | | | | | | |
| WARNE, P F (HM20932) | | | | | | | | | | | | | | | | | | | | | | | | |
| WECK, LYN (HM21096) | | | | | | | | | | | | | | | | | | | | | | | | |
| WEEDON, BRIAN J (HM21101) | | | | | | | | | | | | | | | | | | | | | | | | |
| WELL HOUSE HOLISTIC HLTH CTRE (HM21138) | ● | | | | | | | | | | | | | | | | | | | | | ● | | |
| WELSH, R P (HM21187) | | | | | | | | | | | | | | | | | | | | | | | | |
| WELSH, R P & C J (HM21188) | | | | | | | | | | | | | | | | | | | | | | | | |
| WESSEX OSTEOPATHY CLINIC (HM21211) | | | | | | | | | | | | | | | | | | | | | | | | |
| WHITE, W (HM21383) | | | | | | | | | | | | | | | | | | | | | | | | |
| WILLIAMS, LIZ-BETH (HM21578) | | | | | | | | | | | | | | | | | | | | | | | | |
| WILLOW TREE THERAPEUTIC AGENCY (HM21627) | | | | | | | | | | | | | | | | | | | | | | | | |
| WINCHESTER CHIROPRACTIC CLINIC (HM21691) | | | | | | | | | | | | | | | | | | | | ● | | | | |
| WINCHESTER HOM PRACTICE (HM21692) | | | | ● | | | | | | | | | | | | | | | | | | | | |
| WOODROW, LORRAINE (HM21844) | | | | | | | | | | | | | | | | | | | | | | | | |
| **HEREFORDSHIRE** | | | | | | | | | | | | | | | | | | | | | | | | |
| BEAUTY IS YOURS (HM01999) | | | | | | | | | | | | ● | | | | | | | | | | | | |
| BLACKBURN, ROBERT W (HM02437) | | | | | | | | | | | | | | | | | | | | | | | | |
| BODY PERFECTION (HM02604) | | | | | | | | | | | | | | | | | | ● | | | | | | |
| BROADVIEW NATURAL HEALTH CTRE (HM03119) | ● | | | | | | | | | | | | | | | | | | | | | | | |
| CHARVET, BARBARA (HM04053) | | | | | | | | | | | | | | | | | | | | | | | | |

# O - Z Therapies at Practices/Businesses

| Business by County with Reference no. | Orthotics | Osteomyology | Osteopathy | PAM | Paranormal Therapies | Pattern Therapies | Physiotherapy | Phytotherapy | Pilates | Podiatry | Polarity Therapy | Postural Integration | Primal Therapy | Psionic Therapy | Psychotherapy | Pyramid Power | Pyscho-Synthesis | Reflexology | Reichian Therapy | Reiki | Remedial Massage | Rogerian Therapy | Rolfing | Seichem | Sensitivity Training | Shiatsu | Silva Method | Sound Therapy | Spiritual Healing | Sports Massage | Stress Therapy | Swedish Body Massage | T'ai-Chi Ch'uan | Tantra Therapy | Tera-Mai | Thought Field Therapy | Touch Therapy | Transactional Analysis | Tui-na | Ultrasonics | Vibrational Therapy | Visualisation Therapy | Vitamin Therapy | Voice Therapy | X-Ray | Ying & Yang | Yoga | Zen Therapy | Zero Balancing |
|---|---|---|---|---|---|---|---|---|---|---|---|---|---|---|---|---|---|---|---|---|---|---|---|---|---|---|---|---|---|---|---|---|---|---|---|---|---|---|---|---|---|---|---|---|---|---|---|---|---|
| COOPER, A (HM05085) | | | | | | | | | | | | | | | ● | | | | | | | | | | | | | | | | | | | | | | | | | | | | | | | | | | |
| EVANS, JOANNE (HM06979) | | | | | | | | | | | | | | | | | | ● | | | | | | | | | | | | | | | | | | | | | | | | | | | | | | | |
| GIBSON-FORTY, J (HM08048) | | | ● | | | | | | | | | | | | | | | | | | | | | | | | | | | | | | | | | | | | | | | | | | | | | | |
| HANDOLL & ASSOCIATES (HM08901) | | | ● | | | | | | | | | | | | | | | | | | | | | | | | | | | | | | | | | | | | | | | | | | | | | | |
| HANDOLL, NICHOLAS & ASSOCIATES (HM08902) | | | ● | | | | | | | | | | | | | | | | | | | | | | | | | | | | | | | | | | | | | | | | | | | | | | |
| HANDY, SUSAN (HM08921) | | | | | | | | | | | | | | | ● | | | | | | | | | | | | | | | | | | | | | | | | | | | | | | | | | | |
| HEREFORD CENTRE (HM09677) | | | ● | | | | | | | | | | | | ● | | | ● | | | | | | | | ● | | | ● | | ● | | | | | | | | | | | ● | | | | | | | |
| JONES, KEVIN D G (HM11165) | | | ● | | | | | | | | | | | | | | | | | | | | | | | | | | | | | | | | | | | | | | | | | | | | | | |
| LEDBURY NATURAL HEALTH CENTRE (HM12122) | | | | | | | | | | | | | | | | | | ● | | ● | | | | | | | | | | | | | | | | | | | | | | | | | | | | | ● |
| LEDBURY OSTEOPATHIC PRACTICE (HM12123) | | | ● | | | | | | | | | | | | | | | | | | | | | | | | | | | | | | | | | | | | | | | | | | | | | | |
| LEOMINSTER OSTEOPATHS (HM12221) | | | ● | | | | | | | | | | | | | | | | | | | | | | | | | | | | | | | | | | | | | | | | | | | | | | |
| MOULE, TERRY G (HM14285) | | | ● | | | | | | | | | | | | | | | | | | | | | | | | | | | | | | | | | | | | | | | | | | | | | | |
| OLIVER, JENNY (HM15292) | | | | | | | | | | | | | | | ● | | | | | | | | | | | | | | | | | | | | | | | | | | | | | | | | | | |
| PHILLPOT, ANN (HM16146) | | | | | | | | | | | | | | | | | | ● | | | | | | | | | | | | | | | | | | | | | | | | | | | | | | | |
| WILLCOCKS, T & S (HM21519) | | | | | | | | | | | | | | | | | | ● | | ● | | | | | | | | | ● | | | | | | | | | | | | | | | | | | | | |
| WILLIAMS, VALERIE MOLYNEUX (HM21603) | | | | | | | | | | | | | | | | | | ● | | | | | | | | | | | | | | | | | | | | | | | | | | | | | | | |
| **HERTFORDSHIRE** | | | | | | | | | | | | | | | | | | | | | | | | | | | | | | | | | | | | | | | | | | | | | | | | | |
| ABUNDANCE HEALING (HM00145) | | | | | | | | | | | | | | | | | | ● | | ● | | | | | | | | | | | | | | | | | | | | | | | | | | | | | |
| ALDER, DENNIS (HM00497) | | | | | | | | | | ● | | | | | | | | | | | | | | | | | | | | | | | | | | | | | | | | | | | | | | | |
| ALLEN, JULIE & LEN (HM00613) | | | | | | | | | | | | | | | ● | | | | | | | | | | | | | | | | ● | | | | | | | | | | | | | | | | | | |
| ALTERNATIVE CHOICES (HM00697) | | | | | | | | | | | | | | | | | | | | ● | | | | | | | | | | | | | | | | | | | | | | | | | | | | | |
| AQUARIAN SCHOOL HERTFORDSHIRE (HM00955) | | | | | | | | | | | | | | | | | | ● | | | | | | | | | | | | | | | | | | | | | | | | | | | | | | | |
| ARNOLD, PETER & JACKIE (HM01036) | | | ● | | | | | | | | | | | | | | | | | | | | | | | | | | | | | | | | | | | | | | | | | | | | | | |
| AROMATHERAPY BY ANTONIO (HM01095) | | | | | | | | | | | | | | | | | | ● | | | | | | | | | | | | | | | | | | | | | | | | | | | | | | | |
| ASHDOWN CLINIC (HM01205) | | | ● | | | | ● | | ● | | | | | | | | | ● | | ● | | | | | | ● | | | | | | | | | | | | | | | | | ● | | ● | | | | |
| ASHWELL, MELBOURN & BALDOCK (HM01246) | | | ● | | | | | | | | | | | | | | | | | | | | | | | | | | | | | | | | | | | | | | | | | | | | | | |
| ASSOCIATES HEAD & SHORT (HM01277) | | | | | | | | | | ● | | | | | | | | | | | | | | | | | | | | | | | | | | | | | | | | | | | | | | | |
| ASSOCIATES HEAD & SHORT (HM01276) | | | | | | | | | | ● | | | | | | | | | | | | | | | | | | | | | | | | | | | | | | | | | | | | | | | |
| ASSOCIATION OF STRESS MNGMT (HM01293) | | | | | | | | | | | | | | | | | | | | | | | | | | | | | | | ● | | | | | | | | | | | | | | | | | | |
| BA FOR COUNSELLING (HM01458) | | | | | | | | | | | | | | | ● | | | | | | | | | | | | | | | | | | | | | | | | | | | | | | | | | | |
| BARBER, NICHOLAS J (HM01688) | | | ● | | | | | | | | | | | | | | | | | | | | | | | | | | | | | | | | | | | | | | | | | | | | | | |
| BARRETT, CAROL-ANN (HM01788) | | | | | | | | | | | | | | | | | | ● | | | | | | | | | | | | | | | | | | | | | | | | | | | | | | | |
| BASSETT CLINIC (HM01853) | | | | | | | | | | | | | | | | | | ● | | | | | | | | | | | | | | | | | | | | | | | | | | | ● | | | | |
| BEAUCHAMP BAGENAL (HM01983) | | | | | | | | | | | | | | | | | | | | | | | | | | | | | | | ● | | | | | | | | | | | | | ● | | | | | |

# O - Z Therapies at Practices/Businesses

| Business by County with Reference no. | Orthotics | Osteomyology | Osteopathy | PAM | Paranormal Therapies | Pattern Therapies | Physiotherapy | Phytotherapy | Pilates | Podiatry | Polarity Therapy | Postural Integration | Primal Therapy | Psionic Therapy | Psychotherapy | Pyramid Power | Pyscho-Synthesis | Reflexology | Reichian Therapy | Reiki | Remedial Massage | Rogerian Therapy | Rolfing | Seichem | Sensitivity Training |
|---|---|---|---|---|---|---|---|---|---|---|---|---|---|---|---|---|---|---|---|---|---|---|---|---|---|
| BEDFORD, JANET (HM02039) | | | | | | | | | | | | | | | | | | ● | | | | | | | |
| BENNETT, CHARLES R (HM02138) | | | ● | | | | | | | | | | | | | | | | | | | | | | |
| BENSON, HAZEL (HM02167) | | | | | | | | | | | | | | | | | | ● | | | | | | | |
| BERKHAMSTED PHYSIO CLINIC (HM02193) | | | | | | | ● | | | | | | | | | | | | | | | | | | |
| BERNER, ERICH (HM02199) | | | | | | | | | | | | | | | | | | ● | | | | | | | |
| BETA HEALTH CLINIC (HM02229) | | | ● | | | | ● | | | | | | | | | | | | | | | | | | |
| BETSER, J (HM02231) | | | ● | | | | | | | | | | | | | | | | | | | | | | |
| BODY MECHANICS THERAPY CLINIC (HM02598) | | | | | | | | | | | | | | | ● | | | ● | | | | | | | |
| BRIGGS-WILSON, A (HM03037) | | | | | | | | | | | | | | | | | | ● | | ● | | | | | |
| BRIND, KEVIN (HM03053) | | | | | | | ● | | | | | | | | | | | | | | | | | | |
| BROCKWELL, BADGER (HM03131) | | | | | | | | | | | | | | | ● | | | | | | | | | | |
| BURYHILL PHYSIOTHERAPY (HM03456) | | | | | | | ● | | | | | | | | | | | | | | | | | | |
| BUSHEY PRACTICE (HM03464) | | | ● | | | | | | | | | | | | | | | | | | | | | | |
| BUTTERFIELD, ROBIN (HM03496) | | ● | ● | | | | | | | | | | | | ● | | | | | | | | | | |
| CANNING, LINDA (HM03632) | | | | | | | | | | | | | | | | | | ● | | | | | | | |
| CANNON, VALERIE (HM03635) | | | | | | | | | | | | | | | | | | ● | | ● | | | | | |
| CARTWRIGHT-ADAMS, NATALIE (HM03799) | | | ● | | | | | | | | | | | | | | | | | | | | | | |
| CHAMBERS, AINE (HM03957) | | | | | | | | | | | | | | | ● | | | | | | | | | | |
| CHANDLER, LENA (HM03975) | | | | | | | | | | | | | | | | | | ● | | | | | | | |
| CHAPMAN, ANNA (HM03999) | | | ● | | | | | | | | | | | | | | | | | | | | | | |
| CHESHUNT OSTEOPATHIC CLINIC (HM04118) | | | ● | | | | | | | | | | | | | | | | | | | | | | |
| CHOPRA, S (HM04427) | ● | | | | | | | | | | | | | | | | | | | | | | | | |
| CLARE JAMES HEALTH FOODS (HM04532) | | | | | | | | | | | | | | | | | | | | | | | | | |
| CLARIDGE, PATRICIA (HM04545) | | | | | | | | | | | | | | | | | | ● | | | | | | | |
| CLARK, MICHELLE (HM04573) | | | | | | | | | | | | | | | | | | ● | | | | | | | |
| COE, J NICHOLAS (HM04781) | | | ● | | | | | | | | | | | | | | | | | | | | | | |
| COLLEGE OF OSTEOPATHS (HM04852) | | | ● | | | | | | | | | | | | | | | | | | | | | | |
| CONISTON PHYSIOTHERAPY CLINIC (HM04980) | | | ● | | | | | | | | | | | | | | | | | | | | | | |
| COOPER, FELICITY (HM05101) | | | | | | | | | | ● | | | | | | | | | | | | | | | |
| COX, MADDI (HM05314) | | | | | | | | | | | | | | | | | | ● | | | | | | | |
| COX, T (HM05322) | | | ● | | | | | | | | | | | | | | | | | | | | | | |
| CUSWORTH, BRIAN (HM05641) | | | ● | | | | | | | | | | | | | | | | | | | | | | |
| DAVID HERBERT REFLEXOLOGY (HM05774) | | | | | | | | | | | | | | | | | | ● | | | | | | | |
| DAVIES, JACQUELINE (HM05817) | | | | | | | | | | | | | | | | | | ● | | | | | | | |

| Business by County with Reference no. | Shiatsu | Silva Method | Sound Therapy | Spiritual Healing | Sports Massage | Stress Therapy | Swedish Body Massage | T'ai-Chi Ch'uan | Tantra Therapy | Tera-Mai | Thought Field Therapy | Touch Therapy | Transactional Analysis | Tui-na | Ultrasonics | Vibrational Therapy | Visualisation Therapy | Vitamin Therapy | Voice Therapy | X-Ray | Ying & Yang | Yoga | Zen Therapy | Zero Balancing |
|---|---|---|---|---|---|---|---|---|---|---|---|---|---|---|---|---|---|---|---|---|---|---|---|---|
| BEDFORD, JANET (HM02039) | | | | | | | | | | | | | | | | | | | | | | | | |
| BENNETT, CHARLES R (HM02138) | | | | | | | | | | | | | | | | | | | | | | | | |
| BENSON, HAZEL (HM02167) | | | | | | | | | | | | | | | | | | | | | | | | |
| BERKHAMSTED PHYSIO CLINIC (HM02193) | | | | | | | | | | | | | | | | | | | | | | | | |
| BERNER, ERICH (HM02199) | | | | | | | | | | | | | | | | | | | | | | | | |
| BETA HEALTH CLINIC (HM02229) | ● | | | | | | | | | | | | | | | | | | | | | | | |
| BETSER, J (HM02231) | | | | | | | | | | | | | | | | | | | | | | | | |
| BODY MECHANICS THERAPY CLINIC (HM02598) | | | | | | | | | | | | | | | | | | | | | | | | |
| BRIGGS-WILSON, A (HM03037) | | | | | | | | | | | | | | | | | | | | | | | | |
| BRIND, KEVIN (HM03053) | | | | | | | | | | | | | | | | | | | | | | | | |
| BROCKWELL, BADGER (HM03131) | | | | | | | | | | | | | | | | | | | | | | | | |
| BURYHILL PHYSIOTHERAPY (HM03456) | | | | | | | | | | | | | | | | | | | | | | | | |
| BUSHEY PRACTICE (HM03464) | | | | | | | | | | | | | | | | | | | | | | | | |
| BUTTERFIELD, ROBIN (HM03496) | | | | | | ● | | | ● | | | | | | | | | | | | | | | |
| CANNING, LINDA (HM03632) | | | | | | | | | | | | | | | | | | | | | | | | |
| CANNON, VALERIE (HM03635) | | | | | | | | | | | | | | | | | | | | | | | | |
| CARTWRIGHT-ADAMS, NATALIE (HM03799) | | | | | | | | | | | | | | | | | | | | | | | | |
| CHAMBERS, AINE (HM03957) | | | | | | | | | | | | | | | | | | | | | | | | |
| CHANDLER, LENA (HM03975) | | | | | | | | | | | | | | | | | | | | | | | | |
| CHAPMAN, ANNA (HM03999) | | | | | | | | | | | | | | | | | | | | | | | | |
| CHESHUNT OSTEOPATHIC CLINIC (HM04118) | | | | | | | | | | | | | | | | | | | | | | | | |
| CHOPRA, S (HM04427) | | | | | | | | | | | | | | | | | | | | | | | | |
| CLARE JAMES HEALTH FOODS (HM04532) | | | | | | | | | | | | | | | | | | ● | | | | | | |
| CLARIDGE, PATRICIA (HM04545) | | | | | | | | | | | | | | | | | | | | | | | | |
| CLARK, MICHELLE (HM04573) | | | | | | | | | | | | | | | | | | | | | | | | |
| COE, J NICHOLAS (HM04781) | | | | | | | | | | | | | | | | | | | | | | | | |
| COLLEGE OF OSTEOPATHS (HM04852) | | | | | | | | | | | | | | | | | | | | | | | | |
| CONISTON PHYSIOTHERAPY CLINIC (HM04980) | | | | ● | | ● | | | | | | | | | ● | | | ● | | | | | | |
| COOPER, FELICITY (HM05101) | | | | | | | | | | | | | | | | | | | | | | | | |
| COX, MADDI (HM05314) | | | | | | | | | | | | | | | | | | | | | | | | |
| COX, T (HM05322) | | | | | | | | | | | | | | | | | | | | | | | | |
| CUSWORTH, BRIAN (HM05641) | | | | | | | | | | | | | | | | | | | | | | | | |
| DAVID HERBERT REFLEXOLOGY (HM05774) | | | | | | | | | | | | | | | | | | | | | | | | |
| DAVIES, JACQUELINE (HM05817) | | | | | | | | | | | | | | | | | | | | | | | | |

# O - Z Therapies at Practices/Businesses

| Business by County with Reference no. | Orthotics | Osteomyology | Osteopathy | PAM | Paranormal Therapies | Pattern Therapies | Physiotherapy | Phytotherapy | Pilates | Podiatry | Polarity Therapy | Postural Integration | Primal Therapy | Psionic Therapy | Psychotherapy | Pyramid Power | Pyscho-Synthesis | Reflexology | Reichian Therapy | Reiki | Remedial Massage | Rogerian Therapy | Rolfing | Seichem | Sensitivity Training | Shiatsu | Silva Method | Sound Therapy | Spiritual Healing | Sports Massage | Stress Therapy | Swedish Body Massage | T'ai-Chi Ch'uan | Tantra Therapy | Tera-Mai | Thought Field Therapy | Touch Therapy | Transactional Analysis | Tui-na | Ultrasonics | Vibrational Therapy | Visualisation Therapy | Vitamin Therapy | Voice Therapy | X-Ray | Ying & Yang | Yoga | Zen Therapy | Zero Balancing |
|---|---|---|---|---|---|---|---|---|---|---|---|---|---|---|---|---|---|---|---|---|---|---|---|---|---|---|---|---|---|---|---|---|---|---|---|---|---|---|---|---|---|---|---|---|---|---|---|---|---|
| DAVIS-PARRY, CLARISSA J B (HM05866) | | | ● | | | | | | | | | | | | | | | | | | | | | | | | | | | | | | | | | | | | | | | | | | | | | | |
| DOYLE, AUDREY (HM06257) | | | | | | | ● | | | | | | | | | | | ● | | | | | | | | | | | | | | | | | | | | | | | | | | | | | | | |
| DOYLE, KATH (HM06265) | | | | | | | | | | | | | | | | | | ● | | | | | | | | | | | | | | | | | | | | | | | | | | | | | | | |
| DRYER, DIANA (HM06334) | | | | | | | | | | | | | | | | | | ● | | | | | | | | | | | | | | | | | | | | | | | | | | | | | | | |
| DUDGEON, DELIA (HM06353) | | | | | | | | | | | | | | | | | | ● | | ● | | | | | | | | | | | | | | | | | | | | | | | | | | | | | |
| DUNNE, CAROL (HM06418) | | | | | | | | | | | | | | | ● | | | | | | | | | | | | | | | | | | | | | | | | | | | | | | | | | | |
| EVANS, C (HM06959) | | | ● | | | | | | | | | | | | | | | | | | | | | | | | | | | | | | | | | | | | | | | | | | | | | | |
| EVERITT, ELAINE (HM07006) | | | ● | | | | | | | | | | | | | | | | | | | | | | | | | | | | | | | | | | | | | | | | | | | | | | |
| EVERITT, ELAINE M (HM07007) | | | ● | | | | | | | | | | | | | | | | | | | | | | | | | | | | | | | | | | | | | | | | | | | | | | |
| EXETER, SHARON (HM07024) | | | | | | | | | | | | | | | | | | ● | | | | | | | | | | | | | | | | | | | | | | | | | | | | | | | |
| EYRES, M R (HM07031) | | | ● | | | | | | | | | | | | | | | | | | | | | | | | | | | | | | | | | | | | | | | | | | | | | | |
| FEET RETREAT () | | | | | | | | | | | | | | | | | | ● | | | | | | | | | | | | | | | | | | | | | | | | | | | | | | | |
| FIELD, P M (HM07264) | | | ● | | | | | | | | | | | | | | | | | | | | | | | | | | | | | | | | | | | | | | | | | | | | | | |
| FIELD, PAUL (HM07265) | | | ● | | | | | | | | | | | | | | | | | | | | | | | | | | | | | | | | | | | | | | | | | | | | | | |
| FOX, J P (HM07639) | | | ● | | | | | | | | | | | | | | | | | | | | | | | | | | | | | | | | | | | | | | | | | | | | | | |
| FOZZARD, JOANNA M (HM07648) | | | ● | | | | | | | | | | | | | | | | | | | | | | | | | | | | | | | | | | | | | | | | | | | | | | |
| FOZZARD, JOANNA M (HM07647) | | | ● | | | | | | | | | | | | | | | | | | | | | | | | | | | | | | | | | | | | | | | | | | | | | | |
| GARD, GRAHAM (HM07865) | | | ● | | | | | | | | | | | | | | | | | | | | | | | | | | | | | | | | | | | | | | | | | | | | | | |
| GEMS (HM07969) | | | | | | | | | | | | | | | | | | | | ● | | | | | | | | | | | | | | | | | | | | | | | | | | | | | |
| GENTLE FEET (HM07977) | | | | | | | | | | | | | | | | | | ● | | | | | | | | | | | | | | | | | | | | | | | | | | | | | | | |
| GEOFF THIEL, COUNS & PSYCHO (HM07986) | | | | | | | | | | | | | | | ● | | | | | | | | | | | | | | | | | | | | | | | | | | | | | | | | | | |
| GILLING, LINDA (HM08095) | | | | | | | | | | | | | | | | | | ● | | | | | | | | | | | | | | | | | | | | | | | | | | | | | | | |
| GOODMAN, HENRY (HM08258) | | | | | | | | | | | | | | | ● | | | | | | | | | | | | | | | | ● | | | | | | | | | | | | | | | | | | |
| GOURLAY, B (HM08319) | | | | | | | | | | | | | | | ● | | | | | | | | | | | | | | | | | | | | | | | | | | | | | | | | | | |
| GREEN, K B (HM08466) | | | ● | | | | | | | | | | | | | | | | | | | | | | | | | | | | | | | | | | | | | | | | | | | | | | |
| GREGORIADIS, SUE (HM08516) | | | | | | | | | | | | | | | | | | ● | | | | | | | | | | | | | | | | | | | | | | | | | | | | | | | |
| GROUNDS, L (HM08599) | | | | | | | | | | | | | | | | | | ● | | | | | | | | | | | | | | | | | | | | | | | | | | | | | | | |
| HALFORD, ELIZABETH (HM08749) | | | ● | | | | | | | | | | | | | | | | | | | | | | | | | | | | | | | | | | | | | | | | | | | | | | |
| HALL, JACQUELINE (HM08776) | | | | | | | | | | | | | | | | | | ● | | | | | | | | | | | | | | | | | | | | | | | | | | | | | | | |
| HAMILTON-PETERS, R & J A (HM08849) | | | | | | | | | | | | | | | ● | | | | | | | | | | | | | | | | ● | | | | | | | | | | | | | | | | | | |
| HAMILTON-PLANT, C A (HM08850) | | | ● | | | | | | | | | | | | | | | | | | | | | | | | | | | | | | | | | | | | | | | | | | | | | | |
| HANWELL, TIM (HM08949) | | | ● | | | | | | | | | | | | | | | | | | | | | | | | | | | | | | | | | | | | | | | | | | | | | | |
| HARPENDEM OSTEOPATHIC PRACTICE (HM09035) | | | ● | | | | | | | | | | | | | | | | | | | | | | | | | | | | | | | | | | | | | | | | | | | | | | |
| HARRY, K M (HM09122) | | | ● | | | | | | | | | | | | | | | | | | | | | | | | | | | | | | | | | | | | | | | | | | | | | | |

# O - Z Therapies at Practices/Businesses

| Business by County with Reference no. | Orthotics | Osteomyology | Osteopathy | PAM | Paranormal Therapies | Pattern Therapies | Physiotherapy | Phytotherapy | Pilates | Podiatry | Polarity Therapy | Postural Integration | Primal Therapy | Psionic Therapy | Psychotherapy | Pyramid Power | Pyscho-Synthesis | Reflexology | Reichian Therapy | Reiki | Remedial Massage | Rogerian Therapy | Rolfing | Seichem | Sensitivity Training |
|---|---|---|---|---|---|---|---|---|---|---|---|---|---|---|---|---|---|---|---|---|---|---|---|---|---|
| HEALTH BARN CLINIC (HM09377) | | | ● | | | | | | | | | | | | | | | | | | | | | | |
| HERTFORD NATURAL THERAPY CTRE (HM09690) | | | | | | | ● | | | | | | | | | | | ● | | ● | | | | | |
| HEWITT, P M (HM09707) | | | ● | | | | | | | | | | | | | | | | | | | | | | |
| HODGES, RAY (HM09878) | | | | | | | | | | | | | | | | | | ● | | | | | | | |
| HOLLENBERY, S (HM10019) | | | | | | | ● | | | | | | | | | | | | | | | | | | |
| HUMPHRY, S B (HM10383) | | | ● | | | | | | | | | | | | | | | | | | | | | | |
| IAN COLLANGE ASSOCIATES (HM10558) | | | ● | | | | | | | | | | | | | | | | | | | | | | |
| JACOB, SIMON (HM10856) | | | | | | | | | | | | | | | ● | | | | | | | | | | |
| JEOFFROY, ANNA (HM11013) | | | | | | | | | | | | | | | | | | ● | | | | | | | |
| JOE MILLER SPORTS INJURY (HM11045) | | | ● | | | | | | | | | | | | | | | | | | | | | | |
| KELLETT, DAVID & ASSOCIATES (HM11420) | | | ● | | | | | | | | | | | | | | | | | | | | | | |
| KELLY, EILEEN (HM11430) | | | | | | | | | | | | | | | | | | ● | | | | | | | |
| KENNAN, PHILIPPA (HM11486) | | | | | | | | | | | | | | | | | | ● | | | | | | | |
| KENNON, SUSAN (HM11504) | | | | | | | | | | | | | | | | | | ● | | | | | | | |
| KERSTIN HEALTH & BEAUTY (HM11559) | | | | | | | | | | | | | | | | | | ● | | | | | | | |
| KEW, DEREK (HM11576) | | | | | | | | | | | | | | | ● | | | | | | | ● | | | |
| KING, SANDRA (HM11642) | | | | | | | | | | | | | | | | | | ● | | | | | | | |
| KINGS LANGLEY OSTEO PRACTICE (HM11654) | | | ● | | | | | | | | | | | | | | | | | | | | | | |
| KIRBY, ANNIE (HM11700) | | | | | | | | | | | | | | | | | | ● | | | | | | | |
| KNEBWORTH PHYSIO CLINIC (HM11742) | | | | | | | ● | | | | | | | | | | | | | | | | | | |
| KNIGHT, S L (HM11756) | | | | | | | | | | | | | | | | | | ● | | | | | | | |
| KONTOU, F (HM11784) | | | | | | | | | | | | | | | | | | ● | | | | | | | |
| KRAFT, T (HM11795) | | | | | | | | | | | | | | | ● | | | | | | | | | | |
| LEACOCK, S D (HM12093) | | | ● | | | | | | | | | | | | | | | | | | | | | | |
| LETCHWORTH CENTRE (HM12247) | | | ● | | | | | | | | | | | | | | | | | | | | | | |
| LETCHWORTH-PHYSIOTHERAPY (HM12248) | | | | | | | ● | | | | | | | | | | | | | | | | | | |
| LEWIN, ROCHELLE (HM12273) | | | | | | | | | | | | | | | | | | | | | | | | | |
| LEWIS, BRIAN (HM12282) | | | ● | | | | | | | | | | | | | | | | | | | | | | |
| LIFELINES (HM12355) | | | | | | | | | | | | | | | | | | | | | | | | | |
| LINDY, D (HM12426) | | | ● | | | | | | | | | | | | | | | | | | | | | | |
| MALLARD, CAROLE (HM12976) | | | | | | | | | | | | | | | | | | ● | | | | | | | |
| MARCUS, CLAIRE HANNAH (HM13078) | | | | | | | | | | | | | | | | | | ● | | | | | | | |
| MASON GOODMAN NAT MEDICINE (HM13234) | | | ● | | | | | | | | | | | | | | | | | | | | | | |
| MASON, L C (HM13247) | | | | | | | | | | | | | | | ● | | | | | | | | | | |

| Business by County with Reference no. | Shiatsu | Silva Method | Sound Therapy | Spiritual Healing | Sports Massage | Stress Therapy | Swedish Body Massage | T'ai-Chi Ch'uan | Tantra Therapy | Tera-Mai | Thought Field Therapy | Touch Therapy | Transactional Analysis | Tui-na | Ultrasonics | Vibrational Therapy | Visualisation Therapy | Vitamin Therapy | Voice Therapy | X-Ray | Ying & Yang | Yoga | Zen Therapy | Zero Balancing |
|---|---|---|---|---|---|---|---|---|---|---|---|---|---|---|---|---|---|---|---|---|---|---|---|---|
| HEALTH BARN CLINIC (HM09377) | | | | | | | | | | | | | | | | | | | | | | | | |
| HERTFORD NATURAL THERAPY CTRE (HM09690) | ● | | | | | ● | | | | | | | | | | | | | | | | | | |
| HEWITT, P M (HM09707) | | | | | | | | | | | | | | | | | | | | | | | | |
| HODGES, RAY (HM09878) | | | | | | | | | | | | | | | | | | | | | | | | |
| HOLLENBERY, S (HM10019) | | | | | | | | | | | | | | | | | | | | | | | | |
| HUMPHRY, S B (HM10383) | | | | | | | | | | | | | | | | | | | | | | | | |
| IAN COLLANGE ASSOCIATES (HM10558) | | | | | | | | | | | | | | | | | | | | | | | | |
| JACOB, SIMON (HM10856) | | | | | | | | | | | | | | | | | | | | | | | | |
| JEOFFROY, ANNA (HM11013) | | | | | | | | | | | | | | | | | | | | | | | | |
| JOE MILLER SPORTS INJURY (HM11045) | | | | | | | | | | | | | | | ● | | | | | | | | | |
| KELLETT, DAVID & ASSOCIATES (HM11420) | | | | | | | | | | | | | | | | | | | | | | | | |
| KELLY, EILEEN (HM11430) | | | | | | | | | | | | | | | | | | | | | | | | |
| KENNAN, PHILIPPA (HM11486) | | | | | | | | | | | | | | | | | | | | | | | | |
| KENNON, SUSAN (HM11504) | | | | | | | | | | | | | | | | | | | | | | | | |
| KERSTIN HEALTH & BEAUTY (HM11559) | | | | | | | | | | | | | | | | | | | | | | | | |
| KEW, DEREK (HM11576) | | | | | | ● | | | | | | | ● | | | | ● | | | | | | | |
| KING, SANDRA (HM11642) | | | | | | | | | | | | | | | | | | | | | | | | |
| KINGS LANGLEY OSTEO PRACTICE (HM11654) | | | | | | | | | | | | | | | | | | | | | | | | |
| KIRBY, ANNIE (HM11700) | | | | | | | | | | | | | | | | | | | | | | | | |
| KNEBWORTH PHYSIO CLINIC (HM11742) | | | | | | ● | | | | | | | | | ● | | | | | | | | | |
| KNIGHT, S L (HM11756) | | | | | | | | | | | | | | | | | | | | | | | | |
| KONTOU, F (HM11784) | | | | | | | | | | | | | | | | | | | | | | | | |
| KRAFT, T (HM11795) | | | | | | | | | | | | | | | | | | | | | | | | |
| LEACOCK, S D (HM12093) | | | | | | | | | | | | | | | | | | | | | | | | |
| LETCHWORTH CENTRE (HM12247) | | | | | | | | | | | | | | | | | | | | | | | | |
| LETCHWORTH-PHYSIOTHERAPY (HM12248) | | | | | | | | | | | | | | | | | | | | | | | | |
| LEWIN, ROCHELLE (HM12273) | | | | | | | | | | | | | | | | | ● | | | | | | | |
| LEWIS, BRIAN (HM12282) | | | | | | | | | | | | | | | | | | | | | | | | |
| LIFELINES (HM12355) | | | | ● | | ● | | | | | | | | | | | | | | | | | | |
| LINDY, D (HM12426) | | | | | | | | | | | | | | | | | | | | | | | | |
| MALLARD, CAROLE (HM12976) | | | | | | | | | | | | | | | | | | | | | | | | |
| MARCUS, CLAIRE HANNAH (HM13078) | | | | | | | | | | | | | | | | | | | | | | | | |
| MASON GOODMAN NAT MEDICINE (HM13234) | | | | | | | | | | | | | | | | | | | | | | | | |
| MASON, L C (HM13247) | | | | | | | | | | | | | | | | | ● | | | | | | | |

# O - Z Therapies at Practices/Businesses

| Business by County with Reference no. | Orthotics | Osteomyology | Osteopathy | PAM | Paranormal Therapies | Pattern Therapies | Physiotherapy | Phytotherapy | Pilates | Podiatry | Polarity Therapy | Postural Integration | Primal Therapy | Psionic Therapy | Psychotherapy | Pyramid Power | Pyscho-Synthesis | Reflexology | Reichian Therapy | Reiki | Remedial Massage | Rogerian Therapy | Rolfing | Seichem | Sensitivity Training |
|---|---|---|---|---|---|---|---|---|---|---|---|---|---|---|---|---|---|---|---|---|---|---|---|---|---|
| MAUREEN PRIDDLE (HM13328) | | | | | | | | | | | | | | | | | | ● | | | | | | | |
| MAYOR, DAVID F (HM13359) | | | | | | | | | | | | | | | | | | | | | | | | | |
| MCAVOY, JAMES (HM13373) | | | ● | | | | | | | | | | | | | | | | | | | | | | |
| MCMAHON, STEPHANIE (HM13567) | | | ● | | | | | | | | | | | | | | | | | | | | | | |
| MCTIMONEY CHIROPRACTIC CLINIC (HM13612) | | | | | | | | | | | | | | | | | | ● | | | | | | | |
| MELLERICK, N D (HM13708) | | | ● | | | | | | | | | | | | | | | | | | | | | | |
| MIDAS TOUCH (HM13808) | | | | | | | | | | | | | | | | | | | | ● | | | | | |
| MID-HERTS ALEXANDER CENTRE (HM13827) | | | | | | | | | | | | | | | | | | | | | | | | | |
| MILLHOUSE (HM13910) | | | ● | | | | | | | | | | | | | | | | | | | | | | |
| MOYNIHAN, T (HM14307) | | | ● | | | | | | | | | | | | | | | | | | | | | | |
| MOYNIHAN, T (HM14306) | | | ● | | | | | | | | | | | | | | | | | | | | | | |
| MURRAY, TERESA (HM14415) | | | | | | | | | | | | | | | | | | ● | | | | | | | |
| MURRELL, JANE (HM14419) | | | | | | | | | | | | | | | | | | ● | | | | | | | |
| NATURAL HEALTH CLINIC (HM14589) | | | ● | | | | | | | | | | | | | | | | | | | | | | |
| NATURAL THERAPY PRACTICE (HM14663) | | | ● | | | | | | | | | | | | | | | | | | | | | | |
| O'HARA, JOHN (HM15246) | | | | | | | | | | | | | | | | | | ● | | | | | | | |
| O'NEILL, SUSAN (HM15338) | | | | | | | | | | | | | | | | | | ● | | | | | | | |
| OPEN MINDS (HM15343) | | | | | | | | | | | | | | | | | | | | | | | | | |
| OSTEOPATHIC CLINIC (HM15459) | | | ● | | | | ● | | | ● | | | | | | | | ● | | ● | | | | | |
| OVERINGTON, KEL (HM15512) | | | | | | | | | | | | | | | | | | | | | | | | | |
| PALMER, ELEANOR (HM15602) | | | | | | | | | | | | | | | | | | ● | | | | | | | |
| PARKER, PHILIP (HM15700) | | | ● | | | | | | | | | | | | | | | | | | | | | | |
| PAULS, A (HM15852) | | | ● | | | | | | | | | | | | | | | | | | | | | | |
| PERRY, SJ & GRACE, B (HM16051) | | | ● | | | | | | | | | | | | | | | | | | | | | | |
| PERSONAL REFLECTIONS (HM16061) | | | | | | | | | | | | | | | | | | ● | | ● | | | | | |
| PHILIP, AARONS (HM16121) | | | ● | | | | | | | | | | | | | | | | | | | | | | |
| PHYSIO & SPORTS INJURIES CLNC (HM16177) | | | | | | | | | | | | | | | | | | | | | | | | | |
| PLESHETTE, JANET (HM16367) | | | | | | | | | | | | | | | | | | ● | | | | | | | |
| PREMADASA, L (DR) (HM16535) | | | ● | | | | | | | | | | | | | | | | | | | | | | |
| PRINCE, KAREN (HM16619) | | | ● | | | | | | | | | | | | | | | | | | | | | | |
| PSYCHO & HYPNOTHERAPY CLINIC (HM16697) | | | | | | | | | | | | | | | ● | | | | | | | | | | |
| PSYCHOTHERAPY (HM16726) | | | | | | | | | | | | | | | ● | | | | | | | | | | |
| QUIGLEY, CAROLINE (HM16803) | | | ● | | | | | | | | | | | | | | | | | | | | | | |
| QUYE, KARINA (HM16827) | | | | | | | | | | | | | | | | | | ● | | | | | | | |

| Business by County with Reference no. | Shiatsu | Silva Method | Sound Therapy | Spiritual Healing | Sports Massage | Stress Therapy | Swedish Body Massage | T'ai-Chi Ch'uan | Tantra Therapy | Tera-Mai | Thought Field Therapy | Touch Therapy | Transactional Analysis | Tui-na | Ultrasonics | Vibrational Therapy | Visualisation Therapy | Vitamin Therapy | Voice Therapy | X-Ray | Ying & Yang | Yoga | Zen Therapy | Zero Balancing |
|---|---|---|---|---|---|---|---|---|---|---|---|---|---|---|---|---|---|---|---|---|---|---|---|---|
| MAUREEN PRIDDLE (HM13328) | | | | | | | | | | | | | | | | | | | | | | | | |
| MAYOR, DAVID F (HM13359) | | | | | | | | | | | | | | | | ● | | ● | | | | | | |
| MCAVOY, JAMES (HM13373) | | | | | | | | | | | | | | | | | | | | | | | | |
| MCMAHON, STEPHANIE (HM13567) | | | | | | | | | | | | | | | | | | | | | | | | |
| MCTIMONEY CHIROPRACTIC CLINIC (HM13612) | | | | | | | | | | | | | | | | | | | | | | | | |
| MELLERICK, N D (HM13708) | | | | | | | | | | | | | | | | | | | | | | | | |
| MIDAS TOUCH (HM13808) | | | | | | | | | | | | | | | | | | | | | | | | |
| MID-HERTS ALEXANDER CENTRE (HM13827) | | | | | | ● | | | | | | | | | | | | | ● | | | | | |
| MILLHOUSE (HM13910) | | | | | | | | | | | | | | | | | | | | | | | | |
| MOYNIHAN, T (HM14307) | | | | | | | | | | | | | | | | | | | | | | | | |
| MOYNIHAN, T (HM14306) | | | | | | | | | | | | | | | | | | | | | | | | |
| MURRAY, TERESA (HM14415) | | | | | | | | | | | | | | | | | | | | | | | | |
| MURRELL, JANE (HM14419) | | | | | | | | | | | | | | | | | | | | | | | | |
| NATURAL HEALTH CLINIC (HM14589) | | | | | | | | | | | | | | | | | | | | | | | | |
| NATURAL THERAPY PRACTICE (HM14663) | | | | | | | | | | | | | | | | | | | | | | | | |
| O'HARA, JOHN (HM15246) | | | | | | | | | | | | | | | | | | | | | | | | |
| O'NEILL, SUSAN (HM15338) | | | | | | | | | | | | | | | | | | | | | | | | |
| OPEN MINDS (HM15343) | ● | | | | | | | | | | | | | | | | | | | | | | | |
| OSTEOPATHIC CLINIC (HM15459) | | | | | | | | | | | | | | | | | | | | | | | | |
| OVERINGTON, KEL (HM15512) | ● | | | | | | | | | | | | | | | | | | | | | | | |
| PALMER, ELEANOR (HM15602) | | | | | | | | | | | | | | | | | | | | | | | | |
| PARKER, PHILIP (HM15700) | | | | | | | | | | | | | | | | | | | | | | | | |
| PAULS, A (HM15852) | | | | | | | | | | | | | | | | | | | | | | | | |
| PERRY, SJ & GRACE, B (HM16051) | | | | | | | | | | | | | | | | | | | | | | | | |
| PERSONAL REFLECTIONS (HM16061) | | | | ● | | ● | ● | | | | | | | | | | | | | | | | | |
| PHILIP, AARONS (HM16121) | | | | | | | | | | | | | | | | | | | | | | | | |
| PHYSIO & SPORTS INJURIES CLNC (HM16177) | | | | | | | | | | | | | | | ● | | | | | | | | | |
| PLESHETTE, JANET (HM16367) | | | | | | | | | | | | | | | | | | | | | | | | |
| PREMADASA, L (DR) (HM16535) | | | | | | | | | | | | | | | | | | | | | | | | |
| PRINCE, KAREN (HM16619) | | | | | | | | | | | | | | | | | | | | | | | | |
| PSYCHO & HYPNOTHERAPY CLINIC (HM16697) | | | | | | | | | | | | | | | | | | | | | | | | |
| PSYCHOTHERAPY (HM16726) | | | | | | | | | | | | | | | | | | | | | | | | |
| QUIGLEY, CAROLINE (HM16803) | | | | | | | | | | | | | | | | | | | | | | | | |
| QUYE, KARINA (HM16827) | | | | | | | | | | | | | | | | | | | | | | | | |

# O - Z Therapies at Practices/Businesses

| Business by County with Reference no. | Orthotics | Osteomyology | Osteopathy | PAM | Paranormal Therapies | Pattern Therapies | Physiotherapy | Phytotherapy | Pilates | Podiatry | Polarity Therapy | Postural Integration | Primal Therapy | Psionic Therapy | Psychotherapy | Pyramid Power | Pyscho-Synthesis |
|---|---|---|---|---|---|---|---|---|---|---|---|---|---|---|---|---|---|
| RICARDO, LINDA (HM17238) | | | | | | | | | | | | | | | | | |
| RICHARDS, KATHY (HM17258) | | | | | | | | | | | | | | | | | |
| RICHMOND, CLARE (HM17304) | | | ● | | | | | | | | | | | | | | |
| RICKETT, MARION (HM17311) | | | | | | | | | | | | | | | ● | | |
| RUSHANT, LYNDA (HM17757) | | | | | | | | | | | | | | | | | |
| S K REFLEXOLOGY (HM17811) | | | | | | | | | | | | | | | | | |
| SCOTT, LAURA (HM18122) | | | | | | | | | | | | | | | | | |
| SHAW, CHRISTINE (HM18333) | | | | | | | | | | | | | | | | | |
| SHERIDAN, SARAH (HM18431) | | | | | | | | | | | | | | | | | |
| SMITH, SOPHIA (HM18811) | | | | | | | | | | | | | | | | | |
| SMITH, SUSAN (HM18813) | | | | | | | | | | | | | | | | | |
| SMITH, SUZANNE (HM18815) | | | | | | | | | | | | | | | | | |
| SOLDANO, JOANNE (HM18865) | | | | | | | | | | | | | | | | | |
| SOPWELL OSTEOPATHIC CLINIC (HM18894) | | | ● | | | | | | | | | | | | | | |
| SOUTH, JO (HM18917) | | | | | | | | | | | | | | | | | |
| SPINOZA, DAVID (HM19019) | | | ● | | | | | | | | | | | | | | |
| ST ALBANS CHIROPRACTIC CLINIC (HM19063) | | | | | | | | | | ● | | | | | | | |
| STEVENSON, LEIGH (HM19250) | | | | | | | | | | | | | | | | | |
| STORT COUNS & PSYCHOTHERAPY (HM19351) | | | | | | | | | | | | | | | ● | | |
| STORTFORD GRANGE PHYSIO CENTRE (HM19352) | | | | | | | ● | | | | | | | | | | |
| SWAN & SWAN (HM19572) | | | | | | | | | | ● | | | | | | | |
| TANT, M (HM19694) | | | ● | | | | | | | | | | | | | | |
| THOMPSON, MARK (HM19991) | | | ● | | | | | | | | | | | | | | |
| THOMPSON, MARK () | | | ● | | | | | | | | | | | | | | |
| THORNHILL, WANDA (HM20022) | | | | | | | | | | | | | | | | | |
| THORNTON, MICHAEL (HM20026) | | | ● | | | | | | | | | | | | | | |
| TOSELAND, DOROTHY (HM20175) | | | | | | | | | | | | | | | | | |
| TREEND, NICOLA (HM20312) | | | | | | | | | | | | | | | | | |
| UNERMAN, EVE (HM20503) | | | | | | | | | | | | | | | | | |
| WALKER, NEL (HM20791) | | | | | | | | | | | | | | | ● | | |
| WAYMAN, W N (HM21041) | | | ● | | | | | | | | | | | | | | |
| WEBB, MARCUS (HM21073) | | | ● | | | | | | | | | | | | | | |
| WEBB, MARY (HM21074) | | | ● | | | | | | | | | | | | | | |
| WEBSTER, KAREN (HM21093) | | | | | | | | | | | | | | | | | |

| Business by County with Reference no. | Reflexology | Reichian Therapy | Reiki | Remedial Massage | Rogerian Therapy | Rolfing | Seichem | Sensitivity Training | Shiatsu | Silva Method | Sound Therapy | Spiritual Healing | Sports Massage | Stress Therapy | Swedish Body Massage | T'ai-Chi Ch'uan | Tantra Therapy |
|---|---|---|---|---|---|---|---|---|---|---|---|---|---|---|---|---|---|
| RICARDO, LINDA (HM17238) | ● | | | | | | | | | | | | | | | | |
| RICHARDS, KATHY (HM17258) | ● | | | | | | | | | | | | | | | | |
| RICHMOND, CLARE (HM17304) | | | | | | | | | | | | | | | | | |
| RICKETT, MARION (HM17311) | | | | | | | | | | | | | | | | | |
| RUSHANT, LYNDA (HM17757) | ● | | | | | | | | | | | | | | | | |
| S K REFLEXOLOGY (HM17811) | ● | | | | | | | | | | | ● | | ● | | | |
| SCOTT, LAURA (HM18122) | | | ● | | | | | | | | | | | | | | |
| SHAW, CHRISTINE (HM18333) | ● | | | | | | | | | | | | | | | | |
| SHERIDAN, SARAH (HM18431) | ● | | | | | | | | | | | | | | | | |
| SMITH, SOPHIA (HM18811) | ● | | | | | | | | | | | | | | | | |
| SMITH, SUSAN (HM18813) | ● | | | | | | | | | | | | | | | | |
| SMITH, SUZANNE (HM18815) | ● | | | | | | | | | | | | | | | | |
| SOLDANO, JOANNE (HM18865) | ● | | | | | | | | | | | | | | | | |
| SOPWELL OSTEOPATHIC CLINIC (HM18894) | | | | | | | | | | | | | | | | | |
| SOUTH, JO (HM18917) | ● | | | | | | | | | | | | | | | | |
| SPINOZA, DAVID (HM19019) | | | | | | | | | | | | | | | | ● | |
| ST ALBANS CHIROPRACTIC CLINIC (HM19063) | | | | | | | | | | | | | | | | | |
| STEVENSON, LEIGH (HM19250) | ● | | | | | | | | | | | | | | | | |
| STORT COUNS & PSYCHOTHERAPY (HM19351) | | | | | | | | | | | | | | ● | | | |
| STORTFORD GRANGE PHYSIO CENTRE (HM19352) | | | | | | | | | | | | | | | | | |
| SWAN & SWAN (HM19572) | | | | | | | | | | | | | | | | | |
| TANT, M (HM19694) | | | | | | | | | | | | | | | | | |
| THOMPSON, MARK (HM19991) | | | | | | | | | | | | | | | | | |
| THOMPSON, MARK () | | | | | | | | | | | | | | | | | |
| THORNHILL, WANDA (HM20022) | ● | | | | | | | | | | | | | | | | |
| THORNTON, MICHAEL (HM20026) | | | | | | | | | | | | | | | | | |
| TOSELAND, DOROTHY (HM20175) | ● | | | | | | | | | | | | | | | | |
| TREEND, NICOLA (HM20312) | ● | | | | | | | | | | | | | | | | |
| UNERMAN, EVE (HM20503) | ● | | | | | | | | | | | | | | | | |
| WALKER, NEL (HM20791) | | | | | | | | | | | | | | ● | | | |
| WAYMAN, W N (HM21041) | | | | | | | | | | | | | | | | | |
| WEBB, MARCUS (HM21073) | | | | | | | | | | | | | | | | | |
| WEBB, MARY (HM21074) | | | | | | | | | | | | | | | | | |
| WEBSTER, KAREN (HM21093) | ● | | | | | | | | | | | | | | | | |

| Business by County with Reference no. | Tera-Mai | Thought Field Therapy | Touch Therapy | Transactional Analysis | Tui-na | Ultrasonics | Vibrational Therapy | Visualisation Therapy | Vitamin Therapy | Voice Therapy | X-Ray | Ying & Yang | Yoga | Zen Therapy | Zero Balancing |
|---|---|---|---|---|---|---|---|---|---|---|---|---|---|---|---|
| RICARDO, LINDA (HM17238) | | | | | | | | | | | | | | | |
| RICHARDS, KATHY (HM17258) | | | | | | | | | | | | | | | |
| RICHMOND, CLARE (HM17304) | | | | | | | | | | | | | | | |
| RICKETT, MARION (HM17311) | | | | | | | | | | | | | | | |
| RUSHANT, LYNDA (HM17757) | | | | | | | | | | | | | | | |
| S K REFLEXOLOGY (HM17811) | | | | | | | | | | | | | | | |
| SCOTT, LAURA (HM18122) | | | | | | | | | | | | | | | |
| SHAW, CHRISTINE (HM18333) | | | | | | | | | | | | | ● | | |
| SHERIDAN, SARAH (HM18431) | | | | | | | | | | | | | | | |
| SMITH, SOPHIA (HM18811) | | | | | | | | | | | | | | | |
| SMITH, SUSAN (HM18813) | | | | | | | | | | | | | | | |
| SMITH, SUZANNE (HM18815) | | | | | | | | | | | | | | | |
| SOLDANO, JOANNE (HM18865) | | | | | | | | | | | | | | | |
| SOPWELL OSTEOPATHIC CLINIC (HM18894) | | | | | | | | | | | | | | | |
| SOUTH, JO (HM18917) | | | | | | | | | | | | | | | |
| SPINOZA, DAVID (HM19019) | | | | | | | | | | | | | ● | ● | |
| ST ALBANS CHIROPRACTIC CLINIC (HM19063) | | | | | | | | | | | | | | | |
| STEVENSON, LEIGH (HM19250) | | | | | | | | | | | | | | | |
| STORT COUNS & PSYCHOTHERAPY (HM19351) | | | | | | | | | | | | | | | |
| STORTFORD GRANGE PHYSIO CENTRE (HM19352) | | | | | | | | | | | | | | | |
| SWAN & SWAN (HM19572) | | | | | | | | | | | | | | | |
| TANT, M (HM19694) | | | | | | | | | | | | | | | |
| THOMPSON, MARK (HM19991) | | | | | | | | | | | | | | | |
| THOMPSON, MARK () | | | | | | | | | | | | | | | |
| THORNHILL, WANDA (HM20022) | | | | | | | | | | | | | | | |
| THORNTON, MICHAEL (HM20026) | | | | | | | | | | | | | | | |
| TOSELAND, DOROTHY (HM20175) | | | | | | | | | | | | | | | |
| TREEND, NICOLA (HM20312) | | | | | | | | | | | | | | | |
| UNERMAN, EVE (HM20503) | | | | | | | | | | | | | | | |
| WALKER, NEL (HM20791) | | | | | | | | | | | | | | | |
| WAYMAN, W N (HM21041) | | | | | | | | | | | | | | | |
| WEBB, MARCUS (HM21073) | | | | | | | | | | | | | | | |
| WEBB, MARY (HM21074) | | | | | | | | | | | | | | | |
| WEBSTER, KAREN (HM21093) | | | | | | | | | | | | | | | |

# O - Z Therapies at Practices/Businesses

| Business by County with Reference no. | Orthotics | Osteomyology | Osteopathy | PAM | Paranormal Therapies | Pattern Therapies | Physiotherapy | Phytotherapy | Pilates | Podiatry | Polarity Therapy | Postural Integration | Primal Therapy | Psionic Therapy | Psychotherapy | Pyramid Power | Pyscho-Synthesis | Reflexology | Reichian Therapy | Reiki | Remedial Massage | Rogerian Therapy | Rolfing | Seichem | Sensitivity Training | Shiatsu | Silva Method | Sound Therapy | Spiritual Healing | Sports Massage | Stress Therapy | Swedish Body Massage | T'ai-Chi Ch'uan | Tantra Therapy | Tera-Mai | Thought Field Therapy | Touch Therapy | Transactional Analysis | Tui-na | Ultrasonics | Vibrational Therapy | Visualisation Therapy | Vitamin Therapy | Voice Therapy | X-Ray | Ying & Yang | Yoga | Zen Therapy | Zero Balancing |
|---|---|---|---|---|---|---|---|---|---|---|---|---|---|---|---|---|---|---|---|---|---|---|---|---|---|---|---|---|---|---|---|---|---|---|---|---|---|---|---|---|---|---|---|---|---|---|---|---|---|
| WEEDON, HAZEL (HM21102) | | | | | | | | | | | | | | | | | | ● | | | | | | | | | | | | | | | | | | | | | | | | | | | | | | | |
| WHITE, ELIZABETH (HM21354) | | | | | | | | | | | | | | | | | | ● | | | | | | | | | | | | | | | | | | | | | | | | | | | | | | | |
| WHITE, GRAHAM C (HM21355) | | | | | | | | ● | | | | | | | | | | | | | | | | | | | | | | | | | | | | | | | | | | | | | | | | | |
| WILKIN, P (DR) (HM21497) | | | ● | | | | | | | | | | | | | | | | | | | | | | | | | | | | | | | | | | | | | | | | | | | | | | |
| WILKINSON, ANNE (HM21504) | | | | | | | | | | | | | | | | | | ● | | | | | | | | | | | | | | | | | | | | | | | | | | | | | | | |
| WILLIAMS, HAZEL (HM21562) | | | ● | | | | | | | | | | | | | | | | | | | | | | | | | | | | | | | | | | | | | | | | | | | | | | |
| WILLIAMS, NEVILLE L (HM21582) | | | | | | | | | | | | | | | | | | | | | ● | | | | | | | | | | | | | | | | | | | | | | | | | | | | |
| WILSON, N (HM21662) | | | ● | | | | | | | | | | | | | | | | | | | | | | | | | | | | | | | | | | | | | | | | | | | | | | |
| WISE, ALAN (HM21731) | | | | | | | | | | | | | | | ● | | | | | | | | | | | | | | | | | | | | | | | | | | | | | | | | | | |
| WOOD STREET CHIROPRACTIC CLNC (HM21780) | | | ● | | | | | | | | | | | | | | | | | | | | | | | | | | | | | | | | | | | | | | | | | | | | | | |
| WOOD STREET CLINIC (HM21781) | | | | | | | | | | | | | | | | | | | | | | | | | | | | | | | | | | | | | | | | | ● | | | | | | | | |
| WORDSWORTH, LINDA (HM21890) | | | | | | | | | | | | | | | | | | ● | | ● | | | | | | | | | | | | | | | | | | | | | | | | | | | | | |
| WYNDHAM CLINIC (HM21977) | | | | | | | ● | | | ● | | | | | | | | ● | | | | | | | | | | | | | | | | | | | | | | | | | | | | | | | |
| **HUMBERSIDE** | | | | | | | | | | | | | | | | | | | | | | | | | | | | | | | | | | | | | | | | | | | | | | | | | |
| PRIOSE COLES (HM16635) | | | | | | | | | | | | | | | | | | ● | | | | | | | | | | | | | | | | | | | | | | | | | ● | | | | | | |
| SCUNTHORPE CHIROPRACTIC CLINIC (HM18157) | | | | | | | | | | | | ● | | | | | | | | | | | | | | | | | | | | | | | | | | | | ● | | | | | | | | | |
| STEEPER, P T (HM19184) | | | ● | | | | | | | | | | | | | | | | | | | | | | | | | | | | | | | | | | | | | | | | | | | | | | |
| **HUMBERSIDE (NORTH)** | | | | | | | | | | | | | | | | | | | | | | | | | | | | | | | | | | | | | | | | | | | | | | | | | |
| ACADEMY PHYSIOTHERAPY CLINIC (HM00149) | | | | | | | ● | | | | | | | | | | | | | | | | | | | | | | | | | | | | | | | | | | | | | | | | | | |
| ACORN SCHOOL OF REFLEXOLOGY (HM00180) | | | | | | | | | | | | | | | | | | ● | | | | | | | | | | | | | | | | | | | | | | | | | | | | | | | |
| ALTERNATIVES (HM00739) | | | | | | | | | | | | | | | ● | | | | | | | | | | | | | | | | | | | | | | | | | | | | | | | | | | |
| ASHCROFT, PATSY (HM01202) | | | | | | | | | | | | | | | | | | ● | | | | | | | | | | | | | | | | | | | | | | | | | | | | | | | |
| ATTLESEY, C (HM01337) | | | ● | | | | | | | | | | | | | | | | | | | | | | | | | | | | | | | | | | | | | | | | | | | | | | |
| BAKER, IRENE (HM01585) | | | ● | | | | | | | | | | | | | | | | | | | | | | | | | | | | | | | | | | | | | | | | | | | | | | |
| BRIDLINGTON CHIROPODY SURGERY (HM03018) | | | | | | | | | | ● | | | | | | | | | | | | | | | | | | | | | | | | | | | | | | | | | | | | | | | |
| BRINDLEY, ELAINE (HM03055) | | | | | | | | | | | | | | | ● | | | | | | | | | | | | | | | | | | | | | | | | | | | | | | | | | | |
| CAMPBELL, KRYSTYNA (HM03602) | | | | | | | | | | | | | | | | | | ● | | | | | | | | | | | | | | | | | | | | | | | | | | | | | | | |
| CARMAN, CAROL (HM03704) | | | | | | | | | | | | | | | ● | | | | | | | | | | | | | | | | | | | | | | | | | | | | | | | | | | |
| CULPIN, SANDRA (HM05590) | | | | | | | | | | | | | | | | | | ● | | | | | | | | | | | | | | | | | | | | | | | | | | | | | | | |
| DALCROFT COUNSELLING SERVICES (HM05679) | | | | | | | | | | | | | | | ● | | | | | | | | | | | | | | | | | | | | | | | | | | | | | | | | | | |
| DAMIAN P JOHNS (HM05704) | ● | | | | | | | | | ● | | | | | | | | | | | | | | | | | | | | | | | | | | | | | | | | | | | | | | | |
| EAST RIDING COLLEGE (HM06524) | | | | | | | | | | | | | | | | | | ● | | ● | | | | | | | | | | | | | | | | | | | | | | | | | | | | | |
| GILBERDYKE SPORTS & INJURY (HM08054) | | | | | | | | ● | | | | | | | | | | | | | | | | | | | | | | | | | | | | | | | | | | | | | | | | | |
| HARVEY CLINIC (HM09159) | | | ● | | | | | | | | | | | | | | | | | | | | | | | | | | | | | | | | | | | | | | | | | | | | | | |

# O - Z Therapies at Practices/Businesses

| Business by County with Reference no. | Orthotics | Osteomyology | Osteopathy | PAM | Paranormal Therapies | Pattern Therapies | Physiotherapy | Phytotherapy | Pilates | Podiatry | Polarity Therapy | Postural Integration | Primal Therapy | Psionic Therapy | Psychotherapy | Pyramid Power | Pyscho-Synthesis | Reflexology | Reichian Therapy | Reiki | Remedial Massage | Rogerian Therapy | Rolfing | Seichem | Sensitivity Training | Shiatsu | Silva Method | Sound Therapy | Spiritual Healing | Sports Massage | Stress Therapy | Swedish Body Massage | T'ai-Chi Ch'uan | Tantra Therapy | Tera-Mai | Thought Field Therapy | Touch Therapy | Transactional Analysis | Tui-na | Ultrasonics | Vibrational Therapy | Visualisation Therapy | Vitamin Therapy | Voice Therapy | X-Ray | Ying & Yang | Yoga | Zen Therapy | Zero Balancing |
|---|---|---|---|---|---|---|---|---|---|---|---|---|---|---|---|---|---|---|---|---|---|---|---|---|---|---|---|---|---|---|---|---|---|---|---|---|---|---|---|---|---|---|---|---|---|---|---|---|---|
| HODGSON, M (HM09888) |||●|||||||||||||||||||||||||||||||||||||||||||||||
| LEHAIN, DAN (HM12180) |||||||||||||||●|||||||||||||||||||||||||||||||||||
| NATURAL THERAPIES (HM14629) |||||||||||||||||||||||||||||||||||||||||||●||||●||||
| NATURAL THERAPY CENTRE (HM14653) |||||||||||||||||||||||||||||||●||||||||||||||||||
| OSTEO-MEDIC SERVICES (HM15444) |||●|||||||||||||||||||||||||||||||||||||||||||||||
| SAMANTHA WHITE AROMATICA (HM17877) |||||||||||●|||||||||●|||||||||||●||||||||||||||||||
| STARLIGHT CENTRE (HM19151) ||||||||||||||||||●||||||||||||||||||||||||||||||||
| STEELE, AMANDA (HM19175) ||||||||||||||||||●||||||||||||||||||||||||||||||||
| STOW, A L (HM19362) |||●|||||||||||||||||||||||||||||||||||||||||||||||
| WADSWORTH OSTEOPATHS (HM20731) |||●|||||||||||||||||||||||||||||||||||||||||||||||
| WADSWORTH, ROBERT (HM20732) |||●|||||||||||||||||||||||||||||||||||||||||||||||
| WRIGHT, STEPHEN (HM21950) ||||||||||||||||||●||||||||||||||||||||||||||||||||
| **HUMBERSIDE (SOUTH)** ||||||||||||||||||||||||||||||||||||||||||||||||||
| LOUISE HEALING CENTRE (HM12668) ||||||||||||||||||●|||||||||||●||||●||||||||||||||●|||
| SCARTHO OSTEOPATHIC PRACTICE (HM18007) |||●|||||||||||||||●||||||||||||||||||||||||||||||||
| WALL, R A (HM20819) ||||||||||||||||||●||||||||||||||||||||||||||||||||
| WEBB, C M (HM21057) |●|||||||||●||||||||||||||||||||||||||||||||||||||||
| **ISLE OF WIGHT** ||||||||||||||||||||||||||||||||||||||||||||||||||
| BEISLY, N L (DR) (HM02072) |||●|||||||||||||||||||||||||||||||||||||||||||||||
| CARISBROOKE HEALTH CENTRE (HM03687) ||||||||||●||||||||||||||||||||||||||||||||||||||||
| CROUTEAR, SARAH (HM05496) ||||||||||||||||||●||||||||||||||||||||||||||||||||
| DIDHAM, JUDI (HM06089) ||||||||||||||||||●||||||||||||||||||||||||||||||||
| FOOTSTEPS (HM07510) ||||||||||●||||||||||||||||||||||||||||||||||||||||
| GODDEN, PATRICIA (HM08181) ||||||||||||||||||●||||||||||||||||||||||||||||||||
| GREENFIELD, BRIAN (HM08484) |||||||||||||||||||||||||||||●||●|||||||||||||||||||
| HOPE CLINIC (HM10134) ||||||||||||||||||●||||||||||||||||||||||||||||||||
| LITTLEJOHN CLINIC (HM12471) |||●|||||||||||||||||||||||||||||||||||||||||||||||
| NOIRET, C J P (HM14978) |||●|||||||||||||||||||||||||||||||||||||||||||||||
| NORMAN, NANCY (HM15006) ||||||||||||||||||||●||||||||||||||||||||||||||||||
| P D W PRAGNELL SPINAL THRP (HM15550) |||●|||||||||||||||||||||||||||||||||||||||||||||||
| PSYCHOTHERAPY UNIT (HM16738) |||||||||||||||●|||||||||||||||||||||||||||||||||||
| ROBINSON, MICHAEL (HM17496) |||●|||||||||||||||||||||||||||||||||||||||||||||||
| SAUNDERS, NICHOLAS (HM17959) |||●|||||||||||||||||||||||||||||||||||||||||||||||
| SHEN CLINIC (HM18391) |||||||||||||||●|||||||||||●||||||||||||||||||||||||

# O - Z Therapies at Practices/Businesses

Business by County with Reference no.

| Business | Orthotics | Osteomyology | Osteopathy | PAM | Paranormal Therapies | Pattern Therapies | Physiotherapy | Phytotherapy | Pilates | Podiatry | Polarity Therapy | Postural Integration | Primal Therapy | Psionic Therapy | Psychotherapy | Pyramid Power |
|---|---|---|---|---|---|---|---|---|---|---|---|---|---|---|---|---|
| SIMON, DAVE (HM18568) | | | | | | | | | | | | | | | ● | |
| TOUCH FOR HEALTH (HM20186) | | | | | | | | | | | | | | | | |
| KENT | | | | | | | | | | | | | | | | |
| ABBOTT, LISA (HM00098) | | | | | | | | | | | | | | | | |
| ABBOTT, LISA (HM00100) | | | | | | | | | | | | | | | | |
| ABSOLUTE SOLUTIONS (HM00142) | | | | | | | | | | | | | | | | |
| AMBROSE, YVONNE D (HM00774) | | | | | | | | | | | | | | | | |
| ARTHUR, ALICIA (HM01161) | | | | | | | | | | | | | | | | |
| ASHFORD OSTEOPATHIC CLINIC (HM01217) | | | ● | | | | | | | | | | | | | |
| AYLESFORD MEDICAL CENTRE (HM01426) | | | ● | | | | | | | | | | | | | |
| AYLESFORD OSTEOPATHIC PRACTICE (HM01427) | | | ● | | | | | | | | | | | | | |
| AYLING, GILL (HM01428) | | | | | | | | | | | | | | | | |
| AYLSHAM OSTEOPATHIC PRACTICE (HM01429) | | | ● | | | | | | | | | ● | | | | |
| BAILEY, GILLIAN (HM01547) | | | | | | | | | | | | | | | | |
| BALDWIN, MADELEINE (HM01617) | | | | | | | | | | | | | | | | |
| BARNES & ASSOCIATES (HM01738) | | | ● | | | | | | | | | | | | | |
| BARRETT, ROSEMARY (HM01795) | | | | | | | | | | | | | | | | |
| BAXTER, BEVERLEY J (HM01922) | | | | | | | | | | | | | | | | |
| BELLAMY, K J (HM02096) | | | ● | | | | | | | | | | | | | |
| BENSTED, LUCINDA (HM02171) | | | ● | | | | | | | | | | | | | |
| BERGMANN, MARIA (DR) (HM02190) | | | | | | | | ● | | | | | | | | |
| BERRY, ELIZABETH (HM02208) | | | | | | | | | | | | | | | | |
| BEXLEY OSTEOPATHIC CLINIC (HM02259) | | | ● | | | | | | | | | | | | | |
| BEXLEYHEATH NATURAL HEALTH (HM02262) | | | ● | | | | | | | | | | | | | |
| BIRCH, DIANA (HM02350) | | | | | | | | | | | | | | | | |
| BLACKFEN HYPNOTHERAPY (HM02442) | | | | | | | | | | | | | | | ● | |
| BLACKWOOD, JANE (HM02467) | | | | | | | | | | | | | | | | |
| BOTHA, M E (HM02732) | | | | | | | | | | | | | | | ● | |
| BOWEN, CHRISTINE (HM02779) | | | | | | | | | | | | | | | | |
| BOWLING, ANDREW (HM02798) | | | | | | | | | | | | | | | | |
| BOWYER, MARGARET (HM02807) | | | ● | | | | | | | | | | | | | |
| BREARE, SARAH (HM02938) | | | ● | | | | | | | | | | | | | |
| BROMLEY CHIROPRACTIC CLINIC (HM03143) | | | ● | | | | | | | | | | | | | |
| BROMLEY OSTEOPATHIC CLINIC (HM03145) | | | ● | | | | | | | | | | | | | |

| Business | Pyscho-Synthesis | Reflexology | Reichian Therapy | Reiki | Remedial Massage | Rogerian Therapy | Rolfing | Seichem | Sensitivity Training | Shiatsu | Silva Method | Sound Therapy | Spiritual Healing | Sports Massage | Stress Therapy | Swedish Body Massage |
|---|---|---|---|---|---|---|---|---|---|---|---|---|---|---|---|---|
| SIMON, DAVE (HM18568) | | | | | | | | | | | | | | | | |
| TOUCH FOR HEALTH (HM20186) | | ● | | | | | | | | | | | | | | |
| KENT | | | | | | | | | | | | | | | | |
| ABBOTT, LISA (HM00098) | | ● | | ● | | | | | | ● | | | | | | |
| ABBOTT, LISA (HM00100) | | ● | | | | | | | | | | | | | | |
| ABSOLUTE SOLUTIONS (HM00142) | | | | | | | | | | | | | | | ● | |
| AMBROSE, YVONNE D (HM00774) | | ● | | | | | | | | | | | | | | |
| ARTHUR, ALICIA (HM01161) | | ● | | | | | | | | | | | | | | |
| ASHFORD OSTEOPATHIC CLINIC (HM01217) | | | | | | | | | | | | | | | | |
| AYLESFORD MEDICAL CENTRE (HM01426) | | | | | | | | | | | | | | | | |
| AYLESFORD OSTEOPATHIC PRACTICE (HM01427) | | | | | | | | | | | | | | | | |
| AYLING, GILL (HM01428) | | ● | | | | | | | | | | | | | | |
| AYLSHAM OSTEOPATHIC PRACTICE (HM01429) | | | | | | | | | | | | | | | | |
| BAILEY, GILLIAN (HM01547) | | ● | | | | | | | | | | | | | | |
| BALDWIN, MADELEINE (HM01617) | | ● | | | | | | | | | | | | | | |
| BARNES & ASSOCIATES (HM01738) | | | | | | | | | | | | | | | | |
| BARRETT, ROSEMARY (HM01795) | | ● | | | | | | | | | | | | | | |
| BAXTER, BEVERLEY J (HM01922) | | ● | | | | | | | | | | | | | | |
| BELLAMY, K J (HM02096) | | | | | | | | | | | | | | | | |
| BENSTED, LUCINDA (HM02171) | | | | | | | | | | | | | | | | |
| BERGMANN, MARIA (DR) (HM02190) | | | | | | | | | | | | | | | | |
| BERRY, ELIZABETH (HM02208) | | ● | | | | | | | | | | | | | | |
| BEXLEY OSTEOPATHIC CLINIC (HM02259) | | | | | | | | | | | | | | | | |
| BEXLEYHEATH NATURAL HEALTH (HM02262) | | ● | | | | | | | | | | | | | | |
| BIRCH, DIANA (HM02350) | | ● | | | | | | | | | | | | | | |
| BLACKFEN HYPNOTHERAPY (HM02442) | | | | | | ● | | | | | | | | | ● | |
| BLACKWOOD, JANE (HM02467) | | ● | | | | | | | | | | | | | | |
| BOTHA, M E (HM02732) | | | | | | | | | | | | | | | | |
| BOWEN, CHRISTINE (HM02779) | | ● | | | | | | | | | | | | | | |
| BOWLING, ANDREW (HM02798) | | ● | | | | | | | | | | | | | | |
| BOWYER, MARGARET (HM02807) | | | | | | | | | | | | | | | | |
| BREARE, SARAH (HM02938) | | | | | | | | | | | | | | | | |
| BROMLEY CHIROPRACTIC CLINIC (HM03143) | | | | | | | | | | | | | | | | |
| BROMLEY OSTEOPATHIC CLINIC (HM03145) | | | | | | | | | | | | | | | | |

| Business | T'ai-Chi Ch'uan | Tantra Therapy | Tera-Mai | Thought Field Therapy | Touch Therapy | Transactional Analysis | Tui-na | Ultrasonics | Vibrational Therapy | Visualisation Therapy | Vitamin Therapy | Voice Therapy | X-Ray | Ying & Yang | Yoga | Zen Therapy | Zero Balancing |
|---|---|---|---|---|---|---|---|---|---|---|---|---|---|---|---|---|---|
| SIMON, DAVE (HM18568) | | | | | | | | | | | | | | | | | |
| TOUCH FOR HEALTH (HM20186) | | | | | | | | | | | | | | | | | |
| KENT | | | | | | | | | | | | | | | | | |
| ABBOTT, LISA (HM00098) | | | | | | | | | | | | | | | | | |
| ABBOTT, LISA (HM00100) | | | | | | | | | | | | | | | | | |
| ABSOLUTE SOLUTIONS (HM00142) | | | | | | | | | | | | | | | ● | | |
| AMBROSE, YVONNE D (HM00774) | | | | | | | | | | | | | | | | | |
| ARTHUR, ALICIA (HM01161) | | | | | | | | | | | | | | | | | |
| ASHFORD OSTEOPATHIC CLINIC (HM01217) | | | | | | | | | | | | | | | | | |
| AYLESFORD MEDICAL CENTRE (HM01426) | | | | | | | | | | | | | | | | | |
| AYLESFORD OSTEOPATHIC PRACTICE (HM01427) | | | | | | | | | | | | | | | | | |
| AYLING, GILL (HM01428) | | | | | | | | | | | | | | | | | |
| AYLSHAM OSTEOPATHIC PRACTICE (HM01429) | | | | | | | | | | | | | | | | | |
| BAILEY, GILLIAN (HM01547) | | | | | | | | | | | | | | | | | |
| BALDWIN, MADELEINE (HM01617) | | | | | | | | | | | | | | | | | |
| BARNES & ASSOCIATES (HM01738) | | | | | | | | | | | | | | | | | |
| BARRETT, ROSEMARY (HM01795) | | | | | | | | | | | | | | | | | |
| BAXTER, BEVERLEY J (HM01922) | | | | | | | | | | | | | | | | | |
| BELLAMY, K J (HM02096) | | | | | | | | | | | | | | | | | |
| BENSTED, LUCINDA (HM02171) | | | | | | | | | | | | | | | | | |
| BERGMANN, MARIA (DR) (HM02190) | | | | | | | | | | | | | | | | | |
| BERRY, ELIZABETH (HM02208) | | | | | | | | | | | | | | | | | |
| BEXLEY OSTEOPATHIC CLINIC (HM02259) | | | | | | | | | | | | | | | | | |
| BEXLEYHEATH NATURAL HEALTH (HM02262) | | | | | | | | | | | | | | | | | |
| BIRCH, DIANA (HM02350) | | | | | | | | | | | | | | | | | |
| BLACKFEN HYPNOTHERAPY (HM02442) | | | | | | | | | | | | | | | | | |
| BLACKWOOD, JANE (HM02467) | | | | | | | | | | | | | | | | | |
| BOTHA, M E (HM02732) | | | | | | | | | | | | | | | | | |
| BOWEN, CHRISTINE (HM02779) | | | | | | | | | | | | | | | | | |
| BOWLING, ANDREW (HM02798) | | | | | | | | | | | | | | | | | |
| BOWYER, MARGARET (HM02807) | | | | | | | | | | | | | | | | | |
| BREARE, SARAH (HM02938) | | | | | | | | | | | | | | | | | |
| BROMLEY CHIROPRACTIC CLINIC (HM03143) | | | | | | | | | | | | | | | | | |
| BROMLEY OSTEOPATHIC CLINIC (HM03145) | | | | | | | | | | | | | | | | | |

# O - Z Therapies at Practices/Businesses

| Business by County with Reference no. | BUCKBERRY, TINA (HM03308) | BURGE, ROBERT A (HM03373) | BURGIS, TESSA (HM03383) | BUSH, RON (HM03461) | BUTTERFILL, M T (HM03498) | CALLAGHAN, DENISE (HM03547) | CANTERBURY OSTEOPATHIC CLINIC (HM03641) | CARDWELL, MARTIN (HM03673) | CARTER, AMANDA (HM03774) | CASTLE CLINIC (HM03830) | CENTRE (HM03897) | CHAMPION, ALISON (HM03964) | CHANDRA PDS (HM03982) | CHARTIER, SUSAN (HM04052) | CHENG, MIGGI (HM04103) | CHIDWICK, SAMUEL (HM04160) | CHIROPRACTIC PLUS (HM04402) | CHISLEHURST NATURAL HEALTH (HM04410) | CHISTLEHURST NATURAL HLTH CTRE (HM04411) | CHRISTINE CHINNERY COMP THER (HM04446) | COACH HOUSE CLINIC (HM04749) | COMFORT, STEVEN V (HM04900) | CORRIGAN, PETER (HM05195) | COTTERILL, JENNY (HM05227) | COX, ANGELA (HM05300) | COX, K (HM05309) | COX, KATHERINE (HM05310) | COX, RITA (HM05319) | COYSTEN & ASSOCIATES (HM05332) | CROUCH, JANET (HM05494) | CUMMINGS, ELIZABETH (HM05610) | DARTFORD NATURAL HEALTH CENTRE (HM05751) | DATE, M S (HM05755) | DAVENPORT-FRY, ELIZABETH (HM05766) |
|---|---|---|---|---|---|---|---|---|---|---|---|---|---|---|---|---|---|---|---|---|---|---|---|---|---|---|---|---|---|---|---|---|---|---|
| Zero Balancing | | | | | | | | | | | | | | | | | | | | | | | | | | | | | | | | | | |
| Zen Therapy | | | | | | | | | | | | | | | | | | | | | | | | | | | | | | | | | | |
| Yoga | | | | | | | | | | | | | | | | | | | | | | | | | | | | | | | | | | |
| Ying & Yang | | | | | | | | | | | | | | | | | | | | | | | | | | | | | | | | | | |
| X-Ray | | | | | | | | | | | | | | | | | | | | | | | | | | | | | | | | | | |
| Voice Therapy | | | | | | | | | | | | | | | | | | | | | | | | | | | | | | | | | | |
| Vitamin Therapy | | | | | | | ● | | | | | | | | | | | | | | | | | | | | | | | | | | | |
| Visualisation Therapy | | | | | | | | | | | | | | | | | | | | | | | | | | | | | | | | | | |
| Vibrational Therapy | | | | | | | | | | | | | | | | | | | | | | | | | | | | | | | | | | |
| Ultrasonics | | | | | | | | | | | | | | | | | | | | | | | | | | | | | | | | | | |
| Tui-na | | | | | | | | | | | | | | | | | | | | | | | | | | | | | | | | | | |
| Transactional Analysis | | | | | | | | | | | | | | | | | | | | | | | | | | | | | | | | | | |
| Touch Therapy | | | | | | | | | | | | | | | | | | | | | | | | | | | | | | | | | | |
| Thought Field Therapy | | | | | | | | | | | | | | | | | | | | | | | | | | | | | | | | | | |
| Tera-Mai | | | | | | | | | | | | | | | | | | | | | | | | | | | | | | | | | | |
| Tantra Therapy | | | | | | | | | | | | | | | | | | | | | | | | | | | | | | | | | | |
| T'ai-Chi Ch'uan | | | | | | | | | | | | | | | | | | | | | | | | | | | | | | | | | | |
| Swedish Body Massage | | | | | | | | | | | | | | | | | | | | | | | | | | | | | | | | | | |
| Stress Therapy | | | | | | | | ● | | | | | ● | | | | | | | | | | | | | | | | | | | | | |
| Sports Massage | | | | | | | | | | | | | | | | | | | | | | | | | | | | | | | | | | |
| Spiritual Healing | | | | | | | | ● | | | ● | | | | | | | | | | | | | | | | | | | | | | | |
| Sound Therapy | | | | | | | | | | | | | | | | | | | | | | | | | | | | | | | | | | |
| Silva Method | | | | | | | | | | | | | | | | | | | | | | | | | | | | | | | | | | |
| Shiatsu | | | | | | | | | | | | | | | | | | ● | ● | | | | | | | | | | | | | | | |
| Sensitivity Training | | | | | | | | | | | | | | | | | | | | | | | | | | | | | | | | | | |
| Seichem | | | | | | | | ● | | | | | | | | | | | | | | | | | | | | | | | | | | |
| Rolfing | | | | | | | | | | | | | | | | | | | | | | | | | | | | | | | | | | |
| Rogerian Therapy | | | | | | | | | | | | | | | | | | | | | | | | | | | | | | | | | | |
| Remedial Massage | | | | | | | | | | | | | | | | | | | | | | | | | | | | | | | | | | |
| Reiki | | | | | | | | ● | | | ● | | | | | | ● | | | | | | | | | | | | | | | | | |
| Reichian Therapy | | | | | | | | | | | | | | | | | | | | | | | | | | | | | | | | | | |
| Reflexology | ● | | ● | ● | ● | | | | ● | | ● | ● | ● | ● | ● | ● | | ● | ● | ● | | | ● | ● | ● | | | ● | | ● | ● | | | |
| Pyscho-Synthesis | | | | | | | | | | | | | | | | | | | | | | | | | | | | | | | | | | |
| Pyramid Power | | | | | | | | | | | | | | | | | | | | | | | | | | | | | | | | | | |
| Psychotherapy | | | | | | | | | | ● | | | | | | | | | | | | | | | | | | | | | | | | |
| Psionic Therapy | | | | | | | | | | | | | | | | | | | | | | | | | | | | | | | | | | |
| Primal Therapy | | | | | | | | | | | | | | | | | | | | | | | | | | | | | | | | | | |
| Postural Integration | | | | | | | | | | | | | | | | | | | | | | | | | | | | | ● | | | | | |
| Polarity Therapy | | | | | | | | | | | | | | | | | | | | | | | | | | | | | | | | | | |
| Podiatry | | | | | | | | | | | | | | | | | | | | | | | | | | | | | | | | | | |
| Pilates | | | | | | | | | | | | | | | | | | | | | | | | | | | | | | | | | | |
| Phytotherapy | | | | | | | | | | | | | | | | | | | | | | | | | | | | | | | | | | |
| Physiotherapy | | | | | | | | | | | | | | | | | | | | | | | | | | | | | | | | | | |
| Pattern Therapies | | | | | | | | | | | | | | | | | | | | | | | | | | | | | | | | | | |
| Paranormal Therapies | | | | | | | | | | | | | | | | | | | | | | | | | | | | | | | | | | |
| PAM | | | | | | | | | | | | | | | | | | | | | | | | | | | | | | | | | | |
| Osteopathy | | ● | | | | ● | ● | | | ● | ● | | | | | | | ● | ● | | ● | ● | | | | ● | ● | | ● | | | ● | ● | ● |
| Osteomyology | | | | | | | | | | | | | | | | | | | | | | | | | | | | | | | | | | |
| Orthotics | | | | | | | | | | | | | | | | | | | | | | | | | | | | | | | | | | |

# O - Z Therapies at Practices/Businesses

| Business by County with Reference no. | Orthotics | Osteomyology | Osteopathy | PAM | Paranormal Therapies | Pattern Therapies | Physiotherapy | Phytotherapy | Pilates | Podiatry | Polarity Therapy | Postural Integration | Primal Therapy | Psionic Therapy | Psychotherapy | Pyramid Power | Pyscho-Synthesis | Reflexology |
|---|---|---|---|---|---|---|---|---|---|---|---|---|---|---|---|---|---|---|
| DAVIES, ANGELA (HM05795) | | | | | | | | | | | | | | | | | | ● |
| DAVIES, FIONA (HM05810) | | | | | | | | | | | | | | | | | | ● |
| DEAKIN, T (HM05933) | | | | | | | | | | | | | | | ● | | | |
| DENTON, B (HM05999) | | | ● | | | | | | | | | | | | | | | |
| DICKMAN, ANNIE (HM06080) | | | | | | | | | | | | | | | | | | ● |
| DILLON, MICHAEL (HM06100) | | | | | | | | | | | | | | | ● | | | |
| DIMENT, GORDON L (HM06105) | | | | | | | | | | | | | | | ● | | | |
| DOREY, STELLA (HM06198) | | | | | | | | | | | | | | | | | | ● |
| DOWLING, R (HM06240) | | | ● | | | | | | | | | | | | | | | |
| DUFFY, MELANIE (HM06364) | | | | | | | | | | | | | | | ● | | | |
| DUFFY, MELANIE (HM06365) | | | | | | | | | | | | | | | ● | | | |
| EARL, A (HM06496) | | | | | | | | | | | | | | | ● | | | |
| EAST PECKHAM OSTEO PRACTICE (HM06523) | | | ● | | | | | | | | | | | | | | | |
| EDEN, PATRICIA (HM06593) | | | | | | | | | | | | | | | | | | ● |
| EUROPEAN AYUR-VEDA (HM06944) | | | | | | | | | | | | | | | | | | |
| EUROPEAN SCHOOL OF OSTEOPATHY (HM06949) | | | ● | | | | | | | | | | | | | | | |
| EUROPEAN SCHOOL OF OSTEOPATHY (HM06948) | | | ● | | | | | | | | | | | | | | | |
| EVEGATE CLINIC (HM06996) | | | ● | | | | | | | | | | | | | | | ● |
| EVOLUTION HEALTH (HM07014) | | | | | | | | | | | | | | | | | | ● |
| FALLSHAW, ELIZABETH (HM07078) | | | | | | | | | | | | | | | | | | ● |
| FEET FIRST (HM07167) | | | | | | | | | | | | | | | | | | ● |
| FERGUSON, SUSAN (HM07231) | | | | | | | | | | | | | | | | | | ● |
| FIELD, KATIE (HM07262) | | | | | | | | | | | | | | | | | | ● |
| FOORD, AUDREY (HM07463) | | | | | | | ● | | | | | | | | | | | ● |
| GARDENER, B (HM07868) | | | ● | | | | | | | | | | | | | | | |
| GIBSON, JAN (HM08040) | | | | | | | | | | | | | | | ● | | | |
| GILLINGHAM CLINIC OF COMP MED (HM08097) | | | ● | | | | | | | | | | | | | | | ● |
| GORING-THOMAS, DIANE (HM08290) | | | | | | | | | | | | | | | | | | ● |
| GRAHAM, J (HM08348) | | | ● | | | | | | | | | | | | | | | |
| GREEN, ELIZABETH (HM08454) | | | | | | | | | | | | | | | | | | ● |
| GUNN, JASON (HM08642) | | | ● | | | | | | | | | | | | | | | |
| GUPTA, S (HM08650) | | | ● | | | | | | | | | | | | | | | |
| GUTH & ASSOCIATES (HM08658) | | | ● | | | | | | | | | | | | | | | |
| HANNA, MARK (HM08931) | | | | | | | | | | | | ● | | | ● | | | |

| Business by County with Reference no. | Reichian Therapy | Reiki | Remedial Massage | Rogerian Therapy | Rolfing | Seichem | Sensitivity Training | Shiatsu | Silva Method | Sound Therapy | Spiritual Healing | Sports Massage | Stress Therapy | Swedish Body Massage | T'ai-Chi Ch'uan | Tantra Therapy | Tera-Mai | Thought Field Therapy | Touch Therapy | Transactional Analysis | Tui-na | Ultrasonics | Vibrational Therapy | Visualisation Therapy | Vitamin Therapy | Voice Therapy | X-Ray | Ying & Yang | Yoga | Zen Therapy | Zero Balancing |
|---|---|---|---|---|---|---|---|---|---|---|---|---|---|---|---|---|---|---|---|---|---|---|---|---|---|---|---|---|---|---|---|
| DAVIES, ANGELA (HM05795) | | | | | | | | | | | | | | | | | | | | | | | | | | | | | | | |
| DAVIES, FIONA (HM05810) | | | | | | | | | | | | | | | | | | | | | | | | | | | | | | | |
| DEAKIN, T (HM05933) | | | | | | | | | | | | | | | | | | | | | | | | | | | | | | | |
| DENTON, B (HM05999) | | | | | | | | | | | | | | | | | | | | | | | | | | | | | | | |
| DICKMAN, ANNIE (HM06080) | | | | | | | | | | | | | | | | | | | | | | | | | | | | | ● | | |
| DILLON, MICHAEL (HM06100) | | | | | | | | | | | | | ● | | | | | | | | | | | ● | | | | | | | |
| DIMENT, GORDON L (HM06105) | | | | ● | | | | | | | | | ● | | | | | | | | | | | | | | | | | | |
| DOREY, STELLA (HM06198) | | | | | | | | | | | | | | | | | | | | | | | | | | | | | | | |
| DOWLING, R (HM06240) | | | | | | | | | | | | | | | | | | | | | | | | | | | | | | | |
| DUFFY, MELANIE (HM06364) | | | | | | | | | | | | | | | | | | | | | | | | | | | | | | | |
| DUFFY, MELANIE (HM06365) | | | | | | | | | | | | | | | | | | | | | | | | | | | | | | | |
| EARL, A (HM06496) | | | | | | | | | | | | | | | | | | | | | | | | | | | | | | | |
| EAST PECKHAM OSTEO PRACTICE (HM06523) | | | | | | | | | | | | | | | | | | | | | | | | | | | | | | | |
| EDEN, PATRICIA (HM06593) | | | | | | | | | | | | | | | | | | | | | | | | | | | | | | | |
| EUROPEAN AYUR-VEDA (HM06944) | | | | | | | | | | | | | ● | | | | | | | | | | | | | | | | ● | | |
| EUROPEAN SCHOOL OF OSTEOPATHY (HM06949) | | | | | | | | | | | | | | | | | | | | | | | | | | | | | | | |
| EUROPEAN SCHOOL OF OSTEOPATHY (HM06948) | | | | | | | | | | | | | | | | | | | | | | | | | | | | | | | |
| EVEGATE CLINIC (HM06996) | | ● | | | | | | ● | | | | | | | | | | | | | | | | | | | | | | | |
| EVOLUTION HEALTH (HM07014) | | | | | | | | | | | | | | | | | | | | | | | | | | | | | | | |
| FALLSHAW, ELIZABETH (HM07078) | | | | | | | | | | | | | | | | | | | | | | | | | | | | | | | |
| FEET FIRST (HM07167) | | | | | | | | | | | | | | | | | | | | | | | | | | | | | | | |
| FERGUSON, SUSAN (HM07231) | | | | | | | | | | | | | | | | | | | | | | | | | | | | | | | |
| FIELD, KATIE (HM07262) | | | | | | | | | | | | | | | | | | | | | | | | | | | | | | | |
| FOORD, AUDREY (HM07463) | | | | | | | | | | | | | | | | | | | | | | | | | | | | | | | |
| GARDENER, B (HM07868) | | | | | | | | | | | | | | | | | | | | | | | | | | | | | | | |
| GIBSON, JAN (HM08040) | | | | | | | | | | | ● | | ● | | | | | | | ● | | | | ● | | | | | | | |
| GILLINGHAM CLINIC OF COMP MED (HM08097) | | | | | | | | | | | | | ● | | | | | | | | | | | | | | | | | | |
| GORING-THOMAS, DIANE (HM08290) | | | | | | | | | | | | | | | | | | | | | | | | | | | | | | | |
| GRAHAM, J (HM08348) | | | | | | | | | | | | | | | | | | | | | | | | | | | | | | | |
| GREEN, ELIZABETH (HM08454) | | | | | | | | | | | | | | | | | | | | | | | | | | | | | | | |
| GUNN, JASON (HM08642) | | | | | | | | | | | | | | | | | | | | | | | | | | | | | | | |
| GUPTA, S (HM08650) | | | | | | | | | | | | | | | | | | | | | | | | | | | | | | | |
| GUTH & ASSOCIATES (HM08658) | | | | | | | | | | | | | | | | | | | | | | | | | | | | | | | |
| HANNA, MARK (HM08931) | | | | | | | | | | | | | ● | | | | | | | ● | | | ● | | | | | | ● | | |

# O - Z Therapies at Practices/Businesses

| Business by County with Reference no. | Orthotics | Osteomyology | Osteopathy | PAM | Paranormal Therapies | Pattern Therapies | Physiotherapy | Phytotherapy | Pilates | Podiatry | Polarity Therapy | Postural Integration | Primal Therapy | Psionic Therapy | Psychotherapy | Pyramid Power | Pyscho-Synthesis | Reflexology | Reichian Therapy | Reiki | Remedial Massage | Rogerian Therapy | Rolfing | Seichem | Sensitivity Training | Shiatsu | Silva Method | Sound Therapy | Spiritual Healing | Sports Massage | Stress Therapy | Swedish Body Massage | T'ai-Chi Ch'uan | Tantra Therapy | Tera-Mai | Thought Field Therapy | Touch Therapy | Transactional Analysis | Tui-na | Ultrasonics | Vibrational Therapy | Visualisation Therapy | Vitamin Therapy | Voice Therapy | X-Ray | Ying & Yang | Yoga | Zen Therapy | Zero Balancing |
|---|---|---|---|---|---|---|---|---|---|---|---|---|---|---|---|---|---|---|---|---|---|---|---|---|---|---|---|---|---|---|---|---|---|---|---|---|---|---|---|---|---|---|---|---|---|---|---|---|---|
| HARPER, D (HM09039) | | | ● | | | | | | | | | | | | | | | | | | | | | | | | | | | | | | | | | | | | | | | | | | | | | | |
| HARVEY CLINIC (HM09158) | | | ● | | | | | | | | | | | | | | | | | | | | | | | | | | | | | | | | | | | | | | | | | | | | | | |
| HAWKHURST NATURAL THERAPIES (HM09216) | | | | | | | | | | | | | | | | | | | | ● | | | | | | | | | | | | | | | | | | | | | | | | | | | | | |
| HAYDEN, J T (HM09253) | | | ● | | | | | | | | | | | | | | | | | | | | | | | | | | | | | | | | | | | | | | | | | | | | | | |
| HAYES, JACQUELINE (HM09260) | | | ● | | | | | | | | | | | | | | | | | | | | | | | | | | | | | | | | | | | | | | | | | | | | | | |
| HAZLEWOOD OSTEOPATHIC PRACTICE (HM09297) | | | ● | | | | | | | | | | | | | | | | | | | | | | | | | | | | | | | | | | | | | | | | | | | | | | |
| HEAD TO TOE WELL-BEING (HM09300) | | | | | | | | | | | | | | | | | | ● | | | | | | | | | | | | | | | | | | | | | | | | | | | | | | | |
| HEADON, CHRISTOPHER (HM09307) | | | | | | | | | | | | | | | ● | | | | | | | | | | | | | | | | | | | | | | | | | | | | | | | | | | |
| HEALER, ANDY JOHNSON (HM09319) | | | | | | | | | | | | | | | | | | | | | | | | | | | | | ● | | | | | | | | | | | | | | | | | | | | |
| HEALING AND HERBS (HM09325) | | | | | | | | | | | | | | | | | | | | ● | | | | ● | | | | | ● | | ● | | | | | | ● | | | | | | | | | | | | |
| HEATHSIDE CENTRE (HM09461) | | | | | | | | | | | | | | | | | | ● | | ● | | | | | | | | | | | | | | | | | | | | | | | | | | | | | |
| HEMSLEY, SARAH (HM09538) | | | | | | | | | | | | | | | | | | ● | | | | | | | | | | | | | | | | | | | | | | | | | | | | | | | |
| HERTERICH, NIGEL (HM09688) | | | ● | | | | | | | | | | | | | | | | | | | | | | | | | | | | | | | | | | | | | | | | | | | | | | |
| HILLS, MAURICE J (HM09802) | | | ● | | | | | | | | | | | | | | | | | | | | | | | | | | | | | | | | | | | | | | | | | | | | | | |
| HILTON HEALTH CENTRE (HM09812) | | | ● | | | | | | | | | | | | | | | | | | | | | | | | | | | | | | | | | | | | | | | | | | | | | | |
| HINDE, TERESA (HM09827) | | | | | | | | | | | | | | | | | | ● | | | | | | | | | | | | | | | | | | | | | | | | | | | | | | | |
| HIROKO, KELLY (HM09841) | | | | | | | | | | | | | | | | | | ● | | | | | | | | | | | | | | | | | | | | | | | | | | | | | | | |
| HOAD, A S (HM09849) | | | ● | | | | | | | | | | | | | | | | | | | | | | | | | | | | | | | | | | | | | | | | | | | | | | |
| HOGGARD, J (HM09915) | | | ● | | | | | | | | | | | | | | | | | | | | | | | | | | | | | | | | | | | | | | | | | | | | | | |
| HOLISTIC THERAPIES (HM09993) | | | | | | | | | | | | | | | | | | ● | | | | | | | | | | | | | | | | | | | | | | | | | | | | | | | |
| HOLMDEN, JO-ANNE (HM10034) | | | ● | | | | | | | | | | | | | | | | | | | | | | | | | | | | | | | | | | | | | | | | | | | | | | |
| HOLMES, S A (HM10045) | | | | | | | | | | | | | | | | | | ● | | | | | | | | | | | ● | | | | | | | | | | | | | | | | | | | | |
| HORNER, LINDLEY (HM10179) | | | ● | | | | | | | | | | | | | | | | | | | | | | | | | | | | | | | | | | | | | | | | | | | | | | |
| HUTCHIN, MARK (HM10446) | | | ● | | | | | | | | | | | | | | | | | | | | | | | | | | | | | | | | | | | | | | | | | | | | | | |
| IRONSIDE, YOLANDA (HM10742) | | | | | | | | | | | | | | | | | | ● | | | | | | | | | | | | | | | | | | | | | | | | | | | | | | | |
| ISIS (HM10763) | | | | | | | | | | | | | | | ● | ● | | ● | | | | | | | | | | | ● | | ● | | | | | | | | | | | | | | | ● | ● | ● | |
| JACCQUELINE ELLISON PRACTICE (HM10811) | | | ● | | | | | | | | | | | | | | | | | | | | | | | | | | | | | | | | | | | | | | | | | | | | | | |
| JANSEN, W (HM10924) | | | ● | | | | | | | | | | | | | | | | | | | | | | | | | | | | | | | | | | | | | | | | | | | | | | |
| JOCHIM, ANDREAS (HM11044) | | | ● | | | | | | | | | | | | | | | | | | | | | | | | | | | | | | | | | | | | | | | | | | | | | | |
| JOCHIM, ANDREAS (HM11043) | | | ● | | | | | | | | | | | | | | | | | | | | | | | | | | | | | | | | | | | | | | | | | | | | | | |
| KALTCHEVA-HICKS, DANIELA (HM11300) | | | | | | | | | | | | | | | | | | ● | | | | | | | | | | | | | | | | | | | | | | | | | | | | | | | |
| KANANI, ALPESH (HM11305) | | | ● | | | | | | | | | | | | | | | | | | | | | | | | | | | | | | | | | | | | | | | | | | | | | | |
| KARMERS CLINIQUE (HM11328) | | | | | | | | | | | | | | | | | | ● | | | | | | | | | | | | | | | | | | | | | | | | | | | | | | | |
| KENNERLEY, MAGGIE (HM11499) | | | | | | | | | | | | | | | | | | ● | | | | | | | | | | | | | | | | | | | | | | | | | | | | | | | |

# O - Z Therapies at Practices/Businesses

| Business by County with Reference no. | Orthotics | Osteomyology | Osteopathy | PAM | Paranormal Therapies | Pattern Therapies | Physiotherapy | Phytotherapy | Pilates | Podiatry | Polarity Therapy | Postural Integration | Primal Therapy | Psionic Therapy | Psychotherapy | Pyramid Power | Pyscho-Synthesis | Reflexology | Reichian Therapy | Reiki | Remedial Massage | Rogerian Therapy | Rolfing | Seichem | Sensitivity Training | Shiatsu | Silva Method | Sound Therapy | Spiritual Healing | Sports Massage | Stress Therapy | Swedish Body Massage | T'ai-Chi Ch'uan | Tantra Therapy | Tera-Mai | Thought Field Therapy | Touch Therapy | Transactional Analysis | Tui-na | Ultrasonics | Vibrational Therapy | Visualisation Therapy | Vitamin Therapy | Voice Therapy | X-Ray | Ying & Yang | Yoga | Zen Therapy | Zero Balancing |
|---|---|---|---|---|---|---|---|---|---|---|---|---|---|---|---|---|---|---|---|---|---|---|---|---|---|---|---|---|---|---|---|---|---|---|---|---|---|---|---|---|---|---|---|---|---|---|---|---|---|
| KENT COUNS PSYCHOTHPY UNION (HM11515) | | | | | | | | | | | | | | | ● | | | | | | | | | | | | | | | | | | | | | | | | | | | | | | | | | | |
| KENT OSTEOPATHIC CLINIC (HM11522) | | | ● | | | | | | | | | | | | | | | | | | | | | | | | | | | | | | | | | | | | | | | | | | | | | | |
| KINGSTON, PATRICIA (HM11681) | | | | | | | | | | | | | | | | | | ● | | | | | | | | | | | | | | | | | | | | | | | | | | | | | | | |
| KRAMER, STUART (HM11796) | | | ● | | | | | | | | | | | | | | | | | | | | | | | | | | | | | | | | | | | | | | | | | | | | | | |
| KSC (HM11812) | | | ● | | | | | | | | | | | | ● | | | ● | | | | | | | | | | | | ● | | | | | | | | | | | | | | | | | | | |
| KYRIA, S (HM11836) | | | ● | | | | | | | | | | | | | | | | | | | | | | | | | | | | | | | | | | | | | | | | | | | | | | |
| LAMB, G BRIAN (HM11888) | | | ● | | | | | | | | | | | | ● | | | | | | | | | | | | | | | | ● | | | | | | | | | | | | ● | | | | | | |
| LEBOR, JILL (HM12115) | | | | | | | | | | | | | | | | | | | | ● | | | | | | ● | | | | | | | | | | | | | | | | | | | | | | | |
| LEBRET, A F (HM12117) | | | ● | | | | | | | | | | | | | | | | | | | | | | | | | | | | | | | | | | | | | | | | | | | | | | |
| LEBRET, A F (HM12116) | | | ● | | | | | | | | | | | | | | | | | | | | | | | | | | | | | | | | | | | | | | | | | | | | | | |
| LEGG, PAM (HM12175) | | | | | | | | | | | | | | | | | | ● | | | | | | | | | | | | | | | | | | | | | | | | | | | | | | | |
| LEIGH HOUSE NAT HEALTH CLINIC (HM12184) | | | ● | | | | | | | | | | | | | | | | | | | | | | | | | | | | | | | | | | | | | | | | | | | | | | |
| LEIGH, JON (HM12187) | | | ● | | | | | | | | | | | | | | | | | | | | | | | | | | | | | | | | | | | | | | | | | | | | | | |
| LEIGH, JON H (HM12188) | | | ● | | | | | | | | | | | | | | | | | | | | | | | | | | | | | | | | | | | | | | | | | | | | | | |
| LEIPER, BRUCE M (HM12199) | | | ● | | | | | | | | | | | | | | | | | | | | | | | | | | | | | | | | | | | | | | | | | | | | | | |
| LINCOLN, FRED (HM12410) | | | | | | | | | | | | | | | | | | ● | | | | | | | | | | | | | | | | | | | | | | | | | | | | | | | |
| LOBB, BRIAN W (HM12528) | | | | | | | | | | | | | | | ● | | | | | | | ● | | | | | | | | | ● | | | | | | | ● | | | | ● | | | | | | | |
| LOMAS-HARRIS, ELISABETH (HM12576) | | | | | | | | | | | | | | | | | | ● | | | | | | | | | | | | | | | | | | | | | | | | | | | | | | | |
| LOWE, JANET (HM12696) | | | | | | | | | | | | | | | | | | ● | | | | | | | | | | | | | | | | | | | | | | | | | | | | | | | |
| LYE, JENNY (HM12756) | | | | | | | | | | | | | | | | | | ● | | | | | | | | | | | | | | | | | | | | | | | | | | | | | | | |
| MABBERLEY, KATHIE (HM12812) | | | | | | | | | | | | | | | | | | ● | | | | | | | | | | | | | | | | | | | | | | | | | | | | | | | |
| MABBERLEY, KATHIE (HM12813) | | | | | | | | | | | | | | | | | | ● | | | | | | | | | | | | | | | | | | | | | | | | | | | | | | | |
| MACARI, SALVINA (HM12817) | | | | | | | | | | | | | | | | | | ● | | | | | | | | | | | | | | | | | | | | | | | | | | | | | | | |
| MACLEAN, JANE FERGUSON (HM12863) | | | | | | | | | | | | | | | | | | ● | | | | | | | | | | | | | | | | | | | | | | | | | | | | | | | |
| MAIDSTONE COLLEGE-OSTEOPATHY (HM12937) | | | ● | | | | | | | | | | | | | | | | | | | | | | | | | | | | | | | | | | | | | | | | | | | | | | |
| MARY CANNON - CLINICAL NUTRI (HM13221) | | | | | | | | ● | | | | | | | | | | | | | | | | | | | | | | | ● | | | | | | | | | | | | ● | | | | | | |
| MASON & ASSOCIATES (HM13232) | | | ● | | | | | | | | | | | | | | | | | | | | | | | | | | | | | | | | | | | | | | | | | | | | | | |
| MASON & ASSOCIATES (HM13233) | | | ● | | | | | | | | | | | | | | | | | | | | | | | | | | | | | | | | | | | | | | | | | | | | | | |
| MATTHEWS, S (HM13314) | | | ● | | | | | | | | | | | | | | | | | | | | | | | | | | | | | | | | | | | | | | | | | | | | | | |
| MCCARTHY, C R (HM13394) | | | | | | | | | | | | | | | ● | | | | | | | | | | | | | | | | | | | | | | | | | | | | | | | | | | |
| MEOPHAM CLINIC (HM13732) | | ● | ● | | | | | | | ● | | | | | | | | | | | | | | | | | | | | | | | | | | | | | | | | | | | | | | | |
| MEW, JILL (HM13781) | | | ● | | | | | | | | | | | | | | | | | | | | | | | | | | | | | | | | | | | | | | | | | | | | | | |
| MICHIE, CAROL A (HM13801) | | | ● | | | | | | | | | | | | | | | | | | | | | | | | | | | | | | | | | | | | | | | | | | | | | | |
| MILLER, JENNY (HM13891) | | | | | | | | | | | | | | | | | | ● | | | | | | | | | | | | | | | | | | | | | | | | | | | | | | | |

# O - Z Therapies at Practices/Businesses

| Business by County with Reference no. | Orthotics | Osteomyology | Osteopathy | PAM | Paranormal Therapies | Pattern Therapies | Physiotherapy | Phytotherapy | Pilates | Podiatry | Polarity Therapy | Postural Integration | Primal Therapy | Psionic Therapy | Psychotherapy | Pyramid Power | Pyscho-Synthesis | Reflexology | Reichian Therapy | Reiki | Remedial Massage | Rogerian Therapy | Rolfing | Seichem | Sensitivity Training | Shiatsu | Silva Method | Sound Therapy | Spiritual Healing | Sports Massage | Stress Therapy | Swedish Body Massage | T'ai-Chi Ch'uan | Tantra Therapy | Tera-Mai | Thought Field Therapy | Touch Therapy | Transactional Analysis | Tui-na | Ultrasonics | Vibrational Therapy | Visualisation Therapy | Vitamin Therapy | Voice Therapy | X-Ray | Ying & Yang | Yoga | Zen Therapy | Zero Balancing |
|---|---|---|---|---|---|---|---|---|---|---|---|---|---|---|---|---|---|---|---|---|---|---|---|---|---|---|---|---|---|---|---|---|---|---|---|---|---|---|---|---|---|---|---|---|---|---|---|---|---|
| MUIRHEAD, MARGARET (HM14323) | | | | | | | | | | | | | | | | | | | | | | | | | | | | | | | | | | | | | | | | | | | ● | | | | | | |
| MULVANEY, ALISTAIR (HM14353) | | | | | | | | | | ● | | | | | | | | | | | | | | | | | | | | | | | | | | | | | | | | | | | | | | | |
| MURRELL, CHARLES (HM14418) | | | | | | | | | | | | | | | | | | ● | | | | | | | | | | | | | | | | | | | | | | | | | | | | | | | |
| NASH, MONICA (HM14492) | | | | | | | | | | | | | | | | | | ● | | | | | | | | | | | | | | | | | | | | | | | | | | | | | | | |
| NATURAL HEALTH CENTRE (HM14562) | | | | | | | | | | | | | | | ● | | | | | | | | | | | | | | | | | | | | | | | | | | | | | | | | | | |
| NATURAL HEALTH CENTRE (HM14568) | | | | | | | | | | ● | | | | | | | | ● | | ● | | | | | | ● | | | ● | | | | | | | | | | | | | | | | | | | | |
| NATURAL THERAPIST (HM14635) | | | | | | | | | | | | | | | | | | | | ● | | | | | | | | | | | ● | | | | | | | | | | | | | | | | | | |
| NEUDEGG, KENNETH (HM14792) | | | | | | | | | | | | | | | | | | ● | | | | | | | | | | | | | | | | | | | | | | | | | | | | | | | |
| NICHOLS, SYLVIA (HM14918) | | | | | | | | | | | | | | | | | | ● | | ● | | | | | | | | | | | | | | | | | | | | | | | | | | | | | |
| NOAD, SARA (HM14963) | | | | | | | | | | | | | | | | | | ● | | | | | | | | | | | | | | | | | | | | | | | | | | | | | | | |
| O'DONNELL, ANNEGRET (HM15223) | | | | | | | | | | | | | | | | | | ● | | | | | | | | | | | | | | | | | | | | | | | | | | | | | | | |
| OPTIVAVA (HM15352) | | | ● | | | | | | | | | | | | | | | | | | | | | | | | | | | | | | | | | | | | | | | | | | | | | | |
| ORME, SUE (HM15396) | | | | | | | | | | | | | | | | | | ● | | | | | | | | | | | | | | | | | | | | | | | | | | | | | | | |
| O'ROURKE, LESLEY (HM15401) | | | | | | | | | | | | | | | | | | ● | | | | | | | | | | | | | | | | | | | | | | | | | | | | | | | |
| OSTEOPATHIC CLINIC (HM15461) | | | ● | | | | | | | | | | | | | | | | | | | | | | | | | | | | | | | | | | | | | | | | | | | | | | |
| OSTEOPATHIC PRACTICE (HM15466) | | | ● | | | | | | | | | | | | | | | | | | | | | | | | | | | | | | | | | | | | | | | | | | | | | | |
| PANTALL, A L (HM15638) | | | ● | | | | | | | | | | | | | | | | | | | | | | | | | | | | | | | | | | | | | | | | | | | | | | |
| PASCOE & ASSOCIATES (HM15773) | | | ● | | | | | | | | | | | | | | | | | | | | | | | | | | | | | | | | | | | | | | | | | | | | | | |
| PASSCHIER, CORNELIUS (HM15778) | | | | | | | | | | | | | | | ● | | | | | | | | | | | | | | | | | | | | | | | | | | | | | | | | | | |
| PATEMAN, A R & H G (HM15807) | | | ● | | | | | | | | | | | | | | | | | | | | | | | | | | | | | | | | | | | | | | | | | | | | | | |
| PATERSON, MARGARET (HM15814) | | | | | | | | | | | | | | | | | | ● | | | | | | | | | | | ● | | | | | | | | | | | | | | | | | | | | |
| PEARSON, E (HM15912) | | | | | | | | | | | | | | | | | | ● | | | | | | | | | | | | | | | | | | | | | | | | | | | | | | | |
| PEARTON, GILL (HM15919) | | | | | | | | | | | | | | | | | | ● | | | | | | | | | | | | | | | | | | | | | | | | | | | | | | | |
| PELE, ANDRI (HM15950) | | | | | | | | | | | | | | | ● | | | | | | | | | | | | | | | | | | | | | | | | | | | | | | | | | | |
| PETERS, MATTHEW (HM16089) | | | ● | | | | | | | | | | | | | | | | | | | | | | | | | | | | | | | | | | | | | | | | | | | | | | |
| PHILLIPS, CAROL (HM16127) | | | | | | | | | | | | | | | | | | ● | | | | | | | | | | | | | | | | | | | | | | | | | | | | | | | |
| PHYSIOTHERAPY CENTRE (HM16230) | | | | | | | ● | | | | | | | | | | | | | | | | | | | | | | | | | | | | | | | | | | | | | | | | | | |
| PIKE, DAVINA (HM16285) | | | | | | | | | | | | | | | | | | ● | | | | | | | | | | | | | | | | | | | | | | | | | | | | | | | |
| PITCAIRN-KNOWLES, M (HM16333) | | | ● | | | | | | | | | | | | | | | | | | | | | | | | | | | | | | | | | | | | | | | | | | | | | | |
| PITT, D (HM16345) | | | ● | | | | | | | | | | | | | | | | | | | | | | | | | | | | | | | | | | | | | | | | | | | | | | |
| POWELL, ANNE-MARIE (HM16487) | | | | | | | | | | | | | | | | | | ● | | | | | | | | | | | | | | | | | | | | | | | | | | | | | | | |
| PRICE, GILLIAN (HM16576) | | | | | | | | | | | | | | | | | | ● | | | | | | | | | | | | | | | | | | | | | | | | | | | | | | | |
| PRINCES AVENUE OSTEOPATHIC (HM16623) | | | ● | | | | | | | | | | | | | | | | | | | | | | | | | | | | | | | | | | | | | | | | | | | | | | |
| PRO PHYSIO CLINIC (HM16650) | | | | | | | ● | | | | | | | | | | | | | | | | | | | | | | | | | | | | | | | | | | | | | | | | | | |

# O - Z Therapies at Practices/Businesses

| Business by County with Reference no. | Orthotics | Osteomyology | Osteopathy | PAM | Paranormal Therapies | Pattern Therapies | Physiotherapy | Phytotherapy | Pilates | Podiatry | Polarity Therapy | Postural Integration | Primal Therapy | Psionic Therapy | Psychotherapy | Pyramid Power | Pyscho-Synthesis | Reflexology | Reichian Therapy | Reiki | Remedial Massage | Rogerian Therapy | Rolfing | Seichem | Sensitivity Training | Shiatsu | Silva Method | Sound Therapy | Spiritual Healing | Sports Massage | Stress Therapy | Swedish Body Massage | T'ai-Chi Ch'uan | Tantra Therapy | Tera-Mai | Thought Field Therapy | Touch Therapy | Transactional Analysis | Tui-na | Ultrasonics | Vibrational Therapy | Visualisation Therapy | Vitamin Therapy | Voice Therapy | X-Ray | Ying & Yang | Yoga | Zen Therapy | Zero Balancing |
|---|---|---|---|---|---|---|---|---|---|---|---|---|---|---|---|---|---|---|---|---|---|---|---|---|---|---|---|---|---|---|---|---|---|---|---|---|---|---|---|---|---|---|---|---|---|---|---|---|---|
| PYE, MICHAEL (HM16783) | | | ● | | | | | | | | | | | | | | | | | | | | | | | | | | | | | | | | | | | | | | | | | | | | | | |
| READ, CHARLES REG OSTEOPATH (HM16994) | | | ● | | | | | | | | | | | | | | | | | | | | | | | | | | | | | | | | | | | | | | | | | | | | | | |
| REEVE, ANNA C (HM17058) | | | ● | | | | | | | | | | | | | | | | | | | | | | | | | | | | | | | | | | | | | | | | | | | | | | |
| REEVES, SUSAN (HM17068) | | | | | | | | | | | | | | | | | | ● | | | | | | | | | | | | | | | | | | | | | | | | | | | | | | | |
| REIKI ASSOCIATION (HM17129) | | | | | | | | | | | | | | | | | | | | ● | | | | | | | | | | | | | | | | | | | | | | | | | | | | | |
| REIKI HEALING CENTRE (HM17136) | | | | | | | | | | | | | | | | | | | | ● | | | | | | | | | | | | | | | | | | | | | | | | | | | | | |
| RIJSKIJK, CAROLE (HM17337) | | | ● | | | | | | | | | | | | | | | | | | | | | | | | | | | | | | | | | | | | | | | | | | | | | | |
| ROBERTS, A J (HM17401) | | | ● | | | | | | | | | | | | | | | | | | | | | | | | | | | | | | | | | | | | | | | | | | | | | | |
| ROBERTS, J R (HM17416) | | | ● | | | | | | | | | | | | | | | | | | | | | | | | | | | | | | | | | | | | | | | | | | | | | | |
| ROBERTS, KATE (HM17419) | | | | | | | | | | | | | | | | | | ● | | | | | | | | | | | | | | | | | | | | | | | | | | | | | | | |
| ROCHESTER PHYSIO & SPORTS (HM17520) | | | | | | | ● | | | | | | | | | | | | | | | | | | | | | | | | | | | | | | | | | | | | | | | | | | |
| ROMNEY MARSH OSTEOPATHS (HM17574) | | | ● | | | | | | | | | | | | | | | | | | | | | | | | | | | | | | | | | | | | | | | | | | | | | | |
| ROSE, NAOMI (HM17612) | | | | | | | | | | | | | | | | | | ● | | | | | | | | | | | ● | | | | | | | | ● | | | | | | | | | | | | |
| ROUND ROOM (HM17663) | | | | | | | | | | | | | | | | | | ● | | | | | | | | | | | | | | | | | | | | | | | | | | | | | | | |
| ROUSE, BARBARA (HM17672) | | | | | | | | | | | | | | | | | | ● | | | | | | | | | | | | | | | | | | | | | | | | | | | | | | | |
| ROYLANCE, JOHN (HM17719) | | | | | | | | | | | | | | | ● | | | | | | | | | | | | | | | | | | | | | | | | | | | | | | | | | | |
| RYAN, ANN (HM17788) | | | | | | | | | | | | | | | | | | ● | | | | | | | | | | | | | | | | | | | | | | | | | | | | | | | |
| S J DYSON REFLEX-AROMA (HM17809) | | | | | | | | | | | | | | | | | | ● | | | | | | | | | | | | | | | | | | | | | | | | | | | | | | | |
| SACKS, PATRICA (HM17828) | | | | | | | | | | ● | | | | | | | | | | | | | | | | | | | | | | | | | | | | | | | | | | | | | | | |
| SAINSBURY (HM17842) | | | | | | | | | | | | | | | | | | ● | | | | | | | | | | | | | | | | | | | | | | | | | | | | | | | |
| SAMUELS, CAROLANN (HM17885) | | | | | | | | | | | | | | | | | | ● | | | | | | | | | | | | | | | | | | | | | | | | | | | | | | | |
| SANCTUM HOLISTIC THERAPY CTRE (HM17896) | | | | | | | | | | | | | | | | | | ● | | | | | | | | | | | | | | | | | | | | | | | | | | | | | | | |
| SANDERS, PETER (HM17914) | | | ● | | | | | | | | | | | | | | | | | | | | | | | | | | | | | | | | | | | | | | | | | | | | | | |
| SANDOWN CLINIC FOR COMP MED (HM17926) | | | | | | | | | | | | | | | | | | ● | | ● | | | | | | | | | | | | | | | | | | | | | | | | | | | | | |
| SHARP, JUSTIN (HM18313) | | | ● | | | | | | | | | | | | | | | | | | | | | | | | | | | | | | | | | | | | | | | | | | | | | | |
| SHAWCROSS, ROSALIND (HM18350) | | | | | | | | | | | | | | | | | | ● | | | | | | | | | | | | | | | | | | | | | | | | | | | | | | | |
| SHEARER, GAYLE (HM18357) | | | ● | | | | | | | | | | | | | | | | | | | | | | | | | | | | | | | | | | | | | | | | | | | | | | |
| SHIATSU (HM18451) | | | | | | | | | | | | | | | | | | | | | | | | | | ● | | | ● | | | | | | | | | | | | | | | | | | | | |
| SILLITOE, CHRISTOPHER (HM18537) | | | | | | | | | | | | | | | | | | ● | | | | | | | | | | | | | | | | | | | | | | | | | | | | | | | |
| SMITH, KENNETH (HM18763) | | | | | | | | | | | | | | | | | | ● | | | | | | | | | | | | | | | | | | | | | | | | | | | | | | | |
| SMITH, M (HM18771) | | | ● | | | | | | | | | | | | | | | | | | | | | | | | | | | | | | | | | | | | | | | | | | | | | | |
| SMITH, P (HM18784) | | | ● | | | | | | | | | | | | | | | | | | | | | | | | | | | | | | | | | | | | | | | | | | | | | | |
| SMITH, SUSAN M (HM18814) | | | ● | | | | | | | | | | | | | | | | | | | | | | | | | | | | | | | | | | | | | | | | | | | | | | |
| SOLE PURPOSE (HM18867) | | | | | | | | | | | | | | | | | | ● | | | | | | | | | | | | | | | | | | | | | | | | | | | | | | | |

# O - Z Therapies at Practices/Businesses

Business by County with Reference no.

| Business by County with Reference no. | Orthotics | Osteomyology | Osteopathy | PAM | Paranormal Therapies | Pattern Therapies | Physiotherapy | Phytotherapy | Pilates | Podiatry | Polarity Therapy | Postural Integration | Primal Therapy | Psionic Therapy | Psychotherapy | Pyramid Power | Pyscho-Synthesis |
|---|---|---|---|---|---|---|---|---|---|---|---|---|---|---|---|---|---|
| SOUTAR, GILLIAN (HM18900) | | | | | | | | | | | | | | | | | |
| SOUTH EAST MASSAGE (HM18905) | | | | | | | | | | | | | | | | | |
| SPINAL HEALTH CLINIC (HM19015) | | | ● | | | | | | | | | | | | | | |
| STAPLES, ELAINE (HM19140) | | | | | | | | | | | | | | | | | |
| STARFIELDS HOLISTIC HLTH CTRE (HM19145) | | | | | | | | | | | | | | | | | |
| STEWART, SUSAN (HM19278) | | | | | | | | | | | | | | | | | |
| STONE, CHARLES (HM19334) | | | ● | | | | | | | | | | | | | | |
| STONE, JUNE (HM19337) | | | | | | | | | | | | | | | | | |
| STURGE, DEBBIE (HM19445) | | | | | | | | | | | | | | | | | |
| SWAN, VIVA (HM19575) | | | | | | | ● | | | | | | | | | | |
| T C CLINIC (HM19638) | | | ● | | | | | | | | | | | | | | |
| TAVAKKOLI, KIAN (HM19724) | | | | | | | | | | | | | | | | | |
| THERAPY PLACE (HM19908) | | | | | | | | | | | | | | | ● | | |
| TOLE, J R E (HM20118) | | | | | | | | | | | | | | | ● | | |
| TONBRIDGE CLINIC (HM20151) | | | ● | | | | | | | | | | | | | | |
| TOWLI, BARBARA (HM20198) | | | | | | | | | | | | | | | | | |
| TUNBRIDGE WELLS OSTEO PRACTICE (HM20393) | | | ● | | | | | | | | | | | | | | |
| TURNER, ANDREA (HM20417) | | | | | | | | | | | | | | | | | |
| TURNER, PAULA (HM20433) | | | | | | | | | | | | | | | | | |
| TYLER, VALERIE (HM20467) | | | | | | | | | | | | | | | | | |
| USEFUL THERAPIES (HM20534) | | | | | | | | | | | | | | | | | |
| VARNEY, MONICA (HM20591) | | | | | | | | | | | | | | | | | |
| VILLAGE PHYSIOTHERAPY PRACTICE (HM20667) | | | | | | | ● | | | | | | | | | | |
| VINES REIKI HEALING CENTRE (HM20680) | | | ● | | | | | | | | | | | | | | |
| WARD, FRANCES (HM20901) | | | | | | | | | | | | | | | | | |
| WARD, JAN (HM20905) | | | | | | | | | | | | | | | | | |
| WARWICK, MAUREEN (HM20970) | | | | | | | | | | | | | | | | | |
| WATLING STREET THERAPY CTRE (HM21001) | | | ● | | | | | ● | | | ● | | | | ● | | |
| WEBB, ALAN (HM21055) | | | ● | | | | | | | | | | | | | | |
| WEBB, JENNIFER (HM21067) | | | | | | | | | | | | | | | | | |
| WELLING CLINIC (HM21162) | | | ● | | | | | | | | | | | | | | |
| WELLS PHYSIO & SPORTS CLINIC (HM21168) | | | | | | | ● | | | | | | | | | | |
| WEST, LAINA (HM21252) | | | | | | | | | | | | | | | | | |
| WESTERN, GRAME (HM21266) | | | ● | | | | | | | | | | | | | | |

| Business by County with Reference no. | Reflexology | Reichian Therapy | Reiki | Remedial Massage | Rogerian Therapy | Rolfing | Seichem | Sensitivity Training | Shiatsu | Silva Method | Sound Therapy | Spiritual Healing | Sports Massage | Stress Therapy | Swedish Body Massage | T'ai-Chi Ch'uan |
|---|---|---|---|---|---|---|---|---|---|---|---|---|---|---|---|---|
| SOUTAR, GILLIAN (HM18900) | ● | | | | | | | | | | | | | | | |
| SOUTH EAST MASSAGE (HM18905) | | | | ● | | | | | | | | ● | | | ● | |
| SPINAL HEALTH CLINIC (HM19015) | | | | | | | | | | | | | | | | |
| STAPLES, ELAINE (HM19140) | ● | | | | | | | | | | | | | | | |
| STARFIELDS HOLISTIC HLTH CTRE (HM19145) | | | ● | | | | | | | | | ● | | | | |
| STEWART, SUSAN (HM19278) | ● | | | | | | | | | | | | | | | |
| STONE, CHARLES (HM19334) | ● | | ● | | | | | | | | | ● | | ● | | |
| STONE, JUNE (HM19337) | ● | | | | | | | | | | | | | | | |
| STURGE, DEBBIE (HM19445) | | | | | | | | | | | | | | | | |
| SWAN, VIVA (HM19575) | | | | | | | | | | | | | | | | |
| T C CLINIC (HM19638) | | | | | | | | | | | | | | | | |
| TAVAKKOLI, KIAN (HM19724) | ● | | | | | | | | | | | | | | | |
| THERAPY PLACE (HM19908) | | | | | | | | | | | | | | | | |
| TOLE, J R E (HM20118) | | | | | | | | | | | | | | | | |
| TONBRIDGE CLINIC (HM20151) | | | | | | | | | | | | | | | | |
| TOWLI, BARBARA (HM20198) | ● | | | | | | | | | | | | | | | |
| TUNBRIDGE WELLS OSTEO PRACTICE (HM20393) | | | | | | | | | | | | | | | | |
| TURNER, ANDREA (HM20417) | ● | | | | | | | | | | | | | | | |
| TURNER, PAULA (HM20433) | ● | | | | | | | | | | | | | | | |
| TYLER, VALERIE (HM20467) | ● | | | | | | | | | | | | | | | |
| USEFUL THERAPIES (HM20534) | ● | | ● | | | | | | ● | | | | | | | |
| VARNEY, MONICA (HM20591) | ● | | ● | | | | | | | | | | | | | |
| VILLAGE PHYSIOTHERAPY PRACTICE (HM20667) | | | | | | | | | | | | | | | | |
| VINES REIKI HEALING CENTRE (HM20680) | | | ● | | | | | | | | | | ● | | | ● |
| WARD, FRANCES (HM20901) | ● | | | | | | | | | | | | | | | |
| WARD, JAN (HM20905) | ● | | | | | | | | | | | | | | | |
| WARWICK, MAUREEN (HM20970) | ● | | | | | | | | | | | | | | | |
| WATLING STREET THERAPY CTRE (HM21001) | ● | | ● | | | | | | ● | | | | | ● | | |
| WEBB, ALAN (HM21055) | | | | | | | | | | | | | | | | |
| WEBB, JENNIFER (HM21067) | ● | | | | | | | | | | | | | | | |
| WELLING CLINIC (HM21162) | | | | | | | | | | | | | | | | |
| WELLS PHYSIO & SPORTS CLINIC (HM21168) | | | | | | | | | | | | | | | | |
| WEST, LAINA (HM21252) | ● | | | | | | | | | | | | | | | |
| WESTERN, GRAME (HM21266) | | | | | | | | | | | | | | | | |

| Business by County with Reference no. | Tantra Therapy | Tera-Mai | Thought Field Therapy | Touch Therapy | Transactional Analysis | Tui-na | Ultrasonics | Vibrational Therapy | Visualisation Therapy | Vitamin Therapy | Voice Therapy | X-Ray | Ying & Yang | Yoga | Zen Therapy | Zero Balancing |
|---|---|---|---|---|---|---|---|---|---|---|---|---|---|---|---|---|
| SOUTAR, GILLIAN (HM18900) | | | | | | | | | | | | | | | | |
| SOUTH EAST MASSAGE (HM18905) | | | | | | | | | | | | | | | | |
| SPINAL HEALTH CLINIC (HM19015) | | | | | | | | | | | | | | | | |
| STAPLES, ELAINE (HM19140) | | | | | | | | | | | | | | | | |
| STARFIELDS HOLISTIC HLTH CTRE (HM19145) | | | | | | | | | | ● | | | | | | |
| STEWART, SUSAN (HM19278) | | | | | | | | | | | | | | | | |
| STONE, CHARLES (HM19334) | | | ● | | | | | | | | | | | | | |
| STONE, JUNE (HM19337) | | | | | | | | | | | | | | | | |
| STURGE, DEBBIE (HM19445) | | | | | | | | | | ● | | | | | | |
| SWAN, VIVA (HM19575) | | | | | | | | | | | | | | ● | | |
| T C CLINIC (HM19638) | | | | | | | | | | | | | | | | |
| TAVAKKOLI, KIAN (HM19724) | | | | | | | | | | | | | | | | |
| THERAPY PLACE (HM19908) | | | | | | | | | | | | | | | | |
| TOLE, J R E (HM20118) | | | | | | | | | | | | | | | | |
| TONBRIDGE CLINIC (HM20151) | | | | | | | | | | | | | | | | |
| TOWLI, BARBARA (HM20198) | | | | | | | | | | | | | | | | |
| TUNBRIDGE WELLS OSTEO PRACTICE (HM20393) | | | | | | | | | | | | | | | | |
| TURNER, ANDREA (HM20417) | | | | | | | | | | | | | | | | |
| TURNER, PAULA (HM20433) | | | | | | | | | | | | | | | | |
| TYLER, VALERIE (HM20467) | | | | | | | | | | | | | | | | |
| USEFUL THERAPIES (HM20534) | | | | | | | | | | | | | | | | |
| VARNEY, MONICA (HM20591) | | | | | | | | | | | | | | | | |
| VILLAGE PHYSIOTHERAPY PRACTICE (HM20667) | | | | | | | | | | | | | | | | |
| VINES REIKI HEALING CENTRE (HM20680) | | | | | | | | | | | | | | | | |
| WARD, FRANCES (HM20901) | | | | | | | | | | | | | | | | |
| WARD, JAN (HM20905) | | | | | | | | | | | | | | | | |
| WARWICK, MAUREEN (HM20970) | | | | | | | | | | | | | | | | |
| WATLING STREET THERAPY CTRE (HM21001) | | | | ● | | | | | | ● | | | | | | |
| WEBB, ALAN (HM21055) | | | | | | | | | | | | | | | | |
| WEBB, JENNIFER (HM21067) | | | | | | | | | | | | | | | | |
| WELLING CLINIC (HM21162) | | | | | | | | | | | | | | | | |
| WELLS PHYSIO & SPORTS CLINIC (HM21168) | | | | | | | | | | | | | | | | |
| WEST, LAINA (HM21252) | | | | | | | | | | | | | | | | |
| WESTERN, GRAME (HM21266) | | | | | | | | | | | | | | | | |

# O - Z Therapies at Practices/Businesses

| Business by County with Reference no. | Orthotics | Osteomyology | Osteopathy | PAM | Paranormal Therapies | Pattern Therapies | Physiotherapy | Phytotherapy | Pilates | Podiatry | Polarity Therapy | Postural Integration | Primal Therapy | Psionic Therapy | Psychotherapy | Pyramid Power | Pyscho-Synthesis | Reflexology | Reichian Therapy | Reiki | Remedial Massage | Rogerian Therapy | Rolfing | Seichem | Sensitivity Training | Shiatsu | Silva Method | Sound Therapy | Spiritual Healing | Sports Massage | Stress Therapy | Swedish Body Massage | T'ai-Chi Ch'uan | Tantra Therapy | Tera-Mai | Thought Field Therapy | Touch Therapy | Transactional Analysis | Tui-na | Ultrasonics | Vibrational Therapy | Visualisation Therapy | Vitamin Therapy | Voice Therapy | X-Ray | Ying & Yang | Yoga | Zen Therapy | Zero Balancing |
|---|---|---|---|---|---|---|---|---|---|---|---|---|---|---|---|---|---|---|---|---|---|---|---|---|---|---|---|---|---|---|---|---|---|---|---|---|---|---|---|---|---|---|---|---|---|---|---|---|---|
| WESTGATE OSTEOPATHIC PRACTICE (HM21268) | | | ● | | | | | | | | | | | | | | | | | | | | | | | | | | | | | | | | | | | | | | | | | | | | | | |
| WHATLING, NICOLA (HM21306) | | | | | | | | | | | | | | | | | | ● | | | | | | | | | | | | | | | | | | | | | | | | | | | | | | | |
| WHELAN, P (HM21324) | | | | | | | | | | | | | | | | | | ● | | | | | | | | | | | | | | | | | | | | | | | | | | | | | | | |
| WILLIAMS, SUSAN (HM21595) | | | | | | | | | | | | | | | | | | ● | | | | | | | | | | | | | | | | | | | | | | | | | | | | | | | |
| WILLIAMSON, P A (HM21608) | | | ● | | | | | | | | | | | | | | | | | | | | | | | | | | | | | | | | | | | | | | | | | | | | | | |
| WILSON, VERONICA (HM21678) | | | | | | | | | | | | | | | ● | | | | | | | | | | | | | | | | | | | | | | | | | | | | | | | | | | |
| WOOLF, JOY (HM21871) | | | | | | | | | | | | | | | | | | | | | | | | | | ● | | | | | | | | | | | | | | | | | | | | | | | |
| WYE OSTEOPATHIC PRACTICE (HM21967) | | | ● | | | | | | | | | | | | | | | | | | | | | | | | | | | | | | | | | | | | | | | | | | | | | | |
| YOUNG, CAROLE (HM22066) | | | | | | | | | | | | | | | | | | ● | | | | | | | | | | | | | | | | | | | | | | | | | | | | | | | |
| **LANCASHIRE** | | | | | | | | | | | | | | | | | | | | | | | | | | | | | | | | | | | | | | | | | | | | | | | | | |
| ABERNETHY, HILARY (HM00123) | | | | | | | | | | | | | | | ● | | | ● | | | | | | | ● | | | | | | ● | | | | | | | | | | | | | | | | | | |
| ALDEPHI HOUSE (HM00495) | | | | | | | | | | | | | | | ● | | | | | | | | | | | | | | | | | | | | | | | | | | | | | | | | | | |
| ALTERNATIVE MEDICINE (HM00715) | | | ● | | | | | | | | | | | ● | | | | ● | | | | | | | | | | | | | | | | | | | | | | ● | | | ● | | | | | | |
| ALTERNATIVE MEDICINE PRACTICE (HM00721) | | | ● | | | | | | | | | | | | ● | | | ● | | | | | | | | | | | | | | | | | | | | | | ● | | | ● | | | | | | |
| ALYN, PAUL (HM00758) | | | | | | | | | | | | | | | | | | ● | | | | | | | | | | | | | | | | | | | | | | | | | | | | | | | |
| BEARLEY, CAROL (HM01969) | | | | | | | | | | | | | | | | | | ● | | | | | | | | | | | | | | | | | | | | | | | | | | | | | | | |
| BEESTON, J (HM02061) | | | | | | | | | | | | | | | | | | | | | | | | | | | | | | | | | | | | | | | | ● | | | | | | | | | |
| BENTLEY AND ASSOCIATES (HM02172) | | | | | | | ● | | | ● | | | | | | | | | | | | | | | | | | | | | ● | | | | | | | | | | | | | | | | | | |
| BFMP (HM02265) | | | ● | | | | | | | | | | | | | | | ● | | ● | | | | | | | | | | | ● | | | | | | | | | ● | | | | | | | | | |
| BLACKPOOL OSTEOPATHY CLINIC (HM02459) | | | ● | | | | | | | | | | | | | | | | | | | | | | | | | | | | | | | | | | | | | | | | | | | | | | |
| BOLTON CLINIC OF ACUPUNCTURE (HM02657) | | | ● | | | | | | | | | | | | | | | | | | | | | | | | | | | | | | | | | | | | | | | | | | | | | | |
| BOLTON PHYSIOTHERAPY CLINIC (HM02658) | | | | | | | ● | | | | | | | | | | | | | | | | | | | | | | | | | | | | | | | | | | | | | | | | | | |
| BOLTON THERAPY CENTRE (HM02659) | | | | | | | | | | | | ● | | | | | | ● | | ● | | | | | | | | | | | ● | | | | | | | | | ● | | | | | | | | | |
| BOLTON, VANESSA (HM02665) | | | | | | | | | | | | | | | | | | ● | | | | | | | | | | | | | | | | | | | | | | | | | | | | | | | |
| BOLTON, VANESSA (HM02664) | | | | | | | ● | | | | | | | | ● | | | ● | | | | | | | | | | | | | ● | | | | | | | | | | | | | | | | | | |
| BRADLEY & ASSOCIATES (HM02857) | | | ● | | | | | | | | | | | | | | | | | | | | | | | | | | | | | | | | | | | | | | | | | | | | | | |
| BRADLEY & ASSOCIATES (HM02856) | | | ● | | | | | | | | | | | | | | | | | | | | | | | | | | | | | | | | | | | | | | | | | | | | | | |
| BRUNTON, A (HM03282) | | | ● | | | | | | | | | | | | | | | | | | | | | | | | | | | | | | | | | | | | | | | | | | | | | | |
| BURNLEY CLINIC OF OSTEOPATHY (HM03408) | | | ● | | | | | | | | | | | | | | | | | | | | | | | | | | | | | | | | | | | | | | | | | | | | | | |
| BURSCOUGH PHYSIOTHERAPY (HM03425) | | | | | | ● | | | | | | | | | | | | | | | | | | | | | | | | | | | | | | | | | | | | | | | | | | | |
| CHARTERED PHYSIO & SPORTS (HM04041) | | | | | | | ● | | | | | | | | | | | | | | | | | | | | | | | | | | | | | | | | | | | | | | | | | | |
| CLOUGHS - CHRTRD PHYSIO CLINIC (HM04735) | | | | | | | ● | | | | | | | | | | | | | | | | | | | | | | | | | | | | | | | | | | | | | | | | | | |
| CROOK, G C (HM05470) | | | | | | | | | | | | | | | ● | | | | | | | | | | | | | | | | | | | | | | | | | | | | | | | | | | |
| CRYSTAL & REIKI (HM05524) | | | | | | | | | | | | | | | | | | | | ● | | | | | | | | | | | | | | | | | | | | | | | | | | | | | |

# O - Z Therapies at Practices/Businesses

| Business by County with Reference no. | Orthotics | Osteomyology | Osteopathy | PAM | Paranormal Therapies | Pattern Therapies | Physiotherapy | Phytotherapy | Pilates | Podiatry | Polarity Therapy | Postural Integration | Primal Therapy | Psionic Therapy | Psychotherapy | Pyramid Power | Pyscho-Synthesis | Reflexology | Reichian Therapy | Reiki | Remedial Massage | Rogerian Therapy | Rolfing | Seichem | Sensitivity Training | Shiatsu | Silva Method | Sound Therapy | Spiritual Healing | Sports Massage | Stress Therapy | Swedish Body Massage | T'ai-Chi Ch'uan | Tantra Therapy | Tera-Mai | Thought Field Therapy | Touch Therapy | Transactional Analysis | Tui-na | Ultrasonics | Vibrational Therapy | Visualisation Therapy | Vitamin Therapy | Voice Therapy | X-Ray | Ying & Yang | Yoga | Zen Therapy | Zero Balancing |
|---|---|---|---|---|---|---|---|---|---|---|---|---|---|---|---|---|---|---|---|---|---|---|---|---|---|---|---|---|---|---|---|---|---|---|---|---|---|---|---|---|---|---|---|---|---|---|---|---|---|
|DACRELANDS CLINIC (HM05667)|||●|||||||●|||||●|||●|||●|||||●|||●||||||||||||||||||||||
|DE LOWE, V (HM05913)|||●||||||||||||||||||||||||||||||||||||||||||||||
|DOODY, ANDREW (HM06186)|||●||||||||||||||||||||||||||||||||||||||||||||||
|FERNS, J (HM07242)|||●||||||||||||||||||||||||||||||||||||||||||||||
|FLETCHER, J E (HM07412)|||●||||||||||||||||||||||||||||||||||||||||||||||
|GARSTANG, LINDA (HM07912)||||||||||||||||||●|||||||||||||||||||||||||||||||
|GINSBERG, ANNE (HM08111)|||||●|||||||||||||||||||||||●|||||||||||||●||||||||
|GREENHALGH, A J T (HM08489)||||||||||●|||||||||||||||||||||||||||||||||||||||
|GRIFFITHS, DOROTHY (HM08564)|||●||||||||||||||||||||||||||||||||||||||||||||||
|GUTTERIDGE, DAVID (HM08660)|||●||||||||||||||||||||||||||||||||||||||||||||||
|HARCOMBE, PATRICIA (HM08963)||||||||||||||||||●|||||||||||||||||||||||||||||||
|HARMONIOUS HEALTHCARE (HM09015)||||||||||||||||||●||●|●|||||||||||||||||||||||||||||
|HEALTH SERVICES (HM09401)|||||||||||||||●||||||||||||||||||||||||||||||||||
|HEYWORTH, S (HM09716)||||||||||●|||||||||||||||||||||||||||||||||||||||
|HILTON, PETER (HM09817)|||||||||||||||●||||||||||||||||||||||||||||||||||
|HOLLANDERS, HENRY (DR) (HM10016)|||||||||||||||●||||||||||||||||||||||||||||||||||
|HYNDBURN PRIVATE CLINIC-OSTEO (HM10481)|||●||||||||||||||||||||||||||||||||||||||||||||||
|IBBETSON, JOHN A (HM10563)|||●||||||||||||||||||||||||||||||||||||||||||||||
|JENKINS, JUDITH (HM10988)|||●||||||||||||||||||||||||||||||||||||||||||||||
|JOHN HOLDEN ASSOCIATES (HM11051)||||||||||●|||||||||||||||||||||||||||||||||||||||
|JONES, MARGARET (HM11172)||||||||||||||||||●|||||||||||||||||||||||||||||||
|JOY, ALAN (HM11230)|||●||||||||||||||||||||||||||||||||||||||||||||||
|KEATING, B G (HM11374)||||||||||||||||||●|||||||||||||||||||||||||||||||
|KELLY CHIROPODY (HM11424)|||●||||||||||||●|||●|||||||||||||||||||||||||||||||
|KELSALL, PETER T (HM11451)|||●||||||||||||||||||||||||||||||||||||||||||||||
|KENDEL HOUSE CLINIC (HM11479)|||●|||||||||||||||●|||||||||||●||||||||||||||||||||
|LAYNE, SUSAN G (HM12077)||||||||||||||||||●|||||||||||||||||||||||||||||||
|LEE-CROWTHER, CATHRYN (HM12152)||||||||||||||||||●|||||||||||||||||||||||||||||||
|LEYLAND PHYSIOTHERAPY CENTRE (HM12319)|||||||●||||||||||||||||||||||||||||||||||||||||||
|MALKIN, DK, MANIP THERAPY (HM12975)|||●||||||||||||||||||||||||||||●|||||||||●|||||||||
|METCALF, JOHN (HM13767)|||●||||||||||||||||||||||||||||||||||||||||||||||
|MILLER, SUSAN (HM13903)||||||||||||||||||●|||||||||||||||||||||||||||||||
|MOON, BARBARA (HM14098)|||||||||||||||●||||||||||||||||||||||||||||||||||
|NATURAL HEALTH CENTRE (HM14566)||||||||||||||||||●||●|||||||||||||||||||||||||||||

# O - Z Therapies at Practices/Businesses

Business by County with Reference no.

| Business | Orthotics | Osteomyology | Osteopathy | PAM | Paranormal Therapies | Pattern Therapies | Physiotherapy | Phytotherapy | Pilates | Podiatry | Polarity Therapy | Postural Integration | Primal Therapy | Psionic Therapy | Psychotherapy | Pyramid Power | Pyscho-Synthesis | Reflexology | Reichian Therapy | Reiki | Remedial Massage | Rogerian Therapy | Rolfing | Seichem | Sensitivity Training |
|---|---|---|---|---|---|---|---|---|---|---|---|---|---|---|---|---|---|---|---|---|---|---|---|---|---|
| NELSON, S (HM14782) | | | | | | | | | | | | | | | | | | ● | | | | | | | |
| NORTHERN ACU & OSTEO MED CTRE (HM15056) | | | ● | | | | | | | | | | | | | | | | | | | | | | |
| ONE STOP HEALTH & BEAUTY (HM15323) | | | | | ● | | | | | | ● | ● | | | | | | ● | | ● | | | ● | | |
| O'SHEA, SHEILA & PARTNERS (HM15434) | | | ● | | | | | | | | | | | | | | | | | | | | | | |
| OWEN, GEORGE (HM15523) | | | ● | | | | | | | | | | | | | | | | | | | | | | |
| PENFOLD, LYN (HM15972) | | | | | | | | | | | | | | | | | | ● | | | | | | | |
| PEN-Y-BRYN HOLISTIC THERAPY (HM16003) | | | | | | | | | | | | | | | | | | ● | | ● | ● | | | | |
| PEPPER, JOHN (HM16009) | | | | | | | | | | | | | | | ● | | | | | | | ● | | | |
| PERCIVAL, R W & H A (HM16018) | | | ● | | | | | | | | | | | | | | | | | | | | | | |
| PHYSIO AND SPORTS INJURIES (HM16195) | | | | | | | | | | | | ● | | | | | | | | | | | | | |
| PRESTON THERAPY CENTRE (HM16550) | | | | | | | | | | | | | | | ● | | | | | | | | | | |
| PURCELL, AMANDA (HM16762) | | | ● | | | | | | | | | | | | | | | | | | | | | | |
| PURE HEALTH (HM16765) | | | | | | | | | | | | | | | | | | ● | | | ● | | | | |
| RAFFIT, PHILIPPE (HM16866) | | | ● | | | | | | | | | | | | | | | | | | | | | | |
| RAMSBOTTOM PHYSIO CLINIC (HM16919) | | | | | | | ● | | | | | | | | | | | | | | | | | | |
| RATCLIFFE, MARK (HM16949) | | | ● | | | | | | | | | | | | | | | | | | | | | | |
| RATCLIFFE, MARK (HM16950) | | | ● | | | | | | | | | | | | | | | | | | | | | | |
| REMEDIAL MASSAGE/SPORTS (HM17175) | | | | | | | ● | | | | | | | | | | | | | | ● | | | | |
| ROGERS, HEATHER (HM17547) | | | | | | | | | | | | | | | | | | ● | | | | | | | |
| SEMLEY (HM18223) | | | ● | | | | | | | | | | | | | | | | | | | | | | |
| SOUTHWORTH, L (HM18950) | | | ● | | | | | | | | | | | | | | | | | | | | | | |
| SOWERBUTTS, G H (HM18953) | | | ● | | | | | | | | | | | | | | | | | | | | | | |
| SPIRITUAL THERAPIST (HM19029) | | | | | ● | | | | | | | | | | | | | | | ● | | | | | |
| ST GEORGES MULTI THERAPY CTRE (HM19075) | | | ● | | | | ● | | | | | | | | ● | | | ● | | | | | | | |
| TIP TOES (HM20086) | | | | | | | | | | | | | | | | | | ● | | ● | ● | | | | |
| TOMLINSON ASSOCIATES (HM20139) | | | ● | | | | | | | | | | | | | | | | | | | | | | |
| TOMLINSON, JUDITH (HM20142) | | | | | | | | | | | | | | | | | | ● | | | | | | | |
| TREVITT, ELAINE (HM20323) | | | ● | | | | | | | | | | | | | | | | | | | | | | |
| WARBURTON, G L (HM20894) | | | ● | | | | | | | | | | | | | | | | | | | | | | |
| WARNER, HAZEL (HM20933) | | | | | | | | | | | | | | | | | | ● | | | | | | | |
| WARNER, JEAN (HM20934) | | | ● | | | | | | | | | | | | | | | | | | | | | | |
| WATKINSON, BARBARA (HM20999) | | | | | | | | | | | | | | | | | | ● | | ● | | | | | |
| WHEILDON, SARAH J (HM21322) | | | ● | | | | | | | | | | | | | | | | | | | | | | |
| WILSON, G (HM21656) | | | | | | | | | | | | | | | ● | | | | | | | | | | |

| Business | Shiatsu | Silva Method | Sound Therapy | Spiritual Healing | Sports Massage | Stress Therapy | Swedish Body Massage | T'ai-Chi Ch'uan | Tantra Therapy | Tera-Mai | Thought Field Therapy | Touch Therapy | Transactional Analysis | Tui-na | Ultrasonics | Vibrational Therapy | Visualisation Therapy | Vitamin Therapy | Voice Therapy | X-Ray | Ying & Yang | Yoga | Zen Therapy | Zero Balancing |
|---|---|---|---|---|---|---|---|---|---|---|---|---|---|---|---|---|---|---|---|---|---|---|---|---|
| NELSON, S (HM14782) | | | | | | | | | | | | | | | | | | | | | | | | |
| NORTHERN ACU & OSTEO MED CTRE (HM15056) | | | | | | | | | | | | | | | | | | | | | | | | |
| ONE STOP HEALTH & BEAUTY (HM15323) | | | | ● | | ● | | | | | | ● | | | | ● | | | | | | | | |
| O'SHEA, SHEILA & PARTNERS (HM15434) | | | | | | | | | | | | | | | | | | | | | | | | |
| OWEN, GEORGE (HM15523) | | | | | | | | | | | | | | | | | | | | | | | | |
| PENFOLD, LYN (HM15972) | | | | | | | | | | | | | | | | | | | | | | | | |
| PEN-Y-BRYN HOLISTIC THERAPY (HM16003) | | | | | | ● | | | | | | | | | | | | | | | | | | |
| PEPPER, JOHN (HM16009) | | | | ● | | ● | | | | | | | | | | | ● | | | | | | | |
| PERCIVAL, R W & H A (HM16018) | | | | | | | | | | | | | | | | | | | | | | | | |
| PHYSIO AND SPORTS INJURIES (HM16195) | | | | | | | | | | | | | | | | | | | | | | | | |
| PRESTON THERAPY CENTRE (HM16550) | | | | | | | | | | | | | | | | | | | | | | | | |
| PURCELL, AMANDA (HM16762) | | | | | | | | | | | | | | | | | | | | | | | | |
| PURE HEALTH (HM16765) | | | | | | ● | | | | | | | | | | | | | | | | | | |
| RAFFIT, PHILIPPE (HM16866) | | | | | | | | | | | | | | | | | | | | | | | | |
| RAMSBOTTOM PHYSIO CLINIC (HM16919) | | | | | | | | | | | | | | | | | | | | | | | | |
| RATCLIFFE, MARK (HM16949) | | | | | | | | | | | | | | | | | | | | | | | | |
| RATCLIFFE, MARK (HM16950) | | | | | | | | | | | | | | | | | | | | | | | | |
| REMEDIAL MASSAGE/SPORTS (HM17175) | | | | | | | | | | | | | | | | | | | | | | | | |
| ROGERS, HEATHER (HM17547) | | | | | | | | | | | | | | | | | | | | | | | | |
| SEMLEY (HM18223) | | | | | | | | | | | | | | | | | | | | | | | | |
| SOUTHWORTH, L (HM18950) | | | | | | | | | | | | | | | | | | | | | | | | |
| SOWERBUTTS, G H (HM18953) | | | | | | | | | | | | | | | | | | | | | | | | |
| SPIRITUAL THERAPIST (HM19029) | | | | ● | | | | | | | | | | | | | ● | | | | | | | |
| ST GEORGES MULTI THERAPY CTRE (HM19075) | | | | | | ● | | | | | | | | | | | ● | | | | | | | |
| TIP TOES (HM20086) | | | | | | | ● | | | | | | | | | | | | | | | | | |
| TOMLINSON ASSOCIATES (HM20139) | | | | | | | | | | | | | | | | | | | | | | | | |
| TOMLINSON, JUDITH (HM20142) | | | | | | | | | | | | | | | | | | | | | | ● | | |
| TREVITT, ELAINE (HM20323) | | | | | | | | | | | | | | | | | | | | | | | | |
| WARBURTON, G L (HM20894) | | | | | | | | | | | | | | | | | | | | | | | | |
| WARNER, HAZEL (HM20933) | | | | | | | | | | | | | | | | | | | | | | | | |
| WARNER, JEAN (HM20934) | | | | | | | | | | | | | | | | | | | | | | | | |
| WATKINSON, BARBARA (HM20999) | | | | | | | | | | | | | | | | | | | | | | | | |
| WHEILDON, SARAH J (HM21322) | | | | | | | | | | | | | | | | | | | | | | | | |
| WILSON, G (HM21656) | | | | | | ● | | | | | | | | | | | | | | | | | | |

# O - Z Therapies at Practices/Businesses

| Business by County with Reference no. | Orthotics | Osteomyology | Osteopathy | PAM | Paranormal Therapies | Pattern Therapies | Physiotherapy | Phytotherapy | Pilates | Podiatry | Polarity Therapy | Postural Integration | Primal Therapy | Psionic Therapy | Psychotherapy | Pyramid Power | Pyscho-Synthesis |
|---|---|---|---|---|---|---|---|---|---|---|---|---|---|---|---|---|---|
| WOOD, ALISON (HM21785) | | | | | | | | | | | | | | | | | |
| LEICESTERSHIRE | | | | | | | | | | | | | | | | | |
| ALBANY HOUSE (HM00479) | | | | | | | | | | | | | | | | | |
| ANDREWS, SIMON C (HM00859) | | | | | | | | | | | | | | | | | |
| ARCHWAY HSE NATURAL HLTH CTRE (HM00983) | | | | | | | | | | | | | | | | | |
| ASHFORD, HAYLEY (HM01219) | | | | | | | | | | | | | | | | | |
| AYURVEDIC HERBAL CLINIC (HM01444) | | | | | | | | | | | | | | | ● | | |
| BELLAMY, ELIZABETH (HM02095) | | | | | | | | | | | | | | | | | |
| BIGGIN, ALISON (HM02291) | | | ● | | | | | | | | | | | | | | |
| BODY PRACTICE (HM02605) | | | ● | | | | | | | | | | | | | | |
| BOOTH, JACQUELINE (HM02699) | | | | | | | | | | | | | | | | | |
| BROWN, F H (HM03219) | | | ● | | | | | | | | | | | | | | |
| BROWN, VAL (HM03252) | | | | | | | | | | | | | | | | | |
| CALM WATERS (HM03557) | | | | | | | | | | | | | | | | | |
| CHADWICK, ATOSHA (HM03935) | | | | | | | | | | | | | | | | | |
| CHARLESWORTH, MARIAN (HM04030) | | | | | | | | | | | | | | | | | |
| CONLIFFE, LOUISE (HM04982) | | | | | | | | | | | | | | | | | |
| DEAN, JOSIE (HM05939) | | | | | | | | | | | | | | | | | |
| ELTON, KATHRYN (HM06790) | | | | | | | | | | | | | | | | | |
| FAIRWEATHER, S & E (HM07068) | | | | | | | | | | | | | | | | | |
| GLENFIELD PRACTICE (HM08150) | | | ● | | | | | | | | | | | | | | |
| GLOVER, ELEANOR L (HM08162) | | | ● | | | | | | | | | | | | | | |
| GRAHAM SPOWAGE OSTEOPATHIC SVS (HM08340) | | | ● | | | | | | | | | | | | | | |
| HARBOROUGH OSTEOPATHIC CLINIC (HM08960) | | | ● | | | | | | | | | | | | | | |
| HASSETT, CHARLES (HM09187) | | | ● | | | | | | | | | | | | | | |
| HELIX CENTRE (HM09521) | | | | | | | | | | | | | | | | | |
| HIGGINSON, ANN (HM09731) | | | | | | | | | | | | | | | | | |
| HOWARTH, LYNNE (HM10252) | | | | | | | | | | | | | | | | | |
| HURD, J V (HM10416) | | | | | | | | | | | | | | | ● | | |
| JAYES, CERI (HM10945) | | | | | | | | | | | | | | | | | |
| LORRIMAN, MARGARET (HM12647) | | | | | | | | | | | | | | | | | |
| LOUGHBOROUGH OSTEOPATHIC (HM12660) | | | ● | | | | | | | | | | | | | | |
| MCNULTY, RAAKHEE (HM13588) | | | | | | | | | | | | | | | | | |
| MELTON MOWBRAY PHYSIO CLINIC (HM13717) | | | | | | | ● | | | | | | | | | | |

| Business by County with Reference no. | Reflexology | Reichian Therapy | Reiki | Remedial Massage | Rogerian Therapy | Rolfing | Seichem | Sensitivity Training | Shiatsu | Silva Method | Sound Therapy | Spiritual Healing | Sports Massage | Stress Therapy | Swedish Body Massage | T'ai-Chi Ch'uan |
|---|---|---|---|---|---|---|---|---|---|---|---|---|---|---|---|---|
| WOOD, ALISON (HM21785) | ● | | | | | | | | | | | | | | | |
| LEICESTERSHIRE | | | | | | | | | | | | | | | | |
| ALBANY HOUSE (HM00479) | | | | | | | | | | | | | | | | |
| ANDREWS, SIMON C (HM00859) | ● | | ● | | | | | | | | | | | | | |
| ARCHWAY HSE NATURAL HLTH CTRE (HM00983) | ● | | ● | | | | | | ● | | | | | | | |
| ASHFORD, HAYLEY (HM01219) | ● | | | | | | | | | | | | | | | |
| AYURVEDIC HERBAL CLINIC (HM01444) | ● | | | | | | | | | | | | | ● | | |
| BELLAMY, ELIZABETH (HM02095) | ● | | | | | | | | | | | | | | | |
| BIGGIN, ALISON (HM02291) | | | | | | | | | | | | | | | | |
| BODY PRACTICE (HM02605) | | | | | | | | | | | | | | | | |
| BOOTH, JACQUELINE (HM02699) | ● | | | | | | | | | | | | | | | |
| BROWN, F H (HM03219) | | | | | | | | | | | | | | | | |
| BROWN, VAL (HM03252) | ● | | | | | | | | | | | | | | | |
| CALM WATERS (HM03557) | | | ● | | | | | | | | | | ● | | | |
| CHADWICK, ATOSHA (HM03935) | ● | | | | | | | | | | | | | | | |
| CHARLESWORTH, MARIAN (HM04030) | ● | | | | | | | | | | | | | | | |
| CONLIFFE, LOUISE (HM04982) | ● | | | | | | | | | | | | | | | |
| DEAN, JOSIE (HM05939) | ● | | | | | | | | | | | | | | | |
| ELTON, KATHRYN (HM06790) | ● | | | | | | | | | | | | | | | |
| FAIRWEATHER, S & E (HM07068) | | | | ● | | | | | | | | | | | | |
| GLENFIELD PRACTICE (HM08150) | | | | | | | | | | | | | | | | |
| GLOVER, ELEANOR L (HM08162) | | | | | | | | | | | | | | | | |
| GRAHAM SPOWAGE OSTEOPATHIC SVS (HM08340) | | | | | | | | | | | | | | | | |
| HARBOROUGH OSTEOPATHIC CLINIC (HM08960) | | | | | | | | | | | | | | | | |
| HASSETT, CHARLES (HM09187) | | | | | | | | | | | | | | | | |
| HELIX CENTRE (HM09521) | ● | | ● | ● | | | | | | | | ● | | | | |
| HIGGINSON, ANN (HM09731) | ● | | | | | | | | | | | | | | | |
| HOWARTH, LYNNE (HM10252) | ● | | | | | | | | | | | | | | | |
| HURD, J V (HM10416) | | | | | | | | | | | | | | | | |
| JAYES, CERI (HM10945) | ● | | | | | | | | | | | | | | | |
| LORRIMAN, MARGARET (HM12647) | ● | | | | | | | | | | | | | | | |
| LOUGHBOROUGH OSTEOPATHIC (HM12660) | | | | | | | | | | | | | | | | |
| MCNULTY, RAAKHEE (HM13588) | ● | | | | | | | | | | | | | | | |
| MELTON MOWBRAY PHYSIO CLINIC (HM13717) | | | | | | | | | | | | | | | | |

| Business by County with Reference no. | Tantra Therapy | Tera-Mai | Thought Field Therapy | Touch Therapy | Transactional Analysis | Tui-na | Ultrasonics | Vibrational Therapy | Visualisation Therapy | Vitamin Therapy | Voice Therapy | X-Ray | Ying & Yang | Yoga | Zen Therapy | Zero Balancing |
|---|---|---|---|---|---|---|---|---|---|---|---|---|---|---|---|---|
| WOOD, ALISON (HM21785) | | | | | | | | | | | | | | | | |
| LEICESTERSHIRE | | | | | | | | | | | | | | | | |
| ALBANY HOUSE (HM00479) | | | | | | | | | | | | | | ● | | |
| ANDREWS, SIMON C (HM00859) | | | | | | | | | | | | | | ● | | |
| ARCHWAY HSE NATURAL HLTH CTRE (HM00983) | | | | | | | | | | | | | | | | ● |
| ASHFORD, HAYLEY (HM01219) | | | | | | | | | | | | | | | | |
| AYURVEDIC HERBAL CLINIC (HM01444) | | | | ● | | | | | | ● | | | | ● | | |
| BELLAMY, ELIZABETH (HM02095) | | | | | | | | | | | | | | | | |
| BIGGIN, ALISON (HM02291) | | | | | | | | | | | | | | | | |
| BODY PRACTICE (HM02605) | | | | | | | | | | | | | | | | |
| BOOTH, JACQUELINE (HM02699) | | | | | | | | | | | | | | | | |
| BROWN, F H (HM03219) | | | | | | | | | | | | | | | | |
| BROWN, VAL (HM03252) | | | | | | | | | | | | | | | | |
| CALM WATERS (HM03557) | | | | | | | | | | | | | | | | |
| CHADWICK, ATOSHA (HM03935) | | | | | | | | | | | | | | | | |
| CHARLESWORTH, MARIAN (HM04030) | | | | | | | | | | | | | | | | |
| CONLIFFE, LOUISE (HM04982) | | | | | | | | | | | | | | | | |
| DEAN, JOSIE (HM05939) | | | | | | | | | | | | | | | | |
| ELTON, KATHRYN (HM06790) | | | | | | | | | | | | | | | | |
| FAIRWEATHER, S & E (HM07068) | | | | | | | | | | | | | | | | |
| GLENFIELD PRACTICE (HM08150) | | | | | | | | | | | | | | | | |
| GLOVER, ELEANOR L (HM08162) | | | | | | | | | | | | | | | | |
| GRAHAM SPOWAGE OSTEOPATHIC SVS (HM08340) | | | | | | | | | | | | | | | | |
| HARBOROUGH OSTEOPATHIC CLINIC (HM08960) | | | | | | | | | | | | | | | | |
| HASSETT, CHARLES (HM09187) | | | | | | | | | | | | | | | | |
| HELIX CENTRE (HM09521) | | | | | | | | | | | | | | | | |
| HIGGINSON, ANN (HM09731) | | | | | | | | | | | | | | | | |
| HOWARTH, LYNNE (HM10252) | | | | | | | | | | | | | | | | |
| HURD, J V (HM10416) | | | | | | | | | | | | | | | | |
| JAYES, CERI (HM10945) | | | | | | | | | | | | | | | | |
| LORRIMAN, MARGARET (HM12647) | | | | | | | | | | | | | | | | |
| LOUGHBOROUGH OSTEOPATHIC (HM12660) | | | | | | | | | | | | | | | | |
| MCNULTY, RAAKHEE (HM13588) | | | | | | | | | | | | | | | | |
| MELTON MOWBRAY PHYSIO CLINIC (HM13717) | | | | | | | | | | | | | | | | |

# O - Z Therapies at Practices/Businesses

| Business by County with Reference no. | Orthotics | Osteomyology | Osteopathy | PAM | Paranormal Therapies | Pattern Therapies | Physiotherapy | Phytotherapy | Pilates | Podiatry | Polarity Therapy | Postural Integration | Primal Therapy | Psionic Therapy | Psychotherapy | Pyramid Power | Pyscho-Synthesis |
|---|---|---|---|---|---|---|---|---|---|---|---|---|---|---|---|---|---|
| MERIDIAN HEALTHCARE (HM13743) | | | ● | | | | | | | | | | | | | | |
| MOORE, GINA (HM14123) | | | | | | | | | | | | | | | | | |
| NATURAL WAY HEALTH CENTRE (HM14669) | | | | | | | | | | | | | | | | | |
| NEWELL, JOHN (HM14860) | | | ● | | | | | | | | | | | | | | |
| OADBY HOUSE (HM15140) | | | | | | | ● | | | | | | | | | | |
| OAKHAM OSTEOPATHIC CLINIC (HM15152) | | | ● | | | | | | | | | | | | | | |
| PADBURY, STEPHANIE (HM15561) | | | | | | | | | | | | | | | | | |
| PATEL, DIPTI (HM15786) | | | | | | | | | | | | | | | | | |
| ROBINSON, J H (HM17477) | | | | | | | | | | | | | | | ● | | |
| ROSE, MARCIA (HM17610) | | | | | | | | | | | | | | | | | |
| SCHOOL OF SPIRITUAL KNOWLEDGE (HM18085) | | | | | | | | | | | | | | | | | |
| SIBSON, AVRIL (HM18523) | | | | | | | | | | | | | | | | | |
| SMITH, SHEILA (HM18810) | | | | | | | | | | | | | | | | | |
| STEPHENSON, ANN (HM19206) | | | | | | | | | | | | | | | | | |
| STERN, J (HM19217) | | | | | | | | | | | | | | | ● | | |
| STEVENS, TARA L (HM19240) | | | | | | | | | | | | | | | | | |
| STEWART, LINDSEY (HM19272) | | | ● | | | | | | | | | | | | | | |
| SUE CHARLES AROMATHERAPY (HM19466) | | | | | | | | | | | | | | | | | |
| SUE RICKS COMP THERAPY (HM19467) | | | | | | | | | | | | | | | | | |
| TUCK, JANICE (HM20362) | | | | | | | | | | | | | | | | | |
| VIALS, REBECCA (HM20634) | | | | | | | | | | | | | | | | | |
| VICTORIA CLINIC (HM20650) | | | | | | | | | | | | | | | | | |
| VICTORIA CLINIC (HM20651) | | | ● | | | | | | | | | | | | | | |
| WENDY PRICE HOLISTIC RIDING (HM21198) | | | | | | | | | | | | | | | | | |
| WEST, DIANA (HM21248) | | | | | | | | | | | | | | | | | |
| WILKINSON, GWEN (HM21507) | | | | | | | | | | | | | | | | | |
| WILLMOTT, ISOBEL (HM21621) | | | | | | | | | | | | | | | | | |
| WOOD, WIN (HM21813) | | | | | | | | | | | | | | | ● | | |
| **LINCOLNSHIRE** | | | | | | | | | | | | | | | | | |
| ALEXANDER TECHNIQUE (HM00550) | | | | | | | | | | | | | | | | | |
| BARN HOUSE PHYSIO CLINIC (HM01726) | | | | | | | | | | | | | | | ● | | |
| BEVERLEYS (HM02246) | | | | | | | | | | | | | | | | | |
| BRANSON, H J L (HM02920) | | | ● | | | | | | | | | | | | | | |
| BROAD STREET PRACTICE (HM03107) | | | ● | | | | | | | | | | | | | | |

| Business by County with Reference no. | Reflexology | Reichian Therapy | Reiki | Remedial Massage | Rogerian Therapy | Rolfing | Seichem | Sensitivity Training | Shiatsu | Silva Method | Sound Therapy | Spiritual Healing | Sports Massage | Stress Therapy | Swedish Body Massage | T'ai-Chi Ch'uan |
|---|---|---|---|---|---|---|---|---|---|---|---|---|---|---|---|---|
| MERIDIAN HEALTHCARE (HM13743) | | | | | | | | | | | | | | | | |
| MOORE, GINA (HM14123) | ● | | | | | | | | | | | | | | | |
| NATURAL WAY HEALTH CENTRE (HM14669) | | | ● | | | | | | ● | | | | | | | |
| NEWELL, JOHN (HM14860) | | | | | | | | | | | | | | | | |
| OADBY HOUSE (HM15140) | | | | | | | | | | | | | | | | |
| OAKHAM OSTEOPATHIC CLINIC (HM15152) | | | | | | | | | | | | | | | | |
| PADBURY, STEPHANIE (HM15561) | ● | | | | | | | | | | | | | | | |
| PATEL, DIPTI (HM15786) | ● | | | | | | | | | | | | | | | |
| ROBINSON, J H (HM17477) | | | | | | | | | | | | | | | | |
| ROSE, MARCIA (HM17610) | ● | | | | | | | | | | | | | | | |
| SCHOOL OF SPIRITUAL KNOWLEDGE (HM18085) | | | | | | | | | | | | ● | | | | |
| SIBSON, AVRIL (HM18523) | ● | | | | | | | | | | | | | | | |
| SMITH, SHEILA (HM18810) | ● | | | | | | | | | | | | | | | |
| STEPHENSON, ANN (HM19206) | ● | | | | | | | | | | | | | | | |
| STERN, J (HM19217) | | | | | | | | | | | | | | | | |
| STEVENS, TARA L (HM19240) | ● | | | | | | | | | | | | | | | |
| STEWART, LINDSEY (HM19272) | | | | | | | | | | | | | | | | |
| SUE CHARLES AROMATHERAPY (HM19466) | | | | | | | | | ● | | | | | ● | | |
| SUE RICKS COMP THERAPY (HM19467) | ● | | ● | | | | | | | | | | | | | |
| TUCK, JANICE (HM20362) | ● | | | | | | | | | | | | | | | |
| VIALS, REBECCA (HM20634) | ● | | | | | | | | | | | | | | | |
| VICTORIA CLINIC (HM20650) | | | ● | | | | | | | | | ● | | ● | | |
| VICTORIA CLINIC (HM20651) | | | | | | | | | | | | | | | | |
| WENDY PRICE HOLISTIC RIDING (HM21198) | | | ● | | | | | | | | | ● | | ● | | |
| WEST, DIANA (HM21248) | ● | | | | | | | | | | | | | | | |
| WILKINSON, GWEN (HM21507) | | | | | | | | | | | ● | | | | | |
| WILLMOTT, ISOBEL (HM21621) | ● | | | | | | | | | | | | | | | |
| WOOD, WIN (HM21813) | | | | | | | | | | | | | | | | |
| **LINCOLNSHIRE** | | | | | | | | | | | | | | | | |
| ALEXANDER TECHNIQUE (HM00550) | | | | | | | | | | | | | | | | ● |
| BARN HOUSE PHYSIO CLINIC (HM01726) | | | | | | | | | | | | | | | | |
| BEVERLEYS (HM02246) | ● | | | | | | | | | | | | | | | |
| BRANSON, H J L (HM02920) | | | | | | | | | | | | | | | | |
| BROAD STREET PRACTICE (HM03107) | | | | | | | | | | | | | | | | |

| Business by County with Reference no. | Tantra Therapy | Tera-Mai | Thought Field Therapy | Touch Therapy | Transactional Analysis | Tui-na | Ultrasonics | Vibrational Therapy | Visualisation Therapy | Vitamin Therapy | Voice Therapy | X-Ray | Ying & Yang | Yoga | Zen Therapy | Zero Balancing |
|---|---|---|---|---|---|---|---|---|---|---|---|---|---|---|---|---|
| MERIDIAN HEALTHCARE (HM13743) | | | | | | | | | | | | | | | | |
| MOORE, GINA (HM14123) | | | | | | | | | | | | | | | | |
| NATURAL WAY HEALTH CENTRE (HM14669) | | | | | | | | | | | | | | | | |
| NEWELL, JOHN (HM14860) | | | | | | | | | | | | | | | | |
| OADBY HOUSE (HM15140) | | | | | | | | | | | | | | | | |
| OAKHAM OSTEOPATHIC CLINIC (HM15152) | | | | | | | | | | | | | | | | |
| PADBURY, STEPHANIE (HM15561) | | | | | | | | | | | | | | | | |
| PATEL, DIPTI (HM15786) | | | | | | | | | | | | | | | | |
| ROBINSON, J H (HM17477) | | | | | | | | | | | | | | | | |
| ROSE, MARCIA (HM17610) | | | | | | | | | | | | | | | | |
| SCHOOL OF SPIRITUAL KNOWLEDGE (HM18085) | | | | | | | | | | | | | | | | |
| SIBSON, AVRIL (HM18523) | | | | | | | | | | | | | | | | |
| SMITH, SHEILA (HM18810) | | | | | | | | | | | | | | | | |
| STEPHENSON, ANN (HM19206) | | | | | | | | | | | | | | | | |
| STERN, J (HM19217) | | | | | | | | | | | | | | | | |
| STEVENS, TARA L (HM19240) | | | | | | | | | | | | | | | | |
| STEWART, LINDSEY (HM19272) | | | | | | | | | | | | | | | | |
| SUE CHARLES AROMATHERAPY (HM19466) | | | | ● | | | | | | | | | | | | |
| SUE RICKS COMP THERAPY (HM19467) | | | | | | | | ● | | | | | | | | |
| TUCK, JANICE (HM20362) | | | | | | | | | | | | | | | | |
| VIALS, REBECCA (HM20634) | | | | | | | | | | | | | | | | |
| VICTORIA CLINIC (HM20650) | | | | | | | | | | ● | | | | | | |
| VICTORIA CLINIC (HM20651) | | | | | | | | | | | | | | | | |
| WENDY PRICE HOLISTIC RIDING (HM21198) | | | | | | | | | ● | | | | | | | |
| WEST, DIANA (HM21248) | | | | | | | | | | | | | | | | |
| WILKINSON, GWEN (HM21507) | | | | | | | | | | | | | | | | |
| WILLMOTT, ISOBEL (HM21621) | | | | | | | | | | | | | | | | |
| WOOD, WIN (HM21813) | | | | | | | | | | | | | | | | |
| **LINCOLNSHIRE** | | | | | | | | | | | | | | | | |
| ALEXANDER TECHNIQUE (HM00550) | | | | | | | | | | | | | | | | |
| BARN HOUSE PHYSIO CLINIC (HM01726) | | | | | | | | | | | | | | | | |
| BEVERLEYS (HM02246) | | | | | | | | | | | | | | ● | | |
| BRANSON, H J L (HM02920) | | | | | | | | | | | | | | | | |
| BROAD STREET PRACTICE (HM03107) | | | | | | | | | | | | | | | | |

# O - Z Therapies at Practices/Businesses

| Business by County with Reference no. | Orthotics | Osteomyology | Osteopathy | PAM | Paranormal Therapies | Pattern Therapies | Physiotherapy | Phytotherapy | Pilates | Podiatry | Polarity Therapy | Postural Integration | Primal Therapy | Psionic Therapy | Psychotherapy | Pyramid Power | Pyscho-Synthesis | Reflexology | Reichian Therapy | Reiki | Remedial Massage | Rogerian Therapy | Rolfing | Seichem | Sensitivity Training | Shiatsu | Silva Method | Sound Therapy | Spiritual Healing | Sports Massage | Stress Therapy | Swedish Body Massage | T'ai-Chi Ch'uan | Tantra Therapy | Tera-Mai | Thought Field Therapy | Touch Therapy | Transactional Analysis | Tui-na | Ultrasonics | Vibrational Therapy | Visualisation Therapy | Vitamin Therapy | Voice Therapy | X-Ray | Ying & Yang | Yoga | Zen Therapy | Zero Balancing |
|---|---|---|---|---|---|---|---|---|---|---|---|---|---|---|---|---|---|---|---|---|---|---|---|---|---|---|---|---|---|---|---|---|---|---|---|---|---|---|---|---|---|---|---|---|---|---|---|---|---|
| CASTLEGATE OSTEO PRACTICE (HM03847) | | |●| | | | | | | | | | | | | | | | | | | | | | | | | | | | | | | | | | | | | | | | | | | | | | |
| CHIEN ACUPUNCTURE CLINIC (HM04161) | | | | | | |●| | | | | | | | | | | | | | | | | | | | | | | | | | | | | | | | | | | | | | | | | | |
| CLINIC OF NATURAL MEDICINE (HM04703) | | |●| | | | | | | | | | | | | | | | | | | | | | | | | | | | | | | | | | | | | |●| | | | | | | | |
| COMPLEMENTARY THERAPY CENTRE (HM04946) | | | | | | | | | | | | | | | | | | | |●| | | |●| | | | | | |●| | | |●| | | | | | | | | | | | | | |
| COXON CLINIC (HM05326) | | |●| | | | | | | | | | | | | | | | |●| | | | | | | | | | | | | | | | | | | | | | | | | | | | | |
| DEPARTMENT OF PSYCHOTHERAPY (HM06006) | | | | | | | | | | | | | | |●| | | | | | | | | | | | | | | | | | | | | | | | | | | | | | | | | | |
| GOOD HEALTHKEEPING (HM08241) | | | | | | | | | | | | | |●| | | |●| |●| |●| | | | | |●| | | | | | | | | | | | | | |●| | | |●| | |
| GRANTHAM PHYSIO PRACTICE (HM08394) | | | | | | |●| | | | | | | | | | | | | | | | | | | | | | | | | | | | | | | | | | | | | | | | | | |
| GREENS HEALTH FOODS (HM08494) | | | | | | | | | | | | | | | | | | | | | | | | | | | | | | | | | | | | | | | | | | |●| | | | | | |
| GRESHAM, CLARE (HM08537) | | | | | | | | | | | | | | | | | |●| | | | | | | | | | | | | | | | | | | | | | | | | | | | | | | |
| HALL, ALAN (HM08763) | | | | | | | | | | | | | | | | | |●| | | | | | | | | | | | | | | | | | | | | | | | | | | | | | | |
| HEART TO HEART (HM09443) | | | | |●| | | | | | | | | | | | | | |●| | | | | | | | |●| |●| | | | | | | | | | | | | | | | | | |
| HOBBS, J M (HM09855) | | |●| | | | | | | | | | | | | | | | | | | | | | | | | | | | | | | | | | | | | | | | | | | | | | |
| IRIS VON SASS-HYDE ART THRPY (HM10725) | | | | | | | | | | | | | | |●| | | | | | | | | | | | | | | | | | | | | | | | | | | | | | | | | | |
| JUST JILLS (HM11282) | | | | | | | | | | | | | | | | | |●| | | | | | | | | | | | | | | | | | | | | | | | | | | | | | | |
| MADDICK, ELAINE (HM12895) | | | | | | | | | | | | | | | | | |●| | | | | | | | | | | | | | | | | | | | | | | | | | | | | | | |
| MARK RIDDLE HYPNOTHERAPY (HM13108) | | | | | | | |●| | | | | | | | | | | | | | | | | | | | | | |●| | | | | | | | | | |●| |●| | | | | |
| MASON, W J (HM13253) | | |●| | | | | | | | | | | | | | | | | | | | | | | | | | | | | | | | | | | | | | | | | | | | | | |
| MORLEY-KIRK, JOHN (HM14187) | | | | | | | | | | | | | | | | | |●| | | | | | | | | | | | | | | | | | | | | | | | | | | | | | | |
| MOURTON, JEAN (HM14299) | | | | | | | | | | | | | | | | | |●| | | | | | | | | | | | | | | | | | | | | | | | | | | | | | | |
| NEWLAND CHIROPRACTIC CLINIC (HM14866) | | | | | | | | | | | | | | | | | | | | | | | | | | | | | | | | | | | | | | | | | | | | |●| | | | |
| OSTEOPATHIC CLINIC (HM15460) | | |●| | | | | | | | | | | | | | | | | | | | | | | | | | | | | | | | | | | | | | | | | | | | | | |
| REFLEXOLOGY CLINIC (HM17084) | | | | | | | | | | | | | | | | | |●| |●| | | | | | | | | | | | | | | | | | | | | | | | | | | | | |
| REMEDIES (HM17176) | | | | | | | | | | | | | | | | | | | | |●| | | | | | | | | | | | | | | | | | | | | | | | | | | | |
| ROBINSON, ANN (HM17460) | | | | | | | | | | | | | | | | | |●| | | | | | | | | | | | | | | | | | | | | | | | | | | | | | | |
| SALON, JANIES (HM17863) | | | | | | | | | | | | | | | | | |●| |●| | | | | | | | | | | | | | | | | | | | | | | | | | | | | |
| SPALDING OSTEOPATHIC CLINIC (HM18954) | | |●| | | | | | | | | | | | | | | | | | | | | | | | | | | | | | | | | | | | | | | | | | | | | | |
| STELLA ARDEN ASSOCIATES (HM19191) | | |●| | | | | | | | | | | | | | | | | | | | | | | | | | | | | | | | | | | | | | | | | | | | | | |
| STYAN, JENNY (HM19456) | | | | | | | | | | | | | | | | | |●| | | | | | | | | | | | | | | | | | | | | | | | | | | | | | | |
| TOUCHLINE THERAPIES (HM20190) | | | | | | | | | | | | | | | | | |●| |●| | | | | |●| | | | | | | | | | | | | | | | | | | | | | | |
| WALTON, S K (HM20886) | | |●| | | | | | | | | | | | | | | | | | | | | | | | | | | | | | | | | | | | | | | | | | | | | | |
| WEST PARADE OSTEOPATHS (HM21233) | | |●| | | | | | | | | | | | | | | | | | | | | | | | | | | | | | | | | | | | | | | | | | | | | | |
| WHITE, HEATHER (HM21357) | | | | | | | | | | | | | | |●| | | | | | | | | | | | | | | |●| | | | | | | | | | |●| | | | | | | |
| WINTERTON, SUZANNE (HM21725) | | | | | | | | | | | | | | | | | | | | | | | | | | | | |●| | | | | | | | | | | | | | | | | | | | |

# O - Z Therapies at Practices/Businesses

| Business by County with Reference no. | Orthotics | Osteomyology | Osteopathy | PAM | Paranormal Therapies | Pattern Therapies | Physiotherapy | Phytotherapy | Pilates | Podiatry | Polarity Therapy | Postural Integration | Primal Therapy | Psionic Therapy | Psychotherapy | Pyramid Power | Pyscho-Synthesis | Reflexology | Reichian Therapy | Reiki | Remedial Massage | Rogerian Therapy | Rolfing | Seichem | Sensitivity Training | Shiatsu | Silva Method | Sound Therapy | Spiritual Healing | Sports Massage | Stress Therapy | Swedish Body Massage | T'ai-Chi Ch'uan | Tantra Therapy | Tera-Mai | Thought Field Therapy | Touch Therapy | Transactional Analysis | Tui-na | Ultrasonics | Vibrational Therapy | Visualisation Therapy | Vitamin Therapy | Voice Therapy | X-Ray | Ying & Yang | Yoga | Zen Therapy | Zero Balancing |
|---|---|---|---|---|---|---|---|---|---|---|---|---|---|---|---|---|---|---|---|---|---|---|---|---|---|---|---|---|---|---|---|---|---|---|---|---|---|---|---|---|---|---|---|---|---|---|---|---|---|
| LONDON | | | | | | | | | | | | | | | | | | | | | | | | | | | | | | | | | | | | | | | | | | | | | | | | | |
| HARLEY STREET COMP MEDICINE (HM09001) | | | | | | | | | | | | | | | | | | ● | | ● | | | | | | | | | | | | | | | | | | | | | | | | | | | | | |
| LONDON (GREATER) | | | | | | | | | | | | | | | | | | | | | | | | | | | | | | | | | | | | | | | | | | | | | | | | | |
| 1ST ALTERNATIVE HEALTH CENTRE (HM00002) | | | ● | | | | | | | | | | | | ● | | | | | | | | | | | ● | | | | | | | | | | | | | | | | | | | | | | | |
| A2Z COUNSELLING (HM00054) | | | | | | | | | | | | | | | | | | | | | | | | | | | | | ● | | | | | | | ● | | | | | | | | | | | | | |
| AARON ACUPUNCTURE & OSTEOPATHY (HM00063) | | | ● | | | | | | | | | | | | | | | | | | | | | | | | | | | | | | | | | | | | | | | | | | | | | | |
| ABBEY CENTRE (HM00071) | | | | | | | ● | | | | | | | | ● | | | | | | | | | | | | | | | | ● | | | | | | | | | | | | | | | | | | |
| ABIGAIL'S (HM00126) | | | | | | | | | | | | | | | | | | ● | | | | | | | | | | | | | | | | | | | | | | | | | | | | | | | |
| ABRAHAMS & BENNETT (HM00132) | | | ● | | | | | | | | | | | | | | | | | | | | | | | | | | | | | | | | | | | | | | | | | | | | | | |
| ABRAHAMS & BENNETT (HM00133) | | | ● | | | | | | | | | | | | | | | | | | | | | | | | | | | | | | | | | | | | | | | | | | | | | | |
| ACTIVE BALANCE CLINIC (HM00188) | | | ● | | | | | | | | | | | | | | | | | | | | | | | | | | | | | | | | | | | | | | | | | | | | | | |
| ACTIVE BALANCE CLINIC (HM00190) | | | ● | | | | | | | | | | | | | | | | | | | | | | | | | | | | | | | | | | | | | | | | | | | | | | |
| ACTON PRACTICE (HM00206) | | | ● | | | | | | | | | | | | | | | | | | | | | | | | | | | | | | | | | | | | | | | | | | | | | | |
| ACUMEDIC (HM00217) | | | | | | | | | | | | | | | | | | | | | | | | | | | | | | | | | ● | | | | | | | | | | | | | | | | |
| ACUPUNCTURE CLINIC (HM00287) | | | | | | | | | | | | | | | | | | | | ● | | | | | | | | | | | | | | | | | | | | | | | | | | ● | | | |
| ADATIA, K H (DR) (HM00367) | | | | | | | ● | | | | | | | | | | | | | | | | | | | | | | | | | | | | | | | | | | | | | | | | | | |
| ADEGOKE, ROTIMI (HM00376) | | | ● | | | | | | | | | | | | | | | | | | | | | | | | | | | | | | | | | | | | | | | | | | | | | | |
| AGIUS, ANTHONY JOSEPH (HM00421) | | | ● | | | | | | | | | | | | | | | | | | | | | | | | | | | | | | | | | | | | | | | | | | | | | | |
| AJANTA CENTRE (HM00455) | | | | | | | | | | | | | | | ● | | | | | | | | | | | | | | | | | | | | | | | | | | | | | | | | | | |
| ALLEN, WENDY (HM00623) | | | ● | | | | | | | | | | | | | | | | | | | | | | | | | | | | | | | | | | | | | | | | | | | | | | |
| ALLIANCE OF PSYCHOTHERAPISTS (HM00644) | | | | | | | | | | | | | | | ● | | | | | | | | | | | | | | | | | | | | | | | | | | | | | | | | | | |
| ALTERNATIVE THERAPIES CENTRE (HM00728) | | | ● | | | | | | | | | | | | ● | | ● | ● | | ● | | | | | | ● | | | | | ● | | | | | | ● | | | | | | | | | | | ● | |
| ALTERNATIVES COMP THERAPY CTRE (HM00743) | | | ● | | | | | | | | | | | | ● | | | ● | | ● | | | | | | ● | | | | | ● | | | | | | | | | | | | ● | | | | | | |
| ALTINA, R J (HM00746) | | | ● | | | | | | | | | | | | | | | | | | | | | | | | | | | | | | | | | | | | | | | | | | | | | | |
| AMANN OSTEOPATHIC CLINIC (HM00761) | | | ● | | | | | | | | | | | | | | | | | | | | | | | | | | | | | | | | | | | | | | | | | | | | | | |
| ANDERSON, J (HM00824) | | | | | | | | | | | | | | | ● | | | | | | | | | | | | | | | | | | | | | | | | | | | | | | | | | | |
| ANDERSON, LOUISE (HM00833) | | | | | | | | | | | | | | | | | | ● | | | | | | | | | | | | | | | | | | | | | | | | | | | | | | | |
| ANGEL HEART CENTRE (HM00867) | | | | | | | | | | | | | | | | | | | | ● | | | | | | | | | | | ● | | | | | | | | | | | | | | | | | | |
| ANGEL, LESLEY (HM00871) | | | | | | | | | | | | | | | | | | ● | | | | | | | | | | | | | | | | | | | | | | | | | | | | | | | |
| ANNE WRIGHT & LARA SEYMOUR (HM00903) | | | ● | | | | | | | | | | | | | | | | | | | | | | | | | | | | | | | | | | | | | | | | | | | | | | |
| AP CLINIC OF PHYSICAL MEDICINE (HM00927) | | | ● | | | | | | | | | | | | | | | | | | | | | | | | | | | | | | | | | | | | | | | | | | | | | | |
| ARBOURS ASSOCIATION (HM00966) | | | | | | | | | | | | | | | ● | | | | | | | | | | | | | | | | | | | | | | | | | | | | | | | | | | |
| ARBOURS CRISIS CENTRE (HM00967) | | | | | | | | | | | | | | | ● | | | | | | | | | | | | | | | | | | | | | | | | | | | | | | | | | | |
| ARCHER, SARAH (HM00979) | | | | | | | | | | | | | | | | | | ● | | | | | | | | | | | | | | | | | | | | | | | | | | | | | | | |

# O - Z Therapies at Practices/Businesses

| Business by County with Reference no. | Orthotics | Osteomyology | Osteopathy | PAM | Paranormal Therapies | Pattern Therapies | Physiotherapy | Phytotherapy | Pilates | Podiatry | Polarity Therapy | Postural Integration | Primal Therapy | Psionic Therapy | Psychotherapy | Pyramid Power | Pyscho-Synthesis | Reflexology | Reichian Therapy | Reiki | Remedial Massage | Rogerian Therapy | Rolfing | Seichem | Sensitivity Training |
|---|---|---|---|---|---|---|---|---|---|---|---|---|---|---|---|---|---|---|---|---|---|---|---|---|---|
| ARCHIBALD, VALERIE (HM00981) | | | | | | | | | | | | | | | | | |●| | | | | | | |
| ARMITAGE, PETER (HM01013) | | |●| | | | | | | | | | | | | | | | | | | | | | |
| ARMSTRONG, EVELYN (HM01022) | | | | | | | | | | | | | | | | | |●| | | | | | | |
| ARMSTRONG, JOHN (HM01024) | | |●| | | | | | | | | | | | | | | | | | | | | | |
| ASCLEPION (HM01176) | | | | | | | | | | | | | | |●| | | | | | | | | | |
| ASHLEY, CLIVE (HM01225) | | |●| | | | | | | | | | | | | | | | | | | | | | |
| ASHWIN STREET PRACTICE (HM01247) | | | | | | | | | | | | | | |●| | | | | | | | | | |
| ASS FOR GROUP & IND PSYCHO (HM01259) | | | | | | | | | | | | | | |●| | | | | | | | | | |
| ASS OF IND PSYCHOTHERAPISTS (HM01263) | | | | | | | | | | | | | | |●| | | | | | | | | | |
| ASS OF WOMEN PSYCHOTHERAPISTS (HM01265) | | | | | | | | | | | | | | |●| | | | | | | | | | |
| ASSOCIATION OF CHILD PSYCHO (HM01281) | | | | | | | | | | | | | | |●| | | | | | | | | | |
| ATKINSON, SOPHIE (HM01327) | | | | | | | | | | | | | | | | | |●| | | | | | | |
| AUDSLEY, ADRIAN (HM01347) | | | | | | | | | | | | | | | | | |●| | | | | | | |
| AVATAR (HM01384) | | | | | | | | | | | | | | | | | |●| | | | | | | |
| AVENUE PSYCHOTHERAPY SERVICES (HM01391) | | | | | | | | | | | | | | |●| | | | | | | | | | |
| AYURVED HERBELI (HM01442) | | | | | | | | | | | | | | | | | | | | | | | | | |
| BACK PAIN & SPORTS INJURIES (HM01492) | | |●| | | | | | | | | | | | | | | | | | | | | | |
| BACK PAIN CENTRE (HM01497) | | |●| | | | | | | | | | | | | | | | | | | | | | |
| BACK PAIN CENTRE (HM01498) | | |●| | | | | | | | | | | | | | | | | | | | | | |
| BALDWIN, BERNADETTE (HM01612) | | | | | | | | | | | | | | | | | |●| | | | | | | |
| BALL, SANDRA (HM01631) | | | | | | | | | | | | | | | | | |●| | | | | | | |
| BANSAL, SATPAL (HM01677) | | |●| | | | | | | | | | | | | | | | | | | | | | |
| BARBICAN CENTRE (HM01693) | | | | | | | | | |●| | | | | | | | | | | | | | | |
| BARKER, JOHN (HM01710) | | |●| | | | | | | | | | | | | | | | | | | | | | |
| BARNARD-HADLEY, JEAN (HM01734) | | |●| | | | | | | | | | | | | | | | | | | | | | |
| BARNES CHIROPRACTIC HEALTHCARE (HM01740) | | | | | | | | | | | | | | | | | | | | | | | | | |
| BARNETT, RUTH (HM01759) | | | | | | | | | | | | | | |●| | | | | | | | | | |
| BARNETT, SAMANTHA (HM01760) | | | | | | | | | | | | | | | | | |●| | | | | | | |
| BARRETT, CARMEL (HM01787) | | | | | | | | | | | | | | | | | |●| | | | | | | |
| BARRIE, ALEXANDER (HM01798) | | | | | | | | | | | |●| | | | | | | | | | | | | |
| BARTHROPP, VICTORIA (HM01819) | | | | | | | | | | | | | | | | | |●| | | | | | | |
| BASCOMBE, K E (HM01840) | | |●| | | | | | | | | | | | | | | | | | | | | | |
| BEACH, P J (HM01949) | | |●| | | | | | | | | | | | | | | | | | | | | | |
| BEAVER, STEPHEN (HM02009) | | |●| | | | | | | | | | | | | | | | | | | | | | |

| Business by County with Reference no. | Shiatsu | Silva Method | Sound Therapy | Spiritual Healing | Sports Massage | Stress Therapy | Swedish Body Massage | T'ai-Chi Ch'uan | Tantra Therapy | Tera-Mai | Thought Field Therapy | Touch Therapy | Transactional Analysis | Tui-na | Ultrasonics | Vibrational Therapy | Visualisation Therapy | Vitamin Therapy | Voice Therapy | X-Ray | Ying & Yang | Yoga | Zen Therapy | Zero Balancing |
|---|---|---|---|---|---|---|---|---|---|---|---|---|---|---|---|---|---|---|---|---|---|---|---|---|
| ARCHIBALD, VALERIE (HM00981) | | | | | | | | | | | | | | | | | | | | | | | | |
| ARMITAGE, PETER (HM01013) | | | | | | | | | | | | | | | | | | | | | | | | |
| ARMSTRONG, EVELYN (HM01022) | | | | | | | | | | | | | | | | | | | | | | | | |
| ARMSTRONG, JOHN (HM01024) | | | | | | | | | | | | | | | | | | | | | | | | |
| ASCLEPION (HM01176) | | | | | | | | | | | | | | | | | | | | | | | | |
| ASHLEY, CLIVE (HM01225) | | | | | | | | | | | | | | | | | | | | | | | | |
| ASHWIN STREET PRACTICE (HM01247) | | | | | | | | | | | | | | | | | | | | | | | | |
| ASS FOR GROUP & IND PSYCHO (HM01259) | | | | | | | | | | | | | | | | | | | | | | | | |
| ASS OF IND PSYCHOTHERAPISTS (HM01263) | | | | | | | | | | | | | | | | | | | | | | | | |
| ASS OF WOMEN PSYCHOTHERAPISTS (HM01265) | | | | | | | | | | | | | | | | | | | | | | | | |
| ASSOCIATION OF CHILD PSYCHO (HM01281) | | | | | | | | | | | | | | | | | | | | | | | | |
| ATKINSON, SOPHIE (HM01327) | | | | | | | | | | | | | | | | | | | | | | | | |
| AUDSLEY, ADRIAN (HM01347) | | | | | | | | | | | | | | | | | | | | | | | | |
| AVATAR (HM01384) | | | | | | | | | | | | | | | | | | | | | | | | |
| AVENUE PSYCHOTHERAPY SERVICES (HM01391) | | | | | | | | | | | | | | | | | | | | | | | | |
| AYURVED HERBELI (HM01442) | | | | | | | | | | | | | | | | | | | | | |●| | |
| BACK PAIN & SPORTS INJURIES (HM01492) | | | | | | | | | | | | | | | | | | | | | | | | |
| BACK PAIN CENTRE (HM01497) | | | | | | | | | | | | | | | | | | | | | | | | |
| BACK PAIN CENTRE (HM01498) | | | | | | | | | | | | | | | | | | | | | | | | |
| BALDWIN, BERNADETTE (HM01612) | | | | | | | | | | | | | | | | | | | | | | | | |
| BALL, SANDRA (HM01631) | | | | | | | | | | | | | | | | | | | | | | | | |
| BANSAL, SATPAL (HM01677) | | | | | | | | | | | | | | | | | | | | | | | | |
| BARBICAN CENTRE (HM01693) | | | | | | | | | | | | | | | | | | | | | | | | |
| BARKER, JOHN (HM01710) | | | | | | | | | | | | | | | | | | | | | | | | |
| BARNARD-HADLEY, JEAN (HM01734) | | | | | | | | | | | | | | | | | | | | | | | | |
| BARNES CHIROPRACTIC HEALTHCARE (HM01740) | | | | | | | | | | | | | | | | | | | |●| | | | |
| BARNETT, RUTH (HM01759) | | | | | | | | | | | | | | | | | | | | | | | | |
| BARNETT, SAMANTHA (HM01760) | | | | | | | | | | | | | | | | | | | | | | | | |
| BARRETT, CARMEL (HM01787) | | | | | | | | | | | | | | | | | | | | | | | | |
| BARRIE, ALEXANDER (HM01798) |●| | | | |●| | | | | | | | | | | | | | | |●| | |
| BARTHROPP, VICTORIA (HM01819) | | | | | | | | | | | | | | | | | | | | | | | | |
| BASCOMBE, K E (HM01840) | | | | | | | | | | | | | | | | | | | | | | | | |
| BEACH, P J (HM01949) | | | | | | | | | | | | | | | | | | | | | | | | |
| BEAVER, STEPHEN (HM02009) | | | | | | | | | | | | | | | | | | | | | | | | |

# O - Z Therapies at Practices/Businesses

| Business by County with Reference no. | Orthotics | Osteomyology | Osteopathy | PAM | Paranormal Therapies | Pattern Therapies | Physiotherapy | Phytotherapy | Pilates | Podiatry | Polarity Therapy | Postural Integration | Primal Therapy | Psionic Therapy | Psychotherapy | Pyramid Power | Pyscho-Synthesis | Reflexology | Reichian Therapy | Reiki | Remedial Massage | Rogerian Therapy | Rolfing | Seichem | Sensitivity Training | Shiatsu | Silva Method | Sound Therapy | Spiritual Healing | Sports Massage | Stress Therapy | Swedish Body Massage | T'ai-Chi Ch'uan | Tantra Therapy | Tera-Mai | Thought Field Therapy | Touch Therapy | Transactional Analysis | Tui-na | Ultrasonics | Vibrational Therapy | Visualisation Therapy | Vitamin Therapy | Voice Therapy | X-Ray | Ying & Yang | Yoga | Zen Therapy | Zero Balancing |
|---|---|---|---|---|---|---|---|---|---|---|---|---|---|---|---|---|---|---|---|---|---|---|---|---|---|---|---|---|---|---|---|---|---|---|---|---|---|---|---|---|---|---|---|---|---|---|---|---|
| BECKER, AMELY (HM02021) | | | | | | | | | | | | | | | ● | | | | | | | | | | | | | | | | | | | | | | | | | | | | | | | | | | |
| BEDINGFELD, ANN (HM02044) | | | | | | | | | | | | | | | | | | ● | | | | | | | | | | | | | | | | | | | | | | | | | | | | | | | |
| BEHAVIORAL PSYCHOTHERAPY SVS (HM02065) | | | | | | | | | | | | | | | ● | | | | | | | | | | | | | | | | | | | | | | | | | | | | | | | | | | |
| BELL, LIZ (HM02084) | | | | | | | | | | | | | | | | | | ● | | | | | | | | | | | | | | | | | | | | | | | | | | | | | | | |
| BELLISSIMA (HM02103) | | | | | | | | | | | | | | | | | | ● | | | | | | | | | | | | | | | | | | | | | | | | | | | | | | | |
| BELMONT PHYSIOTHERAPY PRACTICE (HM02108) | | | | | | | ● | | | | | | | | | | | | | | | | | | | | | | | | | | | | | | | | | | | | | | | | | | |
| BENNETT, A (HM02136) | | | ● | | | | | | | | | | | | | | | | | | | | | | | | | | | | | | | | | | | | | | | | | | | | | | |
| BERKE, JOSEPH (HM02191) | | | | | | | | | | | | | | | ● | | | | | | | | | | | | | | | | | | | | | | | | | | | | | | | | | | |
| BERNSTEIN, SAMUEL (HM02204) | | | | | | | | | | | | | | | ● | | | | | | | | | | | | | | | | ● | | | | | | | | | | | ● | | | | | | | |
| BEST, JOHN G E (HM02224) | | | ● | | | | | | | | | | | | | | | | | | | | | | | | | | | | | | | | | | | | | | | | | | | | | | |
| BIRCH, MARGARET (HM02352) | | | | | | | | | | | | | | | | | | ● | | | | | | | | | | | | | | | | | | | | | | | | | | | | | | | |
| BIRD, IAN M (HM02364) | | | ● | | | | | | | | | | | | | | | | | | | | | | | | | | | | | | | | | | | | | | | | | | | | | | |
| BIRD, J K (HM02366) | | | ● | | | | | | | | | | | | | | | | | | | | | | | | | | | | | | | | | | | | | | | | | | | | | | |
| BISDÉE, EMMA (HM02402) | | | | | | | | | | | | | | | | | | ● | | | | | | | | | | | | | | | | | | | | | | | | | | | | | | | |
| BLACKHEATH & BROCKLEY (HM02446) | | | | | | | | | | | | | | | ● | | | | | | | | | | | | | | | | | | | | | | | | | | | | | | | | | | |
| BLISS (HM02507) | | | | | | | | | | | | | | | ● | | | | | | | | | | | | | | | | ● | | | | | | | | | | | | | | | | | | |
| BLOMFIELD, VAL (HM02513) | | | | | | | | | | | | | | | ● | | | | | | | | | | | | | | | | | | | | | | | | | | | | | | | | | | |
| BLOOMSBURY ALEXANDER CENTRE (HM02516) | | | | | | | | | | | | ● | | | ● | | | ● | | | | | | | | | | | | | | | | | | | | | | | | | | | | | | | |
| BLOOMSBURY CLINIC (HM02517) | | | ● | | | | | | | | | | | | | | | | | | | | | | | | | | | | | | | | | | | | | | | | | | | | | | |
| BODY & SOLE REFLEXOLOGY (HM02559) | | | | | | | | | | | | | | | | | | ● | | | | | | | | | | | | | | | | | | | | | | | | | | | | | | | |
| BODY CONTROL STUDIOS (HM02583) | | | | | | | | | ● | | | | | | | | | | | | | | | | | | | | | | | | | | | | | | | | | | | | | | | | |
| BODYCENTRE (HM02616) | | | ● | | | | | | | | | | | | | | | | | | | | | | | | | | | | | | | | | | | | | | | | | | | | | | |
| BODYSPACE (HM02632) | | | | | | | | | | | | | | | ● | | | | | | | | | | | | | | | | | | | | | | | | | | | | | | | | | | |
| BOND, LESLEY (HM02671) | | | | | | | | | | | | | | | ● | | | | | | | | | | | | | | | | | | | | | | | | | | | | | | | | | | |
| BOOTH, JUDY (HM02703) | | | | | | | | | | | | | | | | | | ● | | | ● | | | | | | | | | | | | | | | | | | | | | | | | | | | | |
| BOSTON CHIROPODY CLINIC (HM02725) | | | | | | | | | | ● | | | | | | | | | | | | | | | | | | | | | | | | | | | | | | | | | | | | | | | |
| BOSTON, SANDY (HM02727) | | | | | | | | | | | | | | | | | | ● | | | | | | | | | | | | | | | | | | | | | | | | | | | | | | | |
| BOWLES, LESLEY-ANN (HM02797) | | | | | | | | | | | | | | | | | | ● | | | | | | | | | | | | | | | | | | | | | | | | | | | | | | | |
| BOWYER, MO (HM02808) | | | | | | | | | | | | | | | | | | ● | | | | | | | | | | | | | | | | | | | | | | | | | | | | | | | |
| BRACKENBURY NTRL HEALTH CLNC (HM02837) | | | ● | | | | | | | ● | | | | | ● | | | ● | | ● | | | | | | ● | | | | | | | | | | | | | | | | | | | | | | | |
| BRANDON, NICHOLAS (HM02914) | | | | | | | | | | | | | | | | | | | | | | | | | | | | | | | | | | | | | | | | | | | | | | | ● | | |
| BRENNAN, STANLEY (HM02959) | | | | | | | | | | | | | | | ● | | | | | | | | | | | | | | | | | | | | | | | | | | | | | | | | | | |
| BRESSEY OSTEOPATHIC CLINIC (HM02968) | | | ● | | | | | | | | | | | | | | | | | | | | | | | | | | | | | | | | | | | | | | | | | | | | | | |
| BRIDGE PSYCHOTHERAPY (HM02994) | | | | | | | | | | | | | | | ● | | | | | | | | | | | | | | | | | | | | | | | | | | | | | | | | | | |

# O - Z Therapies at Practices/Businesses

Business by County with Reference no.

| Business | Orthotics | Osteomyology | Osteopathy | PAM | Paranormal Therapies | Pattern Therapies | Physiotherapy | Phytotherapy | Pilates | Podiatry | Polarity Therapy | Postural Integration | Primal Therapy | Psionic Therapy | Psychotherapy | Pyramid Power | Pyscho-Synthesis | Reflexology | Reichian Therapy | Reiki | Remedial Massage | Rogerian Therapy | Rolfing | Seichem | Sensitivity Training | Shiatsu | Silva Method | Sound Therapy | Spiritual Healing | Sports Massage | Stress Therapy | Swedish Body Massage | T'ai-Chi Ch'uan | Tantra Therapy | Tera-Mai | Thought Field Therapy | Touch Therapy | Transactional Analysis | Tui-na | Ultrasonics | Vibrational Therapy | Visualisation Therapy | Vitamin Therapy | Voice Therapy | X-Ray | Ying & Yang | Yoga | Zen Therapy | Zero Balancing |
|---|---|---|---|---|---|---|---|---|---|---|---|---|---|---|---|---|---|---|---|---|---|---|---|---|---|---|---|---|---|---|---|---|---|---|---|---|---|---|---|---|---|---|---|---|---|---|---|---|---|
| BRIDGMONT, NICHOLAS (HM03013) | | | | | | | | | | | | | | | | | | ● | | | | | | | | | | | | | | | | | | | | | | | | | | | | | | | |
| BRITISH ASS OF GROUP PSYCHO (HM03073) | | | | | | | | | | | | | | | ● | | | | | | | | | | | | | | | | | | | | | | | | | | | | | | | | | | |
| BRITISH AUTOGENIC SOCIETY (HM03076) | | | | | | | | | | | | | | | ● | | | | | | | | | | | | | | | | ● | | | | | | | | | | | | | | | | | | |
| BRITISH COLLEGE-NATURO & OSTEO (HM03079) | | | ● | | | | | | | | | | | | | | | | | | | | | | | | | | | | | | | | | | | | | | | | | | | | | | |
| BRITISH CONFEDERATION-PSYCHO (HM03080) | | | | | | | | | | | | | | | ● | | | | | | | | | | | | | | | | | | | | | | | | | | | | | | | | | | |
| BRITISH HYPNOTHERAPY ASS (HM03084) | | | | | | | | | | | | | | | ● | | | | | | | | | | | | | | | | | | | | | | | | | | | | | | | | | | |
| BRIXTON TAI CHI (HM03106) | | | | | | | | | | | | | | | | | | | | | | | | | | | | | | | | | ● | | | | | | | | | | | | | | | | |
| BROEKHOFF, MARIA (HM03137) | | | | | | | | | | | | | | | | | | ● | | | | | | | | | | | | | | | | | | | | | | | | | | | | | | | |
| BROOK GREEN OSTEOPATHY (HM03155) | | | ● | | | | | | | | | | | | | | | | | | | | | | | | | | | | | | | | | | | | | | | | | | | | | | |
| BROOKS, CATHY (HM03175) | | | | | | | | | | | | | | | | | | | | ● | | | | | | | | | | | | | | | | | | | | | | | | | | | | | |
| BROOKS, JANE (HM03177) | | | | | | | | | | | | | | | ● | | | | | | | ● | | | | | | | ● | | ● | | | | | | | | | | | | | | | | | | |
| BROWN, ALISON R (HM03210) | | | ● | | | | | | | | | | | | | | | | | | | | | | | | | | | | | | | | | | | | | | | | | | | | | | |
| BRUGGEMEYER'S (HM03276) | | | ● | | | | | | | | | | | | | | | | | | | | | | | | | | | | | | | | | | | | | | | | | | | | | | |
| BUCHANAN, ANGELA (HM03300) | | | | | | | | ● | | | | | | | | | | | | | | | | | | | | | | | | | | | | | | | | ● | | | | | | | | | |
| BUCKLAND, CAROLINE (HM03313) | | | | | | | | | | | | | | | | | | ● | | | | | | | | | | | | | | | | | | | | | | | | | | | | | | | |
| BUCKLEY, BILLIE (HM03318) | | | | | | | | | | | | | | | ● | | | | | | | | | | | | | | | | ● | | | | | | | | | | | | | | | | | | |
| BUDD, CHRISTINE (HM03322) | | | ● | | | | | | | | | | | | | | | | | | | | | | | | | | | | | | | | | | | | | | | | | | | | | | |
| BUDDEN, CLARE (HM03328) | | | | | | | | | | | | | | | | | | ● | | | | | | | | | | | | | | | | | | | | | | | | | | | | | | | |
| BUILDING FUTURES (HM03335) | | | | | | | | | | | | | | | ● | | | | | | | | | | | | | | | | | | | | | | | | | | | | | | | | | | |
| BURFORD, DOMINIQUE (HM03372) | | | | | | | | | | | | | | | | | | ● | | | | | | | | | | | | | | | | | | | | | | | | | | | | | | | |
| BURGESS, DAVINA (HM03376) | | | | | | | | | | | | | | | | | | ● | | | | | | | | | | | | | | | | | | | | | | | | | | | | | | | |
| BURNS, ALEX (HM03411) | | | | | | | | | | | | | | | ● | | | | | | | | | | | | | | | | | | | | | | | | | | | | | | | | | | |
| BURY, D R (HM03455) | | | | | | | | | | | | | | | ● | | | | | | | | | | | | | | | | | | | | | | | | | | | | | | | | | | |
| BYRNE, JUDY (HM03516) | | | | | | | | | | | | | | | ● | | | | | | | | | | | | | | | | | | | | | | | | | | | | | | | | | | |
| CAMDEN PSYCHOTHERAPY UNIT (HM03579) | | | | | | | | | | | | | | | ● | | | | | | | | | | | | | | | | | | | | | | | | | | | | | | | | | | |
| CAMPBELL & ASSOCIATES (HM03591) | | | ● | | | | | | | | | | | | | | | | | | | | | | | | | | | | | | | | | | | | | | | | | | | | | | |
| CARTER, GERALD R (HM03779) | | | ● | | | | | | | | | | | | | | | | | | | | | | | | | | | | | | | | | | | | | | | | | | | | | | |
| CASSIDY MEDICAL CENTRE (HM03815) | | | ● | | | | | | | | | | | | | | | | | | | | | | | | | | | | | | | | | | | | | | | | | | | | | | |
| CASTLE ROAD OSTEO PRACTICE (HM03835) | | | ● | | | | | | | | | | | | | | | | | | | | | | | | | | | | | | | | | | | | | | | | | | | | | | |
| CENTRE FOR TRANSFORMATION (HM03920) | | | | | | | | | | | | | | | | | | | | ● | | | | | | | | | | | | | | | | | | | | | | | ● | | | | | | |
| CHAPMAN, A G (HM03997) | | | ● | | | | | | | | | | | | | | | | | | | | | | | | | | | | | | | | | | | | | | | | | | | | | | |
| CHAPMAN, RUPERT (HM04009) | | | ● | | | | | | | | | | | | | | | | | | | | | | | | | | | | | | | | | | | | | | | | | | | | | | |
| CHARTERHOUSE PHYSIOTHERAPY (HM04049) | | | | | | | ● | | | | | | | | | | | | | | | | | | | | | | | | | | | | | | | | | | | | | | | | | | |
| CHARTERHOUSE PHYSIOTHERAPY (HM04048) | | | | | | | ● | | | | | | | | | | | | | | | | | | | | | | | | | | | | | | | | | | | | | | | | | | |

# Angling Times

Includes contacts for 1800 tackle suppliers and over 1100 clubs and associations

# The Ultimate Guide to over 5,600 Freshwater Fisheries in the UK & Ireland

www.fishooked.com

Also known as fishooked
The UK & Irish Fisheries Directory

Publishing HCC
An HCC Next Generation Directory

# O - Z Therapies at Practices/Businesses

| Business by County with Reference no. | Orthotics | Osteomyology | Osteopathy | PAM | Paranormal Therapies | Pattern Therapies | Physiotherapy | Phytotherapy | Pilates | Podiatry | Polarity Therapy | Postural Integration | Primal Therapy | Psionic Therapy | Psychotherapy | Pyramid Power | Pyscho-Synthesis | Reflexology | Reichian Therapy | Reiki | Remedial Massage | Rogerian Therapy | Rolfing | Seichem | Sensitivity Training | Shiatsu | Silva Method | Sound Therapy | Spiritual Healing | Sports Massage | Stress Therapy | Swedish Body Massage | T'ai-Chi Ch'uan | Tantra Therapy | Tera-Mai | Thought Field Therapy | Touch Therapy | Transactional Analysis | Tui-na | Ultrasonics | Vibrational Therapy | Visualisation Therapy | Vitamin Therapy | Voice Therapy | X-Ray | Ying & Yang | Yoga | Zen Therapy | Zero Balancing |
|---|---|---|---|---|---|---|---|---|---|---|---|---|---|---|---|---|---|---|---|---|---|---|---|---|---|---|---|---|---|---|---|---|---|---|---|---|---|---|---|---|---|---|---|---|---|---|---|---|---|
| EDGWARE NATURAL HEALTH CENTRE (HM06604) |||●|||||||||||||||●||●|||||||||||●|||||||||||●|●|||||||
| EDGWARE PRACTICE (HM06605) |||●||||||||||||||||||||||||||||||||||||||||||||||
| EDWARDS, JOHN (HM06660) |||||||||||||||●||||||||||||||||||||||||||||||||||
| EGLINTON, DOMINIC (HM06686) |||●||||||||||||||||||||||||||||||||||||||||||||||
| EISENHAUER, G (HM06693) |||||||||||||||●||||||||||||||||||||||||||||||||||
| ELLWOOD, CAROLINE (HM06780) |||●||||||||||||||||||||||||||||||||||||||||||||||
| ELSON, M (HM06785) |||||||||||||||●||||||||||||||||||||||||||||||||||
| ELTHAM HYPNOTHERAPY ANALYSIS (HM06789) |||||||||||||||●|||||||||||||||||●|||||||●||||||||||||
| ENFIELD CLINIC OF HERBAL MED (HM06818) ||||||||●|||||||||||||||||||||||||||||||||||||||||||
| EQUILIBRIUM (HM06869) ||||||||||||||||||●||●||||||●||||||||||||||||||||||||
| EQUILIBRIUM COUNS/THRPY CTRE (HM06873) |||●||||||||||||●||||||||||||||||||||||||||||||||||
| EVANS, ELIZABETH (HM06969) ||||||||||||||||||●|||||||||||||||||||||||||||||||
| FAIR, ANNETTE (HM07048) |||●||||||||||||||||||||||||||||||||||||||||||||||
| FAITH, JAVAD (HM07070) |||●||||||||||||||||||||||||||||||||||||||||||||||
| FARMACIA URBAN HEALING (HM07107) |||●|||||||||||||||●||||||||●||||||●||||||||||||||||||
| FARQUHAR, KATE (HM07116) |||||||||||||||●||||||||||||||||||||||||||||||||||
| FENN, AILEEN (HM07215) |||●||||||||||||||||||||||||||||||||||||||||||||||
| FIELD END COMP HEALTH CLINIC (HM07258) |||●||||||||||||||||||||||||||||||||||||||||||||||
| FINLAYTER, LENNOX (HM07318) |||●||||||||||||||||||||||||||||||||||||||||||||||
| FLEXIBLE HOUR (HM07420) ||||||||||||||||||||||||||●|||||||●||||||||||||||||
| FLOAT WORKS (HM07424) ||||||||||||||||||||●||||||●|||||||●||||||||||||||||
| FOREST COMPLEMENTARY CLINIC (HM07545) |||●||||||||||||||||||||||||||||||||||||||||||||||
| FOREST-HYPNOPSYCHOTHERAPY (HM07551) |||||||||||||||●||||||||||||||||||||||||||||||||||
| FORSYTH, ELNA (HM07575) ||||||||||||||||||●|||||||||||||||||||||||||||||||
| FOX, SOPHIE LANE (HM07641) ||||||||||||||||||●|||||||||||||||||||||||||||||||
| FRANCOISE, JORDAN (HM07680) ||||||||||||||||||●|||||||||||||||||||||||||||||||
| FRASER, ELIZABETH (HM07694) ||||||||||||||||||●|||||||||||||||||||||||||||||||
| FRASER, HUGH ROSS (HM07698) |||||||||||||||●||||||||||||||||||||||||||||||||||
| FREEDMAN, SIMON (HM07713) |||●||||||||||||||||||||||||||||||||||||||||||||||
| FREEGARD, CHANTAL (HM07716) ||||||||||||||||||●|||||||||||||||||||||||||||||||
| FREEGROVE CENTRE (HM07717) |||||||||||||||●||||||||||||||||||||||||||||||||||
| FRENCH, EILEEN (DR) (HM07731) |||||||||||||||●||||||||||||||||||||||||||||||||||
| FRESHWATER, WILLIAM T (HM07739) |||||||||||||||●||||||||||||||||||||||||||||||||||
| FUDGE, JOHN (HM07778) |||●||||||||||||||||||||||||||||||||||||||||||||||

# O - Z Therapies at Practices/Businesses

| Business by County with Reference no. | Orthotics | Osteomyology | Osteopathy | PAM | Paranormal Therapies | Pattern Therapies | Physiotherapy | Phytotherapy | Pilates | Podiatry | Polarity Therapy | Postural Integration | Primal Therapy | Psionic Therapy | Psychotherapy | Pyramid Power | Pyscho-Synthesis | Reflexology | Reichian Therapy | Reiki | Remedial Massage | Rogerian Therapy | Rolfing | Seichem | Sensitivity Training | Shiatsu | Silva Method | Sound Therapy | Spiritual Healing | Sports Massage | Stress Therapy | Swedish Body Massage | T'ai-Chi Ch'uan | Tantra Therapy | Tera-Mai | Thought Field Therapy | Touch Therapy | Transactional Analysis | Tui-na | Ultrasonics | Vibrational Therapy | Visualisation Therapy | Vitamin Therapy | Voice Therapy | X-Ray | Ying & Yang | Yoga | Zen Therapy | Zero Balancing |
|---|---|---|---|---|---|---|---|---|---|---|---|---|---|---|---|---|---|---|---|---|---|---|---|---|---|---|---|---|---|---|---|---|---|---|---|---|---|---|---|---|---|---|---|---|---|---|---|---|---|
| FULHAM CLINIC (HM07781) | | | ● | | | | | | | | | | | | | | | ● | | | | | | | | ● | | | | | | | | | | | | | | | | | | | | | | | |
| FULHAM MEDICAL CENTRE (HM07782) | | | ● | | | | | | | | | | | | | | | | | | | | | | | | | | | | | | | | | | | | | | | | | | | | | | |
| FULHAM OSTEOPATHIC PRACTICE (HM07783) | | | ● | | | | ● | | | | | | | | | | | | | | | | | | | | | | | | | | | | | | | | | | | | | | | | | | |
| G T CONSULTANCY (HM07815) | | | | | | | | | | | | | | | ● | | | | | | | | | | | | | | | | ● | | | | | | | | | | | | | | | | | | |
| GABRIEL PROGRAMME (HM07820) | | | | | | | | | | | | | | | ● | | | | | | | | | | | | | | | | | | | | | | | | | | | | | | | | | | |
| GAITERO-ARROYO, CRISTINA (HM07834) | | | | | | | | | | | | | | | | | | ● | | | | | | | | | | | | | | | | | | | | | | | | | | | | | | | |
| GAJAHARSINGH, GERRY (HM07835) | | | ● | | | | | | | | | | | | | | | | | | | | | | | | | | | | | | | | | | | | | | | | | | | | | | |
| GALGUT, CORDELIA (HM07838) | | | | | | | | | | | | | | | ● | | | | | | | | | | | | | | | | | | | | | | | | | | | | | | | | | | |
| GEOFF PICK PSYCHOTHERAPY (HM07985) | | | | | | | | | | | | | | | ● | | | | | | | | | | | | | | | | | | | | | | | | | | | | | | | | | | |
| GESTALT CENTRE (HM08005) | | | | | | | | ● | | | | | | | | | | | | | | | | | | | | | | | | | | | | | | | | | | | | | | | | | |
| GESTALT CONSORTIUM (HM08006) | | | | | | | | | | | | | | | ● | | | | | | | | | | | | | | | | | | | | | | | | | | | | | | | | | | |
| GESTALT STUDIO (HM08009) | | | | | | | | | | | | | | | ● | | | | | | | | | | | | | | | | | | | | | | | | | | | | | | | | | | |
| GILBEY, BRIGETTE (HM08060) | | | ● | | | | | | | | | | | | | | | | | | | | | | | | | | | | | | | | | | | | | | | | | | | | | | |
| GILBEY, J (HM08061) | | | ● | | | | | | | | | | | | | | | | | | | | | | | | | | | | | | | | | | | | | | | | | | | | | | |
| GILES, KAY (HM08069) | | | | | | | | | | | | | | | | | | ● | | | | | | | | | | | | | | | | | | | | | | | | | | | | | | | |
| GILLY-CRUYSMANS, FABIENNE (HM08103) | | | | | | | | | | | | | | | | | | ● | | | | | | | | | | | | | | | | | | | | | | | | | | | | | | | |
| GOGIA, D R (DR) (HM08196) | | | ● | | | | | | | | | | | | | | | | | | | | | | | | | | | | | | | | | | | | | | | | | | | | | | |
| GOLDIE, L (DR) (HM08216) | | | | | | | | | | | | | | | ● | | | | | | | | | | | | | | | | | | | | | | | | | | | | | | | | | | |
| GOLDIE, SUSIE (HM08219) | | | | | | | | | | | | | | | | | | ● | | | | | | | | | | | | | | | | | | | | | | | | | | | | | | | |
| GOODMAN, JOSEPH & LINDA (HM08260) | | | ● | | | | | | | | | | | | | | | | | | | | | | | | | | | | | | | | | | | | | | | | | | | | | | |
| GOULD, JENNY (HM08317) | | | | | | | | | | | | | | | | | | ● | | | | | | | | | | | | | | | | | | | | | | | | | | | | | | | |
| GOWING, JOSIE (HM08326) | | | | | | | | | | | | | | | | | | ● | | | | | | | | | | | | | | | | | | | | | | | | | | | | | | | |
| GRAHAM, NIGEL (HM08354) | | | ● | | | | | | | | | | | | | | | | | | | | | | | | | | | | | | | | | | | | | | | | | | | | | | |
| GRAHAM, NIGEL (HM08355) | | | ● | | | | | | | | | | | | | | | | | | | | | | | | | | | | | | | | | | | | | | | | | | | | | | |
| GRANT, JANE (HM08380) | | | | | | | | | | | | | | | | | | ● | | | | | | | | | | | | | | | | | | | | | | | | | | | | | | | |
| GRANT, SUE (HM08389) | | | | | | | | | | | | | | | ● | | | | | | | | | | | | | | | | | | | | | | | | | | | | | | | | | | |
| GREEN PARK CLASSICAL OSTEOPATH (HM08439) | | | ● | | | | | | | | | | | | | | | | | | | | | | | | | | | | | | | | | | | | | | | | | | | | | | |
| GREEN, TRACEY (HM08477) | | | | | | | | | | | | | | | | | | ● | | | | | | | | | | | | | | | | | | | | | | | | | | | | | | | |
| GREENWICH NATURAL HEALTH CTRE (HM08500) | | | ● | | | | | | | | | | | | ● | | ● | ● | | ● | | | | | | ● | | | | | ● | | | | | | | | | | | | | | | | | | |
| GREGSON, NEIL R (HM08523) | | | ● | | | | | | | | | | | | | | | | | | | | | | | | | | | | | | | | | | | | | | | | | | | | | | |
| GROFSKI, JANE (HM08591) | | | | | | | | | | | | | | | | | | ● | | | | | | | | | | | | | | | | | | | | | | | | | | | | | | | |
| GROSS, A (HM08595) | | | ● | | | | | | | | | | | | | | | | | | | | | | | | | | | | | | | | | | | | | | | | | | | | | | |
| GROUP ANALYSIS-ROSENDALE (HM08603) | | | | | | | | | | | | | | | ● | | | | | | | | | | | | | | | | | | | | | | | | | | | | | | | | | | |
| GROUP ANALYTIC PRACTICE (HM08605) | | | | | | | | | | | | | | | ● | | | | | | | | | | | | | | | | | | | | | | | | | | | | | | | | | | |

# O - Z Therapies at Practices/Businesses

| Business by County with Reference no. | Orthotics | Osteomyology | Osteopathy | PAM | Paranormal Therapies | Pattern Therapies | Physiotherapy | Phytotherapy | Pilates | Podiatry | Polarity Therapy | Postural Integration | Primal Therapy | Psionic Therapy | Psychotherapy | Pyramid Power | Pyscho-Synthesis |
|---|---|---|---|---|---|---|---|---|---|---|---|---|---|---|---|---|---|
| GROWNEY, SHAUN (HM08618) | | | | | | | | | | | | | | | ● | | |
| GRUNDBERG, SIBYL (HM08620) | | | ● | | | | | | | | | | | | | | |
| GUERRINI, HEATHER (HM08622) | | | | | | | | | | | | | | | | | |
| GUILD OF PSYCHOTHERAPISTS (HM08628) | | | | | | | | | | | | | | | ● | | |
| GUNN, HARRY (HM08641) | | | ● | | | | | | | | | | | | | | |
| GUNTER, MARIGOLD (HM08646) | | | | | | | | | | | | | | | | | |
| GURNET, CATHERINE (HM08651) | | | | | | | | | | | | | | | | | |
| HACKNEY & ISLINGTON PSYCHO (HM08683) | | | | | | | | | | | | | | | ● | | |
| HACKNEY HYPNOTHERAPY (HM08685) | | | | | | | | | | | | | | | ● | | |
| HAIN, PATRICIA (HM08712) | | | | | | | | | | | | | | | | | |
| HAMILTON, FIONA (HM08843) | | | ● | | | | | | | | | | | | | | |
| HAMMETT, JANET (HM08864) | | | | | | | | | | | | | | | | | |
| HARBEN, PAM (HM08959) | | | | | | | | | | | | | | | | | |
| HARDY, THEA (HM08986) | | | ● | | | | | | | | | | | | | | |
| HAREWOOD, MARCIA M (HM08991) | | | ● | | | | | | | | | | | | | | |
| HARLEY ST STRESS MNGMT (HM08999) | | | | | | | | | | | | | | | ● | | |
| HARLEY STREET ACADEMY (HM09000) | | | | | | | | | | | | | | | ● | | |
| HARLEY, KI (HM09006) | | | | | | | | | | | | | | | ● | | |
| HARMON, MIKE (HM09014) | | | | | | | | | | | | | | | | | |
| HARPER, SUZANNE G (HM09041) | | | ● | | | | | | | | | | | | ● | | |
| HARPER, SUZANNE G (HM09042) | | | ● | | | | | | | | | | | | ● | | |
| HARRIS, NESLI (HM09083) | | | ● | | | | | | | | | | | | | | |
| HARROW HEALTH CARE CENTRE (HM09121) | | | ● | | | | | | | | | | | | | | |
| HARVEY-KUMMER, DIANNE (HM09169) | | | ● | | | | | | | | | | | | | | |
| HARWARD, M (HM09171) | | | | | | | | | | | | | | | ● | | |
| HARWICH, ANDREW (HM09172) | | | ● | | | | | | | | | | | | | | |
| HASLAM, PENELOPE J (HM09184) | | | ● | | | | | | | | | | | | | | |
| HATHA YOGA/COUNSELLING (HM09195) | | | | | | | | | | | | | | | | | |
| HAVELOCK-SEARLE, PAULINE (HM09206) | | | | | | | | | | | | | | | | | |
| HAWKINS, JAN (HM09222) | | | | | | | | | | | | | | | ● | | |
| HAWTIN, JANICE (HM09245) | | | | | | | | | | | | | | | | | |
| HEAL, CHRISTIANNE (HM09314) | | | | | | | | | | | | | | | ● | | |
| HEALERS WORLD (HM09320) | | | ● | | | | | | | | ● | | | | ● | | |
| HEALING ARTS UK (HM09326) | | | | | | | | | | | | | | | | | |

| Business by County with Reference no. | Reflexology | Reichian Therapy | Reiki | Remedial Massage | Rogerian Therapy | Rolfing | Seichem | Sensitivity Training | Shiatsu | Silva Method | Sound Therapy | Spiritual Healing | Sports Massage | Stress Therapy | Swedish Body Massage | T'ai-Chi Ch'uan |
|---|---|---|---|---|---|---|---|---|---|---|---|---|---|---|---|---|
| GROWNEY, SHAUN (HM08618) | | | | | | | | | | | | | | | | |
| GRUNDBERG, SIBYL (HM08620) | | | | | | | | | | | | | | | | |
| GUERRINI, HEATHER (HM08622) | ● | | | | | | | | | | | | | | | |
| GUILD OF PSYCHOTHERAPISTS (HM08628) | | | | | | | | | | | | | | | | |
| GUNN, HARRY (HM08641) | | | | | | | | | | | | | | | | |
| GUNTER, MARIGOLD (HM08646) | ● | | | | | | | | | | | | | | | |
| GURNET, CATHERINE (HM08651) | ● | | | | | | | | | | | | | | | |
| HACKNEY & ISLINGTON PSYCHO (HM08683) | | | | | | | | | | | | | | | | |
| HACKNEY HYPNOTHERAPY (HM08685) | | | | | | | | | | | | | | ● | | |
| HAIN, PATRICIA (HM08712) | ● | | | | | | | | | | | | | | | |
| HAMILTON, FIONA (HM08843) | | | | | | | | | | | | | | | | |
| HAMMETT, JANET (HM08864) | ● | | | | | | | | | | | | | | | |
| HARBEN, PAM (HM08959) | ● | | | | | | | | | | | | | | | |
| HARDY, THEA (HM08986) | | | | | | | | | | | | | | | | |
| HAREWOOD, MARCIA M (HM08991) | | | | | | | | | | | | | | | | |
| HARLEY ST STRESS MNGMT (HM08999) | | | | | | | | | | | | | | ● | | |
| HARLEY STREET ACADEMY (HM09000) | | | | | | | | | | | | | | | | |
| HARLEY, KI (HM09006) | | | | | | | | | | | | | | | | |
| HARMON, MIKE (HM09014) | ● | | | | | | | | | | | | | | | |
| HARPER, SUZANNE G (HM09041) | | | ● | | | | | | | | | | | | | |
| HARPER, SUZANNE G (HM09042) | | | ● | | | | | | | | | | | | | |
| HARRIS, NESLI (HM09083) | | | | | | | | | | | | | | | | |
| HARROW HEALTH CARE CENTRE (HM09121) | | | | | | ● | | | | | | | | ● | | |
| HARVEY-KUMMER, DIANNE (HM09169) | | | | | | | | | | | | | | | | |
| HARWARD, M (HM09171) | | | | | | | | | | | | | | | | |
| HARWICH, ANDREW (HM09172) | | | | | | | | | | | | | | | | |
| HASLAM, PENELOPE J (HM09184) | | | | | | | | | | | | | | | | |
| HATHA YOGA/COUNSELLING (HM09195) | | | | | | | | | | | | | | | | |
| HAVELOCK-SEARLE, PAULINE (HM09206) | | | | | | | | | | | | | | | | |
| HAWKINS, JAN (HM09222) | | | | | ● | | | | | | | | | ● | | |
| HAWTIN, JANICE (HM09245) | ● | | | | | | | | | | | | | | | |
| HEAL, CHRISTIANNE (HM09314) | ● | | | | | | | | | | | | | | | |
| HEALERS WORLD (HM09320) | ● | | | | | | | | ● | | | ● | | ● | | ● |
| HEALING ARTS UK (HM09326) | | | ● | | | | | | | | | | ● | | | |

| Business by County with Reference no. | Tantra Therapy | Tera-Mai | Thought Field Therapy | Touch Therapy | Transactional Analysis | Tui-na | Ultrasonics | Vibrational Therapy | Visualisation Therapy | Vitamin Therapy | Voice Therapy | X-Ray | Ying & Yang | Yoga | Zen Therapy | Zero Balancing |
|---|---|---|---|---|---|---|---|---|---|---|---|---|---|---|---|---|
| GROWNEY, SHAUN (HM08618) | | | | | | | | | | | | | | | | |
| GRUNDBERG, SIBYL (HM08620) | | | | | | | | | | | | | | | | |
| GUERRINI, HEATHER (HM08622) | | | | | | | | | | | | | | | | |
| GUILD OF PSYCHOTHERAPISTS (HM08628) | | | | | | | | | | | | | | | | |
| GUNN, HARRY (HM08641) | | | | | | | | | | | | | | | | |
| GUNTER, MARIGOLD (HM08646) | | | | | | | | | | | | | | | | |
| GURNET, CATHERINE (HM08651) | | | | | | | | | | | | | | | | |
| HACKNEY & ISLINGTON PSYCHO (HM08683) | | | | | | | | | | | | | | | | |
| HACKNEY HYPNOTHERAPY (HM08685) | | | | | | | | | | | | | | | | |
| HAIN, PATRICIA (HM08712) | | | | | | | | | | | | | | | | |
| HAMILTON, FIONA (HM08843) | | | | | | | | | | | | | | | | |
| HAMMETT, JANET (HM08864) | | | | | | | | | | | | | | | | |
| HARBEN, PAM (HM08959) | | | | | | | | | | | | | | | | |
| HARDY, THEA (HM08986) | | | | | | | | | | | | | | | | |
| HAREWOOD, MARCIA M (HM08991) | | | | | | | | | | ● | | | | | | |
| HARLEY ST STRESS MNGMT (HM08999) | | | | | | | | | ● | | | | | | | |
| HARLEY STREET ACADEMY (HM09000) | | | | | | | | | | | | | | | | |
| HARLEY, KI (HM09006) | | | | | ● | | | | | | | | | | | |
| HARMON, MIKE (HM09014) | | | | | | | | | | | | | | | | |
| HARPER, SUZANNE G (HM09041) | | | | | | | | | | ● | | | | | | |
| HARPER, SUZANNE G (HM09042) | | | | | | | | | | ● | | | | | | |
| HARRIS, NESLI (HM09083) | | | | | | | | | | | | | | | | |
| HARROW HEALTH CARE CENTRE (HM09121) | | | | | | | | | | ● | | ● | | | | |
| HARVEY-KUMMER, DIANNE (HM09169) | | | | | | | | | | | | | | | | |
| HARWARD, M (HM09171) | | | | | | | | | | | | | | | | |
| HARWICH, ANDREW (HM09172) | | | | | | | | | | | | | | | | |
| HASLAM, PENELOPE J (HM09184) | | | | | | | | | | | | | | | | |
| HATHA YOGA/COUNSELLING (HM09195) | | | | | | | | | | | | | | ● | | |
| HAVELOCK-SEARLE, PAULINE (HM09206) | | | | | | | | | | | | | | ● | | |
| HAWKINS, JAN (HM09222) | | | | | | | | | | | | | | | | |
| HAWTIN, JANICE (HM09245) | | | | | | | | | | | | | | | | |
| HEAL, CHRISTIANNE (HM09314) | | | | | | | | | | | | | | | | |
| HEALERS WORLD (HM09320) | | | | | | | | | ● | ● | | ● | | ● | | |
| HEALING ARTS UK (HM09326) | | | | | | | | | | | | | | | | |

# O - Z Therapies at Practices/Businesses

| Business by County with Reference no. | Orthotics | Osteomyology | Osteopathy | PAM | Paranormal Therapies | Pattern Therapies | Physiotherapy | Phytotherapy | Pilates | Podiatry | Polarity Therapy | Postural Integration | Primal Therapy | Psionic Therapy | Psychotherapy | Pyramid Power | Pyscho-Synthesis | Reflexology | Reichian Therapy | Reiki | Remedial Massage | Rogerian Therapy | Rolfing | Seichem | Sensitivity Training | Shiatsu | Silva Method | Sound Therapy | Spiritual Healing | Sports Massage | Stress Therapy | Swedish Body Massage | T'ai-Chi Ch'uan | Tantra Therapy | Tera-Mai | Thought Field Therapy | Touch Therapy | Transactional Analysis | Tui-na | Ultrasonics | Vibrational Therapy | Visualisation Therapy | Vitamin Therapy | Voice Therapy | X-Ray | Ying & Yang | Yoga | Zen Therapy | Zero Balancing |
|---|---|---|---|---|---|---|---|---|---|---|---|---|---|---|---|---|---|---|---|---|---|---|---|---|---|---|---|---|---|---|---|---|---|---|---|---|---|---|---|---|---|---|---|---|---|---|---|---|---|
| HEALTHWORKS (HM09424) | | | | | | | | | | | | | | | ● | | | | | | | | | | | | | | | | | | | | | | | | | | | | | | | | | | |
| HEATH HEALTH CARE CENTRE (HM09447) | | | ● | | | | | | ● | | | | | | | | | | | | | | | | | | | | | | | | | | | | | | | | | | | | | | | | |
| HEATHROW OSTEOPATHIC CLINIC (HM09459) | | | ● | | | | | | | | | | | | | | | | | | | | | | | | | | | | | | | | | | | | | | | | | | | | | | |
| HEAVENS, SUSAN (HM09479) | | | | | | | | | | | | | | | | | | ● | | | | | | | | | | | | | | | | | | | | | | | | | | | | | | | |
| HEMINGWAY, JENNY (HM09531) | | | ● | | | | | | | | | | | | | | | | | | | | | | | | | | | | | | | | | | | | | | | | | | | | | | |
| HENDERSON, DAVID (HM09546) | | | | | | | | | | | | | | | ● | | | | | | | | | | | | | | | | | | | | | | | | | | | | | | | | | | |
| HENRY, JOHN (HM09569) | | | | | | | | | | | | | | | ● | | | | | | | | | | | | | | | | | | | | | | | | | | | | | | | | | | |
| HENSHAW, COLIN (HM09574) | | | ● | | | | | | | | | | | | | | | | | | | | | | | | | | | | | | | | | | | | | | | | | | | | | | |
| HERBAL TREATMENT CLINIC (HM09638) | | | | | | | | ● | | | | | | | | | | | | | | | | | | | | | | | | | | | | | | | | | | | | | | | | | |
| HERBERT, DARYL (HM09653) | | | ● | | | | | | | | | | | | | | | | | | | | | | | | | | | | | | | | | | | | | | | | | | | | | | |
| HERBMEDIC (HM09663) | | | | | | | | | | | | | | | | | | | | | | | | | | | | | | | | | | | | | | | | | | | | | | ● | | | |
| HERSBORG, TORBEN (HM09687) | | | ● | | | | | | | | | | | | | | | | | | | | | | | | | | | | | | | | | | | | | | | | | | | | | | |
| HEWETT, EMMA (HM09700) | | | | | | | | | | | | | | | | | | ● | | | | | | | | | | | | | | | | | | | | | | | | | | | | | | | |
| HEWSON, JAN (HM09710) | | | | | | | | | | | | | | | | | | ● | | | | | | | | | | | | | | | | | | | | | | | | | | | | | | | |
| HIGHBURY PARK CLINIC (HM09747) | | | ● | | | | | | | | | | | | | | | | | | | | | | | | | | | | | | | | | | | | | | | | | | | | | | |
| HILDRETH & COCKER (HM09767) | | | | | | | | | | | | | | | | | | | | | | | | | | | | | | | | | | | | | | | | | | | ● | | | | | | |
| HILLER, STEPHANIE (HM09794) | | | | | | | | | | | | | | | | | | ● | | | | | | | | | | | | | | | | | | | | | | | | | | | | | | | |
| HINDMARSH, JULIE (HM09830) | | | | | | | | | | | | | | | ● | | | | | | | | | | | | | | | | | | | | | | | | | | | | | | | | | | |
| HINDS, PATRICIA (HM09831) | | | | | | | | | | | | | | | | | | ● | | | | | | | | | | | | | | | | | | | | | | | | | | | | | | | |
| HOARE, ELIZABETH (HM09851) | | | | | | | | | | | | | | | | | | ● | | | | | | | | | | | | | | | | | | | | | | | | | | | | | | | |
| HOBBS, SALLY (HM09858) | | | ● | | | | | | | | | | | | | | | | | | | | | | | | | | | | | | | | | | | | | | | | | | | | | | |
| HOGARTH CLINIC (HM09907) | | | ● | | | | ● | | | | | ● | | | | | | ● | | | | | ● | | | ● | | | | | ● | | | | | | | | | | | | | | ● | | | | |
| HOLE, NIGEL (HM09941) | | | ● | | | | | | | | | | | | | | | | | | | | | | | | | | | | | | | | | | | | | | | | | | | | | | |
| HOLLAND PARK OSTEO PRACTICE (HM10006) | | | ● | | | | | | | | | | | | | | | | | | | | | | | | | | | | | | | | | | | | | | | | | | | | | | |
| HOME VISITING SERVICES (HM10069) | | | | | | | | | | | | | | | ● | | | | | | | | | | | | | | | | | | | | | | | | | | | | | | | | | | |
| HONG TAD ACUPUNCTURE & HERBAL (HM10119) | | | | | | | | | | | | | | | | | | | | | | | | | | | | | ● | | ● | | | | | | | | | | | | ● | | | | | | |
| HOPE, ANN (HM10137) | | | | | | | | | | ● | | | | | | | | | | | | | | | | | | | | | | | | | | | | | | | | | | | | | | | |
| HOPKIN, A N L (HM10144) | | | | | | | | | | | | | | | ● | | | | | | | | | | | | | | | | | | | | | | | | | | | | | | | | | | |
| HORROCKS (HM10183) | | | | | | | | | | | | | | | ● | | | | | | | | | | | | | | | | | | | | | | | | | | | | | | | | | | |
| HOUSE OF MISTRY (HM10220) | | | | | | | | | | | | | | | | | | ● | | | | | | | | ● | | | | | | | | | | | | | | | | | | | | | | | |
| HOWELL, JANE (HM10268) | | | | | | | | | | | | | | | | | | ● | | | | | | | | | | | | | | | | | | | | | | | | | | | | | | | |
| HUBBERS, HILARY (HM10304) | | | ● | | | | | | | | | | | | | | | | | | | | | | | | | | | | | | | | | | | | | | | | | | | | | | |
| HUMPHREY, A (HM10371) | | | | | | | | | | | | | | | ● | | | | | | | | | | | | | | | | | | | | | | | | | | | | | | | | | | |
| HUMPHRIES, JUDITH (HM10379) | | | | | | | | | | | | | | | | | | ● | | | | | | | | | | | | | | | | | | | | | | | | | | | | | | | |

# O - Z Therapies at Practices/Businesses

| Business by County with Reference no. | Orthotics | Osteomyology | Osteopathy | PAM | Paranormal Therapies | Pattern Therapies | Physiotherapy | Phytotherapy | Pilates | Podiatry | Polarity Therapy | Postural Integration | Primal Therapy | Psionic Therapy | Psychotherapy | Pyramid Power | Pyscho-Synthesis | Reflexology | Reichian Therapy | Reiki | Remedial Massage | Rogerian Therapy | Rolfing | Seichem |
|---|---|---|---|---|---|---|---|---|---|---|---|---|---|---|---|---|---|---|---|---|---|---|---|---|
| HUNT, MAGGIE (HM10398) | | | | | | | | | | | | | | | ● | | | | | | | | | |
| HUSSEY, DOMINICK (HM10441) | | | ● | | | | | | | | | | | | | | | | | | | | | |
| HYDE BARKER & ASSOCIATES (HM10469) | | | | | | | | | | ● | | | | | | | | | | | | | | |
| INDEPENDENT PSYCHOLOGY SERVICE (HM10610) | | | | | | | | | | | | | | | ● | | | | | | | ● | | |
| INNERGY YOGA CENTRE (HM10644) | | | | | | | | | | | | | | | | | | | | | | | | |
| ISLINGTON PSYCHOTHERAPY (HM10775) | | | | | | | | | | | | | | | ● | | | | | | | | | |
| IVES, R (HM10781) | | | ● | | | | | | | | | | | | | | | | | | | | | |
| JACKSON, ALISON (HM10820) | | | | | | | | | | | | | | | | | | ● | | | | | | |
| JACKSON, FRANCISCA-IRENE (HM10837) | | | | | | | | | | | | | | | | | | ● | | | | | | |
| JAMES, MAURICE (HM10894) | | | | | | | | | | | | | | | | | | ● | | | | | | |
| JELFS, MARTIN (HM10976) | | | | | | | | | | | | | | | ● | | | | ● | | | ● | | |
| JELFS, MARTIN (HM10977) | | | | | | | | | | | | | | | ● | | | | ● | | | ● | | |
| JEWERS, M S (HM11025) | | | | | | | | | | ● | | | | | | | | | | | | | | |
| JIMENEZ, HILARY (HM11033) | | | | | | | | | | | | | | | | | | ● | | | | | | |
| JINKS, BARBARA (HM11035) | | | ● | | | | | | | | | | | | | | | | | | | | | |
| JOHANSSON, BERIT (HM11048) | | | | | | | | | | | | | | | | | | ● | | | | | | |
| JOHNSON, JAMES D (HM11078) | | | ● | | | | | | | | | | | | | | | | | | | | | |
| JOHNSTON, SALLY (HM11104) | | | ● | | | | | | | | | | | | | | | | | | | | | |
| JONES, DAVE (HM11135) | | | | | | | | | | | | | | | ● | | | | | | | | | |
| JONES, EILUNED (HM11139) | | | | | | | | | | | | | | | | | | ● | | | | | | |
| JONES, JULIE (HM11161) | | | | | | | | | | | | | | | | | | ● | | | | | | |
| JORDAN, A I (HM11208) | | | | | | | | | | | | | | | ● | | | | | | | | | |
| JOSEPH CLINIC (HM11215) | | | ● | | | | | | | | | | | | | | | | | | | | | |
| JOSEPH, BRIAN (HM11217) | | | ● | | | | | | | | | | | | | | | | | | | | | |
| JUDAH, ALISON (HM11244) | | | ● | | | | | | | | | | | | | | | | | | | | | |
| JULAILA, A (HM11254) | | | ● | | | | | | | | | | | | | | | | | | | | | |
| KANANI, ALPESH (HM11306) | | | ● | | | | | | | | | | | | | | | | | | | | | |
| KANE AND ROSS CLINICS (HM11309) | | | ● | | | | | | | | | | | | | | | | | | | | | |
| KEARNEY, JOHN (HM11370) | | | | | | | | | | | | | | | | | | ● | | | | | | |
| KEELING, ERNEST (HM11386) | | | ● | | | | | | | | | | | | | | | | | | | | | |
| KELLY, PENNY (HM11440) | | | ● | | | | | | | | | | | | | | | | | | | | | |
| KENT, JOANNE (HM11526) | | | | | | | | | | | | | | | | | | ● | | | | | | |
| KEPPENS, I (HM11541) | | | | | | | | | | | | | | | ● | | | | | | | | | |
| KERN, MICHAEL (HM11544) | | | ● | | | | | | | | | | | | | | | | | | | | | |

| Business by County with Reference no. | Sensitivity Training | Shiatsu | Silva Method | Sound Therapy | Spiritual Healing | Sports Massage | Stress Therapy | Swedish Body Massage | T'ai-Chi Ch'uan | Tantra Therapy | Tera-Mai | Thought Field Therapy | Touch Therapy | Transactional Analysis | Tui-na | Ultrasonics | Vibrational Therapy | Visualisation Therapy | Vitamin Therapy | Voice Therapy | X-Ray | Ying & Yang | Yoga | Zen Therapy | Zero Balancing |
|---|---|---|---|---|---|---|---|---|---|---|---|---|---|---|---|---|---|---|---|---|---|---|---|---|---|
| HUNT, MAGGIE (HM10398) | | | | | | | | | | | | | | | | | | | | | | | | | |
| HUSSEY, DOMINICK (HM10441) | | | | | | | | | | | | | | | | | | | | | | | | | |
| HYDE BARKER & ASSOCIATES (HM10469) | | | | | | | | | | | | | | | | | | | | | | | | | |
| INDEPENDENT PSYCHOLOGY SERVICE (HM10610) | | | | | | | | | | | | | | | | | | | | | | | | | |
| INNERGY YOGA CENTRE (HM10644) | | | | | | | | | | | | | | | | | | | | | | | ● | | |
| ISLINGTON PSYCHOTHERAPY (HM10775) | | | | | | | | | | | | | | | | | | | | | | | ● | | |
| IVES, R (HM10781) | | | | | | | | | | | | | | | | | | | | | | | | | |
| JACKSON, ALISON (HM10820) | | | | | | | | | | | | | | | | | | | | | | | | | |
| JACKSON, FRANCISCA-IRENE (HM10837) | | | | | | | | | | | | | | | | | | | | | | | | | |
| JAMES, MAURICE (HM10894) | | | | | | | | | | | | | | | | | | | | | | | | | |
| JELFS, MARTIN (HM10976) | | | | | | | | | | ● | | | | | | | | | | | | | | | |
| JELFS, MARTIN (HM10977) | | | | | | | ● | | | ● | | | | | | | | | | | | | | | |
| JEWERS, M S (HM11025) | | | | | | | | | | | | | | | | | | | | | | | | | |
| JIMENEZ, HILARY (HM11033) | | | | | | | | | | | | | | | | | | | | | | | | | |
| JINKS, BARBARA (HM11035) | | | | | | | | | | | | | | | | | | | | | | | | | |
| JOHANSSON, BERIT (HM11048) | | | | | | | | | | | | | | | | | | | | | | | | | |
| JOHNSON, JAMES D (HM11078) | | | | | | | | | | | | | | | | | | | | | | | | | |
| JOHNSTON, SALLY (HM11104) | | | | | | | | | | | | | | | | | | | | | | | | | |
| JONES, DAVE (HM11135) | | | | | | | | | | | | | | | | | | | | | | | | | |
| JONES, EILUNED (HM11139) | | | | | | | | | | | | | | | | | | | | | | | | | |
| JONES, JULIE (HM11161) | | | | | | | | | | | | | | | | | | | | | | | | | |
| JORDAN, A I (HM11208) | | | | | | | | | | | | | | | | | | | | | | | | | |
| JOSEPH CLINIC (HM11215) | | | | | | | | | | | | | | | | | | | | | | | | | |
| JOSEPH, BRIAN (HM11217) | | | | | | | | | | | | | | | | | | | | | | | | | |
| JUDAH, ALISON (HM11244) | | | | | | | | | | | | | | | | | | | | | | | | | |
| JULAILA, A (HM11254) | | | | | | | | | | | | | | | | | | | | | | | | | |
| KANANI, ALPESH (HM11306) | | | | | | | | | | | | | | | | | | | | | | | | | |
| KANE AND ROSS CLINICS (HM11309) | | | | | | | ● | | | | | | | | | | | | | | | | | | |
| KEARNEY, JOHN (HM11370) | | | | | | | | | | | | | | | | | | | | | | | | | |
| KEELING, ERNEST (HM11386) | | | | | | | | | | | | | | | | | | | | | | | | | |
| KELLY, PENNY (HM11440) | | | | | | | | | | | | | | | | | | | | | | | | | |
| KENT, JOANNE (HM11526) | | | | | | | | | | | | | | | | | | | | | | | | | |
| KEPPENS, I (HM11541) | | | | | | | | | | | | | | | | | | | | | | | | | |
| KERN, MICHAEL (HM11544) | | | | | | | | | | | | | | | | | | | | | | | | | |

# O - Z Therapies at Practices/Businesses

| Business by County with Reference no. | Orthotics | Osteomyology | Osteopathy | PAM | Paranormal Therapies | Pattern Therapies | Physiotherapy | Phytotherapy | Pilates | Podiatry | Polarity Therapy | Postural Integration | Primal Therapy | Psionic Therapy | Psychotherapy | Pyramid Power | Pyscho-Synthesis | Reflexology | Reichian Therapy | Reiki | Remedial Massage | Rogerian Therapy | Rolfing | Seichem | Sensitivity Training | Shiatsu | Silva Method | Sound Therapy | Spiritual Healing | Sports Massage | Stress Therapy | Swedish Body Massage | T'ai-Chi Ch'uan | Tantra Therapy | Tera-Mai | Thought Field Therapy | Touch Therapy | Transactional Analysis | Tui-na | Ultrasonics | Vibrational Therapy | Visualisation Therapy | Vitamin Therapy | Voice Therapy | X-Ray | Ying & Yang | Yoga | Zen Therapy | Zero Balancing |
|---|---|---|---|---|---|---|---|---|---|---|---|---|---|---|---|---|---|---|---|---|---|---|---|---|---|---|---|---|---|---|---|---|---|---|---|---|---|---|---|---|---|---|---|---|---|---|---|---|---|
| KIKAI SHIATSU CENTRE (HM11598) | | | | | | | | | | | | | | | | | | | | | | | | | | ● | | | | | | | | | | | | | | | | | | | | | | | |
| KILBRIDE, PETER (HM11600) | | | | | | | | | | | | | | | ● | | | | | | | | | | | | | | | | ● | | | | | | | | | | | ● | | | | | | | |
| KIMIA HEALTH CLINIC (HM11616) | | | | | | | | | | | | | | | ● | | | | | | | | | | | | | | | | | | | | | | | | | | | | | | | | | | |
| KINGSBURY PSYCHOTHERAPY PRAC (HM11660) | | | | | ● | | | | | | | | | | ● | | | | | ● | | | | ● | | | | | | | ● | | | | | | | | | | | | | | | | | | |
| KIRK, ROBIN (HM11711) | | | ● | | | | | | | | | | | | | | | | | | | | | | | | | | | | | | | | | | | | | | | | | | | | | | |
| KIRKPATRICK, W H (HM11720) | | | ● | | | | | | | | | | | | | | | | | | | | | | | | | | | | | | | | | | | | | | | | | | | | | | |
| KIRSH, MALCOLM (DR) (HM11725) | | | | | | | | | | | | | | | ● | | | | | | | | | | | | | | | | | | | | | | | | | | | | | | | | | | |
| KIRSH, MALCOLM (DR) (HM11724) | | | | | | | | | | | | | | | ● | | | | | | | | | | | | | | | | | | | | | | | | | | | | | | | | | | |
| KNOWLAND, VIVIEN (HM11766) | | | | | | | | | | | | | | | | | | ● | | | | | | | | | | | | | | | | | | | | | | | | | | | | | | | |
| KNUDSEN, KIM (HM11774) | | | | | | | | | | | | | | | ● | | | | | | | | | | | | | | | | | | | | | | | | | | | | | | | | | | |
| KRAFT, T (HM11794) | | | | | | | | | | | | | | | ● | | | | | | | | | | | | | | | | | | | | | | | | | | | | | | | | | | |
| KUPRADZE, NADINE (HM11824) | | | | | | | | | | | | | | | | | | ● | | | | | | | | | | | | | | | | | | | | | | | | | | | | | | | |
| KYRIAKI PEROS (HM11837) | | | | | | | | | | | | | | | | | | ● | | | | | | | | | | | | | | | | | | | | | | | | | | | | | | | |
| LAKHANI, B V (HM11877) | | | ● | | | | | | | | | | | | | | | | | | | | | | | | | | | | | | | | | | | | | | | | | | | | | | |
| LAMKIN, CARLA (HM11909) | | | ● | | | | | | | | | | | | | | | | | | | | | | | | | | | | | | | | | | | | | | | | | | | | | | |
| LANGDALE-KING, ROSIE (HM11949) | | | | | | | | | | | | | | | | | | ● | | | | | | | | | | | | | | | | | | | | | | | | | | | | | | | |
| LANKESTER, CHARLES (HM11961) | | | ● | | | | | | | | | | | | | | | | | | | | | | | | | | | | | | | | | | | | | | | | | | | | | | |
| LAWRIE, CAROLINE (HM12059) | | | | | | | | | | | | | | | | | | ● | | | | | | | | | | | | | | | | | | | | | | | | | | | | | | | |
| LAY, VIVIEN & PARTNERS (HM12075) | | | ● | | | | | | | | | | | | | | | | | | | | | | | | | | | | | | | | | | | | | | | | | | | | | | |
| LEDERMAN, E (DR) (HM12127) | | | ● | | | | | | | | | | | | | | | | | | | | | | | | | | | | | | | | | | | | | | | | | | | | | | |
| LEE COMPLEMENTARY HEALTH CTRE (HM12130) | | | ● | | | | | ● | ● | | | | | | | | | ● | | ● | | | | | | | | | | | | | ● | | | | | | | ● | | | ● | | | | ● | | |
| LEE, NICOLA (HM12143) | | | | | | | | | | | | | | | | | | ● | | | | | | | | | | | | | | | | | | | | | | | | | | | | | | | |
| LEONARD, CHRIS (HM12224) | | | ● | | | | | | | | | | | | | | | | | | | | | | | | | | | | | | | | | | | | | | | | | | | | | | |
| LESADD, JENNY (HM12233) | | | | | | | | | | | | | | | ● | | | | | | | | | | | | | | | | | | | | | | | | | | | | | | | | | | |
| LEVER CLINIC (HM12256) | | | ● | | | | | | | | ● | ● | | | | | | ● | | | | | | | | | | | | | ● | | | | | | ● | | | ● | | | | | | | | | |
| LEWIS, BERYL (HM12281) | | | | | | | | | | | | | | | | | | ● | | | | | | | | | | | | | | | | | | | | | | | | | | | | | | | |
| LEWIS, JULIE (HM12300) | | | ● | | | | | | | | | | | | | | | | | | | | | | | | | | | | | | | | | | | | | | | | | | | | | | |
| LEWIS, RICHARD (HM12311) | | | | | | | | | | | | | | | ● | | | | | | | | | | | | | | | | | | | | | | | | | | | | | | | | | | |
| LIGHTFOOT, ANNA (HM12374) | | | | | | | | | | | | | | | | | | ● | | | | | | | | | | | | | | | | | | | | | | | | | | | | | | | |
| LIME STREET OSTEOPATHIC (HM12397) | | | ● | | | | | | | | | | | | | | | | | | | | | | | | | | | | | | | | | | | | | | | | | | | | | | |
| LINCOLN CLINIC-PSYCHOTHERAPY (HM12405) | | | | | | | | | | | | | | | ● | | | | | | | | | | | | | | | | | | | | | | | | | | | | | | | | | | |
| LINDBERG FITNESS (HM12414) | | | | | | | | | ● | | | | | | | | | | | | | | | | | | | | | | | | | | | | | | | | | | | | | | | | |
| LINTONBON, DAVID (HM12445) | | | ● | | | | | | | | | | | | | | | | | | | | | | | | | | | | | | | | | | | | | | | | | | | | | | |
| LISTER, CHRISTINE (HM12462) | | | ● | | | | | | | | | | | | | | | | | | | | | | | | | | | | | | | | | | | | | | | | | | | | | | |

# O - Z Therapies at Practices/Businesses

| Business by County with Reference no. | Orthotics | Osteomyology | Osteopathy | PAM | Paranormal Therapies | Pattern Therapies | Physiotherapy | Phytotherapy | Pilates | Podiatry | Polarity Therapy | Postural Integration | Primal Therapy | Psionic Therapy | Psychotherapy | Pyramid Power | Pyscho-Synthesis | Reflexology | Reichian Therapy | Reiki | Remedial Massage | Rogerian Therapy | Rolfing | Seichem |
|---|---|---|---|---|---|---|---|---|---|---|---|---|---|---|---|---|---|---|---|---|---|---|---|---|
| MONYPENNY, HELEN (HM14091) | | | | | | | | | | | | | | | ● | | | | | | | | | |
| MOORE, ANGELA (HM14115) | | | | | | | | | | | | | | | | | | ● | | | | | | |
| MORRIS, PENNY (HM14211) | | | | | | | | | | | | | | | | | | ● | | | | | | |
| MORRIS, TIMOTHY (HM14218) | | | ● | | | | | | | | | | | | | | | | | | | | | |
| MOSS, PAUL (HM14267) | | | ● | | | | | | | | | | | | | | | | | | | | | |
| MOSS, PAUL W (HM14268) | | | ● | | | | | | | | | | | | | | | | | | | | | |
| MOTE, CHRISTOPHER C (HM14274) | | | ● | | | | | | | | | | | | | | | | | | | | | |
| MOTTRAM, ANN (HM14280) | | | | | | | | | | | | | | | ● | | | | | | | | | |
| MOUNTVIEW NTRL HEALTH CLINIC (HM14296) | | | | | | | | | | | | | | | ● | | | | | | | | | |
| M-POWER (HM14308) | | | | | | | | | | | | | | | ● | | | | | | | | | |
| MULCAHY, TRICIA (HM14332) | | | | | | | | | | | | | | | ● | | | | | | | | | |
| MULCHINOCK, PENNY (HM14333) | | | | | | | | | | | | | | | ● | | | | | | | | | |
| MULLALLY, K (HM14336) | | | ● | | | | | | | | | | | | | | | | | | | | | |
| MURPHY, ALAN (HM14376) | | | | | | | | | | | | | | | ● | | | | | | | | | |
| MURRAY, T A (DR) (HM14414) | | | ● | | | | | | | | | | | | | | | | | | | | | |
| NAFSIYAT-INTER CULTURAL THRPY (HM14458) | | | | | | | | | | | | | | | ● | | | | | | | | | |
| NASH, S (HM14494) | | | | | | | | | | | | | | | ● | | | | | | | | | |
| NATURAL HEALTH CLINIC (HM14575) | | | | | | | | | | | | | | | | | | ● | | | | | | |
| NEEDHAM, A (HM14747) | | | | | | | | | | | | | | | ● | | | | | | | | | |
| NEIL, ERIC G (HM14760) | | | ● | | | | | | | | | | | | | | | | | | | | | |
| NEIL-ASHER, S (HM14761) | | | ● | | | | | | | | | | | | | | | | | | | | | |
| NEILL, VICTORIA (HM14764) | | | | | | | | | ● | | | ● | | | | | | | | | | | | |
| NEVIES, ALAN (HM14797) | | | ● | | | | | | | | | | | | | | | | | | | | | |
| NEW CROSS NATURAL THRPY CTRE (HM14814) | | | ● | | | | | | | | | ● | | | ● | | | ● | | ● | | | | |
| NEWNS, DAVID (HM14878) | | | | | | | | | | | | | | | ● | | | | | | | | | |
| NICKALLS, JILL (HM14922) | | | ● | | | | | | | | | | | | | | | | | | | | | |
| NIEBOER, SARAH (HM14931) | | | | | | | | | | | | | | | ● | | | | | | | | | |
| NIEL-ASHER, S (HM14933) | | | ● | | | | | | | | | | | | | | | | | | | | | |
| NIELSEN, RITA C (HM14935) | | | | | | | | | | | | | | | | | | ● | | | | | | |
| NIXON, MICHAEL (HM14957) | | | ● | | | | | | | | | | | | | | | | | | | | | |
| NIXON, MICHAEL (HM14958) | | | ● | | | | | | | | | | | | | | | | | | | | | |
| NOBLETT, ANN (HM14974) | | | | | | | | | | | | | | | | | | ● | | | | | | |
| NORTH END PRACTICE (HM15028) | | | ● | | | | | | | | | | | | | | | | | | | | | |
| NORTH END ROAD PSYCHO PRACTICE (HM15029) | | | | | | | | | | | | | | | ● | | | | | | | | | |

| Business by County with Reference no. | Sensitivity Training | Shiatsu | Silva Method | Sound Therapy | Spiritual Healing | Sports Massage | Stress Therapy | Swedish Body Massage | T'ai-Chi Ch'uan | Tantra Therapy | Tera-Mai | Thought Field Therapy | Touch Therapy | Transactional Analysis | Tui-na | Ultrasonics | Vibrational Therapy | Visualisation Therapy | Vitamin Therapy | Voice Therapy | X-Ray | Ying & Yang | Yoga | Zen Therapy | Zero Balancing |
|---|---|---|---|---|---|---|---|---|---|---|---|---|---|---|---|---|---|---|---|---|---|---|---|---|---|
| MONYPENNY, HELEN (HM14091) | | | | | | | | | | | | | | | | | | | | | | | | | |
| MOORE, ANGELA (HM14115) | | | | | | | | | | | | | | | | | | | | | | | | | |
| MORRIS, PENNY (HM14211) | | | | | | | | | | | | | | | | | | | | | | | | | |
| MORRIS, TIMOTHY (HM14218) | | | | | | | | | | | | | | | | | | | | | | | | | |
| MOSS, PAUL (HM14267) | | | | | | | | | | | | | | | | | | | | | | | | | |
| MOSS, PAUL W (HM14268) | | | | | | | | | | | | | | | | | | | | | | | | | |
| MOTE, CHRISTOPHER C (HM14274) | | | | | | | | | | | | | | | | | | | | | | | | | |
| MOTTRAM, ANN (HM14280) | | | | | | | | | | | | | | | | | | | | | | | | | |
| MOUNTVIEW NTRL HEALTH CLINIC (HM14296) | | | | | | | | | | | | | | | | | | | | | | | | | |
| M-POWER (HM14308) | | | | | | | ● | | | | | | | | | | | | | | | | | | |
| MULCAHY, TRICIA (HM14332) | | | | | | | | | | | | | | | | | | | | | | | | | |
| MULCHINOCK, PENNY (HM14333) | | | | | | | | | | | | | | | | | | | | | | | | | |
| MULLALLY, K (HM14336) | | | | | | | | | | | | | | | | | | | | | | | | | |
| MURPHY, ALAN (HM14376) | | | | | | | | | | | | | | | | | | | | | | | | | |
| MURRAY, T A (DR) (HM14414) | | | | | | | | | | | | | | | | | | | | | | | | | |
| NAFSIYAT-INTER CULTURAL THRPY (HM14458) | | | | | | | | | | | | | | | | | | | | | | | | | |
| NASH, S (HM14494) | | | | | | | | | | | | | | | | | | | | | | | | | |
| NATURAL HEALTH CLINIC (HM14575) | | ● | | | | | | | | | | | ● | | | | | | ● | | | | | | |
| NEEDHAM, A (HM14747) | | | | | | | | | | | | | | | | | | | | | | | | | |
| NEIL, ERIC G (HM14760) | | | | | | | | | | | | | | | | | | | | | | | | | |
| NEIL-ASHER, S (HM14761) | | | | | | | | | | | | | | | | | | | | | | | | | |
| NEILL, VICTORIA (HM14764) | | | | | | | ● | | | | | | | | | ● | | ● | | | | | | | |
| NEVIES, ALAN (HM14797) | | | | | | | | | | | | | | | | | | | | | | | | | |
| NEW CROSS NATURAL THRPY CTRE (HM14814) | | ● | | | | | | | | | | | | | | | | | | | | | | | |
| NEWNS, DAVID (HM14878) | | | | | | | | | | | | | | | | | | | | | | | | | |
| NICKALLS, JILL (HM14922) | | | | | | | | | | | | | | | | | | | | | | | | | |
| NIEBOER, SARAH (HM14931) | | | | | | | | | | | | | | | | | | | | | | | | | |
| NIEL-ASHER, S (HM14933) | | | | | | | | | | | | | | | | | | | | | | | | | |
| NIELSEN, RITA C (HM14935) | | | | | | | | | | | | | | | | | | | | | | | | | |
| NIXON, MICHAEL (HM14957) | | | | | | | | | | | | | | | | | | | | | | | | | |
| NIXON, MICHAEL (HM14958) | | | | | | | | | | | | | | | | | | | | | | | | | |
| NOBLETT, ANN (HM974) | | | | | | | | | | | | | | | | | | | | | | | | | |
| NORTH END PRACTICE (HM15028) | | | | | | | | | | | | | | | | | | | | | | | | | |
| NORTH END ROAD PSYCHO PRACTICE (HM15029) | | | | | | | | | | | | | | | | | | | | | | | | | |

# O - Z Therapies at Practices/Businesses

| Business by County with Reference no. | Orthotics | Osteomyology | Osteopathy | PAM | Paranormal Therapies | Pattern Therapies | Physiotherapy | Phytotherapy | Pilates | Podiatry | Polarity Therapy | Postural Integration | Primal Therapy | Psionic Therapy | Psychotherapy | Pyramid Power | Pyscho-Synthesis | Reflexology | Reichian Therapy | Reiki | Remedial Massage | Rogerian Therapy | Rolfing | Seichem | Sensitivity Training |
|---|---|---|---|---|---|---|---|---|---|---|---|---|---|---|---|---|---|---|---|---|---|---|---|---|---|
| NORTH LONDON BACK PAIN CLNC (HM15032) | | | ● | | | | | | | | | | | | | | | | | | | | | | |
| NORTH LONDON CTRE-GROUP THRPY (HM15033) | | | | | | | | | | | | | | | ● | | | | | | | | | | |
| NORTH LONDON LINK CONSULTANCY (HM15034) | | | | | | | | | | | | | | | ● | | | | | | | | | | |
| NORTH POLE SCH OF T'AI-CHI (HM15094) | | | | | | | | | | | | | | | | | | | | | | | | | |
| NORTHWOOD CLINIC (HM15067) | | | ● | | | | | ● | | ● | | | | | | | | | | | | | | | |
| NOTTING HILL TRAD ACU CTRE (HM15081) | | | ● | | | | | | | | | | | | | | | | | | | | | | |
| NRTH LONDON PSYCHO COUNS ASS (HM15093) | | | | | | | | | | | | | | | ● | | | | | | | | | | |
| NRTH WST LONDON PSYCHOTHY CTRE (HM15098) | | | | | | | | | | | | | | | ● | | | | | | | | | | |
| NUTRITION FOR LIFE INT (HM15124) | | | | | | | | | | | | | | | | | | | | | | | | | |
| OASIS CENTRE (HM15160) | | | | | | | | | | | | | | | ● | | | | | | | | | | |
| O'DELL, ANNIE (HM15219) | | | | | | | | | | | | | | | | | | ● | | | | | | | |
| OHUCHE, MARGARET (HM15248) | | | ● | | | | | | | | | | | | | | | | | | | | | | |
| ORIENTAL MEDICINE (HM15386) | | | | | | | | | | | | | | | | | | ● | | | | | | | |
| ORMAY, A P (HM15393) | | | | | | | | | | | | | | | ● | | | | | | | | | | |
| OSBORNE, HOLLY (HM15423) | | | | | | | | | | | | | | | | | | ● | | | | | | | |
| OSTEOPATHIC & SPORTS CLINIC (HM15451) | | | ● | | | | | | | | | | | | | | | | | | | | | | |
| OSTEOPATHIC ASSOCIATION CLINIC (HM15453) | | | ● | | | | | | | | | | | | | | | | | | | | | | |
| OSTEOPATHIC EMERGENCY SERVICE (HM15464) | | | ● | | | | | | | | | | | | | | | | | | | | | | |
| OSTEOPATHIC PRACTICE (HM15467) | | | ● | | | | | | | | | | | | | | | | | | | | | | |
| OSTEOPATHIC PRACTICE (HM15473) | | | ● | | | | | | | | | | | | | | | | | | | | | | |
| OSTEOPATHIC PRACTICE (HM15470) | | | ● | | | | | | | | | | | | | | | | | | | | | | |
| OSTEOPATHIC PRACTICE (HM15471) | | | ● | | | | | | | | | | | | | | | | | | | | | | |
| OTREMBA, KATHARINA (HM15496) | | | | | | | | | | | | | | | ● | | | | | | | | | | |
| OUTCOMES (HM15502) | | | | | | | | | | | | | | | ● | | | ● | | ● | | | | | |
| OVESEN, PEER B K (HM15517) | | | | | | | | | | | | | | | | | | ● | | | | | | | |
| PACIFIC WAVES PRODUCTIONS (HM15553) | | | | | | | | | | | | | | | ● | | | | | | | | | | |
| PALACE ROAD OSTEOPATHIC CLINIC (HM15590) | | | ● | | | | | | | | | | | | | | | | | | | | | | |
| PALFREYMAN, SUE (HM15592) | | | ● | | | | | | | | | | | | | | | | | | | | | | |
| PALMER, FIONA (HM15603) | | | ● | | | | | | | | | | | | | | | | | | | | | | |
| PALMER, STEPHEN (HM15616) | | | | | | | | | | | | | | | ● | | | | | | | | | | |
| PAPOUTSIS, MARGARET (HM15642) | | | ● | | | | | | | | | | | | | | | | | | | | | | |
| PARK, JAMES (HM15680) | | | | | | | | | | | | | | | ● | | | | | | | | | | |
| PARKER, JOHN (HM15695) | | | | | | | | | | | | | | | ● | | | | | | | | | | |
| PARKINSON, JUDI (HM15719) | | | | | | | | | | | | | | | ● | | | | | | | | | | |

| Business by County with Reference no. | Shiatsu | Silva Method | Sound Therapy | Spiritual Healing | Sports Massage | Stress Therapy | Swedish Body Massage | T'ai-Chi Ch'uan | Tantra Therapy | Tera-Mai | Thought Field Therapy | Touch Therapy | Transactional Analysis | Tui-na | Ultrasonics | Vibrational Therapy | Visualisation Therapy | Vitamin Therapy | Voice Therapy | X-Ray | Ying & Yang | Yoga | Zen Therapy | Zero Balancing |
|---|---|---|---|---|---|---|---|---|---|---|---|---|---|---|---|---|---|---|---|---|---|---|---|---|
| NORTH LONDON BACK PAIN CLNC (HM15032) | | | | | | | | | | | | | | | | | | | | | | | | |
| NORTH LONDON CTRE-GROUP THRPY (HM15033) | | | | | | | | | | | | | | | | | | | | | | | | |
| NORTH LONDON LINK CONSULTANCY (HM15034) | | | | | | | | | | | | | | | | | | | | | | | | |
| NORTH POLE SCH OF T'AI-CHI (HM15094) | | | | | | | | ● | | | | | | | | | | | | | | | | |
| NORTHWOOD CLINIC (HM15067) | | | | | | | | | | | | | | | | | | | | | | | | |
| NOTTING HILL TRAD ACU CTRE (HM15081) | | | | | | | | | | | | | | | | | | | | | | | | |
| NRTH LONDON PSYCHO COUNS ASS (HM15093) | | | | | | | | | | | | | | | | | | | | | | | | |
| NRTH WST LONDON PSYCHOTHY CTRE (HM15098) | | | | | | | | | | | | | | | | | | | | | | | | |
| NUTRITION FOR LIFE INT (HM15124) | | | | | | | | | | | | | | | | | | ● | | | | | | |
| OASIS CENTRE (HM15160) | | | | | | | | | | | | | | | | | | | | | | | | |
| O'DELL, ANNIE (HM15219) | | | | | | | | | | | | | | | | | | | | | | | | |
| OHUCHE, MARGARET (HM15248) | | | | | | | | | | | | | | | | | | | | | | | | |
| ORIENTAL MEDICINE (HM15386) | | | | | | | | | | | | | | | | | | | | | | | | |
| ORMAY, A P (HM15393) | | | | | | | | | | | | | | | | | | | | | | | | |
| OSBORNE, HOLLY (HM15423) | | | | | | | | | | | | | | | | | | | | | | | | |
| OSTEOPATHIC & SPORTS CLINIC (HM15451) | | | | | | | | | | | | | | | | | | | | | | | | |
| OSTEOPATHIC ASSOCIATION CLINIC (HM15453) | | | | | | | | | | | | | | | | | | | | | | | | |
| OSTEOPATHIC EMERGENCY SERVICE (HM15464) | | | | | | | | | | | | | | | | | | | | | | | | |
| OSTEOPATHIC PRACTICE (HM15467) | | | | | | | | | | | | | | | | | | | | | | | | |
| OSTEOPATHIC PRACTICE (HM15473) | | | | | | | | | | | | | | | | | | | | | | | | |
| OSTEOPATHIC PRACTICE (HM15470) | ● | | | | | | | | | | | | | | ● | | | | | | | ● | | |
| OSTEOPATHIC PRACTICE (HM15471) | | | | | | | | | | | | | | | | | | | | | | | | |
| OTREMBA, KATHARINA (HM15496) | | | | | | ● | | | | | | | | | | | ● | ● | | | | | | |
| OUTCOMES (HM15502) | | | | | | ● | | | | | | | | | | | ● | | | | | | | |
| OVESEN, PEER B K (HM15517) | | | | | | | | | | | | | | | | | | | | | | | | |
| PACIFIC WAVES PRODUCTIONS (HM15553) | | | | | | ● | | | | | | | ● | | | | ● | | | | | | | |
| PALACE ROAD OSTEOPATHIC CLINIC (HM15590) | | | | | | | | | | | | | | | | | | | | | | | | |
| PALFREYMAN, SUE (HM15592) | | | | | | | | | | | | | | | | | | | | | | | | |
| PALMER, FIONA (HM15603) | | | | | | | | | | | | | | | | | | | | | | | | |
| PALMER, STEPHEN (HM15616) | | | | | | | | | | | | | | | | | | | | | | | | |
| PAPOUTSIS, MARGARET (HM15642) | | | | | | | | | | | | | | | | | | | | | | | | |
| PARK, JAMES (HM15680) | | | | | | | | | | | | | | | | | | | | | | | | |
| PARKER, JOHN (HM15695) | | | | | | | | | | | | | | | | | | | | | | | | |
| PARKINSON, JUDI (HM15719) | | | | | | | | | | | | | | | | | | | | | | | | |

# O - Z Therapies at Practices/Businesses

| Business by County with Reference no. | Orthotics | Osteomyology | Osteopathy | PAM | Paranormal Therapies | Pattern Therapies | Physiotherapy | Phytotherapy | Pilates | Podiatry | Polarity Therapy | Postural Integration | Primal Therapy | Psionic Therapy | Psychotherapy | Pyramid Power | Pyscho-Synthesis | Reflexology | Reichian Therapy | Reiki | Remedial Massage | Rogerian Therapy | Rolfing | Seichem | Sensitivity Training | Shiatsu | Silva Method | Sound Therapy | Spiritual Healing | Sports Massage | Stress Therapy | Swedish Body Massage | T'ai-Chi Ch'uan | Tantra Therapy | Tera-Mai | Thought Field Therapy | Touch Therapy | Transactional Analysis | Tui-na | Ultrasonics | Vibrational Therapy | Visualisation Therapy | Vitamin Therapy | Voice Therapy | X-Ray | Ying & Yang | Yoga | Zen Therapy | Zero Balancing |
|---|---|---|---|---|---|---|---|---|---|---|---|---|---|---|---|---|---|---|---|---|---|---|---|---|---|---|---|---|---|---|---|---|---|---|---|---|---|---|---|---|---|---|---|---|---|---|---|---|---|
| PARSIFAL OSTEOPATHIC CLINIC (HM15745) ||| ● ||||||||||||||||||||||||||||||||||||||||||||||
| PASHLEY, MAGGIE (HM15775) ||||||||||||||||| ● || ● |||||| ● ||||||||||||||||||||||||
| PATEL, J C (HM15788) ||||||||| ● ||||||||||||||||||||||||||||||||||||||||
| PATEL, LINA (HM15792) ||||||||||||||||| ● ||||||||||||||||||||||||||||||||
| PATEL, NEIL (HM15796) ||| ● ||||||||||||||||||||||||||||||||||||||||||||||
| PATEL, P (HM15797) ||| ● ||||||||||||||||||||||||||||||||||||||||||||||
| PATEL, PRAGNA (HM15798) ||| ● ||||||||||||||||||||||||||||||||||||||||||||||
| PATERSON, KARETH (HM15810) ||||||||||||||||| ● || ● ||||||||||||||||||||||||||||||
| PAULO, EMMA (HM15850) ||||||||||||||||| ● ||||||||||||||||||||||||||||||||
| PEARCE, R P (HM15900) ||| ● ||||||||||||||||||||||||||||||||||||||||||||||
| PELLIN INSTITUTE (HM15953) |||||||||||||| ● ||||||||||||||||||||||||||||||||||
| PELLING, KAREN (HM15955) ||| ● ||||||||||||||||||||||||||||||||||||||||||||||
| PENFOLD, CHRISTINE (HM15971) ||||||||||||||||| ● ||||||||||||||||||||||||||||||||
| PERICLEOUS, CHRISTINE (HM16024) |||||||||||||| ● ||||||||||||||||||||||||||||||||||
| PERRINA, MARIE (HM16037) ||||||||||||||||| ● ||||||||||||||||||||||||||||||||
| PERSAD, ROBI (HM16054) ||| ● ||||||||||||||||||||||||||||||||||||||||||||||
| PERSON TO PERSON (HM16059) |||||||||||||| ● ||||||||||||||||||||||||||||||||||
| PETER WANLESS & BETTY HOLTROP (HM16077) |||||||||||||| ● ||||||||||||||||||||||||||||||||||
| PHILADELPHIA ASSOCIATION (HM16116) |||||||||||||| ● ||||||||||||||||||||||||||||||||||
| PHILLIPS, HARRY (DR) (HM16130) ||| ● ||||||||||||||||||||||||||||||||||||||||||||||
| PHOKOU, PERI P (HM16159) ||| ● ||||||||||||||||||||||||||||||||||||||||||||||
| PHYSIO ONE (HM16202) ||||||| ● |||||||||||||||||||||||||||||||||||||||||
| PHYSIO SOLUTIONS (HM16205) |||||| ● ||||||||||||||||||||||||||||||||||||||||||
| PHYSIOTHERAPY PRACTICE (HM16253) ||||||| ● |||||||||||| ● ||||||||| ● |||||||| ● || ● ||||||
| PIDD, MARTIN (HM16275) ||| ● ||||||||||||||||||||||||||||||||||||||||||||||
| PIKE, BEA (HM16284) ||| ● ||||||||||||||||||||||||||||||||||||||||||||||
| PINNER ROAD PHYSIOTHERAPY (HM16316) |||||| ● ||||||||||||||||||||||||||||||||||||||||||
| PINSENT, MARIA (HM16318) ||||||||||||||||| ● ||||||||||||||||||||||||||||||||
| PINSKER, SUZANNE (HM16319) ||| ● ||||||||||||||||||||||||||||||||||||||||||||||
| PIPER, ROBIN (HM16326) |||||||||||||| ● ||||||||||||||||||||||||||||||||||
| PIRIE, STEPHEN (HM16329) ||| ● ||||||||||||||||||||||||||||||||||||||||||||||
| PITAMBER, NADINE (HM16331) ||||||||||||||||| ● ||||||||||||||||||||||||||||||||
| PLATT, DEE (HM16363) ||||||||||||||||| ● ||||||||||||||||||||||||||||||||
| PODIATRY CLINIC (HM16393) ||||||||||| ● |||||||||||||||||||||||||||||||||||||

# O - Z Therapies at Practices/Businesses

| Business by County with Reference no. | Orthotics | Osteomyology | Osteopathy | PAM | Paranormal Therapies | Pattern Therapies | Physiotherapy | Phytotherapy | Pilates | Podiatry | Polarity Therapy | Postural Integration | Primal Therapy | Psionic Therapy | Psychotherapy | Pyramid Power | Pyscho-Synthesis | Reflexology | Reichian Therapy | Reiki | Remedial Massage | Rogerian Therapy | Rolfing | Seichem | Sensitivity Training |
|---|---|---|---|---|---|---|---|---|---|---|---|---|---|---|---|---|---|---|---|---|---|---|---|---|---|
| POLAND STREET PRACTICE (HM16401) | | | ● | | | | | | | | | | | | | | | | | | | | | | |
| PRAGNELL, C A (HM16526) | | | ● | | | | | | | | | | | | | | | | | | | | | | |
| PRICE, SANDRA (HM16594) | | | ● | | | | | | | | | | | | | | | | | | | | | | |
| PRICE, SANDRA (HM16595) | | | ● | | | | | | | | | | | | | | | | | | | | | | |
| PRIMROSE HEALING CENTRE (HM16616) | | | ● | | | | | | | | | | | | | | | | | | | | | | |
| PRIVATE HEALTH CLINIC (HM16644) | | | ● | | | | ● | | | | ● | | | | | | | ● | | | | | | | |
| PRIVATE PRACTICE (HM16649) | | | | | | | | | | | | | | | ● | | | | | | | | | | |
| PROPERT, DAVID (HM16666) | | | ● | | | | | | | | | | | | | | | | | | | | | | |
| PROWER, JANET (HM16677) | | | ● | | | | | | | | | | | | | | | | | | | | | | |
| PSYCHOTHERAPY CENTRE (HM16733) | | | | | | | | | | | | | | | ● | | | | | | | | | | |
| PSYCHOTHERAPY CENTRE (HM16734) | | | | | | | | | | | | | | | ● | | | | | | | | | | |
| PSYCHOTHERAPY REFERRAL SERVICE (HM16735) | | | | | | | | | | | | | | | ● | | | | | | | | | | |
| PSYCHOTHERAPY REFERRAL SERVICE (HM16736) | | | | | | | | | | | | | | | ● | | | | | | | | | | |
| PSYCHOTHERAPY SERVICES (HM16737) | | | | | | | | | | | | | | | ● | | | | | | | | | | |
| PUGH, G (HM16747) | | | | | | | | | | | | | | | ● | | | | | | | | | | |
| PUTNEY CHIROPRACTIC (HM16780) | | | | | | | | | | | | | | | | | | | | | | | | | |
| RACHEL YOUNG - HYPNOTHERAPIST (HM16837) | | | | | | | | | | | | | | | ● | | | | | ● | | | | | |
| RAEBURN, JO (HM16865) | | | | | | | | | | | | | | | | | | | | ● | | | | | |
| RAHS, EFFIE (HM16872) | | | | | | | | | | | | | | | | | | ● | | | | | | | |
| RAILTON, CAROLE (HM16873) | | | | | | | | | | | | | | | | | | ● | | | | | | | |
| RANDALL, CAROLINE (HM16926) | | | | | | | | ● | | | | | | | | | | | | | | | | | |
| RATIGAN, SARAH (HM16958) | | | | | | | | | | | | | | | | | | ● | | | | | | | |
| RAVENSCROFT CENTRE (HM16967) | | | | | | | | | | | | | | | ● | | | ● | | | | | | | |
| READ, CHARLES (HM16993) | | | ● | | | | | | | | | | | | | | | | | | | | | | |
| REDLER, LEON (DR) (HM17029) | | | | | | | | | | | | | | | ● | | | | | | | | | | |
| REED, JEAN (HM17042) | | | | | | | | | | | | | | | | | | ● | | | | | | | |
| REFLEXOLOGY (HM17077) | | | | | | | | | | | | | | | | | | ● | | | | | | | |
| REFLEXOLOGY CLINIC (HM17089) | | | | | | | | | | | | | | | | | | ● | | ● | | | | | |
| REGENTS CLINIC (HM17101) | | | ● | | | | | | | | | | | | | | | | | | | | | | |
| REIKI HEALING & TRAINING CTRE (HM17133) | | | | | | | | | | | | | | | | | | | | ● | | | | | |
| REIKI LIGHT SELF HEALING CTRE (HM17139) | | | | | | | | | | | | | | | | | | | | ● | | | | | |
| RELAXING HEALTHY OPTIONS (HM17169) | | | | | | | | | | | ● | | | | | | | ● | | | | | | | |
| REPLINGHAM CLINIC (HM17195) | | | ● | | | | | | | | | | | | ● | | | ● | | | | | | | |
| RIES, GIDEON (HM17326) | | | ● | | | | | | | | | | | | | | | | | | | | | | |

| Business by County with Reference no. | Shiatsu | Silva Method | Sound Therapy | Spiritual Healing | Sports Massage | Stress Therapy | Swedish Body Massage | T'ai-Chi Ch'uan | Tantra Therapy | Tera-Mai | Thought Field Therapy | Touch Therapy | Transactional Analysis | Tui-na | Ultrasonics | Vibrational Therapy | Visualisation Therapy | Vitamin Therapy | Voice Therapy | X-Ray | Ying & Yang | Yoga | Zen Therapy | Zero Balancing |
|---|---|---|---|---|---|---|---|---|---|---|---|---|---|---|---|---|---|---|---|---|---|---|---|---|
| POLAND STREET PRACTICE (HM16401) | | | | | | | | | | | | | | | | | | | | | | | | |
| PRAGNELL, C A (HM16526) | | | | | | | | | | | | | | | | | | | | | | | | |
| PRICE, SANDRA (HM16594) | | | | | | | | | | | | | | | | | | | | | | | | |
| PRICE, SANDRA (HM16595) | | | | | | | | | | | | | | | | | | | | | | | | |
| PRIMROSE HEALING CENTRE (HM16616) | | | | | | | | | | | | | | | | | | | | | | | | |
| PRIVATE HEALTH CLINIC (HM16644) | | | | | | | | | | | | | | | | | | | | | | ● | | |
| PRIVATE PRACTICE (HM16649) | | | | | | | | | | | | | | | | | | | | | | | | |
| PROPERT, DAVID (HM16666) | | | | | | | | | | | | | | | | | | | | | | | | |
| PROWER, JANET (HM16677) | | | | | | | | | | | | | | | | | | | | | | | | |
| PSYCHOTHERAPY CENTRE (HM16733) | | | | | | | | | | | | | | | | | | | | | | | | |
| PSYCHOTHERAPY CENTRE (HM16734) | | | | | | | | | | | | | | | | | | | | | | | | |
| PSYCHOTHERAPY REFERRAL SERVICE (HM16735) | | | | | | | | | | | | | | | | | | | | | | | | |
| PSYCHOTHERAPY REFERRAL SERVICE (HM16736) | | | | | | | | | | | | | | | | | | | | | | | | |
| PSYCHOTHERAPY SERVICES (HM16737) | | | | | | | | | | | | | | | | | | | | | | | | |
| PUGH, G (HM16747) | | | | | | | | | | | | | | | | | | | | | | | | |
| PUTNEY CHIROPRACTIC (HM16780) | | | | | | | | | | | | | | | | | | | | ● | | | | |
| RACHEL YOUNG - HYPNOTHERAPIST (HM16837) | | | | ● | | ● | | | | | | ● | | | | | ● | | | | ● | | | |
| RAEBURN, JO (HM16865) | | | | | | | | | | | | | | | | | | | | | | | | |
| RAHS, EFFIE (HM16872) | | | | | | | | | | | | | | | | | | | | | | | | |
| RAILTON, CAROLE (HM16873) | | | | | | | | | | | | | | | | | | | | | | | | |
| RANDALL, CAROLINE (HM16926) | | | | | | | | | | | | | | | | | | | | | | | | |
| RATIGAN, SARAH (HM16958) | | | | | | | | | | | | | | | | | | | | | | | | |
| RAVENSCROFT CENTRE (HM16967) | | | | ● | | ● | | | | | | | | | | | | | | | | | | |
| READ, CHARLES (HM16993) | | | | | | | | | | | | | | | | | | | | | | | | |
| REDLER, LEON (DR) (HM17029) | | | | | | | | | | | | | | | | | | | | | | | | |
| REED, JEAN (HM17042) | | | | | | | | | | | | | | | | | | | | | | | | |
| REFLEXOLOGY (HM17077) | | | | | | | | | | | | | | | | | | | | | | | | |
| REFLEXOLOGY CLINIC (HM17089) | | | | | | | | | | | | | | | | | | | | | | | | |
| REGENTS CLINIC (HM17101) | | | | | | | | | | | | | | | | | | | | | | | | |
| REIKI HEALING & TRAINING CTRE (HM17133) | | | | | | | | | | | | | | | | | | | | | | | | |
| REIKI LIGHT SELF HEALING CTRE (HM17139) | | | | | | | | | | | | | | | | | | | | | | | | |
| RELAXING HEALTHY OPTIONS (HM17169) | | | | | | | | | | | | | | | | | | | | | | | | |
| REPLINGHAM CLINIC (HM17195) | ● | | | | | | | | | | | | | | | | ● | | | | | | | |
| RIES, GIDEON (HM17326) | | | | | | | | | | | | | | | | | | | | | | | | |

# O - Z Therapies at Practices/Businesses

Business by County with Reference no.

| Business by County with Reference no. | Orthotics | Osteomyology | Osteopathy | PAM | Paranormal Therapies | Pattern Therapies | Physiotherapy | Phytotherapy | Pilates | Podiatry | Polarity Therapy | Postural Integration | Primal Therapy | Psionic Therapy | Psychotherapy | Pyramid Power | Pyscho-Synthesis |
|---|---|---|---|---|---|---|---|---|---|---|---|---|---|---|---|---|---|
| RIVIERE, SUSANNA (HM17384) | | | | | | | | | | | | | | | | | |
| ROBERTSON, FIONA (HM17438) | | | ● | | | | | | | | | | | | | | |
| ROBERTSON, FIONA (HM17440) | | | ● | | | | | | | | | | | | | | |
| ROBERTSON, K & ROWLAND, D (HM17446) | | | ● | | | | | | | | | | | | | | |
| ROCK & ROLL THERAPY (HM17521) | | | | | | | | | | | | | | | ● | | |
| ROEHAMPTON PHYSIO/SPORTS (HM17535) | | | | | | | ● | | | | | | | | | | |
| ROGERS, AMY (HM17544) | | | | | | | | | | | | | | | | | |
| ROHRIG, A (HM17560) | | | | | | | | | | | | | | | ● | | |
| ROSAMBEAU, VALERIE (HM17593) | | | | | | | | | | | | | | | | | |
| ROSE, NICHOLAS (HM17613) | | | ● | | | | | | | | | | | | | | |
| ROW, PATRICIA (HM17679) | | | ● | | | | | | | | | | | | | | |
| RUSSO, HAZEL (HM17773) | | | | | | | | | | | | | | | | | |
| RUSSO, JACQUELINE (HM17774) | | | | | | | | | | | | | | | | | |
| RUTHERFORD, BERWYN (HM17780) | | | ● | | | | | | | | | | | | | | |
| RYAN, ROSEMARY (HM17794) | | | | | | | | | | | | | | | | | |
| S K REFLEXOLOGY & AROMATHERAPY (HM17812) | | | | | | | | | | | | | | | | | |
| S M GORDON ANALYTICAL PSYCH (HM17815) | | | | | | | | | | | | | | | ● | | |
| SACKLIN, CECILIA (HM17827) | | | | | | | | | | | | | | | | | |
| SAGIR, SHARON (HM17839) | | | | | | | | | | | | | | | | | |
| SALISBURY, ERICA (HM17855) | | | ● | | | | | | | | | | | | | | |
| SANDRINGHAM OSTEOPATHY CLINIC (HM17928) | | | ● | | | | | | | | | | | | | | |
| SAUNDERS, P (HM17960) | | | ● | | | | | | | | | | | | | | |
| SAYER CLINIC (HM17993) | | | | | | | | | | | | ● | | | | | |
| SAYERS, FIONA (HM17998) | | | | | | | | | | | | | | | | | |
| SCHOFIELD, IAN (HM18020) | | | ● | | | | | | | | | | | | | | |
| SCHOOL OF PSYCHO & COUNSELLING (HM18084) | | | | | | | | | | | | | | | ● | | |
| SEEAR, MICHAEL (DR) (HM18189) | | | | | | | | | | | | | | ● | ● | | |
| SEYMOUR PRACTICE (HM18257) | | | ● | | | | | | | | | | | | | | |
| SHERWOOD PSYCHO TRAINING INS (HM18442) | | | | | | | | | | | | | | | ● | | |
| SHIATSU PLACE (HM18458) | | | ● | | | | | | | | | | | | | | |
| SHIATSU STUDIO (HM18465) | | | | | | | | | | | | | | | | | |
| SHIPRA, AMIN (HM18481) | | | ● | | | | | | | | | | | | | | |
| SHRUBBERIES (HM18512) | | | | | | | | | | | | | | | ● | | |
| SILVER-LEIGH, V (HM18547) | | | | | | | | | | | | | | | ● | | |

| Business by County with Reference no. | Reflexology | Reichian Therapy | Reiki | Remedial Massage | Rogerian Therapy | Rolfing | Seichem | Sensitivity Training | Shiatsu | Silva Method | Sound Therapy | Spiritual Healing | Sports Massage | Stress Therapy | Swedish Body Massage | T'ai-Chi Ch'uan |
|---|---|---|---|---|---|---|---|---|---|---|---|---|---|---|---|---|
| RIVIERE, SUSANNA (HM17384) | ● | | | | | | | | | | | | | | | |
| ROBERTSON, FIONA (HM17438) | | | | | | | | | | | | | | | | |
| ROBERTSON, FIONA (HM17440) | ● | | | | | | | | | | | | | | | |
| ROBERTSON, K & ROWLAND, D (HM17446) | | | | | | | | | | | | | | | | |
| ROCK & ROLL THERAPY (HM17521) | | | | | | | | | | | | | | | | |
| ROEHAMPTON PHYSIO/SPORTS (HM17535) | | | | | | | | | | | | | | | | |
| ROGERS, AMY (HM17544) | ● | | | | | | | | | | | | | | | |
| ROHRIG, A (HM17560) | | | | | | | | | | | | | | | | |
| ROSAMBEAU, VALERIE (HM17593) | ● | | | | | | | | | | | | | | | |
| ROSE, NICHOLAS (HM17613) | | | | | | | | | | | | | | | | |
| ROW, PATRICIA (HM17679) | | | | | | | | | | | | | | | | |
| RUSSO, HAZEL (HM17773) | ● | | ● | | | | | | | | | | | | | |
| RUSSO, JACQUELINE (HM17774) | ● | | | | | | | | | | | | | | | |
| RUTHERFORD, BERWYN (HM17780) | | | | | | | | | | | | | | | | |
| RYAN, ROSEMARY (HM17794) | ● | | | | | | | | | | | | | | | |
| S K REFLEXOLOGY & AROMATHERAPY (HM17812) | ● | | | | | | | | | | | | | | | |
| S M GORDON ANALYTICAL PSYCH (HM17815) | | | | | | | | | | | | | | | | |
| SACKLIN, CECILIA (HM17827) | ● | | | | | | | | | | | | | | | |
| SAGIR, SHARON (HM17839) | ● | | | | | | | | | | | | | | | |
| SALISBURY, ERICA (HM17855) | | | | | | | | | | | | | | | | |
| SANDRINGHAM OSTEOPATHY CLINIC (HM17928) | | | | | | | | | | | | | | | | |
| SAUNDERS, P (HM17960) | | | | | | | | | | | | | | | | |
| SAYER CLINIC (HM17993) | | | | | | | | | | | | | | | | |
| SAYERS, FIONA (HM17998) | ● | | | | | | | | | | | | | | | |
| SCHOFIELD, IAN (HM18020) | | | | | | | | | | | | | | | | |
| SCHOOL OF PSYCHO & COUNSELLING (HM18084) | | | | | | | | | | | | | | | | |
| SEEAR, MICHAEL (DR) (HM18189) | | | | ● | | | | | | | | | | | | |
| SEYMOUR PRACTICE (HM18257) | | | | | | | | | | | | | | | | |
| SHERWOOD PSYCHO TRAINING INS (HM18442) | | | | | | | | | | | | | | | | |
| SHIATSU PLACE (HM18458) | | | ● | | | | | | ● | | | | | | | ● |
| SHIATSU STUDIO (HM18465) | | | ● | | | | ● | | ● | | | | | | | |
| SHIPRA, AMIN (HM18481) | | | | | | | | | | | | | | | | |
| SHRUBBERIES (HM18512) | | | | | | | | | | | | | | | | |
| SILVER-LEIGH, V (HM18547) | | | | | | | | | | | | | | | | |

| Business by County with Reference no. | Tantra Therapy | Tera-Mai | Thought Field Therapy | Touch Therapy | Transactional Analysis | Tui-na | Ultrasonics | Vibrational Therapy | Visualisation Therapy | Vitamin Therapy | Voice Therapy | X-Ray | Ying & Yang | Yoga | Zen Therapy | Zero Balancing |
|---|---|---|---|---|---|---|---|---|---|---|---|---|---|---|---|---|
| RIVIERE, SUSANNA (HM17384) | | | | | | | | | | | | | | | | |
| ROBERTSON, FIONA (HM17438) | | | | | | | | | | | | | | | | |
| ROBERTSON, FIONA (HM17440) | | | | | | | | | | | | | | | | |
| ROBERTSON, K & ROWLAND, D (HM17446) | | | | | | | | | | | | | | | | |
| ROCK & ROLL THERAPY (HM17521) | | | | | | | | | | | | | | | | |
| ROEHAMPTON PHYSIO/SPORTS (HM17535) | | | | | | | | | | | | | | | | |
| ROGERS, AMY (HM17544) | | | | | | | | | | | | | | | | |
| ROHRIG, A (HM17560) | | | | | | | | | | | | | | | | |
| ROSAMBEAU, VALERIE (HM17593) | | | | | | | | | | | | | | | | |
| ROSE, NICHOLAS (HM17613) | | | | | | | ● | | | | | | | | | |
| ROW, PATRICIA (HM17679) | | | | | | | | | | | | | | | | |
| RUSSO, HAZEL (HM17773) | | | | | | | | | | | | | | | | |
| RUSSO, JACQUELINE (HM17774) | | | | | | | | | | | | | | | | |
| RUTHERFORD, BERWYN (HM17780) | | | | | | | | | | | | | | | | |
| RYAN, ROSEMARY (HM17794) | | | | | | | | | | | | | | | | |
| S K REFLEXOLOGY & AROMATHERAPY (HM17812) | | | | | | | | | | | | | | | | |
| S M GORDON ANALYTICAL PSYCH (HM17815) | | | | | | | | | | | | | | | | |
| SACKLIN, CECILIA (HM17827) | | | | | | | | | | | | | | | | |
| SAGIR, SHARON (HM17839) | | | | | | | | | | | | | | | | |
| SALISBURY, ERICA (HM17855) | | | | | | | | | | | | | | | | |
| SANDRINGHAM OSTEOPATHY CLINIC (HM17928) | | | | | | | | | | | | | | | | |
| SAUNDERS, P (HM17960) | | | | | | | | | | | | | | | | |
| SAYER CLINIC (HM17993) | | | | | | | | | | | | ● | | | | |
| SAYERS, FIONA (HM17998) | | | | | | | | | | | | | | | | |
| SCHOFIELD, IAN (HM18020) | | | | | | | | | | | | | | | | |
| SCHOOL OF PSYCHO & COUNSELLING (HM18084) | | | | | | | | | | | | | | | | |
| SEEAR, MICHAEL (DR) (HM18189) | | | | ● | | | | | | | | | ● | | | |
| SEYMOUR PRACTICE (HM18257) | | | | | | | | | | | | | | | | |
| SHERWOOD PSYCHO TRAINING INS (HM18442) | | | | | | | | | | | | | | | | |
| SHIATSU PLACE (HM18458) | | | | | | | | | | | | | | ● | | |
| SHIATSU STUDIO (HM18465) | | | | | | | | | | | | | | | | |
| SHIPRA, AMIN (HM18481) | | | | | | | | | | | | | | | | |
| SHRUBBERIES (HM18512) | | | | | | | | | | | | | | | | |
| SILVER-LEIGH, V (HM18547) | | | | | | | | | | | | | | | | |

# O - Z Therapies at Practices/Businesses

| Business by County with Reference no. | Orthotics | Osteomyology | Osteopathy | PAM | Paranormal Therapies | Pattern Therapies | Physiotherapy | Phytotherapy | Pilates | Podiatry | Polarity Therapy | Postural Integration | Primal Therapy | Psionic Therapy | Psychotherapy | Pyramid Power | Pyscho-Synthesis | Reflexology | Reichian Therapy | Reiki | Remedial Massage | Rogerian Therapy | Rolfing | Seichem | Sensitivity Training |
|---|---|---|---|---|---|---|---|---|---|---|---|---|---|---|---|---|---|---|---|---|---|---|---|---|---|
| SIMPLY HERBAL CLINIC (HM18577) | | | | | | | | | | | | | | | | | | | | | | | | | |
| SIMPSON, MARGARET (HM18594) | | | | | | | | | | | | | | | | | | ● | | | | | | | |
| SINGH, GURU (HM18609) | | | ● | | | | | | | | | | | | | | | | | | | | | | |
| SLADE OSTEOPATHIC PRACTICE (HM18667) | | | ● | | | | | | | | | | | | | | | | | | | | | | |
| SLADE, JOHN (HM18668) | | | | | | | | | | | | | | | ● | | | | | | | | | | |
| SLESS, DEBORAH (HM18685) | | | | | | | | | | | | | | | ● | | | | | | | | | | |
| SMEED, BEATE (HM18702) | | | | | | | | | | | | | | | | | | ● | | | | | | | |
| SMER, IRENE (HM18703) | | | | | | | | | | | | | | | | | | ● | | | | | | | |
| SMITH, DEBORAH (HM18733) | | | | | | | | | | | | | | | ● | | | | | | | | | | |
| SMITH, RUTHIE (HM18801) | | | | | | | | | | | | | | | ● | | | | | | | | | | |
| SMITH, SHAN (HM18808) | | | | | | | | | | | | | | | | | | ● | | | | | | | |
| SMITH, TRACEY (HM18816) | | | | | | | | | | | | | | | | | | ● | | | | | | | |
| SMITH-OLIVER, J M (HM18823) | | | | | | | | | | | | | | | | | | ● | | | | | | | |
| SOHAL, D S (HM18859) | | | ● | | | | | | | | | | | | | | | | | | | | | | |
| SOLIMENO, MARIE (HM18873) | | | | | | | | | | | | | | | | | | ● | | | | | | | |
| SOUTH LONDON NATURAL HLTH CTRE (HM18911) | | | ● | | | | | | ● | | ● | ● | | | | | | ● | | ● | | | | | |
| SPALL MEDICAL CENTRE (HM18957) | | | | | | | | | | | | | | | | | | | | | | | | | |
| SPECIALIST HEALTH (HM18972) | | | ● | | | | | | | | | | | | | | | | | | | | | | |
| SPECTRUM CENTRE (HM18975) | | | | | | | | | | | | | | | ● | | | | | | | | | | |
| SPENCER, PIERS (HM19001) | | | ● | | | | | | | | | | | | | | | | | | | | | | |
| SPYROS MOUZOURIDES (HM19056) | | | | | | | | | | | | | | | | | | ● | | | | | | | |
| ST JOHN, RUTH MOYRA (HM19081) | | | | | | | | | | | | | | | | | | ● | | | | | | | |
| ST MARTINS LANE PRACTICE (HM19086) | | | ● | | | | | | | | | | | | | | | | | | | | | | |
| STANHOPE-WILLIAMSON, BARBARA (HM19126) | | | | | | | | | | | | | | | | | | ● | | | | | | | |
| STANTON, MARTIN (DR) (HM19138) | | | | | | | | | | | | | | | ● | | | | | | | | | | |
| STEELE, JULIE (HM19180) | | | | | | | | | | | | | | | | | | ● | | | | | | | |
| STEP, SUE (HM19196) | | | ● | | | | | | | | | | | | | | | | | | | | | | |
| STOBEZKI, YAEL (HM19307) | | | | | | | | | | | | | | | ● | | | | | | | | | | |
| STOCKLEY, R (HM19312) | | | | | | | | | | | | | | | ● | | | | | | | | | | |
| STOCKTON, CAROL LESLEY (HM19315) | | | ● | | | | | | | | | | | | | | | | | | | | | | |
| STONE, ANTHONY (HM19330) | | | | | | | | | | | | | | | ● | | | | | | | | | | |
| STRESS MANAGEMENT CENTRE (HM19397) | | | | | | | | | | | | | | | ● | | | | | | | | | | |
| STRONG, STELLA (HM19419) | | | ● | | | | | | | | | | | | | | | | | | | | | | |
| SULLIVAN, DAWN (HM19477) | | | | | | | | | | | | | | | | | | ● | | | | | | | |

| Business by County with Reference no. | Shiatsu | Silva Method | Sound Therapy | Spiritual Healing | Sports Massage | Stress Therapy | Swedish Body Massage | T'ai-Chi Ch'uan | Tantra Therapy | Tera-Mai | Thought Field Therapy | Touch Therapy | Transactional Analysis | Tui-na | Ultrasonics | Vibrational Therapy | Visualisation Therapy | Vitamin Therapy | Voice Therapy | X-Ray | Ying & Yang | Yoga | Zen Therapy | Zero Balancing |
|---|---|---|---|---|---|---|---|---|---|---|---|---|---|---|---|---|---|---|---|---|---|---|---|---|
| SIMPLY HERBAL CLINIC (HM18577) | | | | | | ● | | | | | | | | | | | | | | | | | | |
| SIMPSON, MARGARET (HM18594) | | | | | | | | | | | | | | | | | | | | | | | | |
| SINGH, GURU (HM18609) | | | | | | | | | | | | | | | | | | | | | | | | |
| SLADE OSTEOPATHIC PRACTICE (HM18667) | | | | | | | | | | | | | | | | | | | | | | | | |
| SLADE, JOHN (HM18668) | | | | | | | | | | | | | | | | | | | | | | | | |
| SLESS, DEBORAH (HM18685) | | | | | | | | | | | | | | | | | | | | | | | | |
| SMEED, BEATE (HM18702) | | | | | | | | | | | | | | | | | | | | | | | | |
| SMER, IRENE (HM18703) | | | | | | | | | | | | | | | | | | | | | | | | |
| SMITH, DEBORAH (HM18733) | | | | | | | | | | | | | | | | | | | | | | | | |
| SMITH, RUTHIE (HM18801) | | | | | | | | | | | | | | | | | | | | | | | | |
| SMITH, SHAN (HM18808) | | | | | | | | | | | | | | | | | | | | | | | | |
| SMITH, TRACEY (HM18816) | | | | | | | | | | | | | | | | | | | | | | | | |
| SMITH-OLIVER, J M (HM18823) | | | | | | | | | | | | | | | | | | | | | | | | |
| SOHAL, D S (HM18859) | | | | | | | | | | | | | | | | | | | | | | | | |
| SOLIMENO, MARIE (HM18873) | | | | | | | | | | | | | | | | | | | | | | | | |
| SOUTH LONDON NATURAL HLTH CTRE (HM18911) | ● | | | ● | | ● | | ● | | | | | | | | | | | | | | ● | | |
| SPALL MEDICAL CENTRE (HM18957) | | | | | | ● | | | | | | | | | | | | ● | | | ● | | | |
| SPECIALIST HEALTH (HM18972) | | | | | | | | | | | | | | | | | | | | | | | | |
| SPECTRUM CENTRE (HM18975) | | | | | | | | | | | | | | | | | | | | | | | | |
| SPENCER, PIERS (HM19001) | | | | | | | | | | | | | | | ● | | | | | | | | | |
| SPYROS MOUZOURIDES (HM19056) | | | | | | | | | | | | | | | | | | | | | | | | |
| ST JOHN, RUTH MOYRA (HM19081) | | | | | | | | | | | | | | | | | | | | | | | | |
| ST MARTINS LANE PRACTICE (HM19086) | | | | | | | | | | | | | | | | | | | | | | | | |
| STANHOPE-WILLIAMSON, BARBARA (HM19126) | | | | | | | | | | | | | | | | | | | | | | | | |
| STANTON, MARTIN (DR) (HM19138) | | | | | | | | | | | | | | | | | | | | | | | | |
| STEELE, JULIE (HM19180) | | | | | | | | | | | | | | | | | | | | | | | | |
| STEP, SUE (HM19196) | | | | | | | | | | | | | | | | | | | | | | | | |
| STOBEZKI, YAEL (HM19307) | | | | | | | | | | | | | | | | | | | | | | | | |
| STOCKLEY, R (HM19312) | | | | | | | | | | | | | | | | | | | | | | | | |
| STOCKTON, CAROL LESLEY (HM19315) | | | | | | | | | | | | | | | | | | | | | | | | |
| STONE, ANTHONY (HM19330) | | | | | | | | | | | | | | | | | | | | | | | | |
| STRESS MANAGEMENT CENTRE (HM19397) | | | | | | | | | | | | | | | | | | | | | | | | |
| STRONG, STELLA (HM19419) | | | | | | | | | | | | | | | | | | | | | | | | |
| SULLIVAN, DAWN (HM19477) | | | | | | | | | | | | | | | | | | | | | | | | |

# O - Z Therapies at Practices/Businesses

| Business by County with Reference no. | Orthotics | Osteomyology | Osteopathy | PAM | Paranormal Therapies | Pattern Therapies | Physiotherapy | Phytotherapy | Pilates | Podiatry | Polarity Therapy | Postural Integration | Primal Therapy | Psionic Therapy | Psychotherapy | Pyramid Power | Pyscho-Synthesis | Reflexology | Reichian Therapy | Reiki | Remedial Massage | Rogerian Therapy | Rolfing | Seichem | Sensitivity Training | Shiatsu | Silva Method | Sound Therapy | Spiritual Healing | Sports Massage | Stress Therapy | Swedish Body Massage | T'ai-Chi Ch'uan | Tantra Therapy | Tera-Mai | Thought Field Therapy | Touch Therapy | Transactional Analysis | Tui-na | Ultrasonics | Vibrational Therapy | Visualisation Therapy | Vitamin Therapy | Voice Therapy | X-Ray | Ying & Yang | Yoga | Zen Therapy | Zero Balancing |
|---|---|---|---|---|---|---|---|---|---|---|---|---|---|---|---|---|---|---|---|---|---|---|---|---|---|---|---|---|---|---|---|---|---|---|---|---|---|---|---|---|---|---|---|---|---|---|---|---|---|
| SULLIVAN, MARY (HM19483) |||||||||||||||●|||||||||||||||||||||||||||||||||||
| SWAIN, HILARY ANNE (HM19562) |||●||||||||||||||||||||||||||||||||||||||||||||||
| SYMBIOSIS HEALTH CLINIC (HM19622) |||●||||||||||||||||||||||||||||||||||||||||||||||
| SYMBIOSIS OSTEO/NATURAL HEALTH (HM19623) |||●||||||||||||||||||||||||||||||||||||||||||||||
| SYMONDS, G B (HM19626) |||●||||||||||||||||||||||||||||||||||||||||||||||
| TAI-CHI CHUAN (HM19657) ||||||||||||||||||||||||||||||||●|||||||||||||●||||
| TAMBOLY, KERSI (HM19671) ||||||||||||||||||●||||||||||||||||||||||||||||||||
| TATTON, DAVID (HM19721) |||●||||||||||||||||||||||||||||||||||||||||||||||
| TAYLOR, A J (HM19731) |||||||||||||||●|||||||||||||||||||||||||||||||||||
| TELFORD, JOHN (HM19820) |||●||||||||||||||||||||||||||||||||||||||||||||||
| THIEBAUD, M F (HM19918) |||●||||||||||||||||||||||||||||||||||||||||||||||
| THOMAS HEWETSON (HM19927) |||●||||||||||||||||||||||||||||||||||||||||||||||
| THOMAS HEWETSON (HM19928) |||●||||||||||||||||||||||||||||||||||||||||||||||
| THOMAS, ALAN (HM19930) |||●||||||||||||||||||||||||||||||||||||||||||||||
| THOMPSON, DARRELL (HM19973) ||||||||||||||||||●||||||||||||||||||||||||||||||||
| THOMPSON, DOROTHY (HM19974) ||||||||||||||||||●||||||||||||||||||||||||||||||||
| THOMPSON, MARK (HM19990) |||●||||||||||||||||||||||||||||||||||||||||||||||
| THURGOOD, SIMON (HM20047) |||●||||||||||||||||||||||||||||||||||||||||||||||
| TOIBIN, EILEEN (HM20116) |||||||||||||||●|||||||||||||||||||||||||||||||||||
| TOLMAN, KEITH (DR) (HM20124) |||||||||||||||●|||||||||||||||||||||||||||||||||||
| TORRIDON COMP THERAPY CLINIC (HM20173) ||||||||||||||||||●||●||||||||||||||||||||||||||||||
| TOUCH IN LIVE (HM20187) ||||||||||||||||||●||||||||||||||||||||||||||||||||
| TRAD CHINESE MASSOTHERAPY (HM20215) |||||||||||||||||||||●||||||||||||●||||||●|||||||||||
| TRAINER, G (HM20248) |||●||||||||||||||||||||||||||||||||||||||||||||||
| TRANQUILITY (HM20255) ||||||||||||||||||●||●|||||||||●||●|●|||||●|||||||||||||
| TROHEAR, PATRICIA (HM20345) |||||||||||||||||||||||||||||||●|||||||||||||||||||
| TUGWELL, SUZANNE (HM20380) |||●||||||||||||||||||||||||||||||||||||||||||||||
| TUNMORE, M (HM20399) |||●||||||||||||||||||||||||||||||||||||||||||||||
| TURNBULL, JO (HM20413) ||||||||||||||||||●||||||||||||||||||||||||||||||||
| TURNER, S (HM20436) |||●||||||||||||||||||||||||||||||||||||||||||||||
| TURNER, TERI (HM20438) |||●||||||||||||||||||||||||||||||||||||||||||||||
| TURVEY, D L & BROWNHILL, K (HM20445) |||●||||||||||||||||||||||||||||||||||||||||||||||
| TWICKENHAM PHYSIOFIRST CENTRE (HM20451) |||||||●|||||||||||||||||||||||||||||||||||||||||||
| TYLER, SHARON (HM20464) |||●||||||||||||||||||||||||||||||||||||||||||||||

# O - Z Therapies at Practices/Businesses

| Business by County with Reference no. | Orthotics | Osteomyology | Osteopathy | PAM | Paranormal Therapies | Pattern Therapies | Physiotherapy | Phytotherapy | Pilates | Podiatry | Polarity Therapy | Postural Integration | Primal Therapy | Psionic Therapy | Psychotherapy | Pyramid Power | Pyscho-Synthesis | Reflexology | Reichian Therapy | Reiki | Remedial Massage | Rogerian Therapy | Rolfing | Seichem | Sensitivity Training | Shiatsu | Silva Method | Sound Therapy | Spiritual Healing | Sports Massage | Stress Therapy | Swedish Body Massage | T'ai-Chi Ch'uan | Tantra Therapy | Tera-Mai | Thought Field Therapy | Touch Therapy | Transactional Analysis | Tui-na | Ultrasonics | Vibrational Therapy | Visualisation Therapy | Vitamin Therapy | Voice Therapy | X-Ray | Ying & Yang | Yoga | Zen Therapy | Zero Balancing |
|---|---|---|---|---|---|---|---|---|---|---|---|---|---|---|---|---|---|---|---|---|---|---|---|---|---|---|---|---|---|---|---|---|---|---|---|---|---|---|---|---|---|---|---|---|---|---|---|---|---|
| UKCP (HM20490) | | | | | | | | | | | | | ● | | ● | | ● | | ● | | | ● | | | | | | | | | ● | | | | | | | ● | | | | | | | | | | | |
| UNDERHILL, K (HM20496) | | | ● | | | | | | | | | | | | | | | | | | | | | | | | | | | | | | | | | | | | | | | | | | | | | | |
| UNDERWOOD, MARTIN (HM20500) | | | ● | | | | | | | | | | | | | | | | | | | | | | | | | | | | | | | | | | | | | | | | | | | | | | |
| UNUIS CLINIC (HM20518) | | | ● | | | | | | | | | | | | | | | | | | | | | | | | | | | | | | | | | | | | | | | | | | | | | | |
| VALE PRACTICE (HM20551) | | | ● | | | | | | ● | | | | | | ● | | | ● | | ● | | | | | | ● | | | | | ● | | ● | | | | | | | | | | ● | | | | ● | | |
| VANBRUGH PHYSIOTHERAPY CLINIC (HM20575) | | | | | | | ● | | | | | | | | | | | ● | | ● | | | | | | | | | | ● | | | | | | | | | | | | | | | | | | | |
| VASQUEZ-NALDEN, ESTELA (HM20594) | | | | | | | | | | | | | | | | | | ● | | | | | | | | | | | | | | | | | | | | | | | | | | | | | | | |
| VENN-BROWN, HELEN (HM20615) | | | | | | | | | | | | | | | | | | ● | | | | | | | | | | | | | | | | | | | | | | | | | | | | | | | |
| VILE, CAROL (HM20663) | | | ● | | | | | | | | | | | | | | | | | | | | | | | | | | | | | | | | | | | | | | | | | | | | | | |
| VILE, CAROL (HM20664) | | | ● | | | | | | | | | | | | | | | | | | | | | | | | | | | | | | | | | | | | | | | | | | | | | | |
| VISION, R E (HM20695) | | | | | | | | | | | | | | | ● | | | | | | | | | | | | | | | | | | | | | | | | | | | | | | | | | | |
| VIV HOUSE (HM20707) | | | | | | | | | | | | | | | | | | ● | | | | | | | | | | | | | | | | | | | | | | | | | | | | | | | |
| VOICE THERAPY (HM20709) | | | | | | | | | | | | | | | | | | | | | | | | | | | | | | | | | | | | | | | | | | | | ● | | | | | |
| VOLK & ASSOCIATES (HM20711) | | | | | | | | | | | | | | | ● | | | | | | | | | | | | | | | | | | | | | | | | | | | | | | | | | | |
| W P F COUNSELLING (HM20723) | | | | | | | | | | | | | | | ● | | | | | | | | | | | | | | | | | | | | | | | | | | | | | | | | | | |
| WALK IN BACK RUB (HM20758) | | | | | | | | | | | | | | | | | | | | | | | | | | ● | | | | | | | | | | | | | | | | | | | | | | | |
| WALK IN BACKRUB (HM20760) | | | | | | | | | | | | | | | | | | | | | | | | | | ● | | | | | | | | | | | | | | | | | | | | | | | |
| WALK IN BACKRUB (HM20759) | | | | | | | | | | | | | | | | | | | | | | | | | | ● | | | | | | | | | | | | | | | | | | | | | | | |
| WALKER, DYLANIE (HM20767) | | | | | | | | | | | | | | | ● | | | | | | | | | | | | | | | | | | | | | | | | | | | | | | | | | | |
| WANDSWORTH ASS OF PSYCHO (HM20887) | | | | | | | | | | | | | | | ● | | | | | | | | | | | | | | | | | | | | | | | | | | | | | | | | | | |
| WARD, MARY (HM20909) | | | | | | | | | | | | | | | | | | ● | | | | | | | | | | | | | | | | | | | | | | | | | | | | | | | |
| WARDELL, L (HM20918) | | | ● | | | | | | | | | | | | | | | | | | | | | | | | | | | | | | | | | | | | | | | | | | | | | | |
| WARREN, DAVID (HM20946) | | | ● | | | | | | | | | | | | | | | | | | | | | | | | | | | | | | | | | | | | | | | | | | | | | | |
| WART, D (HM20959) | | | ● | | | | ● | | | | | | | | | | | | | | | | | | | | | | | | | | | | | | | | | | | | | | | | | | |
| WARWICK ALTERNATIVE HEALTH (HM20961) | | | | | | | ● | | | | | | | | | | | ● | | ● | | | | | | | | | | | | | | | | | | | | | | | | | | | | | |
| WEBB, CHARLOTTE (HM21058) | | | ● | | | | | | | | | | | | | | | | | | | | | | | | | | | | | | | | | | | | | | | | | | | | | | |
| WEBB, FIONA (HM21063) | | | | | | | | | | | | | | | | | | ● | | | | | | | | | | | | | | | | | | | | | | | | | | | | | | | |
| WEBER, MARALYN (HM21082) | | | | | | | | | | | | | | | | | | ● | | | | | | | | | | | | | | | | | | | | | | | | | | | | | | | |
| WEBSTER, GEORGINA (HM21086) | | | | | | | | | | | | | | | | | | ● | | | | | | | | | | | | | | | | | | | | | | | | | | | | | | | |
| WEEKES, CHRIS (HM21104) | | | | | | | | | | | | | | | | | | ● | | | | | | | | | | | | | | | | | | | | | | | | | | | | | | | |
| WELLBURN, JOCELYN (HM21155) | | | | | | | | | | | | | | | | | | | | | | | | | | ● | | | | | | | | | | | | | | | | | | | | | | | |
| WERNINCK, RODNEY (HM21203) | | | | | | | | | | | | | | | ● | | | | | | | | | | | | | | | | | | | | | | | | | | | | | | | | | | |
| WEST LONDON HOLISTIC CENTRE (HM21226) | | | | | | | | ● | | | | | | | | | | | | | | ● | | | | | | | ● | | ● | | | | | | | ● | | | ● | ● | | | | ● | | | |
| WEST LONDON PSYCHOTHERAPY (HM21227) | | | | | | | | | | | | | | | ● | | | | | | | | | | | | | | | | | | | | | | | | | | | | | | | | | | |

# O - Z Therapies at Practices/Businesses

Business by County with Reference no.

| Business | Orthotics | Osteomyology | Osteopathy | PAM | Paranormal Therapies | Pattern Therapies | Physiotherapy | Phytotherapy | Pilates | Podiatry | Polarity Therapy | Postural Integration | Primal Therapy | Psionic Therapy | Psychotherapy | Pyramid Power | Pyscho-Synthesis | Reflexology |
|---|---|---|---|---|---|---|---|---|---|---|---|---|---|---|---|---|---|---|
| WEST LONDON YOGA SHALA (HM21228) | | | | | | | | | | | | | | | | | | |
| WESTERN, G (HM21265) | | | ● | | | | | | | | | | | | | | | |
| WHITE HART LANE THERAPY CENTRE (HM21338) | | | ● | | | | ● | | | | | | | | | | | ● |
| WHITE, NULA (HM21370) | | | | | | | | | | | | | | | ● | | | |
| WHITECHAPEL OSTEOPATHS (HM21384) | | | ● | | | | | | | | | | | | | | | |
| WHITTEMORE, JANE (HM21421) | | | | | | | | | | | | | | | | | | ● |
| WIGHAM, A (HM21468) | | | | | | | | | | | | | | | ● | | ● | |
| WILKINS, MARILYN (HM21503) | | | | | | | | | | | | | | | | | | ● |
| WILKINSON, GILL (HM21505) | | | | | | | | | | | | | | | ● | | | |
| WILLETT, OLIVIA (HM21526) | | | | | | | | | | | | | | | | | | ● |
| WILLIAMS, B A (HM21541) | | | | | | | | | | | | | | | | | | ● |
| WILLIAMS, BERNADETTE (HM21542) | | | | | | | | | | | | | | | | | | ● |
| WILLIAMS, MARILYN (HM21580) | | | | | | | | | | | | | | | | | | ● |
| WILLIAMS, RUTH (HM21588) | | | | | | | | | | | | | | | ● | | | |
| WILLMOTT, SUSAN (HM21623) | | | | | | | | | | | | | | | ● | | ● | |
| WILSON, CHRISTOPHER (HM21651) | | | | | | | | | | | | | | | | | | |
| WIMBLEDON CLINIC OF NTRL MED (HM21683) | | | ● | | | | | | | | | | | | | | | |
| WIMBLEDON OSTEO & SPORTS (HM21685) | | | ● | | | | | | | | | | | | | | | |
| WINCHMORE CLINIC OF OSTEOPATHY (HM21694) | | | ● | | | | | | | | | | | | ● | | | ● |
| WINER, J (HM21698) | | | ● | | | | | | | | | | | | | | | |
| WOMEN & MEDICAL PRACTICE (HM21772) | | | | | | | | | | | | | | | ● | | | |
| WOMEN THERAPISTS REFERRAL SV (HM21773) | | | | | | | | | | | | | | | ● | | | |
| WOMENS THERAPY LINK (HM21776) | | | | | | | | | | | | | | | ● | | | |
| WOOD, DEANA (HM21793) | | | | | | | | | | | | | | | | | | ● |
| WOOD, GILLIAN (HM21796) | | | | | | | | | | | | | | | | | | ● |
| WOODBERRY CLINIC (HM21815) | | | ● | | | | | | | | | | | | | | | |
| WOODLEIGH, R M (HM21835) | | | ● | | | | | | | | | | | | | | | |
| WOODSIDE COUNSELLING (HM21858) | | | | | | | | | | | | | | | ● | | | |
| WOOLF, PERRY (HM21872) | | | | | | | | ● | | ● | | | | | | | | |
| WOOLFE, MICHAEL & LESLIE (HM21873) | | | | | | | | | | | | | | | | | | ● |
| WOOLLISCROFT, J (HM21880) | | | | | | | | | | | | | | | ● | | | |
| WORLD OF LIGHT (HM21898) | | | | | | | | | | | | | | | | | | ● |
| WREN CLINIC (HM21919) | | | ● | | | | | | | | | | | | ● | | | ● |
| WRIGHT, JENNY (HM21936) | | | | | | | | | | | | | | | ● | | | |

| Business | Reichian Therapy | Reiki | Remedial Massage | Rogerian Therapy | Rolfing | Seichem | Sensitivity Training | Shiatsu | Silva Method | Sound Therapy | Spiritual Healing | Sports Massage | Stress Therapy | Swedish Body Massage | T'ai-Chi Ch'uan | Tantra Therapy |
|---|---|---|---|---|---|---|---|---|---|---|---|---|---|---|---|---|
| WEST LONDON YOGA SHALA (HM21228) | | | | | | | | | | | | | | | | |
| WESTERN, G (HM21265) | | | | | | | | | | | | | | | | |
| WHITE HART LANE THERAPY CENTRE (HM21338) | | | | | | | | | | | | | | | | |
| WHITE, NULA (HM21370) | | | | | | | | | | | | | | | | |
| WHITECHAPEL OSTEOPATHS (HM21384) | | | | | | | | | | | | | | | | |
| WHITTEMORE, JANE (HM21421) | | | | | | | | | | | | | | | | |
| WIGHAM, A (HM21468) | | | | | | | | | | | | | ● | | | |
| WILKINS, MARILYN (HM21503) | | | | | | | | | | | | | | | | |
| WILKINSON, GILL (HM21505) | | | | | | | | | | | | | | | | |
| WILLETT, OLIVIA (HM21526) | | | | | | | | | | | | | | | | |
| WILLIAMS, B A (HM21541) | | | | | | | | | | | | | | | | |
| WILLIAMS, BERNADETTE (HM21542) | | | | | | | | | | | | | | | | |
| WILLIAMS, MARILYN (HM21580) | | | | | | | | | | | | | | | | |
| WILLIAMS, RUTH (HM21588) | | | | | | | | | | | | | | | | |
| WILLMOTT, SUSAN (HM21623) | | | | | | | | | | | | | | | | |
| WILSON, CHRISTOPHER (HM21651) | | ● | | | | | | | | | | | | | | |
| WIMBLEDON CLINIC OF NTRL MED (HM21683) | | | | | | | | | | | | | | | | |
| WIMBLEDON OSTEO & SPORTS (HM21685) | | | | | | | | | | | | | | | | |
| WINCHMORE CLINIC OF OSTEOPATHY (HM21694) | | | | | | | | ● | | | | | | | | |
| WINER, J (HM21698) | | | | | | | | | | | | | | | | |
| WOMEN & MEDICAL PRACTICE (HM21772) | | | | | | | | | | | | | | | | |
| WOMEN THERAPISTS REFERRAL SV (HM21773) | | | | | | | | | | | | | | | | |
| WOMENS THERAPY LINK (HM21776) | | | | | | | | | | | | | | | | |
| WOOD, DEANA (HM21793) | | | | | | | | | | | | | | | | |
| WOOD, GILLIAN (HM21796) | | | | | | | | | | | | | | | | |
| WOODBERRY CLINIC (HM21815) | | | | | | | | | | | | | | | | |
| WOODLEIGH, R M (HM21835) | | | | | | | | | | | | | | | | |
| WOODSIDE COUNSELLING (HM21858) | | | | | | | | | | | | | | | | |
| WOOLF, PERRY (HM21872) | | | | | | | | | | | | | | | | |
| WOOLFE, MICHAEL & LESLIE (HM21873) | | | | | | | | | | | | | | | | |
| WOOLLISCROFT, J (HM21880) | | | | | | | | | | | | | | | | |
| WORLD OF LIGHT (HM21898) | | ● | | | | | | | | | ● | | | | | |
| WREN CLINIC (HM21919) | | | | | | | | ● | | | | | | | | |
| WRIGHT, JENNY (HM21936) | | | | | | | | | | | | | ● | | | |

| Business | Tera-Mai | Thought Field Therapy | Touch Therapy | Transactional Analysis | Tui-na | Ultrasonics | Vibrational Therapy | Visualisation Therapy | Vitamin Therapy | Voice Therapy | X-Ray | Ying & Yang | Yoga | Zen Therapy | Zero Balancing |
|---|---|---|---|---|---|---|---|---|---|---|---|---|---|---|---|
| WEST LONDON YOGA SHALA (HM21228) | | | | | | | | | | | | | ● | | |
| WESTERN, G (HM21265) | | | | | | | | | | | | | | | |
| WHITE HART LANE THERAPY CENTRE (HM21338) | | | | | | | | | | | | | | | |
| WHITE, NULA (HM21370) | | | | | | | | | | | | | | | |
| WHITECHAPEL OSTEOPATHS (HM21384) | | | | | | | | | | | | | | | |
| WHITTEMORE, JANE (HM21421) | | | | | | | | | | | | | | | |
| WIGHAM, A (HM21468) | | | | | | | | ● | | | | | | | |
| WILKINS, MARILYN (HM21503) | | | | | | | | | | | | | | | |
| WILKINSON, GILL (HM21505) | | | | | | | | | | | | | | | |
| WILLETT, OLIVIA (HM21526) | | | | | | | | | | | | | | | |
| WILLIAMS, B A (HM21541) | | | | | | | | | | | | | | | |
| WILLIAMS, BERNADETTE (HM21542) | | | | | | | | | | | | | | | |
| WILLIAMS, MARILYN (HM21580) | | | | | | | | | | | | | | | |
| WILLIAMS, RUTH (HM21588) | | | | | | | | | | | | | | | |
| WILLMOTT, SUSAN (HM21623) | | | | ● | | | | | | | | | | | |
| WILSON, CHRISTOPHER (HM21651) | | | | | | | | | | | | | | | |
| WIMBLEDON CLINIC OF NTRL MED (HM21683) | | | | | | | | | | | | | | | |
| WIMBLEDON OSTEO & SPORTS (HM21685) | | | | | | | | | | | | | | | |
| WINCHMORE CLINIC OF OSTEOPATHY (HM21694) | | | | ● | | ● | | | | | | | | | |
| WINER, J (HM21698) | | | | | | | | | | | | | | | |
| WOMEN & MEDICAL PRACTICE (HM21772) | | | | | | | | | | | | | | | |
| WOMEN THERAPISTS REFERRAL SV (HM21773) | | | | | | | | | | | | | | | |
| WOMENS THERAPY LINK (HM21776) | | | | | | | | | | | | | | | |
| WOOD, DEANA (HM21793) | | | | | | | | | | | | | | | |
| WOOD, GILLIAN (HM21796) | | | | | | | | | | | | | | | |
| WOODBERRY CLINIC (HM21815) | | | | | | | | | | | | | | | |
| WOODLEIGH, R M (HM21835) | | | | | | | | | | | | | | | |
| WOODSIDE COUNSELLING (HM21858) | | | | | | | | | | | | | | | |
| WOOLF, PERRY (HM21872) | | | | | | ● | | | | | | | | | |
| WOOLFE, MICHAEL & LESLIE (HM21873) | | | | | | | | | | | | | | | |
| WOOLLISCROFT, J (HM21880) | | | | | | | | | | | | | | | |
| WORLD OF LIGHT (HM21898) | | | | | | | | | | | | | | | |
| WREN CLINIC (HM21919) | | | | | | | | | | | | | | | |
| WRIGHT, JENNY (HM21936) | | | | | | | | | | | | | | | |

# O - Z Therapies at Practices/Businesses

| Business by County with Reference no. | Orthotics | Osteomyology | Osteopathy | PAM | Paranormal Therapies | Pattern Therapies | Physiotherapy | Phytotherapy | Pilates | Podiatry | Polarity Therapy | Postural Integration | Primal Therapy | Psionic Therapy | Psychotherapy | Pyramid Power | Pyscho-Synthesis | Reflexology | Reichian Therapy | Reiki | Remedial Massage | Rogerian Therapy | Rolfing | Seichem | Sensitivity Training | Shiatsu | Silva Method | Sound Therapy | Spiritual Healing | Sports Massage | Stress Therapy | Swedish Body Massage | T'ai-Chi Ch'uan | Tantra Therapy | Tera-Mai | Thought Field Therapy | Touch Therapy | Transactional Analysis | Tui-na | Ultrasonics | Vibrational Therapy | Visualisation Therapy | Vitamin Therapy | Voice Therapy | X-Ray | Ying & Yang | Yoga | Zen Therapy | Zero Balancing |
|---|---|---|---|---|---|---|---|---|---|---|---|---|---|---|---|---|---|---|---|---|---|---|---|---|---|---|---|---|---|---|---|---|---|---|---|---|---|---|---|---|---|---|---|---|---|---|---|---|---|
| WYLIE, DIANE (HM21973) |||||||||||||||||||●||||||||||||||||||||||||||||||||
| YING, FRANK (HM22014) ||||●|||||||||||||||||||||||||||||||||||||||||||||||
| YOGA THERAPY CENTRE (HM22033) |||||||||||||||||||||||||||||||||||||||||||||||●|||
| YOGA THERAPY CENTRE (HM22032) |||||||||||||||||||||||||||||||||||||||||||||||●|||
| YOUNGS, BRIAN K (HM22084) ||||●|||||||||||||||||||||||||||||||||||||||||||||||
| YULE, AILEEN (HM22087) |||||||||||||||||||●||||||||||||||||||||||||||||||||
| ZAHNISER, ESTHER (HM22094) ||||||||||||||||●|||||||||||||||||||||||||||||||||||
| ZARBAFI, A (HM22096) ||||||||||||||||●|||||||||||||||||||||||||||||||||||
| ZEN HEALTH CENTRE (HM22100) ||||●|||||||||||||||●||●||||||●|||●||||||||||||||●|||●||●||
| ZEN SHIATSU & HEALING TAO (HM22101) |||||||||||||||||||||||||||●|||||||●|●||||||||||||||||
| ZIA, ROBINA (HM22109) |||||||||||||||||||●||||||||||||||||||||||||||||||||
| ZIELINSKI, KRYSTYNA (HM22111) ||||●|||||||||||||||||||||||||||||||||||||||||||||||
| MANCHESTER (GREATER) ||||||||||||||||||||||||||||||||||||||||||||||||||
| A SIR ROBERTS ALT PLACE (HM00045) ||||●|||||||||●|||●|●||●||||||||●|||●||●||||||●||||●|||||||||
| A6 CHIROPODY PRACTICE (HM00055) |||||||||||||||||||●||||||||||||||||||||||||||||||||
| ACUMEDIC (HM00220) ||||||||||||||||||||||||||||||||||●|||||||||||||||||
| ADVANCED PHYSIOTHERAPY CLINIC (HM00403) ||||||||●|||||||||||●||||||||||||||||||||||●||||||||||
| ALL IN THE MIND (HM00582) ||||||||||||||||||||||||||||||||●|||||||||||●||||||||
| ANDREWS CLINIC (HM00850) ||||●|||||||||||||||||||||||||||||||||||||||||||||||
| ARMITAGE, S (HM01014) ||||●|||||||||||||||||||||||||||||||||||||||||||||||
| AROMATHERAPY LADIES MASSAGE (HM01118) |||||||||||||||||||●||||||||||||||||||||||||||||||||
| ASCOTT, TARA (HM01179) ||||●|||||||||||||||||||||||||||||||||||||||||||||||
| ASTLEY COMPLEMENTARY CENTRE (HM01300) ||||●||||||||||||●|||●||●||||||●|||||●|||||||||||||||||||
| BARLEY, ANDREW (HM01717) ||||||||||||||||●|||||||||||||||||||||||||||||||||||
| BENNETT, MO (HM02152) ||||||||||||||||●|||||||||||||||||||||||||||||||||||
| BRAMHALL CHIROPRACTIC CLINIC (HM02898) ||||||||||||||||||||||||||||||||||||||||||||||●|||||
| BROOKHOUSE, S (HM03168) ||||||||||||||||●|||||||||||||||||||||||||||||||||||
| BROWN & ROBINSON (HM03207) ||||●|||||||||||||||||||||||||||||||||||||||||||||||
| BURGESS, KAREN (HM03377) ||||||||●|||||||||||||||||||||||||||||||||||||||||||
| C CARTLEDGE REFLEXOLOGY (HM03521) |||||||||||||||||||●||||||||||||||||||||||||||||||||
| CENTRE FOR SHIATSU (HM03917) |||||||||||||||||||||||||||●||||||||||||||||||||||||
| CHARTERED PHYSIOTHERAPY CLINIC (HM04046) ||||●||||●|||||||||||||||||||||||||||||||||●||||||||||
| CHORLTON STRESS MANAGEMENT (HM04430) ||||||●||||||||||●|||||●|||||||||||●|||||||||||●||||||||
| CLARENDON CLINIC (HM04540) ||||●|||||||||||||||●||||||||||||||||||||||●|||●|||||||

# O - Z Therapies at Practices/Businesses

| Business by County with Reference no. | Orthotics | Osteomyology | Osteopathy | PAM | Paranormal Therapies | Pattern Therapies | Physiotherapy | Phytotherapy | Pilates | Podiatry | Polarity Therapy | Postural Integration | Primal Therapy | Psionic Therapy | Psychotherapy | Pyramid Power | Pyscho-Synthesis | Reflexology | Reichian Therapy | Reiki | Remedial Massage | Rogerian Therapy | Rolfing | Seichem | Sensitivity Training | Shiatsu | Silva Method | Sound Therapy | Spiritual Healing | Sports Massage | Stress Therapy | Swedish Body Massage | T'ai-Chi Ch'uan | Tantra Therapy | Tera-Mai | Thought Field Therapy | Touch Therapy | Transactional Analysis | Tui-na | Ultrasonics | Vibrational Therapy | Visualisation Therapy | Vitamin Therapy | Voice Therapy | X-Ray | Ying & Yang | Yoga | Zen Therapy | Zero Balancing |
|---|---|---|---|---|---|---|---|---|---|---|---|---|---|---|---|---|---|---|---|---|---|---|---|---|---|---|---|---|---|---|---|---|---|---|---|---|---|---|---|---|---|---|---|---|---|---|---|---|---|
| CLEVERLY, MARAGRET (HM04658) | | | | | | | | | | | | | | | | | | ● | | | | | | | | | | | | | | | | | | | | | | | | | | | | | | | |
| COLLINGE, J C (HM04863) | | | | | | | | ● | | | | | | | | | | | | | | | | | | | | | | | | | | | | | | | | ● | | | | | | | | | |
| COSGROVES PHYSIO-FIT CENTRE (HM05201) | | | | | | | | | | | | | | | | | | | | | | | | | | | | | | | | | | | | | | | | ● | | | | | | | ● | | |
| CROSSWAY CLINIC (HM05491) | | | ● | | | | | | | | | | | | | | | ● | | | | | | | | | | | | | ● | | | | | | | | | | | | | | | | | | |
| DIDSBURY CHIROPRACTIC CLINIC (HM06090) | | | | | | | | | | | | | | | | | | | | | | | | | | | | | | | | | | | | | | | | | | | | | ● | | | | |
| EVANS, DAVID (HM06967) | | | | | | | | | | | | | | | ● | | | | | ● | | | | | | | | | | | ● | | | | | | | | | | | ● | | | | | | | |
| GOGIA, D R (DR) (HM08195) | | | ● | | | | | | | | | | | | | | | | | | | | | | | | | | | | | | | | | | | | | | | | | | | | | | |
| GRAHAM COOMBE - MCTIMONEY (HM08337) | | | | | | | | | | | | | | | | | | | | ● | | | | | | | | | | | | | | | | | | | | | | | | | | | | | |
| GUILD OF PRACTITIONERS (HM08627) | | | | | | | | | | | | | | | | | | | | | | | | | | | | | | | ● | | | | | | ● | | | | ● | | | | | | | | |
| HAMPDEN HOUSE CENTRE (HM08872) | | | | | | | | | | | | | | | ● | | | | | | | | | | | | | | | | | | | | | | | | | | | | | | | | | | |
| HIGH PEAK HOLISTIC CENTRE (HM09738) | | | | | | | | | | | | | | | | | | ● | | | | | | | | | | | | | | | | | | | | | | | | | | | | | | | |
| HODKINSON, EDWINA (HM09891) | | | | | | | | | | | | | | | | | | ● | | | | | | | | | | | | | | | | | | | | | | | | | | | | | | | |
| HOLMED CLINIC (HM10038) | | | ● | | | | | | | | | | | | | | | | | | | | | | | | | | | | | | | | | | | | | | | | | | | | | | |
| HUMAN TOUCH CENTRE (HM10366) | | | | | | | | | | | | | | | ● | | | ● | | ● | | | | | | | | | | | | | | | | | | | | | | | | | | | | | |
| IBBETSON, JOHN A (HM10564) | | | ● | | | | | | | | | | | | | | | | | | | | | | | | | | | | | | | | | | | | | | | | | | | | | | |
| IBBOTSON, GEOFF (DR) (HM10565) | | | | | | | | | | | | | | | ● | | | | | | | | | | | | | | | | | | | | | | | | | | | | | | | | | | |
| KYRIAKOS KAPLANIS (HM11838) | | | | | | | | | | | | | | | | | | ● | | | | | | | | | | | | | | | | | | | | | | | | | | | | | | | |
| M J HAYLETT - PHYSIOTHERAPIST (HM12802) | | | | | | | | | | | | | | | | | | | | | | | | | | | | | | | ● | | | | | | | | | ● | | | | | | | | | |
| MACARTNEY HOUSE PSYCHOTHERAPY (HM12821) | | | | | | | | | | | | | | | ● | | | | | | | | | | | | | | | | | | | | | | | | | | | | | | | | | | |
| MANCHESTER GESTALT CENTRE (HM13001) | | | | | | | | | | | | | | | ● | | | | | | | | | | | | | | | | | | | | | | | | | | | | | | | | | | |
| MANCHESTER INSTITUTE-PSYCHO (HM13003) | | | | | | | | | | | | | | | ● | | | | | | | | | | | | | | | | | | | | | | | | | | | | | | | | | | |
| MANCHESTER SCHOOL OF MASSAGE (HM13004) | | | | | | | | | | | | | | | | | | ● | | | | | | | | | | | | | | | | | | | | | | | | | | | | | | | |
| MILWARD, S J (HM13955) | | | ● | | | | | | | | | | | | | | | | | | | | | | | | | | | | | | | | | | | | | | | | | | | | | | |
| MOBILE COMPLEMENTARY THERAPIES (HM14029) | | | | | | | | | | | | | | | | | | | | | ● | | | | | | | | | | ● | | | | | | | | | | | | | | | | | | |
| MOUNT STREET COMP THERAPIES (HM14291) | | | | | | | | | | | | | | | | | | ● | | | | | | | | ● | | | | | | | | | | | | | | | | | | | | | | | |
| NEWSHAM ASS URMSTON REMEDIAL (HM14889) | | | ● | | | | | | | | | | | | | | | | | | | | | | | | | | | | | | | | | | | | | | | | | | | | | | |
| NICKI HAVES PHYSIO CLINIC (HM14923) | | | | | | | ● | | | | | | | | | | | | | | | | | | | | | | | | | | | | | | | | | | | | | | | | | | |
| NIVERN, D (HM14954) | | | | | | | | | | | | | | | | | | ● | | ● | | | | | | ● | | | | | ● | | | | | | | | | | | | ● | | | ● | | | |
| PHILLIPS, LORRAINE (HM16139) | | | | | | | | | | | | | | | | | | ● | | | | | | | | | | | | | | | | | | | | | | | | | | | | | | | |
| POLLARD, JACQUELINE (HM16406) | | | | | | | | | | | | | | | | | | ● | | | | | | | | | | | | | | | | | | | | | | | | | | | | | | | |
| POSTON, JONATHAN (HM16459) | | | ● | | | | | | | | | | | | | | | | | | | | | | | | | | | | | | | | | | | | | | | | | | | | | | |
| REDHOUSE (HM17027) | | | | | | | | | | | | | | | ● | | | | | | | | | | | | | | | | | | | | | | | | | | | | | | | | | | |
| REFLEXOLOGY & CHIROPODY (HM17079) | | | | | | | | | | | | | | | | | | ● | | | | | | | | | | | | | ● | | | | | | | | | | | | | | | | | | |
| SCHOFIELD, G A (HM18018) | | | | | | | | | | ● | | | | | | | | | | | | | | | | | | | | | | | | | | | | | | | | | | | | | | | |

# O - Z Therapies at Practices/Businesses

| Business by County with Reference no. | Orthotics | Osteomyology | Osteopathy | PAM | Paranormal Therapies | Pattern Therapies | Physiotherapy | Phytotherapy | Pilates | Podiatry | Polarity Therapy | Postural Integration | Primal Therapy | Psionic Therapy | Psychotherapy | Pyramid Power | Pyscho-Synthesis | Reflexology | Reichian Therapy | Reiki | Remedial Massage | Rogerian Therapy | Rolfing | Seichem | Sensitivity Training | Shiatsu | Silva Method | Sound Therapy | Spiritual Healing | Sports Massage | Stress Therapy | Swedish Body Massage | T'ai-Chi Ch'uan | Tantra Therapy | Tera-Mai | Thought Field Therapy | Touch Therapy | Transactional Analysis | Tui-na | Ultrasonics | Vibrational Therapy | Visualisation Therapy | Vitamin Therapy | Voice Therapy | X-Ray | Ying & Yang | Yoga | Zen Therapy | Zero Balancing |
|---|---|---|---|---|---|---|---|---|---|---|---|---|---|---|---|---|---|---|---|---|---|---|---|---|---|---|---|---|---|---|---|---|---|---|---|---|---|---|---|---|---|---|---|---|---|---|---|---|---|
| ST JOHN STREET PHYSIO PRACTICE (HM19080) | | | | | | | | ● | | | | | | | | | | | | | | | | | | | | | | | | | | | | | | | | ● | | | | | | | | | |
| STIRLING, DIANNE (HM19301) | | | | | | | | | | | | | | | | | | ● | | ● | | | | | | | | | | | | | | | | | | | | | | | | | | | | | |
| SWINTON HEALTH FOODS (HM19600) | | | | | | | | ● | | | | | | | | | | ● | | ● | | | | | | | | | | | | | | | | | | | | | | | | | | | | | |
| THERAPY BREAK (HM19891) | | | | | | | ● | | | | | | | | | | | ● | | ● | ● | | | | | | | | ● | | ● | | | | | | | | | | | | | | | | | | |
| WAINWRIGHT, P (HM20739) | | | | | | | | | | ● | | | | | | | | ● | | ● | | | | | | | | | | | | | | | | | | | | | | | | | | | | | |
| WILLIAMS, JANE (HM21569) | | | | | | | | | | | | | | | ● | | | | | | | | | | | | | | | | | | | | | | | | | | | | | | | | | | |
| WILSON, NICOLA (HM21663) | | | | | | | | | | | | | | | | | | ● | | | | | | | | | | | | | | | | | | | | | | | | | | | | | | | |
| **MERSEYSIDE** | | | | | | | | | | | | | | | | | | | | | | | | | | | | | | | | | | | | | | | | | | | | | | | | | |
| ABBEY FOOT CLINIC (HM00083) | | | | | | | | | | ● | | | | | | | | | | | | | | | | | | | | | | | | | | | | | | | | | | | | | | | |
| AINTREE OSTEOPATHIC (HM00439) | ● | | ● | | | | | | | | | | | | | | | ● | | | | | | | | | | | | | | | | | | | | | | | | | | | | | | | |
| AITKEN, ANNE (HM00452) | | | | | | | | | | | | | | | ● | | | | | | | | | | | | | | | | | | | | | | | | | | | | | | | | | | |
| ALLERTON HEALTH CENTRE (HM00639) | | | ● | | | | | | | | | | | | | | | | | | ● | | | | | | | | | | | | | | | | | | | | | | | | | | | | |
| ALLERTON REMEDIAL CLINIC (HM00642) | | | ● | | | | | | | | | | | | | | | | | | | | | | | | | | | | | | | | | | | | | | | | | | | | | | |
| ALTERNATIVE MEDICAL CENTRE (HM00710) | | | ● | | | | | | | | | | | | | | | | | | | | | | | | | | | | | | | | | | | | | | | | | | | | | | |
| ATKINSON, D W (HM01321) | | | ● | | | | | | | | | | | | | | | | | | | | | | | | | | | | | | | | | | | | | | | | | | | | | | |
| ATKINSON, D W (HM01322) | | | ● | | | | | | | | | | | | | | | | | | | | | | | | | | | | | | | | | | | | | | | | | | | | | | |
| BARKER, KAY E (HM01711) | | | ● | | | | | | | | | | | | | | | | | | | | | | | | | | | | | | | | | | | | | | | | | | | | | | |
| BESTEL & ASSOCIATES (HM02227) | | | | | | | | | | | | | | | ● | | | | | | | | | | | | | | | | | | | | | | | | | | | | | | | | | | |
| BIMPSON, PETER (HM02311) | | | | | | | | | | | | | | | | | | ● | | | | | | | | | | | | | | | | | | | | | | | | | | | | | | | |
| BOLTON, TOM (HM02663) | | | | | | | | | | | | | | | ● | | | | | | | | | | | | | | | | | | | | | | | | | | | | | | | | | | |
| BOYLE, ANDREW (HM02826) | ● | | | | | | | | ● | ● | | | | | | | | ● | | ● | | | | | | | | | | | | | | | | | | | | ● | | | | | | | | | |
| BRENNAN, M A (HM02958) | ● | | | | | | | | | ● | | | | | | | | | | | | | | | | | | | | | | | | | | | | | | | | | | | | | | | |
| BRITTAIN, HAL (HM03101) | | | ● | | | | | | | | | | | | | | | | | | | | | | | | | | | | | | | | | | | | | | | | | | | | | | |
| CARMICHAEL, KAREN (HM03710) | | | | | | | | | | | | | | | | | | ● | | | | | | | | | | | | | | | | | | | | | | | | | | | | | | | |
| CARTER, G R (HM03778) | ● | | | | | | | | | ● | | | | | | | | | | | | | | | | | | | | | | | | | | | | | | | | | | | | | | | |
| CAWLEY, TONY (HM03871) | | | | | | | | | | | | | | | ● | | | | | | | ● | | | | | | | | | ● | | | | | | | | | | | ● | | | | | | | |
| CONROY, GILLIAN (HM05008) | | | | | | | | | | | | | | | | | | ● | | | | | | | | | | | | | | | | | | | | | | | | | | | | | | | |
| COUNSELLING CLINIC (HM05251) | | | | | | | | | | | | | | | ● | | | | | | | | | | | | | | | | | | | | | | | | | | | | | | | | | | |
| D A F CLINIC (HM05655) | | | | | | | | | | | | | | | | | | ● | | | | | | | | | | | | | ● | | | | | | | | | | | ● | | | | | | | |
| DARE TO CARE (HM05739) | | | | | | | | | | | | | | | | | | ● | | ● | | | | | | ● | | | | | | | | | | | | | | | | | | | | | ● | | |
| ECCLES CHIROPODY SERVICES (HM06572) | | | | | | | | | | ● | | | | | | | | | | | | | | | | | | | | | | | | | | | | | | | | | | | | | | | |
| FARMER, BARBARA (HM01681) | | | | | | | | ● | | | | | | | | | | | | | | | | | | | | | | | ● | | | | | | | | | ● | | | | | | | | | |
| FRESHLEA PRIVATE CLINICS (HM07738) | | | ● | | | | | | | | | | | | | | | | | | ● | | | | | | | | | | | | | | | | | | | | | | | | | | | | |
| GATEAUD, S (HM07924) | | | ● | | | | | | | | | | | | | | | ● | | ● | | | | | | | | | | | | | | | | | | | | | | | | | | | | | |

# O - Z Therapies at Practices/Businesses

| Business by County with Reference no. | Orthotics | Osteomyology | Osteopathy | PAM | Paranormal Therapies | Pattern Therapies | Physiotherapy | Phytotherapy | Pilates | Podiatry | Polarity Therapy | Postural Integration | Primal Therapy | Psionic Therapy | Psychotherapy | Pyramid Power | Pyscho-Synthesis | Reflexology | Reichian Therapy | Reiki | Remedial Massage | Rogerian Therapy | Rolfing | Seichem | Sensitivity Training |
|---|---|---|---|---|---|---|---|---|---|---|---|---|---|---|---|---|---|---|---|---|---|---|---|---|---|
| GOLDEN SAFFRON (HM08209) | | | | | | | | | | | | | | | | | | | | | | | | | |
| HALSALL, JANET (HM08817) | | | | | | | | | | | | | | | | | |●| | | | | | | |
| HEAL TO TOE (HM09311) | | | | | | | | | | | | | | | | | |●| | | | | | | |
| HILL, LESLEY (HM09781) | | | | | | | | | | | | | | | | | |●| | | | | | | |
| HYPNOCARE (HM10490) | | | | | | | | | | | | | | |●| | | | | | | | | | |
| JABBAR, A (HM10806) | | |●| | | | | | | | | | | | | | | | | | | | | | |
| JACKSONS (HM10854) | | | | | | | |●| | | | | | | | | | | | | | | | | |
| JAMES, ANN (HM10880) |●| | | | | | | | | | | | | | | | | | | | | | | | |
| JARVIS, K R (HM10934) |●| | | | | | | | |●| | | | | | | | | | | | | | | |
| JENKINS, JUDITH (HM10989) | | |●| | | | | | | | | | | | | | | | | | | | | | |
| KARRAN, MARGARETTE (HM11330) | | | | | | | | | | | | | | | | | |●| | | | | | | |
| KNOWLES, JANICE (HM11771) | | | | | | | | | |●| | | | | | | | | | | | | | | |
| LAVENDER, M J (HM12026) | | |●| | | | | | | | | | | | | | | | | | | | | | |
| LYON, A (HM12777) | | |●| | | | | | | | | | | | | | | | | | | | | | |
| MARTIN, JEAN (HM13200) | | | | | | | | | | | | | | | | | |●| | | | | | | |
| MARTLAND, ANNE (HM13218) | | | | | | | | | | | | | | | | | |●| | | | | | | |
| MASSAGE & REFLEXOLOGY (HM13255) | | | | | | | | | | | | | | | | | |●| | | | | | | |
| MCLOUGHLIN, CLAIRE (HM13560) |●| | | | | | | | |●| | | | | | | | | | | | | | | |
| MILLIGAN, RICHARD (HM13915) | | | | | | | | | | | | | | | | | |●| | | | | | | |
| MOON, BARBARA (HM14099) | | | | | | | | | | | | | | | | | |●| | | | | | | |
| NATURAL HEALTH CLINIC (HM14576) | | | | | | | | | | | | | | | | | |●| | | | | | | |
| NATUROPATHIC HEALTH CENTRE (HM14709) | | |●| | | | | | | | | | | | | | |●| | | | |●| | |
| ORR, WILLIAM A (HM15405) | | | | | | |●| | | | | | | | | | | | | | | | | | |
| PSYCHOLOGICAL CONSULTING SVS (HM16704) | | | | | | | | | | | | | | |●| | | | | | | | | | |
| REIKI-4-LIFE (HM17150) | | | | | | | | | | | | | | | | | | | |●| | | | | |
| SANCTUARY NATURAL HEALTH (HM17893) | | | | | | | | | | | | | | | | | |●| |●| | | | | |
| SCOTT, ANDREW (HM18107) | | | | | | | | | | | | | | | | | | | | | | | | | |
| SEFTON PARK NATURAL THRPY CTRE (HM18198) | | | | | | | | | | |●|●| | |●| | | |●| | | | | | |
| SIMPSON CLINIC (HM18584) | | |●| | | | |●| | | | | | | | | | | | | | | | | |
| SOUTHPORT OSTEO & ACUPUNCTURE (HM18942) | | |●| | | | | | | | | | | | | | | | |●| | | | | |
| STEINA SPORTS & PHYSIOTHERAPY (HM19188) | | | | | | |●| | | | | | | | | | |●| | | | | | | |
| TARA SCHOOL OF HYPNOTHERAPY (HM19701) | | | | | | | | | | | | | | | | | | | | | | | | | |
| TAYLOR, KAREN (HM19775) | | | | | | | | | | | | | | | | | |●| | | | | | | |
| THERAPY 21 (HM19890) | | | | | | | | | | | | | | | | | | | |●| | | | | |

| Business by County with Reference no. | Shiatsu | Silva Method | Sound Therapy | Spiritual Healing | Sports Massage | Stress Therapy | Swedish Body Massage | T'ai-Chi Ch'uan | Tantra Therapy | Tera-Mai | Thought Field Therapy | Touch Therapy | Transactional Analysis | Tui-na | Ultrasonics | Vibrational Therapy | Visualisation Therapy | Vitamin Therapy | Voice Therapy | X-Ray | Ying & Yang | Yoga | Zen Therapy | Zero Balancing |
|---|---|---|---|---|---|---|---|---|---|---|---|---|---|---|---|---|---|---|---|---|---|---|---|---|
| GOLDEN SAFFRON (HM08209) | | | | | | | | | | | | | | | | | | | | | | | |●|
| HALSALL, JANET (HM08817) | | | | | | | | | | | | | | | | | | | | | | | | |
| HEAL TO TOE (HM09311) | | | | | | | | | | | | | | | | | | | | | | | | |
| HILL, LESLEY (HM09781) | | | | | | | | | | | | | | | | | | | | | | | | |
| HYPNOCARE (HM10490) | | | | | | | | | | | | | | | | | | | | | | | | |
| JABBAR, A (HM10806) | | | | | | | | | | | | | | | | | | | | | | | | |
| JACKSONS (HM10854) | | | | | | | | | | | | | | | | | | | | | | | | |
| JAMES, ANN (HM10880) | | | | | | | | | | | | | | |●| | | | | | | | | |
| JARVIS, K R (HM10934) | | | | | | | | | | | | | | | | | | | | | | | | |
| JENKINS, JUDITH (HM10989) | | | | | | | | | | | | | | | | | | | | | | | | |
| KARRAN, MARGARETTE (HM11330) | | | | | | | | | | | | | | | | | | | | | | | | |
| KNOWLES, JANICE (HM11771) | | | | | | | | | | | | | | | | | | | | | | | | |
| LAVENDER, M J (HM12026) | | | | | | | | | | | | | | | | | | | | | | | | |
| LYON, A (HM12777) | | | | | | | | | | | | | | | | | | | | | | | | |
| MARTIN, JEAN (HM13200) | | | | | | | | | | | | | | | | | | | | | | | | |
| MARTLAND, ANNE (HM13218) | | | | | | | | | | | | | | | | | | | | | | | | |
| MASSAGE & REFLEXOLOGY (HM13255) | | | | | | | | | | | | | | | | | | | | | | | | |
| MCLOUGHLIN, CLAIRE (HM13560) | | | | | | | | | | | | | | | | | | | | | | | | |
| MILLIGAN, RICHARD (HM13915) | | | | | | | | | | | | | | | | | | | | | | | | |
| MOON, BARBARA (HM14099) | | | | | | | | | | | | | | | | | | | | | | | | |
| NATURAL HEALTH CLINIC (HM14576) | | | | | | | | | | | | | | | | | | | | | | | | |
| NATUROPATHIC HEALTH CENTRE (HM14709) | | | | | | | | | | | | | | |●| | | | | | | | | |
| ORR, WILLIAM A (HM15405) | | | | | | | | | | | | | | | | | | | | | | | | |
| PSYCHOLOGICAL CONSULTING SVS (HM16704) | | | | | | | | | | | | | | | | | | | | | | | | |
| REIKI-4-LIFE (HM17150) | | | | | | | | | | | | | | | | | | | | | | | | |
| SANCTUARY NATURAL HEALTH (HM17893) |●| | | | | | | | | | |●| | | | | | | | | | | | |
| SCOTT, ANDREW (HM18107) |●| | | | | | | | | | | | | | | | | | | | | | | |
| SEFTON PARK NATURAL THRPY CTRE (HM18198) | | | | | | | | | | | | | | | | | | | | | | | | |
| SIMPSON CLINIC (HM18584) | | | | | | | | | | | | | | | | | |●| | |●| | | |
| SOUTHPORT OSTEO & ACUPUNCTURE (HM18942) | | | | | | | | | | | | | | | | | | | | | | | | |
| STEINA SPORTS & PHYSIOTHERAPY (HM19188) | | | | | | | | | | | | | | | | | | | | | | | | |
| TARA SCHOOL OF HYPNOTHERAPY (HM19701) | | | | | | | | | | | | | | | | |●| | | | | | | |
| TAYLOR, KAREN (HM19775) | | | | | | | | | | | | | | | | | | | | | | | | |
| THERAPY 21 (HM19890) |●| | | | |●| | | |●| |●| | | | | | | | | | | | |

# O - Z Therapies at Practices/Businesses

| Business by County with Reference no. | Orthotics | Osteomyology | Osteopathy | PAM | Paranormal Therapies | Pattern Therapies | Physiotherapy | Phytotherapy | Pilates | Podiatry | Polarity Therapy | Postural Integration | Primal Therapy | Psionic Therapy | Psychotherapy | Pyramid Power | Pyscho-Synthesis |
|---|---|---|---|---|---|---|---|---|---|---|---|---|---|---|---|---|---|
| TUEBROOK OSTEOPATHIC CLINIC (HM20375) | | | ● | | | | | | | | | | | | | | |
| TUEBROOK OSTEOPATHIC CLINIC (HM20374) | | | ● | | | | | | | | | | | | | | |
| VAEZZADEH, M (HM20546) | | | ● | | | | | | | | | | | | | | |
| WILLIAMS, T H (HM21597) | | | | | | | | | | ● | | | | | | | |
| WILLIAMS, TECWYN H (HM21598) | | | | | | | | | | ● | | | | | | | |
| **MIDDLESEX** | | | | | | | | | | | | | | | | | |
| CLANRICARDE CLINIC (HM04526) | | | ● | | | | | | | | | | | | | | |
| **MIDLANDS (WEST)** | | | | | | | | | | | | | | | | | |
| ABBEY CLINIC (HM00077) | | | ● | | | | | ● | | | | | | | | | |
| ABBIE HYPNOTHERAPY CENTRE (HM00093) | | | | | | | | | | | | | | | ● | | |
| AION COUNSELLING/PSYCHOTHERAPY (HM00440) | | | | | | | | | | | | | | | ● | | |
| ALDA HOUSE NATURAL THERAPY (HM00492) | | | | | | | | | | | | | | | | | |
| ALDOUS, JOSIE (HM00503) | | | | | | | | | | | | | | | | | |
| ALLEN, ELAINE (HM00608) | | | | | | | | | | | | | | | | | |
| ALTERNATIVE BACK CARE (HM00696) | | | ● | | | | | | | | | | | | | | |
| ARNAOUT, HUDA (HM01030) | | | | | | | | | | | | | | | | | |
| AROMA SANTE (HM01057) | | | | | | | | | | | | | | | | | |
| ARTHURS, BEV (HM01165) | | | | | | | | | | | | | | | | | |
| ASSOCIATION OF STRESS MNGMT (HM01288) | | | | | | | | | | | | | | | | | |
| BACKCARE & ACUPUNCTURE CLINIC (HM01526) | | | ● | | | | | | | | | | | | | | |
| BILLINGHAM, S (HM02301) | | | | | | | | | | | | | | | | | |
| BIOENERGY PARTNERSHIP (HM02334) | | | | | | | | | | | | | | | | | |
| BIRCH, GILLIAN (HM02351) | | | | | | | | | | | | | | | | | |
| BIRD, CAROLINE (HM02358) | | | | | | | | | | | | | | | | | |
| BIRMINGHAM & DISTRICT (HM02381) | | | ● | | | | | | | | | | | | | | |
| BIRMINGHAM HYPNOTHERAPY (HM02386) | | | | | | | | | | | | | | | | | |
| BIRMINGHAM PHYSIO CLINIC (HM02388) | | | | | | | | | | | | | | | ● | | |
| BIRMINGHAM TRAD ACU CENTRE (HM02390) | | | | | | | | | | | | | | | | | |
| BIRMINGHAM WOMENS COUNS (HM02391) | | | | | | | | | | | | | | | ● | | |
| BLAKE, D H (HM02479) | | | ● | | | | | | | | | | | | | | |
| BOLDMERE HYPNOTHERAPY (HM02653) | | | | | | | | | | | | | | | | | |
| BOWEN, MARGARET (HM02782) | | | | | | | | | | | | | | | | | |
| BROWNHILL, D G (HM03257) | | | | | | | | | | | | | | | ● | | |
| BTAC (HM03296) | | | | | | | | | | | ● | | | | | | |

| Business by County with Reference no. | Reflexology | Reichian Therapy | Reiki | Remedial Massage | Rogerian Therapy | Rolfing | Seichem | Sensitivity Training | Shiatsu | Silva Method | Sound Therapy | Spiritual Healing | Sports Massage | Stress Therapy | Swedish Body Massage | T'ai-Chi Ch'uan |
|---|---|---|---|---|---|---|---|---|---|---|---|---|---|---|---|---|
| TUEBROOK OSTEOPATHIC CLINIC (HM20375) | | | | | | | | | | | | | | | | |
| TUEBROOK OSTEOPATHIC CLINIC (HM20374) | | | | | | | | | | | | | | | | |
| VAEZZADEH, M (HM20546) | | | | | | | | | | | | | | | | |
| WILLIAMS, T H (HM21597) | | | | | | | | | | | | | | | | |
| WILLIAMS, TECWYN H (HM21598) | | | | | | | | | | | | | | | | |
| **MIDDLESEX** | | | | | | | | | | | | | | | | |
| CLANRICARDE CLINIC (HM04526) | | | | | | | | | | | | | | | | |
| **MIDLANDS (WEST)** | | | | | | | | | | | | | | | | |
| ABBEY CLINIC (HM00077) | ● | | ● | | | ● | | | ● | | | | | | | |
| ABBIE HYPNOTHERAPY CENTRE (HM00093) | | | | | | | | | | | | | | ● | | |
| AION COUNSELLING/PSYCHOTHERAPY (HM00440) | | | | | | | | | | | | | | | | |
| ALDA HOUSE NATURAL THERAPY (HM00492) | ● | | ● | | | | | | | | | | | ● | | |
| ALDOUS, JOSIE (HM00503) | | | ● | | | | ● | | | | | ● | | | | |
| ALLEN, ELAINE (HM00608) | ● | | | | | | | | | | | | | | | |
| ALTERNATIVE BACK CARE (HM00696) | | | | | | | | | | | | | | | | |
| ARNAOUT, HUDA (HM01030) | ● | | | | | | | | | | | | | | | |
| AROMA SANTE (HM01057) | ● | | ● | | | | | | | | | | | | | |
| ARTHURS, BEV (HM01165) | ● | | | | | | | | | | | | | | | |
| ASSOCIATION OF STRESS MNGMT (HM01288) | | | | | | | | | | | | | | ● | | |
| BACKCARE & ACUPUNCTURE CLINIC (HM01526) | ● | | | | | | | | | | | | | ● | | |
| BILLINGHAM, S (HM02301) | ● | | | | | | | | | | | | | | | |
| BIOENERGY PARTNERSHIP (HM02334) | | | | | | | | | | | | | | | | |
| BIRCH, GILLIAN (HM02351) | ● | | | | | | | | | | | | | | | |
| BIRD, CAROLINE (HM02358) | ● | | | | | | | | | | | | | | | |
| BIRMINGHAM & DISTRICT (HM02381) | | | | | | | | | | | | | | | | |
| BIRMINGHAM HYPNOTHERAPY (HM02386) | | | | | | | | | | | | ● | | ● | | |
| BIRMINGHAM PHYSIO CLINIC (HM02388) | | | | | | | | | | | | | | | | |
| BIRMINGHAM TRAD ACU CENTRE (HM02390) | | | | | | | | | | | | | | | | |
| BIRMINGHAM WOMENS COUNS (HM02391) | | | | | | | | | | | | | | | | |
| BLAKE, D H (HM02479) | | | | | | | | | | | | | | | | |
| BOLDMERE HYPNOTHERAPY (HM02653) | | | | | | | | | | | | | | ● | | |
| BOWEN, MARGARET (HM02782) | ● | | | | | | | | | | | | | | | |
| BROWNHILL, D G (HM03257) | | | | | | | | | | | | | | | | |
| BTAC (HM03296) | ● | | | | | | | | ● | | | ● | | | | ● |

| Business by County with Reference no. | Tantra Therapy | Tera-Mai | Thought Field Therapy | Touch Therapy | Transactional Analysis | Tui-na | Ultrasonics | Vibrational Therapy | Visualisation Therapy | Vitamin Therapy | Voice Therapy | X-Ray | Ying & Yang | Yoga | Zen Therapy | Zero Balancing |
|---|---|---|---|---|---|---|---|---|---|---|---|---|---|---|---|---|
| TUEBROOK OSTEOPATHIC CLINIC (HM20375) | | | | | | | | | | | | | | | | |
| TUEBROOK OSTEOPATHIC CLINIC (HM20374) | | | | | | | | | | | | | | | | |
| VAEZZADEH, M (HM20546) | | | | | | | | | | | | | | | | |
| WILLIAMS, T H (HM21597) | | | | | | | | | | | | | | | | |
| WILLIAMS, TECWYN H (HM21598) | | | | | | | | | | | | | | | | |
| **MIDDLESEX** | | | | | | | | | | | | | | | | |
| CLANRICARDE CLINIC (HM04526) | | | | | | | | | | | | | | | | |
| **MIDLANDS (WEST)** | | | | | | | | | | | | | | | | |
| ABBEY CLINIC (HM00077) | | | | | | | | | | ● | | | | | | |
| ABBIE HYPNOTHERAPY CENTRE (HM00093) | | | | | | | | | | | | | | | | |
| AION COUNSELLING/PSYCHOTHERAPY (HM00440) | | | | | | | | | | | | | | | | |
| ALDA HOUSE NATURAL THERAPY (HM00492) | | | | | | | | | | | | | | | | |
| ALDOUS, JOSIE (HM00503) | | | | | | | | | | | | | | | | |
| ALLEN, ELAINE (HM00608) | | | | | | | | | | | | | | | | |
| ALTERNATIVE BACK CARE (HM00696) | | | | | | | | | | | | | | | | |
| ARNAOUT, HUDA (HM01030) | | | | | | | | | | | | | | | | |
| AROMA SANTE (HM01057) | | | | | | | | | | | | | | | | |
| ARTHURS, BEV (HM01165) | | | | | | | | | | | | | | | | |
| ASSOCIATION OF STRESS MNGMT (HM01288) | | | | | | | | | | | | | | | | |
| BACKCARE & ACUPUNCTURE CLINIC (HM01526) | | | | | | | | | | | | | | | | |
| BILLINGHAM, S (HM02301) | | | | | | | | | | | | | | | | |
| BIOENERGY PARTNERSHIP (HM02334) | | | | | | | | | | | | | | ● | | |
| BIRCH, GILLIAN (HM02351) | | | | | | | | | | | | | | | | |
| BIRD, CAROLINE (HM02358) | | | | | | | | | | | | | | | | |
| BIRMINGHAM & DISTRICT (HM02381) | | | | | | | | | | | | | | | | |
| BIRMINGHAM HYPNOTHERAPY (HM02386) | | | | | | | | | | | | | | | | |
| BIRMINGHAM PHYSIO CLINIC (HM02388) | | | | | | | | | | | | | | | | |
| BIRMINGHAM TRAD ACU CENTRE (HM02390) | | | | | | | | | | | | | | | | ● |
| BIRMINGHAM WOMENS COUNS (HM02391) | | | | | | | | | | | | | | | | |
| BLAKE, D H (HM02479) | | | | | | | | | | | | | | | | |
| BOLDMERE HYPNOTHERAPY (HM02653) | | | | | | | | | | | | | | | | |
| BOWEN, MARGARET (HM02782) | | | | | | | | | | | | | | | | |
| BROWNHILL, D G (HM03257) | | | | | | | | | | | | | | | | |
| BTAC (HM03296) | | | | | | | | | ● | | | | ● | | | |

# O - Z Therapies at Practices/Businesses

| Business by County with Reference no. | Orthotics | Osteomyology | Osteopathy | PAM | Paranormal Therapies | Pattern Therapies | Physiotherapy | Phytotherapy | Pilates | Podiatry | Polarity Therapy | Postural Integration | Primal Therapy | Psionic Therapy | Psychotherapy | Pyramid Power | Pyscho-Synthesis | Reflexology | Reichian Therapy | Reiki | Remedial Massage | Rogerian Therapy | Rolfing | Seichem | Sensitivity Training | Shiatsu | Silva Method | Sound Therapy | Spiritual Healing | Sports Massage | Stress Therapy | Swedish Body Massage | T'ai-Chi Ch'uan | Tantra Therapy | Tera-Mai | Thought Field Therapy | Touch Therapy | Transactional Analysis | Tui-na | Ultrasonics | Vibrational Therapy | Visualisation Therapy | Vitamin Therapy | Voice Therapy | X-Ray | Ying & Yang | Yoga | Zen Therapy | Zero Balancing |
|---|---|---|---|---|---|---|---|---|---|---|---|---|---|---|---|---|---|---|---|---|---|---|---|---|---|---|---|---|---|---|---|---|---|---|---|---|---|---|---|---|---|---|---|---|---|---|---|---|---|
| O'GRADY, MARGARET (HM15242) | | | | | | | | | | | | | | | | | | ● | | | | | | | | | | | | | | | | | | | | | | | | | | | | | | | |
| ORTON, G (HM15413) | | | | | | | | | | | | | | | | | | ● | | | | | | | | | | | | | | | | | | | | | | | | | | | | | | | |
| PARK PRACTICE (HM15672) | | | ● | | | | | | | | | | | | | | | ● | | | | | | | | | | | | | | | | | | | | | | | | | | | | | | | |
| PARKES, VAL (HM15713) | | | | | | | | | | | | | | | ● | | | | | | | | | | | | | | | | | | | | | | | | | | | | | | | | | | |
| PASSEY, F (HM15780) | | | ● | | | | | | | | | | | | | | | | | | | | | | | | | | | | | | | | | | | | | | | | | | | | | | |
| PASSEY, FIONA (HM15781) | | | ● | | | | | | | | | | | | | | | | | | | | | | | | | | | | | | | | | | | | | | | | | | | | | | |
| PERRY, ALICIA (HM16040) | | | | | | | | | | | | | | | | | | ● | | | | | | | | | | | | | | | | | | | | | | | | | | | | | | | |
| PHYSIOTHERAPY CLINIC (HM16241) | | | | | | | ● | | | | | | | | | | | | | | | | | | | | | | | | | | | | | | | | | | | | | | | | | | |
| PLANT, ALISON () | | | | | | | | | | | | | | | | | | ● | | | | | | | | | | | | | | | | | | | | | | | | | | | | | | | |
| POPPLEWELL, SALLY (HM16439) | | | | | | | | | | | | | | | | | | ● | | | | | | | | ● | | | | | | | | | | | | | | | | | | | | | | | |
| PRISM THERAPIES (HM16636) | | | | | | | | | | | | | | | | | | | | ● | | | | | | | | | | | ● | | | | | | | | | | | | | | | | | | |
| PSYCHOTHERAPY ASSOCIATES INT (HM16732) | | | | | | | | | | | | | | | ● | | | | | | | | | | | | | | | | | | | | | | | | | | | | | | | | | | |
| RENTOUL, R W (HM17191) | | | | | | | | | | | | | | | ● | | | | | | | | | | | | | | | | | | | | | | | | | | | | | | | | | | |
| RICHARDSON, CYRIL (HM17273) | | | | | | | | | | ● | | | | | | | | | | | | | | | | | | | | | | | | | | | | | | | | | | | | | | | |
| ROMSLEY PHYSIOTHERAPY PRACTICE (HM17578) | | | | | | | | | | | | | | | | | | ● | | | | | | | | | | | | | | | | | | | | | | | | | | | | | | | |
| ROSEMARY HILL CLINIC (HM17620) | | | ● | | | | | | | | | | | | | | | | | | | | | | | | | | | | | | | | | | | | | | | | | | | | | | |
| RUXTON, HUGH (HM17787) | | | ● | | | | | | | | | | | | | | | | | | | | | | | | | | | | | | | | | | | | | | | | | | | | | | |
| SEITAI/SHIATSU & MANIPULATION (HM18202) | | | | | | | | | | | | | | | | | | | | | | | | | | ● | | | | | | | | | | | | | | | | | | | | | | | |
| SHARMAN, SARAH (HM18305) | | | ● | | | | | | | | | | | | | | | | | | | | | | | | | | | | | | | | | | | | | | | | | | | | | | |
| SIDHOM, A (HM18529) | | | ● | | | | | | | | | | | | ● | | | | | | | | | | | | | | | | | | | | | | | | | | | | | | | | | | |
| SIRDEFIELD, PAUL (HM18619) | | | | | | | | | | | | | | | | | | ● | | | | | | | | | | | | | | | | | | | | | | | | | | | | | | | |
| SMITH, CHERYL (HM18726) | | | | | | | | | | | | | | | | | | ● | | | | | | | | | | | | | | | | | | | | | | | | | | | | | | | |
| SMITH, GILL (HM18744) | | | | | | | | | | | | | | | | | | ● | | | | | | | | | | | | | | | | | | | | | | | | | | | | | | | |
| ST PAULS OSTEOPATHY PRACTICE (HM19094) | | | ● | | | | | | | | | | | | | | | | | ● | | | | | | | | | | | | | | | | | | | | ● | | | | | | | | | |
| STOURBRIDGE ACU & OSTEO CTRE (HM19356) | | | ● | | | | | | | | | | | | | | | | | | | | | | | | | | | | | | | | | | | | | | | | | | | | | | |
| SUCCESSWORKS (HM19461) | | | | | | | | | | | | | | | | | | | | ● | | | | | | | | | ● | | ● | | | | | | | | | | | ● | | | | | | | |
| SUNDERLAND, CYNTHIA (HM19505) | | | | | | | | | | | | | | | ● | | | | | | | | | | | | | | | | | | | | | | | | | | | | | | | | | | |
| SUTTON COLDFIELD HEALTH CLINIC (HM19544) | | | | | | | | | | | | | | | | | | | | | | | | | | | | | | | | | ● | | | | | | | | | | | | | | | | |
| TAPERELL, AVRIL (HM19696) | | | | | | | | | | | | | | | | | | ● | | | | | | | | | | | | | | | | | | | | | | | | | | | | | | | |
| TELLING, MELANIE (HM19822) | | | | | | | | | | | | | | | | | | ● | | ● | | | | | | | | | | | | | | | | | | | | | | | | | | | | | |
| TELLING, MELANIE (HM19823) | | | | | | | | | | | | | | | | | | ● | | ● | | | | | | | | | | | | | | | | | | | | | | | | | | | | | |
| THERAPY TRAINING COLLEGE (HM19911) | | | | | | | | | | | | | | | | | | | | | | | | | | | | | | | ● | | | | | | | | | | | | | | | | | | |
| TILNEY, TONY (HM20072) | | | | | | | | | | | | | | | ● | | | | | | | | | | | | | | | | | | | | | | | | | | | | | | | | | | |
| TUNNICLIFFE, JEANETTE (HM20400) | | | | | | | | | | | | | | | | | | ● | | | | | | | | | | | | | | | | | | | | | | | | | | | | | | | |

# O - Z Therapies at Practices/Businesses

| Business by County with Reference no. | Orthotics | Osteomyology | Osteopathy | PAM | Paranormal Therapies | Pattern Therapies | Physiotherapy | Phytotherapy | Pilates | Podiatry | Polarity Therapy | Postural Integration | Primal Therapy | Psionic Therapy | Psychotherapy | Pyramid Power | Pyscho-Synthesis | Reflexology | Reichian Therapy | Reiki | Remedial Massage | Rogerian Therapy | Rolfing | Seichem | Sensitivity Training | Shiatsu | Silva Method | Sound Therapy | Spiritual Healing | Sports Massage | Stress Therapy | Swedish Body Massage | T'ai-Chi Ch'uan | Tantra Therapy | Tera-Mai | Thought Field Therapy | Touch Therapy | Transactional Analysis | Tui-na | Ultrasonics | Vibrational Therapy | Visualisation Therapy | Vitamin Therapy | Voice Therapy | X-Ray | Ying & Yang | Yoga | Zen Therapy | Zero Balancing |
|---|---|---|---|---|---|---|---|---|---|---|---|---|---|---|---|---|---|---|---|---|---|---|---|---|---|---|---|---|---|---|---|---|---|---|---|---|---|---|---|---|---|---|---|---|---|---|---|---|---|
| TYE, MARIE (HM20460) | | | | | | | | | | | | | | | | | | ● | | | | | | | | | | | | | | | | | | | | | | | | | | | | | | | |
| WALSALL PHYSIOTHERAPY CLINIC (HM20853) | | | | | | | ● | | | | | | | | | | | | | | | | | | | | | | | | | | | | | | | | | | | | | | | | | | |
| WELL NATURAL HEALTH CENTRE (HM21139) | | | | | | | | | | ● | | | | | ● | | | ● | | ● | | | | | | | | | | | ● | ● | | | | | | | | | | | | | | | | | |
| WELL NATURAL HEALTH CENTRE (HM21140) | | | | | | | | ● | | | | | | | | | | ● | | ● | | | | | | | | | ● | | ● | | | | | | | | | | | ● | | | | | | | |
| WEST MIDLAND HYPNOTHERAPY (HM21229) | | | | | | | | | | | | | | | | | | | | ● | | | | | | | | | | | ● | | | | | | | | | | | | | | | | | | |
| WESTON, JOHN (HM21278) | | | ● | | | | | | | | | ● | | | | | | | | | | | | | | | | | | | | | | | | | | | | | | | | | | | | | |
| WESTWOOD, ANGELA (HM21285) | | | | | | | | | | | | | | | | | | ● | | ● | | | | | | | | | | | | | | | | | | | | | | | | | | | | | |
| WHITE, SHELLEY (HM21378) | | | | | | | | | | | | | | | | | | ● | | | | | | | | | | | | | | | | | | | | | | | | | | | | | | | |
| WHITEHOUSE, PAMELA (HM21391) | | | | | | | | | | | | | | | | | | ● | | | | | | | | | | | | | | | | | | | | | | | | | | | | | | | |
| WILLOWS CLNC COMP HEALTH CTRE (HM21630) | | | ● | | | | | ● | | | | | | | ● | | | ● | | | | | | | | | | | | ● | ● | | | | | | | | | | | | | | | ● | | | |
| WITHYMOOR PHYSIOTHERAPY CLINIC (HM21749) | | | | | | | ● | | | | | | | | | | | | | | | | | | | | | | | | | | | | | | | | | | | | | | | | | | |
| YOGA TUITION (HM22034) | | | | | | | | | | | | | | | | | | | | | | | | | | | | | | | | | | | | | | | | | | | | | | | ● | | |
| YOUNG, PATRICIA (HM22078) | | | | | | | | | | | | | | | | | | ● | | | | | | | | | | | | | | | | | | | | | | | | | | | | | | | |
| YOUNG, ROSEMARY (HM22079) | | | | | | | | | | | | | | | | | | ● | | | | | | | | | | | | | | | | | | | | | | | | | | | | | | | |
| ZEN HEALTH & BEAUTY (HM22099) | | | | | | | | | | | | | | | | | | ● | | ● | | | | | | | | | | | | | | | | | | | | | | | | | | | | | |
| NORFOLK | | | | | | | | | | | | | | | | | | | | | | | | | | | | | | | | | | | | | | | | | | | | | | | | | |
| AQUARONE REMY (HM00960) | | | | | | | | | | | | | | | ● | | | | | | | | | | | | | | | | | | | | | | | | | | | | | | | | | | |
| AVIS, JEAN (HM01401) | | | | | | | | | | | | | | | | | | ● | | | | | | | | | | | | | | | | | | | | | | | | | | | | | | | |
| BODY BEAUTIFUL (HM02576) | | | | | | | | | | | | | | | | | | ● | | ● | | | | | | | | | | | | | | | | | | | | | | | | | | | | | |
| BRUNSWICK PHYSIO (HM03280) | | | | | | | ● | | | | | | | | | | | | | | | | | | | | | | | | | | | | | | | | | | | | | | | | | | |
| BURRIDGE, C (HM03421) | | | | | | | | | | | | | | | | | | ● | | | | | | | | | | | | | | | | | | | | | | | | | | | | | | | |
| CHANDLER, ANN (HM03973) | | | | | | | ● | | | | | | | | | | | | | | | | | | | | | | | | | | | | | | | | | | | | | | | | | | |
| CHASE PARK PRACTICE (HM04060) | | | | | | | | | | | | | | | ● | | | | | | | ● | | | | | | | | | | | | | | | | | | | | | | | | | | | |
| CLARKE, RACHEL (HM04600) | | | | | | | | | | | | | | | | | | ● | | | | | | | | | | | | | | | | | | | | | | | | | | | | | | | |
| CLASSICAL OSTEOPATH (HM04611) | | | ● | | | | | | | | | | | | | | | ● | | ● | | | | ● | | | | | | | | | | | ● | | | | | | | | | | | | | | |
| COMER OSTEOPATHIC CLINIC (HM04897) | | | ● | | | | | | | | | | | | | | | | | | | | | | | | | | | | | | | | | | | | | | | | | | | | | | |
| COMPLEMENTARY HEALTH CLINIC (HM04926) | | | ● | | | | | | | | | | | | | | | ● | | | | | | | | | | | | | | | | | | | | | | | | | | | | | | | |
| COOPER, D W (HM05096) | | | ● | | | | | | | | | | | | | | | | | | | | | | | | | | | | | | | | | | | | | | | | | | | | | | |
| COOPER, P W (HM05122) | | | ● | | | | | | | | | | | | | | | | | | | | | | | | | | | | | | | | | | | | | | | | | | | | | | |
| DISS NATURAL HEALTH CLINIC (HM06121) | | | ● | | | | | | | | | | | | | | | ● | | ● | | | | | | | | | | | ● | | | | | | | | | | | | ● | | | | | | |
| DOYLE, JULIA (HM06264) | | | | | | | | | | | | | | | | | | ● | | | | | | | | | | | | | | | | | | | | | | | | | | | | | | | |
| ELEMENTS OF HEALTH (HM06725) | | | | | | | | | | | | ● | | | | | | ● | | ● | | | | | | ● | | | | | ● | | | | | | | | | | | | | | | | | | |
| FISHER, JACK E (HM07355) | | | ● | | | | | | | | | | | | | | | | | | | | | | | | | | | | | | | | | | | | | | | | | | | | | | |
| FORD OSTEOPATHIC CLINIC (HM07521) | | | ● | | | | | | | | | | | | | | | | | ● | | | | | | | | | | | | | | | | | | | | | | | | | | | | | |

# O - Z Therapies at Practices/Businesses

| Business by County with Reference no. | Orthotics | Osteomyology | Osteopathy | PAM | Paranormal Therapies | Pattern Therapies | Physiotherapy | Phytotherapy | Pilates | Podiatry | Polarity Therapy | Postural Integration | Primal Therapy | Psionic Therapy | Psychotherapy | Pyramid Power | Pyscho-Synthesis | Reflexology | Reichian Therapy | Reiki | Remedial Massage | Rogerian Therapy | Rolfing | Seichem | Sensitivity Training | Shiatsu | Silva Method | Sound Therapy | Spiritual Healing | Sports Massage | Stress Therapy | Swedish Body Massage | T'ai-Chi Ch'uan | Tantra Therapy | Tera-Mai | Thought Field Therapy | Touch Therapy | Transactional Analysis | Tui-na | Ultrasonics | Vibrational Therapy | Visualisation Therapy | Vitamin Therapy | Voice Therapy | X-Ray | Ying & Yang | Yoga | Zen Therapy | Zero Balancing |
|---|---|---|---|---|---|---|---|---|---|---|---|---|---|---|---|---|---|---|---|---|---|---|---|---|---|---|---|---|---|---|---|---|---|---|---|---|---|---|---|---|---|---|---|---|---|---|---|---|---|
| GEARY, A G (HM07951) | ● | | | | | | | | | | | | | | | | | | | | | | | | | | | | | | | | | | | | | | | | | | | | | | | | |
| GLYNN, CLAIR (HM08168) | | | | | | | | | | | | | | | | | | ● | | | | | | | | | | | | | | | | | | | | | | | | | | | | | | | |
| HALL, G J (HM08771) | | | ● | | | | | | | | | | | | | | | | | | | | | | | | | | | | | | | | | | | | | | | | | | | | | | |
| HARGHAM HALL OSTEO PRACTICE (HM08992) | | | ● | | | | | | | | | ● | | | | | | | | | | | | | | | | | | | | | | | | | | | | | | | | | | | | | |
| HART, S (HM09133) | | | | | | | | | | | | | | | ● | | | | | | | | | | | | | | | | | | | | | | | | | | | | | | | | | | |
| HAUGHTON, CATHERINE (HM09202) | | | | | | | | | | | | | | | | | | ● | | | | | | | | | | | | | | | | | | | | | | | | | | | | | | | |
| HOMEOPATHIC CLINIC (HM10074) | | | | | | | | | | | | | | | | | | | | ● | | | | | | | | | ● | | | | | | | | | | | | | | | | | | | | |
| JAMES, MALCOLM (HM10892) | | | ● | | | | | | | | | | | | | | | | | | | | | | | | | | | | | | | | | | | | | | | | | | | | | | |
| JENKINS, G M (HM10985) | | | ● | | | | | | | | | | | | | | | | | | | | | | | | | | | | | | | | | | | | | | | | | | | | | | |
| JESSOP CLINIC (HM11021) | | | ● | | | | | | | | | | | | | | | | | | | | | | | | | | | | | | | | | | | | | | | | | | | | | | |
| KING, SIMON (HM11644) | | | | | | ● | | ● | | | | | | | | | | | | | | | | | ● | | | | | | ● | | | | | | | | | | ● | | ● | | | | | | |
| MACKELLAR, D (HM12849) | | | ● | | | | | | | | | | | | | | | | | | | | | | | | | | | | | | | | | | | | | | | | | | | | | | |
| MUSGRAVE-BROWN, LYLEEN (HM14427) | | | | | | | | | | | | | | | | | | ● | | | | | | | | | | | | | | | | | | | | | | | | | | | | | | | |
| NEW MARKET RD PHYSIO PRACTICE (HM14824) | | | | | | | ● | | | | | | | | | | | | | | | | | | | | | | | | | | | | | | | | | | | | | | | | | | |
| NORFOLK CLINIC (HM14993) | | | ● | | | | | | | | | | | | | | | ● | | | | | | | | | | | | | | | | | | | | | | | | | | | | | | | |
| NORFOLK NATURAL HEALTH SERVICE (HM14995) | | | | | | | | ● | | | | | | | ● | | | ● | | ● | | | | | | ● | | | ● | | | | ● | | | | | | | | | | | | | ● | | | |
| NORMAN, A J (HM14999) | | | | | | | | | | | | | | | | | | | | | | | | | | | | | | | ● | | | | | | | | | | | | | | | | | | |
| PARTRIDGE, DEIRDRE (HM15767) | | | | | | | | | | | | | | | | | | ● | | | | | | | | | | | | | | | | | | | | | | | | | | | | | | | |
| PETHER, ANNE (HM16090) | | | | | | | | | | | | | | | | | | ● | | | | | | | | | | | | | | | | | | | | | | | | | | | | | | | |
| PHILPOTT, MONIQUE (HM16149) | | | | | | | | | | | | | | | | | | ● | | ● | | | | | | | | | | | | | | | | | | | | | | | | | | | | | |
| POINTER, TERESA (HM16398) | | | | | | | | | | | | | | | | | | ● | | | | | | | | | | | | | | | | | | | | | | | | | | | | | | | |
| PRIOR-SANDERSON, SARA (HM16630) | | | | | | | | | | | | | | | | | | ● | | | | | | | | | | | | | | | | | | | | | | | | | | | | | | | |
| PSYCHOTHERAPY (HM16727) | | | | | | | | | | | | | | | ● | | | | | | | | | | | | | | | | | | | | | | | | | | | | | | | | | | |
| REID, C R (HM17115) | | | ● | | | | | | | | | | | | | | | | | | | | | | | | | | | | | | | | | | | | | | | | | | | | | | |
| RICHARDSON, ALAN (HM17268) | | | | | | | | ● | | | | | | | ● | | | | | | | | | | | | | | | | ● | | | | | | | | | | | | ● | | | | | | |
| RIGBY COURT CLINIC (HM17331) | | | | | | | | | | | | | | | ● | | | ● | | ● | | | | | | ● | | | | | ● | | | | | | | | | | | | | | | | | | |
| ROSBOTHAM, VALERIE (HM17595) | | | | | | | | | | | | | | | | | | ● | | | | | | | | | | | | | | | | | | | | | | | | | | | | | | | |
| SCOTT-ROBINSON, JAMES (HM18138) | | | ● | | | | | | | | | | | | | | | | | | | | | | | | | | | | | | | | | | | | | | | | | | | | | | |
| SEELY, SUSAN (HM18196) | | | ● | | | | | | | | | | | | | | | | | | | | | | | | | | | | | | | | | | | | | | | | | | | | | | |
| SELLENS DRAKE, ANGELA (HM18216) | | | | | | | | | | | | | | | | | | ● | | | | | | | | | | | | | | | | | | | | | | | | | | | | | | | |
| SHARP, DENISE (HM18307) | | | | | | | | | | | | | | | | | | ● | | | | | | | | | | | | | | | | | | | | | | | | | | | | | | | |
| SHARPE, ISABEL (HM18315) | | | ● | | | | | | | | | | | | | | | | | | | | | | | | | | | | | | | | | | | | | | | | | | | | | | |
| SHIATSU CENTRE (HM18453) | | | | | | | | | | | | | | | | | | | | | | | | | | ● | | | | | | | | | | | | | | | | | | | | | | | |
| SMITH, SANDRA (HM18807) | | | | | | | | | | | | | | | | | | ● | | | | | | | | | | | | | | | | | | | | | | | | | | | | | | | |

# O - Z Therapies at Practices/Businesses

| Business by County with Reference no. | Orthotics | Osteomyology | Osteopathy | PAM | Paranormal Therapies | Pattern Therapies | Physiotherapy | Phytotherapy | Pilates | Podiatry | Polarity Therapy | Postural Integration | Primal Therapy | Psionic Therapy | Psychotherapy | Pyramid Power | Pyscho-Synthesis | Reflexology | Reichian Therapy | Reiki | Remedial Massage | Rogerian Therapy | Rolfing | Seichem | Sensitivity Training | Shiatsu | Silva Method | Sound Therapy | Spiritual Healing | Sports Massage | Stress Therapy | Swedish Body Massage | T'ai-Chi Ch'uan | Tantra Therapy | Tera-Mai | Thought Field Therapy | Touch Therapy | Transactional Analysis | Tui-na | Ultrasonics | Vibrational Therapy | Visualisation Therapy | Vitamin Therapy | Voice Therapy | X-Ray | Ying & Yang | Yoga | Zen Therapy | Zero Balancing |
|---|---|---|---|---|---|---|---|---|---|---|---|---|---|---|---|---|---|---|---|---|---|---|---|---|---|---|---|---|---|---|---|---|---|---|---|---|---|---|---|---|---|---|---|---|---|---|---|---|---|
| ST AUGUSTINES PSYCHOTHRPY CTRE (HM19069) |||||||||||||||●|||||||||||||||||||||||||||||||||||
| ST STEPHENS PRACTICE (HM19099) |||●|||||||||||||||||●|||||||||●|||||||||||||||||||||
| STUDLEY, MARGARET (HM19443) ||||||||||||||||||●||||||||||||||||||||||||||||||||
| THORPE CLINIC (HM20033) |||●||||||||||||||||||||||||||||||||||||||||||||||
| TRAFFORD, DEBORAH (HM20247) ||||||||||||||||||●||||||||||||||||||||||||||||||||
| VIDION, BARBARA (HM20661) ||||||||||||||||||●||||||||||||||||||||||||||||||||
| WALLEN, ANN (HM20835) ||||||||||||||||||●||||||||||||||||||||||||||||||||
| WALTERS, MARGARET (HM20878) ||||||||||||||||||●||||||||||||||||||||||||||||||||
| WATTON PHYSIOTHERAPY CLINIC (HM21033) |||||||●||||||||||||||||||||||||||||||||||||||||||
| WILMOT, D (HM21637) |||||||||||||||●|||||||||||||||||||||||||||||||||||
| WOBURN CLINIC (HM21755) |||●||||||●||||||●|||●||●||||||●|||●||●||||||||||||||||●|||
| WOODEN, SUSAN (HM21822) ||||||||||||||||||●||||||||||||||||||||||||||||||||
| NORTHAMPTONSHIRE ||||||||||||||||||||||||||||||||||||||||||||||||||
| ALLEN HINDE - PHYSIOTHERAPIST (HM00598) ||||||||||||||||||||||||||||||||||||||||●||||||||||
| ANNELISE (HM00906) ||||||||||||||||||●|||||||||||||●|||||||||||||||||||
| ARBOURS (HM00965) |●|||||||||||||||||||||||||||||||||||||||||||||||||
| ARMSTRONG, HEATHER (HM01023) ||||||||||||||||||●||||||||||||||||||||||||||||||||
| BECKWITH, JONATHAN (HM02029) ||||||||||||||||||●||||||||||||||||||||||||||||||||
| BELLINGHAM, JANE (HM02102) |||●||||||||||||||||||||||||||||||||||||||||||||||
| BEVINGTON, ANN (HM02247) ||||||||||||||||||●||||||||||||||||||||||||||||||||
| BROWN, RITA (HM03246) ||||||||||||||||||●||||||||||||||||||||||||||||||||
| C F C M (HM03523) ||||||||||||||||||||||||||||||||||||||||||||||●||||
| CALLIS THERAPY FOUNDATION (HM03555) ||||||||||||||||||●|||●|||||●||||||||||||||||||||||||
| CAMERON, LOUISE E (HM03585) |||●||||||||||||||||||||||||||||||||||||||||||||||
| COLESHILL, AMANDA Y (HM04837) |||●||||||||||||||||||●|||||||||||||||||||||||||||||||
| DAVENTRY NATUREWORKS (HM05768) |||●|||||||||||||||●||||||||||||||||||||||||||||||●|
| DAVIDSON, NIKKI (HM05789) ||||||||||||||||||●||||||||||||||||||||||||||||||||
| DEVON PARADE CLINIC (HM06041) |||●||||●|||||●|||●|||●||||||||||||●|●||||||||||||||●|●||||
| DINNAGE, DAWN (HM06112) ||||||||||||||||||●||||||||||||||||||||||||||||||||
| DON, ANITA (HM06166) ||||||||||||||||||●|||●|||||||||||●||||||||||||||||||
| EASTON, JOSEPHINE (HM06547) ||||||||||||||||||●||||||||||||||||||||||||||||||||
| FINKE, MARTYN (HM07314) ||||||||||||||||||●||||||||||||||||||||||||||||||||
| FINKE, WENDY (HM07315) ||||||||||||||||||●||||||||||||||||||||||||||||||||
| FORSYTH, JILLIAN (HM07577) |||●||||||||||||||||||||||||||||||||||||||||||||||

# O - Z Therapies at Practices/Businesses

| Business by County with Reference no. | Orthotics | Osteomyology | Osteopathy | PAM | Paranormal Therapies | Pattern Therapies | Physiotherapy | Phytotherapy | Pilates | Podiatry | Polarity Therapy | Postural Integration | Primal Therapy | Psionic Therapy | Psychotherapy | Pyramid Power | Pyscho-Synthesis | Reflexology | Reichian Therapy | Reiki | Remedial Massage | Rogerian Therapy | Rolfing | Seichem | Sensitivity Training | Shiatsu | Silva Method | Sound Therapy | Spiritual Healing | Sports Massage | Stress Therapy | Swedish Body Massage | T'ai-Chi Ch'uan | Tantra Therapy | Tera-Mai | Thought Field Therapy | Touch Therapy | Transactional Analysis | Tui-na | Ultrasonics | Vibrational Therapy | Visualisation Therapy | Vitamin Therapy | Voice Therapy | X-Ray | Ying & Yang | Yoga | Zen Therapy | Zero Balancing |
|---|---|---|---|---|---|---|---|---|---|---|---|---|---|---|---|---|---|---|---|---|---|---|---|---|---|---|---|---|---|---|---|---|---|---|---|---|---|---|---|---|---|---|---|---|---|---|---|---|---|
| GARVEY-WILLIAMS, RICHARD (HM07914) | | | ● | | | | | | | | | | | | | | | | | | | | | | | | | | | | | | | | | | | | | | | | | | | | | | |
| GARVEY-WILLIAMS, RICHARD (HM07915) | | | ● | | | | | | | | | | | | | | | | | | | | | | | | | | | | | | | | | | | | | | | | | | | | | | |
| GEDDES, PIPPA (HM07955) | | | | | | | | | | | | | | | | | | ● | | | | | | | | | | | | | | | | | | | | | | | | | | | | | | | |
| HUDSON, ELIZABETH (HM10310) | | | | | | | | | | | | | | | | | | ● | | | | | | | | | | | | | | | | | | | | | | | | | | | | | | | |
| JUST RELAX (HM11285) | | | | | | | | | | | | | | | | | | ● | | | | | | | | | | | | | | ● | | | | | | | | | | | | | | | | | |
| KETTERING OSTEOPATH (HM11568) | | | ● | | | | | | | | | | | | | | | | | | | | | | | | | | | | | | | | | | | | | | | | | | | | | | |
| LAWSON, JANET (HM12067) | | | ● | | | | | | | | | | | | | | | | | | | | | | | | | | | | | | | | | | | | | | | | | | | | | | |
| LAWSON, JANET (HM12065) | | | ● | | | | | | | | | | | | | | | | | | | | | | | | | | | | | | | | | | | | | | | | | | | | | | |
| LAWSON, R O L (HM12071) | | | ● | | | | | | | | | | | | | | | | | | | | | | | | | | | | | | | | | | | | | | | | | | | | | | |
| MAPLE TREE OSTEO PRACTICE (HM13061) | | | ● | | | | | | | | | | | | | | | | | | | | | | | | | | | | | | | | | | | | | | | | | | | | | | |
| MILBORNE, JOHN (HM13852) | | | ● | | | | | | | | | | | | | | | | | | | | | | | | | | | | | | | | | | | | | | | | | | | | | | |
| MULLAN, JENNIFER (HM14339) | | | | | | | | | | | | | | | | | | ● | | | | | | | | | | | | | | | | | | | | | | | | | | | | | | | |
| NENE VALLEY COMP THERAPIES (HM14785) | | | | | | | | | | | | | | | | | | ● | | ● | | | | | | | | | | | | | | | | | | | | | | | | | | | | | |
| PARROTT, LINDA (HM15735) | | | | | | | | | | | | | | | | | | ● | | ● | | | | | | | | | | | | | | | | | | | | | | | | | | | | | |
| PITT, KATHLEEN (HM16348) | | | | | | | | | | | | | | | | | | ● | | | | | | | | | | | | | | | | | | | | | | | | | | | | | | | |
| PROFESSIONAL PSYCHO CENTRE (HM16661) | | | | | | | | | | | | | | | ● | | | | | | | | | | | | | | | | | | | | | | | | | | | | | | | | | | |
| REFLEXOLOGY CLINIC (HM17085) | | | | | | | | | | | | | | | | | | ● | | ● | | | | | | | | | | | | | | | | | | | | | | | | | | | | | |
| SURTEES, JOANNE (HM19525) | | | | | | | | | | | | | | | | | | ● | | | | | | | | | | | | | | | | | | | | | | | | | | | | | | | |
| WILLCOX, JAN (HM21520) | | | | | | | | | | | | | | | | | | ● | | | | | | | | | | | | | | | | | | | | | | | | | | | | | | | |
| WITH COMPLEMENTS (HM21745) | | | | | | | | | | | | | | | | | | | | ● | | | | | | | | | | | | | | | | | | | | | | | | | | | | | |
| **NORTHUMBERLAND** | | | | | | | | | | | | | | | | | | | | | | | | | | | | | | | | | | | | | | | | | | | | | | | | | |
| ACUCARE (HM00209) | | | | | | | | | | | | | | | ● | | | | | | | | | | | | | | | | | | | | | | | | | | | | | | | | | | |
| BRUCE, BOB (HM03265) | | | | | | | | | | | | | | | | | | ● | | | | | | | | | | | | | | | | | | | | | | | | | | | | | | | |
| BURN, I (HM03392) | | | ● | | | | | | | | | | | | | | | | | | | | | | | | | | | | | | | | | | | | | | | | | | | | | | |
| EATON, MAX (HM06564) | | | | | | | | | | | | | | | | | | ● | | | | | | | | | | | | | | | | | | | | | | | | | | | | | | | |
| EVISON, ALEX (HM07012) | | | | | | | | | | | | | | | | | | | | | | | | | | | | | | | ● | | | | | | | | | | | ● | | | | | | | |
| FOTHERGILL, MICHAEL (HM07606) | | | | | | | | | | | | | | | | | | ● | | | | | | | | | | | | | | | | | | | | | | | | | | | | | | | |
| GELSON, C J (HM07968) | | | ● | | | | | | | | | | | | | | | | | | | | | | | | | | | | | | | | | | | | | | | | | | | | | | |
| GREEN BATT PHYSIOTHERAPY (HM08434) | | | | | | | | | | | | | | | | | | | | | | | | | | | | | | | | | | | | | | | | ● | | | | | | | | | |
| KI CLINIC (HM11591) | | | | | | | | | | | | | | | | | | ● | | | | | | | | | | | | | | | | | | | | | | | | | ● | | | | | | |
| PHYSIOTHERAPY & SPORTS CLINIC (HM16223) | | | | | | | ● | | | | | | | | | | | | | | | | | | | | | | | | | | | | | | | | | | | | | | | | | | |
| RINSKE, BARTSTRA (HM17360) | | | ● | | | | | | | | | | | | | | | | | | | | | | | | | | | | | | | | | | | | | | | | | | | | | | |
| **NOTTINGHAMSHIRE** | | | | | | | | | | | | | | | | | | | | | | | | | | | | | | | | | | | | | | | | | | | | | | | | | |
| ADDISON, SYLVIA (HM00373) | | | | | | | | | | | | | | | | | | ● | | | | | | | | | | | | | | | | | | | | | | | | | | | | | | | |

# O - Z Therapies at Practices/Businesses

| Business by County with Reference no. | Orthotics | Osteomyology | Osteopathy | PAM | Paranormal Therapies | Pattern Therapies | Physiotherapy | Phytotherapy | Pilates | Podiatry | Polarity Therapy | Postural Integration | Primal Therapy | Psionic Therapy | Psychotherapy | Pyramid Power | Pyscho-Synthesis | Reflexology | Reichian Therapy | Reiki | Remedial Massage | Rogerian Therapy | Rolfing | Seichem | Sensitivity Training | Shiatsu | Silva Method | Sound Therapy | Spiritual Healing | Sports Massage | Stress Therapy | Swedish Body Massage | T'ai-Chi Ch'uan | Tantra Therapy | Tera-Mai | Thought Field Therapy | Touch Therapy | Transactional Analysis | Tui-na | Ultrasonics | Vibrational Therapy | Visualisation Therapy | Vitamin Therapy | Voice Therapy | X-Ray | Ying & Yang | Yoga | Zen Therapy | Zero Balancing |
|---|---|---|---|---|---|---|---|---|---|---|---|---|---|---|---|---|---|---|---|---|---|---|---|---|---|---|---|---|---|---|---|---|---|---|---|---|---|---|---|---|---|---|---|---|---|---|---|---|---|
| APPLETREE HEALTHY LIVING CTRE (HM00946) |||●||||||||||||||||||||||||||||||||||||||||||||||||
| BEESTON PHYSIO & SPORTS CLNC (HM02060) |||||||●||||||||||||||||||||||||||||||||||||||||||||
| BLOOMFIELD, MICHAEL (HM02515) |||●||||||||||||||||||||||||||||||||||||||||||||||||
| BOND, DIANORA (HM02669) |||●|||||||||||||||●||||||||||||||||||||||●||||||||||
| BRAHMA KUMARIS WORLD (HM02891) |||||||||||||||||||||||||||||||||||||||||||||||●|||
| BROADLEY, RICHARD (HM03116) |||||||||||||||●||||||||||||||||||||||||||||||||||||
| BULLEN-SPICER ASSOCIATES (HM03342) |||||||||||||||●||||||||||||||||●||||||||||||●||||||||
| CARITAS NATURAL HEALTH CLINIC (HM03688) |||●||||||||||||||||||||||||||●||||||||||||||||||||
| CASSIDY, TRISH (HM03820) ||||||||||||||||||●|||||||||||||||||||||||||||||||||
| CENTRE FOR TRANSFORMATION (HM03921) ||||||||||||||||||||●|||||||||||||||||||||||●|||||||
| CHANNON, CHRISTINA (HM03989) |||||||||||||||●||||||||||||||||||||||||||||||||||||
| COOPER, VAUGHAN (HM05131) |||●||||||||||||||||||||||||||||||||||||||||||||||||
| DEAN, MARTIN (HM05942) ||||||||||||||||||●||●||||●|||||||●||||●||||||||||||||||
| DERBY GESTALT CENTRE (HM06012) |||||||||||||||●||||||||||||||||||||||||||||||||||||
| EDWARDS, T W (HM06673) |||●||||||||||||||||||||||||||||||||||||||||||||||||
| GLOVER, ELEANOR L (HM08163) |||●||||||||||||||||||||||||||||||||||||||||||||||||
| GOTHAM VILLAGE PHSYO CLINIC (HM08308) |||||||●||||||||||||||||||||||||||||||||||||||||||||
| GRAHAM, HILARY E (HM08347) |||||||||||||||●||||||||||||||||||||||||||||||||||||
| HANDS ON HEALTH (HM08912) ||||||||||||||||||||||||||||||●||||||||||||||||||||
| HEMINGWAY, IMOGEN (HM09529) |||●||||||||||||||||||||||||||||||||||||||||||||||||
| IMPACT PHYSIO & SPORTS INJURIES (HM10590) |||||||●||||||||||||||||||||||||||||||||||||||||||||
| LIGHT UP YOUR LIFE (HM12370) ||||||||||||||||●||||●||||●||●|||||||||●||||||||||||||||
| MCMAHON MOUGHTIN CONSULTANCY (HM13563) |||||||||||||||●||||||||||||||||||||||||||||||||||||
| MORLEY-KIRK, JOHN (HM14188) ||||||||||||||||||●|||||||||||||||||||||||||||||||||
| MORTIMER, PHILIP (HM14243) |||●||||||||||||||||||||||||||||||||||||||||||||||||
| NATURAL HEALTH (HM14554) |||||||||●||||||||||●|||●||●||||||●|||||●||||||||||||||||●|||
| NATURAL THERAPY CLINIC (HM14654) |||||||||||||||●|||●||●||||||||||||||||||||||||||||||
| NEWARK OSTEOPATHIC CLINIC (HM14842) |||●||||||||||||||||||||||||||||||||||||||||||||||||
| NOTTINGHAM M S THERAPY CTRE (HM15083) ||||||||||||||||||●|||||||||||||||||||||||||||||||||
| NOTTINGHAM NATURAL HEALTH CTRE (HM15084) |||●||||||||||||●|||●||●||||||●||||||||||||||||||||||||●|
| NOTTINGHAM SPORTS INJURY (HM15085) |||||||●||||||||||||||||||||||||||||||||||||||||||||
| OPTIMUM HEALTH (HM15348) |||●|||||||||||||||●||●||||||●||●|●||●||||||||||||||●|||||||
| PARKSIDE STRESS MANAGEMENT (HM15722) ||||||||||||||||||||●|||||||||||||||||||||||●|●||||●|||
| PHYSIO DIRECT (HM16197) |||||||●||||||||||||||||||||||||||||||||||||||||||||

# O - Z Therapies at Practices/Businesses

Business by County with Reference no.

| Business | Orthotics | Osteomyology | Osteopathy | PAM | Paranormal Therapies | Pattern Therapies | Physiotherapy | Phytotherapy | Pilates | Podiatry | Polarity Therapy | Postural Integration | Primal Therapy | Psionic Therapy | Psychotherapy | Pyramid Power |
|---|---|---|---|---|---|---|---|---|---|---|---|---|---|---|---|---|
| PHYSIODIRECT (HM16214) | | | | | | | ● | | | | | | | | | |
| PIGGOTT, R S (HM16281) | | | | | | | | | | | | | | | ● | |
| PLAINS PHYSIO & BACK PAIN (HM16355) | | | | | | | ● | | | | | | | | | |
| RANDHAWA, PAL (HM16937) | | | | | | | | | | | | | | | | |
| RETFORD CHIROPRACTIC CLINIC (HM17200) | | | | | | | | | | | | | | | | |
| RICHARDS, PAUL (HM17263) | | | | | | | | | | | | | | | ● | |
| SEVENTHMOON NATURAL THRPY CTRE (HM18247) | | | | | | | | | | | | | | | | |
| SHEER TECHNIQUE (HM18368) | | | | | | | | | | | ● | ● | | | | |
| SHERWOOD PSYCHO TRAINING INS (HM18441) | | | | | | | | ● | | | | | | | ● | |
| SMITH, SALLY (HM18806) | | | | | | | | | | | | | | | | |
| STEWART, IAN (DR) (HM19268) | | | | | | | | | | | | | | | ● | |
| SUTTON THERAPY CENTRE (HM19550) | | | ● | | | | | | | | | | | | | |
| TOMLIN, NORMAN (HM20131) | | | | ● | | | | | | | | | | | | |
| TRADITIONAL ACUPUNCTURIST (HM20222) | | | | | | | | | | | | | | | | |
| VALENCIA, D (HM20555) | | | | | | | | | | | | | | | ● | |
| VAUGHTON, NORMAN D (HM20601) | | | | | | | | | | | | | | | ● | |
| WELLS, MADELEINE (HM21177) | | | | | | | | | | | | | | | | |
| WHITELEY, CHRIS (HM21398) | | | | | | | | | | | | | | | ● | |
| WOODHEAD, C S (HM21824) | | | ● | | | | | | | | | | | | | |
| **OXFORDSHIRE** | | | | | | | | | | | | | | | | |
| A BODY ORIENTED HUMANISTIC (HM00025) | | | | | | | | | | | | | | | ● | |
| ABRAMS, CAROLINE (HM00136) | | | ● | | | | | | | | | | | | | |
| ASHCROFT CLINIC (HM01198) | | | ● | | | | | | | ● | | | | | | |
| ASWAB (HM01306) | | | | | | | | | | | | | | | ● | |
| BACK IN LINE (HM01481) | | | | | | | | | ● | | | | | | | |
| BACK PAIN & SPORTS CLINIC (HM01490) | | | ● | | | | | | | | | | | | | |
| BAILEY, GILLIAN (HM01548) | | | | | | | | | | | | | | | | |
| BEDFORD, TOM (HM02042) | | | ● | | | | | | | | | | | | | |
| BENNETT, SHEILA (HM02159) | | | | | | | | | | | | | | | | |
| BOBY, KEITH (HM02547) | | | | | | | | | | | | | | | ● | |
| BODY CONTROL PILATES OXFORD (HM02581) | | | | | | | | | ● | | | | | | | |
| BURDEN, GILLIAN (HM03368) | | | | | | | | | | | | | | | | |
| CORKE, AMI (HM05168) | | | | | | | | | | | | | | | | |
| CORRIE REIKI HEALING (HM05192) | | | | | | | | | | | | | | | | |

| Business | Pyscho-Synthesis | Reflexology | Reichian Therapy | Reiki | Remedial Massage | Rogerian Therapy | Rolfing | Seichem | Sensitivity Training | Shiatsu | Silva Method | Sound Therapy | Spiritual Healing | Sports Massage | Stress Therapy | Swedish Body Massage |
|---|---|---|---|---|---|---|---|---|---|---|---|---|---|---|---|---|
| PHYSIODIRECT (HM16214) | | | | | | | | | | | | | | | | |
| PIGGOTT, R S (HM16281) | | | | | | | | | | | | | | | | |
| PLAINS PHYSIO & BACK PAIN (HM16355) | | | | | | | | | | | | | | | | |
| RANDHAWA, PAL (HM16937) | | ● | | | | | | | | | | | | | | |
| RETFORD CHIROPRACTIC CLINIC (HM17200) | | ● | | | | | | | | | | | | | | |
| RICHARDS, PAUL (HM17263) | | | | | | | | | | | | | | | | |
| SEVENTHMOON NATURAL THRPY CTRE (HM18247) | | ● | | ● | ● | | | | | | | | | | ● | |
| SHEER TECHNIQUE (HM18368) | | ● | | ● | | | | ● | | | | | ● | | ● | |
| SHERWOOD PSYCHO TRAINING INS (HM18441) | | | | ● | | ● | | | | | | | ● | | | |
| SMITH, SALLY (HM18806) | | ● | | | | | | | | | | | | | | |
| STEWART, IAN (DR) (HM19268) | | | | | | | | | | | | | | | | |
| SUTTON THERAPY CENTRE (HM19550) | | | | | | | | | | | | | | | | |
| TOMLIN, NORMAN (HM20131) | | | | | | | | | | | | | | | | |
| TRADITIONAL ACUPUNCTURIST (HM20222) | | | | ● | | | | | | | | | | | | |
| VALENCIA, D (HM20555) | | | | | | | | | | | | | | | | |
| VAUGHTON, NORMAN D (HM20601) | | | | | | | | | | | | | | | | |
| WELLS, MADELEINE (HM21177) | | ● | | | | | | | | | | | | | | |
| WHITELEY, CHRIS (HM21398) | | | | | | | | | | | | | | | | |
| WOODHEAD, C S (HM21824) | | | | | | | | | | | | | | | | |
| **OXFORDSHIRE** | | | | | | | | | | | | | | | | |
| A BODY ORIENTED HUMANISTIC (HM00025) | | | | | | | | | | | | | | | | |
| ABRAMS, CAROLINE (HM00136) | | | | | | | | | | | | | | | | |
| ASHCROFT CLINIC (HM01198) | | | | | | | | | | | | | | | ● | |
| ASWAB (HM01306) | | | | | | | | | | | | | | | | |
| BACK IN LINE (HM01481) | | | | | | | | | | | | | | | | |
| BACK PAIN & SPORTS CLINIC (HM01490) | | | | | | | | | | | | | | | | |
| BAILEY, GILLIAN (HM01548) | | ● | | | | | | | | | | | | | | |
| BEDFORD, TOM (HM02042) | | | | | | | | | | | | | | | | |
| BENNETT, SHEILA (HM02159) | | ● | | | | | | | | | | | | | | |
| BOBY, KEITH (HM02547) | | | | | | | | | | | | | | | | |
| BODY CONTROL PILATES OXFORD (HM02581) | | | | | | | | | | | | | | | | |
| BURDEN, GILLIAN (HM03368) | | ● | | | | | | | | | | | | | | |
| CORKE, AMI (HM05168) | | ● | | | | | | | | | | | | | | |
| CORRIE REIKI HEALING (HM05192) | | | | ● | | | | | | | | | | | | |

| Business | T'ai-Chi Ch'uan | Tantra Therapy | Tera-Mai | Thought Field Therapy | Touch Therapy | Transactional Analysis | Tui-na | Ultrasonics | Vibrational Therapy | Visualisation Therapy | Vitamin Therapy | Voice Therapy | X-Ray | Ying & Yang | Yoga | Zen Therapy | Zero Balancing |
|---|---|---|---|---|---|---|---|---|---|---|---|---|---|---|---|---|---|
| PHYSIODIRECT (HM16214) | | | | | | | | | | | | | | | | | |
| PIGGOTT, R S (HM16281) | | | | | | | | | | | | | | | | | |
| PLAINS PHYSIO & BACK PAIN (HM16355) | | | | | | | | | | | | | | | | | |
| RANDHAWA, PAL (HM16937) | | | | | | | | | | | | | | | | | |
| RETFORD CHIROPRACTIC CLINIC (HM17200) | | | | | | | | | | | | | | | | | |
| RICHARDS, PAUL (HM17263) | | | | | | | | | | | | | | | | | |
| SEVENTHMOON NATURAL THRPY CTRE (HM18247) | | | | | | | | | | | | | | | | | |
| SHEER TECHNIQUE (HM18368) | | | | | ● | | | | | ● | | | | | | | |
| SHERWOOD PSYCHO TRAINING INS (HM18441) | | | | | | ● | | | | | | | | | | | |
| SMITH, SALLY (HM18806) | | | | | | | | | | | | | | | | | |
| STEWART, IAN (DR) (HM19268) | | | | | | | | | | | | | | | | | |
| SUTTON THERAPY CENTRE (HM19550) | | | | | | | | | | | | | | | | | |
| TOMLIN, NORMAN (HM20131) | | | | | | | | | | | | | | | | | |
| TRADITIONAL ACUPUNCTURIST (HM20222) | | | | | | | | | | | | | | | | | |
| VALENCIA, D (HM20555) | | | | | | | | | | | | | | | | | |
| VAUGHTON, NORMAN D (HM20601) | | | | | | | | | | ● | | | | | | | |
| WELLS, MADELEINE (HM21177) | | | | | | | | | | | | | | | | | |
| WHITELEY, CHRIS (HM21398) | | | | | | | | | | | | | | | | | |
| WOODHEAD, C S (HM21824) | | | | | | | | | | | | | | | | | |
| **OXFORDSHIRE** | | | | | | | | | | | | | | | | | |
| A BODY ORIENTED HUMANISTIC (HM00025) | | | | | | | | | | | | | | | | | |
| ABRAMS, CAROLINE (HM00136) | | | | | | | | | | | | | | | | | |
| ASHCROFT CLINIC (HM01198) | | | | | | | | ● | ● | | ● | | ● | | | | |
| ASWAB (HM01306) | | | | | | | | | | | | | | | | | |
| BACK IN LINE (HM01481) | | | | | | | | | | | | | | | | | |
| BACK PAIN & SPORTS CLINIC (HM01490) | | | | | | | | | | | | | | | | | |
| BAILEY, GILLIAN (HM01548) | | | | | | | | | | | | | | | | | |
| BEDFORD, TOM (HM02042) | | | | | | | | | | | | | | | | | |
| BENNETT, SHEILA (HM02159) | | | | | | | | | | | | | | | | | |
| BOBY, KEITH (HM02547) | | | | | | | | | | | | | | | | | |
| BODY CONTROL PILATES OXFORD (HM02581) | | | | | | | | | | | | | | | | | |
| BURDEN, GILLIAN (HM03368) | | | | | | | | | | | | | | | | | |
| CORKE, AMI (HM05168) | | | | | | | | | | | | | | | | | |
| CORRIE REIKI HEALING (HM05192) | | | | | | | | | | | | | | | | | |

# O - Z Therapies at Practices/Businesses

| Business by County with Reference no. | Orthotics | Osteomyology | Osteopathy | PAM | Paranormal Therapies | Pattern Therapies | Physiotherapy | Phytotherapy | Pilates | Podiatry | Polarity Therapy | Postural Integration | Primal Therapy | Psionic Therapy | Psychotherapy | Pyramid Power | Pyscho-Synthesis | Reflexology | Reichian Therapy | Reiki | Remedial Massage | Rogerian Therapy | Rolfing | Seichem | Sensitivity Training |
|---|---|---|---|---|---|---|---|---|---|---|---|---|---|---|---|---|---|---|---|---|---|---|---|---|---|
| COTTAGE CLINIC (HM05221) | | | | | | | | | | | | | | | | | | ● | | ● | | | | | |
| DAY, RUKMANI G (HM05896) | | | ● | | | | | | | | | | | | | | | | | | | | | | |
| ELLAM, VALERIE (HM06745) | | | | | | | | | | | | | | | | | | ● | | | | | | | |
| ENGLAND, PAMELA (HM06828) | | | | | | | | | | | | | | | | | | ● | | | | | | | |
| FEET FIRST (HM07179) | | | | | | | | | | | | | | | | | | ● | | | | | | | |
| GILES, CHRISTOPHER (HM08067) | | | | | | | | | | | | | | | | | | ● | | | | | | | |
| GILMORE, V M (HM08106) | | | | | | | | | | | | | | | ● | | | | | | | | | | |
| GODSWELL NATURAL THRPY CTRE (HM08191) | | | | | | | ● | | | | | | | | ● | | | ● | | ● | | | | | |
| GOSS, TOM (HM08303) | | | | | | | | | | | | | | | ● | | | | | | | | | | |
| HANDS-ON-FEET (HM08919) | | | | | | | | | | | | | | | | | | ● | | | | | | | |
| HARRIS, CAROLE (HM09055) | | | | | | | | | | | | | | | | | | ● | | | | | | | |
| HARRIS, JONATHAN (HM09074) | | | | | | | | | | | | | | | ● | | | | | | | | | | |
| HELIX HOUSE (HM09522) | | | ● | | | | | | | | | | | | ● | | | | | | | | | | |
| HILL, ROSIE (HM09789) | | | | | | | | | | | | | | | | | | ● | | | | | | | |
| HUDSON, EMMA (HM10311) | | | ● | | | | | | | | | | | | | | | | | | | | | | |
| HYPNOTHERAPY CENTRE (HM10516) | | | | | | | | | | | | | | | | | | | | | | | | | |
| INGRAM, S (HM10627) | | | ● | | | | | | | | | | | | | | | | | | | | | | |
| ISIS CENTRE (HM10766) | | | | | | | | | | | | | | | ● | | | | | | | | | | |
| ISWARIAH, ROHAN (HM10777) | | | ● | | | | | | | | | | | | | | | | | | | | | | |
| JONES, JANET (HM11157) | | | | | | | | | | | | | | | | | | ● | | | | | | | |
| JONES, PATRICIA JEAN (HM11187) | | | | | | | | | | | | | | | | | | ● | | | | | | | |
| KIDLINGTON OSTEO PRACTICE (HM11596) | | | ● | | | | | | | | | | | | | | | | | | | | ● | | |
| LEWIS, MAGGIE (HM12303) | | | | | | | | | | | | | | | ● | | | | | | | | | | |
| LOCK, ALISON (HM12534) | | | | | | | | | | | | | | | | | | ● | | | | | | | |
| LOW-BEER, F E (HM12689) | | | | | | | | | | | | | | | ● | | | | | | | | | | |
| MANSTON, N (HM13050) | | | ● | | | | | | | | | | | | | | | | | | | | | | |
| MARRIOTT, HUGH (HM13138) | | | ● | | | | | | | | | | | | | | | | | | | | | | |
| MARRIOTT, HUGH (HM13139) | | | ● | | | | | | | | | | | | | | | | | | | | | | |
| MCGREGOR, STUART (HM13503) | | | ● | | | | | | | | | | | | | | | | | | | | | | |
| MILLER, J F (HM13890) | | | | | | | | | | | | | | | ● | | | | | | | | | | |
| MOSSMAN, CELIA (HM14271) | | | | | | | | | | | | | | | | | | ● | | | | | | | |
| O'BRIEN, JOHN (HM15186) | | | ● | | | | | | | | | | | | | | | | | | | | | | |
| O'BRIEN, JOHN C (HM15187) | | | ● | | | | | | | | | | | | | | | | | | | | | | |
| O'DONNELL, ELSPETH (HM15225) | | | | | | | | | | | | | | | | | | | | | | | | | |

| Business by County with Reference no. | Shiatsu | Silva Method | Sound Therapy | Spiritual Healing | Sports Massage | Stress Therapy | Swedish Body Massage | T'ai-Chi Ch'uan | Tantra Therapy | Tera-Mai | Thought Field Therapy | Touch Therapy | Transactional Analysis | Tui-na | Ultrasonics | Vibrational Therapy | Visualisation Therapy | Vitamin Therapy | Voice Therapy | X-Ray | Ying & Yang | Yoga | Zen Therapy | Zero Balancing |
|---|---|---|---|---|---|---|---|---|---|---|---|---|---|---|---|---|---|---|---|---|---|---|---|---|
| COTTAGE CLINIC (HM05221) | ● | | | | | | | | | ● | | | | | | | | | | | | | | |
| DAY, RUKMANI G (HM05896) | | | | | | | | | | | | | | | | | | | | | | | | |
| ELLAM, VALERIE (HM06745) | | | | | | | | | | | | | | | | | | | | | | | | |
| ENGLAND, PAMELA (HM06828) | | | | | | | | | | | | | | | | | | | | | | | | |
| FEET FIRST (HM07179) | | | | | | | | | | | | | | | | | | | | | | | | |
| GILES, CHRISTOPHER (HM08067) | | | | | | | | | | | | | | | | | | | | | | | | |
| GILMORE, V M (HM08106) | | | | | | | | | | | | | | | | | | | | | | | | |
| GODSWELL NATURAL THRPY CTRE (HM08191) | ● | | | | | | | | | | | | | | | | | ● | | | | ● | | |
| GOSS, TOM (HM08303) | | | | | | | | | | | | | | | | | | | | | | | | |
| HANDS-ON-FEET (HM08919) | | | | | | | | | | | | | | | | | | | | | | | | |
| HARRIS, CAROLE (HM09055) | | | | | | | | | | | | | | | | | | | | | | | | |
| HARRIS, JONATHAN (HM09074) | | | | | | | | | | | | | | | | | | | | | | | | |
| HELIX HOUSE (HM09522) | | | | ● | | | | | | | | | | | | | | | | | | | | |
| HILL, ROSIE (HM09789) | | | | | | | | | | | | | | | | | | | | | | | | |
| HUDSON, EMMA (HM10311) | | | | | | | | | | | | | | | | | | | | | | | | |
| HYPNOTHERAPY CENTRE (HM10516) | | | | ● | | | | | | | | | | | | | | | | | | | | |
| INGRAM, S (HM10627) | | | | | | | | | | | | | | | | | | | | | | | | |
| ISIS CENTRE (HM10766) | | | | | | | | | | | | | | | | | | | | | | | | |
| ISWARIAH, ROHAN (HM10777) | | | | | | | | | | | | | | | | | | | | | | | | |
| JONES, JANET (HM11157) | | | | | | | | | | | | | | | | | | | | | | | | |
| JONES, PATRICIA JEAN (HM11187) | | | | | | | | | | | | | | | | | | | | | | | | |
| KIDLINGTON OSTEO PRACTICE (HM11596) | | | | | | | | | | | | | | | ● | | | | | | | | | |
| LEWIS, MAGGIE (HM12303) | | | | | | | | | | | | | | | | | | | | | | | | |
| LOCK, ALISON (HM12534) | | | | | | | | | | | | | | | | | | | | | | | | |
| LOW-BEER, F E (HM12689) | | | | | | | | | | | | | | | | | | | | | | | | |
| MANSTON, N (HM13050) | | | | | | | | | | | | | | | | | | | | | | | | |
| MARRIOTT, HUGH (HM13138) | | | | | | | | | | | | | | | | | | | | | | | | |
| MARRIOTT, HUGH (HM13139) | | | | | | | | | | | | | | | | | | | | | | | | |
| MCGREGOR, STUART (HM13503) | | | | | | | | | | | | | | | | | | | | | | | | |
| MILLER, J F (HM13890) | | | | | | | | | | | | | | | | | | | | | | | | |
| MOSSMAN, CELIA (HM14271) | | | | | | | | | | | | | | | | | | | | | | | | |
| O'BRIEN, JOHN (HM15186) | | | | | | | | | | | | | | | | | | | | | | | | |
| O'BRIEN, JOHN C (HM15187) | | | | | | | | | | | | | | | | | | | | | | | | |
| O'DONNELL, ELSPETH (HM15225) | ● | | | | | | | | | | | | | | | | | | | | | | | |

# O - Z Therapies at Practices/Businesses

| Business by County with Reference no. | Orthotics | Osteomyology | Osteopathy | PAM | Paranormal Therapies | Pattern Therapies | Physiotherapy | Phytotherapy | Pilates | Podiatry | Polarity Therapy | Postural Integration | Primal Therapy | Psionic Therapy | Psychotherapy | Pyramid Power | Pyscho-Synthesis | Reflexology | Reichian Therapy | Reiki | Remedial Massage | Rogerian Therapy | Rolfing | Seichem | Sensitivity Training | Shiatsu | Silva Method | Sound Therapy | Spiritual Healing | Sports Massage | Stress Therapy | Swedish Body Massage | T'ai-Chi Ch'uan | Tantra Therapy | Tera-Mai | Thought Field Therapy | Touch Therapy | Transactional Analysis | Tui-na | Ultrasonics | Vibrational Therapy | Visualisation Therapy | Vitamin Therapy | Voice Therapy | X-Ray | Ying & Yang | Yoga | Zen Therapy | Zero Balancing |
|---|---|---|---|---|---|---|---|---|---|---|---|---|---|---|---|---|---|---|---|---|---|---|---|---|---|---|---|---|---|---|---|---|---|---|---|---|---|---|---|---|---|---|---|---|---|---|---|---|---|
| OXFORD TRANSCENDTL MEDITA CTRE (HM15544) | | | | | | | | | | | | | | | | | | | | | | | | | | | | | | | ● | | | | | | | | | | | | | | | | | | |
| PARSONS STREET CLINIC (HM15747) | | | ● | | | | | | | | | | | | | | | | | | | | | | | | | | | | | | | | | | | | | | | | | | | | | | |
| PITTS, RICHARD (HM16353) | | | | | | | | | | | | | | | | | | ● | | | | | | | | | | | | | | | | | | | | | | | | | | | | | | | |
| POLLOCK, SUSAN (HM16418) | | | | | | | | | | ● | | | | | | | | ● | | | | | | | | | | | | | ● | | | | | | | | | | | | | | | | | | |
| POWER, CLIVE (HM16502) | | | ● | | | | | | | | | | | | | | | | | | | | | | | | | | | | | | | | | | | | | | | | | | | | | | |
| RUDDICK, DAVID (HM17731) | | | ● | | | | | | | | | | | | | | | | | | | | | | | | | | | | | | | | | | | | | | | | | | | | | | |
| SIDEBOTTOM, MARGARET (HM18527) | | | | | | | ● | | | | | | | | | | | | | | | | | | | | | | | | | | | | | | | | | | | | | | | | | | |
| SPARKS, MARTIN ANDREW (HM18962) | | | | | | | | | | | | | | | | | | ● | | | | | | | | | | | | | | | | | | | | | | | | | | | | | | | |
| SUMMERTON CLINIC (HM19498) | | | | | | | | ● | | | | | | | | | | | | | | | | | | | | | | | | | | | | | | | | | | | | | | | | | |
| THAME THERAPY CLINIC (HM19864) | | | ● | | | | | | | | | | | | | | | | | | | | | | | | | | | | | | | | | | | | | | | | | | | | | | |
| THOMPSON, PAT (HM19995) | | | | | | | | | | | | | | | ● | | | | | | | | | | | | | | | | | | | | | | | | | | | | | | | | | | |
| THROWER, MARIANNE (HM20045) | | | | | | | | | | | | | | | | | | ● | | | | | | | | | | | | | | | | | | | | | | | | | | | | | | | |
| TOUCH OF NATURE (HM20188) | | | | | | | | ● | | | | | | | | | | ● | | ● | | | | | | | | | ● | | ● | | | | | | | | | | | | ● | | | | | | |
| TRANS PERSONAL PSYCHOTHERAPIST (HM20263) | | | | | | | | | | | | | | | ● | | | | | | | | | | | | | | | | | | | | | | | | | | | | | | | | | | |
| TWINE, I E (HM20453) | | | ● | | | | | | | | | | | | | | | ● | | | | | | | | | | | | | | | | | | | | | | | | | | | | | | | |
| WANTAGE NATURAL HEALTH CENTRE (HM20891) | | | ● | | | | | | | | | | | | | | | ● | | | | | | | | | | | | | | | | | | | | | | | | | | | | | | | |
| WANTAGE OSTEOPATHIC PRACTICE (HM20892) | | | ● | | | | | | | | | | | | | | | | | | | | | | | | | | | | | | | | | | | | | | | | | | | | | | |
| WEST BAR CLINIC (HM21214) | | | | | | | | | | | | | | | ● | | | | | | | | | | | | | | | | | | | | | | | | | | | | | | | | | | |
| WHEATLEY COMP THERAPY (HM21308) | | | | | | | | | | | | | | | | | | ● | | | ● | | | | | | | | | | | | | | | | | | | | | | | | | | | | |
| WHITMORE, ELIZABETH (HM21412) | | | | | | | | | | | | | | | | | | ● | | | | | | | | | | | | | | | | | | | | | | | | | | | | | | | |
| WINTER, CLAIRE (HM21717) | | | | | | | | | | | | | | | | | | ● | | | | | | | | | | | | | | | | | | | | | | | | | | | | | | | |
| WITNEY CHIROPRACTIC/CHIROPODY (HM21750) | | | | | | | | | | | | | | | | | | | | | | | | | | | | | | | | | | | | | | | | | | | | | ● | | | | |
| WITNEY NATURAL HEALTH CLINIC (HM21751) | | | | | | | | | ● | | | | | | | | | ● | | ● | | | | ● | | ● | | | ● | ● | ● | | ● | | | | | ● | | | | | | | | | ● | | |
| RUTLAND | | | | | | | | | | | | | | | | | | | | | | | | | | | | | | | | | | | | | | | | | | | | | | | | | |
| FINNIS, ELIZABETH (HM07326) | | | | | | | | | | | | | | | | | | ● | | | | | | | | | | | | | | | | | | | | | | | | | | | | | | | |
| SHROPSHIRE | | | | | | | | | | | | | | | | | | | | | | | | | | | | | | | | | | | | | | | | | | | | | | | | | |
| ACUMEDIC (HM00218) | | | | | | | | | | | | | | | | | | | | | | | | | | | | | | | | | ● | | | | | | | | | | | | | | | | |
| ADLARD, FIONA (HM00383) | | | ● | | | | | | | | | | | | | | | | | | | | | | | | | | | | | | | | | | | | | | | | | | | | | | |
| ALLCOCK, RACHAEL (HM00594) | | | | | | | | | | | | | | | | | | ● | | | | | | | | | | | | | | | | | | | | | | | | | | | | | | | |
| ALLEN, RICHARD (HM00615) | | | ● | | | | | | | | | | | | | | | | | | | | | | | | | | | | | | | | | | | | | | | | | | | | | | |
| ANDERSON, BETTY (HM00814) | | | | | | | | | | | | | | | | | | ● | | | | | | | | | | | | | | | | | | | | | | | | | | | | | | | |
| AYRES, JOHN (HM01434) | | | | | | | | | | | | | | | ● | | | | | | | ● | | | | | | | | | ● | | | | | | | | | | | | | | | | | | |
| BENNETT, JANET (HM02144) | | | | | | | | | | | | | | | | | | ● | | | | | | | | | | | | | | | | | | | | | | | | | | | | | | | |
| BODYLIFE CENTRE (HM02622) | | | | | | | | | | | | | | | | | | | | | | | | | | | | | | | | | | | | | | | | | | | | | | | ● | | |

# O-Z Therapies at Practices/Businesses

| Business by County with Reference no. | Orthotics | Osteomyology | Osteopathy | PAM | Paranormal Therapies | Pattern Therapies | Physiotherapy | Phytotherapy | Pilates | Podiatry | Polarity Therapy | Postural Integration |
|---|---|---|---|---|---|---|---|---|---|---|---|---|
| BOOTH, ROBERT (HM02709) | | | | | | | ● | | | | | |
| BROCKBANK, BRETT (HM03129) | | | ● | | | | | | | | | |
| CHAKRAVERTY, R C (DR) (HM03943) | | | ● | | | | | | | | | |
| CHAKRAVERTY, R C (DR) (HM03944) | | | ● | | | | | | | | | |
| COLERIDGE, JUDY (HM04831) | | | | | | | | | | | | |
| CORKE, A J (HM05167) | | | | | | | | | | | | |
| GOODWILLIE, GILL (HM08266) | | | | | | | | | | | | |
| HALES OSTEOPATHIC PRACTICE (HM08743) | | | ● | | | | | | | | | |
| LOUIS, L (HM12664) | | | ● | | | | | | | | | |
| LUDLOW OSTEOPATHIC CLINIC (HM12727) | | | ● | | | | | | | | | |
| MADDOCKS CLINIC (HM12898) | | | | | | | ● | | | | | |
| MEDAYD PHYSIOTHERAPY (HM13645) | | | | | | | ● | | | | | |
| MEDAYD PHYSIOTHERAPY (HM13644) | | | | | | | ● | | | | | |
| NEEDHAM, LYNDA M (HM14751) | | | | | | | | | | | | |
| OSTEOPATHIC (HM15449) | | | ● | | | | | | | | | |
| OSTEOPATHIC PRACTICE (HM15472) | | | ● | | | | | | | | | |
| PARSONS, BRONDA (HM15748) | | | | | | | | | | | | |
| PEARSON, CHRISTINE (HM15911) | | | | | | | | | | | | |
| PHILLIPS, ANN (HM16124) | | | | | | | | | | | | |
| PREES COMPLEMENTARY THERAPIES (HM16533) | | | | | | | | | | | | |
| RUXTON, HUGH (HM17786) | | | ● | | | | | | | | | |
| SPENCER, DIANE (HM18993) | | | | | | | | | | | | |
| STONE, JANET (HM19336) | | | | | | | | | | | | |
| TAN & BEAUTY STUDIO (HM19676) | | | | | | | | | | | | |
| WALMSLEY, RUTH (HM20848) | | | | | | | | | | | | |
| WARREN, SUSAN (HM20952) | | | | | | | | | | | | |
| WESTON, JOHN (HM21279) | | | ● | | | | | | | | | |
| WESTON, JOHN M (HM21280) | | | ● | | | | | | | | | |
| WHITELEY, STEVEN (HM21400) | | | | | | | | | | | | |
| WILLIAMS, J (HM21567) | | | ● | | | | | | | | | |
| **SOMERSET** | | | | | | | | | | | | |
| ALASKAN BACH FLOWER REMEDIES (HM00472) | | | | | | | | | | | | |
| ANSON, BARRIE (HM00916) | | | | | | | | | | | | |
| AUSSENS, MIEKE (HM01359) | | | | | | | | | | | | |

| Business by County with Reference no. | Primal Therapy | Psionic Therapy | Psychotherapy | Pyramid Power | Pyscho-Synthesis | Reflexology | Reichian Therapy | Reiki | Remedial Massage | Rogerian Therapy | Rolfing | Seichem |
|---|---|---|---|---|---|---|---|---|---|---|---|---|
| BOOTH, ROBERT (HM02709) | | | | | | | | | | | | |
| BROCKBANK, BRETT (HM03129) | | | | | | | | | | | | |
| CHAKRAVERTY, R C (DR) (HM03943) | | | | | | | | | | | | |
| CHAKRAVERTY, R C (DR) (HM03944) | | | | | | | | | | | | |
| COLERIDGE, JUDY (HM04831) | | | ● | | | ● | | | | | | |
| CORKE, A J (HM05167) | | | | | | | | | | | | |
| GOODWILLIE, GILL (HM08266) | | | ● | | | | | | | | | |
| HALES OSTEOPATHIC PRACTICE (HM08743) | | | | | | | | | | | | |
| LOUIS, L (HM12664) | | | | | | | | | | | | |
| LUDLOW OSTEOPATHIC CLINIC (HM12727) | | | | | | | | | | | | |
| MADDOCKS CLINIC (HM12898) | | | | | | | | ● | | | | |
| MEDAYD PHYSIOTHERAPY (HM13645) | | | | | | | | | | | | |
| MEDAYD PHYSIOTHERAPY (HM13644) | | | | | | | | | | | | |
| NEEDHAM, LYNDA M (HM14751) | | | | | | | | | | | | |
| OSTEOPATHIC (HM15449) | | | | | | | | | | | ● | |
| OSTEOPATHIC PRACTICE (HM15472) | | | | | | | | | | | | |
| PARSONS, BRONDA (HM15748) | | | | | | ● | | | | | | |
| PEARSON, CHRISTINE (HM15911) | | | | | | ● | | ● | | | | |
| PHILLIPS, ANN (HM16124) | | | | | | ● | | ● | | | | |
| PREES COMPLEMENTARY THERAPIES (HM16533) | | | | | | ● | | | | | | |
| RUXTON, HUGH (HM17786) | | | | | | | | | | | | |
| SPENCER, DIANE (HM18993) | | | | | | ● | | | | | | |
| STONE, JANET (HM19336) | | | | | | ● | | | | | | |
| TAN & BEAUTY STUDIO (HM19676) | | | | | | ● | | | | | | |
| WALMSLEY, RUTH (HM20848) | | | | | | ● | | | | | | |
| WARREN, SUSAN (HM20952) | | | | | | ● | | | | | | |
| WESTON, JOHN (HM21279) | | | | | | | | | | | | |
| WESTON, JOHN M (HM21280) | | | | | | | | | | | | |
| WHITELEY, STEVEN (HM21400) | | | | | | ● | | | | | | |
| WILLIAMS, J (HM21567) | | | | | | | | | | | | |
| **SOMERSET** | | | | | | | | | | | | |
| ALASKAN BACH FLOWER REMEDIES (HM00472) | | | | | | ● | | | | | | |
| ANSON, BARRIE (HM00916) | | | ● | | | | | | | | | |
| AUSSENS, MIEKE (HM01359) | | | | | | | | | | | | |

| Business by County with Reference no. | Sensitivity Training | Shiatsu | Silva Method | Sound Therapy | Spiritual Healing | Sports Massage | Stress Therapy | Swedish Body Massage | T'ai-Chi Ch'uan | Tantra Therapy | Tera-Mai | Thought Field Therapy |
|---|---|---|---|---|---|---|---|---|---|---|---|---|
| BOOTH, ROBERT (HM02709) | | | | | | | | | | | | |
| BROCKBANK, BRETT (HM03129) | | | | | | | | | | | | |
| CHAKRAVERTY, R C (DR) (HM03943) | | | | | | | | | | | | |
| CHAKRAVERTY, R C (DR) (HM03944) | | | | | | | | | | | | |
| COLERIDGE, JUDY (HM04831) | | | | | | | ● | | | | | |
| CORKE, A J (HM05167) | | | | | | | ● | | | | | |
| GOODWILLIE, GILL (HM08266) | | | | | | | | | | | | |
| HALES OSTEOPATHIC PRACTICE (HM08743) | | | | | | | | | | | | |
| LOUIS, L (HM12664) | | | | | | | | | | | | |
| LUDLOW OSTEOPATHIC CLINIC (HM12727) | | | | | | | | | | | | |
| MADDOCKS CLINIC (HM12898) | | | | | | | | | | | | |
| MEDAYD PHYSIOTHERAPY (HM13645) | | | | | | | | | | | | |
| MEDAYD PHYSIOTHERAPY (HM13644) | | | | | | | | | | | | |
| NEEDHAM, LYNDA M (HM14751) | | | | | | | ● | | | | | |
| OSTEOPATHIC (HM15449) | | | | | | | | | | | | |
| OSTEOPATHIC PRACTICE (HM15472) | | | | | | | | | | | | |
| PARSONS, BRONDA (HM15748) | | | | | | | | | | | | |
| PEARSON, CHRISTINE (HM15911) | | | | | | | | | | | | |
| PHILLIPS, ANN (HM16124) | | | | | | | | | | | | |
| PREES COMPLEMENTARY THERAPIES (HM16533) | | | | | | | | | | | | |
| RUXTON, HUGH (HM17786) | | | | | | | | | | | | |
| SPENCER, DIANE (HM18993) | | | | | | | | | | | | |
| STONE, JANET (HM19336) | | | | | | | | | | | | |
| TAN & BEAUTY STUDIO (HM19676) | | | | | | | | | | | | |
| WALMSLEY, RUTH (HM20848) | | | | | | | ● | | | | | |
| WARREN, SUSAN (HM20952) | | | | | | | | | | | | |
| WESTON, JOHN (HM21279) | | | | | | | | | | | | |
| WESTON, JOHN M (HM21280) | | | | | | | | | | | | |
| WHITELEY, STEVEN (HM21400) | | | | | | | | | | | | |
| WILLIAMS, J (HM21567) | | | | | | | | | | | | |
| **SOMERSET** | | | | | | | | | | | | |
| ALASKAN BACH FLOWER REMEDIES (HM00472) | | | | | | | | | | | | |
| ANSON, BARRIE (HM00916) | | | | | ● | | ● | | | | | |
| AUSSENS, MIEKE (HM01359) | | ● | | | | | | | | | | |

| Business by County with Reference no. | Touch Therapy | Transactional Analysis | Tui-na | Ultrasonics | Vibrational Therapy | Visualisation Therapy | Vitamin Therapy | Voice Therapy | X-Ray | Ying & Yang | Yoga | Zen Therapy | Zero Balancing |
|---|---|---|---|---|---|---|---|---|---|---|---|---|---|
| BOOTH, ROBERT (HM02709) | | | | | | | | | | | | | |
| BROCKBANK, BRETT (HM03129) | | | | | | | | | | | | | |
| CHAKRAVERTY, R C (DR) (HM03943) | | | | | | | | | | | | | |
| CHAKRAVERTY, R C (DR) (HM03944) | | | | | | | | | | | | | |
| COLERIDGE, JUDY (HM04831) | ● | | | | | | | | | | | | |
| CORKE, A J (HM05167) | | | | | | | | | | | | | |
| GOODWILLIE, GILL (HM08266) | | | | | | | | | | | | | |
| HALES OSTEOPATHIC PRACTICE (HM08743) | | | | | | | ● | | | | | | |
| LOUIS, L (HM12664) | | | | | | | | | | | | | |
| LUDLOW OSTEOPATHIC CLINIC (HM12727) | | | | | | | | | | | | | |
| MADDOCKS CLINIC (HM12898) | | | | | | | | | | | | | |
| MEDAYD PHYSIOTHERAPY (HM13645) | | | | | | | | | | | | | |
| MEDAYD PHYSIOTHERAPY (HM13644) | | | | | | | | | | | | | |
| NEEDHAM, LYNDA M (HM14751) | | | | | | | | | | | | | |
| OSTEOPATHIC (HM15449) | | | | | | | | | | | | | |
| OSTEOPATHIC PRACTICE (HM15472) | | | | | | | | | | | | | |
| PARSONS, BRONDA (HM15748) | | | | | | | | | | | | | |
| PEARSON, CHRISTINE (HM15911) | | | | | | | | | | | | | |
| PHILLIPS, ANN (HM16124) | | | | | | | | | | | | | |
| PREES COMPLEMENTARY THERAPIES (HM16533) | | | | | | | | | | | | | |
| RUXTON, HUGH (HM17786) | | | | | | | | | | | | | |
| SPENCER, DIANE (HM18993) | | | | | | | | | | | | | |
| STONE, JANET (HM19336) | | | | | | | | | | | | | |
| TAN & BEAUTY STUDIO (HM19676) | | | | | | | | | | | | | |
| WALMSLEY, RUTH (HM20848) | ● | | | | | | | | | | | | |
| WARREN, SUSAN (HM20952) | | | | | | | | | | | | | |
| WESTON, JOHN (HM21279) | | | | | | | | | | | | | |
| WESTON, JOHN M (HM21280) | | | | | | | | | | | | | |
| WHITELEY, STEVEN (HM21400) | | | | | | | | | | | | | |
| WILLIAMS, J (HM21567) | | | | | | | | | | | | | |
| **SOMERSET** | | | | | | | | | | | | | |
| ALASKAN BACH FLOWER REMEDIES (HM00472) | | | | | | | | | | | | | |
| ANSON, BARRIE (HM00916) | | | | | | | ● | | | | | | |
| AUSSENS, MIEKE (HM01359) | | | | | | | | | | | | | |

# O - Z Therapies at Practices/Businesses

Business by County with Reference no.

| Business by County with Reference no. | Orthotics | Osteomyology | Osteopathy | PAM | Paranormal Therapies | Pattern Therapies | Physiotherapy | Phytotherapy | Pilates | Podiatry | Polarity Therapy | Postural Integration | Primal Therapy | Psionic Therapy | Psychotherapy | Pyramid Power |
|---|---|---|---|---|---|---|---|---|---|---|---|---|---|---|---|---|
| AVENUE CLINIC (HM01388) | | | ● | | | | | | | | | | | | | |
| BAILEY, ALISON (HM01540) | | | | | | | | | | | | | | | | |
| BATH BACK CLINIC (HM01891) | | | | | | | | | | | | | | | | |
| BATH NATURAL MEDICAL CENTRE (HM01893) | | | | | | | | | | | | | | | ● | |
| BATH PRACTICE (HM01894) | | | ● | | | | | | | | | | | | | |
| BATHPOOL CHIROPRACTIC CLINIC (HM01900) | | | | | | | | | | | | | | | | |
| BEECH HOUSE CLINIC (HM02046) | | | ● | | | | | | | | | | | | | |
| BOULEVARD PHARMACY (HM02739) | | | | | | | ● | ● | | | | | | | ● | |
| BRIDGET HEALING CENTRE (HM03008) | | | | | | | | | | | | | | | | |
| BROWN, JULIET (HM03231) | | | | | | | | | | | | | | | ● | |
| CAMERON, IAN L (HM03584) | | | ● | | | | | | | | | | | | | |
| CAMPION, RICHARD (HM03615) | | | ● | | | | | | | | | | | | | |
| CASTLE SURGERY (HM03840) | | | ● | | | | | | | | | | | | | |
| CHAMELEON OILS (HM03961) | | | | | | | | | | | | | | | | |
| CHEDDAR COMP MEDICINE CTRE (HM04075) | | | ● | | | | ● | | | | | | | | ● | |
| CHINESE MEDICAL CENTRE (HM04238) | | | | | | | | | | | | | | | | |
| CHIPPER, MARY (HM04278) | | | | | | | | | | | | | | | | |
| CLINIC OF COMP MEDICINE (HM04689) | | | ● | | | | | | | | | | | | | |
| CLISBY, JANE (HM04722) | | | | | | | | | | | | | | | | |
| COBB, JOANNA (HM04760) | | | ● | | | | | | | | | | | | | |
| COUNSULTING ROOMS (HM05253) | | | | | | | | | | | | | | | | |
| DAVIES, SALLY (HM05840) | | | | | | | | | | | | | | | | |
| GAWEN & ASSOCIATES (HM07939) | | | ● | | | | | | | | | | | | | |
| GLASTONBURY CHIROPRACTIC (HM08131) | | | | | | | | | | | | | | | | |
| GLASTONBURY EAST WEST CENTRE (HM08132) | | | ● | | | | | | | | | | | | ● | |
| GOSWELL HOUSE CLINIC (HM08307) | | | ● | | | | | | | | | | | | | |
| GWILT, ANNA (HM08669) | | | ● | | | | | | | | | | | | | |
| HAMAR, KLARE (HM08823) | | | | | | | | | | | | | | | | |
| HAMMET STREET PRACTICE (HM08863) | | | ● | | | | | | | | | | | | | |
| HODGSON, JENNIFER (HM09886) | | | ● | | | | | | | | | | | | | |
| HOLISTIC HEALING CENTRE (HM09962) | | | | | | | | | | | | | | | | |
| HOPKINS, JILL (HM10150) | | | | | | | | | | | | | | | ● | |
| HUDSON, JOHN (HM10315) | | | | | | | | | | | | | | | ● | |
| HUXTABLE, ALISON (HM10461) | | | ● | | | | | | | | | | | | | |

| Business by County with Reference no. | Pyscho-Synthesis | Reflexology | Reichian Therapy | Reiki | Remedial Massage | Rogerian Therapy | Rolfing | Seichem | Sensitivity Training | Shiatsu | Silva Method | Sound Therapy | Spiritual Healing | Sports Massage | Stress Therapy | Swedish Body Massage |
|---|---|---|---|---|---|---|---|---|---|---|---|---|---|---|---|---|
| AVENUE CLINIC (HM01388) | | ● | | | | | | | | ● | | | | | | |
| BAILEY, ALISON (HM01540) | | ● | | | | | | | | | | | | | | |
| BATH BACK CLINIC (HM01891) | | | | | | | | | | | | | | | | |
| BATH NATURAL MEDICAL CENTRE (HM01893) | | | | | | | | | | ● | | | | | | |
| BATH PRACTICE (HM01894) | | | | | | | | | | | | | | | | |
| BATHPOOL CHIROPRACTIC CLINIC (HM01900) | | ● | | | | | | | | | | | | | ● | |
| BEECH HOUSE CLINIC (HM02046) | | | | | | | | | | | | | | | | |
| BOULEVARD PHARMACY (HM02739) | | ● | | ● | | | | | | ● | | | ● | | ● | |
| BRIDGET HEALING CENTRE (HM03008) | | ● | | ● | | | | | | ● | | | | | | |
| BROWN, JULIET (HM03231) | | | | | | | | | | | | | | | | |
| CAMERON, IAN L (HM03584) | | | | | | | | | | | | | | | | |
| CAMPION, RICHARD (HM03615) | | | | | | | | | | | | | | | | |
| CASTLE SURGERY (HM03840) | | ● | | | | | | | | | | | | | | |
| CHAMELEON OILS (HM03961) | | ● | | | | | | | | | | | | | | |
| CHEDDAR COMP MEDICINE CTRE (HM04075) | | | | ● | | | | | | | | | | | | |
| CHINESE MEDICAL CENTRE (HM04238) | | | | | | | | | | | | | | | | |
| CHIPPER, MARY (HM04278) | | | | | | | | | | | | | | | ● | |
| CLINIC OF COMP MEDICINE (HM04689) | | | | | | | | | | | | | | | | |
| CLISBY, JANE (HM04722) | | ● | | | | | | | | | | | | | | |
| COBB, JOANNA (HM04760) | | | | | | | | | | | | | | | | |
| COUNSULTING ROOMS (HM05253) | | | | | | | | | | | | | | | ● | |
| DAVIES, SALLY (HM05840) | | ● | | | | | | | | | | | | | | |
| GAWEN & ASSOCIATES (HM07939) | | | | | | | | | | | | | | | | |
| GLASTONBURY CHIROPRACTIC (HM08131) | | ● | | ● | | | | | | | | | | | | |
| GLASTONBURY EAST WEST CENTRE (HM08132) | | | | | | | | | | ● | | | | | ● | |
| GOSWELL HOUSE CLINIC (HM08307) | | | | | | | | | | | | | | | | |
| GWILT, ANNA (HM08669) | | | | | | | | | | | | | | | | |
| HAMAR, KLARE (HM08823) | | ● | | | | | | | | | | | | | | |
| HAMMET STREET PRACTICE (HM08863) | | | | | | | | | | | | | | | | |
| HODGSON, JENNIFER (HM09886) | | | | | | | | | | | | | | | | |
| HOLISTIC HEALING CENTRE (HM09962) | | ● | | | | | | | | | | | | | | |
| HOPKINS, JILL (HM10150) | | | | | | | | | | | | | | | | |
| HUDSON, JOHN (HM10315) | | | | | | | | | | | | | | | | |
| HUXTABLE, ALISON (HM10461) | | | | | | | | | | | | | | | | |

| Business by County with Reference no. | T'ai-Chi Ch'uan | Tantra Therapy | Tera-Mai | Thought Field Therapy | Touch Therapy | Transactional Analysis | Tui-na | Ultrasonics | Vibrational Therapy | Visualisation Therapy | Vitamin Therapy | Voice Therapy | X-Ray | Ying & Yang | Yoga | Zen Therapy | Zero Balancing |
|---|---|---|---|---|---|---|---|---|---|---|---|---|---|---|---|---|---|
| AVENUE CLINIC (HM01388) | | | | | | | | | | | | | | | | | |
| BAILEY, ALISON (HM01540) | | | | | | | | | | | | | | | | | |
| BATH BACK CLINIC (HM01891) | | | | | | | | | | | | | | | ● | | |
| BATH NATURAL MEDICAL CENTRE (HM01893) | | | | | | | | | | | | | | | | | |
| BATH PRACTICE (HM01894) | | | | | | | | | | | | | | | | | |
| BATHPOOL CHIROPRACTIC CLINIC (HM01900) | | | | | | | | | | | | | | | | | |
| BEECH HOUSE CLINIC (HM02046) | | | | | | | | | | | | | | | | | |
| BOULEVARD PHARMACY (HM02739) | | | | | | | | | | | | | | | ● | | |
| BRIDGET HEALING CENTRE (HM03008) | | | | | | | | | | | | | | | | | |
| BROWN, JULIET (HM03231) | | | | | | | | | | | | | | | | | |
| CAMERON, IAN L (HM03584) | | | | | | | | | | | | | | | | | |
| CAMPION, RICHARD (HM03615) | | | | | | | | | | | | | | | | | |
| CASTLE SURGERY (HM03840) | | | | | | | | | | | | | | | | | |
| CHAMELEON OILS (HM03961) | | | | | | | | | | | | | | | | | |
| CHEDDAR COMP MEDICINE CTRE (HM04075) | | | | | | | | | | | | | | | | | |
| CHINESE MEDICAL CENTRE (HM04238) | ● | | | | | | | | | | | | | | | | |
| CHIPPER, MARY (HM04278) | | | | | | | | | | | | | | | | | |
| CLINIC OF COMP MEDICINE (HM04689) | | | | | | | | | | | | | | | | | |
| CLISBY, JANE (HM04722) | | | | | | | | | | | | | | | | | |
| COBB, JOANNA (HM04760) | | | | | | | | | | | | | | | | | |
| COUNSULTING ROOMS (HM05253) | | | | | | ● | | | | ● | | | | | | | |
| DAVIES, SALLY (HM05840) | | | | | | | | | | | | | | | | | |
| GAWEN & ASSOCIATES (HM07939) | | | | | | | | | | | | | | | | | |
| GLASTONBURY CHIROPRACTIC (HM08131) | | | | | | | | | | | | | | | | | |
| GLASTONBURY EAST WEST CENTRE (HM08132) | | | | | | | | | | | | | | | ● | | |
| GOSWELL HOUSE CLINIC (HM08307) | | | | | | | | | | | | | | | | | |
| GWILT, ANNA (HM08669) | | | | | | | | | | | | | | | | | |
| HAMAR, KLARE (HM08823) | | | | | | | | | | | | | | | | | |
| HAMMET STREET PRACTICE (HM08863) | | | | | | | | | | | | | | | | | |
| HODGSON, JENNIFER (HM09886) | | | | | | | | | | | | | | | | | |
| HOLISTIC HEALING CENTRE (HM09962) | | | | | | | | | | | | | | | | | |
| HOPKINS, JILL (HM10150) | | | | | | | | | | | | | | | | | |
| HUDSON, JOHN (HM10315) | | | | | | | | | | | | | | | | | |
| HUXTABLE, ALISON (HM10461) | | | | | | | | | | | | | | | | | |

# O - Z Therapies at Practices/Businesses

Business by County with Reference no.

| Business by County with Reference no. | Orthotics | Osteomyology | Osteopathy | PAM | Paranormal Therapies | Pattern Therapies | Physiotherapy | Phytotherapy | Pilates | Podiatry | Polarity Therapy | Postural Integration | Primal Therapy | Psionic Therapy | Psychotherapy | Pyramid Power | Pyscho-Synthesis |
|---|---|---|---|---|---|---|---|---|---|---|---|---|---|---|---|---|---|
| JASMINE HOLISTIC HEALTH (HM10937) | | | | | | | | | | | | | | | | | |
| JEFFERY, JO (HM10965) | | | | | | | | | | | | | | | | | |
| JENKINSON, TRISHA (HM11000) | | | | | | | | | | | | | | | | | |
| KALISCH, DAVID (HM11296) | | | | | | | | | | | | | | | ● | | |
| KEARNS, ANTHONY P (HM11372) | | | ● | | | | | | | | | | | | | | |
| KENNARD, S (HM11487) | | | ● | | | | | | | | | | | | | | |
| KHAFAF, TARA (HM11583) | | | | | | | | | | | | | | | | | |
| KIRKMEAD CENTRE (HM11718) | | | | | | | | | | | | | | | | | |
| KNIGHT, ANDREW (HM11746) | | | ● | | | | | | | | | | | | | | |
| KNIGHT, ANDREW M (HM11747) | | | ● | | | | | | | | | | | | | | |
| KUHN, SUE (HM11816) | | | | | | | | | | | | | | | ● | | |
| LANSDOWN PHYSIOTHERAPY CLINIC (HM11964) | | | | | | | | | | | | | | | | | |
| LAUREL PLACE (HM12009) | | | | | | | | | | | | | | | ● | | |
| LEAVEY, J () | | | | | | | | | | | | | | | | | |
| LOGAN, DAVID (HM12566) | | | | | | | | | | | | | | | | | |
| MAYHEW, PAMELA (HM13355) | | | | | | | | | | | | | | | | | |
| MCLOUGHLIN, BRENDAN (HM13559) | | | | | | | | | | | | | | | ● | | |
| MILLER, HELENE (HM13886) | | | | | | | | | | | | | | | | | |
| MILSOM STREET CLINIC (HM13944) | | | ● | | | | | | | | | | | | | | |
| MOIR, GILL (HM14047) | | | | | | | | | | | | | | | | | |
| NATURAL THERAPIES (HM14632) | | | | | | | | | | | | | | | | | |
| NEWCOMBE-JONES, ELAINE (HM14857) | | | | | | | | | | | | | | | | | |
| ORCHARD CLINIC (HM15360) | | | | | | | | | | | | | | | | | |
| O'TOOLE, ALAN (HM15495) | | | ● | | | | | | | | | | | | | | |
| PARK HOUSE CLINIC (HM15666) | | | ● | ● | | | | | | | | | | | | | |
| PEARSON, C (HM15910) | | | ● | | | | | | | | | | | | | | |
| PENNINGTON, PAM (HM15990) | | | | | | | | | | ● | | | | | | | |
| PENNINGTON, PAM V (HM15991) | | | | | | | | | | ● | | | | | | | |
| PITMAN, VICTORIA (HM16343) | | | | | | | | | | | | | | | | | |
| PITT, I T (HM16347) | | | ● | | | | | | | | | ● | | | | | |
| PLUMB, STEPHEN (HM16380) | | | ● | | | | | | | | | | | | | | |
| REED, W A (HM17046) | | | | | | | | | | | | | | | | | |
| ROBERTSON, JULIET (HM17444) | | | | | | | | | | | | | | | | | |
| SCHOOL OF THE LIVING LIGHT (HM18088) | | | | | | | | | | | | | | | | | |

| Business by County with Reference no. | Reflexology | Reichian Therapy | Reiki | Remedial Massage | Rogerian Therapy | Rolfing | Seichem | Sensitivity Training | Shiatsu | Silva Method | Sound Therapy | Spiritual Healing | Sports Massage | Stress Therapy | Swedish Body Massage | T'ai-Chi Ch'uan |
|---|---|---|---|---|---|---|---|---|---|---|---|---|---|---|---|---|
| JASMINE HOLISTIC HEALTH (HM10937) | ● | | | | | | | | | | | | | | | |
| JEFFERY, JO (HM10965) | ● | | | | | | | | | | | | | | | |
| JENKINSON, TRISHA (HM11000) | ● | | | | | | | | | | | | | | | |
| KALISCH, DAVID (HM11296) | | | | | | | | | | | | | | | | |
| KEARNS, ANTHONY P (HM11372) | | | | | | | | | | | | | | | | |
| KENNARD, S (HM11487) | | | | | | | | | | | | | | | | |
| KHAFAF, TARA (HM11583) | ● | | | | | | | | | | | | | | | |
| KIRKMEAD CENTRE (HM11718) | ● | | | | | | | | | | | | | | | |
| KNIGHT, ANDREW (HM11746) | | | | | | | | | | | | | | | | |
| KNIGHT, ANDREW M (HM11747) | | | | | | | | | | | | | | | | |
| KUHN, SUE (HM11816) | | | | | | | | | | | | | | | | |
| LANSDOWN PHYSIOTHERAPY CLINIC (HM11964) | | | | | | | | | | | | | | | | |
| LAUREL PLACE (HM12009) | ● | | ● | | | | | | ● | | | ● | | | | |
| LEAVEY, J () | | | | | | | | | | | | | ● | | | |
| LOGAN, DAVID (HM12566) | | | ● | | | | | | | | | | | ● | | |
| MAYHEW, PAMELA (HM13355) | ● | | | | | | | | | | | | | | | |
| MCLOUGHLIN, BRENDAN (HM13559) | | | | | | | | | | | | | | | | |
| MILLER, HELENE (HM13886) | ● | | | | | | | | | | | | | | | |
| MILSOM STREET CLINIC (HM13944) | ● | | | | | | | | ● | | | | | | | |
| MOIR, GILL (HM14047) | ● | | ● | | | | | | | | | | | ● | ● | |
| NATURAL THERAPIES (HM14632) | | | ● | | | | ● | | | | | | | | | |
| NEWCOMBE-JONES, ELAINE (HM14857) | ● | | | | | | | | | | | | | | | |
| ORCHARD CLINIC (HM15360) | | | | ● | | | | | | | | | | | | |
| O'TOOLE, ALAN (HM15495) | | | | | | | | | | | | | | | | |
| PARK HOUSE CLINIC (HM15666) | | | | | | | | | | | | | | | | |
| PEARSON, C (HM15910) | | | | | | | | | | | | | | | | |
| PENNINGTON, PAM (HM15990) | | | | | | | | | | | | | | | | |
| PENNINGTON, PAM V (HM15991) | | | | | | | | | | | | | | | | |
| PITMAN, VICTORIA (HM16343) | ● | | | | | | | | | | | | | | | |
| PITT, I T (HM16347) | | | | | | | | | | | | | | | | |
| PLUMB, STEPHEN (HM16380) | | | | | | | | | | | | | | | | |
| REED, W A (HM17046) | | | | | | | | | | | | | ● | | | |
| ROBERTSON, JULIET (HM17444) | ● | | | | | | | | | | | | | | | |
| SCHOOL OF THE LIVING LIGHT (HM18088) | | | ● | | | | | | | | | | | | | |

| Business by County with Reference no. | Tantra Therapy | Tera-Mai | Thought Field Therapy | Touch Therapy | Transactional Analysis | Tui-na | Ultrasonics | Vibrational Therapy | Visualisation Therapy | Vitamin Therapy | Voice Therapy | X-Ray | Ying & Yang | Yoga | Zen Therapy | Zero Balancing |
|---|---|---|---|---|---|---|---|---|---|---|---|---|---|---|---|---|
| JASMINE HOLISTIC HEALTH (HM10937) | | | | | | | | | | | | | | | | |
| JEFFERY, JO (HM10965) | | | | | | | | | | | | | | | | |
| JENKINSON, TRISHA (HM11000) | | | | | | | | | | | | | | | | |
| KALISCH, DAVID (HM11296) | | | | | | | | | | | | | | | | |
| KEARNS, ANTHONY P (HM11372) | | | | | | | | | | | | | | | | |
| KENNARD, S (HM11487) | | | | | | | | | | | | | | | | |
| KHAFAF, TARA (HM11583) | | | | | | | | | | | | | | | | |
| KIRKMEAD CENTRE (HM11718) | | | | | | | | | | | | | | | | |
| KNIGHT, ANDREW (HM11746) | | | | | | | | | | | | | | | | |
| KNIGHT, ANDREW M (HM11747) | | | | | | | | | | | | | | | | |
| KUHN, SUE (HM11816) | | | | | | | | | | | | | | | | |
| LANSDOWN PHYSIOTHERAPY CLINIC (HM11964) | | | | | | | ● | | | | | | | | | |
| LAUREL PLACE (HM12009) | | | | | | | | | | | | | | | | |
| LEAVEY, J () | | | | | | | | | | | | | | | | |
| LOGAN, DAVID (HM12566) | | | | | | | | | | | | | | | | |
| MAYHEW, PAMELA (HM13355) | | | | | | | | | | | | | | | | |
| MCLOUGHLIN, BRENDAN (HM13559) | | | | | | | | | | | | | | | | |
| MILLER, HELENE (HM13886) | | | | | | | | | | | | | | | | |
| MILSOM STREET CLINIC (HM13944) | | | | | | | | | | | | | | | | |
| MOIR, GILL (HM14047) | | | | | | | | | | | | | | | | |
| NATURAL THERAPIES (HM14632) | | | | | | | | | | | | | | | | |
| NEWCOMBE-JONES, ELAINE (HM14857) | | | | | | | | | | | | | | | | |
| ORCHARD CLINIC (HM15360) | | | | | | | | | | | | | | | | |
| O'TOOLE, ALAN (HM15495) | | | | | | | | | | | | | | | | |
| PARK HOUSE CLINIC (HM15666) | | | | | | | ● | ● | | | | | | | | |
| PEARSON, C (HM15910) | | | | | | | | | | | | | | | | |
| PENNINGTON, PAM (HM15990) | | | | | | | | | | | | | | | | |
| PENNINGTON, PAM V (HM15991) | | | | | | | | | | | | | | | | |
| PITMAN, VICTORIA (HM16343) | | | | | | | | | | | | | | | | |
| PITT, I T (HM16347) | | | | | | | | | | | | | | | | |
| PLUMB, STEPHEN (HM16380) | | | | | | | | | | | | | | | | |
| REED, W A (HM17046) | | | | | | | | | | | | | | | | |
| ROBERTSON, JULIET (HM17444) | | | | | | | | | | | | | | | | |
| SCHOOL OF THE LIVING LIGHT (HM18088) | | | | | | | | | | | | | | | | |

# O - Z Therapies at Practices/Businesses

| Business by County with Reference no. | Orthotics | Osteomyology | Osteopathy | PAM | Paranormal Therapies | Pattern Therapies | Physiotherapy | Phytotherapy | Pilates | Podiatry | Polarity Therapy | Postural Integration | Primal Therapy | Psionic Therapy | Psychotherapy | Pyramid Power | Pyscho-Synthesis |
|---|---|---|---|---|---|---|---|---|---|---|---|---|---|---|---|---|---|
| SCOVELL, MICHAEL (HM18141) | | | | | | | | | | | | | | | ● | | |
| SEFTON, PHILIP (HM18200) | | | ● | | | | | | | | | | | | | | |
| SHAMBHALA (HM18275) | | | | | | ● | | | | | | | | | | | |
| SHIATSU THERAPY (HM18466) | | | | | | | | | | | | | | | | | |
| SIMS, A (HM18600) | | | ● | | | | | | | | | | | | | | |
| SMITH, ANN (HM18716) | | | | | | | | | | | | | | | | | |
| SPARKES, MARTIN J (HM18961) | | | ● | | | | | | | | | | | | | | |
| ST JAMES'S SURGERY (HM19079) | | | ● | | | | | | | | | | | | | | |
| ST MICHAEL'S HYPNOTHERAPY (HM19090) | | | | | | | | | | | | | | | | | |
| STEWART, SHEILA (HM19277) | | | | | | | | | | | | | | | | | |
| STREET CHIROPRACTIC CLINIC (HM19383) | | | | | | | | | | | | | | | | | |
| STRESS CLINIC & NTRL HLTH CTRE (HM19389) | | | ● | | | | | | | | | | | | ● | | ● |
| SUTCLIFFE, T (HM19534) | | | ● | | | | | | | | | | | | | | |
| TARETH CENTRE (HM19704) | | | | | | | | | | | | | | | | | |
| TAUNTON FOOT SURGERY (HM19722) | | | | | | | | | | ● | | | | | | | |
| TERRACE THRPY PSYCHO/NTRL HLTH (HM19843) | | | | | | | | | | | | | | | ● | | |
| TOME OSTEOPATHIC & SPORTS (HM20128) | | | ● | | | | | | | | | | | | | | |
| TYLER, LIZZY (HM20462) | | | | | | | | | | | | | | | | | |
| WELLSPRING OSTEO/NTRL HEALTH (HM21181) | | | ● | | | | | | | | | | | | | | |
| WHITE, KIM (HM21363) | | | ● | | | | | | | | | | | | | | |
| WILLIAMS, FRANCES (HM21556) | | | | | | | | | | | | | | | | | |
| WOODINGTON, NICHOLAS J (HM21830) | | | ● | | | | | | | | | | | | | | |
| YEOVIL CHIROPRACTIC CLINIC (HM22008) | | | ● | | | | | | | | | | | | | | |
| **STAFFORDSHIRE** | | | | | | | | | | | | | | | | | |
| ALTERNATIVE THERAPY CENTRE (HM00735) | | | ● | | | | | | | | | | | | ● | | |
| ALTERNATIVES (HM00741) | | | | | | | | | | | | | | | | | |
| ANDERSON, G (HM00818) | | | | | | | | | | | | | | | | | |
| BARCROFT, J M (HM01696) | | | | | | | | | | ● | | | | | | | |
| BONNEBAIGT, ANDRE (HM02682) | | | | | | | | ● | | | | | | | | | |
| BORE ST POD & CHIROP PRACTICE (HM02716) | ● | | | | | | | | | | | | | | | | |
| BRADBURY, SHARON (HM02841) | | | ● | | | | | | | | | | | | | | |
| BRADBURY, SHARON (HM02842) | | | ● | | | | | | | | | | | | | | |
| BRAMPTON TREES CLINIC (HM02908) | | | | | | | ● | | | | | | | | | | |
| BRIDGETT, A (HM03011) | | | | | | | | ● | | | | | | | | | |

| Business by County with Reference no. | Reflexology | Reichian Therapy | Reiki | Remedial Massage | Rogerian Therapy | Rolfing | Seichem | Sensitivity Training | Shiatsu | Silva Method | Sound Therapy | Spiritual Healing | Sports Massage | Stress Therapy | Swedish Body Massage | T'ai-Chi Ch'uan |
|---|---|---|---|---|---|---|---|---|---|---|---|---|---|---|---|---|
| SCOVELL, MICHAEL (HM18141) | | | | | | | | | | | | | | | | |
| SEFTON, PHILIP (HM18200) | | | | | | | | | | | | | | | | |
| SHAMBHALA (HM18275) | ● | | ● | | | | | | | | | ● | | | | |
| SHIATSU THERAPY (HM18466) | | | | | | | | | ● | | | | | | | |
| SIMS, A (HM18600) | | | | | | | | | | | | | | | | |
| SMITH, ANN (HM18716) | ● | | | | | | | | | | | | | | | |
| SPARKES, MARTIN J (HM18961) | | | | | | | | | | | | | | | | |
| ST JAMES'S SURGERY (HM19079) | | | | | | | | | | | | | | | | |
| ST MICHAEL'S HYPNOTHERAPY (HM19090) | | | | | | | | | | | | | | ● | | |
| STEWART, SHEILA (HM19277) | ● | | | | | | | | | | | | | | | |
| STREET CHIROPRACTIC CLINIC (HM19383) | | | | | | | | | | | | | | | | |
| STRESS CLINIC & NTRL HLTH CTRE (HM19389) | ● | | ● | | | | | | ● | | | | | ● | | |
| SUTCLIFFE, T (HM19534) | | | | | | | | | | | | | | | | |
| TARETH CENTRE (HM19704) | | | | | | | | | | | | ● | | | | |
| TAUNTON FOOT SURGERY (HM19722) | | | | | | | | | | | | | | | | |
| TERRACE THRPY PSYCHO/NTRL HLTH (HM19843) | ● | | | | | | | | | | | | | | | |
| TOME OSTEOPATHIC & SPORTS (HM20128) | | | | | | | | | | | | | | | | |
| TYLER, LIZZY (HM20462) | ● | | | | | | | | | | | | | | | |
| WELLSPRING OSTEO/NTRL HEALTH (HM21181) | ● | | | | | | | | | | | | | | | |
| WHITE, KIM (HM21363) | | | | | | | | | | | | | | | | |
| WILLIAMS, FRANCES (HM21556) | ● | | | | | | | | | | | | | | | |
| WOODINGTON, NICHOLAS J (HM21830) | | | | | | | | | | | | | | | | |
| YEOVIL CHIROPRACTIC CLINIC (HM22008) | | | | | | | | | | | | | | | | |
| **STAFFORDSHIRE** | | | | | | | | | | | | | | | | |
| ALTERNATIVE THERAPY CENTRE (HM00735) | ● | | | | | | | | | | | ● | | ● | | |
| ALTERNATIVES (HM00741) | ● | | ● | | | | | | | | | | | | | |
| ANDERSON, G (HM00818) | | | ● | | | | | | | | | | | | | |
| BARCROFT, J M (HM01696) | | | | | | | | | | | | | | | | |
| BONNEBAIGT, ANDRE (HM02682) | | | | | | | | | | | | | | | | |
| BORE ST POD & CHIROP PRACTICE (HM02716) | | | | | | | | | | | | | | | | |
| BRADBURY, SHARON (HM02841) | | | | | | | | | | | | | | | | |
| BRADBURY, SHARON (HM02842) | | | | | | | | | | | | | | | | |
| BRAMPTON TREES CLINIC (HM02908) | | | | | | | | | | | | | | | | |
| BRIDGETT, A (HM03011) | | | | | | | | | | | | | | ● | | |

| Business by County with Reference no. | Tantra Therapy | Tera-Mai | Thought Field Therapy | Touch Therapy | Transactional Analysis | Tui-na | Ultrasonics | Vibrational Therapy | Visualisation Therapy | Vitamin Therapy | Voice Therapy | X-Ray | Ying & Yang | Yoga | Zen Therapy | Zero Balancing |
|---|---|---|---|---|---|---|---|---|---|---|---|---|---|---|---|---|
| SCOVELL, MICHAEL (HM18141) | | | | | | | | | | | | | | | | |
| SEFTON, PHILIP (HM18200) | | | | | | | | | | | | | | | | |
| SHAMBHALA (HM18275) | | | | | | | | ● | | | | | | | | |
| SHIATSU THERAPY (HM18466) | | | | | | | | | | | | | | | | |
| SIMS, A (HM18600) | | | | | | | | | | | | | | | | |
| SMITH, ANN (HM18716) | | | | | | | | | | | | | | | | |
| SPARKES, MARTIN J (HM18961) | | | | | | | | | | | | | | | | |
| ST JAMES'S SURGERY (HM19079) | | | | | | | | | | | | | | | | |
| ST MICHAEL'S HYPNOTHERAPY (HM19090) | | | | | | | | | | | | | | | | |
| STEWART, SHEILA (HM19277) | | | | | | | | | | | | | | | | |
| STREET CHIROPRACTIC CLINIC (HM19383) | | | | | | | ● | | | | | ● | | | | |
| STRESS CLINIC & NTRL HLTH CTRE (HM19389) | | | | | | | | | | | | | | ● | | |
| SUTCLIFFE, T (HM19534) | | | | | | | | | | | | | | | | |
| TARETH CENTRE (HM19704) | | | | | | | | | | | | | | | | |
| TAUNTON FOOT SURGERY (HM19722) | | | | | | | | | | | | | | | | |
| TERRACE THRPY PSYCHO/NTRL HLTH (HM19843) | | | | | | | | | | | | | | | | |
| TOME OSTEOPATHIC & SPORTS (HM20128) | | | | | | | | | | | | | | | | |
| TYLER, LIZZY (HM20462) | | | | | | | | | | | | | | | | |
| WELLSPRING OSTEO/NTRL HEALTH (HM21181) | | | | | | | | | | | | | | | | |
| WHITE, KIM (HM21363) | | | | | | | | | | | | | | | | |
| WILLIAMS, FRANCES (HM21556) | | | | | | | | | | | | | | | | |
| WOODINGTON, NICHOLAS J (HM21830) | | | | | | | | | | | | | | | | |
| YEOVIL CHIROPRACTIC CLINIC (HM22008) | | | | | | | | | | | | | | | | |
| **STAFFORDSHIRE** | | | | | | | | | | | | | | | | |
| ALTERNATIVE THERAPY CENTRE (HM00735) | | | | | | | | | ● | ● | | | | | | |
| ALTERNATIVES (HM00741) | | | | | | | | | | | | | | | | |
| ANDERSON, G (HM00818) | | | | | | | | | | | | | | | | |
| BARCROFT, J M (HM01696) | | | | | | | | | | | | | | | | |
| BONNEBAIGT, ANDRE (HM02682) | | | | | | | | | | | | | | | | |
| BORE ST POD & CHIROP PRACTICE (HM02716) | | | | | | | | | | | | | | | | |
| BRADBURY, SHARON (HM02841) | | | | | | | | | | | | | | | | |
| BRADBURY, SHARON (HM02842) | | | | | | | | | | | | | | | | |
| BRAMPTON TREES CLINIC (HM02908) | | | | | | | | | | | | | | | | |
| BRIDGETT, A (HM03011) | | | | | | | | | | | | | | | | |

# O - Z Therapies at Practices/Businesses

| Business by County with Reference no. | Orthotics | Osteomyology | Osteopathy | PAM | Paranormal Therapies | Pattern Therapies | Physiotherapy | Phytotherapy | Pilates | Podiatry | Polarity Therapy | Postural Integration | Primal Therapy | Psionic Therapy | Psychotherapy | Pyramid Power | Pyscho-Synthesis | Reflexology | Reichian Therapy | Reiki | Remedial Massage | Rogerian Therapy | Rolfing | Seichem | Sensitivity Training | Shiatsu | Silva Method | Sound Therapy | Spiritual Healing | Sports Massage | Stress Therapy | Swedish Body Massage | T'ai-Chi Ch'uan | Tantra Therapy | Tera-Mai | Thought Field Therapy | Touch Therapy | Transactional Analysis | Tui-na | Ultrasonics | Vibrational Therapy | Visualisation Therapy | Vitamin Therapy | Voice Therapy | X-Ray | Ying & Yang | Yoga | Zen Therapy | Zero Balancing |
|---|---|---|---|---|---|---|---|---|---|---|---|---|---|---|---|---|---|---|---|---|---|---|---|---|---|---|---|---|---|---|---|---|---|---|---|---|---|---|---|---|---|---|---|---|---|---|---|---|---|
| BURKE, E (HM03385) | | | | | | | | | | | | | | | ● | | | | | | | | | | | | | | | | ● | | | | | | | | | | | ● | | | | | | | |
| CASTLEFIELDS SURGERY (HM03846) | | | ● | | | | | | | | | | | | | | | | | | | | | | | | | | | | | | | | | | | | | | | | | | | | | | |
| CHASE HEALTH FOODS (HM04055) | | | | | | | | | | | | | | | | | | ● | | | | | | | | | | | | | | | | | | | | | | | | | | | | | | | |
| CHASE NATURAL THERAPY CENTRE (HM04059) | | | | | | | | | | | | | | | | | | ● | | ● | | | | | | | | | | | | ● | | | | | | | | | | | | | | | | | |
| COMPLEMENTARY THERAPIES (HM04941) | | | | | | | | | | | | | | | | | | ● | | | | | | | | | | | | | | | | | | | | | | | | | | | | | | | |
| COOPER, DAVID (HM05097) | | | ● | | | | | | | | | | | | | | | | | | | | | | | | | | | | | | | | | | | | | | | | | | | | | | |
| CORKER, E (HM05170) | | | | | | | | | | | | | | | ● | | | | | | | | | | | | | | | | | | | | | | | | | | | | | | | | | | |
| CORNERSTONES PRACTICE (HM05182) | | | | | | | | | | | | | | | ● | | | | | ● | | | | | | | | | | | | | | | | | | | | | | | | | | | | | |
| CRESCENT CLINIC (HM05417) | | | | | | | | | | | | | | | ● | | | ● | | | ● | | | | | | | | | | | | ● | | | | | | | | | | | | | | | | |
| CRESCENT CLINIC FOR COMP MED (HM05418) | | | | | | | ● | | | | | | | | | | | ● | | | ● | | | | | | | | | | | | ● | | | | | | | | | | | | | | | | |
| DAVIES, MARTIN K (HM05829) | | | ● | | | | | | | | | | | | | | | | | | | | | | | | | | | | | | | | | | | | | | | | | | | | | | |
| DOWNEY, FRANCES (HM06248) | | | | | | | | | | | | | | | | | | ● | | | | | | | | | | | | | | | | | | | | | | | | | | | | | | | |
| DRURY, ANNE (HM06329) | | | | | | | | | | | | | | | ● | | | | | | | | | | | | | | | | | | | | | | | | | | | | | | | | | | |
| EASTY, JAYNE (HM06552) | | | ● | | | | | | | | | | | | | | | | | | | | | | | | | | | | | | | | | | | | | | | | | | | | | | |
| ESSENTIAL HEALTH (HM06911) | | | | | | | | | | | | | | | | | | ● | | ● | | | | | | | | | | | | | | | | | | | | | | | | | | | | | |
| EVANS, RICHARD (HM06989) | | | | | | | | | | | | | | | | | | ● | | ● | | | | | | | | | | | | | | | | | | | | | | | | | | | | | |
| FEET FIRST (HM07176) | | | | | | | | | | ● | | | | | | | | | | | | | | | | | | | | | | | | | | | | | | | | | | | | | | | |
| FOOT SOUL & BODYWORKS (HM07487) | | | | | | | | | | | | | | | | | | ● | | ● | | | | | | | | | | | | | | | | | ● | | | | | | | | | | | | |
| FORTEY, C J (HM07579) | | | | | | | | | | ● | | | | | | | | | | | | | | | | | | | | | | | | | | | | | | | | | | | | | | | |
| GASCOIGNE, DOROTHY (HM07917) | | | | | | | | | | | | | | | | | | ● | | | | | | | | | | | | | | | | | | | | | | | | | | | | | | | |
| GASCOYNE, P (HM07920) | | | | | | | | ● | | | | | | | | | | | | | | | | | | | | | | | | | | | | | | | | | | | | | | | | | |
| GORDON, KAREN (HM08279) | | | | | | | | | | | | | | | | | | ● | | | | | | | | | | | | | | | | | | | | | | | | | | | | | | | |
| HALLARD, SHARON (HM08800) | | | | | | | | ● | | | | | | | | | | | | | | | | | | | | | | | | | | | | | | | | | | | | | | | | | |
| HANCHER, LYNNE (HM08892) | | | | | | | | | | | | | | | | | | ● | | | | | | | | | | | | | | | | | | | | | | | | | | | | | | | |
| HARRISON, GRETA (HM09099) | | | | | | | | | | | | | | | | | | ● | | | | | | | | | | | | | | | | | | | | | | | | | | | | | | | |
| HEATH, DAVID (HM09452) | | | ● | | | | | | | | | | | | | | | | | | | | | | | | | | | | | | | | | | | | | | | | | | | | | | |
| HINGORANI, S (HM09833) | | | ● | | | | | | | | | | | | | | | | | | | | | | | | | | | | | | | | | | | | | | | | | | | | | | |
| HOLDCROFT, R A (HM09925) | | | ● | | | | | | | | | | | | | | | | | | | | | | | | | | | | | | | | | | | | | | | | | | | | | | |
| HOLDCROFT, ROSEMARIE A (HM09926) | | | ● | | | | | | | | | | | | | | | | | | | | | | | | | | | | | | | | | | | | | | | | | | | | | | |
| HOLLOWAY, MICHAEL & AMANDA (HM10026) | | | ● | | | | | | | | | | | | | | | | | | | | | | | | | | | | | | | | | | | | | | | | | | | | | | |
| HUGHES, R T (HM10341) | | | ● | | | | | | | | | | | | | | | | | | | | | | | | | | | | | | | | | | | | | | | | | | | | | | |
| IBBS, ROGER (HM10566) | | | | | | | | | | ● | | | | | | | | | | | | | | | | | | | | | | | | | | | | | | | | | | | | | | | |
| ISHTA CENTRE (HM10761) | | | | | | | | | ● | | | | | | | | | ● | | ● | ● | | | | | | | | ● | | | | | | | | | | | | | | ● | | | | | | |
| JOHNSON, JANICE (HM11079) | | | | | | | | | | | | | | | ● | | | | | ● | | | | | | | | | ● | | ● | | | | | | | | | | | ● | | | | | | | |

# O - Z Therapies at Practices/Businesses

| Business by County with Reference no. | Orthotics | Osteomyology | Osteopathy | PAM | Paranormal Therapies | Pattern Therapies | Physiotherapy | Phytotherapy | Pilates | Podiatry | Polarity Therapy | Postural Integration | Primal Therapy | Psionic Therapy | Psychotherapy | Pyramid Power | Pyscho-Synthesis | Reflexology | Reichian Therapy | Reiki | Remedial Massage | Rogerian Therapy | Rolfing | Seichem | Sensitivity Training | Shiatsu | Silva Method | Sound Therapy | Spiritual Healing | Sports Massage | Stress Therapy | Swedish Body Massage | Tai-Chi Ch'uan | Tantra Therapy | Tera-Mai | Thought Field Therapy | Touch Therapy | Transactional Analysis | Tui-na | Ultrasonics | Vibrational Therapy | Visualisation Therapy | Vitamin Therapy | Voice Therapy | X-Ray | Ying & Yang | Yoga | Zen Therapy | Zero Balancing |
|---|---|---|---|---|---|---|---|---|---|---|---|---|---|---|---|---|---|---|---|---|---|---|---|---|---|---|---|---|---|---|---|---|---|---|---|---|---|---|---|---|---|---|---|---|---|---|---|---|---|
| LOMAS, CHRISTINA (HM12573) | | | | | | | | | | | | | | | | | | ● | | | | | | | | | | | | | | | | | | | | | | | | | | | | | | | |
| LOUISE BRITTLE (HM12667) | | | | | | | | | | ● | | | | | | | | | | | | | | | | | | | | | | | | | | | | | | | | | | | | | | | |
| MARSHALL, LYNN (HM13168) | | | | | | | | | | | | | | | | | | ● | | | | | | | | | | | | | | | | | | | | | | | | | | | | | | | |
| MELLOR, J SIMON (HM13709) | | | | | | | | | | ● | | | | | | | | | | | | | | | | | | | | | | | | | | | | | | | | | | | | | | | |
| MILL BANK OSTEOPATHIC CLINIC (HM13865) | | | ● | | | | | | | | | | | | | | | | | | | | | | | | | | | | | | | | | | | | | | | | | | | | | | |
| NARAYAN, MAMTA (HM14486) | | | ● | | | | | | | | | | | | | | | | | | | | | | | | | | | | | | | | | | | | | | | | | | | | | | |
| NORBURY, SUSAN (HM14990) | | | | | | | | | | | | | | | | | | ● | | | | | | | | | | | | | | | | | | | | | | | | | | | | | | | |
| PARSONS, CHRISTINA (HM15752) | | | ● | | | | | | | | | | | | | | | | | | | | | | | | | | | | | | | | | | | | | | | | | | | | | | |
| PEACH, F J (HM15879) | | | | | | | | | | ● | | | | | | | | | | | | | | | | | | | | | | | | | | | | | | | | | | | | | | | |
| PRIORS PODIATRY PRACTICE (HM16629) | | | | | | | | | | | | | | | | | | | | | | | | | | | | | | | | | | | | | | | | | | | | | ● | | | | |
| ROBERTS, KATE (HM17418) | | | | | | | | | | | | | | | ● | | ● | | | | | ● | | | | | | | | | ● | | | | | | | | | | | | | | | | | | |
| RUDD, SUSAN (HM17730) | | | | | | | | | | | | | | | | | | ● | | | | | | | | | | | | | | | | | | | | | | | | | | | | | | | |
| STAFFORD CHIROPRACTIC CLINIC (HM19108) | | | | | | | | | | | | | | | | | | | | | | | | | | | | | | | | | | | | | | | | | | | | | ● | | | | |
| STEVENS, MARGARET (HM19236) | | | | | | | | | | | | | | | ● | | | | | | | | | | | | | | | | | | | | | | | | | | | | | | | | | | |
| SUSAN JAMES CONSULTANCY (HM19527) | | | | | | | | | | | | | | | ● | | | | | | | | | | | | | | ● | | | | | | | | | | | | | | | | | | | | |
| TAMWORTH PHYSIOTHERAPY CLINIC (HM19675) | | | | | | | ● | | | | | | | | | | | | | | | | | | | | | | | | | | | | | | | | | | | | | | | | | | |
| TUNSTALL HYPNOTHERAPY CENTRE (HM20401) | | | | | | | | | | | | | | | | | | | | ● | | | | | | | | | | | | | | | | | | | | | | | | | | | | | |
| WELCH, STEPHEN (HM21127) | | | | | | | | | | | | | | | | | | ● | | | | | | | | | | | | | | | | | | | | | | | | | | | | | | | |
| WHITBY, S E (HM21334) | | | | | | | ● | | | | | | | | | | | | | | | | | | | | | | | | | | | | | | | | | | | | | | | | | | |
| WHYTE, IAN (HM21439) | | | ● | | | | | | | | | | | | | | | | | | | | | | | | | | | | | | | | | | | | | | | | | | | | | | |
| WHYTE, IAN (HM21440) | | | ● | | | | | | | | | | | | | | | | | | | | | | | | | | | | | | | | | | | | | | | | | | | | | | |
| **SUFFOLK** | | | | | | | | | | | | | | | | | | | | | | | | | | | | | | | | | | | | | | | | | | | | | | | | | |
| AJNA (HM00457) | | | | | | | | | | | | | | | | | | | | ● | | | | | | | | | | | | | | | | | | | | | | | | | | | | | |
| BATES, SUSAN (HM01887) | | | | | | | | | | | | | | | | | | ● | | | | | | | | | | | | | | | | | | | | | | | | | | | | | | | |
| BECCLES PSYCHO & COUNS CTRE (HM02014) | | | | | | | | | | | | | | | ● | | | | | | | | | | | | | | | | | | | | | | | | | | | | | | | | | | |
| BODY MECHANICS THERAPY CLINIC (HM02599) | | | | | | | | | | | | | | | ● | | | ● | | | | | | | | | | | | | | | | | | | | | | | | | | | | | | | |
| BULL, C S (HM03337) | | | ● | | | | | | | | | | | | | | | | | | | | | | | | | | | | | | | | | | | | | | | | | | | | | | |
| BURY PRACTICE (HM03451) | | | | | | | | | | | | | | | ● | | | | | | | | | | | | | | | | | | | | | | | | | | | | | | | | | | |
| BYERS, PAULINE (HM03510) | | | | | | | | | | | | | | | | | | ● | | | | | | | | | | | | | | | | | | | | | | | | | | | | | | | |
| CHADWICK, ANTHONY (HM03934) | | | | | | | | | | | | | | | | | | | | ● | | | | | | | | | | | | | | | | | | | | | | | | | | | | | |
| CHARLTON CLINIC (HM04033) | | | | | | | | | ● | | | | | | | | | ● | | | | | | | | | | | | | | | | | | | | | | ● | | | | | | | | | |
| CHURCHMAN & ASS REG OST (HM04475) | | | ● | | | | | | | | | | | | | | | | | | | | | | | | | | | | | | | | | | | | | | | | | | | | | | |
| CHURCHMAN, B (HM04476) | | | ● | | | | | | | | | | | | | | | | | | | | | | | | | | | | | | | | | | | | | | | | | | | | | | |
| CHURCHMAN, BERYL (HM04478) | | | ● | | | | | | | | | | | | | | | | | | | | | | | | | | | | | | | | | | | | | | | | | | | | | | |

# O - Z Therapies at Practices/Businesses

Business by County with Reference no.

| Business | Orthotics | Osteomyology | Osteopathy | PAM | Paranormal Therapies | Pattern Therapies | Physiotherapy | Phytotherapy | Pilates | Podiatry | Polarity Therapy | Postural Integration | Primal Therapy | Psionic Therapy | Psychotherapy | Pyramid Power |
|---|---|---|---|---|---|---|---|---|---|---|---|---|---|---|---|---|
| CLAIRVOYANT SERVICES (HM04518) | | | | | | | | | | | | | | | | |
| COLLINS, JOHN (HM04871) | | | | | | | | | | | | | | | | |
| COSMIC CONNECTIONS (HM05203) | | | | | | | | | | | | | | | | |
| CT & IM LEITH (HM05534) | | | | | | | | | | | | | | | | |
| CUDDEFORD, C (HM05551) | | | ● | | | | | | | | | | | | | |
| CUDDEFORD, C (HM05550) | | | ● | | | | | | | | | | | | | |
| DALTON, EMMA (HM05697) | | | | | | | | | | | | | | | | |
| DENT, TRISH () | | | | | | | | | | | | | | | | |
| EVENKEEL (HM06997) | | | | | | | | | | | | | | | | |
| FELIXSTOWE COUNS & PYSCHO CTRE (HM07201) | | | | | | | | | | | | | | | ● | |
| FELIXSTOWE PHYSIO PRACTICE (HM07203) | | | | | | | ● | | | | | | | | | |
| FENN, JASON (HM07216) | | | | | | | | | | | | | | | | |
| FRESHFIELDS OF ALDEBURGH (HM07737) | | | ● | | | | | | | ● | | | | | | |
| FRIAR, CARL (HM07743) | | | | | | | | | | | | | | | | |
| GILMOUR, PIPER & ASSOCIATES (HM08107) | | | ● | | | | | | | | | | | | | |
| GOLD, STEPHEN (HM08204) | | | ● | | | | | | | | | | | | | |
| GREEN FARM CLINIC (HM08435) | | | | | | | ● | | | | | | | | | |
| GROSVENOR PHYSIOTHERAPY CLINIC (HM08597) | | | | | | | ● | | | | | | | | | |
| HARDY, MICHAEL (HM08984) | | | | | | | | | | | | | | | | |
| HEALING CONNECTIONS (HM09330) | | | | | | | | | | | | | | | | |
| HEALING HANDS (HM09336) | | | | | | | | | | | | | | | | |
| HOPKINS, C J (HM10147) | | | | | | | | | | | | | | | | |
| HUGHES, DOREEN (HM10325) | | | | | | | | | | | | | | | | |
| HUGHES, LINDA (HM10333) | | | | | | | | | | | | | | | ● | |
| IPSWICH CHIROPRACTIC CLINIC (HM10714) | | | | | | | | | | | | | | | | |
| IPSWICH PSYCHOTHERAPY/COUNS (HM10716) | | | | | | | | | | | | | | | ● | |
| JUBY, P (HM11243) | | | ● | | | | | | | | | | | | | |
| KEMP, N J (HM11463) | | | ● | | | | | | | | | | | | | |
| KINNEAR, MARGARET (HM11689) | | | | | | | | | | | | | | | | |
| LAVENDER LODGE CLINIC (HM12023) | | | ● | | ● | | | | | | | | | | ● | |
| LINDOS PSYCHOTHERAPY CENTRE (HM12420) | | | | | | | | | | | | | | | ● | |
| MACFARLANE, CLARE (HM12834) | | | | | | | | | | | | | | | | |
| MALAROC (HM12961) | | | ● | | | | | ● | | | | | | | | |
| MANOR HOUSE (HM13039) | | | ● | | | | | | | ● | | | | | | |

| Business | Pyscho-Synthesis | Reflexology | Reichian Therapy | Reiki | Remedial Massage | Rogerian Therapy | Rolfing | Seichem | Sensitivity Training | Shiatsu | Silva Method | Sound Therapy | Spiritual Healing | Sports Massage | Stress Therapy | Swedish Body Massage |
|---|---|---|---|---|---|---|---|---|---|---|---|---|---|---|---|---|
| CLAIRVOYANT SERVICES (HM04518) | | | | | | | | | | | | | ● | | | |
| COLLINS, JOHN (HM04871) | | | | ● | ● | | | | | | | | | | | |
| COSMIC CONNECTIONS (HM05203) | | | | | | | | | | | | | | | | |
| CT & IM LEITH (HM05534) | | | | ● | | | | | | | | | | | | |
| CUDDEFORD, C (HM05551) | | | | | | | | | | | | | | | | |
| CUDDEFORD, C (HM05550) | | | | | | | | | | | | | | | | |
| DALTON, EMMA (HM05697) | | ● | | | | | | | | | | | | | | |
| DENT, TRISH () | | | | | | | | | | ● | | | | | | |
| EVENKEEL (HM06997) | | | | | | | | | | | | | | | ● | |
| FELIXSTOWE COUNS & PYSCHO CTRE (HM07201) | | | | | | | | | | | | | | | | |
| FELIXSTOWE PHYSIO PRACTICE (HM07203) | | | | | | | | | | | | | | | | |
| FENN, JASON (HM07216) | | ● | | | | | | | | | | | | | | |
| FRESHFIELDS OF ALDEBURGH (HM07737) | | ● | | | | | | | | ● | | | | | | |
| FRIAR, CARL (HM07743) | | ● | | | | | | | | | | | | | | |
| GILMOUR, PIPER & ASSOCIATES (HM08107) | | | | | | | | | | | | | | | | |
| GOLD, STEPHEN (HM08204) | | | | | | | | | | | | | | | | |
| GREEN FARM CLINIC (HM08435) | | | | | | | | | | | | | | | | |
| GROSVENOR PHYSIOTHERAPY CLINIC (HM08597) | | | | | | | | | | | | | | | | |
| HARDY, MICHAEL (HM08984) | | | | | | | | | | ● | | | | | | |
| HEALING CONNECTIONS (HM09330) | | | | ● | | | | | | | | | | | | |
| HEALING HANDS (HM09336) | | ● | | ● | | | | | | | | | | | ● | ● |
| HOPKINS, C J (HM10147) | | | | | | | | | | | | | | | ● | |
| HUGHES, DOREEN (HM10325) | | ● | | | | | | | | | | | | | | |
| HUGHES, LINDA (HM10333) | | | | | | | | | | | | | | | | |
| IPSWICH CHIROPRACTIC CLINIC (HM10714) | | ● | | | | | | | | ● | | | | | | |
| IPSWICH PSYCHOTHERAPY/COUNS (HM10716) | | | | | | | | | | | | | | | | |
| JUBY, P (HM11243) | | | | | | | | | | | | | | | | |
| KEMP, N J (HM11463) | | | | | | | | | | | | | | | | |
| KINNEAR, MARGARET (HM11689) | | ● | | | | | | | | | | | | | | |
| LAVENDER LODGE CLINIC (HM12023) | | ● | | ● | | | | | | | | | ● | | | |
| LINDOS PSYCHOTHERAPY CENTRE (HM12420) | | | | | | | | | | | | | | | | |
| MACFARLANE, CLARE (HM12834) | | ● | | | | | | | | | | | | | | |
| MALAROC (HM12961) | | | | | | | | | | | | | | | | |
| MANOR HOUSE (HM13039) | | | | | | | | | | | | | | | | |

| Business | Tai-Chi Ch'uan | Tantra Therapy | Tera-Mai | Thought Field Therapy | Touch Therapy | Transactional Analysis | Tui-na | Ultrasonics | Vibrational Therapy | Visualisation Therapy | Vitamin Therapy | Voice Therapy | X-Ray | Ying & Yang | Yoga | Zen Therapy | Zero Balancing |
|---|---|---|---|---|---|---|---|---|---|---|---|---|---|---|---|---|---|
| CLAIRVOYANT SERVICES (HM04518) | | | | | | | | | | | | | | | | | |
| COLLINS, JOHN (HM04871) | | | | | | | | | | | | | | | | | |
| COSMIC CONNECTIONS (HM05203) | | | | | | | | | ● | | | | | | | | |
| CT & IM LEITH (HM05534) | | | | | | | | | | | | | ● | | | | |
| CUDDEFORD, C (HM05551) | | | | | | | | | | | | | | | | | |
| CUDDEFORD, C (HM05550) | | | | | | | | | | | | | | | | | |
| DALTON, EMMA (HM05697) | | | | | | | | | | | | | | | | | |
| DENT, TRISH () | | | | | | | | | | | | | | | | | |
| EVENKEEL (HM06997) | | | | | | | | | | | | | | | | | |
| FELIXSTOWE COUNS & PYSCHO CTRE (HM07201) | | | | | | | | | | | | | | | | | |
| FELIXSTOWE PHYSIO PRACTICE (HM07203) | | | | | | | | | | | | | | | | | |
| FENN, JASON (HM07216) | | | | | | | | | | | | | | | | | |
| FRESHFIELDS OF ALDEBURGH (HM07737) | | | | | | | | | | | ● | | | | | | |
| FRIAR, CARL (HM07743) | | | | | | | | | | | | | | | | | |
| GILMOUR, PIPER & ASSOCIATES (HM08107) | | | | | | | | | | | | | | | | | |
| GOLD, STEPHEN (HM08204) | | | | | | | | | | | | | | | | | |
| GREEN FARM CLINIC (HM08435) | | | | | | | | | | | | | | | | | |
| GROSVENOR PHYSIOTHERAPY CLINIC (HM08597) | | | | | | | | | | | | | | | | | |
| HARDY, MICHAEL (HM08984) | | | | | | | | | | | | | | | | | |
| HEALING CONNECTIONS (HM09330) | | | | | | | | | | | | | | | | | |
| HEALING HANDS (HM09336) | | | | | ● | ● | | | | ● | | | | | | | |
| HOPKINS, C J (HM10147) | | | | | | | | | | ● | | | | | | | |
| HUGHES, DOREEN (HM10325) | | | | | | | | | | | | | | | | | |
| HUGHES, LINDA (HM10333) | | | | | | | | | | | | | | | | | |
| IPSWICH CHIROPRACTIC CLINIC (HM10714) | | | | | | | | | | | | | ● | | | | |
| IPSWICH PSYCHOTHERAPY/COUNS (HM10716) | | | | | | | | | | | | | | | | | |
| JUBY, P (HM11243) | | | | | | | | | | | | | | | | | |
| KEMP, N J (HM11463) | | | | | | | | | | | | | | | | | |
| KINNEAR, MARGARET (HM11689) | | | | | | | | | | | | | | | | | |
| LAVENDER LODGE CLINIC (HM12023) | | | | | | | | | | | | | | | | | |
| LINDOS PSYCHOTHERAPY CENTRE (HM12420) | | | | | | | | | | | | | | | | | |
| MACFARLANE, CLARE (HM12834) | | | | | | | | | | | | | | | | | |
| MALAROC (HM12961) | | | | | | | | ● | ● | | | | | | | | |
| MANOR HOUSE (HM13039) | | | | | | | | | | | | | | | | | |

# O - Z Therapies at Practices/Businesses

Business by County with Reference no.

| Business | Orthotics | Osteomyology | Osteopathy | PAM | Paranormal Therapies | Pattern Therapies | Physiotherapy | Phytotherapy | Pilates | Podiatry | Polarity Therapy | Postural Integration | Primal Therapy | Psionic Therapy | Psychotherapy | Pyramid Power |
|---|---|---|---|---|---|---|---|---|---|---|---|---|---|---|---|---|
| MASKERY, M (HM13231) | | | | | | | | | | | | | | | | |
| MASSAGE FOR HEALTH (HM13260) | | | | | | | | | | | | | | | | |
| MILES, JAMES (HM13858) | | | ● | | | | | | | | | | | | | |
| MILLER, PAM (HM13898) | | | | | | | | | | | | | | | | |
| MILLS, SUE (HM13934) | | | | | | | | | | | | | | | | |
| MOHAN, TERRY (HM14046) | | | | | | | | | | | | | | | ● | |
| MORRISON, SUSAN (HM14232) | | | ● | | | | | | | | | | | | | |
| NATURECURES (HM14684) | | | | | | | | | | | | | | | | |
| NOAH'S ARK PSYCHOTHERAPY (HM14964) | | | | | | | | | | | | | | | ● | |
| ORWELL COUNSELLING GROUP (HM15416) | | | | | | | | | | | | | | | ● | |
| PAROLIN, PAUL (HM15728) | | | | | | | | | | | | | | | | |
| PARSONS, CAROL (HM15750) | | | | | | | | | | | | | | | | |
| PARTRIDGE, VERONICA (HM15769) | | | | | | | | | | | | | | | | |
| PIPER, KARREN (HM16324) | | | | | | | | | | | | | | | | |
| QUENTIN-HICKS, M (HM16798) | | | ● | | | | | | | | | | | | | |
| ROWNEY, ERICA (HM17705) | | | | | | | | | | | | | | | | |
| SEAL, RAYMOND (HM18166) | | | | | | | | | | | | | | | ● | |
| SEAL, W (HM18167) | | | | | | | | | | | | | | | | |
| SHEROMA THERAPY (HM18435) | | | | | | | | | | | | | | | | |
| SPALDING, JULIE (HM18955) | | | | | | | | | | | ● | | | | ● | |
| SPALDING, PAUL (HM18956) | | | | | | | | | | | | | | | | |
| SPRINGFIELD LODGE HEALTH CARE (HM19052) | | | ● | | | | ● | | | | | | | | ● | |
| ST MARYS PRACTICE (HM19088) | | | ● | | | | | | | | | | | | | |
| STEWARD, J A (HM19252) | | | ● | | | | | | | | | | | | | |
| STEWARD, J A (HM19253) | | | ● | | | | | | | | | | | | | |
| STICKLAND, PAULINE (HM19287) | | | | | | | | | | | | | | | | |
| STOWMARKET OSTEOPATHS (HM19363) | | | ● | | | | | | | | | | | | | |
| SUDBURY CHIROPRACTIC CLINIC (HM19462) | | | | | | | ● | | | | | | | | | |
| TANSWELL, PHILLIP J (HM19693) | | | ● | | | | | | | | | | | | | |
| WALKER, LINDA (HM20786) | | | | | | | | | | | | | | | | |
| WEI CLINIC (HM21111) | | | | | | | | | | | | | | | | |
| WOODBRIDGE COMP HEALTH CENTRE (HM21816) | | | | | | | | | | | | | | | | |
| WOOLPITPHYSIO (HM21881) | | | | | | | ● | | | | | | | | | |
| WORSLEY, JULIA (HM21904) | | | | | | | | | | | | | | | | |

| Business | Pyscho-Synthesis | Reflexology | Reichian Therapy | Reiki | Remedial Massage | Rogerian Therapy | Rolfing | Seichem | Sensitivity Training | Shiatsu | Silva Method | Sound Therapy | Spiritual Healing | Sports Massage | Stress Therapy | Swedish Body Massage |
|---|---|---|---|---|---|---|---|---|---|---|---|---|---|---|---|---|
| MASKERY, M (HM13231) | | ● | | | | | | | | | | | | | | |
| MASSAGE FOR HEALTH (HM13260) | | | | | | | | | | | | | ● | | | |
| MILES, JAMES (HM13858) | | | | | | | | | | | | | | | | |
| MILLER, PAM (HM13898) | | ● | | | | | | | | | | | | | | |
| MILLS, SUE (HM13934) | | ● | | | | | | | | | | | | | | |
| MOHAN, TERRY (HM14046) | | | | | | ● | | | | | | | | | ● | |
| MORRISON, SUSAN (HM14232) | | | | | | | | | | | | | | | | |
| NATURECURES (HM14684) | | | | | | | | | | ● | | | | | | |
| NOAH'S ARK PSYCHOTHERAPY (HM14964) | | | | | | | | | | | | | | | ● | |
| ORWELL COUNSELLING GROUP (HM15416) | | | | | | | | | | | | | | | | |
| PAROLIN, PAUL (HM15728) | | | | | | | | | | | | | | | | |
| PARSONS, CAROL (HM15750) | | ● | | | | | | | | | | | | | | |
| PARTRIDGE, VERONICA (HM15769) | | ● | | | | | | | | | | | | | | |
| PIPER, KARREN (HM16324) | | ● | | | | | | | | | | | | | | |
| QUENTIN-HICKS, M (HM16798) | | | | | | | | | | | | | | | | |
| ROWNEY, ERICA (HM17705) | | ● | | | | | | | | | | | | | | |
| SEAL, RAYMOND (HM18166) | | | | | | | | | | | | | | | | |
| SEAL, W (HM18167) | | ● | | | | | | | | | | | | | | |
| SHEROMA THERAPY (HM18435) | | ● | ● | ● | | | | | | | | | | | ● | |
| SPALDING, JULIE (HM18955) | | | | | | | | | | | | | | | ● | |
| SPALDING, PAUL (HM18956) | | ● | | | | | | | | | | | | | | |
| SPRINGFIELD LODGE HEALTH CARE (HM19052) | | ● | | ● | | | | | | ● | | | | | | |
| ST MARYS PRACTICE (HM19088) | | | | | | | | | | | | | | | | |
| STEWARD, J A (HM19252) | | | | | | | | | | | | | | | | |
| STEWARD, J A (HM19253) | | | | | | | | | | | | | | | | |
| STICKLAND, PAULINE (HM19287) | | ● | | | | | | | | | | | | | | |
| STOWMARKET OSTEOPATHS (HM19363) | | | | | | | | | | | | | | | | |
| SUDBURY CHIROPRACTIC CLINIC (HM19462) | | | | | | | | | | | | | | | | |
| TANSWELL, PHILLIP J (HM19693) | | | | | | | | | | | | | | | | |
| WALKER, LINDA (HM20786) | | ● | | | | | | | | | | | | | | |
| WEI CLINIC (HM21111) | | ● | | | | | | | | | | | | | | |
| WOODBRIDGE COMP HEALTH CENTRE (HM21816) | | ● | | ● | | | | | | | | | ● | | ● | |
| WOOLPITPHYSIO (HM21881) | | | | | | | | | | | | | | | | |
| WORSLEY, JULIA (HM21904) | | ● | | | | | | | | | | | | | | |

| Business | Tai-Chi Ch'uan | Tantra Therapy | Tera-Mai | Thought Field Therapy | Touch Therapy | Transactional Analysis | Tui-na | Ultrasonics | Vibrational Therapy | Visualisation Therapy | Vitamin Therapy | Voice Therapy | X-Ray | Ying & Yang | Yoga | Zen Therapy | Zero Balancing |
|---|---|---|---|---|---|---|---|---|---|---|---|---|---|---|---|---|---|
| MASKERY, M (HM13231) | | | | | | | | | | | | | | | | | |
| MASSAGE FOR HEALTH (HM13260) | | | | | | | | | | | | | | ● | | | |
| MILES, JAMES (HM13858) | | | | | | | | | | | | | | | | | |
| MILLER, PAM (HM13898) | | | | | | | | | | | | | | | | | |
| MILLS, SUE (HM13934) | | | | | | | | | | | | | | | | | |
| MOHAN, TERRY (HM14046) | | | | | | | | | | ● | | | | | | | |
| MORRISON, SUSAN (HM14232) | | | | | | | | | | | | | | | | | |
| NATURECURES (HM14684) | | | | | | | | | | | | | | | | | |
| NOAH'S ARK PSYCHOTHERAPY (HM14964) | | | | | | ● | | | | | | | | | | | |
| ORWELL COUNSELLING GROUP (HM15416) | | | | | | | | | | | | | | | | | |
| PAROLIN, PAUL (HM15728) | | | | | | | | | | | | | | | ● | | |
| PARSONS, CAROL (HM15750) | | | | | | | | | | | | | | | | | |
| PARTRIDGE, VERONICA (HM15769) | | | | | | | | | | | | | | | | | |
| PIPER, KARREN (HM16324) | | | | | | | | | | | | | | | | | |
| QUENTIN-HICKS, M (HM16798) | | | | | | | | | | | | | | | | | |
| ROWNEY, ERICA (HM17705) | | | | | | | | | | | | | | | | | |
| SEAL, RAYMOND (HM18166) | | | | | | | | | | | | | | | | | |
| SEAL, W (HM18167) | | | | | | | | | | | | | | | | | |
| SHEROMA THERAPY (HM18435) | | | | | | | | | | | | | | | | | |
| SPALDING, JULIE (HM18955) | | | | | | | | | | ● | | | | | | | |
| SPALDING, PAUL (HM18956) | | | | | | | | | | | | | | | | | |
| SPRINGFIELD LODGE HEALTH CARE (HM19052) | | | | | | | | | | | | | | | ● | | |
| ST MARYS PRACTICE (HM19088) | | | | | | | | | | | | | | | | | |
| STEWARD, J A (HM19252) | | | | | | | | | | | | | | | | | |
| STEWARD, J A (HM19253) | | | | | | | | | | | | | | | | | |
| STICKLAND, PAULINE (HM19287) | | | | | | | | | | | | | | | | | |
| STOWMARKET OSTEOPATHS (HM19363) | | | | | | | | | | | | | | | | | |
| SUDBURY CHIROPRACTIC CLINIC (HM19462) | | | | | | | | | | | | | | | | | |
| TANSWELL, PHILLIP J (HM19693) | | | | | | | | | | | | | | | | | |
| WALKER, LINDA (HM20786) | | | | | | | | | | | | | | | | | |
| WEI CLINIC (HM21111) | | | | | | | | | | | | | | | | | |
| WOODBRIDGE COMP HEALTH CENTRE (HM21816) | | | | | | | | | | | | | | | | | |
| WOOLPITPHYSIO (HM21881) | | | | | | | | | | | | | | | | | |
| WORSLEY, JULIA (HM21904) | | | | | | | | | | | | | | | | | |

# O - Z Therapies at Practices/Businesses

| Business by County with Reference no. | Orthotics | Osteomyology | Osteopathy | PAM | Paranormal Therapies | Pattern Therapies | Physiotherapy | Phytotherapy | Pilates | Podiatry | Polarity Therapy | Postural Integration | Primal Therapy | Psionic Therapy | Psychotherapy | Pyramid Power | Pyscho-Synthesis | Reflexology | Reichian Therapy | Reiki | Remedial Massage | Rogerian Therapy | Rolfing | Seichem | Sensitivity Training | Shiatsu | Silva Method | Sound Therapy | Spiritual Healing | Sports Massage | Stress Therapy | Swedish Body Massage | T'ai-Chi Ch'uan | Tantra Therapy | Tera-Mai | Thought Field Therapy | Touch Therapy | Transactional Analysis | Tui-na | Ultrasonics | Vibrational Therapy | Visualisation Therapy | Vitamin Therapy | Voice Therapy | X-Ray | Ying & Yang | Yoga | Zen Therapy | Zero Balancing |
|---|---|---|---|---|---|---|---|---|---|---|---|---|---|---|---|---|---|---|---|---|---|---|---|---|---|---|---|---|---|---|---|---|---|---|---|---|---|---|---|---|---|---|---|---|---|---|---|---|---|
| WRIGHT, J L (HM21935) | | | ● | | | | | | | | | | | | | | | | | | | | | | | | | | | | | | | | | | | | | | | | | | | | | | |
| SURREY | | | | | | | | | | | | | | | | | | | | | | | | | | | | | | | | | | | | | | | | | | | | | | | | | |
| ACE NUTRITION (HM00157) | | | | | | | | | | | | | | | | | | ● | | | | | | | | | | | | | | | | | | | | | | | | | | | | | | | |
| ACHES & PAINS (HM00158) | | | ● | | | | | | | | | | | | | | | | | | | | | | | | | | | | | | | | | | | | | | | | | | | | | | |
| ACORN THERAPY CENTRE (HM00181) | | | | | | | | | | | | | | | | | | | | | | | | | | | | | ● | | ● | | | | | | | | | | | ● | | | | | | | |
| ACUHERBAL CHINESE MEDICINE (HM00214) | | | | | | | | | | | | | | | | | | ● | | | | | | | | | | | | | | | | | | | | | | | | | | | | | | | |
| AGNEW, B K (HM00422) | | | | | | | | | | | | | | | ● | | | | | | | | | | | | | | | | | | | | | | | | | | | | | | | | | | |
| ALTERNATIVES (HM00738) | | | | | | | | | | | | | | | ● | | | | | | | | | | | | | | | | | | | | | | | | | | | | | | | | | | |
| AMBER THERAPEUTIC CLINIC (HM00768) | | | | | | | | | | | | | | | | | | | | | ● | | | | | | | | | | | | | | | | | | | | | | | | | | | | |
| ASCOT HOMEOPATHIC CLINIC (HM01177) | | | | | | | | | | | | | | | | | | | | ● | | | | | | | | | | | | | | | | | | | | | | | | | | | | | |
| ASHFORD OSTEOPATHIC CLINIC (HM01218) | | | ● | | | | | | | | | | | | | | | | | | | | | | | | | | | | | | | | | | | | | | | | | | | | | | |
| ASHTEAD CHARTERED PHYSIO SV (HM01230) | | | | | | | | ● | ● | | | | | | | | | | | | | | | | | | | | | | | | | | | | | | | ● | | | | | | | | | |
| ASHTEAD CLINIC (HM01232) | | | ● | | | | | | | | | | | | | | | ● | | | | | | | | | | | | | | | | | | | | | | | | | | | | | | | |
| ASTON CLINIC (HM01301) | | | ● | | | | ● | | | | | | | | | | | ● | | | | | | | | | | | | | | | | | | | | | | | | | | | | | | | |
| ASW ALLERGY CONSULTANTS (HM01305) | | | | | | | | ● | | | | | | | | | | | | | | | | | | | | | | | | | | | | | | | | | | | | | | | | | |
| AVENUE PHYSIO & SPORTS CLNC (HM01390) | | | | | | | ● | | | | | | | | | | | | | | | | | | | | | | | | | | | | | | | | | | | | | | | | | | |
| BAARTZ, MARIAN (HM01459) | | | | | | | | | | | | | | | | | | ● | | | | | | | | | | | | | | | | | | | | | | | | | | | | | | | |
| BACKCARE CLINIC (HM01527) | | | ● | | | | | | | | | | | | | | | | | | | | | | | | | | | | | | | | | | | | | ● | | | | | | | | | |
| BAILEY, L J (HM01551) | | | ● | | | | | | | | | | | | | | | | | | | | | | | | | | | ● | | | | | | | | | | | | | | | | | | | |
| BARNES, A K R (HM01743) | | | ● | | | | | | | | | | | | | | | | | | | | | | | | | | | | | | | | | | | | | | | | | | | | | | |
| BARNSTEAD VILLAGE CLINIC (HM01769) | | | ● | | | | | | | | | | | | | | | | | | | | | | | | | | | | | | | | | | | | | | | | | | | | | | |
| BARRETT-BOYCE, PATRICK (HM01797) | | | ● | | | | | | | | | | | | | | | | | | | | | | | | | | | | | | | | | | | | | | | | | | | | | | |
| BASSETT, LESLEY (HM01855) | | | | | | | | | | | | | | | | | | ● | | | | | | | | | | | | | | | | | | | | | | | | | | | | | | | |
| BATCHELOR, C (HM01863) | | | | | | | | | | | | | | | ● | | | | | | | | | | | | | | | | | | | | | | | | | | | | | | | | | | |
| BAYLEY, EVA (HM01939) | | | | | | | | | | | | | | | ● | | | | | | | | | | | | | | | | | | | | | | | | | | | | | | | | | | |
| BENNETT, ELIZABETH (HM02139) | | | | | | | | | | | | | | | | | | ● | | | | | | | | | | | | | | | | | | | | | | | | | | | | | | | |
| BERRIE, INGE (HM02205) | | | | | | | | | | | | | | | | | | ● | | | | | | | | | | | | | | | | | | | | | | | | | | | | | | | |
| BILLINGTON, PEGGY (HM02310) | | | ● | | | | | | | | | | | | | | | | | | | | | | | | | | | | | | | | | | | | | | | | | | | | | | |
| BIODYNAMICS (HM02332) | | | | | | | | | | | | | | | | | | | | | | | | | | | | | | | | | | | | | | | | | | | ● | | | | | | |
| BONTHRON, SARAH (HM02687) | | | | | | | | | | | | | | | | | | ● | | | | | | | | | | | | | | | | | | | | | | | | | | | | | | | |
| BORDISS, DEBORAH (HM02715) | | | | | | | | | | | | | | | | | | ● | | | | | | | | | | | | | | | | | | | | | | | | | | | | | | | |
| BOSSERT, ELAINE HARRISON (HM02724) | | | | | | | | | | | | | | | | | | ● | | | | | | | | | | | | | | | | | | | | | | | | | | | | | | | |
| BOULTON, FRANCES (HM02743) | | | | | | | | | | | | | | | | | | ● | | | | | | | | | | | | | | | | | | | | | | | | | | | | | | | |
| BOURNE HEALTH (HM02753) | | | | | | | | | | | | | | | | | | | | ● | ● | | | | | | | | | | | | | | | | | | | | | | | | | | | | |

# O - Z Therapies at Practices/Businesses

| Business by County with Reference no. | Orthotics | Osteomyology | Osteopathy | PAM | Paranormal Therapies | Pattern Therapies | Physiotherapy | Phytotherapy | Pilates | Podiatry | Polarity Therapy | Postural Integration | Primal Therapy | Psionic Therapy | Psychotherapy | Pyramid Power | Pyscho-Synthesis | Reflexology | Reichian Therapy | Reiki | Remedial Massage | Rogerian Therapy | Rolfing | Seichem | Sensitivity Training | Shiatsu | Silva Method | Sound Therapy | Spiritual Healing | Sports Massage | Stress Therapy | Swedish Body Massage | T'ai-Chi Ch'uan | Tantra Therapy | Tera-Mai | Thought Field Therapy | Touch Therapy | Transactional Analysis | Tui-na | Ultrasonics | Vibrational Therapy | Visualisation Therapy | Vitamin Therapy | Voice Therapy | X-Ray | Ying & Yang | Yoga | Zen Therapy | Zero Balancing |
|---|---|---|---|---|---|---|---|---|---|---|---|---|---|---|---|---|---|---|---|---|---|---|---|---|---|---|---|---|---|---|---|---|---|---|---|---|---|---|---|---|---|---|---|---|---|---|---|---|---|
| BOWLER, ANNIE (HM02794) | | | | | | | | | | | | | | | | | | ● | | | | | | | | | | | | | | | | | | | | | | | | | | | | | | | |
| BOWRY, HEATHER (HM02805) | | | | | | | | | | | | | | | | | | ● | | | | | | | | | | | | | | | | | | | | | | | | | | | | | | | |
| BOYD-JONES, KERVIN (DR) (HM02821) | | | ● | | | | | | | | | | | | | | | | | | | | | | | | | | | | | | | | | | | | | | | | | | | | | | |
| BRABANT HOUSE CLINIC (HM02830) | | | ● | | | | | | | | | | | | ● | | | ● | | ● | | | | | | ● | | | ● | | | | | | | | | | | ● | | | | | | | | | |
| BRADLEY, JOANNAH (HM02867) | | | | | | | | | | | | | | | | | | ● | | | | | | | | | | | | | | | | | | | | | | | | | | | | | | | |
| BREWSTER, DAVID J (HM02980) | | | | | | | | | | | | | | | ● | | | | | | | ● | | | | | | | | | ● | | | | | | | | | | | ● | | | | | | | |
| BRIDGE COUNSELLING CENTRE (HM02989) | | | | | | | | | | | | | | | ● | | | | | | | | | | | | | | | | | | | | | | | | | | | | | | | | | | |
| BUSWELL, PRISILLA J (HM03470) | | | ● | | | | | | | | | | | | | | | | | | | | | | | | | | | | | | | | | | | | | | | | | | | | | | |
| BYRNE, ANGELA (HM03515) | | | | | | | | | | | | | | | | | | ● | | | | | | | | | | | | | | | | | | | | | | | | | | | | | | | |
| C PHILIP & J FOSTER & A MULA (HM03526) | | | ● | | | | | | | | | | | | | | | | | | | | | | | | | | | | | | | | | | | | | | | | | | | | | | |
| CAMBERLEY NATURAL THERAPY CTRE (HM03566) | | | | | | | | | | | | | | | | | | ● | | | | | | | | | | | | | | | | | | | | | | | | | | | | | | | |
| CAMPBELL & ASSOCIATES (HM03592) | | | ● | | | | | | | | | | | | | | | | | | | | | | | | | | | | | | | | | | | | | | | | | | | | | | |
| CANE, PAT (HM03626) | | | | | | | | | | | | | | | | | | ● | | | | | | | | | | | | | | | | | | | | | | | | | | | | | | | |
| CARLTON CLINIC (HM03700) | | | ● | | | | | | ● | | | ● | | | ● | | | ● | | ● | | | ● | | | ● | | | ● | | ● | | | | | | | | | ● | ● | | ● | | | | | | |
| CARPANINI, REGINALD & PENELOPE (HM03724) | | | ● | | | | | | | | | | | | | | | | | | | | | | | | | | | | | | | | | | | | | | | | | | | | | | |
| CASTLETON, DAVID (HM03849) | | | | | | | | | | | | | | | ● | | | | | | | | | | | | | | | | | | | | | | | | | | | | | | | | | | |
| CATERHAM OSTEOPATHIC PRACTICE (HM03854) | | | ● | | | | | | | | | | | | | | | | | | | | | | | | | | | | | | | | | | | | | | | | | | | | | | |
| CHANDLER, M D (HM03976) | | | | | | | | | | | | | | | ● | | | | | | | | | | | | | | | | | | | | | | | | | | | | | | | | | | |
| CHI CLINIC (HM04148) | | | | | | | | | | | | | | | | | | ● | | | | | | | | ● | | | | | | | | | | | | | | | | | | | | | | | |
| CHRISTINE KEY HYPNOTHERAPIST (HM04447) | | | | | | | | | | | | | | | ● | | | | | | | | | | | | | | | | | | | | | | | | | | | | | | | | | | |
| CITISPORT (HM04483) | | | | | | | ● | | | ● | | | | | | | | | | | | | | | | | | | | ● | | | | | | | | | | | | | | | | | | | |
| CLARK, JOYCE (HM04561) | | | | | | | | | | | | | | | | | | ● | | | | | | | | | | | | | | | | | | | | | | | | | | | | | | | |
| CLAXTON, VICKI (HM04613) | | | | | | | | | | | | | | | | | | ● | | | | | | | | | | | | | | | | | | | | | | | | | | | | | | | |
| CLEMENTS, CHRISTINE (HM04643) | | | ● | | | | | | | | | | | | | | | | | | | | | | | | | | | | | | | | | | | | | | | | | | | | | | |
| CLEMENTS, J (HM04644) | | | | | | | | | | | | | | | | | | ● | | | | | | | | | | | | | | | | | | | | | | | | | | | | | | | |
| CLEVERLY, BARBARA (HM04657) | | | | | | | | | | | | | | | | | | ● | | | | | | | | | | | | | | | | | | | | | | | | | | | | | | | |
| COHEN, MICHAEL (HM04793) | | | | | | | | | | | | | | | ● | | | | | | | | | | | | | | | | ● | | | | | | | | | | | ● | | | | | | | |
| COOK, ANN (HM05039) | | | ● | | | | | | | | | | | | | | | | | | | | | | | | | | | | | | | | | | | | | | | | | | | | | | |
| COWIESON, MARY (HM05296) | | | | | | | | | | | | | | | | | | ● | | | | | | | | | | | | | | | | | | | | | | | | | | | | | | | |
| COX, JULIET (HM05307) | | | | | | | | | | | | | | | | | | | | | | | | | | | | | | | | | | | | | | | | | | | | ● | | | | | |
| CRAIG-WOOD, SAMANTHA (HM05357) | | | ● | | | | | | | | | | | | | | | | | | | | | | | | | | | | | | | | | | | | | | | | | | | | | | |
| CRANLEIGH CHIROPRACTIC CLINIC (HM05381) | | | | | | | | | | | | | | | | | | ● | | ● | | | | | | | | | | | | | | | | | | | | ● | | | | | ● | | | | |
| CRAVEN, CLAIRE (HM05387) | | | ● | | | | | | | | | | | | | | | | | | | | | | | | | | | | | | | | | | | | | | | | | | | | | | |
| CRITTELL, SANDRA (HM05448) | | | | | | | | | | | | | | | ● | | | | | | | | | | | | | | | | | | | | | | | | | | | | | | | | | | |

# O - Z Therapies at Practices/Businesses

| Business by County with Reference no. | Orthotics | Osteomyology | Osteopathy | PAM | Paranormal Therapies | Pattern Therapies | Physiotherapy | Phytotherapy | Pilates | Podiatry | Polarity Therapy | Postural Integration | Primal Therapy | Psionic Therapy | Psychotherapy | Pyramid Power | Pyscho-Synthesis | Reflexology | Reichian Therapy | Reiki | Remedial Massage | Rogerian Therapy | Rolfing | Seichem | Sensitivity Training | Shiatsu | Silva Method | Sound Therapy | Spiritual Healing | Sports Massage | Stress Therapy | Swedish Body Massage | Tai-Chi Ch'uan | Tantra Therapy | Tera-Mai | Thought Field Therapy | Touch Therapy | Transactional Analysis | Tui-na | Ultrasonics | Vibrational Therapy | Visualisation Therapy | Vitamin Therapy | Voice Therapy | X-Ray | Ying & Yang | Yoga | Zen Therapy | Zero Balancing |
|---|---|---|---|---|---|---|---|---|---|---|---|---|---|---|---|---|---|---|---|---|---|---|---|---|---|---|---|---|---|---|---|---|---|---|---|---|---|---|---|---|---|---|---|---|---|---|---|---|---|
| CROFTON HOUSE OSTEO CLINIC (HM05457) | | | ● | | | | | | | | | | | | | | | | | | | | | | | | | | | | | | | | | | | | | | | | | | | | | | |
| CROWLEY, HEATHER (HM05506) | | | | | | | | | | | | | | | | | | ● | | | | | | | | | | | | | | | | | | | | | | | | | | | | | | | |
| CROYDON HEALING CENTRE (HM05515) | | | | | | | | | | | | | | | | | | | | | | | | | | | | | ● | | | | | | | | | | | | | | | | | | | | |
| CROYDON PRACTICE-PSYCHOTHERAPY (HM05517) | | | | | | | | | | | | | | | ● | | | | | | | | | | | | | | | | | | | | | | | | | | | | | | | | | | |
| CUMBERLIDGE, CAROL (HM05597) | | | | | | | | | | | | | | | | | | ● | | | | | | | | | | | | | | | | | | | | | | | | | | | | | | | |
| CUMMINS, ROZ (HM05617) | | | | | | | | | | | | | | | | | | ● | | ● | | | | | | | | | ● | | | | | | | | | | | | | | | | | | | | |
| DAVIES, ROBERT (HM05837) | | | | | | | | | | | | | | | | | | ● | | | | | | | | | | | | | | | | | | | | | | | | | | | | | | | |
| DE LIMA, RENUKA (HM05911) | | | ● | | | | | | | | | | | | | | | | | | | | | | | | | | | | | | | | | | | | | | | | | | | | | | |
| DIXON, CLAIRE (HM06126) | | | | | | | | | | | | | | | | | | ● | | | | | | | | | | | | | | | | | | | | | | | | | | | | | | | |
| DORCHESTER HOUSE OSTEOPATHY (HM06195) | | | ● | | | | | | | | | | | | | | | | | | | | | | | | | | | | | | | | | | | | | | | | | | | | | | |
| DORKING, PAUL (HM06200) | | | | | | | | ● | | | | | | | | | | | | | | | | | | | | | | | | | | | | | | | | | | | | | | | | | |
| EDWARDS HEALTH CLINIC (HM06639) | | | | | | | | | | | | | | | ● | | | | | | | ● | | | | | ● | | | | | | | | | | | ● | | | | ● | | | | | | | |
| EDWARDS, ZENA (HM06675) | | | | | | | | | | | | | | | | | | ● | | | | | | | | | | | | | | | | | | | | | | | | | | | | | | | |
| EKSTS, ANNE (HM06696) | | | | | | | | | | | | | | | | | | ● | | | | | | | | | | | | | | | | | | | | | | | | | | | | | | | |
| ENOCK-SHORE, ANGELA (HM06845) | | | | | | | | | | | | | | | | | | | | | | | | | | | | | | | ● | | | | | | | | | | | ● | | | | | | | |
| EQUILIBRIUM OSTEOPATHIC (HM06876) | | | ● | | | | | | | | | ● | | | | | | | | | | | | | | | | | | | | | | | | | | | | | | | | | | | | | |
| FEATHER, A J (HM07155) | | | ● | | | | | | | | | | | | | | | | | | | | | | | | | | | | | | | | | | | | | | | | ● | | | | | | |
| FOSTER, ROSALYN (HM07599) | | | ● | | | | | | | | | | | | | | | | | | | | | | | | | | | | | | | | | | | | | | | | | | | | | | |
| FRANKCOM, DAVID J (HM07685) | | | ● | | | | | | | | | | | | | | | | | | | | | | | | | | | | | | | | | | | | | | | | | | | | | | |
| FULLER, MICHAEL A (HM07790) | | | ● | | | | | | | | | | | | | | | | | | | | | | | | | | | | | | | | | | | | | | | | | | | | | | |
| GATEWAYS CENTRE (HM07928) | | | | | | | | | | | | | | | ● | | | | | | | | | | | | | | | | | | | | | | | | | | | | | | | | | | |
| GAUVAIN, TONY (HM07934) | | | | | | | | ● | | | | | | | | | | | | | | | | | | | | | | | ● | | | | | | | | | | | ● | ● | | | | | | |
| GAZELEY, HELEN (HM07948) | | | | | | | | | | | | | | | | | | ● | | | | | | | | | | | | | | | | | | | | | | | | | | | | | | | |
| GILES, ROSEMARY (HM08070) | | | | | | | | | | | | | | | | | | ● | | | | | | | | | | | | | | | | | | | | | | | | | | | | | | | |
| GLAISTER, BRIAN (DR) (HM08120) | | | | | | | | | | | | | | | ● | | | | | | | | | | | | | | | | | | | | | | | | | | | | | | | | | | |
| GLEICH, M T (HM08143) | | | ● | | | | | | | | | | | | | | | | | | | | | | | | | | | | | | | | | | | | | | | | | | | | | | |
| GODDARD, TERRI (HM08180) | | | | | | | | | | | | | | | | | | | | | | | | | | ● | | | | | | | | | | | | | | | | | | | | ● | | | |
| GOODLIFE NATURAL HEALTH CENTRE (HM08256) | | | ● | | | | | | | | | | | | | | | | | | | | | | | | | | | | | | | | | | | | | ● | | | | | | | | | |
| GRAINNE, MULLANY (HM08367) | | | | | | | | | | | | | | | | | | ● | | | | | | | | | | | | | | | | | | | | | | | | | | | | | | | |
| GREEN, S (HM08473) | | | ● | | | | | | | | | | | | | | | | | | | | | | | | | | | | | | | | | | | | | | | | | | | | | | |
| GRIFFITH-WARD, JANE (HM08574) | | | ● | | | | | | | | | | | | | | | | | | | | | | | | | | | | | | | | | | | | | | | | | | | | | | |
| GRIGGS, LESLEY (HM08575) | | | ● | | | | | | | | | | | | | | | | | | | | | | | | | | | | | | | | | | | | | | | | | | | | | | |
| GUILDFORD PHYSIO & SPORTS (HM08632) | | | | | | | ● | | | | | | | | | | | | | | | | | | | | | | | | | | | | | | | | | | | | | | | | | | |
| HALL, CHRISTINE (HM08769) | | | | | | | | | | | | | | | | | | ● | | | | | | | | | | | | | | | | | | | | | | | | | | | | | | | |

# O - Z Therapies at Practices/Businesses

| Business by County with Reference no. | Orthotics | Osteomyology | Osteopathy | PAM | Paranormal Therapies | Pattern Therapies | Physiotherapy | Phytotherapy | Pilates | Podiatry | Polarity Therapy | Postural Integration | Primal Therapy | Psionic Therapy | Psychotherapy | Pyramid Power | Pyscho-Synthesis |
|---|---|---|---|---|---|---|---|---|---|---|---|---|---|---|---|---|---|
| HALLINAN, DEBORAH (HM08810) | | | | | | | | | | | | | | | | | |
| HANFORD, S P (HM08925) | | | | | | | | | | | | | | | | | |
| HARRIS, JOHN R C (HM09073) | | | ● | | | | | | | | | | | | | | |
| HEARN, JUNE (HM09438) | | | | | | | | | | | | | | | ● | | |
| HELIANTHUS PRACTICE (HM09518) | | | | | | | | ● | | | | | | | | | |
| HELLON-HARRIS, HUGH (HM09523) | | | ● | | | | | | | | | | | | | | |
| HILL, CHARLOTTE (HM09774) | | | ● | | | | | | | | | | | | | | |
| HILLVIEW PHYSIO & SPORTS CLNC (HM09809) | | | | | | | ● | | | | | | | | | | |
| HILTON, DOROTHY M (HM09815) | | | ● | | | | | | | | | | | | | | |
| HOBSON, N (HM09866) | | | ● | | | | | | | | | | | | | | |
| HOLISTIC CENTRE (HM09949) | | | ● | | | | | | | | | | | | ● | | |
| HOOD, CHRISTINA (HM10123) | | | ● | | | | | | | | | | | | | | |
| HOPPER, C A (HM10156) | | | | | | | | | | | | | | | ● | | ● |
| HORSFORD, HELENA (HM10189) | | | | | | | | | | | | | | | | | |
| HOUE, DAVID (HM10207) | | | ● | | | | | | | | | | | | | | |
| HOUNSFIELD, BRIAN (HM10214) | | | ● | | | | | | | | | | | | | | |
| HUDSON, ROSEMARY (HM10318) | | | | | | | | | | | | | | | | | |
| HUMAN FOCUS RETURN TO WORK (HM10362) | | | ● | | | | ● | ● | | | | | | | | | |
| INGLEDALE NATURAL HEALTH CTRE (HM10621) | | | ● | | | | | | | | | | | | | | |
| INTERNATIONAL FED OF REFLEX (HM10695) | | | | | | | | | | | | | | | | | |
| JACKSON, ROBIN (HM10849) | | | ● | | | | | | | | | | | | | | |
| JEFFREY & ASSOCIATES (HM10968) | | | ● | | | | | | | | | | | | | | |
| JENNY HOK (HM11008) | | | | | | | | | | | | | | | | | |
| JOHNSON, LOUISE (HM11084) | | | | | | | | | | | | | | | | | |
| KANANI, ALPESH (HM11304) | | | ● | | | | | | | | | | | | | | |
| KATESMARK, R (HM11337) | | | ● | | | | | | | | | | | | | | |
| KATHERINE'S THERAPIES (HM11339) | | | | | | | | | | | | | | | | | |
| KENT CLINIC OF NATURAL MED (HM11514) | | | | | | | | | | | ● | | | | ● | | |
| KEW CHIROPRACTIC CLINIC (HM11575) | | | | | | | | | | | | | | | | | |
| KINGSTON NATURAL HEALING CTRE (HM11677) | | | ● | | | | | | | | | | | | ● | | |
| KINGSTON OSTEOPATHS (HM11679) | | | ● | | | | | | | | | | | | | | |
| KIRTON, CHRISTINE (HM11726) | | | | | | | | | | | | | | | ● | | |
| KOHLER, SUE (HM11778) | | | | | | | | | | | | | | | | | |
| LEWIN, SANDRA (HM12274) | | | | | | | | | | | | | | | | | |

| Business by County with Reference no. | Reflexology | Reichian Therapy | Reiki | Remedial Massage | Rogerian Therapy | Rolfing | Seichem | Sensitivity Training | Shiatsu | Silva Method | Sound Therapy | Spiritual Healing | Sports Massage | Stress Therapy | Swedish Body Massage | T'ai-Chi Ch'uan |
|---|---|---|---|---|---|---|---|---|---|---|---|---|---|---|---|---|
| HALLINAN, DEBORAH (HM08810) | ● | | | | | | | | | | | | | | | |
| HANFORD, S P (HM08925) | ● | | | | | | | | | | | | | | | |
| HARRIS, JOHN R C (HM09073) | | | | | | | | | | | | | | | | |
| HEARN, JUNE (HM09438) | | | | | | | | | | | | | | | | |
| HELIANTHUS PRACTICE (HM09518) | | | | | | | | | | | | | | | | |
| HELLON-HARRIS, HUGH (HM09523) | | | | | | | | | | | | | | | | |
| HILL, CHARLOTTE (HM09774) | | | | | | | | | | | | | | | | |
| HILLVIEW PHYSIO & SPORTS CLNC (HM09809) | | | | | | | | | | | | | | | | |
| HILTON, DOROTHY M (HM09815) | | | | | | | | | | | | | | | | |
| HOBSON, N (HM09866) | | | | | | | | | | | | | | | | |
| HOLISTIC CENTRE (HM09949) | ● | | ● | | | | | | ● | | | | | | | |
| HOOD, CHRISTINA (HM10123) | | | | | | | | | | | | | | | | |
| HOPPER, C A (HM10156) | | | | | | | | | | | | | | | | |
| HORSFORD, HELENA (HM10189) | ● | | | | | | | | | | | | | | | |
| HOUE, DAVID (HM10207) | | | | | | | | | | | | | | | | |
| HOUNSFIELD, BRIAN (HM10214) | | | | | | | | | | | | | | | | |
| HUDSON, ROSEMARY (HM10318) | ● | | | | | | | | | | | | | | | |
| HUMAN FOCUS RETURN TO WORK (HM10362) | | | | | | | | | | | | | | | | |
| INGLEDALE NATURAL HEALTH CTRE (HM10621) | | | | | | | | | | | | | | | | |
| INTERNATIONAL FED OF REFLEX (HM10695) | ● | | | | | | | | | | | | | | | |
| JACKSON, ROBIN (HM10849) | | | | | | | | | | | | | | | | |
| JEFFREY & ASSOCIATES (HM10968) | | | | | | | | | | | | | | | | |
| JENNY HOK (HM11008) | ● | | | | | | | | | | | | | | | |
| JOHNSON, LOUISE (HM11084) | ● | | | | | | | | | | | | | | | |
| KANANI, ALPESH (HM11304) | | | | | | | | | | | | | | | | |
| KATESMARK, R (HM11337) | | | | | | | | | | | | | | | | |
| KATHERINE'S THERAPIES (HM11339) | ● | | | | | | | | | | | | | | ● | |
| KENT CLINIC OF NATURAL MED (HM11514) | ● | | ● | | | | | | | | | ● | | ● | | ● |
| KEW CHIROPRACTIC CLINIC (HM11575) | | | | | | | | | | | | | | | | |
| KINGSTON NATURAL HEALING CTRE (HM11677) | ● | | ● | | | | | | ● | | | ● | | ● | | |
| KINGSTON OSTEOPATHS (HM11679) | | | | | | | | | | | | | | | | |
| KIRTON, CHRISTINE (HM11726) | | | | | | | | | | | | | | | | |
| KOHLER, SUE (HM11778) | ● | | | | | | | | | | | | | | | |
| LEWIN, SANDRA (HM12274) | ● | | | | | | | | | | | | | | | |

| Business by County with Reference no. | Tantra Therapy | Tera-Mai | Thought Field Therapy | Touch Therapy | Transactional Analysis | Tui-na | Ultrasonics | Vibrational Therapy | Visualisation Therapy | Vitamin Therapy | Voice Therapy | X-Ray | Ying & Yang | Yoga | Zen Therapy | Zero Balancing |
|---|---|---|---|---|---|---|---|---|---|---|---|---|---|---|---|---|
| HALLINAN, DEBORAH (HM08810) | | | | | | | | | | | | | | | | |
| HANFORD, S P (HM08925) | | | | | | | | | | | | | | | | |
| HARRIS, JOHN R C (HM09073) | | | | | | | | | | | | | | | | |
| HEARN, JUNE (HM09438) | | | | | | | | | | | | | | | | |
| HELIANTHUS PRACTICE (HM09518) | | | | | | | | | | | | | | | | |
| HELLON-HARRIS, HUGH (HM09523) | | | | | | | | | | | | | | | | |
| HILL, CHARLOTTE (HM09774) | | | | | | | | | | | | | | | | |
| HILLVIEW PHYSIO & SPORTS CLNC (HM09809) | | | | | | | | | | | | | | | | |
| HILTON, DOROTHY M (HM09815) | | | | | | | | | | | | | | | | |
| HOBSON, N (HM09866) | | | | | | | | | | | | | | | | |
| HOLISTIC CENTRE (HM09949) | | | | | | | | | | | | | | ● | | |
| HOOD, CHRISTINA (HM10123) | | | | | | | | | | | | | | | | |
| HOPPER, C A (HM10156) | | | | | | | | | ● | | | | | | | |
| HORSFORD, HELENA (HM10189) | | | | | | | | | | | | | | | | |
| HOUE, DAVID (HM10207) | | | | | | | | | | | | | | | | |
| HOUNSFIELD, BRIAN (HM10214) | | | | | | | | | | | | | | | | |
| HUDSON, ROSEMARY (HM10318) | | | | | | | | | | | | | | | | |
| HUMAN FOCUS RETURN TO WORK (HM10362) | | | | | | | | | | | | | | | | |
| INGLEDALE NATURAL HEALTH CTRE (HM10621) | | | | | | | ● | | | | | | | | | |
| INTERNATIONAL FED OF REFLEX (HM10695) | | | | | | | | | | | | | | | | |
| JACKSON, ROBIN (HM10849) | | | | | | | | | | | | | | | | |
| JEFFREY & ASSOCIATES (HM10968) | | | | | | | | | | | | | | | | |
| JENNY HOK (HM11008) | | | | | | | | | | | | | | | | |
| JOHNSON, LOUISE (HM11084) | | | | | | | | | | | | | | | | |
| KANANI, ALPESH (HM11304) | | | | | | | | | | | | | | | | |
| KATESMARK, R (HM11337) | | | | | | | | | | | | | | | | |
| KATHERINE'S THERAPIES (HM11339) | | | | | | | | | | | | | | | | |
| KENT CLINIC OF NATURAL MED (HM11514) | | | | ● | | | | | | | | | | ● | | |
| KEW CHIROPRACTIC CLINIC (HM11575) | | | | | | | | | | | | ● | | | | |
| KINGSTON NATURAL HEALING CTRE (HM11677) | | | | | | | | | | | | | | | | |
| KINGSTON OSTEOPATHS (HM11679) | | | | | | | | | | | | | | | | |
| KIRTON, CHRISTINE (HM11726) | | | | | | | | | | | | | | | | |
| KOHLER, SUE (HM11778) | | | | | | | | | | | | | | | | |
| LEWIN, SANDRA (HM12274) | | | | | | | | | | | | | | | | |

# O - Z Therapies at Practices/Businesses

| Business by County with Reference no. | Orthotics | Osteomyology | Osteopathy | PAM | Paranormal Therapies | Pattern Therapies | Physiotherapy | Phytotherapy | Pilates | Podiatry | Polarity Therapy | Postural Integration | Primal Therapy | Psionic Therapy | Psychotherapy | Pyramid Power | Pyscho-Synthesis | Reflexology | Reichian Therapy | Reiki | Remedial Massage | Rogerian Therapy | Rolfing | Seichem | Sensitivity Training | Shiatsu | Silva Method | Sound Therapy | Spiritual Healing | Sports Massage | Stress Therapy | Swedish Body Massage | T'ai-Chi Ch'uan | Tantra Therapy | Tera-Mai | Thought Field Therapy | Touch Therapy | Transactional Analysis | Tui-na | Ultrasonics | Vibrational Therapy | Visualisation Therapy | Vitamin Therapy | Voice Therapy | X-Ray | Ying & Yang | Yoga | Zen Therapy | Zero Balancing |
|---|---|---|---|---|---|---|---|---|---|---|---|---|---|---|---|---|---|---|---|---|---|---|---|---|---|---|---|---|---|---|---|---|---|---|---|---|---|---|---|---|---|---|---|---|---|---|---|---|---|
| LIFE STYLE NATURAL HEALTH CTRE (HM12349) | | | | | | | | | | | | | | | ● | | | ● | | | ● | | | | | | | | | | | ● | | | | | | | | | | | | | | | | | |
| LINDSAY, LISA F (HM12424) | | | ● | | | | | | | | | | | | | | | | | | | | | | | | | | | | | | | | | | | | | | | | | | | | | | |
| LONDON SPINE AND JOINT CLINIC (HM12610) | | | | | | | | | | | | | | | | | | ● | | | | | | | | | | | | | | | | | | | | | | | | | | | | | | | |
| LOW, ROYSTON (HM12688) | | | ● | | | | | | | | | | | | | | | | | | | | | | | | | | | | | | | | | | | | | | | | | | | | | | |
| MAHBOOBANI, KATHY (HM12929) | | | | | | | | | | | | | | | | | | ● | | | | | | | | | | | | | | | | | | | | | | | | | | | | | | | |
| MALIPHANT, JACKIE (HM12974) | | | | | | | | | | | | | | | | | | ● | | | | | | | | | | | | | | | | | | | | | | | | | | | | | | | |
| MALONNE, MARIANNE (HM12989) | | | | | | | | | | | | | | | | | | ● | | | | | | | | | | | | | | | | | | | | | | | | | | | | | | | |
| MANGAN PETER & CRAVEN CLAIRE (HM13010) | | | ● | | | | | | | | | | | | | | | | | | | | | | | | | | | | | | | | | | | | | | | | | | | | | | |
| MARKS, DARREN HYPNOTHERAPY (HM13120) | | | | | | | | | | | | | | | | | | | | ● | | | | | | | | | | | | | | | | | | | | | | | | | | | | | |
| MARTIN, HILARY (HM13192) | | | | | | | | | | | | | | | | | | ● | | | | | | | | | | | | | | | | | | | | | | | | | | | | | | | |
| MATTHEW DAV & SAMANTHA TAY (HM13297) | | | ● | | | | | | | | | | | | | | | | | | | | | | | | | | | | | | | | | | | | | | | | | | | | | | |
| MEENEGHAN, TOM (HM13685) | | | | | | | | | | | | | | | | | | | | | | | | | | | | | | | ● | | | | | | | | | | | | | | | | | | |
| MEFFAN, JOHN (HM13688) | | | ● | | | | | | | | | | | | | | | | | | | | | | | | | | | | | | | | | | | | | | | | | | | | | | |
| MERRYDOWN CENTRE (HM13754) | | | | | | | | | | | | | | | ● | | | | | | | | | | | | | | | | | | | | | | | | | | | | | | | | | | |
| MICHIE, CATRIONA (HM13802) | | | | | | | | | | | | | | | | | | ● | | | | | | | | | | | | | | | | | | | | | | | | | | | | | | | |
| MIDDLETON, VALERIE (HM13823) | | | | | | | | | | | | | | | | | | ● | | | | | | | | | | | | | | | | | | | | | | | | | | | | | | | |
| MIDGLEY & ASSOCIATES (HM13825) | | | ● | | | | | | | | | | | | | | | | | | | | | | | | | | | | | | | | | | | | | | | | | | | | | | |
| MILFORD MASSAGE PRACTICE (HM13863) | | | | | | | | | | | | | | | | | | | | | ● | | | | | | | | | | | | | | | | | | | | | | | | | | | | |
| MILLER CONSULTANCY (HM13880) | | | | | | | | | | | | | | | ● | | | | | | | | | | | | | | ● | | | | | | | | | | | | | | | | | | | | |
| MIND AND BODY (HM13958) | | | | | | | | | | | | | | | | | | ● | | ● | | | | | | | | | | | | | | | | | | | | | | | | | | | | | |
| MIST, CORINNE (HM13996) | | | | | | | | | | | | | | | | | | ● | | ● | | | | | | | | | | | | | | | | | | | | | | | | | | | | | |
| MORAN, CARMEL (HM14143) | | | | | | | | | | | | | | | | | | ● | | ● | | | | | | | | | | | | | | | | | | | | | | | | | | | | | |
| MORRISSEY, PAUL (HM14237) | | | ● | | | | | | | | | | | | | | | | | | | | | | | | | | | | | | | | | | | | | | | | | | | | | | |
| MOSS, JANICE (HM14265) | | | ● | | | | | | | | | | | | | | | | | | | | | | | | | | | | | | | | | | | | | | | | | | | | | | |
| MULA, ANIA (HM14329) | | | ● | | | | | | | | | | | | | | | | | | | | | | | | | | | | | | | | | | | | | | | | | | | | | | |
| NATIONAL COUNCIL OF PSYCHO (HM14506) | | | | | | | | | | | | | | | ● | | | | | | | | | | | | | | | | | | | | | | | | | | | | | | | | | | |
| NATURAL HEALING CENTRE (HM14541) | | | | | | | | | | | | | | | | | | ● | | ● | | | | | | | | | ● | | | | | | | | | | | | | | | | | | | | |
| NATURAL HEALING CLINIC (HM14550) | | | | | | | | | | | | | | | | | | ● | | ● | | | | | | | | | | | ● | | | | | | | | | | | | | | | | | | |
| NATURAL HEALTH PRACTICE (HM14594) | | | ● | | | | | | | | | | | | | | | | | | | | | | | | | | | | | | | | | | | | | | | | | | | | | | |
| NATURAL LIFE AROMATHERAPY (HM14608) | | | | | | | | | | | | | | | ● | | | ● | | | ● | | | | | | | | | | | ● | | | | | | | | | | | | | | | | | |
| NICOLA FRY-HEALTH & BEAUTY (HM14927) | | | | | | | | | | | | | | | | | | ● | | ● | | | | | | | | | | | | | | | | | | | | | | | | | | | | | |
| OATLANDS OSTEOPATHIC CLINIC (HM15166) | | | ● | | | | | | | | | | | | | | | | | | | | | | | | | | | | | | | | | | | | | | | | | | | | | | |
| OCEANFLOOD COMPUTERS (HM15201) | | | ● | | | | | | | | | | | | | | | | | | | | | | | | | | | | | | | | | | | | | | | | | | | | | | |
| O'DWYER, ANNEGRET (HM15232) | | | | | | | | | | | | | | | ● | | | | | | | | | | | | | | | | | | | | | | | | | | | | | | | | | | |

# O - Z Therapies at Practices/Businesses

| Business by County with Reference no. | Orthotics | Osteomyology | Osteopathy | PAM | Paranormal Therapies | Pattern Therapies | Physiotherapy | Phytotherapy | Pilates | Podiatry | Polarity Therapy | Postural Integration | Primal Therapy | Psionic Therapy | Psychotherapy | Pyramid Power | Pyscho-Synthesis | Reflexology | Reichian Therapy | Reiki | Remedial Massage | Rogerian Therapy | Rolfing | Seichem | Sensitivity Training | Shiatsu | Silva Method | Sound Therapy | Spiritual Healing | Sports Massage | Stress Therapy | Swedish Body Massage | T'ai-Chi Ch'uan | Tantra Therapy | Tera-Mai | Thought Field Therapy | Touch Therapy | Transactional Analysis | Tui-na | Ultrasonics | Vibrational Therapy | Visualisation Therapy | Vitamin Therapy | Voice Therapy | X-Ray | Ying & Yang | Yoga | Zen Therapy | Zero Balancing |
|---|---|---|---|---|---|---|---|---|---|---|---|---|---|---|---|---|---|---|---|---|---|---|---|---|---|---|---|---|---|---|---|---|---|---|---|---|---|---|---|---|---|---|---|---|---|---|---|---|---|
| OLD WOKING GRANGE (HM15264) | | | ● | | | | | | ● | | | | | | | | | ● | | ● | | | | | | ● | | ● | ● | | ● | | ● | | | | ● | | | | | | ● | | | | ● | ● | |
| O'REILLY, FRANCES (HM15372) | | | | | | | | | | | | | | | | | | ● | | | | | | | | | | | | | | | | | | | | | | | | | | | | | | | |
| OSTEO CLINIC & HEALING CENTRE (HM15443) | | | ● | | | | | | | | | | | | | | | | | | | | | | | | | | | | | | | | | | | | | | | | | | | | | | |
| OSTEOPATHIC CENTRE (HM15457) | | | ● | | | | | | | | | | | | | | | | | | | | | | | | | | | | | | | | | | | | | | | | | | | | | | |
| OSTEOPATHS FOR INDUSTRY (HM15476) | | | ● | | | | | | | | | | | | | | | | | | | | | | | | | | | | | | | | | | | | | | | | | | | | | | |
| OSTEOPATHY (HM15477) | | | ● | | | | | | | | | | | | | | | | | | | | | | | | | | | | | | | | | | | | | | | | | | | | | | |
| OTTERSHAW OSTEOPATHIC PRACTICE (HM15497) | | | ● | | | | | | | | | | | | | | | | | | | | | | | | | | | | | | | | | | | | | | | | | | | | | | |
| PAXTON, JACQUELINE (HM15859) | | | | | | | | | | | | | | | | | | ● | | | | | | | | | | | | | | | | | | | | | | | | | | | | | | | |
| PAYNE, I J (HM15863) | | | ● | | | | | | | | | | | | | | | | | | | | | | | | | | | | | | | | | | | | | | | | | | | | | | |
| PEET, SANDRA (HM15944) | | | | | | | | | | | | | | | ● | | | | | | | | | | | | | | | | | | | | | | | | | | | | | | | | | | |
| PENN, NICOLA (HM15984) | | | ● | | | | | | | | | | | | | | | | | | | | | | | | | | | | | | | | | | | | | | | | | | | | | | |
| PENWARDEN, DAVID (HM15998) | | | ● | | | | | | | | | | | | | | | | | | | | | | | | | | | | | | | | | | | | | | | | | | | | | | |
| PERSONAL/RELATIONSHIP THERAPY (HM16062) | | | | | | | | | | | | | | | ● | | | | | | | | | | | | | | | | | | | | | | | | | | | | | | | | | | |
| PETERS, A J (HM16081) | | | ● | | | | | | | | | | | | | | | | | | | | | | | | | | | | | | | | | | | | | | | | | | | | | | |
| PHILP, CHRISTINE (HM16147) | | | | | | | | | | | | | | | | | | | | ● | | | | | | | | | | | | | | | | | | | | | | | | | | | | | |
| PINCHES, CHRISTOPHER (HM16304) | | | ● | | | | | | | | | | | | | | | | | | | | | | | | | | | | | | | | | | | | | | | | | | | | | | |
| PIRAINO, MARK (HM16327) | | | ● | | | | | | | | | | | | | | | | | | | | | | | | | | | | | | | | | | | | | | | | | | | | | | |
| PLANT, BELINDA (HM16357) | | | | | | | | | | | | | | | | | | ● | | | | | | | | | | | | | | | | | | | | | | | | | | | | | | | |
| PRACTITONERS SCHOOL (HM16524) | | | | | | | | | | | | | | | | | | ● | | | | | | | | | | | | | | | | | | | | | | | | | | | | | | | |
| PRINGLE, AMANDA (HM16627) | | | | | | | | | | | | | | | | | | ● | | | | | | | | | | | | | | | | | | | | | | | | | | | | | | | |
| PRIOR, CYNTHIA (HM16628) | | | | | | | | | | | | | | | | | | ● | | | | | | | | | | | | | | | | | | | | | | | | | | | | | | | |
| PSYCHOLOGICAL & COUNS SVS (HM16700) | | | | | | | | | | | | | | | ● | | | | | | | | | | | | | | | | | | | | | | | | | | | | | | | | | | |
| RASMUSSEN, A C (HM16946) | | | ● | | | | | | | | | | | | | | | | | | | | | | | | | | | | | | | | | | | | | | | | | | | | | | |
| REES, MAUREEN E (HM17051) | | | ● | | | | | | | | | | | | | | | | | | | | | | | | | | | | | | | | | | | | | | | | | | | | | | |
| REIGATE OSTEOPATHIC (HM17123) | | | ● | | | | | | | | | | | | | | | | | | | | | | | | | | | | | | | | | | | | | | | | | | | | | | |
| RICHMOND OSTEOPATHIC (HM17300) | | | ● | | | | | | | | | | | | | | | | | | | | | | | | | | | | | | | | | | | | | | | | | | | | | | |
| RICHMOND PHYSIOTHERAPY (HM17301) | | | | | | | ● | | | | | | | | | | | ● | | | | | | | | | | | | ● | | | | | | | | | | | | | | | | | | | |
| RIGAL, M (HM17330) | | | | | | | | | | | | | | | | | | ● | | | | | | | | | | | | | | | | | | | | | | | | | | | | | | | |
| ROBSHAW, HELEN (HM17509) | | | | | | | | | | | | | | | ● | | | | | | | | | | | | | | | | | | | | | | | | | | | | | | | | | | |
| ROBYNA, ANNETTE (HM17516) | | | | | | | | | | | ● | | | | | | | ● | | ● | | | | | | | | | | | | | | | | | | | | | | | | | | | ● | | |
| ROSE, CYNTHIA J (HM17605) | | | | | | | | | | | | | | | | | | ● | | ● | | | | | | | | | | | | | | | | | | | | | | | | | | | | | |
| ROSE, JILL (HM17608) | | | | | | | | | | | | | | | | | | ● | | | | | | | | | | | | | | | | | | | | | | | | | | | | | | | |
| ROSS, PATRICK (HM17639) | | | ● | | | | | | | | | | | | | | | | | | | | | | | | | | | | | | | | | | | | | | | | | | | | | | |
| ROUX, ANITA DE (HM17678) | | | | | | | | | | | | | | | | | | ● | | | | | | | | | | | | | | | | | | | | | | | | | | | | | | | |

www.healthmyself.com

www.healthmyself.com

# O - Z Therapies at Practices/Businesses

| Business by County with Reference no. | Orthotics | Osteomyology | Osteopathy | PAM | Paranormal Therapies | Pattern Therapies | Physiotherapy | Phytotherapy | Pilates | Podiatry | Polarity Therapy | Postural Integration | Primal Therapy | Psionic Therapy | Psychotherapy | Pyramid Power | Pyscho-Synthesis | Reflexology | Reichian Therapy | Reiki | Remedial Massage | Rogerian Therapy | Rolfing | Seichem | Sensitivity Training | Shiatsu | Silva Method | Sound Therapy | Spiritual Healing | Sports Massage | Stress Therapy | Swedish Body Massage | T'ai-Chi Ch'uan | Tantra Therapy | Tera-Mai | Thought Field Therapy | Touch Therapy | Transactional Analysis | Tui-na | Ultrasonics | Vibrational Therapy | Visualisation Therapy | Vitamin Therapy | Voice Therapy | X-Ray | Ying & Yang | Yoga | Zen Therapy | Zero Balancing |
|---|---|---|---|---|---|---|---|---|---|---|---|---|---|---|---|---|---|---|---|---|---|---|---|---|---|---|---|---|---|---|---|---|---|---|---|---|---|---|---|---|---|---|---|---|---|---|---|---|---|
| RUDENKO, MARIEA (HM17734) | | | | | | | | | | | | | | | | | | ● | | | | | | | | | | | | | | | | | | | | | | | | | | | | | | | |
| RUTH WHITE YOGA CENTRE (HM17776) | | | | | | | | | | | | | | | | | | | | | | | | | | | | | | | | | | | | | | | | | | | | | | | ● | | |
| SAAG, INGRID (HM17820) | | | | | | | | | | | | | | | | | | ● | | | | | | | | | | | | | | | | | | | | | | | | | | | | | | | |
| SALMON, PHILIP (HM17859) | | | | | | | | | | | | | | | | | | ● | | | | | | | | | | | | | | | | | | | | | | | | | | | | | | | |
| SAMMUT & SAMMUT ASSOCIATES (HM17881) | | | ● | | | | | | | | | | | | | | | | | | | | | | | | | | | | | | | | | | | | | | | | | | | | | | |
| SCHONBERG, VERA (HM18078) | | | | | | | | | | | | | | | | | | ● | | ● | | | | ● | | | | | ● | | | | | | | | | | | | | | ● | | | | | | |
| SCHOOL OF YOGA (HM18089) | | | | | | | | | | | | | | | ● | | | | | | | | | | | | | | | | | | | | | | | | | | | | | | | | ● | | |
| SCIATICA CENTRE (HM18097) | | | ● | | | | | | | | | | | | | | | | | | | | | | | | | | | | | | | | | | | | | | | | | | | | | | |
| SCORPIO PHYSIOTHERAPY (HM18103) | | | ● | | | | ● | | ● | | | | | | | | | | | | | | | | | | | | | | | | | | | | | | | | | | | | | | | | |
| SEAMER, R (HM18170) | | | ● | | | | | | | | | | | | | | | | | | | | | | | | | | | | | | | | | | | | | | | | | | | | | | |
| SELSDON COMP/RESP CLINIC (HM18220) | | | | | | | | | | | | | | | ● | | | | | ● | | | | | | | | | ● | | | | | | | | | | | | | ● | ● | | | | | | |
| SEVEN SIGHS (HM18244) | | | | | | | | | | | | | | | | | | ● | | ● | | | | | | | | | | | | | | | | | | | | | | | | | | | | | |
| SHEPHERD, DIANNE (HM18410) | | | ● | | | | | | | | | | | | | | | | | | | | | | | | | | | | | | | | | | | | | | | | | | | | | | |
| SHEPPERTON PHYSIOFIRST CENTRE (HM18425) | | | | | | | ● | | | | | | | | | | | | | | | | | | | | | | | | | | | | | | | | | | | | | | | | | | |
| SIDDELL, ANGELA (HM18526) | | | | | | | | | | | | | | | ● | | | | | | | | | | | | | | | | | | | | | | | | | | | | | | | | | | |
| SIMMERLING, LUNIA (HM18551) | | | | | | | | | | | | | | | | | | ● | | | | | | | | | | | | | | | | | | | | | | | | | | | | | | | |
| SIMMONS, R (HM18562) | | | ● | | | | | | | | | | | | | | | | | | | | | | | | | | | | | | | | | | | | | | | | | | | | | | |
| SIMMS, KATHERINE (HM18564) | | | | | | | | | ● | | | | | | | | | ● | | | | | | | | | | | | | | | | | | | | | | | | | | | | | ● | | |
| SMALLBROOK CLINIC (HM18695) | | | ● | | | | | | | | | | | | | | | | | | | | | | | | | | | | | | | | | | | | | | | | | | | | | | |
| SMITH, CHARLES (HM18725) | | | ● | | | | | | | | | | | | | | | | | | | | | | | | | | | | | | | | | | | | | | | | | | | | | | |
| SMITH, S J (HM18804) | | | ● | | | | | | | | | | | | | | | | | | | | | | | | | | | | | | | | | | | | | | | | | | | | | | |
| SOUND MIND & BODY REFLEXOLOGY (HM18899) | | | | | | | | | | | | | | | | | | ● | | | | | | | | | | | | | | | | | | | | | | | | | | | | | | | |
| SOUTH LONDON PSYCH GROUP (HM18912) | | | | | | | | | | | | | | | ● | | | | | | | | | | | | | | | | | | | | | | | | | | | | | | | | | | |
| SQUIRE, ELIZABETH (HM19059) | | | | | | | | | | | | | | | | | | ● | | | | | | | | | | | | | | | | | | | | | | | | | | | | | | | |
| STEVENS, NIGEL GATES (HM19237) | | | ● | | | | | | | | | | | | | | | | | | | | | | | | | | | | | | | | | | | | | | | | | | | | | | |
| STRIKE, SUE (HM19406) | | | | | | | | | | | | | | | | | | ● | | | | | | | | | | | | | | | | | | | | | | | | | | | | | | | |
| SULLIVAN, MARGARET (HM19482) | | | | | | | | | | | | | | | | | | ● | | | | | | | | | | | | | | | | | | | | | | | | | | | | | | | |
| SURBITON NATURAL HEALTH CENTRE (HM19514) | | | ● | | | | | | | | | | | | | | | ● | | | | | | | | | | | | | | | | | | | | | | | | | | | | | | | |
| SURREY HEALING SANCTUARY (HM19522) | | | | | | | | ● | | | | | | | | | | ● | | | | | | | | | | | ● | | | | | | | | | | | | | | | | | | | | |
| SUTHERLAND, JENNY (HM19539) | | | | | | | | | | | | | | | | | | ● | | ● | | | | | | | | | | | | | | | | | | | | | | | | | | | | | |
| SUTTON CHIROPRACTIC CLINIC (HM19543) | | | ● | | | | | | | | | | | | | | | | | | | | | | | | | | | | | | | | | | | | | | | | | | | | | | |
| SUTTON, HELEN (HM19552) | | | | | | | | | | | | | | | | | | ● | | | | | | | | | | | | | | | | | | | | | | | | | | | | | | | |
| TANG, SIMON (HM19683) | | | ● | | | | | | | | | | | | | | | | | | | | | | | | | | | | | | | | | | | | | | | | | | | | | | |
| TANSILL, LUCY (HM19689) | | | ● | | | | | | | | | | | | | | | | | | | | | | | | | | | | | | | | | | | | | | | | | | | | | | |

# O - Z Therapies at Practices/Businesses

| Business by County with Reference no. | Orthotics | Osteomyology | Osteopathy | PAM | Paranormal Therapies | Pattern Therapies | Physiotherapy | Phytotherapy | Pilates | Podiatry | Polarity Therapy | Postural Integration | Primal Therapy | Psionic Therapy | Psychotherapy | Pyramid Power | Pyscho-Synthesis | Reflexology | Reichian Therapy | Reiki | Remedial Massage | Rogerian Therapy | Rolfing | Seichem | Sensitivity Training | Shiatsu | Silva Method | Sound Therapy | Spiritual Healing | Sports Massage | Stress Therapy | Swedish Body Massage | T'ai-Chi Ch'uan | Tantra Therapy | Tera-Mai | Thought Field Therapy | Touch Therapy | Transactional Analysis | Tui-na | Ultrasonics | Vibrational Therapy | Visualisation Therapy | Vitamin Therapy | Voice Therapy | X-Ray | Ying & Yang | Yoga | Zen Therapy | Zero Balancing |
|---|---|---|---|---|---|---|---|---|---|---|---|---|---|---|---|---|---|---|---|---|---|---|---|---|---|---|---|---|---|---|---|---|---|---|---|---|---|---|---|---|---|---|---|---|---|---|---|---|---|
| TAYLOR, DESMOND (HM19754) | | | ● | | | | | | | | | | | | | | | | | | | | | | | | | | | | | | | | | | | | | | | | | | | | | | |
| TAYLOR, L (HM19776) | | | ● | | | | | | | | | | | | | | | | | | | | | | | | | | | | | | | | | | | | | | | | | | | | | | |
| TELLING, PAUL (HM19824) | | | | | | | | | | | | | | | | | | | | ● | | | | | | | | | | | | | | | | | | | | | | | | | | | | | |
| TIESDELL-SMITH, DOREEN (HM20062) | | | | | | | | | | | | | | | | | | ● | | | | | | | | | | | | | | | | | | | | | | | | | | | | | | | |
| TOWNS, KATE (HM20202) | | | | | | | | | | | | | | | | | | | | | | | | | | | | | | | ● | | | | | | | | | | | | | | | | | | |
| TRADITIONAL CHINESE MEDICINE (HM20225) | | | | | | | | | | | | | | | ● | | | | | | | | | | | | | | | | | | | | | | | | | | | | | | | | | | |
| TREFSER, SIGFRIED (DR) (HM20314) | | | ● | | | | | | | | | | | | | | | | | | | | | | | | | | | | | | | | | | | | | | | | | | | | | | |
| TROTMAN, SALLY (HM20346) | | | | | | | | | | | | | | | | | | ● | | | | | | | | | | | | | | | | | | | | | | | | | | | | | | | |
| TUCKER, JOCELYN (HM20365) | | | | | | | | | | | | | | | | | | ● | | | | | | | | | | | | | | | | | | | | | | | | | | | | | | | |
| TURNER, R E (HM20435) | | | ● | | | | | | | | | | | | | | | | | | | | | | | | | | | | | | | | | | | | | | | | | | | | | | |
| TWINE, RAY (HM20456) | | | | | | | | | | | | | | | ● | | | | | | | | | | | | | | | | | | | | | | | | | | | | | | | | | | |
| TWO STEPS REFLEXOLOGY (HM20458) | | | | | | | | | | | | | | | | | | ● | | | | | | | | | | | | | | | | | | | | | | | | | | | | | | | |
| UNWIN LAMBERT, B & PEGG, E (HM20520) | | | ● | | | | | | | | | | | | | | | | | | | | | | | | | | | | | | | | | | | | | | | | | | | | | | |
| VESEY, JOHN M (HM20631) | | | ● | | | | | | | | | | | | | | | | | | | | | | | | | | | | | | | | | | | | | | | | | | | | | | |
| WALLACE, SUE (HM20832) | | | | | | | | | | | | | | | | | | | | | | | | | | ● | | | ● | | | | | | | | | | | | | | | | | | | | |
| WHITWORTH, MICHAEL T (HM21431) | ● | | | | | | | | | ● | | | | | | | | | | | | | | | | | | | | | | | | | | | | | | | | | | | | | | | |
| WICKER, GEMMA (HM21447) | | | | | | | | | | | | | | | | | | ● | | | | | | | | | | | | | | | | | | | | | | | | | | | | | | | |
| WILLIS, SALLY (HM21618) | | | | | | | | | | | | | | | ● | | | | | | | | | | | | | | | | | | | | | | | | | | | | | | | | | | |
| WILLSON, AUDREY (HM21635) | | | | | | | | | | | | | | | | | | ● | | | | | | | | | | | | | | | | | | | | | | | | | | | | | | | |
| WILSON-SMITH, ANDREW (HM21681) | | | ● | | | | | | | | | | | | | | | | | | | | | | | | | | | | | | | | | | | | | | | | | | | | | | |
| WINGROVE, ROSEMARY (HM21705) | | | | | | | | | | | | | | | | | | ● | | | | | | | | | | | | | | | | | | | | | | | | | | | | | | | |
| WINTER, DAVID (HM21718) | | | | | | | | | | | | | | | | | | | | | | | | | | ● | | | | | | | | | | | | | | | | | | | | | | | |
| WOOD, SAMANTHA CRAIG (HM21807) | | | ● | | | | | | | | | | | | | | | | | | | | | | | | | | | | | | | | | | | | | | | | | | | | | | |
| WOODLANDS NATURAL HLTH THERAPY (HM21832) | | | | | | | | | | | | | | | | | | ● | | | | | | | | | | | | | | | | | | | | | | | | | | | | | | | |
| WYATT, JOANNA (HM21965) | | | ● | | | | | | | | | | | | | | | | | | | | | | | | | | | | | | | | | | | | | | | | | | | | | | |
| YARNTON, C (HM21990) | | | | | | | | | | | | | | | ● | | | | | | | | | | | | | | | | | | | | | | | | | | | | | | | | | | |
| **SUSSEX (EAST)** | | | | | | | | | | | | | | | | | | | | | | | | | | | | | | | | | | | | | | | | | | | | | | | | | |
| ACADEMY OF HOLISTIC STUDIES (HM00148) | | | | | | | | | | | | | | | | | | | | ● | | | | | | | | | | | | | | | | | | | | | | | | | | | | | |
| ALBION CLINIC (HM00483) | | | | | | | | | | | | | | | | | | | | | | | | | | ● | | | | | | | | | | | | | | | | | | | | | | | |
| ALEXANDER, LAUREL (HM00566) | | | | | | | | | | | | | | | | | | ● | | | | | | | | | | | | | | | | | | | | | | | | | | | | | | | |
| ALLCHORN, MAGGIE (HM00593) | | | | | | | | | | | | | | | | | | ● | | | | | | | | | | | | | | | | | | | | | | | | | | | | | | | |
| ALPHA HYPNOTHERAPY (HM00684) | | | | | | | | | | | | | | | ● | | | | | | | | | | | | | | | | | | | | | | | | | | | | | | | | | | |
| ANDERSON, A J (HM00811) | | | | | | | | | | | | | | | ● | | | | | | | | | | | | | | | | | | | | | | | | | | | | | | | | | | |
| ARDERN FOOT & HEALTH CLINIC (HM00992) | | | | | | | | | | ● | | | | | | | | ● | | | | | | | | | | | | | | | | | | | | | | | | | | | | | | | |

# O - Z Therapies at Practices/Businesses

| Business by County with Reference no. | Orthotics | Osteomyology | Osteopathy | PAM | Paranormal Therapies | Pattern Therapies | Physiotherapy | Phytotherapy | Pilates | Podiatry | Polarity Therapy | Postural Integration | Primal Therapy | Psionic Therapy | Psychotherapy | Pyramid Power | Pyscho-Synthesis | Reflexology | Reichian Therapy | Reiki |
|---|---|---|---|---|---|---|---|---|---|---|---|---|---|---|---|---|---|---|---|---|
| AROMA HAIR (HM01047) | | | | | | | | | | | | | | | | | | ● | | ● |
| ASHDOWN OSTEOPATHIC CENTRE (HM01206) | | | ● | | | | | | ● | | | ● | | | ● | | | | | ● |
| BAIRD, DAVID (HM01569) | | | ● | | | | ● | | ● | | | | | | ● | | | ● | | ● |
| BARKWORTH & ASSOCIATES (HM01716) | | | ● | | | | | | | | | | | | | | | | | |
| BASSETT, N S (HM01857) | | | ● | | | | | | | | | | | | | | | | | |
| BELL, DERYN (HM02082) | | | ● | | | | | | | | | | | | | | | | | |
| BELVAIN, E (HM02118) | | | | | | | | | | | | | | | | | | ● | | |
| BEXHILL CHIROPRACTIC (HM02255) | | | | | | | | | | | | | | | | | | ● | | |
| BEXHILL OSTEOPATHIC PRACTICE (HM02257) | | | ● | | | | | | | | | | | | | | | | | |
| BOURNE, JOHN (HM02755) | | | | | | | | | | | | | | | | | | ● | | |
| BRIGHTON & HOVE SPORTS CLINIC (HM03041) | | | | | | | ● | | | | | | | | | | | | | |
| BRIGHTON HEALTH & RACQUET CLUB (HM03045) | | | | | | | ● | | | | | | | | | | | | | |
| BRIGHTON PHYSIOTHERAPY CLINIC (HM03048) | | | | | | | ● | | | | | | | | | | | | | |
| BROOKS, M (HM03179) | | | ● | | | | | | | | | | | | | | | | | |
| BRYANT, JACQUELINE (HM03288) | | | | | | | | | | | | | | | | | | ● | | |
| BUTLER, CHERYL (HM03484) | | | | | | | | | | | | | | | | | | ● | | |
| BUXTED OSTEOPATHIC PRACTICE (HM03502) | | | ● | | | | | | | | | | | | | | | | | |
| CHAPEL HOUSE CLINIC (HM03993) | | | ● | | | | | | | | | | | | | | | | | |
| CHARTERS PHYSIO & SPORTS (HM04050) | | | | | | | ● | | | | | | | | | | | | | |
| CLARK, M D C (HM04570) | | | ● | | | | | | | | | | | | | | | | | |
| CLARK, MALCOLM (HM04572) | | | ● | | | | | | | | | | | | | | | | | |
| CLINCH, ADELE (HM04675) | | | | | | | | | | ● | | | | | | | | | | |
| CLINIC OF PHYSICAL MEDICINE (HM04707) | | | ● | | | | | | | | | | | | | | | | | |
| CLINICAL CENTRE OF CHINESE MED (HM04712) | | | ● | | | | | | | | | | | | | | | | | |
| COLE, B (HM04812) | | | | | | | | | | | | | | | ● | | | | | |
| COLLEGE OF PHYTOTHERAPY (HM04853) | | | | | | | | ● | | | | | | | | | | | | |
| COMP THERAPY & TRAINING CENTRE (HM04915) | | | | | | | | ● | | | | | | | | | | ● | | ● |
| CONCEPTS PHYSIO & NUTRITION (HM04970) | | | | | | | ● | | | | ● | | | | | | | ● | | ● |
| COUSSENS, C A (HM05276) | | | ● | | | | | | | | | | | | | | | | | |
| COX, JULIET (HM05308) | | | | | | | | | | | | | | | | | | | | |
| COXHEAD, ANN (HM05325) | | | ● | | | | | | | | | | | | | | | | | |
| CRESENT CLINIC (HM05422) | | | ● | | | | ● | | | | | | | | | | | ● | | |
| CROSSLEY CLINIC (HM05488) | | | ● | | | | | | | | | | | | | | | | | |
| CROWBOROUGH CHIRO/COMP HLTH (HM05498) | | | | | | | | | | | | | | | | | | ● | | ● |

| Business by County with Reference no. | Remedial Massage | Rogerian Therapy | Rolfing | Seichem | Sensitivity Training | Shiatsu | Silva Method | Sound Therapy | Spiritual Healing | Sports Massage | Stress Therapy | Swedish Body Massage | T'ai-Chi Ch'uan | Tantra Therapy | Tera-Mai | Thought Field Therapy | Touch Therapy | Transactional Analysis | Tui-na | Ultrasonics | Vibrational Therapy | Visualisation Therapy | Vitamin Therapy | Voice Therapy | X-Ray | Ying & Yang | Yoga | Zen Therapy | Zero Balancing |
|---|---|---|---|---|---|---|---|---|---|---|---|---|---|---|---|---|---|---|---|---|---|---|---|---|---|---|---|---|---|
| AROMA HAIR (HM01047) | | | | | | | | | | | | | | | | | | | | | | | | | | | | | |
| ASHDOWN OSTEOPATHIC CENTRE (HM01206) | | | | | | | | | | | | | | | | | | | | ● | | | | | | | | | |
| BAIRD, DAVID (HM01569) | | | | | | ● | | | | | | | | | | | | | | | | | | | | | ● | | |
| BARKWORTH & ASSOCIATES (HM01716) | | | | | | | | | | | | | | | | | | | | | | | | | | | | | |
| BASSETT, N S (HM01857) | | | | | | ● | | | | | | | | | | | | | | | | | | | | | | | |
| BELL, DERYN (HM02082) | | | | | | | | | | | | | | | | | | | | | | | | | | | | | |
| BELVAIN, E (HM02118) | | | | | | ● | | | | | | | | | | | | | | | | | | | | | | | |
| BEXHILL CHIROPRACTIC (HM02255) | | | | | | | | | | | ● | | | | | | | | | | | | | | | | | | |
| BEXHILL OSTEOPATHIC PRACTICE (HM02257) | | | | | | ● | | | | | | | | | | | | | | | | | | | | | | | |
| BOURNE, JOHN (HM02755) | | | | | | | | | | | | | | | | | | | | | | | | | | | | | |
| BRIGHTON & HOVE SPORTS CLINIC (HM03041) | | | | | | | | | | | | | | | | | | | | | | | | | | | | | |
| BRIGHTON HEALTH & RACQUET CLUB (HM03045) | | | | | | | | | | | | | | | | | | | | | | | | | | | | | |
| BRIGHTON PHYSIOTHERAPY CLINIC (HM03048) | | | | | | | | | | | | | | | | | | | | | | | | | | | | | |
| BROOKS, M (HM03179) | | | | | | | | | | | | | | | | | | | | | | | | | | | | | |
| BRYANT, JACQUELINE (HM03288) | | | | | | | | | | | | | | | | | | | | | | | | | | | | | |
| BUTLER, CHERYL (HM03484) | | | | | | | | | | | | | | | | | | | | | | | | | | | | | |
| BUXTED OSTEOPATHIC PRACTICE (HM03502) | | | | | | | | | | | | | | | | | | | | | | | | | | | | | |
| CHAPEL HOUSE CLINIC (HM03993) | | | | | | | | | | | | | | | | | | | | | | | | | | | | | |
| CHARTERS PHYSIO & SPORTS (HM04050) | | | | | | | | | | | | | | | | | | | | | | | | | | | | | |
| CLARK, M D C (HM04570) | | | | | | | | | | | | | | | | | | | | | | | | | | | | | |
| CLARK, MALCOLM (HM04572) | | | | | | | | | | | | | | | | | | | | | | | | | | | | | |
| CLINCH, ADELE (HM04675) | | | | | | | | | | | | | | | | | | | | | | | | | | | | | |
| CLINIC OF PHYSICAL MEDICINE (HM04707) | | | | | | | | | | | | | | | | | | | | | | | | | | | | | |
| CLINICAL CENTRE OF CHINESE MED (HM04712) | | | | | | ● | | | | | | | | | | | | | | | | | | | | | | | |
| COLE, B (HM04812) | | | | | | | | | | | | | | | | | | | | | | | | | | | | | |
| COLLEGE OF PHYTOTHERAPY (HM04853) | | | | | | | | | | | | | | | | | | | | | | | | | | | | | |
| COMP THERAPY & TRAINING CENTRE (HM04915) | | | | | | ● | | | | | | | | | | | | | | | | | | | | | | | |
| CONCEPTS PHYSIO & NUTRITION (HM04970) | | | | ● | | | | | | | ● | | | | | | ● | | | ● | | | ● | | | | | | |
| COUSSENS, C A (HM05276) | | | | | | | | | | | | | | | | | | | | | | | | | | | | | |
| COX, JULIET (HM05308) | | | | | | | | | | | | | | | | | | | | | | | | ● | | | | | |
| COXHEAD, ANN (HM05325) | | | | | | | | | | | | | | | | | | | | | | | | | | | | | |
| CRESENT CLINIC (HM05422) | | | | | | | | | | | | | | | | | | | | ● | | | | | | | | | |
| CROSSLEY CLINIC (HM05488) | | | | | | | | | | | | | | | | | | | | | | | | | | | | | |
| CROWBOROUGH CHIRO/COMP HLTH (HM05498) | | | | | | | | | | | | | ● | | | | | | | | | ● | | | | | | | |

# O - Z Therapies at Practices/Businesses

Business by County with Reference no.

| Business by County with Reference no. | Orthotics | Osteomyology | Osteopathy | PAM | Paranormal Therapies | Pattern Therapies | Physiotherapy | Phytotherapy | Pilates | Podiatry | Polarity Therapy | Postural Integration | Primal Therapy | Psionic Therapy | Psychotherapy | Pyramid Power | Pyscho-Synthesis | Reflexology | Reichian Therapy | Reiki | Remedial Massage | Rogerian Therapy | Rolfing | Seichem | Sensitivity Training |
|---|---|---|---|---|---|---|---|---|---|---|---|---|---|---|---|---|---|---|---|---|---|---|---|---|---|
| CROWBOROUGH COMP THERAPISTS (HM05499) | | | | | | | | | | | | | | | | | | ● | | ● | | | | | |
| CUDLIPP, G (HM05552) | | | ● | | | | | | | | | | | | | | | | | | | | | | |
| CULL, BEN (HM05556) | | | ● | | | | | | | | | | | | | | | | | | | | | | |
| DALE-ROBERTS, PAULETTE (HM05688) | | | | | | | | | | | | | | | | | | ● | | | | | | | |
| DE TUTE, MARY (HM05920) | | | | | | | | | | | | | | | | | | ● | | | | | | | |
| DRIVE OSTEO AND SPORTS CLINIC (HM06314) | | | ● | | | | | | | | | | | | | | | | | | | | | | |
| DRYDEN, B A (HM06332) | | | | | | | | | | | | | | | ● | | | | | | | | | | |
| DYKE ROAD NATURAL HEALTH (HM06450) | | | ● | | | | | | | | | | | | | | | ● | | | | | | | |
| EAST BOURNE CLINIC (HM06509) | | | | | | | | | | | | | | | | | | ● | | | ● | | | | |
| EATON, MARION (HM06563) | | | | | | | | | | | | | | | | | | | | ● | | | | | |
| FAIRCHILD, HAZEL (HM07052) | | | | | | | | | | | | | | | | | | | | | | | | | |
| FAMILY FIRST (HM07087) | | | | | | | | | | | | | | | ● | | | | | ● | | | | | |
| FIVEWAYS OSTEOPATHIC PRACTICE (HM07382) | | | ● | | | | | | | | | ● | | | | | | | | | | | | | |
| FOREST ROW OSTEOPATHIC CLINIC (HM07550) | | | ● | | | | | | | | | | | | | | | | | | | | | | |
| FOUNDATION, ANGELGATE (HM07615) | | | | | | | | | | | | | | | | | | ● | | ● | | | | | |
| FOX, JACKY (HM07640) | | | | | | | | | | | | | | | | | | | | ● | | | | | |
| GATEHOUSE THERAPY CENTRE (HM07925) | | | | | | | | | | | | | | | ● | | | | | | | | | | |
| GLENDINNING, CATHERINE (HM08148) | | | | | | | | | | | | | | | | | | ● | | | | | | | |
| GOLDINGHAM, ROMEY (HM08223) | | | | | | | | | | | | | | | | | | ● | | | | | | | |
| GOLDSTONE CLINIC (HM08230) | | | | | | | | | | | | | | | | | | | | | | | | | |
| GOSSET & HALES (HM08304) | | | ● | | | | | | | | | | | | | | | | | | | | | | |
| GOSSET, N E (HM08305) | | | ● | | | | | | | | | | | | | | | | | | | | | | |
| GRIFFITHS, J (HM08567) | | | | | | | | | | | | | | | | | | | | | ● | | | | |
| HALPIN, P J (HM08816) | | | | | | | | | | | | | | | ● | | | | | | | | | | |
| HAMILTON, ANITA (HM08841) | | | | | | | | | | | | | | | | | | ● | | | | | | | |
| HAWKINS, LUKE (HM09224) | | | | | | | | | | ● | | | | | | | | | | | | | | | |
| HELESFAY-EVANS, JO (HM09517) | | | | | | | | | | | | | | | | | | ● | | | | | | | |
| HERBAL HEALTH CLINIC (HM09617) | | | | | | | | ● | | | | | | | ● | | | ● | | | | | | | |
| HEWERDINE, VICTORIA (HM09698) | | | | | | | | | | | | | | | | | | ● | | | | | | | |
| HOLDEN NATURAL HEALTH CLINIC (HM09927) | | | | | | | | | | | | | | | | | | ● | | | | | | | |
| HOVE OSTEOPATHIC CLINIC (HM10228) | | | ● | | | | | | | | | | | | | | | | | | | | | | |
| HUMPHRIES, CARL (HM10378) | | | ● | | | | | | | | | | | | | | | | | | | | | | |
| JOY, JANET (HM11231) | | | | | | | | | | | | | | | ● | | | | | | | | | | |
| JURY, YAEL (HM11276) | | | | | | | | | | | | | | | | | | ● | | | | | | | |

| Business by County with Reference no. | Shiatsu | Silva Method | Sound Therapy | Spiritual Healing | Sports Massage | Stress Therapy | Swedish Body Massage | T'ai-Chi Ch'uan | Tantra Therapy | Tera-Mai | Thought Field Therapy | Touch Therapy | Transactional Analysis | Tui-na | Ultrasonics | Vibrational Therapy | Visualisation Therapy | Vitamin Therapy | Voice Therapy | X-Ray | Ying & Yang | Yoga | Zen Therapy | Zero Balancing |
|---|---|---|---|---|---|---|---|---|---|---|---|---|---|---|---|---|---|---|---|---|---|---|---|---|
| CROWBOROUGH COMP THERAPISTS (HM05499) | | | | | | | | | | | | | | | | | | | | | | | | |
| CUDLIPP, G (HM05552) | | | | | | | | | | | | | | | | | | | | | | | | |
| CULL, BEN (HM05556) | | | | | | | | | | | | | | | | | | | | | | | | |
| DALE-ROBERTS, PAULETTE (HM05688) | | | | | | | | | | | | | | | | | | | | | | | | |
| DE TUTE, MARY (HM05920) | | | | | | | | | | | | | | | | | | | | | | | | |
| DRIVE OSTEO AND SPORTS CLINIC (HM06314) | | | | | | | | | | | | | | | | | | | | | | | | |
| DRYDEN, B A (HM06332) | | | | | | | | | | | | | | | | | | | | | | | | |
| DYKE ROAD NATURAL HEALTH (HM06450) | ● | | | | | | | | | | | | | | | | | | | | | | | |
| EAST BOURNE CLINIC (HM06509) | | | | | | | | | | | | | | | | | | | | | | | | |
| EATON, MARION (HM06563) | | | | | | | | | | | | | | | | | | | | | | | | |
| FAIRCHILD, HAZEL (HM07052) | | | | | | ● | | | | | | | | | | | ● | | | | | | | |
| FAMILY FIRST (HM07087) | | | | | | | | | | | | | | | | | | | | | | | | |
| FIVEWAYS OSTEOPATHIC PRACTICE (HM07382) | | | | | | | | | | | | | | | | | | | | | | | | |
| FOREST ROW OSTEOPATHIC CLINIC (HM07550) | | | | | | | | | | | | | | | | | | | | | | | | |
| FOUNDATION, ANGELGATE (HM07615) | | | | ● | | | | | | | | ● | | | | | | | | | | | | |
| FOX, JACKY (HM07640) | | | | | | | | | | | | | | | | | | | | | | | | |
| GATEHOUSE THERAPY CENTRE (HM07925) | | | | | | | | | | | | | | | | | | | | | | | | |
| GLENDINNING, CATHERINE (HM08148) | | | | | | | | | | | | | | | | | | | | | | | | |
| GOLDINGHAM, ROMEY (HM08223) | | | | | | | | | | | | | | | | | | | | | | | | |
| GOLDSTONE CLINIC (HM08230) | ● | | | | | | | | | | | | | | | | | | | | | | | |
| GOSSET & HALES (HM08304) | | | | | | | | | | | | | | | | | | | | | | | | |
| GOSSET, N E (HM08305) | | | | | | | | | | | | | | | | | | | | | | | | |
| GRIFFITHS, J (HM08567) | | | | | | | | | | | | | | | | | | | | | | | | |
| HALPIN, P J (HM08816) | | | | | | | | | | | | | | | | | | | | | | | | |
| HAMILTON, ANITA (HM08841) | | | | | | | | | | | | | | | | | | | | | | | | |
| HAWKINS, LUKE (HM09224) | | | | | | | | | | | | | | | | | | | | | | | | |
| HELESFAY-EVANS, JO (HM09517) | | | | | | | | | | | | | | | | | | | | | | | | |
| HERBAL HEALTH CLINIC (HM09617) | | | | ● | | ● | | | | | | | | | | | ● | ● | | | | | | |
| HEWERDINE, VICTORIA (HM09698) | | | | | | | | | | | | | | | | | | | | | | | | |
| HOLDEN NATURAL HEALTH CLINIC (HM09927) | | | | | | | | | | | | | | | | | | | | | | | | |
| HOVE OSTEOPATHIC CLINIC (HM10228) | | | | | | | | | | | | | | | | | | | | | | | | |
| HUMPHRIES, CARL (HM10378) | | | | | | | | | | | | | | | | | | | | | | | | |
| JOY, JANET (HM11231) | | | | | | ● | | | | | | | | | | | ● | | | | | | | |
| JURY, YAEL (HM11276) | | | | | | | | | | | | | | | | | | | | | | | | |

# O - Z Therapies at Practices/Businesses

| Business by County with Reference no. | Orthotics | Osteomyology | Osteopathy | PAM | Paranormal Therapies | Pattern Therapies | Physiotherapy | Phytotherapy | Pilates | Podiatry | Polarity Therapy | Postural Integration | Primal Therapy | Psionic Therapy | Psychotherapy | Pyramid Power | Pyscho-Synthesis | Reflexology | Reichian Therapy | Reiki | Remedial Massage | Rogerian Therapy | Rolfing | Seichem | Sensitivity Training |
|---|---|---|---|---|---|---|---|---|---|---|---|---|---|---|---|---|---|---|---|---|---|---|---|---|---|
| KRISTANA (HM11806) | | | | | | | | | | | | | | | | | | | | | | | | | |
| LEECH, JUNE & EASTAUGH, MIRIAM (HM12151) | | | ● | | | | | | | | | | | | | | | | | | | | | | |
| LEWES CHIROPRACTIC CLINIC (HM12271) | | | | | | | | | | | | | | | | | | | | | | | | | |
| LINTON, CHERRIE (HM12442) | | | | | | | | | | | | | | | | | | ● | | | | | | | |
| LONDON SCHOOL OF SPRTS MASSAGE (HM12606) | | | | | | | | | | | | | | | | | | | | | | | | | |
| MACALEVEY, MIKE (HM12814) | | | ● | | | | | | | | | | | | | | | | | | | | | | |
| MEADOWS, ERIC (HM13632) | | | | | | | | | | | | | | | | | | ● | | | | | | | |
| MENELAUS, CHERYL T (DR) (HM13724) | | | | | | | | | | | | | | | ● | | | | | | | | | | |
| MEREDITH, C A (HM13736) | | | ● | | | | | | | | | | | | | | | | | | | | | | |
| MOONCIE, BENEDICT (HM14102) | | | | | | | | | | | | | | | ● | | | | | | | | | | |
| MORRIS, STEPHEN (HM14216) | | | ● | | | | | | | | | | | | | | | | | | | | | | |
| NEAT FEET (HM14742) | | | | | | | | | | ● | | | | | | | | | | | | | | | |
| NEWHAM, DAVID (HM14863) | | | | | | | | | | | | | | | | | | ● | | | | | | | |
| NEWHAVEN OSTEOPATHIC CLINIC (HM14864) | | | ● | | | | | | | | | | | | | | | | | | | | | | |
| NEWICK PHYSIOTHERAPY CLINIC (HM14865) | | | | | | | ● | | | | | | | | | | | | | | | | | | |
| PACKER, COLIN (HM15556) | | | | | | | | | | | | | | | | | | ● | | | | | | | |
| PAVEL VITEK (HM15853) | | | | | | | | | | | | | | | | | | ● | | | | | | | |
| PEVENSEY BAY NTRL HEALING (HM16105) | | | | | | | | | | | | | | | | | | ● | | | ● | | | | |
| PICHLER, JOHN F (HM16263) | | | ● | | | | | | | | | | | | | | | | | | | | | | |
| PIPER, C (HM16322) | | | ● | | | | | | | | | | | | | | | | | | | | | | |
| PIPER, CLAIRE (HM16323) | | | ● | | | | | | | | | | | | | | | | | | | | | | |
| PLUCKROSE, S N (HM16378) | | | ● | | | | | | | | | | | | | | | | | | | | | | |
| POINTON, RICHARD (HM16399) | | | ● | | | | | | | | | | | | | | | | | | | | | | |
| POSTLETHWAITE, CAROLINE (HM16458) | | | ● | | | | | | | | | | | | | | | | | | | | | | |
| PREECE, ELLA (HM16530) | | | | | | | | | | | | | | | | | | ● | | | | | | | |
| RAINBOW PATHWAYS (HM16882) | | | | | | | | | | | | | | | | | | ● | | ● | | | | | |
| RAWLINGS, MAXINE (HM16970) | | | | | | | | | | | | | | | | | | ● | | | | | | | |
| REDFORD, SARAH (HM17022) | | | | | | | | | | | | | | | | | | ● | | | | | | | |
| REES, PAULINE (HM17052) | | | | | | | | | | | | | | | | | | ● | | | | | | | |
| REEVES, ALAN (HM17062) | | | | | | | | | | | | | | | ● | | | | | | | | | | |
| REFLEXOLOGY FOR HEALTH (HM17095) | | | | | | | | | | | | | | | | | | ● | | | | | | | |
| REIKI MASTER (HM17140) | | | | | | | | | | | | | | | | | | | | ● | | | | | |
| RETIEF & ASSOCIATES (HM17201) | | | ● | | | | | | | | | | | | | | | | | | | | | | |
| REYNOLDS, MARION (HM17213) | | | | | | | | | | | | | | | | | | ● | | | | | | | |

| Business by County with Reference no. | Shiatsu | Silva Method | Sound Therapy | Spiritual Healing | Sports Massage | Stress Therapy | Swedish Body Massage | T'ai-Chi Ch'uan | Tantra Therapy | Tera-Mai | Thought Field Therapy | Touch Therapy | Transactional Analysis | Tui-na | Ultrasonics | Vibrational Therapy | Visualisation Therapy | Vitamin Therapy | Voice Therapy | X-Ray | Ying & Yang | Yoga | Zen Therapy | Zero Balancing |
|---|---|---|---|---|---|---|---|---|---|---|---|---|---|---|---|---|---|---|---|---|---|---|---|---|
| KRISTANA (HM11806) | | | | ● | | | | | | | | | | | | | | | | | | | | |
| LEECH, JUNE & EASTAUGH, MIRIAM (HM12151) | | | | | | | | | | | | | | | | | | | | | | | | |
| LEWES CHIROPRACTIC CLINIC (HM12271) | | | | | | | | | | | | | | | | | | | | ● | | | | |
| LINTON, CHERRIE (HM12442) | | | | | | | | | | | | | | | | | | | | | | | | |
| LONDON SCHOOL OF SPRTS MASSAGE (HM12606) | | | | | ● | | | | | | | | | | | | | | | | | | | |
| MACALEVEY, MIKE (HM12814) | | | | | | | | | | | | | | | | | | | | | | | | |
| MEADOWS, ERIC (HM13632) | | | | | | | | | | | | | | | | | | | | | | | | |
| MENELAUS, CHERYL T (DR) (HM13724) | | | | | | | | | | | | | | | | | | | | | | | | |
| MEREDITH, C A (HM13736) | | | | | | | | | | | | | | | | | | | | | | | | |
| MOONCIE, BENEDICT (HM14102) | | | | | | | | | | | | | | | | | | | | | | | | |
| MORRIS, STEPHEN (HM14216) | | | | | | | | | | | | | | | | | | | | | | | | |
| NEAT FEET (HM14742) | | | | | | | | | | | | | | | | | | | | | | | | |
| NEWHAM, DAVID (HM14863) | | | | | | | | | | | | | | | | | | | | | | | | |
| NEWHAVEN OSTEOPATHIC CLINIC (HM14864) | | | | | | | | | | | | | | | | | | | | | | | | |
| NEWICK PHYSIOTHERAPY CLINIC (HM14865) | | | | | | | | | | | | | | | | | | | | | | | | |
| PACKER, COLIN (HM15556) | | | | | | | | | | | | | | | | | | | | | | | | |
| PAVEL VITEK (HM15853) | | | | | | | | | | | | | | | | | | | | | | | | |
| PEVENSEY BAY NTRL HEALING (HM16105) | | | | | | | | | | | | | | | | | | | | | | | | |
| PICHLER, JOHN F (HM16263) | | | | | | | | | | | | | | | | | | | | | | | | |
| PIPER, C (HM16322) | | | | | | | | | | | | | | | | | | | | | | | | |
| PIPER, CLAIRE (HM16323) | | | | | | | | | | | | | | | | | | | | | | | | |
| PLUCKROSE, S N (HM16378) | | | | | | | | | | | | | | | | | | | | | | | | |
| POINTON, RICHARD (HM16399) | | | | | | | | | | | | | | | | | | | | | | | | |
| POSTLETHWAITE, CAROLINE (HM16458) | | | | | | | | | | | | | | | | | | | | | | | | |
| PREECE, ELLA (HM16530) | | | | | | | | | | | | | | | | | | | | | | | | |
| RAINBOW PATHWAYS (HM16882) | | | | | | | | | | | | | | | | | | | | | | | | |
| RAWLINGS, MAXINE (HM16970) | | | | | | | | | | | | | | | | | | | | | | | | |
| REDFORD, SARAH (HM17022) | | | | | | | | | | | | | | | | | | | | | | | | |
| REES, PAULINE (HM17052) | | | | | | | | | | | | | | | | | | | | | | | | |
| REEVES, ALAN (HM17062) | | | | | | | | | | | | | | | | | | | | | | | | |
| REFLEXOLOGY FOR HEALTH (HM17095) | | | | | | | | | | | | | | | | | | | | | | | | |
| REIKI MASTER (HM17140) | | | | | | | | | | | | | | | | | | | | | | | | |
| RETIEF & ASSOCIATES (HM17201) | | | | | | | | | | | | | | | | | | | | | | | | |
| REYNOLDS, MARION (HM17213) | | | | | | | | | | | | | | | | | | | | | | | | |

# O - Z Therapies at Practices/Businesses

| Business by County with Reference no. | Orthotics | Osteomyology | Osteopathy | PAM | Paranormal Therapies | Pattern Therapies | Physiotherapy | Phytotherapy | Pilates | Podiatry | Polarity Therapy | Postural Integration | Primal Therapy | Psionic Therapy | Psychotherapy | Pyramid Power | Pyscho-Synthesis | Reflexology | Reichian Therapy | Reiki | Remedial Massage | Rogerian Therapy | Rolfing | Seichem | Sensitivity Training | Shiatsu | Silva Method | Sound Therapy | Spiritual Healing | Sports Massage | Stress Therapy | Swedish Body Massage | T'ai-Chi Ch'uan | Tantra Therapy | Tera-Mai | Thought Field Therapy | Touch Therapy | Transactional Analysis | Tui-na | Ultrasonics | Vibrational Therapy | Visualisation Therapy | Vitamin Therapy | Voice Therapy | X-Ray | Ying & Yang | Yoga | Zen Therapy | Zero Balancing |
|---|---|---|---|---|---|---|---|---|---|---|---|---|---|---|---|---|---|---|---|---|---|---|---|---|---|---|---|---|---|---|---|---|---|---|---|---|---|---|---|---|---|---|---|---|---|---|---|---|---|
| RIHAL, PAMELA (HM17336) | | | | | | | | | | | | | | | | | | ● | | | | | | | | | | | | | | | | | | | | | | | | | | | | | | | |
| ROBINSON, JACQUELINE (HM17481) | | | | | | | | | | | | | | | | | | ● | | | | | | | | | | | | | | | | | | | | | | | | | | | | | | | |
| ROMANINI, ADRIANO (HM17570) | | | | | | | | | | | | | | | | | | ● | | | | | | | | | | | | | | | | | | | | | | | | | | | | | | | |
| RUMBALL, ALMA (HM17746) | | | | | | | | | | | | | | | ● | | | | | | | | | | | | | | | | | | | | | | | | | | | | | | | | | | |
| SANDERS, PETER (HM17915) | | | | | | | | | | | | | | | ● | | | | | | | | | | | | | | | | | | | | | | | | | | | | | | | | | | |
| SCHOLL CENTRE (HM18032) | | | | | | | | | | ● | | | | | | | | | | | | | | | | | | | | | | | | | | | | | | | | | | | | | | | |
| SEPHTON, ANN (HM18231) | | | | | | | | | | | | | | | | | | ● | | | | | | | | | | | | | | | | | | | | | | | | | | | | | | | |
| STARK, J (HM19146) | | | ● | | | | | | | | | | | | | | | | | | | | | | | | | | | | | | | | | | | | | | | | | | | | | | |
| STEPNEY, NICK (HM19212) | | | | | | | | | | | | | | | ● | | | | | | | | | | | | | | | | | | | | | | | | | | | | | | | | | | |
| STOCKDALE, MEL (HM19309) | | | | | | | | | | | | | | | ● | | | | | | | | | | | | | | | | | | | | | | | | | | | | | | | | | | |
| TEALE, PAUL (HM19809) | | | ● | | | | | | | | | | | | | | | | | | | | | | | | | | | | | | | | | | | | | | | | | | | | | | |
| THOMSON, B L (HM20001) | | | ● | | | | | | | | | | | | | | | | | | | | | | | | | | | | | | | | | | | | | | | | | | | | | | |
| TRENCHARD, ABIGAIL (HM20319) | | | | | ● | | | | | | | | | | | | | | | | | | | | | | | | | | ● | | | | | | | | | | | | | | | | | | |
| TROUSDELL, PETA (HM20348) | | | | | | | | | | | | | | | | | | ● | | | | | | | | | | | | | | | | | | | | | | | | | | | | | | | |
| TURNER, WENDY (HM20440) | | | | | | | | | | | | | | | | | | ● | | | | | | | | | | | | | | | | | | | | | | | | | | | | | | | |
| VALENCE ROAD OSTEOPATHS (HM20554) | | | | | | | | | | | | | | | | | | ● | | | | | | | | | | | | | | | | | | | | | | | | | | | | | | | |
| VARA, J & ASSOCIATES (HM20583) | | | ● | | | | | | | | | | | | | | | | | | | | | | | | | | | | | | | | | | | | | | | | | | | | | | |
| WADHURST PHYSIO/SPORTS CLNC (HM20730) | | | | | | | ● | | | | | | | | | | | | | | | | | | | | | | | | | | | | | | | | | | | | | | | | | | |
| WADHURST PHYSIO/SPORTS CLNC (HM20729) | | | | | | | ● | | | | | | | | | | | | | | | | | | | | | | | | | | | | | | | | | | | | | | | | | | |
| WALKER, KRISTINE (HM20783) | | | | | | | | | | | | | | | | | | ● | | | | | | | | | | | | | | | | | | | | | | | | | | | | | | | |
| WALSH, M J (HM20865) | | | ● | | | | | | | | | | | | | | | | | | | | | | | | | | | | | | | | | | | | | | | | | | | | | | |
| WELBOURNE, SONIA D (HM21122) | | | ● | | | | | | | | | | | | | | | | | | | | | | | | | | | | | | | | | | | | | | | | | | | | | | |
| WHIPPY, TESSA (HM21330) | | | | | | | | | | | | | | | | | | ● | | | | | | | | | | | | | | | | | | | | | | | | | | | | | | | |
| WILBURY PHYSIOTHERAPY (HM21480) | | | | | | | ● | | | ● | | | | | | | | | | | | | | | | ● | | | | | | | | | | | | | | | | | | | | | | | |
| WINSKELL, HEIDI (HM21713) | | | | | | | | | | | | | | | | | | ● | | | | | | | | | | | | | | | | | | | | | | | | | | | | | | | |
| WOODWARD, CHRISTINE (HM21863) | | | | | | | | | | | | | | | | | | ● | | | | | | | | | | | | | | | | | | | | | | | | | | | | | | | |
| WRIGHT, P A (HM21946) | | | | | | | | | | ● | | | | | | | | | | | | | | | | | | | | | | | | | | | | | | | | | | | | | | | |
| **SUSSEX (WEST)** | | | | | | | | | | | | | | | | | | | | | | | | | | | | | | | | | | | | | | | | | | | | | | | | | |
| A G PUSEY & ASSOCIATES (HM00033) | | | ● | | | | | | | | | | | | | | | | | | | | | | | | | | | | | | | | | | | | | | | | | | | | | | |
| A G PUSEY & ASSOCIATES (HM00034) | | | ● | | | | | | | | | | | | | | | | | | | | | | | | | | | | | | | | | | | | | | | | | | | | | | |
| ACKLAND, MAUREEN (HM00167) | | | | | | | | | | | | | | | | | | ● | | | | | | | | | | | | | | | | | | | | | | | | | | | | | | | |
| ACORN CENTRE (HM00171) | | | | | | | | | | | | | | | ● | | | ● | | | | | | | | ● | | | ● | | | | | | | | | | | | | | | | | | | | |
| ALAN SMITH CHIROPRACTOR (HM00470) | | | | | | | | | | | | | | | | | | | | ● | | | | | | | | | | | | | | | | | | | | | | | | | | | | | |
| ALDRED, HELEN (HM00505) | | | | | | | | | | | | | | | | | | ● | | | | | | | | | | | | | | | | | | | | | | | | | | | | | | | |

# O - Z Therapies at Practices/Businesses

| Business by County with Reference no. | Orthotics | Osteomyology | Osteopathy | PAM | Paranormal Therapies | Pattern Therapies | Physiotherapy | Phytotherapy | Pilates | Podiatry | Polarity Therapy | Postural Integration | Primal Therapy | Psionic Therapy | Psychotherapy | Pyramid Power | Pyscho-Synthesis | Reflexology | Reichian Therapy | Reiki | Remedial Massage | Rogerian Therapy | Rolfing | Seichem | Sensitivity Training | Shiatsu | Silva Method | Sound Therapy | Spiritual Healing | Sports Massage | Stress Therapy | Swedish Body Massage | T'ai-Chi Ch'uan | Tantra Therapy | Tera-Mai | Thought Field Therapy | Touch Therapy | Transactional Analysis | Tui-na | Ultrasonics | Vibrational Therapy | Visualisation Therapy | Vitamin Therapy | Voice Therapy | X-Ray | Ying & Yang | Yoga | Zen Therapy | Zero Balancing |
|---|---|---|---|---|---|---|---|---|---|---|---|---|---|---|---|---|---|---|---|---|---|---|---|---|---|---|---|---|---|---|---|---|---|---|---|---|---|---|---|---|---|---|---|---|---|---|---|---|---|
| ANDREW BATHIE PRACTICE (HM00846) | | | | | | | | | | | | | | | ● | | | | | | | | | | | | | | | | ● | | | | | | | | | | | ● | | | | | | | |
| ANGELA (HM00872) | | | | | | | | | | | | | | | | | | | | | | | | | | | | | ● | | | | | | | | | | | | | | | | | | | | |
| AVALON HEALTH CENTRE (HM01380) | | | ● | | | | ● | | | | | | | | | | | | | | | | | | | | | | | | | | | | | | | | | | | | | | | | | | |
| B O P (HM01452) | | | ● | | | | | | | | | | | | | | | ● | | | | | | | | | | | | | | | | | | | | | | ● | | | | | | | | | |
| BABBAGE-CLARK, SACHA (HM01462) | | | ● | | | | | | | | | | | | | | | | | | | | | | | | | | | | | | | | | | | | | | | | | | | | | | |
| BALOOMBE OSTEOPATHIC & SPORTS (HM01641) | | | ● | | | | | | | | | | | | | | | | | | | | | | | | | | | | | | | | | | | | | | | | | | | | | | |
| BARTHOLOMEW WAY CLINIC (HM01818) | ● | | ● | | | | ● | | | ● | | | | | | | | | | | | | | | | | | | | | | | | | | | | | | | | | | | ● | | | | |
| BELLAMY PARTNERSHIP (HM02093) | | | ● | | | | | | | | | | | | | | | | | | | | | | | | | | | | | | | | | | | | | | | | | | | | | | |
| BELLAMY, ANTHO A P (HM02094) | | | ● | | | | | | | | | | | | | | | | | | | | | | | | | | | | | | | | | | | | | | | | | | | | | | |
| BEVIS, J P (HM02248) | | | ● | | | | | | | | | | | | | | | | | | | | | | | | | | | | | | | | | | | | | | | | | | | | | | |
| BILLINGTON, P J (HM02309) | | | ● | | | | | | | | | | | | | | | | | | | | | | | | | | | | | | | | | | | | | | | | | | | | | | |
| BODYGUIDE ALTERNATE (HM02619) | | | | | | | | | | | | | | | | | | ● | | ● | | | | | | | | | | | | | | | | | | | | | | | | | | | | | |
| BOHNET, CAROLE (HM02648) | | | | | | | | | | | | | | | | | | ● | | ● | ● | | | | | | | | | | | | | | | | | | | | | | | | | | | | |
| BROADBENT, S (HM03111) | | | ● | | | | | | | | | | | | | | | | | | | | | | | | | | | | | | | | | | | | | | | | | | | | | | |
| BROADBENT, SUSAN (HM03112) | | | ● | | | | | | | | | | | | | | | | | | | | | | | | | | | | | | | | | | | | | | | | | | | | | | |
| BULL, MARGARET (HM03339) | | | | | | | | | | | | | | | | | | ● | | | | | | | | | | | | | | | | | | | | | | | | | | | | | | | |
| BUNGAY, SHERILYN (HM03352) | | | ● | | | | | | | | | | | | | | | | | | | | | | | | | | | | | | | | | | | | | | | | | | | | | | |
| BURNS, L C (HM03417) | | | | | | | ● | | | | | | | | | | | | | | | | | | | | | | | | | | | | | | | | | | | | | | | | | | |
| CARTEY, SARAH (HM03792) | | | | | | | | | | | | | | | | | | ● | | | | | | | | | | | | | | | | | | | | | | | | | | | | | | | |
| CARTLAND, ANN (HM03794) | | | | | | | | | | ● | | | | | | | | | | | | | | | | | | | | | | | | | | | | | | | | | | | | | | | |
| CHANGES (HM03985) | | | | | | | | | | | | | | | | | | ● | | | | | | | | | | | ● | | | | | | | | | | | | | | ● | | | | | | |
| CLAIRVOYANT - MEDIUM - HEALER (HM04514) | | | | | | | | | | | | | | | | | | | | | | | | | | | | | ● | | | | | | | | | | | | | | | | | | | | |
| CLARK, GERALD (HM04557) | | | ● | | | | | | | | | | | | | | | | | | | | | | | | | | | | | | | | | | | | | | | | | | | | | | |
| CLARKE, STEVEN (HM04604) | | | | | | | | | | | | | | | ● | | | | | | | | | | | | | | | | ● | | | | | | | | | | | | | | | | | | |
| CONNOLLY COUNSELLING (HM04998) | | | | | | | | | | | | | | | ● | | | | | | | | | | | | | | | | | | | | | | | | | | | | | | | | | | |
| CORNERWEIGHS (HM05183) | | | | | | | | ● | | | | | | | | | | | | | | | | | | | | | | | | | | | | | | | | | | | ● | | | | | | |
| COYSTEN, T (HM05333) | | | ● | | | | | | | | | | | | | | | | | | | | | | | | | | | | | | | | | | | | | | | | | | | | | | |
| DALLAS, PETER (HM05691) | | | | | | | | | | | | | | | | | | | | | | | | | | ● | | | | | | | ● | | | | | | | | | | | | | | | | |
| DIEBSCHLAG, FRANCESCA (HM06091) | | | | | | | | | | | | | | | ● | | | | | | | | | | | | | | | | | | | | | | | | | | | | | | | | | | |
| DORON, LORRAINE (HM06203) | | | | | | | | | | | | | | | | | | ● | | | | | | | | | | | | | | | | | | | | | | | | | | | | | | | |
| DUNLOP, JOAN (HM06412) | | | | | | | | | | | | | | | ● | | | | | | | | | | | | | | | | | | | | | | | | | | | | | | | | | | |
| DURRANT, NICOLA (HM06437) | | | | | | | | | | | | | | | | | | ● | | | | | | | | | | | | | | | | | | | | | | | | | | | | | | | |
| DYER & ASSOCIATES (HM06444) | | | ● | | | | | | | | | | | | | | | | | | | | | | | | | | | ● | | | | | | | | | | | | | | | | | | | |
| EMINATIONS ACUPUNCTURE CLINIC (HM06805) | | | | | | | | | | | | | | | | | | | | | | | | | | | | | ● | | | | | | | | | | | | | | | | | | | | |

# O - Z Therapies at Practices/Businesses

| Business by County with Reference no. | Orthotics | Osteomyology | Osteopathy | PAM | Paranormal Therapies | Pattern Therapies | Physiotherapy | Phytotherapy | Pilates | Podiatry | Polarity Therapy | Postural Integration | Primal Therapy | Psionic Therapy | Psychotherapy | Pyramid Power |
|---|---|---|---|---|---|---|---|---|---|---|---|---|---|---|---|---|
| FELPHAM NATURAL HEALTH CLINIC (HM07206) | | | | | | | | | | | | | | | | |
| FORSHAW, ROBYN S (HM07567) | | | | | | | | | | | | | | | | |
| FROST, CHARLES (HM07760) | | | | | | | | | | | | | | | | |
| FURNACE GREEN CHIRO CTRE (HM07800) | | | | | | | | | | | | | | | | |
| G & G FOOD SUPPLIES (HM07807) | | | | | | | | | | | | | | | | |
| GADD, A (HM07822) | | | ● | | | | | | | | | | | | | |
| GREEN, GEOFFREY C (HM08455) | | | ● | | | | | | | | | | | | | |
| GREENFIELD, KAREN (HM08486) | | | | | | | | | | | | | | | | |
| GURNEY, CHRISTINE (HM08652) | | | | | | | | | | | | | | | | |
| HARDY, ELIZABETH (HM08980) | | | | | | | | | | | | | | | | |
| HEALTH IS HAPPINESS REFLEX (HM09390) | | | | | | | | | | | | | | | | |
| HEELER CENTRE (HM09498) | | | ● | | | | | | ● | ● | | ● | | | ● | |
| HILDER, MONICA (HM09765) | | | | | | | | | | | | | | | | |
| HOLDEN, ELFRIEDE (HM09930) | | | | | | | | | | | | | | | | |
| HORSHAM OSTEOPATHS (HM10192) | | | ● | | | | | | | | | | | | | |
| HORTON, JONATHAN (HM10195) | | | ● | | | | | | | | | | | | | |
| HUMPHRIES, C (HM10377) | | | ● | | | | | | | | | | | | | |
| I C O M (HM10548) | | | | | | | | | | | | | | | | |
| JONES, NIGEL (HM11182) | | | ● | | | | | | | | | | | | | |
| LARKIN, JILL (HM11976) | | | | | | | | | | | | | | | | |
| LAUNDON, J (HM12005) | | | ● | | | | | | | | | | | | | |
| LITTLEHAMPTON NAT HLTH CTRE (HM12470) | | | ● | | | | | | | ● | | | | | ● | |
| MACHIN, KAREN (HM12839) | | | | | | | | | | | | | | | | |
| MARTIN, LYN (HM13203) | | | | | | | | | | | | | | | | |
| MCCORMICK, KITTY (HM13425) | | | | | | | | | | | | | | | | |
| MID SUSSEX CHIROPRACTIC CLINIC (HM13805) | | | | | | | | | | | | | | | | |
| MILLS, B J (HM13926) | | | ● | | | | | | | | | | | | | |
| NORRIS, MARIA (HM15013) | | | | | | | | | | | | | | | ● | |
| OASIS CLINICS (HM15162) | | | ● | | | | | | | | | | | | | |
| OSTEOPATHY AT ESQUIRE'S (HM15479) | | | ● | | | | | | | | | | | | | |
| PAIN & PARALYSIS SPECIALIST (HM15578) | | | | | | | | | | | | | | | | |
| PALMER, GAYLE (HM15605) | | | ● | | | | | | | | | ● | | | | |
| PALMER, GAYLE (HM15606) | | | ● | | | | | | | | | | | | | |
| PALMER, SIMON (HM15615) | | | ● | | | | | | | | | | | | | |

| Business by County with Reference no. | Pyscho-Synthesis | Reflexology | Reichian Therapy | Reiki | Remedial Massage | Rogerian Therapy | Rolfing | Seichem | Sensitivity Training | Shiatsu | Silva Method | Sound Therapy | Spiritual Healing | Sports Massage | Stress Therapy | Swedish Body Massage |
|---|---|---|---|---|---|---|---|---|---|---|---|---|---|---|---|---|
| FELPHAM NATURAL HEALTH CLINIC (HM07206) | | ● | | | | | | | | | | | ● | | ● | |
| FORSHAW, ROBYN S (HM07567) | | ● | | | | | | | | | | | | | | |
| FROST, CHARLES (HM07760) | | | | | | ● | | | | | | | | | ● | |
| FURNACE GREEN CHIRO CTRE (HM07800) | | | | | | | | | | | | | | | | |
| G & G FOOD SUPPLIES (HM07807) | | | | | | | | | | | | | | | | |
| GADD, A (HM07822) | | | | | | | | | | | | | | | | |
| GREEN, GEOFFREY C (HM08455) | | | | | | | | | | | | | | | | |
| GREENFIELD, KAREN (HM08486) | | ● | | | | | | | | | | | | | | |
| GURNEY, CHRISTINE (HM08652) | | ● | | | | | | | | | | | | | | |
| HARDY, ELIZABETH (HM08980) | | ● | | | | | | | | | | | | | | |
| HEALTH IS HAPPINESS REFLEX (HM09390) | | ● | | | | | | | | | | | | | | |
| HEELER CENTRE (HM09498) | | ● | | ● | | | | | | ● | | | | ● | | |
| HILDER, MONICA (HM09765) | | ● | | | | | | | | | | | | | | |
| HOLDEN, ELFRIEDE (HM09930) | | ● | | | | | | | | | | | | | | |
| HORSHAM OSTEOPATHS (HM10192) | | | | | | | | | | | | | | | | |
| HORTON, JONATHAN (HM10195) | | | | | | | | | | | | | | | | |
| HUMPHRIES, C (HM10377) | | | | | | | | | | | | | | | | |
| I C O M (HM10548) | | | | | | | | | | | | | | | | |
| JONES, NIGEL (HM11182) | | | | | | | | | | | | | | | | |
| LARKIN, JILL (HM11976) | | | | ● | | | | | | | | | | | | |
| LAUNDON, J (HM12005) | | | | | | | | | | | | | | | | |
| LITTLEHAMPTON NAT HLTH CTRE (HM12470) | | ● | | ● | | | | | | ● | | | ● | | ● | |
| MACHIN, KAREN (HM12839) | | ● | | | | | | | | | | | | | | |
| MARTIN, LYN (HM13203) | | ● | | | | | | | | | | | | | | |
| MCCORMICK, KITTY (HM13425) | | ● | | | | | | | | | | | | | | |
| MID SUSSEX CHIROPRACTIC CLINIC (HM13805) | | | | | | | | | | | | | | | | |
| MILLS, B J (HM13926) | | | | | | | | | | | | | | | | |
| NORRIS, MARIA (HM15013) | | | | | | | | | | | | | | | | |
| OASIS CLINICS (HM15162) | | | | | | | | | | | | | | | | |
| OSTEOPATHY AT ESQUIRE'S (HM15479) | | | | | | | | | | | | | | | | |
| PAIN & PARALYSIS SPECIALIST (HM15578) | | | | ● | | | | | | | | | | | ● | |
| PALMER, GAYLE (HM15605) | | | | ● | | | | | | | | | | | ● | |
| PALMER, GAYLE (HM15606) | | | | ● | | | | | | | | | | | ● | |
| PALMER, SIMON (HM15615) | | | | | | | | | | | | | | | | |

| Business by County with Reference no. | T'ai-Chi Ch'uan | Tantra Therapy | Tera-Mai | Thought Field Therapy | Touch Therapy | Transactional Analysis | Tui-na | Ultrasonics | Vibrational Therapy | Visualisation Therapy | Vitamin Therapy | Voice Therapy | X-Ray | Ying & Yang | Yoga | Zen Therapy | Zero Balancing |
|---|---|---|---|---|---|---|---|---|---|---|---|---|---|---|---|---|---|
| FELPHAM NATURAL HEALTH CLINIC (HM07206) | | | | | | | | | | | | | | | | | |
| FORSHAW, ROBYN S (HM07567) | | | | | | | | | | | | | | | | | |
| FROST, CHARLES (HM07760) | | | | | | | | | | ● | | | | | | | |
| FURNACE GREEN CHIRO CTRE (HM07800) | | | | | | | | | | | ● | | | | | | |
| G & G FOOD SUPPLIES (HM07807) | | | | | | | | | | | ● | | | | | | |
| GADD, A (HM07822) | | | | | | | | | | | | | | | | | |
| GREEN, GEOFFREY C (HM08455) | | | | | | | | | | | | | | | | | |
| GREENFIELD, KAREN (HM08486) | | | | | | | | | | | | | | | | | |
| GURNEY, CHRISTINE (HM08652) | | | | | | | | | | | | | | | | | |
| HARDY, ELIZABETH (HM08980) | | | | | | | | | | | | | | | | | |
| HEALTH IS HAPPINESS REFLEX (HM09390) | | | | | | | | | | | | | | | | | |
| HEELER CENTRE (HM09498) | | | | | | | | | | | ● | | | | ● | | |
| HILDER, MONICA (HM09765) | | | | | | | | | | | | | | | | | |
| HOLDEN, ELFRIEDE (HM09930) | | | | | | | | | | | | | | | | | |
| HORSHAM OSTEOPATHS (HM10192) | | | | | | | | | | | | | | | | | |
| HORTON, JONATHAN (HM10195) | | | | | | | | | | | | | | | | | |
| HUMPHRIES, C (HM10377) | | | | | | | | | | | | | | | | | |
| I C O M (HM10548) | | | | | | | | | | | | | | ● | | | |
| JONES, NIGEL (HM11182) | | | | | | | | | | | | | | | | | |
| LARKIN, JILL (HM11976) | | | | | | | | | | | | | | | | | |
| LAUNDON, J (HM12005) | | | | | | | | | | | | | | | | | |
| LITTLEHAMPTON NAT HLTH CTRE (HM12470) | ● | | | | | | | | | ● | | | | ● | ● | | |
| MACHIN, KAREN (HM12839) | | | | | | | | | | | | | | | | | |
| MARTIN, LYN (HM13203) | | | | | | | | | | | | | | | | | |
| MCCORMICK, KITTY (HM13425) | | | | | | | | | | | | | | | | | |
| MID SUSSEX CHIROPRACTIC CLINIC (HM13805) | | | | | | | | | | | ● | | ● | | | | |
| MILLS, B J (HM13926) | | | | | | | | | | | | | | | | | |
| NORRIS, MARIA (HM15013) | | | | | | | | | | | | | | | | | |
| OASIS CLINICS (HM15162) | | | | | | | | | | | | | | | | | |
| OSTEOPATHY AT ESQUIRE'S (HM15479) | | | | | | | | | | | | | | | | | |
| PAIN & PARALYSIS SPECIALIST (HM15578) | | | | | | | | | | | ● | | | | | | |
| PALMER, GAYLE (HM15605) | | | | | | | | | | | ● | | | | | | |
| PALMER, GAYLE (HM15606) | | | | | | | | | | | ● | | | | | | |
| PALMER, SIMON (HM15615) | | | | | | | | | | | | | | | | | |

# O - Z Therapies at Practices/Businesses

| Business by County with Reference no. | Orthotics | Osteomyology | Osteopathy | PAM | Paranormal Therapies | Pattern Therapies | Physiotherapy | Phytotherapy | Pilates | Podiatry | Polarity Therapy | Postural Integration | Primal Therapy | Psionic Therapy | Psychotherapy | Pyramid Power | Pyscho-Synthesis |
|---|---|---|---|---|---|---|---|---|---|---|---|---|---|---|---|---|---|
| PALMER, STEPHEN R (HM15617) | | | ● | | | | | | | | | | | | | | |
| PEARSON, YASMIN (HM15918) | | | | | | | | | | | | | | | | | |
| PICHLER, JOHN (HM16262) | | | ● | | | | | | | | | | | | | | |
| POLLARD, SALLY (HM16410) | | | | | | | | | | | | | | | ● | | |
| PORTLAND PHYSIOTHERAPY CLINIC (HM16451) | | | | | | | ● | | | | | | | | | | |
| POTHECARY, I C (DR) (HM16463) | | | ● | | | | | | | | | | | | | | |
| RICHARDS OSTEOPATHIC CLINIC (HM17246) | | | ● | | | | | | | | | | | | | | |
| RICHARDSON, BRIAN J (HM17269) | ● | | | | | | | | | | | | | | | | |
| ROOM FOR HEALING (HM17585) | | | | | | | | | | | | | | | | | |
| ROSS, PATRICK M (HM17641) | | | ● | | | | | | | | | | | | | | |
| SCHOLEY, PAMELA (HM18024) | | | | | | | | | | | | | | | | | |
| SCOTT, JANE (HM18116) | | | | | | | | | | | | | | | | | |
| SEVENTH HEAVEN (HM18246) | | | | | | | | | | | | | | | | | |
| SILVER GREY CLINIC (HM18540) | | | ● | | | | | | | | | | | | | | |
| SMALLCORN, KAREN A (HM18696) | | | ● | | | | | | | | | | | | | | |
| STOTT-DURHAM, ANDREW (HM19355) | | | | | | | | | | | | | | | | | |
| STURGESS, ELAINE (HM19448) | | | ● | | | | | | | | | | | | | | |
| SWAN, LAURIE C (HM19574) | | | | | | | | | | | | | | | | | |
| TAYLOR, ELIZABETH (HM19758) | | | | | | | | | | | | | | | | | |
| TRANQUILLITY (HM20260) | | | | | | | | | | | | | | | | | |
| TUGNUTT, SALLY (HM20378) | | | | | | | | | | | | | | | | | |
| TURNER, JANET (HM20427) | | | | | | | | | | | | | | | | | |
| TURNER, JULIA (HM20428) | | | ● | | | | | | | | | | | | | | |
| TYRIE, M (HM20475) | | | ● | | | | | | | | | | | | | | |
| URQUHART-PULLEN, MARINA (HM20532) | | | ● | | | | | | | | | | | | | | |
| WARD, SANDRA (HM20913) | | | | | | | | | | | | | | | | | |
| WEST, MARCUS (HM21253) | | | | | | | | | | | | | | | ● | | |
| WILSON, AVIS (HM21646) | | | | | | | | | | | | | | | | | |
| WOOD, J G (HM21798) | | | | | | | | | ● | | | ● | | | | | |
| WORTHING CLINIC OF ACUPUNCTURE (HM21908) | | | | | | | | | | | | | | | ● | | |
| YOUNG, LINDA (HM22077) | | | | | | | | | | | | | | | | | |
| **TYNE AND WEAR** | | | | | | | | | | | | | | | | | |
| ACUPUNCTURE & NAT MED CLINIC (HM00243) | | | ● | | | | | | | | | | | | | | |
| B WIGRAM HEALING & REFLEXOLOGY (HM01455) | | | | | | | | | | | | | | | | | |

| Business by County with Reference no. | Reflexology | Reichian Therapy | Reiki | Remedial Massage | Rogerian Therapy | Rolfing | Seichem | Sensitivity Training | Shiatsu | Silva Method | Sound Therapy | Spiritual Healing | Sports Massage | Stress Therapy | Swedish Body Massage | T'ai-Chi Ch'uan |
|---|---|---|---|---|---|---|---|---|---|---|---|---|---|---|---|---|
| PALMER, STEPHEN R (HM15617) | | | | | | | | | | | | | | | | |
| PEARSON, YASMIN (HM15918) | ● | | | | | | | | | | | | | | | |
| PICHLER, JOHN (HM16262) | | | | | | | | | | | | | | | | |
| POLLARD, SALLY (HM16410) | | | | | | | | | | | | | | | | |
| PORTLAND PHYSIOTHERAPY CLINIC (HM16451) | | | | | | | | | | | | | | | | |
| POTHECARY, I C (DR) (HM16463) | | | | | | | | | | | | | | | | |
| RICHARDS OSTEOPATHIC CLINIC (HM17246) | | | | | | | | | | | | | | | | |
| RICHARDSON, BRIAN J (HM17269) | | | | | | | | | | | | | | | | |
| ROOM FOR HEALING (HM17585) | ● | | ● | | | | | | | | | | | | | |
| ROSS, PATRICK M (HM17641) | | | | | | | | | | | | | | | | |
| SCHOLEY, PAMELA (HM18024) | ● | | | | | | | | | | | | | | | |
| SCOTT, JANE (HM18116) | ● | | | | | | | | | | | | | | | |
| SEVENTH HEAVEN (HM18246) | | | ● | | | | | | | | | | | | | |
| SILVER GREY CLINIC (HM18540) | | | | | | | | | | | | | | | | |
| SMALLCORN, KAREN A (HM18696) | | | | | | | | | | | | | | | | |
| STOTT-DURHAM, ANDREW (HM19355) | | | | | | | | | ● | | | | | | | |
| STURGESS, ELAINE (HM19448) | | | | | | | | | | | | | | | | |
| SWAN, LAURIE C (HM19574) | | | | | | | | | | | | | | ● | | |
| TAYLOR, ELIZABETH (HM19758) | ● | | | | | | | | | | | | | | | |
| TRANQUILLITY (HM20260) | | | ● | | | | ● | | | | | | | ● | | |
| TUGNUTT, SALLY (HM20378) | ● | | | | | | | | | | | | | | | |
| TURNER, JANET (HM20427) | ● | | | | | | | | | | | | | | | |
| TURNER, JULIA (HM20428) | | | | | | | | | | | | | | | | |
| TYRIE, M (HM20475) | | | | | | | | | | | | | | | | |
| URQUHART-PULLEN, MARINA (HM20532) | | | | | | | | | | | | | | | | |
| WARD, SANDRA (HM20913) | ● | | | | | | | | | | | | | | | |
| WEST, MARCUS (HM21253) | | | | | | | | | | | | | | | | |
| WILSON, AVIS (HM21646) | ● | | | | | | | | | | | | | | | |
| WOOD, J G (HM21798) | | | | | | | | | | | | | | ● | | |
| WORTHING CLINIC OF ACUPUNCTURE (HM21908) | | | | | | | | | | | | | | | | |
| YOUNG, LINDA (HM22077) | ● | | | | | | | | | | | | | | | |
| **TYNE AND WEAR** | | | | | | | | | | | | | | | | |
| ACUPUNCTURE & NAT MED CLINIC (HM00243) | | | | | | | | | ● | | | | | | | |
| B WIGRAM HEALING & REFLEXOLOGY (HM01455) | ● | | | | | | | | | | | ● | | | | |

| Business by County with Reference no. | Tantra Therapy | Tera-Mai | Thought Field Therapy | Touch Therapy | Transactional Analysis | Tui-na | Ultrasonics | Vibrational Therapy | Visualisation Therapy | Vitamin Therapy | Voice Therapy | X-Ray | Ying & Yang | Yoga | Zen Therapy | Zero Balancing |
|---|---|---|---|---|---|---|---|---|---|---|---|---|---|---|---|---|
| PALMER, STEPHEN R (HM15617) | | | | | | | | | | | | | | | | |
| PEARSON, YASMIN (HM15918) | | | | | | | | | | | | | | | | |
| PICHLER, JOHN (HM16262) | | | | | | | | | | | | | | | | |
| POLLARD, SALLY (HM16410) | | | | | | | | | | | | | | | | |
| PORTLAND PHYSIOTHERAPY CLINIC (HM16451) | | | | | | | | | | | | | | | | |
| POTHECARY, I C (DR) (HM16463) | | | | | | | | | | | | | | | | |
| RICHARDS OSTEOPATHIC CLINIC (HM17246) | | | | | | | | | | | | | | | | |
| RICHARDSON, BRIAN J (HM17269) | | | | | | | | | | | | | | | | |
| ROOM FOR HEALING (HM17585) | | | | | | | | | | | | | | | | |
| ROSS, PATRICK M (HM17641) | | | | | | | | | | | | | | | | |
| SCHOLEY, PAMELA (HM18024) | | | | | | | | | | | | | | | | |
| SCOTT, JANE (HM18116) | | | | | | | | | | | | | | | | |
| SEVENTH HEAVEN (HM18246) | | | | | | | | | | | | | | | | |
| SILVER GREY CLINIC (HM18540) | | | | | | | | | | | | | | | | |
| SMALLCORN, KAREN A (HM18696) | | | | | | | | | | | | | | | | |
| STOTT-DURHAM, ANDREW (HM19355) | | | | | | | | | | | | | | | | |
| STURGESS, ELAINE (HM19448) | | | | | | | | | | | | | | | | |
| SWAN, LAURIE C (HM19574) | | | | | | | | | | | | | | | | |
| TAYLOR, ELIZABETH (HM19758) | | | | | | | | | | | | | | | | |
| TRANQUILLITY (HM20260) | | ● | | | | | | | ● | | | | | | | |
| TUGNUTT, SALLY (HM20378) | | | | | | | | | | | | | | | | |
| TURNER, JANET (HM20427) | | | | | | | | | | | | | | | | |
| TURNER, JULIA (HM20428) | | | | | | | | | | | | | | | | |
| TYRIE, M (HM20475) | | | | | | | | | | | | | | | | |
| URQUHART-PULLEN, MARINA (HM20532) | | | | | | | | | | | | | | | | |
| WARD, SANDRA (HM20913) | | | | | | | | | | | | | | | | |
| WEST, MARCUS (HM21253) | | | | | | | | | | | | | | | | |
| WILSON, AVIS (HM21646) | | | | | | | | | | | | | | | | |
| WOOD, J G (HM21798) | | | | | | | ● | | | | | | | | | |
| WORTHING CLINIC OF ACUPUNCTURE (HM21908) | | | | | | | | | | | | | | | | |
| YOUNG, LINDA (HM22077) | | | | | | | | | | | | | | | | |
| **TYNE AND WEAR** | | | | | | | | | | | | | | | | |
| ACUPUNCTURE & NAT MED CLINIC (HM00243) | | | | | | | | | | ● | | | | | | |
| B WIGRAM HEALING & REFLEXOLOGY (HM01455) | | | | | | | | | ● | | | | | | | |

# O - Z Therapies at Practices/Businesses

Business by County with Reference no.

| Business by County with Reference no. | Orthotics | Osteomyology | Osteopathy | PAM | Paranormal Therapies | Pattern Therapies | Physiotherapy | Phytotherapy | Pilates | Podiatry | Polarity Therapy | Postural Integration | Primal Therapy | Psionic Therapy | Psychotherapy | Pyramid Power | Pyscho-Synthesis | Reflexology | Reichian Therapy | Reiki | Remedial Massage | Rogerian Therapy | Rolfing | Seichem |
|---|---|---|---|---|---|---|---|---|---|---|---|---|---|---|---|---|---|---|---|---|---|---|---|---|
| BALMORAL PHYSIOTHERAPY (HM01640) | | | | | | | ● | | | | | | | | | | | | | | | | | |
| BANNISTER, M (HM01672) | | | ● | | | | | | | | | | | | | | | | | | | | | |
| BASS, MIKE (HM01850) | | | | | | | | | | | | | | | | | | ● | | | | | | |
| BIANCARDI, J (HM02272) | | | | | | | | | | | | | | | ● | | | | | | | | | |
| BUXTON, PETER (HM03505) | | | ● | | | | | | | | | | | | | | | | | | | | | |
| CARLSON, PATRICIA (HM03699) | | | | | | | | | | | | | | | | | | ● | | | | | | |
| CHIROPODY CLINIC (HM04324) | ● | | | | | | | | | ● | | | | | | | | ● | | | | | | |
| CONNECT PHYSICAL HEALTH CTRE (HM04989) | | | | | | | ● | | ● | ● | | ● | | | | | | ● | | | | | | |
| DENTON, A (HM05998) | | | | | | | | | | | | | | | | | | ● | | | | | | |
| DERWENT CENTRE (HM06020) | | | | | | | | | | | | | | | | | | | | | | | | |
| DYER, RICHARD J (HM06449) | | | ● | | | | | | | | | | | | | | | | | | | | | |
| EARDLEY, D & J (HM06492) | | | | | | | | | | | | | | | | | | ● | | | | | | |
| EIGENWELT, AMIDA (HM06688) | | | | | | | | | | | | | | | ● | | | | | | | | | |
| FARTHING, ANN (HM07136) | | | ● | | | | | | | | | | | | | | | | | | | | | |
| FEEL GOOD AROMATHERAPY (HM07164) | | | | | | | | | | | | | | | ● | | | | | | | | | |
| FOGGIN, SYLVIA (HM07455) | | | | | | | | | | | | | | | | | | ● | | | | | | |
| FOWLER, CHRISTINE (HM07628) | | | | | | | | | | | | | | | | | | | | ● | | | | |
| FRANCIS, A (HM07667) | | | ● | | | | | | | | | | | | | | | | | | | | | |
| GATESHEAD COMPLEMENTARY HEALTH (HM07927) | | | | | | | | | | | | | | | | | | ● | | | | | | |
| GRAHAM, G S (HM08344) | | | | | | | | | | | | | | | ● | | | | | | | | | |
| GRIMES, JUNE (HM08576) | | | | | | | | | | | | | | | | | | ● | | | | | | |
| HANCOCK, S & NESS, A (HM08897) | | | | | | | | | | | | | | | | | | ● | | | | | | |
| HERBAL GARDEN AROMATHERAPY (HM09612) | | | | | | | | ● | | | | | | | | | | | | | | | | |
| HEWITT, STEPHEN J (HM09708) | | | ● | | | | | | | | | | | | | | | | | | | | | |
| HOLISTIC CHIROPRACTOR (HM09951) | | | | | | | | | | | | ● | | | | | | | | | | | | |
| HOWARTH, C D (HM10247) | | | ● | | | | | | | | | | | | | | | | | | | | | |
| HYPNOTHERAPY AND COUNSELLING (HM10514) | | | | | | | | | | | | | | | ● | | | | | | | | | |
| LILBURN, JESSICA (HM12390) | | | | | | | | | | | | | | | | | | ● | | | | | | |
| MOSS, OLGA (HM14266) | | | | | | | | | | | | | | | | | | ● | | | | | | |
| MULLINS, MARJORIE (HM14349) | | | | | | | | | | | | | | | | | | ● | | | | | | |
| NEW LIFE NATURAL HEALTH CARE (HM14820) | | | | | | | | | ● | | | | | | | | | ● | | | | | | |
| NEWCASTLE SPRTS INJ/THRPY CTRE (HM14855) | | | | | | | ● | | | | | | | | | | | | | | ● | | | |
| OSBORNE CLINIC (HM15420) | | | ● | | | | | | ● | | | | | | | | | ● | | | | | | |
| PETCH, MARIAN (HM16070) | | | | | | | | | | | | | | | | | | ● | | | | | | |

| Business by County with Reference no. | Sensitivity Training | Shiatsu | Silva Method | Sound Therapy | Spiritual Healing | Sports Massage | Stress Therapy | Swedish Body Massage | T'ai-Chi Ch'uan | Tantra Therapy | Tera-Mai | Thought Field Therapy | Touch Therapy | Transactional Analysis | Tui-na | Ultrasonics | Vibrational Therapy | Visualisation Therapy | Vitamin Therapy | Voice Therapy | X-Ray | Ying & Yang | Yoga | Zen Therapy | Zero Balancing |
|---|---|---|---|---|---|---|---|---|---|---|---|---|---|---|---|---|---|---|---|---|---|---|---|---|---|
| BALMORAL PHYSIOTHERAPY (HM01640) | | | | | | | | | | | | | | | | | | | | | | | | | |
| BANNISTER, M (HM01672) | | | | | | | | | | | | | | | | | | | | | | | | | |
| BASS, MIKE (HM01850) | | | | | | | | | | | | | | | | | | | | | | | | | |
| BIANCARDI, J (HM02272) | | | | | | | | | | | | | | | | | | | | | | | | | |
| BUXTON, PETER (HM03505) | | | | | | | | | | | | | | | | | | | | | | | | | |
| CARLSON, PATRICIA (HM03699) | | | | | | | | | | | | | | | | | | | | | | | | | |
| CHIROPODY CLINIC (HM04324) | | | | | | | | | | | | | | | | | | | | | | | | | |
| CONNECT PHYSICAL HEALTH CTRE (HM04989) | | | | | | | | | | | | | | | | | | | | | | | | | |
| DENTON, A (HM05998) | | | | | | | | | | | | | | | | | | | | | | | | | |
| DERWENT CENTRE (HM06020) | | | | | ● | | | | | | | | | | | | | | | | | | | | |
| DYER, RICHARD J (HM06449) | | | | | | | | | | | | | | | | | | | | | | | | | |
| EARDLEY, D & J (HM06492) | | | | | | | | | | | | | | | | | | | | | | | | | |
| EIGENWELT, AMIDA (HM06688) | | | | | | | | | | | | | | | | | | | | | | | | | |
| FARTHING, ANN (HM07136) | | | | | | | | | | | | | | | | | | | | | | | | | |
| FEEL GOOD AROMATHERAPY (HM07164) | | | | | | | | | | | | | | | | | | | ● | | | | | | |
| FOGGIN, SYLVIA (HM07455) | | | | | | | | | | | | | | | | | | | | | | | | | |
| FOWLER, CHRISTINE (HM07628) | | | | | | | | | | | | | | | | | | | | | | | | | |
| FRANCIS, A (HM07667) | | | | | | | | | | | | | | | | | | | | | | | | | |
| GATESHEAD COMPLEMENTARY HEALTH (HM07927) | | | | | | | | | | | | | | | | | | | | | | | | | |
| GRAHAM, G S (HM08344) | | | | | | | | | | | | | | | | | | | | | | | | | |
| GRIMES, JUNE (HM08576) | | | | | | | | | | | | | | | | | | | | | | | | | |
| HANCOCK, S & NESS, A (HM08897) | | | | | | | | | | | | | | | | | | | | | | | | | |
| HERBAL GARDEN AROMATHERAPY (HM09612) | | | | | | | ● | | | | | | | | | | | | | | | | | | |
| HEWITT, STEPHEN J (HM09708) | | | | | | | | | | | | | | | | | | | | | | | | | |
| HOLISTIC CHIROPRACTOR (HM09951) | | | | | | | | | ● | | | | | | | | | | | | | | | | |
| HOWARTH, C D (HM10247) | | | | | | | | | | | | | | | | | | | | | | | | | |
| HYPNOTHERAPY AND COUNSELLING (HM10514) | | | | | | | ● | | | | | | | | | | | | | | | | | | |
| LILBURN, JESSICA (HM12390) | | | | | | | | | | | | | | | | | | | | | | | | | |
| MOSS, OLGA (HM14266) | | | | | | | | | | | | | | | | | | | | | | | | | |
| MULLINS, MARJORIE (HM14349) | | | | | | | | | | | | | | | | | | | | | | | | | |
| NEW LIFE NATURAL HEALTH CARE (HM14820) | | | | | | | | | | | | | | | | | | | | | | | | | |
| NEWCASTLE SPRTS INJ/THRPY CTRE (HM14855) | | | | | | | | | | | | | | | | | | | | | | | | | |
| OSBORNE CLINIC (HM15420) | | | | | | | ● | | | | | | | | | ● | | | | | | | | | |
| PETCH, MARIAN (HM16070) | | | | | | | | | | | | | | | | | | | | | | | | | |

# O - Z Therapies at Practices/Businesses

Business by County with Reference no.

| Business by County with Reference no. | Orthotics | Osteomyology | Osteopathy | PAM | Paranormal Therapies | Pattern Therapies | Physiotherapy | Phytotherapy | Pilates | Podiatry | Polarity Therapy | Postural Integration | Primal Therapy | Psionic Therapy | Psychotherapy | Pyramid Power | Pyscho-Synthesis | Reflexology | Reichian Therapy | Reiki | Remedial Massage | Rogerian Therapy | Rolfing | Seichem |
|---|---|---|---|---|---|---|---|---|---|---|---|---|---|---|---|---|---|---|---|---|---|---|---|---|
| RAINBOW, RICHARD S (HM16887) |  |  |  |  |  |  |  |  |  |  |  |  |  |  | ● |  |  |  |  |  |  |  |  |  |
| RICHARDSON, DEBORAH (HM17276) |  |  |  |  |  |  |  |  |  | ● |  |  |  |  |  |  |  |  |  |  |  |  |  |  |
| SCHOLL FOOTWEAR CENTRE (HM18077) |  |  |  |  |  |  |  |  |  | ● |  |  |  |  |  |  |  |  |  |  |  |  |  |  |
| SMITH, R (HM18796) |  |  | ● |  |  |  |  |  |  |  |  |  |  |  |  |  |  |  |  |  |  |  |  |  |
| SMITH, ROY (HM18800) |  |  | ● |  |  |  |  |  |  |  |  |  |  |  |  |  |  |  |  |  |  |  |  |  |
| STAINSBY, TRICIA S (HM19115) |  |  | ● |  |  |  |  |  |  |  |  |  |  |  |  |  |  |  |  |  |  |  |  |  |
| STEVENSON, G (HM19245) |  |  | ● |  |  |  |  |  |  |  |  |  |  |  |  |  |  |  |  |  |  |  |  |  |
| THERAPEUTIC MASSAGE (HM19881) |  |  | ● |  |  |  |  |  |  |  |  |  |  |  |  |  |  |  |  |  |  |  |  |  |
| WALLSEND CLINIC (HM20846) |  |  | ● |  |  |  |  |  |  |  |  |  |  |  |  |  |  |  |  |  |  |  |  |  |
| WESTOE PRACTICE (HM21277) |  |  |  |  |  |  |  |  |  | ● |  |  |  |  |  |  |  |  |  |  |  |  |  |  |
| WHITLEY BAY OSTEOPATHIC CENTRE (HM21407) |  |  | ● |  |  |  |  |  |  |  |  |  |  |  |  |  |  |  |  |  |  |  |  |  |
| **WARWICKSHIRE** |  |  |  |  |  |  |  |  |  |  |  |  |  |  |  |  |  |  |  |  |  |  |  |  |
| ACUPUNCTURE CLINIC (HM00279) |  |  |  |  |  |  |  |  |  |  |  |  |  |  |  |  |  |  |  |  |  |  |  |  |
| AROMATHERAPY MASSAGE/REFLEX (HM01120) |  |  |  |  |  |  |  |  |  |  |  |  |  |  |  |  |  | ● |  |  |  |  |  |  |
| BARRATT'S HOMEOPATHY (HM01780) |  |  |  |  |  |  |  | ● |  |  |  |  |  |  |  |  |  |  |  |  |  |  |  |  |
| BIRTWELL, ANDREW (HM02400) |  |  |  |  |  |  |  |  |  |  |  |  |  |  | ● |  |  |  |  |  |  | ● |  |  |
| BRIEF COUNS & PSYCHOTHERAPY SV (HM03020) |  |  |  |  |  |  |  |  |  |  |  |  |  |  | ● |  |  |  |  |  |  | ● |  |  |
| BUCKLE, WENDY-ANNE (HM03315) |  |  |  |  |  |  |  |  |  |  |  |  |  |  |  |  |  | ● |  |  |  |  |  |  |
| CHURCH LAWFORD CHIRO CLINIC (HM04463) |  |  |  |  |  |  |  |  |  |  |  | ● |  |  |  |  |  |  |  | ● |  |  |  |  |
| CLARKE, ROSEMARY (HM04602) |  |  |  |  |  |  |  |  |  |  |  |  |  |  | ● |  |  |  |  |  |  |  |  |  |
| CLIFTON OSTEOPATHIC PRACTICE (HM04669) |  |  | ● |  |  |  |  |  |  |  |  |  |  |  |  |  |  |  |  |  |  |  |  |  |
| COLLINS & ASSOCIATES (HM04867) |  |  | ● |  |  |  |  |  |  |  |  |  |  |  |  |  |  |  |  |  |  |  |  |  |
| CREATIVE HEALTH CENTRE (HM05397) |  |  |  |  |  |  |  |  |  |  |  |  |  |  | ● |  |  |  |  |  |  |  |  |  |
| DAVID HOPE PERSONAL DEV (HM05775) |  |  |  |  |  |  |  |  |  |  |  |  |  |  | ● |  |  |  |  |  |  |  |  |  |
| DEWDNEY, JOSEPHINE (HM06047) |  |  |  |  |  |  |  |  |  |  |  |  |  |  |  |  |  | ● |  |  |  |  |  |  |
| FIGHT (HM07282) |  |  | ● |  |  |  |  |  |  | ● |  |  |  |  |  |  |  |  |  |  |  |  | ● |  |
| FRANCIS, JAKKI (HM07672) |  |  |  |  |  |  |  |  |  |  |  |  |  |  |  |  |  | ● |  |  |  |  |  |  |
| GREIG, E (HM08527) |  |  |  |  |  |  |  |  |  |  |  |  |  |  |  |  |  | ● |  |  |  |  |  |  |
| HAYES, CAROLE (HM09258) |  |  |  |  |  |  |  |  |  |  |  |  |  |  |  |  |  | ● |  |  |  |  |  |  |
| HEART OF ENGLAND SHIATSU (HM09442) |  |  |  |  |  |  |  |  |  |  |  |  |  |  |  |  |  |  |  |  |  |  |  |  |
| HEARTLANDS (HM09445) |  |  |  |  |  |  |  |  |  |  |  |  |  |  |  |  |  |  |  | ● |  |  |  | ● |
| HOLYCOMBE (HM10060) |  |  |  |  |  |  |  |  |  |  |  |  |  |  | ● |  |  |  |  | ● |  |  |  |  |
| HOUGHTON, REBECCA (HM10213) |  |  | ● |  |  |  |  |  |  |  |  |  |  |  |  |  |  |  |  |  |  |  |  |  |
| JAN LLOYD AROMATHERAPY (HM10913) |  |  |  |  |  |  |  |  |  |  |  |  |  |  |  |  |  |  |  | ● |  |  |  |  |

| Business by County with Reference no. | Sensitivity Training | Shiatsu | Silva Method | Sound Therapy | Spiritual Healing | Sports Massage | Stress Therapy | Swedish Body Massage | T'ai-Chi Ch'uan | Tantra Therapy | Tera-Mai | Thought Field Therapy | Touch Therapy | Transactional Analysis | Tui-na | Ultrasonics | Vibrational Therapy | Visualisation Therapy | Vitamin Therapy | Voice Therapy | X-Ray | Ying & Yang | Yoga | Zen Therapy | Zero Balancing |
|---|---|---|---|---|---|---|---|---|---|---|---|---|---|---|---|---|---|---|---|---|---|---|---|---|---|
| RAINBOW, RICHARD S (HM16887) |  |  |  |  |  |  | ● |  |  |  |  |  |  |  |  |  |  | ● |  |  |  |  |  |  |  |
| RICHARDSON, DEBORAH (HM17276) |  |  |  |  |  |  |  |  |  |  |  |  |  |  |  |  |  |  |  |  |  |  |  |  |  |
| SCHOLL FOOTWEAR CENTRE (HM18077) |  |  |  |  |  |  |  |  |  |  |  |  |  |  |  |  |  |  |  |  |  |  |  |  |  |
| SMITH, R (HM18796) |  |  |  |  |  |  |  |  |  |  |  |  |  |  |  |  |  |  |  |  |  |  |  |  |  |
| SMITH, ROY (HM18800) |  |  |  |  |  |  |  |  |  |  |  |  |  |  |  |  |  |  |  |  |  |  |  |  |  |
| STAINSBY, TRICIA S (HM19115) |  |  |  |  |  |  |  |  |  |  |  |  |  |  |  |  |  |  |  |  |  |  |  |  |  |
| STEVENSON, G (HM19245) |  |  |  |  |  |  |  |  |  |  |  |  |  |  |  |  |  |  |  |  |  |  |  |  |  |
| THERAPEUTIC MASSAGE (HM19881) |  |  |  |  |  |  |  |  |  |  |  |  |  |  |  |  |  |  |  |  |  |  |  |  |  |
| WALLSEND CLINIC (HM20846) |  |  |  |  |  |  |  |  |  |  |  |  |  |  |  |  |  |  |  |  |  |  |  |  |  |
| WESTOE PRACTICE (HM21277) |  |  |  |  |  |  |  |  |  |  |  |  |  |  |  |  |  |  |  |  |  |  |  |  |  |
| WHITLEY BAY OSTEOPATHIC CENTRE (HM21407) |  |  |  |  |  |  |  |  |  |  |  |  |  |  |  |  |  |  |  |  |  |  |  |  |  |
| **WARWICKSHIRE** |  |  |  |  |  |  |  |  |  |  |  |  |  |  |  |  |  |  |  |  |  |  |  |  |  |
| ACUPUNCTURE CLINIC (HM00279) |  | ● |  |  |  |  |  |  |  |  |  |  |  |  |  |  |  |  |  |  |  |  |  |  |  |
| AROMATHERAPY MASSAGE/REFLEX (HM01120) |  |  |  |  |  |  |  |  |  |  |  |  |  |  |  |  |  |  |  |  |  |  |  |  |  |
| BARRATT'S HOMEOPATHY (HM01780) |  |  |  |  |  |  |  |  |  |  |  |  |  |  |  |  |  |  | ● |  |  |  |  |  |  |
| BIRTWELL, ANDREW (HM02400) |  |  |  |  |  |  | ● |  |  |  |  |  |  |  |  |  |  |  |  |  |  |  |  |  |  |
| BRIEF COUNS & PSYCHOTHERAPY SV (HM03020) |  |  |  |  |  |  | ● |  |  |  |  |  |  |  |  |  |  |  |  |  |  |  |  |  |  |
| BUCKLE, WENDY-ANNE (HM03315) |  |  |  |  |  |  |  |  |  |  |  |  |  |  |  |  |  |  |  |  |  |  |  |  |  |
| CHURCH LAWFORD CHIRO CLINIC (HM04463) |  |  |  |  |  |  |  |  |  |  |  |  |  |  |  |  |  |  |  |  |  |  |  |  |  |
| CLARKE, ROSEMARY (HM04602) |  |  |  |  |  |  |  |  |  |  |  |  |  |  |  |  |  |  |  |  |  |  |  |  |  |
| CLIFTON OSTEOPATHIC PRACTICE (HM04669) |  |  |  |  |  |  |  |  |  |  |  |  |  |  |  |  |  |  |  |  |  |  |  |  |  |
| COLLINS & ASSOCIATES (HM04867) |  |  |  |  |  |  |  |  |  |  |  |  |  |  |  |  |  |  |  |  |  |  |  |  |  |
| CREATIVE HEALTH CENTRE (HM05397) |  | ● |  |  |  |  |  |  |  |  |  |  |  |  |  |  |  |  |  |  |  |  | ● |  |  |
| DAVID HOPE PERSONAL DEV (HM05775) |  |  |  |  |  |  |  |  |  |  |  |  |  |  |  |  |  |  |  |  |  |  |  |  |  |
| DEWDNEY, JOSEPHINE (HM06047) |  |  |  |  |  |  |  |  |  |  |  |  |  |  |  |  |  |  |  |  |  |  |  |  |  |
| FIGHT (HM07282) |  | ● |  |  |  |  |  |  |  |  |  |  |  |  |  |  |  |  | ● |  |  |  |  |  |  |
| FRANCIS, JAKKI (HM07672) |  |  |  |  |  |  |  |  |  |  |  |  |  |  |  |  |  |  |  |  |  |  |  |  |  |
| GREIG, E (HM08527) |  |  |  |  |  |  | ● |  |  |  |  |  |  |  |  |  |  | ● |  |  |  |  |  |  |  |
| HAYES, CAROLE (HM09258) |  |  |  |  |  |  |  |  |  |  |  |  |  |  |  |  |  |  |  |  |  |  |  |  |  |
| HEART OF ENGLAND SHIATSU (HM09442) |  | ● |  |  |  |  |  |  |  |  |  |  |  |  |  |  |  |  |  |  |  |  | ● |  |  |
| HEARTLANDS (HM09445) |  | ● | ● |  |  |  | ● |  |  |  |  |  |  |  |  |  |  | ● | ● |  |  | ● | ● |  |  |
| HOLYCOMBE (HM10060) |  | ● |  |  | ● |  | ● |  |  |  |  |  |  |  |  |  |  |  |  |  |  |  |  |  |  |
| HOUGHTON, REBECCA (HM10213) |  |  |  |  |  |  |  |  |  |  |  |  |  |  |  |  |  |  |  |  |  |  |  |  |  |
| JAN LLOYD AROMATHERAPY (HM10913) |  |  |  |  |  |  |  |  |  |  |  |  |  |  |  |  |  |  |  |  |  |  |  |  |  |

# O - Z Therapies at Practices/Businesses

| Business by County with Reference no. | Orthotics | Osteomyology | Osteopathy | PAM | Paranormal Therapies | Pattern Therapies | Physiotherapy | Phytotherapy | Pilates | Podiatry | Polarity Therapy | Postural Integration | Primal Therapy | Psionic Therapy | Psychotherapy | Pyramid Power | Pyscho-Synthesis | Reflexology | Reichian Therapy | Reiki | Remedial Massage | Rogerian Therapy | Rolfing | Seichem | Sensitivity Training | Shiatsu | Silva Method | Sound Therapy | Spiritual Healing | Sports Massage | Stress Therapy | Swedish Body Massage | T'ai-Chi Ch'uan | Tantra Therapy | Tera-Mai | Thought Field Therapy | Touch Therapy | Transactional Analysis | Tui-na | Ultrasonics | Vibrational Therapy | Visualisation Therapy | Vitamin Therapy | Voice Therapy | X-Ray | Ying & Yang | Yoga | Zen Therapy | Zero Balancing |
|---|---|---|---|---|---|---|---|---|---|---|---|---|---|---|---|---|---|---|---|---|---|---|---|---|---|---|---|---|---|---|---|---|---|---|---|---|---|---|---|---|---|---|---|---|---|---|---|---|---|
| KITCHEN, H J (DR)/KITCHEN, J A (HM11728) | | | ● | | | | | | | | | | | | | | | | | | | | | | | | | | | | | | | | | | | | | | | | | | | | | | |
| LAKHANI, B V (HM11878) | | | ● | | | | | | | | | | | | | | | | | | | | | | | | | | | | | | | | | | | | | | | | | | | | | | |
| LAVENDER HOUSE (HM12022) | | | | | | | | | | | | | | | | | | | | | | | | | | ● | | | | | | | | | | | | | | | | | | | | | | | |
| MACWHINNIE, IAN (HM12882) | | | | | | | | | | | | | | | | | | | | | | | | | | ● | | | | | | | | | | | | | | | | | | | | | | | |
| MCCREA, SUE (HM13430) | | | | | | | | | | | | | | | | | | ● | | | | | | | | | | | | | | | | | | | | | | | | | | | | | | | |
| MCDERMOTT, T P (HM13450) | | | | | | | | | | | | | | | ● | | | | | | | | | | | | | | | | | | | | | | | | | | | | | | | | | | |
| MULLALLY, K (HM14337) | | | ● | | | | | | | | | | | | | | | | | | | | | | | | | | | | | | | | | | | | | | | | | | | | | | |
| MYERS, MARION (HM14437) | | | | | | | | | | | | | | | ● | | | | | | | | | | | | | | | | | | | | | | | | | | | | | | | | | | |
| NATURAL HEALTH CENTRE (HM14567) | | | ● | | | | | | | | | | | | | | | ● | | ● | | | | ● | | | | | | ● | ● | | | | | | | | | | | | | | | | | | |
| NEWEY, RACHEL (HM14862) | | | | | | | | | | | | | | | | | | | | ● | | | | | | | | | | | | | | | | | | | | | | | | | | | | | |
| NUNEATON CHIROPRACTIC CLINIC (HM15104) | | | | | | | | | | | | | | | | | | | | ● | | | | | | | | | | | | | | | | | | | | | | | | | | | | | |
| OVERTON, PETER J (HM15514) | | | ● | | | | | | | | | | | | | | | | | | | | | | | | | | | | | | | | | | | | | | | | | | | | | | |
| PETERS, EVERARD (HM16085) | | | ● | | | | | | | | | | | | | | | | | | | | | | | | | | | | | | | | | | | | | | | | | | | | | | |
| PREISLER, TONI TYE (HM16534) | | | | | | | | | | | | | | | ● | | | | | | | | | | | | | | | | | | | | | | | | | | | | | | | | | | |
| REDFERN, JOY (HM17021) | | | | | | | | | | | | | | | | | | ● | | | | | | | | | | | | | | | | | | | | | | | | | | | | | | | |
| REFLEXOLOGY CLINIC (HM17091) | | | | | | | | | | | | | | | | | | ● | | | | | | | | | | | | | | | | | | | | | | | | | | | | | | | |
| ROGERS, REBECCA (HM17553) | | | | | | | | | | | | | | | | | | ● | | | | | | | | | | | | | | | | | | | | | | | | | | | | | | | |
| SAVAGE, GERALD (HM17966) | | | | | | | | ● | | | | | | | | | | | | | | | | | | | | | | | ● | | | | | | | ● | | | | | | | | | | | |
| SHAWE AVENUE OSTEO PRACTICE (HM18351) | | | ● | | | | | | | | | | | | | | | | | | | | ● | | | | | | | | | | | | | | | | | | | | ● | | | | | | |
| SHERIDAN & AST (HM18429) | | | ● | | | | | | | | | | | | | | | | | | | | | | | | | | | | | | | | | | | | | | | | | | | | | | |
| SHIATSU SOCIETY (HM18464) | | | | | | | | | | | | | | | | | | | | | | | | | | ● | | | | | | | | | | | | | | | | | | | | | | | |
| SMALLWOOD, P (HM18698) | ● | | | | | | | | | ● | | | | | | | | | | | | | | | | | | | | | | | | | | | | | | | | | | | | | | | |
| STRATFORD ACU & HOLISTIC HLTH (HM19369) | | | | | | | | | | | | | | | | | | ● | | ● | | | | | | | | | | | | | | | | | | | | | | | | | | | | | |
| STRATFORD PHYSIO CLINIC (HM19370) | | | | | | | ● | | | | | | | | | | | | | | | | | | | | | | | | | | | | | | | | | | | | | | | | | | |
| STUDLEY PHYSIOTHERAPY CENTRE (HM19442) | | | | | | | ● | | ● | | | ● | | | | | | | | | | | | | | | | | | | | | | | | | | | | ● | | | | | | | | | |
| TE VELDE, JOHANNA (HM19804) | | | | | | | | | | | | | | | ● | | | | | | | | | | | | | | | | | | | | | | | | | | | | | | | | | | |
| TERYLENA REFLEXOLOGY (HM19850) | | | | | | | | | | | | | | | | | | ● | | | | | | | | | | | | | | | | | | | | | | | | | | | | | | | |
| TRADITIONAL ACUPUNCTURE GROUP (HM20221) | | | | | | | | | | | | | | | | | | ● | | | | | | | | | | | | | | | | | | | | | | | | | | | | | | | |
| WARWICK OSTEOPATHIC PRACTICE (HM20966) | | | ● | | | | | | | | | | | | | | | | | | | | | | | | | | | | | | | | | | | | | | | | | | | | | | |
| WREN, PAULINE (HM21922) | | | | | | | | | | | | | | | ● | | | | | ● | | ● | | | | | | | ● | | ● | | | | | | | | | | | ● | | | | | | | |
| **WILTSHIRE** | | | | | | | | | | | | | | | | | | | | | | | | | | | | | | | | | | | | | | | | | | | | | | | | | |
| ASTBURY, PENNIE (HM01297) | | | | | | | | | | | | | | | | | | ● | | | | | | | | | | | | | | | | | | | | | | | | | | | | | | | |
| ASTILL-SMITH, A (HM01299) | | | ● | | | | | | | | | | | | | | | | | | | | | | | | | | | | | | | | | | | | | | | | | | | | | | |
| BANKS, RONALD (HM01668) | | | | | | | | | | | | | | | ● | | | | | | | | | | | | | | | | | | | | | | | | | | | | | | | | | | |

# O - Z Therapies at Practices/Businesses

Business by County with Reference no.

| Business by County with Reference no. | Orthotics | Osteomyology | Osteopathy | PAM | Paranormal Therapies | Pattern Therapies | Physiotherapy | Phytotherapy | Pilates | Podiatry | Polarity Therapy | Postural Integration | Primal Therapy | Psionic Therapy | Psychotherapy | Pyramid Power | Pyscho-Synthesis |
|---|---|---|---|---|---|---|---|---|---|---|---|---|---|---|---|---|---|
| BARNES, JONATHAN P (HM01749) | | | ● | | | | | | | | | | | | | | |
| BLUNSDON ABBEY PHYSIOTHERAPY (HM02533) | | | | | | | ● | | | ● | | | | | | | |
| BRUNSKILL, DAVID (HM03279) | | | ● | | | | | | | | | | | | | | |
| BURNETT, KIM (HM03402) | | | ● | | | | | | | | | | | | | | |
| CRICKLADE ROAD PRACTICE (HM05439) | | | ● | | | | | | | | | | | | | | |
| DECLERCQ, LAURENCE (HM05954) | | | ● | | | | | | | | | | | | | | |
| DIRECT HEALING (HM06114) | | | | | | | | | | | | | | | | | |
| EASE MANAGEMENT CENTRE (HM06506) | | | | | | | | | | | | | | | ● | | |
| ENGLISH, JOHN M (DR) (HM06834) | | | | | | | | | | | | | | | | | |
| HARRISON, SUSAN (HM09109) | | | | | | | | | | | | | | | | | |
| HEALTH HYDRO (HM09389) | | | ● | | | | | | | | | ● | | | | | |
| HYPNOTHERAPY CENTRE (HM10529) | | | | | | | | | | | | | | | ● | | |
| KERLEY, JEAN (HM11543) | | | | | | | | | | | | | | | ● | | |
| LEIGHTON REFLEXOLOGY CLINIC (HM12196) | | | | | | | | | | | | | | | | | |
| LIFE-ENERGIES (HM12352) | | | | | | | | | | | | | | | | | |
| LYON, P (HM12783) | | | | | | | | | | | | ● | | | | | |
| MAGNO PULSE (HM12919) | | | | | | | | | | | ● | | | | | | |
| MARLBOROUGH NATURAL HLTH CTRE (HM13123) | | | | | | | | | | | | | | | ● | | |
| MATHER, PAULINE (HM13280) | | | ● | | | | | | ● | | | | | | | | |
| MICHAEL, DAVID (HM13793) | | | | | | | | | | | | | | | ● | | |
| MULTI-THERAPY CENTRE (HM14352) | | | | | | | | | | | | | | | | | |
| NATURAL THERAPY CENTRE (HM14639) | | | | | | | | ● | | | | ● | | | | | |
| NEWTON, KAREN (HM14900) | | | | | | | | | | | | | | | | | |
| OATS, A J (HM15167) | | | ● | | | | | | | | | | | | | | |
| OSTEOPATHS (HM15475) | | | ● | | | | | | | | | | | | | | |
| PALMER, LORRAINE (HM15609) | | | | | | | | | | | | | | | | | |
| PETER & CAROLINE (HM16071) | | | | | | | | | | | | | | | | | |
| PETRAMAN, FRANCOISE (HM16092) | | | | | | | | | | | | | | | | | |
| PETTIFER, JUSTINA (HM16095) | | | | | | | | | | | | | | | ● | | |
| PHYSIOTHERAPY CLINIC (HM16247) | | | | | | | ● | | | | | | | | | | |
| RIGBY, T L (HM17333) | | | ● | | | | | | | | | | | | | | |
| SARUM PHYSIOTHERAPY CENTRE (HM17947) | | | | | | | ● | | | | | | | | | | |
| SHAFTSBURY PRACTICE (HM18266) | | | ● | | | | | | | ● | | | | | | | |
| SPIRITUAL HEALER (HM19026) | | | | | | | | | | | | | | | | | |

| Business by County with Reference no. | Reflexology | Reichian Therapy | Reiki | Remedial Massage | Rogerian Therapy | Rolfing | Seichem | Sensitivity Training | Shiatsu | Silva Method | Sound Therapy | Spiritual Healing | Sports Massage | Stress Therapy | Swedish Body Massage |
|---|---|---|---|---|---|---|---|---|---|---|---|---|---|---|---|
| BARNES, JONATHAN P (HM01749) | | | | | | | | | | | | | | | |
| BLUNSDON ABBEY PHYSIOTHERAPY (HM02533) | | | | | | | | | | | | | | | |
| BRUNSKILL, DAVID (HM03279) | | | | | | | | | | | | | | | |
| BURNETT, KIM (HM03402) | | | | | | | | | | | | | | | |
| CRICKLADE ROAD PRACTICE (HM05439) | | | | | | | | | | | | | | | |
| DECLERCQ, LAURENCE (HM05954) | | | | | | | | | | | | | | | |
| DIRECT HEALING (HM06114) | | | ● | | | | | | | | | | | | |
| EASE MANAGEMENT CENTRE (HM06506) | | | | | ● | | | | | | | | | ● | |
| ENGLISH, JOHN M (DR) (HM06834) | | | | | | | | | | | | | | | |
| HARRISON, SUSAN (HM09109) | ● | | | | | | | | | | | | | | |
| HEALTH HYDRO (HM09389) | ● | | | | | | | | | | | | | | |
| HYPNOTHERAPY CENTRE (HM10529) | | | | | | | | | | | | | | ● | |
| KERLEY, JEAN (HM11543) | | | | | | | | | | | | | | | |
| LEIGHTON REFLEXOLOGY CLINIC (HM12196) | ● | | ● | | | | | | | | | | | ● | |
| LIFE-ENERGIES (HM12352) | ● | | | | | | | | | | | | | ● | |
| LYON, P (HM12783) | | | | | | | | | | | | | | | |
| MAGNO PULSE (HM12919) | | | | | | | | | | | | | | | |
| MARLBOROUGH NATURAL HLTH CTRE (HM13123) | | | | | | | | | ● | | | | | | |
| MATHER, PAULINE (HM13280) | | | | | | | | | | | | | | ● | |
| MICHAEL, DAVID (HM13793) | | | | | | | | | | | | | | | |
| MULTI-THERAPY CENTRE (HM14352) | ● | | ● | | | | | | | | | | | | |
| NATURAL THERAPY CENTRE (HM14639) | ● | | ● | | | | | | | | | ● | | ● | |
| NEWTON, KAREN (HM14900) | ● | | | | | | | | | | | | | | |
| OATS, A J (HM15167) | | | | | | | | | | | | | | | |
| OSTEOPATHS (HM15475) | | | | | | | | | | | | | | | |
| PALMER, LORRAINE (HM15609) | ● | | | | | | | | | | | | | | |
| PETER & CAROLINE (HM16071) | | | | | | | | | | | | ● | | | |
| PETRAMAN, FRANCOISE (HM16092) | ● | | | | | | | | | | | | | | |
| PETTIFER, JUSTINA (HM16095) | | | ● | | | | | | ● | | | | | ● | |
| PHYSIOTHERAPY CLINIC (HM16247) | | | | | | | | | | | | | | | |
| RIGBY, T L (HM17333) | | | | | | | | | | | | | | | |
| SARUM PHYSIOTHERAPY CENTRE (HM17947) | | | | | | | | | | | | | | | |
| SHAFTSBURY PRACTICE (HM18266) | ● | | | | | | | | | | | | | | |
| SPIRITUAL HEALER (HM19026) | | | | | | | | | | | | ● | | | |

| Business by County with Reference no. | T'ai-Chi Ch'uan | Tantra Therapy | Tera-Mai | Thought Field Therapy | Touch Therapy | Transactional Analysis | Tui-na | Ultrasonics | Vibrational Therapy | Visualisation Therapy | Vitamin Therapy | Voice Therapy | X-Ray | Ying & Yang | Yoga | Zen Therapy | Zero Balancing |
|---|---|---|---|---|---|---|---|---|---|---|---|---|---|---|---|---|---|
| BARNES, JONATHAN P (HM01749) | | | | | | | | | | | | | | | | | |
| BLUNSDON ABBEY PHYSIOTHERAPY (HM02533) | | | | | | | | | | | | | | | | | |
| BRUNSKILL, DAVID (HM03279) | | | | | | | | | | | | | | | | | |
| BURNETT, KIM (HM03402) | | | | | | | | | | | | | | | | | |
| CRICKLADE ROAD PRACTICE (HM05439) | | | | | | | | | | | | | | | | | |
| DECLERCQ, LAURENCE (HM05954) | | | | | | | | | | | | | | | | | |
| DIRECT HEALING (HM06114) | | | | | | | | | | | | | | | | | |
| EASE MANAGEMENT CENTRE (HM06506) | | | | | | ● | | | | | | | | | | | |
| ENGLISH, JOHN M (DR) (HM06834) | | | | | | | | | | ● | | | | | | | |
| HARRISON, SUSAN (HM09109) | | | | | | | | | | | | | | | | | |
| HEALTH HYDRO (HM09389) | | | | | | | | | | | | | | | | | |
| HYPNOTHERAPY CENTRE (HM10529) | | | | | | | | | | ● | | | | | | | |
| KERLEY, JEAN (HM11543) | | | | | | | | | | | | | | | | | |
| LEIGHTON REFLEXOLOGY CLINIC (HM12196) | | | | | ● | | | | | | | | | ● | | | |
| LIFE-ENERGIES (HM12352) | | | | | | | | | | | ● | | | | ● | | |
| LYON, P (HM12783) | | | | | | | | | | | | | | | | | |
| MAGNO PULSE (HM12919) | | | | | | | | | | | | | | | | | |
| MARLBOROUGH NATURAL HLTH CTRE (HM13123) | | | | | | | | | | | | | | | | | |
| MATHER, PAULINE (HM13280) | | | | | | | | | | | ● | | | | | | |
| MICHAEL, DAVID (HM13793) | | | | | | | | | | | | | | | | | |
| MULTI-THERAPY CENTRE (HM14352) | ● | | | | | | | | | | | | | | | | |
| NATURAL THERAPY CENTRE (HM14639) | | | | | ● | | | | | ● | | | | | | | |
| NEWTON, KAREN (HM14900) | | | | | | | | | | | | | | | | | |
| OATS, A J (HM15167) | | | | | | | | | | | | | | | | | |
| OSTEOPATHS (HM15475) | | | | | | | | | | | | | | | | | |
| PALMER, LORRAINE (HM15609) | | | | | | | | | | | | | | | | | |
| PETER & CAROLINE (HM16071) | | | | | | | | | ● | ● | | | | | | | |
| PETRAMAN, FRANCOISE (HM16092) | | | | | | | | | | | | | | | | | |
| PETTIFER, JUSTINA (HM16095) | | | | | | | | | | | | | | | | | |
| PHYSIOTHERAPY CLINIC (HM16247) | | | | | | | | | | | | | | | | | |
| RIGBY, T L (HM17333) | | | | | | | | | | | | | | | | | |
| SARUM PHYSIOTHERAPY CENTRE (HM17947) | | | | | | | | | | | | | | | | | |
| SHAFTSBURY PRACTICE (HM18266) | | | | | | | | | | | | | | | | | |
| SPIRITUAL HEALER (HM19026) | | | | | | | | | | | | | | | | | |

# O - Z Therapies at Practices/Businesses

| Business by County with Reference no. | Orthotics | Osteomyology | Osteopathy | PAM | Paranormal Therapies | Pattern Therapies | Physiotherapy | Phytotherapy | Pilates | Podiatry | Polarity Therapy | Postural Integration | Primal Therapy | Psionic Therapy | Psychotherapy | Pyramid Power | Pyscho-Synthesis | Reflexology | Reichian Therapy | Reiki | Remedial Massage | Rogerian Therapy | Rolfing | Seichem | Sensitivity Training | Shiatsu | Silva Method | Sound Therapy | Spiritual Healing | Sports Massage | Stress Therapy | Swedish Body Massage | T'ai-Chi Ch'uan | Tantra Therapy | Tera-Mai | Thought Field Therapy | Touch Therapy | Transactional Analysis | Tui-na | Ultrasonics | Vibrational Therapy | Visualisation Therapy | Vitamin Therapy | Voice Therapy | X-Ray | Ying & Yang | Yoga | Zen Therapy | Zero Balancing |
|---|---|---|---|---|---|---|---|---|---|---|---|---|---|---|---|---|---|---|---|---|---|---|---|---|---|---|---|---|---|---|---|---|---|---|---|---|---|---|---|---|---|---|---|---|---|---|---|---|---|
| SULLIVAN, CHRISTIAN (HM19475) |||●|||||||||||||||||||||||||||||||||||||||||||||||
| TILLEY, D S (HM20068) |||●|||||||||||||||||||||||||||||||||||||||||||||||
| TISBURY OSTEOPATHIC PRACTICE (HM20094) |||●|||||||||||||||||||||||||||||||||||||||||||||||
| WARMINSTER OSTEOPATHIC CLINIC (HM20929) |||●||||||||||||●|||●||●||||||||||||||||||||●||||||||||
| WATSON, RHIAN (HM21022) |||●|||||||||||||||||||||||||||||||||||||||||||||||
| WATSON'S COURT CLINIC (HM21025) |●||||||||||||||||●|||||||||||||||||||||||||||||||
| WESSEX OSTEOPATHY CLINIC (HM21210) |||●|||||||||||||||||||||||||||||||||||||||||||||||
| WESTBURY REFLEXOLOGY CLINIC (HM21260) ||||||||||||||||||●|||||||||||||||||||||||||||||||
| WILLIS, JANET (HM21615) ||||||||||||||||||●|||||||||||||||||||||||||||||||
| WOOTTON BASSETT (HM21885) ||||||||||||||||||||||||||||||||||||||||●||||||||||
| WORCESTERSHIRE ||||||||||||||||||||||||||||||||||||||||||||||||||
| AINSLEY, S (HM00433) |●||||||||||||||||||||||||||||||||||||||||||||||||
| ANNE JORDAN CLINIC (HM00899) ||||||||||||||||||●|||||||||||||||||||||||||||||||
| ASTRID, KELLY (HM01303) ||||||||||||||||||●|||||||||||||||||||||||||||||||
| BERESFORD, GUY S (HM02181) |||●|||||||||||||||||||||||||||||||||||||||||||||||
| BRETFORDTON CLINIC (HM02969) |||●||||||||||||●|||●||||||||||●||||||||||||||●||||||||||
| BROOKS, KENNETH (HM03178) |||●|||||||||||||||||||||||||||||||||||||||||||||||
| CARTER, SUSAN (HM03786) ||||||||||||||||||●|||||||||||||||||||||||||||||||
| CAWLEY, LOUISE (HM03869) ||||||||||||||||||●|||||||||||||||||||||||||||||||
| DAVIDSON, SUSAN (HM05790) ||||||||||||||||||●|||||||||||||||||||||||||||||||
| DAVIES PODIATRY (HM05792) ||||||||||●|||||||||||||||||||||||||||||||||||||||
| EDWARDS, J E (HM06658) |||●|||||||||||||||||||||||||||||||||||||||||||||||
| EVESHAM NATURAL HEALTH CENTRE (HM07009) |||●||||||||||||●|||●||●|||||||||||||||||||||||||||●|||
| FIELDSEND, SARAH (HM07278) ||||||||||||||||||●|||||||||||||||||||||||||||||||
| FRONTIA (HM07757) |||||||||||||||●|||●||●|||||||||●||●||||||||||||●||||||||
| GREEN, PETER J (HM08472) |||●|||||||||||||||||||||||||||||||||||||||||||||||
| HIGGINS, ADRIAN R (HM09728) |||●|||||||||||||||||||||||||||||||||||||||||||||||
| HOLDEN, NINA (HM09933) ||||||||||||||||||●|||||||||||||||||||||||||||||||
| HOWARD, KAREN (HM10237) ||||||||||||||||||●|||||||||||||||||||||||||||||||
| IN THE PINK (HM10598) ||||||||||||||||||●|||||||||||||||||||||||||||||||
| IRVING, GORDON R (HM10746) |||●|||||||||||||||||||||||||||||||||||||||||||||||
| IRVING, GORDON R (HM10747) |||●|||||||||||||||||||||||||||||||||||||||||||||||
| KAVANAGH, N (HM11346) |||●|||||||||||||||||||||||||||||||||||||||||||||||
| KAVANAGH, NIGEL (HM11347) |||●|||||||||||||||||||||||||||||||||||||||||||||||

# O - Z Therapies at Practices/Businesses

| Business by County with Reference no. | Orthotics | Osteomyology | Osteopathy | PAM | Paranormal Therapies | Pattern Therapies | Physiotherapy | Phytotherapy | Pilates | Podiatry | Polarity Therapy | Postural Integration | Primal Therapy | Psionic Therapy | Psychotherapy | Pyramid Power | Pyscho-Synthesis | Reflexology | Reichian Therapy | Reiki | Remedial Massage | Rogerian Therapy | Rolfing | Seichem | Sensitivity Training |
|---|---|---|---|---|---|---|---|---|---|---|---|---|---|---|---|---|---|---|---|---|---|---|---|---|---|
| KITSON, P (HM11730) | | | ● | | | | | | | | | | | | | | | ● | | | | | | | |
| KITSON, PAUL (HM11731) | | | ● | | | | | | | | | | | | | | | | | | | | | | |
| LAMBON, MICHELE (HM11902) | | | | | | | | | | | | | | | | | | ● | | | | | | | |
| LEWINTON, EVELYN (HM12275) | | | | | | | | | | | | | | | | | | ● | | | | | | | |
| LISON, CAROLINE (HM12456) | | | | | | | | | | | | | | | | | | ● | | | | | | | |
| MALVERN NATURAL HEALTH CENTRE (HM12998) | | | | | | | | | | | | | | | | | | ● | | ● | | | | ● | |
| MALVERN OSTEOPATHIC CLINIC (HM12999) | | | ● | | | | | | | | | | | | | | | | | | | | | | |
| MARSTON, SUE (HM13179) | | | | | | | | | | | | | | | | | | | | ● | | | | | |
| MATTHEWS, SUSAN (HM13315) | | | ● | | | | | | | | | | | | | | | | | | | | | | |
| MEAKIN, D W (HM13637) | | | ● | | | | | | | | | | | | | | | | | | | | | | |
| MEYER, ANDREA (HM13786) | | | ● | | | | | | | | | | | | | | | | | | | | | | |
| NOTTINGHAM, STUART (HM15086) | | | | | | | | | ● | | | | | | | | | | | | | | | | |
| NURCHIR (HM15110) | | | | | | | | | | | | | | | | | | | | | | | | | |
| PERSHORE NAT THERAPY CLINIC (HM16057) | | | | | | | | | | | | | | | | | | ● | | ● | | | | | |
| PRETTY, RUTH (HM16565) | | | | | | | | | | | | | | | | | | ● | | | | | | | |
| PSYCHOTHERAPY & COUNS SVS (HM16729) | | | | | | | | | | | | | | | ● | | | | | | | | | | |
| R C C M (HM16829) | | | ● | | | | | | | | | | | | | | | ● | | | | | | | |
| REIKI HEALING BY TRICIA (HM17135) | | | | | | | | | | | | | | | | | | | | ● | | | | | |
| RICHARDSON, NAOMI (HM17285) | | | | | | | | | | | | | | | ● | | | | | | | | | | |
| SHIATSU SCHOOL (HM18462) | | | | | | | | | | | | | | | | | | | | | | | | | |
| SINGLETON, MARI (HM18611) | | | | | | | | | | | | | | | | | | ● | | | | | | | |
| SMITH, AMANDA (HM18714) | | | | | | | | | | | | | | | | | | ● | | | | | | | |
| SMITH, K C (HM18760) | | | ● | | | | | | | | | | | | | | | | | | | | | | |
| SOUTH WORCESTERSHIRE HYP (HM18915) | | | | | | | | | | | | | | | | | | | | | | | | | |
| SPENCER, BARBARA (HM18992) | | | | | | | | | | | | | | | | | | ● | | | | | | | |
| STOKES, TERRY (HM19325) | | | ● | | | | | | | | | | | | | | | ● | | | | | | | |
| STONE, ANNE L (HM19329) | | | | | | | | | | | | ● | | | | | | | | | | | | | |
| SZAWEJKO, MARGARET (HM19635) | | | | | | | | | | | | | | | | | | ● | | | | | | | |
| VINE MEWS CLINIC (HM20678) | | | ● | | | | | | | | | | | | | | | | | | | | | | |
| WARREN, CAROL (HM20945) | | | | | | | | | | | | | | | | | | ● | | | | | | | |
| WICKS, DIANE (HM21453) | | | | | | | | | | | | | | | | | | ● | | | | | | | |
| WORCESTER NATURAL THERAPY CTRE (HM21886) | | | ● | | | | | | | | | | | | | | | ● | | ● | | | | | |
| YOUNG, JOANNA (HM22075) | | | ● | | | | | | | | | | | | | | | | | | | | | | |

| Business by County with Reference no. | Shiatsu | Silva Method | Sound Therapy | Spiritual Healing | Sports Massage | Stress Therapy | Swedish Body Massage | T'ai-Chi Ch'uan | Tantra Therapy | Tera-Mai | Thought Field Therapy | Touch Therapy | Transactional Analysis | Tui-na | Ultrasonics | Vibrational Therapy | Visualisation Therapy | Vitamin Therapy | Voice Therapy | X-Ray | Ying & Yang | Yoga | Zen Therapy | Zero Balancing |
|---|---|---|---|---|---|---|---|---|---|---|---|---|---|---|---|---|---|---|---|---|---|---|---|---|
| KITSON, P (HM11730) | | | | | | | | | | | | | | | | | | | | | | | | |
| KITSON, PAUL (HM11731) | | | | | | | | | | | | | | | | | | | | | | | | |
| LAMBON, MICHELE (HM11902) | | | | | | | | | | | | | | | | | | | | | | | | |
| LEWINTON, EVELYN (HM12275) | | | | | | | | | | | | | | | | | | | | | | | | |
| LISON, CAROLINE (HM12456) | | | | | | | | | | | | | | | | | | | | | | | | |
| MALVERN NATURAL HEALTH CENTRE (HM12998) | | | | | | | | ● | | | | | | | | | | | | | | | | ● |
| MALVERN OSTEOPATHIC CLINIC (HM12999) | | | | | | | | | | | | | | | ● | | | | | | | | | |
| MARSTON, SUE (HM13179) | | | | | | | | | | | | | | | | | | | | | | | | |
| MATTHEWS, SUSAN (HM13315) | | | | | | | | | | | | | | | | | | | | | | | | |
| MEAKIN, D W (HM13637) | | | | | | | | | | | | | | | | | | | | | | | | |
| MEYER, ANDREA (HM13786) | | | | | | | | | | | | | | | | | | | | | | | | |
| NOTTINGHAM, STUART (HM15086) | | | | | | | | | | | | | | | ● | ● | | | | | | | | |
| NURCHIR (HM15110) | | | | | | | | | | | | | | | ● | | | | | | | | | |
| PERSHORE NAT THERAPY CLINIC (HM16057) | | | | ● | | | | | | | | | | | | | | | | | | | | |
| PRETTY, RUTH (HM16565) | | | | | | | | | | | | | | | | | | | | | | | | |
| PSYCHOTHERAPY & COUNS SVS (HM16729) | | | | | | | | | | | | | | | | | | | | | | | | |
| R C C M (HM16829) | | | | | | | | | | | | | | | | | | | | | | | | |
| REIKI HEALING BY TRICIA (HM17135) | | | | | | | | | | | | | | | | | | | | | | | | |
| RICHARDSON, NAOMI (HM17285) | | | | | | | | | | | | | | | | | | | | | | | | |
| SHIATSU SCHOOL (HM18462) | ● | | | | | | | | | | | | | | | | | | | | | | | |
| SINGLETON, MARI (HM18611) | | | | | | | | | | | | | | | | | | | | | | | | |
| SMITH, AMANDA (HM18714) | | | | | | | | | | | | | | | | | | | | | | | | |
| SMITH, K C (HM18760) | | | | | | | | | | | | | | | | | | | | | | | | |
| SOUTH WORCESTERSHIRE HYP (HM18915) | | | | | | ● | | | | | | | | | | | | | | | | | | |
| SPENCER, BARBARA (HM18992) | | | | | | | | | | | | | | | | | | | | | | | | |
| STOKES, TERRY (HM19325) | | | | | | | | | | | | | | | | | | | | | | | | |
| STONE, ANNE L (HM19329) | | | | | | | | | | | | | | | ● | | | | | | | | | |
| SZAWEJKO, MARGARET (HM19635) | | | | | | | | | | | | | | | | | | | | | | | | |
| VINE MEWS CLINIC (HM20678) | | | | | | | | | | | | | | | | | | | | | | | | |
| WARREN, CAROL (HM20945) | | | | | | | | | | | | | | | | | | | | | | | | |
| WICKS, DIANE (HM21453) | | | | | | | | | | | | | | | | | | | | | | | | |
| WORCESTER NATURAL THERAPY CTRE (HM21886) | ● | | | | | | | | | | | | | | | | | | | | | | | |
| YOUNG, JOANNA (HM22075) | | | | | | | | | | | | | | | | | | | | | | | | |

# O - Z Therapies at Practices/Businesses

Business by County with Reference no.

| YORKSHIRE (NORTH) | Orthotics | Osteomyology | Osteopathy | PAM | Paranormal Therapies | Pattern Therapies | Physiotherapy | Phytotherapy | Pilates | Podiatry | Polarity Therapy | Postural Integration | Primal Therapy | Psionic Therapy | Psychotherapy | Pyramid Power | Pyscho-Synthesis |
|---|---|---|---|---|---|---|---|---|---|---|---|---|---|---|---|---|---|
| A TACTILE BUSINESS (HM00046) | | | | | | | | | | | | | | | | | |
| ASHTON SCHOOL OF REFLEXOLOGY (HM01236) | | | | | | | | | | | | | | | | | |
| BAKER, LINDA (HM01587) | | | | | | | | | | | | | | | | | |
| BARLOW, J A (HM01722) | | | ● | | | | | | | | | | | | | | |
| BARNARD, SIMON (HM01731) | | | ● | | | | | | | | | | | | | | |
| BARRASS, K I (HM01778) | ● | | | | | | | | | ● | | | | | | | |
| BEVERLEY, SHEILA (HM02245) | | | | | | | | | | | | | | | | | |
| BROADHEAD, J N & M (HM03114) | | | | | | | | | | ● | | | | | | | |
| BULLOCK, WILLIAM (HM03345) | | | | | | | | | | | | | | | | | |
| BUSWELL, RONA (HM03471) | | | | | | | | | | | | | | | | | |
| CHINESE THERAPY CLINIC (HM04270) | | | | | | | | | | | | | | | | | |
| CRAVEN CLINIC (HM05384) | | | ● | | | | | | | | | | | | ● | | |
| CREE, TOM (HM05409) | | | ● | | | | | | | | | | | | | | |
| CROFT HOUSE CLINIC (HM05452) | | | ● | | | | | | | | | | | | | | |
| DAIRY PSYCHOTHERAPY (HM05676) | | | | | | | | | | | | | | | ● | | |
| DOVE COURT CENTRE (HM06225) | | | | | | | | | | | | | | | | | |
| EASY WAY YORKSHIRE (HM06557) | | | | | | | | | | | | | | | ● | | |
| ELLIOTT, KATHRYN L (HM06756) | | | ● | | | | | | | | | | | | | | |
| EVETTS-SECKER, JOSEPHINE (HM07010) | | | | | | | | | | | | | | | ● | | |
| FROBISHER, LYNDA (HM07754) | | | | | | | | | | | | | | | | | |
| GRIFFITHS, SAIDA K (HM08573) | | | | | | | | | | | | | | | ● | | |
| HARROGATE HOLISTIC HEALTH CTRE (HM09116) | | | | | | | | | | | | | | | ● | | |
| HEALING CLINIC (HM09328) | | | | | | | | | | | ● | | | | | | |
| HESCOTT, J D (HM09692) | ● | | | | | | | | | | | | | | | | |
| HIGHTHORN PHYSIOTHERAPY CLINIC (HM09759) | | | | | | | | | | | | | | | ● | | |
| HOBSON, I K (HM09863) | | | | | | | | | | ● | | | | | | | |
| HODGSON, DAPHNE (HM09885) | | | ● | | | | | | | | | | | | | | |
| HOWELL, SHIRLEY (HM10270) | | | | | | | | | | | | | | | ● | | |
| HUYTON, CHRISTOPHER P (HM10464) | | | ● | | | | | | | | | | | | | | |
| KNIGHT, SYLVIA (HM11758) | | | | | | | | | | | | | | | | | |
| LIFESUPPORT (HM12366) | | | | | | | | | | | | | | | | | |
| MACARTHUR, T (HM12820) | | | ● | | | | | | | | | | | | | | |
| MACHADO, LOUISA (HM12838) | | | | | | | | | | | | | | | | | |

| YORKSHIRE (NORTH) | Reflexology | Reichian Therapy | Reiki | Remedial Massage | Rogerian Therapy | Rolfing | Seichem | Sensitivity Training | Shiatsu | Silva Method | Sound Therapy | Spiritual Healing | Sports Massage | Stress Therapy | Swedish Body Massage | T'ai-Chi Ch'uan |
|---|---|---|---|---|---|---|---|---|---|---|---|---|---|---|---|---|
| A TACTILE BUSINESS (HM00046) | ● | | | | | | | | | | | | | | | |
| ASHTON SCHOOL OF REFLEXOLOGY (HM01236) | ● | | | | | | | | | | | | | | | |
| BAKER, LINDA (HM01587) | ● | | ● | | | | | | | | | | | | | |
| BARLOW, J A (HM01722) | | | | | | | | | | | | | | | | |
| BARNARD, SIMON (HM01731) | | | | | | | | | | | | | | | | |
| BARRASS, K I (HM01778) | | | | | | | | | | | | | | | | |
| BEVERLEY, SHEILA (HM02245) | ● | | | | | | | | | | | | | | | |
| BROADHEAD, J N & M (HM03114) | | | | | | | | | | | | | | | | |
| BULLOCK, WILLIAM (HM03345) | ● | | | | | | | | | | | | | | | |
| BUSWELL, RONA (HM03471) | ● | | | ● | | | | | | | | | | | | |
| CHINESE THERAPY CLINIC (HM04270) | | | | | | | | | ● | | | | | | | ● |
| CRAVEN CLINIC (HM05384) | ● | | ● | | | | | ● | ● | | | ● | | ● | | ● |
| CREE, TOM (HM05409) | | | | | | | | | | | | | | | | |
| CROFT HOUSE CLINIC (HM05452) | ● | | | | | | | | | | | | | | | |
| DAIRY PSYCHOTHERAPY (HM05676) | | | | | | | | | | | | | | | | |
| DOVE COURT CENTRE (HM06225) | | | | | | | | | | | | | | | ● | |
| EASY WAY YORKSHIRE (HM06557) | | | | | | | | | | | | | | | | |
| ELLIOTT, KATHRYN L (HM06756) | | | | | | | | | | | | | | | | |
| EVETTS-SECKER, JOSEPHINE (HM07010) | | | | | | | | | | | | | | | | |
| FROBISHER, LYNDA (HM07754) | ● | | | | | | | | | | | | | | | |
| GRIFFITHS, SAIDA K (HM08573) | | | | | | | | | | | | | | | | |
| HARROGATE HOLISTIC HEALTH CTRE (HM09116) | ● | | ● | | | | | | ● | | | | | | | |
| HEALING CLINIC (HM09328) | ● | | ● | | | | | | ● | | | | | | | ● |
| HESCOTT, J D (HM09692) | | | | | | | | | | | | | | | | |
| HIGHTHORN PHYSIOTHERAPY CLINIC (HM09759) | | | | | | | | | | | | | | | | |
| HOBSON, I K (HM09863) | | | | | | | | | | | | | | | | |
| HODGSON, DAPHNE (HM09885) | | | | | | | | | | | | | | | | |
| HOWELL, SHIRLEY (HM10270) | | | | | | | | | | | | | | | | |
| HUYTON, CHRISTOPHER P (HM10464) | | | | | | | | | | | | | | | | |
| KNIGHT, SYLVIA (HM11758) | ● | | | | | | | | | | | | | | | |
| LIFESUPPORT (HM12366) | ● | | ● | | | | ● | | | | | | | ● | | |
| MACARTHUR, T (HM12820) | | | | | | | | | | | | | | | | |
| MACHADO, LOUISA (HM12838) | ● | | | | | | | | | | | | | | | |

| YORKSHIRE (NORTH) | Tantra Therapy | Tera-Mai | Thought Field Therapy | Touch Therapy | Transactional Analysis | Tui-na | Ultrasonics | Vibrational Therapy | Visualisation Therapy | Vitamin Therapy | Voice Therapy | X-Ray | Ying & Yang | Yoga | Zen Therapy | Zero Balancing |
|---|---|---|---|---|---|---|---|---|---|---|---|---|---|---|---|---|
| A TACTILE BUSINESS (HM00046) | | | | | | | | | | | | | | | | |
| ASHTON SCHOOL OF REFLEXOLOGY (HM01236) | | | | | | | | | | | | | | | | |
| BAKER, LINDA (HM01587) | | | | | | | | | | | | | | | | |
| BARLOW, J A (HM01722) | | | | | | | | | | | | | | | | |
| BARNARD, SIMON (HM01731) | | | | | | | | | | | | | | | | |
| BARRASS, K I (HM01778) | | | | | | | | | | | | | | | | |
| BEVERLEY, SHEILA (HM02245) | | | | | | | | | | | | | | | | |
| BROADHEAD, J N & M (HM03114) | | | | | | | | | | | | | | | | |
| BULLOCK, WILLIAM (HM03345) | | | | | | | | | | | | | | | | |
| BUSWELL, RONA (HM03471) | | | | | | | | | | | | | | | | |
| CHINESE THERAPY CLINIC (HM04270) | | | | | | | | | | | | | | | | |
| CRAVEN CLINIC (HM05384) | | | | ● | | | | | | | | | | | | |
| CREE, TOM (HM05409) | | | | | | | | | | | | | | | | |
| CROFT HOUSE CLINIC (HM05452) | | | | | | | | | | | | | | | | |
| DAIRY PSYCHOTHERAPY (HM05676) | | | | | | | | | | | | | | | | |
| DOVE COURT CENTRE (HM06225) | | | | | | | | | | | | | | | | |
| EASY WAY YORKSHIRE (HM06557) | | | | | | | | | | | | | | | | |
| ELLIOTT, KATHRYN L (HM06756) | | | | | | | | | | | | | | | | |
| EVETTS-SECKER, JOSEPHINE (HM07010) | | | | | | | | | | | | | | | | |
| FROBISHER, LYNDA (HM07754) | | | | | | | | | | | | | | | | |
| GRIFFITHS, SAIDA K (HM08573) | | | | | | | | | | | | | | | | |
| HARROGATE HOLISTIC HEALTH CTRE (HM09116) | | | | | | | | | | | | | | | | |
| HEALING CLINIC (HM09328) | | | | | | | | | | ● | | | | | | |
| HESCOTT, J D (HM09692) | | | | | | | | | | | | | | | | |
| HIGHTHORN PHYSIOTHERAPY CLINIC (HM09759) | | | | | | | | | | | | | | | | |
| HOBSON, I K (HM09863) | | | | | | | | | | | | | | | | |
| HODGSON, DAPHNE (HM09885) | | | | | | | | | | | | | | | | |
| HOWELL, SHIRLEY (HM10270) | | | | | | | | | | | | | | | | |
| HUYTON, CHRISTOPHER P (HM10464) | | | | | | | | | | | | | | | | |
| KNIGHT, SYLVIA (HM11758) | | | | | | | | | | | | | | | | |
| LIFESUPPORT (HM12366) | | ● | | | | | | | ● | | | | | ● | | |
| MACARTHUR, T (HM12820) | | | | | | | | | | | | | | | | |
| MACHADO, LOUISA (HM12838) | | | | | | | | | | | | | | | | |

# O - Z Therapies at Practices/Businesses

| Business by County with Reference no. | Orthotics | Osteomyology | Osteopathy | PAM | Paranormal Therapies | Pattern Therapies | Physiotherapy | Phytotherapy | Pilates | Podiatry | Polarity Therapy | Postural Integration | Primal Therapy | Psionic Therapy | Psychotherapy | Pyramid Power | Pyscho-Synthesis | Reflexology | Reichian Therapy | Reiki | Remedial Massage | Rogerian Therapy | Rolfing | Seichem | Sensitivity Training |
|---|---|---|---|---|---|---|---|---|---|---|---|---|---|---|---|---|---|---|---|---|---|---|---|---|---|
| MCARTHUR, JILL (HM13369) | | | | | | | | | | | | | | | | | | ● | | | | | | | |
| MORTON, P J (HM14252) | | | ● | | | | | | | | | | | | | | | | | | | | | | |
| MORTON, PETER J (HM14253) | | | ● | | | | | | | | | | | | | | | | | | | | | | |
| NANCY METCALFE MOBILE CONSULT (HM14468) | | | | | | | | | | | | | | | | | | | | | | | | | |
| PERSAUD, PENNEY & PARTNERS (HM16055) | | | ● | | | | | | | | | | | | | | | | | | | | | | |
| PSYCHOTHERAPY & COUNSELLING SV (HM16730) | | | | | | | | | | | | | | | ● | | | | | | | | | | |
| RATHBONE, DONNA (HM16955) | | | | | | | | | | | | | | | | | | | | ● | | | | | |
| RIPON NATURAL HEALTH CENTRE (HM17365) | | | ● | | | | | | | | | | | | | | | | | ● | | | | | |
| ROSE, MARTIN J (HM17611) | | | ● | | | | | | | | | | | | | | | | | | | | | | |
| RUSSELL, CAROLINE (HM17764) | | | | | | | | | | | | | | | | | | ● | | | | | | | |
| RYEDALE CLINIC (HM17803) | | | | | | | | | | | | | | | | | | ● | | | | | | | |
| SHACKLETON, MAUREEN (HM18264) | | | | | | | | | | | | | | | ● | | | | | | | | | | |
| SHAH, ATUL (HM18268) | | | | | | | | | | | | | | | | | | | | | | | | | |
| SHARROCKS, LYNN (HM18323) | | | | | | | | | | | | | | | | | | ● | | | | | | | |
| SHEEHAN, NICHOLAS (HM18363) | | | ● | | | | | | | | | | | | | | | | | | | | | | |
| SI SHEN CLINIC (HM18519) | | | | | | | | | | | | | | | | | | ● | | | | | | | |
| STRATTON, FIONA (HM19372) | | | | | | | | | | | | | | | | | | ● | | | | | | | |
| TERRY ANNE (HM19845) | | | | | | | | | | | | | | | ● | | | | | | | | | | |
| THOMPSON, CAROLINE (HM19970) | | | ● | | | | | | | | | | | | | | | | | | | | | | |
| TIDSWELL, SUSAN (HM20059) | | | | | | | | | | | | | | | | | | ● | | | | | | | |
| TUKE CENTRE (HM20381) | | | | | | | | | | | | | | | ● | | | | | | | | | | |
| WALLACE, GENEVIEVE (HM20822) | | | | | | | | | | | | | | | | | | ● | | | | | | | |
| WATSON, J (HM21012) | | | | | | | | | | | | | | | | | | ● | | | | | | | |
| WHEELER, J (HM21315) | | | ● | | | | | | | | | | | | | | | | | | | | | | |
| YOGA FOR ALL (HM22026) | | | | | | | | | | | | | | | | | | | | | | | | | |
| YORK CHIROPRACTIC CLINIC (HM22039) | | | | | | | | | | | | | | | | | | | | | | | | | |
| YORK CLINIC (HM22040) | | | ● | | | | | | | ● | | | | | | | | ● | | | | | | | |
| YORK COUNSELLING (HM22042) | | | | | | | | | | | | | | | ● | | | | | | | ● | | | |
| YORK SCHOOL OF COMP MEDICINE (HM22050) | | | | | | | | | | | | | | | | | | ● | | | | | | | |
| **YORKSHIRE (SOUTH)** | | | | | | | | | | | | | | | | | | | | | | | | | |
| ALTERNATIVES (HM00742) | | | | | | | | | | | | | | | | | | ● | | | | | | | |
| ALTON & JAMES MED HERBAL (HM00748) | | | | | | | | ● | | | | | | | | | | | | | | | | | |
| ANDERSON, A DUDLEY (HM00810) | | | | | | | | | | | | | | | ● | | | | | ● | | | | | |
| BAWTRY PHYSIOTHERAPY PRACTICE (HM01918) | | | | | | | ● | | | | | | | | | | | | | | | | | | |

| Business by County with Reference no. | Shiatsu | Silva Method | Sound Therapy | Spiritual Healing | Sports Massage | Stress Therapy | Swedish Body Massage | T'ai-Chi Ch'uan | Tantra Therapy | Tera-Mai | Thought Field Therapy | Touch Therapy | Transactional Analysis | Tui-na | Ultrasonics | Vibrational Therapy | Visualisation Therapy | Vitamin Therapy | Voice Therapy | X-Ray | Ying & Yang | Yoga | Zen Therapy | Zero Balancing |
|---|---|---|---|---|---|---|---|---|---|---|---|---|---|---|---|---|---|---|---|---|---|---|---|---|
| MCARTHUR, JILL (HM13369) | | | | | | | | | | | | | | | | | | | | | | | | |
| MORTON, P J (HM14252) | | | | | | | | | | | | | | | | | | | | | | | | |
| MORTON, PETER J (HM14253) | | | | | | | | | | | | | | | | | | | | | | | | |
| NANCY METCALFE MOBILE CONSULT (HM14468) | | | | | | ● | | | | | | ● | | | | ● | | | | | | | | |
| PERSAUD, PENNEY & PARTNERS (HM16055) | | | | | | | | | | | | | | | | | | | | | | | | |
| PSYCHOTHERAPY & COUNSELLING SV (HM16730) | | | | | | | | | | | | | | | | | | | | | | | | |
| RATHBONE, DONNA (HM16955) | | | | | | | | | | | | | | | | | | | | | | | | |
| RIPON NATURAL HEALTH CENTRE (HM17365) | ● | | | | | ● | | | | | | ● | | | | | | | | | | | | |
| ROSE, MARTIN J (HM17611) | | | | | | | | | | | | | | | | | | | | | | | | |
| RUSSELL, CAROLINE (HM17764) | | | | | | | | | | | | | | | | | | | | | | | | |
| RYEDALE CLINIC (HM17803) | | | | | | | | | | | | | | | | | | | | | | | | |
| SHACKLETON, MAUREEN (HM18264) | | | | | | | | | | | | | | | | | | | | | | | | |
| SHAH, ATUL (HM18268) | | | | | | ● | | | | | | | | | | | | | | | | | | |
| SHARROCKS, LYNN (HM18323) | | | | | | | | | | | | | | | | | | | | | | | | |
| SHEEHAN, NICHOLAS (HM18363) | | | | | | | | | | | | | | | | | | | | | | | | |
| SI SHEN CLINIC (HM18519) | | | | | | | | | | | | | | | | | | | | | | | | |
| STRATTON, FIONA (HM19372) | | | | ● | | | | | | | | | | | | | | | | | | | | |
| TERRY ANNE (HM19845) | | | | | | ● | | | | | | | | | | | ● | | | | | | | |
| THOMPSON, CAROLINE (HM19970) | | | | | | | | | | | | | | | | | | | | | | | | |
| TIDSWELL, SUSAN (HM20059) | | | | | | | | | | | | | | | | | | | | | | | | |
| TUKE CENTRE (HM20381) | | | | | | | | | | | | | | | | | | | | | | | | |
| WALLACE, GENEVIEVE (HM20822) | | | | | | | | | | | | | | | | | | | | | | | | |
| WATSON, J (HM21012) | | | | | | | | | | | | | | | | | | | | | | | | |
| WHEELER, J (HM21315) | | | | | | | | | | | | | | | | | | | | | | | | |
| YOGA FOR ALL (HM22026) | | | | | | | | | | | | | | | | | | | | | | ● | | |
| YORK CHIROPRACTIC CLINIC (HM22039) | | | | | | | | | | | | | | | | | | | | ● | | | | |
| YORK CLINIC (HM22040) | | | | | | | | | | | | | | | | | | | | | | | | |
| YORK COUNSELLING (HM22042) | | | | | | ● | | | | | | | | | | | | | | | | | | |
| YORK SCHOOL OF COMP MEDICINE (HM22050) | | | | | | | | | | | | | | | | | | | | | | | | |
| **YORKSHIRE (SOUTH)** | | | | | | | | | | | | | | | | | | | | | | | | |
| ALTERNATIVES (HM00742) | | | | ● | | | | | | | | | | | | | | | | | | | | |
| ALTON & JAMES MED HERBAL (HM00748) | | | | | | | | | | | | | | | | | | | | | | | | |
| ANDERSON, A DUDLEY (HM00810) | | | | | | ● | | | | | | ● | | | | | ● | | | | | | | |
| BAWTRY PHYSIOTHERAPY PRACTICE (HM01918) | | | | | | | | | | | | | | | | | | | | | | | | |

# O - Z Therapies at Practices/Businesses

Business by County with Reference no.

| Business by County with Reference no. | Orthotics | Osteomyology | Osteopathy | PAM | Paranormal Therapies | Pattern Therapies | Physiotherapy | Phytotherapy | Pilates | Podiatry | Polarity Therapy | Postural Integration | Primal Therapy | Psionic Therapy | Psychotherapy | Pyramid Power |
|---|---|---|---|---|---|---|---|---|---|---|---|---|---|---|---|---|
| SMITH, JANET (HM18751) | | | | | | | | | | | | | | | | |
| SPENCE, SYLVIA (HM18986) | | | | | | | | | | | | | | | | |
| STEAD, JULIE ANN (HM19164) | | | | | | | | | | | | | | | | |
| STEVEN, PAUL (HM19223) | | | | | | | | | | | | | | | ● | |
| STOREY, RACHEL (HM19348) | | | | | | | | | | | | | | | | |
| SURGERY (HM19519) | | | | | | | ● | | | ● | | | | | | |
| SWAINE, PAULA (HM19565) | | | | | | | | | | ● | | | | | | |
| TAYLOR, JULIE (HM19772) | | | | | | | | | | | | | | | | |
| TORNTON, HOWARD (HM20172) | | | ● | | | | | | | | | | | | | |
| TUEL LANE PHYSIOTHERAPY CLINIC (HM20376) | | | | | | | ● | | | | | | | | | |
| TUNE, VICTORIA (HM20396) | | | | | | | | | | | | | | | | |
| UNDERWOOD, TRISH (HM20502) | | | | | | | | | | | | | | | | |
| WARING, D (HM20928) | | | ● | | | | | | | | | | | | | |
| WATKINS, JEAN (HM20996) | | | | | | | | | | | | | | | | |
| WEBB, JOAN (HM21068) | | | | | | | | | | | | | | | ● | |
| WEST YORKSHIRE CLINIC (HM21242) | | | ● | | | | | | | | | | | | | |
| WEST YORKSHIRE PHYSIO CENTRE (HM21244) | | | | | | | ● | | | | | | | | | |
| WETHERBY PHYSIO PRACTICE (HM21290) | | | | | | | ● | | | | | | | | | |
| WHITE, JACQUELINE (HM21359) | | | | | | | | | | | | | | | | |
| WHITLEY, JILL (HM21409) | | | | | | | | | | | | | | | | |
| WILCOX & ASSOCIATES (HM21486) | | | ● | | | | | | | | | | | | | |
| WILLMOTT, BERYL (HM21619) | | | | | | | | | | | | | | | | |
| WISE, CAROL (HM21732) | | | | | | | | | | | | | | | | |
| WISZNIEWSKI, H (HM21741) | | | ● | | | | | | | | | | | | | |
| WOMENS COUNS & THERAPY SV (HM21774) | | | | | | | | | | | | | | | ● | |
| WOOD, TRACY (HM21810) | | | | | | | | | | | | | | | | |
| WOODHOUSE CLINIC (HM21826) | | | ● | | | | | | | | | | | | | |
| WRIGHT, GEORGINA (HM21932) | | | | | | | | | | | | | | | | |
| YEHIA, CHRISTINE (HM22000) | | | | | | | | | | | | | | | | |
| YORKSHIRE ASS - PSYCHO (HM22055) | | | | | | | | | | | | | | | ● | |
| YORKSHIRE SCHOOL OF SHIATSU (HM22057) | | | | | | | | | | | | | | | | |

| Business by County with Reference no. | Pyscho-Synthesis | Reflexology | Reichian Therapy | Reiki | Remedial Massage | Rogerian Therapy | Rolfing | Seichem | Sensitivity Training | Shiatsu | Silva Method | Sound Therapy | Spiritual Healing | Sports Massage | Stress Therapy | Swedish Body Massage |
|---|---|---|---|---|---|---|---|---|---|---|---|---|---|---|---|---|
| SMITH, JANET (HM18751) | | | | ● | | | | | | | | | | | | |
| SPENCE, SYLVIA (HM18986) | | ● | | | | | | | | | | | | | | |
| STEAD, JULIE ANN (HM19164) | | ● | | ● | | | | | | | | | | | | |
| STEVEN, PAUL (HM19223) | | | | | | | | | | | | | | | | |
| STOREY, RACHEL (HM19348) | | ● | | | | | | | | | | | | | | |
| SURGERY (HM19519) | | | | | | | | | | | | | | | | |
| SWAINE, PAULA (HM19565) | | | | | | | | | | | | | | | | |
| TAYLOR, JULIE (HM19772) | | ● | | | | | | | | | | | | | | |
| TORNTON, HOWARD (HM20172) | | | | | | | | | | | | | | | | |
| TUEL LANE PHYSIOTHERAPY CLINIC (HM20376) | | | | | | | | | | | | | | ● | | |
| TUNE, VICTORIA (HM20396) | | ● | | | | | | | | | | | | | | |
| UNDERWOOD, TRISH (HM20502) | | ● | | | | | | | | | | | | | | |
| WARING, D (HM20928) | | | | | | | | | | | | | | | | |
| WATKINS, JEAN (HM20996) | | ● | | | | | | | | | | | | | | |
| WEBB, JOAN (HM21068) | | | | | | | | | | | | | | | | |
| WEST YORKSHIRE CLINIC (HM21242) | | | | | | | | | | ● | | | | | ● | |
| WEST YORKSHIRE PHYSIO CENTRE (HM21244) | | | | | | | | | | | | | | ● | | |
| WETHERBY PHYSIO PRACTICE (HM21290) | | | | | | | | | | | | | | | | |
| WHITE, JACQUELINE (HM21359) | | ● | | | | | | | | | | | | | | |
| WHITLEY, JILL (HM21409) | | ● | | | | | | | | | | | | | | |
| WILCOX & ASSOCIATES (HM21486) | | | | | | | | | | | | | | | | |
| WILLMOTT, BERYL (HM21619) | | ● | | | | | | | | | | | | | | |
| WISE, CAROL (HM21732) | | | | | | | | | | | | | | | | |
| WISZNIEWSKI, H (HM21741) | | | | | | | | | | | | | | | | |
| WOMENS COUNS & THERAPY SV (HM21774) | | | | | | | | | | | | | | | | |
| WOOD, TRACY (HM21810) | | ● | | | | | | | | | | | | | | |
| WOODHOUSE CLINIC (HM21826) | | | | | | | | | | | | | | | | |
| WRIGHT, GEORGINA (HM21932) | | ● | | | | | | | | | | | | | | |
| YEHIA, CHRISTINE (HM22000) | | ● | | | | | | | | | | | | | | |
| YORKSHIRE ASS - PSYCHO (HM22055) | | | | | | | | | | | | | | | | |
| YORKSHIRE SCHOOL OF SHIATSU (HM22057) | | | | | | | | | | ● | | | | | | |

| Business by County with Reference no. | T'ai-Chi Ch'uan | Tantra Therapy | Tera-Mai | Thought Field Therapy | Touch Therapy | Transactional Analysis | Tui-na | Ultrasonics | Vibrational Therapy | Visualisation Therapy | Vitamin Therapy | Voice Therapy | X-Ray | Ying & Yang | Yoga | Zen Therapy | Zero Balancing |
|---|---|---|---|---|---|---|---|---|---|---|---|---|---|---|---|---|---|
| SMITH, JANET (HM18751) | | | | | | | | | | | | | | | ● | | |
| SPENCE, SYLVIA (HM18986) | | | | | | | | | | | | | | | | | |
| STEAD, JULIE ANN (HM19164) | | | | | | | | | | | | | | | | | |
| STEVEN, PAUL (HM19223) | | | | | | | | | | | | | | | | | |
| STOREY, RACHEL (HM19348) | | | | | | | | | | | | | | | | | |
| SURGERY (HM19519) | | | | | | | | ● | | | ● | | | | | | |
| SWAINE, PAULA (HM19565) | | | | | | | | | | | | | | | | | |
| TAYLOR, JULIE (HM19772) | | | | | | | | | | | | | | | | | |
| TORNTON, HOWARD (HM20172) | | | | | | | | | | | | | | | | | |
| TUEL LANE PHYSIOTHERAPY CLINIC (HM20376) | | | | | | | | | | | | | | | | | |
| TUNE, VICTORIA (HM20396) | | | | | | | | | | | | | | | | | |
| UNDERWOOD, TRISH (HM20502) | | | | | | | | | | | | | | | | | |
| WARING, D (HM20928) | | | | | | | | | | | | | | | | | |
| WATKINS, JEAN (HM20996) | | | | | | | | | | | | | | | | | |
| WEBB, JOAN (HM21068) | | | | | | | | | | | | | | | | | |
| WEST YORKSHIRE CLINIC (HM21242) | | | | | | | | | | | | | | | | | |
| WEST YORKSHIRE PHYSIO CENTRE (HM21244) | | | | | | | | | | | | | | | | | |
| WETHERBY PHYSIO PRACTICE (HM21290) | | | | | | | | | | | | | | | | | |
| WHITE, JACQUELINE (HM21359) | | | | | | | | | | | | | | | | | |
| WHITLEY, JILL (HM21409) | | | | | | | | | | | | | | | | | |
| WILCOX & ASSOCIATES (HM21486) | | | | | | | | | | | | | | | | | |
| WILLMOTT, BERYL (HM21619) | | | | | | | | | | | | | | | | | |
| WISE, CAROL (HM21732) | ● | | | | | | | | | | | | | | | | |
| WISZNIEWSKI, H (HM21741) | | | | | | | | | | | | | | | | | |
| WOMENS COUNS & THERAPY SV (HM21774) | | | | | | | | | | | | | | | | | |
| WOOD, TRACY (HM21810) | | | | | | | | | | | | | | | | | |
| WOODHOUSE CLINIC (HM21826) | | | | | | | | | | | | | | | | | |
| WRIGHT, GEORGINA (HM21932) | | | | | | | | | | | | | | | | | |
| YEHIA, CHRISTINE (HM22000) | | | | | | | | | | | | | | | | | |
| YORKSHIRE ASS - PSYCHO (HM22055) | | | | | | | | | | | | | | | | | |
| YORKSHIRE SCHOOL OF SHIATSU (HM22057) | | | | | | | | | | | | | | | | | |

# O - Z Therapies at Practices/Businesses

Business by County with Reference no.

| Business by County with Reference no. | Orthotics | Osteomyology | Osteopathy | PAM | Paranormal Therapies | Pattern Therapies | Physiotherapy | Phytotherapy | Pilates | Podiatry | Polarity Therapy | Postural Integration | Primal Therapy | Psionic Therapy | Psychotherapy | Pyramid Power | Pyscho-Synthesis | Reflexology | Reichian Therapy | Reiki | Remedial Massage | Rogerian Therapy | Rolfing | Seichem | Sensitivity Training |
|---|---|---|---|---|---|---|---|---|---|---|---|---|---|---|---|---|---|---|---|---|---|---|---|---|---|
| IRELAND | | | | | | | | | | | | | | | | | | | | | | | | | |
| COUNTY CLARE | | | | | | | | | | | | | | | | | | | | | | | | | |
| SIMONS, ROBERT ALLEN (DR) (HM18572) | | | | | | | | | | | | | | | ● | | | | | | | ● | | | |
| COUNTY CORK | | | | | | | | | | | | | | | | | | | | | | | | | |
| ANNAPURNA NATURAL HEALTHCARE (HM00894) | | | | | | | | | | | | | | | | | | ● | | ● | | | | | |
| BANDON CHIROPRACTIC CLINIC (HM01653) | | | | | | | | | | | | | | | | | | | | | | | | | |
| BROOKFIELD PHYSIOTHERAPY (HM03167) | | | | | | | | | | | | | | | | | | | | ● | | | | | |
| EAST CORK PHYSIOTHERAPY (HM06511) | | | | | | | | | | | | | | | | | | | | | | | | | |
| HATTERSLEY, LAURENCE (HM09200) | | | ● | | | | | | | | | | | | | | | | | ● | | | | | |
| HEALING THERAPIES (HM09354) | | | | | | | | | | | | | | | | | | | | ● | | | | ● | |
| INS-CLINICAL HYP & PSYCHO (HM10661) | | | | | | | | | | | | | | | ● | | | | | | | | | | |
| JONES, COLEEN (HM11131) | | | | | | | | | | | | | | | ● | | | | | | | | | | |
| KEATING, MARY (HM11379) | | | | | | | | | | | | | | | | | | | | ● | | | | | |
| MOORE-GROACKE, GILLIAN (DR) (HM14136) | | | | | | | | | | | | | | | ● | | | | | | | | | | |
| PAUL DENNEHY - HYPNOTHERAPIST (HM15842) | | | | | | | | | | | ● | | | | ● | | ● | | | | | ● | | | ● |
| SHIATSU (HM18452) | | | | | | | | | | | | | | | | | | | | | | | | | |
| COUNTY DUBLIN | | | | | | | | | | | | | | | | | | | | | | | | | |
| ALBANY CLINIC (HM00478) | | | ● | | | | | | | | | | | | | | | | | | | | | | |
| ARDAGH ACUPUNCTURE CLINIC (HM00988) | | | | | | | | | | | | | | | | | | | | ● | | | | | |
| ARDUNA COUNS & PSYCHOTHPY CTRE (HM00995) | | | | | | | | | | | | | | | ● | | | | | | | | | | |
| BREE, JOHN (HM02947) | | | | | | | | | | | | | | | | | | | | ● | | | | | |
| B-WELL HYPNOTHERAPY CLINIC (HM03506) | | | | | | | | | | | | | | | ● | | | | | ● | | | | ● | |
| CHADHA, PRADEEP K (DR) (HM03933) | | | | | | | | | | | | | | | ● | | | | | | | | | | |
| DUN LAOIRE HEALING ROOM (HM06389) | | | | | | | | | | | | | | | | | | | | | | | | | |
| FAIRVIEW THERAPY CENTRE (HM07066) | | | | | | | | | | | | | | | ● | | | ● | | ● | | ● | | | |
| FINISHING TOUCHES (HM07313) | | | | | | | | | | | | | | | | | | | | | | | | | |
| FITZGERALD HYP-PSYCHOTHERAPY (HM07364) | | | | | | | | | | | | | | | ● | | | | | | | ● | | | |
| HEALING PLACE (HM09347) | | | | | | | | | | | | | | | | | | | | | | | | | |
| HEALING ROOM - DRUMCONDRA (HM09351) | | | | | | | | | | | | | | | | | | ● | | ● | | | | | |
| HEALTH COUNSEL (HM09384) | | | | | | | | | | | | | | | | | | | | | | | | | |
| HERBAL & ACUPUNCTURE (HM09595) | | | | | | | | | | | | | | | | | | | | | | | | | |
| HOWTH COUNSELLING SERVICE (HM10294) | | | | | | | | | | | | | | | ● | | | | | | | ● | | | |
| INNER CIRCLE HEALING CENTRE (HM10635) | | | | | ● | | | | ● | | ● | | | | ● | | | ● | | ● | | | | ● | |

| Business by County with Reference no. | Shiatsu | Silva Method | Sound Therapy | Spiritual Healing | Sports Massage | Stress Therapy | Swedish Body Massage | T'ai-Chi Ch'uan | Tantra Therapy | Tera-Mai | Thought Field Therapy | Touch Therapy | Transactional Analysis | Tui-na | Ultrasonics | Vibrational Therapy | Visualisation Therapy | Vitamin Therapy | Voice Therapy | X-Ray | Ying & Yang | Yoga | Zen Therapy | Zero Balancing |
|---|---|---|---|---|---|---|---|---|---|---|---|---|---|---|---|---|---|---|---|---|---|---|---|---|
| IRELAND | | | | | | | | | | | | | | | | | | | | | | | | |
| COUNTY CLARE | | | | | | | | | | | | | | | | | | | | | | | | |
| SIMONS, ROBERT ALLEN (DR) (HM18572) | | | | | | | | | | | | | | | | | | | | | | | | |
| COUNTY CORK | | | | | | | | | | | | | | | | | | | | | | | | |
| ANNAPURNA NATURAL HEALTHCARE (HM00894) | | | | | | | | | | | | | | | | | | | | | | | | |
| BANDON CHIROPRACTIC CLINIC (HM01653) | | | | | | | | | | | | | | | ● | | | | | | | | | |
| BROOKFIELD PHYSIOTHERAPY (HM03167) | | | | | | | | | | | | | | | | | | | | | | | | |
| EAST CORK PHYSIOTHERAPY (HM06511) | | | | | | ● | | | | | | ● | | | ● | ● | | ● | | | | | | |
| HATTERSLEY, LAURENCE (HM09200) | | | | | | | | | | | | | | | | | | | | | | | | |
| HEALING THERAPIES (HM09354) | | | | ● | | ● | | | | ● | | ● | | | | | ● | | | | | | | |
| INS-CLINICAL HYP & PSYCHO (HM10661) | | | | ● | | ● | | | | | | | | | | | ● | | | | | | | |
| JONES, COLEEN (HM11131) | | | | | | | | | | | | | | | | | | | | | | | | |
| KEATING, MARY (HM11379) | | | | | | | | | | | | | | | | | | | | | | | | |
| MOORE-GROACKE, GILLIAN (DR) (HM14136) | | | | | | | | | | | | | | | | | | | | | | | | |
| PAUL DENNEHY - HYPNOTHERAPIST (HM15842) | | | ● | ● | | ● | | | | | | ● | ● | | | | | | ● | | ● | | | |
| SHIATSU (HM18452) | ● | | | | | | | | | | | | | | | | | | | | | | | |
| COUNTY DUBLIN | | | | | | | | | | | | | | | | | | | | | | | | |
| ALBANY CLINIC (HM00478) | | | | | | | | | | | | | | | | | | | | | | | | |
| ARDAGH ACUPUNCTURE CLINIC (HM00988) | | | | | | | | | | | | | | | | | | | | | ● | | | |
| ARDUNA COUNS & PSYCHOTHPY CTRE (HM00995) | | | | | | | | | | | | | | | | | | | | | | | | |
| BREE, JOHN (HM02947) | | | | | | ● | | | | | | | | | | | | | | | | | | |
| B-WELL HYPNOTHERAPY CLINIC (HM03506) | | | | ● | | | | | | ● | | | | | | | | | | | | | | |
| CHADHA, PRADEEP K (DR) (HM03933) | | | | | | | | | | | | | | | | | | | | | | | | |
| DUN LAOIRE HEALING ROOM (HM06389) | | | | ● | | | | | | | | | | | | | | | | | | | | |
| FAIRVIEW THERAPY CENTRE (HM07066) | ● | | | | | | | | | | | | | | | | | | | | | | | |
| FINISHING TOUCHES (HM07313) | | | | ● | | ● | | | | | | ● | | | | | | | | | | | | |
| FITZGERALD HYP-PSYCHOTHERAPY (HM07364) | | | | | | ● | | | | | | | | | | | | | | | | | | |
| HEALING PLACE (HM09347) | ● | | | | | | | | | | | | | | | | | | | | | | | |
| HEALING ROOM - DRUMCONDRA (HM09351) | ● | | | | | | | | | | | | | | | | | | | | | | | |
| HEALTH COUNSEL (HM09384) | | ● | | | | ● | | | | | | | | | | | | | | | | | | |
| HERBAL & ACUPUNCTURE (HM09595) | ● | | | | | | | | | | | | | | | | | | | | | | | |
| HOWTH COUNSELLING SERVICE (HM10294) | | | | | | ● | | | | | | | | | | | | | | | | | | |
| INNER CIRCLE HEALING CENTRE (HM10635) | | | | ● | | ● | | | | | | | | | | | | | | | | | | |

# O - Z Therapies at Practices/Businesses

Business by County with Reference no.

| Business | Orthotics | Osteomology | Osteopathy | PAM | Paranormal Therapies | Pattern Therapies | Physiotherapy | Phytotherapy | Pilates | Podiatry | Polarity Therapy | Postural Integration | Primal Therapy | Psionic Therapy | Psychotherapy | Pyramid Power | Psycho-Synthesis | Reflexology | Reichian Therapy | Reiki | Remedial Massage | Rogerian Therapy | Rolfing | Seichem | Sensitivity Training |
|---|---|---|---|---|---|---|---|---|---|---|---|---|---|---|---|---|---|---|---|---|---|---|---|---|---|
| INSTITUTE OF PSYCHOSOCIAL MED (HM10678) | | | | | | | | | | | | | | | ● | | | | | | | | | | |
| KELLY, ANGELINA (HM11427) | | | | | | | | ● | | | | | | | | | | ● | | | | | | | |
| LALLOO'S ACUPUNCTURE CLINIC (HM11881) | | | | | | | | | | | ● | | | | | | | ● | | ● | | | | | |
| LITTLEJOHN CLINIC (HM12472) | | | ● | | | | | | | | | | | | | | | | | | | | | | |
| MACLIAM, FIONNULA (HM12867) | | | | | | | | | | | | | | | ● | | | | | | | | | | |
| MCHUGH HYPNOSIS & REFLEXOLOGY (HM13509) | | | | | | | | | | | | | | | ● | | | ● | | | | | | | |
| MELT/TEMPLE BAR NATURAL (HM13716) | | | | | | | | | ● | | ● | | | | | | | ● | | ● | | | | ● | |
| NATURAL SOLUTIONS (HM14625) | | | | | | | | | | | | | | | ● | | | | | ● | | | | | |
| NUALA WOULFE BEAUTY SALON (HM15101) | | | | | | | | | | | | | | | | | | ● | | | | | | | |
| T C M CENTRE (HM19639) | | | | | | | | | | | | | | | | | | | | | | | | | |
| THERAPEUTICS (HM19888) | | | | | | | | | | | | | | | | | | ● | | | | | | | |
| TOBIN, ROSALEEN (HM20105) | | | | | | | | | | | | | | | | | | | | ● | | | | ● | |
| TRAD CHINESE MEDICINE/MASSAGE (HM20216) | | | | | | | | | | | | | | | | | | ● | | | | | | | |
| TROY, ROSEMARY (HM20349) | | | | | | | | | | | | | | | ● | | | | | | | | | | |
| COUNTY GALWAY | | | | | | | | | | | | | | | | | | | | | | | | | |
| BODYWATCH (HM02636) | | | | | | | | | ● | | | | | | ● | | | | | | | | | | |
| IRWIN, MARY (HM10752) | | | | | | | | | | | | | | | | | | ● | | | | | | | |
| PRENDERGAST, KARL (HM16542) | | | ● | | | | | | | | | | | | | | | | | | | | | | |
| PSYCHOL & FAMILY THRPY PRACT (HM16699) | | | | | | | | | | | | | | | ● | | | | | | | | | | |
| COUNTY KERRY | | | | | | | | | | | | | | | | | | | | | | | | | |
| WOODLAWN HOLISTIC THERAPY CTRE (HM21834) | | | ● | | | | | | | | | | | | | | | ● | | ● | | | | | |
| COUNTY KILDARE | | | | | | | | | | | | | | | | | | | | | | | | | |
| GREEN ROAD HEALING CENTRE (HM08441) | | | | | | | | | | | | | | | | | | ● | | | | | | | |
| SHENANDOAH HEALING (HM18395) | | | | | | | | | | | | | | | | | | | | | | | | | |
| COUNTY KILKENNY | | | | | | | | | | | | | | | | | | | | | | | | | |
| BLUE ROOM (HM02528) | | | | | ● | | | ● | | | | | | | ● | | | | ● | ● | | | | | ● |
| HOLISTIC HEALING CENTRE (HM09965) | | | | | | | | | | | ● | | | | ● | | | ● | | ● | | | | | |
| COUNTY LIMERICK | | | | | | | | | | | | | | | | | | | | | | | | | |
| HOLISTIC HEALING (HM09960) | | | | | | | | | | | | | | | | | | ● | | ● | | | | ● | |
| COUNTY LOUTH | | | | | | | | | | | | | | | | | | | | | | | | | |
| HOLISTIC SOL NTRL HEALING CTRE (HM09989) | | | | | | | | | | | | | | | ● | | | | | ● | | | | | |
| COUNTY MAYO | | | | | | | | | | | | | | | | | | | | | | | | | |
| NATURAL HEALING CENTRE (HM14547) | | | | | | | | | | | | ● | | | ● | | | ● | | ● | | | | | ● |
| TOBAR PHADRAIC (HM20102) | | | | | | | | | | | | | | | | | | ● | | ● | | | | | |

| Business | Shiatsu | Silva Method | Sound Therapy | Spiritual Healing | Sports Massage | Stress Therapy | Swedish Body Massage | T'ai-Chi Ch'uan | Tantra Therapy | Tera-Mai | Thought Field Therapy | Touch Therapy | Transactional Analysis | Tui-na | Ultrasonics | Vibrational Therapy | Visualisation Therapy | Vitamin Therapy | Voice Therapy | X-Ray | Ying & Yang | Yoga | Zen Therapy | Zero Balancing |
|---|---|---|---|---|---|---|---|---|---|---|---|---|---|---|---|---|---|---|---|---|---|---|---|---|
| INSTITUTE OF PSYCHOSOCIAL MED (HM10678) | | | | ● | | | | | | | | | | | | | | | | | | | | |
| KELLY, ANGELINA (HM11427) | | | | | | | | ● | | | | | | | | | | | | | | | | |
| LALLOO'S ACUPUNCTURE CLINIC (HM11881) | | | | | | ● | | | | ● | | ● | | | | | | ● | | | ● | | | |
| LITTLEJOHN CLINIC (HM12472) | | | | | | | | | | | | | | | | | | | | | | | | |
| MACLIAM, FIONNULA (HM12867) | | | | | | | | | | | | | | | | | | | | | | | | |
| MCHUGH HYPNOSIS & REFLEXOLOGY (HM13509) | | | | | | | | | | | | | | | | | | | | | | | | |
| MELT/TEMPLE BAR NATURAL (HM13716) | ● | | | | | ● | | ● | | | | | | | | ● | | ● | | | | ● | | |
| NATURAL SOLUTIONS (HM14625) | | | | | | | | | | | | | | | | | | | ● | | | | | |
| NUALA WOULFE BEAUTY SALON (HM15101) | | | | | | | | | | | | | | | | | | | | | | | | |
| T C M CENTRE (HM19639) | | | | | | ● | | | | | | | | | | ● | | | | | ● | | | |
| THERAPEUTICS (HM19888) | | | | | | | | | | | | | | | | | | | | | | | | |
| TOBIN, ROSALEEN (HM20105) | | | | ● | | | | | | ● | | | | | | | | | | | | | | |
| TRAD CHINESE MEDICINE/MASSAGE (HM20216) | ● | | | | | | | | | | | | | | | | | | | | | | | |
| TROY, ROSEMARY (HM20349) | | | | | | | | | | | | | | | | | | | | | | | | |
| COUNTY GALWAY | | | | | | | | | | | | | | | | | | | | | | | | |
| BODYWATCH (HM02636) | | | | | | | | | | | | | | | | | | | | | | | | |
| IRWIN, MARY (HM10752) | | | | | | | | | | | | | | | | | | | | | | | | |
| PRENDERGAST, KARL (HM16542) | | | | | | | | | | | | | | | | | | | | | | | | |
| PSYCHOL & FAMILY THRPY PRACT (HM16699) | | | | | | | | | | | | | | | | | | | | | | | | |
| COUNTY KERRY | | | | | | | | | | | | | | | | | | | | | | | | |
| WOODLAWN HOLISTIC THERAPY CTRE (HM21834) | | | | | | ● | | | | | | | | | | ● | | | | | | | | |
| COUNTY KILDARE | | | | | | | | | | | | | | | | | | | | | | | | |
| GREEN ROAD HEALING CENTRE (HM08441) | | | | | | | | | | | | ● | | | | | | | | | | | | |
| SHENANDOAH HEALING (HM18395) | | | | ● | | | | | | | | ● | | | | | | | | | | | | |
| COUNTY KILKENNY | | | | | | | | | | | | | | | | | | | | | | | | |
| BLUE ROOM (HM02528) | | | ● | ● | | ● | | | ● | | | ● | | | | | ● | ● | ● | | | ● | | |
| HOLISTIC HEALING CENTRE (HM09965) | | | | | | | | | | | | ● | | | | | | | | | | | | |
| COUNTY LIMERICK | | | | | | | | | | | | | | | | | | | | | | | | |
| HOLISTIC HEALING (HM09960) | | | | ● | | | | | | | | | | | | | | | | | | | | |
| COUNTY LOUTH | | | | | | | | | | | | | | | | | | | | | | | | |
| HOLISTIC SOL NTRL HEALING CTRE (HM09989) | | | | | | ● | | | | | | | | | | | | | | | | | | |
| COUNTY MAYO | | | | | | | | | | | | | | | | | | | | | | | | |
| NATURAL HEALING CENTRE (HM14547) | | | ● | ● | | ● | | | | | | ● | | | | | ● | | ● | | ● | | | |
| TOBAR PHADRAIC (HM20102) | | | | | | | | | | | | | | | | | | | | | | ● | | |

# O - Z Therapies at Practices/Businesses

| Business by County with Reference no. | Orthotics | Osteomyology | Osteopathy | PAM | Paranormal Therapies | Pattern Therapies | Physiotherapy | Phytotherapy | Pilates | Podiatry | Polarity Therapy | Postural Integration | Primal Therapy | Psionic Therapy |
|---|---|---|---|---|---|---|---|---|---|---|---|---|---|---|
| **COUNTY MONAGHAN** | | | | | | | | | | | | | | |
| HEALTHY CHOICES (HM09426) | | | | | | | | | | | | ● | | |
| NORTHAMBER (HM15050) | | | ● | | | | | | | | | | | |
| **COUNTY ROSCOMMON** | | | | | | | | | | | | | | |
| HOLISTIC HEALTH FARM (HM09980) | | | | | | ● | | | | | | | | |
| **COUNTY SLIGO** | | | | | | | | | | | | | | |
| ANAM CHARA COUNSELLING (HM00802) | | | | | | | | | | | | | | |
| SLIGO CHIROPRACTIC (HM18686) | | | | | | | | | | | | | | |
| **COUNTY TIPPERARY** | | | | | | | | | | | | | | |
| KINSELLA, MARIE (HM11693) | | | | | | | | | | | | | | |
| **COUNTY WESTMEATH** | | | | | | | | | | | | | | |
| HOWE, JAN (HM10263) | | | | | | | | | | | | | | |
| **COUNTY WEXFORD** | | | | | | | | | | | | | | |
| JEFFARIES, PHILIP (HM10958) | | | ● | | | | | | | | | | | |
| JEFFARIES, PHILIP (HM10957) | | | ● | | | | | | | | | | | |
| MURPHY, MARY (HM14388) | | | | | | ● | | | | | | | | |
| OSTEOPATHIC PRACTICE (HM15474) | | | ● | | | | | | | | | | | |
| **COUNTY WICKLOW** | | | | | | | | | | | | | | |
| HOLISTIC OPTIONS (HM09985) | | | | | | | | | | | | | | |
| JAMESON PERSONAL EXCELLENCE (HM10903) | | | | | | | | | | | | | | |
| MARK GOULDING - ACUPUNCTURIST (HM13107) | | | | | | | | | | | | | | |

| Business by County with Reference no. | Psychotherapy | Pyramid Power | Pyscho-Synthesis | Reflexology | Reichian Therapy | Reiki | Remedial Massage | Rogerian Therapy | Rolfing | Seichem | Sensitivity Training | Shiatsu | Silva Method | Sound Therapy | Spiritual Healing |
|---|---|---|---|---|---|---|---|---|---|---|---|---|---|---|---|
| **COUNTY MONAGHAN** | | | | | | | | | | | | | | | |
| HEALTHY CHOICES (HM09426) | | | | ● | | ● | | | | | | | | | ● |
| NORTHAMBER (HM15050) | ● | | | ● | | | | | | | | | | | |
| **COUNTY ROSCOMMON** | | | | | | | | | | | | | | | |
| HOLISTIC HEALTH FARM (HM09980) | | | | ● | | ● | | | | | | | | | |
| **COUNTY SLIGO** | | | | | | | | | | | | | | | |
| ANAM CHARA COUNSELLING (HM00802) | ● | | | | | | | ● | | | | | | | |
| SLIGO CHIROPRACTIC (HM18686) | | | | | | | | | | | | | | | |
| **COUNTY TIPPERARY** | | | | | | | | | | | | | | | |
| KINSELLA, MARIE (HM11693) | | | | | | | | | | | | | | | |
| **COUNTY WESTMEATH** | | | | | | | | | | | | | | | |
| HOWE, JAN (HM10263) | | | | | | | | | | | | ● | | | |
| **COUNTY WEXFORD** | | | | | | | | | | | | | | | |
| JEFFARIES, PHILIP (HM10958) | | | | | | | | | | | | | | | |
| JEFFARIES, PHILIP (HM10957) | | | | | | | | | | | | | | | |
| MURPHY, MARY (HM14388) | ● | | | | | | | ● | | | ● | | | | |
| OSTEOPATHIC PRACTICE (HM15474) | | | | | | | | | | | | | | | |
| **COUNTY WICKLOW** | | | | | | | | | | | | | | | |
| HOLISTIC OPTIONS (HM09985) | | | | ● | | | | | | | | | | | |
| JAMESON PERSONAL EXCELLENCE (HM10903) | ● | | | | | ● | | | | ● | | | | | ● |
| MARK GOULDING - ACUPUNCTURIST (HM13107) | | | | | | | | | | | | | | | |

| Business by County with Reference no. | Sports Massage | Stress Therapy | Swedish Body Massage | Tai-Chi Ch'uan | Tantra Therapy | Tera-Mai | Thought Field Therapy | Touch Therapy | Transactional Analysis | Tui-na | Ultrasonics | Vibrational Therapy | Visualisation Therapy | Vitamin Therapy | Voice Therapy | X-Ray | Ying & Yang | Yoga | Zen Therapy | Zero Balancing |
|---|---|---|---|---|---|---|---|---|---|---|---|---|---|---|---|---|---|---|---|---|
| **COUNTY MONAGHAN** | | | | | | | | | | | | | | | | | | | | |
| HEALTHY CHOICES (HM09426) | | ● | | | | | | | | | ● | | | ● | | | | | | |
| NORTHAMBER (HM15050) | | ● | | | | | | | | | | ● | | ● | | | | | | |
| **COUNTY ROSCOMMON** | | | | | | | | | | | | | | | | | | | | |
| HOLISTIC HEALTH FARM (HM09980) | | | | | | | | | | | | | | | | | | | | |
| **COUNTY SLIGO** | | | | | | | | | | | | | | | | | | | | |
| ANAM CHARA COUNSELLING (HM00802) | | | | | | | | | | | | | | | | | | | | |
| SLIGO CHIROPRACTIC (HM18686) | | | | | | | | | | | | | | | | ● | | | | |
| **COUNTY TIPPERARY** | | | | | | | | | | | | | | | | | | | | |
| KINSELLA, MARIE (HM11693) | | ● | | | | | | | | | | | | | | | | | | |
| **COUNTY WESTMEATH** | | | | | | | | | | | | | | | | | | | | |
| HOWE, JAN (HM10263) | | | | | | | | | | | | | | | | | | | | |
| **COUNTY WEXFORD** | | | | | | | | | | | | | | | | | | | | |
| JEFFARIES, PHILIP (HM10958) | | | | | | | | | | | | | | | | | | | | |
| JEFFARIES, PHILIP (HM10957) | | | | | | | | | | | | | | | | | | | | |
| MURPHY, MARY (HM14388) | | ● | | | | | | | ● | | | | | | | | | | | |
| OSTEOPATHIC PRACTICE (HM15474) | | | | | | | | | | | | | | | | | | | | |
| **COUNTY WICKLOW** | | | | | | | | | | | | | | | | | | | | |
| HOLISTIC OPTIONS (HM09985) | | ● | | | | | | | | | | | | | | | | | | |
| JAMESON PERSONAL EXCELLENCE (HM10903) | | ● | | | | | | ● | | | | | ● | | | | | | | |
| MARK GOULDING - ACUPUNCTURIST (HM13107) | | ● | | | | | | | | | | | | | | | | | | |

# O - Z Therapies at Practices/Businesses

Business by County with Reference no.

| Business | Orthotics | Osteomyology | Osteopathy | PAM | Paranormal Therapies | Pattern Therapies | Physiotherapy | Phytotherapy | Pilates | Podiatry | Polarity Therapy | Postural Integration | Primal Therapy | Psionic Therapy | Psychotherapy | Pyramid Power | Pyscho-Synthesis | Reflexology | Reichian Therapy | Reiki | Remedial Massage | Rogerian Therapy | Rolfing | Seichem | Sensitivity Training |
|---|---|---|---|---|---|---|---|---|---|---|---|---|---|---|---|---|---|---|---|---|---|---|---|---|---|
| **NORTHERN IRELAND** | | | | | | | | | | | | | | | | | | | | | | | | | |
| **COUNTY ANTRIM** | | | | | | | | | | | | | | | | | | | | | | | | | |
| ACTIVE BALANCE CLINIC (HM00189) | | | ● | | | | | ● | | | | | | | | | | | | | | | | | |
| BAILIE, EILEEN (HM01556) | | | | | | | | | | | | | | | | | | ● | | | | | | | |
| BROWN, AVRIL (HM03215) | | | | | | | | | | | | | | | ● | | | | | | | | | | |
| CLARKE, LORRAINE (HM04591) | | | | | | | | | | | | | | | | | | ● | | | | | | | |
| DOHERTY, COLIN (HM06153) | | | | | | | | | | | | | | | | | | ● | | | | | | | |
| EAKIN, LINDA (HM06482) | | | | | | | | | | | | | | | | | | ● | | | | | | | |
| EARLS, JAMES (HM06497) | | | | | | | | | | | | | | | | | | ● | | | | | | | |
| FARRELL, BARBARA (HM07127) | | | | | | | | | | | | | | | | | | ● | | | | | | | |
| FLANIGAN, JANICE (HM07392) | | | | | | | | | | | | | | | | | | ● | | | | | | | |
| FLORENCE SHARPE CHIROPODIST (HM07431) | | | | | | | | | | ● | | | | | | | | | | | | | | | |
| FRAMAR NATURAL HEALTH CLINIC (HM07654) | | | ● | | | | | ● | | | | | | | | | | ● | | ● | | | | | |
| GIBSON, A E (HM08035) | | | ● | | | | | | | | | | | | | | | | | | | | | | |
| GIVEN, CLIVE (HM08115) | | | | | | | | | | | | | | | | | | ● | | ● | | | | | |
| HAYHURST, GEOFFREY A (HM09267) | | | ● | | | | | | | | | | | | | | | | | | | | | | |
| HOSWELL, CHRISTINE (HM10205) | | | | | | | | | | | | | | | | | | ● | | | | | | | |
| HYPNOTHERAPY CENTRE (HM10521) | | | | | | | ● | | | | | | | | | | | | | | | | | | |
| LAMBERT, RACHEL (HM11901) | | | | | | | | | | | | | | | | | | ● | | ● | | | | | |
| MAXWELL, MARY (HM13337) | | | | | | | | | | | | | | | | | | ● | | | | | | | |
| MCCARTNEY, W J (HM13401) | | | | | | | | | | ● | | | | | | | | | | | | | | | |
| MCCRYSTALS NATUROPATHIC CENTRE (HM13436) | | | | | | | | | | | | | | | | | | ● | | | | | | | |
| MCMULLAN, MARITA (HM13575) | | | | | | | | | | | | | | | | | | ● | | | | | | | |
| MYSTIC SCHEHERAZADE (HM14445) | | | | | | | | | | | | | | | | | | | | | | | | | |
| O'RAWE, IVY (HM15358) | | | | | | | | | | | | | | | | | | ● | | | | | | | |
| W M RYAN AND SON (HM20722) | | | | | | | | | | | | | | | | | | ● | | | | | | | |
| WRAY, CAROLE (HM21917) | | | | | | | | | | | | | | | | | | ● | | | | | | | |
| YOGA BIOMEDICAL TRUST (HM22021) | | | | | | | | | | | | | | | | | | | | | | | | | |
| **COUNTY ARMAGH** | | | | | | | | | | | | | | | | | | | | | | | | | |
| MCCRORY, GERALDINE (HM13434) | | | | | | | | | | | | | | | | | | ● | | | | | | | |
| MITCHELL, DEIRDRE (HM14004) | | | | | | | | | | | | | | | | | | ● | | | | | | | |
| O'NEILL, MARIA (HM15333) | | | | | | | | | | | | | | | | | | ● | | | | | | | |
| WHITTOCK, ANNE (HM21426) | | | | | | | | | | | | | | | | | | ● | | | | | | | |

| Business | Shiatsu | Silva Method | Sound Therapy | Spiritual Healing | Sports Massage | Stress Therapy | Swedish Body Massage | T'ai-Chi Ch'uan | Tantra Therapy | Tera-Mai | Thought Field Therapy | Touch Therapy | Transactional Analysis | Tui-na | Ultrasonics | Vibrational Therapy | Visualisation Therapy | Vitamin Therapy | Voice Therapy | X-Ray | Ying & Yang | Yoga | Zen Therapy | Zero Balancing |
|---|---|---|---|---|---|---|---|---|---|---|---|---|---|---|---|---|---|---|---|---|---|---|---|---|
| **NORTHERN IRELAND** | | | | | | | | | | | | | | | | | | | | | | | | |
| **COUNTY ANTRIM** | | | | | | | | | | | | | | | | | | | | | | | | |
| ACTIVE BALANCE CLINIC (HM00189) | | | | | | ● | | | | | | | | | | | | ● | | | | | | |
| BAILIE, EILEEN (HM01556) | | | | | | | | | | | | | | | | | | | | | | | | |
| BROWN, AVRIL (HM03215) | | | | | | | | | | | | | | | | | | | | | | | | |
| CLARKE, LORRAINE (HM04591) | | | | | | | | | | | | | | | | | | | | | | | | |
| DOHERTY, COLIN (HM06153) | | | | | | | | | | | | | | | | | | | | | | | | |
| EAKIN, LINDA (HM06482) | | | | | | | | | | | | | | | | | | | | | | | | |
| EARLS, JAMES (HM06497) | | | | | | | | | | | | | | | | | | | | | | | | |
| FARRELL, BARBARA (HM07127) | | | | | | | | | | | | | | | | | | | | | | | | |
| FLANIGAN, JANICE (HM07392) | | | | | | | | | | | | | | | | | | | | | | | | |
| FLORENCE SHARPE CHIROPODIST (HM07431) | | | | | | | | | | | | | | | | | | | | | | | | |
| FRAMAR NATURAL HEALTH CLINIC (HM07654) | | | | | | | | | | | | | | | | | | ● | | | | | | |
| GIBSON, A E (HM08035) | | | | | | | | | | | | | | | | | | | | | | | | |
| GIVEN, CLIVE (HM08115) | | | | | | | | | | | | | | | | | | | | | | | | |
| HAYHURST, GEOFFREY A (HM09267) | | | | | | | | | | | | | | | | | | | | | | | | |
| HOSWELL, CHRISTINE (HM10205) | | | | | | | | | | | | | | | | | | | | | | | | |
| HYPNOTHERAPY CENTRE (HM10521) | | | | | | | | | | | | | | | | | | | | | | | | |
| LAMBERT, RACHEL (HM11901) | | | | | | | | | | | | | | | | | | | | | | | | |
| MAXWELL, MARY (HM13337) | | | | | | | | | | | | | | | | | | | | | | | | |
| MCCARTNEY, W J (HM13401) | | | | | | | | | | | | | | | | | | | | | | | | |
| MCCRYSTALS NATUROPATHIC CENTRE (HM13436) | | | | | | ● | | | | | | ● | | | | | | ● | | | | | | |
| MCMULLAN, MARITA (HM13575) | | | | | | | | | | | | | | | | | | | | | | | | |
| MYSTIC SCHEHERAZADE (HM14445) | | | | ● | | | | | | | | | | | | | | | | | | | | |
| O'RAWE, IVY (HM15358) | | | | | | | | | | | | | | | | | | | | | | | | |
| W M RYAN AND SON (HM20722) | | | | | | | | | | | | | | | | | | | | | | | | |
| WRAY, CAROLE (HM21917) | | | | | | | | | | | | | | | | | | | | | | | | |
| YOGA BIOMEDICAL TRUST (HM22021) | | | | | | | | | | | | | | | | | | | | | ● | | | |
| **COUNTY ARMAGH** | | | | | | | | | | | | | | | | | | | | | | | | |
| MCCRORY, GERALDINE (HM13434) | | | | | | | | | | | | | | | | | | | | | | | | |
| MITCHELL, DEIRDRE (HM14004) | | | | | | | | | | | | | | | | | | | | | | | | |
| O'NEILL, MARIA (HM15333) | | | | | | | | | | | | | | | | | | | | | | | | |
| WHITTOCK, ANNE (HM21426) | | | | | | | | | | | | | | | | | | | | | | | | |

# O - Z Therapies at Practices/Businesses

| Business by County with Reference no. | Orthotics | Osteomyology | Osteopathy | PAM | Paranormal Therapies | Pattern Therapies | Physiotherapy | Phytotherapy | Pilates | Podiatry | Polarity Therapy | Postural Integration | Primal Therapy | Psionic Therapy | Psychotherapy | Pyramid Power | Pyscho-Synthesis | Reflexology | Reichian Therapy | Reiki | Remedial Massage | Rogerian Therapy | Rolfing | Seichem | Sensitivity Training | Shiatsu | Silva Method | Sound Therapy | Spiritual Healing | Sports Massage | Stress Therapy | Swedish Body Massage | T'ai-Chi Ch'uan | Tantra Therapy | Tera-Mai | Thought Field Therapy | Touch Therapy | Transactional Analysis | Tui-na | Ultrasonics | Vibrational Therapy | Visualisation Therapy | Vitamin Therapy | Voice Therapy | X-Ray | Ying & Yang | Yoga | Zen Therapy | Zero Balancing |
|---|---|---|---|---|---|---|---|---|---|---|---|---|---|---|---|---|---|---|---|---|---|---|---|---|---|---|---|---|---|---|---|---|---|---|---|---|---|---|---|---|---|---|---|---|---|---|---|---|---|
| WILLIS, IAN (HM21614) | | | | | | | | | | ● | | | | | | | | | | | | | | | | | | | | | | | | | | | | | | | | | | | | | | | | |
| COUNTY DOWN | | | | | | | | | | | | | | | | | | | | | | | | | | | | | | | | | | | | | | | | | | | | | | | | | | |
| BANGOR OSTEOPATHIC CLINIC (HM01660) | | | ● | | | | | | | | | | | | | | | | | | | | | | | | | | | | | | | | | | | | | | | | | | | | | | | |
| CHIROPRACTICE (HM04405) | | | | | | | | | | ● | | | | | | | | | | | | | | | | | | | | | | | | | | | | | | | | | | | | | | | | |
| GIBSON, A E (HM08034) | | | ● | | | | | | | | | | | | | | | | | | | | | | | | | | | | | | | | | | | | | | | | | | | | | | | |
| HADDEN, MARLENE (HM08687) | | | | | | | | | | | | | | | | | | ● | | | | | | | | | | | | | | | | | | | | | | | | | | | | | | | | |
| KIRK, DONNA (HM11706) | | | | | | | | | | | | | | | | | | ● | | | | | | | | | | | | | | | | | | | | | | | | | | | | | | | | |
| LYCIUM CENTRE (HM12755) | | | | | | | | | | | | | | | | | | ● | | | | | | | | | | | | | | | | | | | | | | | | | | | | | | | | |
| MCCARTAN, DEBORAH (HM13392) | | | | | | | | | | ● | | | | | | | | | | | | | | | | | | | | | | | | | | | | | | | | | | | | | | | | |
| MCCOY, DOLORES (HM13428) | | | | | | | | | | | | | | | | | | ● | | | | | | | | | | | | | | | | | | | | | | | | | | | | | | | | |
| MCCUTCHEON, R M (HM13440) | | | ● | | | | | | | | | | | | | | | | | | | | | | | | | | | | | | | | | | | | | | | | | | | | | | | |
| MCCUTCHEON, TINA (HM13441) | | | ● | | | | | | | | | | | | | | | | | | | | | | | | | | | | | | | | | | | | | | | | | | | | | | | |
| MCGUIGGAN, MARY (HM13506) | | | | | | | | | | | | | | | | | | ● | | | | | | | | | | | | | | | | | | | | | | | | | | | | | | | | |
| NORTH DOWN CLINIC (HM15023) | | | ● | | | | | | | | | | | | | | | | | | | | | | | | | | | | | | | | | | | | | | | | | | | | | | | |
| PRINGLE CHIROPRACTIC (HM16626) | | | | | | | | | ● | | | | | | | | | ● | | ● | | | ● | | | ● | | | | | | | ● | | | | | | | | | | | | ● | ● | | | |
| PUNDYKE, MARIA (HM16758) | | | | | | | | | | | | | | | | | | ● | | | | | | | | | | | | | | | | | | | | | | | | | | | | | | | | |
| QUINN, BARBARA (HM16808) | | | ● | | | | | | | | | | | | | | | | | | | | | | | | | | | | | | | | | | | | | | | | | | | | | | | |
| REFLEXOLOGY CLINIC (HM17092) | | | | | | | | | | | | | | | | | | ● | | | | | | | | | | | | | | | | | | | | | | | | | | | | | | | | |
| ROYLANCE, HEATHER (HM17718) | | | | | | | | | | | | | | | | | | ● | | | | | | | | | | | | | | | | | | | | | | | | | | | | | | | | |
| TUDOR REFLEXOLOGY (HM20372) | | | | | | | | | | | | | | | | | | ● | | | | | | | | | | | | | | | | | | | | | | | | | | | | | | | | |
| YOGA CENTRE OF IRELAND (HM22023) | | | | | | | | | | | | | | | | | | | | | | | | | | | | | | | | | | | | | | | | | | | | | | | ● | | |
| COUNTY LONDONDERRY | | | | | | | | | | | | | | | | | | | | | | | | | | | | | | | | | | | | | | | | | | | | | | | | | | |
| CURRAN, MAUREEN (HM05630) | | | | | | | | | | | | | | | | | | ● | | ● | | | | | | | | | | | ● | | | | | | | | | | | | | | | | | | | |
| DISPENSERY (HM06117) | | | | | | | | | | | | | | | | | | ● | | ● | | | | | | ● | | | | ● | | | | | | | | | | | | | | | | | ● | | |
| EQUILIBRIUM HOLISTIC CLINIC (HM06875) | | | | | | | | | | | | | | | | | | ● | | ● | | | | | | | | | | | | | ● | | | | | | | | | | | | | | ● | | |
| FEET FIRST (HM07174) | | | | | | | | | | ● | | | | | | | | | | | | | | | | | | | | | | | | | | | | | | | | | | | | | | | | |
| FOYLE HYPNOTHERAPY CENTRE (HM07646) | | | | | | | | | | | | | | | ● | | | | | | | | | | | | | | | | ● | | | | | | | | | | | ● | | | | ● | | | |
| MCBRINE, HAZEL (HM13374) | | | | | | | | | | | | | | | | | | ● | | | | | | | | | | | | | | | | | | | | | | | | | | | | | | | | |
| COUNTY TYRONE | | | | | | | | | | | | | | | | | | | | | | | | | | | | | | | | | | | | | | | | | | | | | | | | | | |
| BRADLEY, R M (HM02871) | | | | | | | | | | ● | | | | | | | | | | | | | | | | | | | | | | | | | | | | | | | | | | | | | | | | |
| ROSEWOOD HEALTH CLINIC (HM17630) | | | | | | | | | | | | | | | | | | ● | | | | | | | | | | | | | | | | | | | | | | | | | | | | | | | | |

# O - Z Therapies at Practices/Businesses

| Business by County with Reference no. | Orthotics | Osteomyology | Osteopathy | PAM | Paranormal Therapies | Pattern Therapies | Physiotherapy | Phytotherapy | Pilates | Podiatry | Polarity Therapy | Postural Integration | Primal Therapy | Psionic Therapy | Psychotherapy | Pyramid Power | Pyscho-Synthesis | Reflexology | Reichian Therapy | Reiki | Remedial Massage | Rogerian Therapy | Rolfing | Seichem | Sensitivity Training | Shiatsu | Silva Method | Sound Therapy | Spiritual Healing | Sports Massage | Stress Therapy | Swedish Body Massage | T'ai-Chi Ch'uan | Tantra Therapy | Tera-Mai | Thought Field Therapy | Touch Therapy | Transactional Analysis | Tui-na | Ultrasonics | Vibrational Therapy | Visualisation Therapy | Vitamin Therapy | Voice Therapy | X-Ray | Ying & Yang | Yoga | Zen Therapy | Zero Balancing |
|---|---|---|---|---|---|---|---|---|---|---|---|---|---|---|---|---|---|---|---|---|---|---|---|---|---|---|---|---|---|---|---|---|---|---|---|---|---|---|---|---|---|---|---|---|---|---|---|---|---|
| **SCOTLAND** | | | | | | | | | | | | | | | | | | | | | | | | | | | | | | | | | | | | | | | | | | | | | | | | | |
| **ABERDEENSHIRE** | | | | | | | | | | | | | | | | | | | | | | | | | | | | | | | | | | | | | | | | | | | | | | | | | |
| ALTERNATIVE PRACTICE (HM00723) | | | | | | | | | | | | | | | | | | ● | | ● | | | | | | | | | | | | | | | | | | | | | | | | | | | | | |
| ANTHONY, JOHN (HM00918) | | | | | | | | | | | | | | | ● | | | | | | | | | | | | | | | | | | | | | | | | | | | | | | | | | | |
| BEECHGROVE CLINIC (HM02050) | | | ● | | | | | | | | | ● | | | | | | | | | | | | | | | | | | | | | | | | | | | | ● | | | | | | | ● | | |
| BIRNIE, KATHLEEN (HM02394) | | | | | | | | | | | | | | | | | | ● | | | | | | | | | | | | | | | | | | | | | | | | | | | | | | | |
| CHELSEA HOUSE CLINIC (HM04090) | | | | | | | | | | ● | | | | | | | | ● | | ● | | | | | | | | | | | | | | | | | | | | | | | | | | | | | |
| CLAIRBAUX CLINIC (HM04506) | | | | | | | ● | | | | | | | | | | | | | | | | | | | | | | | | | | | | | | | | | | | | | | | | | | |
| CLAIRBAUX CLINIC (HM04505) | | | | | | | ● | | | | | | | | | | | | | | | | | | | | | | | | | | | | | | | | | | | | | | | | | | |
| CRAN, LORAINE (HM05366) | | | | | | | | | | | | | | | | | | ● | | | | | | | | | | | | | | | | | | | | | | | | | | | | | | | |
| DAVISON, FIONA (HM05865) | | | ● | | | | | | | | | | | | | | | | | | | | | | | | | | | | | | | | | | | | | | | | | | | | | | |
| GRAY, SHEILA (HM08419) | | | | | | | | | | | | | | | | | | ● | | ● | | | | | | | | | | | | | | | | | | | | | | | | | | | | | |
| MCPHERSON, MALCOLM (HM13589) | | | | | | | | | | | | | | | ● | | | | | | | | | | | | | | | | | | | | | | | | | | | | | | | | | | |
| MITCHELL, GILLIAN M (HM14007) | | | ● | | | | | | | | | | | | | | | | | | | | | | | | | | | | | | | | | | | | | | | | | | | | | | |
| REIKI TRAINING CENTRE (HM17149) | | | | | | | | | | | | | | | | | | | | ● | | | | | | | | | | | | | | | | | | | | | | | | | | | | | |
| RICHARDSON, ROSEMARY (HM17288) | | | | | | | | | | | | | | | | | | ● | | | | | | | | | | | | | | | | | | | | | | | | | | | | | | | |
| RIVERSIDE CHIROPRACTIC CLINIC (HM17378) | | | | | | | | | | | | ● | | | | | | | | | | | | | | | | | | | | | | | | | | | | | | | ● | | | | | | |
| ROBINSON, ELIZABETH (HM17469) | | | ● | | | | | | | | | | | | | | | | | | | | | | | | | | | | | | | | | | | | | | | | | | | | | | |
| ROSEMOUNT CENTRE (HM17623) | | | | | | | | | | | | | | | ● | | | ● | | ● | | | | | | ● | | | | | | | | | | | | | | | | | | | | | | | |
| ROSEMOUNT OSTEOPATHY (HM17625) | | | ● | | | | | | | | | | | | | | | | | | | | | | | | | | | | | | | | | | | | | | | | | | | | | | |
| ROSS, COLIN R (HM17634) | | | ● | | | | | | | | | | | | | | | | | | | | | | | | | | | | | | | | | | | | | | | | | | | | | | |
| SAWYER, KEN (HM17985) | | | | | | | | | | | | | | | ● | | | | | | | | | | | | | | | | | | | | | | | | | | | | | | | | | | |
| SERENDIPITY (HM18232) | | | | | | | | | | | | | | | | | | ● | | ● | | | | | | | | | | | | | | | | | | | | | | | | | | | | | |
| TAGGART, RUTH (HM19652) | | | | | | | | | | | | | | | | | | | | | ● | | | | | | | | | | ● | | | | | | | | | | | | | | | | | | |
| TOE TO HEEL - REFLEXOLOGY (HM20110) | | | | | | | | | | | | | | | | | | ● | | | | | | | | | | | | | | | | | | | | | | | | | | | | | | | |
| WEST END PHYSIOTHERAPY (HM21219) | | | | | | | ● | | | | | | | | | | | | | | | | | | | | | | | | | | | | | | | | | | | | | | | | | | |
| WILKEN, ANGEL (HM21492) | | | | | | | | | | | | | | | | | | ● | | | | | | | | | | | | | ● | | | | | | | | | | | | | | | | | | |
| WILSON, R (HM21666) | | | ● | | | | | | | | | | | | | | | | | | | | | | | | | | | | | | | | | | | | | | | | | | | | | | |
| **ANGUS** | | | | | | | | | | | | | | | | | | | | | | | | | | | | | | | | | | | | | | | | | | | | | | | | | |
| BAKER, P T (HM01593) | | | ● | | | | | | | | | | | | | | | | | | | | | | | | | | | | | | | | | | | | | | | | | | | | | | |
| FALCONER, N (HM07072) | | | ● | | | | | | | | | | | | | | | | | | | | | | | | | | | | | | | | | | | | | | | | | | | | | | |
| FRASER, SANDY (HM07700) | | | ● | | | | | | | | | | | | | | | | | | | | | | | | | | | | | | | | | | | | | | | | | | | | | | |
| HOLISTIC HEALING CENTRE (HM09964) | | | ● | | | | | | | | | | | | | | | | | | | | | | | | | | | | | | | | | | | | | | | | | | | | | | |

# O - Z Therapies at Practices/Businesses

| Business by County with Reference no. | Orthotics | Osteomyology | Osteopathy | PAM | Paranormal Therapies | Pattern Therapies | Physiotherapy | Phytotherapy | Pilates | Podiatry | Polarity Therapy | Postural Integration | Primal Therapy | Psionic Therapy | Psychotherapy | Pyramid Power | Pyscho-Synthesis | Reflexology | Reichian Therapy | Reiki | Remedial Massage | Rogerian Therapy | Rolfing | Seichem | Sensitivity Training |
|---|---|---|---|---|---|---|---|---|---|---|---|---|---|---|---|---|---|---|---|---|---|---|---|---|---|
| KIRRIEMUIR PHYSIO CLINIC (HM11723) | | | | | | | ● | | | | | | | | | | | | | | | | | | |
| MIND BODY SOUL & ASSOCIATES (HM13960) | | | ● | | | | | | | | | | | | | | | ● | | ● | ● | | | | |
| NEILSON, J R (HM14767) | | | | | | | | | | | | | | | ● | | | | | | | | | | |
| NEWAYS INDEPENDENT CONSULTANT (HM14844) | | | | | | | | | | | | | | | | | | | | | | | | | |
| NICOLL, ELAINE (HM14929) | | | | | | | | | | ● | | | | | | | | | | | | | | | |
| ARGYLL AND BUTE | | | | | | | | | | | | | | | | | | | | | | | | | |
| BRIMELOW, KEITH (HM03052) | | | ● | | | | | | | | | | | | | | | | | | | | | | |
| COMPLEMENTARY HEALTH CENTRE (HM04922) | | | ● | | | | | | | | | | | | | | | | | | | | | | |
| GIBSON, RONALD J (HM08045) | | | | | | | | | | ● | | | | | | | | ● | | | | | | | |
| GRAPEVINE (HM08398) | | | | | | | | | | | | | | | | | | | | ● | | | | | |
| HOMEOPATHIC PODIATRIST/REFLEX (HM10078) | | | | | | | | | | | | | | | | | | ● | | | | | | | |
| LINTON, THERESA (HM12443) | | | | | | | | | | | | | | | | | | ● | | | | | | | |
| NATURAL THERAPY CENTRE (HM14648) | | | ● | | | | | | | | | | | | | | | ● | | | | | | | |
| REIKI LIGHT (HM17138) | | | | | | | | | | | | | | | | | | | | ● | | | | | |
| AYRSHIRE (EAST) | | | | | | | | | | | | | | | | | | | | | | | | | |
| LITTLEJOHN, S (HM12473) | | | | | | | | | | ● | | | | | | | | | | | | | | | |
| LYNN BROWN CLINICAL AROM (HM12772) | | | | | | | | | | | | | | | | | | ● | | | | | | | |
| REID, ELIZABETH (HM17117) | | | | | | | | | | | | | | | | | | ● | | ● | | | | | |
| AYRSHIRE (NORTH) | | | | | | | | | | | | | | | | | | | | | | | | | |
| REID, E (HM17116) | | | | | | | | | | | | | | | | | | ● | | | | | | | |
| AYRSHIRE (SOUTH) | | | | | | | | | | | | | | | | | | | | | | | | | |
| BELL, W DOUGLAS (HM02091) | | | | | | | | | | | | | | | | | | ● | | | | | | | |
| CARRICK CLINIC (HM03742) | | | ● | | | | | | | | | | | | | | | ● | | | | | | | |
| ESSENCE OF HEALTH (HM06890) | | | | | | | | | | | | | | | | | | ● | | ● | | | | ● | |
| HARDIE, ANNE (HM08966) | | | | | | | ● | | | | | | | | | | | | | | | | | | |
| HEARTLAKE PHYSIOTHERAPY (HM09444) | | | | | | | ● | | | | | | | | | | | | | | | | | | |
| HODGE, IAN (HM09874) | | | | | ● | | | | | | | | | | ● | | | | | | | ● | | | |
| SCOTTISH SCHOOL OF REFLEXOLOGY (HM18136) | | | | | | | | | | | | | | | | | | ● | | | | | | | |
| SMITH, ALICIA (HM18712) | | | | | | | | | | | | | | | ● | | | ● | | | | | | | |
| STEWART, ALAN (HM19257) | | | | | | | | | | | | | | | | | | | | ● | | | | | |
| CLACKMANNANSHIRE | | | | | | | | | | | | | | | | | | | | | | | | | |
| ALTERNATIVE MEDICAL CLINIC (HM00711) | | | | | | | | | | | | | | | | | | ● | | | ● | | | | |
| DUMFRIES AND GALLOWAY | | | | | | | | | | | | | | | | | | | | | | | | | |
| BURTON, VICKY (HM03447) | | | | | | | | | | | | | | | | | | ● | | ● | | | | | |

| Business by County with Reference no. | Shiatsu | Silva Method | Sound Therapy | Spiritual Healing | Sports Massage | Stress Therapy | Swedish Body Massage | T'ai-Chi Ch'uan | Tantra Therapy | Tera-Mai | Thought Field Therapy | Touch Therapy | Transactional Analysis | Tui-na | Ultrasonics | Vibrational Therapy | Visualisation Therapy | Vitamin Therapy | Voice Therapy | X-Ray | Ying & Yang | Yoga | Zen Therapy | Zero Balancing |
|---|---|---|---|---|---|---|---|---|---|---|---|---|---|---|---|---|---|---|---|---|---|---|---|---|
| KIRRIEMUIR PHYSIO CLINIC (HM11723) | | | | | | | | | | | | | | | | | | | | | | | | |
| MIND BODY SOUL & ASSOCIATES (HM13960) | ● | | | | | ● | ● | | | | | | | | | | | | | | | | | |
| NEILSON, J R (HM14767) | | | | | | | | | | | | | | | | | | | | | | | | |
| NEWAYS INDEPENDENT CONSULTANT (HM14844) | | | | | | | | | | | | | | | | | | ● | | | | | | |
| NICOLL, ELAINE (HM14929) | | | | | | | | | | | | | | | | | | | | | | | | |
| ARGYLL AND BUTE | | | | | | | | | | | | | | | | | | | | | | | | |
| BRIMELOW, KEITH (HM03052) | | | | | | | | | | | | | | | | | | | | | | | | |
| COMPLEMENTARY HEALTH CENTRE (HM04922) | | | | | | | | | | | | | | | | | | | | | | | | |
| GIBSON, RONALD J (HM08045) | | | | | | | | | | | | | | | | | | | | | | | | |
| GRAPEVINE (HM08398) | | | | ● | | | | | | | | | | | | | | | | | | | | |
| HOMEOPATHIC PODIATRIST/REFLEX (HM10078) | | | | | | | | | | | | | | | | | | | | | | | | |
| LINTON, THERESA (HM12443) | | | | | | | | | | | | | | | | | | | | | | | | |
| NATURAL THERAPY CENTRE (HM14648) | | | | | | ● | | | | | | | | | | | | | | | | | | |
| REIKI LIGHT (HM17138) | | | | | | | | | | | | | | | | | | | | | | | | |
| AYRSHIRE (EAST) | | | | | | | | | | | | | | | | | | | | | | | | |
| LITTLEJOHN, S (HM12473) | | | | | | | | | | | | | | | | | | | | | | | | |
| LYNN BROWN CLINICAL AROM (HM12772) | | | | | | | | | | | | | | | | | | | | | | | | |
| REID, ELIZABETH (HM17117) | | | | | | ● | | | | | | | | | | | | | | | | | | |
| AYRSHIRE (NORTH) | | | | | | | | | | | | | | | | | | | | | | | | |
| REID, E (HM17116) | | | | | | | | | | | | | | | | | | | | | | | | |
| AYRSHIRE (SOUTH) | | | | | | | | | | | | | | | | | | | | | | | | |
| BELL, W DOUGLAS (HM02091) | | | | | | | | | | | | | | | | | | | | | | | | |
| CARRICK CLINIC (HM03742) | | | | | | | | | | | | | | | ● | | | ● | | | | | | |
| ESSENCE OF HEALTH (HM06890) | ● | | | ● | | | | | | | | | | | | | | | | | | | | |
| HARDIE, ANNE (HM08966) | | | | | | | | | | | | | | | | | | | | | | | | |
| HEARTLAKE PHYSIOTHERAPY (HM09444) | | | | | | | | | | | | | | | | | | | | | | | | |
| HODGE, IAN (HM09874) | | | | | | ● | | | | | | | | | | | ● | | | | | ● | | |
| SCOTTISH SCHOOL OF REFLEXOLOGY (HM18136) | | | | | | | | | | | | | | | | | | | | | | | | |
| SMITH, ALICIA (HM18712) | | | | | | ● | | | | | | | | | | | | | | | | | | |
| STEWART, ALAN (HM19257) | | | | | | | ● | | | | | | | | | | | | | | | | | |
| CLACKMANNANSHIRE | | | | | | | | | | | | | | | | | | | | | | | | |
| ALTERNATIVE MEDICAL CLINIC (HM00711) | | | | | | | | | | | | | | | | | | | | | | | | |
| DUMFRIES AND GALLOWAY | | | | | | | | | | | | | | | | | | | | | | | | |
| BURTON, VICKY (HM03447) | | | | | | | | | | | | | | | | | | | | | | | | |

# O - Z Therapies at Practices/Businesses

| Business by County with Reference no. | Orthotics | Osteomyology | Osteopathy | PAM | Paranormal Therapies | Pattern Therapies | Physiotherapy | Phytotherapy | Pilates | Podiatry | Polarity Therapy | Postural Integration | Primal Therapy | Psionic Therapy | Psychotherapy | Pyramid Power | Pyscho-Synthesis | Reflexology | Reichian Therapy | Reiki | Remedial Massage | Rogerian Therapy | Rolfing | Seichem | Sensitivity Training | Shiatsu | Silva Method | Sound Therapy | Spiritual Healing | Sports Massage | Stress Therapy | Swedish Body Massage | T'ai-Chi Ch'uan | Tantra Therapy | Tera-Mai | Thought Field Therapy | Touch Therapy | Transactional Analysis | Tui-na | Ultrasonics | Vibrational Therapy | Visualisation Therapy | Vitamin Therapy | Voice Therapy | X-Ray | Ying & Yang | Yoga | Zen Therapy | Zero Balancing |
|---|---|---|---|---|---|---|---|---|---|---|---|---|---|---|---|---|---|---|---|---|---|---|---|---|---|---|---|---|---|---|---|---|---|---|---|---|---|---|---|---|---|---|---|---|---|---|---|---|---|
| DUMFRIES HOLISTIC HEALTH CTRE (HM06386) | | | ● | | | | | | | | | | | | ● | | | ● | | | ● | | | | | | | | ● | | | | | | | | | | | | | | | | | | | | |
| DUNLOP, JAMES R W (HM06410) | | | ● | | | | | | | | | | | | | | | | | | | | | | | | | | | | | | | | | | | | | | | | | | | | | | |
| HEALTH STRESS & INJURIES CLNC (HM09405) | | | | | | | | | | | | | | | ● | | | | | | | | | | | | | | ● | | | | | | | | | | | | | | | | | | | | |
| HEPPEL, V (HM09583) | | | | | | | | | | | | | | | ● | | | | | | | | | | | | | | | | | | | | | | | | | | | | | | | | | | |
| MCCLYMOUNT, JENNIFER (HM13416) | | | | | | | | | | ● | | | | | | | | | | | | | | | | | | | | | | | | | | | | | | | | | | | | | | | |
| WILLIAMS, KELLY (HM21576) | | | | | | | | | | | | | | | | | | ● | | | | | | | | | | | | | | | | | | | | | | | | | | | | | | | |
| **EDINBURGH (CITY OF)** | | | | | | | | | | | | | | | | | | | | | | | | | | | | | | | | | | | | | | | | | | | | | | | | | |
| ACTIVE OSTEOPATHS (HM00200) | | | ● | | | | | | | | | | | | | | | | | | | | | | | | | | | | | | | | | | | | | | | | | | | | | | |
| BLACKHALL PHYSIOTHERAPY CLINIC (HM02445) | | | | | | | | | | | | | | | ● | | | | | | | | | | | | | | | | | | | | | | | | | | | | | | | | | | |
| BLAIR, RICHARD (HM02475) | | | | | | | | | | | | | | | | | | | | | | | | | | ● | | | | | | | | | | | | | | | | | | | | | | | |
| BOYD, A (HM02817) | | | | | | | | | | | | | | | ● | | | | | | | | | | | | | | | | | | | | | | | | | | | | | | | | | | |
| CARRS, ALLEN (HM03762) | | | | | | | | | | | | | | | ● | | | | | | | | | | | | | | | | | | | | | | | | | | | | | | | | | | |
| CHRISTIE, ADRIAN (HM04438) | | | | | | | | | | | | | | | ● | | | | | | | | | | | | | | | | | | | | | | | | | | | | | | | | | | |
| DRUMMOND, TARA W (HM06328) | | | ● | | | | | | | | | | | | | | | | | | | | | | | | | | | | | | | | | | | | | | | | | | | | | | |
| E G H P (HM06468) | | | | | | | | | | | | | | | ● | | | | | | | | | | | | | | | | | | | | | | | | | | | ● | | | | | | | |
| EDINBURGH FLOATARIUM (HM06611) | | | | | | | | | | | | | | | | | | ● | | ● | | | | | | ● | | | | | | | | | | | | | | | | | | | | | | | |
| EDINBURGH OSTEOPATHIC SURGERY (HM06615) | | | ● | | | | | | | | | | | | | | | | | | | | | | | | | | | | | | | | | | | | | | | | | | | | | | |
| EXCLUSIVE HYPNOTHERAPY (HM07019) | | | | | | | | | | | | | | | ● | | | | | | | ● | | | | | | | | | | | | | | | | | | | | | | | | | | | |
| GARDINER, F (HM07872) | | | | | | | | | | | | | | | | | | ● | | | | | | | | | | | | | | | | | | | | | | | | | | | | | | | |
| HOLDEN, SHEENA (HM09934) | | | | | | | | | | | | | | | | | | ● | | | | | | | | | | | | | | | | | | | | | | | | | | | | | | | |
| HOW, HELEN F (HM10231) | | | ● | | | | | | | | | | | | | | | | | | | | | | | | | | | | | | | | | | | | | | | | | | | | | | |
| J W PHYSIOTHERAPY & SPORTS (HM10804) | | | | | | | | | | ● | | | | | | | | | | | | | | | | | | | | | | | | | | | | | | ● | | | | | | | | | |
| J W PHYSIOTHERAPY & SPORTS (HM10805) | | | | | | | | | | ● | | | | | | | | | | | | | | | | | | | | | | | | | | | | | | ● | | | | | | | | | |
| JENAI (HM10980) | | | | | | | | | | | | | | | | | | ● | | | | | | | | | | | | | | | | | | | | | | | | | | | | | | | |
| LIVING MIND (HM12487) | | | | | | | | | | | | | | | | | | | | | | | | | | | | | | | ● | | | | | | | | | | | | | | | | | | |
| LOGAN, CAROL (HM12565) | | | | | | | | | | | | | | | ● | | | | | | | ● | | | | | | | | | | | | | | | | | | | | | | | | | | | |
| MARCHMONT PHYSIOTHERAPY CLINIC (HM13073) | | | | | | | ● | | | | | | | | | | | | | | | | | | | | | | | | | | | | | | | | | | | | | | | | | | |
| MCDONALD, DAVID S (HM13456) | | | | | | | | | | ● | | | | | | | | | | | | | | | | | | | | | | | | | | | | | | | | | | | | | | | |
| MCVITTIE, D (HM13623) | | | | | | | | | | | | | | | | | | ● | | | | | | | | | | | | | | | | | | | | | | | | | | | | | | | |
| MOBILE CHIROPODY SERVICES (HM14028) | | | | | | | | | | ● | | | | | | | | | | | | | | | | | | | | | | | | | | | | | | | | | | | | | | | |
| MORNINGSIDE PODIATRY SERVICE (HM14192) | | | | | | | | | | ● | | | | | | | | | | | | | | | | | | | | | | | | | | | | | | | | | | | | | | | |
| MORRISON, SANDRA (HM14231) | | | | | | | | | | | | | | | | | | ● | | | | | | | | | | | | | | | | | | | | | | | | | | | | | | | |
| PSYCHIC AND LIFE SOLUTIONS (HM16685) | | | | | | | | | | | | | | | | | | | | | | | | | | | | ● | ● | | | | | | | | | | | | | | | | | | | | |
| RADIANT HEALTH (HM16848) | | | | | | | | | | | | | | | | | | | | | | | | | | | | | | | | | ● | | | | | | | | | | | | | | | | |

# O - Z Therapies at Practices/Businesses

| Business by County with Reference no. | Orthotics | Osteomyology | Osteopathy | PAM | Paranormal Therapies | Pattern Therapies | Physiotherapy | Phytotherapy | Pilates | Podiatry | Polarity Therapy | Postural Integration | Primal Therapy | Psionic Therapy | Psychotherapy | Pyramid Power | Pyscho-Synthesis |
|---|---|---|---|---|---|---|---|---|---|---|---|---|---|---|---|---|---|
| RICHARDSON, SALLY (HM17290) | | | | | | | | | | | | | | | | | |
| ROBERT STONE THERAPEUTICS (HM17398) | | | | | | | | | | | | | | | | | |
| RUMNEY, KATHLEEN (HM17748) | | | | | | | | | | | | | | | | | |
| SCOTTISH CENTRE (HM18130) | | | | | | | | | | | | | | | ● | | |
| SMITH, MATTHEW (HM18779) | | | ● | | | | | | | | | | | | | | |
| STOBIE, JENNY (HM19308) | | | | | | | | | | | | | | | | | |
| TARA ROKPA ENDINBURGH (HM19699) | | | | | | | | | | | | | | | ● | | |
| TEAMWORK (HM19811) | | | | | | | | | | | | | | | ● | | |
| WELLBEING (HM21146) | | | | | | | | | | | | | | | | | |
| WELLSPRING (HM21179) | | | | | | | | | | | | | | | ● | | |
| FALKIRK | | | | | | | | | | | | | | | | | |
| ANGUS WILLIAMSON CLINIC (HM00885) | | | | | | | | | | | | | | | | | |
| GRANT, LESLIE & DAWN (HM08385) | | | | | | | | | | ● | | | | | | | |
| GRANT, LESLIE AND DAWN (HM08386) | | | | | | | | | | ● | | | | | | | |
| KELIMAR CLINIC (HM11416) | | | | | | | | | | | | | | | | | |
| NATURAL HEALING CENTRE (HM14543) | | | | | | | | | | | | | | | | | |
| FIFE | | | | | | | | | | | | | | | | | |
| BODYNEEDS (HM02629) | | | | | | | | | | | | | | | | | |
| BRYCE, EDWARD (HM03290) | | | ● | | | | | | | | | | | | | | |
| CAMERON, WILLIAM (HM03588) | | | | | | | | | | ● | | | | | | | |
| CAMILLA HEY HOLISTIC PRACTICE (HM03590) | | | | | | | | | | | | | | | | | |
| CAROLE'S MOBILE THERAPIST (HM03718) | | | | | | | | | | | | | | | | | |
| COMPLEMENTARY THERAPY CLINIC (HM04949) | | | | | | | | | | | | | | | ● | | |
| CUMMINS, LYNN (HM05615) | | | | | | | | | | | | | | | | | |
| DAVIDSON, ANGELA (HM05785) | | | | | | | | | | ● | | | | | | | |
| FORD, MARGARET (HM07525) | | | | | | | | | | | | | | | | | |
| FOUNDATION HEALTH (HM07613) | | | | | | | | | | | | | | | | | |
| HEALING HANDS (HM09337) | | | | | | | | | | | | | | | | | |
| LEUTER, PAM () | | | | | | | | | | | | | | | | | |
| NATURAL REMEDY CLINIC (HM14621) | | | ● | | | | | | | | | | | | | | |
| NEAT FEET (HM14743) | | | | | | | | | | | | | | | | | |
| PAUL'S (HM15851) | | | | | | | | | | | | | | | ● | | |
| SHEERINS, ROZ (HM18370) | | | | | | | | | | ● | | | | | | | |
| ST ANDREWS OSTEOPATHS (HM19065) | | | ● | | | | | | | | | | | | | | |

| Business by County with Reference no. | Reflexology | Reichian Therapy | Reiki | Remedial Massage | Rogerian Therapy | Rolfing | Seichem | Sensitivity Training | Shiatsu | Silva Method | Sound Therapy | Spiritual Healing | Sports Massage | Stress Therapy | Swedish Body Massage | T'ai-Chi Ch'uan |
|---|---|---|---|---|---|---|---|---|---|---|---|---|---|---|---|---|
| RICHARDSON, SALLY (HM17290) | ● | | | | | | | | | | | | | | | |
| ROBERT STONE THERAPEUTICS (HM17398) | ● | | | | | | | | | | | | | | | |
| RUMNEY, KATHLEEN (HM17748) | ● | | ● | | | | | | | | | | | | | |
| SCOTTISH CENTRE (HM18130) | | | | | | | | | | | | | | | | |
| SMITH, MATTHEW (HM18779) | | | | | | | | | | | | | | | | |
| STOBIE, JENNY (HM19308) | ● | | | | | | | | | | | | | | | |
| TARA ROKPA ENDINBURGH (HM19699) | | | | | | | | | | | | | | | | |
| TEAMWORK (HM19811) | | | | | | | | | | | | | | | | |
| WELLBEING (HM21146) | | | ● | | | | | | | | | | | | | |
| WELLSPRING (HM21179) | | | | | | | | | | | | | | | | |
| FALKIRK | | | | | | | | | | | | | | | | |
| ANGUS WILLIAMSON CLINIC (HM00885) | ● | | | | | | | | | | | | | | | |
| GRANT, LESLIE & DAWN (HM08385) | | | | | | | | | | | | | | | | |
| GRANT, LESLIE AND DAWN (HM08386) | | | | | | | | | | | | | | | | |
| KELIMAR CLINIC (HM11416) | | | | ● | | | | | | | | | | | | |
| NATURAL HEALING CENTRE (HM14543) | | | ● | | | | | | | | | | | | | |
| FIFE | | | | | | | | | | | | | | | | |
| BODYNEEDS (HM02629) | ● | | | | | | | | | | | | ● | | ● | |
| BRYCE, EDWARD (HM03290) | | | | | | | | | | | | | | | | |
| CAMERON, WILLIAM (HM03588) | | | | | | | | | | | | | | | | |
| CAMILLA HEY HOLISTIC PRACTICE (HM03590) | | | | ● | | | | | | | | | | | | |
| CAROLE'S MOBILE THERAPIST (HM03718) | | | ● | | | | | | | | | | | | | |
| COMPLEMENTARY THERAPY CLINIC (HM04949) | | | ● | | | | | | | | | | | ● | | ● |
| CUMMINS, LYNN (HM05615) | ● | | | | | | | | | | | | | | | |
| DAVIDSON, ANGELA (HM05785) | ● | | ● | | | | | | | | | | | | | |
| FORD, MARGARET (HM07525) | ● | | | | | | | | | | | | | | | |
| FOUNDATION HEALTH (HM07613) | | | | | | | | | | | | | | | | |
| HEALING HANDS (HM09337) | ● | | ● | | | | | | | | | | | | | |
| LEUTER, PAM () | | | ● | | | | | | | | | | | | | |
| NATURAL REMEDY CLINIC (HM14621) | ● | | ● | | | | | | | | | ● | | ● | | |
| NEAT FEET (HM14743) | ● | | ● | | | | | | | | | | | | | |
| PAUL'S (HM15851) | | | | | | | | | | | | | | | | |
| SHEERINS, ROZ (HM18370) | | | | | | | | | | | | | | | | |
| ST ANDREWS OSTEOPATHS (HM19065) | | | | | | | | | | | | | | | | |

| Business by County with Reference no. | Tantra Therapy | Tera-Mai | Thought Field Therapy | Touch Therapy | Transactional Analysis | Tui-na | Ultrasonics | Vibrational Therapy | Visualisation Therapy | Vitamin Therapy | Voice Therapy | X-Ray | Ying & Yang | Yoga | Zen Therapy | Zero Balancing |
|---|---|---|---|---|---|---|---|---|---|---|---|---|---|---|---|---|
| RICHARDSON, SALLY (HM17290) | | | | | | | | | | | | | | | | |
| ROBERT STONE THERAPEUTICS (HM17398) | | | | | | | | | | | | | | | | |
| RUMNEY, KATHLEEN (HM17748) | | | | | | | | | | | | | | | | |
| SCOTTISH CENTRE (HM18130) | | | | | | | | | | | | | | | | |
| SMITH, MATTHEW (HM18779) | | | | | | | | | | | | | | | | |
| STOBIE, JENNY (HM19308) | | | | | | | | | | | | | | | | |
| TARA ROKPA ENDINBURGH (HM19699) | | | | | | | | | | | | | | ● | | |
| TEAMWORK (HM19811) | | | | | | | | | | | | | | | | |
| WELLBEING (HM21146) | | | | | | | | | | | | | | | | |
| WELLSPRING (HM21179) | | | | | | | | | | | | | | | | |
| FALKIRK | | | | | | | | | | | | | | | | |
| ANGUS WILLIAMSON CLINIC (HM00885) | | | | | | | | | | | | | | | | |
| GRANT, LESLIE & DAWN (HM08385) | | | | | | | | | | | | | | | | |
| GRANT, LESLIE AND DAWN (HM08386) | | | | | | | | | | | | | | | | |
| KELIMAR CLINIC (HM11416) | | | | | | | | | | | | | | | | |
| NATURAL HEALING CENTRE (HM14543) | | | | | | | | | | | | | | | | |
| FIFE | | | | | | | | | | | | | | | | |
| BODYNEEDS (HM02629) | | | | | | | | | | | | | | | | |
| BRYCE, EDWARD (HM03290) | | | | | | | | | | | | | | | | |
| CAMERON, WILLIAM (HM03588) | | | | | | | | | | | | | | | | |
| CAMILLA HEY HOLISTIC PRACTICE (HM03590) | | | | | | | | | | | | | | | | |
| CAROLE'S MOBILE THERAPIST (HM03718) | | | | | | | | | | | | | | | | |
| COMPLEMENTARY THERAPY CLINIC (HM04949) | | | | ● | ● | | | | | ● | | | | | | |
| CUMMINS, LYNN (HM05615) | | | | | | | | | | | | | | | | |
| DAVIDSON, ANGELA (HM05785) | | | | | | | | | | | | | | | | |
| FORD, MARGARET (HM07525) | | | | | | | | | | | | | | | | |
| FOUNDATION HEALTH (HM07613) | | | | | | | | | | ● | | | | | | |
| HEALING HANDS (HM09337) | | | | | | | | | | | | | | | | |
| LEUTER, PAM () | | | | | | | | | | | | | | | | |
| NATURAL REMEDY CLINIC (HM14621) | | | | | | | | | | | | | | | | |
| NEAT FEET (HM14743) | | | | | | | | | | | | | | | | |
| PAUL'S (HM15851) | | | | | | | | | | | | | | | | |
| SHEERINS, ROZ (HM18370) | | | | | | | | | | | | | | | | |
| ST ANDREWS OSTEOPATHS (HM19065) | | | | | | | | | | | | | | | | |

# O - Z Therapies at Practices/Businesses

| Business by County with Reference no. | Orthotics | Osteomyology | Osteopathy | PAM | Paranormal Therapies | Pattern Therapies | Physiotherapy | Phytotherapy | Pilates | Podiatry | Polarity Therapy | Postural Integration | Primal Therapy | Psionic Therapy | Psychotherapy | Pyramid Power | Pyscho-Synthesis | Reflexology | Reichian Therapy | Reiki | Remedial Massage | Rogerian Therapy | Rolfing | Seichem | Sensitivity Training | Shiatsu | Silva Method | Sound Therapy | Spiritual Healing | Sports Massage | Stress Therapy | Swedish Body Massage | T'ai-Chi Ch'uan | Tantra Therapy | Tera-Mai | Thought Field Therapy | Touch Therapy | Transactional Analysis | Tui-na | Ultrasonics | Vibrational Therapy | Visualisation Therapy | Vitamin Therapy | Voice Therapy | X-Ray | Ying & Yang | Yoga | Zen Therapy | Zero Balancing |
|---|---|---|---|---|---|---|---|---|---|---|---|---|---|---|---|---|---|---|---|---|---|---|---|---|---|---|---|---|---|---|---|---|---|---|---|---|---|---|---|---|---|---|---|---|---|---|---|---|---|
| TOLBOOTH HOUSE (HM20117) | | | ● | | | | | | | ● | | | | | | | | ● | | ● | | | | | | | | | | | | | | | | | | | | | | | | | | | | | |
| **GLASGOW (CITY OF)** | | | | | | | | | | | | | | | | | | | | | | | | | | | | | | | | | | | | | | | | | | | | | | | | | |
| ANDERSON DOE PODIATRY CLINIC (HM00809) | | | | | | | ● | | | ● | | | | | | | | | | | | | | | | | | | | | | | | | | | | | | | | | | | | | | | |
| ANNE PENMAN THERAPY (HM00900) | | | | | | | | | | | | | | | | | | | | ● | | | | | | | | | | | | | | | | | | | | | | | | | | | | | |
| ASHE, SHIRLEY (HM01208) | | | | | | | | | | | | | | | | | | ● | | | | | | | | | | | | | | | | | | | | | | | | | | | | | | | |
| BEHIND THE VEIL (HM02068) | | | | | | | | | | | | | | | | | | | | ● | | | | | | | | | ● | | | | | | | | | | | | | | | | | | | | |
| BLACK, JIM (HM02424) | | | | | | | | | | ● | | | | | | | | | | | | | | | | | | | | | | | | | | | | | | | | | | | | | | | |
| BOTHWELL PHYSIOTHERAPY (HM02733) | | | | | | | ● | | | | | | | | | | | | | | | | | | | | | | | | | | | | | | | | | | | | | | | | | | |
| BRAZENALL, A R (HM02934) | | ● | ● | | | | ● | | | | | | | | | | | | | | | | | | | | | | | | | | | | | | | | | | | | | | | | | | |
| BUCKINGHAM CLINIC (HM03311) | | | ● | | | | | | | | | | | | | | | | | | | | | | | | | | | | | | | | | | | | | | | | | | | | | | |
| CARRICK STREET PHYSIO & SPORT (HM03743) | | | | | | | ● | | | | | | | | | | | | | | | | | | | | | | | | | | | | | | | | | | | | | | | | | | |
| CRAM, ALEXANDER (HM05358) | | | ● | | | | | | | | | | | | | | | | | | | | | | | | | | | | | | | | | | | | | | | | | | | | | | |
| CRAM, D (HM05359) | | | ● | | | | | | | | | | | | | | | | | | | | | | | | | | | | | | | | | | | | | | | | | | | | | | |
| CRAM, DENNIS (HM05360) | | | ● | | | | | | | | | | | | | | | | | | | | | | | | | | | | | | | | | | | | | | | | | | | | | | |
| ESSENTIAL BEAUTY (HM06897) | | | | | | | | | | | | | | | | | | ● | | | | | | | | | | | | | | | | | | | | | | | | | | | | | | | |
| FAIRBAIRN, KAREN (HM07050) | | | | | | | | | | | | | | | | | | ● | | | | | | | | | | | | | | | | | | | | | | | | | | | | | | | |
| FITZPATRICK, J H (HM07374) | | | | | | | | | | ● | | | | | | | | | | | | | | | | | | | | | | | | | | | | | | | | | | | | | | | |
| FLETCHER, KATIE (HM07413) | | | ● | | | | | | | | | | | | | | | | | | | | | | | | | | | | | | | | | | | | | | | | | | | | | | |
| GARNETHILL CENTRE (HM07896) | | | | | | | | | | | | | | | ● | | | | | | | | | | | | | | | | | | | | | | | | | | | | | | | | | | |
| GRAHAM, JANE (HM08349) | | | | | | | | | | | | | | | | | | ● | | | | | | | | | | | | | | | | | | | | | | | | | | | | | | | |
| HARVEST CLINIC (HM09152) | | | | | | | | | | | ● | | | | ● | | | ● | | ● | | ● | | | | | | | | | ● | | | | | | | | | | | | ● | | | | | | |
| HEALTH & VITALITY (HM09374) | | | | | | | | | | | | | | | | | | ● | | ● | | | | | | | | | | | | | | | | | | | | | | | | | | | | | |
| HOLISTIC HEALING & HYP (HM09961) | | | | | | | | | | | | | | | ● | | | ● | | ● | | | | | | | | | | | | | | | | | | | | | | | | | | | | | |
| HUMAN PERFORMANCE CLINIC (HM10364) | | | | | | | | | | | | | | | ● | | | | | | | | | | | | | | | | | | | | | | | | | | | | | | | | | | |
| KNOX, HELEN (HM11773) | | | | | | | | | | | | | | | | | | ● | | | | | | | | | | | | | | | | | | | | | | | | | | | | | | | |
| LAMBERT, C W (HM11895) | ● | | | | | | | | | ● | | | | | | | | | | | | | | | | | | | | | | | | | | | | | | | | | | | | | | | |
| LOBO, MARIETTE (HM12531) | | | | | | | | | | | | | | | | | | ● | | | | | | | | | | | | | | | | | | | | | | | | | | | | | | | |
| LONG RIVER TAI CHI CIRCLE (HM12617) | | | | | | | | | | | | | | | | | | | | | | | | | | | | | | | | | ● | | | | | | | | | | | | | | | | |
| MARY HERAGHTY AT HEALTHY FEET (HM13222) | | | | | | | | | | | | | | | | | | ● | | | | | | | | | | | | | | | | | | | | | | | | | | | | | | | |
| MCLAREN, CATH RENA (HM13539) | | | | | | | | | | | | | | | | | | ● | | ● | | | | | | | | | | | | | | | | | | | | | | | | | | | | | |
| NUTRITION WORLD (HM15126) | | | | | | | ● | | | | | | | | | | | ● | | | | | | | | ● | | | | | | | | | | | | | | | | | ● | | | | ● | | |
| PLUIDGE, MARK (HM16379) | | | | | | | | | | ● | | | | | | | | | | | | | | | | | | | | | | | | | | | | | | | | | | | | | | | |
| PSYCHIC & HEALING CENTRE (HM16684) | | | | | | | | | | | | | | | | | | | | ● | | | | | | | | | | | | | | | | | | | | | | | | | | | | | |
| RAMONA, SUE (HM16916) | | | | | | | | | | | | | | | ● | | | | | | | | | | | | | | | | | | | | | | | | | | | | | | | | | | |

# O - Z Therapies at Practices/Businesses

| Business by County with Reference no. | Orthotics | Osteomyology | Osteopathy | PAM | Paranormal Therapies | Pattern Therapies | Physiotherapy | Phytotherapy | Pilates | Podiatry | Polarity Therapy | Postural Integration | Primal Therapy | Psionic Therapy | Psychotherapy | Pyramid Power | Pyscho-Synthesis | Reflexology | Reichian Therapy | Reiki | Remedial Massage | Rogerian Therapy | Rolfing | Seichem | Sensitivity Training | Shiatsu | Silva Method | Sound Therapy | Spiritual Healing | Sports Massage | Stress Therapy | Swedish Body Massage | T'ai-Chi Ch'uan | Tantra Therapy | Tera-Mai | Thought Field Therapy | Touch Therapy | Transactional Analysis | Tui-na | Ultrasonics | Vibrational Therapy | Visualisation Therapy | Vitamin Therapy | Voice Therapy | X-Ray | Ying & Yang | Yoga | Zen Therapy | Zero Balancing |
|---|---|---|---|---|---|---|---|---|---|---|---|---|---|---|---|---|---|---|---|---|---|---|---|---|---|---|---|---|---|---|---|---|---|---|---|---|---|---|---|---|---|---|---|---|---|---|---|---|---|
| SCHOLL CENTRE (HM18039) | | | | | | | | | | ● | | | | | | | | | | | | | | | | | | | | | | | | | | | | | | | | | | | | | | | |
| SCOTTISH INSTITUTE-HUMAN REL (HM18133) | | | | | | | | | | | | | | | ● | | | | | | | | | | | | | | | | | | | | | | | | | | | | | | | | | | |
| STEWART, JIM (DR) (HM19270) | | | | | | | | | | | | | | | ● | | | | | | | | | | | | | | | | ● | | | | | | | | | | | ● | | | | | | | |
| THERAPY CENTRE (HM19895) | | | ● | | | | | | | | | | | | | | | | | | | | | | | | | | | | | | | | | | | | | | | | | | | | | | |
| VAHEY, G (HM20547) | | | | | | | | | | | | | | | ● | | | | | | | | | | | | | | | | | | | | | | | | | | | | | | | | | | |
| VOY, JOAN (HM20714) | | | | | | | | | | | | | | | | | | ● | | | | | | | | | | | | | | | | | | | | | | | | | | | | | | | |
| WEST END THERAPY CENTRE (HM21221) | | | | | | | | | | | | | | | | | | ● | | ● | | | | | | | | | | | | | | | | | | | | | | | | | | | | | |
| **HIGHLAND** | | | | | | | | | | | | | | | | | | | | | | | | | | | | | | | | | | | | | | | | | | | | | | | | | |
| BUMBLE - BEE'S PHYSIO (HM03347) | | | | | | | ● | | | | | | | | | | | ● | | | | | | | | | | | | | | | | | | | | | | | | | | | | | | | |
| GENTLE WAYS (HM07980) | | | | | | | | | | | | | | | | | | ● | | ● | | | | | | | | | | | | | | | | | | | | | | | | | | | | | |
| HARMONOLOGY CENTRE (HM09017) | | | | | | | | | | | | | | | | | | | | | | | | | | | | | ● | | | | | | | | | | | | | | | | | | | | |
| HEALTH CORNER (HM09383) | | | | | | | | | | | | | | | | | | ● | | ● | | | | | | ● | | | ● | | ● | | | | | | | | | | | | | | | | ● | | |
| MACKENZIE, J D (HM12853) | | | ● | | | | | | | | | | | | | | | | | | | | | | | | | | | | | | | | | | | | | | | | | | | | | | |
| MCILWRAITH, B G (HM13510) | | | ● | | | | | | | | | | | | | | | | | | | | | | | | | | | | | | | | | | | | | | | | | | | | | | |
| MORNING LIGHT (HM14189) | | | | | | | | | | | | | | | ● | | | | | | | | | | | | | | | | | | | | | | | | | | | | | | | | | | |
| PUFFIN HYDROTHERAPY POOL (HM16743) | | | | | | | ● | | | | | | | | | | | | | | | | | | | | | | | | | | | | | | | | | | | | | | | | | | |
| TAYLOR, JUNE (HM19773) | | | | | | | | | | | | | | | | | | ● | | ● | | | | | | | | | | | | | | | | | | | | | | | | | | | | | |
| WAH, G (HM20735) | | | | | | | | | | | | | | | | | | ● | | | | | | | | | | | | | | | | | | | | | | | | | | | | | | | |
| **INVERCLYDE** | | | | | | | | | | | | | | | | | | | | | | | | | | | | | | | | | | | | | | | | | | | | | | | | | |
| INVERCLYDE OSTEOPATHIC CLINIC (HM10704) | | | ● | | | | | | | | | | | | | | | ● | | | | | | | | | | | | | | | | | | | | | | | | | | | | | | | |
| KELLERMANS (HM11418) | | | ● | | | | | ● | | | | | | | ● | | | ● | | ● | | | | | | ● | | | ● | | ● | | | | | | | | | | | | | | | | | | |
| **LANARKSHIRE (NORTH)** | | | | | | | | | | | | | | | | | | | | | | | | | | | | | | | | | | | | | | | | | | | | | | | | | |
| SEMPRE LIBERA (HM18224) | | | | | | | | | | | | | | | | | | ● | | | | | | | | | | | | | | | | | | | | | | | | | | | | | | | |
| SMITH, IRENE B (HM18748) | | | | | | | | | | | | | | | | | | | | ● | ● | | | | | | | | | ● | | | | | | | | | | | | | | | | | | | |
| STRATH NATURAL THERAPIES (HM19371) | | | | | | | | | | | | | | | | | | ● | | | | | | | | | | | | | ● | | | | | | | | | | | | | | | | | | |
| WORLD OF HEALTH (HM21897) | | | | | | | | | | | | | | | | | | | | | | | | | | | | | | | | | | | | | | | | | | | ● | | | | | | |
| **LANARKSHIRE (SOUTH)** | | | | | | | | | | | | | | | | | | | | | | | | | | | | | | | | | | | | | | | | | | | | | | | | | |
| MEEK, ROSLYN (HM13682) | | | ● | | | | | | | | | | | | | | | | | | | | | | | | | | | | | | | | | | | | | | | | | | | | | | |
| WILSON, S A (HM21669) | | | ● | | | | | | | | | | | | | | | | | | | | | | | | | | | | | | | | | | | | | | | | | | | | | | |
| **LOTHIAN (EAST)** | | | | | | | | | | | | | | | | | | | | | | | | | | | | | | | | | | | | | | | | | | | | | | | | | |
| AROMA (HM01042) | | | | | | | | | | | | | | | | | | | | ● | | | | | | | | | | | | | | | | | | | | | | | | | | | | | |
| DUNBAR PHYSIOTHERAPY (HM06391) | | | ● | | | | | | | | | | | | | | | | | | | | | | | | | | | | | | | | | | | | | | | | | | | | | | |
| EAST LOTHIAN PHYSIO CENTRE (HM06518) | | | | | | | ● | | | | | | | | | | | | | | | | | | | | | | | | ● | | | | | | | | | ● | | | | | | | | | |
| FRASER, GORDON (HM07696) | | | | | | | | | | | | | | | | | | | | ● | | | | | | ● | | | | | | | | | | | | | | | | | | | | | | | |

# O - Z Therapies at Practices/Businesses

| Business by County with Reference no. | Orthotics | Osteomyology | Osteopathy | PAM | Paranormal Therapies | Pattern Therapies | Physiotherapy | Phytotherapy | Pilates | Podiatry | Polarity Therapy | Postural Integration | Primal Therapy | Psionic Therapy | Psychotherapy | Pyramid Power | Pyscho-Synthesis | Reflexology | Reichian Therapy | Reiki | Remedial Massage | Rogerian Therapy | Rolfing | Seichem | Sensitivity Training |
|---|---|---|---|---|---|---|---|---|---|---|---|---|---|---|---|---|---|---|---|---|---|---|---|---|---|
| LOGAN, K (HM12567) | | | | | | | | | | | | | | | | | | ● | | | | | | | |
| LOTHIAN (MID) | | | | | | | | | | | | | | | | | | | | | | | | | |
| CRYSTAL SANCTUARY (HM05532) | | | | | | | | | | | | | | | | | | ● | | ● | | | | | |
| HAMILTON, JAMES (HM08844) | | | | | | | | | | | | | | | | | | ● | | | | | | | |
| NATURAL HEALTH CENTRE (HM14573) | | | | | | | | | | | | | | | | | | | | ● | ● | | | | |
| PEASTON, S (HM15920) | | | | | | | | | | | | | | | | | | ● | | | | | | | |
| WYLIE, DORIS (HM21974) | | | | | | | | | | | | | | | | | | ● | | | | | | | |
| LOTHIAN (WEST) | | | | | | | | | | | | | | | | | | | | | | | | | |
| CORMACK, SUSAN (HM05176) | | | | | | | | | | | | | | | | | | ● | | | | | | | |
| GILL, SHIRLEY (HM08080) | | | | | | | | | | | | | | | | | | ● | | | | | | | |
| LINLITHGOW PHYSIO PRACTICE (HM12438) | | | | | | | ● | | | | | | | | | | | | | | | | | | |
| MORRISON, R D (HM14230) | | | ● | | | | | | | | | | | | | | | | | | | | | | |
| VINCES, DENISE (HM20674) | | | | | | | | | | | | | | | | | | ● | | ● | | | | | |
| MORAY | | | | | | | | | | | | | | | | | | | | | | | | | |
| HEALTHWORKS (HM09422) | | | ● | | | | | | | | | | | | | | | ● | | ● | | | | | |
| NORTH COLLEGE OSTEO PRACTICE (HM15022) | | | ● | | | | | | | | | | | | | | | | | | | | | | |
| ROBINSON, ELIZABETH (HM17471) | | | ● | | | | | | | | | | | | | | | | | | | | | | |
| TRUJILLO, DR ORLANDO (HM20352) | | | | | | | | | | | | | | | ● | | | | | | | | | | |
| YOUNG, COURTENAY (HM22067) | | | | | | | | | | | | | | | ● | | | | | | | | | | |
| NORTHUMBERLAND | | | | | | | | | | | | | | | | | | | | | | | | | |
| SOLAR- PLEXUS (HM18864) | | | | | | | | | | | | | | | | | | ● | | | | | | | |
| PERTH AND KINROSS | | | | | | | | | | | | | | | | | | | | | | | | | |
| ARMFIELD, L S (HM01010) | | | ● | | | | | | | | | | | | | | | | | | | | | | |
| AUCHTERARDER CHIROPODY (HM01343) | ● | | | | | | | | | ● | | | | | | | | | | | | | | | |
| BACK PAIN & SPORTS CLINIC (HM01491) | | | | | | | | | | | | | | | | | | | | | | | | | |
| BAND, NEIL M (HM01651) | | | ● | | | | | | | | | | | | | | | | | | | | | | |
| BARRON, DEIRDRE (HM01803) | | | | | | | | | | | | | | | | | | ● | | | | | | | |
| HOWIE, TOM R (HM10283) | | | | | | | | | | ● | | | | | | | | | | | | | | | |
| HOWIE, TOM R (HM10284) | | | | | | | | | | ● | | | | | | | | | | | | | | | |
| LENDRICK LODGE (HM12210) | | | | | | | | | | | | | | | | | | | | ● | | | | | |
| MACKENZIE, BOYD (HM12850) | | | ● | | | | | | | | | | | | | | | | | | | | | | |
| STEVENSON, IAN W (HM19246) | | | | | | | | | | ● | | | | | | | | | | | | | | | |
| TAYLOR, D (HM19749) | | | | | | | | | | | | | | | ● | | | | | | | | | | |

| Business by County with Reference no. | Shiatsu | Silva Method | Sound Therapy | Spiritual Healing | Sports Massage | Stress Therapy | Swedish Body Massage | T'ai-Chi Ch'uan | Tantra Therapy | Tera-Mai | Thought Field Therapy | Touch Therapy | Transactional Analysis | Tui-na | Ultrasonics | Vibrational Therapy | Visualisation Therapy | Vitamin Therapy | Voice Therapy | X-Ray | Ying & Yang | Yoga | Zen Therapy | Zero Balancing |
|---|---|---|---|---|---|---|---|---|---|---|---|---|---|---|---|---|---|---|---|---|---|---|---|---|
| LOGAN, K (HM12567) | | | | | | | | | | | | | | | | | | | | | | | | |
| LOTHIAN (MID) | | | | | | | | | | | | | | | | | | | | | | | | |
| CRYSTAL SANCTUARY (HM05532) | | | | | | | | | | | | | | | | | | | | | | | | |
| HAMILTON, JAMES (HM08844) | | | | | | | | | | | | | | | | | | | | | | | | |
| NATURAL HEALTH CENTRE (HM14573) | ● | | | | ● | | | | | | | | | | | | | | | | | | | |
| PEASTON, S (HM15920) | | | | | | | | | | | | | | | | | | | | | | | | |
| WYLIE, DORIS (HM21974) | | | | | | | | | | | | | | | | | | | | | | | | |
| LOTHIAN (WEST) | | | | | | | | | | | | | | | | | | | | | | | | |
| CORMACK, SUSAN (HM05176) | | | | | | | | | | | | | | | | | | | | | | | | |
| GILL, SHIRLEY (HM08080) | | | | | | | | | | | | | | | | | | | | | | | | |
| LINLITHGOW PHYSIO PRACTICE (HM12438) | | | | | | | | | | | | | | | | | | | | | | | | |
| MORRISON, R D (HM14230) | | | | | | | | | | | | | | | | | | | | | | | | |
| VINCES, DENISE (HM20674) | | | | | | | | | | | | | | | | | | | | | | | | |
| MORAY | | | | | | | | | | | | | | | | | | | | | | | | |
| HEALTHWORKS (HM09422) | ● | | | ● | | | | | | | | | | | | | | | | | | | | |
| NORTH COLLEGE OSTEO PRACTICE (HM15022) | | | | | | | | | | | | | | | | | | | | | | | | |
| ROBINSON, ELIZABETH (HM17471) | | | | | | | | | | | | | | | | | | | | | | | | |
| TRUJILLO, DR ORLANDO (HM20352) | | | | | | | | | | | | | | | | | | | | | | | | |
| YOUNG, COURTENAY (HM22067) | | | | | | | | | | | | | | | | | | | | | | | | |
| NORTHUMBERLAND | | | | | | | | | | | | | | | | | | | | | | | | |
| SOLAR- PLEXUS (HM18864) | | | | | | | | | | | | | | | | | | | | | | | | |
| PERTH AND KINROSS | | | | | | | | | | | | | | | | | | | | | | | | |
| ARMFIELD, L S (HM01010) | | | | | | | | | | | | | | | | | | | | | | | | |
| AUCHTERARDER CHIROPODY (HM01343) | | | | | | | | | | | | | | | | | | | | | | | | |
| BACK PAIN & SPORTS CLINIC (HM01491) | | | | | | | | | | | | | | | ● | | | | | | | | | |
| BAND, NEIL M (HM01651) | | | | | | | | | | | | | | | | | | | | | | | | |
| BARRON, DEIRDRE (HM01803) | | | | | | | | | | | | | | | | | | | | | | | | |
| HOWIE, TOM R (HM10283) | | | | | | | | | | | | | | | | | | | | | | | | |
| HOWIE, TOM R (HM10284) | | | | | | | | | | | | | | | | | | | | | | | | |
| LENDRICK LODGE (HM12210) | | | | | | | | | | | | | | | | | | | | | | ● | | |
| MACKENZIE, BOYD (HM12850) | | | | | | | | | | | | | | | | | | | | | | | | |
| STEVENSON, IAN W (HM19246) | | | | | | | | | | | | | | | | | | | | | | | | |
| TAYLOR, D (HM19749) | | | | | | | | | | | | | | | | | | | | | | | | |

# O - Z Therapies at Practices/Businesses

| Business by County with Reference no. | Orthotics | Osteomyology | Osteopathy | PAM | Paranormal Therapies | Pattern Therapies | Physiotherapy | Phytotherapy | Pilates | Podiatry | Polarity Therapy | Postural Integration | Primal Therapy | Psionic Therapy | Psychotherapy | Pyramid Power | Pyscho-Synthesis | Reflexology | Reichian Therapy | Reiki | Remedial Massage | Rogerian Therapy | Rolfing | Seichem | Sensitivity Training | Shiatsu | Silva Method | Sound Therapy | Spiritual Healing | Sports Massage | Stress Therapy | Swedish Body Massage | T'ai-Chi Ch'uan | Tantra Therapy | Tera-Mai | Thought Field Therapy | Touch Therapy | Transactional Analysis | Tui-na | Ultrasonics | Vibrational Therapy | Visualisation Therapy | Vitamin Therapy | Voice Therapy | X-Ray | Ying & Yang | Yoga | Zen Therapy | Zero Balancing |
|---|---|---|---|---|---|---|---|---|---|---|---|---|---|---|---|---|---|---|---|---|---|---|---|---|---|---|---|---|---|---|---|---|---|---|---|---|---|---|---|---|---|---|---|---|---|---|---|---|---|
| RENFREWSHIRE | | | | | | | | | | | | | | | | | | | | | | | | | | | | | | | | | | | | | | | | | | | | | | | | | |
| ALBA CENTRE (HM00473) | | | | | | | | | | | | | | | | | | ● | | ● | | | | | | | | | ● | | | | | | | | | | | | | | | | | | | | |
| BLACKHALL PARK CENTRE (HM02444) | | | | | | | | | | | | | | | | | | ● | | ● | | | | | | | | | | | | | | | | | | | | | | | | | | | | | |
| DOUGLAS, ANNE S (HM06212) | | | | | | | ● | | | | | | | | | | | | | ● | | | | | | | | | | | | | | | | | | | | | | | | | | | | | |
| GILLON, RACHEL (HM08102) | | | | | | | | | | | | | | | | | | ● | | | | | | | | | | | | | | | | | | | | | | | | | | | | | | | |
| MITCHELL, CAROLE (HM14003) | | | ● | | | | | | | | | | | | | | | | | | | | | | | | | | | | | | | | | | | | | | | | | | | | | | |
| PAISLEY CHIROPRACTIC CLINIC (HM15587) | | | | | | | | | | | | | | | | | | | | | | | | | | | | | | | ● | | | | | | | | | | | | ● | | ● | | | | |
| PAISLEY NATURAL THERAPY CENTRE (HM15588) | | | ● | | | | | | | | ● | | | | | | | ● | | ● | | | | | | | | | | | | | | | | | | | | | | | | | | | | | |
| PAISLEY PHYSIOTHERAPY CENTRE (HM15589) | | | ● | | | | | | | | | | | | | | | | | | | | | | | | | ● | | | | | | | | | | | | ● | | | | | | | | | |
| RAINEY, MARTHA (HM16890) | | | | | | | | | | | | | | | | | | ● | | | | | | | | | | | | | | | | | | | | | | | | | | | | | | | |
| SCOTTISH BORDERS | | | | | | | | | | | | | | | | | | | | | | | | | | | | | | | | | | | | | | | | | | | | | | | | | |
| L W FOOTCARE (HM11844) | | | | | | | | | | ● | | | | | | | | | | | | | | | | | | | | | | | | | | | | | | | | | | | | | | | |
| LAMBERT, IAN (HM11897) | | | ● | | | | | | | | | | | | | | | | | | | | | | | | | | | | | | | | | | | | | | | | | | | | | | |
| MOROZZO, RUTH (HM14195) | | | | | | | | | | | | | | | | | | ● | | | | | | | | | | | | | | | | | | | | | | | | | | | | | | | |
| MURRELL, R J (HM14422) | | | ● | | | | | | | | | | | | | | | | | | | | | | | | | | | | | | | | | | | | | | | | | | | | | | |
| NATURAL THERAPY CENTRE (HM14647) | | | ● | | | | | | | | | | | | | | | | | | | | | | | | | | | | | | | | | | | | | | | | | | | | | | |
| WISHING WELL (HM21738) | | | | | | | | ● | | | | | | | | | | ● | | ● | | | | | | | | | | | ● | | | | | | | | | | | | | | | | | | |
| SHETLAND ISLANDS | | | | | | | | | | | | | | | | | | | | | | | | | | | | | | | | | | | | | | | | | | | | | | | | | |
| LERWICK CHIROPRACTIC CLINIC (HM12231) | | | | | | | | | | | | ● | | | | | | | | | | | | | | | | | | | | | | | | | | | | | | | ● | | | | | | |
| STIRLING | | | | | | | | | | | | | | | | | | | | | | | | | | | | | | | | | | | | | | | | | | | | | | | | | |
| ROBERTSON, K (HM17445) | | | ● | | | | | | | | | | | | | | | | | | | | | | | | | | | | | | | | | | | | | | | | | | | | | | |
| WILSON, R A (HM21667) | | | ● | | | | | | | | | | | | | | | | | | | | | | | | | | | | | | | | | | | | | | | | | | | | | | |

# O - Z Therapies at Practices/Businesses

| Business by County with Reference no. | Orthotics | Osteomyology | Osteopathy | PAM | Paranormal Therapies | Pattern Therapies | Physiotherapy | Phytotherapy | Pilates | Podiatry | Polarity Therapy | Postural Integration | Primal Therapy | Psionic Therapy | Psychotherapy | Pyramid Power | Pyscho-Synthesis | Reflexology | Reichian Therapy | Reiki | Remedial Massage | Rogerian Therapy | Rolfing | Seichem | Sensitivity Training | Shiatsu | Silva Method | Sound Therapy | Spiritual Healing | Sports Massage | Stress Therapy | Swedish Body Massage | T'ai-Chi Ch'uan | Tantra Therapy | Tera-Mai | Thought Field Therapy | Touch Therapy | Transactional Analysis | Tui-na | Ultrasonics | Vibrational Therapy | Visualisation Therapy | Vitamin Therapy | Voice Therapy | X-Ray | Ying & Yang | Yoga | Zen Therapy | Zero Balancing |
|---|---|---|---|---|---|---|---|---|---|---|---|---|---|---|---|---|---|---|---|---|---|---|---|---|---|---|---|---|---|---|---|---|---|---|---|---|---|---|---|---|---|---|---|---|---|---|---|---|---|
| **WALES** | | | | | | | | | | | | | | | | | | | | | | | | | | | | | | | | | | | | | | | | | | | | | | | | | |
| **BLAENAU GWENT** | | | | | | | | | | | | | | | | | | | | | | | | | | | | | | | | | | | | | | | | | | | | | | | | | |
| ABERTILLERY PHYSIOTHERAPY (HM00125) | | | | | | | ● | | | | | | | | | | | | | | | | | | | | | | | | | | | | | | | | | | | | | | | | | | |
| CLASSIC CLINIC (HM04606) | | | | | | | | | | | | | | | | | | | | | | | | | | | | | | ● | | | | | | | | | | | | | | | | | | | |
| **BRIDGEND** | | | | | | | | | | | | | | | | | | | | | | | | | | | | | | | | | | | | | | | | | | | | | | | | | |
| ADEGOKE, ROTIMI (HM00377) | | | ● | | | | | | | | | | | | | | | | | | | | | | | | | | | | | | | | | | | | | | | | | | | | | | |
| ALTERNATIVE HEALING CENTRE (HM00698) | | | | | | | | | | | | | | | ● | | | | | ● | | | | | | | | | | | ● | | | | | | | | | | | ● | | | | | | | |
| GRIFFITHS, IAN (HM08565) | | | ● | | | | | | | | | | | | | | | | | | | | | | | | | | | | | | | | | | | | | | | | | | | | | | |
| SMITH, ALLAN (HM18713) | | | ● | | | | | | | | | | | | | | | | | | | | | | | | | | | | | | | | | | | | | | | | | | | | | | |
| **CAERPHILLY** | | | | | | | | | | | | | | | | | | | | | | | | | | | | | | | | | | | | | | | | | | | | | | | | | |
| DAVIES, N G (HM05832) | | | ● | | | | | | | | | | | | | | | | | | | | | | | | | | | | | | | | | | | | | | | | | | | | | | |
| OAKFIELD NATURAL HEALTH CENTRE (HM15151) | | | | | | | | | | | | | | | | | | ● | | | | | | | | | | | | | | | | | | | | | | | | | | | | | | | |
| **CARMARTHENSHIRE** | | | | | | | | | | | | | | | | | | | | | | | | | | | | | | | | | | | | | | | | | | | | | | | | | |
| ASHTON, HAZEL (HM01239) | | | | | | | | | | | | | | | | | | ● | | | | | | | | | | | | | | | | | | | | | | | | | | | | | | | |
| EVANS, HELEN (HM06977) | | | | | | | | | | | | | | | | | | ● | | | | | | | | | | | | | | | | | | | | | | | | | | | | | | | |
| GREENWAY CONSULTANCY (HM08495) | | | | | | | | | | | | | | | ● | | | | | | | | | | | | | | ● | | ● | | | | | | ● | | | | | | | ● | | | | | |
| GRIFFITHS, IAN (HM08566) | | | ● | | | | | | | | | | | | | | | | | | | | | | | | | | | | | | | | | | | | | | | | | | | | | | |
| HALFORD, ELIZABETH (HM08750) | | | ● | | | | | | | | | | | | | | | | | | | | | | | | | | | | | | | | | | | | | | | | | | | | | | |
| HAZELBY, TRACY (HM09291) | | | | | | | | | | | | | | | | | | ● | | | | | | | | | | | | | | | | | | | | | | | | | | | | | | | |
| HEALING HANDS (HM09339) | | | | | | | | | | | | | | | | | | | | ● | | | | | | | | | | | | | | | | | | | | | | | | | | | | | |
| JONES, J G (HM11153) | | | ● | | | | | | | | | | | | | | | | | | | | | | | | | | | | | | | | | | | | | | | | | | | | | | |
| KACHA-STONES.COM (HM11292) | | | | | ● | | | | | | | | | | | ● | | | | | | | | | | | | | | | ● | | | | | | | | | | | | | | | | ● | | |
| KENWARD, SANDRA (HM11535) | | | | | | | | | | | | | | | | | | ● | | | | | | | | | | | | | | | | | | | | | | | | | | | | | | | |
| POWNER, MARGARET (HM16514) | | | | | | | | | | | | | | | | | | ● | | | | | | | | | | | | | | | | | | | | | | | | | | | | | | | |
| SPENCER AROMATHERAPY (HM18990) | | | | | | | | | | | | | | | | | | ● | | | | | | | | | | | | ● | | | | | | | | | | | | | | | | | | | |
| TONY'S HAIR & HEALTH CENTRE (HM20158) | | | ● | | | | | | | | | | | | | | | | | | | | | | | | | | | | | | | | | | | | | | | | | | | | | | |
| WAINWRIGHT, MARY (HM20738) | | | | | | | | | | | | | | | | | | | | ● | | | | ● | | | | | | | | | | | | | | | | | | | | | | | | | |
| **CEREDIGION** | | | | | | | | | | | | | | | | | | | | | | | | | | | | | | | | | | | | | | | | | | | | | | | | | |
| FFYNNONWEN NATURAL THRPY CTRE (HM07256) | | | | | | | | ● | | | | | | | | | | ● | ● | | | | | | | | | | | | | | | | | | | | | | | | | | | | | | |
| WILLIAMS, A (HM21535) | | | | | | | | | | | | | | | ● | | | | | | | | | | | | | | | | | | | | | | | | | | | | | | | | | | |
| **CONWY** | | | | | | | | | | | | | | | | | | | | | | | | | | | | | | | | | | | | | | | | | | | | | | | | | |
| CARR, R N D (HM03741) | | | ● | | | | | | | | | | | | | | | | | | | | | | | | | | | | | | | | | | | | | | | | | | | | | | |
| DEGANWY OSTEOPATHIC CLINIC (HM05961) | | | ● | | | | | | | | | | | | | | | | | | | | | | | | | | | | | | | | | | | | | | | | | | | | | | |

# O - Z Therapies at Practices/Businesses

Business by County with Reference no.

| Business | Orthotics | Osteomyology | Osteopathy | PAM | Paranormal Therapies | Pattern Therapies | Physiotherapy | Phytotherapy | Pilates | Podiatry | Polarity Therapy | Postural Integration | Primal Therapy | Psionic Therapy | Psychotherapy | Pyramid Power | Pyscho-Synthesis | Reflexology | Reichian Therapy | Reiki | Remedial Massage | Rogerian Therapy | Rolfing | Seichem |
|---|---|---|---|---|---|---|---|---|---|---|---|---|---|---|---|---|---|---|---|---|---|---|---|---|
| DREW, DAVID (HM06305) | | | | | ● | | | | | | | | | | | | | | | | | | | |
| GREENHALGH, KEITH (HM08490) | | | ● | | | | | | | | | | | | | | | | | | | | | |
| GREENHALGH, P (HM08491) | | | ● | | | | | | | | | | | | | | | | | | | | | |
| HERBS FOR EVERYONE (HM09669) | | | ● | | | | | ● | | | | | | | | | | ● | | ● | ● | | | |
| MELA CENTRE OF OSTEOPATHY (HM13702) | | | ● | | | | | | | | | ● | | | | | | | | | | | | |
| NORTH WALES YOGA/NAT THRPY (HM15039) | | | | | | | | | | | | | | | | | | | | | | | | |
| PARKHOUSE, R (HM15715) | | | ● | | | | | | | | | | | | | | | | | | | | | |
| DENBIGHSHIRE | | | | | | | | | | | | | | | | | | | | | | | | |
| ALLIED PHYSIOTHERAPY (HM00646) | | | ● | | | | | | | | | | | | | | | | | | | | | |
| CONSTABLE, JOY (HM05010) | | | | | | | | | | | | | | | | | | ● | | | | | | |
| DEWBERRY, MAY (HM06046) | | | | | | | | | | | | | | | | | | ● | | | | | | |
| HARNWELL, J P (HM09034) | | | | | | | | | | | | | | | ● | | | | | | | | | |
| HEALING WAYS (HM09359) | | | | | | | | | | | | | | | | | | ● | | | | | | |
| HURD, JOAN (HM10417) | | | | | | | | | | | | | | | ● | | | | | | | | | |
| MCGILL, L (HM13484) | | | | | | | | | | | | | | | | | | | | ● | | | | |
| PITSTOW, S P (HM16344) | | | ● | | | | | | | | | | | | | | | | | | | | | |
| POWELL, IANTO D (HM16494) | | | ● | | | | | | | | | | | | | | | | | | | | | |
| ROY MORRIS CLINIC (HM17709) | | | | | | | | | | | | | | | | | | ● | | | | | | |
| FLINTSHIRE | | | | | | | | | | | | | | | | | | | | | | | | |
| A L J RILEY ASSOCIATES (HM00038) | | | | | | | | | | | | | | | | | | | | | | | | |
| BOOTS HEALTHCARE SERVICES (HM02711) | | | | | | | | | | ● | | | | | | | | | | | | | | |
| CHIROPODISTS SURGERY (HM04298) | | | | | | | | | | ● | | | | | | | | | | | | | | |
| DUGGAN, NORA (HM06370) | | | | | | | | | | | | | | | | | | ● | | | | | | |
| GAFFNEY, ALMA (HM07827) | ● | | | | | | | | | ● | | | | | | | | | | | | | | |
| HYPNOTHERAPY CENTRE (HM10528) | | | | | | | | | | | | | | | ● | | | | | | | | | |
| OSTEOPATHY & ACUPUNCTURE (HM15478) | | | ● | | | | | | | | | | | | | | | | | | | | | |
| POWELL, IANTO D (HM16495) | | | ● | | | | | | | | | | | | | | | | | | | | | |
| REECE, JULIE (HM17038) | ● | | | | | | | | | | | | | | | | | | | | | | | |
| GLAMORGAN (VALE OF) | | | | | | | | | | | | | | | | | | | | | | | | |
| AMETHYST HEALING CENTRE (HM00784) | | | | | | | | | | | | | | | | | | ● | | | | | | |
| ARCOS, LYNNE (HM00986) | | | | | | | | | | | | | | | | | | ● | | | | | | |
| AROMATHERAPY CLINIC (HM01105) | | | | | | | | | | | | | | | | | | ● | | ● | | | | |
| BARRY OSTEOPATHIC CLINIC (HM01809) | | | ● | | | | | | | | | | | | | | | | | | | | | |
| BRITISH SCHOOL OF SHIATSU-DO (HM03093) | | | | | | | | | | | | | | | | | | | | | | | | |

| Business | Sensitivity Training | Shiatsu | Silva Method | Sound Therapy | Spiritual Healing | Sports Massage | Stress Therapy | Swedish Body Massage | T'ai-Chi Ch'uan | Tantra Therapy | Tera-Mai | Thought Field Therapy | Touch Therapy | Transactional Analysis | Tui-na | Ultrasonics | Vibrational Therapy | Visualisation Therapy | Vitamin Therapy | Voice Therapy | X-Ray | Ying & Yang | Yoga | Zen Therapy | Zero Balancing |
|---|---|---|---|---|---|---|---|---|---|---|---|---|---|---|---|---|---|---|---|---|---|---|---|---|---|
| DREW, DAVID (HM06305) | | | | | ● | | ● | | | | | | | | | | | | | | | | | | |
| GREENHALGH, KEITH (HM08490) | | | | | | | | | | | | | | | | | | | | | | | | | |
| GREENHALGH, P (HM08491) | | | | | | | | | | | | | | | | | | | | | | | | | |
| HERBS FOR EVERYONE (HM09669) | | | | | | ● | | | | | | | | | | | | | | | | | | | |
| MELA CENTRE OF OSTEOPATHY (HM13702) | | | | | | | | | | | | | | | | | | | | | | | | | |
| NORTH WALES YOGA/NAT THRPY (HM15039) | | | | | | | | | | | | | | | | | | | | | | | ● | | |
| PARKHOUSE, R (HM15715) | | | | | | | | | | | | | | | | | | | | | | | | | |
| DENBIGHSHIRE | | | | | | | | | | | | | | | | | | | | | | | | | |
| ALLIED PHYSIOTHERAPY (HM00646) | | | | | | | | | | | | | | | | | | | | | | | | | |
| CONSTABLE, JOY (HM05010) | | | | | | | | | | | | | | | | | | | | | | | | | |
| DEWBERRY, MAY (HM06046) | | | | | | | | | | | | | | | | | | | | | | | | | |
| HARNWELL, J P (HM09034) | | | | | | | | | | | | | | | | | | | | | | | | | |
| HEALING WAYS (HM09359) | | | | | | | ● | | | | | | | | | | | | | | | | | | |
| HURD, JOAN (HM10417) | | | | | | | | | | | | | | | | | | | | | | | | | |
| MCGILL, L (HM13484) | | | | | ● | | | | | | | | | | | | | | | | | | | | |
| PITSTOW, S P (HM16344) | | | | | | | | | | | | | | | | | | | | | | | | | |
| POWELL, IANTO D (HM16494) | | | | | | | | | | | | | | | | | | | | | | | | | |
| ROY MORRIS CLINIC (HM17709) | | ● | | | | | | | | | | | | | | | | | | | | | | | |
| FLINTSHIRE | | | | | | | | | | | | | | | | | | | | | | | | | |
| A L J RILEY ASSOCIATES (HM00038) | | | | | | | | | | | | | | | | | | | ● | | | | | | |
| BOOTS HEALTHCARE SERVICES (HM02711) | | | | | | | | | | | | | | | | | | | | | | | | | |
| CHIROPODISTS SURGERY (HM04298) | | | | | | | | | | | | | | | | | | | | | | | | | |
| DUGGAN, NORA (HM06370) | | | | | | | | | | | | | | | | | | | | | | | | | |
| GAFFNEY, ALMA (HM07827) | | | | | | | | | | | | | | | | | | | | | | | | | |
| HYPNOTHERAPY CENTRE (HM10528) | | | | | | | | | | | | | | | | | | | | | | | | | |
| OSTEOPATHY & ACUPUNCTURE (HM15478) | | | | | | | | | | | | | | | | | | | | | | | | | |
| POWELL, IANTO D (HM16495) | | | | | | | | | | | | | | | | | | | | | | | | | |
| REECE, JULIE (HM17038) | | | | | | | | | | | | | | | | | | | | | | | | | |
| GLAMORGAN (VALE OF) | | | | | | | | | | | | | | | | | | | | | | | | | |
| AMETHYST HEALING CENTRE (HM00784) | | | | | | | | | | | | | | | | | | | | | | | | | |
| ARCOS, LYNNE (HM00986) | | | | | | | | | | | | | | | | | | | | | | | | | |
| AROMATHERAPY CLINIC (HM01105) | | | | | | | | | | | | | | | | | | | | | | | | | |
| BARRY OSTEOPATHIC CLINIC (HM01809) | | | | | | | | | | | | | | | | | | | | | | | | | |
| BRITISH SCHOOL OF SHIATSU-DO (HM03093) | | ● | | | | | | | | | | | | | | | | | | | | | | | |

# O - Z Therapies at Practices/Businesses

Business by County with Reference no.

| Business by County with Reference no. | Orthotics | Osteomyology | Osteopathy | PAM | Paranormal Therapies | Pattern Therapies | Physiotherapy | Phytotherapy | Pilates | Podiatry | Polarity Therapy | Postural Integration | Primal Therapy | Psionic Therapy | Psychotherapy | Pyramid Power | Pyscho-Synthesis | Reflexology | Reichian Therapy | Reiki | Remedial Massage | Rogerian Therapy | Rolfing | Seichem | Sensitivity Training | Shiatsu | Silva Method | Sound Therapy | Spiritual Healing | Sports Massage | Stress Therapy | Swedish Body Massage | T'ai-Chi Ch'uan | Tantra Therapy | Tera-Mai | Thought Field Therapy | Touch Therapy | Transactional Analysis | Tui-na | Ultrasonics | Vibrational Therapy | Visualisation Therapy | Vitamin Therapy | Voice Therapy | X-Ray | Ying & Yang | Yoga | Zen Therapy | Zero Balancing |
|---|---|---|---|---|---|---|---|---|---|---|---|---|---|---|---|---|---|---|---|---|---|---|---|---|---|---|---|---|---|---|---|---|---|---|---|---|---|---|---|---|---|---|---|---|---|---|---|---|---|
| BRITTON, JAN (HM03104) | | | | | | | | | | | | | | | | | | ● | | | | | | | | | | | | | | | | | | | | | | | | | | | | | | | |
| BROWN, ANNE (HM03214) | | | | | | | | ● | | | | | | | | | | | | | | | | | | | | | | | | | | | | | | | | | | | | | | | | | |
| BROWN, HELEN (HM03224) | | | | | | | | | | | | | | | | | | ● | | | | | | | | | | | | | | | | | | | | | | | | | | | | | | | |
| BROWN, VICTORIA (HM03253) | | | | | | | | | | | | | | | | | | ● | | | | | | | | | | | | | | | | | | | | | | | | | | | | | | | |
| COWBRIDGE OSTEOPATH CLINIC (HM05290) | | | ● | | | | | | | | | | | | | | | | | | | | | | | | | | | | | | | | | | | | | | | | | | | | | | |
| ELIAS, IAN R (HM06733) | | | ● | | | | | | | | | | | | | | | | | | | | | | | | | | | | | | | | | | | | | | | | | | | | | | |
| EVANS, MARI (HM06984) | | | ● | | | | | | | | | | | | | | | | | | | | | | | | | | | | | | | | | | | | | | | | | | | | | | |
| EVANS, STEVE (HM06990) | | | | | | | ● | | | | | | | | | | | | | | | | | | | | | | | | | | | | | | | | | | | | | | | | | | |
| GLAMORGAN HEALTH & RACQUET (HM08122) | | | | | | | ● | | | | | | | | | | | | | | | | | | | | | | | | | | | | | | | | | | | | | | | | | | |
| GREENWOOD, CLARE (HM08504) | | | | | | | | | | | | | | | | | | ● | | | | | | | | | | | | | | | | | | | | | | | | | | | | | | | |
| GRIMWADE, S (HM08586) | | | ● | | | | | | | | | | | | | | | | | | | | | | | | | | | | | | | | | | | | | | | | | | | | | | |
| GRIMWADE, S (HM08587) | | | ● | | | | | | | | | | | | | | | | | | | | | | | | | | | | | | | | | | | | | | | | | | | | | | |
| HANCOCK, C B (HM08893) | | | ● | | | | | | | | | | | | | | | | | | | | | | | | | | | | | | | | | | | | | | | | | | | | | | |
| HENRIETTA CTRE FOR COMP THRPY (HM09565) | | | | | | | | | | | | | | | ● | | | ● | | ● | | | | | | ● | | | | | | | | | | | | | | | | | | | | | | | |
| JOHNSON, C (HM11070) | | | | | | | | | | | | | | | | | | ● | | | | | | | | | | | | | | | | | | | | | | | | | | | | | | | |
| JUDY COURIE - REFLEX & AROMA (HM11250) | | | | | | | | | | | | | | | | | | ● | | | | | | | | | | | | ● | | | | | | | | | | | | | | | | | | | |
| LLANISHEN PHYSIOTHERAPY CLINIC (HM12501) | | | | | | | ● | | | | | | | | | | | | | | | | | | | | | | | | | | | | | | | | | | | | | | | | | | |
| MOBILE FOOTWORKS (HM14031) | | | | | | | | | | | | | | | | | | ● | | | | | | | | | | | | | | | | | | | | | | | | | | | | | | | |
| MORGAN-AYRES, PAUL (PROF) (HM14178) | | | | | ● | | | | | | | | | | ● | | | | | | | | | | | | | | ● | | ● | | | | | | | ● | | | | ● | | | | | | | |
| MULLINS, JOHN (HM14348) | | | | | | | ● | | | | | | | | | | | | | | | | | | | ● | | | | ● | | | | | | | | | | | | | | | | | | | |
| NATURAL HEALTHCARE (HM14601) | | | | | | | | | | | | | | | | | | ● | | ● | | | | | | | | | | | | | | | | | | | | | | | | | | | ● | | |
| PALMER, G A PETER (HM15604) | | | ● | | | | | | | | | | | | | | | | | | | | | | | | | | | | | | | | | | | | | | | | | | | | | | |
| PALMER, PETER G A (HM15612) | | | ● | | | | | | | | | | | | | | | | | | | | | | | | | | | | | | | | | | | | | | | | | | | | | | |
| PARRY, PHIL (HM15741) | | | ● | | | | | | | | | | | | | | | | | | | | | | | | | | | | | | | | | | | | | | | | | | | | | | |
| PENYLAN PODIATRIC CENTRE (HM16005) | | | | | | | ● | | | ● | | | | | | | | | | | | | | | | | | | | | | | | | | | | | | | | | | | | | | | |
| POLLEY, LYNDON (HM16414) | | | | | | | | | | ● | | | | | | | | | | | | | | | | | | | | | | | | | | | | | | | | | | | | | | | |
| POLLEY, LYNDON (HM16413) | | | | | | | | | | ● | | | | | | | | | | | | | | | | | | | | | | | | | | | | | | | | | | | | | | | |
| POLLEY, LYNDON (HM16415) | | | | | | | | | | ● | | | | | | | | | | | | | | | | | | | | | | | | | | | | | | | | | | | | | | | |
| RAJA YOGA MEDITATION (HM16897) | | | | | | | | | | | | | | | | | | | | | | | | | | | | | | | | | | | | | | | | | | | | | | | ● | | |
| RENWICK, SARAH NADINE (HM17192) | | | | | | | | ● | ● | | | | | | | | | ● | | ● | | | | | | ● | | | ● | | ● | | | | | | | | | | | | | | | ● | ● | ● | |
| RIDGE, D (HM17316) | | | ● | | | | | | | | | | | | | | | | | | | | | | | | | | | | | | | | | | | | | | | | | | | | | | |
| RIDGE, D (HM17315) | | | ● | | | | | | | | | | | | | | | | | | | | | | | | | | | | | | | | | | | | | | | | | | | | | | |
| RIVENDELL NAT THERAPY CLINIC (HM17375) | | | | | | | | | | | | | | | | | | ● | | ● | | | | | | | | | | | | | | | | | | | | | | | | | | | | | |
| SAWDAY, CAROLINE (HM17983) | | | | | | | | | | | | | | | | | | ● | | | | | | | | | | | | | | | | | | | | | | | | | | | | | | | |

www.healthmyself.com

# O - Z Therapies at Practices/Businesses

| Business by County with Reference no. | Orthotics | Osteomyology | Osteopathy | PAM | Paranormal Therapies | Pattern Therapies | Physiotherapy | Phytotherapy | Pilates | Podiatry | Polarity Therapy | Postural Integration | Primal Therapy | Psionic Therapy | Psychotherapy | Pyramid Power | Pyscho-Synthesis | Reflexology | Reichian Therapy | Reiki | Remedial Massage | Rogerian Therapy | Rolfing | Seichem | Sensitivity Training | Shiatsu | Silva Method | Sound Therapy | Spiritual Healing | Sports Massage | Stress Therapy | Swedish Body Massage | T'ai-Chi Ch'uan | Tantra Therapy | Tera-Mai | Thought Field Therapy | Touch Therapy | Transactional Analysis | Tui-na | Ultrasonics | Vibrational Therapy | Visualisation Therapy | Vitamin Therapy | Voice Therapy | X-Ray | Ying & Yang | Yoga | Zen Therapy | Zero Balancing |
|---|---|---|---|---|---|---|---|---|---|---|---|---|---|---|---|---|---|---|---|---|---|---|---|---|---|---|---|---|---|---|---|---|---|---|---|---|---|---|---|---|---|---|---|---|---|---|---|---|---|
| SELIGMAN, PHILIPPA (HM18210) ||||||||||||||||●||||||||||||||||||||||||||||||||||||
| STEELE, ASHLEY (HM19176) |||||||||||||||||||●|||||||||||||||||||||||||||||||||
| SWANSEA VALLEY PHYSIO PRACTICE (HM19579) ||||||||||||||||||||||||||||||||||||||||●||||||||||
| THOMAS, ANGELA (HM19931) |||||||||||||||||||●|||||||||||||||||||||||||||||||||
| WEBBORN, S H P (HM21081) ||||●||||||||||||||||||||||||||||||||||||||||||||||
| WHATLEY, JUDITH (HM21303) |||||||||||||||||||●|||||||||||||||||||||||||||||||||
| GWYNEDD |||||||||||||||||||||||||||||||||||||||||||||||||||
| COLE, HARVEY M (HM04815) ||||●||||||||||||||||||||||||||||||||||||||||||||||
| HALL, ALISON (HM08764) ||||●||||||||||||||||||||||||||||||||||||||||||||||
| NATURAL THERAPY CLINIC (HM14660) |||||||||||||||||||●||●||||||●||||||||||||||||||||||||
| NORTH DOWN CLINIC (HM15024) ||||●||||||||||||||||||||||||||||||||||||||||||||||
| O'NEIL, L (HM15325) ||||||||||||||||●||||||||||||||||||||||||||||||||||||
| ISLE OF ANGLESEY |||||||||||||||||||||||||||||||||||||||||||||||||||
| CHALMERS, D G (HM03951) ||||||||||||||||||||||||||||||||||||||||●||||||||||
| EPHRAIM, NONA (HM06851) ||||||||||||||||●||||||||||||||||||||||||||||||||||||
| LORD, WENDY (HM12641) |||||||||||||||||||●|||||||||||||||||||||||||||||||||
| MAY, ADAM (HM13340) ||||||||||||||||●||||||||||||||||||||||||||||||||||||
| MILLS, A R (HM13924) ||||●||||||||||||||||||||||||||||||||||||||||||||||
| OSTEOPATHIC CENTRE (HM15456) ||||●||||||||||||||||||||||||||||||||||||||||||||||
| MONMOUTHSHIRE |||||||||||||||||||||||||||||||||||||||||||||||||||
| ABERGAVENNY THERAPY CTRE (HM00121) |||||||||||||||||||●|||||||||||||||||||||||||||||||||
| AGINCOURT OSTEOPATHIC CLINIC (HM00419) ||||●||||||||||||||||||||||||||||||||||||||||||||||
| BROOKSIDE PHYSIO PRACTICE (HM03184) ||||||||●|||||||||||||||||||||||||||||||||●||||||||||
| CRAM, F (HM05361) |||||||||●||||||||||||||||||||||||||||||||||||||||||
| GARRATT, L J (HM07901) ||||●||||||||||||||||||||||||||||||||||||||||||||||
| HARMONY (HM09020) |||||||||||||||||||●||●||||||||||||||||||||||||||||||
| LEWIS, ANDREW J (HM12279) ||||●||||||||||||||||||||||||||||||||||||||||||||||
| NICHOLS, JONATHAN (HM14917) ||||●||||||||||||||||||||||||||||||||||||||||||||||
| SKINNER, G (HM18652) ||||●||||||||||||||||||||||||||||||||||||||||||||||
| TURFAEN CHIROPODY CLINIC (HM20407) |||||||||||●|||||||||||||||||||||||||||||||||||||||
| NEATH PORT TALBOT |||||||||||||||||||||||||||||||||||||||||||||||||||
| DAWSON, KAREN (HM05884) |||||||||||||||||||●|||||||||||||||||||||||||||||||||
| ST JAMES MEDICAL CENTRE (HM19078) ||||||||||||||||●||||||||||||||||||||||||||||||||||||

# O - Z Therapies at Practices/Businesses

| Business by County with Reference no. | Orthotics | Osteomyology | Osteopathy | PAM | Paranormal Therapies | Pattern Therapies | Physiotherapy | Phytotherapy | Pilates | Podiatry | Polarity Therapy | Postural Integration | Primal Therapy | Psionic Therapy | Psychotherapy | Pyramid Power | Pyscho-Synthesis | Reflexology | Reichian Therapy | Reiki | Remedial Massage | Rogerian Therapy | Rolfing | Seichem | Sensitivity Training | Shiatsu | Silva Method | Sound Therapy | Spiritual Healing | Sports Massage | Stress Therapy | Swedish Body Massage | T'ai-Chi Ch'uan | Tantra Therapy | Tera-Mai | Thought Field Therapy | Touch Therapy | Transactional Analysis | Tui-na | Ultrasonics | Vibrational Therapy | Visualisation Therapy | Vitamin Therapy | Voice Therapy | X-Ray | Ying & Yang | Yoga | Zen Therapy | Zero Balancing |
|---|---|---|---|---|---|---|---|---|---|---|---|---|---|---|---|---|---|---|---|---|---|---|---|---|---|---|---|---|---|---|---|---|---|---|---|---|---|---|---|---|---|---|---|---|---|---|---|---|---|
| **NEWPORT** | | | | | | | | | | | | | | | | | | | | | | | | | | | | | | | | | | | | | | | | | | | | | | | | | |
| BAJJADA, JUNE (HM01572) | | | | | | | | | | | | | | | | | | ● | | | | | | | | | | | | | ● | | | | | | | | | | | | | | | | | | |
| BEIGHTON, J W (HM02069) | | | | | | | | | | | | | | | | | | ● | | | | | | | | | | | | | | | | | | | | | | | | | | | | | | | |
| BOWKETT, LYN (HM02792) | | | | | | | | | | | | | | | | | | ● | | ● | | | | | | | | | | | | | | | | | | | | | | | | | | | | | |
| CLINIC OF HOLISTIC HEALTH (HM04693) | | | ● | | | | | | | | | | | | ● | | | ● | | | | | | | | ● | | | | | | | | | | | | | | | | | | | | | | | |
| MOXLEY, SHIRLEY (HM14304) | | | | | | | | | | | | | | | | | | ● | | | | | | | | | | | | | | | | | | | | | | | | | | | | | | | |
| OLIVER, MARION (HM15294) | | | | | | | | | | | | | | | | | | ● | | | | | | | | | | | | | | | | | | | | | | | | | | | | | | | |
| **PEMBROKESHIRE** | | | | | | | | | | | | | | | | | | | | | | | | | | | | | | | | | | | | | | | | | | | | | | | | | |
| BLACKLAW-JONES, R (HM02453) | | | ● | | | | | | | | | | | | | | | | | | | | | | | | | | | | | | | | | | | | | | | | | | | | | | |
| BRIERLEY, ANTHONY (HM03021) | | | | | | | | | | | | | | | | | | ● | | | | | | | | | | | | | | | | | | | | | | | | | | | | | | | |
| CENTRE OF TRADITIONAL HEALING (HM03926) | | | | | | | | | | | | | | | | | | ● | | | | | | | | ● | | | | | | | | | | | | | | | | | | | | | | | |
| CLUTTERBUCK, B (HM04745) | | | | | | | | | | | | | | | | | | ● | | | | | | | | | | | | | | | | | | | | | | | | | | | | | | | |
| **POWYS** | | | | | | | | | | | | | | | | | | | | | | | | | | | | | | | | | | | | | | | | | | | | | | | | | |
| BRECON CLINIC (HM02944) | | | | | | | | | | | | | | | | | | | | ● | | | | | | | | | | | | | | | | | | | | | | | | | | | | | |
| BRECON COMPLEMENTARY MED CTRE (HM02945) | | | | | | | | | | | | | | | | | | ● | | ● | | | | ● | | | | | | | | | | | | | | | | | | | | | | | | | |
| CHAMBERS, HANNAH (HM03958) | | | | | | | | | | | | | | | | | | ● | | | | | | | | | | | | | | | | | | | | | | | | | | | | | | | |
| CONROY, CHRISTINE (HM05007) | | | ● | | | | | | | | | | | | | | | | | | | | | | | | | | | | | | | | | | | | | | | | | | | | | | |
| COVENT HOUSE NTRL HEALTH CTRE (HM05280) | | | | | | | | | | | | | | | | | ● | ● | | | | | | | | ● | | | | | | | | | | | | | | | | | | | | | | | |
| DAVIES, E (HM05808) | | | ● | | | | | | | | | | | | | | | | | | | | | | | | | | | | | | | | | | | | | | | | | | | | | | |
| DUNNE, TERESA (HM06421) | | | ● | | | | | | | | | | | | | | | | | | | | | | | | | | | | | | | | | | | | | | | | | | | | | | |
| FISHER, SUSAN (HM07359) | | | | | | | | | | | | | | | | | | ● | | | | | | | | | | | | | | | | | | | | | | | | | | | | | | | |
| FRANCIS, HELEN (HM07671) | | | | | | | | | | | | | | | | | | ● | | | | | | | | | | | | | | | | | | | | | | | | | | | | | | | |
| HEALTH FOCUS (HM09386) | | | ● | | | | | | | | | | | | | | | ● | | ● | | | | | | | | | | | | | | | | | | | | | | | | | | | | | |
| KILGOUR, KATHARINE () | | | | | | | | | | | | ● | | | | | | | | | | | | | | | | | | | | | | | | | | | | | | | | | | | | | |
| LLANDINAM COUNSELLING (HM12498) | | | | | | | | | | | | | | | ● | | | | | | | | | | | | | | | | | | | | | | | | | | | | | | | | | | |
| LLANDRINDOD WELLS SPA TOWN (HM12499) | | | ● | | | | | | | | | | | | ● | | | | | ● | | | | | | | | | | | | | | | | | | | | | | | | | | | | | |
| PEACE CLINIC (HM15876) | | | | | | | | | | | | | | | ● | | | | | | | | | | | | | | | | | | | | | | | | | | | | | | | | | | |
| PRITCHARD, AUDREY (HM16637) | | | | | | | | | | | | | | | | | | ● | | | | | | | | | | | | | | | | | | | | | | | | | | | | | | | |
| REFLEXOLOGY & ALLERGY THERAPY (HM17078) | | | | | | | | | | | | | | | | | | ● | | | | | | | | | | | | | | | | | | | | | | | | | | | | | | | |
| RODWAY, D J (HM17532) | | | ● | | | | | | | | | | | | | | | | | | | | | | | | | | | | | | | | | | | | | | | | | | | | | | |
| SHEPPARD, HELEN (HM18421) | | | | | | | | | | | | | | | | | | ● | | | | | | | | | | | | | | | | | | | | | | | | | | | | | | | |
| STEPHENS, JANE (HM19203) | | | | | | | | | | | | | | | | | | ● | | | | | | | | | | | | | | | | | | | | | | | | | | | | | | | |
| WILDEN, J D (HM21490) | | | ● | | | | | | | | | | | | | | | | | | | | | | | | | | | | | | | | | | | | | | | | | | | | | | |

# O - Z Therapies at Practices/Businesses

| Business by County with Reference no. | Orthotics | Osteomyology | Osteopathy | PAM | Paranormal Therapies | Pattern Therapies | Physiotherapy | Phytotherapy | Pilates | Podiatry | Polarity Therapy | Postural Integration | Primal Therapy | Psionic Therapy | Psychotherapy | Pyramid Power | Pyscho-Synthesis | Reflexology | Reichian Therapy | Reiki | Remedial Massage | Rogerian Therapy | Rolfing | Seichem | Sensitivity Training | Shiatsu | Silva Method | Sound Therapy | Spiritual Healing | Sports Massage | Stress Therapy | Swedish Body Massage | T'ai-Chi Ch'uan | Tantra Therapy | Tera-Mai | Thought Field Therapy | Touch Therapy | Transactional Analysis | Tui-na | Ultrasonics | Vibrational Therapy | Visualisation Therapy | Vitamin Therapy | Voice Therapy | X-Ray | Ying & Yang | Yoga | Zen Therapy | Zero Balancing |
|---|---|---|---|---|---|---|---|---|---|---|---|---|---|---|---|---|---|---|---|---|---|---|---|---|---|---|---|---|---|---|---|---|---|---|---|---|---|---|---|---|---|---|---|---|---|---|---|---|---|
| RHONDDA CYNON TAFF | | | | | | | | | | | | | | | | | | | | | | | | | | | | | | | | | | | | | | | | | | | | | | | | | |
| CAVIL, A J (HM03867) | | | ● | | | | | | | | | | | | | | | | | | | | | | | | | | | | | | | | | | | | | | | | | | | | | | |
| HUNT, JOHN (HM10395) | | | ● | | | | | | | | | | | | | | | | | | | | | | | | | | | | | | | | | | | | | | | | | | | | | | |
| POLLEY, LYNDON (HM16416) | | | | | | | | | | ● | | | | | | | | | | | | | | | | | | | | | | | | | | | | | | | | | | | | | | | |
| VAUGHAN OWEN, JENI (HM20595) | | | | | | | | | | | | | | | | | | ● | | | | | | | | | | | | | | | | | | | | | | | | | | | | | | | |
| WILLIAMS, ANDREA (HM21537) | | | | | | | | | | | | | | | | | | ● | | | | | | | | | | | | | | | | | | | | | | | | | | | | | | | |
| SWANSEA | | | | | | | | | | | | | | | | | | | | | | | | | | | | | | | | | | | | | | | | | | | | | | | | | |
| ABERTAWE PHYSIOTHERAPY CLINIC (HM00124) | | | | | | | ● | | | | | | | | | | | | | | | | | | | | | | | | | | | | | | | | | ● | | | | | | | | | |
| BEYNON, MARTIN (HM02264) | | | ● | | | | | | | | | | | | | | | | | | | | | | | | | | | | | | | | | | | | | | | | | | | | | | |
| BLACKLAW-JONES, RICHARD (HM02454) | | | ● | | | | | | | | | | | | | | | | | | | | | | | | | | | | | | | | | | | | | | | | | | | | | | |
| BURDEN, RICHARD (HM03370) | | | ● | | | | | | | | | | | | | | | | | | | | | | | | | | | | | | | | | | | | | | | | | | | | | | |
| HALE, SUE (HM08742) | | | | | | | | | | | | | | | ● | | | | | | | | | | | | | | | | | | | | | | | | | | | | | | | | | | |
| RODWAY & ASSOCIATES (HM17531) | | | ● | | | | | | | | | | | | | | | | | | | | | | | | | | | | | | | | | | | | | | | | | | | | | | |
| STEPHENS, G F (HM19202) | | | ● | | | | | | | | | | | | | | | | | | | | | | | | | | | | | | | | | | | | | | | | | | | | | | |
| TORFAEN | | | | | | | | | | | | | | | | | | | | | | | | | | | | | | | | | | | | | | | | | | | | | | | | | |
| CLUB INDIGO (HM04741) | | | | | | | ● | | | | | | | | | | | | | | | | | | | | | | | | | | | | | | | | | | | | | | | | | | |
| PUGH, VIV (HM16749) | | | ● | | | | | | | | | | | | | | | | | | | | | | | | | | | | | | | | | | | | | | | | | | | | | | |
| WREXHAM | | | | | | | | | | | | | | | | | | | | | | | | | | | | | | | | | | | | | | | | | | | | | | | | | |
| DYKINS, PAUL (HM06451) | | | ● | | | | | | | | | | | | | | | | | | | | | | | | | | | | | | | | | | | | | | | | | | | | | | |
| EATON, MARGARET (HM06562) | | | | | | | | | | | | | | | | | | ● | | | | | | | | | | | | | | | | | | | | | | | | | | | | | | | |
| FREEDOM WITHIN (HM07715) | | | | | | | | | | | | | | | ● | | | | | | | | | | | | | | | | | | | | | | | | | | | | | | | | | | |
| HARMONY IN HEALTH (HM09028) | | | | | | | | | | | | | | | | | | | | ● | | | | | | | | | ● | | | | | | | | | | | | | | | | | | | | |
| LATHAM, PATRICIA (HM11995) | | | | | | | | | | | | | | | | | | ● | | | | | | | | | | | | | | | | | | | | | | | | | | | | | | | |
| PRICE, VICTORIA (HM16598) | | | | | | | | | | | | | | | | | | ● | | | | | | | | | | | | | | | | | | | | | | | | | | | | | | | |
| RHONE, B (HM17233) | | | ● | | | | | | | | | | | | | | | | | | | | | | | | | | | | | | | | | | | | | | | | | | | | | | |
| SENSORAMA (HM18229) | | | | | | | | | | | | | | | | | | ● | | | | | | | | | | | | | | | | | | | | | | | | | | | | | | | |
| SHEPHERD, STEVEN (HM18417) | | | ● | | | | | | | | | | | | | | | | | | | | | | | | | | | | | | | | | | | | | | | | | | | | | | |
| SLATER, GISELE (HM18673) | | | | | | | | | | | | | | | | | | ● | | | | | | | | | | | | | | | | | | | | | | | | | | | | | | | |
| WARR, V W & D L (HM20940) | | | ● | | | | | | | | | | | | | | | | | | | | | | | | | | | | | | | | | | | | | | | | | | | | | | |

HEALTH MYSELF

# SECTION 4a

## A-C of Conditions treated at Practices

# A - C Conditions treated at Practices/Businesses

Business by County with Reference no.

## ENGLAND

### BEDFORDSHIRE

| Business by County with Reference no. | Acne | Addiction | Adenoids | Aids | Alcoholism | Allergy | Alzheimer's Disease | Amnesia | Anaemia | Angina | Anorexia | Anxiety | Arthritis | Asthma | Athletes Foot | Autism | Back Pain |
|---|---|---|---|---|---|---|---|---|---|---|---|---|---|---|---|---|---|
| ALOE VERA SPECIALISTS (HM00681) | ● | | | | | ● | ● | | | | | | ● | ● | ● | | ● |
| ALTERNATIVE THERAPY AT WORK (HM00732) | | | | | | | | | | | | ● | | | | | ● |
| AMPTHILL & FLITWICK CLINIC (HM00795) | | | | | | | | | | | | | ● | | | | ● |
| BEDFORD ACUPUNCTURE CLINIC (HM02032) | ● | | | | | ● | | | | | | | ● | | | | ● |
| BEDFORD CHIROPRACTIC SURGERY (HM02033) | | | | | | | | | | | | | ● | | | | ● |
| BEDFORD PHYSIOTHERAPY CENTRE (HM02035) | | | | | | | | | | | | | ● | | | | ● |
| BELLAMY, R D (HM02097) | | | | | | | | | | | | | ● | ● | | | ● |
| BOYCE, MICHAEL (HM02814) | | | | | | ● | | | | | | ● | | | | | |
| BURTON, MERILYNN (HM03444) | | | | | | | | | | | | | | | ● | | |
| CHARTERED PHYSIOTHERAPIST (HM04042) | | | | | | | | | | | | | ● | | | | ● |
| CLNC OF ACU & CHINESE HERB MED (HM04726) | ● | ● | | ● | | | | | | | | ● | ● | | | | ● |
| COULSTOCK, JUDY (HM05239) | | | | | | | | | | | ● | ● | ● | ● | | | ● |
| DA SILVA, CAROLE (HM05665) | | | | | | | | | | | | ● | ● | | | | ● |
| DISS, KATHRYN (HM06122) | ● | | | | | ● | | | | | | ● | ● | | | | ● |
| DUNTON CTRE-COUN/PSYCHOTHERAPY (HM06428) | | ● | | | ● | | | | | | ● | ● | | | | | |
| GOUGH, E & P T (HM08314) | | | | | | | | | | | | | | | ● | | |
| GROVE NATURAL THERAPY CLINIC (HM08610) | ● | ● | | | ● | ● | | ● | | | ● | ● | ● | | | ● | ● |
| HEALES CHIROPRACTIC CLINIC (HM09321) | | | | | | | | | | | | | ● | | | | ● |
| HOLISTIC HYPNOTHERAPY (HM09983) | | ● | | | ● | ● | | | | ● | ● | ● | ● | ● | | | ● |
| INWARD BOUND THERAPIES (HM10707) | | | | | | | | | | | | ● | | | | | |
| JENNIFER K HOUGH - PHYSIO (HM11004) | | | | | | | | | | | | | ● | ● | | | ● |
| JOHNSON, ANNE (HM11068) | | | | | | | | | | | | | ● | | | | ● |
| JOHNSTONS CHIROPODIST (HM11107) | | | | | | | | | | | | | ● | | | | |
| KEMPSTON CHIROPRACTIC CLINIC (HM11469) | | | | | | | | | | | | | ● | | | | ● |
| MAGNETS 4 HEALTH (HM12918) | | | | | | | | | | | | ● | ● | | | | ● |
| MULTIPLE SCLEROSIS THRPY CTRE (HM14351) | | | | | | | | | | | | ● | ● | | | | ● |
| OSBORN, HELEN (HM15418) | | | | | | | | | | | | | ● | | | | ● |
| PRICE, SARAH (HM16596) | | | | | | | | | | | | ● | ● | | | ● | ● |
| SCHOOL OF ICASA (HM18082) | | | | | | | | | | | | ● | | | | | |
| SHEER PERFECTION (HM18367) | | | | | | | | | | | | ● | ● | | | | ● |
| SPECTRUM HEALTH TRUST (HM18976) | ● | ● | | | ● | ● | ● | | ● | ● | | ● | ● | ● | ● | | ● |

| Business by County with Reference no. | Bacterial Infections | Baldness | Bereavement | Bladder Problems | Blood Pressure | Boils | Bowel Problems | Breast Problems | Breathing Problems | Bronchitis | Bruising | Bulimia | Bunions | Bursitis | Callices | Cancers |
|---|---|---|---|---|---|---|---|---|---|---|---|---|---|---|---|---|
| ALOE VERA SPECIALISTS (HM00681) | ● | | | | | ● | ● | | | ● | | | | | | |
| ALTERNATIVE THERAPY AT WORK (HM00732) | | | | | | | | | | | | | | | | |
| AMPTHILL & FLITWICK CLINIC (HM00795) | | | | | | | | | | | | | | | | |
| BEDFORD ACUPUNCTURE CLINIC (HM02032) | | | | | | | | | | | | | | | | |
| BEDFORD CHIROPRACTIC SURGERY (HM02033) | | | | | ● | | | | | | | | | | | |
| BEDFORD PHYSIOTHERAPY CENTRE (HM02035) | | | | | | | | | | | ● | | | | | |
| BELLAMY, R D (HM02097) | | | | | | | ● | | ● | | | | | | | |
| BOYCE, MICHAEL (HM02814) | | | | | ● | | | | | | | | | | | |
| BURTON, MERILYNN (HM03444) | | | | | | | | | | | | | | | ● | |
| CHARTERED PHYSIOTHERAPIST (HM04042) | | | | | | | | | | | | | | ● | | |
| CLNC OF ACU & CHINESE HERB MED (HM04726) | | | | ● | ● | | ● | | ● | ● | | | | ● | | |
| COULSTOCK, JUDY (HM05239) | | | | ● | ● | | ● | ● | ● | | | | | | | ● |
| DA SILVA, CAROLE (HM05665) | | | | | ● | | | | ● | | | | | | | |
| DISS, KATHRYN (HM06122) | | | | | ● | | | | ● | ● | | | | | | |
| DUNTON CTRE-COUN/PSYCHOTHERAPY (HM06428) | | | | | | | ● | | | | | | | | | |
| GOUGH, E & P T (HM08314) | | | | | | | | | | | | | | | ● | |
| GROVE NATURAL THERAPY CLINIC (HM08610) | | | | ● | ● | | | | ● | ● | | ● | | | | |
| HEALES CHIROPRACTIC CLINIC (HM09321) | | | | | | | | | | | | | | | | |
| HOLISTIC HYPNOTHERAPY (HM09983) | | | | | | | | | | | ● | ● | | ● | | ● |
| INWARD BOUND THERAPIES (HM10707) | | | | | | | | | | | | | | | | |
| JENNIFER K HOUGH - PHYSIO (HM11004) | | | | ● | ● | | | | ● | | | | | ● | | |
| JOHNSON, ANNE (HM11068) | | | | | | | | | | | | | | | | |
| JOHNSTONS CHIROPODIST (HM11107) | | | | | | | | | | | | | | | | |
| KEMPSTON CHIROPRACTIC CLINIC (HM11469) | | | | | | | | | | | | | | | | |
| MAGNETS 4 HEALTH (HM12918) | | | | | | | | | | | | | | ● | | |
| MULTIPLE SCLEROSIS THRPY CTRE (HM14351) | | | | | | | | | | | | | | | | |
| OSBORN, HELEN (HM15418) | | | | | | | | | | | | | | | | |
| PRICE, SARAH (HM16596) | | | | | ● | | | | | | | | | | | ● |
| SCHOOL OF ICASA (HM18082) | | | | | | | | | | | | | | | | |
| SHEER PERFECTION (HM18367) | | | | ● | ● | | | | ● | | | | | | | |
| SPECTRUM HEALTH TRUST (HM18976) | ● | | | ● | ● | ● | ● | ● | ● | ● | | | | ● | | ● |

| Business by County with Reference no. | Cataracts | Catarrh | Cerebral Palsy | Circulation Problems | Cold Sores | Colds | Colic | Colitis | Conjunctivitis | Constipation | Convulsions | Corns | Coughs | Cramp | Cystitis |
|---|---|---|---|---|---|---|---|---|---|---|---|---|---|---|---|
| ALOE VERA SPECIALISTS (HM00681) | | | | ● | ● | ● | ● | ● | ● | ● | | | | ● | ● |
| ALTERNATIVE THERAPY AT WORK (HM00732) | | | | | | | | | | ● | | | | | |
| AMPTHILL & FLITWICK CLINIC (HM00795) | | | | | | | | | | | | | | | |
| BEDFORD ACUPUNCTURE CLINIC (HM02032) | | | | | | | | | | ● | | | | | |
| BEDFORD CHIROPRACTIC SURGERY (HM02033) | | | | ● | | | ● | | | | | | | | |
| BEDFORD PHYSIOTHERAPY CENTRE (HM02035) | | | | | | | | | | | | | | | |
| BELLAMY, R D (HM02097) | | | | ● | | | | | | ● | | | | ● | |
| BOYCE, MICHAEL (HM02814) | | | | | | | | | | | | | | | |
| BURTON, MERILYNN (HM03444) | | | | | | | | | | | | ● | | | |
| CHARTERED PHYSIOTHERAPIST (HM04042) | | | | | | | | | | | | | | ● | |
| CLNC OF ACU & CHINESE HERB MED (HM04726) | | ● | | ● | | | | ● | | ● | | | ● | | ● |
| COULSTOCK, JUDY (HM05239) | | | | ● | | | | | | | | | | | |
| DA SILVA, CAROLE (HM05665) | | | | | | | | | | | | | | | |
| DISS, KATHRYN (HM06122) | | ● | | ● | | | ● | | | | | | | | |
| DUNTON CTRE-COUN/PSYCHOTHERAPY (HM06428) | | | | | | | | | | | | | | | |
| GOUGH, E & P T (HM08314) | | | | | | | | | | | | ● | | | |
| GROVE NATURAL THERAPY CLINIC (HM08610) | | ● | | ● | | | | | | ● | | | | | |
| HEALES CHIROPRACTIC CLINIC (HM09321) | | | | ● | | | ● | | | | | | | | |
| HOLISTIC HYPNOTHERAPY (HM09983) | | | | ● | | | | | | | | | | | |
| INWARD BOUND THERAPIES (HM10707) | | | | | | | | | | | | | | | |
| JENNIFER K HOUGH - PHYSIO (HM11004) | | | | ● | | | | | | ● | | | | | |
| JOHNSON, ANNE (HM11068) | | | | | | | ● | | | | | | | | |
| JOHNSTONS CHIROPODIST (HM11107) | | | | ● | | | | | | | | | | | |
| KEMPSTON CHIROPRACTIC CLINIC (HM11469) | | | | ● | | | ● | | | | | | | | |
| MAGNETS 4 HEALTH (HM12918) | | | | ● | | | | | | | | | | ● | |
| MULTIPLE SCLEROSIS THRPY CTRE (HM14351) | | | | | | | | | | | | | | | |
| OSBORN, HELEN (HM15418) | | | | ● | | | ● | | | | | | | | |
| PRICE, SARAH (HM16596) | | | | ● | | | | | | | | | | | |
| SCHOOL OF ICASA (HM18082) | | | | | | | | | | | | | | | |
| SHEER PERFECTION (HM18367) | | | | ● | | | | | | ● | | | | | |
| SPECTRUM HEALTH TRUST (HM18976) | ● | ● | | ● | ● | ● | ● | ● | ● | ● | ● | | ● | ● | ● |

# A - C Conditions treated at Practices/Businesses

| Business by County with Reference no. | Acne | Addiction | Adenoids | Aids | Alcoholism | Allergy | Alzheimer's Disease | Amnesia | Anaemia | Angina | Anorexia | Anxiety | Arthritis | Asthma | Athletes Foot | Autism | Back Pain | Bacterial Infections | Baldness | Bereavement | Bladder Problems | Blood Pressure | Boils | Bowel Problems | Breast Problems | Breathing Problems | Bronchitis | Bruising | Bulimia | Bunions | Bursitis | Callices | Cancers | Cataracts | Catarrh | Cerebral Palsy | Circulation Problems | Cold Sores | Colds | Colic | Colitis | Conjunctivitis | Constipation | Convulsions | Corns | Coughs | Cramp | Cystitis |
|---|---|---|---|---|---|---|---|---|---|---|---|---|---|---|---|---|---|---|---|---|---|---|---|---|---|---|---|---|---|---|---|---|---|---|---|---|---|---|---|---|---|---|---|---|---|---|---|---|
| SPORT, ALEXANDER (HM19041) | | | | | | | | | | | | | | | | | ● | | | | | | | | | ● | | | | | | | | | | | ● | | | | | | ● | | | | ● | |
| SWEET BREEZE (HM19584) | ● | ● | ● | ● | ● | ● | ● | ● | ● | ● | ● | ● | ● | ● | ● | ● | ● | ● | ● | | ● | ● | ● | ● | ● | ● | ● | ● | ● | | ● | ● | ● | ● | ● | | ● | ● | ● | ● | ● | ● | ● | ● | ● | ● | ● | ● |
| THERAPY CENTRE (HM19894) | | | | | | | | | | | | | ● | | | | ● | | | | | | | | | | | | | | | | | | | | | | | | | | | | | | | |
| THOMPSON, MARTIN (HM19992) | | | | | | | | | | | | | ● | | ● | | | | | | | | | | | | | | | ● | | ● | | | | | | | | | | | | | ● | | | |
| WINTER, SALLY (HM21721) | | | | | | | | | | | | | | | ● | | | | | | | | | | | | | | | | | ● | | | | | | | | | | | | | ● | | | |
| WOODSIDE CLINIC (HM21857) | | | | | | ● | | | | | | ● | ● | ● | | | ● | | | | | ● | | ● | | | | | | | ● | | | | | | | | | ● | ● | | ● | | | | | |
| BERKSHIRE | | | | | | | | | | | | | | | | | | | | | | | | | | | | | | | | | | | | | | | | | | | | | | | | |
| 1ST CHIROPRACTIC CLINIC (HM00004) | | | | | | | | | | | | | ● | | | | ● | | | | | ● | | | | | | | | | | | | | | | ● | | | ● | | | | | | | | |
| ANABELLE'S THERAPEUTIC MASSAGE (HM00798) | | | | | | | | | | | | | | | | | ● | | | | | | | | | | | | | | | | | | | | | | | | | | | | | | | |
| ASCOT PHYSIOFIRST CENTRE (HM01178) | | | | | | | | | | | | | ● | | | | ● | | | | | | | | | | | ● | | | | | | | | | | | | | | | | | | | ● | |
| BACK TO HEALTH - WINDSOR (HM01516) | | | | | | | | | | | | | ● | | | | ● | | | | | | | | | | | | | | | | | | | | ● | | | ● | | | | | | | | |
| BERKSHIRE CHIROPRACTIC (HM02195) | | | | | | ● | | | | | | | ● | ● | | | ● | | | | | ● | | ● | | ● | | ● | | | ● | | | | | | ● | | | ● | | | ● | | | ● | ● | |
| BODY & SOUL (HM02561) | | | | | | | | | | | | | ● | | | | | | | | | | | | | | | | | | | | | | | | | | | | | | | | | | | |
| BRACKNELL CHIROPRACTIC CLINIC (HM02838) | | | | | | | | | | | | | ● | | | | ● | | | | | | | | | | | | | | | | | | | | ● | | | ● | | | | | | | | |
| BRUCE, ANN (HM03264) | | ● | | | ● | | | ● | | | ● | ● | | | | | | | | | | | | ● | | | | | ● | | | | | | | | | | | | | | | | | | | |
| BURNHAM CHIROPRACTIC CLINIC (HM03404) | | | | | | | | | | | | | ● | | | | ● | | | | | ● | | | | | | | | | | | | | | | ● | | | ● | | | | | | | | |
| CAMPBELL, ELSPETH (HM03597) | ● | ● | | | ● | ● | ● | ● | | ● | ● | ● | ● | ● | | ● | ● | ● | | | | ● | | ● | | ● | | | ● | | | | ● | | ● | | ● | | ● | ● | ● | | ● | | | ● | | ● |
| CASTLE HILL CLINIC (HM03833) | ● | ● | | | ● | ● | | | ● | ● | ● | ● | ● | ● | ● | | ● | ● | ● | | ● | ● | ● | ● | ● | ● | ● | ● | ● | | ● | | | | ● | | ● | ● | ● | ● | ● | ● | ● | ● | | ● | ● | ● |
| CAVERSHAM CHIROPRACTIC CLINC (HM03864) | | | | | | | | | | | | | ● | | | | ● | | | | | ● | | | | | | | | | | | | | | | ● | | | ● | | | | | | | | |
| CAVERSHAM FOOT CLINIC (HM03866) | | | | | | ● | | | | | | ● | ● | | ● | | ● | | | | | ● | | | | | | | | | ● | | | | | | | | | | | | | | | | | |
| CHEFLAND, GERTI (HM04084) | ● | | | | | ● | | | | | | ● | ● | ● | | | ● | | | | ● | ● | | ● | ● | ● | ● | ● | | | | | ● | | ● | | ● | | ● | ● | | | ● | | | ● | ● | ● |
| CHEUNG, JAMES T (DR) (HM04142) | | | | | | | | | | | | | ● | ● | | | ● | | | | | | | | | | | | | | | | | | | | | | ● | | | | ● | | | ● | | ● |
| COOKHAM CHIROPRACTIC CLINIC (HM05068) | | | | | | | | ● | | | | ● | ● | ● | | ● | ● | | | | | | | | | | | | | | | | | | ● | | ● | | | ● | | | ● | | | | ● | |
| COPPERTHWAITE, ERIC (HM05147) | | | | | | | | | | | | ● | | | | | | | | | | | | | | | | | | | | | | | | | | | | | | | | | | | | |
| DEAN RUSSELL & BRYDGES ROBERT (HM05936) | | | | | | | | | | | | | ● | | | | ● | | | | | | | | | | | | | | | | | | | | ● | | | ● | | | | | | | | |
| DEJODE, SONIA (HM05962) | | | | | | | | | | | | | ● | | | | ● | | | | | ● | | | | | | | | | | | | | | | ● | | | ● | | | | | | | | |
| EDNEY, C S (HM06625) | | | | | | | | | | | | ● | ● | ● | | | ● | | | | | | | | | | ● | | | | | | | | ● | | ● | | | | | | | | | | | |
| EDWARDS, JOHN (HM06659) | | | | | | | | | | | | ● | | | | | | | | | | | | | | | | | | | | | | | | | | | | | | | | | | | | |
| EIGHAN, PENELOPE (HM06689) | | | | | | | | | | | | ● | ● | ● | ● | | ● | | | | ● | ● | | ● | | ● | | | | | ● | | | | ● | | ● | | | ● | ● | | ● | | | ● | ● | |
| EIGHT WINDS ACUPUNCTURE (HM06690) | | | | | | ● | | | | | | ● | ● | ● | | | ● | | | | | | | | | | | | | | | | | | | | | | | | | | ● | | | | | ● |
| FAIRBOURNE CLINIC (HM07051) | ● | ● | | | | ● | | | | | | ● | | | ● | | ● | | | | | ● | | | ● | | | | | | | | | | | | | | | ● | | | | | | | | ● |
| FEET TREAT (HM07186) | | | | | | ● | | | | | | ● | ● | | | | ● | | | | ● | ● | | ● | | ● | | | | | | | | | | | ● | | ● | | | | ● | | | | ● | ● |
| FERINGA, MARLIES (HM07233) | | | | | | | | | | | | ● | ● | ● | ● | | ● | | | | ● | | | ● | | ● | ● | | | | | | | | ● | | ● | ● | ● | | ● | | ● | | | ● | ● | ● |
| HALL, BEVERLEY (HM08767) | | | | | | | | | | | | ● | ● | | | | ● | | | | | ● | | | | ● | ● | | | | | | | | | | | | | | | | | | | | | |

# A - C Conditions treated at Practices/Businesses

Business by County with Reference no.

| Condition | HALL, GRACE (HM08773) | HAZEL'S HOLISTIC HEALTH CARE (HM09294) | HEWITT, ANDREW (HM09703) | HILLSIDE OSTEOPATHIC PRACTICE (HM09806) | KENT, JANET (HM11524) | KINGFISHERS COMP HEALTH CARE (HM11650) | LANE, CORINNE (HM11931) | LANGLEY CHIROPRACTORS CLINIC (HM11953) | LAVENDER, S (HM12029) | LIFE GUIDANCE (HM12344) | LISSADELL HOUSE PRACTICE (HM12457) | MAIDENHEAD CHIROPRACTIC (HM12933) | MAIDENHEAD PHYSIO & SPORTS (HM12934) | MCGREGOR, TONY (HM13504) | NASEBY ACUPUNCTURE CLINIC (HM14487) | NATURAL HEALTH CONSULTANCY (HM14591) | NATURAL THERAPY CLINIC (HM14656) | NATURAL THERAPY CLINIC (HM14655) | NEWBURY CHIROPRACTIC CENTRE (HM14851) | NEWBURY PHYSIOTHERAPY (HM14852) | NS3UK NUTRITION SERVICES (HM15099) | PETERS, JEAN (HM16086) | PIM HEALTH CLINIC (HM16301) | ROSEDALE CLINIC (HM17616) | SANDALL, S (HM17898) | SLOUGH SPORTS INJURIES CLINIC (HM18690) | SMETHURST, ALISON (HM18704) | SOUTH LODGE CONSULTING (HM18909) | STRINGER, FRANCES (HM19407) | SUNNINGDALE HEALING CENTRE (HM19509) | THATCHAM CHIROPRACTIC CLINIC (HM19867) | TSENG, PATRICIA (HM20359) | WINNERSH HYPNOTHERAPY PRACTICE (HM21711) | WOOD, JEANIE M (HM21801) |
|---|---|---|---|---|---|---|---|---|---|---|---|---|---|---|---|---|---|---|---|---|---|---|---|---|---|---|---|---|---|---|---|---|---|---|
| Cystitis | | | | | | | | | | | ● | | | | ● | ● | ● | ● | | | ● | | | | | | ● | | | | | | | |
| Cramp | ● | | | | | ● | | | | | ● | | ● | | ● | | ● | ● | | | | | | | | ● | | | | | | ● | | |
| Coughs | | | | | | | | | | | ● | | | | ● | ● | ● | ● | | | | | | | | | ● | | | | | ● | | |
| Corns | | | | | | | | | ● | | | | | | | | ● | ● | | | | | | | | | | | | | | | | |
| Convulsions | | | | | | | | | | | | | | | ● | | ● | | | | | | | | | | | | | | | | | |
| Constipation | | ● | | | | ● | | | | | ● | | | | ● | ● | ● | ● | | | ● | ● | | ● | | | ● | | | | | ● | | |
| Conjunctivitis | | | | | | | | | | | | | | | ● | | ● | ● | | | | | | | | | | | | | | | | |
| Colitis | | | | | | | | | | | | | | | ● | ● | ● | ● | ● | | | | | | | | ● | | | | | | | |
| Colic | | | ● | | | | | ● | | | ● | ● | | | ● | ● | ● | ● | | | | | | | | | | | ● | | ● | ● | | ● |
| Colds | | | | | | | | | | | | | | | ● | ● | ● | ● | | | ● | | ● | | | | ● | | | | | ● | | |
| Cold Sores | | | | | | | | | | | ● | | | | ● | ● | ● | ● | | | | | ● | | | | | | | | | | | |
| Circulation Problems | ● | ● | ● | | | ● | | ● | | | ● | ● | | | ● | ● | ● | ● | ● | | ● | ● | ● | ● | | | ● | | ● | | ● | ● | | ● |
| Cerebral Palsy | | | | | | | | | | | | | | | | | | | | | | | | | | | | | | | | | | |
| Catarrh | | | | | | ● | | | | | ● | | | | ● | ● | ● | ● | | | | | ● | | | | | | | | | | | |
| Cataracts | | | | | | | | | | | | | | | ● | | ● | ● | | | | | | | | | | | | | | | | |
| Cancers | | | | | | | | | | | | | | | ● | | ● | | | | | | | | | | | | | ● | | ● | | |
| Callices | | | | | | | | | ● | | | | | | | | ● | ● | | | | | | | | | | | | | | | | |
| Bursitis | | | | | | | | | | | ● | | | | ● | | ● | ● | | | | | | | | | | ● | | | | ● | | |
| Bunions | | | | | | | | | | | | | | | | | | | | | | | | | ● | | | | | | | | | |
| Bulimia | | | | | | | | | | | | | | ● | | | ● | ● | | | ● | | | | | | | | | | | ● | ● | |
| Bruising | | | | | | | | | | | ● | | ● | | ● | ● | ● | ● | | ● | | | | ● | | ● | | ● | | | | | | |
| Bronchitis | | | | | | | | | | | ● | | | | ● | ● | ● | ● | | | | | ● | | | | ● | | ● | | | ● | | |
| Breathing Problems | | ● | | | | ● | | | | | ● | | | | ● | ● | ● | ● | | | | | ● | | | | ● | | ● | | | ● | | |
| Breast Problems | | | | | | ● | | | | | | | | | ● | | ● | ● | | | ● | | | | | | | | | | | | | |
| Bowel Problems | | | | | | ● | | | | | ● | | | | ● | ● | ● | ● | | | ● | ● | | | | | ● | | | | | ● | | |
| Boils | | | | | | | | | | | ● | | | | | | ● | ● | | | | | | | | | | | | | | | | |
| Blood Pressure | | | | | ● | ● | | ● | | | | | | | ● | ● | ● | ● | ● | | | ● | ● | | | | ● | | ● | | ● | ● | | |
| Bladder Problems | | ● | | | | | | | | | | | | | ● | ● | ● | ● | | | | ● | | | | | ● | | | | | | | |
| Bereavement | | | | | | | | | | | | | | | | | | | | | | | | | | | | | | | | | | |
| Baldness | | | | | | | | | | | | | | | | | ● | ● | | | | | | | | | | | | | | | | |
| Bacterial Infections | | | | | | | | | | | ● | | | | | ● | ● | ● | | | ● | | | | ● | | | | | | | ● | | |
| Back Pain | | ● | ● | ● | | ● | | ● | | | ● | ● | ● | | ● | ● | ● | ● | ● | ● | | ● | ● | ● | ● | ● | ● | ● | ● | | ● | ● | | ● |
| Autism | | | | | | | | | | | | | | | | | ● | | | | ● | | | | | | | | | | | | | |
| Athletes Foot | | | | | | | | | ● | | ● | | | | | ● | ● | | | | | ● | | | ● | | ● | | | | | ● | | |
| Asthma | | ● | | | ● | | | | | | ● | | | | ● | ● | ● | ● | | | ● | | | | | | ● | | | | | ● | | |
| Arthritis | | ● | ● | | | ● | | ● | | | ● | ● | ● | | ● | ● | ● | ● | ● | ● | | | ● | ● | ● | ● | ● | ● | ● | | ● | ● | | ● |
| Anxiety | ● | ● | | | ● | ● | ● | | | | ● | | | ● | ● | ● | ● | ● | | | | ● | ● | | | | ● | | | | | ● | ● | |
| Anorexia | | | | | ● | | | | | | | | | | | | ● | ● | | | | | | | | | | | | | | ● | | |
| Angina | | | | | | | | | | | | | | | ● | | ● | ● | | | | ● | | | | | | | | | | ● | | |
| Anaemia | | | | | | | | | | | | | | | | | ● | ● | | | ● | | | | | | | | | | | | | |
| Amnesia | | | | | ● | | | | | | | | | | | | ● | ● | | | | | | | | | | | | | | | | |
| Alzheimer's Disease | | | | | | | | | | | | | | | | | ● | | | | | | | | | | | | | | | | | |
| Allergy | | | | | | ● | | | | | ● | | | | | ● | ● | ● | | | | | ● | ● | | | ● | | | | | ● | | |
| Alcoholism | | | | | ● | | | | | ● | | | | | | | ● | ● | | | | | | | | | | | | | | | | |
| Aids | | | | | | | | | | | | | | | | | ● | ● | | | | | | | | | | | | | | ● | | |
| Adenoids | | | | | | | | | | | | | | | | ● | ● | ● | | | | | | | | | | | | | | | | |
| Addiction | | | | | ● | | ● | | | ● | | | | | ● | | ● | ● | | | | | ● | | | | | | | | | ● | | |
| Acne | | | | | | ● | | | | | ● | | | | | ● | ● | ● | | | ● | | ● | ● | | | | | | | | ● | | |

England (by County)

CONDITIONS TREATED

A-C

www.healthmyself.com

# A - C Conditions treated at Practices/Businesses

| Business by County with Reference no. | Acne | Addiction | Adenoids | Aids | Alcoholism | Allergy | Alzheimer's Disease | Amnesia | Anaemia | Angina | Anorexia | Anxiety | Arthritis | Asthma | Athletes Foot | Autism |
|---|---|---|---|---|---|---|---|---|---|---|---|---|---|---|---|---|
| WOODLEY HEALING CENTRE (HM21836) | ● | ● | | | | ● | ● | | ● | ● | ● | ● | ● | ● | ● | |
| **BRISTOL** | | | | | | | | | | | | | | | | |
| ANDERSON, KEITH (HM00830) | | | | | | | | | | | | | ● | ● | | |
| AQUARIUS HEALTH CENTRE (HM00959) | ● | ● | ● | ● | ● | ● | ● | ● | ● | ● | ● | ● | ● | ● | ● | ● |
| ARMSTRONG, ELIZABETH (HM01021) | | | | | | | | | | | | | ● | | | |
| ASS-DANCE MOVEMENT THERAPY (HM01268) | | ● | | | ● | | ● | | | | ● | ● | | | | |
| AVON COMPLEMENTARY MEDICINE (HM01404) | | | | | | ● | | | | | | | | | | |
| BAGGLEY, J M (HM01536) | | | | | | | | | | | | | | | ● | |
| BEVAN, RUSS (HM02242) | ● | | | | | ● | | ● | ● | ● | ● | ● | ● | ● | | |
| BRISTOL HYPNOTHERAPY CLINIC (HM03063) | | | | | | | | | | | | ● | | | | |
| BRISTOL NATURAL HEALTH SERVICE (HM03064) | ● | ● | | | | ● | | | | ● | ● | ● | ● | ● | ● | |
| CASTLE CHIROPODY CLINIC (HM03828) | | | | | | | | | | | | | | | ● | |
| CHARLES CLINIC (HM04020) | | | | | | | | | | | | | ● | | | |
| CHERINGTON PRACTICE (HM04106) | | | | | | | | | | | | | ● | | | |
| CLARK, LYN (HM04566) | | | | | | | | | | | | | | | | |
| CLIFTON CHIROPRACTIC CLINIC (HM04666) | | | | | | | | | | | | | ● | ● | | |
| CLIFTON PRACTICE (HM04670) | | | | | | | | | | | | ● | | | | |
| CLINIC OF NATURAL MEDICINE (HM04704) | | | | | | ● | | | | | | ● | | ● | | |
| CROSS HANDS CHIRO CLINIC (HM05478) | | | | | | ● | | | | | | | ● | | | |
| CTRE FOR KINESIOLOGY (HM05542) | ● | ● | ● | | | ● | | | ● | | | | ● | ● | ● | |
| DANCE VOICE THERAPY CENTRE (HM05709) | | ● | | | ● | | ● | | | | ● | ● | | | | ● |
| DOWRY CHIROPRACTIC CLINIC (HM06255) | | | | | | | | | | | | | ● | | | |
| FILE, CHRISTINE (HM07288) | | | | | | ● | | | | | | ● | | ● | | |
| FRANCIS, PATRICIA (HM07675) | | | | | | | | | | | | | | | | |
| FREEMAN, ANN (HM07719) | ● | | | | | ● | ● | ● | ● | ● | | ● | ● | ● | ● | |
| GARLAND, C (HM07889) | | | | | | | | | | | | ● | ● | | | |
| HARCOURT, A (HM08964) | | | | | | | | | | | | | ● | | | |
| HEALING WITH GABRIELLE TWINE (HM09360) | ● | | | | | ● | | | | | | ● | ● | ● | ● | |
| HEALTH & HEALING (HM09371) | ● | ● | ● | ● | ● | ● | ● | ● | ● | ● | ● | ● | ● | ● | ● | ● |
| HOPLEY, DENISE (HM10154) | | | | | | | | | | | | ● | ● | | | |
| HUDSON, JOHN (HM10313) | | | | | | | | | | | ● | ● | | | | |
| KEYNSHAM CHIROPRACTIC CLINÍC (HM11580) | | | | | | | | | | | | | ● | | | |
| KINGSWOOD CHIROPRACTIC CLINIC (HM11682) | | | | | | | | | | | | | ● | | | |
| KNIGHTSWOOD CLINIC (HM11762) | | | | | | | | | | | | | ● | | | |

| Business by County with Reference no. | Back Pain | Bacterial Infections | Baldness | Bereavement | Bladder Problems | Blood Pressure | Boils | Bowel Problems | Breast Problems | Breathing Problems | Bronchitis | Bruising | Bulimia | Bunions | Bursitis | Callices |
|---|---|---|---|---|---|---|---|---|---|---|---|---|---|---|---|---|
| WOODLEY HEALING CENTRE (HM21836) | ● | ● | ● | | ● | ● | ● | ● | ● | ● | ● | ● | | | | |
| **BRISTOL** | | | | | | | | | | | | | | | | |
| ANDERSON, KEITH (HM00830) | | | | | | | | | | | | | | | | |
| AQUARIUS HEALTH CENTRE (HM00959) | ● | ● | ● | | ● | ● | ● | ● | ● | ● | ● | ● | ● | | ● | ● |
| ARMSTRONG, ELIZABETH (HM01021) | ● | | | | | | | | | | | | | | | |
| ASS-DANCE MOVEMENT THERAPY (HM01268) | | | | | | | | | | | | | ● | | | |
| AVON COMPLEMENTARY MEDICINE (HM01404) | | | | | | | | | | | | | | | | |
| BAGGLEY, J M (HM01536) | | | | | | | | | | | | | | | | |
| BEVAN, RUSS (HM02242) | ● | | | | ● | ● | ● | ● | ● | ● | | | ● | | | |
| BRISTOL HYPNOTHERAPY CLINIC (HM03063) | | | | | | ● | | ● | | | | | ● | | | |
| BRISTOL NATURAL HEALTH SERVICE (HM03064) | ● | ● | | | ● | ● | ● | ● | | | ● | | ● | | | |
| CASTLE CHIROPODY CLINIC (HM03828) | | | | | | | | | | | | | | | | ● |
| CHARLES CLINIC (HM04020) | ● | | | | | ● | | | | | | | | | | |
| CHERINGTON PRACTICE (HM04106) | ● | | | | | | | | | | | | | | | |
| CLARK, LYN (HM04566) | ● | | | | | | | | | | | | | | | |
| CLIFTON CHIROPRACTIC CLINIC (HM04666) | ● | | | | | ● | | ● | | ● | | | | | | |
| CLIFTON PRACTICE (HM04670) | | | | | | | | | | | | | | | | |
| CLINIC OF NATURAL MEDICINE (HM04704) | ● | | | | | ● | | | | ● | | | | | | |
| CROSS HANDS CHIRO CLINIC (HM05478) | ● | | | | | | | ● | | | | | | | | |
| CTRE FOR KINESIOLOGY (HM05542) | ● | ● | | | ● | ● | | ● | ● | ● | | | | | | |
| DANCE VOICE THERAPY CENTRE (HM05709) | | | | | | | | | | | | | ● | | | |
| DOWRY CHIROPRACTIC CLINIC (HM06255) | ● | | | | | | | | | | | | | | ● | |
| FILE, CHRISTINE (HM07288) | ● | | | | | ● | | | | ● | | | | | | |
| FRANCIS, PATRICIA (HM07675) | ● | | | | | | | | | | | | | | | |
| FREEMAN, ANN (HM07719) | | ● | | | ● | ● | | ● | ● | ● | ● | ● | | | | |
| GARLAND, C (HM07889) | ● | | | | | | | | | | | | | | | |
| HARCOURT, A (HM08964) | ● | | | | | ● | | | | | | | | | | |
| HEALING WITH GABRIELLE TWINE (HM09360) | ● | | | | ● | ● | ● | ● | ● | ● | ● | ● | | | | |
| HEALTH & HEALING (HM09371) | ● | ● | ● | | ● | ● | ● | ● | ● | ● | ● | ● | ● | | ● | ● |
| HOPLEY, DENISE (HM10154) | ● | | | | | | | | | | | ● | | | ● | |
| HUDSON, JOHN (HM10313) | | | | | | | | | | | | | ● | | | |
| KEYNSHAM CHIROPRACTIC CLINÍC (HM11580) | ● | | | | | | | | | | | | | | | |
| KINGSWOOD CHIROPRACTIC CLINIC (HM11682) | ● | | | | | | | | | | | | | | | |
| KNIGHTSWOOD CLINIC (HM11762) | ● | | | | | | | | | | | | | | | |

| Business by County with Reference no. | Cancers | Cataracts | Catarrh | Cerebral Palsy | Circulation Problems | Cold Sores | Colds | Colic | Colitis | Conjunctivitis | Constipation | Convulsions | Corns | Coughs | Cramp | Cystitis |
|---|---|---|---|---|---|---|---|---|---|---|---|---|---|---|---|---|
| WOODLEY HEALING CENTRE (HM21836) | ● | ● | ● | | ● | ● | ● | ● | ● | ● | ● | | | ● | ● | ● |
| **BRISTOL** | | | | | | | | | | | | | | | | |
| ANDERSON, KEITH (HM00830) | | | ● | | | | | | | | ● | | | | | |
| AQUARIUS HEALTH CENTRE (HM00959) | ● | ● | ● | | ● | ● | ● | ● | ● | ● | ● | ● | ● | ● | ● | ● |
| ARMSTRONG, ELIZABETH (HM01021) | | | | | ● | | | | | | | | | | | |
| ASS-DANCE MOVEMENT THERAPY (HM01268) | | | | | | | | | | | | | | | | |
| AVON COMPLEMENTARY MEDICINE (HM01404) | | | | | | | | | | | | | | | | |
| BAGGLEY, J M (HM01536) | | | | | | | | | | | | | | | | |
| BEVAN, RUSS (HM02242) | | | ● | | ● | ● | ● | | ● | | | | | | ● | ● |
| BRISTOL HYPNOTHERAPY CLINIC (HM03063) | ● | | | | | | | | | | | | | | | |
| BRISTOL NATURAL HEALTH SERVICE (HM03064) | | | ● | | ● | ● | ● | ● | ● | | ● | | | ● | ● | ● |
| CASTLE CHIROPODY CLINIC (HM03828) | | | | | | | | | | | | | ● | | | |
| CHARLES CLINIC (HM04020) | | | | | | | | | | | | | | | | |
| CHERINGTON PRACTICE (HM04106) | | | | | | | | | | | | | | | | |
| CLARK, LYN (HM04566) | ● | | | | | | | | | | | | | | | |
| CLIFTON CHIROPRACTIC CLINIC (HM04666) | | | | | ● | ● | | | | | ● | | | | | |
| CLIFTON PRACTICE (HM04670) | | | | | | | | | | | | | | | | |
| CLINIC OF NATURAL MEDICINE (HM04704) | | | | | ● | | | | | | | | | | | |
| CROSS HANDS CHIRO CLINIC (HM05478) | | | | | ● | | | | | | ● | | | | | |
| CTRE FOR KINESIOLOGY (HM05542) | | | ● | | ● | ● | ● | ● | ● | ● | ● | | | ● | ● | ● |
| DANCE VOICE THERAPY CENTRE (HM05709) | | | | | | | | | | | | | | | | |
| DOWRY CHIROPRACTIC CLINIC (HM06255) | | | | | ● | | | | | | | | | | | |
| FILE, CHRISTINE (HM07288) | | | | | ● | | | | | | | | | | | |
| FRANCIS, PATRICIA (HM07675) | | | | | | | | | | | | | | | | |
| FREEMAN, ANN (HM07719) | | | ● | | ● | ● | ● | | ● | ● | ● | | | ● | ● | ● |
| GARLAND, C (HM07889) | | | | | | | | | | | | | | | | |
| HARCOURT, A (HM08964) | | | | | ● | | | | | | | | | | | |
| HEALING WITH GABRIELLE TWINE (HM09360) | ● | | ● | | ● | ● | | | | ● | ● | ● | | ● | ● | ● |
| HEALTH & HEALING (HM09371) | ● | ● | ● | | ● | ● | ● | ● | ● | ● | ● | ● | ● | ● | ● | ● |
| HOPLEY, DENISE (HM10154) | | | | | | | | | | | | | | | | |
| HUDSON, JOHN (HM10313) | | | | | | | | | | | | | | | | |
| KEYNSHAM CHIROPRACTIC CLINÍC (HM11580) | | | | | ● | | | ● | | | | | | | | |
| KINGSWOOD CHIROPRACTIC CLINIC (HM11682) | | | | | ● | | | ● | | | | | | | | |
| KNIGHTSWOOD CLINIC (HM11762) | | | | | | | | | | | | | | | | |

# A - C Conditions treated at Practices/Businesses

Business by County with Reference no.

| Business | Acne | Addiction | Adenoids | Aids | Alcoholism | Allergy | Alzheimer's Disease | Amnesia | Anaemia | Angina | Anorexia | Anxiety | Arthritis | Asthma | Athletes Foot | Autism | Back Pain | Bacterial Infections | Baldness | Bereavement | Bladder Problems | Blood Pressure | Boils | Bowel Problems |
|---|---|---|---|---|---|---|---|---|---|---|---|---|---|---|---|---|---|---|---|---|---|---|---|---|
| NAILSEA CHIROPRACTIC CLINIC (HM14460) | | | | | | | | | | | | |●| | | |●| | | | | | | |
| NAYDLER, NICK (HM14711) | | | | | | | | | | | |●| | | | | | | | | | | | |
| ORCHARD MEDICAL CENTRE (HM15364) | | | | | |●| | | | | |●|●|●|●| |●| | | | |●| | |
| ORIENTAL MEDICINE PRACTICE (HM15387) |●| |●|●| |●|●| | |●| |●|●|●| | |●| | | | |●| |●|
| PARKER CLINIC (HM15683) | | | | | | | | | | | | |●| | | |●| | | | | | | |
| POCOCK, A (HM16391) | | | | | | | | | | | | | | |●| | | | | | | | | |
| REDLANDS HOUSE CLINIC (HM17028) | | | | | | | | | | | | |●| | | |●| | | | | | | |
| REDMOND, CAROLINE (HM17031) |●|●|●|●|●|●|●|●|●|●|●|●|●|●|●|●|●|●|●| |●|●|●|●|
| RICHARD GIBBONS - ACUPUNCT (HM17244) | |●| | |●|●| | | | | |●|●|●| | |●| | | |●|●| |●|
| STEVENS, BEN (HM19225) | | | | | |●| | | | | |●|●|●| | |●| | | | | | | |
| STIRLING, P (HM19302) |●|●|●|●|●|●|●|●|●|●|●|●|●|●|●|●|●|●|●| |●|●|●|●|
| STYLES, PATRICIA (HM19458) | | | | | | | | | | | | | | |●| | | | | | | | | |
| THOMAS, TRUDY (HM19958) | | | | | | | | | | | | | | |●| | | | | | | | | |
| TOLL HOUSE CLINIC (HM20120) | | | | | | | | | | | | | |●| | |●| | | |●| | | |
| BUCKINGHAMSHIRE | | | | | | | | | | | | | | | | | | | | | | | | |
| ALTERNATE WAYS (HM00692) | | | | | | | | | | | | | | | | | | | | | | | | |
| ALTERNATIVE THERAPIES TRAINING (HM00730) |●|●|●|●|●|●|●|●|●|●|●|●|●|●|●|●|●|●|●| |●|●|●|●|
| AMERSHAM CHIROPRACTIC CLINIC (HM00779) | | | | | | | | | | | | |●| | | |●| | | | |●| | |
| AMERSHAM OSTEOPATHIC CLINIC (HM00780) | | |●| | |●| | | | | |●|●|●| |●|●| | | | | | |●|
| ASHBERRY PHYSIOTHERAPY CLINIC (HM01188) | | | | | | | | | | | | |●| | | |●| | | | | | | |
| AYLESBURY CHIROPRACTIC CLINIC (HM01422) | | | | | | | | | | | | |●| | | |●| | | | | | | |
| AYLESBURY COMPLEMENTARY HEALTH (HM01423) | | | | | | | | | | |●|●|●|●|●| |●| | | | |●| | |
| AYLESBURY VALE THERAPY (HM01425) |●|●| | |●| | | | | | |●| |●| | | | | | | |●| |●|
| BANFIELD, KATIE (HM01657) | | | | | |●| | | | | | |●|●| | |●| | | | | | |●|
| BEACONSFIELD CHIRO CLINIC (HM01954) | | | | | | | | | | | | |●| | | |●| | | | |●| | |
| BIGGS, SYLVIA (HM02294) | | | | | | | | | | |●| | |●| | |●| | | |●|●| | |
| BODY & SOUL (HM02565) |●| | | | | | | | | | |●|●| | | |●| | | | | | | |
| BREEZE, T (HM02951) | | | | | | | | | | | | | | | | |●| | | | | | | |
| BUCKINGHAM CHIROPRACTIC CLINIC (HM03310) | | | | | | | | | | | |●|●| | | |●| | | | | | | |
| CAMPBELL, LOUISE (HM03604) | | | | | | | | | | | |●| |●| | | | | | | | | | |
| CAMPBELL, NIKKI (HM03605) | |●| | |●|●|●| | | |●|●|●|●| |●|●| | | | |●| |●|
| CARMA HEALING SANCTUARY (HM03703) | | | | | | | | | | | | | | | | |●| | | | | | | |
| CASTLE STREET CLINIC (HM03837) | | | | | |●| | | | | |●|●|●| | |●| | | | | | |●|
| CHILTERN AROMATHERAPY (HM04172) | | | | | | | | | | | | |●| | | |●| | | | | | | |

| Business | Breast Problems | Breathing Problems | Bronchitis | Bruising | Bulimia | Bunions | Bursitis | Callices | Cancers | Cataracts | Catarrh | Cerebral Palsy | Circulation Problems | Cold Sores | Colds | Colic | Colitis | Conjunctivitis | Constipation | Convulsions | Corns | Coughs | Cramp | Cystitis |
|---|---|---|---|---|---|---|---|---|---|---|---|---|---|---|---|---|---|---|---|---|---|---|---|---|
| NAILSEA CHIROPRACTIC CLINIC (HM14460) | | | | | | | | | | | | | | | | | | | | | | | | |
| NAYDLER, NICK (HM14711) | | | | | | | | | | | | | | | | | | | | | | | | |
| ORCHARD MEDICAL CENTRE (HM15364) | | |●| | | | | | | | | |●| | | | | | | | | | | |
| ORIENTAL MEDICINE PRACTICE (HM15387) |●|●|●|●| | | | | | |●| |●|●|●|●|●|●|●| | |●|●|●|
| PARKER CLINIC (HM15683) | | | | | | | | | | | | |●| | | | | | | | | | | |
| POCOCK, A (HM16391) | | | | | | | |●| | | | | | | | | | | | |●| | | |
| REDLANDS HOUSE CLINIC (HM17028) | | | | | | | | | | | | |●| | | | | | | | | | | |
| REDMOND, CAROLINE (HM17031) |●|●|●|●|●| |●|●|●|●|●| |●|●|●|●|●|●|●|●|●|●|●|●|
| RICHARD GIBBONS - ACUPUNCT (HM17244) | | | | | | | | | | |●| |●| | | |●| |●| | |●| | |
| STEVENS, BEN (HM19225) | | | |●| | | | | | | | | | | | | | |●| | | |●|●|
| STIRLING, P (HM19302) |●|●|●|●|●| |●|●|●|●|●| |●|●|●|●|●|●|●|●|●|●|●|●|
| STYLES, PATRICIA (HM19458) | | | | | | | |●| | | | | | | | | | | | |●| | | |
| THOMAS, TRUDY (HM19958) | | | | | | | |●| | | | | | | | | | | | |●| | | |
| TOLL HOUSE CLINIC (HM20120) | | | | | | | | | | | | | | | | | | | | | | | | |
| BUCKINGHAMSHIRE | | | | | | | | | | | | | | | | | | | | | | | | |
| ALTERNATE WAYS (HM00692) | |●| | | | | | | | | | |●| | | | | | | | | | | |
| ALTERNATIVE THERAPIES TRAINING (HM00730) |●|●|●|●|●| |●|●|●|●|●| |●|●|●|●|●|●|●|●|●|●|●|●|
| AMERSHAM CHIROPRACTIC CLINIC (HM00779) | | | | | | |●| | | | | |●| | |●| | | | | | | | |
| AMERSHAM OSTEOPATHIC CLINIC (HM00780) | |●|●|●| | |●| | | |●| | | |●|●|●|●|●| | |●| |●|
| ASHBERRY PHYSIOTHERAPY CLINIC (HM01188) | | | |●| | | | | | | | | | | | | | | | | | | | |
| AYLESBURY CHIROPRACTIC CLINIC (HM01422) | | | | | | | | | | | | |●| | |●| | | | | | | | |
| AYLESBURY COMPLEMENTARY HEALTH (HM01423) | | | | | | | | |●| | | |●|●|●| | | |●| | |●| | |
| AYLESBURY VALE THERAPY (HM01425) | |●| | |●| | | |●| | | | | | | | | |●| | | | | |
| BANFIELD, KATIE (HM01657) | | | | | | | | | | |●| | | | |●| | |●| | | | |●|
| BEACONSFIELD CHIRO CLINIC (HM01954) | | | | | | | | | | | | |●| | |●| | | | | | | | |
| BIGGS, SYLVIA (HM02294) | | | | | | | | | | |●| |●| | | | | |●| | | | | |
| BODY & SOUL (HM02565) | | | | | | | | | | | | | | | | | | | | | | | | |
| BREEZE, T (HM02951) | | | | | | | | | | | | | | | | | | | | | | | | |
| BUCKINGHAM CHIROPRACTIC CLINIC (HM03310) | | | | | | | | | | | | |●| | |●| | | | | | | | |
| CAMPBELL, LOUISE (HM03604) | | | | | | | | | | | | |●| |●| | | | | | | | | |
| CAMPBELL, NIKKI (HM03605) |●|●| | |●| | | | | |●| |●| | |●|●| | | | | | | |
| CARMA HEALING SANCTUARY (HM03703) | | | | | | | | |●| | | | | | | | | | | | | | | |
| CASTLE STREET CLINIC (HM03837) | | |●|●| | |●| | | | | | | | |●|●| |●| | | | |●|
| CHILTERN AROMATHERAPY (HM04172) | | | | | | | | | | | | | | | | | | | | | | | | |

# A - C Conditions treated at Practices/Businesses

Business by County with Reference no.

| | COACHING FOR SUCCESS (HM04750) | COLDWELL, VERONICA (HM04810) | COMPLEMENTARY HEALTH (HM04921) | COMPLEMENTARY HEALTH CENTRE (HM04923) | DOIG, PAUL (HM06158) | DOWDELL, FIONA K (HM06234) | EDWARDS, EMMA (HM06650) | ELAINE MCCARTHY REFLEXOLOGIST (HM06698) | ENFIELD, CLAUDIA (HM06820) | FIRMAN, BARBARA (HM07332) | FLEET, BARBARA (HM07402) | GERRARDS CROSS SPORTS & BACK (HM08004) | HEATH, SUSAN (HM09454) | HOBBS, SALLY (HM09857) | HOLISTIC HEALING (HM09959) | HULCOTT END PRACTICE (HM10352) | J J COUNSELLING SERVICES (HM10798) | JOHNSON, HELEN (HM11074) | K BANFIELD NATUROPATHY/OSTEO (HM11288) | KENTISH, LORNE (HM11531) | LONG CRENDON OSTEOPATHS (HM12614) | MATTHEWS, FRANK (HM13306) | MIDDLE WAY RE-EDUCATION CTRE (HM13813) | MIND AND BODY (HM13959) | MIRZOEFF, PETER (HM13992) | MORRISSEY, BLANCHE (HM14236) | O'NEIL, PAULA (HM15326) | OXFORDSHIRE BOWEN CLINIC (HM15545) | PATON, BARBARA (HM15823) | PHYSIO FIRST PRACTICE (HM16199) | PINEWOOD CHIROPODY PRACTICE (HM16312) | PRESTWOOD PHYSIOTHERAPY CLINIC (HM16562) | RUNDLE, RICHARD (HM17752) | SHAW, FIONA (HM18335) |
|---|---|---|---|---|---|---|---|---|---|---|---|---|---|---|---|---|---|---|---|---|---|---|---|---|---|---|---|---|---|---|---|---|---|---|
| Acne | | ● | | | ● | | | ● | | ● | | | | ● | | ● | | ● | | | | | | | | | ● | | | | | | ● | |
| Addiction | | ● | | | | | | ● | | ● | | | | ● | | | ● | ● | | | | | | | | | | | | | | | ● | |
| Adenoids | | ● | | | | | | ● | | | | | | ● | | | | ● | | | | | | | | | | | | | | | | |
| Aids | | ● | | | | | | ● | | | | | | ● | | | | | | | | | | | | | | | | | | | ● | |
| Alcoholism | | ● | | | | | | ● | | | | | | ● | | | | ● | | | | | | | | | | | | | | | ● | |
| Allergy | | ● | | ● | ● | | | ● | | ● | | | | ● | | | | ● | ● | | | | | | | | ● | | | | | | ● | |
| Alzheimer's Disease | | ● | | | | | | ● | | | | | | ● | | | | ● | | | | | | | | | | | | | | | | |
| Amnesia | | ● | | | | | | ● | | | | | | ● | | | | | | | | | | | | | | | | | | | | |
| Anaemia | | ● | | | ● | | | ● | | | | | | ● | | | | ● | | | | | | | | | | | | | | | ● | |
| Angina | | ● | | | ● | | | | | | | | | ● | | | | ● | | | | | | | | | | | | | | | | |
| Anorexia | | ● | ● | ● | ● | | | ● | | ● | | | ● | ● | | | ● | ● | | | | ● | | | | | | | | | | | | |
| Anxiety | ● | ● | ● | ● | ● | | ● | ● | ● | ● | | | ● | ● | ● | ● | ● | ● | | ● | | ● | ● | ● | ● | | | | | | | | ● | ● |
| Arthritis | | ● | ● | ● | ● | ● | | ● | ● | ● | ● | ● | | ● | ● | ● | | ● | ● | | ● | | | | | | ● | ● | ● | ● | | ● | ● | ● |
| Asthma | | ● | ● | ● | ● | | ● | ● | ● | ● | | | | ● | ● | | | ● | ● | | | | | | | | ● | ● | ● | | | | ● | |
| Athletes Foot | | ● | ● | ● | ● | | | ● | | ● | | | | ● | | | | ● | | ● | | | | | | | | | | | ● | | ● | |
| Autism | | ● | | | ● | | | | | ● | | | | ● | | | | ● | | | | | | | | | | | | | | | | |
| Back Pain | | ● | ● | ● | | ● | | ● | | ● | ● | ● | | ● | ● | ● | | ● | ● | ● | | | ● | ● | | | ● | ● | ● | ● | ● | ● | ● | ● |
| Bacterial Infections | | ● | | | | | | ● | | | | | | ● | | | | ● | | | | | | | | | | | | | | | ● | |
| Baldness | | ● | | | | | | | | | | | | ● | | | | ● | | | | | | | | | | | | | | | ● | |
| Bereavement | | | | | | | | | | | | | | | | | ● | ● | | | | | | | | | | | | | | | | |
| Bladder Problems | | ● | | | ● | | ● | ● | ● | | | | | ● | | | | ● | | | | | | | | | | | | ● | | | ● | ● |
| Blood Pressure | | ● | ● | | ● | | | ● | ● | ● | | | | ● | | ● | | ● | | ● | | | | ● | | | | ● | ● | | | | ● | ● |
| Boils | | ● | | | ● | | | | | | | | | ● | | | | ● | | | | | | | | | | | | | | | ● | |
| Bowel Problems | | ● | | ● | ● | | | ● | ● | ● | | | | ● | | | | ● | ● | ● | | | | | | | ● | ● | ● | | | | ● | ● |
| Breast Problems | | ● | | | ● | | | ● | | ● | | | ● | ● | | | | ● | | | | | | | | | | ● | | | | | ● | |
| Breathing Problems | | ● | | | | | ● | ● | ● | ● | | | ● | ● | | | | ● | | ● | | | ● | | | | | ● | ● | | | | ● | ● |
| Bronchitis | | ● | | | ● | | ● | ● | | ● | | | | ● | | | | ● | | | | | | | | | | | ● | | | | ● | |
| Bruising | | ● | | | ● | | | ● | | | | ● | | ● | | | | ● | | | | | | | | | | | | ● | | | ● | |
| Bulimia | | ● | ● | ● | ● | | | ● | | ● | | | | ● | | | | ● | | | | ● | | | ● | | | | | | | | ● | |
| Bunions | | | | | | | | | | | | | | | | | | ● | | | | | | | | ● | | | | | | | | |
| Bursitis | | ● | | | | | | ● | | | | ● | | ● | | ● | | ● | | | | | | | | | | ● | ● | ● | ● | | ● | |
| Callices | | ● | | | | | | | | | | | | | | | | ● | | ● | | | | | | ● | | | | | | | | |
| Cancers | | ● | ● | ● | ● | | | ● | | | | | ● | ● | | | | ● | | | | | | | | | | | | | | | ● | |
| Cataracts | | ● | | | | | | ● | | | | | | ● | | | | ● | | | | | | | | | | | | | | | ● | |
| Catarrh | | ● | | | ● | | | ● | | ● | | | | ● | | | | ● | ● | | | | | | | | | | | | | | ● | |
| Cerebral Palsy | | | | | | | | | | | | | | | | | | | | | | | | | | | | | | | | | | |
| Circulation Problems | | ● | ● | ● | ● | | ● | ● | ● | ● | | | | ● | ● | | | ● | | ● | | | | | | | | | ● | | | | ● | ● |
| Cold Sores | | ● | ● | ● | ● | | | | | | | | | ● | | | | ● | | | | | | | | | | | | | | | ● | |
| Colds | | ● | ● | ● | ● | | ● | ● | | ● | | | | ● | | | | ● | | ● | | | | | | | | | | | | | ● | |
| Colic | | ● | | | ● | ● | | ● | | | | | | ● | | | | ● | ● | | | | | | | | | | | | | | ● | |
| Colitis | ● | ● | | | ● | | | ● | | ● | | | | ● | | | | ● | | | | | | | | | ● | | | | | | ● | |
| Conjunctivitis | | ● | | | ● | | | ● | | | | | | ● | | | | ● | | | | | | | | | ● | | | | | | | |
| Constipation | | ● | ● | ● | ● | | ● | ● | ● | ● | | | ● | ● | | | | ● | ● | ● | | | | | | | ● | ● | ● | | | | ● | ● |
| Convulsions | | ● | | | ● | | | ● | | | | | | ● | | | | ● | | | | | | | | | | | | | | | | |
| Corns | | ● | | | | | | | | | | | | | | | | ● | | ● | | | | | | ● | | | | | | | | |
| Coughs | | ● | ● | ● | ● | | | | | | | | | ● | | | | ● | | | | | | | | | | ● | | | | | ● | |
| Cramp | | ● | | ● | ● | | | ● | | | | | | ● | | | | ● | | | | | | | | | | ● | | | ● | | ● | |
| Cystitis | | ● | | | ● | | | ● | | ● | | | | ● | | | | ● | ● | | | | | | | | | | | | | | ● | |

# A - C Conditions treated at Practices/Businesses

| Business by County with Reference no. | Acne | Addiction | Adenoids | Aids | Alcoholism | Allergy | Alzheimer's Disease | Amnesia | Anaemia | Angina | Anorexia | Anxiety | Arthritis | Asthma | Athletes Foot | Autism |
|---|---|---|---|---|---|---|---|---|---|---|---|---|---|---|---|---|
| SHENLEY CHIROPRACTIC CLINIC (HM18399) | | | | | | | | | | | | | ● | | | |
| STEINBERG, PAMELA (HM19189) | ● | ● | ● | ● | ● | ● | ● | ● | ● | ● | ● | ● | ● | ● | ● | ● |
| TAYLOR, IAN E (HM19763) | | | | | | | | | | | | | | | ● | |
| TEACHERS OF ALEXNDR TECH (HM19806) | | | | | | | | | | | | ● | ● | | | |
| TODD, PAUL (HM20107) | | | | | | | | | | | | | | | ● | |
| TOMLIN, SUSAN M (HM20136) | | | | | | ● | | | | | ● | ● | ● | ● | | |
| TUDOR HOUSE CLINIC (HM20371) | | | | | | | | | | | | | ● | | | |
| WARDLAW, MICHAEL (HM20921) | | | | | | | | | | | | | | | ● | |
| WELLBURN (HM21154) | | | ● | ● | ● | ● | ● | ● | ● | ● | ● | ● | ● | ● | ● | |
| WELLER, JACK (HM21156) | | ● | | | ● | | | | | | ● | ● | | | | |
| WEST WYCOMBE CHIRO CLINIC (HM21240) | | | | | | | | | | | | | ● | | | |
| WESTWOOD, TERRY (HM21287) | | ● | | | ● | | | | | | ● | | | | | |
| WOODWARD, MARGARET (HM21866) | | | | | | | | | | | | | | | | |
| **CAMBRIDGESHIRE** | | | | | | | | | | | | | | | | |
| ACHILLES PHYSIOTHERAPY CLINIC (HM00161) | | | | | | | | | | | | | ● | | | |
| ANDERSON, M (HM00834) | | | | | | | | | | | | | ● | | | |
| ANDERSON, PAUL (HM00836) | | | | | | | | | | | | | | | ● | |
| ARJUNA NATURAL HEALTH CENTRE (HM01000) | ● | ● | ● | ● | ● | ● | ● | ● | ● | ● | ● | ● | ● | ● | ● | ● |
| BACK ON TRACK (HM01488) | | | | | | | | | | | | | ● | | | |
| BACK ON TRACK (HM01486) | | | | | | | | | | | | | ● | | | |
| BACK ON TRACK (HM01487) | | | | | | | | | | | | | ● | | | |
| BENSON, HUGH (HM02168) | ● | ● | ● | | ● | ● | ● | ● | ● | ● | ● | ● | ● | ● | ● | ● |
| BRAMPTON CHIROPRACTIC CLINIC (HM02906) | | | | | | ● | | | | | | ● | ● | ● | | |
| CAMBRIDGE CHIROPRACTIC CENTRE (HM03572) | | | | | | | | | | | | | ● | | | |
| CAMBRIDGE NUTRITIONAL SCIENCES (HM03575) | | | | | | ● | | | | | | | | | | |
| CAMBRIDGE TRAD ACUPUNC CENTRE (HM03578) | | | | | | ● | | | | | | ● | ● | ● | | |
| CHIROPRATIC & HOM HEALTH CTRE (HM04408) | | | | | | | | | | ● | ● | ● | ● | ● | | |
| COMPLEMENTARY HEALTH CLINIC (HM04927) | ● | ● | | | ● | | | | | | | ● | ● | ● | | |
| COXELL REMEDIAL CLINIC (HM05324) | | | | | | | | | | | | | ● | | | |
| CUTTING, VALERIE (HM05648) | | | | | | | | | | | | ● | | | | |
| FAULKNER, CINDY (HM07141) | | | | | | | | | ● | ● | | ● | ● | ● | ● | |
| GILBERT RD OSTEOPATHIC (HM08055) | | | | | | | | | | | | | ● | | | |
| HEAL, CHRISTIANNE (HM09313) | | | | | | | | | | | | | | | | |
| HEALTH TEAM (HM09406) | ● | ● | | | | ● | | ● | ● | ● | ● | ● | ● | ● | ● | ● |

| Business by County with Reference no. | Back Pain | Bacterial Infections | Baldness | Bereavement | Bladder Problems | Blood Pressure | Boils | Bowel Problems | Breast Problems | Breathing Problems | Bronchitis | Bruising | Bulimia | Bunions | Bursitis | Callices |
|---|---|---|---|---|---|---|---|---|---|---|---|---|---|---|---|---|
| SHENLEY CHIROPRACTIC CLINIC (HM18399) | ● | | | | | ● | | | | | | | | | | |
| STEINBERG, PAMELA (HM19189) | ● | ● | ● | | ● | ● | ● | ● | ● | ● | ● | ● | ● | | ● | ● |
| TAYLOR, IAN E (HM19763) | | | | | | | | | | | | | | ● | ● | |
| TEACHERS OF ALEXNDR TECH (HM19806) | ● | | | | | ● | | | | | | | | | | |
| TODD, PAUL (HM20107) | | | | | | | | | | | | | | | | ● |
| TOMLIN, SUSAN M (HM20136) | ● | | | | ● | | | ● | ● | ● | ● | | | | | |
| TUDOR HOUSE CLINIC (HM20371) | ● | | | | | | | | | | | ● | | | | |
| WARDLAW, MICHAEL (HM20921) | | ● | | | | | | | | | | | | | | ● |
| WELLBURN (HM21154) | ● | ● | ● | | ● | ● | ● | ● | ● | ● | ● | ● | ● | | | |
| WELLER, JACK (HM21156) | | | | | | | | | | | | | ● | | | |
| WEST WYCOMBE CHIRO CLINIC (HM21240) | ● | | | | | ● | | | | | | | | | | |
| WESTWOOD, TERRY (HM21287) | | | | | | | | | | | | | ● | | | |
| WOODWARD, MARGARET (HM21866) | ● | | | | | | | | | | | | | | | |
| **CAMBRIDGESHIRE** | | | | | | | | | | | | | | | | |
| ACHILLES PHYSIOTHERAPY CLINIC (HM00161) | ● | | | | | | | | | | | | | | | |
| ANDERSON, M (HM00834) | ● | | | | | | | | | | | | | | | |
| ANDERSON, PAUL (HM00836) | | | | | | | | | | | | | | | | ● |
| ARJUNA NATURAL HEALTH CENTRE (HM01000) | ● | ● | ● | | ● | ● | ● | ● | ● | ● | ● | ● | ● | | ● | |
| BACK ON TRACK (HM01488) | ● | | | | | | | | | | | | | | | |
| BACK ON TRACK (HM01486) | ● | | | | | | | | | | | | | | | |
| BACK ON TRACK (HM01487) | ● | | | | | | | | | | | | | | | |
| BENSON, HUGH (HM02168) | ● | ● | ● | | ● | ● | ● | ● | ● | ● | ● | ● | ● | | ● | ● |
| BRAMPTON CHIROPRACTIC CLINIC (HM02906) | ● | | | | ● | ● | | | | ● | | | | | | |
| CAMBRIDGE CHIROPRACTIC CENTRE (HM03572) | ● | | | | | | | | | | | | | | | |
| CAMBRIDGE NUTRITIONAL SCIENCES (HM03575) | | | | | | | | | | | | | | | | |
| CAMBRIDGE TRAD ACUPUNC CENTRE (HM03578) | ● | | | | | | | | | | | ● | | | | |
| CHIROPRATIC & HOM HEALTH CTRE (HM04408) | ● | | | | ● | | | | | ● | | | | | | |
| COMPLEMENTARY HEALTH CLINIC (HM04927) | ● | | | | | ● | | ● | | | ● | | | | | |
| COXELL REMEDIAL CLINIC (HM05324) | ● | | | | | | | | | ● | | | | | | |
| CUTTING, VALERIE (HM05648) | ● | | | | | ● | | | | | | | | | | |
| FAULKNER, CINDY (HM07141) | ● | | | | ● | ● | | ● | | ● | ● | | | | | |
| GILBERT RD OSTEOPATHIC (HM08055) | ● | | | | | | | | | | | | | | | |
| HEAL, CHRISTIANNE (HM09313) | | | | ● | | | | | | | | | | | | |
| HEALTH TEAM (HM09406) | ● | ● | | | ● | ● | ● | ● | ● | ● | | | ● | | ● | |

| Business by County with Reference no. | Cancers | Cataracts | Catarrh | Cerebral Palsy | Circulation Problems | Cold Sores | Colds | Colic | Colitis | Conjunctivitis | Constipation | Convulsions | Corns | Coughs | Cramp | Cystitis |
|---|---|---|---|---|---|---|---|---|---|---|---|---|---|---|---|---|
| SHENLEY CHIROPRACTIC CLINIC (HM18399) | | | | | | | | ● | | | | | | | | |
| STEINBERG, PAMELA (HM19189) | ● | ● | ● | | ● | ● | ● | ● | ● | ● | ● | ● | ● | ● | ● | ● |
| TAYLOR, IAN E (HM19763) | | | | | | | | | | | | | ● | | | |
| TEACHERS OF ALEXNDR TECH (HM19806) | | | | | ● | | | ● | | | | | | | | |
| TODD, PAUL (HM20107) | | | | | | | | | | | | | ● | | | |
| TOMLIN, SUSAN M (HM20136) | | | ● | | ● | | | ● | ● | | ● | | | | ● | ● |
| TUDOR HOUSE CLINIC (HM20371) | | | | | | | | | | | | | | | ● | |
| WARDLAW, MICHAEL (HM20921) | | | | | | | | | | | | | ● | | | |
| WELLBURN (HM21154) | ● | ● | ● | | ● | ● | ● | ● | ● | ● | ● | | | ● | ● | ● |
| WELLER, JACK (HM21156) | | | | | | | | | | | | | | | | |
| WEST WYCOMBE CHIRO CLINIC (HM21240) | | | | | | | | ● | | | | | | | | |
| WESTWOOD, TERRY (HM21287) | | | | | | | | | | | | | | | | |
| WOODWARD, MARGARET (HM21866) | | | | | ● | | | | | | ● | | | | | |
| **CAMBRIDGESHIRE** | | | | | | | | | | | | | | | | |
| ACHILLES PHYSIOTHERAPY CLINIC (HM00161) | | | | | | | | | | | | | | | | |
| ANDERSON, M (HM00834) | | | | | ● | | | | | | | | | | | |
| ANDERSON, PAUL (HM00836) | | | | | | | | | | | | | ● | | | |
| ARJUNA NATURAL HEALTH CENTRE (HM01000) | ● | ● | ● | | ● | ● | ● | ● | ● | ● | ● | ● | | ● | ● | ● |
| BACK ON TRACK (HM01488) | | | | | | | | | | | | | | | | |
| BACK ON TRACK (HM01486) | | | | | | | | | | | | | | | | |
| BACK ON TRACK (HM01487) | | | | | | | | | | | | | | | | |
| BENSON, HUGH (HM02168) | | ● | ● | | ● | ● | ● | ● | ● | ● | ● | ● | ● | ● | ● | ● |
| BRAMPTON CHIROPRACTIC CLINIC (HM02906) | | | ● | | | | | ● | | | ● | | | | ● | |
| CAMBRIDGE CHIROPRACTIC CENTRE (HM03572) | | | | | ● | | | | | | | | | | | |
| CAMBRIDGE NUTRITIONAL SCIENCES (HM03575) | | | | | | | | | | | | | | | | |
| CAMBRIDGE TRAD ACUPUNC CENTRE (HM03578) | | | | | ● | | | | | | ● | | | | ● | ● |
| CHIROPRATIC & HOM HEALTH CTRE (HM04408) | | | ● | | ● | | | | | | ● | | | | ● | |
| COMPLEMENTARY HEALTH CLINIC (HM04927) | | | ● | | | | | | ● | | ● | | | ● | ● | |
| COXELL REMEDIAL CLINIC (HM05324) | | | | | | | | | | | | | | | | |
| CUTTING, VALERIE (HM05648) | | | | | ● | | | | | | | | | | | |
| FAULKNER, CINDY (HM07141) | | | ● | | ● | | ● | | ● | | | | | | ● | ● |
| GILBERT RD OSTEOPATHIC (HM08055) | | | | | | | | | | | | | | | | |
| HEAL, CHRISTIANNE (HM09313) | | | | | | | | | | | | | | | | |
| HEALTH TEAM (HM09406) | ● | | ● | | ● | | ● | ● | ● | | ● | | | | ● | ● |

# A - C Conditions treated at Practices/Businesses

| Business by County with Reference no. | Acne | Addiction | Adenoids | Aids | Alcoholism | Allergy | Alzheimer's Disease | Amnesia | Anaemia | Angina | Anorexia | Anxiety | Arthritis | Asthma | Athletes Foot | Autism |
|---|---|---|---|---|---|---|---|---|---|---|---|---|---|---|---|---|
| HYPNOSIS AND HEALTH (HM10495) | | ● | | | ● | | | | | | ● | ● | | | | |
| LIFELINE (HM12354) | | | | | | | | | | | | ● | | | | |
| LIZ HALE HANDSON HEALTH (HM12495) | | | | | | | | | | | | | ● | | | |
| LY, THI PHUNG (DR) (HM12754) | ● | ● | ● | | ● | ● | | | ● | ● | ● | ● | ● | ● | ● | |
| MATHIESON, M A (HM13290) | | | | | | | | | | | | | | | ● | |
| MAYNARD, SUSANNE (HM13358) | | | | | | | | | | | | | ● | | | |
| OUTSIDE IN (HM15507) | | | | | | | ● | | | | | | | | | |
| OXBOROUGH, JOY (HM15536) | ● | | | | | ● | | | | ● | | ● | ● | ● | | |
| PHIL SEAL PSYCHOTHERAPY (HM16115) | | | | | | | | | | | | ● | | | | |
| PRESTONS CHRTRD PHYSIOTHERAPY (HM16560) | | | | | | | | | | | | | ● | | | |
| REID, SUSAN (HM17121) | | | | | | | | | | | | | ● | | | |
| ROBINSON-ZEL, B (HM17508) | | | | | | | | | | | ● | ● | | | | |
| SMITH, JEANETTE (HM18752) | | | | | | | | | | | | ● | | ● | | |
| SPENCE, ALEX (HM18982) | | | | | | | | | | | | | ● | | | |
| TONG, JENNY (HM20154) | | | | | | | | | | | | ● | ● | ● | | |
| TRANSCENDENTAL MEDITATION (HM20286) | | | | | | | | | | | | | | | | |
| WASS, ANNETTE (HM20975) | ● | | ● | | | ● | | | ● | ● | ● | ● | ● | ● | ● | |
| WILKINSON, GLYNNIS (HM21506) | | | | | | | | | | | | | | | ● | |
| **CHANNEL ISLANDS** | | | | | | | | | | | | | | | | |
| ST SAMPSON'S MEDICAL CENTRE (HM19098) | | | | | | | | | | | | | | | | |
| **CHESHIRE** | | | | | | | | | | | | | | | | |
| A & H PAIN CLINIC (HM00016) | ● | ● | | | ● | ● | | | ● | ● | | ● | ● | ● | | |
| ADULT & CHILD FOOT CLINIC (HM00391) | | | | | | | | | | | | | ● | | ● | |
| AROMASPHERE (HM01083) | | | | | | | | | | | | ● | ● | | | |
| BACHE CHIROPODY (HM01471) | | | | | | | | | | | | | | | ● | |
| BACK PAIN CLINIC (HM01500) | | | | | | | | | | | | | ● | | | |
| BATES VISION EDUCATION (HM01878) | | | | | | | | | | | | ● | | | | |
| BAXTER, GILLIAN (HM01927) | | | | | | | | | | | | | | | ● | |
| BERESFORD, KATHLEEN (HM02183) | | | | | | | | | | | ● | ● | | ● | | |
| BLOCH, PETER (HM02510) | | | | | | | | | | | | | ● | | | |
| BODY ESSENCES (HM02586) | | | | | | | | | | | | ● | ● | | | |
| BRAMHALL PARK PHYSIO CLINIC (HM02899) | | | | | | | | | | | | | ● | | | |
| BURTON, J S (HM03436) | | | | | | | | | | | | | | | ● | |
| CARMICHAEL CLINIC (HM03708) | | | | | | | | | | | | ● | ● | | | |

| Business by County with Reference no. | Back Pain | Bacterial Infections | Baldness | Bereavement | Bladder Problems | Blood Pressure | Boils | Bowel Problems | Breast Problems | Breathing Problems | Bronchitis | Bruising | Bulimia | Bunions | Bursitis | Callices |
|---|---|---|---|---|---|---|---|---|---|---|---|---|---|---|---|---|
| HYPNOSIS AND HEALTH (HM10495) | | | | | | ● | | | | | | | ● | | | |
| LIFELINE (HM12354) | | | | | | | | | | | | | | | | |
| LIZ HALE HANDSON HEALTH (HM12495) | ● | | | | | | | | | ● | ● | | | | ● | |
| LY, THI PHUNG (DR) (HM12754) | ● | ● | | | ● | ● | ● | ● | ● | ● | ● | ● | ● | | ● | |
| MATHIESON, M A (HM13290) | | | | | | | | | | | | | | | | ● |
| MAYNARD, SUSANNE (HM13358) | ● | | | | | | | | | | | ● | | | | |
| OUTSIDE IN (HM15507) | | | | | | | | | | | | | | | | |
| OXBOROUGH, JOY (HM15536) | ● | ● | ● | | ● | ● | ● | ● | ● | ● | ● | ● | | | | |
| PHIL SEAL PSYCHOTHERAPY (HM16115) | | | | | | ● | | ● | | | | | | | | |
| PRESTONS CHRTRD PHYSIOTHERAPY (HM16560) | ● | | | | | | | | | | | ● | | | | |
| REID, SUSAN (HM17121) | ● | | | | | ● | | | | ● | ● | | | | | |
| ROBINSON-ZEL, B (HM17508) | | | | | | | | | | | | | | | | |
| SMITH, JEANETTE (HM18752) | ● | | | | ● | | | | ● | ● | ● | | | | | |
| SPENCE, ALEX (HM18982) | ● | | | | | | | | | | | | | | | |
| TONG, JENNY (HM20154) | ● | | | | ● | ● | | | ● | ● | ● | | | | | |
| TRANSCENDENTAL MEDITATION (HM20286) | | | | | | ● | | | | | | | | | | |
| WASS, ANNETTE (HM20975) | | ● | | | ● | ● | ● | ● | ● | ● | ● | ● | | | ● | |
| WILKINSON, GLYNNIS (HM21506) | | | | | | | | | | | | | | | | ● |
| **CHANNEL ISLANDS** | | | | | | | | | | | | | | | | |
| ST SAMPSON'S MEDICAL CENTRE (HM19098) | ● | | | | | | | | | | | | | | | |
| **CHESHIRE** | | | | | | | | | | | | | | | | |
| A & H PAIN CLINIC (HM00016) | ● | | ● | | ● | ● | ● | ● | | ● | ● | | | | | |
| ADULT & CHILD FOOT CLINIC (HM00391) | ● | | | | | | | | | | | | | | | |
| AROMASPHERE (HM01083) | | | | | | | | | | | | | | | | |
| BACHE CHIROPODY (HM01471) | | | | | | | | | | | | | | | | ● |
| BACK PAIN CLINIC (HM01500) | ● | | | | | | | | | | | | | | | |
| BATES VISION EDUCATION (HM01878) | | | | | | | | | | | | | | | | |
| BAXTER, GILLIAN (HM01927) | | | | | | | | | | | | | | | | ● |
| BERESFORD, KATHLEEN (HM02183) | ● | | | | | ● | | ● | | ● | | | | | | |
| BLOCH, PETER (HM02510) | ● | | | | | | | | | | | | | | | |
| BODY ESSENCES (HM02586) | | | | | | | | | | | | | | | | |
| BRAMHALL PARK PHYSIO CLINIC (HM02899) | ● | | | | | | | | | | | ● | | | | |
| BURTON, J S (HM03436) | | | | | | | | | | | | | | | | ● |
| CARMICHAEL CLINIC (HM03708) | ● | | | | | | | ● | | | | | | | ● | |

| Business by County with Reference no. | Cancers | Cataracts | Catarrh | Cerebral Palsy | Circulation Problems | Cold Sores | Colds | Colic | Colitis | Conjunctivitis | Constipation | Convulsions | Corns | Coughs | Cramp | Cystitis |
|---|---|---|---|---|---|---|---|---|---|---|---|---|---|---|---|---|
| HYPNOSIS AND HEALTH (HM10495) | ● | | | | | | | | | | | | | | | |
| LIFELINE (HM12354) | | | | | | | | | | | | | | | | |
| LIZ HALE HANDSON HEALTH (HM12495) | | | ● | | ● | ● | ● | ● | ● | | | | | ● | ● | |
| LY, THI PHUNG (DR) (HM12754) | | | ● | | ● | | ● | ● | ● | ● | ● | | | ● | ● | ● |
| MATHIESON, M A (HM13290) | | | | | | | | | | | | | ● | | | |
| MAYNARD, SUSANNE (HM13358) | | | | | | | | | | | | | | | | |
| OUTSIDE IN (HM15507) | | | | | | | | | | | | | | | | |
| OXBOROUGH, JOY (HM15536) | ● | | ● | | ● | ● | ● | ● | ● | ● | | ● | | ● | ● | |
| PHIL SEAL PSYCHOTHERAPY (HM16115) | | | | | | | | | | | | | | | | |
| PRESTONS CHRTRD PHYSIOTHERAPY (HM16560) | | | | | | | | | | | | | | | | |
| REID, SUSAN (HM17121) | | | | | ● | | | ● | | | | | | | | |
| ROBINSON-ZEL, B (HM17508) | | | | | | | | | | | | | | | | |
| SMITH, JEANETTE (HM18752) | | | | | ● | | | | | | ● | | | | | |
| SPENCE, ALEX (HM18982) | | | | | | | | | | | | | | | | |
| TONG, JENNY (HM20154) | | | | | ● | | | | | | ● | | | | | |
| TRANSCENDENTAL MEDITATION (HM20286) | | | | | | | | | | | | | | | | |
| WASS, ANNETTE (HM20975) | | | ● | | ● | ● | ● | ● | ● | ● | ● | | | ● | ● | ● |
| WILKINSON, GLYNNIS (HM21506) | | | | | | | | | | | | | ● | | | |
| **CHANNEL ISLANDS** | | | | | | | | | | | | | | | | |
| ST SAMPSON'S MEDICAL CENTRE (HM19098) | | | | | | | | ● | | | | | | | | |
| **CHESHIRE** | | | | | | | | | | | | | | | | |
| A & H PAIN CLINIC (HM00016) | ● | | ● | | ● | | ● | | ● | | ● | | | ● | | ● |
| ADULT & CHILD FOOT CLINIC (HM00391) | | | | | ● | | | | | | | | ● | | | |
| AROMASPHERE (HM01083) | | | | | | | | | | | | | | | | |
| BACHE CHIROPODY (HM01471) | | | | | | | | | | | | | ● | | | |
| BACK PAIN CLINIC (HM01500) | | | | | ● | | | ● | | | | | | | | |
| BATES VISION EDUCATION (HM01878) | | ● | | | | | | | | | | | | | | |
| BAXTER, GILLIAN (HM01927) | | | | | | | | | | | | | ● | | | |
| BERESFORD, KATHLEEN (HM02183) | | | | | ● | | ● | | | | | | | | | |
| BLOCH, PETER (HM02510) | | | | | ● | | | | ● | | | | | | | |
| BODY ESSENCES (HM02586) | | | | | | | | | | | | | | | | |
| BRAMHALL PARK PHYSIO CLINIC (HM02899) | | | | | | | | | | | | | | | ● | |
| BURTON, J S (HM03436) | | | | | | | | | | | | | ● | | | |
| CARMICHAEL CLINIC (HM03708) | | | ● | | | | | | | | ● | | | | | |

# A - C Conditions treated at Practices/Businesses

Business by County with Reference no.

| Business | Acne | Addiction | Adenoids | Aids | Alcoholism | Allergy | Alzheimer's Disease | Amnesia | Anaemia | Angina | Anorexia | Anxiety | Arthritis | Asthma | Athletes Foot | Autism |
|---|---|---|---|---|---|---|---|---|---|---|---|---|---|---|---|---|
| CHEADLE HULME NATURAL HEALTH (HM04070) | | | | | | | | | | | | ● | ● | ● | | |
| CHESHIRE HEALTH CLINIC (HM04115) | | | | | | | | | | | | | ● | | | |
| CHESTER ALEXANDER TECH ST (HM04125) | | | | | | | | | | | | | ● | | | |
| CHESTER CHIROPODY (HM04126) | | | | | | | | | | | | | | | ● | |
| CHESTER CHIROPRACTIC CLINIC (HM04127) | | | | | | | | | | | | | ● | | | |
| CHESTER CLINIC (HM04128) | ● | ● | | ● | | ● | | | ● | | | ● | ● | ● | | |
| CHESTER HEALTH (HM04129) | | | | | | | | | | | | ● | ● | ● | | |
| CHESTER HEALTH & BEAUTY STUDIO (HM04130) | | | | | | | | | | | | ● | ● | ● | | |
| CHESTER HOMEOPATHIC CLINIC (HM04131) | ● | ● | ● | | ● | ● | ● | | ● | ● | ● | ● | ● | ● | ● | ● |
| CHESTER THERAPY CENTRE (HM04134) | | ● | | | | | | | | | | | | | | |
| CHINESE MEDICINE CENTRE (HM04257) | ● | | | | ● | ● | | | | ● | | ● | ● | ● | | |
| CHIROPODIST SURGERY (HM04295) | | | | | | | | | | | | | ● | | ● | |
| CHIROPODY CORNER (HM04330) | | | | | | | | | | | | | ● | | ● | |
| CLINIC OF ACUPUNCTURE (HM04684) | | ● | | | | ● | | | | ● | | ● | ● | ● | | |
| COLHOUN, PETER (HM04842) | | | | | | | | | | | | | | | ● | |
| CONGLETON COUNSELLING PRACTICE (HM04977) | | ● | | | ● | | | | | | | ● | | | | |
| CONSTANTINE, J C (HM05012) | | | | | | | | | | | | | ● | | | |
| CREWE & NANT PHYSIO CLINIC (HM05431) | | | | | | | | | | | | | ● | | | |
| CROPPER, AGNES (HM05473) | | | | | | | | | | | | ● | ● | ● | | |
| DAVIES & ASSOCIATES (HM05791) | | | | | | | | | | | | | | | | |
| DEWHURST, PATRICA A (HM06049) | ● | | ● | | ● | ● | ● | | ● | ● | | ● | ● | ● | | |
| EDDIE, DAVID (HM06585) | | | | | | | | | | | | ● | ● | | | |
| EVANS, DI (HM06968) | | ● | ● | | | | | | | ● | | ● | ● | | | |
| FAGAN, B W (HM07042) | | | | | | | | | | | | | ● | | | |
| FEET FIRST MOBILE CHIROPODY SV (HM07183) | | | | | | | | | | | | | | | ● | |
| FIELD VIEW SURGERY (HM07259) | | | | | | | | | | | | | | | ● | |
| FINCH, WENDY (HM07302) | | | | | | | | | | | | ● | | | | |
| FIVE WAYS OSTEOPATHIC SURGERY (HM07381) | | | | | | | | | | | | | ● | | | |
| GENTLE TOUCH (HM07979) | | | | | | | | | | | | | | | | |
| GRACE & ASSOCIATES (HM08331) | | | | | | | | | | | | | ● | | ● | |
| GRAHAM COOMBE - MCTIMONEY (HM08338) | | | | | | | | | | | | | | ● | | |
| HANDS ON PHYSIOTHERAPY (HM08913) | | | | | | | | | | | | | ● | | | |
| HAZELDENE, BARBARA (HM09292) | | | | | | | | | | | | ● | | | | |
| HEALD, M T (HM09316) | | | | | | | | | | | | | | | ● | |

| Business | Back Pain | Bacterial Infections | Baldness | Bereavement | Bladder Problems | Blood Pressure | Boils | Bowel Problems | Breast Problems | Breathing Problems | Bronchitis | Bruising | Bulimia | Bunions | Bursitis |
|---|---|---|---|---|---|---|---|---|---|---|---|---|---|---|---|
| CHEADLE HULME NATURAL HEALTH (HM04070) | ● | | | | ● | ● | | | ● | ● | | | | | |
| CHESHIRE HEALTH CLINIC (HM04115) | ● | | | | | | | | | | | | | | |
| CHESTER ALEXANDER TECH ST (HM04125) | ● | | | | | | | | | ● | | | | | |
| CHESTER CHIROPODY (HM04126) | | | | | | | | | | | | | | | |
| CHESTER CHIROPRACTIC CLINIC (HM04127) | ● | | | | | | | | | | | | | | |
| CHESTER CLINIC (HM04128) | ● | ● | | | ● | ● | ● | ● | ● | ● | ● | ● | | | ● |
| CHESTER HEALTH (HM04129) | ● | | | | | ● | | ● | | ● | | ● | ● | | ● |
| CHESTER HEALTH & BEAUTY STUDIO (HM04130) | ● | | | | | ● | | ● | | ● | | ● | ● | | ● |
| CHESTER HOMEOPATHIC CLINIC (HM04131) | ● | ● | ● | | ● | ● | ● | ● | ● | ● | ● | ● | ● | | ● |
| CHESTER THERAPY CENTRE (HM04134) | | | | | | | | | | | | | | | |
| CHINESE MEDICINE CENTRE (HM04257) | ● | ● | | ● | ● | ● | | ● | | ● | ● | ● | ● | ● | ● |
| CHIROPODIST SURGERY (HM04295) | | | | | | | ● | | | | | | | | |
| CHIROPODY CORNER (HM04330) | | ● | | | | | | | | | | | | | |
| CLINIC OF ACUPUNCTURE (HM04684) | ● | | | | ● | | | ● | | ● | | ● | | | |
| COLHOUN, PETER (HM04842) | ● | | | | | | | | | | | | | | ● |
| CONGLETON COUNSELLING PRACTICE (HM04977) | | | | | | | | | | | | | ● | | |
| CONSTANTINE, J C (HM05012) | ● | | | | | | | | | | | | | | ● |
| CREWE & NANT PHYSIO CLINIC (HM05431) | ● | | | | | | | | | | | ● | | | |
| CROPPER, AGNES (HM05473) | ● | | | | | ● | | | | ● | | | | | |
| DAVIES & ASSOCIATES (HM05791) | ● | | | | | | | | | ● | | | | | |
| DEWHURST, PATRICA A (HM06049) | ● | ● | ● | | ● | ● | ● | ● | ● | ● | ● | ● | | | ● |
| EDDIE, DAVID (HM06585) | ● | | | | | | | | | | | | | | |
| EVANS, DI (HM06968) | ● | | | | ● | ● | | | ● | ● | | | | | |
| FAGAN, B W (HM07042) | ● | | | | | | | | | | ● | ● | | | |
| FEET FIRST MOBILE CHIROPODY SV (HM07183) | | | | | | | | | | | | | | | |
| FIELD VIEW SURGERY (HM07259) | | ● | | | | | | | | | | | | ● | ● |
| FINCH, WENDY (HM07302) | ● | | | | | | | | | | | | | | ● |
| FIVE WAYS OSTEOPATHIC SURGERY (HM07381) | ● | | | | | | | | | ● | | | | | ● |
| GENTLE TOUCH (HM07979) | | | | | | | | | | | | | | | |
| GRACE & ASSOCIATES (HM08331) | | ● | | | | | | | | | | | | ● | |
| GRAHAM COOMBE - MCTIMONEY (HM08338) | ● | | | | | | | ● | | ● | | | | | ● |
| HANDS ON PHYSIOTHERAPY (HM08913) | ● | | | | | | | | | | | ● | | | |
| HAZELDENE, BARBARA (HM09292) | ● | | | | | ● | | | | ● | | | | | |
| HEALD, M T (HM09316) | | | | | | | | | | | | | | | |

| Business | Callices | Cancers | Cataracts | Catarrh | Cerebral Palsy | Circulation Problems | Cold Sores | Colds | Colic | Colitis | Conjunctivitis | Constipation | Convulsions | Corns | Coughs | Cramp | Cystitis |
|---|---|---|---|---|---|---|---|---|---|---|---|---|---|---|---|---|---|
| CHEADLE HULME NATURAL HEALTH (HM04070) | | | | | | ● | ● | ● | | | | | | | ● | | |
| CHESHIRE HEALTH CLINIC (HM04115) | ● | | | | | ● | | | | | | | | ● | | | |
| CHESTER ALEXANDER TECH ST (HM04125) | | | | | | ● | | | | | | | | | | ● | |
| CHESTER CHIROPODY (HM04126) | | | | | | | | | | | | | | | | | |
| CHESTER CHIROPRACTIC CLINIC (HM04127) | | | | | | | | | | | | | | | | | |
| CHESTER CLINIC (HM04128) | | ● | | ● | | ● | ● | ● | ● | ● | ● | ● | | | ● | ● | ● |
| CHESTER HEALTH (HM04129) | | | | ● | | ● | ● | ● | ● | | | ● | | | ● | | ● |
| CHESTER HEALTH & BEAUTY STUDIO (HM04130) | | | | ● | | ● | ● | ● | ● | | | ● | | | ● | | ● |
| CHESTER HOMEOPATHIC CLINIC (HM04131) | | ● | | ● | | ● | ● | ● | ● | ● | ● | ● | ● | | ● | ● | ● |
| CHESTER THERAPY CENTRE (HM04134) | | | | | | | | | | | | | | | | | |
| CHINESE MEDICINE CENTRE (HM04257) | ● | ● | ● | ● | | ● | ● | ● | | | | | | ● | | | |
| CHIROPODIST SURGERY (HM04295) | ● | | | | | | | | | | | | | ● | | | |
| CHIROPODY CORNER (HM04330) | ● | | | | | | | | | | | | | ● | | | |
| CLINIC OF ACUPUNCTURE (HM04684) | | | | ● | | ● | ● | ● | | ● | | ● | | | ● | ● | ● |
| COLHOUN, PETER (HM04842) | ● | | | | | ● | | | | | | | | ● | | ● | |
| CONGLETON COUNSELLING PRACTICE (HM04977) | | | | | | | | | | | | | | | | | |
| CONSTANTINE, J C (HM05012) | | | | ● | | ● | | | ● | | | | | | | | |
| CREWE & NANT PHYSIO CLINIC (HM05431) | | | | | | | | | | | | | | | | | |
| CROPPER, AGNES (HM05473) | | | | | | ● | | | | | | | | | | | |
| DAVIES & ASSOCIATES (HM05791) | | | | | | | | | | | | | | | | | |
| DEWHURST, PATRICA A (HM06049) | | ● | ● | ● | | ● | ● | ● | ● | ● | ● | ● | ● | | ● | ● | ● |
| EDDIE, DAVID (HM06585) | | | | | | ● | | | | | | | | | | ● | |
| EVANS, DI (HM06968) | | | | | | ● | | | | | | ● | | | | | |
| FAGAN, B W (HM07042) | | | | | | | | | | | | | | | | | |
| FEET FIRST MOBILE CHIROPODY SV (HM07183) | | | | | | | | | | | | | | | | | |
| FIELD VIEW SURGERY (HM07259) | | | | | | ● | | | | | | | | | | | |
| FINCH, WENDY (HM07302) | | | ● | | | ● | | | | | | | | | | | |
| FIVE WAYS OSTEOPATHIC SURGERY (HM07381) | | | | | | | | | | | | | | | | | |
| GENTLE TOUCH (HM07979) | | ● | | | | | | | | | | | | | | | |
| GRACE & ASSOCIATES (HM08331) | ● | | | | | | | | | | | | | ● | | | |
| GRAHAM COOMBE - MCTIMONEY (HM08338) | | | | | | | | | | | | ● | | | | ● | |
| HANDS ON PHYSIOTHERAPY (HM08913) | | | | | | | | | | | | | | | | ● | |
| HAZELDENE, BARBARA (HM09292) | | | | | | ● | | | | | | | | | | | |
| HEALD, M T (HM09316) | ● | | | | | | | | | | | | | ● | | | |

www.healthmyself.com

# A - C Conditions treated at Practices/Businesses

| Business by County with Reference no. | Acne | Addiction | Adenoids | Aids | Alcoholism | Allergy | Alzheimer's Disease | Amnesia | Anaemia | Angina | Anorexia | Anxiety |
|---|---|---|---|---|---|---|---|---|---|---|---|---|
| HIGHLEY, T J (HM09757) | | | | | | | | | | | | |
| HOWE, BARBARA (HM10261) | | | | | | | | | | | | ● |
| HUSKISSON, EILEEN (HM10434) | | | | | | | | | | | | |
| HYPNOS PRACTICE (HM10492) | | ● | | | | | | | | | | ● |
| IPHOFEN, RON (DR) (HM10712) | | | | | | | | | | | | ● |
| JANE HAMMOND THERAPY (HM10916) | | | | | | | | | | | | ● |
| JENKINSON, LEILA (HM10999) | ● | ● | ● | | ● | ● | ● | ● | ● | ● | | ● |
| JONES, J W (HM11155) | | | | | | | | | | | | |
| KNUTSFORD CHIROPRACTIC CLINIC (HM11775) | ● | | | | | ● | | ● | | ● | ● | ● |
| LEGGE, PAT (HM12176) | | | | | | | | | | | | ● |
| LOMAS, CLIFFORD (HM12574) | | | | | | | | | | | | |
| MACALLAN, STEPHEN (HM12815) | ● | | | | | ● | | | ● | ● | ● | ● |
| MARSH, F W (HM13147) | | | | | | | | | | | | |
| MEDICINE WHEEL (HM13670) | | | | | | | | | | | | ● |
| MEHTA HYPNOTHERAPY (HM13695) | ● | ● | | | ● | ● | | | | | | ● |
| MIDDLETON & ASSOCIATES (HM13817) | ● | ● | | | | ● | | | | | | ● |
| MORTON, J V (HM14251) | | | | | | | | | | | | |
| NEEDHAM, ANGELA (HM14749) | ● | ● | ● | | ● | ● | ● | ● | ● | ● | ● | ● |
| NEW LIFE NATURAL HEALTH CARE (HM14821) | ● | ● | ● | ● | ● | ● | ● | ● | ● | ● | ● | ● |
| NEWTON, J C (HM14898) | | | | | | | | | | | | |
| NUTRITION AND ALLERGY CLINIC (HM15121) | ● | ● | ● | ● | ● | ● | | | ● | ● | ● | ● |
| OLD HALL CLINIC (HM15256) | ● | | ● | | | ● | | ● | ● | ● | ● | ● |
| PATON, W A (HM15825) | | | | | | | | | | | | |
| PENNYCOOK, AMANDA (HM15996) | | | | | | | | | | | | |
| PHOENIX CENTRE (HM16154) | | ● | | | | | | | | | | ● |
| PHYSIO & SPORTS INJURY CLINIC (HM16181) | ● | | | | | | | | | | | |
| PHYSIO PLUS (HM16203) | | | | | | | | | | | | |
| PHYSIO SPORTS INJURY CLINIC (HM16209) | | | | | | | | | | | | |
| POYNTON CHIROPRACTIC CLINIC (HM16519) | | | | | | | | | | | | |
| PREW, BEVERLEY (HM16566) | | | | | | | | | | | | |
| PRINCE, TANIA A (HM16622) | | ● | | | ● | ● | | | | | ● | ● |
| REDGRAVE, KENNETH (HM17025) | | | | | | | | | | | ● | ● |
| RICHARDS, DAVID (HM17250) | | | | | | | | | | | | |
| RICHARDS, KERRY L (HM17260) | | | | | | | | | | | | |

| Business by County with Reference no. | Arthritis | Asthma | Athletes Foot | Autism | Back Pain | Bacterial Infections | Baldness | Bereavement | Bladder Problems | Blood Pressure | Boils | Bowel Problems |
|---|---|---|---|---|---|---|---|---|---|---|---|---|
| HIGHLEY, T J (HM09757) | | | ● | | | | | | | | | |
| HOWE, BARBARA (HM10261) | | | | | ● | | | | | | | |
| HUSKISSON, EILEEN (HM10434) | ● | | ● | | | ● | | | | | | |
| HYPNOS PRACTICE (HM10492) | | ● | | | | | | ● | | | | ● |
| IPHOFEN, RON (DR) (HM10712) | | | | | ● | | | | | | | |
| JANE HAMMOND THERAPY (HM10916) | | | | | | | | | | | | |
| JENKINSON, LEILA (HM10999) | ● | ● | ● | ● | ● | | ● | | ● | ● | ● | ● |
| JONES, J W (HM11155) | | | ● | | | ● | | | | | | |
| KNUTSFORD CHIROPRACTIC CLINIC (HM11775) | ● | ● | | | ● | | | | | ● | | ● |
| LEGGE, PAT (HM12176) | ● | | | | ● | | | | | | | |
| LOMAS, CLIFFORD (HM12574) | | | | | ● | | | | | | | |
| MACALLAN, STEPHEN (HM12815) | ● | ● | ● | | ● | ● | | | ● | ● | ● | ● |
| MARSH, F W (HM13147) | | | ● | | | ● | | | | | | |
| MEDICINE WHEEL (HM13670) | ● | | | | ● | | | | | | | |
| MEHTA HYPNOTHERAPY (HM13695) | ● | ● | | | ● | | | | ● | ● | | ● |
| MIDDLETON & ASSOCIATES (HM13817) | ● | | | | ● | | | | | ● | | |
| MORTON, J V (HM14251) | | | | | | | | | | | | |
| NEEDHAM, ANGELA (HM14749) | ● | ● | | ● | | ● | | | ● | ● | ● | ● |
| NEW LIFE NATURAL HEALTH CARE (HM14821) | ● | ● | ● | ● | ● | ● | ● | | ● | ● | ● | ● |
| NEWTON, J C (HM14898) | | | ● | | | | | | | | | |
| NUTRITION AND ALLERGY CLINIC (HM15121) | ● | ● | ● | ● | ● | | ● | | ● | ● | ● | ● |
| OLD HALL CLINIC (HM15256) | ● | ● | ● | ● | ● | ● | ● | | ● | ● | ● | ● |
| PATON, W A (HM15825) | ● | | | | ● | | | | | | | |
| PENNYCOOK, AMANDA (HM15996) | | | ● | | | | | | | | | |
| PHOENIX CENTRE (HM16154) | | | | | ● | | | | | | | |
| PHYSIO & SPORTS INJURY CLINIC (HM16181) | ● | ● | | | ● | | | | ● | | | |
| PHYSIO PLUS (HM16203) | ● | | | | ● | | | | | | | |
| PHYSIO SPORTS INJURY CLINIC (HM16209) | ● | | | | ● | | | | | | | |
| POYNTON CHIROPRACTIC CLINIC (HM16519) | ● | ● | | | ● | | | | | | | |
| PREW, BEVERLEY (HM16566) | | | | | | | | | | | | |
| PRINCE, TANIA A (HM16622) | | ● | | | ● | | | | | ● | | |
| REDGRAVE, KENNETH (HM17025) | | | | | | | | | | | | |
| RICHARDS, DAVID (HM17250) | | | ● | | | | | | | | | |
| RICHARDS, KERRY L (HM17260) | | | ● | | | | | | | | | |

| Business by County with Reference no. | Breast Problems | Breathing Problems | Bronchitis | Bruising | Bulimia | Bunions | Bursitis | Callices | Cancers | Cataracts | Catarrh | Cerebral Palsy |
|---|---|---|---|---|---|---|---|---|---|---|---|---|
| HIGHLEY, T J (HM09757) | | | | | | | | | | | | |
| HOWE, BARBARA (HM10261) | | | | | | | | | | | | |
| HUSKISSON, EILEEN (HM10434) | | | | | | ● | | ● | | | | |
| HYPNOS PRACTICE (HM10492) | | | | | | | | | | | | |
| IPHOFEN, RON (DR) (HM10712) | | | | | | | | | | | | |
| JANE HAMMOND THERAPY (HM10916) | | | | | | | | | | | | |
| JENKINSON, LEILA (HM10999) | ● | ● | ● | ● | ● | | ● | ● | ● | ● | ● | |
| JONES, J W (HM11155) | | | | | | | | ● | | | | |
| KNUTSFORD CHIROPRACTIC CLINIC (HM11775) | | ● | ● | | | | ● | | | | ● | |
| LEGGE, PAT (HM12176) | | | | | | | | | | | | |
| LOMAS, CLIFFORD (HM12574) | | | | | | | | | | | | |
| MACALLAN, STEPHEN (HM12815) | ● | ● | ● | ● | | | | | | | ● | |
| MARSH, F W (HM13147) | | | | | | ● | | ● | | | | |
| MEDICINE WHEEL (HM13670) | | | | | | | | | | | | |
| MEHTA HYPNOTHERAPY (HM13695) | | | ● | | | | | | ● | | | |
| MIDDLETON & ASSOCIATES (HM13817) | | ● | ● | | | | | | | | | |
| MORTON, J V (HM14251) | | | | | | | ● | | | | | |
| NEEDHAM, ANGELA (HM14749) | ● | ● | ● | ● | ● | | ● | ● | | | ● | |
| NEW LIFE NATURAL HEALTH CARE (HM14821) | ● | ● | ● | ● | ● | | ● | ● | ● | ● | ● | |
| NEWTON, J C (HM14898) | | | | | | ● | | ● | | | | |
| NUTRITION AND ALLERGY CLINIC (HM15121) | ● | ● | | ● | ● | | ● | | ● | ● | ● | |
| OLD HALL CLINIC (HM15256) | ● | ● | ● | ● | ● | | ● | | ● | | ● | |
| PATON, W A (HM15825) | | | | | | | | | | | | |
| PENNYCOOK, AMANDA (HM15996) | | | | | | | | ● | | | | |
| PHOENIX CENTRE (HM16154) | | | | | | | | | | | | |
| PHYSIO & SPORTS INJURY CLINIC (HM16181) | | ● | ● | ● | | | ● | | | | | |
| PHYSIO PLUS (HM16203) | | | | | | | | | | | | |
| PHYSIO SPORTS INJURY CLINIC (HM16209) | | | | | | | | | | | | |
| POYNTON CHIROPRACTIC CLINIC (HM16519) | | | | | | | | | | | | |
| PREW, BEVERLEY (HM16566) | | | | | | | | | | | | |
| PRINCE, TANIA A (HM16622) | | | | | | | | | ● | | | |
| REDGRAVE, KENNETH (HM17025) | | | | | | | | | | | | |
| RICHARDS, DAVID (HM17250) | | | | | | | | ● | | | | |
| RICHARDS, KERRY L (HM17260) | | | | | | | | ● | | | | |

| Business by County with Reference no. | Circulation Problems | Cold Sores | Colds | Colic | Colitis | Conjunctivitis | Constipation | Convulsions | Corns | Coughs | Cramp | Cystitis |
|---|---|---|---|---|---|---|---|---|---|---|---|---|
| HIGHLEY, T J (HM09757) | | | | | | | | | | | | |
| HOWE, BARBARA (HM10261) | ● | | | | | | | | | | | |
| HUSKISSON, EILEEN (HM10434) | | | | | | | | | ● | | | |
| HYPNOS PRACTICE (HM10492) | | | | | | | | | | | | |
| IPHOFEN, RON (DR) (HM10712) | | | | | | | | | | | | |
| JANE HAMMOND THERAPY (HM10916) | | | | | | | | | | | | |
| JENKINSON, LEILA (HM10999) | ● | ● | ● | ● | ● | ● | ● | ● | | ● | ● | ● |
| JONES, J W (HM11155) | ● | | | | | | | | ● | | | |
| KNUTSFORD CHIROPRACTIC CLINIC (HM11775) | ● | | | ● | ● | | ● | | | ● | ● | |
| LEGGE, PAT (HM12176) | | | | | | | | | | | | |
| LOMAS, CLIFFORD (HM12574) | | | | | | | | | | | | |
| MACALLAN, STEPHEN (HM12815) | ● | ● | ● | ● | ● | ● | ● | | | ● | ● | ● |
| MARSH, F W (HM13147) | | | | | | | | | ● | | | |
| MEDICINE WHEEL (HM13670) | | | | | | | | | | | | |
| MEHTA HYPNOTHERAPY (HM13695) | | | | | | | | | | | | |
| MIDDLETON & ASSOCIATES (HM13817) | ● | | ● | ● | | | ● | | | ● | ● | |
| MORTON, J V (HM14251) | ● | | | | | | | | | | | |
| NEEDHAM, ANGELA (HM14749) | ● | ● | ● | ● | ● | ● | ● | ● | ● | ● | ● | ● |
| NEW LIFE NATURAL HEALTH CARE (HM14821) | ● | ● | ● | ● | ● | ● | ● | ● | ● | ● | ● | ● |
| NEWTON, J C (HM14898) | | | | | | | | | ● | | | |
| NUTRITION AND ALLERGY CLINIC (HM15121) | ● | ● | ● | ● | ● | | ● | ● | | ● | ● | ● |
| OLD HALL CLINIC (HM15256) | ● | ● | ● | ● | ● | ● | ● | ● | | ● | ● | ● |
| PATON, W A (HM15825) | | | | | | | | | | | | |
| PENNYCOOK, AMANDA (HM15996) | | | | | | | | | ● | | | |
| PHOENIX CENTRE (HM16154) | | | | | | | | | | | | |
| PHYSIO & SPORTS INJURY CLINIC (HM16181) | ● | | | | | | | | | | ● | |
| PHYSIO PLUS (HM16203) | | | | | | | | | | | | |
| PHYSIO SPORTS INJURY CLINIC (HM16209) | | | | | | | | | | | | |
| POYNTON CHIROPRACTIC CLINIC (HM16519) | | | | ● | | | | | | | | |
| PREW, BEVERLEY (HM16566) | ● | | | | | | | | | | | |
| PRINCE, TANIA A (HM16622) | | | | | | | | | | | | |
| REDGRAVE, KENNETH (HM17025) | | | | | | | ● | | | | | |
| RICHARDS, DAVID (HM17250) | | | | | | | | | ● | | | |
| RICHARDS, KERRY L (HM17260) | | | | | | | | | ● | | | |

# A - C Conditions treated at Practices/Businesses

| Business by County with Reference no. | Acne | Addiction | Adenoids | Aids | Alcoholism | Allergy | Alzheimer's Disease | Amnesia | Anaemia | Angina | Anorexia | Anxiety | Arthritis | Asthma | Athletes Foot | Autism | Back Pain | Bacterial Infections | Baldness | Bereavement | Bladder Problems | Blood Pressure | Boils | Bowel Problems | Breast Problems | Breathing Problems | Bronchitis | Bruising | Bulimia | Bunions | Bursitis | Callices | Cancers | Cataracts | Catarrh | Cerebral Palsy | Circulation Problems | Cold Sores | Colds | Colic | Colitis | Conjunctivitis | Constipation | Convulsions | Corns | Coughs | Cramp | Cystitis |
|---|---|---|---|---|---|---|---|---|---|---|---|---|---|---|---|---|---|---|---|---|---|---|---|---|---|---|---|---|---|---|---|---|---|---|---|---|---|---|---|---|---|---|---|---|---|---|---|---|
| SANDBACH HYPNOSIS CLINIC (HM17899) | | |●| | | | | | | | |●| | | | | | | | | | | | | | | | | | | | | | | | | | | | | | | | | | | | |
| SAXELBY, M (HM17990) | | | | | | | | | | | | |●| |●| | | | | | | | | | | | | | |●| |●| | | | | | | | | | | | |●| | | |
| SCENTED GARDENS (HM18011) | | | | | | | | | | | |●|●| | | |●| | | | | | | | | | | | | | | | | | | | | | | | | | | | | | | |
| TEDSTONE, ALISON (HM19815) | | | | | | | | | | | | |●| |●| | | | | | | | | | | | | | |●| |●| | | | | | | | | | | | |●| | | |
| THOMAS, BEVERLEY (HM19933) | | | | | | | | | | | | | | |●| | | | | | | | | | | | | | | | |●| | | | | | | | | | | | |●| | | |
| THORNBER, A A (HM20016) | | | | | | | | | | | | |●| |●| |●| | | | | | | | | | | | | | |●| | | | | | | | | | | | |●| | | |
| TIPLING, L (HM20087) | | | | | | | | | | | | |●| |●| | | | | | | | | | | | | | |●| | | | | | | | | | | | | | | | | | |
| TRINITY HOUSE PRACTICE (HM20339) | | | | | | | | | | | | |●| | | |●| | | | | | | | | | | | | |●| | | | | | | | | | | | | | | | | |
| TULLY, CHARLES (HM20388) | | | | | | | | | | | |●|●|●| | |●| | | | |●| | | |●| | | | | | | | | | |●| | | | | | | | | |●| |
| TYRER, HELEN R (HM20473) | | | | | | | | | | | | |●| |●| | | | | | | | | | | | | | |●| |●| | | | | | | | | | | | |●| | | |
| VALE ROYAL CHIROPRACTIC CLINIC (HM20552) | | | | | | | | | | | | |●| | | |●| | | | |●| | | | | | | | | | | | | | |●| | |●| | | | | | | | |
| VALE ROYAL CHIROPRACTIC CLINIC (HM20553) | | | | | | | | | | | | |●| | | |●| | | | |●| | | | | | | | | | | | | | |●| | |●| | | | | | | | |
| WARRINGTON CHIROPRACTIC CLINIC (HM20957) | | | | | |●| | | | | | |●|●| | |●| | | |●|●| |●| |●| | | | |●| | | | | |●| | |●| | |●| | | | | |
| WEAVER HOUSE CLINIC (HM21049) |●|●| | |●|●| | | | |●|●|●|●|●|●|●| | | |●| |●|●|●|●|●|●|●| |●| | | |●| |●|●|●|●|●|●|●| | |●|●|●|
| WIDNES OSTEOPATHIC CLINIC (HM21459) | | | | | | | | | | | | |●| | | |●| | | | | | | | | | | | | | | | | | | | | | | | | | | | | | | |
| WILLIAMS OSTEOPATHIC CLINIC (HM21532) | | | | | | | | | | | |●| | | | |●| | | | | | | | | | | | | | | | | | | | | | | | | | | | | | | |
| WOOLLEY, M E (HM21878) | | | | | | | | | | | | | | |●| | | | | | | | | | | | | | |●| |●| | | | | | | | | | | | |●| | | |
| CLEVELAND | | | | | | | | | | | | | | | | | | | | | | | | | | | | | | | | | | | | | | | | | | | | | | | | |
| ALEXANDER TECHNIQUE (HM00548) | |●| | | | | | | | |●|●|●|●| | |●| | | | |●| |●| |●| | |●| | | | | | | | | | | | | |●| | | | |●| |
| BARNARD, SIMON (HM01732) | | | | | | | | | | | | |●|●| | |●| | | | | | | | |●| | | | | | | | | | | | | | | | | | | | | | |
| BODY BALANCE (HM02570) | | | | | | | | | | | | |●| | | |●| | | | | | | | | | | | | | | | | | | | | | | | | | | | | | | |
| ELLISON, TIM (HM06777) | | | | | | | | | | | | | | |●| | | | | | | | | | | | | | |●| |●| | | | | | | | | | | | |●| | | |
| HARTLEPOOL CHIROPRACTIC CLINIC (HM09138) | | | | | | | | | | | | |●| | | |●| | | | | | | | | | | | | | | | | | | |●| | | | | | | | | | | |
| MERMAID CHIROPRACTIC PRACTICE (HM13749) | | | | | | | | | | | | |●| | | |●| | | | | | | | | | | | | | | | | | | |●| | |●| | | | | | | | |
| NATURAL THERAPY CENTRE (HM14637) | | | | | |●| | | | | | |●| |●| |●| | | | | | | | | | | | | | | | | | | |●| |●| | | |●| | | | | |
| NORTHERN GUILD-PSYCHOTHERAPY (HM15061) | |●| | |●| | | | | |●|●| | | | | | | | | | | | | | | | |●| | | | | | | | | | | | | | | | | | | |
| RAINBOW BRIDGE SCHOOL (HM16875) |●|●|●|●|●|●|●|●|●|●|●|●|●|●|●|●|●|●|●| |●|●|●|●|●|●|●|●|●| |●|●|●|●|●| |●|●|●|●|●|●|●|●|●|●|●|●|
| REDCAR PHYSIO & SPORTS (HM17007) | | | | | | | | | | | | |●| | | |●| | | | | | | | | | | | | | | | | | | | | | | | | | | | | | | |
| RUSH, DENNIS (HM17754) |●|●| | |●|●| | | | | |●| |●| | | | | | |●|●| | | | | | |●| | | | | | | | | | | | | | | | | | | |
| SKIPPINGS & ASSOCIATES (HM18657) | | | | | | | | | | | | |●| | | |●| | | | | | | | | | | | | | | | | | | |●| | |●| | | | | | | | |
| STRESS COUNSELLING (HM19391) | |●| | | | | | | | | |●| | | | | | | | | | | | | | | | | | | | | | | | | | | | | | | | | | | | |
| CORNWALL | | | | | | | | | | | | | | | | | | | | | | | | | | | | | | | | | | | | | | | | | | | | | | | | |
| AROMATICA (HM01135) | | | | | | | | | | | |●| | |●| |●| | | |●| | | | | |●|●| | | | | | | | |●|●|●| | | |●| | |●|●| |
| BANBURY, A E (HM01646) | | | | | | | | | | | | |●|●| | |●| | | | | | | | |●|●| | | |●| | | |●| |●| | | |●| |●| | | | | |

www.healthmyself.com

# A - C Conditions treated at Practices/Businesses

| Business by County with Reference no. | Acne | Addiction | Adenoids | Aids | Alcoholism | Allergy | Alzheimer's Disease | Amnesia | Anaemia | Angina | Anorexia | Anxiety | Arthritis | Asthma | Athletes Foot | Autism |
|---|---|---|---|---|---|---|---|---|---|---|---|---|---|---|---|---|
| BARNETT, ANN (HM01763) | | | | | | ● | | | | ● | | ● | ● | ● | | |
| BEARE, M E (HM01968) | | | | | | | | | | | | | ● | | ● | |
| CARADON CHIROPRACTIC CLINIC (HM03656) | | | | | | | | | | | | | ● | | | |
| CHIROPODIST/PODIATRIST (HM04296) | | | | | | | | | | | | | ● | | ● | |
| COMP HEALTH INITIATIVE (HM04912) | ● | ● | ● | ● | ● | ● | ● | ● | ● | ● | ● | ● | ● | ● | ● | ● |
| FEET FIRST (HM07180) | ● | | | | ● | ● | | | ● | | | | ● | ● | ● | |
| FOOTCARE (HM07492) | | | | | | | | | | | | | | | ● | |
| FORCE, GAYLE (HM07520) | | | | | | ● | ● | | ● | ● | ● | ● | ● | ● | | |
| HALL, PETER (HM08787) | | | | | | | | | | | | | | | | |
| HAWKSLAND PHYSIOTHERAPY CENTRE (HM09233) | | | | | | | | | | | | | ● | | | |
| LIFE 'N' LIMB (HM12345) | ● | ● | ● | ● | ● | ● | ● | ● | ● | ● | ● | ● | ● | ● | ● | ● |
| LIFE 'N' LIMB (HM12346) | ● | | | | | | ● | | | | | ● | ● | ● | ● | ● |
| LIFE-WORK POTENTIAL (HM12368) | ● | | | | | ● | | | | | | ● | ● | ● | ● | |
| LISKEARD CHIROPRACTIC CLINIC (HM12453) | | | | | | | | | | | | | ● | | | |
| LISTER NATURAL HEALTH PRACTICE (HM12461) | ● | ● | ● | ● | ● | ● | | ● | ● | ● | ● | ● | ● | ● | ● | ● |
| MASTERS, B (HM13273) | | | | | | ● | | | | | | | ● | ● | | ● |
| MORSE, EMMA (HM14239) | ● | | | | | | | | | | | | ● | | | |
| NEWQUAY CHIROPRACTIC CLINIC (HM14883) | | ● | | | | ● | | | | | | ● | ● | ● | ● | |
| OSTEOPATHIC FAMILY CENTRE (HM15465) | | | | | | ● | | | | | | ● | ● | ● | | |
| PENZANCE NATURAL HEALTH CENTRE (HM16006) | | | | | | ● | | | | | | | ● | ● | | |
| REEVES, J (HM17066) | | | | | | | | | | | | | | | ● | |
| ST AUSTELL CHIROPRACTIC CLINIC (HM19070) | | | | | | ● | | | | | | ● | ● | ● | | |
| TRURO CHIROPRACTIC CLINIC (HM20354) | | | | | | ● | | | | | | ● | ● | ● | | |
| TRURO OSTEOPATHIC PRACTICE (HM20356) | | | | | | | | | | | | | ● | | | |
| VERA BOYES ACUPUNCTURE (HM20618) | | ● | | | | ● | | | | | | ● | ● | ● | | |
| WEATHERHOGG, D J (HM21046) | | | | | | | | | | | | | ● | | | |
| WILLS, JONATHAN (HM21632) | | | | | | | | | | | | | ● | | | |
| WRIGHT, CYNTHIA (HM21929) | | ● | | | ● | | | | | | ● | ● | | | | |
| COUNTY DURHAM | | | | | | | | | | | | | | | | |
| ALOE VERA ADVICE CENTRE (HM00670) | | | | | | | | | | | | | | | | |
| BALANCE HOLISTIC HEALTHCARE (HM01606) | | ● | | | ● | ● | | | | | ● | ● | ● | ● | | ● |
| BODYWORK HEALTH CLUB & CLINIC (HM02639) | | | | | | | | | | | | ● | ● | | | |
| CALLAGHAN, M M (HM03548) | | | | | | | | | | | | | | | ● | |
| EVANS, BRUCE (DR) (HM06958) | | | | | | | | | | | | | ● | | | |

| Business by County with Reference no. | Back Pain | Bacterial Infections | Baldness | Bereavement | Bladder Problems | Blood Pressure | Boils | Bowel Problems | Breast Problems | Breathing Problems | Bronchitis | Bruising | Bulimia | Bunions | Bursitis | Callices |
|---|---|---|---|---|---|---|---|---|---|---|---|---|---|---|---|---|
| BARNETT, ANN (HM01763) | | | | | ● | | | | | ● | | | | | | |
| BEARE, M E (HM01968) | | | | | | | | | | | | | | ● | | ● |
| CARADON CHIROPRACTIC CLINIC (HM03656) | ● | | | | | ● | | | | | | | | | | |
| CHIROPODIST/PODIATRIST (HM04296) | | ● | | | | | | | | | | | | ● | | ● |
| COMP HEALTH INITIATIVE (HM04912) | ● | ● | ● | | ● | ● | ● | ● | ● | ● | ● | ● | ● | | ● | ● |
| FEET FIRST (HM07180) | ● | | | | ● | ● | | ● | ● | ● | ● | ● | | | | |
| FOOTCARE (HM07492) | | | | | | | | | | | | | | ● | | ● |
| FORCE, GAYLE (HM07520) | ● | ● | | | ● | ● | | ● | ● | ● | | | ● | | | |
| HALL, PETER (HM08787) | | | | | | ● | | ● | | | | | | | | |
| HAWKSLAND PHYSIOTHERAPY CENTRE (HM09233) | ● | | | | | | | | | | | ● | | | | |
| LIFE 'N' LIMB (HM12345) | ● | ● | ● | | ● | ● | ● | ● | ● | ● | ● | ● | ● | | ● | ● |
| LIFE 'N' LIMB (HM12346) | ● | ● | | | ● | ● | ● | ● | | ● | ● | ● | | | ● | |
| LIFE-WORK POTENTIAL (HM12368) | | ● | | | | | ● | ● | | ● | ● | ● | | | | |
| LISKEARD CHIROPRACTIC CLINIC (HM12453) | ● | | | | | ● | | | | | | | | | | |
| LISTER NATURAL HEALTH PRACTICE (HM12461) | ● | | ● | | ● | ● | ● | ● | ● | ● | ● | ● | ● | | ● | |
| MASTERS, B (HM13273) | ● | | | | ● | ● | | ● | | ● | ● | | | | ● | |
| MORSE, EMMA (HM14239) | ● | | | | | | | | | | | | | | | |
| NEWQUAY CHIROPRACTIC CLINIC (HM14883) | ● | | | | | ● | | ● | | ● | | | | | ● | |
| OSTEOPATHIC FAMILY CENTRE (HM15465) | ● | | | | ● | | | ● | | ● | ● | | | | ● | |
| PENZANCE NATURAL HEALTH CENTRE (HM16006) | ● | | | | | ● | | | | | | | | | | |
| REEVES, J (HM17066) | | | | | | | | | | | | | | ● | | ● |
| ST AUSTELL CHIROPRACTIC CLINIC (HM19070) | ● | | | | ● | ● | | | | ● | | | | | | |
| TRURO CHIROPRACTIC CLINIC (HM20354) | ● | | | | ● | ● | | ● | | ● | ● | | | | | |
| TRURO OSTEOPATHIC PRACTICE (HM20356) | ● | | | | | | | | | | | | | | ● | |
| VERA BOYES ACUPUNCTURE (HM20618) | ● | | | | | | | ● | | | | | | | | |
| WEATHERHOGG, D J (HM21046) | ● | | | | | | | | | | | | | | | |
| WILLS, JONATHAN (HM21632) | ● | | | | | | | | | | | | | | ● | |
| WRIGHT, CYNTHIA (HM21929) | | | | | ● | | | | | | | | | | | |
| COUNTY DURHAM | | | | | | | | | | | | | | | | |
| ALOE VERA ADVICE CENTRE (HM00670) | ● | | | | | | | | | | | | | | | |
| BALANCE HOLISTIC HEALTHCARE (HM01606) | ● | | | | | | | ● | | | | | ● | | | |
| BODYWORK HEALTH CLUB & CLINIC (HM02639) | ● | | | | | | | | | | | | | | | |
| CALLAGHAN, M M (HM03548) | | | | | | | | | | | | | | | | ● |
| EVANS, BRUCE (DR) (HM06958) | ● | | | | | | | | | | | | | | ● | |

| Business by County with Reference no. | Cancers | Cataracts | Catarrh | Cerebral Palsy | Circulation Problems | Cold Sores | Colds | Colic | Colitis | Conjunctivitis | Constipation | Convulsions | Corns | Coughs | Cramp | Cystitis |
|---|---|---|---|---|---|---|---|---|---|---|---|---|---|---|---|---|
| BARNETT, ANN (HM01763) | ● | | | | ● | | | | | | ● | | | | | |
| BEARE, M E (HM01968) | | | | | | | | | | | | | ● | | | |
| CARADON CHIROPRACTIC CLINIC (HM03656) | | | | | ● | | | ● | | | | | | | | |
| CHIROPODIST/PODIATRIST (HM04296) | | | | | | | | | | | | | ● | | | |
| COMP HEALTH INITIATIVE (HM04912) | ● | ● | ● | | ● | ● | ● | ● | ● | ● | ● | ● | ● | ● | ● | ● |
| FEET FIRST (HM07180) | ● | | ● | | ● | | | | ● | ● | ● | | | ● | ● | ● |
| FOOTCARE (HM07492) | | | | | | | | | | | | | ● | | | |
| FORCE, GAYLE (HM07520) | ● | | | | ● | | | ● | ● | | ● | ● | | ● | ● | |
| HALL, PETER (HM08787) | | | | | ● | | | | ● | | ● | | | | | |
| HAWKSLAND PHYSIOTHERAPY CENTRE (HM09233) | | | | | | | | | | | | | | | | |
| LIFE 'N' LIMB (HM12345) | ● | ● | ● | | ● | ● | ● | ● | ● | ● | ● | ● | ● | ● | ● | ● |
| LIFE 'N' LIMB (HM12346) | | | ● | | ● | ● | ● | ● | ● | | ● | | | ● | ● | ● |
| LIFE-WORK POTENTIAL (HM12368) | | | ● | | ● | ● | ● | ● | ● | ● | ● | | | ● | ● | ● |
| LISKEARD CHIROPRACTIC CLINIC (HM12453) | | | | | ● | | | ● | | | | | | | | |
| LISTER NATURAL HEALTH PRACTICE (HM12461) | ● | | ● | | ● | ● | ● | ● | ● | ● | ● | | | ● | ● | ● |
| MASTERS, B (HM13273) | | | ● | | ● | | | ● | ● | | ● | ● | | | ● | ● |
| MORSE, EMMA (HM14239) | | | | | | | | | | | | | | | ● | |
| NEWQUAY CHIROPRACTIC CLINIC (HM14883) | | | | | ● | | | ● | ● | | ● | | | | ● | |
| OSTEOPATHIC FAMILY CENTRE (HM15465) | | | | | ● | | | ● | ● | | ● | | | | | ● |
| PENZANCE NATURAL HEALTH CENTRE (HM16006) | ● | | | | ● | | | | ● | | | | | ● | | |
| REEVES, J (HM17066) | | | | | | | | | | | | | ● | | | |
| ST AUSTELL CHIROPRACTIC CLINIC (HM19070) | | | | | ● | | | ● | | | ● | | | | | |
| TRURO CHIROPRACTIC CLINIC (HM20354) | | | | | ● | | | ● | | | ● | | | | | |
| TRURO OSTEOPATHIC PRACTICE (HM20356) | | | | | | | | | | | | | | | | |
| VERA BOYES ACUPUNCTURE (HM20618) | | | | | | | | ● | ● | | ● | | | | | |
| WEATHERHOGG, D J (HM21046) | | | | | | | | | | | | | | | | |
| WILLS, JONATHAN (HM21632) | | | | | | | | | | | | | | | | |
| WRIGHT, CYNTHIA (HM21929) | | | | | | | | | | | | | | | | |
| COUNTY DURHAM | | | | | | | | | | | | | | | | |
| ALOE VERA ADVICE CENTRE (HM00670) | | | | | | | | | | | | | | | | |
| BALANCE HOLISTIC HEALTHCARE (HM01606) | | | | | | | | | | | ● | | | | | ● |
| BODYWORK HEALTH CLUB & CLINIC (HM02639) | | | | | | | | | | | | | | | | |
| CALLAGHAN, M M (HM03548) | | | | | | | | | | | | | ● | | | |
| EVANS, BRUCE (DR) (HM06958) | | | | | | | | | | | | | | | | |

# A - C Conditions treated at Practices/Businesses

| Business by County with Reference no. | Acne | Addiction | Adenoids | Aids | Alcoholism | Allergy | Alzheimer's Disease | Amnesia | Anaemia | Angina | Anorexia | Anxiety | Arthritis | Asthma | Athletes Foot | Autism | Back Pain | Bacterial Infections | Baldness | Bereavement | Bladder Problems | Blood Pressure | Boils | Bowel Problems | Breast Problems | Breathing Problems | Bronchitis | Bruising | Bulimia | Bunions | Bursitis | Callices | Cancers | Cataracts | Catarrh | Cerebral Palsy | Circulation Problems | Cold Sores | Colds | Colic | Colitis | Conjunctivitis | Constipation | Convulsions | Corns | Coughs | Cramp | Cystitis |
|---|---|---|---|---|---|---|---|---|---|---|---|---|---|---|---|---|---|---|---|---|---|---|---|---|---|---|---|---|---|---|---|---|---|---|---|---|---|---|---|---|---|---|---|---|---|---|---|
| FIONA OTTEWELL CHRTRD PHYSIO (HM07329) | | | | | | | | | | | | |●| | | | |●| | | | | | | | | | | | | | | | | | | | | | | | | | | | | | | |
| FOOTPRINTS (HM07507) | | | | | | | | | | | | | | | |●| | | | | | | | | | | | | | | | | |●| | | | | | | | | | | | | |●| | | | |
| HIND, CAROLE (HM09824) | | | | | | | | | | | | |●|●| | | | |●| | | | |●|●| |●|●|●| | | | | | | | | | |●| |●| | | | | | |●| | |●|●|●|
| HOBSON, I K (HM09864) | | | | | | | | | | | | | | | |●| | | | | | | | | | | | | | | | | | | | | | | | | | | | | | | | |
| NEWCASTLE/NE TRANS MEDITA CTRE (HM14856) | |●| | |●|●| | | | | | |●| |●| | | | | | | | |●| | | | | | | | | | | | | | | | | | | | | | | | | |
| OLD PIT PRACTICE (HM15260) | | | | | |●| | | | | | |●|●| | | | |●| | | | | | | | | | | | |●| | | |●| | | | | | | | | | | | | |●| | | | |
| SPOORS, L & D (HM19039) | | | | | | | | | | | | | |●| | | |●| | | | |●| | | | | | | | | | | | | | | |●| | | | | | | | | | | | |
| TEESDALE OSTEOPATHIC CLINIC (HM19817) | | | | | | | | | | | | | |●| | | |●| | | | |●| | | | | | | | | | | | | | | |●| | | | | | | | | | | | |
| TREATMENT ROOM (HM20302) | | | | | | | | | | | |●|●| | | | |●| | | | | | | | | | | | | |●| | | | | | | | | | | | | | | | | |
| WARWICK, ANDREA (HM20967) | | | | | |●| | | | | |●|●|●| | | |●| | | | | | |●| |●| | |●| | | | | | | | |●| | | | | |●| | | |●| |
| **CUMBRIA** | | | | | | | | | | | | | | | | | | | | | | | | | | | | | | | | | | | | | | | | | | | | | | | | |
| CUMBRIA PHYSIO & SPORTS CLINIC (HM05598) | | | | | | | | | | | | |●| | | | |●| | | | | | | | | | | | | | | | | | | | | | | | | | | | |●| |
| DEERING, CHRISTINE (HM05959) | | | | | | | | | | | |●| | | | | | | | | | | | | | | | |●| | | | | | | | | | | | | | | | | | | |
| EDWARDS, D E (HM06648) | | | | | | | | | | |●|●| | | | | | | |●| | | | | | | | |●| | | | | | | | | | | | | | | | | | | |
| FOOTWORKS (HM07515) | | | | | | | | | | | | | | |●| | | | | | | | | | | | | | | | |●| | | | | | | | | | | | |●| | | |
| GARNETT, JANE (HM07897) | |●| | | | | | | | | |●| | | | |●| | | | | | | | | | | | | | | | | | | | | | | | | | | | | | | |
| HERBS AND HELPERS (HM09668) |●| | | | |●| | | | | |●|●|●| | | | | | |●|●|●|●|●|●|●| | | | | |●| |●| |●|●| | |●| |●| | |●|●|●|
| HYPNOTHERAPY CENTRE (HM10525) | | | | | | | | | | | |●| | | | | | | | | | | | | | | | | | | | | | | | | | | | | | | | | | | | |
| LIBRA THERAPY CENTRE (HM12328) | | | | | |●| | | | | |●|●|●| | |●| | | | | | | | | | | | | | | | | | | | | | | | | | | | | | | |
| MCWATT, LIZ (HM13624) |●| | | | |●| | | | | |●|●| | | |●| | | | |●| |●| | | | | | | | |●| |●| |●| | |●| | |●| | | | | |●|
| PETER STREET CLINIC (HM16075) | | | | | | | | | | | | | | |●| | | | | | | | | | | | | | | | |●| | | | | | | | | | | | |●| | | |
| RHAM, TRICIA (HM17217) | | | | | | | | | | | |●|●|●| |●|●| | | | |●| |●| |●| | | | | | | | | | |●| | |●| | | | | | |●| |
| RUBINSTEIN, ADAM (HM17724) | | | | | | | | | | |●| | | | |●|●| | | |●|●| | | |●| | |●| | | | | | | |●| | |●| | |●| | | |●| |
| RUBINSTEIN, ADAM (HM17725) | | | | | | | | | | |●| | | | |●|●| | | |●|●| | | |●| | |●| | | | | | | |●| | |●| | |●| | | |●| |
| SINGLETON, POLLY (HM18612) |●|●|●|●|●|●|●|●|●|●|●|●|●|●|●|●|●|●| | |●|●|●|●|●|●|●|●|●| |●|●|●|●|●| |●|●|●|●|●|●|●|●|●|●|●|●|
| STRAWBERRY HOW CLINIC (HM19378) | | | | | |●| | |●| |●|●|●| | | |●| | | | | | | | | |●| |●| | | | | |●| | | | | |●| |●|●| |●| |●|
| SWINDALE, TESSA (HM19594) | | | | | | | | | | | | | | |●| | | | | | | | | | | | | | | | |●| | | | | | | | | | | | |●| | | |
| THERAPY CENTRE (HM19898) |●|●| | | |●| | |●|●| |●|●|●| | |●|●|●| |●|●|●|●|●|●|●|●| | |●| |●| |●| |●|●|●|●|●|●|●|●| |●|●|●|
| VULCANS LANE CHIROPODY (HM20720) | | | | | | | | | | | | | | | | |●| | | | | | |●| | | | | | | | | | | | | | | | | | |●| | | | | |
| WILSON, P M (HM21664) | | | | | | | | | | | | | | |●| | | | | | | | | | | | | | | | |●| | | | | | | | | | | | |●| | | |
| **DERBYSHIRE** | | | | | | | | | | | | | | | | | | | | | | | | | | | | | | | | | | | | | | | | | | | | | | | | |
| ACUPUNCTURE CLINIC (HM00270) | | | | | | | | | | | |●|●|●| | |●| | | | | | | | | | | | | | | | | | | | | |●| | | |●| | |●| |●|
| ALTER-MED (HM00690) |●|●|●|●|●|●|●|●|●|●|●|●|●|●|●|●|●|●|●| |●|●|●|●|●|●|●|●|●| |●|●|●|●|●| |●|●|●|●|●|●|●|●|●|●|●|●|
| AROMATHERAPY & REFLEX CTRE (HM01090) |●|●|●|●|●|●|●|●|●|●|●|●|●|●|●|●|●|●|●| |●|●|●|●|●|●|●|●|●| |●|●|●|●|●| |●|●|●|●|●|●|●|●|●|●|●|●|

www.healthmyself.com

Healthmyself Directory

A-C CONDITIONS TREATED England (by County)

# A - C Conditions treated at Practices/Businesses

| Business by County with Reference no. | Acne | Addiction | Adenoids | Aids | Alcoholism | Allergy | Alzheimer's Disease | Amnesia | Anaemia | Angina | Anorexia | Anxiety |
|---|---|---|---|---|---|---|---|---|---|---|---|---|
| BACH FLOWER REMEDIES (HM01469) | | | | | | | | | | | | ● |
| BANKS, LINDA (HM01665) | | | | | | | | | | | | ● |
| BARROWCLIFFE, GRAHAM (DR) (HM01806) | ● | ● | | | ● | | | | | | ● | ● |
| BELPER BACKPAIN CLINIC (HM02110) | | | | | | | | | | ● | | |
| BELPER HOMEOPATHY (HM02111) | ● | | ● | | | ● | | | ● | ● | ● | ● |
| BELPER NATURAL HEALTH CENTRE (HM02112) | ● | ● | ● | ● | ● | ● | ● | ● | ● | ● | ● | ● |
| BRADSHAW, P J (HM02878) | | ● | | | ● | | | ● | | | ● | ● |
| CARRICK-SMITH, L (HM03744) | | | | | | | | | | | | ● |
| CHIROPODY & PHYSIOTHERAPY (HM04303) | | | | | | | | | | | | |
| CONTOUR DESIGNS (HM05021) | | ● | | | | | | | | | | ● |
| COVERLEY PHYSIOTHERAPY CLINIC (HM05284) | | | | | | | | | | | | |
| DARBY, ANN (HM05735) | | | | | | | | | | | | |
| DERBYSHIRE SPORTS INJURIES (HM06014) | | | | | | | | | | | | |
| DRONFIELD PHYSIOTHERAPY CLINIC (HM06320) | | | | | | | | | | | | |
| ENJOY SPORT (HM06836) | | | | | | | | | | | | |
| GARRISON-TODD, WENDY (HM07905) | ● | ● | ● | ● | ● | ● | | ● | ● | ● | ● | ● |
| HARDING, MANDY (HM08971) | | | | | | | | | | | | |
| HATHERSAGE HEALTH & THRPY CTRE (HM09198) | | | | | | | | | | | | ● |
| HIGGS, ANN (HM09734) | ● | ● | | | ● | ● | | | ● | | ● | ● |
| HOUSE OF AROMATHERAPY (HM10216) | | | | | | | | | | | | ● |
| ILKESTONE OSTEO & MED CTRE (HM10580) | | | | | | | | | | | | |
| JOHNSON, MELVYN (HM11086) | | | | | | | | | | | | |
| KARDAHJI, F C (HM11319) | | | | | | | | | | | | |
| KEMP, G D (HM11460) | | | | | | | | | | | | |
| KEMP, GILLIAN (HM11461) | | | | | | | | | | | | ● |
| LANCASHIRE, A W (HM11915) | | | | | | | | | | | | |
| LIFESOLUTIONS (HM12359) | | ● | | | | | | | | | ● | ● |
| MATLOCK PHYSIOTHERAPY CENTRE (HM13293) | ● | ● | ● | ● | ● | ● | ● | ● | ● | ● | ● | ● |
| MATTHEWS, A (HM13299) | ● | ● | ● | | | ● | ● | ● | ● | ● | ● | ● |
| MATTHEWS, AMANDA (HM13301) | ● | ● | ● | | | ● | ● | ● | ● | ● | ● | ● |
| NATURAL HEALTH CLINIC (HM14577) | | | | | | | | | | | | |
| PHILIP STOCK - PHYSIOTHERAPIST (HM16120) | | | | | | | | | | | | |
| PHYSIO ACTIVE (HM16193) | ● | ● | ● | | ● | ● | | | | ● | ● | ● |
| SMITH, ALAN P (HM18711) | | | | | | | | | | | | |

| Business by County with Reference no. | Arthritis | Asthma | Athletes Foot | Autism | Back Pain | Bacterial Infections | Baldness | Bereavement | Bladder Problems | Blood Pressure | Boils | Bowel Problems |
|---|---|---|---|---|---|---|---|---|---|---|---|---|
| BACH FLOWER REMEDIES (HM01469) | | | | | | | | | | | | |
| BANKS, LINDA (HM01665) | ● | ● | | | ● | | | | | ● | | ● |
| BARROWCLIFFE, GRAHAM (DR) (HM01806) | | | | | ● | | | | | ● | | ● |
| BELPER BACKPAIN CLINIC (HM02110) | ● | ● | | | ● | | | | | | | |
| BELPER HOMEOPATHY (HM02111) | ● | ● | ● | ● | | ● | | | ● | ● | ● | ● |
| BELPER NATURAL HEALTH CENTRE (HM02112) | ● | ● | ● | | ● | ● | ● | | ● | ● | ● | ● |
| BRADSHAW, P J (HM02878) | | | | | | | | | | | | |
| CARRICK-SMITH, L (HM03744) | | | | | | | | | | | | |
| CHIROPODY & PHYSIOTHERAPY (HM04303) | ● | | ● | | | | | | | ● | | |
| CONTOUR DESIGNS (HM05021) | | | | | | | | | | | | |
| COVERLEY PHYSIOTHERAPY CLINIC (HM05284) | ● | | | | ● | | | | | | | |
| DARBY, ANN (HM05735) | ● | | | | | | | | | | | |
| DERBYSHIRE SPORTS INJURIES (HM06014) | ● | | | | ● | | | | | | | |
| DRONFIELD PHYSIOTHERAPY CLINIC (HM06320) | ● | | | | ● | | | | | | | |
| ENJOY SPORT (HM06836) | ● | | | | ● | | | | | | | |
| GARRISON-TODD, WENDY (HM07905) | ● | ● | ● | | ● | ● | ● | | ● | ● | ● | ● |
| HARDING, MANDY (HM08971) | | | ● | | | | | | | | | |
| HATHERSAGE HEALTH & THRPY CTRE (HM09198) | ● | | | | ● | | | | | | | |
| HIGGS, ANN (HM09734) | ● | ● | | | | | | | ● | ● | | |
| HOUSE OF AROMATHERAPY (HM10216) | ● | | | | ● | | | | | | | |
| ILKESTONE OSTEO & MED CTRE (HM10580) | ● | | | | ● | | | | | ● | | ● |
| JOHNSON, MELVYN (HM11086) | ● | | | | ● | | | | | ● | | |
| KARDAHJI, F C (HM11319) | ● | | ● | | | | | | | | | |
| KEMP, G D (HM11460) | | | ● | | | | | | | | | |
| KEMP, GILLIAN (HM11461) | ● | | | | ● | | | | | | | |
| LANCASHIRE, A W (HM11915) | ● | | | | ● | | | | | ● | | |
| LIFESOLUTIONS (HM12359) | | | | | | | | | | ● | | ● |
| MATLOCK PHYSIOTHERAPY CENTRE (HM13293) | ● | ● | ● | ● | ● | ● | ● | | ● | ● | ● | ● |
| MATTHEWS, A (HM13299) | ● | ● | ● | ● | ● | ● | | | ● | ● | ● | ● |
| MATTHEWS, AMANDA (HM13301) | ● | ● | ● | ● | ● | ● | ● | | ● | ● | ● | ● |
| NATURAL HEALTH CLINIC (HM14577) | ● | | | | ● | | | | | | | |
| PHILIP STOCK - PHYSIOTHERAPIST (HM16120) | ● | | | | ● | | | | | | | |
| PHYSIO ACTIVE (HM16193) | ● | ● | ● | ● | ● | ● | | | ● | ● | ● | ● |
| SMITH, ALAN P (HM18711) | ● | | | | ● | | | | | ● | | |

| Business by County with Reference no. | Breast Problems | Breathing Problems | Bronchitis | Bruising | Bulimia | Bunions | Bursitis | Callices | Cancers | Cataracts | Catarrh | Cerebral Palsy |
|---|---|---|---|---|---|---|---|---|---|---|---|---|
| BACH FLOWER REMEDIES (HM01469) | | | | | | | | | | | | |
| BANKS, LINDA (HM01665) | | | | | | | | | ● | | | |
| BARROWCLIFFE, GRAHAM (DR) (HM01806) | | | ● | | ● | | | | | | | |
| BELPER BACKPAIN CLINIC (HM02110) | | | | | | | | | | | | |
| BELPER HOMEOPATHY (HM02111) | ● | ● | ● | ● | ● | | ● | | ● | ● | ● | |
| BELPER NATURAL HEALTH CENTRE (HM02112) | ● | ● | ● | ● | ● | | ● | ● | ● | ● | ● | |
| BRADSHAW, P J (HM02878) | | | | | ● | | | | | | | |
| CARRICK-SMITH, L (HM03744) | | | | | | | | | | | | |
| CHIROPODY & PHYSIOTHERAPY (HM04303) | | | | | | | | | | | | |
| CONTOUR DESIGNS (HM05021) | | | | | | | | | | | | |
| COVERLEY PHYSIOTHERAPY CLINIC (HM05284) | | | | ● | | | | | | | | |
| DARBY, ANN (HM05735) | | | | | | | | | | | | |
| DERBYSHIRE SPORTS INJURIES (HM06014) | | | | ● | | | | | | | | |
| DRONFIELD PHYSIOTHERAPY CLINIC (HM06320) | | | | | | | | | | | | |
| ENJOY SPORT (HM06836) | | ● | | ● | | | ● | | | | | |
| GARRISON-TODD, WENDY (HM07905) | ● | ● | ● | ● | ● | | | ● | | ● | ● | |
| HARDING, MANDY (HM08971) | | | | | | | | ● | | | | |
| HATHERSAGE HEALTH & THRPY CTRE (HM09198) | | | | | | | | | | | | |
| HIGGS, ANN (HM09734) | | ● | ● | | ● | | | | ● | | | |
| HOUSE OF AROMATHERAPY (HM10216) | | | | | | | | | | | | |
| ILKESTONE OSTEO & MED CTRE (HM10580) | | | | | | | | | | | | |
| JOHNSON, MELVYN (HM11086) | | | | | | | | | | | | |
| KARDAHJI, F C (HM11319) | | | | | | | | ● | | | | |
| KEMP, G D (HM11460) | | | | | | | | | | | | |
| KEMP, GILLIAN (HM11461) | | | | | | | | | | | | |
| LANCASHIRE, A W (HM11915) | | | | | | | | | | | | |
| LIFESOLUTIONS (HM12359) | | | | | ● | | | | | | | |
| MATLOCK PHYSIOTHERAPY CENTRE (HM13293) | ● | ● | ● | ● | ● | | ● | | ● | ● | ● | |
| MATTHEWS, A (HM13299) | ● | ● | ● | ● | | | ● | | ● | | | |
| MATTHEWS, AMANDA (HM13301) | ● | ● | ● | ● | | | ● | ● | | | | |
| NATURAL HEALTH CLINIC (HM14577) | | | | | | | | | | | | |
| PHILIP STOCK - PHYSIOTHERAPIST (HM16120) | | | | | | | ● | | | | | |
| PHYSIO ACTIVE (HM16193) | ● | ● | ● | | ● | | ● | | | | ● | |
| SMITH, ALAN P (HM18711) | | | | | | | | | | | | |

| Business by County with Reference no. | Circulation Problems | Cold Sores | Colds | Colic | Colitis | Conjunctivitis | Constipation | Convulsions | Corns | Coughs | Cramp | Cystitis |
|---|---|---|---|---|---|---|---|---|---|---|---|---|
| BACH FLOWER REMEDIES (HM01469) | | | | | | | | | | | | |
| BANKS, LINDA (HM01665) | ● | | | | | | ● | | | | | |
| BARROWCLIFFE, GRAHAM (DR) (HM01806) | | | | | ● | | ● | | | | | |
| BELPER BACKPAIN CLINIC (HM02110) | | | | | | | | | | | | |
| BELPER HOMEOPATHY (HM02111) | ● | ● | ● | ● | ● | ● | ● | ● | ● | ● | ● | ● |
| BELPER NATURAL HEALTH CENTRE (HM02112) | ● | ● | ● | ● | ● | ● | ● | ● | ● | ● | ● | ● |
| BRADSHAW, P J (HM02878) | | | | | | | | | | | | |
| CARRICK-SMITH, L (HM03744) | | | | | | | | | | | | |
| CHIROPODY & PHYSIOTHERAPY (HM04303) | | | | | | | | | | | | |
| CONTOUR DESIGNS (HM05021) | | | | | | | | | | | | |
| COVERLEY PHYSIOTHERAPY CLINIC (HM05284) | | | | | | | | | | | ● | |
| DARBY, ANN (HM05735) | ● | | | | | | | | | | ● | ● |
| DERBYSHIRE SPORTS INJURIES (HM06014) | | | | | | | | | | | ● | |
| DRONFIELD PHYSIOTHERAPY CLINIC (HM06320) | | | | | | | | | | | | |
| ENJOY SPORT (HM06836) | | | | | | | | | | | | |
| GARRISON-TODD, WENDY (HM07905) | ● | ● | ● | ● | ● | ● | ● | | ● | ● | ● | ● |
| HARDING, MANDY (HM08971) | | | | | | | | | ● | | | |
| HATHERSAGE HEALTH & THRPY CTRE (HM09198) | | | | | | | | | | | | |
| HIGGS, ANN (HM09734) | ● | | | | ● | | ● | | | | | ● |
| HOUSE OF AROMATHERAPY (HM10216) | | | | | | | | | | | | |
| ILKESTONE OSTEO & MED CTRE (HM10580) | ● | | | | | | | | | | | |
| JOHNSON, MELVYN (HM11086) | ● | | | | | | | | | | | |
| KARDAHJI, F C (HM11319) | | | | | | | | | ● | | | |
| KEMP, G D (HM11460) | | | | | | | | | ● | | | |
| KEMP, GILLIAN (HM11461) | | | | | | | | | | | | |
| LANCASHIRE, A W (HM11915) | | | | | | | | | | | | |
| LIFESOLUTIONS (HM12359) | | | | | | | | | | | | |
| MATLOCK PHYSIOTHERAPY CENTRE (HM13293) | ● | ● | ● | ● | ● | ● | ● | ● | | ● | ● | ● |
| MATTHEWS, A (HM13299) | ● | ● | ● | ● | ● | ● | ● | | | ● | ● | ● |
| MATTHEWS, AMANDA (HM13301) | ● | ● | ● | ● | ● | ● | ● | | ● | ● | ● | ● |
| NATURAL HEALTH CLINIC (HM14577) | | | | | | | | | | | | |
| PHILIP STOCK - PHYSIOTHERAPIST (HM16120) | | | | | | | | | | | ● | |
| PHYSIO ACTIVE (HM16193) | ● | ● | ● | ● | ● | ● | ● | ● | | ● | ● | ● |
| SMITH, ALAN P (HM18711) | ● | | | | | | | | | | | |

# A - C Conditions treated at Practices/Businesses

Business by County with Reference no.

| Business | Acne | Addiction | Adenoids | Aids | Alcoholism | Allergy | Alzheimer's Disease | Amnesia | Anaemia | Angina | Anorexia | Anxiety | Arthritis | Asthma | Athletes Foot | Autism | Back Pain | Bacterial Infections | Baldness | Bereavement | Bladder Problems | Blood Pressure | Boils | Bowel Problems |
|---|---|---|---|---|---|---|---|---|---|---|---|---|---|---|---|---|---|---|---|---|---|---|---|---|
| SPINK, BERNADETTE (HM19017) | | | | | | | | | | | | |●| |●| |●|●| | |●|●| |●|
| SPIRAC PHYSIOTHERAPY (HM19020) | | | | | | | | | | | | |●| | | |●| | | | | | | |
| STEVENSON, JACKIE (HM19249) |●|●|●|●|●|●|●|●|●|●|●|●|●|●|●|●|●|●|●| |●|●|●|●|
| SYKES, PETER W (HM19617) | | | | | | | | | | | | |●| |●| | | | | | | | | |
| TAYLOR, E F (HM19756) | | | | | | | | | | | | |●| | | |●| | | | | | | |
| TAYLOR, E F (HM19757) | | | | | | | | | | | | |●| | | |●| | | | | | | |
| TREEWICKS (HM20313) | | | | | | | | | | | |●|●| | | |●| | | | | | | |
| WHITEING CHIROPODISTS (HM21392) | | | | | | | | | | | | |●| |●| | | | | | | | | |
| WHITTLE, S (HM21425) | | | | | | | | | | | | |●| |●| | | | | | | | | |
| **DEVON** | | | | | | | | | | | | | | | | | | | | | | | | |
| ABBEYMEAD NATURAL HEALTH CTRE (HM00090) |●| | | | | | | | | | | |●|●| | |●| | | | | | | |
| ACUPUNCTURE CLINIC (HM00276) |●|●|●|●|●|●|●|●|●|●|●|●|●|●|●| |●|●| | |●|●|●|●|
| ALISON MORTON PHYSIOTHERAPY (HM00579) | | | | | |●| | | | | |●|●| | | |●| | | | | | | |
| ANNE RAWLINGS HYPNOTHERAPY (HM00901) | |●| | |●|●| |●| | |●|●| |●| | | | | | | |●| | |
| ASSOCIATED CHIROPODY SERVICES (HM01270) | | | | | | | | | | | | | | |●| | |●| | | | | | |
| AWARENESS CENTRE (HM01415) |●|●|●|●|●|●|●|●|●|●|●|●|●|●|●|●|●|●|●| |●|●|●|●|
| BALL, ADRIAN (HM01624) | | | | | | | | | | | | | | | | |●| | | | | | | |
| BARRETT, J (HM01790) | | | | | | | | | | | | | | |●| | | | | | | | | |
| BINMORE, F (HM02318) | | | | | |●| | | | | |●|●|●| | |●| | | | | | | |
| BRIXHAM HEALING HANDS CENTRE (HM03105) | | | | | | | | | | | |●|●| | | |●| | | | | | | |
| CARPENTER, PAUL (HM03734) | | |●| | | | | | | | |●|●|●|●| |●|●| | |●|●| |●|
| CASTLE CHIROPRACTIC CLINIC (HM03829) | | | | | | | | | | | | | | | | |●| | | | | | | |
| CASTLEBRIDGE CHIRO & REFLEX (HM03844) | | | | | | | | | | | | | | |●| | | | | | | | | |
| CHELSTON CHIROPODY PRACTICE (HM04092) | | | | | | | | | | | |●|●|●|●| |●|●| | |●|●| |●|
| CHEMIN, CHRISTIAN (HM04098) | | | | | | | | | | | |●| | | | |●| | | | | | | |
| CLINIC OF CHINESE MEDICINE (HM04687) | | | | | |●| | | | | |●| |●| | |●| | | | | | | |
| COLLEGE OF NATURAL NUTRITION (HM04851) |●| | | | | | | | | |●| |●|●| | |●| | | |●|●| |●|
| COPE, ANNE (HM05134) | | | | | | | | | | | | |●|●| | |●|●| | | | | |●|
| COX, MIRANDA (HM05316) | |●| | |●| | | | | |●|●| | | |●| | | | | | | | |
| DEVONSHIRE HEALTH & RAQUET (HM06043) | | | | | | | | | | | | |●| | | |●| | | | | | | |
| EAST DEVON CONSULTANCY (HM06512) |●| | | | |●| | | | | | |●| | | | | | | | | |●|●|
| ELDON HEALTH CLINIC (HM06705) |●| | | | |●| | |●|●|●|●|●|●| | |●|●| | | |●| |●|
| ELLIS, SUE (HM06773) | | | | | |●| | | |●| | |●|●| | |●| | | |●| | |●|
| FOOT CLINIC & THERAPY ROOM (HM07474) | | | | | | | | | | | | | | |●| | | | | | | | | |

| Business | Breast Problems | Breathing Problems | Bronchitis | Bruising | Bulimia | Bunions | Bursitis | Callices | Cancers | Cataracts | Catarrh | Cerebral Palsy | Circulation Problems | Cold Sores | Colds | Colic | Colitis | Conjunctivitis | Constipation | Convulsions | Corns | Coughs | Cramp | Cystitis |
|---|---|---|---|---|---|---|---|---|---|---|---|---|---|---|---|---|---|---|---|---|---|---|---|---|
| SPINK, BERNADETTE (HM19017) |●| |●|●| | | | | | |●| |●|●|●| | | | |●| |●|●|●|
| SPIRAC PHYSIOTHERAPY (HM19020) | | | |●| | | | | | | | | | | | | | | | | | |●| |
| STEVENSON, JACKIE (HM19249) |●|●|●|●|●| |●|●|●|●|●| |●|●|●|●|●|●|●|●|●|●|●|●|
| SYKES, PETER W (HM19617) | | | | | |●| |●| | | | | | | | | | | | |●| | | |
| TAYLOR, E F (HM19756) | | | | | | | | | | | | |●| | | | | | | | | | | |
| TAYLOR, E F (HM19757) | | | | | | | | | | | | |●| | | | | | | | | | | |
| TREEWICKS (HM20313) | |●| | | | | | | | | | | | | | | | | | | | | | |
| WHITEING CHIROPODISTS (HM21392) | | | | | | | |●| | | | | | | | | | | | |●| | | |
| WHITTLE, S (HM21425) | | | | | |●| |●| | | | | | | | | | | | |●| | | |
| **DEVON** | | | | | | | | | | | | | | | | | | | | | | | | |
| ABBEYMEAD NATURAL HEALTH CTRE (HM00090) | | | | | | | | | | | | |●| |●|●| | | | | | | | |
| ACUPUNCTURE CLINIC (HM00276) |●|●|●|●|●| |●|●|●| |●| |●|●|●|●|●|●|●|●|●|●|●|●|
| ALISON MORTON PHYSIOTHERAPY (HM00579) | | | | | | | | | | | | | | | | | | |●| | | | | |
| ANNE RAWLINGS HYPNOTHERAPY (HM00901) | | | | |●| | | | | | | | | | | | | | | | | | | |
| ASSOCIATED CHIROPODY SERVICES (HM01270) | | | | | |●| |●| | | | | | | | | | | | |●| | | |
| AWARENESS CENTRE (HM01415) |●|●|●|●|●| |●|●|●|●|●| |●|●|●|●|●|●|●|●|●|●|●|●|
| BALL, ADRIAN (HM01624) | | | | | | |●| | | | | | | | | | | | | | | | | |
| BARRETT, J (HM01790) | | | | | |●| |●| | | | | | | | | | | | |●| | | |
| BINMORE, F (HM02318) | |●| | | | | | | | |●| |●| | | | | |●| | | |●| |
| BRIXHAM HEALING HANDS CENTRE (HM03105) | | | | | | | | | | | | |●| | | | | | | | | | | |
| CARPENTER, PAUL (HM03734) |●|●| | | | | | | | | | |●| | | | | | | | | | | |
| CASTLE CHIROPRACTIC CLINIC (HM03829) | | | | | | | | | | | | | | | |●| | | | | | | | |
| CASTLEBRIDGE CHIRO & REFLEX (HM03844) | | | | | | |●| | | | | | | | | | | | | | | | | |
| CHELSTON CHIROPODY PRACTICE (HM04092) |●|●| | | | | | | | | | |●| |●| | | | | | | | | |
| CHEMIN, CHRISTIAN (HM04098) | | | | | | | | | | | | | | | | | | | | | | | | |
| CLINIC OF CHINESE MEDICINE (HM04687) | | | | | | | | | | | | | | | | | | |●| | | | | |
| COLLEGE OF NATURAL NUTRITION (HM04851) |●| | | | | | | | | | | |●| | | | | |●| | | |●|●|
| COPE, ANNE (HM05134) | |●| | | | | | | | |●| |●| | | | | |●| | | | | |
| COX, MIRANDA (HM05316) | | | | | | | | | | | | | | | | | | | | | | | | |
| DEVONSHIRE HEALTH & RAQUET (HM06043) | | | | | | | | | | | | | | | | | | | | | | | | |
| EAST DEVON CONSULTANCY (HM06512) | |●|●| | | | | | | |●| | | | | | | |●| | | | |●|
| ELDON HEALTH CLINIC (HM06705) |●|●| | |●| |●| | | | | |●|●| | |●| |●| | | |●|●|
| ELLIS, SUE (HM06773) | | | | | | |●| | | | | |●| | | | | | | | | |●| |
| FOOT CLINIC & THERAPY ROOM (HM07474) | | | | | | | | | | | | | | | | | | | | | | | | |

# A - C Conditions treated at Practices/Businesses

Business by County with Reference no.

| Condition | FOOTEC MEDICAL (HM07500) | FUDGE, H (HM07777) | GARRETTLEY, U (HM07902) | HEALTH CONSULTANCY (HM09382) | HEALTH WAVES (HM09408) | HUME, PETER D (HM10370) | IRIDOLOGY/NUTRITIONAL THER (HM10723) | J T SERVICES (HM10802) | JANE HYDE CHRTRD PHYSIO (HM10917) | JEFFRIES, BARBARA (HM10972) | JOHNSON, MICHAEL (HM11087) | JULIE ADAMS REFLEXOLOGIST (HM11256) | KINGSBRIDGE COMP HLTH PRACTICE (HM11658) | KINGSBRIDGE PHYSICAL THERAPY (HM11659) | LIGHT TOUCH THERAPY TRAINING (HM12369) | LINDEMAN, A J (HM12415) | LION HOUSE SURGERY (HM12446) | MALLARDO, RENEE (HM12977) | MASON, MARCUS (HM13248) | MASSAGE RELAXING THERAPEUTIC (HM13262) | MONSHIN, DEBORAH J (HM14075) | NELSON, PAUL (HM14781) | NETHERWAY, JEAN (HM14789) | PAIGNTON PHYSIOTHERAPY (HM15576) | PANNELL, R J (HM15636) | PLAYERS, MEGAN (HM16365) | PLYMOUTH OSTEOPATHS (HM16388) | REFLEXOLOGY CENTRE (HM17083) | RENDLE, S (HM17182) | RIVERSIDE CHIROPRACTIC CLINIC (HM17379) | ROSE & CROWN CLINIC (HM17598) | SANDERS, RACHEL (HM17916) | SCURR, PETER M (HM18160) | SEELEY, JANICE (HM18194) |
|---|---|---|---|---|---|---|---|---|---|---|---|---|---|---|---|---|---|---|---|---|---|---|---|---|---|---|---|---|---|---|---|---|---|---|
| Acne | | | |●| | |●| | | | | |●| |●|●|●| | | |●|●| | | |●| | | | |●| | |●|
| Addiction | | | |●| | |●| | |●|●| |●| | | |●|●| | |●| | | |●|●| | | | |●| | | |
| Adenoids | | | | | | |●| | | | | |●| | | | | | | | | | | | | | | | | |●| | | |
| Aids | | | | | | |●| | | | | | | | | | | | | | | | | | | | | | | |●| | | |
| Alcoholism | | | | | | |●| | |●| | |●| | | | | | | | | | | |●|●| | | | |●| | | |
| Allergy | | | |●| | |●| | | |●|●|●| | |●|●| |●| |●| | | |●|●| | | | |●| | |●|
| Alzheimer's Disease | | | |●| | |●| | | | | |●| | | | | | | | | | | | | | | | | |●| | |●|
| Amnesia | | | | | | |●| | | | | |●| | | | |●| | | | | | | |●| | | | |●| | | |
| Anaemia | | | |●| | |●| | | | | |●| | |●| | |●| | |●| | | |●| | | | |●| | |●|
| Angina | | | |●| | |●| | | |●| |●| |●|●| | |●| | |●| | |●|●| | | | |●| | |●|
| Anorexia | |●| |●| | |●| | |●| | |●| | |●| | |●| | | | | |●|●| | | | |●| | |●|
| Anxiety | |●|●|●| | |●| | |●| |●|●| |●|●|●|●|●|●|●|●|●| |●|●| |●| | |●| | |●|
| Arthritis |●| |●|●| |●|●|●|●| |●| |●|●|●|●|●| |●| | | | |●|●|●|●|●|●|●|●|●|●|●|
| Asthma | | |●|●| | |●|●| | | |●|●| |●|●|●| |●| |●|●|●| |●|●| | | | |●| | |●|
| Athletes Foot |●| | |●| |●|●| | | | | |●| | |●| | | | | |●| | |●|●| | |●| |●|●|●|●|
| Autism | | | |●| | |●| | | | | |●| | |●| | | | | | | | | |●| | | | |●| | |●|
| Back Pain | |●|●|●|●| |●|●|●| |●|●|●|●|●| |●| |●|●| | |●|●|●|●|●|●| |●|●| | | |
| Bacterial Infections | | | |●| | |●| | | | | |●| | |●| | | | | |●| | |●|●| | | | |●| |●|●|
| Baldness | | | | | | |●| | | | | | | |●|●| | |●| | | | | | |●| | | | |●| | |●|
| Bereavement | | | | | | |●| | | | | |●| | | | | | | | | | | | | | | | | | | | | |
| Bladder Problems | | |●|●| | |●| | | |●| |●| |●|●| | |●| | |●|●| | |●| | | | |●| | |●|
| Blood Pressure | | | |●| | |●|●| | |●|●|●| |●|●|●| |●| | |●| | |●|●| |●| | |●| | |●|
| Boils | | | | | | |●| | | | | |●| |●|●| | | | | |●| | | |●| | | | |●| | |●|
| Bowel Problems | | | |●| | |●| | | |●|●|●| |●|●|●|●|●| | |●| | | |●| |●| | |●| | |●|
| Breast Problems | | | |●| | |●| | | | | |●| |●|●| | |●| | |●| | | |●| | | | |●| | |●|
| Breathing Problems | | |●|●| | |●|●| | | | |●| |●|●|●|●|●| | |●|●| |●|●| | | | |●| | |●|
| Bronchitis | | | |●| | |●| | | | | |●| |●|●|●| |●| | |●| | | |●| | | | |●| | |●|
| Bruising | | | |●| | |●|●| | | | |●| |●|●| | | | | |●| |●| |●| | | | |●| | | |
| Bulimia | |●| |●| | |●| | | | | |●| | | | | |●| | | | | |●| | | | | |●| | | |
| Bunions |●| | | | |●|●| | | | | |●| | | | | | | | | | | | | | | |●| | | |●| |
| Bursitis | | | |●| | |●| |●| | | | | |●| | | | | | |●| | | |●| | | | |●| | | |
| Callices |●| | | | |●|●| | | | | |●| | | | | | | | | | | | |●| | |●| |●|●|●| |
| Cancers | | | |●| | |●| | | | | | | | | | | |●| | |●| | | |●| | | | |●| | |●|
| Cataracts | | | |●| | |●| | | | | | | | |●| | | | | | | | | | | | | | |●| | |●|
| Catarrh | | |●|●| | |●| | | | | |●| |●|●|●| |●| | |●| | | |●| | | | |●| | |●|
| Cerebral Palsy | | | | | | | | | | | | | | | | | | | | | | | | | | | | | | | | | | |
| Circulation Problems | | |●|●| | |●|●| | |●| |●| |●|●|●| |●| |●|●|●| |●|●| |●| | |●| | |●|
| Cold Sores | | | |●| | |●| | | | | |●| |●|●| | | | | |●| | | |●| | | | |●| | |●|
| Colds | | | | | | |●| | | | | |●| |●| | | |●| | | | | | |●| | | | |●| | |●|
| Colic | | | |●| | |●| | | | | |●| |●|●|●| |●| | |●| | | |●| | | |●|●| | |●|
| Colitis | | | |●| | |●| | | | | |●| |●|●| | |●| | |●| | | |●| | | | |●| | |●|
| Conjunctivitis | | | | | | |●| | | | | |●| |●|●| | | | | |●| | | |●| | | | |●| | |●|
| Constipation | | |●|●| | |●| | | | |●|●| |●| |●| |●| |●|●| | | |●| |●| | |●| | |●|
| Convulsions | | | |●| | |●| | | | | | | |●|●| | | | | | | | | |●| | | | |●| | |●|
| Corns |●| | | | |●|●| | | | | |●| | | | | | | | | | | | |●| | |●| |●|●|●| |
| Coughs | | | |●| | |●| | | | | |●| |●|●| | |●| | |●| | | |●| | | | |●| | |●|
| Cramp | |●|●|●| | |●|●| | | | | | |●| | | |●| | |●| | |●|●|●| | | |●| | |●|
| Cystitis | | | |●| | |●| | | |●| |●| |●|●| | |●| | |●| | | |●| | | | |●| | |●|

# A - C Conditions treated at Practices/Businesses

| Business by County with Reference no. | Acne | Addiction | Adenoids | Aids | Alcoholism | Allergy | Alzheimer's Disease | Amnesia | Anaemia | Angina | Anorexia | Anxiety | Arthritis | Asthma | Athletes Foot | Autism |
|---|---|---|---|---|---|---|---|---|---|---|---|---|---|---|---|---|
| SERENITY (HM18233) | ● | ● | ● | ● | ● | ● | ● | ● | ● | ● | ● | ● | ● | ● | ● | ● |
| STIMULUS FOR CHANGE (HM19296) | ● | | | | | | | | | | | ● | ● | ● | | |
| TRANCE - FORMATIONS HEALING (HM20250) | | ● | | | ● | ● | | ● | | | ● | ● | | ● | | |
| VITAL TOUCH (HM20703) | | | | | | | | | | | | ● | | | | |
| WALTERS, RICHARD (HM20880) | | | | | | ● | | | | | | | ● | ● | | |
| WALTERS, RICHARD (HM20882) | | | | | | ● | | | | | | | ● | ● | | |
| WILKINSON, MARY (HM21512) | | | | | | | | | | | | | | | ● | |
| WILLIAMS CLINIC (HM21531) | | | | | | ● | | | | | | | ● | | | |
| WILLSHER, ERNEST R (HM21633) | | | | | | | | | | | | | | | ● | |
| YOGA HEALTH STUDIO (HM22028) | | | | | ● | | | | | | | ● | ● | ● | | |
| YORK HOUSE CHIROPODY (HM22044) | | | | | | | | | | | | | ● | | ● | |
| YORK HOUSE CHIROPRACTIC CLINIC (HM22045) | | | | | | | | | | | | | | | | |
| **DORSET** | | | | | | | | | | | | | | | | |
| ABBEY VIEW COMP CLINIC (HM00088) | ● | ● | ● | | ● | ● | ● | ● | ● | ● | ● | ● | ● | ● | ● | ● |
| ALTERNATIVE APPROACH (HM00694) | | | | | | | | | | | | | ● | | | |
| ARCHIBALD, LIZ (HM00980) | | ● | | | | | | | | | | ● | | | | |
| AROMA TRANQUILITY (HM01064) | ● | | | | | | | | | | | ● | | ● | | |
| ART OF REFLEXOLOGY (HM01154) | | | | | | | | | | | | | | | | |
| AWDRY, ROBERT (HM01416) | ● | | | | | ● | | | | | ● | ● | ● | ● | ● | |
| BACK IN BALANCE (HM01479) | | | | | | | | | | | | | ● | | | |
| BACK IN FORM (HM01480) | | | | | | | | | | | | | ● | | | |
| BELTAIN CENTRE (HM02117) | | ● | | | | | | | | | ● | ● | | | | |
| BELTAIN CENTRE (HM02116) | | | | | | | | | | | | ● | ● | ● | | |
| BOURNEMOUTH CTRE FOR COMP MED (HM02761) | ● | ● | ● | ● | ● | ● | ● | ● | ● | ● | ● | ● | ● | ● | ● | |
| BOURNEMOUTH PHYSIO CLINIC (HM02762) | | | | | | | | | | | | | | | | |
| BOWEN CLINIC (HM02771) | | | | | | | | | | | | ● | ● | ● | | |
| BOWOOD HEALTH & BEAUTY CENTRE (HM02804) | | | | | | | | | | | | ● | | | | |
| BRANDON, DAVE (HM02912) | ● | ● | ● | ● | ● | ● | ● | ● | ● | ● | ● | ● | ● | ● | ● | ● |
| BRIDPORT COMP MEDICINE CTRE (HM03019) | ● | ● | ● | ● | ● | ● | ● | ● | ● | ● | ● | ● | ● | ● | ● | ● |
| BRIGHTER FUTURE (HM03039) | | | | | | | | | | | | ● | | | | |
| BRIGHTER FUTURE (HM03040) | | | | | | | | | | | | ● | | | | |
| BROADSTONE CENTRE COMP MED (HM03117) | ● | ● | | ● | | | | | ● | ● | ● | ● | ● | ● | | |
| BROADSTONE CENTRE OF COMP MED (HM03118) | ● | ● | ● | ● | ● | ● | ● | ● | ● | ● | ● | ● | ● | ● | ● | ● |
| BROWN, A D (HM03208) | | | | | | | | | | | | | | | ● | |

| Business by County with Reference no. | Back Pain | Bacterial Infections | Baldness | Bereavement | Bladder Problems | Blood Pressure | Boils | Bowel Problems | Breast Problems | Breathing Problems | Bronchitis | Bruising | Bulimia | Bunions | Bursitis | Callices |
|---|---|---|---|---|---|---|---|---|---|---|---|---|---|---|---|---|
| SERENITY (HM18233) | ● | ● | ● | | ● | ● | ● | ● | ● | ● | ● | ● | ● | | ● | ● |
| STIMULUS FOR CHANGE (HM19296) | | | | | | ● | ● | ● | ● | ● | ● | ● | | | | |
| TRANCE - FORMATIONS HEALING (HM20250) | | | | | | ● | | ● | | | | | ● | | | |
| VITAL TOUCH (HM20703) | ● | | | | | | | | | ● | | | | | | |
| WALTERS, RICHARD (HM20880) | | | | | | | | | | | | | | | | |
| WALTERS, RICHARD (HM20882) | | | | | | | | | | | | | | | | |
| WILKINSON, MARY (HM21512) | ● | | | | ● | | | ● | | | | | | | | |
| WILLIAMS CLINIC (HM21531) | ● | | | | | | | | | | | | | | | |
| WILLSHER, ERNEST R (HM21633) | | ● | | | | | | | | | | | | | | ● |
| YOGA HEALTH STUDIO (HM22028) | ● | | | | | ● | | | | | ● | | | | | |
| YORK HOUSE CHIROPODY (HM22044) | | ● | | | | | | | | | | | | ● | | ● |
| YORK HOUSE CHIROPRACTIC CLINIC (HM22045) | ● | | | | | | | | | | | | | | | |
| **DORSET** | | | | | | | | | | | | | | | | |
| ABBEY VIEW COMP CLINIC (HM00088) | ● | ● | ● | | ● | ● | ● | ● | ● | ● | ● | ● | ● | | ● | |
| ALTERNATIVE APPROACH (HM00694) | ● | | | | | | | | | | | | | | | |
| ARCHIBALD, LIZ (HM00980) | | | | | | | | | | | | | | | | |
| AROMA TRANQUILITY (HM01064) | ● | | | | | | | | | ● | ● | | | | | |
| ART OF REFLEXOLOGY (HM01154) | ● | | | | | | | | | ● | | | | | | |
| AWDRY, ROBERT (HM01416) | | | | | ● | ● | ● | ● | ● | ● | ● | ● | | | | |
| BACK IN BALANCE (HM01479) | ● | | | | | | | | | | | | | | | |
| BACK IN FORM (HM01480) | ● | | | | | | | | | | | | | | | |
| BELTAIN CENTRE (HM02117) | | | | | | ● | | ● | | ● | | | ● | | | |
| BELTAIN CENTRE (HM02116) | ● | | | | | | | ● | | | | | | | | |
| BOURNEMOUTH CTRE FOR COMP MED (HM02761) | ● | ● | ● | | ● | ● | ● | ● | ● | ● | ● | ● | ● | | ● | ● |
| BOURNEMOUTH PHYSIO CLINIC (HM02762) | ● | | | | | | | | | | | | | | | |
| BOWEN CLINIC (HM02771) | ● | | | | ● | ● | | ● | ● | ● | ● | | | | | |
| BOWOOD HEALTH & BEAUTY CENTRE (HM02804) | | | | | | | | | | | | | | | | |
| BRANDON, DAVE (HM02912) | ● | ● | ● | | ● | ● | ● | ● | ● | ● | ● | ● | ● | | ● | |
| BRIDPORT COMP MEDICINE CTRE (HM03019) | ● | ● | ● | | ● | ● | ● | ● | ● | ● | ● | ● | ● | | ● | ● |
| BRIGHTER FUTURE (HM03039) | | | | | | | | | | | | | | | | |
| BRIGHTER FUTURE (HM03040) | | | | | | | | | | | | | | | | |
| BROADSTONE CENTRE COMP MED (HM03117) | ● | | | | ● | ● | ● | ● | ● | ● | ● | | ● | | | |
| BROADSTONE CENTRE OF COMP MED (HM03118) | ● | ● | ● | | ● | ● | ● | ● | ● | ● | ● | ● | ● | | ● | ● |
| BROWN, A D (HM03208) | | | | | | | | | | | | | | | | |

| Business by County with Reference no. | Cancers | Cataracts | Catarrh | Cerebral Palsy | Circulation Problems | Cold Sores | Colds | Colic | Colitis | Conjunctivitis | Constipation | Convulsions | Corns | Coughs | Cramp | Cystitis |
|---|---|---|---|---|---|---|---|---|---|---|---|---|---|---|---|---|
| SERENITY (HM18233) | ● | ● | ● | | ● | ● | ● | ● | ● | ● | ● | ● | ● | ● | ● | ● |
| STIMULUS FOR CHANGE (HM19296) | | | ● | | | ● | ● | ● | ● | ● | ● | | | ● | ● | ● |
| TRANCE - FORMATIONS HEALING (HM20250) | | | | | | | | | ● | | | | | | | |
| VITAL TOUCH (HM20703) | | | | | | | | ● | | | ● | | | | ● | |
| WALTERS, RICHARD (HM20880) | | | | | | | | | | | ● | | | | | ● |
| WALTERS, RICHARD (HM20882) | | | | | | | | | | | ● | | | | | ● |
| WILKINSON, MARY (HM21512) | | | | | | | | | | | ● | | | | | |
| WILLIAMS CLINIC (HM21531) | | | | | | | | | | | ● | | | | | ● |
| WILLSHER, ERNEST R (HM21633) | | | | | | | | | | | | | ● | | | |
| YOGA HEALTH STUDIO (HM22028) | ● | | | | | | | | | | | | | | | |
| YORK HOUSE CHIROPODY (HM22044) | | | | | | | | | | | | | ● | | | |
| YORK HOUSE CHIROPRACTIC CLINIC (HM22045) | | | | | | | | | | | | | | | | |
| **DORSET** | | | | | | | | | | | | | | | | |
| ABBEY VIEW COMP CLINIC (HM00088) | | ● | ● | | ● | ● | ● | ● | ● | ● | ● | ● | | ● | ● | ● |
| ALTERNATIVE APPROACH (HM00694) | | | | | ● | | | | | | | | | | | |
| ARCHIBALD, LIZ (HM00980) | | | | | | | | | | | | | | | | |
| AROMA TRANQUILITY (HM01064) | | | | | ● | | | | | | | | | | | |
| ART OF REFLEXOLOGY (HM01154) | | | | | ● | | | | | | | | | | | |
| AWDRY, ROBERT (HM01416) | ● | | ● | | ● | ● | ● | ● | ● | ● | ● | | | ● | ● | ● |
| BACK IN BALANCE (HM01479) | | | | | ● | | | ● | | | | | | | | |
| BACK IN FORM (HM01480) | | | | | ● | | | | | | | | | | | |
| BELTAIN CENTRE (HM02117) | | | | | ● | | | | | | | | | | | |
| BELTAIN CENTRE (HM02116) | ● | | | | | | | | | | | | | | | |
| BOURNEMOUTH CTRE FOR COMP MED (HM02761) | | | ● | | ● | ● | ● | ● | ● | ● | ● | ● | ● | ● | ● | ● |
| BOURNEMOUTH PHYSIO CLINIC (HM02762) | | | | | | | | | | | | | | | | |
| BOWEN CLINIC (HM02771) | | | ● | | ● | | | ● | | | ● | | | ● | ● | |
| BOWOOD HEALTH & BEAUTY CENTRE (HM02804) | | | | | | | | | | | | | | | | |
| BRANDON, DAVE (HM02912) | ● | ● | ● | | ● | ● | ● | ● | ● | ● | ● | ● | | ● | ● | ● |
| BRIDPORT COMP MEDICINE CTRE (HM03019) | ● | ● | ● | | ● | ● | ● | ● | ● | ● | ● | ● | ● | ● | ● | ● |
| BRIGHTER FUTURE (HM03039) | | | | | | | | | | | | | | | | |
| BRIGHTER FUTURE (HM03040) | | | | | | | | | | | | | | | | |
| BROADSTONE CENTRE COMP MED (HM03117) | ● | | ● | | ● | ● | ● | ● | ● | ● | ● | | | ● | ● | ● |
| BROADSTONE CENTRE OF COMP MED (HM03118) | ● | ● | ● | | ● | ● | ● | ● | ● | ● | ● | ● | ● | ● | ● | ● |
| BROWN, A D (HM03208) | | | | | | | | | | | | | | | | |

# A - C Conditions treated at Practices/Businesses

| Business by County with Reference no. | Acne | Addiction | Adenoids | Aids | Alcoholism | Allergy | Alzheimer's Disease | Amnesia | Anaemia | Angina | Anorexia | Anxiety | Arthritis | Asthma | Athletes Foot | Autism |
|---|---|---|---|---|---|---|---|---|---|---|---|---|---|---|---|---|
| BURT, S (HM03429) | ● | | | | ● | ● | ● | | ● | ● | ● | ● | ● | ● | ● | |
| BWT PODIATRY (HM03508) | | | | | | | | | | | | | ● | | ● | |
| CARBERY PRACTICE (HM03657) | | | | | | | | | | | ● | ● | | | | |
| CHARMINSTER CHIRO CLINIC (HM04036) | | | | | | | | | | | | | ● | | | |
| CHINESE MEDICINE CENTRE (HM04254) | | | | | | | | | | | | | | | | |
| CHINESE MEDICINE CLINIC (HM04258) | | | | | | | | | | | | | ● | | | |
| CHIROPODY SERVICES (HM04338) | | | | | | | | | | | | | | | ● | |
| CHIROPRACTIC TREATMENT CENTRE (HM04403) | | | | | | | | | | | | | ● | | | |
| CHRISTCHURCH CHIROPRACTIC CTRE (HM04435) | | | | | | | | | | | | ● | ● | | | |
| CHRISTCHURCH PHYSIO PRACTICE (HM04436) | | | | | | | | | | | | | ● | | | |
| CLARK, LYNN (HM04568) | | | | | | | | | | | | | | | ● | |
| COLLINWOOD, LOUIS (HM04884) | | | | | | ● | | | | | | | ● | ● | | ● |
| COMMUNITY CHIROPRACTIC CLINIC (HM04906) | | | | | | | | | | | | | ● | | | |
| DLP HYPNOTHERAPY CENTRE (HM06134) | | ● | | | ● | | | ● | | | | ● | | | | |
| DORSET RACQUETS & HEALTH CLUB (HM06205) | | | | | | | | | | | | ● | | | | |
| EVANS, REBECCA MARY (HM06988) | | | | | | | | | | | | | | | | |
| FEET FIRST (HM07171) | | | | | | | | | | | | | | | ● | |
| FERNDOWN CHIROPRACTIC CLINIC (HM07239) | | | | | | | | | | | | | ● | | | |
| FREESPIRIT (HM07724) | ● | ● | ● | ● | | ● | ● | | ● | ● | ● | ● | ● | ● | | ● |
| FULL SPECTRUM THERAPY CENTRE (HM07786) | ● | ● | ● | ● | ● | ● | ● | ● | ● | ● | ● | ● | ● | ● | ● | ● |
| GLENCAIRE CLINIC (HM08145) | | | | | | | | | | | | | ● | | | |
| GODFREY, BRIAN (HM08184) | | | | | ● | ● | | | | | ● | ● | | | | |
| HAMPTON, ANNE (HM08886) | | | | | | | | | | | | | | | ● | |
| HARLING, MARIANNE (DR) (HM09010) | ● | | ● | | | ● | | ● | ● | ● | ● | ● | ● | ● | ● | |
| HIGHCLIFFE CHIROPRACTIC CLINIC (HM09748) | | | | | | | | | | | | | ● | | | |
| HIGHCLIFFE CHIROPRACTIC CLINIC (HM09749) | | | | | | | | | | | | | ● | | | |
| HOLISTIC HEALTH CENTRE (HM09973) | ● | ● | ● | ● | ● | ● | | ● | ● | ● | ● | ● | ● | ● | ● | |
| HOMEOPATHY HEALS (HM10081) | ● | | | | | ● | | | ● | | | | ● | ● | ● | |
| HOPKINS, H G (HM10149) | | | | | | | | | | | | | ● | | | |
| HORNE, SUE (HM10175) | | | | | | ● | | | | | | ● | ● | ● | ● | |
| JACKSON, A E (HM10817) | ● | ● | ● | ● | ● | ● | ● | ● | ● | ● | ● | ● | ● | ● | ● | ● |
| JELFS, MARTIN (HM10975) | | | | | | | | | | | | ● | | | | |
| KENNEDY, EDWARD (HM11491) | | | | | | | | | | | | | | | | |
| LEVER, I J (HM12261) | | | | | | | | | | | | | ● | | | |

| Business by County with Reference no. | Back Pain | Bacterial Infections | Baldness | Bereavement | Bladder Problems | Blood Pressure | Boils | Bowel Problems | Breast Problems | Breathing Problems | Bronchitis | Bruising | Bulimia | Bunions | Bursitis | Callices |
|---|---|---|---|---|---|---|---|---|---|---|---|---|---|---|---|---|
| BURT, S (HM03429) | ● | ● | | | ● | ● | ● | ● | ● | ● | ● | ● | ● | | | |
| BWT PODIATRY (HM03508) | | | | | | | | | | | | | | | ● | |
| CARBERY PRACTICE (HM03657) | ● | | | | ● | ● | | | | | | | ● | | | |
| CHARMINSTER CHIRO CLINIC (HM04036) | ● | | | | | | | | | | | | | | | |
| CHINESE MEDICINE CENTRE (HM04254) | ● | | | | | | | | | | | | | | | |
| CHINESE MEDICINE CLINIC (HM04258) | | | | | | | | | | | | | | | | |
| CHIROPODY SERVICES (HM04338) | | | | | | | | | | | | | | | | |
| CHIROPRACTIC TREATMENT CENTRE (HM04403) | ● | | | | | | | | | | | | | | | |
| CHRISTCHURCH CHIROPRACTIC CTRE (HM04435) | ● | | | | | | | ● | | | | | | | | |
| CHRISTCHURCH PHYSIO PRACTICE (HM04436) | ● | | | | | | | | | | | | | | ● | |
| CLARK, LYNN (HM04568) | | | | | | | | | | | | | | | | ● |
| COLLINWOOD, LOUIS (HM04884) | ● | | | | ● | ● | | ● | | ● | ● | | | | | |
| COMMUNITY CHIROPRACTIC CLINIC (HM04906) | ● | | | | | | | | | | | | | | | |
| DLP HYPNOTHERAPY CENTRE (HM06134) | | | | | ● | | | ● | | | | | | | | |
| DORSET RACQUETS & HEALTH CLUB (HM06205) | ● | | | | | | | | | | | | | | | |
| EVANS, REBECCA MARY (HM06988) | ● | | | | | | | | | | | | | | | |
| FEET FIRST (HM07171) | | | | | | | | | | | | | | | | |
| FERNDOWN CHIROPRACTIC CLINIC (HM07239) | ● | | | | | | | | | | | | | | | |
| FREESPIRIT (HM07724) | ● | | | | ● | ● | | ● | | | | ● | | | | |
| FULL SPECTRUM THERAPY CENTRE (HM07786) | ● | ● | ● | | ● | ● | ● | ● | ● | ● | ● | ● | ● | | ● | ● |
| GLENCAIRE CLINIC (HM08145) | ● | | | | | ● | | | | | | | | | | |
| GODFREY, BRIAN (HM08184) | ● | | | | ● | ● | | ● | | | | | ● | | | |
| HAMPTON, ANNE (HM08886) | | | | | | | | | | | | | | | | ● |
| HARLING, MARIANNE (DR) (HM09010) | ● | ● | ● | ● | ● | ● | ● | ● | ● | ● | ● | ● | ● | ● | ● | ● |
| HIGHCLIFFE CHIROPRACTIC CLINIC (HM09748) | ● | | | | | | | | | | | | | | | |
| HIGHCLIFFE CHIROPRACTIC CLINIC (HM09749) | ● | | | | | | | | | | | | | | | |
| HOLISTIC HEALTH CENTRE (HM09973) | ● | ● | ● | | ● | ● | ● | ● | ● | ● | ● | ● | ● | | | ● |
| HOMEOPATHY HEALS (HM10081) | | ● | | | ● | ● | ● | ● | ● | ● | ● | | | | ● | ● |
| HOPKINS, H G (HM10149) | ● | | | | | ● | | | | | | | | | | |
| HORNE, SUE (HM10175) | ● | | | | ● | ● | ● | | | ● | ● | | | | | |
| JACKSON, A E (HM10817) | ● | ● | ● | | ● | ● | ● | ● | ● | ● | ● | ● | ● | | ● | ● |
| JELFS, MARTIN (HM10975) | | | | | | | | | | | | | | | | |
| KENNEDY, EDWARD (HM11491) | ● | | | | | | | | | | | | | | | |
| LEVER, I J (HM12261) | ● | | | | | | | | | | | | | | | |

| Business by County with Reference no. | Cancers | Cataracts | Catarrh | Cerebral Palsy | Circulation Problems | Cold Sores | Colds | Colic | Colitis | Conjunctivitis | Constipation | Convulsions | Corns | Coughs | Cramp | Cystitis |
|---|---|---|---|---|---|---|---|---|---|---|---|---|---|---|---|---|
| BURT, S (HM03429) | | ● | ● | | ● | ● | ● | ● | ● | ● | ● | ● | | ● | ● | ● |
| BWT PODIATRY (HM03508) | | | | | ● | | | | | | | | | | | |
| CARBERY PRACTICE (HM03657) | | | | | ● | | | | | | ● | | | | | |
| CHARMINSTER CHIRO CLINIC (HM04036) | | | | | ● | | | | | | | | | | | |
| CHINESE MEDICINE CENTRE (HM04254) | | | | | | | | | | | | | | | | |
| CHINESE MEDICINE CLINIC (HM04258) | | | | | | | | | | | | | | | | |
| CHIROPODY SERVICES (HM04338) | | | | | | | | | | | | | | | | |
| CHIROPRACTIC TREATMENT CENTRE (HM04403) | | | | | ● | | | | | | | | | | | |
| CHRISTCHURCH CHIROPRACTIC CTRE (HM04435) | | | | | | | | ● | ● | | ● | | | | | |
| CHRISTCHURCH PHYSIO PRACTICE (HM04436) | | | | | | | | | | | | | | | | |
| CLARK, LYNN (HM04568) | | | | | | | | | | | | | ● | | | |
| COLLINWOOD, LOUIS (HM04884) | | | | | ● | | | ● | | | | | | | | |
| COMMUNITY CHIROPRACTIC CLINIC (HM04906) | | | | | ● | | | | | | | | | | | |
| DLP HYPNOTHERAPY CENTRE (HM06134) | | | | | | | | | | | | | | | | |
| DORSET RACQUETS & HEALTH CLUB (HM06205) | | | | | | | | | | | | | | | | |
| EVANS, REBECCA MARY (HM06988) | | | | | | | | | | | | | | | | |
| FEET FIRST (HM07171) | | | | | | | | | | | | | | | | |
| FERNDOWN CHIROPRACTIC CLINIC (HM07239) | | | | | ● | | | ● | | | | | | | | |
| FREESPIRIT (HM07724) | ● | | | | ● | | | | | | | | | | ● | ● |
| FULL SPECTRUM THERAPY CENTRE (HM07786) | ● | ● | ● | | ● | ● | ● | ● | ● | ● | ● | ● | ● | ● | ● | ● |
| GLENCAIRE CLINIC (HM08145) | | | | | ● | | | | | | | | | | | |
| GODFREY, BRIAN (HM08184) | ● | | ● | | | | | | | | ● | | | | | |
| HAMPTON, ANNE (HM08886) | | | | | | | | | | | | | ● | | | |
| HARLING, MARIANNE (DR) (HM09010) | ● | | ● | | ● | ● | ● | ● | ● | ● | | ● | ● | ● | ● | ● |
| HIGHCLIFFE CHIROPRACTIC CLINIC (HM09748) | | | | | ● | | | ● | | | | | | | | |
| HIGHCLIFFE CHIROPRACTIC CLINIC (HM09749) | | | | | | | | | | | | | | | | |
| HOLISTIC HEALTH CENTRE (HM09973) | ● | | ● | | ● | ● | ● | ● | ● | ● | ● | | ● | ● | ● | ● |
| HOMEOPATHY HEALS (HM10081) | ● | ● | ● | | ● | ● | ● | ● | ● | ● | ● | ● | ● | ● | ● | ● |
| HOPKINS, H G (HM10149) | | | | | ● | | | | ● | | | | | | | |
| HORNE, SUE (HM10175) | | | ● | | ● | | ● | | ● | | ● | | | ● | ● | ● |
| JACKSON, A E (HM10817) | ● | ● | ● | | ● | ● | ● | ● | ● | ● | ● | ● | ● | ● | ● | ● |
| JELFS, MARTIN (HM10975) | | | | | | | | | | | | | | | | |
| KENNEDY, EDWARD (HM11491) | | | | | | | | | | | | | | | | |
| LEVER, I J (HM12261) | | | | | ● | | | | | | | | | | | |

# A - C Conditions treated at Practices/Businesses

| Business by County with Reference no. | LOCK, ROBERT (HM12538) | MOTCOMBE PARK PHYSIOTHERAPY (HM14273) | NATURAL HEALTH CONSULTANCY (HM14592) | NEIJIA (HM14759) | PARTNERSHIP, BAKER (DR) (HM15764) | PHYSIO, MASSAGE & PR ACU (HM16210) | PRIDEAUX-BRUNE, COLETTE (HM16604) | PRIDMORE, JOSEPHINE (HM16605) | PROSPECT HEALTH (HM16667) | ROBSON, VANESSA (HM17514) | ROLLS MILL COMP HEALTH CENTRE (HM17567) | ROWE, PENNY (HM17689) | ROY, COLLEEN (HM17710) | SHEBORNE CHIROPRACTIC CENTRE (HM18361) | SKELTON, JAN (HM18635) | SOUTHBOURNE HERBAL CLINIC (HM18924) | SOUTHBOURNE NATURAL HLTH CTRE (HM18925) | STANDISH-HAYES, QUENTIN (HM19125) | STEELE, T M (HM19183) | THORNTONS PHARMACY (HM20029) | TREAT FEET (HM20301) | TRUNDELL, C (HM20353) | WALTERS, RICHARD (HM20881) | WESSEX HEALTHY LIVING FOUND (HM21208) | WEST MOORS CHIROPRACTIC CLINIC (HM21230) | WIMBORNE CHIROPODY SURGERY (HM21687) | YELLOW HOUSE (HM22005) | ESSEX | A M R THERAPIES (HM00040) | ABBOT, LISA (HM00095) | ABBOTT, LISA (HM00099) | AEQUILIBRIUM (HM00407) | ARC HEALTHCARE (HM00968) | AROMATHERAPY CLINIC (HM01107) |
|---|---|---|---|---|---|---|---|---|---|---|---|---|---|---|---|---|---|---|---|---|---|---|---|---|---|---|---|---|---|---|---|---|---|---|
| Cystitis | ● | | ● | ● | | | ● | ● | | | | ● | ● | | | ● | ● | | | ● | | | ● | ● | | | ● | | | | | ● | ● | |
| Cramp | ● | | ● | ● | | ● | ● | ● | | | | ● | ● | | | ● | ● | | | ● | | | | ● | | | ● | | | | | ● | | |
| Coughs | ● | | ● | ● | | | ● | ● | | | | ● | ● | | | ● | ● | | | ● | | | | ● | | | ● | | | | | ● | | |
| Corns | | | ● | | | | ● | | | ● | | ● | ● | | | | ● | | | ● | ● | | | | | | ● | | | | | | | |
| Convulsions | ● | | ● | | | | ● | | | | | ● | ● | | | | ● | | | ● | | | | ● | | | ● | | | | | | | |
| Constipation | ● | | ● | ● | | ● | ● | ● | | | ● | ● | ● | | | ● | ● | | | ● | | | ● | ● | | | ● | | | ● | ● | ● | | |
| Conjunctivitis | | | ● | ● | | | ● | ● | | | | ● | ● | | | ● | ● | | | ● | | | | ● | | | ● | | | | | ● | | |
| Colitis | ● | | ● | ● | | | ● | ● | | | ● | ● | ● | | | ● | ● | | | ● | | | | ● | | | ● | | | | | | ● | |
| Colic | | | ● | ● | | | ● | ● | ● | | ● | ● | ● | | | ● | ● | | | ● | | | | ● | ● | | ● | | | | | ● | | |
| Colds | | | ● | ● | | ● | ● | ● | | | | ● | ● | | | ● | ● | | | ● | | | | ● | | | ● | | | | | ● | | ● |
| Cold Sores | | | ● | ● | | | ● | ● | | | | ● | ● | | | ● | ● | | | ● | | | | ● | | | ● | | | | | | | |
| Circulation Problems | ● | | ● | ● | | ● | ● | ● | ● | | | ● | ● | | ● | ● | ● | ● | ● | ● | | | | ● | ● | | ● | | | ● | ● | ● | | |
| Cerebral Palsy | | | | | | | | | | | | | | | | | | | | | | | | | | | | | | | | | | |
| Catarrh | | | ● | ● | | ● | ● | ● | | | | ● | ● | | ● | ● | ● | | | ● | | | | ● | | | ● | | | | | ● | | ● |
| Cataracts | | | ● | ● | | | ● | | | | | ● | ● | | | | ● | | | ● | | | | | | | ● | | | | | ● | | |
| Cancers | | | ● | | | | ● | ● | | | ● | ● | ● | | | ● | ● | | | ● | | | | ● | | | ● | | | | | | | |
| Callices | | | ● | | | | ● | | | ● | | ● | ● | | | | ● | | | ● | ● | | | | | | ● | | | | | | | |
| Bursitis | | | ● | | | ● | ● | | | | | ● | ● | ● | | ● | ● | | | ● | | | | ● | | | ● | | | | | | | |
| Bunions | | | | | | | | | | | | | | | | | | | | | | | | | | | | | | | | | | |
| Bulimia | ● | | ● | | | | ● | ● | | | | ● | ● | | | | ● | | | ● | | | | ● | | | ● | | | | | | | |
| Bruising | ● | ● | ● | ● | | ● | ● | | | | | ● | ● | | | | ● | | | ● | | | | ● | | | ● | | | | | | | |
| Bronchitis | ● | | ● | ● | | ● | ● | ● | | | | ● | ● | | | ● | ● | | | ● | | | | ● | | | ● | | | | | ● | | |
| Breathing Problems | ● | | ● | ● | | ● | ● | ● | | | | ● | ● | ● | | ● | ● | | | ● | | | | | | | ● | | | ● | ● | ● | | |
| Breast Problems | | | ● | ● | | | ● | ● | | | | ● | ● | | | | ● | | | ● | | | | | | | ● | | | | | ● | | |
| Bowel Problems | ● | | ● | ● | | ● | ● | ● | | | ● | ● | ● | | | ● | ● | | | ● | | | | ● | | | ● | | | ● | ● | ● | ● | |
| Boils | | | ● | | | | ● | ● | | | | ● | ● | | | ● | ● | | | ● | | | | ● | | | ● | | | | | ● | | |
| Blood Pressure | ● | | ● | ● | | ● | ● | ● | | | | ● | ● | | | ● | ● | | ● | ● | | | | ● | ● | | ● | | | ● | ● | | | |
| Bladder Problems | ● | | ● | ● | | | ● | ● | | | | ● | ● | | | ● | ● | | | ● | | | | ● | | | ● | | | | | ● | | |
| Bereavement | | | | | | | | | | | | | | | | | | | | | | | | | | | | | | | | | | |
| Baldness | | | ● | | | | ● | | | | | ● | ● | | | | ● | | | ● | | | | | | | ● | | | | | | | |
| Bacterial Infections | | | ● | ● | | | ● | | | | | ● | ● | | | ● | ● | | | ● | | | | ● | | | ● | | | | | | ● | |
| Back Pain | ● | ● | ● | ● | | ● | ● | ● | ● | | ● | ● | ● | ● | ● | | ● | ● | ● | ● | | | | ● | ● | | ● | | ● | ● | ● | ● | | |
| Autism | | | ● | ● | | | ● | | | | | ● | ● | | | | ● | | | ● | | | | ● | | | ● | | | | | | ● | |
| Athletes Foot | | | ● | | | ● | ● | | ● | ● | | ● | ● | | | ● | ● | | | ● | ● | ● | | ● | | ● | ● | | | | | ● | | |
| Asthma | ● | | ● | ● | | ● | ● | ● | ● | | | ● | ● | ● | | ● | ● | | | ● | | | ● | ● | | | ● | | | | | ● | | |
| Arthritis | ● | ● | ● | ● | | ● | ● | ● | ● | | ● | ● | ● | ● | ● | ● | ● | ● | ● | ● | | | ● | ● | ● | | ● | | ● | | | ● | | ● |
| Anxiety | ● | | ● | ● | ● | ● | ● | ● | ● | | | ● | ● | | | ● | ● | | | ● | | | | ● | | | ● | | | ● | ● | ● | | ● |
| Anorexia | ● | | ● | | | | ● | ● | | | | ● | ● | | | | ● | | | ● | | | | ● | | | ● | | | | | ● | | |
| Angina | ● | | ● | ● | | | ● | ● | | | | ● | ● | | | ● | ● | | | ● | | | | ● | | | ● | | | | | | | |
| Anaemia | ● | | ● | ● | | | ● | ● | ● | | | ● | ● | | | | ● | | | ● | | | | ● | | | ● | | | | | | | |
| Amnesia | | | ● | | | | ● | | | | | ● | ● | | | | ● | | | ● | | | | ● | | | ● | | | | | | | |
| Alzheimer's Disease | | | ● | ● | | | ● | | | | | ● | ● | | | | ● | | | ● | | | | ● | | | ● | | | | | | | |
| Allergy | ● | | ● | ● | | | ● | ● | ● | | ● | ● | ● | ● | | ● | ● | | | ● | | | ● | ● | | | ● | | | | | ● | ● | |
| Alcoholism | | | ● | ● | | ● | ● | | | | | ● | ● | | | ● | ● | | | ● | | | | | | | ● | | | | | | | |
| Aids | | | ● | | | | ● | ● | | | | ● | ● | | | | ● | | | ● | | | | | | | ● | | | | | | | |
| Adenoids | | | ● | | | | ● | | ● | | | ● | ● | | | | ● | | | ● | | | | | | | ● | | | | | ● | | |
| Addiction | ● | | ● | ● | | ● | ● | ● | ● | | | ● | ● | | | | ● | | | ● | | | | ● | | | ● | | | | | | | |
| Acne | ● | | ● | ● | | | ● | ● | ● | | | ● | ● | | | ● | ● | | | ● | | | | ● | | | ● | | | | | ● | | |

# A - C Conditions treated at Practices/Businesses

Business by County with Reference no.

| Condition | ASHBY & ASSOCIATES (HM01194) | AVART, GILLIAN (HM01383) | BARKING PHYSICAL THERAPY CTRE (HM01715) | BAXTER, LISA (HM01929) | BENEDICTA (HM02125) | BE-WELL CLINIC (HM02251) | BODY BALANCE HEALTH SOLUTIONS (HM02571) | BRENTWOOD CHIROPODY SURGERY (HM02963) | BRITISH INSTITUTE-HYPNOTHERAPY (HM03085) | BURNHAM PHYSIOTHERAPY CLINIC (HM03405) | CAIN, SHEILA (HM03538) | CATON, PETER (HM03859) | CHAKRA ROSE (HM03942) | CHRIS MOSLIN HYPNOTHERAPIST (HM04433) | CLACTON CHIROPRACTIC CLINIC (HM04501) | CLARKE, M R (HM04593) | COKER, EILEEN (HM04800) |
|---|---|---|---|---|---|---|---|---|---|---|---|---|---|---|---|---|---|
| Cystitis | | ● | | ● | | | | | | | ● | | | | | | ● |
| Cramp | | | ● | ● | | | | | | | ● | | | | | | ● |
| Coughs | | ● | | ● | | | | | | | ● | | | | | | ● |
| Corns | ● | ● | | | | | ● | ● | | | | | | | | | |
| Convulsions | | | | | | | | | | | | | | | | | |
| Constipation | | ● | | ● | | | | | | | ● | | ● | | | | ● |
| Conjunctivitis | | | | | | | | | | | | | | | | | |
| Colitis | | | | | | | | | | | ● | | | | | | ● |
| Colic | | ● | | | | | | | | | ● | | | | | | ● |
| Colds | | | | ● | ● | | | | | | ● | | | | | | ● |
| Cold Sores | | ● | | ● | ● | | | | | | ● | | ● | | | | ● |
| Circulation Problems | | ● | | ● | ● | | | | | | ● | | ● | | ● | | ● |
| Cerebral Palsy | | | | | | | | | | | | | | | | | |
| Catarrh | | ● | | ● | ● | | | | | | ● | | | | | | |
| Cataracts | | | | | | | | | | | | | | | | | |
| Cancers | | | | | | | | | | | ● | | ● | | | | |
| Callices | ● | | | | | | ● | ● | | | | | | | | | |
| Bursitis | | | | | | | | | | | | | | | | | ● |
| Bunions | | | | | | | | | | | | | | | | | |
| Bulimia | | | | | | | | | | | | | | | | | ● |
| Bruising | | ● | ● | | | | | | | | ● | | | | | | ● |
| Bronchitis | | ● | | | | | | | | | ● | | | | | | ● |
| Breathing Problems | | ● | | ● | | | | | | | ● | | | ● | | | ● |
| Breast Problems | | | | | | | | | | | ● | | | | | | ● |
| Bowel Problems | | | | ● | | | | | | | ● | | ● | ● | | | ● |
| Boils | | | | | | | | | | | | | | | | | ● |
| Blood Pressure | | ● | | ● | ● | | | | | | ● | | | | | | ● |
| Bladder Problems | | | | ● | | | | | | | ● | | | | | | ● |
| Bereavement | | | | | | | | | | | | | | | | | |
| Baldness | | | | | | | | | | | | | | | | | ● |
| Bacterial Infections | | ● | | ● | | | | | | | | | | | | | ● |
| Back Pain | | ● | ● | ● | ● | | ● | | | ● | ● | | | | ● | ● | ● |
| Autism | | | | | | | | | | | | | | | | | ● |
| Athletes Foot | ● | ● | | ● | | | ● | ● | | | | | | | | | ● |
| Asthma | | ● | | ● | ● | | | | | | ● | | ● | ● | | | ● |
| Arthritis | | ● | ● | ● | ● | | ● | | | | ● | | ● | | ● | | ● |
| Anxiety | | ● | | ● | ● | | | | ● | | | ● | ● | ● | | | ● |
| Anorexia | | | | | | | | | ● | | ● | | | | | | |
| Angina | | | | | | | | | | | ● | | | | | | |
| Anaemia | | | | | | | | | | | | | | | | | |
| Amnesia | | | | | | | | | | | | | | | | | |
| Alzheimer's Disease | | | | | | | | | | | | | ● | | | | |
| Allergy | | | | ● | | ● | | | | | ● | | ● | | | | |
| Alcoholism | | | | | | | | | ● | | | ● | ● | ● | | | |
| Aids | | | | | | | | | | | | | | | | | |
| Adenoids | | | | ● | | | | | | | | | | | | | |
| Addiction | | | | ● | | | | | ● | | | ● | | ● | | | |
| Acne | | ● | | ● | | | | | | | | | | ● | | | |

| Condition | COMPLETE CHIROPRACTIC (HM04957) | COOK, JOE (HM05048) | COOPER, FELICITY (HM05104) | CROSS HANDS CHIRO CLINIC (HM05479) | CROWN CHIROPRACTIC CLINIC (HM05508) | CROWN CHIROPRACTIC CLINIC (HM05507) | DICKASON, J T (HM06067) | E A O C (HM06465) | EDWARDS, G E (HM06651) | EDWARDS, G E (HM06652) | ELMER CHIROPODY & PODIATRY SVS (HM06781) | EPPING OSTEOPATHY AND SPORTS (HM06854) | EPPING PHYSIOTHERAPY PRACTICE (HM06855) | ESSEX PHYSIO & SPORTS INJ CTRE (HM06938) | FARROW, VICKI (HM07135) | FLEUROMA (HM07418) | FOOT HEALTH CLINIC (HM07482) |
|---|---|---|---|---|---|---|---|---|---|---|---|---|---|---|---|---|---|
| Cystitis | | | | | | | | | | | | | | | | | |
| Cramp | | | | | | | | | | | | | ● | ● | | | ● |
| Coughs | | | | | | | | | | | | | | | | | |
| Corns | | | | | | | | | ● | ● | ● | | | | | | |
| Convulsions | | | | | | | | | | | | | | | | | |
| Constipation | | ● | | | | | | | | | | | | | ● | | |
| Conjunctivitis | | | | | | | | | | | | | | | | | |
| Colitis | | | | | | | | | | | | | | | | | |
| Colic | | | | | | | | | | | | | | | | ● | |
| Colds | | | | | | | | | | | | | | | | | |
| Cold Sores | | | | | | | | | | | | | | | | | |
| Circulation Problems | ● | | | | | | | ● | | | | | | ● | ● | ● | |
| Cerebral Palsy | | | | | | | | | | | | | | | | | |
| Catarrh | | | | | | | | | | | | | | | | | |
| Cataracts | | | | | | | | | | | | | | | | | |
| Cancers | | | | | | | | | | | | | | | ● | | |
| Callices | | | | | | | | | ● | ● | ● | | | | | | |
| Bursitis | | | | | | | | ● | | | | ● | | | | | |
| Bunions | | | | | | | | | ● | ● | | | | | | | |
| Bulimia | | ● | | | | | | | | | | | | | | | |
| Bruising | | | | | | | | | | | | | | ● | | | |
| Bronchitis | | | | | | | | | | | | | | | | ● | |
| Breathing Problems | | | | | | | | | | | | | | | | ● | |
| Breast Problems | | | | | | | | | | | | | | | | | |
| Bowel Problems | | | | | | | | | | | | | | | | ● | |
| Boils | | | | | | | | | | | | | | | | | |
| Blood Pressure | | ● | | | ● | ● | | ● | | | | | | | | | |
| Bladder Problems | | | | | | | | | | | | | | | | | |
| Bereavement | | | | | | | | | | | | | | | | | |
| Baldness | | | | | | | | | | | | | | | | | |
| Bacterial Infections | | | | | | | | | | | | | | | | | |
| Back Pain | ● | | | ● | ● | ● | ● | ● | | | | ● | | ● | ● | ● | ● |
| Autism | | | | | | | | | | | | | | | | | |
| Athletes Foot | | | ● | | | | | | ● | ● | ● | | | | | | ● |
| Asthma | | ● | | | | | | | | | | ● | ● | | | ● | |
| Arthritis | ● | ● | ● | ● | ● | ● | ● | | ● | ● | ● | ● | ● | ● | ● | ● | |
| Anxiety | | ● | | | | | | | | | | | | | ● | ● | |
| Anorexia | | ● | | | | | | | | | | | | | | | |
| Angina | | | | | | | | | | | | | | | | | |
| Anaemia | | | | | | | | | | | | | | | | | |
| Amnesia | | | | | | | | | | | | | | | | | |
| Alzheimer's Disease | | | | | | | | | | | | | | | | | |
| Allergy | | | | | | | | | | | | | | | | | |
| Alcoholism | | ● | | | | | | | | | | | | | | | |
| Aids | | | | | | | | | | | | | | | ● | | |
| Adenoids | | | | | | | | | | | | | | | | | |
| Addiction | | ● | | | | | | | | | | | | | ● | | |
| Acne | | | | | | | | | | | | | | | | ● | |

# A - C Conditions treated at Practices/Businesses

Business by County with Reference no.

| Business by County with Reference no. | Acne | Addiction | Adenoids | Aids | Alcoholism | Allergy | Alzheimer's Disease | Amnesia | Anaemia | Angina | Anorexia | Anxiety |
|---|---|---|---|---|---|---|---|---|---|---|---|---|
| FOULKES, GEOFFREY LLOYD (HM07609) | ● | ● | ● | ● | ● | ● | ● | ● | ● | ● | ● | ● |
| FROST, JANICE (HM07761) | ● | ● | ● | | | ● | | | | | | ● |
| FULTON, A J (HM07796) | | | | | | | | | | | | |
| FULTON, A J (HM07795) | | | | | | | | | | | | |
| GENT, WENDY (HM07973) | | | | | | | | | | | | ● |
| GRAY, P A (HM08417) | | | | | | | | | | | | |
| HADLEIGH PODIATRY CLINIC (HM08695) | | | | | | | | | | | | |
| HARLOW OSTEOPATHIC PRACTICE (HM09011) | | | | | | | | | | | | |
| HEALING ROOM (HM09349) | | | | | | | | | | | | |
| HYPNOTHERAPY & PSYCHO CONS (HM10508) | | | | | | | | | | | | ● |
| HYPNOTHERAPY CENTRE (HM10532) | | ● | | | | | | | | | | ● |
| HYPNOTHERAPY CENTRE (HM10530) | | ● | | | | | | | | | | ● |
| ISIS HOUSE THERAPY CENTRE (HM10768) | | | | | | | | | | | | ● |
| JACKSON, CYRIL (HM10832) | | | | | | | | | | | | ● |
| JOYNES, IAN (HM11239) | | | | | | | | | | | | |
| KELLY, GILLIAN (HM11431) | | | | | | ● | | | | | | ● |
| LAING, RICHARD (DR) (HM11866) | ● | | ● | | | ● | | | ● | ● | | ● |
| LA-SANTE AROMATHERAPY (HM11981) | | | | | | | | | | | | |
| LEIGH, MARTIN (HM12189) | | | | | | | | | | ● | | ● |
| LEVY, PAUL (HM12269) | | | | | | | | | | | | |
| LINGWOOD CLINIC (HM12435) | | | | | | ● | | | | | | ● |
| LONDON ROAD PHYSIO PRACTICE (HM12603) | | | | | | | | | | | | |
| MARTIN, LEIGH (HM13202) | | | | | | | | | | ● | | ● |
| MEDELY CLINIC (HM13647) | | | | | | | | | | | | ● |
| MILES, C J (HM13855) | | | | | | | | | | | | |
| MOONSTONE HEALING CENTRE (HM14111) | | | | | | | | | | ● | ● | ● |
| MOORE, SUSAN (HM14134) | | | | | | | | | | | | |
| MOUCHET, F (HM14282) | | | | | | | | | | | | ● |
| NATURAL REMEDY CENTRE (HM14620) | ● | ● | | | | ● | | | ● | ● | ● | ● |
| PALMER, DAVID J (HM15600) | | | | | | ● | | | | | | ● |
| PARVEZ, SHAUKAT (HM15771) | ● | ● | | | | | | | | | | ● |
| PEPPER, SUSAN (HM16010) | | | | | | | | | | | | |
| PHARMACARE (HM16109) | ● | | ● | | ● | ● | ● | ● | ● | ● | ● | ● |
| PHYSIO & SPORTS INJURY CLINIC (HM16186) | | | | | | | | | | | | |

| Business by County with Reference no. | Arthritis | Asthma | Athletes Foot | Autism | Back Pain | Bacterial Infections | Baldness | Bereavement | Bladder Problems | Blood Pressure | Boils | Bowel Problems |
|---|---|---|---|---|---|---|---|---|---|---|---|---|
| FOULKES, GEOFFREY LLOYD (HM07609) | ● | ● | ● | ● | ● | ● | ● | | ● | ● | ● | ● |
| FROST, JANICE (HM07761) | ● | ● | ● | | ● | | | | ● | ● | ● | ● |
| FULTON, A J (HM07796) | | | ● | | | ● | | | | | | |
| FULTON, A J (HM07795) | | | ● | | | ● | | | | | | |
| GENT, WENDY (HM07973) | | | | | ● | | | | | | | |
| GRAY, P A (HM08417) | | | ● | | | | | | | | | |
| HADLEIGH PODIATRY CLINIC (HM08695) | ● | | ● | | | ● | | | | | | |
| HARLOW OSTEOPATHIC PRACTICE (HM09011) | ● | | | | ● | | | | | | | |
| HEALING ROOM (HM09349) | ● | | | | ● | | | | | | | ● |
| HYPNOTHERAPY & PSYCHO CONS (HM10508) | | | | | | | | | | | | |
| HYPNOTHERAPY CENTRE (HM10532) | | | | | | | | | | | | |
| HYPNOTHERAPY CENTRE (HM10530) | | | | | | | | | | | | |
| ISIS HOUSE THERAPY CENTRE (HM10768) | | | | | ● | | | | | ● | | |
| JACKSON, CYRIL (HM10832) | | | | | | | | | | | | |
| JOYNES, IAN (HM11239) | | | ● | | | | | | | | | |
| KELLY, GILLIAN (HM11431) | ● | ● | | | ● | | | | | | | |
| LAING, RICHARD (DR) (HM11866) | ● | ● | ● | ● | ● | ● | | | ● | ● | ● | ● |
| LA-SANTE AROMATHERAPY (HM11981) | ● | | | | | | | | | | | |
| LEIGH, MARTIN (HM12189) | | | | ● | ● | | | | | | | |
| LEVY, PAUL (HM12269) | | | ● | | | | | | | | | |
| LINGWOOD CLINIC (HM12435) | ● | ● | | | ● | | | | | | | |
| LONDON ROAD PHYSIO PRACTICE (HM12603) | ● | | | | ● | | | | | | | |
| MARTIN, LEIGH (HM13202) | | | | | ● | | | | | | | |
| MEDELY CLINIC (HM13647) | | | | | ● | | | | | | | |
| MILES, C J (HM13855) | | | ● | | | ● | | | | | | |
| MOONSTONE HEALING CENTRE (HM14111) | ● | ● | | | ● | | | | | ● | | ● |
| MOORE, SUSAN (HM14134) | | | ● | | ● | | | | | | | |
| MOUCHET, F (HM14282) | | | | | | | | | | | | |
| NATURAL REMEDY CENTRE (HM14620) | ● | ● | ● | ● | ● | ● | ● | | ● | ● | ● | ● |
| PALMER, DAVID J (HM15600) | | ● | | | ● | | | | | | | ● |
| PARVEZ, SHAUKAT (HM15771) | ● | ● | ● | ● | ● | | | | ● | ● | ● | ● |
| PEPPER, SUSAN (HM16010) | | | | | ● | | | | | | | |
| PHARMACARE (HM16109) | ● | ● | ● | | ● | ● | ● | | ● | ● | ● | ● |
| PHYSIO & SPORTS INJURY CLINIC (HM16186) | ● | | | | ● | | | | ● | | | |

| Business by County with Reference no. | Breast Problems | Breathing Problems | Bronchitis | Bruising | Bulimia | Bunions | Bursitis | Callices | Cancers | Cataracts | Catarrh | Cerebral Palsy |
|---|---|---|---|---|---|---|---|---|---|---|---|---|
| FOULKES, GEOFFREY LLOYD (HM07609) | ● | ● | ● | ● | ● | | ● | | | ● | ● | |
| FROST, JANICE (HM07761) | ● | ● | ● | ● | | | ● | ● | | | ● | |
| FULTON, A J (HM07796) | | | | | | ● | | ● | | | | |
| FULTON, A J (HM07795) | | | | | | ● | | ● | | | | |
| GENT, WENDY (HM07973) | | ● | | | | | | | | | | |
| GRAY, P A (HM08417) | | | | | | | | ● | | | | |
| HADLEIGH PODIATRY CLINIC (HM08695) | | | | | | | | ● | | | | |
| HARLOW OSTEOPATHIC PRACTICE (HM09011) | | | | | | | ● | | | | | |
| HEALING ROOM (HM09349) | | | | | | | | | | | ● | |
| HYPNOTHERAPY & PSYCHO CONS (HM10508) | | | | | | | | | | | | |
| HYPNOTHERAPY CENTRE (HM10532) | | | | | | | | | | | | |
| HYPNOTHERAPY CENTRE (HM10530) | | | | | | | | | | | | |
| ISIS HOUSE THERAPY CENTRE (HM10768) | | | | | | | | | | | | |
| JACKSON, CYRIL (HM10832) | | | | | | | | | | | | |
| JOYNES, IAN (HM11239) | | | | | | | | | | | | |
| KELLY, GILLIAN (HM11431) | | | | ● | | | | | | | | |
| LAING, RICHARD (DR) (HM11866) | ● | ● | ● | ● | | | ● | | | | ● | |
| LA-SANTE AROMATHERAPY (HM11981) | | | | | | | | | | | | |
| LEIGH, MARTIN (HM12189) | | | | | | | | | | | | |
| LEVY, PAUL (HM12269) | | | | | | | | ● | | | | |
| LINGWOOD CLINIC (HM12435) | | | | | | | | | | | | |
| LONDON ROAD PHYSIO PRACTICE (HM12603) | | | | ● | | | | ● | | | | |
| MARTIN, LEIGH (HM13202) | | | | | | | | | | | | |
| MEDELY CLINIC (HM13647) | | | | | | | | | | | | |
| MILES, C J (HM13855) | | | | | | ● | | ● | | | | |
| MOONSTONE HEALING CENTRE (HM14111) | | ● | ● | ● | ● | | | | ● | | ● | |
| MOORE, SUSAN (HM14134) | | | | | | | | | | | | |
| MOUCHET, F (HM14282) | | | | | | | | | | | | |
| NATURAL REMEDY CENTRE (HM14620) | ● | ● | ● | ● | ● | | ● | | ● | | ● | |
| PALMER, DAVID J (HM15600) | ● | | | ● | | | | | | | | |
| PARVEZ, SHAUKAT (HM15771) | ● | ● | ● | ● | ● | | ● | | ● | | | |
| PEPPER, SUSAN (HM16010) | | ● | | | | | | | | | | |
| PHARMACARE (HM16109) | ● | ● | ● | ● | | | ● | | ● | ● | ● | |
| PHYSIO & SPORTS INJURY CLINIC (HM16186) | | | | ● | | | | | | | | |

| Business by County with Reference no. | Circulation Problems | Cold Sores | Colds | Colic | Colitis | Conjunctivitis | Constipation | Convulsions | Corns | Coughs | Cramp | Cystitis |
|---|---|---|---|---|---|---|---|---|---|---|---|---|
| FOULKES, GEOFFREY LLOYD (HM07609) | ● | ● | ● | ● | ● | ● | ● | ● | | ● | ● | ● |
| FROST, JANICE (HM07761) | ● | ● | ● | ● | ● | ● | ● | ● | ● | ● | ● | ● |
| FULTON, A J (HM07796) | | | | | | | | | ● | | | |
| FULTON, A J (HM07795) | | | | | | | | | ● | | | |
| GENT, WENDY (HM07973) | | | | | | | | | | | | |
| GRAY, P A (HM08417) | | | | | | | | | ● | | | |
| HADLEIGH PODIATRY CLINIC (HM08695) | | | | | | | | | ● | | | |
| HARLOW OSTEOPATHIC PRACTICE (HM09011) | | | | | | | | | | | ● | |
| HEALING ROOM (HM09349) | | | ● | | | | ● | | | ● | | |
| HYPNOTHERAPY & PSYCHO CONS (HM10508) | | | | | | | | | | | | |
| HYPNOTHERAPY CENTRE (HM10532) | | | | | | | | | | | | |
| HYPNOTHERAPY CENTRE (HM10530) | | | | | | | | | | | | |
| ISIS HOUSE THERAPY CENTRE (HM10768) | | | | | | | | | | | | |
| JACKSON, CYRIL (HM10832) | | | | | | | | | | | | |
| JOYNES, IAN (HM11239) | | | | | | | | | | | | |
| KELLY, GILLIAN (HM11431) | | | ● | | | | ● | | | ● | | ● |
| LAING, RICHARD (DR) (HM11866) | ● | ● | ● | ● | ● | ● | ● | ● | | ● | ● | ● |
| LA-SANTE AROMATHERAPY (HM11981) | | | | | | | | | | | | |
| LEIGH, MARTIN (HM12189) | ● | | | ● | | | ● | | | | ● | |
| LEVY, PAUL (HM12269) | | | | | | | | | ● | | | |
| LINGWOOD CLINIC (HM12435) | ● | | | ● | | | | | | | | |
| LONDON ROAD PHYSIO PRACTICE (HM12603) | | | | | | | | | ● | | ● | |
| MARTIN, LEIGH (HM13202) | ● | | | ● | | | ● | | | | ● | |
| MEDELY CLINIC (HM13647) | ● | | | | | | | | | | | |
| MILES, C J (HM13855) | | | | | | | | | ● | | | |
| MOONSTONE HEALING CENTRE (HM14111) | ● | | | | ● | | ● | | | ● | ● | ● |
| MOORE, SUSAN (HM14134) | ● | | | | | | | | | | | |
| MOUCHET, F (HM14282) | | | | | | | | | | | | |
| NATURAL REMEDY CENTRE (HM14620) | ● | ● | ● | ● | ● | ● | ● | ● | | ● | ● | ● |
| PALMER, DAVID J (HM15600) | ● | | | | | | | | | | | |
| PARVEZ, SHAUKAT (HM15771) | ● | ● | ● | ● | ● | ● | ● | ● | | ● | ● | ● |
| PEPPER, SUSAN (HM16010) | | | | | | | | | | | | |
| PHARMACARE (HM16109) | ● | ● | ● | ● | ● | ● | ● | ● | | ● | ● | ● |
| PHYSIO & SPORTS INJURY CLINIC (HM16186) | | | | | | | | | | | ● | |

# A - C Conditions treated at Practices/Businesses

| Business by County with Reference no. | Acne | Addiction | Adenoids | Aids | Alcoholism | Allergy | Alzheimer's Disease | Amnesia | Anaemia | Angina | Anorexia | Anxiety | Arthritis | Asthma | Athletes Foot | Autism | Back Pain | Bacterial Infections | Baldness | Bereavement | Bladder Problems | Blood Pressure | Boils | Bowel Problems |
|---|---|---|---|---|---|---|---|---|---|---|---|---|---|---|---|---|---|---|---|---|---|---|---|---|
| PINEWOOD PHYSIOTHERAPY CLINIC (HM16313) | | | | | | | ● | | | | | | ● | | | | ● | | | | | | | |
| PISCES NATURAL THERAPY CENTRE (HM16330) | | | | | | | | | | | | ● | | | | | | | | | | | | |
| PRICE, G J (HM16572) | ● | | | | | | | | | | | ● | ● | ● | | | ● | | | | ● | ● | ● | ● |
| PRIVATE HEALTH CENTRE CLINIC (HM16643) | ● | ● | ● | ● | ● | ● | ● | ● | ● | ● | ● | ● | ● | ● | ● | ● | ● | ● | ● | | ● | ● | ● | ● |
| REFLEXOLOGY CLINIC (HM17088) | | ● | | | | ● | | | | | | ● | ● | ● | | | ● | | | | ● | ● | | ● |
| ROBINSON, DAVID (HM17466) | | ● | | | | | | | | | | ● | | | | | | | | | | | | |
| SANDERS, G (HM17909) | | | | | | | | | | | | | ● | | ● | | | ● | | | | | | |
| SCOTT, MARY (HM18124) | ● | ● | ● | ● | ● | ● | ● | ● | ● | ● | ● | ● | ● | ● | ● | ● | ● | ● | ● | | ● | ● | ● | ● |
| SELF AWARENESS HEALING (HM18204) | | ● | | | | | | | | | | ● | | | | | | | | | | | | |
| SELVES, KATIE (HM18222) | ● | | | | | ● | | | | ● | ● | ● | ● | ● | ● | | | ● | | | ● | ● | ● | ● |
| SEYMOUR, LOUISE (HM18259) | | | | | | | | | | | | | | | ● | | | | | | | | | |
| SHELDON, PEGGY (HM18380) | | | | | | ● | | | | | | ● | | | | | | | | | ● | ● | | ● |
| SOUTH, JO (HM18918) | ● | ● | ● | ● | ● | ● | ● | ● | ● | ● | ● | ● | ● | ● | ● | ● | ● | ● | ● | | ● | ● | ● | ● |
| TRINITY CENTRE (HM20338) | ● | ● | ● | ● | ● | ● | ● | ● | ● | ● | ● | ● | ● | ● | ● | ● | ● | ● | ● | | ● | ● | ● | ● |
| WADDINGTON, R M (HM20726) | | | | | | | | | | | | | ● | | ● | | | ● | | | | | | |
| WAYNE-WRIGHT, M S (HM21043) | | | | | | | | | | | | | | | ● | | | | | | | | | |
| WELLS HYPNOTHERAPY CLINIC (HM21167) | | | | | | | | | | | | ● | | | | | | | | | | | | |
| WENTWORTH HEALTH CLINIC (HM21201) | ● | | | | | | | | | | | ● | ● | ● | | ● | ● | | | | | ● | | |
| WETHERALL, STUART (HM21289) | | | | | | | | | | | | ● | | | | | | | | | | | | |
| WHEELER, M A (HM21316) | | | | | | | | | | | | ● | ● | | ● | | ● | | | | | ● | | |
| WHEELER, M A (HM21317) | | | | | | | | | | | | | ● | | ● | | | | | | | | | |
| WHITE WATER HEALING CENTRE (HM21345) | | ● | | ● | | | | | | | | ● | | | | | ● | | | | | | | |
| WOODSIDE NATURAL HEALTH (HM21859) | | ● | | | | | | | | | | ● | ● | ● | | | ● | | | | | | | |
| GLOUCESTERSHIRE | | | | | | | | | | | | | | | | | | | | | | | | |
| ACUPUNCTURE CLINIC (HM00262) | | | | | | ● | | | | | ● | ● | ● | ● | | | ● | | | | ● | ● | | ● |
| ADAMS, PETER (HM00360) | ● | ● | ● | ● | ● | ● | | ● | ● | ● | ● | ● | ● | ● | ● | ● | ● | ● | ● | | ● | ● | ● | ● |
| AGASCAR, ROBIN (HM00416) | | | | | | | | | | | | ● | | | | | | | | | | | | |
| ARTICHOKE NATURAL HEALTH (HM01168) | ● | ● | | | | ● | | | ● | | | ● | ● | ● | ● | ● | ● | | | | ● | ● | ● | ● |
| BISHOPS CLEEVE PHYSIO & SPORTS (HM02413) | | | | | | | | | | | | | ● | | | | ● | | | | | | | |
| BUNTON, LYNN (HM03354) | | ● | | | ● | ● | | | | | | | ● | ● | | | ● | | | | | ● | | ● |
| BURKE, JAYNE (HM03388) | | | | | | | | | | | | ● | ● | ● | | | ● | | | | | ● | | ● |
| CHELTENHAM HOLISTIC HLTH CTRE (HM04094) | ● | ● | ● | ● | ● | ● | ● | ● | ● | ● | ● | ● | ● | ● | ● | ● | ● | ● | ● | | ● | ● | ● | ● |
| CHELTENHAM HYPNOTHERAPY (HM04096) | | ● | | | | ● | | ● | | | | ● | | ● | | | | | | | | | | |
| CHELTENHAM PHYSIO/SPRTS CLNC (HM04097) | | | | | | | | | | | | | ● | | | | ● | | | | | | | |

| Business by County with Reference no. | Breast Problems | Breathing Problems | Bronchitis | Bruising | Bulimia | Bunions | Bursitis | Callices | Cancers | Cataracts | Catarrh | Cerebral Palsy | Circulation Problems | Cold Sores | Colds | Colic | Colitis | Conjunctivitis | Constipation | Convulsions | Corns | Coughs | Cramp | Cystitis |
|---|---|---|---|---|---|---|---|---|---|---|---|---|---|---|---|---|---|---|---|---|---|---|---|---|
| PINEWOOD PHYSIOTHERAPY CLINIC (HM16313) | | | | ● | | | ● | | | | | | ● | | | | | | | | | | | |
| PISCES NATURAL THERAPY CENTRE (HM16330) | | | | | | | | | | | | | | | | | | | | | | | | |
| PRICE, G J (HM16572) | | ● | ● | ● | | | | | | | ● | | ● | ● | ● | ● | ● | | ● | | | | ● | ● |
| PRIVATE HEALTH CENTRE CLINIC (HM16643) | ● | ● | ● | ● | ● | | ● | ● | ● | ● | ● | | ● | ● | ● | ● | ● | ● | ● | ● | ● | ● | ● | ● |
| REFLEXOLOGY CLINIC (HM17088) | | ● | | | | | ● | | | | | | ● | | | | ● | | ● | | | | ● | ● |
| ROBINSON, DAVID (HM17466) | | | | | | | | | | | | | | | | | | | | | | | | |
| SANDERS, G (HM17909) | | | | | | ● | | ● | | | | | | | | | | | | | ● | | | |
| SCOTT, MARY (HM18124) | ● | ● | ● | ● | ● | | ● | ● | ● | ● | ● | | ● | ● | ● | ● | ● | ● | ● | ● | ● | ● | ● | ● |
| SELF AWARENESS HEALING (HM18204) | | | | | | | | | | | | | | | | | | | | | | | | |
| SELVES, KATIE (HM18222) | ● | ● | ● | ● | ● | | ● | | ● | | ● | | ● | ● | ● | ● | ● | ● | | ● | | ● | ● | ● |
| SEYMOUR, LOUISE (HM18259) | | | | | | | | ● | | | | | | | | | | | | | ● | | | |
| SHELDON, PEGGY (HM18380) | ● | | | | | | | | | | | | ● | | | | | | ● | | | | | |
| SOUTH, JO (HM18918) | ● | ● | ● | ● | ● | | ● | | ● | ● | ● | | ● | ● | ● | ● | ● | ● | ● | ● | | ● | ● | ● |
| TRINITY CENTRE (HM20338) | ● | ● | ● | ● | ● | | ● | ● | | | ● | | ● | ● | ● | ● | ● | ● | ● | ● | ● | ● | ● | ● |
| WADDINGTON, R M (HM20726) | | | | | | ● | | ● | | | | | | | | | | | | | ● | | | |
| WAYNE-WRIGHT, M S (HM21043) | | | | | | | | ● | | | | | | | | | | | | | ● | | | |
| WELLS HYPNOTHERAPY CLINIC (HM21167) | | | | | | | | | | | | | | | | | | | | | | | | |
| WENTWORTH HEALTH CLINIC (HM21201) | | ● | | | | | | | | | | | ● | | | | | | ● | | | | | |
| WETHERALL, STUART (HM21289) | | | | | | | | | | | | | | | | | | | | | | | | |
| WHEELER, M A (HM21316) | | | | | | | | | | | | | ● | | | | | | | | | | ● | |
| WHEELER, M A (HM21317) | | | | | | | | ● | | | | | | | | | | | | | ● | | | |
| WHITE WATER HEALING CENTRE (HM21345) | | | ● | | | | | | ● | | | | | | | | | | | | | | | |
| WOODSIDE NATURAL HEALTH (HM21859) | | ● | ● | | | | | | | | ● | | ● | | ● | | | | ● | | | | | ● |
| GLOUCESTERSHIRE | | | | | | | | | | | | | | | | | | | | | | | | |
| ACUPUNCTURE CLINIC (HM00262) | | ● | ● | | | | | | | | ● | | ● | | | | ● | | ● | | | ● | | |
| ADAMS, PETER (HM00360) | ● | ● | ● | ● | ● | | ● | ● | ● | ● | ● | | ● | ● | ● | ● | ● | ● | ● | ● | ● | ● | ● | ● |
| AGASCAR, ROBIN (HM00416) | | | | | | | | | | | | | | | | | | | | | | | | |
| ARTICHOKE NATURAL HEALTH (HM01168) | ● | ● | ● | ● | ● | | | | | | ● | | ● | | | ● | | | ● | | | ● | | |
| BISHOPS CLEEVE PHYSIO & SPORTS (HM02413) | | | | | | | | | | | | | | | | | | | | | | | | |
| BUNTON, LYNN (HM03354) | | ● | ● | | | | | | | | | | | | | | | | | | | | | |
| BURKE, JAYNE (HM03388) | ● | ● | | | | | | | | | ● | | ● | | ● | | | | | | | | | |
| CHELTENHAM HOLISTIC HLTH CTRE (HM04094) | ● | ● | ● | ● | ● | | ● | ● | ● | ● | ● | | ● | ● | ● | ● | ● | ● | ● | ● | ● | ● | ● | ● |
| CHELTENHAM HYPNOTHERAPY (HM04096) | | | | | | | | | | | | | | | | | | | | | | | | |
| CHELTENHAM PHYSIO/SPRTS CLNC (HM04097) | | | | | | | | | | | | | | | | | | | | | | | | |

# A - C Conditions treated at Practices/Businesses

Business by County with Reference no.

| Business | Acne | Addiction | Adenoids | Aids | Alcoholism | Allergy | Alzheimer's Disease | Amnesia | Anaemia | Angina | Anorexia | Anxiety | Arthritis | Asthma | Athletes Foot | Autism | Back Pain | Bacterial Infections | Baldness | Bereavement | Bladder Problems | Blood Pressure | Boils | Bowel Problems |
|---|---|---|---|---|---|---|---|---|---|---|---|---|---|---|---|---|---|---|---|---|---|---|---|---|
| COMPLEMENTARY TOUCH (HM04950) | | | | | | ● | | | | | | ● | ● | | | | ● | | | | ● | ● | | ● |
| COOPER, ANGELA (HM05089) | | ● | | | | | | | | | | ● | | | | | | | | | | | | |
| COOPER, ANN (HM05090) | | | | | | | ● | | | | | | ● | ● | | | | | | | | | | ● |
| COTSWOLD PHYSIOTHERAPY CENTRE (HM05215) | | | | | | | | | | | | | ● | ● | | | ● | | | | | | | |
| ESSENTIAL BODYWORKS COMPANY (HM06899) | | | | | | | | | | | | | | | | | ● | | ● | | | ● | | |
| GREENWELL, DAVID (HM08498) | | ● | | | | | | | | | | ● | | ● | | | | | | | | ● | | ● |
| HYGEIA COLLEGE-COLOUR THERAPY (HM10476) | | | | | | | | | | | | | | | | | ● | | | | | | | |
| JOANNA SMITH AROMATHERAPY (HM11040) | | | | | | | | | | | | ● | ● | ● | | | ● | | | | | | | |
| LAWLER, R & G (HM12041) | | | | | | ● | | | | | | ● | ● | ● | | | ● | | | | | ● | | |
| LECKHAMPTON CHIROPRACTIC CLNC (HM12119) | | | | | | | | | | | | | ● | | | | ● | | | | | | | |
| MYERS, MERRILYN (HM14438) | | | | | | | | | | | | ● | | | | | | | | | | | | |
| NATURAL THERAPIES CLINIC (HM14633) | ● | ● | | | ● | ● | | ● | | ● | ● | ● | ● | ● | ● | ● | ● | | | | ● | ● | | ● |
| NATURAL THERAPY CENTRE (HM14649) | | | | | | ● | | | | | ● | ● | ● | ● | | ● | ● | | | | ● | ● | | ● |
| OLD CONVENT (HM15255) | | | | | | | | | | | | ● | ● | | | | ● | | | | | | | |
| OSTEOPATH (HM15445) | | | | | | | | | | | | | | | | | ● | | | | | | | |
| PENACHE (HM15960) | | | | | | | | | | | | ● | ● | | | | ● | | | | | | | |
| SHIATSU PRACTICE (HM18460) | | ● | | ● | ● | | | | | ● | ● | ● | ● | ● | | | ● | | | | ● | ● | | ● |
| SLATER, D C (HM18672) | | | | | | | | | | | | ● | | | | | | | | | | | | |
| SMYTH, DAVID (HM18830) | ● | ● | | | ● | ● | | | | ● | ● | ● | ● | ● | | ● | ● | ● | ● | | ● | ● | ● | ● |
| STOUT, HEATHER (HM19359) | ● | | | | | ● | | | | ● | | ● | ● | ● | | ● | ● | ● | | | ● | ● | ● | ● |
| STROUD NATURAL HEALTH CLINIC (HM19422) | ● | ● | ● | ● | ● | ● | ● | ● | ● | ● | ● | ● | ● | ● | ● | ● | ● | ● | ● | | ● | ● | ● | ● |
| TREE OF LIFE CENTRE (HM20307) | | | | | | | | | | | | ● | ● | ● | | | ● | | | | | ● | | |
| VILLAGE CLINIC (HM20665) | | | | | | | | | | | | | ● | | ● | | ● | ● | | | | | | |
| VINEY HALL PHYSIOTHERAPY (HM20683) | | | | | | | | | | | | | ● | | | | ● | | | | | | | |
| WELLS, GEORGINA (HM21172) | ● | | | | | | | | | | | ● | ● | | ● | | ● | ● | | | | ● | ● | ● |
| YOGA DRUVAM JIVAN YOGA SOCIETY (HM22024) | | | | | | | | | | | | | | | | | ● | | | | | ● | | |
| **HAMPSHIRE** | | | | | | | | | | | | | | | | | | | | | | | | |
| ACUPUNCTURE & PHYSIO CLINIC (HM00245) | ● | ● | | | ● | | | | | | | | ● | | | | | | | | | ● | | |
| ALL - HEAL ACU & HERB CENTRE (HM00581) | ● | ● | | | ● | ● | | | ● | ● | ● | ● | ● | ● | ● | | ● | ● | ● | | ● | ● | ● | ● |
| ALLERGY THERAPY (HM00637) | ● | ● | ● | ● | ● | ● | ● | ● | ● | ● | ● | ● | ● | ● | ● | ● | ● | ● | ● | | ● | ● | ● | ● |
| ARTEMIS (HM01156) | | ● | | | ● | | | | | | | | | | | | | | | | | | | |
| AVENUE CLINIC (HM01389) | | | | | | | | | | | | | ● | ● | | | ● | | | | ● | ● | | ● |
| BOLDICK, KATHLEEN (HM02652) | | | | | | | | | | | | ● | ● | | | | ● | | | | ● | | | |
| BRADFORD HOUSE CHIRO CLINIC (HM02849) | | | | | | | | | | | | | ● | | | | ● | | | | | | | |

| Business | Breast Problems | Breathing Problems | Bronchitis | Bruising | Bulimia | Bunions | Bursitis | Callices | Cancers | Cataracts | Catarrh | Cerebral Palsy | Circulation Problems | Cold Sores | Colds | Colic | Colitis | Conjunctivitis | Constipation | Convulsions | Corns | Coughs | Cramp | Cystitis |
|---|---|---|---|---|---|---|---|---|---|---|---|---|---|---|---|---|---|---|---|---|---|---|---|---|
| COMPLEMENTARY TOUCH (HM04950) | | ● | | | | | | | | | | | ● | | | | | | | | | | | |
| COOPER, ANGELA (HM05089) | | | | | | | | | | | | | | | | | | | | | | | | |
| COOPER, ANN (HM05090) | ● | ● | | | | | | | | | | | ● | | | | | | | | | | | |
| COTSWOLD PHYSIOTHERAPY CENTRE (HM05215) | | ● | | | | | ● | | | | ● | | | | | | | | | | | | | |
| ESSENTIAL BODYWORKS COMPANY (HM06899) | | ● | | | | | ● | | | | ● | | ● | | ● | | | | | | | | ● | |
| GREENWELL, DAVID (HM08498) | | | | | | | | | | | | | | | | | | | | | | | | |
| HYGEIA COLLEGE-COLOUR THERAPY (HM10476) | | | | | | | | | | | | | | | | | | | | | | | | |
| JOANNA SMITH AROMATHERAPY (HM11040) | | ● | | | | | | | | | ● | | | | | | | | | | | | | |
| LAWLER, R & G (HM12041) | | ● | | | | | | | | | | | ● | | ● | | | | ● | | | | | |
| LECKHAMPTON CHIROPRACTIC CLNC (HM12119) | | | | | | | | | | | | | | | | | | | | | | | | |
| MYERS, MERRILYN (HM14438) | | | | | | | | | | | | | | | | | | | | | | | | |
| NATURAL THERAPIES CLINIC (HM14633) | | ● | | ● | | | | | | | ● | | ● | | ● | | | | ● | ● | | | ● | ● |
| NATURAL THERAPY CENTRE (HM14649) | | | | | | | | | ● | | | ● | ● | | ● | ● | | | | | | | | |
| OLD CONVENT (HM15255) | | | | | | | | | | | | | | | | | | | | | | | | |
| OSTEOPATH (HM15445) | | | | | | | | | | | | | | | | | | | | | | | | |
| PENACHE (HM15960) | | | | | | | | | | | | | | | | | | | | | | | | |
| SHIATSU PRACTICE (HM18460) | ● | ● | ● | | ● | | ● | | ● | | | | ● | | ● | | ● | | ● | | | ● | ● | ● |
| SLATER, D C (HM18672) | | | | | | | | | | | | | | | | | | | | | | | | |
| SMYTH, DAVID (HM18830) | ● | ● | ● | ● | ● | | ● | ● | ● | ● | ● | | ● | ● | ● | ● | ● | ● | ● | ● | ● | ● | ● | ● |
| STOUT, HEATHER (HM19359) | ● | ● | | | | | ● | | | | ● | | | ● | ● | ● | ● | ● | ● | | | ● | ● | ● |
| STROUD NATURAL HEALTH CLINIC (HM19422) | ● | ● | ● | ● | ● | | ● | ● | ● | ● | ● | | ● | ● | ● | ● | ● | ● | ● | ● | ● | ● | ● | ● |
| TREE OF LIFE CENTRE (HM20307) | ● | ● | | | | | | | | ● | | | ● | ● | | | | | ● | | | | | |
| VILLAGE CLINIC (HM20665) | | | | | | | ● | | | | | | ● | | | | | | | | ● | | | |
| VINEY HALL PHYSIOTHERAPY (HM20683) | | | | | | | ● | | | | | | | | | | | | | | | | | |
| WELLS, GEORGINA (HM21172) | | | ● | ● | | | | | | | | | ● | ● | ● | | | | | | | | ● | |
| YOGA DRUVAM JIVAN YOGA SOCIETY (HM22024) | | | | | | | | | | | | | ● | | | | | | | | | | | |
| **HAMPSHIRE** | | | | | | | | | | | | | | | | | | | | | | | | |
| ACUPUNCTURE & PHYSIO CLINIC (HM00245) | | ● | ● | ● | | | ● | | | | | | | | | | | | ● | | | ● | ● | |
| ALL - HEAL ACU & HERB CENTRE (HM00581) | ● | ● | ● | ● | ● | | | | ● | | ● | | ● | ● | ● | | ● | | ● | | | ● | ● | ● |
| ALLERGY THERAPY (HM00637) | ● | ● | ● | ● | ● | | ● | ● | ● | ● | ● | | ● | ● | ● | ● | ● | ● | ● | ● | ● | ● | ● | ● |
| ARTEMIS (HM01156) | | | | | | | | | | | | | | | | | | | | | | | | |
| AVENUE CLINIC (HM01389) | | | | | | | ● | | | | | | | | | | | | | | | | ● | |
| BOLDICK, KATHLEEN (HM02652) | | ● | | | | | | | | | ● | | ● | | | | | | ● | | | | | |
| BRADFORD HOUSE CHIRO CLINIC (HM02849) | | | | | | | | | | | | | ● | | | ● | | | | | | | | |

# A - C Conditions treated at Practices/Businesses

| Business by County with Reference no. | Acne | Addiction | Adenoids | Aids | Alcoholism | Allergy | Alzheimer's Disease | Amnesia | Anaemia | Angina | Anorexia | Anxiety | Arthritis | Asthma | Athletes Foot | Autism |
|---|---|---|---|---|---|---|---|---|---|---|---|---|---|---|---|---|
| BUCK, PETER (HM03306) | | | | | | | | | | | | | | | ● | |
| CARMICHAEL, GORDON (HM03709) | | | | | | | | | | | | | | | | |
| CASSELL, JOHN (HM03814) | ● | ● | ● | ● | ● | ● | ● | ● | ● | ● | ● | ● | ● | ● | ● | ● |
| CENTRE FOR COMP MEDICINE (HM03901) | ● | | ● | | ● | ● | ● | | ● | ● | ● | ● | ● | ● | ● | ● |
| CHILTERN COTTAGE CLINIC (HM04175) | ● | | ● | | | ● | | | | | | ● | | ● | | |
| CLEMENTS, CHRISTINE (HM04642) | | | | | | | | | | | | | | | | |
| COAST CLINIC (HM04752) | | | | | | | | | | | | ● | | | | |
| COLVILE, RICHARD (HM04895) | ● | | | | | | | | | | | | ● | ● | | |
| COMPLETE ANGEL HEALING CENTRE (HM04955) | | | | | | | | | | | | ● | ● | ● | | |
| CORELLO, LOUISE (HM05161) | | | | | | | | | | ● | | ● | ● | ● | | |
| CRAIG, PETER (HM05353) | | | | | | | | | | | | | | | ● | |
| CRANIOSACRAL THERAPY (HM05377) | | ● | | | | | | | | | | ● | | ● | | |
| CTRE FOR THE STUDY OF COMP MED (HM05543) | ● | | ● | | | ● | | | | | | ● | ● | ● | | ● |
| DOLPHIN STUDIOS (HM06165) | | | | | | | | | | | | ● | | | | |
| EASTLEIGH OSTEOPATHIC CLINIC (HM06544) | | | | | | | | | | | | | ● | | | |
| EDGAR, A (HM06596) | | | | | | | | | | | | | | | ● | |
| ENERGY EXCHANGE HOLISTIC CTRE (HM06816) | | | | | | | | | | | | ● | | | | |
| EVANS (HM06953) | | | | | | | | | | | | | | | ● | |
| FAIRFIELDS LANE WEST (HM07059) | ● | | | | | ● | | | | | ● | ● | ● | ● | | |
| FAMILY CHIRO & ALT MED CTRE (HM07081) | ● | ● | | ● | | ● | ● | | ● | ● | ● | ● | ● | ● | ● | ● |
| FIT FEET CHIROPODY (HM07361) | | | | | | | | | | | | ● | ● | ● | ● | |
| FLEET & DISTRICT HYP CENTRE (HM07399) | | ● | | | | | | | | | ● | ● | | | | |
| FOOT SHOP (HM07486) | | | | | | | | | | | | | | | ● | |
| FOREVER LIVING PRODUCTS (HM07555) | ● | | | | | | | | | | | ● | ● | | | |
| FOSTER, JAMES M ASSOCIATES (HM07593) | | | | | | | | | | | | | ● | | ● | |
| FOX, ANTONY D (DR) (HM07631) | ● | | ● | | | ● | | | ● | ● | ● | ● | ● | ● | ● | ● |
| GEE, L (HM07958) | | | | | | | | | | | | | | | | |
| GROVE NATURAL THERAPY CENTRE (HM08609) | | | | | | ● | | | | | | | | | | |
| HANTSCARE (HM08947) | | | | | | | | | | | | | ● | | | |
| HAYLING ISLAND CHIRO CLINIC (HM09268) | | | | | | | | | | | | | ● | | | |
| HEAL-ALL HERB AND ACU CTRE (HM09315) | ● | ● | | | ● | ● | | | ● | ● | ● | ● | ● | ● | ● | |
| HEARNE, BRIAN (HM09440) | | | | | | | | | | | | | | | ● | |
| HERB MEDIC (HM09592) | ● | | | | | | | | | | | | | | | |
| HIGH STREET CLINIC (HM09742) | | | | | | | | | | | | ● | | | ● | |

| Business by County with Reference no. | Back Pain | Bacterial Infections | Baldness | Bereavement | Bladder Problems | Blood Pressure | Boils | Bowel Problems | Breast Problems | Breathing Problems | Bronchitis | Bruising | Bulimia | Bunions | Bursitis | Callices |
|---|---|---|---|---|---|---|---|---|---|---|---|---|---|---|---|---|
| BUCK, PETER (HM03306) | | | | | | | | | | | | | | | | |
| CARMICHAEL, GORDON (HM03709) | ● | | | | | | | | | ● | | | | | | |
| CASSELL, JOHN (HM03814) | ● | ● | ● | | ● | ● | ● | ● | ● | ● | ● | ● | ● | | ● | ● |
| CENTRE FOR COMP MEDICINE (HM03901) | ● | ● | ● | ● | ● | ● | ● | ● | ● | ● | ● | ● | ● | ● | ● | ● |
| CHILTERN COTTAGE CLINIC (HM04175) | | ● | | | ● | | | ● | | | ● | ● | | | | |
| CLEMENTS, CHRISTINE (HM04642) | ● | | | | | | | | | | | | | | | |
| COAST CLINIC (HM04752) | ● | | | | | | | | | | | | | | | |
| COLVILE, RICHARD (HM04895) | | | | | | ● | | | | | | | | | | |
| COMPLETE ANGEL HEALING CENTRE (HM04955) | ● | | | | ● | | | ● | | ● | | | | | | |
| CORELLO, LOUISE (HM05161) | ● | | | | ● | ● | | ● | ● | | | | | | ● | |
| CRAIG, PETER (HM05353) | | | | | | | | | | | | | | | | |
| CRANIOSACRAL THERAPY (HM05377) | ● | | | | | ● | | ● | | ● | ● | | | | | |
| CTRE FOR THE STUDY OF COMP MED (HM05543) | ● | ● | | | ● | ● | ● | ● | ● | ● | ● | ● | | | ● | |
| DOLPHIN STUDIOS (HM06165) | ● | | | | | | | | | | | | | | | |
| EASTLEIGH OSTEOPATHIC CLINIC (HM06544) | ● | | | | | | | | | | | | | | ● | |
| EDGAR, A (HM06596) | | | | | | | | | | | | | | ● | | ● |
| ENERGY EXCHANGE HOLISTIC CTRE (HM06816) | ● | | | | | | | | | | | | | | | |
| EVANS (HM06953) | | | | | | | | | | | | | | | | ● |
| FAIRFIELDS LANE WEST (HM07059) | ● | | | | | | | | | | | | ● | | | |
| FAMILY CHIRO & ALT MED CTRE (HM07081) | ● | | | | ● | ● | ● | ● | | ● | ● | ● | ● | | ● | |
| FIT FEET CHIROPODY (HM07361) | ● | | | | ● | ● | | ● | | ● | | | | | | ● |
| FLEET & DISTRICT HYP CENTRE (HM07399) | | | | | | | | | | | | | ● | | | |
| FOOT SHOP (HM07486) | | | | | | | | | | | | | | | | |
| FOREVER LIVING PRODUCTS (HM07555) | | | | | | | | | | | | | | | | |
| FOSTER, JAMES M ASSOCIATES (HM07593) | | | | | | | | | | | | | | | | |
| FOX, ANTONY D (DR) (HM07631) | ● | ● | | | ● | ● | ● | ● | ● | ● | ● | ● | | | | |
| GEE, L (HM07958) | ● | | | | | | | | | | | | | | | |
| GROVE NATURAL THERAPY CENTRE (HM08609) | | | | | | | | | | | | | | | | |
| HANTSCARE (HM08947) | ● | | | | | | | | | | | ● | | | ● | |
| HAYLING ISLAND CHIRO CLINIC (HM09268) | ● | | | | | | | | | | | | | | ● | |
| HEAL-ALL HERB AND ACU CTRE (HM09315) | ● | ● | ● | | ● | ● | ● | ● | ● | ● | ● | ● | ● | | | |
| HEARNE, BRIAN (HM09440) | | | | | | | | | | | | | | | | ● |
| HERB MEDIC (HM09592) | | | | | | ● | | | | | | | | | | |
| HIGH STREET CLINIC (HM09742) | ● | | | | | ● | | ● | | ● | | | | | | |

| Business by County with Reference no. | Cancers | Cataracts | Catarrh | Cerebral Palsy | Circulation Problems | Cold Sores | Colds | Colic | Colitis | Conjunctivitis | Constipation | Convulsions | Corns | Coughs | Cramp | Cystitis |
|---|---|---|---|---|---|---|---|---|---|---|---|---|---|---|---|---|
| BUCK, PETER (HM03306) | | | | | | | | | | | | | | | | |
| CARMICHAEL, GORDON (HM03709) | | | | | | | | | | | | | | | ● | |
| CASSELL, JOHN (HM03814) | ● | ● | ● | | ● | ● | ● | ● | ● | ● | ● | ● | ● | ● | ● | ● |
| CENTRE FOR COMP MEDICINE (HM03901) | ● | ● | ● | | ● | ● | ● | ● | ● | ● | ● | ● | ● | ● | ● | ● |
| CHILTERN COTTAGE CLINIC (HM04175) | | | ● | | | | ● | ● | ● | ● | ● | ● | | ● | | ● |
| CLEMENTS, CHRISTINE (HM04642) | | | | | | | | | | | | | | | | |
| COAST CLINIC (HM04752) | | | | | | | | | | | | | | | | |
| COLVILE, RICHARD (HM04895) | | | | | | | | | | | | | | | | ● |
| COMPLETE ANGEL HEALING CENTRE (HM04955) | ● | | ● | | ● | | | | | | ● | | | | ● | ● |
| CORELLO, LOUISE (HM05161) | | | ● | | ● | ● | ● | | | ● | ● | | | | ● | ● |
| CRAIG, PETER (HM05353) | | | | | | | | | | | | | | | | |
| CRANIOSACRAL THERAPY (HM05377) | | | | | ● | | | | ● | | ● | | | | | |
| CTRE FOR THE STUDY OF COMP MED (HM05543) | ● | | ● | | ● | ● | ● | ● | ● | ● | ● | ● | | ● | ● | ● |
| DOLPHIN STUDIOS (HM06165) | | | | | | | | | | | | | | | | |
| EASTLEIGH OSTEOPATHIC CLINIC (HM06544) | | | | | | | | ● | | | | | | | | |
| EDGAR, A (HM06596) | | | | | | | | | | | | | ● | | | |
| ENERGY EXCHANGE HOLISTIC CTRE (HM06816) | | | | | ● | | | | | | | | | | | |
| EVANS (HM06953) | | | | | | | | | | | | | ● | | | |
| FAIRFIELDS LANE WEST (HM07059) | | | | | | | | | | | | | | | | |
| FAMILY CHIRO & ALT MED CTRE (HM07081) | ● | | ● | | ● | ● | ● | ● | ● | | ● | | | ● | ● | ● |
| FIT FEET CHIROPODY (HM07361) | | | | | ● | | | | | | | | ● | | ● | |
| FLEET & DISTRICT HYP CENTRE (HM07399) | | | | | | | | | | | | | | | | |
| FOOT SHOP (HM07486) | | | | | | | | | | | | | | | | |
| FOREVER LIVING PRODUCTS (HM07555) | | | | | | | ● | | | | | | | | | |
| FOSTER, JAMES M ASSOCIATES (HM07593) | | | | | | | | | | | | | | | | |
| FOX, ANTONY D (DR) (HM07631) | | ● | ● | | ● | ● | ● | ● | ● | ● | ● | ● | | ● | ● | ● |
| GEE, L (HM07958) | | | | | | | | | | | | | | | | |
| GROVE NATURAL THERAPY CENTRE (HM08609) | | | | | | | | | | | | | | | | |
| HANTSCARE (HM08947) | | | | | | | | | | | | | | | | |
| HAYLING ISLAND CHIRO CLINIC (HM09268) | | | | | | | | | ● | | ● | | | | | |
| HEAL-ALL HERB AND ACU CTRE (HM09315) | ● | | ● | | ● | ● | ● | | ● | | ● | | | ● | ● | ● |
| HEARNE, BRIAN (HM09440) | | | | | | | | | | | | | ● | | | |
| HERB MEDIC (HM09592) | | | | | | | ● | | | | | | | | | |
| HIGH STREET CLINIC (HM09742) | | | ● | | ● | | | | | | ● | | | | ● | |

# A - C Conditions treated at Practices/Businesses

| Business by County with Reference no. | Acne | Addiction | Adenoids | Aids | Alcoholism | Allergy | Alzheimer's Disease | Amnesia | Anaemia | Angina | Anorexia | Anxiety | Arthritis | Asthma | Athletes Foot | Autism | Back Pain | Bacterial Infections | Baldness | Bereavement | Bladder Problems | Blood Pressure | Boils | Bowel Problems |
|---|---|---|---|---|---|---|---|---|---|---|---|---|---|---|---|---|---|---|---|---|---|---|---|---|
| HOBBS, T J (HM09860) | | | | | | | | | | | | ● | ● | ● | | | ● | | | | ● | | | ● |
| HOLISTIC ARTS STUDIOS (HM09948) | | | | | | | | | | | | ● | | | | | ● | | | | | ● | | |
| HOMOEOPATHIC CLINIC (HM10088) | | | | | | | | | | | | | ● | ● | | | ● | | | | | | | ● |
| HUTCHINGS, MARGARET (HM10448) | | | | | | | | | | | | ● | | | | | ● | | | | | | | |
| HYPNOSIS & STRESS COUNSELLING (HM10494) | | | | | | | | | | | | ● | | | | | | | | | | | | |
| HYPNOTHRPY FOR POSITIVE CHANGE (HM10542) | ● | ● | | | ● | ● | | ● | | | | ● | | ● | | | ● | | | | | | ● | ● |
| INLPTA (HM10633) | | ● | | | ● | | | | | | | ● | | | | | | | | | | | | |
| INNER WHISPERS & THERAPY CTRE (HM10643) | | | | | | | | | | | | ● | ● | ● | | | ● | | | | | | | |
| JENKINS, RUSSELL (HM10994) | ● | ● | ● | ● | ● | ● | ● | ● | ● | ● | ● | ● | ● | ● | ● | ● | ● | ● | ● | | ● | ● | ● | ● |
| JOYCE, HELEN G M (HM11236) | | | | | | | | | | | | | ● | | | | ● | | | | | | | |
| KAY SILVER HYPNOTHERAPY (HM11349) | | | | | | | | | | | ● | ● | | | | | | | | | | | | ● |
| KD PHYSIOTHERAPY (HM11363) | | | | | | | | | | | | | ● | | | | ● | | | | | | | |
| LEACH, TRICIA (HM12091) | | | | | | | | | | | | ● | ● | | | | ● | | | | | | | |
| LEWIS, D J S (HM12288) | ● | ● | ● | | ● | ● | ● | ● | ● | ● | ● | ● | ● | ● | ● | ● | ● | ● | ● | ● | ● | ● | ● | ● |
| LISLE, THOMAS (HM12455) | | | | | | | | | | | | | | | ● | | | | | | | | | |
| LOCKHAMS THERAPY CENTRE (HM12545) | | | | | | | | | | | | ● | ● | ● | | | | | | | | ● | | |
| LOWE, KENNETH (HM12699) | | | | | | | | | | | | | ● | | | | ● | | | | | | | |
| LYMINGTON CHIROPRACTIC CLINIC (HM12759) | | ● | | | ● | | | | ● | | | ● | ● | ● | | | ● | | | | ● | ● | | ● |
| MARLOR, J (HM13127) | | | | | | | | | | | | | | | ● | | | | | | | | | |
| MELHUISH, J I (DR) (HM13705) | | | | | | | | | | | | | ● | | | | ● | | | | | ● | | |
| MINDWORKS HYPNOTHERAPY CLINIC (HM13969) | ● | ● | | | ● | | | | | | ● | ● | | | | | ● | | | | | ● | | ● |
| NATURAL HEALTH SERVICE (HM14595) | ● | ● | ● | ● | ● | ● | ● | ● | ● | ● | ● | ● | ● | ● | ● | ● | ● | ● | ● | ● | ● | ● | ● | ● |
| NATURES GATE (HM14688) | | | | | | | | | | | | | ● | | | | ● | | | | | | | |
| NEW MILTON CHIROPRACTIC CLINIC (HM14825) | | | | | | | | | | | | | ● | | | | ● | | | | | | | |
| NORMAN, J M (HM15004) | | | | | | | | | | | | | | | | | | | | | | | | |
| NORSWORTHY, CLAIRE (HM15017) | | | | | | | | | | | | ● | | ● | | | ● | | | | | | | |
| PARCHMENT STREET CLINIC (HM15646) | ● | ● | | ● | | ● | | | ● | ● | ● | ● | ● | ● | | | ● | | | | ● | ● | | ● |
| PHOENIX HOLISTIC CENTRE (HM16156) | | | | | | | | | | | | ● | ● | | | | ● | | | | | | | |
| PHYSIOTHERAPY CENTRE (HM16233) | | | | | | | | | | | | | ● | | ● | | ● | | | | | | | |
| REIKI NATURAL HEALING CENTRE (HM17142) | ● | ● | ● | ● | ● | ● | ● | ● | ● | ● | ● | ● | ● | ● | ● | ● | ● | ● | ● | | ● | ● | ● | ● |
| RICHARDS, CLAIRE (HM17249) | | | | | | | | | | | | ● | | | | | ● | | | | | | | |
| RINGWOOD CHIROPRACTIC CLINIC (HM17355) | | | | | | | | | | | | | ● | | | | ● | | | | | | | |
| RINGWOOD NATURAL HEALTH CLINIC (HM17357) | ● | | | | | ● | | | ● | ● | | ● | ● | ● | | | ● | ● | | | ● | ● | | ● |
| RINGWOOD PHYSIOTHERAPY CENTRE (HM17358) | | | | | | | | | | | | | ● | | | | ● | | | | | | | |

| Business by County with Reference no. | Breast Problems | Breathing Problems | Bronchitis | Bruising | Bulimia | Bunions | Bursitis | Callices | Cancers | Cataracts | Catarrh | Cerebral Palsy | Circulation Problems | Cold Sores | Colds | Colic | Colitis | Conjunctivitis | Constipation | Convulsions | Corns | Coughs | Cramp | Cystitis |
|---|---|---|---|---|---|---|---|---|---|---|---|---|---|---|---|---|---|---|---|---|---|---|---|---|
| HOBBS, T J (HM09860) | | | | | | | | | | | ● | | ● | | | | | | ● | | | | ● | |
| HOLISTIC ARTS STUDIOS (HM09948) | | | | | | | | | | | | | ● | | | | | | | | | ● | ● | |
| HOMOEOPATHIC CLINIC (HM10088) | | ● | | | | | ● | | | | | | | | | | ● | | ● | | | | | |
| HUTCHINGS, MARGARET (HM10448) | | | | | | | | | | | | | | | | | | | | | | | | |
| HYPNOSIS & STRESS COUNSELLING (HM10494) | | | | | ● | | | | | | | | | | | | | | | | | | | |
| HYPNOTHRPY FOR POSITIVE CHANGE (HM10542) | | ● | | | ● | | | | | | | | ● | | | | | | | | | | | |
| INLPTA (HM10633) | | | | | | | | | | | | | | | | | | | | | | | | |
| INNER WHISPERS & THERAPY CTRE (HM10643) | | | | | | | | | ● | | | | | | | | | | | | | | | |
| JENKINS, RUSSELL (HM10994) | ● | ● | ● | ● | ● | | ● | ● | ● | ● | ● | | ● | ● | ● | ● | ● | ● | ● | ● | ● | ● | ● | ● |
| JOYCE, HELEN G M (HM11236) | | | | | | | | | | | | | | | | | | | | | | | | |
| KAY SILVER HYPNOTHERAPY (HM11349) | | | | | ● | | | | | | | | | | | | ● | | ● | | | | | |
| KD PHYSIOTHERAPY (HM11363) | | | | | | | | | | | | | | | | | | | | | | | | |
| LEACH, TRICIA (HM12091) | | ● | | | | | | | | | ● | | ● | | | | | | ● | | | | ● | |
| LEWIS, D J S (HM12288) | ● | ● | ● | ● | ● | ● | ● | ● | ● | ● | ● | | ● | ● | ● | ● | ● | ● | ● | ● | ● | ● | ● | ● |
| LISLE, THOMAS (HM12455) | | | | | | | | ● | | | | | | | | | | | | | ● | | | |
| LOCKHAMS THERAPY CENTRE (HM12545) | | ● | | | | | | | ● | | | | | | | | | | | | | | | |
| LOWE, KENNETH (HM12699) | | | | | | | | | | | | | | | | | | | | | | | | |
| LYMINGTON CHIROPRACTIC CLINIC (HM12759) | | | | | | | ● | | | | | | | | | ● | | | | | | | ● | |
| MARLOR, J (HM13127) | | | | | | | | ● | | | | | | | | | | | | | ● | | | |
| MELHUISH, J I (DR) (HM13705) | | | | | | | | | | | | | | | | ● | | | | | | | | |
| MINDWORKS HYPNOTHERAPY CLINIC (HM13969) | | | | | | | | | ● | | | | | | | | | | ● | | | | | |
| NATURAL HEALTH SERVICE (HM14595) | ● | ● | ● | ● | ● | | ● | ● | ● | ● | ● | | ● | ● | ● | ● | ● | ● | ● | ● | ● | ● | ● | ● |
| NATURES GATE (HM14688) | | | | | | | | | | | | | | | | | | | | | | | | |
| NEW MILTON CHIROPRACTIC CLINIC (HM14825) | | | | | | | ● | | | | | | ● | | | | | | | | | | ● | |
| NORMAN, J M (HM15004) | | | | | | | | | | | | | ● | | | | | | ● | | | | | |
| NORSWORTHY, CLAIRE (HM15017) | | ● | | | | | | | | | | | ● | | | | | | ● | | | | | |
| PARCHMENT STREET CLINIC (HM15646) | | ● | ● | ● | ● | | | | | | ● | | ● | | ● | ● | ● | | ● | | | ● | ● | ● |
| PHOENIX HOLISTIC CENTRE (HM16156) | | | | | | | | | ● | | | | | | | | | | ● | | | | | |
| PHYSIOTHERAPY CENTRE (HM16233) | | | | | | | | ● | | | | | | | | | | | | | ● | | | |
| REIKI NATURAL HEALING CENTRE (HM17142) | ● | ● | ● | ● | ● | | ● | ● | ● | ● | ● | | ● | ● | ● | ● | ● | ● | ● | ● | ● | ● | ● | ● |
| RICHARDS, CLAIRE (HM17249) | | | | | | | | | | | ● | | ● | | | | | | | | | | | |
| RINGWOOD CHIROPRACTIC CLINIC (HM17355) | | | | | | | | | | | | | ● | | | ● | | | | | | | | |
| RINGWOOD NATURAL HEALTH CLINIC (HM17357) | | ● | ● | ● | | | | | | | ● | | ● | ● | ● | ● | ● | ● | ● | | | ● | ● | ● |
| RINGWOOD PHYSIOTHERAPY CENTRE (HM17358) | | | | | | | | | | | | | | | | | | | | | | | | |

www.healthmyself.com

# A - C Conditions treated at Practices/Businesses

| Business by County with Reference no. | Acne | Addiction | Adenoids | Aids | Alcoholism | Allergy | Alzheimer's Disease | Amnesia | Anaemia | Angina | Anorexia | Anxiety | Arthritis | Asthma | Athletes Foot | Autism | Back Pain | Bacterial Infections | Baldness | Bereavement | Bladder Problems | Blood Pressure | Boils | Bowel Problems | Breast Problems | Breathing Problems | Bronchitis | Bruising | Bulimia | Bunions | Bursitis | Callices | Cancers | Cataracts | Catarrh | Cerebral Palsy | Circulation Problems | Cold Sores | Colds | Colic | Colitis | Conjunctivitis | Constipation | Convulsions | Corns | Coughs | Cramp | Cystitis |
|---|---|---|---|---|---|---|---|---|---|---|---|---|---|---|---|---|---|---|---|---|---|---|---|---|---|---|---|---|---|---|---|---|---|---|---|---|---|---|---|---|---|---|---|---|---|---|---|---|
| S E E D INSTITUTE (HM17805) | | | | | | | | | | | |●|●| | | |●| | | | | | | | | | | | | | | | | | | | | | | | | | | | | | | |
| SCANDINAVIAN CHIROPRACTIC CTRE (HM18002) | | | | | | | | | | | | |●| | | |●| | | | |●| | | | | | | | | | | | | | |●| | |●| | | | | | | | |
| SIMCOE CLINIC (HM18549) |●| | | | | | | |●| | | |●|●|●| |●| | | |●|●| |●| |●|●| | | |●| | | |●| |●| |●|●|●| |●| | | |●|●|
| SIMMONDS, J (HM18555) |●| | | | |●| | |●|●| |●|●|●| |●|●|●| | |●|●| |●|●|●|●| | | | | |●|●|●| |●|●|●|●|●|●|●| | |●|●| |
| SOLENT CHIROPRACTIC CLINIC (HM18871) | | | | | | | | | | | | |●| | | |●| | | | | | | | | | | | | | | | | | | | | | | | | | | | | | | |
| SOUTHGATE NAT THERAPY CLINIC (HM18937) | | | | |●|●| | |●|●| |●|●|●| | |●|●| | |●|●| |●|●|●|●|●| | | | |●| |●| |●| |●|●|●| |●| | |●|●|●|
| SOUTHSEA CENTRE FOR COMP MED (HM18943) |●|●|●|●|●|●|●|●| |●|●|●|●|●|●|●|●|●| | |●|●|●|●|●|●|●|●|●| |●| |●|●|●| |●| |●|●|●| |●| | |●|●|●|
| THOMA, ANDREW (HM19923) | | | | | | | | | | | | | | | | |●| | | | | | | | | | | | | |●| | | | | | | | | | | | | | | |●| |
| TURNER, CATHY (HM20420) |●|●|●|●|●|●|●|●|●|●|●|●|●|●|●|●|●|●|●| |●|●|●|●|●|●|●|●|●| |●| |●|●|●| |●|●|●|●|●|●|●|●| |●|●|●|
| TWESLEDOWN PHYSIOTHERAPY (HM20449) | | | | | | | | | | | | |●| | | |●| | | | | | | | | | | | | | | | | | | | | | | | | | | | | | | |
| VINCE, LINDA (HM20668) | | | | | | | | | | | | |●| | | | | | | | | | | | | | | | | | |●| | | | | | | | | | | | |●| | | |
| WELL HOUSE HOLISTIC HLTH CTRE (HM21138) |●|●|●|●|●|●|●|●|●|●|●|●|●|●|●|●|●|●|●| |●|●|●|●|●|●|●|●|●| |●|●|●|●|●| |●|●|●|●|●|●|●|●|●|●|●|●|
| WINCHESTER CHIROPRACTIC CLINIC (HM21691) | | | | | | | | | | | | |●| | | |●| | | |●| | | | | | | | | | | | | | | | | | | | | | | | | | | |
| WINCHESTER HOM PRACTICE (HM21692) |●|●|●|●|●|●| |●|●|●|●|●|●|●|●|●|●|●|●| |●|●|●|●|●|●|●|●|●| |●| |●|●|●| |●|●|●|●|●|●|●|●| |●|●|●|
| HEREFORDSHIRE | | | | | | | | | | | | | | | | | | | | | | | | | | | | | | | | | | | | | | | | | | | | | | | | |
| BEAUTY IS YOURS (HM01999) |●| | | | | | | | | | | |●|●| | |●| | | | |●| |●| |●| | | | | | | | | | | | | | |●| | | | | | | |
| BROADVIEW NATURAL HEALTH CTRE (HM03119) | |●| | | |●| | | | | |●|●|●| | |●| | | | | | | | | | | | | | | | | | | | | | | | | | | | | | | |
| HEREFORD CENTRE (HM09677) |●|●| |●|●|●| |●|●|●|●|●|●|●|●| |●|●| |●|●|●|●|●|●|●|●|●|●|●| |●| | |●| |●|●|●|●|●|●|●|●|●|●|●|●|
| HEREFORD CHIROPRACTIC CLINIC (HM09678) | | | | | | | | | | | | |●| | | |●| | | | |●| | | | | | | | | | | | | | |●| | |●| | | | | | | | |
| JONES, KEVIN D G (HM11165) | | | | | | | | | | | | | | | | |●| | | | | | | | | | | | | | | | | | | | | | | | | | | | | |●| |
| LEDBURY NATURAL HEALTH CENTRE (HM12122) |●|●|●|●|●|●|●|●|●|●|●|●|●|●|●|●|●|●|●| |●|●|●|●|●|●|●|●|●| |●|●|●|●|●| |●|●|●|●|●|●|●|●|●|●|●|●|
| LEOMINSTER OSTEOPATHS (HM12221) | | | | | |●| | | | | |●|●|●| | |●| | | | | | | | |●| | | | | | | | | | |●| | |●| | |●| | | | | |
| TEDDER, CATHRINE (HM19814) | | | | | | | | | | | | | | |●| | | | | | | | | | | | | | | | |●| | | | | | | | | | | |●| | | |
| WILLCOCKS, T & S (HM21519) | | | | | | | | | | | | | |●| | |●| | | | | | | | | | | | | | | | | | | | | | | | | | | | | | | |
| HERTFORDSHIRE | | | | | | | | | | | | | | | | | | | | | | | | | | | | | | | | | | | | | | | | | | | | | | | | |
| ALDER, DENNIS (HM00497) | | | | | | | | | | | | |●| |●| | | | | | | | | | | | | | | |●| |●| | | | | | | | | | | |●| | | |
| ALLEN, JULIE & LEN (HM00613) |●|●| | | |●| |●|●| |●|●|●|●|●| |●|●|●| |●|●|●| |●|●|●|●|●| |●| |●|●|●| |●| |●|●|●|●| |●| |●|●|●|
| ALTERNATIVE CHOICES (HM00697) |●|●| | | |●| | | |●| |●|●|●| | |●| | | |●|●|●|●|●|●|●| | | | | | | | | | | |●|●| |●| | | | | | |
| ARNOLD, PETER & JACKIE (HM01036) |●| | | | | | | | | | |●|●|●| | |●| | | | |●| | | | | |●| | |●| | | |●| |●| |●| | |●|●| | | | | |
| AROMA ROOM (HM01055) | | | | | | | | | | | |●| | | | |●| | | | | | |●| | | | | | | | | | | | | | | | | | | | | | | | |
| AROMATHERAPY BY ANTONIO (HM01095) | | | | | | | | | | | |●| | | | |●| | | | | | | | | | | | | | | | | | | | | | | | | | | | | | | |
| ASHDOWN CLINIC (HM01205) | | | | | |●| | | | | |●|●| |●| |●|●| | |●|●| |●| |●|●| | |●|●| | | |●| |●|●|●| | | |●| | |●|●|●|
| ASHWELL, MELBOURN & BALDOCK (HM01246) | | | | | | | | | | | | |●| | | |●| | | | | | | | | | |●| | |●| | | | | | | | | | | | | | | |●| |
| ASSOCIATES HEAD & SHORT (HM01276) | | | |●| | |●| | | | | |●| |●| | | | | | | | | | | | | | | | |●| | | | | | | | | | | | |●| | | |

# A - C Conditions treated at Practices/Businesses

Business by County with Reference no.

| Business | Acne | Addiction | Adenoids | Aids | Alcoholism | Allergy | Alzheimer's Disease | Amnesia | Anaemia | Angina | Anorexia | Anxiety | Arthritis | Asthma | Athletes Foot | Autism |
|---|---|---|---|---|---|---|---|---|---|---|---|---|---|---|---|---|
| ASSOCIATES HEAD & SHORT (HM01277) | | | | ● | | | ● | | | | | | ● | | ● | |
| ASSOCIATION OF STRESS MNGMT (HM01293) | | | | | | | | | | | | ● | ● | ● | | |
| AUTOGENIC TRAINING (HM01372) | ● | | ● | ● | | ● | | | | ● | | ● | ● | ● | | |
| BARNET CHIROPODY SURGERY (HM01757) | | | | | | | | | | | | | | | ● | |
| BASSETT CLINIC (HM01853) | | | | | | | | | | | | | ● | | | |
| BEAUCHAMP BAGENAL (HM01983) | | | | | | | | | | | | ● | ● | ● | | |
| BERKHAMSTED PHYSIO CLINIC (HM02193) | | | | | | | | | | | | | ● | | | |
| BETA HEALTH CLINIC (HM02229) | | | | | | ● | | | | | | | ● | ● | ● | |
| BISHOP'S STORTFORD HOMEOPATHIC (HM02416) | ● | | | | | ● | | | | | | | ● | | ● | ● |
| BODY MECHANICS THERAPY CLINIC (HM02598) | | | | | | | | | | | | | ● | ● | | |
| BOREHAMWOOD CHIRO CLINIC (HM02717) | | | | | | | | | | | | | ● | | | |
| BRIGGS-WILSON, A (HM03037) | | | | | | | | | | | | | | | | |
| BRIND, KEVIN (HM03053) | | | | | | | | | | | | | ● | | | |
| BURYHILL PHYSIOTHERAPY (HM03456) | | | | | | | | | | | | | ● | | | |
| BUTTERFIELD, ROBIN (HM03496) | | | | | | | | | | | | | ● | | | |
| CANNON, VALERIE (HM03635) | | | | | | | | | | | | ● | ● | | | |
| CHAUHAN, D K (HM04065) | ● | ● | ● | ● | ● | ● | ● | ● | ● | ● | ● | ● | ● | ● | ● | ● |
| CHOPRA, S (HM04427) | | | | | | | | | | | | | ● | | ● | |
| CHOPRA, S (HM04426) | | | | | | | | | | | | | ● | | ● | |
| CLARE JAMES HEALTH FOODS (HM04532) | | | | | | | | | | | | | ● | | ● | |
| CLNC OF ACU & CHINESE HRBL MED (HM04727) | ● | ● | | ● | | | | | | | | ● | ● | | | |
| CONISTON PHYSIOTHERAPY CLINIC (HM04980) | | | | | | | | | | | | | ● | | | |
| COOPER, FELICITY (HM05101) | | | | | | | | | | | | | ● | | ● | |
| DAVID HERBERT REFLEXOLOGY (HM05774) | | | | | | | | | | ● | ● | ● | ● | ● | | |
| DEVINE, MARY (HM06036) | | | | | | | | | | | | | | | ● | |
| DOYLE, AUDREY (HM06257) | ● | ● | ● | | | ● | ● | ● | ● | ● | ● | ● | ● | ● | ● | |
| DUDGEON, DELIA (HM06353) | | | | | | | | | | | | ● | | | | |
| EVANS, HELEN (HM06975) | | | | | | | | | | | | | | | ● | |
| EVANS, HELEN (HM06976) | | | | | | | | | | | | | | | ● | |
| FEET RETREAT () | | | | | | ● | | | | | | | ● | | | |
| FREEMAN, FRANCES (HM07721) | ● | ● | ● | ● | ● | ● | ● | ● | ● | ● | ● | ● | ● | ● | ● | ● |
| GEMS (HM07969) | | ● | | | | | | | | | | ● | | | | |
| GENTLE FEET (HM07977) | ● | ● | ● | | | ● | ● | ● | ● | ● | ● | ● | ● | ● | | |
| GEOFF THIEL, COUNS & PSYCHO (HM07986) | | | | | | | | | | | | ● | | | | |

| Business | Back Pain | Bacterial Infections | Baldness | Bereavement | Bladder Problems | Blood Pressure | Boils | Bowel Problems | Breast Problems | Breathing Problems | Bronchitis | Bruising | Bulimia | Bunions | Bursitis | Callices |
|---|---|---|---|---|---|---|---|---|---|---|---|---|---|---|---|---|
| ASSOCIATES HEAD & SHORT (HM01277) | | | | | | | | | | | | | | | | ● |
| ASSOCIATION OF STRESS MNGMT (HM01293) | ● | | | | | | | | | | | | | | | |
| AUTOGENIC TRAINING (HM01372) | ● | | | | ● | ● | ● | ● | | ● | | | | | ● | |
| BARNET CHIROPODY SURGERY (HM01757) | | | | | | | | | | | | | | | | ● |
| BASSETT CLINIC (HM01853) | ● | | | | | | | | | | | | | | | |
| BEAUCHAMP BAGENAL (HM01983) | ● | | | | | ● | | | | ● | | | | | | |
| BERKHAMSTED PHYSIO CLINIC (HM02193) | ● | | | | | | | | | | | ● | | | | |
| BETA HEALTH CLINIC (HM02229) | ● | | | | | | | | | | | ● | | | | ● |
| BISHOP'S STORTFORD HOMEOPATHIC (HM02416) | | | | | ● | ● | | ● | | ● | ● | ● | | | | |
| BODY MECHANICS THERAPY CLINIC (HM02598) | | | | | | | | | | | | | | | | |
| BOREHAMWOOD CHIRO CLINIC (HM02717) | ● | | | | | | | | | | | | | | | |
| BRIGGS-WILSON, A (HM03037) | ● | | | | | | | | | | | | | | | |
| BRIND, KEVIN (HM03053) | ● | | | | | | | | | | | ● | | | | |
| BURYHILL PHYSIOTHERAPY (HM03456) | ● | | | | | | | | | | | ● | | | | |
| BUTTERFIELD, ROBIN (HM03496) | ● | | | | | | | | | | | | | | | |
| CANNON, VALERIE (HM03635) | ● | | | | ● | | | | | ● | | | | | | |
| CHAUHAN, D K (HM04065) | ● | ● | ● | | ● | ● | ● | ● | ● | ● | ● | ● | ● | | ● | ● |
| CHOPRA, S (HM04427) | | | | | | | | | | | | | | ● | | ● |
| CHOPRA, S (HM04426) | | | | | | | | | | | | | | ● | | ● |
| CLARE JAMES HEALTH FOODS (HM04532) | | | | | | | | ● | | | | ● | | | | |
| CLNC OF ACU & CHINESE HRBL MED (HM04727) | ● | | | | ● | ● | | ● | | ● | ● | | | | ● | |
| CONISTON PHYSIOTHERAPY CLINIC (HM04980) | ● | | | | | | | | | | | ● | | | ● | |
| COOPER, FELICITY (HM05101) | | | | | | | | | | | | | | | | ● |
| DAVID HERBERT REFLEXOLOGY (HM05774) | ● | | | | ● | ● | | ● | | ● | ● | | | | ● | |
| DEVINE, MARY (HM06036) | | | | | | | | | | | | | | | | |
| DOYLE, AUDREY (HM06257) | ● | | | | ● | ● | | ● | ● | ● | ● | | ● | ● | ● | ● |
| DUDGEON, DELIA (HM06353) | ● | | | | | | | ● | | ● | | | | | | |
| EVANS, HELEN (HM06975) | | | | | | | | | | | | | | | | |
| EVANS, HELEN (HM06976) | | | | | | | | | | | | | | | | |
| FEET RETREAT () | ● | | | | ● | ● | | | | ● | ● | | | | | |
| FREEMAN, FRANCES (HM07721) | ● | ● | ● | | ● | ● | ● | ● | ● | ● | ● | ● | ● | | ● | |
| GEMS (HM07969) | | | | | | | | | | | | | | | | |
| GENTLE FEET (HM07977) | ● | | | | ● | ● | | ● | ● | ● | ● | | ● | | ● | |
| GEOFF THIEL, COUNS & PSYCHO (HM07986) | | | | | | | | | | | | | | | | |

| Business | Cancers | Cataracts | Catarrh | Cerebral Palsy | Circulation Problems | Cold Sores | Colds | Colic | Colitis | Conjunctivitis | Constipation | Convulsions | Corns | Coughs | Cramp | Cystitis |
|---|---|---|---|---|---|---|---|---|---|---|---|---|---|---|---|---|
| ASSOCIATES HEAD & SHORT (HM01277) | | | | | | | | | | | | | ● | | | |
| ASSOCIATION OF STRESS MNGMT (HM01293) | | | | | | | | | | | | | | | | |
| AUTOGENIC TRAINING (HM01372) | | | | | ● | ● | ● | ● | ● | ● | ● | | | ● | ● | ● |
| BARNET CHIROPODY SURGERY (HM01757) | | | | | | | | | | | | | ● | | | |
| BASSETT CLINIC (HM01853) | | | | | | | | ● | | | | | | | ● | |
| BEAUCHAMP BAGENAL (HM01983) | | | | | ● | | | | | | | | | | ● | |
| BERKHAMSTED PHYSIO CLINIC (HM02193) | | | | | | | | | | | | | | | ● | |
| BETA HEALTH CLINIC (HM02229) | | | | | | | | | | | ● | | ● | | ● | |
| BISHOP'S STORTFORD HOMEOPATHIC (HM02416) | | | ● | | ● | ● | ● | ● | ● | | ● | | | ● | | ● |
| BODY MECHANICS THERAPY CLINIC (HM02598) | | | | | ● | | | | | | | | | | ● | |
| BOREHAMWOOD CHIRO CLINIC (HM02717) | | | | | | | | | | | | | | | | |
| BRIGGS-WILSON, A (HM03037) | | | | | | | | | | | ● | | | | | |
| BRIND, KEVIN (HM03053) | | | | | | | | | | | | | | | | |
| BURYHILL PHYSIOTHERAPY (HM03456) | | | | | | | | | | | | | | | | |
| BUTTERFIELD, ROBIN (HM03496) | | | | | | | | | | | | | | | | |
| CANNON, VALERIE (HM03635) | | | ● | | ● | | | | | | ● | | | | ● | |
| CHAUHAN, D K (HM04065) | ● | ● | ● | | ● | ● | ● | ● | ● | ● | ● | ● | ● | ● | ● | ● |
| CHOPRA, S (HM04427) | | | | | | | | | | | | | ● | | | |
| CHOPRA, S (HM04426) | | | | | | | | | | | | | ● | | | |
| CLARE JAMES HEALTH FOODS (HM04532) | | | ● | | ● | | ● | | | | | | | ● | ● | |
| CLNC OF ACU & CHINESE HRBL MED (HM04727) | | ● | ● | | | | | | ● | | ● | | | ● | | ● |
| CONISTON PHYSIOTHERAPY CLINIC (HM04980) | | | | | ● | | | | | | | | | | ● | |
| COOPER, FELICITY (HM05101) | | | | | | | | | | | | | ● | | | |
| DAVID HERBERT REFLEXOLOGY (HM05774) | | | ● | | ● | | ● | | ● | | ● | | | | | ● |
| DEVINE, MARY (HM06036) | | | | | | | | | | | | | | | | |
| DOYLE, AUDREY (HM06257) | ● | | ● | | ● | | ● | | ● | | ● | | ● | ● | ● | ● |
| DUDGEON, DELIA (HM06353) | | | | | ● | | | | ● | | | | | | | |
| EVANS, HELEN (HM06975) | | | | | | | | | | | | | | | | |
| EVANS, HELEN (HM06976) | | | | | | | | | | | | | | | | |
| FEET RETREAT () | | | | | ● | | ● | | | | ● | | | | | |
| FREEMAN, FRANCES (HM07721) | ● | ● | ● | | ● | ● | ● | ● | ● | ● | ● | ● | | ● | ● | ● |
| GEMS (HM07969) | | | | | | | | | | | | | | | | |
| GENTLE FEET (HM07977) | ● | | ● | | ● | | ● | ● | ● | | ● | | | ● | ● | ● |
| GEOFF THIEL, COUNS & PSYCHO (HM07986) | | | | | | | | | | | | | | | | |

# A - C Conditions treated at Practices/Businesses

| Business by County with Reference no. | Acne | Addiction | Adenoids | Aids | Alcoholism | Allergy | Alzheimer's Disease | Amnesia | Anaemia | Angina | Anorexia | Anxiety | Arthritis | Asthma | Athletes Foot | Autism |
|---|---|---|---|---|---|---|---|---|---|---|---|---|---|---|---|---|
| GILLING, LINDA (HM08095) | ● | | ● | | | ● | | | ● | | | ● | ● | ● | | |
| GOODMAN, HENRY (HM08258) | | ● | | | | | | | | | | ● | | | | |
| GRAHAM & KERSTIN ELLIOTT (HM08336) | | | | | | | | | | | | | ● | | | |
| GROUNDS, L (HM08599) | ● | ● | | | | ● | | ● | ● | ● | ● | ● | ● | ● | | |
| HALAHAN, ELISABETH (HM08722) | ● | | ● | | ● | ● | | ● | ● | ● | ● | ● | ● | ● | ● | |
| HAMILTON-PETERS, R & J A (HM08849) | | ● | | | | | | | | | | ● | ● | ● | | |
| HARPENDEM OSTEOPATHIC PRACTICE (HM09035) | | | | | | | | | | | | | ● | | | |
| HARPENDEN CHIROPRACTIC CLINIC (HM09036) | | | | | | | | | | | | | ● | | | |
| HATHAWAY, ELIZABETH (HM09196) | | | | | | | | | | | | | ● | | | |
| HEALES CHIROPRACTIC CLINIC (HM09322) | | | | | | | | | | | | | ● | | | |
| HEALTHY AND WISE (HM09425) | ● | | | | | ● | | | | | | ● | ● | ● | | |
| HERTFORD NATURAL THERAPY CTRE (HM09690) | ● | | | | | ● | | | | | | ● | ● | ● | | |
| HODSDON, L M (HM09893) | | | | | | | | | | | | | | | ● | |
| HOLLENBERY, S (HM10019) | | | | | | | | | | | | | | | | |
| JACKSON, BARBARA (HM10830) | | ● | | | ● | | | | | | ● | | | | | |
| JENNIFER SAJIR PAED PHYSIO (HM11005) | | | | | | | | | | | | | | ● | | |
| JOE MILLER SPORTS INJURY (HM11045) | | | | | | | | | | | | | ● | | | |
| JONES, ALAN (HM11115) | | | | | | | | | | | | | ● | | ● | |
| KEW, DEREK (HM11576) | | | | | | | | | | | | ● | | | | |
| KNEBWORTH PHYSIO CLINIC (HM11742) | | | | | | | | | | | | | ● | ● | | |
| LETCHWORTH-PHYSIOTHERAPY (HM12248) | | | | | | | | | | | | | ● | | | |
| LEWIN, ROCHELLE (HM12273) | | | | | | | | | | | ● | ● | | | | |
| LIFELINES (HM12355) | | | | | | | | | | | | ● | | | | |
| LINDY, D (HM12426) | | | | | | | | | | | | | ● | | | |
| MASON, L C (HM13247) | | ● | | | ● | ● | | | | | ● | ● | | ● | | |
| MAUREEN PRIDDLE (HM13328) | | | | | | | | | | | | ● | ● | | | |
| MAYOR, DAVID F (HM13359) | ● | ● | | | | ● | | ● | | ● | | ● | ● | ● | | |
| MCTIMONEY CHIROPRACTIC CLINIC (HM13612) | | | | | | | | | | | | | | | | |
| MELLERICK, N D (HM13708) | | | | | | | | | | | | | ● | | | |
| MIDAS TOUCH (HM13808) | ● | | | ● | | | | | | | | ● | | | | |
| MID-HERTS ALEXANDER CENTRE (HM13827) | | | | | | | | | | | | ● | ● | ● | | |
| NATURAL HEALTH CLINIC (HM14589) | | | | | | | | | | | | ● | ● | | | |
| NATURAL-BALANCE CO UK (HM14672) | ● | | | | | ● | | | | | | ● | ● | ● | | ● |
| O'HARA, JOHN (HM15246) | | | | | | | | | | | | | ● | | | |

| Business by County with Reference no. | Back Pain | Bacterial Infections | Baldness | Bereavement | Bladder Problems | Blood Pressure | Boils | Bowel Problems | Breast Problems | Breathing Problems | Bronchitis | Bruising | Bulimia | Bunions | Bursitis |
|---|---|---|---|---|---|---|---|---|---|---|---|---|---|---|---|
| GILLING, LINDA (HM08095) | ● | ● | | | ● | ● | ● | ● | ● | ● | ● | ● | | | ● |
| GOODMAN, HENRY (HM08258) | | | | | | | | | | | | | | | |
| GRAHAM & KERSTIN ELLIOTT (HM08336) | ● | | | | | | | | | | | | | | |
| GROUNDS, L (HM08599) | ● | | | | ● | ● | ● | ● | ● | ● | | | ● | | ● |
| HALAHAN, ELISABETH (HM08722) | ● | ● | | | ● | ● | ● | ● | ● | ● | ● | ● | ● | | ● |
| HAMILTON-PETERS, R & J A (HM08849) | ● | | | | | ● | | ● | | | ● | | ● | | |
| HARPENDEM OSTEOPATHIC PRACTICE (HM09035) | | | | | | | | | | | | | | | |
| HARPENDEN CHIROPRACTIC CLINIC (HM09036) | ● | | | | | | | | | | | | | | |
| HATHAWAY, ELIZABETH (HM09196) | ● | | | | | ● | | | | | | | | | |
| HEALES CHIROPRACTIC CLINIC (HM09322) | ● | | | | | | | | | | | | | | |
| HEALTHY AND WISE (HM09425) | | | | | | | | | | ● | ● | | | | |
| HERTFORD NATURAL THERAPY CTRE (HM09690) | ● | | | | | | | | | | | ● | | | |
| HODSDON, L M (HM09893) | | | | | | | | | | | | | | | |
| HOLLENBERY, S (HM10019) | ● | | | | | | | | | | | ● | | | |
| JACKSON, BARBARA (HM10830) | | | | ● | | | | | | | | | | | |
| JENNIFER SAJIR PAED PHYSIO (HM11005) | | | | | | | | | | | | | | | |
| JOE MILLER SPORTS INJURY (HM11045) | ● | | | | | | | | | | | ● | | | ● |
| JONES, ALAN (HM11115) | | | | | | | | | | | | | | ● | |
| KEW, DEREK (HM11576) | | | | | | ● | | ● | | | | | ● | | |
| KNEBWORTH PHYSIO CLINIC (HM11742) | ● | | | | ● | | | | | ● | | | | | ● |
| LETCHWORTH-PHYSIOTHERAPY (HM12248) | ● | | | | | | | | | | | | | | |
| LEWIN, ROCHELLE (HM12273) | | | | | | | | | | | | | ● | | |
| LIFELINES (HM12355) | | | | | | | | | | | | | | | |
| LINDY, D (HM12426) | ● | | | | | | | | | | | | | | |
| MASON, L C (HM13247) | ● | | | | | ● | | ● | | | | | ● | | |
| MAUREEN PRIDDLE (HM13328) | ● | | | | | | | | | | | | | | |
| MAYOR, DAVID F (HM13359) | ● | ● | | | ● | ● | | ● | | ● | | | | | ● |
| MCTIMONEY CHIROPRACTIC CLINIC (HM13612) | ● | | | | | | | | | | | | | | |
| MELLERICK, N D (HM13708) | ● | | | | | | | | | | | | | | |
| MIDAS TOUCH (HM13808) | ● | | | | | | | ● | | | | | | | |
| MID-HERTS ALEXANDER CENTRE (HM13827) | ● | | | | | ● | | | | ● | | | | | |
| NATURAL HEALTH CLINIC (HM14589) | ● | | | | | | | | | | | | | | |
| NATURAL-BALANCE CO UK (HM14672) | | | | | | | | | ● | | | ● | ● | | |
| O'HARA, JOHN (HM15246) | ● | | | | | ● | | ● | | ● | ● | | | | |

| Business by County with Reference no. | Callices | Cancers | Cataracts | Catarrh | Cerebral Palsy | Circulation Problems | Cold Sores | Colds | Colic | Colitis | Conjunctivitis | Constipation | Convulsions | Corns | Coughs | Cramp | Cystitis |
|---|---|---|---|---|---|---|---|---|---|---|---|---|---|---|---|---|---|
| GILLING, LINDA (HM08095) | | ● | | ● | | ● | ● | ● | ● | ● | ● | ● | | | ● | ● | ● |
| GOODMAN, HENRY (HM08258) | | | | | | | | | | | | | | | | | |
| GRAHAM & KERSTIN ELLIOTT (HM08336) | | | | | | ● | | | ● | | | | | | | | |
| GROUNDS, L (HM08599) | | ● | ● | ● | | ● | | | ● | ● | ● | ● | | | ● | ● | ● |
| HALAHAN, ELISABETH (HM08722) | | ● | | ● | | ● | ● | ● | ● | ● | ● | ● | ● | | ● | ● | ● |
| HAMILTON-PETERS, R & J A (HM08849) | | | | | | | | ● | | ● | | | | | ● | | |
| HARPENDEM OSTEOPATHIC PRACTICE (HM09035) | | | | | | | | | | | | ● | | | | | |
| HARPENDEN CHIROPRACTIC CLINIC (HM09036) | | | | | | | | | | ● | | | | | | | |
| HATHAWAY, ELIZABETH (HM09196) | | | | | | ● | | | | | | | | | | | |
| HEALES CHIROPRACTIC CLINIC (HM09322) | | | | | | ● | | | ● | | | | | | | | |
| HEALTHY AND WISE (HM09425) | | | | ● | | | ● | ● | ● | | ● | ● | | | ● | | |
| HERTFORD NATURAL THERAPY CTRE (HM09690) | | | | | | ● | | ● | | | | ● | | | ● | ● | ● |
| HODSDON, L M (HM09893) | | | | | | | | | | | | | | | | | |
| HOLLENBERY, S (HM10019) | | | | | | | | | | | | | | | | | |
| JACKSON, BARBARA (HM10830) | | | | | | | | | | | | | | | | | |
| JENNIFER SAJIR PAED PHYSIO (HM11005) | | | | | ● | | | | | | | | | | | | |
| JOE MILLER SPORTS INJURY (HM11045) | | | | | | | | | | | | | | | | ● | |
| JONES, ALAN (HM11115) | ● | | | | | | | | | | | | | ● | | | |
| KEW, DEREK (HM11576) | | | | | | | | | | | | ● | | | | | |
| KNEBWORTH PHYSIO CLINIC (HM11742) | | | | | | | | | | | | | | | | | |
| LETCHWORTH-PHYSIOTHERAPY (HM12248) | | | | | | | | | | | | | | | | | |
| LEWIN, ROCHELLE (HM12273) | | | | | | | | | | | | | | | | | |
| LIFELINES (HM12355) | | | | | | | | | | | | | | | | | |
| LINDY, D (HM12426) | | | | | | | | | | | | | | | | | |
| MASON, L C (HM13247) | | | | | | | | | | ● | | ● | | | | | |
| MAUREEN PRIDDLE (HM13328) | | | | | | | | | | | | | | | | | |
| MAYOR, DAVID F (HM13359) | | | | ● | | ● | | ● | | ● | ● | ● | | | ● | ● | ● |
| MCTIMONEY CHIROPRACTIC CLINIC (HM13612) | | | | | | | | | | | | | | | | | |
| MELLERICK, N D (HM13708) | | | | | | | | | | | | | | | | | |
| MIDAS TOUCH (HM13808) | | | | | | | ● | ● | | | | ● | | | | | |
| MID-HERTS ALEXANDER CENTRE (HM13827) | | | | | | ● | | | | | | | | | | ● | |
| NATURAL HEALTH CLINIC (HM14589) | | | | | | ● | | | | | | | | | | | |
| NATURAL-BALANCE CO UK (HM14672) | | | | ● | | | ● | ● | ● | | ● | ● | | | ● | | ● |
| O'HARA, JOHN (HM15246) | | ● | | ● | | | | | | | | | | | | | |

# A - C Conditions treated at Practices/Businesses

| Business by County with Reference no. | Acne | Addiction | Adenoids | Aids | Alcoholism | Allergy | Alzheimer's Disease | Amnesia | Anaemia | Angina | Anorexia | Anxiety | Arthritis | Asthma | Athletes Foot | Autism |
|---|---|---|---|---|---|---|---|---|---|---|---|---|---|---|---|---|
| OPEN MINDS (HM15343) | | | | | | | | | | | | ● | | | | |
| OSTEOPATHIC CLINIC (HM15459) | | | | | | ● | | | | | | | ● | | | |
| OVERINGTON, KEL (HM15512) | | | | | | | | | | | | ● | | | | |
| PEEDLE, DAVID R (HM15938) | | | | | | | | | | | | | | | ● | |
| PERRY, KAREN (HM16049) | | | | | | | | | | | | | ● | | ● | |
| PERSONAL REFLECTIONS (HM16061) | | | | | | | | | | | | ● | ● | ● | | |
| PHYSIO & SPORTS INJURIES CLNC (HM16177) | | | | | | | | | | | | | ● | | | |
| PRIDDLE, PATRICK (HM16602) | | | | | | | | | | | | ● | | | | |
| PSYCHOTHERAPY (HM16726) | | ● | | | ● | ● | | ● | | | | ● | | ● | | |
| PURLYS (HM16769) | | | | | | | | | | | | ● | | | | |
| ROWLAND, JETHRO (HM17692) | ● | ● | | ● | ● | ● | | | | ● | ● | ● | ● | ● | | |
| S K REFLEXOLOGY (HM17811) | | | | | | | | | | | | ● | | | | |
| SHAW, CHRISTINE (HM18333) | | | | | | | | | | | | ● | ● | ● | | |
| SMITH, SUSAN (HM18813) | | | | | | | | | | | | ● | ● | ● | | |
| SOPWELL OSTEOPATHIC CLINIC (HM18894) | | | | | | | | | | | | ● | | | | |
| SOUTH, JO (HM18917) | ● | ● | ● | ● | ● | ● | ● | ● | ● | ● | ● | ● | ● | ● | ● | ● |
| SOUTHDOWN CHIROPODY PRACTICE (HM18929) | | | | | | | | | | | | | | | ● | |
| SPINOZA, DAVID (HM19019) | | | | | | | | | | | | | | | | |
| ST ALBANS CHIROPRACTIC CLINIC (HM19063) | | | | | | ● | | | | | | | ● | | | |
| STORT COUNS & PSYCHOTHERAPY (HM19351) | | | | | | | | | | | | ● | | | | |
| STORTFORD GRANGE PHYSIO CENTRE (HM19352) | | | | | | | | | | | | | ● | | | |
| SURVIVAL TRUST SURGERY (HM19526) | ● | ● | ● | ● | ● | ● | ● | ● | ● | ● | ● | ● | ● | ● | ● | ● |
| SWAN & SWAN (HM19572) | | | | | | | | | | | | | | | ● | |
| THOMPSON, MARK (HM19991) | | | | | | | | | | ● | | | ● | ● | | |
| THOMPSON, MARK () | | | | | | | | | | ● | | | ● | ● | | |
| WALKER, NEL (HM20791) | | | | | | | | | | | ● | ● | | | | |
| WALKER, RICHARD (HM20798) | | | | | | ● | | | | ● | ● | ● | ● | ● | | |
| WATSON, KATHRYN (HM21015) | ● | | | ● | | | ● | | ● | ● | | ● | | ● | ● | |
| WELWYN CHIROPRACTIC CLINIC (HM21192) | | | | | | | | | | | | | ● | | | |
| WHITE, GRAHAM C (HM21355) | ● | ● | ● | | ● | ● | ● | ● | ● | ● | ● | ● | ● | ● | ● | |
| WOOD STREET CHIROPRACTIC CLNC (HM21780) | | | | | | | | | | | | | ● | ● | | |
| WOOD STREET CLINIC (HM21781) | | ● | | | | ● | | | ● | | | | | ● | | |
| WORDSWORTH, LINDA (HM21890) | | | | | | | | | | | | ● | ● | ● | | |
| WRIGHT, DOREEN (HM21931) | ● | ● | ● | ● | ● | ● | ● | ● | ● | ● | ● | ● | ● | ● | | |

| Business by County with Reference no. | Back Pain | Bacterial Infections | Baldness | Bereavement | Bladder Problems | Blood Pressure | Boils | Bowel Problems | Breast Problems | Breathing Problems | Bronchitis | Bruising | Bulimia | Bunions | Bursitis | Callices |
|---|---|---|---|---|---|---|---|---|---|---|---|---|---|---|---|---|
| OPEN MINDS (HM15343) | ● | | | | | | | | | | | | | | | |
| OSTEOPATHIC CLINIC (HM15459) | ● | | | | | | | | | | | | | | ● | |
| OVERINGTON, KEL (HM15512) | ● | | | | ● | | | | | ● | | | | | | |
| PEEDLE, DAVID R (HM15938) | | | | | | | | | | | | | | | | ● |
| PERRY, KAREN (HM16049) | | | | | | | | | | | | | | ● | | ● |
| PERSONAL REFLECTIONS (HM16061) | ● | | | | ● | | | ● | | ● | | | | | | |
| PHYSIO & SPORTS INJURIES CLNC (HM16177) | ● | | | | ● | | | | | ● | ● | | | | ● | |
| PRIDDLE, PATRICK (HM16602) | | | | | | | | | | | | | | | | |
| PSYCHOTHERAPY (HM16726) | ● | | | ● | | | | | | | | | ● | | | |
| PURLYS (HM16769) | | | | | | | | | | | | | | | | |
| ROWLAND, JETHRO (HM17692) | ● | ● | ● | | ● | ● | ● | ● | ● | ● | ● | | ● | | ● | |
| S K REFLEXOLOGY (HM17811) | ● | | | | ● | | | ● | | ● | | | | | | |
| SHAW, CHRISTINE (HM18333) | ● | | | | | | | ● | | ● | | | | | | |
| SMITH, SUSAN (HM18813) | ● | | | | ● | | | | | ● | | | | | | |
| SOPWELL OSTEOPATHIC CLINIC (HM18894) | ● | | | | | | | ● | | ● | ● | | | | ● | |
| SOUTH, JO (HM18917) | ● | ● | ● | | ● | ● | ● | ● | ● | ● | ● | ● | ● | | ● | |
| SOUTHDOWN CHIROPODY PRACTICE (HM18929) | | | | | | | | | | | | | | | | |
| SPINOZA, DAVID (HM19019) | ● | | ● | | | | | | | ● | | | | | | |
| ST ALBANS CHIROPRACTIC CLINIC (HM19063) | ● | | | | | ● | | | | | | | | | | |
| STORT COUNS & PSYCHOTHERAPY (HM19351) | | | | | | | | | | | | | | | | |
| STORTFORD GRANGE PHYSIO CENTRE (HM19352) | ● | | | | | | | | | | | | | | | |
| SURVIVAL TRUST SURGERY (HM19526) | ● | ● | ● | | ● | ● | ● | ● | ● | ● | ● | ● | ● | | ● | |
| SWAN & SWAN (HM19572) | | | | | | | | | | | | | | | | ● |
| THOMPSON, MARK (HM19991) | ● | | | | | ● | | ● | | ● | | | | | | |
| THOMPSON, MARK () | ● | | | | | ● | | ● | | ● | | | | | | |
| WALKER, NEL (HM20791) | | | | | | | | | | | | | ● | | | |
| WALKER, RICHARD (HM20798) | ● | | | | ● | ● | | ● | | ● | | | ● | | | |
| WATSON, KATHRYN (HM21015) | | ● | | | ● | ● | ● | ● | ● | ● | ● | ● | | | | |
| WELWYN CHIROPRACTIC CLINIC (HM21192) | ● | | | | | | | | | | | | | | | |
| WHITE, GRAHAM C (HM21355) | ● | ● | | | ● | ● | ● | ● | ● | ● | ● | ● | ● | | ● | |
| WOOD STREET CHIROPRACTIC CLNC (HM21780) | ● | | | | | | | | | | | | | | | |
| WOOD STREET CLINIC (HM21781) | | ● | | | ● | ● | | ● | ● | ● | ● | ● | | | ● | |
| WORDSWORTH, LINDA (HM21890) | ● | | | | ● | ● | | ● | | | | | | | ● | |
| WRIGHT, DOREEN (HM21931) | ● | | | | ● | ● | ● | ● | ● | ● | ● | ● | | | ● | |

| Business by County with Reference no. | Cancers | Cataracts | Catarrh | Cerebral Palsy | Circulation Problems | Cold Sores | Colds | Colic | Colitis | Conjunctivitis | Constipation | Convulsions | Corns | Coughs | Cramp | Cystitis |
|---|---|---|---|---|---|---|---|---|---|---|---|---|---|---|---|---|
| OPEN MINDS (HM15343) | | | | | | | | | | | | | | | | |
| OSTEOPATHIC CLINIC (HM15459) | | | | | ● | | | | | | | | | | ● | |
| OVERINGTON, KEL (HM15512) | | | | | ● | | | | | | | | | | | |
| PEEDLE, DAVID R (HM15938) | | | | | | | | | | | | | ● | | | |
| PERRY, KAREN (HM16049) | | | | | | | | | | | | | ● | | | |
| PERSONAL REFLECTIONS (HM16061) | | | ● | | ● | | | | | | ● | | | | | |
| PHYSIO & SPORTS INJURIES CLNC (HM16177) | | | | | ● | | | | | | | | | | | |
| PRIDDLE, PATRICK (HM16602) | | | | | | | | | | | | | | | | |
| PSYCHOTHERAPY (HM16726) | | | | | | | | | | | | | | | | |
| PURLYS (HM16769) | | | | | | | | | | | | | | | | |
| ROWLAND, JETHRO (HM17692) | ● | ● | ● | | ● | ● | ● | ● | ● | ● | ● | ● | | ● | ● | ● |
| S K REFLEXOLOGY (HM17811) | | | | | ● | | | | | | | | | | | |
| SHAW, CHRISTINE (HM18333) | | | ● | | ● | | ● | | ● | | ● | | | | | ● |
| SMITH, SUSAN (HM18813) | | | ● | | ● | | | | | | ● | | | | | |
| SOPWELL OSTEOPATHIC CLINIC (HM18894) | | | ● | | ● | | ● | | ● | | ● | | | ● | | |
| SOUTH, JO (HM18917) | ● | ● | ● | | ● | ● | ● | ● | ● | ● | ● | ● | | ● | ● | ● |
| SOUTHDOWN CHIROPODY PRACTICE (HM18929) | | | | | | | | | | | | | | | | |
| SPINOZA, DAVID (HM19019) | | | | | ● | | | | | | | | | | | |
| ST ALBANS CHIROPRACTIC CLINIC (HM19063) | | | | | ● | | | | | | | | | | | |
| STORT COUNS & PSYCHOTHERAPY (HM19351) | | | | | | | | | | | | | | | | |
| STORTFORD GRANGE PHYSIO CENTRE (HM19352) | | | | | | | | | | | | | | | | |
| SURVIVAL TRUST SURGERY (HM19526) | ● | ● | ● | | ● | ● | ● | ● | ● | ● | ● | ● | | ● | ● | ● |
| SWAN & SWAN (HM19572) | | | | | | | | | | | | | ● | | | |
| THOMPSON, MARK (HM19991) | | | | | ● | | | ● | | | ● | | | ● | | |
| THOMPSON, MARK () | | | | | ● | | | ● | | | ● | | | ● | | |
| WALKER, NEL (HM20791) | | | | | | | | | | | | | | | | |
| WALKER, RICHARD (HM20798) | ● | | | | ● | | | | | | ● | | | | | |
| WATSON, KATHRYN (HM21015) | | | ● | | ● | ● | ● | ● | ● | ● | ● | ● | | ● | ● | ● |
| WELWYN CHIROPRACTIC CLINIC (HM21192) | | | | | ● | | | ● | | | | | | | | |
| WHITE, GRAHAM C (HM21355) | ● | | ● | | ● | ● | ● | ● | ● | ● | ● | ● | | ● | ● | ● |
| WOOD STREET CHIROPRACTIC CLNC (HM21780) | | | | | | | | ● | | | | | | | | |
| WOOD STREET CLINIC (HM21781) | | | ● | | ● | ● | ● | ● | ● | ● | ● | | | ● | | ● |
| WORDSWORTH, LINDA (HM21890) | | | | | ● | | | | ● | | ● | | | | | |
| WRIGHT, DOREEN (HM21931) | | ● | ● | | ● | ● | ● | ● | ● | ● | ● | ● | | ● | ● | ● |

www.healthmyself.com

# A - C Conditions treated at Practices/Businesses

| Business by County with Reference no. | Acne | Addiction | Adenoids | Aids | Alcoholism | Allergy | Alzheimer's Disease | Amnesia | Anaemia | Angina | Anorexia | Anxiety | Arthritis | Asthma | Athletes Foot | Autism | Back Pain | Bacterial Infections | Baldness | Bereavement | Bladder Problems | Blood Pressure | Boils | Bowel Problems |
|---|---|---|---|---|---|---|---|---|---|---|---|---|---|---|---|---|---|---|---|---|---|---|---|---|
| WRIGHT, KAREN (HM21940) | | | | | | | | | | | | | | | ● | | | | | | | | | |
| WYE, DEBORAH (HM21969) | | | | | | | | | | | | | | | ● | | | | | | | | | |
| WYNDHAM CLINIC (HM21977) | ● | | ● | | | ● | | | | | | ● | ● | ● | ● | ● | ● | ● | | | ● | ● | ● | ● |
| **HUMBERSIDE** | | | | | | | | | | | | | | | | | | | | | | | | |
| BATH, ANN (HM01899) | ● | | | | | | | | | | | ● | ● | | | | ● | | | | | | | |
| BRIGG CHIROPRACTIC CLINIC (HM03028) | | | | | | | | | | | | | ● | | | | ● | | | | | | | |
| BRIGG SKIN SURGERY (HM03030) | ● | | | | | | | | | | | | | | | | | | | | | | | |
| MESSINGHAM CHIROPODIST SURGERY (HM13761) | | | | | | | | | | | | | | | ● | | | | | | | | | |
| PRIOSE COLES (HM16635) | ● | | | | | ● | | | ● | | | ● | ● | ● | | | ● | | | | ● | ● | | |
| SCUNTHORPE CHIROPRACTIC CLINIC (HM18157) | | | | | | | | | | | | | ● | | | | ● | | | | | | | |
| **HUMBERSIDE (NORTH)** | | | | | | | | | | | | | | | | | | | | | | | | |
| ACADEMY PHYSIOTHERAPY CLINIC (HM00149) | | | | | | | | | | | | | ● | | | | ● | | | | | | | |
| BEVERLEY CHIROPRACTIC CLINIC (HM02243) | | | | | | | | | | | | | ● | | | | ● | | | | | | | |
| BRIDLINGTON CHIROPODY SURGERY (HM03018) | | | | | | | | | | | | | ● | | ● | | | ● | | | | | | |
| DAMIAN P JOHNS (HM05704) | | | | | | | | | | | | | | | ● | | | | | | | | | |
| GILBERDYKE SPORTS & INJURY (HM08054) | | | | | | | | | | | | | ● | | | | ● | | | | | | | |
| NATURAL THERAPIES (HM14629) | | ● | | | | ● | | | | | | ● | ● | ● | | | ● | | | | ● | ● | | ● |
| NATURAL THERAPY CENTRE (HM14653) | | ● | | ● | ● | ● | | | | | ● | ● | ● | ● | | | | | | | | ● | | |
| SAMANTHA WHITE AROMATICA (HM17877) | | | | | | | | | | | | ● | ● | ● | ● | | ● | ● | | | ● | ● | ● | ● |
| STARLIGHT CENTRE (HM19151) | | | | | | ● | | | | | | | | | | | | | | | | | | |
| **HUMBERSIDE (SOUTH)** | | | | | | | | | | | | | | | | | | | | | | | | |
| DAVIES, MICHAEL (HM05831) | | | | | | | | | | | | | ● | | | | ● | | | | | | | |
| HARRISON-WILLIAMS (HM09113) | | | | | | | | | | | | | | | ● | | | | | | | | | |
| HARRISON-WILLIAMS CHIROPODIST (HM09114) | | | | | | | | | | | | | | | ● | | | | | | | | | |
| LOUISE HEALING CENTRE (HM12668) | | ● | | | | ● | | | | | | ● | ● | ● | | | ● | | | | ● | ● | ● | ● |
| ROBINSON, KEITH (HM17488) | | | | | | | | | | | | | | | ● | | | | | | | | | |
| SCARTHO OSTEOPATHIC PRACTICE (HM18007) | | | | | | | | | | | | | ● | | | | ● | | | | | | | |
| WALL, R A (HM20819) | | | | | | | | | | | | | ● | | | | ● | | | | | | | |
| WEBB, C M (HM21057) | | | | | | | | | | | | | | | ● | | | | | | | | | |
| **ISLE OF WIGHT** | | | | | | | | | | | | | | | | | | | | | | | | |
| BURROWS, MARY (HM03424) | | | | | | | | | | | | | | | ● | | | ● | | | | | | |
| CARISBROOKE HEALTH CENTRE (HM03687) | | | | | | | | | | | | | | | ● | | ● | ● | | | | | | |
| F VON - MEHREN (HM07034) | | | | | | | | | | | | | | | ● | | | | | | | | | |
| FLANDERS, H (HM07391) | | | | | | | | | | | | | | | ● | | | ● | | | | | | |

| Business by County with Reference no. | Breast Problems | Breathing Problems | Bronchitis | Bruising | Bulimia | Bunions | Bursitis | Callices | Cancers | Cataracts | Catarrh | Cerebral Palsy | Circulation Problems | Cold Sores | Colds | Colic | Colitis | Conjunctivitis | Constipation | Convulsions | Corns | Coughs | Cramp | Cystitis |
|---|---|---|---|---|---|---|---|---|---|---|---|---|---|---|---|---|---|---|---|---|---|---|---|---|
| WRIGHT, KAREN (HM21940) | | | | | | | | | | | | | | | | | | | | | | | | |
| WYE, DEBORAH (HM21969) | | | | | | | | ● | | | | | | | | | | | | | ● | | | |
| WYNDHAM CLINIC (HM21977) | ● | ● | ● | | | | | | ● | | ● | | | ● | ● | ● | ● | | ● | | | ● | ● | ● |
| **HUMBERSIDE** | | | | | | | | | | | | | | | | | | | | | | | | |
| BATH, ANN (HM01899) | | | | | | | | | | | | | | | | | | | | | | | | |
| BRIGG CHIROPRACTIC CLINIC (HM03028) | | | | | | | | | | | | | ● | | | | | | | | | | | |
| BRIGG SKIN SURGERY (HM03030) | | | | | | | | | | | | | | | | | | | | | | | | |
| MESSINGHAM CHIROPODIST SURGERY (HM13761) | | | | | | | | ● | | | | | | | | | | | | | ● | | | |
| PRIOSE COLES (HM16635) | | ● | | | | | | | | | ● | | ● | ● | | ● | ● | | ● | | | | | ● |
| SCUNTHORPE CHIROPRACTIC CLINIC (HM18157) | | | | | | | ● | | | | | | | | | | | | | | | | | |
| **HUMBERSIDE (NORTH)** | | | | | | | | | | | | | | | | | | | | | | | | |
| ACADEMY PHYSIOTHERAPY CLINIC (HM00149) | | | | | | | | | | | | | | | | | | | | | | | | |
| BEVERLEY CHIROPRACTIC CLINIC (HM02243) | | | | | | | | | | | | | ● | | | | | | | | | | ● | |
| BRIDLINGTON CHIROPODY SURGERY (HM03018) | | | | | | ● | | ● | | | | | | | | | | | | | ● | | | |
| DAMIAN P JOHNS (HM05704) | | | | | | | | ● | | | | | | | | | | | | | ● | | | |
| GILBERDYKE SPORTS & INJURY (HM08054) | | | | ● | | | | | | | | | | | | | | | | | | | ● | |
| NATURAL THERAPIES (HM14629) | | ● | | | | | | | ● | | ● | | ● | | ● | | ● | | ● | ● | | ● | | ● |
| NATURAL THERAPY CENTRE (HM14653) | | ● | ● | | ● | | | | ● | | | | | | | | | | ● | | | | | |
| SAMANTHA WHITE AROMATICA (HM17877) | | | ● | | | | | | | | ● | | ● | ● | ● | | ● | | ● | | | | | ● |
| STARLIGHT CENTRE (HM19151) | | | | | | | | | | | | | | | | | | | | | | | | |
| **HUMBERSIDE (SOUTH)** | | | | | | | | | | | | | | | | | | | | | | | | |
| DAVIES, MICHAEL (HM05831) | | | | ● | | | ● | | | | | | | | | | | | | | | | | |
| HARRISON-WILLIAMS (HM09113) | | | | | | | | ● | | | | | | | | | | | | | ● | | | |
| HARRISON-WILLIAMS CHIROPODIST (HM09114) | | | | | | | | | | | | | | | | | | | | | | | | |
| LOUISE HEALING CENTRE (HM12668) | | ● | | ● | | | ● | | ● | | ● | | ● | | | ● | ● | | ● | | | | | |
| ROBINSON, KEITH (HM17488) | | | | | | | | ● | | | | | | | | | | | | | ● | | | |
| SCARTHO OSTEOPATHIC PRACTICE (HM18007) | | | | | | | ● | | | | | | | | | | | | | | | | ● | |
| WALL, R A (HM20819) | | | | | | | | | | | | | | | | | | | | | | | | |
| WEBB, C M (HM21057) | | | | | | | | ● | | | | | | | | | | | | | ● | | | |
| **ISLE OF WIGHT** | | | | | | | | | | | | | | | | | | | | | | | | |
| BURROWS, MARY (HM03424) | | | | | | ● | | ● | | | | | | | | | | | | | ● | | | |
| CARISBROOKE HEALTH CENTRE (HM03687) | | ● | | | | ● | | ● | | | | | | | | | | | | | ● | | | |
| F VON - MEHREN (HM07034) | | | | | | ● | | ● | | | | | | | | | | | | | ● | | | |
| FLANDERS, H (HM07391) | | | | | | ● | | ● | | | | | | | | | | | | | ● | | | |

# A - C Conditions treated at Practices/Businesses

| Business by County with Reference no. | Acne | Addiction | Adenoids | Aids | Alcoholism | Allergy | Alzheimer's Disease | Amnesia | Anaemia | Angina | Anorexia | Anxiety | Arthritis | Asthma | Athletes Foot | Autism | Back Pain | Bacterial Infections | Baldness | Bereavement | Bladder Problems | Blood Pressure | Boils | Bowel Problems | Breast Problems | Breathing Problems | Bronchitis | Bruising | Bulimia | Bunions | Bursitis | Callices | Cancers | Cataracts | Catarrh | Cerebral Palsy | Circulation Problems | Cold Sores | Colds | Colic | Colitis | Conjunctivitis | Constipation | Convulsions | Corns | Coughs | Cramp | Cystitis |
|---|---|---|---|---|---|---|---|---|---|---|---|---|---|---|---|---|---|---|---|---|---|---|---|---|---|---|---|---|---|---|---|---|---|---|---|---|---|---|---|---|---|---|---|---|---|---|---|---|
| FOOTSTEPS (HM07510) | | | | | | | | | | | | | | | ● | | | ● | | | | | | | | | | | | ● | | | | | | | | | | | | | | | | | | |
| FOOTSTEPS THERAPY CENTRE (HM07513) | | | | | | | | | | | | | | | ● | | | ● | | | | | | | | | | | | ● | | ● | | | | | | | | | | | | | ● | | | |
| GREENFIELD, BRIAN (HM08484) | | | | | | | | | | | | ● | ● | ● | | | ● | | | | | ● | | | | ● | | | | | | | ● | | ● | | ● | | | | | | | | | | ● | |
| HOPE CLINIC (HM10134) | ● | ● | ● | ● | ● | ● | ● | ● | ● | ● | ● | ● | ● | ● | ● | ● | ● | ● | ● | | ● | ● | ● | ● | ● | ● | ● | ● | ● | | ● | ● | ● | ● | ● | | ● | ● | ● | ● | ● | ● | ● | ● | ● | ● | ● | ● |
| HYPNOTHERAPY CONSULTANCY (HM10537) | | ● | | | ● | | | ● | | | ● | ● | | ● | | | | | | | | ● | | ● | | | | | ● | | | | | | | | ● | | | | | | | | | | | |
| SHEN CLINIC (HM18391) | | | | | | | | | | | | ● | ● | ● | | | ● | | | | | | | | | ● | | | | | | | | | | | | | | | | | | | | | | |
| TAYLOR, S A (HM19791) | | | | | | | | | | | | | | | ● | | | ● | | | | | | | | | | | | | | ● | | | | | | | | | | | | | ● | | | |
| TOUCH FOR HEALTH (HM20186) | | | | | | | | | | | | | | | | | ● | | | | | | | | | | | | | | | | | | | | | | | | | | | | | | | |
| WRIGLEY, BARBARA (HM21956) | | | | | | | | | | | | ● | ● | | | | ● | | | | | | | | | | | | | | | | | | | | | | | | | | | | | | | |
| **KENT** | | | | | | | | | | | | | | | | | | | | | | | | | | | | | | | | | | | | | | | | | | | | | | | | |
| ABBOTT, LISA (HM00098) | | | | | | | | | | | | ● | | | | | ● | | | | | ● | | ● | | ● | | | | | | | | | | | ● | | | | | | ● | | | | | |
| ABSOLUTE SOLUTIONS (HM00142) | | ● | | | ● | | | | | ● | | ● | | ● | | | ● | | | | | ● | | | | | | | ● | | | | | | | | | | ● | | | | | | | | | |
| ALEXANDER TECHNIQUE (HM00553) | | | | | | | | | | | | | | | | | ● | | | | | | | | | | | | | | | | | | | | | | | | | | | | | | | |
| ASHFORD CLINIC (HM01216) | | | | | | ● | | | | | | ● | | | | | ● | | | | | | | | | | | | | | | | | | | | ● | | | | | | | | | | | |
| ASHFORD OSTEOPATHIC CLINIC (HM01217) | | | | | | | | | | | | | ● | | | | ● | | | | | | | | | | | | | | | | | | | | | | | | | | | | | | | |
| AYLSHAM OSTEOPATHIC PRACTICE (HM01429) | | | | | | | | | | | | | ● | ● | | | ● | | | | | | | ● | | | | | | | ● | | | | | | | | | ● | | | | | | | | |
| BECKENHAM & BROMLEY (HM02017) | | | | | | | | | | | | | ● | | | | ● | | | | | | | | | | | | | | | | | | | | ● | | | ● | | | | | | | | |
| BENNETT, J P (HM02143) | | | | | | | | | | | | ● | | | | | | | | | | | | | | | | | | | | | | | | | | | | | | | | | | | | |
| BERGMANN, MARIA (DR) (HM02190) | ● | | | | | | | | | | | | | | | | | | | | | | | | | | | | | | | | ● | | | | ● | | | | | | | | | | | |
| BEXLEY OSTEOPATHIC CLINIC (HM02259) | | | | | | | | | | | | | ● | | | | ● | | | | | | | | | | | | | | | | | | | | | | | | | | | | | | | |
| BEXLEYHEATH NATURAL HEALTH (HM02262) | ● | ● | ● | ● | ● | ● | ● | ● | ● | ● | ● | ● | ● | ● | ● | ● | ● | ● | ● | | ● | ● | ● | ● | ● | ● | ● | ● | ● | | ● | ● | ● | ● | ● | | ● | ● | ● | ● | ● | ● | ● | ● | ● | ● | ● | ● |
| BISHOP, SARAH (HM02411) | | | | | | | | | | | | | | | | | ● | | | | | | | | | ● | | | | | | | | | | | | | | | | | | | | | | |
| BLACKFEN HYPNOTHERAPY (HM02442) | ● | ● | | | ● | | | | | ● | ● | ● | | ● | | | | | | | ● | ● | | ● | | | | | ● | | | | | | | | | | | | ● | | | | | | ● | |
| BLOSSOM AROMATHERAPY CENTRE (HM02521) | | | | | | | | | | | | ● | ● | | | | ● | | | | | | | | | | | | | | | | | | | | | | | | | | | | | | | |
| BROMLEY CHIROPODY CENTRE (HM03142) | | | | | | | | | | | | | | | ● | | | | | | | | | | | | | | | | | ● | | | | | | | | | | | | | ● | | | |
| BROMLEY CHIROPRACTIC CLINIC (HM03143) | | ● | | | ● | ● | | | | | | ● | ● | | | | ● | | | | | | | | | ● | | | | | | | | | | | ● | | | | | | | | | | | |
| BROMLEY OSTEOPATHIC CLINIC (HM03145) | | | | | | | | | | | | | ● | | | | ● | | | | | ● | | | | | | | | | | | | | | | ● | | | | | | | | | | | |
| CANTERBURY OSTEOPATHIC CLINIC (HM03641) | | | ● | | | ● | | | ● | | | ● | ● | ● | ● | ● | ● | ● | | | | ● | | ● | ● | ● | ● | | | | ● | | ● | | ● | | ● | | ● | ● | ● | | ● | ● | | ● | | ● |
| CARDWELL, MARTIN (HM03673) | | ● | ● | ● | ● | ● | ● | ● | ● | ● | ● | ● | ● | ● | | ● | ● | | | | ● | ● | | ● | | ● | ● | ● | ● | | | ● | ● | | ● | | ● | | | | | ● | ● | ● | ● | ● | ● | ● |
| CASTLE CLINIC (HM03830) | ● | ● | ● | | ● | ● | ● | ● | ● | ● | ● | ● | ● | ● | ● | ● | ● | ● | ● | | ● | ● | ● | ● | ● | ● | ● | ● | ● | | ● | ● | | ● | ● | | ● | ● | ● | ● | ● | ● | ● | ● | ● | ● | ● | ● |
| CENTRE (HM03897) | ● | ● | ● | ● | ● | ● | ● | ● | ● | ● | ● | ● | ● | ● | ● | ● | ● | ● | ● | | ● | ● | ● | ● | ● | ● | ● | ● | ● | | ● | ● | ● | ● | ● | | ● | ● | ● | ● | ● | ● | ● | ● | ● | ● | ● | ● |
| CHANDRA PDS (HM03982) | | ● | | | ● | ● | | | | | | ● | | | | | | | | | | | | | | | | | | | | | | | | | | | | | | | | | | | | |
| CHANGE OF LIFE (HM03984) | ● | | | | | | | | ● | ● | | | ● | ● | | | | | | | | | | ● | | | | | | | | | | | | | | | | | | | | | | | | |
| CHINESE HERBAL MED & HLTH CARE (HM04200) | | | | | | | | | | | | | ● | | | | | | | | | | | | | | | | | | | | | | | | | | | | | | | | | | | |

www.healthmyself.com

# A - C Conditions treated at Practices/Businesses

| Business by County with Reference no. | Acne | Addiction | Adenoids | Aids | Alcoholism | Allergy | Alzheimer's Disease | Amnesia | Anaemia | Angina | Anorexia | Anxiety | Arthritis | Asthma | Athletes Foot | Autism | Back Pain | Bacterial Infections | Baldness | Bereavement | Bladder Problems | Blood Pressure | Boils | Bowel Problems | Breast Problems | Breathing Problems | Bronchitis | Bruising | Bulimia | Bunions | Bursitis | Callices | Cancers | Cataracts | Catarrh | Cerebral Palsy | Circulation Problems | Cold Sores | Colds | Colic | Colitis | Conjunctivitis | Constipation | Convulsions | Corns | Coughs | Cramp | Cystitis |
|---|---|---|---|---|---|---|---|---|---|---|---|---|---|---|---|---|---|---|---|---|---|---|---|---|---|---|---|---|---|---|---|---|---|---|---|---|---|---|---|---|---|---|---|---|---|---|---|
| CHINESE HERBAL MED ACU CTRE (HM04205) | | | | | | | | | | | | | ● | ● | | | | | | | | | | | | | | | | | | | | | | | | | | | | | | | | | | |
| CHIROPRACTIC PLUS (HM04402) | ● | ● | ● | ● | ● | ● | ● | ● | ● | ● | ● | ● | ● | ● | ● | ● | ● | ● | ● | | ● | ● | ● | ● | ● | ● | ● | ● | ● | | ● | ● | | ● | ● | | ● | ● | ● | ● | ● | ● | ● | ● | ● | ● | ● | ● |
| CHISLEHURST NATURAL HEALTH (HM04410) | ● | ● | ● | ● | ● | ● | ● | ● | ● | ● | ● | ● | ● | ● | ● | ● | ● | ● | ● | | ● | ● | ● | ● | ● | ● | ● | ● | ● | | ● | ● | ● | ● | ● | | ● | ● | ● | ● | ● | ● | ● | ● | ● | ● | ● | ● |
| CHISTLEHURST NATURAL HLTH CTRE (HM04411) | ● | ● | ● | ● | ● | ● | ● | ● | ● | ● | ● | ● | ● | ● | ● | ● | ● | ● | ● | | ● | ● | ● | ● | ● | ● | ● | ● | ● | | ● | ● | ● | ● | ● | | ● | ● | ● | ● | ● | ● | ● | ● | ● | ● | ● | ● |
| CHRISTINE CHINNERY COMP THER (HM04446) | ● | | | | | | | | ● | | | ● | ● | ● | ● | | ● | ● | | | ● | | ● | ● | ● | ● | ● | ● | | | | | ● | | | | ● | | ● | ● | ● | | ● | | | ● | ● | ● |
| CORRIGAN, PETER (HM05195) | | | | | | | | | | | | ● | | | | | | | | | | | | | | | | | | | | | | | | | | | | | | | | | | | | |
| COURT, SUSAN (HM05266) | | | | | | | | | | | | | ● | | | | ● | | | | ● | ● | | ● | | | | | | | | | | | | | | | | | | | ● | | | | ● | ● |
| COURT, SUSAN (HM05265) | | | | | | | | | | | | | ● | | | | ● | | | | ● | ● | | ● | | | | | | | | | | | | | | | | | | | ● | | | | ● | ● |
| COYSTEN & ASSOCIATES (HM05332) | | | | | | | | | | ● | | ● | ● | ● | | ● | ● | | | | ● | ● | | ● | | ● | | | | | ● | | | | | | ● | | | ● | ● | | ● | ● | | | ● | ● |
| CROIX, LINDA LA (HM05460) | | | | | | | | | | | | ● | ● | | | | | | | | | | | | | | | | | | | | | | | | | | | | | | | | | | | |
| DELTA MEDI CLINIC (HM05969) | | | | | | | | | | | | | ● | | | | ● | | | | ● | | | | | | | | | | ● | | | | | | | | | | | | | | | | | |
| DICKMAN, ANNIE (HM06080) | ● | | ● | | | ● | | | | | | ● | ● | ● | ● | | ● | ● | | | ● | ● | ● | ● | | ● | ● | ● | | | ● | | | | ● | | ● | ● | ● | ● | | | ● | | | ● | ● | ● |
| DILLON, MICHAEL (HM06100) | | | | | | | | | | | | ● | | | | | | | | | | | | | | | | | | | | | | | | | | | | | | | | | | | | |
| DIMENT, GORDON L (HM06105) | | ● | | | | | | | | | ● | ● | | | | | | | | | | | | ● | | | | | ● | | | | | | | | | | | | | | | | | | | |
| EARL, A (HM06496) | | | | | | | | | | | | ● | | | | | | | | | | | | | | | | | | | | | | | | | | | | | | | | | | | | |
| EDWARDS, R (HM06668) | | | | | | | | | | | | | ● | | | | ● | | | | | | | | | | | | | | | | | | | | ● | | | | | | | | | | | |
| EDWARDS, R, HERNE BAY (HM06670) | | | | | | | | | | | | | ● | | | | ● | | | | | | | | | | | | | | | | | | | | ● | | | | | | | | | | | |
| ELIZABETH ANNE (HM06736) | | ● | | | ● | | | | | | ● | ● | | | | | | | | | | | | | | | | | | | | | | | | | | | | | ● | | ● | | | | | |
| EUROPEAN AYUR-VEDA (HM06944) | | | | | | ● | | | | | | ● | ● | | | | ● | | | | | ● | | | | | | | | | | | | | | | | | | | | | ● | | | | | |
| EVEGATE CLINIC (HM06996) | ● | ● | ● | ● | ● | ● | ● | ● | ● | ● | ● | ● | ● | ● | ● | ● | ● | ● | ● | | ● | ● | ● | ● | ● | ● | ● | ● | ● | | ● | | ● | ● | ● | | ● | ● | ● | ● | ● | ● | ● | ● | | ● | ● | ● |
| EVOLUTION HEALTH (HM07014) | | | | | | | | | | | | | | | | | ● | | | | | | | | | | | | | | | | | | | | | | | ● | | | | | | | | |
| FALCONER, PATRICIA (HM07073) | | | | | | | | | | | | ● | | | | | ● | | | | | | | | | | | | | | | | | | | | | | | | | | | | | | | |
| FEET FIRST (HM07167) | | | | | | | | | | | | ● | ● | ● | | | | | | | | ● | | ● | | ● | | | | | | | ● | | | | ● | | | | ● | | ● | | | | | |
| FRANCIS-JONES, TREVOR (DR) (HM07679) | | | | | | | | | | | | | ● | | | | ● | | | | | | | | | | | | | | | | | | | | | | | | | | | | | | | |
| GIBSON, JAN (HM08040) | | ● | | | ● | | | | | | | ● | | ● | | | ● | | | | | | | ● | | ● | | | ● | | | | | | | | ● | | | | | | ● | | | | | |
| GILLINGHAM CLINIC OF COMP MED (HM08097) | ● | | | | | ● | | | | ● | | | ● | ● | | | ● | | | | | ● | | ● | ● | ● | ● | ● | | | ● | | | | ● | | ● | ● | ● | ● | ● | ● | ● | | | ● | ● | ● |
| GRAVESEND HOMOEOPATHY CLINIC (HM08404) | ● | | ● | | | ● | | | ● | | | ● | ● | ● | ● | ● | ● | | | | ● | ● | ● | ● | ● | ● | ● | ● | ● | | ● | ● | | | ● | | ● | ● | ● | ● | ● | ● | ● | | ● | ● | ● | ● |
| GUNN, JASON (HM08642) | | | | | | | | | | | | | ● | | | | ● | | | | | | | | | | | | | | | | | | | | | | | | | | | | | | | |
| HANNA, MARK (HM08931) | | ● | | | ● | ● | | | | | | ● | | ● | | | | | | | | ● | | ● | | ● | | | ● | | | | | | | | | | | | | | | | | | | |
| HAYES, JACQUELINE (HM09260) | | | | | | ● | | | | | | ● | ● | ● | | ● | ● | | | | ● | ● | | ● | ● | ● | ● | | | | | | ● | | ● | | ● | | | ● | ● | | ● | ● | | ● | ● | |
| HAZLEWOOD OSTEOPATHIC PRACTICE (HM09297) | | | | | | | | | | | | | ● | ● | | | ● | | | | | | | | | | | | | | | | | | | | | | | | | | | | | | | |
| HEAD TO TOE WELL-BEING (HM09300) | | | | | | | | | | | | ● | | | | | ● | | | | | ● | | | | | | | | | | | | | | | ● | | | | | | | | | | | |
| HEALING AND HERBS (HM09325) | ● | ● | | ● | ● | ● | ● | | ● | ● | ● | ● | ● | ● | | | ● | ● | | | ● | ● | ● | ● | | ● | ● | ● | ● | | | | ● | | ● | | ● | ● | ● | ● | | | ● | | | | | ● |
| HEATHSIDE CENTRE (HM09461) | ● | ● | ● | ● | ● | ● | ● | ● | ● | ● | ● | ● | ● | ● | ● | ● | ● | ● | ● | | ● | ● | ● | ● | ● | ● | ● | ● | ● | | ● | ● | ● | ● | ● | | ● | ● | ● | ● | ● | ● | ● | ● | ● | ● | ● | ● |

# A - C Conditions treated at Practices/Businesses

| Business by County with Reference no. | Acne | Addiction | Adenoids | Aids | Alcoholism | Allergy | Alzheimer's Disease | Amnesia | Anaemia | Angina | Anorexia | Anxiety | Arthritis | Asthma | Athletes Foot | Autism | Back Pain | Bacterial Infections | Baldness | Bereavement | Bladder Problems | Blood Pressure | Boils | Bowel Problems | Breast Problems | Breathing Problems | Bronchitis | Bruising | Bulimia | Bunions | Bursitis | Callices | Cancers | Cataracts | Catarrh | Cerebral Palsy | Circulation Problems | Cold Sores | Colds | Colic | Colitis | Conjunctivitis | Constipation | Convulsions | Corns | Coughs | Cramp | Cystitis |
|---|---|---|---|---|---|---|---|---|---|---|---|---|---|---|---|---|---|---|---|---|---|---|---|---|---|---|---|---|---|---|---|---|---|---|---|---|---|---|---|---|---|---|---|---|---|---|---|---|
| HERTERICH, NIGEL (HM09688) | | | | | | | | | | | | | | | | |●| | | | | | | | | | | | | | | | | | | | | | | | | | | | | | | |
| HOFFMAN, BRIAN ASSOCIATES (HM09900) | | | | | | | | | | | | |●| | | |●| | | | | | | | | | |●| | | | | | | | |●| | | | | | | | | |●| |
| HOLMES, S A (HM10045) | | | | | | | | | | | |●|●| | | | | | | |●|●| |●| |●| | | | | | | | | | |●| | | | | | | | | | | |
| HOPE CHIROPRACTIC (HM10133) | | | | | | | | | | | | |●| | | | | | | | | | | | | | | | | | | | | | | |●| | | | | | | | | | | |
| JACCQUELINE ELLISON PRACTICE (HM10811) | | | | | | | | | | | | | | | | |●| | | | | | | | | | | | | | | | | | | | | | | | | | | | | | | |
| KARMERS CLINIQUE (HM11328) |●| | | | |●| | | | | | | | | | |●| | | | | | | | | | | | | | | |●| |●| |●| | | | | | | | | | | |
| KENT HOUSE CHIROPRACTIC CLINIC (HM11520) | | | | | | | | | | | | |●| | | | | | | | | | | | | | | | | | | | | | | |●| | | | | | | | | | | |
| KENT HOUSE CHIROPRACTIC CLINIC (HM11517) | | | | | | | | | | | | |●| | | |●| | | | | | | | | | | | | | | | | | | |●| | | | | | | | | | | |
| KENT HOUSE CHIROPRACTIC CLINIC (HM11518) | | | | | | | | | | | | |●| | | | | | | | | | | | | | | | | | | | | | | |●| | | | | | | | | | | |
| KENT HOUSE CHIROPRACTIC CLINIC (HM11519) | | | | | | | | | | | | |●| | | |●| | | | | | | | | | | | | | | | | | | |●| | |●| | | | | | | | |
| KSC (HM11812) |●|●|●|●|●|●|●|●|●|●|●|●|●|●|●|●|●|●|●| |●|●|●|●|●|●|●|●|●| |●|●|●|●|●| |●|●|●|●|●|●|●|●|●|●|●|●|
| LAMB, G BRIAN (HM11888) |●| |●| | | | | |●|●| |●|●|●|●| |●|●|●|●|●|●|●|●| |●|●|●| | |●| | | |●| |●|●|●|●|●|●|●| | |●|●|●|
| LAVINGOTN, A (HM12034) |●| | | | | | | | | | |●|●| | | |●| | | | | | | | | | | | | | | | | | | | | | | | | | | | | | | |
| LEBOR, JILL (HM12115) | |●| | | |●| | | |●| |●|●|●| | |●| | | |●|●| |●|●|●|●| | | | | |●| |●| |●| |●|●|●| |●| | |●|●| |
| LIVING WELL CLINIC (HM12488) | | | | | | | | | | | | |●| | | |●| | | | | | | | | | | | | | | | | | | |●| | | | | | | | | | | |
| LOBB, BRIAN W (HM12528) | | | | | | | | | | | |●| | | | | | | | | | | | | | | | | | | | | | | | | | | | | | | | | | | | |
| LUGG, G (HM12732) | | | | | |●| | | | | |●|●|●|●|●|●|●| | |●|●|●|●| | | |●| | | | | | |●| |●| | | | | | | | | | | |
| MABBERLEY, KATHIE (HM12812) |●| | | | | | | | | | | |●|●| | |●| | | | | | |●| | | | | | | | | | |●| |●| | | | | | | | | | | |
| MAIDSTONE ACUPUNCTURE CLINIC (HM12935) |●|●| |●|●|●|●| | |●|●|●|●|●| | |●| |●| |●|●|●|●|●|●|●|●|●| |●| | | |●| |●|●|●|●|●|●|●|●| |●|●|●|
| MARY CANNON - CLINICAL NUTRI (HM13221) |●| | | | |●| | | |●|●|●|●|●|●| | |●| | | |●|●|●|●|●|●|●| | | | | | |●| |●|●|●|●|●|●|●| | |●|●|●|
| MASON & ASSOCIATES (HM13232) | | | | | | | | | | | | |●| | | |●| | | | |●| | | | | | | | | | | | | | | | | | | | | | | | | | |
| MASON & ASSOCIATES (HM13233) | | | | | | | | | | | | |●| | | |●| | | | |●| | | | | | | | | | | | | | | | | | | | | | | | | | |
| MATHER, SUE (HM13281) |●|●|●|●|●|●|●|●|●|●|●|●|●|●|●|●|●|●|●| |●|●|●|●|●|●|●|●|●| |●|●|●|●|●| |●|●|●|●|●|●|●|●|●|●|●|●|
| MCDOWELL, S (HM13467) | | | | | | | | | | | | | | | | |●| | | | | | | | | | | | | | | | | | | | | | | | | | | | | | | |
| MEADOWS (HM13630) | | | | | | | | | | | | | | | | | | | | | | | | | | | | | | | | | | | | | | |●| | | | | | | | | |
| MEOPHAM CLINIC (HM13732) | | | | | | | | | | | | |●| | | |●| | | | |●| | | | | | | | | | | | | | |●| | | | | | | | | | | |
| MUIRHEAD, MARGARET (HM14323) |●|●|●|●|●|●|●|●|●|●|●|●|●|●|●|●|●|●|●| |●|●|●|●|●|●|●|●|●| |●|●|●| |●| |●|●|●|●|●|●|●|●|●|●|●|●|
| MULVANEY, ALISTAIR (HM14353) | | | | | | | | | | | | | | |●| | | | | | | | | | | | | | | | |●| | | | | | | | | | | | |●| | | |
| NATURAL HEALTH CENTRE (HM14568) |●|●|●|●|●|●|●|●|●|●|●|●|●|●|●|●|●|●|●| |●|●|●|●|●|●|●|●|●| |●|●|●|●|●| |●|●|●|●|●|●|●|●|●|●|●|●|
| NATURAL HEALTH CENTRE (HM14562) | |●| | |●| | | | | | | | | | | | | | |●| | | | | | | | |●| | | | | | | | | | | | | | | | | | | |
| NATURAL THERAPIST (HM14635) |●| | | |●| | |●|●|●| |●|●|●| | |●| | | | |●| |●| | |●|●| | |●| | | |●| |●| | | | | |●| | | |●| |
| NATURAL THERAPY CENTRE (HM14643) | | | | | |●| | | | | | |●| | | | | | | | | | | | | | | | | | | | | | | | | | | | | | | | | | | |
| OPTIVAVA (HM15352) | | | | | | | | | | | | | | | | |●| | | | | | | | | | | | | | | | | | | | | | | | | | | | | | | |
| OSTEOPATHIC CLINIC (HM15461) | | | | | | | | | | | | |●| | | |●| | | | | | | | | | | | | | | | | | | |●| | | | | | | | | | | |

www.healthmyself.com

# A - C Conditions treated at Practices/Businesses

| Business by County with Reference no. | Acne | Addiction | Adenoids | Aids | Alcoholism | Allergy | Alzheimer's Disease | Amnesia | Anaemia | Angina | Anorexia | Anxiety | Arthritis | Asthma | Athletes Foot | Autism |
|---|---|---|---|---|---|---|---|---|---|---|---|---|---|---|---|---|
| OSTEOPATHIC PRACTICE (HM15466) | | | | | | | | | | | | | | | | |
| PASSCHIER, MAREANNE SASSEN (HM15779) | ● | ● | ● | ● | ● | ● | ● | ● | ● | ● | ● | ● | ● | ● | ● | ● |
| PATERSON, MARGARET (HM15814) | | | | | | | | | | | ● | ● | ● | ● | | |
| PEARTON, GILL (HM15919) | | ● | | | | ● | | | ● | ● | ● | ● | ● | ● | | |
| PELE, ANDRI (HM15950) | | ● | | | ● | | | | | | ● | ● | | | | |
| PHYSIOTHERAPY CENTRE (HM16230) | | | | | | | | | | | | | ● | | ● | |
| PRINCES AVENUE OSTEOPATHIC (HM16623) | | | | | | | | | | | | | ● | ● | | |
| RALPH & EVANS (HM16906) | ● | ● | | | | ● | | | ● | ● | | ● | ● | ● | ● | |
| READ, CHARLES REG OSTEOPATH (HM16994) | | | | | | | | | | | | | ● | | | |
| REVEREND CAROL HADDERSLEY (HM17204) | ● | ● | ● | ● | ● | ● | ● | ● | ● | ● | ● | ● | ● | ● | ● | |
| RIDLEY, VICKY (HM17324) | ● | | ● | ● | | ● | ● | | ● | ● | ● | ● | ● | ● | ● | |
| ROCHESTER PHYSIO & SPORTS (HM17520) | | | | | | | | | | | | | ● | | | |
| ROMNEY MARSH OSTEOPATHS (HM17574) | | | | | | ● | | | | | | | ● | ● | | |
| ROSE, NAOMI (HM17612) | | | | | | | | | | | | ● | | ● | | |
| ROUND ROOM (HM17663) | ● | | | | | ● | | | | | | ● | ● | ● | | |
| SACKS, PATRICA (HM17828) | | | | | | | | | | | | | | | ● | |
| SANCTUM HOLISTIC THERAPY CTRE (HM17896) | | | | | | | | | | | | ● | | | | |
| SANDERS, PETER (HM17914) | | | | | | | | | | | | | | | | |
| SANDOWN CLINIC FOR COMP MED (HM17926) | ● | ● | ● | ● | ● | ● | ● | ● | ● | ● | ● | ● | ● | ● | ● | ● |
| SHEARER, GAYLE (HM18357) | | | | | | | | | | | | | | | | |
| SHIATSU (HM18451) | | | | | | | | | | | | ● | | | | |
| SOUTH LONDON HYPNOTHERAPY CTRE (HM18910) | | ● | | | ● | | | ● | | ● | | | | ● | | |
| SOUTHCOTE CHIROPRACTIC CLINIC (HM18927) | | | | | | | | | | | | | ● | | | |
| STARFIELDS HOLISTIC HLTH CTRE (HM19145) | ● | ● | ● | ● | ● | ● | ● | ● | ● | ● | ● | ● | ● | ● | ● | ● |
| STONE, CHARLES (HM19334) | | ● | | | | | | | | | ● | ● | | | | |
| STURGE, DEBBIE (HM19445) | ● | | | | | | | | | | | | ● | ● | | |
| SWAN, VIVA (HM19575) | ● | ● | ● | ● | ● | ● | ● | ● | ● | ● | ● | ● | ● | ● | ● | ● |
| SYCAMORE, TONI (HM19606) | | | | | | | | | | | | | ● | ● | ● | |
| TONBRIDGE CLINIC (HM20151) | | | | | | ● | | | | | ● | ● | | | ● | |
| TOWN, BERNICE (HM20199) | | | | | | | | | | | | | | | ● | |
| TURNER, ANDREA (HM20417) | | | ● | | | ● | | | ● | ● | ● | ● | ● | ● | | |
| VARNEY, MONICA (HM20591) | | | | | | | | | | | | ● | ● | ● | | |
| VILLAGE PHYSIOTHERAPY PRACTICE (HM20667) | | | | | | | | | | | | | | | | |
| VINCENT, EUNICE (HM20671) | | | | | | | | | | | | | | | | |

| Business by County with Reference no. | Back Pain | Bacterial Infections | Baldness | Bereavement | Bladder Problems | Blood Pressure | Boils | Bowel Problems | Breast Problems | Breathing Problems | Bronchitis | Bruising | Bulimia | Bunions | Bursitis | Callices |
|---|---|---|---|---|---|---|---|---|---|---|---|---|---|---|---|---|
| OSTEOPATHIC PRACTICE (HM15466) | ● | | | | | | | | | | | | | | | |
| PASSCHIER, MAREANNE SASSEN (HM15779) | ● | ● | ● | | ● | ● | ● | ● | ● | ● | ● | ● | ● | | ● | ● |
| PATERSON, MARGARET (HM15814) | ● | | | | ● | ● | | ● | | ● | ● | | ● | | | |
| PEARTON, GILL (HM15919) | ● | | | | ● | ● | ● | ● | ● | ● | ● | | | | | ● |
| PELE, ANDRI (HM15950) | | | | ● | | | | | | | | | ● | | | |
| PHYSIOTHERAPY CENTRE (HM16230) | | | | | | | | | | | | | | | | ● |
| PRINCES AVENUE OSTEOPATHIC (HM16623) | ● | | | | | | | ● | | | | | | | ● | |
| RALPH & EVANS (HM16906) | | ● | | | ● | ● | ● | ● | ● | ● | ● | | | | ● | |
| READ, CHARLES REG OSTEOPATH (HM16994) | ● | | | | | | | | | | | | | | ● | |
| REVEREND CAROL HADDERSLEY (HM17204) | ● | ● | ● | | ● | ● | ● | ● | ● | ● | ● | ● | ● | | ● | ● |
| RIDLEY, VICKY (HM17324) | | ● | | | ● | ● | ● | ● | ● | ● | ● | ● | | | ● | |
| ROCHESTER PHYSIO & SPORTS (HM17520) | ● | | | | | | | | | | | ● | | | | |
| ROMNEY MARSH OSTEOPATHS (HM17574) | ● | | | | ● | ● | | ● | | ● | ● | | | | | |
| ROSE, NAOMI (HM17612) | ● | | | | | ● | | ● | | | | | | | | |
| ROUND ROOM (HM17663) | | | | | | | | | | | | | | | | |
| SACKS, PATRICA (HM17828) | | | | | | | | | | | | | | | | ● |
| SANCTUM HOLISTIC THERAPY CTRE (HM17896) | ● | | | | | | | | | | | | | | | |
| SANDERS, PETER (HM17914) | ● | | | | | | | | | | | | | | | |
| SANDOWN CLINIC FOR COMP MED (HM17926) | ● | ● | ● | | ● | ● | ● | ● | ● | ● | ● | ● | ● | | ● | ● |
| SHEARER, GAYLE (HM18357) | ● | | | | | | | | | | | | | | | |
| SHIATSU (HM18451) | ● | | | | | | | | | | | | | | | |
| SOUTH LONDON HYPNOTHERAPY CTRE (HM18910) | ● | | | | | ● | | ● | | | | | ● | | | |
| SOUTHCOTE CHIROPRACTIC CLINIC (HM18927) | ● | | | | | | | | | | | | | | ● | |
| STARFIELDS HOLISTIC HLTH CTRE (HM19145) | ● | ● | | ● | ● | ● | ● | ● | ● | ● | ● | ● | ● | ● | ● | ● |
| STONE, CHARLES (HM19334) | | | | | | | | | | | | | ● | | | |
| STURGE, DEBBIE (HM19445) | | | | | | | | ● | | | | | | | | |
| SWAN, VIVA (HM19575) | ● | ● | ● | | ● | ● | ● | ● | ● | ● | ● | ● | ● | | ● | ● |
| SYCAMORE, TONI (HM19606) | | | | | | | | | | | | | | | | |
| TONBRIDGE CLINIC (HM20151) | ● | | | | | | | | | | | | | | | |
| TOWN, BERNICE (HM20199) | | | | | | | | | | | | | | | | ● |
| TURNER, ANDREA (HM20417) | ● | | | | | | | | | ● | | | | | | |
| VARNEY, MONICA (HM20591) | ● | | | | | ● | | ● | | ● | | | | | | |
| VILLAGE PHYSIOTHERAPY PRACTICE (HM20667) | ● | | | | | | | | | | | | | | | |
| VINCENT, EUNICE (HM20671) | ● | | | | | | | | | | | | | | | |

| Business by County with Reference no. | Cancers | Cataracts | Catarrh | Cerebral Palsy | Circulation Problems | Cold Sores | Colds | Colic | Colitis | Conjunctivitis | Constipation | Convulsions | Corns | Coughs | Cramp | Cystitis |
|---|---|---|---|---|---|---|---|---|---|---|---|---|---|---|---|---|
| OSTEOPATHIC PRACTICE (HM15466) | | | | | ● | | | | | | | | | | ● | |
| PASSCHIER, MAREANNE SASSEN (HM15779) | ● | ● | ● | | ● | ● | ● | ● | ● | ● | ● | ● | ● | ● | ● | ● |
| PATERSON, MARGARET (HM15814) | ● | | ● | | ● | | | | | | ● | | | ● | | |
| PEARTON, GILL (HM15919) | | | ● | | ● | | ● | | ● | | ● | | ● | ● | | ● |
| PELE, ANDRI (HM15950) | | | | | | | | | | | | | | | | |
| PHYSIOTHERAPY CENTRE (HM16230) | | | | | | | | | | | | | ● | | | |
| PRINCES AVENUE OSTEOPATHIC (HM16623) | | | | | ● | | | ● | | | ● | | | | | |
| RALPH & EVANS (HM16906) | | | ● | | ● | ● | ● | ● | ● | ● | ● | | | ● | ● | ● |
| READ, CHARLES REG OSTEOPATH (HM16994) | | | | | | | | | | | | | | | ● | |
| REVEREND CAROL HADDERSLEY (HM17204) | ● | ● | ● | | ● | ● | ● | ● | ● | ● | ● | ● | ● | ● | ● | ● |
| RIDLEY, VICKY (HM17324) | ● | | ● | | ● | ● | ● | ● | ● | ● | ● | | | ● | ● | ● |
| ROCHESTER PHYSIO & SPORTS (HM17520) | | | | | | | | | | | | | | | | |
| ROMNEY MARSH OSTEOPATHS (HM17574) | | | ● | | ● | | ● | ● | ● | | ● | | | ● | ● | ● |
| ROSE, NAOMI (HM17612) | | | ● | | ● | | | ● | ● | | ● | | | | ● | |
| ROUND ROOM (HM17663) | | | ● | | ● | | | | | | ● | | | | | |
| SACKS, PATRICA (HM17828) | | | | | | | | | | | | | ● | | | |
| SANCTUM HOLISTIC THERAPY CTRE (HM17896) | | | | | | | | | | | | | | | | |
| SANDERS, PETER (HM17914) | | | | | | | | | | | | | | | | |
| SANDOWN CLINIC FOR COMP MED (HM17926) | ● | ● | ● | | ● | ● | ● | ● | ● | ● | ● | ● | ● | ● | ● | ● |
| SHEARER, GAYLE (HM18357) | | | | | | | | | | | | | | | | |
| SHIATSU (HM18451) | | | | | | | | | | | | | | | | |
| SOUTH LONDON HYPNOTHERAPY CTRE (HM18910) | | | | | ● | | | | ● | | ● | | | | | ● |
| SOUTHCOTE CHIROPRACTIC CLINIC (HM18927) | | | | | | | | | | | | | | | | |
| STARFIELDS HOLISTIC HLTH CTRE (HM19145) | ● | ● | ● | | ● | ● | ● | ● | ● | ● | ● | ● | ● | ● | ● | ● |
| STONE, CHARLES (HM19334) | | | | | | | | | | | | | | | | |
| STURGE, DEBBIE (HM19445) | | | | | | | | | | | ● | | | | | |
| SWAN, VIVA (HM19575) | ● | ● | ● | | ● | ● | ● | ● | ● | ● | ● | ● | ● | ● | ● | ● |
| SYCAMORE, TONI (HM19606) | | | | | | | | | | | | | | | | |
| TONBRIDGE CLINIC (HM20151) | | | | | | | | | | | | | | | | |
| TOWN, BERNICE (HM20199) | | | | | | | | | | | | | ● | | | |
| TURNER, ANDREA (HM20417) | ● | | | | ● | | | | | | ● | | | | | |
| VARNEY, MONICA (HM20591) | ● | | | | | | | | | | ● | | | | | |
| VILLAGE PHYSIOTHERAPY PRACTICE (HM20667) | | | | | | | | | | | | | | | | |
| VINCENT, EUNICE (HM20671) | | | | | | | | | | | | | | | | |

# A - C Conditions treated at Practices/Businesses

| Business by County with Reference no. | Acne | Addiction | Adenoids | Aids | Alcoholism | Allergy | Alzheimer's Disease | Amnesia | Anaemia | Angina | Anorexia | Anxiety | Arthritis | Asthma | Athletes Foot | Autism | Back Pain | Bacterial Infections | Baldness | Bereavement | Bladder Problems | Blood Pressure | Boils | Bowel Problems |
|---|---|---|---|---|---|---|---|---|---|---|---|---|---|---|---|---|---|---|---|---|---|---|---|---|
| VINES REIKI HEALING CENTRE (HM20680) | ● | ● | ● | ● | ● | ● | ● | ● | ● | ● | ● | ● | ● | ● | ● | ● | ● | ● | ● |  | ● | ● | ● | ● |
| WATLING STREET THERAPY CTRE (HM21001) | ● | ● |  |  |  | ● |  |  |  |  |  | ● | ● | ● | ● |  | ● |  |  |  |  |  | ● |  |
| WEBB, JENNIFER (HM21067) |  |  |  |  |  |  |  |  |  |  |  |  | ● |  |  |  | ● |  |  |  |  | ● |  |  |
| WELLS PHYSIO & SPORTS CLINIC (HM21168) |  |  |  |  |  |  |  |  |  |  |  |  | ● |  |  |  | ● |  |  |  |  |  |  |  |
| WOLFE, ROBERT (HM21762) |  |  |  |  |  |  |  |  |  |  |  |  |  |  | ● |  |  |  |  |  |  |  |  |  |
| WOOLF, JOY (HM21871) |  |  |  |  |  |  |  |  |  |  |  |  |  |  |  |  | ● |  |  |  |  |  |  |  |
| LANCASHIRE |  |  |  |  |  |  |  |  |  |  |  |  |  |  |  |  |  |  |  |  |  |  |  |  |
| ABERNETHY, HILARY (HM00123) |  |  |  |  |  |  |  |  |  |  |  | ● | ● |  |  |  | ● |  |  |  |  | ● |  | ● |
| ACUPUNCTURE PRIVATE CLINIC (HM00317) |  |  |  |  |  |  |  |  |  |  |  |  |  |  |  |  | ● |  |  |  |  |  |  |  |
| ALPHAWAVE (HM00685) |  | ● |  |  |  |  |  |  |  |  | ● | ● |  |  |  |  |  |  |  |  |  |  |  |  |
| ALTERNATIVE MEDICINE (HM00715) | ● | ● | ● |  |  | ● |  |  | ● | ● | ● | ● | ● | ● | ● |  | ● |  |  |  | ● | ● | ● | ● |
| ALTERNATIVE MEDICINE PRACTICE (HM00721) | ● | ● | ● |  |  | ● |  |  | ● | ● | ● | ● | ● | ● | ● |  | ● |  |  |  | ● | ● | ● | ● |
| BARRETT & LIPTROTT (HM01783) |  |  |  |  |  |  |  |  |  |  |  |  |  |  | ● |  |  |  |  |  |  |  |  |  |
| BEARLEY, CAROL (HM01969) |  |  |  |  |  | ● |  |  |  |  |  | ● | ● | ● |  |  | ● |  |  |  |  |  |  |  |
| BEESTON, J (HM02061) |  |  |  |  |  |  |  |  |  |  |  |  | ● | ● |  |  | ● |  |  |  |  |  |  |  |
| BENTLEY AND ASSOCIATES (HM02172) |  | ● |  |  | ● |  |  |  |  |  |  | ● | ● |  | ● |  | ● |  |  |  |  |  |  |  |
| BFMP (HM02265) | ● |  |  |  |  | ● |  |  | ● |  |  | ● | ● | ● |  |  | ● |  | ● |  |  |  |  |  |
| BIOS NATURE CLINIC (HM02344) |  |  |  |  |  |  |  |  |  |  |  |  |  |  |  |  |  |  |  |  |  |  |  |  |
| BOLTON CHIROPRATIC CLINIC (HM02656) |  |  |  |  |  |  |  |  |  |  |  |  | ● |  |  |  | ● |  |  |  |  |  |  |  |
| BOLTON CLINIC OF ACUPUNCTURE (HM02657) |  |  |  |  |  |  |  |  |  |  |  | ● | ● | ● |  |  | ● |  |  |  |  |  |  |  |
| BOLTON PHYSIOTHERAPY CLINIC (HM02658) |  |  |  |  |  |  |  |  |  |  |  |  | ● |  |  |  | ● |  |  |  |  |  |  |  |
| BOLTON THERAPY CENTRE (HM02659) |  |  |  |  |  | ● |  |  |  |  |  | ● | ● | ● |  |  | ● |  |  |  |  | ● |  | ● |
| BOLTON, VANESSA (HM02664) |  |  | ● |  |  | ● |  |  |  | ● |  | ● | ● | ● |  |  | ● |  |  |  | ● | ● |  | ● |
| BRIDGWATER, K A (HM03016) | ● | ● | ● | ● | ● | ● | ● | ● | ● | ● | ● | ● | ● | ● | ● | ● | ● | ● | ● |  | ● | ● | ● | ● |
| BROOKES, MICHAEL (HM03163) | ● |  |  |  |  | ● |  |  |  |  |  |  | ● | ● | ● |  |  |  |  |  |  |  |  | ● |
| CHARTERED PHYSIO & SPORTS (HM04041) |  |  |  |  |  |  |  |  |  |  |  |  | ● |  |  |  | ● |  |  |  |  |  |  |  |
| CLOUGHS - CHRTRD PHYSIO CLINIC (HM04735) |  |  |  |  |  |  |  |  |  |  |  |  | ● |  |  |  | ● |  |  |  |  |  |  |  |
| COLES, RONNIE (HM04836) |  |  |  |  |  |  |  |  |  |  |  |  |  |  | ● |  |  |  |  |  |  |  |  |  |
| COMPLEMENTARY HEALTH SERVICES (HM04929) |  |  |  |  |  |  |  |  |  |  |  |  | ● |  |  |  | ● |  |  |  |  |  |  |  |
| COTTAM, O N (HM05224) |  |  |  |  |  |  |  |  |  |  |  |  |  |  | ● |  |  |  |  |  |  |  |  |  |
| CRYSTAL & REIKI (HM05524) |  |  |  |  |  |  |  |  |  |  |  |  | ● |  |  |  | ● |  |  |  |  |  |  |  |
| DAVIES, JOHNATHON (HM05819) |  |  |  |  |  |  |  |  |  |  |  |  |  |  | ● |  |  |  |  |  |  |  |  |  |
| DOUGLAS, CAROLINE (HM06213) |  |  |  |  |  |  |  |  |  |  |  |  | ● |  | ● |  |  | ● |  |  |  |  |  |  |
| DUCKWORTH, JEAN (HM06347) | ● | ● | ● |  | ● | ● | ● |  | ● | ● |  | ● | ● | ● | ● | ● | ● | ● | ● |  | ● | ● | ● | ● |

| Business by County with Reference no. | Breast Problems | Breathing Problems | Bronchitis | Bruising | Bulimia | Bunions | Bursitis | Callices | Cancers | Cataracts | Catarrh | Cerebral Palsy | Circulation Problems | Cold Sores | Colds | Colic | Colitis | Conjunctivitis | Constipation | Convulsions | Corns | Coughs | Cramp | Cystitis |
|---|---|---|---|---|---|---|---|---|---|---|---|---|---|---|---|---|---|---|---|---|---|---|---|---|
| VINES REIKI HEALING CENTRE (HM20680) | ● | ● | ● | ● | ● |  | ● | ● | ● | ● | ● |  | ● | ● | ● | ● | ● | ● | ● | ● | ● | ● | ● | ● |
| WATLING STREET THERAPY CTRE (HM21001) |  |  |  |  |  |  |  |  |  |  |  |  |  | ● | ● |  | ● | ● | ● |  |  | ● | ● | ● |
| WEBB, JENNIFER (HM21067) |  |  |  |  |  |  |  |  |  |  |  |  |  |  |  |  |  |  |  |  |  |  |  |  |
| WELLS PHYSIO & SPORTS CLINIC (HM21168) |  |  |  | ● |  |  |  |  |  |  |  |  |  |  |  |  |  |  |  |  |  |  |  |  |
| WOLFE, ROBERT (HM21762) |  |  |  |  |  |  |  |  |  |  |  |  |  |  |  |  |  |  |  |  |  |  |  |  |
| WOOLF, JOY (HM21871) |  |  |  |  |  |  |  |  |  |  |  |  |  |  |  |  |  |  |  |  |  |  |  |  |
| LANCASHIRE |  |  |  |  |  |  |  |  |  |  |  |  |  |  |  |  |  |  |  |  |  |  |  |  |
| ABERNETHY, HILARY (HM00123) |  |  |  |  |  |  |  |  |  |  |  |  | ● | ● |  |  |  |  |  |  |  |  |  |  |
| ACUPUNCTURE PRIVATE CLINIC (HM00317) |  |  |  |  |  |  |  |  |  |  |  |  |  |  |  |  |  |  |  |  |  |  |  |  |
| ALPHAWAVE (HM00685) |  |  |  |  | ● |  |  |  |  |  |  |  |  |  |  |  |  |  |  |  |  |  |  |  |
| ALTERNATIVE MEDICINE (HM00715) |  | ● | ● |  | ● |  | ● |  |  |  | ● |  | ● | ● | ● | ● | ● |  | ● |  |  | ● | ● | ● |
| ALTERNATIVE MEDICINE PRACTICE (HM00721) |  | ● | ● |  | ● |  |  |  |  |  | ● |  | ● | ● | ● | ● | ● | ● | ● |  |  | ● | ● | ● |
| BARRETT & LIPTROTT (HM01783) |  |  |  |  |  |  |  | ● |  |  |  |  |  |  |  |  |  |  |  |  | ● |  |  |  |
| BEARLEY, CAROL (HM01969) |  |  |  |  |  |  |  |  |  |  |  |  | ● |  |  |  |  |  |  |  |  |  |  |  |
| BEESTON, J (HM02061) |  |  |  | ● |  |  | ● |  |  |  |  |  | ● |  |  |  |  |  |  |  |  |  | ● |  |
| BENTLEY AND ASSOCIATES (HM02172) |  |  |  | ● |  |  | ● |  |  |  |  |  |  |  |  |  |  |  |  |  |  |  |  |  |
| BFMP (HM02265) |  | ● | ● |  |  |  |  |  |  |  |  |  | ● |  |  |  |  |  | ● |  |  |  |  |  |
| BIOS NATURE CLINIC (HM02344) |  |  |  |  |  |  |  |  | ● |  |  |  |  |  |  |  |  |  |  |  |  |  |  |  |
| BOLTON CHIROPRATIC CLINIC (HM02656) |  |  |  |  |  |  |  |  |  |  |  |  | ● |  |  | ● |  |  |  |  |  |  |  |  |
| BOLTON CLINIC OF ACUPUNCTURE (HM02657) |  |  |  |  | ● |  |  |  |  |  |  |  |  |  |  |  |  |  | ● |  |  |  |  |  |
| BOLTON PHYSIOTHERAPY CLINIC (HM02658) |  |  |  |  |  |  |  |  |  |  |  |  |  |  |  |  |  |  |  |  |  |  |  |  |
| BOLTON THERAPY CENTRE (HM02659) |  | ● |  |  |  |  | ● |  |  |  | ● |  |  |  |  |  | ● |  | ● |  |  |  |  | ● |
| BOLTON, VANESSA (HM02664) | ● | ● |  |  |  |  |  |  |  |  | ● |  | ● | ● |  |  | ● | ● | ● |  |  |  | ● | ● |
| BRIDGWATER, K A (HM03016) | ● | ● | ● | ● | ● |  | ● | ● | ● | ● | ● |  | ● | ● | ● | ● | ● | ● | ● | ● | ● | ● | ● | ● |
| BROOKES, MICHAEL (HM03163) |  |  |  |  |  |  |  |  |  |  | ● |  |  |  |  |  | ● |  | ● |  |  |  |  |  |
| CHARTERED PHYSIO & SPORTS (HM04041) |  |  |  |  |  |  |  |  |  |  |  |  |  |  |  |  |  |  |  |  |  |  |  |  |
| CLOUGHS - CHRTRD PHYSIO CLINIC (HM04735) |  |  |  |  |  |  |  |  |  |  |  |  |  |  |  |  |  |  |  |  |  |  |  |  |
| COLES, RONNIE (HM04836) |  |  |  |  |  |  |  | ● |  |  |  |  |  |  |  |  |  |  |  |  | ● |  |  |  |
| COMPLEMENTARY HEALTH SERVICES (HM04929) |  |  |  |  |  |  |  |  |  |  |  |  |  |  |  |  |  |  |  |  |  |  |  |  |
| COTTAM, O N (HM05224) |  |  |  |  |  |  |  | ● |  |  |  |  |  |  |  |  |  |  |  |  | ● |  |  |  |
| CRYSTAL & REIKI (HM05524) |  |  |  |  |  |  |  |  |  |  |  |  |  |  |  |  |  |  |  |  |  |  |  |  |
| DAVIES, JOHNATHON (HM05819) |  |  |  |  |  |  |  |  |  |  |  |  |  |  |  |  |  |  |  |  |  |  |  |  |
| DOUGLAS, CAROLINE (HM06213) |  |  |  |  |  | ● |  | ● |  |  |  |  |  |  |  |  |  |  |  |  | ● |  |  |  |
| DUCKWORTH, JEAN (HM06347) | ● | ● |  | ● |  |  |  |  | ● |  | ● |  | ● | ● | ● | ● | ● | ● | ● | ● |  | ● | ● | ● |

# A - C Conditions treated at Practices/Businesses

| Business by County with Reference no. | Acne | Addiction | Adenoids | Aids | Alcoholism | Allergy | Alzheimer's Disease | Amnesia | Anaemia | Angina | Anorexia | Anxiety | Arthritis | Asthma | Athletes Foot | Autism | Back Pain | Bacterial Infections | Baldness | Bereavement | Bladder Problems | Blood Pressure | Boils | Bowel Problems |
|---|---|---|---|---|---|---|---|---|---|---|---|---|---|---|---|---|---|---|---|---|---|---|---|---|
| GEE, D (HM07957) |  |  |  |  |  |  |  |  |  |  |  |  |  |  | ● |  |  | ● |  |  |  |  |  |  |
| GREENHALGH, A J T (HM08489) |  |  |  |  |  |  |  |  |  |  |  |  |  |  | ● |  |  |  |  |  |  |  |  |  |
| GROGAN, DIANA E (HM08592) |  |  |  |  |  |  |  |  |  | ● |  |  | ● | ● | ● |  | ● |  |  |  | ● | ● |  | ● |
| HAMPSOM, JAMES (HM08878) |  |  |  |  |  | ● |  |  |  |  |  | ● | ● |  |  |  | ● |  |  |  |  |  |  |  |
| HARDMAN, ALAN (HM08974) |  |  |  |  |  |  |  |  |  |  |  |  |  |  | ● |  |  |  |  |  |  |  |  |  |
| HARMONIOUS HEALTHCARE (HM09015) | ● |  | ● |  |  |  |  |  |  | ● |  | ● | ● | ● | ● |  | ● | ● |  |  | ● |  | ● | ● |
| HAYDOCK, CLAIRE (HM09254) |  |  |  |  |  |  |  |  |  |  |  |  |  |  | ● |  |  |  |  |  |  |  |  |  |
| HEAVENS SCENT AROMATHERAPY (HM09478) | ● |  |  |  |  |  |  |  |  |  |  | ● |  |  |  |  |  |  |  |  |  |  |  |  |
| HEYWORTH, S (HM09716) |  |  |  |  |  |  |  |  |  |  |  |  |  |  | ● |  |  |  |  |  |  |  |  |  |
| HOLDEN, JOHN H (HM09932) |  |  |  |  |  |  |  |  |  |  |  |  |  |  | ● |  |  |  |  |  |  |  |  |  |
| JOHN HOLDEN ASSOCIATES (HM11051) |  |  |  |  |  |  |  |  |  |  |  |  |  |  | ● |  |  |  |  |  |  |  |  |  |
| KELLY CHIROPODY (HM11424) |  |  |  |  |  | ● |  |  |  |  |  | ● |  | ● | ● |  | ● |  |  |  |  |  |  |  |
| KENDEL HOUSE CLINIC (HM11479) |  |  |  |  |  |  |  |  |  |  |  |  | ● |  |  |  | ● |  |  |  |  |  |  |  |
| LAYNE, SUSAN G (HM12077) | ● | ● |  |  |  | ● |  |  | ● | ● |  | ● | ● | ● |  |  | ● |  |  |  | ● | ● | ● | ● |
| LEYLAND PHYSIOTHERAPY CENTRE (HM12319) |  |  |  |  |  |  |  |  |  |  |  |  | ● |  |  |  | ● |  |  |  |  |  |  |  |
| MALKIN, DK, MANIP THERAPY (HM12975) |  |  |  |  |  |  |  |  |  |  |  | ● | ● | ● |  |  | ● |  |  |  |  |  |  |  |
| MOBILE CHIROPODIST (HM14027) |  |  |  |  |  |  |  |  |  |  |  |  |  |  | ● |  |  |  |  |  |  |  |  |  |
| NATURAL HEALTH CENTRE (HM14566) | ● |  |  |  |  | ● |  |  | ● |  |  | ● | ● | ● | ● |  | ● |  | ● |  | ● | ● | ● | ● |
| NELSON, S (HM14782) |  |  |  |  |  | ● |  |  |  | ● |  | ● | ● | ● |  |  | ● | ● |  |  | ● | ● |  | ● |
| ONE STOP HEALTH & BEAUTY (HM15323) | ● | ● | ● | ● | ● | ● | ● | ● | ● | ● | ● | ● | ● | ● | ● | ● | ● | ● | ● | ● | ● | ● | ● | ● |
| PEPPER, JOHN (HM16009) |  |  |  |  |  |  |  |  |  |  |  | ● | ● | ● |  |  | ● |  |  |  |  | ● |  | ● |
| PHYSIO AND SPORTS INJURIES (HM16195) |  |  |  |  |  |  |  |  |  |  |  |  | ● |  |  |  | ● |  |  |  |  |  |  |  |
| PURCELL, AMANDA (HM16762) |  |  |  |  |  |  |  |  |  |  |  |  | ● |  |  |  | ● |  |  |  |  |  |  |  |
| RAMSBOTTOM PHYSIO CLINIC (HM16919) |  |  |  |  |  |  |  |  |  |  |  |  | ● |  |  |  | ● |  |  |  |  |  |  |  |
| RATCLIFFE, MARK (HM16949) |  |  |  |  |  |  |  |  |  |  |  |  | ● |  |  |  | ● |  |  |  |  |  |  |  |
| REMEDIAL MASSAGE/SPORTS (HM17175) |  |  |  |  |  |  |  |  |  |  |  |  |  |  |  |  | ● |  |  |  |  |  |  |  |
| SMITH, CHRISTOPHER (DR) (HM18728) |  |  |  |  |  |  |  |  |  |  |  |  | ● |  |  |  | ● |  |  |  |  |  |  |  |
| SPIRITUAL THERAPIST (HM19029) |  |  |  |  |  |  |  |  |  |  |  | ● |  |  |  |  |  |  |  |  |  |  |  |  |
| ST GEORGES MULTI THERAPY CTRE (HM19075) |  | ● |  |  | ● | ● |  |  |  |  | ● | ● |  |  | ● |  | ● |  |  |  |  |  |  |  |
| ST MARY'S CLINIC (HM19087) |  |  |  |  |  |  |  |  |  |  |  |  | ● |  | ● |  | ● |  |  |  |  |  |  |  |
| TATTERSALL, KAREN (HM19719) |  |  |  |  |  |  |  |  |  |  |  |  |  |  | ● |  |  |  |  |  |  |  |  |  |
| TINKER, D C (HM20083) |  |  |  |  |  |  |  |  |  |  |  |  |  |  | ● |  |  |  |  |  |  |  |  |  |
| TIP TOES (HM20086) |  |  |  |  |  |  |  |  |  |  |  | ● | ● |  |  |  | ● |  |  |  | ● | ● |  | ● |
| TRADITIONAL ACUPUNCTURE CLINIC (HM20220) |  |  |  |  |  |  |  |  |  |  |  | ● | ● | ● |  |  | ● |  |  |  | ● | ● |  | ● |

| Business by County with Reference no. | Breast Problems | Breathing Problems | Bronchitis | Bruising | Bulimia | Bunions | Bursitis | Callices | Cancers | Cataracts | Catarrh | Cerebral Palsy | Circulation Problems | Cold Sores | Colds | Colic | Colitis | Conjunctivitis | Constipation | Convulsions | Corns | Coughs | Cramp | Cystitis |
|---|---|---|---|---|---|---|---|---|---|---|---|---|---|---|---|---|---|---|---|---|---|---|---|---|
| GEE, D (HM07957) |  |  |  |  |  | ● |  | ● |  |  |  |  |  |  |  |  |  |  |  |  | ● |  |  |  |
| GREENHALGH, A J T (HM08489) |  |  |  |  |  |  |  | ● |  |  |  |  |  |  |  |  |  |  |  |  | ● |  |  |  |
| GROGAN, DIANA E (HM08592) |  | ● | ● |  |  |  |  |  |  |  | ● |  |  |  |  |  | ● |  | ● |  |  | ● |  | ● |
| HAMPSOM, JAMES (HM08878) |  |  |  |  |  |  |  |  |  |  |  |  | ● |  |  |  |  |  | ● |  |  |  |  |  |
| HARDMAN, ALAN (HM08974) |  |  |  |  |  |  |  |  |  |  |  |  |  |  |  |  |  |  |  |  |  |  |  |  |
| HARMONIOUS HEALTHCARE (HM09015) |  |  |  |  |  |  | ● |  |  |  |  |  | ● |  | ● | ● | ● |  | ● |  |  |  |  | ● |
| HAYDOCK, CLAIRE (HM09254) |  |  |  |  |  |  |  | ● |  |  |  |  |  |  |  |  |  |  |  |  | ● |  |  |  |
| HEAVENS SCENT AROMATHERAPY (HM09478) |  |  |  |  |  |  |  |  |  |  |  |  | ● |  |  |  |  |  | ● |  |  |  |  | ● |
| HEYWORTH, S (HM09716) |  |  |  |  |  |  |  | ● |  |  |  |  |  |  |  |  |  |  |  |  | ● |  |  |  |
| HOLDEN, JOHN H (HM09932) |  |  |  |  |  |  |  |  |  |  |  |  |  |  |  |  |  |  |  |  |  |  |  |  |
| JOHN HOLDEN ASSOCIATES (HM11051) |  |  |  |  |  |  |  | ● |  |  |  |  |  |  |  |  |  |  |  |  | ● |  |  |  |
| KELLY CHIROPODY (HM11424) |  |  |  |  |  |  |  |  |  |  |  |  | ● |  |  |  |  |  |  |  |  |  |  |  |
| KENDEL HOUSE CLINIC (HM11479) |  |  |  | ● |  |  |  |  | ● |  |  |  |  |  |  |  |  |  |  |  |  |  |  |  |
| LAYNE, SUSAN G (HM12077) | ● | ● | ● |  |  |  |  |  |  |  | ● |  | ● |  |  | ● | ● |  | ● |  |  |  |  | ● |
| LEYLAND PHYSIOTHERAPY CENTRE (HM12319) |  | ● |  |  |  |  |  |  |  |  |  |  |  |  |  |  |  |  |  |  |  |  |  |  |
| MALKIN, DK, MANIP THERAPY (HM12975) |  | ● |  |  |  |  |  |  |  |  |  |  | ● |  |  |  |  |  | ● |  |  |  |  |  |
| MOBILE CHIROPODIST (HM14027) |  |  |  |  |  |  |  |  |  |  |  |  |  |  |  |  |  |  |  |  |  |  |  |  |
| NATURAL HEALTH CENTRE (HM14566) |  | ● | ● |  |  |  |  |  |  |  | ● |  | ● | ● | ● |  |  |  | ● |  |  | ● |  |  |
| NELSON, S (HM14782) |  | ● | ● |  |  |  |  |  |  |  | ● |  | ● | ● | ● | ● | ● | ● | ● |  |  | ● | ● | ● |
| ONE STOP HEALTH & BEAUTY (HM15323) | ● | ● | ● | ● | ● | ● | ● | ● | ● | ● | ● |  | ● | ● | ● | ● | ● | ● | ● | ● | ● | ● | ● | ● |
| PEPPER, JOHN (HM16009) |  | ● |  |  |  |  |  |  | ● |  |  |  |  |  | ● |  | ● |  |  |  |  |  |  |  |
| PHYSIO AND SPORTS INJURIES (HM16195) |  |  |  |  |  |  |  |  |  |  |  |  |  |  |  |  |  |  |  |  |  |  |  |  |
| PURCELL, AMANDA (HM16762) |  |  |  |  |  |  |  |  |  |  |  |  |  |  |  |  |  |  |  |  |  |  |  |  |
| RAMSBOTTOM PHYSIO CLINIC (HM16919) |  |  |  | ● |  |  |  |  |  |  |  |  |  |  |  |  |  |  |  |  |  |  | ● |  |
| RATCLIFFE, MARK (HM16949) |  | ● |  |  |  |  |  |  |  |  |  |  |  |  |  |  |  |  |  |  |  |  |  |  |
| REMEDIAL MASSAGE/SPORTS (HM17175) |  |  |  |  |  |  |  |  |  |  |  |  |  |  |  |  |  |  |  |  |  |  |  |  |
| SMITH, CHRISTOPHER (DR) (HM18728) |  |  |  |  |  |  |  |  |  |  |  |  | ● |  |  |  |  |  |  |  |  |  |  |  |
| SPIRITUAL THERAPIST (HM19029) |  |  |  |  |  |  |  |  |  |  |  |  |  |  |  |  |  |  |  |  |  |  |  |  |
| ST GEORGES MULTI THERAPY CTRE (HM19075) |  |  |  |  | ● |  |  |  |  |  |  |  |  |  |  |  |  |  |  |  |  |  |  |  |
| ST MARY'S CLINIC (HM19087) |  |  |  | ● |  |  |  |  |  |  |  |  |  |  |  |  |  |  |  |  |  |  | ● |  |
| TATTERSALL, KAREN (HM19719) |  |  |  |  |  |  |  | ● |  |  |  |  |  |  |  |  |  |  |  |  | ● |  |  |  |
| TINKER, D C (HM20083) |  |  |  |  |  |  |  | ● |  |  |  |  |  |  |  |  |  |  |  |  | ● |  |  |  |
| TIP TOES (HM20086) |  | ● |  |  |  |  |  |  |  |  |  |  | ● |  | ● |  |  |  | ● |  |  |  | ● |  |
| TRADITIONAL ACUPUNCTURE CLINIC (HM20220) |  | ● | ● |  |  |  |  |  |  |  |  |  | ● |  |  |  | ● |  | ● |  |  |  | ● | ● |

# A - C Conditions treated at Practices/Businesses

| Business by County with Reference no. | Acne | Addiction | Adenoids | Aids | Alcoholism | Allergy | Alzheimer's Disease | Amnesia | Anaemia | Angina | Anorexia | Anxiety | Arthritis | Asthma | Athletes Foot | Autism | Back Pain | Bacterial Infections | Baldness | Bereavement | Bladder Problems | Blood Pressure | Boils | Bowel Problems | Breast Problems | Breathing Problems | Bronchitis | Bruising | Bulimia | Bunions | Bursitis | Callices | Cancers | Cataracts | Catarrh | Cerebral Palsy | Circulation Problems | Cold Sores | Colds | Colic | Colitis | Conjunctivitis | Constipation | Convulsions | Corns | Coughs | Cramp | Cystitis |
|---|---|---|---|---|---|---|---|---|---|---|---|---|---|---|---|---|---|---|---|---|---|---|---|---|---|---|---|---|---|---|---|---|---|---|---|---|---|---|---|---|---|---|---|---|---|---|---|
| TRADITIONAL CHINESE MED CTRE (HM20223) |●||||||||||||●||||●||||●||||●||||●|||||||||●||●|||||||●|||●|●|●|
| UPHAM, GILL (HM20522) ||||||●|||||||●|||||||||||||●||●||●||||||||●||●|||●|||●|||||
| WATKINSON, BARBARA (HM20999) ||||||||||||||●|●|||●||||||||||||||||||||||||||||||||
| WEST LANCS MCTIMONEY (HM21224) |||||||||||||||●|●||●||||||||||||||||||||||||||||||||
| WILSON, G (HM21656) ||||||||||||||●|||||||||||||||||||||||||||||||||||||
| YEAMAN, DAVID (HM21996) ||||||||||||||||●|||●||||||||||||||●||●|||||||||||||●||||
| LEICESTERSHIRE |||||||||||||||||||||||||||||||||||||||||||||||||
| ACUPUNCTURE SERVICES (HM00320) ||●||||●|||||●|●|●|||●|||||||●||●||||||||||||||●||||||||
| ALBANY HOUSE (HM00479) |●||||||||||||●|●|●||||||||||||||||||||●|||●|||||||||||||
| ANDREWS, SIMON C (HM00859) |●|●|●|●|●|●|●|●|●|●|●|●|●|●|●|●|●|●|||●|●|●|●|●|●|●|●|●||●|●|●|●|●||●|●|●|●|●|●|●|●|●|●|●|●|
| ARCHWAY HSE NATURAL HLTH CTRE (HM00983) |||||||||||||●|●|||||||||||||||||||||||●||||||||||
| AROMATHERAPY INTERNATIONAL (HM01115) ||||||||||||●|●|||●||||||||||||||||||||||||||||||||
| AYURVEDIC HERBAL CLINIC (HM01444) |●|●|●|●|●|●|●||●|●|●|●|●|●|●|●|●|●|●||●|●|●|●|●|●|●|●|●||●||●|●|●||●|●|●|●|●|●|●|●||●|●|●|
| BROWN, RAY (HM03245) |||||||||||||●||||●|||||||||||||||||||||||||||||||||
| CALM WATERS (HM03557) |●|●|●|●|●|●|●|●|●|●|●|●|●|●|●|●|●|●|●||●|●|●|●|●|●|●|●|●||●|●|●|●|●||●|●|●|●|●|●|●|●|●|●|●|●|
| CHIROPRACTIC CENTRE (HM04381) |||||||||||||●||||●|||||||||||||||||||||||||||||||||
| CONLIFFE, LOUISE (HM04982) |●|||||●||||||●||●|||●|||||●||●|●|●|||||||||●||●|●|●|●||●|●|||●||●|
| DEADMAN, P J (HM05932) ||||||||||||●|||||||||||||||||||||||||||||||||||||
| FAIRWEATHER, S & E (HM07068) ||||||||||||●|||||●|||●||||||||||||||||||||||||||||
| GRAHAM SPOWAGE OSTEOPATHIC SVS (HM08340) |||||||||||||●||||●||||||||||||||●|||||||||||||||||
| HASSETT, CHARLES (HM09187) |||||||||||||●||||●|||||||||||||||||||||||||||||||||
| JACQUI BATES COUNSELLING (HM10866) ||||||||||||●|||||||||||||||||||||||||||||||||||||
| LEWIS, JACQUELINE (HM12296) |||||||||||||||||●|||||||||||||||||||||||||||||||||
| LOUGHBOROUGH OSTEOPATHIC (HM12660) |||||||||||||●||||●|||||||||||||||||||||||||||||||||
| MELTON MOWBRAY PHYSIO CLINIC (HM13717) |||||||||||||||||●||||||||||||●|||||||||||||||||||||
| NATURAL WAY HEALTH CENTRE (HM14669) ||||||●||||||||||●||||||||||||||||||||||||||●|||||
| OADBY HOUSE (HM15140) |||||||||||||●||||●|||||||||||||||||||||||||||||||||
| SCHOOL OF SPIRITUAL KNOWLEDGE (HM18085) ||||●||●|●||●|●||●|●|●|||●||||●|●||●|●|●|●||●||||●|●|●||●||●||||●|||●||●|
| SHIRLEY FRANKLIN AROMATHERAPY (HM18485) ||●||||||||||●|●|||●|||||●|||||||||||||||●||||||●|||||
| STERN, J (HM19217) ||||||||||||●|||||||||||||||||||||||||||||||||||||
| SUE CHARLES AROMATHERAPY (HM19466) |●|||●|||||||●||●|●|||●|||||●|||||||●||||||●||●||●|||||||||●||
| SUE RICKS COMP THERAPY (HM19467) |●||||||||●|●|●|●|●|●||●||||●|●|●|●|●|●|●|●|●|||●|●|●|●||●|●|●|●|●|●|●|●|●|●|●|●|
| VICTORIA CLINIC (HM20650) ||●|||●|●||||●|●|●|●|||●|||||●|||●||||●||||||●||●|||||●||||●||
| WENDY PRICE HOLISTIC RIDING (HM21198) ||●|||●||||||●|||||||||||||||||||||||||||||||||||||

www.healthmyself.com

# A - C Conditions treated at Practices/Businesses

| Business by County with Reference no. | Acne | Addiction | Adenoids | Aids | Alcoholism | Allergy | Alzheimer's Disease | Amnesia | Anaemia | Angina | Anorexia | Anxiety | Arthritis | Asthma | Athletes Foot | Autism | Back Pain | Bacterial Infections | Baldness | Bereavement | Bladder Problems | Blood Pressure | Boils | Bowel Problems | Breast Problems | Breathing Problems | Bronchitis | Bruising | Bulimia | Bunions | Bursitis | Callices | Cancers | Cataracts | Catarrh | Cerebral Palsy | Circulation Problems | Cold Sores | Colds | Colic | Colitis | Conjunctivitis | Constipation | Convulsions | Corns | Coughs | Cramp | Cystitis |
|---|---|---|---|---|---|---|---|---|---|---|---|---|---|---|---|---|---|---|---|---|---|---|---|---|---|---|---|---|---|---|---|---|---|---|---|---|---|---|---|---|---|---|---|---|---|---|---|---|
| WOHL, M (DR) (HM21758) | | ● | | | ● | | | | | ● | ● | ● | ● | ● | | | ● | | | | | ● | | ● | | ● | | | ● | | | | | | | | ● | | | | | | | | | | ● | |
| **LINCOLNSHIRE** | | | | | | | | | | | | | | | | | | | | | | | | | | | | | | | | | | | | | | | | | | | | | | | | |
| ALEXANDER TECHNIQUE (HM00550) | | | | | | | | | | | | | ● | | | | ● | | | | | | | | | ● | | | | | | | | | | | | | | | | | | | | | | |
| BARN HOUSE PHYSIO CLINIC (HM01726) | | | | | | | | | | | | | ● | | | | ● | | | | | | | | | | | | | | | | | | | | | | | | | | | | | | | |
| BEVERLEYS (HM02246) | ● | ● | ● | ● | ● | ● | ● | ● | ● | ● | ● | ● | ● | ● | ● | ● | ● | ● | ● | | ● | ● | ● | ● | ● | ● | ● | ● | ● | | ● | ● | ● | ● | ● | | ● | ● | ● | ● | ● | ● | ● | ● | ● | ● | ● | ● |
| BOSTON CHIROPRACTIC CLINIC (HM02726) | | | | | | | | | | | | | ● | | | | ● | | | | | | | | | | | | | | | | | | | | ● | | | ● | | | | | | | | |
| CASTLEGATE OSTEO PRACTICE (HM03847) | | | | | | | | | | | | | ● | | | | ● | | | | | | | | | | | | | | ● | | | | | | | | | ● | | | ● | | | | ● | |
| CHIEN ACUPUNCTURE CLINIC (HM04161) | | | | | | ● | | | | | | ● | ● | ● | | | ● | | | | | | | | | | | ● | | | | | | | | | | | | | | | ● | | | | | ● |
| CLINIC OF NATURAL MEDICINE (HM04703) | | | | | | ● | | | | | | | | ● | ● | ● | ● | | | | ● | ● | | ● | | | ● | | | | ● | | | | | | ● | ● | ● | ● | ● | | ● | | | ● | | ● |
| COMPLEMENTARY THERAPY CENTRE (HM04946) | | | | | | | | | | | | ● | ● | | | | ● | | | | | ● | | | | | | | | | | | | | | | | | | | | | | | | | | |
| COXON CLINIC (HM05326) | ● | | | | | ● | | | | | | | ● | ● | | | ● | ● | | | | | | ● | | | | | | | | | | | | | | | | | | | ● | | | | ● | |
| DORMAN, KARL (HM06201) | | | | | | | | | | | | | ● | | | | ● | | | | | | | | | | | | | | | | | | | | | | | | | | | | | | | |
| EASTGATE HYPNOTHERAPY CENTRE (HM06541) | | | | | | | | | | | | ● | | | | | | | | | | | | | | | | | | | | | ● | | | | | | | | | | | | | | | |
| GOOD HEALTHKEEPING (HM08241) | ● | | ● | | | ● | ● | | ● | ● | | ● | ● | ● | ● | | ● | ● | ● | | ● | ● | ● | ● | ● | ● | ● | ● | | | ● | | ● | | ● | | ● | ● | ● | ● | ● | ● | ● | ● | | ● | ● | ● |
| GRANTHAM PHYSIO PRACTICE (HM08394) | | | | | | | | | | | | | ● | | | | ● | | | | | | | | | | | | | | ● | | | | | | | | | | | | | | | | | |
| HARRISON, FIONA (HM09098) | ● | | | | | | | | | | | ● | ● | | | | ● | | | | | | | | | | | | | | | | | | | | | | | | | | | | | | | |
| HEART TO HEART (HM09443) | | | | | | | | | | | | ● | | | | | | | | | | | | | | | | | | | | | | | | | | | | | | | | | | | | |
| HORNCASTLE WAR MEMORIAL CENTRE (HM10172) | | | | | | | | | | | | | ● | | | | ● | | | | | | | | | | | | | | | | | | | | ● | | | ● | | | | | | | | |
| JUST JILLS (HM11282) | ● | | | | | ● | | | | | | ● | ● | ● | | | | ● | | | ● | ● | | ● | | | ● | ● | | | | | | | | | | ● | ● | ● | ● | | ● | | | ● | ● | ● |
| KESTEVEN NATURAL HEALTH CENTRE (HM11564) | ● | ● | ● | ● | ● | ● | ● | ● | ● | ● | ● | ● | ● | ● | ● | ● | ● | ● | ● | | ● | ● | ● | ● | ● | ● | ● | ● | ● | | ● | ● | ● | ● | ● | | ● | ● | ● | ● | ● | ● | ● | ● | ● | ● | ● | ● |
| LINCOLN HERBAL TREATMENT CTRE (HM12407) | ● | ● | ● | | | ● | | | ● | ● | | ● | ● | ● | ● | | ● | ● | | | ● | ● | ● | ● | ● | ● | ● | ● | | | | ● | ● | | ● | | ● | ● | ● | ● | ● | | ● | ● | ● | ● | ● | ● |
| LIVING HEALTH (HM12485) | | | | | | | | | | | | ● | ● | | | | ● | | | | | | | | | | | | | | | | | | | | ● | | | ● | | | | | | | | |
| MARK RIDDLE HYPNOTHERAPY (HM13108) | | ● | | | ● | | | ● | | | ● | ● | | | | | | | | | | | | | | | | | ● | | | | | | | | | | | | | | | | | | | |
| MORLEY-KIRK, JOHN (HM14187) | ● | | | | | ● | | | | ● | ● | ● | ● | ● | | | ● | ● | | | ● | ● | | ● | ● | ● | ● | ● | ● | | ● | | ● | | ● | | ● | | | | ● | ● | ● | | | ● | ● | ● |
| NEWLAND CHIROPRACTIC CLINIC (HM14866) | | | | | | | | | | | | | ● | ● | | | ● | | | | | | | | | | | | | | ● | | | | ● | | ● | | | ● | | | | | | | ● | |
| REFLEXOLOGY CLINIC (HM17084) | | ● | | | ● | | | | | | | ● | ● | ● | | | ● | | | | | ● | | ● | ● | ● | ● | | | | | | ● | | | | ● | | | | ● | | ● | | | ● | ● | |
| REMEDIES (HM17176) | | | | | | | | | | | | | ● | | | | ● | | | | | | | | | | | | | | | | | | | | | | | | | | | | | | | |
| SALON, JANIES (HM17863) | ● | | | | | | | | | | | ● | | | | | ● | | | | | | | | | | | | | | | | | | | | | | | | | | | | | | | |
| SMITH, MICHAEL (HM18780) | | | | | ● | | | | | | ● | ● | | | | | | | | | | | | ● | | | | | ● | | | | | | | | | | | | | | | | | | | |
| WHITE, HEATHER (HM21357) | | ● | | | ● | ● | | | | | | ● | | ● | | | ● | | | | | ● | | ● | | ● | | | | | | | ● | | | | ● | | | | | | ● | | | | | |
| **LONDON** | | | | | | | | | | | | | | | | | | | | | | | | | | | | | | | | | | | | | | | | | | | | | | | | |
| FIRST PATH HYPNOTHERAPY (HM07338) | | ● | | | | | | | | | | ● | | | | | | | | | | | | ● | | | | | | | | | | | | | | | | | | | | | | | | |
| HARLEY STREET COMP MEDICINE (HM09001) | ● | ● | ● | ● | ● | ● | ● | ● | ● | ● | ● | ● | ● | ● | ● | ● | ● | ● | ● | | ● | ● | ● | ● | ● | ● | ● | ● | ● | | ● | ● | ● | ● | ● | | ● | ● | ● | ● | ● | ● | ● | ● | ● | ● | ● | ● |
| **LONDON (GREATER)** | | | | | | | | | | | | | | | | | | | | | | | | | | | | | | | | | | | | | | | | | | | | | | | | |

# A - C Conditions treated at Practices/Businesses

Business by County with Reference no.

| Business | Acne | Addiction | Adenoids | Aids | Alcoholism | Allergy | Alzheimer's Disease | Amnesia | Anaemia | Angina | Anorexia | Anxiety | Arthritis | Asthma | Athletes Foot | Autism |
|---|---|---|---|---|---|---|---|---|---|---|---|---|---|---|---|---|
| 1ST ALTERNATIVE HEALTH CENTRE (HM00002) | ● | | | | | ● | | | | | | ● | ● | ● | | |
| ABBEY CENTRE (HM00071) | | ● | | | | | | | | | ● | ● | | ● | | |
| ABBEYWOOD CHIROPODY CLINIC (HM00091) | | | | | | | | | | | | ● | | | ● | |
| ABIGAIL'S (HM00126) | ● | | | | | | | | | | | ● | ● | | | |
| ABRAHAMS & BENNETT (HM00132) | | | | | | | | | | | | | ● | | | |
| ABRAHAMS & BENNETT (HM00133) | | | | | | | | | | | | | ● | | | |
| ACORN THERAPY CENTRE (HM00182) | | ● | | | | | | | | | | ● | | | | |
| ACUMEDIC (HM00217) | ● | ● | | | | ● | | | | | ● | ● | ● | ● | | |
| ACUPUNCTURE & HERBAL CLINIC (HM00240) | ● | | | | | ● | | | | | | ● | ● | | | |
| ACUPUNCTURE CLINIC (HM00287) | ● | ● | ● | ● | ● | ● | ● | ● | ● | ● | ● | ● | ● | ● | ● | ● |
| AGAINST ALLERGY (HM00415) | | | | | | ● | | | | | | | | | | |
| ALEXANDER TECHNIQUE (HM00545) | | | | | | | | | | | | ● | | | | |
| ALEXANDER TECHNIQUE (HM00547) | | | | | | | | | | | | ● | ● | | | |
| ALEXANDER TECHNIQUE CENTRE (HM00555) | | ● | ● | | ● | ● | | | | | | ● | ● | ● | ● | ● |
| ALTERNATIVE HEALTH CENTRE (HM00705) | | | | | | ● | | | | | | | | | | |
| ALTERNATIVE THERAPIES CENTRE (HM00728) | | | | | | ● | | | | | | ● | ● | ● | ● | |
| ALTERNATIVES COMP THERAPY CTRE (HM00743) | ● | | | | | | | | | | | ● | ● | ● | ● | |
| ANGEL HEART CENTRE (HM00867) | | | | | | | | | | | | ● | | | | |
| AUSTERBERRY, HELEN (HM01363) | ● | | | | | ● | | | | | | ● | ● | ● | ● | |
| AUSTERBERRY, HELEN (HM01362) | ● | | | | | ● | | | | | | ● | ● | ● | ● | |
| AVALON CHINESE MEDICINE CLINIC (HM01377) | ● | ● | | | ● | ● | ● | ● | ● | ● | ● | ● | ● | ● | | |
| AVATAR (HM01384) | | ● | | | ● | | | ● | | | ● | ● | ● | | | |
| AVENUE PSYCHOTHERAPY SERVICES (HM01391) | | ● | | ● | ● | | | ● | | | ● | ● | | ● | | ● |
| AYURVED HERBELI (HM01442) | ● | | | | | ● | | | ● | ● | | ● | ● | ● | ● | |
| BACK PAIN CENTRE (HM01497) | | | | | | | | | | | | | ● | | | |
| BACK PAIN CENTRE (HM01499) | | | | | | | | | | | | | ● | | | |
| BACK PAIN CENTRE (HM01498) | | | | | | | | | | | | | ● | | | |
| BACK PAIN CLINIC (HM01503) | ● | | | | | ● | | | | ● | | | | ● | | |
| BACK TO HEALTH - CHISWICK (HM01510) | | | | | | | | | | | | | ● | | | |
| BACK TO HEALTH - KINGSTON (HM01512) | | | | | | | | | | | | | ● | | | |
| BACK TO HEALTH - NORTH FINCHLEY (HM01513) | | | | | | | | | | | | | ● | | | |
| BACK TO HEALTH CHIRO CLINIC (HM01518) | | | | | | | | | | | | | ● | | | |
| BACK TO HEALTH-EALING (HM01519) | | | | | | | | | | | | | ● | | | |
| BARBICAN CENTRE (HM01693) | | | | | | | | | | | | | ● | | ● | |

| Business | Back Pain | Bacterial Infections | Baldness | Bereavement | Bladder Problems | Blood Pressure | Boils | Bowel Problems | Breast Problems | Breathing Problems | Bronchitis | Bruising | Bulimia | Bunions | Bursitis | Callices |
|---|---|---|---|---|---|---|---|---|---|---|---|---|---|---|---|---|
| 1ST ALTERNATIVE HEALTH CENTRE (HM00002) | ● | | | | | ● | ● | | | ● | | | | | ● | |
| ABBEY CENTRE (HM00071) | | | | | | | | | | | | | | | | |
| ABBEYWOOD CHIROPODY CLINIC (HM00091) | | | | | | | | | | | | | | | | ● |
| ABIGAIL'S (HM00126) | ● | | | | | | | | | | | | | | | |
| ABRAHAMS & BENNETT (HM00132) | ● | | | | | | | | | ● | | | | | | |
| ABRAHAMS & BENNETT (HM00133) | ● | | | | | | | | | | | | | | | |
| ACORN THERAPY CENTRE (HM00182) | | | | | | | | | | | | | | | | |
| ACUMEDIC (HM00217) | ● | | | | ● | ● | | ● | | | | | | | | |
| ACUPUNCTURE & HERBAL CLINIC (HM00240) | ● | | | | | | | | | | | | | | | |
| ACUPUNCTURE CLINIC (HM00287) | ● | ● | | | ● | ● | ● | ● | ● | ● | ● | ● | ● | | ● | |
| AGAINST ALLERGY (HM00415) | | | | | | | | | | | | | | | | |
| ALEXANDER TECHNIQUE (HM00545) | ● | | | | | | | | | ● | | | | | ● | |
| ALEXANDER TECHNIQUE (HM00547) | ● | | | | | ● | | | | | | | | | ● | |
| ALEXANDER TECHNIQUE CENTRE (HM00555) | ● | | | | ● | ● | | ● | | ● | ● | | | | ● | |
| ALTERNATIVE HEALTH CENTRE (HM00705) | | | | | | | | | | | | | | | | |
| ALTERNATIVE THERAPIES CENTRE (HM00728) | ● | | | | ● | ● | | ● | | ● | ● | | | | | |
| ALTERNATIVES COMP THERAPY CTRE (HM00743) | ● | | | | | ● | | ● | | ● | | | | | | |
| ANGEL HEART CENTRE (HM00867) | | | | | | | | | | | | | | | | |
| AUSTERBERRY, HELEN (HM01363) | | ● | | | ● | | ● | ● | ● | ● | ● | ● | | | | |
| AUSTERBERRY, HELEN (HM01362) | | ● | | | ● | | ● | ● | ● | ● | ● | ● | | | | |
| AVALON CHINESE MEDICINE CLINIC (HM01377) | ● | ● | | | ● | ● | ● | ● | ● | ● | ● | ● | ● | | ● | |
| AVATAR (HM01384) | ● | | | | ● | ● | | ● | | ● | | | ● | | | |
| AVENUE PSYCHOTHERAPY SERVICES (HM01391) | | | | ● | | | | | | | | | ● | | | |
| AYURVED HERBELI (HM01442) | ● | ● | | | | ● | | ● | | ● | ● | | | | | |
| BACK PAIN CENTRE (HM01497) | ● | | | | | ● | | | | | | | | | | |
| BACK PAIN CENTRE (HM01499) | ● | | | | | ● | | | | | | | | | | |
| BACK PAIN CENTRE (HM01498) | ● | | | | | ● | | | | | | | | | | |
| BACK PAIN CLINIC (HM01503) | ● | | | | ● | ● | ● | | | ● | ● | | | | ● | |
| BACK TO HEALTH - CHISWICK (HM01510) | ● | | | | | | | | | | | | | | | |
| BACK TO HEALTH - KINGSTON (HM01512) | ● | | | | | | | | | | | | | | | |
| BACK TO HEALTH - NORTH FINCHLEY (HM01513) | ● | | | | | | | | | | | | | | | |
| BACK TO HEALTH CHIRO CLINIC (HM01518) | | | | | | | | | | | | | | | | |
| BACK TO HEALTH-EALING (HM01519) | ● | | | | | ● | | | | | | | | | | |
| BARBICAN CENTRE (HM01693) | | | | | | | | | | | | | | | | ● |

| Business | Cancers | Cataracts | Catarrh | Cerebral Palsy | Circulation Problems | Cold Sores | Colds | Colic | Colitis | Conjunctivitis | Constipation | Convulsions | Corns | Coughs | Cramp | Cystitis |
|---|---|---|---|---|---|---|---|---|---|---|---|---|---|---|---|---|
| 1ST ALTERNATIVE HEALTH CENTRE (HM00002) | | | | | | | | ● | | | | | | | ● | |
| ABBEY CENTRE (HM00071) | | | | | | | | | | | | | | | | |
| ABBEYWOOD CHIROPODY CLINIC (HM00091) | | | | | | | | | | | | | ● | | | |
| ABIGAIL'S (HM00126) | | | | | | | | | | | | | | | | |
| ABRAHAMS & BENNETT (HM00132) | | | | | | | | | | | | | | | | |
| ABRAHAMS & BENNETT (HM00133) | | | | | | | | | | | | | | | | |
| ACORN THERAPY CENTRE (HM00182) | | | | | | | | | | | | | | | | |
| ACUMEDIC (HM00217) | | | | | ● | | | | | | ● | | | | ● | |
| ACUPUNCTURE & HERBAL CLINIC (HM00240) | | | | | ● | | | | | | ● | | | | | |
| ACUPUNCTURE CLINIC (HM00287) | ● | | ● | | ● | ● | ● | ● | ● | ● | ● | ● | | ● | ● | ● |
| AGAINST ALLERGY (HM00415) | | | | | | | | | | | | | | | | |
| ALEXANDER TECHNIQUE (HM00545) | | | | | | | | | | | | | | | | |
| ALEXANDER TECHNIQUE (HM00547) | | | | | | | | | | | | | | | | |
| ALEXANDER TECHNIQUE CENTRE (HM00555) | | | ● | | ● | | | ● | | ● | ● | ● | | ● | ● | ● |
| ALTERNATIVE HEALTH CENTRE (HM00705) | | | | | | | | | | | | | | | | |
| ALTERNATIVE THERAPIES CENTRE (HM00728) | | | ● | | ● | ● | ● | ● | ● | ● | ● | | | ● | ● | ● |
| ALTERNATIVES COMP THERAPY CTRE (HM00743) | | | ● | | ● | | ● | | | | ● | | | ● | | |
| ANGEL HEART CENTRE (HM00867) | | | | | | | | | | | | | | | | |
| AUSTERBERRY, HELEN (HM01363) | | | ● | | | ● | ● | ● | ● | ● | ● | | | ● | | ● |
| AUSTERBERRY, HELEN (HM01362) | | | ● | | | ● | ● | ● | ● | ● | ● | | | ● | | ● |
| AVALON CHINESE MEDICINE CLINIC (HM01377) | ● | | ● | | ● | ● | ● | ● | ● | | ● | ● | | ● | ● | ● |
| AVATAR (HM01384) | | | | | ● | | | | ● | | ● | | | | | |
| AVENUE PSYCHOTHERAPY SERVICES (HM01391) | | | | | | | | | | | | ● | | | | |
| AYURVED HERBELI (HM01442) | | | ● | | | | ● | ● | ● | | ● | | | ● | | ● |
| BACK PAIN CENTRE (HM01497) | | | | | ● | | | | | | | | | | | |
| BACK PAIN CENTRE (HM01499) | | | | | ● | | | | | | | | | | | |
| BACK PAIN CENTRE (HM01498) | | | | | ● | | | | | | | | | | | |
| BACK PAIN CLINIC (HM01503) | | | ● | | | | ● | ● | ● | ● | ● | | | ● | ● | ● |
| BACK TO HEALTH - CHISWICK (HM01510) | | | | | ● | | | ● | | | | | | | | |
| BACK TO HEALTH - KINGSTON (HM01512) | | | | | ● | | | ● | | | | | | | | |
| BACK TO HEALTH - NORTH FINCHLEY (HM01513) | | | | | ● | | | ● | | | | | | | | |
| BACK TO HEALTH CHIRO CLINIC (HM01518) | | | | | ● | | | ● | | | | | | | | |
| BACK TO HEALTH-EALING (HM01519) | | | | | ● | | | ● | | | | | | | | |
| BARBICAN CENTRE (HM01693) | | | | | | | | | | | | | ● | | | |

# A - C Conditions treated at Practices/Businesses

| Business by County with Reference no. | Acne | Addiction | Adenoids | Aids | Alcoholism | Allergy | Alzheimer's Disease | Amnesia | Anaemia | Angina | Anorexia | Anxiety | Arthritis | Asthma | Athletes Foot | Autism | Back Pain | Bacterial Infections | Baldness | Bereavement | Bladder Problems | Blood Pressure | Boils | Bowel Problems | Breast Problems | Breathing Problems | Bronchitis | Bruising | Bulimia | Bunions | Bursitis | Callices | Cancers | Cataracts | Catarrh | Cerebral Palsy | Circulation Problems | Cold Sores | Colds | Colic | Colitis | Conjunctivitis | Constipation | Convulsions | Corns | Coughs | Cramp | Cystitis |
|---|---|---|---|---|---|---|---|---|---|---|---|---|---|---|---|---|---|---|---|---|---|---|---|---|---|---|---|---|---|---|---|---|---|---|---|---|---|---|---|---|---|---|---|---|---|---|---|
| BARBICAN PODIATRY PRACTICE (HM01694) | | | | | | | | | | | | | | | ● | | ● | | | | | | | | | | | | | | | | | | | | | | | | | | | | | | | |
| BARNES CHIROPRACTIC HEALTHCARE (HM01740) | | | | | | ● | | | | | | | ● | ● | | | ● | | | | | | | ● | | ● | | | | | ● | | | | | | ● | | | ● | | | ● | | | | ● | |
| BARRIE, ALEXANDER (HM01798) | | | | | | | | | | | | | | | | | ● | | | | ● | ● | | ● | | ● | ● | | | | ● | | | | | | ● | | ● | ● | ● | | ● | | | ● | | |
| BAXTER, STEPHEN (HM01934) | | | | | | | | | | | | | ● | ● | | | ● | | | | | | | | | | | | | | | | | | | | | | | | | | | | | | | |
| BECKER, AMELY (HM02021) | | ● | | | | | | | | | ● | ● | | | | | | | | ● | | | | | | | | | ● | | | | | | | | | | | | | | | | | | | |
| BELMONT PHYSIOTHERAPY PRACTICE (HM02108) | | | | | | | | | | | | | ● | | | | ● | | | | | | | | | | | | | | | | | | | | | | | | | | | | | | | |
| BERNSTEIN, SAMUEL (HM02204) | | ● | | | ● | | | | | | ● | ● | | | | | | | | | | | | | | | | | ● | | | | | | | | | | | | | | | | | | | |
| BEVERLEY CLINIC (HM02244) | | | | | | | | | | | | | | | | | ● | | | | | | | | | | | | | | | | | | | | | | | | | | | | | | | |
| BLACKHEATH COMP THERAPIES CTRE (HM02450) | | ● | | | | | | | | | | | | | | | ● | | | | | | | | | | | | | | | | | | | | | | | | | | | | | | | |
| BLOOMSBURY ALEXANDER CENTRE (HM02516) | ● | ● | ● | ● | ● | ● | ● | ● | ● | ● | ● | ● | ● | ● | ● | ● | ● | ● | ● | | ● | ● | ● | ● | ● | ● | ● | ● | ● | | ● | | ● | ● | ● | | ● | ● | ● | ● | ● | ● | ● | ● | | ● | ● | ● |
| BLOOMSBURY THERAPY CENTRE (HM02518) | ● | ● | ● | ● | ● | ● | ● | ● | ● | ● | ● | ● | ● | ● | ● | ● | ● | ● | ● | | ● | ● | ● | ● | ● | ● | ● | ● | ● | | ● | | ● | ● | ● | | ● | ● | ● | ● | ● | ● | ● | ● | | ● | ● | ● |
| BOCOCK, RICHARD (HM02548) | ● | | | | | | | | | | | | | | | | | ● | | | | | ● | ● | | | | | | | | | | | | | | ● | | | | | | | | | | |
| BODYSPACE (HM02632) | | | | | | | | | | | | ● | | | | | | | | | | | | | | | | | | | | | | | | | | | | | | | | | | | | |
| BODYWISE (HM02637) | ● | | ● | | | ● | ● | | ● | ● | ● | ● | ● | ● | ● | | ● | ● | | | ● | ● | ● | ● | ● | ● | ● | ● | ● | | ● | | ● | ● | ● | | ● | ● | ● | ● | ● | ● | ● | ● | | ● | ● | ● |
| BOSTON CHIROPODY CLINIC (HM02725) | | | | | | | | | | | | | ● | | ● | | ● | ● | | | | | | | | | | | | | | | | | | | ● | | | | | | | | | | ● | |
| BRACKENBURY NTRL HEALTH CLNC (HM02837) | | | | | | ● | | | | | | | ● | ● | ● | | ● | | | | | | | | | | | | | | | | | | | | ● | | ● | | | | ● | | | ● | | |
| BRAHMA KUMARIS INNER SPACE (HM02886) | | | | | | | | | | | | ● | | | | | | | | | | | | | | | | | | | | | | | | | | | | | | | | | | | | |
| BRITISH AUTOGENIC SOCIETY (HM03076) | ● | | | ● | | ● | | | | ● | ● | ● | ● | | | | | | | | | ● | | ● | | ● | | | ● | | | | | | ● | | ● | | | | | | ● | | | ● | | |
| BRITISH HYPNOTHERAPY ASS (HM03084) | | ● | | | ● | ● | | | | | | ● | | ● | | | | | | | | | | | | | | | | | | | | | | | | | | | | | | | | | | |
| BRIXTON TAI CHI (HM03106) | | | | | | | | | | | | | | | | | ● | | | | | | | | | ● | | | | | | | | | | | | | | | | | | | | | | |
| BROOK GREEN OSTEOPATHY (HM03155) | | | | | | | | | | | | | ● | ● | | | ● | | | | ● | | | ● | | ● | | | | | ● | | | | | | | | | | ● | | ● | | | | ● | |
| BROOKS, CATHY (HM03175) | ● | | | | | ● | | | | | ● | | ● | ● | ● | | ● | | | | ● | ● | ● | ● | ● | ● | ● | ● | | | | | | | ● | | ● | ● | ● | ● | | ● | ● | ● | | ● | | |
| BROOKS, JANE (HM03177) | | | | | ● | ● | | | | | | ● | | | | | | | | | | | | | | | | | | | | | | | | | | | | | | | | | | | | |
| BROWN, ALISON R (HM03210) | | | | | | | | | | | | | ● | | | | ● | | | | | | | | | | | | | | | | | | | | ● | | | | | | | | | | | |
| BST FOUNDATION (HM03295) | | | | | | | | | | | | ● | | | | | | | | | | | | | | | | | | | | | | | | | | | | | | | | | | | | |
| BUCHANAN, ANGELA (HM03300) | | | | | | | | | | | | | ● | | | | ● | | | | | | | | | ● | | | | | ● | | | | | | | | | | | | | | | | | |
| BUCKLEY, BILLIE (HM03318) | | ● | | | | | | | | | | ● | | | | | | | | | | | | | | | | | ● | | | | | | | | | | | | | | | | | | | |
| BUREN, VAN (HM03371) | | | | | | | | | | | | ● | | | | | | | | | | | | | | | | | | | | | | | | | | | | | | | | | | | | |
| BYRNE, JUDY (HM03516) | ● | ● | | ● | ● | | | ● | | | | ● | | | | | | | | | | ● | | | | | | | ● | | | | | | | | | | | | | | ● | | | | | |
| CASSIDY MEDICAL CENTRE (HM03815) | | | | | | | | | | | | | | | | | ● | | | | | | | | | | | | | | | | | | | | | | | | | | | | | | | |
| CENTRE FOR TRANSFORMATION (HM03920) | ● | | | | | ● | | | ● | ● | ● | ● | ● | ● | ● | ● | ● | | | | ● | | | ● | ● | ● | ● | ● | ● | | ● | | ● | ● | ● | | ● | ● | ● | ● | ● | ● | ● | ● | | ● | ● | ● |
| CHAPMAN, RUPERT (HM04009) | | | | | | | | | | | | | ● | ● | | | ● | | | | | | | | | ● | ● | ● | | | ● | | | | | | | | | | | | ● | | | | | |
| CHARTERHOUSE PHYSIOTHERAPY (HM04049) | | | | | | | | | | | | | ● | | | | ● | | | | | | | | | | | | | | | | | | | | | | | | | | | | | | | |
| CHARTERHOUSE PHYSIOTHERAPY (HM04048) | | | | | | | | | | | | | ● | | | | ● | | | | | | | | | | | | | | | | | | | | | | | | | | | | | | | |

# A - C Conditions treated at Practices/Businesses

Business by County with Reference no.

| Condition | CHATSWORTH CLINIC (HM04063) | CHINESE MEDICAL CTRE OF LONDON (HM04245) | CHINESE SHOP (HM04269) | CHIROPRACTIC CLINIC (HM04393) | CHISWICK CHIROPRACTIC CLINIC (HM04412) | CITY HEALTH CENTRE (HM04496) | CLAIRE CHOUDHURY HERBAL PRAC (HM04507) | CLASSICAL OSTEOPATH (HM04610) | CLINIC FOR COUNSELLING (HM04681) | CLINIC FOR COUNSELLING (HM04680) | COLLEGE-PRACTICAL HOMEOPATHY (HM04855) | COMP MEDI ASS (HM04913) | COMPLETE HEALTH CARE (HM04958) | CONNAUGHT SQUARE HYPNOTHERAPY (HM04986) | CONWAY, JONATHAN (HM05028) | CONWAY, JONATHON (HM05029) | COUNSELLING & PSYCHOTHERAPY (HM05246) |
|---|---|---|---|---|---|---|---|---|---|---|---|---|---|---|---|---|---|
| Cystitis | ● | ● | | | | ● | ● | ● | | | | | ● | | | | |
| Cramp | ● | ● | | | ● | ● | ● | ● | | | | | ● | | | | |
| Coughs | ● | ● | ● | | | ● | ● | ● | | | | | ● | | | | |
| Corns | | | | | | | | | | | | | | | | | |
| Convulsions | | ● | ● | | | ● | | | | | | | | | | | |
| Constipation | ● | ● | | | ● | ● | ● | ● | | | | | ● | | | | |
| Conjunctivitis | ● | ● | | | | | ● | | | | | | ● | | | | |
| Colitis | ● | ● | | | | ● | ● | ● | | | | | ● | | | | |
| Colic | ● | ● | | ● | ● | ● | ● | ● | | | | | ● | | | | |
| Colds | ● | ● | ● | | | ● | ● | ● | | | | | | | | | |
| Cold Sores | ● | ● | | | | | ● | | | | | | ● | | | | |
| Circulation Problems | ● | ● | ● | ● | | ● | ● | ● | | | | | ● | | | | |
| Cerebral Palsy | | | | | | | | | | | | | | | | | |
| Catarrh | ● | ● | | | | ● | ● | ● | | | | | ● | | | | |
| Cataracts | | ● | | | | | | | | | | | | | | | |
| Cancers | | ● | | | | | | | | | | | | | | | |
| Callices | | | | | | | | | | | | | | | | | |
| Bursitis | ● | ● | ● | | | ● | | | | | | | ● | | | | |
| Bunions | | | | | | | | | | | | | | | | | |
| Bulimia | | | | | | | | | | | | | ● | ● | | | |
| Bruising | ● | ● | | | | | | | | | | | ● | | | | |
| Bronchitis | ● | ● | | | | ● | ● | ● | | | | | ● | | | | |
| Breathing Problems | ● | ● | ● | | | ● | ● | ● | | | | | ● | | | | |
| Breast Problems | ● | ● | | | | ● | ● | | | | | | ● | | | | |
| Bowel Problems | ● | ● | ● | | ● | ● | ● | ● | | | | | ● | | | | |
| Boils | ● | ● | | | | | ● | | | | | | ● | | | | |
| Blood Pressure | ● | ● | ● | | | ● | ● | ● | | | | | ● | | | | |
| Bladder Problems | ● | ● | ● | ● | ● | ● | ● | ● | | | | | ● | | | | |
| Bereavement | | | | | | | | | | | | | | | | | |
| Baldness | | ● | | | | | | | | | | | | | | | |
| Bacterial Infections | | ● | | | | | ● | | | | | | ● | | | | |
| Back Pain | ● | ● | ● | ● | | ● | | ● | | | ● | | ● | | | | ● |
| Autism | ● | | | | | | | | | | | | | | | | |
| Athletes Foot | ● | ● | | | | | ● | | | | | | | | | | |
| Asthma | ● | ● | ● | | ● | ● | ● | | | | | | ● | | | | |
| Arthritis | ● | ● | ● | ● | ● | ● | ● | ● | | | ● | | ● | | | | |
| Anxiety | ● | ● | ● | | | ● | ● | ● | ● | ● | ● | | ● | | ● | ● | ● |
| Anorexia | | ● | | | | | | | | | | | ● | | | | |
| Angina | ● | ● | ● | | | | ● | | | | | | ● | | | | |
| Anaemia | ● | ● | ● | | | | ● | | | | | | | | | | |
| Amnesia | | | | | | | | | | | | | | | | | |
| Alzheimer's Disease | | | | | | | | | | | | | | | | | |
| Allergy | ● | ● | ● | | | ● | ● | | | | | ● | ● | | | | |
| Alcoholism | | ● | | | | | ● | | | | | | ● | | | | |
| Aids | ● | ● | | | | | | | | | | | | | | | ● |
| Adenoids | ● | ● | | | | | ● | ● | | | | | | | | | |
| Addiction | | ● | ● | | | | | | ● | ● | | | ● | ● | ● | ● | ● |
| Acne | ● | ● | ● | | | | ● | | | | | | ● | | | | |

| Condition | COUNSELLING SERVICE (HM05252) | CRAVEN CLINIC (HM05385) | CREATIVE INSIGHTS (HM05399) | CRISTA GALLI OSTEOPATHS (HM05446) | CTRE FOR CRANIO-SACRAL THERAPY (HM05540) | CTRE FOR THE STUDY OF COMP MED (HM05544) | DALTON, HELEN (HM05698) | DAVID WEISS HOMEOPATHY (HM05781) | DAVIS, JULIA (HM05854) | DAWSON, DAVID (DR) (HM05880) | DE BURGH, JULIE (HM05904) | DELROY, SANDRA (DR) (HM05968) | DENNIS MICHAEL PRACTICE (HM05990) | DENNISON, IAN (HM05996) | DISTANT HEALING (HM06123) | DOCKLANDS DENTAL/COMP HLTH (HM06141) | DREAM LINE (HM06296) |
|---|---|---|---|---|---|---|---|---|---|---|---|---|---|---|---|---|---|
| Cystitis | | | | ● | ● | ● | ● | | ● | | | | | | ● | | |
| Cramp | | | | ● | ● | ● | ● | | ● | | | | | ● | ● | | |
| Coughs | | | | ● | ● | ● | ● | ● | ● | | | | | | | | |
| Corns | | | | | | | | | | | | | | | | | |
| Convulsions | | | | ● | | ● | | | ● | | | | | | | | |
| Constipation | | ● | | ● | ● | ● | ● | ● | ● | | | | ● | | | | |
| Conjunctivitis | | | | | | ● | ● | ● | ● | | | | | | ● | | |
| Colitis | | | | ● | ● | ● | ● | ● | ● | | | | | | ● | | |
| Colic | | | | ● | ● | ● | ● | ● | ● | | | | | | | | |
| Colds | | | | | | ● | ● | ● | ● | | | | | | | | |
| Cold Sores | | | | | | ● | ● | ● | ● | | | | | | | | |
| Circulation Problems | | | | ● | ● | ● | ● | | ● | | | | | ● | ● | ● | |
| Cerebral Palsy | | | | | | | | | | | | | | | | | |
| Catarrh | | | | ● | ● | ● | ● | ● | ● | | | | | | ● | | |
| Cataracts | | | | | | | | | ● | | | | | | ● | | |
| Cancers | | | | | | ● | | | ● | | | | | | ● | | |
| Callices | | | | | | | | | | | | | | | | | |
| Bursitis | | | | ● | ● | ● | ● | | ● | | | | | | | | |
| Bunions | | | | | | | | | | | | | | | | | |
| Bulimia | | | | ● | ● | | | | ● | | | | | | | | |
| Bruising | | ● | | | ● | ● | ● | | ● | | | | | | | | |
| Bronchitis | | | | ● | ● | ● | ● | ● | ● | | | | | | ● | | |
| Breathing Problems | | | | ● | ● | ● | ● | | ● | | | | | | ● | | |
| Breast Problems | | | | ● | | ● | ● | | ● | | | | | | ● | | ● |
| Bowel Problems | | | ● | ● | ● | ● | ● | ● | ● | | | | ● | | ● | | |
| Boils | | | | | | ● | ● | | ● | | | | | | ● | | |
| Blood Pressure | | | | ● | ● | ● | ● | ● | ● | | | | | | ● | ● | |
| Bladder Problems | | | | ● | ● | ● | ● | | ● | | | | | | ● | | |
| Bereavement | ● | | | | | | | | | | | ● | | | | | |
| Baldness | | | | | | | | | ● | | | | | | | | |
| Bacterial Infections | | | | ● | | ● | ● | | ● | | | | | | | | |
| Back Pain | | ● | ● | ● | ● | ● | ● | ● | ● | | | | | ● | ● | ● | |
| Autism | | | | ● | ● | ● | | ● | ● | | | | | | ● | | |
| Athletes Foot | | | | | | | ● | | ● | | | | | | ● | | |
| Asthma | | ● | | ● | ● | ● | ● | ● | ● | | | | | | ● | | |
| Arthritis | | ● | | ● | ● | ● | ● | ● | ● | | | | ● | ● | ● | ● | |
| Anxiety | ● | ● | ● | ● | ● | ● | ● | ● | ● | | ● | ● | | | ● | | |
| Anorexia | | | ● | ● | | | | | ● | | | | | | | | |
| Angina | | | | ● | | | ● | | ● | | | | | | ● | | |
| Anaemia | | | | | | | ● | | ● | | | | | | ● | | |
| Amnesia | | | | | ● | | | | ● | | | | | | ● | | |
| Alzheimer's Disease | | | | | | | | | ● | | | | | | ● | | |
| Allergy | | ● | ● | ● | ● | ● | ● | ● | ● | ● | | | | | ● | | ● |
| Alcoholism | | | ● | | | | | ● | ● | | | | | | ● | | |
| Aids | | | | ● | | | | | ● | | | | | | ● | | |
| Adenoids | | | | ● | | ● | ● | | ● | | | | | | | | |
| Addiction | | | | | | | | ● | ● | | ● | | | | ● | | |
| Acne | | | | | | ● | ● | ● | ● | | | | | | ● | | |

www.healthmyself.com

# A - C Conditions treated at Practices/Businesses

| Business by County with Reference no. | Acne | Addiction | Adenoids | Aids | Alcoholism | Allergy | Alzheimer's Disease | Amnesia | Anaemia | Angina | Anorexia | Anxiety | Arthritis | Asthma | Athletes Foot | Autism | Back Pain | Bacterial Infections | Baldness | Bereavement |
|---|---|---|---|---|---|---|---|---|---|---|---|---|---|---|---|---|---|---|---|---|
| DREAMCATCHER (HM06298) | | | | | | | | | | | | | | | | | | | | |
| DULWICH PHYSIOTHERAPY (HM06383) | | | | | | | | | | | | | | | | | ● | | | |
| E.LONDON COMPLEMENTARY HEALTH (HM06479) | ● | | | | ● | ● | | | ● | ● | ● | ● | ● | ● | ● | ● | ● | ● | ● | |
| EALING COUNS & THERAPY CTRE (HM06488) | ● | ● | | | | ● | | | | | | ● | ● | | | | | | | |
| EAST WEST HERB SHOP (HM06527) | ● | | | | | ● | | | | | | ● | ● | ● | | | ● | | | |
| EAST WEST THERAPIES (HM06529) | | ● | | | | | | | | | | ● | ● | | | | ● | | | |
| EDGELL, MARJORY (HM06599) | | | | | ● | | | | | | | ● | ● | | | | | | | |
| EDGWARE NATURAL HEALTH CENTRE (HM06604) | ● | | | | | ● | | | ● | ● | | ● | ● | ● | ● | | ● | ● | | |
| ELLWOOD, CAROLINE (HM06780) | | | | | | | | | | | | | | | | | ● | | | |
| ELTHAM HYPNOTHERAPY ANALYSIS (HM06789) | | ● | | | ● | | | | | | ● | ● | | | | ● | ● | | | |
| ENFIELD CLINIC OF HERBAL MED (HM06818) | ● | | | | | | | | ● | ● | ● | ● | ● | ● | ● | | | ● | | |
| ENFIELD HYP & COUNSELLING (HM06819) | | ● | | | | | | | | | | ● | ● | | | | ● | | | ● |
| EQUILIBRIUM (HM06869) | | | | | | ● | | | | | | ● | ● | ● | | | ● | | ● | |
| EQUILIBRIUM COUNS/THRPY CTRE (HM06873) | | ● | | | ● | | | | | | | ● | ● | | | | ● | | | |
| FAIR, ANNETTE (HM07048) | | | | | | | | | | | | | ● | | | | ● | | | |
| FARMACIA URBAN HEALING (HM07107) | | | | | | ● | | | | | | | | | | | | | | |
| FELDENKRAIS CENTRE (HM07190) | | | | | | | | | | | | | | | | | ● | | | |
| FLETCHER, CLARE (HM07410) | | | | | | ● | | | | | | | | | | | ● | | | |
| FLEXIBLE HOUR (HM07420) | | | | | | | | | | | | | ● | | | | ● | | | |
| FLOAT WORKS (HM07424) | | ● | | | ● | | | | | | | ● | ● | | | | ● | | | |
| FRY, HOWARD (HM07772) | | | | | | | | | | | | | | | ● | | | | | |
| FULHAM CLINIC (HM07781) | ● | ● | | | | ● | | | ● | | ● | ● | ● | ● | | | ● | ● | | |
| G T CONSULTANCY (HM07815) | | ● | | | ● | | | | | | | ● | | | | | | | | |
| GEE, PHILL (HM07959) | | | | | | | | | | | | ● | | | | | | | | |
| GEORGE (HM07987) | | | | | | | | | | | | | ● | | ● | | | | | |
| GLASSMAN, DAVID (HM08128) | | ● | ● | | ● | ● | | | | | | ● | ● | ● | ● | ● | ● | | | |
| GODWIN, ROME (HM08194) | | | | | | | | | | | | | ● | ● | | | ● | | | |
| GREENWICH NATURAL HEALTH CTRE (HM08500) | | | | | | | | | | | | ● | ● | ● | | | ● | | | |
| GREIDINGER, CLIVE (HM08524) | | | | | | | | | | | | ● | | | | | | | | |
| HACKNEY HYPNOTHERAPY (HM08685) | | ● | | | | | | ● | | | ● | ● | | | | | | | | |
| HAIN, PATRICIA (HM08712) | ● | ● | | | | ● | ● | | ● | ● | ● | ● | ● | ● | ● | ● | ● | ● | | |
| HAMILTON, FIONA (HM08843) | | | | | | | | | | | | | | | | | ● | | | |
| HAMPSTEAD ACU/CHINESE HBL MED (HM08881) | | | | | | ● | | | | | | | ● | ● | | | | | | |
| HAREWOOD, MARCIA M (HM08991) | ● | | | | | ● | | | ● | | | | ● | ● | | | ● | | | |

| Business by County with Reference no. | Bladder Problems | Blood Pressure | Boils | Bowel Problems | Breast Problems | Breathing Problems | Bronchitis | Bruising | Bulimia | Bunions | Bursitis | Callices | Cancers | Cataracts | Catarrh | Cerebral Palsy |
|---|---|---|---|---|---|---|---|---|---|---|---|---|---|---|---|---|
| DREAMCATCHER (HM06298) | | | | | | | | | | | | | | | | |
| DULWICH PHYSIOTHERAPY (HM06383) | | | | | | | | | | | | | | | | |
| E.LONDON COMPLEMENTARY HEALTH (HM06479) | ● | ● | ● | ● | ● | ● | ● | ● | ● | | ● | ● | ● | ● | ● | |
| EALING COUNS & THERAPY CTRE (HM06488) | | | | | | | | | | | | | | | | |
| EAST WEST HERB SHOP (HM06527) | | | | ● | | ● | | | | | | | | | | |
| EAST WEST THERAPIES (HM06529) | ● | ● | | ● | | ● | | | | | | | | ● | | |
| EDGELL, MARJORY (HM06599) | | | | | | | | | | | | | ● | | | |
| EDGWARE NATURAL HEALTH CENTRE (HM06604) | ● | ● | ● | ● | | ● | | | | | | | | | | |
| ELLWOOD, CAROLINE (HM06780) | | | | | | | | ● | | | | | | | | |
| ELTHAM HYPNOTHERAPY ANALYSIS (HM06789) | | | | | | | | | ● | | | | | | | |
| ENFIELD CLINIC OF HERBAL MED (HM06818) | ● | ● | ● | ● | | ● | ● | ● | ● | | | | | | ● | |
| ENFIELD HYP & COUNSELLING (HM06819) | | | | | | | | | | | | | | | | |
| EQUILIBRIUM (HM06869) | | ● | | ● | ● | | | | | | | | | | | |
| EQUILIBRIUM COUNS/THRPY CTRE (HM06873) | | | | | | | | | ● | | | | | | | |
| FAIR, ANNETTE (HM07048) | | ● | | | | | | | | | | | | | | |
| FARMACIA URBAN HEALING (HM07107) | | | | | | | | | | | | | | | | |
| FELDENKRAIS CENTRE (HM07190) | | | | | | | | | | | | | | | | |
| FLETCHER, CLARE (HM07410) | | | | | | | | | | | | | | | | |
| FLEXIBLE HOUR (HM07420) | | | | | | | | | | | | | | | | |
| FLOAT WORKS (HM07424) | | | | | | | | | | | | | | | | |
| FRY, HOWARD (HM07772) | | | | | | | | | | | | ● | | | | |
| FULHAM CLINIC (HM07781) | ● | | | ● | | ● | ● | | | | | | | | | |
| G T CONSULTANCY (HM07815) | | | | ● | | | | | | | | | | | | |
| GEE, PHILL (HM07959) | | | | | | | | | | | | | | | | |
| GEORGE (HM07987) | | | | | | | | | | ● | | | | | | |
| GLASSMAN, DAVID (HM08128) | ● | ● | | ● | | ● | ● | ● | | | ● | | | | ● | |
| GODWIN, ROME (HM08194) | | | | | | | | | | | | | | | | |
| GREENWICH NATURAL HEALTH CTRE (HM08500) | | ● | | ● | | | | | | | ● | | ● | | | |
| GREIDINGER, CLIVE (HM08524) | | ● | | | | | | | | | | | | | | |
| HACKNEY HYPNOTHERAPY (HM08685) | | | | | | | | | ● | | | | ● | | | |
| HAIN, PATRICIA (HM08712) | ● | ● | ● | ● | ● | ● | ● | | ● | | | | ● | | ● | |
| HAMILTON, FIONA (HM08843) | | | | ● | | ● | | | | | | | | | | |
| HAMPSTEAD ACU/CHINESE HBL MED (HM08881) | | | | | | | ● | | | | | | | | | |
| HAREWOOD, MARCIA M (HM08991) | ● | ● | ● | ● | ● | | | | | | ● | | | | ● | |

| Business by County with Reference no. | Circulation Problems | Cold Sores | Colds | Colic | Colitis | Conjunctivitis | Constipation | Convulsions | Corns | Coughs | Cramp | Cystitis |
|---|---|---|---|---|---|---|---|---|---|---|---|---|
| DREAMCATCHER (HM06298) | ● | | | | | | | | | | | |
| DULWICH PHYSIOTHERAPY (HM06383) | | | | | | | | | | | | |
| E.LONDON COMPLEMENTARY HEALTH (HM06479) | ● | ● | ● | ● | ● | ● | ● | ● | ● | ● | ● | ● |
| EALING COUNS & THERAPY CTRE (HM06488) | | | ● | | | | | | | ● | | |
| EAST WEST HERB SHOP (HM06527) | ● | | ● | ● | | | ● | | | ● | | ● |
| EAST WEST THERAPIES (HM06529) | ● | | | | ● | | ● | | | ● | | |
| EDGELL, MARJORY (HM06599) | | | | | | | | | | | | |
| EDGWARE NATURAL HEALTH CENTRE (HM06604) | | | | | | | ● | | | ● | | ● |
| ELLWOOD, CAROLINE (HM06780) | | | ● | | | | | | | | | |
| ELTHAM HYPNOTHERAPY ANALYSIS (HM06789) | | | | | | | | | | | | |
| ENFIELD CLINIC OF HERBAL MED (HM06818) | ● | ● | ● | ● | ● | ● | ● | | | ● | ● | ● |
| ENFIELD HYP & COUNSELLING (HM06819) | | | ● | | | | | | | | | |
| EQUILIBRIUM (HM06869) | ● | | ● | ● | | | ● | | | | | |
| EQUILIBRIUM COUNS/THRPY CTRE (HM06873) | | | | | | | | | | | | |
| FAIR, ANNETTE (HM07048) | ● | | | | | | | | | | | |
| FARMACIA URBAN HEALING (HM07107) | | | | | | | | | | | | |
| FELDENKRAIS CENTRE (HM07190) | | | | | | | | | | | | |
| FLETCHER, CLARE (HM07410) | | | | | | | ● | | | | | |
| FLEXIBLE HOUR (HM07420) | | | | | | | | | | | | |
| FLOAT WORKS (HM07424) | | | | | | | | | | | | |
| FRY, HOWARD (HM07772) | | | | | | | | | ● | | | |
| FULHAM CLINIC (HM07781) | ● | | ● | | | | ● | | | | ● | ● |
| G T CONSULTANCY (HM07815) | | | | | | | | | | | | |
| GEE, PHILL (HM07959) | | | | | | | | | | | | |
| GEORGE (HM07987) | | | | | | | | | | | | |
| GLASSMAN, DAVID (HM08128) | ● | | | ● | | ● | ● | ● | | ● | ● | ● |
| GODWIN, ROME (HM08194) | ● | | | | | | | | | | | |
| GREENWICH NATURAL HEALTH CTRE (HM08500) | | | | | | | | | | | | |
| GREIDINGER, CLIVE (HM08524) | | | | | ● | | | | | | | |
| HACKNEY HYPNOTHERAPY (HM08685) | | | | | | | | | | | | |
| HAIN, PATRICIA (HM08712) | ● | | ● | ● | ● | | ● | | | ● | | ● |
| HAMILTON, FIONA (HM08843) | ● | | | | | | ● | | | | ● | |
| HAMPSTEAD ACU/CHINESE HBL MED (HM08881) | ● | | ● | | ● | | ● | | | | | |
| HAREWOOD, MARCIA M (HM08991) | ● | | ● | ● | ● | | ● | | | | ● | ● |

# A - C Conditions treated at Practices/Businesses

Business by County with Reference no.

| Business | Acne | Addiction | Adenoids | Aids | Alcoholism | Allergy | Alzheimer's Disease | Amnesia | Anaemia | Angina | Anorexia | Anxiety | Arthritis | Asthma | Athletes Foot | Autism |
|---|---|---|---|---|---|---|---|---|---|---|---|---|---|---|---|---|
| HARLEY ST STRESS MNGMT (HM08999) | | ● | | | | | | | | | ● | ● | | | | ● |
| HARLEY, KI (HM09006) | | | | | | | | | | | | ● | | | | |
| HARPER, SUZANNE G (HM09041) | ● | ● | | | | ● | | | | | ● | ● | ● | ● | | |
| HARPER, SUZANNE G (HM09042) | ● | ● | | | | ● | | | | | ● | ● | | ● | | |
| HARROW HEALTH CARE CENTRE (HM09121) | | ● | | | | | | | | | | | ● | ● | ● | |
| HATHA YOGA/COUNSELLING (HM09195) | | | | | | | | | | | | ● | | ● | | |
| HAVELOCK-SEARLE, PAULINE (HM09206) | | ● | | | ● | | | ● | | | ● | ● | | | | |
| HAWKINS, JAN (HM09222) | | ● | | | ● | | | | | | ● | ● | | | | |
| HEAL, CHRISTIANNE (HM09314) | | | | | | | | | | | ● | ● | | | | |
| HEALERS WORLD (HM09320) | ● | ● | ● | ● | ● | ● | ● | ● | ● | ● | ● | ● | ● | ● | ● | ● |
| HEALING ARTS UK (HM09326) | | | | ● | | | | | | | | ● | ● | | | |
| HEALTHY LIVING CENTRE (HM09429) | ● | ● | ● | ● | ● | ● | ● | ● | ● | ● | ● | ● | ● | ● | ● | ● |
| HERBAL CARE (HM09601) | ● | ● | | | ● | ● | | | ● | ● | ● | ● | ● | ● | ● | |
| HERBAL CARE (HM09600) | ● | ● | | | ● | ● | | | ● | ● | ● | ● | ● | ● | ● | |
| HERBMEDIC (HM09663) | ● | ● | | ● | ● | ● | | | ● | ● | | ● | ● | ● | ● | |
| HETHERTON, ANNE (HM09697) | ● | | ● | | ● | ● | | ● | ● | ● | ● | ● | ● | ● | ● | ● |
| HIGHBURY CENTRE (HM09746) | | | | | | | | | | | | | | | | |
| HILDRETH & COCKER (HM09767) | | | | | | | | | | | | | ● | | | |
| HOGARTH CLINIC (HM09907) | | ● | | | | | | | | ● | | ● | ● | ● | | |
| HOLMES, DAVID (HM10040) | | | | | | | | | | | | | | | ● | |
| HOME VISITING SERVICES (HM10069) | ● | ● | ● | ● | ● | | | | | | | ● | ● | ● | ● | |
| HONG TAD ACUPUNCTURE & HERBAL (HM10119) | ● | ● | | | ● | ● | ● | | ● | ● | ● | ● | ● | ● | ● | |
| HOPE, ANN (HM10137) | | | | | | | | | | | | | | | ● | |
| HOUSE OF MISTRY (HM10220) | ● | | | | | ● | | | | | | | ● | ● | ● | |
| HOWARD, LYNNE (HM10240) | ● | ● | ● | ● | ● | ● | ● | ● | ● | ● | ● | ● | ● | ● | ● | ● |
| HUGHES, PAUL (HM10339) | ● | | | | | ● | | | | | | ● | ● | ● | | |
| HYDE BARKER & ASSOCIATES (HM10469) | | | | | | | | | | | | | ● | ● | ● | |
| INDEPENDENT PSYCHOLOGY SERVICE (HM10610) | | | | | ● | | | | | | ● | ● | | | | |
| INSIDE STORY (HM10650) | | | | | | ● | | | | | | | ● | ● | | ● |
| JACOBS, BRIAN M (HM10858) | | | | | | | | | | | ● | ● | | | | |
| JELFS, MARTIN (HM10976) | | | | | | | | | | | | ● | | | | |
| JELFS, MARTIN (HM10977) | | | | | | | | | | | | ● | | | | |
| JEWERS, M S (HM11025) | | | | | | | | | | | | | | | ● | |
| JOSEPH CLINIC (HM11215) | | | | | | | | | | | | | ● | ● | ● | |

| Business | Back Pain | Bacterial Infections | Baldness | Bereavement | Bladder Problems | Blood Pressure | Boils | Bowel Problems | Breast Problems | Breathing Problems | Bronchitis | Bruising | Bulimia | Bunions | Bursitis | Callices |
|---|---|---|---|---|---|---|---|---|---|---|---|---|---|---|---|---|
| HARLEY ST STRESS MNGMT (HM08999) | | | | | | ● | | ● | | ● | | | ● | | | |
| HARLEY, KI (HM09006) | | | | ● | | | | | | | | | | | | |
| HARPER, SUZANNE G (HM09041) | ● | | | | ● | ● | | ● | ● | ● | | ● | | | ● | |
| HARPER, SUZANNE G (HM09042) | ● | | | | ● | ● | | ● | ● | ● | | ● | | | ● | |
| HARROW HEALTH CARE CENTRE (HM09121) | ● | | | | | ● | | | | | ● | | | | ● | |
| HATHA YOGA/COUNSELLING (HM09195) | ● | | | | | | | | | ● | | | | | | |
| HAVELOCK-SEARLE, PAULINE (HM09206) | | | | | | | | | | | | | ● | | | |
| HAWKINS, JAN (HM09222) | | | | | | ● | | | | ● | | | ● | | | |
| HEAL, CHRISTIANNE (HM09314) | | | | ● | | | | | | | | | | | | |
| HEALERS WORLD (HM09320) | ● | ● | ● | | ● | ● | ● | ● | ● | ● | ● | ● | ● | | ● | ● |
| HEALING ARTS UK (HM09326) | ● | | | | | | | | | | | | | | ● | |
| HEALTHY LIVING CENTRE (HM09429) | ● | ● | ● | | ● | ● | ● | ● | ● | ● | ● | ● | ● | | ● | |
| HERBAL CARE (HM09601) | ● | ● | ● | | ● | ● | ● | ● | ● | ● | ● | ● | | | | |
| HERBAL CARE (HM09600) | ● | ● | ● | | ● | ● | ● | ● | ● | ● | ● | ● | | | | ● |
| HERBMEDIC (HM09663) | ● | ● | ● | | ● | ● | ● | ● | ● | ● | ● | ● | ● | | | |
| HETHERTON, ANNE (HM09697) | ● | ● | ● | | ● | ● | ● | ● | ● | ● | ● | ● | ● | | ● | |
| HIGHBURY CENTRE (HM09746) | ● | | | | | | | | | | | | | | | |
| HILDRETH & COCKER (HM09767) | | | | | | | | | | | | | | | | |
| HOGARTH CLINIC (HM09907) | ● | | | | | ● | | | | ● | ● | | | | ● | |
| HOLMES, DAVID (HM10040) | | | | | | | | | | | | | | | | ● |
| HOME VISITING SERVICES (HM10069) | ● | | | | | ● | ● | ● | ● | ● | ● | | | | | |
| HONG TAD ACUPUNCTURE & HERBAL (HM10119) | ● | | | | ● | ● | ● | ● | ● | ● | ● | ● | | | ● | |
| HOPE, ANN (HM10137) | | | | | | | | | | | | | | | | |
| HOUSE OF MISTRY (HM10220) | ● | ● | | | ● | ● | ● | ● | | | | ● | | | | |
| HOWARD, LYNNE (HM10240) | ● | ● | ● | | ● | ● | ● | ● | ● | ● | ● | ● | ● | | ● | ● |
| HUGHES, PAUL (HM10339) | ● | ● | | | ● | ● | ● | ● | ● | ● | | ● | | | | |
| HYDE BARKER & ASSOCIATES (HM10469) | ● | ● | | | | | | | | | | ● | | | ● | ● |
| INDEPENDENT PSYCHOLOGY SERVICE (HM10610) | | | | | | | | | | | | | ● | | | |
| INSIDE STORY (HM10650) | | | | | | | | | | | | | | | | |
| JACOBS, BRIAN M (HM10858) | | | | | | | | | | | | | | | | |
| JELFS, MARTIN (HM10976) | | | | | | | | | | | | | | | | |
| JELFS, MARTIN (HM10977) | | | | | | | | | | | | | | | | |
| JEWERS, M S (HM11025) | | ● | | | | | | | | | | | | ● | | ● |
| JOSEPH CLINIC (HM11215) | ● | | | | | | | | | | | | | | | |

| Business | Cancers | Cataracts | Catarrh | Cerebral Palsy | Circulation Problems | Cold Sores | Colds | Colic | Colitis | Conjunctivitis | Constipation | Convulsions | Corns | Coughs | Cramp | Cystitis |
|---|---|---|---|---|---|---|---|---|---|---|---|---|---|---|---|---|
| HARLEY ST STRESS MNGMT (HM08999) | ● | | | | | | | | | | ● | | | | | |
| HARLEY, KI (HM09006) | | | | | | | | | | | | | | | | |
| HARPER, SUZANNE G (HM09041) | | | ● | | ● | ● | ● | ● | ● | | ● | | | ● | ● | ● |
| HARPER, SUZANNE G (HM09042) | | | ● | | ● | ● | ● | ● | ● | | ● | | | ● | ● | |
| HARROW HEALTH CARE CENTRE (HM09121) | | | | | | | | ● | ● | | ● | | | | ● | ● |
| HATHA YOGA/COUNSELLING (HM09195) | | | | | | | | | | | | | | | | |
| HAVELOCK-SEARLE, PAULINE (HM09206) | | | | | | | | | | | | | | | | |
| HAWKINS, JAN (HM09222) | | | | | | | | | | | | ● | | | | |
| HEAL, CHRISTIANNE (HM09314) | | | | | | | | | | | | | | | | |
| HEALERS WORLD (HM09320) | ● | ● | ● | | ● | ● | ● | ● | ● | ● | ● | ● | ● | ● | ● | ● |
| HEALING ARTS UK (HM09326) | | | | | ● | | | | | | | | | | ● | |
| HEALTHY LIVING CENTRE (HM09429) | ● | ● | ● | | ● | ● | ● | ● | ● | ● | ● | ● | | ● | ● | ● |
| HERBAL CARE (HM09601) | | | ● | | ● | ● | ● | | ● | ● | ● | | | ● | ● | ● |
| HERBAL CARE (HM09600) | | | ● | | ● | ● | ● | | ● | ● | ● | | ● | ● | ● | ● |
| HERBMEDIC (HM09663) | ● | ● | ● | | ● | ● | ● | ● | ● | ● | ● | ● | | ● | ● | ● |
| HETHERTON, ANNE (HM09697) | ● | | ● | | ● | ● | ● | ● | ● | ● | ● | ● | | ● | ● | ● |
| HIGHBURY CENTRE (HM09746) | | | | | | | | | | | | | | | | |
| HILDRETH & COCKER (HM09767) | | | | | | | | | | | | | | | | |
| HOGARTH CLINIC (HM09907) | | | | | ● | | | ● | ● | | ● | | | | ● | ● |
| HOLMES, DAVID (HM10040) | | | | | | | | | | | | | ● | | | |
| HOME VISITING SERVICES (HM10069) | | | | | ● | ● | ● | | ● | | ● | | | ● | ● | ● |
| HONG TAD ACUPUNCTURE & HERBAL (HM10119) | ● | | ● | | ● | ● | ● | ● | ● | ● | ● | ● | | ● | ● | ● |
| HOPE, ANN (HM10137) | | | | | | | | | | | | | | | | |
| HOUSE OF MISTRY (HM10220) | | | ● | | ● | ● | ● | ● | ● | ● | ● | | | ● | ● | ● |
| HOWARD, LYNNE (HM10240) | ● | ● | ● | | ● | ● | ● | ● | ● | ● | ● | ● | ● | ● | ● | ● |
| HUGHES, PAUL (HM10339) | ● | | ● | | ● | ● | ● | ● | ● | ● | ● | | | ● | | ● |
| HYDE BARKER & ASSOCIATES (HM10469) | | | | | ● | | | | | | | | ● | | | |
| INDEPENDENT PSYCHOLOGY SERVICE (HM10610) | | | | | | | | | | | | | | | | |
| INSIDE STORY (HM10650) | | | | | | | | ● | ● | | ● | | | | | |
| JACOBS, BRIAN M (HM10858) | | | | | | | | | | | | | | | | |
| JELFS, MARTIN (HM10976) | | | | | | | | | | | | | | | | |
| JELFS, MARTIN (HM10977) | | | | | | | | | | | | | | | | |
| JEWERS, M S (HM11025) | | | | | | | | | | | | | ● | | | |
| JOSEPH CLINIC (HM11215) | | | | | | | | | | | | | | | ● | |

www.healthmyself.com

# A - C Conditions treated at Practices/Businesses

| Business by County with Reference no. | Acne | Addiction | Adenoids | Aids | Alcoholism | Allergy | Alzheimer's Disease | Amnesia | Anaemia | Angina | Anorexia | Anxiety |
|---|---|---|---|---|---|---|---|---|---|---|---|---|
| KALLAS, JEMIMA (HM11297) | ● | ● | | | ● | ● | | | ● | | ● | ● |
| KANE AND ROSS CLINICS (HM11309) | | | | | | | | | | | | ● |
| KEITH EGLETON HYPNOTHERAPY (HM11412) | | ● | | | ● | | | ● | | | ● | |
| KERN, MICHAEL (HM11544) | | | | | | | ● | | | | | ● |
| KIKAI SHIATSU CENTRE (HM11598) | | ● | | ● | ● | | | | | | | ● |
| KILBRIDE, PETER (HM11600) | | | | | | | | | | | | ● |
| KINGSBURY PSYCHOTHERAPY PRAC (HM11660) | | ● | | | | | | | | | ● | ● |
| KINGSGATE ACUPUNCTURE PRACTICE (HM11663) | ● | ● | | ● | ● | | | | ● | | ● | |
| KIRSH, MALCOLM (DR) (HM11725) | | | | | | | | | | | | ● |
| KIRSH, MALCOLM (DR) (HM11724) | | | | | | | | | | | | ● |
| KLEIN, JEMMA (HM11737) | | | | | | | | | | | | |
| LASSMAN, J (HM11986) | | | | | | ● | | | | | | |
| LEE COMPLEMENTARY HEALTH CTRE (HM12130) | | | | | | | | | | | | |
| LEVER CLINIC (HM12256) | | | | | | | | | | | | |
| LITTLE VENICE CHIROPODY (HM12469) | | | | | | | | | | | | |
| LIVING CENTRE CLINIC (HM12483) | ● | | | | | ● | | | | | | ● |
| LIZ DAWSON - PSYCHOTHERAPIST (HM12494) | | ● | | | ● | | | | | | ● | ● |
| LONDON FLOAT CENTRE (HM12597) | | | | | | ● | | | | | | |
| LONDON INDIAN CHAMPISSAGE CTRE (HM12599) | | | | | | | | | | | | |
| LONDON SCHOOL OF OSTEOPATHY (HM12604) | | | | | | | | | | | | |
| LONDON SPINE AND JOINT CLINIC (HM12611) | | | | | | | | | | | | |
| LONGARETTI, ANTHONY (HM12623) | | | | | | | | | | | | |
| LOTUS CLINIC (HM12653) | ● | ● | ● | | ● | | | | ● | | ● | ● |
| LOW, JANET (DR) (HM12686) | | | | | | | | | | | | ● |
| LUXTON, PAULINE (HM12752) | | | | | | | | | | | | ● |
| MANLEY CLINIC (HM13016) | ● | | ● | | ● | ● | | ● | ● | ● | ● | ● |
| MARIE, SOUTA (HM13099) | | | | | | | | | | | | ● |
| MARKS, DARREN HYPNOTHERAPY (HM13119) | | ● | | ● | | | | | | | | ● |
| MARLBOROUGH THERAPY PRACTICE (HM13125) | | ● | | | | | | | | | ● | ● |
| MATTHEWS, ROBERT (HM13312) | | ● | | | ● | | | | | | ● | ● |
| MCCAFFREY, GERARDINE (HM13380) | | | | | | ● | | | | | | ● |
| MCCLOSKEY, P J (HM13409) | | | | | | | | | | | | |
| MEDICAL SCIENCES TECH CORP (HM13654) | | | | | | ● | | | | | | |
| MEYERSON, SIMON (HM13789) | | | | | | | | | | | | ● |

| Business by County with Reference no. | Arthritis | Asthma | Athletes Foot | Autism | Back Pain | Bacterial Infections | Baldness | Bereavement | Bladder Problems | Blood Pressure | Boils | Bowel Problems |
|---|---|---|---|---|---|---|---|---|---|---|---|---|
| KALLAS, JEMIMA (HM11297) | | ● | ● | | | | | | ● | ● | ● | ● |
| KANE AND ROSS CLINICS (HM11309) | ● | | | | ● | | | | | | | |
| KEITH EGLETON HYPNOTHERAPY (HM11412) | | ● | | | | | | | ● | ● | | ● |
| KERN, MICHAEL (HM11544) | ● | ● | | | ● | | | | ● | ● | | ● |
| KIKAI SHIATSU CENTRE (HM11598) | ● | | | | ● | | | | | | | ● |
| KILBRIDE, PETER (HM11600) | | | | | | | | | | | | ● |
| KINGSBURY PSYCHOTHERAPY PRAC (HM11660) | | | | | | | | | | | | |
| KINGSGATE ACUPUNCTURE PRACTICE (HM11663) | ● | ● | | | ● | | | | ● | ● | | ● |
| KIRSH, MALCOLM (DR) (HM11725) | | | | | | | | | | | | |
| KIRSH, MALCOLM (DR) (HM11724) | | | | | | | | | | | | |
| KLEIN, JEMMA (HM11737) | ● | | ● | | | | | | | | | |
| LASSMAN, J (HM11986) | ● | | | | ● | | | | | | | |
| LEE COMPLEMENTARY HEALTH CTRE (HM12130) | ● | | | | ● | | | | | | | |
| LEVER CLINIC (HM12256) | ● | ● | | | ● | | | | | | | |
| LITTLE VENICE CHIROPODY (HM12469) | | | ● | | ● | | | | | | | |
| LIVING CENTRE CLINIC (HM12483) | ● | ● | ● | | ● | | | | ● | ● | ● | ● |
| LIZ DAWSON - PSYCHOTHERAPIST (HM12494) | | | | | | | | ● | | | | |
| LONDON FLOAT CENTRE (HM12597) | | | | | | | | | | | | |
| LONDON INDIAN CHAMPISSAGE CTRE (HM12599) | | | | | ● | | | | | | | |
| LONDON SCHOOL OF OSTEOPATHY (HM12604) | ● | ● | | | ● | | | | | | | |
| LONDON SPINE AND JOINT CLINIC (HM12611) | ● | | | | ● | | | | | | | |
| LONGARETTI, ANTHONY (HM12623) | | | | | ● | | | | | | | |
| LOTUS CLINIC (HM12653) | ● | ● | ● | | | ● | | | ● | ● | ● | ● |
| LOW, JANET (DR) (HM12686) | | | | | | | | | | | | |
| LUXTON, PAULINE (HM12752) | | | ● | | | | | | | | | |
| MANLEY CLINIC (HM13016) | ● | ● | ● | ● | ● | ● | ● | | ● | ● | ● | ● |
| MARIE, SOUTA (HM13099) | | | | | | | | ● | | | | |
| MARKS, DARREN HYPNOTHERAPY (HM13119) | | | | | | | | | | | | |
| MARLBOROUGH THERAPY PRACTICE (HM13125) | | | | | | | | | | | | ● |
| MATTHEWS, ROBERT (HM13312) | | ● | | | | | | | | ● | | ● |
| MCCAFFREY, GERARDINE (HM13380) | ● | ● | ● | | ● | | | | | ● | | ● |
| MCCLOSKEY, P J (HM13409) | | | ● | | ● | | | | | | | |
| MEDICAL SCIENCES TECH CORP (HM13654) | | | | | | | | | | | | |
| MEYERSON, SIMON (HM13789) | | | | | | | | | | | | |

| Business by County with Reference no. | Breast Problems | Breathing Problems | Bronchitis | Bruising | Bulimia | Bunions | Bursitis | Callices | Cancers | Cataracts | Catarrh | Cerebral Palsy |
|---|---|---|---|---|---|---|---|---|---|---|---|---|
| KALLAS, JEMIMA (HM11297) | ● | ● | ● | ● | ● | | ● | | | | ● | |
| KANE AND ROSS CLINICS (HM11309) | | | | | | | | | | | | |
| KEITH EGLETON HYPNOTHERAPY (HM11412) | | ● | | | ● | | | | | | | |
| KERN, MICHAEL (HM11544) | | ● | ● | | | | | | | | ● | |
| KIKAI SHIATSU CENTRE (HM11598) | ● | ● | ● | | | | | | ● | | | |
| KILBRIDE, PETER (HM11600) | | ● | | | | | | | | | | |
| KINGSBURY PSYCHOTHERAPY PRAC (HM11660) | | | | | | | | | | | | |
| KINGSGATE ACUPUNCTURE PRACTICE (HM11663) | | | ● | | | | ● | | | | | |
| KIRSH, MALCOLM (DR) (HM11725) | | | | | | | | | | | | |
| KIRSH, MALCOLM (DR) (HM11724) | | | | | | | | | | | | |
| KLEIN, JEMMA (HM11737) | | | | | | ● | | ● | | | | |
| LASSMAN, J (HM11986) | | | | ● | | | | | | | | |
| LEE COMPLEMENTARY HEALTH CTRE (HM12130) | | | | | | | | | | | | |
| LEVER CLINIC (HM12256) | | | | ● | | | ● | | | | | |
| LITTLE VENICE CHIROPODY (HM12469) | | | | | | | | | | | | |
| LIVING CENTRE CLINIC (HM12483) | | | ● | | | | | | | | ● | |
| LIZ DAWSON - PSYCHOTHERAPIST (HM12494) | | | | | | | | | | | | |
| LONDON FLOAT CENTRE (HM12597) | | | | | | | | | | | | |
| LONDON INDIAN CHAMPISSAGE CTRE (HM12599) | | | | | | | | | | | | |
| LONDON SCHOOL OF OSTEOPATHY (HM12604) | | | | | | | | | | | | |
| LONDON SPINE AND JOINT CLINIC (HM12611) | | | | ● | | | ● | | | | | |
| LONGARETTI, ANTHONY (HM12623) | | | | | | | | | | | | |
| LOTUS CLINIC (HM12653) | ● | ● | ● | ● | ● | | ● | | | | ● | |
| LOW, JANET (DR) (HM12686) | | | | | | | | | | | | |
| LUXTON, PAULINE (HM12752) | | | | | | | | | | | | |
| MANLEY CLINIC (HM13016) | ● | ● | ● | ● | ● | | ● | | ● | | ● | |
| MARIE, SOUTA (HM13099) | | | | | | | | | | | | |
| MARKS, DARREN HYPNOTHERAPY (HM13119) | | | | | | | | | ● | | | |
| MARLBOROUGH THERAPY PRACTICE (HM13125) | | | | | | | | | | | | |
| MATTHEWS, ROBERT (HM13312) | | | | | ● | | | | | | | |
| MCCAFFREY, GERARDINE (HM13380) | ● | ● | | | | | ● | ● | | | | |
| MCCLOSKEY, P J (HM13409) | | | | ● | | ● | ● | | | | | |
| MEDICAL SCIENCES TECH CORP (HM13654) | | | | | | | | | | | | |
| MEYERSON, SIMON (HM13789) | | | | | | | | | | | | |

| Business by County with Reference no. | Circulation Problems | Cold Sores | Colds | Colic | Colitis | Conjunctivitis | Constipation | Convulsions | Corns | Coughs | Cramp | Cystitis |
|---|---|---|---|---|---|---|---|---|---|---|---|---|
| KALLAS, JEMIMA (HM11297) | ● | ● | ● | ● | | ● | ● | | | ● | ● | ● |
| KANE AND ROSS CLINICS (HM11309) | | | | | | | | | | | | |
| KEITH EGLETON HYPNOTHERAPY (HM11412) | ● | | | | | | ● | | | | ● | |
| KERN, MICHAEL (HM11544) | ● | | ● | ● | ● | | ● | | | | ● | ● |
| KIKAI SHIATSU CENTRE (HM11598) | ● | | ● | | ● | | ● | | | | ● | |
| KILBRIDE, PETER (HM11600) | | | | ● | ● | | | | | | ● | |
| KINGSBURY PSYCHOTHERAPY PRAC (HM11660) | | | | | | | | | | | | |
| KINGSGATE ACUPUNCTURE PRACTICE (HM11663) | ● | ● | ● | ● | | | ● | | | ● | ● | ● |
| KIRSH, MALCOLM (DR) (HM11725) | | | | | | | | | | | | |
| KIRSH, MALCOLM (DR) (HM11724) | | | | | | | | | | | | |
| KLEIN, JEMMA (HM11737) | | | | | | | | | ● | | | |
| LASSMAN, J (HM11986) | | | | | | | ● | | | | | |
| LEE COMPLEMENTARY HEALTH CTRE (HM12130) | | | | ● | | | | | | | | |
| LEVER CLINIC (HM12256) | ● | ● | | | | | | | | | ● | |
| LITTLE VENICE CHIROPODY (HM12469) | | | | | | | | | ● | | | |
| LIVING CENTRE CLINIC (HM12483) | ● | ● | ● | ● | ● | ● | ● | | | ● | ● | ● |
| LIZ DAWSON - PSYCHOTHERAPIST (HM12494) | | | | | | | | | | | | |
| LONDON FLOAT CENTRE (HM12597) | | | | | | | | | | | | |
| LONDON INDIAN CHAMPISSAGE CTRE (HM12599) | | | | | | | | | | | | |
| LONDON SCHOOL OF OSTEOPATHY (HM12604) | | | | | | | | | | | | |
| LONDON SPINE AND JOINT CLINIC (HM12611) | | | | ● | | | | | | | ● | |
| LONGARETTI, ANTHONY (HM12623) | | | | | | | | | | | | |
| LOTUS CLINIC (HM12653) | ● | ● | ● | ● | ● | ● | ● | | | ● | ● | ● |
| LOW, JANET (DR) (HM12686) | | | | | | | | | | | | |
| LUXTON, PAULINE (HM12752) | | | | | | | | | | | | |
| MANLEY CLINIC (HM13016) | ● | ● | ● | ● | ● | ● | ● | ● | | ● | ● | ● |
| MARIE, SOUTA (HM13099) | | | | | | | | | | | | |
| MARKS, DARREN HYPNOTHERAPY (HM13119) | | | | | | | | | | | | |
| MARLBOROUGH THERAPY PRACTICE (HM13125) | | | | | | | | | | | | |
| MATTHEWS, ROBERT (HM13312) | | | | | ● | | | | | | | |
| MCCAFFREY, GERARDINE (HM13380) | ● | | ● | | | | ● | | ● | | | ● |
| MCCLOSKEY, P J (HM13409) | ● | | | | | | | | | | | |
| MEDICAL SCIENCES TECH CORP (HM13654) | | | | | | | | | | | | |
| MEYERSON, SIMON (HM13789) | | | | | | | | | | | | |

# A - C Conditions treated at Practices/Businesses

| Business by County with Reference no. | Acne | Addiction | Adenoids | Aids | Alcoholism | Allergy | Alzheimer's Disease | Amnesia | Anaemia | Angina | Anorexia | Anxiety | Arthritis | Asthma | Athletes Foot | Autism | Back Pain | Bacterial Infections | Baldness | Bereavement | Bladder Problems | Blood Pressure | Boils | Bowel Problems | Breast Problems | Breathing Problems | Bronchitis | Bruising | Bulimia | Bunions | Bursitis | Callices | Cancers | Cataracts | Catarrh | Cerebral Palsy | Circulation Problems | Cold Sores | Colds | Colic | Colitis | Conjunctivitis | Constipation | Convulsions | Corns | Coughs | Cramp | Cystitis |
|---|---|---|---|---|---|---|---|---|---|---|---|---|---|---|---|---|---|---|---|---|---|---|---|---|---|---|---|---|---|---|---|---|---|---|---|---|---|---|---|---|---|---|---|---|---|---|---|---|
| MIDDLETON, IAN W (HM13821) | ● |  |  |  |  | ● |  |  |  |  | ● | ● | ● | ● |  |  |  | ● |  |  | ● | ● |  | ● |  |  | ● |  |  |  |  |  |  |  | ● |  | ● | ● | ● |  | ● |  | ● |  |  | ● |  | ● |
| MILLS DE-WIN STUDIOS (HM13922) | ● |  |  |  |  |  |  |  |  |  |  |  | ● | ● |  | ● | ● |  |  |  | ● | ● |  |  | ● | ● | ● |  |  |  | ● |  |  |  | ● |  | ● | ● | ● | ● | ● |  | ● |  |  | ● |  | ● |
| MONTSERRAT CLINIC (HM14090) | ● |  | ● |  |  | ● | ● | ● | ● | ● | ● | ● | ● | ● | ● |  | ● | ● | ● |  | ● | ● | ● | ● | ● | ● | ● | ● | ● |  | ● | ● |  | ● | ● |  | ● | ● | ● | ● | ● | ● | ● | ● | ● | ● | ● | ● |
| MOTHERSOLE, VINETA (HM20682) |  |  |  |  |  |  |  |  |  |  |  |  |  |  | ● |  |  | ● |  |  |  |  |  |  |  |  |  | ● |  |  | ● |  |  |  |  |  | ● |  |  |  |  |  |  |  |  |  |  |  |
| MOTTINGHAM HYPNOTHERAPY CTRE (HM14279) | ● |  |  |  | ● | ● |  | ● |  |  | ● | ● |  | ● |  |  |  |  |  |  |  | ● |  | ● |  | ● |  |  | ● |  |  |  |  |  |  |  |  | ● |  |  | ● |  | ● |  |  |  |  |  |
| M-POWER (HM14308) |  | ● |  |  |  |  |  |  |  |  |  | ● |  |  |  |  |  |  |  |  |  |  |  |  |  |  |  |  |  |  |  |  |  |  |  |  |  |  |  |  |  |  |  |  |  |  |  |  |
| NEIL-ASHER, S (HM14761) |  |  |  |  |  |  |  |  |  |  |  |  | ● |  |  |  | ● |  |  |  |  | ● |  |  |  |  |  |  |  |  |  |  |  |  |  |  | ● |  |  |  |  |  |  |  |  |  |  |  |
| NEILL, VICTORIA (HM14764) |  |  |  |  |  |  |  |  |  |  |  | ● | ● | ● |  |  | ● |  |  |  |  |  |  |  |  | ● | ● | ● |  |  | ● |  | ● |  |  |  |  |  |  |  |  |  |  |  |  |  |  |  |
| NIEL-ASHER, S (HM14933) |  |  |  |  |  |  |  |  |  |  |  |  | ● |  |  |  | ● |  |  |  |  | ● |  |  |  |  |  |  |  |  |  |  |  |  |  |  | ● |  |  |  |  |  |  |  |  |  |  |  |
| NIELSEN, RITA C (HM14935) |  |  |  |  |  |  |  |  |  |  |  | ● | ● | ● |  |  | ● |  |  |  | ● |  |  |  |  | ● |  |  |  |  |  |  |  |  | ● |  | ● |  |  |  |  |  | ● | ● |  |  |  |  |
| NORTH POLE SCH OF T'AI-CHI (HM15094) |  |  |  |  |  |  |  |  |  |  |  | ● | ● |  |  |  |  |  |  |  |  | ● |  |  |  |  |  |  |  |  |  |  |  |  |  |  | ● |  |  |  |  |  |  |  |  |  |  |  |
| NORTHWOOD CLINIC (HM15067) |  |  |  |  |  |  |  |  |  |  |  |  | ● |  | ● |  | ● | ● |  |  |  |  |  |  |  |  |  |  |  |  |  | ● |  |  |  |  |  |  |  |  |  |  |  |  | ● |  |  |  |
| NOTTING HILL TRAD ACU CTRE (HM15081) | ● |  |  |  |  | ● |  |  |  |  | ● | ● | ● | ● |  |  | ● |  |  |  |  |  |  |  |  |  |  | ● |  |  |  |  |  |  |  |  |  |  |  |  |  |  | ● |  |  |  |  | ● |
| NRTH LONDON ALEXANDER PRACTICE (HM15092) |  |  |  |  |  |  |  |  |  |  |  |  |  |  |  |  | ● |  |  |  |  |  |  |  |  | ● |  |  |  |  |  |  |  |  |  |  |  |  |  |  |  |  |  |  |  |  |  |  |
| NUTRITION FOR LIFE INT (HM15124) |  |  |  |  |  | ● | ● |  |  |  |  | ● | ● | ● |  |  | ● | ● |  |  | ● | ● |  | ● |  | ● |  |  |  |  |  |  | ● | ● |  |  | ● |  | ● |  |  |  |  |  |  |  |  | ● |
| O'CONNOR, PENNY (HM15214) |  |  |  |  |  |  |  |  |  |  |  | ● |  |  |  |  | ● |  |  |  |  |  |  |  |  | ● |  |  |  |  |  |  |  |  |  |  |  |  |  |  |  |  |  |  |  |  |  |  |
| ORIENTAL MEDICINE (HM15386) | ● | ● |  | ● | ● | ● | ● | ● | ● | ● | ● | ● | ● | ● | ● |  | ● | ● | ● |  | ● | ● | ● | ● | ● | ● | ● | ● |  |  | ● |  | ● | ● | ● |  | ● | ● | ● | ● | ● | ● | ● | ● |  | ● | ● | ● |
| OSTEOPATHIC ASSOCIATION CLINIC (HM15453) |  |  |  |  |  |  |  |  |  |  |  |  |  |  |  |  | ● |  |  |  |  |  |  |  |  |  |  |  |  |  |  |  |  |  |  |  |  |  |  |  |  |  |  |  |  |  |  |  |
| OSTEOPATHIC PRACTICE (HM15467) |  |  |  |  |  |  |  |  |  |  |  |  | ● |  |  |  | ● |  |  |  |  |  |  |  |  |  |  |  |  |  | ● |  |  |  |  |  |  |  |  |  |  |  |  |  |  |  |  |  |
| OSTEOPATHIC PRACTICE (HM15473) |  |  |  |  |  |  |  |  |  |  |  |  |  |  |  |  | ● |  |  |  |  |  |  |  |  |  |  |  |  |  |  |  |  |  |  |  |  |  |  |  |  |  |  |  |  |  |  |  |
| OSTEOPATHIC PRACTICE (HM15471) |  |  |  |  |  |  |  |  |  |  |  |  | ● |  |  |  | ● |  |  |  |  |  |  |  |  |  |  |  |  |  |  |  |  |  | ● |  |  |  |  |  |  |  | ● |  |  |  |  |  |
| OSTEOPATHIC PRACTICE (HM15470) |  | ● |  |  | ● |  |  |  |  |  |  |  |  | ● |  | ● | ● |  |  |  |  |  |  | ● |  | ● | ● |  |  |  |  |  |  |  |  |  |  | ● | ● | ● | ● |  |  |  |  | ● |  | ● |
| OTREMBA, KATHARINA (HM15496) | ● | ● |  |  |  | ● |  |  |  |  | ● | ● |  | ● |  | ● | ● | ● | ● |  | ● |  |  | ● |  | ● | ● | ● | ● |  |  |  |  |  | ● |  | ● | ● | ● |  | ● |  | ● | ● |  | ● | ● | ● |
| OUTCOMES (HM15502) | ● | ● |  | ● | ● | ● |  |  |  |  | ● | ● | ● | ● |  |  |  |  |  |  | ● | ● | ● | ● | ● | ● | ● |  | ● |  | ● |  | ● |  |  |  |  |  |  |  |  |  | ● |  |  |  |  |  |
| PACIFIC WAVES PRODUCTIONS (HM15553) | ● | ● |  |  | ● | ● |  | ● |  |  | ● | ● | ● | ● |  |  | ● |  |  |  |  | ● |  | ● |  | ● |  |  | ● |  |  |  |  |  |  |  | ● |  |  |  |  |  | ● |  |  |  |  |  |
| PALACE ROAD OSTEOPATHIC CLINIC (HM15590) |  |  |  |  |  |  |  |  |  |  |  |  |  |  |  |  | ● |  |  |  |  |  |  |  |  |  |  |  |  |  |  |  |  |  |  |  |  |  |  |  |  |  |  |  |  |  |  |  |
| PALFREYMAN, SUE (HM15592) |  |  |  |  |  |  |  |  |  |  |  |  | ● | ● |  |  | ● |  |  |  |  |  |  | ● |  | ● |  |  |  |  |  |  |  |  |  |  |  |  |  |  |  |  |  |  |  |  |  |  |
| PAPOUTSIS, MARGARET (HM15642) |  |  |  |  |  |  |  |  |  |  |  |  | ● |  |  |  | ● |  |  |  |  |  |  |  |  |  |  |  |  |  |  |  |  |  |  |  |  |  |  |  |  |  |  |  |  |  |  |  |
| PATEL, J C (HM15788) |  |  |  |  |  |  |  |  |  |  |  |  | ● |  | ● |  |  | ● |  |  |  |  |  |  |  |  |  |  |  |  |  |  |  |  |  |  |  |  |  |  |  |  |  |  |  |  |  |  |
| PHYSIO ONE (HM16202) |  |  |  |  |  |  |  |  |  |  |  |  | ● |  | ● |  | ● |  |  |  |  |  |  |  |  |  |  |  |  |  |  |  |  |  |  |  |  |  |  |  |  |  |  |  |  |  |  |  |
| PHYSIO SOLUTIONS (HM16205) |  |  |  |  |  |  |  |  |  |  |  |  | ● |  |  |  | ● |  |  |  |  |  |  |  |  |  |  | ● |  |  | ● |  |  |  |  |  |  |  |  |  |  |  |  |  |  |  |  |  |
| PHYSIOTHERAPY PRACTICE (HM16253) |  |  |  |  |  |  |  |  |  |  |  |  | ● |  |  |  | ● |  |  |  |  |  |  |  |  |  |  |  |  |  | ● |  |  |  |  |  |  |  |  |  |  |  |  |  |  |  |  |  |
| PINNER ROAD PHYSIOTHERAPY (HM16316) |  |  |  |  |  |  |  |  |  |  |  |  | ● |  |  |  | ● |  |  |  |  |  |  |  |  |  |  |  |  |  |  |  |  |  |  |  |  |  |  |  |  |  |  |  |  |  |  |  |
| PODIATRY CLINIC (HM16393) |  |  |  |  |  |  |  |  |  |  |  |  |  |  | ● |  | ● | ● |  |  |  |  |  |  |  |  |  |  |  |  |  |  |  |  |  |  |  |  |  |  |  |  |  |  |  |  |  |  |

 

# A - C Conditions treated at Practices/Businesses

| Business by County with Reference no. | Acne | Addiction | Adenoids | Aids | Alcoholism | Allergy | Alzheimer's Disease | Amnesia | Anaemia | Angina | Anorexia | Anxiety | Arthritis | Asthma | Athletes Foot | Autism | Back Pain | Bacterial Infections | Baldness | Bereavement | Bladder Problems | Blood Pressure | Boils | Bowel Problems |
|---|---|---|---|---|---|---|---|---|---|---|---|---|---|---|---|---|---|---|---|---|---|---|---|---|
| PRICE, GILLIAN (HM16575) | ● | ● | ● |  | ● | ● | ● |  | ● | ● |  | ● | ● | ● |  |  | ● | ● | ● |  | ● | ● | ● | ● |
| PRICE, SANDRA (HM16594) |  |  |  |  |  |  |  |  |  |  |  |  | ● |  |  |  | ● |  |  |  |  |  |  |  |
| PRICE, SANDRA (HM16595) |  |  |  |  |  |  |  |  |  |  |  |  | ● |  |  |  | ● |  |  |  |  |  |  |  |
| PRIMROSE HEALING CENTRE (HM16616) |  | ● |  |  |  |  |  |  |  |  |  | ● |  |  |  |  |  |  |  |  |  |  |  | ● |
| PRIVATE HEALTH CLINIC (HM16644) | ● | ● | ● | ● | ● | ● | ● | ● | ● | ● | ● | ● | ● | ● | ● | ● | ● | ● | ● |  | ● | ● | ● | ● |
| PRIVATE PRACTICE (HM16649) |  |  |  |  |  |  |  |  |  |  | ● | ● |  |  |  |  |  |  |  |  |  |  |  |  |
| PSYCHOTHERAPY CENTRE (HM16734) | ● | ● |  |  | ● | ● |  | ● |  |  |  | ● |  | ● |  |  |  |  |  |  |  |  |  |  |
| PSYCHOTHERAPY SERVICES (HM16737) |  |  |  |  |  |  |  |  |  |  |  | ● |  |  |  |  |  |  |  |  |  |  |  |  |
| PUTNEY CHIROPRACTIC (HM16780) |  |  |  |  |  |  |  |  |  |  |  |  | ● | ● |  |  | ● |  |  |  |  |  |  |  |
| RACHEL YOUNG - HYPNOTHERAPIST (HM16837) |  |  |  |  |  | ● |  |  |  | ● | ● | ● | ● | ● |  |  | ● |  |  |  | ● | ● |  | ● |
| RAEBURN, JO (HM16865) | ● |  |  | ● |  |  |  |  |  |  |  | ● | ● | ● | ● |  | ● | ● | ● |  | ● | ● | ● | ● |
| RANDALL, CAROLINE (HM16926) | ● | ● | ● | ● | ● | ● | ● | ● | ● | ● | ● | ● | ● | ● | ● | ● | ● | ● | ● |  | ● | ● | ● | ● |
| RAVENSCROFT CENTRE (HM16967) |  |  |  |  |  |  |  |  |  |  |  | ● |  |  |  |  |  |  |  |  |  |  |  |  |
| READ, CHARLES (HM16993) |  |  |  |  |  |  |  |  |  |  |  |  | ● |  |  |  | ● |  |  |  |  |  |  |  |
| REEVE, MALCOLM (HM17060) |  |  |  |  |  | ● |  |  |  |  |  |  |  |  |  |  | ● |  |  |  |  |  |  |  |
| REFLEXOLOGY (HM17077) |  |  | ● |  | ● |  |  |  | ● |  |  | ● | ● |  |  |  |  |  |  |  | ● | ● |  | ● |
| REFLEXOLOGY CLINIC (HM17089) |  |  |  |  |  |  |  |  |  |  |  |  |  |  |  |  | ● |  |  |  |  | ● |  |  |
| RELAXATION PLACE (HM17166) | ● |  |  |  |  |  |  |  |  |  |  | ● | ● |  |  |  | ● |  |  |  |  |  |  |  |
| REPLINGHAM CLINIC (HM17195) | ● | ● |  |  | ● | ● |  |  | ● |  | ● | ● | ● | ● |  | ● | ● |  |  |  | ● | ● |  | ● |
| ROBERTS, MATT (HM17420) |  | ● |  |  |  |  |  |  |  |  | ● | ● |  |  |  |  |  |  |  |  |  |  |  | ● |
| ROBINSON, GABIE (HM17473) | ● |  |  |  |  |  |  |  |  |  |  | ● | ● | ● |  |  |  |  |  |  | ● | ● |  | ● |
| ROEHAMPTON PHYSIO/SPORTS (HM17535) |  |  |  |  |  |  |  |  |  |  |  |  | ● |  |  |  | ● |  |  |  |  |  |  |  |
| ROSE, NICHOLAS (HM17613) |  |  |  |  |  |  |  |  |  |  |  |  | ● |  |  |  | ● |  |  |  |  |  |  | ● |
| RUTHERFORD, BERWYN (HM17780) | ● |  | ● |  |  | ● |  |  |  |  |  |  | ● | ● | ● |  | ● |  |  |  | ● | ● | ● | ● |
| SALTER, LIZ (HM17869) | ● |  |  |  |  | ● |  |  |  |  | ● | ● | ● | ● | ● | ● | ● | ● | ● |  | ● | ● | ● | ● |
| SAYER CLINIC (HM17993) |  |  |  |  |  |  |  |  |  |  |  |  | ● | ● |  |  | ● |  |  |  |  |  |  | ● |
| SAYER CLINIC (HM17994) |  |  |  |  |  |  |  |  |  |  |  |  | ● |  |  |  |  |  |  |  |  |  |  |  |
| SEARBY, JOE (HM18174) |  |  |  |  |  |  |  |  |  |  |  | ● | ● |  |  |  | ● |  |  |  |  |  |  |  |
| SEEAR, MICHAEL (DR) (HM18189) | ● | ● | ● | ● | ● |  |  | ● | ● | ● | ● | ● | ● | ● |  |  | ● |  |  |  | ● | ● |  | ● |
| SEYMOUR PRACTICE (HM18257) |  |  |  |  |  |  |  |  |  |  |  |  |  |  |  |  | ● |  |  |  |  |  |  |  |
| SHIATSU PLACE (HM18458) |  | ● |  |  |  | ● |  |  |  |  |  | ● | ● | ● |  |  | ● |  |  |  | ● | ● |  | ● |
| SHIATSU STUDIO (HM18465) |  |  |  |  |  |  |  |  |  |  |  | ● |  |  |  |  | ● |  |  |  |  |  |  |  |
| SIMON, CAROLYN (HM18567) |  |  |  |  |  |  |  |  |  |  |  | ● |  |  |  |  | ● |  |  |  |  |  |  |  |
| SIMPLY HERBAL CLINIC (HM18577) | ● | ● | ● |  |  | ● | ● |  | ● | ● | ● | ● | ● | ● | ● | ● | ● | ● | ● |  | ● | ● | ● | ● |

| Business by County with Reference no. | Breast Problems | Breathing Problems | Bronchitis | Bruising | Bulimia | Bunions | Bursitis | Callices | Cancers | Cataracts | Catarrh | Cerebral Palsy | Circulation Problems | Cold Sores | Colds | Colic | Colitis | Conjunctivitis | Constipation | Convulsions | Corns | Coughs | Cramp | Cystitis |
|---|---|---|---|---|---|---|---|---|---|---|---|---|---|---|---|---|---|---|---|---|---|---|---|---|
| PRICE, GILLIAN (HM16575) | ● | ● | ● | ● | ● |  | ● | ● |  | ● | ● |  | ● | ● | ● | ● | ● | ● | ● | ● | ● | ● | ● | ● |
| PRICE, SANDRA (HM16594) |  |  |  |  |  |  |  |  |  |  |  |  |  |  |  |  |  |  |  |  |  |  |  |  |
| PRICE, SANDRA (HM16595) |  |  |  |  |  |  |  |  |  |  |  |  |  |  |  | ● |  |  |  |  |  |  |  |  |
| PRIMROSE HEALING CENTRE (HM16616) |  |  |  |  |  |  |  |  |  |  |  |  |  |  |  |  |  |  |  |  |  |  |  |  |
| PRIVATE HEALTH CLINIC (HM16644) | ● | ● | ● | ● | ● |  | ● | ● | ● | ● | ● |  | ● | ● | ● | ● | ● | ● | ● | ● | ● | ● | ● | ● |
| PRIVATE PRACTICE (HM16649) |  |  |  |  | ● |  |  |  |  |  |  |  |  |  |  |  |  |  |  |  |  |  |  |  |
| PSYCHOTHERAPY CENTRE (HM16734) |  |  |  |  |  |  |  |  |  |  |  |  |  |  |  |  |  |  |  |  |  |  |  |  |
| PSYCHOTHERAPY SERVICES (HM16737) |  |  |  |  |  |  |  |  |  |  |  |  |  |  |  |  |  |  |  |  |  |  |  |  |
| PUTNEY CHIROPRACTIC (HM16780) |  |  |  |  |  |  |  |  |  |  |  |  |  |  |  | ● |  |  |  |  |  |  |  |  |
| RACHEL YOUNG - HYPNOTHERAPIST (HM16837) |  | ● | ● |  | ● |  |  |  | ● |  | ● |  | ● |  |  | ● | ● |  | ● |  |  | ● | ● | ● |
| RAEBURN, JO (HM16865) |  |  | ● | ● |  |  |  |  | ● |  | ● |  | ● | ● | ● | ● | ● |  | ● |  |  | ● |  | ● |
| RANDALL, CAROLINE (HM16926) | ● | ● | ● | ● | ● |  | ● | ● | ● | ● | ● |  | ● | ● | ● | ● | ● | ● | ● | ● | ● | ● | ● | ● |
| RAVENSCROFT CENTRE (HM16967) |  |  |  |  |  |  |  |  |  |  |  |  |  |  |  |  |  |  |  |  |  |  |  |  |
| READ, CHARLES (HM16993) |  |  |  |  |  |  | ● |  |  |  |  |  |  |  |  |  |  |  |  |  |  |  | ● |  |
| REEVE, MALCOLM (HM17060) |  |  |  | ● |  |  |  |  |  |  |  |  |  |  |  |  |  |  |  |  |  |  | ● |  |
| REFLEXOLOGY (HM17077) |  | ● |  |  |  |  |  |  |  |  |  |  | ● |  |  |  |  |  |  |  |  |  |  | ● |
| REFLEXOLOGY CLINIC (HM17089) |  |  |  |  |  |  |  |  |  |  |  |  | ● |  |  |  |  |  | ● |  |  |  |  |  |
| RELAXATION PLACE (HM17166) |  |  |  |  |  |  |  |  |  |  |  |  |  |  |  |  |  |  |  |  |  |  |  |  |
| REPLINGHAM CLINIC (HM17195) |  |  | ● |  |  |  |  |  |  |  | ● |  | ● |  | ● | ● |  |  | ● |  |  | ● |  |  |
| ROBERTS, MATT (HM17420) |  |  |  |  |  |  |  |  |  |  |  |  |  |  |  |  |  |  |  |  |  |  |  |  |
| ROBINSON, GABIE (HM17473) |  | ● | ● |  |  |  |  |  |  |  |  |  | ● |  | ● |  |  |  |  |  |  |  |  |  |
| ROEHAMPTON PHYSIO/SPORTS (HM17535) |  |  |  | ● |  |  |  |  |  |  |  |  |  |  |  |  |  |  |  |  |  |  |  |  |
| ROSE, NICHOLAS (HM17613) |  |  |  |  |  |  | ● |  |  |  |  |  | ● |  |  |  |  |  |  |  |  |  | ● |  |
| RUTHERFORD, BERWYN (HM17780) |  | ● | ● |  |  |  | ● |  |  |  | ● |  | ● |  |  |  |  |  | ● |  |  |  |  | ● |
| SALTER, LIZ (HM17869) | ● | ● | ● | ● | ● |  |  |  | ● |  | ● |  | ● | ● | ● | ● | ● | ● | ● | ● |  | ● | ● | ● |
| SAYER CLINIC (HM17993) |  | ● |  |  |  |  |  |  |  |  |  |  | ● |  |  |  |  |  | ● |  |  |  |  | ● |
| SAYER CLINIC (HM17994) |  |  |  |  |  |  |  |  |  |  |  |  | ● |  |  |  |  |  |  |  |  |  |  |  |
| SEARBY, JOE (HM18174) |  | ● |  |  |  |  |  |  |  |  |  |  | ● |  |  |  |  |  |  |  |  |  |  |  |
| SEEAR, MICHAEL (DR) (HM18189) |  | ● | ● |  | ● |  | ● |  | ● |  | ● |  | ● |  | ● |  |  | ● | ● |  |  | ● | ● | ● |
| SEYMOUR PRACTICE (HM18257) |  | ● |  |  |  |  | ● |  |  |  |  |  |  |  |  |  |  |  |  |  |  |  |  |  |
| SHIATSU PLACE (HM18458) |  | ● | ● |  |  |  | ● |  | ● |  |  |  | ● |  |  | ● | ● |  | ● |  |  | ● |  | ● |
| SHIATSU STUDIO (HM18465) |  | ● |  |  |  |  |  |  |  |  |  |  |  |  |  |  |  |  |  |  |  |  |  |  |
| SIMON, CAROLYN (HM18567) |  | ● |  |  |  |  |  |  |  |  |  |  |  |  |  |  |  |  |  |  |  |  |  |  |
| SIMPLY HERBAL CLINIC (HM18577) | ● | ● | ● | ● | ● |  | ● | ● | ● | ● | ● |  | ● | ● | ● | ● | ● | ● | ● | ● | ● | ● | ● | ● |

# A - C Conditions treated at Practices/Businesses

Business by County with Reference no.

| Condition | SIMPSON, STELLA (HM18599) | SLADE OSTEOPATHIC PRACTICE (HM18667) | SOUTH LONDON NATURAL HLTH CTRE (HM18911) | SOUTHFIELDS CLINIC (HM18935) | SPALL MEDICAL CENTRE (HM18957) | SPECIALIST HEALTH (HM18972) | SPYROS MOUZOURIDES (HM19056) | STANMORE PHYSIO PRACTICE (HM19132) | STOBEZKI, YAEL (HM19307) | STRONG, STELLA (HM19419) | T C M HEALTHCARE (HM19640) | THOMPSON, MARK (HM19990) | THURGOOD, SIMON (HM20047) | TORRIDON COMP THERAPY CLINIC (HM20173) | TRADITIONAL ACUPUNCTURE CENTRE (HM20218) | TRANQUILITY (HM20255) | TROHEAR, PATRICIA (HM20345) | TURMAINE, VICKI (HM20410) | TURNBULL, JO (HM20413) | TURNER, TERI (HM20438) | TWICKENHAM PHYSIOFIRST CENTRE (HM20451) | UKCP (HM20490) | UNDERHILL, K (HM20496) | VALE PRACTICE (HM20551) | VANBRUGH PHYSIOTHERAPY CLINIC (HM20575) | WALK IN BACK RUB (HM20758) | WALK IN BACKRUB (HM20760) | WALK IN BACKRUB (HM20759) | WART, D (HM20959) | WARWICK ALTERNATIVE HEALTH (HM20961) | WEBER, MARALYN (HM21082) | WELL BEING (HM21131) | WEST LONDON HOLISTIC CENTRE (HM21226) | WEST LONDON PSYCHOTHERAPY (HM21227) |
|---|---|---|---|---|---|---|---|---|---|---|---|---|---|---|---|---|---|---|---|---|---|---|---|---|---|---|---|---|---|---|---|---|---|---|
| Cystitis | ● | | ● | | ● | | ● | | | | | | | | ● | ● | | ● | ● | | | | | ● | | | | | | | ● | ● | | |
| Cramp | ● | | ● | | ● | | ● | | | | | | | ● | ● | ● | | ● | | | | | | ● | ● | | | | | | ● | | | |
| Coughs | ● | | ● | | ● | | ● | | | | | ● | | | | ● | | ● | ● | | | | | ● | | | | | | | ● | ● | | |
| Corns | | | | | | | | | | | | | | | | | | | | | | | | ● | | | | | | | ● | | | |
| Convulsions | ● | | ● | | | | ● | | | | | | | | | | | | | | | | | ● | | | | | | | | | | |
| Constipation | ● | | ● | ● | ● | | ● | | | | | ● | | ● | ● | ● | | ● | ● | | | | | ● | | | | | | | ● | ● | | |
| Conjunctivitis | | | ● | | | | ● | | | | | | | | | ● | | ● | | | | | | ● | | | | | | | ● | ● | | |
| Colitis | ● | | ● | | | | ● | | | | | | | | | ● | | ● | | | | | | ● | | | | | | | ● | | | |
| Colic | ● | | ● | | ● | | ● | | | | | ● | | | | ● | | ● | ● | | | | | ● | | | | | | | | | | |
| Colds | ● | | ● | | ● | | ● | | | | | | | | | ● | | ● | ● | | | | | ● | | | | | | | ● | | | |
| Cold Sores | | | ● | | | | ● | | | | | | | | | ● | | ● | | | | | | ● | | | | | | | ● | | | |
| Circulation Problems | ● | ● | ● | | | | ● | | | | | ● | | ● | | ● | | ● | ● | ● | | | | ● | | | | | | ● | ● | | | |
| Cerebral Palsy | | | | | | | | | | | | | | | | | | | | | | | | | | | | | | | | | | |
| Catarrh | ● | | ● | | ● | | ● | | | | | | | ● | | ● | | ● | | | | | | ● | | | | | | | ● | ● | | |
| Cataracts | | | ● | | | | ● | | | | | | | | | | | | | | | | | | | | | | | | | | | |
| Cancers | ● | | ● | | | | ● | | | | | | | | | | | | | | | | | | | | | | | | ● | ● | | |
| Callices | | | | | | | | | | | | | | | | | | | | | | | | ● | | | | | | | ● | | | |
| Bursitis | ● | | ● | | | ● | ● | ● | | | | | | | | | | | | | | | | ● | | | | | | | ● | | | |
| Bunions | | | | | | | | | | | | | | | | | | | | | | | | | | | | | | | | | | |
| Bulimia | | | ● | | | | ● | | ● | | | | | ● | | ● | | | | | | ● | | ● | | | | | | | ● | | ● | |
| Bruising | | | ● | ● | | | ● | | | | | | | | ● | ● | | ● | | | ● | | | ● | ● | | | | | | ● | ● | | |
| Bronchitis | ● | | ● | | | | ● | | | | | | | | | ● | | | ● | | | | | ● | | | | | | | ● | | | |
| Breathing Problems | ● | | ● | | | | ● | | | | | ● | | ● | | ● | | | ● | | | | | ● | | | | | | | ● | | | |
| Breast Problems | ● | | ● | | | | ● | | | | | | | | | | | ● | | | | | | ● | | | | | | | ● | ● | | |
| Bowel Problems | ● | | ● | | | | ● | | | | | ● | | | | ● | | ● | ● | | | | | ● | | | | | | | ● | | | |
| Boils | | | ● | | | | ● | | | | | | | | | | | | | | | | | ● | | | | | | | ● | | | |
| Blood Pressure | ● | ● | ● | | ● | | ● | | | | | ● | | | | ● | | | ● | ● | | | | ● | | | | | | | ● | ● | | |
| Bladder Problems | ● | | ● | | | | ● | | | | | | | | | ● | | ● | ● | | | | | ● | | | | | | | ● | | | |
| Bereavement | | | | | | | | | ● | | | | | | | | | | | | | | | | | | | | | | | | | ● |
| Baldness | | | ● | | ● | | ● | | | | | | | | | | | | | | | | | | | | | | | | ● | | | |
| Bacterial Infections | | | ● | | | | ● | | | | | | | | | ● | | | | | | | | ● | | | | | | | ● | | | |
| Back Pain | ● | ● | ● | ● | | ● | ● | ● | | ● | ● | ● | ● | ● | ● | ● | | ● | ● | ● | ● | | ● | ● | ● | ● | ● | ● | ● | ● | ● | | | |
| Autism | | | ● | | | | ● | | | | | | | | | | | | | | | | | ● | | | | | | | | | | |
| Athletes Foot | | | ● | | | | ● | | | | | | | | | | | | | | | | | ● | | | | | | | | | | |
| Asthma | ● | | ● | ● | ● | | ● | | | | | ● | | | ● | ● | | | ● | | | | | ● | | | | | | | ● | ● | ● | |
| Arthritis | ● | ● | ● | ● | ● | ● | ● | ● | | | ● | ● | ● | ● | ● | ● | | ● | | ● | ● | | ● | ● | ● | | | | ● | | ● | ● | ● | |
| Anxiety | ● | | ● | | | | ● | | ● | ● | ● | | | ● | ● | ● | ● | ● | ● | | | ● | | ● | | | | | | ● | ● | ● | ● | |
| Anorexia | | | ● | | | | ● | | ● | | | | | ● | | ● | | | | | | ● | | ● | | | | | | | ● | ● | | |
| Angina | ● | | ● | | ● | | ● | | | | | ● | | | | | | | | | | | | ● | | | | | | | ● | | | |
| Anaemia | ● | | ● | | | | ● | | | | | | | | | | | | | | | | | ● | | | | | | | ● | | | |
| Amnesia | | | ● | | | | ● | | | | | | | | | | | ● | | | | | | ● | | | | | | | | | | |
| Alzheimer's Disease | | | ● | | | | ● | | | | | | | | | | | | | | | | | | | | | | | | | | | |
| Allergy | ● | | ● | ● | | ● | ● | | | | | | | | ● | ● | | ● | ● | | | | | ● | ● | | | | | | ● | | ● | |
| Alcoholism | ● | | ● | | | | ● | | ● | | | | | | | | | | | | | ● | | ● | | | | | | | | | | |
| Aids | ● | | ● | | | | | | | | | | | | | | | | ● | | | | | ● | | | | | | | | | | |
| Adenoids | ● | | ● | | | | ● | | | | | | | | | | | | | | | | | ● | | | | | | | ● | | | |
| Addiction | ● | | ● | | | | ● | | ● | | | | | | | ● | | | ● | | | ● | | ● | | | | | | | ● | | ● | |
| Acne | ● | | ● | ● | ● | | ● | | | | | | | | ● | | | ● | ● | | | | | ● | | | | | | | ● | | | |

www.healthmyself.com

England (by County)

CONDITIONS TREATED

A-C

# A - C Conditions treated at Practices/Businesses

| Business by County with Reference no. | Acne | Addiction | Adenoids | Aids | Alcoholism | Allergy | Alzheimer's Disease | Amnesia | Anaemia | Angina | Anorexia | Anxiety | Arthritis | Asthma | Athletes Foot | Autism | Back Pain | Bacterial Infections | Baldness | Bereavement | Bladder Problems | Blood Pressure | Boils | Bowel Problems |
|---|---|---|---|---|---|---|---|---|---|---|---|---|---|---|---|---|---|---|---|---|---|---|---|---|
| WEST LONDON YOGA SHALA (HM21228) | | ● | | | | | | | | | ● | ● | ● | ● | | | ● | | | | ● | ● | | ● |
| WESTERN, G (HM21265) | | | | | | | | | | | | | ● | | | | ● | | | | | | | |
| WHITE HART LANE THERAPY CENTRE (HM21338) | | | | | | | | | | | | | ● | | ● | | ● | | | | | | | |
| WHOLE-BEING INTERACTIVE HYP (HM21435) | | ● | | | ● | | | | | | | ● | | | | | | | | | | | | |
| WIGHAM, A (HM21468) | | | | | | | | | | | | ● | | | | | | | | | | | | |
| WILKINSON, GILL (HM21505) | | | | | ● | | | | | | | ● | | | | | | | | | | | | |
| WILLIAMS, B A (HM21541) | | | | | | ● | | | | | | | ● | | ● | | ● | | | | | | | |
| WILLIAMS, IAN (HM21565) | | | | | | | | | | | | | | | ● | | | ● | | | | | | |
| WILLIAMS, RUTH (HM21588) | | | | | | | | | | | | | | | | | | | | | | | | |
| WILLMOTT, SUSAN (HM21623) | | ● | | | ● | | | ● | | | | ● | | | | | | | | | | | | |
| WINCHMORE CLINIC OF OSTEOPATHY (HM21694) | | | | | | | | | | | | ● | ● | | | | ● | | | | | | | |
| WOODBERRY CLINIC (HM21815) | | | | | | | | | | | | | ● | | | | | | | | | | | |
| WOOLF, PERRY (HM21872) | | | | | | | | | | | | | ● | | ● | | | | | | | | | |
| WORLD OF LIGHT (HM21898) | ● | ● | ● | ● | ● | ● | ● | ● | ● | ● | ● | ● | ● | ● | ● | ● | ● | ● | ● | | ● | ● | ● | ● |
| WREN, ANTHONY (HM21920) | | | | | | | | | | | | | | | | | | | | | | | | |
| WRIGHT, JENNY (HM21936) | | ● | | | | | | | | | ● | ● | | | | | | | | | | ● | | ● |
| WYNNE-SIMMONS, A (DR) (HM21979) | ● | | ● | | | ● | | | ● | ● | ● | ● | ● | ● | ● | ● | ● | ● | ● | | ● | ● | ● | ● |
| YING, FRANK (HM22014) | | | | | | | | | | | | | ● | ● | | | ● | | | | | | | |
| YOGA THERAPY CENTRE (HM22033) | | | | | | | | | | | | | | ● | | | ● | | | | | | | |
| ZEN HEALTH CENTRE (HM22100) | ● | ● | | ● | ● | ● | | | ● | | ● | ● | ● | ● | ● | | ● | ● | ● | | ● | ● | ● | ● |
| ZEN SHIATSU & HEALING TAO (HM22101) | | | | | | | | | | | | ● | ● | ● | | | ● | | | | | | | ● |
| MANCHESTER (GREATER) | | | | | | | | | | | | | | | | | | | | | | | | |
| A SIR ROBERTS ALT PLACE (HM00045) | ● | ● | | | ● | ● | | | | ● | ● | ● | ● | | | | ● | | | | | ● | | |
| A6 CHIROPODY PRACTICE (HM00055) | | | | | | | | | | | | | ● | | ● | | | | | | | | | |
| ACUMEDIC (HM00220) | ● | ● | | | | ● | | | | | ● | ● | ● | ● | | | ● | | | | ● | ● | | ● |
| ACUPUNCTURE CENTRE (HM00252) | | | | | | | | | | ● | | | ● | ● | | | ● | | | | ● | | | ● |
| ADVANCED CHIROPODY SURGERY (HM00394) | | | | | | | | | | | | | | | ● | | | | | | | | | |
| ADVANCED PHYSIOTHERAPY CLINIC (HM00403) | | | | | | | | | | | | | ● | ● | | | | | | | | | | |
| ALL IN THE MIND (HM00582) | | ● | | | | | | | | | | ● | | | | | | | | | | | | |
| AROMATHERAPY BY SARA (HM01098) | | | | | | | | | | | | ● | | | | | | | | | | | | |
| AROMATHERAPY LADIES MASSAGE (HM01118) | ● | ● | ● | ● | ● | ● | ● | ● | ● | ● | ● | ● | ● | ● | ● | ● | ● | ● | ● | | ● | ● | ● | ● |
| ASTLEY COMPLEMENTARY CENTRE (HM01300) | | ● | | | | ● | | | | | ● | ● | ● | ● | | | ● | | | | | | | ● |
| BRAMHALL CHIROPRACTIC CLINIC (HM02898) | | | | | | | | | | | | ● | ● | | | | ● | | | | | | | ● |
| BURGESS, KAREN (HM03377) | | | | | | | | | | | | | ● | ● | ● | | ● | | | | | | | |

| Business by County with Reference no. | Breast Problems | Breathing Problems | Bronchitis | Bruising | Bulimia | Bunions | Bursitis | Callices | Cancers | Cataracts | Catarrh | Cerebral Palsy | Circulation Problems | Cold Sores | Colds | Colic | Colitis | Conjunctivitis | Constipation | Convulsions | Corns | Coughs | Cramp | Cystitis |
|---|---|---|---|---|---|---|---|---|---|---|---|---|---|---|---|---|---|---|---|---|---|---|---|---|
| WEST LONDON YOGA SHALA (HM21228) | ● | | | | | | | | | | | | ● | | ● | | | | | | | | | |
| WESTERN, G (HM21265) | | | | | | | | | | | | | | | | | | | | | | | | |
| WHITE HART LANE THERAPY CENTRE (HM21338) | | | | ● | | | | | | | | | | | | | | | | | | | ● | |
| WHOLE-BEING INTERACTIVE HYP (HM21435) | | | | | | | | | | | | | | | | | | | | | | | | ● |
| WIGHAM, A (HM21468) | | | | | | | | | | | | | | | | | | | | | | | | |
| WILKINSON, GILL (HM21505) | | | | | ● | | | | | | | | | | | | | | | | | | | |
| WILLIAMS, B A (HM21541) | | | | | | | | | | | | | | | | | | | ● | | | | | ● |
| WILLIAMS, IAN (HM21565) | | | | | | | | ● | | | | | | | | | | | | | ● | | | |
| WILLIAMS, RUTH (HM21588) | | | | | ● | | | | | | | | | | | | | | | | | | | |
| WILLMOTT, SUSAN (HM21623) | | | | | ● | | | | | | | | | | | | | | | | | | | |
| WINCHMORE CLINIC OF OSTEOPATHY (HM21694) | | | | ● | | | ● | | | | | | | | | ● | | | | | | | | |
| WOODBERRY CLINIC (HM21815) | | | | | | | | | | | | | | | | | | | | | | | | |
| WOOLF, PERRY (HM21872) | | | | | | ● | ● | ● | | | | | ● | | | | | | | | ● | | | |
| WORLD OF LIGHT (HM21898) | ● | ● | ● | ● | ● | | ● | | ● | ● | ● | | ● | ● | ● | ● | ● | ● | ● | ● | | ● | ● | ● |
| WREN, ANTHONY (HM21920) | | | | | | | | | | | | | ● | | | | | | | | | | | |
| WRIGHT, JENNY (HM21936) | | | | | ● | | | | | | | | | | | | | | | | | | | |
| WYNNE-SIMMONS, A (DR) (HM21979) | ● | ● | ● | ● | | | | | ● | | ● | | | ● | ● | ● | ● | ● | ● | ● | | ● | ● | ● |
| YING, FRANK (HM22014) | | | | | | | ● | | | | | | | | | | | | | | | | | |
| YOGA THERAPY CENTRE (HM22033) | | | | | | | | | ● | | | | | | | | | | | | | | | |
| ZEN HEALTH CENTRE (HM22100) | ● | ● | ● | ● | ● | | ● | | ● | ● | ● | | ● | ● | ● | ● | ● | ● | ● | | | ● | ● | ● |
| ZEN SHIATSU & HEALING TAO (HM22101) | ● | ● | | | | | | | ● | | | | ● | | | | ● | | ● | | | | | |
| MANCHESTER (GREATER) | | | | | | | | | | | | | | | | | | | | | | | | |
| A SIR ROBERTS ALT PLACE (HM00045) | | ● | ● | ● | ● | | | | ● | | | | ● | | | | | | | | | | ● | ● |
| A6 CHIROPODY PRACTICE (HM00055) | | | | | | | | ● | | | | | | | | | | | | | ● | | | |
| ACUMEDIC (HM00220) | | | | | | | | | | | | | ● | | | | | | ● | | | | ● | |
| ACUPUNCTURE CENTRE (HM00252) | ● | | | | | | | | | | | | | | | ● | ● | | ● | | | | | ● |
| ADVANCED CHIROPODY SURGERY (HM00394) | | | | | | | | | | | | | | | | | | | | | | | | |
| ADVANCED PHYSIOTHERAPY CLINIC (HM00403) | | | ● | | | | | | | | | | | | | | | | | | | | | |
| ALL IN THE MIND (HM00582) | | | | | | | | | | | | | | | | | | | | | | | | |
| AROMATHERAPY BY SARA (HM01098) | | | | | | | | | | | | | | | | | | | | | | | | |
| AROMATHERAPY LADIES MASSAGE (HM01118) | ● | ● | ● | ● | ● | | ● | ● | ● | ● | ● | | ● | ● | ● | ● | ● | ● | ● | ● | ● | ● | ● | ● |
| ASTLEY COMPLEMENTARY CENTRE (HM01300) | | | | | ● | | | | | | ● | | | | | | ● | | | | | | | |
| BRAMHALL CHIROPRACTIC CLINIC (HM02898) | | | | | | | ● | | | | | | | | | | | | | | | | | |
| BURGESS, KAREN (HM03377) | | ● | ● | ● | | | ● | | | | | | ● | | | | | | | | | | | |

# A - C Conditions treated at Practices/Businesses

Business by County with Reference no.

| Business by County with Reference no. | Acne | Addiction | Adenoids | Aids | Alcoholism | Allergy | Alzheimer's Disease | Amnesia | Anaemia | Angina | Anorexia | Anxiety | Arthritis | Asthma | Athletes Foot | Autism | Back Pain | Bacterial Infections | Baldness | Bereavement | Bladder Problems | Blood Pressure | Boils | Bowel Problems |
|---|---|---|---|---|---|---|---|---|---|---|---|---|---|---|---|---|---|---|---|---|---|---|---|---|
| C CARTLEDGE REFLEXOLOGY (HM03521) | ● | ● | ● | ● | ● | ● | ● | ● | ● | ● | ● | ● | ● | ● | ● | ● | ● | ● | ● |  | ● | ● | ● | ● |
| CHARTERED PHYSIOTHERAPY CLINIC (HM04046) |  |  |  |  |  |  |  |  |  |  |  |  | ● |  |  |  | ● |  |  |  |  |  |  |  |
| CHORLTON STRESS MANAGEMENT (HM04430) |  | ● |  |  |  |  |  |  |  |  | ● | ● |  |  |  |  |  |  |  |  |  |  |  |  |
| CLARENDON CLINIC (HM04540) |  |  |  |  |  | ● |  |  |  |  |  |  | ● | ● |  |  | ● |  |  |  |  |  |  |  |
| COHEN, D (DR) (HM04789) |  |  |  |  |  | ● |  |  |  |  |  | ● |  |  |  |  |  |  |  |  | ● |  |  |  |
| COLLINGE, J C (HM04863) |  |  |  |  |  |  |  |  |  |  |  | ● |  |  |  |  | ● |  |  |  | ● |  |  | ● |
| COSGROVES PHYSIO-FIT CENTRE (HM05201) |  |  |  |  |  |  |  |  |  |  |  |  |  |  |  |  | ● |  |  |  |  |  |  |  |
| CROSSWAY CLINIC (HM05491) |  | ● |  |  |  | ● |  |  |  |  |  | ● | ● | ● | ● |  | ● |  |  |  |  | ● |  |  |
| DAVEENA ASSOCIATES (HM05763) |  |  |  |  |  |  |  |  |  |  |  | ● |  |  |  |  |  |  |  |  |  |  |  |  |
| DIDSBURY CHIROPRACTIC CLINIC (HM06090) |  |  |  |  |  |  |  |  |  |  |  |  | ● |  |  |  | ● |  |  |  |  |  |  |  |
| EVANS, DAVID (HM06967) | ● | ● |  |  | ● | ● |  | ● |  | ● | ● | ● |  | ● |  |  | ● |  | ● |  | ● | ● |  | ● |
| GOGIA, D R (DR) (HM08195) |  |  |  |  |  |  |  |  |  |  |  |  |  |  |  |  | ● |  |  |  |  |  |  |  |
| GRAHAM COOMBE - MCTIMONEY (HM08337) |  |  |  |  |  |  |  |  |  |  |  |  |  | ● |  |  | ● |  |  |  |  |  |  | ● |
| GUILD OF PRACTITIONERS (HM08627) |  |  |  |  |  |  |  |  |  |  |  |  | ● |  |  |  | ● |  |  |  |  |  |  |  |
| HOLMED CLINIC (HM10038) |  |  |  |  |  |  |  |  |  |  |  |  | ● |  |  |  | ● |  |  |  |  |  |  |  |
| HORRIDGE, S P (HM10182) |  |  |  |  |  |  |  |  |  |  |  |  | ● |  | ● |  |  |  |  |  |  |  |  |  |
| HUMAN TOUCH CENTRE (HM10366) |  |  |  |  |  |  |  |  |  |  |  | ● | ● | ● |  |  | ● |  |  |  |  |  |  |  |
| IBBOTSON, GEOFF (DR) (HM10565) |  |  |  |  |  |  |  |  |  |  | ● | ● |  | ● |  |  |  |  |  |  |  |  |  |  |
| M J HAYLETT - PHYSIOTHERAPIST (HM12802) |  |  |  |  |  |  |  |  |  |  |  | ● | ● |  |  |  | ● |  |  |  |  |  |  |  |
| MOBILE COMPLEMENTARY THERAPIES (HM14029) |  |  |  |  |  |  |  |  |  |  |  | ● |  |  |  |  | ● |  | ● |  |  |  |  |  |
| MOUNT STREET COMP THERAPIES (HM14291) |  |  |  |  |  |  |  |  |  |  |  | ● | ● |  |  |  | ● |  |  |  |  |  |  |  |
| NICKI HAVES PHYSIO CLINIC (HM14923) |  |  |  |  |  |  |  |  |  |  |  |  | ● |  |  |  | ● |  |  |  |  |  |  |  |
| NIVERN, D (HM14954) | ● |  |  |  |  |  |  |  |  |  |  | ● | ● | ● | ● |  | ● | ● |  |  |  | ● |  |  |
| REJUVENATION (HM17154) |  |  |  |  |  |  |  |  |  |  |  |  |  |  |  |  | ● |  |  |  |  |  |  |  |
| SCHOFIELD, G A (HM18018) | ● | ● | ● | ● | ● | ● | ● | ● | ● | ● | ● | ● | ● | ● | ● |  | ● |  |  |  | ● | ● |  | ● |
| SHANGHAI ACUPUNCTURE CLINIC (HM18280) | ● | ● | ● | ● | ● | ● | ● | ● | ● | ● | ● | ● | ● | ● | ● | ● | ● | ● | ● |  | ● | ● | ● | ● |
| ST JOHN STREET PHYSIO PRACTICE (HM19080) |  |  |  |  |  |  |  |  |  |  |  |  | ● | ● |  |  | ● |  |  |  |  |  |  |  |
| STIRLING, DIANNE (HM19301) |  |  |  |  |  |  |  |  |  |  |  | ● |  |  |  |  |  |  |  |  |  |  |  |  |
| SWINTON HEALTH FOODS (HM19600) |  |  |  |  |  | ● |  |  |  |  |  | ● | ● |  |  |  |  |  | ● |  |  | ● |  | ● |
| WAINWRIGHT, P (HM20739) |  |  |  |  |  |  |  |  |  |  |  |  | ● |  | ● |  | ● | ● |  |  |  |  |  |  |
| **MERSEYSIDE** |  |  |  |  |  |  |  |  |  |  |  |  |  |  |  |  |  |  |  |  |  |  |  |  |
| ABBEY FOOT CLINIC (HM00083) |  |  |  |  |  |  |  |  |  |  |  |  |  |  | ● |  |  |  |  |  |  |  |  |  |
| ACUPUNCTURE CLINIC (HM00263) |  |  |  |  |  | ● |  |  |  | ● |  | ● | ● | ● |  |  | ● |  |  |  | ● | ● |  | ● |
| AIGBURTH MCTIMONEY CLINIC (HM00427) |  |  |  |  |  |  |  |  |  |  |  |  | ● | ● |  |  | ● |  |  |  |  |  |  | ● |

| Business by County with Reference no. | Breast Problems | Breathing Problems | Bronchitis | Bruising | Bulimia | Bunions | Bursitis | Callices | Cancers | Cataracts | Catarrh | Cerebral Palsy | Circulation Problems | Cold Sores | Colds | Colic | Colitis | Conjunctivitis | Constipation | Convulsions | Corns | Coughs | Cramp | Cystitis |
|---|---|---|---|---|---|---|---|---|---|---|---|---|---|---|---|---|---|---|---|---|---|---|---|---|
| C CARTLEDGE REFLEXOLOGY (HM03521) | ● | ● | ● | ● | ● |  | ● |  | ● | ● | ● |  | ● | ● | ● | ● | ● | ● | ● | ● |  | ● | ● | ● |
| CHARTERED PHYSIOTHERAPY CLINIC (HM04046) |  | ● |  |  |  |  | ● |  |  |  |  |  | ● |  |  |  |  |  |  |  |  |  |  |  |
| CHORLTON STRESS MANAGEMENT (HM04430) |  |  |  |  | ● |  |  |  |  |  |  |  |  |  |  |  |  |  |  |  |  |  |  |  |
| CLARENDON CLINIC (HM04540) |  |  |  |  |  |  | ● |  |  |  |  |  |  |  | ● |  |  |  |  |  |  | ● |  | ● |
| COHEN, D (DR) (HM04789) |  |  | ● |  |  |  |  |  |  | ● | ● |  |  | ● |  |  |  | ● | ● |  |  |  | ● | ● |
| COLLINGE, J C (HM04863) |  |  | ● |  |  |  |  |  |  |  |  |  |  |  |  |  |  |  | ● |  |  |  |  |  |
| COSGROVES PHYSIO-FIT CENTRE (HM05201) |  |  |  |  |  |  |  |  |  |  |  |  |  |  |  |  |  |  |  |  |  |  |  |  |
| CROSSWAY CLINIC (HM05491) |  |  |  |  |  |  | ● |  |  |  |  |  |  |  |  |  |  |  |  |  |  |  |  |  |
| DAVEENA ASSOCIATES (HM05763) |  |  |  |  |  |  |  |  |  |  |  |  |  |  |  |  |  |  |  |  |  |  |  |  |
| DIDSBURY CHIROPRACTIC CLINIC (HM06090) |  |  |  |  |  |  |  |  |  |  |  |  |  |  |  |  |  |  |  |  |  |  |  |  |
| EVANS, DAVID (HM06967) |  | ● |  |  | ● |  |  |  | ● |  |  |  | ● |  |  |  | ● |  | ● |  |  |  | ● |  |
| GOGIA, D R (DR) (HM08195) |  |  |  |  |  |  |  |  |  |  |  |  |  |  |  |  |  |  |  |  |  |  |  |  |
| GRAHAM COOMBE - MCTIMONEY (HM08337) |  | ● |  |  |  |  | ● |  |  |  |  |  |  |  |  |  |  |  | ● |  |  |  | ● |  |
| GUILD OF PRACTITIONERS (HM08627) |  |  |  |  |  |  |  |  |  |  |  |  |  |  |  |  |  |  |  |  |  |  |  |  |
| HOLMED CLINIC (HM10038) |  |  |  |  |  |  |  |  |  |  |  |  | ● |  |  | ● |  |  |  |  |  |  |  |  |
| HORRIDGE, S P (HM10182) |  |  |  |  |  |  |  | ● |  |  |  |  |  |  |  |  |  |  |  |  | ● |  |  |  |
| HUMAN TOUCH CENTRE (HM10366) |  |  |  |  |  |  |  |  | ● |  |  |  |  |  |  |  |  |  |  |  |  |  |  |  |
| IBBOTSON, GEOFF (DR) (HM10565) |  |  |  |  | ● |  |  |  |  |  |  |  |  |  |  |  |  |  |  |  |  |  |  |  |
| M J HAYLETT - PHYSIOTHERAPIST (HM12802) |  |  |  |  |  |  |  |  |  |  |  |  |  |  |  |  |  |  |  |  |  |  |  |  |
| MOBILE COMPLEMENTARY THERAPIES (HM14029) |  |  |  |  |  |  |  |  |  |  |  |  | ● |  |  |  |  |  |  |  |  |  |  |  |
| MOUNT STREET COMP THERAPIES (HM14291) |  |  |  |  |  |  |  |  |  |  |  |  |  |  |  |  |  |  |  |  |  |  |  |  |
| NICKI HAVES PHYSIO CLINIC (HM14923) |  |  |  |  |  |  |  |  |  |  |  |  |  |  |  |  |  |  |  |  |  |  |  |  |
| NIVERN, D (HM14954) |  |  | ● |  |  |  |  |  |  |  | ● |  | ● | ● | ● |  |  |  | ● |  |  | ● |  | ● |
| REJUVENATION (HM17154) |  |  |  |  |  |  |  |  |  |  |  |  |  |  |  |  |  |  |  |  |  |  |  |  |
| SCHOFIELD, G A (HM18018) |  | ● | ● |  |  | ● | ● |  | ● |  | ● |  | ● |  | ● |  |  |  | ● |  |  |  | ● | ● |
| SHANGHAI ACUPUNCTURE CLINIC (HM18280) | ● | ● | ● | ● | ● |  | ● | ● | ● | ● | ● |  | ● | ● | ● | ● | ● | ● | ● | ● | ● | ● | ● | ● |
| ST JOHN STREET PHYSIO PRACTICE (HM19080) | ● |  |  |  |  |  | ● |  |  |  |  |  |  |  |  |  |  |  |  |  |  |  |  |  |
| STIRLING, DIANNE (HM19301) |  |  |  |  |  |  |  |  |  |  |  |  |  |  |  |  |  |  |  |  |  |  |  |  |
| SWINTON HEALTH FOODS (HM19600) |  | ● |  |  |  |  |  |  |  |  |  |  | ● |  |  |  |  |  | ● |  |  |  |  |  |
| WAINWRIGHT, P (HM20739) |  |  |  |  |  |  | ● |  |  |  |  |  | ● |  |  |  |  |  |  |  |  |  |  |  |
| **MERSEYSIDE** |  |  |  |  |  |  |  |  |  |  |  |  |  |  |  |  |  |  |  |  |  |  |  |  |
| ABBEY FOOT CLINIC (HM00083) |  |  |  |  |  |  |  | ● |  |  |  |  |  |  |  |  |  |  |  |  | ● |  |  |  |
| ACUPUNCTURE CLINIC (HM00263) |  | ● | ● |  |  |  |  |  |  |  |  |  | ● |  |  |  | ● |  | ● |  |  |  | ● | ● |
| AIGBURTH MCTIMONEY CLINIC (HM00427) |  | ● |  |  |  |  | ● |  |  |  |  |  | ● |  |  |  |  |  |  |  |  |  |  |  |

# A - C Conditions treated at Practices/Businesses

| Business by County with Reference no. | Acne | Addiction | Adenoids | Aids | Alcoholism | Allergy | Alzheimer's Disease | Amnesia | Anaemia | Angina | Anorexia | Anxiety | Arthritis | Asthma | Athletes Foot | Autism | Back Pain | Bacterial Infections |
|---|---|---|---|---|---|---|---|---|---|---|---|---|---|---|---|---|---|---|
| AINTREE OSTEOPATHIC (HM00439) | | | | | | | | | | | | ● | | | | | ● | |
| ALLERTON HEALTH CENTRE (HM00639) | | | | | | ● | | | | | | | ● | ● | ● | | ● | |
| BIMPSON, PETER (HM02311) | | | | | | | | | | | | ● | ● | | | | ● | |
| BOLTON, TOM (HM02663) | | ● | | | | | | | | | | ● | | | | | | |
| BOYLE, ANDREW (HM02826) | | | | | | | | | | | | ● | ● | ● | ● | | ● | ● |
| BRENNAN, M A (HM02958) | | | | | | | | | | | | | | | ● | | | |
| CARTER, G R (HM03778) | | | | | | | | | | | | | | | ● | | | |
| CAWLEY, TONY (HM03871) | | ● | | | ● | | | | | | ● | ● | | | | | | |
| CONCANNON, DEIRDRE (HM04965) | | | | | | | | | | | | | ● | | | | ● | |
| D A F CLINIC (HM05655) | | ● | | | ● | | | | | | | ● | | | ● | | | |
| DARE TO CARE (HM05739) | | | | | | ● | | | | | | | ● | ● | | | ● | |
| ECCLES CHIROPODY SERVICES (HM06572) | | | | | | | | | | | | | ● | | ● | | | |
| FARMER, BARBARA (HM01681) | | | | | | | | | | | | ● | ● | | ● | | ● | |
| FRESHLEA PRIVATE CLINICS (HM07738) | | | | | | | | | | | | | ● | | | | ● | |
| GATEAUD, S (HM07924) | ● | | | | | ● | | | | | | | ● | ● | | | ● | |
| GROUNDS, L (HM08600) | | | | | | | | | | | | | | | ● | | | |
| HEAL TO TOE (HM09311) | ● | ● | ● | | ● | ● | ● | ● | ● | ● | ● | ● | ● | ● | | | ● | ● |
| HOLISTIC HEALTH CENTRE (HM09975) | ● | | ● | | | ● | | | | | | ● | ● | ● | | | ● | ● |
| HOPE STREET NATURAL HLTH CTRE (HM10136) | | | | | | ● | | | | | | ● | ● | | | | ● | |
| HYPNOCARE (HM10490) | | | | | | | | | | | ● | ● | | | | | | |
| JAMES, ANN (HM10880) | | | | ● | | ● | ● | | | | | | ● | | ● | | ● | ● |
| JARVIS, K R (HM10934) | | | | | | | | | | | | | | | ● | | | |
| KNOWLES, JANICE (HM11771) | | | | | | | | | | | | | ● | | ● | | | ● |
| MARKET STREET CHIROPODY CLINIC (HM13113) | | | | | | | | | | | | | | | ● | | | |
| MARSH, E C (HM13146) | | | | | | | | | | | | ● | | | ● | | | ● |
| MCLOUGHLIN, CLAIRE (HM13560) | | | | | | | | | | | | | | | ● | | | |
| NATURAL HEALTH CLINIC (HM14576) | ● | | ● | | | ● | | | | ● | ● | ● | ● | ● | ● | ● | ● | ● |
| NATUROPATHIC HEALTH CENTRE (HM14709) | | | | | | | | | | | | | | | | | | |
| NELSON, PATRICIA (HM14780) | | | | | | | | | | | | | | | ● | | | |
| PURE ESSENTIALS DIRECT (HM16764) | ● | | | | | | | | | | | | | | | | | |
| SANCTUARY NATURAL HEALTH (HM17893) | | | | | | | | | | | | | ● | | | | ● | |
| SCOTT, ANDREW (HM18107) | | | | | | | | | | | | ● | ● | ● | | | ● | |
| SEFTON PARK NATURAL THRPY CTRE (HM18198) | | | | | | | | | | | | ● | ● | ● | | | | |
| SIMPSON CLINIC (HM18584) | ● | | | | | ● | ● | ● | ● | ● | | ● | ● | ● | ● | | ● | ● |

| Business by County with Reference no. | Baldness | Bereavement | Bladder Problems | Blood Pressure | Boils | Bowel Problems | Breast Problems | Breathing Problems | Bronchitis | Bruising | Bulimia | Bunions | Bursitis | Callices | Cancers | Cataracts | Catarrh | Cerebral Palsy |
|---|---|---|---|---|---|---|---|---|---|---|---|---|---|---|---|---|---|---|
| AINTREE OSTEOPATHIC (HM00439) | | | | | | | | | | | | | | | | | | |
| ALLERTON HEALTH CENTRE (HM00639) | | | | | | | | | | | | | | | | | | |
| BIMPSON, PETER (HM02311) | | | | | | | | | | | | | | | | | | |
| BOLTON, TOM (HM02663) | | ● | | | | | | | | | | | | | | | | |
| BOYLE, ANDREW (HM02826) | | | ● | | | ● | | ● | | ● | | | ● | | ● | | | |
| BRENNAN, M A (HM02958) | | | | | | | | | | | | | | ● | | | | |
| CARTER, G R (HM03778) | | | | | | | | | | | | | | ● | | | | |
| CAWLEY, TONY (HM03871) | | | | | | | | | | | ● | | | | | | | |
| CONCANNON, DEIRDRE (HM04965) | | | | ● | | | | | | | | | | | | | | |
| D A F CLINIC (HM05655) | | | | ● | | | | | | | | | | | | | | |
| DARE TO CARE (HM05739) | | | | | | | | | | | | | | | | | | |
| ECCLES CHIROPODY SERVICES (HM06572) | | | | | | | | | | | | | | | | | | |
| FARMER, BARBARA (HM01681) | | | | | | | | ● | ● | | | | ● | | | | | |
| FRESHLEA PRIVATE CLINICS (HM07738) | | | | | | | | | | | | | | | | | | |
| GATEAUD, S (HM07924) | | | | ● | | | | | | | | | | | | | | |
| GROUNDS, L (HM08600) | | | | | | | | | | | | | | ● | | | | |
| HEAL TO TOE (HM09311) | | | ● | ● | ● | ● | ● | ● | ● | ● | ● | | | ● | ● | ● | ● | |
| HOLISTIC HEALTH CENTRE (HM09975) | | | ● | | ● | ● | ● | ● | ● | ● | | | ● | | | | ● | |
| HOPE STREET NATURAL HLTH CTRE (HM10136) | | | | | | | | | | | | | | | | | | |
| HYPNOCARE (HM10490) | | | | | | | | | | | ● | | | | | | | |
| JAMES, ANN (HM10880) | | | | | ● | | | | | ● | | | ● | ● | | | | |
| JARVIS, K R (HM10934) | | | | | | | | | | | | | | | | | | |
| KNOWLES, JANICE (HM11771) | | | | | | | | | | | | ● | | ● | | | | |
| MARKET STREET CHIROPODY CLINIC (HM13113) | | | | | | | | | | | | | | ● | | | | |
| MARSH, E C (HM13146) | | | | | | | | | | | | ● | | ● | | | | |
| MCLOUGHLIN, CLAIRE (HM13560) | | | | | | | | | | | | | | ● | | | | |
| NATURAL HEALTH CLINIC (HM14576) | | | ● | ● | | ● | ● | ● | ● | ● | | | | | | | ● | |
| NATUROPATHIC HEALTH CENTRE (HM14709) | | | | | | ● | | | | | | | | | | | | |
| NELSON, PATRICIA (HM14780) | | | | | | | | | | | | | | ● | | | | |
| PURE ESSENTIALS DIRECT (HM16764) | | | | | | | | ● | | | | | | | | | | |
| SANCTUARY NATURAL HEALTH (HM17893) | | | | | | | | | | | | | | | | | | |
| SCOTT, ANDREW (HM18107) | | | ● | | | ● | | ● | | | | | ● | | | | ● | |
| SEFTON PARK NATURAL THRPY CTRE (HM18198) | | | | | | | | | | | ● | | | | | | | |
| SIMPSON CLINIC (HM18584) | | | ● | ● | ● | ● | ● | ● | ● | ● | | | ● | | ● | ● | ● | |

| Business by County with Reference no. | Circulation Problems | Cold Sores | Colds | Colic | Colitis | Conjunctivitis | Constipation | Convulsions | Corns | Coughs | Cramp | Cystitis |
|---|---|---|---|---|---|---|---|---|---|---|---|---|
| AINTREE OSTEOPATHIC (HM00439) | ● | | | | | | | | | | | |
| ALLERTON HEALTH CENTRE (HM00639) | | | | | | | ● | | | | | |
| BIMPSON, PETER (HM02311) | | | | | | | | | | | | |
| BOLTON, TOM (HM02663) | | | | | | | | | | | | |
| BOYLE, ANDREW (HM02826) | | | | | ● | | ● | | | | ● | |
| BRENNAN, M A (HM02958) | | | | | | | | | ● | | | |
| CARTER, G R (HM03778) | | | | | | | | | ● | | | |
| CAWLEY, TONY (HM03871) | | | | | | | | | | | | |
| CONCANNON, DEIRDRE (HM04965) | ● | | | | | | | | | | | |
| D A F CLINIC (HM05655) | | | | | | | ● | | | | | |
| DARE TO CARE (HM05739) | | | | | | | | | | | | |
| ECCLES CHIROPODY SERVICES (HM06572) | | | | | | | | | | | | |
| FARMER, BARBARA (HM01681) | ● | | | | | | | | | | | |
| FRESHLEA PRIVATE CLINICS (HM07738) | | | | | | | | | | | | |
| GATEAUD, S (HM07924) | | | | | | | ● | | | | | |
| GROUNDS, L (HM08600) | | | | | | | | | ● | | | |
| HEAL TO TOE (HM09311) | ● | ● | ● | ● | ● | ● | ● | ● | ● | ● | ● | ● |
| HOLISTIC HEALTH CENTRE (HM09975) | ● | ● | | | ● | | ● | | | ● | ● | ● |
| HOPE STREET NATURAL HLTH CTRE (HM10136) | ● | | | | | | ● | | | | | |
| HYPNOCARE (HM10490) | | | | | | | | | | | | |
| JAMES, ANN (HM10880) | ● | | | | | | | | ● | | ● | |
| JARVIS, K R (HM10934) | | | | | | | | | | | | |
| KNOWLES, JANICE (HM11771) | | | | | | | | | ● | | | |
| MARKET STREET CHIROPODY CLINIC (HM13113) | | | | | | | | | ● | | | |
| MARSH, E C (HM13146) | | | | | | | | | ● | | | |
| MCLOUGHLIN, CLAIRE (HM13560) | | | | | | | | | ● | | | |
| NATURAL HEALTH CLINIC (HM14576) | ● | ● | ● | ● | ● | ● | ● | | | ● | ● | ● |
| NATUROPATHIC HEALTH CENTRE (HM14709) | | | | | | | | | | | | |
| NELSON, PATRICIA (HM14780) | | | | | | | | | ● | | | |
| PURE ESSENTIALS DIRECT (HM16764) | ● | | ● | | | | | | | | | |
| SANCTUARY NATURAL HEALTH (HM17893) | | | | | | | | | | | | |
| SCOTT, ANDREW (HM18107) | ● | | | | | | ● | | | ● | ● | |
| SEFTON PARK NATURAL THRPY CTRE (HM18198) | | | | | | | | | | | | |
| SIMPSON CLINIC (HM18584) | ● | ● | ● | ● | ● | ● | ● | ● | | ● | ● | ● |

# A - C Conditions treated at Practices/Businesses

| Business by County with Reference no. | Acne | Addiction | Adenoids | Aids | Alcoholism | Allergy | Alzheimer's Disease | Amnesia | Anaemia | Angina | Anorexia | Anxiety | Arthritis | Asthma | Athletes Foot | Autism | Back Pain | Bacterial Infections | Baldness | Bereavement | Bladder Problems | Blood Pressure | Boils | Bowel Problems | Breast Problems | Breathing Problems | Bronchitis | Bruising | Bulimia | Bunions | Bursitis | Callices | Cancers | Cataracts | Catarrh | Cerebral Palsy | Circulation Problems | Cold Sores | Colds | Colic | Colitis | Conjunctivitis | Constipation | Convulsions | Corns | Coughs | Cramp | Cystitis |
|---|---|---|---|---|---|---|---|---|---|---|---|---|---|---|---|---|---|---|---|---|---|---|---|---|---|---|---|---|---|---|---|---|---|---|---|---|---|---|---|---|---|---|---|---|---|---|---|---|
| SOUTHPORT OSTEO & ACUPUNCTURE (HM18942) | | | | | | | | | | | | |●| | | |●| | | | | | | | | | | | | | | | | | | | | | | | | | | | | | | |
| STEINA SPORTS & PHYSIOTHERAPY (HM19188) | | | | | | | | | | | | |●| | | |●| | | | | | | | | | | | | | | | | | | | | | | | | | | | | | | |
| SUMMERS, ALFRED A (HM19487) | | | | | | | | | | | | | | |●| | | | | | | | | | | | | | | | |●| | | | | | | | | | | | |●| | | |
| TARA SCHOOL OF HYPNOTHERAPY (HM19701) | | | | | | | | | | | |●| | | | | | | | | | | | | | | | | | | | | | | | | | | | | | | | | | | | |
| THERAPY 21 (HM19890) | | | | | | | | | | | |●|●|●|●| |●| | | | |●| | | |●| | | | | | | | |●| |●|●|●| | | | | | |●| | |
| WEST WIRRAL CHIROPRACTIC (HM21239) | | | | | | | | | | | | |●| | | |●| | | | | | | | | | | | | | | | | | | |●| | | | | | | | | | | |
| WILLIAMS CHIROPODY SERVICE (HM21530) | | | | | | | | | | | | | | |●| | | | | | | | | | | | | | | | |●| | | | | | | | | | | | |●| | | |
| WILLIAMS, CATHERINE (HM21546) | | | | | | | | | | | | | | |●| |●| | | | | | | | | | | | | | |●| | | | | | | | | | | | |●| | | |
| WILLIAMS, T H (HM21597) | | | | | | | | | | | | | | |●| | | | | | | | | | | | | | | | |●| | | | | | | | | | | | |●| | | |
| WILLIAMS, TECWYN H (HM21598) | | | | | | | | | | | | | | |●| | | | | | | | | | | | | | | | |●| | | | | | | | | | | | |●| | | |
| WIRRALL CLINIC (HM21730) | | | | | |●| | | | | | |●| | | |●| | | | | | | | | | | | | | | | | | | | | | | | | |●| | | | | |
| **MIDDLESEX** | | | | | | | | | | | | | | | | | | | | | | | | | | | | | | | | | | | | | | | | | | | | | | | | |
| CLANRICARDE CLINIC (HM04526) | | |●| | | |●| |●|●|●| |●|●|●| |●|●| | |●|●| |●|●|●|●| | | |●| |●| | | | |●|●| |●| |●| | | | |●|
| **MIDLANDS (WEST)** | | | | | | | | | | | | | | | | | | | | | | | | | | | | | | | | | | | | | | | | | | | | | | | |
| 1ST CHIROPRACTIC UK (HM00005) | | | | | | | | | | | | |●| | | |●| | | | | | | | | | | | | | | | | | | |●| | |●| | | | | | | | |
| 1ST CHIROPRACTIC UK (HM00006) | | | | | | | | | | | | |●| | | |●| | | | | | | | | | | | | | | | | | | | | | |●| | | | | | | | |
| A Q C H (HM00044) |●|●| | |●|●| |●| | |●|●|●|●| | | | |●| |●|●| | | |●| | |●| | | |●| |●| |●|●| | |●| |●|●| | |●|●|
| ABBEY CLINIC (HM00077) | | | | | | | | | | | | |●|●| | |●| | | | | | |●| | | | | | |●| | | | | | | | |●| | |●| | | | | |
| ABBIE HYPNOTHERAPY CENTRE (HM00093) | |●| | |●|●| |●| | |●|●| |●| |●|●| | | | |●| |●| |●| | |●| | | |●| | | | | | | | | | | | | | | |
| ACUPUNCTURE HEALTH CLINIC (HM00312) | | | | | |●| | | | | |●|●|●| | |●| | | | | | | | | | | | | | | | | | | | | |●| | | |●| | |●| |●|
| ALCOCK, E C (HM00490) | | | | | | | | | | | | |●| |●| | | | | | | | | | | | | | | | | | | | | | | | | | | | | | | | |
| ALDA HOUSE NATURAL THERAPY (HM00492) | |●| | | |●| | |●|●| |●|●|●|●| |●|●| | |●|●|●|●|●|●|●|●| | | | | | |●| |●|●|●|●|●|●|●| | |●|●|●|
| ALLEN, ELAINE (HM00608) | | | | | | | | | | | |●|●| | | |●| | | | | | | | | | | | | | | | | | | | | | | | | | | | | | |
| AROMA SANTE (HM01057) |●|●|●|●|●|●|●|●|●|●|●|●|●|●|●|●|●|●|●| |●|●|●|●|●|●|●|●|●| |●|●|●|●|●| |●|●|●|●|●|●|●|●|●|●|●|●|
| ARROW BANK CHIROPRACTIC CLINIC (HM01149) | | | | | | | | | | | | |●| | | |●| | | | | | | | | | | | | | | | | | | | | | | | | | | | | | |
| ASSOCIATION OF STRESS MNGMT (HM01288) | |●| | |●|●| |●| |●|●|●|●|●| | |●| | | | |●| | | | | | |●| | | | | | | | | | | | | | | | | | | |
| BACKCARE & ACUPUNCTURE CLINIC (HM01526) |●|●| |●|●|●| | |●|●| |●|●|●|●| |●|●|●| | |●| |●| | | |●| | | | | | |●| |●| |●|●|●| |●| | | |●|●|
| BEAUTIFORM COLLEGE (HM01992) |●| | | | | | | | | | |●| | | | |●| | | | |●| | | | | | | | | | | | | | | | | | | | |●| | | |●| |
| BILLINGHAM, S (HM02301) | | | | | | | | | | | |●|●| | | |●| | | | | | | | |●| | | | | | |●| |●| |●| | | | | |●| | | | | |
| BIOENERGY PARTNERSHIP (HM02334) | | | | | |●| | | | | | | |●| | |●| | | | | | | | | | | | | | | | | | | | | | | | | | | | | | | |
| BIRMINGHAM ACU/CHIRO CLNC (HM02382) |●|●|●|●|●|●|●|●|●|●|●|●|●|●|●|●|●|●|●| |●|●|●|●|●|●|●|●|●| |●| | |●|●| |●|●|●|●|●|●|●|●| |●|●|●|
| BIRMINGHAM PHYSIO CLINIC (HM02388) | | | | | | | | | | | | |●| | | |●| | | | | | | | | | | | | | | | | | | | | | | | | | | | | | |
| BIRMINGHAM TRAD ACU CENTRE (HM02390) | | | | | | | | | | | | |●| | | |●| | | | | | | | | | | | | | | | | | | |●| | | | | | | | | | | |
| BLAKE, D H (HM02479) | | | | | | | | | | | | |●| | | |●| | | | |●| | | | | | | | | | | | | | |●| | | | | | | | | | | |

# A - C Conditions treated at Practices/Businesses

| Business by County with Reference no. | Acne | Addiction | Adenoids | Aids | Alcoholism | Allergy | Alzheimer's Disease | Amnesia | Anaemia | Angina | Anorexia | Anxiety | Arthritis | Asthma | Athletes Foot | Autism | Back Pain | Bacterial Infections | Baldness | Bereavement | Bladder Problems | Blood Pressure | Boils | Bowel Problems | Breast Problems | Breathing Problems | Bronchitis | Bruising | Bulimia | Bunions | Bursitis | Callices | Cancers | Cataracts | Catarrh | Cerebral Palsy | Circulation Problems | Cold Sores | Colds | Colic | Colitis | Conjunctivitis | Constipation | Convulsions | Corns | Coughs | Cramp | Cystitis |
|---|---|---|---|---|---|---|---|---|---|---|---|---|---|---|---|---|---|---|---|---|---|---|---|---|---|---|---|---|---|---|---|---|---|---|---|---|---|---|---|---|---|---|---|---|---|---|---|---|
| BOLDMERE HYPNOTHERAPY (HM02653) | ● | ● |  |  | ● |  |  |  |  |  |  |  |  |  |  |  |  |  |  |  |  |  |  | ● |  |  |  |  |  |  |  |  |  |  |  |  |  |  |  |  | ● |  |  |  |  |  |  |  |
| BROWNHILL, D G (HM03257) |  | ● |  |  |  |  |  |  |  |  | ● | ● |  |  |  |  |  |  |  |  |  |  |  |  |  |  |  |  |  |  |  |  |  |  |  |  |  |  |  |  |  |  |  |  |  |  |  |  |
| BTAC (HM03296) | ● | ● |  |  |  |  |  |  |  |  | ● | ● | ● | ● |  |  | ● |  |  |  |  | ● |  | ● |  | ● |  |  | ● |  | ● |  |  |  | ● |  | ● |  | ● |  | ● |  | ● |  |  | ● | ● | ● |
| BULLOCK, JULIE (HM03344) |  |  |  |  |  |  |  |  |  |  |  |  | ● |  | ● |  |  |  |  |  |  |  |  |  |  |  |  |  |  | ● |  |  |  |  |  |  |  |  |  |  |  |  |  |  |  |  |  |  |
| CALLAGHAN, R M & J (HM03549) |  |  |  |  |  |  |  |  |  |  |  |  |  |  | ● |  |  |  |  |  |  |  |  |  |  |  |  |  |  |  |  |  |  |  |  |  |  |  |  |  |  |  |  |  |  |  |  |  |
| CARPENTER, DAVID (HM03727) |  | ● |  |  | ● | ● |  | ● |  | ● |  | ● | ● | ● |  |  | ● |  |  |  |  | ● |  | ● | ● | ● |  |  | ● |  |  |  | ● |  |  |  |  | ● |  | ● | ● |  | ● |  |  |  | ● |  |
| CENTRAL CHIROPODY CLINIC (HM03888) |  |  |  |  |  |  |  |  |  |  |  |  |  |  | ● |  |  |  |  |  |  |  |  |  |  |  |  |  |  |  |  | ● |  |  |  |  |  |  |  |  |  |  |  |  | ● |  |  |  |
| CENTRE FOR NATURAL THERAPIES (HM03913) | ● | ● | ● | ● | ● | ● | ● | ● | ● | ● | ● | ● | ● | ● | ● | ● | ● | ● | ● |  | ● | ● | ● | ● | ● | ● | ● | ● | ● |  | ● | ● | ● | ● | ● |  | ● | ● | ● | ● | ● | ● | ● | ● | ● | ● | ● | ● |
| CHEER, MARIE (HM04082) |  |  |  |  |  |  |  |  |  |  |  | ● |  |  |  |  | ● |  |  |  |  |  |  |  |  |  |  |  |  |  |  |  |  |  |  |  |  |  |  |  |  |  |  |  |  |  |  |  |
| CHELMSLEY WOOD FOOT CLINIC (HM04086) |  |  |  |  |  |  |  |  |  |  |  |  |  |  | ● |  |  |  |  |  |  |  |  |  |  |  |  |  |  |  |  |  |  |  |  |  |  |  |  |  |  |  |  |  |  |  |  |  |
| CHEYLESMORE PHYSIO CLINIC (HM04147) |  |  |  |  |  |  |  |  |  |  |  |  |  |  |  |  | ● |  |  |  |  |  |  |  |  |  |  |  |  |  |  |  |  |  |  |  |  |  |  |  |  |  |  |  |  |  |  |  |
| CHIRO MED (HM04283) | ● | ● |  | ● |  | ● |  |  |  |  |  | ● | ● | ● |  |  | ● |  |  |  | ● | ● |  | ● |  |  |  |  |  |  | ● |  |  |  | ● |  | ● | ● | ● | ● | ● |  | ● |  |  |  | ● |  |
| CHIROPRACTIC CLINIC (HM04388) |  |  |  |  |  |  |  |  |  |  |  |  | ● |  |  |  | ● |  |  |  |  |  |  |  |  |  |  |  |  |  |  |  |  |  |  |  | ● |  |  |  |  |  |  |  |  |  |  |  |
| CHIROPRACTORS OF WARWICK ROAD (HM04407) |  |  |  |  |  |  |  |  |  |  |  |  | ● |  |  |  | ● |  |  |  |  |  |  |  |  |  |  |  |  |  |  |  |  |  |  |  | ● |  |  |  |  |  |  |  |  |  |  |  |
| CODSALL COMP THERAPIES (HM04778) | ● |  |  |  |  | ● |  |  |  |  |  | ● |  |  |  |  |  |  |  |  |  |  |  |  |  |  |  |  |  |  |  |  |  |  |  |  |  |  |  |  |  |  |  |  |  |  |  |  |
| COMPLEMENTARY HEALING CENTRE (HM04919) |  |  |  |  |  |  |  |  |  |  |  | ● |  |  |  |  |  |  |  |  |  |  |  |  |  |  |  |  |  |  |  |  |  |  |  |  |  |  |  |  |  |  |  |  |  |  |  |  |
| COMPLEMENTARY MEDICINE CENTRE (HM04937) |  |  |  |  |  |  |  |  |  |  |  |  |  |  |  |  |  |  |  |  |  | ● |  |  |  |  |  |  |  |  |  |  |  |  |  |  |  |  |  |  |  |  |  |  |  |  |  |  |
| COMPLEMENTARY THERAPY CENTRE (HM04943) |  |  |  |  |  |  |  |  |  |  |  |  | ● |  |  |  | ● |  |  |  |  |  |  |  |  |  |  |  |  |  |  |  |  |  |  |  |  |  |  |  |  |  |  |  |  |  |  |  |
| COMPLEMENTARY THERAPY CENTRE (HM04947) |  |  |  |  |  |  |  |  |  |  |  |  | ● |  |  |  | ● |  |  |  |  |  |  |  |  |  |  |  |  |  |  |  |  |  |  |  |  |  |  |  |  |  |  |  |  |  |  |  |
| CREATIVE HEALTH CENTRE (HM05398) | ● |  |  |  |  | ● |  |  | ● | ● | ● | ● |  | ● |  |  | ● |  |  |  |  |  |  |  |  |  | ● |  |  |  |  |  |  |  |  |  |  |  | ● |  | ● |  | ● |  |  |  | ● |  |
| CROFT, ANGELA (HM05453) |  |  |  |  |  | ● |  |  |  |  |  |  |  |  |  |  |  |  |  |  |  |  |  |  |  |  |  |  |  |  |  |  |  |  |  |  |  |  |  |  |  |  |  |  |  |  |  |  |
| CRYSTAL CLEAR PRACTICE (HM05528) | ● | ● | ● | ● | ● | ● | ● | ● | ● | ● | ● | ● | ● | ● | ● | ● | ● | ● | ● |  | ● | ● | ● | ● | ● | ● | ● | ● | ● |  | ● | ● | ● | ● | ● |  | ● | ● | ● | ● | ● | ● | ● | ● | ● | ● | ● | ● |
| CTRE-REFLEX & AROMATHERAPY (HM05549) | ● |  |  |  |  |  |  |  |  |  |  | ● | ● | ● |  |  | ● |  |  |  |  |  |  | ● |  |  |  |  |  |  |  |  |  |  | ● |  | ● | ● |  |  | ● |  |  |  |  |  | ● |  |
| DAVIS A STARKEY REM THERAP (HM05846) |  |  |  |  |  |  |  |  |  |  |  |  | ● |  |  |  | ● |  |  |  |  | ● |  | ● |  |  |  |  |  |  |  |  |  |  |  |  |  |  |  |  |  |  |  |  |  |  |  |  |
| DHANA, P N (HM06053) |  |  |  |  |  |  |  |  |  |  |  |  |  |  | ● |  |  |  |  |  |  |  |  |  |  |  |  |  |  |  |  | ● |  |  |  |  |  |  |  |  |  |  |  |  | ● |  |  |  |
| DUDLEY PHYSIOTHERAPY CLINIC (HM06354) |  |  |  |  |  |  |  |  |  |  |  |  | ● |  |  |  | ● |  |  |  |  |  |  |  |  |  |  |  |  |  |  |  |  |  |  |  |  |  |  |  |  |  |  |  |  |  |  |  |
| ERDINGTHON NATURAL HEALTH CLNC (HM06880) | ● | ● | ● | ● | ● | ● | ● | ● | ● | ● | ● | ● | ● | ● | ● | ● | ● | ● | ● |  | ● | ● | ● | ● | ● | ● | ● | ● | ● |  | ● |  | ● | ● | ● |  | ● | ● | ● | ● | ● | ● | ● | ● |  | ● | ● | ● |
| ESSENTIAL HEALTH (HM06909) | ● |  |  |  |  |  |  |  |  |  |  | ● |  |  |  |  | ● |  |  |  |  |  |  |  |  | ● | ● |  |  |  |  |  |  |  |  |  | ● |  |  |  |  |  |  |  |  |  |  |  |
| FAIRFAX PRIVATE THERAPY (HM07056) | ● | ● |  |  |  | ● |  |  | ● |  | ● | ● | ● | ● |  |  | ● | ● |  |  | ● | ● | ● |  |  | ● | ● | ● | ● |  |  |  |  |  | ● |  | ● | ● | ● | ● |  |  |  |  |  | ● | ● |  |
| FLETCHER, VICTOR JOHN (HM07416) |  |  |  |  |  |  |  |  |  |  |  |  |  |  | ● |  |  |  |  |  |  |  |  |  |  |  |  |  |  |  |  |  |  |  |  |  |  |  |  |  |  |  |  |  |  |  |  |  |
| FORD, MARIA (HM07526) |  |  |  |  |  |  |  |  |  |  |  |  |  |  |  |  |  |  |  |  |  |  |  |  |  |  |  |  |  |  |  |  |  |  |  |  | ● |  |  |  |  |  |  |  |  |  |  |  |
| FRESHWINDS CHARITABLE TRUST (HM07740) | ● | ● | ● | ● | ● | ● | ● | ● | ● | ● | ● | ● | ● | ● | ● | ● | ● | ● | ● |  | ● | ● | ● | ● | ● | ● | ● | ● | ● |  | ● | ● | ● | ● | ● |  | ● | ● | ● | ● | ● |  | ● | ● | ● | ● | ● | ● |
| GOLDEN PALMS (HM08207) | ● |  |  |  |  |  |  |  |  |  |  |  | ● | ● |  |  | ● |  |  |  | ● | ● |  | ● |  | ● |  |  |  |  |  |  |  |  |  |  |  |  |  |  |  |  |  |  |  |  |  |  |
| GREAT BARR OSTEO PRACTICE (HM08430) |  |  |  |  |  |  |  |  |  |  |  |  |  | ● |  |  | ● |  |  |  |  |  |  |  |  |  |  |  |  |  |  |  |  |  |  |  |  |  |  |  |  |  |  |  |  |  |  |  |

# A - C Conditions treated at Practices/Businesses

| Business by County with Reference no. | Acne | Addiction | Adenoids | Aids | Alcoholism | Allergy | Alzheimer's Disease | Amnesia | Anaemia | Angina | Anorexia | Anxiety | Arthritis | Asthma | Athletes Foot | Autism | Back Pain | Bacterial Infections | Baldness | Bereavement | Bladder Problems | Blood Pressure | Boils | Bowel Problems | Breast Problems | Breathing Problems | Bronchitis | Bruising | Bulimia | Bunions | Bursitis | Callices | Cancers | Cataracts | Catarrh | Cerebral Palsy | Circulation Problems | Cold Sores | Colds | Colic | Colitis | Conjunctivitis | Constipation | Convulsions | Corns | Coughs | Cramp | Cystitis |
|---|---|---|---|---|---|---|---|---|---|---|---|---|---|---|---|---|---|---|---|---|---|---|---|---|---|---|---|---|---|---|---|---|---|---|---|---|---|---|---|---|---|---|---|---|---|---|---|---|
| GREEN VALLEY THERAPY CENTRE (HM08443) | ● | ● | ● | ● | ● | ● | ● | ● | ● | ● | ● | ● | ● | ● | ● | ● | ● | ● | ● | | ● | ● | ● | ● | ● | ● | ● | ● | ● | | ● | | ● | ● | ● | | ● | ● | ● | ● | ● | ● | ● | ● | | ● | ● | ● |
| GURPAL SINGH AROMA/REFLEX (HM08655) | | | | | | | | | | | | ● | ● | | | | ● | | | | | | | | | | | | | | | | | | | | | | | | | | | | | | | |
| HAGLEY CENTRE OF COMP MED (HM08701) | ● | ● | | | | ● | | | | | | ● | ● | ● | | | ● | | | | ● | | ● | | | | ● | | | | | | ● | | | | ● | | | | | | | | | ● | | |
| HALE ASSOCIATES (HM08727) | | | | | | | | | | | | | ● | | | | ● | | | | | | | | | | | | | | | | | | | | | | | | | | | | | | | |
| HALE, GEOFF (HM08732) | | | | | | | | | | | | | ● | | | | ● | | | | | | | | | | | | | | | | | | | | | | | | | | | | | | | |
| HALL GREEN ALTERN PRACTICE (HM08760) | ● | ● | ● | ● | ● | ● | ● | ● | ● | ● | ● | ● | ● | ● | ● | ● | ● | ● | ● | | ● | ● | ● | ● | ● | ● | ● | ● | ● | | ● | | ● | ● | ● | | ● | ● | ● | ● | ● | ● | ● | ● | | ● | ● | ● |
| HALL, SUSAN (HM08790) | ● | ● | ● | | | | | | | | | ● | ● | ● | ● | | ● | ● | | | ● | ● | | ● | ● | ● | ● | | | | | ● | | | ● | | ● | | ● | | | ● | ● | | ● | ● | ● | ● |
| HARTNESS, R (HM09149) | | | | | | | | | | | | | ● | | ● | | | | | | | | | | | | | | | ● | | | | | | | | | | | | | | | | | | |
| HEALTH SHOP (HM09402) | ● | | | | | ● | | | | | | ● | ● | ● | ● | | ● | | | | ● | ● | ● | ● | | | ● | ● | | | | | | ● | | | ● | ● | ● | ● | | | ● | | | ● | ● | ● |
| HERBAL PHARMACY (HM09632) | | | | | | ● | | | ● | ● | ● | ● | ● | ● | ● | | ● | ● | | | ● | ● | ● | ● | ● | ● | ● | ● | ● | | | | | | | | ● | ● | ● | ● | | ● | ● | ● | | ● | ● | ● |
| HIGGS, R W (HM09737) | | | | | | | | | | | | | | | ● | | | | | | | | | | | | | | | | | | | | | | | | | | | | | | | | | |
| HOGG, DEBBI (HM09913) | ● | ● | ● | | | ● | ● | | ● | ● | ● | ● | ● | ● | ● | | ● | ● | | | ● | ● | ● | ● | ● | ● | ● | | ● | | | | ● | ● | ● | | ● | ● | ● | ● | ● | ● | ● | ● | | ● | ● | ● |
| HOLISTIC HEALTH CENTRE (HM09972) | | | | | | ● | | | | | | ● | ● | | | | | | | | | | | | | | | | | | | | ● | | | | | | | | | | | | | | | |
| HOLLOWAY, P (HM10027) | | | | | | | | | | | | ● | | ● | | | | | | | | | | | | ● | | | | | | | | | | | | | | | | | | | | | | |
| HOLLY COTTAGE CHIRO CLINIC (HM10029) | | | | | | | | | | | | | ● | | | | ● | | | | | | | | | | | | | | | | | | | | ● | | | ● | | | | | | | | |
| HOMOEOPATHIC CLINIC/PHARMACY (HM10090) | ● | | | | | | | ● | | | ● | ● | ● | | | | ● | | | | ● | | | ● | | | | | | | | | | | ● | | ● | | | | | ● | ● | | | | | |
| HOT-PAK (HM10206) | | | | | | | | | | | | | | | | | ● | | | | | | | | | | | | | | | | | | | | | | | | | | | | | | | |
| HUSBANDS, STEVE (HM10432) | ● | ● | ● | ● | ● | ● | ● | ● | ● | ● | ● | ● | ● | ● | ● | ● | ● | ● | ● | | ● | ● | ● | ● | ● | ● | ● | ● | ● | | ● | | ● | ● | ● | | ● | ● | ● | ● | ● | ● | ● | ● | | ● | ● | ● |
| INGRAM, CLARE (HM10624) | | | | | | ● | | | | | | ● | ● | ● | ● | | ● | ● | | | ● | ● | ● | ● | ● | ● | ● | ● | | | | | | | ● | | ● | ● | ● | ● | ● | | ● | | | ● | ● | ● |
| INNERSENSE (HM10647) | | | | | | | | | | | | | ● | | | | ● | | | | | | | | | | | | | | | | | | | | | | | | | | | | | | | |
| J BENSON CHIROPODIST (HM10793) | | | | | | | | | | | | | ● | | ● | | | ● | | | | | | | | | | | | | ● | | | | | | | | | | | | | | | | | |
| JOHNSON FOOTCARE (HM11061) | | | | | | | | | | | | | | | ● | | | | | | | | | | | | | | | | | ● | | | | | | | | | | | | | ● | | | |
| KEMPSON, STEVE (HM11468) | | | | | | ● | | | | | | ● | | | | | ● | | | | | | | | | | | | | | | | | | | | | | | | | | | | | | | |
| KEVIN FISHER CHIROPODY (HM11573) | | | | | | | | | | | | | ● | | ● | | | | | | | | | | | | | | | ● | | ● | | | | | | | | | | | | | ● | | | |
| LEWIS, MYRA (HM12305) | | | | | | | | | | | | ● | | | | | ● | | | | | | | | | | | | | | | | | | | | | | | | | | | | | | | |
| LIFE'S OPTION (HM12358) | | | | | | | | | | | | ● | | | | | | | | | | | | | | | | | | | | | | | | | | | | | | | | | | | | |
| LONGFORD PHYSIO & SPORTS (HM12627) | | | | | | | | | | | | | ● | ● | | | ● | | | | | | | | | | | | | | | | | | | | ● | | | | | | | | | | ● | |
| MAPES, JANET (HM13059) | | | | | | | | | | | | | ● | | | | ● | | | | | | | | | | | | | | | | ● | | | | | | | | | | | | | | | |
| MCDERMOTT, J V (HM13447) | | | | | | | | | | | | | ● | | | | ● | | | | | | | | | | | | | | | | | | | | | | | | | | | | | | | |
| MIDLAND HYPNOTHERAPY CENTRE (HM13831) | ● | ● | | | ● | ● | ● | ● | ● | | ● | ● | ● | ● | | | ● | | ● | | ● | ● | ● | ● | ● | ● | ● | | ● | | ● | | ● | | ● | | ● | ● | ● | ● | ● | | ● | ● | | ● | ● | ● |
| MIDLAND HYPNOTHERAPY CENTRE (HM13830) | ● | | | | ● | ● | ● | ● | ● | | ● | ● | ● | ● | | | ● | | | | ● | ● | ● | ● | ● | ● | ● | | ● | | ● | | ● | | ● | | ● | ● | ● | ● | ● | | ● | ● | | ● | ● | ● |
| MIDLAND MEDICAL HOM PRACTICE (HM13832) | ● | ● | ● | ● | ● | ● | ● | ● | ● | ● | ● | ● | ● | ● | ● | ● | ● | ● | ● | | ● | ● | ● | ● | ● | ● | ● | ● | ● | | ● | | ● | ● | ● | | ● | ● | ● | ● | ● | ● | ● | ● | | ● | ● | ● |
| MIDLAND MEDICAL HOM PRACTICE (HM13833) | ● | ● | ● | ● | ● | ● | ● | ● | ● | ● | ● | ● | ● | ● | ● | ● | ● | ● | ● | | ● | ● | ● | ● | ● | ● | ● | ● | ● | | ● | | ● | ● | ● | | ● | ● | ● | ● | ● | ● | ● | ● | | ● | ● | ● |
| MIDLAND MEDICAL HOM PRACTICE (HM13834) | ● | ● | ● | ● | ● | ● | ● | ● | ● | ● | ● | ● | ● | ● | ● | ● | ● | ● | ● | | ● | ● | ● | ● | ● | ● | ● | ● | ● | | ● | | ● | ● | ● | | ● | ● | ● | ● | ● | ● | ● | ● | | ● | ● | ● |

# A - C Conditions treated at Practices/Businesses

| Business by County with Reference no. | Acne | Addiction | Adenoids | Aids | Alcoholism | Allergy | Alzheimer's Disease | Amnesia | Anaemia | Angina | Anorexia | Anxiety | Arthritis | Asthma | Athletes Foot | Autism | Back Pain | Bacterial Infections | Baldness | Bereavement | Bladder Problems | Blood Pressure | Boils | Bowel Problems | Breast Problems | Breathing Problems | Bronchitis | Bruising | Bulimia | Bunions | Bursitis | Callices | Cancers | Cataracts | Catarrh | Cerebral Palsy | Circulation Problems | Cold Sores | Colds | Colic | Colitis | Conjunctivitis | Constipation | Convulsions | Corns | Coughs | Cramp | Cystitis |
|---|---|---|---|---|---|---|---|---|---|---|---|---|---|---|---|---|---|---|---|---|---|---|---|---|---|---|---|---|---|---|---|---|---|---|---|---|---|---|---|---|---|---|---|---|---|---|---|---|
| MIDLAND MEDICAL OSTEO PRACTICE (HM13837) | | | | | | | | | | | | | | | | | ● | | | | | | | | | | | | | | | | | | | | | | | | | | | | | | | |
| MIDLAND MEDICAL OSTEO PRACTICE (HM13835) | | | | | | | | | | | | | | | | | ● | | | | | | | | | | | | | | | | | | | | | | | | | | | | | | | |
| MIDLAND MEDICAL OSTEO PRACTICE (HM13836) | | | | | | | | | | | | | | | | | ● | | | | | | | | | | | | | | | | | | | | | | | | | | | | | | | |
| MORGAN, VALERIE (HM14177) | ● | | | | | ● | | | | | | | ● | ● | | | ● | | | | ● | | | | | | ● | | | | | | | | ● | | ● | ● | ● | | ● | | ● | | | ● | | ● |
| MORRIS, CLAIRE (HM14202) | | | | | | | | | | | | | | | ● | | | | | | | | | | | | | | | | | ● | | | | | | | | | | | | | ● | | | |
| MYATT, ANITA (HM14432) | ● | ● | ● | ● | ● | ● | ● | ● | ● | ● | ● | ● | ● | ● | ● | ● | ● | ● | ● | | ● | ● | ● | ● | ● | ● | ● | ● | ● | | ● | ● | ● | ● | ● | | ● | ● | ● | ● | ● | ● | ● | ● | ● | ● | ● | ● |
| NATURAL HEALTH CENTRE (HM14574) | | | | | | ● | | | | | | | | | | | | | | | | | | | | | | | | | | | | | | | ● | | | | | | ● | | | | | |
| NEWBRIDGE PHARMACY (HM14850) | ● | ● | | | ● | ● | | | | ● | ● | ● | ● | ● | | | | ● | ● | | | ● | ● | ● | | ● | ● | ● | ● | | ● | | ● | | ● | | ● | | ● | ● | ● | | ● | | | ● | ● | ● |
| OULTON FOOT CLINIC (HM15499) | | | | | | | | | | | | | | | ● | | | | | | | | | | | | | | | | | | | | | | | | | | | | | | | | | |
| PARK PRACTICE (HM15672) | ● | ● | ● | ● | ● | ● | ● | ● | ● | ● | ● | ● | ● | ● | ● | ● | ● | ● | ● | | ● | ● | ● | ● | ● | ● | ● | ● | ● | | ● | ● | ● | ● | ● | | ● | ● | ● | ● | ● | ● | ● | ● | ● | ● | ● | ● |
| PAUL MAWER PSYCHOLGICAL SVS (HM15843) | | | | | | | | | | | | ● | | | | ● | | | | | | | | | | | | | | | | | | | | | | | | | | | | | | | | |
| PHYSIOTHERAPY CLINIC (HM16241) | | | | | | | | | | | | | ● | | | | ● | | | | | | | | | | | | | | | | | | | | | | | | | | | | | | | |
| PIKE, ELIZABETH G & J K (HM16286) | | | | | | | | | | | | | | | ● | | | | | | | | | | | | | | | | | | | | | | | | | | | | | | | | | |
| PILLATH, CHRISTINE (HM16297) | | | | | | | | | | | | | ● | | | | ● | | | | | | | | | | | | | | | | | | | | ● | | | | | | | | | | | |
| PLANT, ALISON () | | | | | | | | | | | | ● | ● | | | | ● | | | | | ● | | | | | ● | | | | | | | | ● | | ● | ● | | | | | ● | | | | | |
| PRISM THERAPIES (HM16636) | | ● | | | | | | ● | | | ● | ● | ● | | | | ● | | | | | ● | | ● | | | | | ● | | ● | | | | | | ● | | | | | | ● | | | | | |
| REMEDIAL MASSAGE THERAPY (HM17174) | | | | | | | | | | | | | ● | | | | ● | | | | | | | ● | ● | | | | | | ● | | | | | | | | | | | | | | | | | |
| RICHARDSON, CYRIL (HM17273) | | | | | | | | | | | | | | | ● | | | | | | | | | | | | | | | | | ● | | | | | | | | | | | | | ● | | | |
| ROBINSON, JOHN (HM17484) | | | | | | | | | | | | | | | ● | | | | | | | | | | | | | | | | | ● | | | | | | | | | | | | | ● | | | |
| ROMSLEY PHYSIOTHERAPY PRACTICE (HM17578) | | | | | | | | | | | | | ● | | | | ● | | | | | | | | | | | ● | | | | | | | | | | | | | | | ● | | | | | ● |
| SEITAI/SHIATSU & MANIPULATION (HM18202) | | | | | | | | | | | | | ● | | | | ● | | | | | | | | | | | | | | | | | | | | | | | | | | | | | | | |
| SIDHOM, A (HM18529) | | | | | | | | | | | | | ● | | | | ● | | | | | | | | | | | | | | | | | | | | | | | | | | | | | | | |
| SOLIHULL CHIROPRACTIC CLINIC (HM18872) | | | | | | | | | | | | | ● | | | | ● | | | | | | | | | | | | | | | | | | | | ● | | | ● | | | | | | | | |
| SOMEWAY HERBAL CLINIC (HM18883) | ● | | | | | ● | | | | | | | | | | | | | | | | | | | | | | | | | | | | | | | | | | | | | | | | | | |
| ST PAULS OSTEOPATHY PRACTICE (HM19094) | | | | | | ● | | | | | | | ● | ● | | | ● | | | | | | | | | ● | | | | | ● | | | | ● | | ● | | | ● | | | | | | | ● | |
| STARKEY, DAVID (HM19147) | | | | | | | | | | | | | ● | | | | ● | | | | | | | ● | | | | | | | | | | | | | | | | | | | | | | | | |
| STOURBRIDGE ACU & OSTEO CTRE (HM19356) | | | | | | | | | | | | | ● | | | | ● | | | | | | | | | | | | | | | | | | | | | | | | | | | | | | | |
| SUCCESSWORKS (HM19461) | | | | | | | | | | | | ● | | | | | ● | | | | | | | | | | | | | | | | | | | | | | | | | | | | | | | |
| SUTTON COLDFIELD HEALTH CLINIC (HM19544) | | ● | | | ● | ● | | | ● | ● | | ● | ● | ● | | | ● | | | | ● | ● | | ● | | ● | ● | | | | | | | | | | ● | | ● | | ● | | ● | | | | ● | ● |
| TELLING, MELANIE (HM19822) | | | | | | | | | | | | ● | | ● | | | ● | | | | ● | ● | | | | ● | | | | | | | ● | | | | ● | | | | | | ● | | | | | |
| TELLING, MELANIE (HM19823) | | | | | | ● | | | | | | ● | ● | ● | | | ● | | | | ● | ● | | | ● | ● | ● | | | | | | ● | | | | ● | | | | | | ● | | | | | |
| THERAPY TRAINING COLLEGE (HM19911) | | ● | | | ● | ● | | | | | ● | ● | | ● | | | | | | | | ● | | ● | | | | | ● | | | | | | | | | | | | | | | | | | | |
| WALSALL PHYSIOTHERAPY CLINIC (HM20853) | | | | | | | | | | | | | ● | | | | ● | | | | | | | | | | | | | | | | | | | | | | | | | | | | | | | |
| WALSGRAVE CHIROPRACTIC CLINIC (HM20855) | | | | | | | | | | | | | ● | | | | ● | | | | | | | | | | | | | | | | | | | | ● | | | | | | | | | | | |

# A - C Conditions treated at Practices/Businesses

| Business by County with Reference no. | Acne | Addiction | Adenoids | Aids | Alcoholism | Allergy | Alzheimer's Disease | Amnesia | Anaemia | Angina | Anorexia | Anxiety | Arthritis | Asthma | Athletes Foot | Autism | Back Pain | Bacterial Infections | Baldness | Bereavement | Bladder Problems | Blood Pressure | Boils | Bowel Problems | Breast Problems | Breathing Problems | Bronchitis | Bruising | Bulimia | Bunions | Bursitis | Callices | Cancers | Cataracts | Catarrh | Cerebral Palsy | Circulation Problems | Cold Sores | Colds | Colic | Colitis | Conjunctivitis | Constipation | Convulsions | Corns | Coughs | Cramp | Cystitis |
|---|---|---|---|---|---|---|---|---|---|---|---|---|---|---|---|---|---|---|---|---|---|---|---|---|---|---|---|---|---|---|---|---|---|---|---|---|---|---|---|---|---|---|---|---|---|---|---|---|
| WARD, JAQUELINE (HM20906) | | | | | | | | | | | | ● | | | | | | | | | | | | | | | | | | | | | | | | | | | | | | | | | | | | |
| WELL NATURAL HEALTH CENTRE (HM21139) | ● | ● | ● | ● | ● | ● | ● | ● | ● | ● | ● | ● | ● | ● | ● | ● | ● | ● | ● | | ● | ● | ● | ● | | ● | ● | ● | ● | | ● | ● | ● | ● | ● | | ● | ● | ● | ● | ● | ● | ● | ● | ● | ● | ● | ● |
| WELL NATURAL HEALTH CENTRE (HM21140) | ● | ● | ● | ● | ● | ● | ● | ● | ● | ● | ● | ● | ● | ● | ● | ● | ● | ● | ● | | ● | ● | ● | ● | ● | ● | ● | ● | ● | | ● | | ● | ● | ● | | ● | ● | ● | ● | ● | ● | ● | ● | | ● | ● | ● |
| WEST MIDLAND HYPNOTHERAPY (HM21229) | | | | | | | | | | | | ● | | | | | | | | | | | | | | | | | | | | | | | | | | | | | | | | | | | | |
| WESTON, JOHN (HM21278) | | | | | | | | | | | | | ● | | | | ● | | | | | | | | | | | | | | | | | | | | | | | | | | | | | | | |
| WESTWOOD, ANGELA (HM21285) | | | | | | ● | | | | | | | ● | | | | ● | | | | ● | | | | | ● | ● | | | | | | | | | | ● | | ● | | | | ● | | | | | |
| WHITE, SHELLEY (HM21378) | ● | | | | | ● | | | ● | | | ● | ● | ● | | | | | | | ● | | | | | | | | | | | | | | | | | | | | | | | | | | | |
| WHITEHALL, CAROL (HM21385) | | | | | | | | | | | | | | | ● | | | | | | | | | | | | | | | ● | | | | | | | | | | | | | | | | | | |
| WILLOWS CLNC COMP HEALTH CTRE (HM21630) | ● | ● | | | ● | ● | | | ● | ● | ● | ● | ● | ● | ● | | ● | ● | ● | | ● | ● | | ● | ● | ● | ● | ● | ● | ● | ● | ● | | | ● | | ● | ● | ● | ● | ● | ● | ● | | ● | ● | ● | ● |
| WITHYMOOR PHYSIOTHERAPY CLINIC (HM21749) | | | | | | | | | | | | | ● | | | | ● | | | | | | | | | | | | | | | | | | | | | | | | | | | | | | | |
| WOLVERHAMPTON CHINESE MED CTRE (HM21765) | ● | ● | | ● | ● | ● | | | | | | ● | ● | ● | | | ● | | ● | | ● | ● | | ● | | ● | ● | | | | | | ● | | | | ● | ● | ● | | ● | | ● | | | ● | | ● |
| ZEN HEALTH & BEAUTY (HM22099) | | | | | | | | | | | | ● | | | | | ● | | | | | | | | | | | | | | | | | | | | | | | | | | | | | | | |
| **NORFOLK** | | | | | | | | | | | | | | | | | | | | | | | | | | | | | | | | | | | | | | | | | | | | | | | | |
| ALTERNATIVE HEALTH CARE (HM00702) | ● | | | | | | ● | | | | | ● | ● | ● | | | | | | | ● | | | | | | ● | | | | | | ● | | ● | | ● | | | | | | ● | | | | | |
| AMALA CHIROPODY CENTRE (HM00760) | | | | | | | | | | | | ● | | | ● | | | | | | | | | | | | | | | | | ● | | | | | | | | | | | | | ● | | | |
| BODY BEAUTIFUL (HM02576) | ● | | | | | | ● | | | | | ● | ● | | ● | | ● | ● | | | | | | ● | | | | | | | | | | | | | ● | ● | ● | | | | ● | | | ● | | |
| BRUNSWICK PHYSIO (HM03280) | | | | | | | | | | | | | ● | | | | ● | | | | | | | | | | | | | | | | | | | | | | | | | | | | | | | |
| CARSON, KAREN (HM03770) | | | | | | | | | | | | | | | ● | | | ● | | | | | | | | | | | | | | ● | | | | | | | | | | | | | ● | | | |
| CHANDLER, ANN (HM03973) | | | | | | | | | | | | | ● | | | | ● | | | | | | | | | | | ● | | | | | | | | | | | | | | | | | | | | |
| CHASE PARK PRACTICE (HM04060) | | | | | | | | | | | ● | ● | | | | | | | | ● | | | | | | | | | ● | | | | | | | | | | | | | | | | | | | |
| CHIROPODIST (HM04291) | | | | | | | | | | | | | | | ● | | | ● | | | | | | | | | | | | | | ● | | | | | | | | | | | | | ● | | | |
| CHIROPODISTS (HM04297) | | | | | | | | | | | | | | | ● | | | ● | | | | | | | | | | | | | | ● | | | | | | | | | | | | | ● | | | |
| CLASSICAL OSTEOPATH (HM04611) | | | ● | | | | | | | | | ● | ● | ● | | | ● | | | | ● | ● | | ● | | ● | ● | | | | | | | | ● | | ● | | ● | ● | ● | | ● | | | ● | ● | ● |
| COMER OSTEOPATHIC CLINIC (HM04897) | | | | | | | | | | | | | ● | ● | | | ● | | | | | | | ● | | | | | | | ● | | | | ● | | | | | ● | ● | | ● | | | | | |
| COMPLEMENTARY HEALTH CLINIC (HM04926) | ● | ● | | | ● | | | | | | | ● | ● | ● | | | ● | | | | | ● | | ● | | | ● | | | | | | | | ● | | | | | | ● | | ● | | | ● | ● | |
| COTTAGE CHIROPRACTIC CLINIC (HM05217) | | | | | | | | | | | | | ● | | | | ● | | | | | ● | | | | | | | | | | | | | | | ● | | | ● | | | | | | | | |
| COTTAGE CLINIC (HM05220) | ● | | | | | ● | | | ● | ● | | ● | ● | ● | ● | | | ● | | | ● | ● | ● | ● | ● | ● | ● | ● | | | ● | | ● | ● | ● | | ● | ● | ● | ● | ● | ● | ● | | | ● | ● | ● |
| COUNTY HEALTH (HM05259) | ● | ● | ● | | | ● | | | ● | | | ● | ● | ● | | | | | | | ● | ● | | ● | | ● | | ● | | | | | | | ● | | | ● | ● | ● | ● | ● | ● | | | ● | | ● |
| DISS NATURAL HEALTH CLINIC (HM06121) | ● | | | | | ● | | | | | | ● | ● | ● | ● | | ● | ● | | | | | ● | ● | | ● | ● | | | | ● | | | | ● | | ● | ● | ● | ● | ● | | ● | | | ● | ● | ● |
| ELEMENTS OF HEALTH (HM06725) | ● | ● | ● | ● | ● | ● | | ● | ● | ● | ● | ● | ● | ● | ● | | ● | ● | | | ● | ● | ● | ● | ● | ● | ● | ● | ● | | ● | | | | ● | | ● | ● | ● | ● | ● | ● | ● | ● | | ● | ● | ● |
| ELLIS, STEPHEN (HM06772) | | | | | | | | | | | | ● | ● | ● | | | ● | | | | | | | | | | | | | | | | | | | | | | | | | | | | | | | |
| FIRST STEP FOOTCARE (HM07340) | | | | | | | | | | | | | | | ● | | | ● | | | | | | | | | | | | ● | | ● | | | | | | | | | | | | | ● | | | |
| FISHER, JACK E (HM07355) | | | | | | | | | | | | | ● | | | | ● | | | | | | | | | | | | | | | | | | | | | | | | | | | | | | | |
| FORD OSTEOPATHIC CLINIC (HM07521) | | | | | | | | | | | | ● | ● | ● | | | ● | | | | | | | | | | | | | | ● | | | | | | | | | | | | | | | | | |

www.healthmyself.com

# A - C Conditions treated at Practices/Businesses

| Business by County with Reference no. | Acne | Addiction | Adenoids | Aids | Alcoholism | Allergy | Alzheimer's Disease | Amnesia | Anaemia | Angina | Anorexia | Anxiety | Arthritis | Asthma | Athletes Foot | Autism | Back Pain | Bacterial Infections | Baldness | Bereavement | Bladder Problems | Blood Pressure | Boils | Bowel Problems | Breast Problems | Breathing Problems | Bronchitis | Bruising | Bulimia | Bunions | Bursitis | Callices | Cancers | Cataracts | Catarrh | Cerebral Palsy | Circulation Problems | Cold Sores | Colds | Colic | Colitis | Conjunctivitis | Constipation | Convulsions | Corns | Coughs | Cramp | Cystitis |
|---|---|---|---|---|---|---|---|---|---|---|---|---|---|---|---|---|---|---|---|---|---|---|---|---|---|---|---|---|---|---|---|---|---|---|---|---|---|---|---|---|---|---|---|---|---|---|---|---|
| GEARY, A G (HM07951) | | | | | | | | | | | | | | | ● | | | ● | | | | | | | | | | | | | | ● | | | | | | | | | | | | | ● | | | |
| GT YARMOUTH PHYSICAL THERAPY (HM08330) | | | | | | | | | | | | | ● | | | | ● | | | | | | | | | | | | | | ● | | | | | | | | | | | | | | | | | |
| HARGHAM HALL OSTEO PRACTICE (HM08992) | | | | | | | | | | | | | ● | ● | | | ● | | | | | | | ● | | | | | | | ● | | | | | | | | | ● | | | | | | | | |
| HOBSON, L A (HM09865) | | | | | | | | | | | | | | | ● | | | ● | | | | | | | | | | | | | | ● | | | | | | | | | | | | | ● | | | |
| HOMEOPATHIC CLINIC (HM10074) | ● | ● | ● | ● | ● | ● | ● | | ● | ● | ● | ● | ● | ● | ● | ● | ● | ● | ● | | ● | ● | ● | ● | ● | ● | ● | ● | ● | | ● | ● | ● | ● | ● | | ● | ● | ● | ● | ● | ● | ● | ● | ● | ● | ● | ● |
| JAMES, LINDA (HM10890) | | | | | | | | | | | | ● | ● | | | | ● | | | | | | | | | | | | | | | | | | | | | | | | | | | | | | | |
| JESSOP CLINIC (HM11021) | | | | | | | | | | | | | ● | ● | | | ● | | | | | | | | | | | | | | | | | | | | ● | | | | | | | | | | | |
| KING, SIMON (HM11644) | | ● | | | ● | | | ● | ● | ● | ● | ● | | ● | | | | ● | | | ● | ● | | ● | ● | ● | ● | ● | ● | | | ● | | ● | ● | | ● | ● | | ● | ● | ● | ● | | ● | ● | ● | ● |
| MONSON, J L B (HM14076) | | | | | | | | | | | | ● | | | | | | | | | | | | | | | | | | | | | | | | | | | | | | | | | | | | |
| NEW MARKET RD PHYSIO PRACTICE (HM14824) | | | | | | | | | | | | | ● | | | | ● | | | | | | | | | | | ● | | | | | | | | | | | | | | | | | | | | |
| NORFOLK CLINIC (HM14993) | ● | | | | | ● | | | | ● | | ● | ● | ● | ● | | ● | | | | ● | ● | ● | ● | | | ● | | | | | | | | ● | | ● | ● | ● | ● | | ● | ● | | | ● | ● | ● |
| NORFOLK NATURAL HEALTH SERVICE (HM14995) | | | | ● | | ● | | | | | | | ● | ● | | | ● | ● | | | ● | ● | | ● | | ● | | ● | | | | | | | | | ● | | ● | | ● | | ● | | | ● | | ● |
| NORMAN, A J (HM14999) | | | | | | | | | | | | ● | ● | | | | ● | | | | | ● | | | | | | | | | | | | | | | ● | | | ● | | | | | | | | |
| OLIVE GROVE BODY SCIENCE (HM15281) | | | | | | | | | | | | | ● | | ● | | | | | | | | | | | | | | | | | ● | | | | | | | | | | | | | ● | | | |
| PARK PHYSIOTHERAPY (HM15669) | | | | | | | | | | | | | ● | | | | ● | | | | | | | | | | | | | | | | | | | | | | | | | | | | | | | |
| QUEENS SQUARE SURGERY (HM16796) | ● | ● | ● | ● | ● | ● | ● | ● | ● | ● | ● | ● | ● | ● | ● | ● | ● | ● | ● | | ● | ● | ● | ● | ● | ● | ● | ● | ● | | ● | ● | ● | ● | ● | | ● | ● | ● | ● | ● | ● | ● | ● | ● | ● | ● | ● |
| RICHARDSON, ALAN (HM17268) | | | | | | ● | | | | | | ● | ● | | | | ● | | | | | | | | | | | | | | | | | | | | | | | | ● | | ● | | | | | ● |
| RIGBY COURT CLINIC (HM17331) | ● | ● | | | ● | ● | | | ● | | | ● | ● | ● | | | ● | | | | ● | ● | ● | ● | ● | ● | ● | | | | ● | | | | ● | | ● | ● | ● | ● | ● | ● | ● | ● | | ● | ● | ● |
| SHARP, DENISE (HM18307) | | | | | | | | | | ● | | ● | ● | ● | | | ● | | | | | ● | | | | ● | | | | | | | | | ● | | ● | | | | | | ● | | | | ● | |
| SHIATSU CENTRE (HM18453) | | | | | | | | | | | | | ● | ● | | | ● | | | | | | | | | | | | | | | | | | | | | | | | | | | | | | | |
| ST STEPHENS PRACTICE (HM19099) | | | | | | | | | | | | ● | ● | ● | ● | | ● | | | | | | | | | | | | | | | | | | | | | | ● | | | | ● | | | | | ● |
| WATTON PHYSIOTHERAPY CLINIC (HM21033) | | | | | | | | | | | | | ● | | | | ● | | | | | | | | | | | | | | | | | | | | | | | | | | | | | | | |
| WENDY JILLEY - MEDICAL HERB (HM21197) | ● | | | | | ● | | | | ● | | ● | ● | ● | ● | | | ● | | | ● | ● | ● | ● | ● | ● | ● | ● | | | | | | | ● | | ● | ● | ● | ● | ● | | ● | | | ● | ● | ● |
| WOBURN CLINIC (HM21755) | | ● | | | | ● | | | | | | ● | ● | | | | ● | | | | | ● | | ● | | ● | | | | | | | | | | | ● | | | ● | | | ● | | | ● | ● | |
| NORTHAMPTONSHIRE | | | | | | | | | | | | | | | | | | | | | | | | | | | | | | | | | | | | | | | | | | | | | | | | |
| ACUPUNCTURE CLINIC (HM00275) | ● | ● | | | | ● | | | | | ● | ● | ● | ● | | | ● | | | | | | | | | | | | ● | | | | | | | | | | | | | | ● | | | | | |
| ALLEN HINDE - PHYSIOTHERAPIST (HM00598) | | | | | | | | | | | | | ● | | | | ● | | | | | | | | | ● | ● | ● | | | ● | | | | | | | | | | | | | | | ● | ● | |
| ANDREWS, S C (HM00857) | ● | ● | ● | ● | ● | ● | ● | ● | ● | ● | ● | ● | ● | ● | ● | ● | ● | ● | ● | ● | ● | ● | ● | ● | ● | ● | ● | ● | ● | ● | ● | ● | ● | ● | ● | | ● | ● | ● | ● | ● | ● | ● | ● | ● | ● | ● | ● |
| ANDREWS, SIMON C (HM00860) | ● | ● | ● | ● | ● | ● | ● | ● | ● | ● | ● | ● | ● | ● | ● | ● | ● | ● | | | ● | ● | ● | ● | ● | ● | ● | ● | ● | | ● | | ● | ● | ● | | ● | ● | ● | ● | ● | ● | ● | ● | | ● | ● | ● |
| ANNELISE (HM00906) | | | | | | | | | | | | ● | ● | | | | ● | | | | | ● | | ● | | | | | | | | | | | | | | | | | | | | | | | | |
| ARBOURS (HM00965) | | | | | | | | | | | | | ● | | ● | | | ● | | | | | | | | | | | | | | ● | | | | | | | | | | | | | ● | | | |
| C F C M (HM03523) | ● | ● | | | | ● | | | | ● | | ● | ● | ● | | | ● | ● | ● | | ● | ● | ● | ● | ● | ● | ● | ● | | | ● | | | ● | ● | | ● | ● | ● | ● | ● | ● | ● | ● | | ● | ● | ● |
| CALLIS THERAPY FOUNDATION (HM03555) | ● | ● | ● | ● | ● | ● | ● | ● | ● | ● | ● | ● | ● | ● | ● | ● | ● | ● | ● | | ● | ● | ● | ● | ● | ● | ● | ● | ● | | ● | ● | ● | ● | ● | | ● | ● | ● | ● | ● | ● | ● | ● | ● | ● | ● | ● |
| CLINTON HOUSE CHIROPODY (HM04719) | | | | | | | | | | | | | | | ● | | | ● | | | | | | | | | | | | | | ● | | | | | | | | | | | | | ● | | | |

# A - C Conditions treated at Practices/Businesses

Business by County with Reference no.

| Business | Acne | Addiction | Adenoids | Aids | Alcoholism | Allergy | Alzheimer's Disease | Amnesia | Anaemia | Angina | Anorexia | Anxiety | Arthritis | Asthma | Athletes Foot | Autism |
|---|---|---|---|---|---|---|---|---|---|---|---|---|---|---|---|---|
| DAVENTRY NATUREWORKS (HM05768) | | | | | | ● | | | | | | | ● | | | |
| DEVON PARADE CLINIC (HM06041) | ● | ● | ● | | ● | | | | | | ● | ● | ● | ● | ● | |
| ESSERY, TRICIA (HM06933) | | | | | | | | | | | | ● | ● | ● | | |
| GARVEY-WILLIAMS, RICHARD (HM07915) | | | | | | ● | ● | | | | | ● | ● | ● | | |
| GARVEY-WILLIAMS, RICHARD (HM07914) | | | | | | | | | | | | | ● | | | |
| GEDDES, PIPPA (HM07955) | ● | | ● | | | ● | | | | | ● | ● | ● | ● | ● | |
| JUST RELAX (HM11285) | ● | ● | ● | | | ● | | | | ● | | ● | ● | ● | | |
| LEE, STEPHEN (HM12146) | ● | | | | | ● | | | | | | ● | ● | ● | | |
| MAPLE TREE OSTEO PRACTICE (HM13061) | | | | | | | | | | ● | | ● | ● | ● | | |
| MOTLEY, MAUREEN (HM14277) | ● | | | | | | ● | | | | | | ● | | | |
| NENE VALLEY COMP THERAPIES (HM14785) | | | | | | | | | | | | ● | ● | ● | | |
| NORTHAMPTON CHIROPRACTIC (HM15051) | | | | | | | | | | | | | ● | | | |
| NORTHAMPTON CLINIC (HM15052) | | | | | | | | | | | | ● | | | | |
| REFLEXOLOGY CLINIC (HM17085) | ● | ● | ● | | ● | ● | | ● | ● | ● | ● | ● | ● | ● | | |
| TOWCESTER CHIROPRACTIC CLINIC (HM20194) | | | | | | | | | | | | | | | | |
| **NORTHUMBERLAND** | | | | | | | | | | | | | | | | |
| ACUCARE (HM00209) | ● | ● | | | | ● | | | | | ● | ● | ● | ● | | |
| AYRES, ELIZABETH (HM01433) | | | | | | | | | | | | | | | ● | |
| BOWEN TECHNIQUE STUDIO (HM02775) | | | | | | | | | | | | | | | | |
| EVISON, ALEX (HM07012) | | ● | | | | | | | | | | ● | | | | |
| FORSTER, LINDA (HM07570) | | | | | | | | | | | ● | | | | | |
| GREEN BATT PHYSIOTHERAPY (HM08434) | | | | | | | | | | | | | | | | |
| KI CLINIC (HM11591) | ● | ● | | | | ● | | | | | | ● | ● | ● | ● | |
| MEAD, BRUCE (HM13626) | | | | | | | | | | | | | | | ● | |
| PHYSIOTHERAPY & SPORTS CLINIC (HM16223) | | | | | | | | | | | | | ● | | | |
| **NOTTINGHAMSHIRE** | | | | | | | | | | | | | | | | |
| ACUPUNCTURE CLINIC (HM00264) | ● | | | | | ● | | | | | ● | ● | ● | | | |
| BEESTON PHYSIO & SPORTS CLNC (HM02060) | | | | | | | | | | | | | ● | | | |
| BOND, DIANORA (HM02669) | ● | | | | | | | | | | | | ● | ● | | |
| BRAHMA KUMARIS WORLD (HM02891) | | | | | | | | | | | | ● | | | | |
| BROADLEY, RICHARD (HM03116) | | | | | | | | | | | | | | | | |
| BULLEN-SPICER ASSOCIATES (HM03342) | | ● | | | ● | | | | | | ● | ● | | | | ● |
| CARITAS NATURAL HEALTH CLINIC (HM03688) | | | | | | | | | | | | ● | ● | ● | | |
| CENTRE FOR TRANSFORMATION (HM03921) | ● | | | | | ● | | | ● | ● | ● | ● | ● | ● | ● | ● |

| Business | Back Pain | Bacterial Infections | Baldness | Bereavement | Bladder Problems | Blood Pressure | Boils | Bowel Problems | Breast Problems | Breathing Problems | Bronchitis | Bruising | Bulimia | Bunions | Bursitis | Callices |
|---|---|---|---|---|---|---|---|---|---|---|---|---|---|---|---|---|
| DAVENTRY NATUREWORKS (HM05768) | ● | | | | | | | | | | | ● | | | | |
| DEVON PARADE CLINIC (HM06041) | ● | | | | ● | | | ● | | ● | | ● | | | ● | ● |
| ESSERY, TRICIA (HM06933) | | | | | | ● | | | | ● | | | | | | |
| GARVEY-WILLIAMS, RICHARD (HM07915) | ● | | | | | ● | | ● | | | | | | | | |
| GARVEY-WILLIAMS, RICHARD (HM07914) | ● | | | | | | | | | | | | | | | |
| GEDDES, PIPPA (HM07955) | ● | ● | | | ● | ● | | ● | ● | ● | ● | | | | ● | |
| JUST RELAX (HM11285) | ● | ● | | | ● | ● | | ● | | ● | | | | | | |
| LEE, STEPHEN (HM12146) | ● | | | | | | | | | | ● | | | | | |
| MAPLE TREE OSTEO PRACTICE (HM13061) | ● | | | | ● | | | ● | | ● | | | | | ● | |
| MOTLEY, MAUREEN (HM14277) | | | | | | | | | | | | | | | | |
| NENE VALLEY COMP THERAPIES (HM14785) | ● | | | | | | | | | ● | | | | | | |
| NORTHAMPTON CHIROPRACTIC (HM15051) | ● | | | | | ● | | | | | | | | | | |
| NORTHAMPTON CLINIC (HM15052) | | | | | | | | | | | | | | | | |
| REFLEXOLOGY CLINIC (HM17085) | ● | ● | ● | | ● | ● | | ● | ● | ● | ● | ● | ● | | | |
| TOWCESTER CHIROPRACTIC CLINIC (HM20194) | ● | | | | | | | | | | | | | | | |
| **NORTHUMBERLAND** | | | | | | | | | | | | | | | | |
| ACUCARE (HM00209) | ● | | | | | | | | | | | | | | | |
| AYRES, ELIZABETH (HM01433) | | ● | | | | | | | | | | | | | | ● |
| BOWEN TECHNIQUE STUDIO (HM02775) | ● | | | | | | | | | | | | | | | |
| EVISON, ALEX (HM07012) | | | | | | ● | | ● | | | | | | | | |
| FORSTER, LINDA (HM07570) | | | | | | | | | | | | | ● | | | |
| GREEN BATT PHYSIOTHERAPY (HM08434) | ● | | | | | | | | | ● | ● | ● | | | ● | |
| KI CLINIC (HM11591) | ● | ● | | | | ● | | ● | | ● | ● | | | | | |
| MEAD, BRUCE (HM13626) | | ● | | | | | | | | | | | | | | ● |
| PHYSIOTHERAPY & SPORTS CLINIC (HM16223) | ● | | | | | | | | | | | ● | | | | |
| **NOTTINGHAMSHIRE** | | | | | | | | | | | | | | | | |
| ACUPUNCTURE CLINIC (HM00264) | ● | | | | | | | | | | | | | | | |
| BEESTON PHYSIO & SPORTS CLNC (HM02060) | ● | | | | | | | | | | | | | | | |
| BOND, DIANORA (HM02669) | ● | | | | ● | | | | | | ● | ● | | | ● | |
| BRAHMA KUMARIS WORLD (HM02891) | | | | | | | | | | | | | | | | |
| BROADLEY, RICHARD (HM03116) | | | | ● | | | | | | | | | | | | |
| BULLEN-SPICER ASSOCIATES (HM03342) | | | | | | ● | | ● | | ● | | | ● | | | |
| CARITAS NATURAL HEALTH CLINIC (HM03688) | ● | | | | ● | | | ● | | ● | | | | | | |
| CENTRE FOR TRANSFORMATION (HM03921) | ● | | | | ● | | | ● | ● | ● | ● | ● | ● | | ● | |

| Business | Cancers | Cataracts | Catarrh | Cerebral Palsy | Circulation Problems | Cold Sores | Colds | Colic | Colitis | Conjunctivitis | Constipation | Convulsions | Corns | Coughs | Cramp | Cystitis |
|---|---|---|---|---|---|---|---|---|---|---|---|---|---|---|---|---|
| DAVENTRY NATUREWORKS (HM05768) | | | | | | | | | | | ● | | | | | |
| DEVON PARADE CLINIC (HM06041) | | | | | ● | | | ● | | | ● | | ● | | ● | |
| ESSERY, TRICIA (HM06933) | | | ● | | ● | | | | | | ● | | | | ● | |
| GARVEY-WILLIAMS, RICHARD (HM07915) | | | | | | | ● | ● | ● | | ● | | | | ● | |
| GARVEY-WILLIAMS, RICHARD (HM07914) | | | | | | | | | | | ● | | | | ● | |
| GEDDES, PIPPA (HM07955) | | | ● | | ● | ● | ● | ● | ● | ● | ● | | | ● | ● | ● |
| JUST RELAX (HM11285) | ● | ● | ● | | ● | | ● | | ● | ● | ● | | | ● | | ● |
| LEE, STEPHEN (HM12146) | | | | | | | | | ● | | ● | | | ● | | ● |
| MAPLE TREE OSTEO PRACTICE (HM13061) | | | | | ● | | ● | ● | ● | | | | | | | ● |
| MOTLEY, MAUREEN (HM14277) | | | | | | | | | | | | | | | | |
| NENE VALLEY COMP THERAPIES (HM14785) | | | ● | | ● | | | | | | ● | | | | | |
| NORTHAMPTON CHIROPRACTIC (HM15051) | | | | | | | | ● | | | | | | | | |
| NORTHAMPTON CLINIC (HM15052) | | | | | | | | | | | | | | | | |
| REFLEXOLOGY CLINIC (HM17085) | ● | | ● | | ● | ● | ● | ● | ● | ● | ● | ● | | ● | ● | ● |
| TOWCESTER CHIROPRACTIC CLINIC (HM20194) | | | | | | | | | | | | | | | | |
| **NORTHUMBERLAND** | | | | | | | | | | | | | | | | |
| ACUCARE (HM00209) | | | | | | | | | | | ● | | | | | |
| AYRES, ELIZABETH (HM01433) | | | | | | | | | | | | | ● | | | |
| BOWEN TECHNIQUE STUDIO (HM02775) | | | | | | | | | | | | | | | | |
| EVISON, ALEX (HM07012) | | | | | | | | | | | | | | | | |
| FORSTER, LINDA (HM07570) | | | | | | | | | | | | | | | | |
| GREEN BATT PHYSIOTHERAPY (HM08434) | | | | | | | | | | | | | | | | |
| KI CLINIC (HM11591) | ● | | ● | | ● | ● | ● | ● | ● | ● | ● | | | ● | ● | ● |
| MEAD, BRUCE (HM13626) | | | | | | | | | | | | | ● | | | |
| PHYSIOTHERAPY & SPORTS CLINIC (HM16223) | | | | | | | | | | | | | | | ● | |
| **NOTTINGHAMSHIRE** | | | | | | | | | | | | | | | | |
| ACUPUNCTURE CLINIC (HM00264) | | | | | | | | | | | ● | | | | | |
| BEESTON PHYSIO & SPORTS CLNC (HM02060) | | | | | | | | | | | | | | | | |
| BOND, DIANORA (HM02669) | | | | | ● | | | | | | | | | | | |
| BRAHMA KUMARIS WORLD (HM02891) | | | | | | | | | | | | | | | | |
| BROADLEY, RICHARD (HM03116) | | | | | | | | | | | | | | | | |
| BULLEN-SPICER ASSOCIATES (HM03342) | | | | | | | | | | | | | | | | |
| CARITAS NATURAL HEALTH CLINIC (HM03688) | | | | | ● | | | | | | | | | | ● | |
| CENTRE FOR TRANSFORMATION (HM03921) | ● | ● | ● | | ● | ● | ● | ● | ● | ● | ● | ● | | ● | ● | ● |

# A - C Conditions treated at Practices/Businesses

| Business by County with Reference no. | Acne | Addiction | Adenoids | Aids | Alcoholism | Allergy | Alzheimer's Disease | Amnesia | Anaemia | Angina | Anorexia | Anxiety | Arthritis | Asthma | Athletes Foot | Autism |
|---|---|---|---|---|---|---|---|---|---|---|---|---|---|---|---|---|
| DEAN, MARTIN (HM05942) | | | | | | | | | | | | ● | ● | ● | | |
| EAST BRIDGEFORD PHYSIO NEEDS (HM06510) | | | | | | | | | | | | | ● | | | |
| GOTHAM VILLAGE PHSYO CLINIC (HM08308) | | | | | | | | | | | | | ● | | | |
| GREENWOOD, JULIA (HM08507) | | | | | | | | | | | | | | | ● | |
| HANDS ON HEALTH (HM08912) | | | | | | | | | | | | ● | ● | ● | | |
| IMPACT PHYSIO & SPORTS INJURIES (HM10590) | | | | | | | | | | | | | ● | | | |
| LIGHT UP YOUR LIFE (HM12370) | | | | | | | | | | | | | | | | |
| MANSFIELD CHIROPODY (HM13046) | | | | | | | | | | | | | | | ● | |
| MORLEY-KIRK, JOHN (HM14188) | ● | | | | | ● | | | | ● | ● | ● | ● | ● | | |
| NATURAL HEALTH (HM14554) | ● | ● | | | ● | ● | | ● | ● | ● | ● | ● | ● | ● | ● | |
| NATURAL THERAPY CLINIC (HM14654) | ● | ● | ● | | | ● | | | ● | ● | ● | ● | ● | ● | ● | |
| NOTTINGHAM M S THERAPY CTRE (HM15083) | | | | | | | | | | ● | | ● | ● | ● | | |
| NOTTINGHAM NATURAL HEALTH CTRE (HM15084) | ● | ● | ● | ● | ● | ● | ● | ● | ● | ● | ● | ● | ● | ● | ● | ● |
| NOTTINGHAM SPORTS INJURY (HM15085) | | | | | | | | | | | | | ● | | | |
| OPTIMUM HEALTH (HM15348) | ● | ● | ● | ● | ● | ● | ● | ● | ● | ● | ● | ● | ● | ● | ● | ● |
| PARKSIDE STRESS MANAGEMENT (HM15722) | ● | ● | | | | ● | | | | | | | ● | ● | ● | |
| PHYSIO DIRECT (HM16197) | | | | | | | | | | | | | ● | | | |
| PHYSIODIRECT (HM16214) | | | | | | | | | | | | | ● | | | |
| PLAINS PHYSIO & BACK PAIN (HM16355) | | | | | | | | | | | | | ● | | | |
| RETFORD CHIROPRACTIC CLINIC (HM17200) | | | | | | ● | | | | | | ● | ● | ● | | |
| SEVENTHMOON NATURAL THRPY CTRE (HM18247) | | | | | | | | | | | | ● | | | | |
| SHEER TECHNIQUE (HM18368) | ● | ● | | | | ● | | ● | ● | | ● | ● | ● | ● | ● | |
| SHERWOOD PSYCHO TRAINING INS (HM18441) | | ● | | | ● | | | | | | ● | ● | | | | |
| SKELTON, CATHERINE () | ● | ● | ● | | | ● | ● | | ● | | | ● | ● | ● | ● | ● |
| SOUTHWELL ACUPUNCTURE CLINIC (HM18948) | | | | | | ● | | | | ● | | ● | ● | ● | | |
| TODD, S J (HM20108) | | | | | | ● | | | ● | ● | | ● | ● | ● | ● | |
| TOMLIN, NORMAN (HM20131) | | | | | | | | | | | | | | | | |
| TRADITIONAL ACUPUNCTURIST (HM20222) | | | | | | ● | | | ● | | | ● | ● | ● | | |
| VAUGHTON, NORMAN D (HM20601) | | | | | | | | | | | ● | ● | | | | |
| WELLBEING CENTRE (HM21149) | | | | | | | | | | | | ● | | | | |
| OXFORDSHIRE | | | | | | | | | | | | | | | | |
| ASHCROFT CLINIC (HM01198) | | | | | | ● | | | | | | | ● | | | |
| BACK IN LINE (HM01481) | | | | | | | | | | | | | ● | | | |
| BACK TO NORMAL CHIRO CLINIC (HM01522) | | | | | | | | | | | | | ● | | | |

| Business by County with Reference no. | Back Pain | Bacterial Infections | Baldness | Bereavement | Bladder Problems | Blood Pressure | Boils | Bowel Problems | Breast Problems | Breathing Problems | Bronchitis | Bruising | Bulimia | Bunions | Bursitis | Callices |
|---|---|---|---|---|---|---|---|---|---|---|---|---|---|---|---|---|
| DEAN, MARTIN (HM05942) | ● | | | | ● | ● | | ● | | ● | | | | | | |
| EAST BRIDGEFORD PHYSIO NEEDS (HM06510) | ● | | | | | | | | | | | | | | | |
| GOTHAM VILLAGE PHSYO CLINIC (HM08308) | ● | | | | | | | | | | | | | | | |
| GREENWOOD, JULIA (HM08507) | | | | | | | | | | | | | | | | |
| HANDS ON HEALTH (HM08912) | ● | | | | ● | | | ● | | ● | | | | | | |
| IMPACT PHYSIO & SPORTS INJURIES (HM10590) | ● | | | | | | | | | | | | | | | |
| LIGHT UP YOUR LIFE (HM12370) | ● | | | | | ● | | ● | ● | ● | ● | ● | | | | |
| MANSFIELD CHIROPODY (HM13046) | | ● | | | | | | | | | | | | | | ● |
| MORLEY-KIRK, JOHN (HM14188) | ● | ● | | | ● | ● | | ● | ● | ● | ● | ● | ● | | ● | |
| NATURAL HEALTH (HM14554) | ● | ● | ● | | ● | ● | ● | ● | ● | ● | ● | ● | ● | | ● | |
| NATURAL THERAPY CLINIC (HM14654) | ● | ● | | | ● | ● | ● | ● | ● | ● | ● | ● | ● | | ● | |
| NOTTINGHAM M S THERAPY CTRE (HM15083) | ● | | | | ● | | | | | | | | | | | |
| NOTTINGHAM NATURAL HEALTH CTRE (HM15084) | ● | ● | ● | | ● | ● | ● | ● | ● | ● | ● | ● | ● | | ● | ● |
| NOTTINGHAM SPORTS INJURY (HM15085) | ● | | | | | | | | | | | | | | | |
| OPTIMUM HEALTH (HM15348) | ● | ● | ● | | ● | ● | ● | ● | ● | ● | ● | ● | ● | | ● | ● |
| PARKSIDE STRESS MANAGEMENT (HM15722) | ● | ● | | | ● | ● | ● | ● | | ● | ● | ● | ● | | | |
| PHYSIO DIRECT (HM16197) | ● | | | | | | | | | | | ● | | | | |
| PHYSIODIRECT (HM16214) | ● | | | | | | | | | | | ● | | | | |
| PLAINS PHYSIO & BACK PAIN (HM16355) | ● | | | | | | | | | | | ● | | | | |
| RETFORD CHIROPRACTIC CLINIC (HM17200) | ● | | | | | ● | | ● | | | | | | | ● | |
| SEVENTHMOON NATURAL THRPY CTRE (HM18247) | ● | | | | ● | ● | | ● | | ● | | | | | | |
| SHEER TECHNIQUE (HM18368) | ● | ● | | | ● | ● | ● | ● | ● | ● | ● | ● | ● | | | |
| SHERWOOD PSYCHO TRAINING INS (HM18441) | | | | | | | | | | | | | ● | | | |
| SKELTON, CATHERINE () | ● | ● | | | ● | ● | ● | ● | ● | ● | ● | | | | | |
| SOUTHWELL ACUPUNCTURE CLINIC (HM18948) | ● | | | | ● | ● | | ● | | ● | ● | ● | | | | |
| TODD, S J (HM20108) | ● | ● | | | ● | ● | | ● | ● | ● | ● | | | | ● | |
| TOMLIN, NORMAN (HM20131) | ● | | | | | | | | | | | | | | | |
| TRADITIONAL ACUPUNCTURIST (HM20222) | ● | | | | ● | | | ● | | ● | ● | | | | | |
| VAUGHTON, NORMAN D (HM20601) | | | | ● | | | | ● | | ● | | | ● | | | |
| WELLBEING CENTRE (HM21149) | | | | | | | | | | | | | | | | |
| OXFORDSHIRE | | | | | | | | | | | | | | | | |
| ASHCROFT CLINIC (HM01198) | ● | | | | | | | ● | | | | | | | | |
| BACK IN LINE (HM01481) | ● | | | | | | | | | | | | | | | |
| BACK TO NORMAL CHIRO CLINIC (HM01522) | ● | | | | | | | | | | | | | | | |

| Business by County with Reference no. | Cancers | Cataracts | Catarrh | Cerebral Palsy | Circulation Problems | Cold Sores | Colds | Colic | Colitis | Conjunctivitis | Constipation | Convulsions | Corns | Coughs | Cramp | Cystitis |
|---|---|---|---|---|---|---|---|---|---|---|---|---|---|---|---|---|
| DEAN, MARTIN (HM05942) | | | ● | | | | ● | | ● | | ● | | | ● | ● | ● |
| EAST BRIDGEFORD PHYSIO NEEDS (HM06510) | | | | | | | | | | | | | | | | |
| GOTHAM VILLAGE PHSYO CLINIC (HM08308) | | | | | | | | | | | | | | | | |
| GREENWOOD, JULIA (HM08507) | | | | | | | | | | | | | | | | |
| HANDS ON HEALTH (HM08912) | | | | | ● | | | | | | | | | | ● | |
| IMPACT PHYSIO & SPORTS INJURIES (HM10590) | | | | | | | | | | | | | | | | |
| LIGHT UP YOUR LIFE (HM12370) | ● | | ● | | ● | | | ● | ● | | ● | | | ● | ● | |
| MANSFIELD CHIROPODY (HM13046) | | | | | | | | | | | | | ● | | | |
| MORLEY-KIRK, JOHN (HM14188) | ● | | ● | | ● | | | | ● | ● | ● | | | ● | ● | ● |
| NATURAL HEALTH (HM14554) | | ● | ● | | ● | ● | ● | ● | ● | ● | ● | ● | | ● | ● | ● |
| NATURAL THERAPY CLINIC (HM14654) | | | ● | | ● | ● | ● | ● | ● | ● | ● | | | ● | ● | ● |
| NOTTINGHAM M S THERAPY CTRE (HM15083) | | | ● | | ● | | | | | | ● | | | | | |
| NOTTINGHAM NATURAL HEALTH CTRE (HM15084) | ● | ● | ● | | ● | ● | ● | ● | ● | ● | ● | ● | ● | ● | ● | ● |
| NOTTINGHAM SPORTS INJURY (HM15085) | | | | | | | | | | | | | | | | |
| OPTIMUM HEALTH (HM15348) | ● | ● | ● | | ● | ● | ● | ● | ● | ● | ● | ● | ● | ● | ● | ● |
| PARKSIDE STRESS MANAGEMENT (HM15722) | | | ● | | ● | ● | ● | ● | ● | ● | ● | | | ● | ● | ● |
| PHYSIO DIRECT (HM16197) | | | | | | | | | | | | | | | | |
| PHYSIODIRECT (HM16214) | | | | | | | | | | | | | | | | |
| PLAINS PHYSIO & BACK PAIN (HM16355) | | | | | | | | | | | | | | | | |
| RETFORD CHIROPRACTIC CLINIC (HM17200) | | | ● | | ● | | | ● | ● | | ● | | | | | |
| SEVENTHMOON NATURAL THRPY CTRE (HM18247) | | | | | ● | ● | | | | | | | | | | ● |
| SHEER TECHNIQUE (HM18368) | ● | | ● | | ● | ● | ● | ● | ● | ● | ● | | | ● | ● | ● |
| SHERWOOD PSYCHO TRAINING INS (HM18441) | | | | | | | | | | | | | | | | |
| SKELTON, CATHERINE () | | | ● | | ● | ● | ● | ● | ● | ● | ● | | | ● | ● | ● |
| SOUTHWELL ACUPUNCTURE CLINIC (HM18948) | | | ● | | ● | | ● | ● | | | ● | | | ● | ● | ● |
| TODD, S J (HM20108) | ● | | ● | | ● | | | | ● | | ● | | | | ● | ● |
| TOMLIN, NORMAN (HM20131) | | | | | | | | | | | ● | | | | | |
| TRADITIONAL ACUPUNCTURIST (HM20222) | | | ● | | ● | | ● | | | ● | ● | | | ● | | ● |
| VAUGHTON, NORMAN D (HM20601) | | | | | | | | | | | | | | | | |
| WELLBEING CENTRE (HM21149) | | | | | | | | | | | | | | | | |
| OXFORDSHIRE | | | | | | | | | | | | | | | | |
| ASHCROFT CLINIC (HM01198) | | | | | ● | | | | ● | | ● | | | | | |
| BACK IN LINE (HM01481) | | | | | ● | | | ● | | | | | | | | |
| BACK TO NORMAL CHIRO CLINIC (HM01522) | | | | | ● | | | | | | | | | | ● | |

# A - C Conditions treated at Practices/Businesses

Business by County with Reference no.

| Business by County with Reference no. | Acne | Addiction | Adenoids | Aids | Alcoholism | Allergy | Alzheimer's Disease | Amnesia | Anaemia | Angina | Anorexia | Anxiety | Arthritis | Asthma | Athletes Foot | Autism |
|---|---|---|---|---|---|---|---|---|---|---|---|---|---|---|---|---|
| BLISS REMEDIES (HM02508) | | | | | | | | | | ● | | ● | ● | ● | ● | |
| COOPER, STEPHEN (HM05128) | | | | | | | | | | | | ● | ● | ● | | |
| CORRIE REIKI HEALING (HM05192) | ● | | | | | | | | | | | | | | | |
| COTTAGE CLINIC (HM05221) | | | | | | | | | | | | ● | | | | |
| EDULJEE, STELLA (HM06638) | | | | | | | | | | | | ● | ● | ● | | ● |
| FEET FIRST (HM07179) | | | | | | | | | | | | ● | ● | ● | ● | ● |
| FYSON, MELANIE (HM07806) | ● | | | | | ● | | | ● | | | ● | ● | ● | ● | |
| HANDS ON THERAPY (HM08915) | | | | | | | | | | | | | | | | |
| HELIX HOUSE (HM09522) | | | | | | | | | | | | | ● | ● | | |
| HUDSON, EMMA (HM10311) | | | | | | | | | | | | | | ● | | |
| HYPNOTHERAPY CENTRE (HM10516) | | ● | | | ● | | | ● | | | | ● | | | | |
| KIDLINGTON CHIROPRACTIC (HM11594) | | | | | | | | | | | | | ● | | | |
| KIDLINGTON HERBAL PRACTICE (HM11595) | ● | | | | | ● | | ● | | ● | ● | ● | ● | ● | ● | |
| KIDLINGTON OSTEO PRACTICE (HM11596) | | | | | | | | | | | | | | | | |
| MARRIOTT, HUGH (HM13138) | | | | | | | | | | | | | | | | |
| MIDSUMMER COTTAGE CLINIC (HM13845) | ● | | | | | | | | ● | ● | ● | ● | ● | ● | ● | |
| O'BRIEN, FRANCES (HM15179) | ● | ● | | | | ● | | | | | | ● | ● | | | |
| O'DONNELL, ELSPETH (HM15225) | | | | | | | | | | | | | | | | |
| OXFORD NUTRITION & ALLRGY CTRE (HM15541) | ● | ● | | | ● | ● | ● | | ● | | ● | ● | ● | ● | ● | |
| OXFORD TRANSCENDTL MEDITA CTRE (HM15544) | ● | ● | | | ● | ● | | | | ● | | ● | ● | ● | | |
| PARSONS STREET CLINIC (HM15747) | | ● | | | ● | ● | | | | | | ● | ● | | | |
| PLESTED, JOHN (HM16368) | | | | | | | | | | | | | ● | | | |
| POLLOCK, SUSAN (HM16418) | ● | ● | | | | ● | | | | | | ● | ● | ● | ● | |
| SIDEBOTTOM, MARGARET (HM18527) | | | | | | | | | | | | | ● | | | |
| SUMMERTON CLINIC (HM19498) | ● | | ● | | | ● | | | | ● | | ● | ● | ● | ● | |
| TOUCH OF NATURE (HM20188) | | | | | | | | | | | | | ● | | | |
| TWINE, I E (HM20453) | ● | ● | | | | ● | | ● | | ● | ● | ● | ● | ● | | |
| WANTAGE NATURAL HEALTH CENTRE (HM20891) | ● | ● | ● | ● | ● | ● | ● | ● | ● | ● | ● | ● | ● | ● | ● | ● |
| WANTAGE OSTEOPATHIC PRACTICE (HM20892) | | | | | | | | | | | | | ● | ● | | |
| WHEATLEY COMP THERAPY (HM21308) | ● | | | | | ● | | | | | | ● | | | | |
| WITNEY CHIROPRACTIC/CHIROPODY (HM21750) | | | | | | | | | | | | | ● | | | |
| WITNEY NATURAL HEALTH CLINIC (HM21751) | ● | ● | ● | ● | ● | ● | | | ● | ● | ● | ● | ● | ● | ● | ● |
| **SHROPSHIRE** | | | | | | | | | | | | | | | | |
| ACUMEDIC (HM00218) | ● | ● | | | | ● | | | | | ● | ● | ● | ● | | |

| Business by County with Reference no. | Back Pain | Bacterial Infections | Baldness | Bereavement | Bladder Problems | Blood Pressure | Boils | Bowel Problems | Breast Problems | Breathing Problems | Bronchitis | Bruising | Bulimia | Bunions | Bursitis | Callices |
|---|---|---|---|---|---|---|---|---|---|---|---|---|---|---|---|---|
| BLISS REMEDIES (HM02508) | ● | | | | ● | | | | | ● | | | | | | |
| COOPER, STEPHEN (HM05128) | ● | | | | | ● | | | | ● | | | | | | |
| CORRIE REIKI HEALING (HM05192) | | | | | | | | | | | | | | | | |
| COTTAGE CLINIC (HM05221) | ● | | | | | | | | | | | | | | | |
| EDULJEE, STELLA (HM06638) | ● | | | | ● | | | ● | ● | ● | | | | | | |
| FEET FIRST (HM07179) | ● | | | | ● | ● | | ● | | | | | | | ● | |
| FYSON, MELANIE (HM07806) | | | | | ● | ● | | | | | | ● | | | | |
| HANDS ON THERAPY (HM08915) | | | | | | | | | | | | | | | | |
| HELIX HOUSE (HM09522) | ● | | | | ● | | | | | ● | | | | | | |
| HUDSON, EMMA (HM10311) | ● | | | | | | | | | | | | | | ● | |
| HYPNOTHERAPY CENTRE (HM10516) | | | | | | | | | | | | | ● | | | |
| KIDLINGTON CHIROPRACTIC (HM11594) | ● | | | | | ● | | | | ● | | | | | | |
| KIDLINGTON HERBAL PRACTICE (HM11595) | ● | ● | | | ● | ● | ● | ● | ● | ● | ● | ● | | | | |
| KIDLINGTON OSTEO PRACTICE (HM11596) | ● | | | | | | | | | | | ● | | | | |
| MARRIOTT, HUGH (HM13138) | ● | | | | | | | | | ● | | | | | | |
| MIDSUMMER COTTAGE CLINIC (HM13845) | ● | | | | ● | ● | ● | ● | ● | ● | ● | ● | ● | | ● | |
| O'BRIEN, FRANCES (HM15179) | ● | | | | | | | | | | | | ● | | | |
| O'DONNELL, ELSPETH (HM15225) | ● | | | | | | | | | | | ● | | | | |
| OXFORD NUTRITION & ALLRGY CTRE (HM15541) | | ● | ● | | ● | ● | ● | ● | ● | | | | ● | | | |
| OXFORD TRANSCENDTL MEDITA CTRE (HM15544) | | | | | | ● | | ● | | ● | | | | | | |
| PARSONS STREET CLINIC (HM15747) | ● | | | | | | | | | | | | | | | |
| PLESTED, JOHN (HM16368) | ● | | | | | | | | | | | | | | | |
| POLLOCK, SUSAN (HM16418) | | ● | | | | | | | | | | | | | | |
| SIDEBOTTOM, MARGARET (HM18527) | ● | | | | | | | | | | | | | | | |
| SUMMERTON CLINIC (HM19498) | | ● | | | ● | ● | ● | ● | ● | ● | ● | ● | | | | |
| TOUCH OF NATURE (HM20188) | ● | | | | | | | | | | | | | | | |
| TWINE, I E (HM20453) | ● | | | | | ● | | | | | | | ● | | | |
| WANTAGE NATURAL HEALTH CENTRE (HM20891) | ● | ● | ● | | ● | ● | ● | ● | ● | ● | ● | ● | ● | | ● | |
| WANTAGE OSTEOPATHIC PRACTICE (HM20892) | ● | | | | | | | ● | | | | | | | ● | |
| WHEATLEY COMP THERAPY (HM21308) | ● | | | | | | ● | | | | | | | | | |
| WITNEY CHIROPRACTIC/CHIROPODY (HM21750) | ● | | | | | | | | | | | | | | | |
| WITNEY NATURAL HEALTH CLINIC (HM21751) | ● | ● | ● | | ● | ● | ● | ● | ● | ● | ● | ● | ● | | ● | |
| **SHROPSHIRE** | | | | | | | | | | | | | | | | |
| ACUMEDIC (HM00218) | ● | | | | ● | ● | | ● | | | | | | | | |

| Business by County with Reference no. | Cancers | Cataracts | Catarrh | Cerebral Palsy | Circulation Problems | Cold Sores | Colds | Colic | Colitis | Conjunctivitis | Constipation | Convulsions | Corns | Coughs | Cramp | Cystitis |
|---|---|---|---|---|---|---|---|---|---|---|---|---|---|---|---|---|
| BLISS REMEDIES (HM02508) | ● | | | | | | ● | | | | | | | ● | | |
| COOPER, STEPHEN (HM05128) | | | | | ● | | | | | | | | | | | |
| CORRIE REIKI HEALING (HM05192) | | | | | | | | | | | | | | | | |
| COTTAGE CLINIC (HM05221) | | | | | | | | | | | ● | | | | ● | |
| EDULJEE, STELLA (HM06638) | | | ● | | ● | | | | | | ● | | | | | |
| FEET FIRST (HM07179) | ● | | ● | | ● | | ● | ● | | ● | ● | | | ● | | ● |
| FYSON, MELANIE (HM07806) | | | ● | | ● | ● | ● | ● | ● | ● | ● | | | ● | ● | ● |
| HANDS ON THERAPY (HM08915) | | | | | ● | | | | | | | | | | | |
| HELIX HOUSE (HM09522) | | | | | | | | | | | | | | | | |
| HUDSON, EMMA (HM10311) | | | | | | | | | | | | | | | | |
| HYPNOTHERAPY CENTRE (HM10516) | | | | | | | | | | | | | | | ● | |
| KIDLINGTON CHIROPRACTIC (HM11594) | | | | | | | | ● | | | | | | | | |
| KIDLINGTON HERBAL PRACTICE (HM11595) | | | ● | | ● | | ● | ● | ● | | ● | | | ● | ● | ● |
| KIDLINGTON OSTEO PRACTICE (HM11596) | | | | | | | | | | | ● | | | | ● | |
| MARRIOTT, HUGH (HM13138) | | | | | | | | | | | | | | | | |
| MIDSUMMER COTTAGE CLINIC (HM13845) | ● | ● | | | ● | ● | ● | ● | ● | ● | ● | | | ● | ● | ● |
| O'BRIEN, FRANCES (HM15179) | | | | | | | | | | | ● | | | | | |
| O'DONNELL, ELSPETH (HM15225) | | | | | | | | | | | | | | | | |
| OXFORD NUTRITION & ALLRGY CTRE (HM15541) | | | ● | | ● | ● | ● | ● | ● | ● | ● | | | ● | | ● |
| OXFORD TRANSCENDTL MEDITA CTRE (HM15544) | | | | | | | | | | | | | | | | |
| PARSONS STREET CLINIC (HM15747) | | | | | | | | | | | | | | | | |
| PLESTED, JOHN (HM16368) | | | | | ● | | | | | | | | | | ● | |
| POLLOCK, SUSAN (HM16418) | | | | | ● | | | | | | | | | | ● | |
| SIDEBOTTOM, MARGARET (HM18527) | | | | | | | | | | | | | | | | |
| SUMMERTON CLINIC (HM19498) | | | ● | | ● | ● | ● | ● | ● | | ● | | | ● | ● | ● |
| TOUCH OF NATURE (HM20188) | | | | | ● | | | | | | ● | | | | | ● |
| TWINE, I E (HM20453) | | | ● | | ● | | | ● | | | ● | | | ● | ● | ● |
| WANTAGE NATURAL HEALTH CENTRE (HM20891) | ● | ● | ● | | ● | ● | ● | ● | ● | ● | ● | ● | | ● | ● | ● |
| WANTAGE OSTEOPATHIC PRACTICE (HM20892) | | | | | | | | | | | | | | | | |
| WHEATLEY COMP THERAPY (HM21308) | | | | | ● | | ● | | | | | | | | | |
| WITNEY CHIROPRACTIC/CHIROPODY (HM21750) | | | | | | | | | | | | | | | | |
| WITNEY NATURAL HEALTH CLINIC (HM21751) | ● | ● | ● | | ● | ● | ● | ● | ● | ● | ● | ● | | ● | ● | ● |
| **SHROPSHIRE** | | | | | | | | | | | | | | | | |
| ACUMEDIC (HM00218) | | | | | ● | | | | | | ● | | | | ● | |

www.healthmyself.com

# A - C Conditions treated at Practices/Businesses

| Business by County with Reference no. | Acne | Addiction | Adenoids | Aids | Alcoholism | Allergy | Alzheimer's Disease | Amnesia | Anaemia | Angina | Anorexia | Anxiety | Arthritis | Asthma | Athletes Foot | Autism | Back Pain | Bacterial Infections | Baldness | Bereavement | Bladder Problems | Blood Pressure | Boils | Bowel Problems | Breast Problems | Breathing Problems | Bronchitis | Bruising | Bulimia | Bunions | Bursitis | Callices | Cancers | Cataracts | Catarrh | Cerebral Palsy | Circulation Problems | Cold Sores | Colds | Colic | Colitis | Conjunctivitis | Constipation | Convulsions | Corns | Coughs | Cramp | Cystitis |
|---|---|---|---|---|---|---|---|---|---|---|---|---|---|---|---|---|---|---|---|---|---|---|---|---|---|---|---|---|---|---|---|---|---|---|---|---|---|---|---|---|---|---|---|---|---|---|---|
| AYRES, JOHN (HM01434) |●|||●|||||●|●|||||||||||||||||●||||||||||||||||||||
| BEATTIE, R G (HM01979) |||||||||||||||●|||||||||||||||●||●|||||||||||||●||||
| BODYLIFE CENTRE (HM02622) ||●|||||||||●|●||||●||||||||||●|||||||||||●|||||||||||
| BOOTH, ROBERT (HM02709) |||||||||||||●||||●|||||||||||||||||||||||||||||||
| COLERIDGE, JUDY (HM04831) |||||||||||●|||||●|||||||●|||||||||||||●||||||●|||||
| CORKE, A J (HM05167) |||||||||||●||||||||||||||||||||||||||||||||||||
| FULLERTON, N P (HM07792) |||||||||||||●|●|||●|||||||||●||||||||||||||●|||||||●||
| HALES OSTEOPATHIC PRACTICE (HM08743) |●|●|||●|●|●||●||●|●|●|●||●|●||||●|●||●|●|●|||●||●||||●||●|●||●|●||●|||●|●|●|
| HEALING FOUNDATION (HM09334) |||||||||||●|●|●|||●|||||●|||||●||||||||||●|||||||●||||●||
| LUDLOW OSTEOPATHIC CLINIC (HM12727) ||||||●|||||||●||||●|●||||||||||||||●||||||||||●||||||||
| MADDOCKS CLINIC (HM12898) |||||||||||||||||●|||||||||||||||||||||||||||||||
| MEDAYD PHYSIOTHERAPY (HM13645) |||||||||||||●||||●|||||||||||||||||||||||||||||||
| MEDAYD PHYSIOTHERAPY (HM13644) |||||||||||||●||||●|||||||||||||||||||||||||||||||
| NEEDHAM, LYNDA M (HM14751) ||●||||||●||||●|●||||●|||||||●|||||||||||||||||||●|||||
| OSTEOPATHIC (HM15449) |●|||||||||||●|●|●|||●||●||●|||●|●||||||||||||●||●|||●|●||●||||●|●|
| OSTLE, SAMANTHA (HM15480) |||||||||||||●||||●|||||||||●|||||||||||●|||||||||||
| PEARSON, CHRISTINE (HM15911) |●|●|●|●|●|●|●|●|●|●|●|●|●|●|●|●|●|●|●||●|●|●|●|●|●|●|●|●||●|●|●|●|●||●|●|●|●|●|●|●|●|●|●|●|●|
| PHILLIPS, ANN (HM16124) |||||||||||●||●|||●||||||||●|●|||||||●||||●|||||||||||
| PREES COMPLEMENTARY THERAPIES (HM16533) ||||||||||●|●|||||●||||||||||||●|||||||||||||||||||
| REYNOLDS, TESS (HM17216) ||●||||●|||●|●||●|●|●|||●|||||●|●||●||●|●|●|||||||●||●||●||●||●|||●|●||
| SHREWSBURY SOLE CARE (HM18507) |||||||||||||●||●|||●||||||||||||||●|||||||||||||●||||
| STONE, JANET (HM19336) |●|●|●|●|●|●|●|●|●|●|●|●|●|●|●|●|●|●|●||●|●|●|●|●|●|●|●|●||●|●|●|●|●||●|●|●|●|●|●|●|●|●|●|●|●|
| TAN & BEAUTY STUDIO (HM19676) ||||||||||●||●|●|●|||●||||●||||||●||||||||●||●||||||●||||●||
| WALMSLEY, RUTH (HM20848) |||||||||||●|●|●|||●||||●|●||●||●|●|||||||●||||●||||●||●||||●||
| WESTON, JOHN (HM21279) |||||||||||||●||||●|||||||||||||||||||||||||||||||
| WHITELEY, STEVEN (HM21400) |●|●|●|●|●|●|●|●|●|●|●|●|●|●|●|●|●|●|●||●|●|●|●|●|●|●|●|●||●|●|●|●|●||●|●|●|●|●|●|●|●|●|●|●|●|
| WILD ROSE (HM21488) ||●|||||||||●|●|●|||●|||||●|||||●|●|||||||●||||●|||●|●|||||||
| WILSON, AMANDA (HM21644) |||||||||||||●||●||||||||||||||●||||||||||||||||||
| SOMERSET |||||||||||||||||||||||||||||||||||||||||||||||||
| ABBEY CHIROPODY SERVICES (HM00074) |||||||||||||||●|||||||||||||||||||||||||||||||||
| ALASKAN BACH FLOWER REMEDIES (HM00472) |||||||||||●|||||●|||||||||||||||||||||||||||||||
| ANDERSON, DAVID (HM00816) |||||||||||||||●||||||||||||||||●|||||||||||||●||||
| ANSON, BARRIE (HM00916) |●|●|●|||●|||●|●|●|●|●|●|●||●||||●|●|●|●||●||●|●||●||●||●||●|●|●|●|●|●|●|●||●|●|●|
| AUSSENS, MIEKE (HM01359) |||||||||||●|||●|||●||||||||||||●||||||||●||||||||||||

# A - C Conditions treated at Practices/Businesses

| Business by County with Reference no. | Acne | Addiction | Adenoids | Aids | Alcoholism | Allergy | Alzheimer's Disease | Amnesia | Anaemia | Angina | Anorexia | Anxiety | Arthritis | Asthma | Athletes Foot | Autism | Back Pain | Bacterial Infections | Baldness | Bereavement | Bladder Problems | Blood Pressure | Boils | Bowel Problems |
|---|---|---|---|---|---|---|---|---|---|---|---|---|---|---|---|---|---|---|---|---|---|---|---|---|
| AVENUE CLINIC (HM01388) |●|●|●|●|●|●|●|●|●|●|●|●|●|●|●|●|●|●|●|●|●|●|●|●|
| BAILEY, LINDA R (HM01552) |●| | | | |●| | | | | |●| | |●| | |●| | |●| | |●|
| BATH ALEXANDER TECHNIQUE (HM01890) | | | | | | | | | | | | |●|●| | |●| | | | |●| | |
| BATH NATURAL MEDICAL CENTRE (HM01893) | | | | | |●| | | | | | |●|●| | |●| | | | | | | |
| BATHPOOL CHIROPRACTIC CLINIC (HM01900) | | | | | |●| | | | | |●|●| | | |●| | | | |●| |●|
| BEECH HOUSE CLINIC (HM02046) | | | | | | | | | | | | |●| | | |●| | | | | | | |
| BOULEVARD PHARMACY (HM02739) | |●| | |●|●| | | |●|●|●|●|●|●| |●|●| | |●|●|●|●|
| BRIDGET HEALING CENTRE (HM03008) |●|●|●|●|●|●|●|●|●|●|●|●|●|●|●|●|●|●|●| |●|●|●|●|
| CASTLE SURGERY (HM03840) | | | | | | | | | | | | |●| | | |●| | | | | | | |
| CHAMELEON OILS (HM03961) |●| | | | | | | | | | |●|●| |●| |●|●| | | | | | |
| CHEDDAR COMP MEDICINE CTRE (HM04075) |●|●| | | |●| | | | |●|●|●|●|●| |●| | | | | | | |
| CHINESE MEDICAL CENTRE (HM04238) |●|●| | | |●| | | | |●|●|●|●| | |●| | | |●|●| |●|
| CHIPPER, MARY (HM04278) | | | | | | | | | | | | | | | | |●| | | | | | | |
| CHIROPODY SURGERY (HM04344) | | | | | | | | | | | | |●| |●| | | | | | | | | |
| CLARKE GAIL & RAWLINSON MIKE (HM04581) | | | | | | | | | | | |●| |●| | |●| | | | | | | |
| CLINIC OF COMP MEDICINE (HM04689) |●| |●| | |●| | |●|●|●|●|●|●| | |●| | | |●|●|●|●|
| CLISBY, JANE (HM04722) | | | | | | | | | | | |●| |●| | | | | | | | | | |
| COMPLEMENTARY THERAPY (HM04942) | | | | | |●| | | | | | | | | | | | | | | | | | |
| COOK, COLIN (HM05041) | | | | | | | | | | | | |●| | | |●| | | | | | | |
| COUNSULTING ROOMS (HM05253) | | | | | |●| | | | | |●| |●| | | | | | | |●| |●|
| DAVIES, SALLY (HM05840) | | | | | | | | | | | |●|●| | | |●| | | | | | | |
| DEVONSHIRE SURGERY (HM06044) | | | | | | | | | | | | |●| | | |●| | | | | | | |
| EUROPEAN COLLEGE-BOWEN STUDIES (HM06946) | | | | | |●| | | | | |●| |●| | |●| | | |●|●| |●|
| FRANCES-WHITAKER, J A (HM07665) | | | | | | | | | | | | | | |●| | | | | | | | | |
| GLASTONBURY CHIROPRACTIC (HM08131) |●|●| | | |●| | | | | |●|●| | | |●| | | | |●| | |
| GLASTONBURY EAST WEST CENTRE (HM08132) |●|●|●| |●|●| |●|●|●| |●|●|●|●| |●|●| | |●|●|●|●|
| HELEN SMITH CHIROPODIST (HM09515) | | | | | | | | | | | | | | |●| | | | | | | | | |
| HOLISTIC HEALING CENTRE (HM09962) | | | | | | | | | | | |●|●|●| | |●| | | |●| | | |
| HUDSON, JOHN (HM10315) | | | | | | | | | | |●|●| | | | | | | | | | | | |
| HUXTABLE, ALISON (HM10461) | | | | | | | | | | | | |●| | | |●| | | | | | | |
| JONES, BECKY (HM11125) | |●| | | | | | | | | | |●|●| | | | | | |●| | |●|
| JONES, RAYMOND (HM11190) | | | | | | | | | | | | |●| | | |●| | | | | | | |
| KIRKMEAD CENTRE (HM11718) | | | | | | | | | | | |●|●| | | |●| | | | | | | |
| LANSDOWN PHYSIOTHERAPY CLINIC (HM11964) | | | | | | | | | | | | |●| | | |●| | | | | | | |

| Business by County with Reference no. | Breast Problems | Breathing Problems | Bronchitis | Bruising | Bulimia | Bunions | Bursitis | Callices | Cancers | Cataracts | Catarrh | Cerebral Palsy | Circulation Problems | Cold Sores | Colds | Colic | Colitis | Conjunctivitis | Constipation | Convulsions | Corns | Coughs | Cramp | Cystitis |
|---|---|---|---|---|---|---|---|---|---|---|---|---|---|---|---|---|---|---|---|---|---|---|---|---|
| AVENUE CLINIC (HM01388) |●|●|●|●|●|●|●|●|●|●|●| |●|●|●|●|●|●|●|●|●|●|●|●|
| BAILEY, LINDA R (HM01552) | | | | | | | | | | | | | | | | | | |●| | | |●|●|
| BATH ALEXANDER TECHNIQUE (HM01890) | |●| | | | | | | | | | | | | | | | | | | | |●| |
| BATH NATURAL MEDICAL CENTRE (HM01893) | | | | | | | | | | | | | | | | | | | | | | | | |
| BATHPOOL CHIROPRACTIC CLINIC (HM01900) | | | | | | | | | | | | | | | | | | | | | | | | |
| BEECH HOUSE CLINIC (HM02046) | | | | | | |●| | | | | |●| | |●| | | | | | | | |
| BOULEVARD PHARMACY (HM02739) |●|●|●|●| | |●|●| | |●| |●|●|●|●|●|●|●| |●|●|●|●|
| BRIDGET HEALING CENTRE (HM03008) |●|●|●|●|●| |●|●|●|●|●| |●|●|●|●|●|●|●|●|●|●|●|●|
| CASTLE SURGERY (HM03840) | | | | | | | | | | | | |●| | | | | | | | | | | |
| CHAMELEON OILS (HM03961) | | | | | | | | | | | | |●| |●| | | | | | |●| | |
| CHEDDAR COMP MEDICINE CTRE (HM04075) | | | | |●| | |●| | | | |●| | | | | |●| |●| | | |
| CHINESE MEDICAL CENTRE (HM04238) | | | | | | | | | | | | |●| | | | | |●| | | |●| |
| CHIPPER, MARY (HM04278) | | | | | | | | | | | | | | | | | | | | | | | | |
| CHIROPODY SURGERY (HM04344) | | | | | |●| |●| | | | | | | | | | | | |●| | | |
| CLARKE GAIL & RAWLINSON MIKE (HM04581) | |●| | | | | | | | | | | | | | | | | | | | | | |
| CLINIC OF COMP MEDICINE (HM04689) |●|●|●|●| | |●| | | |●| |●|●|●|●|●|●|●|●| |●|●|●|
| CLISBY, JANE (HM04722) | | | | | | | | | | | | |●| | | | | | | | | | | |
| COMPLEMENTARY THERAPY (HM04942) | | | | | | | | | | | | | | | | | | | | | | | | |
| COOK, COLIN (HM05041) | | | | | | |●| | | | | | | | | | | | | | | | | |
| COUNSULTING ROOMS (HM05253) | | | | | | | | | | | | | | | | | | | | | | | | |
| DAVIES, SALLY (HM05840) | | | | | | | | | | | | | | | | | | | | | | | | |
| DEVONSHIRE SURGERY (HM06044) | | | | | | | | | | | | |●| | |●| | | | | | | | |
| EUROPEAN COLLEGE-BOWEN STUDIES (HM06946) |●|●|●| | | |●| | | |●| |●| | | |●| |●| | |●|●|●|
| FRANCES-WHITAKER, J A (HM07665) | | | | | | | | | | | | | | | | | | | | | | | | |
| GLASTONBURY CHIROPRACTIC (HM08131) | |●|●| | | | | | | | | |●| | |●| | |●| | |●|●| |
| GLASTONBURY EAST WEST CENTRE (HM08132) |●|●|●|●|●| |●|●| |●|●| |●|●|●|●|●|●|●|●|●|●|●|●|
| HELEN SMITH CHIROPODIST (HM09515) | | | | | | | |●| | | | | | | | | | | | |●| | | |
| HOLISTIC HEALING CENTRE (HM09962) | |●| | | | | | | |●| | | | | | | | | | | | |●| |
| HUDSON, JOHN (HM10315) | | | | |●| | | | | | | | | | | | | | | | | | | |
| HUXTABLE, ALISON (HM10461) | | | | | | | | | | | | | | | | | | | | | | | | |
| JONES, BECKY (HM11125) | |●| | |●| | | |●| | | |●| | | | | | | | | |●| |
| JONES, RAYMOND (HM11190) | | | | | | | | | | | | |●| | | | | | | | | | | |
| KIRKMEAD CENTRE (HM11718) | | | | | | | | | | | | | | | | | | | | | | | | |
| LANSDOWN PHYSIOTHERAPY CLINIC (HM11964) | | | | | | | | | | | | | | | | | | | | | | | | |

# A - C Conditions treated at Practices/Businesses

| Business by County with Reference no. | Acne | Addiction | Adenoids | Aids | Alcoholism | Allergy | Alzheimer's Disease | Amnesia | Anaemia | Angina | Anorexia | Anxiety | Arthritis | Asthma | Athletes Foot | Autism |
|---|---|---|---|---|---|---|---|---|---|---|---|---|---|---|---|---|
| LAUREL PLACE (HM12009) | | | | | | ● | | | | | | | | | | |
| LEAVEY, J () | | | | | | | | | | | | ● | ● | | | |
| LOGAN, DAVID (HM12566) | | | | | | | | | | | ● | | | ● | | |
| MARY WILKINSON - MCTIMONEY (HM13225) | | | | | | | | | | | | | | | ● | |
| MARY WILKINSON - MCTIMONEY (HM13226) | | | | | | | | | | | | | | | ● | |
| MCLOUGHLIN, BRENDAN (HM13559) | | | | | | | | | | | | ● | | | | |
| MIDSOMER NORTON CHIROPRACTIC (HM13844) | | | | | | | | | | | | | ● | | | |
| MILSOM STREET CLINIC (HM13944) | | | | | | | | | | | | | ● | | | |
| NATURAL SPIRITUAL HEALING (HM14626) | | | | ● | | | | | | | | ● | ● | | | |
| NATURAL THERAPIES (HM14632) | | | | | | | | | | | | ● | ● | | | |
| NORSO BIOMAGNETICS UK (HM15016) | | | | | | | | | | | | ● | ● | ● | | |
| NUTRITION FOR LIFE (HM15123) | ● | | | | | ● | ● | ● | ● | ● | ● | ● | ● | ● | | |
| ORCHARD CLINIC (HM15360) | ● | ● | | | | ● | | | | | | ● | ● | | | |
| PARK HOUSE CLINIC (HM15666) | | | | | | | | | | | | | ● | | | |
| PARNELL, R H (HM15727) | | | | | | | | | | | ● | ● | ● | ● | | |
| PARRY, J M (HM15738) | | | | | | | | | | | | | ● | | ● | |
| PENNINGTON, PAM (HM15990) | | | | | | | | | | | | | | | ● | |
| PENNINGTON, PAM V (HM15991) | | | | | | | | | | | | | | | ● | |
| PERKINS, L (HM16026) | | | | | | | | | | | | | ● | | | |
| PITT, I T (HM16347) | | | | | | ● | | | | | | | ● | ● | ● | |
| PRESSURE WORKS (HM16544) | | | | | | | | | | | | | | | | |
| REED, W A (HM17046) | | | | | | | | | | | | ● | ● | | | |
| RICHARDS, M J (HM17261) | | | | | | | | | | | | | | | ● | |
| SHAMBHALA (HM18275) | | ● | | | ● | | | | | | | ● | ● | | | |
| SNOWDON, JANET (HM18843) | ● | ● | ● | ● | ● | ● | ● | ● | ● | ● | ● | ● | ● | ● | ● | ● |
| ST JAMES'S SURGERY (HM19079) | | | | | | | | | | | | | ● | | | |
| ST MICHAELS CHIROPRACTIC (HM19089) | | | | | | | | | | | | | | | | |
| ST MICHAEL'S HYPNOTHERAPY (HM19090) | | ● | | | | | | | | | | ● | | | | |
| STANLEY COURT SURGERY (HM19127) | | | | | | | | | | | | | ● | | | |
| STREET CHIROPRACTIC CLINIC (HM19382) | | | | | | | | | | | | | ● | | ● | |
| STREET CHIROPRACTIC CLINIC (HM19383) | | | | | | | | | | | | | ● | | | |
| STRESS CLINIC & NTRL HLTH CTRE (HM19389) | ● | ● | ● | | | ● | | | | | ● | ● | ● | ● | | ● |
| TARETH CENTRE (HM19704) | ● | ● | ● | ● | ● | ● | ● | ● | ● | ● | ● | ● | ● | ● | ● | ● |
| TAUNTON FOOT SURGERY (HM19722) | | | | | | | | | | | | | ● | | ● | |

| Business by County with Reference no. | Back Pain | Bacterial Infections | Baldness | Bereavement | Bladder Problems | Blood Pressure | Boils | Bowel Problems | Breast Problems | Breathing Problems | Bronchitis | Bruising | Bulimia | Bunions | Bursitis | Callices |
|---|---|---|---|---|---|---|---|---|---|---|---|---|---|---|---|---|
| LAUREL PLACE (HM12009) | | | | | | | | | | | | | | | | |
| LEAVEY, J () | ● | | | | | | | | | | | | | | | |
| LOGAN, DAVID (HM12566) | | | | ● | | ● | | | | | | | ● | | | |
| MARY WILKINSON - MCTIMONEY (HM13225) | ● | | | | ● | | | ● | | | | | | | | |
| MARY WILKINSON - MCTIMONEY (HM13226) | ● | | | | ● | | | ● | | | | | | | | |
| MCLOUGHLIN, BRENDAN (HM13559) | | | | | | | | | | | | | | | | |
| MIDSOMER NORTON CHIROPRACTIC (HM13844) | ● | | | | | | | | | | | | | | | |
| MILSOM STREET CLINIC (HM13944) | ● | | | | | | | | | | | | | | | |
| NATURAL SPIRITUAL HEALING (HM14626) | ● | | | | ● | ● | | ● | ● | ● | | | | | | |
| NATURAL THERAPIES (HM14632) | ● | | ● | | | ● | | | | | | | | | | |
| NORSO BIOMAGNETICS UK (HM15016) | ● | | | | | | | ● | | ● | ● | ● | | | | |
| NUTRITION FOR LIFE (HM15123) | ● | ● | | | | ● | | ● | | ● | ● | | | | | |
| ORCHARD CLINIC (HM15360) | ● | | | | | ● | | ● | | ● | ● | | | | | |
| PARK HOUSE CLINIC (HM15666) | ● | | | | | | | | | | | | | | | |
| PARNELL, R H (HM15727) | ● | | | | | | | | | | | | ● | | | |
| PARRY, J M (HM15738) | | | | | | | | | | | | | | ● | | ● |
| PENNINGTON, PAM (HM15990) | | | | | | | | | | | | | | | | ● |
| PENNINGTON, PAM V (HM15991) | | | | | | | | | | | | | | | | ● |
| PERKINS, L (HM16026) | | ● | | | | | | | | | | | | ● | | ● |
| PITT, I T (HM16347) | ● | | | | | | | ● | | | | | | | | |
| PRESSURE WORKS (HM16544) | ● | | | | | | | | | | | | | | | |
| REED, W A (HM17046) | ● | | | | | | | | | | | | | | | |
| RICHARDS, M J (HM17261) | | | | | | | | | | | | | | | | |
| SHAMBHALA (HM18275) | ● | ● | | | | ● | | ● | | ● | | | ● | | | |
| SNOWDON, JANET (HM18843) | ● | ● | ● | | ● | ● | ● | ● | ● | ● | ● | ● | ● | | ● | |
| ST JAMES'S SURGERY (HM19079) | ● | | | | | | | | | ● | | | | | | |
| ST MICHAELS CHIROPRACTIC (HM19089) | ● | | | | | | | | | | | | | | | |
| ST MICHAEL'S HYPNOTHERAPY (HM19090) | | | | | | | | | | | | | | | | |
| STANLEY COURT SURGERY (HM19127) | ● | | | | | ● | | | | | | | | | | |
| STREET CHIROPRACTIC CLINIC (HM19382) | ● | | | | | | | | | | | | | | | ● |
| STREET CHIROPRACTIC CLINIC (HM19383) | ● | | | | | | | | | | | | | | | |
| STRESS CLINIC & NTRL HLTH CTRE (HM19389) | ● | | | | ● | ● | ● | ● | | ● | | | ● | | | |
| TARETH CENTRE (HM19704) | ● | ● | ● | | ● | ● | ● | ● | ● | ● | ● | ● | ● | | ● | ● |
| TAUNTON FOOT SURGERY (HM19722) | | | | | | | | | | | | | | ● | | |

| Business by County with Reference no. | Cancers | Cataracts | Catarrh | Cerebral Palsy | Circulation Problems | Cold Sores | Colds | Colic | Colitis | Conjunctivitis | Constipation | Convulsions | Corns | Coughs | Cramp | Cystitis |
|---|---|---|---|---|---|---|---|---|---|---|---|---|---|---|---|---|
| LAUREL PLACE (HM12009) | | | | | | | | | | | | | | | | |
| LEAVEY, J () | | | | | | | | | | | | | | | | |
| LOGAN, DAVID (HM12566) | | | | | | | | | | | | | | | | |
| MARY WILKINSON - MCTIMONEY (HM13225) | | | | | | | | | | | ● | | | | | |
| MARY WILKINSON - MCTIMONEY (HM13226) | | | | | | | | | | | ● | | | | | |
| MCLOUGHLIN, BRENDAN (HM13559) | | | | | | | | | | | | | | | | |
| MIDSOMER NORTON CHIROPRACTIC (HM13844) | | | | | ● | | | | | | | | | | | |
| MILSOM STREET CLINIC (HM13944) | | | | | | | | | | | | | | | | |
| NATURAL SPIRITUAL HEALING (HM14626) | ● | | | | | | | | ● | | ● | | | | | ● |
| NATURAL THERAPIES (HM14632) | | | | | ● | | | | | | | | | | | |
| NORSO BIOMAGNETICS UK (HM15016) | | | | | ● | | | | | | | | | | ● | |
| NUTRITION FOR LIFE (HM15123) | | | ● | | ● | ● | ● | | ● | | ● | | | ● | ● | ● |
| ORCHARD CLINIC (HM15360) | | | ● | | ● | | | ● | | | ● | | | | | |
| PARK HOUSE CLINIC (HM15666) | | | | | | | | | | | | | | | | |
| PARNELL, R H (HM15727) | | | | | | | | | | | ● | | | | | |
| PARRY, J M (HM15738) | | | | | | | | | | | | | ● | | | |
| PENNINGTON, PAM (HM15990) | | | | | | | | | | | | | ● | | | |
| PENNINGTON, PAM V (HM15991) | | | | | | | | | | | | | ● | | | |
| PERKINS, L (HM16026) | | | | | | | | | | | | | ● | | | |
| PITT, I T (HM16347) | | | ● | | | | | | | | | | | | | |
| PRESSURE WORKS (HM16544) | | | | | ● | | | | | | | | | | | |
| REED, W A (HM17046) | | | | | | | | | | | | | | | | |
| RICHARDS, M J (HM17261) | | | | | | | | | | | | | | | | |
| SHAMBHALA (HM18275) | | | | | ● | | | | | | | | | | | |
| SNOWDON, JANET (HM18843) | ● | ● | ● | | ● | ● | ● | ● | ● | ● | ● | | | | | |
| ST JAMES'S SURGERY (HM19079) | | | | | | | | | | | | | | | | |
| ST MICHAELS CHIROPRACTIC (HM19089) | | | | | ● | | | | | | | | | | | |
| ST MICHAEL'S HYPNOTHERAPY (HM19090) | | | | | | | | | | | | | | | | |
| STANLEY COURT SURGERY (HM19127) | | | | | ● | | | ● | | | | | | | | |
| STREET CHIROPRACTIC CLINIC (HM19382) | | | | | ● | | | | | | | | ● | | | |
| STREET CHIROPRACTIC CLINIC (HM19383) | | | | | | | | | | | | | | | | |
| STRESS CLINIC & NTRL HLTH CTRE (HM19389) | | | ● | | ● | ● | ● | ● | ● | ● | ● | | | ● | ● | ● |
| TARETH CENTRE (HM19704) | ● | ● | ● | | ● | ● | ● | ● | ● | ● | ● | ● | ● | ● | ● | ● |
| TAUNTON FOOT SURGERY (HM19722) | | | | | | | | | | | | | | | | |

# A - C Conditions treated at Practices/Businesses

| Business by County with Reference no. | Acne | Addiction | Adenoids | Aids | Alcoholism | Allergy | Alzheimer's Disease | Amnesia | Anaemia | Angina | Anorexia | Anxiety | Arthritis | Asthma | Athletes Foot | Autism | Back Pain | Bacterial Infections | Baldness | Bereavement | Bladder Problems | Blood Pressure | Boils | Bowel Problems | Breast Problems | Breathing Problems | Bronchitis | Bruising | Bulimia | Bunions | Bursitis | Callices | Cancers | Cataracts | Catarrh | Cerebral Palsy | Circulation Problems | Cold Sores | Colds | Colic | Colitis | Conjunctivitis | Constipation | Convulsions | Corns | Coughs | Cramp | Cystitis |
|---|---|---|---|---|---|---|---|---|---|---|---|---|---|---|---|---|---|---|---|---|---|---|---|---|---|---|---|---|---|---|---|---|---|---|---|---|---|---|---|---|---|---|---|---|---|---|---|---|
| TAYLOR, GILLIAN (HM19760) |  |  |  |  |  |  |  |  |  |  |  |  |  |  | ● |  |  |  |  |  |  |  |  |  |  |  |  |  |  |  |  | ● |  |  |  |  |  |  |  |  |  |  |  |  | ● |  |  |  |
| THOMPSON, G W (DR) (HM19978) |  |  |  |  |  |  |  |  |  |  |  |  | ● |  |  |  | ● |  |  |  |  |  |  |  |  |  |  |  |  |  |  |  |  |  |  |  |  |  |  | ● |  |  |  |  |  |  |  |  |
| TURNPIKE SURGERY (HM20441) |  |  |  |  |  |  |  |  |  |  |  |  | ● |  |  |  | ● |  |  |  |  | ● |  |  |  |  |  |  |  |  |  |  |  |  |  |  | ● |  |  | ● |  |  |  |  |  |  |  |  |
| WELLSPRING OSTEO/NTRL HEALTH (HM21181) | ● | ● | ● |  |  | ● |  |  |  |  | ● | ● | ● | ● |  |  | ● |  |  |  |  | ● |  | ● |  | ● | ● |  |  |  | ● |  |  |  | ● |  | ● |  |  | ● | ● |  | ● |  |  | ● |  | ● |
| WESTERN CHIROPRACTIC CLINIC (HM21263) |  |  |  |  |  | ● |  |  |  | ● |  | ● | ● | ● |  | ● | ● |  | ● |  | ● | ● |  | ● | ● | ● | ● | ● |  |  |  |  |  |  | ● |  | ● |  | ● | ● | ● |  | ● | ● |  | ● | ● | ● |
| WILKINSON, MARY (HM21511) |  |  |  |  |  |  |  |  |  |  |  |  |  |  | ● |  | ● |  |  |  | ● |  |  | ● |  |  |  |  |  |  |  |  |  |  |  |  |  |  |  |  |  |  | ● |  |  |  |  |  |
| WINCANTON CHIROPRACTIC CLINIC (HM21690) |  |  |  |  |  |  |  |  |  |  |  |  | ● |  |  |  | ● |  |  |  |  |  |  |  |  |  |  |  |  |  |  |  |  |  |  |  | ● |  |  |  |  |  |  |  |  |  |  |  |
| YELLOW EMPEROR CORP (HM22004) |  |  |  |  |  |  |  |  |  |  | ● |  | ● | ● |  |  | ● |  |  |  |  |  |  |  |  |  |  |  | ● |  |  |  |  |  |  |  |  |  |  |  |  |  |  |  |  |  |  |  |
| YEOVIL CHIROPRACTIC CLINIC (HM22008) |  |  |  |  |  |  |  |  |  |  |  |  | ● |  |  |  | ● |  |  |  |  |  |  |  |  |  |  |  |  |  |  |  |  |  |  |  | ● |  |  |  |  |  |  |  |  |  |  |  |
| **STAFFORDSHIRE** |  |  |  |  |  |  |  |  |  |  |  |  |  |  |  |  |  |  |  |  |  |  |  |  |  |  |  |  |  |  |  |  |  |  |  |  |  |  |  |  |  |  |  |  |  |  |  |  |
| ALTERNATIVE THERAPY CENTRE (HM00735) | ● | ● |  |  |  | ● |  |  |  |  |  | ● | ● | ● |  |  | ● |  |  |  | ● | ● | ● | ● |  |  |  |  |  |  | ● |  |  |  | ● |  | ● |  | ● |  | ● |  | ● |  |  | ● | ● | ● |
| ALTERNATIVES (HM00741) | ● | ● | ● | ● | ● | ● | ● | ● | ● | ● | ● | ● | ● | ● | ● | ● | ● | ● | ● |  | ● | ● | ● | ● | ● | ● | ● | ● | ● |  | ● | ● | ● | ● | ● |  | ● | ● | ● | ● | ● | ● | ● | ● | ● | ● | ● | ● |
| ANDERSON, G (HM00818) |  |  |  |  |  |  |  |  |  |  |  | ● |  |  |  |  | ● |  |  |  |  |  |  |  |  |  |  |  |  |  |  |  |  |  |  |  |  |  |  |  |  |  |  |  |  |  |  |  |
| BARCROFT, J M (HM01696) |  |  |  |  |  |  |  |  |  |  |  | ● | ● |  | ● |  |  | ● |  |  |  |  |  |  |  |  |  |  |  | ● |  |  |  |  |  |  |  |  |  |  |  |  |  |  |  |  |  |  |
| BASFORD CHIROPRACTIC CLINIC (HM01842) |  |  |  |  |  |  |  |  |  |  |  |  | ● |  |  |  | ● |  |  |  |  |  |  |  |  |  |  |  |  |  |  |  |  |  |  |  | ● |  |  | ● |  |  |  |  |  |  |  |  |
| BLANK, CHRISTOPHER (HM02499) |  |  |  |  |  |  |  |  |  |  |  |  | ● |  | ● |  |  | ● |  |  |  |  |  |  |  |  |  |  |  | ● |  | ● |  |  |  |  |  |  |  |  |  |  |  |  | ● |  |  |  |
| BONNEBAIGT, ANDRE (HM02682) |  |  |  |  |  |  |  |  |  |  |  | ● |  |  |  |  |  |  |  |  |  |  |  |  |  |  |  |  |  |  |  |  |  |  |  |  |  |  |  |  |  |  |  |  |  |  |  |  |
| BORE ST POD & CHIROP PRACTICE (HM02716) |  |  |  |  |  |  |  |  |  |  |  |  |  |  | ● |  |  |  |  |  |  |  |  |  |  |  |  |  |  | ● | ● |  |  |  |  |  |  |  |  |  |  |  |  |  |  |  |  |  |
| BRADBURY, SHARON (HM02842) |  |  |  |  |  |  |  |  |  |  |  |  | ● | ● |  |  | ● |  |  |  |  |  |  |  |  |  |  |  |  |  | ● |  |  |  |  |  |  |  |  |  |  |  |  |  |  |  |  |  |
| BRAMPTON TREES CLINIC (HM02908) |  |  |  |  |  |  |  |  |  |  |  |  | ● |  |  |  | ● |  |  |  |  |  |  |  |  |  |  |  |  |  |  |  |  |  |  |  |  |  |  |  |  |  |  |  |  |  |  |  |
| BRIDGETT, A (HM03011) |  |  |  |  |  |  |  |  |  |  |  |  | ● |  |  |  |  |  |  |  |  | ● |  |  |  | ● |  | ● |  |  |  |  |  |  |  |  |  |  |  |  |  |  |  |  |  |  | ● |  |
| BURKE, E (HM03385) |  | ● |  |  | ● |  |  |  |  |  |  | ● |  |  |  |  |  |  |  |  |  |  |  |  |  |  |  |  | ● |  |  |  |  |  |  |  |  |  |  |  |  |  |  |  |  |  |  |  |
| CASTLEFIELDS SURGERY (HM03846) |  |  |  |  |  |  |  |  |  |  |  |  | ● |  |  |  | ● |  |  |  |  |  |  |  |  |  |  |  |  |  |  |  |  |  |  |  |  |  |  | ● |  |  |  |  |  |  |  |  |
| CHASE HEALTH FOODS (HM04055) | ● | ● | ● |  | ● | ● | ● | ● | ● | ● | ● | ● | ● | ● | ● | ● | ● | ● | ● |  | ● | ● | ● | ● | ● | ● | ● | ● | ● |  | ● |  | ● | ● | ● |  | ● | ● | ● | ● | ● | ● | ● | ● |  | ● | ● | ● |
| CHASE NATURAL THERAPY CENTRE (HM04059) | ● | ● | ● | ● | ● | ● | ● | ● | ● | ● | ● | ● | ● | ● | ● | ● | ● | ● | ● |  | ● | ● | ● | ● | ● | ● | ● | ● | ● |  | ● | ● | ● | ● | ● |  | ● | ● | ● | ● | ● | ● | ● | ● | ● | ● | ● | ● |
| CITY CHIROPRACTIC CLINIC (HM04492) | ● | ● |  |  |  | ● |  |  |  |  |  | ● | ● |  | ● |  | ● |  |  |  |  | ● |  | ● |  | ● | ● | ● |  |  |  |  |  |  |  |  | ● |  |  | ● |  |  |  |  |  |  |  |  |
| CORNERSTONES PRACTICE (HM05182) | ● | ● | ● | ● | ● | ● | ● | ● | ● | ● | ● | ● | ● | ● | ● | ● | ● | ● | ● |  | ● | ● | ● | ● | ● | ● | ● | ● | ● |  | ● | ● | ● | ● | ● |  | ● | ● | ● | ● | ● | ● | ● | ● | ● | ● | ● | ● |
| CRESCENT CLINIC (HM05417) | ● | ● | ● | ● | ● | ● | ● | ● | ● | ● | ● | ● | ● | ● | ● | ● | ● | ● | ● |  | ● | ● | ● | ● | ● | ● | ● | ● | ● |  | ● | ● | ● | ● | ● |  | ● | ● | ● | ● | ● | ● | ● | ● | ● | ● | ● | ● |
| CRESCENT CLINIC FOR COMP MED (HM05418) |  | ● |  |  |  | ● |  |  |  |  |  | ● | ● | ● |  |  | ● |  |  |  |  |  |  |  |  |  |  |  |  |  |  |  |  |  |  |  |  |  |  |  |  |  | ● |  |  |  |  |  |
| EDWARDS, ALLYN (HM06641) |  |  |  |  |  |  |  |  |  |  |  |  | ● | ● |  |  | ● |  |  |  |  | ● |  | ● |  |  |  |  |  |  |  |  |  |  |  |  | ● |  |  |  |  |  | ● |  |  |  |  |  |
| ESSENTIAL HEALTH (HM06911) | ● | ● |  |  |  | ● | ● | ● |  |  |  |  |  |  |  |  |  |  |  |  |  |  |  |  |  |  |  |  |  |  |  |  |  |  |  |  |  |  |  |  |  |  |  |  |  |  |  |  |
| EVANS, RICHARD (HM06989) |  |  |  |  |  |  |  |  | ● | ● |  | ● | ● | ● |  |  | ● | ● |  |  | ● | ● |  | ● | ● | ● |  |  |  |  |  |  | ● |  | ● |  | ● |  | ● |  |  |  | ● |  |  | ● | ● | ● |
| FEET FIRST (HM07176) |  |  |  |  |  |  |  |  |  |  |  |  |  |  | ● |  |  | ● |  |  |  |  |  |  |  |  |  |  |  | ● |  | ● |  |  |  |  |  |  |  |  |  |  |  |  | ● |  |  |  |
| FOOT SOUL & BODYWORKS (HM07487) |  |  |  |  |  |  |  |  |  |  |  | ● | ● | ● |  |  | ● |  |  |  |  |  |  | ● |  | ● | ● |  |  |  |  |  |  |  | ● |  |  | ● | ● | ● | ● |  | ● |  |  | ● | ● | ● |

www.healthmyself.com

# A - C Conditions treated at Practices/Businesses

| Business by County with Reference no. | Acne | Addiction | Adenoids | Aids | Alcoholism | Allergy | Alzheimer's Disease | Amnesia | Anaemia | Angina | Anorexia | Anxiety | Arthritis | Asthma | Athletes Foot | Autism |
|---|---|---|---|---|---|---|---|---|---|---|---|---|---|---|---|---|
| FORTEY, C J (HM07579) | | | | | | | | | | | | | | | | |
| GASCOIGNE, DOROTHY (HM07917) | | ● | | | | | | | | | | | | | | |
| GASCOYNE, P (HM07920) | | | | | | | | | | | | | ● | | ● | |
| HALLARD, SHARON (HM08800) | | | | | | | | | | | | ● | | | | |
| IBBS, ROGER (HM10566) | | | | | | | | | | | | | ● | | ● | |
| ISHTA CENTRE (HM10761) | ● | ● | ● | | ● | ● | ● | ● | ● | ● | ● | ● | ● | ● | ● | ● |
| JOHNSON, JANICE (HM11079) | | ● | | | ● | | | | | | | ● | | | | |
| LOUISE BRITTLE (HM12667) | | | | | | | | | | | | | | ● | ● | |
| MARCONI, L R (HM13076) | | | | | | | | | | | | | ● | | ● | |
| MELLOR, J SIMON (HM13709) | | | | | | | | | | | | | ● | | ● | |
| MILL BANK OSTEOPATHIC CLINIC (HM13865) | | | | | | | | | | | | | ● | | | |
| NARAYAN, MAMTA (HM14486) | | | | | | | | | | | | | ● | | | |
| NORBURY, SUSAN (HM14990) | ● | ● | | | | ● | ● | ● | ● | ● | ● | ● | ● | ● | ● | ● |
| O'CALLAGHAN, STEVE (HM15193) | | | | | | | | | | | | ● | ● | | | |
| PAYTON, ANTHONY (HM15875) | | | | | | | | | | | | | | | ● | |
| PEACEHAVEN AROMATHERAPY (HM15877) | | | | | | | | | | | | ● | ● | | | |
| PEACH, F J (HM15879) | | | | | | | | | | | | | ● | | ● | |
| PLANT, R M (HM16359) | | | | | | | | | | | | | | | ● | |
| PRIORS PODIATRY PRACTICE (HM16629) | | | | | | | | | | | | | ● | | ● | |
| REECE, P & BRADSHAW, J (HM17039) | | | | | | | | | | | | | | | ● | |
| ROBERTS, KATE (HM17418) | | | | | | | | | | | | ● | | | | |
| SAGGU, S (HM17838) | | | | | | | | | | | | | | | ● | |
| STAFFORD CHIROPRACTIC CLINIC (HM19108) | | | | | | | | | | | | | ● | | | |
| STAFFORDSHIRE MCTIMONEY (HM19111) | | | | | | ● | | | | | | | ● | ● | | |
| SUSAN JAMES CONSULTANCY (HM19527) | | | | | | | | | | | ● | ● | | | | ● |
| TAMWORTH PHYSIOTHERAPY CLINIC (HM19675) | | | | | | | | | | | | | ● | | | |
| TE NOSCE (HM19803) | ● | ● | | | | ● | ● | | ● | ● | | ● | ● | ● | | |
| TUNSTALL HYPNOTHERAPY CENTRE (HM20401) | | | | | | | | | | | | | ● | | | |
| WATSON, G T (HM21008) | | | | | | | | | | | | | | | ● | |
| WHITBY, S E (HM21334) | | | | | | | | | | | | | ● | | | |
| YARNFIELD PARK- HEALTH/SPORTS (HM21989) | ● | ● | ● | ● | ● | ● | ● | ● | ● | ● | ● | ● | ● | ● | ● | ● |
| SUFFOLK | | | | | | | | | | | | | | | | |
| AJNA (HM00457) | | | | | | | | | | | | ● | | | | |
| BODY MECHANICS THERAPY CLINIC (HM02599) | | | | | | | | | | | | | | | | |

| Business by County with Reference no. | Back Pain | Bacterial Infections | Baldness | Bereavement | Bladder Problems | Blood Pressure | Boils | Bowel Problems | Breast Problems | Breathing Problems | Bronchitis | Bruising | Bulimia | Bunions | Bursitis | Callices |
|---|---|---|---|---|---|---|---|---|---|---|---|---|---|---|---|---|
| FORTEY, C J (HM07579) | ● | | | | | | | | | | | | | | | |
| GASCOIGNE, DOROTHY (HM07917) | | | | | | | | | | | | | | | | |
| GASCOYNE, P (HM07920) | | | | | | | | | | | | | | | | ● |
| HALLARD, SHARON (HM08800) | | | | | | | | | | | | | | | | |
| IBBS, ROGER (HM10566) | | | | | | | | | | | | | | ● | | ● |
| ISHTA CENTRE (HM10761) | ● | ● | ● | | ● | ● | ● | ● | ● | ● | ● | ● | ● | | ● | ● |
| JOHNSON, JANICE (HM11079) | | | | | | ● | | | | | | | | | | |
| LOUISE BRITTLE (HM12667) | | | | | | | | | | | | | | | | ● |
| MARCONI, L R (HM13076) | | ● | | | | | | | | | | | | ● | | ● |
| MELLOR, J SIMON (HM13709) | | | | | | | | | | | | | | ● | | |
| MILL BANK OSTEOPATHIC CLINIC (HM13865) | ● | | | | | | | | | ● | | | | | ● | |
| NARAYAN, MAMTA (HM14486) | ● | | | | | | | | | | | | | | | |
| NORBURY, SUSAN (HM14990) | ● | | ● | | ● | ● | ● | ● | ● | ● | ● | ● | | | ● | ● |
| O'CALLAGHAN, STEVE (HM15193) | ● | | | | | ● | | | | ● | ● | | | | | |
| PAYTON, ANTHONY (HM15875) | | ● | | | | | | | | | | | | ● | | ● |
| PEACEHAVEN AROMATHERAPY (HM15877) | ● | | | | | ● | | | | | | | | | | |
| PEACH, F J (HM15879) | | | | | | | | | | | | | | ● | | ● |
| PLANT, R M (HM16359) | | ● | | | | | | | | | | | | ● | | ● |
| PRIORS PODIATRY PRACTICE (HM16629) | ● | | | | | | | | | | | | | ● | | |
| REECE, P & BRADSHAW, J (HM17039) | | | | | | | | | | | | | | ● | | ● |
| ROBERTS, KATE (HM17418) | | | | | | | | | | | | | | | | |
| SAGGU, S (HM17838) | | ● | | | | | | | | | | | | | | ● |
| STAFFORD CHIROPRACTIC CLINIC (HM19108) | ● | | | | | | | | | | | | | | | |
| STAFFORDSHIRE MCTIMONEY (HM19111) | ● | | | | | | | | | | | | | | | |
| SUSAN JAMES CONSULTANCY (HM19527) | | | | | | | | | | | | | | | | |
| TAMWORTH PHYSIOTHERAPY CLINIC (HM19675) | ● | | | | | | | | | | | ● | | | | |
| TE NOSCE (HM19803) | ● | ● | ● | | ● | ● | | ● | | | ● | | | | ● | |
| TUNSTALL HYPNOTHERAPY CENTRE (HM20401) | | | | | | | | ● | | | | | | | | |
| WATSON, G T (HM21008) | | | | | | | | | | | | | | ● | | ● |
| WHITBY, S E (HM21334) | ● | | | | | | | | | | | | | | | |
| YARNFIELD PARK- HEALTH/SPORTS (HM21989) | ● | ● | ● | | ● | ● | ● | ● | ● | ● | ● | ● | ● | | ● | ● |
| SUFFOLK | | | | | | | | | | | | | | | | |
| AJNA (HM00457) | | | | | | | | | | | | | | | | |
| BODY MECHANICS THERAPY CLINIC (HM02599) | ● | | | | | | | | | | | ● | | | | |

| Business by County with Reference no. | Cancers | Cataracts | Catarrh | Cerebral Palsy | Circulation Problems | Cold Sores | Colds | Colic | Colitis | Conjunctivitis | Constipation | Convulsions | Corns | Coughs | Cramp | Cystitis |
|---|---|---|---|---|---|---|---|---|---|---|---|---|---|---|---|---|
| FORTEY, C J (HM07579) | | | | | | | | | | | | | | | | |
| GASCOIGNE, DOROTHY (HM07917) | | | | | | | | | | | | | | | | |
| GASCOYNE, P (HM07920) | | | | | | | | | | | | | ● | | | |
| HALLARD, SHARON (HM08800) | | | | | | | | | | | | | | | | |
| IBBS, ROGER (HM10566) | | | | | | | | | | | | | ● | | | |
| ISHTA CENTRE (HM10761) | ● | ● | ● | | ● | ● | ● | ● | ● | ● | ● | ● | | ● | ● | ● |
| JOHNSON, JANICE (HM11079) | | | | | | | | | | | | | | | | |
| LOUISE BRITTLE (HM12667) | | | | | | | | | | | | | ● | | | |
| MARCONI, L R (HM13076) | | | | | | | | | | | | | ● | | | |
| MELLOR, J SIMON (HM13709) | | | | | | | | | | | | | | | | |
| MILL BANK OSTEOPATHIC CLINIC (HM13865) | | | | | ● | | | ● | ● | | | | | | | |
| NARAYAN, MAMTA (HM14486) | | | | | | | | | | | | | | | | |
| NORBURY, SUSAN (HM14990) | ● | ● | ● | | ● | ● | ● | ● | ● | ● | ● | ● | ● | ● | ● | ● |
| O'CALLAGHAN, STEVE (HM15193) | | | | | ● | | | | | | ● | | | | ● | |
| PAYTON, ANTHONY (HM15875) | | | | | | | | | | | | | ● | | | |
| PEACEHAVEN AROMATHERAPY (HM15877) | | | | | ● | | | | | | | | | | | |
| PEACH, F J (HM15879) | | | | | | | | | | | | | ● | | | |
| PLANT, R M (HM16359) | | | | | | | | | | | | | ● | | | |
| PRIORS PODIATRY PRACTICE (HM16629) | | | | | ● | | | | | | | | | | ● | |
| REECE, P & BRADSHAW, J (HM17039) | | | | | | | | | | | | | ● | | | |
| ROBERTS, KATE (HM17418) | | | | | | | | | | | | | | | | |
| SAGGU, S (HM17838) | | | | | | | | | | | | | ● | | | |
| STAFFORD CHIROPRACTIC CLINIC (HM19108) | | | | | ● | | | ● | | | | | | | | |
| STAFFORDSHIRE MCTIMONEY (HM19111) | | | | | ● | | | ● | ● | | | | | | | |
| SUSAN JAMES CONSULTANCY (HM19527) | | | | | | | | | | | | | | | | |
| TAMWORTH PHYSIOTHERAPY CLINIC (HM19675) | | | | | | | | | | | | | | | ● | |
| TE NOSCE (HM19803) | | ● | ● | | ● | | ● | | ● | | ● | | | | | ● |
| TUNSTALL HYPNOTHERAPY CENTRE (HM20401) | | | | | | | | | | | | | | | | |
| WATSON, G T (HM21008) | | | | | | | | | | | | | ● | | | |
| WHITBY, S E (HM21334) | | | | | | | | | | | | | | | | |
| YARNFIELD PARK- HEALTH/SPORTS (HM21989) | ● | ● | ● | | ● | ● | ● | ● | ● | ● | ● | ● | ● | ● | ● | ● |
| SUFFOLK | | | | | | | | | | | | | | | | |
| AJNA (HM00457) | | | | | | | | | | | | | | | | |
| BODY MECHANICS THERAPY CLINIC (HM02599) | | | | | | | | | | | | | | | ● | |

# A - C Conditions treated at Practices/Businesses

| Business by County with Reference no. | Acne | Addiction | Adenoids | Aids | Alcoholism | Allergy | Alzheimer's Disease | Amnesia | Anaemia | Angina | Anorexia | Anxiety | Arthritis | Asthma | Athletes Foot | Autism | Back Pain | Bacterial Infections | Baldness | Bereavement | Bladder Problems | Blood Pressure | Boils | Bowel Problems |
|---|---|---|---|---|---|---|---|---|---|---|---|---|---|---|---|---|---|---|---|---|---|---|---|---|
| CHARLTON CLINIC (HM04033) | | | | | | | | | | | | | ● | | | | ● | | | | | | | |
| CHURCHMAN & ASS REG OST (HM04475) | | | | | | | | | | | | | ● | | | | ● | | | | | | | |
| CHURCHMAN, BERYL (HM04478) | | | | | | | | | | | | | ● | | | | ● | | | | | | | |
| COLEBROOK, G (HM04820) | | | | | | | | | | | | ● | | | ● | | | ● | | | ● | | | |
| COOPER, A R (HM05088) | | | | | | | | | | | | | | | ● | | | | | | | | | |
| CT & IM LEITH (HM05534) | | | | | | ● | | | ● | | | ● | ● | | | | ● | | | | ● | | | ● |
| DENT, TRISH () | | | | | | | | | | | | ● | ● | ● | | | ● | | | | | | | ● |
| EVENKEEL (HM06997) | | ● | | | | | | | | | | | | | | | ● | | | | | | | |
| FELIXSTOWE PHYSIO PRACTICE (HM07203) | | | | | | | | | | | | | ● | | | | ● | | | | | | | |
| FRESHFIELDS OF ALDEBURGH (HM07737) | ● | ● | ● | | ● | ● | ● | ● | ● | ● | ● | | ● | ● | ● | ● | ● | ● | ● | | ● | ● | ● | ● |
| GREEN FARM CLINIC (HM08435) | | | | | | | | | | | | | ● | | | | ● | | | | | | | |
| GROSVENOR PHYSIOTHERAPY CLINIC (HM08597) | | | | | | | | | | | | | ● | | | | ● | | | | | | | |
| HARDY, MICHAEL (HM08984) | | | | | | | | | | | | | | ● | | | ● | | | | | | | |
| HEALING CONNECTIONS (HM09330) | ● | ● | ● | ● | | ● | ● | ● | ● | ● | ● | ● | ● | ● | ● | | ● | ● | ● | | ● | ● | | ● |
| HEALING HANDS (HM09336) | | | | | | | | | | | | ● | ● | ● | ● | | ● | ● | | | ● | ● | | ● |
| HITCHINS, ROSIE (HM09847) | | | | | | | | | | | | ● | ● | | | | ● | | | | | | | |
| HOPKINS, C J (HM10147) | | | | | | | | | | | | ● | | | | | ● | | | | | | | |
| INNER SPACE SUFFOLK (HM10641) | | | | | | ● | | | | | | ● | ● | | | | ● | | | | ● | | | ● |
| IPSWICH CHIROPRACTIC CLINIC (HM10714) | | | | | | | | | | | | ● | | ● | | | ● | | | | | ● | | ● |
| IPSWICH PHYSIOTHERAPY PRACTICE (HM10715) | | | | | | | | | | | | | ● | | | | ● | | | | | | | |
| LAVENDER LODGE CLINIC (HM12023) | | | | | | | | | | | | | | | | ● | ● | | | | | | | |
| MALAROC (HM12961) | | | | | | | | | | | | | ● | | | | ● | | | | | | | |
| MANOR HOUSE (HM13039) | | | | | | | | | | | | | ● | | ● | | ● | | | | | | | |
| MARK CHURCH AROMATHERAPY (HM13106) | ● | | | | | | | | | | | | ● | | | | ● | | | | | | | |
| MASSAGE FOR HEALTH (HM13260) | | | | | | | | | | | | | ● | | | | ● | | | | | | | |
| MCTIMONEY CHIROPRACTIC CLINIC (HM13607) | | | | | | | | | | | | ● | | ● | ● | | ● | | | | ● | | | |
| MOHAN, TERRY (HM14046) | | ● | | | | | | | | | | ● | | | | | ● | | | | | ● | | |
| NATURECURES (HM14684) | | ● | | | | ● | | | | | | ● | ● | ● | | | ● | | | | | ● | | ● |
| NOAH'S ARK PSYCHOTHERAPY (HM14964) | | ● | | | ● | | | | | | ● | ● | | | | | | | | | | | | |
| PAGE, COLIN J (HM15570) | | | | | | | | | | | | ● | | | | | | | | | | | | |
| PAROLIN, PAUL (HM15728) | | | | | | | | | | | | ● | ● | ● | | ● | ● | | | | ● | ● | | ● |
| SHEROMA THERAPY (HM18435) | | ● | | | | | | | | | | ● | ● | | | | ● | | | | | | | |
| SPALDING, JULIE (HM18955) | ● | ● | | | ● | ● | | ● | | | | ● | | | | | ● | | | | ● | | | ● |
| SPRINGFIELD LODGE HEALTH CARE (HM19052) | ● | ● | ● | ● | ● | ● | ● | ● | ● | ● | ● | ● | ● | ● | ● | ● | ● | ● | ● | | ● | ● | ● | ● |

| Business by County with Reference no. | Breast Problems | Breathing Problems | Bronchitis | Bruising | Bulimia | Bunions | Bursitis | Callices | Cancers | Cataracts | Catarrh | Cerebral Palsy | Circulation Problems | Cold Sores | Colds | Colic | Colitis | Conjunctivitis | Constipation | Convulsions | Corns | Coughs | Cramp | Cystitis |
|---|---|---|---|---|---|---|---|---|---|---|---|---|---|---|---|---|---|---|---|---|---|---|---|---|
| CHARLTON CLINIC (HM04033) | | | | ● | | | ● | | | | | | ● | | | | | | | | | | ● | |
| CHURCHMAN & ASS REG OST (HM04475) | | | | | | | | | | | | | | | | | | | | | | | | |
| CHURCHMAN, BERYL (HM04478) | | | | | | | | | | | | | | | | | | | | | | | | |
| COLEBROOK, G (HM04820) | | ● | | | | | | | | | | | | | | | | | | | | | | |
| COOPER, A R (HM05088) | | | | | | | | ● | | | | | | | | | | | | | ● | | | |
| CT & IM LEITH (HM05534) | | ● | ● | ● | | | ● | | | | ● | | ● | ● | | | | | | | | | ● | ● |
| DENT, TRISH () | | ● | | | | | | | | | | | | | | | | | ● | | | | | |
| EVENKEEL (HM06997) | | | | | | | | | | | | | | | | | | | | | | | ● | |
| FELIXSTOWE PHYSIO PRACTICE (HM07203) | | | | | | | | | | | | | | | | | | | | | | | | |
| FRESHFIELDS OF ALDEBURGH (HM07737) | ● | ● | ● | ● | ● | | | ● | | | ● | | ● | ● | ● | ● | ● | ● | ● | ● | ● | ● | ● | ● |
| GREEN FARM CLINIC (HM08435) | | | | ● | | | ● | | | | | | | | | | | | | | | | | |
| GROSVENOR PHYSIOTHERAPY CLINIC (HM08597) | | | | ● | | | | | | | | | | | | | | | | | | | | |
| HARDY, MICHAEL (HM08984) | | ● | | | | | | | | | | | ● | | | | | | | | | | | |
| HEALING CONNECTIONS (HM09330) | ● | ● | ● | ● | ● | | ● | ● | ● | | ● | | ● | ● | ● | ● | ● | ● | ● | ● | ● | ● | ● | ● |
| HEALING HANDS (HM09336) | | ● | ● | | | | | | | | | | ● | | | | | | ● | | | | | ● |
| HITCHINS, ROSIE (HM09847) | | | | | | | | | | | | | | | | | | | | | | | | |
| HOPKINS, C J (HM10147) | | | | | | | | | | | | | | | | | | | | | | | | |
| INNER SPACE SUFFOLK (HM10641) | | | | | | | | | | | | | | | | ● | | | | | | | | |
| IPSWICH CHIROPRACTIC CLINIC (HM10714) | | ● | | | | | ● | | | | | | ● | | | ● | ● | | ● | | | | ● | |
| IPSWICH PHYSIOTHERAPY PRACTICE (HM10715) | | | | | | | | | | | | | | | | | | | | | | | | |
| LAVENDER LODGE CLINIC (HM12023) | | ● | | | | | | | | | | | ● | | | | | | ● | | | | | |
| MALAROC (HM12961) | | | | ● | | | | | | | | | | | | | | | | | | | | |
| MANOR HOUSE (HM13039) | | | | | | | | | | | | | | | | | | | | | | | | |
| MARK CHURCH AROMATHERAPY (HM13106) | | | | ● | | | | | ● | | | | ● | | ● | | | | | | | | | |
| MASSAGE FOR HEALTH (HM13260) | | | | | | | | | | | | | | | | | | | | | | | | |
| MCTIMONEY CHIROPRACTIC CLINIC (HM13607) | | | | | | | | | | | | | | | | | | | ● | | | ● | ● | ● |
| MOHAN, TERRY (HM14046) | | | | | | | | | | | | | | | | | | | | | | | | |
| NATURECURES (HM14684) | | ● | ● | | | | | | | | | | ● | | | | | | ● | | | | | ● |
| NOAH'S ARK PSYCHOTHERAPY (HM14964) | | ● | | | | | | | | | | | | | | | | | | | | | | |
| PAGE, COLIN J (HM15570) | | | | | | | | | | | | | | | | | | | | | | | | |
| PAROLIN, PAUL (HM15728) | | ● | ● | | | | ● | | | | | | ● | | | ● | | | ● | | | ● | ● | |
| SHEROMA THERAPY (HM18435) | | | | | | | | | | | | | ● | | | | | | | | | | | |
| SPALDING, JULIE (HM18955) | ● | | | | ● | | | | | | | | | | | | ● | | | | | | | |
| SPRINGFIELD LODGE HEALTH CARE (HM19052) | ● | ● | ● | ● | ● | | ● | ● | ● | ● | ● | | ● | ● | ● | ● | ● | ● | ● | ● | ● | ● | ● | ● |

# A - C Conditions treated at Practices/Businesses

| Business by County with Reference no. | Acne | Addiction | Adenoids | Aids | Alcoholism | Allergy | Alzheimer's Disease | Amnesia | Anaemia | Angina | Anorexia | Anxiety | Arthritis | Asthma | Athletes Foot | Autism | Back Pain | Bacterial Infections | Baldness | Bereavement |
|---|---|---|---|---|---|---|---|---|---|---|---|---|---|---|---|---|---|---|---|---|
| ST MARYS PRACTICE (HM19088) | | | | | | | | | | | | | ● | | ● | | ● | | | |
| STEPHEN GORDON (HM19197) | ● | | ● | | ● | ● | | | ● | ● | ● | ● | ● | ● | ● | ● | ● | ● | | |
| STOWMARKET OSTEOPATHS (HM19363) | | | | | | | | | | | | | ● | ● | | | ● | | | |
| SUDBURY CHIROPRACTIC CLINIC (HM19462) | | | | | | | | | | | | | | | | | ● | | | |
| UNITY HEALTH CENTRE (HM20510) | | | | | | ● | | | | | | | | | | | | | | |
| WEI CLINIC (HM21111) | ● | | | | | ● | | | ● | | | ● | ● | ● | | | ● | | | |
| WOOLPITPHYSIO (HM21881) | | | | | | | | | | | | | | | | | ● | | | |
| **SURREY** | | | | | | | | | | | | | | | | | | | | |
| ACE NUTRITION (HM00157) | ● | | | | | ● | | | | | | ● | ● | | | | ● | ● | | |
| ACORN HEALTH CLINIC (HM00177) | | ● | | | | ● | | | | | | ● | ● | | | | | | | |
| ACORN THERAPY CENTRE (HM00181) | | ● | | | ● | | | | | | | ● | | | | | | | | ● |
| ACUHERBAL CHINESE MEDICINE (HM00214) | | | | | | | | | | | | | | | | | ● | | | |
| ASCOT HOMEOPATHIC CLINIC (HM01177) | | ● | | | | ● | | | ● | ● | | ● | | ● | | ● | | ● | | |
| ASHTEAD CHARTERED PHYSIO SV (HM01230) | | | | | | | | | | | | | ● | | | | ● | | | |
| ASHTEAD CLINIC (HM01232) | | | | | | | | | | | | | ● | | | | ● | | | |
| ASTON CLINIC (HM01301) | | | | | | ● | | | | | | | ● | | | | ● | | | |
| ASW ALLERGY CONSULTANTS (HM01305) | ● | | | | | ● | | | | | | ● | ● | ● | ● | | | | | |
| AVENUE PHYSIO & SPORTS CLNC (HM01390) | | | | | | | | | | | | | ● | | | | ● | | | |
| BACK TO HEALTH (HM01508) | | | | | | | | | | | | | ● | | | | ● | | | |
| BACK TO HEALTH - GUILDFORD (HM01511) | | | | | | | | | | | | | ● | | | | ● | | | |
| BACK TO HEALTH - RICHMOND (HM01514) | | | | | | | | | | | | | ● | | | | ● | | | |
| BACK TO HEALTH - SUTTON (HM01515) | | | | | | | | | | | | | ● | | | | | | | |
| BACKCARE CLINIC (HM01527) | | | | | | | | | | | | | | ● | | | ● | | | |
| BAILEY, L J (HM01551) | | | | | | | | | | | | | ● | ● | | | ● | | | |
| BARNES, A K R (HM01743) | | | | | | | | | | | | | ● | | | | ● | | | |
| BARNSTEAD VILLAGE CLINIC (HM01769) | | | | | | ● | | | | | | | ● | | ● | | ● | | | |
| BATCHELOR, C (HM01863) | | | | | | | | | | | | ● | | | | | | | | |
| BAXTER, STEPHEN (HM01933) | | | | | | | | | | | | | | ● | | | ● | | | |
| BIGWOOD, SIMON (HM02295) | | | | | | ● | | | | | | | | | | | ● | | | |
| BIODYNAMICS (HM02332) | | | | ● | | ● | ● | ● | ● | ● | ● | ● | ● | ● | | | ● | ● | ● | |
| BOURNE HEALTH (HM02753) | | | | | | | | | | | | ● | ● | | | | | | | |
| BRABANT HOUSE CLINIC (HM02830) | ● | | | | | ● | | | | ● | ● | ● | ● | ● | ● | | ● | | ● | |
| BREWSTER, DAVID J (HM02980) | | ● | | | ● | | | ● | | | ● | ● | | | | | | | | |
| BST FOUNDATION (HM03294) | | | | | | | | | | | | ● | | | | | | | | |

| Business by County with Reference no. | Bladder Problems | Blood Pressure | Boils | Bowel Problems | Breast Problems | Breathing Problems | Bronchitis | Bruising | Bulimia | Bunions | Bursitis | Callices | Cancers | Cataracts | Catarrh | Cerebral Palsy | Circulation Problems | Cold Sores | Colds | Colic | Colitis | Conjunctivitis | Constipation | Convulsions | Corns | Coughs | Cramp | Cystitis |
|---|---|---|---|---|---|---|---|---|---|---|---|---|---|---|---|---|---|---|---|---|---|---|---|---|---|---|---|---|
| ST MARYS PRACTICE (HM19088) | | | | | | | | | | | | | | | | | | | | | | | | | | | | |
| STEPHEN GORDON (HM19197) | ● | ● | ● | ● | ● | ● | ● | ● | ● | | ● | | | | ● | | ● | ● | ● | ● | ● | ● | ● | ● | | ● | ● | ● |
| STOWMARKET OSTEOPATHS (HM19363) | | | | | | | | | | | | | | | | | | | | | | | | | | | | |
| SUDBURY CHIROPRACTIC CLINIC (HM19462) | | | | | | | | | | | | | | | | | | | | | | | | | | | | |
| UNITY HEALTH CENTRE (HM20510) | | | | | | | | | | | | | | | | | | | | | | | | | | | | |
| WEI CLINIC (HM21111) | ● | ● | | | | ● | | | | | | | | | ● | | ● | | ● | ● | ● | ● | ● | | | ● | ● | ● |
| WOOLPITPHYSIO (HM21881) | | | | | | | | | | | | | | | | | | | | | | | | | | | | |
| **SURREY** | | | | | | | | | | | | | | | | | | | | | | | | | | | | |
| ACE NUTRITION (HM00157) | ● | ● | | ● | ● | | | ● | | | | | | | | | | | | | ● | | ● | | | | | |
| ACORN HEALTH CLINIC (HM00177) | | | | | | | | | | | | | | | | | | | | | | | ● | | | | | ● |
| ACORN THERAPY CENTRE (HM00181) | | | | | | ● | | | | | | | | | | | | | | | | | | | | | | |
| ACUHERBAL CHINESE MEDICINE (HM00214) | | | | | | | | | | | | | | | | | | | | | | | | | | | | |
| ASCOT HOMEOPATHIC CLINIC (HM01177) | ● | ● | ● | ● | ● | ● | ● | ● | ● | | ● | | | | ● | | ● | ● | ● | ● | ● | ● | ● | ● | | ● | ● | ● |
| ASHTEAD CHARTERED PHYSIO SV (HM01230) | | | | | | | | | | | ● | | | | | | | | | | | | | | | | | |
| ASHTEAD CLINIC (HM01232) | | | | | | | | | | | | | | | | | | | | | | | | | | | | |
| ASTON CLINIC (HM01301) | | | | | | | | ● | | | | | | | | | ● | | ● | | | | ● | | | ● | ● | ● |
| ASW ALLERGY CONSULTANTS (HM01305) | ● | ● | | ● | | ● | | | | | | | | | ● | | ● | | | | | | ● | | | ● | | ● |
| AVENUE PHYSIO & SPORTS CLNC (HM01390) | | | | | | | | | | | | | | | | | | | | | | | | | | | | |
| BACK TO HEALTH (HM01508) | | | | | | | | | | | | | | | | | ● | | | ● | | | | | | | | |
| BACK TO HEALTH - GUILDFORD (HM01511) | | | | | | | | | | | | | | | | | | | | ● | | | | | | | | |
| BACK TO HEALTH - RICHMOND (HM01514) | | | | | | | | | | | | | | | | | ● | | | ● | | | | | | | | |
| BACK TO HEALTH - SUTTON (HM01515) | | | | | | | | | | | | | | | | | | | | ● | | | | | | | | |
| BACKCARE CLINIC (HM01527) | | | | | | ● | | | | | | | | | | | ● | | | | | | | | | | | |
| BAILEY, L J (HM01551) | | | | ● | | ● | ● | ● | | | ● | | | | ● | | ● | | | | | | ● | | | | | |
| BARNES, A K R (HM01743) | | | | | | ● | | | | | ● | | | | | | | | | | | | | | | | | |
| BARNSTEAD VILLAGE CLINIC (HM01769) | | | | | | | | | | | | ● | | | | | | | | | | | ● | | ● | | | |
| BATCHELOR, C (HM01863) | | | | | | | | | | | | | | | | | | | | | | | | | | | | |
| BAXTER, STEPHEN (HM01933) | | | | | | | | | | | | | | | | | | | | | | | | | | | | |
| BIGWOOD, SIMON (HM02295) | | | | | | | | | | | | | | | | | ● | | | | | | ● | | | | | |
| BIODYNAMICS (HM02332) | ● | ● | | | ● | ● | ● | ● | ● | | | | ● | ● | ● | | ● | | ● | ● | ● | ● | | | | ● | ● | |
| BOURNE HEALTH (HM02753) | | | | | | | | | | | | | | | | | ● | | | | | | | | | | ● | |
| BRABANT HOUSE CLINIC (HM02830) | ● | ● | | ● | | ● | | | | | ● | | | | ● | | ● | ● | ● | ● | ● | | ● | | | ● | | ● |
| BREWSTER, DAVID J (HM02980) | | | | ● | | | | | ● | | | | | | | | | | | | ● | | ● | | | | | |
| BST FOUNDATION (HM03294) | | | | | | | | | | | | | | | | | | | | | | | | | | | | |

# A - C Conditions treated at Practices/Businesses

Business by County with Reference no.

| Business | Acne | Addiction | Adenoids | Aids | Alcoholism | Allergy | Alzheimer's Disease | Amnesia | Anaemia | Angina | Anorexia | Anxiety | Arthritis | Asthma | Athletes Foot | Autism | Back Pain | Bacterial Infections | Baldness | Bereavement | Bladder Problems | Blood Pressure | Boils | Bowel Problems |
|---|---|---|---|---|---|---|---|---|---|---|---|---|---|---|---|---|---|---|---|---|---|---|---|---|
| CAMBERLEY NATURAL THERAPY CTRE (HM03566) | ● | | | | | ● | | | | | | ● | ● | ● | | | ● | | | | ● | ● | | ● |
| CARLTON CLINIC (HM03700) | ● | ● | ● | | ● | ● | | ● | ● | ● | ● | ● | ● | ● | ● | | ● | ● | | | | ● | ● | ● |
| CATERHAM CHIROPRACTIC CLINIC (HM03853) | | | | | | | | | | | | | ● | | | | ● | | | | | | | |
| CHART LANE CLINIC (HM04039) | ● | | ● | | ● | ● | ● | ● | ● | ● | ● | ● | ● | ● | ● | ● | ● | ● | | | ● | ● | ● | ● |
| CHI CLINIC (HM04148) | ● | ● | ● | ● | ● | ● | ● | ● | ● | ● | ● | ● | ● | ● | ● | ● | ● | ● | ● | | ● | ● | ● | ● |
| CHIROPRACTIC CENTRE (HM04382) | | | | | | | | | | | | | ● | | | | ● | | | | | | | |
| CHRISTINE KEY HYPNOTHERAPIST (HM04447) | | ● | | | ● | | | | | | ● | ● | | | | | | | | | | | | |
| CITISPORT (HM04483) | | | | | | | | | | | | | ● | | | | ● | | | | | ● | | ● |
| CLEMENTS, J (HM04644) | | | | | | | | | | | | ● | ● | | | | | | | | ● | ● | | ● |
| COHEN, MICHAEL (HM04793) | | | | | | | | | | | | ● | | | | | | | | | | | | |
| CONFIDENTIAL COUNSELLING SVS (HM04975) | | | | | | | | | | | | ● | | | | | | | | | | | | |
| COX, JULIET (HM05307) | | | | | | | | | | | | ● | ● | ● | | | ● | | | | | ● | | |
| CROYDON HEALING CENTRE (HM05515) | ● | ● | ● | ● | ● | ● | ● | ● | ● | ● | ● | ● | ● | ● | ● | ● | ● | ● | ● | | ● | ● | ● | ● |
| CROYDON HYPNOTHERAPY (HM05516) | ● | | | | ● | ● | | ● | | | ● | ● | | ● | | | | | | | | ● | | ● |
| CUMMINS, ROZ (HM05617) | | | | | | ● | | | | ● | | | | ● | | | ● | | | | ● | | | |
| DORCHESTER HOUSE OSTEOPATHY (HM06195) | ● | ● | ● | ● | ● | ● | ● | ● | ● | ● | ● | ● | ● | ● | ● | ● | ● | ● | ● | | ● | ● | ● | ● |
| DORKING, PAUL (HM06200) | | | | | | | | | | | ● | ● | | | | | | | | | | | | |
| ECONS, A (DR) (HM06583) | | | | | | ● | | | | | | | | | | | | | | | | | | |
| EDWARDS HEALTH CLINIC (HM06639) | ● | ● | | | | | | ● | | | | | | | | | ● | | | | ● | ● | ● | ● |
| ENOCK-SHORE, ANGELA (HM06845) | ● | ● | | | | ● | | | | | | ● | | ● | | | ● | | | | | ● | | |
| EPSOM CHIROPRACTIC CLINIC (HM06857) | | | | | | | | | | | | | ● | | | | ● | | | | | | | |
| EQUILIBRIUM OSTEOPATHIC (HM06876) | ● | | ● | | | ● | | | ● | | | | ● | ● | | | ● | | | | ● | ● | | ● |
| FARNBOROUGH CHIRO CLINIC (HM07111) | | | | | | | | | | | | | ● | | | | ● | | | | | | | |
| FOOT CARE CENTRE (HM07466) | | | | | | | | | | | | | | | ● | | | | | | | | | |
| GATEWAYS CENTRE (HM07928) | | | | | | | | | | | | ● | | | | | | | | | | | | |
| GAUVAIN, TONY (HM07934) | | | | | | | | | | | | ● | | | | | | | | ● | | | | |
| GLAISTER, BRIAN (DR) (HM08120) | | | | | | | | | | | | ● | | | | | | | | | | | | |
| GODDARD, TERRI (HM08180) | | | | | | | | | | | | ● | ● | | | | ● | | | | | | | |
| GOODLIFE NATURAL HEALTH CENTRE (HM08256) | | | | | | | | | | | | | ● | | | | ● | | | | | | | |
| GORDON, SARAH (HM08282) | | | | | | | | | | | | ● | ● | | | | ● | | | | | | | |
| GRAVELL, NICOLA (HM08401) | | | | | | | | | | | | ● | | | | | | | | | | | | |
| GUILDFORD PHYSIO & SPORTS (HM08632) | | | | | | | | | | | | | | | | | ● | | | | | | | |
| HAM CHIROPRACTIC CLINIC (HM08822) | | | | | | | | | | | | | | | | | ● | | | | | | | |
| HANDS ON HEALTH (HM08911) | | | | | | | | | | | | | ● | | ● | | ● | | | | | | | |

| Business | Breast Problems | Breathing Problems | Bronchitis | Bruising | Bulimia | Bunions | Bursitis | Callices | Cancers | Cataracts | Catarrh | Cerebral Palsy | Circulation Problems | Cold Sores | Colds | Colic | Colitis | Conjunctivitis | Constipation | Convulsions | Corns | Coughs | Cramp | Cystitis |
|---|---|---|---|---|---|---|---|---|---|---|---|---|---|---|---|---|---|---|---|---|---|---|---|---|
| CAMBERLEY NATURAL THERAPY CTRE (HM03566) | | | | | | | ● | | | | ● | | ● | ● | ● | ● | | ● | ● | | | ● | ● | ● |
| CARLTON CLINIC (HM03700) | | ● | ● | ● | ● | | ● | | | | ● | | ● | ● | ● | ● | ● | ● | ● | | | | ● | ● |
| CATERHAM CHIROPRACTIC CLINIC (HM03853) | | | | | | | | | | | | | ● | | | | | | | | | | | |
| CHART LANE CLINIC (HM04039) | ● | ● | ● | ● | ● | | ● | ● | ● | ● | ● | | ● | ● | ● | ● | ● | ● | ● | | ● | ● | ● | ● |
| CHI CLINIC (HM04148) | ● | ● | ● | ● | ● | | ● | ● | ● | ● | ● | | ● | ● | ● | ● | ● | ● | ● | ● | ● | ● | ● | ● |
| CHIROPRACTIC CENTRE (HM04382) | | | | | | | | | | | | | ● | | | | | | | | | | | |
| CHRISTINE KEY HYPNOTHERAPIST (HM04447) | | | | | ● | | | | | | | | | | | | | | | | | | | |
| CITISPORT (HM04483) | | | | | | | ● | | | | | | | | | | ● | | ● | | | | | |
| CLEMENTS, J (HM04644) | | ● | | | | | | | | | | | ● | | | | | | | | | | | |
| COHEN, MICHAEL (HM04793) | | | | | ● | | | | | | | | | | | | | | | | | | | |
| CONFIDENTIAL COUNSELLING SVS (HM04975) | | | | | | | | | | | | | | | | | | | | | | | | |
| COX, JULIET (HM05307) | | ● | | | | | | | | | | | | | | | | | | | | | | |
| CROYDON HEALING CENTRE (HM05515) | ● | ● | ● | ● | ● | | ● | | ● | ● | ● | | ● | ● | ● | ● | ● | ● | ● | ● | | ● | ● | ● |
| CROYDON HYPNOTHERAPY (HM05516) | | ● | | | ● | | | | | | | | | ● | | | ● | | ● | | | | | |
| CUMMINS, ROZ (HM05617) | | ● | | | | | | | | | ● | | ● | | | | | | ● | | | | ● | |
| DORCHESTER HOUSE OSTEOPATHY (HM06195) | ● | ● | ● | ● | ● | | ● | ● | ● | ● | ● | | ● | ● | ● | ● | ● | ● | ● | ● | ● | ● | ● | ● |
| DORKING, PAUL (HM06200) | | | | | ● | | | | | | | | | | | | | | | | | | | |
| ECONS, A (DR) (HM06583) | | | | | | | | | | | | | | | | | | | | | | | | |
| EDWARDS HEALTH CLINIC (HM06639) | ● | | | | ● | | | | | | | | ● | | | | | | ● | | | | | |
| ENOCK-SHORE, ANGELA (HM06845) | | ● | | | ● | | | | | | ● | | ● | | | | ● | | | | | | | |
| EPSOM CHIROPRACTIC CLINIC (HM06857) | | | | | | | | | | | | | ● | | | | | | | | | | | |
| EQUILIBRIUM OSTEOPATHIC (HM06876) | | | | ● | | | ● | | | | | | | | ● | ● | ● | | ● | | | | ● | |
| FARNBOROUGH CHIRO CLINIC (HM07111) | | | | | | | | | | | | | | | | ● | | | | | | | | |
| FOOT CARE CENTRE (HM07466) | | | | | | | | | | | | | | | | | | | | | | | | |
| GATEWAYS CENTRE (HM07928) | | | | | | | | | | | | | | | | | | | | | | | | |
| GAUVAIN, TONY (HM07934) | | | | | | | | | | | | | | | | | | | | | | | | |
| GLAISTER, BRIAN (DR) (HM08120) | | | | | | | | | | | | | | | | | | | | | | | | |
| GODDARD, TERRI (HM08180) | | ● | | | | | | | | | | | | | | | | | | | | | ● | |
| GOODLIFE NATURAL HEALTH CENTRE (HM08256) | | | | | | | ● | | | | | | | | | | | | | | | | | |
| GORDON, SARAH (HM08282) | | | | | | | | | | | | | | | | | | | | | | | | |
| GRAVELL, NICOLA (HM08401) | | | | | | | | | | | | | | | | | | | | | | | | |
| GUILDFORD PHYSIO & SPORTS (HM08632) | | | | | | | | | | | | | | | | | | | | | | | | |
| HAM CHIROPRACTIC CLINIC (HM08822) | | | | | | | ● | | | | | | | | | | | | | | | | | |
| HANDS ON HEALTH (HM08911) | | | | | | | | | | | | | | | | ● | | | | | | | | |

# A - C Conditions treated at Practices/Businesses

| Business by County with Reference no. | Acne | Addiction | Adenoids | Aids | Alcoholism | Allergy | Alzheimer's Disease | Amnesia | Anaemia | Angina | Anorexia | Anxiety | Arthritis | Asthma | Athletes Foot | Autism | Back Pain | Bacterial Infections | Baldness | Bereavement | Bladder Problems | Blood Pressure | Boils | Bowel Problems |
|---|---|---|---|---|---|---|---|---|---|---|---|---|---|---|---|---|---|---|---|---|---|---|---|---|
| HANFORD, S P (HM08925) | | | | | | | | | | | | ● | ● | ● | | | ● | | | | ● | ● | | ● |
| HARDY, JACK E (HM08981) | | ● | | | ● | | | | | | | | | | | | | | | ● | | | | |
| HARTLEY, GILL (HM09140) | | | | | | | | | | | | ● | ● | | | | ● | | | | | | | ● |
| HEAVEN MOUNTAIN TAIJI QUAN (HM09472) | | | | | | | | | | | | | | ● | | | ● | | | | | | | |
| HELIANTHUS PRACTICE (HM09518) | ● | | | | | ● | | | ● | ● | | ● | ● | ● | ● | | ● | ● | | | ● | ● | ● | ● |
| HERBAL KING (HM09628) | ● | | | | | ● | | | | | | | ● | ● | | | | | | | | | | |
| HERBALS (HM09647) | ● | | ● | | ● | ● | ● | ● | ● | ● | ● | ● | ● | ● | ● | ● | ● | ● | ● | | ● | ● | ● | ● |
| HILL, CHARLOTTE (HM09774) | | | | | | | | | | | | | ● | | | | | | | | | | | |
| HILLVIEW PHYSIO & SPORTS CLNC (HM09809) | | | | | | | | | | | | | ● | | | | ● | | | | | | | |
| HOLISTIC CENTRE (HM09949) | ● | ● | ● | ● | ● | ● | ● | ● | ● | ● | ● | ● | ● | ● | ● | ● | ● | ● | ● | | ● | ● | ● | ● |
| HOLISTIC HEALTH CENTRE (HM09971) | | ● | | | | ● | | | | | | ● | ● | | | | | | | | | | | |
| HOPPER, C A (HM10156) | | | | | | | | | | | | ● | | | | | | | | | | | | |
| HUMAN FOCUS RETURN TO WORK (HM10362) | | | | | | | | | | | | ● | | | | | ● | | | | | | | |
| INGLEDALE NATURAL HEALTH CTRE (HM10621) | | | | | | | | | | | | | ● | | | | ● | | | | | | | |
| INTEGRAL HEALTH (HM10690) | ● | ● | ● | ● | ● | ● | ● | ● | ● | ● | ● | ● | ● | ● | ● | ● | ● | ● | ● | | ● | ● | ● | ● |
| J V ASSOCIATES (HM10803) | ● | | | | | | ● | | | | | | ● | ● | | | ● | | | | | ● | | |
| KENT CLINIC OF NATURAL MED (HM11514) | ● | ● | ● | ● | ● | ● | ● | ● | ● | ● | ● | ● | ● | ● | ● | ● | ● | ● | ● | | ● | ● | ● | ● |
| KEW CHIROPRACTIC CLINIC (HM11575) | | | | | | | | | | | | | ● | | | | ● | | | | | | | |
| KINGSTON NATURAL HEALING CTRE (HM11677) | ● | ● | | | | ● | | | | | | ● | ● | ● | ● | ● | ● | | | | | | | ● |
| KINGSTON OSTEOPATHS (HM11679) | | | | | | | | | | | | | ● | ● | | | ● | | | | ● | ● | | ● |
| KOLTHAMMER, JOHN (HM11780) | | | | | | | | | | | | | | | | | ● | | | | | | | |
| LEATHERHEAD CHIRO CLINIC (HM12114) | | | | | | | | | | | | ● | ● | | | | | ● | | | | | | |
| LIFE STYLE NATURAL HEALTH CTRE (HM12349) | | | | | | ● | | | | | | | | | | | | | | | | | | |
| LONDON SPINE AND JOINT CLINIC (HM12610) | | | | | | | | | | | | | | | | | ● | | | | | | | |
| LOW, ROYSTON (HM12688) | | | | | | ● | | | | ● | | ● | ● | ● | | | ● | | | | ● | ● | | ● |
| MARKS, DARREN HYPNOTHERAPY (HM13120) | | ● | | ● | | | | | | | | ● | | | | | | | | | | | | |
| MARSON, JOY (HM13178) | | | | | ● | ● | | | ● | | ● | | ● | ● | | | | | | | | ● | | ● |
| MEDICAL HYPNOTHERAPY CLINIC (HM13653) | | | | | | | | | | | | ● | | | | | | | | | | | | |
| MEEKS, FIONA (HM13683) | | | | | | ● | | | | | | | | ● | | | | | | | ● | | | |
| MEENEGHAN, TOM (HM13685) | ● | ● | ● | | ● | ● | | | ● | ● | ● | ● | ● | ● | ● | | ● | ● | | | ● | ● | ● | ● |
| MILFORD MASSAGE PRACTICE (HM13863) | | | | | | | | | | | | | ● | | | | ● | | | | | | | |
| MILLER CONSULTANCY (HM13880) | | | | | ● | ● | | | ● | | ● | ● | | ● | | ● | ● | | | ● | ● | ● | | ● |
| MIND AND BODY (HM13958) | | | | | | ● | | | | | | ● | ● | ● | ● | | ● | | | | | | | ● |
| MIST, CORINNE (HM13996) | ● | | | | | | | | | | | | ● | | | | | | | | ● | ● | | ● |

| Business by County with Reference no. | Breast Problems | Breathing Problems | Bronchitis | Bruising | Bulimia | Bunions | Bursitis | Callices | Cancers | Cataracts | Catarrh | Cerebral Palsy | Circulation Problems | Cold Sores | Colds | Colic | Colitis | Conjunctivitis | Constipation | Convulsions | Corns | Coughs | Cramp | Cystitis |
|---|---|---|---|---|---|---|---|---|---|---|---|---|---|---|---|---|---|---|---|---|---|---|---|---|
| HANFORD, S P (HM08925) | | | | | | | ● | | | | ● | | ● | | | | | | ● | | | | | |
| HARDY, JACK E (HM08981) | | | | | | | | | | | | | | | | | | | | | | | | |
| HARTLEY, GILL (HM09140) | | ● | | | | | | | | | | | ● | | | ● | | | ● | | | | ● | |
| HEAVEN MOUNTAIN TAIJI QUAN (HM09472) | | ● | | | | | | | | | | | | | | | | | | | | | | |
| HELIANTHUS PRACTICE (HM09518) | ● | ● | ● | ● | ● | | ● | | ● | | ● | | ● | ● | ● | ● | ● | ● | ● | | | ● | ● | ● |
| HERBAL KING (HM09628) | | ● | ● | | | | | | ● | | | | ● | | | | | | | | | | | |
| HERBALS (HM09647) | ● | ● | ● | ● | ● | | ● | | | | ● | | ● | ● | ● | ● | ● | ● | ● | | | ● | ● | ● |
| HILL, CHARLOTTE (HM09774) | | | | | | | | | | | | | | | | ● | | | | | | | | |
| HILLVIEW PHYSIO & SPORTS CLNC (HM09809) | | | | | | | | | | | | | | | | | | | | | | | | |
| HOLISTIC CENTRE (HM09949) | ● | ● | ● | ● | ● | | ● | ● | ● | ● | ● | | ● | ● | ● | ● | ● | ● | ● | ● | ● | ● | ● | ● |
| HOLISTIC HEALTH CENTRE (HM09971) | | | | | | | | | | | | | | | | | | | ● | | | | | ● |
| HOPPER, C A (HM10156) | | ● | | | | | | | | | | | | | | | | | | | | | | |
| HUMAN FOCUS RETURN TO WORK (HM10362) | | | | | | | | | | | | | | | | | | | | | | | | |
| INGLEDALE NATURAL HEALTH CTRE (HM10621) | | | | | | | ● | | | | | | | | | | | | | | | | | |
| INTEGRAL HEALTH (HM10690) | ● | ● | ● | ● | ● | | ● | ● | ● | ● | ● | | ● | ● | ● | ● | ● | ● | ● | ● | ● | ● | ● | ● |
| J V ASSOCIATES (HM10803) | | ● | | | | | | | | | | | ● | | | | | | | | | | | |
| KENT CLINIC OF NATURAL MED (HM11514) | ● | ● | ● | ● | ● | | ● | | ● | ● | ● | | ● | ● | ● | ● | ● | ● | ● | ● | | ● | ● | ● |
| KEW CHIROPRACTIC CLINIC (HM11575) | | | | | | | ● | | | | | | ● | | | | | | ● | | | | ● | |
| KINGSTON NATURAL HEALING CTRE (HM11677) | | ● | | | | | ● | | | | ● | | ● | | ● | ● | | | ● | | | ● | | |
| KINGSTON OSTEOPATHS (HM11679) | ● | ● | ● | | | | ● | | | | | | ● | | ● | ● | ● | | ● | | | ● | | |
| KOLTHAMMER, JOHN (HM11780) | | | | | | | | | | | | | | | | | | | | | | | | |
| LEATHERHEAD CHIRO CLINIC (HM12114) | | | | | | | | | | | | | | | | | ● | | | | | | | |
| LIFE STYLE NATURAL HEALTH CTRE (HM12349) | | | | | | | | | | | | | | | | | | | | | | | | |
| LONDON SPINE AND JOINT CLINIC (HM12610) | | | | | | | ● | | | | | | | | | | | | | | | | | |
| LOW, ROYSTON (HM12688) | | ● | ● | | | | ● | | | | ● | | ● | | | ● | ● | | | | | | | ● |
| MARKS, DARREN HYPNOTHERAPY (HM13120) | | | | | | | | | ● | | | | | | | | | | | | | | | |
| MARSON, JOY (HM13178) | | | | | | | | | ● | | ● | | ● | ● | | | ● | | ● | | | | | ● |
| MEDICAL HYPNOTHERAPY CLINIC (HM13653) | | | | | | | | | | | | | | | | | | | | | | | | |
| MEEKS, FIONA (HM13683) | | ● | | | | | | | | | | ● | | | | | | | | | | | | |
| MEENEGHAN, TOM (HM13685) | ● | ● | ● | ● | ● | | ● | | ● | | ● | | ● | ● | ● | ● | ● | ● | ● | ● | | ● | ● | ● |
| MILFORD MASSAGE PRACTICE (HM13863) | | | | | | | | | | | | | | | | | | | | | | | | |
| MILLER CONSULTANCY (HM13880) | | ● | ● | | ● | | | | | | | | ● | | | ● | | | ● | | | | ● | ● |
| MIND AND BODY (HM13958) | | | | | | | ● | | | | | | | | | | ● | | ● | | | | ● | |
| MIST, CORINNE (HM13996) | | ● | | | | | | | | | | | ● | | | | | | ● | | | | | |

# A - C Conditions treated at Practices/Businesses

Business by County with Reference no.

| Business | Acne | Addiction | Adenoids | Aids | Alcoholism | Allergy | Alzheimer's Disease | Amnesia | Anaemia | Angina | Anorexia | Anxiety | Arthritis | Asthma | Athletes Foot | Autism |
|---|---|---|---|---|---|---|---|---|---|---|---|---|---|---|---|---|
| NATURAL HEALING CENTRE (HM14541) | | | | | | | | | | ● | ● | ● | ● | ● | | |
| NATURAL HEALING CLINIC (HM14550) | | | | | | | | | | | | | | | | |
| NATURAL HEALTH PRACTICE (HM14594) | | | | | | | | | | ● | | | ● | | | |
| NATURAL LIFE AROMATHERAPY (HM14608) | | | | | | ● | | | | | | | | | | |
| NICHOLLS, VERITY (HM14915) | | | | | | | | | | | | | | | ● | |
| NICOLA FRY-HEALTH & BEAUTY (HM14927) | ● | | | | | | | | | | | ● | | | | |
| OLD WOKING GRANGE (HM15264) | ● | ● | | | ● | ● | | | | | ● | ● | ● | | | |
| OSTEOPATHY (HM15477) | | | | | | | | | | | | | ● | | | |
| PHILP, CHRISTINE (HM16147) | | | | | | | | | | | | ● | ● | | | |
| POWER, DAVID J (HM16503) | | | | | | | | | | | | | | | ● | |
| PRICE, SANDRA (HM16593) | | | | | | | | | | | | | ● | | | |
| RICHMOND PHYSIOTHERAPY (HM17301) | | | | | | | | | | | | | ● | | | |
| ROBYNA, ANNETTE (HM17516) | | | | | | ● | | | | | ● | ● | | ● | | |
| ROUNDABOUT DRAMA/MOVEMENT (HM17665) | | | | | | | | | | | | | | | | ● |
| SARAH BOGUE HOMEOPATH (HM17944) | | | | | | | | | | | | ● | | ● | | |
| SAUMEEL PATEL ACU CLINIC (HM17950) | | | | | | ● | | | | | ● | ● | ● | | | |
| SAYER CLINIC (HM17992) | | | | | | | | | | | | | ● | | | |
| SCHONBERG, VERA (HM18078) | ● | ● | | | ● | | | | | | | ● | ● | ● | | |
| SCHOOL OF YOGA (HM18089) | | | | | | | | | | | | | | ● | | |
| SCORPIO PHYSIOTHERAPY (HM18103) | | | | | | | | | | | | | ● | | | |
| SELSDON COMP/RESP CLINIC (HM18220) | ● | ● | ● | ● | ● | ● | ● | ● | ● | ● | ● | ● | ● | ● | | |
| SEVEN SIGHS (HM18244) | | | | | | ● | | | | | | ● | ● | ● | | |
| SHEPPERTON PHYSIOFIRST CENTRE (HM18425) | | | | | | | | | | | | | ● | | | |
| SIMMS, KATHERINE (HM18564) | | | | | | | | | | | | ● | | | | |
| SLATTERY, BRIDGET (HM18677) | | | | | | | | | | | | | | | | |
| STEWART, I (HM19267) | | | | | | | | | | | | | | | ● | |
| SURBITON NATURAL HEALTH CENTRE (HM19514) | ● | ● | | | | ● | | | | | | ● | ● | ● | | |
| SURREY HEALING SANCTUARY (HM19522) | ● | ● | ● | | | ● | ● | ● | ● | ● | ● | ● | ● | ● | ● | ● |
| SUTHERLAND, JENNY (HM19539) | | | | | | | | | | | | ● | ● | | | |
| SUTTON CHIROPRACTIC CLINIC (HM19543) | | | | | | | | | | | | | | | | |
| TANSILL, LUCY (HM19689) | | | | | | | | | ● | | | | | | | |
| TELLING, PAUL (HM19824) | | | | | | | | | | | | ● | | | | |
| TOWNS, KATE (HM20202) | ● | ● | | | | | | | | | ● | ● | | | | |
| TRADITIONAL CHINESE MEDICINE (HM20225) | | | | | | | | | | | | ● | ● | ● | | |

| Business | Back Pain | Bacterial Infections | Baldness | Bereavement | Bladder Problems | Blood Pressure | Boils | Bowel Problems | Breast Problems | Breathing Problems | Bronchitis | Bruising | Bulimia | Bunions | Bursitis | Callices |
|---|---|---|---|---|---|---|---|---|---|---|---|---|---|---|---|---|
| NATURAL HEALING CENTRE (HM14541) | ● | | | | ● | ● | | | | ● | | | | | | |
| NATURAL HEALING CLINIC (HM14550) | ● | | | | | | | | | | | | | | | |
| NATURAL HEALTH PRACTICE (HM14594) | ● | | | | | | | | | | | | | | ● | |
| NATURAL LIFE AROMATHERAPY (HM14608) | | | | | | | | | | | | | | | | |
| NICHOLLS, VERITY (HM14915) | | | | | | | | | | | | | | ● | | ● |
| NICOLA FRY-HEALTH & BEAUTY (HM14927) | ● | | | | | | | | | | ● | ● | | | | |
| OLD WOKING GRANGE (HM15264) | | ● | | | ● | ● | | ● | | ● | | | ● | | | |
| OSTEOPATHY (HM15477) | ● | | | | | | | | | | | | | | | |
| PHILP, CHRISTINE (HM16147) | ● | | | | | ● | | | | | | | | | | |
| POWER, DAVID J (HM16503) | | | | | | | | | | | | | | | | ● |
| PRICE, SANDRA (HM16593) | ● | | | | | | | | | | | | | | | |
| RICHMOND PHYSIOTHERAPY (HM17301) | ● | | | | | | | | | | | ● | | | | |
| ROBYNA, ANNETTE (HM17516) | ● | | | | | ● | | | | ● | | | | | | |
| ROUNDABOUT DRAMA/MOVEMENT (HM17665) | | | | | | | | | | | | | | | | |
| SARAH BOGUE HOMEOPATH (HM17944) | | | | | | | | ● | | | | | | | | |
| SAUMEEL PATEL ACU CLINIC (HM17950) | ● | | | | | | | | | | | | ● | | | |
| SAYER CLINIC (HM17992) | | | | | | | | | | | | | | | | |
| SCHONBERG, VERA (HM18078) | ● | | | | | ● | | | | | | | ● | | | |
| SCHOOL OF YOGA (HM18089) | ● | | | | | | | | | ● | | | | | | |
| SCORPIO PHYSIOTHERAPY (HM18103) | ● | | | | | | | ● | | | | | | | ● | |
| SELSDON COMP/RESP CLINIC (HM18220) | ● | ● | | | ● | ● | ● | ● | | ● | ● | ● | ● | | ● | ● |
| SEVEN SIGHS (HM18244) | ● | | | | | ● | | | | | | | | | | |
| SHEPPERTON PHYSIOFIRST CENTRE (HM18425) | ● | | | | | | | | | | | ● | | | | |
| SIMMS, KATHERINE (HM18564) | ● | | | | | ● | | | | ● | | | | | | |
| SLATTERY, BRIDGET (HM18677) | | | | ● | | | | | | | | | | | | |
| STEWART, I (HM19267) | | | | | | | | | | | | | | ● | | |
| SURBITON NATURAL HEALTH CENTRE (HM19514) | ● | | | | | | | | | | | | | | | |
| SURREY HEALING SANCTUARY (HM19522) | ● | ● | ● | | ● | ● | ● | ● | ● | ● | ● | ● | ● | | ● | |
| SUTHERLAND, JENNY (HM19539) | ● | | | | ● | | | | | ● | | | | | | |
| SUTTON CHIROPRACTIC CLINIC (HM19543) | ● | | | | | | | | | | | | | | | |
| TANSILL, LUCY (HM19689) | ● | | | | ● | ● | | ● | | | | | | | | |
| TELLING, PAUL (HM19824) | ● | | | | | | | | | | | | | | | |
| TOWNS, KATE (HM20202) | | | ● | | | | | | | | | | | | | |
| TRADITIONAL CHINESE MEDICINE (HM20225) | ● | | | | | | | | | ● | | | | | | |

| Business | Cancers | Cataracts | Catarrh | Cerebral Palsy | Circulation Problems | Cold Sores | Colds | Colic | Colitis | Conjunctivitis | Constipation | Convulsions | Corns | Coughs | Cramp | Cystitis |
|---|---|---|---|---|---|---|---|---|---|---|---|---|---|---|---|---|
| NATURAL HEALING CENTRE (HM14541) | | | ● | | ● | | | | | | ● | | | | ● | |
| NATURAL HEALING CLINIC (HM14550) | | | | | | | | | | | | | | | | |
| NATURAL HEALTH PRACTICE (HM14594) | | | | | | | ● | ● | ● | | ● | | | | | |
| NATURAL LIFE AROMATHERAPY (HM14608) | | | | | | | | | | | | | | | | |
| NICHOLLS, VERITY (HM14915) | | | | | | | | | | | | | ● | | | |
| NICOLA FRY-HEALTH & BEAUTY (HM14927) | | | ● | | ● | | | | | | | | | | | |
| OLD WOKING GRANGE (HM15264) | ● | | | | | | | | ● | | ● | | | | | ● |
| OSTEOPATHY (HM15477) | | | | | | | | | | | | | | | | |
| PHILP, CHRISTINE (HM16147) | | | | | | | | | | | | | | | | |
| POWER, DAVID J (HM16503) | | | | | | | | | | | | | ● | | | |
| PRICE, SANDRA (HM16593) | | | | | | | | | | | | | | | | |
| RICHMOND PHYSIOTHERAPY (HM17301) | | | | | | | | | | | | | | | | |
| ROBYNA, ANNETTE (HM17516) | | | | | ● | | | | | | ● | | | | ● | |
| ROUNDABOUT DRAMA/MOVEMENT (HM17665) | | | | | | | | | | | | | | | | |
| SARAH BOGUE HOMEOPATH (HM17944) | | | ● | | | | ● | | | | | | | ● | | ● |
| SAUMEEL PATEL ACU CLINIC (HM17950) | | | | | | | | | | | ● | | | | | |
| SAYER CLINIC (HM17992) | | | | | ● | | | | | | | | | | | |
| SCHONBERG, VERA (HM18078) | | | | | | | | | | | | | | | | |
| SCHOOL OF YOGA (HM18089) | | | | | | | | | | | | | | | ● | |
| SCORPIO PHYSIOTHERAPY (HM18103) | | | | | | | | | | | ● | | | | | |
| SELSDON COMP/RESP CLINIC (HM18220) | ● | | ● | | ● | ● | ● | ● | ● | ● | ● | | ● | ● | ● | ● |
| SEVEN SIGHS (HM18244) | | | | | | | | | | | | | | | | |
| SHEPPERTON PHYSIOFIRST CENTRE (HM18425) | | | | | | | | | | | | | | | | |
| SIMMS, KATHERINE (HM18564) | | | | | | | | | | | | | | | | |
| SLATTERY, BRIDGET (HM18677) | | | | | | | | | | | | | | | | |
| STEWART, I (HM19267) | | | | | | | | | | | | | | | | |
| SURBITON NATURAL HEALTH CENTRE (HM19514) | | | | | | | | | | | ● | | | | | |
| SURREY HEALING SANCTUARY (HM19522) | ● | ● | ● | | ● | ● | ● | ● | ● | | ● | ● | | ● | ● | ● |
| SUTHERLAND, JENNY (HM19539) | | | ● | | ● | | | | | | ● | | | | ● | |
| SUTTON CHIROPRACTIC CLINIC (HM19543) | | | | | | | | | | | | | | | | |
| TANSILL, LUCY (HM19689) | | | | | ● | | | | | | | | | | | |
| TELLING, PAUL (HM19824) | | | | | | | | | | | | | | | | |
| TOWNS, KATE (HM20202) | | | | | | | | | | | | | | | | |
| TRADITIONAL CHINESE MEDICINE (HM20225) | | | ● | | ● | | | | | | ● | | | | ● | |

# A - C Conditions treated at Practices/Businesses

| Business by County with Reference no. | Acne | Addiction | Adenoids | Aids | Alcoholism | Allergy | Alzheimer's Disease | Amnesia | Anaemia | Angina | Anorexia | Anxiety | Arthritis | Asthma | Athletes Foot | Autism | Back Pain | Bacterial Infections | Baldness | Bereavement | Bladder Problems | Blood Pressure | Boils | Bowel Problems | Breast Problems | Breathing Problems | Bronchitis | Bruising | Bulimia | Bunions | Bursitis | Callices | Cancers | Cataracts | Catarrh | Cerebral Palsy | Circulation Problems | Cold Sores | Colds | Colic | Colitis | Conjunctivitis | Constipation | Convulsions | Corns | Coughs | Cramp | Cystitis |
|---|---|---|---|---|---|---|---|---|---|---|---|---|---|---|---|---|---|---|---|---|---|---|---|---|---|---|---|---|---|---|---|---|---|---|---|---|---|---|---|---|---|---|---|---|---|---|---|---|
| TRANSCENDENTAL MEDITATION (HM20266) | | ● | | | ● | | | | | | | ● | | | | | | | | | | ● | | | | | | | | | | | | | | | | | | | | | | | | | | |
| TURNER, R E (HM20435) | | | | | | | | | | | | | ● | | | | ● | | | | | | | | | | | | | | | | | | | | | | | | | | | | | | ● | |
| TWO STEPS REFLEXOLOGY (HM20458) | ● | | ● | | | ● | | | | | ● | ● | ● | ● | | | ● | ● | | | ● | ● | ● | ● | | | ● | ● | | | | | | | ● | | ● | | ● | ● | | | ● | | | ● | ● | ● |
| WALKER, SARAH (HM20803) | | | | | | | | | | | | | ● | | | | ● | | | | | ● | | | | | | | | | | | | | | | ● | | | | | | | | | | | |
| WALLACE, SUE (HM20832) | | | | | | | | | | | | | ● | | | | ● | | | | | ● | | | | | | | | | | | | | | | | | | | ● | | ● | | | | | |
| WEYBRIDGE CHIROPRACTIC CLINIC (HM21293) | | | | | | | | | | | | | | | | | ● | | | | | | | | | | | | | | | | | | | | | | | | | | | | | | | |
| WHITWORTH, MICHAEL T (HM21431) | | | | | | | | | | | | | | | ● | | | | | | | | | | | | | | | | | ● | | | | | | | | | | | | | ● | | | |
| WILKINSON, LESLEY (HM21510) | | | | ● | | ● | | | ● | | ● | ● | ● | ● | ● | | | | | | | ● | ● | ● | ● | ● | ● | ● | ● | | | | ● | ● | ● | | ● | ● | ● | ● | ● | ● | ● | ● | | ● | ● | ● |
| WILLIS, SALLY (HM21618) | | ● | | | ● | | | | | | ● | ● | | | | | | | | | | | | | | | | | ● | | | | | | | | | | | | | | | | | | | |
| WINTER, DAVID (HM21718) | ● | ● | ● | ● | ● | ● | ● | ● | ● | ● | ● | ● | ● | ● | ● | ● | ● | ● | ● | | ● | ● | ● | ● | ● | ● | ● | ● | ● | | ● | ● | ● | ● | ● | | ● | ● | ● | ● | ● | ● | ● | ● | ● | ● | ● | ● |
| WOOD, VALERIE (HM21811) | | | | | | | | | | | | ● | ● | | | | ● | | | | | | | | | | | | | | | | | | | | | | | | | | | | | | | |
| WOODLANDS NATURAL HLTH THERAPY (HM21832) | ● | | | | | ● | | | | | | ● | ● | ● | | | ● | | | | ● | ● | | ● | | ● | | | | | | | | | | | ● | | | | | | ● | | | | | ● |
| **SUSSEX (EAST)** | | | | | | | | | | | | | | | | | | | | | | | | | | | | | | | | | | | | | | | | | | | | | | | | |
| ALBION CLINIC (HM00483) | | | | | | | | | | | | ● | ● | ● | | | ● | | | | | ● | | ● | | ● | ● | | | | | | | ● | ● | | ● | | ● | ● | | | ● | | | | | |
| ALEXANDER TECHNIQUE (HM00549) | | | | | | | | | | | | ● | ● | ● | | | ● | | | | | ● | | | | ● | | | | | ● | | | | | | | | | | | | | | | | | |
| ALPHA HYPNOTHERAPY (HM00684) | | ● | | | | | | | | | | ● | | | | | | | | | | | | | | | | | | | | | | | | | | | | | | | | | | | | |
| ANGELA MATTHEWS HOMEOPATH (HM00873) | | ● | | | ● | ● | | | | | | | | ● | | | | | | | ● | ● | | | | | | | | | | | | | | | | | | | | | ● | | | ● | | ● |
| ARDERN FOOT & HEALTH CLINIC (HM00992) | ● | | | | | | | | | | | | ● | | ● | | ● | | | | | | | | | ● | | | | | | | | | | | ● | | | | | | ● | | | | | |
| AROMA HAIR (HM01047) | | | | | | | | | | | | ● | ● | | | | ● | | | | | | | | | | | | | | | | | | | | | | | | | | | | | | | |
| ASHDOWN OSTEOPATHIC CENTRE (HM01206) | | | | | | | | | | | | ● | ● | ● | | | ● | | | | | | | | | | | | | | ● | | | | | | | | | | | | | | | | | |
| BAIRD, DAVID (HM01569) | | | | | | ● | | | | | | | | | | | | | | | | | | | | | | | | | | | | | | | | | | | | | | | | | | |
| BASSETT, N S (HM01857) | | | | | | | | | | | | | | | | | ● | | | | | ● | | | | ● | | ● | | | ● | | | | | | | | | | | | | | | | ● | |
| BELVAIN, E (HM02118) | | | | | | | | | | | | | ● | ● | | | | | | | | | | | | | | | | | | | | | | | | | | | ● | | | | | | | |
| BEXHILL CHIROPRACTIC (HM02255) | | | | | | | | | | | | ● | ● | | | | ● | | | | | ● | | ● | | ● | | | | | | | | | | | ● | | | | | | ● | | | | | |
| BEXHILL OSTEOPATHIC PRACTICE (HM02257) | | | | | | ● | | | | | | ● | ● | ● | | | ● | | | | | | | | | ● | | | | | ● | | | | ● | | | | | | | | | | | | ● | |
| BLACKER, JOHN (HM02441) | | | | | | | | | | | | ● | | | | | | | | | | | | | | | | | | | | | | | | | | | | | | | | | | | | |
| BRIGHTON & HOVE SPORTS CLINIC (HM03041) | | | | | | | | | | | | | ● | | | | ● | | | | | | | | | | | | | | | | | | | | | | | | | | | | | | | |
| BRIGHTON ACUPUNCTURE CLINIC (HM03042) | ● | | | | | | | | | | | ● | | | | | ● | | | | ● | ● | | ● | | ● | ● | | | | | | | | ● | | ● | | | | | | | | | | | ● |
| BRIGHTON ALEXANDER TRAINING (HM03043) | | | | | | | | | | | | | | | | | ● | | | | | | | | | | | | | | | | | | | | ● | | | | | | | | | | | |
| BRIGHTON CHIROPRACTIC CLINIC (HM03044) | | | | | | | | | | | | | ● | | | | ● | | | | | | | | | | | | | | | | | | | | ● | | | | | | ● | | | | ● | |
| BRIGHTON HEALTH & RACQUET CLUB (HM03045) | | | | | | | | | | | | | ● | | | | ● | | | | | | | | | | | | | | | | | | | | | | | | | | | | | | | |
| BRIGHTON PHYSIOTHERAPY CLINIC (HM03048) | | | | | | | | | | | | | ● | | | | ● | | | | | | | | | | | | | | | | | | | | | | | | | | | | | | | |
| CANTERLA, MARGARET (HM03643) | ● | ● | ● | ● | ● | ● | ● | ● | ● | ● | ● | ● | ● | ● | ● | ● | ● | ● | ● | | ● | ● | ● | ● | ● | ● | ● | ● | ● | | ● | ● | ● | ● | ● | | ● | ● | ● | ● | ● | ● | ● | ● | ● | ● | ● | ● |
| CHARTERS PHYSIO & SPORTS (HM04050) | | | | | | | | | | | | | ● | | | | ● | | | | | | | | | | | | | | | | | | | | | | | | | | | | | | | |

# A - C Conditions treated at Practices/Businesses

| Business by County with Reference no. | Acne | Addiction | Adenoids | Aids | Alcoholism | Allergy | Alzheimer's Disease | Amnesia | Anaemia | Angina | Anorexia | Anxiety | Arthritis | Asthma | Athletes Foot | Autism | Back Pain | Bacterial Infections | Baldness | Bereavement | Bladder Problems | Blood Pressure | Boils | Bowel Problems | Breast Problems | Breathing Problems | Bronchitis | Bruising | Bulimia | Bunions | Bursitis | Callices | Cancers | Cataracts | Catarrh | Cerebral Palsy | Circulation Problems | Cold Sores | Colds | Colic | Colitis | Conjunctivitis | Constipation | Convulsions | Corns | Coughs | Cramp | Cystitis |
|---|---|---|---|---|---|---|---|---|---|---|---|---|---|---|---|---|---|---|---|---|---|---|---|---|---|---|---|---|---|---|---|---|---|---|---|---|---|---|---|---|---|---|---|---|---|---|---|---|
| CLINCH, ADELE (HM04675) | | | | | | | | | | | | | | |●| | | | | | | | | | | | | | | | |●| | | | | | | | | | | | |●| | | |
| CLINIC OF CHINESE MED & ACU (HM04685) | | | | | |●| | | | | | | | | | |●| | | | | | | | | | | | | | | | | | | | | | | | | |●| | | | | |
| COMP THERAPY & TRAINING CENTRE (HM04915) |●|●|●|●|●|●|●|●|●|●|●|●|●|●|●|●|●|●|●| |●|●|●|●|●|●|●|●|●| |●|●|●|●|●| |●|●|●|●|●|●|●|●|●|●|●|●|
| CONCEPTS PHYSIO & NUTRITION (HM04970) |●|●| | |●|●| | |●|●|●|●|●|●|●| |●| | | |●|●|●|●|●|●|●|●|●| |●| |●| |●| |●|●|●|●|●|●|●|●| |●|●|●|
| COOK, ELAINE (HM05042) | |●| | | |●| | |●| | |●|●|●| | |●| | | |●|●| |●|●|●|●| | | | | | | |●| |●| |●| | | | | | |●| | |
| COX, JULIET (HM05308) | | | | | | | | | | | |●|●|●| | |●| | | | |●| | | |●| | | | | | | | | | | | | | | | | | | | | | |
| CRESENT CLINIC (HM05422) | |●| | | |●| | | | | |●|●|●| | |●| | | |●|●|●|●|●|●|●|●|●| |●| | | |●| |●|●|●|●|●|●|●| | |●| |●|
| CROWBOROUGH CHIRO/COMP HLTH (HM05498) | | | | | | | | | | | | |●| | | |●| | | | | | | | | | | | | | | | | | | | | | | | | | | | | | | |
| CROWBOROUGH COMP THERAPISTS (HM05499) | | | | | | | | | | | |●|●|●| | |●| | | | |●| | |●|●| | | | | | | | |●| |●| | | | | |●| | | |●| |
| CULL, BEN (HM05556) | |●| | |●|●| |●| |●| |●|●|●| | |●| | | |●|●| | | |●| | | | | | | | | | | | | |●|●| | | | | | | |
| DADSWELL, CLAIRE (HM05670) |●|●|●| | |●| | | |●|●|●|●|●|●|●| |●|●| |●|●|●|●|●|●|●|●|●| | |●|●|●|●| |●|●|●|●|●|●|●|●|●|●|●|●|
| DEEKS, STUART (HM05956) | |●| | | |●| | | | | |●| |●| | | | | | |●|●|●|●|●|●|●|●|●| | | | | |●| |●| |●|●|●|●|●| | |●| |●|
| DRIVE OSTEO AND SPORTS CLINIC (HM06314) | | | | | | | | | | | | |●|●| | |●| | | | |●| | | | | | | | |●| | | | | |●| | |●| | | | | | |●| |
| DRYDEN, B A (HM06332) | | | | | | | | | | | |●| | | | | | | | | | | | | | | | |●| | | | | | | | | | | | | | | | | | |
| DYKE ROAD NATURAL HEALTH (HM06450) |●|●|●|●|●|●|●|●|●|●|●|●|●|●|●|●|●|●|●| |●|●|●|●|●|●|●|●|●| |●| |●|●|●| |●|●|●|●|●|●|●|●| |●|●|●|
| EAST BOURNE CLINIC (HM06509) | | | | | | | | | | | | |●| | | |●| | | | | | | | | | | | | | | | | | | |●| | | | | | | | | | | |
| EASTBOURNE CHIROPRACTIC CLINIC (HM06535) | | | | | | | | | | | | |●| | | |●| | | | | | | | | | | | | | | | | | | |●| | | | | | | | | | | |
| FAIRCHILD, HAZEL (HM07052) | | | | | | | | | | | |●| | | | | | | | | | | | | | | | | | | | | | | | | | | | | | | | | | | |
| FAMILY FIRST (HM07087) | |●| | |●| | | | | | | | |●| | |●| | | | | | | | | | | | | | | | | | | | | | | | | | | | | | |
| FIVEWAYS OSTEOPATHIC PRACTICE (HM07382) | | | | | | | | | | | | |●| | | |●| | | | | | | | | | | | | |●| | | | | | | | | | | | | | | | |
| FLOYD, MICHELLE (HM07438) |●| |●| | |●| | |●|●|●|●|●|●| |●|●|●| | |●|●|●|●|●|●|●|●|●| |●|●|●|●|●| |●|●|●|●|●|●|●|●|●|●|●|●|
| FOUNDATION, ANGELGATE (HM07615) | | | |●| | |●| | | | | |●|●|●| |●| |●| | | | |●| | |●| | | | | | |●|●| | | |●|●|●| |●| | | | |●|
| GATEHOUSE THERAPY CENTRE (HM07925) | | | | | | | | | | | |●| | | | | | | | | | | | | | | | | | | | | | | | | | | | | | | | | | | |
| GEIGES, STEPHANIE (HM07967) | | | | | | | | | | | | |●| | | |●| | | | | | | | | | | | | | | | | | | |●| | | | | | | | | | | |
| GOLDSTONE CLINIC (HM08230) | | | | | | | | | | | |●|●| | | |●| | | | | | | | | | | | | | | | | | | | | | | | | | | | | | | |
| GOLDSTONE CLINIC (HM08229) | |●| | |●|●| | | | | | |●| | | |●| | | | | | | | | | | | | | | | | | | |●| | | | | | | | | | | |
| GONZALEZ, SOHANI (HM08237) |●|●|●| | |●| | |●|●|●|●|●|●|●|●| |●| | |●|●|●|●|●|●|●|●|●| |●|●|●| |●| |●|●|●|●|●|●|●|●|●|●|●|●|
| GRIFFITHS, J (HM08567) | | | | | | | | | | | |●|●| | | |●| | | | | | | | |●| | | | | | | | | | |●| | | | | | | | | |●| |
| HART, RONALD (HM09130) | | | | | | | | | | | | | | |●| | | | | | | | | | | | | | | | |●| | | | | | | | | | | | |●| | | |
| HART, RONALD (HM09131) | | | | | | | | | | | | | |●| | | | | | | | | | | | | | | | | |●| | | | | | | | | | | | |●| | | |
| HAWKINS, LUKE (HM09224) | | | | | | | | | | | | | | |●| | | | | | | | | | | | | | | | |●| | | | | | | | | | | | |●| | | |
| HEMMINGWAY CHIROPODIST (HM09537) | | | | | | | | | | | | | | |●| | | | | | | | | | | | | | | | |●| | | | |●| | | | | | | |●| | | |
| HERBAL HEALTH CLINIC (HM09617) |●| |●| | |●| | | |●|●|●|●|●|●| |●|●| | |●|●| |●| |●|●|●| | |●| | | |●| |●|●|●|●|●|●|●| | |●|●|●|
| HOLDEN NATURAL HEALTH CLINIC (HM09927) | | | | | | | | | | | | | |●|●| | |●| | | |●| | | |●|●| | | | | | | | | | | |●| | | |●| | | |●| |

www.healthmyself.com

# A - C Conditions treated at Practices/Businesses

| Business by County with Reference no. | Acne | Addiction | Adenoids | Aids | Alcoholism | Allergy | Alzheimer's Disease | Amnesia | Anaemia | Angina | Anorexia | Anxiety | Arthritis | Asthma | Athletes Foot | Autism |
|---|---|---|---|---|---|---|---|---|---|---|---|---|---|---|---|---|
| HOVE CHIROPRACTIC CLINIC (HM10227) | | | | | | | | | | | | | ● | | | |
| HUGHES, CLARE (HM10324) | | | | | | | | | | | | | ● | | | |
| HYSLOP, C P (HM10543) | ● | ● | ● | ● | ● | ● | ● | ● | ● | ● | ● | ● | ● | ● | ● | ● |
| JEMPSON, NICOLA (HM10978) | | | | | | | | | | | | | ● | | | |
| JOY, JANET (HM11231) | | | | | | | | | | | | ● | | | | |
| LEWES CHIROPRACTIC CLINIC (HM12271) | | | | | | | | | | | | | ● | | | |
| MCKEOWN, KAY (HM13532) | | | | | | | | | | | | | | | | |
| MEADOWSWEET (HM13634) | | | | | | | | | | | | | ● | | | |
| MURPHY, KEVIN (HM14387) | | | | | | ● | | | | | | | | ● | | |
| NEAT FEET (HM14742) | | | | | | | | | | | | | | | ● | |
| NEWICK PHYSIOTHERAPY CLINIC (HM14865) | | | | | | | | | | | | | | | | |
| OLD TOWN CHIROPRACTIC CLINIC (HM15263) | | | | | | | | | | | | | | | | |
| PRICE, JAMES (HM16583) | | | | | | | | | | | | | | | ● | |
| PRIORY HEIGHTS (HM16633) | | | | | | | | | | | ● | ● | ● | | | |
| REEVES, ALAN (HM17062) | | | | | | | | | | | | ● | | | | |
| REFLEXOLOGY FOR HEALTH (HM17095) | | | | | | | | | | | | | | ● | | |
| SANDERSON & ELEMENT (HM17919) | | | | | | | | | | | | | ● | | | |
| SANDERSON & ELEMENT (HM17920) | | | | | | | | | | | | | ● | | | |
| SANDERSON & ELEMENT (HM17922) | | | | | | | | | | | | | ● | | | |
| SCHOLL CENTRE (HM18032) | | | | | | | | | | | | | | | ● | |
| SUNDIAL HOUSE CHIROPRACTIC (HM19506) | | | | | | | | | | | | | ● | | | |
| TEALE, PAUL (HM19809) | | | | | | | | | | | | | ● | ● | | |
| TISSERAND (HM20095) | | | | | | | | | | | | ● | ● | | | |
| TRENCHARD, ABIGAIL (HM20319) | | | | | | | | | | | | ● | | | | |
| VALENCE ROAD OSTEOPATHS (HM20554) | | | | | | | | | | | | | | | | |
| WADHURST PHYSIO/SPORTS CLNC (HM20729) | | | | | | | | | | | | | ● | | | |
| WADHURST PHYSIO/SPORTS CLNC (HM20730) | | | | | | | | | | | | | ● | | | |
| WALSH, M J (HM20865) | | | | | | | | | | | | | ● | | | |
| WEDLAKE-GRIFFITHS, J (HM21097) | | | | | | | | | | | | | ● | | | |
| WILBURY PHYSIOTHERAPY (HM21480) | | | | | | | | | | | | | ● | | | |
| WRIGHT, P A (HM21946) | | | | | | | | | | | | | | | ● | |
| SUSSEX (WEST) | | | | | | | | | | | | | | | | |
| ACORN CENTRE (HM00171) | | | | | | ● | | | | | | | ● | ● | | |
| ALAN SMITH CHIROPRACTOR (HM00470) | | | | | | | | | | | | | ● | | | |

| Business by County with Reference no. | Back Pain | Bacterial Infections | Baldness | Bereavement | Bladder Problems | Blood Pressure | Boils | Bowel Problems | Breast Problems | Breathing Problems | Bronchitis | Bruising | Bulimia | Bunions | Bursitis |
|---|---|---|---|---|---|---|---|---|---|---|---|---|---|---|---|
| HOVE CHIROPRACTIC CLINIC (HM10227) | | | | | | | | | | | | | | | |
| HUGHES, CLARE (HM10324) | ● | | | | | | | | | | | | | | |
| HYSLOP, C P (HM10543) | ● | ● | ● | | ● | ● | ● | ● | ● | ● | ● | ● | ● | | ● |
| JEMPSON, NICOLA (HM10978) | ● | | | | | | | | | | | | | | |
| JOY, JANET (HM11231) | | | | ● | | | | ● | | | | | | | |
| LEWES CHIROPRACTIC CLINIC (HM12271) | ● | | | | | | | | | | | | | | ● |
| MCKEOWN, KAY (HM13532) | ● | | | | | | | | | ● | | | | | |
| MEADOWSWEET (HM13634) | ● | | | | | | | ● | | | | | | | |
| MURPHY, KEVIN (HM14387) | ● | | | | | | | | | | | | | | |
| NEAT FEET (HM14742) | | | | | | | | | | | | | | | |
| NEWICK PHYSIOTHERAPY CLINIC (HM14865) | ● | | | | | | | | | | | ● | | | |
| OLD TOWN CHIROPRACTIC CLINIC (HM15263) | ● | | | | | | | | | | | | | | |
| PRICE, JAMES (HM16583) | | | | | | | | | | | | | | | |
| PRIORY HEIGHTS (HM16633) | ● | | | | | | | | | | | | ● | | |
| REEVES, ALAN (HM17062) | | | | | | | | | | | | | | | |
| REFLEXOLOGY FOR HEALTH (HM17095) | ● | | | | ● | ● | | ● | ● | | | | | | ● |
| SANDERSON & ELEMENT (HM17919) | ● | | | | | | | | | | | | | | |
| SANDERSON & ELEMENT (HM17920) | ● | | | | | | | | | | | | | | |
| SANDERSON & ELEMENT (HM17922) | ● | | | | | | | | | | | | | | |
| SCHOLL CENTRE (HM18032) | | | | | | | | | | | | | | | |
| SUNDIAL HOUSE CHIROPRACTIC (HM19506) | ● | | | | | | | | | | | | | | |
| TEALE, PAUL (HM19809) | ● | | | | | | | | | | | | | | ● |
| TISSERAND (HM20095) | | | | | | | | | | | | | | | |
| TRENCHARD, ABIGAIL (HM20319) | | | | | | | | | | | | | | | |
| VALENCE ROAD OSTEOPATHS (HM20554) | ● | | | | | | | | | | | | | | ● |
| WADHURST PHYSIO/SPORTS CLNC (HM20729) | ● | | | | | | | | | | | ● | | | |
| WADHURST PHYSIO/SPORTS CLNC (HM20730) | ● | | | | | | | | | | | | | | |
| WALSH, M J (HM20865) | ● | | | | | | | | | | | | | | |
| WEDLAKE-GRIFFITHS, J (HM21097) | ● | | | | | | | | | | | | | | |
| WILBURY PHYSIOTHERAPY (HM21480) | ● | | | | | | | | | | | ● | | | |
| WRIGHT, P A (HM21946) | | | | | | | | | | | | | | | |
| SUSSEX (WEST) | | | | | | | | | | | | | | | |
| ACORN CENTRE (HM00171) | ● | | | | | ● | | ● | | | | | | | ● |
| ALAN SMITH CHIROPRACTOR (HM00470) | ● | | | | ● | | | | | | | | | | ● |

| Business by County with Reference no. | Callices | Cancers | Cataracts | Catarrh | Cerebral Palsy | Circulation Problems | Cold Sores | Colds | Colic | Colitis | Conjunctivitis | Constipation | Convulsions | Corns | Coughs | Cramp | Cystitis |
|---|---|---|---|---|---|---|---|---|---|---|---|---|---|---|---|---|---|
| HOVE CHIROPRACTIC CLINIC (HM10227) | | | | | | ● | | | | | | | | | | | |
| HUGHES, CLARE (HM10324) | | | | | | ● | | | | | | | | | | | |
| HYSLOP, C P (HM10543) | ● | ● | ● | ● | | ● | ● | ● | ● | ● | ● | ● | ● | ● | ● | ● | ● |
| JEMPSON, NICOLA (HM10978) | | | | | | ● | | | | | | | | | | | |
| JOY, JANET (HM11231) | | | | | | | | | | | | | | | | | |
| LEWES CHIROPRACTIC CLINIC (HM12271) | | | | | | | | | ● | | | | | | | ● | |
| MCKEOWN, KAY (HM13532) | | | | | | | | | | | | | | | | | |
| MEADOWSWEET (HM13634) | | | | | | ● | | | ● | | | | | | | ● | |
| MURPHY, KEVIN (HM14387) | | | | | | | | | | | | | | | | ● | |
| NEAT FEET (HM14742) | ● | | | | | | | | | | | | | ● | | | |
| NEWICK PHYSIOTHERAPY CLINIC (HM14865) | | | | | | | | | | | | | | | | ● | |
| OLD TOWN CHIROPRACTIC CLINIC (HM15263) | | | | | | | | | ● | | | | | | | | |
| PRICE, JAMES (HM16583) | | | | | | ● | | | | | | | | | | | |
| PRIORY HEIGHTS (HM16633) | | | | | | | | | | | | ● | | | | | |
| REEVES, ALAN (HM17062) | | | | | | | | | | | | | | | | | |
| REFLEXOLOGY FOR HEALTH (HM17095) | | | | | | ● | | | | | | ● | | | | | ● |
| SANDERSON & ELEMENT (HM17919) | | | | | | ● | | | | | | | | | | | |
| SANDERSON & ELEMENT (HM17920) | | | | | | ● | | | | | | | | | | | |
| SANDERSON & ELEMENT (HM17922) | | | | | | | | | | | | | | | | | |
| SCHOLL CENTRE (HM18032) | ● | | | | | | | | | | | | | ● | | | |
| SUNDIAL HOUSE CHIROPRACTIC (HM19506) | | | | | | ● | | | | | | | | | | | |
| TEALE, PAUL (HM19809) | | | | | | | | | | | | | | | | | |
| TISSERAND (HM20095) | | | | | | | | | | | | | | | | | |
| TRENCHARD, ABIGAIL (HM20319) | | | | | | | | | | | | | | | | | |
| VALENCE ROAD OSTEOPATHS (HM20554) | | | | | | | | | | | | | | | | | |
| WADHURST PHYSIO/SPORTS CLNC (HM20729) | | | | | | | | | | | | | | | | ● | |
| WADHURST PHYSIO/SPORTS CLNC (HM20730) | | | | | | | | | | | | | | | | | |
| WALSH, M J (HM20865) | | | | | | | | | | | | | | | | | |
| WEDLAKE-GRIFFITHS, J (HM21097) | | | | | | | | | | | | | | | | | |
| WILBURY PHYSIOTHERAPY (HM21480) | | | | | | | | | | | | | | | | ● | |
| WRIGHT, P A (HM21946) | ● | | | | | | | | | | | | | ● | | | |
| SUSSEX (WEST) | | | | | | | | | | | | | | | | | |
| ACORN CENTRE (HM00171) | | | | | | | | | | | | ● | | | ● | | |
| ALAN SMITH CHIROPRACTOR (HM00470) | | | | | | | | | | | | | | | | | |

# A - C Conditions treated at Practices/Businesses

England (by County)



| Business by County with Reference no. | ANDREW BATHIE PRACTICE (HM00846) | ANGELA (HM00872) | AUROMA (HM01357) | AVALON HEALTH CENTRE (HM01380) | B O P (HM01452) | BACK 2 FITNESS CHIROPRACTIC (HM01476) | BALOOMBE OSTEOPATHIC & SPORTS (HM01641) | BARTHOLOMEW WAY CLINIC (HM01818) | BELLAMY PARTNERSHIP (HM02093) | BLACK, PAULINE (HM02425) | BODYGUIDE ALTERNATE (HM02619) | BOHNET, CAROLE (HM02648) | BRITCHIRO CLINIC (HM03068) | BURNS, L C (HM03417) | CARTLAND, ANN (HM03794) | CASH, G G (HM03811) | CHANGES (HM03985) | CHASE, PETER (HM04061) | CHICHESTER NATURAL HEALTH CTRE (HM04156) | CHIROPODIST () | CLAIRVOYANT - MEDIUM - HEALER (HM04514) | CLARKE, STEVEN (HM04604) | CORNERWEIGHS (HM05183) | DALLAS, PETER (HM05691) | DYER & ASSOCIATES (HM06444) | EMINATIONS ACUPUNCTURE CLINIC (HM06805) | FELPHAM NATURAL HEALTH CLINIC (HM07206) | FROST, CHARLES (HM07760) | FURNACE GREEN CHIRO CTRE (HM07800) | GARDINER, SAM (HM07876) | GRAVILLE, CHRIS (HM08405) | GREENFIELD, KAREN (HM08486) | HARRIS, PAUL A E (HM09084) | HEALTH IS HAPPINESS REFLEX (HM09390) |
|---|---|---|---|---|---|---|---|---|---|---|---|---|---|---|---|---|---|---|---|---|---|---|---|---|---|---|---|---|---|---|---|---|---|---|
| Cystitis | | | | ● | | | | | | ● | ● | | | | | | ● | | ● | | ● | | ● | ● | | ● | | | ● | | | | | |
| Cramp | | | | ● | ● | | | | | ● | ● | | | ● | | | | | ● | | ● | | | | | | | | ● | | | | | |
| Coughs | | | | ● | | | | | | ● | ● | | | | | | | | ● | | ● | | ● | ● | | ● | | | ● | | | | | |
| Corns | | | | ● | | | | | | ● | ● | | | | ● | ● | | ● | | ● | | | | | | | | | ● | | | | | |
| Convulsions | | | | ● | | | | | | ● | ● | | | | | | | | ● | | | | | | | ● | | | ● | | | | | |
| Constipation | ● | | | ● | | | | | | ● | ● | ● | | | | | ● | | ● | | | | ● | ● | | ● | | | ● | | | ● | | ● |
| Conjunctivitis | | | | ● | | | | | | ● | ● | | | | | | ● | | ● | | | | ● | | | ● | | | ● | | | | | |
| Colitis | ● | | | ● | ● | | | | | ● | ● | | | | | | ● | | ● | | ● | | | ● | | | | | ● | | | | | |
| Colic | | | | ● | | | | | | ● | ● | | ● | | | | ● | | ● | | ● | | | | | | | | ● | | | | | |
| Colds | | | | ● | | | | | | ● | ● | | | | | | ● | | ● | | ● | | ● | | | ● | | | ● | | | | | |
| Cold Sores | | | | ● | | | | | | ● | ● | | | | | | ● | | ● | | | | | | | | | | ● | | | | | |
| Circulation Problems | | ● | | ● | | ● | | ● | | ● | ● | ● | ● | | | | ● | | ● | | ● | | | ● | | ● | | | ● | | | | ● | ● |
| Cerebral Palsy | | | | | | | | | | | | | | | | | | | | | ● | | | | | | | | | | | | | |
| Catarrh | | | | ● | | | | | | ● | ● | | | | | | ● | | ● | | ● | | | ● | | | | | ● | | | | | ● |
| Cataracts | | | | ● | | | | | | ● | ● | | | | | | | | ● | | ● | | | | | | | | ● | | | | | |
| Cancers | | | | ● | | | | | | ● | ● | | | | | | ● | | ● | | ● | | | | | | ● | | ● | ● | | | | |
| Callices | | | | ● | | | | | | ● | ● | | | | ● | ● | | ● | | ● | | | | | | | | | ● | | | | | |
| Bursitis | | | | ● | ● | | | ● | | ● | ● | | | | | | | | ● | | | | | | | | | | ● | | | | | |
| Bunions | | | | | | | | | | | | | | | | ● | | ● | | | | | | | | | | | | | | | | |
| Bulimia | ● | | | ● | | | | | | ● | ● | | | | | | | | ● | | | | | | | | | ● | ● | ● | | | | |
| Bruising | | | | ● | ● | | | | | ● | ● | | | ● | | | ● | | ● | | ● | | | | | | ● | | ● | | | | | |
| Bronchitis | | | | ● | | | | | | ● | ● | ● | | | | | | | ● | | ● | | | | | | | | ● | | | ● | | |
| Breathing Problems | | | | ● | ● | | ● | | | ● | ● | ● | | | | | | | ● | | ● | | | ● | | ● | | | ● | ● | | | | ● |
| Breast Problems | | | | ● | | | | | | ● | ● | | | | | | ● | | ● | | ● | | | | | | | | ● | | | | | |
| Bowel Problems | ● | | | ● | ● | | | | | ● | ● | ● | | | | | ● | | ● | | ● | | ● | | | ● | | | ● | ● | | | | |
| Boils | | | | ● | | | | | | ● | ● | | | | | | | | ● | | ● | | | | | | | | ● | | | | | |
| Blood Pressure | ● | | | ● | | | | | | ● | ● | ● | ● | | | | | | ● | | ● | ● | ● | ● | | ● | | ● | ● | ● | | | | |
| Bladder Problems | ● | | | ● | | | | | | ● | ● | ● | | | | | ● | | ● | | ● | | | ● | | ● | | | ● | | | | | |
| Bereavement | | | | | | | | | | | | | | | | | | | | | | | | | | | | | | | | | | |
| Baldness | | | | ● | | | | | | ● | ● | | | | | | | | ● | | | | | | | | | | ● | | | | | |
| Bacterial Infections | | | | ● | | | | ● | | ● | ● | | | | | ● | | ● | ● | | ● | | ● | | | ● | | | ● | | | | | |
| Back Pain | | | ● | ● | ● | ● | ● | ● | ● | ● | ● | ● | ● | ● | | | | | ● | | ● | | | ● | ● | ● | ● | | ● | ● | | ● | ● | ● |
| Autism | | | | ● | | | | | | ● | ● | | | | | | | | ● | | | | | | | | | | ● | | | | | |
| Athletes Foot | | | | ● | | | | ● | | ● | ● | | | | ● | ● | ● | ● | ● | ● | ● | | ● | | | | | | ● | | | | | |
| Asthma | ● | | | ● | ● | | ● | | | ● | ● | ● | | | | | ● | | ● | | ● | | | ● | | ● | | ● | ● | | | ● | | |
| Arthritis | ● | ● | ● | ● | ● | ● | ● | ● | | ● | ● | | ● | ● | | | ● | | ● | | ● | | | ● | ● | ● | | | ● | | ● | | ● | ● |
| Anxiety | ● | ● | ● | ● | | | ● | | | ● | ● | ● | | | | | ● | | ● | | ● | | | ● | | ● | ● | ● | ● | | ● | ● | | ● |
| Anorexia | ● | | | ● | | | | | | ● | ● | | | | | | | | ● | | | | | ● | | | | | ● | ● | | | | |
| Angina | | | | ● | | | | | | ● | ● | | | | | | ● | | ● | | ● | | | ● | | | | | ● | | | | | |
| Anaemia | | | | ● | | | | | | ● | ● | | | | | | ● | | ● | | ● | | | ● | | ● | | | ● | | | | | |
| Amnesia | | | | ● | | | | | | | ● | | | | | | | | | | | | | | | | | | ● | | | | | |
| Alzheimer's Disease | | | | ● | | | | | | | ● | | | | | | | | ● | | | | | | | | | | ● | | | | | |
| Allergy | | | | ● | | | | | | ● | ● | | | | | | ● | | ● | | | | | | | ● | | | ● | | | | | ● |
| Alcoholism | | | | ● | | | | | | ● | ● | | | | | | | | ● | | | | | | | | | | ● | | | | | |
| Aids | | | | ● | | | | | | | ● | | | | | | | | | | | | | | | | | | ● | ● | | | | |
| Adenoids | | | | ● | | | | | | ● | ● | | | | | | | | ● | | | | | | | | | | ● | | | | | |
| Addiction | ● | | | ● | | | | | | ● | ● | | | | | | | | | | | | | | | ● | | | ● | | | | | |
| Acne | | | | ● | | | | | | ● | ● | | | | | | | | ● | | | | ● | | | | | | ● | | | ● | | |

# A - C Conditions treated at Practices/Businesses

Business by County with Reference no.

| Business | Acne | Addiction | Adenoids | Aids | Alcoholism | Allergy | Alzheimer's Disease | Amnesia | Anaemia | Angina | Anorexia | Anxiety | Arthritis | Asthma | Athletes Foot | Autism |
|---|---|---|---|---|---|---|---|---|---|---|---|---|---|---|---|---|
| HEELER CENTRE (HM09498) | ● | ● | | | | ● | | | | | | ● | ● | ● | ● | |
| HORSHAM CHIROPRACTIC CENTRE (HM10191) | | | | | | | | | | | | | ● | | | |
| I C O M (HM10548) | | | | | | ● | | | ● | ● | ● | ● | ● | ● | | |
| JONES, NIGEL (HM11182) | | | | | | | | | | | | | ● | | | |
| JONES, WENDY (HM11203) | | | | | | | | | | | | | ● | | | |
| LITTLEHAMPTON NAT HLTH CTRE (HM12470) | ● | ● | ● | ● | ● | ● | ● | ● | ● | ● | ● | ● | ● | ● | ● | ● |
| MAYNARD, MARTIN A (HM13357) | | | | | | | | | | | | | | | ● | |
| MID SUSSEX CHIROPRACTIC CLINIC (HM13805) | ● | | ● | | | | | | | | | | ● | ● | | |
| MID SUSSEX HOMEOPATHIC CLINIC (HM13806) | ● | | | | | ● | | | ● | | | ● | ● | ● | | ● |
| MILLENNIUM HOMEOPATHY (HM13877) | ● | ● | ● | ● | ● | ● | ● | ● | ● | ● | ● | ● | ● | ● | ● | ● |
| MIND WORK SOLUTIONS (HM13967) | ● | ● | ● | ● | ● | ● | ● | ● | ● | ● | ● | ● | ● | ● | ● | ● |
| NUNN, SALLY (HM15108) | ● | ● | ● | | ● | ● | ● | ● | ● | ● | ● | ● | ● | ● | ● | ● |
| OSTEOPATHY AT ESQUIRE'S (HM15479) | | | | | | | | | | | | | ● | ● | | |
| PAIN & PARALYSIS SPECIALIST (HM15578) | | | | | | | | | | | | ● | ● | | | |
| PALMER, GAYLE (HM15605) | | | | | | ● | ● | ● | ● | ● | ● | ● | ● | ● | | ● |
| PALMER, GAYLE (HM15606) | | | | | | | | | | ● | | ● | ● | ● | | ● |
| PITT, KATHY (HM16349) | ● | ● | ● | ● | ● | ● | ● | ● | ● | ● | ● | ● | ● | ● | ● | ● |
| PORTLAND PHYSIOTHERAPY CLINIC (HM16451) | | | | | | | | | | | | | ● | | | |
| RICHARDSON, BRIAN J (HM17269) | | | | | | | | | | | | | ● | | ● | |
| RICHARDSON, JANET (HM17282) | | | | | | | | | | | | | ● | | ● | |
| ROOM FOR HEALING (HM17585) | | | | | | ● | | | | ● | | ● | ● | ● | ● | |
| SANDERSON & ELEMENT (HM17921) | | | | | | | | | | | | | ● | | | |
| SANDON, PATER H G (DR) (HM17925) | ● | ● | ● | ● | ● | ● | ● | ● | ● | ● | ● | ● | ● | ● | ● | ● |
| SMITH, BARBARA (HM18720) | | | | | | | | | | | | | | | ● | |
| STEVENS, PAT (HM19238) | | | | | | | | | | | | | | | | |
| STOTT-DURHAM, ANDREW (HM19355) | | | | | | | | | | | | | ● | | | |
| SWAN, LAURIE C (HM19574) | ● | ● | ● | | | ● | | | ● | | | | | | ● | |
| TAYLOR, CHRISTIAN (HM19744) | ● | ● | ● | ● | ● | ● | ● | ● | ● | ● | ● | ● | ● | ● | ● | ● |
| TRANQUILLITY (HM20260) | | | | | | | | | | | | ● | ● | | | |
| WESTACOTT, EILEEN (HM21256) | | | | | | | | | | | | | | | | |
| WILSON, AVIS (HM21646) | ● | | | | | | | | | | | | | | | |
| WOOD, J G (HM21798) | | | | | | | | | | | | | ● | ● | | |
| WORSFOLD, CHRISTINE (HM21903) | | | | | | | | | | | | | | | ● | |
| WORTHING CHIROPRACTIC CLINIC (HM21907) | | | | | | | | | | | | ● | | | | |

| Business | Back Pain | Bacterial Infections | Baldness | Bereavement | Bladder Problems | Blood Pressure | Boils | Bowel Problems | Breast Problems | Breathing Problems | Bronchitis | Bruising | Bulimia | Bunions | Bursitis | Callices |
|---|---|---|---|---|---|---|---|---|---|---|---|---|---|---|---|---|
| HEELER CENTRE (HM09498) | ● | ● | | | ● | | | ● | | ● | ● | ● | | | ● | |
| HORSHAM CHIROPRACTIC CENTRE (HM10191) | ● | | | | | ● | | | | | | | | | | |
| I C O M (HM10548) | ● | | | | ● | ● | | ● | ● | ● | | | ● | | ● | |
| JONES, NIGEL (HM11182) | ● | | | | | | | | | | | | | | ● | |
| JONES, WENDY (HM11203) | ● | | | | | | | | | | | ● | | | ● | |
| LITTLEHAMPTON NAT HLTH CTRE (HM12470) | ● | ● | ● | | ● | ● | ● | ● | ● | ● | ● | ● | ● | | ● | |
| MAYNARD, MARTIN A (HM13357) | | | | | | | | | | | | | | | ● | |
| MID SUSSEX CHIROPRACTIC CLINIC (HM13805) | ● | | | | ● | ● | | ● | | ● | ● | | | | ● | |
| MID SUSSEX HOMEOPATHIC CLINIC (HM13806) | ● | | | | ● | ● | ● | ● | ● | ● | ● | ● | | | ● | |
| MILLENNIUM HOMEOPATHY (HM13877) | ● | ● | ● | | ● | ● | ● | ● | ● | ● | ● | ● | ● | | ● | ● |
| MIND WORK SOLUTIONS (HM13967) | ● | ● | ● | | ● | ● | ● | ● | ● | ● | ● | ● | ● | | ● | ● |
| NUNN, SALLY (HM15108) | ● | ● | ● | | ● | ● | ● | ● | ● | ● | ● | ● | ● | | ● | ● |
| OSTEOPATHY AT ESQUIRE'S (HM15479) | ● | | | | | | | | | | | | | | ● | |
| PAIN & PARALYSIS SPECIALIST (HM15578) | ● | | | | | | | | | ● | | ● | | | | |
| PALMER, GAYLE (HM15605) | ● | | | | | | | ● | | ● | ● | ● | | | ● | |
| PALMER, GAYLE (HM15606) | ● | | | | ● | ● | | ● | | ● | ● | | | | | |
| PITT, KATHY (HM16349) | ● | ● | ● | | ● | ● | ● | ● | ● | ● | ● | ● | ● | | ● | ● |
| PORTLAND PHYSIOTHERAPY CLINIC (HM16451) | ● | | | | | | | | | | | | | | | |
| RICHARDSON, BRIAN J (HM17269) | | | | | | | | | | | | | | | ● | |
| RICHARDSON, JANET (HM17282) | | ● | | | | | | | | | | | | ● | | ● |
| ROOM FOR HEALING (HM17585) | ● | ● | | | ● | ● | | ● | | ● | ● | ● | | | ● | |
| SANDERSON & ELEMENT (HM17921) | ● | | | | | | | | | | | | | | | |
| SANDON, PATER H G (DR) (HM17925) | ● | ● | ● | | ● | ● | ● | ● | ● | ● | ● | ● | ● | | ● | ● |
| SMITH, BARBARA (HM18720) | | ● | | | | | | | | | | | | ● | | ● |
| STEVENS, PAT (HM19238) | ● | | | | ● | | | | | | | | | | | |
| STOTT-DURHAM, ANDREW (HM19355) | | | | | | | | | | | | | | | | |
| SWAN, LAURIE C (HM19574) | ● | ● | | | ● | ● | ● | ● | ● | | | | | | | |
| TAYLOR, CHRISTIAN (HM19744) | ● | ● | ● | | ● | ● | ● | ● | ● | ● | ● | ● | ● | | ● | ● |
| TRANQUILLITY (HM20260) | ● | | | | | | | | | | | | | | | |
| WESTACOTT, EILEEN (HM21256) | ● | | | | | | | | | | | | | | | |
| WILSON, AVIS (HM21646) | ● | | | | | | | | | | | | | | | |
| WOOD, J G (HM21798) | ● | | | | | | | | | ● | ● | ● | | | ● | |
| WORSFOLD, CHRISTINE (HM21903) | | | | | | | | | | | | | | | | ● |
| WORTHING CHIROPRACTIC CLINIC (HM21907) | ● | | | | | | | | | | | | | | | |

| Business | Cancers | Cataracts | Catarrh | Cerebral Palsy | Circulation Problems | Cold Sores | Colds | Colic | Colitis | Conjunctivitis | Constipation | Convulsions | Corns | Coughs | Cramp | Cystitis |
|---|---|---|---|---|---|---|---|---|---|---|---|---|---|---|---|---|
| HEELER CENTRE (HM09498) | | | | | ● | | | ● | ● | | ● | | | | | ● |
| HORSHAM CHIROPRACTIC CENTRE (HM10191) | | | | | ● | | | ● | | | | | | | | |
| I C O M (HM10548) | | | | | ● | | | | | | | | | | | |
| JONES, NIGEL (HM11182) | | | | | | | | | | | | | | | | |
| JONES, WENDY (HM11203) | | | | | | | | | | | | | | | | |
| LITTLEHAMPTON NAT HLTH CTRE (HM12470) | ● | ● | ● | | ● | ● | ● | ● | ● | ● | ● | ● | | ● | ● | ● |
| MAYNARD, MARTIN A (HM13357) | | | | | | | | | | | | | | | | |
| MID SUSSEX CHIROPRACTIC CLINIC (HM13805) | | | | | | | | | | | ● | | | ● | | |
| MID SUSSEX HOMEOPATHIC CLINIC (HM13806) | | | ● | | ● | ● | ● | ● | ● | ● | ● | | | ● | ● | ● |
| MILLENNIUM HOMEOPATHY (HM13877) | ● | ● | ● | | ● | ● | ● | ● | ● | ● | ● | ● | ● | ● | ● | ● |
| MIND WORK SOLUTIONS (HM13967) | ● | ● | ● | | ● | ● | ● | ● | ● | ● | ● | ● | ● | ● | ● | ● |
| NUNN, SALLY (HM15108) | | ● | ● | | ● | ● | ● | ● | ● | ● | ● | ● | ● | ● | ● | ● |
| OSTEOPATHY AT ESQUIRE'S (HM15479) | | | | | | | | ● | | | | | | | | |
| PAIN & PARALYSIS SPECIALIST (HM15578) | | | | | ● | | | | | | ● | | | | | |
| PALMER, GAYLE (HM15605) | | ● | ● | | ● | | ● | ● | ● | ● | ● | ● | | ● | ● | ● |
| PALMER, GAYLE (HM15606) | | ● | ● | ● | ● | | ● | ● | ● | ● | ● | ● | | ● | ● | ● |
| PITT, KATHY (HM16349) | ● | ● | ● | | ● | ● | ● | ● | ● | ● | ● | ● | ● | ● | ● | ● |
| PORTLAND PHYSIOTHERAPY CLINIC (HM16451) | | | | | | | | | | | | | | | | |
| RICHARDSON, BRIAN J (HM17269) | | | | | | | | | | | | | | | | |
| RICHARDSON, JANET (HM17282) | | | | | | | | | | | | | ● | | | |
| ROOM FOR HEALING (HM17585) | ● | ● | ● | | ● | ● | ● | | ● | ● | ● | ● | | ● | | ● |
| SANDERSON & ELEMENT (HM17921) | | | | | ● | | | | | | | | | | | |
| SANDON, PATER H G (DR) (HM17925) | ● | ● | ● | | ● | ● | ● | ● | ● | ● | ● | ● | ● | ● | ● | ● |
| SMITH, BARBARA (HM18720) | | | | | | | | | | | | | ● | | | |
| STEVENS, PAT (HM19238) | | | | | | | | | | | | | | | | |
| STOTT-DURHAM, ANDREW (HM19355) | | | | | ● | | | | | | | | | | | |
| SWAN, LAURIE C (HM19574) | | | ● | | ● | | | | | | | | | | ● | |
| TAYLOR, CHRISTIAN (HM19744) | ● | ● | ● | | ● | ● | ● | ● | ● | ● | ● | ● | ● | ● | ● | ● |
| TRANQUILLITY (HM20260) | | | | | | | | | | | | | | | | |
| WESTACOTT, EILEEN (HM21256) | | | | | | | | | | | | | | | | |
| WILSON, AVIS (HM21646) | | | | | | | | | | | | | | | | |
| WOOD, J G (HM21798) | | | | | ● | | | | | | | | | | ● | |
| WORSFOLD, CHRISTINE (HM21903) | | | | | | | | | | | | | ● | | | |
| WORTHING CHIROPRACTIC CLINIC (HM21907) | | | | | ● | | | | | | | | | | | |

# A - C Conditions treated at Practices/Businesses

| Business by County with Reference no. | Acne | Addiction | Adenoids | Aids | Alcoholism | Allergy | Alzheimer's Disease | Amnesia | Anaemia | Angina | Anorexia | Anxiety | Arthritis | Asthma | Athletes Foot | Autism | Back Pain | Bacterial Infections | Baldness | Bereavement | Bladder Problems | Blood Pressure | Boils | Bowel Problems | Breast Problems | Breathing Problems | Bronchitis | Bruising | Bulimia | Bunions | Bursitis | Callices | Cancers | Cataracts | Catarrh | Cerebral Palsy | Circulation Problems | Cold Sores | Colds | Colic | Colitis | Conjunctivitis | Constipation | Convulsions | Corns | Coughs | Cramp | Cystitis |
|---|---|---|---|---|---|---|---|---|---|---|---|---|---|---|---|---|---|---|---|---|---|---|---|---|---|---|---|---|---|---|---|---|---|---|---|---|---|---|---|---|---|---|---|---|---|---|---|---|
| WORTHING CLINIC OF ACUPUNCTURE (HM21908) | | | | | | | | | | | ● | ● | ● | ● | | | ● | | | | | | | ● | | | | | ● | | | | | | | | | | | | | | ● | | | | | |
| YORK, TIM (HM22054) | | | | | | | | | | | | ● | | | | | ● | | | | | | | | | | | | | | | | | | | | | | | | | | | | | | | |
| **TYNE AND WEAR** | | | | | | | | | | | | | | | | | | | | | | | | | | | | | | | | | | | | | | | | | | | | | | | | |
| ACUPUNCTURE & NAT MED CLINIC (HM00243) | ● | ● | ● | ● | ● | ● | ● | ● | ● | ● | ● | ● | ● | ● | ● | ● | ● | ● | ● | | ● | ● | ● | ● | ● | ● | ● | ● | ● | | ● | | ● | ● | ● | | ● | ● | ● | ● | ● | ● | ● | ● | | ● | ● | ● |
| AROMATHERAPY IN PRACTICE (HM01114) | | | | | | | | | | | | ● | ● | | | | ● | | | | | | | | | | | | | | | | | | | | | | | | | | | | | | | |
| B WIGRAM HEALING & REFLEXOLOGY (HM01455) | | | | | | | | | | ● | | ● | ● | | | | | | | | | | | | | | | | | | | | ● | | | | | | | | | | | | | | | |
| BALMORAL PHYSIOTHERAPY (HM01640) | | | | | | | | | | | | | ● | | | | ● | | | | | | | | | | | ● | | | | | | | | | | | | | | | | | | | ● | |
| BASS, MIKE (HM01850) | ● | ● | ● | ● | ● | ● | ● | ● | ● | ● | ● | ● | ● | ● | ● | ● | ● | ● | | | ● | ● | ● | ● | ● | ● | ● | | ● | | | | ● | | ● | | ● | | ● | ● | ● | ● | ● | | | ● | ● | ● |
| BODY BALANCE HOLISTIC THERAPY (HM02572) | | | | | | | | | | | | ● | ● | | | | ● | | | | | | | | | | | | | | | | | | | | | | | | | | | | | | | |
| CHIROPODY CLINIC (HM04324) | | | | | | | | | | | | ● | ● | ● | ● | | ● | | | | ● | | | | | ● | | | | | | ● | | | | | ● | | | | | | ● | | ● | | | |
| CONNECT PHYSICAL HEALTH CTRE (HM04989) | | | | | | | | | | | | | | | ● | | ● | ● | | | | | | | | | | | | | | | | | | | | | | | | | | | | | | |
| COOP, JOE (HM05082) | | ● | | | | | | | | | | | | | | | | | | | | | | | | | | | | | | | | | | | | | | | | | | | | | | |
| DENTON, A (HM05998) | | | | | | ● | | | | | | ● | ● | ● | | | ● | | | | | | | ● | ● | ● | | | | | | | | | | | ● | ● | | | | | ● | | | | ● | ● |
| DERWENT CENTRE (HM06020) | ● | ● | ● | ● | ● | ● | ● | ● | ● | ● | ● | ● | ● | ● | ● | ● | ● | ● | ● | ● | ● | ● | ● | ● | ● | ● | ● | ● | ● | ● | ● | ● | ● | ● | ● | | ● | ● | ● | ● | ● | ● | ● | ● | ● | ● | ● | ● |
| EQUILIBRIUM (HM06867) | | | | | | | | | | | | | | | | ● | | | | | | | | | | | | | | | | | | | | | | | | | | | | | | | | |
| FAMILY CHIRO WELLNESS CENTRE (HM07083) | | | | | | ● | | ● | | | | ● | ● | ● | ● | ● | ● | ● | | | ● | ● | | | | ● | ● | ● | | | ● | | | | | | ● | | ● | ● | ● | | ● | ● | | ● | ● | ● |
| FEEL GOOD AROMATHERAPY (HM07164) | ● | | | | | ● | | | ● | ● | ● | ● | ● | ● | ● | | ● | ● | ● | | ● | ● | ● | ● | ● | ● | ● | ● | | | ● | | ● | | ● | | ● | ● | ● | ● | | | ● | | | ● | ● | ● |
| FOWLER, CHRISTINE (HM07628) | ● | ● | ● | ● | ● | ● | ● | ● | ● | ● | ● | ● | ● | ● | ● | ● | ● | ● | ● | | ● | ● | ● | ● | ● | ● | ● | ● | ● | | ● | ● | ● | ● | ● | | ● | ● | ● | ● | ● | ● | ● | ● | ● | ● | ● | ● |
| GATESHEAD COMPLEMENTARY HEALTH (HM07927) | | ● | | | | | | | | | | ● | | | | | ● | | | | | | | | | | | | | | | | | | | | | | | | | | | | | | | |
| HEALTH ALLIANCE CENTRE (HM09375) | | | | | | | | | | | | | ● | | | | ● | | | | | | | | | | | | | | ● | | | | | | | | | | | | | | | | | |
| HERBAL GARDEN AROMATHERAPY (HM09612) | ● | | | | | ● | | | | | | ● | ● | ● | ● | | ● | ● | | | | ● | | ● | | | | ● | | | | | | | | | ● | ● | ● | ● | | ● | ● | | | ● | ● | ● |
| HOLISTIC CHIROPRACTOR (HM09951) | | | | | | | | | | | | ● | ● | | | | ● | | | | | | | | | ● | | | | | | | | | | | ● | | | | | | | | | | | |
| HON, ARTHUR M R (HM10111) | | | | | | | | | | | | | | | | | ● | | | | | | | | | | | | | | | | | | | | | | | | | | | | | | | |
| HYPNOTHERAPY AND COUNSELLING (HM10514) | | | | | | | | | | | | ● | | ● | | | | | | | | ● | | | | | | | | | | | | | | | | | | | | | | | | | | |
| MCANELLY, J L (HM13368) | | ● | | | | | | | | | | ● | | | | | | | | | | | | | | | | | | | | | | | | | | | | | | | | | | | | |
| NATURAL SELECTION (HM14623) | ● | | | | | ● | | | | | | ● | | | | | | | | | | | | | | | ● | | | | | | | | | | | | ● | | | | | | | ● | | |
| NEW LIFE NATURAL HEALTH CARE (HM14820) | ● | ● | ● | ● | ● | ● | ● | ● | ● | ● | ● | ● | ● | ● | ● | ● | ● | ● | ● | | ● | ● | ● | ● | ● | ● | ● | ● | ● | | ● | ● | ● | ● | ● | | ● | ● | ● | ● | ● | ● | ● | ● | ● | ● | ● | ● |
| NEWCASTLE SPRTS INJ/THRPY CTRE (HM14855) | ● | | | | | ● | | | | | ● | ● | ● | | ● | | ● | | | | | | | | | | | | ● | | | ● | | | | | | | | | | | ● | | ● | | | |
| OSBORNE CLINIC (HM15420) | | ● | | | | | | | | | | | | | | | ● | | | | ● | | | ● | | ● | | | | | ● | | | | | | | | | | | | ● | | | | | |
| RAINBOW, RICHARD S (HM16887) | | ● | | | | | | | | | | ● | | | | | | | | | | | | | | | | | | | | | | | | | | | | | | | | | | | | |
| SCHOLL FOOTWEAR CENTRE (HM18077) | | | | | | | | | | | | | | | ● | | | ● | | | | | | | | | | | | | | ● | | | | | | | | | | | | | ● | | | |
| SHEN HOLISTIC THERAPIES (HM18392) | | | | | | | | | | | | | | ● | | | ● | | | | | | | | | | | | | | | | | | | | | | | | | | | | | | | |
| WESTOE PRACTICE (HM21277) | | | | | | | | | | | | | | | ● | | | ● | | | | | | | | | | | | | | ● | | | | | | | | | | | | | ● | | | |
| WHITLEY BAY CHIROPRACTOR (HM21406) | | | | | | | | | | | | | | | | | ● | | | | | | | | | | | | | | | | | | | | | | | | | | | | | | ● | |

# A - C Conditions treated at Practices/Businesses

| Business by County with Reference no. | Acne | Addiction | Adenoids | Aids | Alcoholism | Allergy | Alzheimer's Disease | Amnesia | Anaemia | Angina | Anorexia | Anxiety | Arthritis | Asthma | Athletes Foot | Autism | Back Pain | Bacterial Infections | Baldness | Bereavement | Bladder Problems | Blood Pressure | Boils | Bowel Problems |
|---|---|---|---|---|---|---|---|---|---|---|---|---|---|---|---|---|---|---|---|---|---|---|---|---|
| WARWICKSHIRE | | | | | | | | | | | | | | | | | | | | | | | | |
| ACUPUNCTURE CLINIC (HM00279) | | | | | | ● | | | | | | | ● | ● | | | ● | | | | | | | |
| BARRATT'S HOMEOPATHY (HM01780) | ● | ● | ● | ● | ● | ● | ● | ● | ● | ● | ● | ● | ● | ● | ● | ● | ● | ● | | | ● | ● | ● | ● |
| BIRTWELL, ANDREW (HM02400) | | ● | | | ● | | | | | | ● | ● | | | | | | | | | | | | |
| BRIEF COUNS & PSYCHOTHERAPY SV (HM03020) | | | | | | | | | | | ● | ● | | | | | | | | ● | | | | |
| CHURCH LAWFORD CHIRO CLINIC (HM04463) | | | | | | | | | | | | | ● | | | | ● | | | | | ● | | |
| CLIFTON OSTEOPATHIC PRACTICE (HM04669) | ● | | ● | | | ● | | | | | | ● | ● | ● | | | ● | | | | ● | ● | ● | ● |
| EDWARDS, IRENE & PETER (HM06656) | | ● | | | | | | | | | | ● | ● | | | | | | | | | | | |
| FIGHT (HM07282) | ● | | | | | | | | | | | ● | ● | | | | ● | | | | | | | |
| GREIG, E (HM08527) | | | | | | | | | | | | ● | ● | | | | | | | | | ● | | |
| HEALTHPOINT (HM09414) | ● | | | | | | | | | ● | | ● | ● | ● | | | ● | | | | | | | |
| HEART OF ENGLAND SHIATSU (HM09442) | ● | | | ● | | | | | | ● | | ● | ● | ● | | | ● | | | | ● | ● | | ● |
| HEARTLANDS (HM09445) | | ● | | | ● | | | | | | ● | ● | | ● | | | | | | | | ● | | ● |
| HERBAL ONE (HM09631) | ● | ● | ● | ● | ● | ● | ● | ● | ● | ● | ● | ● | ● | ● | ● | ● | ● | ● | ● | | ● | ● | ● | ● |
| HOLYCOMBE (HM10060) | | | | | | | | | | | | | | | | | ● | | | | | | | ● |
| JAN LLOYD AROMATHERAPY (HM10913) | ● | | | | | | | | | | | ● | ● | | | | ● | | | | | ● | | |
| LEAMINGTON SPA CHIRO CLINIC (HM12104) | ● | | | | | ● | | | | | | ● | ● | | | | ● | | | | | | | |
| LIFE-WAYS (HM12367) | ● | ● | ● | | ● | ● | ● | ● | ● | ● | ● | ● | ● | ● | ● | ● | ● | ● | ● | | ● | ● | ● | ● |
| NATURAL HEALTH CENTRE (HM14567) | ● | ● | | | ● | ● | ● | | | ● | | ● | ● | ● | | | ● | | | | ● | ● | | ● |
| NATURAL THERAPY CENTRE (HM14651) | | ● | ● | | | ● | | | ● | ● | | ● | ● | ● | ● | | ● | ● | | | ● | ● | ● | ● |
| NEWEY, RACHEL (HM14862) | | | | | | | | | | | | ● | | ● | | | ● | | | | | | | ● |
| NUNEATON CHIROPRACTIC CLINIC (HM15104) | | | | | | ● | | ● | | | | ● | ● | | | | ● | | | | | | | |
| PETERS, EVERARD (HM16085) | | | ● | | | | | | | | | ● | ● | ● | | ● | ● | | | | | | | |
| REFLEXOLOGY CLINIC (HM17091) | | | | | | | | | | ● | | ● | ● | | | | ● | | | | ● | ● | | ● |
| REVITALIZE (HM17205) | | | | | | | | | | | | ● | ● | | | | ● | | | | | | | |
| RUSSELL, COLIN (HM17766) | | | | | | | | | | | | | | | ● | | | | | | | | | |
| SAVAGE, GERALD (HM17966) | | ● | | | ● | ● | | ● | | | ● | ● | | | | | | | | | | | | |
| SHAWE AVENUE OSTEO PRACTICE (HM18351) | | | | | | | | | | | | | ● | ● | | | ● | | | | | | | ● |
| SHIATSU SOCIETY (HM18464) | | | | | | | | | | | | | | ● | | | ● | | | | ● | ● | | ● |
| SMALLWOOD, P (HM18698) | | | | | | | | | | | | | | | ● | | | | | | | | | |
| STRATFORD PHYSIO CLINIC (HM19370) | | | | | | | | | | | | | ● | | | | ● | | | | | | | |
| STUDLEY PHYSIOTHERAPY CENTRE (HM19442) | | | | | | | | | | | | | ● | | | | ● | | | | ● | | | |
| TOWERS, DIANA (HM20195) | | ● | | | ● | ● | | ● | | | ● | ● | ● | | | | ● | | | | | ● | | ● |
| TRADITIONAL ACUPUNCTURE GROUP (HM20221) | ● | ● | | | ● | ● | | | ● | ● | | ● | ● | ● | | | ● | | | | ● | ● | ● | ● |

| Business by County with Reference no. | Breast Problems | Breathing Problems | Bronchitis | Bruising | Bulimia | Bunions | Bursitis | Callices | Cancers | Cataracts | Catarrh | Cerebral Palsy | Circulation Problems | Cold Sores | Colds | Colic | Colitis | Conjunctivitis | Constipation | Convulsions | Corns | Coughs | Cramp | Cystitis |
|---|---|---|---|---|---|---|---|---|---|---|---|---|---|---|---|---|---|---|---|---|---|---|---|---|
| WARWICKSHIRE | | | | | | | | | | | | | | | | | | | | | | | | |
| ACUPUNCTURE CLINIC (HM00279) | | | | | | | | | | | | | | | ● | | | | ● | | | ● | ● | ● |
| BARRATT'S HOMEOPATHY (HM01780) | ● | ● | ● | ● | ● | | ● | | ● | ● | ● | | ● | ● | ● | ● | ● | ● | ● | ● | | ● | ● | ● |
| BIRTWELL, ANDREW (HM02400) | | | | | ● | | | | | | | | | | | | | | | | | | | |
| BRIEF COUNS & PSYCHOTHERAPY SV (HM03020) | | | | | | | | | | | | | | | | | | | | | | | | |
| CHURCH LAWFORD CHIRO CLINIC (HM04463) | | | | | | | | | | | | | ● | | | ● | | | | | | | | |
| CLIFTON OSTEOPATHIC PRACTICE (HM04669) | ● | ● | ● | ● | | | ● | | | | ● | | ● | ● | ● | ● | ● | ● | ● | | | ● | ● | ● |
| EDWARDS, IRENE & PETER (HM06656) | | | | | | | | | | | | | | | | | | | | | | | | |
| FIGHT (HM07282) | | ● | | | | | | | | | | | ● | | | | | | | | | | ● | |
| GREIG, E (HM08527) | | | | | | | | | | | | | | | | | | | | | | | | |
| HEALTHPOINT (HM09414) | | | ● | | | | | | | | | | ● | | | | ● | ● | ● | | | ● | ● | |
| HEART OF ENGLAND SHIATSU (HM09442) | ● | ● | | | | | | | ● | | | | ● | | | | ● | ● | ● | | | | | ● |
| HEARTLANDS (HM09445) | | | | | ● | | | | | | | | | | | | ● | | ● | | | | | |
| HERBAL ONE (HM09631) | ● | ● | ● | ● | ● | | ● | | ● | ● | ● | | ● | ● | ● | ● | ● | ● | ● | ● | | ● | ● | ● |
| HOLYCOMBE (HM10060) | | ● | | | | | | | | | | | ● | | | | | | ● | | | | | |
| JAN LLOYD AROMATHERAPY (HM10913) | | | | | | | | | | | ● | | | | | | | | | | | | ● | |
| LEAMINGTON SPA CHIRO CLINIC (HM12104) | | | | | | | | | | | | | ● | | | ● | | | | | | | | |
| LIFE-WAYS (HM12367) | ● | ● | ● | ● | ● | | ● | ● | ● | ● | ● | | ● | ● | ● | ● | ● | ● | ● | ● | ● | ● | ● | ● |
| NATURAL HEALTH CENTRE (HM14567) | ● | ● | ● | | | | ● | | | | ● | | ● | ● | ● | | ● | | ● | | | ● | | ● |
| NATURAL THERAPY CENTRE (HM14651) | ● | ● | ● | ● | | | | | | | ● | | ● | ● | ● | ● | ● | ● | ● | | | ● | ● | ● |
| NEWEY, RACHEL (HM14862) | | | | ● | | | ● | | | | | | | | | | | | ● | | | | ● | |
| NUNEATON CHIROPRACTIC CLINIC (HM15104) | | ● | ● | | | | | | | | | | ● | | | | | | | | | | | |
| PETERS, EVERARD (HM16085) | | ● | | | | | ● | | | | ● | | | | | ● | | | | | | | | |
| REFLEXOLOGY CLINIC (HM17091) | ● | ● | ● | | | | | | | | ● | | ● | | | | | | ● | | | | | |
| REVITALIZE (HM17205) | | | | | | | | | | | | | | | | | | | | | | | | |
| RUSSELL, COLIN (HM17766) | | | | | | | | | | | | | | | | | | | | | | | | |
| SAVAGE, GERALD (HM17966) | | | | | ● | | | | | | | | | | | | | | | | | | | |
| SHAWE AVENUE OSTEO PRACTICE (HM18351) | | | | | | | | | | | | | ● | | | ● | | | ● | | | | | |
| SHIATSU SOCIETY (HM18464) | | ● | ● | ● | | | | | | | | | ● | | ● | | | | ● | | | ● | ● | ● |
| SMALLWOOD, P (HM18698) | | | | | | | | ● | | | | | | | | | | | | | ● | | | |
| STRATFORD PHYSIO CLINIC (HM19370) | | | | ● | | | | | | | | | | | | | | | | | | | ● | |
| STUDLEY PHYSIOTHERAPY CENTRE (HM19442) | | ● | | | | | ● | | | | | | | | | | | | | | | | | |
| TOWERS, DIANA (HM20195) | | | | | ● | | | | ● | | | | | | | | | | ● | | | | | |
| TRADITIONAL ACUPUNCTURE GROUP (HM20221) | ● | ● | ● | ● | ● | | ● | | ● | | ● | | ● | ● | ● | ● | ● | | ● | ● | | ● | ● | ● |

# A - C Conditions treated at Practices/Businesses

Business by County with Reference no.

| Business | Acne | Addiction | Adenoids | Aids | Alcoholism | Allergy | Alzheimer's Disease | Amnesia | Anaemia | Angina | Anorexia | Anxiety | Arthritis | Asthma | Athletes Foot | Autism |
|---|---|---|---|---|---|---|---|---|---|---|---|---|---|---|---|---|
| WARWICK OSTEOPATHIC PRACTICE (HM20966) | ● | | ● | | | ● | | | | | | ● | ● | ● | | |
| WREN, PAULINE (HM21922) | | ● | | | | | | | | | | ● | | | | |
| **WILTSHIRE** | | | | | | | | | | | | | | | | |
| AMESBURY ABBEY CLINIC (HM00781) | | | | | | | | | | | | | | | | |
| ANDREWS, HAZEL (HM00852) | | | | | | ● | | | | ● | | ● | ● | ● | | |
| AVEBURY HYPNOTHERAPY PRACTICE (HM01386) | | | | | ● | ● | | | | | | | | | | |
| 'BACK IN LINE' (HM01482) | | | | | | | | | | | | | | | | |
| BLUNSDON ABBEY PHYSIOTHERAPY (HM02533) | | | | | | | | | | | | | ● | | | |
| CASTLE STREET CHIRO CLINIC (HM03836) | | | | | | | | | | | | | ● | | | |
| CRICKLADE ROAD PRACTICE (HM05439) | | | | | | ● | | | | | | | ● | | | |
| EASE MANAGEMENT CENTRE (HM06506) | | | | | | | | | | | ● | ● | | | | |
| ENGLISH, JOHN M (DR) (HM06834) | ● | | | | | ● | | | | | ● | ● | ● | ● | | |
| HEALTH HYDRO (HM09389) | ● | ● | | | ● | ● | | | | | ● | ● | ● | ● | | |
| HIGHWORTH PHYSIOTHERAPY CLINIC (HM09761) | | | | | | | | | | | | | ● | | | |
| HYPNOTHERAPY CENTRE (HM10529) | | ● | | | | ● | | | | | ● | ● | | ● | | |
| JENKINS, RUSSELL S (HM10996) | | | | | | | | | | | | | | | | |
| LEIGHTON REFLEXOLOGY CLINIC (HM12196) | | | | | | | | | | | | ● | ● | | | |
| LIFE-ENERGIES (HM12352) | ● | | | ● | | | ● | | ● | ● | | | ● | ● | | |
| LYON, P (HM12783) | | | | | | | | | | | | ● | | | | |
| MAGNO PULSE (HM12919) | | | | | | | | | | ● | | | ● | ● | | |
| MALMESBURY CHIROPRACTIC CLINIC (HM12982) | | | | | | | | | | | | | ● | | | |
| MARLBOROUGH CHIRO CLINIC (HM13122) | | | | | | | | | | | | | | | | |
| MARLBOROUGH NATURAL HLTH CTRE (HM13123) | ● | ● | ● | ● | ● | ● | ● | ● | ● | ● | ● | ● | ● | ● | ● | ● |
| MATHER, PAULINE (HM13280) | | | | | | ● | | | | | | | ● | | | |
| MOURANT, JENNIFER L (HM14298) | | | | | | | | | | | | ● | | | | |
| MULTI-THERAPY CENTRE (HM14352) | ● | ● | | | | ● | | | | | | ● | ● | ● | | |
| NATURAL THERAPY CENTRE (HM14639) | | | | | | | | | | | | ● | ● | ● | | |
| NATURALLY NUTRITION (HM14673) | ● | ● | | | | ● | ● | | ● | | ● | | ● | ● | | |
| OSTEOPATHS (HM15475) | | | | | | | | | | | | | ● | ● | | |
| PETER & CAROLINE (HM16071) | | | | | | | | | | | | ● | ● | | | |
| PETTIFER, JUSTINA (HM16095) | | | | | | | | | | | | ● | | | | |
| PHYSIOTHERAPY CLINIC (HM16247) | | | | | | | | | | | | | ● | | | |
| QUIRKE, G (HM16820) | | ● | | | | | | | | | ● | | | | | |
| RAINBOW NATURAL THERAPIES (HM16880) | | | | | | | | | | | | ● | | | | |

| Business | Back Pain | Bacterial Infections | Baldness | Bereavement | Bladder Problems | Blood Pressure | Boils | Bowel Problems | Breast Problems | Breathing Problems | Bronchitis | Bruising | Bulimia | Bunions | Bursitis | Callices |
|---|---|---|---|---|---|---|---|---|---|---|---|---|---|---|---|---|
| WARWICK OSTEOPATHIC PRACTICE (HM20966) | ● | | | | ● | ● | ● | ● | ● | ● | ● | ● | | | ● | |
| WREN, PAULINE (HM21922) | | | | | | | | | | | | | ● | | | |
| **WILTSHIRE** | | | | | | | | | | | | | | | | |
| AMESBURY ABBEY CLINIC (HM00781) | ● | | | | | | | | | | | | | | | |
| ANDREWS, HAZEL (HM00852) | ● | | | | ● | ● | | ● | | ● | | | | | ● | |
| AVEBURY HYPNOTHERAPY PRACTICE (HM01386) | | | | | | | | ● | | | | | | | | |
| 'BACK IN LINE' (HM01482) | ● | | | | | | | | | | | | | | | |
| BLUNSDON ABBEY PHYSIOTHERAPY (HM02533) | ● | | | | | | | | | | | ● | | | | |
| CASTLE STREET CHIRO CLINIC (HM03836) | ● | | | | | | | | | | | | | | | |
| CRICKLADE ROAD PRACTICE (HM05439) | ● | | | | | | | | | ● | | | | | ● | |
| EASE MANAGEMENT CENTRE (HM06506) | | | | | | | | | | | | | ● | | | |
| ENGLISH, JOHN M (DR) (HM06834) | ● | ● | | | ● | | ● | ● | ● | ● | ● | ● | ● | | ● | |
| HEALTH HYDRO (HM09389) | ● | | | | | | ● | ● | | ● | ● | | | | | |
| HIGHWORTH PHYSIOTHERAPY CLINIC (HM09761) | ● | | | | | | | | | | | | | | ● | |
| HYPNOTHERAPY CENTRE (HM10529) | ● | | | | | ● | | ● | ● | ● | | | | | | |
| JENKINS, RUSSELL S (HM10996) | ● | | | | | | | | | | | | | | | |
| LEIGHTON REFLEXOLOGY CLINIC (HM12196) | ● | | ● | | | ● | | ● | | | | | | | | |
| LIFE-ENERGIES (HM12352) | ● | ● | | | ● | ● | ● | ● | | ● | ● | ● | | | ● | |
| LYON, P (HM12783) | ● | | | | | | | | | ● | | | | | | |
| MAGNO PULSE (HM12919) | ● | | | | | ● | | ● | | | | ● | | | | |
| MALMESBURY CHIROPRACTIC CLINIC (HM12982) | ● | | | | | ● | | | | | | | | | | |
| MARLBOROUGH CHIRO CLINIC (HM13122) | ● | | | | | | | | | | | | | | | |
| MARLBOROUGH NATURAL HLTH CTRE (HM13123) | ● | ● | ● | | ● | ● | ● | ● | ● | ● | ● | ● | ● | | ● | ● |
| MATHER, PAULINE (HM13280) | ● | ● | | | | | | ● | | | | | | | ● | |
| MOURANT, JENNIFER L (HM14298) | | | | | | | | | | | | | | | | |
| MULTI-THERAPY CENTRE (HM14352) | ● | | | | | ● | ● | ● | ● | ● | ● | ● | | | | |
| NATURAL THERAPY CENTRE (HM14639) | ● | | | | ● | ● | | ● | | ● | ● | ● | | | ● | |
| NATURALLY NUTRITION (HM14673) | | | | | | ● | | ● | | | | | | | | |
| OSTEOPATHS (HM15475) | ● | | | | | | | | | | | | | | ● | |
| PETER & CAROLINE (HM16071) | | | | | ● | | | | | | | | | | | |
| PETTIFER, JUSTINA (HM16095) | | | | | | | | | | | | | | | | |
| PHYSIOTHERAPY CLINIC (HM16247) | ● | | | | | | | | | | | | | | | |
| QUIRKE, G (HM16820) | | | | | | | | ● | | | | | ● | | | |
| RAINBOW NATURAL THERAPIES (HM16880) | | | | | | | | | | | | | | | | |

| Business | Cancers | Cataracts | Catarrh | Cerebral Palsy | Circulation Problems | Cold Sores | Colds | Colic | Colitis | Conjunctivitis | Constipation | Convulsions | Corns | Coughs | Cramp | Cystitis |
|---|---|---|---|---|---|---|---|---|---|---|---|---|---|---|---|---|
| WARWICK OSTEOPATHIC PRACTICE (HM20966) | | | ● | | ● | ● | ● | ● | ● | ● | ● | | | ● | ● | ● |
| WREN, PAULINE (HM21922) | | | | | | | | | | | | | | | | |
| **WILTSHIRE** | | | | | | | | | | | | | | | | |
| AMESBURY ABBEY CLINIC (HM00781) | | | | | | | | | | | | | | | | |
| ANDREWS, HAZEL (HM00852) | | | ● | | ● | | ● | | ● | ● | ● | | | ● | ● | ● |
| AVEBURY HYPNOTHERAPY PRACTICE (HM01386) | | | | | | | | | | | | | | | | |
| 'BACK IN LINE' (HM01482) | | | | | ● | | | | | | ● | | | | ● | |
| BLUNSDON ABBEY PHYSIOTHERAPY (HM02533) | | | | | | | | | | | | | | | | |
| CASTLE STREET CHIRO CLINIC (HM03836) | | | | | | | | | | | | | | | | |
| CRICKLADE ROAD PRACTICE (HM05439) | | | | | ● | | | | | | | | | | | |
| EASE MANAGEMENT CENTRE (HM06506) | | | | | | | | | | | | | | | | |
| ENGLISH, JOHN M (DR) (HM06834) | ● | | ● | | ● | ● | ● | ● | ● | ● | ● | | | ● | ● | ● |
| HEALTH HYDRO (HM09389) | | | ● | | ● | ● | | | ● | | ● | | | | ● | |
| HIGHWORTH PHYSIOTHERAPY CLINIC (HM09761) | | | | | | | | | | | | | | | | |
| HYPNOTHERAPY CENTRE (HM10529) | | | ● | | | | | | | | ● | | | | | |
| JENKINS, RUSSELL S (HM10996) | | | | | | | | | | | | | | | ● | |
| LEIGHTON REFLEXOLOGY CLINIC (HM12196) | | | ● | | ● | | ● | | | | ● | | | | ● | ● |
| LIFE-ENERGIES (HM12352) | | | | | ● | ● | ● | ● | ● | | ● | | | ● | ● | ● |
| LYON, P (HM12783) | | | | | | | | | | | | | | | | |
| MAGNO PULSE (HM12919) | | | | | ● | | | | | | | | | | | |
| MALMESBURY CHIROPRACTIC CLINIC (HM12982) | | | | | ● | | | | | | | | | | | |
| MARLBOROUGH CHIRO CLINIC (HM13122) | | | | | | | | | | | | | | | ● | |
| MARLBOROUGH NATURAL HLTH CTRE (HM13123) | ● | ● | ● | | ● | ● | ● | ● | ● | ● | ● | ● | ● | ● | ● | ● |
| MATHER, PAULINE (HM13280) | | | | | | | | | | | | | | | | |
| MOURANT, JENNIFER L (HM14298) | | | | | | ● | | | | | | | | | | |
| MULTI-THERAPY CENTRE (HM14352) | | | ● | | ● | ● | ● | ● | ● | ● | ● | | | ● | ● | ● |
| NATURAL THERAPY CENTRE (HM14639) | | | ● | | | | ● | | ● | | ● | | | ● | ● | ● |
| NATURALLY NUTRITION (HM14673) | | | | | ● | ● | ● | | | | ● | | | ● | | ● |
| OSTEOPATHS (HM15475) | | | | | | | | | | | | | | | | |
| PETER & CAROLINE (HM16071) | | | | | ● | | | | | | | | | | | ● |
| PETTIFER, JUSTINA (HM16095) | | | | | | | | | | | | | | | | |
| PHYSIOTHERAPY CLINIC (HM16247) | | | | | ● | | | | | | | | | | | |
| QUIRKE, G (HM16820) | | | | | | | | | | | | | | | | |
| RAINBOW NATURAL THERAPIES (HM16880) | | | | | | | | | | | | | | | | |

# A - C Conditions treated at Practices/Businesses

| Business by County with Reference no. | Acne | Addiction | Adenoids | Aids | Alcoholism | Allergy | Alzheimer's Disease | Amnesia | Anaemia | Angina | Anorexia | Anxiety | Arthritis | Asthma | Athletes Foot | Autism | Back Pain | Bacterial Infections | Baldness | Bereavement | Bladder Problems | Blood Pressure | Boils | Bowel Problems | Breast Problems | Breathing Problems | Bronchitis | Bruising | Bulimia | Bunions | Bursitis | Callices | Cancers | Cataracts | Catarrh | Cerebral Palsy | Circulation Problems | Cold Sores | Colds | Colic | Colitis | Conjunctivitis | Constipation | Convulsions | Corns | Coughs | Cramp | Cystitis |
|---|---|---|---|---|---|---|---|---|---|---|---|---|---|---|---|---|---|---|---|---|---|---|---|---|---|---|---|---|---|---|---|---|---|---|---|---|---|---|---|---|---|---|---|---|---|---|---|---|
| SARUM PHYSIOTHERAPY CENTRE (HM17947) | | | | | | | | | | | | | ● | | | | ● | | | | | | | | | | | ● | | | | | | | | | | | | | | | | | | | ● | |
| SAWAYA, ALICIA (HM17982) | ● | ● | ● | ● | ● | ● | ● | ● | ● | ● | ● | ● | ● | ● | ● | ● | ● | ● | ● | | ● | ● | ● | ● | ● | ● | ● | ● | ● | | ● | | ● | ● | ● | | ● | ● | ● | ● | ● | ● | ● | ● | | ● | ● | ● |
| SHAFTSBURY PRACTICE (HM18266) | ● | ● | ● | ● | ● | ● | ● | ● | ● | ● | ● | ● | ● | ● | ● | ● | ● | ● | ● | | ● | ● | ● | ● | ● | ● | ● | ● | ● | | ● | | ● | ● | ● | | ● | ● | ● | ● | ● | ● | ● | ● | | ● | ● | ● |
| SHAVE, G M (HM18325) | | | | | | | | | | | | | | | ● | | | ● | | | | | | | | | | | | ● | | ● | | | | | | | | | | | | | ● | | | |
| SPIRITUAL HEALER (HM19026) | | | | | | | | | | | | | ● | | | | ● | | | | | | | | | | | | | | | | | | | | ● | | | | | | | | | | | |
| SWINDON CHIROPRACTIC CLINIC (HM19595) | | | | | | | | | | | | | ● | | | | ● | | | | | | | | | | | | | | | | | | | | | | | | | | | | | | | |
| TISBURY OSTEOPATHIC PRACTICE (HM20094) | | | | | | | | | | | | | | ● | | | ● | | | | | | | | | ● | | | | | ● | | | | | | | | | ● | | | ● | | | | | |
| WARMINSTER OSTEOPATHIC CLINIC (HM20929) | | | | | | ● | | | ● | | ● | ● | | ● | | ● | ● | | | | ● | ● | ● | ● | ● | ● | | | ● | | ● | | | | ● | | ● | | ● | | ● | | ● | | | ● | ● | |
| WATSON'S COURT CLINIC (HM21025) | | | | | | | | | | | | | ● | | ● | | ● | ● | | | | | | | | | | | | ● | ● | ● | | | | | | | | | | | | | ● | | | |
| WELLS, HENRIETTA (HM21175) | ● | ● | ● | ● | ● | ● | ● | ● | ● | ● | ● | ● | ● | ● | ● | ● | ● | ● | ● | | ● | ● | ● | ● | ● | ● | ● | ● | ● | | ● | ● | ● | ● | ● | | ● | ● | ● | ● | ● | ● | ● | ● | ● | ● | ● | ● |
| WESTBURY CHIROPRACTIC (HM21258) | | | | | | | | | | | | | ● | | | | ● | | | | | ● | | | | | | | | | | | | | | | ● | | | ● | | | | | | | | |
| WESTBURY REFLEXOLOGY CLINIC (HM21260) | | | | | | ● | | | | | | ● | ● | ● | | | ● | | | | | | | | | | | | | | | | | | | | | | | | | | | | | | | |
| WOOTTON BASSETT (HM21885) | | | | | | | | | | | | | ● | | | | ● | | | | | | | | | | | ● | | | | | | | | | | | | | | | | | | | | |
| **WORCESTERSHIRE** | | | | | | | | | | | | | | | | | | | | | | | | | | | | | | | | | | | | | | | | | | | | | | | | |
| 1ST CHIROPRACTIC UK (HM00007) | | | | | | | | | | | | | ● | | | | ● | | | | | | | | | | | | | | | | | | | | ● | | | ● | | | | | | | | |
| AINSLEY, S (HM00433) | | | | | | | | | | | | | ● | | ● | | ● | | | | | | | | | | | | | | ● | | | | | | | | | | | | | | | | | |
| BRETFORDTON CLINIC (HM02969) | | | | ● | | | ● | | | | | | ● | ● | ● | | ● | | | | | ● | | ● | | ● | ● | ● | | | | | | | | | ● | | | | | | ● | | | | | |
| BROMSGROVE CHIROPRACTIC CLINIC (HM03151) | | | | | | | | | | | | | ● | | | | ● | | | | | | | | | | | | | | | | | | | | ● | | | ● | | | | | | | | |
| CARYL, M D (HM03804) | | | | | | | | | | | | | | | ● | | | | | | | | | | | | | | | ● | | ● | | | | | | | | | | | | | ● | | | |
| DAVIES PODIATRY (HM05792) | | | | | | | | | | | | | | | ● | | | ● | | | | | | | | | | | | ● | | ● | | | | | | | | | | | | | ● | | | |
| EVESHAM NATURAL HEALTH CENTRE (HM07009) | | ● | | | | ● | | ● | ● | ● | ● | ● | ● | ● | ● | | ● | ● | | | | ● | ● | ● | | ● | ● | ● | ● | | ● | | | | ● | | ● | ● | ● | ● | ● | ● | ● | | | ● | ● | |
| FRONTIA (HM07757) | | | | ● | | ● | | | | | | ● | ● | ● | ● | | ● | | | | ● | ● | | ● | | ● | ● | ● | | | | | | | | | | ● | ● | ● | ● | ● | ● | | | ● | ● | ● |
| GIBBINS, JONATHAN (HM08022) | | | | | | | | | | | | | ● | ● | | | ● | | | | ● | | | ● | | ● | | | | | ● | | | | | | | | | | | | ● | | | | ● | |
| HINKS, MAXINE (HM09834) | | | | | | | | | | | | ● | ● | | | | ● | | | | | | | | | | | | | | | | | | | | | | | | | | | | | | | |
| HOLDEN, NINA (HM09933) | | | | | | ● | | ● | | | | ● | ● | ● | | | ● | | | | ● | ● | | | | ● | | | | | | | | | | | | | | ● | | | ● | | | | | |
| JONES, VAL (HM11200) | | | | | | | | | | | | | | | ● | | | | | | | | | | | | | | | | | | | | | | | | | | | | | | | | | |
| KITSON, P (HM11730) | | | | | | | | | | | | | ● | | | | ● | | | | | | | | | | | | | | | | | | | | | | | | | | | | | | | |
| KRISS, ADRIAN D (HM11803) | | | | | | | | | | | | | | | ● | | | | | | | | | | | | | | | | | | | | | | | | | | | | | | | | | |
| M THORLOW CHIROPODY (HM12810) | | | | | | | | | | | | | | | ● | | | | | | | | | | | | | | | ● | | ● | | | | | | | | | | | | | ● | | | |
| MALVERN NATURAL HEALTH CENTRE (HM12998) | ● | ● | ● | ● | ● | ● | ● | ● | ● | ● | ● | ● | ● | ● | ● | ● | ● | ● | ● | | ● | ● | ● | ● | ● | ● | ● | ● | ● | | ● | ● | ● | ● | ● | | ● | ● | ● | ● | ● | ● | ● | ● | ● | ● | ● | ● |
| MALVERN OSTEOPATHIC CLINIC (HM12999) | | | | | | | | | | | | | | | | | ● | | | | | | | | | | | | | | | | | | | | | | | | | | | | | | | |
| MARSTON, SUE (HM13179) | | | | | | ● | | | | | | ● | ● | | | | ● | | | | | | | | | | | ● | | | | | | | | | ● | | | | | | ● | | | | | |
| MEAKIN, D W (HM13637) | | | | | | | | | | | | | ● | | | | ● | | | | | | | | | | | | | | | | | | | | | | | | | | | | | | | |
| NATURAL HEALTH CENTRE (HM14564) | ● | | | | | | | | ● | ● | | ● | ● | ● | | | ● | | | | | | | | | | ● | | | | | | | | | | | | ● | | ● | | ● | | | | | ● |

# A - C Conditions treated at Practices/Businesses

| Business by County with Reference no. | Acne | Addiction | Adenoids | Aids | Alcoholism | Allergy | Alzheimer's Disease | Amnesia | Anaemia | Angina | Anorexia | Anxiety | Arthritis | Asthma | Athletes Foot | Autism | Back Pain | Bacterial Infections | Baldness | Bereavement | Bladder Problems | Blood Pressure | Boils | Bowel Problems | Breast Problems | Breathing Problems | Bronchitis | Bruising | Bulimia | Bunions | Bursitis | Callices | Cancers | Cataracts | Catarrh | Cerebral Palsy | Circulation Problems | Cold Sores | Colds | Colic | Colitis | Conjunctivitis | Constipation | Convulsions | Corns | Coughs | Cramp | Cystitis |
|---|---|---|---|---|---|---|---|---|---|---|---|---|---|---|---|---|---|---|---|---|---|---|---|---|---|---|---|---|---|---|---|---|---|---|---|---|---|---|---|---|---|---|---|---|---|---|---|
| NOTTINGHAM, STUART (HM15086) | | | | | | | | | | | | | ● | | | | ● | | | | | | | | | | | ● | | | ● | | | | | | | | | | | | | | | | | |
| NURCHIR (HM15110) | | | | | | | | | | | | | | | ● | | | ● | | | | | | | | | | | | ● | | ● | | | | | ● | | | | | | | | ● | | | |
| NUTRIMED (HM15118) | | | | | | ● | | | | | | | | | | | | | | | | | | | | | | | | | | | | | | | | | | | | | | | | | | |
| OAKFIELD CLINIC (HM15150) | | | | | | ● | | | | ● | | ● | | ● | | | | | | | | ● | | | | ● | ● | | | | | | | | | | | | | | | | | | | | | |
| PARDOE, DIANA T (HM15648) | | ● | | | | | | | | | | ● | | | | | | | | | | ● | | | | | | | | | | | | | | | | | | | | | | | | | | |
| PERSHORE NAT THERAPY CLINIC (HM16057) | ● | ● | ● | ● | ● | ● | ● | ● | ● | ● | ● | ● | ● | ● | ● | ● | ● | ● | ● | | ● | ● | ● | ● | ● | ● | ● | ● | ● | | ● | ● | ● | ● | ● | | ● | ● | ● | ● | ● | ● | ● | ● | ● | ● | ● | ● |
| R C C M (HM16829) | | | | | | | | | | | | | ● | | | | ● | | | | | | | | | | | | | | | | | | | | | | | | | | | | | | | |
| REDDITCH CHIROPRACTIC CLINIC (HM17013) | | | | | | | | | | | | | ● | | | | ● | | | | | | | | | | | | | | | | | | | | ● | | | ● | | | | | | | | |
| REDDITCH FOOTCARE SURGERY (HM17014) | | | | | | | | | | | | | | | ● | | | | | | | | | | | | | | | | | | | | | | | | | | | | | | | | | |
| ROBINSON, MIG (HM17498) | | | | | | | | | | | | | | | | | | | | ● | | | | | | | | | | | | | | | | | | | | | | | | | | | | |
| SOUTH WORCESTERSHIRE HYP (HM18915) | | | | | | ● | | | | | ● | ● | | ● | | | | | | | | | | ● | | | | | | | | | | | | | | | | | ● | | ● | | | | | |
| STOKES, TERRY (HM19325) | | | | | | ● | | | ● | | ● | ● | ● | ● | ● | | ● | | | | ● | | ● | ● | ● | ● | ● | ● | | | | | ● | | ● | | ● | ● | | ● | | ● | ● | | | ● | | ● |
| STONE, ANNE L (HM19329) | | | | | | | | | | | | | ● | | | | ● | | | | | | | | | ● | | | | | ● | | | | | | | | | | | | | | | | | |
| WORCESTER NATURAL THERAPY CTRE (HM21886) | ● | ● | ● | ● | ● | ● | ● | ● | ● | ● | ● | ● | ● | ● | ● | ● | ● | ● | ● | | ● | ● | ● | ● | ● | ● | ● | ● | ● | | ● | ● | ● | ● | ● | | ● | ● | ● | ● | ● | ● | ● | ● | ● | ● | ● | ● |
| YOUNG, JOANNA (HM22075) | | | | | | | | | | | | | | | | ● | ● | | | | | | | | | | | | | | | | | | | | ● | | | ● | | | | | | | | |
| **YORKSHIRE (NORTH)** | | | | | | | | | | | | | | | | | | | | | | | | | | | | | | | | | | | | | | | | | | | | | | | | |
| A TACTILE BUSINESS (HM00046) | | | | | | | | | | | | | | | | | ● | | | | | ● | | | | | | | | | | | | | | | | | | | | | | | | | | |
| BARRASS, K I (HM01778) | | | | | | | | | | | | | | | ● | | | | | | | | | | | | | | | ● | | | | | | | | | | | | | | | | | | |
| BLACK, SAUL (HM02428) | | | | | | | | | | | | | ● | | ● | | | | | | | | | | | | | | | | | ● | | | | | | | | | | | | | ● | | | |
| BROADHEAD, J N & M (HM03114) | | | | | | | | | | | | | | | ● | | | | | | | | | | | | | | | ● | | ● | | | | | | | | | | | | | ● | | | |
| BUSWELL, RONA (HM03471) | | | | | | | | | | | | ● | ● | | | | | | | | ● | ● | | | | ● | | | | | | | | | | | ● | | | | | | ● | | | | | |
| CHIROPODIST (HM04292) | | | | | | | | | | | | | | | ● | | | | | | | | | | | | | | | ● | | ● | | | | | | | | | | | | | ● | | | |
| CORDEL, MICHAEL (HM05160) | | ● | | | | | | | | ● | | ● | ● | | | | ● | | | | ● | ● | | ● | | ● | ● | | | | ● | | | | | | ● | | ● | | ● | ● | ● | | | ● | | ● |
| CRAVEN CLINIC (HM05384) | ● | ● | ● | | ● | ● | | | ● | ● | ● | ● | ● | ● | ● | ● | ● | ● | ● | | ● | ● | ● | ● | ● | ● | ● | ● | ● | | ● | | ● | ● | ● | | ● | ● | ● | ● | ● | ● | ● | ● | | ● | ● | ● |
| CROFT HOUSE CLINIC (HM05452) | | | | | | | | | | | | | ● | ● | | | ● | | | | | | | | | | | ● | | | | | | | | | | | | ● | | | | | | | | |
| DOVE COURT CENTRE (HM06225) | ● | ● | ● | ● | ● | ● | ● | ● | ● | ● | ● | ● | ● | ● | ● | ● | ● | ● | ● | | ● | ● | ● | ● | ● | ● | ● | ● | ● | | ● | ● | ● | ● | ● | | ● | ● | ● | ● | ● | ● | ● | ● | ● | ● | ● | ● |
| EASY WAY YORKSHIRE (HM06557) | | ● | | | ● | | | | | | | | | | | | | | | | | | | | | | | | | | | | | | | | | | | | | | | | | | | |
| GRIFFIN, TRICIA (HM08555) | ● | | | | | ● | | | | | | ● | ● | ● | | | | | | | ● | | | ● | | | | | | | | | | | | | | ● | | ● | | | ● | | | | | ● |
| HARROGATE HOLISTIC HEALTH CTRE (HM09116) | | ● | | | | ● | | | | | | | | | | | ● | | | | | | | ● | | | | | | | | | | | | | | | | | | | | | | | | |
| HEALING CLINIC (HM09328) | | ● | ● | ● | | ● | | | ● | ● | | ● | ● | ● | ● | ● | ● | ● | | | ● | ● | ● | ● | ● | ● | ● | ● | | | ● | | ● | | ● | | ● | ● | ● | ● | ● | ● | ● | | | ● | ● | ● |
| HESCOTT, J D (HM09692) | | | | | | | | | | | | | | | ● | | | | | | | | | | | | | | | | | ● | | | | | | | | | | | | | ● | | | |
| HIGHTHORN PHYSIOTHERAPY CLINIC (HM09759) | | | | | | | | | | | | | ● | | | | ● | | | | | | | | | | | ● | | | | | | | | | | | | | | | | | | | ● | |
| HOBSON, I K (HM09863) | | | | | | | | | | | | | | | ● | | | | | | | | | | | | | | | | | | | | | | | | | | | | | | | | | |
| KNOWLES, J (HM11770) | | | | | | | | | | | | | ● | | ● | | | | | | | | | | | | | | | ● | | ● | | | | | | | | | | | | | ● | | | |

# A - C Conditions treated at Practices/Businesses

| Business by County with Reference no. | Acne | Addiction | Adenoids | Aids | Alcoholism | Allergy | Alzheimer's Disease | Amnesia | Anaemia | Angina | Anorexia | Anxiety | Arthritis | Asthma | Athletes Foot | Autism |
|---|---|---|---|---|---|---|---|---|---|---|---|---|---|---|---|---|
| LESZCZUK, PAULA (HM12246) | ● | ● | ● | | ● | ● | ● | | ● | ● | ● | ● | ● | ● | ● | |
| LESZCZUK, PAULA (HM12245) | ● | ● | ● | | ● | ● | ● | ● | | ● | ● | ● | ● | ● | ● | |
| LIFESUPPORT (HM12366) | ● | ● | | | ● | ● | | | | | | ● | ● | ● | ● | |
| NANCY METCALFE MOBILE CONSULT (HM14468) | | | | | | | | | | | | ● | ● | | | |
| NATURAL BALANCE (HM14515) | | | | | | | | | | | | ● | | | | |
| PANACEA ACUPUNCTURE CLINIC (HM15628) | | | | | | ● | | | | | | | | | | |
| PAULA LESZCZUK (HM15849) | ● | ● | ● | | ● | ● | ● | | ● | ● | ● | ● | ● | ● | ● | |
| RATHBONE, DONNA (HM16955) | | | | | | | | | | | | | | | ● | |
| RIPON NATURAL HEALTH CENTRE (HM17365) | ● | | | | | ● | | | | ● | ● | ● | ● | ● | | ● |
| SHACKLETON, MAUREEN (HM18264) | | | | | | | | | | | | | | | | |
| SHAH, ATUL (HM18268) | ● | ● | ● | | | ● | | | ● | ● | | ● | ● | ● | ● | |
| SHEEHAN, NICHOLAS (HM18363) | | | | | | | | | | | | | ● | | | |
| SI SHEN CLINIC (HM18519) | | | | | | | | | | | | ● | | | | |
| SKIPTON CHIROPODY CENTRE (HM18658) | | | | | | | | | | | | | | | ● | |
| SMITH, C J (HM18723) | | | | | | | | | | | | | ● | | | |
| STATHER, M (HM19160) | | | | | | | | | | | | | ● | | ● | |
| STRATTON, FIONA (HM19372) | | | | | | | | | | | | ● | ● | | ● | |
| TERRY ANNE (HM19845) | ● | ● | ● | | | ● | | | | | ● | ● | ● | ● | | |
| YOGA FOR ALL (HM22026) | | | | | | | | | | | | ● | | ● | | |
| YORK CHIROPRACTIC CLINIC (HM22039) | | | | | | | | | | | | | ● | | | |
| YORK CLINIC (HM22040) | ● | ● | ● | ● | ● | ● | ● | ● | ● | ● | ● | ● | ● | ● | ● | ● |
| YORK COUNSELLING (HM22042) | ● | ● | | | | | | ● | | | ● | ● | | ● | | |
| **YORKSHIRE (SOUTH)** | | | | | | | | | | | | | | | | |
| ALTON & JAMES MED HERBAL (HM00748) | ● | | | | | ● | | | | | | | ● | ● | ● | |
| ANDERSON, A DUDLEY (HM00810) | | ● | | | | | | | | | | ● | | | | |
| BAWTRY PHYSIOTHERAPY PRACTICE (HM01918) | | | | | | | | | | | | | ● | | | |
| BLUFF, ANN (HM02529) | | | | | | | | | | | | | ● | | ● | |
| BONESETTER AND MANIPULATOR (HM02676) | | | | | | | | | | | | | | | | |
| BOON, G M (HM02690) | | | | | | | | | | | | | ● | | ● | |
| BRAMLEY HALL CLINIC (HM02902) | ● | | | | | ● | ● | | | | | | ● | | | |
| BRANKIN, M & K (HM02917) | | | | | | | | | | | | | ● | | ● | |
| BRANKLIN, M & K (HM02918) | | | | | | | | | | | | | ● | | ● | |
| BROOMHILL MEDICAL CENTRE (HM03193) | | | | | | | | | | | | ● | ● | | | |
| CARING CLINIC (HM03682) | ● | | | | | ● | | | ● | ● | | ● | ● | ● | ● | |

| Business by County with Reference no. | Back Pain | Bacterial Infections | Baldness | Bereavement | Bladder Problems | Blood Pressure | Boils | Bowel Problems | Breast Problems | Breathing Problems | Bronchitis | Bruising | Bulimia | Bunions | Bursitis | Callices |
|---|---|---|---|---|---|---|---|---|---|---|---|---|---|---|---|---|
| LESZCZUK, PAULA (HM12246) | ● | ● | | | ● | ● | ● | ● | ● | ● | ● | ● | ● | | ● | |
| LESZCZUK, PAULA (HM12245) | ● | ● | | | ● | ● | ● | ● | ● | ● | ● | ● | ● | | ● | |
| LIFESUPPORT (HM12366) | ● | | | | ● | ● | | ● | | | ● | | | | ● | |
| NANCY METCALFE MOBILE CONSULT (HM14468) | ● | | | | | | | | | | | | | | | |
| NATURAL BALANCE (HM14515) | ● | | | | | | | | | | | | | | | |
| PANACEA ACUPUNCTURE CLINIC (HM15628) | | | | | | | | | | | | | | | | |
| PAULA LESZCZUK (HM15849) | ● | ● | | | ● | ● | ● | ● | ● | ● | ● | ● | ● | | ● | |
| RATHBONE, DONNA (HM16955) | | | | | | | | | | | | | | | | ● |
| RIPON NATURAL HEALTH CENTRE (HM17365) | ● | | | | ● | ● | ● | ● | ● | ● | | ● | ● | | ● | |
| SHACKLETON, MAUREEN (HM18264) | | | | | | | | | | | | | | | | |
| SHAH, ATUL (HM18268) | ● | ● | | | ● | ● | ● | ● | ● | ● | ● | ● | | | ● | |
| SHEEHAN, NICHOLAS (HM18363) | ● | | | | | | | | | ● | | | | | | |
| SI SHEN CLINIC (HM18519) | ● | | | | | | | | | | | | | | | |
| SKIPTON CHIROPODY CENTRE (HM18658) | | | | | | | | | | | | | | | | |
| SMITH, C J (HM18723) | ● | | | | | | | | | | | | | | | |
| STATHER, M (HM19160) | | | | | | | | | | | | | | | | ● |
| STRATTON, FIONA (HM19372) | ● | ● | | | ● | | | ● | ● | ● | | | | | | |
| TERRY ANNE (HM19845) | ● | | | | ● | ● | | | | ● | | | | | | |
| YOGA FOR ALL (HM22026) | ● | | | | | ● | | ● | | ● | | | | | | |
| YORK CHIROPRACTIC CLINIC (HM22039) | ● | | | | | | | | | | | | | | | |
| YORK CLINIC (HM22040) | ● | ● | ● | | ● | ● | ● | ● | ● | ● | ● | ● | ● | | ● | ● |
| YORK COUNSELLING (HM22042) | | | | ● | | ● | | | | | | | ● | | | |
| **YORKSHIRE (SOUTH)** | | | | | | | | | | | | | | | | |
| ALTON & JAMES MED HERBAL (HM00748) | | ● | | | ● | ● | ● | ● | | | ● | | | | | |
| ANDERSON, A DUDLEY (HM00810) | | | | | | | | | | | | | | | | |
| BAWTRY PHYSIOTHERAPY PRACTICE (HM01918) | ● | | | | | | | | | | | | | | | |
| BLUFF, ANN (HM02529) | | | | | | | | | | | | | | | | ● |
| BONESETTER AND MANIPULATOR (HM02676) | ● | | | | | | | | | | | | | | | |
| BOON, G M (HM02690) | | ● | | | | | | | | | | | | ● | | |
| BRAMLEY HALL CLINIC (HM02902) | ● | ● | | | ● | ● | | ● | | ● | ● | | | | ● | ● |
| BRANKIN, M & K (HM02917) | | | | | | | | | | | | | | | | ● |
| BRANKLIN, M & K (HM02918) | | ● | | | | | | | | | | | | | | ● |
| BROOMHILL MEDICAL CENTRE (HM03193) | ● | | | | | | | | | | | | | | | |
| CARING CLINIC (HM03682) | | ● | | | | ● | ● | ● | | ● | ● | ● | ● | | ● | |

| Business by County with Reference no. | Cancers | Cataracts | Catarrh | Cerebral Palsy | Circulation Problems | Cold Sores | Colds | Colic | Colitis | Conjunctivitis | Constipation | Convulsions | Corns | Coughs | Cramp | Cystitis |
|---|---|---|---|---|---|---|---|---|---|---|---|---|---|---|---|---|
| LESZCZUK, PAULA (HM12246) | ● | ● | ● | | ● | ● | ● | ● | ● | ● | ● | ● | | ● | ● | ● |
| LESZCZUK, PAULA (HM12245) | ● | ● | ● | | ● | ● | ● | ● | ● | ● | ● | ● | | ● | ● | ● |
| LIFESUPPORT (HM12366) | | | ● | | ● | ● | ● | | | | ● | | | ● | ● | ● |
| NANCY METCALFE MOBILE CONSULT (HM14468) | | | | | ● | | | | | | | | | | ● | |
| NATURAL BALANCE (HM14515) | | | | | | | | | | | | | | | | |
| PANACEA ACUPUNCTURE CLINIC (HM15628) | | | | | | | | | | | ● | | | | | |
| PAULA LESZCZUK (HM15849) | ● | ● | ● | | ● | ● | ● | ● | ● | ● | ● | ● | | ● | ● | ● |
| RATHBONE, DONNA (HM16955) | | | | | | | | | | | | | ● | | | |
| RIPON NATURAL HEALTH CENTRE (HM17365) | ● | ● | ● | | ● | ● | ● | ● | ● | ● | ● | ● | | ● | ● | ● |
| SHACKLETON, MAUREEN (HM18264) | ● | | | | | | | | | | | | | | | |
| SHAH, ATUL (HM18268) | | ● | ● | | ● | ● | ● | ● | ● | ● | ● | | | ● | ● | ● |
| SHEEHAN, NICHOLAS (HM18363) | | | | | | | | | | | | | | | | |
| SI SHEN CLINIC (HM18519) | | | | | | | | | | | | | | | | |
| SKIPTON CHIROPODY CENTRE (HM18658) | | | | | | | | | | | | | | | | |
| SMITH, C J (HM18723) | | | | | ● | | | ● | | | | | | | | |
| STATHER, M (HM19160) | | | | | | | | | | | | | ● | | | |
| STRATTON, FIONA (HM19372) | ● | | ● | | ● | | ● | | | | ● | | | | ● | ● |
| TERRY ANNE (HM19845) | | | ● | | ● | | | | | | ● | | | | | |
| YOGA FOR ALL (HM22026) | | | | | ● | | | | | | ● | | | | | |
| YORK CHIROPRACTIC CLINIC (HM22039) | | | | | | | | | | | | | | | | |
| YORK CLINIC (HM22040) | ● | ● | ● | | ● | ● | ● | ● | ● | ● | ● | ● | ● | ● | ● | ● |
| YORK COUNSELLING (HM22042) | | | | | | | | | | | | | | | | |
| **YORKSHIRE (SOUTH)** | | | | | | | | | | | | | | | | |
| ALTON & JAMES MED HERBAL (HM00748) | | | ● | | ● | | ● | | ● | | ● | | | ● | ● | ● |
| ANDERSON, A DUDLEY (HM00810) | | | | | | | | | | | | | | | | |
| BAWTRY PHYSIOTHERAPY PRACTICE (HM01918) | | | | | | | | | | | | | | | ● | |
| BLUFF, ANN (HM02529) | | | | | | | | | | | | | ● | | | |
| BONESETTER AND MANIPULATOR (HM02676) | | | | | | | | | | | | | | | | |
| BOON, G M (HM02690) | | | | | | | | | | | | | | | | |
| BRAMLEY HALL CLINIC (HM02902) | ● | | ● | | ● | ● | ● | ● | ● | | ● | | | | | ● |
| BRANKIN, M & K (HM02917) | | | | | | | | | | | | | ● | | | |
| BRANKLIN, M & K (HM02918) | | | | | | | | | | | | | ● | | | |
| BROOMHILL MEDICAL CENTRE (HM03193) | | | | | | | | | | | | | | | | |
| CARING CLINIC (HM03682) | ● | | ● | | ● | ● | ● | | ● | ● | ● | | | | | ● |

# A - C Conditions treated at Practices/Businesses

| Business by County with Reference no. | Acne | Addiction | Adenoids | Aids | Alcoholism | Allergy | Alzheimer's Disease | Amnesia | Anaemia | Angina | Anorexia | Anxiety | Arthritis | Asthma | Athletes Foot | Autism | Back Pain | Bacterial Infections | Baldness | Bereavement | Bladder Problems |
|---|---|---|---|---|---|---|---|---|---|---|---|---|---|---|---|---|---|---|---|---|---|
| CHIROPODY SURGERY (HM04342) | | | | | | | | | | | | | | | | | | | | | |
| CLAIRE LOUISE (HM04510) | | | | | | | | | | | | | | | ● | | | ● | | | |
| COUNTRY PRACTICE (HM05256) | ● | | | | | | | | | | | ● | ● | | ● | | ● | | | | |
| DORE PHYSIOTHERAPY PRACTICE (HM06196) | | | | | | | | | | | | | ● | | | | ● | | | | |
| EATON, T C (HM06565) | | | | | | | | | | | | | ● | | | | | ● | | | |
| ESSENTIAL HARMONY (HM06907) | ● | | | | | | | | | | | ● | | | | | | | | | |
| FISHER, CHRISTINE A (HM07349) | | | | | | | | | | | | | | | ● | | | | | | |
| GORNEY, C (HM08296) | | | | | | | | | | | | | | | | | | | | ● | |
| GRAPEVINE HEALTH (HM08399) | ● | ● | ● | ● | ● | ● | ● | ● | ● | ● | ● | ● | ● | ● | ● | ● | ● | ● | ● | | ● |
| GRENOSIDE PHYSIOTHERAPY (HM08536) | | | | | | | | | | | | | ● | | | | ● | | | | |
| GYALTSABJE BUDDHIST CENTRE (HM08672) | | | | | | | | | | | | ● | | | | | | | | | |
| HALLAMSHIRE NATURAL HLTH CTRE (HM08798) | | | | | | ● | | | | | | ● | | | | ● | ● | ● | | | |
| HEALTHY FEET (HM09427) | | | | | | | | | | | | | ● | | ● | | ● | ● | | | |
| HINCHLIFFE, JACKIE (HM09822) | ● | | | | | | | | | | | ● | ● | ● | ● | | ● | ● | | | |
| HYPNOTHERAPY CENTRE (HM10515) | ● | ● | | | ● | ● | | ● | | | ● | ● | | | | | | | | | |
| KIRBY, M (HM11702) | ● | ● | ● | ● | | | ● | ● | ● | ● | | ● | ● | ● | | | ● | ● | ● | | ● |
| LAISTER, MARTIN (HM11868) | | | | | | | | | | | | | | | ● | | | ● | | | |
| LLEWELLYN CONSULTANCY (HM12502) | ● | ● | | | | ● | ● | ● | | ● | ● | ● | ● | ● | | ● | ● | ● | | | ● |
| M & B SERVICES (HM12794) | | ● | | | ● | ● | | | | | ● | ● | ● | ● | | ● | ● | ● | | | ● |
| MEDICAL HERBALIST (HM13652) | ● | ● | ● | ● | ● | ● | ● | ● | ● | ● | ● | ● | ● | ● | ● | ● | ● | ● | ● | | ● |
| MILLINGTON, JANET (HM13917) | | ● | | | ● | ● | | | | | | ● | | | | | | | | | |
| MOORGATE NATURAL HEALING CTRE (HM14138) | ● | ● | ● | ● | ● | ● | ● | ● | ● | ● | ● | ● | ● | ● | ● | ● | ● | ● | ● | | ● |
| NIGHTINGALE PHYSIO PRACTICE (HM14937) | | | | | | | | | | | | | ● | | | | ● | | | | |
| PAUL BOIZOT AROMATHERAPY (HM15839) | | | | | | | | | | | | | ● | | | | ● | | | | |
| SCHOLL CENTRE (HM18046) | | | | | | | | | | | | | | | ● | | | | | | |
| SEASONS BEAUTY CENTRE (HM18178) | ● | ● | ● | ● | | ● | | ● | ● | ● | ● | ● | ● | ● | ● | ● | ● | ● | | | ● |
| SHARRON CHIROPODY CLINIC (HM18324) | | | | | | | | | | | | | ● | | ● | | | ● | | | |
| SHEFFIELD NATURAL HEALTH CTRE (HM18372) | ● | ● | ● | ● | ● | ● | ● | ● | ● | ● | ● | ● | ● | ● | ● | ● | ● | ● | ● | | ● |
| SIMPSON, SARAH E (HM18598) | | | | | | | | | | | | | | | ● | | | | | | |
| STONES, KAREN (HM19343) | | ● | | ● | | ● | | | ● | ● | | ● | ● | ● | ● | | ● | ● | ● | | ● |
| TRIGG, REBECCA (HM20334) | | | | | | ● | | | | | | | | | | | ● | | | | |
| VINSON, CAROL (HM20686) | | | | | | | | | | | | ● | | | ● | | | | | | |
| WELLFORCE (HM21160) | ● | | ● | | | ● | ● | ● | ● | ● | ● | ● | ● | ● | ● | ● | ● | ● | ● | | ● |
| WELSH CHIROPRACTIC (HM21183) | | | | | | | | | | | | | ● | ● | | | ● | | | | |

| Business by County with Reference no. | Blood Pressure | Boils | Bowel Problems | Breast Problems | Breathing Problems | Bronchitis | Bruising | Bulimia | Bunions | Bursitis | Callices | Cancers | Cataracts | Catarrh | Cerebral Palsy | Circulation Problems | Cold Sores | Colds | Colic | Colitis | Conjunctivitis | Constipation | Convulsions | Corns | Coughs | Cramp | Cystitis |
|---|---|---|---|---|---|---|---|---|---|---|---|---|---|---|---|---|---|---|---|---|---|---|---|---|---|---|---|
| CHIROPODY SURGERY (HM04342) | | | | | | | | | | | ● | | | | | | | | | | | | | ● | | | |
| CLAIRE LOUISE (HM04510) | | | | | | | | | | | | | | | | | | | | | | | | | | | |
| COUNTRY PRACTICE (HM05256) | ● | | | | | | | | | ● | | | | ● | | ● | | | | | | | | | | | |
| DORE PHYSIOTHERAPY PRACTICE (HM06196) | | | | | | | | | | | | | | | | | | | | | | | | | | | |
| EATON, T C (HM06565) | | | | | | | | | | | ● | | | | | | | | | | | | | ● | | | |
| ESSENTIAL HARMONY (HM06907) | ● | | | | | | | | | | | | | ● | | ● | ● | ● | ● | | | ● | | | ● | | |
| FISHER, CHRISTINE A (HM07349) | | | | | | | | | | | ● | | | | | | | | | | | | | ● | | | |
| GORNEY, C (HM08296) | | | | | | | | | | | | | | | | | | | | | | | | | | | |
| GRAPEVINE HEALTH (HM08399) | ● | ● | ● | ● | ● | ● | ● | ● | | ● | ● | ● | ● | ● | | ● | ● | ● | ● | ● | ● | ● | ● | ● | ● | ● | ● |
| GRENOSIDE PHYSIOTHERAPY (HM08536) | | | | | | | | | | | | | | | | | | | | | | | | | | | |
| GYALTSABJE BUDDHIST CENTRE (HM08672) | | | | | | | | | | | | | | | | | | | | | | | | | | | |
| HALLAMSHIRE NATURAL HLTH CTRE (HM08798) | | | ● | | | | | | | | | | | | | | | | | ● | | ● | | | | | |
| HEALTHY FEET (HM09427) | | | | | | | | | | ● | | | | | | ● | | | | | | | | ● | | | |
| HINCHLIFFE, JACKIE (HM09822) | ● | ● | | | | | | | | | | | | ● | | | | ● | | | | ● | | | ● | | ● |
| HYPNOTHERAPY CENTRE (HM10515) | ● | | ● | ● | | | | ● | | | | | | | | | | | | | | | | | | | |
| KIRBY, M (HM11702) | ● | | ● | ● | ● | ● | ● | | | ● | ● | ● | | ● | | ● | ● | ● | ● | ● | ● | ● | | ● | ● | ● | ● |
| LAISTER, MARTIN (HM11868) | | | | | | | | | | | ● | | | | | | | | | | | | | ● | | | |
| LLEWELLYN CONSULTANCY (HM12502) | ● | ● | ● | | ● | ● | ● | ● | | ● | ● | ● | | ● | | ● | ● | ● | ● | ● | ● | ● | | ● | ● | ● | ● |
| M & B SERVICES (HM12794) | ● | | ● | | ● | ● | ● | ● | | | | ● | ● | ● | | ● | ● | ● | ● | ● | ● | ● | ● | | | ● | ● |
| MEDICAL HERBALIST (HM13652) | ● | ● | ● | ● | ● | ● | ● | ● | | ● | ● | ● | ● | ● | | ● | ● | ● | ● | ● | ● | ● | ● | ● | ● | ● | ● |
| MILLINGTON, JANET (HM13917) | ● | | ● | | | | | | | | | | | | | | | | | ● | | ● | | | | | |
| MOORGATE NATURAL HEALING CTRE (HM14138) | ● | ● | ● | ● | ● | ● | ● | ● | | ● | | ● | ● | ● | | ● | ● | ● | ● | ● | ● | ● | ● | | ● | ● | ● |
| NIGHTINGALE PHYSIO PRACTICE (HM14937) | | | | | | | | | | | | | | | | | | | | | | | | | | ● | |
| PAUL BOIZOT AROMATHERAPY (HM15839) | | | ● | | | | | | | | | | | | | | | ● | ● | | | | | | | | |
| SCHOLL CENTRE (HM18046) | | | | | | | | | | | ● | | | | | | | | | | | | | ● | | | |
| SEASONS BEAUTY CENTRE (HM18178) | ● | | ● | ● | ● | ● | ● | ● | | ● | ● | ● | | ● | | ● | ● | ● | ● | ● | ● | ● | | ● | ● | ● | ● |
| SHARRON CHIROPODY CLINIC (HM18324) | | | | | | | | | | | ● | | | | | | | | | | | | | ● | | | |
| SHEFFIELD NATURAL HEALTH CTRE (HM18372) | ● | ● | ● | ● | ● | ● | ● | ● | | ● | ● | ● | ● | ● | | ● | ● | ● | ● | ● | ● | ● | ● | ● | ● | ● | ● |
| SIMPSON, SARAH E (HM18598) | | | | | | | | | | | ● | | | | | | | | | | | | | ● | | | |
| STONES, KAREN (HM19343) | ● | | ● | ● | ● | ● | ● | | | ● | ● | | ● | ● | | ● | ● | ● | ● | ● | ● | ● | ● | ● | ● | ● | ● |
| TRIGG, REBECCA (HM20334) | | | | | | | | | | | | | | | | | | | | | | ● | | | | | |
| VINSON, CAROL (HM20686) | | | | | | | | | | | ● | | | | | | | | | | | | | ● | | | |
| WELLFORCE (HM21160) | ● | ● | ● | ● | ● | ● | ● | ● | | | | ● | | ● | | ● | ● | ● | ● | ● | ● | ● | | | ● | ● | ● |
| WELSH CHIROPRACTIC (HM21183) | | | ● | | | ● | | | | ● | | ● | | | | ● | | | ● | | | ● | | | | ● | |

www.healthmyself.com

# A - C Conditions treated at Practices/Businesses

| Business by County with Reference no. | Acne | Addiction | Adenoids | Aids | Alcoholism | Allergy | Alzheimer's Disease | Amnesia | Anaemia | Angina | Anorexia | Anxiety | Arthritis | Asthma | Athletes Foot | Autism | Back Pain | Bacterial Infections | Baldness | Bereavement | Bladder Problems | Blood Pressure | Boils | Bowel Problems | Breast Problems | Breathing Problems | Bronchitis | Bruising | Bulimia | Bunions | Bursitis | Callices | Cancers | Cataracts | Catarrh | Cerebral Palsy | Circulation Problems | Cold Sores | Colds | Colic | Colitis | Conjunctivitis | Constipation | Convulsions | Corns | Coughs | Cramp | Cystitis |
|---|---|---|---|---|---|---|---|---|---|---|---|---|---|---|---|---|---|---|---|---|---|---|---|---|---|---|---|---|---|---|---|---|---|---|---|---|---|---|---|---|---|---|---|---|---|---|---|---|
| WHITEING, J P (HM21393) | | | | | | | | | | | | | ● | | ● | | | | | | | | | | | | | | | ● | | ● | | | | | | | | | | | | | ● | | | |
| WILSON, JOHN PAUL (HM21658) | | | | | | | | | | | | | ● | | ● | | | ● | | | | | | | | | | | | | | ● | | | | | | | | | | | | | ● | | | |
| WOMBWELL ACUPUNCTURE CLINIC (HM21770) | | | | | | | | | | | | | | | | | ● | | | | | | | | | | | | | | | | | | | | | | | | | | | | | | | |
| **YORKSHIRE (WEST)** | | | | | | | | | | | | | | | | | | | | | | | | | | | | | | | | | | | | | | | | | | | | | | | | |
| A BARCHAM REFLEXOLOGY (HM00024) | | | ● | | | ● | | | ● | ● | | ● | ● | ● | ● | | ● | ● | | | ● | ● | | ● | ● | ● | ● | ● | ● | | | | ● | | ● | | ● | ● | | | ● | | ● | | | ● | ● | ● |
| ACTIVE MINDS (HM00199) | | | | | | | ● | | | | | ● | | | | | | | | | | | | | | | | | | | | | | | | | | | | | | | | | | | | |
| AIREDALE ALLERGY CENTRE (HM00441) | ● | | | | | ● | ● | | ● | | | | ● | ● | ● | | | | | | ● | | | ● | | ● | | | | | | | | | ● | | | ● | | ● | ● | | ● | | | ● | | ● |
| ALEX TECH TEACHING CENTRE (HM00513) | | | | | | | | | | | | | ● | ● | | | ● | | | | | | | | | ● | | | | | | | | | | | ● | | | | | | | | | | | |
| AMETHYST HEALING CENTRE (HM00783) | ● | ● | ● | ● | ● | ● | | ● | ● | ● | ● | ● | ● | ● | | | | ● | | | ● | ● | ● | ● | ● | ● | ● | ● | ● | | ● | | ● | | ● | | ● | ● | ● | ● | ● | | ● | | | ● | ● | ● |
| ARDENTE CHIROPODY SERVICE (HM00991) | | | | | | | | | | | | | | | | | | ● | | | | | | | | | | | | | ● | | | | | | | | | | | | | | | | | |
| ASH, STACEY (HM01183) | ● | | | | | ● | | | | | | ● | ● | | | | ● | | | | | | | | | | | | | | | | | | | | | | | | | | | | | | | |
| ASPEN CLINIC (HM01255) | | | | | | | | | | | | | ● | | | | ● | | | | | | | | | | | | | | | | | | | | | | | | | | | | | | | |
| BAILEY FLOWER ESSENCES (HM01539) | | | | | | | | | | | | ● | | | | | | | | | | | | | | | | | | | | | | | | | | | | | | | | | | | | |
| BENTLEY, J H (HM02173) | | | | | | | | | | | ● | ● | | | | | | | | | | | | | | | | | | | | | | | | | | | | | | | | | | | | |
| BINGLEY HOMOEOPATHIC PRACTICE (HM02315) | ● | ● | ● | ● | ● | ● | ● | ● | ● | ● | ● | ● | ● | ● | ● | ● | ● | ● | ● | | ● | ● | ● | ● | ● | ● | ● | ● | ● | | ● | ● | ● | ● | ● | | ● | ● | ● | ● | ● | ● | ● | ● | ● | ● | ● | ● |
| BODY ESSENCE (HM02585) | | | | | | | | | | | | ● | ● | | | | ● | | | | | | | | | | | | | | | | | | | | | | | | | | | | | | | |
| BOYD HYPNOTHERAPY (HM02816) | ● | ● | | | ● | | | ● | | | ● | ● | ● | ● | | | | | | | | | | | | | | | | | | | | | | | | | | | | | | | | | | |
| BRADFORD CHIROPODY & BIO CLNC (HM02846) | | | | | | | | | | | | | | | ● | | | | | | | | | | | | | | | | | | | | | | | | | | | | | | | | | |
| BRADFORD CLINIC OF ALT MED (HM02848) | ● | ● | ● | ● | ● | ● | ● | ● | ● | ● | ● | ● | ● | ● | ● | ● | ● | ● | ● | | ● | ● | ● | ● | ● | ● | ● | ● | ● | | ● | ● | ● | ● | ● | | ● | ● | ● | ● | ● | ● | ● | ● | ● | ● | ● | ● |
| BRAMIN CLINIC (HM02900) | | | | | | | | | | | | | ● | | | | ● | | | | | | | | | | | | | | | | | | | | ● | | | | | | | | | | | |
| BRAMLEY COMP THERAPY CLINIC (HM02901) | ● | ● | | | ● | ● | | | | ● | ● | ● | ● | ● | ● | | ● | ● | | | ● | ● | ● | ● | ● | ● | ● | ● | ● | | ● | | ● | | ● | | ● | ● | ● | ● | ● | ● | ● | | | ● | ● | ● |
| BRAY, D N (HM02928) | | | | | | | | | | | | | | | | | ● | | | | | | | | | | | | | | | | | | | | | | | | | | | | | | | |
| BROWN, PAT (HM03243) | | | | | | | | | | | | | | | | | | | | | | | | | | ● | | | | | | | | | | | | | | | | | | | | | | |
| CALVERLEY ACUPUNCTURE CLINIC (HM03561) | | | | | | | | | ● | | | ● | ● | | | | ● | | | | | ● | | ● | | | | | | | | | | | | | | | | | | | ● | | | | | |
| CHAMPANERIA, S K (HM03963) | | | | | | ● | | | | | | | | ● | | | ● | ● | | | | | | | | ● | ● | | | | | | | | | | | | | | | | | | | | | |
| CHOICE AROMAS (HM04421) | ● | | | | | | | | | | | ● | ● | ● | ● | | ● | | | | ● | | ● | ● | | ● | ● | | | | | | | | ● | | ● | | ● | | | | ● | | | ● | ● | |
| CLARKE, DON (HM04586) | | | | | | ● | | | | | | ● | | | | | ● | | | | | | | | | | | ● | | | | | | | | | | | | | | | ● | | | | | |
| COOPER, SAFFRON (HM05126) | ● | | ● | | | ● | | | ● | | | ● | ● | ● | ● | | ● | ● | | | ● | ● | ● | ● | ● | ● | ● | ● | ● | | ● | | | | ● | | ● | ● | ● | ● | ● | ● | ● | | | ● | ● | ● |
| DESIGNING CHANGE (HM06022) | | ● | | | ● | | | | | | | ● | | | | | | | | | | | | | | | | | | | | | | | | | | | | | | | | | | | | |
| DRURY, WENDY (HM06331) | | | | | | ● | ● | | ● | | | ● | ● | | | | ● | | | | ● | ● | | ● | ● | ● | ● | | | | | | | | ● | | ● | | | ● | | | ● | | | | | ● |
| DUFFIELD (HM06360) | | | | | | ● | | | | | | ● | | ● | | | ● | | | | | | | ● | | | | | | | | | | | ● | | ● | | | | | | ● | | | | | |
| EQUA-LIBRA (HM06863) | ● | | | | | | | | | | | ● | ● | | | | ● | | | | | | | | | | | | | | | | | | | | | | | | | | | | | | | |
| FIGURA, CATHERINE MARIA (HM07283) | | | | | | | | | | | | ● | ● | | | | ● | | | | | | | | | | | | | | | | | | | | | | | | | | | | | | | |
| GILLETT, LIZ (HM08088) | | | | | | | | | | | | | ● | ● | | | ● | | | | | | | | | | | | | | | | | | | | | | | | | | | | | | | |

# A - C Conditions treated at Practices/Businesses

Business by County with Reference no.

| Business | Acne | Addiction | Adenoids | Aids | Alcoholism | Allergy | Alzheimer's Disease | Amnesia | Anaemia | Angina | Anorexia | Anxiety | Arthritis | Asthma | Athletes Foot | Autism |
|---|---|---|---|---|---|---|---|---|---|---|---|---|---|---|---|---|
| HAMER-BLOOM, S (HM08832) | | | | | | | | | | | | | | | | |
| HAMNETT, SHEILA (HM08870) | | | | | | | | | | | | | ● | | | |
| HANSON, S C (HM08944) | | | | | | | | | | | | | ● | | ● | |
| HEBDEN BRIDGE CENTRE (HM09487) | | ● | | | ● | | | | | | | ● | | | | |
| HERMITAGE OILS (HM09684) | ● | | | | | | | | | | | | ● | ● | ● | |
| HOBSON, ANNE (HM09862) | | | | | | | | | | | | ● | ● | | | |
| HOLME VALLEY SPORTS CLINIC (HM10036) | | | | | | | | | | | | | | | | |
| HOLMFIRTH PHYSIO/SPORTS INJURY (HM10048) | | | | | | | | | | | | ● | | | | |
| HOMEOPATHIC MEDICAL PRACTICE (HM10076) | ● | | | | | ● | | | | | | ● | | ● | | |
| HUNTER, REBECCA (HM10408) | | ● | ● | ● | ● | ● | | | | | | ● | ● | ● | | |
| J & J HARROP (HM10792) | | | | | | | | | | | | | | | ● | |
| JACKSON, ROGER D (HM10850) | | | | | | | | | | | | | | | | |
| KANG DA CLINIC (HM11313) | ● | ● | ● | | ● | ● | ● | ● | ● | ● | ● | ● | ● | ● | ● | ● |
| KINGSMITH, ANNE-MARIE (HM11673) | | | | | | | | | | | | | | | | |
| KINNAIRD, F M (HM11686) | | ● | | | ● | | | ● | | | ● | ● | | | | |
| LEEDS CHINESE MEDICAL CENTRE (HM12154) | ● | ● | ● | ● | ● | ● | ● | ● | ● | ● | ● | ● | ● | ● | ● | ● |
| LEEDS COUNSELLING & PSYCHO SVS (HM12158) | | | | | | | | | | | ● | ● | | | | |
| LPS TRAINING & CONSULTANCY (HM12713) | | | | | | | | | | | | | ● | | | |
| MOORFIELD FLOATATION (HM14137) | | | | | | | | | | | | | | | | |
| MORGAN, J D (DR) (HM14167) | | ● | | | ● | | | ● | | | | ● | | | | |
| MORLEY ACUPUNCTURE CLINIC (HM14180) | ● | ● | | | | ● | | | | | ● | ● | ● | ● | | ● |
| MORNINGTON PHYSIOTHERAPY (HM14193) | | | | | | | | | | | | | ● | | | |
| NATURES WORKROOM (HM14705) | ● | ● | ● | ● | ● | ● | ● | ● | ● | ● | ● | ● | ● | ● | ● | ● |
| NEILL-HIGGINS, CHRISTINA (HM14765) | | | | | | ● | | | | ● | | ● | ● | ● | ● | |
| NRTH LEEDS PHYSIO/SPRTS INJ (HM15091) | | | | | | | | | | | | | ● | | | |
| OWENS, PAULINE (HM15533) | | | | | | ● | | | | | | ● | | ● | | |
| PALLAS, ANDREW (HM15595) | | | | | | ● | | | | ● | | ● | ● | ● | ● | |
| PARKS, HILARY (HM15720) | | | | | | | | | | | | ● | | ● | | |
| PAYNE, AUDREY (HM15861) | | | | | | ● | | | | | | | ● | | | |
| POPPLEWELL, MARK (HM16437) | | | | | | | | | | | | ● | ● | ● | | |
| PRESTON, CATHY (HM16551) | | ● | | | | | | ● | | | ● | ● | | | | |
| RAINTREE HEALTH (HM16893) | ● | | | ● | ● | ● | | | | | | ● | ● | ● | | |
| RICHARDSON CLINIC (HM17266) | ● | ● | ● | ● | ● | ● | ● | ● | ● | ● | ● | ● | ● | ● | ● | ● |
| ROTHWELL SPORTS CENTRE (HM17658) | | | | | | | | | | | | | ● | | | |

| Business | Back Pain | Bacterial Infections | Baldness | Bereavement | Bladder Problems | Blood Pressure | Boils | Bowel Problems | Breast Problems | Breathing Problems | Bronchitis | Bruising | Bulimia | Bunions | Bursitis | Callices |
|---|---|---|---|---|---|---|---|---|---|---|---|---|---|---|---|---|
| HAMER-BLOOM, S (HM08832) | | ● | | | | | | | | | | | | | ● | |
| HAMNETT, SHEILA (HM08870) | ● | | | | | | | | | | | | | | | |
| HANSON, S C (HM08944) | ● | ● | | | | | | | | | | ● | | | ● | |
| HEBDEN BRIDGE CENTRE (HM09487) | | | | ● | | | | | | | | | ● | | | |
| HERMITAGE OILS (HM09684) | | | | | | | | | | | | | | | | |
| HOBSON, ANNE (HM09862) | ● | | | | | | | | | | | | | | | |
| HOLME VALLEY SPORTS CLINIC (HM10036) | ● | | | | | | | | | | | | | | | |
| HOLMFIRTH PHYSIO/SPORTS INJURY (HM10048) | ● | | | | | | | | | | | | | | | |
| HOMEOPATHIC MEDICAL PRACTICE (HM10076) | | | | | | | | ● | ● | | | | | | | |
| HUNTER, REBECCA (HM10408) | ● | ● | | | ● | ● | ● | ● | ● | ● | ● | ● | | | ● | |
| J & J HARROP (HM10792) | | | | | | | | | | | | | | | | |
| JACKSON, ROGER D (HM10850) | ● | | | | | | | | | | | ● | | | ● | |
| KANG DA CLINIC (HM11313) | ● | ● | ● | | ● | ● | ● | ● | ● | ● | ● | ● | ● | | | |
| KINGSMITH, ANNE-MARIE (HM11673) | | | | | | | | | | | | | | | | ● |
| KINNAIRD, F M (HM11686) | | | | | | | | ● | | ● | | | ● | | | |
| LEEDS CHINESE MEDICAL CENTRE (HM12154) | ● | ● | ● | | ● | ● | ● | ● | ● | ● | ● | | | | | |
| LEEDS COUNSELLING & PSYCHO SVS (HM12158) | | | | | | | | | | | | | ● | | | |
| LPS TRAINING & CONSULTANCY (HM12713) | ● | | | | | | | | | | | | | | | |
| MOORFIELD FLOATATION (HM14137) | ● | | | | | | | | | | | | | | | |
| MORGAN, J D (DR) (HM14167) | | | | | ● | | | ● | | | | | | | | |
| MORLEY ACUPUNCTURE CLINIC (HM14180) | ● | ● | | | ● | ● | ● | ● | ● | ● | ● | | ● | | ● | |
| MORNINGTON PHYSIOTHERAPY (HM14193) | ● | | | | | | | | | | | ● | | | ● | |
| NATURES WORKROOM (HM14705) | ● | ● | ● | | ● | ● | ● | ● | ● | ● | ● | ● | ● | | ● | ● |
| NEILL-HIGGINS, CHRISTINA (HM14765) | ● | ● | | | ● | ● | ● | ● | ● | ● | ● | ● | | | | |
| NRTH LEEDS PHYSIO/SPRTS INJ (HM15091) | ● | | | | | | | | | | | | | | ● | |
| OWENS, PAULINE (HM15533) | ● | | | | ● | ● | | ● | ● | ● | ● | | | | | |
| PALLAS, ANDREW (HM15595) | ● | ● | | | | ● | | ● | | ● | ● | | | | ● | |
| PARKS, HILARY (HM15720) | | | | | ● | ● | | ● | | ● | | | | | | |
| PAYNE, AUDREY (HM15861) | ● | | | | | | | ● | | | | | | | | |
| POPPLEWELL, MARK (HM16437) | ● | | | | ● | ● | | ● | | ● | ● | | | | ● | |
| PRESTON, CATHY (HM16551) | | | | | | | | ● | | | | | ● | | | |
| RAINTREE HEALTH (HM16893) | ● | ● | ● | | ● | ● | ● | ● | ● | ● | ● | | | | | |
| RICHARDSON CLINIC (HM17266) | ● | ● | ● | | ● | ● | ● | ● | ● | ● | ● | ● | ● | | ● | ● |
| ROTHWELL SPORTS CENTRE (HM17658) | ● | | | | | | | | | | | | | | | |

| Business | Cancers | Cataracts | Catarrh | Cerebral Palsy | Circulation Problems | Cold Sores | Colds | Colic | Colitis | Conjunctivitis | Constipation | Convulsions | Corns | Coughs | Cramp | Cystitis |
|---|---|---|---|---|---|---|---|---|---|---|---|---|---|---|---|---|
| HAMER-BLOOM, S (HM08832) | | | | | | | | | | | | | | | | |
| HAMNETT, SHEILA (HM08870) | | | | | ● | | | | | | | | | | | |
| HANSON, S C (HM08944) | | | | | ● | | | | | | | | | | | |
| HEBDEN BRIDGE CENTRE (HM09487) | | | | | | | | | | | | | | | | |
| HERMITAGE OILS (HM09684) | | | | | | ● | | | | | | | | | | |
| HOBSON, ANNE (HM09862) | | | | | | | | | | | | | | | | |
| HOLME VALLEY SPORTS CLINIC (HM10036) | | | | | | | | | | | | | | | | |
| HOLMFIRTH PHYSIO/SPORTS INJURY (HM10048) | | | | | | | | | | | | | | | | |
| HOMEOPATHIC MEDICAL PRACTICE (HM10076) | ● | | | | | | | ● | ● | | ● | | | ● | | ● |
| HUNTER, REBECCA (HM10408) | | | ● | | ● | ● | ● | ● | ● | ● | ● | | | ● | ● | ● |
| J & J HARROP (HM10792) | | | | | | | | | | | | | | | | |
| JACKSON, ROGER D (HM10850) | | | | | | | | | | | | | | | | |
| KANG DA CLINIC (HM11313) | ● | ● | ● | | ● | ● | ● | | ● | ● | ● | | | ● | ● | ● |
| KINGSMITH, ANNE-MARIE (HM11673) | | | | | | | | | | | | | ● | | | |
| KINNAIRD, F M (HM11686) | | | | | | | | | | | | | | | | |
| LEEDS CHINESE MEDICAL CENTRE (HM12154) | | | | | | | | | | | | | | | | |
| LEEDS COUNSELLING & PSYCHO SVS (HM12158) | | | | | | | | | | | | | | | | |
| LPS TRAINING & CONSULTANCY (HM12713) | | | | | | | | | | | | | | | | |
| MOORFIELD FLOATATION (HM14137) | | | | | | | | | | | | | | | | |
| MORGAN, J D (DR) (HM14167) | | | | | | | | | | | | | | | | |
| MORLEY ACUPUNCTURE CLINIC (HM14180) | | | ● | | ● | ● | ● | ● | ● | ● | ● | | | ● | ● | ● |
| MORNINGTON PHYSIOTHERAPY (HM14193) | | | | | | | | | | | | | | | ● | |
| NATURES WORKROOM (HM14705) | ● | ● | ● | | ● | ● | ● | ● | ● | ● | ● | ● | ● | ● | ● | ● |
| NEILL-HIGGINS, CHRISTINA (HM14765) | ● | | ● | | ● | ● | | | ● | | ● | | | ● | | ● |
| NRTH LEEDS PHYSIO/SPRTS INJ (HM15091) | | | | | | | | | | | | | | | | |
| OWENS, PAULINE (HM15533) | | | | | ● | | | | | | ● | | | | | |
| PALLAS, ANDREW (HM15595) | | | ● | | ● | | ● | ● | | | ● | | | ● | ● | ● |
| PARKS, HILARY (HM15720) | | | | | ● | | | | | | ● | | | | | |
| PAYNE, AUDREY (HM15861) | | | ● | | | | | | | | ● | | | | | |
| POPPLEWELL, MARK (HM16437) | | | ● | | ● | | ● | | | | ● | | | ● | | ● |
| PRESTON, CATHY (HM16551) | | | | | | | | | | | | | | | | |
| RAINTREE HEALTH (HM16893) | ● | | ● | | ● | | ● | ● | ● | ● | ● | ● | | ● | ● | ● |
| RICHARDSON CLINIC (HM17266) | ● | ● | ● | | ● | ● | ● | ● | ● | ● | ● | ● | ● | ● | ● | ● |
| ROTHWELL SPORTS CENTRE (HM17658) | | | | | | | | | | | | | | | | |

# A - C Conditions treated at Practices/Businesses

Business by County with Reference no.

| Condition | ROUNDHAY CHIROPRACTIC CLINIC (HM17667) | SALTAIRE COMP HEALTH STUDIO (HM17864) | SHACKLETON, JOHN A (HM18263) | SHERQIA, DARULSHAFA (HM18436) | SMITH, JANET (HM18751) | STEAD, JULIE ANN (HM19164) | SURGERY (HM19519) | SWAINE, PAULA (HM19565) | SYKES CLINIC (HM19610) | TORNTON, HOWARD (HM20172) | TRANSCENDENTAL MEDITATION (HM20285) | TUEL LANE PHYSIOTHERAPY CLINIC (HM20376) | WATKINS, JEAN (HM20996) | WEST YORKSHIRE CLINIC (HM21242) | WEST YORKSHIRE M S THRPY CTRE (HM21243) | WEST YORKSHIRE PHYSIO CENTRE (HM21244) | WETHERBY PHYSIO PRACTICE (HM21290) | WIDDOPP, BRIAN (HM21455) | WISE, CAROL (HM21732) | WOODHOUSE CLINIC (HM21826) |
|---|---|---|---|---|---|---|---|---|---|---|---|---|---|---|---|---|---|---|---|---|
| Acne | | ● | | ● | | | | | | | | | | ● | | | | | ● | ● |
| Addiction | | ● | | | | | ● | | | | | | | ● | | | | | ● | |
| Adenoids | | ● | | | | | | | | | | | | | | | | | ● | |
| Aids | | ● | | | | | | | | | | | | ● | | | | | ● | |
| Alcoholism | | ● | | | | | ● | | | | | | | | | | | | ● | |
| Allergy | | ● | | ● | ● | | | | ● | | | | | ● | | | | | ● | |
| Alzheimer's Disease | | ● | | | | | | | | | | | | | ● | | | | ● | |
| Amnesia | | ● | | ● | | | | | | | | | | | | | | | ● | |
| Anaemia | | ● | | ● | | | | | | | | | | ● | | | | | ● | |
| Angina | | ● | | ● | | | | | | | | | | ● | ● | | | | ● | |
| Anorexia | | ● | | ● | | | | | | | | | | ● | | | | | ● | |
| Anxiety | | ● | | ● | ● | ● | ● | | ● | | ● | | ● | ● | | | | ● | ● | |
| Arthritis | ● | ● | | ● | ● | ● | ● | | ● | ● | | ● | ● | ● | ● | ● | ● | ● | ● | ● |
| Asthma | ● | ● | | ● | ● | ● | ● | | ● | | | | ● | ● | ● | | | | ● | ● |
| Athletes Foot | | ● | ● | ● | | ● | ● | ● | | | | | | ● | | | | | ● | ● |
| Autism | | ● | | | | | | | | | | | | | ● | | | | ● | |
| Back Pain | ● | ● | | ● | ● | | ● | | ● | ● | | ● | | ● | | ● | ● | ● | ● | ● |
| Bacterial Infections | | ● | | | | | | | | | | | | | | | | | ● | |
| Baldness | | ● | | | | | | | | | | | | | | | | | ● | |
| Bereavement | | | | | | | | | | | | | | | | | | | | |
| Bladder Problems | | ● | | ● | | | | | | | | | ● | ● | | | | | ● | |
| Blood Pressure | | ● | | | | ● | | | ● | | | | ● | ● | | | | | ● | |
| Boils | | ● | | ● | | | | | | | | | | ● | | | | | ● | |
| Bowel Problems | | ● | | ● | ● | | | | | | | | ● | ● | | | | | ● | |
| Breast Problems | | ● | | | | | | | | | | | | | | | | | ● | ● |
| Breathing Problems | | ● | | ● | | ● | | | | | | | ● | ● | | | | ● | ● | |
| Bronchitis | | ● | | ● | | | ● | | | | | | | ● | | | | | ● | |
| Bruising | | ● | | | | | | | | | | | | ● | | | | | ● | |
| Bulimia | | ● | | | | | | | | | | | | ● | | | | | ● | |
| Bunions | | | | | | | | | | | | | | | | | | | | |
| Bursitis | | ● | | | | | ● | | | | | | | ● | | | | | ● | ● |
| Callices | | ● | ● | | | | | ● | | | | | | | | | | | ● | |
| Cancers | | ● | | | | | | | | | | | | | | | | | ● | |
| Cataracts | | ● | | | ● | | | | | | | | | | | | | | ● | |
| Catarrh | | ● | | ● | | ● | | | | | | | | ● | | | | | ● | |
| Cerebral Palsy | | | | | | | | | | | | | | | ● | | | | | |
| Circulation Problems | | ● | | ● | | ● | | | | | | | ● | ● | | | | ● | ● | |
| Cold Sores | | ● | | ● | | | | | | | | | | ● | | | | | ● | |
| Colds | | ● | | ● | ● | | | | | | | | | ● | | | | | ● | |
| Colic | ● | ● | | ● | | | | | ● | | | | | ● | | | | | ● | ● |
| Colitis | | ● | | ● | ● | | | | | | | | | ● | | | | | ● | |
| Conjunctivitis | | ● | | | | | | | | | | | | | | | | | ● | |
| Constipation | | ● | | ● | | | | | | | | | | ● | | | | | ● | |
| Convulsions | | ● | | | | | | | | | | | | ● | | | | | ● | |
| Corns | | ● | ● | | | | | ● | | | | | | | | | | | ● | |
| Coughs | | ● | | ● | ● | | | | | | | | | ● | | | | | ● | |
| Cramp | | ● | | ● | | ● | | | | | | | | ● | | | | | ● | |
| Cystitis | | ● | | ● | | | | | | | | | ● | ● | | | | | ● | ● |

# A - C Conditions treated at Practices/Businesses

Business by County with Reference no.

| Business by County with Reference no. | Acne | Addiction | Adenoids | Aids | Alcoholism | Allergy | Alzheimer's Disease | Amnesia | Anaemia | Angina | Anorexia | Anxiety | Arthritis | Asthma | Athletes Foot | Autism |
|---|---|---|---|---|---|---|---|---|---|---|---|---|---|---|---|---|
| **IRELAND** | | | | | | | | | | | | | | | | |
| **COUNTY CAVAN** | | | | | | | | | | | | | | | | |
| BI-AURA THERAPY (HM02274) | ● | | | | | ● | | | ● | ● | ● | ● | ● | ● | | ● |
| **COUNTY CORK** | | | | | | | | | | | | | | | | |
| ANNAPURNA NATURAL HEALTHCARE (HM00894) | | | | | | | | | | | | ● | ● | | | ● |
| BANDON CHIROPRACTIC CLINIC (HM01653) | | | | | | | | | | | | | ● | | | |
| BROOKFIELD PHYSIOTHERAPY (HM03167) | | | | | | | | | | | | | | | | |
| EAST CORK PHYSIOTHERAPY (HM06511) | ● | ● | | | | | | | | | | ● | ● | ● | | |
| HATTERSLEY, LAURENCE (HM09200) | | | | | | | | | | | | ● | ● | ● | | ● |
| HEALING THERAPIES (HM09354) | | | | | | | | | | | | ● | | | | |
| INS-CLINICAL HYP & PSYCHO (HM10661) | | ● | | ● | ● | ● | | ● | | | ● | ● | ● | ● | | |
| JONES, COLEEN (HM11131) | | | | | | | | | | | ● | ● | | | | |
| KEATING, MARY (HM11379) | | ● | | | | | | | | | | ● | ● | ● | | |
| MOORE-GROACKE, GILLIAN (DR) (HM14136) | | ● | | ● | | ● | | | | | ● | ● | | | | |
| PAUL DENNEHY - HYPNOTHERAPIST (HM15842) | ● | ● | | | ● | ● | | ● | | | ● | ● | | ● | | |
| RAVEN HILL CHIROPRACTIC CLINIC (HM16964) | ● | | | | | ● | | | | | | ● | ● | ● | ● | |
| SHIATSU (HM18452) | | | | | | | | | ● | | ● | ● | ● | ● | | |
| **COUNTY DUBLIN** | | | | | | | | | | | | | | | | |
| ABELIA COUNSELLING (HM00110) | | | | | | | | | | | | ● | | | | |
| ARDAGH ACUPUNCTURE CLINIC (HM00988) | | | | | | ● | ● | ● | | | | | | | | |
| ARDUNA COUNS & PSYCHOTHPY CTRE (HM00995) | | ● | | ● | ● | | | | | | | ● | | | | |
| BREE, JOHN (HM02947) | ● | ● | ● | ● | | ● | ● | ● | ● | ● | ● | ● | ● | ● | ● | ● |
| B-WELL HYPNOTHERAPY CLINIC (HM03506) | ● | ● | ● | ● | ● | ● | ● | ● | ● | ● | ● | ● | ● | ● | ● | ● |
| CHADHA, PRADEEP K (DR) (HM03933) | | ● | | | ● | | | | | | ● | ● | | | | |
| DUN LAOIRE HEALING ROOM (HM06389) | | | | | | | | | | | | ● | | | | |
| FAIRVIEW THERAPY CENTRE (HM07066) | | | | | | ● | | | | ● | ● | ● | ● | ● | | |
| FINISHING TOUCHES (HM07313) | ● | | | | | | | | | | | | ● | | | |
| FITZGERALD HYP-PSYCHOTHERAPY (HM07364) | | | | | | | | | | | | ● | | | | |
| HEALING PLACE (HM09347) | | | | | | | | | | | | | ● | ● | | |
| HEALING ROOM - DRUMCONDRA (HM09351) | | | | | | | | | | ● | | ● | ● | ● | | |
| HEALTH COUNSEL (HM09384) | | | | | | ● | | | | | | ● | | | | |
| HERBAL & ACUPUNCTURE (HM09595) | ● | | | ● | | | | | | | | ● | ● | ● | ● | |
| HOWTH COUNSELLING SERVICE (HM10294) | | | | | | | | | | | | ● | | | | |

| Business by County with Reference no. | Back Pain | Bacterial Infections | Baldness | Bereavement | Bladder Problems | Blood Pressure | Boils | Bowel Problems | Breast Problems | Breathing Problems | Bronchitis | Bruising | Bulimia | Bunions | Bursitis | Callices |
|---|---|---|---|---|---|---|---|---|---|---|---|---|---|---|---|---|
| **IRELAND** | | | | | | | | | | | | | | | | |
| **COUNTY CAVAN** | | | | | | | | | | | | | | | | |
| BI-AURA THERAPY (HM02274) | ● | ● | ● | | ● | ● | ● | ● | ● | ● | ● | ● | | | | |
| **COUNTY CORK** | | | | | | | | | | | | | | | | |
| ANNAPURNA NATURAL HEALTHCARE (HM00894) | ● | | | | | | | | | | | | | | | |
| BANDON CHIROPRACTIC CLINIC (HM01653) | ● | | | | | | | | | | | | | | | |
| BROOKFIELD PHYSIOTHERAPY (HM03167) | ● | | | | | ● | | | ● | ● | ● | | | | | |
| EAST CORK PHYSIOTHERAPY (HM06511) | ● | | | | ● | ● | | ● | | ● | ● | ● | | | ● | |
| HATTERSLEY, LAURENCE (HM09200) | ● | | | | | | | | | ● | | | | | | |
| HEALING THERAPIES (HM09354) | ● | | | ● | | ● | | | | ● | | | | | | |
| INS-CLINICAL HYP & PSYCHO (HM10661) | ● | | | | ● | ● | | ● | ● | ● | | | ● | | | |
| JONES, COLEEN (HM11131) | | | | | | | | | | | | | ● | | | |
| KEATING, MARY (HM11379) | ● | | | | ● | | | | ● | | | | | | | |
| MOORE-GROACKE, GILLIAN (DR) (HM14136) | ● | | | | | ● | | | | ● | | | ● | | | |
| PAUL DENNEHY - HYPNOTHERAPIST (HM15842) | | | | | ● | ● | ● | ● | | | | | ● | | | |
| RAVEN HILL CHIROPRACTIC CLINIC (HM16964) | ● | ● | | | | | ● | ● | | ● | ● | ● | | | ● | |
| SHIATSU (HM18452) | ● | | | | | ● | | ● | ● | ● | | | | | | |
| **COUNTY DUBLIN** | | | | | | | | | | | | | | | | |
| ABELIA COUNSELLING (HM00110) | | | | | | | | | | | | | | | | |
| ARDAGH ACUPUNCTURE CLINIC (HM00988) | ● | | | | | | | ● | | ● | ● | | | | | |
| ARDUNA COUNS & PSYCHOTHPY CTRE (HM00995) | | | | | | | | | | | | | ● | | | |
| BREE, JOHN (HM02947) | ● | ● | | | ● | ● | ● | ● | ● | ● | ● | ● | | | | |
| B-WELL HYPNOTHERAPY CLINIC (HM03506) | ● | ● | ● | | ● | ● | ● | ● | ● | ● | ● | ● | ● | | ● | |
| CHADHA, PRADEEP K (DR) (HM03933) | | | | | | ● | | ● | | | | | ● | | | |
| DUN LAOIRE HEALING ROOM (HM06389) | | | | | | | | | | | | | | | | |
| FAIRVIEW THERAPY CENTRE (HM07066) | ● | | | | ● | | | ● | | | | | ● | | | |
| FINISHING TOUCHES (HM07313) | ● | | | | | | | | | | | | | | | |
| FITZGERALD HYP-PSYCHOTHERAPY (HM07364) | | | | | | | | | | | | | | | | |
| HEALING PLACE (HM09347) | ● | | | | | | | ● | | | ● | ● | | | ● | |
| HEALING ROOM - DRUMCONDRA (HM09351) | ● | | | | | ● | | ● | | ● | | | | | ● | |
| HEALTH COUNSEL (HM09384) | | | | | | | | | | | | | | | | |
| HERBAL & ACUPUNCTURE (HM09595) | ● | ● | | | ● | ● | ● | ● | | ● | ● | ● | | | | |
| HOWTH COUNSELLING SERVICE (HM10294) | | | | | | | | | | ● | | | ● | | | |

| Business by County with Reference no. | Cancers | Cataracts | Catarrh | Cerebral Palsy | Circulation Problems | Cold Sores | Colds | Colic | Colitis | Conjunctivitis | Constipation | Convulsions | Corns | Coughs | Cramp | Cystitis |
|---|---|---|---|---|---|---|---|---|---|---|---|---|---|---|---|---|
| **IRELAND** | | | | | | | | | | | | | | | | |
| **COUNTY CAVAN** | | | | | | | | | | | | | | | | |
| BI-AURA THERAPY (HM02274) | ● | ● | | | ● | | ● | ● | ● | | ● | ● | | ● | ● | ● |
| **COUNTY CORK** | | | | | | | | | | | | | | | | |
| ANNAPURNA NATURAL HEALTHCARE (HM00894) | | | | | | | | | | | ● | | | | | |
| BANDON CHIROPRACTIC CLINIC (HM01653) | | | | | | | | | | | | | | | | |
| BROOKFIELD PHYSIOTHERAPY (HM03167) | ● | | | | | | ● | | | | ● | | | | ● | |
| EAST CORK PHYSIOTHERAPY (HM06511) | ● | | ● | | ● | | ● | | | ● | ● | | | ● | ● | ● |
| HATTERSLEY, LAURENCE (HM09200) | ● | | | | | | | | | | | | | | | |
| HEALING THERAPIES (HM09354) | | | | | | | ● | | | | | | | | | |
| INS-CLINICAL HYP & PSYCHO (HM10661) | ● | | | | | | | | ● | | | | | | | |
| JONES, COLEEN (HM11131) | | | | | | | | | | | | | | | | |
| KEATING, MARY (HM11379) | | | | | | | | | | | | | | | | |
| MOORE-GROACKE, GILLIAN (DR) (HM14136) | | ● | | | | | | | | | | | | | | |
| PAUL DENNEHY - HYPNOTHERAPIST (HM15842) | ● | | | | ● | | | | | | ● | | | | ● | |
| RAVEN HILL CHIROPRACTIC CLINIC (HM16964) | | | ● | | ● | ● | | ● | | | ● | | | ● | ● | ● |
| SHIATSU (HM18452) | | | ● | | ● | | ● | | | | ● | | | ● | ● | ● |
| **COUNTY DUBLIN** | | | | | | | | | | | | | | | | |
| ABELIA COUNSELLING (HM00110) | | | | | | | | | | | | | | | | |
| ARDAGH ACUPUNCTURE CLINIC (HM00988) | | | | | | | | | | | ● | | | ● | | |
| ARDUNA COUNS & PSYCHOTHPY CTRE (HM00995) | | | | | | | | | | | | | | | | |
| BREE, JOHN (HM02947) | ● | ● | ● | | ● | ● | ● | ● | ● | ● | | | | ● | ● | ● |
| B-WELL HYPNOTHERAPY CLINIC (HM03506) | ● | ● | ● | | ● | ● | ● | ● | ● | ● | ● | ● | | ● | ● | ● |
| CHADHA, PRADEEP K (DR) (HM03933) | | | | | | | | | | | | | | | | |
| DUN LAOIRE HEALING ROOM (HM06389) | ● | | | | | | | | | | | | | | | |
| FAIRVIEW THERAPY CENTRE (HM07066) | | | ● | | | | ● | | ● | | ● | | | ● | | |
| FINISHING TOUCHES (HM07313) | | | | | | | | | | | | | | | | |
| FITZGERALD HYP-PSYCHOTHERAPY (HM07364) | | | | | | | | | | | | | | | | |
| HEALING PLACE (HM09347) | | | ● | | | | | | ● | | ● | | | | ● | ● |
| HEALING ROOM - DRUMCONDRA (HM09351) | | | | | | | | | ● | | ● | | | | | ● |
| HEALTH COUNSEL (HM09384) | | | | | | | | | | | | | | | | |
| HERBAL & ACUPUNCTURE (HM09595) | | | ● | | ● | ● | ● | | | ● | ● | | | ● | | |
| HOWTH COUNSELLING SERVICE (HM10294) | | | | | | | | | | | | | | | | |

# A - C Conditions treated at Practices/Businesses

| Business by County with Reference no. | Acne | Addiction | Adenoids | Aids | Alcoholism | Allergy | Alzheimer's Disease | Amnesia | Anaemia | Angina | Anorexia | Anxiety | Arthritis | Asthma | Athletes Foot | Autism |
|---|---|---|---|---|---|---|---|---|---|---|---|---|---|---|---|---|
| INNER CIRCLE HEALING CENTRE (HM10635) | | ● | | | ● | ● | | | | | ● | ● | | ● | | |
| KELLY, ANGELINA (HM11427) | ● | ● | | | | ● | | | | | | ● | ● | ● | ● | |
| LALLOO'S ACUPUNCTURE CLINIC (HM11881) | ● | ● | ● | | ● | ● | | | ● | | | ● | ● | ● | ● | |
| LITTLEJOHN CLINIC (HM12472) | | | | | | | | | | | | ● | | ● | | |
| MACLIAM, FIONNULA (HM12867) | | | | | | | | | | | | ● | | | | |
| MCHUGH HYPNOSIS & REFLEXOLOGY (HM13509) | | ● | | | | | | | | | | ● | ● | ● | | |
| MELT/TEMPLE BAR NATURAL (HM13716) | ● | ● | ● | | ● | ● | ● | | | ● | ● | ● | ● | ● | | ● |
| NATURAL SOLUTIONS (HM14625) | | | | | ● | ● | | ● | | | ● | ● | | | | |
| NUALA WOULFE BEAUTY SALON (HM15101) | ● | | | | | | | | | | | | | | | |
| RATHMINES CHIROPRACTIC CENTRE (HM16957) | | | | | | | | | | | | | | | | |
| T C M CENTRE (HM19639) | ● | ● | | ● | ● | ● | | | | | | ● | ● | ● | ● | |
| THERAPEUTICS (HM19888) | | | | | | | ● | | | | | | | | | |
| THEW, NIN (HM19916) | | ● | | | | | | ● | ● | ● | | ● | ● | | ● | |
| TOBIN, ROSALEEN (HM20105) | | ● | | | | | | | | | | ● | | | | |
| TRAD CHINESE MEDICINE/MASSAGE (HM20216) | | | | | | | | | | | | ● | | ● | | |
| COUNTY GALWAY | | | | | | | | | | | | | | | | |
| ALEXANDER TECHNIQUE CENTRE (HM00557) | | | | | | | | | | | | ● | ● | ● | | |
| BODYWATCH (HM02636) | | | | | | | | | | | | ● | | | | |
| O'COLMAIN, AIDAN (DR) (HM15203) | | | | | | | | | | | | ● | ● | | | |
| PRENDERGAST, KARL (HM16542) | | | | | | | | | | | | | | | | |
| COUNTY KERRY | | | | | | | | | | | | | | | | |
| ACUPUNCTURE CLINIC (HM00286) | ● | ● | ● | | | | | | ● | ● | | ● | ● | ● | | |
| WOODLAWN HOLISTIC THERAPY CTRE (HM21834) | ● | ● | | | | | | | | | | | | | | |
| COUNTY KILDARE | | | | | | | | | | | | | | | | |
| GREEN ROAD HEALING CENTRE (HM08441) | | | | | | | | | | | | ● | ● | ● | ● | |
| SHENANDOAH HEALING (HM18395) | | | | | | ● | | | | | | ● | | | ● | |
| COUNTY KILKENNY | | | | | | | | | | | | | | | | |
| BLUE ROOM (HM02528) | | | | | | | | | | | | ● | | | | |
| DULCAMARA (HM06375) | ● | | | | | ● | | | | ● | | | ● | ● | | |
| HOLISTIC HEALING CENTRE (HM09965) | | | | | | | | | | | | | ● | ● | | |
| COUNTY LIMERICK | | | | | | | | | | | | | | | | |
| HOLISTIC HEALING (HM09960) | | | | | | ● | | | | | ● | ● | ● | ● | ● | |
| COUNTY LONGFORD | | | | | | | | | | | | | | | | |
| LONGFORD BEAUTY CLINIC (HM12626) | ● | | | | | | | | | | | | | | | |

| Business by County with Reference no. | Back Pain | Bacterial Infections | Baldness | Bereavement | Bladder Problems | Blood Pressure | Boils | Bowel Problems | Breast Problems | Breathing Problems | Bronchitis | Bruising | Bulimia | Bunions | Bursitis | Callices |
|---|---|---|---|---|---|---|---|---|---|---|---|---|---|---|---|---|
| INNER CIRCLE HEALING CENTRE (HM10635) | ● | | | | | | | ● | | | | | | | | |
| KELLY, ANGELINA (HM11427) | ● | | | | | ● | | | | ● | ● | ● | | | | |
| LALLOO'S ACUPUNCTURE CLINIC (HM11881) | ● | ● | ● | | ● | ● | ● | ● | ● | ● | ● | ● | ● | | ● | |
| LITTLEJOHN CLINIC (HM12472) | ● | | | | | | | | | ● | ● | | | | | |
| MACLIAM, FIONNULA (HM12867) | | | | | | | | | | | | | ● | | | |
| MCHUGH HYPNOSIS & REFLEXOLOGY (HM13509) | ● | | | | ● | ● | | ● | | ● | | | | | | |
| MELT/TEMPLE BAR NATURAL (HM13716) | ● | | ● | | | ● | ● | ● | ● | | ● | | ● | | | |
| NATURAL SOLUTIONS (HM14625) | | | | | | | | | | | | | | | | |
| NUALA WOULFE BEAUTY SALON (HM15101) | ● | | | | | | | ● | | | | | | | ● | |
| RATHMINES CHIROPRACTIC CENTRE (HM16957) | ● | | | | | | | | | | | | | | | |
| T C M CENTRE (HM19639) | ● | ● | ● | | ● | ● | ● | ● | ● | ● | ● | | | | | |
| THERAPEUTICS (HM19888) | | | | | | | | | | | | | | | | |
| THEW, NIN (HM19916) | ● | ● | ● | | ● | ● | ● | ● | ● | ● | ● | | | | | |
| TOBIN, ROSALEEN (HM20105) | | | | | | | | | | | | | ● | | | |
| TRAD CHINESE MEDICINE/MASSAGE (HM20216) | ● | | | | ● | ● | | ● | | ● | ● | | | | ● | |
| COUNTY GALWAY | | | | | | | | | | | | | | | | |
| ALEXANDER TECHNIQUE CENTRE (HM00557) | ● | | | | | ● | | | | ● | | | | | | |
| BODYWATCH (HM02636) | | | | | | | | | | | | | | | | |
| O'COLMAIN, AIDAN (DR) (HM15203) | ● | | | | | | | | | | | | | | ● | |
| PRENDERGAST, KARL (HM16542) | ● | | | | | | | | | | | | | | | |
| COUNTY KERRY | | | | | | | | | | | | | | | | |
| ACUPUNCTURE CLINIC (HM00286) | ● | | | | | ● | ● | ● | ● | ● | ● | ● | | | ● | |
| WOODLAWN HOLISTIC THERAPY CTRE (HM21834) | ● | | | | | | | | | | | | | | | |
| COUNTY KILDARE | | | | | | | | | | | | | | | | |
| GREEN ROAD HEALING CENTRE (HM08441) | ● | | | | | ● | | ● | | ● | ● | ● | | | | |
| SHENANDOAH HEALING (HM18395) | ● | | | | | ● | | | | | | | | | | |
| COUNTY KILKENNY | | | | | | | | | | | | | | | | |
| BLUE ROOM (HM02528) | ● | | | | | ● | | ● | | ● | ● | | | | | |
| DULCAMARA (HM06375) | | | | | | ● | ● | ● | ● | ● | ● | | | | | |
| HOLISTIC HEALING CENTRE (HM09965) | ● | | | | | | | | | | | | | | ● | |
| COUNTY LIMERICK | | | | | | | | | | | | | | | | |
| HOLISTIC HEALING (HM09960) | ● | | | | ● | ● | | ● | ● | ● | | | | | | |
| COUNTY LONGFORD | | | | | | | | | | | | | | | | |
| LONGFORD BEAUTY CLINIC (HM12626) | | | | | | | | | | | | | | | | |

| Business by County with Reference no. | Cancers | Cataracts | Catarrh | Cerebral Palsy | Circulation Problems | Cold Sores | Colds | Colic | Colitis | Conjunctivitis | Constipation | Convulsions | Corns | Coughs | Cramp | Cystitis |
|---|---|---|---|---|---|---|---|---|---|---|---|---|---|---|---|---|
| INNER CIRCLE HEALING CENTRE (HM10635) | | | | | | | | | | | | | | | | |
| KELLY, ANGELINA (HM11427) | | | | | ● | ● | ● | | | | | | | ● | ● | ● |
| LALLOO'S ACUPUNCTURE CLINIC (HM11881) | | | ● | | ● | | ● | ● | ● | ● | ● | ● | | ● | ● | ● |
| LITTLEJOHN CLINIC (HM12472) | | | | | | | ● | | | | | | | ● | | |
| MACLIAM, FIONNULA (HM12867) | | | | | | | | | | | | | | | | |
| MCHUGH HYPNOSIS & REFLEXOLOGY (HM13509) | ● | | | | | | | | ● | | ● | | | | | |
| MELT/TEMPLE BAR NATURAL (HM13716) | ● | ● | | | | | ● | | | | ● | | | ● | | ● |
| NATURAL SOLUTIONS (HM14625) | | | | | | | | | | | | | | | | |
| NUALA WOULFE BEAUTY SALON (HM15101) | | | | | ● | | | | | | ● | | | | | |
| RATHMINES CHIROPRACTIC CENTRE (HM16957) | | | | | | | | | | | | | | | | |
| T C M CENTRE (HM19639) | ● | | ● | | ● | ● | ● | ● | ● | ● | ● | | | ● | ● | ● |
| THERAPEUTICS (HM19888) | | | | | | | | | | | | | | | | |
| THEW, NIN (HM19916) | | | ● | | ● | | ● | | ● | | | | | ● | ● | ● |
| TOBIN, ROSALEEN (HM20105) | | | | | | | | | | | ● | | | | | |
| TRAD CHINESE MEDICINE/MASSAGE (HM20216) | | | ● | | ● | | ● | | | | ● | | | ● | | ● |
| COUNTY GALWAY | | | | | | | | | | | | | | | | |
| ALEXANDER TECHNIQUE CENTRE (HM00557) | | | | | | | | | | | | | | | ● | |
| BODYWATCH (HM02636) | | | | | | | | | | | | | | | | |
| O'COLMAIN, AIDAN (DR) (HM15203) | | | | | | | | | | | | | | | | |
| PRENDERGAST, KARL (HM16542) | | | | | | | | | | | | | | | ● | |
| COUNTY KERRY | | | | | | | | | | | | | | | | |
| ACUPUNCTURE CLINIC (HM00286) | | | ● | | ● | | ● | ● | | | ● | | | ● | ● | ● |
| WOODLAWN HOLISTIC THERAPY CTRE (HM21834) | | | ● | | | | ● | | | | ● | | | | | |
| COUNTY KILDARE | | | | | | | | | | | | | | | | |
| GREEN ROAD HEALING CENTRE (HM08441) | | | ● | | ● | ● | ● | ● | ● | | ● | | | ● | ● | ● |
| SHENANDOAH HEALING (HM18395) | | | | | | | | | | | ● | | | | | |
| COUNTY KILKENNY | | | | | | | | | | | | | | | | |
| BLUE ROOM (HM02528) | ● | | | | ● | | | | | | | | | | | |
| DULCAMARA (HM06375) | ● | | ● | | ● | ● | ● | | ● | | | | | ● | | ● |
| HOLISTIC HEALING CENTRE (HM09965) | | | | | ● | | | | | | ● | | | | ● | |
| COUNTY LIMERICK | | | | | | | | | | | | | | | | |
| HOLISTIC HEALING (HM09960) | | | | | ● | | | ● | | | ● | | | | | |
| COUNTY LONGFORD | | | | | | | | | | | | | | | | |
| LONGFORD BEAUTY CLINIC (HM12626) | | | | | | | | | | | | | | | | |

# A - C Conditions treated at Practices/Businesses

| Business by County with Reference no. | Acne | Addiction | Adenoids | Aids | Alcoholism | Allergy | Alzheimer's Disease | Amnesia | Anaemia | Angina | Anorexia | Anxiety | Arthritis | Asthma | Athletes Foot | Autism | Back Pain | Bacterial Infections | Baldness | Bereavement | Bladder Problems | Blood Pressure | Boils | Bowel Problems |
|---|---|---|---|---|---|---|---|---|---|---|---|---|---|---|---|---|---|---|---|---|---|---|---|---|
| COUNTY LOUTH | | | | | | | | | | | | | | | | | | | | | | | | |
| HOLISTIC SOL NTRL HEALING CTRE (HM09989) | | ● | | | | | | | | | ● | ● | | | | | | | | | | | | |
| COUNTY MAYO | | | | | | | | | | | | | | | | | | | | | | | | |
| NATURAL HEALING CENTRE (HM14547) | ● | ● | ● | | ● | ● | | | ● | ● | | ● | ● | ● | ● | | ● | ● | | | ● | ● | ● | ● |
| TOBAR PHADRAIC (HM20102) | | | | | | | | | | | | ● | | ● | | | ● | | | | | | | ● |
| COUNTY MEATH | | | | | | | | | | | | | | | | | | | | | | | | |
| NATURAL MEDICINE CENTRE (HM14610) | ● | | | | | ● | | | ● | ● | | ● | ● | ● | ● | | ● | ● | | | ● | ● | ● | ● |
| COUNTY MONAGHAN | | | | | | | | | | | | | | | | | | | | | | | | |
| AROMA - ZONE (HM01043) | ● | | | | | | | | | | | | ● | | | | ● | | | | | | | |
| HEALTHY CHOICES (HM09426) | ● | | | | | ● | | | | | | | ● | ● | | | ● | | | | | | | ● |
| NORTHAMBER (HM15050) | ● | ● | | | ● | ● | ● | ● | ● | ● | ● | ● | ● | ● | ● | | ● | ● | ● | | ● | ● | ● | ● |
| COUNTY ROSCOMMON | | | | | | | | | | | | | | | | | | | | | | | | |
| HOLISTIC HEALTH FARM (HM09980) | | | | | | ● | | | | | | | | | | | ● | | | | | | | ● |
| COUNTY SLIGO | | | | | | | | | | | | | | | | | | | | | | | | |
| ANAM CHARA COUNSELLING (HM00802) | | | | | | | | | | | | ● | | | | | | | | ● | | | | |
| SLIGO CHIROPRACTIC (HM18686) | | ● | ● | | ● | ● | | ● | | | ● | ● | ● | ● | | ● | ● | | | | ● | ● | | ● |
| COUNTY TIPPERARY | | | | | | | | | | | | | | | | | | | | | | | | |
| KINSELLA, MARIE (HM11693) | | ● | | | ● | | | | | | | | | | | | | | | ● | | | | |
| COUNTY WESTMEATH | | | | | | | | | | | | | | | | | | | | | | | | |
| HOWE, JAN (HM10263) | | | | | | | | | | | | | | | | | ● | | | | ● | ● | | |
| COUNTY WEXFORD | | | | | | | | | | | | | | | | | | | | | | | | |
| FOURTH MOUNTAIN HOM AND ACU (HM07622) | ● | ● | ● | | | ● | | | | | | ● | ● | ● | ● | ● | ● | | | | ● | ● | ● | ● |
| JEFFARIES, PHILIP (HM10958) | | | | | | | | | | | | | ● | | | | ● | | | | | | | |
| JEFFARIES, PHILIP (HM10957) | | | | | | | | | | | | | ● | | | | ● | | | | | | | |
| MURPHY, MARY (HM14388) | | | | | | | | | | | | ● | | | | | | | | | | | | |
| OSTEOPATHIC PRACTICE (HM15474) | | | | | | | | | | | | | ● | ● | | | ● | | | | | | | ● |
| COUNTY WICKLOW | | | | | | | | | | | | | | | | | | | | | | | | |
| ARKLOW NATURAL HEALING CENTRE (HM01007) | ● | | | | | | | | | | | | | ● | ● | | | | ● | | | | ● | ● |
| HOLISTIC OPTIONS (HM09985) | | | | | ● | | | | | | | ● | ● | ● | ● | | ● | | ● | | ● | ● | ● | ● |
| JAMESON PERSONAL EXCELLENCE (HM10903) | | ● | | | ● | ● | | | | | | ● | | ● | | | ● | | | | | | | ● |
| MARK GOULDING - ACUPUNCTURIST (HM13107) | ● | ● | | ● | ● | ● | | | ● | ● | ● | ● | ● | ● | | | ● | | | | ● | ● | ● | ● |

| Business by County with Reference no. | Breast Problems | Breathing Problems | Bronchitis | Bruising | Bulimia | Bunions | Bursitis | Callices | Cancers | Cataracts | Catarrh | Cerebral Palsy | Circulation Problems | Cold Sores | Colds | Colic | Colitis | Conjunctivitis | Constipation | Convulsions | Corns | Coughs | Cramp | Cystitis |
|---|---|---|---|---|---|---|---|---|---|---|---|---|---|---|---|---|---|---|---|---|---|---|---|---|
| COUNTY LOUTH | | | | | | | | | | | | | | | | | | | | | | | | |
| HOLISTIC SOL NTRL HEALING CTRE (HM09989) | | | | | | | | | ● | | | | | | | | | | | | | | | |
| COUNTY MAYO | | | | | | | | | | | | | | | | | | | | | | | | |
| NATURAL HEALING CENTRE (HM14547) | ● | ● | ● | ● | | | | ● | ● | ● | ● | | ● | ● | ● | ● | ● | ● | ● | | ● | ● | ● | ● |
| TOBAR PHADRAIC (HM20102) | | ● | ● | | | | | | | | | | | | | | | | ● | | | | | |
| COUNTY MEATH | | | | | | | | | | | | | | | | | | | | | | | | |
| NATURAL MEDICINE CENTRE (HM14610) | ● | ● | ● | ● | | | | | ● | | ● | | ● | ● | ● | ● | ● | ● | ● | | | ● | ● | ● |
| COUNTY MONAGHAN | | | | | | | | | | | | | | | | | | | | | | | | |
| AROMA - ZONE (HM01043) | | | ● | | | | | | | | ● | | | ● | ● | | | | ● | | | ● | ● | |
| HEALTHY CHOICES (HM09426) | | | | | | | ● | | | | | | | | | ● | ● | | ● | | | | | ● |
| NORTHAMBER (HM15050) | ● | ● | ● | ● | ● | | ● | | ● | | ● | | ● | ● | ● | ● | ● | ● | ● | ● | | ● | ● | ● |
| COUNTY ROSCOMMON | | | | | | | | | | | | | | | | | | | | | | | | |
| HOLISTIC HEALTH FARM (HM09980) | | ● | | | | | | | | | | | | | | | | | ● | | | | | |
| COUNTY SLIGO | | | | | | | | | | | | | | | | | | | | | | | | |
| ANAM CHARA COUNSELLING (HM00802) | | | | | | | | | ● | | | | | | | | | | | | | | | |
| SLIGO CHIROPRACTIC (HM18686) | | ● | ● | | | | | | | | | | ● | | ● | ● | | | ● | | | | ● | ● |
| COUNTY TIPPERARY | | | | | | | | | | | | | | | | | | | | | | | | |
| KINSELLA, MARIE (HM11693) | | | | | | | | | | | | | | | | | | | | | | | | |
| COUNTY WESTMEATH | | | | | | | | | | | | | | | | | | | | | | | | |
| HOWE, JAN (HM10263) | | | | | | | | | | | | | | | | | | | ● | | | | | |
| COUNTY WEXFORD | | | | | | | | | | | | | | | | | | | | | | | | |
| FOURTH MOUNTAIN HOM AND ACU (HM07622) | ● | ● | ● | ● | | | | | | | ● | | ● | ● | ● | ● | ● | ● | ● | | | ● | ● | ● |
| JEFFARIES, PHILIP (HM10958) | | | | | | | | | | | | | | | | | | | | | | | | |
| JEFFARIES, PHILIP (HM10957) | | | | | | | | | | | | | | | | | | | | | | | | |
| MURPHY, MARY (HM14388) | | | | | | | | | | | | | | | | | | | | | | | | |
| OSTEOPATHIC PRACTICE (HM15474) | | ● | | | | | | | | | | | | | | | | | ● | | | | | |
| COUNTY WICKLOW | | | | | | | | | | | | | | | | | | | | | | | | |
| ARKLOW NATURAL HEALING CENTRE (HM01007) | | | | ● | | | | | | | ● | | | ● | ● | ● | | ● | ● | | | ● | ● | ● |
| HOLISTIC OPTIONS (HM09985) | | ● | ● | | ● | | | | | | ● | | ● | ● | ● | | ● | | ● | | | ● | | ● |
| JAMESON PERSONAL EXCELLENCE (HM10903) | | | | | ● | | | | | | | | | | | | ● | | ● | | | | | |
| MARK GOULDING - ACUPUNCTURIST (HM13107) | ● | ● | ● | | | | ● | | | | ● | | ● | ● | ● | ● | ● | ● | ● | | | ● | ● | ● |

# A - C Conditions treated at Practices/Businesses

| Business by County with Reference no. | Acne | Addiction | Adenoids | Aids | Alcoholism | Allergy | Alzheimer's Disease | Amnesia | Anaemia | Angina | Anorexia | Anxiety | Arthritis | Asthma | Athletes Foot | Autism | Back Pain | Bacterial Infections | Baldness | Bereavement | Bladder Problems | Blood Pressure | Boils | Bowel Problems | Breast Problems | Breathing Problems | Bronchitis | Bruising | Bulimia | Bunions | Bursitis | Callices | Cancers | Cataracts | Catarrh | Cerebral Palsy | Circulation Problems | Cold Sores | Colds | Colic | Colitis | Conjunctivitis | Constipation | Convulsions | Corns | Coughs | Cramp | Cystitis |
|---|---|---|---|---|---|---|---|---|---|---|---|---|---|---|---|---|---|---|---|---|---|---|---|---|---|---|---|---|---|---|---|---|---|---|---|---|---|---|---|---|---|---|---|---|---|---|---|---|
| **NORTHERN IRELAND** | | | | | | | | | | | | | | | | | | | | | | | | | | | | | | | | | | | | | | | | | | | | | | | | |
| **COUNTY ANTRIM** | | | | | | | | | | | | | | | | | | | | | | | | | | | | | | | | | | | | | | | | | | | | | | | | |
| ACTIVE BALANCE CLINIC (HM00189) | ● | | | | | | | | | ● | | ● | ● | ● | | | ● | ● | | | ● | ● | | ● | ● | | ● | | | | ● | | | | ● | | ● | | | ● | ● | ● | ● | | | | ● | ● |
| ALOE VERA (HM00669) | | | | | | | ● | ● | | | | | ● | ● | ● | | ● | ● | | | ● | ● | ● | ● | | | ● | ● | | | | | | | | | ● | ● | ● | ● | ● | ● | ● | | | ● | ● | |
| ANTRIM CHIROPRACTIC CLINIC (HM00923) | | | | | | | | | | | | | ● | | | | ● | | | | | | | | | | | | | | | | | | | | | | | | | | | | | | | |
| BALLYCLARE CHIROPRACTIC CLINIC (HM01636) | | | | | | | | | | | | | ● | | | | ● | | | | | ● | | | | | | | | | | | | | | | | | | | | | | | | | | |
| BALLYMONEY CHIROPRACTIC CLINIC (HM01639) | | | | | | | | | | | | | ● | | | | ● | | | | | | | | | | | | | | | | | | | | ● | | | | | | | | | | | |
| BROWN, AVRIL (HM03215) | | | | | | | | | | | | ● | | | | | | | | | | | | | | | | | | | | | | | | | | | | | | | | | | | | |
| CHIROPODIST (HM04290) | | | | | | | | | | | | | | | ● | | | | | | | | | | | | | | | | | | | | | | | | | | | | | | | | | |
| CRAWFORD, J G (HM05392) | | | | | | | | | | | | | | | | | | | | | | | | | | | | | | | | ● | | | | | | | | | | | | | ● | | | |
| CREGAGH CHIROPRACTIC CLINIC (HM05412) | | | | | | | | | | | | | ● | | | | ● | | | | | | | | | | | | | | | | | | | | ● | | | | | | | | | | | |
| EARLS, JAMES (HM06497) | | | | | | | | | | | | | | | | | ● | | | | | | | | | | | | | | | | | | | | ● | | | | | | | | | | | |
| FINAGHY CHIROPRACTIC CLINIC (HM07295) | | | | | | | | | | | | | ● | | | | ● | | | | | | | | | | | | | | | | | | | | ● | | | | | | | | | | | |
| FLORENCE SHARPE CHIROPODIST (HM07431) | | | | | | | | | | | | | | | ● | | | | | | | | | | | | | | | | | ● | | | | | | | | | | | | | ● | | | |
| FRAMAR NATURAL HEALTH CLINIC (HM07654) | ● | | | | | ● | | | | ● | | ● | ● | ● | ● | | ● | | ● | | ● | ● | ● | ● | ● | ● | ● | ● | ● | | ● | | ● | ● | ● | | ● | ● | ● | ● | ● | ● | ● | | | ● | ● | ● |
| GIVEN, CLIVE (HM08115) | ● | ● | ● | ● | ● | ● | ● | ● | ● | ● | ● | ● | ● | ● | ● | ● | ● | ● | ● | | ● | ● | ● | ● | ● | ● | ● | ● | ● | | ● | ● | ● | ● | ● | | ● | ● | ● | ● | ● | ● | ● | ● | ● | ● | ● | ● |
| GLENGORMLEY CHIRO CLINIC (HM08151) | | | | | | | | | | | | | ● | | | | ● | | | | | | | | | | | | | | | | | | | | ● | | | | | | | | | | | |
| HYPNOTHERAPY CENTRE (HM10521) | | ● | | | | | | | | | ● | | | | | | | | | | | | | | | | | | ● | | | | | | | | | | | | | | | | | | | |
| LAMBERT, RACHEL (HM11901) | ● | | | | | | | | | | | ● | | | | | ● | | | | | | | | | | | | | | | | | | | | ● | | | | | | | | | | | |
| LISBURN CHIROPRACTIC CLINIC (HM12452) | | | | | | | | | | | | | ● | | | | | | | | | | | | | | | | | | | | | | | | ● | | | | | | | | | | | |
| MAXWELL, MARY (HM13337) | | | | | | | | | | | | ● | ● | ● | ● | | ● | | | | ● | ● | | | ● | ● | | | | | | | | | | | ● | | | | | | ● | | | | | |
| MCCARTNEY, W J (HM13401) | | | | | | | | | | | | | | | ● | | | | | | | | | | | | | | | | | ● | | | | | | | | | | | | | ● | | | |
| MCCRYSTALS NATUROPATHIC CENTRE (HM13436) | ● | | | | | ● | | | | | | ● | ● | ● | ● | | ● | | | | ● | ● | ● | ● | ● | ● | ● | ● | | | ● | | | | ● | | ● | ● | ● | ● | ● | ● | ● | ● | | ● | ● | ● |
| MCCULLY, JOAN (HM13437) | | | | | | | | | | | | | | | ● | | | | | | | | | | | | | | | | | | | | | | | | | | | | | | | | | |
| MYSTIC SCHEHERAZADE (HM14445) | | | | | | | | | | | | | ● | | | | ● | | | | | | | | | | | | | | | | | | | | | | | | | | | | | | | |
| NTH IRELAND MUSIC THER TRUST (HM15100) | | | | | | | | | | | | ● | | | | ● | | | | | | | | | | | | | | | | | | | | | | | | | | | | | | | | |
| REAY, H (HM17004) | | | | | | | | | | | | | | | ● | | | | | | | | | | | | | | | | | | | | | | | | | | | | | | | | | |
| SCRABO HEALTH PRODUCTS (HM18143) | ● | | | | | ● | | | ● | ● | | ● | ● | ● | ● | | ● | ● | ● | | ● | ● | ● | ● | ● | ● | ● | ● | | | ● | | | ● | ● | | ● | ● | ● | ● | ● | ● | ● | | | ● | ● | ● |
| STEWART, S (HM19276) | | | | | | | | | | | | | | | ● | | | | | | | | | | | | | | | | | ● | | | | | | | | | | | | | ● | | | |
| TODD, TREVOR (HM20109) | | | | | | | | | | | | | | | ● | | | | | | | | | | | | | | | | | ● | | | | | | | | | | | | | ● | | | |
| W M RYAN AND SON (HM20722) | | | | | | | | | | | | | | | | | ● | | | | | | | | | | | | | | | | | | | | | | | | | | | | | | | |
| YARO (HM21991) | | | | | | | | | | | | ● | ● | | | | ● | | | | | | | | | | | | | | | | ● | | | | | | | | | | | | | | | |

# A - C Conditions treated at Practices/Businesses

Business by County with Reference no.

| Business | Acne | Addiction | Adenoids | Aids | Alcoholism | Allergy | Alzheimer's Disease | Amnesia | Anaemia | Angina | Anorexia | Anxiety | Arthritis | Asthma | Athletes Foot | Autism | Back Pain | Bacterial Infections | Baldness | Bereavement | Bladder Problems | Blood Pressure | Boils | Bowel Problems |
|---|---|---|---|---|---|---|---|---|---|---|---|---|---|---|---|---|---|---|---|---|---|---|---|---|
| **COUNTY ARMAGH** | | | | | | | | | | | | | | | | | | | | | | | | |
| CAMPBELL, FIONA (HM03598) | | | | | | | | | | | | | | | ● | | | | | | | | | |
| CRAIGAVON CHIROPRACTIC CLINIC (HM05355) | | | | | | | | | | | | | ● | | | | ● | | | | | | | |
| LYON, HARRIETTE (HM12780) | | | | | | | | | | | | | | | ● | | | | | | | | | |
| WILLIS, IAN (HM21614) | | | | | | | | | | | | | | | ● | | | | | | | | | |
| **COUNTY DOWN** | | | | | | | | | | | | | | | | | | | | | | | | |
| ARDS CHIROPRACTIC CLINIC (HM00993) | | | | | | | | | | | | | ● | | | | ● | | | | | | | |
| BANGOR CHIROPRACTIC CLINIC (HM01659) | | | | | | | | | | | | | ● | | | | | | | | | | | |
| BANGOR OSTEOPATHIC CLINIC (HM01660) | | | | | | | | | | | | | | | | | ● | | | | | | | |
| CHIROPRACTICE (HM04405) | | | | | | | | | | | | | ● | | ● | | ● | | | | | | | |
| COCHRANE, NIALL (HM04764) | | | | | | | | | | | | | | | ● | | | | | | | | | |
| HADDEN, MARLENE (HM08687) | | | | | | | | | | | | | ● | ● | ● | | ● | | | | ● | ● | | ● |
| LYCIUM CENTRE (HM12755) | ● | | | | | ● | | | ● | ● | | | ● | ● | ● | | ● | | | | ● | ● | | ● |
| MCCARTAN, DEBORAH (HM13392) | | | | | | | | | | | | | | | ● | | | | | | | | | |
| MCCLURG, T A (HM13412) | | | | | | | | | | | | | | | ● | | | | | | | | | |
| MCCUTCHEON, TINA (HM13441) | | | | | | | | | | | | ● | ● | ● | | | ● | | | | ● | | | ● |
| NEWRY CHIROPRACTIC CLINIC (HM14886) | | | | | | | | | | | | | ● | | | | ● | | | | | | | |
| NOBLE, ANDREW (DR) (HM14968) | | | | | | | | | | | | | ● | | | | ● | | | | | | | |
| NORTH DOWN CLINIC (HM15023) | | | | | | | | | | | | | | | | ● | ● | | | | | | | |
| PRINGLE CHIROPRACTIC (HM16626) | | | | | | ● | | | | | | ● | ● | ● | | | ● | | | | ● | ● | | ● |
| QUINN, BARBARA (HM16808) | | | | | | | | | | | | | ● | | | | ● | | | | | | | |
| REFLEXOLOGY CLINIC (HM17092) | | | | | | | | | | | | ● | | ● | | | ● | | | | | ● | | ● |
| YOGA CENTRE OF IRELAND (HM22023) | | | | | | | | | | | | | | | | | | | | | | ● | | |
| **COUNTY FERMANAGH** | | | | | | | | | | | | | | | | | | | | | | | | |
| ENNISKILLEN CHIRO CLINIC (HM06844) | | | | | | | | | | | | | ● | | | | ● | | | | | | | |
| **COUNTY LONDONDERRY** | | | | | | | | | | | | | | | | | | | | | | | | |
| CLARENDON CHIROPRACTIC CLINIC (HM04539) | | | | | | | | | | | | | ● | | | | ● | | | | | | | |
| CLAUDY CHIROPRACTIC CLINIC (HM04612) | | | | | | | | | | | | | ● | | | | ● | | | | | | | |
| CURRAN, MAUREEN (HM05630) | ● | | | | | | | | | | | | | | | | ● | | | | | | | |
| DISPENSERY (HM06117) | ● | | ● | | | ● | | ● | ● | ● | ● | ● | ● | ● | ● | | ● | ● | ● | | ● | ● | ● | ● |
| EQUILIBRIUM HOLISTIC CLINIC (HM06875) | | | | | | | | | | | | ● | ● | | | | ● | | | | | | | |
| FEET FIRST (HM07174) | | | | | | | | | | | | | | | ● | | | | | | | | | |
| FOYLE HYPNOTHERAPY CENTRE (HM07646) | | ● | | | ● | | | ● | | | ● | ● | | ● | | | ● | | | | | | | ● |
| LIFE TREE (HM12350) | | | | | | ● | | | | | | | ● | ● | ● | | | ● | | | | ● | | ● |

| Business | Breast Problems | Breathing Problems | Bronchitis | Bruising | Bulimia | Bunions | Bursitis | Callices | Cancers | Cataracts | Catarrh | Cerebral Palsy | Circulation Problems | Cold Sores | Colds | Colic | Colitis | Conjunctivitis | Constipation | Convulsions | Corns | Coughs | Cramp | Cystitis |
|---|---|---|---|---|---|---|---|---|---|---|---|---|---|---|---|---|---|---|---|---|---|---|---|---|
| **COUNTY ARMAGH** | | | | | | | | | | | | | | | | | | | | | | | | |
| CAMPBELL, FIONA (HM03598) | | | | | | | | ● | | | | | | | | | | | | | ● | | | |
| CRAIGAVON CHIROPRACTIC CLINIC (HM05355) | | | | | | | | | | | | | | | | | | | | | | | | |
| LYON, HARRIETTE (HM12780) | | | | | | | | ● | | | | | | | | | | | | | ● | | | |
| WILLIS, IAN (HM21614) | | | | | | | | | | | | | | | | | | | | | | | | |
| **COUNTY DOWN** | | | | | | | | | | | | | | | | | | | | | | | | |
| ARDS CHIROPRACTIC CLINIC (HM00993) | | | | | | | | | | | | | ● | | | | | | | | | | | |
| BANGOR CHIROPRACTIC CLINIC (HM01659) | | | | | | | | | | | | | ● | | | | | | | | | | | |
| BANGOR OSTEOPATHIC CLINIC (HM01660) | | | | | | | | | | | | | | | | | | | | | | | | |
| CHIROPRACTICE (HM04405) | | | | | | | | | | | | | ● | | | | | | | | | | | |
| COCHRANE, NIALL (HM04764) | | | | | | | | ● | | | | | | | | | | | | | ● | | | |
| HADDEN, MARLENE (HM08687) | ● | ● | ● | | | | | | | | | | ● | | | | | | ● | | | | | |
| LYCIUM CENTRE (HM12755) | | | | | | | | | | | ● | | ● | | ● | | | | ● | | | ● | | ● |
| MCCARTAN, DEBORAH (HM13392) | | | | | | | | ● | | | | | | | | | | | | | ● | | | |
| MCCLURG, T A (HM13412) | | | | | | | ● | | | | | | ● | | | | | | | | | | | |
| MCCUTCHEON, TINA (HM13441) | | | | | | | | | | | | | ● | | | | ● | | | | | ● | ● | ● |
| NEWRY CHIROPRACTIC CLINIC (HM14886) | | | | | | | | | | | | | ● | | | | | | | | | | | |
| NOBLE, ANDREW (DR) (HM14968) | | | | | | | | | | | | | ● | | | | | | | | | | | |
| NORTH DOWN CLINIC (HM15023) | | | | | | | | | | | | | ● | | | | ● | | ● | | | | | |
| PRINGLE CHIROPRACTIC (HM16626) | | ● | | | | | | | | | ● | | ● | | | ● | ● | | ● | | | | ● | |
| QUINN, BARBARA (HM16808) | | | | | | | | | | | | | ● | | | | | | ● | | | | ● | |
| REFLEXOLOGY CLINIC (HM17092) | | ● | | | | | | | | | ● | | ● | | | | ● | | ● | | | | | |
| YOGA CENTRE OF IRELAND (HM22023) | | | | | | | | | | | | | | | | | | | | | | | | |
| **COUNTY FERMANAGH** | | | | | | | | | | | | | | | | | | | | | | | | |
| ENNISKILLEN CHIRO CLINIC (HM06844) | | | | | | | | | | | | | | | | ● | | | | | | | | |
| **COUNTY LONDONDERRY** | | | | | | | | | | | | | | | | | | | | | | | | |
| CLARENDON CHIROPRACTIC CLINIC (HM04539) | | | | | | | | | | | | | ● | | | | | | | | | | | |
| CLAUDY CHIROPRACTIC CLINIC (HM04612) | | | | | | | | | | | | | ● | | | | | | | | | | | |
| CURRAN, MAUREEN (HM05630) | | | | | | | | | | | | | | | | | | | | | | | | |
| DISPENSERY (HM06117) | ● | ● | ● | ● | ● | | ● | ● | ● | ● | ● | | ● | ● | ● | ● | ● | ● | ● | ● | ● | ● | ● | ● |
| EQUILIBRIUM HOLISTIC CLINIC (HM06875) | | | | | | | | | | | | | | | | | | | | | | | | |
| FEET FIRST (HM07174) | | | | | | | | ● | | | | | | | | | | | | | ● | | | |
| FOYLE HYPNOTHERAPY CENTRE (HM07646) | | | | | ● | | | | | | | | | | | | | | | | | | | |
| LIFE TREE (HM12350) | | ● | | | | | | | | | ● | | ● | ● | ● | ● | | | ● | | | ● | | ● |

www.healthmyself.com

# A - C Conditions treated at Practices/Businesses

| Business by County with Reference no. | Acne | Addiction | Adenoids | Aids | Alcoholism | Allergy | Alzheimer's Disease | Amnesia | Anaemia | Angina | Anorexia | Anxiety |
|---|---|---|---|---|---|---|---|---|---|---|---|---|
| MAGHERAFELT CHIRO CLINIC (HM12906) | | | | | | | | | | | | |
| **COUNTY TYRONE** | | | | | | | | | | | | |
| BRADLEY, R M (HM02871) | | | | | | | | | | | | |
| COOKSTOWN HERBAL CLINIC (HM05073) | ● | ● | ● | ● | ● | ● | ● | ● | ● | ● | ● | ● |
| DUNGANNON CHIROPRACTIC CLINIC (HM06405) | | | | | | | | | | | | |
| ROSEWOOD HEALTH CLINIC (HM17630) | ● | ● | ● | ● | ● | ● | ● | ● | ● | ● | ● | ● |

| Business by County with Reference no. | Arthritis | Asthma | Athletes Foot | Autism | Back Pain | Bacterial Infections | Baldness | Bereavement | Bladder Problems | Blood Pressure | Boils | Bowel Problems |
|---|---|---|---|---|---|---|---|---|---|---|---|---|
| MAGHERAFELT CHIRO CLINIC (HM12906) | | | | | ● | | | | | | | |
| **COUNTY TYRONE** | | | | | | | | | | | | |
| BRADLEY, R M (HM02871) | | | ● | | | | | | | | | |
| COOKSTOWN HERBAL CLINIC (HM05073) | ● | ● | ● | ● | ● | ● | ● | | ● | ● | ● | ● |
| DUNGANNON CHIROPRACTIC CLINIC (HM06405) | ● | | | | ● | | | | | | | |
| ROSEWOOD HEALTH CLINIC (HM17630) | ● | ● | ● | ● | ● | ● | ● | | ● | ● | ● | ● |

| Business by County with Reference no. | Breast Problems | Breathing Problems | Bronchitis | Bruising | Bulimia | Bunions | Bursitis | Callices | Cancers | Cataracts | Catarrh | Cerebral Palsy |
|---|---|---|---|---|---|---|---|---|---|---|---|---|
| MAGHERAFELT CHIRO CLINIC (HM12906) | | | | | | | | | | | | |
| **COUNTY TYRONE** | | | | | | | | | | | | |
| BRADLEY, R M (HM02871) | | | | | | | | ● | | | | |
| COOKSTOWN HERBAL CLINIC (HM05073) | ● | ● | ● | ● | ● | | ● | ● | ● | ● | ● | |
| DUNGANNON CHIROPRACTIC CLINIC (HM06405) | | | | | | | | | | | | |
| ROSEWOOD HEALTH CLINIC (HM17630) | ● | ● | ● | ● | ● | | ● | ● | ● | ● | ● | |

| Business by County with Reference no. | Circulation Problems | Cold Sores | Colds | Colic | Colitis | Conjunctivitis | Constipation | Convulsions | Corns | Coughs | Cramp | Cystitis |
|---|---|---|---|---|---|---|---|---|---|---|---|---|
| MAGHERAFELT CHIRO CLINIC (HM12906) | | | | | | | | | | | | |
| **COUNTY TYRONE** | | | | | | | | | | | | |
| BRADLEY, R M (HM02871) | | | | | | | | | ● | | | |
| COOKSTOWN HERBAL CLINIC (HM05073) | ● | ● | ● | ● | ● | ● | ● | ● | ● | ● | ● | ● |
| DUNGANNON CHIROPRACTIC CLINIC (HM06405) | ● | | | | | | | | | | | |
| ROSEWOOD HEALTH CLINIC (HM17630) | ● | ● | ● | ● | ● | ● | ● | ● | ● | ● | ● | ● |

# A - C Conditions treated at Practices/Businesses

Business by County with Reference no.

| Business | Acne | Addiction | Adenoids | Aids | Alcoholism | Allergy | Alzheimer's Disease | Amnesia | Anaemia | Angina | Anorexia | Anxiety | Arthritis | Asthma | Athletes Foot | Autism |
|---|---|---|---|---|---|---|---|---|---|---|---|---|---|---|---|---|
| **SCOTLAND** | | | | | | | | | | | | | | | | |
| **ABERDEENSHIRE** | | | | | | | | | | | | | | | | |
| A WAY WITH THE FAERIES (HM00051) | | | | | | | | | | | | ● | | | | |
| ABERDEEN CHIROPRACTIC CLINIC (HM00114) | | | | | | | | | | | | | ● | | | |
| ALTERNATIVE PRACTICE (HM00723) | ● | ● | | | | | | | | | | | | | | |
| BANCHORY CHIROPODY PRACTICE (HM01649) | | | | | | | | | | | | | | | ● | |
| BEECHGROVE CLINIC (HM02050) | | | | | | | | | | | | | ● | | | |
| BON-ACCORD CHIROPODY (HM02667) | | | | | | | | | | | | | | | ● | |
| CHELSEA HOUSE CLINIC (HM04090) | | | | | | | | | | | | ● | ● | | | |
| CITY BEACH (HM04486) | ● | | | | | | | | | | | | | | | |
| CLAIRBAUX CLINIC (HM04505) | | | | | | | | | | | | | ● | ● | | |
| CLAIRBAUX CLINIC (HM04506) | | | | | | | | | | | | | ● | ● | | |
| DAVISON, FIONA (HM05865) | | | | | | | | | | | | | | | | |
| DEEVIEW AROMATHERAPY (HM05960) | | | | | | | | | | | | ● | ● | | | |
| GRAY, SHEILA (HM08419) | | | | | | | | | | | | ● | | ● | | |
| HUNTLY CHIROPRACTIC CLINIC (HM10412) | | | | | | | | | | | | | ● | | | |
| LEAL, DOUGLAS (HM12102) | | | | | | | | | | | | | | | ● | |
| MOSS PHARMACY (HM14262) | | | | | | | | | | | | | | | ● | |
| REIKI TRAINING CENTRE (HM17149) | | ● | | | | | | | | | | ● | | | | |
| RIVERSIDE CHIROPRACTIC CLINIC (HM17378) | | | | | | | | | | | | | ● | | | |
| ROSEMOUNT CENTRE (HM17623) | ● | ● | | | ● | ● | | | | | ● | ● | ● | ● | | ● |
| SAWYER, KEN (HM17985) | | ● | | | ● | ● | | | | | ● | ● | | | | |
| SERENDIPITY (HM18232) | | | | | | | | | | | | ● | | ● | | |
| STEPHENSON, L (HM19208) | | | | | | | | | | | | | | | ● | |
| TAGGART, RUTH (HM19652) | | | | | | | | | | | | ● | ● | ● | | |
| TOE TO HEEL - REFLEXOLOGY (HM20110) | ● | | | | | ● | | | | ● | | ● | ● | ● | | |
| TURRIFF CHIROPRACTIC CLINIC (HM20443) | | | | | | | | | | | | | ● | | | |
| WEST END PHYSIOTHERAPY (HM21219) | | | | | | | | | | | | | | | | |
| WILKEN, ANGEL (HM21492) | | | | | | | | | | | | ● | | ● | | |
| WOOD, A R (HM21783) | | | | | | | | | | | | | | | ● | |
| **ANGUS** | | | | | | | | | | | | | | | | |
| BAKER, P T (HM01593) | | | | | | | | | | | | | ● | | | |
| DRYDEN, PHILIP (HM06333) | | | | | | | | | | | | | | | ● | |

| Business | Back Pain | Bacterial Infections | Baldness | Bereavement | Bladder Problems | Blood Pressure | Boils | Bowel Problems | Breast Problems | Breathing Problems | Bronchitis | Bruising | Bulimia | Bunions | Bursitis | Callices |
|---|---|---|---|---|---|---|---|---|---|---|---|---|---|---|---|---|
| **SCOTLAND** | | | | | | | | | | | | | | | | |
| **ABERDEENSHIRE** | | | | | | | | | | | | | | | | |
| A WAY WITH THE FAERIES (HM00051) | ● | | | | | | | | | | | | | | | |
| ABERDEEN CHIROPRACTIC CLINIC (HM00114) | ● | | | | | | | | | | | | | | | |
| ALTERNATIVE PRACTICE (HM00723) | ● | | | | | | | | | | | | | | | |
| BANCHORY CHIROPODY PRACTICE (HM01649) | | | | | | | | | | | | | | | | |
| BEECHGROVE CLINIC (HM02050) | ● | | | | ● | | | | | | | ● | | | ● | |
| BON-ACCORD CHIROPODY (HM02667) | | | | | | | | | | | | | | | | ● |
| CHELSEA HOUSE CLINIC (HM04090) | ● | | | | | | | | | | | | | | | |
| CITY BEACH (HM04486) | | | | | | | | | | | | | | | | |
| CLAIRBAUX CLINIC (HM04505) | ● | | | | | | | | | | | ● | | | | |
| CLAIRBAUX CLINIC (HM04506) | ● | | | | | | | | | | | ● | | | | |
| DAVISON, FIONA (HM05865) | ● | | | | | | | | | | | | | | | |
| DEEVIEW AROMATHERAPY (HM05960) | ● | | | | | ● | | ● | | | | | | | | |
| GRAY, SHEILA (HM08419) | ● | | | | | | | ● | | | | | | | | |
| HUNTLY CHIROPRACTIC CLINIC (HM10412) | ● | | | | | | | | | | | | | | | |
| LEAL, DOUGLAS (HM12102) | | | | | | | | | | | | | | | | |
| MOSS PHARMACY (HM14262) | | | | | | | | | | | | | | | | |
| REIKI TRAINING CENTRE (HM17149) | | | | | | | | | | | | | | | | |
| RIVERSIDE CHIROPRACTIC CLINIC (HM17378) | ● | | | | | | | | | | | | | | | |
| ROSEMOUNT CENTRE (HM17623) | ● | | ● | | ● | ● | ● | ● | ● | ● | | | ● | | | |
| SAWYER, KEN (HM17985) | | | | | | | | | | | | | ● | | | |
| SERENDIPITY (HM18232) | ● | | | | | | | | | | | | | | | |
| STEPHENSON, L (HM19208) | | | | | | | | | | | | | | | | |
| TAGGART, RUTH (HM19652) | ● | | | | | | | | | ● | | | | | | |
| TOE TO HEEL - REFLEXOLOGY (HM20110) | ● | | | | ● | ● | | ● | ● | | | | | | ● | |
| TURRIFF CHIROPRACTIC CLINIC (HM20443) | ● | | | | | | | | | | | | | | | |
| WEST END PHYSIOTHERAPY (HM21219) | ● | | | | | | | | | | | | | | | |
| WILKEN, ANGEL (HM21492) | ● | | | | | | | | | ● | | | | | | |
| WOOD, A R (HM21783) | | | | | | | | | | | | | | | | |
| **ANGUS** | | | | | | | | | | | | | | | | |
| BAKER, P T (HM01593) | ● | | | | | ● | | | | | | | | | | |
| DRYDEN, PHILIP (HM06333) | | | | | | | | | | | | | | | | ● |

| Business | Cancers | Cataracts | Catarrh | Cerebral Palsy | Circulation Problems | Cold Sores | Colds | Colic | Colitis | Conjunctivitis | Constipation | Convulsions | Corns | Coughs | Cramp | Cystitis |
|---|---|---|---|---|---|---|---|---|---|---|---|---|---|---|---|---|
| **SCOTLAND** | | | | | | | | | | | | | | | | |
| **ABERDEENSHIRE** | | | | | | | | | | | | | | | | |
| A WAY WITH THE FAERIES (HM00051) | | | | | | | | | | | | | | | | |
| ABERDEEN CHIROPRACTIC CLINIC (HM00114) | | | | | ● | | | ● | | | | | | | | |
| ALTERNATIVE PRACTICE (HM00723) | | | | | | | | | | | | | | | | |
| BANCHORY CHIROPODY PRACTICE (HM01649) | | | | | | | | | | | | | | | | |
| BEECHGROVE CLINIC (HM02050) | | | | | | | | | | | | | | | | |
| BON-ACCORD CHIROPODY (HM02667) | | | | | | | | | | | | | ● | | | |
| CHELSEA HOUSE CLINIC (HM04090) | | | | | | | | | | | | | | | | |
| CITY BEACH (HM04486) | | | | | | | | | | | | | | | | |
| CLAIRBAUX CLINIC (HM04505) | | | | | | | | | | | ● | | | | ● | |
| CLAIRBAUX CLINIC (HM04506) | | | | | | | | | | | ● | | | | ● | |
| DAVISON, FIONA (HM05865) | | | | | | | | | | | | | | | | |
| DEEVIEW AROMATHERAPY (HM05960) | | | | | ● | | | | ● | | | | | | | |
| GRAY, SHEILA (HM08419) | | | ● | | ● | | | | | | ● | | | | | |
| HUNTLY CHIROPRACTIC CLINIC (HM10412) | | | | | ● | | | ● | | | | | | | | |
| LEAL, DOUGLAS (HM12102) | | | | | | | | | | | | | | | | |
| MOSS PHARMACY (HM14262) | | | | | | | | | | | | | | | | |
| REIKI TRAINING CENTRE (HM17149) | | | | | | | | | | | | | | | | |
| RIVERSIDE CHIROPRACTIC CLINIC (HM17378) | | | | | | | | ● | | | | | | | | |
| ROSEMOUNT CENTRE (HM17623) | ● | ● | ● | | | ● | ● | ● | ● | ● | ● | | | | ● | |
| SAWYER, KEN (HM17985) | | | | | | | | | | | | | | | | |
| SERENDIPITY (HM18232) | | | | | | | | | | | | | | | | |
| STEPHENSON, L (HM19208) | | | | | | | | | | | | | | | | |
| TAGGART, RUTH (HM19652) | ● | | | | | | | | | | | | | | | |
| TOE TO HEEL - REFLEXOLOGY (HM20110) | ● | | ● | | ● | | | ● | ● | | ● | | | | ● | ● |
| TURRIFF CHIROPRACTIC CLINIC (HM20443) | | | | | | | | | | | | | | | | |
| WEST END PHYSIOTHERAPY (HM21219) | | | | | | | | | | | | | | | | |
| WILKEN, ANGEL (HM21492) | | | | | ● | | | | | | | | | | | |
| WOOD, A R (HM21783) | | | | | | | | | | | | | | | | |
| **ANGUS** | | | | | | | | | | | | | | | | |
| BAKER, P T (HM01593) | | | | | ● | | | | | | | | | | | |
| DRYDEN, PHILIP (HM06333) | | | | | | | | | | | | | ● | | | |

# A - C Conditions treated at Practices/Businesses

| Business by County with Reference no. | Acne | Addiction | Adenoids | Aids | Alcoholism | Allergy | Alzheimer's Disease | Amnesia | Anaemia | Angina | Anorexia | Anxiety | Arthritis | Asthma | Athletes Foot | Autism | Back Pain | Bacterial Infections | Baldness | Bereavement |
|---|---|---|---|---|---|---|---|---|---|---|---|---|---|---|---|---|---|---|---|---|
| FOGGIE, MARGARET (HM07454) | | | | | | | | | | | | | | | ● | | | | | |
| HOLISTIC HEALING CENTRE (HM09964) | | | | | | | | | | | | | ● | | | | ● | | | |
| KIRRIEMUIR PHYSIO CLINIC (HM11723) | | | | | | | | | | | | | ● | | | | ● | | | |
| NATURAL HEALTH & CHIROPODY (HM14558) | | | | | | | | | | | | | | | | | | | | |
| NICOLL, ELAINE (HM14929) | | | | | | | | | | | | | | | ● | | | | | |
| **ARGYLL AND BUTE** | | | | | | | | | | | | | | | | | | | | |
| ACTIVE CHIROPRACTIC (HM00195) | | | | | | | | | | | | | ● | | | | ● | | | |
| COMPLEMENTARY HEALTH CENTRE (HM04922) | | | | | | | | | | | | ● | | | ● | | ● | | | |
| GIBSON, RONALD J (HM08045) | | | | | | | | | | | | ● | ● | | ● | | ● | | | |
| HOMEOPATHIC PODIATRIST/REFLEX (HM10078) | | ● | | | | | | | | | | ● | ● | | | | ● | | | |
| NATURAL THERAPY CENTRE (HM14648) | | | | | | | | | | | | | ● | ● | ● | | ● | | | |
| REIKI LIGHT (HM17138) | | | | | | | | | | | | ● | | | | | ● | | | |
| **AYRSHIRE (EAST)** | | | | | | | | | | | | | | | | | | | | |
| CRUISE, M & M (HM05520) | | | | | | | | | | | | | | | ● | | | | | |
| LITTLEJOHN, S (HM12473) | | | | | | | | | | | | | | | ● | | | | | |
| LYNN BROWN CLINICAL AROM (HM12772) | ● | ● | | | ● | ● | | | | | | ● | ● | ● | ● | | ● | | | |
| MCCABE, P J (HM13376) | | | | | | | | | | | | | | | ● | | | | | |
| **AYRSHIRE (NORTH)** | | | | | | | | | | | | | | | | | | | | |
| BODYSCENTS (HM02631) | | | | | | | | | | | | ● | ● | | | | ● | | | |
| BURNS, ALAN STEWART (HM03410) | | | | | | | | | | | | | | | ● | | | | | |
| CHIRO HEALTH CARE CLINIC (HM04282) | | | | | | ● | | | | | | ● | ● | ● | | | ● | | | |
| HANDS FOR FEET (HM08905) | | | | | | | | | | | | | | | ● | | | | | |
| PATON, MARY S (HM15824) | | | | | | | | | | | | | | | ● | | | | | |
| REID, E (HM17116) | | | | | | | | | | | | ● | ● | ● | ● | | ● | | | |
| **AYRSHIRE (SOUTH)** | | | | | | | | | | | | | | | | | | | | |
| BELL, W DOUGLAS (HM02091) | ● | ● | ● | ● | ● | ● | ● | ● | ● | ● | ● | ● | ● | ● | ● | ● | ● | ● | ● | |
| CARRICK CLINIC (HM03742) | | | | | | ● | | | | | | ● | ● | ● | | | ● | | | |
| CRUISE, M & M (HM05522) | | | | | | | | | | | | | | | ● | | | | | |
| ESSENCE OF HEALTH (HM06890) | ● | ● | ● | ● | ● | ● | ● | ● | ● | ● | ● | ● | ● | ● | ● | ● | ● | ● | ● | |
| HARDIE, ANNE (HM08966) | | | | | | | | | | | | ● | ● | | | | ● | | | |
| HEALTH STRESS & INJURIES (HM09404) | | ● | | | | ● | | | | | | ● | ● | | | | ● | | | |
| HEARTLAKE PHYSIOTHERAPY (HM09444) | | | | | | | | | | | | | ● | | | | ● | | | |
| HODGE, IAN (HM09874) | | ● | | | ● | | | ● | | | ● | ● | ● | ● | | | ● | | | |
| ORIENTAL HEALTH CENTRE (HM15381) | | | | | | | | | | ● | | | | ● | | | ● | | | |

| Business by County with Reference no. | Bladder Problems | Blood Pressure | Boils | Bowel Problems | Breast Problems | Breathing Problems | Bronchitis | Bruising | Bulimia | Bunions | Bursitis | Callices | Cancers | Cataracts | Catarrh | Cerebral Palsy | Circulation Problems | Cold Sores | Colds | Colic | Colitis | Conjunctivitis | Constipation | Convulsions | Corns | Coughs | Cramp | Cystitis |
|---|---|---|---|---|---|---|---|---|---|---|---|---|---|---|---|---|---|---|---|---|---|---|---|---|---|---|---|---|
| FOGGIE, MARGARET (HM07454) | | | | | | | | | | | | ● | | | | | | | | | | | | | ● | | | |
| HOLISTIC HEALING CENTRE (HM09964) | | | | | | | | | | | | | | | | | ● | | | | | | | | | | | |
| KIRRIEMUIR PHYSIO CLINIC (HM11723) | | | | | | | | | | | | | | | | | | | | | | | | | | | | |
| NATURAL HEALTH & CHIROPODY (HM14558) | | | | | | | | | | | | | | | | | ● | | | | | | | | | | | |
| NICOLL, ELAINE (HM14929) | | | | | | | | | | | | ● | | | | | | | | | | | | | ● | | | |
| **ARGYLL AND BUTE** | | | | | | | | | | | | | | | | | | | | | | | | | | | | |
| ACTIVE CHIROPRACTIC (HM00195) | | | | | | | | ● | | | ● | | | | | | | | | ● | | | | | | | | |
| COMPLEMENTARY HEALTH CENTRE (HM04922) | | | | | | | | | | | | ● | | | | | | | | | | | | | ● | | | |
| GIBSON, RONALD J (HM08045) | | ● | | | | | | | | | ● | | | | | | ● | | | | | | ● | | | | ● | |
| HOMEOPATHIC PODIATRIST/REFLEX (HM10078) | ● | ● | ● | ● | | ● | | ● | | | ● | | | | ● | | ● | | | | | | ● | | | | ● | |
| NATURAL THERAPY CENTRE (HM14648) | ● | ● | | ● | | | ● | ● | | | ● | | | | | | ● | | | | | | ● | | | | | |
| REIKI LIGHT (HM17138) | | | | | | | | | | | | | ● | | | | | | | | | | | | | | | |
| **AYRSHIRE (EAST)** | | | | | | | | | | | | | | | | | | | | | | | | | | | | |
| CRUISE, M & M (HM05520) | | | | | | | | | | | | ● | | | | | | | | | | | | | ● | | | |
| LITTLEJOHN, S (HM12473) | | | | | | | | | | | | ● | | | | | | | | | | | | | ● | | | |
| LYNN BROWN CLINICAL AROM (HM12772) | ● | ● | ● | ● | ● | ● | ● | | | | | | | | | | ● | ● | ● | ● | ● | | ● | | | ● | ● | ● |
| MCCABE, P J (HM13376) | | | | | | | | | | | | ● | | | | | | | | | | | | | ● | | | |
| **AYRSHIRE (NORTH)** | | | | | | | | | | | | | | | | | | | | | | | | | | | | |
| BODYSCENTS (HM02631) | | | | | | | | | | | | | | | | | | | | | | | | | | | | |
| BURNS, ALAN STEWART (HM03410) | | | | | | | | | | | | | | | | | | | | | | | | | | | | |
| CHIRO HEALTH CARE CLINIC (HM04282) | ● | ● | | ● | ● | ● | ● | | | | | | | | | | ● | | | ● | ● | | ● | | | | | |
| HANDS FOR FEET (HM08905) | | | | | | | | | | | | | | | | | | | | | | | | | | | | |
| PATON, MARY S (HM15824) | | | | | | | | | | | | ● | | | | | | | | | | | | | ● | | | |
| REID, E (HM17116) | ● | ● | | | | ● | | | | | | ● | | | | | ● | | | | | | ● | | ● | | | |
| **AYRSHIRE (SOUTH)** | | | | | | | | | | | | | | | | | | | | | | | | | | | | |
| BELL, W DOUGLAS (HM02091) | ● | ● | ● | ● | ● | ● | ● | ● | ● | | ● | ● | ● | ● | ● | | ● | ● | ● | ● | ● | ● | ● | ● | ● | ● | ● | ● |
| CARRICK CLINIC (HM03742) | ● | ● | | ● | | | ● | ● | | | ● | | | | ● | | ● | | ● | | | | ● | | | ● | ● | ● |
| CRUISE, M & M (HM05522) | | | | | | | | | | | | ● | | | | | | | | | | | | | ● | | | |
| ESSENCE OF HEALTH (HM06890) | ● | ● | ● | ● | ● | ● | ● | ● | ● | | ● | ● | ● | ● | ● | | ● | ● | ● | ● | ● | ● | ● | ● | ● | ● | ● | ● |
| HARDIE, ANNE (HM08966) | | | | | | | | | | | | | | | | | | | | | | | | | | | | |
| HEALTH STRESS & INJURIES (HM09404) | | ● | | | | | ● | | | | | | | | ● | | ● | | ● | ● | | | | | | | ● | |
| HEARTLAKE PHYSIOTHERAPY (HM09444) | | | | | | | | | | | | | | | | | | | | | | | | | | | | |
| HODGE, IAN (HM09874) | | ● | | ● | | | | | ● | | | | | | | | | | ● | | | | ● | | | ● | | |
| ORIENTAL HEALTH CENTRE (HM15381) | | | | | | | | | | | | | | | | | | | | | | | | | | | | |

# A - C Conditions treated at Practices/Businesses

| Business by County with Reference no. | Acne | Addiction | Adenoids | Aids | Alcoholism | Allergy | Alzheimer's Disease | Amnesia | Anaemia | Angina | Anorexia | Anxiety | Arthritis | Asthma | Athletes Foot | Autism |
|---|---|---|---|---|---|---|---|---|---|---|---|---|---|---|---|---|
| REID, A (HM17112) | | | | | | | | | | | | | | | | |
| SMITH, ALICIA (HM18712) | | ● | | | ● | | | | | | | ● | | | | |
| STEVENSON, SCOTT (HM19251) | | | | | | | | | | | | ● | ● | | | |
| **CLACKMANNANSHIRE** | | | | | | | | | | | | | | | | |
| ALTERNATIVE MEDICAL CLINIC (HM00711) | | | | | | | | | | | | ● | ● | | | |
| **DUMFRIES AND GALLOWAY** | | | | | | | | | | | | | | | | |
| BURTON, VICKY (HM03447) | | | | | | | | | | | | ● | | | | |
| CHLOE'S HERBS (HM04419) | ● | | | | | | | | | ● | | ● | ● | ● | ● | |
| DAVIDSON, MORAG (HM05788) | | | | | | | | | | | | | | | ● | |
| DUMFRIES HOLISTIC HEALTH CTRE (HM06386) | ● | ● | ● | ● | ● | ● | ● | ● | ● | ● | ● | ● | ● | ● | ● | ● |
| HEALTH STRESS & INJURIES CLNC (HM09405) | ● | ● | ● | ● | ● | ● | ● | ● | ● | ● | ● | ● | ● | ● | ● | ● |
| MCCLUNE, LORNA (HM13410) | | | | | | | | | | | | | ● | | ● | |
| MCCLYMOUNT, JENNIFER (HM13416) | | | | | | | | | | | | | | | ● | |
| RANKINE, VANORA (HM16939) | | | | | | | | | | | | | | | ● | |
| SHARP, LINDA A (HM18314) | ● | | | | | ● | | | | ● | | ● | ● | ● | | |
| **EDINBURGH (CITY OF)** | | | | | | | | | | | | | | | | |
| ACTIVE OSTEOPATHS (HM00200) | | | | | | | | | | | | | ● | ● | | |
| ALEXANDER TECHNIQUE (HM00517) | | | | | | | | | | | | ● | | ● | | |
| BABY HOLISTIC & MASSAGE (HM01464) | | | | | | | | | | | | | | | | |
| BIORADIANT HEALTH (HM02343) | | | | | | | | | | | | ● | | | | |
| BLACKHALL PHYSIOTHERAPY CLINIC (HM02445) | | | | | | | | | | | | | ● | | | |
| BLAIR, RICHARD (HM02475) | | | | ● | | | | ● | | | | ● | ● | ● | | |
| CHRISTIE, ADRIAN (HM04438) | | | | | | | | | | | | ● | | | | |
| DRUMMOND, IAN (HM06326) | | | | | | | | | | | | ● | | | | |
| E G H P (HM06468) | | ● | | | | | | | | | | ● | | | | |
| EDINBURGH ALEXANDER CENTRE (HM06606) | | | | | | | | | | | | ● | | | | |
| EDINBURGH FLOATARIUM (HM06611) | | | | | | | | | | | | | | | | |
| EDINBURGH HOMEOPATHIC CENTRE (HM06613) | | | | | | ● | | | | | | | ● | | | |
| EDINBURGH OSTEOPATHIC SURGERY (HM06615) | | | | | | | | | | | | | | | | |
| EDINBURGH PHYSIOTHERAPY CENTRE (HM06616) | | | | | | | | | | | | | | | ● | |
| EXCLUSIVE HYPNOTHERAPY (HM07019) | | ● | | | | | | | | | | ● | | | | |
| GARDINER, F (HM07872) | | ● | | | | | | | | | | ● | ● | | | |
| HAZEL, J M (HM09290) | | | | | | | | | | | | | | | ● | |
| HOLDEN, SHEENA (HM09934) | | | | | | | | | | | | ● | | | | |

| Business by County with Reference no. | Back Pain | Bacterial Infections | Baldness | Bereavement | Bladder Problems | Blood Pressure | Boils | Bowel Problems | Breast Problems | Breathing Problems | Bronchitis | Bruising | Bulimia | Bunions | Bursitis | Callices |
|---|---|---|---|---|---|---|---|---|---|---|---|---|---|---|---|---|
| REID, A (HM17112) | | | | | | | | | | | | | | | | ● |
| SMITH, ALICIA (HM18712) | | | | | | | | | | | | | | | | |
| STEVENSON, SCOTT (HM19251) | ● | | | | | | | | | | | | | | | |
| **CLACKMANNANSHIRE** | | | | | | | | | | | | | | | | |
| ALTERNATIVE MEDICAL CLINIC (HM00711) | ● | | ● | | | ● | | ● | | ● | | | | | | |
| **DUMFRIES AND GALLOWAY** | | | | | | | | | | | | | | | | |
| BURTON, VICKY (HM03447) | ● | | | | ● | | | ● | | ● | | | | | | |
| CHLOE'S HERBS (HM04419) | ● | ● | | | ● | | | ● | | ● | ● | | | | | |
| DAVIDSON, MORAG (HM05788) | | | | | | | | | | | | | | | | ● |
| DUMFRIES HOLISTIC HEALTH CTRE (HM06386) | ● | ● | ● | | ● | ● | ● | ● | ● | ● | ● | ● | ● | | ● | ● |
| HEALTH STRESS & INJURIES CLNC (HM09405) | ● | ● | ● | | ● | ● | ● | ● | ● | ● | ● | ● | ● | | ● | ● |
| MCCLUNE, LORNA (HM13410) | | | | | | | | | | | | | | ● | | ● |
| MCCLYMOUNT, JENNIFER (HM13416) | | | | | | | | | | | | | | | | ● |
| RANKINE, VANORA (HM16939) | | | | | | | | | | | | | | | | ● |
| SHARP, LINDA A (HM18314) | ● | | | | ● | ● | | ● | ● | ● | ● | ● | | | ● | |
| **EDINBURGH (CITY OF)** | | | | | | | | | | | | | | | | |
| ACTIVE OSTEOPATHS (HM00200) | ● | | | | | | | | | | | | | | | |
| ALEXANDER TECHNIQUE (HM00517) | ● | | | | | | | | | ● | | | | | | |
| BABY HOLISTIC & MASSAGE (HM01464) | | | | | | | | | | | | | | | | |
| BIORADIANT HEALTH (HM02343) | ● | | | | | | | | | | | | | | | |
| BLACKHALL PHYSIOTHERAPY CLINIC (HM02445) | ● | | | | | | | | | | | | | | | |
| BLAIR, RICHARD (HM02475) | ● | | | | ● | | | ● | ● | ● | | | | | ● | |
| CHRISTIE, ADRIAN (HM04438) | | | | | | | | | | | | | | | | |
| DRUMMOND, IAN (HM06326) | | | | | | | | | | | | | | | | |
| E G H P (HM06468) | ● | | | | | ● | | ● | | | | | | | | |
| EDINBURGH ALEXANDER CENTRE (HM06606) | ● | | | | | ● | | | | | | | | | | |
| EDINBURGH FLOATARIUM (HM06611) | | | | | | | | | | | | | | | | |
| EDINBURGH HOMEOPATHIC CENTRE (HM06613) | ● | | | | | | | | | | | | | | | |
| EDINBURGH OSTEOPATHIC SURGERY (HM06615) | ● | | | | | | | | | | | | | | | |
| EDINBURGH PHYSIOTHERAPY CENTRE (HM06616) | ● | | | | | | | | | | | | | | | |
| EXCLUSIVE HYPNOTHERAPY (HM07019) | | | | | ● | | | | | | | | | | | |
| GARDINER, F (HM07872) | ● | | | | ● | ● | | ● | | ● | | | | | | |
| HAZEL, J M (HM09290) | | | | | | | | | | | | | | | | |
| HOLDEN, SHEENA (HM09934) | | | | | | ● | | ● | | | | | | | | |

| Business by County with Reference no. | Cancers | Cataracts | Catarrh | Cerebral Palsy | Circulation Problems | Cold Sores | Colds | Colic | Colitis | Conjunctivitis | Constipation | Convulsions | Corns | Coughs | Cramp | Cystitis |
|---|---|---|---|---|---|---|---|---|---|---|---|---|---|---|---|---|
| REID, A (HM17112) | | | | | | | | | | | | | ● | | | |
| SMITH, ALICIA (HM18712) | | | | | | | | | | | | | | | | |
| STEVENSON, SCOTT (HM19251) | | | | | | | | | | | | | | | | |
| **CLACKMANNANSHIRE** | | | | | | | | | | | | | | | | |
| ALTERNATIVE MEDICAL CLINIC (HM00711) | ● | | | | ● | | | | | | ● | | | | ● | ● |
| **DUMFRIES AND GALLOWAY** | | | | | | | | | | | | | | | | |
| BURTON, VICKY (HM03447) | | | | | ● | | ● | | | | ● | | | | | |
| CHLOE'S HERBS (HM04419) | ● | | ● | | ● | ● | ● | ● | ● | ● | ● | | | ● | ● | ● |
| DAVIDSON, MORAG (HM05788) | | | | | | | | | | | | | ● | | | |
| DUMFRIES HOLISTIC HEALTH CTRE (HM06386) | ● | ● | ● | | ● | ● | ● | ● | ● | ● | ● | ● | ● | ● | ● | ● |
| HEALTH STRESS & INJURIES CLNC (HM09405) | ● | ● | ● | | ● | ● | ● | ● | ● | ● | ● | ● | ● | ● | ● | ● |
| MCCLUNE, LORNA (HM13410) | | | | | | | | | | | | | ● | | | |
| MCCLYMOUNT, JENNIFER (HM13416) | | | | | | | | | | | | | ● | | | |
| RANKINE, VANORA (HM16939) | | | | | | | | | | | | | ● | | | |
| SHARP, LINDA A (HM18314) | ● | | ● | | ● | ● | ● | ● | ● | | ● | | | ● | | ● |
| **EDINBURGH (CITY OF)** | | | | | | | | | | | | | | | | |
| ACTIVE OSTEOPATHS (HM00200) | | | | | | | | | | | | | | | | |
| ALEXANDER TECHNIQUE (HM00517) | | | | | | | | | | | | | | | | |
| BABY HOLISTIC & MASSAGE (HM01464) | | | | | | | | ● | | | ● | | | | | |
| BIORADIANT HEALTH (HM02343) | | | | | ● | | | | | | | | | | | |
| BLACKHALL PHYSIOTHERAPY CLINIC (HM02445) | | | | | | | | | | | | | | | | |
| BLAIR, RICHARD (HM02475) | | ● | ● | | ● | | ● | | | | ● | | | | | |
| CHRISTIE, ADRIAN (HM04438) | | | | | | | | | | | | | | | | |
| DRUMMOND, IAN (HM06326) | | | | | | | | | | | | | | | | |
| E G H P (HM06468) | | | | | | | | | | | | | | | | |
| EDINBURGH ALEXANDER CENTRE (HM06606) | | | | | | | | | | | | | | | | |
| EDINBURGH FLOATARIUM (HM06611) | | | | | | | | | | | | | ● | | | |
| EDINBURGH HOMEOPATHIC CENTRE (HM06613) | | | | | | | | | | | | | | | | ● |
| EDINBURGH OSTEOPATHIC SURGERY (HM06615) | | | | | | | | | | | | | | | ● | |
| EDINBURGH PHYSIOTHERAPY CENTRE (HM06616) | | | | | | | | | | | | | | | | |
| EXCLUSIVE HYPNOTHERAPY (HM07019) | | | | | | | | | | | | | | | | |
| GARDINER, F (HM07872) | | | | | ● | | ● | | | | ● | | | | | |
| HAZEL, J M (HM09290) | | | | | | | | | | | | | | | | |
| HOLDEN, SHEENA (HM09934) | | | | | | | | | | | ● | | | | | |

# A - C Conditions treated at Practices/Businesses

| Business by County with Reference no. | Acne | Addiction | Adenoids | Aids | Alcoholism | Allergy | Alzheimer's Disease | Amnesia | Anaemia | Angina | Anorexia | Anxiety | Arthritis | Asthma | Athletes Foot | Autism |
|---|---|---|---|---|---|---|---|---|---|---|---|---|---|---|---|---|
| IN HARMONY AROMATHERAPY (HM10595) | | | | | | | | | | | | ● | ● | | | |
| J W PHYSIOTHERAPY & SPORTS (HM10804) | | | | | | | | | | | | | ● | | | |
| J W PHYSIOTHERAPY & SPORTS (HM10805) | | | | | | | | | | | | | ● | | | |
| JENAI (HM10980) | | | | | | | | | | | | ● | ● | | | |
| KELLY, T G (HM11447) | | | | | | | | | | | | | | | ● | |
| KELLY, T G (HM11446) | | | | | | | | | | | | | | | ● | |
| LIVING MIND (HM12487) | | ● | | | | | | | | | | ● | | | | |
| LOGAN, CAROL (HM12565) | | | | | | | | | | | | ● | | ● | | |
| MACPHERSON, R G (HM12877) | | | | | | | | | | | | | | | ● | |
| MARCHMONT PHYSIOTHERAPY CLINIC (HM13073) | | | | | | | | | | | | | ● | | | |
| MARIPOSA AROMATHERAPY (HM13103) | | | | | | | | | | | | ● | ● | | | |
| MARSHALL, S C (HM13171) | | | | | | | | | | | | | | | ● | |
| MCDONALD, DAVID S (HM13456) | | | | | | | | | | | | | | | ● | |
| MCVITTIE, D (HM13623) | | | | | | | | | | | | ● | ● | ● | | |
| MOBILE CHIROPODY SERVICES (HM14028) | | | | | | | | | | | | | | | ● | |
| MORNINGSIDE PODIATRY SERVICE (HM14192) | | | | | | | | | | | | | | | ● | |
| N H S (HM14449) | | | | | | | | | | | | | | | ● | |
| OLIVER & STODDARD (HM15285) | | | | | | ● | | | | | | ● | | | | |
| PATTERSON, YVONNE (HM15833) | | | | | | | | | | | | ● | ● | | | |
| PSYCHIC AND LIFE SOLUTIONS (HM16685) | | | | | | | | | | | | ● | | | | |
| ROBERT STONE THERAPEUTICS (HM17398) | | | | ● | | | | | | | | ● | | | | |
| RUMNEY, KATHLEEN (HM17748) | ● | ● | ● | ● | ● | ● | ● | ● | ● | ● | ● | ● | ● | ● | ● | ● |
| SHENTON, DIANNE (HM18402) | | | | | | | | | | | | | | | ● | |
| SKEDD, L A (HM18629) | | | | | | | | | | | | | | | ● | |
| TARA ROKPA ENDINBURGH (HM19699) | ● | | | | | | | | | | | ● | | | | |
| WARD, ELIZABETH (HM20900) | | | | | | | | | | | | ● | ● | ● | | |
| WELLBEING (HM21146) | | | | | | | | | | | | ● | | | | |
| **FALKIRK** | | | | | | | | | | | | | | | | |
| AESTHETICA TOTAL SKIN & BODY (HM00411) | | | | | | | | | | | | ● | ● | | | |
| ANGUS WILLIAMSON CLINIC (HM00885) | | | | | | | | | | | | ● | | | | |
| FALKIRK CHIROPRACTIC CLINIC (HM07074) | | | | | | | | | | | | | ● | | | |
| GRANT, LESLIE & DAWN (HM08385) | | | | | | | | | | | | | | | ● | |
| GRANT, LESLIE AND DAWN (HM08386) | | | | | | | | | | | | | | | ● | |
| KELIMAR CLINIC (HM11416) | | | | | | | | | | | | | | | | |

| Business by County with Reference no. | Back Pain | Bacterial Infections | Baldness | Bereavement | Bladder Problems | Blood Pressure | Boils | Bowel Problems | Breast Problems | Breathing Problems | Bronchitis | Bruising | Bulimia | Bunions | Bursitis | Callices |
|---|---|---|---|---|---|---|---|---|---|---|---|---|---|---|---|---|
| IN HARMONY AROMATHERAPY (HM10595) | ● | | | | | | | | | | | | | | | |
| J W PHYSIOTHERAPY & SPORTS (HM10804) | ● | | | | | | | | | | | | | | ● | |
| J W PHYSIOTHERAPY & SPORTS (HM10805) | ● | | | | | | | | | | | | | | ● | |
| JENAI (HM10980) | ● | | | | | | | | | | | | | | | |
| KELLY, T G (HM11447) | | | | | | | | | | | | | | | | ● |
| KELLY, T G (HM11446) | | | | | | | | | | | | | | | | ● |
| LIVING MIND (HM12487) | ● | | | | | | | ● | | | | | | | | |
| LOGAN, CAROL (HM12565) | ● | | | | | ● | | ● | | | | | ● | | | |
| MACPHERSON, R G (HM12877) | | | | | | | | | | | | | | | | ● |
| MARCHMONT PHYSIOTHERAPY CLINIC (HM13073) | ● | | | | | | | | | | | | | | | |
| MARIPOSA AROMATHERAPY (HM13103) | ● | | | | | | | | | | | | | | | |
| MARSHALL, S C (HM13171) | | | | | | | | | | | | | | | | ● |
| MCDONALD, DAVID S (HM13456) | | | | | | | | | | | | | | | | ● |
| MCVITTIE, D (HM13623) | ● | | | | ● | ● | | ● | | | | | | | | |
| MOBILE CHIROPODY SERVICES (HM14028) | | | | | | | | | | | | | | | | |
| MORNINGSIDE PODIATRY SERVICE (HM14192) | | | | | | | | | | | | | | | | ● |
| N H S (HM14449) | | | | | | | | | | | | | | | | ● |
| OLIVER & STODDARD (HM15285) | | ● | | | ● | ● | | ● | | | | | | | | |
| PATTERSON, YVONNE (HM15833) | ● | | | | | | | | | | | | | | | |
| PSYCHIC AND LIFE SOLUTIONS (HM16685) | | | | | | | | | | | | | | | | |
| ROBERT STONE THERAPEUTICS (HM17398) | ● | | | | | | | | | | | | | | | |
| RUMNEY, KATHLEEN (HM17748) | ● | ● | ● | | ● | ● | ● | ● | ● | ● | ● | ● | ● | | ● | ● |
| SHENTON, DIANNE (HM18402) | | | | | | | | | | | | | | | | ● |
| SKEDD, L A (HM18629) | | | | | | | | | | | | | | | | |
| TARA ROKPA ENDINBURGH (HM19699) | | | | | ● | ● | | | | ● | | | | | | |
| WARD, ELIZABETH (HM20900) | ● | | | | | | | | | | | | | | | |
| WELLBEING (HM21146) | ● | | | | | | | | | | | | | | | |
| **FALKIRK** | | | | | | | | | | | | | | | | |
| AESTHETICA TOTAL SKIN & BODY (HM00411) | ● | | | | | | | | | | | | | | | |
| ANGUS WILLIAMSON CLINIC (HM00885) | ● | | | | | | | | | | | | | | | |
| FALKIRK CHIROPRACTIC CLINIC (HM07074) | ● | | | | | | | | | | | | | | | |
| GRANT, LESLIE & DAWN (HM08385) | | | | | | | | | | | | | | | | ● |
| GRANT, LESLIE AND DAWN (HM08386) | | | | | | | | | | | | | | | | ● |
| KELIMAR CLINIC (HM11416) | ● | | | | | | | | | | | | | | | |

| Business by County with Reference no. | Cancers | Cataracts | Catarrh | Cerebral Palsy | Circulation Problems | Cold Sores | Colds | Colic | Colitis | Conjunctivitis | Constipation | Convulsions | Corns | Coughs | Cramp | Cystitis |
|---|---|---|---|---|---|---|---|---|---|---|---|---|---|---|---|---|
| IN HARMONY AROMATHERAPY (HM10595) | | | | | | | | | | | | | | | | |
| J W PHYSIOTHERAPY & SPORTS (HM10804) | | | | | | | | | | | | | | | | |
| J W PHYSIOTHERAPY & SPORTS (HM10805) | | | | | | | | | | | | | | | | |
| JENAI (HM10980) | | | | | | | | | | | | | | | | |
| KELLY, T G (HM11447) | | | | | | | | | | | | | ● | | | |
| KELLY, T G (HM11446) | | | | | | | | | | | | | ● | | | |
| LIVING MIND (HM12487) | ● | | | | | | ● | | | | ● | | | | ● | |
| LOGAN, CAROL (HM12565) | | | | | | | | | | | | | | | | |
| MACPHERSON, R G (HM12877) | | | | | | | | | | | | | ● | | | |
| MARCHMONT PHYSIOTHERAPY CLINIC (HM13073) | | | | | | | | | | | | | | | | |
| MARIPOSA AROMATHERAPY (HM13103) | | | | | | | | | | | | | | | | |
| MARSHALL, S C (HM13171) | | | | | | | | | | | | | ● | | | |
| MCDONALD, DAVID S (HM13456) | | | | | | | | | | | | | ● | | | |
| MCVITTIE, D (HM13623) | | | | | ● | | | | | | ● | | | | | |
| MOBILE CHIROPODY SERVICES (HM14028) | | | | | | | | | | | | | | | | |
| MORNINGSIDE PODIATRY SERVICE (HM14192) | | | | | | | | | | | | | ● | | | |
| N H S (HM14449) | | | | | | | | | | | | | ● | | | |
| OLIVER & STODDARD (HM15285) | | | | | ● | | | | | | ● | | | | | |
| PATTERSON, YVONNE (HM15833) | | | | | | | | | | | | | | | | |
| PSYCHIC AND LIFE SOLUTIONS (HM16685) | | | | | | | | | | | | | | | | |
| ROBERT STONE THERAPEUTICS (HM17398) | | | | | ● | | | | | | | | | | | |
| RUMNEY, KATHLEEN (HM17748) | ● | ● | ● | | ● | ● | ● | ● | ● | ● | ● | ● | ● | ● | ● | ● |
| SHENTON, DIANNE (HM18402) | | | | | | | | | | | | | ● | | | |
| SKEDD, L A (HM18629) | | | | | | | | | | | | | | | | |
| TARA ROKPA ENDINBURGH (HM19699) | | | | | | | | | | | | | | | | |
| WARD, ELIZABETH (HM20900) | | | | | | | | | | | | | | | | |
| WELLBEING (HM21146) | ● | | | | | | | | | | | | | | | |
| **FALKIRK** | | | | | | | | | | | | | | | | |
| AESTHETICA TOTAL SKIN & BODY (HM00411) | | | | | | | | | | | | | | | | |
| ANGUS WILLIAMSON CLINIC (HM00885) | | | | | | | | | | | | | | | | |
| FALKIRK CHIROPRACTIC CLINIC (HM07074) | | | | | ● | | | | | | | | | | | |
| GRANT, LESLIE & DAWN (HM08385) | | | | | | | | | | | | | ● | | | |
| GRANT, LESLIE AND DAWN (HM08386) | | | | | | | | | | | | | ● | | | |
| KELIMAR CLINIC (HM11416) | | | | | | | | | | | | | | | | |

# A - C Conditions treated at Practices/Businesses

| Business by County with Reference no. | Acne | Addiction | Adenoids | Aids | Alcoholism | Allergy | Alzheimer's Disease | Amnesia | Anaemia | Angina | Anorexia | Anxiety | Arthritis | Asthma | Athletes Foot | Autism |
|---|---|---|---|---|---|---|---|---|---|---|---|---|---|---|---|---|
| NATURAL HEALING CENTRE (HM14543) | | | | | | | | | | | | ● | ● | ● | | |
| **FIFE** | | | | | | | | | | | | | | | | |
| BODYNEEDS (HM02629) | ● | ● | ● | ● | ● | ● | ● | ● | ● | ● | ● | ● | ● | ● | ● | ● |
| CAMERON, WILLIAM (HM03588) | | | | | | | | | | | | | | | ● | |
| CAROLE'S MOBILE THERAPIST (HM03718) | | | | | | | | | | | | ● | ● | | | |
| COMPLEMENTARY THERAPY CLINIC (HM04949) | ● | ● | | | ● | | | | | | | ● | ● | ● | ● | |
| DAVIDSON, ANGELA (HM05785) | | ● | | | | | | | | ● | ● | ● | ● | ● | ● | |
| KEEP IN STEP (HM11394) | | | | | | | | | | | | | | | ● | |
| LEUTER, PAM () | | | | | | | | | | | | | | | | |
| NEAT FEET (HM14743) | | ● | | ● | ● | | | | | ● | ● | ● | ● | ● | | |
| O'BRIAN, D (HM15171) | | | | | | | | | | | | | | | ● | |
| SHEERINS, ROZ (HM18370) | | | | | | | | | | | | | | | ● | |
| ST ANDREWS OSTEOPATHS (HM19065) | | | | | | | | | | | | | | ● | | |
| TOLBOOTH HOUSE (HM20117) | ● | ● | | | | ● | | | | | | ● | ● | | ● | |
| TWA ACRES HYPNO TRAINING CTRE (HM20447) | ● | ● | | | | ● | | | | | | ● | | ● | | |
| **GLASGOW (CITY OF)** | | | | | | | | | | | | | | | | |
| ABOUT FACE (HM00131) | | | | | | | | | | | | | | | | |
| ACTIVE CHIROPRACTIC (HM00194) | | | | | | | | | | | | | ● | | | |
| ANDERSON DOE PODIATRY CLINIC (HM00809) | | | | | | | | | | | | | ● | | ● | |
| ANNE PENMAN THERAPY (HM00900) | | ● | | | | | | | | | | ● | | | | |
| BEARSDEN CHIROPRACTIC CLINIC (HM01971) | | | | | | | | | | | | | | | | |
| BEHIND THE VEIL (HM02068) | ● | | | | | ● | | | | | | ● | ● | ● | | |
| BLACK, JIM (HM02424) | | | | | | | | | | | | | | | ● | |
| BOTHWELL PHYSIOTHERAPY (HM02733) | | | | | | | | | | | | | ● | | | |
| CARRICK STREET PHYSIO & SPORT (HM03743) | | | | | | | | | | | | | ● | | | |
| CLINIC AT CHARING CROSS (HM04679) | ● | | | | | | | | | | | | | | | |
| CONWAY, VALERIE (DR) (HM05034) | ● | | ● | | | ● | | | | ● | | ● | ● | ● | | |
| CONWAY, VALERIE A (DR) (HM05035) | ● | | ● | | | ● | | | | ● | | ● | ● | ● | | |
| FITZPATRICK, J H (HM07374) | | | | | | | | | | | | | | | ● | |
| HARVEST CLINIC (HM09152) | ● | ● | | | ● | ● | | | | | ● | ● | ● | | | |
| HOLISTIC HEALING & HYP (HM09961) | | ● | | | | | | | | | | | | | | |
| HUMAN PERFORMANCE CLINIC (HM10364) | | ● | | | ● | | | | | | ● | ● | | | | |
| LAMBERT, C W (HM11895) | | | | | | | | | | | | | | | ● | |
| LASER THERAPY CENTRE (HM11984) | | | | | | | | | | | | ● | | | | |

| Business by County with Reference no. | Back Pain | Bacterial Infections | Baldness | Bereavement | Bladder Problems | Blood Pressure | Boils | Bowel Problems | Breast Problems | Breathing Problems | Bronchitis | Bruising | Bulimia | Bunions | Bursitis |
|---|---|---|---|---|---|---|---|---|---|---|---|---|---|---|---|
| NATURAL HEALING CENTRE (HM14543) | ● | | | | | ● | | | | | | | | | |
| **FIFE** | | | | | | | | | | | | | | | |
| BODYNEEDS (HM02629) | ● | ● | ● | | ● | ● | ● | ● | ● | ● | ● | ● | ● | | ● |
| CAMERON, WILLIAM (HM03588) | | | | | | | | | | | | | | | |
| CAROLE'S MOBILE THERAPIST (HM03718) | ● | | | | | | | | | | | | | | |
| COMPLEMENTARY THERAPY CLINIC (HM04949) | ● | ● | | ● | ● | | ● | ● | | ● | | ● | | | |
| DAVIDSON, ANGELA (HM05785) | ● | | | | | ● | | ● | | ● | | | | | ● |
| KEEP IN STEP (HM11394) | | | | | | | | | | | | | | | |
| LEUTER, PAM () | | | | | | | | | | | | | | | |
| NEAT FEET (HM14743) | ● | | | | | ● | | ● | | ● | | | ● | | |
| O'BRIAN, D (HM15171) | | | | | | | | | | | | | | | |
| SHEERINS, ROZ (HM18370) | | | | | | | | | | | | | | | |
| ST ANDREWS OSTEOPATHS (HM19065) | ● | | | | | | | ● | | ● | | | | | |
| TOLBOOTH HOUSE (HM20117) | ● | | | | | | | ● | | | | | | | |
| TWA ACRES HYPNO TRAINING CTRE (HM20447) | | | | | ● | ● | | ● | ● | ● | | | ● | | |
| **GLASGOW (CITY OF)** | | | | | | | | | | | | | | | |
| ABOUT FACE (HM00131) | | | | | | ● | | | | | | | | | |
| ACTIVE CHIROPRACTIC (HM00194) | ● | | | | | | | | | | | ● | | | ● |
| ANDERSON DOE PODIATRY CLINIC (HM00809) | ● | | | | | | | | | | | ● | | | |
| ANNE PENMAN THERAPY (HM00900) | | | | | | | | | | | | | | | |
| BEARSDEN CHIROPRACTIC CLINIC (HM01971) | ● | | | | | | | | | | | | | | |
| BEHIND THE VEIL (HM02068) | ● | | | | | ● | | | | ● | ● | | | | |
| BLACK, JIM (HM02424) | | | | | | | | | | | | | | | |
| BOTHWELL PHYSIOTHERAPY (HM02733) | ● | | | | | | | | | | | | | | |
| CARRICK STREET PHYSIO & SPORT (HM03743) | ● | | | | | | | | | | | | | | |
| CLINIC AT CHARING CROSS (HM04679) | ● | | | | | | | | ● | | | | | | |
| CONWAY, VALERIE (DR) (HM05034) | ● | ● | | | ● | ● | ● | ● | ● | ● | ● | ● | | | ● |
| CONWAY, VALERIE A (DR) (HM05035) | ● | ● | | | ● | ● | ● | ● | ● | ● | ● | ● | | | ● |
| FITZPATRICK, J H (HM07374) | | | | | | | | | | | | | | | |
| HARVEST CLINIC (HM09152) | ● | | | | | ● | | ● | | | ● | | ● | | |
| HOLISTIC HEALING & HYP (HM09961) | | | | | | | | | | | | | ● | | |
| HUMAN PERFORMANCE CLINIC (HM10364) | | | | | ● | ● | | ● | | | | | ● | | |
| LAMBERT, C W (HM11895) | | | | | | | | | | | | | | | |
| LASER THERAPY CENTRE (HM11984) | | | | | | | | | | | | | | | |

| Business by County with Reference no. | Callices | Cancers | Cataracts | Catarrh | Cerebral Palsy | Circulation Problems | Cold Sores | Colds | Colic | Colitis | Conjunctivitis | Constipation | Convulsions | Corns | Coughs | Cramp | Cystitis |
|---|---|---|---|---|---|---|---|---|---|---|---|---|---|---|---|---|---|
| NATURAL HEALING CENTRE (HM14543) | | | | ● | | ● | | ● | | | | ● | | | | ● | ● |
| **FIFE** | | | | | | | | | | | | | | | | | |
| BODYNEEDS (HM02629) | ● | ● | ● | ● | | ● | ● | ● | ● | ● | ● | ● | ● | ● | ● | ● | ● |
| CAMERON, WILLIAM (HM03588) | ● | | | | | | | | | | | | | ● | | | |
| CAROLE'S MOBILE THERAPIST (HM03718) | | | | | | | | | | | | | | | | | |
| COMPLEMENTARY THERAPY CLINIC (HM04949) | | | | | | ● | ● | ● | | ● | ● | ● | | | | ● | |
| DAVIDSON, ANGELA (HM05785) | | ● | | | | ● | | | | ● | | ● | | | | | |
| KEEP IN STEP (HM11394) | ● | | | | | | | | | | | | | ● | | | |
| LEUTER, PAM () | | | | | | ● | | | | | | | | | | ● | |
| NEAT FEET (HM14743) | | ● | | | | ● | | ● | | | | ● | | | | ● | ● |
| O'BRIAN, D (HM15171) | ● | | | | | | | | | | | | | ● | | | |
| SHEERINS, ROZ (HM18370) | ● | | | | | | | | | | | | | ● | | | |
| ST ANDREWS OSTEOPATHS (HM19065) | | | | | | | | | | | | | | | | | |
| TOLBOOTH HOUSE (HM20117) | | | | | | | | | | | | | | | ● | | |
| TWA ACRES HYPNO TRAINING CTRE (HM20447) | | ● | | | | | | | | | | | | | | | |
| **GLASGOW (CITY OF)** | | | | | | | | | | | | | | | | | |
| ABOUT FACE (HM00131) | | | | | | | | | | | | ● | | | | | |
| ACTIVE CHIROPRACTIC (HM00194) | | | | | | | | | ● | | | | | | | | |
| ANDERSON DOE PODIATRY CLINIC (HM00809) | ● | | | | | | | | | | | | | ● | | ● | |
| ANNE PENMAN THERAPY (HM00900) | | | | | | | | | | | | | | | | | |
| BEARSDEN CHIROPRACTIC CLINIC (HM01971) | | | | | | | | | | | | | | | | | |
| BEHIND THE VEIL (HM02068) | | | | | | ● | | | | | | ● | | | ● | ● | |
| BLACK, JIM (HM02424) | ● | | | | | | | | | | | | | ● | | | |
| BOTHWELL PHYSIOTHERAPY (HM02733) | | | | | | | | | | | | | | | | | |
| CARRICK STREET PHYSIO & SPORT (HM03743) | | | | | | | | | | | | | | | | | |
| CLINIC AT CHARING CROSS (HM04679) | | | | | | | ● | | | | | | | | | | |
| CONWAY, VALERIE (DR) (HM05034) | | | | ● | | ● | ● | ● | ● | ● | ● | ● | | | ● | ● | ● |
| CONWAY, VALERIE A (DR) (HM05035) | | | | ● | | ● | ● | ● | ● | ● | ● | ● | | | ● | ● | ● |
| FITZPATRICK, J H (HM07374) | | | | | | | | | | | | | | | | | |
| HARVEST CLINIC (HM09152) | | ● | | ● | | ● | ● | ● | | | | ● | | | ● | ● | ● |
| HOLISTIC HEALING & HYP (HM09961) | | | | | | | | | | | | | | | | | |
| HUMAN PERFORMANCE CLINIC (HM10364) | | | | | | | | | | | | | | | | | |
| LAMBERT, C W (HM11895) | ● | | | | | | | | | | | | | ● | | | |
| LASER THERAPY CENTRE (HM11984) | | | | | | | | | | | | | | | | | |

# A - C Conditions treated at Practices/Businesses

| Business by County with Reference no. | Acne | Addiction | Adenoids | Aids | Alcoholism | Allergy | Alzheimer's Disease | Amnesia | Anaemia | Angina | Anorexia | Anxiety | Arthritis | Asthma | Athletes Foot | Autism | Back Pain | Bacterial Infections | Baldness | Bereavement | Bladder Problems | Blood Pressure | Boils | Bowel Problems |
|---|---|---|---|---|---|---|---|---|---|---|---|---|---|---|---|---|---|---|---|---|---|---|---|---|
| LAURIE, A (HM12015) | | | | | | | | | | | | | | | ● | | | | | | | | | |
| LONG RIVER TAI CHI CIRCLE (HM12617) | | | | | | | | | | | | ● | ● | | | | | | | | | ● | | |
| MARY HERAGHTY AT HEALTHY FEET (HM13222) | | | | | | | | | | | | | | | ● | | | | | | ● | ● | | |
| MCLAREN, CATH RENA (HM13539) | ● | ● | | | | ● | | | | | | ● | ● | ● | | | ● | | | | ● | ● | | ● |
| MCLEAN, A M (HM13551) | | | | | | | | | | | | | ● | | ● | | ● | ● | | | | | | |
| MCTIMONEY CHIROPRACTIC CLINIC (HM13611) | | | | | | | | | | | | | | | | | ● | | | | | | | |
| NUTRITION WORLD (HM15126) | ● | ● | | ● | ● | ● | ● | | ● | ● | ● | ● | ● | ● | ● | ● | ● | ● | ● | | ● | ● | ● | ● |
| PLUIDGE, MARK (HM16379) | | | | | | | | | | | | | | | ● | | | | | | | | | |
| RHODIE, ANDREA (HM17231) | | | | | | | | | | | | ● | ● | | | | | | | | | | | |
| ROLLAND, C R (HM17563) | | | | | | | | | | | | | | | ● | | | | | | | | | |
| SCHOLL CENTRE (HM18039) | | | | | | | | | | | | | | | ● | | | | | | | | | |
| SHAWLANDS HYPNOTHERAPY CLINIC (HM18352) | | | | | | ● | | | | | | ● | | | | | | | | | | ● | | |
| SINO-HERBAL CLINIC (HM18615) | ● | | | | | ● | | | | | | ● | ● | ● | ● | | ● | ● | | | ● | ● | | |
| STEWART, JIM (DR) (HM19270) | | | | | | | | | | | ● | ● | | | | | | | | | | | | ● |
| THERAPY OF LIFE CLINIC (HM19905) | ● | ● | | ● | ● | ● | | ● | | | | ● | ● | ● | ● | | ● | ● | | | | ● | ● | ● |
| WEST END THERAPY CENTRE (HM21221) | ● | ● | ● | ● | ● | ● | ● | ● | ● | ● | ● | ● | ● | ● | ● | ● | ● | ● | ● | | ● | ● | ● | ● |
| **HIGHLAND** | | | | | | | | | | | | | | | | | | | | | | | | |
| BUMBLE - BEE'S PHYSIO (HM03347) | | | | | | | | | | | | | ● | | | | ● | | | | | ● | | |
| GENTLE WAYS (HM07980) | | | | | | | | | | | | ● | | | | | | | | | | | | |
| HARMONOLOGY CENTRE (HM09017) | | | | | | | | | | | | | | | | | | | | | | | | |
| HEALTH CORNER (HM09383) | | ● | | | | ● | | | | | | ● | ● | ● | | ● | ● | | | | ● | ● | | ● |
| PUFFIN HYDROTHERAPY POOL (HM16743) | | | | | | | | | | | | | | | | | ● | | | | | | | |
| TAYLOR, JUNE (HM19773) | | | | | | | | | | ● | | ● | ● | ● | | | ● | ● | | | ● | ● | | |
| WAH, G (HM20735) | | | | | | | | | | ● | | ● | ● | ● | | ● | ● | ● | | | ● | ● | | |
| **INVERCLYDE** | | | | | | | | | | | | | | | | | | | | | | | | |
| INVERCLYDE OSTEOPATHIC CLINIC (HM10704) | ● | | | | | | | | | | | ● | | ● | | ● | ● | | | | | | | |
| KELLERMANS (HM11418) | | | | | | | | | | | | ● | ● | ● | | | ● | | | | ● | | | |
| **LANARKSHIRE (NORTH)** | | | | | | | | | | | | | | | | | | | | | | | | |
| REGISTERED HOMEOPATH (HM17103) | ● | | ● | | | ● | ● | ● | ● | ● | ● | ● | ● | ● | | ● | ● | ● | | | ● | ● | ● | ● |
| SEMPRE LIBERA (HM18224) | | | | | | | | | | | | ● | ● | | | | ● | | | | | | | |
| STRATH NATURAL THERAPIES (HM19371) | | | | | | | | | | | | ● | | | | | ● | | | | | ● | | ● |
| **LANARKSHIRE (SOUTH)** | | | | | | | | | | | | | | | | | | | | | | | | |
| QUINN, JIM (HM16810) | ● | ● | ● | | | ● | ● | ● | ● | ● | ● | ● | ● | ● | ● | ● | ● | ● | ● | ● | ● | ● | ● | ● |
| ROBB, A (DR) (HM17387) | ● | ● | ● | ● | ● | ● | ● | ● | ● | ● | ● | ● | ● | ● | ● | ● | ● | ● | ● | | ● | ● | ● | ● |

| Business by County with Reference no. | Breast Problems | Breathing Problems | Bronchitis | Bruising | Bulimia | Bunions | Bursitis | Callices | Cancers | Cataracts | Catarrh | Cerebral Palsy | Circulation Problems | Cold Sores | Colds | Colic | Colitis | Conjunctivitis | Constipation | Convulsions | Corns | Coughs | Cramp | Cystitis |
|---|---|---|---|---|---|---|---|---|---|---|---|---|---|---|---|---|---|---|---|---|---|---|---|---|
| LAURIE, A (HM12015) | | | | | | | | ● | | | | | | | | | | | | | ● | | | |
| LONG RIVER TAI CHI CIRCLE (HM12617) | | ● | | | | | | | | | | | ● | | | | | | | | | | | |
| MARY HERAGHTY AT HEALTHY FEET (HM13222) | | | | | | | | | | | | | ● | | | | | | | | | | | |
| MCLAREN, CATH RENA (HM13539) | | ● | | | | | | | | | ● | | ● | | ● | ● | ● | ● | ● | | | ● | ● | ● |
| MCLEAN, A M (HM13551) | | | | ● | | | ● | | | | | | ● | | | | | | | | | | ● | |
| MCTIMONEY CHIROPRACTIC CLINIC (HM13611) | | | | | | | | | | | | | | | | | | | | | | | | |
| NUTRITION WORLD (HM15126) | ● | ● | ● | ● | ● | | ● | | ● | ● | ● | | ● | ● | ● | ● | ● | ● | ● | ● | | ● | ● | ● |
| PLUIDGE, MARK (HM16379) | | | | | | | | ● | | | | | | | | | | | | | ● | | | |
| RHODIE, ANDREA (HM17231) | | | | | | | | | | | | | | | | | | | | | | | | |
| ROLLAND, C R (HM17563) | | | | | | | | | | | | | | | | | | | | | | | | |
| SCHOLL CENTRE (HM18039) | | | | | | | | ● | | | | | | | | | | | | | ● | | | |
| SHAWLANDS HYPNOTHERAPY CLINIC (HM18352) | | | | | | | | | | | | | | | | | | | | | | | | |
| SINO-HERBAL CLINIC (HM18615) | | | ● | | | | | | ● | | ● | | | ● | | | | | | | | ● | ● | ● |
| STEWART, JIM (DR) (HM19270) | | | | | ● | | | | ● | | | | | | | | | | | | | | | |
| THERAPY OF LIFE CLINIC (HM19905) | | ● | ● | ● | | | | | ● | | ● | | ● | ● | ● | ● | | | ● | | | ● | ● | ● |
| WEST END THERAPY CENTRE (HM21221) | ● | ● | ● | ● | ● | | ● | ● | ● | ● | ● | | ● | ● | ● | ● | ● | ● | ● | ● | ● | ● | ● | ● |
| **HIGHLAND** | | | | | | | | | | | | | | | | | | | | | | | | |
| BUMBLE - BEE'S PHYSIO (HM03347) | | ● | ● | | | | | | | | | | ● | | | | | | ● | | | | | |
| GENTLE WAYS (HM07980) | | | | | | | | | | | | | | | | | | | | | | | | |
| HARMONOLOGY CENTRE (HM09017) | | | | | | | | | ● | | | | | | | | | | | | | | | |
| HEALTH CORNER (HM09383) | | ● | ● | | | | | | | | | | ● | | ● | | | | ● | | | | | ● |
| PUFFIN HYDROTHERAPY POOL (HM16743) | | | | | | | | | | | | ● | | | | | | | | | | | | |
| TAYLOR, JUNE (HM19773) | ● | ● | | | ● | | | | ● | | | | ● | | ● | | | | ● | | | ● | ● | ● |
| WAH, G (HM20735) | | ● | ● | | ● | | | | ● | | ● | | | | | | | | ● | | | ● | ● | ● |
| **INVERCLYDE** | | | | | | | | | | | | | | | | | | | | | | | | |
| INVERCLYDE OSTEOPATHIC CLINIC (HM10704) | | | ● | ● | | | | | | | ● | | ● | ● | ● | ● | | | ● | | | | | ● |
| KELLERMANS (HM11418) | ● | ● | | | | | | | | | ● | | ● | | | | | | ● | | | | | |
| **LANARKSHIRE (NORTH)** | | | | | | | | | | | | | | | | | | | | | | | | |
| REGISTERED HOMEOPATH (HM17103) | ● | ● | ● | ● | ● | | ● | ● | ● | | ● | | ● | ● | ● | ● | ● | ● | ● | ● | ● | ● | ● | ● |
| SEMPRE LIBERA (HM18224) | | | | | | | | | | | | | | | | | | | | | | | | |
| STRATH NATURAL THERAPIES (HM19371) | | | | | | | | | | | | | | | | | | | ● | | | | | |
| **LANARKSHIRE (SOUTH)** | | | | | | | | | | | | | | | | | | | | | | | | |
| QUINN, JIM (HM16810) | ● | ● | ● | ● | ● | ● | ● | ● | ● | ● | ● | | ● | ● | ● | ● | ● | ● | ● | ● | ● | ● | ● | ● |
| ROBB, A (DR) (HM17387) | ● | ● | ● | ● | ● | | ● | ● | ● | ● | ● | | ● | ● | ● | ● | ● | ● | ● | ● | ● | ● | ● | ● |

# A - C Conditions treated at Practices/Businesses

Business by County with Reference no.

| Business by County with Reference no. | Acne | Addiction | Adenoids | Aids | Alcoholism | Allergy | Alzheimer's Disease | Amnesia | Anaemia | Angina | Anorexia | Anxiety | Arthritis | Asthma | Athletes Foot | Autism | Back Pain | Bacterial Infections | Baldness | Bereavement | Bladder Problems | Blood Pressure | Boils | Bowel Problems |
|---|---|---|---|---|---|---|---|---|---|---|---|---|---|---|---|---|---|---|---|---|---|---|---|---|
| **LOTHIAN (EAST)** | | | | | | | | | | | | | | | | | | | | | | | | |
| AROMA (HM01042) | ● | ● | ● | ● | ● | ● | ● | ● | ● | ● | ● | ● | ● | ● | ● | ● | ● | ● | ● | | ● | ● | ● | ● |
| EAST LOTHIAN PHYSIO CENTRE (HM06518) | | | | | | | | | | | | | ● | | | | ● | | | | | | | |
| FRASER, GORDON (HM07696) | ● | ● | ● | ● | ● | ● | ● | ● | ● | ● | ● | ● | ● | ● | ● | ● | ● | ● | ● | | ● | ● | ● | ● |
| **LOTHIAN (MID)** | | | | | | | | | | | | | | | | | | | | | | | | |
| CRYSTAL SANCTUARY (HM05532) | | | | | | | | | | | | ● | | | | | | | | | ● | ● | | ● |
| HAMILTON, JAMES (HM08844) | | | | | | | | | | | | ● | ● | ● | ● | | ● | | | | | ● | | |
| NATURAL HEALTH CENTRE (HM14573) | ● | ● | ● | ● | ● | ● | ● | ● | ● | ● | ● | ● | ● | ● | ● | ● | ● | ● | ● | | ● | ● | ● | ● |
| NEW DUNDAS CLINIC (HM14817) | | | | | | | | | | | | | ● | | | | ● | | | | | | | |
| RADIANT COLOUR (HM16847) | | ● | | | | ● | | | | | ● | ● | | | | | | | | | | | | |
| SCOTTISH KINESIOLOGY CENTRE (HM18134) | ● | ● | ● | ● | ● | ● | ● | ● | ● | ● | ● | ● | ● | ● | ● | ● | ● | ● | ● | | ● | ● | ● | ● |
| **LOTHIAN (WEST)** | | | | | | | | | | | | | | | | | | | | | | | | |
| DUIGNAN, KAREN (HM06372) | | ● | | | | | | | | | | ● | | | | | | | | | | | | |
| GILL, SHIRLEY (HM08080) | | | | | | | | | | | | ● | ● | ● | | | | | | | ● | ● | | ● |
| LINLITHGOW PHYSIO PRACTICE (HM12438) | | | | | | | | | | | | | ● | | | | ● | | | | | | | |
| VINCES, DENISE (HM20674) | | | | | | | | | | | | ● | ● | | | | | | | | ● | ● | | ● |
| **MORAY** | | | | | | | | | | | | | | | | | | | | | | | | |
| AROMANTIC (HM01080) | ● | | | | | ● | | | | | | | ● | | ● | | ● | | | | | | | |
| ELGIN CHIROPRACTIC CLINIC (HM06729) | | | | | | | | | | | | | ● | | | | ● | | | | | | | |
| FINDHORN FLOWER ESSENCES (HM07307) | | | | | | | | | | | | ● | | | | | | | | | | | | |
| HEALTHWORKS (HM09422) | ● | ● | | | | ● | | | | ● | ● | ● | ● | ● | ● | | ● | ● | | | ● | ● | ● | ● |
| **NORTHUMBERLAND** | | | | | | | | | | | | | | | | | | | | | | | | |
| SOLAR- PLEXUS (HM18864) | | | | | | | ● | | | | | ● | | | | | ● | | | | | | | |
| **ORKNEY ISLES** | | | | | | | | | | | | | | | | | | | | | | | | |
| A D S THOM (HM00030) | | | | | | | | | | | | | | | ● | | | | | | | | | |
| **PERTH AND KINROSS** | | | | | | | | | | | | | | | | | | | | | | | | |
| ACUPUNCTURE CLINIC (HM00288) | | | | | | | | | | ● | | ● | ● | ● | | | ● | | | | ● | ● | | ● |
| ACUPUNCTURE CLINIC DUNKELD (HM00289) | | | | | | | | | | ● | | ● | ● | ● | | | ● | | | | ● | ● | | ● |
| AUCHTERARDER CHIROPODY (HM01343) | | | | | | | | | | | | | ● | | ● | | | ● | | | | | | |
| BACK PAIN & SPORTS CLINIC (HM01491) | | | | | | | | | | | | | ● | ● | | | ● | | | | | | | |
| HOWIE, TOM R (HM10283) | | | | | | | | | | | | | ● | | ● | | | ● | | | | | | |
| HOWIE, TOM R (HM10284) | | | | | | | | | | | | | ● | | ● | | | ● | | | | | | |
| LENDRICK LODGE (HM12210) | | | | | | | | | | | | ● | | | | | | | | | | | | |
| STEVENSON, IAN W (HM19246) | | | | | | | | | | | | | ● | | ● | | | ● | | | | | | |

| Business by County with Reference no. | Breast Problems | Breathing Problems | Bronchitis | Bruising | Bulimia | Bunions | Bursitis | Callices | Cancers | Cataracts | Catarrh | Cerebral Palsy | Circulation Problems | Cold Sores | Colds | Colic | Colitis | Conjunctivitis | Constipation | Convulsions | Corns | Coughs | Cramp | Cystitis |
|---|---|---|---|---|---|---|---|---|---|---|---|---|---|---|---|---|---|---|---|---|---|---|---|---|
| **LOTHIAN (EAST)** | | | | | | | | | | | | | | | | | | | | | | | | |
| AROMA (HM01042) | ● | ● | ● | ● | ● | | ● | ● | ● | ● | ● | | ● | ● | ● | ● | ● | ● | ● | ● | ● | ● | ● | ● |
| EAST LOTHIAN PHYSIO CENTRE (HM06518) | | | | | | | ● | | | | | | | | | | | | | | | | | |
| FRASER, GORDON (HM07696) | ● | ● | ● | ● | ● | | | ● | ● | ● | ● | | ● | ● | ● | ● | ● | ● | ● | ● | ● | ● | ● | ● |
| **LOTHIAN (MID)** | | | | | | | | | | | | | | | | | | | | | | | | |
| CRYSTAL SANCTUARY (HM05532) | | ● | | | | | | | | | | | ● | | | | | | ● | | | | | |
| HAMILTON, JAMES (HM08844) | | ● | ● | | | | | ● | | | | | ● | | | | | | ● | | ● | | | |
| NATURAL HEALTH CENTRE (HM14573) | ● | ● | ● | ● | ● | | | ● | ● | ● | ● | | ● | ● | ● | ● | ● | ● | ● | ● | ● | ● | ● | ● |
| NEW DUNDAS CLINIC (HM14817) | | | | ● | | | ● | | | | | | | | | | | | | | | | | |
| RADIANT COLOUR (HM16847) | | | | | | | | | | | | | | | | | | | | | | | | |
| SCOTTISH KINESIOLOGY CENTRE (HM18134) | ● | ● | ● | ● | ● | | ● | ● | ● | ● | ● | | ● | ● | ● | ● | ● | ● | ● | ● | ● | ● | ● | ● |
| **LOTHIAN (WEST)** | | | | | | | | | | | | | | | | | | | | | | | | |
| DUIGNAN, KAREN (HM06372) | | | | | | | | | | | | | | | | | | | | | | | | |
| GILL, SHIRLEY (HM08080) | | ● | | | | | | | | | | | ● | | | | | | | | | | | |
| LINLITHGOW PHYSIO PRACTICE (HM12438) | | | | ● | | | | | | | | | | | | | | | | | | | | |
| VINCES, DENISE (HM20674) | | ● | | | | | | | | | | | ● | | ● | | | | ● | | | | | |
| **MORAY** | | | | | | | | | | | | | | | | | | | | | | | | |
| AROMANTIC (HM01080) | | | | | | | | | | | | | | | | | | | | | | | | |
| ELGIN CHIROPRACTIC CLINIC (HM06729) | | | | | | | | | | | | | ● | | | ● | | | | | | | | |
| FINDHORN FLOWER ESSENCES (HM07307) | | | | | | | | | | | | | | | | | | | | | | | | |
| HEALTHWORKS (HM09422) | ● | ● | ● | ● | | | | | ● | | ● | | ● | ● | ● | ● | ● | | ● | ● | | ● | ● | ● |
| **NORTHUMBERLAND** | | | | | | | | | | | | | | | | | | | | | | | | |
| SOLAR- PLEXUS (HM18864) | | | | | | | | | | | | | ● | | | | | | ● | | | | | |
| **ORKNEY ISLES** | | | | | | | | | | | | | | | | | | | | | | | | |
| A D S THOM (HM00030) | | | | | | | | ● | | | | | | | | | | | | | ● | | | |
| **PERTH AND KINROSS** | | | | | | | | | | | | | | | | | | | | | | | | |
| ACUPUNCTURE CLINIC (HM00288) | ● | ● | ● | ● | | | ● | | | | ● | | ● | | ● | ● | ● | ● | ● | | | ● | ● | ● |
| ACUPUNCTURE CLINIC DUNKELD (HM00289) | ● | ● | ● | ● | | | ● | | | | ● | | ● | | ● | ● | ● | ● | ● | | | ● | ● | ● |
| AUCHTERARDER CHIROPODY (HM01343) | | | | | | ● | | ● | | | | | | | | | | | | | ● | | | |
| BACK PAIN & SPORTS CLINIC (HM01491) | | | | | | | ● | | | | | | | | | | | | ● | | | | ● | |
| HOWIE, TOM R (HM10283) | | | | | | ● | | ● | | | | | | | | | | | | | ● | | | |
| HOWIE, TOM R (HM10284) | | | | | | ● | | ● | | | | | | | | | | | | | ● | | | |
| LENDRICK LODGE (HM12210) | | | | | | | | | ● | | | | ● | | | | | | | | | | | |
| STEVENSON, IAN W (HM19246) | | | | | | ● | | ● | | | | | | | | | | | | | ● | | | |

Healthmyself Directory

# A - C Conditions treated at Practices/Businesses

| Business by County with Reference no. | Acne | Addiction | Adenoids | Aids | Alcoholism | Allergy | Alzheimer's Disease | Amnesia | Anaemia | Angina | Anorexia | Anxiety | Arthritis | Asthma | Athletes Foot | Autism | Back Pain | Bacterial Infections | Baldness | Bereavement | Bladder Problems | Blood Pressure | Boils | Bowel Problems | Breast Problems | Breathing Problems | Bronchitis | Bruising | Bulimia | Bunions | Bursitis | Callices | Cancers | Cataracts | Catarrh | Cerebral Palsy | Circulation Problems | Cold Sores | Colds | Colic | Colitis | Conjunctivitis | Constipation | Convulsions | Corns | Coughs | Cramp | Cystitis |
|---|---|---|---|---|---|---|---|---|---|---|---|---|---|---|---|---|---|---|---|---|---|---|---|---|---|---|---|---|---|---|---|---|---|---|---|---|---|---|---|---|---|---|---|---|---|---|---|---|
| TAYLOR, D (HM19749) | | ● | | ● | ● | | | | | | ● | | | | | | | | | | | ● | | ● | | | | | ● | | | | | | | | | | | | | | | | | | | |
| **RENFREWSHIRE** | | | | | | | | | | | | | | | | | | | | | | | | | | | | | | | | | | | | | | | | | | | | | | | | |
| ALBA CENTRE (HM00473) | | | | | | | | | | | | ● | ● | | | | ● | | | ● | | | | | | | | | | | | | ● | | | | ● | | | | | | | | | | | |
| BLACKHALL PARK CENTRE (HM02444) | | | | | | ● | | | | ● | | ● | ● | ● | | | ● | | | | | ● | | | | ● | ● | | | | | | | | ● | | ● | | | | | | ● | | | | ● | |
| DOUGLAS, ANNE S (HM06212) | | | | | | | | | | | | | ● | | | | ● | | | | | | | | | | | | | | | | | | | | | | | | | | | | | | | |
| FANNING, M W (HM07095) | | | | | | | | | | | | ● | | ● | | | ● | | | | | ● | | | | | | | | | | | ● | | | | ● | | | | | | | | | | ● | |
| LINTON, UNNA (HM12444) | | | | | | | | | | | | | ● | | ● | | | | | | | | | | | | | | | ● | | ● | | | | | | | | | | | | | ● | | | |
| PAISLEY CHIROPRACTIC CLINIC (HM15587) | | | | | | ● | | | | | | | | ● | | | ● | | | | | | | ● | | ● | | | | | ● | | | | | | ● | | | ● | | | ● | | | | | |
| PAISLEY NATURAL THERAPY CENTRE (HM15588) | | ● | | | | ● | | | | ● | | ● | ● | ● | ● | | ● | | | | | ● | ● | ● | | ● | ● | ● | | | ● | | | | | | | | | ● | ● | ● | ● | | | ● | ● | ● |
| PAISLEY PHYSIOTHERAPY CENTRE (HM15589) | | | | | | | | | | | | | ● | | | | ● | | | | | | | | | | | ● | | | ● | | | | | | | | | | | | | | | | | |
| RAINEY, MARTHA (HM16890) | | | | ● | | | ● | | | ● | | ● | ● | ● | | | ● | | | | ● | ● | | ● | | | ● | | | | | | | | ● | | ● | | | | | | | ● | | ● | | |
| ROSEWOOD AROMATHERAPY ROOM (HM17629) | ● | | | | | | | | | | | ● | ● | | | | ● | | | | | | | | | | | | | | | | | | | | | | | | | | | | | | | |
| **SCOTTISH BORDERS** | | | | | | | | | | | | | | | | | | | | | | | | | | | | | | | | | | | | | | | | | | | | | | | | |
| HOGARTH, JAMES (HM09908) | | | | | | | | | | | | | ● | | ● | | | | | | | | | | | | | | | ● | | ● | | | | | | | | | | | | | ● | | | |
| L W FOOTCARE (HM11844) | | | | | | | | | | | | | ● | | ● | | | | | | | | | | | | | | | ● | | ● | | | | | | | | | | | | | ● | | | |
| NATURES TOUCH (HM14698) | | | | | | | | | | | | ● | ● | | | | | | | | | | | | | | | | | | | | | | | | | | | | | | | | | | | |
| NATURES WAY (HM14702) | | | | | | ● | | | | | | | ● | | | | | | | | | | | | | | | | | | | | | | | | | | ● | | | | | | | | | |
| ST BOSWELLS CHIRO CLINIC (HM19072) | | | | | | ● | | | | | | | ● | | | | ● | ● | | | | | | | | | | | | | | | | | | | | | ● | ● | | | | | | | ● | |
| WATT, A S (HM21028) | | | | | | | | | | | | | | | ● | | | | | | | | | | | | | | | | | ● | | | | | | | | | | | | | ● | | | |
| WISHING WELL (HM21738) | ● | ● | | | ● | ● | | | ● | | ● | ● | ● | ● | | | ● | ● | | | ● | ● | ● | ● | | ● | | ● | | | ● | | ● | | ● | | ● | | ● | ● | ● | | ● | | | ● | ● | ● |
| **SHETLAND ISLANDS** | | | | | | | | | | | | | | | | | | | | | | | | | | | | | | | | | | | | | | | | | | | | | | | | |
| LERWICK CHIROPRACTIC CLINIC (HM12231) | | | | | | | | | | | | | ● | | | | ● | | | | | | | | | | | | | | | | | | | | | | | ● | | | | | | | | |

# A - C Conditions treated at Practices/Businesses

Business by County with Reference no.

| Business by County with Reference no. | Acne | Addiction | Adenoids | Aids | Alcoholism | Allergy | Alzheimer's Disease | Amnesia | Anaemia | Angina | Anorexia | Anxiety | Arthritis | Asthma | Athletes Foot | Autism | Back Pain | Bacterial Infections | Baldness | Bereavement | Bladder Problems | Blood Pressure | Boils | Bowel Problems |
|---|---|---|---|---|---|---|---|---|---|---|---|---|---|---|---|---|---|---|---|---|---|---|---|---|
| **WALES** | | | | | | | | | | | | | | | | | | | | | | | | |
| **BLAENAU GWENT** | | | | | | | | | | | | | | | | | | | | | | | | |
| ABERTILLERY PHYSIOTHERAPY (HM00125) | | | | | | | | | | | | | ● | | | | ● | | | | | | | |
| CLASSIC CLINIC (HM04606) | ● | | | | | | | | | | ● | ● | ● | | | | ● | | | | | ● | | |
| **BRIDGEND** | | | | | | | | | | | | | | | | | | | | | | | | |
| JENKINS, JOHN (HM10987) | | | | | | | | | | | ● | ● | | | | | | | | | | | | |
| PARKWOOD CHIROPRACTIC CLINIC (HM15725) | | | | | | | | | | | | | ● | | | | ● | | | | | | | |
| **CAERPHILLY** | | | | | | | | | | | | | | | | | | | | | | | | |
| OAKFIELD NATURAL HEALTH CENTRE (HM15151) | ● | ● | ● | ● | ● | ● | ● | ● | ● | ● | ● | ● | ● | ● | ● | ● | ● | ● | ● | | ● | ● | ● | ● |
| PARKWOOD CHIROPRACTIC CLINIC (HM15723) | | | | | | | | | | | | | ● | | | | ● | | | | | | | |
| **CARMARTHENSHIRE** | | | | | | | | | | | | | | | | | | | | | | | | |
| GREENWAY CONSULTANCY (HM08495) | ● | ● | | ● | ● | ● | | | | | | ● | ● | ● | ● | | ● | ● | | | | ● | ● | ● |
| HEALING HANDS (HM09339) | | | | | | | | | | | | | ● | | | | ● | | | | | | | |
| JABROO, C (HM10808) | ● | ● | ● | ● | ● | ● | ● | ● | ● | ● | ● | ● | ● | ● | ● | ● | ● | ● | ● | | ● | ● | ● | ● |
| SPENCER AROMATHERAPY (HM18990) | | | | | | | | | | | | ● | ● | | | | | | | | | | | |
| WAINWRIGHT, MARY (HM20738) | ● | ● | ● | | ● | ● | ● | ● | ● | ● | ● | ● | ● | ● | ● | ● | ● | ● | ● | | ● | ● | ● | ● |
| **CEREDIGION** | | | | | | | | | | | | | | | | | | | | | | | | |
| AMIES, SUSAN (HM00785) | | | | | | | | | | | | | | | ● | | | | | | | | | |
| CHERRY TREE CTRE FOR NTRL MED (HM04109) | ● | ● | ● | ● | ● | ● | ● | ● | ● | ● | ● | ● | ● | ● | ● | ● | ● | ● | ● | | ● | ● | ● | ● |
| COCKSEDGE, JOHN M (HM04774) | | | | | | | | | | | | | ● | | ● | | | ● | | | | | | |
| FFYNNONWEN NATURAL THRPY CTRE (HM07256) | ● | | | | | ● | | | | | ● | ● | | | | | ● | | | | | | | ● |
| JONES, B E (HM11122) | | | | | | | | | | | | | | | ● | | | | | | | | | |
| LEWIS, D MICHAEL (HM12289) | | | | | | | | | | | | | ● | | ● | | | | | | | | | |
| **CONWY** | | | | | | | | | | | | | | | | | | | | | | | | |
| DREW, DAVID (HM06305) | | | | | | | | | | ● | ● | ● | ● | ● | | | ● | | | | ● | ● | | |
| HERBS FOR EVERYONE (HM09669) | ● | ● | ● | ● | ● | ● | ● | | ● | ● | ● | ● | ● | ● | ● | | ● | ● | | | ● | ● | ● | ● |
| MELA CENTRE OF OSTEOPATHY (HM13702) | | | | | | | | | | | | | ● | | | | ● | | | | | | | |
| MEWIS, R J (HM13782) | | | | | | | | | | | | | | | | | ● | | | | | ● | | |
| **DENBIGHSHIRE** | | | | | | | | | | | | | | | | | | | | | | | | |
| ALLIED PHYSIOTHERAPY (HM00646) | | | | | | | | | | | | | | | ● | | ● | | | | | | | |
| HEALING WAYS (HM09359) | ● | ● | ● | ● | ● | ● | ● | ● | ● | ● | ● | ● | ● | ● | ● | ● | ● | ● | ● | | ● | ● | ● | ● |
| MCGILL, L (HM13484) | | | | | | ● | | | | | | | | | | | ● | | | | | | | |
| ROY MORRIS CLINIC (HM17709) | ● | | | | | | ● | | ● | ● | ● | ● | ● | ● | ● | | ● | | | | ● | ● | | ● |

| Business by County with Reference no. | Breast Problems | Breathing Problems | Bronchitis | Bruising | Bulimia | Bunions | Bursitis | Callices | Cancers | Cataracts | Catarrh | Cerebral Palsy | Circulation Problems | Cold Sores | Colds | Colic | Colitis | Conjunctivitis | Constipation | Convulsions | Corns | Coughs | Cramp | Cystitis |
|---|---|---|---|---|---|---|---|---|---|---|---|---|---|---|---|---|---|---|---|---|---|---|---|---|
| **WALES** | | | | | | | | | | | | | | | | | | | | | | | | |
| **BLAENAU GWENT** | | | | | | | | | | | | | | | | | | | | | | | | |
| ABERTILLERY PHYSIOTHERAPY (HM00125) | | | | | | | ● | | | | | | | | | | | | | | | | | |
| CLASSIC CLINIC (HM04606) | | | | | | | | | | | | | | | | | | | | | | | | |
| **BRIDGEND** | | | | | | | | | | | | | | | | | | | | | | | | |
| JENKINS, JOHN (HM10987) | | | | | ● | | | | | | | | | | | | | | | | | | | |
| PARKWOOD CHIROPRACTIC CLINIC (HM15725) | | | | | | | | | | | | | ● | | | | | | | | | | | |
| **CAERPHILLY** | | | | | | | | | | | | | | | | | | | | | | | | |
| OAKFIELD NATURAL HEALTH CENTRE (HM15151) | ● | ● | ● | ● | ● | | ● | ● | ● | ● | ● | | ● | ● | ● | ● | ● | ● | ● | ● | ● | ● | ● | ● |
| PARKWOOD CHIROPRACTIC CLINIC (HM15723) | | ● | | | | | | | | | | | | | | | | | | | | | ● | |
| **CARMARTHENSHIRE** | | | | | | | | | | | | | | | | | | | | | | | | |
| GREENWAY CONSULTANCY (HM08495) | ● | ● | ● | ● | ● | | | | | | ● | | ● | ● | ● | ● | ● | | ● | | | ● | ● | ● |
| HEALING HANDS (HM09339) | | | | | | | | | | | | | | | | | | | | | | | | |
| JABROO, C (HM10808) | ● | ● | ● | ● | ● | | ● | ● | ● | ● | ● | | ● | ● | ● | ● | ● | ● | ● | ● | ● | ● | ● | ● |
| SPENCER AROMATHERAPY (HM18990) | | | | | | | | | ● | | | | | | | | | | | | | | | |
| WAINWRIGHT, MARY (HM20738) | ● | ● | ● | ● | ● | | ● | ● | ● | ● | ● | | ● | ● | ● | ● | ● | ● | ● | ● | ● | ● | ● | ● |
| **CEREDIGION** | | | | | | | | | | | | | | | | | | | | | | | | |
| AMIES, SUSAN (HM00785) | | | | | | | | | | | | | | | | | | | | | ● | | | |
| CHERRY TREE CTRE FOR NTRL MED (HM04109) | ● | ● | ● | ● | ● | | ● | ● | ● | ● | ● | | ● | ● | ● | ● | ● | ● | ● | ● | ● | ● | ● | ● |
| COCKSEDGE, JOHN M (HM04774) | | | | | | ● | | ● | | | | | | | | | | | | | ● | | | |
| FFYNNONWEN NATURAL THRPY CTRE (HM07256) | | ● | | | | | | | | | ● | | | ● | | | ● | | ● | | | | | |
| JONES, B E (HM11122) | | | | | | ● | | ● | | | | | | | | | | | | | ● | | | |
| LEWIS, D MICHAEL (HM12289) | | | | | | ● | | ● | | | | | | | | | | | | | ● | | | |
| **CONWY** | | | | | | | | | | | | | | | | | | | | | | | | |
| DREW, DAVID (HM06305) | ● | ● | | | ● | | | | ● | | | | | | | | | | | | | | | |
| HERBS FOR EVERYONE (HM09669) | ● | ● | ● | ● | ● | | ● | | | ● | ● | | ● | ● | ● | ● | ● | ● | ● | ● | | ● | ● | ● |
| MELA CENTRE OF OSTEOPATHY (HM13702) | | | | | | | ● | | | | | | | | | | | | | | | | | |
| MEWIS, R J (HM13782) | | | | | | | | | | | | | | | | | | | | | | | | |
| **DENBIGHSHIRE** | | | | | | | | | | | | | | | | | | | | | | | | |
| ALLIED PHYSIOTHERAPY (HM00646) | | | | | | | | | | | | | | | | | | | | | | | | |
| HEALING WAYS (HM09359) | ● | ● | ● | ● | ● | | ● | ● | ● | ● | ● | | ● | ● | ● | ● | ● | ● | ● | ● | ● | ● | ● | ● |
| MCGILL, L (HM13484) | | | | | | | | | | | | | | | | | | | | | | | | |
| ROY MORRIS CLINIC (HM17709) | ● | ● | ● | ● | ● | | ● | ● | | | ● | | ● | ● | ● | ● | ● | ● | ● | | ● | ● | ● | ● |

# A - C Conditions treated at Practices/Businesses

| Business by County with Reference no. | Acne | Addiction | Adenoids | Aids | Alcoholism | Allergy | Alzheimer's Disease | Amnesia | Anaemia | Angina | Anorexia | Anxiety | Arthritis | Asthma | Athletes Foot | Autism | Back Pain | Bacterial Infections | Baldness | Bereavement | Bladder Problems | Blood Pressure | Boils | Bowel Problems | Breast Problems | Breathing Problems | Bronchitis | Bruising | Bulimia | Bunions | Bursitis | Callices | Cancers | Cataracts | Catarrh | Cerebral Palsy | Circulation Problems | Cold Sores | Colds | Colic | Colitis | Conjunctivitis | Constipation | Convulsions | Corns | Coughs | Cramp | Cystitis |
|---|---|---|---|---|---|---|---|---|---|---|---|---|---|---|---|---|---|---|---|---|---|---|---|---|---|---|---|---|---|---|---|---|---|---|---|---|---|---|---|---|---|---|---|---|---|---|---|---|
| **FLINTSHIRE** | | | | | | | | | | | | | | | | | | | | | | | | | | | | | | | | | | | | | | | | | | | | | | | | |
| A L J RILEY ASSOCIATES (HM00038) | ● | | | | | ● | | | ● | | | ● | ● | ● | ● | | ● | ● | | | ● | ● | ● | ● | ● | ● | ● | ● | | | | | | | | | ● | ● | ● | ● | ● | | ● | | | ● | | |
| BOOTS HEALTHCARE SERVICES (HM02711) | | | | | | | | | | | | | | | ● | | | | | | | | | | | | | | | | | ● | | | | | | | | | | | | | ● | | ● | |
| CHIROPODISTS SURGERY (HM04298) | | | | | | | | | | | | | | | ● | | | | | | | | | | | | | | | | | | | | | | | | | | | | | | | | | |
| GAFFNEY, ALMA (HM07827) | | | | | | | | | | | | | | | ● | | | | | | | | | | | | | | | | | ● | | | | | | | | | | | | | ● | | | |
| HYPNOTHERAPY CENTRE (HM10528) | | ● | | | ● | | | | | | ● | | | | | | | | | | | ● | | | | | | | ● | | | | | | | | | | | | | | | | | | | |
| REECE, JULIE (HM17038) | | | | | | | | | | | | | | | ● | | | | | | | | | | | | | | | | | ● | | | | | | | | | | | | | ● | | | |
| **GLAMORGAN (VALE OF)** | | | | | | | | | | | | | | | | | | | | | | | | | | | | | | | | | | | | | | | | | | | | | | | | |
| ALEXANDER TECHNIQUE (HM00546) | | | | | | | | | | | | | ● | | | | ● | | | | | | | | | | | | | | | | | | | | | | | | | | | | | | | |
| ALEXANDER TECHNIQUE (HM00551) | | | | | | | | | | | | | ● | | | | ● | | | | | | | | | | | | | | | | | | | | ● | | | | | | | | | | | |
| AMETHYST HEALING CENTRE (HM00784) | | | | | | | | | | | | ● | ● | | | | | | | | | | | | | | | | | | | | | | | | | | | | | | | | | | | |
| AROMATHERAPY CLINIC (HM01105) | | | | | | | | | | | | | ● | | | | ● | | | | | | | | | | | | | | | | | | | | | | | | | | | | | | | |
| AYRE CENTRE OF HYPNOTHERAPY (HM01430) | | ● | | | | | | | | | ● | ● | | | | | | | | | | | | | | | | | ● | | | | | | | | | | | | | | | | | | | |
| BARRY OSTEOPATHIC CLINIC (HM01809) | | | | | | | | | | | | | | | | | ● | | | | | | | | | | | | | | | | | | | | | | | | | | | | | | | |
| BODY ESSENTIALS (HM02587) | | | | | | | | | | | | ● | ● | | | | | | | | | | | | | | | | | | | | | | | | | | | | | | | | | | | |
| BROWN, ANNE (HM03214) | | | | | | | | | | | | | ● | | | | ● | | | | | | | | | | | | | | ● | | | | | | | | | | | | | | | | | |
| CARDIFF CHIROPRACTIC CLINIC (HM03666) | | | | | | | | | | | | | ● | | | | ● | | | | | | | | | | | | | | | | | | | | ● | | | | | | | | | | | |
| CARDIFF HEALTH PRACTICE (HM03670) | | | | | | | | | | | | | ● | | | | ● | | | | | | | | | | | | | | | | | | | | ● | | | | | | | | | | | |
| CARDIFF HOMEOPATHIC CLINIC (HM03671) | ● | ● | ● | ● | ● | ● | ● | ● | ● | ● | ● | ● | ● | ● | ● | ● | ● | ● | ● | | ● | ● | ● | ● | ● | ● | ● | ● | ● | | ● | ● | ● | ● | ● | | ● | ● | ● | ● | ● | ● | ● | ● | ● | ● | ● | ● |
| CITY CENTRE CHIRO CLINIC (HM04488) | | | | | | | | | | | | | ● | | | | ● | | | | | | | | | | | | | | | | | | | | ● | | | | | | | | | | | |
| COWBRIDGE CHIRO/SPINAL REHAB (HM05289) | ● | ● | ● | ● | ● | ● | ● | ● | ● | ● | ● | ● | ● | ● | ● | ● | ● | ● | | | ● | ● | ● | ● | ● | ● | ● | ● | ● | | ● | ● | | | ● | | ● | ● | ● | ● | ● | ● | ● | ● | ● | ● | ● | ● |
| COWBRIDGE OSTEOPATH CLINIC (HM05290) | | | | | | | | | | | | | ● | | | | ● | | | | | | | | | | | | | | ● | | | | | | | | | | | | | | | | | |
| EVANS, STEVE (HM06990) | | | | | | | | | | | | | ● | | | | ● | | | | | | | | | | | | | | | | | | | | | | | | | | | | | | | |
| GLAMORGAN HEALTH & RACQUET (HM08122) | | | | | | | | | | | | | ● | | | | ● | | | | | | | | | | | | | | | | | | | | | | | | | | | | | | | |
| GRIMWADE, S (HM08586) | | | | | | | | | | | | | | | | | ● | | | | | | | | | | | | | | | | | | | | | | | | | | | | | | | |
| HENRIETTA CTRE FOR COMP THRPY (HM09565) | | | | | | | | | | | | ● | | | | | | | | | | | | | | | | | | | | | | | | | | | | | | | | | | | | |
| LLANISHEN PHYSIOTHERAPY CLINIC (HM12501) | | | | | | | | | | | | | ● | | | | ● | | | | | | | | | | | | | | | | | | | | | | | | | | | | | | | |
| MILES, ANDREW (HM13854) | | | | | | | | | | | | | ● | | | | ● | | | | | | | | | | | | | | | | | | | | ● | | | | | | | | | | | |
| MOBILE FOOTWORKS (HM14031) | | | | | | | | | | | | ● | ● | | ● | | ● | ● | | | | ● | | ● | | ● | | | | | | | | | | | ● | | | | | | | | | | | |
| MORGAN-AYRES, PAUL (PROF) (HM14178) | | ● | | | ● | ● | | ● | | | ● | ● | | | | | | | | | | | | ● | | | | | ● | | | | ● | | | | | | | | ● | | | | | | | |
| MULLINS, JOHN (HM14348) | | | | | | | | | | | | | | | | | ● | | | | | | | | | | | | | | | | | | | | | | | | | | | | | | | |
| NATURAL HEALTHCARE (HM14601) | | | | | | | | | | | | ● | ● | | | ● | ● | ● | ● | | ● | ● | | ● | ● | | | | | | | | | | | | ● | | | | ● | ● | ● | | | | ● | |
| PARKWOOD CHIROPRACTIC CLINIC (HM15724) | | | | | | | | | | | | | ● | | | | ● | | | | | | | | | | | | | | | | | | | | ● | | | | | | | | | | | |
| PARKWOOD CHIROPRACTIC CLINIC (HM15726) | | | | | | | | | | | | | ● | | | | ● | | | | | | | | | | | | | | | | | | | | ● | | | | | | | | | | | |

# A - C Conditions treated at Practices/Businesses

| Business by County with Reference no. | Acne | Addiction | Adenoids | Aids | Alcoholism | Allergy | Alzheimer's Disease | Amnesia | Anaemia | Angina | Anorexia | Anxiety | Arthritis | Asthma | Athletes Foot | Autism | Back Pain | Bacterial Infections | Baldness | Bereavement | Bladder Problems | Blood Pressure | Boils | Bowel Problems | Breast Problems | Breathing Problems | Bronchitis | Bruising | Bulimia | Bunions | Bursitis | Callices | Cancers | Cataracts | Catarrh | Cerebral Palsy | Circulation Problems | Cold Sores | Colds | Colic | Colitis | Conjunctivitis | Constipation | Convulsions | Corns | Coughs | Cramp | Cystitis |
|---|---|---|---|---|---|---|---|---|---|---|---|---|---|---|---|---|---|---|---|---|---|---|---|---|---|---|---|---|---|---|---|---|---|---|---|---|---|---|---|---|---|---|---|---|---|---|---|---|
| PENARTH CHIROPRACTIC CLINIC (HM15961) | | | | | | | | | | | | | | | | | ● | | | | | | | | | ● | | | | | | | | | | | ● | | | | | | | | | | | |
| PENARTH HOMEOPATHY CLINIC (HM15962) | ● | ● | ● | | ● | ● | ● | ● | ● | ● | ● | ● | ● | ● | ● | ● | ● | ● | ● | | ● | ● | ● | ● | ● | ● | ● | ● | ● | | ● | ● | | ● | ● | | ● | ● | ● | ● | ● | ● | ● | ● | ● | ● | ● | ● |
| PENYLAN PODIATRIC CENTRE (HM16005) | | | | | | | | | | | | | | | ● | | | | | | | | | | | | | | | | | ● | | | | | | | | | | | | | ● | | | |
| PHYSIO FIRST CENTRE (HM16198) | | | | | | | | | | | | | ● | | | | ● | | | | | | | | | | | | | | | | | | | | | | | | | | | | | | | |
| POLLEY, LYNDON (HM16415) | | | | | | | | | | | | | | | ● | | | | | | | | | | | | | | | | | ● | | | | | | | | | | | | | ● | | | |
| POLLEY, LYNDON (HM16413) | | | | | | | | | | | | | | | ● | | | | | | | | | | | | | | | | | ● | | | | | | | | | | | | | ● | | | |
| POLLEY, LYNDON (HM16414) | | | | | | | | | | | | | | | ● | | | | | | | | | | | | | | | | | ● | | | | | | | | | | | | | ● | | | |
| RENWICK, SARAH NADINE (HM17192) | ● | ● | | | ● | | | | | | | | ● | ● | | | ● | | | | | ● | | ● | | ● | | | | | | | | | | | | | | | | | | | | | | |
| RIDGE, D (HM17316) | | | | | | | | | | | | | ● | | | | ● | | | | | | | | | | | | | | ● | | | | | | | | | | | | | | | | | |
| RIDGE, D (HM17315) | | | | | | | | | | | | | ● | | | | ● | | | | | | | | | | | | | | ● | | | | | | | | | | | | | | | | ● | |
| SIMS, TRACEY (HM18602) | | | | | | | | | | | | | | | ● | | | | | | | | | | | | | | | | | ● | | | | | | | | | | | | | ● | | | |
| WALSH, J A (HM20859) | | | | | | | | | | | | | | | ● | | | | | | | | | | | | | | | | | ● | | | | | | | | | | | | | ● | | | |
| **GWYNEDD** | | | | | | | | | | | | | | | | | | | | | | | | | | | | | | | | | | | | | | | | | | | | | | | | |
| CENTRE FOR WELL BEING (HM03922) | | | | | | | | | | | | ● | | | | | | | | | | | | | | | | | | | | | | | | | | | | | | | | | | | | |
| MOSSHILL HOLISTIC CENTRE (HM14270) | ● | ● | ● | ● | ● | ● | ● | ● | ● | ● | ● | ● | ● | ● | ● | ● | ● | ● | ● | | ● | ● | ● | ● | ● | ● | ● | ● | ● | | ● | ● | ● | ● | ● | | ● | ● | ● | ● | ● | ● | ● | ● | ● | ● | ● | ● |
| NATURAL THERAPY CLINIC (HM14660) | ● | ● | | | ● | ● | | | ● | | ● | ● | ● | ● | | | ● | | | | | ● | | ● | | ● | | | ● | | | | ● | | ● | | ● | | | | | | ● | | | | | |
| O'NEIL, L (HM15325) | | | | | | | | | | | | ● | | | | | | | | | | | | | | | | | | | | | | | | | | | | | | | | | | | | |
| **ISLE OF ANGLESEY** | | | | | | | | | | | | | | | | | | | | | | | | | | | | | | | | | | | | | | | | | | | | | | | | |
| CHALMERS, D G (HM03951) | | | | | | | | | | | | ● | ● | | | | ● | | | | | | | | | | | ● | | | ● | | | | | | ● | | | | | | | | | | | |
| EPHRAIM, NONA (HM06851) | | | | | | | | | | | | ● | | | | | | | | | | | | | | | | | | | | | | | | | | | | | | | | | | | | |
| **MONMOUTHSHIRE** | | | | | | | | | | | | | | | | | | | | | | | | | | | | | | | | | | | | | | | | | | | | | | | | |
| ABERGAVENNY THERAPY CTRE (HM00121) | | | | | | | | | | | | ● | ● | ● | | | ● | | | | ● | | | | | ● | ● | | | | | | | | ● | | ● | | | | | | | | | | ● | |
| BROOKSIDE PHYSIO PRACTICE (HM03184) | | | | | | | | | | | | | ● | | | | ● | | | | | | | | | | | | | | ● | | | | | | | | | | | | | | | | | |
| ELECTROMAGNETIC PRODUCTS (HM06721) | | | | | | | | | | | | | ● | | | | ● | | | | | | | | | | | | | | | | | | | | ● | | | | | | | | | | ● | |
| HARMONY (HM09020) | ● | | ● | | | ● | | ● | ● | ● | | ● | ● | ● | ● | ● | ● | ● | | | ● | ● | ● | ● | ● | ● | ● | ● | | | | ● | ● | | ● | | ● | ● | ● | ● | ● | | ● | ● | ● | ● | ● | ● |
| NUTRITION CLINIC (HM15122) | | | | | | ● | | | ● | ● | ● | ● | ● | ● | ● | | ● | ● | | | ● | ● | | ● | ● | ● | | | ● | | | ● | ● | | ● | | ● | ● | ● | ● | ● | | ● | | ● | | ● | ● |
| TURFAEN CHIROPODY CLINIC (HM20407) | | | | | | | | | | | | | | | ● | | ● | | | | | | | | | | | | | | | | | | | | | | | | | | | | | | | |
| **NEATH PORT TALBOT** | | | | | | | | | | | | | | | | | | | | | | | | | | | | | | | | | | | | | | | | | | | | | | | | |
| ST JAMES MEDICAL CENTRE (HM19078) | ● | ● | ● | ● | ● | ● | ● | ● | ● | ● | ● | ● | ● | ● | ● | ● | ● | ● | ● | | ● | ● | ● | ● | ● | ● | ● | ● | ● | | ● | ● | ● | ● | ● | | ● | ● | ● | ● | ● | ● | ● | ● | ● | ● | ● | ● |
| YNODDFA MARKETING (HM22017) | | | | | | | | | | | | | | | | | | | | | | | | | | | | | | | | | ● | | | | | | | | | | | | | | | |
| **NEWPORT** | | | | | | | | | | | | | | | | | | | | | | | | | | | | | | | | | | | | | | | | | | | | | | | | |
| BAJJADA, JUNE (HM01572) | | ● | | | ● | | | | | | | ● | ● | ● | | | ● | | | | ● | ● | | ● | | ● | | | | | ● | | | | ● | | ● | | ● | | ● | | | | | ● | ● | |
| BEIGHTON, J W (HM02069) | ● | | | | | | | | | | | ● | | ● | ● | ● | ● | ● | | | ● | ● | ● | ● | ● | ● | ● | ● | | | ● | | ● | | ● | | ● | ● | ● | ● | ● | ● | ● | ● | | ● | ● | ● |
| BOWKETT, LYN (HM02792) | ● | ● | ● | ● | ● | ● | ● | ● | ● | ● | ● | ● | ● | ● | ● | ● | ● | ● | ● | | ● | ● | ● | ● | ● | ● | ● | ● | ● | | ● | ● | ● | ● | ● | | ● | ● | ● | ● | ● | ● | ● | ● | ● | ● | ● | ● |

www.healthmyself.com

# A - C Conditions treated at Practices/Businesses

| Business by County with Reference no. | Acne | Addiction | Adenoids | Aids | Alcoholism | Allergy | Alzheimer's Disease | Amnesia | Anaemia | Angina | Anorexia | Anxiety | Arthritis | Asthma | Athletes Foot | Autism | Back Pain | Bacterial Infections | Baldness | Bereavement | Bladder Problems | Blood Pressure | Boils | Bowel Problems | Breast Problems | Breathing Problems | Bronchitis | Bruising | Bulimia | Bunions | Bursitis | Callices | Cancers | Cataracts | Catarrh | Cerebral Palsy | Circulation Problems | Cold Sores | Colds | Colic | Colitis | Conjunctivitis | Constipation | Convulsions | Corns | Coughs | Cramp | Cystitis |
|---|---|---|---|---|---|---|---|---|---|---|---|---|---|---|---|---|---|---|---|---|---|---|---|---|---|---|---|---|---|---|---|---|---|---|---|---|---|---|---|---|---|---|---|---|---|---|---|---|
| CLINIC OF HOLISTIC HEALTH (HM04693) | ● | ● | ● | ● | ● | ● | ● | ● | ● | ● | ● | ● | ● | ● | ● | ● | ● | ● | ● | | ● | ● | ● | ● | ● | ● | ● | ● | ● | | ● | ● | ● | ● | ● | | ● | ● | ● | ● | ● | ● | ● | ● | ● | ● | ● | ● |
| MOXLEY, SHIRLEY (HM14304) | ● | | | | | ● | | | | ● | | ● | ● | ● | | | ● | | | | ● | ● | | ● | | ● | ● | | | | | | ● | | ● | | ● | | | ● | ● | | ● | | | | ● | |
| OLIVER, MARION (HM15294) | | | | | | ● | ● | | | | | ● | ● | ● | ● | | ● | | | | ● | ● | | ● | ● | ● | ● | | | | | | ● | | ● | | ● | | | ● | ● | ● | ● | | | ● | ● | ● |
| **PEMBROKESHIRE** | | | | | | | | | | | | | | | | | | | | | | | | | | | | | | | | | | | | | | | | | | | | | | | | |
| CENTRE OF TRADITIONAL HEALING (HM03926) | | | | | | | | | | | | ● | | | | | ● | | | | | | | | | | | | | | | | | | | | | | | | | | | | | | | |
| JABROO, C (HM10809) | ● | ● | ● | ● | ● | ● | ● | ● | ● | ● | ● | ● | ● | ● | ● | ● | ● | ● | ● | | ● | ● | ● | ● | ● | ● | ● | ● | ● | | ● | ● | ● | ● | ● | | ● | ● | ● | ● | ● | ● | ● | ● | ● | ● | ● | ● |
| **POWYS** | | | | | | | | | | | | | | | | | | | | | | | | | | | | | | | | | | | | | | | | | | | | | | | | |
| BRECON CLINIC (HM02944) | ● | ● | | | ● | ● | | ● | ● | | ● | ● | ● | ● | | | ● | | | | ● | ● | ● | ● | ● | ● | ● | | ● | | ● | | | | ● | | ● | | ● | ● | ● | | ● | | | | ● | ● |
| BRECON COMPLEMENTARY MED CTRE (HM02945) | ● | ● | ● | ● | ● | ● | ● | ● | ● | ● | ● | ● | ● | ● | ● | ● | ● | ● | ● | | ● | ● | ● | ● | ● | ● | ● | ● | ● | | ● | ● | ● | ● | ● | | ● | ● | ● | ● | ● | ● | ● | ● | ● | ● | ● | ● |
| CONROY, CHRISTINE (HM05007) | | | | | | | | | | | | | | | | | ● | | | | | | | | | ● | | | | | | | | | | | | | | | | | | | | | | |
| COVENT HOUSE NTRL HEALTH CTRE (HM05280) | ● | ● | | | | ● | | | ● | ● | ● | ● | ● | ● | ● | ● | ● | ● | ● | | ● | ● | ● | ● | ● | ● | ● | ● | ● | | ● | | ● | ● | ● | | ● | ● | ● | ● | ● | ● | ● | ● | | ● | ● | ● |
| GROVES, FRAN (HM08614) | | | | | | | | | | | | | | | | | ● | | | | | | | | | | | | | | | | | | | | ● | | | | | | | | | | | |
| HEALTH FOCUS (HM09386) | ● | ● | ● | | | ● | | | | | | ● | ● | ● | ● | | ● | ● | | | ● | ● | ● | ● | ● | ● | ● | ● | ● | | ● | ● | | | | | ● | ● | ● | ● | ● | | ● | ● | ● | ● | ● | ● |
| HERBAL HELPLINE (HM09619) | | ● | | | ● | | | | | ● | ● | | | | | | | ● | | | | ● | | ● | | | ● | | ● | | | | ● | | | | | | | | | | | | | | | |
| KILGOUR, KATHARINE () | | | | | | | | | | | | | ● | | | | ● | | | | | | | | | | | ● | | | | | | | | | | | | | | | | | | | | |
| LLANDRINDOD WELLS SPA TOWN (HM12499) | ● | ● | ● | ● | ● | ● | ● | ● | ● | ● | ● | ● | ● | ● | ● | ● | ● | ● | ● | | ● | ● | ● | ● | ● | ● | ● | ● | ● | | ● | ● | ● | ● | ● | | ● | ● | ● | ● | ● | ● | ● | ● | ● | ● | ● | ● |
| PEACE CLINIC (HM15876) | | ● | | | | | | ● | | | ● | ● | | | | | | | | | | | | ● | | ● | | | ● | | | | | | | | | | | | ● | | ● | | | | | |
| REFLEXOLOGY & ALLERGY THERAPY (HM17078) | | | | | | ● | | | | | | ● | ● | | | | | | | | ● | ● | | ● | | ● | | | | | | | | | | | ● | | | | | | | | | | | |
| SHEPPARD, HELEN (HM18421) | ● | | ● | | | | | | ● | ● | ● | ● | ● | ● | ● | ● | ● | ● | | | ● | ● | | ● | ● | ● | ● | | | | ● | | | | ● | | ● | | ● | ● | ● | | ● | | | ● | ● | ● |
| **RHONDDA CYNON TAFF** | | | | | | | | | | | | | | | | | | | | | | | | | | | | | | | | | | | | | | | | | | | | | | | | |
| POLLEY, LYNDON (HM16416) | | | | | | | | | | | | | | | ● | | | | | | | | | | | | | | | | | ● | | | | | | | | | | | | | ● | | | |
| **SWANSEA** | | | | | | | | | | | | | | | | | | | | | | | | | | | | | | | | | | | | | | | | | | | | | | | | |
| ABERTAWE PHYSIOTHERAPY CLINIC (HM00124) | | | | | | | | | | | | | ● | | | | ● | | | | | | | | | | | | | | ● | | | | | | | | | | | | | | | | | |
| ACUPUNCTURE CENTRE (HM00254) | | | | | | ● | | | | | | | ● | ● | | | ● | | | | | | | | | | | ● | | | | | | | | | | | | | | | ● | | | | | ● |
| BURDEN, RICHARD (HM03370) | ● | | | | | | | | | | | | ● | | | | ● | | | | | | | ● | | | | ● | | | | | | | | | | | ● | | ● | | ● | | | | ● | ● |
| CONTINENTAL SKIN CLINIC (HM05020) | ● | | | | | | | | | | | | | | | | | | | | | | | | | | | | | | | | | | | | | | | | | | | | | | | |
| PEDORTHICS FOOT SGY PRACTICE (HM15935) | | | | | | | | | | | | | | | ● | | ● | | | | | | | | | | | | | | | | | | | | | | | | | | | | | | | |
| RODWAY & ASSOCIATES (HM17531) | | | | | | | | | | | | | ● | | | | ● | | | | | | | | | | | | | | | | | | | | | | | | | | | | | | | |
| **TORFAEN** | | | | | | | | | | | | | | | | | | | | | | | | | | | | | | | | | | | | | | | | | | | | | | | | |
| CLUB INDIGO (HM04741) | | | | | | | | | | | | | ● | | | | ● | | | | | | | | | | | | | | | | | | | | | | | | | | | | | | | |
| **WREXHAM** | | | | | | | | | | | | | | | | | | | | | | | | | | | | | | | | | | | | | | | | | | | | | | | | |
| HARMONY IN HEALTH (HM09028) | | | | | | | | | ● | | | ● | ● | ● | | | ● | | | | | | | | | | | | | | | | | | | | | | | | | | | | | | | |
| SENSORAMA (HM18229) | | | | | | | | | | | | ● | ● | | | | ● | | | | | | | | | | | | | | | | | | | | | | | | | | | | | | | |

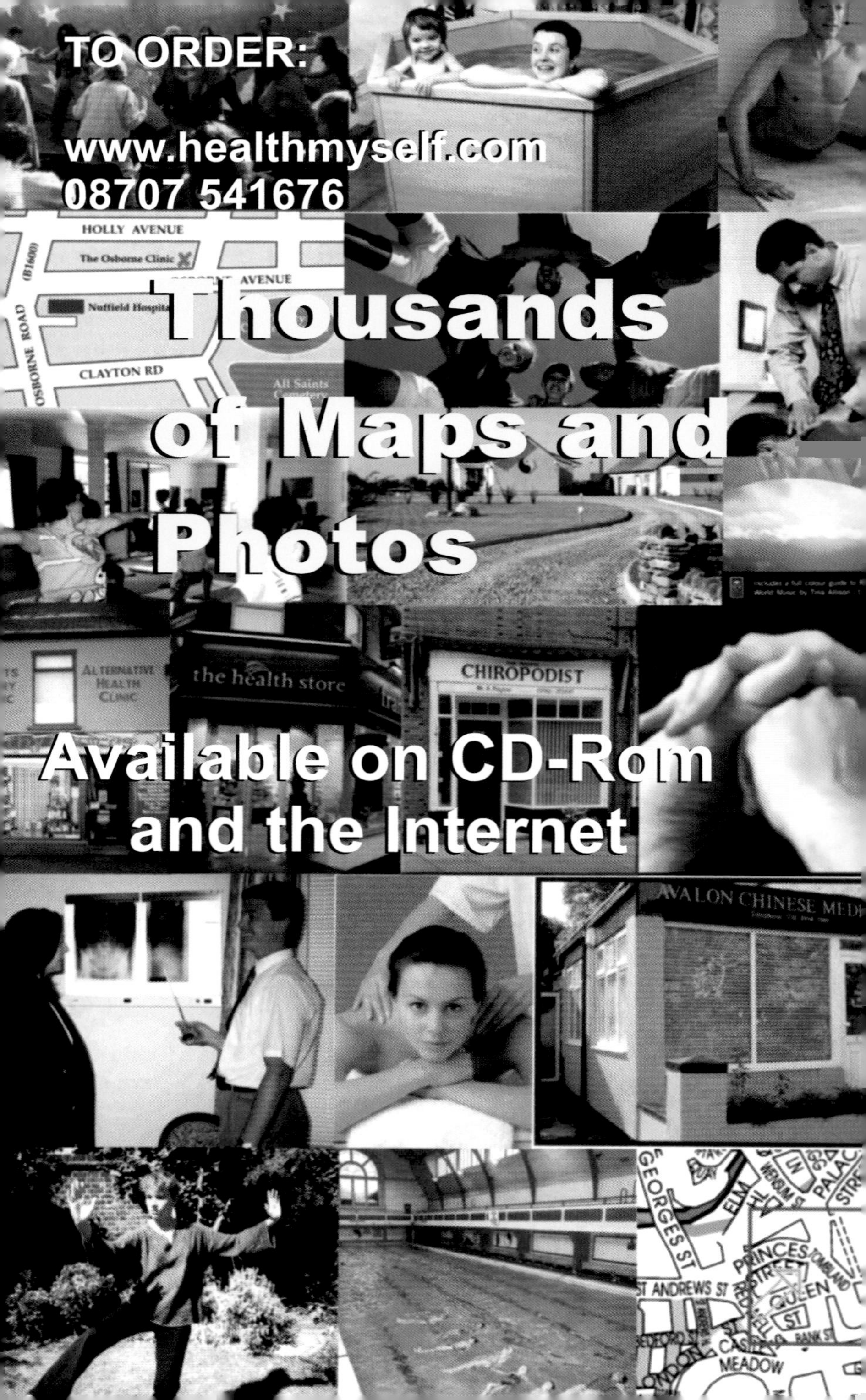
TO ORDER:
www.healthmyself.com
08707 541676
Thousands of Maps and Photos
Available on CD-Rom and the Internet
HOLLY AVENUE
The Osborne Clinic
OSBORNE ROAD
(B1600)
CLAYTON RD
ALTERNATIVE HEALTH CLINIC
the health store
CHIROPODIST
GEORGES ST
ST ANDREWS ST
PRINCES STREET
QUEEN ST
MEADOW

HEALTH MYSELF

# SECTION 4b

## D-I of Conditions treated at Practices

# D - I Conditions treated at Practices/Businesses

Business by County with Reference no.

## ENGLAND

### BEDFORDSHIRE

| Business | Dandruff | Deafness | Depression | Diabetes | Diarrhoea | Digestive Problems | Diverticulitis | Dizziness | Dyslexia | Dyspraxia | Ear Disorders | Eczema | ENT Disorders | Epilepsy | Eye Disorders | Fatigue | Fears | Fertility Problems | Fever | Fibroids | Flatulence | Foot Problems | Fractures | Fungal Infections | Gallstones | Gastrointestinal Problems | Genital Herpes | Gingivitis | Glandular Fever | Glaucoma | Gout | Gum Disease | Hair Problems | Halitosis | Hand Problems | Hay Fever | Headaches | Hearing Problems | High Blood Pressure | Hip Complaints | Hyperactivity | Hypoglycaemia | Impotence | Incontinence | Indigestion | Infertility | Influenza | Ingrowing Toenails |
|---|---|---|---|---|---|---|---|---|---|---|---|---|---|---|---|---|---|---|---|---|---|---|---|---|---|---|---|---|---|---|---|---|---|---|---|---|---|---|---|---|---|---|---|---|---|---|---|
| ALOE VERA SPECIALISTS (HM00681) | | ● | ● | | ● | ● | ● | | | | | ● | | | | ● | | | | | ● | | | ● | | ● | | ● | ● | | ● | ● | ● | ● | | ● | ● | | | | ● | | | | ● | | ● | |
| ALTERNATIVE THERAPY AT WORK (HM00732) | | | ● | | | ● | | | | | | | | | | ● | | | | | | | | | | | | | | | | | | | | | ● | | | | | | | | | | | |
| AMPTHILL & FLITWICK CLINIC (HM00795) | | | | | | | | | | | | | | | | | | | | | | | ● | | | | | | | | | | | | | | | | | ● | | | | | | | | |
| BEDFORD ACUPUNCTURE CLINIC (HM02032) | | | | | ● | | | | | | | ● | | ● | | | | ● | | | | | | | | | | | | | | | | | | ● | ● | | | | | | | | | ● | | |
| BEDFORD CHIROPRACTIC SURGERY (HM02033) | | | | | | | | | | | | | | | | | | | | | | | ● | | | | | | | | | | | | | | ● | | | ● | | | | | | | | |
| BEDFORD PHYSIOTHERAPY CENTRE (HM02035) | | | | | | | | | | | | | | | | | | | | | | | ● | | | | | | | | | | | | | | | | | ● | | | | | | | | |
| BELLAMY, R D (HM02097) | | | | | | ● | | | | | | | | | | ● | | | | | | ● | ● | | | | | | | | | | | | ● | | ● | | | ● | | | | | | | | |
| BOYCE, MICHAEL (HM02814) | | | | | | ● | | | | | | | | | | ● | | | | | | | | | | | | | | | | | | | | | ● | | ● | ● | | | | | | | | |
| BURTON, MERILYNN (HM03444) | | | | | | | | | | | | | | | | | | | | | | ● | | ● | | | | | | | | | | | | | | | | | | | | | | | | ● |
| CHARTERED PHYSIOTHERAPIST (HM04042) | | | | | | | | ● | | ● | | | | | | | | | | | | ● | ● | | | | | | | | | | | | ● | | ● | | | ● | | | | | | | | |
| CLNC OF ACU & CHINESE HERB MED (HM04726) | | | | | ● | ● | ● | ● | | | | ● | | | | ● | | ● | | ● | | | | | | ● | | | | | | | ● | | | ● | ● | | ● | | | | ● | | | ● | | |
| COULSTOCK, JUDY (HM05239) | | | ● | | | ● | | | | | | | | | | ● | | | | | | | | | | | | | | | ● | | | | | ● | ● | | ● | | | | | ● | ● | ● | | |
| DA SILVA, CAROLE (HM05665) | | | | | | ● | | | | | | | | | | | | | | | | | | | | | | | | | | | | | | | ● | | ● | | | | | | ● | | | |
| DISS, KATHRYN (HM06122) | | | ● | | | | | | | | | | | | | | | | | | | ● | ● | | | | | | | | ● | | | | | | ● | | ● | ● | | | | | ● | | | |
| DUNTON CTRE-COUN/PSYCHOTHERAPY (HM06428) | | | ● | | | | | | | | | | | | | ● | | ● | | | | | | | | | | | | | | | | | | | | | | | | | | | | | | |
| GOUGH, E & P T (HM08314) | | | | | | | | | | | | | | | | | | | | | | ● | | | | | | | | | | | | | | | | | | | | | | | | | | |
| GROVE NATURAL THERAPY CLINIC (HM08610) | | | ● | | | ● | | | | | | | | | | ● | ● | | ● | | ● | | | | | | | | | | | | ● | | | | ● | | ● | ● | ● | | | | ● | | | |
| HEALES CHIROPRACTIC CLINIC (HM09321) | | | | | | | | | | | | | | | | | | | | | | | | | | | | | | | | | | | | | ● | | | ● | | | | | | | | |
| HOLISTIC HYPNOTHERAPY (HM09983) | | | ● | ● | | | | | ● | | | ● | | | | ● | ● | | | | | | ● | | | | | | | | ● | | | | | ● | ● | | | | ● | | ● | | ● | | | |
| INWARD BOUND THERAPIES (HM10707) | | | ● | | | | | | | | | | | | | | | | | | | | | | | | | | | | | | | | | | | | | | | | | | | | | |
| JENNIFER K HOUGH - PHYSIO (HM11004) | | | ● | | | | | | | ● | | | | | | | | | | | | ● | | | | | | | | | ● | | | | | | ● | | ● | ● | | | | ● | | | | |
| JOHNSON, ANNE (HM11068) | | | | | | | | | | | | | | | | | | | | | | | | | | | | | | | | | | | ● | | | | | ● | | | | | | | | |
| JOHNSTONS CHIROPODIST (HM11107) | | | | ● | | | | | | | | | | | | | | | | | | | | | | | | | | | | | | | | | | | | | | | | | | | | |
| KEMPSTON CHIROPRACTIC CLINIC (HM11469) | | | | | | | | | | | | | | | | | | | | | | | | | | | | | | | | | | | | | ● | | | ● | | | | | | | | |
| MAGNETS 4 HEALTH (HM12918) | | | | | | | | | | | | | | | | ● | | | | | | ● | ● | | | | | | | | | | | | ● | | ● | | | | | | | | | | | |
| OSBORN, HELEN (HM15418) | | | ● | | | | | | | | | | | | | | | | | | | | | | | | | | | | | | | | | | ● | | ● | ● | | | | | | | | |
| PRICE, SARAH (HM16596) | | | ● | | | | | | | | | | | | | ● | | | | | | | | | | | | | | | | | | | | | ● | | ● | | | | | | | | | |
| SCHOOL OF ICASA (HM18082) | | | | | | | | | | | | | | | | | | | | | | | | | | | | | | | | | | | | | | | | | | | ● | | | | | |
| SHEER PERFECTION (HM18367) | | | ● | | ● | ● | | | | | | | | | | ● | | | | | | | | | | | | | | | | | | | | | ● | | ● | | | | | ● | ● | | | |
| SPECTRUM HEALTH TRUST (HM18976) | ● | ● | ● | ● | ● | ● | ● | ● | | | ● | ● | | ● | ● | ● | ● | ● | ● | ● | ● | ● | ● | ● | ● | ● | | ● | | ● | ● | ● | | ● | ● | ● | ● | ● | ● | ● | ● | ● | | | ● | ● | ● | |
| SPORT, ALEXANDER (HM19041) | | | | | | ● | | ● | | ● | | | | | | ● | | | | | | | | | | | | | | | | | | | | | ● | | | ● | | | | | ● | | | |

# D - I Conditions treated at Practices/Businesses

| Business by County with Reference no. | Dandruff | Deafness | Depression | Diabetes | Diarrhoea | Digestive Problems | Diverticulitis | Dizziness | Dyslexia | Dyspraxia | Ear Disorders | Eczema | ENT Disorders | Epilepsy | Eye Disorders | Fatigue | Fears | Fertility Problems | Fever | Fibroids | Flatulence | Foot Problems | Fractures | Fungal Infections | Gallstones | Gastrointestinal Problems | Genital Herpes | Gingivitis | Glandular Fever | Glaucoma | Gout | Gum Disease | Hair Problems | Halitosis | Hand Problems | Hay Fever | Headaches | Hearing Problems | High Blood Pressure | Hip Complaints | Hyperactivity | Hypoglycaemia | Impotence | Incontinence | Indigestion | Infertility | Influenza | Ingrowing Toenails |
|---|---|---|---|---|---|---|---|---|---|---|---|---|---|---|---|---|---|---|---|---|---|---|---|---|---|---|---|---|---|---|---|---|---|---|---|---|---|---|---|---|---|---|---|---|---|---|---|---|
| SWEET BREEZE (HM19584) | ● | ● | ● | ● | ● | ● | ● | ● | ● | ● | ● | ● | ● | ● | ● | ● | ● | ● | ● | ● | ● | ● | ● | ● | ● | ● | ● | ● | ● | ● | ● | ● | ● | ● | ● | ● | ● | ● | ● | ● | ● | ● | ● | ● | ● | ● | ● |  |
| THERAPY CENTRE (HM19894) |  |  |  |  |  |  |  |  |  |  |  |  |  |  |  |  |  |  |  |  |  |  | ● |  |  |  |  |  |  |  |  |  |  |  |  |  |  |  |  | ● |  |  |  |  |  |  |  |  |
| THOMPSON, MARTIN (HM19992) |  |  |  |  |  |  |  |  |  |  |  |  |  |  |  |  |  |  |  |  |  |  |  |  |  |  |  |  |  |  |  |  |  |  |  |  |  |  |  |  |  |  |  |  |  |  |  | ● |
| WINTER, SALLY (HM21721) |  |  |  |  |  |  |  |  |  |  |  |  |  |  |  |  |  |  |  |  |  |  |  |  |  |  |  |  |  |  |  |  |  |  |  |  |  |  |  |  |  |  |  |  |  |  |  | ● |
| WOODSIDE CLINIC (HM21857) |  |  | ● |  |  | ● |  | ● |  |  |  | ● |  |  |  | ● |  |  |  |  |  | ● | ● |  |  | ● |  |  |  |  |  |  |  |  | ● | ● | ● |  | ● | ● |  |  |  |  | ● |  |  |  |
| BERKSHIRE |  |  |  |  |  |  |  |  |  |  |  |  |  |  |  |  |  |  |  |  |  |  |  |  |  |  |  |  |  |  |  |  |  |  |  |  |  |  |  |  |  |  |  |  |  |  |  |  |
| 1ST CHIROPRACTIC CLINIC (HM00004) |  |  |  |  |  |  |  |  |  |  |  |  |  |  |  |  |  |  |  |  |  |  |  |  |  |  |  |  |  |  |  |  |  |  |  |  | ● |  |  | ● |  |  |  |  |  |  |  |  |
| ASCOT PHYSIOFIRST CENTRE (HM01178) |  |  |  |  |  |  |  |  |  |  |  |  |  |  |  |  |  |  |  |  |  |  | ● |  |  |  |  |  |  |  |  |  |  |  |  |  |  |  |  | ● |  |  |  |  |  |  |  |  |
| BACK TO HEALTH - WINDSOR (HM01516) |  |  |  |  |  |  |  |  |  |  |  |  |  |  |  |  |  |  |  |  |  |  |  |  |  |  |  |  |  |  |  |  |  |  |  |  | ● |  |  | ● |  |  |  |  |  |  |  |  |
| BERKSHIRE CHIROPRACTIC (HM02195) |  |  |  | ● | ● | ● |  | ● |  |  |  |  |  |  | ● | ● |  |  |  |  |  |  | ● |  |  | ● |  |  |  |  | ● |  |  |  | ● |  | ● | ● |  | ● |  |  |  |  | ● |  |  |  |
| BRACKNELL CHIROPRACTIC CLINIC (HM02838) |  |  |  |  |  |  |  |  |  |  |  |  |  | ● |  |  |  |  |  |  |  |  |  |  |  |  |  |  |  |  |  |  |  |  |  |  | ● |  |  | ● |  |  |  |  |  |  |  |  |
| BRUCE, ANN (HM03264) |  |  | ● |  |  |  |  |  |  |  |  |  |  |  |  |  | ● |  |  |  |  |  |  |  |  |  |  |  |  |  |  |  |  |  |  |  |  |  |  |  |  |  |  |  |  | ● |  |  |
| BURNHAM CHIROPRACTIC CLINIC (HM03404) |  |  |  |  |  |  |  |  |  |  |  |  |  |  |  |  |  |  |  |  |  |  |  |  |  |  |  |  |  |  |  |  |  |  |  |  | ● |  | ● | ● |  |  |  |  |  |  |  |  |
| CAMPBELL, ELSPETH (HM03597) |  |  | ● |  | ● | ● |  | ● | ● |  |  |  |  |  |  | ● | ● | ● |  |  | ● |  |  | ● |  | ● |  |  |  |  |  |  |  |  |  | ● | ● |  | ● | ● | ● |  | ● |  | ● | ● |  |  |
| CASTLE HILL CLINIC (HM03833) | ● | ● | ● | ● | ● | ● | ● | ● | ● |  | ● | ● | ● | ● | ● | ● | ● |  | ● |  | ● | ● |  | ● |  | ● | ● | ● | ● | ● | ● | ● | ● | ● | ● | ● | ● |  | ● | ● | ● | ● | ● | ● | ● |  | ● |  |
| CAVERSHAM CHIROPRACTIC CLINC (HM03864) |  |  |  |  |  |  |  |  |  |  |  |  |  |  |  |  |  |  |  |  |  |  |  |  |  |  |  |  |  |  |  |  |  |  |  |  | ● |  |  | ● |  |  |  |  |  |  |  |  |
| CAVERSHAM FOOT CLINIC (HM03866) |  |  |  | ● |  |  |  |  |  |  |  |  |  |  |  |  |  |  |  |  |  | ● |  | ● |  |  |  |  |  |  |  |  |  |  |  |  |  |  |  |  |  |  |  |  |  |  |  |  |
| CHEFLAND, GERTI (HM04084) |  |  | ● |  | ● | ● | ● |  |  |  |  | ● |  |  |  | ● | ● | ● | ● |  | ● | ● |  |  | ● | ● |  |  |  |  |  |  |  |  |  |  | ● |  | ● | ● |  |  |  |  | ● | ● | ● |  |
| CHEUNG, JAMES T (DR) (HM04142) |  |  |  |  | ● |  |  |  |  |  |  |  |  |  |  |  |  |  |  |  |  |  |  |  |  |  |  |  |  |  |  |  |  |  |  | ● |  |  |  |  | ● |  |  |  |  |  |  |  |
| COOKHAM CHIROPRACTIC CLINIC (HM05068) |  | ● | ● |  |  |  |  | ● | ● |  |  | ● |  |  |  | ● |  |  |  |  |  |  |  |  |  |  |  |  |  |  |  |  |  |  |  | ● | ● | ● | ● | ● | ● |  |  |  |  | ● |  |  |
| COPPERTHWAITE, ERIC (HM05147) |  |  | ● |  |  |  |  |  |  |  |  |  |  |  |  |  |  |  |  |  |  |  |  |  |  |  |  |  |  |  |  |  |  |  |  |  |  |  |  |  |  |  |  |  |  |  |  |  |
| DEAN RUSSELL & BRYDGES ROBERT (HM05936) |  |  |  |  |  |  |  |  |  |  |  |  |  |  |  |  |  |  |  |  |  |  |  |  |  |  |  |  |  |  |  |  |  |  |  |  | ● |  |  | ● |  |  |  |  |  |  |  |  |
| DEJODE, SONIA (HM05962) |  |  |  |  |  |  |  |  |  |  |  |  |  |  |  |  |  |  |  |  |  |  |  |  |  |  |  |  |  |  |  |  |  |  |  |  | ● |  |  | ● |  |  |  |  |  |  |  |  |
| EDNEY, C S (HM06625) |  |  | ● |  |  | ● |  |  |  |  |  |  |  |  |  | ● |  |  |  |  |  |  |  |  |  |  |  |  |  |  |  |  |  |  |  |  |  |  |  |  |  |  |  |  |  |  |  |  |
| EDWARDS, JOHN (HM06659) |  |  |  |  |  |  |  |  |  |  |  |  |  |  |  |  | ● |  |  |  |  |  |  |  |  |  |  |  |  |  |  |  |  |  |  |  |  |  |  |  |  |  |  |  |  |  |  |  |
| EIGHAN, PENELOPE (HM06689) |  |  |  |  | ● | ● | ● |  |  |  | ● | ● | ● |  |  |  |  |  |  | ● | ● | ● |  |  |  |  |  |  |  |  |  |  |  |  | ● |  | ● |  | ● | ● |  |  |  |  | ● |  |  |  |
| EIGHT WINDS ACUPUNCTURE (HM06690) |  |  | ● |  |  |  |  |  |  |  |  |  |  |  |  | ● |  |  |  |  |  |  |  |  |  |  |  |  |  |  |  |  |  |  |  | ● | ● |  |  | ● |  |  |  |  | ● |  |  |  |
| FAIRBOURNE CLINIC (HM07051) |  |  |  |  |  |  |  |  |  |  | ● |  |  |  |  |  |  | ● |  |  |  | ● |  |  |  |  |  |  |  |  |  |  |  |  |  |  | ● |  |  |  |  |  |  |  |  |  |  |  |
| FEET TREAT (HM07186) |  |  | ● | ● | ● | ● | ● |  |  |  |  | ● |  |  |  | ● |  | ● |  |  |  |  |  |  |  | ● |  |  |  |  |  |  |  |  |  | ● | ● |  | ● | ● |  |  |  |  | ● | ● |  |  |
| FERINGA, MARLIES (HM07233) | ● |  | ● | ● | ● | ● | ● |  |  |  |  |  |  |  |  |  |  |  |  |  | ● |  |  |  |  |  |  |  |  |  | ● |  | ● | ● |  |  | ● |  | ● |  |  |  |  |  | ● |  |  |  |
| HALL, BEVERLEY (HM08767) |  |  | ● |  |  | ● |  |  |  |  |  |  |  |  |  |  |  |  |  |  |  | ● | ● |  |  |  |  |  |  |  |  |  |  |  | ● |  | ● |  | ● | ● |  |  |  |  |  |  |  |  |
| HALL, GRACE (HM08773) |  |  | ● |  | ● |  |  |  |  |  |  |  |  |  |  |  |  |  |  |  |  |  |  |  |  |  |  |  |  |  |  |  |  |  |  |  |  |  |  | ● |  |  |  |  |  |  |  |  |
| HAZEL'S HOLISTIC HEALTH CARE (HM09294) |  |  | ● |  |  | ● |  |  |  |  |  |  |  |  |  |  |  |  |  |  |  |  |  |  |  |  |  |  |  |  |  |  |  |  |  |  | ● |  |  |  |  |  |  |  | ● |  |  |  |
| HEWITT, ANDREW (HM09703) |  |  |  |  |  |  |  |  |  |  |  |  |  |  |  |  |  |  |  |  |  | ● | ● |  |  |  |  |  |  |  |  |  |  |  |  |  | ● |  |  | ● |  |  |  |  |  |  |  |  |

# D - I Conditions treated at Practices/Businesses

| Business by County with Reference no. | Dandruff | Deafness | Depression | Diabetes | Diarrhoea | Digestive Problems | Diverticulitis | Dizziness | Dyslexia | Dyspraxia | Ear Disorders | Eczema | ENT Disorders | Epilepsy | Eye Disorders | Fatigue | Fears | Fertility Problems | Fever | Fibroids | Flatulence | Foot Problems | Fractures | Fungal Infections |
|---|---|---|---|---|---|---|---|---|---|---|---|---|---|---|---|---|---|---|---|---|---|---|---|---|
| HILLSIDE OSTEOPATHIC PRACTICE (HM09806) | | | | | | | | | | | | | | | | | | | | | | ● | | |
| KENT, JANET (HM11524) | | | ● | | | | | | | | | | | | | ● | | | | | | | | |
| KINGFISHERS COMP HEALTH CARE (HM11650) | | | ● | | | ● | | | | | | ● | | | | ● | | ● | | | | | | |
| LANE, CORINNE (HM11931) | | | ● | | | | | | | | | | | | | ● | | | | | | | | |
| LANGLEY CHIROPRACTORS CLINIC (HM11953) | | | | | | | | | | | | | | | | | | | | | | | | |
| LAVENDER, S (HM12029) | | | ● | | | | | | | | | | | | | | | | | | | ● | | ● |
| LIFE GUIDANCE (HM12344) | | | | | | ● | | | | | | | | | | | ● | | | | | | | |
| LISSADELL HOUSE PRACTICE (HM12457) | | | ● | | ● | ● | ● | ● | | | | ● | | | | ● | ● | ● | | | ● | | | |
| MAIDENHEAD CHIROPRACTIC (HM12933) | | | | | | | | | | | | | | | | | | | | | | | | |
| MAIDENHEAD PHYSIO & SPORTS (HM12934) | | | | | | | | | | | | | | | | | | | | | | | | |
| MCGREGOR, TONY (HM13504) | | | ● | | | | | | | | | | | | | | ● | | | | | | | |
| NASEBY ACUPUNCTURE CLINIC (HM14487) | | | ● | | ● | ● | ● | ● | | | ● | ● | | | | ● | ● | ● | ● | ● | ● | ● | | |
| NATURAL HEALTH CONSULTANCY (HM14591) | ● | | ● | ● | ● | ● | | ● | | | ● | ● | ● | | | ● | ● | | ● | ● | ● | | | ● |
| NATURAL THERAPY CLINIC (HM14656) | ● | ● | ● | ● | ● | ● | ● | ● | ● | ● | ● | ● | ● | ● | ● | ● | ● | ● | ● | ● | ● | ● | ● | ● |
| NATURAL THERAPY CLINIC (HM14655) | ● | ● | ● | ● | ● | ● | | ● | ● | | ● | ● | ● | | | ● | ● | ● | ● | ● | ● | ● | | ● |
| NEWBURY CHIROPRACTIC CENTRE (HM14851) | | | | | | ● | | | | | | | | | | | | | | | | | | |
| NEWBURY PHYSIOTHERAPY (HM14852) | | | | | | | | | | | | | | | | | | | | | | ● | ● | |
| NS3UK NUTRITION SERVICES (HM15099) | ● | | ● | | ● | ● | ● | ● | ● | ● | ● | ● | ● | | | ● | | ● | | ● | ● | | | ● |
| PETERS, JEAN (HM16086) | | | ● | | | ● | | | | | | | | | | ● | | | | | | ● | | ● |
| PIM HEALTH CLINIC (HM16301) | | | ● | | | ● | | | | | | | | | | ● | ● | | | | | | | |
| ROSEDALE CLINIC (HM17616) | | | ● | | ● | ● | | | | | | | | | | ● | | | | | | | | |
| SANDALL, S (HM17898) | | | | ● | | | | | | | | | | | | | | | | | | ● | | |
| SLOUGH SPORTS INJURIES CLINIC (HM18690) | | | | | | | | | | | | | | | | | | | | | | | | |
| SMETHURST, ALISON (HM18704) | | | ● | ● | | ● | | | | | | ● | | | | ● | | ● | | | | ● | | |
| SOUTH LODGE CONSULTING (HM18909) | | | | | | | | | | | | | | | | | | | | | | ● | ● | |
| STRINGER, FRANCES (HM19407) | | | | | | ● | | | | | | | | | | ● | ● | | | | | | | |
| SUNNINGDALE HEALING CENTRE (HM19509) | | | | | | | | | | | | | | | | | | | | | | | | |
| THATCHAM CHIROPRACTIC CLINIC (HM19867) | | | | | | | | | | | | | | ● | | | | | | | | | | |
| TSENG, PATRICIA (HM20359) | | | ● | | | | | | | | | ● | | | | ● | ● | | | | | | | |
| WINNERSH HYPNOTHERAPY PRACTICE (HM21711) | | | | | | | | | | | | | | | | | ● | | | | | | | |
| WOOD, JEANIE M (HM21801) | | | ● | | | ● | | | | | | | | | | | | | | | | | | |
| WOODLEY HEALING CENTRE (HM21836) | ● | | ● | ● | ● | ● | ● | ● | | | | ● | | | | ● | | ● | | ● | ● | ● | | ● |
| **BRISTOL** | | | | | | | | | | | | | | | | | | | | | | | | |
| ANDERSON, KEITH (HM00830) | | | | | | | | | | | | ● | | | | | | | | | | | | |

| Business by County with Reference no. | Gallstones | Gastrointestinal Problems | Genital Herpes | Gingivitis | Glandular Fever | Glaucoma | Gout | Gum Disease | Hair Problems | Halitosis | Hand Problems | Hay Fever | Headaches | Hearing Problems | High Blood Pressure | Hip Complaints | Hyperactivity | Hypoglycaemia | Impotence | Incontinence | Indigestion | Infertility | Influenza | Ingrowing Toenails |
|---|---|---|---|---|---|---|---|---|---|---|---|---|---|---|---|---|---|---|---|---|---|---|---|---|
| HILLSIDE OSTEOPATHIC PRACTICE (HM09806) | | | | | | | | | | | ● | | ● | | | ● | | | | | | | | |
| KENT, JANET (HM11524) | | | | | | | | | | | | | ● | | ● | | | | ● | ● | | | | |
| KINGFISHERS COMP HEALTH CARE (HM11650) | ● | | | | | | | | | | | | ● | | ● | | | | | | ● | | | |
| LANE, CORINNE (HM11931) | | | | | | | | | | | | | | | | | | | | | | | | |
| LANGLEY CHIROPRACTORS CLINIC (HM11953) | | | | | | | | | | | | | ● | | ● | ● | | | | | | | | |
| LAVENDER, S (HM12029) | | | | | | | | | | | | | | | | | | | | | | | | |
| LIFE GUIDANCE (HM12344) | | | | | | | | | | | | | | | | | ● | | | | ● | | | |
| LISSADELL HOUSE PRACTICE (HM12457) | | ● | | | | | ● | | | ● | ● | ● | ● | ● | ● | ● | | ● | ● | | ● | ● | | |
| MAIDENHEAD CHIROPRACTIC (HM12933) | | | | | | | | | | | | | ● | | | ● | | | | | | | | |
| MAIDENHEAD PHYSIO & SPORTS (HM12934) | | | | | | | | | | | | | | | | ● | | | | | | | | |
| MCGREGOR, TONY (HM13504) | | | | | | | | | | | | | | | | | | | | | | | | |
| NASEBY ACUPUNCTURE CLINIC (HM14487) | ● | ● | ● | ● | ● | ● | ● | | | ● | ● | ● | ● | | ● | ● | ● | ● | ● | ● | ● | ● | ● | |
| NATURAL HEALTH CONSULTANCY (HM14591) | | ● | | | ● | | ● | | | ● | | ● | ● | ● | ● | ● | ● | ● | ● | | ● | | ● | |
| NATURAL THERAPY CLINIC (HM14656) | ● | ● | ● | ● | ● | ● | ● | ● | ● | ● | ● | ● | ● | ● | ● | ● | ● | ● | ● | ● | ● | ● | ● | |
| NATURAL THERAPY CLINIC (HM14655) | ● | ● | ● | ● | ● | | ● | ● | ● | ● | | ● | ● | ● | ● | ● | ● | ● | ● | ● | ● | ● | ● | |
| NEWBURY CHIROPRACTIC CENTRE (HM14851) | | | | | | | | | | | | | ● | | ● | ● | | | | | ● | | | |
| NEWBURY PHYSIOTHERAPY (HM14852) | | | | | | | | | | | | | | | | ● | | | | | | | | |
| NS3UK NUTRITION SERVICES (HM15099) | | ● | | ● | | | ● | | | ● | | | ● | | | | ● | ● | | | ● | ● | | |
| PETERS, JEAN (HM16086) | | | | | | | | | | | | ● | ● | | ● | ● | ● | | | | ● | | | ● |
| PIM HEALTH CLINIC (HM16301) | | | | | | | | | | | | | ● | | ● | ● | | | | | ● | | | |
| ROSEDALE CLINIC (HM17616) | | | | | | | | | | | | ● | ● | | ● | ● | | | | | | | | |
| SANDALL, S (HM17898) | | | | | | | | | | | | | ● | | | ● | | | | | | | | |
| SLOUGH SPORTS INJURIES CLINIC (HM18690) | | | | | | | | | | | | | | | | ● | | | | | | | | |
| SMETHURST, ALISON (HM18704) | | | | | | | | | | | | | ● | | ● | | | | | | ● | ● | | |
| SOUTH LODGE CONSULTING (HM18909) | | | | | | | | | | | | | | | | | | | | | | | | |
| STRINGER, FRANCES (HM19407) | | | | | | | | | | | | | ● | | ● | ● | | | | | | | | |
| SUNNINGDALE HEALING CENTRE (HM19509) | | | | | | | | | | | | | | | | ● | | | | | | | | |
| THATCHAM CHIROPRACTIC CLINIC (HM19867) | | | | | | | | | | | | | | | | ● | | | | | | | | |
| TSENG, PATRICIA (HM20359) | | | | | | | | | | | | | ● | | ● | ● | | | | | | | | |
| WINNERSH HYPNOTHERAPY PRACTICE (HM21711) | | | | | | | | | | | | | ● | | | | | | | | | | | |
| WOOD, JEANIE M (HM21801) | | | | | | | | | | | | | ● | | ● | ● | | | | | | | | |
| WOODLEY HEALING CENTRE (HM21836) | ● | ● | | ● | ● | | ● | ● | ● | ● | ● | ● | ● | | ● | ● | ● | ● | ● | ● | ● | ● | ● | |
| **BRISTOL** | | | | | | | | | | | | | | | | | | | | | | | | |
| ANDERSON, KEITH (HM00830) | | | | | | | | | | | | | | | | | | | | | | | | |

# D - I Conditions treated at Practices/Businesses

| Business by County with Reference no. | Dandruff | Deafness | Depression | Diabetes | Diarrhoea | Digestive Problems | Diverticulitis | Dizziness | Dyslexia | Dyspraxia | Ear Disorders | Eczema | ENT Disorders | Epilepsy | Eye Disorders | Fatigue | Fears | Fertility Problems | Fever | Fibroids | Flatulence | Foot Problems | Fractures | Fungal Infections | Gallstones | Gastrointestinal Problems | Genital Herpes | Gingivitis | Glandular Fever | Glaucoma | Gout | Gum Disease | Hair Problems | Halitosis | Hand Problems | Hay Fever | Headaches | Hearing Problems | High Blood Pressure | Hip Complaints | Hyperactivity | Hypoglycaemia | Impotence | Incontinence | Indigestion | Infertility | Influenza | Ingrowing Toenails |
|---|---|---|---|---|---|---|---|---|---|---|---|---|---|---|---|---|---|---|---|---|---|---|---|---|---|---|---|---|---|---|---|---|---|---|---|---|---|---|---|---|---|---|---|---|---|---|---|---|
| AQUARIUS HEALTH CENTRE (HM00959) | ● | ● | ● | ● | ● | ● | ● | ● | ● | ● | ● | ● | ● | ● | ● | ● | ● | ● | ● | ● | ● | ● | ● | ● | ● | ● | ● | ● | ● | ● | ● | ● | ● | ● | ● | ● | ● | ● | ● | ● | ● | ● | ● | ● | ● | ● | ● | |
| ARMSTRONG, ELIZABETH (HM01021) | | | | | | | | | | | | | | | | | | | | | | | | | | | | | | | | | | | | | ● | | | ● | | | | | | | | |
| ASS-DANCE MOVEMENT THERAPY (HM01268) | | | ● | | | | | | ● | ● | | | | | | ● | ● | | | | | | | | | | | | | | | | | | | | | | | | ● | | | | | | | |
| AVON COMPLEMENTARY MEDICINE (HM01404) | | | | | | | | | | | | | | | | | | | | | | | | | | | | | | | | | | | | | | | | | ● | | | | | | | |
| BAGGLEY, J M (HM01536) | | | | | | | | | | | | | | | | | | | | | | ● | | ● | | | | | | | | | | | | | | | | | | | | | | | | |
| BEVAN, RUSS (HM02242) | ● | | ● | ● | ● | ● | | ● | ● | | ● | ● | ● | | | ● | ● | ● | ● | | ● | ● | | | | ● | | | ● | | ● | | ● | ● | | ● | ● | | ● | ● | ● | ● | ● | ● | ● | ● | | |
| BRISTOL HYPNOTHERAPY CLINIC (HM03063) | | | ● | | | | | | | | | | | | | | ● | | | | | | | | | | | | | | | | | | | | ● | | ● | | | | | | | | | |
| BRISTOL NATURAL HEALTH SERVICE (HM03064) | ● | | ● | ● | ● | ● | | ● | | | | ● | ● | | | ● | ● | ● | | | | | | | | | | | | | | | | ● | | ● | ● | ● | ● | ● | ● | | ● | ● | ● | ● | ● | |
| CASTLE CHIROPODY CLINIC (HM03828) | | | | | | | | | | | | | | | | | | | | | | ● | | ● | | | | | | | | | | | | | | | | | | | | | | | | |
| CHARLES CLINIC (HM04020) | | | | | | | | | | | | | | | | | | | | | | | | | | | | | | | | | | | | | ● | | | ● | | | | | | | | |
| CLARK, LYN (HM04566) | | | ● | | | | | | | | | | | | | | | ● | | | | | | | | | | | | | | | | | | | | | | | | | | | | | | |
| CLIFTON CHIROPRACTIC CLINIC (HM04666) | | | | ● | | ● | | ● | | | ● | ● | | | | | | | | | | ● | | | | ● | | | | | ● | ● | | | | | ● | | | ● | | | | | ● | | | |
| CLIFTON PRACTICE (HM04670) | | | ● | | | | | | | | | | | | | | | | | | | | | | | | | | | | | | | | | | | | | | | | | | | | | |
| CLINIC OF NATURAL MEDICINE (HM04704) | | | ● | ● | | ● | | | | | | | | | | | | | | | | | | | | | | | | | | | | | | | ● | | | | | | | | ● | | | |
| CROSS HANDS CHIRO CLINIC (HM05478) | | | | | | ● | | | | | | | | | | | | | | | | | ● | | | | | | | | | | | | | | ● | | | ● | | | | | | | | |
| CTRE FOR KINESIOLOGY (HM05542) | ● | | ● | ● | ● | ● | ● | ● | | | ● | ● | | | | ● | ● | ● | | ● | ● | ● | | ● | | ● | | | | | ● | | | ● | | ● | ● | ● | ● | ● | ● | ● | | | ● | ● | | |
| DANCE VOICE THERAPY CENTRE (HM05709) | | | ● | | | | | | | | | | | | | ● | ● | | | | | | | | | | | | | | | | | | | | | | | | ● | | | | | | | |
| DOWRY CHIROPRACTIC CLINIC (HM06255) | | | | | | | | | | | | | | | | | | | | | | | | | | | | | | | | | | | | | ● | | | ● | | | | | | | | |
| FILE, CHRISTINE (HM07288) | | | ● | ● | | ● | | | | | | ● | | | | | | | | | | | | | | | | | | | | | | | | | ● | | | | | | | | | | | |
| FREEMAN, ANN (HM07719) | ● | | ● | | ● | ● | ● | ● | | | | ● | ● | | | ● | ● | ● | ● | ● | ● | ● | | ● | ● | ● | ● | ● | | | ● | ● | ● | ● | ● | ● | ● | ● | ● | | ● | ● | | ● | ● | ● | ● | |
| GARLAND, C (HM07889) | | | ● | | | | | | | | | | | | | | | | | | | | | | | | | | | | | | | | | | ● | | | | | | | | | | | |
| HARCOURT, A (HM08964) | | | | | | | | | | | | | | | | | | | | | | | | | | | | | | | | | | | | | ● | | | ● | | | | | | | | |
| HEALING WITH GABRIELLE TWINE (HM09360) | | | ● | | ● | ● | ● | | | | | ● | | ● | ● | ● | ● | ● | ● | ● | ● | ● | ● | | | ● | ● | | ● | | ● | ● | | | ● | ● | ● | | ● | ● | | | | ● | ● | ● | | |
| HEALTH & HEALING (HM09371) | ● | ● | ● | ● | ● | ● | ● | ● | ● | ● | ● | ● | ● | ● | ● | ● | ● | ● | ● | ● | ● | ● | ● | ● | ● | ● | ● | ● | ● | ● | ● | ● | ● | ● | ● | ● | ● | ● | ● | ● | ● | ● | ● | ● | ● | ● | ● | |
| HUDSON, JOHN (HM10313) | | | ● | | | | | | | | | | | | | | | | | | | | | | | | | | | | | | | | | | | | | | | | | | | | | |
| KEYNSHAM CHIROPRACTIC CLINIC (HM11580) | | | | | | | | | | | | | | | | | | | | | | | | | | | | | | | | | | | | | ● | | | ● | | | | | | | | |
| KINGSWOOD CHIROPRACTIC CLINIC (HM11682) | | | | | | | | | | | | | | | | | | | | | | | | | | | | | | | | | | | | | ● | | | ● | | | | | | | | |
| NAILSEA CHIROPRACTIC CLINIC (HM14460) | | | | | | | | | | | | | | | | | | | | | | | | | | | | | | | | | | | | | ● | | | ● | | | | | | | | |
| NAYDLER, NICK (HM14711) | | | ● | | | | | | | | | | | | | | | | | | | | | | | | | | | | | | | | | | | | | | | | | | | | | |
| ORCHARD MEDICAL CENTRE (HM15364) | | | ● | ● | | ● | | ● | | | | | | | | | | | | | | ● | | ● | | | | | | | | | | | ● | | ● | | ● | ● | | | ● | ● | | | | |
| ORIENTAL MEDICINE PRACTICE (HM15387) | | | ● | ● | ● | ● | ● | ● | | | | ● | ● | | ● | ● | ● | ● | ● | ● | ● | ● | ● | ● | ● | ● | ● | ● | ● | ● | ● | ● | | ● | ● | ● | ● | ● | ● | ● | ● | ● | ● | ● | ● | ● | | |
| PARKER CLINIC (HM15683) | | | | | | | | | | | | | | | | | | | | | | | ● | | | | | | | | | | | | | | ● | | | ● | | | | | | | | |
| POCOCK, A (HM16391) | | | | | | | | | | | | | | | | | | | | | | ● | | ● | | | | | | | | | | | | | | | | | | | | | | | | |
| REDLANDS HOUSE CLINIC (HM17028) | | | | | | | | | | | | | | | | | | | | | | | ● | | | | | | | | | | | | | | ● | | | ● | | | | | | | | |

# D - I Conditions treated at Practices/Businesses

| Business by County with Reference no. | Dandruff | Deafness | Depression | Diabetes | Diarrhoea | Digestive Problems | Diverticulitis | Dizziness | Dyslexia | Dyspraxia | Ear Disorders | Eczema | ENT Disorders | Epilepsy | Eye Disorders | Fatigue | Fears | Fertility Problems | Fever | Fibroids | Flatulence | Foot Problems | Fractures | Fungal Infections | Gallstones | Gastrointestinal Problems | Genital Herpes | Gingivitis | Glandular Fever | Glaucoma | Gout | Gum Disease | Hair Problems | Halitosis | Hand Problems | Hay Fever | Headaches | Hearing Problems | High Blood Pressure | Hip Complaints | Hyperactivity | Hypoglycaemia | Impotence | Incontinence | Indigestion | Infertility | Influenza | Ingrowing Toenails |
|---|---|---|---|---|---|---|---|---|---|---|---|---|---|---|---|---|---|---|---|---|---|---|---|---|---|---|---|---|---|---|---|---|---|---|---|---|---|---|---|---|---|---|---|---|---|---|---|---|
| ENFIELD, CLAUDIA (HM06820) | | | | | ● | ● | | | | | | | | | | ● | | | | | | | | | | ● | | | | | ● | | | | | | ● | | ● | ● | | | ● | | ● | ● | | |
| FIRMAN, BARBARA (HM07332) | | | ● | ● | | ● | ● | ● | | | ● | ● | ● | | | ● | ● | ● | | | | ● | | | | | | | ● | | | | | | | | | | ● | ● | ● | | ● | | ● | ● | | |
| FLEET, BARBARA (HM07402) | | | ● | | | ● | | | | | | ● | | | | ● | ● | | | | | | | | | | | | | | | | | | | | | | | | | | | | | | | |
| GERRARDS CROSS SPORTS & BACK (HM08004) | | | | | | | | | | | | | | | | | | | | | | ● | ● | | | | | | | | | | | | | | | | | | | | | | | | | |
| HOBBS, SALLY (HM09857) | ● | ● | ● | ● | ● | ● | ● | ● | ● | ● | ● | ● | ● | ● | ● | ● | ● | ● | ● | ● | ● | ● | ● | ● | ● | ● | ● | ● | ● | ● | ● | ● | ● | ● | ● | ● | ● | ● | ● | ● | ● | ● | ● | ● | ● | ● | ● | |
| HOLISTIC HEALING (HM09959) | | | ● | | | | | | | | | | | | | ● | | | | | | | | | | | | | | | | | | | ● | ● | ● | | ● | ● | ● | | | | ● | | | |
| HULCOTT END PRACTICE (HM10352) | | | ● | | | | | | | ● | | ● | | | | | | | | | | ● | ● | | | ● | | | | | | | | | ● | | ● | | | ● | | | | | | | | |
| J J COUNSELLING SERVICES (HM10798) | | | ● | | | | | | | | | | | | | ● | | | | | | | | | | | | | | | | | | | | | | | | | | | ● | | | | | |
| JOHNSON, HELEN (HM11074) | ● | ● | ● | ● | ● | ● | ● | ● | ● | ● | ● | ● | ● | ● | ● | ● | ● | ● | ● | ● | ● | ● | ● | ● | ● | ● | ● | ● | ● | ● | ● | ● | ● | ● | ● | ● | ● | ● | ● | ● | ● | ● | ● | ● | ● | ● | ● | ● |
| K BANFIELD NATUROPATHY/OSTEO (HM11288) | | | | | ● | ● | ● | | | | ● | | | | | ● | | | | | ● | ● | | | ● | ● | | | | | ● | | | | ● | | ● | | | ● | ● | ● | | | ● | | | |
| KENTISH, LORNE (HM11531) | | ● | | | | ● | | ● | | | | | | | | ● | | | | | | ● | | ● | | | | | | | | | | | | ● | ● | | ● | | | | | | ● | | ● | ● |
| LONG CRENDON OSTEOPATHS (HM12614) | | | | | | | | | | | | | | | | | | | | | | ● | | | | | | | | | | | | | | | ● | | | ● | | | | | | | | |
| MATTHEWS, FRANK (HM13306) | | | | | | | | | | | | | | | | | ● | | | | | | | | | | | | | | | | | | | | | | | | | | | | | | | |
| MIDDLE WAY RE-EDUCATION CTRE (HM13813) | | | | | | | | | ● | ● | ● | | | | | | ● | | | | | | | | | | | | | | | | | | | | | ● | | | ● | | | | | | | |
| MIND AND BODY (HM13959) | | | | | | ● | | | | | | | | | | ● | ● | | | | | | | | | | | | | | | | ● | | | | ● | | ● | | | | | | | | | |
| MIRZOEFF, PETER (HM13992) | | | ● | | | | | | | | | | | | | | ● | | | | | | | | | | | | | | | | | | | | | | | | | | | | | | | |
| MORRISSEY, BLANCHE (HM14236) | | | | | | | | | | | | | | | | | | | | | | ● | | | | | | | | | | | | | | | | | | | | | | | | | | |
| O'NEIL, PAULA (HM15326) | | | | | ● | ● | ● | | | | ● | ● | | | ● | ● | | ● | | | ● | | | | | ● | | | | | ● | | | | ● | ● | ● | ● | | | | | | | ● | ● | | |
| OXFORDSHIRE BOWEN CLINIC (HM15545) | | | | | | ● | | ● | | | ● | | | | | | | | | | | | | | | ● | | | | | | | | | | | | | ● | ● | | | | | ● | | | |
| PATON, BARBARA (HM15823) | | | ● | | | ● | | | | | | | | | | ● | | | | | | ● | | | | | | | | | | | | | ● | | ● | | ● | ● | ● | | | | ● | | | |
| PHYSIO FIRST PRACTICE (HM16199) | | | | | | | | | | | | | | | | | | | | | | | ● | | | | | | | | | | | | | | | | | | | | | | | | | |
| PINEWOOD CHIROPODY PRACTICE (HM16312) | | | | ● | | | | | | | | | | | | | | | | | | ● | | ● | | | | | | | ● | | | | | | | | | | | | | | | | | ● |
| PRESTWOOD PHYSIOTHERAPY CLINIC (HM16562) | | | | | | | | | | | | | | | | | | | | | | | ● | | | | | | | | | | | | | | | | | | | | | | | | | |
| REIKI HEALTH CENTRE (HM17137) | | | | | | | | | | | | | | ● | | | | | | | | | | | | | | | | | | | | | | | ● | | | | | | | | | | | |
| RUNDLE, RICHARD (HM17752) | ● | ● | ● | ● | ● | ● | ● | ● | | | ● | ● | ● | ● | ● | ● | ● | ● | ● | ● | ● | ● | ● | ● | ● | ● | ● | ● | ● | ● | ● | ● | ● | ● | ● | ● | ● | ● | ● | ● | ● | ● | ● | ● | ● | ● | ● | |
| SHAW, FIONA (HM18335) | | | ● | | ● | ● | | | | | | | | | | ● | | | | | | | | | | | | | | | | | | | | | ● | | | | | | | ● | ● | | | |
| SHENLEY CHIROPRACTIC CLINIC (HM18399) | | | | | | | | | | | | | | | | | | | | | | | | | | | | | | | | | | | | | ● | | | ● | | | | | | | | |
| STEINBERG, PAMELA (HM19189) | ● | ● | ● | ● | ● | ● | ● | ● | ● | ● | ● | ● | ● | ● | ● | ● | ● | ● | ● | ● | ● | ● | ● | ● | ● | ● | ● | ● | ● | ● | ● | ● | ● | ● | ● | ● | ● | ● | ● | ● | ● | ● | ● | ● | ● | ● | ● | |
| TAYLOR, IAN E (HM19763) | | | | | | | | | | | | | | | | | | | | | | ● | | | | | | | | | ● | | | | | | | | | | | | | | | | | ● |
| TEACHERS OF ALEXNDR TECH (HM19806) | | | | | | ● | | | | | | | | | | | ● | | | | | | | | | | | | | | | | | | | | ● | | | ● | | | | | | | | |
| TODD, PAUL (HM20107) | | | | | | | | | | | | | | | | | | | | | | ● | | ● | | | | | | | | | | | | | | | | | | | | | | | | |
| TOMLIN, SUSAN M (HM20136) | | | ● | | ● | ● | ● | | | | ● | | ● | | ● | ● | | ● | | | ● | | | | ● | ● | | ● | | ● | ● | ● | | | | ● | ● | ● | | | ● | | ● | | ● | ● | | |
| TUDOR HOUSE CLINIC (HM20371) | | | | | | | | | | | | | | | | | | | | | | | ● | | | | | | | | | | | | | | | | | ● | | | | | | | | |
| WARDLAW, MICHAEL (HM20921) | | | | | | | | | | | | | | | | | | | | | | ● | | | | | | | | | | | | | | | | | | | | | | | | | | |

# D - I Conditions treated at Practices/Businesses

| Business by County with Reference no. | Dandruff | Deafness | Depression | Diabetes | Diarrhoea | Digestive Problems | Diverticulitis | Dizziness | Dyslexia | Dyspraxia | Ear Disorders | Eczema | ENT Disorders | Epilepsy | Eye Disorders | Fatigue | Fears | Fertility Problems | Fever | Fibroids | Flatulence | Foot Problems | Fractures | Fungal Infections | Gallstones | Gastrointestinal Problems | Genital Herpes | Gingivitis | Glandular Fever | Glaucoma | Gout | Gum Disease | Hair Problems | Halitosis | Hand Problems | Hay Fever | Headaches | Hearing Problems | High Blood Pressure | Hip Complaints | Hyperactivity | Hypoglycaemia | Impotence | Incontinence | Indigestion | Infertility | Influenza | Ingrowing Toenails |
|---|---|---|---|---|---|---|---|---|---|---|---|---|---|---|---|---|---|---|---|---|---|---|---|---|---|---|---|---|---|---|---|---|---|---|---|---|---|---|---|---|---|---|---|---|---|---|---|
| REDMOND, CAROLINE (HM17031) | ● | ● | ● | ● | ● | ● | ● | ● | ● | ● | ● | ● | ● | ● | ● | ● | ● | ● | ● | ● | ● | ● | ● | ● | ● | ● | ● | ● | ● | ● | ● | ● | ● | ● | ● | ● | ● | ● | ● | ● | ● | ● | ● | ● | ● | ● | ● | |
| RICHARD GIBBONS - ACUPUNCT (HM17244) | | | ● | | ● | ● | | ● | | | | ● | | | | ● | | ● | | | | | | | ● | | | | | | | | | | | ● | ● | | ● | ● | | | ● | ● | ● | ● | | |
| STEVENS, BEN (HM19225) | | | ● | | ● | ● | | | | | | | | | | | | ● | | | | | | | | | | | | | | | | | | ● | ● | | | | | | | | | ● | | |
| STIRLING, P (HM19302) | ● | ● | ● | ● | ● | ● | ● | ● | ● | ● | ● | ● | ● | ● | ● | ● | ● | ● | ● | ● | ● | ● | ● | ● | ● | ● | ● | ● | ● | ● | ● | ● | ● | ● | ● | ● | ● | ● | ● | ● | ● | ● | ● | ● | ● | ● | ● | |
| STYLES, PATRICIA (HM19458) | | | | | | | | | | | | | | | | | | | | | | ● | | ● | | | | | | | | | | | | | | | | | | | | | | | | |
| THOMAS, TRUDY (HM19958) | | | | | | | | | | | | | | | | | | | | | | ● | | ● | | | | | | | | | | | | | | | | | | | | | | | | |
| TOLL HOUSE CLINIC (HM20120) | | | ● | | | | | | | | | | | | | | | | | | | ● | ● | | | ● | | | | | | | | | | | | | | ● | | | | ● | | | | |
| **BUCKINGHAMSHIRE** | | | | | | | | | | | | | | | | | | | | | | | | | | | | | | | | | | | | | | | | | | | | | | | | |
| ALTERNATE WAYS (HM00692) | | | | | | | | | | | | | | | | ● | | | | | | | | | | | | | | | | | | | | | ● | | | | | | | | | | | |
| ALTERNATIVE THERAPIES TRAINING (HM00730) | ● | ● | ● | ● | ● | ● | ● | ● | ● | ● | ● | ● | ● | ● | ● | ● | ● | ● | ● | ● | ● | ● | ● | ● | ● | ● | ● | ● | ● | ● | ● | ● | ● | ● | ● | ● | ● | ● | ● | ● | ● | ● | ● | ● | ● | ● | ● | |
| AMERSHAM CHIROPRACTIC CLINIC (HM00779) | | | | | | | | ● | | ● | | | | | | | | | | | | ● | | | | | | | | | | | | | | | ● | | | ● | ● | | | | | | | |
| AMERSHAM OSTEOPATHIC CLINIC (HM00780) | | | | | | ● | | | ● | ● | ● | ● | ● | ● | | ● | | | | | | | ● | | | ● | | | | | | | | | ● | | ● | | | ● | ● | | | | | | ● | |
| ASHBERRY PHYSIOTHERAPY CLINIC (HM01188) | | | | | | | | | | | | | | | | | | | | | | | | | | | | | | | | | | | | | | | | ● | | | | | | | | |
| AYLESBURY CHIROPRACTIC CLINIC (HM01422) | | | | | | | | | | | | | | | | | | | | | | | | | | | | | | | | | | | | | ● | | | ● | | | | | | | | |
| AYLESBURY COMPLEMENTARY HEALTH (HM01423) | | | ● | | | | | | ● | ● | | ● | | | | ● | ● | | | | | | | | | | | | | | | | | | | | ● | | ● | | | | ● | | ● | | | |
| AYLESBURY VALE THERAPY (HM01425) | | | ● | | | ● | | | | | | | | | | ● | ● | ● | | | | | | | | ● | | | | | | | | | | | ● | | ● | | ● | | ● | ● | | ● | | |
| BANFIELD, KATIE (HM01657) | | | | | ● | ● | ● | | | | ● | | | | | ● | | | | | ● | ● | | | ● | ● | | | | | ● | | | | ● | | ● | | | ● | ● | ● | | | ● | | | |
| BEACONSFIELD CHIRO CLINIC (HM01954) | | | | | | | | | | | | | | | | | | | | | | | | | | | | | | | | | | | | | ● | | | ● | | | | | | | | |
| BIGGS, SYLVIA (HM02294) | | | ● | | | ● | | | | | | | | | | | | | | | | | | | | | | | | | | | | | | ● | ● | | | ● | ● | | | | ● | | | |
| BODY & SOUL (HM02565) | | | ● | | | | | | | | | ● | | | | | | | | | | | | | | | | | | | | | | | | | ● | | | | | | | | | | | |
| BREEZE, T (HM02951) | | | | | | | | | | | | | | | | | | | | | | | | | | | | | | | | | | | | | ● | | | | | | | | | | | |
| BUCKINGHAM CHIROPRACTIC CLINIC (HM03310) | | | | | | | | | | | | | | | | | | | | | | | | | | | | | | | | | | | | | ● | | ● | ● | | | | | | | | |
| CAMPBELL, LOUISE (HM03604) | | ● | | | | ● | | | | | | | | | | ● | | | | | | | | | | | | | | | | | | | | ● | ● | | | | | | | | ● | | | |
| CAMPBELL, NIKKI (HM03605) | | ● | ● | ● | | ● | | ● | ● | ● | ● | | ● | | ● | ● | ● | ● | | | | | | | | | | ● | | | | ● | | | | | ● | ● | ● | ● | ● | | | | | | | |
| CASTLE STREET CLINIC (HM03837) | | | | | ● | ● | | | | | | | | | | | | ● | | | | ● | | | ● | ● | | | ● | | | | | | ● | ● | ● | | ● | ● | | ● | | | ● | ● | | |
| CHILTERN AROMATHERAPY (HM04172) | | | | | | | | | | | | | | | | ● | | | | | | | | | | | | | | | | | | | | | ● | | | | | | | | | | | |
| COACHING FOR SUCCESS (HM04750) | | | | | | ● | | | | | | | | | | ● | ● | | | | | | | | | ● | | | | | | | | | | | ● | | | | | | | | | | | |
| COLDWELL, VERONICA (HM04810) | ● | ● | ● | ● | ● | ● | ● | ● | ● | ● | ● | ● | ● | ● | ● | ● | ● | ● | ● | ● | ● | ● | ● | ● | ● | ● | ● | ● | ● | ● | ● | ● | ● | ● | ● | ● | ● | ● | ● | ● | ● | ● | ● | ● | ● | ● | ● | |
| COMPLEMENTARY HEALTH (HM04921) | | | ● | | | | | | ● | ● | | ● | | | | ● | ● | | | | | | | | | | | | | | | | | | | | ● | | ● | | | | ● | | ● | | | |
| COMPLEMENTARY HEALTH CENTRE (HM04923) | | | ● | | ● | | ● | | ● | ● | | ● | | | | ● | ● | ● | | | | | | | | | | | | | | | | | | | ● | | ● | | | ● | ● | | ● | | | |
| DOIG, PAUL (HM06158) | | | ● | ● | ● | ● | ● | ● | | | | ● | | ● | | ● | ● | ● | ● | ● | ● | ● | | ● | ● | ● | | | | | ● | | | ● | | ● | ● | | ● | | ● | | | | ● | ● | | |
| DOWDELL, FIONA K (HM06234) | | | | | | | | | | | | | | | | | | | | | | | | | | | | | | | | | | | | | ● | | | ● | | | | | | | | |
| EDWARDS, EMMA (HM06650) | | | ● | | | ● | | ● | | | | | | | | ● | | | | | | | | | | | | | | | | | | | ● | ● | ● | | ● | | | | | ● | ● | | ● | |
| ELAINE MCCARTHY REFLEXOLOGIST (HM06698) | | ● | ● | ● | ● | ● | ● | ● | | | ● | ● | ● | ● | ● | ● | ● | ● | ● | ● | ● | ● | | ● | | ● | ● | | ● | ● | ● | ● | | | ● | ● | ● | ● | ● | ● | ● | ● | ● | ● | ● | ● | ● | |

# D - I Conditions treated at Practices/Businesses

| Business by County with Reference no. | Dandruff | Deafness | Depression | Diabetes | Diarrhoea | Digestive Problems | Diverticulitis | Dizziness | Dyslexia | Dyspraxia | Ear Disorders | Eczema | ENT Disorders | Epilepsy | Eye Disorders | Fatigue | Fears | Fertility Problems | Fever | Fibroids | Flatulence | Foot Problems | Fractures | Fungal Infections | Gallstones | Gastrointestinal Problems | Genital Herpes | Gingivitis | Glandular Fever | Glaucoma | Gout | Gum Disease | Hair Problems | Halitosis | Hand Problems | Hay Fever | Headaches | Hearing Problems | High Blood Pressure | Hip Complaints | Hyperactivity | Hypoglycaemia | Impotence | Incontinence | Indigestion | Infertility | Influenza | Ingrowing Toenails |
|---|---|---|---|---|---|---|---|---|---|---|---|---|---|---|---|---|---|---|---|---|---|---|---|---|---|---|---|---|---|---|---|---|---|---|---|---|---|---|---|---|---|---|---|---|---|---|---|---|
| WELLBURN (HM21154) |●|●|●|●|●|●|●|●|●|●|●|●|●|●|●|●|●|●| |●|●|●|●|●|●|●|●|●|●| |●|●|●|●|●|●|●|●|●|●|●|●|●|●|●|●|●| |
| WELLER, JACK (HM21156) | | |●| | | | | | | | | | | | | | ●| | | | | | | | | | | | | | | | | | | | | | | | | | | | | | | |
| WEST WYCOMBE CHIRO CLINIC (HM21240) | | | | | | | | | | | | | | | | | | | | | | | | | | | | | | | | | | | | |●| | |●| | | | | | | | |
| WESTWOOD, TERRY (HM21287) | | |●| | | | | | | | | | | | | | ●| | | | | | | | | | | | | | | | | | | | | | | | | | | | | | | |
| WOODWARD, MARGARET (HM21866) | | | | | |●| | | | | | | | | | | |●| |●| | | | | | ●| | | | | | | | | | |●| | | | | | | | |●| | |
| CAMBRIDGESHIRE | | | | | | | | | | | | | | | | | | | | | | | | | | | | | | | | | | | | | | | | | | | | | | | | |
| ANDERSON, M (HM00834) | | | | | | | | | | | | | | | | | | | | | | | | | | | | | | | | | | | | |●| | |●| | | | | | | | |
| ANDERSON, PAUL (HM00836) | | | | | | | | | | | | | | | | | | | | | |●| |●| | | | | | | | | | | | | | | | | | | | | | | | |
| ARJUNA NATURAL HEALTH CENTRE (HM01000) |●|●|●|●|●|●|●|●|●|●|●|●|●|●|●|●|●|●|●|●|●|●|●|●|●|●|●|●|●|●|●|●|●|●|●|●|●|●|●|●|●|●|●|●|●|●|●| |
| BACK ON TRACK (HM01486) | | | | | | | | | | | | | | | | | | | | | | |●| | | | | | | | | | | | | | | | | | | | | | | | | |
| BACK ON TRACK (HM01487) | | | | | | | | | | | | | | | | | | | | | | |●| | | | | | | | | | | | | | | | | | | | | | | | | |
| BACK ON TRACK (HM01488) | | | | | | | | | | | | | | | | | | | | | | |●| | | | | | | | | | | | | | | | | | | | | | | | | |
| BENSON, HUGH (HM02168) |●|●|●|●|●|●|●|●|●|●|●|●|●|●|●|●|●|●|●|●|●|●| |●|●|●|●|●|●|●|●|●|●|●|●|●|●|●|●|●|●|●|●|●|●|●|●| |
| BRAMPTON CHIROPRACTIC CLINIC (HM02906) | | |●| | | | |●| | | | | | | |●| | | | | |●| | | | | | | | | | | | |●|●|●| | |●|●| | | | |●|●| | |
| CAMBRIDGE CHIROPRACTIC CENTRE (HM03572) | | | | | | | | | | | | | | | | | | | | | | | | | | | | | | | | | | | | |●| | |●| | | | | | | | |
| CAMBRIDGE TRAD ACUPUNC CENTRE (HM03578) | | |●| |●|●| | | | | | | | | |●| | | | | | | | | | | | | | | | | | | |●|●| | | | | | | | | | | |
| CHIROPRATIC & HOM HEALTH CTRE (HM04408) | | |●| |●|●| |●| | | |●| | | |●| | | | | | |●| | | | | | | | | | | |●|●|●|●|●|●|●| | | | |●| | | |
| COMPLEMENTARY HEALTH CLINIC (HM04927) | | |●| | |●| | | | | | | | | |●|●| | | | | | | |●| | | |●| | | | | | | |●| |●|●| |●| | | |●| | |
| COXELL REMEDIAL CLINIC (HM05324) | | |●| | | | |●| | | | | | | |●| | | | | | | | | | | | | | | | | | |●| |●| | |●| | | | | | | | |
| CUTTING, VALERIE (HM05648) | | |●| | |●| | | | | | | | | |●| | | | | |●| | | | | | | | | | | | | |●|●| |●| | | | | |●| | | |
| FAULKNER, CINDY (HM07141) | | |●| |●|●|●|●| | | | | | | |●|●|●| |●|●| | | |●| | | | | | |●| | | | |●|●| | |●| |●|●|●|●| | |
| GILBERT RD OSTEOPATHIC (HM08055) | | | | | | | | | | | | | | | | | | | | | |●| | | | | | | | | | | | | | |●| | |●| | | | | | | | |
| HEALTH TEAM (HM09406) | |●|●| |●|●|●|●|●|●|●|●|●|●|●|●|●|●|●|●|●|●| |●|●|●| |●| | |●|●|●|●|●|●|●|●|●|●|●|●|●|●|●|●|●| |
| HYPNOSIS AND HEALTH (HM10495) | | |●| | |●| | | | | | | | | | | |●| | | | | | | | | | | | | | | | | | |●| |●| | | |●| | |●| | |
| LIFELINE (HM12354) | | | | | | | | | | | | | | | | |●| | | | | | | | | | | | | | | | | | | | | | | | | | | | | | | |
| LIZ HALE HANDSON HEALTH (HM12495) | |●|●| | |●|●|●| | | |●| | | |●| | | | | | | |●| | | | | | | | | | |●|●|●| | |●| | | |●| |●|●| |
| LY, THI PHUNG (DR) (HM12754) | | |●| |●|●|●|●| | |●|●|●|●|●|●|●|●|●|●|●|●|●| |●|●|●|●|●| |●|●| | |●|●|●|●|●|●| | |●|●|●|●|●| |
| MATHIESON, M A (HM13290) | | | | | | | | | | | | | | | | | | | | | |●| |●| | | | | | | | | | | | | | | | | | | | | | | | |
| MAYNARD, SUSANNE (HM13358) | | | | | | | | | | | | | | | | | | | | | | | | | | | | | | | | | | | | | | | |●| | | | | | | | |
| OUTSIDE IN (HM15507) | | |●| | | | | | | | | | | | | | | | | | | | | | | | | | | | | | | | | | | | | | | | | | | | | |
| OXBOROUGH, JOY (HM15536) |●|●|●|●|●|●|●|●|●|●|●|●| | |●|●| |●| |●|●|●|●|●|●|●| |●|●|●|●|●|●|●|●|●|●| |●| | | | | | |●|●| | |
| PHIL SEAL PSYCHOTHERAPY (HM16115) | | |●| | | | | | | | | | | | | |●| | | | | | | | | | | | | | | | | | | |●| |●| | | | | | | | | |
| PRESTONS CHRTRD PHYSIOTHERAPY (HM16560) | | | | | | | | | | | | | | | | | | | | | | | | | | | | | | | | | | | | | | | |●| | | | | | | | |
| REID, SUSAN (HM17121) | | |●| | |●| |●| | | | | | | |●|●| | | |●|●|●| | | | | | | | | | | | | |●| |●|●| | | | |●| | | |

www.healthmyself.com

# D - I Conditions treated at Practices/Businesses

| Business by County with Reference no. | Dandruff | Deafness | Depression | Diabetes | Diarrhoea | Digestive Problems | Diverticulitis | Dizziness | Dyslexia | Dyspraxia | Ear Disorders | Eczema | ENT Disorders | Epilepsy | Eye Disorders | Fatigue | Fears | Fertility Problems | Fever | Fibroids | Flatulence | Foot Problems | Fractures | Fungal Infections |
|---|---|---|---|---|---|---|---|---|---|---|---|---|---|---|---|---|---|---|---|---|---|---|---|---|
| ROBINSON-ZEL, B (HM17508) | | | ● | | | | | | | | | | | | | | | | | | | | | |
| SMITH, JEANETTE (HM18752) | | | | | | ● | | | | | | | | | | | | | | | | ● | | |
| SPENCE, ALEX (HM18982) | | | | | | | | | | | | | | | | | | | | | | | | |
| TONG, JENNY (HM20154) | | | ● | ● | | ● | | ● | | | | ● | | | | ● | | | | | | ● | | |
| WASS, ANNETTE (HM20975) | ● | | ● | | ● | ● | ● | | | | ● | ● | ● | | | ● | | ● | ● | ● | ● | | | ● |
| WILKINSON, GLYNNIS (HM21506) | | | | | | | | | | | | | | | | | | | | | | ● | | ● |
| **CHANNEL ISLANDS** | | | | | | | | | | | | | | | | | | | | | | | | |
| ST SAMPSON'S MEDICAL CENTRE (HM19098) | | | | | | | | | | | | | | | | | | | | | | | | |
| **CHESHIRE** | | | | | | | | | | | | | | | | | | | | | | | | |
| A & H PAIN CLINIC (HM00016) | | ● | ● | | ● | ● | | ● | | | ● | ● | | ● | ● | ● | ● | ● | | | ● | | | |
| ADULT & CHILD FOOT CLINIC (HM00391) | | | | ● | | | | | | | | | | | | | | | | | | | | |
| ADVANCED SKIN THERAPY CLINIC (HM00404) | | | | | | | | | | | | | | | | | | | | | | | | |
| AROMASPHERE (HM01083) | | | ● | | | | | | | | | | | | | | | | | | | | | |
| BACHE CHIROPODY (HM01471) | | | | | | | | | | | | | | | | | | | | | | ● | | ● |
| BACK PAIN CLINIC (HM01500) | | | | | | | | | | | | | | | | | | | | | | | | |
| BATES VISION EDUCATION (HM01878) | | ● | | | | | | | | | | | | | ● | | | | | | | | | |
| BAXTER, GILLIAN (HM01927) | | | | | | | | | | | | | | | | | | | | | | ● | | ● |
| BERESFORD, KATHLEEN (HM02183) | | ● | ● | | | ● | | | | | | | | | | ● | | | | | | ● | | |
| BLOCH, PETER (HM02510) | | | | | | | | | | | | | | | | | | | | | | | | |
| BODY ESSENCES (HM02586) | | | ● | | | ● | | | | | | | | | | | | | | | | | | |
| BRAMHALL PARK PHYSIO CLINIC (HM02899) | | | | | | | | | | | | | | | | | | | | | | | | |
| BURTON, J S (HM03436) | | | | | | | | | | | | | | | | | | | | | | ● | | ● |
| CARMICHAEL CLINIC (HM03708) | | | | | ● | ● | | | | | | ● | | | | | | | | | | ● | ● | |
| CHEADLE HULME NATURAL HEALTH (HM04070) | | ● | ● | ● | ● | | | | | | | | | | | ● | | | | | | | | |
| CHESHIRE HEALTH CLINIC (HM04115) | | | ● | | | | | | | | | | | | | | | | | | | | | |
| CHESTER ALEXANDER TECH ST (HM04125) | | | | | | | | | | | | | | | | | ● | | | | | | | |
| CHESTER CHIROPODY (HM04126) | | | | | | | | | | | | | | | | | | | | | | ● | | ● |
| CHESTER CHIROPRACTIC CLINIC (HM04127) | | | | | | | | | | | | | | | | | | | | | | | | |
| CHESTER CLINIC (HM04128) | ● | | ● | | ● | ● | ● | ● | | | ● | ● | ● | | ● | ● | ● | ● | | ● | | ● | | ● |
| CHESTER HEALTH (HM04129) | ● | | ● | | | ● | ● | ● | | | | ● | | | | ● | | ● | | | | | | ● |
| CHESTER HEALTH & BEAUTY STUDIO (HM04130) | ● | | ● | | | ● | ● | ● | | | | ● | | | | ● | | ● | | | | | | ● |
| CHESTER HOMEOPATHIC CLINIC (HM04131) | ● | ● | ● | | ● | ● | ● | | | | ● | ● | ● | | | ● | ● | ● | ● | ● | ● | | | ● |
| CHINESE MEDICINE CENTRE (HM04257) | ● | ● | ● | ● | ● | ● | | | | | ● | ● | | ● | ● | ● | | | ● | ● | ● | ● | ● | ● |
| CHIROPODIST SURGERY (HM04295) | | | | ● | | | | | | | | | | | | | | | | | | ● | | ● |

| Business by County with Reference no. | Gallstones | Gastrointestinal Problems | Genital Herpes | Gingivitis | Glandular Fever | Glaucoma | Gout | Gum Disease | Hair Problems | Halitosis | Hand Problems | Hay Fever | Headaches | Hearing Problems | High Blood Pressure | Hip Complaints | Hyperactivity | Hypoglycaemia | Impotence | Incontinence | Indigestion | Infertility | Influenza | Ingrowing Toenails |
|---|---|---|---|---|---|---|---|---|---|---|---|---|---|---|---|---|---|---|---|---|---|---|---|---|
| ROBINSON-ZEL, B (HM17508) | | | | | | | | | | | | | | | | | | | | | | | | |
| SMITH, JEANETTE (HM18752) | | | | | | | | | | | ● | | | | ● | | | | | | | | | |
| SPENCE, ALEX (HM18982) | | | | | | | | | | | | | ● | | | ● | | | | | | | | |
| TONG, JENNY (HM20154) | | | | | | | | | | | ● | | ● | | ● | | | | | | ● | | | |
| WASS, ANNETTE (HM20975) | ● | ● | ● | ● | ● | | ● | ● | ● | ● | | ● | ● | | ● | | | ● | | | ● | ● | ● | |
| WILKINSON, GLYNNIS (HM21506) | | | | | | | | | | | | | | | | | | | | | | | | |
| **CHANNEL ISLANDS** | | | | | | | | | | | | | | | | | | | | | | | | |
| ST SAMPSON'S MEDICAL CENTRE (HM19098) | | | | | | | | | | | ● | | ● | | | ● | | | | | | | | |
| **CHESHIRE** | | | | | | | | | | | | | | | | | | | | | | | | |
| A & H PAIN CLINIC (HM00016) | | ● | | | | | | ● | ● | | | ● | ● | ● | ● | ● | | | ● | | ● | ● | | |
| ADULT & CHILD FOOT CLINIC (HM00391) | | | | | | | ● | | | | | | | | | ● | | | | | | | | ● |
| ADVANCED SKIN THERAPY CLINIC (HM00404) | | | | | | | | | ● | | | | | | | | | | | | | | | |
| AROMASPHERE (HM01083) | | | | | | | | | | | | | ● | | | | | | | | | | | |
| BACHE CHIROPODY (HM01471) | | | | | | | | | | | | | | | | | | | | | | | | |
| BACK PAIN CLINIC (HM01500) | | | | | | | | | | | | | ● | | ● | ● | | | | | | | | |
| BATES VISION EDUCATION (HM01878) | | | | | | ● | | | | | | | ● | ● | | | | | | | | | | |
| BAXTER, GILLIAN (HM01927) | | | | | | | | | | | | | | | | | | | | | | | | |
| BERESFORD, KATHLEEN (HM02183) | | | | | | | | | | | | ● | ● | ● | | | | | | | ● | | | |
| BLOCH, PETER (HM02510) | | | | | | | | | | | | | ● | | | ● | | | | | | | | |
| BODY ESSENCES (HM02586) | | | | | | | | | | | | | ● | | | | | | | | | | | |
| BRAMHALL PARK PHYSIO CLINIC (HM02899) | | | | | | | | | | | | | | | | ● | | | | | | | | |
| BURTON, J S (HM03436) | | | | | | | | | | | | | | | | | | | | | | | | ● |
| CARMICHAEL CLINIC (HM03708) | | ● | | | | | | | | | ● | | ● | | | ● | | | ● | | | | | |
| CHEADLE HULME NATURAL HEALTH (HM04070) | | | | | | | ● | | | | ● | ● | ● | | ● | ● | ● | | | ● | ● | | | |
| CHESHIRE HEALTH CLINIC (HM04115) | | | | | | | | | | | | | ● | | | ● | | | | | | | | |
| CHESTER ALEXANDER TECH ST (HM04125) | | | | | | | | | | | | | ● | | ● | ● | | | | | | | | |
| CHESTER CHIROPODY (HM04126) | | | | | | | | | | | | | | | | | | | | | | | | |
| CHESTER CHIROPRACTIC CLINIC (HM04127) | | | | | | | | | | | | | ● | | | ● | | | | | | | | |
| CHESTER CLINIC (HM04128) | ● | ● | | ● | ● | | ● | ● | | ● | ● | ● | ● | ● | ● | ● | ● | ● | ● | | ● | ● | ● | |
| CHESTER HEALTH (HM04129) | | | | | | | | | ● | | | ● | ● | | ● | | | ● | | | | | | |
| CHESTER HEALTH & BEAUTY STUDIO (HM04130) | | | | | | | | | ● | | | ● | ● | | ● | | | ● | | | | | | |
| CHESTER HOMEOPATHIC CLINIC (HM04131) | | ● | | ● | ● | | | ● | | ● | | ● | ● | ● | ● | | ● | | | | ● | ● | ● | |
| CHINESE MEDICINE CENTRE (HM04257) | ● | ● | ● | ● | ● | ● | ● | ● | ● | ● | ● | ● | ● | ● | ● | ● | ● | ● | ● | ● | ● | ● | ● | ● |
| CHIROPODIST SURGERY (HM04295) | | | | | | | | | | | | | | | | | | | | | | | | ● |

# D - I Conditions treated at Practices/Businesses

Business by County with Reference no.

| | CHIROPODY CORNER (HM04330) | CLINIC OF ACUPUNCTURE (HM04684) | COLHOUN, PETER (HM04842) | CONGLETON COUNSELLING PRACTICE (HM04977) | CONSTANTINE, J C (HM05012) | CREWE & NANT PHYSIO CLINIC (HM05431) | CROPPER, AGNES (HM05473) | DAVIES & ASSOCIATES (HM05791) | DEWHURST, PATRICA A (HM06049) | EDDIE, DAVID (HM06585) | EVANS, DI (HM06968) | FAGAN, B W (HM07042) | FEET FIRST MOBILE CHIROPODY SV (HM07183) | FIELD VIEW SURGERY (HM07259) | FINCH, WENDY (HM07302) | FIVE WAYS OSTEOPATHIC SURGERY (HM07381) | GENTLE TOUCH (HM07979) | GRACE & ASSOCIATES (HM08331) | GRAHAM COOMBE - MCTIMONEY (HM08338) | HANDS ON PHYSIOTHERAPY (HM08913) | HAZELDENE, BARBARA (HM09292) | HEALD, M T (HM09316) | HIGHLEY, T J (HM09757) | HOWE, BARBARA (HM10261) | HUSKISSON, EILEEN (HM10434) | HYPNOS PRACTICE (HM10492) | IPHOFEN, RON (DR) (HM10712) | JANE HAMMOND THERAPY (HM10916) | JENKINSON, LEILA (HM10999) | JONES, J W (HM11155) | KNUTSFORD CHIROPRACTIC CLINIC (HM11775) | LEGGE, PAT (HM12176) | LOMAS, CLIFFORD (HM12574) | MACALLAN, STEPHEN (HM12815) |
|---|---|---|---|---|---|---|---|---|---|---|---|---|---|---|---|---|---|---|---|---|---|---|---|---|---|---|---|---|---|---|---|---|---|---|
| Ingrowing Toenails | ● | | ● | | | | | | | | | | | | | | | | | | | | | | ● | | | | | | | | | |
| Influenza | | | | | | | | | ● | | | | | | | | | | | | | | | | | | | | ● | | ● | | | ● |
| Infertility | | ● | | | | | | | ● | | ● | | | | | | | | | | | | | | | | | | ● | | ● | | | ● |
| Indigestion | | ● | | | | | ● | | ● | | ● | | | | | | ● | | | | ● | | | | | | | | ● | | ● | | | ● |
| Incontinence | | | | | | | | | ● | | ● | | | | | | | | | | | | | | | | | | ● | | ● | | | |
| Impotence | | | | | | | | | ● | | ● | | | | | | | | | | | | | | | ● | | | ● | | ● | | | ● |
| Hypoglycaemia | | | ● | | | | | | ● | | | | | | | | | | | | | | | | | | | | ● | | | | | ● |
| Hyperactivity | | | | | ● | | | | ● | | | | | | | | | | | | ● | | | | | | | | ● | | | | | ● |
| Hip Complaints | | ● | | | ● | ● | | | ● | ● | | ● | | ● | | ● | | | ● | ● | | | | | | | | | ● | | ● | | ● | |
| High Blood Pressure | | ● | | | | | ● | | ● | | | | | | | | | | | | ● | | | | | | | | ● | | ● | | | ● |
| Hearing Problems | | | | | | | | | | | | | | | | | | | | | | | | | | | | | ● | | ● | | | |
| Headaches | | ● | | | ● | | ● | ● | ● | ● | ● | ● | | | ● | ● | | | ● | | ● | | | | | ● | ● | | ● | | ● | ● | ● | ● |
| Hay Fever | | ● | | | ● | | ● | | ● | | | | | | | | | | | | ● | | | | | | | | ● | | | | | ● |
| Hand Problems | | ● | | | | | | ● | | | ● | ● | | | | ● | | | | | ● | | | | | | | | ● | | ● | | | ● |
| Halitosis | | | | | | | | | ● | | | | | | | | | | | | | | | | | | | | ● | | ● | | | ● |
| Hair Problems | | ● | | | | | | | ● | | | | | | | | ● | | | | | | | | | | | | ● | | | | | |
| Gum Disease | | | | | | | | | ● | | | | | | | | ● | | | | | | | | | | | | ● | | | | | ● |
| Gout | | ● | ● | | | | | | ● | | | ● | | | | | | | | | | | | | | | | | ● | ● | ● | | | |
| Glaucoma | | | | | | | | | | | | | | | ● | | | | | | | | | | | | | | ● | | | | | |
| Glandular Fever | | | | | | | | | ● | | | | | | | | | | | | | | | | | | | | ● | | ● | | | ● |
| Gingivitis | | | | | | | | | ● | | | | | | | | ● | | | | | | | | | | | | ● | | | | | ● |
| Genital Herpes | | | | | | | | | ● | | | | | | | | | | | | | | | | | | | | ● | | | | | ● |
| Gastrointestinal Problems | | ● | | | | | | | ● | | | | | | | | | | | | | | | | | ● | | | ● | | ● | | | ● |
| Gallstones | | | | | | | | | ● | | | | | | | | | | | | | | | | | | | | ● | | ● | | | ● |
| Fungal Infections | | | ● | | | | | | ● | | | | ● | ● | | | | | | | | ● | ● | | | | | | ● | ● | | | | ● |
| Fractures | | | | | ● | | | | | | | ● | | | | | | | | | | | | | | | | | | | ● | | | |
| Foot Problems | ● | | ● | | ● | | | ● | | | | ● | ● | ● | ● | ● | | ● | | | | ● | ● | | ● | | | | ● | ● | ● | | ● | |
| Flatulence | | ● | | | | | | | ● | | | | | | | | | | | | | | | | | | | | ● | | | | | ● |
| Fibroids | | | | | | | | | ● | | | | | | | | | | | | | | | | | | | | ● | | | | | ● |
| Fever | | ● | | | | | | | ● | | | | | | | | | | | | | | | | | | | | ● | | ● | | | ● |
| Fertility Problems | | ● | | | | | | | ● | | | | | | | | | | | | | | | | | | | | ● | | ● | | | ● |
| Fears | | ● | | ● | | | | | ● | | | | | | | | | | | | | | | | | ● | ● | ● | ● | | ● | | | |
| Fatigue | | ● | | | | | | | ● | | ● | | | | | | | | | | ● | | | ● | | | | | ● | | ● | | | ● |
| Eye Disorders | | | | | | | | | ● | | | | | | ● | | | | | | | | | | | | | | ● | | | | | |
| Epilepsy | | | | | | | | | ● | | | | | | | | | | | | | | | | | | | | ● | | | | | |
| ENT Disorders | | ● | | | ● | | | ● | ● | | | | | | | | | | | | | | | | | | | | ● | | ● | | ● | ● |
| Eczema | | ● | ● | | | | | | ● | | | | | | | | | | | | | | | | | ● | | | ● | ● | | | | ● |
| Ear Disorders | | | | | ● | | | | ● | | | | | | | | | | | | | | | | | | | | ● | | ● | | | ● |
| Dyspraxia | | | | | ● | | | | | | | | | | | | | | | | | | | | | | | | ● | | | | | |
| Dyslexia | | | | | ● | | | | | | | | | | | | | | | | | | | | | | | | ● | | | | | |
| Dizziness | | ● | | | | | | ● | ● | | ● | | | | | ● | | | ● | | | | | | | | | | ● | | ● | | | ● |
| Diverticulitis | | ● | | | | | | | ● | | | | | | | | | | | | | | | | | | | | ● | | | | | ● |
| Digestive Problems | | ● | | | | | ● | | ● | | ● | | | | | | ● | | ● | | ● | | | | | ● | | | ● | | ● | | | ● |
| Diarrhoea | | ● | | | | | | | ● | | | | | | | | | | | | | | | | | | | | ● | | | | | ● |
| Diabetes | | | ● | | | | | | ● | | | | | | | | | ● | | | | | | | | | | | ● | ● | | | | ● |
| Depression | | ● | | ● | | | ● | | ● | ● | ● | | | | | | | | | | ● | | | | | ● | | ● | ● | | ● | ● | | ● |
| Deafness | | | | | | | | | | | | | | | | | | | | | | | | | | | | | ● | | ● | | | |
| Dandruff | | | | | | | | | | | | | | | | | | | | | | | | | | | | | ● | | | | | ● |

# D - I Conditions treated at Practices/Businesses

| Business by County with Reference no. | Dandruff | Deafness | Depression | Diabetes | Diarrhoea | Digestive Problems | Diverticulitis | Dizziness | Dyslexia | Dyspraxia | Ear Disorders | Eczema |
|---|---|---|---|---|---|---|---|---|---|---|---|---|
| MARSH, F W (HM13147) | | | | | | | | | | | | |
| MEDICINE WHEEL (HM13670) | | | ● | | | | | | | | ● | |
| MEHTA HYPNOTHERAPY (HM13695) | | | ● | | | | | | | | | |
| MIDDLETON & ASSOCIATES (HM13817) | | | ● | | | | | | | | | |
| MISSION, CHAITANYA (HM13995) | | | ● | | | | | | | | | |
| MORTON, J V (HM14251) | | | | ● | | | | | | | | |
| NEEDHAM, ANGELA (HM14749) | ● | ● | ● | ● | ● | ● | ● | ● | ● | | ● | ● |
| NEW LIFE NATURAL HEALTH CARE (HM14821) | ● | | ● | ● | ● | ● | ● | ● | | | ● | ● |
| NEWTON, J C (HM14898) | | | | | | | | | | | | |
| NUTRITION AND ALLERGY CLINIC (HM15121) | | ● | ● | ● | ● | ● | | ● | ● | | ● | ● |
| OLD HALL CLINIC (HM15256) | ● | ● | ● | | ● | ● | ● | ● | ● | ● | ● | ● |
| PATON, W A (HM15825) | | | | | | | | | | | | |
| PENNYCOOK, AMANDA (HM15996) | | | | | | | | | | | | |
| PHOENIX CENTRE (HM16154) | | | ● | | | | | | | | | ● |
| PHYSIO & SPORTS INJURY CLINIC (HM16181) | | | | | | | | | | | | ● |
| PHYSIO PLUS (HM16203) | | | | | | | | | | | | |
| POYNTON CHIROPRACTIC CLINIC (HM16519) | | | | | | | | ● | | | | |
| PRINCE, TANIA A (HM16622) | | | ● | | | | | | ● | | | ● |
| RICHARDS, DAVID (HM17250) | | | | | | | | | | | | |
| RICHARDS, KERRY L (HM17260) | | | | | | | | | | | | |
| SAXELBY, M (HM17990) | | | | ● | | | | | | | | |
| SCENTED GARDENS (HM18011) | | | ● | | | | | | | | | |
| TEDSTONE, ALISON (HM19815) | | | | ● | | | | | | | | |
| THOMAS, BEVERLEY (HM19933) | | | | | | | | | | | | |
| THORNBER, A A (HM20016) | | | | | | | | | | | | |
| TIPLING, L (HM20087) | | | | ● | | | | | | | | |
| TRINITY HOUSE PRACTICE (HM20339) | | | | | | | | | | | | |
| TULLY, CHARLES (HM20388) | | | | | | | | | | | | |
| TYRER, HELEN R (HM20473) | | | | ● | | | | | | | | |
| VALE ROYAL CHIROPRACTIC CLINIC (HM20552) | | | | | | | | | | | | |
| VALE ROYAL CHIROPRACTIC CLINIC (HM20553) | | | | | | | | | | | | |
| WARRINGTON CHIROPRACTIC CLINIC (HM20957) | | | | | | ● | | ● | | | ● | |
| WEAVER HOUSE CLINIC (HM21049) | ● | | ● | ● | ● | ● | ● | | | | ● | ● |
| WIDNES OSTEOPATHIC CLINIC (HM21459) | | | ● | | | | | | | | | |

| Business by County with Reference no. | ENT Disorders | Epilepsy | Eye Disorders | Fatigue | Fears | Fertility Problems | Fever | Fibroids | Flatulence | Foot Problems | Fractures | Fungal Infections |
|---|---|---|---|---|---|---|---|---|---|---|---|---|
| MARSH, F W (HM13147) | | | | | | | | | | ● | | |
| MEDICINE WHEEL (HM13670) | | | | | | | | | | | | |
| MEHTA HYPNOTHERAPY (HM13695) | | | | | ● | | | | | | | |
| MIDDLETON & ASSOCIATES (HM13817) | | ● | | ● | | | | | | | | |
| MISSION, CHAITANYA (HM13995) | | | | ● | | | | | | | | |
| MORTON, J V (HM14251) | | | | | | | | | | ● | | ● |
| NEEDHAM, ANGELA (HM14749) | ● | ● | ● | ● | ● | ● | ● | ● | ● | ● | | ● |
| NEW LIFE NATURAL HEALTH CARE (HM14821) | ● | ● | ● | ● | ● | ● | ● | ● | ● | ● | | ● |
| NEWTON, J C (HM14898) | | | | | | | | | | ● | | |
| NUTRITION AND ALLERGY CLINIC (HM15121) | ● | ● | ● | ● | | ● | | | ● | | ● | ● |
| OLD HALL CLINIC (HM15256) | ● | ● | ● | ● | ● | ● | ● | ● | ● | ● | | ● |
| PATON, W A (HM15825) | | | | | | | | | | | ● | |
| PENNYCOOK, AMANDA (HM15996) | | | | | | | | | | ● | | ● |
| PHOENIX CENTRE (HM16154) | | | | | ● | | | | | | | |
| PHYSIO & SPORTS INJURY CLINIC (HM16181) | | | | | | | | | | ● | ● | |
| PHYSIO PLUS (HM16203) | | | | | | | | | | | | |
| POYNTON CHIROPRACTIC CLINIC (HM16519) | | | | | | | | | | ● | | |
| PRINCE, TANIA A (HM16622) | | | | | ● | ● | | | | | | |
| RICHARDS, DAVID (HM17250) | | | | | | | | | | ● | | ● |
| RICHARDS, KERRY L (HM17260) | | | | | | | | | | ● | | ● |
| SAXELBY, M (HM17990) | | | | | | | | | | ● | | |
| SCENTED GARDENS (HM18011) | | | | ● | | | | | | | | |
| TEDSTONE, ALISON (HM19815) | | | | | | | | | | ● | | |
| THOMAS, BEVERLEY (HM19933) | | | | | | | | | | ● | | ● |
| THORNBER, A A (HM20016) | | | | | | | | | | ● | | ● |
| TIPLING, L (HM20087) | | | | | | | | | | ● | | ● |
| TRINITY HOUSE PRACTICE (HM20339) | | | | | | | | | | ● | | |
| TULLY, CHARLES (HM20388) | ● | | | | | | | | | | | |
| TYRER, HELEN R (HM20473) | | | | | | | | | | ● | | ● |
| VALE ROYAL CHIROPRACTIC CLINIC (HM20552) | | | | | | | | | | | | |
| VALE ROYAL CHIROPRACTIC CLINIC (HM20553) | | | | | | | | | | | | |
| WARRINGTON CHIROPRACTIC CLINIC (HM20957) | | | | | | | | | | ● | | |
| WEAVER HOUSE CLINIC (HM21049) | ● | | | ● | ● | | | | ● | | | ● |
| WIDNES OSTEOPATHIC CLINIC (HM21459) | | | | | | | | | | | | |

| Business by County with Reference no. | Gallstones | Gastrointestinal Problems | Genital Herpes | Gingivitis | Glandular Fever | Glaucoma | Gout | Gum Disease | Hair Problems | Halitosis | Hand Problems | Hay Fever |
|---|---|---|---|---|---|---|---|---|---|---|---|---|
| MARSH, F W (HM13147) | | | | | | | | | | | | |
| MEDICINE WHEEL (HM13670) | | | | | | | | | | | | |
| MEHTA HYPNOTHERAPY (HM13695) | | | | | | | | | | | | |
| MIDDLETON & ASSOCIATES (HM13817) | | | | | | | | | | | ● | ● |
| MISSION, CHAITANYA (HM13995) | | | | | | | | | | | | |
| MORTON, J V (HM14251) | | | | | | | | | | | | |
| NEEDHAM, ANGELA (HM14749) | ● | ● | ● | ● | ● | | ● | ● | ● | ● | | ● |
| NEW LIFE NATURAL HEALTH CARE (HM14821) | ● | ● | | ● | ● | ● | ● | ● | ● | ● | ● | ● |
| NEWTON, J C (HM14898) | | | | | | | | | | | | |
| NUTRITION AND ALLERGY CLINIC (HM15121) | ● | ● | ● | ● | ● | | ● | ● | ● | ● | ● | ● |
| OLD HALL CLINIC (HM15256) | ● | ● | | ● | ● | | ● | ● | ● | ● | ● | ● |
| PATON, W A (HM15825) | | | | | | | | | | | | |
| PENNYCOOK, AMANDA (HM15996) | | | | | | | | | | | | |
| PHOENIX CENTRE (HM16154) | | | | | | | | | | | | |
| PHYSIO & SPORTS INJURY CLINIC (HM16181) | | | | | | | | | | | ● | |
| PHYSIO PLUS (HM16203) | | | | | | | | | | | | |
| POYNTON CHIROPRACTIC CLINIC (HM16519) | | | | | | | | | | | | |
| PRINCE, TANIA A (HM16622) | | | | | | | | | | | | |
| RICHARDS, DAVID (HM17250) | | | | | | | | | | | | |
| RICHARDS, KERRY L (HM17260) | | | | | | | | | | | | |
| SAXELBY, M (HM17990) | | | | | | | | | | | | |
| SCENTED GARDENS (HM18011) | | | | | | | | | | | | |
| TEDSTONE, ALISON (HM19815) | | | | | | | | | | | | |
| THOMAS, BEVERLEY (HM19933) | | | | | | | | | | | | |
| THORNBER, A A (HM20016) | | | | | | | | | | | | |
| TIPLING, L (HM20087) | | | | | | | | | | | | |
| TRINITY HOUSE PRACTICE (HM20339) | | | | | | | | | | | | |
| TULLY, CHARLES (HM20388) | | | | | | | | | | | ● | |
| TYRER, HELEN R (HM20473) | | | | | | | | | | | | |
| VALE ROYAL CHIROPRACTIC CLINIC (HM20552) | | | | | | | | | | | | |
| VALE ROYAL CHIROPRACTIC CLINIC (HM20553) | | | | | | | | | | | | |
| WARRINGTON CHIROPRACTIC CLINIC (HM20957) | | ● | | | | | | | | | ● | |
| WEAVER HOUSE CLINIC (HM21049) | | | ● | ● | | | | | | ● | ● | ● |
| WIDNES OSTEOPATHIC CLINIC (HM21459) | | | | | | | | | | | | |

| Business by County with Reference no. | Headaches | Hearing Problems | High Blood Pressure | Hip Complaints | Hyperactivity | Hypoglycaemia | Impotence | Incontinence | Indigestion | Infertility | Influenza | Ingrowing Toenails |
|---|---|---|---|---|---|---|---|---|---|---|---|---|
| MARSH, F W (HM13147) | | | | | | | | | | | | ● |
| MEDICINE WHEEL (HM13670) | ● | | | | | | | | | | | |
| MEHTA HYPNOTHERAPY (HM13695) | ● | | ● | | | | | | | | | |
| MIDDLETON & ASSOCIATES (HM13817) | ● | | ● | ● | | | | | ● | | ● | |
| MISSION, CHAITANYA (HM13995) | ● | | | | | | | | | | | |
| MORTON, J V (HM14251) | | | | | | | | | | | | |
| NEEDHAM, ANGELA (HM14749) | ● | ● | ● | | ● | ● | ● | ● | ● | ● | ● | |
| NEW LIFE NATURAL HEALTH CARE (HM14821) | ● | ● | ● | ● | ● | ● | ● | ● | ● | ● | ● | |
| NEWTON, J C (HM14898) | | | | | | | | | | | | |
| NUTRITION AND ALLERGY CLINIC (HM15121) | ● | ● | ● | ● | ● | ● | ● | ● | ● | ● | ● | |
| OLD HALL CLINIC (HM15256) | ● | ● | | ● | ● | ● | ● | ● | ● | ● | ● | |
| PATON, W A (HM15825) | | | | ● | | | | | | | | |
| PENNYCOOK, AMANDA (HM15996) | | | | | | | | | | | | ● |
| PHOENIX CENTRE (HM16154) | ● | | | | | | | | | | | |
| PHYSIO & SPORTS INJURY CLINIC (HM16181) | ● | | | ● | | | | | | | | |
| PHYSIO PLUS (HM16203) | | | | ● | | | | | | | | |
| POYNTON CHIROPRACTIC CLINIC (HM16519) | ● | | | ● | | | | | | | | |
| PRINCE, TANIA A (HM16622) | | | ● | | | | ● | | | ● | | |
| RICHARDS, DAVID (HM17250) | | | | | | | | | | | | |
| RICHARDS, KERRY L (HM17260) | | | | | | | | | | | | ● |
| SAXELBY, M (HM17990) | | | | | | | | | | | | |
| SCENTED GARDENS (HM18011) | ● | | | | | | | | | | | |
| TEDSTONE, ALISON (HM19815) | | | | | | | | | | | | ● |
| THOMAS, BEVERLEY (HM19933) | | | | | | | | | | | | ● |
| THORNBER, A A (HM20016) | | | | ● | | | | | | | | |
| TIPLING, L (HM20087) | | | | | | | | | | | | |
| TRINITY HOUSE PRACTICE (HM20339) | | | | | | | | | | | | |
| TULLY, CHARLES (HM20388) | ● | | ● | ● | | | | | | | | |
| TYRER, HELEN R (HM20473) | | | | | | | | | | | | |
| VALE ROYAL CHIROPRACTIC CLINIC (HM20552) | ● | | | ● | | | | | | | | |
| VALE ROYAL CHIROPRACTIC CLINIC (HM20553) | ● | | | ● | | | | | | | | |
| WARRINGTON CHIROPRACTIC CLINIC (HM20957) | ● | | ● | ● | | | | | ● | | | |
| WEAVER HOUSE CLINIC (HM21049) | ● | | | ● | ● | | ● | ● | ● | | | |
| WIDNES OSTEOPATHIC CLINIC (HM21459) | | | | | | | | | | | | |

# D - I Conditions treated at Practices/Businesses

Business by County with Reference no.

| Business | Dandruff | Deafness | Depression | Diabetes | Diarrhoea | Digestive Problems | Diverticulitis | Dizziness | Dyslexia | Dyspraxia | Ear Disorders | Eczema | ENT Disorders | Epilepsy | Eye Disorders | Fatigue | Fears | Fertility Problems | Fever | Fibroids | Flatulence | Foot Problems | Fractures | Fungal Infections |
|---|---|---|---|---|---|---|---|---|---|---|---|---|---|---|---|---|---|---|---|---|---|---|---|---|
| WILLIAMS OSTEOPATHIC CLINIC (HM21532) | | | | | | | | | | | | | | | | | | | | | | ● | | |
| WOOLLEY, M E (HM21878) | | | | | | | | | | | | | | | | | | | | | | ● | | ● |
| **CLEVELAND** | | | | | | | | | | | | | | | | | | | | | | | | |
| ALEXANDER TECHNIQUE (HM00548) | | | ● | | | ● | | ● | ● | ● | | | | | | ● | ● | | | | | | | |
| BARNARD, SIMON (HM01732) | | | | | | | | | | | | | | | | | | | | | | | | |
| BODY BALANCE (HM02570) | | | | | | | | | | | | | | | | | | | | | | ● | | |
| ELLISON, TIM (HM06777) | | | | ● | | | | | | | | | | | | | | | | | | ● | | ● |
| HARTLEPOOL CHIROPRACTIC CLINIC (HM09138) | | | | | | | | | | | | | | | | | | | | | | | | |
| MERMAID CHIROPRACTIC PRACTICE (HM13749) | | | | | | | | | ● | | | | | | | | | | | | | | | |
| NATURAL THERAPY CENTRE (HM14637) | | | | | ● | ● | | | | | | | | | | ● | ● | | | | | ● | | ● |
| NORTHERN GUILD-PSYCHOTHERAPY (HM15061) | | | ● | | | | | | | | | | | | | | ● | | | | | | | |
| RAINBOW BRIDGE SCHOOL (HM16875) | ● | ● | ● | ● | ● | ● | ● | ● | ● | ● | ● | ● | ● | ● | ● | ● | ● | ● | ● | ● | ● | ● | ● | ● |
| REDCAR PHYSIO & SPORTS (HM17007) | | | | | | | | | | | | | | | | | | | | | | | | |
| RUSH, DENNIS (HM17754) | | | ● | | | | | | | | | ● | | | | ● | ● | ● | | | | | | |
| SKIPPINGS & ASSOCIATES (HM18657) | | | | | | | | | | | | | | | | | | | | | | | | |
| STRESS COUNSELLING (HM19391) | | | ● | | | | | | | | | | | | | ● | ● | | | | | | | |
| **CORNWALL** | | | | | | | | | | | | | | | | | | | | | | | | |
| AROMATICA (HM01135) | | | ● | | | ● | | ● | | | | ● | | | | ● | ● | | | | | ● | | ● |
| BANBURY, A E (HM01646) | | | | | | | | | | | | | | | | | | | | | | | | |
| BARNNETT, ANN (HM01763) | | | ● | | | ● | | | | ● | | | | | | ● | | | | | | ● | | |
| BEARE, M E (HM01968) | | | | ● | | | | | | | | | | | | | | | | | | | | |
| CARADON CHIROPRACTIC CLINIC (HM03656) | | | | | | | | | | | | | | | | | | | | | | | | |
| CHIROPODIST/PODIATRIST (HM04296) | | | | | | | | | | | | | | | | | | | | | | ● | | |
| COMP HEALTH INITIATIVE (HM04912) | ● | ● | ● | ● | ● | ● | ● | ● | ● | ● | ● | ● | ● | ● | ● | ● | ● | ● | ● | ● | ● | ● | ● | ● |
| FEET FIRST (HM07180) | | | ● | | ● | ● | ● | ● | | | ● | ● | | | | ● | ● | ● | | ● | ● | ● | | ● |
| FOOTCARE (HM07492) | | | | | | | | | | | | | | | | | | | | | | ● | | |
| FORCE, GAYLE (HM07520) | | ● | ● | | | ● | ● | ● | | | ● | ● | | ● | ● | ● | ● | ● | | ● | ● | ● | | ● |
| HALL, PETER (HM08787) | | | | | ● | | ● | ● | ● | | | ● | | | | ● | ● | ● | | | ● | | | ● |
| HAWKSLAND PHYSIOTHERAPY CENTRE (HM09233) | | | | | | | | | | | | | | | | | | | | | | ● | | |
| LIFE 'N' LIMB (HM12345) | ● | ● | ● | ● | ● | ● | ● | ● | ● | ● | ● | ● | ● | ● | ● | ● | ● | ● | ● | ● | ● | ● | ● | ● |
| LIFE 'N' LIMB (HM12346) | ● | | ● | | ● | ● | | | | | | ● | | ● | | ● | ● | | ● | | ● | ● | | ● |
| LIFE-WORK POTENTIAL (HM12368) | ● | | | | ● | ● | ● | ● | ● | ● | ● | ● | | ● | ● | ● | ● | ● | | | ● | ● | | ● |
| LISKEARD CHIROPRACTIC CLINIC (HM12453) | | | | | | | | | | | | | | | | | | | | | | | | |
| LISTER NATURAL HEALTH PRACTICE (HM12461) | | ● | ● | ● | ● | ● | ● | ● | ● | ● | ● | ● | ● | | | ● | ● | ● | ● | ● | ● | ● | | ● |

| Business | Gallstones | Gastrointestinal Problems | Genital Herpes | Gingivitis | Glandular Fever | Glaucoma | Gout | Gum Disease | Hair Problems | Halitosis | Hand Problems | Hay Fever | Headaches | Hearing Problems | High Blood Pressure | Hip Complaints | Hyperactivity | Hypoglycaemia | Impotence | Incontinence | Indigestion | Infertility | Influenza | Ingrowing Toenails |
|---|---|---|---|---|---|---|---|---|---|---|---|---|---|---|---|---|---|---|---|---|---|---|---|---|
| WILLIAMS OSTEOPATHIC CLINIC (HM21532) | | | | | | | | | | | | | ● | | | | | | | | | | | |
| WOOLLEY, M E (HM21878) | | | | | | | | | | | | | | | | | | | | | | | | |
| **CLEVELAND** | | | | | | | | | | | | | | | | | | | | | | | | |
| ALEXANDER TECHNIQUE (HM00548) | | | | | | | | | | | ● | | ● | ● | ● | ● | | | | | ● | | | |
| BARNARD, SIMON (HM01732) | | | | | | | | | | | | | ● | | | ● | | | | | | | | |
| BODY BALANCE (HM02570) | | | | | | | | | | | ● | | | | | | | | | | | | | |
| ELLISON, TIM (HM06777) | | | | | | | ● | | | | | | | | | | | ● | | | | | | ● |
| HARTLEPOOL CHIROPRACTIC CLINIC (HM09138) | | | | | | | | | | | | | ● | | | ● | | | | | | | | |
| MERMAID CHIROPRACTIC PRACTICE (HM13749) | | | | | | | | | | | | | ● | | | ● | | | | | | | | |
| NATURAL THERAPY CENTRE (HM14637) | | | | | | | | | | | | ● | ● | | | ● | | | | | | | | |
| NORTHERN GUILD-PSYCHOTHERAPY (HM15061) | | | | | | | | | | | | | | | | | | | | | | | | |
| RAINBOW BRIDGE SCHOOL (HM16875) | ● | ● | ● | ● | ● | ● | ● | ● | ● | ● | ● | ● | ● | ● | ● | ● | ● | ● | ● | ● | ● | ● | ● | |
| REDCAR PHYSIO & SPORTS (HM17007) | | | | | | | | | | | | | | | | ● | | | | | | | | |
| RUSH, DENNIS (HM17754) | | | | | | | | | | | | | ● | | ● | | | | ● | | | | | |
| SKIPPINGS & ASSOCIATES (HM18657) | | | | | | | | | | | | | ● | | | ● | | | | | | | | |
| STRESS COUNSELLING (HM19391) | | | | | | | | | | | | | ● | | | | | | | | | | | |
| **CORNWALL** | | | | | | | | | | | | | | | | | | | | | | | | |
| AROMATICA (HM01135) | | | | | | | | | ● | | ● | ● | ● | | | | | | | | ● | | | |
| BANBURY, A E (HM01646) | | ● | | | | | | | | | | | ● | | | ● | | | | | ● | | | |
| BARNNETT, ANN (HM01763) | | | | | | | | | | | ● | ● | ● | | ● | | ● | | | | | | | |
| BEARE, M E (HM01968) | | | | | | | | | | | | | | | | | | | | | | | | |
| CARADON CHIROPRACTIC CLINIC (HM03656) | | | | | | | | | | | | | ● | | | ● | | | | | | | | |
| CHIROPODIST/PODIATRIST (HM04296) | | | | | | | | | | | | | | | | | | | | | | | | ● |
| COMP HEALTH INITIATIVE (HM04912) | ● | ● | ● | ● | ● | ● | ● | ● | ● | ● | ● | ● | ● | ● | ● | ● | ● | ● | ● | ● | ● | ● | ● | |
| FEET FIRST (HM07180) | ● | ● | | | | | ● | | ● | | ● | | ● | ● | ● | ● | ● | | ● | | ● | ● | | |
| FOOTCARE (HM07492) | | | | | | | | | | | | | | | | | | | | | | | | |
| FORCE, GAYLE (HM07520) | ● | ● | | | ● | | | | ● | ● | ● | ● | ● | ● | ● | | ● | | ● | ● | ● | ● | | |
| HALL, PETER (HM08787) | | | | | | | | | | | | | | | ● | | | | ● | | ● | ● | | |
| HAWKSLAND PHYSIOTHERAPY CENTRE (HM09233) | | | | | | | | | | | ● | | ● | | | ● | | | | | | | | |
| LIFE 'N' LIMB (HM12345) | ● | ● | ● | ● | ● | ● | ● | ● | ● | ● | ● | ● | ● | ● | ● | ● | ● | ● | ● | ● | ● | ● | ● | |
| LIFE 'N' LIMB (HM12346) | ● | ● | | ● | | | ● | ● | ● | ● | ● | | ● | | ● | ● | ● | | ● | | ● | | ● | |
| LIFE-WORK POTENTIAL (HM12368) | | ● | ● | ● | ● | | | ● | ● | ● | | ● | ● | | | | ● | ● | | ● | ● | | ● | |
| LISKEARD CHIROPRACTIC CLINIC (HM12453) | | | | | | | | | | | | | ● | | | ● | | | | | | | | |
| LISTER NATURAL HEALTH PRACTICE (HM12461) | ● | ● | ● | ● | ● | | ● | ● | ● | ● | ● | ● | ● | ● | ● | ● | ● | ● | ● | ● | ● | ● | ● | |

www.healthmyself.com

# D - I Conditions treated at Practices/Businesses

| Business by County with Reference no. | Dandruff | Deafness | Depression | Diabetes | Diarrhoea | Digestive Problems | Diverticulitis | Dizziness | Dyslexia | Dyspraxia | Ear Disorders | Eczema | ENT Disorders | Epilepsy | Eye Disorders | Fatigue |
|---|---|---|---|---|---|---|---|---|---|---|---|---|---|---|---|---|
| MASTERS, B (HM13273) | | | ● | | | ● | ● | ● | | | | | | ● | | |
| MORSE, EMMA (HM14239) | | | | | | | | | | | | | | | | |
| NEWQUAY CHIROPRACTIC CLINIC (HM14883) | | | ● | | | ● | | ● | ● | | | ● | | | | ● |
| OSTEOPATHIC FAMILY CENTRE (HM15465) | | | | | | ● | | ● | ● | ● | ● | ● | ● | | | ● |
| PENZANCE NATURAL HEALTH CENTRE (HM16006) | | | ● | | | ● | ● | | | | | | | | | ● |
| REEVES, J (HM17066) | | | | | | | | | | | | | | | | |
| ST AUSTELL CHIROPRACTIC CLINIC (HM19070) | | | ● | | | | | | | | | | | | | ● |
| TRURO CHIROPRACTIC CLINIC (HM20354) | | | ● | | | | | | | | | | | | | ● |
| TRURO OSTEOPATHIC PRACTICE (HM20356) | | | | | | | | | | | | | | | | |
| VERA BOYES ACUPUNCTURE (HM20618) | | | ● | | | ● | | ● | | | | | | | | ● |
| WEATHERHOGG, D J (HM21046) | | | | | | | | | | | | | | | | |
| WILLS, JONATHAN (HM21632) | | | | | | | | | | | | | | | | |
| WRIGHT, CYNTHIA (HM21929) | | | ● | | | | | | | | | | | | | ● |
| **COUNTY DURHAM** | | | | | | | | | | | | | | | | |
| BALANCE HOLISTIC HEALTHCARE (HM01606) | | | ● | | | ● | ● | | | | | | | | | |
| CALLAGHAN, M M (HM03548) | | | | | | | | | | | | | | | | |
| EVANS, BRUCE (DR) (HM06958) | | | | | | | | | | | | | | | | |
| FIONA OTTEWELL CHRTRD PHYSIO (HM07329) | | | | | | | | | | | | | | | | |
| FOOTPRINTS (HM07507) | | | | | | | | | | | | | | | | |
| HIND, CAROLE (HM09824) | | | ● | | | ● | ● | | | | ● | | ● | | | ● |
| HOBSON, I K (HM09864) | | | | | | | | | | | | | | | | |
| NEWCASTLE/NE TRANS MEDITA CTRE (HM14856) | | | ● | ● | | | | | | | | | | | | ● |
| OLD PIT PRACTICE (HM15260) | | | ● | | | ● | | | | | | | | | | |
| SPOORS, L & D (HM19039) | | | | | | | | | | | | | | | | |
| TEESDALE OSTEOPATHIC CLINIC (HM19817) | | | | | | | | | | | | | | | | |
| TREATMENT ROOM (HM20302) | | | | | | | | | | | | | | | | |
| WARWICK, ANDREA (HM20967) | | | ● | | ● | ● | ● | | | | ● | ● | | | | ● |
| **CUMBRIA** | | | | | | | | | | | | | | | | |
| CUMBRIA PHYSIO & SPORTS CLINIC (HM05598) | | | | | | | | | | | | | | | | |
| DEERING, CHRISTINE (HM05959) | | | ● | | | | | | | | | | | | | |
| FOOTWORKS (HM07515) | | | | | | | | | | | | | | | | |
| GARNETT, JANE (HM07897) | | | | | | | | | | | | | | | | |
| HERBS AND HELPERS (HM09668) | | | ● | ● | ● | ● | ● | ● | | | | ● | ● | | | ● |
| HYPNOTHERAPY CENTRE (HM10525) | | | | | | | | | | | | | | | | |

| Business by County with Reference no. | Fears | Fertility Problems | Fever | Fibroids | Flatulence | Foot Problems | Fractures | Fungal Infections | Gallstones | Gastrointestinal Problems | Genital Herpes | Gingivitis | Glandular Fever | Glaucoma | Gout | Gum Disease |
|---|---|---|---|---|---|---|---|---|---|---|---|---|---|---|---|---|
| MASTERS, B (HM13273) | | | | | | ● | | | | | | | | | ● | |
| MORSE, EMMA (HM14239) | | | | | | | | | | | | | | | | |
| NEWQUAY CHIROPRACTIC CLINIC (HM14883) | | | | | ● | ● | | ● | | ● | | | | | | |
| OSTEOPATHIC FAMILY CENTRE (HM15465) | ● | | | | | ● | | | | ● | | | | | | |
| PENZANCE NATURAL HEALTH CENTRE (HM16006) | | | | ● | | | | | | | | | | | | |
| REEVES, J (HM17066) | | | | | | ● | | | | | | | | | | |
| ST AUSTELL CHIROPRACTIC CLINIC (HM19070) | ● | | | | ● | ● | ● | | | | | | | | | |
| TRURO CHIROPRACTIC CLINIC (HM20354) | ● | | | | ● | ● | ● | | | | | | | | | |
| TRURO OSTEOPATHIC PRACTICE (HM20356) | | | | | | ● | | | | | | | | | | |
| VERA BOYES ACUPUNCTURE (HM20618) | | | | | | | | | | ● | | | | | | |
| WEATHERHOGG, D J (HM21046) | | | | | | ● | | | | | | | | | | |
| WILLS, JONATHAN (HM21632) | | | | | | ● | | | | | | | | | | |
| WRIGHT, CYNTHIA (HM21929) | | | | | | | | | | | | | | | | |
| **COUNTY DURHAM** | | | | | | | | | | | | | | | | |
| BALANCE HOLISTIC HEALTHCARE (HM01606) | ● | | | | | | | ● | | | | | | | | |
| CALLAGHAN, M M (HM03548) | | | | | | ● | | ● | | | | | | | | |
| EVANS, BRUCE (DR) (HM06958) | | | | | | ● | | | | | | | | | | |
| FIONA OTTEWELL CHRTRD PHYSIO (HM07329) | | | | | | | ● | | | | | | | | | |
| FOOTPRINTS (HM07507) | | | | | | ● | | ● | | | | | | | | |
| HIND, CAROLE (HM09824) | | ● | | | | | | | | | | | | | | |
| HOBSON, I K (HM09864) | | | | | | ● | | ● | | | | | | | | |
| NEWCASTLE/NE TRANS MEDITA CTRE (HM14856) | ● | | | | | | | | | | | | | | | |
| OLD PIT PRACTICE (HM15260) | | | | | | ● | | ● | | | | | | | | |
| SPOORS, L & D (HM19039) | | | | | | | | | | | | | | | | |
| TEESDALE OSTEOPATHIC CLINIC (HM19817) | | | | | | | | | | | | | | | | |
| TREATMENT ROOM (HM20302) | | | | | | ● | ● | | | | | | | | ● | |
| WARWICK, ANDREA (HM20967) | ● | | | | ● | | | | | ● | | | | | | |
| **CUMBRIA** | | | | | | | | | | | | | | | | |
| CUMBRIA PHYSIO & SPORTS CLINIC (HM05598) | | | | | | | ● | | | | | | | | | |
| DEERING, CHRISTINE (HM05959) | ● | | | | | | | | | | | | | | | |
| FOOTWORKS (HM07515) | | | | | | ● | | ● | | | | | | | | |
| GARNETT, JANE (HM07897) | ● | | | | | | | | | | | | | | | |
| HERBS AND HELPERS (HM09668) | | ● | | ● | | | | | | ● | | ● | ● | | | |
| HYPNOTHERAPY CENTRE (HM10525) | | | | | | | | | | | | | | | | |

| Business by County with Reference no. | Hair Problems | Halitosis | Hand Problems | Hay Fever | Headaches | Hearing Problems | High Blood Pressure | Hip Complaints | Hyperactivity | Hypoglycaemia | Impotence | Incontinence | Indigestion | Infertility | Influenza | Ingrowing Toenails |
|---|---|---|---|---|---|---|---|---|---|---|---|---|---|---|---|---|
| MASTERS, B (HM13273) | | | ● | | ● | | ● | ● | | | | | | | | |
| MORSE, EMMA (HM14239) | | | | | ● | | | | | | | | | | | |
| NEWQUAY CHIROPRACTIC CLINIC (HM14883) | | | ● | | ● | | ● | | | | | | ● | | | |
| OSTEOPATHIC FAMILY CENTRE (HM15465) | | | ● | ● | ● | | | ● | ● | | | | ● | | | |
| PENZANCE NATURAL HEALTH CENTRE (HM16006) | | | | | | | | | | | | | | | | |
| REEVES, J (HM17066) | | | | | | | | | | | | | | | | ● |
| ST AUSTELL CHIROPRACTIC CLINIC (HM19070) | | | | | ● | | | ● | | | | | | | | |
| TRURO CHIROPRACTIC CLINIC (HM20354) | | | | | ● | | | ● | | | | | | | | |
| TRURO OSTEOPATHIC PRACTICE (HM20356) | | | ● | | ● | | | ● | | | | | | | | |
| VERA BOYES ACUPUNCTURE (HM20618) | | | | ● | ● | | | ● | | | | | | | | |
| WEATHERHOGG, D J (HM21046) | | | ● | | ● | | | ● | | | | | | | | |
| WILLS, JONATHAN (HM21632) | | | | | ● | | | ● | | | | | | | | |
| WRIGHT, CYNTHIA (HM21929) | | | | | ● | | | | | | | ● | | | | |
| **COUNTY DURHAM** | | | | | | | | | | | | | | | | |
| BALANCE HOLISTIC HEALTHCARE (HM01606) | | | | | | | | | | | | | | | | |
| CALLAGHAN, M M (HM03548) | | | | | | | | | | | | | | | | ● |
| EVANS, BRUCE (DR) (HM06958) | | | ● | | | | | ● | | | | | | | | |
| FIONA OTTEWELL CHRTRD PHYSIO (HM07329) | | | | | | | | | | | | | | | | |
| FOOTPRINTS (HM07507) | | | | | | | | | | | | | | | | ● |
| HIND, CAROLE (HM09824) | | | | | ● | | ● | ● | | | | | ● | ● | | |
| HOBSON, I K (HM09864) | | | | | | | | ● | | | | | | | | |
| NEWCASTLE/NE TRANS MEDITA CTRE (HM14856) | | | | | ● | | ● | | | | | | | | | |
| OLD PIT PRACTICE (HM15260) | | | | | ● | | | ● | | | | | | | | |
| SPOORS, L & D (HM19039) | | | | | ● | | | ● | | | | | | | | |
| TEESDALE OSTEOPATHIC CLINIC (HM19817) | | | | | ● | | | ● | | | | | | | | |
| TREATMENT ROOM (HM20302) | | | | | ● | | | | | | | | | | | |
| WARWICK, ANDREA (HM20967) | | | | | ● | | ● | ● | | | | | ● | ● | | |
| **CUMBRIA** | | | | | | | | | | | | | | | | |
| CUMBRIA PHYSIO & SPORTS CLINIC (HM05598) | | | | | | | | ● | | | | | | | | |
| DEERING, CHRISTINE (HM05959) | | | | | | | | | ● | | | | | | | |
| FOOTWORKS (HM07515) | | | | | | | | | | | | | | | | |
| GARNETT, JANE (HM07897) | | | | | | | | | | | | | | | | |
| HERBS AND HELPERS (HM09668) | ● | | | ● | ● | | ● | | | ● | ● | | ● | ● | | |
| HYPNOTHERAPY CENTRE (HM10525) | | | | | ● | | | | | | | | | | | |

# D - I Conditions treated at Practices/Businesses

| Business by County with Reference no. | Dandruff | Deafness | Depression | Diabetes | Diarrhoea | Digestive Problems | Diverticulitis | Dizziness | Dyslexia | Dyspraxia | Ear Disorders | Eczema | ENT Disorders | Epilepsy | Eye Disorders | Fatigue | Fears | Fertility Problems | Fever | Fibroids | Flatulence | Foot Problems | Fractures | Fungal Infections | Gallstones | Gastrointestinal Problems | Genital Herpes | Gingivitis | Glandular Fever | Glaucoma | Gout | Gum Disease | Hair Problems | Halitosis | Hand Problems | Hay Fever | Headaches | Hearing Problems | High Blood Pressure | Hip Complaints | Hyperactivity | Hypoglycaemia | Impotence | Incontinence | Indigestion | Infertility | Influenza | Ingrowing Toenails |
|---|---|---|---|---|---|---|---|---|---|---|---|---|---|---|---|---|---|---|---|---|---|---|---|---|---|---|---|---|---|---|---|---|---|---|---|---|---|---|---|---|---|---|---|---|---|---|---|---|
| LIBRA THERAPY CENTRE (HM12328) | | | ● | | | | | | | | | | | | | | | | | | | | | | | | | | | | | | | | | | | | | | | | | | | | | |
| MCWATT, LIZ (HM13624) | | | ● | | ● | ● | ● | | | | | ● | | | | ● | ● | | | | ● | | | ● | | ● | | | | | | | | ● | | | ● | | ● | | ● | ● | | | ● | | | |
| PETER STREET CLINIC (HM16075) | | | | | | | | | | | | | | | | | | | | | | ● | | ● | | | | | | | | | | | | | | | | | | | | | | | | |
| RHAM, TRICIA (HM17217) | | ● | ● | | | ● | | ● | ● | | ● | | ● | | | ● | ● | | | | ● | ● | | | | ● | | | | | | | | | ● | | ● | ● | ● | ● | ● | | | | | | | |
| RUBINSTEIN, ADAM (HM17724) | | | ● | ● | | ● | | ● | ● | ● | ● | | ● | | | ● | ● | | | | | | | | | ● | | | | | | | | | ● | | ● | ● | ● | | ● | | | ● | | | | |
| RUBINSTEIN, ADAM (HM17725) | | | ● | ● | | ● | | ● | ● | ● | ● | | ● | | | ● | ● | | | | | | | | | ● | | | | | | | | | ● | | ● | ● | ● | | ● | | | ● | | | | |
| SINGLETON, POLLY (HM18612) | ● | ● | ● | ● | ● | ● | ● | ● | ● | ● | ● | ● | ● | ● | ● | ● | ● | ● | ● | ● | ● | ● | ● | ● | ● | ● | ● | ● | ● | ● | ● | ● | ● | ● | ● | ● | ● | ● | ● | ● | ● | ● | ● | ● | ● | ● | ● | |
| STRAWBERRY HOW CLINIC (HM19378) | | | ● | | ● | | | | | | | | | | | | | ● | | | | | | | ● | | | | | | | | | | | ● | ● | | | | | | | | ● | ● | ● | |
| SWINDALE, TESSA (HM19594) | | | | | | | | | | | | | | | | | | | | | | ● | | ● | | | | | | | | | | | | | | | | | | | | | | | | |
| THERAPY CENTRE (HM19898) | | ● | ● | | ● | ● | ● | ● | | | ● | ● | ● | ● | ● | ● | ● | ● | ● | ● | | ● | ● | ● | ● | ● | ● | ● | ● | | ● | ● | ● | | ● | ● | ● | ● | ● | ● | | | ● | | ● | ● | | |
| VULCANS LANE CHIROPODY (HM20720) | | | ● | | | | | | | | | | | | | | | | | | | ● | | ● | | | | | | | | | | | | | | | | | | | | | | | | |
| WILSON, P M (HM21664) | | | | | | | | | | | | | | | | | | | | | | ● | | ● | | | | | | | | | | | | | | | | | | | | | | | | |
| **DERBYSHIRE** | | | | | | | | | | | | | | | | | | | | | | | | | | | | | | | | | | | | | | | | | | | | | | | | |
| ACUPUNCTURE CLINIC (HM00270) | | | ● | | | ● | | | | | | | | | | ● | | | | | | | | | | | | | | | | | | | | ● | ● | | | ● | | | | | | | | |
| ALTER-MED (HM00690) | ● | ● | ● | ● | ● | ● | ● | ● | ● | ● | ● | ● | ● | ● | ● | ● | ● | ● | ● | ● | ● | ● | ● | ● | ● | ● | ● | ● | ● | ● | ● | ● | ● | ● | ● | ● | ● | ● | ● | ● | ● | ● | ● | ● | ● | ● | ● | |
| AROMATHERAPY & REFLEX CTRE (HM01090) | ● | ● | ● | ● | ● | ● | ● | ● | ● | ● | ● | ● | ● | ● | ● | ● | ● | ● | ● | ● | ● | ● | ● | ● | ● | ● | ● | ● | ● | ● | ● | ● | ● | ● | ● | ● | ● | ● | ● | ● | ● | ● | ● | ● | ● | ● | ● | |
| BACH FLOWER REMEDIES (HM01469) | | | ● | | | | | | | | | | | | | | | | | | | | | | | | | | | | | | | | | | | | | | | | | | | | | |
| BANKS, LINDA (HM01665) | | | ● | | | ● | | | | | ● | | | | | ● | | | | | | | | | ● | | | | | | | | | | | ● | ● | | ● | | | ● | | | ● | | | |
| BARROWCLIFFE, GRAHAM (DR) (HM01806) | | | ● | | | | | | | | | | | | | | | ● | | | | | | | | | | | | | | | | | | | | | ● | | | | ● | | | ● | | |
| BELPER BACKPAIN CLINIC (HM02110) | | ● | | | | | | | | | ● | | | | | | | | | | | | | | | | | | | | ● | | | | ● | | | ● | | ● | | | | | | | | |
| BELPER HOMEOPATHY (HM02111) | ● | ● | ● | ● | ● | ● | ● | ● | ● | ● | ● | ● | ● | ● | ● | ● | ● | ● | ● | ● | ● | ● | ● | ● | ● | ● | ● | ● | ● | ● | ● | ● | ● | ● | ● | ● | ● | ● | ● | ● | ● | ● | ● | ● | ● | ● | ● | |
| BELPER NATURAL HEALTH CENTRE (HM02112) | ● | ● | ● | ● | ● | ● | ● | ● | ● | ● | ● | ● | ● | ● | ● | ● | ● | ● | ● | ● | ● | ● | ● | ● | ● | ● | ● | ● | ● | ● | ● | ● | ● | ● | ● | ● | ● | ● | ● | ● | ● | ● | ● | ● | ● | ● | ● | |
| BRADSHAW, P J (HM02878) | | | ● | | | | | | | | | | | | | ● | ● | | | | | | | | | | | | | | | | | | | | | | | | | | | | | | | |
| CARRICK-SMITH, L (HM03744) | | | ● | | | | | | | | | | | | | | | | | | | | | | | | | | | | | | | | | | | | | | | | | | | | | |
| CHIROPODY & PHYSIOTHERAPY (HM04303) | | | | | | | | | | | | | | | | | | | | | | ● | | ● | | | | | | | | | | | | | | | ● | | | | | | | | | |
| COVERLEY PHYSIOTHERAPY CLINIC (HM05284) | | | | | | | | | | | | | | | | | | | | | | | | | | | | | | | | | | | | | | | | ● | | | | | | | | |
| DARBY, ANN (HM05735) | | | ● | ● | | | | | | | | | | ● | | | | | | | | | | | | | | | | | | | | | | | ● | | ● | | | | | | | | | |
| DERBYSHIRE SPORTS INJURIES (HM06014) | | | | | | | | | | | | | | | | | | | | | | | | | | | | | | | | | | | | | | | | ● | | | | | | | | |
| DRONFIELD PHYSIOTHERAPY CLINIC (HM06320) | | | | | | | | | | | | | | | | | | | | | | | | | | | | | | | | | | | | | | | | ● | | | | | | | | |
| ENJOY SPORT (HM06836) | | | | | | | | ● | | | | | | | | | | | | | | ● | | | | | | | | | | | | | ● | | | | | ● | | | | | | | | |
| GARRISON-TODD, WENDY (HM07905) | ● | ● | ● | ● | ● | ● | ● | ● | | | ● | ● | ● | | ● | ● | ● | ● | ● | ● | ● | ● | ● | ● | | ● | ● | ● | ● | ● | ● | ● | ● | ● | ● | ● | ● | ● | ● | ● | ● | ● | ● | ● | ● | ● | ● | |
| HARDING, MANDY (HM08971) | | | | | | | | | | | | | | | | | | | | | | ● | | ● | | | | | | | | | | | | | | | | | | | | | | | | |
| HATHERSAGE HEALTH & THRPY CTRE (HM09198) | | | | | | | | | | | | | | | | | | | | | | ● | | | | | | | | | | | | | | | ● | | | | | | | | | | | |
| HIGGS, ANN (HM09734) | | ● | ● | ● | ● | ● | ● | | | | ● | | ● | | | ● | ● | ● | | ● | ● | | | | ● | ● | | | | | ● | | ● | | | | ● | | ● | | ● | ● | ● | ● | ● | ● | | |

www.healthmyself.com

# D - I Conditions treated at Practices/Businesses

| Business by County with Reference no. | Dandruff | Deafness | Depression | Diabetes | Diarrhoea | Digestive Problems | Diverticulitis | Dizziness | Dyslexia | Dyspraxia | Ear Disorders | Eczema | ENT Disorders | Epilepsy | Eye Disorders | Fatigue | Fears | Fertility Problems | Fever | Fibroids | Flatulence | Foot Problems | Fractures | Fungal Infections | Gallstones | Gastrointestinal Problems | Genital Herpes | Gingivitis | Glandular Fever | Glaucoma | Gout | Gum Disease | Hair Problems | Halitosis | Hand Problems | Hay Fever | Headaches | Hearing Problems | High Blood Pressure | Hip Complaints | Hyperactivity | Hypoglycaemia | Impotence | Incontinence | Indigestion | Infertility | Influenza | Ingrowing Toenails |
|---|---|---|---|---|---|---|---|---|---|---|---|---|---|---|---|---|---|---|---|---|---|---|---|---|---|---|---|---|---|---|---|---|---|---|---|---|---|---|---|---|---|---|---|---|---|---|---|---|
| HOUSE OF AROMATHERAPY (HM10216) | | |●| | | | | | | | | | | | |●| | | | | | | | | | | | | | | | | | | | | | | | | | | | | | | | |
| ILKESTONE OSTEO & MED CTRE (HM10580) | | | | | | | |●| | | | | | | | | | | | | | | | | | | | | | | | | | | | |●| |●|●| | | | | |●| | |
| JOHNSON, MELVYN (HM11086) | | | | | | | | | | | | | | | | | | | | | | | | | | | | | | | | | | | | |●| | |●| | | | | | | | |
| KARDAHJI, F C (HM11319) | | | |●| | | | | | | | | | | | | | | | | |●| | | | | | | | | | | | | | | | | | | | | | | | | |●|
| KEMP, G D (HM11460) | | | | | | | | | | | | | | | | | | | | | |●| |●| | | | | | | | | | | | | | | | | | | | | | | |●|
| KEMP, GILLIAN (HM11461) | | |●| | | | | | | | | | | | |●|●| | | | | | | | | | | | | | | | | | | | | | | | | | | | | | | |
| LANCASHIRE, A W (HM11915) | | | | | | | | | | | | | | | | | | | | | | | | | | | | | | | | | | | | |●| | |●| | | | | | | | |
| LIFESOLUTIONS (HM12359) | | |●| | |●| |●| | | | | | | |●|●|●| | | | | | | | | | | | | | | | | | |●| | | | | |●| | | | | |
| MATLOCK PHYSIOTHERAPY CENTRE (HM13293) |●|●|●|●|●|●|●|●|●|●|●|●|●|●|●|●|●|●|●|●|●|●|●|●|●|●|●|●|●|●|●|●|●|●|●|●|●|●|●|●|●|●|●|●|●|●|●| |
| MATTHEWS, A (HM13299) | |●|●|●|●|●|●|●|●| |●|●|●|●|●|●|●|●|●|●|●|●| |●|●|●| | | |●|●| | | | |●|●|●|●|●|●|●|●|●|●|●|●| |
| MATTHEWS, AMANDA (HM13301) |●|●|●|●|●|●|●|●| | |●|●|●|●|●|●|●|●|●|●|●|●| |●|●|●| | | |●|●| | | | |●|●|●|●|●|●|●|●|●|●|●|●| |
| NATURAL HEALTH CLINIC (HM14577) | | | | | | | | | | | | | | | | |●| | | | | | | | | | | | | | | | | | | | | | | | | | | | | | | |
| PHILIP STOCK - PHYSIOTHERAPIST (HM16120) | | | | | | | |●| | | | | | | | | | | | | |●|●| | | | | | | |●| | | |●| |●| | |●| | | | | | | | |
| PHYSIO ACTIVE (HM16193) | | |●| |●|●|●|●| | |●|●|●|●| |●|●|●|●|●|●| | |●| |●|●|●|●|●|●|●| | | |●|●| |●|●|●|●| |●|●|●|●| |
| SMITH, ALAN P (HM18711) | | | | | | | | | | | | | | | | | | | | | | | | | | | | | | | | | | | | |●| | |●| | | | | | | | |
| SPINK, BERNADETTE (HM19017) | | |●| |●|●| | | | | |●| | | |●|●| |●|●| |●|●|●| | | |●| | |●|●| | |●|●|●| |●|●| | | | |●| |●| |
| SPIRAC PHYSIOTHERAPY (HM19020) | | | | | | | | | | | | | | | | | | | | | | | | | | | | | | | | | | | | | | |●| | | | | | | | |
| STEVENSON, JACKIE (HM19249) |●|●|●|●|●|●|●|●|●|●|●|●|●|●|●|●|●|●|●|●|●|●|●|●|●|●|●|●|●|●|●|●|●|●|●|●|●|●|●|●|●|●|●|●|●|●|●| |
| SYKES, PETER W (HM19617) | | | | | | | | | | | | | | | | | | | | | | | | | | | | | | | | | | | | | | | | | | | | | | | |●|
| TAYLOR, E F (HM19757) | | | | | | | |●| | | | | | | | | | | | | | | | | | | | | | | | | | | | |●| | |●| | | | | | | | |
| TAYLOR, E F (HM19756) | | | | | | | |●| | | | | | | | | | | | | | | | | | | | | | | | | | | | |●| | |●| | | | | | | | |
| TREEWICKS (HM20313) | | |●| | | | | | | | | | | | |●|●| | | | | | | | | | | | | | | | | | | | | | | | | | | | | | | |
| WHITEING CHIROPODISTS (HM21392) | | | |●| | | | | | | | | | | | | | | | | |●| | | | | | | | | | | | | | | | | | | | | | | | | | |
| WHITTLE, S (HM21425) | | | |●| | | | | | | | | | | | | | | | | |●| |●| | | | | | | | | | | | | | | | | | | | | | | | |
| **DEVON** | | | | | | | | | | | | | | | | | | | | | | | | | | | | | | | | | | | | | | | | | | | | | | | | |
| ABBEYMEAD NATURAL HEALTH CTRE (HM00090) | | | | | | | |●| | |●|●|●| | |●|●| | | | | | | | |●| | | | | | | |●| | |●| |●| | |●| | | | |●| |
| ACUPUNCTURE CLINIC (HM00276) |●|●|●|●|●|●|●|●| | |●|●|●|●|●|●|●|●|●|●|●|●|●|●|●|●|●|●|●|●|●|●|●|●|●|●|●|●|●|●|●|●|●|●|●|●|●| |
| ALISON MORTON PHYSIOTHERAPY (HM00579) | | |●| |●| | | | | | |●| | | | | | | | | | | | | | | | | | | | | | | |●|●| | |●| | | | | | | | |
| ANNE RAWLINGS HYPNOTHERAPY (HM00901) | | |●| | |●| | | | | |●| | | |●|●|●| | | | | | | | | | | | | | | | | | |●| |●| | | |●| | | | | |
| ASSOCIATED CHIROPODY SERVICES (HM01270) | | | |●| | | | | | | | | | | | | | | | | |●| | | | | | | | | | | | | | | | | | | | | | | | | | |
| AWARENESS CENTRE (HM01415) |●|●|●|●|●|●|●|●|●|●|●|●|●|●|●|●|●|●|●|●|●|●|●|●|●|●|●|●|●|●|●|●|●|●|●|●|●|●|●|●|●|●|●|●|●|●|●| |
| BALL, ADRIAN (HM01624) | | | | | | | | | | | | | | | | | | | | | | | | | | | | | | | | | | | | |●| | |●| | | | | | | | |
| BARRETT, J (HM01790) | | | | | | | | | | | | | | | | | | | | | | | | | | | | | | | | | | | | | | | | | | | | | | | |●|
| BINMORE, F (HM02318) | | |●| | |●| |●| | | | | | | |●| |●| | | | | | | | | | | | | | | | |●|●|●| |●|●|●| | | |●| |●| |

# D - I Conditions treated at Practices/Businesses

| Business by County with Reference no. | Dandruff | Deafness | Depression | Diabetes | Diarrhoea | Digestive Problems | Diverticulitis | Dizziness | Dyslexia | Dyspraxia | Ear Disorders | Eczema | ENT Disorders | Epilepsy | Eye Disorders | Fatigue | Fears | Fertility Problems | Fever | Fibroids | Flatulence | Foot Problems | Fractures | Fungal Infections | Gallstones | Gastrointestinal Problems | Genital Herpes | Gingivitis | Glandular Fever | Glaucoma | Gout | Gum Disease | Hair Problems | Halitosis | Hand Problems | Hay Fever | Headaches | Hearing Problems | High Blood Pressure | Hip Complaints | Hyperactivity | Hypoglycaemia | Impotence | Incontinence | Indigestion | Infertility | Influenza | Ingrowing Toenails |
|---|---|---|---|---|---|---|---|---|---|---|---|---|---|---|---|---|---|---|---|---|---|---|---|---|---|---|---|---|---|---|---|---|---|---|---|---|---|---|---|---|---|---|---|---|---|---|---|---|
| BRIXHAM HEALING HANDS CENTRE (HM03105) | | | ● | | | | | | | | | | | | | | | | | | | | | | | | | | | | | | | | | | ● | | ● | | | | | | ● | | | |
| CARPENTER, PAUL (HM03734) | | | ● | | ● | ● | ● | | | | | | | ● | | ● | | | | | ● | ● | | ● | | ● | | | | | | | | | | | ● | | ● | | | | | | ● | | | |
| CASTLE CHIROPRACTIC CLINIC (HM03829) | | | | | | | | | ● | | | | | | | | | | | | | ● | | | | | | | | | | | | | ● | | ● | | | ● | | | | | | | | |
| CASTLEBRIDGE CHIRO & REFLEX (HM03844) | | | ● | | | | | | | | | | | | | | | | | | | ● | | | | | | | | | | | | | | | | | | | | | | | | | | |
| CHELSTON CHIROPODY PRACTICE (HM04092) | | | ● | ● | ● | ● | | | | | | | | | | ● | | | | | | ● | | | | | | | | | | | | | | | ● | | ● | | | | | | ● | | | ● |
| CHEMIN, CHRISTIAN (HM04098) | | | ● | | | | | ● | | | | | ● | | | ● | | | | | | | | | | | | | | | | | | | | | ● | | | ● | ● | | | | | | | |
| CLINIC OF CHINESE MEDICINE (HM04687) | | | ● | | ● | ● | | | | | | ● | | | | ● | | | | | | | | | | | | | | | | | | | | ● | ● | | | | | | | | | | | |
| COLLEGE OF NATURAL NUTRITION (HM04851) | | | ● | | ● | ● | | | ● | | | ● | | | | ● | | ● | | | | | | | ● | | | | | | | | ● | | | ● | ● | | ● | | ● | | ● | | ● | ● | | |
| COPE, ANNE (HM05134) | | | | | | ● | | | | | | | ● | | | | | | | | | ● | ● | | | ● | | | | | | | | | ● | | ● | | | ● | | | | | ● | | | |
| COX, MIRANDA (HM05316) | | | ● | | | | | | | | | | | | | | | | | | | | | | | | | | | | | | | | | | | | | | | | | | | | | |
| EAST DEVON CONSULTANCY (HM06512) | | | ● | | ● | ● | ● | ● | | | ● | ● | ● | | | ● | | | | | ● | | | | | ● | | ● | | | | ● | | ● | | ● | ● | | ● | | ● | | | | ● | ● | | |
| ELDON HEALTH CLINIC (HM06705) | | | ● | | ● | ● | ● | ● | | | | ● | | | | ● | | ● | | | ● | ● | | | ● | ● | | ● | | | ● | ● | | | ● | | ● | | ● | ● | | ● | | | ● | ● | ● | |
| ELLIS, SUE (HM06773) | | | | | | ● | | ● | | | | | | | | | | | | | | ● | | | | | | | | | | | | | ● | ● | ● | | | ● | | | | | | | | |
| FOOT CLINIC & THERAPY ROOM (HM07474) | | | | ● | | | | | | | | | | | | | | | | | | ● | | ● | | | | | | | ● | | | | | | | | | | | | | | | | | |
| FOOTEC MEDICAL (HM07500) | | | | ● | | | | | | | | | | | | | | | | | | ● | | | | | | | | | | | | | | | | | | | | | | | | | | |
| FUDGE, H (HM07777) | | | ● | | | | | | | | | | | | | | | | | | | ● | | | | | | | | | | | | | ● | | ● | | | ● | | | | | | | | |
| GARRETTLEY, U (HM07902) | | | | | | ● | | ● | | | | | | | | ● | | | | | | | | | | | | | | | | | | | ● | ● | ● | | ● | | | | | | ● | | | |
| HEALTH CONSULTANCY (HM09382) | | | ● | ● | ● | ● | ● | ● | | | ● | ● | ● | ● | | ● | ● | | | ● | ● | | | ● | ● | ● | | | ● | ● | ● | | | | ● | ● | ● | | ● | | | | ● | ● | ● | ● | | |
| HUME, PETER D (HM10370) | | | | ● | | | | | | | | | | | | | | | | | | ● | | ● | | | | | | | | | | | | | | | | | | | | | | | | ● |
| IRIDOLOGY/NUTRITIONAL THER (HM10723) | ● | ● | ● | ● | ● | ● | ● | ● | ● | ● | ● | ● | ● | ● | ● | ● | ● | ● | ● | ● | ● | ● | ● | ● | ● | ● | ● | ● | ● | ● | ● | ● | ● | ● | ● | ● | ● | ● | ● | ● | ● | ● | ● | ● | ● | ● | ● | ● |
| J T SERVICES (HM10802) | | | | ● | | | | | | | | ● | | | | ● | | | | | | ● | | | | | | | | | | | | | ● | | ● | | ● | ● | ● | | | | | | | |
| JANE HYDE CHRTRD PHYSIO (HM10917) | | | | | | | | | | | | | | | | | | | | | | ● | | | | | | | | | | | | | ● | | ● | | | | | | | | | | | |
| JEFFRIES, BARBARA (HM10972) | | | ● | | | | | | | | | | | | | | ● | | | | | | | | | | | | | | | | | | | | | | | | | | | | | | | |
| JOHNSON, MICHAEL (HM11087) | | | | | ● | | | | | | ● | ● | | | | | ● | ● | | | | | | | | | | | ● | | ● | | | | | | ● | | ● | | | | ● | | | ● | | |
| JULIE ADAMS REFLEXOLOGIST (HM11256) | | | | | | ● | ● | | | | | | | | | | | | | | ● | | | | | | | | | | | | | | | | | | ● | | | | | | ● | | | |
| KINGSBRIDGE COMP HLTH PRACTICE (HM11658) | | ● | ● | ● | ● | ● | ● | ● | ● | ● | ● | ● | ● | | ● | ● | ● | ● | ● | ● | ● | ● | ● | ● | | ● | ● | ● | ● | | | ● | | ● | ● | ● | ● | ● | ● | ● | ● | ● | ● | ● | ● | ● | ● | ● |
| KINGSBRIDGE PHYSICAL THERAPY (HM11659) | | | | | | | | | | | | | | | | | | | | | | | | | | | | | | | | | | | | | | | | ● | | | | | | | | |
| LIGHT TOUCH THERAPY TRAINING (HM12369) | | | ● | | ● | ● | ● | ● | | | ● | ● | ● | | ● | ● | ● | ● | ● | ● | | | ● | | ● | ● | ● | | ● | | ● | | ● | | | ● | ● | | ● | | | | ● | ● | ● | ● | ● | |
| LINDEMAN, A J (HM12415) | ● | ● | ● | | ● | ● | ● | ● | | | ● | ● | ● | | ● | ● | | ● | ● | ● | ● | ● | | ● | ● | ● | ● | ● | ● | | ● | ● | ● | ● | ● | ● | ● | ● | ● | ● | ● | ● | ● | ● | ● | ● | ● | |
| LION HOUSE SURGERY (HM12446) | | | ● | | ● | ● | | | ● | | | | ● | ● | | | | | | | | | | | | | | | | | | | | | | | ● | | ● | ● | | | | | ● | | | |
| MALLARDO, RENEE (HM12977) | | | ● | | | | | | | | | | | | | ● | ● | ● | | | | | | | | | | | | | | | | | | | | | | | | | | | | | | |
| MASON, MARCUS (HM13248) | | | ● | ● | ● | ● | ● | ● | | | ● | ● | ● | | | ● | ● | ● | ● | ● | ● | | | | ● | ● | | | ● | | ● | | | | | ● | ● | | ● | ● | ● | ● | ● | ● | ● | ● | ● | |
| MASSAGE RELAXING THERAPEUTIC (HM13262) | | | ● | | | | | | | | | | | | | ● | | | | | | | | | | | | | | | | | | | | | ● | | | | | | | | | | | |
| MONSHIN, DEBORAH J (HM14075) | | | ● | | ● | ● | | | | | | ● | | | | ● | ● | | | | | | | | | ● | | | | | | | | | | ● | ● | | | | | | | | | | | |

# D - I Conditions treated at Practices/Businesses

| Business by County with Reference no. | Dandruff | Deafness | Depression | Diabetes | Diarrhoea | Digestive Problems | Diverticulitis | Dizziness | Dyslexia | Dyspraxia | Ear Disorders | Eczema | ENT Disorders | Epilepsy | Eye Disorders | Fatigue | Fears | Fertility Problems | Fever | Fibroids | Flatulence | Foot Problems | Fractures | Fungal Infections | Gallstones | Gastrointestinal Problems | Genital Herpes | Gingivitis | Glandular Fever | Glaucoma | Gout | Gum Disease | Hair Problems | Halitosis | Hand Problems | Hay Fever | Headaches | Hearing Problems | High Blood Pressure | Hip Complaints | Hyperactivity | Hypoglycaemia | Impotence | Incontinence | Indigestion | Infertility | Influenza | Ingrowing Toenails |
|---|---|---|---|---|---|---|---|---|---|---|---|---|---|---|---|---|---|---|---|---|---|---|---|---|---|---|---|---|---|---|---|---|---|---|---|---|---|---|---|---|---|---|---|---|---|---|---|---|
| NELSON, PAUL (HM14781) |  | ● | ● |  | ● | ● | ● | ● |  |  | ● | ● | ● |  | ● | ● | ● | ● | ● | ● | ● | ● | ● | ● | ● | ● | ● | ● | ● |  | ● | ● |  | ● | ● | ● | ● | ● | ● |  | ● | ● | ● |  | ● | ● | ● |  |
| NETHERWAY, JEAN (HM14789) |  |  | ● |  |  |  |  | ● |  |  |  |  |  |  |  |  | ● |  |  |  |  |  |  |  |  |  |  |  |  |  |  |  |  |  |  |  | ● |  | ● |  |  |  |  |  | ● |  |  |  |
| PAIGNTON PHYSIOTHERAPY (HM15576) |  |  |  |  |  |  |  |  |  |  |  |  |  |  |  |  |  |  |  |  |  |  | ● |  |  |  |  |  |  |  |  |  |  |  |  |  |  |  |  | ● |  |  |  |  |  |  |  |  |
| PANNELL, R J (HM15636) |  |  | ● |  |  |  |  |  |  |  |  |  |  |  |  | ● |  |  |  |  |  | ● |  |  |  |  |  |  |  |  |  |  |  |  | ● |  | ● |  |  | ● |  |  |  |  |  |  |  |  |
| PLAYERS, MEGAN (HM16365) | ● | ● | ● | ● | ● | ● | ● | ● | ● |  | ● | ● | ● | ● | ● | ● | ● | ● | ● | ● | ● | ● | ● | ● | ● | ● |  | ● |  | ● | ● | ● | ● | ● | ● | ● | ● | ● | ● | ● | ● | ● | ● | ● | ● | ● | ● |  |
| PLYMOUTH OSTEOPATHS (HM16388) |  |  |  |  |  |  |  |  |  |  |  |  |  |  |  |  |  |  |  |  |  | ● |  |  |  |  |  |  |  |  |  |  |  |  |  |  | ● |  |  | ● |  |  |  |  |  |  |  |  |
| REFLEXOLOGY CENTRE (HM17083) |  |  |  |  |  | ● |  |  |  |  |  |  |  |  |  |  |  | ● |  |  | ● |  |  |  |  |  |  |  |  |  |  |  |  |  |  |  |  |  |  |  |  |  |  |  | ● |  |  |  |
| RENDLE, S (HM17182) |  |  |  | ● |  |  |  |  |  |  |  |  |  |  |  |  |  |  |  |  |  | ● |  | ● |  |  |  |  |  |  |  |  |  |  |  |  |  |  |  |  |  |  |  |  |  |  |  |  |
| RIVERSIDE CHIROPRACTIC CLINIC (HM17379) |  |  |  |  |  |  |  | ● |  |  |  |  |  |  |  |  |  |  |  |  |  |  |  |  |  |  |  |  |  |  |  |  |  |  |  |  | ● |  |  | ● |  |  |  |  |  |  |  |  |
| ROSE & CROWN CLINIC (HM17598) | ● | ● | ● | ● | ● | ● | ● | ● | ● | ● | ● | ● | ● | ● | ● | ● | ● | ● | ● | ● | ● | ● | ● | ● | ● | ● | ● | ● | ● | ● | ● | ● | ● | ● | ● | ● | ● | ● | ● | ● | ● | ● | ● | ● | ● | ● | ● |  |
| SANDERS, RACHEL (HM17916) |  |  |  | ● |  |  |  |  |  |  |  |  |  |  |  |  |  |  |  |  |  |  |  |  |  |  |  |  |  |  |  |  |  |  |  |  |  |  |  |  |  |  |  |  |  |  |  |  |
| SCURR, PETER M (HM18160) |  |  |  | ● |  |  |  |  |  |  |  |  |  |  |  |  |  |  |  |  |  | ● |  |  |  |  |  |  |  |  |  |  |  |  |  |  |  |  |  |  |  |  |  |  |  |  |  | ● |
| SEELEY, JANICE (HM18194) |  |  | ● | ● | ● | ● | ● | ● |  |  | ● | ● |  |  | ● | ● |  | ● | ● | ● | ● | ● |  | ● | ● | ● | ● | ● | ● | ● | ● | ● |  | ● | ● | ● | ● | ● | ● | ● | ● | ● | ● | ● | ● | ● | ● |  |
| SERENITY (HM18233) | ● | ● | ● | ● | ● | ● | ● | ● | ● | ● | ● | ● | ● | ● | ● | ● | ● | ● | ● | ● | ● | ● | ● | ● | ● | ● | ● | ● | ● | ● | ● | ● | ● | ● | ● | ● | ● | ● | ● | ● | ● | ● | ● | ● | ● | ● | ● |  |
| STIMULUS FOR CHANGE (HM19296) |  |  | ● |  | ● | ● |  |  |  |  | ● | ● | ● |  |  | ● | ● | ● | ● |  | ● |  | ● |  |  | ● | ● |  | ● |  |  |  |  |  |  | ● | ● |  |  |  |  |  |  | ● | ● |  | ● |  |
| TRANCE - FORMATIONS HEALING (HM20250) |  |  | ● |  |  |  |  |  |  |  |  | ● |  |  |  | ● | ● |  |  |  |  |  |  |  |  |  |  |  |  |  |  |  |  |  |  |  | ● |  | ● |  | ● |  | ● |  |  | ● |  |  |
| VITAL TOUCH (HM20703) |  |  |  |  |  | ● |  |  |  |  |  |  |  |  |  | ● |  | ● |  |  |  |  |  |  |  |  |  |  |  |  |  |  |  |  |  |  | ● |  |  |  |  |  |  |  |  |  |  |  |
| WALTERS, RICHARD (HM20882) |  |  |  |  | ● |  |  | ● |  |  |  |  |  |  |  | ● |  |  |  |  |  |  |  |  |  |  |  |  |  |  |  |  |  |  |  | ● | ● |  |  | ● |  |  |  |  |  |  |  |  |
| WALTERS, RICHARD (HM20880) |  |  |  |  | ● | ● |  | ● |  |  |  |  |  |  |  | ● |  |  |  |  |  |  |  |  |  |  |  |  |  |  |  |  |  |  |  | ● | ● |  |  | ● |  |  |  |  |  |  |  |  |
| WILKINSON, MARY (HM21512) |  |  |  |  |  |  |  |  |  |  |  |  |  |  |  |  |  |  |  |  |  |  |  |  |  |  |  |  |  |  |  |  |  |  |  |  | ● |  |  | ● |  |  |  | ● |  |  |  |  |
| WILLIAMS CLINIC (HM21531) |  |  | ● |  | ● | ● |  | ● |  |  |  |  |  |  |  | ● |  |  |  |  |  |  |  |  |  |  |  |  |  |  |  |  |  |  |  | ● | ● |  |  |  |  |  |  |  |  |  |  |  |
| WILLSHER, ERNEST R (HM21633) |  |  |  |  |  |  |  |  |  |  |  |  |  |  |  |  |  |  |  |  |  | ● |  |  |  |  |  |  |  |  |  |  |  |  |  |  |  |  |  |  |  |  |  |  |  |  |  | ● |
| YOGA HEALTH STUDIO (HM22028) |  |  | ● | ● |  |  |  |  |  |  |  |  |  |  |  | ● |  |  |  |  |  |  |  |  |  |  |  |  |  |  |  |  |  |  |  |  |  |  |  |  |  |  |  |  |  |  |  |  |
| YORK HOUSE CHIROPODY (HM22044) |  |  |  |  |  |  |  |  |  |  |  |  |  |  |  |  |  |  |  |  |  | ● |  |  |  |  |  |  |  |  |  |  |  |  |  |  |  |  |  |  |  |  |  |  |  |  |  |  |
| **DORSET** |  |  |  |  |  |  |  |  |  |  |  |  |  |  |  |  |  |  |  |  |  |  |  |  |  |  |  |  |  |  |  |  |  |  |  |  |  |  |  |  |  |  |  |  |  |  |  |  |
| ABBEY VIEW COMP CLINIC (HM00088) | ● | ● | ● | ● | ● | ● | ● | ● | ● | ● | ● | ● | ● | ● | ● | ● | ● | ● | ● | ● | ● | ● | ● | ● | ● | ● | ● | ● | ● | ● | ● | ● | ● | ● | ● | ● | ● | ● | ● | ● | ● | ● | ● | ● | ● | ● | ● |  |
| ALTERNATIVE APPROACH (HM00694) |  |  |  |  |  |  |  |  |  |  |  |  |  |  |  |  |  |  |  |  |  |  | ● |  |  |  |  |  |  |  |  |  |  |  |  |  | ● |  |  | ● |  |  |  |  |  |  |  |  |
| ARCHIBALD, LIZ (HM00980) |  |  | ● |  |  |  |  |  |  |  |  |  |  |  |  |  | ● |  |  |  |  |  |  |  |  |  |  |  |  |  |  |  |  |  |  |  |  |  |  |  |  |  |  |  |  |  |  |  |
| ARNDALE CHIROPRACTIC (HM01031) |  |  |  |  |  |  |  |  |  |  |  |  |  |  |  |  |  |  |  |  |  |  |  |  |  |  |  |  |  |  |  |  |  |  |  |  | ● |  |  |  |  |  |  |  |  |  |  |  |
| AROMA TRANQUILITY (HM01064) |  |  | ● |  |  |  |  |  |  |  |  | ● |  |  |  | ● |  |  |  |  |  |  |  | ● |  |  |  |  |  |  |  |  |  |  |  |  |  |  | ● |  |  |  |  |  |  |  |  |  |
| ART OF REFLEXOLOGY (HM01154) |  |  |  |  |  | ● |  |  |  |  |  |  |  |  |  |  |  |  |  |  |  |  |  |  |  |  |  |  |  |  |  |  |  |  |  |  |  |  |  |  |  |  |  |  |  |  |  |  |
| AWDRY, ROBERT (HM01416) | ● |  | ● |  | ● | ● | ● | ● |  |  | ● | ● | ● | ● | ● | ● | ● | ● | ● | ● | ● | ● | ● | ● | ● | ● | ● | ● | ● |  | ● | ● | ● | ● | ● | ● | ● |  | ● | ● | ● | ● | ● |  | ● | ● | ● |  |
| BACK IN BALANCE (HM01479) |  |  |  |  |  |  |  |  |  |  |  |  |  |  |  |  |  |  |  |  |  |  |  |  |  |  |  |  |  |  |  |  |  |  |  |  | ● |  |  | ● |  |  |  |  |  |  |  |  |
| BACK IN FORM (HM01480) |  |  |  |  |  |  |  |  |  |  |  |  |  |  |  |  |  |  |  |  |  |  | ● |  |  |  |  |  |  |  |  |  |  |  |  |  | ● |  |  | ● |  |  |  |  |  |  |  |  |

# D - I Conditions treated at Practices/Businesses

Business by County with Reference no.

| Business | Dandruff | Deafness | Depression | Diabetes | Diarrhoea | Digestive Problems | Diverticulitis | Dizziness | Dyslexia | Dyspraxia | Ear Disorders | Eczema | ENT Disorders | Epilepsy | Eye Disorders | Fatigue | Fears | Fertility Problems | Fever | Fibroids | Flatulence | Foot Problems | Fractures | Fungal Infections |
|---|---|---|---|---|---|---|---|---|---|---|---|---|---|---|---|---|---|---|---|---|---|---|---|---|
| BELTAIN CENTRE (HM02117) | | | ● | | | ● | | | | | | ● | | | | ● | ● | | | | | | | |
| BELTAIN CENTRE (HM02116) | | | | | | | | | | | | | | | | ● | ● | | | | | | | |
| BOURNEMOUTH CTRE FOR COMP MED (HM02761) | ● | ● | ● | ● | ● | ● | ● | ● | ● | ● | ● | ● | ● | ● | ● | ● | ● | ● | ● | ● | ● | ● | ● | ● |
| BOURNEMOUTH PHYSIO CLINIC (HM02762) | | | | | | | | | | | | | | | | | | | | | | | ● | |
| BOWEN CLINIC (HM02771) | | | | | | ● | | | | ● | | ● | | | | ● | | ● | | | ● | | ● | |
| BRANDON, DAVE (HM02912) | ● | ● | ● | ● | ● | ● | ● | ● | ● | ● | ● | ● | ● | ● | ● | ● | ● | ● | ● | ● | ● | ● | | ● |
| BRIDPORT COMP MEDICINE CTRE (HM03019) | ● | ● | ● | ● | ● | ● | ● | ● | ● | ● | ● | ● | ● | ● | ● | ● | ● | ● | ● | ● | ● | ● | ● | ● |
| BRIGHTER FUTURE (HM03040) | | | ● | | | | | | | | | | | | | | ● | | | | | | | |
| BRIGHTER FUTURE (HM03039) | | | ● | | | | | | | | | | | | | | ● | | | | | | | |
| BROADSTONE CENTRE COMP MED (HM03117) | | | ● | | ● | ● | ● | ● | | | | ● | ● | | | ● | ● | ● | | ● | ● | | | |
| BROADSTONE CENTRE OF COMP MED (HM03118) | ● | ● | ● | ● | ● | ● | ● | ● | ● | ● | ● | ● | ● | ● | ● | ● | ● | ● | ● | ● | ● | ● | ● | ● |
| BROWN, A D (HM03208) | | | | | | | | | | | | | | | | | | | | | | ● | | ● |
| BURT, S (HM03429) | | ● | ● | ● | ● | ● | ● | ● | | | | ● | | | ● | ● | ● | ● | ● | ● | ● | ● | | ● |
| BWT PODIATRY (HM03508) | | | | ● | | | | | | | | | | | | | | | | | | ● | | ● |
| CARBERY PRACTICE (HM03657) | | | ● | | | | | ● | | | | | | | | ● | ● | ● | | | | | | |
| CHARMINSTER CHIRO CLINIC (HM04036) | | | | | | | | | | | | | | | | | | | | | | | | |
| CHINESE MEDICINE CENTRE (HM04254) | | | ● | | | | | | | | | | | | | | | | | | | | | |
| CHINESE MEDICINE CLINIC (HM04258) | | | | | | | | | | | | ● | | | | | | | | | | | | |
| CHIROPODY SERVICES (HM04338) | | | | | | | | | | | | | | | | | | | | | | ● | | ● |
| CHIROPRACTIC TREATMENT CENTRE (HM04403) | | | | | | | | | | | | | | | | | | | | | | | | |
| CHRISTCHURCH CHIROPRACTIC CTRE (HM04435) | | | | | | ● | ● | | | | | | | | | ● | | | | | | | | |
| CHRISTCHURCH PHYSIO PRACTICE (HM04436) | | | | | | | | | | | | | | | | | | | | | | ● | ● | |
| CLARK, LYNN (HM04568) | | | | | | | | | | | | | | | | | | | | | | ● | | ● |
| COLLINWOOD, LOUIS (HM04884) | | | ● | | | | | | | ● | | | | ● | | ● | | | | | | | | |
| COMMUNITY CHIROPRACTIC CLINIC (HM04906) | | | | | | | | | | | | | | | | | | | | | | | | |
| DLP HYPNOTHERAPY CENTRE (HM06134) | | | ● | | | | | | | | | ● | | | | ● | ● | | | | | | | |
| FEET FIRST (HM07171) | | | | | | | | | | | | | | | | | | | | | | ● | | ● |
| FERNDOWN CHIROPRACTIC CLINIC (HM07239) | | | | | | | | | | | | | | | | | | | | | | | | |
| FREESPIRIT (HM07724) | | ● | ● | | | ● | | | | | ● | ● | ● | | | ● | ● | | | ● | | ● | | |
| FULL SPECTRUM THERAPY CENTRE (HM07786) | ● | ● | ● | ● | ● | ● | ● | ● | ● | ● | ● | ● | ● | ● | ● | ● | ● | ● | ● | ● | ● | ● | ● | ● |
| GLENCAIRE CLINIC (HM08145) | | | | | | | | | | | | | | | | | | | | | | | | |
| GODFREY, BRIAN (HM08184) | | | | | ● | | | | | | | | | | | | ● | ● | | | | | | |
| HAMPTON, ANNE (HM08886) | | | | | | | | | | | | | | | | | | | | | | ● | | ● |
| HARLING, MARIANNE (DR) (HM09010) | ● | ● | ● | ● | ● | ● | ● | ● | | | | ● | ● | ● | | ● | ● | ● | ● | ● | ● | ● | | ● |

| Business | Gallstones | Gastrointestinal Problems | Genital Herpes | Gingivitis | Glandular Fever | Glaucoma | Gout | Gum Disease | Hair Problems | Halitosis | Hand Problems | Hay Fever | Headaches | Hearing Problems | High Blood Pressure | Hip Complaints | Hyperactivity | Hypoglycaemia | Impotence | Incontinence | Indigestion | Infertility | Influenza | Ingrowing Toenails |
|---|---|---|---|---|---|---|---|---|---|---|---|---|---|---|---|---|---|---|---|---|---|---|---|---|
| BELTAIN CENTRE (HM02117) | | | | | | | | | | | | | ● | | ● | | | | | | ● | | | |
| BELTAIN CENTRE (HM02116) | | | | | | | | | | | | | ● | ● | | | | | | | | | | |
| BOURNEMOUTH CTRE FOR COMP MED (HM02761) | ● | ● | ● | ● | ● | ● | ● | ● | ● | ● | ● | ● | ● | ● | ● | ● | ● | ● | | ● | ● | ● | ● | |
| BOURNEMOUTH PHYSIO CLINIC (HM02762) | | | | | | | | | | | | | | | | | | | | | | | | |
| BOWEN CLINIC (HM02771) | | ● | | | | | ● | | | | ● | | ● | | ● | ● | | | | | ● | | | |
| BRANDON, DAVE (HM02912) | ● | ● | ● | ● | ● | ● | ● | ● | ● | ● | ● | ● | ● | ● | ● | ● | ● | ● | ● | ● | ● | ● | ● | |
| BRIDPORT COMP MEDICINE CTRE (HM03019) | ● | ● | ● | ● | ● | ● | ● | ● | ● | ● | ● | ● | ● | ● | ● | ● | ● | ● | ● | ● | ● | ● | ● | |
| BRIGHTER FUTURE (HM03040) | | | | | | | | | | | | | ● | | | | | | | | | | | |
| BRIGHTER FUTURE (HM03039) | | | | | | | | | | | | | ● | | | | | | | | | | | |
| BROADSTONE CENTRE COMP MED (HM03117) | ● | | | | ● | | ● | | | ● | ● | ● | ● | ● | ● | ● | ● | ● | ● | ● | ● | ● | ● | |
| BROADSTONE CENTRE OF COMP MED (HM03118) | ● | ● | ● | ● | ● | ● | ● | ● | ● | ● | ● | ● | ● | ● | ● | ● | ● | ● | ● | ● | ● | ● | ● | |
| BROWN, A D (HM03208) | | | | | | | | | | | | | | | | | | | | | | | | |
| BURT, S (HM03429) | ● | ● | ● | ● | ● | ● | ● | ● | ● | ● | ● | ● | ● | ● | ● | | | ● | ● | ● | ● | ● | ● | |
| BWT PODIATRY (HM03508) | | | | | | | ● | | | | | | | | | | | | | | | | | |
| CARBERY PRACTICE (HM03657) | | | | | | | | | | | | | ● | | ● | ● | | | | | | | | |
| CHARMINSTER CHIRO CLINIC (HM04036) | | | | | | | | | | | | | ● | | | ● | | | | | | | | |
| CHINESE MEDICINE CENTRE (HM04254) | | | | | | | | | | | | | | | | | | | | | | | | |
| CHINESE MEDICINE CLINIC (HM04258) | | | | | | | | | | | | ● | | | | | | | | | | | | |
| CHIROPODY SERVICES (HM04338) | | | | | | | | | | | | | | | | | | | | | | | | |
| CHIROPRACTIC TREATMENT CENTRE (HM04403) | | | | | | | | | | | | | ● | | | ● | | | | | | | | |
| CHRISTCHURCH CHIROPRACTIC CTRE (HM04435) | | ● | | | | | | | | | | | ● | | | ● | | ● | | | ● | | | |
| CHRISTCHURCH PHYSIO PRACTICE (HM04436) | | | | | | | | | | | ● | | ● | | | | | | | | | | | |
| CLARK, LYNN (HM04568) | | | | | | | | | | | | | | | | | | | | | | | | |
| COLLINWOOD, LOUIS (HM04884) | | | | | | | | | | | | | ● | | | ● | ● | | | | | | | |
| COMMUNITY CHIROPRACTIC CLINIC (HM04906) | | | | | | | | | | | | | ● | | | ● | | | | | | | | |
| DLP HYPNOTHERAPY CENTRE (HM06134) | | | | | | | | | | | | | ● | | | | | | ● | | | | | |
| FEET FIRST (HM07171) | | | | | | | | | | | | | | | | | | | | | | | | |
| FERNDOWN CHIROPRACTIC CLINIC (HM07239) | | | | | | | | | | | | | ● | | | ● | | | | | | | | |
| FREESPIRIT (HM07724) | | | | | | | | | | | ● | | ● | ● | ● | ● | ● | | | | | | | |
| FULL SPECTRUM THERAPY CENTRE (HM07786) | ● | ● | ● | ● | ● | ● | ● | ● | ● | ● | ● | ● | ● | ● | ● | ● | ● | ● | ● | ● | ● | ● | ● | |
| GLENCAIRE CLINIC (HM08145) | | | | | | | | | | | | | ● | | | ● | | | | | | | | |
| GODFREY, BRIAN (HM08184) | | ● | | | | | | | | | | ● | ● | | ● | ● | | | | | | | | |
| HAMPTON, ANNE (HM08886) | | | | | | | | | | | | | | | | | | | | | | | | |
| HARLING, MARIANNE (DR) (HM09010) | ● | ● | ● | ● | ● | | ● | ● | ● | ● | ● | ● | ● | ● | ● | | ● | ● | ● | ● | ● | ● | ● | ● |

# D - I Conditions treated at Practices/Businesses

| Business by County with Reference no. | Dandruff | Deafness | Depression | Diabetes | Diarrhoea | Digestive Problems | Diverticulitis | Dizziness | Dyslexia | Dyspraxia | Ear Disorders | Eczema | ENT Disorders | Epilepsy | Eye Disorders | Fatigue | Fears | Fertility Problems | Fever | Fibroids | Flatulence | Foot Problems | Fractures | Fungal Infections |
|---|---|---|---|---|---|---|---|---|---|---|---|---|---|---|---|---|---|---|---|---|---|---|---|---|
| HIGHCLIFFE CHIROPRACTIC CLINIC (HM09748) | | | | | | | | | | | | | | | | | | | | | | | | |
| HIGHCLIFFE CHIROPRACTIC CLINIC (HM09749) | | | | | | | | | | | | | | | | | | | | | | ● | | |
| HOLISTIC HEALTH CENTRE (HM09973) | ● | | ● | ● | ● | ● | ● | ● | | | ● | ● | ● | ● | | ● | ● | ● | ● | ● | ● | ● | | ● |
| HOMEOPATHY HEALS (HM10081) | ● | | ● | ● | ● | ● | ● | | | ● | ● | ● | | ● | ● | ● | ● | ● | ● | ● | ● | ● | ● | ● |
| HOPKINS, H G (HM10149) | | | | | | | | | | | | | | | | | | | | | | | | |
| HORNE, SUE (HM10175) | ● | | ● | ● | | ● | | | | | | ● | | | | ● | ● | ● | ● | | ● | | | |
| JACKSON, A E (HM10817) | ● | ● | ● | ● | ● | ● | ● | ● | ● | ● | ● | ● | ● | ● | ● | ● | ● | ● | ● | ● | ● | ● | ● | ● |
| JELFS, MARTIN (HM10975) | | | ● | | | | | | | | | | | | | | | | | | | | | |
| KENNEDY, EDWARD (HM11491) | | | | | | | | | | | | | | | | | | | | | | | | |
| LEVER, I J (HM12261) | | | | | | | | ● | | | | | | | | | | | | | | | | |
| LOCK, ROBERT (HM12538) | ● | | ● | | ● | ● | | | | | | ● | | ● | | ● | ● | ● | ● | | ● | | | |
| MOTCOMBE PARK PHYSIOTHERAPY (HM14273) | | | | | | | | | | | | | | | | | | | | | | | | |
| NATURAL HEALTH CONSULTANCY (HM14592) | ● | ● | ● | ● | ● | ● | ● | ● | ● | ● | ● | ● | ● | ● | ● | ● | ● | ● | ● | ● | ● | ● | ● | ● |
| NEIJIA (HM14759) | ● | ● | ● | | ● | ● | | ● | ● | | ● | ● | ● | ● | ● | ● | ● | ● | ● | ● | ● | ● | ● | ● |
| PARTNERSHIP, BAKER (DR) (HM15764) | | | ● | | | | | | | | | | | | | | ● | | | | | | | |
| PHYSIO, MASSAGE & PR ACU (HM16210) | | | ● | | | | | ● | | | | ● | | | | ● | ● | | | | | | ● | |
| PRIDEAUX-BRUNE, COLETTE (HM16604) | ● | ● | ● | ● | ● | ● | ● | ● | ● | ● | ● | ● | ● | ● | ● | ● | ● | ● | ● | ● | ● | ● | ● | ● |
| PRIDMORE, JOSEPHINE (HM16605) | | | ● | | ● | ● | ● | ● | | | | ● | ● | | | ● | ● | ● | | ● | ● | | | |
| PROSPECT HEALTH (HM16667) | | | ● | | | | | | | | | | | | | ● | ● | | | | | ● | | |
| ROBSON, VANESSA (HM17514) | | | | | | | | | | | | | | | | | | | | | | ● | | ● |
| ROLLS MILL COMP HEALTH CENTRE (HM17567) | | | | | | ● | | | | | | ● | | | | ● | | | | | | | | |
| ROWE, PENNY (HM17689) | ● | ● | ● | ● | ● | ● | ● | ● | ● | ● | ● | ● | ● | ● | ● | ● | ● | ● | ● | ● | ● | ● | ● | ● |
| ROY, COLLEEN (HM17710) | ● | ● | ● | ● | ● | ● | ● | ● | ● | ● | ● | ● | ● | ● | ● | ● | ● | ● | ● | ● | ● | ● | ● | ● |
| SHEBORNE CHIROPRACTIC CENTRE (HM18361) | | | | | | | | ● | | | | | | | | | | | | | ● | ● | | |
| SKELTON, JAN (HM18635) | | | | | | | | | | | | | | | | | | | | | | | | |
| SOUTHBOURNE HERBAL CLINIC (HM18924) | | | ● | | | ● | ● | ● | | | | ● | | | | ● | | ● | | | ● | | | ● |
| SOUTHBOURNE NATURAL HLTH CTRE (HM18925) | ● | ● | ● | ● | ● | ● | ● | ● | ● | ● | ● | ● | ● | ● | ● | ● | ● | ● | ● | ● | ● | ● | ● | ● |
| STANDISH-HAYES, QUENTIN (HM19125) | | | | | | | | | | | | | | | | | | | | | | | | |
| STEELE, T M (HM19183) | | | | | | | | | | | | | | | | | | | | | | | | |
| THORNTONS PHARMACY (HM20029) | ● | ● | ● | ● | ● | ● | ● | ● | ● | ● | ● | ● | ● | ● | ● | ● | ● | ● | ● | ● | ● | ● | ● | ● |
| TREAT FEET (HM20301) | | | | | | | | | | | | | | | | | | | | | | ● | | ● |
| TRUNDELL, C (HM20353) | | | | | | | | | | | | | | | | | | | | | | ● | | ● |
| WALTERS, RICHARD (HM20881) | | | | | ● | | | ● | | | | | | | | ● | | | | | | | | |
| WESSEX HEALTHY LIVING FOUND (HM21208) | ● | | ● | | ● | ● | ● | ● | | | ● | ● | ● | | | ● | ● | | ● | ● | | ● | | ● |

| Business by County with Reference no. | Gallstones | Gastrointestinal Problems | Genital Herpes | Gingivitis | Glandular Fever | Glaucoma | Gout | Gum Disease | Hair Problems | Halitosis | Hand Problems | Hay Fever | Headaches | Hearing Problems | High Blood Pressure | Hip Complaints | Hyperactivity | Hypoglycaemia | Impotence | Incontinence | Indigestion | Infertility | Influenza | Ingrowing Toenails |
|---|---|---|---|---|---|---|---|---|---|---|---|---|---|---|---|---|---|---|---|---|---|---|---|---|
| HIGHCLIFFE CHIROPRACTIC CLINIC (HM09748) | | | | | | | | | | | | | ● | | | ● | | | | | | | | |
| HIGHCLIFFE CHIROPRACTIC CLINIC (HM09749) | | | | | | | | | | | ● | | ● | | | ● | | | | | | | | |
| HOLISTIC HEALTH CENTRE (HM09973) | ● | ● | ● | ● | ● | | ● | ● | ● | ● | ● | ● | ● | ● | ● | ● | ● | ● | ● | ● | ● | ● | ● | |
| HOMEOPATHY HEALS (HM10081) | | ● | ● | ● | ● | ● | ● | ● | ● | ● | ● | ● | ● | ● | ● | | ● | ● | ● | ● | ● | ● | ● | |
| HOPKINS, H G (HM10149) | | | | | | | | | | | | | ● | | | ● | | | | | | | | |
| HORNE, SUE (HM10175) | | ● | | | | | ● | | | | | | ● | | ● | | | | | | ● | | | |
| JACKSON, A E (HM10817) | ● | ● | ● | ● | ● | ● | ● | ● | ● | ● | ● | ● | ● | ● | ● | ● | ● | ● | ● | ● | ● | ● | ● | |
| JELFS, MARTIN (HM10975) | | | | | | | | | | | | | | | | | | | | | | | | |
| KENNEDY, EDWARD (HM11491) | | | | | | | | | | | | | ● | | | ● | | | | | | | | |
| LEVER, I J (HM12261) | | | | | | | | | | | | | ● | | | ● | | | | | | | | |
| LOCK, ROBERT (HM12538) | ● | ● | | | | | | ● | | ● | | ● | ● | | ● | ● | ● | | | | ● | ● | | |
| MOTCOMBE PARK PHYSIOTHERAPY (HM14273) | | | | | | | | | | | | | | | | ● | | | | | | | | |
| NATURAL HEALTH CONSULTANCY (HM14592) | ● | ● | ● | ● | ● | ● | ● | ● | ● | ● | ● | ● | ● | ● | ● | ● | ● | ● | ● | ● | ● | ● | ● | |
| NEIJIA (HM14759) | ● | ● | ● | | ● | ● | ● | ● | ● | ● | ● | ● | ● | ● | ● | ● | ● | | ● | ● | ● | ● | ● | |
| PARTNERSHIP, BAKER (DR) (HM15764) | | | | | | | | | | | | | | | | | | | | | | | | |
| PHYSIO, MASSAGE & PR ACU (HM16210) | | | | | | | | | | | ● | ● | ● | | ● | ● | | | | | | | | |
| PRIDEAUX-BRUNE, COLETTE (HM16604) | ● | ● | ● | ● | ● | ● | ● | ● | ● | ● | ● | ● | ● | ● | ● | ● | ● | ● | ● | ● | ● | ● | ● | |
| PRIDMORE, JOSEPHINE (HM16605) | ● | | | | ● | | ● | | | ● | ● | ● | ● | ● | ● | ● | ● | ● | ● | ● | ● | ● | ● | |
| PROSPECT HEALTH (HM16667) | | | | ● | | | | ● | | ● | | | | | | | | | | | | | | |
| ROBSON, VANESSA (HM17514) | | | | | | | | | | | | | | | | | | | | | | | | |
| ROLLS MILL COMP HEALTH CENTRE (HM17567) | | | | | | | | | | | | | ● | | | ● | | | | | | | | |
| ROWE, PENNY (HM17689) | ● | ● | ● | ● | ● | ● | ● | ● | ● | ● | ● | ● | ● | ● | ● | ● | ● | ● | ● | ● | ● | ● | ● | |
| ROY, COLLEEN (HM17710) | ● | ● | ● | ● | ● | ● | ● | ● | ● | ● | ● | ● | ● | ● | ● | ● | ● | ● | ● | ● | ● | ● | ● | |
| SHEBORNE CHIROPRACTIC CENTRE (HM18361) | | | | | | | | | | | ● | | ● | | | | | | | | ● | | | |
| SKELTON, JAN (HM18635) | | | | | | | | | | | | | ● | | | | | | | | | | | |
| SOUTHBOURNE HERBAL CLINIC (HM18924) | ● | ● | ● | | ● | | ● | ● | | | | ● | ● | | ● | | | ● | ● | | ● | ● | ● | |
| SOUTHBOURNE NATURAL HLTH CTRE (HM18925) | ● | ● | ● | ● | ● | ● | ● | ● | ● | ● | ● | ● | ● | ● | ● | ● | ● | ● | ● | ● | ● | ● | ● | |
| STANDISH-HAYES, QUENTIN (HM19125) | | | | | | | | | | | | | ● | | | ● | | | | | | | | |
| STEELE, T M (HM19183) | | | | | | | | | | | | | ● | | | ● | | | | | | | | |
| THORNTONS PHARMACY (HM20029) | ● | ● | ● | ● | ● | ● | ● | ● | ● | ● | ● | ● | ● | ● | ● | ● | ● | ● | ● | ● | ● | ● | ● | |
| TREAT FEET (HM20301) | | | | | | | | | | | | | | | | | | | | | | | | |
| TRUNDELL, C (HM20353) | | | | | | | | | | | | | | | | | | | | | | | | |
| WALTERS, RICHARD (HM20881) | | | | | | | | | | | | ● | ● | | | ● | | | | | | | | |
| WESSEX HEALTHY LIVING FOUND (HM21208) | | | | ● | ● | | | ● | | ● | ● | ● | ● | | ● | | ● | ● | | | ● | | ● | |

# D - I Conditions treated at Practices/Businesses

| Business by County with Reference no. | Dandruff | Deafness | Depression | Diabetes | Diarrhoea | Digestive Problems | Diverticulitis | Dizziness | Dyslexia | Dyspraxia | Ear Disorders | Eczema | ENT Disorders | Epilepsy | Eye Disorders | Fatigue | Fears | Fertility Problems | Fever | Fibroids | Flatulence | Foot Problems | Fractures | Fungal Infections | Gallstones | Gastrointestinal Problems | Genital Herpes | Gingivitis | Glandular Fever | Glaucoma | Gout | Gum Disease | Hair Problems | Halitosis | Hand Problems | Hay Fever | Headaches | Hearing Problems | High Blood Pressure | Hip Complaints | Hyperactivity | Hypoglycaemia | Impotence | Incontinence | Indigestion | Infertility | Influenza | Ingrowing Toenails |
|---|---|---|---|---|---|---|---|---|---|---|---|---|---|---|---|---|---|---|---|---|---|---|---|---|---|---|---|---|---|---|---|---|---|---|---|---|---|---|---|---|---|---|---|---|---|---|---|
| WEST MOORS CHIROPRACTIC CLINIC (HM21230) | | | | | | | | | | | | | | | | | | | | | | | | | | | | | | | | | | | | | ● | | | ● | | | | | | | | |
| WIMBORNE CHIROPODY SURGERY (HM21687) | | | | | | | | | | | | | | | | | | | | | | ● | | ● | | | | | | | | | | | | | | | | | | | | | | | | |
| YELLOW HOUSE (HM22005) | ● | ● | ● | ● | ● | ● | ● | ● | ● | ● | ● | ● | ● | ● | ● | ● | ● | ● | ● | ● | ● | ● | ● | ● | ● | ● | ● | ● | ● | ● | ● | ● | ● | ● | ● | ● | ● | ● | ● | ● | ● | ● | ● | ● | ● | ● | ● | |
| **ESSEX** | | | | | | | | | | | | | | | | | | | | | | | | | | | | | | | | | | | | | | | | | | | | | | | | |
| ABBOT, LISA (HM00095) | | | ● | | | ● | | | | | | | | | | ● | | | | | | | | | | | | | | | | | | | | | ● | | ● | | | | | | | | | |
| ABBOTT, LISA (HM00099) | | | ● | | | ● | | | | | | | | | | ● | | | | | | | | | | | | | | | | | | | | | ● | | ● | | | | | | | | | |
| AEQUILIBRIUM (HM00407) | | | ● | ● | ● | ● | ● | | | | ● | ● | ● | | ● | ● | | | | | ● | | | ● | ● | ● | | | | | ● | | | | | ● | ● | ● | | ● | ● | ● | | ● | ● | | ● | |
| ARC HEALTHCARE (HM00968) | | | | | | ● | | | | | | | | | | ● | | | | ● | | | | ● | | | | | | | | | | | | ● | ● | | | | | | | | | ● | | |
| AROMATHERAPY CLINIC (HM01107) | | | ● | | | | | | | | | ● | | | | ● | | | ● | | | | | | | | | | | | | | | | | | | | | | | | | | ● | | | |
| ASHBY & ASSOCIATES (HM01194) | | | | | | | | | | | | | | | | | | | | | | ● | | ● | | | | | | | | | | | | | | | | | | | | | | | | |
| AVART, GILLIAN (HM01383) | ● | | ● | | | ● | | | | | | ● | | | | ● | | | | | ● | | | | | ● | | ● | | | | ● | ● | | ● | ● | ● | | ● | ● | | | | | ● | | ● | |
| BARKING PHYSICAL THERAPY CTRE (HM01715) | | | | | | | | | | | | | | | | | | | | | | | | | | | | | | | | | | | | | | | | ● | | | | | | | | |
| BAXTER, LISA (HM01929) | | | ● | ● | ● | ● | | | | | ● | ● | ● | | | ● | | ● | ● | | | ● | | | | ● | | | | | | | | | ● | ● | ● | | ● | | | | | | ● | ● | | |
| BENEDICTA (HM02125) | | | ● | | | ● | | | | | | ● | | | | ● | | | | | | | | | | | | | | | | | | | | | | ● | ● | | | | | | | | | |
| BODY BALANCE HEALTH SOLUTIONS (HM02571) | | | | | | | | | | | | | | | | | | | | | | ● | | | | | | | | | | | | | | | ● | | | | | | | | | | | |
| BRENTWOOD CHIROPODY SURGERY (HM02963) | | | | | | | | | | | | | | | | | | | | | | ● | | ● | | | | | | | | | | | | | | | | | | | | | | | | |
| BRITISH INSTITUTE-HYPNOTHERAPY (HM03085) | | | ● | | | | | | | | | | | | | | ● | | | | | | | | | | | | | | | | | | | | ● | | | | | | ● | | | | | |
| BURNHAM PHYSIOTHERAPY CLINIC (HM03405) | | | | | | | | | | | | | | | | | | | | | | | | | | | | | | | | | | | | | | | | ● | | | | | | | | |
| CAIN, SHEILA (HM03538) | | | ● | ● | ● | ● | ● | | ● | ● | ● | ● | ● | ● | | ● | ● | ● | | | ● | ● | | | | | | | ● | | ● | | | | ● | ● | ● | | ● | ● | ● | ● | ● | | ● | ● | ● | |
| CATON, PETER (HM03859) | | | ● | | | | | | | | | | | | | ● | | | | | | | | | | | | | | | | | | | | | ● | | | | | | | | | | | |
| CHAKRA ROSE (HM03942) | | | ● | | | ● | | | | | | | | | | | ● | | | | | | | | | | | | | | | | ● | | | | ● | | | | | | | | | | | |
| CHRIS MOSLIN HYPNOTHERAPIST (HM04433) | | | ● | | | | | | | | | | | | | ● | ● | | | | | | | | | | | | | | | | | | | | ● | | | | | | | | | | | |
| CLACTON CHIROPRACTIC CLINIC (HM04501) | | | | | | | | | | | | | | | | | | | | | | | | | | | | | | | | | | | | | ● | | | ● | | | | | | | | |
| CLARKE, M R (HM04593) | | | | | | | | | | | | | | | | | | | | | | | | | | | | | | | | | | | | | ● | | | | | | | | | | | |
| COKER, EILEEN (HM04800) | ● | | ● | | ● | ● | ● | | | | | ● | ● | | | ● | ● | ● | ● | ● | ● | ● | | ● | | ● | ● | | ● | | ● | | ● | ● | ● | | ● | | ● | | ● | | ● | | ● | ● | | |
| COMPLETE CHIROPRACTIC (HM04957) | | | | | | | | | | | | | | | | | | | | | | | | | | | | | | | | | | | | | ● | | | ● | | | | | | | | |
| COOK, JOE (HM05048) | | | ● | | ● | | | | ● | | | ● | | | | | ● | | | | | | | | | | | | | | | | | | | | ● | | ● | | ● | | ● | | | | | |
| COOPER, FELICITY (HM05104) | | | | ● | | | | | | | | | | | | | | | | | | ● | | ● | | | | | | | ● | | | | | | | | | | | | | | | | | |
| CROWN CHIROPRACTIC CLINIC (HM05508) | | | | | | | | | | | | | | | | | | | | | | | | | | | | | | | | | | | | | ● | | | ● | | | | | | | | |
| CROWN CHIROPRACTIC CLINIC (HM05507) | | | | | | | | | | | | | | | | | | | | | | | | | | | | | | | | | | | | | ● | | | ● | | | | | | | | |
| DICKASON, J T (HM06067) | | | | | | | | | | | | | | | | | | | | | | | | | | | | | | | | | | | | | ● | | | ● | | | | | | | | |
| E A O C (HM06465) | | | | | | | | ● | | | | | | | | ● | | | | | | | | | | | | | | | | | | | | ● | ● | | ● | ● | | | | | | | | |
| EDWARDS, G E (HM06651) | | | | ● | | | | | | | | | | | | | | | | | | ● | | ● | | | | | | | | | | | | | | | | | | | | | | | | |
| EDWARDS, G E (HM06652) | | | | | | | | | | | | | | | | | | | | | | ● | | ● | | | | | | | | | | | | | | | | | | | | | | | | |

# D - I Conditions treated at Practices/Businesses

| Business by County with Reference no. | Dandruff | Deafness | Depression | Diabetes | Diarrhoea | Digestive Problems | Diverticulitis | Dizziness | Dyslexia | Dyspraxia | Ear Disorders | Eczema | ENT Disorders | Epilepsy | Eye Disorders | Fatigue | Fears | Fertility Problems | Fever | Fibroids | Flatulence | Foot Problems | Fractures | Fungal Infections | Gallstones | Gastrointestinal Problems | Genital Herpes | Gingivitis | Glandular Fever | Glaucoma | Gout | Gum Disease | Hair Problems | Halitosis | Hand Problems | Hay Fever | Headaches | Hearing Problems | High Blood Pressure | Hip Complaints | Hyperactivity | Hypoglycaemia | Impotence | Incontinence | Indigestion | Infertility | Influenza | Ingrowing Toenails |
|---|---|---|---|---|---|---|---|---|---|---|---|---|---|---|---|---|---|---|---|---|---|---|---|---|---|---|---|---|---|---|---|---|---|---|---|---|---|---|---|---|---|---|---|---|---|---|---|---|
| ELECTROLYSIS CLINIC (HM06716) | | | | | | | | | | | | | | | | | | | | | | | | | | | | | | | | | ● | | | | | | | | | | | | | | | |
| ELMER CHIROPODY & PODIATRY SVS (HM06781) | | | | ● | | | | | | | | | | | | | | | | | | ● | | ● | | | | | | | ● | | | | | | | | | | | | | | | | | |
| EPPING OSTEOPATHY AND SPORTS (HM06854) | | | | | | | | | | | | | | | | | | | | | | ● | | | | | | | | | | | | | | | ● | | | ● | | | | | | | | |
| EPPING PHYSIOTHERAPY PRACTICE (HM06855) | | | ● | | | ● | | ● | | | | | | | | ● | | | | | | | | | | | | | | | | | | | | ● | ● | | | | | | | | | | | |
| ESSEX PHYSIO & SPORTS INJ CTRE (HM06938) | | | | | | | | | | | | | | | | ● | | | | | | | | | | | | | | | | | | | | | | | | ● | | | | | ● | | | |
| FARROW, VICKI (HM07135) | | | ● | | | ● | | | | | | | | | | ● | | | | | | | | | | | | | | | | | | | | | ● | | | | | | | | | | | |
| FLEUROMA (HM07418) | | | | | | ● | | | | | | ● | ● | | | | | ● | | | ● | ● | | | | | | | | | | | | | ● | | ● | | ● | | | | | | ● | | | |
| FOOT HEALTH CLINIC (HM07482) | | | | | | | | | | | | | | | | | | | | | | ● | | ● | | | | | | | | | | | | | | | | | | | | | | | | |
| FOULKES, GEOFFREY LLOYD (HM07609) | ● | ● | ● | ● | ● | ● | ● | ● | ● | ● | ● | ● | ● | ● | ● | ● | ● | ● | ● | ● | ● | ● | ● | ● | ● | ● | ● | ● | ● | ● | ● | ● | ● | ● | ● | ● | ● | ● | ● | ● | ● | ● | ● | ● | ● | ● | ● | |
| FROST, JANICE (HM07761) | ● | ● | ● | ● | ● | ● | ● | ● | | ● | ● | ● | ● | | ● | ● | ● | ● | ● | ● | ● | ● | | ● | ● | ● | ● | ● | ● | ● | ● | ● | | ● | ● | ● | ● | ● | ● | ● | ● | ● | ● | ● | ● | ● | ● | |
| FULTON, A J (HM07795) | | | | | | | | | | | | | | | | | | | | | | ● | | | | | | | | | | | | | | | | | | | | | | | | | | |
| FULTON, A J (HM07796) | | | | | | | | | | | | | | | | | | | | | | ● | | | | | | | | | | | | | | | | | | | | | | | | | | |
| GENT, WENDY (HM07973) | | | ● | | | | | | | | | | | | | | | | | | | ● | | | | | | | | | | | | | ● | | ● | | | | | | | | | | | |
| GRAY, P A (HM08417) | | | | | | | | | | | | | | | | | | | | | | ● | ● | | | | | | | | | | | | | | | | | | | | | | | | | |
| HADLEIGH PODIATRY CLINIC (HM08695) | | | | | | | | | | | | | | | | | | | | | | ● | | | | | | | | | | | | | | | | | | | | | | | | | | |
| HARLOW OSTEOPATHIC PRACTICE (HM09011) | | | | | | | | | | | | | | | | | | | | | | ● | | | | | | | | | | | | | ● | | | | | ● | | | | | | | | |
| HEALING ROOM (HM09349) | | | ● | | | ● | | | | | | ● | | | | ● | | ● | | | | ● | | | | ● | | | ● | | | | | | ● | | ● | | ● | ● | | | | | | ● | | |
| ISIS HOUSE THERAPY CENTRE (HM10768) | | | ● | | | | | | | | | | | | | ● | ● | | | | | | | | | | | | | | | | | | | | | | | | | | | | | | | |
| JOYNES, IAN (HM11239) | | | | | | | | | | | | | | | | | | | | | | ● | | ● | | | | | | | | | | | | | | | | | | | | | | | | ● |
| KELLY, GILLIAN (HM11431) | | | ● | | ● | ● | | | | | | | | | | ● | | | | | | | | | | | | | | | | | | | | ● | ● | | | ● | | | | | | | | |
| LAING, RICHARD (DR) (HM11866) | ● | ● | ● | | ● | ● | ● | ● | | | ● | ● | ● | | ● | ● | ● | ● | ● | ● | ● | | | ● | ● | ● | ● | ● | ● | ● | ● | ● | | ● | | ● | ● | | ● | | ● | ● | | | ● | ● | ● | |
| LEIGH, MARTIN (HM12189) | | | | | ● | ● | | ● | | | | | | | | ● | | | | | | | | | | ● | | | | | | | | | | | ● | | ● | ● | | | | | ● | | | |
| LEVY, PAUL (HM12269) | | | | | | | | | | | | | | | | | | | | | | ● | | ● | | | | | | | | | | | | | | | | | | | | | | | | ● |
| LINGWOOD CLINIC (HM12435) | | | ● | | | ● | | | | | | ● | | | | ● | | | | | | | | | | | | | | | | | | | | ● | ● | | ● | ● | ● | | | | | ● | | |
| LONDON ROAD PHYSIO PRACTICE (HM12603) | | | | | | | | | | | | | | | | | | | | | | ● | ● | ● | | | | | | | | | | | | | | | | | | | | | | | | |
| MARTIN, LEIGH (HM13202) | | | | | ● | ● | | ● | | | | | | | | ● | | | | | | | | | | ● | | | | | | | | | | | ● | | ● | ● | | | | | ● | | | |
| MEDELY CLINIC (HM13647) | | | | | | | | | | | | | | | | | | | | | | | | | | | | | | | | | | | | | ● | | | | | | | | | | | |
| MILES, C J (HM13855) | | | | ● | | | | | | | | | | | | | | | | | | ● | | | | | | | | | | | | | | | | | | | | | | | | | | |
| MOONSTONE HEALING CENTRE (HM14111) | | | ● | | | ● | ● | ● | | | | ● | | | | ● | ● | | ● | | | ● | | | ● | ● | | | | | | | | | | ● | ● | | ● | | ● | | | | ● | | ● | |
| MOORE, SUSAN (HM14134) | | | ● | | | ● | | | | | | | | | | | | | | | | ● | | ● | | | | | | | | | | | | | ● | | ● | | | | | | | | | ● |
| NATURAL REMEDY CENTRE (HM14620) | ● | | ● | ● | ● | ● | ● | ● | | | | ● | ● | ● | | ● | ● | ● | ● | ● | ● | ● | | ● | ● | ● | ● | ● | ● | | ● | ● | ● | ● | ● | ● | ● | | ● | ● | ● | | ● | ● | ● | ● | ● | |
| PALMER, DAVID J (HM15600) | | | | | | ● | | | | | ● | | ● | | | ● | | ● | | | | | | | | | | | | | | | | | ● | ● | ● | | | ● | | | ● | | | ● | | |
| PALMIST (HM15620) | | | ● | | | | | | | | | | | | | | | | | | | | | | | | | | | | | | | | | | | | | | | | | | | | | |
| PARVEZ, SHAUKAT (HM15771) | | | ● | ● | ● | ● | ● | ● | | | ● | ● | ● | ● | ● | ● | ● | ● | | ● | | ● | | | | ● | | | | | ● | | | | ● | ● | ● | | ● | ● | ● | | ● | ● | ● | ● | | |

# D-I Conditions treated at Practices/Businesses

| Business by County with Reference no. | Dandruff | Deafness | Depression | Diabetes | Diarrhoea | Digestive Problems | Diverticulitis | Dizziness | Dyslexia | Dyspraxia | Ear Disorders | Eczema | ENT Disorders | Epilepsy | Eye Disorders | Fatigue | Fears | Fertility Problems | Fever | Fibroids | Flatulence | Foot Problems | Fractures | Fungal Infections | Gallstones | Gastrointestinal Problems | Genital Herpes | Gingivitis | Glandular Fever | Glaucoma | Gout | Gum Disease | Hair Problems | Halitosis | Hand Problems | Hay Fever | Headaches | Hearing Problems | High Blood Pressure | Hip Complaints | Hyperactivity | Hypoglycaemia | Impotence | Incontinence | Indigestion | Infertility | Influenza | Ingrowing Toenails |
|---|---|---|---|---|---|---|---|---|---|---|---|---|---|---|---|---|---|---|---|---|---|---|---|---|---|---|---|---|---|---|---|---|---|---|---|---|---|---|---|---|---|---|---|---|---|---|---|---|
| PEPPER, SUSAN (HM16010) | | | | | | | | | | | | | | | | | | | | | | | | | | | | | | | | | | | | | ● | | | | | | | | | | | |
| PHARMACARE (HM16109) | ● | ● | ● | ● | ● | ● | ● | ● | | ● | ● | ● | ● | ● | ● | ● | | ● | ● | | ● | ● | ● | ● | ● | ● | | ● | | ● | ● | ● | ● | ● | ● | ● | ● | ● | ● | ● | ● | ● | ● | ● | ● | ● | ● | |
| PHYSIO & SPORTS INJURY CLINIC (HM16186) | | | | | | | | ● | | | | | | | | | | | | | | ● | ● | | | | | | | | | | | | ● | | ● | | | ● | | | | ● | | | | |
| PINEWOOD PHYSIOTHERAPY CLINIC (HM16313) | | | | | | | | | | | | | | | | | | | | | | ● | | | | | | | | | ● | | | | | | ● | | | ● | | | | | | | | |
| PISCES NATURAL THERAPY CENTRE (HM16330) | | | | | | | | | | | | | | | | ● | ● | | | | | | | | | | | | | | | | | | | | | | | | | | | | | | | |
| PRICE, G J (HM16572) | | | ● | ● | ● | ● | | ● | | | | ● | | | | ● | | | | | ● | | | | | ● | | | | | ● | | | | ● | ● | ● | | ● | ● | ● | | | | ● | | | |
| PRIVATE HEALTH CENTRE CLINIC (HM16643) | ● | ● | ● | ● | ● | ● | ● | ● | ● | ● | ● | ● | ● | ● | ● | ● | ● | ● | ● | ● | ● | ● | ● | ● | ● | ● | ● | ● | ● | ● | ● | ● | ● | ● | ● | ● | ● | ● | ● | ● | ● | ● | ● | ● | ● | ● | ● | |
| REFLEXOLOGY CLINIC (HM17088) | | | | ● | | ● | ● | | | | ● | | | | ● | ● | ● | ● | | | | ● | | | | ● | | | | | | | | | | | | | ● | ● | | | | | ● | ● | | |
| SANDERS, G (HM17909) | | | | ● | | | | | | | | | | | | | | | | | | ● | | | | | | | | | | | | | | | | | | | | | | | | | | |
| SCOTT, MARY (HM18124) | ● | ● | ● | ● | ● | ● | ● | ● | ● | ● | ● | ● | ● | ● | ● | ● | ● | ● | ● | ● | ● | ● | ● | ● | ● | ● | ● | ● | ● | ● | ● | ● | ● | ● | ● | ● | ● | ● | ● | ● | ● | ● | ● | ● | ● | ● | ● | |
| SELF AWARENESS HEALING (HM18204) | | | ● | | | | | | | | | | | | | ● | ● | | | | | | | | | | | | | | | | | | | | | | | | | | | | | | | |
| SELVES, KATIE (HM18222) | ● | ● | ● | | ● | ● | ● | ● | | | ● | ● | ● | | ● | ● | ● | ● | ● | ● | ● | ● | | ● | | ● | | | ● | | ● | | | | | ● | ● | | ● | | ● | | | | ● | ● | ● | |
| SEYMOUR, LOUISE (HM18259) | | | | | | | | | | | | | | | | | | | | | | ● | | ● | | | | | | | | | | | | | | | | | | | | | | | | |
| SHELDON, PEGGY (HM18380) | | | ● | | ● | ● | | | | | | | | | | ● | | | | | | | | | | ● | | | | | ● | | | | | | ● | | ● | ● | | | | ● | ● | | | |
| SOUTH, JO (HM18918) | ● | ● | ● | ● | ● | ● | ● | ● | ● | ● | ● | ● | ● | ● | ● | ● | ● | ● | ● | ● | ● | ● | ● | ● | ● | ● | ● | ● | ● | ● | ● | ● | ● | ● | ● | ● | ● | ● | ● | ● | ● | ● | ● | ● | ● | ● | ● | |
| TRINITY CENTRE (HM20338) | ● | ● | ● | | ● | ● | ● | ● | ● | ● | ● | ● | ● | ● | ● | ● | ● | ● | ● | ● | ● | ● | ● | ● | ● | ● | ● | ● | ● | ● | ● | ● | ● | ● | ● | ● | ● | ● | ● | ● | ● | ● | ● | ● | ● | ● | ● | |
| WADDINGTON, R M (HM20726) | | | | | | | | | | | | | | | | | | | | | | ● | | | | | | | | | | | | | | | | | | | | | | | | | | |
| WAYNE-WRIGHT, M S (HM21043) | | | | | | | | | | | | | | | | | | | | | | ● | | ● | | | | | | | | | | | | | | | | | | | | | | | | |
| WENTWORTH HEALTH CLINIC (HM21201) | | | ● | | | ● | | | | | | | | | | | | ● | | | ● | | | | | | | | | | | | | | ● | | ● | | ● | | | | | | ● | | | |
| WHEELER, M A (HM21317) | | | | ● | | | | | | | | | | | | | | | | | | ● | | ● | | | | | | | | | | | | | | | | | | | | | | | | |
| WHEELER, M A (HM21316) | | | | ● | | | | | | | | | | | | | | | | | | | | ● | | | | | | | | | | | | | | | ● | ● | | | | | | | | |
| WHITE WATER HEALING CENTRE (HM21345) | | | ● | | | | | | | | ● | | | | | ● | ● | | | | | | | | | | | | | | | | | | ● | | ● | | | | | | | | | | | |
| WOODSIDE NATURAL HEALTH (HM21859) | ● | | ● | | | ● | ● | | | | | | | | | ● | ● | | | ● | ● | | | ● | | | | | | | | | | | | ● | ● | | | | ● | ● | ● | | ● | | | |
| **GLASGOW (CITY OF)** | | | | | | | | | | | | | | | | | | | | | | | | | | | | | | | | | | | | | | | | | | | | | | | | |
| TAI CHI UNION FOR GB (HM19655) | | | | | | | | | | | | | | | | | | | | | | | | | | | | | | | | | | | | | | | ● | | | | | | | | | |
| **GLOUCESTERSHIRE** | | | | | | | | | | | | | | | | | | | | | | | | | | | | | | | | | | | | | | | | | | | | | | | | |
| ACUPUNCTURE CLINIC (HM00262) | | | ● | | ● | ● | ● | ● | | | | ● | | | | | ● | ● | | | ● | | ● | | | ● | | | ● | | | | ● | | | ● | ● | | ● | ● | ● | | | ● | ● | ● | | |
| ADAMS, PETER (HM00360) | ● | ● | ● | ● | ● | ● | ● | ● | ● | ● | ● | ● | ● | ● | ● | ● | ● | ● | ● | ● | ● | ● | ● | ● | ● | ● | ● | ● | ● | ● | ● | ● | ● | ● | ● | ● | ● | ● | ● | ● | ● | ● | ● | ● | ● | ● | ● | |
| ARTICHOKE NATURAL HEALTH (HM01168) | | | ● | | | ● | | | | ● | | ● | | | | ● | ● | | | | | ● | | | | ● | | | | | | | | | | | ● | | | ● | ● | | | | ● | | | |
| BISHOPS CLEEVE PHYSIO & SPORTS (HM02413) | | | | | | | | | | | | | | | | | | | | | | | | | | | | | | | | | | | | | | | | ● | | | | | | | | |
| BUNTON, LYNN (HM03354) | | | ● | | | | | | | | | | | | | | | ● | | | | | | | | | | | | | | | | | | ● | | | ● | | | | ● | | | | ● | |
| BURKE, JAYNE (HM03388) | | | ● | | | ● | | | | | | | | | | ● | | | | | | | | | | | | | | | ● | | | | ● | ● | ● | ● | ● | | ● | | | ● | ● | | ● | |
| CHELTENHAM HOLISTIC HLTH CTRE (HM04094) | ● | ● | ● | ● | ● | ● | ● | ● | ● | ● | ● | ● | ● | ● | ● | ● | ● | ● | ● | ● | ● | ● | ● | ● | ● | ● | ● | ● | ● | ● | ● | ● | ● | ● | ● | ● | ● | ● | ● | ● | ● | ● | ● | ● | ● | ● | ● | |
| CHELTENHAM HYPNOTHERAPY (HM04096) | | | ● | | | | | | | | | | | | | | ● | | | | | | | | | | | | | | | | | | | | | | | | | | | | | | | |

# D - I Conditions treated at Practices/Businesses

| Business by County with Reference no. | Dandruff | Deafness | Depression | Diabetes | Diarrhoea | Digestive Problems | Diverticulitis | Dizziness | Dyslexia | Dyspraxia | Ear Disorders | Eczema | ENT Disorders | Epilepsy | Eye Disorders | Fatigue |
|---|---|---|---|---|---|---|---|---|---|---|---|---|---|---|---|---|
| CHELTENHAM PHYSIO/SPRTS CLNC (HM04097) | | | | | | | | | | | | | | | | |
| COMPLEMENTARY TOUCH (HM04950) | | | ● | | | ● | | | | | | | | | | ● |
| COOPER, ANGELA (HM05089) | | | ● | | | | | | | | | | | | ● | ● |
| COOPER, ANN (HM05090) | | | ● | | | ● | | | | | | | | | | |
| COTSWOLD PHYSIOTHERAPY CENTRE (HM05215) | | | | | | | | ● | | | ● | | | | | |
| ESSENTIAL BODYWORKS COMPANY (HM06899) | | | ● | | | | | | | | ● | | | | | |
| GREENWELL, DAVID (HM08498) | | | ● | | | | | | | | | ● | | | | ● |
| HYGEIA COLLEGE-COLOUR THERAPY (HM10476) | | | ● | | | | | | | | | | | | | |
| JOANNA SMITH AROMATHERAPY (HM11040) | | | | | | | | | | | | | | | | ● |
| LAWLER, R & G (HM12041) | | | ● | | | ● | | | | | | | | | | ● |
| LECKHAMPTON CHIROPRACTIC CLNC (HM12119) | | | | | | | | | | | | | | | | |
| NATURAL THERAPIES CLINIC (HM14633) | | | ● | | ● | | | ● | | | | | | | | ● |
| NATURAL THERAPY CENTRE (HM14649) | | | ● | | | ● | | | ● | | | | | ● | | ● |
| OLD CONVENT (HM15255) | | | | | | | | | | | | | | | | |
| OSTEOPATH (HM15445) | | | | | | | | | | | | | | | | |
| PENACHE (HM15960) | | | ● | | | | | | | | | | | | | |
| SHIATSU PRACTICE (HM18460) | | | ● | ● | ● | ● | ● | ● | | | ● | | | | | ● |
| SLATER, D C (HM18672) | | | ● | | | | | | | | | | | | | |
| SMYTH, DAVID (HM18830) | ● | ● | ● | ● | ● | ● | ● | ● | ● | ● | ● | ● | ● | ● | ● | ● |
| STOUT, HEATHER (HM19359) | | | ● | | ● | ● | ● | ● | | | ● | ● | ● | | | ● |
| STROUD NATURAL HEALTH CLINIC (HM19422) | ● | ● | ● | ● | ● | ● | ● | ● | ● | ● | ● | ● | ● | ● | ● | ● |
| TREE OF LIFE CENTRE (HM20307) | | | ● | | | ● | | | | | | | | | | ● |
| VILLAGE CLINIC (HM20665) | | | | ● | | | | | | | | | | | | |
| VINEY HALL PHYSIOTHERAPY (HM20683) | | | | | | | | | | | | | | | | |
| WELLS, GEORGINA (HM21172) | | | ● | | | ● | | | | | | ● | | ● | | ● |
| YOGA DRUVAM JIVAN YOGA SOCIETY (HM22024) | | | ● | | | | | | | | | | | | | ● |
| **HAMPSHIRE** | | | | | | | | | | | | | | | | |
| ACUPUNCTURE & PHYSIO CLINIC (HM00245) | | ● | ● | | ● | ● | ● | | | | ● | ● | ● | | ● | ● |
| ALL - HEAL ACU & HERB CENTRE (HM00581) | ● | ● | ● | ● | ● | ● | ● | ● | | | | ● | | ● | | ● |
| ALLERGY THERAPY (HM00637) | ● | ● | ● | ● | ● | ● | ● | ● | ● | ● | ● | ● | ● | ● | ● | ● |
| ARTEMIS (HM01156) | | | ● | | | | | | | | | | | | | |
| AVENUE CLINIC (HM01389) | | | | | | ● | | ● | ● | ● | | | | | | |
| BOLDICK, KATHLEEN (HM02652) | | | ● | | | | | | | | | | | | | ● |
| BRADFORD HOUSE CHIRO CLINIC (HM02849) | | | | | | | | ● | | | | | | | | |

| Business by County with Reference no. | Fears | Fertility Problems | Fever | Fibroids | Flatulence | Foot Problems | Fractures | Fungal Infections | Gallstones | Gastrointestinal Problems | Genital Herpes | Gingivitis | Glandular Fever | Glaucoma | Gout | Gum Disease |
|---|---|---|---|---|---|---|---|---|---|---|---|---|---|---|---|---|
| CHELTENHAM PHYSIO/SPRTS CLNC (HM04097) | | | | | | | ● | | | | | | | | | |
| COMPLEMENTARY TOUCH (HM04950) | ● | | | | | | | | | | | | | | | |
| COOPER, ANGELA (HM05089) | ● | | | | | | | | | | | | | | | |
| COOPER, ANN (HM05090) | | | | | | | | | | ● | | | | | ● | |
| COTSWOLD PHYSIOTHERAPY CENTRE (HM05215) | | | | | | ● | | | | | | | | | ● | |
| ESSENTIAL BODYWORKS COMPANY (HM06899) | | | | | | ● | | | | ● | | | | | | |
| GREENWELL, DAVID (HM08498) | | | | | | | | | | | | | | | | |
| HYGEIA COLLEGE-COLOUR THERAPY (HM10476) | | | | | | | | | | | | | | | | |
| JOANNA SMITH AROMATHERAPY (HM11040) | | | | | | | | | | | | | | | | |
| LAWLER, R & G (HM12041) | | | | | | | | | | | | | | | | |
| LECKHAMPTON CHIROPRACTIC CLNC (HM12119) | | | | | | | | | | | | | | | | |
| NATURAL THERAPIES CLINIC (HM14633) | ● | | | | ● | | | | | | | | | | ● | |
| NATURAL THERAPY CENTRE (HM14649) | ● | ● | | | | | | | | ● | | | | | | |
| OLD CONVENT (HM15255) | | | | | | ● | | | | | | | | | | |
| OSTEOPATH (HM15445) | | | | | | | | | | | | | | | ● | |
| PENACHE (HM15960) | | | | | | | | | | | | | | | | |
| SHIATSU PRACTICE (HM18460) | ● | ● | | | ● | ● | | | | | | | | | | |
| SLATER, D C (HM18672) | ● | | | | | | | | | | | | | | | |
| SMYTH, DAVID (HM18830) | ● | ● | ● | ● | ● | ● | ● | ● | ● | ● | ● | ● | ● | ● | ● | ● |
| STOUT, HEATHER (HM19359) | ● | ● | ● | ● | ● | ● | | | | ● | | | ● | | ● | |
| STROUD NATURAL HEALTH CLINIC (HM19422) | ● | ● | ● | ● | ● | ● | ● | ● | ● | ● | ● | ● | ● | ● | ● | ● |
| TREE OF LIFE CENTRE (HM20307) | | | | | | | | | | | | | | | ● | |
| VILLAGE CLINIC (HM20665) | | | | | | ● | ● | | | | | | | | | |
| VINEY HALL PHYSIOTHERAPY (HM20683) | | | | | | ● | ● | | | | | | | | | |
| WELLS, GEORGINA (HM21172) | ● | | ● | | ● | | | | | | | ● | | | | ● |
| YOGA DRUVAM JIVAN YOGA SOCIETY (HM22024) | | | | | | | | | | | | | | | | |
| **HAMPSHIRE** | | | | | | | | | | | | | | | | |
| ACUPUNCTURE & PHYSIO CLINIC (HM00245) | ● | ● | ● | | ● | ● | ● | | | ● | | | ● | | | |
| ALL - HEAL ACU & HERB CENTRE (HM00581) | ● | | ● | ● | ● | ● | | ● | | | | ● | | | ● | |
| ALLERGY THERAPY (HM00637) | ● | ● | ● | ● | ● | ● | ● | ● | ● | ● | ● | ● | ● | ● | ● | ● |
| ARTEMIS (HM01156) | ● | | | | | | | | | | | | | | | |
| AVENUE CLINIC (HM01389) | | | | | | | | | | | | | | | | |
| BOLDICK, KATHLEEN (HM02652) | | | | | | | | | | | | | | | | |
| BRADFORD HOUSE CHIRO CLINIC (HM02849) | | | | | | ● | | | | | | | | | | |

| Business by County with Reference no. | Hair Problems | Halitosis | Hand Problems | Hay Fever | Headaches | Hearing Problems | High Blood Pressure | Hip Complaints | Hyperactivity | Hypoglycaemia | Impotence | Incontinence | Indigestion | Infertility | Influenza | Ingrowing Toenails |
|---|---|---|---|---|---|---|---|---|---|---|---|---|---|---|---|---|
| CHELTENHAM PHYSIO/SPRTS CLNC (HM04097) | | | | | | | | ● | | | | | | | | |
| COMPLEMENTARY TOUCH (HM04950) | | | | | ● | | ● | ● | | | | ● | ● | | | |
| COOPER, ANGELA (HM05089) | | | | | | | | | | | | | | | | |
| COOPER, ANN (HM05090) | | | | | ● | | | ● | ● | | | ● | | | | |
| COTSWOLD PHYSIOTHERAPY CENTRE (HM05215) | | | ● | | ● | | | ● | | | | ● | | | | |
| ESSENTIAL BODYWORKS COMPANY (HM06899) | | | ● | | ● | | ● | | | | | | | | | |
| GREENWELL, DAVID (HM08498) | | | | | ● | | ● | | | | ● | | | | | |
| HYGEIA COLLEGE-COLOUR THERAPY (HM10476) | | | | | | | | | | | | | | | | |
| JOANNA SMITH AROMATHERAPY (HM11040) | | | | ● | ● | | | | | | | | | | | |
| LAWLER, R & G (HM12041) | | | ● | ● | ● | ● | ● | | ● | | | | ● | | | |
| LECKHAMPTON CHIROPRACTIC CLNC (HM12119) | | | | | ● | | | ● | | | | | | | | |
| NATURAL THERAPIES CLINIC (HM14633) | | | ● | ● | | | ● | | ● | | | ● | ● | | | |
| NATURAL THERAPY CENTRE (HM14649) | | | | | ● | | | ● | ● | | ● | | | ● | | |
| OLD CONVENT (HM15255) | | | | | ● | | | | | | | | | | | |
| OSTEOPATH (HM15445) | | | ● | | ● | | | | | | | | | | | |
| PENACHE (HM15960) | | | | | ● | | | | | | | | | | | |
| SHIATSU PRACTICE (HM18460) | | | ● | ● | ● | | ● | ● | | | ● | ● | ● | ● | | |
| SLATER, D C (HM18672) | | | | | | | | | | | | | | | | |
| SMYTH, DAVID (HM18830) | ● | ● | ● | ● | ● | ● | ● | ● | ● | ● | ● | ● | ● | ● | ● | |
| STOUT, HEATHER (HM19359) | | | | ● | ● | | ● | ● | ● | | | | ● | ● | ● | |
| STROUD NATURAL HEALTH CLINIC (HM19422) | ● | ● | ● | ● | ● | ● | ● | ● | ● | ● | ● | ● | ● | ● | ● | |
| TREE OF LIFE CENTRE (HM20307) | | | ● | ● | | ● | ● | | ● | | | ● | ● | | ● | |
| VILLAGE CLINIC (HM20665) | | | ● | | ● | | | ● | | | | | | | | |
| VINEY HALL PHYSIOTHERAPY (HM20683) | | | | | ● | | | ● | | | | | | | | |
| WELLS, GEORGINA (HM21172) | | | | | | | | | | | | | | | | |
| YOGA DRUVAM JIVAN YOGA SOCIETY (HM22024) | | | | | | | | | | | | | | | | |
| **HAMPSHIRE** | | | | | | | | | | | | | | | | |
| ACUPUNCTURE & PHYSIO CLINIC (HM00245) | | ● | ● | ● | ● | ● | ● | ● | | | ● | ● | ● | ● | ● | |
| ALL - HEAL ACU & HERB CENTRE (HM00581) | ● | ● | | ● | ● | | ● | ● | ● | ● | ● | | ● | ● | ● | |
| ALLERGY THERAPY (HM00637) | ● | ● | ● | ● | ● | ● | ● | ● | ● | ● | ● | ● | ● | ● | ● | |
| ARTEMIS (HM01156) | | | | | | | | | | | | | | | | |
| AVENUE CLINIC (HM01389) | | | ● | | ● | ● | | | | | ● | ● | | | | |
| BOLDICK, KATHLEEN (HM02652) | | | ● | ● | ● | | ● | | | | | | ● | | | |
| BRADFORD HOUSE CHIRO CLINIC (HM02849) | | | ● | | ● | | | ● | | | | | | | | |

# D - I Conditions treated at Practices/Businesses

Business by County with Reference no.

| | BUCK, PETER (HM03306) | CARMICHAEL, GORDON (HM03709) | CASSELL, JOHN (HM03814) | CENTRE FOR COMP MEDICINE (HM03901) | CHILTERN COTTAGE CLINIC (HM04175) | CLEMENTS, CHRISTINE (HM04642) | COAST CLINIC (HM04752) | COLVILE, RICHARD (HM04895) | COMPLETE ANGEL HEALING CENTRE (HM04955) | CORELLO, LOUISE (HM05161) | CRAIG, PETER (HM05353) | CRANIOSACRAL THERAPY (HM05377) | CTRE FOR THE STUDY OF COMP MED (HM05543) | DOLPHIN STUDIOS (HM06165) | EASTLEIGH OSTEOPATHIC CLINIC (HM06544) | EDGAR, A (HM06596) | ENERGY EXCHANGE HOLISTIC CTRE (HM06816) | EVANS (HM06953) | FAIRFIELDS LANE WEST (HM07059) | FAMILY CHIRO & ALT MED CTRE (HM07081) | FIT FEET CHIROPODY (HM07361) | FLEET & DISTRICT HYP CENTRE (HM07399) | FOOT SHOP (HM07486) | FOREVER LIVING PRODUCTS (HM07555) | FOSSEY, LYNETTE (HM07585) | FOSTER, JAMES M ASSOCIATES (HM07593) | FOX, ANTONY D (DR) (HM07631) | HANTSCARE (HM08947) | HAYLING ISLAND CHIRO CLINIC (HM09268) | HEAL-ALL HERB AND ACU CTRE (HM09315) | HEARNE, BRIAN (HM09440) | HERB MEDIC (HM09592) | HIGH STREET CLINIC (HM09742) | HOBBS, T J (HM09860) |
|---|---|---|---|---|---|---|---|---|---|---|---|---|---|---|---|---|---|---|---|---|---|---|---|---|---|---|---|---|---|---|---|---|---|---|
| Ingrowing Toenails |●| | |●| | | | | | | | | | | |●| |●| | | | | | | | | | | | | | | | |
| Influenza | | |●|●|●| | | | | | | |●| | | | | | |●| | | | | | |●| | |●| | | |●|
| Infertility | | |●|●|●| | | | | | | |●| | | | | |●| | | | | | | |●| | |●| |●| | |
| Indigestion | | |●|●|●| | | |●|●| |●|●| |●| | | | |●|●| | | | | |●| | |●| | |●|●|
| Incontinence | | |●|●|●| | | | | | | |●| | | | | | |●|●| | | | | |●| | | | | | | |
| Impotence | | |●|●| | | | | | | | |●| | | | | | |●| |●| | | | |●| | |●| | | | |
| Hypoglycaemia | | |●|●| | | | | |●| | |●| | | | | | | |●| | | | | |●| | |●| | | | |
| Hyperactivity | | |●|●|●| | |●|●|●| |●|●| | | | | | |●|●| | | | | |●| | |●| | |●|●|
| Hip Complaints | |●|●|●| |●| |●|●|●| |●|●| |●| | | | |●| | | | | | |●| |●|●| | |●|●|
| High Blood Pressure | | |●|●| | | |●|●|●| |●|●| | | | | | |●|●| | | | | |●| | |●| |●|●|●|
| Hearing Problems | | |●|●|●| | | | | | | | | | | | | | | | | | | | | |●| | | | | | | |
| Headaches | | |●|●|●|●|●| |●|●| |●|●|●|●| |●| | |●|●| | |●| | |●|●|●|●| | |●|●|
| Hay Fever | | |●|●|●| | | |●| | | |●| | | | | |●|●| | | | | | |●| | |●| | |●|●|
| Hand Problems | | |●|●| | | | |●| | | | | | | | | | |●| | | | | | |●|●|●| | | | |●|
| Halitosis | | |●|●| | | | | | | | |●| | | | | | |●| | | | | | |●| | |●| | | | |
| Hair Problems | | |●|●| | | | | | | | | | | | | | | | | | | |●| | |●| | |●| | | | |
| Gum Disease | | |●|●| | | | | | | | | | | | | | | |●| | | | | | |●| | | | | | | |
| Gout | | |●|●| | | | |●|●| | |●| | | | | | |●| | | | | | |●| | |●| | | | |
| Glaucoma | | |●|●| | | | | | | | | | | | | | | | | | | | | | |●| | | | | | | |
| Glandular Fever | | |●|●|●| | | | |●| | |●| | | | | | | | | | | | | |●| | | | | | | |
| Gingivitis | | |●|●| | | | | | | | | | | | | | | |●| | | | | | |●| | |●| | | | |
| Genital Herpes | | |●|●| | | | | | | | |●| | | | | | | | | | | | | |●| | | | | | | |
| Gastrointestinal Problems | | |●|●|●| | | | | | |●|●| |●| | | | | |●| | | | | |●| | | | | | | |
| Gallstones | | |●|●|●| | | | | | | | | | | | | | | | | | | | | |●| | | | | | | |
| Fungal Infections |●| |●|●|●| | | | | |●| |●|●| | | |●| |●|●| |●| | | |●| | |●|●| |●| |
| Fractures | | |●|●| | | | | | | | | | | | | | | |●| | | | | | |●|●| | | | | | |
| Foot Problems |●|●|●|●| | | | | |●|●| | | | |●| |●| |●|●| |●| | |●|●|●|●|●|●| |●| |
| Flatulence | | |●|●| | | | | | | |●|●| | | | | | |●|●| | | | | |●| | |●| | | | |
| Fibroids | | |●|●|●| | | | | | |●|●| | | | | | | | | | | | | |●| | |●| |●| | |
| Fever | | |●|●|●| | | | | | | | | | | | | | | | | | | | | |●| | |●| | | | |
| Fertility Problems | | |●|●|●| | | | |●| | |●| | | | | |●| | | | | | | |●| | | | | | | |
| Fears | | |●|●|●| | | | |●| |●|●| | | |●| | |●| |●| | | | |●| | |●| | | | |
| Fatigue | | |●|●|●| | |●|●|●| |●|●| | | |●| |●|●|●| | | | | |●| | |●| | |●|●|
| Eye Disorders | | |●|●| | | | | | | |●| | | | | | | | | | | | | | |●| | | | | | | |
| Epilepsy | | |●|●| | | |●| | | |●|●| | | | | | | | | | | | | |●| | |●| | | | |
| ENT Disorders | | |●|●|●| | | | | | | |●| | | | | | |●| | | | | | |●| | | | | | | |
| Eczema | | |●|●|●| | |●| | | |●|●| | | | | |●|●| | | |●| | |●| | |●| |●| | |
| Ear Disorders | | |●|●|●| | | | | | |●|●| | | | | | |●| | | | | | |●| | | | | | | |
| Dyspraxia | | |●|●|●| | | | | | |●| | | | | | | |●| | | | | | |●| | | | | | | |
| Dyslexia | | |●|●| | | | | | | |●| | | | | | | |●| | | | | | |●| | | | | | | |
| Dizziness | | |●|●|●| | | | |●| |●|●| | | | | | |●| | | | | | |●| | |●| | | | |
| Diverticulitis | | |●|●|●| | | | | | | |●| | | | | | |●| | | | | | |●| | |●| | | | |
| Digestive Problems | | |●|●|●| | |●|●|●| |●|●|●|●| | | | |●|●| | |●| | |●| |●|●| | | |●|
| Diarrhoea | | |●|●|●| | | |●|●| | |●| | | | | | | |●| | | | | |●| | |●| | |●| |
| Diabetes | | |●|●| | | | | | |●| |●| | |●| | | |●|●| |●| | |●|●| | |●| | | | |
| Depression | | |●|●|●| | | |●|●| |●|●|●| | |●| |●|●|●|●| | |●| |●| | |●| | |●|●|
| Deafness | | |●|●| | | | | | | | | | | | | | | | | | | | | | |●| | |●| | | | |
| Dandruff | | |●|●| | | |●| | | | | | | | | | | |●| | | | | | |●| | |●| | | | |

www.healthmyself.com

England (by County)

CONDITIONS TREATED

D-I

# D - I Conditions treated at Practices/Businesses

| Business by County with Reference no. | Dandruff | Deafness | Depression | Diabetes | Diarrhoea | Digestive Problems | Diverticulitis | Dizziness | Dyslexia | Dyspraxia | Ear Disorders | Eczema | ENT Disorders | Epilepsy | Eye Disorders | Fatigue | Fears | Fertility Problems | Fever | Fibroids | Flatulence | Foot Problems | Fractures | Fungal Infections |
|---|---|---|---|---|---|---|---|---|---|---|---|---|---|---|---|---|---|---|---|---|---|---|---|---|
| HOLISTIC ARTS STUDIOS (HM09948) | | | ● | | | ● | | | | | | | | | | ● | | | | | ● | | | |
| HOMOEOPATHIC CLINIC (HM10088) | | | | | | | | | | | | | | | | | | | | | | ● | | |
| HUTCHINGS, MARGARET (HM10448) | | | ● | | | | | | | | | | | | | | | | | | | | | |
| HYPNOTHRPY FOR POSITIVE CHANGE (HM10542) | | | ● | | | | | | ● | | | ● | | | | ● | ● | | | | | | | |
| INLPTA (HM10633) | | | ● | | | | | | ● | | | | | | | ● | ● | | | | | | | |
| INNER WHISPERS & THERAPY CTRE (HM10643) | | | ● | | | | | | | | | | | | | ● | | | | | | | | |
| JENKINS, RUSSELL (HM10994) | ● | ● | ● | ● | ● | ● | ● | ● | ● | ● | ● | ● | ● | ● | ● | ● | ● | ● | ● | ● | ● | ● | ● | ● |
| JOYCE, HELEN G M (HM11236) | | | | | | | | | | | | | | | | | | | | | | ● | | |
| KAY SILVER HYPNOTHERAPY (HM11349) | | | ● | | ● | ● | ● | | | | | | | | ● | ● | ● | | | | ● | | | |
| KD PHYSIOTHERAPY (HM11363) | | | | | | | | | | | | | | | | | | | | | | | ● | |
| LEACH, TRICIA (HM12091) | | | ● | | | ● | | | | | | | | | | ● | | | | | | | | |
| LEWIS, D J S (HM12288) | ● | ● | ● | ● | ● | ● | ● | ● | ● | ● | ● | ● | ● | ● | ● | ● | ● | ● | ● | ● | ● | ● | ● | ● |
| LISLE, THOMAS (HM12455) | | | | | | | | | | | | | | | | | | | | | | ● | | ● |
| LOCKHAMS THERAPY CENTRE (HM12545) | | | ● | | | | | | | | | | | | | | ● | | | | | | | |
| LOWE, KENNETH (HM12699) | | | | | | | | | | | | | | | | ● | | | | | | | | |
| LYMINGTON CHIROPRACTIC CLINIC (HM12759) | | | ● | | ● | ● | ● | ● | | | | | | | | ● | ● | | | | ● | ● | | ● |
| MARLOR, J (HM13127) | | | | | | | | | | | | | | | | | | | | | | ● | | ● |
| MELHUISH, J I (DR) (HM13705) | | | | | | | | | | | | | | | | | | | | | | | | |
| MINDWORKS HYPNOTHERAPY CLINIC (HM13969) | | | ● | | | | | ● | | | | | | | | ● | | | | | | | | |
| NATURAL HEALTH SERVICE (HM14595) | ● | ● | ● | ● | ● | ● | ● | ● | ● | ● | ● | ● | ● | ● | ● | ● | ● | ● | ● | ● | ● | ● | ● | ● |
| NEW MILTON CHIROPRACTIC CLINIC (HM14825) | | | | | | | | ● | | | | | | | | | | | | | | ● | ● | ● |
| NORMAN, J M (HM15004) | | | | | | ● | | | | | | | | | | | | | | | | | | |
| NORSWORTHY, CLAIRE (HM15017) | | | ● | | | ● | | | | | | | | | | ● | | | | | | | | |
| PARCHMENT STREET CLINIC (HM15646) | | | ● | ● | ● | ● | | ● | | | ● | ● | ● | ● | ● | ● | ● | ● | | ● | ● | ● | | |
| PHOENIX HOLISTIC CENTRE (HM16156) | | | ● | | | ● | | | | | | | | | | ● | ● | | | | | | | |
| PHYSIOTHERAPY CENTRE (HM16233) | | | | | | | | | | | | | | | | | | | | | | ● | ● | ● |
| REIKI NATURAL HEALING CENTRE (HM17142) | ● | ● | ● | ● | ● | ● | ● | ● | ● | ● | ● | ● | ● | ● | ● | ● | ● | ● | ● | ● | ● | ● | ● | ● |
| RICHARDS, CLAIRE (HM17249) | | | ● | | | | | | | | | | | | | ● | | | | | | | | |
| RINGWOOD CHIROPRACTIC CLINIC (HM17355) | | | | | | | | | | | | | | | | | | | | | | | | |
| RINGWOOD NATURAL HEALTH CLINIC (HM17357) | | | ● | | ● | ● | | ● | | | | ● | | | | ● | ● | | ● | | ● | | | ● |
| RINGWOOD PHYSIOTHERAPY CENTRE (HM17358) | | | | | | | | | | | | | | | | | | | | | | | ● | |
| S E E D INSTITUTE (HM17805) | | | ● | | | | | | | | | | | | | | | | | | | | | |
| SCANDINAVIAN CHIROPRACTIC CTRE (HM18002) | | | | | | | | | | | | | | | | | | | | | | | | |
| SIMCOE CLINIC (HM18549) | | | ● | | | ● | ● | ● | | | ● | ● | ● | | | ● | | ● | | | ● | ● | | ● |

| Business by County with Reference no. | Gallstones | Gastrointestinal Problems | Genital Herpes | Gingivitis | Glandular Fever | Glaucoma | Gout | Gum Disease | Hair Problems | Halitosis | Hand Problems | Hay Fever | Headaches | Hearing Problems | High Blood Pressure | Hip Complaints | Hyperactivity | Hypoglycaemia | Impotence | Incontinence | Indigestion | Infertility | Influenza | Ingrowing Toenails |
|---|---|---|---|---|---|---|---|---|---|---|---|---|---|---|---|---|---|---|---|---|---|---|---|---|
| HOLISTIC ARTS STUDIOS (HM09948) | | | | | | | | | | | | | ● | | | | | | | | | | | |
| HOMOEOPATHIC CLINIC (HM10088) | | | | | | | | | | | ● | | ● | | | ● | | | | | | | | |
| HUTCHINGS, MARGARET (HM10448) | | | | | | | | | | | | | | | | | | | | | | | | |
| HYPNOTHRPY FOR POSITIVE CHANGE (HM10542) | | | | | | | | | | | | ● | ● | | | | | | | ● | | | | |
| INLPTA (HM10633) | | | | | | | | | | | | | ● | | | | | | | | | | | |
| INNER WHISPERS & THERAPY CTRE (HM10643) | | | | | | | | | | | | | ● | | | | | | | | | | | |
| JENKINS, RUSSELL (HM10994) | ● | ● | ● | ● | ● | ● | ● | ● | ● | ● | ● | ● | ● | ● | ● | ● | ● | ● | ● | ● | ● | ● | ● | |
| JOYCE, HELEN G M (HM11236) | | | | | | | | | | | | | ● | | | ● | | | | | | | | |
| KAY SILVER HYPNOTHERAPY (HM11349) | | | | | | | | | | | | | | | | | | | | | ● | | | |
| KD PHYSIOTHERAPY (HM11363) | | | | | | | | | | | | | | | | ● | | | | | | | | |
| LEACH, TRICIA (HM12091) | | | | | | | | | | | ● | ● | ● | | ● | | ● | | | | ● | | | |
| LEWIS, D J S (HM12288) | ● | ● | ● | ● | ● | ● | ● | ● | ● | ● | ● | ● | ● | ● | ● | | ● | ● | ● | ● | ● | ● | ● | ● |
| LISLE, THOMAS (HM12455) | | | | | | | | | | | | | | | | | | | | | | | | ● |
| LOCKHAMS THERAPY CENTRE (HM12545) | | | | | | | | | | | | | ● | | ● | ● | | | | | | | | |
| LOWE, KENNETH (HM12699) | | | | | | | | | | | | | | | | | | | | | | | | |
| LYMINGTON CHIROPRACTIC CLINIC (HM12759) | | ● | | | | | | | | ● | ● | | ● | | ● | ● | ● | ● | | | ● | | | |
| MARLOR, J (HM13127) | | | | | | | | | | | | | | | | | | | | | | | | ● |
| MELHUISH, J I (DR) (HM13705) | | | | | | | | | | | | | ● | | | ● | | | | | | | | |
| MINDWORKS HYPNOTHERAPY CLINIC (HM13969) | | | | | | | | | | | | | | | | | | | ● | | | | | |
| NATURAL HEALTH SERVICE (HM14595) | ● | ● | ● | ● | ● | ● | ● | ● | ● | ● | ● | ● | ● | ● | ● | ● | ● | ● | ● | ● | ● | ● | ● | |
| NEW MILTON CHIROPRACTIC CLINIC (HM14825) | | | | | | | ● | | | | ● | | ● | | | ● | | | | | | | | |
| NORMAN, J M (HM15004) | | | | | | | | | | | | | ● | | | | | | | | | | | |
| NORSWORTHY, CLAIRE (HM15017) | | | | | | | | | | | ● | ● | ● | | ● | ● | ● | | | | ● | | ● | |
| PARCHMENT STREET CLINIC (HM15646) | | ● | | | ● | | ● | | ● | ● | | ● | ● | ● | ● | | ● | ● | ● | ● | ● | ● | | |
| PHOENIX HOLISTIC CENTRE (HM16156) | | | | | | | | | ● | | | | ● | | | | ● | | ● | | ● | | | |
| PHYSIOTHERAPY CENTRE (HM16233) | | | | | | | | | | | | | | | | ● | | | | | | | | |
| REIKI NATURAL HEALING CENTRE (HM17142) | ● | ● | ● | ● | ● | ● | ● | ● | ● | ● | ● | ● | ● | ● | ● | ● | ● | ● | ● | ● | ● | ● | ● | |
| RICHARDS, CLAIRE (HM17249) | | | | | | | | | | | | | ● | | | | | | | | | | | |
| RINGWOOD CHIROPRACTIC CLINIC (HM17355) | | | | | | | | | | | | | ● | | | ● | | | | | | | | |
| RINGWOOD NATURAL HEALTH CLINIC (HM17357) | ● | ● | | | ● | | | | | ● | | ● | ● | | ● | ● | ● | | | | ● | ● | ● | |
| RINGWOOD PHYSIOTHERAPY CENTRE (HM17358) | | | | | | | | | | | | | | | | | | | | | | | | |
| S E E D INSTITUTE (HM17805) | | | | | | | | | | | | | ● | | | | | | | | | | | |
| SCANDINAVIAN CHIROPRACTIC CTRE (HM18002) | | | | | | | | | | | | | ● | | | ● | | | | | | | | |
| SIMCOE CLINIC (HM18549) | ● | ● | | | ● | | | | ● | ● | ● | ● | ● | | ● | ● | | | | | ● | ● | | |

# D - I Conditions treated at Practices/Businesses

Business by County with Reference no.

| Business | Dandruff | Deafness | Depression | Diabetes | Diarrhoea | Digestive Problems | Diverticulitis | Dizziness | Dyslexia | Dyspraxia | Ear Disorders | Eczema |
|---|---|---|---|---|---|---|---|---|---|---|---|---|
| SIMMONDS, J (HM18555) | | ● | ● | ● | ● | ● | ● | ● | | | ● | ● |
| SOLENT CHIROPRACTIC CLINIC (HM18871) | | | | | | | | | | | | |
| SOUTHGATE NAT THERAPY CLINIC (HM18937) | | | ● | | ● | ● | ● | ● | ● | | | ● |
| SOUTHSEA CENTRE FOR COMP MED (HM18943) | ● | ● | ● | ● | ● | ● | ● | ● | ● | ● | ● | ● |
| THOMA, ANDREW (HM19923) | | | | | | | | ● | | | | |
| TURNER, CATHY (HM20420) | ● | ● | ● | ● | ● | ● | ● | ● | ● | ● | ● | ● |
| TWESLEDOWN PHYSIOTHERAPY (HM20449) | | | | | | | | | | | | |
| VINCE, LINDA (HM20668) | | | | ● | | | | | | | | |
| WELL HOUSE HOLISTIC HLTH CTRE (HM21138) | ● | ● | ● | ● | ● | ● | ● | ● | ● | ● | ● | ● |
| WINCHESTER CHIROPRACTIC CLINIC (HM21691) | | | | | | | | ● | | | | |
| WINCHESTER HOM PRACTICE (HM21692) | ● | ● | ● | ● | ● | ● | ● | ● | ● | ● | ● | ● |
| **HEREFORDSHIRE** | | | | | | | | | | | | |
| BEAUTY IS YOURS (HM01999) | | | | | | ● | ● | | | | | ● |
| BROADVIEW NATURAL HEALTH CTRE (HM03119) | | | ● | | | ● | | | | | | ● |
| HEREFORD CENTRE (HM09677) | ● | | ● | ● | ● | ● | ● | ● | | | ● | ● |
| HEREFORD CHIROPRACTIC CLINIC (HM09678) | | | | | | | | | | | | |
| JONES, KEVIN D G (HM11165) | | | | | | | | ● | | | | |
| LEDBURY NATURAL HEALTH CENTRE (HM12122) | ● | ● | ● | ● | ● | ● | ● | ● | ● | ● | ● | ● |
| LEOMINSTER OSTEOPATHS (HM12221) | | | | | | ● | | ● | | | ● | ● |
| TEDDER, CATHRINE (HM19814) | | | | | | | | | | | | |
| WILLCOCKS, T & S (HM21519) | | | | | | | | | | | | |
| **HERTFORDSHIRE** | | | | | | | | | | | | |
| ALDER, DENNIS (HM00497) | | | | ● | | | | | | | | |
| ALLEN, JULIE & LEN (HM00613) | ● | ● | ● | ● | ● | ● | ● | ● | | | ● | ● |
| ALTERNATIVE CHOICES (HM00697) | | ● | ● | ● | ● | ● | | | | | | |
| ARNOLD, PETER & JACKIE (HM01036) | | | ● | ● | | | | | | | | ● |
| AROMA ROOM (HM01055) | | | ● | | | | | | | | | |
| AROMATHERAPY BY ANTONIO (HM01095) | | | ● | | | | | | | | | |
| ASHDOWN CLINIC (HM01205) | | | ● | | ● | ● | ● | ● | | | ● | ● |
| ASHWELL, MELBOURN & BALDOCK (HM01246) | | | | | | | | | | | | |
| ASSOCIATES HEAD & SHORT (HM01277) | | | | ● | | | | | | | | |
| ASSOCIATES HEAD & SHORT (HM01276) | | | | ● | | | | | | | | |
| ASSOCIATION OF STRESS MNGMT (HM01293) | | | | | | | | | | | | |
| AUTOGENIC TRAINING (HM01372) | | | | ● | ● | ● | ● | ● | | | | |

| Business | ENT Disorders | Epilepsy | Eye Disorders | Fatigue | Fears | Fertility Problems | Fever | Fibroids | Flatulence | Foot Problems | Fractures | Fungal Infections |
|---|---|---|---|---|---|---|---|---|---|---|---|---|
| SIMMONDS, J (HM18555) | ● | ● | ● | ● | ● | ● | | | | | | |
| SOLENT CHIROPRACTIC CLINIC (HM18871) | | | | | | | | | | | | |
| SOUTHGATE NAT THERAPY CLINIC (HM18937) | | | | ● | ● | ● | ● | | | | ● | |
| SOUTHSEA CENTRE FOR COMP MED (HM18943) | ● | ● | ● | ● | ● | ● | ● | ● | ● | ● | ● | ● |
| THOMA, ANDREW (HM19923) | | | | | | | | | | | | |
| TURNER, CATHY (HM20420) | ● | ● | ● | ● | ● | ● | ● | ● | ● | ● | ● | ● |
| TWESLEDOWN PHYSIOTHERAPY (HM20449) | | | | | | | | | | | ● | |
| VINCE, LINDA (HM20668) | | | | | | | | | | ● | | |
| WELL HOUSE HOLISTIC HLTH CTRE (HM21138) | ● | ● | ● | ● | ● | ● | ● | ● | ● | ● | ● | ● |
| WINCHESTER CHIROPRACTIC CLINIC (HM21691) | | | | | | | | | | ● | | |
| WINCHESTER HOM PRACTICE (HM21692) | ● | ● | ● | ● | ● | ● | ● | ● | ● | ● | ● | ● |
| **HEREFORDSHIRE** | | | | | | | | | | | | |
| BEAUTY IS YOURS (HM01999) | | | | | | | | | | | | |
| BROADVIEW NATURAL HEALTH CTRE (HM03119) | | | | | | | | | | | | |
| HEREFORD CENTRE (HM09677) | ● | | | ● | ● | ● | ● | ● | ● | ● | | ● |
| HEREFORD CHIROPRACTIC CLINIC (HM09678) | | | | | | | | | | | | |
| JONES, KEVIN D G (HM11165) | | | | | | | | | | ● | | |
| LEDBURY NATURAL HEALTH CENTRE (HM12122) | ● | ● | ● | ● | ● | ● | ● | ● | ● | ● | ● | ● |
| LEOMINSTER OSTEOPATHS (HM12221) | | ● | | ● | | ● | | | | | | |
| TEDDER, CATHRINE (HM19814) | | | | | | | | | | ● | | ● |
| WILLCOCKS, T & S (HM21519) | | | | ● | | | | | | | | |
| **HERTFORDSHIRE** | | | | | | | | | | | | |
| ALDER, DENNIS (HM00497) | | | | | | | | | | ● | | ● |
| ALLEN, JULIE & LEN (HM00613) | ● | ● | | ● | ● | ● | ● | ● | ● | ● | | ● |
| ALTERNATIVE CHOICES (HM00697) | | ● | | ● | | | ● | ● | | ● | | |
| ARNOLD, PETER & JACKIE (HM01036) | | | | | | | | | ● | ● | | |
| AROMA ROOM (HM01055) | | | | | | | | | | | | |
| AROMATHERAPY BY ANTONIO (HM01095) | | | | | | | | | | | | |
| ASHDOWN CLINIC (HM01205) | | | | ● | ● | | | ● | ● | ● | | ● |
| ASHWELL, MELBOURN & BALDOCK (HM01246) | | | | | | | | | | | ● | |
| ASSOCIATES HEAD & SHORT (HM01277) | | | | | | | | | | | | ● |
| ASSOCIATES HEAD & SHORT (HM01276) | | | | | | | | | | | | ● |
| ASSOCIATION OF STRESS MNGMT (HM01293) | | | | | | | | | | | | |
| AUTOGENIC TRAINING (HM01372) | | | | ● | ● | ● | | | ● | | | |

| Business | Gallstones | Gastrointestinal Problems | Genital Herpes | Gingivitis | Glandular Fever | Glaucoma | Gout | Gum Disease | Hair Problems | Halitosis | Hand Problems | Hay Fever |
|---|---|---|---|---|---|---|---|---|---|---|---|---|
| SIMMONDS, J (HM18555) | | ● | | | | ● | ● | | | | ● | ● |
| SOLENT CHIROPRACTIC CLINIC (HM18871) | | | | | | | | | | | | |
| SOUTHGATE NAT THERAPY CLINIC (HM18937) | ● | ● | | | ● | | ● | | | | ● | ● |
| SOUTHSEA CENTRE FOR COMP MED (HM18943) | ● | ● | ● | ● | ● | ● | ● | ● | ● | | | ● |
| THOMA, ANDREW (HM19923) | | | | | | | | | | | | |
| TURNER, CATHY (HM20420) | ● | ● | ● | ● | ● | ● | ● | ● | ● | ● | ● | ● |
| TWESLEDOWN PHYSIOTHERAPY (HM20449) | | | | | | | | | | | | |
| VINCE, LINDA (HM20668) | | | | | | | | | | | | |
| WELL HOUSE HOLISTIC HLTH CTRE (HM21138) | ● | ● | ● | ● | ● | ● | ● | ● | ● | ● | ● | ● |
| WINCHESTER CHIROPRACTIC CLINIC (HM21691) | | | | | | | | | | | | |
| WINCHESTER HOM PRACTICE (HM21692) | ● | ● | ● | ● | ● | ● | ● | ● | ● | ● | ● | ● |
| **HEREFORDSHIRE** | | | | | | | | | | | | |
| BEAUTY IS YOURS (HM01999) | | | | | | | | | | | ● | |
| BROADVIEW NATURAL HEALTH CTRE (HM03119) | | | | | | | | | | | | ● |
| HEREFORD CENTRE (HM09677) | ● | ● | ● | ● | ● | ● | ● | ● | ● | ● | ● | ● |
| HEREFORD CHIROPRACTIC CLINIC (HM09678) | | | | | | | | | | | | |
| JONES, KEVIN D G (HM11165) | | | | | | | | | | | ● | |
| LEDBURY NATURAL HEALTH CENTRE (HM12122) | ● | ● | ● | ● | ● | ● | ● | ● | ● | ● | ● | ● |
| LEOMINSTER OSTEOPATHS (HM12221) | | | | | ● | ● | ● | | | | | ● |
| TEDDER, CATHRINE (HM19814) | | | | | | | | | | | | |
| WILLCOCKS, T & S (HM21519) | | | | | | | | | | | ● | |
| **HERTFORDSHIRE** | | | | | | | | | | | | |
| ALDER, DENNIS (HM00497) | | | | | | | | | | | | |
| ALLEN, JULIE & LEN (HM00613) | ● | ● | ● | ● | ● | | ● | ● | ● | ● | ● | |
| ALTERNATIVE CHOICES (HM00697) | | | | | | | ● | | | | ● | ● |
| ARNOLD, PETER & JACKIE (HM01036) | | | | | | | | | | | ● | ● |
| AROMA ROOM (HM01055) | | | | | | | | | | | | |
| AROMATHERAPY BY ANTONIO (HM01095) | | | | | | | | | | | | |
| ASHDOWN CLINIC (HM01205) | | | | | | | ● | | | | ● | ● |
| ASHWELL, MELBOURN & BALDOCK (HM01246) | | | | | | | | | | | ● | |
| ASSOCIATES HEAD & SHORT (HM01277) | | | | | | | ● | | | | | |
| ASSOCIATES HEAD & SHORT (HM01276) | | | | | | | ● | | | | | |
| ASSOCIATION OF STRESS MNGMT (HM01293) | | | | | | | | | | | | |
| AUTOGENIC TRAINING (HM01372) | | ● | | | ● | | | | | | | ● |

| Business | Headaches | Hearing Problems | High Blood Pressure | Hip Complaints | Hyperactivity | Hypoglycaemia | Impotence | Incontinence | Indigestion | Infertility | Influenza | Ingrowing Toenails |
|---|---|---|---|---|---|---|---|---|---|---|---|---|
| SIMMONDS, J (HM18555) | ● | ● | ● | ● | ● | ● | ● | ● | ● | ● | | |
| SOLENT CHIROPRACTIC CLINIC (HM18871) | ● | | | ● | | | | | | | | |
| SOUTHGATE NAT THERAPY CLINIC (HM18937) | ● | | ● | ● | | ● | | | ● | ● | ● | |
| SOUTHSEA CENTRE FOR COMP MED (HM18943) | ● | ● | ● | ● | ● | ● | ● | ● | ● | | | |
| THOMA, ANDREW (HM19923) | ● | | | | | | | | | | | |
| TURNER, CATHY (HM20420) | ● | ● | ● | ● | ● | ● | ● | ● | ● | ● | ● | |
| TWESLEDOWN PHYSIOTHERAPY (HM20449) | | | | ● | | | | | | | | |
| VINCE, LINDA (HM20668) | | | | | | | | | | | | |
| WELL HOUSE HOLISTIC HLTH CTRE (HM21138) | ● | ● | ● | ● | ● | ● | ● | ● | ● | ● | ● | |
| WINCHESTER CHIROPRACTIC CLINIC (HM21691) | ● | | | ● | | | | | ● | | | |
| WINCHESTER HOM PRACTICE (HM21692) | ● | ● | ● | ● | ● | ● | ● | ● | ● | ● | ● | |
| **HEREFORDSHIRE** | | | | | | | | | | | | |
| BEAUTY IS YOURS (HM01999) | ● | | ● | ● | | | | | ● | | | |
| BROADVIEW NATURAL HEALTH CTRE (HM03119) | ● | | | | | | | | ● | | | |
| HEREFORD CENTRE (HM09677) | ● | ● | ● | ● | ● | ● | ● | ● | ● | ● | ● | ● |
| HEREFORD CHIROPRACTIC CLINIC (HM09678) | ● | | | ● | | | | | | | | |
| JONES, KEVIN D G (HM11165) | ● | | | | | | | | | | | |
| LEDBURY NATURAL HEALTH CENTRE (HM12122) | ● | ● | ● | ● | ● | ● | ● | ● | ● | ● | ● | |
| LEOMINSTER OSTEOPATHS (HM12221) | ● | | | | ● | ● | | ● | ● | ● | | |
| TEDDER, CATHRINE (HM19814) | | | | | | | | | | | | ● |
| WILLCOCKS, T & S (HM21519) | | | | ● | | | | | | | | |
| **HERTFORDSHIRE** | | | | | | | | | | | | |
| ALDER, DENNIS (HM00497) | | | | | | | | | | | | |
| ALLEN, JULIE & LEN (HM00613) | ● | ● | ● | ● | ● | ● | ● | ● | ● | ● | ● | |
| ALTERNATIVE CHOICES (HM00697) | ● | ● | | | | | ● | | ● | | | |
| ARNOLD, PETER & JACKIE (HM01036) | ● | | | | | | | | ● | | ● | |
| AROMA ROOM (HM01055) | | | | | | | | | | | | |
| AROMATHERAPY BY ANTONIO (HM01095) | | | | | | | | | | | | |
| ASHDOWN CLINIC (HM01205) | ● | | ● | ● | | | | | ● | | | |
| ASHWELL, MELBOURN & BALDOCK (HM01246) | ● | | | ● | | | | | | | | |
| ASSOCIATES HEAD & SHORT (HM01277) | | | | | | | | | | | | |
| ASSOCIATES HEAD & SHORT (HM01276) | | | ● | | | | | | | | | |
| ASSOCIATION OF STRESS MNGMT (HM01293) | | | | | | | ● | | | | | |
| AUTOGENIC TRAINING (HM01372) | ● | | ● | | | | | | ● | ● | | |

www.healthmyself.com

# D - I Conditions treated at Practices/Businesses

Business by County with Reference no.

| | BARNET CHIROPODY SURGERY (HM01757) | BASSETT CLINIC (HM01853) | BEAUCHAMP BAGENAL (HM01983) | BERKHAMSTED PHYSIO CLINIC (HM02193) | BETA HEALTH CLINIC (HM02229) | BISHOP'S STORTFORD HOMEOPATHIC (HM02416) | BODY MECHANICS THERAPY CLINIC (HM02598) | BOREHAMWOOD CHIRO CLINIC (HM02717) | BRIGGS-WILSON, A (HM03037) | BRIND, KEVIN (HM03053) | BURYHILL PHYSIOTHERAPY (HM03456) | BUTTERFIELD, ROBIN (HM03496) | CANNON, VALERIE (HM03635) | CHAUHAN, D K (HM04065) | CHOPRA, S (HM04427) | CHOPRA, S (HM04426) | CLARE JAMES HEALTH FOODS (HM04532) | CLINC OF ACU & CHINESE HRBL MED (HM04727) | CONISTON PHYSIOTHERAPY CLINIC (HM04980) | COOPER, FELICITY (HM05101) | DAVID HERBERT REFLEXOLOGY (HM05774) | DEVINE, MARY (HM06036) | DOYLE, AUDREY (HM06257) | DUDGEON, DELIA (HM06353) | EVANS, HELEN (HM06975) | EVANS, HELEN (HM06976) | FEET RETREAT () | FREEMAN, FRANCES (HM07721) | GEMS (HM07969) | GENTLE FEET (HM07977) | GEOFF THIEL, COUNS & PSYCHO (HM07986) | GILLING, LINDA (HM08095) | GOODMAN, HENRY (HM08258) | GRAHAM & KERSTIN ELLIOTT (HM08336) |
|---|---|---|---|---|---|---|---|---|---|---|---|---|---|---|---|---|---|---|---|---|---|---|---|---|---|---|---|---|---|---|---|---|---|---|
| Ingrowing Toenails | | | | | | | | | | | | | | | ● | ● | | | | | | | | | | | | | | | | | | |
| Influenza | | | | | | ● | | | | | | | | ● | | | | ● | | | | | | | | | | ● | | | | ● | | |
| Infertility | | | | | | ● | | | | | | ● | | ● | | | | ● | | | ● | | ● | ● | | | | ● | | ● | | ● | | |
| Indigestion | | | | | | ● | | | | | | | ● | ● | | | | | | | ● | | ● | ● | | | | ● | | ● | | ● | | |
| Incontinence | | | | | | | | | | | | | | ● | | | | | | | ● | | ● | | | | | ● | | ● | | | | |
| Impotence | | | | | | | | | | | | ● | | ● | | | | ● | | | | | ● | | | | | ● | | ● | | | ● | |
| Hypoglycaemia | | | | | | | | | | | | | | ● | | | | | | | | | | | | | | ● | | | | ● | | |
| Hyperactivity | | | | | | | | ● | | | | | ● | ● | | | | | | | | | | | | | | ● | | | | ● | | |
| Hip Complaints | | ● | ● | ● | ● | | ● | ● | | ● | ● | | ● | ● | | | | | ● | | | | ● | ● | | | ● | ● | | ● | | | | ● |
| High Blood Pressure | | | | | | | ● | | | | | | ● | ● | | | | ● | | | ● | | ● | ● | | | | ● | | ● | | ● | | |
| Hearing Problems | | | | | | ● | | | | | | | | ● | | | | | | | | | | | | | | ● | | | | | | |
| Headaches | | ● | ● | | ● | ● | ● | ● | ● | | | | ● | ● | | | | ● | ● | | ● | | ● | ● | | | ● | ● | | ● | | ● | | ● |
| Hay Fever | | | | | ● | | | | | | | | ● | ● | | | | ● | | | ● | | ● | | | | ● | ● | | ● | | ● | | |
| Hand Problems | | ● | | | | | | ● | | | | ● | | ● | | | | | ● | | | | | | | | | ● | | | | ● | | |
| Halitosis | | | | | | ● | | | | | | | | ● | | | | | | | | | | | | | | ● | | | | ● | | |
| Hair Problems | | | | | | | | | | | | | | ● | | | | ● | | | ● | | ● | | | | | ● | | ● | | ● | | |
| Gum Disease | | | | | | | | | | | | | | ● | | | | | | | | | | | | | | ● | | | | ● | | |
| Gout | | | | | | ● | | | | | | | | ● | | | | | | ● | | | ● | | | | | ● | | ● | | ● | | |
| Glaucoma | | | | | | | | | | | | | | ● | | | | | | | | | | | | | | ● | | | | ● | | |
| Glandular Fever | | | | | | | | | | | | | | ● | | | | | | | | | | | | | | ● | | | | ● | | |
| Gingivitis | | | | | | | | | | | | | | ● | | | | | | | | | | | | | | ● | | | | ● | | |
| Genital Herpes | | | | | | | | | | | | | | ● | | | | | | | | | ● | | | | | ● | | ● | | | | |
| Gastrointestinal Problems | | | | | | | | ● | | | | | | ● | | | | ● | | | ● | | ● | ● | | | | ● | | ● | | ● | | |
| Gallstones | | | | | | | | | | | | | | ● | | | | | | | | | ● | | | | ● | ● | | ● | | ● | | |
| Fungal Infections | ● | | | | ● | ● | | | | | | | | ● | ● | ● | | | | ● | | ● | | | ● | ● | | ● | | | | ● | | |
| Fractures | | | | ● | | | | | | | | | | ● | | | | | ● | | | | | | | | | | | | | ● | | |
| Foot Problems | ● | ● | | | ● | | | ● | | | | | | ● | ● | ● | | | ● | ● | | ● | | | ● | ● | ● | ● | | | | | | |
| Flatulence | | | | | | ● | | | | | | | | ● | | | | | | | ● | | | | | | | ● | | ● | | ● | | |
| Fibroids | | | | | | | | | | | | | | ● | | | | ● | | | | | ● | | | | | ● | | ● | | ● | | |
| Fever | | | | | | ● | | | | | | | | ● | | | | | | | | | | | | | | ● | | | | ● | | |
| Fertility Problems | | | | | | ● | | | | | | | | ● | | | | ● | | | ● | | ● | ● | | | | ● | | ● | | ● | | |
| Fears | | | | | | ● | | | | | | | | ● | | | ● | | | | | | ● | | | | | ● | | ● | ● | | ● | |
| Fatigue | | | | | ● | ● | | | | | | | ● | ● | | | | ● | ● | | ● | | ● | ● | | | ● | ● | ● | ● | | ● | ● | ● |
| Eye Disorders | | | | | | | | | | | | | | ● | | | | | | | | | | | | | | ● | | | | ● | | |
| Epilepsy | | | | | | | | | | | | | | ● | | | | | | | | | ● | | | | | ● | | ● | | | | |
| ENT Disorders | | | ● | | | | | | | | | | | ● | | | | | | | | | ● | | | | | ● | | ● | | ● | | |
| Eczema | | | | | | | | | | | | | | ● | | | ● | ● | | | ● | | ● | | | | | ● | | ● | | ● | | |
| Ear Disorders | | | | | | | | | | | | | | ● | | | | | | | | | ● | | | | | ● | | ● | | ● | | |
| Dyspraxia | | | | | | | | | | | | | | ● | | | | | | | | | | | | | | ● | | | | | | |
| Dyslexia | | | | | | | | | | | | | | ● | | | | | | | | | | | | | | ● | | | | | | |
| Dizziness | | | | | | | | | | | | | | ● | | | | ● | ● | | | | ● | | | | ● | ● | | ● | | ● | | |
| Diverticulitis | | | | | | ● | | | | | | | | ● | | | | ● | | | ● | | ● | ● | | | | ● | | ● | | ● | | |
| Digestive Problems | | | | | ● | ● | | | | | | | ● | ● | | | | ● | | | ● | | ● | ● | | | ● | ● | | ● | | ● | | |
| Diarrhoea | | | | | ● | | | | | | | | ● | ● | | | | ● | | | ● | | ● | | | | | ● | | ● | | ● | | |
| Diabetes | | | | | | | | | | | | | | ● | | | | | | ● | | | ● | | | | | ● | | ● | | | | |
| Depression | | | | | ● | ● | | | ● | | | | ● | ● | | | | | | | ● | | ● | | | | ● | ● | | ● | ● | ● | ● | |
| Deafness | | | | | | | | | | | | | | ● | | | | | | | | | | | | | | ● | | | | | | |
| Dandruff | | | | | | | | | | | | | | ● | | | | | | | ● | | ● | | | | | ● | | ● | | ● | | |

# D - I Conditions treated at Practices/Businesses

Business by County with Reference no.

| | GROUNDS, L (HM08599) | HALAHAN, ELISABETH (HM08722) | HAMILTON-PETERS, R & J A (HM08849) | HARPENDEM OSTEOPATHIC PRACTICE (HM09035) | HARPENDEN CHIROPRACTIC CLINIC (HM09036) | HATHAWAY, ELIZABETH (HM09196) | HEALES CHIROPRACTIC CLINIC (HM09322) | HEALTHY AND WISE (HM09425) | HERTFORD NATURAL THERAPY CTRE (HM09690) | HODSDON, L M (HM09893) | HOLLENBERY, S (HM10019) | JACKSON, BARBARA (HM10830) | JENNIFER SAJIR PAED PHYSIO (HM11005) | JOE MILLER SPORTS INJURY (HM11045) | JONES, ALAN (HM11115) | KEW, DEREK (HM11576) | KNEBWORTH PHYSIO CLINIC (HM11742) | LETCHWORTH-PHYSIOTHERAPY (HM12248) | LEWIN, ROCHELLE (HM12273) | LIFELINES (HM12355) | LINDY, D (HM12426) | MASON, L C (HM13247) | MAUREEN PRIDDLE (HM13328) | MAYOR, DAVID F (HM13359) | MELLERICK, N D (HM13708) | MIDAS TOUCH (HM13808) | MID-HERTS ALEXANDER CENTRE (HM13827) | NATURAL HEALTH CLINIC (HM14589) | NATURAL-BALANCE CO UK (HM14672) | O'HARA, JOHN (HM15246) | OPEN MINDS (HM15343) | OSTEOPATHIC CLINIC (HM15459) | OVERINGTON, KEL (HM15512) | PEEDLE, DAVID R (HM15938) |
|---|---|---|---|---|---|---|---|---|---|---|---|---|---|---|---|---|---|---|---|---|---|---|---|---|---|---|---|---|---|---|---|---|---|---|
| Ingrowing Toenails | | | | | | | | | | | | | | | ● | | | | | | | | | | | | | | | | | | | |
| Influenza | ● | ● | | | | | | | | | | | | | | | | | | | | | | | | | | | ● | | | | | |
| Infertility | ● | ● | ● | | | | | | | | | | | | | | | | | | | | | ● | | | | | | | | | ● | |
| Indigestion | ● | ● | | | | | | ● | | | | | | | | ● | | | | | | ● | ● | ● | | ● | | | | ● | | | ● | |
| Incontinence | ● | ● | ● | | | | | | | | | | | | | | ● | | | | | | | | | | | | ● | | | | | |
| Impotence | ● | ● | | | | | | | | | | | | | | | | | | | | | | | | | | | ● | | | | | |
| Hypoglycaemia | | ● | | | | | | | | | | | | | | | | | | | | | | ● | | | | | ● | | | | | |
| Hyperactivity | | ● | ● | | | | | | | | | | | | | | | | | | | | | | | | | | ● | | | | | |
| Hip Complaints | | ● | | | ● | ● | ● | | ● | | ● | | | ● | | | ● | ● | | | ● | | | ● | ● | | ● | | | ● | | | | |
| High Blood Pressure | | ● | ● | | | | | | ● | | | | | | | ● | | | | ● | | ● | | ● | | | | | | ● | | | ● | |
| Hearing Problems | | ● | | | | | | | | | | | | | | | | | | | | | | ● | | | | | ● | | | | | |
| Headaches | ● | ● | ● | | ● | ● | ● | ● | ● | | | | | | | ● | | | | ● | ● | ● | ● | ● | ● | ● | ● | ● | ● | ● | | ● | ● | |
| Hay Fever | | ● | | | | | | ● | ● | | | | | | | | | | | | | | | ● | | | | | ● | | | | | |
| Hand Problems | | ● | | | | | | | | | | | | ● | | | ● | | | | | | | ● | | | | | | | | | | |
| Halitosis | | ● | | | | | | | | | | | | | | | | | | | | | | | | | | | | | | | | |
| Hair Problems | | ● | | | | | | | | | | | | | | | | | | | | | | | | | | | | | | | | |
| Gum Disease | ● | ● | | | | | | | | | | | | | | | | | | | | | | | | | | | ● | | | | | |
| Gout | ● | ● | | | | | | | | | | | | | | | | | | | | | | ● | | | | | | | | | | |
| Glaucoma | ● | | | | | | | | | | | | | | | | | | | | | | | ● | | | | | | | | | | |
| Glandular Fever | ● | ● | | | | | | ● | | | | | | | | | | | | | | | | | | | | | ● | | | | | |
| Gingivitis | ● | ● | | | | | | | | | | | | | | | | | | | | | | | | | | | ● | | | | | |
| Genital Herpes | | ● | | | | | | | | | | | | | | | | | | | | | | | | ● | | | | | | | | |
| Gastrointestinal Problems | ● | ● | | | | | | | | | | | | | | ● | | | | | | | | ● | | | | | ● | | | | | |
| Gallstones | ● | ● | | | | | | | | | | | | | | | | | | | | | | ● | | | | | | | | | | |
| Fungal Infections | | ● | | | | | | ● | | ● | | | | | | | | | | | | | | ● | | ● | | | ● | | | | | ● |
| Fractures | | ● | | | | | | | | | | | | | | | ● | | | | | | | ● | | | | | | | | | | |
| Foot Problems | ● | ● | | ● | | | | | | ● | | | ● | ● | | | ● | | | | | | | ● | | | | | | | | ● | | ● |
| Flatulence | ● | ● | | | | | | | | | | | | | | ● | | | | | | | | ● | | ● | | | ● | | | | | |
| Fibroids | ● | ● | | | | | | ● | | | | | | | | | | | | | | | | ● | | | | | | | | | | |
| Fever | ● | ● | | | | | | | | | | | | | | | | | | | | | | ● | | | | | | | | | | |
| Fertility Problems | ● | ● | ● | | | | | | | | | | | | | | | | | | | ● | | ● | | | | | ● | | | | | |
| Fears | ● | ● | ● | | | | | ● | ● | | | | | | | | | | ● | | | ● | | | | | | | ● | | | | | |
| Fatigue | ● | ● | ● | | | | | | ● | | | | | | | ● | | | | | | ● | ● | ● | | ● | | | ● | | | | | |
| Eye Disorders | ● | ● | | | | | | | | | | | | | | | | | | | | | | ● | | | | | | | | | | |
| Epilepsy | | ● | | | | | | ● | | | | | | | | | | | | | | | | | | | | | ● | | | | | |
| ENT Disorders | ● | ● | | | | | | ● | | | | | | | | | | | | | | | | ● | | | ● | | ● | | | | | |
| Eczema | ● | ● | ● | | | | | ● | ● | | | | | | | ● | | | | | | ● | | ● | | ● | | | ● | | | ● | | |
| Ear Disorders | ● | | | | | | | ● | | | | | | | | | | | | | | | | ● | | | | | ● | | | | | |
| Dyspraxia | | | | | | | | | | | | | ● | | | | | | | | | | | | | | | | ● | | | | | |
| Dyslexia | | | | | | | | | | | | | | | | | | | | | | ● | | | | | | | ● | | | | | |
| Dizziness | ● | ● | | ● | | | | | | | | | | | | | | | | | | | | ● | | | | | | | | | ● | |
| Diverticulitis | ● | | | | | | | | | | | | | | | ● | | | | | | | | ● | | | | | | | | | | |
| Digestive Problems | ● | ● | ● | | | | | ● | ● | | | | | | | ● | | | | | | ● | | ● | | ● | | | ● | ● | | ● | | |
| Diarrhoea | ● | ● | | | | | | ● | ● | | | | | | | ● | | | | | | ● | | ● | | | | | ● | | | | | |
| Diabetes | ● | | | | | | | | | | | | | | ● | | | | | | | | | | | | | | | | | | | |
| Depression | ● | ● | ● | | | | | ● | ● | | | ● | | | | ● | | | ● | ● | | ● | ● | ● | | | | ● | ● | | ● | ● | ● | |
| Deafness | ● | | | | | | | | | | | | | | | | | | | | | | | | | | | | | | | | | |
| Dandruff | | ● | | | | | | | | | | | | | | | | | | | | | | | | | | | | | | | | |

www.healthmyself.com

# D - I Conditions treated at Practices/Businesses

| Business by County with Reference no. | Dandruff | Deafness | Depression | Diabetes | Diarrhoea | Digestive Problems | Diverticulitis | Dizziness | Dyslexia | Dyspraxia | Ear Disorders | Eczema | ENT Disorders | Epilepsy | Eye Disorders | Fatigue | Fears | Fertility Problems | Fever | Fibroids | Flatulence | Foot Problems | Fractures | Fungal Infections |
|---|---|---|---|---|---|---|---|---|---|---|---|---|---|---|---|---|---|---|---|---|---|---|---|---|
| PERRY, KAREN (HM16049) | | | | ● | | | | | | | | | | | | | | | | | | ● | | ● |
| PERSONAL REFLECTIONS (HM16061) | | | ● | | ● | ● | | | | | | | | | | ● | ● | | | | | | | |
| PHYSIO & SPORTS INJURIES CLNC (HM16177) | | | | | | | | | | | | | | | | | | | | | | ● | ● | |
| PRIDDLE, PATRICK (HM16602) | | | ● | | | | | | | | | | | | | ● | ● | | | | | | | |
| PSYCHOTHERAPY (HM16726) | | | ● | | | | | | | | | ● | | | | ● | | ● | | | | | | |
| PURLYS (HM16769) | | | | | | | | | | | | | | | | | | | | | | | | |
| ROWLAND, JETHRO (HM17692) | | | ● | ● | ● | ● | ● | ● | ● | ● | ● | ● | ● | ● | ● | ● | ● | | ● | ● | ● | | | |
| S K REFLEXOLOGY (HM17811) | | | | | | ● | | | | | | ● | | | | | | | | | | | | |
| SHAW, CHRISTINE (HM18333) | | | | ● | ● | ● | ● | | | | ● | | ● | | | ● | | ● | | ● | ● | | | |
| SMITH, SUSAN (HM18813) | | | ● | | | ● | | | | | | | | | | ● | | | | | | | | |
| SOPWELL OSTEOPATHIC CLINIC (HM18894) | | | | | ● | ● | ● | | | | ● | | | | | | | | | | | | | |
| SOUTH, JO (HM18917) | ● | ● | ● | ● | ● | ● | ● | ● | ● | ● | ● | ● | ● | ● | ● | ● | ● | ● | ● | ● | ● | ● | ● | ● |
| SOUTHDOWN CHIROPODY PRACTICE (HM18929) | | | | | | | | | | | | | | | | | | | | | | ● | | ● |
| SPINOZA, DAVID (HM19019) | ● | | | | | | | | | | | ● | | | | | | | | | | | | |
| ST ALBANS CHIROPRACTIC CLINIC (HM19063) | | | | | | | | | | | | | | | | | | | | | | | | |
| STORT COUNS & PSYCHOTHERAPY (HM19351) | | | ● | | | | | | | | | | | | | | ● | | | | | | | |
| STORTFORD GRANGE PHYSIO CENTRE (HM19352) | | | | | | | | | | | | | | | | | | | | | | | ● | |
| SURVIVAL TRUST SURGERY (HM19526) | ● | ● | ● | ● | ● | ● | ● | ● | ● | ● | ● | ● | ● | ● | ● | ● | ● | ● | ● | ● | ● | ● | | ● |
| SWAN & SWAN (HM19572) | | | | ● | | | | | | | | | | | | | | | | | | ● | | ● |
| THOMPSON, MARK () | | | ● | ● | ● | ● | ● | | | | | | | | | ● | | ● | | | ● | ● | ● | |
| THOMPSON, MARK (HM19991) | | | ● | ● | ● | ● | ● | | | | | | | | | ● | | ● | | | ● | ● | ● | |
| WALKER, NEL (HM20791) | | | ● | | | | | | | | | | | | | | ● | | | | | | | |
| WALKER, RICHARD (HM20798) | | | ● | | | | | | | | ● | ● | | | | | ● | ● | | | | | | |
| WATSON, KATHRYN (HM21015) | ● | | ● | | ● | ● | ● | | | | ● | ● | ● | | | ● | | ● | | | ● | | | ● |
| WELWYN CHIROPRACTIC CLINIC (HM21192) | | | | | | | | | | | | | | | | | | | | | | | | |
| WHITE, GRAHAM C (HM21355) | ● | ● | ● | ● | ● | ● | ● | ● | | ● | ● | ● | ● | ● | ● | ● | ● | ● | ● | ● | ● | ● | ● | ● |
| WOOD STREET CHIROPRACTIC CLNC (HM21780) | | | | | | | | | | | | | | | | | | | | | | | | |
| WOOD STREET CLINIC (HM21781) | | | | | ● | ● | ● | | | | | ● | ● | | | ● | | | ● | | ● | | | ● |
| WORDSWORTH, LINDA (HM21890) | | ● | ● | ● | | | ● | ● | | | ● | | | | | ● | ● | ● | | | ● | | | |
| WRIGHT, DOREEN (HM21931) | ● | ● | ● | ● | ● | ● | ● | ● | ● | ● | ● | ● | ● | ● | ● | ● | ● | ● | ● | ● | ● | ● | ● | ● |
| WRIGHT, KAREN (HM21940) | | | | | | | | | | | | | | | | | | | | | | ● | | ● |
| WYE, DEBORAH (HM21969) | | | | | | | | | | | | | | | | | | | | | | ● | | ● |
| WYNDHAM CLINIC (HM21977) | | | ● | | ● | ● | ● | ● | | | ● | ● | ● | | | ● | | ● | | ● | ● | | | ● |

| Business by County with Reference no. | Gallstones | Gastrointestinal Problems | Genital Herpes | Gingivitis | Glandular Fever | Glaucoma | Gout | Gum Disease | Hair Problems | Halitosis | Hand Problems | Hay Fever | Headaches | Hearing Problems | High Blood Pressure | Hip Complaints | Hyperactivity | Hypoglycaemia | Impotence | Incontinence | Indigestion | Infertility | Influenza | Ingrowing Toenails |
|---|---|---|---|---|---|---|---|---|---|---|---|---|---|---|---|---|---|---|---|---|---|---|---|---|
| PERRY, KAREN (HM16049) | | | | | | | | | | | | | | | | | | | | | | | | |
| PERSONAL REFLECTIONS (HM16061) | | | | | | | | | | | ● | ● | ● | | ● | ● | ● | | | | ● | ● | | |
| PHYSIO & SPORTS INJURIES CLNC (HM16177) | | | | | | | | | | | | | | | | ● | | | | ● | | | | |
| PRIDDLE, PATRICK (HM16602) | | | | | | | | | | | | | | | | | | | | | | | | |
| PSYCHOTHERAPY (HM16726) | | | | | | | | | | | | | ● | | | | ● | | ● | | | ● | | |
| PURLYS (HM16769) | | | | ● | | | | ● | | | | | ● | | | | | | | | | | | |
| ROWLAND, JETHRO (HM17692) | ● | ● | ● | ● | ● | | ● | ● | ● | ● | ● | ● | ● | | ● | | ● | ● | ● | ● | ● | ● | ● | |
| S K REFLEXOLOGY (HM17811) | | | | | | | | | | | | | ● | | | | | | ● | | | | | |
| SHAW, CHRISTINE (HM18333) | | ● | | | ● | ● | | | | | | ● | ● | | ● | ● | | | | | ● | | | |
| SMITH, SUSAN (HM18813) | | | | | | | | | | | | ● | ● | | ● | | ● | | | | ● | | | |
| SOPWELL OSTEOPATHIC CLINIC (HM18894) | | | | | | | | | | | | ● | ● | ● | | ● | | | | | ● | | | |
| SOUTH, JO (HM18917) | ● | ● | ● | ● | ● | ● | ● | ● | ● | ● | ● | ● | ● | ● | ● | ● | ● | ● | ● | ● | ● | ● | ● | |
| SOUTHDOWN CHIROPODY PRACTICE (HM18929) | | | | | | | | | | | | | | | | | | | | | | | | |
| SPINOZA, DAVID (HM19019) | | | | | | | | | ● | | | | | | | | | | | | | | | |
| ST ALBANS CHIROPRACTIC CLINIC (HM19063) | | | | | | | | | | | | | ● | | ● | ● | | | | | | | | |
| STORT COUNS & PSYCHOTHERAPY (HM19351) | | | | | | | | | | | | | | | | | | | | | | | | |
| STORTFORD GRANGE PHYSIO CENTRE (HM19352) | | | | | | | | | | | | | | | | ● | | | | | | | | |
| SURVIVAL TRUST SURGERY (HM19526) | ● | ● | ● | ● | ● | ● | ● | ● | ● | ● | ● | ● | ● | ● | ● | ● | ● | ● | ● | ● | ● | ● | ● | |
| SWAN & SWAN (HM19572) | | | | | | | | | | | | | | | | | | | | | | | | ● |
| THOMPSON, MARK () | ● | ● | | | | | | ● | | | | | ● | | ● | ● | ● | ● | ● | ● | ● | ● | | |
| THOMPSON, MARK (HM19991) | ● | ● | | | | | | ● | | | | | ● | | ● | ● | ● | ● | ● | ● | ● | ● | | |
| WALKER, NEL (HM20791) | | | | | | | | | | | | | | | | | | | | | | | | |
| WALKER, RICHARD (HM20798) | | | | | | | | | | | | | ● | | ● | | | | ● | | | ● | | |
| WATSON, KATHRYN (HM21015) | | ● | | ● | ● | | ● | ● | | ● | | ● | ● | | ● | | ● | ● | ● | ● | ● | ● | ● | |
| WELWYN CHIROPRACTIC CLINIC (HM21192) | | | | | | | | | | | | | ● | | | ● | | | | | | | | |
| WHITE, GRAHAM C (HM21355) | ● | ● | ● | ● | ● | ● | ● | ● | ● | ● | ● | ● | ● | ● | ● | ● | ● | ● | ● | ● | ● | ● | ● | |
| WOOD STREET CHIROPRACTIC CLNC (HM21780) | | | | | | | | | | | | | ● | | | ● | | | | | | | | |
| WOOD STREET CLINIC (HM21781) | ● | ● | ● | ● | ● | | ● | ● | | ● | | ● | ● | | ● | | ● | ● | | ● | ● | | ● | |
| WORDSWORTH, LINDA (HM21890) | | | | | | | | | | | | | ● | | ● | | | ● | ● | | ● | ● | | |
| WRIGHT, DOREEN (HM21931) | ● | ● | | ● | ● | ● | ● | ● | ● | ● | ● | ● | ● | ● | ● | ● | | ● | ● | ● | ● | ● | ● | |
| WRIGHT, KAREN (HM21940) | | | | | | | | | | | | | | | | | | | | | | | | |
| WYE, DEBORAH (HM21969) | | | | | | | | | | | | | | | | | | | | | | | | |
| WYNDHAM CLINIC (HM21977) | | ● | | ● | ● | | ● | ● | | ● | | ● | ● | | ● | | ● | ● | | | ● | ● | | |

# D - I Conditions treated at Practices/Businesses

Business by County with Reference no.

| Business | Dandruff | Deafness | Depression | Diabetes | Diarrhoea | Digestive Problems | Diverticulitis | Dizziness | Dyslexia | Dyspraxia | Ear Disorders | Eczema | ENT Disorders | Epilepsy | Eye Disorders | Fatigue | Fears | Fertility Problems | Fever |
|---|---|---|---|---|---|---|---|---|---|---|---|---|---|---|---|---|---|---|---|
| **HUMBERSIDE** | | | | | | | | | | | | | | | | | | | |
| BATH, ANN (HM01899) | | | | | | | | | | | | ● | | | | | | | |
| BRIGG CHIROPRACTIC CLINIC (HM03028) | | | | | | | | | | | | | | | | | | | |
| BRIGG SKIN SURGERY (HM03030) | | | | | | | | | | | | ● | | | | | | | |
| MESSINGHAM CHIROPODIST SURGERY (HM13761) | | | | | | | | | | | | | | | | | | | |
| PRIOSE COLES (HM16635) | | | ● | | | ● | | | | | | ● | | | | ● | | | |
| SCUNTHORPE CHIROPRACTIC CLINIC (HM18157) | | | | | | | | | | | | | | | | | | | |
| **HUMBERSIDE (NORTH)** | | | | | | | | | | | | | | | | | | | |
| BEVERLEY CHIROPRACTIC CLINIC (HM02243) | | | | | | | | ● | | | ● | | | | | | | | |
| BRIDLINGTON CHIROPODY SURGERY (HM03018) | | | | | | | | | | | | | | | | | | | |
| DAMIAN P JOHNS (HM05704) | | | | | | | | | | | | | | | | | | | |
| GILBERDYKE SPORTS & INJURY (HM08054) | | | | | | | | | | | | | | | | | | | |
| NATURAL THERAPIES (HM14629) | | | ● | ● | ● | ● | ● | ● | | | ● | ● | ● | ● | | ● | ● | ● | |
| NATURAL THERAPY CENTRE (HM14653) | | | ● | | ● | ● | | | | | | | | | | ● | ● | ● | |
| SAMANTHA WHITE AROMATICA (HM17877) | | | ● | | | | | | | | | | | | | ● | | | |
| **HUMBERSIDE (SOUTH)** | | | | | | | | | | | | | | | | | | | |
| HARRISON-WILLIAMS (HM09113) | | | | | | | | | | | | | | | | | | | |
| HARRISON-WILLIAMS CHIROPODIST (HM09114) | | | | | | | | | | | | | | | | | | | |
| LOUISE HEALING CENTRE (HM12668) | | ● | ● | ● | | ● | ● | | | | | ● | | | | ● | ● | ● | |
| ROBINSON, KEITH (HM17488) | | | | | | | | | | | | | | | | | | | |
| SCARTHO OSTEOPATHIC PRACTICE (HM18007) | | | | | | | | | | | | | | | | | | | |
| WALL, R A (HM20819) | | | | | | | | | | | | | | | | | | | |
| WEBB, C M (HM21057) | | | | | | | | | | | | | | | | | | | |
| **ISLE OF WIGHT** | | | | | | | | | | | | | | | | | | | |
| BURROWS, MARY (HM03424) | | | | | | | | | | | | | | | | | | | |
| CARISBROOKE HEALTH CENTRE (HM03687) | | | | | | ● | | | | | | | | | | | ● | | |
| F VON - MEHREN (HM07034) | | | | | | | | | | | | | | | | | | | |
| FLANDERS, H (HM07391) | | | | | | | | | | | | | | | | | | | |
| FOOTSTEPS (HM07510) | | | | | | | | | | | | | | | | | | | |
| FOOTSTEPS THERAPY CENTRE (HM07513) | | | | | | | | | | | | | | | | | | | |
| GREENFIELD, BRIAN (HM08484) | | | ● | | | | | | | | ● | | | | | ● | | | |
| HOPE CLINIC (HM10134) | ● | ● | ● | ● | ● | ● | ● | ● | ● | ● | ● | ● | ● | ● | ● | ● | ● | ● | ● |
| HYPNOTHERAPY CONSULTANCY (HM10537) | | | ● | | | ● | ● | | | | | ● | | | | ● | ● | ● | |
| SHEN CLINIC (HM18391) | | | ● | | | | | | | | | | | | | ● | | | |

| Business | Fibroids | Flatulence | Foot Problems | Fractures | Fungal Infections | Gallstones | Gastrointestinal Problems | Genital Herpes | Gingivitis | Glandular Fever | Glaucoma | Gout | Gum Disease | Hair Problems | Halitosis | Hand Problems | Hay Fever | Headaches | Hearing Problems | High Blood Pressure | Hip Complaints | Hyperactivity | Hypoglycaemia | Impotence | Incontinence | Indigestion | Infertility | Influenza | Ingrowing Toenails |
|---|---|---|---|---|---|---|---|---|---|---|---|---|---|---|---|---|---|---|---|---|---|---|---|---|---|---|---|---|---|
| **HUMBERSIDE** | | | | | | | | | | | | | | | | | | | | | | | | | | | | | |
| BATH, ANN (HM01899) | | | | | | | | | | | | | | | | | | ● | | | | | | | | | | | |
| BRIGG CHIROPRACTIC CLINIC (HM03028) | | | | | | | | | | | | | | | | | | ● | | | ● | | | | | | | | |
| BRIGG SKIN SURGERY (HM03030) | | | | | | | | | | | | | | | | | | | | | | | | | | | | | |
| MESSINGHAM CHIROPODIST SURGERY (HM13761) | | | ● | | ● | | | | | | | | | | | | | | | | | | | | | | | | |
| PRIOSE COLES (HM16635) | | ● | ● | | | | ● | | | | | | | | | | ● | ● | | ● | | | ● | | | ● | | | |
| SCUNTHORPE CHIROPRACTIC CLINIC (HM18157) | | | ● | | | | | | | | | | | | | | | ● | | | ● | | | | | | | | |
| **HUMBERSIDE (NORTH)** | | | | | | | | | | | | | | | | | | | | | | | | | | | | | |
| BEVERLEY CHIROPRACTIC CLINIC (HM02243) | | | ● | | | | | | | | | | | | | ● | | ● | ● | | ● | | | | | | | | |
| BRIDLINGTON CHIROPODY SURGERY (HM03018) | | | ● | | ● | | | | | | | | | | ● | | | | | | | | | | | | | | |
| DAMIAN P JOHNS (HM05704) | | | ● | | ● | | | | | | | | | | | | | | | | | | | | | | | | ● |
| GILBERDYKE SPORTS & INJURY (HM08054) | | | | | | | | | | | | | | | | | | | | | ● | | | | | | | | |
| NATURAL THERAPIES (HM14629) | | ● | ● | | ● | | ● | | | | | ● | | | | ● | ● | ● | | ● | | | | ● | ● | ● | ● | | |
| NATURAL THERAPY CENTRE (HM14653) | | ● | | | | | | | | | | | | | | | ● | ● | | ● | | | | ● | ● | ● | ● | | |
| SAMANTHA WHITE AROMATICA (HM17877) | | | | | ● | | | | | | | | | | | | | ● | | ● | | | | | | | | ● | |
| **HUMBERSIDE (SOUTH)** | | | | | | | | | | | | | | | | | | | | | | | | | | | | | |
| HARRISON-WILLIAMS (HM09113) | | | ● | | ● | | | | | | | | | | | | | | | | | | | | | | | | |
| HARRISON-WILLIAMS CHIROPODIST (HM09114) | | | ● | | ● | | | | | | | | | | | | | | | | | | | | | | | | |
| LOUISE HEALING CENTRE (HM12668) | | | ● | | | | ● | | | | | | | | | | | ● | | ● | ● | ● | | | | | | | |
| ROBINSON, KEITH (HM17488) | | | ● | | ● | | | | | | | | | | | | | | | | | | | | | | | | |
| SCARTHO OSTEOPATHIC PRACTICE (HM18007) | | | ● | | | | | | | | | | | | | ● | | ● | | | ● | | | | | | | | |
| WALL, R A (HM20819) | | | ● | | ● | | | | | | | | | | | | | | | | | | | | | | | | |
| WEBB, C M (HM21057) | | | ● | | ● | | | | | | | | | | | | | | | | | | | | | | | | |
| **ISLE OF WIGHT** | | | | | | | | | | | | | | | | | | | | | | | | | | | | | |
| BURROWS, MARY (HM03424) | | | ● | | | | | | | | | | | | | | | | | | | | | | | | | | ● |
| CARISBROOKE HEALTH CENTRE (HM03687) | | | ● | | | | | | | | | | | | | | | ● | | | ● | | | | | | | | |
| F VON - MEHREN (HM07034) | | | ● | | | | | | | | | | | | | | | | | | | | | | | | | | |
| FLANDERS, H (HM07391) | | | ● | | | | | | | | | | | | | | | | | | | | | | | | | | ● |
| FOOTSTEPS (HM07510) | | | ● | | | | | | | | | | | | | | | | | | | | | | | | | | |
| FOOTSTEPS THERAPY CENTRE (HM07513) | | | ● | | | | | | | | | | | | | | | | | | | | | | | | | | |
| GREENFIELD, BRIAN (HM08484) | | | | | | | | | | | | | | | | | | ● | | ● | | | | | | | | | |
| HOPE CLINIC (HM10134) | ● | ● | ● | ● | ● | ● | ● | ● | ● | ● | ● | ● | ● | ● | ● | ● | ● | ● | ● | ● | ● | ● | ● | ● | ● | ● | ● | ● | |
| HYPNOTHERAPY CONSULTANCY (HM10537) | | | | | | | | | | | | | | | | | | ● | | ● | | | | ● | | ● | | | |
| SHEN CLINIC (HM18391) | ● | | ● | | | | | | | | | | | | | ● | | ● | | ● | | | | | | | | | |

www.healthmyself.com

# D - I Conditions treated at Practices/Businesses

| Business by County with Reference no. | Dandruff | Deafness | Depression | Diabetes | Diarrhoea | Digestive Problems | Diverticulitis | Dizziness | Dyslexia | Dyspraxia | Ear Disorders | Eczema | ENT Disorders | Epilepsy | Eye Disorders | Fatigue | Fears | Fertility Problems | Fever | Fibroids | Flatulence | Foot Problems | Fractures |
|---|---|---|---|---|---|---|---|---|---|---|---|---|---|---|---|---|---|---|---|---|---|---|---|
| TAYLOR, S A (HM19791) | | | | | | | | | | | | | | | | | | | | | | ● | |
| WRIGLEY, BARBARA (HM21956) | | | ● | | | | | | | | | | | | | | | | | | | | |
| **KENT** | | | | | | | | | | | | | | | | | | | | | | | |
| ABBOTT, LISA (HM00098) | | | ● | | | ● | | | | | | | | | | ● | | | | | | | |
| ABSOLUTE SOLUTIONS (HM00142) | | | ● | | | | | | | | | | | | | ● | ● | | | | | | |
| ALEXANDER TECHNIQUE (HM00553) | | | | | | | | | | | | | | | | | | | | | | | |
| ASHFORD CLINIC (HM01216) | | | ● | | | | | | | | | | | | | | | | | | | | |
| ASHFORD OSTEOPATHIC CLINIC (HM01217) | | | | | | | | ● | | | | | | | | | | | | | | | |
| AYLESFORD MEDICAL CENTRE (HM01426) | | | | | | | | | | | | | | | | | | | | | | | |
| AYLSHAM OSTEOPATHIC PRACTICE (HM01429) | | | | | | ● | | ● | | | | | | | | | | | | | | | |
| BECKENHAM & BROMLEY (HM02017) | | | | | | | | | | | | | | | | | | | | | | | |
| BECKENHAM CHINESE MED CTRE (HM02019) | | | | | | ● | | | | | | | | | | | | ● | | | | | |
| BENNETT, J P (HM02143) | | | ● | | | | | | | | | | | | | | ● | | | | | | |
| BERGMANN, MARIA (DR) (HM02190) | | | | | | ● | | | | | | | | | | | | | | | | | |
| BEXLEY OSTEOPATHIC CLINIC (HM02259) | | | | | | | | | | | | | | | | | | | | | | | |
| BEXLEYHEATH NATURAL HEALTH (HM02262) | ● | ● | ● | ● | ● | ● | ● | ● | ● | ● | ● | ● | ● | ● | ● | ● | ● | ● | ● | ● | ● | ● | ● |
| BISHOP, SARAH (HM02411) | | | | | | | | | | | | | | | | | | | | | | | |
| BLACKFEN HYPNOTHERAPY (HM02442) | | | ● | | | | | | | | | ● | | | | ● | ● | | | | | | |
| BLOSSOM AROMATHERAPY CENTRE (HM02521) | | | ● | | | ● | | | | | | | | | | | | | | | | | |
| BROMLEY CHIROPODY CENTRE (HM03142) | | | | | | | | | | | | | | | | | | | | | | ● | |
| BROMLEY CHIROPRACTIC CLINIC (HM03143) | | | | | | | | | | | | | | | | ● | | | | | | | |
| BROMLEY OSTEOPATHIC CLINIC (HM03145) | | | | | | | | | | | | | | | | | | | | | | | |
| CANTERBURY OSTEOPATHIC CLINIC (HM03641) | | | | ● | ● | ● | ● | ● | | ● | ● | ● | ● | ● | | ● | ● | | ● | | | ● | |
| CARDWELL, MARTIN (HM03673) | | ● | ● | ● | | ● | | ● | | | ● | ● | | ● | ● | ● | ● | ● | | ● | ● | ● | ● |
| CASTLE CLINIC (HM03830) | ● | ● | ● | ● | ● | ● | ● | ● | ● | ● | ● | ● | ● | ● | ● | ● | ● | ● | ● | ● | ● | ● | ● |
| CENTRE (HM03897) | ● | ● | ● | ● | ● | ● | ● | ● | ● | ● | ● | ● | ● | ● | ● | ● | ● | ● | ● | ● | ● | ● | ● |
| CHANGE OF LIFE (HM03984) | | | | ● | ● | | ● | | | | | ● | | | | ● | | | | | | | |
| CHINESE HERBAL MED & HLTH CARE (HM04200) | | | ● | | | | | | | | | | | | | | | ● | | | | | |
| CHINESE HERBAL MED ACU CTRE (HM04205) | | | | | | | | | | | | ● | | | | | | | | | | | |
| CHIROPRACTIC PLUS (HM04402) | ● | ● | ● | ● | ● | ● | ● | ● | ● | ● | ● | ● | ● | | ● | ● | ● | ● | ● | ● | ● | ● | ● |
| CHISLEHURST NATURAL HEALTH (HM04410) | ● | ● | ● | ● | ● | ● | ● | ● | ● | ● | ● | ● | ● | ● | ● | ● | ● | ● | ● | ● | ● | ● | ● |
| CHISTLEHURST NATURAL HLTH CTRE (HM04411) | ● | ● | ● | ● | ● | ● | ● | ● | ● | ● | ● | ● | ● | ● | ● | ● | ● | ● | ● | ● | ● | ● | ● |
| CHRISTINE CHINNERY COMP THER (HM04446) | | | ● | ● | ● | ● | ● | ● | | | | ● | | | | ● | ● | ● | ● | ● | ● | ● | ● |
| CORRIGAN, PETER (HM05195) | | | ● | | | | | | | | | | | | | | | | | | | | |

| Business by County with Reference no. | Fungal Infections | Gallstones | Gastrointestinal Problems | Genital Herpes | Gingivitis | Glandular Fever | Glaucoma | Gout | Gum Disease | Hair Problems | Halitosis | Hand Problems | Hay Fever | Headaches | Hearing Problems | High Blood Pressure | Hip Complaints | Hyperactivity | Hypoglycaemia | Impotence | Incontinence | Indigestion | Infertility | Influenza | Ingrowing Toenails |
|---|---|---|---|---|---|---|---|---|---|---|---|---|---|---|---|---|---|---|---|---|---|---|---|---|---|
| TAYLOR, S A (HM19791) | | | | | | | | | | | | | | | | | | | | | | | | | ● |
| WRIGLEY, BARBARA (HM21956) | | | | | | | | | | | | | | ● | | | | | | | | | | | |
| **KENT** | | | | | | | | | | | | | | | | | | | | | | | | | |
| ABBOTT, LISA (HM00098) | | | | | | | | | | | | | | ● | | ● | | | | | | | | | |
| ABSOLUTE SOLUTIONS (HM00142) | | | | | | | | | | | | | | ● | | ● | | | | | | | | | |
| ALEXANDER TECHNIQUE (HM00553) | | | | | | | | | | | | | | | | | ● | | | | | | | | |
| ASHFORD CLINIC (HM01216) | | | | | | | | | | | | | | ● | | | | | | | | | | | |
| ASHFORD OSTEOPATHIC CLINIC (HM01217) | | | | | | | | | | | | | | ● | | | | | | | | | | | |
| AYLESFORD MEDICAL CENTRE (HM01426) | | | | | | | | | | | | | | ● | | | | | | | | ● | | | |
| AYLSHAM OSTEOPATHIC PRACTICE (HM01429) | | | | | | | | | | | | | | | | | ● | | | | | | | | |
| BECKENHAM & BROMLEY (HM02017) | | | | | | | | | | | | | | ● | | | ● | | | | | | | | |
| BECKENHAM CHINESE MED CTRE (HM02019) | | | | | | | | | | | | | | | | | | | | | | | ● | | |
| BENNETT, J P (HM02143) | | | | | | | | | | | | | | | | | | | | ● | | | | | |
| BERGMANN, MARIA (DR) (HM02190) | | | | | | | | | | | | | | | | | | | | | | | | | |
| BEXLEY OSTEOPATHIC CLINIC (HM02259) | | | | | | | | | | | | | | ● | | | ● | | | | | | | | |
| BEXLEYHEATH NATURAL HEALTH (HM02262) | ● | ● | ● | ● | ● | ● | ● | ● | ● | ● | ● | ● | ● | ● | ● | ● | ● | ● | ● | ● | ● | ● | ● | ● | |
| BISHOP, SARAH (HM02411) | | | | | | | | | | | | | | ● | | | ● | | | | | | | | |
| BLACKFEN HYPNOTHERAPY (HM02442) | | | | | | | | | | | | | | ● | | ● | | | | ● | | ● | | | |
| BLOSSOM AROMATHERAPY CENTRE (HM02521) | | | | | | | | | | | | | | | | | | | | | | | | | |
| BROMLEY CHIROPODY CENTRE (HM03142) | ● | | | | | | | | | | | | | | | | | | | | | | | | |
| BROMLEY CHIROPRACTIC CLINIC (HM03143) | | | | | | | | | | | | | | ● | | | ● | | | | | | | | |
| BROMLEY OSTEOPATHIC CLINIC (HM03145) | | | | | | | | | | | | | | ● | | | ● | | | | | | | | |
| CANTERBURY OSTEOPATHIC CLINIC (HM03641) | ● | | ● | | ● | ● | | | ● | | | ● | ● | ● | | ● | ● | ● | ● | | | ● | | ● | |
| CARDWELL, MARTIN (HM03673) | | | | | | ● | | ● | | | | ● | ● | ● | ● | ● | ● | ● | ● | ● | ● | ● | ● | | |
| CASTLE CLINIC (HM03830) | ● | ● | ● | ● | ● | ● | ● | ● | ● | ● | ● | ● | ● | ● | ● | ● | ● | ● | ● | ● | ● | ● | ● | ● | |
| CENTRE (HM03897) | ● | ● | ● | ● | ● | ● | ● | ● | ● | ● | ● | ● | ● | ● | ● | ● | ● | ● | ● | ● | ● | ● | ● | ● | |
| CHANGE OF LIFE (HM03984) | | | | | | | | | | | | | | | | | | ● | | | | | | | |
| CHINESE HERBAL MED & HLTH CARE (HM04200) | | | | | | | | | | | | | | | | | | | | | | | | | |
| CHINESE HERBAL MED ACU CTRE (HM04205) | | | | | | | | | | | | | | | | | | | | | | | ● | | |
| CHIROPRACTIC PLUS (HM04402) | ● | | ● | ● | ● | ● | ● | ● | ● | ● | ● | ● | ● | ● | ● | ● | ● | ● | ● | ● | ● | ● | ● | ● | |
| CHISLEHURST NATURAL HEALTH (HM04410) | ● | ● | ● | ● | ● | ● | ● | ● | ● | ● | ● | ● | ● | ● | ● | ● | ● | ● | ● | ● | ● | ● | ● | ● | |
| CHISTLEHURST NATURAL HLTH CTRE (HM04411) | ● | ● | ● | ● | ● | ● | ● | ● | ● | ● | ● | ● | ● | ● | ● | ● | ● | ● | ● | ● | ● | ● | ● | ● | |
| CHRISTINE CHINNERY COMP THER (HM04446) | ● | ● | | | | ● | | | | | | ● | ● | ● | | ● | ● | | | ● | ● | ● | ● | ● | |
| CORRIGAN, PETER (HM05195) | | | | | | | | | | | | | | | | | | | | | | | | | |

# D - I Conditions treated at Practices/Businesses

Business by County with Reference no.

| Condition | COURT, SUSAN (HM05265) | COURT, SUSAN (HM05266) | COYSTEN & ASSOCIATES (HM05332) | CROIX, LINDA LA (HM05460) | DELTA MEDI CLINIC (HM05969) | DICKMAN, ANNIE (HM06080) | DILLON, MICHAEL (HM06100) | DIMENT, GORDON L (HM06105) | EDWARDS, R (HM06668) | EDWARDS, R, HERNE BAY (HM06670) | ELIZABETH ANNE (HM06736) | EUROPEAN AYUR-VEDA (HM06944) | EVEGATE CLINIC (HM06996) | EVOLUTION HEALTH (HM07014) | FALCONER, PATRICIA (HM07073) | FEET FIRST (HM07167) | FRANCIS-JONES, TREVOR (DR) (HM07679) | GIBSON, JAN (HM08040) | GILLINGHAM CLINIC OF COMP MED (HM08097) | GRAVESEND HOMOEOPATHY CLINIC (HM08404) | GUNN, JASON (HM08642) | HANNA, MARK (HM08931) | HAYES, JACQUELINE (HM09260) | HAZLEWOOD OSTEOPATHIC PRACTICE (HM09297) | HEAD TO TOE WELL-BEING (HM09300) | HEALING AND HERBS (HM09325) | HEATHSIDE CENTRE (HM09461) | HOFFMAN, BRIAN ASSOCIATES (HM09900) | HOLMES, S A (HM10045) | HOPE CHIROPRACTIC (HM10133) | KARMERS CLINIQUE (HM11328) | KENT HOUSE CHIROPRACTIC CLINIC (HM11520) | KENT HOUSE CHIROPRACTIC CLINIC (HM11519) | KENT HOUSE CHIROPRACTIC CLINIC (HM11518) |
|---|---|---|---|---|---|---|---|---|---|---|---|---|---|---|---|---|---|---|---|---|---|---|---|---|---|---|---|---|---|---|---|---|---|---|
| Dandruff | | | | | | ● | | | | | | | ● | | | | | | | ● | | | | | | | ● | | | | | | | |
| Deafness | | | | | | | | | | | | | ● | | | | | | | | | | | | | | ● | | | | | | | |
| Depression | | | | ● | | ● | ● | ● | | | ● | | ● | | | | | ● | | ● | | ● | ● | | | ● | ● | | ● | | | | | |
| Diabetes | | | | | | | | | | | | | ● | | | | | | ● | ● | | | ● | | | | ● | | | | | | | |
| Diarrhoea | | | ● | | | ● | | | | | | | ● | | | | | | ● | ● | | | | | | ● | ● | | ● | | | | | |
| Digestive Problems | ● | ● | ● | | | ● | | | | | | ● | ● | | | ● | | | ● | ● | | | ● | | ● | ● | ● | | ● | | ● | | | |
| Diverticulitis | | | ● | | | ● | | | | | ● | | ● | | | ● | | | ● | ● | | | | | | | ● | | | | ● | | | |
| Dizziness | | | ● | | | ● | | | | | | | ● | | | | | | ● | ● | | | ● | | | ● | ● | | | | ● | | | |
| Dyslexia | | | | | | | | | | | | | ● | | | | | | | ● | | | ● | | | | ● | | | | | | | |
| Dyspraxia | | | | | | | | | | | | | ● | | | | | | ● | ● | | | ● | | | | ● | | | | | | | |
| Ear Disorders | | | ● | | | | | | | | | | ● | | | | | | ● | ● | | | ● | | | ● | ● | | | | | | | |
| Eczema | | | | | | ● | | | | | | ● | ● | | | | | | ● | ● | | | | | | ● | ● | | | | ● | | | |
| ENT Disorders | | | | | | | | | | | | | ● | | | | | | ● | ● | | | ● | | | ● | ● | | | | | | | |
| Epilepsy | | | | | | | | | | | | | ● | | | | | | | ● | | | ● | | | | ● | | | | | | | |
| Eye Disorders | | | | | | | | | | | | | ● | | | | | | | ● | | | | | | | ● | | | | ● | | | |
| Fatigue | | | ● | | | ● | | | | | | ● | ● | | | | | ● | ● | ● | | ● | ● | | | ● | ● | ● | ● | | | | | |
| Fears | | | | | | ● | ● | | | | ● | ● | ● | | | | | ● | | ● | | ● | | | | ● | ● | | | | | | | |
| Fertility Problems | | | ● | | | ● | | | | | | | ● | | | | | ● | | ● | | | ● | | | | ● | | | | | | | |
| Fever | | | | | | | | | | | | | ● | | | | | | ● | ● | | | | | | | ● | | | | | | | |
| Fibroids | | | | | | | | | | | | | ● | | | | | | | ● | | | ● | | | ● | ● | | | | | | | |
| Flatulence | | | | | | ● | | | | | | | ● | | | | | | ● | ● | | | ● | | | | ● | | | | | | | |
| Foot Problems | ● | ● | ● | | | ● | | | | | | | ● | ● | | | | | ● | ● | | | ● | | | | ● | | | | | | | |
| Fractures | | | | | | | | | | | | | ● | | | | | | | ● | | | ● | | | | ● | | | | | | | |
| Fungal Infections | | | | | | ● | | | | | | | ● | | | | | | | ● | | | | | | | ● | | | | | | | |
| Gallstones | | | | | | | | | | | | | ● | | | | | | | ● | | | ● | | | ● | ● | | | | | | | |
| Gastrointestinal Problems | | | ● | | | ● | | | | | | | ● | | | | | | ● | ● | | | ● | | | | ● | | ● | | | | | |
| Genital Herpes | | | | | | | | | | | | | ● | | | | | | | ● | | | | | | | ● | | | | | | | |
| Gingivitis | | | | | | | | | | | | | ● | | | | | | | ● | | | | | | | ● | | | | | | | |
| Glandular Fever | | | | | | | | | | | | | ● | | | | | | ● | ● | | | ● | | | | ● | | | | ● | | | |
| Glaucoma | | | | | | | | | | | | | ● | | | | | | ● | ● | | | | | | | ● | | | | | | | |
| Gout | | | | | | | | | | | | | ● | | | | | | ● | ● | | | | | | | ● | ● | ● | | | | | |
| Gum Disease | | | | | | | | | | | | | ● | | | | | | | ● | | | | | | | ● | | | | | | | |
| Hair Problems | | | | | | | | | | | | | ● | | | | | | | ● | | | | | | | ● | | | | | | | |
| Halitosis | | | | | | | | | | | | | ● | | | | | | | ● | | | | | | | ● | | | | | | | |
| Hand Problems | ● | ● | ● | | | ● | | | | | | | ● | | | | | | | ● | | | ● | | | | ● | | | | | | | |
| Hay Fever | | | | | | ● | | | | | | | ● | | | ● | | ● | ● | ● | | | | | | | ● | | | | | | | |
| Headaches | ● | ● | ● | ● | | ● | ● | | ● | ● | | | ● | ● | ● | ● | ● | ● | ● | ● | ● | ● | ● | | | | ● | | ● | ● | ● | ● | ● | ● |
| Hearing Problems | | | | | | | | | | | | | ● | | | | | | | ● | | | | | | | ● | | | | ● | | | |
| High Blood Pressure | | | ● | | | ● | ● | | | | | ● | ● | | | ● | | | ● | ● | | ● | ● | | ● | ● | ● | | ● | | | | | |
| Hip Complaints | ● | ● | ● | | ● | | | | ● | ● | | | ● | | | | | | ● | ● | ● | | ● | ● | | | ● | | | ● | | ● | ● | ● |
| Hyperactivity | | | ● | | | ● | | | | | | | ● | | | | | | | ● | | ● | ● | | | | ● | | | | | | | |
| Hypoglycaemia | | | | | | | | | | | | | ● | | | | | | | ● | | | | | | | ● | | | | | | | |
| Impotence | | | | | | | ● | ● | | | ● | | ● | | | | | ● | | ● | | ● | | | | | ● | | | | | | | |
| Incontinence | | | | | | ● | | | | | | | ● | | | | | ● | ● | ● | | | ● | | | | ● | | ● | | | | | |
| Indigestion | | | ● | | | ● | | | | | | | ● | | | ● | | | ● | ● | | | ● | | | ● | ● | | ● | | | | | |
| Infertility | | | | | | ● | | | | | | | ● | | | | | ● | | ● | | | ● | | | | ● | | | | | | | |
| Influenza | | | | | | | | | | | | | ● | | | | | | ● | ● | | | | | | | ● | | | | | | | |
| Ingrowing Toenails | | | | | | | | | | | | | | | | | | | | | | | | | | | | | | | | | | |

# D - I Conditions treated at Practices/Businesses

Business by County with Reference no.

| Business by County with Reference no. | Dandruff | Deafness | Depression | Diabetes | Diarrhoea | Digestive Problems | Diverticulitis | Dizziness | Dyslexia | Dyspraxia | Ear Disorders | Eczema | ENT Disorders | Epilepsy | Eye Disorders | Fatigue |
|---|---|---|---|---|---|---|---|---|---|---|---|---|---|---|---|---|
| KENT HOUSE CHIROPRACTIC CLINIC (HM11517) | | | | | | | | | | | | | | | | |
| KSC (HM11812) | ● | ● | ● | ● | ● | ● | ● | ● | ● | ● | ● | ● | ● | ● | ● | ● |
| LAMB, G BRIAN (HM11888) | ● | | ● | | ● | ● | ● | ● | | | ● | ● | ● | | ● | ● |
| LAVINGOTN, A (HM12034) | | | ● | | | ● | | | | | | | | | | ● |
| LEBOR, JILL (HM12115) | | | ● | | | ● | | ● | | | ● | ● | ● | | | ● |
| LIVING WELL CLINIC (HM12488) | | | | | | | | | | | | | | | | |
| LOBB, BRIAN W (HM12528) | | | ● | | | | | | | | | | | | | |
| LUGG, G (HM12732) | | | ● | ● | | ● | | | | | | ● | | | | |
| MABBERLEY, KATHIE (HM12812) | | | ● | | | | | | | | | | | | | ● |
| MAIDSTONE ACUPUNCTURE CLINIC (HM12935) | ● | ● | ● | ● | ● | ● | ● | ● | ● | | ● | ● | ● | ● | ● | ● |
| MARY CANNON - CLINICAL NUTRI (HM13221) | ● | | ● | | ● | ● | ● | | | | | ● | ● | | | ● |
| MASON & ASSOCIATES (HM13232) | | | | | | | | ● | | | | | | | | |
| MASON & ASSOCIATES (HM13233) | | | | | | | | ● | | | | | | | | |
| MATHER, SUE (HM13281) | ● | ● | ● | ● | ● | ● | ● | ● | ● | ● | ● | ● | ● | ● | ● | ● |
| MCDOWELL, S (HM13467) | | | | | | | | | | | | | | | | |
| MEADOWS (HM13630) | | | | | | | | | | | | ● | | | | |
| MEOPHAM CLINIC (HM13732) | | | | | | | | | | | | | | | | |
| MUIRHEAD, MARGARET (HM14323) | ● | ● | ● | ● | ● | ● | ● | ● | | ● | ● | ● | ● | ● | ● | ● |
| MULVANEY, ALISTAIR (HM14353) | | | | | | | | | | | | | | | | |
| NATURAL HEALTH CENTRE (HM14562) | | | ● | | | | | ● | | ● | | ● | | | | ● |
| NATURAL HEALTH CENTRE (HM14568) | ● | ● | ● | ● | ● | ● | ● | ● | ● | ● | ● | ● | ● | ● | ● | ● |
| NATURAL THERAPIST (HM14635) | | ● | ● | ● | | ● | ● | | | | ● | | | ● | | ● |
| NATURAL THERAPY CENTRE (HM14643) | | | | | | | | | | | | | | | | |
| OPTIVAVA (HM15352) | | | | | | | | | | | | | | | | |
| OSTEOPATHIC CLINIC (HM15461) | | | | | | | | | | | | | | | | |
| OSTEOPATHIC PRACTICE (HM15466) | | | | | | | | | | | | | | | | |
| PASSCHIER, MAREANNE SASSEN (HM15779) | ● | ● | ● | ● | ● | ● | ● | ● | ● | ● | ● | ● | ● | ● | ● | ● |
| PATERSON, MARGARET (HM15814) | | | | ● | | ● | ● | | | | | ● | | | | ● |
| PEARTON, GILL (HM15919) | | | ● | ● | ● | | ● | ● | | | ● | ● | ● | ● | | |
| PELE, ANDRI (HM15950) | | | ● | | | | | ● | | ● | | ● | | | | ● |
| PRINCES AVENUE OSTEOPATHIC (HM16623) | | | | | ● | ● | | ● | | | | | | | | |
| RALPH & EVANS (HM16906) | ● | | | | ● | ● | ● | ● | | | | ● | ● | | | ● |
| READ, CHARLES REG OSTEOPATH (HM16994) | | | | | | | | | | | | | | | | |
| REVEREND CAROL HADDERSLEY (HM17204) | | ● | ● | ● | ● | ● | ● | ● | | | ● | ● | ● | ● | ● | ● |

| Business by County with Reference no. | Fears | Fertility Problems | Fever | Fibroids | Flatulence | Foot Problems | Fractures | Fungal Infections | Gallstones | Gastrointestinal Problems | Genital Herpes | Gingivitis | Glandular Fever | Glaucoma | Gout | Gum Disease |
|---|---|---|---|---|---|---|---|---|---|---|---|---|---|---|---|---|
| KENT HOUSE CHIROPRACTIC CLINIC (HM11517) | | | | | | | | | | | | | | | | |
| KSC (HM11812) | ● | ● | ● | ● | ● | ● | ● | ● | ● | ● | ● | ● | ● | ● | ● | ● |
| LAMB, G BRIAN (HM11888) | ● | | ● | | ● | ● | | ● | ● | ● | | ● | | | ● | ● |
| LAVINGOTN, A (HM12034) | | | | | | | | | | | | | | | | |
| LEBOR, JILL (HM12115) | ● | ● | | ● | ● | ● | ● | | ● | ● | | | ● | | ● | |
| LIVING WELL CLINIC (HM12488) | | | | | | | ● | | | | | | | | | |
| LOBB, BRIAN W (HM12528) | | | | | | | | | | | | | | | | |
| LUGG, G (HM12732) | | | | | | ● | | ● | | ● | | | | | ● | |
| MABBERLEY, KATHIE (HM12812) | | | | | | | | | | | | | | | | |
| MAIDSTONE ACUPUNCTURE CLINIC (HM12935) | ● | ● | ● | ● | ● | ● | | ● | ● | ● | | ● | | | ● | |
| MARY CANNON - CLINICAL NUTRI (HM13221) | | ● | ● | ● | ● | | ● | ● | ● | ● | ● | ● | ● | | ● | ● |
| MASON & ASSOCIATES (HM13232) | | | | | | | | | | | | | | | | |
| MASON & ASSOCIATES (HM13233) | | | | | | | | | | | | | | | | |
| MATHER, SUE (HM13281) | ● | ● | ● | ● | ● | ● | ● | ● | ● | ● | ● | ● | ● | ● | ● | ● |
| MCDOWELL, S (HM13467) | | | | | | | | | | | | | | | | |
| MEADOWS (HM13630) | | | | | | | | | | | | | | | | |
| MEOPHAM CLINIC (HM13732) | | | | | | | | | | | | | | | | |
| MUIRHEAD, MARGARET (HM14323) | ● | ● | ● | ● | ● | ● | | ● | ● | ● | ● | ● | ● | ● | ● | ● |
| MULVANEY, ALISTAIR (HM14353) | | | | | | ● | | ● | | | | | | | | |
| NATURAL HEALTH CENTRE (HM14562) | ● | | | | | | | | | | | | | | | |
| NATURAL HEALTH CENTRE (HM14568) | ● | ● | ● | ● | ● | ● | ● | ● | ● | ● | ● | ● | ● | ● | ● | ● |
| NATURAL THERAPIST (HM14635) | ● | | | ● | ● | | | | | | | | | | ● | |
| NATURAL THERAPY CENTRE (HM14643) | | | | | | | | | | ● | | | | | | |
| OPTIVAVA (HM15352) | | | | | | | | | | | | | | | | |
| OSTEOPATHIC CLINIC (HM15461) | | | | | | | | | | | | | | | | |
| OSTEOPATHIC PRACTICE (HM15466) | | | | | | ● | | | | | | | | | | |
| PASSCHIER, MAREANNE SASSEN (HM15779) | ● | ● | ● | ● | ● | ● | ● | ● | ● | ● | ● | ● | ● | ● | ● | ● |
| PATERSON, MARGARET (HM15814) | ● | ● | | | ● | | | | | ● | | | ● | | | |
| PEARTON, GILL (HM15919) | | ● | ● | ● | ● | ● | | | ● | ● | | | | | ● | |
| PELE, ANDRI (HM15950) | ● | | | | | | | | | | | | | | | |
| PRINCES AVENUE OSTEOPATHIC (HM16623) | | | | | | ● | | | | | | | | | | |
| RALPH & EVANS (HM16906) | ● | ● | | ● | | | | ● | ● | ● | | ● | ● | | ● | |
| READ, CHARLES REG OSTEOPATH (HM16994) | | | | | | ● | | | | | | | | | | |
| REVEREND CAROL HADDERSLEY (HM17204) | ● | ● | ● | ● | ● | ● | ● | ● | ● | ● | ● | ● | ● | ● | ● | ● |

| Business by County with Reference no. | Hair Problems | Halitosis | Hand Problems | Hay Fever | Headaches | Hearing Problems | High Blood Pressure | Hip Complaints | Hyperactivity | Hypoglycaemia | Impotence | Incontinence | Indigestion | Infertility | Influenza | Ingrowing Toenails |
|---|---|---|---|---|---|---|---|---|---|---|---|---|---|---|---|---|
| KENT HOUSE CHIROPRACTIC CLINIC (HM11517) | | | | | ● | | | ● | | | | | | | | |
| KSC (HM11812) | ● | ● | ● | ● | ● | ● | ● | ● | ● | ● | ● | ● | ● | ● | ● | |
| LAMB, G BRIAN (HM11888) | ● | ● | ● | ● | ● | | ● | ● | ● | | ● | ● | ● | | | |
| LAVINGOTN, A (HM12034) | | | | | ● | | | | | | | | | | | |
| LEBOR, JILL (HM12115) | | | ● | ● | ● | | ● | ● | ● | ● | ● | ● | ● | ● | | |
| LIVING WELL CLINIC (HM12488) | | | | | ● | | | ● | | | | | | | | |
| LOBB, BRIAN W (HM12528) | | | | | ● | | | | | | | | | | | |
| LUGG, G (HM12732) | | | | ● | ● | | ● | | | | | | ● | | | |
| MABBERLEY, KATHIE (HM12812) | | | | | ● | | | | ● | | | | | | | |
| MAIDSTONE ACUPUNCTURE CLINIC (HM12935) | ● | ● | ● | ● | ● | ● | ● | ● | ● | ● | ● | ● | ● | ● | ● | |
| MARY CANNON - CLINICAL NUTRI (HM13221) | | ● | | ● | ● | | ● | | ● | ● | | | ● | ● | ● | |
| MASON & ASSOCIATES (HM13232) | | | | | ● | | | ● | | | | | | | | |
| MASON & ASSOCIATES (HM13233) | | | | | ● | | | ● | | | | | | | | |
| MATHER, SUE (HM13281) | ● | ● | ● | ● | ● | ● | ● | ● | ● | ● | ● | ● | ● | ● | ● | |
| MCDOWELL, S (HM13467) | | | | | | | | ● | | | | | | | | |
| MEADOWS (HM13630) | | | | | ● | | | | | | | | | | | |
| MEOPHAM CLINIC (HM13732) | | | | | ● | | | ● | | | | | | | | |
| MUIRHEAD, MARGARET (HM14323) | ● | ● | ● | ● | ● | ● | ● | ● | ● | ● | ● | ● | ● | ● | ● | |
| MULVANEY, ALISTAIR (HM14353) | | | | | | | | | | | | | | | | ● |
| NATURAL HEALTH CENTRE (HM14562) | ● | | | | | | | | | | | | | | | |
| NATURAL HEALTH CENTRE (HM14568) | ● | ● | ● | ● | ● | ● | ● | ● | ● | ● | ● | ● | ● | ● | ● | |
| NATURAL THERAPIST (HM14635) | | | | | ● | ● | ● | ● | ● | | | | ● | ● | | |
| NATURAL THERAPY CENTRE (HM14643) | | | | | | | | | | | | | | | | |
| OPTIVAVA (HM15352) | | | | | ● | | | | | | | | | | | |
| OSTEOPATHIC CLINIC (HM15461) | | | | | ● | | | ● | | | | | | | | |
| OSTEOPATHIC PRACTICE (HM15466) | | | | | ● | | | | | | | | | | | |
| PASSCHIER, MAREANNE SASSEN (HM15779) | ● | ● | ● | ● | ● | ● | ● | ● | ● | ● | ● | ● | ● | ● | ● | |
| PATERSON, MARGARET (HM15814) | | | | | ● | | ● | | | | | | ● | ● | | |
| PEARTON, GILL (HM15919) | | | | ● | ● | ● | ● | ● | ● | | ● | | ● | ● | ● | |
| PELE, ANDRI (HM15950) | ● | | | | | | | | | | | | | | | |
| PRINCES AVENUE OSTEOPATHIC (HM16623) | | | | | ● | | | ● | | | | | ● | | | |
| RALPH & EVANS (HM16906) | | ● | | ● | ● | | ● | | ● | ● | | | ● | ● | ● | |
| READ, CHARLES REG OSTEOPATH (HM16994) | | | ● | | ● | | | ● | | | | | | | | |
| REVEREND CAROL HADDERSLEY (HM17204) | ● | ● | ● | ● | ● | ● | ● | ● | ● | ● | ● | ● | ● | ● | ● | |

# D - I Conditions treated at Practices/Businesses

Business by County with Reference no.

| Business | Dandruff | Deafness | Depression | Diabetes | Diarrhoea | Digestive Problems | Diverticulitis | Dizziness | Dyslexia | Dyspraxia | Ear Disorders | Eczema | ENT Disorders | Epilepsy | Eye Disorders | Fatigue | Fears | Fertility Problems | Fever | Fibroids | Flatulence | Foot Problems | Fractures | Fungal Infections |
|---|---|---|---|---|---|---|---|---|---|---|---|---|---|---|---|---|---|---|---|---|---|---|---|---|
| RIDLEY, VICKY (HM17324) | ● | | ● | ● | ● | ● | ● | ● | | | ● | ● | ● | ● | ● | ● | ● | ● | ● | ● | ● | ● | ● | ● |
| ROCHESTER PHYSIO & SPORTS (HM17520) | | | | | | | | | | | | | | | | | | | | | | | ● | |
| ROMNEY MARSH OSTEOPATHS (HM17574) | | ● | ● | | ● | ● | ● | ● | | | ● | ● | ● | ● | | ● | | | | | ● | ● | | |
| ROSE, NAOMI (HM17612) | | | ● | | | ● | | ● | | ● | ● | | | | | ● | | ● | | | | ● | | ● |
| ROUND ROOM (HM17663) | | | ● | | | ● | | | | | | ● | | | | ● | | | | | | | | |
| SACKS, PATRICA (HM17828) | | | | | | | | | | | | | | | | | | | | | | ● | | ● |
| SANCTUM HOLISTIC THERAPY CTRE (HM17896) | | | ● | | | | | | | | | | | | | | | | | | | | | |
| SANDOWN CLINIC FOR COMP MED (HM17926) | ● | ● | ● | ● | ● | ● | ● | ● | ● | ● | ● | ● | ● | ● | ● | ● | ● | ● | ● | ● | ● | ● | ● | ● |
| SHEARER, GAYLE (HM18357) | | | | | | | | ● | | | | | | | | | | | | | | | | |
| SHIATSU (HM18451) | | | ● | | | ● | | | | | | | | | | ● | ● | | | | | | | |
| SOUTH LONDON HYPNOTHERAPY CTRE (HM18910) | | | ● | | | ● | | | | | | ● | | ● | | ● | ● | | | | ● | | | |
| SOUTHCOTE CHIROPRACTIC CLINIC (HM18927) | | | | | | | | | | ● | | | | | | | | | | | | ● | | |
| STARFIELDS HOLISTIC HLTH CTRE (HM19145) | ● | ● | ● | ● | ● | ● | ● | ● | ● | ● | ● | ● | ● | ● | ● | ● | ● | ● | ● | ● | ● | ● | ● | ● |
| STONE, CHARLES (HM19334) | | | ● | | | | | | | | | | | | | | ● | | | | | | | |
| STURGE, DEBBIE (HM19445) | | | | | | ● | | | | | | ● | | | | ● | | ● | | | ● | | | |
| SWAN, VIVA (HM19575) | ● | ● | ● | ● | ● | ● | ● | ● | ● | ● | ● | ● | ● | ● | ● | ● | ● | ● | ● | ● | ● | ● | ● | ● |
| SYCAMORE, TONI (HM19606) | | | | | | | | | | | | ● | | | | | | | | | | | | |
| TONBRIDGE CLINIC (HM20151) | | | ● | | | | | | | | | ● | | | | ● | | | | | | ● | ● | |
| TOWN, BERNICE (HM20199) | | | | | | | | | | | | | | | | | | | | | | ● | | ● |
| TURNER, ANDREA (HM20417) | | | | | | | | | | | | | ● | | | | | ● | | | | | | |
| TURNER, PENNY (HM20434) | | | ● | | | | | | | | | | | | | | | | | | | | | |
| VARNEY, MONICA (HM20591) | | | ● | | | | ● | | | | | | | | | ● | | | | | ● | ● | | |
| VILLAGE PHYSIOTHERAPY PRACTICE (HM20667) | | | | | | | | | | | | | | | | | | | | | | | | |
| VINCENT, EUNICE (HM20671) | | | | | | | | | | | | | | | | | | | | | | | | |
| VINES REIKI HEALING CENTRE (HM20680) | ● | ● | ● | ● | ● | ● | ● | ● | ● | ● | ● | ● | ● | ● | ● | ● | ● | ● | ● | ● | ● | ● | ● | ● |
| WATLING STREET THERAPY CTRE (HM21001) | ● | | ● | | | ● | | ● | | | ● | ● | | | | ● | | | | | ● | ● | | ● |
| WEBB, JENNIFER (HM21067) | | | | | | ● | | | | | | | | | | ● | | | | | | | | |
| WELLS PHYSIO & SPORTS CLINIC (HM21168) | | | | | | | | | | | | | | | | | | | | | | | | |
| WOLFE, ROBERT (HM21762) | | | | | | | | | | | | | | | | | | | | | | ● | | ● |
| **LANCASHIRE** | | | | | | | | | | | | | | | | | | | | | | | | |
| ABERNETHY, HILARY (HM00123) | | | ● | | ● | ● | | | | | | | | | | ● | ● | | | | | | | ● |
| ALPHAWAVE (HM00685) | | | ● | | | | | | | | | | | | | | | | | | | | | |
| ALTERNATIVE MEDICINE (HM00715) | ● | | ● | | ● | ● | ● | ● | | | | ● | ● | | | ● | ● | ● | | | | ● | | ● |
| ALTERNATIVE MEDICINE PRACTICE (HM00721) | | | ● | | ● | ● | ● | | | | | ● | ● | | | ● | ● | ● | | | ● | | | ● |

| Business | Gallstones | Gastrointestinal Problems | Genital Herpes | Gingivitis | Glandular Fever | Glaucoma | Gout | Gum Disease | Hair Problems | Halitosis | Hand Problems | Hay Fever | Headaches | Hearing Problems | High Blood Pressure | Hip Complaints | Hyperactivity | Hypoglycaemia | Impotence | Incontinence | Indigestion | Infertility | Influenza | Ingrowing Toenails |
|---|---|---|---|---|---|---|---|---|---|---|---|---|---|---|---|---|---|---|---|---|---|---|---|---|
| RIDLEY, VICKY (HM17324) | ● | ● | ● | ● | ● | | ● | ● | ● | ● | | ● | ● | ● | ● | ● | ● | ● | ● | ● | ● | ● | ● | |
| ROCHESTER PHYSIO & SPORTS (HM17520) | | | | | | | | | | | | | | | | ● | | | | | | | | |
| ROMNEY MARSH OSTEOPATHS (HM17574) | | ● | | | | | | | | | ● | ● | ● | ● | | ● | ● | | | | ● | | ● | |
| ROSE, NAOMI (HM17612) | | ● | | | | | | | | | | | ● | ● | ● | ● | ● | | | | | ● | | |
| ROUND ROOM (HM17663) | | | | | | | | | | | | ● | ● | | ● | | ● | | | | ● | | | |
| SACKS, PATRICA (HM17828) | | | | | | | | | | | | | | | | | | | | | | | | |
| SANCTUM HOLISTIC THERAPY CTRE (HM17896) | | | | | | | | | | | | | ● | | | | | | | | | | | |
| SANDOWN CLINIC FOR COMP MED (HM17926) | ● | ● | ● | ● | ● | ● | ● | ● | ● | ● | ● | ● | ● | ● | ● | ● | ● | ● | ● | ● | ● | ● | ● | |
| SHEARER, GAYLE (HM18357) | | | | | | | | | | | | | | | | ● | | | | | | | | |
| SHIATSU (HM18451) | | | | | | | | | | | | | ● | | | | | | | | | | | |
| SOUTH LONDON HYPNOTHERAPY CTRE (HM18910) | | | | | | | | | ● | | | ● | ● | | ● | | ● | | | ● | | ● | | |
| SOUTHCOTE CHIROPRACTIC CLINIC (HM18927) | | | | | | | | | | | ● | | ● | | | ● | | | | | | | | |
| STARFIELDS HOLISTIC HLTH CTRE (HM19145) | ● | ● | ● | ● | ● | ● | ● | ● | ● | ● | ● | ● | ● | ● | ● | ● | ● | ● | ● | ● | ● | ● | ● | ● |
| STONE, CHARLES (HM19334) | | | | | | | | | | | | | | | | | | | | | | | | |
| STURGE, DEBBIE (HM19445) | | ● | | | | | | | | | | | | | | | | ● | | | ● | ● | | |
| SWAN, VIVA (HM19575) | ● | ● | ● | ● | ● | ● | ● | ● | ● | ● | ● | ● | ● | ● | ● | ● | ● | ● | ● | ● | ● | ● | ● | |
| SYCAMORE, TONI (HM19606) | | | | | | | | | | | | | | | | | | | | | ● | | | |
| TONBRIDGE CLINIC (HM20151) | | | | | | | | | | | | | | | | ● | | | | | | | | |
| TOWN, BERNICE (HM20199) | | | | | | | | | | | | | | | | | | | | | | | | |
| TURNER, ANDREA (HM20417) | | | | | | | | | | | | | ● | | | | | | | | | ● | | |
| TURNER, PENNY (HM20434) | | | | | | | | | | | | | | | | | | | | | | | | |
| VARNEY, MONICA (HM20591) | ● | | | | | | | | | | | | ● | | ● | ● | | | | | | | | |
| VILLAGE PHYSIOTHERAPY PRACTICE (HM20667) | | | | | | | | | | | | | | | | ● | | | | | | | | |
| VINCENT, EUNICE (HM20671) | | | | | | | | | | | | | ● | | | | | | | | | | | |
| VINES REIKI HEALING CENTRE (HM20680) | ● | ● | ● | ● | ● | ● | ● | ● | ● | ● | ● | ● | ● | ● | ● | ● | ● | ● | ● | ● | ● | ● | ● | |
| WATLING STREET THERAPY CTRE (HM21001) | | ● | | ● | | | | | | | | ● | ● | | ● | | ● | ● | | | ● | | ● | |
| WEBB, JENNIFER (HM21067) | | | | | | | | | | | | | | | ● | | | | | | | | | |
| WELLS PHYSIO & SPORTS CLINIC (HM21168) | | | | | | | | | | | | | | | | ● | | | | | | | | |
| WOLFE, ROBERT (HM21762) | | | | | | | | | | | | | | | | | | | | | | | | |
| **LANCASHIRE** | | | | | | | | | | | | | | | | | | | | | | | | |
| ABERNETHY, HILARY (HM00123) | | | | | | | | | | | | | | | | | | | | | | | | |
| ALPHAWAVE (HM00685) | | | | | | | | | | | | | | | | | | | | | | | | |
| ALTERNATIVE MEDICINE (HM00715) | ● | ● | | | ● | | ● | | | ● | | ● | ● | | ● | ● | ● | ● | ● | ● | ● | ● | ● | |
| ALTERNATIVE MEDICINE PRACTICE (HM00721) | ● | ● | | | ● | | ● | | | ● | | ● | ● | | ● | ● | ● | ● | ● | | ● | ● | | |

# D - I Conditions treated at Practices/Businesses

| Business by County with Reference no. | Dandruff | Deafness | Depression | Diabetes | Diarrhoea | Digestive Problems | Diverticulitis | Dizziness | Dyslexia | Dyspraxia | Ear Disorders | Eczema | ENT Disorders | Epilepsy | Eye Disorders | Fatigue | Fears | Fertility Problems | Fever | Fibroids | Flatulence | Foot Problems | Fractures | Fungal Infections |
|---|---|---|---|---|---|---|---|---|---|---|---|---|---|---|---|---|---|---|---|---|---|---|---|---|
| BARRETT & LIPTROTT (HM01783) | | | | | | | | | | | | | | | | | | | | | | ● | | ● |
| BEARLEY, CAROL (HM01969) | | | | | | ● | | | | | | | | | | ● | | | | | | | | |
| BEESTON, J (HM02061) | | | | | | | | | | | | | | | | | | | | | | ● | | |
| BENTLEY AND ASSOCIATES (HM02172) | | | ● | ● | | | | | | | | | | | | | ● | | | | | ● | ● | ● |
| BFMP (HM02265) | ● | | ● | | | ● | ● | | | | | ● | | | | ● | | | | | ● | ● | | |
| BOLTON CHIROPRATIC CLINIC (HM02656) | | | | | | | | | | | | | | | | | | | | | | | ● | |
| BOLTON CLINIC OF ACUPUNCTURE (HM02657) | | | ● | | ● | | | | | | | | | ● | | | | | | | | | | |
| BOLTON PHYSIOTHERAPY CLINIC (HM02658) | | | | | | | | | | | | | | | | | | | | | | | ● | |
| BOLTON THERAPY CENTRE (HM02659) | | | ● | | | ● | ● | ● | | | | ● | | | | ● | | | | | | ● | ● | |
| BOLTON, VANESSA (HM02664) | | | ● | ● | | ● | ● | | | | ● | ● | ● | | ● | ● | ● | ● | | ● | ● | ● | | |
| BRIDGWATER, K A (HM03016) | ● | ● | ● | ● | ● | ● | ● | ● | ● | ● | ● | ● | ● | ● | ● | ● | ● | ● | ● | ● | ● | ● | ● | ● |
| BROOKES, MICHAEL (HM03163) | ● | | ● | | ● | ● | ● | | | | | ● | | | | ● | | | | | ● | | | ● |
| CHARTERED PHYSIO & SPORTS (HM04041) | | | | | | | | | | | | | | | | | | | | | | | | |
| CLOUGHS - CHRTRD PHYSIO CLINIC (HM04735) | | | | | | | | | | | | | | | | | | | | | | | ● | |
| COLES, RONNIE (HM04836) | | | | | | | | | | | | | | | | | | | | | | ● | | ● |
| COMPLEMENTARY HEALTH SERVICES (HM04929) | | | | | | | | | | | | | | | | | | | | | | | | |
| COTTAM, O N (HM05224) | | | | | | | | | | | | | | | | | | | | | | ● | | ● |
| CRYSTAL & REIKI (HM05524) | | | ● | | | | | | | | | | | | | ● | | | | | | | | |
| DAVIES, JOHNATHON (HM05819) | | | | | | | | | | | | | | | | | | | | | | ● | | ● |
| DOUGLAS, CAROLINE (HM06213) | | | | ● | | | | | | | | | | | | | | | | | | ● | | |
| DUCKWORTH, JEAN (HM06347) | | | ● | ● | ● | ● | ● | ● | | | ● | ● | ● | | ● | ● | ● | ● | ● | ● | | ● | ● | ● |
| GEE, D (HM07957) | | | | | | | | | | | | | | | | | | | | | | ● | | ● |
| GREENHALGH, A J T (HM08489) | | | | | | | | | | | | | | | | | | | | | | ● | | ● |
| GROGAN, DIANA E (HM08592) | | | | | ● | ● | ● | ● | | | | ● | | | | ● | | ● | | | | ● | | |
| HAMPSOM, JAMES (HM08878) | | | ● | | | ● | | | | | | | | | | ● | | | | | | | | |
| HARDMAN, ALAN (HM08974) | | | | | | | | | | | | | | | | | | | | | | ● | | ● |
| HARMONIOUS HEALTHCARE (HM09015) | | ● | ● | | ● | ● | ● | ● | | | ● | ● | ● | | | ● | | ● | | | ● | ● | | ● |
| HAYDOCK, CLAIRE (HM09254) | | | | | | | | | | | | | | | | | | | | | | ● | | ● |
| HEAVENS SCENT AROMATHERAPY (HM09478) | | | | | | ● | | | | | | ● | | | | ● | | | | | | | | ● |
| HEYWORTH, S (HM09716) | | | | | | | | | | | | | | | | | | | | | | ● | | ● |
| HOLDEN, JOHN H (HM09932) | | | | | | | | | | | | | | | | | | | | | | ● | | ● |
| JOHN HOLDEN ASSOCIATES (HM11051) | | | | | | | | | | | | | | | | | | | | | | ● | | ● |
| KELLY CHIROPODY (HM11424) | | | ● | | | ● | | | | | | | | | | | | | | | | ● | | ● |
| KENDEL HOUSE CLINIC (HM11479) | | | ● | | | | | | | | | | | | | ● | ● | | | | | ● | | |

| Business by County with Reference no. | Gallstones | Gastrointestinal Problems | Genital Herpes | Gingivitis | Glandular Fever | Glaucoma | Gout | Gum Disease | Hair Problems | Halitosis | Hand Problems | Hay Fever | Headaches | Hearing Problems | High Blood Pressure | Hip Complaints | Hyperactivity | Hypoglycaemia | Impotence | Incontinence | Indigestion | Infertility | Influenza | Ingrowing Toenails |
|---|---|---|---|---|---|---|---|---|---|---|---|---|---|---|---|---|---|---|---|---|---|---|---|---|
| BARRETT & LIPTROTT (HM01783) | | | | | | | | | | | | | | | | | | | | | | | | |
| BEARLEY, CAROL (HM01969) | | | | | | | | | | | | | ● | | | | | | | | | | | |
| BEESTON, J (HM02061) | | | | | | | ● | | | | | | ● | | | ● | | | | | | | | |
| BENTLEY AND ASSOCIATES (HM02172) | | | | | | | ● | | | | ● | | ● | | | ● | | | | | | | | |
| BFMP (HM02265) | | ● | | | ● | | ● | | ● | | | ● | | | | | ● | ● | | ● | ● | ● | ● | |
| BOLTON CHIROPRATIC CLINIC (HM02656) | | | | | | | | | | | | | ● | | | ● | | | | | | | | |
| BOLTON CLINIC OF ACUPUNCTURE (HM02657) | | | | | | | | | | | | ● | ● | | | | | | | | | | | |
| BOLTON PHYSIOTHERAPY CLINIC (HM02658) | | | | | | | | | | | | | | | | | | | | | | | | |
| BOLTON THERAPY CENTRE (HM02659) | | | | | | | | | | | ● | ● | ● | | ● | ● | | | | | ● | | | |
| BOLTON, VANESSA (HM02664) | | ● | | | | | ● | ● | | ● | | | ● | ● | ● | ● | | ● | | | ● | | | |
| BRIDGWATER, K A (HM03016) | ● | ● | ● | ● | ● | ● | ● | ● | ● | ● | ● | ● | ● | ● | ● | ● | ● | ● | ● | ● | ● | ● | ● | |
| BROOKES, MICHAEL (HM03163) | | ● | | | | | | | | | | ● | ● | | | | ● | ● | | | ● | | | |
| CHARTERED PHYSIO & SPORTS (HM04041) | | | | | | | | | | | | | | | | ● | | | | | | | | |
| CLOUGHS - CHRTRD PHYSIO CLINIC (HM04735) | | | | | | | | | | | | | | | | ● | | | | | | | | |
| COLES, RONNIE (HM04836) | | | | | | | | | | | | | | | | | | | | | | | | |
| COMPLEMENTARY HEALTH SERVICES (HM04929) | | | | | | | | | | | ● | | ● | | | ● | | | | | | | | |
| COTTAM, O N (HM05224) | | | | | | | | | | | | | | | | | | | | | | | | |
| CRYSTAL & REIKI (HM05524) | | | | | | | | | | | | | | | | | | | | | | | | |
| DAVIES, JOHNATHON (HM05819) | | | | | | | | | | | | | | | | | | | | | | | | |
| DOUGLAS, CAROLINE (HM06213) | | | | | | | | | | | | | | | | | | | | | | | | |
| DUCKWORTH, JEAN (HM06347) | ● | ● | ● | ● | ● | ● | ● | ● | ● | ● | ● | ● | ● | ● | ● | ● | ● | | ● | ● | ● | ● | ● | |
| GEE, D (HM07957) | | | | | | | | | | | | | | | | | | | | | | | | ● |
| GREENHALGH, A J T (HM08489) | | | | | | | | | | | | | | | | | | | | | | | | |
| GROGAN, DIANA E (HM08592) | | ● | | | | | | | | | ● | | ● | | ● | | | | | | ● | ● | | |
| HAMPSOM, JAMES (HM08878) | | | | | | | | | | | | ● | ● | | ● | | | | | | | | | |
| HARDMAN, ALAN (HM08974) | | | | | | | | | | | | | | | | | | | | | | | | |
| HARMONIOUS HEALTHCARE (HM09015) | | ● | | | ● | | | | ● | | ● | ● | ● | ● | | ● | ● | | | ● | ● | ● | ● | |
| HAYDOCK, CLAIRE (HM09254) | | | | | | | | | | | | | | | | | | | | | | | | |
| HEAVENS SCENT AROMATHERAPY (HM09478) | | | | | | | | | | | ● | ● | ● | | ● | | | | | | | | | |
| HEYWORTH, S (HM09716) | | | | | | | | | | | | | | | | | | | | | | | | |
| HOLDEN, JOHN H (HM09932) | | | | | | | | | | | | | | | | | | | | | | | | |
| JOHN HOLDEN ASSOCIATES (HM11051) | | | | | | | | | | | | | | | | | | | | | | | | |
| KELLY CHIROPODY (HM11424) | | | | | | | | | | | | | ● | | | | | | | | | | | |
| KENDEL HOUSE CLINIC (HM11479) | | | | | | | | | | | | ● | ● | ● | | ● | ● | | | | ● | | | |

# D - I Conditions treated at Practices/Businesses

| Business by County with Reference no. | Dandruff | Deafness | Depression | Diabetes | Diarrhoea | Digestive Problems | Diverticulitis | Dizziness | Dyslexia | Dyspraxia | Ear Disorders | Eczema | ENT Disorders | Epilepsy | Eye Disorders | Fatigue | Fears | Fertility Problems | Fever | Fibroids | Flatulence | Foot Problems | Fractures | Fungal Infections | Gallstones | Gastrointestinal Problems | Genital Herpes | Gingivitis | Glandular Fever | Glaucoma | Gout | Gum Disease | Hair Problems | Halitosis | Hand Problems | Hay Fever | Headaches | Hearing Problems | High Blood Pressure | Hip Complaints | Hyperactivity | Hypoglycaemia | Impotence | Incontinence | Indigestion | Infertility | Influenza | Ingrowing Toenails |
|---|---|---|---|---|---|---|---|---|---|---|---|---|---|---|---|---|---|---|---|---|---|---|---|---|---|---|---|---|---|---|---|---|---|---|---|---|---|---|---|---|---|---|---|---|---|---|---|---|
| LAYNE, SUSAN G (HM12077) | |●|●| | | | |●| |●|●|●| | | |●|●|●| | |●| | | | | | | | | | |●|●| |●| |●|●| |●|●|●|●|●| |●|●| | |
| LEYLAND PHYSIOTHERAPY CENTRE (HM12319) | | | | | | | | | | | | | | | | | | | | | | | | | | | | | | | | | | | | | | |●| | | | | | | | |
| MALKIN, DK, MANIP THERAPY (HM12975) | | | | | |●| | | | | | | | | | | | | | | | | | | | | | | | | | | | | | |●| | | | | | | |●| | | |
| MOBILE CHIROPODIST (HM14027) | | | | | | | | | | | | | | | | | | | | | |●| |●| | | | | | | | | | | | | | | | | | | | | | | | |
| NATURAL HEALTH CENTRE (HM14566) | | | | | | | | | | | |●| | | |●| | | | |●|●| |●| | | | |●| | |●|●| | |●|●| |●| | | | | |●| |●| |
| NELSON, S (HM14782) | |●|●|●|●|●|●|●| | |●|●|●| |●|●|●|●| |●|●| | | | |●| |●|●|●|●|●| |●| |●|●| |●|●| | | | |●|●| | |
| ONE STOP HEALTH & BEAUTY (HM15323) |●|●|●|●|●|●|●|●|●|●|●|●|●|●|●|●|●|●|●|●|●|●|●|●|●|●|●|●|●|●|●|●|●|●|●|●|●|●|●|●|●|●|●|●|●|●|●|●|
| PEPPER, JOHN (HM16009) | | |●| | |●| | | | | |●| | | |●|●| | | |●| | | | |●| | | | | | | | | | |●| |●| |●| | | |●| | | |
| PHYSIO AND SPORTS INJURIES (HM16195) | | | | | | | | | | | | | | | | | | | | | | | | | | | | | | | | | | |●| |●| | |●| | | | | | | | |
| PURCELL, AMANDA (HM16762) | | | | | | | | | | | | | | | | | | | | | | | | | | | | | | | | | | | | | | |●| | | | | | | | |
| RAMSBOTTOM PHYSIO CLINIC (HM16919) | | | | | | | | | | | | | | | | | | | | | | | | | | | | | | | | | | | | | | |●| | | | | | | | |
| RATCLIFFE, MARK (HM16949) | | | | | | | | | | | | | | | | | | | | | |●| | | | | | | | | | | | | | |●| | |●| | | | |●| | | |
| REMEDIAL MASSAGE/SPORTS (HM17175) | | | | | | | | | | | | | | | | | | | | | | |●| | | | | | | | | | | | | | | | | | | | | | | | | |
| SMITH, CHRISTOPHER (DR) (HM18728) | | | | | | | | | | | | | | | | | | | | | | | | | | | | | | | | | | | | |●| | |●| | | | | | | | |
| SPIRITUAL THERAPIST (HM19029) | | |●| | | | | | | | | | | | | |●| | | | | | | | | | | | | | | | | | | | | | | | | | | | | | | |
| ST GEORGES MULTI THERAPY CTRE (HM19075) | | |●| | |●| | | | | | | | | | | | | | | |●| |●| | | | | | | | | | | |●|●| | | | | | | | | | | |
| ST MARY'S CLINIC (HM19087) | | | | | | | | | | | | | | | |●| | | | | |●| | | | | | | | | | | | | | |●| | |●| | | | | | | | |
| TATTERSALL, KAREN (HM19719) | | | | | | | | | | | | | | | | | | | | | |●| | | | | | | | | | | | | | | | | | | | | | | | | | |
| TINKER, D C (HM20083) | | | | | | | | | | | | | | | | | | | | | |●| |●| | | | | | | | | | | | | | | | | | | | | | | | |
| TIP TOES (HM20086) | | |●| | |●| | | | | | | | | |●| | | | | |●| | | |●| | | | | | |●| | |●|●| |●| | | | |●|●| | | |
| TRADITIONAL ACUPUNCTURE CLINIC (HM20220) | | |●| |●|●|●|●| | | |●| | | |●|●|●| |●|●| | | | |●| | | | | | | | |●|●|●| |●|●| | |●|●|●|●| | |
| TRADITIONAL CHINESE MED CTRE (HM20223) | | | | |●|●| |●| | |●|●| | | |●| |●| | |●| | |●| |●| | | | |●| | | | |●|●| | |●| | | |●|●|●| | |
| UPHAM, GILL (HM20522) |●|●|●| |●|●| | | |●|●|●| | | |●|●| | | |●| | | | |●| | | | | | | | | |●|●|●| | |●| | | |●| |●| |
| WATKINSON, BARBARA (HM20999) | | |●| | |●| | | | | | | | | |●|●|●| | | | | | | | | | | | | | | | | | |●| |●|●| | | | | |●| | |
| WEST LANCS MCTIMONEY (HM21224) | | | | | | | |●| | | | | | | | | | | | | | | | | | | | | | | | | | | | |●| | |●| | | | | | | | |
| WILSON, G (HM21656) | | |●| | | | | | | | | | | | | |●| | | | | | | | | | | | | | | | | | | | | | | | | | | | | | | |
| YEAMAN, DAVID (HM21996) | | | | | | | | | | | | | | | | | | | | | |●| | | | | | | | | | | | | | | | | | | | | | | | | | |
| **LEICESTERSHIRE** | | | | | | | | | | | | | | | | | | | | | | | | | | | | | | | | | | | | | | | | | | | | | | | | |
| ACUPUNCTURE SERVICES (HM00320) | | |●| | |●|●| | | | | | | | |●|●| | | | | | | | |●| | | | | | | | | |●|●| | | | | | | | | | | |
| ALBANY HOUSE (HM00479) | | |●| | | | | | | | |●| | | | | | | | | | | |●| | | | | | | | | |●| |●|●| | | | | | | | | | | |
| ANDREWS, SIMON C (HM00859) |●|●|●|●|●|●|●|●| | |●|●|●|●|●|●|●|●|●|●|●| | |●|●|●|●|●|●|●|●|●|●|●| |●|●|●|●|●|●|●|●|●|●|●|●| |
| ARCHWAY HSE NATURAL HLTH CTRE (HM00983) | | |●| | | | | | | | | | | | |●|●| | |●| | | | | | | | | | |●| | | | | | | | | | | | | |●|●| | |
| AROMATHERAPY INTERNATIONAL (HM01115) | | |●| | | | | | | | | | | | | | | | | | | | | | | | | | | | | | | | | |●| |●| | | | | | | | | |
| AYURVEDIC HERBAL CLINIC (HM01444) |●|●|●|●|●|●|●|●|●|●|●|●|●|●|●|●|●|●|●|●|●|●| |●|●|●|●|●|●|●|●|●|●| | | | | | | | | | | | | | | |

www.healthmyself.com

# D - I Conditions treated at Practices/Businesses

| Business by County with Reference no. | Dandruff | Deafness | Depression | Diabetes | Diarrhoea | Digestive Problems | Diverticulitis | Dizziness | Dyslexia | Dyspraxia | Ear Disorders | Eczema | ENT Disorders | Epilepsy | Eye Disorders | Fatigue | Fears | Fertility Problems | Fever | Fibroids | Flatulence | Foot Problems | Fractures | Fungal Infections | Gallstones | Gastrointestinal Problems | Genital Herpes | Gingivitis | Glandular Fever | Glaucoma | Gout | Gum Disease | Hair Problems | Halitosis | Hand Problems | Hay Fever | Headaches | Hearing Problems | High Blood Pressure | Hip Complaints | Hyperactivity | Hypoglycaemia | Impotence | Incontinence | Indigestion | Infertility | Influenza | Ingrowing Toenails |
|---|---|---|---|---|---|---|---|---|---|---|---|---|---|---|---|---|---|---|---|---|---|---|---|---|---|---|---|---|---|---|---|---|---|---|---|---|---|---|---|---|---|---|---|---|---|---|---|---|
| CALM WATERS (HM03557) | ● | ● | ● | ● | ● | ● | ● | ● | ● | ● | ● | ● | ● | ● | ● | ● | ● | ● | ● | ● | ● | ● | ● | ● | ● | ● | ● | ● | ● | ● | ● | ● | ● | ● | ● | ● | ● | ● | ● | ● | ● | ● | ● | ● | ● | ● | ● | |
| CHIROPRACTIC CENTRE (HM04381) | | | | | | | | | | | | | | | | | | | | | | ● | | | | | | | | | | | | | ● | | ● | | | ● | | | | | | | | |
| CONLIFFE, LOUISE (HM04982) | | | ● | | ● | ● | | ● | | | ● | ● | | | | ● | ● | ● | ● | | ● | | | | | | | | ● | | | | ● | | | ● | ● | | ● | | | | | ● | ● | | ● | |
| DEADMAN, P J (HM05932) | | | ● | | | | | | | | | | | | | | | | | | | | | | | | | | | | | | | | | | | | | | | | | | | | | |
| FAIRWEATHER, S & E (HM07068) | | | ● | | | | | | | | | | | | | | | | | | | | | | | | | | | | | | | | | | | | | | | | | | | | | |
| GRAHAM SPOWAGE OSTEOPATHIC SVS (HM08340) | | | | | | | | ● | | | | | | | | | | | | | | ● | | | | | | | | | | | | | ● | | ● | | | ● | | | | | | | | |
| HASSETT, CHARLES (HM09187) | | | | | | | | | | | | | | | | | | | | | | ● | | | | | | | | | | | | | | | ● | | | ● | | | | | | | | |
| JACQUI BATES COUNSELLING (HM10866) | | | ● | | | | | | | | | | | | | | ● | | | | | | | | | | | | | | | | | | | | | | | | | | | | | | | |
| LEWIS, JACQUELINE (HM12296) | | | ● | | | | | | | | | | | | | | | | | | | | | | | | | | | | | | | | | | ● | | | | | | | | | | | |
| LOUGHBOROUGH OSTEOPATHIC (HM12660) | | | | | | | | | | | | | | | | | | | | | | ● | | | | | | | | | | | | | | | ● | | | | | | | | | | | |
| MELTON MOWBRAY PHYSIO CLINIC (HM13717) | | | | | | | | | | | | | | | | | | | | | | | | | | | | | | | | | | | | | | | | ● | | | | | | | | |
| NATURAL WAY HEALTH CENTRE (HM14669) | | | | | ● | ● | | | | | | | | | | ● | | | | | | | | | | | | | | | | | | | | ● | ● | | | | | | | | | | | |
| SCHOOL OF SPIRITUAL KNOWLEDGE (HM18085) | | ● | | ● | | ● | ● | | | ● | | ● | ● | ● | ● | ● | ● | | | ● | | ● | ● | | | ● | ● | | | ● | ● | | | | ● | ● | ● | ● | ● | ● | ● | | | | | | ● | |
| SHIRLEY FRANKLIN AROMATHERAPY (HM18485) | | | ● | | | | | | | | | ● | | | | ● | ● | | | | | | | | | | | | | | | | | | | | ● | | | | | | | | | | | |
| STERN, J (HM19217) | | | ● | | | | | | | | | | | | | | | | | | | | | | | | | | | | | | | | | | | | | | | | | | | | | |
| SUE CHARLES AROMATHERAPY (HM19466) | | | ● | | | | | | | | | ● | | | | ● | ● | | | | | | | ● | | | | | | | ● | | | | | | | | | | | | | | | | | |
| SUE RICKS COMP THERAPY (HM19467) | ● | ● | ● | ● | ● | ● | ● | ● | ● | ● | ● | ● | ● | ● | ● | ● | ● | ● | ● | ● | ● | ● | ● | ● | ● | ● | ● | ● | ● | ● | ● | ● | ● | ● | ● | ● | ● | ● | ● | ● | ● | ● | ● | ● | ● | ● | ● | |
| VICTORIA CLINIC (HM20650) | | | ● | | | | | ● | ● | | | | | | | ● | ● | | | | | ● | | | | | | | | | | | | | ● | ● | ● | | ● | ● | ● | | | | | | | |
| WENDY PRICE HOLISTIC RIDING (HM21198) | | | ● | | | | | | | | | | | | | ● | ● | | | | | | | | | | | | | | | | | | | | | | | | | | | | | | | |
| WILKINSON, GWEN (HM21507) | | | | | | | | | ● | ● | | | | | | | | | | | | | | | | | | | | | | | | | | | | | | | | | | | | | | |
| WOHL, M (DR) (HM21758) | | | ● | | | ● | | | ● | ● | | | | | | ● | ● | | | | | | | | | | | | | | | | | | ● | | ● | | ● | ● | | | | | ● | | | |
| LINCOLNSHIRE | | | | | | | | | | | | | | | | | | | | | | | | | | | | | | | | | | | | | | | | | | | | | | | | |
| ALEXANDER TECHNIQUE (HM00550) | | | | | | | | | | | | | | | | | | | | | | | | | | | | | | | | | | | | | ● | | | | | | | | | | | |
| BARN HOUSE PHYSIO CLINIC (HM01726) | | | | | | | | | | | | | | | | | | | | | | | | | | | | | | | | | | | | | | | | ● | | | | | | | | |
| BEVERLEYS (HM02246) | ● | ● | ● | ● | ● | ● | ● | ● | ● | ● | ● | ● | ● | ● | ● | ● | ● | ● | ● | ● | ● | ● | ● | ● | ● | ● | ● | ● | ● | ● | ● | ● | ● | ● | ● | ● | ● | ● | ● | ● | ● | ● | ● | ● | ● | ● | ● | |
| BOSTON CHIROPRACTIC CLINIC (HM02726) | | | | | | | | | | | | | | | | | | | | | | | | | | | | | | | | | | | | | ● | | ● | ● | | | | | | | | |
| CASTLEGATE OSTEO PRACTICE (HM03847) | | | | | | ● | | ● | | | | | | | | | | | | | | ● | ● | | | | | | | | | | | | ● | | ● | ● | | ● | | | | | | | | |
| CHIEN ACUPUNCTURE CLINIC (HM04161) | | | ● | | ● | | | ● | | | | ● | | | | ● | | | | | | | ● | | | | | | | | | | | | | ● | | | | ● | | | | | ● | | | |
| CLINIC OF NATURAL MEDICINE (HM04703) | | | | | ● | ● | | | | | | | ● | | | ● | | | | | | ● | | ● | | ● | | | | | | | | | | ● | ● | | | ● | ● | | ● | ● | ● | ● | ● | |
| COMPLEMENTARY THERAPY CENTRE (HM04946) | | | ● | | | | | | | | | | | | | | | | | | | | | | | | | | | | | | | | | | ● | | ● | ● | | | | | | | | |
| COXON CLINIC (HM05326) | | | | | ● | ● | | | | | | | | | | | | | | | | ● | | | | | | | | | | | | | | ● | | | | ● | | | | | ● | | | |
| EASTGATE HYPNOTHERAPY CENTRE (HM06541) | | | ● | | | ● | | | | | | | | | | | ● | | | | | | | | | | | | | | | | | | | | | | | | | | | | | | | |
| GOOD HEALTHKEEPING (HM08241) | ● | | ● | ● | ● | ● | ● | ● | | | ● | ● | ● | ● | | ● | ● | ● | ● | ● | ● | | | ● | ● | ● | | ● | ● | | ● | ● | ● | ● | | ● | ● | | ● | | ● | ● | ● | ● | ● | ● | ● | |
| GRANTHAM PHYSIO PRACTICE (HM08394) | | | | | | | | | | | | | | | | | | | | | | ● | ● | | | | | | | | | | | | | | | | | ● | | | | | | | | |

# D - I Conditions treated at Practices/Businesses

| Business by County with Reference no. | BROOK GREEN OSTEOPATHY (HM03155) | BROOKS, CATHY (HM03175) | BROOKS, JANE (HM03177) | BROWN, ALISON R (HM03210) | BST FOUNDATION (HM03295) | BUCHANAN, ANGELA (HM03300) | BUCKLEY, BILLIE (HM03318) | BYRNE, JUDY (HM03516) | CASSIDY MEDICAL CENTRE (HM03815) | CENTRE FOR TRANSFORMATION (HM03920) | CHAPMAN, RUPERT (HM04009) | CHARTERHOUSE PHYSIOTHERAPY (HM04049) | CHARTERHOUSE PHYSIOTHERAPY (HM04048) | CHATSWORTH CLINIC (HM04063) | CHINESE MEDICAL CTRE OF LONDON (HM04245) | CHINESE SHOP (HM04269) | CHIROPRACTIC CLINIC (HM04393) | CHISWICK CHIROPRACTIC CLINIC (HM04412) | CITY HEALTH CENTRE (HM04496) | CLAIRE CHOUDHURY HERBAL PRAC (HM04507) | CLASSICAL OSTEOPATH (HM04610) | CLINIC FOR COUNSELLING (HM04681) | CLINIC FOR COUNSELLING (HM04680) | COLLEGE-PRACTICAL HOMEOPATHY (HM04855) | COMPLETE HEALTH CARE (HM04958) | COUNSELLING & PSYCHOTHERAPY (HM05246) | COUNSELLING SERVICE (HM05252) | CRAVEN CLINIC (HM05385) | CREATIVE INSIGHTS (HM05399) | CRISTA GALLI OSTEOPATHS (HM05446) | CTRE FOR CRANIO-SACRAL THERAPY (HM05540) | CTRE FOR THE STUDY OF COMP MED (HM05544) | DALTON, HELEN (HM05698) | DAVID WEISS HOMEOPATHY (HM05781) |
|---|---|---|---|---|---|---|---|---|---|---|---|---|---|---|---|---|---|---|---|---|---|---|---|---|---|---|---|---|---|---|---|---|---|---|
| Ingrowing Toenails |  |  |  |  |  |  |  |  |  |  |  |  |  |  |  |  |  |  |  |  |  |  |  |  |  |  |  |  |  |  |  |  |  |  |
| Influenza |  | ● |  |  |  |  |  |  |  |  |  |  |  | ● | ● | ● |  |  | ● | ● | ● |  |  |  |  |  |  |  |  | ● |  | ● | ● |  |
| Infertility |  | ● |  |  |  |  |  |  |  | ● |  |  |  | ● | ● | ● |  |  | ● | ● |  |  |  |  | ● |  |  |  |  | ● | ● | ● | ● |  |
| Indigestion | ● | ● |  |  |  |  |  |  |  | ● |  |  |  | ● | ● | ● |  |  | ● | ● | ● |  |  |  | ● |  |  | ● |  | ● | ● | ● | ● |  |
| Incontinence | ● | ● |  |  |  |  |  |  |  |  |  |  |  | ● | ● |  |  |  | ● |  | ● |  |  |  |  |  |  |  |  | ● |  | ● |  |  |
| Impotence |  |  |  |  |  |  |  |  |  | ● |  |  |  | ● | ● |  |  |  |  |  | ● |  |  |  | ● |  |  |  |  |  | ● | ● |  |  |
| Hypoglycaemia |  |  |  |  |  |  |  |  |  |  |  |  |  |  | ● |  |  |  |  | ● |  |  |  |  | ● |  |  |  |  | ● | ● | ● | ● |  |
| Hyperactivity |  | ● |  |  |  |  |  |  |  |  |  |  |  |  | ● |  |  |  | ● |  |  |  |  |  |  |  |  |  |  | ● | ● | ● | ● | ● |
| Hip Complaints | ● |  |  | ● |  | ● |  |  |  |  | ● | ● | ● |  | ● |  | ● | ● | ● |  |  |  |  |  | ● |  |  | ● |  | ● | ● | ● |  |  |
| High Blood Pressure |  | ● |  |  |  |  |  |  |  |  |  |  |  | ● | ● | ● |  |  | ● | ● | ● |  |  |  | ● |  |  |  |  | ● | ● | ● | ● | ● |
| Hearing Problems |  | ● |  |  |  |  |  |  |  |  |  |  |  |  | ● |  |  |  | ● |  |  |  |  |  |  |  |  |  |  | ● | ● |  | ● |  |
| Headaches | ● | ● |  |  |  |  |  |  | ● | ● | ● |  |  | ● | ● | ● | ● | ● | ● | ● | ● |  |  | ● | ● |  |  | ● | ● | ● | ● | ● | ● | ● |
| Hay Fever |  | ● |  |  |  |  |  |  |  | ● |  |  |  | ● | ● | ● |  |  | ● | ● |  |  |  |  | ● |  |  | ● |  |  | ● | ● | ● | ● |
| Hand Problems | ● |  |  |  |  | ● |  |  |  | ● | ● |  |  |  | ● |  |  |  | ● |  | ● |  |  |  | ● |  |  |  |  | ● | ● |  |  |  |
| Halitosis |  |  |  |  |  |  |  |  |  |  |  |  |  | ● |  |  |  |  |  | ● |  |  |  |  | ● |  |  |  |  |  |  | ● |  |  |
| Hair Problems |  | ● |  |  |  |  |  |  |  | ● |  |  |  |  | ● | ● |  |  |  |  |  |  |  |  |  |  |  |  |  |  |  |  | ● |  |
| Gum Disease |  | ● |  |  |  |  |  |  |  | ● |  |  |  | ● | ● |  |  |  |  | ● |  |  |  |  | ● |  |  |  |  |  |  |  | ● |  |
| Gout |  |  |  |  |  |  |  |  |  | ● |  |  |  | ● | ● | ● |  |  |  | ● |  |  |  |  | ● |  |  |  |  |  |  | ● | ● |  |
| Glaucoma |  |  |  |  |  |  |  |  |  |  |  |  |  | ● | ● |  |  |  | ● |  |  |  |  |  |  |  |  |  |  |  |  |  |  |  |
| Glandular Fever |  | ● |  |  |  |  |  |  |  | ● |  |  |  | ● | ● |  |  |  |  | ● | ● |  |  |  | ● |  |  |  |  | ● | ● | ● | ● |  |
| Gingivitis |  |  |  |  |  |  |  |  |  | ● |  |  |  | ● | ● |  |  |  |  | ● |  |  |  |  |  |  |  |  |  |  |  |  | ● |  |
| Genital Herpes |  | ● |  |  |  |  |  |  |  |  |  |  |  | ● | ● |  |  |  |  |  |  |  |  |  | ● |  |  |  |  |  |  | ● | ● |  |
| Gastrointestinal Problems | ● | ● |  |  |  |  |  |  |  | ● |  |  |  | ● | ● |  |  |  | ● | ● | ● |  |  |  | ● |  |  |  |  | ● | ● | ● | ● | ● |
| Gallstones |  |  |  |  |  |  |  |  |  |  |  |  |  | ● | ● |  |  |  | ● | ● |  |  |  |  |  |  |  |  |  | ● |  |  |  |  |
| Fungal Infections |  | ● |  |  |  |  |  |  |  |  |  |  |  |  | ● | ● |  |  |  | ● |  |  |  |  |  |  |  |  |  |  |  | ● | ● |  |
| Fractures | ● | ● |  |  |  | ● |  |  |  |  |  |  |  |  | ● |  |  |  |  |  |  |  |  |  |  |  |  |  |  | ● |  |  | ● |  |
| Foot Problems | ● |  |  |  |  | ● |  |  | ● | ● | ● |  |  |  | ● |  |  |  | ● |  | ● |  |  |  | ● |  |  |  |  | ● | ● |  | ● |  |
| Flatulence | ● | ● |  |  |  |  |  |  |  | ● |  |  |  | ● | ● | ● |  |  | ● | ● | ● |  |  |  | ● |  |  |  |  | ● |  | ● | ● |  |
| Fibroids |  |  |  |  |  |  |  |  |  | ● |  |  |  | ● | ● | ● |  |  | ● | ● |  |  |  |  | ● |  |  |  |  | ● | ● | ● | ● |  |
| Fever |  |  |  |  |  |  |  |  |  |  |  |  |  | ● | ● |  |  |  | ● | ● | ● |  |  |  |  |  |  |  |  | ● |  |  | ● |  |
| Fertility Problems |  | ● |  |  |  |  |  |  |  | ● |  |  |  | ● | ● | ● |  |  | ● | ● |  |  |  |  | ● |  |  |  |  | ● | ● | ● | ● |  |
| Fears |  | ● | ● |  | ● |  | ● |  |  | ● |  |  |  | ● | ● |  |  |  |  |  |  | ● | ● |  | ● |  |  | ● | ● |  |  | ● | ● |  |
| Fatigue | ● | ● |  |  |  |  |  |  |  | ● |  |  |  | ● | ● | ● |  |  | ● | ● | ● |  |  |  | ● | ● |  | ● |  | ● | ● | ● | ● | ● |
| Eye Disorders |  |  |  |  |  |  |  |  |  | ● |  |  |  | ● | ● |  |  |  | ● |  | ● |  |  |  |  |  |  |  |  | ● | ● |  |  |  |
| Epilepsy |  |  |  |  |  |  |  |  |  |  |  |  |  |  | ● |  |  |  | ● |  |  |  |  |  |  |  |  |  |  | ● | ● | ● |  |  |
| ENT Disorders |  | ● |  |  |  |  |  |  |  | ● |  |  |  | ● | ● |  |  |  | ● |  | ● |  |  |  | ● |  |  |  |  | ● | ● | ● | ● | ● |
| Eczema |  | ● |  |  |  |  |  | ● |  | ● |  |  |  | ● | ● | ● |  |  | ● | ● |  |  |  |  | ● |  |  | ● |  |  | ● | ● | ● | ● |
| Ear Disorders |  | ● |  |  |  |  |  |  |  | ● |  |  |  | ● | ● |  |  |  | ● |  | ● |  |  |  |  |  |  |  |  | ● | ● | ● | ● | ● |
| Dyspraxia |  |  |  |  |  |  |  |  |  |  |  |  |  |  |  |  |  |  | ● |  |  |  |  |  |  |  |  |  |  | ● | ● |  |  |  |
| Dyslexia |  |  |  |  |  |  |  |  |  | ● |  |  |  |  | ● |  |  |  | ● |  |  |  |  |  |  |  |  |  | ● | ● | ● |  |  |  |
| Dizziness | ● | ● |  | ● |  |  |  |  |  | ● |  |  |  | ● | ● |  |  | ● | ● | ● | ● |  |  |  | ● |  |  |  |  | ● | ● | ● |  |  |
| Diverticulitis |  | ● |  |  |  |  |  |  |  | ● |  |  |  | ● |  | ● |  |  | ● | ● | ● |  |  |  | ● |  |  |  |  | ● | ● | ● |  |  |
| Digestive Problems |  | ● |  |  |  |  |  |  |  | ● | ● |  |  | ● | ● |  |  | ● | ● | ● | ● |  |  |  | ● |  |  | ● |  | ● | ● | ● | ● | ● |
| Diarrhoea |  | ● |  |  |  |  |  | ● |  | ● |  |  |  | ● | ● |  |  |  | ● | ● | ● |  |  |  | ● |  |  | ● |  | ● | ● | ● | ● | ● |
| Diabetes |  |  |  |  |  |  |  |  |  |  |  |  |  |  | ● | ● |  |  |  |  |  |  |  |  | ● |  |  |  |  |  |  | ● |  |  |
| Depression |  | ● | ● |  |  |  | ● | ● |  | ● |  |  |  | ● | ● |  |  |  | ● | ● |  | ● | ● |  | ● | ● | ● | ● | ● |  | ● | ● | ● | ● |
| Deafness |  | ● |  |  |  |  |  |  |  |  |  |  |  |  | ● |  |  |  | ● |  |  |  |  |  |  |  |  |  |  | ● | ● |  | ● |  |
| Dandruff |  | ● |  |  |  |  |  |  |  |  |  |  |  |  | ● |  |  |  |  | ● |  |  |  |  | ● |  |  |  |  |  |  |  | ● |  |

# D - I Conditions treated at Practices/Businesses

Business by County with Reference no.

| Business by County with Reference no. | Dandruff | Deafness | Depression | Diabetes | Diarrhoea | Digestive Problems | Diverticulitis | Dizziness | Dyslexia | Dyspraxia | Ear Disorders | Eczema | ENT Disorders | Epilepsy | Eye Disorders | Fatigue | Fears | Fertility Problems | Fever | Fibroids | Flatulence |
|---|---|---|---|---|---|---|---|---|---|---|---|---|---|---|---|---|---|---|---|---|---|
| DAVIS, JULIA (HM05854) | ● | ● | ● | ● | ● | ● | ● | ● | ● | ● | ● | ● | ● | ● | ● | ● | ● | ● | ● | ● | ● |
| DAWSON, DAVID (DR) (HM05880) | | | | | | | | | | | | | | | | | | | | | |
| DE BURGH, JULIE (HM05904) | | | ● | | | | | | | | | | | | | | ● | | | | |
| DELROY, SANDRA (DR) (HM05968) | | | ● | | | | | | | | | | | | | | ● | | | | |
| DENNIS MICHAEL PRACTICE (HM05990) | | | | | | | | | | | | | | | | | | | | | |
| DENNISON, IAN (HM05996) | | | | | | | | | | | | | | | | | | | | | |
| DISTANT HEALING (HM06123) | | | ● | ● | | ● | | | | | ● | | | | ● | ● | ● | | | ● | |
| DOCKLANDS DENTAL/COMP HLTH (HM06141) | | | | | | | | | | | | | | | | | | | | | |
| DREAM LINE (HM06296) | | | ● | | | | | | | | | | | | | ● | ● | | | ● | |
| DREAMCATCHER (HM06298) | | | | | | ● | | | | | | | | | | | | | | | |
| DULWICH PHYSIOTHERAPY (HM06383) | | | | | | | | | | | | | | | | | | | | | |
| E.LONDON COMPLEMENTARY HEALTH (HM06479) | | | ● | ● | ● | ● | ● | ● | ● | ● | ● | ● | ● | ● | ● | ● | ● | ● | ● | ● | ● |
| EALING COUNS & THERAPY CTRE (HM06488) | | | | | ● | ● | | | | | | ● | | | | | | ● | | | ● |
| EAST WEST HERB SHOP (HM06527) | | | | | ● | ● | ● | ● | | | | ● | | | | ● | | ● | | | |
| EAST WEST THERAPIES (HM06529) | | | ● | | | ● | | | | | | ● | | | ● | ● | ● | ● | | | ● |
| EDGELL, MARJORY (HM06599) | | | ● | | | | | | | | | ● | | | | ● | ● | | | | |
| EDGWARE NATURAL HEALTH CENTRE (HM06604) | | | ● | | | ● | ● | | | | | ● | | | | ● | ● | | | | ● |
| ELLWOOD, CAROLINE (HM06780) | | | | | | ● | | | | | | | | | | ● | | | | | ● |
| ELTHAM HYPNOTHERAPY ANALYSIS (HM06789) | | | ● | | | | | | | | | | | ● | | | | | | | |
| ENFIELD CLINIC OF HERBAL MED (HM06818) | ● | | ● | | ● | ● | ● | | | | | ● | ● | | | ● | | ● | ● | ● | ● |
| ENFIELD HYP & COUNSELLING (HM06819) | | | ● | | | | | | | | | | | | | | ● | | | | |
| EQUILIBRIUM (HM06869) | | | ● | | | ● | | ● | | | | ● | | | | ● | | ● | | | |
| EQUILIBRIUM COUNS/THRPY CTRE (HM06873) | | | ● | | | | | | | | | | | | | | ● | | | | |
| FAIR, ANNETTE (HM07048) | | | | | | | | | | | | | | | | | | | | | |
| FELDENKRAIS CENTRE (HM07190) | | | | | | | | | | | | | | | | | | | | | |
| FERTILITY ENTHERAPY GROUP (HM07247) | | | | | | | | | | | | | | | | | | | | | |
| FLETCHER, CLARE (HM07410) | | | | | ● | ● | | | | | | | | | | ● | | | | | |
| FLEXIBLE HOUR (HM07420) | | | | | | ● | | | | | | | | | | ● | | | | | ● |
| FLOAT WORKS (HM07424) | | | | | | | | | | | | | | | | | ● | | | | |
| FRY, HOWARD (HM07772) | | | | | | | | | | | | | | | | | | | | | |
| FULHAM CLINIC (HM07781) | | | | | | ● | | | | | ● | ● | | | | ● | | ● | | | |
| G T CONSULTANCY (HM07815) | | | ● | | | | | | ● | | | ● | | | | | ● | | | | |
| GEE, PHILL (HM07959) | | | | | | | | | | | | | | | | | ● | | | | |
| GEORGE (HM07987) | | | | ● | | | | | | | | | | | | | | | | | |

| Business by County with Reference no. | Foot Problems | Fractures | Fungal Infections | Gallstones | Gastrointestinal Problems | Genital Herpes | Gingivitis | Glandular Fever | Glaucoma | Gout | Gum Disease | Hair Problems | Halitosis | Hand Problems | Hay Fever | Headaches | Hearing Problems | High Blood Pressure | Hip Complaints | Hyperactivity | Hypoglycaemia | Impotence | Incontinence | Indigestion | Infertility | Influenza | Ingrowing Toenails |
|---|---|---|---|---|---|---|---|---|---|---|---|---|---|---|---|---|---|---|---|---|---|---|---|---|---|---|---|
| DAVIS, JULIA (HM05854) | ● | ● | ● | ● | ● | ● | ● | ● | ● | ● | ● | ● | ● | ● | ● | ● | ● | ● | ● | ● | ● | ● | ● | ● | ● | ● | |
| DAWSON, DAVID (DR) (HM05880) | | | | | | | | | | | | | | | | | | | | ● | | | | | | | |
| DE BURGH, JULIE (HM05904) | | | | | | | | | | | | | | | | | | | | | | | | | | | |
| DELROY, SANDRA (DR) (HM05968) | | | | | | | | | | | | | | | | | | | | | | | | | | | |
| DENNIS MICHAEL PRACTICE (HM05990) | | | | | | | | | | | | | | | | ● | | | ● | | | | | | | | |
| DENNISON, IAN (HM05996) | | | | | | | | | | | | | | | | | | | ● | | | | | | | | |
| DISTANT HEALING (HM06123) | ● | | ● | ● | ● | | | | | | | ● | | ● | | ● | ● | ● | | ● | | | | ● | ● | | |
| DOCKLANDS DENTAL/COMP HLTH (HM06141) | ● | | | | | | | | | | | | | | | ● | | | ● | | | | | | | | |
| DREAM LINE (HM06296) | | | | | | | | | | | | | | | | | | | | | | | | | | | |
| DREAMCATCHER (HM06298) | | | | | | | | | | | | | | | | | | | | | | | | | | | |
| DULWICH PHYSIOTHERAPY (HM06383) | | | | | | | | | | | | | | | | | | | ● | | | | | | | | |
| E.LONDON COMPLEMENTARY HEALTH (HM06479) | ● | ● | ● | ● | ● | ● | ● | ● | ● | ● | ● | ● | ● | ● | ● | ● | ● | ● | ● | ● | ● | ● | ● | ● | ● | ● | |
| EALING COUNS & THERAPY CTRE (HM06488) | | | | | ● | | | ● | | | | | | | | ● | | ● | | | | | | | ● | ● | |
| EAST WEST HERB SHOP (HM06527) | | | | | ● | | | | | | | | | | ● | ● | | | | | | | | ● | ● | | |
| EAST WEST THERAPIES (HM06529) | ● | | | | ● | | | | | | | ● | | | | ● | | ● | ● | | | ● | | ● | | | |
| EDGELL, MARJORY (HM06599) | | | | | | | | | | | | | | | | | | ● | | | | | | ● | | | |
| EDGWARE NATURAL HEALTH CENTRE (HM06604) | | | ● | | ● | | | | | ● | | | | | | ● | | ● | | | | | | ● | | ● | |
| ELLWOOD, CAROLINE (HM06780) | | | ● | | ● | | | | | | | | | | | ● | | | | | | | | ● | | | |
| ELTHAM HYPNOTHERAPY ANALYSIS (HM06789) | | | | | | | | | | | | | | | | ● | | ● | | ● | | ● | | | | | |
| ENFIELD CLINIC OF HERBAL MED (HM06818) | | | ● | | ● | | ● | ● | | ● | ● | | ● | | ● | ● | | ● | | ● | ● | ● | ● | ● | ● | ● | |
| ENFIELD HYP & COUNSELLING (HM06819) | | | | | | | | | | | | | | | | ● | | | | | | | | | | | |
| EQUILIBRIUM (HM06869) | | | | | | | | | | | | | | | | ● | | ● | | | | | | ● | ● | ● | |
| EQUILIBRIUM COUNS/THRPY CTRE (HM06873) | | | | | | | | | | | | | | | | ● | | ● | | | | | | | | | |
| FAIR, ANNETTE (HM07048) | ● | | | | | | | | | | | | | | | ● | | | ● | | | | | | | | |
| FELDENKRAIS CENTRE (HM07190) | ● | | | | | | | | | | | | | | | | | | ● | | | | | | | | |
| FERTILITY ENTHERAPY GROUP (HM07247) | | | | | | | | | | | | | | | | | | | | | | | | | ● | | |
| FLETCHER, CLARE (HM07410) | | | | | | | | | | | | | | | ● | ● | | | ● | | | | | | | | |
| FLEXIBLE HOUR (HM07420) | | | | | | | | | | | | | | | | ● | | | | | | | | ● | | | |
| FLOAT WORKS (HM07424) | | | | | | | | | | | | | | | | | | | | | | | | | | | |
| FRY, HOWARD (HM07772) | ● | | ● | | | | | | | | | | | | | | | | | | | | | | | | |
| FULHAM CLINIC (HM07781) | ● | | ● | ● | | | | | | ● | | | | | ● | ● | | ● | ● | | | | | ● | ● | | |
| G T CONSULTANCY (HM07815) | | | | | | | | | | | | | | | | | | | | | | ● | | | | | |
| GEE, PHILL (HM07959) | | | | | | | | | | | | | | | | | | | | | | | | | | | |
| GEORGE (HM07987) | ● | | | | | | | | | | | | | | | | | | | | | | | | | | ● |

# D - I Conditions treated at Practices/Businesses

Business by County with Reference no.

| Business by County with Reference no. | Dandruff | Deafness | Depression | Diabetes | Diarrhoea | Digestive Problems | Diverticulitis | Dizziness | Dyslexia | Dyspraxia | Ear Disorders | Eczema | ENT Disorders | Epilepsy | Eye Disorders | Fatigue | Fears | Fertility Problems | Fever | Fibroids | Flatulence | Foot Problems | Fractures | Fungal Infections |
|---|---|---|---|---|---|---|---|---|---|---|---|---|---|---|---|---|---|---|---|---|---|---|---|---|
| GLASSMAN, DAVID (HM08128) | | ● | ● | ● | ● | ● | ● | ● | ● | ● | ● | ● | ● | ● | ● | ● | ● | | | | ● | ● | | |
| GODWIN, ROME (HM08194) | | | ● | | | | | | | | | | | | | ● | ● | | | | | | | |
| GREENWICH NATURAL HEALTH CTRE (HM08500) | | | | | | ● | | | | | | ● | | | | | | | | | | ● | | |
| GREIDINGER, CLIVE (HM08524) | | | | | | | | | | | | | | | | | | ● | | | | | | |
| HACKNEY HYPNOTHERAPY (HM08685) | | | ● | | | | | | | | | | | | | ● | ● | | | | | | | |
| HAIN, PATRICIA (HM08712) | | ● | ● | ● | ● | ● | ● | ● | | | ● | ● | ● | | | ● | | ● | ● | ● | ● | | | ● |
| HAMILTON, FIONA (HM08843) | | | | | | ● | | | | | | | | | | | | | | | | ● | | |
| HAMPSTEAD ACU/CHINESE HBL MED (HM08881) | | | | | ● | ● | | | | | | | | | | ● | | ● | | | | | | |
| HAREWOOD, MARCIA M (HM08991) | ● | | | | ● | ● | ● | | | | ● | ● | ● | | | ● | | ● | ● | | ● | ● | | |
| HARLEY ST STRESS MNGMT (HM08999) | | | ● | | | ● | | ● | ● | ● | | | | | | ● | ● | | | | | | | |
| HARLEY STREET TCM FERTILITY (HM09003) | | | | | | | | | | | | | | | | | | ● | | | | | | |
| HARLEY, KI (HM09006) | | | ● | | | | | | | | | | | | | | | | | | | | | |
| HARPER, SUZANNE G (HM09041) | | | ● | | ● | ● | ● | ● | | | ● | | ● | | | ● | ● | ● | | | | | | |
| HARPER, SUZANNE G (HM09042) | | | ● | ● | ● | ● | ● | ● | | | ● | | ● | | | ● | ● | ● | | | | | | |
| HARROW HEALTH CARE CENTRE (HM09121) | | | ● | | | ● | | ● | | | | ● | | | | ● | | ● | | | | ● | | |
| HAVELOCK-SEARLE, PAULINE (HM09206) | | | ● | | | | | | | | | | | | | ● | ● | | | | | | | |
| HAWKINS, JAN (HM09222) | | | ● | ● | | | | | | | | | | ● | | ● | | ● | | | | | | |
| HEAL, CHRISTIANNE (HM09314) | | | | | | | | | | | | | | | | | ● | | | | | | | |
| HEALERS WORLD (HM09320) | ● | ● | ● | ● | ● | ● | ● | ● | ● | ● | ● | ● | ● | ● | ● | ● | ● | ● | ● | ● | ● | ● | ● | ● |
| HEALING ARTS UK (HM09326) | | | ● | | | | | | | | | | | | | ● | | | | | | ● | | |
| HEALTHY LIVING CENTRE (HM09429) | ● | ● | ● | ● | ● | ● | ● | ● | ● | ● | ● | ● | ● | ● | ● | ● | ● | ● | ● | ● | ● | ● | ● | ● |
| HERBAL CARE (HM09600) | ● | ● | ● | ● | ● | ● | ● | ● | | | ● | ● | ● | | ● | ● | | ● | ● | ● | | ● | | ● |
| HERBAL CARE (HM09601) | ● | ● | ● | ● | ● | ● | ● | ● | | | ● | ● | ● | | ● | ● | | ● | ● | ● | | ● | | ● |
| HERBMEDIC (HM09663) | ● | ● | ● | ● | ● | ● | | ● | | | ● | ● | ● | ● | ● | ● | ● | ● | ● | ● | ● | ● | ● | ● |
| HETHERTON, ANNE (HM09697) | ● | ● | ● | | ● | ● | ● | ● | ● | ● | ● | ● | ● | ● | ● | ● | ● | ● | ● | ● | ● | ● | ● | ● |
| HIGHBURY CENTRE (HM09746) | | | | | | | | | | | ● | | | | | | | | | | | | | |
| HILDRETH & COCKER (HM09767) | | | | | | | | | | | | | | | | | | | | | | | | |
| HOGARTH CLINIC (HM09907) | | | ● | | | ● | | ● | | | | ● | | ● | | ● | | ● | ● | | | | ● | |
| HOLMES, DAVID (HM10040) | | | | | | | | | | | | | | | | | | | | | | ● | | ● |
| HOME VISITING SERVICES (HM10069) | ● | ● | ● | ● | ● | ● | ● | ● | | | ● | ● | ● | ● | | ● | ● | ● | | ● | ● | ● | | ● |
| HONG TAD ACUPUNCTURE & HERBAL (HM10119) | ● | ● | ● | ● | ● | ● | ● | ● | | | | ● | ● | ● | | ● | ● | ● | ● | ● | ● | ● | ● | ● |
| HOPE, ANN (HM10137) | | | | | | | | | | | | | | | | | | | | | | ● | | |
| HOUSE OF MISTRY (HM10220) | ● | | | ● | ● | ● | | ● | | | ● | ● | | | | ● | | | ● | ● | ● | ● | | ● |
| HOWARD, LYNNE (HM10240) | ● | ● | ● | ● | ● | ● | ● | ● | ● | ● | ● | ● | ● | ● | ● | ● | ● | ● | ● | ● | ● | ● | ● | ● |

| Business by County with Reference no. | Gallstones | Gastrointestinal Problems | Genital Herpes | Gingivitis | Glandular Fever | Glaucoma | Gout | Gum Disease | Hair Problems | Halitosis | Hand Problems | Hay Fever | Headaches | Hearing Problems | High Blood Pressure | Hip Complaints | Hyperactivity | Hypoglycaemia | Impotence | Incontinence | Indigestion | Infertility | Influenza | Ingrowing Toenails |
|---|---|---|---|---|---|---|---|---|---|---|---|---|---|---|---|---|---|---|---|---|---|---|---|---|
| GLASSMAN, DAVID (HM08128) | | ● | | | | ● | | | | ● | ● | ● | ● | ● | ● | ● | | | | ● | ● | | | |
| GODWIN, ROME (HM08194) | | | | | | | | | | | | | ● | | | | | | | | ● | | | |
| GREENWICH NATURAL HEALTH CTRE (HM08500) | | | | | | | | | | | | ● | | | | | | | | | | ● | | |
| GREIDINGER, CLIVE (HM08524) | | | | | | | | | | | | | ● | | | | | | ● | | | | | |
| HACKNEY HYPNOTHERAPY (HM08685) | | | | | | | | | | | | | | | | | | | ● | | | | | |
| HAIN, PATRICIA (HM08712) | ● | ● | | | | | ● | | ● | ● | | ● | ● | ● | ● | ● | ● | ● | | | ● | ● | ● | |
| HAMILTON, FIONA (HM08843) | | | | | | | | | | | ● | | ● | | | ● | | | | | ● | | | |
| HAMPSTEAD ACU/CHINESE HBL MED (HM08881) | | | | | | | | | | | | ● | ● | | | ● | | | | | | ● | | |
| HAREWOOD, MARCIA M (HM08991) | ● | ● | | | | | | | | | | | ● | | ● | | | ● | | | ● | ● | | |
| HARLEY ST STRESS MNGMT (HM08999) | | | | | | | | | | | | | ● | | ● | | ● | | ● | ● | ● | | | |
| HARLEY STREET TCM FERTILITY (HM09003) | | | | | | | | | | | | | | | | | | | | | | | | |
| HARLEY, KI (HM09006) | | | | | | | | | | | | | | | | | | | | | | | | |
| HARPER, SUZANNE G (HM09041) | ● | ● | ● | | | | ● | | | | ● | ● | ● | ● | ● | ● | ● | ● | | | ● | ● | ● | |
| HARPER, SUZANNE G (HM09042) | ● | ● | ● | | | | ● | | | | ● | ● | ● | ● | ● | ● | ● | ● | | | ● | ● | ● | |
| HARROW HEALTH CARE CENTRE (HM09121) | | | | | | | ● | | | | ● | ● | ● | | ● | ● | | | ● | | ● | | | |
| HAVELOCK-SEARLE, PAULINE (HM09206) | | | | | | | | | | | | | | | | | | | ● | | | | | |
| HAWKINS, JAN (HM09222) | | | | | | | | | | | | | | | | | | | ● | | | ● | | |
| HEAL, CHRISTIANNE (HM09314) | | | | | | | | | | | | | | | | | | | | | | | | |
| HEALERS WORLD (HM09320) | ● | ● | ● | ● | ● | ● | ● | ● | ● | ● | ● | ● | ● | ● | ● | ● | ● | ● | ● | ● | ● | ● | ● | |
| HEALING ARTS UK (HM09326) | | | | | | | | | | | ● | | ● | | | ● | | | | | | | | |
| HEALTHY LIVING CENTRE (HM09429) | ● | ● | ● | ● | ● | ● | ● | ● | ● | ● | ● | ● | ● | ● | ● | ● | ● | ● | ● | ● | ● | ● | ● | |
| HERBAL CARE (HM09600) | ● | ● | ● | ● | ● | | ● | ● | ● | | ● | ● | ● | ● | ● | ● | ● | | ● | ● | ● | ● | ● | |
| HERBAL CARE (HM09601) | ● | ● | ● | ● | ● | | ● | ● | ● | | ● | ● | ● | ● | ● | ● | ● | | ● | ● | ● | ● | ● | |
| HERBMEDIC (HM09663) | ● | ● | ● | | ● | | ● | ● | ● | ● | ● | ● | ● | ● | ● | ● | ● | ● | ● | ● | ● | ● | ● | |
| HETHERTON, ANNE (HM09697) | ● | ● | ● | ● | ● | | ● | ● | ● | ● | ● | ● | ● | ● | ● | ● | ● | ● | ● | ● | ● | ● | ● | |
| HIGHBURY CENTRE (HM09746) | | | | | | | | | | | ● | | ● | ● | | | | | | | | | | |
| HILDRETH & COCKER (HM09767) | | | | | | | | | | | | | | | | ● | | | | | | | | |
| HOGARTH CLINIC (HM09907) | | ● | | | | | ● | | | | | ● | ● | ● | ● | ● | ● | | ● | ● | ● | ● | | |
| HOLMES, DAVID (HM10040) | | | | | | | | | | | | | | | | | | | | | | | | |
| HOME VISITING SERVICES (HM10069) | ● | ● | ● | ● | ● | | ● | ● | ● | | | ● | ● | ● | ● | ● | ● | ● | ● | ● | ● | ● | ● | |
| HONG TAD ACUPUNCTURE & HERBAL (HM10119) | ● | ● | ● | | ● | | ● | | ● | ● | ● | ● | ● | ● | ● | ● | ● | ● | ● | ● | ● | ● | ● | |
| HOPE, ANN (HM10137) | | | | | | | | | | | | | | | | | | | | | | | | |
| HOUSE OF MISTRY (HM10220) | ● | ● | | ● | | | ● | ● | ● | ● | ● | ● | ● | | ● | | | | | ● | ● | | ● | |
| HOWARD, LYNNE (HM10240) | ● | ● | ● | ● | ● | ● | ● | ● | ● | ● | ● | ● | ● | ● | ● | ● | ● | ● | ● | ● | ● | ● | ● | |

www.healthmyself.com

# D - I Conditions treated at Practices/Businesses

| Business by County with Reference no. | Dandruff | Deafness | Depression | Diabetes | Diarrhoea | Digestive Problems | Diverticulitis | Dizziness | Dyslexia | Dyspraxia | Ear Disorders | Eczema | ENT Disorders | Epilepsy | Eye Disorders | Fatigue |
|---|---|---|---|---|---|---|---|---|---|---|---|---|---|---|---|---|
| HUGHES, PAUL (HM10339) | | | ● | | ● | ● | | ● | ● | ● | ● | ● | ● | ● | | ● |
| HYDE BARKER & ASSOCIATES (HM10469) | | | | | | | | | | | | | | | | |
| INDEPENDENT PSYCHOLOGY SERVICE (HM10610) | | | ● | | | | | | ● | | | | | | | |
| INSIDE STORY (HM10650) | | | ● | ● | ● | ● | ● | | | | | ● | ● | | | ● |
| JACOBS, BRIAN M (HM10858) | | | ● | | | | | | | | | | | | | |
| JELFS, MARTIN (HM10976) | | | ● | | | | | | | | | | | | | |
| JELFS, MARTIN (HM10977) | | | ● | | | | | | | | | | | | | |
| JEWERS, M S (HM11025) | | | | | | | | | | | | | | | | |
| JOSEPH CLINIC (HM11215) | | | | | | | | ● | | | | | | | | |
| KALLAS, JEMIMA (HM11297) | ● | | ● | | ● | ● | ● | ● | ● | | | ● | ● | | | ● |
| KANE AND ROSS CLINICS (HM11309) | | | | | | | | | | | | | | | | ● |
| KEITH EGLETON HYPNOTHERAPY (HM11412) | | | ● | ● | ● | ● | | ● | ● | | | ● | | | | ● |
| KERN, MICHAEL (HM11544) | | ● | ● | | | ● | | ● | ● | ● | ● | | | ● | ● | ● |
| KIKAI SHIATSU CENTRE (HM11598) | | | | | ● | ● | ● | | | | | | | | | ● |
| KILBRIDE, PETER (HM11600) | | | ● | | | | | | | | | | | | | ● |
| KINGSBURY PSYCHOTHERAPY PRAC (HM11660) | | | ● | | | | | | | | | | | | | |
| KINGSGATE ACUPUNCTURE PRACTICE (HM11663) | | | ● | | ● | ● | | ● | | | | ● | ● | | ● | ● |
| KLEIN, JEMMA (HM11737) | | | | ● | | | | | | | | | | | | |
| LASSMAN, J (HM11986) | | | | | ● | ● | | | | | | | | | | ● |
| LEE COMPLEMENTARY HEALTH CTRE (HM12130) | | | ● | | | | | | | | | | | | | |
| LEVER CLINIC (HM12256) | | | ● | | | | | | | | | | | | | ● |
| LITTLE VENICE CHIROPODY (HM12469) | | | | | | | | | | | | | | | | |
| LIVING CENTRE CLINIC (HM12483) | | | ● | | ● | ● | | ● | | | | ● | | | | ● |
| LIZ DAWSON - PSYCHOTHERAPIST (HM12494) | | | ● | | | | | | | | | | | | | ● |
| LOCKE, ANNA (HM12539) | | | | | | | | | | | | | | | | |
| LONDON ASS OF PRIMAL PSYCHO (HM12583) | | | ● | | | | | | | | | | | | | |
| LONDON INDIAN CHAMPISSAGE CTRE (HM12599) | | | | | | | | | | | | | | | | |
| LONDON SCHOOL OF OSTEOPATHY (HM12604) | | | | | | | | | | | | | | | | |
| LONDON SPINE AND JOINT CLINIC (HM12611) | | | | | | | | | | | | | | | | |
| LONGARETTI, ANTHONY (HM12623) | | | | | | | | | | | | | | | | |
| LOTUS CLINIC (HM12653) | ● | | ● | | ● | ● | ● | ● | ● | | ● | ● | ● | | | ● |
| LOW, JANET (DR) (HM12686) | | | ● | | | | | | | | | | | | | |
| LUXTON, PAULINE (HM12752) | | | | | | | | | | | | | | | | |
| MANLEY CLINIC (HM13016) | ● | ● | ● | | ● | ● | ● | ● | ● | ● | ● | ● | ● | ● | ● | ● |

| Business by County with Reference no. | Fears | Fertility Problems | Fever | Fibroids | Flatulence | Foot Problems | Fractures | Fungal Infections | Gallstones | Gastrointestinal Problems | Genital Herpes | Gingivitis | Glandular Fever | Glaucoma | Gout | Gum Disease |
|---|---|---|---|---|---|---|---|---|---|---|---|---|---|---|---|---|
| HUGHES, PAUL (HM10339) | ● | ● | ● | ● | ● | | | | | ● | | | ● | | ● | ● |
| HYDE BARKER & ASSOCIATES (HM10469) | | | | | | ● | | ● | | | | | | | | |
| INDEPENDENT PSYCHOLOGY SERVICE (HM10610) | | ● | | | | | | | | | | | | | | |
| INSIDE STORY (HM10650) | | | | | ● | | | ● | | ● | | | | | | |
| JACOBS, BRIAN M (HM10858) | | | | | | | | | | | | | | | | |
| JELFS, MARTIN (HM10976) | | | | | | | | | | | | | | | | |
| JELFS, MARTIN (HM10977) | | | | | | | | | | | | | | | | |
| JEWERS, M S (HM11025) | | | | | | ● | | | | | | | | | | |
| JOSEPH CLINIC (HM11215) | | | | | | ● | | | | | | | | | | |
| KALLAS, JEMIMA (HM11297) | ● | ● | | ● | ● | ● | | | ● | ● | ● | ● | ● | | | ● |
| KANE AND ROSS CLINICS (HM11309) | | | | | | | | | | ● | | | | | | |
| KEITH EGLETON HYPNOTHERAPY (HM11412) | ● | ● | | | | | | | | | | | | | | |
| KERN, MICHAEL (HM11544) | ● | ● | ● | | | ● | ● | | | | | | ● | | | |
| KIKAI SHIATSU CENTRE (HM11598) | | | | | | ● | | | | | | | | | | |
| KILBRIDE, PETER (HM11600) | ● | ● | | | | | | | | | | | | | | |
| KINGSBURY PSYCHOTHERAPY PRAC (HM11660) | ● | | | | | | | | | | | | | | | |
| KINGSGATE ACUPUNCTURE PRACTICE (HM11663) | | ● | ● | ● | ● | | | | ● | ● | ● | ● | | | | ● |
| KLEIN, JEMMA (HM11737) | | | | | | ● | | | | | | | | | | |
| LASSMAN, J (HM11986) | | | | | | | | | | | | | | | | |
| LEE COMPLEMENTARY HEALTH CTRE (HM12130) | | | | | | | | | | | | | | | | |
| LEVER CLINIC (HM12256) | | | | | | ● | | | | | | | | | ● | |
| LITTLE VENICE CHIROPODY (HM12469) | | | | | | ● | | ● | | | | | | | ● | |
| LIVING CENTRE CLINIC (HM12483) | ● | ● | | ● | ● | ● | ● | ● | | ● | | | ● | | | |
| LIZ DAWSON - PSYCHOTHERAPIST (HM12494) | | | | | | | | | | | | | | | | |
| LOCKE, ANNA (HM12539) | | | | | | | | | | | | | | | | |
| LONDON ASS OF PRIMAL PSYCHO (HM12583) | ● | | | | | | | | | | | | | | | |
| LONDON INDIAN CHAMPISSAGE CTRE (HM12599) | | | | | | | | | | | | | | | | |
| LONDON SCHOOL OF OSTEOPATHY (HM12604) | | | | | | | | | | | | | | | | |
| LONDON SPINE AND JOINT CLINIC (HM12611) | | | | | | ● | | | | | | | | | | |
| LONGARETTI, ANTHONY (HM12623) | | | | | | ● | | | | | | | | | | |
| LOTUS CLINIC (HM12653) | ● | ● | | ● | ● | | | ● | ● | ● | ● | ● | ● | | | ● |
| LOW, JANET (DR) (HM12686) | ● | | | | | | | | | | | | | | | |
| LUXTON, PAULINE (HM12752) | | | | | | ● | | ● | | | | | | | | |
| MANLEY CLINIC (HM13016) | ● | ● | ● | ● | ● | ● | ● | ● | ● | ● | ● | ● | ● | | ● | ● |

| Business by County with Reference no. | Hair Problems | Halitosis | Hand Problems | Hay Fever | Headaches | Hearing Problems | High Blood Pressure | Hip Complaints | Hyperactivity | Hypoglycaemia | Impotence | Incontinence | Indigestion | Infertility | Influenza | Ingrowing Toenails |
|---|---|---|---|---|---|---|---|---|---|---|---|---|---|---|---|---|
| HUGHES, PAUL (HM10339) | | | | ● | ● | | ● | | ● | | ● | | ● | ● | ● | |
| HYDE BARKER & ASSOCIATES (HM10469) | | | | | | | | | | | | | | | | |
| INDEPENDENT PSYCHOLOGY SERVICE (HM10610) | | | | | | | | | | | ● | | | ● | | |
| INSIDE STORY (HM10650) | | ● | | ● | ● | | ● | | ● | | | | ● | | | |
| JACOBS, BRIAN M (HM10858) | | | | | | | | | | | | | | | | |
| JELFS, MARTIN (HM10976) | | | | | | | | | | | | | | | | |
| JELFS, MARTIN (HM10977) | | | | | | | | | | | | | | | | |
| JEWERS, M S (HM11025) | | | | | | | | | | | | | | | | |
| JOSEPH CLINIC (HM11215) | | | ● | | ● | | | ● | | | | | | | | |
| KALLAS, JEMIMA (HM11297) | ● | ● | | ● | ● | | ● | ● | ● | | ● | ● | ● | ● | ● | |
| KANE AND ROSS CLINICS (HM11309) | | | | | | | | | | | | | | | | |
| KEITH EGLETON HYPNOTHERAPY (HM11412) | | | | | | | ● | | | | ● | ● | ● | ● | | |
| KERN, MICHAEL (HM11544) | | | | | ● | ● | ● | ● | ● | | ● | | | ● | | |
| KIKAI SHIATSU CENTRE (HM11598) | | | ● | | ● | | | | | | | | ● | | | |
| KILBRIDE, PETER (HM11600) | ● | | | | ● | | | | | | ● | | | | | |
| KINGSBURY PSYCHOTHERAPY PRAC (HM11660) | | | | | | | | | | | | | | | | |
| KINGSGATE ACUPUNCTURE PRACTICE (HM11663) | | | | ● | ● | | ● | ● | | | ● | | ● | ● | | |
| KLEIN, JEMMA (HM11737) | | | | | | | | | | | | | | | | |
| LASSMAN, J (HM11986) | | | | ● | ● | | ● | ● | | | | | | | | |
| LEE COMPLEMENTARY HEALTH CTRE (HM12130) | | | | | | | | | | | | | | | | |
| LEVER CLINIC (HM12256) | | | ● | | ● | | | ● | | | | | | | | |
| LITTLE VENICE CHIROPODY (HM12469) | | | | | | | | | | | | | | | | ● |
| LIVING CENTRE CLINIC (HM12483) | ● | | | ● | ● | | ● | ● | ● | | ● | ● | ● | ● | ● | |
| LIZ DAWSON - PSYCHOTHERAPIST (HM12494) | | | | | | | | | | | ● | | | | | |
| LOCKE, ANNA (HM12539) | ● | | | | | | | | | | | | | | | |
| LONDON ASS OF PRIMAL PSYCHO (HM12583) | | | | | | | | | | | | | | | | |
| LONDON INDIAN CHAMPISSAGE CTRE (HM12599) | ● | | | | ● | | | | | | | | | | | |
| LONDON SCHOOL OF OSTEOPATHY (HM12604) | | | ● | | | | | | | | | | | | | |
| LONDON SPINE AND JOINT CLINIC (HM12611) | | | ● | | ● | | | ● | | | | | | | | |
| LONGARETTI, ANTHONY (HM12623) | | | ● | | | | | ● | | | | | | | | |
| LOTUS CLINIC (HM12653) | ● | ● | ● | ● | ● | | | | ● | | ● | ● | ● | ● | ● | |
| LOW, JANET (DR) (HM12686) | | | | | | | | | | | ● | | | | | |
| LUXTON, PAULINE (HM12752) | | | | | | | ● | | | | | | | | | |
| MANLEY CLINIC (HM13016) | ● | ● | ● | ● | ● | ● | ● | ● | ● | ● | ● | ● | ● | ● | ● | |

# D - I Conditions treated at Practices/Businesses

| Business by County with Reference no. | Dandruff | Deafness | Depression | Diabetes | Diarrhoea | Digestive Problems | Diverticulitis | Dizziness | Dyslexia | Dyspraxia | Ear Disorders | Eczema | ENT Disorders | Epilepsy | Eye Disorders | Fatigue | Fears | Fertility Problems | Fever | Fibroids | Flatulence | Foot Problems | Fractures | Fungal Infections | Gallstones | Gastrointestinal Problems | Genital Herpes | Gingivitis | Glandular Fever | Glaucoma | Gout | Gum Disease | Hair Problems | Halitosis | Hand Problems | Hay Fever | Headaches | Hearing Problems | High Blood Pressure | Hip Complaints | Hyperactivity | Hypoglycaemia | Impotence | Incontinence | Indigestion | Infertility | Influenza | Ingrowing Toenails |
|---|---|---|---|---|---|---|---|---|---|---|---|---|---|---|---|---|---|---|---|---|---|---|---|---|---|---|---|---|---|---|---|---|---|---|---|---|---|---|---|---|---|---|---|---|---|---|---|---|
| MARIE, SOUTA (HM13099) | | |●| | | | | | | | | | | | | | | | | | | | | | | | | | | | | | | | | | | | | | | | | | | | | |
| MARKS, DARREN HYPNOTHERAPY (HM13119) | | |●| | | | | | | | | | | | | | | | | | | | | | | | | | | | | | | | | | | | | | | | | | | | | |
| MARLBOROUGH THERAPY PRACTICE (HM13125) | | |●| | | | | | | | | | | | | | | | | | | | | | | | | | | | | | | | | | | | | | | | | | | | | |
| MATTHEWS, ROBERT (HM13312) | | |●| | | | | | | | |●| | | |●|●|●| | | | | | | | | | | | | | | | | | | | |●| | | |●| | |●| | |
| MCCAFFREY, GERARDINE (HM13380) | | |●| | |●| | | | | | | | | |●|●|●| | |●|●| | | |●| | | | | | | | | | |●| | | | | | | | |●| |●|
| MCCLOSKEY, P J (HM13409) | | | |●| | | | | | | |●| | | | | | | | | |●|●|●| | | | | | |●| | | | | | | | |●| | | | | | | |●|
| MEYERSON, SIMON (HM13789) | | |●| | | | | | | | | | | | | | | | | | | | | | | | | | | | | | | | | | | | | | | | | | | | | |
| MIDDLETON, IAN W (HM13821) | | |●| |●|●|●| | | | |●| | | |●| |●| |●| | | |●|●|●| | |●| |●| | | | |●|●| |●| | |●|●| |●|●| | |
| MILLS DE-WIN STUDIOS (HM13922) | |●| | |●|●|●|●| |●|●| | | | |●| | | | |●|●| | |●|●| | | | | | | | |●|●|●|●|●| |●| | |●|●|●| | |
| MONTSERRAT CLINIC (HM14090) | | |●|●|●|●|●|●|●|●|●|●|●| |●|●|●|●|●|●|●|●| |●|●|●|●| |●| |●| |●|●|●|●|●| |●|●|●|●| |●|●| |●| |
| MOTHERSOLE, VINETA (HM20682) | | | | | | | | | | | | | | | | | | | | | |●|●|●| | | | | | |●| | | | | | | | |●| | | | | | | | |
| MOTTINGHAM HYPNOTHERAPY CTRE (HM14279) | | |●| |●|●| |●|●| | |●| | | | | | | | | | | | | | | | | | | | | | | |●|●| |●| | | |●| | | | | |
| M-POWER (HM14308) | | |●| | | | | |●| | | | | | | |●| | | | | | | | | | | | | | | | | | | | | | | | | | | | | | | |
| NEIL-ASHER, S (HM14761) | | | | | | | | | | | | | | | | | | | | | | | | | | | | | | | | | | | | |●| | |●| | | | | | | | |
| NEILL, VICTORIA (HM14764) | | |●| | | | |●| | | | | | | |●| | | | | |●|●| | |●| | | | |●| | | |●| |●| | |●| | | | | | | | |
| NIEL-ASHER, S (HM14933) | | | | | | | | | | | | | | | | | | | | | | | | | | | | | | | | | | | | |●| | |●| | | | | | | | |
| NIELSEN, RITA C (HM14935) | | |●| | |●| | | | | | | | | |●| | | | | | | | | | | | | | | | | | | |●|●| |●|●|●| | | |●| | | |
| NORTH POLE SCH OF T'AI-CHI (HM15094) | | |●| | | | | | | | | | | | |●| | | | | | | | | | | | | | | | | | | | | | |●| |●| | | | | | | |
| NORTHWOOD CLINIC (HM15067) | | | | | | | | | | | | | | | | | | | | | |●| | | | | | | | | | | | | | | | | | | | | | | | | |●|
| NOTTING HILL TRAD ACU CTRE (HM15081) | | |●| |●|●| | | | | | | | | | | |●| | | | | | | | | | | | | | | | | |●|●| | |●| | | | | |●| | |
| NUTRITION FOR LIFE INT (HM15124) |●| | |●| |●| | | | | |●| | |●|●| |●| |●| | | |●| | | |●| |●|●|●|●| | |●|●| |●| |●|●|●| |●| |●| |
| O'CONNOR, PENNY (HM15214) | | | | | | | | | | | | | | | | | | | | | | | | | | | | | | | | | | | | |●| | | | | | | | | | | |
| ORIENTAL MEDICINE (HM15386) |●|●|●|●|●|●|●|●| |●|●|●|●|●|●|●| |●|●|●|●|●|●|●|●|●|●|●|●|●|●|●|●|●|●|●|●|●|●|●|●|●|●|●|●|●|●| |
| OSTEOPATHIC ASSOCIATION CLINIC (HM15453) | | | | | | | | | | | | | | | | | | | | | |●| | | | | | | | | | | | |●| |●| | |●| | | | | | | | |
| OSTEOPATHIC PRACTICE (HM15471) | | | | | | | | | | | | | | | | | | | | | | | | | | | | | | | | | | | | |●| | |●| |●| | | | | | |
| OSTEOPATHIC PRACTICE (HM15470) | | |●|●| |●|●|●| |●| | | | | |●| |●| | | | | | | | | | | | |●| | | | |●|●|●|●|●| | |●|●|●|●| | |
| OSTEOPATHIC PRACTICE (HM15467) | | | | | | | | | | | | | | | | | | | | | |●| | | | | | | | | | | | | | | | | | | | | | | | | | |
| OSTEOPATHIC PRACTICE (HM15473) | | | | | | | | | | | | | | | | | | | | | |●| | | | | | | | | | | | | | | | | | | | | | | | | | |
| OTREMBA, KATHARINA (HM15496) |●| |●| |●|●| | |●| | |●| | | |●|●|●|●|●|●|●| |●| | |●| |●| | | |●| | |●|●|●|●| |●| |●|●|●|●|●| |
| OUTCOMES (HM15502) | | |●|●|●|●| |●|●| | |●| | | |●|●|●| | | | | | | |●| | | | | | | | | |●|●| |●| | |●|●| |●|●| | |
| PACIFIC WAVES PRODUCTIONS (HM15553) | | |●| |●|●| |●| | | |●| | | |●|●|●| | |●| | | | |●| | | | | | | | | | |●| |●| | | |●|●|●|●| | |
| PALFREYMAN, SUE (HM15592) | | | | | |●| | | | | | | | | | | | | | | |●| | | |●| | | | | | | | |●| |●| | |●| | | | |●| | | |
| PAPOUTSIS, MARGARET (HM15642) | | | | | | | | | | | | | | | | | | | | | |●| | | | | | | | | | | | |●| | | | |●| | | | | | | | |
| PATEL, J C (HM15788) | | | |●| | | | | | | | | | | | | | | | | |●| | | | | | | | | | | | | | | | | | | | | | | | | | |

www.healthmyself.com

Healthmyself Directory

D-I **CONDITIONS TREATED** England (by County)

# D - I Conditions treated at Practices/Businesses

| Business by County with Reference no. | Dandruff | Deafness | Depression | Diabetes | Diarrhoea | Digestive Problems | Diverticulitis | Dizziness | Dyslexia | Dyspraxia | Ear Disorders | Eczema | ENT Disorders | Epilepsy | Eye Disorders | Fatigue |
|---|---|---|---|---|---|---|---|---|---|---|---|---|---|---|---|---|
| PHYSIO ONE (HM16202) | | | | | | | | ● | | | | | | | | |
| PHYSIO SOLUTIONS (HM16205) | | | | | | | | | | | | | | | | |
| PINNER ROAD PHYSIOTHERAPY (HM16316) | | | | | | | | | | | | | | | | |
| PODIATRY CLINIC (HM16393) | | | | ● | | | | | | | | | | | | |
| PRICE, GILLIAN (HM16575) | | | ● | ● | ● | ● | ● | ● | | | ● | ● | ● | ● | ● | ● |
| PRICE, SANDRA (HM16594) | | | | | | | | | | | | | | | | |
| PRICE, SANDRA (HM16595) | | | | | | | | | | | | | | | | |
| PRIMROSE HEALING CENTRE (HM16616) | | | | | | | | | | | | | | | | |
| PRIVATE HEALTH CLINIC (HM16644) | ● | ● | ● | ● | ● | ● | ● | ● | ● | ● | ● | ● | ● | ● | ● | ● |
| PRIVATE PRACTICE (HM16649) | | | ● | | | | | | | | | | | | | ● |
| PSYCHOTHERAPY CENTRE (HM16734) | | | ● | | | | | | | | | ● | | | | |
| PSYCHOTHERAPY SERVICES (HM16737) | | | ● | | | | | | | | | | | | | |
| PUTNEY CHIROPRACTIC (HM16780) | | | | | | ● | | ● | | | | | | | | |
| RACHEL YOUNG - HYPNOTHERAPIST (HM16837) | | ● | ● | ● | ● | ● | ● | | | | | ● | | | | ● |
| RAEBURN, JO (HM16865) | ● | | ● | | ● | ● | ● | | | | | ● | ● | | | ● |
| RANDALL, CAROLINE (HM16926) | ● | ● | ● | ● | ● | ● | ● | ● | ● | ● | ● | ● | ● | ● | ● | ● |
| RAVENSCROFT CENTRE (HM16967) | | | ● | | | | | | | | | | | | | ● |
| READ, CHARLES (HM16993) | | | | | | | | | | | | | | | | |
| REEVE, MALCOLM (HM17060) | | | | | | | | | | | | | | | | |
| REFLEXOLOGY (HM17077) | | | ● | | ● | ● | ● | | | | | | | | | ● |
| REFLEXOLOGY CLINIC (HM17089) | | | | | | ● | | | | | | | | | | |
| RELAXATION PLACE (HM17166) | | | | | | | | | | | | ● | | | | |
| REPLINGHAM CLINIC (HM17195) | | | ● | ● | ● | ● | | | | | ● | ● | | | | ● |
| ROBERTS, MATT (HM17420) | | | ● | | | | | | | | | | | | | |
| ROBINSON, GABIE (HM17473) | | | ● | | | ● | | | | | | ● | | | | ● |
| ROEHAMPTON PHYSIO/SPORTS (HM17535) | | | | | | | | | | | | | | | | |
| ROSE, NICHOLAS (HM17613) | | | | | | | | | | | | | | | | |
| RUTHERFORD, BERWYN (HM17780) | | | | | | | | | | | | | | | | ● |
| SALTER, LIZ (HM17869) | ● | | ● | | ● | ● | ● | ● | ● | ● | ● | ● | ● | | ● | ● |
| SAYER CLINIC (HM17994) | | | | | | | | | | | | | | | | |
| SAYER CLINIC (HM17993) | | | | | | | | ● | | | | | | | | |
| SEARBY, JOE (HM18174) | | | | | | ● | | ● | | | | | | | | ● |
| SEEAR, MICHAEL (DR) (HM18189) | | | ● | ● | | ● | ● | ● | | | ● | ● | ● | | ● | ● |
| SEYMOUR PRACTICE (HM18257) | | | | | | | | | | | | | | | | |

| Business by County with Reference no. | Fears | Fertility Problems | Fever | Fibroids | Flatulence | Foot Problems | Fractures | Fungal Infections | Gallstones | Gastrointestinal Problems | Genital Herpes | Gingivitis | Glandular Fever | Glaucoma | Gout | Gum Disease |
|---|---|---|---|---|---|---|---|---|---|---|---|---|---|---|---|---|
| PHYSIO ONE (HM16202) | | | | | | ● | | | | | | | | | | |
| PHYSIO SOLUTIONS (HM16205) | | | | | | | ● | | | | | | | | | |
| PINNER ROAD PHYSIOTHERAPY (HM16316) | | | | | | | ● | | | | | | | | | |
| PODIATRY CLINIC (HM16393) | | | | | | ● | ● | ● | | | | | | | ● | |
| PRICE, GILLIAN (HM16575) | ● | ● | ● | ● | ● | ● | ● | | ● | ● | ● | ● | ● | ● | ● | ● |
| PRICE, SANDRA (HM16594) | | | | | | | | | | | | | | | | |
| PRICE, SANDRA (HM16595) | | | | | | | | | | | | | | | | |
| PRIMROSE HEALING CENTRE (HM16616) | ● | | | | | | | | | | | | | | | |
| PRIVATE HEALTH CLINIC (HM16644) | ● | ● | ● | ● | ● | ● | ● | ● | ● | ● | ● | ● | ● | ● | ● | ● |
| PRIVATE PRACTICE (HM16649) | ● | | | | | | | | | | | | | | | |
| PSYCHOTHERAPY CENTRE (HM16734) | ● | | | | | | | | | | | | | | | |
| PSYCHOTHERAPY SERVICES (HM16737) | | | | | | | | | | | | | | | | |
| PUTNEY CHIROPRACTIC (HM16780) | | | | | | | | | | | | | | | | |
| RACHEL YOUNG - HYPNOTHERAPIST (HM16837) | ● | ● | | | ● | | | | ● | ● | | | ● | | | |
| RAEBURN, JO (HM16865) | ● | | | | ● | ● | | ● | | ● | | | | | | |
| RANDALL, CAROLINE (HM16926) | ● | ● | ● | ● | ● | ● | ● | ● | ● | ● | ● | ● | ● | ● | ● | ● |
| RAVENSCROFT CENTRE (HM16967) | ● | | | | | | | | | | | | | | | |
| READ, CHARLES (HM16993) | | | | | | ● | | | | | | | | | | |
| REEVE, MALCOLM (HM17060) | | | | | | | | | | | | | | | | |
| REFLEXOLOGY (HM17077) | | ● | | | ● | | | | | | | | | | | |
| REFLEXOLOGY CLINIC (HM17089) | | | | | | | | | | | | | | | | |
| RELAXATION PLACE (HM17166) | | ● | | | | | | | | | | | | | | |
| REPLINGHAM CLINIC (HM17195) | ● | ● | | | | ● | | | | ● | ● | | ● | | | |
| ROBERTS, MATT (HM17420) | ● | | | | | | | | | | | | | | | |
| ROBINSON, GABIE (HM17473) | | | | | | | | | | ● | | | | | | |
| ROEHAMPTON PHYSIO/SPORTS (HM17535) | | | | | | | | | | | | | | | | |
| ROSE, NICHOLAS (HM17613) | | | | | | | | | | ● | | | | | | |
| RUTHERFORD, BERWYN (HM17780) | | | | | | | | | | | | | | | | |
| SALTER, LIZ (HM17869) | ● | ● | ● | ● | ● | ● | | ● | ● | ● | ● | ● | ● | ● | ● | ● |
| SAYER CLINIC (HM17994) | | | | | | | | | | | | | | | | |
| SAYER CLINIC (HM17993) | | | | | | ● | ● | | | | | | | | | |
| SEARBY, JOE (HM18174) | ● | | | | | | ● | | | ● | | | | | | |
| SEEAR, MICHAEL (DR) (HM18189) | ● | ● | | | | ● | | | | ● | | | | | | |
| SEYMOUR PRACTICE (HM18257) | | | | | | | | | | | | | | | | |

| Business by County with Reference no. | Hair Problems | Halitosis | Hand Problems | Hay Fever | Headaches | Hearing Problems | High Blood Pressure | Hip Complaints | Hyperactivity | Hypoglycaemia | Impotence | Incontinence | Indigestion | Infertility | Influenza | Ingrowing Toenails |
|---|---|---|---|---|---|---|---|---|---|---|---|---|---|---|---|---|
| PHYSIO ONE (HM16202) | | | | | ● | | | ● | | | | | | | | |
| PHYSIO SOLUTIONS (HM16205) | | | | | ● | | | | | | | | | | | |
| PINNER ROAD PHYSIOTHERAPY (HM16316) | | | | | | | | | | | | | | | | |
| PODIATRY CLINIC (HM16393) | | | | | | | | ● | | | | | | | | |
| PRICE, GILLIAN (HM16575) | ● | ● | ● | ● | ● | ● | ● | ● | ● | ● | ● | ● | ● | ● | ● | |
| PRICE, SANDRA (HM16594) | | | | | ● | | | ● | | | | | | | | |
| PRICE, SANDRA (HM16595) | | | | | ● | | | ● | | | | | | | | |
| PRIMROSE HEALING CENTRE (HM16616) | | | | | | | | | | | ● | | | | | |
| PRIVATE HEALTH CLINIC (HM16644) | ● | ● | ● | ● | ● | ● | ● | ● | ● | ● | ● | ● | ● | ● | ● | |
| PRIVATE PRACTICE (HM16649) | | | | | | | | | | | | | | | | |
| PSYCHOTHERAPY CENTRE (HM16734) | | | | ● | ● | | | | | | ● | | | ● | | |
| PSYCHOTHERAPY SERVICES (HM16737) | | | | | | | | | | | | | | | | |
| PUTNEY CHIROPRACTIC (HM16780) | | | | | ● | | | ● | | | | | ● | | | |
| RACHEL YOUNG - HYPNOTHERAPIST (HM16837) | ● | | | ● | ● | ● | ● | ● | | | ● | | ● | ● | ● | |
| RAEBURN, JO (HM16865) | ● | | ● | ● | ● | | ● | | | | | | ● | | ● | |
| RANDALL, CAROLINE (HM16926) | ● | ● | ● | ● | ● | ● | ● | ● | ● | ● | ● | ● | ● | ● | ● | |
| RAVENSCROFT CENTRE (HM16967) | | | | | ● | | | | | | | | | | | |
| READ, CHARLES (HM16993) | | | ● | | ● | | | ● | | | | | | | | |
| REEVE, MALCOLM (HM17060) | | | | | | | | ● | | | | | | | | |
| REFLEXOLOGY (HM17077) | | | | | ● | | ● | | ● | ● | ● | ● | ● | ● | | |
| REFLEXOLOGY CLINIC (HM17089) | | | | | ● | | | | | | | | | | | |
| RELAXATION PLACE (HM17166) | | | | | ● | | | | | | | | | | | |
| REPLINGHAM CLINIC (HM17195) | | | | ● | ● | | ● | ● | ● | | ● | | ● | ● | ● | |
| ROBERTS, MATT (HM17420) | | | | | | | | | | | ● | | | | | |
| ROBINSON, GABIE (HM17473) | | | | | ● | | ● | | | | | | ● | | | |
| ROEHAMPTON PHYSIO/SPORTS (HM17535) | | | | | | | | ● | | | | | | | | |
| ROSE, NICHOLAS (HM17613) | | | | | ● | | | ● | | | | | | | | |
| RUTHERFORD, BERWYN (HM17780) | | | ● | | ● | | | ● | | | | | | | | |
| SALTER, LIZ (HM17869) | ● | ● | ● | ● | ● | ● | ● | | ● | ● | ● | ● | ● | ● | ● | |
| SAYER CLINIC (HM17994) | | | | | ● | | | ● | | | | | | | | |
| SAYER CLINIC (HM17993) | | | ● | | ● | | | ● | | | | | | | | |
| SEARBY, JOE (HM18174) | | | ● | | ● | | ● | ● | | | | | | | | |
| SEEAR, MICHAEL (DR) (HM18189) | | | ● | ● | ● | | ● | ● | | | ● | | ● | ● | | |
| SEYMOUR PRACTICE (HM18257) | | | | ● | ● | | | ● | | | | | | | | |

# D - I Conditions treated at Practices/Businesses

| Business by County with Reference no. | Dandruff | Deafness | Depression | Diabetes | Diarrhoea | Digestive Problems | Diverticulitis | Dizziness | Dyslexia | Dyspraxia | Ear Disorders | Eczema | ENT Disorders | Epilepsy | Eye Disorders | Fatigue | Fears | Fertility Problems | Fever | Fibroids | Flatulence | Foot Problems | Fractures | Fungal Infections | Gallstones | Gastrointestinal Problems | Genital Herpes | Gingivitis | Glandular Fever | Glaucoma | Gout | Gum Disease | Hair Problems | Halitosis | Hand Problems | Hay Fever | Headaches | Hearing Problems | High Blood Pressure | Hip Complaints | Hyperactivity | Hypoglycaemia | Impotence | Incontinence | Indigestion | Infertility | Influenza | Ingrowing Toenails |
|---|---|---|---|---|---|---|---|---|---|---|---|---|---|---|---|---|---|---|---|---|---|---|---|---|---|---|---|---|---|---|---|---|---|---|---|---|---|---|---|---|---|---|---|---|---|---|---|
| SHIATSU PLACE (HM18458) | | | ● | | ● | ● | | | | | | ● | | | | ● | ● | ● | | ● | ● | ● | | | | | | | | | | | | | ● | ● | ● | ● | ● | ● | | | ● | ● | ● | ● | | |
| SHIATSU STUDIO (HM18465) | | | ● | | | ● | | | | | | | | | | | | | | | | | | | | | | | | | | | | | | | | | | | | | | | | | | |
| SIMON, CAROLYN (HM18567) | | | | | | ● | | | | | | | | | | ● | | | | | | | | | | | | | | | | | | | | | | | | | | | | | | | | |
| SIMPLY HERBAL CLINIC (HM18577) | ● | ● | ● | ● | ● | ● | ● | ● | ● | ● | ● | ● | ● | ● | ● | ● | ● | ● | ● | ● | ● | ● | | ● | ● | ● | ● | ● | ● | ● | ● | ● | ● | ● | ● | ● | ● | ● | ● | ● | ● | ● | ● | ● | ● | ● | ● | |
| SIMPSON, STELLA (HM18599) | | | ● | | ● | ● | ● | ● | | | ● | ● | ● | ● | ● | ● | ● | ● | | | ● | ● | ● | ● | ● | ● | ● | | ● | | ● | | | | | ● | ● | | ● | ● | | ● | ● | | ● | ● | ● | |
| SLADE OSTEOPATHIC PRACTICE (HM18667) | | | | | | | | | | | | | | | | | | | | | | | | | | | | | | | | | | | | | ● | | | ● | | | | | | | | |
| SOUTH LONDON NATURAL HLTH CTRE (HM18911) | ● | ● | ● | ● | ● | ● | ● | ● | ● | ● | ● | ● | ● | ● | ● | ● | ● | ● | ● | ● | ● | ● | ● | ● | ● | ● | ● | ● | ● | ● | ● | ● | ● | ● | ● | ● | ● | ● | ● | ● | ● | ● | ● | ● | ● | ● | ● | |
| SOUTHFIELDS CLINIC (HM18935) | | | ● | | ● | | | | | | | | | | | ● | | | | | | | | | | | | | | | | | | | | ● | ● | | | | | | | | ● | | | |
| SPALL MEDICAL CENTRE (HM18957) | ● | | ● | ● | ● | ● | | | | | | ● | | | | ● | ● | ● | | | | | | | ● | ● | ● | | | | ● | | ● | | | ● | ● | | ● | | | | ● | ● | ● | ● | | |
| SPECIALIST HEALTH (HM18972) | | | | | | | | | | | | | | | | | | | | | | ● | | | | | | | | | | | | | ● | | ● | | | ● | | | | | | | | |
| SPENCER, PIERS (HM19001) | | | | | | | | | | | | | | | | | | | | | | | | | | | | | | | | | | | | | | | | ● | | | | | | | | |
| SPYROS MOUZOURIDES (HM19056) | ● | ● | ● | ● | ● | ● | ● | ● | ● | ● | ● | ● | ● | ● | ● | ● | ● | ● | ● | ● | ● | ● | | ● | ● | ● | ● | ● | ● | ● | ● | ● | ● | ● | ● | ● | ● | ● | ● | ● | ● | ● | ● | ● | ● | ● | ● | |
| STANMORE PHYSIO PRACTICE (HM19132) | | | | | | | | | | | | | | | | | | | | | | | | | | | | | | | | | | | ● | | | | | ● | | | | | | | | |
| STOBEZKI, YAEL (HM19307) | | | ● | | | | | | | | | | | | | | ● | | | | | | | | | | | | | | | | | | | | | | | | | | | | | | | |
| STRONG, STELLA (HM19419) | | | | | | | | | | | | | | | | ● | | | | | | | | | | ● | | | | | | | | | ● | | | | | | | | | | | | | |
| T C M HEALTHCARE (HM19640) | | | ● | | | | | | | | | | | | | | | | | | | | | | | | | | | | | | | | | | | | ● | | | | | | | | | |
| THOMPSON, MARK (HM19990) | | | ● | ● | ● | ● | ● | | | | | | | | | ● | | ● | | | ● | ● | | | ● | ● | | | | | | ● | | | | | ● | | ● | ● | ● | ● | | | ● | ● | | |
| THURGOOD, SIMON (HM20047) | | | | | | | | | | | | | | | | | | | | | | | | | | | | | | | | | | | | | ● | | | | | | | | | | | |
| TORRIDON COMP THERAPY CLINIC (HM20173) | | | ● | | | ● | | | | | | | | | | | | | | | | | | ● | | | | | | | | | | | | ● | ● | | | | ● | | | | ● | | | |
| TRADITIONAL ACUPUNCTURE CENTRE (HM20218) | | | ● | | | | | ● | | | | | | | | ● | | | | | | | | | | | | | | | | | | | | ● | ● | | | ● | | | | | ● | | | |
| TRANQUILITY (HM20255) | | | ● | | ● | ● | | ● | | | ● | ● | | | ● | ● | ● | ● | ● | ● | ● | ● | | | ● | ● | | ● | ● | | ● | ● | ● | ● | ● | ● | ● | | ● | | ● | ● | | ● | ● | ● | ● | |
| TROHEAR, PATRICIA (HM20345) | | | | | | | | | | | | | | | | | ● | | | | | | | | | | | | | | | | | | | | | | | | | | | | | | | |
| TURMAINE, VICKI (HM20410) | ● | | ● | | ● | ● | ● | ● | | | ● | ● | ● | | | | ● | ● | ● | ● | ● | | ● | ● | ● | ● | | ● | ● | | | ● | ● | ● | ● | ● | ● | | | | ● | | ● | ● | ● | ● | ● | |
| TURNBULL, JO (HM20413) | | ● | ● | ● | ● | ● | | | ● | ● | ● | | ● | | | ● | ● | ● | ● | ● | ● | | ● | | ● | ● | | | ● | | ● | | | | | | ● | ● | ● | ● | ● | ● | ● | | ● | ● | ● | |
| TURNER, TERI (HM20438) | | | | | | | | | | | | | | | | | | | | | | | | | | | | | | | | | | | | | ● | | | ● | | | | | | | | |
| TWICKENHAM PHYSIOFIRST CENTRE (HM20451) | | | | | | | | | | | | | | | | | | | | | | | | | | | | | | | | | | | | | | | | ● | | | | | | | | |
| UKCP (HM20490) | | | ● | | | | | | | | | | | | | ● | ● | | | | | | | | | | | | | | | | | | | | | | | | ● | | | | | | | |
| UNDERHILL, K (HM20496) | | | | | | | | ● | | | | | | | | | | | | | | | | | | | | | | | | | | | | | ● | | | | | | | | | | | |
| VALE PRACTICE (HM20551) | ● | ● | ● | ● | ● | ● | ● | ● | ● | ● | ● | ● | ● | ● | ● | ● | ● | ● | ● | ● | ● | ● | ● | ● | ● | ● | ● | ● | ● | ● | ● | ● | ● | ● | ● | ● | ● | ● | ● | ● | ● | ● | ● | ● | ● | ● | ● | |
| VANBRUGH PHYSIOTHERAPY CLINIC (HM20575) | | | | | | ● | | | | | | | | | | | | | | | | | | | | | | | | | | | | | | | ● | | | ● | | | | | | | | |
| WART, D (HM20959) | | | | | | | | | | | | | | | | | | | | | | | | | | | | | | | | | | | | | ● | | | ● | | | | | | | | |
| WARWICK ALTERNATIVE HEALTH (HM20961) | | | ● | | | | | | | | | | | | | | ● | | | | | | | | | | | | | | | | | | | | ● | | | ● | | | | | | | | |
| WEBER, MARALYN (HM21082) | | ● | ● | ● | ● | ● | ● | ● | | | ● | ● | ● | | ● | ● | ● | ● | | ● | ● | ● | | ● | ● | ● | | ● | | ● | ● | ● | | | ● | ● | ● | ● | ● | ● | ● | ● | ● | ● | ● | ● | ● | |
| WELL BEING (HM21131) | | | ● | | ● | ● | | ● | | | ● | ● | | | | ● | ● | ● | ● | ● | ● | | | | | ● | | | | | | | | | | ● | ● | ● | ● | | ● | | | | ● | ● | ● | |

# D - I Conditions treated at Practices/Businesses

| Business by County with Reference no. | Dandruff | Deafness | Depression | Diabetes | Diarrhoea | Digestive Problems | Diverticulitis | Dizziness | Dyslexia | Dyspraxia | Ear Disorders | Eczema | ENT Disorders | Epilepsy | Eye Disorders | Fatigue | Fears | Fertility Problems | Fever | Fibroids | Flatulence | Foot Problems | Fractures | Fungal Infections | Gallstones | Gastrointestinal Problems | Genital Herpes | Gingivitis | Glandular Fever | Glaucoma | Gout | Gum Disease | Hair Problems | Halitosis | Hand Problems | Hay Fever | Headaches | Hearing Problems | High Blood Pressure | Hip Complaints | Hyperactivity | Hypoglycaemia | Impotence | Incontinence | Indigestion | Infertility | Influenza | Ingrowing Toenails |
|---|---|---|---|---|---|---|---|---|---|---|---|---|---|---|---|---|---|---|---|---|---|---|---|---|---|---|---|---|---|---|---|---|---|---|---|---|---|---|---|---|---|---|---|---|---|---|---|
| WEST LONDON HOLISTIC CENTRE (HM21226) | | | ● | ● | | ● | | | | | | ● | | | | | | | | | | | | | | | | | | | | | | | | | | | | | ● | | ● | | | | | |
| WEST LONDON PSYCHOTHERAPY (HM21227) | | | ● | | | | | | | | | | | | | | | | | | | | | | | | | | | | | | | | | | | | | | | | | | | | | |
| WEST LONDON YOGA SHALA (HM21228) | | | ● | | | | | ● | | | | | | | | ● | ● | ● | | | | ● | | | | | | | | | | | | | | | | | ● | | | | | | | | | |
| WESTERN, G (HM21265) | | | | | | | | | | | | | | | | | | | | | | | | | | | | | | | | | | | | | ● | | | ● | | | | | | | | |
| WHITE HART LANE THERAPY CENTRE (HM21338) | | | | | | | | | | | | | | | | | | | | | | ● | | | | | | | | | | | | | | | ● | | | ● | | | | | | | | |
| WIGHAM, A (HM21468) | | | ● | | | | | | | | | | | | | | ● | | | | | | | | | | | | | | | | | | | | | | | | | | | | | | | |
| WILKINSON, GILL (HM21505) | | | ● | | | | | | | | | | | | | | ● | | | | | | | | | | | | | | | | | | | | | | | | | | | | | | | |
| WILLIAMS, B A (HM21541) | | | ● | | ● | | | | | | | | | | | ● | | | | | | ● | | | | | | | | | | | | | | ● | ● | | | ● | | | | | | | | |
| WILLIAMS, IAN (HM21565) | | | | | | | | | | | | | | | | | | | | | | | | | | | | | | | | | | | | | | | | | | | | | | | | ● |
| WILLIAMS, RUTH (HM21588) | | | ● | | | | | | | | | | | | | | ● | | | | | | | | | | | | | | | | | | | | | | | | | | | | | | | |
| WILLMOTT, SUSAN (HM21623) | | | ● | | | | | | | | | | | | | | ● | | | | | | | | | | | | | | | | | | | | | | | | | | | | | | | |
| WILSON, CHRISTOPHER (HM21651) | | | | | | | | | | | | | | | | | | | | | | ● | | | | | | | | | | | | | | | | | | | | | | | | | | |
| WINCHMORE CLINIC OF OSTEOPATHY (HM21694) | | | | | | | | ● | | | | | | | | | | | | | | | | | | | | | | | | | | | ● | | ● | | | ● | | | | | | | | |
| WOODBERRY CLINIC (HM21815) | | | | | | | | | | | | | | | | | | | | | | | | | | | | | | | | | | | | | ● | | | | | | | | | | | |
| WOOLF, PERRY (HM21872) | | | | ● | | | | | | | | | | | | | | | | | | ● | | ● | | | | | | | ● | | | | | | | | | | | | | | | | | ● |
| WORLD OF LIGHT (HM21898) | ● | ● | ● | ● | ● | ● | ● | ● | ● | ● | ● | ● | ● | ● | ● | ● | ● | ● | ● | ● | ● | ● | ● | ● | ● | ● | ● | ● | ● | ● | ● | ● | ● | ● | ● | ● | ● | ● | ● | ● | ● | ● | ● | ● | ● | ● | ● | |
| WREN, ANTHONY (HM21920) | | | ● | | | ● | | | | | | | | | ● | ● | | | | | | | | | | | | | | | | | | | | | ● | | | | ● | | | | | | | |
| WRIGHT, JENNY (HM21936) | | | ● | | | | | | | | | | | | | ● | ● | | | | | | | | | | | | | | | | | | | | | | ● | | | | | | | | | |
| WYNNE-SIMMONS, A (DR) (HM21979) | ● | | ● | ● | ● | ● | ● | ● | | | ● | ● | ● | ● | | ● | ● | ● | ● | ● | ● | ● | ● | ● | | ● | ● | | ● | | ● | | | | ● | ● | ● | | ● | | ● | | ● | ● | ● | ● | ● | |
| YING, FRANK (HM22014) | | | | | | | | | | | | | | | | | | | | | | ● | | | | | | | | | | | | | ● | | ● | | | ● | | | | | | | | |
| YOGA THERAPY CENTRE (HM22033) | | | | | | ● | | | | | | | | | | ● | | | | | | | | | | | | | | | | | | | | | | | | | | | | | | | | |
| ZEN HEALTH CENTRE (HM22100) | ● | | ● | ● | ● | ● | ● | ● | | | ● | ● | | ● | ● | ● | ● | ● | ● | | ● | ● | ● | ● | ● | ● | ● | ● | ● | | ● | ● | ● | | ● | ● | ● | ● | ● | ● | ● | ● | ● | ● | ● | ● | ● | |
| ZEN SHIATSU & HEALING TAO (HM22101) | ● | | ● | | ● | | | | | | | | | ● | | ● | ● | ● | | ● | ● | | | | ● | ● | | | | | | | | | | | ● | | | ● | | | | | | ● | | |
| **MANCHESTER (GREATER)** | | | | | | | | | | | | | | | | | | | | | | | | | | | | | | | | | | | | | | | | | | | | | | | | |
| A SIR ROBERTS ALT PLACE (HM00045) | ● | | ● | | | | ● | | | | | ● | | ● | | ● | ● | ● | | | | | | | ● | | | | | | | | ● | | | | ● | | ● | | ● | | ● | | | ● | | |
| ACUMEDIC (HM00220) | | | | | | ● | | | | | | ● | | | | ● | | ● | | | | | | | | | | | | | | | | ● | | ● | ● | | ● | | | | ● | | | | | |
| ACUPUNCTURE CENTRE (HM00252) | | | ● | | ● | ● | | ● | | | ● | | | | | ● | | ● | | | ● | | | | | ● | | | | | ● | | | | | ● | ● | | ● | | | | | | ● | ● | | |
| ADVANCED CHIROPODY SURGERY (HM00394) | | | | | | | | | | | | | | | | | | | | | | ● | | ● | | | | | | | | | | | | | | | | | | | | | | | | |
| ADVANCED PHYSIOTHERAPY CLINIC (HM00403) | | | | | | | | | | | | | | | | | | | | | | ● | ● | | | | | | | | | | | | ● | | | | | ● | | | | | | | | |
| ALL IN THE MIND (HM00582) | | | ● | | | | | | | | | | | | | ● | ● | ● | | | | | | | | | | | | | | | | | | | | | ● | | | | | | | ● | | |
| AROMATHERAPY BY SARA (HM01098) | | | | | | | | | | | | | | | | | | | | | | | | | | | | | | | | | | | | | ● | | | | | | | | | | | |
| AROMATHERAPY LADIES MASSAGE (HM01118) | ● | ● | ● | ● | ● | ● | ● | ● | ● | ● | ● | ● | ● | ● | ● | ● | ● | ● | ● | ● | ● | ● | ● | ● | ● | ● | ● | ● | ● | ● | ● | ● | ● | ● | ● | ● | ● | ● | ● | ● | ● | ● | ● | ● | ● | ● | ● | |
| ASTLEY COMPLEMENTARY CENTRE (HM01300) | | | ● | | | ● | | | | | | | | | | | ● | | | | ● | | | | | | | | | | | | | ● | | | | | | | ● | | | | ● | | | |
| BEAUTY THERAPY CENTRE (HM02006) | | | ● | | | | | | | | | | | | | | | | | | | | | | | | | | | | | | | | | | ● | | | | | | | | | | | |

# D - I Conditions treated at Practices/Businesses

Business by County with Reference no.

| Business | Dandruff | Deafness | Depression | Diabetes | Diarrhoea | Digestive Problems | Diverticulitis | Dizziness | Dyslexia | Dyspraxia | Ear Disorders | Eczema | ENT Disorders | Epilepsy | Eye Disorders | Fatigue | Fears | Fertility Problems | Fever | Fibroids | Flatulence | Foot Problems |
|---|---|---|---|---|---|---|---|---|---|---|---|---|---|---|---|---|---|---|---|---|---|---|
| BRAMHALL CHIROPRACTIC CLINIC (HM02898) | | | ● | | | | | ● | | | | | | | | ● | ● | | | | | ● |
| BURGESS, KAREN (HM03377) | | | | | | | | | | | | | | | | | | | | | | ● |
| C CARTLEDGE REFLEXOLOGY (HM03521) | ● | ● | ● | ● | ● | ● | ● | ● | ● | ● | ● | ● | ● | ● | ● | ● | ● | ● | ● | ● | ● | ● |
| CHARTERED PHYSIOTHERAPY CLINIC (HM04046) | | | | | | | | ● | | | | | | | | | | | | | | ● |
| CHORLTON STRESS MANAGEMENT (HM04430) | | | ● | | | | | | | | | ● | | | | | ● | | | | | |
| CLARENDON CLINIC (HM04540) | | | ● | | | | | | | | | | | | | ● | | | | | | ● |
| COHEN, D (DR) (HM04789) | | | | | | ● | | | | | | ● | ● | | | | | ● | | | | |
| COLLINGE, J C (HM04863) | | | | | | | | | | | | | | | | | | | | | | ● |
| CROSSWAY CLINIC (HM05491) | | | ● | | | | | | | | | | | | | | ● | | | | | ● |
| DAVEENA ASSOCIATES (HM05763) | | | ● | | | | | | | | | | | | | ● | ● | | | | | |
| DIDSBURY CHIROPRACTIC CLINIC (HM06090) | | | | | | | | | | | | | | | | | | | | | | ● |
| EVANS, DAVID (HM06967) | | | ● | ● | ● | ● | ● | ● | | | | ● | | ● | | ● | ● | ● | | | | |
| GRAHAM COOMBE - MCTIMONEY (HM08337) | | | | | | ● | | ● | | | | | | | | | | | | | | |
| GUILD OF PRACTITIONERS (HM08627) | | | | | | | | | | | | | | | | | | | | | | |
| HOLMED CLINIC (HM10038) | | | | | | | | | | | | | | | | | | | | | | |
| HORRIDGE, S P (HM10182) | | | | ● | | | | | | | | | | | | | | | | | | |
| HUMAN TOUCH CENTRE (HM10366) | | | | | | | | | | | | ● | | | | ● | | | | | | |
| IBBOTSON, GEOFF (DR) (HM10565) | | | ● | | | ● | | | | | | ● | | | | ● | | | | | | |
| M J HAYLETT - PHYSIOTHERAPIST (HM12802) | | | | | | | | | | | | | | | | | | | | | | |
| MOBILE COMPLEMENTARY THERAPIES (HM14029) | | | ● | | | | | | | | | | | | | ● | | | | | | |
| MOUNT STREET COMP THERAPIES (HM14291) | | | ● | | | ● | | | | | | | | | | ● | | | | ● | | |
| NICKI HAVES PHYSIO CLINIC (HM14923) | | | | | | | | | | | | | | | | | | | | | | |
| NIVERN, D (HM14954) | | | ● | | | | | | | | | | | | | ● | ● | | | | ● | |
| SCHOFIELD, G A (HM18018) | | | ● | ● | ● | ● | ● | ● | | | ● | ● | ● | ● | | ● | ● | ● | ● | | ● | ● |
| SHANGHAI ACUPUNCTURE CLINIC (HM18280) | ● | ● | ● | ● | ● | ● | ● | ● | ● | ● | ● | ● | ● | ● | ● | ● | ● | ● | ● | ● | ● | ● |
| ST JOHN STREET PHYSIO PRACTICE (HM19080) | | | | | | | | | | | | | | | | | | | | | | |
| STIRLING, DIANNE (HM19301) | | | ● | | | | | | | | | | | | | ● | | | | | | |
| SWINTON HEALTH FOODS (HM19600) | | | ● | | ● | ● | | | | | | | | | | ● | ● | | | | ● | |
| WAINWRIGHT, P (HM20739) | | | | ● | | | | | | | | | | | | | | | | | | ● |
| **MERSEYSIDE** | | | | | | | | | | | | | | | | | | | | | | |
| ABBEY FOOT CLINIC (HM00083) | | | | | | | | | | | | | | | | | | | | | | ● |
| ACUPUNCTURE CLINIC (HM00263) | | | ● | | | ● | ● | ● | | | | | ● | | | ● | ● | | | | | ● |
| AIGBURTH MCTIMONEY CLINIC (HM00427) | | | | | | ● | | ● | ● | ● | ● | | | | | ● | | | | | | |
| AINTREE OSTEOPATHIC (HM00439) | | | ● | | | | | ● | | | ● | | | | | | | | | | | ● |

| Business | Fractures | Fungal Infections | Gallstones | Gastrointestinal Problems | Genital Herpes | Gingivitis | Glandular Fever | Glaucoma | Gout | Gum Disease | Hair Problems | Halitosis | Hand Problems | Hay Fever | Headaches | Hearing Problems | High Blood Pressure | Hip Complaints | Hyperactivity | Hypoglycaemia | Impotence | Incontinence | Indigestion | Infertility | Influenza | Ingrowing Toenails |
|---|---|---|---|---|---|---|---|---|---|---|---|---|---|---|---|---|---|---|---|---|---|---|---|---|---|---|
| BRAMHALL CHIROPRACTIC CLINIC (HM02898) | | | | | | | | | | | | | ● | | ● | | | ● | | | | | | | | |
| BURGESS, KAREN (HM03377) | | ● | | | | | | | ● | | | | ● | | | | | | | | | | | | | |
| C CARTLEDGE REFLEXOLOGY (HM03521) | ● | ● | ● | ● | ● | ● | ● | ● | ● | ● | ● | ● | ● | ● | ● | ● | ● | ● | ● | ● | ● | ● | ● | ● | ● | |
| CHARTERED PHYSIOTHERAPY CLINIC (HM04046) | ● | | | | | | | | | | | | | | ● | | | | | | | | | | | |
| CHORLTON STRESS MANAGEMENT (HM04430) | | | | | | | | | | | | | | | | | | | | | ● | | | | | |
| CLARENDON CLINIC (HM04540) | ● | | | | | | | | | | | | ● | | ● | | | ● | | | | | ● | | | |
| COHEN, D (DR) (HM04789) | | | | | | | ● | | | | | | | | | | | | | | | | | | | |
| COLLINGE, J C (HM04863) | | | | | | | | | ● | | | | | | ● | | | | | | | ● | | | | |
| CROSSWAY CLINIC (HM05491) | | | | | | | | | | | | | ● | | ● | | | ● | | | | | | | | |
| DAVEENA ASSOCIATES (HM05763) | | | | | | | | | | | | | | | | | | | | | | | | | | |
| DIDSBURY CHIROPRACTIC CLINIC (HM06090) | | | | | | | | | | | | | | | ● | | | | | | | | | | | |
| EVANS, DAVID (HM06967) | | | ● | ● | | | | | | | ● | | | ● | ● | | ● | | ● | | ● | ● | ● | ● | | |
| GRAHAM COOMBE - MCTIMONEY (HM08337) | | | | | | | | | | | | | | | ● | | | ● | | | | | | | | |
| GUILD OF PRACTITIONERS (HM08627) | ● | | | | | | | | | | | | | | ● | | | | | | | | | | | |
| HOLMED CLINIC (HM10038) | | | | | | | | | | | | | | | ● | | | ● | | | | | | | | |
| HORRIDGE, S P (HM10182) | | | | | | | | | | | | | | | | | | | | | | | | | | |
| HUMAN TOUCH CENTRE (HM10366) | | | | | | | | | | | | | | | ● | | | | | | | | | ● | | |
| IBBOTSON, GEOFF (DR) (HM10565) | | | | | | | | | | | | | | | ● | | | | | | ● | | | | | |
| M J HAYLETT - PHYSIOTHERAPIST (HM12802) | ● | | | | | | | | | | | | | | ● | | | | | | | | | | | |
| MOBILE COMPLEMENTARY THERAPIES (HM14029) | | | | | | | | | | | | | | | ● | | | | | | | | | | | |
| MOUNT STREET COMP THERAPIES (HM14291) | | | | | | | | | | | | | | | | | | | | | | | | ● | | |
| NICKI HAVES PHYSIO CLINIC (HM14923) | | | | | | | | | | | | | | | | | | ● | | | | | | | | |
| NIVERN, D (HM14954) | | ● | | | | | | | ● | | ● | | ● | | ● | | ● | ● | | | ● | | ● | | ● | |
| SCHOFIELD, G A (HM18018) | | ● | ● | ● | | | | | ● | | | | | | ● | ● | ● | ● | | | | ● | ● | ● | | |
| SHANGHAI ACUPUNCTURE CLINIC (HM18280) | ● | ● | ● | ● | ● | ● | ● | ● | ● | ● | ● | ● | ● | ● | ● | ● | ● | ● | ● | ● | ● | ● | ● | ● | ● | |
| ST JOHN STREET PHYSIO PRACTICE (HM19080) | ● | | | | | | | | | | | | | | | | | | | | | | | | | |
| STIRLING, DIANNE (HM19301) | | | | | | | | | | | | | | | ● | | | | | | | | | | | |
| SWINTON HEALTH FOODS (HM19600) | | | | ● | | ● | | | ● | ● | ● | | | | ● | | ● | | ● | ● | | ● | ● | | | |
| WAINWRIGHT, P (HM20739) | | ● | | | | | | | ● | | | | | | | | | | | | | | | | | |
| **MERSEYSIDE** | | | | | | | | | | | | | | | | | | | | | | | | | | |
| ABBEY FOOT CLINIC (HM00083) | | ● | | | | | | | | | | | | | | | | | | | | | | | | |
| ACUPUNCTURE CLINIC (HM00263) | | | | | | | | | ● | | | | ● | ● | ● | | ● | ● | | | | | ● | | | |
| AIGBURTH MCTIMONEY CLINIC (HM00427) | | | | ● | | | | | ● | | | | | | ● | ● | ● | ● | ● | | | | | | | |
| AINTREE OSTEOPATHIC (HM00439) | | | | ● | | | | | | | | | ● | ● | ● | | ● | ● | | | | | ● | | | |

# D - I Conditions treated at Practices/Businesses

| Business by County with Reference no. | Dandruff | Deafness | Depression | Diabetes | Diarrhoea | Digestive Problems | Diverticulitis | Dizziness | Dyslexia | Dyspraxia | Ear Disorders | Eczema | ENT Disorders | Epilepsy | Eye Disorders | Fatigue | Fears | Fertility Problems | Fever | Fibroids | Flatulence | Foot Problems | Fractures | Fungal Infections | Gallstones | Gastrointestinal Problems | Genital Herpes | Gingivitis | Glandular Fever | Glaucoma | Gout | Gum Disease | Hair Problems | Halitosis | Hand Problems | Hay Fever | Headaches | Hearing Problems | High Blood Pressure | Hip Complaints | Hyperactivity | Hypoglycaemia | Impotence | Incontinence | Indigestion | Infertility | Influenza | Ingrowing Toenails |
|---|---|---|---|---|---|---|---|---|---|---|---|---|---|---|---|---|---|---|---|---|---|---|---|---|---|---|---|---|---|---|---|---|---|---|---|---|---|---|---|---|---|---|---|---|---|---|---|---|
| ALLERTON HEALTH CENTRE (HM00639) |  |  | ● |  | ● | ● |  | ● |  |  |  |  |  |  |  | ● |  |  |  |  |  | ● |  | ● |  |  |  |  |  |  |  |  |  |  |  | ● | ● |  |  |  |  |  |  |  |  |  |  |  |
| BIMPSON, PETER (HM02311) |  |  | ● |  |  |  |  |  |  |  |  |  |  |  |  | ● |  |  |  |  |  |  |  |  |  |  |  |  |  |  |  |  |  |  |  |  | ● |  |  |  |  |  |  |  |  |  |  |  |
| BOLTON, TOM (HM02663) |  |  | ● |  |  |  |  |  |  |  |  |  |  |  |  |  |  |  |  |  |  |  |  |  |  |  |  |  |  |  |  |  |  |  |  |  |  |  |  |  |  |  |  |  |  |  |  |  |
| BOYLE, ANDREW (HM02826) |  |  | ● | ● | ● | ● | ● | ● |  |  |  | ● |  |  |  | ● | ● | ● |  |  |  | ● | ● | ● |  | ● |  |  |  |  | ● |  | ● |  | ● | ● | ● |  |  | ● | ● |  |  |  | ● | ● |  |  |
| BRENNAN, M A (HM02958) |  |  |  |  |  |  |  |  |  |  |  |  |  |  |  |  |  |  |  |  |  | ● |  | ● |  |  |  |  |  |  |  |  |  |  |  |  |  |  |  |  |  |  |  |  |  |  |  |  |
| CARTER, G R (HM03778) |  |  |  |  |  |  |  |  |  |  |  |  |  |  |  |  |  |  |  |  |  | ● |  | ● |  |  |  |  |  |  |  |  |  |  |  |  |  |  |  |  |  |  |  |  |  |  |  | ● |
| CAWLEY, TONY (HM03871) |  |  | ● |  |  |  |  |  |  |  |  |  |  |  |  |  | ● |  |  |  |  |  |  |  |  |  |  |  |  |  |  |  |  |  |  |  |  |  |  |  |  |  |  |  |  |  |  |  |
| CONCANNON, DEIRDRE (HM04965) |  |  |  |  |  |  |  |  |  |  |  |  |  |  |  |  |  |  |  |  |  |  |  |  |  |  |  |  |  |  |  |  |  |  |  |  | ● |  |  | ● |  |  |  |  |  |  |  |  |
| D A F CLINIC (HM05655) |  |  | ● |  |  |  |  | ● |  |  |  |  |  |  |  | ● |  |  |  |  |  | ● |  |  |  |  |  |  |  |  |  |  |  |  |  |  |  |  | ● |  |  |  | ● |  |  |  |  |  |
| DARE TO CARE (HM05739) |  |  | ● |  |  |  |  |  |  |  |  |  |  |  |  |  |  |  |  |  |  |  |  |  |  |  |  |  |  |  |  |  |  |  |  |  | ● |  |  |  |  |  |  |  |  |  |  |  |
| ECCLES CHIROPODY SERVICES (HM06572) |  |  |  |  |  |  |  |  |  |  |  |  |  |  |  |  |  |  |  |  |  | ● |  |  |  |  |  |  |  |  |  |  |  |  |  |  |  |  |  |  |  |  |  |  |  |  |  |  |
| FARMER, BARBARA (HM01681) |  |  |  |  |  |  |  | ● |  |  |  |  |  |  |  |  |  |  |  |  |  | ● | ● |  |  |  |  |  |  |  |  |  |  |  | ● |  | ● |  |  | ● |  |  |  |  |  |  |  |  |
| FRESHLEA PRIVATE CLINICS (HM07738) |  |  |  |  |  |  |  |  |  |  |  |  |  |  |  |  |  |  |  |  |  |  |  |  |  |  |  |  |  |  |  |  |  |  |  |  | ● |  |  | ● |  |  |  |  |  |  |  |  |
| GATEAUD, S (HM07924) |  |  |  | ● |  |  |  |  |  |  |  | ● |  |  |  |  |  |  |  |  |  |  |  |  |  |  |  |  |  |  |  |  |  |  |  |  | ● |  | ● | ● |  |  |  |  |  |  |  |  |
| GROUNDS, L (HM08600) |  |  |  |  |  |  |  |  |  |  |  |  |  |  |  |  |  |  |  |  |  | ● |  |  |  |  |  |  |  |  |  |  |  |  |  |  |  |  |  |  |  |  |  |  |  |  |  |  |
| HEAL TO TOE (HM09311) |  | ● | ● | ● | ● | ● | ● | ● |  | ● | ● | ● | ● |  | ● | ● | ● | ● | ● | ● | ● | ● |  |  | ● | ● | ● | ● | ● | ● | ● | ● | ● | ● | ● | ● | ● | ● | ● | ● | ● | ● | ● | ● | ● | ● |  |  |
| HOLISTIC HEALTH CENTRE (HM09975) | ● |  |  |  |  | ● |  | ● |  |  |  | ● |  |  |  | ● | ● | ● |  |  | ● | ● |  |  | ● | ● |  |  |  |  | ● |  |  | ● | ● | ● | ● |  |  | ● | ● |  |  |  |  | ● |  |  |
| HOPE STREET NATURAL HLTH CTRE (HM10136) |  |  | ● |  | ● | ● |  |  |  |  |  |  |  |  |  | ● |  |  |  |  |  |  |  |  |  |  |  |  |  |  |  |  |  |  |  | ● | ● |  |  |  |  |  |  |  |  |  |  |  |
| JAMES, ANN (HM10880) |  |  |  | ● |  |  |  |  |  |  |  | ● |  |  |  | ● |  |  |  |  |  | ● | ● | ● |  |  |  |  |  |  | ● |  |  |  | ● |  |  |  |  |  |  |  |  |  |  |  |  |  |
| JARVIS, K R (HM10934) |  |  |  |  |  |  |  |  |  |  |  |  |  |  |  |  |  |  |  |  |  | ● |  | ● |  |  |  |  |  |  |  |  |  |  |  |  |  |  |  |  |  |  |  |  |  |  |  |  |
| KNOWLES, JANICE (HM11771) |  |  |  |  |  |  |  |  |  |  |  |  |  |  |  |  |  |  |  |  |  | ● |  |  |  |  |  |  |  |  |  |  |  |  |  |  |  |  |  |  |  |  |  |  |  |  |  | ● |
| MARKET STREET CHIROPODY CLINIC (HM13113) |  |  |  |  |  |  |  |  |  |  |  |  |  |  |  |  |  |  |  |  |  | ● |  | ● |  |  |  |  |  |  |  |  |  |  |  |  |  |  |  |  |  |  |  |  |  |  |  |  |
| MARSH, E C (HM13146) |  |  |  |  |  |  |  |  |  |  |  |  |  |  |  |  |  |  |  |  |  | ● |  |  |  |  |  |  |  |  |  |  |  |  |  |  |  |  |  |  |  |  |  |  |  |  |  | ● |
| MCLOUGHLIN, CLAIRE (HM13560) |  |  |  |  |  |  |  |  |  |  |  |  |  |  |  |  |  |  |  |  |  | ● |  | ● |  |  |  |  |  |  |  |  |  |  |  |  |  |  |  |  |  |  |  |  |  |  |  |  |
| NATURAL HEALTH CLINIC (HM14576) | ● |  | ● |  | ● | ● | ● | ● | ● |  | ● | ● | ● |  | ● | ● | ● | ● | ● | ● | ● | ● |  |  | ● | ● | ● | ● | ● | ● | ● | ● | ● | ● | ● | ● | ● | ● | ● | ● | ● |  | ● |  | ● | ● | ● |  |
| NELSON, PATRICIA (HM14780) |  |  |  |  |  |  |  |  |  |  |  |  |  |  |  |  |  |  |  |  |  | ● |  | ● |  |  |  |  |  |  |  |  |  |  |  |  |  |  |  |  |  |  |  |  |  |  |  | ● |
| PURE ESSENTIALS DIRECT (HM16764) |  |  |  |  |  | ● |  |  |  |  |  |  |  | ● |  | ● |  |  |  |  |  |  |  |  |  |  |  |  |  |  |  |  |  |  |  |  |  |  |  |  |  |  |  |  |  |  |  |  |
| SANCTUARY NATURAL HEALTH (HM17893) |  |  |  |  |  |  |  |  |  |  |  |  |  |  |  |  |  |  |  |  |  |  |  |  |  |  |  |  |  |  |  |  |  |  |  |  | ● |  |  |  |  |  |  |  |  |  |  |  |
| SCOTT, ANDREW (HM18107) |  |  | ● |  | ● | ● |  | ● |  |  |  |  |  |  |  | ● |  | ● |  |  | ● | ● |  |  |  |  |  |  |  |  |  |  |  |  | ● | ● | ● |  |  | ● |  |  | ● | ● | ● | ● |  |  |
| SEFTON PARK NATURAL THRPY CTRE (HM18198) |  |  |  |  |  | ● |  |  |  |  |  |  |  |  |  | ● | ● |  |  |  | ● |  |  |  |  | ● |  |  |  |  |  |  |  |  |  |  |  |  |  |  |  |  |  |  |  |  |  |  |
| SIMPSON CLINIC (HM18584) | ● | ● | ● | ● | ● | ● | ● | ● | ● | ● | ● | ● | ● |  | ● | ● | ● | ● | ● | ● | ● | ● | ● | ● | ● | ● | ● | ● | ● |  | ● | ● |  | ● | ● | ● | ● | ● | ● | ● | ● | ● | ● |  | ● | ● |  |  |
| SOUTHPORT OSTEO & ACUPUNCTURE (HM18942) |  |  |  |  |  |  |  |  |  |  |  |  |  |  |  |  |  |  |  |  |  |  |  |  |  |  |  |  |  |  |  |  |  |  |  |  | ● |  |  | ● |  |  |  |  |  |  |  |  |
| STEINA SPORTS & PHYSIOTHERAPY (HM19188) |  |  |  |  |  |  |  |  |  |  |  |  |  |  |  |  |  |  |  |  |  |  |  |  |  |  |  |  |  |  |  |  |  |  |  |  |  |  |  | ● |  |  |  |  |  |  |  |  |
| SUMMERS, ALFRED A (HM19487) |  |  |  |  |  |  |  |  |  |  |  |  |  |  |  |  |  |  |  |  |  | ● |  | ● |  |  |  |  |  |  |  |  |  |  |  |  |  |  |  |  |  |  |  |  |  |  |  |  |

# D - I Conditions treated at Practices/Businesses

| Business by County with Reference no. | Dandruff | Deafness | Depression | Diabetes | Diarrhoea | Digestive Problems | Diverticulitis | Dizziness | Dyslexia | Dyspraxia | Ear Disorders | Eczema | ENT Disorders | Epilepsy | Eye Disorders | Fatigue | Fears | Fertility Problems | Fever | Fibroids | Flatulence | Foot Problems | Fractures | Fungal Infections |
|---|---|---|---|---|---|---|---|---|---|---|---|---|---|---|---|---|---|---|---|---|---|---|---|---|
| TARA SCHOOL OF HYPNOTHERAPY (HM19701) | | |●| | | | | | | | | | | | | |●| | | | | | | |
| THERAPY 21 (HM19890) |●| |●| | | | | | | | |●| | | | | | | | | |●| |●|
| WILLIAMS CHIROPODY SERVICE (HM21530) | | | | | | | | | | | | | | | | | | | | | |●| |●|
| WILLIAMS, CATHERINE (HM21546) | | | | | | | | | | | | | | | | | | | | | |●| | |
| WILLIAMS, T H (HM21597) | | | | | | | | | | | | | | | | | | | | | |●| |●|
| WILLIAMS, TECWYN H (HM21598) | | | | | | | | | | | | | | | | | | | | | |●| |●|
| WIRRALL CLINIC (HM21730) | | | | |●| | | | | | | | | | | | | | | | | | | |
| MIDDLESEX | | | | | | | | | | | | | | | | | | | | | | | | |
| CLANRICARDE CLINIC (HM04526) | | |●|●|●|●|●|●|●| |●| |●|●| | | |●| | | |●|●|●|
| MIDLANDS (WEST) | | | | | | | | | | | | | | | | | | | | | | | | |
| 1ST CHIROPRACTIC UK (HM00005) | | | | | | | | | | | | | | | | | | | | | | | | |
| 1ST CHIROPRACTIC UK (HM00006) | | | | | | | | | | | | | | | | | | | | | | | | |
| A Q C H (HM00044) | | |●|●|●|●|●|●|●| | |●| | | |●|●|●| | |●| | | |
| ABBEY CLINIC (HM00077) | | | | | | | |●| | | | | | | | | | | | | |●|●| |
| ABBIE HYPNOTHERAPY CENTRE (HM00093) | | |●| | |●| |●|●| | | | | | |●|●| | | | | | | |
| ACUPUNCTURE HEALTH CLINIC (HM00312) | | | | |●| | | | | | | | | | |●| |●| | | | | | |
| ALCOCK, E C (HM00490) | | | | | | | | | | | | | | | | | | | | | |●| |●|
| ALDA HOUSE NATURAL THERAPY (HM00492) | | |●| |●|●|●|●| | |●|●|●| |●|●|●|●|●|●|●|●| |●|
| ALDOUS, JOSIE (HM00503) | | |●| | | | | | | | | | | | | | | | | | | | | |
| ALLEN, ELAINE (HM00608) | | |●| | | | | | | | | | | | | | | | | | | | | |
| AROMA SANTE (HM01057) |●|●|●|●|●|●|●|●|●|●|●|●|●|●|●|●|●|●|●|●|●|●|●|●|
| ARROW BANK CHIROPRACTIC CLINIC (HM01149) | | | | | | | | | | | | | | | | | | | | | | | | |
| ASSOCIATION OF STRESS MNGMT (HM01288) | | |●| | | | | | | | | | | | |●|●| | | | | | | |
| BACKCARE & ACUPUNCTURE CLINIC (HM01526) | | |●| |●|●|●|●|●| | |●|●| | |●|●|●|●|●|●|●| |●|
| BEAUTIFORM COLLEGE (HM01992) | | | | | |●| | | | | | | | | | | | | | | | | | |
| BILLINGHAM, S (HM02301) | | | | | |●|●| | | | |●| | | |●| | | | | |●| | |
| BIOENERGY PARTNERSHIP (HM02334) | | | | | | | | | | | |●| | | | | | | | | | | | |
| BIRMINGHAM ACU/CHIRO CLNC (HM02382) |●|●|●|●|●|●|●|●|●|●|●|●|●|●|●|●|●|●|●|●|●|●|●|●|
| BIRMINGHAM PHYSIO CLINIC (HM02388) | | | | | | | | | | | | | | | | | | | | | | | | |
| BIRMINGHAM TRAD ACU CENTRE (HM02390) | | | | | | | | | | | | | | | |●| | | | | | | | |
| BLAKE, D H (HM02479) | | | | | | | | | | | | | | | | | | | | | | | | |
| BOLDMERE HYPNOTHERAPY (HM02653) | | |●| | |●| | | | | | | | | |●| | | | | | | | |
| BROWNHILL, D G (HM03257) | | |●| | | | | | | | | | | | | |●| | | | | | | |
| BTAC (HM03296) | | |●| |●|●| |●| | | |●| | | |●|●|●| |●|●| | | |

| Business by County with Reference no. | Gallstones | Gastrointestinal Problems | Genital Herpes | Gingivitis | Glandular Fever | Glaucoma | Gout | Gum Disease | Hair Problems | Halitosis | Hand Problems | Hay Fever | Headaches | Hearing Problems | High Blood Pressure | Hip Complaints | Hyperactivity | Hypoglycaemia | Impotence | Incontinence | Indigestion | Infertility | Influenza | Ingrowing Toenails |
|---|---|---|---|---|---|---|---|---|---|---|---|---|---|---|---|---|---|---|---|---|---|---|---|---|
| TARA SCHOOL OF HYPNOTHERAPY (HM19701) | | | | | | | | | | | | | | | | | | | | | | | | |
| THERAPY 21 (HM19890) | | | | | | | | | | |●| |●| |●| | | | | | | |●| |
| WILLIAMS CHIROPODY SERVICE (HM21530) | | | | | | | | | | | | | | | | | | | | | | | | |
| WILLIAMS, CATHERINE (HM21546) | | | | | | | | | | | | | | | | | | | | | | | | |
| WILLIAMS, T H (HM21597) | | | | | | | | | | | | | | | | | | | | | | | |●|
| WILLIAMS, TECWYN H (HM21598) | | | | | | | | | | | | | | | | | | | | | | | |●|
| WIRRALL CLINIC (HM21730) | | | | | | | | | | | |●|●| | |●| | | | | | | | |
| MIDDLESEX | | | | | | | | | | | | | | | | | | | | | | | | |
| CLANRICARDE CLINIC (HM04526) |●|●| | | | |●| | | | |●|●|●|●|●| |●|●|●|●| | | |
| MIDLANDS (WEST) | | | | | | | | | | | | | | | | | | | | | | | | |
| 1ST CHIROPRACTIC UK (HM00005) | | | | | | | | | | | | |●| | |●| | | | | | | | |
| 1ST CHIROPRACTIC UK (HM00006) | | | | | | | | | | | | |●| | |●| | | | | | | | |
| A Q C H (HM00044) | | |●| | | | | | |●| |●|●| |●| |●| |●|●|●|●| | |
| ABBEY CLINIC (HM00077) | | | | | | | | | | |●| | | | |●| | | | | | | | |
| ABBIE HYPNOTHERAPY CENTRE (HM00093) | | | | | | | | | | | | |●| | | |●| |●|●| |●| | |
| ACUPUNCTURE HEALTH CLINIC (HM00312) | | | | | | | | | | | | |●| | |●| | | | | |●| | |
| ALCOCK, E C (HM00490) | | | | | | |●| | | | | | | | | | | | | | | | | |
| ALDA HOUSE NATURAL THERAPY (HM00492) | |●|●|●|●| |●|●| |●| |●|●|●|●|●|●|●|●|●|●|●|●| |
| ALDOUS, JOSIE (HM00503) | | | | | | | | | | | | | | | | | | | | | | | | |
| ALLEN, ELAINE (HM00608) | | | | | | | | | | | | |●| | | | | | | | | | | |
| AROMA SANTE (HM01057) |●|●|●|●|●|●|●|●|●|●|●|●|●|●|●|●|●|●|●|●|●|●|●| |
| ARROW BANK CHIROPRACTIC CLINIC (HM01149) | | | | | | | | | | | | |●| | |●| | | | | | | | |
| ASSOCIATION OF STRESS MNGMT (HM01288) | | | | | | | | | | | |●|●| |●| | | |●| | | | | |
| BACKCARE & ACUPUNCTURE CLINIC (HM01526) | |●| | | | |●| | | |●|●|●| |●|●|●| | | |●|●|●| |
| BEAUTIFORM COLLEGE (HM01992) | | | | | | | | |●| |●| | | | | | | | | | | | | |
| BILLINGHAM, S (HM02301) | | | | | | | | | | | | |●| | | |●| | | | | | | |
| BIOENERGY PARTNERSHIP (HM02334) | | | | | | | | | | | | |●| | | | | | | | | | | |
| BIRMINGHAM ACU/CHIRO CLNC (HM02382) |●|●|●|●|●|●|●|●|●|●|●|●|●|●|●|●|●|●|●|●|●|●|●| |
| BIRMINGHAM PHYSIO CLINIC (HM02388) | | | | | | | | | | | | | | | |●| | | | | | | | |
| BIRMINGHAM TRAD ACU CENTRE (HM02390) | | | | | | | | | | | | |●| |●| | | | | | | | | |
| BLAKE, D H (HM02479) | | | | | | | | | | | | |●| | |●| | | | | | | | |
| BOLDMERE HYPNOTHERAPY (HM02653) | |●| | | | | | | | | | |●| |●| | | | | | | | | |
| BROWNHILL, D G (HM03257) | | | | | | | | | | | | | | | | | | |●| | | | | |
| BTAC (HM03296) | |●| | | | | | | | | |●|●| |●|●| |●|●| |●|●| | |

www.healthmyself.com

England (by County)

**CONDITIONS TREATED**

**D-I**

# D - I Conditions treated at Practices/Businesses

| Business by County with Reference no. | Dandruff | Deafness | Depression | Diabetes | Diarrhoea | Digestive Problems | Diverticulitis | Dizziness | Dyslexia | Dyspraxia | Ear Disorders | Eczema | ENT Disorders | Epilepsy | Eye Disorders | Fatigue | Fears | Fertility Problems | Fever | Fibroids | Flatulence | Foot Problems | Fractures | Fungal Infections | Gallstones | Gastrointestinal Problems | Genital Herpes | Gingivitis | Glandular Fever | Glaucoma | Gout | Gum Disease | Hair Problems | Halitosis | Hand Problems | Hay Fever | Headaches | Hearing Problems | High Blood Pressure | Hip Complaints | Hyperactivity | Hypoglycaemia | Impotence | Incontinence | Indigestion | Infertility | Influenza | Ingrowing Toenails |
|---|---|---|---|---|---|---|---|---|---|---|---|---|---|---|---|---|---|---|---|---|---|---|---|---|---|---|---|---|---|---|---|---|---|---|---|---|---|---|---|---|---|---|---|---|---|---|---|---|
| BULLOCK, JULIE (HM03344) | | | | ● | | | | | | | | | | | | | | | | | | ● | | ● | | | | | | | | | | | | | | | | | | | | | | | | |
| CALLAGHAN, R M & J (HM03549) | | | | | | | | | | | | | | | | | | | | | | ● | | ● | | | | | | | | | | | | | | | | | | | | | | | | |
| CARPENTER, DAVID (HM03727) | | | ● | | ● | ● | | ● | | | | ● | | ● | | ● | ● | ● | | ● | | | | | | ● | | | | | | | | | | ● | ● | | ● | | ● | | ● | | ● | ● | | |
| CENTRAL CHIROPODY CLINIC (HM03888) | | | | | | | | | | | | | | | | | | | | | | ● | | ● | | | | | | | | | | | | | | | | | | | | | | | | ● |
| CENTRE FOR NATURAL THERAPIES (HM03913) | ● | ● | ● | ● | ● | ● | ● | ● | ● | ● | ● | ● | ● | ● | ● | ● | ● | ● | ● | ● | ● | ● | ● | ● | ● | ● | ● | ● | ● | ● | ● | ● | ● | ● | ● | ● | ● | ● | ● | ● | ● | ● | ● | ● | ● | ● | ● | |
| CHELMSLEY WOOD FOOT CLINIC (HM04086) | | | | | | | | | | | | | | | | | | | | | | ● | | ● | | | | | | | | | | | | | | | | | | | | | | | | |
| CHIRO MED (HM04283) | | | ● | | ● | ● | ● | ● | | | | ● | | | | ● | ● | | | | ● | ● | | | | ● | | | ● | | | | | | ● | ● | ● | | ● | ● | ● | ● | | ● | | ● | ● | |
| CHIROPRACTIC CLINIC (HM04388) | | | | | | | | | | | | | | | | | | | | | | | ● | | | | | | | | | | | | | | ● | | | ● | | | | | | | | |
| CHIROPRACTORS OF WARWICK ROAD (HM04407) | | | | | | | | | | | ● | | | | | | | | | | | | | | | | | | | | | | | | | | ● | | | ● | | | | | | | | |
| CODSALL COMP THERAPIES (HM04778) | | | | | | ● | | | | | | ● | | | | ● | ● | | | ● | | | | | | | | | | | | | | | | ● | ● | | | | | | | | | | | |
| COMPLEMENTARY HEALING CENTRE (HM04919) | | | ● | | | | | | | | | | | | | | | | | | | | | | | | | | | | | | | | | | | | | | | | | | | | | |
| CREATIVE HEALTH CENTRE (HM05398) | | | ● | ● | ● | | | ● | | | | ● | | | | | ● | | | | | | | | | | | | | | | | | | | ● | ● | | ● | | | | | | ● | ● | ● | |
| CROFT, ANGELA (HM05453) | | | | | | ● | | | | | | | | | | | | | | | | | | | | ● | | | | | | | | | | | | | ● | | | | | | | | | |
| CRYSTAL CLEAR PRACTICE (HM05528) | ● | ● | ● | ● | ● | ● | ● | ● | ● | ● | ● | ● | ● | ● | ● | ● | ● | ● | ● | ● | ● | ● | ● | ● | ● | ● | ● | ● | ● | ● | ● | ● | ● | ● | ● | ● | ● | ● | ● | ● | ● | ● | ● | ● | ● | ● | ● | |
| CTRE-REFLEX & AROMATHERAPY (HM05549) | | | | | | | | | | | | | | | | ● | | ● | | | | ● | | | | | | | | | ● | | | | | ● | ● | | | ● | | | | | | ● | | |
| DAVIS A STARKEY REM THERAP (HM05846) | | | | | | | | | | | | | | | | | | | | | | | | | | | | | | | | | | | | | ● | | ● | ● | | | | | | | | |
| DHANA, P N (HM06053) | | | | | | | | | | | | | | | | | | | | | | ● | | ● | | | | | | | | | | | | | | | | | | | | | | | | ● |
| DUDLEY PHYSIOTHERAPY CLINIC (HM06354) | | | | | | | | | | | | | | | | | | | | | | | | | | | | | | | | | | | | | | | | ● | | | | | | | | |
| ERDINGTHON NATURAL HEALTH CLNC (HM06880) | ● | ● | ● | ● | ● | ● | ● | ● | ● | ● | ● | ● | ● | ● | ● | ● | ● | ● | ● | ● | ● | | | | ● | ● | ● | ● | ● | ● | ● | ● | ● | ● | ● | ● | ● | ● | ● | ● | ● | ● | ● | ● | ● | ● | ● | |
| ESSENTIAL HEALTH (HM06909) | | ● | | | | ● | | | | | ● | | ● | | | | | | | | | | | | | | | | | | | | | | | | ● | | | | | | | | | | | |
| FAIRFAX PRIVATE THERAPY (HM07056) | | | ● | | | ● | | | | | | ● | | | | ● | | ● | | | ● | ● | | ● | | | | | | | | | | | | ● | ● | | ● | | ● | | ● | | ● | ● | | |
| FLETCHER, VICTOR JOHN (HM07416) | | | | | | | | | | | | | | | | | | | | | | ● | | ● | | | | | | | | | | | | | | | | | | | | | | | | |
| FORD, MARIA (HM07526) | | | ● | | | | | | | | | | | | | | | | | | | | | | | | | | | | | | | | | | | | | | | | | | | | | |
| FRESHWINDS CHARITABLE TRUST (HM07740) | ● | ● | ● | ● | ● | ● | ● | ● | ● | ● | ● | ● | ● | ● | ● | ● | ● | ● | ● | ● | ● | ● | ● | ● | ● | ● | ● | ● | ● | ● | ● | ● | ● | ● | ● | ● | ● | ● | ● | ● | ● | ● | ● | ● | ● | ● | ● | |
| GOLDEN PALMS (HM08207) | | | ● | | | ● | | | | | | | | | | ● | | | | | | | | ● | | | | | | | | | ● | | | | ● | | ● | | | | | | | | | |
| GREAT BARR OSTEO PRACTICE (HM08430) | | | | | | | | | | | | | | | | | | | | | | ● | | | | | | | | | | | | | ● | | ● | | | | | | | | | | | |
| GREEN VALLEY THERAPY CENTRE (HM08443) | ● | ● | ● | ● | ● | ● | ● | ● | ● | ● | ● | ● | ● | ● | ● | ● | ● | ● | ● | ● | ● | ● | ● | ● | ● | ● | ● | ● | ● | ● | ● | ● | ● | ● | ● | ● | ● | ● | ● | ● | ● | ● | ● | ● | ● | ● | ● | |
| GURPAL SINGH AROMA/REFLEX (HM08655) | | | ● | | | | | | | | | | | | | ● | | | | | | | | | | | | | | | | | | | | | | | | | | | | | | | | |
| HAGLEY CENTRE OF COMP MED (HM08701) | | | ● | | | | | | | | | ● | | | | ● | ● | | | | ● | | | ● | | | | | | | | | | | | ● | ● | | | | | | | | | | | |
| HALE ASSOCIATES (HM08727) | | | | | | | | | | | | | | | | | | | | | | | | | | | | | | | | | | | | | ● | | | | | | | | | | | |
| HALE, GEOFF (HM08732) | | | | | | | | | | | | | | | | | | | | | | | | | | | | | | | | | | | | | ● | | | | | | | | | | | |
| HALL GREEN ALTERN PRACTICE (HM08760) | ● | ● | ● | ● | ● | ● | ● | ● | ● | ● | ● | ● | ● | ● | ● | ● | ● | ● | ● | ● | ● | | | | ● | ● | ● | ● | ● | ● | ● | ● | ● | ● | ● | ● | ● | ● | ● | ● | ● | ● | ● | ● | ● | ● | ● | |
| HALL, SUSAN (HM08790) | | | ● | ● | ● | ● | ● | ● | | | ● | ● | ● | | | ● | | ● | | | ● | ● | | ● | | ● | | | | | ● | | | ● | | ● | ● | ● | ● | ● | | | | | ● | | ● | |
| HARTNESS, R (HM09149) | | | | ● | | | | | | | | | | | | | | | | | | ● | | ● | | | | | | | | | | | | | | | | | | | | | | | | |

# D - I Conditions treated at Practices/Businesses

| Business by County with Reference no. | HEALTH SHOP (HM09402) | HERBAL PHARMACY (HM09632) | HIGGS, R W (HM09737) | HOGG, DEBBI (HM09913) | HOLISTIC HEALTH CENTRE (HM09972) | HOLLOWAY, P (HM10027) | HOLLY COTTAGE CHIRO CLINIC (HM10029) | HOMOEOPATHIC CLINIC/PHARMACY (HM10090) | HOT-PAK (HM10206) | HUSBANDS, STEVE (HM10432) | INGRAM, CLARE (HM10624) | J BENSON CHIROPODIST (HM10793) | JOHNSON FOOTCARE (HM11061) | KEMPSON, STEVE (HM11468) | KEVIN FISHER CHIROPODY (HM11573) | LEWIS, MYRA (HM12305) | LIFE'S OPTION (HM12358) | LONGFORD PHYSIO & SPORTS (HM12627) | MCDERMOTT, J V (HM13447) | MIDLAND HYPNOTHERAPY CENTRE (HM13831) | MIDLAND HYPNOTHERAPY CENTRE (HM13830) | MIDLAND MEDICAL HOM PRACTICE (HM13834) | MIDLAND MEDICAL HOM PRACTICE (HM13832) | MIDLAND MEDICAL HOM PRACTICE (HM13833) | MIDLAND MEDICAL OSTEO PRACTICE (HM13837) | MIDLAND MEDICAL OSTEO PRACTICE (HM13836) | MIDLAND MEDICAL OSTEO PRACTICE (HM13835) | MORGAN, VALERIE (HM14177) | MORRIS, CLAIRE (HM14202) | MYATT, ANITA (HM14432) | NATURAL HEALTH CENTRE (HM14574) | NEWBRIDGE PHARMACY (HM14850) | OULTON FOOT CLINIC (HM15499) | PARK PRACTICE (HM15672) |
|---|---|---|---|---|---|---|---|---|---|---|---|---|---|---|---|---|---|---|---|---|---|---|---|---|---|---|---|---|---|---|---|---|---|---|
| Ingrowing Toenails | | | | | | | | | | | | | | |●| | | | | | | | | | | | | | | | | | | |
| Influenza |●|●| |●| | | |●| |●|●| | | | | | | | | |●|●|●|●| | | |●| |●| | | |●|
| Infertility | |●| |●|●| | | | |●|●| | | | | | | | |●|●|●|●|●| | | |●| |●| | | |●|
| Indigestion |●|●| |●| | | |●| |●|●| | | | | | | | |●|●|●|●|●| | | |●| |●| |●| |●|
| Incontinence | |●| |●| | | |●| |●| | | | | | | |●| |●|●|●|●|●| | | | | |●| |●| |●|
| Impotence | |●| |●| | | |●| |●| | | | | | | | | |●|●|●|●|●| | | | | |●| | | |●|
| Hypoglycaemia | |●| |●| | | | | |●|●| | | | | | | | |●|●|●|●|●| | | | | |●| | | |●|
| Hyperactivity |●|●| |●| | | | | |●|●| | | | | | | | |●|●|●|●|●| | | |●| |●| | | |●|
| Hip Complaints | | | |●| | |●|●| |●|●| | | | | | |●|●| | |●|●|●| | | |●| |●| |●| |●|
| High Blood Pressure |●|●| |●| | | |●| |●|●| | | | | | | | |●|●|●|●|●| | | | | |●| |●| |●|
| Hearing Problems | |●| |●| | | |●| |●|●| | | | | | | | |●|●|●|●|●| | | | | |●| | | |●|
| Headaches |●|●| |●| | |●| |●|●|●| | |●| | |●|●|●|●|●|●|●|●|●|●|●|●| |●|●|●| |●|
| Hay Fever |●|●| |●| | | |●| |●|●| | | | | | | | |●|●|●|●|●| | | |●| |●|●|●| |●|
| Hand Problems |●|●| |●| | | | | |●|●| | | | | | | | |●|●|●|●|●| | | | | |●| | | |●|
| Halitosis | | | |●| | | | | |●| | | | | | | | | |●|●|●|●|●| | | | | |●| | | |●|
| Hair Problems |●|●| |●| | | | | |●| | | | | | | | | |●|●|●|●|●| | | | | |●| | | |●|
| Gum Disease |●|●| |●| | | |●| |●| | | | | | | | | | | |●|●|●| | | | | |●| | | |●|
| Gout | |●| |●| | | |●| |●|●| | | | | | | | | | |●|●|●| | | |●| |●| |●| |●|
| Glaucoma | | | |●| | | | | |●| | | | | | | | | | | |●|●|●| | | | | |●| | | |●|
| Glandular Fever | | | |●| | | | | |●| | | | | | | | | | | |●|●|●| | | |●| |●| | | |●|
| Gingivitis |●|●| |●| | | |●| |●| | | | | | | | | | | |●|●|●| | | | | |●| | | |●|
| Genital Herpes | | | | | | | | | |●| | | | | | | | | |●| |●|●|●| | | | | |●| |●| |●|
| Gastrointestinal Problems | | | |●| | | |●| |●|●| | | | | | | | |●|●|●|●|●| | | |●| |●| |●| |●|
| Gallstones | |●| |●| | | |●| |●| | | | | | | | | | | |●|●|●| | | |●| |●| |●| |●|
| Fungal Infections |●|●|●|●| | | |●| |●|●| |●| |●| | | | |●|●|●|●|●| | | |●|●|●| | |●|●|
| Fractures | | | |●| | | | | | | | | | | | | |●| | | |●|●|●| | | | | |●| |●| |●|
| Foot Problems |●|●|●|●| | |●| |●| | |●|●| |●| | |●| | | |●|●|●| | | | |●|●| | |●|●|
| Flatulence |●|●| |●| |●| |●| |●|●| | | | | | | | |●|●|●|●|●| | | |●| |●| |●| |●|
| Fibroids | |●| |●| | | |●| |●| | | | | | | | | | | |●|●|●| | | |●| |●| |●| |●|
| Fever |●|●| | | | | | | |●| | | | | | | | | |●|●|●|●|●| | | |●| |●| | | |●|
| Fertility Problems | |●| |●|●| | | | |●|●| | | | | | | | |●|●|●|●|●| | | |●| |●| |●| |●|
| Fears |●|●| |●|●| | | | |●|●| | | | | | | | |●|●|●|●|●| | | |●| |●| |●| |●|
| Fatigue |●|●| |●|●| | | | |●|●| | |●| |●| | | |●|●|●|●|●|●| | | |●| |●|●|●| |●|
| Eye Disorders | | | |●|●| | |●| |●| | | | | | | | | |●|●|●|●|●| | | | | |●| | | |●|
| Epilepsy | | | | | | | | | |●| | | | | | | | | |●|●|●|●|●| | | | | |●| |●| |●|
| ENT Disorders | |●| |●| | | |●| |●| | | | | | | | | | | |●|●|●| | | | | |●| |●| |●|
| Eczema |●|●| |●| | | |●| |●|●| | | | | | | | |●|●|●|●|●| | | |●| |●| |●| |●|
| Ear Disorders |●|●| |●| | | |●| |●| | | | | | | | | |●|●|●|●|●| | | |●| |●| | | |●|
| Dyspraxia | |●| | | | | | | |●| | | | | | | | | |●|●|●|●|●| | | | | |●| | | |●|
| Dyslexia | | | |●| | | | | |●| | | | | | | | | |●|●|●|●|●| | | | | |●| | | |●|
| Dizziness |●|●| |●| | | | | |●|●| | | | | | | | |●|●|●|●|●| | | |●| |●| | | |●|
| Diverticulitis |●| | |●| | | |●| |●|●| | | | | | | | |●|●|●|●|●| | | |●| |●| |●| |●|
| Digestive Problems |●|●| |●| | | |●| |●|●| | | | | | | | |●|●|●|●|●| | | |●| |●|●|●| |●|
| Diarrhoea |●|●| |●| | | |●| |●|●| | | | | | | | |●|●|●|●|●| | | |●| |●|●|●| |●|
| Diabetes | | | |●| | | | | |●| | | | |●| | | | |●|●|●|●|●| | | | | |●| | | |●|
| Depression |●|●| |●|●|●| |●| |●|●| | |●| |●|●| | |●|●|●|●|●| | | |●| |●| |●| |●|
| Deafness | | | | | | | | | |●| | | | | | | | | |●|●|●|●|●| | | | | |●| | | |●|
| Dandruff |●| | | | | | | | |●|●| | | | | | | | |●|●|●|●|●| | | | | |●| | | |●|

www.healthmyself.com

Healthmyself Directory

England (by County)

CONDITIONS TREATED

D-I

# D - I Conditions treated at Practices/Businesses

| Business by County with Reference no. | Dandruff | Deafness | Depression | Diabetes | Diarrhoea | Digestive Problems | Diverticulitis | Dizziness | Dyslexia | Dyspraxia | Ear Disorders | Eczema | ENT Disorders | Epilepsy | Eye Disorders | Fatigue | Fears | Fertility Problems | Fever | Fibroids | Flatulence | Foot Problems | Fractures | Fungal Infections | Gallstones | Gastrointestinal Problems | Genital Herpes | Gingivitis | Glandular Fever | Glaucoma | Gout | Gum Disease | Hair Problems | Halitosis | Hand Problems | Hay Fever | Headaches | Hearing Problems | High Blood Pressure | Hip Complaints | Hyperactivity | Hypoglycaemia | Impotence | Incontinence | Indigestion | Infertility | Influenza | Ingrowing Toenails |
|---|---|---|---|---|---|---|---|---|---|---|---|---|---|---|---|---|---|---|---|---|---|---|---|---|---|---|---|---|---|---|---|---|---|---|---|---|---|---|---|---|---|---|---|---|---|---|---|---|
| PHYSIOTHERAPY CLINIC (HM16241) | | | | | | | | | | | | | | | | | | | | | | | | | | | | | | | | | | | | | | | | ● | | | | | | | | |
| PIKE, ELIZABETH G & J K (HM16286) | | | | | | | | | | | | | | | | | | | | | | ● | | ● | | | | | | | | | | | | | | | | | | | | | | | | |
| PILLATH, CHRISTINE (HM16297) | | | | | | | | | | | | | | | | | | | | | | | | | | | | | | | | | | | | | ● | | | ● | | | | | | | | |
| PLANT, ALISON () | | | ● | | | | | | | | | | | | | ● | | | | | | | | | | | | | | | | | | | | | ● | | ● | | | | | | | | | |
| PRISM THERAPIES (HM16636) | | | ● | | | | | | | | | | | | | ● | ● | ● | | | | ● | | | | | | | | | | | | | ● | | ● | | ● | ● | | | | | | ● | | |
| REMEDIAL MASSAGE THERAPY (HM17174) | | | | ● | | ● | | | | | | | | | | | | | | | | | | | | | | | | | | | | | ● | | | | | ● | | | | | ● | | | |
| RICHARDSON, CYRIL (HM17273) | | | | | | | | | | | | | | | | | | | | | | ● | | ● | | | | | | | | | | | | | | | | | | | | | | | | |
| ROBINSON, JOHN (HM17484) | | | | | | | | | | | | | | | | | | | | | | ● | | ● | | | | | | | | | | | | | | | | | | | | | | | | |
| ROMSLEY PHYSIOTHERAPY PRACTICE (HM17578) | | | | | | | ● | | | | | | | | | | | | | | | ● | ● | | | | | | | | | | | | | ● | ● | | | ● | | | | | | | | |
| SEITAI/SHIATSU & MANIPULATION (HM18202) | | | | | | | | | | | | | | | | | | | | | | | | | | | | | | | | | | | | | ● | | | | | | | | | | | |
| SIDHOM, A (HM18529) | | | | | | | | | | | | | | | | | | | | | | | | | | | | | | | | | | | | | ● | | | | | | | | | | | |
| SOLIHULL CHIROPRACTIC CLINIC (HM18872) | | | | | | | | | | | | | | | | | | | | | | | | | | | | | | | | | | | | | ● | | | ● | | | | | | | | |
| SOMEWAY HERBAL CLINIC (HM18883) | | | | | | | | | | | | ● | | | | ● | | | | | | | | | | | | | | | | | | | | ● | ● | | | ● | | | | | | | | |
| ST PAULS OSTEOPATHY PRACTICE (HM19094) | | | | | | | | ● | | | ● | | ● | | | | | | | | | ● | ● | | | | | | | | | | | | | | ● | | | ● | ● | | | | ● | | | |
| STARKEY, DAVID (HM19147) | | | | | | | | | | | | | | | | | | | | | | | | | | | | | | | | | | | | | ● | | ● | ● | | | | | | | | |
| SUCCESSWORKS (HM19461) | | | ● | | | | | ● | | | | | | | | ● | ● | | | | | | | | | | | | | | | | | | | | ● | | | | | | | | | | | |
| SUTTON COLDFIELD HEALTH CLINIC (HM19544) | | ● | ● | ● | ● | ● | ● | | | | | ● | | | | ● | | ● | | | | | | | ● | ● | | | | | | | | | ● | ● | ● | | ● | ● | | | | | ● | | | |
| TELLING, MELANIE (HM19823) | | | ● | | | ● | | | | | ● | | | | | ● | | | | | | | | | | | | | | | | | | | ● | ● | ● | ● | ● | | | | | | | | | |
| TELLING, MELANIE (HM19822) | | | ● | | | ● | | ● | | | ● | | | | | ● | | | | | | | | | | | | | | | | | | | ● | ● | ● | ● | ● | | | | | ● | ● | | | |
| THERAPY TRAINING COLLEGE (HM19911) | | | ● | | | ● | | | | | | | | | | ● | ● | ● | | | | | | | | | | | | | | | | | | ● | ● | | ● | | | | ● | | | ● | | |
| WALSALL PHYSIOTHERAPY CLINIC (HM20853) | | | | | | | | | | | | | | | | | | | | | | | | | | | | | | | | | | | | | | | | ● | | | | | | | | |
| WALSGRAVE CHIROPRACTIC CLINIC (HM20855) | | | | | | | | | | | | | | | | | | | | | | | | | | | | | | | | | | | | | ● | | | | | | | | | | | |
| WARD, JAQUELINE (HM20906) | | | | | | | | | | | | | | | | | ● | | | | | | | | | | | | | | | | | | | | ● | | | | | | | | | | | |
| WELL NATURAL HEALTH CENTRE (HM21139) | ● | ● | ● | ● | ● | ● | ● | ● | ● | ● | ● | ● | ● | ● | ● | ● | ● | ● | ● | ● | ● | ● | | ● | ● | ● | ● | ● | ● | ● | ● | ● | ● | ● | ● | ● | ● | ● | ● | ● | ● | ● | ● | ● | ● | ● | ● | |
| WELL NATURAL HEALTH CENTRE (HM21140) | ● | ● | ● | ● | ● | ● | ● | ● | ● | ● | ● | ● | ● | ● | ● | ● | ● | ● | ● | ● | ● | ● | ● | ● | ● | ● | ● | ● | ● | ● | ● | ● | ● | ● | ● | ● | ● | ● | ● | ● | ● | ● | ● | ● | ● | ● | ● | |
| WEST MIDLAND HYPNOTHERAPY (HM21229) | | | ● | | | | | | | | | | | | | | ● | | | | | | | | | | | | | | | | | | | | | | | | | | | | | | | |
| WESTON, JOHN (HM21278) | | | | | | | | | | | | | | | | | | | | | | | | | | | | | | | | | | | ● | | ● | | | ● | | | | | | | | |
| WESTWOOD, ANGELA (HM21285) | | | ● | | | | | ● | | | ● | | | | | | | ● | | | | ● | | | | | | | | | | | | | | | ● | | | ● | | | | | | ● | | |
| WHITE, SHELLEY (HM21378) | | | ● | | | ● | | | | | | | | | | ● | | | | | | ● | | | | | | | | | | | | | | | ● | | | | | | | | | | | |
| WHITEHALL, CAROL (HM21385) | | | | | | | | | | | | | | | | | | | | | | ● | | ● | | | | | | | | | | | | | | | | | | | | | | | | |
| WILLOWS CLNC COMP HEALTH CTRE (HM21630) | ● | | ● | ● | ● | ● | ● | ● | | | ● | ● | ● | ● | ● | ● | ● | ● | | ● | ● | ● | | ● | ● | ● | ● | | | | ● | | ● | | ● | ● | ● | | ● | ● | ● | ● | ● | ● | ● | ● | | |
| WOLVERHAMPTON CHINESE MED CTRE (HM21765) | | | ● | ● | | ● | | ● | | | | ● | | ● | | ● | | ● | ● | ● | | | | | | ● | ● | | | | | | ● | | | ● | ● | | ● | | ● | | ● | | ● | ● | ● | |
| ZEN HEALTH & BEAUTY (HM22099) | | | ● | | | | | | | | | | | | | | | | | | | | | | | | | | | | | | | | | | | | | | | | | | | | | |

# D - I Conditions treated at Practices/Businesses

Business by County with Reference no.

NORFOLK

| | ALTERNATIVE HEALTH CARE (HM00702) | AMALA CHIROPODY CENTRE (HM00760) | BODY BEAUTIFUL (HM02576) | BRUNSWICK PHYSIO (HM03280) | CARSON, KAREN (HM03770) | CHANDLER, ANN (HM03973) | CHASE PARK PRACTICE (HM04060) | CHIROPODIST (HM04291) | CHIROPODISTS (HM04297) | CLASSICAL OSTEOPATH (HM04611) | COMER OSTEOPATHIC CLINIC (HM04897) | COMPLEMENTARY HEALTH CLINIC (HM04926) | COTTAGE CHIROPRACTIC CLINIC (HM05217) | COTTAGE CLINIC (HM05220) | COTTAGE NTRL HEALTH CLINIC (HM05222) | COUNTY HEALTH (HM05259) | DISS NATURAL HEALTH CLINIC (HM06121) |
|---|---|---|---|---|---|---|---|---|---|---|---|---|---|---|---|---|---|
| Ingrowing Toenails | | ● | | | ● | | | ● | ● | | | | | | | | |
| Influenza | | | | | | | | | | ● | | | | ● | | ● | |
| Infertility | | | | | | | | | | | | ● | | ● | | ● | |
| Indigestion | ● | | | | | | | | | ● | ● | | | ● | | ● | ● |
| Incontinence | ● | | | | | | | | | ● | | | | ● | | | |
| Impotence | | | | | | | ● | | | ● | | | | ● | | | |
| Hypoglycaemia | | | | | | | | | | | | ● | | ● | | ● | |
| Hyperactivity | | | | | | | | | | | | | | ● | | ● | ● |
| Hip Complaints | | | | ● | | ● | | | | ● | ● | ● | ● | | | | ● |
| High Blood Pressure | ● | | ● | | | | | | | ● | ● | ● | | ● | | ● | |
| Hearing Problems | | | | | | | | | | | ● | | | | | | |
| Headaches | ● | | | | | | | | | ● | ● | ● | ● | ● | ● | ● | ● |
| Hay Fever | ● | | | | | | | | | | ● | | | ● | | ● | ● |
| Hand Problems | | | | | | | | | | ● | ● | | | | | | ● |
| Halitosis | | | | | | | | | | | | | | ● | | | ● |
| Hair Problems | | | | | | | | | | | | | | | | | |
| Gum Disease | | | | | | | | | | | | | | ● | | | |
| Gout | | | | | | | | | | | ● | | | ● | | ● | |
| Glaucoma | | | | | | | | | | | | | | | | | |
| Glandular Fever | | | | | | | | | | ● | | ● | | ● | | ● | |
| Gingivitis | | | | | | | | | | | | | | ● | | | |
| Genital Herpes | | | | | | | | | | | | | | | | ● | |
| Gastrointestinal Problems | | | | | | | | | | ● | ● | | | | | ● | |
| Gallstones | | | | | | | | | | | | ● | | ● | | ● | |
| Fungal Infections | | | ● | | | | | | | | | | | ● | | | ● |
| Fractures | | | | ● | | | | | | | | | | | | ● | |
| Foot Problems | | | | | ● | | | ● | ● | ● | ● | | | | | | ● |
| Flatulence | | | | | | | | | | ● | | | | ● | | ● | ● |
| Fibroids | | | | | | | | | | | | | | ● | | ● | |
| Fever | | | | | | | | | | ● | | | | ● | | ● | |
| Fertility Problems | | | | | | | | | | | | | | ● | | ● | |
| Fears | | | | | | | | | | | | ● | | ● | | ● | ● |
| Fatigue | | | | | | | ● | | | ● | ● | ● | | ● | | ● | ● |
| Eye Disorders | | | | | | | | | | ● | | | | ● | | | |
| Epilepsy | | | | | | | | | | | | | | | | | |
| ENT Disorders | | | | | | | | | | ● | ● | | | | | ● | |
| Eczema | | | | | | | | | | | ● | | | ● | | ● | ● |
| Ear Disorders | | | | | | | | | | ● | ● | | | ● | | ● | ● |
| Dyspraxia | | | | | | | | | | | ● | | | | | | ● |
| Dyslexia | | | | | | | | | | | | | | | | | ● |
| Dizziness | ● | | | | | | | | | ● | ● | | | ● | | ● | ● |
| Diverticulitis | | | | | | | | | | ● | ● | | | ● | | ● | |
| Digestive Problems | | | | | | | | | | ● | ● | ● | | ● | | ● | ● |
| Diarrhoea | | | ● | | | | | | | ● | ● | | | ● | | ● | ● |
| Diabetes | | ● | | | | | | ● | | | | | | ● | | | |
| Depression | ● | | ● | | | | ● | | | | | ● | | ● | | ● | ● |
| Deafness | | | | | | | | | | | ● | | | | | | |
| Dandruff | | | | | | | | | | | | | | ● | | ● | ● |

| | ELEMENTS OF HEALTH (HM06725) | ELLIS, STEPHEN (HM06772) | FIRST STEP FOOTCARE (HM07340) | FISHER, JACK E (HM07355) | FORD OSTEOPATHIC CLINIC (HM07521) | GEARY, A G (HM07951) | GT YARMOUTH PHYSICAL THERAPY (HM08330) | HARGHAM HALL OSTEO PRACTICE (HM08992) | HOBSON, L A (HM09865) | HOMEOPATHIC CLINIC (HM10074) | JAMES, LINDA (HM10890) | JESSOP CLINIC (HM11021) | KING, SIMON (HM11644) | MONSON, J L B (HM14076) | NEW MARKET RD PHYSIO PRACTICE (HM14824) | NORFOLK CLINIC (HM14993) |
|---|---|---|---|---|---|---|---|---|---|---|---|---|---|---|---|---|
| Ingrowing Toenails | | | | | | | | | ● | | | | | | | |
| Influenza | ● | | | | | | | | | ● | | | ● | | | |
| Infertility | ● | | | | | | | | | ● | | | ● | | | |
| Indigestion | ● | | | | | | | | | ● | ● | | ● | | | ● |
| Incontinence | ● | | | | | | | | | ● | | | ● | | | |
| Impotence | ● | | | | | | | | | ● | | | ● | | | |
| Hypoglycaemia | ● | | | | | | | | | ● | | | ● | | | |
| Hyperactivity | ● | | | | | | | | | ● | | | ● | | | |
| Hip Complaints | | | | | ● | | ● | ● | | ● | | | | | | |
| High Blood Pressure | ● | | | | | | | | | ● | ● | ● | ● | | | ● |
| Hearing Problems | | | | | | | | | | ● | | | | | | |
| Headaches | ● | ● | | ● | ● | | ● | | | ● | ● | ● | ● | | | ● |
| Hay Fever | ● | ● | | | | | | | | ● | | | ● | | | ● |
| Hand Problems | ● | | | | ● | | | | | ● | | | | | | |
| Halitosis | ● | | | | | | | | | ● | | | | | | ● |
| Hair Problems | ● | | | | | | | | | ● | | | | | | |
| Gum Disease | ● | | | | | | | | | ● | | | ● | | | |
| Gout | ● | | | | | | | | | ● | | | | | | |
| Glaucoma | | | | | | | | | | ● | | | | | | |
| Glandular Fever | | | | | | | | | | ● | | | ● | | | |
| Gingivitis | ● | | | | | | | | | ● | | | ● | | | |
| Genital Herpes | | | | | | | | | | ● | | | ● | | | |
| Gastrointestinal Problems | | | | | | | | | | ● | | | ● | | | |
| Gallstones | | | | | | | | | | ● | | | | | | |
| Fungal Infections | ● | | | | | | | | | ● | | | ● | | | |
| Fractures | | | | | | | | | | ● | | | | | ● | |
| Foot Problems | ● | | ● | ● | ● | ● | | | ● | ● | | | | | | ● |
| Flatulence | ● | | | | | | | | | ● | | | ● | | | ● |
| Fibroids | ● | | | | | | | | | ● | | | ● | | | ● |
| Fever | ● | | | | | | | | | ● | | | ● | | | ● |
| Fertility Problems | ● | ● | | | | | | | | ● | | | ● | | | ● |
| Fears | ● | | | | | | | | | ● | | | ● | | | ● |
| Fatigue | ● | | | | ● | | | | | ● | ● | | ● | | | ● |
| Eye Disorders | | | | | | | | | | ● | | | ● | | | |
| Epilepsy | | | | | | | | | | ● | | | | | | |
| ENT Disorders | ● | | | | | | | | | ● | | | ● | | | |
| Eczema | ● | ● | | | | | | | | ● | | | ● | | | ● |
| Ear Disorders | ● | | | | | | | | | ● | | | ● | | | |
| Dyspraxia | | | | | | | | | | ● | | | | | | |
| Dyslexia | | | | | | | | | | ● | | | | | | |
| Dizziness | ● | | | | | | | ● | | ● | | | ● | | | ● |
| Diverticulitis | ● | | | | | | | | | ● | | | ● | | | ● |
| Digestive Problems | ● | | | | | | | ● | | ● | ● | | ● | | | ● |
| Diarrhoea | ● | | | | | | | | | ● | | | ● | | | ● |
| Diabetes | | | | | | | | | | ● | | | | | | |
| Depression | ● | ● | | | | | | | | ● | ● | | ● | ● | | ● |
| Deafness | ● | | | | | | | | | ● | | | | | | |
| Dandruff | ● | | | | | | | | | ● | | | | | | ● |

www.healthmyself.com

England (by County)

D-I CONDITIONS TREATED

# D - I Conditions treated at Practices/Businesses

| Business by County with Reference no. | Dandruff | Deafness | Depression | Diabetes | Diarrhoea | Digestive Problems | Diverticulitis | Dizziness | Dyslexia | Dyspraxia | Ear Disorders | Eczema | ENT Disorders | Epilepsy | Eye Disorders | Fatigue | Fears | Fertility Problems | Fever | Fibroids | Flatulence | Foot Problems | Fractures | Fungal Infections |
|---|---|---|---|---|---|---|---|---|---|---|---|---|---|---|---|---|---|---|---|---|---|---|---|---|
| NORFOLK NATURAL HEALTH SERVICE (HM14995) | | | ● | | | ● | | | | | ● | ● | | | | ● | | ● | | | ● | | | |
| NORMAN, A J (HM14999) | | | ● | | | ● | | | | | | | | | | | | | | | | | | |
| OLIVE GROVE BODY SCIENCE (HM15281) | | | | ● | | | | | | | | ● | | | | | | | | | | ● | | |
| PARK PHYSIOTHERAPY (HM15669) | | | | | | | | | | | | | | | | | | | | | | | | |
| QUEENS SQUARE SURGERY (HM16796) | ● | ● | ● | ● | ● | ● | ● | ● | ● | ● | ● | ● | ● | ● | ● | ● | ● | ● | ● | ● | ● | ● | ● | ● |
| RICHARDSON, ALAN (HM17268) | | | | | | | ● | | | | | ● | | | | ● | | | | | | | | |
| RIGBY COURT CLINIC (HM17331) | ● | | ● | ● | ● | ● | ● | ● | | | ● | ● | ● | ● | ● | ● | ● | ● | | ● | ● | ● | | ● |
| SHARP, DENISE (HM18307) | | | ● | | | ● | | | | | | | | | | | | | | | | | | |
| SHIATSU CENTRE (HM18453) | | | ● | | | | | | | | | | | | | | | | | | | | | |
| ST STEPHENS PRACTICE (HM19099) | | | ● | | ● | ● | | ● | | | | | | | | | | | | | | ● | | ● |
| WATTON PHYSIOTHERAPY CLINIC (HM21033) | | | | | | | | | | | | | | | | | | | | | | | | |
| WENDY JILLEY - MEDICAL HERB (HM21197) | ● | | ● | | ● | ● | ● | ● | | | | ● | ● | | | ● | | ● | ● | | ● | | | ● |
| WOBURN CLINIC (HM21755) | | | ● | | ● | ● | | | ● | | | ● | | | | ● | ● | | | | | ● | | |
| **NORTHAMPTONSHIRE** | | | | | | | | | | | | | | | | | | | | | | | | |
| ACUPUNCTURE CLINIC (HM00275) | | | ● | | ● | ● | | | | | | ● | | | | ● | | ● | | | | | | |
| ALLEN HINDE - PHYSIOTHERAPIST (HM00598) | | | | | | | | | | | | | | | | | | | | | | ● | ● | |
| ANDREWS, S C (HM00857) | ● | ● | ● | ● | ● | ● | ● | ● | | | ● | ● | ● | ● | ● | ● | ● | ● | ● | ● | ● | | | ● |
| ANDREWS, SIMON C (HM00860) | ● | ● | ● | ● | ● | ● | ● | ● | | | ● | ● | ● | ● | ● | ● | ● | ● | ● | ● | ● | | | ● |
| ANNELISE (HM00906) | | | ● | | | ● | | | | | ● | | ● | | | ● | | | | | | | | ● |
| ARBOURS (HM00965) | | | | ● | | | | | | | | | | | | | | | | | | ● | | |
| C F C M (HM03523) | ● | | ● | ● | ● | ● | ● | ● | | | ● | ● | ● | ● | ● | ● | | ● | ● | ● | ● | | ● | ● |
| CALLIS THERAPY FOUNDATION (HM03555) | ● | ● | ● | ● | ● | ● | ● | ● | ● | ● | ● | ● | ● | ● | ● | ● | ● | ● | ● | ● | ● | ● | ● | ● |
| CLINTON HOUSE CHIROPODY (HM04719) | | | | ● | | | | | | | | | | | | | | | | | | ● | | |
| DAVENTRY NATUREWORKS (HM05768) | | | ● | | ● | ● | | | | | | | | | | ● | | | | | | | | |
| DEVON PARADE CLINIC (HM06041) | | | ● | | | ● | ● | ● | | | | ● | ● | | | ● | ● | ● | | ● | ● | ● | ● | |
| ESSERY, TRICIA (HM06933) | | | ● | | ● | ● | | | | | | | | | | ● | | | | | | | | |
| GARVEY-WILLIAMS, RICHARD (HM07915) | | | ● | ● | | ● | ● | | | | | ● | | | | ● | ● | | | | | | | |
| GARVEY-WILLIAMS, RICHARD (HM07914) | | | | | | | | | | | | | | | | ● | | | | | | | | |
| GEDDES, PIPPA (HM07955) | | ● | ● | | ● | ● | | ● | | | ● | ● | ● | | ● | ● | | ● | | ● | ● | ● | | ● |
| JUST RELAX (HM11285) | ● | | ● | | ● | ● | ● | ● | | | ● | | | | | ● | | | | | ● | | | |
| LEE, STEPHEN (HM12146) | | | ● | | ● | | | ● | | | | ● | | | | | | | | | | | | |
| MAPLE TREE OSTEO PRACTICE (HM13061) | | | ● | | | ● | | | | | ● | | ● | | | ● | ● | | | | | | | |
| MOTLEY, MAUREEN (HM14277) | | | ● | | | | | | | | | ● | | | | ● | | | | | | | | |
| NENE VALLEY COMP THERAPIES (HM14785) | | | ● | | | ● | | | | | | | | | | ● | | | | | | | | |

| Business by County with Reference no. | Gallstones | Gastrointestinal Problems | Genital Herpes | Gingivitis | Glandular Fever | Glaucoma | Gout | Gum Disease | Hair Problems | Halitosis | Hand Problems | Hay Fever | Headaches | Hearing Problems | High Blood Pressure | Hip Complaints | Hyperactivity | Hypoglycaemia | Impotence | Incontinence | Indigestion | Infertility | Influenza | Ingrowing Toenails |
|---|---|---|---|---|---|---|---|---|---|---|---|---|---|---|---|---|---|---|---|---|---|---|---|---|
| NORFOLK NATURAL HEALTH SERVICE (HM14995) | | ● | | | | | | | | | | ● | ● | | ● | | | | | | ● | ● | ● | |
| NORMAN, A J (HM14999) | | | | | | | | | | | | | ● | | | ● | | | | | ● | | | |
| OLIVE GROVE BODY SCIENCE (HM15281) | | | | | | | | | | | | | | | | | | | | | | | | |
| PARK PHYSIOTHERAPY (HM15669) | | | | | | | | | | | | | | | | ● | | | | | | | | |
| QUEENS SQUARE SURGERY (HM16796) | ● | ● | ● | ● | ● | ● | ● | ● | ● | ● | ● | ● | ● | ● | ● | ● | ● | ● | ● | ● | ● | ● | ● | |
| RICHARDSON, ALAN (HM17268) | | ● | | | | | | | | | | | | | ● | | | ● | | | ● | | | |
| RIGBY COURT CLINIC (HM17331) | | ● | ● | | | | | ● | ● | | ● | ● | ● | ● | ● | ● | | ● | ● | ● | ● | ● | ● | |
| SHARP, DENISE (HM18307) | | | | | | | | | | | ● | ● | ● | | ● | | ● | | | | ● | | ● | |
| SHIATSU CENTRE (HM18453) | | | | | | | | | | | | | | | | | | | | | | | | |
| ST STEPHENS PRACTICE (HM19099) | | | | | | | | | | | | ● | ● | | | | ● | | | | | | | |
| WATTON PHYSIOTHERAPY CLINIC (HM21033) | | | | | | | | | | | | | | | | ● | | | | | | | | |
| WENDY JILLEY - MEDICAL HERB (HM21197) | ● | ● | | ● | ● | | ● | ● | ● | ● | | ● | ● | | ● | | ● | | ● | | ● | ● | ● | |
| WOBURN CLINIC (HM21755) | | | | | | | | | | | ● | | ● | | ● | ● | ● | | | | ● | | ● | |
| **NORTHAMPTONSHIRE** | | | | | | | | | | | | | | | | | | | | | | | | |
| ACUPUNCTURE CLINIC (HM00275) | | | | | | | | | | | | ● | ● | | | | | | | | ● | ● | | |
| ALLEN HINDE - PHYSIOTHERAPIST (HM00598) | | | | | | | | | | | ● | | ● | | | ● | | | | | | | | |
| ANDREWS, S C (HM00857) | ● | ● | ● | ● | ● | ● | ● | ● | ● | ● | | ● | ● | ● | ● | | ● | ● | ● | ● | ● | ● | ● | ● |
| ANDREWS, SIMON C (HM00860) | ● | ● | ● | ● | ● | ● | ● | ● | ● | ● | | ● | ● | ● | ● | ● | ● | ● | ● | ● | ● | ● | ● | |
| ANNELISE (HM00906) | | | | | | | | | | | | | ● | | ● | | | | | | | | | |
| ARBOURS (HM00965) | | | | | | | | | | | | | | | | | | | | | | | | ● |
| C F C M (HM03523) | ● | ● | ● | ● | ● | ● | ● | | | | ● | ● | ● | | ● | ● | ● | | ● | ● | ● | ● | ● | |
| CALLIS THERAPY FOUNDATION (HM03555) | ● | ● | ● | ● | ● | ● | ● | ● | ● | ● | ● | ● | ● | ● | ● | ● | ● | ● | ● | ● | ● | ● | ● | |
| CLINTON HOUSE CHIROPODY (HM04719) | | | | | | | | | | | | | | | | | | | | | | | | ● |
| DAVENTRY NATUREWORKS (HM05768) | | | | | | | | | | | | ● | ● | | | ● | | | | | | | | |
| DEVON PARADE CLINIC (HM06041) | | ● | | | | | ● | | | | ● | | ● | | | | | | ● | ● | ● | | | ● |
| ESSERY, TRICIA (HM06933) | | | | | | | ● | | | | ● | ● | ● | | ● | ● | | | | | ● | | ● | |
| GARVEY-WILLIAMS, RICHARD (HM07915) | ● | | | | ● | | | | | | | ● | ● | | ● | ● | | | | | ● | | ● | |
| GARVEY-WILLIAMS, RICHARD (HM07914) | | | | | | | | | | | | | ● | | ● | ● | | | | | | | | |
| GEDDES, PIPPA (HM07955) | ● | ● | | | | | | | | | | ● | ● | | ● | ● | | ● | ● | ● | ● | ● | | |
| JUST RELAX (HM11285) | ● | | | ● | ● | | ● | ● | ● | | | ● | ● | ● | ● | ● | ● | | | | ● | ● | | |
| LEE, STEPHEN (HM12146) | | | | | | | | | | | | ● | ● | | | | | | | ● | ● | ● | | |
| MAPLE TREE OSTEO PRACTICE (HM13061) | | | | | | | | | | | ● | | | | ● | ● | ● | | | | ● | | | |
| MOTLEY, MAUREEN (HM14277) | | | | | | | | | | | | | ● | | | | | | | | | | | |
| NENE VALLEY COMP THERAPIES (HM14785) | | | | | | | | | | | ● | ● | ● | | ● | | ● | | | | ● | | | |

# D - I Conditions treated at Practices/Businesses

| Business by County with Reference no. | NORTHAMPTON CHIROPRACTIC (HM15051) | NORTHAMPTON CLINIC (HM15052) | REFLEXOLOGY CLINIC (HM17085) | TOWCESTER CHIROPRACTIC CLINIC (HM20194) | NORTHUMBERLAND | ACUCARE (HM00209) | AYRES, ELIZABETH (HM01433) | BOWEN TECHNIQUE STUDIO (HM02775) | EVISON, ALEX (HM07012) | GREEN BATT PHYSIOTHERAPY (HM08434) | KI CLINIC (HM11591) | MEAD, BRUCE (HM13626) | PHYSIOTHERAPY & SPORTS CLINIC (HM16223) | NOTTINGHAMSHIRE | ACUPUNCTURE CLINIC (HM00264) | BEESTON PHYSIO & SPORTS CLNC (HM02060) | BOND, DIANORA (HM02669) | BRAHMA KUMARIS WORLD (HM02891) | BULLEN-SPICER ASSOCIATES (HM03342) | CARITAS NATURAL HEALTH CLINIC (HM03688) | CENTRE FOR TRANSFORMATION (HM03921) | DEAN, MARTIN (HM05942) | EAST BRIDGEFORD PHYSIO NEEDS (HM06510) | GOTHAM VILLAGE PHYSO CLINIC (HM08308) | GREENWOOD, JULIA (HM08507) | HANDS ON HEALTH (HM08912) | IMPACT PHYSIO & SPORTS INJURIES (HM10590) | LIGHT UP YOUR LIFE (HM12370) | MANSFIELD CHIROPODY (HM13046) | MORLEY-KIRK, JOHN (HM14188) | NATURAL HEALTH (HM14554) | NATURAL THERAPY CLINIC (HM14654) | NOTTINGHAM M S THERAPY CTRE (HM15083) | NOTTINGHAM NATURAL HEALTH CTRE (HM15084) |
|---|---|---|---|---|---|---|---|---|---|---|---|---|---|---|---|---|---|---|---|---|---|---|---|---|---|---|---|---|---|---|---|---|---|---|
| Ingrowing Toenails | | | | | | |●| | | | |●| | | | | | | | | | | | |●| | | |●| |●| | | |
| Influenza | | |●| | | | | | | |●| | | | | | | | | | |●| | | | | | | | |●|●|●|●|
| Infertility | | |●| | | | | | | |●| | | |●| | | | | |●| | | | | | | | |●|●|●| |●|
| Indigestion | |●|●| | | | | |●| |●| | | | | | | |●| |●|●| | | | | |●| |●|●|●|●|●|
| Incontinence | | | | | | | | | |●| | | | | | |●| | | | | | | | | | | | | |●| | |●|
| Impotence | | | | | | | | |●| |●| | | | | | | |●| |●| | | | | | |●| |●|●|●| |●|
| Hypoglycaemia | | |●| | | | | | | |●| | | | | | | | | | | | | | | | | | |●| |●| |●|
| Hyperactivity | | |●| | | | | | | |●| | | | | | | |●| | | | | | | | | | | |●|●|●|●|
| Hip Complaints |●| |●|●| | | |●| | | | |●| | |●|●| | | | | |●|●|●| | |●|●| | |●|●| |●|
| High Blood Pressure | | |●| | | | | |●| |●| | | | | | | |●| | |●| | | | | |●| |●|●|●|●|●|
| Hearing Problems | | |●| | | | | | | |●| | | | | | | | | | | | | | | | |●| | |●| | |●|
| Headaches |●|●|●|●| |●| | |●| |●| | | |●| | | |●| | | | | | | | |●| |●|●|●|●|●|
| Hay Fever | | |●| | |●| | | | |●| | | |●| | | | | |●| | | | | | | | |●|●|●|●|●|
| Hand Problems | | | |●| | | | | |●|●| | | | | | | | | |●|●| | | | | |●| | |●|●|●|●|
| Halitosis | | | | | | | | | | |●| | | | | | | | | | | | | | | | | | | |●|●| |●|
| Hair Problems | | | | | | | | | | |●| | | | | | | | | |●| | | | | | | | | |●|●| |●|
| Gum Disease | | | | | | | | | | |●| | | | | | | | | |●| | | | | | |●| | |●|●| |●|
| Gout | | | | | | | | | | | | | | | | | | | | |●| | | | | | |●| | |●|●|●|●|
| Glaucoma | | | | | | | | | | | | | | | | | | | | | | | | | | | | | | |●| | |●|
| Glandular Fever | | | | | | | | | | | | | | | | | | | | |●| | | | | | | | | |●|●| |●|
| Gingivitis | | | | | | | | | | |●| | | | | | | | | |●| | | | | | |●| | |●|●| |●|
| Genital Herpes | | | | | | | | | | |●| | | | | | | | | | | | | | | | | | | |●| | |●|
| Gastrointestinal Problems | | |●| | | | | | | |●| | | | | | | | | |●|●| | | | | |●| |●|●|●| |●|
| Gallstones | | |●| | | | | | | | | | | | | | | | | | | | | | | | | | | | |●| |●|
| Fungal Infections | | | | | | | | | | |●| | | | | | | | | | | | | | | | | | | |●|●| |●|
| Fractures | | |●| | | | | | | | | | | | |●|●| | | | | | |●|●| | | | | | |●| | |●|
| Foot Problems | | | | | | |●| | |●| |●| | | | |●| | |●|●| | | |●|●| | |●| |●|●| |●|
| Flatulence | | | | | | | | | | |●| | | | | | | | | |●|●| | | | | | | |●|●|●| |●|
| Fibroids | | |●| | | | | | | |●| | | | | | | | | |●| | | | | | | | | |●|●| |●|
| Fever | | |●| | | | | | | |●| | | | | | | | | | | | | | | | | | |●|●|●| |●|
| Fertility Problems | | |●| | | | | | | |●| | | |●| | | | | |●| | | | | | | | |●|●|●| |●|
| Fears | | |●| | |●| | |●| |●| | | | | | |●|●| |●|●| | | | | |●| | |●|●| |●|
| Fatigue | | |●| | | | | | | |●| | | | | | | |●| |●|●| | | | | |●| |●|●|●|●|●|
| Eye Disorders | | | | | | | | | | |●| | | | | | | | | |●| | | | | | | | | |●|●| |●|
| Epilepsy | | |●| | | | | | | | | | | | | | | | | | | | | | | | | | | | | | |●|
| ENT Disorders | | |●| | | | | | | |●| | | | | | | | | |●| | | | | | | | | |●|●| |●|
| Eczema | | |●| | | | | | | |●| | | |●| | | | | |●|●| | | | | | | |●|●|●| |●|
| Ear Disorders | | |●| | | | | | | |●| | | | | | | | | |●| | | | | | |●| |●|●|●| |●|
| Dyspraxia | | | | | | | | | | |●| | | | | | | | | | | | | | | | | | | |●| | |●|
| Dyslexia | | | | | | | | | | |●| | | | | | | | | |●| | | | | | | | | |●|●| |●|
| Dizziness | | |●| | | | | | | |●| | | | | | | | | |●|●| | | | | | | | |●|●| |●|
| Diverticulitis | | | | | | | | | | |●| | | | | | | | |●|●|●| | | |●| |●| |●|●|●| |●|
| Digestive Problems | | |●| | |●| | |●| |●| | | | | | | | | |●|●| | | | | |●| |●|●|●|●|●|
| Diarrhoea | | |●| | |●| | | | |●| | | |●| | | | | |●|●| | | | | | | |●|●|●| |●|
| Diabetes | | |●| | | | | | | |●| | | | | | | | | | | | | |●| | | | | | | | |●|
| Depression | |●|●| | |●| | |●| |●| | | |●| | |●|●| |●|●| | | | | |●| |●|●|●|●|●|
| Deafness | | | | | | | | | | |●| | | | | | | | | | | | | | | | | | | |●| | |●|
| Dandruff | | | | | | | | | | |●| | | | | | | | | | | | | | | | | | | |●|●| |●|

www.healthmyself.com

# D - I Conditions treated at Practices/Businesses

| Business by County with Reference no. | Dandruff | Deafness | Depression | Diabetes | Diarrhoea | Digestive Problems | Diverticulitis | Dizziness | Dyslexia | Dyspraxia | Ear Disorders | Eczema | ENT Disorders | Epilepsy | Eye Disorders | Fatigue |
|---|---|---|---|---|---|---|---|---|---|---|---|---|---|---|---|---|
| NOTTINGHAM SPORTS INJURY (HM15085) | | | | | | | | | | | | | | | | |
| OPTIMUM HEALTH (HM15348) | ● | ● | ● | ● | ● | ● | ● | ● | ● | ● | ● | ● | ● | ● | ● | ● |
| PARKSIDE STRESS MANAGEMENT (HM15722) | ● | ● | ● | | ● | ● | ● | ● | | | | ● | | | | ● |
| PHYSIO DIRECT (HM16197) | | | | | | | | | | | | | | | | |
| PHYSIODIRECT (HM16214) | | | | | | | | | | | | | | | | |
| PLAINS PHYSIO & BACK PAIN (HM16355) | | | | | | | | | | | | | | | | |
| RETFORD CHIROPRACTIC CLINIC (HM17200) | | | ● | | | ● | | | ● | ● | | ● | | | | ● |
| SEVENTHMOON NATURAL THRPY CTRE (HM18247) | | | ● | | | | | | | | | ● | | | | ● |
| SHEER TECHNIQUE (HM18368) | ● | ● | ● | ● | ● | ● | ● | ● | ● | | ● | ● | ● | | ● | ● |
| SHERWOOD PSYCHO TRAINING INS (HM18441) | | | ● | | | | | | | | | | | | | |
| SKELTON, CATHERINE () | | ● | | | | ● | | | | | ● | | ● | | | ● |
| SOUTHWELL ACUPUNCTURE CLINIC (HM18948) | | | ● | | ● | ● | ● | ● | | | | ● | | | | ● |
| TODD, S J (HM20108) | | | ● | | | ● | | ● | | | | | | | | ● |
| TOMLIN, NORMAN (HM20131) | | | | | | | | | | | | | | | | |
| TRADITIONAL ACUPUNCTURIST (HM20222) | | | ● | | ● | ● | | ● | | | | ● | | | | ● |
| VAUGHTON, NORMAN D (HM20601) | | | ● | | | ● | | | | | | ● | | | | |
| WELLBEING CENTRE (HM21149) | | | ● | | | | | | | | | | | | | |
| **OXFORDSHIRE** | | | | | | | | | | | | | | | | |
| ASHCROFT CLINIC (HM01198) | | | | | | ● | ● | | | | | | | | | ● |
| BACK IN LINE (HM01481) | | | | | | | | | | | | | | | | |
| BACK TO NORMAL CHIRO CLINIC (HM01522) | | | | | | | | | | | | | | | | |
| BLISS REMEDIES (HM02508) | | | | | ● | ● | | ● | | | | ● | | | | |
| COOPER, STEPHEN (HM05128) | | | | | | | | | | | | | | | | ● |
| COTTAGE CLINIC (HM05221) | | | ● | | ● | ● | | | | | | | | | | ● |
| EDULJEE, STELLA (HM06638) | | | ● | | ● | ● | | ● | | | | | | | | |
| FEET FIRST (HM07179) | | | | ● | ● | ● | | | | | ● | ● | | | | ● |
| FYSON, MELANIE (HM07806) | | | ● | ● | ● | ● | | ● | | | ● | ● | ● | | | ● |
| HANDS ON THERAPY (HM08915) | | | | | | | | | | | | | | | | |
| HELIX HOUSE (HM09522) | | | ● | | | ● | | | ● | ● | | | | | | ● |
| HUDSON, EMMA (HM10311) | | | | | | | | | | | | | | | | |
| HYPNOTHERAPY CENTRE (HM10516) | | | ● | | | | | | | | | | | | | |
| KIDLINGTON CHIROPRACTIC (HM11594) | | | | | | | | | | | | | | | | ● |
| KIDLINGTON HERBAL PRACTICE (HM11595) | | | ● | ● | | ● | ● | ● | | | | ● | ● | | | ● |
| KIDLINGTON OSTEO PRACTICE (HM11596) | | | | | | | | | | | | | | | | |

| Business by County with Reference no. | Fears | Fertility Problems | Fever | Fibroids | Flatulence | Foot Problems | Fractures | Fungal Infections | Gallstones | Gastrointestinal Problems | Genital Herpes | Gingivitis | Glandular Fever | Glaucoma | Gout | Gum Disease |
|---|---|---|---|---|---|---|---|---|---|---|---|---|---|---|---|---|
| NOTTINGHAM SPORTS INJURY (HM15085) | | | | | | | ● | | | | | | | | | |
| OPTIMUM HEALTH (HM15348) | ● | ● | ● | ● | ● | ● | ● | ● | ● | ● | ● | ● | ● | ● | ● | ● |
| PARKSIDE STRESS MANAGEMENT (HM15722) | ● | ● | | | ● | ● | | ● | ● | ● | | | | | ● | |
| PHYSIO DIRECT (HM16197) | | | | | | | | | | | | | | | | |
| PHYSIODIRECT (HM16214) | | | | | | | | | | | | | | | | |
| PLAINS PHYSIO & BACK PAIN (HM16355) | | | | | | | ● | | | | | | | | | |
| RETFORD CHIROPRACTIC CLINIC (HM17200) | | ● | | | | | | | | ● | | | | | | |
| SEVENTHMOON NATURAL THRPY CTRE (HM18247) | ● | ● | | ● | | ● | | | | | | | | | | |
| SHEER TECHNIQUE (HM18368) | ● | ● | ● | ● | ● | ● | ● | ● | ● | ● | | ● | | ● | ● | ● |
| SHERWOOD PSYCHO TRAINING INS (HM18441) | | | | | | | | | | | | | | | | |
| SKELTON, CATHERINE () | ● | ● | | ● | ● | ● | | ● | | | | | ● | | ● | |
| SOUTHWELL ACUPUNCTURE CLINIC (HM18948) | ● | ● | ● | ● | ● | | | | ● | ● | | | ● | | ● | |
| TODD, S J (HM20108) | | ● | | | | ● | ● | ● | | | | | | | | |
| TOMLIN, NORMAN (HM20131) | | | | | | | | | | | | | | | | |
| TRADITIONAL ACUPUNCTURIST (HM20222) | ● | ● | | | ● | | | | | | | | | | ● | |
| VAUGHTON, NORMAN D (HM20601) | ● | | | | | | | | | ● | | | | | | |
| WELLBEING CENTRE (HM21149) | | | | | | | | | | | | | | | | |
| **OXFORDSHIRE** | | | | | | | | | | | | | | | | |
| ASHCROFT CLINIC (HM01198) | | | | | | ● | | | | ● | | | | | | |
| BACK IN LINE (HM01481) | | | | | | ● | ● | | | | | | | | | |
| BACK TO NORMAL CHIRO CLINIC (HM01522) | | | | | | | | | | | | | | | | |
| BLISS REMEDIES (HM02508) | | | | | ● | ● | | ● | | | | | | | | |
| COOPER, STEPHEN (HM05128) | ● | | | | | | | | | | | | | | | |
| COTTAGE CLINIC (HM05221) | ● | | | | | | | | | | | | | | | |
| EDULJEE, STELLA (HM06638) | | | | | | ● | | | | | | | | | | |
| FEET FIRST (HM07179) | | ● | | ● | ● | ● | | ● | ● | | | | | | ● | |
| FYSON, MELANIE (HM07806) | ● | ● | ● | ● | ● | | | ● | ● | ● | | | ● | | | |
| HANDS ON THERAPY (HM08915) | | | | | | | | | | | | | | | | |
| HELIX HOUSE (HM09522) | ● | | | | | ● | | | | | | | | | | |
| HUDSON, EMMA (HM10311) | | | | | | ● | | | | | | | | | | |
| HYPNOTHERAPY CENTRE (HM10516) | ● | | | | | | | | | | | | | | | |
| KIDLINGTON CHIROPRACTIC (HM11594) | | | | | | | | | | | | | | | | |
| KIDLINGTON HERBAL PRACTICE (HM11595) | | | ● | ● | ● | | | ● | | ● | | ● | ● | | ● | ● |
| KIDLINGTON OSTEO PRACTICE (HM11596) | | | | | | ● | ● | | | | | | | | | |

| Business by County with Reference no. | Hair Problems | Halitosis | Hand Problems | Hay Fever | Headaches | Hearing Problems | High Blood Pressure | Hip Complaints | Hyperactivity | Hypoglycaemia | Impotence | Incontinence | Indigestion | Infertility | Influenza | Ingrowing Toenails |
|---|---|---|---|---|---|---|---|---|---|---|---|---|---|---|---|---|
| NOTTINGHAM SPORTS INJURY (HM15085) | | | | | | | | ● | | | | | | | | |
| OPTIMUM HEALTH (HM15348) | ● | ● | ● | ● | ● | ● | ● | ● | ● | ● | ● | ● | ● | ● | ● | |
| PARKSIDE STRESS MANAGEMENT (HM15722) | | | ● | ● | ● | ● | ● | | ● | ● | | | ● | | ● | |
| PHYSIO DIRECT (HM16197) | | | | | | | | ● | | | | | | | | |
| PHYSIODIRECT (HM16214) | | | | | | | | ● | | | | | | | | |
| PLAINS PHYSIO & BACK PAIN (HM16355) | | | | | | | | | | | | | | | | |
| RETFORD CHIROPRACTIC CLINIC (HM17200) | | | | | ● | | ● | ● | | | | | ● | | | |
| SEVENTHMOON NATURAL THRPY CTRE (HM18247) | | | | ● | ● | ● | ● | ● | | | | | ● | ● | | |
| SHEER TECHNIQUE (HM18368) | ● | ● | ● | ● | ● | ● | ● | ● | ● | ● | ● | ● | ● | ● | ● | |
| SHERWOOD PSYCHO TRAINING INS (HM18441) | | | | | | | | | | | | | | | | |
| SKELTON, CATHERINE () | | | | | ● | ● | ● | | | | | ● | ● | ● | ● | |
| SOUTHWELL ACUPUNCTURE CLINIC (HM18948) | | | | ● | ● | | ● | ● | ● | ● | ● | ● | ● | ● | ● | |
| TODD, S J (HM20108) | | | | | | | | | | | | | | | | |
| TOMLIN, NORMAN (HM20131) | | | | | ● | | | ● | | | | | | | | |
| TRADITIONAL ACUPUNCTURIST (HM20222) | ● | | | ● | ● | | | ● | | ● | ● | | ● | ● | ● | |
| VAUGHTON, NORMAN D (HM20601) | | | | | ● | | | | | | | | | | | |
| WELLBEING CENTRE (HM21149) | | | | | | | | | | | | | | | | |
| **OXFORDSHIRE** | | | | | | | | | | | | | | | | |
| ASHCROFT CLINIC (HM01198) | | | ● | | ● | | | ● | | | | | ● | | | |
| BACK IN LINE (HM01481) | | | | | ● | | | ● | | | | | | | | |
| BACK TO NORMAL CHIRO CLINIC (HM01522) | | | ● | | ● | | | | | | | | | | | |
| BLISS REMEDIES (HM02508) | | | | ● | | | | | ● | | | | ● | | ● | ● |
| COOPER, STEPHEN (HM05128) | | | | | ● | | ● | | | | | | | | | |
| COTTAGE CLINIC (HM05221) | | | | | | | | | | | | | | | | |
| EDULJEE, STELLA (HM06638) | | | ● | ● | ● | ● | ● | ● | | | | | ● | | | |
| FEET FIRST (HM07179) | | | | | ● | | ● | ● | | | | | ● | ● | | |
| FYSON, MELANIE (HM07806) | | | | ● | ● | | ● | | ● | ● | | | ● | ● | ● | |
| HANDS ON THERAPY (HM08915) | | | | | ● | | | | | | | | | | | |
| HELIX HOUSE (HM09522) | | | | | ● | | | ● | | ● | | ● | | | | |
| HUDSON, EMMA (HM10311) | | | | | ● | | | ● | | | | | | | | |
| HYPNOTHERAPY CENTRE (HM10516) | | | | | | | ● | | | | | | | | | |
| KIDLINGTON CHIROPRACTIC (HM11594) | | | | | ● | | | ● | | | | | | | | |
| KIDLINGTON HERBAL PRACTICE (HM11595) | | | | ● | ● | | ● | | ● | ● | ● | ● | ● | | ● | |
| KIDLINGTON OSTEO PRACTICE (HM11596) | | | ● | | ● | | | ● | | | | | | | | |

# D - I Conditions treated at Practices/Businesses

| Business by County with Reference no. | Dandruff | Deafness | Depression | Diabetes | Diarrhoea | Digestive Problems | Diverticulitis | Dizziness | Dyslexia | Dyspraxia | Ear Disorders | Eczema | ENT Disorders | Epilepsy | Eye Disorders | Fatigue | Fears | Fertility Problems | Fever | Fibroids | Flatulence | Foot Problems | Fractures | Fungal Infections |
|---|---|---|---|---|---|---|---|---|---|---|---|---|---|---|---|---|---|---|---|---|---|---|---|---|
| MARRIOTT, HUGH (HM13138) | | | | | | | | | | |●| |●| | | | | | | | | | | |
| MIDSUMMER COTTAGE CLINIC (HM13845) |●| |●| |●|●|●|●| | |●|●|●| | |●| |●|●|●|●| | |●|
| O'BRIEN, FRANCES (HM15179) | | |●| |●| | | | | | |●| | | | | | | | | | | | |
| O'DONNELL, ELSPETH (HM15225) | | | | | | | | | | | | | | | | | | | | | |●|●| |
| OXFORD NUTRITION & ALLRGY CTRE (HM15541) | | |●|●|●|●|●|●|●| |●|●| | | |●| |●| | |●| | |●|
| OXFORD TRANSCENDTL MEDITA CTRE (HM15544) | | |●| | |●| | | | | | | | | |●| | | | | | | | |
| PARSONS STREET CLINIC (HM15747) | | | | | | | | | | |●| | | | | | | | | | | | | |
| POLLOCK, SUSAN (HM16418) | | |●|●| |●| | | | | |●| | | |●| | | | | |●| |●|
| SIDEBOTTOM, MARGARET (HM18527) | | | | | | | | | | | | | | | | | | | | | | | | |
| SUMMERTON CLINIC (HM19498) |●|●|●| |●|●|●|●| | |●|●|●| | |●|●|●|●|●|●|●|●|●|
| TOUCH OF NATURE (HM20188) | | | | | | | | | | | |●| | | |●| | | | | | | | |
| TWINE, I E (HM20453) | | |●| | |●| |●|●|●| |●| | |●|●|●| | | |●| | | |
| WANTAGE NATURAL HEALTH CENTRE (HM20891) |●|●|●|●|●|●|●|●|●|●|●|●|●|●|●|●|●|●|●|●|●|●|●|●|
| WANTAGE OSTEOPATHIC PRACTICE (HM20892) | | | | | | | |●| | | | | | | | | | | | | | | | |
| WHEATLEY COMP THERAPY (HM21308) | | |●| |●|●| | | |●| |●| | | | |●| | | | | | | |
| WITNEY CHIROPRACTIC/CHIROPODY (HM21750) | | | | | | | | | | | | | | | | | | | | | |●| | |
| WITNEY NATURAL HEALTH CLINIC (HM21751) |●|●|●|●|●|●| |●|●|●|●|●|●|●|●|●|●|●|●|●|●|●|●|●|
| **SHROPSHIRE** | | | | | | | | | | | | | | | | | | | | | | | | |
| ACUMEDIC (HM00218) | | | | | |●| | | | | |●| | | |●| |●| | | | | | |
| AYRES, JOHN (HM01434) | | |●| | | | | | | | | | | | | |●| | | | | | | |
| BEATTIE, R G (HM01979) | | | | | | | | | | | | | | | | | | | | | |●| |●|
| BODYLIFE CENTRE (HM02622) | | |●| | | | | | | | | | | | |●|●| | | | | | | |
| BOOTH, ROBERT (HM02709) | | | | | | | | | | | | | | | | | | | | | | | | |
| COLERIDGE, JUDY (HM04831) | | |●| | | | | | | | | | | | |●|●| | | | |●| | |
| CORKE, A J (HM05167) | | | | | | | | | | | | | | | | | | | | | | | | |
| FULLERTON, N P (HM07792) | | | | | | | |●| | | | | | | | | | | | | | | | |
| HALES OSTEOPATHIC PRACTICE (HM08743) |●| |●|●|●|●|●|●| | |●|●|●|●| |●|●| | |●|●|●|●| |
| HEALING FOUNDATION (HM09334) | | |●| | |●| |●| | | | | | | | | | | | | | | | |
| LUDLOW OSTEOPATHIC CLINIC (HM12727) | | | | | | | | | | | |●| | | |●| | | | | |●| |●|
| MEDAYD PHYSIOTHERAPY (HM13644) | | | | | | | | | | | | | | | | | | | | | | | | |
| MEDAYD PHYSIOTHERAPY (HM13645) | | | | | | | | | | | | | | | | | | | | | | |●| |
| NEEDHAM, LYNDA M (HM14751) | |●|●| | | | | | | | | | | | |●|●| | | |●| | | |
| OSTEOPATHIC (HM15449) |●| |●| | |●| |●| | |●| | | | |●| | | | |●|●| | |
| OSTLE, SAMANTHA (HM15480) | | | | | | | |●| | | | | | | |●| | | | | |●| | |

| Business by County with Reference no. | Gallstones | Gastrointestinal Problems | Genital Herpes | Gingivitis | Glandular Fever | Glaucoma | Gout | Gum Disease | Hair Problems | Halitosis | Hand Problems | Hay Fever | Headaches | Hearing Problems | High Blood Pressure | Hip Complaints | Hyperactivity | Hypoglycaemia | Impotence | Incontinence | Indigestion | Infertility | Influenza | Ingrowing Toenails |
|---|---|---|---|---|---|---|---|---|---|---|---|---|---|---|---|---|---|---|---|---|---|---|---|---|
| MARRIOTT, HUGH (HM13138) | | | | | | | | | | | | |●| | | | | | | | | | | |
| MIDSUMMER COTTAGE CLINIC (HM13845) |●|●|●| |●|●|●| |●|●| |●|●| |●|●|●|●|●|●|●|●|●| |
| O'BRIEN, FRANCES (HM15179) | | | | | | | | | | | |●|●| | |●| | | | | | | | |
| O'DONNELL, ELSPETH (HM15225) | | | | | | | | | | | | | | | |●| | | | | | | | |
| OXFORD NUTRITION & ALLRGY CTRE (HM15541) |●|●| |●|●| |●|●|●|●| |●|●| |●| |●|●|●| |●|●|●| |
| OXFORD TRANSCENDTL MEDITA CTRE (HM15544) | | | | | | | | | | | | |●| |●| |●| | | | | | | |
| PARSONS STREET CLINIC (HM15747) | | | | | | | | | | | | |●| |●|●| | | | | |●| | |
| POLLOCK, SUSAN (HM16418) | | | | | | |●| | | |●| |●| | |●| | | | | | | | |
| SIDEBOTTOM, MARGARET (HM18527) | | | | | | | | | | | | | | | |●| | | | | | | | |
| SUMMERTON CLINIC (HM19498) |●|●|●|●|●|●|●|●|●|●|●|●|●|●|●|●|●|●|●|●|●|●|●| |
| TOUCH OF NATURE (HM20188) | | | | | | | | |●| | | | | | | | | | | | | | | |
| TWINE, I E (HM20453) | | | | |●| |●| | | |●|●|●| |●|●|●| | | |●| | | |
| WANTAGE NATURAL HEALTH CENTRE (HM20891) |●|●|●|●|●|●|●|●|●|●|●|●|●|●|●|●|●|●|●|●|●|●|●| |
| WANTAGE OSTEOPATHIC PRACTICE (HM20892) | | | | | | | | | | | | |●| | |●| | | | | | | | |
| WHEATLEY COMP THERAPY (HM21308) | | | | | | | | | | | | | | |●| | | | | |●| | | |
| WITNEY CHIROPRACTIC/CHIROPODY (HM21750) | | | | | | | | | | |●| |●| | |●| | | | | | | | |
| WITNEY NATURAL HEALTH CLINIC (HM21751) |●|●|●|●|●|●|●|●|●|●|●|●|●|●|●|●|●|●|●|●|●|●|●| |
| **SHROPSHIRE** | | | | | | | | | | | | | | | | | | | | | | | | |
| ACUMEDIC (HM00218) | | | | | | | | | |●| |●|●| |●| | | |●| | | | | |
| AYRES, JOHN (HM01434) | | | | | | | | | | | | | | | | | | | | | | | | |
| BEATTIE, R G (HM01979) | | | | | | | | | | | | | | | | | | | | | | | | |
| BODYLIFE CENTRE (HM02622) | | | | | | | | | | | | |●| | | | | | | | | | | |
| BOOTH, ROBERT (HM02709) | | | | | | | | | | | | | | | |●| | | | | | | | |
| COLERIDGE, JUDY (HM04831) | | | | | | | | | | | | |●| | | | | | | | | | | |
| CORKE, A J (HM05167) | | | | | | | | | | | | | | |●| | | | | | | | | |
| FULLERTON, N P (HM07792) | | | | | | | | | | | | |●| | |●| | | | | | | | |
| HALES OSTEOPATHIC PRACTICE (HM08743) |●|●| |●| |●|●|●|●|●|●|●|●|●|●|●|●|●| |●|●| | | |
| HEALING FOUNDATION (HM09334) | | | | | | | | | | | | | | |●| |●| | | | | | | |
| LUDLOW OSTEOPATHIC CLINIC (HM12727) | |●| | | | | | | | | | | | | | | | | | | | | | |
| MEDAYD PHYSIOTHERAPY (HM13644) | | | | | | | | | | | | | | | |●| | | | | | | | |
| MEDAYD PHYSIOTHERAPY (HM13645) | | | | | | | | | | | | | | | |●| | | | | | | | |
| NEEDHAM, LYNDA M (HM14751) | | | | | | | | | | | | | |●| | | | |●| | | | | |
| OSTEOPATHIC (HM15449) | | | | |●| | | |●| |●| |●| | |●| | | | |●| | | |
| OSTLE, SAMANTHA (HM15480) | | | | | | | | | | |●| |●| | |●| | | | | | | | |

www.healthmyself.com

# D - I Conditions treated at Practices/Businesses

| Business by County with Reference no. | Dandruff | Deafness | Depression | Diabetes | Diarrhoea | Digestive Problems | Diverticulitis | Dizziness | Dyslexia | Dyspraxia | Ear Disorders | Eczema | ENT Disorders | Epilepsy | Eye Disorders | Fatigue | Fears | Fertility Problems | Fever | Fibroids | Flatulence | Foot Problems | Fractures | Fungal Infections |
|---|---|---|---|---|---|---|---|---|---|---|---|---|---|---|---|---|---|---|---|---|---|---|---|---|
| PEARSON, CHRISTINE (HM15911) | ● | ● | ● | ● | ● | ● | ● | ● | ● | ● | ● | ● | ● | ● | ● | ● | ● | ● | ● | ● | ● | ● | ● | ● |
| PHILLIPS, ANN (HM16124) |  |  | ● |  |  |  |  |  |  |  |  |  |  |  |  | ● |  |  |  |  |  |  |  |  |
| PREES COMPLEMENTARY THERAPIES (HM16533) |  |  | ● |  |  |  |  |  |  |  |  |  |  |  |  |  | ● |  |  |  |  |  |  |  |
| REYNOLDS, TESS (HM17216) |  |  | ● |  | ● | ● |  | ● |  |  | ● | ● | ● |  | ● | ● | ● | ● | ● |  |  |  |  |  |
| SHREWSBURY SOLE CARE (HM18507) |  |  |  | ● |  |  |  |  |  |  |  |  |  |  |  |  |  |  |  |  |  | ● |  |  |
| STONE, JANET (HM19336) | ● | ● | ● | ● | ● | ● | ● | ● | ● | ● | ● | ● | ● | ● | ● | ● | ● | ● | ● | ● | ● | ● | ● | ● |
| TAN & BEAUTY STUDIO (HM19676) |  |  |  |  |  | ● |  |  |  |  |  |  |  |  |  | ● |  |  |  |  |  |  |  |  |
| WALMSLEY, RUTH (HM20848) |  |  | ● |  |  | ● | ● |  |  |  |  |  |  |  |  | ● |  |  |  |  |  |  |  |  |
| WESTON, JOHN (HM21279) |  |  |  |  |  |  |  | ● |  |  |  |  |  |  |  |  |  |  |  |  |  | ● |  |  |
| WHITELEY, STEVEN (HM21400) | ● | ● | ● | ● | ● | ● | ● | ● | ● | ● | ● | ● | ● | ● | ● | ● | ● | ● | ● | ● | ● | ● | ● | ● |
| WILD ROSE (HM21488) |  |  |  |  |  |  |  |  |  |  |  |  |  |  |  |  |  |  |  |  |  |  |  |  |
| WILSON, AMANDA (HM21644) |  |  |  |  |  |  |  |  |  |  |  |  |  |  |  |  |  |  |  |  |  | ● |  |  |
| **SOMERSET** |  |  |  |  |  |  |  |  |  |  |  |  |  |  |  |  |  |  |  |  |  |  |  |  |
| ABBEY CHIROPODY SERVICES (HM00074) |  |  |  |  |  |  |  |  |  |  |  |  |  |  |  |  |  |  |  |  |  | ● |  | ● |
| ALASKAN BACH FLOWER REMEDIES (HM00472) |  |  | ● |  |  | ● |  |  |  |  |  | ● |  |  |  |  |  |  |  |  |  |  |  |  |
| ANDERSON, DAVID (HM00816) |  |  |  |  |  |  |  |  |  |  |  |  |  |  |  |  |  |  |  |  |  | ● |  | ● |
| ANSON, BARRIE (HM00916) |  | ● | ● | ● | ● | ● | ● | ● |  |  | ● | ● | ● |  |  | ● | ● | ● | ● | ● | ● | ● |  | ● |
| AUSSENS, MIEKE (HM01359) |  |  | ● |  |  |  |  |  |  |  |  |  |  |  |  |  |  |  |  |  |  |  |  |  |
| AVENUE CLINIC (HM01388) | ● | ● | ● | ● | ● | ● | ● | ● | ● | ● | ● | ● | ● | ● | ● | ● | ● | ● | ● | ● | ● | ● | ● | ● |
| BAILEY, LINDA R (HM01552) |  |  |  |  | ● |  | ● |  |  |  |  |  |  |  |  |  |  |  |  |  | ● |  |  |  |
| BATH ALEXANDER TECHNIQUE (HM01890) |  |  |  |  |  |  |  |  |  |  |  |  |  |  |  | ● |  |  |  |  |  |  |  |  |
| BATH NATURAL MEDICAL CENTRE (HM01893) |  |  |  |  |  |  |  |  |  |  |  |  |  |  |  |  |  |  |  |  |  |  |  |  |
| BATHPOOL CHIROPRACTIC CLINIC (HM01900) |  |  | ● |  |  |  |  |  |  |  |  |  |  |  |  |  |  |  |  |  |  |  |  |  |
| BEECH HOUSE CLINIC (HM02046) |  |  |  |  |  |  |  |  |  |  |  |  |  |  |  |  |  |  |  |  |  |  |  |  |
| BOULEVARD PHARMACY (HM02739) | ● |  | ● | ● | ● | ● | ● | ● |  |  |  | ● | ● |  |  | ● | ● |  | ● |  | ● | ● |  | ● |
| BRIDGET HEALING CENTRE (HM03008) | ● | ● | ● | ● | ● | ● | ● | ● | ● | ● | ● | ● | ● | ● | ● | ● | ● | ● | ● | ● | ● | ● | ● | ● |
| CASTLE SURGERY (HM03840) |  |  |  |  |  |  |  |  |  |  |  |  |  |  |  |  |  |  |  |  |  |  |  |  |
| CHAMELEON OILS (HM03961) |  |  | ● |  |  | ● |  |  |  |  |  | ● |  |  |  | ● | ● |  |  |  |  |  |  | ● |
| CHEDDAR COMP MEDICINE CTRE (HM04075) |  |  | ● |  |  | ● |  |  |  |  |  | ● |  | ● |  | ● |  | ● |  |  |  | ● | ● | ● |
| CHINESE MEDICAL CENTRE (HM04238) |  |  |  |  |  | ● |  |  |  |  |  | ● |  |  |  | ● |  | ● |  |  |  |  |  |  |
| CHIPPER, MARY (HM04278) |  |  |  |  |  |  |  |  |  |  |  |  | ● |  |  |  |  |  |  |  |  |  |  |  |
| CHIROPODY SURGERY (HM04344) |  |  |  |  |  |  |  |  |  |  |  |  |  |  |  |  |  |  |  |  |  |  |  |  |
| CLARKE GAIL & RAWLINSON MIKE (HM04581) |  |  | ● |  |  |  |  |  |  | ● |  |  |  |  |  |  |  |  |  |  |  |  |  |  |
| CLINIC OF COMP MEDICINE (HM04689) |  |  | ● |  | ● | ● | ● | ● |  |  | ● | ● | ● |  | ● | ● | ● |  | ● | ● | ● | ● |  | ● |

| Business by County with Reference no. | Gallstones | Gastrointestinal Problems | Genital Herpes | Gingivitis | Glandular Fever | Glaucoma | Gout | Gum Disease | Hair Problems | Halitosis | Hand Problems | Hay Fever | Headaches | Hearing Problems | High Blood Pressure | Hip Complaints | Hyperactivity | Hypoglycaemia | Impotence | Incontinence | Indigestion | Infertility | Influenza | Ingrowing Toenails |
|---|---|---|---|---|---|---|---|---|---|---|---|---|---|---|---|---|---|---|---|---|---|---|---|---|
| PEARSON, CHRISTINE (HM15911) | ● | ● | ● | ● | ● | ● | ● | ● | ● | ● | ● | ● | ● | ● | ● | ● | ● | ● | ● | ● | ● | ● | ● |  |
| PHILLIPS, ANN (HM16124) |  |  |  |  |  |  |  |  |  |  |  |  | ● |  | ● |  | ● |  |  |  | ● |  |  |  |
| PREES COMPLEMENTARY THERAPIES (HM16533) |  |  |  |  |  |  |  |  |  |  |  |  |  |  |  |  |  |  |  |  |  |  |  |  |
| REYNOLDS, TESS (HM17216) | ● | ● |  |  |  |  |  |  |  |  |  | ● | ● | ● | ● | ● | ● |  | ● |  | ● | ● | ● |  |
| SHREWSBURY SOLE CARE (HM18507) |  |  |  |  |  |  |  |  |  |  |  |  |  |  |  |  |  |  |  |  |  |  |  |  |
| STONE, JANET (HM19336) | ● | ● | ● | ● | ● | ● | ● | ● | ● | ● | ● | ● | ● | ● | ● | ● | ● | ● | ● | ● | ● | ● | ● |  |
| TAN & BEAUTY STUDIO (HM19676) |  |  |  |  |  |  |  |  |  |  | ● | ● | ● | ● | ● |  | ● |  |  |  | ● |  |  |  |
| WALMSLEY, RUTH (HM20848) |  |  |  |  |  |  |  |  |  |  | ● |  | ● |  | ● | ● |  |  |  |  | ● |  |  |  |
| WESTON, JOHN (HM21279) |  |  |  |  |  |  |  |  |  |  | ● |  | ● |  |  | ● |  |  |  |  |  |  |  |  |
| WHITELEY, STEVEN (HM21400) | ● | ● | ● | ● | ● | ● | ● | ● | ● | ● | ● | ● | ● | ● | ● | ● | ● | ● | ● | ● | ● | ● | ● |  |
| WILD ROSE (HM21488) |  |  |  |  |  |  |  |  |  |  |  |  | ● |  | ● | ● |  |  |  |  |  |  |  |  |
| WILSON, AMANDA (HM21644) |  |  |  |  |  |  |  |  |  |  |  |  |  |  |  |  |  |  |  |  |  |  |  |  |
| **SOMERSET** |  |  |  |  |  |  |  |  |  |  |  |  |  |  |  |  |  |  |  |  |  |  |  |  |
| ABBEY CHIROPODY SERVICES (HM00074) |  |  |  |  |  |  |  |  |  |  |  |  |  |  |  |  |  |  |  |  |  |  |  |  |
| ALASKAN BACH FLOWER REMEDIES (HM00472) |  |  |  |  |  |  |  |  |  |  |  |  |  |  | ● |  |  |  |  |  |  |  |  |  |
| ANDERSON, DAVID (HM00816) |  |  |  |  |  |  |  |  |  |  |  |  |  |  |  |  |  |  |  |  |  |  |  |  |
| ANSON, BARRIE (HM00916) | ● | ● | ● | ● | ● |  | ● | ● |  | ● |  | ● | ● | ● | ● |  | ● | ● | ● | ● | ● | ● | ● |  |
| AUSSENS, MIEKE (HM01359) |  |  |  |  |  |  |  |  |  |  |  |  | ● |  |  |  |  |  |  |  |  |  |  |  |
| AVENUE CLINIC (HM01388) | ● | ● | ● | ● | ● | ● | ● | ● | ● | ● | ● | ● | ● | ● | ● | ● | ● | ● | ● | ● | ● | ● | ● | ● |
| BAILEY, LINDA R (HM01552) |  |  |  |  |  |  |  |  |  |  |  |  | ● |  | ● |  |  |  |  |  |  |  |  |  |
| BATH ALEXANDER TECHNIQUE (HM01890) |  |  |  |  |  |  |  |  |  |  | ● |  | ● |  |  |  |  |  |  |  |  |  |  |  |
| BATH NATURAL MEDICAL CENTRE (HM01893) |  |  |  |  |  |  |  |  |  |  |  |  |  |  |  |  |  |  |  |  |  | ● |  |  |
| BATHPOOL CHIROPRACTIC CLINIC (HM01900) |  |  |  |  |  |  |  |  |  |  | ● |  | ● |  | ● | ● |  |  |  |  |  |  |  |  |
| BEECH HOUSE CLINIC (HM02046) |  |  |  |  |  |  |  |  |  |  |  |  | ● |  |  | ● |  |  |  |  |  |  |  |  |
| BOULEVARD PHARMACY (HM02739) |  | ● |  | ● | ● |  | ● | ● |  | ● |  | ● | ● |  | ● | ● | ● | ● | ● | ● | ● |  | ● |  |
| BRIDGET HEALING CENTRE (HM03008) | ● | ● | ● | ● | ● | ● | ● | ● | ● | ● | ● | ● | ● | ● | ● | ● | ● | ● | ● | ● | ● | ● | ● |  |
| CASTLE SURGERY (HM03840) |  |  |  |  |  |  |  |  |  |  |  |  | ● |  |  | ● |  |  |  |  |  |  |  |  |
| CHAMELEON OILS (HM03961) |  |  |  |  |  |  |  |  |  |  |  |  | ● |  |  |  |  |  |  |  |  |  |  |  |
| CHEDDAR COMP MEDICINE CTRE (HM04075) |  |  |  |  |  |  |  |  |  |  |  | ● | ● |  |  | ● |  |  |  |  | ● | ● |  |  |
| CHINESE MEDICAL CENTRE (HM04238) |  |  |  |  |  |  |  |  |  | ● |  | ● | ● |  | ● |  |  |  | ● |  |  |  |  |  |
| CHIPPER, MARY (HM04278) |  |  |  |  |  |  |  |  |  |  |  |  | ● |  |  |  |  |  |  |  |  |  |  |  |
| CHIROPODY SURGERY (HM04344) |  |  |  |  |  |  |  |  |  |  |  |  |  |  |  |  |  |  |  |  |  |  |  | ● |
| CLARKE GAIL & RAWLINSON MIKE (HM04581) |  |  |  |  |  |  |  |  |  |  | ● |  | ● |  |  | ● | ● |  |  |  |  |  |  |  |
| CLINIC OF COMP MEDICINE (HM04689) | ● | ● | ● |  | ● |  | ● |  |  | ● | ● | ● | ● |  | ● | ● | ● |  |  | ● | ● |  | ● |  |

# D - I Conditions treated at Practices/Businesses

Business by County with Reference no.

| Business | Dandruff | Deafness | Depression | Diabetes | Diarrhoea | Digestive Problems | Diverticulitis | Dizziness | Dyslexia | Dyspraxia | Ear Disorders | Eczema |
|---|---|---|---|---|---|---|---|---|---|---|---|---|
| CLISBY, JANE (HM04722) | | | ● | ● | | ● | | ● | | | | |
| COMPLEMENTARY THERAPY (HM04942) | | | | | | | | | | | | |
| COOK, COLIN (HM05041) | | | | | | | | | | | | |
| COUNSULTING ROOMS (HM05253) | | | ● | | | ● | | | | | | ● |
| DAVIES, SALLY (HM05840) | | | ● | | | | | | | | | |
| DEVONSHIRE SURGERY (HM06044) | | | | | | | | | | | | |
| EUROPEAN COLLEGE-BOWEN STUDIES (HM06946) | | | | | | ● | | ● | | | | ● |
| FRANCES-WHITAKER, J A (HM07665) | | | | | | | | | | | | |
| GLASTONBURY CHIROPRACTIC (HM08131) | | | ● | | | | | | | | | |
| GLASTONBURY EAST WEST CENTRE (HM08132) | ● | ● | ● | ● | ● | ● | ● | ● | ● | ● | ● | ● |
| HELEN SMITH CHIROPODIST (HM09515) | | | | | | | | | | | | |
| HOLISTIC HEALING CENTRE (HM09962) | | | ● | | | ● | | | | | | |
| HUDSON, JOHN (HM10315) | | | ● | | | | | | | | | |
| HUXTABLE, ALISON (HM10461) | | | | | | | | | | | | |
| JONES, BECKY (HM11125) | | | ● | | | | | | | | | |
| JONES, RAYMOND (HM11190) | | | | | | | | | | | | |
| KIRKMEAD CENTRE (HM11718) | | | ● | | | ● | | | | | | |
| LANSDOWN PHYSIOTHERAPY CLINIC (HM11964) | | | | | | | | | | | | |
| LEAVEY, J () | | | | | | | | | | | | |
| LOGAN, DAVID (HM12566) | | | ● | | | | | | | | | ● |
| MARY WILKINSON - MCTIMONEY (HM13226) | | | | | | | | | | | | |
| MARY WILKINSON - MCTIMONEY (HM13225) | | | | | | | | | | | | |
| MCLOUGHLIN, BRENDAN (HM13559) | | | ● | | | | | | | | | |
| MIDSOMER NORTON CHIROPRACTIC (HM13844) | | | | | | | | | | | | |
| MILSOM STREET CLINIC (HM13944) | | | | | | | | | | | | |
| NATURAL SPIRITUAL HEALING (HM14626) | | | ● | ● | | ● | | | | | | |
| NATURAL THERAPIES (HM14632) | ● | | ● | | | | | | | | | |
| NORSO BIOMAGNETICS UK (HM15016) | | | ● | ● | | ● | | | | | | |
| NUTRITION FOR LIFE (HM15123) | | | ● | ● | ● | ● | ● | | | | | ● |
| ORCHARD CLINIC (HM15360) | | | ● | | ● | ● | | | | | | |
| PARK HOUSE CLINIC (HM15666) | | | | | | | | | | | | |
| PARNELL, R H (HM15727) | | | ● | | ● | | | | | | | ● |
| PARRY, J M (HM15738) | | | | | | | | | | | | |
| PENNINGTON, PAM (HM15990) | | | | | | | | | | | | |

| Business | ENT Disorders | Epilepsy | Eye Disorders | Fatigue | Fears | Fertility Problems | Fever | Fibroids | Flatulence | Foot Problems | Fractures | Fungal Infections |
|---|---|---|---|---|---|---|---|---|---|---|---|---|
| CLISBY, JANE (HM04722) | | | | ● | | | | | | ● | | |
| COMPLEMENTARY THERAPY (HM04942) | | | | | | | | | | | | |
| COOK, COLIN (HM05041) | | | | | | | | | | ● | | |
| COUNSULTING ROOMS (HM05253) | | | | ● | ● | ● | | | ● | | | |
| DAVIES, SALLY (HM05840) | | | | | | | | | | | | |
| DEVONSHIRE SURGERY (HM06044) | | | | | | | | | | | | |
| EUROPEAN COLLEGE-BOWEN STUDIES (HM06946) | | | | ● | | ● | | | | ● | | |
| FRANCES-WHITAKER, J A (HM07665) | | | | | | | | | | ● | | ● |
| GLASTONBURY CHIROPRACTIC (HM08131) | | ● | | ● | ● | | | | ● | | | |
| GLASTONBURY EAST WEST CENTRE (HM08132) | ● | ● | ● | ● | ● | ● | ● | ● | ● | ● | | ● |
| HELEN SMITH CHIROPODIST (HM09515) | | | | | | | | | | ● | | |
| HOLISTIC HEALING CENTRE (HM09962) | | | | ● | | | | | | | | |
| HUDSON, JOHN (HM10315) | | | | | | | | | | | | |
| HUXTABLE, ALISON (HM10461) | | | | | | | | | | | | |
| JONES, BECKY (HM11125) | | | | ● | ● | | | | | | | |
| JONES, RAYMOND (HM11190) | | | | | | | | | | | | |
| KIRKMEAD CENTRE (HM11718) | | | | ● | ● | | | | | | | |
| LANSDOWN PHYSIOTHERAPY CLINIC (HM11964) | | | | | | | | | | ● | ● | |
| LEAVEY, J () | | | | | | | | | | | | |
| LOGAN, DAVID (HM12566) | | | | | | | | | | | | |
| MARY WILKINSON - MCTIMONEY (HM13226) | | | | | | | | | | | | |
| MARY WILKINSON - MCTIMONEY (HM13225) | | | | | | | | | | | | |
| MCLOUGHLIN, BRENDAN (HM13559) | | | | | | | | | | | | |
| MIDSOMER NORTON CHIROPRACTIC (HM13844) | | | | | | | | | | | | |
| MILSOM STREET CLINIC (HM13944) | | | | | | | | | | | | |
| NATURAL SPIRITUAL HEALING (HM14626) | | ● | | | ● | ● | | | | | | |
| NATURAL THERAPIES (HM14632) | | | | ● | ● | | | | | | | |
| NORSO BIOMAGNETICS UK (HM15016) | | | | ● | | | | | | ● | ● | |
| NUTRITION FOR LIFE (HM15123) | ● | | ● | ● | | | ● | | ● | | | ● |
| ORCHARD CLINIC (HM15360) | ● | ● | | ● | ● | | | | | | | |
| PARK HOUSE CLINIC (HM15666) | | | | | | | | | | | | |
| PARNELL, R H (HM15727) | | ● | | ● | | | | | | | | |
| PARRY, J M (HM15738) | | | | | | | | | | ● | | |
| PENNINGTON, PAM (HM15990) | | | | | | | | | | ● | | ● |

| Business | Gallstones | Gastrointestinal Problems | Genital Herpes | Gingivitis | Glandular Fever | Glaucoma | Gout | Gum Disease | Hair Problems | Halitosis | Hand Problems | Hay Fever |
|---|---|---|---|---|---|---|---|---|---|---|---|---|
| CLISBY, JANE (HM04722) | | | | | | | | | | | ● | |
| COMPLEMENTARY THERAPY (HM04942) | | | | | | | | | | | | |
| COOK, COLIN (HM05041) | | | | | | | | | | | ● | |
| COUNSULTING ROOMS (HM05253) | | | | | | | | | | | | |
| DAVIES, SALLY (HM05840) | | | | | | | | | | | | |
| DEVONSHIRE SURGERY (HM06044) | | | | | | | | | | | | |
| EUROPEAN COLLEGE-BOWEN STUDIES (HM06946) | | | | | | | | | | | | |
| FRANCES-WHITAKER, J A (HM07665) | | | | | | | | | | | | |
| GLASTONBURY CHIROPRACTIC (HM08131) | | | | | | | | | | | ● | |
| GLASTONBURY EAST WEST CENTRE (HM08132) | ● | ● | ● | ● | ● | ● | ● | ● | ● | ● | ● | ● |
| HELEN SMITH CHIROPODIST (HM09515) | | | | | | | | | | | | |
| HOLISTIC HEALING CENTRE (HM09962) | | | | | | | | | | | ● | ● |
| HUDSON, JOHN (HM10315) | | | | | | | | | | | | |
| HUXTABLE, ALISON (HM10461) | | | | | | | | | | | | |
| JONES, BECKY (HM11125) | | | | | | | | | | | | |
| JONES, RAYMOND (HM11190) | | | | | | | | | | | | |
| KIRKMEAD CENTRE (HM11718) | | | | | | | | | | | | |
| LANSDOWN PHYSIOTHERAPY CLINIC (HM11964) | | | | | | | | | | | | |
| LEAVEY, J () | | | | | | | | | | | | |
| LOGAN, DAVID (HM12566) | | | | | | | | | | | | |
| MARY WILKINSON - MCTIMONEY (HM13226) | | | | | | | | | | | | |
| MARY WILKINSON - MCTIMONEY (HM13225) | | | | | | | | | | | | |
| MCLOUGHLIN, BRENDAN (HM13559) | | | | | | | | | | | | |
| MIDSOMER NORTON CHIROPRACTIC (HM13844) | | | | | | | | | | | | |
| MILSOM STREET CLINIC (HM13944) | | | | | | | | | | | | |
| NATURAL SPIRITUAL HEALING (HM14626) | | ● | | | | | | | ● | | | |
| NATURAL THERAPIES (HM14632) | | | | | | | | | ● | | | |
| NORSO BIOMAGNETICS UK (HM15016) | | | | | | | ● | | | | | |
| NUTRITION FOR LIFE (HM15123) | | ● | | ● | | | ● | ● | | | ● | ● |
| ORCHARD CLINIC (HM15360) | | | | | | | | | | | | |
| PARK HOUSE CLINIC (HM15666) | | | | | | | ● | | | | | |
| PARNELL, R H (HM15727) | | | | | | | | | | | | |
| PARRY, J M (HM15738) | | | | | | | | | | | | |
| PENNINGTON, PAM (HM15990) | | | | | | | | | | | | |

| Business | Headaches | Hearing Problems | High Blood Pressure | Hip Complaints | Hyperactivity | Hypoglycaemia | Impotence | Incontinence | Indigestion | Infertility | Influenza | Ingrowing Toenails |
|---|---|---|---|---|---|---|---|---|---|---|---|---|
| CLISBY, JANE (HM04722) | ● | | ● | | | | | ● | ● | | | |
| COMPLEMENTARY THERAPY (HM04942) | | | | | ● | | | | | | | |
| COOK, COLIN (HM05041) | ● | | | ● | | | | | | | | |
| COUNSULTING ROOMS (HM05253) | ● | | ● | | | | ● | | ● | ● | | |
| DAVIES, SALLY (HM05840) | ● | | | | | | | | | | | |
| DEVONSHIRE SURGERY (HM06044) | ● | | | ● | | | | | | | | |
| EUROPEAN COLLEGE-BOWEN STUDIES (HM06946) | ● | | ● | ● | ● | | | ● | | ● | | |
| FRANCES-WHITAKER, J A (HM07665) | | | | | | | | | | | | |
| GLASTONBURY CHIROPRACTIC (HM08131) | ● | | ● | ● | | | | | ● | | | |
| GLASTONBURY EAST WEST CENTRE (HM08132) | ● | ● | ● | ● | ● | ● | ● | ● | ● | ● | ● | |
| HELEN SMITH CHIROPODIST (HM09515) | | | | | | | | | | | | |
| HOLISTIC HEALING CENTRE (HM09962) | ● | | ● | | ● | | | | ● | | | |
| HUDSON, JOHN (HM10315) | | | | | | | | | | | | |
| HUXTABLE, ALISON (HM10461) | ● | | | ● | | | | | | | | |
| JONES, BECKY (HM11125) | ● | | ● | | | | | | | | | |
| JONES, RAYMOND (HM11190) | ● | | | ● | | | | | | | | |
| KIRKMEAD CENTRE (HM11718) | ● | | | | | | | | | | | |
| LANSDOWN PHYSIOTHERAPY CLINIC (HM11964) | ● | | | | | | | | | | | |
| LEAVEY, J () | ● | | | | | | | | | | | |
| LOGAN, DAVID (HM12566) | | | | | ● | | | | | | | |
| MARY WILKINSON - MCTIMONEY (HM13226) | ● | | | ● | | | | ● | | | | |
| MARY WILKINSON - MCTIMONEY (HM13225) | ● | | | ● | | | | | | | | |
| MCLOUGHLIN, BRENDAN (HM13559) | | | | | | | ● | | | | | |
| MIDSOMER NORTON CHIROPRACTIC (HM13844) | ● | | | ● | | | | | | | | |
| MILSOM STREET CLINIC (HM13944) | ● | | | ● | | | | | | | | |
| NATURAL SPIRITUAL HEALING (HM14626) | ● | | ● | | | | | | | ● | | |
| NATURAL THERAPIES (HM14632) | ● | | ● | | | | | | | | | |
| NORSO BIOMAGNETICS UK (HM15016) | | | | ● | | | | | | | | |
| NUTRITION FOR LIFE (HM15123) | ● | | ● | | | | | | ● | | ● | |
| ORCHARD CLINIC (HM15360) | ● | | ● | ● | | | | | ● | | | |
| PARK HOUSE CLINIC (HM15666) | | | | | | | | | | | | |
| PARNELL, R H (HM15727) | ● | | | | | | | | | | | |
| PARRY, J M (HM15738) | | | | | | | | | | | | ● |
| PENNINGTON, PAM (HM15990) | | | | | | | | | | | | |

# D - I Conditions treated at Practices/Businesses

| Business by County with Reference no. | Dandruff | Deafness | Depression | Diabetes | Diarrhoea | Digestive Problems | Diverticulitis | Dizziness | Dyslexia | Dyspraxia | Ear Disorders | Eczema | ENT Disorders | Epilepsy | Eye Disorders | Fatigue | Fears | Fertility Problems | Fever | Fibroids | Flatulence | Foot Problems | Fractures | Fungal Infections | Gallstones | Gastrointestinal Problems | Genital Herpes | Gingivitis | Glandular Fever | Glaucoma | Gout | Gum Disease | Hair Problems | Halitosis | Hand Problems | Hay Fever | Headaches | Hearing Problems | High Blood Pressure | Hip Complaints | Hyperactivity | Hypoglycaemia | Impotence | Incontinence | Indigestion | Infertility | Influenza | Ingrowing Toenails |
|---|---|---|---|---|---|---|---|---|---|---|---|---|---|---|---|---|---|---|---|---|---|---|---|---|---|---|---|---|---|---|---|---|---|---|---|---|---|---|---|---|---|---|---|---|---|---|---|---|
| PENNINGTON, PAM V (HM15991) | | | | | | | | | | | | | | | | | | | | | |●| |●| | | | | | | | | | | | | | | | | | | | | | | | |
| PERKINS, L (HM16026) | | | | | | | | | | | | | | | | | | | | | |●| | | | | | | | | | | | | | | | | | | | | | | | | | |
| PRESSURE WORKS (HM16544) | | | | | | | | | | | | | | | | | | | | | | | | | | | | | | | | | | | | |●| | | | | | | | | | | |
| REED, W A (HM17046) | | |●| | |●| | | | | | | | | |●|●| | | | | | | | | | | | | | | | | | | |●| | | | | | | | | | | |
| RICHARDS, M J (HM17261) | | | | | | | | | | | | | | | | | | | | | |●| |●| | | | | | | | | | | | | | | | | | | | | | | | |
| SHAMBHALA (HM18275) | | |●| | |●|●| | | | | | | | |●|●| | |●| |●| | | |●| | | | | | | | | | |●| | | |●| | | |●| | | |
| SNOWDON, JANET (HM18843) | | | | | | | | | | | | | | |●|●|●|●|●|●|●|●|●|●|●|●|●|●|●|●|●|●|●|●|●|●|●|●|●|●|●|●|●|●|●|●|●| |
| ST JAMES'S SURGERY (HM19079) | | | | | | | | | | | | | | | | | | | | | |●| | | | | | |●| | | | | |●| |●| | |●| | | | | | | | |
| ST MICHAELS CHIROPRACTIC (HM19089) | | | | | | | | | | | | | | | | | | | | | | | | | | | | | | | | | | | | |●| | |●| | | | | | | | |
| ST MICHAEL'S HYPNOTHERAPY (HM19090) | | |●| | | | | | | | | | | | |●|●| | | | | | | | | | | | | | | | | | | | | | | | | | | | | | | |
| STANLEY COURT SURGERY (HM19127) | | | | | | | | | | | | | | | | | | | | | | | | | | | | | | | | | | | | |●| | |●| | | | | | | | |
| STREET CHIROPRACTIC CLINIC (HM19382) | | | | | | | | | | | | | | | | | | | | | |●| |●| | | | | | | | | | | | |●| | | | | | | | | | | |
| STREET CHIROPRACTIC CLINIC (HM19383) | | | | | | | | | | | | | | | | | | | | | | | | | | | | | | | | | | | | |●| | |●| | | | | | | | |
| STRESS CLINIC & NTRL HLTH CTRE (HM19389) | | |●| |●|●|●|●| | |●|●|●| |●|●|●|●| | |●|●| |●| |●| | |●| |●| | | |●|●|●| |●|●|●| |●|●|●|●| | |
| TARETH CENTRE (HM19704) |●|●|●|●|●|●|●|●|●|●|●|●|●|●|●|●|●|●|●|●|●|●|●|●|●|●|●|●|●|●|●|●|●|●|●|●|●|●|●|●|●|●|●|●|●|●|●| |
| TAUNTON FOOT SURGERY (HM19722) | | | |●| | | | | | | | | | | | | | | | | |●| | | | | | | | | | | | | | | | | | | | | | | | | |●|
| TAYLOR, GILLIAN (HM19760) | | | | | | | | | | | | | | | | | | | | | |●| |●| | | | | | | | | | | | | | | | | | | | | | | | |
| THOMPSON, G W (DR) (HM19978) | | | | | | | | | | | | | | | | | | | | | | | | | | | | | | | | | | | | |●| | |●| | | | | | | | |
| TURNPIKE SURGERY (HM20441) | | | | | | | | | | | | | | | | | | | | | | | | | | | | | | | | | | | | |●| | |●| | | | | | | | |
| WELLSPRING OSTEO/NTRL HEALTH (HM21181) | | |●| | |●| |●| |●|●| |●| | |●|●| | | |●|●|●| | |●| | | | | | | | |●|●|●|●|●|●|●| | | | | | | |
| WESTERN CHIROPRACTIC CLINIC (HM21263) | |●|●|●|●|●|●|●|●|●|●|●|●|●| |●|●|●|●| | |●|●| | |●| | |●| |●| | | |●|●|●|●|●| |●|●| |●|●| | | |
| WILKINSON, MARY (HM21511) | | | | | | | | | | | | | | | | | | | | | | | | | | | | | | | | | | | | |●| | |●| | | | | | | | |
| WINCANTON CHIROPRACTIC CLINIC (HM21690) | | | | | | | | | | | | | | | | | | | | | | | | | | | | | | | | | | | | |●| | |●| | | | | | | | |
| YELLOW EMPEROR CORP (HM22004) | | |●| |●| | | | | | |●| | | | | |●| | | | | | | | | | | | | | | | | |●| | | | | | | | | | | | |
| YEOVIL CHIROPRACTIC CLINIC (HM22008) | | | | | | | | | | | | | | | | | | | | | | | | | | | | | | | | | | | | |●| | |●| | | | | | | | |
| **STAFFORDSHIRE** | | | | | | | | | | | | | | | | | | | | | | | | | | | | | | | | | | | | | | | | | | | | | | | | |
| ALTERNATIVE THERAPY CENTRE (HM00735) | |●|●| |●|●|●|●| | |●|●|●| |●|●|●|●| | |●|●|●| | |●| | |●| |●| |●|●|●|●|●|●|●|●|●| | | |●|●| | |
| ALTERNATIVES (HM00741) |●|●|●|●|●|●|●|●|●|●|●|●|●|●|●|●|●|●|●|●|●|●|●|●|●|●|●|●|●|●|●|●|●|●|●|●|●|●|●|●|●|●|●|●|●|●|●| |
| ANDERSON, G (HM00818) | | | | | | | | | | | | | | | | |●| | | | | | | | | | | | | | | | | | | | | | | | | | | | | | | |
| BARCROFT, J M (HM01696) | | | |●| | | | | | | | | | | | | | | | | |●| | | | | | | | | | | | | | |●| | |●| | | | | | | | |
| BASFORD CHIROPRACTIC CLINIC (HM01842) | | | | | | | | | | | | | | | | | | | | | | | | | | | | | | | | | | | | |●| | |●| | | | | | | | |
| BLANK, CHRISTOPHER (HM02499) | | | |●| | | | | | | | | | | | | | | | | |●| |●| | | | | | | | | | | | | | | | | | | | | | | | |
| BONNEBAIGT, ANDRE (HM02682) | | |●| | | | | | | | | | | | | |●| | | | | | | | | | | | | | | | | | | |●| | | | | | | | | | | |
| BORE ST POD & CHIROP PRACTICE (HM02716) | | | | | | | | | | | | | | | | | | | | | | | |●| | | | | | | | | | | | | | | | | | | | | | | |●|

# D - I Conditions treated at Practices/Businesses

| Business by County with Reference no. | Dandruff | Deafness | Depression | Diabetes | Diarrhoea | Digestive Problems | Diverticulitis | Dizziness | Dyslexia | Dyspraxia | Ear Disorders | Eczema | ENT Disorders | Epilepsy | Eye Disorders | Fatigue | Fears | Fertility Problems | Fever | Fibroids | Flatulence | Foot Problems |
|---|---|---|---|---|---|---|---|---|---|---|---|---|---|---|---|---|---|---|---|---|---|---|
| BRADBURY, SHARON (HM02842) | | | | | | | | ● | | | | | | | | | | | | | | |
| BRAMPTON TREES CLINIC (HM02908) | | | | | | | | | | | | | | | | | | | | | | |
| BRIDGETT, A (HM03011) | | | | | | ● | | | | | | | | | | | | | | ● | | |
| BURKE, E (HM03385) | | | ● | | | | ● | | | | | | | | | ● | ● | | | | | |
| CASTLEFIELDS SURGERY (HM03846) | | | | | | | | | | | | | | | | | | | | | | ● |
| CHASE HEALTH FOODS (HM04055) | ● | ● | ● | ● | ● | ● | ● | ● | ● | ● | ● | ● | ● | ● | ● | ● | ● | ● | ● | ● | ● | ● |
| CHASE NATURAL THERAPY CENTRE (HM04059) | ● | ● | ● | ● | ● | ● | ● | ● | ● | ● | ● | ● | ● | ● | ● | ● | ● | ● | ● | ● | ● | ● |
| CITY CHIROPRACTIC CLINIC (HM04492) | | | ● | | | ● | | | | | | | | | | ● | | | | | | ● |
| CORNERSTONES PRACTICE (HM05182) | ● | ● | ● | ● | ● | ● | ● | ● | ● | ● | ● | ● | ● | ● | ● | ● | ● | ● | ● | ● | ● | ● |
| CRESCENT CLINIC (HM05417) | ● | ● | ● | ● | ● | ● | ● | ● | ● | ● | ● | ● | ● | ● | ● | ● | ● | ● | ● | ● | ● | ● |
| CRESCENT CLINIC FOR COMP MED (HM05418) | | | | | ● | ● | | | | | | ● | | | | | | | | | | ● |
| EDWARDS, ALLYN (HM06641) | | | | | | ● | | | | | | | | | | | | | | | | |
| EVANS, RICHARD (HM06989) | | | ● | | ● | ● | ● | ● | | | ● | ● | ● | ● | | ● | ● | ● | | ● | ● | ● |
| FEET FIRST (HM07176) | | | | | | | | | | | | | | | | | | | | | | ● |
| FOOT SOUL & BODYWORKS (HM07487) | ● | | | | ● | ● | | | | | | | | | | ● | | | | | ● | |
| FORTEY, C J (HM07579) | | | | ● | | | | | | | | | | | | | | | | | | ● |
| GASCOYNE, P (HM07920) | | | | ● | | | | | | | | | | | | | | | | | | ● |
| HALLARD, SHARON (HM08800) | | | ● | | | | | | | | | | | | | | ● | | | | | |
| IBBS, ROGER (HM10566) | | | | ● | | | | | | | | | | | | | | | | | | ● |
| ISHTA CENTRE (HM10761) | ● | ● | ● | ● | ● | ● | ● | ● | ● | ● | ● | ● | ● | ● | ● | ● | ● | ● | ● | ● | ● | ● |
| JOHNSON, JANICE (HM11079) | | | ● | | | | | | | | | | | | | | | | | | | |
| LOUISE BRITTLE (HM12667) | | | | ● | | | | | | | | | | | | | | | | | | |
| MARCONI, L R (HM13076) | | | | ● | | | | | | | | | | | | | | | | | | ● |
| MELLOR, J SIMON (HM13709) | | | | ● | | | | | | | | | | | | | | | | | | ● |
| MILL BANK OSTEOPATHIC CLINIC (HM13865) | | | | | | | | | | | ● | | | | | | | | | | | ● |
| NARAYAN, MAMTA (HM14486) | | | | | | | | | | | | | | | | | | | | | | |
| NORBURY, SUSAN (HM14990) | ● | ● | ● | ● | ● | ● | ● | ● | ● | ● | ● | ● | ● | ● | ● | ● | ● | ● | ● | ● | ● | ● |
| O'CALLAGHAN, STEVE (HM15193) | | | ● | | | ● | | | | | | | | | | ● | ● | | | | | ● |
| PAYTON, ANTHONY (HM15875) | | | | | | | | | | | | | | | | | | | | | | ● |
| PEACEHAVEN AROMATHERAPY (HM15877) | | | ● | | | ● | | | | | | ● | | | | ● | ● | | | | | |
| PEACH, F J (HM15879) | | | | | | | | | | | | | | | | | | | | | | ● |
| PLANT, R M (HM16359) | | | | | | | | | | | | | | | | | | | | | | ● |
| PRIORS PODIATRY PRACTICE (HM16629) | | | | ● | | | | | | | | | | | | | | | | | | ● |
| REECE, P & BRADSHAW, J (HM17039) | | | | ● | | | | | | | | | | | | | | | | | | ● |

| Business by County with Reference no. | Fractures | Fungal Infections | Gallstones | Gastrointestinal Problems | Genital Herpes | Gingivitis | Glandular Fever | Glaucoma | Gout | Gum Disease | Hair Problems | Halitosis | Hand Problems | Hay Fever | Headaches | Hearing Problems | High Blood Pressure | Hip Complaints | Hyperactivity | Hypoglycaemia | Impotence | Incontinence | Indigestion | Infertility | Influenza | Ingrowing Toenails |
|---|---|---|---|---|---|---|---|---|---|---|---|---|---|---|---|---|---|---|---|---|---|---|---|---|---|---|
| BRADBURY, SHARON (HM02842) | | | | | | | | | | | | | ● | | | | | | | | | | | | | |
| BRAMPTON TREES CLINIC (HM02908) | | | | | | | | | | | | | | | | | | ● | | | | | | | | |
| BRIDGETT, A (HM03011) | | | | | | | | | | | | | | | | | ● | | | | | | | | | |
| BURKE, E (HM03385) | | | | | | | | | | | | | | | | | | | | | | | | | | |
| CASTLEFIELDS SURGERY (HM03846) | | | | | | | | | | | | | | ● | | | | | | | | | | | | |
| CHASE HEALTH FOODS (HM04055) | | ● | ● | ● | ● | | ● | ● | ● | | ● | ● | ● | ● | ● | ● | ● | ● | ● | ● | ● | ● | ● | ● | ● | |
| CHASE NATURAL THERAPY CENTRE (HM04059) | ● | ● | ● | ● | ● | ● | ● | ● | ● | ● | ● | ● | ● | ● | ● | ● | ● | ● | ● | ● | ● | ● | ● | ● | ● | |
| CITY CHIROPRACTIC CLINIC (HM04492) | ● | | | | | | | | | | | | ● | | ● | | | ● | | | | | ● | | | |
| CORNERSTONES PRACTICE (HM05182) | ● | ● | ● | ● | ● | ● | ● | ● | ● | ● | ● | ● | ● | ● | ● | ● | ● | ● | ● | ● | ● | ● | ● | ● | ● | |
| CRESCENT CLINIC (HM05417) | ● | ● | ● | ● | ● | ● | ● | ● | ● | ● | ● | ● | ● | ● | ● | ● | ● | ● | ● | ● | ● | ● | ● | ● | ● | |
| CRESCENT CLINIC FOR COMP MED (HM05418) | ● | | | | | | | | | | | | | ● | ● | | | ● | | | | | | | | |
| EDWARDS, ALLYN (HM06641) | | | | | | | | | | | | | | | ● | | | ● | | | | | | | | |
| EVANS, RICHARD (HM06989) | | | ● | ● | | | | | ● | | ● | | ● | ● | ● | ● | ● | ● | ● | ● | | | ● | ● | | |
| FEET FIRST (HM07176) | | | | | | | | | | | | | | | | | | | | | | | | | | |
| FOOT SOUL & BODYWORKS (HM07487) | | | | | | | | | | | | | | ● | ● | | | ● | | | | | | | | |
| FORTEY, C J (HM07579) | | | | | | | | | | | | | | | | | | ● | | | | | | | | |
| GASCOYNE, P (HM07920) | | | | | | | | | | | | | | | | | | ● | | | | | | | | |
| HALLARD, SHARON (HM08800) | | | | | | | | | | | | | | | | | | | | | | | | | | |
| IBBS, ROGER (HM10566) | | | | | | | | | | | | | | | | | | | | | | | | | | |
| ISHTA CENTRE (HM10761) | | ● | ● | ● | | | ● | ● | ● | | ● | ● | ● | ● | ● | ● | ● | ● | ● | ● | ● | ● | ● | ● | ● | |
| JOHNSON, JANICE (HM11079) | | | | | | | | | | | | | | | | | ● | | | | | | | | | |
| LOUISE BRITTLE (HM12667) | | | | | | | | | ● | | | | | | | | | | | | | | | | | |
| MARCONI, L R (HM13076) | | | | | | | | | | | | | | | | | | | | | | | | | | |
| MELLOR, J SIMON (HM13709) | | | | | | | | | | | | | | | | | | | | | | | | | | |
| MILL BANK OSTEOPATHIC CLINIC (HM13865) | | | | | | | | | | | | | ● | | ● | | | ● | | | | | | | | |
| NARAYAN, MAMTA (HM14486) | | | | | | | | | | | | | | | ● | | | | | | | | | | | |
| NORBURY, SUSAN (HM14990) | | ● | ● | ● | ● | ● | ● | ● | ● | ● | ● | ● | ● | ● | ● | ● | ● | ● | ● | ● | ● | ● | ● | ● | ● | |
| O'CALLAGHAN, STEVE (HM15193) | | | | | | | | | | | | | | | ● | | ● | ● | | | | | ● | | | |
| PAYTON, ANTHONY (HM15875) | | | | | | | | | | | | | | | | | | | | | | | | | | |
| PEACEHAVEN AROMATHERAPY (HM15877) | | | | | | | | | | | | | | | | | ● | | | | | | | | | |
| PEACH, F J (HM15879) | | | | | | | | | | | | | | | | | | | | | | | | | | |
| PLANT, R M (HM16359) | | | | | | | | | | | | | | | | | | | | | | | | | | |
| PRIORS PODIATRY PRACTICE (HM16629) | | | | | | | | | ● | | | | | | | | | | | | | | | | | |
| REECE, P & BRADSHAW, J (HM17039) | | ● | | | | | | | | | | | | | | | | | | | | | | | | |

www.healthmyself.com

# D - I Conditions treated at Practices/Businesses

| Business by County with Reference no. | Dandruff | Deafness | Depression | Diabetes | Diarrhoea | Digestive Problems | Diverticulitis | Dizziness | Dyslexia | Dyspraxia | Ear Disorders | Eczema | ENT Disorders | Epilepsy | Eye Disorders | Fatigue | Fears | Fertility Problems | Fever | Fibroids | Flatulence | Foot Problems | Fractures | Fungal Infections | Gallstones | Gastrointestinal Problems | Genital Herpes | Gingivitis | Glandular Fever | Glaucoma | Gout | Gum Disease | Hair Problems | Halitosis | Hand Problems | Hay Fever | Headaches | Hearing Problems | High Blood Pressure | Hip Complaints | Hyperactivity | Hypoglycaemia | Impotence | Incontinence | Indigestion | Infertility | Influenza | Ingrowing Toenails |
|---|---|---|---|---|---|---|---|---|---|---|---|---|---|---|---|---|---|---|---|---|---|---|---|---|---|---|---|---|---|---|---|---|---|---|---|---|---|---|---|---|---|---|---|---|---|---|---|
| ROBERTS, KATE (HM17418) |||●||||||||||||||||||||||||||||||||||||||||||||||
| SAGGU, S (HM17838) |||||||||||||||||||||||●||||||||||||||||||||||||||
| STAFFORD CHIROPRACTIC CLINIC (HM19108) |||||||||||||||||||||||||||||||||||●||●|||●|||||||||
| STAFFORDSHIRE MCTIMONEY (HM19111) |||||●||●|●|●||||||●|||||||||||●|||||||||||||●|||●|||||||||
| SUSAN JAMES CONSULTANCY (HM19527) ||||||||||||||||||●||||||||||||||||||||||||||||●|||
| TAMWORTH PHYSIOTHERAPY CLINIC (HM19675) |||||||||||||||||||||||●||||||||||||||||||●|||||||||
| TE NOSCE (HM19803) |●||●|●|●|●|●||||●|||●|●||●|||●|||●||●||●|●|●|●|●|●|●||●|●||●|●||●|●|●|●|||●|●|●||
| TUNSTALL HYPNOTHERAPY CENTRE (HM20401) |||●|||||||||||||||||||||||||||||||||||||||●||||||
| WATSON, G T (HM21008) |||||||||||||||||||||||●||●||||||||||||||||||||||||||
| WHITBY, S E (HM21334) |||||||||||||||||||||||●|●||||||||||||●|||||●|||||||||
| YARNFIELD PARK- HEALTH/SPORTS (HM21989) |●|●|●|●|●|●|●|●|●|●|●|●|●|●|●|●|●|●|●|●|●|●|●|●|●|●|●|●|●|●|●|●|●|●|●|●|●|●|●|●|●|●|●|●|●|●|●||
| **SUFFOLK** |||||||||||||||||||||||||||||||||||||||||||||||||
| AJNA (HM00457) |||||||||||||||||||||||||||||||||||||●|||||||||||
| BODY MECHANICS THERAPY CLINIC (HM02599) |||||||||||||||||||||||●||||||||||||||||||●|||||||||
| CHARLTON CLINIC (HM04033) ||||||||||||||||●||||||●||||||||||||||●||●|||●|||||||||
| CHURCHMAN & ASS REG OST (HM04475) |||||||||||||||||||||||●||||||||||||||||●|||●|||||||||
| CHURCHMAN, BERYL (HM04478) |||||||||||||||||||||||●||||||||||||||||●|||●|||||||||
| COLEBROOK, G (HM04820) ||||||||||||●||||●|||||●|||||||||||||||||●||||||||●|||||
| COOPER, A R (HM05088) |||||||||||||||||||||||●||●||||||||||||||||||||||||
| CT & IM LEITH (HM05534) |||●|||●||||||●||||●|●|||||●||||●|||●||||||●|●|●|||●|||||||●||
| DENT, TRISH () |||●|||●||||||||||●|||||||||||||||||||||●|||||||||||
| EVENKEEL (HM06997) |||||||||||●|||||●||||||●||||||||||||||||●|||●|||||||||
| FRESHFIELDS OF ALDEBURGH (HM07737) |●||●|●|●|●||●|●||●|●|●|||●|●|●|●|●|●|●|●|●||●|●|●|●||●|●|●||●|●|●|●|●|●|●|●|●|●|●|●|●|●||
| GREEN FARM CLINIC (HM08435) ||||||||||||||||||||||||●|||||||||||●|||||●|||||||||
| GROSVENOR PHYSIOTHERAPY CLINIC (HM08597) |||||||||||||||||||||||||||||||||||||||||●|||||||||
| HARDY, MICHAEL (HM08984) |||●|||●||||||||||||||||||||||||||||||||||||||||||
| HEALING CONNECTIONS (HM09330) |●|●|●|●|●|●|●|●|●|●|●|●|●|●|●|●|●|●|●|●|●|●|●|●|●|●||●|●||●|●|●|●|●|●|●|●|●|●|●||●|●|●|●|●||
| HEALING HANDS (HM09336) |||●|||||||||●||||●|●||||●|●||●||●|||||||||||●||●||●|||●||●||||
| HITCHINS, ROSIE (HM09847) |||||||||||||||||||||||||||||||||||||●|||||||||||
| HOPKINS, C J (HM10147) |||||||||||||||||●|||||||||||||||||||||||||||||||
| INNER SPACE SUFFOLK (HM10641) ||||||●||●||||||||||●||||||●|||●|||||||||||●|●|||●|||||●||||
| IPSWICH CHIROPRACTIC CLINIC (HM10714) ||●|●||●|●|●|●|||●|●|●|||●|●|●|||●|●|||||●||||||●|||●||||●||||●||||||||
| LAVENDER LODGE CLINIC (HM12023) |||●||||||||||||●|●|||||●|||||||||||||●||●|||●|||||||||
| MALAROC (HM12961) |||||||||||||||||||||||||||||||||||||●|||●|||||||||

# D - I Conditions treated at Practices/Businesses

| Business by County with Reference no. | Dandruff | Deafness | Depression | Diabetes | Diarrhoea | Digestive Problems | Diverticulitis | Dizziness | Dyslexia | Dyspraxia | Ear Disorders | Eczema | ENT Disorders | Epilepsy | Eye Disorders | Fatigue | Fears | Fertility Problems | Fever | Fibroids | Flatulence | Foot Problems | Fractures | Fungal Infections | Gallstones | Gastrointestinal Problems | Genital Herpes | Gingivitis | Glandular Fever | Glaucoma | Gout | Gum Disease | Hair Problems | Halitosis | Hand Problems | Hay Fever | Headaches | Hearing Problems | High Blood Pressure | Hip Complaints | Hyperactivity | Hypoglycaemia | Impotence | Incontinence | Indigestion | Infertility | Influenza | Ingrowing Toenails |
|---|---|---|---|---|---|---|---|---|---|---|---|---|---|---|---|---|---|---|---|---|---|---|---|---|---|---|---|---|---|---|---|---|---|---|---|---|---|---|---|---|---|---|---|---|---|---|---|---|
| MANOR HOUSE (HM13039) |  |  |  |  |  |  |  |  |  |  |  |  |  |  |  |  |  |  |  |  |  | ● |  | ● |  |  |  |  |  |  |  |  |  |  |  |  | ● |  |  | ● |  |  |  |  |  |  |  |  |
| MARK CHURCH AROMATHERAPY (HM13106) |  |  | ● |  |  | ● |  |  | ● |  |  | ● |  |  |  | ● |  |  |  |  |  |  |  |  |  |  |  |  |  |  |  |  |  |  |  |  | ● |  | ● |  |  |  |  |  | ● |  |  |  |
| MASSAGE FOR HEALTH (HM13260) |  |  |  |  |  |  |  |  |  |  |  |  |  |  |  |  |  |  |  |  |  |  |  |  |  |  |  |  |  |  | ● |  |  |  |  |  | ● |  |  |  |  |  |  |  |  |  |  |  |
| MCTIMONEY CHIROPRACTIC CLINIC (HM13607) |  |  | ● |  | ● | ● |  | ● |  |  |  | ● |  |  |  |  |  |  |  |  | ● |  |  |  |  |  |  |  |  |  |  |  |  |  |  |  | ● |  |  | ● |  |  |  |  | ● |  |  |  |
| MOHAN, TERRY (HM14046) |  |  | ● |  |  |  |  |  |  |  |  |  |  |  |  |  | ● |  |  |  |  |  |  |  |  |  |  |  |  |  |  |  |  |  |  |  |  |  | ● |  |  |  |  |  |  |  |  |  |
| NATURECURES (HM14684) |  |  | ● |  |  | ● |  | ● |  |  | ● | ● |  |  |  | ● | ● |  |  |  |  |  |  |  |  | ● |  |  |  |  |  |  |  |  | ● |  | ● | ● | ● | ● |  |  |  |  | ● | ● |  |  |
| NOAH'S ARK PSYCHOTHERAPY (HM14964) |  |  | ● |  |  |  |  |  | ● |  |  |  |  |  |  |  | ● |  |  |  |  |  |  |  |  |  |  |  |  |  |  |  |  |  |  |  | ● |  |  |  | ● |  | ● |  |  |  |  |  |
| PAGE, COLIN J (HM15570) |  |  |  |  |  |  |  |  |  |  |  |  |  |  |  |  | ● |  |  |  |  |  |  |  |  |  |  |  |  |  |  |  |  |  |  |  |  |  |  |  |  |  |  |  |  |  |  |  |
| PAROLIN, PAUL (HM15728) |  |  | ● |  |  | ● |  | ● | ● | ● | ● |  |  |  | ● | ● | ● |  |  |  |  | ● |  |  |  | ● |  |  |  |  |  |  |  |  | ● |  | ● | ● | ● | ● | ● |  |  |  | ● |  |  |  |
| SPALDING, JULIE (HM18955) |  |  | ● | ● |  |  |  |  | ● |  |  | ● |  |  |  | ● | ● |  |  |  |  |  |  |  |  |  |  |  |  |  |  |  |  |  |  |  | ● |  |  |  | ● | ● | ● |  |  |  |  |  |
| SPRINGFIELD LODGE HEALTH CARE (HM19052) | ● | ● | ● | ● | ● | ● | ● | ● | ● | ● | ● | ● | ● | ● | ● | ● | ● | ● | ● | ● | ● | ● | ● | ● | ● | ● | ● | ● | ● | ● | ● | ● | ● | ● | ● | ● | ● | ● | ● | ● | ● | ● | ● | ● | ● | ● | ● |  |
| ST MARYS PRACTICE (HM19088) |  |  |  |  |  |  |  |  |  |  |  |  |  |  |  |  |  |  |  |  |  | ● |  | ● |  |  |  |  |  |  |  |  |  |  |  |  | ● |  |  | ● |  |  |  |  |  |  |  |  |
| STEPHEN GORDON (HM19197) | ● |  | ● |  | ● | ● | ● | ● | ● | ● | ● | ● | ● | ● | ● | ● | ● | ● | ● | ● | ● | ● | ● | ● | ● | ● | ● | ● | ● | ● | ● | ● | ● | ● |  |  |  |  |  |  |  |  |  |  |  |  |  |  |
| STOWMARKET OSTEOPATHS (HM19363) |  |  |  |  |  |  |  | ● |  |  |  |  | ● |  |  |  |  |  |  |  |  | ● |  |  |  |  |  |  |  |  |  |  |  |  | ● |  | ● |  |  | ● |  |  |  |  |  |  |  |  |
| WEI CLINIC (HM21111) |  |  | ● |  | ● | ● | ● | ● |  |  |  | ● |  |  | ● | ● | ● | ● | ● | ● | ● |  |  |  | ● | ● |  |  |  | ● | ● | ● |  |  |  | ● | ● |  | ● |  |  | ● |  |  | ● | ● |  |  |
| SURREY |  |  |  |  |  |  |  |  |  |  |  |  |  |  |  |  |  |  |  |  |  |  |  |  |  |  |  |  |  |  |  |  |  |  |  |  |  |  |  |  |  |  |  |  |  |  |  |  |
| ACE NUTRITION (HM00157) |  |  | ● |  | ● | ● | ● |  |  |  |  | ● |  |  |  | ● |  | ● |  | ● | ● |  |  |  | ● | ● |  | ● |  |  | ● | ● |  | ● |  | ● | ● |  | ● | ● | ● | ● |  |  | ● | ● |  |  |
| ACORN HEALTH CLINIC (HM00177) |  |  |  |  | ● | ● |  |  |  |  |  |  |  |  |  | ● |  |  |  |  |  |  |  |  |  |  |  |  |  |  |  |  |  |  |  | ● | ● |  |  | ● |  |  |  |  |  |  |  |  |
| ACORN THERAPY CENTRE (HM00181) |  |  | ● |  |  |  |  |  |  |  |  |  |  |  |  | ● | ● |  |  |  |  |  |  |  |  |  |  |  |  |  |  |  |  |  |  |  | ● |  |  |  |  |  | ● |  |  |  |  |  |
| ACUHERBAL CHINESE MEDICINE (HM00214) |  |  | ● |  |  |  |  |  |  |  |  |  |  |  |  |  |  |  |  |  |  |  |  |  |  |  |  |  |  |  |  |  |  |  |  |  |  |  |  |  |  |  |  |  |  |  |  |  |
| ASCOT HOMEOPATHIC CLINIC (HM01177) | ● |  | ● |  | ● | ● |  | ● |  |  | ● | ● | ● | ● |  | ● | ● | ● | ● | ● | ● | ● | ● |  | ● | ● | ● | ● | ● |  |  | ● |  |  |  | ● | ● |  | ● |  | ● | ● | ● | ● | ● | ● | ● |  |
| ASHTEAD CHARTERED PHYSIO SV (HM01230) |  |  |  |  |  |  |  |  |  |  |  |  |  |  |  |  |  |  |  |  |  | ● | ● |  |  |  |  |  |  |  |  |  |  |  | ● |  |  |  |  | ● |  |  |  |  |  |  |  |  |
| ASHTEAD CLINIC (HM01232) |  |  |  |  |  |  |  |  |  |  |  |  |  |  |  |  |  |  |  |  |  |  |  |  |  |  |  |  |  |  |  |  |  |  |  |  | ● |  |  |  |  |  |  |  |  |  |  |  |
| ASTON CLINIC (HM01301) |  |  | ● |  | ● | ● |  |  |  |  |  |  |  |  |  | ● | ● |  |  |  |  | ● |  | ● |  |  |  |  |  |  |  |  |  |  |  | ● | ● |  | ● | ● |  |  |  |  |  |  |  |  |
| ASW ALLERGY CONSULTANTS (HM01305) |  |  | ● |  | ● | ● | ● |  |  |  | ● | ● |  |  | ● | ● |  |  |  |  | ● |  |  | ● | ● | ● |  |  |  |  |  |  |  |  |  | ● | ● |  |  |  | ● |  |  |  | ● |  |  |  |
| BACK TO HEALTH (HM01508) |  |  |  |  |  |  |  |  |  |  |  |  |  |  |  |  |  |  |  |  |  |  |  |  |  |  |  |  |  |  |  |  |  |  |  |  | ● |  |  | ● |  |  |  |  |  |  |  |  |
| BACK TO HEALTH - GUILDFORD (HM01511) |  |  |  |  |  |  |  |  |  |  |  |  |  |  |  |  |  |  |  |  |  |  |  |  |  |  |  |  |  |  |  |  |  |  |  |  | ● |  |  | ● |  |  |  |  |  |  |  |  |
| BACK TO HEALTH - RICHMOND (HM01514) |  |  |  |  |  |  |  |  |  |  |  |  |  |  |  |  |  |  |  |  |  |  |  |  |  |  |  |  |  |  |  |  |  |  |  |  | ● |  |  | ● |  |  |  |  |  |  |  |  |
| BACK TO HEALTH - SUTTON (HM01515) |  |  |  |  |  |  |  |  |  |  |  |  |  |  |  |  |  |  |  |  |  |  |  |  |  |  |  |  |  |  |  |  |  |  |  |  | ● |  |  | ● |  |  |  |  |  |  |  |  |
| BACKCARE CLINIC (HM01527) |  |  |  |  |  |  |  |  |  |  |  |  |  |  |  |  |  |  |  |  |  | ● |  |  |  |  |  |  |  |  |  |  |  |  |  |  |  |  |  |  |  |  |  |  |  |  |  |  |
| BAILEY, L J (HM01551) |  |  |  |  |  |  |  |  |  |  |  |  |  |  |  |  |  |  |  |  |  | ● |  |  |  |  |  |  |  |  |  |  |  |  |  |  | ● |  |  | ● |  |  |  |  |  |  |  |  |
| BARNES, A K R (HM01743) |  |  |  |  |  |  |  | ● |  |  |  |  |  |  |  |  |  |  |  |  |  | ● |  |  |  |  |  |  |  |  |  |  |  |  | ● |  | ● |  |  | ● |  |  |  |  |  |  |  |  |
| BARNSTEAD VILLAGE CLINIC (HM01769) |  |  |  |  | ● | ● |  |  |  |  |  |  |  |  |  | ● |  |  |  |  |  | ● |  | ● |  |  |  |  |  |  |  |  |  |  |  | ● | ● |  |  | ● |  |  |  |  |  |  |  |  |
| BATCHELOR, C (HM01863) |  |  | ● |  |  |  |  |  |  |  |  |  |  |  |  |  |  |  |  |  |  |  |  |  |  |  |  |  |  |  |  |  |  |  |  |  | ● |  |  |  |  |  |  |  |  |  |  |  |

www.healthmyself.com

# D - I Conditions treated at Practices/Businesses

| Business by County with Reference no. | BIGWOOD, SIMON (HM02295) | BIODYNAMICS (HM02332) | BOURNE HEALTH (HM02753) | BRABANT HOUSE CLINIC (HM02830) | BREWSTER, DAVID J (HM02980) | BST FOUNDATION (HM03294) | CAMBERLEY NATURAL THERAPY CTRE (HM03566) | CARLTON CLINIC (HM03700) | CATERHAM CHIROPRACTIC CLINIC (HM03853) | CHART LANE CLINIC (HM04039) | CHI CLINIC (HM04148) | CHIROPRACTIC CENTRE (HM04382) | CHRISTINE KEY HYPNOTHERAPIST (HM04447) | CITISPORT (HM04483) | CLEMENTS, J (HM04644) | COHEN, MICHAEL (HM04793) | COX, JULIET (HM05307) | CROYDON HEALING CENTRE (HM05515) | CROYDON HYPNOTHERAPY (HM05516) | CUMMINS, ROZ (HM05617) | DORCHESTER HOUSE OSTEOPATHY (HM06195) | DORKING, PAUL (HM06200) | EDWARDS HEALTH CLINIC (HM06639) | ENOCK-SHORE, ANGELA (HM06845) | EPSOM CHIROPRACTIC CLINIC (HM06857) | EQUILIBRIUM OSTEOPATHIC (HM06876) | FEATHER, A J (HM07155) | FOOT CARE CENTRE (HM07466) | GATEWAYS CENTRE (HM07928) | GAUVAIN, TONY (HM07934) | GLAISTER, BRIAN (DR) (HM08120) | GODDARD, TERRI (HM08180) | GOODLIFE NATURAL HEALTH CENTRE (HM08256) | GORDON, SARAH (HM08282) |
|---|---|---|---|---|---|---|---|---|---|---|---|---|---|---|---|---|---|---|---|---|---|---|---|---|---|---|---|---|---|---|---|---|---|---|
| Ingrowing Toenails | | | | | | | | | | | | | | | | | | | | | | | | | | | | | | | | | | |
| Influenza | | ● | | | | | ● | ● | | ● | ● | | | | | | | ● | | | ● | | | | | | | | | | | | | |
| Infertility | | ● | | | ● | | | | | ● | ● | | | | | | | ● | | | ● | | | ● | | ● | | | | | | | | |
| Indigestion | ● | ● | | ● | | | | ● | | ● | ● | | | ● | ● | | | ● | | ● | ● | | ● | ● | | ● | | | | | | ● | | |
| Incontinence | | ● | | | ● | | | ● | | ● | ● | | | | ● | | | ● | | | ● | | | | | ● | | | | ● | | | | |
| Impotence | | ● | | | ● | | | ● | | ● | ● | | ● | | | | | ● | ● | | ● | | ● | | | | | | | | | | | |
| Hypoglycaemia | | ● | | | | | | ● | | ● | ● | | | | | | | ● | | | ● | | | | | | | | | | | | | |
| Hyperactivity | | ● | | ● | | | | ● | | ● | ● | | | | | | ● | ● | | ● | ● | | | ● | | ● | | | | | | | | |
| Hip Complaints | | ● | | ● | | | | ● | ● | ● | ● | ● | | ● | | | ● | ● | | ● | ● | | | | ● | ● | ● | | | | | ● | | |
| High Blood Pressure | | ● | | ● | | | | ● | | ● | ● | | | ● | ● | | ● | ● | ● | ● | ● | | ● | ● | | ● | | | | | | | | |
| Hearing Problems | | ● | | | | | | ● | | ● | ● | | | | | | | ● | | | ● | | | | | | | | | | | ● | | |
| Headaches | ● | ● | ● | ● | | | ● | ● | ● | ● | ● | ● | | ● | ● | ● | ● | ● | ● | ● | ● | | ● | ● | ● | ● | | | | | ● | ● | ● | ● |
| Hay Fever | ● | ● | | ● | | | ● | ● | | ● | ● | | | | | | | ● | ● | ● | ● | | | | | ● | | | | | | | | |
| Hand Problems | | | | | | | | ● | | ● | ● | | | ● | | | ● | ● | | ● | ● | | | | | ● | | | | | | | | |
| Halitosis | | | | | | | | | | ● | ● | | | | | | | ● | | | ● | | | | | | | | | | | | | |
| Hair Problems | | ● | | ● | | | | | | ● | ● | | | | | | | ● | | | ● | | ● | | | | | | | | | | | |
| Gum Disease | | ● | | | | | | | | ● | ● | | | | | | | ● | | | ● | | | | | | | | | | | | | |
| Gout | | ● | | ● | | | ● | ● | | ● | ● | | | ● | | | | ● | | | ● | | | | | | | | | | | | | |
| Glaucoma | | ● | | | | | | ● | | ● | ● | | | | | | | ● | | | ● | | | | | | | | | | | | | |
| Glandular Fever | | ● | | ● | | | | ● | | ● | ● | | | | | | | ● | | | ● | | | | | ● | | | | | | | | |
| Gingivitis | | ● | | | | | | | | ● | ● | | | | | | | ● | | | ● | | | | | | | | | | | | | |
| Genital Herpes | | ● | | | | | | | | ● | ● | | | | | | | ● | | | ● | | | | | | | | | | | | | |
| Gastrointestinal Problems | | | | ● | | | | ● | | ● | ● | | | ● | | | | ● | | | ● | | ● | ● | | ● | | | | | | ● | | |
| Gallstones | | | | | | | | ● | | ● | ● | | | | | | | ● | | | ● | | | | | | | | | | | | | |
| Fungal Infections | | ● | | ● | | | | ● | | ● | ● | | | | | | | ● | | | ● | | | | | | | ● | | | | | | |
| Fractures | | | | | | | | ● | | ● | ● | | | | | | | ● | | | ● | | | | | | | | | | | | | |
| Foot Problems | | | | | | | | ● | | ● | ● | | | ● | | | | ● | | | ● | | | | | ● | | ● | | | | | | |
| Flatulence | | | | | | | | ● | | ● | ● | | | | | | | ● | | | ● | | | | | ● | | | | | | | | |
| Fibroids | | ● | | | | | | ● | | ● | ● | | | | | | | ● | | | ● | | | | | | | | | | | | | |
| Fever | | ● | | | | | | ● | | ● | ● | | | | | | | ● | | | ● | | | | | | | | | | | | | |
| Fertility Problems | | ● | | | | | | ● | | ● | ● | | | | | | | ● | | | ● | | ● | | | ● | | | | | | | | |
| Fears | | ● | | ● | ● | ● | | ● | | ● | ● | | ● | | | ● | ● | ● | | | ● | ● | ● | | | | | | ● | | ● | | | |
| Fatigue | | ● | | ● | | | ● | ● | | ● | ● | | | ● | ● | | ● | ● | | ● | ● | | ● | ● | | ● | | | | ● | ● | ● | | ● |
| Eye Disorders | | ● | | | | | | ● | | ● | ● | | | | | | | ● | | | ● | | | | | | | | | | | | | |
| Epilepsy | | ● | | | | | | | | | ● | | | | | | | ● | | | ● | | | | | | | | | | | | | |
| ENT Disorders | | ● | | | | | ● | ● | | ● | ● | | | | | | | ● | | | ● | | | | | | | | | | | ● | | |
| Eczema | | | | ● | | | ● | ● | | ● | ● | | | | | | | ● | ● | | ● | | | ● | | | | | | | | | | |
| Ear Disorders | | ● | | | | | | ● | | ● | ● | | | | | | | ● | | | ● | | | | | | | | | | | ● | | |
| Dyspraxia | | ● | | | | | | ● | | ● | ● | | | | | | | ● | | | ● | | | | | | | | | | | | | |
| Dyslexia | | ● | | | | | | ● | | ● | ● | | | | | | | ● | ● | | ● | | | | | | | | | | | | | |
| Dizziness | | ● | | | | | | ● | | ● | ● | | | | | | | ● | ● | ● | ● | | ● | | | ● | | | | | | ● | | |
| Diverticulitis | | ● | | ● | | | | ● | | ● | ● | | | ● | | | | ● | | | ● | | | | | | | | | | | | | |
| Digestive Problems | ● | ● | ● | ● | | | ● | ● | | ● | ● | | | ● | ● | | | ● | ● | | ● | | ● | ● | | ● | | | | | | ● | | ● |
| Diarrhoea | ● | ● | | ● | ● | | | ● | | ● | ● | | | ● | ● | | | ● | ● | ● | ● | | | | | ● | | | | | | | | |
| Diabetes | | ● | | | | | | ● | | ● | ● | | | ● | | | | ● | | ● | ● | | | | | | | | | | | | | |
| Depression | ● | ● | | ● | ● | | | ● | | ● | ● | | ● | | ● | ● | ● | ● | ● | ● | ● | ● | ● | ● | | | | | ● | ● | ● | | | ● |
| Deafness | | ● | | | | | | ● | | ● | ● | | | | | | | ● | | ● | ● | | | | | | | | | | | | | |
| Dandruff | | | | ● | | | ● | ● | | ● | ● | | | | | | | ● | | | ● | | | | | | | | | | | | | |

# D - I Conditions treated at Practices/Businesses

Business by County with Reference no.

| | Dandruff | Deafness | Depression | Diabetes | Diarrhoea | Digestive Problems | Diverticulitis | Dizziness | Dyslexia | Dyspraxia | Ear Disorders | Eczema | ENT Disorders | Epilepsy | Eye Disorders | Fatigue | Fears | Fertility Problems | Fever | Fibroids | Flatulence | Foot Problems | Fractures | Fungal Infections | Gallstones | Gastrointestinal Problems | Genital Herpes | Gingivitis | Glandular Fever | Glaucoma | Gout | Gum Disease | Hair Problems | Halitosis | Hand Problems | Hay Fever | Headaches | Hearing Problems | High Blood Pressure | Hip Complaints | Hyperactivity | Hypoglycaemia | Impotence | Incontinence | Indigestion | Infertility | Influenza | Ingrowing Toenails |
|---|---|---|---|---|---|---|---|---|---|---|---|---|---|---|---|---|---|---|---|---|---|---|---|---|---|---|---|---|---|---|---|---|---|---|---|---|---|---|---|---|---|---|---|---|---|---|---|---|
| GRAVELL, NICOLA (HM08401) | | | | | | | | | | | | | | | | ● | | | | | | | | | | | | | | | | | | | | ● | | | | | | | | | | | | |
| GUILDFORD PHYSIO & SPORTS (HM08632) | | | | | | | | | | | | | | | | | | | | | | | | | | | | | | | | | | | | | | | | ● | | | | | | | | |
| HAM CHIROPRACTIC CLINIC (HM08822) | | | | | | | | ● | | | | | | | | | | | | | | | | | | | | | | | | | | | | | ● | | | ● | | | | | | | | |
| HANDS ON HEALTH (HM08911) | | | | | | | | ● | | | ● | | ● | | | | | | | | | ● | | | | | | | | | | | | | ● | | ● | | | ● | ● | | | | | | | |
| HANFORD, S P (HM08925) | | | ● | | | ● | | | | | | | | | | ● | | | | | | | | | | | | | | | | | | | | | ● | | | ● | | | | | ● | | | |
| HARDY, JACK E (HM08981) | | | | | | | | | | | | | | | | | ● | | | | | | | | | | | | | | | | | | | | | | | | | | | | | | | |
| HARTLEY, GILL (HM09140) | | | ● | | | ● | | | | | ● | | ● | | | ● | | | | | | | | | | ● | | | | | | | | | ● | | ● | ● | ● | ● | ● | | | | | | | |
| HEAVEN MOUNTAIN TAIJI QUAN (HM09472) | | | | | | | | | | | | | | | | ● | | | | | | | | | | | | | | | | | | | | | ● | | ● | | | | | | | | | |
| HELIANTHUS PRACTICE (HM09518) | | | ● | ● | ● | ● | | ● | | ● | ● | ● | ● | | ● | ● | ● | ● | ● | ● | ● | ● | ● | ● | ● | ● | | ● | ● | ● | ● | ● | ● | ● | ● | ● | ● | | ● | ● | ● | ● | ● | ● | ● | ● | ● | |
| HERBAL KING (HM09628) | | | | ● | | ● | | | | | | | ● | | | ● | | ● | | | | | | | | | | | | | | | | | | | ● | | ● | | | | ● | | ● | ● | | |
| HERBALS (HM09647) | ● | ● | ● | | ● | ● | ● | | | | ● | ● | ● | | | ● | | ● | | ● | ● | ● | ● | ● | ● | ● | | ● | ● | | ● | ● | ● | ● | | ● | ● | | ● | | ● | ● | ● | ● | ● | ● | ● | |
| HILL, CHARLOTTE (HM09774) | | | | | | | | | | | | | | | | | | | | | | | | | | | | | | | | | | | | | ● | | | ● | | | | | | | | |
| HOLISTIC CENTRE (HM09949) | ● | ● | ● | ● | ● | ● | ● | ● | ● | ● | ● | ● | ● | ● | ● | ● | ● | ● | ● | ● | ● | ● | ● | ● | ● | ● | ● | ● | ● | ● | ● | ● | ● | ● | ● | ● | ● | ● | ● | ● | ● | ● | ● | ● | ● | ● | ● | |
| HOLISTIC HEALTH CENTRE (HM09971) | | | ● | | ● | ● | | | | | | | | | | ● | | | | | | | | | | | | | | | | | | | | ● | ● | | | ● | | | | | | | | |
| HOPPER, C A (HM10156) | | | ● | | | | | | | | | | | | | | ● | | | | | | | | | | | | | | | | | | | | | | | | | | | | | | | |
| HUMAN FOCUS RETURN TO WORK (HM10362) | | | ● | | | | | | | | | | | | | ● | ● | | | | | | | | | | | | | | | | | | | | | | | ● | | | | | | | | |
| INGLEDALE NATURAL HEALTH CTRE (HM10621) | | | | | | | | | | | | | | | | | | | | | | | | | | | | | | | | | | | | | ● | | | | | | | | | | | |
| INTEGRAL HEALTH (HM10690) | ● | ● | ● | ● | ● | ● | ● | ● | ● | ● | ● | ● | ● | ● | ● | ● | ● | ● | ● | ● | ● | ● | ● | ● | ● | ● | ● | ● | ● | ● | ● | ● | ● | ● | ● | ● | ● | ● | ● | ● | ● | ● | ● | ● | ● | ● | ● | |
| J V ASSOCIATES (HM10803) | | | | ● | | ● | | | | | | | | | | ● | | | | | | | | | | | | | | | ● | | | | | | ● | | ● | | | | | | ● | | | |
| KENT CLINIC OF NATURAL MED (HM11514) | ● | ● | ● | ● | ● | ● | ● | ● | ● | ● | ● | ● | ● | ● | ● | ● | ● | ● | ● | ● | ● | ● | ● | ● | ● | ● | ● | ● | ● | ● | ● | ● | ● | ● | ● | ● | ● | ● | ● | ● | ● | ● | ● | ● | ● | ● | ● | |
| KEW CHIROPRACTIC CLINIC (HM11575) | | | | | | | | ● | | | | | | | | | | | | | | | | | | | | | | | | | | | | | ● | | | ● | | | | | | | | |
| KINGSTON NATURAL HEALING CTRE (HM11677) | | | | | ● | ● | | ● | ● | | | ● | ● | | | ● | ● | ● | | | | ● | | | | ● | | | ● | | | | | | | ● | ● | | | ● | ● | ● | | ● | ● | ● | | |
| KINGSTON OSTEOPATHS (HM11679) | | | | | ● | ● | ● | | | | | | | | | | | ● | | | ● | ● | ● | | | ● | | | | | | | | | | | | | ● | ● | | | | | ● | ● | ● | |
| KOLTHAMMER, JOHN (HM11780) | | | | | | | | | | | | | | | | | | | | | | | | | | | | | | | | | | | | | ● | | | ● | | | | | | | | |
| LEATHERHEAD CHIRO CLINIC (HM12114) | | | | | ● | | | | | | | | | | | | | | | | | ● | | | | | | | | | | | | | | | | | | | | | | | | | | |
| LONDON SPINE AND JOINT CLINIC (HM12610) | | | | | | | | | | | | | | | | | | | | | | ● | | | | | | | | | | | | | ● | | ● | | | ● | | | | | | | | |
| LOW, ROYSTON (HM12688) | | | ● | | ● | ● | ● | | | | | ● | | | | ● | | | | ● | | ● | | | | ● | | | ● | | | | | | ● | ● | ● | | ● | ● | | | | | ● | | | |
| MARKS, DARREN HYPNOTHERAPY (HM13120) | | | ● | | | | | | | | | | | | | | | | | | | | | | | | | | | | | | | | | | | | | | | | | | | | | |
| MARSON, JOY (HM13178) | | | ● | ● | | ● | | | | | | ● | | | | ● | | ● | | ● | ● | | | ● | | ● | | | | | ● | | | ● | | ● | ● | | ● | | ● | ● | | | ● | ● | | |
| MEEKS, FIONA (HM13683) | | | | | | ● | | ● | | ● | ● | | | | | | | | | | | ● | | | | | | | | | | | | | | | ● | | | ● | | | | ● | | | | |
| MEENEGHAN, TOM (HM13685) | | | ● | | ● | ● | ● | ● | | | ● | ● | ● | | | ● | ● | ● | ● | ● | ● | ● | | ● | ● | ● | ● | | ● | | ● | | | | ● | ● | ● | | ● | ● | ● | ● | | | ● | ● | ● | |
| MILFORD MASSAGE PRACTICE (HM13863) | | | | | | | | | | | | | | | | | | | | | | | | | | | | | | | | | | | | | ● | | | | | | | | | | | |
| MILLER CONSULTANCY (HM13880) | | | ● | ● | | ● | | | ● | | | ● | | ● | | ● | ● | ● | | | | | | | | | | | | | ● | | | | | ● | ● | | | ● | ● | | ● | | ● | ● | | |
| MIND AND BODY (HM13958) | | | ● | | | ● | | | | | | ● | | | | ● | ● | | | | | | | | | | | | | | | | | | ● | | ● | | | ● | | | | | ● | | | |

# D - I Conditions treated at Practices/Businesses

| Business by County with Reference no. | Dandruff | Deafness | Depression | Diabetes | Diarrhoea | Digestive Problems | Diverticulitis | Dizziness | Dyslexia | Dyspraxia | Ear Disorders | Eczema | ENT Disorders | Epilepsy | Eye Disorders | Fatigue | Fears | Fertility Problems | Fever | Fibroids |
|---|---|---|---|---|---|---|---|---|---|---|---|---|---|---|---|---|---|---|---|---|
| MIST, CORINNE (HM13996) | | | | | | ● | | | | | | ● | | | | ● | | | | |
| MOSS PHARMACY PODIATRY (HM14263) | | | | | | | | | | | | | | | | | | | | |
| NATURAL HEALING CENTRE (HM14541) | | | ● | | | ● | | ● | | | | | | | | ● | | | | |
| NATURAL HEALING CLINIC (HM14550) | | | | | | | | | | | | | | | | | | | | |
| NATURAL HEALTH PRACTICE (HM14594) | | | | | | ● | | | | | | | | | | ● | | | | |
| NICHOLLS, VERITY (HM14915) | | | | | | | | | | | | | | | | | | | | |
| NICOLA FRY-HEALTH & BEAUTY (HM14927) | | | | | | | | | | | | ● | | | | ● | | | | |
| OLD WOKING GRANGE (HM15264) | | | ● | | | ● | ● | | | | | ● | | | | ● | ● | | | |
| OSTEOPATHY (HM15477) | | | | | | | | ● | | | | | | | | | | | | |
| PHILP, CHRISTINE (HM16147) | | | ● | | | | | | | | | | | | | | | | | |
| POWER, DAVID J (HM16503) | | | | | | | | | | | | | | | | | | | | |
| PRICE, SANDRA (HM16593) | | | | | | | | | | | | | | | | | | | | |
| RICHMOND PHYSIOTHERAPY (HM17301) | | | | | | | | | | | | | | | | | | | | |
| RIGAL, M (HM17330) | | | | | | | | | | | | | | | | | | | | |
| ROBYNA, ANNETTE (HM17516) | | | ● | | | ● | | | | | | ● | | | | ● | ● | ● | | |
| SARAH BOGUE HOMEOPATH (HM17944) | | | ● | | | ● | | | | | ● | ● | | | | ● | ● | ● | | |
| SAUMEEL PATEL ACU CLINIC (HM17950) | | | ● | | ● | | | | | | | | | ● | | ● | | ● | | |
| SAYER CLINIC (HM17992) | | | | | | | | | | | | | | | | | | | | |
| SCHONBERG, VERA (HM18078) | | | ● | | ● | | | | | | | ● | | | | | | | | |
| SCHOOL OF YOGA (HM18089) | | | | | | | | | | | | | | | | ● | ● | | | |
| SCORPIO PHYSIOTHERAPY (HM18103) | | | | | | | | | | | | | | | | | | | | |
| SELSDON COMP/RESP CLINIC (HM18220) | ● | ● | ● | ● | ● | ● | ● | ● | ● | ● | ● | ● | ● | ● | ● | ● | ● | ● | ● | |
| SEVEN SIGHS (HM18244) | | | | | | | | | | | | | | | | | | | | |
| SHEPPERTON PHYSIOFIRST CENTRE (HM18425) | | | | | | | | | | | | | | | | | | | | |
| SIMMS, KATHERINE (HM18564) | | | | | | | | | | | | | | | | | | | | |
| STEWART, I (HM19267) | | | | | | | | | | | | | | | | | | | | |
| SURBITON NATURAL HEALTH CENTRE (HM19514) | | | | | ● | ● | | | | | | ● | | | | ● | | | | |
| SURREY HEALING SANCTUARY (HM19522) | ● | ● | ● | ● | ● | ● | ● | ● | ● | ● | ● | ● | ● | | | ● | | ● | ● | ● |
| SUTHERLAND, JENNY (HM19539) | | | ● | | ● | ● | | | | | | | | | | ● | | | | |
| SUTTON CHIROPRACTIC CLINIC (HM19543) | | | | | | | | | | | | | | | | | | | | |
| TANSILL, LUCY (HM19689) | | | | | | | | ● | | | | | | | | | | | | |
| TOWNS, KATE (HM20202) | | | ● | | | | | | | | | ● | | | | ● | ● | | | |
| TRADITIONAL CHINESE MEDICINE (HM20225) | | | ● | | | ● | | | | | | | | | | ● | | | | |
| TRANSCENDENTAL MEDITATION (HM20266) | | | ● | | | | | | | | | | | | | ● | | | | |

| Business by County with Reference no. | Flatulence | Foot Problems | Fractures | Fungal Infections | Gallstones | Gastrointestinal Problems | Genital Herpes | Gingivitis | Glandular Fever | Glaucoma | Gout | Gum Disease | Hair Problems | Halitosis | Hand Problems | Hay Fever | Headaches | Hearing Problems | High Blood Pressure | Hip Complaints | Hyperactivity | Hypoglycaemia | Impotence | Incontinence | Indigestion | Infertility | Influenza | Ingrowing Toenails |
|---|---|---|---|---|---|---|---|---|---|---|---|---|---|---|---|---|---|---|---|---|---|---|---|---|---|---|---|---|
| MIST, CORINNE (HM13996) | | | | | | ● | | | | | ● | | | | | | ● | | ● | | | | | | | | | |
| MOSS PHARMACY PODIATRY (HM14263) | | | | | | | | | | | | | | | | | | | | | | | | | | | | ● |
| NATURAL HEALING CENTRE (HM14541) | | | | | | | | | | | | | | | | ● | ● | | ● | ● | ● | | | | ● | | | |
| NATURAL HEALING CLINIC (HM14550) | | | | | | | | | | | | | | | | | ● | | | ● | | | | | | | | |
| NATURAL HEALTH PRACTICE (HM14594) | | ● | | | | | | | | | | | | | ● | | ● | | | ● | | | | | | | | |
| NICHOLLS, VERITY (HM14915) | | ● | | | | | | | | | | | | | | | | | | | | | | | | | | |
| NICOLA FRY-HEALTH & BEAUTY (HM14927) | | | | | | | | | | | | | | | | | ● | | | | | | | | | | | |
| OLD WOKING GRANGE (HM15264) | ● | | | ● | ● | ● | | | | | | | | | | | | | | | | ● | | | ● | | | |
| OSTEOPATHY (HM15477) | | ● | | | | | | | | | | | | | ● | | ● | | | ● | | | | | | | | |
| PHILP, CHRISTINE (HM16147) | | | | | | | | | | | | | | | | | ● | | ● | | | | | | | | | |
| POWER, DAVID J (HM16503) | | ● | | ● | | | | | | | | | | | | | | | | | | | | | | | | |
| PRICE, SANDRA (HM16593) | | | | | | | | | | | | | | | | | ● | | | ● | | | | | | | | |
| RICHMOND PHYSIOTHERAPY (HM17301) | | | | | | | | | | | | | | | | | | | | ● | | | | | | | | |
| RIGAL, M (HM17330) | | ● | | | | | | | | | | | | | ● | | | | | | | | | | | | | |
| ROBYNA, ANNETTE (HM17516) | ● | | | | | | | | | | | | | | | | ● | | ● | | | | | | ● | | | |
| SARAH BOGUE HOMEOPATH (HM17944) | | | | | | ● | | | ● | | | | | | | ● | ● | | | | ● | ● | | | ● | ● | | |
| SAUMEEL PATEL ACU CLINIC (HM17950) | | | | | | | | | | | | | | | | ● | ● | | | | ● | | | | | ● | | |
| SAYER CLINIC (HM17992) | | | | | | | | | | | | | | | | | ● | | | ● | | | | | | | | |
| SCHONBERG, VERA (HM18078) | | | | | | | | | | | | | | | | | ● | | | ● | | | ● | | | | | |
| SCHOOL OF YOGA (HM18089) | | | | | | | | | | | | | | | | ● | ● | | ● | | | | | | | | | |
| SCORPIO PHYSIOTHERAPY (HM18103) | | ● | ● | | | | | | | | | | | | ● | | | | | ● | | | | | | | | |
| SELSDON COMP/RESP CLINIC (HM18220) | ● | ● | ● | ● | ● | ● | | ● | ● | | ● | ● | | ● | ● | ● | ● | ● | ● | ● | ● | ● | ● | ● | ● | ● | ● | |
| SEVEN SIGHS (HM18244) | | | | | | | | | | | | | | | | | | | ● | | | | | | | | | |
| SHEPPERTON PHYSIOFIRST CENTRE (HM18425) | | | | | | | | | | | | | | | | | | | | ● | | | | | | | | |
| SIMMS, KATHERINE (HM18564) | | | | | | | | | | | | | | | | | | | ● | | | | | | | | | |
| STEWART, I (HM19267) | | ● | | ● | | | | | | | | | | | | | | | | | | | | | | | | |
| SURBITON NATURAL HEALTH CENTRE (HM19514) | | | | | | | | | | | | | | | | ● | | | | ● | | | | | ● | | | |
| SURREY HEALING SANCTUARY (HM19522) | ● | ● | | ● | ● | ● | | | ● | ● | ● | | | | ● | ● | ● | ● | ● | ● | ● | | | | ● | ● | ● | |
| SUTHERLAND, JENNY (HM19539) | | | | | | | | | | | | | | | ● | ● | ● | | ● | ● | ● | | | | ● | | | |
| SUTTON CHIROPRACTIC CLINIC (HM19543) | | | | | | | | | | | | | | | | | ● | | | ● | | | | | | | | |
| TANSILL, LUCY (HM19689) | | | | | | | | | | | | | | | | | ● | | | | | | | | | | | |
| TOWNS, KATE (HM20202) | | | | | | | | | | | | | | | | ● | ● | | | | ● | | | | | | | |
| TRADITIONAL CHINESE MEDICINE (HM20225) | | | | | | | | | | | | | | | | ● | | | | | ● | | | | ● | | | |
| TRANSCENDENTAL MEDITATION (HM20266) | | | | | | | | | | | | | | | | | ● | | ● | | | | | | | | | |

# D - I Conditions treated at Practices/Businesses

| Business by County with Reference no. | Dandruff | Deafness | Depression | Diabetes | Diarrhoea | Digestive Problems | Diverticulitis | Dizziness | Dyslexia | Dyspraxia | Ear Disorders | Eczema | ENT Disorders | Epilepsy | Eye Disorders | Fatigue | Fears | Fertility Problems | Fever | Fibroids | Flatulence | Foot Problems | Fractures | Fungal Infections |
|---|---|---|---|---|---|---|---|---|---|---|---|---|---|---|---|---|---|---|---|---|---|---|---|---|
| TURNER, R E (HM20435) | | | | | | | |●| | | | | | | | | | | | | | | | |
| TWO STEPS REFLEXOLOGY (HM20458) | | |●| |●|●| |●| | | | |●| | |●|●|●| | |●| | | |
| WALKER, SARAH (HM20803) | | |●| |●|●| | | | | | | | | | | | | | |●| | | |
| WALLACE, SUE (HM20832) | | | | | |●| | | | | | | | | |●| | | | | | | | |
| WEYBRIDGE CHIROPRACTIC CLINIC (HM21293) | | | | | | | | | | | | | | | | | | | | | | | | |
| WHITWORTH, MICHAEL T (HM21431) | | | | | | | | | | | | | | | | | | | | | |●| |●|
| WILKINSON, LESLEY (HM21510) |●|●|●| |●|●|●|●|●|●|●|●|●|●| |●|●|●| |●|●|●| |●|
| WILLIS, SALLY (HM21618) | | |●| | | | | | | | | | | | | |●| | | | | | | |
| WINTER, DAVID (HM21718) |●|●|●|●|●|●|●|●|●|●|●|●|●|●|●|●|●|●|●|●|●|●|●|●|
| WOOD, VALERIE (HM21811) | | |●| | |●| | | | | | | | | | | | | | | | | | |
| WOODLANDS NATURAL HLTH THERAPY (HM21832) | | |●|●|●|●|●|●| | |●|●| | | |●|●| | |●|●| | |●|
| SUSSEX (EAST) | | | | | | | | | | | | | | | | | | | | | | | | |
| ALBION CLINIC (HM00483) | | |●| |●|●|●|●| | | | | | | |●|●| |●| |●|●|●| |
| ALEXANDER TECHNIQUE (HM00549) | | |●| | |●| | | |●| | | | | |●| | | | | | | | |
| ALPHA HYPNOTHERAPY (HM00684) | | |●| | | | | | | | | | | | | | | | | | | | | |
| ANGELA MATTHEWS HOMEOPATH (HM00873) | | |●| | |●| | | | |●|●| | | |●|●| | |●|●| | | |
| ARDERN FOOT & HEALTH CLINIC (HM00992) | | |●| | | | |●| | | |●| | | |●| | | | | |●| |●|
| AROMA HAIR (HM01047) | | |●| | | | | | | | | | | | | | | | | | | | | |
| ASHDOWN OSTEOPATHIC CENTRE (HM01206) | | | | | |●| |●| | | | | | | | | | | | | |●|●| |
| BASSETT, N S (HM01857) | | | | | | | |●| | |●| | | | | | | | | | | |●| |
| BELVAIN, E (HM02118) | | | | | |●| | | | | |●| | | | | | | | | | | | |
| BEXHILL CHIROPRACTIC (HM02255) | | | | |●|●| | | | | | | | | |●| |●| | |●| | | |
| BEXHILL OSTEOPATHIC PRACTICE (HM02257) | | | | | |●| | | | | |●| | | |●| | | | | |●| | |
| BRIGHTON & HOVE SPORTS CLINIC (HM03041) | | | | | | | | | | | | | | | | | | | | | | | | |
| BRIGHTON ACUPUNCTURE CLINIC (HM03042) | | | | | |●| | | | | |●| | | |●| |●| | | | | | |
| BRIGHTON ALEXANDER TRAINING (HM03043) | | | | | | | | | | | | | | | | | | | | | | | | |
| BRIGHTON CHIROPRACTIC CLINIC (HM03044) | | | | | |●| | | | | | | | | |●| | | | | | |●| |
| BRIGHTON HEALTH & RACQUET CLUB (HM03045) | | | | | | | | | | | | | | | | | | | | | | |●| |
| CANTERLA, MARGARET (HM03643) |●|●|●|●|●|●|●|●|●|●|●|●|●|●|●|●|●|●|●|●|●|●|●|●|
| CLINCH, ADELE (HM04675) | | | | | | | | | | | | | | | | | | | | | |●| |●|
| CLINIC OF CHINESE MED & ACU (HM04685) | | | | |●| | | | | | | | | | |●| | | | | | | | |
| COMP THERAPY & TRAINING CENTRE (HM04915) |●|●|●|●|●|●|●|●|●|●|●|●|●|●|●|●|●|●|●|●|●|●|●|●|
| CONCEPTS PHYSIO & NUTRITION (HM04970) |●|●|●|●|●|●|●|●| | |●|●|●|●|●|●|●|●|●|●|●|●|●|●|
| COOK, ELAINE (HM05042) | | |●| |●|●| |●| | |●|●| | | |●|●|●|●| |●| | | |

| Business by County with Reference no. | Gallstones | Gastrointestinal Problems | Genital Herpes | Gingivitis | Glandular Fever | Glaucoma | Gout | Gum Disease | Hair Problems | Halitosis | Hand Problems | Hay Fever | Headaches | Hearing Problems | High Blood Pressure | Hip Complaints | Hyperactivity | Hypoglycaemia | Impotence | Incontinence | Indigestion | Infertility | Influenza | Ingrowing Toenails |
|---|---|---|---|---|---|---|---|---|---|---|---|---|---|---|---|---|---|---|---|---|---|---|---|---|
| TURNER, R E (HM20435) | | | | | | | | | | | | |●| | |●| | | | | | | | |
| TWO STEPS REFLEXOLOGY (HM20458) | | | | |●| | | | | | |●|●| |●| |●|●|●| |●|●| | |
| WALKER, SARAH (HM20803) | |●| | | | | | | | | | |●| | | | | | |●| | | | |
| WALLACE, SUE (HM20832) | |●| | | | | | | | | | | | | | | | | | |●| | | |
| WEYBRIDGE CHIROPRACTIC CLINIC (HM21293) | | | | | | | | | | | | |●| | | | | | | | | | | |
| WHITWORTH, MICHAEL T (HM21431) | | | | | | | | | | | | | | | | | | | | | | | |●|
| WILKINSON, LESLEY (HM21510) | |●|●|●|●| | |●| | |●|●| | | | | |●|●|●|●|●|●| |
| WILLIS, SALLY (HM21618) | | | | | | | | | | | | | | | | | | | | | | | | |
| WINTER, DAVID (HM21718) |●|●|●|●|●|●|●|●|●|●|●|●|●|●|●|●|●|●|●|●|●|●|●| |
| WOOD, VALERIE (HM21811) | | | | | | | | | | | | |●| | | | | | | |●| | | |
| WOODLANDS NATURAL HLTH THERAPY (HM21832) | |●| | | | |●| | | | |●|●| |●| |●|●| | |●| | | |
| SUSSEX (EAST) | | | | | | | | | | | | | | | | | | | | | | | | |
| ALBION CLINIC (HM00483) | | | | | | |●| | | | | |●| |●|●| | | | |●| | | |
| ALEXANDER TECHNIQUE (HM00549) | | | | | | | | | | | | | | | |●| | | | | | | | |
| ALPHA HYPNOTHERAPY (HM00684) | | | | | | | | | | | | | | | | | | | | | | | | |
| ANGELA MATTHEWS HOMEOPATH (HM00873) | |●| | | | | | | | | |●|●| | | | | | | | | |●| |
| ARDERN FOOT & HEALTH CLINIC (HM00992) | | | | | | | | | | | | |●| |●|●| | | |●|●| | | |
| AROMA HAIR (HM01047) | | | | | | | | | | | | |●| | | | | | | | | | | |
| ASHDOWN OSTEOPATHIC CENTRE (HM01206) | |●| | | | | | | | |●| |●| | |●|●| | | | | | | |
| BASSETT, N S (HM01857) | | | | | | |●| | | | | |●| |●|●| | | | | | | | |
| BELVAIN, E (HM02118) | | | | | | | | | | | | | | | | | | | | | | | | |
| BEXHILL CHIROPRACTIC (HM02255) | |●| | | | | | | | | | |●| |●|●| | | |●|●| | | |
| BEXHILL OSTEOPATHIC PRACTICE (HM02257) | | | | | | | | | | |●| |●| | |●| | | | | | | | |
| BRIGHTON & HOVE SPORTS CLINIC (HM03041) | | | | | | | | | | | | | | | |●| | | | | | | | |
| BRIGHTON ACUPUNCTURE CLINIC (HM03042) | |●| | |●| | | | | | | |●| |●|●| | | | | |●| | |
| BRIGHTON ALEXANDER TRAINING (HM03043) | | | | | | | | | | | | |●| | | | | | | | | | | |
| BRIGHTON CHIROPRACTIC CLINIC (HM03044) | | | | | | | | | | | | |●| | |●| | | | | | | | |
| BRIGHTON HEALTH & RACQUET CLUB (HM03045) | | | | | | | | | | | | | | | | | | | | | | | | |
| CANTERLA, MARGARET (HM03643) |●|●|●|●|●|●|●|●|●|●|●|●|●|●|●|●|●|●|●|●|●|●|●| |
| CLINCH, ADELE (HM04675) | | | | | | | | | | | | | | | | | | | | | | | | |
| CLINIC OF CHINESE MED & ACU (HM04685) | | | | | | | | | | | |●|●| |●| | | | | | | | | |
| COMP THERAPY & TRAINING CENTRE (HM04915) |●|●|●|●|●|●|●|●|●|●|●|●|●|●|●|●|●|●|●|●|●|●|●| |
| CONCEPTS PHYSIO & NUTRITION (HM04970) |●|●|●|●|●|●|●|●|●|●|●|●|●|●|●|●|●|●|●|●|●|●|●| |
| COOK, ELAINE (HM05042) | | |●| | | | | | | | |●|●|●|●|●| | | | |●|●|●| |

# D - I Conditions treated at Practices/Businesses

| Business by County with Reference no. | Dandruff | Deafness | Depression | Diabetes | Diarrhoea | Digestive Problems | Diverticulitis | Dizziness | Dyslexia | Dyspraxia | Ear Disorders | Eczema | ENT Disorders | Epilepsy | Eye Disorders | Fatigue |
|---|---|---|---|---|---|---|---|---|---|---|---|---|---|---|---|---|
| COX, JULIET (HM05308) | | | ● | | | | | | | | | | | | | ● |
| CRESENT CLINIC (HM05422) | | | ● | ● | ● | ● | ● | ● | | | ● | ● | ● | ● | | ● |
| CROWBOROUGH CHIRO/COMP HLTH (HM05498) | | | | | | | | | | | | | | | | ● |
| CROWBOROUGH COMP THERAPISTS (HM05499) | | | ● | | | ● | | ● | | | | | | | | ● |
| CULL, BEN (HM05556) | | | | | | | | | | | | | | | | ● |
| DADSWELL, CLAIRE (HM05670) | ● | ● | ● | ● | ● | ● | ● | ● | ● | ● | ● | ● | ● | ● | ● | ● |
| DEEKS, STUART (HM05956) | | | ● | ● | ● | ● | ● | ● | | | ● | ● | ● | ● | | ● |
| DRIVE OSTEO AND SPORTS CLINIC (HM06314) | | | | | | | | | | | | | | | | |
| DRYDEN, B A (HM06332) | | | | | | | | | | | | | | | | |
| DYKE ROAD NATURAL HEALTH (HM06450) | ● | ● | ● | ● | ● | ● | ● | ● | ● | ● | ● | ● | ● | ● | ● | ● |
| EAST BOURNE CLINIC (HM06509) | | | | | | | | | | | | | | | | |
| EASTBOURNE CHIROPRACTIC CLINIC (HM06535) | | | | | | | | | | | | | | | | |
| FAIRCHILD, HAZEL (HM07052) | | | ● | | | | | | | | | | | | | |
| FAMILY FIRST (HM07087) | | | ● | | | | | | | | | | | | | |
| FIVEWAYS OSTEOPATHIC PRACTICE (HM07382) | | | | | | | | | | | | | | | | |
| FLOYD, MICHELLE (HM07438) | ● | ● | ● | ● | ● | ● | ● | ● | ● | ● | ● | ● | ● | ● | ● | ● |
| FOUNDATION, ANGELGATE (HM07615) | ● | | | ● | ● | ● | ● | | | | | ● | | | ● | ● |
| GEIGES, STEPHANIE (HM07967) | | | | | | | | | | | | | | | | |
| GOLDSTONE CLINIC (HM08229) | | | | | | | | ● | | | | ● | | ● | | |
| GOLDSTONE CLINIC (HM08230) | | | | | | | | | | | | | | | | |
| GONZALEZ, SOHANI (HM08237) | ● | ● | ● | ● | ● | ● | ● | ● | ● | ● | ● | ● | ● | ● | ● | ● |
| GRIFFITHS, J (HM08567) | | | | | | | | ● | | | | | | | | |
| HART, RONALD (HM09131) | | | | | | | | | | | | | | | | |
| HART, RONALD (HM09130) | | | | | | | | | | | | | | | | |
| HAWKINS, LUKE (HM09224) | | | | | | | | | | | | | | | | |
| HEMMINGWAY CHIROPODIST (HM09537) | | | | | | | | | | | | | | | | |
| HERBAL HEALTH CLINIC (HM09617) | ● | | ● | | ● | ● | ● | ● | ● | | ● | ● | ● | | | ● |
| HOLDEN NATURAL HEALTH CLINIC (HM09927) | | | | | | | | | | | ● | | | | | ● |
| HOVE CHIROPRACTIC CLINIC (HM10227) | | | | | | | | | | | | | | | | |
| HOVE OSTEOPATHIC CLINIC (HM10228) | | | | | | | | | | | | | | | | |
| HUGHES, CLARE (HM10324) | | | | | | | | | | | | | | | | |
| HYSLOP, C P (HM10543) | ● | ● | ● | ● | ● | ● | ● | ● | ● | ● | ● | ● | ● | ● | ● | ● |
| JEMPSON, NICOLA (HM10978) | | | ● | | | | | | | | | | | | | |
| JOY, JANET (HM11231) | | | ● | | | | | | | | | | | | | |

| Business by County with Reference no. | Fears | Fertility Problems | Fever | Fibroids | Flatulence | Foot Problems | Fractures | Fungal Infections | Gallstones | Gastrointestinal Problems | Genital Herpes | Gingivitis | Glandular Fever | Glaucoma | Gout | Gum Disease |
|---|---|---|---|---|---|---|---|---|---|---|---|---|---|---|---|---|
| COX, JULIET (HM05308) | ● | | | | | | | | | | | | | | | |
| CRESENT CLINIC (HM05422) | ● | ● | ● | ● | ● | ● | ● | ● | | ● | ● | ● | ● | | ● | ● |
| CROWBOROUGH CHIRO/COMP HLTH (HM05498) | | | | | ● | ● | | | | | | | | | | |
| CROWBOROUGH COMP THERAPISTS (HM05499) | | | | | | | | | | | | | | | | |
| CULL, BEN (HM05556) | ● | | | | | ● | ● | | | ● | | | | | | |
| DADSWELL, CLAIRE (HM05670) | ● | ● | ● | ● | ● | ● | ● | ● | ● | ● | ● | ● | ● | ● | ● | ● |
| DEEKS, STUART (HM05956) | ● | ● | ● | ● | ● | | | ● | | ● | ● | ● | ● | | ● | ● |
| DRIVE OSTEO AND SPORTS CLINIC (HM06314) | | | | | | ● | ● | | | ● | | | | | | |
| DRYDEN, B A (HM06332) | ● | | | | | | | | | | | | | | | |
| DYKE ROAD NATURAL HEALTH (HM06450) | ● | ● | ● | ● | ● | ● | ● | ● | ● | ● | ● | ● | ● | ● | ● | ● |
| EAST BOURNE CLINIC (HM06509) | | | | | | ● | ● | ● | | | | | | | | |
| EASTBOURNE CHIROPRACTIC CLINIC (HM06535) | | | | | | ● | ● | | | | | | | | | |
| FAIRCHILD, HAZEL (HM07052) | ● | | | | | | | | | | | | | | | |
| FAMILY FIRST (HM07087) | ● | | | | | | | | | | | | | | | |
| FIVEWAYS OSTEOPATHIC PRACTICE (HM07382) | | | | | | ● | | | | | | | | | | |
| FLOYD, MICHELLE (HM07438) | ● | ● | ● | ● | ● | ● | ● | | ● | ● | ● | ● | ● | ● | ● | ● |
| FOUNDATION, ANGELGATE (HM07615) | | | | | ● | ● | | ● | ● | | | | | ● | ● | |
| GEIGES, STEPHANIE (HM07967) | | | | | | | | | | | | | | | | |
| GOLDSTONE CLINIC (HM08229) | | | | | | | ● | | | | | | | | | |
| GOLDSTONE CLINIC (HM08230) | | | | | | | | | | | | | | | | |
| GONZALEZ, SOHANI (HM08237) | ● | ● | ● | ● | ● | ● | ● | ● | ● | ● | ● | ● | ● | ● | ● | ● |
| GRIFFITHS, J (HM08567) | | | | | | | | | | | | | | | | |
| HART, RONALD (HM09131) | | | | | | ● | | ● | | | | | | | | |
| HART, RONALD (HM09130) | | | | | | ● | | ● | | | | | | | | |
| HAWKINS, LUKE (HM09224) | | | | | | ● | | ● | | | | | | | | |
| HEMMINGWAY CHIROPODIST (HM09537) | | | | | | ● | | ● | | | | | | | | |
| HERBAL HEALTH CLINIC (HM09617) | ● | ● | | | ● | | | ● | | ● | | ● | | | | ● |
| HOLDEN NATURAL HEALTH CLINIC (HM09927) | | | | | ● | | | ● | | | | | | | | |
| HOVE CHIROPRACTIC CLINIC (HM10227) | | | | | | | | | | | | | | | | |
| HOVE OSTEOPATHIC CLINIC (HM10228) | | | | | | | | | | | | | | | | |
| HUGHES, CLARE (HM10324) | | | | | | | | | | | | | | | | |
| HYSLOP, C P (HM10543) | ● | ● | ● | ● | ● | ● | ● | ● | ● | ● | ● | ● | ● | ● | ● | ● |
| JEMPSON, NICOLA (HM10978) | | | | | | | | | | | | | | | | |
| JOY, JANET (HM11231) | ● | | | | | | | | | | | | | | | |

| Business by County with Reference no. | Hair Problems | Halitosis | Hand Problems | Hay Fever | Headaches | Hearing Problems | High Blood Pressure | Hip Complaints | Hyperactivity | Hypoglycaemia | Impotence | Incontinence | Indigestion | Infertility | Influenza | Ingrowing Toenails |
|---|---|---|---|---|---|---|---|---|---|---|---|---|---|---|---|---|
| COX, JULIET (HM05308) | | | ● | | ● | | ● | ● | ● | | | | | | | |
| CRESENT CLINIC (HM05422) | ● | ● | ● | ● | ● | | ● | ● | ● | | ● | | ● | ● | ● | |
| CROWBOROUGH CHIRO/COMP HLTH (HM05498) | | | ● | | ● | | | | | | | | ● | | | |
| CROWBOROUGH COMP THERAPISTS (HM05499) | | | ● | ● | ● | | ● | ● | ● | | | | ● | | | |
| CULL, BEN (HM05556) | | | ● | | ● | | ● | ● | | | | | | | | |
| DADSWELL, CLAIRE (HM05670) | ● | ● | ● | ● | ● | ● | ● | ● | ● | ● | ● | ● | ● | ● | ● | |
| DEEKS, STUART (HM05956) | ● | ● | | ● | ● | | ● | | ● | | ● | | ● | ● | ● | |
| DRIVE OSTEO AND SPORTS CLINIC (HM06314) | | | | | | | | ● | | | | | ● | | | |
| DRYDEN, B A (HM06332) | | | | | | | | | | | | | | | | |
| DYKE ROAD NATURAL HEALTH (HM06450) | ● | ● | ● | ● | ● | ● | ● | ● | ● | ● | ● | ● | ● | ● | ● | |
| EAST BOURNE CLINIC (HM06509) | | | | | ● | | ● | ● | | | | | ● | | | |
| EASTBOURNE CHIROPRACTIC CLINIC (HM06535) | | | | | ● | | | ● | | | | | | | | |
| FAIRCHILD, HAZEL (HM07052) | | | | | | | | | | | | | | | | |
| FAMILY FIRST (HM07087) | | | | | | | | | | | | | | | | |
| FIVEWAYS OSTEOPATHIC PRACTICE (HM07382) | | | | | ● | | | ● | | | | | | | | |
| FLOYD, MICHELLE (HM07438) | | | | ● | ● | | ● | | ● | ● | ● | ● | ● | ● | ● | |
| FOUNDATION, ANGELGATE (HM07615) | ● | | | | ● | | | ● | ● | | | | ● | | | |
| GEIGES, STEPHANIE (HM07967) | | | | | ● | | | ● | | | | | | | | |
| GOLDSTONE CLINIC (HM08229) | | | | | ● | | | ● | | | | | | | | |
| GOLDSTONE CLINIC (HM08230) | | | | | ● | | | | | | | | | | | |
| GONZALEZ, SOHANI (HM08237) | ● | ● | ● | ● | ● | ● | ● | ● | ● | ● | ● | ● | ● | ● | ● | |
| GRIFFITHS, J (HM08567) | | | ● | ● | ● | | | | | | | | | | | |
| HART, RONALD (HM09131) | | | | | | | | | | | | | | | | |
| HART, RONALD (HM09130) | | | | | | | | | | | | | | | | |
| HAWKINS, LUKE (HM09224) | | | | | | | | | | | | | | | | |
| HEMMINGWAY CHIROPODIST (HM09537) | | | | | | | | | | | | | | | | |
| HERBAL HEALTH CLINIC (HM09617) | | ● | | ● | ● | | ● | | ● | ● | | ● | ● | | ● | |
| HOLDEN NATURAL HEALTH CLINIC (HM09927) | | | | | ● | | ● | | | | | | ● | ● | | |
| HOVE CHIROPRACTIC CLINIC (HM10227) | | | | | ● | | | ● | | | | | | | | |
| HOVE OSTEOPATHIC CLINIC (HM10228) | | | | | ● | | | | | | | | | | | |
| HUGHES, CLARE (HM10324) | | | | | ● | | | ● | | | | | | | | |
| HYSLOP, C P (HM10543) | ● | ● | ● | ● | ● | | ● | ● | ● | ● | ● | ● | ● | ● | ● | |
| JEMPSON, NICOLA (HM10978) | | | | | | | | | | | | | | | | |
| JOY, JANET (HM11231) | | | | | ● | | | | | | | | | | | |

# D - I Conditions treated at Practices/Businesses

| Business by County with Reference no. | Dandruff | Deafness | Depression | Diabetes | Diarrhoea | Digestive Problems | Diverticulitis | Dizziness | Dyslexia | Dyspraxia | Ear Disorders | Eczema | ENT Disorders | Epilepsy | Eye Disorders | Fatigue | Fears | Fertility Problems | Fever | Fibroids | Flatulence | Foot Problems | Fractures | Fungal Infections | Gallstones | Gastrointestinal Problems | Genital Herpes | Gingivitis | Glandular Fever | Glaucoma | Gout | Gum Disease | Hair Problems | Halitosis | Hand Problems | Hay Fever | Headaches | Hearing Problems | High Blood Pressure | Hip Complaints | Hyperactivity | Hypoglycaemia | Impotence | Incontinence | Indigestion | Infertility | Influenza | Ingrowing Toenails |
|---|---|---|---|---|---|---|---|---|---|---|---|---|---|---|---|---|---|---|---|---|---|---|---|---|---|---|---|---|---|---|---|---|---|---|---|---|---|---|---|---|---|---|---|---|---|---|---|---|
| LEWES CHIROPRACTIC CLINIC (HM12271) | | | | | | | | ● | | | | | | | | | | | | | | ● | ● | | | | | | | | | | | | ● | | ● | | | ● | | | | | | | | |
| MCKEOWN, KAY (HM13532) | | | | | | ● | | | | | | | | | | | | | | | | | | | | | | | | | | | | | | | ● | | | ● | | | | | | | | |
| MEADOWSWEET (HM13634) | | | | | | | | ● | | | | | | | | | | | | | | ● | | | | | | | | | | | | | ● | | ● | | | ● | | | | | | | | |
| MURPHY, KEVIN (HM14387) | | | ● | | | | | | ● | | | | | | | ● | | | | | | ● | ● | | | | | | | | ● | | | | ● | | ● | | | ● | | | | | | | | |
| NEAT FEET (HM14742) | | | | | | | | | | | | | | | | | | | | | | ● | | ● | | | | | | | | | | | | | | | | | | | | | | | | |
| NEWICK PHYSIOTHERAPY CLINIC (HM14865) | | | | | | | | | | | | | | | | | | | | | | | | | | | | | | | | | | | | | | | | ● | | | | | | | | |
| OLD TOWN CHIROPRACTIC CLINIC (HM15263) | | | | | | | | | | | | | | | | | | | | | | | | | | | | | | | | | | | ● | | ● | | | ● | | | | | | | | |
| PRICE, JAMES (HM16583) | | | | | | | | | | | | | | | | | | | | | | ● | | ● | | | | | | | | | | | | | | | | | | | | | | | | |
| PRIORY HEIGHTS (HM16633) | | | ● | | | | | | | | | ● | | ● | | | | | | | | | | | | | | | | | | | | | | ● | ● | | | | | | | | | | | |
| REEVES, ALAN (HM17062) | | | ● | | | | | | | | | | | | | | | | | | | | | | | | | | | | | | | | | | | | | | | | | | | | | |
| REFLEXOLOGY FOR HEALTH (HM17095) | | | ● | ● | | ● | | | | | ● | | | | | ● | | ● | | | ● | ● | | | ● | | | | | | | | | | | | ● | | ● | ● | | | | | ● | ● | | |
| SANDERSON & ELEMENT (HM17919) | | | | | | | | | | | | | | | | ● | | | | | | | | | | | | | | | | | | | | | ● | | | ● | | | | | | | | |
| SANDERSON & ELEMENT (HM17920) | | | | | | | | | | | | | | | | ● | | | | | | | | | | | | | | | | | | | | | ● | | | ● | | | | | | | | |
| SANDERSON & ELEMENT (HM17922) | | | | | | | | | | | | | | | | ● | | | | | | | | | | | | | | | | | | | | | ● | | | ● | | | | | | | | |
| SCHOLL CENTRE (HM18032) | | | | | | | | | | | | | | | | | | | | | | ● | | ● | | | | | | | | | | | | | | | | | | | | | | | | |
| SUNDIAL HOUSE CHIROPRACTIC (HM19506) | | | | | | | | | | | | | | | | | | | | | | | ● | | | | | | | | | | | | | | ● | | | ● | | | | | | | | |
| TEALE, PAUL (HM19809) | | | | | | | | | | | | | | | | | | | | | | ● | | | | | | | | | | | | | ● | | ● | | | ● | | | | | | | | |
| TISSERAND (HM20095) | | | ● | | | | | | | | | | | | | | | | | | | | | | | | | | | | | | | | | | ● | | | | | | | | | | | |
| TRENCHARD, ABIGAIL (HM20319) | | | ● | | | | | | | | | | | | | | ● | | | | | | | | | | | | | | | | | | | | | | | | | | | | | | | |
| VALENCE ROAD OSTEOPATHS (HM20554) | | | | | | | | | | | | | | | | | | | | | | | | | | | | | | | | | | | | | ● | | | | | | | | | | | |
| WADHURST PHYSIO/SPORTS CLNC (HM20729) | | | | | | | | | | | | | | | | | | | | | | | | | | | | | | | | | | | | | | | | ● | | | | | | | | |
| WADHURST PHYSIO/SPORTS CLNC (HM20730) | | | | | | | | | | | | | | | | | | | | | | | | | | | | | | | | | | | | | | | | ● | | | | | | | | |
| WALSH, M J (HM20865) | | | | | | | | | | | | | | | | | | | | | | ● | | | | | | | | | | | | | ● | | ● | | | ● | | | | | | | | |
| WEDLAKE-GRIFFITHS, J (HM21097) | | | | | | | | | | | | | | | | | | | | | | ● | | | | | | | | | | | | | | | | | | ● | | | | | | | | |
| WILBURY PHYSIOTHERAPY (HM21480) | | | | | | | | | | | | | | | | | ● | | | | | | | | | | | | | | | | | | | | | | | ● | | | | | | | | |
| WRIGHT, P A (HM21946) | | | | | | | | | | | | | | | | | | | | | | | | ● | | | | | | | | | | | | | | | | | | | | | | | | |
| **SUSSEX (WEST)** | | | | | | | | | | | | | | | | | | | | | | | | | | | | | | | | | | | | | | | | | | | | | | | | |
| ACORN CENTRE (HM00171) | | | ● | | | | | | | | | ● | | ● | | ● | | | | | | | ● | | | | | | | | | | | | | | ● | | | | | | | | ● | | | |
| ALAN SMITH CHIROPRACTOR (HM00470) | | | | | | | | | | | | | | | | ● | | | | | | | | | | | | | | | | | | | | | ● | | | | | | | | | | | |
| ANDREW BATHIE PRACTICE (HM00846) | | | ● | | | ● | | ● | | | | | | | | ● | ● | | | | | | | | | | | | | | | | | | | | ● | | ● | | | | | | | | | |
| ANGELA (HM00872) | | | ● | | | | | | | | | | | | | | | | | | | | | | | | | | | | | | | | | | ● | | | | | | | | | | | |
| AUROMA (HM01357) | | | ● | | | | | | | | | | | | | | | | | | | | | | | | | | | | | | | | | | | | | | | | | | | | | |
| AVALON HEALTH CENTRE (HM01380) | ● | ● | ● | ● | ● | ● | ● | ● | ● | ● | ● | ● | ● | ● | ● | ● | ● | ● | ● | ● | ● | ● | ● | ● | ● | ● | ● | ● | ● | ● | ● | ● | ● | ● | ● | ● | ● | ● | ● | ● | ● | ● | ● | ● | ● | ● | ● | |
| B O P (HM01452) | | | | | | ● | | ● | | | | | | | | ● | | | | | | ● | | | | | | | | | ● | | | | ● | | ● | | | ● | | | | | ● | | | |

# D - I Conditions treated at Practices/Businesses

| Business by County with Reference no. | Dandruff | Deafness | Depression | Diabetes | Diarrhoea | Digestive Problems | Diverticulitis | Dizziness | Dyslexia | Dyspraxia | Ear Disorders | Eczema | ENT Disorders | Epilepsy | Eye Disorders | Fatigue | Fears | Fertility Problems | Fever | Fibroids | Flatulence | Foot Problems | Fractures | Fungal Infections |
|---|---|---|---|---|---|---|---|---|---|---|---|---|---|---|---|---|---|---|---|---|---|---|---|---|
| BACK 2 FITNESS CHIROPRACTIC (HM01476) | | | | | | | | | | | | | | | | | | | | | | | ● | |
| BALOOMBE OSTEOPATHIC & SPORTS (HM01641) | | | | | | | | | | | | | | | | | | | | | | | | |
| BARTHOLOMEW WAY CLINIC (HM01818) | | | | ● | | | | | | | | | | | | | | | | | | ● | ● | ● |
| BELLAMY PARTNERSHIP (HM02093) | | | | | | | | | | | | | | | | | | | | | | ● | | |
| BLACK, PAULINE (HM02425) | ● | ● | ● | ● | ● | ● | ● | ● | ● | ● | ● | ● | ● | ● | ● | ● | ● | ● | ● | ● | ● | ● | ● | ● |
| BODYGUIDE ALTERNATE (HM02619) | ● | ● | ● | ● | ● | ● | ● | ● | ● | ● | ● | ● | ● | ● | ● | ● | ● | ● | ● | ● | ● | ● | ● | ● |
| BOHNET, CAROLE (HM02648) | | | | | | ● | ● | | | | | | | | | ● | | ● | | | | | | |
| BRITCHIRO CLINIC (HM03068) | | | | | | | | | | | | | | | | | | | | | | | | |
| BURNS, L C (HM03417) | | | | | | | | | | | | | | | | | | | | | | | | |
| CARTLAND, ANN (HM03794) | | | | | | | | | | | | | | | | | | | | | | ● | | ● |
| CASH, G G (HM03811) | | | | | | | | | | | | | | | | | | | | | | ● | | ● |
| CHANGES (HM03985) | ● | | ● | ● | | ● | ● | ● | | | ● | ● | | | ● | ● | ● | ● | | ● | ● | | | ● |
| CHASE, PETER (HM04061) | | | | | | | | | | | | | | | | | | | | | | ● | | |
| CHICHESTER NATURAL HEALTH CTRE (HM04156) | ● | ● | ● | ● | ● | ● | ● | ● | ● | ● | ● | ● | ● | ● | ● | ● | ● | ● | ● | ● | ● | ● | ● | ● |
| CHIROPODIST () | | | | | | | | | | | | | | | | | | | | | | | | |
| CLAIRVOYANT - MEDIUM - HEALER (HM04514) | | ● | ● | | | ● | | ● | ● | | | | | ● | ● | ● | ● | ● | ● | ● | ● | ● | ● | ● |
| CLARKE, STEVEN (HM04604) | | | ● | | | | | | | | | | | | | ● | ● | | | | | | | |
| CORNERWEIGHS (HM05183) | ● | | ● | ● | ● | ● | ● | | | | | ● | | | | | | | | | | | | |
| DALLAS, PETER (HM05691) | | | ● | | ● | ● | | ● | | | | ● | | | | ● | ● | | | | ● | | | |
| DYER & ASSOCIATES (HM06444) | | | | | | | | | | | | | | | | | | | | | | | | |
| EMINATIONS ACUPUNCTURE CLINIC (HM06805) | | | ● | ● | ● | ● | ● | ● | | | ● | ● | | | ● | ● | ● | ● | ● | | | | | |
| FELPHAM NATURAL HEALTH CLINIC (HM07206) | | | ● | | | | | | | | | | | | | | | | | | | | | |
| FROST, CHARLES (HM07760) | | | ● | | | | | | | | | | | | | | ● | | | | | | | |
| FURNACE GREEN CHIRO CTRE (HM07800) | ● | ● | ● | ● | ● | ● | ● | ● | ● | ● | ● | ● | ● | ● | ● | ● | ● | ● | ● | ● | ● | ● | ● | ● |
| G & G FOOD SUPPLIES (HM07807) | | | | | | ● | | | | | | | | | | ● | | | | | | | | ● |
| GARDINER, SAM (HM07876) | | | ● | | | | | | | | | | | | | ● | ● | | | | | | | |
| GRAVILLE, CHRIS (HM08405) | | | | | | ● | | | | | | | | | | | | | | | | | | |
| GREENFIELD, KAREN (HM08486) | | | ● | | | ● | | ● | | | | | | | | ● | ● | | | | | | | |
| HARRIS, PAUL A E (HM09084) | | | | | | | | | | | | | | | | | | | | | | | ● | |
| HEALTH IS HAPPINESS REFLEX (HM09390) | | | ● | | | ● | | | | | | | | | | ● | | | | | | | | |
| HEELER CENTRE (HM09498) | | | ● | | | ● | ● | | | | ● | ● | | | | | ● | | | | | ● | | ● |
| HORSHAM CHIROPRACTIC CENTRE (HM10191) | | | | | | | | | | | | | | | | | | | | | | | | |
| I C O M (HM10548) | | ● | ● | ● | | ● | ● | ● | | | ● | ● | | ● | | ● | ● | ● | | ● | ● | ● | | |
| JONES, NIGEL (HM11182) | | | | | | | | | | | | | | | | | | | | | | | | |

| Business by County with Reference no. | Gallstones | Gastrointestinal Problems | Genital Herpes | Gingivitis | Glandular Fever | Glaucoma | Gout | Gum Disease | Hair Problems | Halitosis | Hand Problems | Hay Fever | Headaches | Hearing Problems | High Blood Pressure | Hip Complaints | Hyperactivity | Hypoglycaemia | Impotence | Incontinence | Indigestion | Infertility | Influenza | Ingrowing Toenails |
|---|---|---|---|---|---|---|---|---|---|---|---|---|---|---|---|---|---|---|---|---|---|---|---|---|
| BACK 2 FITNESS CHIROPRACTIC (HM01476) | | | | | | | | | | | | | ● | | | ● | | | | | | | | |
| BALOOMBE OSTEOPATHIC & SPORTS (HM01641) | | | | | | | | | | | | | ● | | | | | | | | | | | |
| BARTHOLOMEW WAY CLINIC (HM01818) | | | | | | | ● | | | | | | | | | ● | | | | | | | | |
| BELLAMY PARTNERSHIP (HM02093) | | | | | | | | | | | | | ● | | | ● | | | | | | | | |
| BLACK, PAULINE (HM02425) | ● | ● | ● | ● | ● | ● | ● | ● | ● | ● | ● | ● | ● | ● | ● | ● | ● | ● | ● | ● | ● | ● | ● | |
| BODYGUIDE ALTERNATE (HM02619) | ● | ● | ● | ● | ● | ● | ● | ● | ● | ● | ● | ● | ● | ● | ● | ● | ● | ● | ● | ● | ● | ● | ● | |
| BOHNET, CAROLE (HM02648) | | | | | | | | | | | | | ● | | ● | ● | | | | | | ● | | |
| BRITCHIRO CLINIC (HM03068) | | | | | | | | | | | | | ● | | | ● | | | | | | | | |
| BURNS, L C (HM03417) | | | | | | | | | | | | | | | | ● | | | | | | | | |
| CARTLAND, ANN (HM03794) | | | | | | | | | | | | | | | | | | | | | | | | |
| CASH, G G (HM03811) | | | | | | | | | | | | | | | | | | | | | | | | |
| CHANGES (HM03985) | | ● | ● | | ● | | ● | | | | | ● | ● | | | | ● | ● | | ● | ● | ● | ● | |
| CHASE, PETER (HM04061) | | | | | | | | | | | | | | | | | | | | | | | | |
| CHICHESTER NATURAL HEALTH CTRE (HM04156) | ● | ● | ● | ● | ● | ● | ● | ● | ● | ● | ● | ● | ● | ● | ● | ● | ● | ● | ● | ● | ● | ● | ● | |
| CHIROPODIST () | | | | | | | | | | | | | | | | | | | | | | | | ● |
| CLAIRVOYANT - MEDIUM - HEALER (HM04514) | | | ● | | ● | ● | | ● | | | ● | | ● | ● | ● | ● | ● | | ● | ● | ● | ● | ● | |
| CLARKE, STEVEN (HM04604) | | | | | | | | | | | | | | | ● | | | | | | | | | |
| CORNERWEIGHS (HM05183) | | | | | | | | | | ● | | | ● | | | | | ● | | | ● | | ● | |
| DALLAS, PETER (HM05691) | | | | | | | | | | | | | ● | | ● | ● | | | ● | | ● | | | |
| DYER & ASSOCIATES (HM06444) | | | | | | | | | | | | | ● | | | ● | | | | | | | | |
| EMINATIONS ACUPUNCTURE CLINIC (HM06805) | | ● | | ● | ● | | ● | | | ● | ● | ● | ● | ● | ● | ● | ● | | ● | ● | ● | ● | ● | |
| FELPHAM NATURAL HEALTH CLINIC (HM07206) | | | | | | | | | | | | | ● | | | | | | | | | | | |
| FROST, CHARLES (HM07760) | | | | | | | | | | | | | | | | | | | ● | | | | | |
| FURNACE GREEN CHIRO CTRE (HM07800) | ● | ● | ● | ● | ● | ● | ● | ● | ● | ● | ● | ● | ● | ● | ● | ● | ● | ● | ● | ● | ● | ● | ● | |
| G & G FOOD SUPPLIES (HM07807) | | ● | | | | | | | | | | | | | | | | | | | | | | |
| GARDINER, SAM (HM07876) | | | | | | | | | | | | | ● | | ● | | | | ● | | | | | |
| GRAVILLE, CHRIS (HM08405) | | | | | | | | | | | | | ● | | | | | | | | | | | |
| GREENFIELD, KAREN (HM08486) | | | | | | | | | | | | | ● | | | | | | ● | ● | | | | |
| HARRIS, PAUL A E (HM09084) | | | | | | | | | | | | | ● | | | ● | | | | | | | | |
| HEALTH IS HAPPINESS REFLEX (HM09390) | | | | | | | ● | | | | ● | ● | ● | ● | ● | ● | ● | | | | ● | | ● | |
| HEELER CENTRE (HM09498) | | ● | | | | | ● | | | | ● | | ● | | ● | | ● | | | | ● | | | |
| HORSHAM CHIROPRACTIC CENTRE (HM10191) | | | | | | | | | | | | | ● | | | ● | | | | | | | | |
| I C O M (HM10548) | ● | ● | | | ● | | ● | | | ● | ● | ● | ● | ● | ● | ● | ● | ● | ● | ● | ● | ● | | |
| JONES, NIGEL (HM11182) | | | | | | | | | | | | | ● | | | ● | | | | | | | | |

# D - I Conditions treated at Practices/Businesses

| Business by County with Reference no. | Dandruff | Deafness | Depression | Diabetes | Diarrhoea | Digestive Problems | Diverticulitis | Dizziness | Dyslexia | Dyspraxia | Ear Disorders | Eczema | ENT Disorders | Epilepsy | Eye Disorders | Fatigue | Fears | Fertility Problems | Fever | Fibroids | Flatulence | Foot Problems | Fractures | Fungal Infections |
|---|---|---|---|---|---|---|---|---|---|---|---|---|---|---|---|---|---|---|---|---|---|---|---|---|
| JONES, WENDY (HM11203) | | | | | | | | | | | | | | | | | | | | | | | | |
| LITTLEHAMPTON NAT HLTH CTRE (HM12470) | ● | ● | ● | ● | ● | ● | ● | ● | ● | ● | ● | ● | ● | ● | ● | ● | ● | ● | ● | ● | ● | ● | ● | ● |
| MAYNARD, MARTIN A (HM13357) | | | | | | | | | | | | | | | | | | | | | | ● | | ● |
| MID SUSSEX CHIROPRACTIC CLINIC (HM13805) | | ● | | ● | ● | ● | ● | ● | | | ● | ● | ● | ● | ● | ● | | ● | | | ● | | | |
| MID SUSSEX HOMEOPATHIC CLINIC (HM13806) | | | ● | | ● | ● | ● | ● | | | ● | ● | ● | ● | ● | ● | ● | | | | ● | | | |
| MILLENNIUM HOMEOPATHY (HM13877) | ● | ● | ● | ● | ● | ● | ● | ● | ● | ● | ● | ● | ● | ● | ● | ● | ● | ● | ● | ● | ● | ● | ● | ● |
| MIND WORK SOLUTIONS (HM13967) | ● | ● | ● | ● | ● | ● | ● | ● | ● | ● | ● | ● | ● | ● | ● | ● | ● | ● | ● | ● | ● | ● | ● | ● |
| NUNN, SALLY (HM15108) | ● | ● | ● | ● | ● | ● | ● | ● | ● | ● | ● | ● | ● | ● | ● | ● | ● | ● | ● | ● | ● | ● | ● | ● |
| OSTEOPATHY AT ESQUIRE'S (HM15479) | | | | | | | | ● | | ● | ● | | | | | | | ● | | | | ● | | |
| PAIN & PARALYSIS SPECIALIST (HM15578) | | | ● | | | | | | | | | | | | | ● | | | | | | ● | ● | |
| PALMER, GAYLE (HM15606) | | | ● | | ● | ● | ● | ● | ● | ● | ● | | ● | ● | ● | ● | ● | | ● | | | ● | ● | |
| PALMER, GAYLE (HM15605) | | | ● | | ● | ● | ● | ● | ● | ● | ● | | ● | ● | ● | ● | | | ● | | ● | ● | ● | |
| PITT, KATHY (HM16349) | ● | ● | ● | ● | ● | ● | ● | ● | ● | ● | ● | ● | ● | ● | ● | ● | ● | ● | ● | ● | ● | ● | ● | ● |
| PORTLAND PHYSIOTHERAPY CLINIC (HM16451) | | | | | | | | | | | | | | | | | | | | | | | | |
| RICHARDSON, BRIAN J (HM17269) | | | | ● | | | | | | | | | | | | | | | | | | ● | | ● |
| RICHARDSON, JANET (HM17282) | | | | ● | | | | | | | | | | | | | | | | | | ● | | |
| ROOM FOR HEALING (HM17585) | | ● | ● | ● | ● | ● | ● | ● | | | ● | ● | | ● | ● | ● | ● | ● | ● | ● | ● | | | ● |
| SANDERSON & ELEMENT (HM17921) | | | | | | | | | | | | | | | | ● | | | | | | | | |
| SANDON, PATER H G (DR) (HM17925) | ● | ● | ● | ● | ● | ● | ● | ● | ● | ● | ● | ● | ● | ● | ● | ● | ● | ● | ● | ● | ● | ● | ● | ● |
| SMITH, BARBARA (HM18720) | | | | | | | | | | | | | | | | | | | | | | ● | | ● |
| STEVENS, PAT (HM19238) | | | | | | | | | | | | | | | | | | | | | | | | |
| STOTT-DURHAM, ANDREW (HM19355) | | | | | | | | | | | | | | | | | | | | | | | | |
| SWAN, LAURIE C (HM19574) | | | | | | ● | | | | | | | | | | ● | ● | | | | ● | | | |
| TAYLOR, CHRISTIAN (HM19744) | ● | ● | | ● | ● | ● | ● | ● | ● | ● | ● | ● | ● | ● | ● | ● | ● | ● | ● | ● | ● | ● | ● | ● |
| TRANQUILLITY (HM20260) | | | ● | | | | | | | | | | | | | ● | ● | | | | | | | |
| WESTACOTT, EILEEN (HM21256) | | | ● | | | | | | | | | | | | | | | | | | | | | |
| WILSON, AVIS (HM21646) | | | | | | | | | | | | | | | | | | | | | | | | |
| WOOD, J G (HM21798) | | | | | | | | ● | | | | | | | | | | | | | | ● | ● | |
| WORSFOLD, CHRISTINE (HM21903) | | | | | | | | | | | | | | | | | | | | | | ● | | ● |
| WORTHING CHIROPRACTIC CLINIC (HM21907) | | | | | | | | | | | | | | | | | | | | | | | | |
| WORTHING CLINIC OF ACUPUNCTURE (HM21908) | | | ● | | ● | | | | | | | ● | | | | | | | | | | | | |
| **TYNE AND WEAR** | | | | | | | | | | | | | | | | | | | | | | | | |
| ACUPUNCTURE & NAT MED CLINIC (HM00243) | ● | ● | ● | ● | ● | ● | ● | ● | ● | ● | ● | ● | ● | ● | ● | ● | ● | ● | ● | ● | ● | ● | ● | ● |
| AROMATHERAPY IN PRACTICE (HM01114) | | ● | | | | | | | | | | | | | | ● | | | | | | | | |

| Business by County with Reference no. | Gallstones | Gastrointestinal Problems | Genital Herpes | Gingivitis | Glandular Fever | Glaucoma | Gout | Gum Disease | Hair Problems | Halitosis | Hand Problems | Hay Fever | Headaches | Hearing Problems | High Blood Pressure | Hip Complaints | Hyperactivity | Hypoglycaemia | Impotence | Incontinence | Indigestion | Infertility | Influenza | Ingrowing Toenails |
|---|---|---|---|---|---|---|---|---|---|---|---|---|---|---|---|---|---|---|---|---|---|---|---|---|
| JONES, WENDY (HM11203) | | | | | | | | | | | | | ● | | | ● | | | | | | | | |
| LITTLEHAMPTON NAT HLTH CTRE (HM12470) | ● | ● | ● | ● | ● | ● | ● | ● | ● | ● | ● | ● | ● | ● | ● | ● | ● | ● | ● | ● | ● | ● | ● | |
| MAYNARD, MARTIN A (HM13357) | | | | | | | | | | | | | | | | | | | | | | | | ● |
| MID SUSSEX CHIROPRACTIC CLINIC (HM13805) | | ● | | | | | | | | | ● | ● | ● | ● | ● | ● | ● | ● | ● | ● | ● | ● | ● | |
| MID SUSSEX HOMEOPATHIC CLINIC (HM13806) | ● | ● | | ● | ● | | ● | ● | ● | | | ● | ● | | ● | ● | ● | ● | | ● | ● | | ● | |
| MILLENNIUM HOMEOPATHY (HM13877) | ● | ● | ● | ● | ● | ● | ● | ● | ● | ● | ● | ● | ● | ● | ● | ● | ● | ● | ● | ● | ● | ● | ● | |
| MIND WORK SOLUTIONS (HM13967) | ● | ● | ● | ● | ● | ● | ● | ● | ● | ● | ● | ● | ● | ● | ● | ● | ● | ● | ● | ● | ● | ● | ● | |
| NUNN, SALLY (HM15108) | ● | ● | ● | ● | ● | ● | ● | ● | ● | ● | ● | ● | ● | ● | ● | ● | ● | ● | ● | ● | ● | ● | ● | |
| OSTEOPATHY AT ESQUIRE'S (HM15479) | | | | | | | | | | | ● | | ● | | | ● | ● | | | | | ● | | |
| PAIN & PARALYSIS SPECIALIST (HM15578) | | | | | | | | | | | ● | | | | | ● | | | | | | | | |
| PALMER, GAYLE (HM15606) | | ● | | | ● | ● | | | | | ● | ● | ● | ● | ● | ● | ● | ● | ● | ● | ● | ● | ● | |
| PALMER, GAYLE (HM15605) | | ● | | | | ● | | | | | ● | ● | ● | ● | ● | ● | ● | ● | ● | ● | ● | ● | | |
| PITT, KATHY (HM16349) | ● | ● | ● | ● | ● | ● | ● | ● | ● | ● | ● | ● | ● | ● | ● | ● | ● | ● | ● | ● | ● | ● | ● | |
| PORTLAND PHYSIOTHERAPY CLINIC (HM16451) | | | | | | | | | | | | | | | | ● | | | | | | | | |
| RICHARDSON, BRIAN J (HM17269) | | | | | | | ● | | | | | | | | | | | | | | | | | |
| RICHARDSON, JANET (HM17282) | | | | | | | | | | | | | | | | | | | | | | | | ● |
| ROOM FOR HEALING (HM17585) | ● | ● | | ● | ● | ● | ● | ● | | | | ● | ● | ● | ● | ● | ● | ● | | | ● | ● | | |
| SANDERSON & ELEMENT (HM17921) | | | | | | | | | | | | | ● | | | ● | | | | | | | | |
| SANDON, PATER H G (DR) (HM17925) | ● | ● | ● | ● | ● | ● | ● | ● | ● | ● | ● | ● | ● | ● | ● | ● | ● | ● | ● | ● | ● | ● | ● | |
| SMITH, BARBARA (HM18720) | | | | | | | | | | | | | | | | | | | | | | | | |
| STEVENS, PAT (HM19238) | | | | | | | | | ● | | | | | | | | | | | | | | | |
| STOTT-DURHAM, ANDREW (HM19355) | | | | | | | | | | | | | | | | ● | | | | | | | | |
| SWAN, LAURIE C (HM19574) | | | | | | | | | | | | | | | | | | | | | ● | | | |
| TAYLOR, CHRISTIAN (HM19744) | ● | ● | ● | ● | ● | ● | ● | ● | ● | ● | ● | ● | ● | ● | ● | ● | ● | ● | ● | ● | ● | ● | ● | |
| TRANQUILLITY (HM20260) | | | | | | | | | | | | | | | | | | | ● | | | | | |
| WESTACOTT, EILEEN (HM21256) | | | | | | | | | | | | | ● | | | | | | | | | | | |
| WILSON, AVIS (HM21646) | | | | | | | | | ● | | | | | | | ● | | | | | | | | |
| WOOD, J G (HM21798) | | | | | | | ● | | | | ● | ● | ● | | | ● | | | | ● | | | | |
| WORSFOLD, CHRISTINE (HM21903) | | | | | | | | | | | | | | | | | | | | | | | | |
| WORTHING CHIROPRACTIC CLINIC (HM21907) | | | | | | | | | | | | | ● | | | ● | | | | | | | | |
| WORTHING CLINIC OF ACUPUNCTURE (HM21908) | | | | | | | | | | | | ● | ● | | | | | | | | | | | |
| **TYNE AND WEAR** | | | | | | | | | | | | | | | | | | | | | | | | |
| ACUPUNCTURE & NAT MED CLINIC (HM00243) | ● | ● | ● | ● | ● | ● | ● | ● | ● | ● | ● | ● | ● | ● | ● | ● | ● | ● | ● | ● | ● | ● | ● | |
| AROMATHERAPY IN PRACTICE (HM01114) | | | | | | | | | | | | | ● | | | | | | | | | | | |

# D - I Conditions treated at Practices/Businesses

| Business by County with Reference no. | Dandruff | Deafness | Depression | Diabetes | Diarrhoea | Digestive Problems | Diverticulitis | Dizziness | Dyslexia | Dyspraxia | Ear Disorders | Eczema | ENT Disorders | Epilepsy | Eye Disorders | Fatigue | Fears | Fertility Problems | Fever | Fibroids | Flatulence | Foot Problems | Fractures | Fungal Infections |
|---|---|---|---|---|---|---|---|---|---|---|---|---|---|---|---|---|---|---|---|---|---|---|---|---|
| B WIGRAM HEALING & REFLEXOLOGY (HM01455) | | | ● | | | | | | | | | | | | | | ● | | | | | | | |
| BALMORAL PHYSIOTHERAPY (HM01640) | | | | | | | | | | | | | | | | | | | | | | | ● | |
| BASS, MIKE (HM01850) | | | ● | ● | ● | ● | ● | ● | ● | | | ● | ● | | | ● | ● | ● | | ● | ● | | | |
| BODY BALANCE HOLISTIC THERAPY (HM02572) | | | ● | | | | | | | | ● | | | | | ● | ● | | | | | | | |
| CHIROPODY CLINIC (HM04324) | | | ● | | | | | ● | | | | | | | | | | | | | | ● | | ● |
| CONNECT PHYSICAL HEALTH CTRE (HM04989) | | | | | | | | | | | | | | | | | | | | | | ● | | ● |
| DENTON, A (HM05998) | | | ● | | | ● | | | | | | | | | | ● | | | | | | ● | | |
| DERWENT CENTRE (HM06020) | ● | ● | ● | ● | ● | ● | ● | ● | ● | ● | ● | ● | ● | ● | ● | ● | ● | ● | ● | ● | ● | ● | ● | ● |
| FAMILY CHIRO WELLNESS CENTRE (HM07083) | | ● | ● | ● | ● | ● | | ● | ● | ● | ● | ● | | ● | | ● | ● | ● | ● | | ● | ● | ● | |
| FEEL GOOD AROMATHERAPY (HM07164) | ● | | ● | | | ● | ● | | | | ● | ● | | | | ● | ● | ● | | | | ● | | ● |
| FOWLER, CHRISTINE (HM07628) | ● | ● | ● | ● | ● | ● | ● | ● | ● | ● | ● | ● | ● | ● | ● | ● | ● | ● | ● | ● | ● | ● | ● | ● |
| HEALTH ALLIANCE CENTRE (HM09375) | | | | | | | | | | | | | | | | | | | | | | | | |
| HERBAL GARDEN AROMATHERAPY (HM09612) | ● | | ● | | | | | | | | | ● | | | | ● | ● | ● | ● | | ● | | | ● |
| HOLISTIC CHIROPRACTOR (HM09951) | | | | | | ● | | | | | ● | | | | | | | | | | | | | |
| HON, ARTHUR M R (HM10111) | | | | | | | | | | | | | | | | | | | | | | | | |
| HYPNOTHERAPY AND COUNSELLING (HM10514) | | | ● | | | | | | | | | | | | | | | | | | | | | |
| MCANELLY, J L (HM13368) | | | ● | | | | | | | | | | | | | | | | | | | | | |
| NATURAL SELECTION (HM14623) | | | | | | | | | | | | | | | | ● | | | | | | | | |
| NEW LIFE NATURAL HEALTH CARE (HM14820) | ● | ● | ● | ● | ● | ● | ● | ● | ● | ● | ● | ● | ● | ● | ● | ● | ● | ● | ● | ● | ● | ● | ● | ● |
| NEWCASTLE SPRTS INJ/THRPY CTRE (HM14855) | | | ● | | ● | | | | | | | ● | | | | | | | | | | ● | ● | ● |
| OSBORNE CLINIC (HM15420) | | | | | ● | | ● | | | | | ● | | | | | | | | | ● | | ● | |
| RAINBOW, RICHARD S (HM16887) | | | ● | | | | | | | | | | | | | | ● | | | | | | | |
| SCHOLL FOOTWEAR CENTRE (HM18077) | | | | | | | | | | | | | | | | | | | | | | ● | | |
| SHEN HOLISTIC THERAPIES (HM18392) | | | ● | | | ● | | | | | | | | | | ● | | ● | | | | | | |
| WESTOE PRACTICE (HM21277) | | | | | | | | | | | | | | | | | | | | | | ● | | |
| WHITLEY BAY CHIROPRACTOR (HM21406) | | | | | | | | | | | | | | | | | | | | | | | | |
| **WARWICKSHIRE** | | | | | | | | | | | | | | | | | | | | | | | | |
| ACUPUNCTURE CLINIC (HM00279) | | | ● | | ● | | | ● | | | | | | | | ● | | | | | | | | |
| BARRATT'S HOMEOPATHY (HM01780) | ● | ● | ● | ● | ● | ● | ● | ● | | | ● | ● | ● | ● | ● | ● | ● | ● | ● | ● | ● | ● | ● | ● |
| BIRTWELL, ANDREW (HM02400) | | | ● | | | | | | | | | | | | | | ● | | | | | | | |
| BRIEF COUNS & PSYCHOTHERAPY SV (HM03020) | | | ● | | | | | | | | | | | | | | ● | | | | | | | |
| CHURCH LAWFORD CHIRO CLINIC (HM04463) | | | | | | ● | | ● | | | | | | | | ● | | | | | | ● | | |
| CLIFTON OSTEOPATHIC PRACTICE (HM04669) | ● | | | | ● | ● | ● | ● | | ● | ● | ● | ● | | ● | ● | | ● | ● | ● | ● | ● | | |
| EDWARDS, IRENE & PETER (HM06656) | | | ● | | | | | | | | | | | | | | | | | | | | | |

| Business by County with Reference no. | Gallstones | Gastrointestinal Problems | Genital Herpes | Gingivitis | Glandular Fever | Glaucoma | Gout | Gum Disease | Hair Problems | Halitosis | Hand Problems | Hay Fever | Headaches | Hearing Problems | High Blood Pressure | Hip Complaints | Hyperactivity | Hypoglycaemia | Impotence | Incontinence | Indigestion | Infertility | Influenza | Ingrowing Toenails |
|---|---|---|---|---|---|---|---|---|---|---|---|---|---|---|---|---|---|---|---|---|---|---|---|---|
| B WIGRAM HEALING & REFLEXOLOGY (HM01455) | | | | | | | | | | | | | ● | | | | | | | | | | | |
| BALMORAL PHYSIOTHERAPY (HM01640) | | | | | | | | | | | | | | | | ● | | | | | | | | |
| BASS, MIKE (HM01850) | ● | ● | | | | | | | | | | ● | ● | | ● | | ● | | | | ● | ● | ● | |
| BODY BALANCE HOLISTIC THERAPY (HM02572) | | | | | | | | | | | | | ● | | | | | | | | | | | |
| CHIROPODY CLINIC (HM04324) | | | | | | | | | | | ● | ● | ● | | ● | | ● | | | | ● | | | |
| CONNECT PHYSICAL HEALTH CTRE (HM04989) | | | | | | | | | | | ● | | ● | | | ● | | | | | | | | |
| DENTON, A (HM05998) | | | | | | | | | | | ● | ● | ● | ● | ● | ● | ● | | | | ● | | ● | |
| DERWENT CENTRE (HM06020) | ● | ● | ● | ● | ● | ● | ● | ● | ● | ● | ● | ● | ● | ● | ● | ● | ● | ● | ● | ● | ● | ● | ● | ● |
| FAMILY CHIRO WELLNESS CENTRE (HM07083) | ● | ● | ● | | | ● | ● | | | | | ● | ● | ● | ● | ● | ● | ● | ● | ● | ● | ● | ● | |
| FEEL GOOD AROMATHERAPY (HM07164) | ● | ● | | ● | | | ● | ● | ● | ● | ● | ● | ● | | ● | ● | | ● | | ● | ● | ● | ● | |
| FOWLER, CHRISTINE (HM07628) | ● | ● | ● | ● | ● | ● | ● | ● | ● | ● | ● | ● | ● | ● | ● | ● | ● | ● | ● | ● | ● | ● | ● | |
| HEALTH ALLIANCE CENTRE (HM09375) | | | | | | | | | | | | | ● | | | ● | | | | | | | | |
| HERBAL GARDEN AROMATHERAPY (HM09612) | | ● | | | ● | | | | | | | ● | ● | | ● | | | | | | ● | ● | ● | |
| HOLISTIC CHIROPRACTOR (HM09951) | | | | | | | | | | | ● | | | | | | | | | | ● | | | |
| HON, ARTHUR M R (HM10111) | | | | | | | | | | | ● | | ● | | | | | | | | | | | |
| HYPNOTHERAPY AND COUNSELLING (HM10514) | | | | | | | | | | | | | | | | | | | | | | | | |
| MCANELLY, J L (HM13368) | | | | | | | | | | | | | | | | | | | | | | | | |
| NATURAL SELECTION (HM14623) | | | | | | | | | | | | ● | ● | | | | | | | | | | | |
| NEW LIFE NATURAL HEALTH CARE (HM14820) | ● | ● | ● | ● | ● | ● | ● | ● | ● | ● | ● | ● | ● | ● | ● | ● | ● | ● | ● | ● | ● | ● | ● | |
| NEWCASTLE SPRTS INJ/THRPY CTRE (HM14855) | | | | | | | | | | | | ● | ● | | | ● | | | | | | | | |
| OSBORNE CLINIC (HM15420) | | | | | | | | | | | ● | | ● | | | ● | | | | ● | | | | |
| RAINBOW, RICHARD S (HM16887) | | | | | | | | | | | | | | | | | | | ● | | | | | |
| SCHOLL FOOTWEAR CENTRE (HM18077) | | | | | | | | | | | | | | | | | | | | | | | | |
| SHEN HOLISTIC THERAPIES (HM18392) | | | | | | | | | | | | | ● | | | | | | | | | | | |
| WESTOE PRACTICE (HM21277) | | | | | | | | | | | | | | | | | | | | | | | | |
| WHITLEY BAY CHIROPRACTOR (HM21406) | | | | | | | | | | | | | ● | | | ● | | | | | | | | |
| **WARWICKSHIRE** | | | | | | | | | | | | | | | | | | | | | | | | |
| ACUPUNCTURE CLINIC (HM00279) | | | | | | | | | | | | ● | ● | | ● | ● | | | | | | | | |
| BARRATT'S HOMEOPATHY (HM01780) | ● | ● | | ● | ● | | ● | ● | ● | ● | ● | ● | ● | ● | ● | ● | ● | ● | ● | ● | ● | ● | ● | |
| BIRTWELL, ANDREW (HM02400) | | | | | | | | | | | | | | | | | | | | | | | | |
| BRIEF COUNS & PSYCHOTHERAPY SV (HM03020) | | | | | | | | | | | | | | | | | | | | | | | | |
| CHURCH LAWFORD CHIRO CLINIC (HM04463) | | | | | | | | | | | | | ● | | | | | | | | | | | |
| CLIFTON OSTEOPATHIC PRACTICE (HM04669) | ● | ● | | | ● | | ● | ● | | | ● | ● | ● | | ● | ● | ● | | | ● | ● | ● | ● | |
| EDWARDS, IRENE & PETER (HM06656) | | | | | | | | | | | | | | | | | | | | | | | | |

# D - I Conditions treated at Practices/Businesses

Business by County with Reference no.

| Business by County with Reference no. | Dandruff | Deafness | Depression | Diabetes | Diarrhoea | Digestive Problems | Diverticulitis | Dizziness | Dyslexia | Dyspraxia | Ear Disorders | Eczema |
|---|---|---|---|---|---|---|---|---|---|---|---|---|
| FIGHT (HM07282) | | | | | | | | | | | | |
| GREIG, E (HM08527) | | | | | | ● | | | | | | |
| HEALTHPOINT (HM09414) | | | ● | | ● | | | | | | ● | ● |
| HEART OF ENGLAND SHIATSU (HM09442) | | ● | ● | | | ● | ● | ● | | | ● | |
| HEARTLANDS (HM09445) | | | ● | | | ● | | | | | | |
| HERBAL ONE (HM09631) | ● | ● | ● | ● | ● | ● | ● | ● | ● | ● | ● | ● |
| HOLYCOMBE (HM10060) | | | ● | | | ● | | | | | | |
| JAN LLOYD AROMATHERAPY (HM10913) | | | | | | | | | | | | ● |
| LEAMINGTON SPA CHIRO CLINIC (HM12104) | | | | | | ● | | | | | | |
| LIFE-WAYS (HM12367) | ● | ● | ● | ● | ● | ● | ● | ● | ● | ● | ● | ● |
| NATURAL HEALTH CENTRE (HM14567) | | | ● | | ● | ● | ● | ● | | ● | ● | ● |
| NATURAL THERAPY CENTRE (HM14651) | | | ● | | ● | ● | ● | ● | ● | | ● | ● |
| NEWEY, RACHEL (HM14862) | | | ● | | ● | ● | | ● | | | | |
| NUNEATON CHIROPRACTIC CLINIC (HM15104) | | | ● | | | | | | | | | |
| PETERS, EVERARD (HM16085) | | | ● | | | | | | | ● | ● | |
| REFLEXOLOGY CLINIC (HM17091) | | ● | | | | ● | | | | | ● | |
| REVITALIZE (HM17205) | | | ● | | | | ● | | | | | ● |
| RUSSELL, COLIN (HM17766) | | | | | | | | | | | | |
| SAVAGE, GERALD (HM17966) | | | ● | | | | | | | | | |
| SHAWE AVENUE OSTEO PRACTICE (HM18351) | | | | | | | | ● | | | | |
| SHIATSU SOCIETY (HM18464) | | | ● | | ● | ● | ● | ● | | | | ● |
| SMALLWOOD, P (HM18698) | | | | | | | | | | | | |
| STRATFORD PHYSIO CLINIC (HM19370) | | | | | | | | | | | | |
| STUDLEY PHYSIOTHERAPY CENTRE (HM19442) | | | | | | | | | | | | |
| TOWERS, DIANA (HM20195) | | | ● | | | ● | | | | | | |
| TRADITIONAL ACUPUNCTURE GROUP (HM20221) | | | ● | | | ● | ● | ● | | | ● | ● |
| WARWICK OSTEOPATHIC PRACTICE (HM20966) | ● | | | | ● | ● | ● | ● | | ● | ● | ● |
| WREN, PAULINE (HM21922) | | | ● | | | ● | | | | | | |
| **WILTSHIRE** | | | | | | | | | | | | |
| AMESBURY ABBEY CLINIC (HM00781) | | | | | | | | | | | | |
| ANDREWS, HAZEL (HM00852) | | | ● | | ● | ● | | ● | | | ● | ● |
| AVEBURY HYPNOTHERAPY PRACTICE (HM01386) | | | ● | | ● | ● | | | | | | ● |
| 'BACK IN LINE' (HM01482) | | | ● | | | | | | | | | |
| BLUNSDON ABBEY PHYSIOTHERAPY (HM02533) | | | | | | | | | | | | |

| Business by County with Reference no. | ENT Disorders | Epilepsy | Eye Disorders | Fatigue | Fears | Fertility Problems | Fever | Fibroids | Flatulence | Foot Problems | Fractures | Fungal Infections |
|---|---|---|---|---|---|---|---|---|---|---|---|---|
| FIGHT (HM07282) | | | | | | | | | | ● | ● | |
| GREIG, E (HM08527) | | | | | ● | | | | | | | |
| HEALTHPOINT (HM09414) | | | | | | | ● | | | ● | | |
| HEART OF ENGLAND SHIATSU (HM09442) | | | ● | ● | ● | | | ● | ● | | | |
| HEARTLANDS (HM09445) | | | | ● | ● | | | | | | | |
| HERBAL ONE (HM09631) | ● | ● | ● | ● | ● | ● | ● | ● | ● | ● | ● | ● |
| HOLYCOMBE (HM10060) | | | | ● | | | | | | | | |
| JAN LLOYD AROMATHERAPY (HM10913) | ● | | | ● | | | | | | | | |
| LEAMINGTON SPA CHIRO CLINIC (HM12104) | | | | | | | | | | | | |
| LIFE-WAYS (HM12367) | ● | ● | ● | ● | ● | ● | ● | ● | ● | ● | ● | ● |
| NATURAL HEALTH CENTRE (HM14567) | | | | ● | ● | | | | ● | | | |
| NATURAL THERAPY CENTRE (HM14651) | ● | ● | | | ● | ● | ● | ● | ● | ● | | ● |
| NEWEY, RACHEL (HM14862) | | | | ● | | | | | | ● | | |
| NUNEATON CHIROPRACTIC CLINIC (HM15104) | | | | ● | | | | | | | | |
| PETERS, EVERARD (HM16085) | | | | ● | | | | | | ● | | |
| REFLEXOLOGY CLINIC (HM17091) | | ● | | | | ● | | | | | | |
| REVITALIZE (HM17205) | | | | ● | ● | ● | | | | | | |
| RUSSELL, COLIN (HM17766) | | | | | | | | | | ● | | ● |
| SAVAGE, GERALD (HM17966) | | | | ● | ● | | | | | | | |
| SHAWE AVENUE OSTEO PRACTICE (HM18351) | | | | | | | | | | ● | ● | |
| SHIATSU SOCIETY (HM18464) | | | | ● | ● | ● | | | ● | | | |
| SMALLWOOD, P (HM18698) | | | | | | | | | | ● | | ● |
| STRATFORD PHYSIO CLINIC (HM19370) | | | | | | | | | | | | |
| STUDLEY PHYSIOTHERAPY CENTRE (HM19442) | | | | | | | | | | | | |
| TOWERS, DIANA (HM20195) | | | | ● | ● | ● | | | | | | |
| TRADITIONAL ACUPUNCTURE GROUP (HM20221) | | | | ● | ● | | ● | | ● | | | |
| WARWICK OSTEOPATHIC PRACTICE (HM20966) | ● | | ● | ● | | ● | ● | ● | ● | ● | | |
| WREN, PAULINE (HM21922) | | | | | ● | | | | | | | |
| **WILTSHIRE** | | | | | | | | | | | | |
| AMESBURY ABBEY CLINIC (HM00781) | | | | | | | | | | | | |
| ANDREWS, HAZEL (HM00852) | ● | | ● | ● | | ● | | | | ● | | |
| AVEBURY HYPNOTHERAPY PRACTICE (HM01386) | | | | ● | ● | | | | | | | |
| 'BACK IN LINE' (HM01482) | | | | ● | | | | | | | | |
| BLUNSDON ABBEY PHYSIOTHERAPY (HM02533) | | | | | | | | | | ● | | |

| Business by County with Reference no. | Gallstones | Gastrointestinal Problems | Genital Herpes | Gingivitis | Glandular Fever | Glaucoma | Gout | Gum Disease | Hair Problems | Halitosis | Hand Problems | Hay Fever |
|---|---|---|---|---|---|---|---|---|---|---|---|---|
| FIGHT (HM07282) | | | | | | | | | | | ● | |
| GREIG, E (HM08527) | | | | | | | | | | | | |
| HEALTHPOINT (HM09414) | | | | | | | | | | | | ● |
| HEART OF ENGLAND SHIATSU (HM09442) | | ● | | | | | | | | | | |
| HEARTLANDS (HM09445) | ● | | | | | | | | | | | |
| HERBAL ONE (HM09631) | ● | ● | ● | ● | ● | ● | ● | ● | ● | ● | ● | ● |
| HOLYCOMBE (HM10060) | | | | | | | | | | | | |
| JAN LLOYD AROMATHERAPY (HM10913) | | | | | | | | | | | | |
| LEAMINGTON SPA CHIRO CLINIC (HM12104) | | | | | | | | | | | ● | ● |
| LIFE-WAYS (HM12367) | ● | ● | ● | ● | ● | ● | ● | ● | ● | ● | ● | ● |
| NATURAL HEALTH CENTRE (HM14567) | | ● | | | | | ● | | ● | ● | | ● |
| NATURAL THERAPY CENTRE (HM14651) | | ● | ● | ● | ● | | ● | ● | | ● | ● | ● |
| NEWEY, RACHEL (HM14862) | | | | | | | | | | | ● | |
| NUNEATON CHIROPRACTIC CLINIC (HM15104) | | | | | | | | | | | | |
| PETERS, EVERARD (HM16085) | | | | | | | | | | | ● | |
| REFLEXOLOGY CLINIC (HM17091) | | | | | | | | | | | | ● |
| REVITALIZE (HM17205) | | | | | | | | | | | | |
| RUSSELL, COLIN (HM17766) | | | | | | | | | | | | |
| SAVAGE, GERALD (HM17966) | | | | | | | | | | | | |
| SHAWE AVENUE OSTEO PRACTICE (HM18351) | | | | | | | | | | | ● | |
| SHIATSU SOCIETY (HM18464) | ● | ● | | | | | | | | | ● | ● |
| SMALLWOOD, P (HM18698) | | | | | | | | | | | | |
| STRATFORD PHYSIO CLINIC (HM19370) | | | | | | | | | | | | |
| STUDLEY PHYSIOTHERAPY CENTRE (HM19442) | | | | | | | | | | | | |
| TOWERS, DIANA (HM20195) | | | | | | | | | | | | ● |
| TRADITIONAL ACUPUNCTURE GROUP (HM20221) | ● | ● | | | | | ● | | | | ● | ● |
| WARWICK OSTEOPATHIC PRACTICE (HM20966) | ● | ● | | | ● | | ● | ● | | | ● | ● |
| WREN, PAULINE (HM21922) | | | | | | | | | | | | |
| **WILTSHIRE** | | | | | | | | | | | | |
| AMESBURY ABBEY CLINIC (HM00781) | | | | | | | | | | | | |
| ANDREWS, HAZEL (HM00852) | | | | | | | ● | | | | ● | |
| AVEBURY HYPNOTHERAPY PRACTICE (HM01386) | | | | | | | | ● | ● | | | |
| 'BACK IN LINE' (HM01482) | | | | | | | | | | | | |
| BLUNSDON ABBEY PHYSIOTHERAPY (HM02533) | | | | | | | | | | | | |

| Business by County with Reference no. | Headaches | Hearing Problems | High Blood Pressure | Hip Complaints | Hyperactivity | Hypoglycaemia | Impotence | Incontinence | Indigestion | Infertility | Influenza | Ingrowing Toenails |
|---|---|---|---|---|---|---|---|---|---|---|---|---|
| FIGHT (HM07282) | ● | | | ● | | | | | | | | |
| GREIG, E (HM08527) | ● | | ● | | | | | | ● | | | |
| HEALTHPOINT (HM09414) | ● | | ● | ● | ● | | | | | | | |
| HEART OF ENGLAND SHIATSU (HM09442) | ● | ● | ● | ● | | | | | | | | |
| HEARTLANDS (HM09445) | ● | | ● | | | | | | ● | | | |
| HERBAL ONE (HM09631) | ● | ● | ● | ● | ● | ● | ● | ● | ● | ● | ● | |
| HOLYCOMBE (HM10060) | ● | | ● | | | | | | ● | | | |
| JAN LLOYD AROMATHERAPY (HM10913) | ● | | ● | ● | | | | | | | | |
| LEAMINGTON SPA CHIRO CLINIC (HM12104) | ● | | ● | ● | ● | | | | ● | | | |
| LIFE-WAYS (HM12367) | ● | ● | ● | ● | ● | ● | ● | ● | ● | ● | ● | |
| NATURAL HEALTH CENTRE (HM14567) | ● | | ● | ● | ● | ● | | | ● | ● | | |
| NATURAL THERAPY CENTRE (HM14651) | ● | | ● | ● | ● | ● | ● | ● | ● | ● | ● | |
| NEWEY, RACHEL (HM14862) | ● | | | | | | | | ● | | | |
| NUNEATON CHIROPRACTIC CLINIC (HM15104) | ● | | | ● | | | | | | | | |
| PETERS, EVERARD (HM16085) | ● | | | ● | ● | | | | | | | |
| REFLEXOLOGY CLINIC (HM17091) | ● | | ● | ● | | | | ● | | | | |
| REVITALIZE (HM17205) | ● | | | | | | | | | | | |
| RUSSELL, COLIN (HM17766) | | | | | | | | | | | | |
| SAVAGE, GERALD (HM17966) | ● | | | | | | ● | | | | | |
| SHAWE AVENUE OSTEO PRACTICE (HM18351) | | | | ● | | | | | | | | |
| SHIATSU SOCIETY (HM18464) | ● | ● | ● | ● | ● | ● | ● | ● | ● | ● | | |
| SMALLWOOD, P (HM18698) | | | | | | | | | | | | ● |
| STRATFORD PHYSIO CLINIC (HM19370) | | | | ● | | | | | | | | |
| STUDLEY PHYSIOTHERAPY CENTRE (HM19442) | ● | | | ● | | | | | | | | |
| TOWERS, DIANA (HM20195) | ● | | | | | | ● | | | | | |
| TRADITIONAL ACUPUNCTURE GROUP (HM20221) | ● | ● | ● | | ● | | | ● | ● | | | |
| WARWICK OSTEOPATHIC PRACTICE (HM20966) | ● | | ● | ● | ● | | | ● | ● | ● | ● | |
| WREN, PAULINE (HM21922) | | | | | | | | | | | | |
| **WILTSHIRE** | | | | | | | | | | | | |
| AMESBURY ABBEY CLINIC (HM00781) | | | | ● | | | | | | | | |
| ANDREWS, HAZEL (HM00852) | ● | | ● | ● | | | | ● | ● | ● | | |
| AVEBURY HYPNOTHERAPY PRACTICE (HM01386) | ● | | | | | | ● | | | | | |
| 'BACK IN LINE' (HM01482) | ● | | | | | | | | | | | |
| BLUNSDON ABBEY PHYSIOTHERAPY (HM02533) | | | | ● | | | | | | | | |

# D - I Conditions treated at Practices/Businesses

| Business by County with Reference no. | Dandruff | Deafness | Depression | Diabetes | Diarrhoea | Digestive Problems | Diverticulitis | Dizziness | Dyslexia | Dyspraxia | Ear Disorders | Eczema | ENT Disorders | Epilepsy | Eye Disorders | Fatigue | Fears | Fertility Problems | Fever | Fibroids | Flatulence | Foot Problems | Fractures | Fungal Infections | Gallstones | Gastrointestinal Problems | Genital Herpes | Gingivitis | Glandular Fever | Glaucoma | Gout | Gum Disease | Hair Problems | Halitosis | Hand Problems | Hay Fever | Headaches | Hearing Problems | High Blood Pressure | Hip Complaints | Hyperactivity | Hypoglycaemia | Impotence | Incontinence | Indigestion | Infertility | Influenza | Ingrowing Toenails |
|---|---|---|---|---|---|---|---|---|---|---|---|---|---|---|---|---|---|---|---|---|---|---|---|---|---|---|---|---|---|---|---|---|---|---|---|---|---|---|---|---|---|---|---|---|---|---|---|
| CASTLE STREET CHIRO CLINIC (HM03836) | | | | | | | | | | | | | | | | | | | | | | | | | | | | | | | | | | | | |●| | |●| | | | | | | | |
| CRICKLADE ROAD PRACTICE (HM05439) | | | | | | | | | | | |●| | | | | | | | | |●| | | |●| | | | | | | | |●| |●| | |●| | | | | | | | |
| EASE MANAGEMENT CENTRE (HM06506) | | |●| | | | | | | | | | | | |●|●| | | | | | | | | | | | | | | | | | | | | | | | | | | | | | | |
| ENGLISH, JOHN M (DR) (HM06834) | | |●|●|●|●|●|●|●| |●|●|●| |●|●|●|●| |●|●|●| | |●|●|●|●|●| |●|●| |●| |●|●| | |●|●|●|●|●|●|●|●| |
| HEALTH HYDRO (HM09389) | | |●|●|●|●|●| | | | |●| | | |●|●| | | |●| | | | |●| |●| | | | | |●| |●|●| | | | | | | |●| | | |
| HIGHWORTH PHYSIOTHERAPY CLINIC (HM09761) | | | | | | | | | | | | | | | | | | | | | | | | | | | | | | | | | | |●| |●| | |●| | | | | | | | |
| HYPNOTHERAPY CENTRE (HM10529) | | |●| |●|●| | | | | |●| | | |●|●|●| | |●| | | | |●| | | | | | | | | | |●| |●| | | | | |●| | | |
| JENKINS, RUSSELL S (HM10996) | | | | | | | | | | | | | | | | | | | | | |●| | | | | | | | | | | | | | | | | |●| | | | | | | | |
| LEIGHTON REFLEXOLOGY CLINIC (HM12196) |●| |●| |●|●| | | | | | | | | |●| |●| | | | | | |●|●| | | | | | |●| | |●|●| |●| |●| | | |●|●| | |
| LIFE-ENERGIES (HM12352) | |●| | |●| |●|●| | |●|●|●|●|●|●| |●|●|●| |●|●|●|●|●| |●|●|●|●|●| | |●|●|●|●|●|●| | |●| | |●|●| |
| LYON, P (HM12783) | | |●| | | | | | | | | | | | | | | | | | | | | | | | | | | | | | | | | | | | | | | | | | | | | |
| MAGNO PULSE (HM12919) | | | |●| |●| | | | | |●| | | | | |●| | | |●|●| | | | | | | |●| | | |●| |●|●|●|●| | |●| | |●| | |
| MALMESBURY CHIROPRACTIC CLINIC (HM12982) | | | | | | | | | | | | | | | | | | | | | | | | | | | | | | | | | | | | |●| | |●| | | | | | | | |
| MARLBOROUGH CHIRO CLINIC (HM13122) | | | | | | | | | | | | | | | | | | | | | |●| | | | | | | | | | | | |●| |●| | | | | | | | | | | |
| MARLBOROUGH NATURAL HLTH CTRE (HM13123) |●|●|●|●|●|●|●|●|●|●|●|●|●|●|●|●|●|●|●|●|●|●|●|●|●|●|●|●|●|●|●|●|●|●|●|●|●|●|●|●|●|●|●|●|●|●|●| |
| MATHER, PAULINE (HM13280) | | | | | |●| | | | | | | | | |●| | | | | |●| | | |●| | | | | | | | | | |●| | |●| |●| | | | | | |
| MOURANT, JENNIFER L (HM14298) | | |●| | | | | | | | | | | | |●| | | | | | | | | | | | | | | | | | | | |●| | | | | | | | | | | |
| MULTI-THERAPY CENTRE (HM14352) | |●|●|●|●|●| | | | |●|●| | | |●|●|●|●| |●| | |●| |●| | |●| | | | | | |●|●| |●| |●| | | |●|●|●| |
| NATURAL THERAPY CENTRE (HM14639) | | |●| | |●| | | | |●|●| | | |●|●| | | |●|●| | | |●| | | | | | | | |●|●|●| |●|●| | | | |●| | | |
| NATURALLY NUTRITION (HM14673) | | |●|●|●|●|●| | | | |●| | | |●| |●| | |●| | | | |●| | | | |●| | |●| |●|●| |●| |●|●| | |●|●|●| |
| OSTEOPATHS (HM15475) | | | | | | | | | | | | | | | | | | | | | |●| | | | | | | | | | | | | | |●| | |●| | | | | | | | |
| PETER & CAROLINE (HM16071) | | | | | | | | | | | | | | | | | | | | | | | | | | | | | | | | | | | | |●| | |●| | | | | | | | |
| PETTIFER, JUSTINA (HM16095) | | |●| | | | | | | | | | | | |●| | | | | | | | | | | | | | | | | | | | | | | | | | |●| | | | | |
| PHYSIOTHERAPY CLINIC (HM16247) | | | | | | | | | | | | | | | | | | | | | | | | | | | | | | | | | | | | | | | |●| | | | | | | | |
| QUIRKE, G (HM16820) | | |●| | | | | | | | | | | | | |●| | | | | | | | | | | | | | | | | | | | | | | | | | | | | | | |
| RAINBOW NATURAL THERAPIES (HM16880) | | |●| | | | | | | | | | | | | | | | | | | | | | | | | | | | | | | | | |●| | | | | | | | | | | |
| SARUM PHYSIOTHERAPY CENTRE (HM17947) | | | | | | | | | | | | | | | | | | | | | | | | | | | | | | | | | | | | | | | |●| | | | | | | | |
| SAWAYA, ALICIA (HM17982) |●|●|●|●|●|●|●|●|●|●|●|●|●|●|●|●|●|●|●|●|●|●|●|●|●|●|●|●|●|●|●|●|●|●|●|●|●|●|●|●|●|●|●|●|●|●|●| |
| SHAFTSBURY PRACTICE (HM18266) |●|●|●|●|●|●|●|●|●|●|●|●|●|●|●|●|●|●|●|●|●| | | |●|●|●|●|●|●|●|●|●|●|●|●|●|●|●|●|●|●|●|●|●|●|●| |
| SHAVE, G M (HM18325) | | | | | | | | | | | | | | | | | | | | | |●| | | | | | | | | | | | | | | | | | | | | | | | | |●|
| SPIRITUAL HEALER (HM19026) | | |●| | | | | | | | | | | | | | | | | | | | | | | | | | | | | | | | | | | | | | | | | | | | | |
| SWINDON CHIROPRACTIC CLINIC (HM19595) | | | | | | | |●| | | | | | | | | | | | | | | | | | | | | | | | | | | | |●| | |●| | | | | | | | |
| TISBURY OSTEOPATHIC PRACTICE (HM20094) | | | | | |●| |●| | |●| | | | | | | | | | | | | | | | | | | | | | | | | |●| | |●| | | | | | | | |
| WARMINSTER OSTEOPATHIC CLINIC (HM20929) | | |●| | | | | | | | |●| |●|●|●|●|●| |●|●| | | | |●| | |●| | | | | |●|●|●| |●|●|●|●|●| |●|●| | |

# D - I Conditions treated at Practices/Businesses

| Business by County with Reference no. | Dandruff | Deafness | Depression | Diabetes | Diarrhoea | Digestive Problems | Diverticulitis | Dizziness | Dyslexia | Dyspraxia | Ear Disorders | Eczema | ENT Disorders | Epilepsy | Eye Disorders | Fatigue | Fears | Fertility Problems | Fever | Fibroids | Flatulence | Foot Problems | Fractures | Fungal Infections | Gallstones | Gastrointestinal Problems | Genital Herpes | Gingivitis | Glandular Fever | Glaucoma | Gout | Gum Disease | Hair Problems | Halitosis | Hand Problems | Hay Fever | Headaches | Hearing Problems | High Blood Pressure | Hip Complaints | Hyperactivity | Hypoglycaemia | Impotence | Incontinence | Indigestion | Infertility | Influenza | Ingrowing Toenails |
|---|---|---|---|---|---|---|---|---|---|---|---|---|---|---|---|---|---|---|---|---|---|---|---|---|---|---|---|---|---|---|---|---|---|---|---|---|---|---|---|---|---|---|---|---|---|---|---|
| WATSON'S COURT CLINIC (HM21025) | | | | ● | | | | | | | | | | | | | | | | | | ● | | ● | | | | | | | ● | | | | | | | | | ● | | | | | | | | ● |
| WELLS, HENRIETTA (HM21175) | ● | ● | ● | ● | ● | ● | ● | ● | ● | ● | ● | ● | ● | ● | ● | ● | ● | ● | ● | ● | ● | ● | ● | ● | ● | ● | ● | ● | ● | ● | ● | ● | ● | ● | ● | ● | ● | ● | ● | ● | ● | ● | ● | ● | ● | ● | ● | |
| WESTBURY CHIROPRACTIC (HM21258) | | | | | | | | | | | | | | | | | | | | | | | | | | | | | | | | | | | | | ● | | | ● | | | | | | | | |
| WESTBURY REFLEXOLOGY CLINIC (HM21260) | | | ● | | | ● | | ● | | | | | | | | ● | | | | | | ● | | | | | | | | | | | | | | ● | ● | | ● | | | | | | ● | ● | | |
| WOOTTON BASSETT (HM21885) | | | | | | | | | | | | | | | | | | | | | | ● | ● | | | | | | | | | | | | | | | | | | | | | ● | | | | |
| **WORCESTERSHIRE** | | | | | | | | | | | | | | | | | | | | | | | | | | | | | | | | | | | | | | | | | | | | | | | | |
| 1ST CHIROPRACTIC UK (HM00007) | | | | | | | | | | | | | | | | | | | | | | | | | | | | | | | | | | | | | ● | | | ● | | | | | | | | |
| AINSLEY, S (HM00433) | | | | | | | | | | | | | | | | | | | | | | ● | | ● | | | | | | | | | | | | | | | | ● | | | | | | | | ● |
| BRETFORDTON CLINIC (HM02969) | | | ● | | | | | | | | | | | | | ● | | | | | | ● | ● | | | | | | | | | | | | | | ● | | ● | ● | ● | | | | | | | |
| BROMSGROVE CHIROPRACTIC CLINIC (HM03151) | | | | | | | | | | | | | | | | | | | | | | | | | | | | | | | | | | | | | ● | | | ● | | | | | | | | |
| CARYL, M D (HM03804) | | | | | | | | | | | | | | | | | | | | | | ● | | | | | | | | | | | | | | | | | | | | | | | | | | ● |
| DAVIES PODIATRY (HM05792) | | | | | | | | | | | | | | | | | | | | | | ● | | ● | | | | | | | | | | | | | | | | | | | | | | | | |
| EVESHAM NATURAL HEALTH CENTRE (HM07009) | | | ● | | ● | ● | ● | ● | | | | ● | | | | ● | | ● | | | ● | ● | | ● | ● | ● | | | | | ● | | | | ● | ● | ● | | ● | ● | | | ● | | ● | ● | | |
| FRONTIA (HM07757) | | | | | ● | ● | ● | ● | | | ● | ● | ● | | | ● | ● | ● | | | | | | | ● | ● | | | ● | | ● | | | | | ● | ● | | ● | ● | ● | | ● | ● | ● | ● | | |
| GIBBINS, JONATHAN (HM08022) | | | | | ● | ● | | ● | | | | | | | | | | | | | | | | | | ● | | | | | | | | | | | ● | | | ● | | | | ● | | | | |
| HINKS, MAXINE (HM09834) | | | ● | | | | | | | | | | | | | ● | | | | | | | | | | | | | | | | | | | | | ● | | | | | | | | | | | |
| HOLDEN, NINA (HM09933) | | | ● | | | ● | | ● | | | ● | | | | ● | | | | | | | | | | | | | | | | | | | | | | ● | | | | | | | | | | | |
| JONES, VAL (HM11200) | | | | | | | | | | | | | | | | | | | | | | ● | | ● | | | | | | | | | | | | | | | | | | | | | | | | |
| KITSON, P (HM11730) | | | | | | | | | | | | | | | | | | | | | | | | | | | | | | | | | | | | | ● | | | ● | | | | | | | | |
| KRISS, ADRIAN D (HM11803) | | | | | | | | | | | | | | | | | | | | | | ● | ● | ● | | | | | | | | | | | | | | | | | | | | | | | | |
| M THORLOW CHIROPODY (HM12810) | | | | | | | | | | | | | | | | | | | | | | ● | | ● | | | | | | | | | | | | | | | | | | | | | | | | ● |
| MALVERN NATURAL HEALTH CENTRE (HM12998) | ● | ● | ● | ● | ● | ● | ● | ● | ● | ● | ● | ● | ● | ● | ● | ● | ● | ● | ● | ● | ● | ● | ● | ● | ● | ● | ● | ● | ● | ● | ● | ● | ● | ● | ● | ● | ● | ● | ● | ● | ● | ● | ● | ● | ● | ● | ● | |
| MALVERN OSTEOPATHIC CLINIC (HM12999) | | | | | | | | | | | | | | | | | | | | | | | | | | | | | | | | | | | | | ● | | | | | | | | | | | |
| MARSTON, SUE (HM13179) | | | ● | | ● | ● | | | | | | | | | | ● | | | | | | | | | | | | | | | | | | | | ● | ● | | ● | ● | | | | | | | | |
| MEAKIN, D W (HM13637) | | | | | | | | | | | | | | | | | | | | | | | | | | | | | | | | | | | | | ● | | | ● | | | | | | | | |
| NATURAL HEALTH CENTRE (HM14564) | | | ● | ● | ● | | | ● | | | | ● | | | | | | ● | | | | | | | | | | | | | | | | | | ● | ● | | ● | | | | | | ● | ● | ● | |
| NOTTINGHAM, STUART (HM15086) | | | | | | | | | | | | | | | | | | | | | | ● | ● | | | | | | | | | | | | ● | | ● | | | ● | | | | | | | | |
| NURCHIR (HM15110) | | | | ● | | | | | | | | | | | | | | | | | | ● | | ● | | | | | | | | | | | | | | | | | | | | | | | | ● |
| OAKFIELD CLINIC (HM15150) | | | | | | | | | | | | ● | | | | | | | | | | | | | | | | | | | | | | | | ● | | | ● | | | | | | | | | |
| PARDOE, DIANA T (HM15648) | | | ● | | | | | | | | | ● | | | | | | | | | | | | | | | | | | | | | | | | | ● | | ● | | | | | | | | | |
| PERSHORE NAT THERAPY CLINIC (HM16057) | ● | ● | ● | ● | ● | ● | ● | ● | ● | ● | ● | ● | ● | ● | ● | ● | ● | ● | ● | ● | ● | ● | ● | ● | ● | ● | ● | ● | ● | ● | ● | ● | ● | ● | ● | ● | ● | ● | ● | ● | ● | ● | ● | ● | ● | ● | ● | |
| R C C M (HM16829) | | | | | | | | | | | | | | | | | | | | | | | | | | | | | | | | | | | | | ● | | | ● | | | | | | | | |
| REDDITCH CHIROPRACTIC CLINIC (HM17013) | | | | | | | | | | | | | | | | | | | | | | | | | | | | | | | | | | | | | ● | | | ● | | | | | | | | |
| REDDITCH FOOTCARE SURGERY (HM17014) | | | | | | | | | | | | | | | | | | | | | | ● | | ● | | | | | | | | | | | | | | | | | | | | | | | | |

# D - I Conditions treated at Practices/Businesses

| Business by County with Reference no. | Dandruff | Deafness | Depression | Diabetes | Diarrhoea | Digestive Problems | Diverticulitis | Dizziness | Dyslexia | Dyspraxia | Ear Disorders | Eczema | ENT Disorders | Epilepsy | Eye Disorders | Fatigue | Fears | Fertility Problems | Fever | Fibroids | Flatulence | Foot Problems | Fractures | Fungal Infections | Gallstones | Gastrointestinal Problems | Genital Herpes | Gingivitis | Glandular Fever | Glaucoma | Gout | Gum Disease | Hair Problems | Halitosis | Hand Problems | Hay Fever | Headaches | Hearing Problems | High Blood Pressure | Hip Complaints | Hyperactivity | Hypoglycaemia | Impotence | Incontinence | Indigestion | Infertility | Influenza | Ingrowing Toenails |
|---|---|---|---|---|---|---|---|---|---|---|---|---|---|---|---|---|---|---|---|---|---|---|---|---|---|---|---|---|---|---|---|---|---|---|---|---|---|---|---|---|---|---|---|---|---|---|---|---|
| SOUTH WORCESTERSHIRE HYP (HM18915) | | | | | ● | | | | | | | | | | | ● | ● | | | | | | | | | | | | | | | | | | | | | | ● | | | | ● | | | | | |
| STOKES, TERRY (HM19325) | | | | | ● | ● | | | | | ● | ● | | | | ● | ● | ● | ● | | ● | ● | | | ● | ● | | | ● | | | | | | | ● | ● | | | | | | ● | ● | ● | ● | ● | |
| STONE, ANNE L (HM19329) | | | | | | | | | | | | | | | | | | | | | | | ● | | | | | | | | | | | | | | ● | | | ● | | | | ● | | | | |
| WORCESTER NATURAL THERAPY CTRE (HM21886) | ● | ● | ● | ● | ● | ● | ● | ● | ● | ● | ● | ● | ● | ● | ● | ● | ● | ● | ● | ● | ● | ● | ● | ● | ● | ● | ● | ● | ● | ● | ● | ● | ● | ● | ● | ● | ● | ● | ● | ● | ● | ● | ● | ● | ● | ● | ● | |
| YOUNG, JOANNA (HM22075) | | | | | | | | | ● | ● | ● | | ● | ● | | ● | | ● | | | | | ● | | | | | | ● | | | | | | ● | | ● | ● | | | ● | | | | ● | | | |
| YORKSHIRE (NORTH) | | | | | | | | | | | | | | | | | | | | | | | | | | | | | | | | | | | | | | | | | | | | | | | | |
| A TACTILE BUSINESS (HM00046) | | | | | | | | | | | | ● | | | | | | ● | | | | | | | | | | | | | | | | | | | | | | | | | | | | | | |
| BARRASS, K I (HM01778) | | | | | | | | | | | | | | | | | | | | | | ● | | | | | | | | | | | | | | | | | | | | | | | | | | |
| BLACK, SAUL (HM02428) | | | | ● | | | | | | | | | | | | | | | | | | ● | | | | | | | | | | | | | | | | | | | | | | | | | | ● |
| BROADHEAD, J N & M (HM03114) | | | | | | | | | | | | | | | | | | | | | | ● | | ● | | | | | | | | | | | | | | | | | | | | | | | | |
| BUSWELL, RONA (HM03471) | | | ● | | ● | ● | | | | | | ● | | | | ● | | | | | | | | | | | | | | | | | | | | | ● | | ● | | | | | | ● | | | |
| CHIROPODIST (HM04292) | | | | | | | | | | | | | | | | | | | | | | ● | | ● | | | | | | | | | | | | | | | | | | | | | | | | |
| CORDEL, MICHAEL (HM05160) | | | ● | | ● | ● | ● | | | | ● | | | | ● | ● | | ● | | | ● | | | | | ● | | | | ● | ● | | | | ● | | ● | | ● | ● | ● | | ● | | ● | ● | ● | |
| CRAVEN CLINIC (HM05384) | ● | ● | ● | ● | ● | ● | ● | ● | ● | ● | ● | ● | ● | ● | ● | ● | ● | ● | ● | ● | ● | ● | ● | ● | ● | ● | ● | ● | ● | ● | ● | ● | ● | ● | ● | ● | ● | ● | ● | ● | ● | ● | ● | ● | ● | ● | ● | |
| CROFT HOUSE CLINIC (HM05452) | | | | | | ● | | | | | | ● | | | | ● | | | | | | | | | | | | | | | | | | | | ● | ● | | | | | | | | | | | |
| DOVE COURT CENTRE (HM06225) | ● | ● | ● | ● | ● | ● | ● | ● | ● | ● | ● | ● | ● | ● | ● | ● | ● | ● | ● | ● | ● | ● | ● | ● | ● | ● | ● | ● | ● | ● | ● | ● | ● | ● | ● | ● | ● | ● | ● | ● | ● | ● | ● | ● | ● | ● | ● | |
| GRIFFIN, TRICIA (HM08555) | | | | | ● | ● | | | | | | | ● | | | | | | | ● | ● | | | | | ● | | | ● | | | | | | | ● | ● | | | | | | | | ● | | | |
| HARROGATE HOLISTIC HEALTH CTRE (HM09116) | | | | | | ● | | | | | | ● | | | | | | | | | ● | | | | | | | | | | | | | | | | | | | | | | | | | | | |
| HEALING CLINIC (HM09328) | ● | ● | ● | | ● | ● | ● | ● | ● | ● | ● | ● | ● | ● | ● | ● | ● | ● | ● | ● | ● | ● | | ● | ● | ● | ● | ● | ● | | | ● | | ● | ● | ● | ● | ● | ● | ● | ● | ● | | ● | ● | ● | ● | |
| HIGHTHORN PHYSIOTHERAPY CLINIC (HM09759) | | | | | | | | | | | | | | | | | | | | | | | | | | | | | | | | | | | | | | | | ● | | | | | | | | |
| HOBSON, I K (HM09863) | | | | | | | | | | | | | | | | | | | | | | | | | | | | | | | | | | | | | | | | ● | | | | | | | | |
| KNOWLES, J (HM11770) | | | | ● | | | | | | | | | | | | | | | | | | ● | | ● | | | | | | | | | | | | | | | | | | | | | | | | |
| LESZCZUK, PAULA (HM12245) | | | ● | ● | ● | ● | ● | ● | | ● | ● | ● | ● | ● | ● | ● | ● | ● | ● | ● | ● | ● | | ● | ● | ● | ● | ● | ● | | ● | ● | | ● | ● | ● | ● | | ● | ● | ● | ● | ● | | ● | ● | ● | |
| LESZCZUK, PAULA (HM12246) | | | ● | ● | ● | ● | ● | ● | | ● | ● | ● | ● | ● | ● | ● | ● | ● | ● | ● | ● | ● | | ● | ● | ● | ● | ● | ● | | ● | ● | | ● | ● | ● | ● | | ● | ● | ● | ● | ● | | ● | ● | ● | |
| LIFESUPPORT (HM12366) | | ● | ● | ● | ● | ● | ● | | | | ● | ● | | | ● | ● | ● | | | | ● | ● | | ● | | | | | ● | | ● | ● | ● | | | ● | ● | ● | ● | ● | ● | | ● | ● | ● | | ● | |
| NANCY METCALFE MOBILE CONSULT (HM14468) | | | ● | | | | | | | | | | | | | | | | | | | | | | | | | | | | | | | | | | ● | | | | | | | | | | | |
| NATURAL BALANCE (HM14515) | | | | | | | | | | | | | | | | | | | | | | | | | | | | | | | | | | | | | ● | | | | | | | | | | | |
| PANACEA ACUPUNCTURE CLINIC (HM15628) | | | | | ● | ● | | | | | | | | | | | | | | | | | | | | | | | | | | | | | | ● | ● | | ● | | | | | | | | | |
| PAULA LESZCZUK (HM15849) | | | ● | ● | ● | ● | ● | ● | | ● | ● | ● | ● | ● | ● | ● | ● | ● | ● | ● | ● | ● | | ● | ● | ● | ● | ● | ● | | ● | ● | | ● | ● | ● | ● | | ● | ● | ● | ● | ● | | ● | ● | ● | |
| RATHBONE, DONNA (HM16955) | | | | | | | | | | | | | | | | | | | | | | ● | | ● | | | | | | | | | | | | | | | | | | | | | | | | |
| RIPON NATURAL HEALTH CENTRE (HM17365) | | ● | ● | ● | ● | ● | ● | ● | ● | | ● | ● | | | ● | ● | ● | | ● | | | | | | ● | ● | | | ● | | ● | | | | ● | ● | ● | ● | ● | ● | ● | | | ● | ● | | ● | |
| SHAH, ATUL (HM18268) | ● | ● | ● | ● | ● | ● | ● | ● | ● | ● | ● | ● | ● | | ● | ● | ● | ● | ● | ● | ● | ● | | ● | ● | ● | | ● | ● | | ● | ● | ● | ● | ● | ● | ● | ● | ● | ● | ● | ● | ● | ● | ● | ● | ● | |
| SHEEHAN, NICHOLAS (HM18363) | | | | | | | | | | | | | | | | | | | | | | | | | | | | | | | | | | | | | ● | | | | | | | | | | | |
| SI SHEN CLINIC (HM18519) | | | | | | | | | | | | | | | | | | | | | | ● | | | | | | | | | | | | | | | | | | | | | | | | | | |

# D - I Conditions treated at Practices/Businesses

Business by County with Reference no.

| Condition | SKIPTON CHIROPODY CENTRE (HM18658) | SMITH, C J (HM18723) | STATHER, M (HM19160) | STRATTON, FIONA (HM19372) | TERRY ANNE (HM19845) | YOGA FOR ALL (HM22026) | YORK CHIROPRACTIC CLINIC (HM22039) | YORK CLINIC (HM22040) | YORK COUNSELLING (HM22042) |
|---|---|---|---|---|---|---|---|---|---|
| Dandruff | | | | | | | | ● | |
| Deafness | | | | | | | | ● | |
| Depression | | | | ● | ● | ● | | ● | ● |
| Diabetes | | | | | | | | ● | |
| Diarrhoea | | | | | | ● | | ● | |
| Digestive Problems | | | | ● | ● | ● | | ● | |
| Diverticulitis | | | | | ● | | | ● | |
| Dizziness | | | | | ● | | ● | ● | |
| Dyslexia | | | | | | | | ● | |
| Dyspraxia | | | | | | | | ● | |
| Ear Disorders | | | | | ● | | | ● | |
| Eczema | | | | ● | ● | | | ● | |
| ENT Disorders | | | | | ● | | | ● | |
| Epilepsy | | | | | | | | ● | |
| Eye Disorders | | | | | ● | | | ● | |
| Fatigue | | | | ● | | ● | | ● | ● |
| Fears | | | | ● | | | | ● | ● |
| Fertility Problems | | | | ● | | | | ● | |
| Fever | | | | | | | | ● | |
| Fibroids | | | | ● | | | | ● | |
| Flatulence | | | | | | ● | | ● | |
| Foot Problems | ● | | ● | | | | | ● | |
| Fractures | | | | | | | | ● | |
| Fungal Infections | ● | | ● | | | | | ● | |
| Gallstones | | | | | | | | ● | |
| Gastrointestinal Problems | | | | ● | | | | ● | |
| Genital Herpes | | | | | | | | ● | |
| Gingivitis | | | | | | | | ● | |
| Glandular Fever | | | | | | | | ● | |
| Glaucoma | | | | | | | | ● | |
| Gout | | | | | | | | ● | |
| Gum Disease | | | | | | | | ● | |
| Hair Problems | | | | | ● | | | ● | |
| Halitosis | | | | | | | | ● | |
| Hand Problems | | | | | | | | ● | |
| Hay Fever | | | | | ● | | | ● | |
| Headaches | | ● | | ● | ● | ● | ● | ● | ● |
| Hearing Problems | | | | | ● | | | ● | |
| High Blood Pressure | | | | ● | ● | ● | | ● | |
| Hip Complaints | | ● | | ● | | | ● | ● | |
| Hyperactivity | | | | | | | | ● | |
| Hypoglycaemia | | | | | | | | ● | |
| Impotence | | | | | ● | | | ● | |
| Incontinence | | | | ● | ● | ● | | ● | |
| Indigestion | | | | ● | ● | ● | | ● | |
| Infertility | | | | ● | | | | ● | |
| Influenza | | | | | | | | ● | |
| Ingrowing Toenails | | | | | | | | | |

YORKSHIRE (SOUTH)

| Condition | ALTON & JAMES MED HERBAL (HM00748) | ANDERSON, A DUDLEY (HM00810) | BLUFF, ANN (HM02529) | BOON, G M (HM02690) | BRAMLEY HALL CLINIC (HM02902) | BRANKIN, M & K (HM02917) | BRANKLIN, M & K (HM02918) | BROOMHILL MEDICAL CENTRE (HM03193) | CARING CLINIC (HM03682) | CLAIRE LOUISE (HM04510) | COUNTRY PRACTICE (HM05256) | DORE PHYSIOTHERAPY PRACTICE (HM06196) | EATON, T C (HM06565) | ESSENTIAL HARMONY (HM06907) | FISHER, CHRISTINE A (HM07349) | GRAPEVINE HEALTH (HM08399) | GRENOSIDE PHYSIOTHERAPY (HM08536) | GYALTSABJE BUDDHIST CENTRE (HM08672) | HALLAMSHIRE NATURAL HLTH CTRE (HM08798) | HEALTHY FEET (HM09427) | HINCHLIFFE, JACKIE (HM09822) | HYPNOTHERAPY CENTRE (HM10515) | KIRBY, M (HM11702) | LAISTER, MARTIN (HM11868) |
|---|---|---|---|---|---|---|---|---|---|---|---|---|---|---|---|---|---|---|---|---|---|---|---|---|
| Dandruff | | | | | | | | | | | | | | ● | | ● | | | | | | | ● | |
| Deafness | | | | | | | | | | | | | | | | | | | | | | | ● | |
| Depression | ● | ● | | | ● | | | | ● | | ● | | | ● | | ● | | ● | | | | ● | ● | |
| Diabetes | | | ● | | ● | ● | ● | | ● | | ● | | ● | | | ● | | | | ● | | | ● | |
| Diarrhoea | ● | | | | | | | | | | | | | | | ● | | | | | | ● | ● | |
| Digestive Problems | ● | | | | ● | | | | ● | | | | | ● | | ● | | | ● | | | ● | ● | |
| Diverticulitis | ● | | | | ● | | | | ● | | | | | | | ● | | | | | | | ● | |
| Dizziness | ● | | | | | | | | | | | ● | | | | ● | | | | | | ● | ● | |
| Dyslexia | | | | | ● | | | | | | | | | | | ● | | | | | | | | |
| Dyspraxia | | | | | | | | | | | | | | | | ● | | | | | | | ● | |
| Ear Disorders | | | | | | | | | | | | | | | | ● | | | | | | | ● | |
| Eczema | ● | | | | ● | | | | ● | | | | | ● | | ● | | | ● | | ● | | ● | |
| ENT Disorders | | | | | | | | | ● | | | | | | | ● | | | ● | | | | ● | |
| Epilepsy | | | | | | | | | | | | | | | | ● | | | | | | | ● | |
| Eye Disorders | | | | | | | | | | | | | | | | ● | | | | | | | ● | |
| Fatigue | ● | | | | ● | | | | ● | | ● | | | ● | | ● | | | ● | | ● | ● | ● | |
| Fears | | ● | | | | | | | ● | | | | | | | ● | | | ● | | | ● | ● | |
| Fertility Problems | ● | | | | ● | | | | ● | | | | | | | ● | | | ● | | | ● | ● | |
| Fever | ● | | | | | | | | | | | | | | | ● | | | | | | | ● | |
| Fibroids | ● | | | | ● | | | | ● | | | | | | | ● | | | | | | | ● | |
| Flatulence | ● | | | | ● | | | | ● | | | | | | | ● | | | ● | | | | ● | |
| Foot Problems | | | ● | ● | | | ● | | | ● | ● | | ● | | ● | ● | | | | ● | | | ● | |
| Fractures | | | | | | | | | | | | | | | | ● | | | | ● | | ● | | |
| Fungal Infections | ● | | | ● | ● | | | | ● | ● | ● | | | | | ● | | | ● | ● | ● | | ● | |
| Gallstones | ● | | | | | | | | ● | | | | | | | ● | | | | | | | ● | |
| Gastrointestinal Problems | ● | | | | ● | | | | ● | | | | | | | ● | | | ● | | | | ● | |
| Genital Herpes | | | | | ● | | | | | | | | | | | ● | | | | | | | | |
| Gingivitis | ● | | | | | | | | | | ● | | | | | ● | | | | | | | | |
| Glandular Fever | ● | | | | | | | | ● | | | | | | | ● | | | ● | | | | ● | |
| Glaucoma | | | | | | | | | ● | | | | | | | ● | | | | | | | ● | |
| Gout | | | | | ● | | | | ● | | | | | | | ● | | | | ● | | | ● | |
| Gum Disease | | | | | | | | | ● | | | | | | | ● | | | | | | | | |
| Hair Problems | | | | | ● | | | | | | | | | | | ● | | | | | | ● | | |
| Halitosis | | | | | ● | | | | ● | | | | | | | ● | | | | | | | ● | |
| Hand Problems | | | | | | | | | | | | | | | | ● | | | ● | | | | ● | |
| Hay Fever | ● | | | | ● | | | | ● | | | | | ● | | ● | | | | | ● | | ● | |
| Headaches | ● | | | | ● | | | ● | ● | | ● | ● | | ● | | ● | | | ● | | ● | ● | ● | |
| Hearing Problems | | | | | | | | | | | | | | | | ● | | | | | | | ● | |
| High Blood Pressure | ● | | | | ● | | | | ● | | | | | ● | | ● | | | ● | | ● | ● | ● | |
| Hip Complaints | | | | | ● | | | | | | | ● | | | | ● | ● | | ● | ● | | | ● | |
| Hyperactivity | ● | | | | ● | | | | ● | | | | | | | ● | | | ● | | | | | |
| Hypoglycaemia | ● | | | | ● | | | | ● | | | | | | | ● | | | ● | | | | ● | |
| Impotence | | | | | ● | | | | | | | | | | | ● | | | | | | ● | | |
| Incontinence | | | | | | | | | | | | | | | | ● | | | | | | | ● | |
| Indigestion | ● | | | | ● | | | | ● | | | | | | | ● | | | ● | | ● | | ● | |
| Infertility | ● | | | | ● | | | | ● | | | | | | | ● | | | ● | | | ● | ● | |
| Influenza | ● | | | | ● | | | | | | | | | | | ● | | | | | | | ● | |
| Ingrowing Toenails | | | | | | | ● | | | | | | ● | | | | | | | ● | | | | ● |

# D - I Conditions treated at Practices/Businesses

| Business by County with Reference no. | Dandruff | Deafness | Depression | Diabetes | Diarrhoea | Digestive Problems | Diverticulitis | Dizziness | Dyslexia | Dyspraxia | Ear Disorders | Eczema | ENT Disorders | Epilepsy | Eye Disorders | Fatigue | Fears | Fertility Problems | Fever | Fibroids | Flatulence | Foot Problems | Fractures | Fungal Infections | Gallstones | Gastrointestinal Problems | Genital Herpes | Gingivitis | Glandular Fever | Glaucoma | Gout | Gum Disease | Hair Problems | Halitosis | Hand Problems | Hay Fever | Headaches | Hearing Problems | High Blood Pressure | Hip Complaints | Hyperactivity | Hypoglycaemia | Impotence | Incontinence | Indigestion | Infertility | Influenza | Ingrowing Toenails |
|---|---|---|---|---|---|---|---|---|---|---|---|---|---|---|---|---|---|---|---|---|---|---|---|---|---|---|---|---|---|---|---|---|---|---|---|---|---|---|---|---|---|---|---|---|---|---|---|---|
| LLEWELLYN CONSULTANCY (HM12502) | | | ● | | ● | ● | ● | ● | ● | ● | ● | ● | ● | | ● | ● | ● | ● | | | ● | | | | | ● | | ● | ● | | | ● | | ● | | ● | ● | | ● | | ● | ● | ● | ● | ● | ● | ● | |
| M & B SERVICES (HM12794) | | | ● | ● | ● | ● | | ● | | | ● | ● | ● | ● | ● | ● | ● | ● | | | ● | ● | ● | | ● | ● | | | | ● | ● | | | | ● | ● | ● | | ● | ● | | | ● | | ● | ● | ● | |
| MEDICAL HERBALIST (HM13652) | ● | ● | ● | ● | ● | ● | ● | ● | ● | ● | ● | ● | ● | ● | ● | ● | ● | ● | ● | ● | ● | ● | ● | ● | ● | ● | ● | ● | ● | ● | ● | ● | ● | ● | ● | ● | ● | ● | ● | ● | ● | ● | ● | ● | ● | ● | ● | |
| MILLINGTON, JANET (HM13917) | | | ● | | | ● | | | | | | ● | | | | | ● | | | | | | | | | | | | | | | | | | | ● | | | ● | | | | | | | | | |
| MOORGATE NATURAL HEALING CTRE (HM14138) | ● | ● | ● | ● | ● | ● | ● | ● | ● | ● | ● | ● | ● | ● | ● | ● | ● | ● | ● | ● | ● | ● | ● | ● | ● | ● | ● | ● | ● | ● | ● | ● | ● | ● | ● | ● | ● | ● | ● | ● | ● | ● | ● | ● | ● | ● | ● | |
| NIGHTINGALE PHYSIO PRACTICE (HM14937) | | | | | | | | | | | | | | | | | | | | | | | | | | | | | | | | | | | | | | | | ● | | | | | | | | |
| PAUL BOIZOT AROMATHERAPY (HM15839) | | | | | | ● | | | | | | ● | | | | | | | | | | | | ● | | | | | | | | | | | | | ● | | | | | | | | ● | | | |
| SCHOLL CENTRE (HM18046) | | | | | | | | | | | | | | | | | | | | | | ● | | ● | | | | | | | | | | | | | | | | | | | | | | | | |
| SEASONS BEAUTY CENTRE (HM18178) | | ● | ● | ● | ● | ● | ● | ● | ● | ● | ● | ● | ● | ● | ● | ● | ● | ● | ● | ● | ● | ● | | ● | ● | ● | | | ● | ● | ● | | | ● | ● | ● | ● | ● | ● | ● | ● | ● | | ● | ● | ● | ● | |
| SHARRON CHIROPODY CLINIC (HM18324) | | | | ● | | | | | | | | | | | | | | | | | | ● | | | | | | | | | | | | | | | | | | | | | | | | | | |
| SHEFFIELD NATURAL HEALTH CTRE (HM18372) | ● | ● | ● | ● | ● | ● | ● | ● | ● | ● | ● | ● | ● | ● | ● | ● | ● | ● | ● | ● | ● | ● | ● | ● | ● | ● | ● | ● | ● | ● | ● | ● | ● | ● | ● | ● | ● | ● | ● | ● | ● | ● | ● | ● | ● | ● | ● | |
| SIMPSON, SARAH E (HM18598) | | | | | | | | | | | | | | | | | | | | | | ● | | ● | | | | | | | | | | | | | | | | | | | | | | | | ● |
| STONES, KAREN (HM19343) | ● | ● | ● | ● | ● | ● | ● | ● | ● | ● | ● | ● | ● | | ● | ● | ● | ● | ● | ● | ● | ● | | ● | ● | ● | | ● | ● | ● | | ● | ● | ● | ● | ● | ● | ● | | ● | ● | ● | | ● | ● | ● | ● | |
| TRIGG, REBECCA (HM20334) | | | | | ● | | | | | | | | | | | ● | | | | | | | | | | | | | | | | | | | | ● | ● | | | | | | | | | | | |
| VINSON, CAROL (HM20686) | | | | ● | | | | | | | | | | | | | | | | | | ● | | | | | | | | | | | | | | | | | | | | | | | | | | ● |
| WELLFORCE (HM21160) | ● | | ● | | ● | ● | ● | ● | ● | | ● | ● | | | ● | ● | ● | ● | ● | ● | ● | ● | ● | ● | ● | ● | ● | ● | ● | | ● | ● | ● | ● | ● | ● | ● | ● | ● | ● | ● | ● | ● | ● | ● | ● | ● | |
| WELSH CHIROPRACTIC (HM21183) | | | | ● | ● | ● | | ● | | | | | ● | | | | | ● | | | | | | | | ● | | | | | | | | | ● | | ● | | | ● | | | | | ● | | | |
| WHITEING, J P (HM21393) | | | | ● | | | | | | | | | | | | | | | | | | | | | | | | | | | | | | | | | | | | | | | | | | | | |
| WILSON, JOHN PAUL (HM21658) | | | | ● | | | | | | | | | | | | | | | | | | ● | | | | | | | | | | | | | | | | | | | | | | | | | | ● |
| WOMBWELL ACUPUNCTURE CLINIC (HM21770) | | | | | | ● | | | | | | | | | | | | | | | | | | | | | | | | | | | | | | | | | | ● | | | | | | | | |
| **YORKSHIRE (WEST)** | | | | | | | | | | | | | | | | | | | | | | | | | | | | | | | | | | | | | | | | | | | | | | | | |
| A BARCHAM REFLEXOLOGY (HM00024) | | | ● | ● | ● | ● | ● | ● | | ● | ● | ● | ● | ● | | ● | ● | ● | | ● | ● | ● | | ● | | ● | | | | | ● | | | | | ● | ● | | ● | | ● | ● | ● | ● | ● | ● | | |
| ACTIVE MINDS (HM00199) | | ● | | | | | | | | | | | | | | | | | | | | | | | | | | | | | | | | | | | | | | | | | | | | | | |
| AIREDALE ALLERGY CENTRE (HM00441) | | | | | ● | ● | ● | | | | | ● | | | | ● | | | | | ● | | | ● | | ● | | | | | | | | | | ● | ● | | | | ● | | | | ● | | | |
| ALEX TECH TEACHING CENTRE (HM00513) | | | | | | ● | | | | | | | | | | ● | | | | | | | | | | | | | | | | | | | ● | | ● | | | | | | | | | | | |
| AMETHYST HEALING CENTRE (HM00783) | | | ● | | ● | ● | ● | ● | ● | | ● | | | | | | ● | ● | ● | | ● | | ● | | | | | | | | | | | | | | | | | | | | | | | | | |
| ARDENTE CHIROPODY SERVICE (HM00991) | | | | | | | | | | | | | | | | | | | | | | ● | | ● | | | | | | | | | | | | | | | | | | | | | | | | |
| ASH, STACEY (HM01183) | | | | | | | | | | | | ● | | | | | | ● | | | | | | | | | | | | | | | | | | ● | ● | | | | | | | | | ● | | |
| ASPEN CLINIC (HM01255) | | | | | | | | | | | | | | | | | | | | | | | | | | | | | | | | | | | | | | | | ● | | | | | | | | |
| BAILEY FLOWER ESSENCES (HM01539) | | | ● | | | | | | | | | | | | | | | | | | | | | | | | | | | | | | | | | | | | | | | | | | | | | |
| BENTLEY, J H (HM02173) | | | | | | | | | | | | | | | | | | | | | | | | | | | | | | | | | | | | | ● | | | | | | | | | | | |
| BINGLEY HOMOEOPATHIC PRACTICE (HM02315) | ● | ● | ● | ● | ● | ● | ● | ● | ● | ● | ● | ● | ● | ● | ● | ● | ● | ● | ● | ● | ● | ● | ● | ● | ● | ● | ● | ● | ● | ● | ● | ● | ● | ● | ● | ● | ● | ● | ● | ● | ● | ● | ● | ● | ● | ● | ● | |
| BODY ESSENCE (HM02585) | | | ● | | | | | | | | | | | | | | | | | | | | | | | | | | | | | | | | | | ● | | ● | | | | | | ● | | | |
| BOYD HYPNOTHERAPY (HM02816) | | | ● | | | ● | | | | | | ● | | | | ● | ● | | | | | | | | | | | | | | | | | | | | | | | | | | ● | ● | ● | | | |

# D - I Conditions treated at Practices/Businesses

| Business by County with Reference no. | Dandruff | Deafness | Depression | Diabetes | Diarrhoea | Digestive Problems | Diverticulitis | Dizziness | Dyslexia | Dyspraxia | Ear Disorders | Eczema | ENT Disorders | Epilepsy | Eye Disorders | Fatigue | Fears | Fertility Problems | Fever | Fibroids | Flatulence | Foot Problems | Fractures | Fungal Infections | Gallstones | Gastrointestinal Problems | Genital Herpes | Gingivitis | Glandular Fever | Glaucoma | Gout | Gum Disease | Hair Problems | Halitosis | Hand Problems | Hay Fever | Headaches | Hearing Problems | High Blood Pressure | Hip Complaints | Hyperactivity | Hypoglycaemia | Impotence | Incontinence | Indigestion | Infertility | Influenza | Ingrowing Toenails |
|---|---|---|---|---|---|---|---|---|---|---|---|---|---|---|---|---|---|---|---|---|---|---|---|---|---|---|---|---|---|---|---|---|---|---|---|---|---|---|---|---|---|---|---|---|---|---|---|---|
| BRADFORD CHIROPODY & BIO CLNC (HM02846) |||||||||||||||||||||||●||●|||||||||||||||||||||||||
| BRADFORD CLINIC OF ALT MED (HM02848) |●|●|●|●|●|●|●|●|●|●|●|●|●|●|●|●|●|●|●|●|●|●|●|●|●|●|●|●|●|●|●|●|●|●|●|●|●|●|●|●|●|●|●|●|●|●|●||
| BRAMIN CLINIC (HM02900) |||||||||||||||||||||||●|||||||||||||||●|||●|||||||||
| BRAMLEY COMP THERAPY CLINIC (HM02901) |||●||●|●|●|●||●||●||||●|●|●|●|●|●|●|●|●|●||●|●||●||●||●|●||●|●||●|●|●||●||●||●||
| BROWN, PAT (HM03243) |||●||||||||||||||||||||||||||||||||||||||||||||||
| CALVERLEY ACUPUNCTURE CLINIC (HM03561) |||●||●|●|●|●||||||||●||●||||●|||||||||||||||●||●|●||||||●|●|||
| CHAMPANERIA, S K (HM03963) |||||●|●|●|||||●||||●||||||||●||●|||||||||●|||●|||||||●||||
| CHOICE AROMAS (HM04421) |||●|||●|||||||●||||●|●||||●|||●|||||||●|||||●|●|||||||●||●||||
| CLARKE, DON (HM04586) |||||●|●||||||||||●||●|||||||||||||||||||●|●||●||||||||||
| COOPER, SAFFRON (HM05126) ||●|●||●|●||●||||●|●|●||●|●|●|●|●|●|●|●|●||●||●|●|●|●||●|●|●|●|●|●|●|●|●|●|●||●|●||●|●||●||
| DESIGNING CHANGE (HM06022) |||||||||||||||||●|●|||||||||||||||||||||||||||||||
| DRURY, WENDY (HM06331) |||||●|●|●|||||●|●|●||●|●|●||||●|||||||●|||||||||||●|●||●|●|||||●||||
| DUFFIELD (HM06360) ||||||●||||||||||●|||||||||||||||||||||●||●|||||●||||
| EQUA-LIBRA (HM06863) |||●|||●||||||||||||||||||||||||||||||●|||||||||||||
| FIGURA, CATHERINE MARIA (HM07283) |||●||||||||||||||||||||||||||||||||||●|||||||||||||
| GILLETT, LIZ (HM08088) |||||||||||||||||||||||||||||||||||||●|||||||||||||
| HAMER-BLOOM, S (HM08832) |||||||||||||||||||||||●||●|||||||||||||||||||||||||
| HAMNETT, SHEILA (HM08870) ||||||●||||||||||||||||||||||||||||||●|||●||||||||||
| HANSON, S C (HM08944) ||||●||||||||●||||||||||●|●|●|||||||●||||●|||||●||●|||||||
| HEBDEN BRIDGE CENTRE (HM09487) |||●||||||||||||||●|||||||||||||||||||||||||||||||
| HERMITAGE OILS (HM09684) |●|||||||||||●||||||||||||●|||||||●|||||||||||||||||||
| HOBSON, ANNE (HM09862) |||●||||||||||||||||||||||||||||||||||●|||||||||||||
| HOLMFIRTH PHYSIO/SPORTS INJURY (HM10048) |||●|||●|||||||||||||||||||||||||||||||||||||||||||
| HOMEOPATHIC MEDICAL PRACTICE (HM10076) ||||||●||||||●|●|●||●|●|||●|●|||●||||●||●|||●|||||||●|●||●|||||||●||||
| HUNTER, REBECCA (HM10408) ||●|●||●|●|●|●|||●|●|●||●|●|●|●|●||●|●||||●|●||●||||●|●|●|●|●|●|●|●|●|●|●||●|●|●||
| J & J HARROP (HM10792) |||||||||||||||||||||||●||●|||||||||||||||||||||||||
| KANG DA CLINIC (HM11313) |●|●|●|●|●||●|●|●||●|●|●|●|●|●|●|●|●|●|●|●|●|●|●|●|●||●|●|●|●|●||●|●|●|●|●|●|●|●|●|●|●|●|●|●||
| KINGSMITH, ANNE-MARIE (HM11673) ||||||||||||||||||||||||||||||||||||||||||||||||●|
| KINNAIRD, F M (HM11686) |||●|||●||||||||||●|●|||||||||||||||||||||●||||||●||●||||
| LEEDS COUNSELLING & PSYCHO SVS (HM12158) |||●||||||||||||||●|||||||||||||||||||||||||||||||
| LPS TRAINING & CONSULTANCY (HM12713) ||||||||||||||||||||||||||||||||||||||||●||||||||
| MORGAN, J D (DR) (HM14167) |||●|||||||||||||||||||||||●|||||||||||●||●|||||●|●|||||
| MORLEY ACUPUNCTURE CLINIC (HM14180) ||●|●||●|●|●|●|||●|●|●|●|●|●|●|●|●|●|●|●|●|●|●|●||●|●|●|●|●||●|●|●|●|●|●|●|●|●|●|●|●|●|●||
| MORNINGTON PHYSIOTHERAPY (HM14193) |||||||||||||||||||||||●|●||||||||●||||●||●|||●||||||||

www.healthmyself.com

# D - I Conditions treated at Practices/Businesses

| Business by County with Reference no. | Dandruff | Deafness | Depression | Diabetes | Diarrhoea | Digestive Problems | Diverticulitis | Dizziness | Dyslexia | Dyspraxia | Ear Disorders | Eczema | ENT Disorders | Epilepsy | Eye Disorders | Fatigue |
|---|---|---|---|---|---|---|---|---|---|---|---|---|---|---|---|---|
| NATURES WORKROOM (HM14705) | ● | ● | ● | ● | ● | ● | ● | ● | ● | ● | ● | ● | ● | ● | ● | ● |
| NEILL-HIGGINS, CHRISTINA (HM14765) | | | ● | ● | | ● | ● | | | | | ● | | | | ● |
| NRTH LEEDS PHYSIO/SPRTS INJ (HM15091) | | | | | | | | | | | | | | | | |
| OWENS, PAULINE (HM15533) | | ● | ● | ● | ● | ● | | ● | | | ● | | | | | |
| PALLAS, ANDREW (HM15595) | | ● | ● | | ● | ● | ● | ● | | | ● | ● | ● | | | ● |
| PARKS, HILARY (HM15720) | | | ● | | ● | ● | | | | | | | | | | ● |
| PAYNE, AUDREY (HM15861) | | | ● | | | | | | | | | | | | | |
| POPPLEWELL, MARK (HM16437) | | | ● | | ● | ● | | ● | | | | | | | | ● |
| PRESTON, CATHY (HM16551) | | | ● | | | | | | | | | | | | | ● |
| RAINTREE HEALTH (HM16893) | ● | ● | ● | ● | ● | ● | | | | | | ● | | ● | | ● |
| RICHARDSON CLINIC (HM17266) | ● | ● | ● | ● | ● | ● | ● | ● | ● | ● | ● | ● | ● | ● | ● | ● |
| ROTHWELL SPORTS CENTRE (HM17658) | | | | | | | | | | | | | | | | |
| ROUNDHAY CHIROPRACTIC CLINIC (HM17667) | | | | | | | | | | | | | | | | |
| SALTAIRE COMP HEALTH STUDIO (HM17864) | ● | ● | ● | ● | ● | ● | ● | ● | ● | ● | ● | ● | ● | ● | ● | ● |
| SHACKLETON, JOHN A (HM18263) | | | | | | | | | | | | | | | | |
| SHERQIA, DARULSHAFA (HM18436) | | | ● | | ● | ● | ● | ● | | | | ● | | | | ● |
| SMITH, JANET (HM18751) | | | ● | | | ● | | | | | | | | | | ● |
| STEAD, JULIE ANN (HM19164) | | | | | | ● | | | | | | | | | | |
| SURGERY (HM19519) | | | | | | | | | | | | | | | | |
| SWAINE, PAULA (HM19565) | | | | | | | | | | | | | | | | |
| SYKES CLINIC (HM19610) | | | ● | | | ● | | | | | | ● | | | | ● |
| TORNTON, HOWARD (HM20172) | | | | | | | | ● | | | | | | | | |
| TRANSCENDENTAL MEDITATION (HM20285) | | | ● | | | | | | | | | | | | | |
| WATKINS, JEAN (HM20996) | | | ● | ● | ● | ● | ● | | | | ● | | ● | ● | | ● |
| WEST YORKSHIRE CLINIC (HM21242) | ● | ● | ● | ● | ● | ● | ● | ● | | ● | ● | ● | ● | ● | ● | ● |
| WEST YORKSHIRE M S THRPY CTRE (HM21243) | | | | ● | | | | | | | | | | ● | | |
| WEST YORKSHIRE PHYSIO CENTRE (HM21244) | | | | | | | | | | | | | | | | |
| WETHERBY PHYSIO PRACTICE (HM21290) | | | | | | | | | | | | | | | | |
| WISE, CAROL (HM21732) | ● | ● | ● | ● | ● | ● | ● | ● | ● | ● | ● | ● | ● | ● | ● | ● |
| WOODHOUSE CLINIC (HM21826) | | | | | | ● | | ● | | | | | | | | ● |

| Business by County with Reference no. | Fears | Fertility Problems | Fever | Fibroids | Flatulence | Foot Problems | Fractures | Fungal Infections | Gallstones | Gastrointestinal Problems | Genital Herpes | Gingivitis | Glandular Fever | Glaucoma | Gout | Gum Disease |
|---|---|---|---|---|---|---|---|---|---|---|---|---|---|---|---|---|
| NATURES WORKROOM (HM14705) | ● | ● | ● | ● | ● | ● | ● | ● | ● | ● | ● | ● | ● | ● | ● | ● |
| NEILL-HIGGINS, CHRISTINA (HM14765) | ● | ● | | | ● | | | ● | | ● | | | | | | |
| NRTH LEEDS PHYSIO/SPRTS INJ (HM15091) | | | | | | ● | ● | | | | | | | | | |
| OWENS, PAULINE (HM15533) | | | | | | | | | | | | | | | | |
| PALLAS, ANDREW (HM15595) | ● | | ● | | ● | ● | | ● | | ● | | | | | ● | |
| PARKS, HILARY (HM15720) | | | | | | | | | | ● | | | | | | |
| PAYNE, AUDREY (HM15861) | | | | | | | | | | | | | | | | |
| POPPLEWELL, MARK (HM16437) | | ● | | | ● | | | | | | | | | | | |
| PRESTON, CATHY (HM16551) | ● | | | | | | | | | | | | | | | |
| RAINTREE HEALTH (HM16893) | ● | ● | ● | | | | | ● | ● | ● | ● | | | | | ● |
| RICHARDSON CLINIC (HM17266) | ● | ● | ● | ● | ● | ● | ● | ● | ● | ● | ● | ● | ● | ● | ● | ● |
| ROTHWELL SPORTS CENTRE (HM17658) | | | | | | | | | | | | | | | | |
| ROUNDHAY CHIROPRACTIC CLINIC (HM17667) | | | | | | | | | | | | | | | | |
| SALTAIRE COMP HEALTH STUDIO (HM17864) | ● | ● | ● | ● | ● | ● | ● | ● | ● | ● | ● | ● | ● | ● | ● | ● |
| SHACKLETON, JOHN A (HM18263) | | | | | | ● | | ● | | | | | | | | |
| SHERQIA, DARULSHAFA (HM18436) | ● | ● | ● | | ● | | | ● | ● | ● | | | | | ● | |
| SMITH, JANET (HM18751) | | | | | | | | | | | | | | | | |
| STEAD, JULIE ANN (HM19164) | | | | | | ● | | ● | | | | | | | | |
| SURGERY (HM19519) | | | | | | ● | ● | ● | | | | | | | | |
| SWAINE, PAULA (HM19565) | | | | | | ● | | ● | | | | | | | | |
| SYKES CLINIC (HM19610) | ● | | | | | | | | | | | | | | | |
| TORNTON, HOWARD (HM20172) | | | | | | ● | | | | | | | | | | |
| TRANSCENDENTAL MEDITATION (HM20285) | | | | | | | | | | | | | | | | |
| WATKINS, JEAN (HM20996) | | | | | ● | | | | | | | | | | ● | |
| WEST YORKSHIRE CLINIC (HM21242) | ● | ● | ● | ● | ● | ● | | ● | ● | ● | | ● | ● | | ● | ● |
| WEST YORKSHIRE M S THRPY CTRE (HM21243) | | | | | | | | | | | | ● | | | | |
| WEST YORKSHIRE PHYSIO CENTRE (HM21244) | | | | | | | | | | | | | | | | |
| WETHERBY PHYSIO PRACTICE (HM21290) | | | | | | | ● | | | | | | | | | |
| WISE, CAROL (HM21732) | ● | ● | ● | ● | ● | ● | ● | ● | ● | ● | ● | ● | ● | ● | ● | ● |
| WOODHOUSE CLINIC (HM21826) | | | | | | ● | | ● | | | | | | | | |

| Business by County with Reference no. | Hair Problems | Halitosis | Hand Problems | Hay Fever | Headaches | Hearing Problems | High Blood Pressure | Hip Complaints | Hyperactivity | Hypoglycaemia | Impotence | Incontinence | Indigestion | Infertility | Influenza | Ingrowing Toenails |
|---|---|---|---|---|---|---|---|---|---|---|---|---|---|---|---|---|
| NATURES WORKROOM (HM14705) | ● | ● | ● | ● | ● | ● | ● | ● | ● | ● | ● | ● | ● | ● | ● | |
| NEILL-HIGGINS, CHRISTINA (HM14765) | | | | ● | ● | | ● | | | | | | ● | ● | ● | |
| NRTH LEEDS PHYSIO/SPRTS INJ (HM15091) | | | ● | | | | | ● | | | | | | | | |
| OWENS, PAULINE (HM15533) | | | ● | ● | ● | ● | | ● | | | | | ● | | ● | |
| PALLAS, ANDREW (HM15595) | | | ● | ● | ● | ● | ● | ● | | ● | | | ● | | ● | |
| PARKS, HILARY (HM15720) | | | | | ● | | ● | | | | | | ● | | | |
| PAYNE, AUDREY (HM15861) | | | | ● | ● | | | | | | | | | | | |
| POPPLEWELL, MARK (HM16437) | | | ● | ● | ● | | ● | ● | | | | ● | ● | ● | | |
| PRESTON, CATHY (HM16551) | | | | | ● | | | | | | | | | | | |
| RAINTREE HEALTH (HM16893) | ● | | | ● | | | ● | | ● | | ● | | ● | | | |
| RICHARDSON CLINIC (HM17266) | ● | ● | ● | ● | ● | ● | ● | ● | ● | ● | ● | ● | ● | ● | ● | |
| ROTHWELL SPORTS CENTRE (HM17658) | | | | | | | | ● | | | | | | | | |
| ROUNDHAY CHIROPRACTIC CLINIC (HM17667) | | | | | ● | | | | | | | | | | | |
| SALTAIRE COMP HEALTH STUDIO (HM17864) | ● | ● | ● | ● | ● | ● | ● | ● | ● | ● | ● | ● | ● | ● | ● | |
| SHACKLETON, JOHN A (HM18263) | | | | | | | | | | | | | | | | |
| SHERQIA, DARULSHAFA (HM18436) | | ● | | ● | ● | | | | | | ● | ● | ● | ● | ● | |
| SMITH, JANET (HM18751) | | | | ● | ● | | | ● | | | | | | | | |
| STEAD, JULIE ANN (HM19164) | | | ● | ● | ● | | ● | | | | | | | | | ● |
| SURGERY (HM19519) | | | ● | | ● | | | ● | | | | | | | | |
| SWAINE, PAULA (HM19565) | | | | | | | | | | | | | | | | ● |
| SYKES CLINIC (HM19610) | | | | | ● | | ● | | | | | | ● | | | |
| TORNTON, HOWARD (HM20172) | | | | | ● | | | ● | | | | | | | | |
| TRANSCENDENTAL MEDITATION (HM20285) | | | | | ● | | | | | | | | | | | |
| WATKINS, JEAN (HM20996) | | | | | ● | | ● | | ● | ● | | ● | ● | | | |
| WEST YORKSHIRE CLINIC (HM21242) | ● | ● | ● | ● | ● | ● | ● | ● | ● | ● | ● | ● | ● | ● | ● | |
| WEST YORKSHIRE M S THRPY CTRE (HM21243) | | | | | ● | | | | | | | | | | | |
| WEST YORKSHIRE PHYSIO CENTRE (HM21244) | | | | | | | | ● | | | | | | | | |
| WETHERBY PHYSIO PRACTICE (HM21290) | | | | | | | | | | | | | | | | |
| WISE, CAROL (HM21732) | ● | ● | ● | ● | ● | ● | ● | ● | ● | ● | ● | ● | ● | ● | ● | |
| WOODHOUSE CLINIC (HM21826) | | | ● | | ● | | | ● | | | | | | | | |

# D - I Conditions treated at Practices/Businesses

Business by County with Reference no.

| Business | Dandruff | Deafness | Depression | Diabetes | Diarrhoea | Digestive Problems | Diverticulitis | Dizziness | Dyslexia | Dyspraxia | Ear Disorders | Eczema | ENT Disorders | Epilepsy | Eye Disorders | Fatigue | Fears | Fertility Problems | Fever | Fibroids | Flatulence | Foot Problems | Fractures |
|---|---|---|---|---|---|---|---|---|---|---|---|---|---|---|---|---|---|---|---|---|---|---|---|
| **IRELAND** | | | | | | | | | | | | | | | | | | | | | | | |
| **COUNTY CAVAN** | | | | | | | | | | | | | | | | | | | | | | | |
| BI-AURA THERAPY (HM02274) | | ● | ● | ● | ● | ● | | ● | ● | | ● | ● | | ● | ● | ● | ● | ● | | ● | ● | | ● |
| **COUNTY CORK** | | | | | | | | | | | | | | | | | | | | | | | |
| ANNAPURNA NATURAL HEALTHCARE (HM00894) | | | ● | | | | | | | | | | | | | ● | ● | | | | | | |
| BROOKFIELD PHYSIOTHERAPY (HM03167) | | | | | | | | | | | | | | | | ● | ● | ● | | | | | ● |
| EAST CORK PHYSIOTHERAPY (HM06511) | | | ● | | ● | ● | | ● | | | | ● | | | ● | ● | ● | ● | ● | ● | | ● | ● |
| HATTERSLEY, LAURENCE (HM09200) | | | | | | | | | | | | | | ● | | | | | | | | | |
| HEALING THERAPIES (HM09354) | | | ● | | | | | | | | | | | | | ● | ● | | | | | | |
| INS-CLINICAL HYP & PSYCHO (HM10661) | | | ● | | | | | | ● | | ● | ● | | | | ● | ● | ● | | | | | |
| JONES, COLEEN (HM11131) | | | ● | | | | | | | | | | | | | | ● | | | | | | |
| KEATING, MARY (HM11379) | | | | | | | | | | | | | | | | | | | | | | ● | |
| MOORE-GROACKE, GILLIAN (DR) (HM14136) | | | ● | | | | | | | | | | | | | | ● | ● | | | | | |
| PAUL DENNEHY - HYPNOTHERAPIST (HM15842) | ● | | ● | | ● | ● | | | ● | ● | | ● | | | | ● | ● | | | | | | |
| RAVEN HILL CHIROPRACTIC CLINIC (HM16964) | | | ● | | ● | ● | ● | ● | | | | ● | | | | ● | ● | ● | | | ● | | |
| SHIATSU (HM18452) | | | ● | | ● | ● | | ● | | | | | | | | ● | ● | | | | ● | | |
| **COUNTY DUBLIN** | | | | | | | | | | | | | | | | | | | | | | | |
| ABELIA COUNSELLING (HM00110) | | | ● | | | | | | | | | | | | | | ● | | | | | | |
| ARDAGH ACUPUNCTURE CLINIC (HM00988) | | | | | ● | ● | | | | | | ● | | | | ● | | ● | | | ● | ● | |
| ARDUNA COUNS & PSYCHOTHPY CTRE (HM00995) | | | ● | | | | | | ● | ● | | | | | | | ● | | | | | | |
| BREE, JOHN (HM02947) | | ● | ● | ● | | ● | ● | ● | | | ● | ● | ● | ● | ● | ● | ● | ● | ● | ● | | ● | |
| B-WELL HYPNOTHERAPY CLINIC (HM03506) | ● | ● | ● | ● | ● | ● | ● | ● | ● | ● | ● | ● | ● | ● | ● | ● | ● | ● | ● | ● | ● | ● | ● |
| CHADHA, PRADEEP K (DR) (HM03933) | | | ● | | | | | | | | | | | | | | ● | | | | | | |
| DUN LAOIRE HEALING ROOM (HM06389) | | | ● | | | | | | | | | | | | | ● | ● | | | | | | |
| FAIRVIEW THERAPY CENTRE (HM07066) | | | ● | ● | | ● | | ● | | | ● | | | | | ● | ● | | | | | | |
| FINISHING TOUCHES (HM07313) | | | | | | | | | | | | | | | | ● | | | | | | | |
| FITZGERALD HYP-PSYCHOTHERAPY (HM07364) | | | ● | | | | | | | | | | | | | ● | ● | | | | | | |
| HEALING PLACE (HM09347) | | | | | ● | ● | ● | | ● | | | | ● | | | ● | | | | | ● | ● | |
| HEALING ROOM - DRUMCONDRA (HM09351) | | | ● | | ● | ● | ● | | | | | | | | | ● | ● | | | | ● | | |
| HEALTH COUNSEL (HM09384) | | | ● | | | | | | | | | | | | | | | | | | | | |
| HERBAL & ACUPUNCTURE (HM09595) | | | | | ● | ● | ● | ● | | | | ● | | | | ● | | ● | | | | | |
| HOWTH COUNSELLING SERVICE (HM10294) | | | ● | | | | | | | | | | | | | | ● | | | | | | |
| INNER CIRCLE HEALING CENTRE (HM10635) | | | ● | | | | ● | | | | | | | | | | ● | | | | | ● | |

| Business | Fungal Infections | Gallstones | Gastrointestinal Problems | Genital Herpes | Gingivitis | Glandular Fever | Glaucoma | Gout | Gum Disease | Hair Problems | Halitosis | Hand Problems | Hay Fever | Headaches | Hearing Problems | High Blood Pressure | Hip Complaints | Hyperactivity | Hypoglycaemia | Impotence | Incontinence | Indigestion | Infertility | Influenza | Ingrowing Toenails |
|---|---|---|---|---|---|---|---|---|---|---|---|---|---|---|---|---|---|---|---|---|---|---|---|---|---|
| **IRELAND** | | | | | | | | | | | | | | | | | | | | | | | | | |
| **COUNTY CAVAN** | | | | | | | | | | | | | | | | | | | | | | | | | |
| BI-AURA THERAPY (HM02274) | | ● | | | | ● | | | | ● | | ● | ● | ● | ● | ● | ● | ● | | ● | ● | ● | ● | ● | |
| **COUNTY CORK** | | | | | | | | | | | | | | | | | | | | | | | | | |
| ANNAPURNA NATURAL HEALTHCARE (HM00894) | | | | | | | | | | | | | | | | | | | | | | | | | |
| BROOKFIELD PHYSIOTHERAPY (HM03167) | | | | | | | | | | | | ● | | ● | | ● | | | | | | ● | ● | | |
| EAST CORK PHYSIOTHERAPY (HM06511) | | | ● | | | | | | | ● | | ● | ● | ● | | ● | ● | | | | ● | ● | ● | | |
| HATTERSLEY, LAURENCE (HM09200) | | | | | | | | | | | | | | ● | | | | | | ● | | | | | |
| HEALING THERAPIES (HM09354) | | | | | | | | | | | | | | ● | | ● | | | | | | | | | |
| INS-CLINICAL HYP & PSYCHO (HM10661) | | | ● | | | | | | | | | | ● | ● | | ● | | | | ● | ● | | ● | | |
| JONES, COLEEN (HM11131) | | | | | | | | | | | | | | | | | | | | | | | | | |
| KEATING, MARY (HM11379) | | | | | | | | | | | | | | | | | ● | | | | | | | | |
| MOORE-GROACKE, GILLIAN (DR) (HM14136) | | | | | | | | | | | | | | ● | | ● | | | | | | | | | |
| PAUL DENNEHY - HYPNOTHERAPIST (HM15842) | | | ● | | | | | ● | | | ● | ● | | ● | | ● | | ● | | ● | ● | ● | ● | | |
| RAVEN HILL CHIROPRACTIC CLINIC (HM16964) | | | ● | | | | | ● | | | ● | ● | ● | ● | ● | ● | ● | | | ● | | ● | ● | | |
| SHIATSU (HM18452) | | | ● | | | | | | | | ● | ● | | ● | | ● | ● | ● | ● | | ● | ● | | ● | |
| **COUNTY DUBLIN** | | | | | | | | | | | | | | | | | | | | | | | | | |
| ABELIA COUNSELLING (HM00110) | | | | | | | | | | | | | | | | | | | | ● | | | | | |
| ARDAGH ACUPUNCTURE CLINIC (HM00988) | | | ● | | | | | | | | | | ● | ● | | | | | | | | ● | | | |
| ARDUNA COUNS & PSYCHOTHPY CTRE (HM00995) | | | | | | | | | | | | | | | | | | | | | | | | | |
| BREE, JOHN (HM02947) | ● | ● | ● | ● | | ● | ● | ● | | | | | ● | ● | ● | ● | ● | ● | | ● | ● | ● | ● | ● | |
| B-WELL HYPNOTHERAPY CLINIC (HM03506) | ● | ● | ● | ● | ● | ● | ● | ● | ● | ● | ● | ● | ● | ● | ● | ● | ● | ● | ● | ● | ● | ● | ● | ● | |
| CHADHA, PRADEEP K (DR) (HM03933) | | | ● | | | | | | | | | | | ● | | ● | | | | ● | | | | | |
| DUN LAOIRE HEALING ROOM (HM06389) | | | | | | | | | | | | | | | | | | | | | | | | | |
| FAIRVIEW THERAPY CENTRE (HM07066) | | | | | | | | | | | | | | ● | | | | ● | | | ● | ● | | | |
| FINISHING TOUCHES (HM07313) | | | | | | | | | | | | | | | | | | | | | | | | | |
| FITZGERALD HYP-PSYCHOTHERAPY (HM07364) | | | | | | | | | | | | | | | | | | ● | | | | | | | |
| HEALING PLACE (HM09347) | | | ● | | | | | ● | | | | | | ● | | | ● | | ● | | | ● | | | |
| HEALING ROOM - DRUMCONDRA (HM09351) | | ● | ● | | | ● | | | | | ● | | | ● | | ● | | | | | | ● | | | |
| HEALTH COUNSEL (HM09384) | | | | | | | | | | | | | | | | | | | | | | | | | |
| HERBAL & ACUPUNCTURE (HM09595) | ● | ● | ● | ● | | ● | | | | ● | ● | | | ● | | ● | ● | | ● | | | | ● | ● | |
| HOWTH COUNSELLING SERVICE (HM10294) | | | | | | | | | | | | | | | | | | ● | | | | | | | |
| INNER CIRCLE HEALING CENTRE (HM10635) | | | | | | | | | | | | | | | | | | | | | | | | | |

# D - I Conditions treated at Practices/Businesses

| Business by County with Reference no. | Dandruff | Deafness | Depression | Diabetes | Diarrhoea | Digestive Problems | Diverticulitis | Dizziness | Dyslexia | Dyspraxia | Ear Disorders | Eczema | ENT Disorders | Epilepsy | Eye Disorders | Fatigue |
|---|---|---|---|---|---|---|---|---|---|---|---|---|---|---|---|---|
| INSTITUTE OF PSYCHOSOCIAL MED (HM10678) | | | ● | | | | | | | | | | | | | |
| KELLY, ANGELINA (HM11427) | | | ● | | ● | ● | | ● | | | | ● | | | | ● |
| LALLOO'S ACUPUNCTURE CLINIC (HM11881) | ● | ● | ● | ● | ● | ● | ● | ● | | | | ● | | | | ● |
| LITTLEJOHN CLINIC (HM12472) | | | | | | ● | | ● | | | ● | | | | | |
| MACLIAM, FIONNULA (HM12867) | | | ● | | | | | | | | | | | | | |
| MCHUGH HYPNOSIS & REFLEXOLOGY (HM13509) | | | ● | | | ● | ● | | | | | | | | | ● |
| MELT/TEMPLE BAR NATURAL (HM13716) | ● | | ● | ● | ● | ● | | ● | | | ● | ● | | ● | ● | ● |
| NATURAL SOLUTIONS (HM14625) | | | ● | | | ● | | | ● | ● | | | | | | ● |
| NUALA WOULFE BEAUTY SALON (HM15101) | | | | | | ● | | | | | | | | | | ● |
| RATHMINES CHIROPRACTIC CENTRE (HM16957) | | | | | | | | | | | | | | | | |
| T C M CENTRE (HM19639) | | | ● | ● | ● | ● | ● | ● | | | ● | ● | ● | | ● | ● |
| THERAPEUTICS (HM19888) | | | ● | | ● | | | | | | | | | | | |
| THEW, NIN (HM19916) | | | ● | | ● | ● | | ● | | | | ● | ● | | ● | ● |
| TOBIN, ROSALEEN (HM20105) | | | ● | | | | | | | | | | | | | ● |
| TRAD CHINESE MEDICINE/MASSAGE (HM20216) | | | | | ● | ● | ● | ● | | | | | | | | ● |
| TROY, ROSEMARY (HM20349) | | | ● | | | | | | | | | | | | | |
| COUNTY GALWAY | | | | | | | | | | | | | | | | |
| ALEXANDER TECHNIQUE CENTRE (HM00557) | | | ● | | | ● | | | | | | | | | | ● |
| BODYWATCH (HM02636) | | | | | | | | | | | | | | | | |
| PRENDERGAST, KARL (HM16542) | | | | | | | | | | | ● | | | | | |
| COUNTY KERRY | | | | | | | | | | | | | | | | |
| ACUPUNCTURE CLINIC (HM00286) | ● | | ● | | ● | ● | | ● | | | ● | ● | ● | ● | | ● |
| WOODLAWN HOLISTIC THERAPY CTRE (HM21834) | | | ● | | | | | | | | | | | | | ● |
| COUNTY KILDARE | | | | | | | | | | | | | | | | |
| GREEN ROAD HEALING CENTRE (HM08441) | ● | | ● | | ● | ● | ● | | | | | ● | | | | ● |
| SHENANDOAH HEALING (HM18395) | | | ● | | | | | | | | | ● | ● | | | ● |
| COUNTY KILKENNY | | | | | | | | | | | | | | | | |
| BLUE ROOM (HM02528) | | | ● | | | ● | | ● | | | | | | | | ● |
| DULCAMARA (HM06375) | | | | | | ● | | | | | | ● | | | | ● |
| HOLISTIC HEALING CENTRE (HM09965) | | | ● | | | ● | | | | | | | | | | ● |
| COUNTY LIMERICK | | | | | | | | | | | | | | | | |
| HOLISTIC HEALING (HM09960) | | | ● | ● | | ● | | ● | | | ● | | | | | ● |
| COUNTY LOUTH | | | | | | | | | | | | | | | | |
| HOLISTIC SOL NTRL HEALING CTRE (HM09989) | | | ● | | | | | | | | | | | | | ● |

| Business by County with Reference no. | Fears | Fertility Problems | Fever | Fibroids | Flatulence | Foot Problems | Fractures | Fungal Infections | Gallstones | Gastrointestinal Problems | Genital Herpes | Gingivitis | Glandular Fever | Glaucoma | Gout | Gum Disease |
|---|---|---|---|---|---|---|---|---|---|---|---|---|---|---|---|---|
| INSTITUTE OF PSYCHOSOCIAL MED (HM10678) | ● | | | | | | | | | | | | | | | |
| KELLY, ANGELINA (HM11427) | ● | | ● | | ● | ● | | ● | | ● | | | | | ● | |
| LALLOO'S ACUPUNCTURE CLINIC (HM11881) | ● | | ● | | ● | ● | | | | ● | | | | | ● | |
| LITTLEJOHN CLINIC (HM12472) | | | | | | ● | ● | | | | | | | | | |
| MACLIAM, FIONNULA (HM12867) | ● | | | | | | | | | | | | | | | |
| MCHUGH HYPNOSIS & REFLEXOLOGY (HM13509) | ● | | | | | | | | ● | ● | | | | | | |
| MELT/TEMPLE BAR NATURAL (HM13716) | ● | | | ● | ● | | | ● | | ● | ● | | | ● | ● | |
| NATURAL SOLUTIONS (HM14625) | ● | | | | | | | ● | | | | | | | | |
| NUALA WOULFE BEAUTY SALON (HM15101) | | | | | | | | | | | | | | | | |
| RATHMINES CHIROPRACTIC CENTRE (HM16957) | | | | | | | | | | | | | | | | |
| T C M CENTRE (HM19639) | | ● | ● | ● | ● | ● | ● | ● | ● | ● | | ● | ● | | ● | ● |
| THERAPEUTICS (HM19888) | | | | | | | | | | | | | | | | |
| THEW, NIN (HM19916) | ● | ● | | ● | ● | ● | | | | ● | | | ● | | ● | |
| TOBIN, ROSALEEN (HM20105) | ● | | | | | | | | | | | | | | | |
| TRAD CHINESE MEDICINE/MASSAGE (HM20216) | | | | | ● | | | | ● | | | | | | ● | |
| TROY, ROSEMARY (HM20349) | ● | | | | | | | | | | | | | | | |
| COUNTY GALWAY | | | | | | | | | | | | | | | | |
| ALEXANDER TECHNIQUE CENTRE (HM00557) | ● | | | | | | | | | | | | | | | |
| BODYWATCH (HM02636) | ● | | | | | | | | | | | | | | | |
| PRENDERGAST, KARL (HM16542) | | | | | | ● | | | | | | | | | | |
| COUNTY KERRY | | | | | | | | | | | | | | | | |
| ACUPUNCTURE CLINIC (HM00286) | | ● | ● | ● | ● | | | | ● | ● | | | ● | | ● | |
| WOODLAWN HOLISTIC THERAPY CTRE (HM21834) | | | | | | | | | | | | | | | | |
| COUNTY KILDARE | | | | | | | | | | | | | | | | |
| GREEN ROAD HEALING CENTRE (HM08441) | | | ● | | ● | | | ● | ● | ● | | | | | ● | |
| SHENANDOAH HEALING (HM18395) | ● | | | | | ● | ● | | | | | | | | | |
| COUNTY KILKENNY | | | | | | | | | | | | | | | | |
| BLUE ROOM (HM02528) | ● | | | | | | | | | ● | | | | | | |
| DULCAMARA (HM06375) | | ● | ● | | | | | | ● | ● | | | ● | | ● | |
| HOLISTIC HEALING CENTRE (HM09965) | ● | | | | | ● | | | | | | | | | | |
| COUNTY LIMERICK | | | | | | | | | | | | | | | | |
| HOLISTIC HEALING (HM09960) | | | | | | | | | | | | | | | | |
| COUNTY LOUTH | | | | | | | | | | | | | | | | |
| HOLISTIC SOL NTRL HEALING CTRE (HM09989) | ● | | | | | | | | | | | | | | | |

| Business by County with Reference no. | Hair Problems | Halitosis | Hand Problems | Hay Fever | Headaches | Hearing Problems | High Blood Pressure | Hip Complaints | Hyperactivity | Hypoglycaemia | Impotence | Incontinence | Indigestion | Infertility | Influenza | Ingrowing Toenails |
|---|---|---|---|---|---|---|---|---|---|---|---|---|---|---|---|---|
| INSTITUTE OF PSYCHOSOCIAL MED (HM10678) | | | | | | | | | | | | | | | | |
| KELLY, ANGELINA (HM11427) | | | | ● | ● | | | | ● | | | | ● | | ● | |
| LALLOO'S ACUPUNCTURE CLINIC (HM11881) | ● | ● | ● | ● | ● | ● | ● | ● | ● | | ● | | ● | | ● | |
| LITTLEJOHN CLINIC (HM12472) | | | | | ● | | | ● | | | | | | | | |
| MACLIAM, FIONNULA (HM12867) | | | | | | | | | | | ● | | | | | |
| MCHUGH HYPNOSIS & REFLEXOLOGY (HM13509) | | | | | ● | | ● | ● | | | | | | | | |
| MELT/TEMPLE BAR NATURAL (HM13716) | | | | ● | | ● | ● | | | | ● | | ● | ● | | |
| NATURAL SOLUTIONS (HM14625) | | | | | | | ● | | ● | ● | ● | | | | | |
| NUALA WOULFE BEAUTY SALON (HM15101) | | | | | | | | | | | | | ● | | | |
| RATHMINES CHIROPRACTIC CENTRE (HM16957) | | | | | | | | ● | | | | | | | | |
| T C M CENTRE (HM19639) | ● | ● | ● | ● | ● | | ● | ● | ● | ● | ● | ● | ● | ● | ● | |
| THERAPEUTICS (HM19888) | | | | ● | | | | | | | | | | | | |
| THEW, NIN (HM19916) | | | ● | | | | ● | | | | ● | ● | ● | ● | | |
| TOBIN, ROSALEEN (HM20105) | | | | | ● | | | | | | | | | | | |
| TRAD CHINESE MEDICINE/MASSAGE (HM20216) | | | | ● | ● | | | | | | | | | | | |
| TROY, ROSEMARY (HM20349) | | | | | | | | | | | | | | | | |
| COUNTY GALWAY | | | | | | | | | | | | | | | | |
| ALEXANDER TECHNIQUE CENTRE (HM00557) | | | | | ● | | ● | | | | | | ● | | | |
| BODYWATCH (HM02636) | | | | | | | | | | | | | | | | |
| PRENDERGAST, KARL (HM16542) | | | ● | | ● | | | ● | | | | | | | | |
| COUNTY KERRY | | | | | | | | | | | | | | | | |
| ACUPUNCTURE CLINIC (HM00286) | | ● | | ● | ● | | ● | ● | ● | ● | ● | | ● | ● | ● | |
| WOODLAWN HOLISTIC THERAPY CTRE (HM21834) | | | | | ● | | ● | | | | | | | | | |
| COUNTY KILDARE | | | | | | | | | | | | | | | | |
| GREEN ROAD HEALING CENTRE (HM08441) | | ● | | ● | ● | | ● | | ● | | | | ● | | ● | |
| SHENANDOAH HEALING (HM18395) | | | | | ● | | ● | | | | | | | | | |
| COUNTY KILKENNY | | | | | | | | | | | | | | | | |
| BLUE ROOM (HM02528) | | | | | | | ● | | | | | | ● | | | |
| DULCAMARA (HM06375) | | | | ● | ● | | ● | | | | | | | ● | ● | |
| HOLISTIC HEALING CENTRE (HM09965) | | | ● | ● | ● | | ● | ● | | | | | | | | |
| COUNTY LIMERICK | | | | | | | | | | | | | | | | |
| HOLISTIC HEALING (HM09960) | | | | ● | ● | | ● | | | | | | ● | | | |
| COUNTY LOUTH | | | | | | | | | | | | | | | | |
| HOLISTIC SOL NTRL HEALING CTRE (HM09989) | | | | | | | | | | | | | | | | |

# D - I Conditions treated at Practices/Businesses

| Business by County with Reference no. | Dandruff | Deafness | Depression | Diabetes | Diarrhoea | Digestive Problems | Diverticulitis | Dizziness | Dyslexia | Dyspraxia | Ear Disorders | Eczema | ENT Disorders | Epilepsy | Eye Disorders | Fatigue | Fears | Fertility Problems | Fever | Fibroids | Flatulence | Foot Problems | Fractures | Fungal Infections |
|---|---|---|---|---|---|---|---|---|---|---|---|---|---|---|---|---|---|---|---|---|---|---|---|---|
| COUNTY MAYO | | | | | | | | | | | | | | | | | | | | | | | | |
| NATURAL HEALING CENTRE (HM14547) | | ● | ● | ● | ● | ● | | ● | ● | | ● | ● | ● | | ● | ● | ● | ● | ● | ● | ● | ● | ● | ● |
| TOBAR PHADRAIC (HM20102) | | | | | | | | | | | | | | | | | | | | | | | | |
| COUNTY MEATH | | | | | | | | | | | | | | | | | | | | | | | | |
| NATURAL MEDICINE CENTRE (HM14610) | ● | | ● | | ● | ● | ● | ● | | | ● | ● | ● | ● | ● | ● | | ● | ● | ● | ● | | | ● |
| COUNTY MONAGHAN | | | | | | | | | | | | | | | | | | | | | | | | |
| AROMA - ZONE (HM01043) | | | | | | | | | | | | | | | | | | | | | | ● | | |
| HEALTHY CHOICES (HM09426) | | | | | ● | ● | | | | | | | | | | ● | | | | | ● | ● | | ● |
| NORTHAMBER (HM15050) | ● | ● | ● | ● | ● | ● | ● | ● | | | ● | ● | ● | ● | ● | ● | ● | ● | ● | ● | ● | ● | ● | ● |
| COUNTY ROSCOMMON | | | | | | | | | | | | | | | | | | | | | | | | |
| HOLISTIC HEALTH FARM (HM09980) | | | | | | ● | | | | | | | | | | ● | ● | ● | | | | ● | | |
| COUNTY SLIGO | | | | | | | | | | | | | | | | | | | | | | | | |
| ANAM CHARA COUNSELLING (HM00802) | | | ● | | | | | | | | | | | ● | | ● | ● | | | | | | | |
| SLIGO CHIROPRACTIC (HM18686) | | ● | ● | | ● | ● | | ● | ● | | | | ● | | | ● | | ● | | | | ● | | |
| COUNTY TIPPERARY | | | | | | | | | | | | | | | | | | | | | | | | |
| KINSELLA, MARIE (HM11693) | | | ● | | | | | | | | | | | | | | | | | | | | | |
| COUNTY WESTMEATH | | | | | | | | | | | | | | | | | | | | | | | | |
| HOWE, JAN (HM10263) | | | | | | ● | | | | | | | | | | ● | | | | | | | | |
| COUNTY WEXFORD | | | | | | | | | | | | | | | | | | | | | | | | |
| FOURTH MOUNTAIN HOM AND ACU (HM07622) | ● | | ● | ● | ● | ● | ● | ● | | | ● | ● | ● | | ● | ● | ● | ● | ● | ● | ● | ● | | ● |
| JEFFARIES, PHILIP (HM10958) | | | | | | | | ● | | | | | | | | | | | | | | ● | | |
| JEFFARIES, PHILIP (HM10957) | | | | | | | | ● | | | | | | | | | | | | | | ● | | |
| MURPHY, MARY (HM14388) | | | ● | | | | | | | | | | | | | ● | ● | | | | | | | |
| OSTEOPATHIC PRACTICE (HM15474) | | | | | | | | | | | | | | | | | | | | | | | | |
| COUNTY WICKLOW | | | | | | | | | | | | | | | | | | | | | | | | |
| ARKLOW NATURAL HEALING CENTRE (HM01007) | ● | | ● | ● | ● | ● | | ● | | | | ● | | | | ● | ● | ● | ● | ● | ● | ● | ● | ● |
| HOLISTIC OPTIONS (HM09985) | ● | ● | ● | ● | ● | ● | ● | ● | ● | ● | | ● | ● | | | ● | ● | ● | | ● | ● | ● | ● | ● |
| JAMESON PERSONAL EXCELLENCE (HM10903) | | | ● | | | | | | | | ● | ● | | | | ● | ● | | | | | | | |
| MARK GOULDING - ACUPUNCTURIST (HM13107) | | | ● | ● | ● | ● | ● | ● | | | ● | ● | ● | | ● | ● | ● | ● | ● | ● | ● | | | |

| Business by County with Reference no. | Gallstones | Gastrointestinal Problems | Genital Herpes | Gingivitis | Glandular Fever | Glaucoma | Gout | Gum Disease | Hair Problems | Halitosis | Hand Problems | Hay Fever | Headaches | Hearing Problems | High Blood Pressure | Hip Complaints | Hyperactivity | Hypoglycaemia | Impotence | Incontinence | Indigestion | Infertility | Influenza | Ingrowing Toenails |
|---|---|---|---|---|---|---|---|---|---|---|---|---|---|---|---|---|---|---|---|---|---|---|---|---|
| COUNTY MAYO | | | | | | | | | | | | | | | | | | | | | | | | |
| NATURAL HEALING CENTRE (HM14547) | ● | ● | | ● | ● | ● | ● | ● | | | ● | ● | ● | ● | ● | ● | ● | | ● | ● | ● | ● | ● | |
| TOBAR PHADRAIC (HM20102) | | | | | | | | | | | | ● | ● | | | | | | | | | | | |
| COUNTY MEATH | | | | | | | | | | | | | | | | | | | | | | | | |
| NATURAL MEDICINE CENTRE (HM14610) | ● | ● | ● | ● | ● | | ● | ● | ● | ● | | ● | ● | | ● | ● | ● | | ● | ● | ● | ● | ● | |
| COUNTY MONAGHAN | | | | | | | | | | | | | | | | | | | | | | | | |
| AROMA - ZONE (HM01043) | | | | | | | | | ● | | | | ● | | | | | | | | | | | |
| HEALTHY CHOICES (HM09426) | ● | ● | | | | | ● | | | | ● | ● | ● | | | ● | | | | | ● | | | |
| NORTHAMBER (HM15050) | ● | ● | ● | ● | ● | | ● | ● | ● | ● | ● | ● | ● | ● | ● | ● | ● | ● | ● | ● | ● | ● | ● | |
| COUNTY ROSCOMMON | | | | | | | | | | | | | | | | | | | | | | | | |
| HOLISTIC HEALTH FARM (HM09980) | | | | | | | | | | | | | ● | | | | | | | | | | | |
| COUNTY SLIGO | | | | | | | | | | | | | | | | | | | | | | | | |
| ANAM CHARA COUNSELLING (HM00802) | | | | | | | | | | | | | | | | | | | ● | | | | | |
| SLIGO CHIROPRACTIC (HM18686) | ● | ● | | | | | | | | | ● | ● | ● | ● | ● | ● | ● | | ● | ● | ● | ● | ● | |
| COUNTY TIPPERARY | | | | | | | | | | | | | | | | | | | | | | | | |
| KINSELLA, MARIE (HM11693) | | | | | | | | | | | | | | | | | | | | | | ● | | |
| COUNTY WESTMEATH | | | | | | | | | | | | | | | | | | | | | | | | |
| HOWE, JAN (HM10263) | | ● | | | | | | | | | | | ● | | | | | ● | | | | | | |
| COUNTY WEXFORD | | | | | | | | | | | | | | | | | | | | | | | | |
| FOURTH MOUNTAIN HOM AND ACU (HM07622) | | ● | ● | ● | ● | | ● | ● | ● | ● | ● | ● | ● | | ● | ● | ● | | | | ● | ● | ● | |
| JEFFARIES, PHILIP (HM10958) | | | | | | | | | | | ● | | | | | | | | | | | | | |
| JEFFARIES, PHILIP (HM10957) | | | | | | | | | | | ● | | | | | | | | | | | | | |
| MURPHY, MARY (HM14388) | | | | | | | | | | | | | ● | | ● | | | | | | | | | |
| OSTEOPATHIC PRACTICE (HM15474) | | ● | | | | | | | | | ● | | ● | | | ● | | | | | | | | |
| COUNTY WICKLOW | | | | | | | | | | | | | | | | | | | | | | | | |
| ARKLOW NATURAL HEALING CENTRE (HM01007) | | ● | ● | | | | | | ● | | | ● | ● | | ● | | | | | | ● | ● | ● | |
| HOLISTIC OPTIONS (HM09985) | ● | ● | | | | ● | ● | ● | ● | ● | ● | ● | ● | ● | ● | ● | ● | | | | ● | | ● | |
| JAMESON PERSONAL EXCELLENCE (HM10903) | | ● | | | | | | | | | | | ● | | | | | | ● | ● | | | | |
| MARK GOULDING - ACUPUNCTURIST (HM13107) | ● | ● | | | | | ● | ● | | | ● | ● | ● | ● | ● | ● | ● | | ● | ● | ● | ● | ● | |

# D - I Conditions treated at Practices/Businesses

| Business by County with Reference no. | Dandruff | Deafness | Depression | Diabetes | Diarrhoea | Digestive Problems | Diverticulitis | Dizziness | Dyslexia | Dyspraxia | Ear Disorders | Eczema | ENT Disorders | Epilepsy | Eye Disorders | Fatigue | Fears | Fertility Problems | Fever | Fibroids | Flatulence | Foot Problems | Fractures | Fungal Infections | Gallstones | Gastrointestinal Problems | Genital Herpes | Gingivitis | Glandular Fever | Glaucoma | Gout | Gum Disease | Hair Problems | Halitosis | Hand Problems | Hay Fever | Headaches | Hearing Problems | High Blood Pressure | Hip Complaints | Hyperactivity | Hypoglycaemia | Impotence | Incontinence | Indigestion | Infertility | Influenza | Ingrowing Toenails |
|---|---|---|---|---|---|---|---|---|---|---|---|---|---|---|---|---|---|---|---|---|---|---|---|---|---|---|---|---|---|---|---|---|---|---|---|---|---|---|---|---|---|---|---|---|---|---|---|---|
| NORTHERN IRELAND | | | | | | | | | | | | | | | | | | | | | | | | | | | | | | | | | | | | | | | | | | | | | | | | |
| COUNTY ANTRIM | | | | | | | | | | | | | | | | | | | | | | | | | | | | | | | | | | | | | | | | | | | | | | | | |
| ACTIVE BALANCE CLINIC (HM00189) | | ● | ● | ● | ● | ● | ● | ● | | | ● | ● | ● | | ● | ● | ● | | | ● | ● | ● | | | ● | | | ● | | | ● | ● | | ● | ● | | ● | ● | ● | ● | ● | ● | | ● | ● | | | |
| ALOE VERA (HM00669) | ● | | ● | ● | ● | ● | ● | ● | | | ● | ● | | | ● | ● | | ● | ● | | | | | ● | ● | | ● | ● | | | ● | ● | ● | | ● | ● | ● | ● | ● | ● | | | | | ● | | ● | |
| ANTRIM CHIROPRACTIC CLINIC (HM00923) | | | | | | | | | | | | | | | | | | | | | | | | | | | | | | | | | | | | | ● | | | ● | | | | | | | | |
| BALLYCLARE CHIROPRACTIC CLINIC (HM01636) | | | | | | | | | | | | | | | | | | | | | | | | | | | | | | | | | | | | | ● | | | ● | | | | | | | | |
| BALLYMONEY CHIROPRACTIC CLINIC (HM01639) | | | | ● | | | | | | | ● | | | | | | | | | | | | | | | | | | | | | | | | | | ● | | | ● | | | | | | | | |
| CHIROPODIST (HM04290) | | | | | | | | | | | | | | | | | | | | | | ● | | ● | | | | | | | | | | | | | | | | | | | | | | | | |
| CREGAGH CHIROPRACTIC CLINIC (HM05412) | | | | | | | | | | | | | | | | | | | | | | | | | | | | | | | | | | | | | ● | | | ● | | | | | | | | |
| EARLS, JAMES (HM06497) | | | | | | | | | | | | | | | | | | | | | | | | | | | | | | | | | | | | | | | ● | ● | | | | | | | | |
| FINAGHY CHIROPRACTIC CLINIC (HM07295) | | | | | | | | | | | | | | | | | | | | | | | | | | | | | | | | | | | | | ● | | | ● | | | | | | | | |
| FLORENCE SHARPE CHIROPODIST (HM07431) | | | | | | | | | | | | | | | | | | | | | | ● | | ● | | | | | | | | | | | | | | | | | | | | | | | | |
| FRAMAR NATURAL HEALTH CLINIC (HM07654) | ● | | ● | ● | ● | ● | ● | ● | | | ● | ● | | | ● | ● | | ● | | | ● | ● | | ● | ● | ● | | ● | | | ● | | ● | ● | | ● | ● | | ● | | | | ● | | ● | ● | ● | |
| GIVEN, CLIVE (HM08115) | ● | ● | ● | ● | ● | ● | ● | ● | ● | ● | ● | ● | ● | ● | ● | ● | ● | ● | ● | ● | ● | ● | ● | ● | ● | ● | ● | ● | ● | ● | ● | ● | ● | ● | ● | ● | ● | ● | ● | ● | ● | ● | ● | ● | ● | ● | ● | |
| GLENGORMLEY CHIRO CLINIC (HM08151) | | | | | | | | | | | | | | | | | | | | | | | | | | | | | | | | | | | | | ● | | | ● | | | | | | | | |
| LAMBERT, RACHEL (HM11901) | | | ● | | | | | | | | | | | | | ● | | | | | | | | | | | | | | | | | | | | | ● | | | | | | | | ● | | | |
| LISBURN CHIROPRACTIC CLINIC (HM12452) | | | | | | | | | | | | | | | | | | | | | | | | | | | | | | | | | | | | | ● | | | ● | | | | | | | | |
| MAXWELL, MARY (HM13337) | | | ● | ● | | ● | | | | | | | | | | ● | | | | | | ● | | ● | | | | | | | | | | | | | | | ● | ● | | | | | ● | | | |
| MCCARTNEY, W J (HM13401) | | | | | | | | | | | | | | | | | | | | | | ● | | ● | | | | | | | | | | | | | | | | | | | | | | | | |
| MCCRYSTALS NATUROPATHIC CENTRE (HM13436) | ● | | ● | | ● | ● | ● | ● | | | ● | ● | ● | ● | ● | ● | ● | ● | ● | ● | ● | ● | ● | ● | ● | ● | ● | ● | ● | | ● | ● | ● | ● | ● | ● | ● | ● | ● | ● | ● | ● | ● | ● | ● | ● | ● | |
| MCCULLY, JOAN (HM13437) | | | | | | | | | | | | | | | | | | | | | | ● | | ● | | | | | | | | | | | | | | | | | | | | | | | | |
| MYSTIC SCHEHERAZADE (HM14445) | | | ● | | | | | | | | | | | | | | | | | | | | | | | | | | | | | | | | | | | | | | | | | | | | | |
| REAY, H (HM17004) | | | | | | | | | | | | | | | | | | | | | | ● | ● | | | | | | | | | | | | | | | | | | | | | | | | | |
| SCRABO HEALTH PRODUCTS (HM18143) | ● | ● | ● | | ● | ● | ● | | | | ● | ● | ● | | ● | ● | ● | ● | ● | ● | ● | ● | | ● | ● | ● | | ● | ● | | ● | ● | ● | ● | ● | ● | ● | | ● | | ● | ● | ● | ● | ● | ● | ● | |
| STEWART, S (HM19276) | | | | | | | | | | | | | | | | | | | | | | ● | | ● | | | | | | | | | | | | | | | | | | | | | | | | |
| TODD, TREVOR (HM20109) | | | | | | | | | | | | | | | | | | | | | | ● | | ● | | | | | | | | | | | | | | | | | | | | | | | | |
| W M RYAN AND SON (HM20722) | | | | | | | | ● | | | | | | | | | | | | | | ● | | | | | | | | | | | | | | | ● | | | | | | | | | | | |
| YARO (HM21991) | | | ● | | | ● | | | | | | | | | | | | | | | | | | | | | | | | | | | | | | | ● | | | | | | | | | | | |
| COUNTY ARMAGH | | | | | | | | | | | | | | | | | | | | | | | | | | | | | | | | | | | | | | | | | | | | | | | | |
| CAMPBELL, FIONA (HM03598) | | | | | | | | | | | | | | | | | | | | | | | | | | | | | | | | | | | | | | | | ● | | | | | | | | |
| CRAIGAVON CHIROPRACTIC CLINIC (HM05355) | | | | | | | | | | | | | | | | | | | | | | | ● | | | | | | | | | | | | | | ● | | | ● | | | | | | | | |
| LYON, HARRIETTE (HM12780) | | | | | | | | | | | | | | | | | | | | | | ● | | ● | | | | | | | | | | | | | | | | | | | | | | | | |
| WILLIS, IAN (HM21614) | | | | ● | | | | | | | | | | | | | | | | | | ● | | ● | | | | | | | | | | | | | | | | | | | | | | | | |

# D - I Conditions treated at Practices/Businesses

Business by County with Reference no.

| Business | Dandruff | Deafness | Depression | Diabetes | Diarrhoea | Digestive Problems | Diverticulitis | Dizziness | Dyslexia | Dyspraxia | Ear Disorders | Eczema | ENT Disorders | Epilepsy | Eye Disorders | Fatigue | Fears | Fertility Problems | Fever | Fibroids | Flatulence | Foot Problems | Fractures | Fungal Infections |
|---|---|---|---|---|---|---|---|---|---|---|---|---|---|---|---|---|---|---|---|---|---|---|---|---|
| **COUNTY DOWN** | | | | | | | | | | | | | | | | | | | | | | | | |
| ARDS CHIROPRACTIC CLINIC (HM00993) | | | | | | | | | | | | | | | | | | | | | | | | |
| BANGOR CHIROPRACTIC CLINIC (HM01659) | | | | | | | | | | | | | | | | | | | | | | | | |
| BANGOR OSTEOPATHIC CLINIC (HM01660) | | | | | | | | | | | | | | | | | | | | | | | | |
| CHIROPRACTICE (HM04405) | | | | | | | | | | | | | | | | | | | | | | ● | | ● |
| COCHRANE, NIALL (HM04764) | | | | | | | | | | | | | | | | | | | | | | ● | | ● |
| HADDEN, MARLENE (HM08687) | | | ● | | ● | ● | | ● | | | | ● | | ● | | ● | | ● | | | | | | |
| LYCIUM CENTRE (HM12755) | | | | | ● | ● | | | | | | ● | | | | ● | | | | ● | ● | ● | | |
| MCCARTAN, DEBORAH (HM13392) | | | | | | | | | | | | | | | | | | | | | | ● | | ● |
| MCCLURG, T A (HM13412) | | | | ● | | | | | | | | | | | | | | | | | | ● | ● | ● |
| MCCUTCHEON, TINA (HM13441) | | | ● | | | ● | ● | | | | | | | | | ● | | | | | | | | |
| NEWRY CHIROPRACTIC CLINIC (HM14886) | | | | | | | | | | | | | | | | | | | | | | | ● | |
| NOBLE, ANDREW (DR) (HM14968) | | | | | | | | | | | | | | | | | | | | | | | | |
| NORTH DOWN CLINIC (HM15023) | | | | | | | | | ● | | | | | ● | | ● | | | | | | | | |
| PRINGLE CHIROPRACTIC (HM16626) | | | ● | | | ● | | ● | | | | | | | | ● | | | | | | ● | | |
| QUINN, BARBARA (HM16808) | | | | | | ● | | | | | | | | | | | | | | | | ● | | |
| REFLEXOLOGY CLINIC (HM17092) | | | | | | ● | ● | | | | | | | | | | | ● | | | | | | |
| YOGA CENTRE OF IRELAND (HM22023) | | | | | | | | | | | | | | | | | | | | | | | | |
| **COUNTY FERMANAGH** | | | | | | | | | | | | | | | | | | | | | | | | |
| ENNISKILLEN CHIRO CLINIC (HM06844) | | | | | | | | | | | | | | | | | | | | | | | | |
| **COUNTY LONDONDERRY** | | | | | | | | | | | | | | | | | | | | | | | | |
| CLARENDON CHIROPRACTIC CLINIC (HM04539) | | | | | | | | | | | | | | | | | | | | | | | | |
| CLAUDY CHIROPRACTIC CLINIC (HM04612) | | | | | | | | | | | | | | | | | | | | | | | | |
| CURRAN, MAUREEN (HM05630) | | | | | | | | | | | | | ● | | | | | | | | | | | |
| DISPENSERY (HM06117) | ● | ● | ● | | ● | ● | ● | ● | ● | ● | ● | ● | ● | ● | ● | ● | ● | ● | ● | ● | ● | ● | ● | ● |
| EQUILIBRIUM HOLISTIC CLINIC (HM06875) | | | ● | | | | | | | | | | | | | ● | | | | | | | | |
| FEET FIRST (HM07174) | | | | | | | | | | | | | | | | | | | | | | ● | | ● |
| FOYLE HYPNOTHERAPY CENTRE (HM07646) | | | ● | | | | | | | | | ● | | | | ● | ● | ● | | | | | | |
| LIFE TREE (HM12350) | | | ● | | | | | | | | | ● | | | ● | ● | ● | | | | ● | | | ● |
| MAGHERAFELT CHIRO CLINIC (HM12906) | | | | | | | | | | | | | | | | | | | | | | | | |
| **COUNTY TYRONE** | | | | | | | | | | | | | | | | | | | | | | | | |
| COOKSTOWN HERBAL CLINIC (HM05073) | ● | ● | ● | ● | ● | ● | ● | ● | ● | ● | ● | ● | ● | ● | ● | ● | ● | ● | ● | ● | ● | ● | ● | ● |
| DUNGANNON CHIROPRACTIC CLINIC (HM06405) | | | | | | | | | | | | | | | | | | | | | | | | |
| ROSEWOOD HEALTH CLINIC (HM17630) | ● | ● | ● | ● | ● | ● | ● | ● | ● | ● | ● | ● | ● | ● | ● | ● | ● | ● | ● | ● | ● | ● | ● | ● |

| Business | Gallstones | Gastrointestinal Problems | Genital Herpes | Gingivitis | Glandular Fever | Glaucoma | Gout | Gum Disease | Hair Problems | Halitosis | Hand Problems | Hay Fever | Headaches | Hearing Problems | High Blood Pressure | Hip Complaints | Hyperactivity | Hypoglycaemia | Impotence | Incontinence | Indigestion | Infertility | Influenza | Ingrowing Toenails |
|---|---|---|---|---|---|---|---|---|---|---|---|---|---|---|---|---|---|---|---|---|---|---|---|---|
| **COUNTY DOWN** | | | | | | | | | | | | | | | | | | | | | | | | |
| ARDS CHIROPRACTIC CLINIC (HM00993) | | | | | | | | | | | | | ● | | | ● | | | | | | | | |
| BANGOR CHIROPRACTIC CLINIC (HM01659) | | | | | | | | | | | | | ● | | | ● | | | | | | | | |
| BANGOR OSTEOPATHIC CLINIC (HM01660) | | | | | | | | | | | | | ● | | | | | | | | | | | |
| CHIROPRACTICE (HM04405) | | | | | | | | | | | | | ● | | | ● | | | | | | | | |
| COCHRANE, NIALL (HM04764) | | | | | | | | | | | | | | | | | | | | | | | | |
| HADDEN, MARLENE (HM08687) | | | | | | | | | | | | | ● | ● | ● | | | | | | | | | |
| LYCIUM CENTRE (HM12755) | | ● | | | | | | | | | | ● | ● | | ● | | | | | | | | | |
| MCCARTAN, DEBORAH (HM13392) | | | | | | | | | | | | | | | | | | | | | | | | |
| MCCLURG, T A (HM13412) | | | | | | | ● | | | | | | | | | ● | | | | | | | | |
| MCCUTCHEON, TINA (HM13441) | | | | | | | | | | | | | | | | ● | | ● | | | ● | | | |
| NEWRY CHIROPRACTIC CLINIC (HM14886) | | | | | | | | | | | | | ● | | | ● | | | | | | | | |
| NOBLE, ANDREW (DR) (HM14968) | | | | | | | | | | | | | ● | | | ● | | | | | | | | |
| NORTH DOWN CLINIC (HM15023) | | | | | | | | | | | | | ● | | | | | | | | | ● | | |
| PRINGLE CHIROPRACTIC (HM16626) | | | | | | | | | | | ● | ● | ● | | | ● | | | | | ● | | | |
| QUINN, BARBARA (HM16808) | | | | | | | | | | | | | ● | | | ● | | | | | | | | |
| REFLEXOLOGY CLINIC (HM17092) | | | | | | | | | | | | ● | ● | | ● | | | | | | | | | |
| YOGA CENTRE OF IRELAND (HM22023) | | | | | | | | | | | | | ● | | | | | | | | | | | |
| **COUNTY FERMANAGH** | | | | | | | | | | | | | | | | | | | | | | | | |
| ENNISKILLEN CHIRO CLINIC (HM06844) | | | | | | | | | | | | | ● | | | | | | | | | | | |
| **COUNTY LONDONDERRY** | | | | | | | | | | | | | | | | | | | | | | | | |
| CLARENDON CHIROPRACTIC CLINIC (HM04539) | | | | | | | | | | | | | ● | | | ● | | | | | | | | |
| CLAUDY CHIROPRACTIC CLINIC (HM04612) | | | | | | | | | | | | | ● | | | ● | | | | | | | | |
| CURRAN, MAUREEN (HM05630) | | | | | | | | | ● | | | | | | | | | | | | | | | |
| DISPENSERY (HM06117) | ● | ● | ● | ● | ● | ● | ● | ● | ● | ● | ● | ● | ● | ● | ● | ● | ● | ● | ● | ● | ● | ● | ● | |
| EQUILIBRIUM HOLISTIC CLINIC (HM06875) | | | | | | | | | | | | | | | | | | | | | | | | |
| FEET FIRST (HM07174) | | | | | | | | | | | | | | | | | | | | | | | | |
| FOYLE HYPNOTHERAPY CENTRE (HM07646) | | | | ● | | | | ● | | | | | ● | | | | ● | | ● | | | | | |
| LIFE TREE (HM12350) | ● | | | | ● | | | | | | | | ● | | ● | | | | | | | | | |
| MAGHERAFELT CHIRO CLINIC (HM12906) | | | | | | | | | | | ● | ● | | | | ● | | | | | | | | |
| **COUNTY TYRONE** | | | | | | | | | | | | | | | | | | | | | | | | |
| COOKSTOWN HERBAL CLINIC (HM05073) | ● | ● | ● | ● | ● | ● | ● | ● | ● | ● | ● | ● | ● | ● | ● | ● | ● | ● | ● | ● | ● | ● | ● | |
| DUNGANNON CHIROPRACTIC CLINIC (HM06405) | | | | | | | | | | | | | ● | | | ● | | | | | | | | |
| ROSEWOOD HEALTH CLINIC (HM17630) | ● | ● | ● | ● | ● | ● | ● | ● | ● | ● | ● | ● | ● | ● | ● | ● | ● | ● | ● | ● | ● | ● | ● | |

# D - I Conditions treated at Practices/Businesses

| Business by County with Reference no. | Dandruff | Deafness | Depression | Diabetes | Diarrhoea | Digestive Problems | Diverticulitis | Dizziness | Dyslexia | Dyspraxia | Ear Disorders | Eczema | ENT Disorders | Epilepsy | Eye Disorders | Fatigue |
|---|---|---|---|---|---|---|---|---|---|---|---|---|---|---|---|---|
| **SCOTLAND** | | | | | | | | | | | | | | | | |
| **ABERDEENSHIRE** | | | | | | | | | | | | | | | | |
| A WAY WITH THE FAERIES (HM00051) | | | | | | ● | | | | | | | | | | |
| ABERDEEN CHIROPRACTIC CLINIC (HM00114) | | | | | | | | | | | | | | | | |
| ALTERNATIVE PRACTICE (HM00723) | | | ● | | | | | | | | | | | | | |
| BANCHORY CHIROPODY PRACTICE (HM01649) | | | | | | | | | | | | | | | | |
| BEECHGROVE CLINIC (HM02050) | | | | | | | | | | | | | | | | ● |
| BON-ACCORD CHIROPODY (HM02667) | | | | | | | | | | | | | | | | |
| CHELSEA HOUSE CLINIC (HM04090) | | | ● | | | | | | | | | | | | | ● |
| CITY BEACH (HM04486) | | | | | | | | | | | | | | | | |
| CLAIRBAUX CLINIC (HM04505) | | | | | ● | ● | | | | | | | | | | |
| CLAIRBAUX CLINIC (HM04506) | | | | | ● | ● | | | | | | | | | | |
| DEEVIEW AROMATHERAPY (HM05960) | | | ● | | | ● | | | | | | | | | | ● |
| GRAY, SHEILA (HM08419) | | | ● | | ● | ● | | | | | | | | | | ● |
| HUNTLY CHIROPRACTIC CLINIC (HM10412) | | | | | | | | | | | | | | | | |
| LEAL, DOUGLAS (HM12102) | | | | | | | | | | | | | | | | |
| MOSS PHARMACY (HM14262) | | | | | | | | | | | | | | | | |
| REIKI TRAINING CENTRE (HM17149) | | | ● | | | | | | | | | | | | | |
| RIVERSIDE CHIROPRACTIC CLINIC (HM17378) | | | | | | ● | | | | | | | | | | |
| ROSEMOUNT CENTRE (HM17623) | | ● | ● | ● | ● | ● | | ● | | | ● | ● | | ● | ● | ● |
| SAWYER, KEN (HM17985) | | | ● | | | | | | | | | | | | | |
| SERENDIPITY (HM18232) | | | ● | | | ● | | | | | | | | | | |
| STEPHENSON, L (HM19208) | | | | | | | | | | | | | | | | |
| TOE TO HEEL - REFLEXOLOGY (HM20110) | | | ● | ● | | ● | ● | ● | | | ● | ● | | | | ● |
| TURRIFF CHIROPRACTIC CLINIC (HM20443) | | | | | | | | | | | | | | | | |
| WEST END PHYSIOTHERAPY (HM21219) | | | | | | | | | | | | | | | | |
| WILKEN, ANGEL (HM21492) | | | ● | | | ● | | | | | | ● | | | | |
| WOOD, A R (HM21783) | | | | | | | | | | | | | | | | |
| **ANGUS** | | | | | | | | | | | | | | | | |
| BAKER, P T (HM01593) | | | | | | | | ● | | | | | | | | |
| DRYDEN, PHILIP (HM06333) | | | | | | | | | | | | | | | | |
| FOGGIE, MARGARET (HM07454) | | | | | | | | | | | | | | | | |
| HOLISTIC HEALING CENTRE (HM09964) | | | | | | | | | | | | | | | | |

| Business by County with Reference no. | Fears | Fertility Problems | Fever | Fibroids | Flatulence | Foot Problems | Fractures | Fungal Infections | Gallstones | Gastrointestinal Problems | Genital Herpes | Gingivitis | Glandular Fever | Glaucoma | Gout | Gum Disease |
|---|---|---|---|---|---|---|---|---|---|---|---|---|---|---|---|---|
| **SCOTLAND** | | | | | | | | | | | | | | | | |
| **ABERDEENSHIRE** | | | | | | | | | | | | | | | | |
| A WAY WITH THE FAERIES (HM00051) | | | | | | | | | | | | | | | | |
| ABERDEEN CHIROPRACTIC CLINIC (HM00114) | | | | | | | | | | | | | | | | |
| ALTERNATIVE PRACTICE (HM00723) | | | | | | | | | | | | | | | | |
| BANCHORY CHIROPODY PRACTICE (HM01649) | | | | | | ● | | ● | | | | | | | | |
| BEECHGROVE CLINIC (HM02050) | | | | | | ● | ● | | | | | | | | ● | |
| BON-ACCORD CHIROPODY (HM02667) | | | | | | ● | | ● | | | | | | | | |
| CHELSEA HOUSE CLINIC (HM04090) | | | | | | | | | | | | | | | | |
| CITY BEACH (HM04486) | | | | | | ● | | | | | | | | | | |
| CLAIRBAUX CLINIC (HM04505) | | | | | | | | | | | | | | | | |
| CLAIRBAUX CLINIC (HM04506) | | | | | | | | | | | | | | | | |
| DEEVIEW AROMATHERAPY (HM05960) | ● | | | | | | | | | | | | | | | |
| GRAY, SHEILA (HM08419) | | | | | | | | | | ● | | | | | | |
| HUNTLY CHIROPRACTIC CLINIC (HM10412) | | | | | | | | | | | | | | | | |
| LEAL, DOUGLAS (HM12102) | | | | | | ● | | ● | | | | | | | | |
| MOSS PHARMACY (HM14262) | | | | | | ● | | ● | | | | | | | | |
| REIKI TRAINING CENTRE (HM17149) | | | | | | | | | | | | | | | | |
| RIVERSIDE CHIROPRACTIC CLINIC (HM17378) | | | | | | | | | | | | | | | | |
| ROSEMOUNT CENTRE (HM17623) | ● | ● | ● | ● | | ● | | | | | | ● | | | ● | ● |
| SAWYER, KEN (HM17985) | ● | | | | | | | | | | | | | | | |
| SERENDIPITY (HM18232) | | | | | | | | | | | | | | | | |
| STEPHENSON, L (HM19208) | | | | | | ● | | ● | | | | | | | | |
| TOE TO HEEL - REFLEXOLOGY (HM20110) | | ● | | | | ● | | | ● | | | | | | ● | |
| TURRIFF CHIROPRACTIC CLINIC (HM20443) | | | | | | | | | | | | | | | | |
| WEST END PHYSIOTHERAPY (HM21219) | | | | | | | ● | | | | | | | | | |
| WILKEN, ANGEL (HM21492) | | | | | | | | | | | | | | | | |
| WOOD, A R (HM21783) | | | | | | ● | | ● | | | | | | | | |
| **ANGUS** | | | | | | | | | | | | | | | | |
| BAKER, P T (HM01593) | | | | | | | | | | | | | | | | |
| DRYDEN, PHILIP (HM06333) | | | | | | ● | | ● | | | | | | | | |
| FOGGIE, MARGARET (HM07454) | | | | | | ● | | | | | | | | | | |
| HOLISTIC HEALING CENTRE (HM09964) | | | | | | | | | | | | | | | | |

| Business by County with Reference no. | Hair Problems | Halitosis | Hand Problems | Hay Fever | Headaches | Hearing Problems | High Blood Pressure | Hip Complaints | Hyperactivity | Hypoglycaemia | Impotence | Incontinence | Indigestion | Infertility | Influenza | Ingrowing Toenails |
|---|---|---|---|---|---|---|---|---|---|---|---|---|---|---|---|---|
| **SCOTLAND** | | | | | | | | | | | | | | | | |
| **ABERDEENSHIRE** | | | | | | | | | | | | | | | | |
| A WAY WITH THE FAERIES (HM00051) | | | | | | | | | | | | | | | | |
| ABERDEEN CHIROPRACTIC CLINIC (HM00114) | | | | | ● | | | ● | | | | | | | | |
| ALTERNATIVE PRACTICE (HM00723) | | | | | | | | | | | | | | | | |
| BANCHORY CHIROPODY PRACTICE (HM01649) | | | | | | | | | | | | | | | | |
| BEECHGROVE CLINIC (HM02050) | | | ● | | ● | | | ● | | | | ● | | | | |
| BON-ACCORD CHIROPODY (HM02667) | | | | | | | | | | | | | | | | |
| CHELSEA HOUSE CLINIC (HM04090) | | | | | ● | | | | | | | | | | | |
| CITY BEACH (HM04486) | ● | | ● | | | | | | | | | | | | | |
| CLAIRBAUX CLINIC (HM04505) | | | | ● | ● | | | ● | | | | | | | | |
| CLAIRBAUX CLINIC (HM04506) | | | | ● | ● | | | ● | | | | | | | | |
| DEEVIEW AROMATHERAPY (HM05960) | | | ● | | ● | | ● | | | | | | | | | |
| GRAY, SHEILA (HM08419) | | | | ● | ● | | ● | | | | | | ● | | | |
| HUNTLY CHIROPRACTIC CLINIC (HM10412) | | | | | ● | | | ● | | | | | | | | |
| LEAL, DOUGLAS (HM12102) | | | | | | | | | | | | | | | | |
| MOSS PHARMACY (HM14262) | | | | | | | | | | | | | | | | |
| REIKI TRAINING CENTRE (HM17149) | | | | | | | | | | | | | | | | |
| RIVERSIDE CHIROPRACTIC CLINIC (HM17378) | | | | | ● | ● | | ● | | | | | | | | |
| ROSEMOUNT CENTRE (HM17623) | ● | | ● | ● | ● | | ● | | ● | | | | | ● | ● | |
| SAWYER, KEN (HM17985) | | | | | | | | | | | | | | | | |
| SERENDIPITY (HM18232) | | | | | | | | | | | | | | | | |
| STEPHENSON, L (HM19208) | | | | | | | | | | | | | | | | |
| TOE TO HEEL - REFLEXOLOGY (HM20110) | | | | ● | ● | | ● | ● | | ● | | | ● | ● | | |
| TURRIFF CHIROPRACTIC CLINIC (HM20443) | | | | | ● | | | ● | | | | | | | | |
| WEST END PHYSIOTHERAPY (HM21219) | | | | | | | | | | | | | | | | |
| WILKEN, ANGEL (HM21492) | | | | | ● | | | | | | | | | | | |
| WOOD, A R (HM21783) | | | | | | | | | | | | | | | | |
| **ANGUS** | | | | | | | | | | | | | | | | |
| BAKER, P T (HM01593) | | | | | ● | | | ● | | | | | | | | |
| DRYDEN, PHILIP (HM06333) | | | | | | | | | | | | | | | | |
| FOGGIE, MARGARET (HM07454) | | | | | | | | | | | | | | | | |
| HOLISTIC HEALING CENTRE (HM09964) | | | | | | | | ● | | | | | | | | |

# D - I Conditions treated at Practices/Businesses

Business by County with Reference no.

| Business | Dandruff | Deafness | Depression | Diabetes | Diarrhoea | Digestive Problems | Diverticulitis | Dizziness | Dyslexia | Dyspraxia | Ear Disorders | Eczema | ENT Disorders | Epilepsy | Eye Disorders | Fatigue |
|---|---|---|---|---|---|---|---|---|---|---|---|---|---|---|---|---|
| KIRRIEMUIR PHYSIO CLINIC (HM11723) | | | | | | | | | | | | | | | | |
| NATURAL HEALTH & CHIROPODY (HM14558) | | | | | | | | | | | | | | | | ● |
| NICOLL, ELAINE (HM14929) | | | | | | | | | | | | | | | | |
| **ARGYLL AND BUTE** | | | | | | | | | | | | | | | | |
| ACTIVE CHIROPRACTIC (HM00195) | | | | | | | | ● | | | | | | | | ● |
| COMPLEMENTARY HEALTH CENTRE (HM04922) | | | ● | | | | | | | | | | | | | |
| GIBSON, RONALD J (HM08045) | | | ● | | | | | | | | | | | | | ● |
| HOMEOPATHIC PODIATRIST/REFLEX (HM10078) | | | ● | ● | | ● | | | | | | | | | | ● |
| NATURAL THERAPY CENTRE (HM14648) | | | | | | | ● | | | | | | ● | | | ● |
| REIKI LIGHT (HM17138) | | | ● | | | | | | | | | | | | | |
| **AYRSHIRE (EAST)** | | | | | | | | | | | | | | | | |
| CRUISE, M & M (HM05520) | | | | | | | | | | | | | | | | |
| LITTLEJOHN, S (HM12473) | | | | | | | | | | | | | | | | |
| LYNN BROWN CLINICAL AROM (HM12772) | ● | | ● | | | ● | ● | | | | | ● | | | | ● |
| MCCABE, P J (HM13376) | | | | | | | | | | | | | | | | |
| **AYRSHIRE (NORTH)** | | | | | | | | | | | | | | | | |
| BODYSCENTS (HM02631) | | | ● | | | | | | | | | | | | | ● |
| BURNS, ALAN STEWART (HM03410) | | | | | | | | | | | | | | | | |
| CHIRO HEALTH CARE CLINIC (HM04282) | | | ● | | | ● | ● | ● | ● | | | | | | | ● |
| HANDS FOR FEET (HM08905) | | | | | | | | | | | | | | | | |
| PATON, MARY S (HM15824) | | | | | | | | | | | | | | | | |
| REID, E (HM17116) | | | ● | | | ● | | ● | | | | | | | | ● |
| **AYRSHIRE (SOUTH)** | | | | | | | | | | | | | | | | |
| BELL, W DOUGLAS (HM02091) | ● | ● | ● | ● | ● | ● | ● | ● | ● | ● | ● | ● | ● | ● | ● | ● |
| CARRICK CLINIC (HM03742) | ● | | ● | | ● | ● | ● | | | | | ● | | | | ● |
| CRUISE, M & M (HM05522) | | | | | | | | | | | | | | | | |
| ESSENCE OF HEALTH (HM06890) | ● | ● | ● | ● | ● | ● | ● | ● | ● | ● | ● | ● | ● | ● | ● | ● |
| HARDIE, ANNE (HM08966) | | | ● | | | ● | | | | | | | | | | ● |
| HEALTH STRESS & INJURIES (HM09404) | | | ● | | | | | | | | | | | | | ● |
| HEARTLAKE PHYSIOTHERAPY (HM09444) | | | | | | | | | | | | | | | | |
| HODGE, IAN (HM09874) | | | ● | | | ● | | | | | | | | | | ● |
| SMITH, ALICIA (HM18712) | | | ● | | | | | | | | | ● | | | | |
| STEVENSON, SCOTT (HM19251) | | | ● | | | | | | | | | | | | | |

| Business | Fears | Fertility Problems | Fever | Fibroids | Flatulence | Foot Problems | Fractures | Fungal Infections | Gallstones | Gastrointestinal Problems | Genital Herpes | Gingivitis | Glandular Fever | Glaucoma | Gout | Gum Disease |
|---|---|---|---|---|---|---|---|---|---|---|---|---|---|---|---|---|
| KIRRIEMUIR PHYSIO CLINIC (HM11723) | | | | | | | | | | | | | | | | |
| NATURAL HEALTH & CHIROPODY (HM14558) | | | | | | | | | | | | | | | | |
| NICOLL, ELAINE (HM14929) | | | | | | ● | | ● | | | | | | | | |
| **ARGYLL AND BUTE** | | | | | | | | | | | | | | | | |
| ACTIVE CHIROPRACTIC (HM00195) | | | | | | | | | | | | | | | | |
| COMPLEMENTARY HEALTH CENTRE (HM04922) | | | | | | ● | | ● | | | | | | | | |
| GIBSON, RONALD J (HM08045) | | | | | | ● | | | | | | | | | ● | |
| HOMEOPATHIC PODIATRIST/REFLEX (HM10078) | ● | ● | | | | ● | ● | ● | | | | | | | ● | |
| NATURAL THERAPY CENTRE (HM14648) | | | | | | ● | ● | | | | | | | | | |
| REIKI LIGHT (HM17138) | | | | | | | | | | | | | | | | |
| **AYRSHIRE (EAST)** | | | | | | | | | | | | | | | | |
| CRUISE, M & M (HM05520) | | | | | | ● | | ● | | | | | | | | |
| LITTLEJOHN, S (HM12473) | | | | | | | | | | | | | | | | |
| LYNN BROWN CLINICAL AROM (HM12772) | ● | | | | ● | ● | | ● | | ● | | | | | ● | |
| MCCABE, P J (HM13376) | | | | | | ● | | ● | | | | | | | | |
| **AYRSHIRE (NORTH)** | | | | | | | | | | | | | | | | |
| BODYSCENTS (HM02631) | | | | | | | | | | | | | | | | |
| BURNS, ALAN STEWART (HM03410) | | | | | | ● | | ● | | | | | | | | |
| CHIRO HEALTH CARE CLINIC (HM04282) | ● | | | | ● | ● | ● | ● | | ● | | | | | ● | |
| HANDS FOR FEET (HM08905) | | | | | | ● | | ● | | | | | | | | |
| PATON, MARY S (HM15824) | | | | | | ● | | ● | | | | | | | | |
| REID, E (HM17116) | | | | | | ● | | ● | | | | | | | | |
| **AYRSHIRE (SOUTH)** | | | | | | | | | | | | | | | | |
| BELL, W DOUGLAS (HM02091) | ● | ● | ● | ● | ● | ● | ● | ● | ● | ● | ● | ● | ● | ● | ● | ● |
| CARRICK CLINIC (HM03742) | | | | | ● | | ● | | | ● | | | | | | |
| CRUISE, M & M (HM05522) | | | | | | ● | | ● | | | | | | | | |
| ESSENCE OF HEALTH (HM06890) | ● | ● | ● | ● | ● | ● | ● | ● | ● | ● | ● | ● | ● | ● | ● | ● |
| HARDIE, ANNE (HM08966) | | | | | | | | | | | | | | | | |
| HEALTH STRESS & INJURIES (HM09404) | | | | | ● | | | | | | | | | | | |
| HEARTLAKE PHYSIOTHERAPY (HM09444) | | | | | | | ● | | | | | | | | | |
| HODGE, IAN (HM09874) | ● | | | | | | | | | | | | | | | |
| SMITH, ALICIA (HM18712) | ● | | | | | | | | | | | | | | | |
| STEVENSON, SCOTT (HM19251) | ● | | | | | | | | | | | | | | | |

| Business | Hair Problems | Halitosis | Hand Problems | Hay Fever | Headaches | Hearing Problems | High Blood Pressure | Hip Complaints | Hyperactivity | Hypoglycaemia | Impotence | Incontinence | Indigestion | Infertility | Influenza | Ingrowing Toenails |
|---|---|---|---|---|---|---|---|---|---|---|---|---|---|---|---|---|
| KIRRIEMUIR PHYSIO CLINIC (HM11723) | | | | | | | | ● | | | | | | | | |
| NATURAL HEALTH & CHIROPODY (HM14558) | | | | | ● | | | | | | | | | | | |
| NICOLL, ELAINE (HM14929) | | | | | | | | | | | | | | | | |
| **ARGYLL AND BUTE** | | | | | | | | | | | | | | | | |
| ACTIVE CHIROPRACTIC (HM00195) | | | | | ● | | | ● | | | | | | | | |
| COMPLEMENTARY HEALTH CENTRE (HM04922) | | | | | | | | | | | | | | | | |
| GIBSON, RONALD J (HM08045) | | | | | ● | | ● | ● | ● | | | | | | | |
| HOMEOPATHIC PODIATRIST/REFLEX (HM10078) | | | | | | | ● | ● | | ● | | | ● | ● | | |
| NATURAL THERAPY CENTRE (HM14648) | | | | | ● | | ● | | | | | | ● | | ● | |
| REIKI LIGHT (HM17138) | | | | | ● | | | | | | | | | | | |
| **AYRSHIRE (EAST)** | | | | | | | | | | | | | | | | |
| CRUISE, M & M (HM05520) | | | | | | | | | | | | | | | | |
| LITTLEJOHN, S (HM12473) | | | | | | | | | | | | | | | | ● |
| LYNN BROWN CLINICAL AROM (HM12772) | | | ● | ● | ● | | ● | | | | | | ● | | | |
| MCCABE, P J (HM13376) | | | | | | | | | | | | | | | | |
| **AYRSHIRE (NORTH)** | | | | | | | | | | | | | | | | |
| BODYSCENTS (HM02631) | | | | | ● | | ● | | | | | | ● | | | |
| BURNS, ALAN STEWART (HM03410) | | | | | | | | | | | | | | | | |
| CHIRO HEALTH CARE CLINIC (HM04282) | ● | | | | ● | ● | ● | ● | ● | | | | ● | | | |
| HANDS FOR FEET (HM08905) | | | | | | | | | | | | | | | | |
| PATON, MARY S (HM15824) | | | | | | | | | | | | | | | | |
| REID, E (HM17116) | | | ● | ● | ● | | ● | ● | | | ● | ● | ● | | | |
| **AYRSHIRE (SOUTH)** | | | | | | | | | | | | | | | | |
| BELL, W DOUGLAS (HM02091) | ● | ● | ● | ● | ● | ● | ● | ● | ● | ● | ● | ● | ● | ● | ● | |
| CARRICK CLINIC (HM03742) | ● | | ● | ● | ● | | ● | ● | | | | | ● | | ● | |
| CRUISE, M & M (HM05522) | | | | | | | | | | | | | | | | |
| ESSENCE OF HEALTH (HM06890) | ● | ● | ● | ● | ● | ● | ● | ● | ● | ● | ● | ● | ● | ● | ● | |
| HARDIE, ANNE (HM08966) | | | | | | | ● | | | | | | | | | |
| HEALTH STRESS & INJURIES (HM09404) | | | | | ● | | ● | ● | | | | | ● | | | |
| HEARTLAKE PHYSIOTHERAPY (HM09444) | | | | | | | | ● | | | | | | | | |
| HODGE, IAN (HM09874) | | | | | | | ● | | | | ● | | | | | |
| SMITH, ALICIA (HM18712) | | | | | | | | | | | | | | | | |
| STEVENSON, SCOTT (HM19251) | | | | | | | | | | | | | | | | |

# D - I Conditions treated at Practices/Businesses

| Business by County with Reference no. | Dandruff | Deafness | Depression | Diabetes | Diarrhoea | Digestive Problems | Diverticulitis | Dizziness | Dyslexia | Dyspraxia | Ear Disorders | Eczema | ENT Disorders | Epilepsy | Eye Disorders | Fatigue | Fears | Fertility Problems | Fever | Fibroids | Flatulence | Foot Problems | Fractures | Fungal Infections |
|---|---|---|---|---|---|---|---|---|---|---|---|---|---|---|---|---|---|---|---|---|---|---|---|---|
| **CLACKMANNANSHIRE** | | | | | | | | | | | | | | | | | | | | | | | | |
| ALTERNATIVE MEDICAL CLINIC (HM00711) | | | ● | ● | | ● | ● | | | | | | | | | ● | ● | ● | | | | ● | | |
| **DUMFRIES AND GALLOWAY** | | | | | | | | | | | | | | | | | | | | | | | | |
| BURTON, VICKY (HM03447) | | | ● | | | ● | | | | | | | | | | ● | | | | | | | | |
| CHLOE'S HERBS (HM04419) | ● | | ● | | ● | ● | ● | | | | ● | ● | | | | ● | | ● | ● | | ● | | | ● |
| DAVIDSON, MORAG (HM05788) | | | | | | | | | | | | | | | | | | | | | | ● | | ● |
| DUMFRIES HOLISTIC HEALTH CTRE (HM06386) | ● | ● | ● | ● | ● | ● | ● | ● | ● | ● | ● | ● | ● | ● | ● | ● | ● | ● | ● | ● | ● | ● | ● | ● |
| HEALTH STRESS & INJURIES CLNC (HM09405) | ● | ● | ● | ● | ● | ● | ● | ● | ● | ● | ● | ● | ● | ● | ● | ● | ● | ● | ● | ● | ● | ● | ● | ● |
| MCCLUNE, LORNA (HM13410) | | | | ● | | | | | | | | | | | | | | | | | | ● | | |
| MCCLYMOUNT, JENNIFER (HM13416) | | | | | | | | | | | | | | | | | | | | | | ● | | ● |
| RANKINE, VANORA (HM16939) | | | | | | | | | | | | | | | | | | | | | | ● | | ● |
| SHARP, LINDA A (HM18314) | | | ● | ● | ● | ● | ● | ● | | | ● | ● | ● | | ● | ● | | ● | | | ● | ● | | ● |
| **EDINBURGH (CITY OF)** | | | | | | | | | | | | | | | | | | | | | | | | |
| ACTIVE OSTEOPATHS (HM00200) | | | | | | | | | | | | | | | | | | | | | | | | |
| ALEXANDER TECHNIQUE (HM00517) | | | ● | | | | | | | | | | | | | | | | | | | | | |
| BABY HOLISTIC & MASSAGE (HM01464) | | | | | | | | | | | | | | | | | | | | | | | | |
| BIORADIANT HEALTH (HM02343) | | | | | | | | | | | | | | | | ● | | | | | | | | |
| BLAIR, RICHARD (HM02475) | | | ● | | ● | ● | | ● | | | ● | | | | | ● | | | | | | | | |
| E G H P (HM06468) | | | ● | | | ● | | | | | | ● | | | | ● | ● | ● | | | ● | | | |
| EDINBURGH ALEXANDER CENTRE (HM06606) | | | | | | | | | | | | | | | | | | | | | | | | |
| EDINBURGH HOMEOPATHIC CENTRE (HM06613) | | | | | | | | | | | | | | | | ● | | | | | | | | |
| EDINBURGH OSTEOPATHIC SURGERY (HM06615) | | | | | | | | | | | | | | | | | | | | | | | | |
| EDINBURGH PHYSIOTHERAPY CENTRE (HM06616) | | | | | | | | | | | | | | | | | | | | | | ● | | |
| EXCLUSIVE HYPNOTHERAPY (HM07019) | | | | | | | | | | | | | | | | ● | | | | | | | | |
| GARDINER, F (HM07872) | | | ● | ● | ● | ● | | | | | | | | | | ● | | | | | ● | | | |
| HAZEL, J M (HM09290) | | | | | | | | | | | | | | | | | | | | | | ● | | ● |
| HOLDEN, SHEENA (HM09934) | | | | | | ● | ● | | | | | | | | | | | | | | | | | |
| IN HARMONY AROMATHERAPY (HM10595) | | | ● | | | ● | | | | | | | | | | ● | | | | | | | | |
| J W PHYSIOTHERAPY & SPORTS (HM10805) | | | | | | | | | | | | | | | | | | | | | | | ● | |
| J W PHYSIOTHERAPY & SPORTS (HM10804) | | | | | | | | | | | | | | | | | | | | | | | ● | |
| JENAI (HM10980) | | | ● | | | | | | | | | ● | | | | ● | | | | | | | | |
| KELLY, T G (HM11446) | | | | | | | | | | | | | | | | | | | | | | ● | | ● |
| KELLY, T G (HM11447) | | | | | | | | | | | | | | | | | | | | | | ● | | ● |
| LIVING MIND (HM12487) | | | ● | | | ● | | | | | | | | | | ● | ● | | | | | | | |

| Business by County with Reference no. | Gallstones | Gastrointestinal Problems | Genital Herpes | Gingivitis | Glandular Fever | Glaucoma | Gout | Gum Disease | Hair Problems | Halitosis | Hand Problems | Hay Fever | Headaches | Hearing Problems | High Blood Pressure | Hip Complaints | Hyperactivity | Hypoglycaemia | Impotence | Incontinence | Indigestion | Infertility | Influenza | Ingrowing Toenails |
|---|---|---|---|---|---|---|---|---|---|---|---|---|---|---|---|---|---|---|---|---|---|---|---|---|
| **CLACKMANNANSHIRE** | | | | | | | | | | | | | | | | | | | | | | | | |
| ALTERNATIVE MEDICAL CLINIC (HM00711) | | ● | | | | | | | ● | | ● | ● | ● | | ● | ● | ● | ● | ● | ● | ● | ● | | |
| **DUMFRIES AND GALLOWAY** | | | | | | | | | | | | | | | | | | | | | | | | |
| BURTON, VICKY (HM03447) | | | | | | | | | | | ● | ● | ● | | ● | | | | | ● | ● | | ● | |
| CHLOE'S HERBS (HM04419) | ● | ● | ● | ● | ● | | ● | ● | | ● | | | | | | ● | ● | ● | | | ● | ● | ● | |
| DAVIDSON, MORAG (HM05788) | | | | | | | | | | | | | | | | | | | | | | | | |
| DUMFRIES HOLISTIC HEALTH CTRE (HM06386) | ● | ● | ● | ● | ● | ● | ● | ● | ● | ● | ● | ● | ● | ● | ● | ● | ● | ● | ● | ● | ● | ● | ● | |
| HEALTH STRESS & INJURIES CLNC (HM09405) | ● | ● | ● | ● | ● | ● | ● | ● | ● | ● | ● | ● | ● | ● | ● | ● | ● | ● | ● | ● | ● | ● | ● | |
| MCCLUNE, LORNA (HM13410) | | | | | | | | | | | | | | | | | | | | | | | | |
| MCCLYMOUNT, JENNIFER (HM13416) | | | | | | | | | | | | | | | | | | | | | | | | ● |
| RANKINE, VANORA (HM16939) | | | | | | | | | | | | | | | | | | | | | | | | |
| SHARP, LINDA A (HM18314) | | ● | | | | | | | | | | ● | ● | | ● | | | ● | | ● | ● | ● | | |
| **EDINBURGH (CITY OF)** | | | | | | | | | | | | | | | | | | | | | | | | |
| ACTIVE OSTEOPATHS (HM00200) | | | | | | | | | | | | | ● | | | | | | | | | | | |
| ALEXANDER TECHNIQUE (HM00517) | | | | | | | | | | | | | ● | | | | | | | | | | | |
| BABY HOLISTIC & MASSAGE (HM01464) | | ● | | | | | | | | | | | | | | | | | | | | | | |
| BIORADIANT HEALTH (HM02343) | | | | | | | | | | | | | ● | | | | | | | | | | | |
| BLAIR, RICHARD (HM02475) | | | | | | | | | | | | | | | | ● | | | | | | | | |
| E G H P (HM06468) | | | | | | | | | | | | | ● | | ● | | ● | | ● | | | ● | | |
| EDINBURGH ALEXANDER CENTRE (HM06606) | | | | | | | | | | | | | | | ● | | | | | | | | | |
| EDINBURGH HOMEOPATHIC CENTRE (HM06613) | | | | | | | | | | | | ● | ● | | | | | | | | | | | |
| EDINBURGH OSTEOPATHIC SURGERY (HM06615) | | | | | | | | | | | | | ● | | | ● | | | | | | | | |
| EDINBURGH PHYSIOTHERAPY CENTRE (HM06616) | | | | | | | | | | | | | | | | ● | | | | | | | | |
| EXCLUSIVE HYPNOTHERAPY (HM07019) | | | | | | | | | ● | | | | | | | | | | ● | | | | | |
| GARDINER, F (HM07872) | | ● | | | | | ● | | | | | | ● | | ● | | | | | ● | ● | ● | | |
| HAZEL, J M (HM09290) | | | | | | | | | | | | | | | | | | | | | | | | |
| HOLDEN, SHEENA (HM09934) | | | | | | | | | | | | | ● | | ● | | | | | | | | | |
| IN HARMONY AROMATHERAPY (HM10595) | | | | | | | | | | | | | ● | | | | | | | | | | | |
| J W PHYSIOTHERAPY & SPORTS (HM10805) | | | | | | | | | | | | | ● | | | ● | | | | | | | | |
| J W PHYSIOTHERAPY & SPORTS (HM10804) | | | | | | | | | | | | | ● | | | ● | | | | | | | | |
| JENAI (HM10980) | | | | | | | | | | | | | ● | | ● | | | | | | | | | |
| KELLY, T G (HM11446) | | | | | | | | | | | | | | | | | | | | | | | | |
| KELLY, T G (HM11447) | | | | | | | | | | | | | | | | | | | | | | | | |
| LIVING MIND (HM12487) | | ● | | | | | | | | | | | ● | | | | | | | | | | | |

# D - I Conditions treated at Practices/Businesses

| Business by County with Reference no. | Dandruff | Deafness | Depression | Diabetes | Diarrhoea | Digestive Problems | Diverticulitis | Dizziness | Dyslexia | Dyspraxia | Ear Disorders | Eczema | ENT Disorders | Epilepsy | Eye Disorders | Fatigue | Fears | Fertility Problems | Fever | Fibroids | Flatulence | Foot Problems | Fractures | Fungal Infections | Gallstones | Gastrointestinal Problems | Genital Herpes | Gingivitis | Glandular Fever | Glaucoma | Gout | Gum Disease | Hair Problems | Halitosis | Hand Problems | Hay Fever | Headaches | Hearing Problems | High Blood Pressure | Hip Complaints | Hyperactivity | Hypoglycaemia | Impotence | Incontinence | Indigestion | Infertility | Influenza | Ingrowing Toenails |
|---|---|---|---|---|---|---|---|---|---|---|---|---|---|---|---|---|---|---|---|---|---|---|---|---|---|---|---|---|---|---|---|---|---|---|---|---|---|---|---|---|---|---|---|---|---|---|---|---|
| LOGAN, CAROL (HM12565) | | | ● | | | ● | | | | | | | | | | ● | ● | | | | | | | | | ● | | | | | | | | | | | ● | | ● | | | | | | | | | |
| MACPHERSON, R G (HM12877) | | | | | | | | | | | | | | | | | | | | | | ● | | ● | | | | | | | | | | | | | | | | | | | | | | | | |
| MARIPOSA AROMATHERAPY (HM13103) | | | ● | | | ● | | | | | | | | | | ● | | | | | | | | | | | | | | | | | | | | | ● | | | | | | | | | | | |
| MARSHALL, S C (HM13171) | | | | | | | | | | | | | | | | | | | | | | ● | | ● | | | | | | | | | | | | | | | | | | | | | | | | |
| MCDONALD, DAVID S (HM13456) | | | | | | | | | | | | | | | | | | | | | | ● | | ● | | | | | | | | | | | | | | | | | | | | | | | | |
| MCVITTIE, D (HM13623) | | | ● | | | ● | ● | | | | | ● | | | | ● | | ● | | | ● | | | | | ● | | | | | | | | | | | ● | ● | ● | ● | | | | ● | ● | ● | | |
| MOBILE CHIROPODY SERVICES (HM14028) | | | | | | | | | | | | | | | | | | | | | | ● | | ● | | | | | | | | | | | | | | | | | | | | | | | | |
| MORNINGSIDE PODIATRY SERVICE (HM14192) | | | | | | | | | | | | | | | | | | | | | | ● | | ● | | | | | | | | | | | | | | | | | | | | | | | | |
| N H S (HM14449) | | | | | | | | | | | | | | | | | | | | | | ● | | ● | | | | | | | | | | | | | | | | | | | | | | | | |
| OLIVER & STODDARD (HM15285) | | | ● | ● | ● | ● | | | | | | | | | | ● | | | | ● | ● | | | | | ● | | | | | ● | | | | | | ● | | ● | | ● | | | | ● | | | |
| PATTERSON, YVONNE (HM15833) | | | ● | | | | | | | | | | | | | | | | | | | | | | | | | | | | | | | | | | ● | | | | | | | | | | | |
| RUMNEY, KATHLEEN (HM17748) | ● | ● | ● | ● | ● | ● | ● | ● | ● | ● | ● | ● | ● | ● | ● | ● | ● | ● | ● | ● | ● | ● | ● | ● | ● | ● | ● | ● | ● | ● | ● | ● | ● | ● | ● | ● | ● | ● | ● | ● | ● | ● | ● | ● | ● | ● | ● | |
| SHENTON, DIANNE (HM18402) | | | | | | | | | | | | | | | | | | | | | | ● | | ● | | | | | | | | | | | | | | | | | | | | | | | | |
| SKEDD, L A (HM18629) | | | | | | | | | | | | | | | | | | | | | | ● | | ● | | | | | | | | | | | | | | | | | | | | | | | | |
| TARA ROKPA ENDINBURGH (HM19699) | | | ● | | | ● | | | | | | | | | | ● | | | | | | | | | | | | | | | | | | | | | ● | | ● | | | | | ● | ● | | | |
| WARD, ELIZABETH (HM20900) | | | ● | | | | | | | | | | | | | ● | | | | | | | | | | | | | | | | | | | | | | | | | | | | | | | | |
| WELLBEING (HM21146) | | | | | | | | | | | | | | | | | | | | | | | | | | | | | | | | | | | | | ● | | | | | | | | | | | |
| **FALKIRK** | | | | | | | | | | | | | | | | | | | | | | | | | | | | | | | | | | | | | | | | | | | | | | | | |
| AESTHETICA TOTAL SKIN & BODY (HM00411) | | | ● | | | | | | | | | | | | | | | | | | | | | | | | | | | | | | | | | | ● | | | | | | | | | | | |
| ANGUS WILLIAMSON CLINIC (HM00885) | | | | | | | | | | | | | | | | | | | | | | ● | | | | | | | | | | | | | ● | | | | | | | | | | | | | |
| FALKIRK CHIROPRACTIC CLINIC (HM07074) | | | | | | | | | | | | | | | | | | | | | | | | | | | | | | | | | | | | | ● | | | ● | | | | | | | | |
| GRANT, LESLIE & DAWN (HM08385) | | | | | | | | | | | | | | | | | | | | | | ● | | ● | | | | | | | | | | | | | | | | | | | | | | | | |
| GRANT, LESLIE AND DAWN (HM08386) | | | | | | | | | | | | | | | | | | | | | | ● | | ● | | | | | | | | | | | | | | | | | | | | | | | | |
| KELIMAR CLINIC (HM11416) | | | | | | | | | | | | | | | | ● | | | | | | ● | | | | | | | | | | | | | ● | | | | | | | | | | | | | |
| NATURAL HEALING CENTRE (HM14543) | | | | | | ● | | | | | | | | | | ● | ● | | | | | | | | | | | | | | | | | | | | ● | | ● | | | | | | ● | ● | | |
| **FIFE** | | | | | | | | | | | | | | | | | | | | | | | | | | | | | | | | | | | | | | | | | | | | | | | | |
| BODYNEEDS (HM02629) | ● | ● | ● | ● | ● | ● | ● | ● | ● | ● | ● | ● | ● | ● | ● | ● | ● | ● | ● | ● | ● | ● | ● | ● | ● | ● | ● | ● | ● | ● | ● | ● | ● | ● | ● | ● | ● | ● | ● | ● | ● | ● | ● | ● | ● | ● | ● | |
| CAMERON, WILLIAM (HM03588) | | | | | | | | | | | | | | | | | | | | | | ● | | ● | | | | | | | | | | | | | | | | | | | | | | | | |
| COMPLEMENTARY THERAPY CLINIC (HM04949) | | ● | ● | | | ● | | ● | | | | ● | | | | ● | ● | | | | | | | ● | | | | | | | | | | | | | ● | ● | ● | ● | | | | ● | ● | | | |
| DAVIDSON, ANGELA (HM05785) | | ● | ● | | ● | ● | | ● | | | ● | ● | ● | ● | ● | ● | | | | | | ● | | ● | ● | ● | | | | | ● | | | | | ● | ● | ● | ● | ● | | | ● | ● | ● | | | |
| KEEP IN STEP (HM11394) | | | | | | | | | | | | | | | | | | | | | | ● | | ● | | | | | | | | | | | | | | | | | | | | | | | | |
| LEUTER, PAM () | | | | | | | | | | | | | | | | ● | | | | | | | | | | | | | | | | | | | | | ● | | | | | | | | | | | |
| NEAT FEET (HM14743) | | | ● | ● | ● | ● | | | | | | ● | ● | ● | | ● | | ● | ● | ● | ● | ● | | | | | | | | | | | | | | ● | ● | | ● | ● | ● | | | | ● | | | |
| O'BRIAN, D (HM15171) | | | | | | | | | | | | | | | | | | | | | | ● | | ● | | | | | | | | | | | | | | | | | | | | | | | | |

# D - I Conditions treated at Practices/Businesses

| Business by County with Reference no. | Dandruff | Deafness | Depression | Diabetes | Diarrhoea | Digestive Problems | Diverticulitis | Dizziness | Dyslexia | Dyspraxia | Ear Disorders | Eczema | ENT Disorders | Epilepsy | Eye Disorders | Fatigue | Fears | Fertility Problems | Fever | Fibroids | Flatulence | Foot Problems | Fractures | Fungal Infections | Gallstones | Gastrointestinal Problems | Genital Herpes | Gingivitis | Glandular Fever | Glaucoma | Gout | Gum Disease | Hair Problems | Halitosis | Hand Problems | Hay Fever | Headaches | Hearing Problems | High Blood Pressure | Hip Complaints | Hyperactivity | Hypoglycaemia | Impotence | Incontinence | Indigestion | Infertility | Influenza | Ingrowing Toenails |
|---|---|---|---|---|---|---|---|---|---|---|---|---|---|---|---|---|---|---|---|---|---|---|---|---|---|---|---|---|---|---|---|---|---|---|---|---|---|---|---|---|---|---|---|---|---|---|---|---|
| SHEERINS, ROZ (HM18370) | | | | | | | | | | | | | | | | | | | | | | ● | | ● | | | | | | | | | | | | | | | | | | | | | | | | |
| ST ANDREWS OSTEOPATHS (HM19065) | | | | | | ● | | | | | | | | | | ● | | ● | | | | ● | ● | | | | | | | | | | | | ● | | | | | | | | | | ● | ● | | |
| TOLBOOTH HOUSE (HM20117) | | | ● | | | | | | | | | ● | | | | | | ● | | | | ● | | ● | | | | | | | | | | | | ● | ● | | | | | | | | | ● | | |
| TWA ACRES HYPNO TRAINING CTRE (HM20447) | ● | | ● | ● | | | | | | | | ● | | | | | ● | ● | | | | | | | | | | | | | | | ● | | | | ● | | | | | | ● | | | | | |
| GLASGOW (CITY OF) | | | | | | | | | | | | | | | | | | | | | | | | | | | | | | | | | | | | | | | | | | | | | | | | |
| ABOUT FACE (HM00131) | | | ● | | | | | | | | | | | | | | | | | | | | | | | | | | | | | | ● | | | | ● | | ● | | | | | | | | | |
| ACTIVE CHIROPRACTIC (HM00194) | | | | | | | | ● | | | | | | | | ● | | | | | | | | | | | | | | | | | | | | | ● | | | ● | | | | | | | | |
| ANDERSON DOE PODIATRY CLINIC (HM00809) | | | | | | | | | | | | | | | | | | | | | | | | | | | | | | | | | | | | | | | | | ● | | | | | | | |
| ANNE PENMAN THERAPY (HM00900) | | | | | | | | | | | | | | | | | ● | | | | | | | | | | | | | | | | | | | | ● | | | | | | | | | | | |
| BEHIND THE VEIL (HM02068) | | | ● | | | ● | | ● | | | | | | | | ● | ● | | | | | | | | | | | | | | | | | | | | ● | | ● | ● | ● | | | | ● | | | |
| BLACK, JIM (HM02424) | | | | | | | | | | | | | | | | | | | | | | ● | | ● | | | | | | | | | | | | | | | | | | | | | | | | |
| BOTHWELL PHYSIOTHERAPY (HM02733) | | | | | | | | | | | | | | | | | | | | | | | | | | | | | | | | | | | | | ● | | | ● | | | | | | | | |
| CLINIC AT CHARING CROSS (HM04679) | | | | | | | | | | | | | | | | ● | | ● | | | | | | | | | | | | | | | | | | | ● | | ● | | | | ● | | | | | |
| CONWAY, VALERIE (DR) (HM05034) | | | ● | | ● | ● | ● | ● | | | ● | ● | ● | | ● | ● | ● | | | ● | ● | ● | | ● | ● | ● | | | ● | | ● | | | | ● | ● | ● | | ● | ● | | | | ● | ● | | ● | |
| CONWAY, VALERIE A (DR) (HM05035) | | | ● | | ● | ● | ● | ● | | | ● | ● | ● | | ● | ● | ● | | | ● | ● | ● | | ● | ● | ● | | | ● | | ● | | | | ● | ● | ● | | ● | ● | | | | ● | ● | | ● | |
| FITZPATRICK, J H (HM07374) | | | | | | | | | | | | | | | | | | | | | | ● | | ● | | | | | | | | | | | | | | | | | | | | | | | | |
| FOOTSURE (HM07514) | | | | | | | | | | | | | | | | | | | | | | ● | | | | | | | | | | | | | | | | | | | | | | | | | | |
| HARVEST CLINIC (HM09152) | ● | | ● | ● | ● | ● | ● | | | | | ● | | | | ● | ● | ● | | | | ● | | | | | | | | | | | ● | | | ● | ● | | ● | | | ● | ● | | ● | | ● | |
| HOLISTIC HEALING & HYP (HM09961) | | | | | | | | | | | | | | | | | ● | | | | | | | | | | | | | | | | | | | | | | | | | | | | | | | |
| HUMAN PERFORMANCE CLINIC (HM10364) | | | ● | | | | | ● | | | | | | | | | ● | | | | | | | | | | | | | | | | | | | | ● | | ● | | | | ● | | | | | |
| LAMBERT, C W (HM11895) | | | | | | | | | | | | | | | | | | | | | | ● | | ● | | | | | | | | | | | | | | | | | | | | | | | | |
| LASER THERAPY CENTRE (HM11984) | | | ● | | | | | | | | | | | | | | | | | | | | | | | | | | | | | | | | | | | | | | | | | | | | | |
| LAURIE, A (HM12015) | | | | ● | | | | | | | | | | | | | | | | | | ● | | ● | | | | | | | | | | | | | | | | | | | | | | | | |
| LONG RIVER TAI CHI CIRCLE (HM12617) | | | ● | | | | | | | | | | | | | ● | | | | | | | | | | | | | | | | | | | | | ● | | ● | | | | | | | | | |
| MARY HERAGHTY AT HEALTHY FEET (HM13222) | | | ● | ● | | | | | | | | | | | | | | | | | ● | ● | | ● | | | | | | | | | | | | | ● | | ● | | ● | | | | | ● | | |
| MCLAREN, CATH RENA (HM13539) | | ● | ● | | ● | ● | ● | ● | | | ● | | ● | | | ● | | | | | ● | | | | | ● | | | | | | | ● | | | | ● | ● | ● | ● | | | | | ● | | | |
| MCLEAN, A M (HM13551) | | | | ● | | | | | | | | ● | | | | | | | | | | ● | ● | ● | | | | | | | ● | | | | | | | | | ● | | | | | | | | |
| MCTIMONEY CHIROPRACTIC CLINIC (HM13611) | | | | | | | | | ● | ● | | | | | | | | | | | | | | | | | | | | | | | | | | | | | | | | | | | | | | |
| NUTRITION WORLD (HM15126) | ● | ● | ● | ● | ● | ● | ● | ● | ● | | ● | ● | ● | ● | ● | ● | ● | ● | ● | ● | ● | ● | ● | ● | ● | ● | ● | ● | ● | ● | ● | ● | ● | ● | ● | ● | ● | ● | ● | ● | ● | ● | ● | ● | ● | ● | ● | |
| PLUIDGE, MARK (HM16379) | | | | | | | | | | | | | | | | | | | | | | ● | | ● | | | | | | | | | | | | | | | | | | | | | | | | |
| RHODIE, ANDREA (HM17231) | | | ● | | | ● | | | | | | | | | | ● | | | | | | | | | | | | | | | | | | | | | ● | | | | | | | | | | | |
| ROLLAND, C R (HM17563) | | | | | | | | | | | | | | | | | | | | | | ● | | ● | | | | | | | | | | | | | | | | | | | | | | | | |
| SCHOLL CENTRE (HM18039) | | | | | | | | | | | | | | | | | | | | | | ● | | ● | | | | | | | | | | | | | | | | | | | | | | | | |
| SHAWLANDS HYPNOTHERAPY CLINIC (HM18352) | | | ● | | | | | | ● | | | ● | | | | | ● | | | | | | | | | | | | | | | | | | | ● | | | | | | | ● | | | | | |

# D - I Conditions treated at Practices/Businesses

| Business by County with Reference no. | Dandruff | Deafness | Depression | Diabetes | Diarrhoea | Digestive Problems | Diverticulitis | Dizziness | Dyslexia | Dyspraxia | Ear Disorders | Eczema | ENT Disorders | Epilepsy | Eye Disorders | Fatigue | Fears | Fertility Problems | Fever | Fibroids | Flatulence | Foot Problems | Fractures | Fungal Infections | Gallstones | Gastrointestinal Problems | Genital Herpes | Gingivitis | Glandular Fever | Glaucoma | Gout | Gum Disease | Hair Problems | Halitosis | Hand Problems | Hay Fever | Headaches | Hearing Problems | High Blood Pressure | Hip Complaints | Hyperactivity | Hypoglycaemia | Impotence | Incontinence | Indigestion | Infertility | Influenza | Ingrowing Toenails |
|---|---|---|---|---|---|---|---|---|---|---|---|---|---|---|---|---|---|---|---|---|---|---|---|---|---|---|---|---|---|---|---|---|---|---|---|---|---|---|---|---|---|---|---|---|---|---|---|---|
| SINO-HERBAL CLINIC (HM18615) | | | ● | ● | ● | ● | | ● | | | | ● | | | ● | ● | ● | ● | ● | | | ● | | ● | | | | | | | | | ● | | ● | ● | ● | ● | ● | ● | ● | | ● | | ● | ● | | |
| STEWART, JIM (DR) (HM19270) | | | ● | | | | | | | | | ● | | | | | ● | | | | | | | | | | | | | | | | | | | | ● | | | | | | | | | | | |
| THERAPY OF LIFE CLINIC (HM19905) | ● | | ● | | | ● | | | | | | ● | | | | ● | ● | | ● | | | ● | | ● | | ● | | | | | ● | | ● | | ● | ● | ● | | ● | ● | ● | | | | ● | | ● | |
| WEST END THERAPY CENTRE (HM21221) | ● | ● | ● | ● | ● | ● | ● | ● | ● | ● | ● | ● | ● | ● | ● | ● | ● | ● | ● | ● | ● | ● | ● | ● | ● | ● | ● | ● | ● | ● | ● | ● | ● | ● | ● | ● | ● | ● | ● | ● | ● | ● | ● | ● | ● | ● | ● | |
| HIGHLAND | | | | | | | | | | | | | | | | | | | | | | | | | | | | | | | | | | | | | | | | | | | | | | | | |
| BUMBLE - BEE'S PHYSIO (HM03347) | | | | | | | | | | | | | | | | | | | | | ● | | | | | | | | | | | | | | | | ● | | | ● | | | | | | | | |
| GENTLE WAYS (HM07980) | | | ● | | | | | | | | | | | | | ● | ● | | | | | | | | ● | | | | | | | | | | | | | ● | ● | | | | | | | | | |
| HARMONOLOGY CENTRE (HM09017) | | | | | | | | | | | | | | | | ● | | | | | | | | | | | | | | | | | | | | | ● | | | | | | | | | | | |
| HEALTH CORNER (HM09383) | | | | | | ● | | | ● | | | | ● | | | | | ● | | | | | | | | | | | | | | | | | | | ● | | ● | | | | | | | | | |
| TAYLOR, JUNE (HM19773) | | ● | ● | ● | | ● | | ● | | | ● | ● | ● | | | ● | | ● | ● | ● | | | | | | ● | | | ● | | | | | | ● | ● | ● | ● | ● | ● | ● | | | | ● | ● | ● | |
| WAH, G (HM20735) | | ● | ● | ● | | ● | | ● | | | ● | ● | ● | | | ● | | ● | ● | ● | | | | | | ● | | | ● | | | | | | ● | ● | ● | ● | ● | ● | ● | | ● | | ● | ● | ● | |
| INVERCLYDE | | | | | | | | | | | | | | | | | | | | | | | | | | | | | | | | | | | | | | | | | | | | | | | | |
| INVERCLYDE OSTEOPATHIC CLINIC (HM10704) | | | ● | | | | | ● | | | | ● | | | | ● | ● | ● | | ● | | ● | | | | ● | | | ● | | ● | | | | | ● | | | ● | ● | | | | | ● | ● | ● | |
| KELLERMANS (HM11418) | | | ● | | ● | ● | | | | | | | | | | ● | | | | | | | | | | | | | | | | | | | ● | ● | ● | | ● | | | | | | | | | |
| LANARKSHIRE (NORTH) | | | | | | | | | | | | | | | | | | | | | | | | | | | | | | | | | | | | | | | | | | | | | | | | |
| REGISTERED HOMEOPATH (HM17103) | | ● | ● | ● | ● | ● | ● | ● | ● | | ● | ● | ● | ● | ● | ● | ● | ● | ● | ● | ● | ● | | ● | ● | ● | ● | ● | ● | | ● | | ● | ● | ● | ● | ● | ● | ● | ● | ● | ● | ● | ● | ● | ● | ● | |
| SEMPRE LIBERA (HM18224) | | | ● | | | | | | | | | | | | | | | | | | | | | | | | | | | | | | | | | | ● | | | | | | | | | | | |
| STRATH NATURAL THERAPIES (HM19371) | | | ● | | | | | | | | | | | | | | | | | | | | | | | | | | | | | | | | | | | | ● | | | | | | | | | |
| LANARKSHIRE (SOUTH) | | | | | | | | | | | | | | | | | | | | | | | | | | | | | | | | | | | | | | | | | | | | | | | | |
| QUINN, JIM (HM16810) | ● | ● | ● | ● | ● | ● | ● | ● | ● | | ● | ● | ● | ● | ● | ● | ● | ● | ● | ● | ● | ● | ● | ● | ● | ● | ● | ● | ● | ● | ● | ● | ● | ● | ● | ● | ● | ● | ● | ● | ● | ● | ● | ● | ● | ● | ● | ● |
| ROBB, A (DR) (HM17387) | ● | ● | ● | ● | ● | ● | ● | ● | ● | ● | ● | ● | ● | ● | ● | ● | ● | ● | ● | ● | ● | ● | ● | ● | ● | ● | ● | ● | ● | ● | ● | ● | ● | ● | ● | ● | ● | ● | ● | ● | ● | ● | ● | ● | ● | ● | ● | |
| LOTHIAN (EAST) | | | | | | | | | | | | | | | | | | | | | | | | | | | | | | | | | | | | | | | | | | | | | | | | |
| AROMA (HM01042) | ● | ● | ● | ● | ● | ● | ● | ● | ● | ● | ● | ● | ● | ● | ● | ● | ● | ● | ● | ● | ● | ● | ● | ● | ● | ● | ● | ● | ● | ● | ● | ● | ● | ● | ● | ● | ● | ● | ● | ● | ● | ● | ● | ● | ● | ● | ● | |
| EAST LOTHIAN PHYSIO CENTRE (HM06518) | | | | | | | | | | | | | | | | | | | | | | ● | ● | | | | | | | | | | | | ● | | ● | | | ● | | | | ● | | | | |
| FRASER, GORDON (HM07696) | ● | ● | ● | ● | ● | ● | ● | ● | ● | ● | ● | ● | ● | ● | ● | ● | ● | ● | ● | ● | ● | ● | ● | ● | ● | ● | ● | ● | ● | ● | ● | ● | ● | ● | ● | ● | ● | ● | ● | ● | ● | ● | ● | ● | ● | ● | ● | |
| LOTHIAN (MID) | | | | | | | | | | | | | | | | | | | | | | | | | | | | | | | | | | | | | | | | | | | | | | | | |
| CRYSTAL SANCTUARY (HM05532) | | | ● | | ● | ● | | | | | | | | | | ● | | | | | ● | | | | | ● | | | | | | | | | | | ● | | ● | | | | | | ● | | | |
| HAMILTON, JAMES (HM08844) | | | ● | ● | | ● | | ● | | | | | | | | ● | | | | | | ● | | ● | | | | | | | | | | | | ● | ● | | ● | | | | ● | ● | ● | | | |
| NATURAL HEALTH CENTRE (HM14573) | ● | ● | ● | ● | ● | ● | ● | ● | ● | ● | ● | ● | ● | ● | ● | ● | ● | ● | ● | ● | ● | ● | ● | ● | ● | ● | ● | ● | ● | ● | ● | ● | ● | ● | ● | ● | ● | ● | ● | ● | ● | ● | ● | ● | ● | ● | ● | |
| NEW DUNDAS CLINIC (HM14817) | | | | | | | | | | | | | | | | | | | | | | ● | | | | | | | | | | | | | | | | | | ● | | | | | | | | |
| RADIANT COLOUR (HM16847) | | | | | | | | | | | | | | | | ● | | | | | | | | | | | | | | | | | | | | | ● | | | | | | | | | | | |
| SCOTTISH KINESIOLOGY CENTRE (HM18134) | ● | ● | ● | ● | ● | ● | ● | ● | ● | ● | ● | ● | ● | ● | ● | ● | ● | ● | ● | ● | ● | ● | ● | ● | ● | ● | ● | ● | ● | ● | ● | ● | ● | ● | ● | ● | ● | ● | ● | ● | ● | ● | ● | ● | ● | ● | ● | |
| LOTHIAN (WEST) | | | | | | | | | | | | | | | | | | | | | | | | | | | | | | | | | | | | | | | | | | | | | | | | |
| GILL, SHIRLEY (HM08080) | | | ● | | | ● | | | | | | | | | | | | | | | | | | | | ● | | | | | | | | | | | ● | | ● | | | | | ● | ● | | | |

# D - I Conditions treated at Practices/Businesses

| Business by County with Reference no. | Dandruff | Deafness | Depression | Diabetes | Diarrhoea | Digestive Problems | Diverticulitis | Dizziness | Dyslexia | Dyspraxia | Ear Disorders | Eczema | ENT Disorders | Epilepsy | Eye Disorders | Fatigue | Fears | Fertility Problems | Fever | Fibroids | Flatulence | Foot Problems | Fractures | Fungal Infections | Gallstones | Gastrointestinal Problems | Genital Herpes | Gingivitis | Glandular Fever | Glaucoma | Gout | Gum Disease | Hair Problems | Halitosis | Hand Problems | Hay Fever | Headaches | Hearing Problems | High Blood Pressure | Hip Complaints | Hyperactivity | Hypoglycaemia | Impotence | Incontinence | Indigestion | Infertility | Influenza | Ingrowing Toenails |
|---|---|---|---|---|---|---|---|---|---|---|---|---|---|---|---|---|---|---|---|---|---|---|---|---|---|---|---|---|---|---|---|---|---|---|---|---|---|---|---|---|---|---|---|---|---|---|---|---|
| LINLITHGOW PHYSIO PRACTICE (HM12438) |  |  |  |  |  |  |  |  |  |  |  |  |  |  |  |  |  |  |  |  |  |  |  |  |  |  |  |  |  |  |  |  |  |  |  |  |  |  |  |  | ● |  |  |  |  |  |  |  |  |
| VINCES, DENISE (HM20674) |  |  | ● |  | ● | ● |  |  |  |  |  |  |  |  |  | ● |  |  |  |  |  | ● |  |  | ● | ● |  |  |  |  | ● |  |  |  |  |  | ● |  | ● |  |  |  |  |  | ● |  |  |  |
| **MORAY** |  |  |  |  |  |  |  |  |  |  |  |  |  |  |  |  |  |  |  |  |  |  |  |  |  |  |  |  |  |  |  |  |  |  |  |  |  |  |  |  |  |  |  |  |  |  |  |  |
| AROMANTIC (HM01080) |  |  |  |  |  |  |  |  |  |  |  | ● |  |  |  |  |  |  |  |  |  | ● |  | ● |  |  |  |  |  |  |  | ● | ● |  |  |  |  |  |  |  |  |  |  |  |  |  |  |  |
| ELGIN CHIROPRACTIC CLINIC (HM06729) |  |  |  |  |  |  |  |  |  |  |  |  |  |  |  |  |  |  |  |  |  |  |  |  |  |  |  |  |  |  |  |  |  |  |  |  | ● |  |  | ● |  |  |  |  |  |  |  |  |
| FINDHORN FLOWER ESSENCES (HM07307) |  |  | ● |  |  |  |  |  |  |  |  |  |  |  |  |  | ● |  |  |  |  |  |  |  |  |  |  |  |  |  |  |  |  |  |  |  |  | ● |  |  |  |  |  |  |  |  |  |  |
| HEALTHWORKS (HM09422) | ● | ● | ● | ● | ● | ● |  | ● |  |  |  | ● |  |  |  | ● | ● | ● | ● | ● | ● | ● |  |  | ● | ● |  |  | ● |  |  |  |  |  | ● | ● | ● |  | ● |  |  |  |  |  | ● |  | ● |  |
| **NORTHUMBERLAND** |  |  |  |  |  |  |  |  |  |  |  |  |  |  |  |  |  |  |  |  |  |  |  |  |  |  |  |  |  |  |  |  |  |  |  |  |  |  |  |  |  |  |  |  |  |  |  |  |
| SOLAR- PLEXUS (HM18864) |  |  | ● |  |  | ● |  |  |  |  |  |  |  |  |  | ● |  |  |  |  |  |  |  |  |  |  |  |  |  |  |  |  |  |  |  |  | ● |  | ● |  | ● |  |  |  | ● |  |  |  |
| **ORKNEY ISLES** |  |  |  |  |  |  |  |  |  |  |  |  |  |  |  |  |  |  |  |  |  |  |  |  |  |  |  |  |  |  |  |  |  |  |  |  |  |  |  |  |  |  |  |  |  |  |  |  |
| A D S THOM (HM00030) |  |  |  |  |  |  |  |  |  |  |  |  |  |  |  |  |  |  |  |  |  | ● |  | ● |  |  |  |  |  |  |  |  |  |  |  |  |  |  |  |  |  |  |  |  |  |  |  |  |
| **PERTH AND KINROSS** |  |  |  |  |  |  |  |  |  |  |  |  |  |  |  |  |  |  |  |  |  |  |  |  |  |  |  |  |  |  |  |  |  |  |  |  |  |  |  |  |  |  |  |  |  |  |  |  |
| ACUPUNCTURE CLINIC (HM00288) |  |  | ● |  | ● | ● | ● | ● |  |  | ● | ● | ● |  | ● | ● | ● | ● | ● | ● | ● |  |  |  | ● | ● |  |  | ● |  |  |  |  |  | ● | ● | ● |  | ● | ● | ● |  | ● | ● | ● | ● | ● |  |
| ACUPUNCTURE CLINIC DUNKELD (HM00289) |  |  | ● |  | ● | ● | ● | ● |  |  | ● | ● | ● |  |  | ● | ● | ● | ● | ● | ● |  |  |  | ● | ● |  |  | ● |  |  |  |  |  | ● | ● | ● |  | ● | ● | ● |  | ● | ● | ● | ● | ● |  |
| AUCHTERARDER CHIROPODY (HM01343) |  |  |  |  |  |  |  |  |  |  |  |  |  |  |  |  |  |  |  |  |  | ● |  |  |  |  |  |  |  |  |  |  |  |  |  |  |  |  |  |  |  |  |  |  |  |  |  | ● |
| BACK PAIN & SPORTS CLINIC (HM01491) |  |  |  |  |  |  |  |  |  |  |  |  |  |  |  |  |  |  |  |  |  | ● |  |  |  |  |  |  |  |  |  |  |  |  |  |  | ● |  |  | ● |  |  |  |  |  |  |  |  |
| HOWIE, TOM R (HM10284) |  |  |  |  |  |  |  |  |  |  |  |  |  |  |  |  |  |  |  |  |  | ● |  |  |  |  |  |  |  |  |  |  |  |  |  |  |  |  |  |  |  |  |  |  |  |  |  |  |
| HOWIE, TOM R (HM10283) |  |  |  |  |  |  |  |  |  |  |  |  |  |  |  |  |  |  |  |  |  | ● |  |  |  |  |  |  |  |  |  |  |  |  |  |  |  |  |  |  |  |  |  |  |  |  |  |  |
| LENDRICK LODGE (HM12210) |  |  |  |  |  |  |  |  |  |  |  |  |  |  |  |  | ● |  |  |  |  |  |  |  |  |  |  |  |  |  |  |  |  |  |  |  |  |  |  |  |  |  |  |  |  |  |  |  |
| STEVENSON, IAN W (HM19246) |  |  |  |  |  |  |  |  |  |  |  |  |  |  |  |  |  |  |  |  |  |  | ● |  |  |  |  |  |  |  |  |  |  |  |  |  |  |  |  |  |  |  |  |  |  |  |  |  |
| TAYLOR, D (HM19749) |  |  | ● |  |  |  |  |  |  |  |  | ● |  |  |  |  | ● |  |  |  |  |  |  |  |  |  |  |  |  |  |  |  |  |  |  |  |  |  | ● |  |  |  | ● |  |  |  |  |  |
| **RENFREWSHIRE** |  |  |  |  |  |  |  |  |  |  |  |  |  |  |  |  |  |  |  |  |  |  |  |  |  |  |  |  |  |  |  |  |  |  |  |  |  |  |  |  |  |  |  |  |  |  |  |  |
| ALBA CENTRE (HM00473) |  |  | ● |  |  |  |  |  |  |  |  |  |  |  |  |  | ● |  |  |  |  |  |  |  |  |  |  |  |  |  |  |  |  |  |  |  |  |  |  |  |  |  |  |  |  |  |  |  |
| BLACKHALL PARK CENTRE (HM02444) |  |  | ● |  | ● | ● |  | ● |  |  |  | ● |  |  |  | ● |  |  |  |  |  |  |  |  |  |  |  |  |  |  | ● |  |  |  | ● | ● | ● |  | ● | ● | ● |  |  |  | ● |  |  |  |
| DOUGLAS, ANNE S (HM06212) |  |  |  |  |  |  |  |  |  |  |  |  |  |  |  |  |  |  |  |  |  |  | ● |  |  |  |  |  |  |  |  |  |  |  |  |  |  |  |  | ● |  |  |  |  |  |  |  |  |
| FANNING, M W (HM07095) |  |  | ● |  |  |  |  |  |  |  |  |  |  |  |  |  |  |  |  |  |  |  |  |  |  |  |  |  |  |  |  |  |  |  |  |  | ● |  |  |  |  |  |  |  |  |  |  |  |
| LINTON, UNNA (HM12444) |  |  |  | ● |  |  |  |  |  |  |  |  |  |  |  |  |  |  |  |  |  | ● |  |  |  |  |  |  |  |  |  |  |  |  |  |  |  |  |  |  |  |  |  |  |  |  |  |  |
| PAISLEY CHIROPRACTIC CLINIC (HM15587) |  |  | ● |  | ● | ● | ● | ● |  |  | ● |  |  |  |  | ● | ● | ● |  |  |  | ● |  |  |  | ● |  |  |  |  |  |  |  |  | ● |  | ● |  |  | ● |  |  |  |  | ● |  |  |  |
| PAISLEY NATURAL THERAPY CENTRE (HM15588) |  |  | ● |  | ● | ● | ● | ● |  | ● | ● | ● |  |  |  | ● | ● |  |  |  | ● |  |  | ● |  | ● |  | ● | ● | ● | ● | ● | ● | ● | ● | ● | ● |  | ● | ● | ● | ● | ● | ● | ● |  | ● |  |
| PAISLEY PHYSIOTHERAPY CENTRE (HM15589) |  |  |  |  |  |  |  | ● |  |  |  |  |  |  |  |  |  |  |  |  |  | ● | ● |  |  |  |  |  |  |  | ● |  |  |  | ● |  | ● |  |  | ● |  |  |  | ● |  |  |  |  |
| RAINEY, MARTHA (HM16890) |  |  | ● | ● | ● | ● |  | ● |  |  | ● |  | ● |  |  | ● |  | ● |  |  |  |  |  |  |  | ● |  |  |  | ● |  |  |  |  |  |  | ● |  | ● | ● |  |  |  |  | ● |  |  |  |
| ROSEWOOD AROMATHERAPY ROOM (HM17629) |  |  | ● |  |  | ● |  |  |  |  |  | ● |  |  |  |  |  |  |  |  |  |  |  |  |  |  |  |  |  |  |  |  |  |  |  |  | ● |  |  |  |  |  |  |  |  |  |  |  |
| **SCOTTISH BORDERS** |  |  |  |  |  |  |  |  |  |  |  |  |  |  |  |  |  |  |  |  |  |  |  |  |  |  |  |  |  |  |  |  |  |  |  |  |  |  |  |  |  |  |  |  |  |  |  |  |
| HOGARTH, JAMES (HM09908) |  |  |  | ● |  |  |  |  |  |  |  |  |  |  |  |  |  |  |  |  |  | ● |  |  |  |  |  |  |  |  |  |  |  |  |  |  |  |  |  |  |  |  |  |  |  |  |  | ● |

# D - I Conditions treated at Practices/Businesses

Business by County with Reference no.

| Condition | L W FOOTCARE (HM11844) | NATURES TOUCH (HM14698) | NATURES WAY (HM14702) | ST BOSWELLS CHIRO CLINIC (HM19072) | WATT, A S (HM21028) | WISHING WELL (HM21738) | SHETLAND ISLANDS | LERWICK CHIROPRACTIC CLINIC (HM12231) |
|---|---|---|---|---|---|---|---|---|
| Ingrowing Toenails | ● | | | | | | | |
| Influenza | | | ● | | | ● | | |
| Infertility | | | | | | ● | | |
| Indigestion | | | | | | ● | | |
| Incontinence | | | | | | ● | | |
| Impotence | | | | | | ● | | |
| Hypoglycaemia | | | | | | | | |
| Hyperactivity | | | | | | ● | | |
| Hip Complaints | | | | | | | | ● |
| High Blood Pressure | | | | | | | | |
| Hearing Problems | | | | | | | | ● |
| Headaches | | | | ● | | ● | | ● |
| Hay Fever | | | | | | ● | | |
| Hand Problems | | | | ● | | ● | | |
| Halitosis | | | | | | ● | | |
| Hair Problems | | | | | | | | |
| Gum Disease | | | | | | | | |
| Gout | | | | | | | | |
| Glaucoma | | | | | | | | |
| Glandular Fever | | | | | | | | |
| Gingivitis | | | | | | | | |
| Genital Herpes | | | | | | | | |
| Gastrointestinal Problems | | | | | | ● | | |
| Gallstones | | | | | | | | |
| Fungal Infections | | | | | ● | | | |
| Fractures | | | | | | | | |
| Foot Problems | ● | | | ● | ● | ● | | |
| Flatulence | | | | | | ● | | |
| Fibroids | | | | | | | | |
| Fever | | | | | | | | |
| Fertility Problems | | | | | | ● | | |
| Fears | | | | | | ● | | |
| Fatigue | | | | | | ● | | |
| Eye Disorders | | | | | | | | |
| Epilepsy | | | | | | | | |
| ENT Disorders | | | | | | ● | | |
| Eczema | | | | | | ● | | |
| Ear Disorders | | | | | | ● | | |
| Dyspraxia | | | | | | | | |
| Dyslexia | | | | | | | | |
| Dizziness | | | | ● | | ● | | |
| Diverticulitis | | | | | | ● | | |
| Digestive Problems | | | | ● | | ● | | ● |
| Diarrhoea | | | | | | ● | | |
| Diabetes | ● | | | | | | | |
| Depression | | ● | | | | ● | | |
| Deafness | | | | | | | | |
| Dandruff | | | | | | ● | | |

# D - I Conditions treated at Practices/Businesses

| Business by County with Reference no. | Dandruff | Deafness | Depression | Diabetes | Diarrhoea | Digestive Problems | Diverticulitis | Dizziness | Dyslexia | Dyspraxia | Ear Disorders | Eczema | ENT Disorders | Epilepsy | Eye Disorders | Fatigue | Fears | Fertility Problems | Fever | Fibroids | Flatulence | Foot Problems | Fractures | Fungal Infections | Gallstones | Gastrointestinal Problems | Genital Herpes | Gingivitis | Glandular Fever | Glaucoma | Gout | Gum Disease | Hair Problems | Halitosis | Hand Problems | Hay Fever | Headaches | Hearing Problems | High Blood Pressure | Hip Complaints | Hyperactivity | Hypoglycaemia | Impotence | Incontinence | Indigestion | Infertility | Influenza | Ingrowing Toenails |
|---|---|---|---|---|---|---|---|---|---|---|---|---|---|---|---|---|---|---|---|---|---|---|---|---|---|---|---|---|---|---|---|---|---|---|---|---|---|---|---|---|---|---|---|---|---|---|---|---|
| WALES | | | | | | | | | | | | | | | | | | | | | | | | | | | | | | | | | | | | | | | | | | | | | | | | |
| BLAENAU GWENT | | | | | | | | | | | | | | | | | | | | | | | | | | | | | | | | | | | | | | | | | | | | | | | | |
| ABERTILLERY PHYSIOTHERAPY (HM00125) | | | | | | | | | | | | | | | | | | | | | | | ● | | | | | | | | | | | | ● | | | | | | | | | | | | | |
| CLASSIC CLINIC (HM04606) | | | ● | | | ● | | | | | | ● | | | | ● | | | | | | | | | | | | | | | | | | | | | ● | | ● | | | | | | | | | |
| BRIDGEND | | | | | | | | | | | | | | | | | | | | | | | | | | | | | | | | | | | | | | | | | | | | | | | | |
| PARKWOOD CHIROPRACTIC CLINIC (HM15725) | | | | | | | | | | | | | | | | | | | | | | | | | | | | | | | | | | | | | ● | | | ● | | | | | | | | |
| CAERPHILLY | | | | | | | | | | | | | | | | | | | | | | | | | | | | | | | | | | | | | | | | | | | | | | | | |
| OAKFIELD NATURAL HEALTH CENTRE (HM15151) | ● | ● | ● | ● | ● | ● | ● | ● | ● | ● | ● | ● | ● | ● | ● | ● | ● | ● | ● | ● | ● | ● | ● | ● | ● | ● | ● | ● | ● | ● | ● | ● | ● | ● | ● | ● | ● | ● | ● | ● | ● | ● | ● | ● | ● | ● | ● | |
| PARKWOOD CHIROPRACTIC CLINIC (HM15723) | | | | | | | | ● | | | | | | | | | | | | | | | | | | | | | | | | | | | ● | | ● | | | ● | | | | | | | | |
| CARMARTHENSHIRE | | | | | | | | | | | | | | | | | | | | | | | | | | | | | | | | | | | | | | | | | | | | | | | | |
| GREENWAY CONSULTANCY (HM08495) | ● | | ● | | ● | ● | ● | ● | | | | ● | | | | ● | ● | | ● | | | | | | ● | ● | | | | | | | ● | ● | ● | ● | ● | | ● | | ● | ● | | ● | ● | | ● | |
| HEALING HANDS (HM09339) | | | | | | | | | | | | | | | | ● | | | | | | ● | | | | | | | | | | | | | | | ● | | ● | | | | | | ● | | | |
| JABROO, C (HM10808) | ● | ● | ● | ● | ● | ● | ● | ● | ● | ● | ● | ● | ● | ● | ● | ● | ● | ● | ● | ● | ● | ● | ● | ● | ● | ● | ● | ● | ● | ● | ● | ● | ● | ● | ● | ● | ● | ● | ● | ● | ● | ● | ● | ● | ● | ● | ● | |
| SPENCER AROMATHERAPY (HM18990) | | | ● | | | | | | | | | | | | | | | ● | | | | | | | | | | | | | | | | | | | | | | | | | | | | | | |
| WAINWRIGHT, MARY (HM20738) | ● | ● | ● | ● | ● | ● | ● | ● | ● | ● | ● | ● | ● | ● | ● | ● | ● | ● | ● | ● | ● | ● | ● | ● | ● | ● | ● | ● | ● | ● | ● | ● | ● | ● | ● | ● | ● | ● | ● | ● | ● | ● | ● | ● | ● | ● | ● | |
| CEREDIGION | | | | | | | | | | | | | | | | | | | | | | | | | | | | | | | | | | | | | | | | | | | | | | | | |
| AMIES, SUSAN (HM00785) | | | | | | | | | | | | | | | | | | | | | | ● | | ● | | | | | | | | | | | | | | | | | | | | | | | | ● |
| CHERRY TREE CTRE FOR NTRL MED (HM04109) | ● | ● | ● | ● | ● | ● | ● | ● | ● | ● | ● | ● | ● | ● | ● | ● | ● | ● | ● | ● | ● | ● | ● | ● | ● | ● | ● | ● | ● | ● | ● | ● | ● | ● | ● | ● | ● | ● | ● | ● | ● | ● | ● | ● | ● | ● | ● | |
| COCKSEDGE, JOHN M (HM04774) | | | | ● | | | | | | | | | | | | | | | | | | ● | | | | | | | | | | | | | | | | | | | | | | | | | | ● |
| FFYNNONWEN NATURAL THRPY CTRE (HM07256) | | | | | ● | | | | | | | ● | | | | ● | ● | | | | | | | | | | | | ● | | | | | | | ● | ● | | | | ● | | | | | | | |
| LEWIS, D MICHAEL (HM12289) | | | | ● | | | | | | | | | | | | | | | | | | | | | | | | | | | | | | | | | | | | | | | | | | | | ● |
| CONWY | | | | | | | | | | | | | | | | | | | | | | | | | | | | | | | | | | | | | | | | | | | | | | | | |
| DREW, DAVID (HM06305) | | | ● | | | | ● | | | | | ● | | | | ● | ● | ● | | | | | | | | | ● | | | | | | | | | | ● | | ● | | | | ● | | | ● | | |
| HERBS FOR EVERYONE (HM09669) | ● | ● | ● | ● | ● | ● | ● | ● | | | ● | ● | ● | ● | | ● | ● | ● | ● | ● | ● | | | ● | ● | ● | ● | ● | ● | ● | ● | ● | ● | | | ● | ● | | ● | | ● | ● | ● | ● | ● | ● | ● | |
| MELA CENTRE OF OSTEOPATHY (HM13702) | | | | | | | | | | | | | | | | | | | | | | ● | | | | | | | | | | | | | ● | | ● | | | ● | | | | | | | | |
| MEWIS, R J (HM13782) | | | | | | | | | | | | | | | | | | | | | | | | | | | | | | | | | | | | | ● | | | ● | | | | | | | | |
| DENBIGHSHIRE | | | | | | | | | | | | | | | | | | | | | | | | | | | | | | | | | | | | | | | | | | | | | | | | |
| ALLIED PHYSIOTHERAPY (HM00646) | | | | | | | | | | | | | | | | | | | | | | ● | | | | | | | | | | | | | | | | | | | | | | | | | | |
| HEALING WAYS (HM09359) | ● | ● | ● | ● | ● | ● | ● | ● | ● | ● | ● | ● | ● | ● | ● | ● | ● | ● | ● | ● | ● | ● | ● | ● | ● | ● | ● | ● | ● | ● | ● | ● | ● | ● | ● | ● | ● | ● | ● | ● | ● | ● | ● | ● | ● | ● | ● | |
| ROY MORRIS CLINIC (HM17709) | ● | ● | ● | ● | ● | ● | ● | ● | | | ● | ● | ● | ● | ● | ● | ● | ● | ● | | ● | ● | | ● | ● | ● | | ● | | ● | ● | ● | | ● | ● | ● | ● | ● | ● | ● | ● | ● | ● | | ● | ● | ● | |
| FLINTSHIRE | | | | | | | | | | | | | | | | | | | | | | | | | | | | | | | | | | | | | | | | | | | | | | | | |
| A L J RILEY ASSOCIATES (HM00038) | ● | | ● | ● | ● | ● | ● | | | | | ● | | | | ● | | | | | ● | | | ● | | ● | | | | | ● | | ● | ● | ● | ● | ● | | ● | | | | | | ● | ● | ● | |
| BOOTS HEALTHCARE SERVICES (HM02711) | | ● | | ● | | | | | | | | | | ● | | | | | | | | ● | ● | ● | | | | | | | ● | | | | | | | | | | | ● | | | | | | |

# D - I Conditions treated at Practices/Businesses

| Business by County with Reference no. | Dandruff | Deafness | Depression | Diabetes | Diarrhoea | Digestive Problems | Diverticulitis | Dizziness | Dyslexia | Dyspraxia | Ear Disorders | Eczema | ENT Disorders | Epilepsy | Eye Disorders | Fatigue | Fears | Fertility Problems | Fever | Fibroids | Flatulence | Foot Problems | Fractures | Fungal Infections | Gallstones | Gastrointestinal Problems | Genital Herpes | Gingivitis | Glandular Fever | Glaucoma | Gout | Gum Disease | Hair Problems | Halitosis | Hand Problems | Hay Fever | Headaches | Hearing Problems | High Blood Pressure | Hip Complaints | Hyperactivity | Hypoglycaemia | Impotence | Incontinence | Indigestion | Infertility | Influenza | Ingrowing Toenails |
|---|---|---|---|---|---|---|---|---|---|---|---|---|---|---|---|---|---|---|---|---|---|---|---|---|---|---|---|---|---|---|---|---|---|---|---|---|---|---|---|---|---|---|---|---|---|---|---|
| CHIROPODISTS SURGERY (HM04298) |||||||||||||||||||||||●||●|||||||||||||||||||||||||●|
| GAFFNEY, ALMA (HM07827) |||||||||||||||||||||||●||●|||||||||||||||||||||||||●|
| HYPNOTHERAPY CENTRE (HM10528) ||●||||||||||||||||||||||||||||||||||||●||||||||||
| REECE, JULIE (HM17038) |||||||||||||||||||||||●||●|||||||||||||||||||||||||●|
| GLAMORGAN (VALE OF) ||||||||||||||||||||||||||||||||||||||||||||||||||
| ALEXANDER TECHNIQUE (HM00546) |||||||||||||||||||||||||||||||||||||●|||●|||||||||
| ALEXANDER TECHNIQUE (HM00551) |||||||||||||||||||||||||||||||||||||●|||●|||||||||
| AMETHYST HEALING CENTRE (HM00784) ||●||||||||||||||||●|||||||||||||||||||●||||||||||||
| AROMATHERAPY CLINIC (HM01105) |||||||||||||||||||||||||||||||||||||●|||●||||||●|||
| BARRY OSTEOPATHIC CLINIC (HM01809) |||||||||||||||||||||||||||||||||||||●|||●|||||||||
| BODY ESSENTIALS (HM02587) ||●||||||||||||||||||||||||||||||||||●||||||||||||
| BROWN, ANNE (HM03214) |||||||||||||||||||||||●|||||||||||||||||●|||||||||
| CARDIFF CHIROPRACTIC CLINIC (HM03666) |||||||||||||||||||||||||||||||||||||●|||●|||||||||
| CARDIFF HEALTH PRACTICE (HM03670) |||||||||||||||||||||||||||||||||||||●|||●|||||||||
| CARDIFF HOMEOPATHIC CLINIC (HM03671) |●|●|●|●|●|●|●|●|●|●|●|●|●|●|●|●|●|●|●|●|●|●|●|●|●|●|●|●|●|●|●|●|●|●|●|●|●|●|●|●|●|●|●|●|●|●|●||
| CITY CENTRE CHIRO CLINIC (HM04488) |||||||||||||||||||||||||||||||||||||●|||●|||||||||
| COWBRIDGE CHIRO/SPINAL REHAB (HM05289) |●|●|●|●|●|●|●|●|●|●|●|●|●|●|●|●|●|●|●|●|●|●|●|●|●|●|●|●|●|●|●|●|●|●|●|●|●|●|●|●|●|●|●|●|●|●|●||
| COWBRIDGE OSTEOPATH CLINIC (HM05290) |||||||||||||||||||||||||||||||||||||●|||●|||||||||
| EVANS, STEVE (HM06990) ||||||||||||||||||||||||||||||||||||||||●|||||||||
| GRIMWADE, S (HM08586) |||||●|||||●|||||●|||||||||||||||||||||●|||●|||||||||
| HENRIETTA CTRE FOR COMP THRPY (HM09565) ||●|||||||||||||||●||||||||||||||||||||||||||||||
| LLANISHEN PHYSIOTHERAPY CLINIC (HM12501) ||||||||||||||||||||||||||||||||||||||||●|||||||||
| MILES, ANDREW (HM13854) |||||||||||||||||||||||||||||||||||||●|||●|||||||||
| MOBILE FOOTWORKS (HM14031) |||||●||||||||||●||●||||●||●|||||||●||||●||●||||||||●||||
| MORGAN-AYRES, PAUL (PROF) (HM14178) ||●|||●||||||||||●|●|||||||||●||||||||||||●||●||●||||||||
| MULLINS, JOHN (HM14348) |||||●|||||||||||||||||●|●||||||||||||||||●|||●|||||●||||
| NATURAL HEALTHCARE (HM14601) |●|●|●|●|●|●|●|●||||||||●|●|●|●|●|●||||||||||||●|●||||||||●|●|●|●|||||||||
| PARKWOOD CHIROPRACTIC CLINIC (HM15724) |||||||||||||||||||||||||||||||||||||●|||●|||||||||
| PARKWOOD CHIROPRACTIC CLINIC (HM15726) |||||||||||||||||||||||||||||||||||||●|||●|||||||||
| PENARTH CHIROPRACTIC CLINIC (HM15961) ||●|||||||||●||||||||||●|●||||||||||||||●||●|●||●|||||●||||
| PENARTH HOMEOPATHY CLINIC (HM15962) |●|●|●|●|●|●|●|●|●|●|●|●|●|●|●|●|●|●|●|●|●|●|●|●|●|●|●|●|●|●|●|●|●|●|●|●|●|●|●|●|●|●|●|●|●|●|●||
| PENYLAN PODIATRIC CENTRE (HM16005) |||||||||||||||||||||||●||●||||||||||||||||||||||||||
| PHYSIO FIRST CENTRE (HM16198) ||||||||||||||||||||||||||||||||||||||||●|||||||||
| POLLEY, LYNDON (HM16413) |||||||||||||||||||||||●||●||||||||||||||||||||||||||

# D - I Conditions treated at Practices/Businesses

| Business by County with Reference no. | Dandruff | Deafness | Depression | Diabetes | Diarrhoea | Digestive Problems | Diverticulitis | Dizziness | Dyslexia | Dyspraxia | Ear Disorders | Eczema | ENT Disorders | Epilepsy | Eye Disorders | Fatigue | Fears | Fertility Problems | Fever | Fibroids | Flatulence | Foot Problems | Fractures | Fungal Infections | Gallstones | Gastrointestinal Problems | Genital Herpes | Gingivitis | Glandular Fever | Glaucoma | Gout | Gum Disease | Hair Problems | Halitosis | Hand Problems | Hay Fever | Headaches | Hearing Problems | High Blood Pressure | Hip Complaints | Hyperactivity | Hypoglycaemia | Impotence | Incontinence | Indigestion | Infertility | Influenza | Ingrowing Toenails |
|---|---|---|---|---|---|---|---|---|---|---|---|---|---|---|---|---|---|---|---|---|---|---|---|---|---|---|---|---|---|---|---|---|---|---|---|---|---|---|---|---|---|---|---|---|---|---|---|---|
| POLLEY, LYNDON (HM16415) | | | | | | | | | | | | | | | | | | | | | | ● | | ● | | | | | | | | | | | | | | | | | | | | | | | | |
| POLLEY, LYNDON (HM16414) | | | | | | | | | | | | | | | | | | | | | | ● | | ● | | | | | | | | | | | | | | | | | | | | | | | | |
| RENWICK, SARAH NADINE (HM17192) | | | | | | | | | | | ● | ● | | | | ● | | ● | | | | | | | | | | | | | | | | | | | ● | | | | | | ● | | ● | | | |
| RIDGE, D (HM17316) | | | | | | | | | | | | | | | | | | | | | | ● | | | | | | | | | | | | | | | | | | ● | | | | | | | | |
| RIDGE, D (HM17315) | | | | | | | | | | | | | | | | | | | | | | ● | | | | | | | | | | | | | | | ● | | | ● | | | | | | | | |
| SIMS, TRACEY (HM18602) | | | | | | | | | | | | | | | | | | | | | | ● | | ● | | | | | | | | | | | | | | | | | | | | | | | | |
| SWANSEA VALLEY PHYSIO PRACTICE (HM19579) | | | | | | | | | | | | | | | | | | | | | | ● | ● | | | | | | | | | | | | | | | | | | | | | | | | | |
| WALSH, J A (HM20859) | | | | | | | | | | | | | | | | | | | | | | ● | | ● | | | | | | | | | | | | | | | | | | | | | | | | |
| **GWYNEDD** | | | | | | | | | | | | | | | | | | | | | | | | | | | | | | | | | | | | | | | | | | | | | | | | |
| CENTRE FOR WELL BEING (HM03922) | | | ● | | | | | | | | | | | | | | | | | | | | | | | | | | | | | | | | | | | | | | | | | | | | | |
| MOSSHILL HOLISTIC CENTRE (HM14270) | ● | ● | ● | ● | ● | ● | ● | ● | ● | ● | ● | ● | ● | ● | ● | ● | ● | ● | ● | ● | ● | ● | ● | ● | ● | ● | ● | ● | ● | ● | ● | ● | ● | ● | ● | ● | ● | ● | ● | ● | ● | ● | ● | ● | ● | ● | ● | |
| NATURAL THERAPY CLINIC (HM14660) | | | | ● | | ● | | | | | | ● | | | | ● | | ● | | | | | ● | ● | | | | | | | | | | | | | ● | | | | | | | | | ● | | |
| O'NEIL, L (HM15325) | | | | | | | | | | | | | | | | ● | ● | | | | | | | | | | | | | | | | | | | | ● | | | | | | ● | | | ● | | |
| **ISLE OF ANGLESEY** | | | | | | | | | | | | | | | | | | | | | | | | | | | | | | | | | | | | | | | | | | | | | | | | |
| CHALMERS, D G (HM03951) | | | | | | | | | | | | | | | | | | | | | | ● | | | | | | | | | | | | | | | | | | ● | | | | | | | | |
| EPHRAIM, NONA (HM06851) | | | ● | | | | | | | | | | | | | | | | | | | | | | | | | | | | | | | | | | | | | | | | | | | | | |
| **MONMOUTHSHIRE** | | | | | | | | | | | | | | | | | | | | | | | | | | | | | | | | | | | | | | | | | | | | | | | | |
| ABERGAVENNY THERAPY CTRE (HM00121) | | | ● | | ● | ● | | | | | | ● | | | | ● | | | | | | | | | | | | | | | | | | | | | | | | | | | | | | | | |
| BROOKSIDE PHYSIO PRACTICE (HM03184) | | | | | | | | | | | | | | | | | | | | | | ● | | | | | | | | | | | | | ● | | ● | | | ● | | | | | | | | |
| ELECTROMAGNETIC PRODUCTS (HM06721) | | | | | | | | | | | | | | | | | | | | | | | | | | | | | | | ● | | | | | | ● | | | | | | | | | | | |
| HARMONY (HM09020) | | ● | ● | ● | ● | ● | ● | ● | | | ● | ● | ● | ● | ● | ● | ● | ● | ● | ● | ● | ● | | ● | ● | ● | ● | ● | ● | | | ● | ● | ● | ● | ● | ● | ● | ● | ● | ● | ● | ● | ● | ● | ● | ● | |
| NUTRITION CLINIC (HM15122) | ● | ● | ● | ● | ● | ● | ● | ● | ● | | ● | ● | ● | | | ● | ● | ● | | ● | ● | | ● | ● | ● | ● | ● | | ● | | ● | | | ● | ● | ● | ● | ● | ● | | ● | ● | ● | | ● | ● | | |
| TURFAEN CHIROPODY CLINIC (HM20407) | | | | ● | | | | | | | | | | | | | | | | | | ● | | ● | | | | | | | ● | | | | | | | | | | | | | | | | | |
| **NEATH PORT TALBOT** | | | | | | | | | | | | | | | | | | | | | | | | | | | | | | | | | | | | | | | | | | | | | | | | |
| ST JAMES MEDICAL CENTRE (HM19078) | ● | ● | ● | ● | ● | ● | ● | ● | ● | ● | ● | ● | ● | ● | ● | ● | ● | ● | ● | ● | ● | ● | ● | ● | ● | ● | ● | ● | ● | ● | ● | ● | ● | ● | ● | ● | ● | ● | ● | ● | ● | ● | ● | ● | ● | ● | ● | |
| **NEWPORT** | | | | | | | | | | | | | | | | | | | | | | | | | | | | | | | | | | | | | | | | | | | | | | | | |
| BAJJADA, JUNE (HM01572) | | | ● | | | ● | ● | ● | | | | ● | | | | ● | ● | | | | ● | ● | | | | ● | | | | | ● | | | | ● | ● | ● | | ● | ● | | | | | ● | | | |
| BEIGHTON, J W (HM02069) | | | ● | ● | ● | ● | ● | ● | ● | | ● | ● | ● | ● | ● | ● | ● | ● | ● | | ● | ● | ● | ● | ● | ● | ● | ● | ● | ● | ● | ● | ● | ● | ● | ● | ● | ● | ● | ● | ● | ● | ● | | ● | ● | ● | |
| BOWKETT, LYN (HM02792) | ● | ● | ● | ● | ● | ● | ● | ● | ● | ● | ● | ● | ● | ● | ● | ● | ● | ● | ● | ● | ● | ● | ● | ● | ● | ● | ● | ● | ● | ● | ● | ● | ● | ● | ● | ● | ● | ● | ● | ● | ● | ● | ● | ● | ● | ● | ● | |
| CLINIC OF HOLISTIC HEALTH (HM04693) | ● | ● | ● | ● | ● | ● | ● | ● | ● | ● | ● | ● | ● | ● | ● | ● | ● | ● | ● | ● | ● | ● | ● | ● | ● | ● | ● | ● | ● | ● | ● | ● | ● | ● | ● | ● | ● | ● | ● | ● | ● | ● | ● | ● | ● | ● | ● | |
| MOXLEY, SHIRLEY (HM14304) | | | ● | ● | | ● | | | | | | ● | | | | ● | | | | | | | ● | | ● | ● | | | | | | | | | | ● | ● | | | | | | | | ● | | | |
| OLIVER, MARION (HM15294) | | | ● | ● | ● | ● | ● | | | | ● | ● | ● | | | ● | ● | | | | ● | ● | | ● | | ● | | ● | ● | | ● | ● | | ● | ● | ● | ● | | ● | ● | ● | | | ● | ● | | | |
| **PEMBROKESHIRE** | | | | | | | | | | | | | | | | | | | | | | | | | | | | | | | | | | | | | | | | | | | | | | | | |
| CENTRE OF TRADITIONAL HEALING (HM03926) | | | ● | | | | | | | | | ● | | | | | | | | | | | | | | | | | | | | | | | | | ● | | | | | | | | | | | |

# D - I Conditions treated at Practices/Businesses

| Business by County with Reference no. | Dandruff | Deafness | Depression | Diabetes | Diarrhoea | Digestive Problems | Diverticulitis | Dizziness | Dyslexia | Dyspraxia | Ear Disorders | Eczema |
|---|---|---|---|---|---|---|---|---|---|---|---|---|
| JABROO, C (HM10809) | ● | ● | ● | ● | ● | ● | ● | ● | ● | ● | ● | ● |
| **POWYS** | | | | | | | | | | | | |
| BRECON CLINIC (HM02944) | | | ● | ● | ● | ● | ● | ● | | | ● | ● |
| BRECON COMPLEMENTARY MED CTRE (HM02945) | ● | ● | ● | ● | ● | ● | ● | ● | ● | ● | ● | ● |
| CONROY, CHRISTINE (HM05007) | | | | | | | | | | | | |
| COVENT HOUSE NTRL HEALTH CTRE (HM05280) | ● | ● | ● | ● | ● | ● | ● | ● | ● | ● | ● | ● |
| GROVES, FRAN (HM08614) | | | | | | | | | | | | |
| HEALTH FOCUS (HM09386) | | | ● | ● | ● | ● | ● | ● | | | ● | ● |
| KILGOUR, KATHARINE () | | | | | | | | | | | | |
| LLANDRINDOD WELLS SPA TOWN (HM12499) | ● | ● | ● | ● | ● | ● | ● | ● | ● | ● | ● | ● |
| PEACE CLINIC (HM15876) | | | ● | | | | | | | | | ● |
| REFLEXOLOGY & ALLERGY THERAPY (HM17078) | | | ● | | ● | ● | | | | | | |
| SHEPPARD, HELEN (HM18421) | | | | | | ● | ● | ● | | | ● | ● |
| **RHONDDA CYNON TAFF** | | | | | | | | | | | | |
| POLLEY, LYNDON (HM16416) | | | | | | | | | | | | |
| **SWANSEA** | | | | | | | | | | | | |
| ABERTAWE PHYSIOTHERAPY CLINIC (HM00124) | | | | | | | | ● | | | | |
| ACUPUNCTURE CENTRE (HM00254) | | | ● | | ● | ● | | ● | | | | |
| BURDEN, RICHARD (HM03370) | | | ● | | ● | ● | ● | | | | | |
| PEDORTHICS FOOT SGY PRACTICE (HM15935) | | | | ● | | | | | | | | |
| RODWAY & ASSOCIATES (HM17531) | | | | | | | | | | | | |
| **WREXHAM** | | | | | | | | | | | | |
| HARMONY IN HEALTH (HM09028) | | | ● | | | | | | | | | |
| SENSORAMA (HM18229) | | | ● | | | | | | | | | |

| Business by County with Reference no. | ENT Disorders | Epilepsy | Eye Disorders | Fatigue | Fears | Fertility Problems | Fever | Fibroids | Flatulence | Foot Problems | Fractures | Fungal Infections |
|---|---|---|---|---|---|---|---|---|---|---|---|---|
| JABROO, C (HM10809) | ● | ● | ● | ● | ● | ● | ● | ● | ● | ● | ● | ● |
| **POWYS** | | | | | | | | | | | | |
| BRECON CLINIC (HM02944) | ● | | | ● | ● | ● | | ● | ● | ● | ● | |
| BRECON COMPLEMENTARY MED CTRE (HM02945) | ● | ● | ● | ● | ● | ● | ● | ● | ● | ● | ● | ● |
| CONROY, CHRISTINE (HM05007) | | | | | | | | | | | | |
| COVENT HOUSE NTRL HEALTH CTRE (HM05280) | ● | ● | ● | ● | ● | ● | ● | ● | ● | ● | ● | ● |
| GROVES, FRAN (HM08614) | | | | | | | | | | | | |
| HEALTH FOCUS (HM09386) | ● | | ● | ● | ● | ● | ● | ● | ● | ● | | ● |
| KILGOUR, KATHARINE () | | | | | | | | | | ● | ● | |
| LLANDRINDOD WELLS SPA TOWN (HM12499) | ● | ● | ● | ● | ● | ● | ● | ● | ● | ● | ● | ● |
| PEACE CLINIC (HM15876) | | | | | ● | | | | | | | |
| REFLEXOLOGY & ALLERGY THERAPY (HM17078) | | | | ● | | ● | | | | | | |
| SHEPPARD, HELEN (HM18421) | | | | ● | ● | ● | | ● | ● | ● | | |
| **RHONDDA CYNON TAFF** | | | | | | | | | | | | |
| POLLEY, LYNDON (HM16416) | | | | | | | | | | ● | | ● |
| **SWANSEA** | | | | | | | | | | | | |
| ABERTAWE PHYSIOTHERAPY CLINIC (HM00124) | | | | | | | | | | ● | ● | |
| ACUPUNCTURE CENTRE (HM00254) | | | | ● | | ● | | | | | | |
| BURDEN, RICHARD (HM03370) | | | | ● | | | | | ● | | | |
| PEDORTHICS FOOT SGY PRACTICE (HM15935) | | | | | | | | | | ● | | |
| RODWAY & ASSOCIATES (HM17531) | | | | | | | | | | | | |
| **WREXHAM** | | | | | | | | | | | | |
| HARMONY IN HEALTH (HM09028) | | | | ● | | ● | | ● | | | | |
| SENSORAMA (HM18229) | | | | ● | | | | | | | | |

| Business by County with Reference no. | Gallstones | Gastrointestinal Problems | Genital Herpes | Gingivitis | Glandular Fever | Glaucoma | Gout | Gum Disease | Hair Problems | Halitosis | Hand Problems | Hay Fever |
|---|---|---|---|---|---|---|---|---|---|---|---|---|
| JABROO, C (HM10809) | ● | ● | ● | ● | ● | ● | ● | ● | ● | ● | ● | ● |
| **POWYS** | | | | | | | | | | | | |
| BRECON CLINIC (HM02944) | ● | ● | | | ● | ● | ● | ● | | ● | ● | ● |
| BRECON COMPLEMENTARY MED CTRE (HM02945) | ● | ● | ● | ● | ● | ● | ● | ● | ● | ● | ● | ● |
| CONROY, CHRISTINE (HM05007) | | | | | | | | | | | | |
| COVENT HOUSE NTRL HEALTH CTRE (HM05280) | ● | ● | ● | ● | ● | ● | ● | ● | ● | ● | ● | ● |
| GROVES, FRAN (HM08614) | | | | | | | | | | | | |
| HEALTH FOCUS (HM09386) | | | | | | | | | | | | ● |
| KILGOUR, KATHARINE () | | | | | | | | | | | | |
| LLANDRINDOD WELLS SPA TOWN (HM12499) | ● | ● | ● | ● | ● | ● | ● | ● | ● | ● | ● | ● |
| PEACE CLINIC (HM15876) | | | | | | | | | | | | |
| REFLEXOLOGY & ALLERGY THERAPY (HM17078) | | ● | | | | | ● | | | | | ● |
| SHEPPARD, HELEN (HM18421) | ● | ● | | | | | ● | | | | ● | ● |
| **RHONDDA CYNON TAFF** | | | | | | | | | | | | |
| POLLEY, LYNDON (HM16416) | | | | | | | | | | | | |
| **SWANSEA** | | | | | | | | | | | | |
| ABERTAWE PHYSIOTHERAPY CLINIC (HM00124) | | | | | | | | | | | ● | |
| ACUPUNCTURE CENTRE (HM00254) | | | | | | | | | | | | ● |
| BURDEN, RICHARD (HM03370) | | ● | | | | | | | | | | |
| PEDORTHICS FOOT SGY PRACTICE (HM15935) | | | | | | | | | | | | |
| RODWAY & ASSOCIATES (HM17531) | | | | | | | | | | | | |
| **WREXHAM** | | | | | | | | | | | | |
| HARMONY IN HEALTH (HM09028) | ● | | | | | | | | | | | |
| SENSORAMA (HM18229) | | | | | | | | | | | | |

| Business by County with Reference no. | Headaches | Hearing Problems | High Blood Pressure | Hip Complaints | Hyperactivity | Hypoglycaemia | Impotence | Incontinence | Indigestion | Infertility | Influenza | Ingrowing Toenails |
|---|---|---|---|---|---|---|---|---|---|---|---|---|
| JABROO, C (HM10809) | ● | ● | ● | ● | ● | ● | ● | ● | ● | ● | ● | |
| **POWYS** | | | | | | | | | | | | |
| BRECON CLINIC (HM02944) | ● | ● | ● | ● | ● | ● | ● | ● | ● | ● | | |
| BRECON COMPLEMENTARY MED CTRE (HM02945) | ● | ● | ● | ● | ● | ● | ● | ● | ● | ● | ● | |
| CONROY, CHRISTINE (HM05007) | ● | | | ● | | | | | | | | |
| COVENT HOUSE NTRL HEALTH CTRE (HM05280) | ● | ● | ● | ● | ● | ● | ● | ● | ● | ● | ● | |
| GROVES, FRAN (HM08614) | ● | | | ● | | | | | | | | |
| HEALTH FOCUS (HM09386) | ● | | ● | ● | ● | | | | | ● | | |
| KILGOUR, KATHARINE () | ● | | | | | | | | | | | |
| LLANDRINDOD WELLS SPA TOWN (HM12499) | ● | ● | ● | ● | ● | ● | ● | ● | ● | ● | ● | |
| PEACE CLINIC (HM15876) | ● | | ● | | | | ● | | | | | |
| REFLEXOLOGY & ALLERGY THERAPY (HM17078) | ● | | ● | | ● | | | | ● | | | |
| SHEPPARD, HELEN (HM18421) | ● | | ● | ● | ● | ● | ● | | ● | ● | | |
| **RHONDDA CYNON TAFF** | | | | | | | | | | | | |
| POLLEY, LYNDON (HM16416) | | | | | | | | | | | | |
| **SWANSEA** | | | | | | | | | | | | |
| ABERTAWE PHYSIOTHERAPY CLINIC (HM00124) | ● | | | ● | | | | | | | | |
| ACUPUNCTURE CENTRE (HM00254) | ● | | | ● | | | | | ● | ● | | |
| BURDEN, RICHARD (HM03370) | ● | | | ● | | ● | | | ● | | | |
| PEDORTHICS FOOT SGY PRACTICE (HM15935) | | | | | | | | | | | | |
| RODWAY & ASSOCIATES (HM17531) | ● | | | ● | | | | | | | | |
| **WREXHAM** | | | | | | | | | | | | |
| HARMONY IN HEALTH (HM09028) | ● | | | | ● | | | | | | | |
| SENSORAMA (HM18229) | ● | | | | | | | | | | | |

HEALTH MYSELF

# SECTION 4c

## I-S of Conditions treated at Practices

# I - S Conditions treated at Practices/Businesses

Business by County with Reference no.

## ENGLAND

### BEDFORDSHIRE

| Business | Insomnia | Irritable Bowel Syndrome | Itching | Jet Lag | Joint Pain | Kidney Complaints | Lactose Intolerance | Laryngitis | Lethargy | Liver Disorders | Low Blood Pressure | Lung Problems |
|---|---|---|---|---|---|---|---|---|---|---|---|---|
| ALOE VERA SPECIALISTS (HM00681) | ● | ● | ● | | ● | | | ● | | | | |
| ALTERNATIVE THERAPY AT WORK (HM00732) | ● | | | | | | | | ● | | | |
| AMPTHILL & FLITWICK CLINIC (HM00795) | | | | | ● | | | | | | | |
| BEDFORD ACUPUNCTURE CLINIC (HM02032) | | | | | ● | | | | | | | |
| BEDFORD CHIROPRACTIC SURGERY (HM02033) | | ● | | | ● | | | | | | | |
| BEDFORD PHYSIOTHERAPY CENTRE (HM02035) | | | | | ● | | | | | | | |
| BELLAMY, R D (HM02097) | | ● | | | ● | | | | | | | |
| BOYCE, MICHAEL (HM02814) | | | | | ● | | | | | | | |
| BURTON, MERILYNN (HM03444) | | | | | | | | | | | | |
| CHARTERED PHYSIOTHERAPIST (HM04042) | | | | | ● | | | | | | ● | |
| CLNC OF ACU & CHINESE HERB MED (HM04726) | ● | ● | | | ● | | | | ● | | | |
| COULSTOCK, JUDY (HM05239) | ● | ● | | | ● | | | | ● | | ● | |
| DA SILVA, CAROLE (HM05665) | | ● | | | ● | | | ● | | | | |
| DISS, KATHRYN (HM06122) | | ● | | | ● | | | | | | | |
| DUNTON CTRE-COUN/PSYCHOTHERAPY (HM06428) | | ● | | | | | | | | | | |
| GROVE NATURAL THERAPY CLINIC (HM08610) | | ● | | | ● | | | | | | | |
| HEALES CHIROPRACTIC CLINIC (HM09321) | | ● | | | ● | | | | | | | |
| HOLISTIC HYPNOTHERAPY (HM09983) | ● | ● | ● | | ● | | | | ● | ● | | |
| INWARD BOUND THERAPIES (HM10707) | | | | | | | | | | | | |
| JENNIFER K HOUGH - PHYSIO (HM11004) | | | | | ● | | | | | | ● | ● |
| JOHNSON, ANNE (HM11068) | | | | | ● | | | | | | | |
| KEMPSTON CHIROPRACTIC CLINIC (HM11469) | | ● | | | ● | | | | | | | |
| MAGNETS 4 HEALTH (HM12918) | | | | | ● | | | | ● | | | |
| MULTIPLE SCLEROSIS THRPY CTRE (HM14351) | | | | | | | | | | | | |
| OSBORN, HELEN (HM15418) | | ● | | | ● | | | | | | | |
| PRICE, SARAH (HM16596) | ● | | | | | | | | ● | | ● | |
| SCHOOL OF ICASA (HM18082) | | | | | | | | | | | | |
| SHEER PERFECTION (HM18367) | | ● | | | | | | | ● | ● | ● | |
| SPECTRUM HEALTH TRUST (HM18976) | ● | ● | ● | ● | ● | ● | ● | ● | ● | ● | ● | ● |
| SPORT, ALEXANDER (HM19041) | ● | | | | ● | | | | ● | | | |
| SWEET BREEZE (HM19584) | ● | ● | ● | ● | ● | ● | ● | ● | ● | ● | ● | ● |

| Business | ME | Menopause | Migraine | Motion Sickness | Mouth Disorders | Mouth Ulcers | Multiple Sclerosis | Muscular Dystrophy | Musculo-skeletal | Nail Health | Nausea | Nerve Disorders |
|---|---|---|---|---|---|---|---|---|---|---|---|---|
| ALOE VERA SPECIALISTS (HM00681) | ● | | | | | | | | | ● | | |
| ALTERNATIVE THERAPY AT WORK (HM00732) | | | ● | | | | | | | | | |
| AMPTHILL & FLITWICK CLINIC (HM00795) | | | | | | | ● | | | | | |
| BEDFORD ACUPUNCTURE CLINIC (HM02032) | | ● | ● | | | | ● | | | | | |
| BEDFORD CHIROPRACTIC SURGERY (HM02033) | ● | | ● | | | | | | | | | ● |
| BEDFORD PHYSIOTHERAPY CENTRE (HM02035) | | | | | | | ● | | | | | |
| BELLAMY, R D (HM02097) | ● | | | | | | | | | | | |
| BOYCE, MICHAEL (HM02814) | | | ● | | | | | | | | | |
| BURTON, MERILYNN (HM03444) | | | | | | | | | | ● | | |
| CHARTERED PHYSIOTHERAPIST (HM04042) | | | | | | | ● | ● | | | | ● |
| CLNC OF ACU & CHINESE HERB MED (HM04726) | ● | ● | ● | | | | ● | | | | | |
| COULSTOCK, JUDY (HM05239) | | | ● | | | | ● | | | | ● | ● |
| DA SILVA, CAROLE (HM05665) | ● | | ● | | | | | | | | | |
| DISS, KATHRYN (HM06122) | ● | | | | | | | ● | | | | ● |
| DUNTON CTRE-COUN/PSYCHOTHERAPY (HM06428) | ● | ● | | | | | | | | | | |
| GROVE NATURAL THERAPY CLINIC (HM08610) | ● | ● | ● | | | | | | | | | ● |
| HEALES CHIROPRACTIC CLINIC (HM09321) | | | | | | | | | | | | ● |
| HOLISTIC HYPNOTHERAPY (HM09983) | ● | | ● | ● | | | ● | | | | ● | |
| INWARD BOUND THERAPIES (HM10707) | | | | | | | | | | | | |
| JENNIFER K HOUGH - PHYSIO (HM11004) | | | | | | | ● | ● | | | ● | ● |
| JOHNSON, ANNE (HM11068) | | | ● | | | | | | | | | |
| KEMPSTON CHIROPRACTIC CLINIC (HM11469) | ● | | | | | | | | | | | ● |
| MAGNETS 4 HEALTH (HM12918) | | | ● | | | | ● | ● | | | | |
| MULTIPLE SCLEROSIS THRPY CTRE (HM14351) | | | | | | | ● | | | | | |
| OSBORN, HELEN (HM15418) | ● | | ● | | | | | | | | | ● |
| PRICE, SARAH (HM16596) | ● | ● | | | | | | | | | | |
| SCHOOL OF ICASA (HM18082) | | | | | | | | | | | | |
| SHEER PERFECTION (HM18367) | | ● | | | | | | | | | | |
| SPECTRUM HEALTH TRUST (HM18976) | ● | ● | ● | ● | ● | ● | ● | | | | ● | ● |
| SPORT, ALEXANDER (HM19041) | ● | | ● | | | | | | | | | |
| SWEET BREEZE (HM19584) | ● | ● | ● | ● | ● | ● | ● | ● | | ● | ● | ● |

| Business | Nervous Disorders | Neuralgia | Obesity | Osteoporosis | Pain | Palpitations | Panic Attacks | Parkinson's Disease | Period Problems | Phobias | Piles | PMT |
|---|---|---|---|---|---|---|---|---|---|---|---|---|
| ALOE VERA SPECIALISTS (HM00681) | | ● | ● | ● | ● | | | | | | ● | ● |
| ALTERNATIVE THERAPY AT WORK (HM00732) | | | | | | | | | | | | |
| AMPTHILL & FLITWICK CLINIC (HM00795) | | | | | ● | | | | | | | |
| BEDFORD ACUPUNCTURE CLINIC (HM02032) | | | | | ● | | | | | | | ● |
| BEDFORD CHIROPRACTIC SURGERY (HM02033) | | | | ● | ● | | | | | | | |
| BEDFORD PHYSIOTHERAPY CENTRE (HM02035) | | | | | ● | | | | | | | |
| BELLAMY, R D (HM02097) | | | | | ● | | | | | | | |
| BOYCE, MICHAEL (HM02814) | | | | | | | | | | | | |
| BURTON, MERILYNN (HM03444) | | | | | | | | | | | | |
| CHARTERED PHYSIOTHERAPIST (HM04042) | | | | ● | ● | | | ● | | | | |
| CLNC OF ACU & CHINESE HERB MED (HM04726) | | | | ● | ● | ● | | | | | ● | ● |
| COULSTOCK, JUDY (HM05239) | ● | | | | | | | | | | | ● |
| DA SILVA, CAROLE (HM05665) | | | | | | | | | | | | |
| DISS, KATHRYN (HM06122) | ● | ● | | ● | ● | | | | | | | ● |
| DUNTON CTRE-COUN/PSYCHOTHERAPY (HM06428) | | | | | | | | | | ● | | ● |
| GROVE NATURAL THERAPY CLINIC (HM08610) | ● | | | ● | ● | | | | ● | ● | | ● |
| HEALES CHIROPRACTIC CLINIC (HM09321) | | | | | ● | | | | | | | |
| HOLISTIC HYPNOTHERAPY (HM09983) | | | ● | | ● | ● | ● | | ● | ● | | ● |
| INWARD BOUND THERAPIES (HM10707) | | | | | | | ● | | | ● | | |
| JENNIFER K HOUGH - PHYSIO (HM11004) | ● | ● | | ● | ● | ● | | ● | | | | |
| JOHNSON, ANNE (HM11068) | | | | | | | | | | | | |
| KEMPSTON CHIROPRACTIC CLINIC (HM11469) | | | | | ● | | | | | | | |
| MAGNETS 4 HEALTH (HM12918) | | ● | | | ● | | | | ● | | ● | |
| MULTIPLE SCLEROSIS THRPY CTRE (HM14351) | | | | | | | | | | | | |
| OSBORN, HELEN (HM15418) | ● | | | | ● | | | | | | | ● |
| PRICE, SARAH (HM16596) | | | | ● | ● | | | | | | | |
| SCHOOL OF ICASA (HM18082) | | | | | | | | | | ● | | |
| SHEER PERFECTION (HM18367) | | | | | | | | | | | | ● |
| SPECTRUM HEALTH TRUST (HM18976) | ● | ● | ● | ● | ● | ● | | ● | ● | ● | ● | ● |
| SPORT, ALEXANDER (HM19041) | | ● | | | ● | | | ● | | ● | | |
| SWEET BREEZE (HM19584) | ● | ● | ● | ● | ● | ● | | ● | ● | ● | ● | ● |

| Business | Pneumonia | Postural Problems | Pregnancy Help | Prostate Problems | Psoriasis | Raynaud's Disease | Recurrent Infections | Restless Legs | Rheumatoid Arthritis | Schizophrenia | Sciatica | Sexual Problems |
|---|---|---|---|---|---|---|---|---|---|---|---|---|
| ALOE VERA SPECIALISTS (HM00681) | | | | | ● | ● | ● | | ● | | ● | |
| ALTERNATIVE THERAPY AT WORK (HM00732) | | | | | | | | | | | | |
| AMPTHILL & FLITWICK CLINIC (HM00795) | | | | | | | | | | | | |
| BEDFORD ACUPUNCTURE CLINIC (HM02032) | | | | | | | | | | | | |
| BEDFORD CHIROPRACTIC SURGERY (HM02033) | | | | | | | | | | | ● | |
| BEDFORD PHYSIOTHERAPY CENTRE (HM02035) | | | | | | | | | | | | |
| BELLAMY, R D (HM02097) | | | | | | | | ● | | | ● | |
| BOYCE, MICHAEL (HM02814) | | | | | | | | | | | | |
| BURTON, MERILYNN (HM03444) | | | | | | | | | | | | |
| CHARTERED PHYSIOTHERAPIST (HM04042) | | ● | | | | | | | ● | | ● | |
| CLNC OF ACU & CHINESE HERB MED (HM04726) | | | | ● | ● | ● | | | ● | | ● | ● |
| COULSTOCK, JUDY (HM05239) | | | | | | | | | ● | | | |
| DA SILVA, CAROLE (HM05665) | | | | | | | | | | | ● | |
| DISS, KATHRYN (HM06122) | | ● | | | | | | | ● | | ● | |
| DUNTON CTRE-COUN/PSYCHOTHERAPY (HM06428) | | | ● | | | | | | | ● | | ● |
| GROVE NATURAL THERAPY CLINIC (HM08610) | | | | | | | | | | | ● | |
| HEALES CHIROPRACTIC CLINIC (HM09321) | | | | | | | | | | | ● | |
| HOLISTIC HYPNOTHERAPY (HM09983) | | | | | ● | ● | | ● | ● | | ● | ● |
| INWARD BOUND THERAPIES (HM10707) | | | | | | | | | | | | |
| JENNIFER K HOUGH - PHYSIO (HM11004) | | | | | | ● | | | ● | | ● | |
| JOHNSON, ANNE (HM11068) | | | ● | | | | | | | | | |
| KEMPSTON CHIROPRACTIC CLINIC (HM11469) | | | | | | | | | | | ● | |
| MAGNETS 4 HEALTH (HM12918) | | | | ● | | ● | | | ● | | ● | |
| MULTIPLE SCLEROSIS THRPY CTRE (HM14351) | | | | | | | | | | | | |
| OSBORN, HELEN (HM15418) | | | ● | | | | | | | | ● | |
| PRICE, SARAH (HM16596) | | | | | | | | | | | ● | |
| SCHOOL OF ICASA (HM18082) | | | | ● | | | | | | | | ● |
| SHEER PERFECTION (HM18367) | | | | | | | | | | | | |
| SPECTRUM HEALTH TRUST (HM18976) | ● | | ● | ● | ● | ● | ● | ● | ● | ● | ● | ● |
| SPORT, ALEXANDER (HM19041) | | | | | | | | | | | ● | |
| SWEET BREEZE (HM19584) | ● | | ● | ● | ● | ● | ● | ● | ● | ● | ● | ● |

# I - S Conditions treated at Practices/Businesses

| Business by County with Reference no. | Insomnia | Irritable Bowel Syndrome | Itching | Jet Lag | Joint Pain | Kidney Complaints | Lactose Intolerance | Laryngitis | Lethargy | Liver Disorders | Low Blood Pressure | Lung Problems | ME | Menopause | Migraine | Motion Sickness | Mouth Disorders | Mouth Ulcers | Multiple Sclerosis | Muscular Dystrophy | Musculo-skeletal | Nail Health | Nausea | Nerve Disorders | Nervous Disorders | Neuralgia | Obesity | Osteoporosis | Pain | Palpitations | Panic Attacks | Parkinson's Disease | Period Problems | Phobias | Piles | PMT | Pneumonia | Postural Problems | Pregnancy Help | Prostate Problems | Psoriasis | Raynaud's Disease | Recurrent Infections | Restless Legs | Rheumatoid Arthritis | Schizophrenia | Sciatica | Sexual Problems |
|---|---|---|---|---|---|---|---|---|---|---|---|---|---|---|---|---|---|---|---|---|---|---|---|---|---|---|---|---|---|---|---|---|---|---|---|---|---|---|---|---|---|---|---|---|---|---|---|---|
| THERAPY CENTRE (HM19894) | | | | |●| | | | | | | | | | | | | |●| | | | | | | | | |●| | | | | | | | | | | | | | | | | | | |
| WOODSIDE CLINIC (HM21857) | |●|●| |●| | | | | | | | | | | | | |●|●| | | |●| |●| | |●| | |●|●| | |●| | | | | | | | |●| |●| |
| BERKSHIRE | | | | | | | | | | | | | | | | | | | | | | | | | | | | | | | | | | | | | | | | | | | | | | | | |
| 1ST CHIROPRACTIC CLINIC (HM00004) | |●| | |●| | | | | | | |●| | | | | | | | | | |●|●| | |●|●| | | | | | | | | | | | | | | | | |●| |
| ANABELLE'S THERAPEUTIC MASSAGE (HM00798) | | | | |●| | | | | | | | | | | | | | | | | | | | | | | | | | | | | | | | | | | | | | | | | | | |
| ASCOT PHYSIOFIRST CENTRE (HM01178) | | | | |●| | | | | | | | | | | | | |●| | | | | | | | | |●| | | | | | | | | | | | | | | | | | | |
| BACK TO HEALTH - WINDSOR (HM01516) | |●| | |●| | | | | | | |●| |●| | | | | | | | |●| | | | |●| | | | | | | | | | | | | | | | | |●| |
| BERKSHIRE CHIROPRACTIC (HM02195) |●|●| | |●|●| | | | |●| |●| |●| | | | | | | | |●|●|●|●|●|●|●| | |●| | |●| | |●| | | | | |●| | |●| |
| BODY & SOUL (HM02561) | | | | | | | | | | | | | | | | | | | | | | | | | | | |●| | | | | | | | | | | | | | | | | | | |
| BRACKNELL CHIROPRACTIC CLINIC (HM02838) | |●| | |●| | | | | | | |●| |●| | | |●| | | | |●|●|●| |●|●| | | | | | | | | | | | | | | | |●| |●| |
| BRUCE, ANN (HM03264) |●|●| | | | | | | | | | | | |●| | | | | | | | | |●| |●| |●| | | | |●| | | | | | | | | | | | | |●|
| BURNHAM CHIROPRACTIC CLINIC (HM03404) | |●| | |●| | | | | | | |●| |●| | | |●| | | | |●|●| | | |●| | | | | | | | | | | | | | | | | |●| |
| CAMPBELL, ELSPETH (HM03597) |●|●|●|●|●|●| | |●| |●|●|●| |●|●| | | | | | |●|●|●|●|●|●|●|●| |●|●|●| |●| | | | |●|●|●|●|●| | |●|
| CASTLE HILL CLINIC (HM03833) |●|●|●|●|●|●|●|●|●|●|●|●|●|●|●|●|●|●| | | |●|●|●|●|●|●|●|●|●| |●|●|●|●|●|●| |●|●|●|●|●|●|●|●|●|●|
| CAVERSHAM CHIROPRACTIC CLINC (HM03864) | |●| | |●| | | | | | | |●| | | | | | | | | | |●|●| | | |●| | | | | | | | | | | | | | | | | |●| |
| CAVERSHAM FOOT CLINIC (HM03866) | | | | | | | | | | | | | | | | | | | | | | | | | | | |●| | | | | | | | | | | | | | | | | | | |
| CHEFLAND, GERTI (HM04084) |●|●|●| |●|●| | |●|●|●|●|●|●|●| | | | | | | |●|●|●|●|●|●|●|●| | |●|●| |●| | |●|●| | |●|●|●| |●|●|
| CHEUNG, JAMES T (DR) (HM04142) | | | | |●| | | |●| | | | | |●| | | |●| | | | | | | | | | | | | | | | | | | | | | | | | | | | | |
| COOKHAM CHIROPRACTIC CLINIC (HM05068) |●|●| | |●| | | |●| | | |●|●|●| | | |●|●| | | |●|●|●| |●|●|●| | | | | |●| | |●| |●|●| |●| | |●| |
| COPPERTHWAITE, ERIC (HM05147) | | | | | | | | | | | | |●| | | | | |●| | | | | | | | | | | | | | | | | | | | | | | | | | | | | |
| DEAN RUSSELL & BRYDGES ROBERT (HM05936) | |●| | |●| | | | | | | |●| |●| | | | | | | | |●|●| | | | | | | | | | | | | | | | | | | | | |●| |
| DEJODE, SONIA (HM05962) | |●| | |●| | | | | | | |●| |●| | | |●| | | | |●|●| | |●|●| | | | | | | | | |●| | | | | | | |●| |
| EDNEY, C S (HM06625) |●| | | | | | | | | | | | | | | | | | | | | | | | | | | | | | | | | | | | | |●| | | | | | | |●| |
| EDWARDS, JOHN (HM06659) | | | | | | | | | | | | | | | | | | | | | | | |●| | | | | |●| | |●| | | | | | | | | | | | | | |
| EIGHAN, PENELOPE (HM06689) |●|●| |●|●| | | |●| |●|●|●|●|●| | | | | | | |●|●|●| |●|●|●| |●|●|●| |●| | |●| |●| | |●|●| |●| |
| EIGHT WINDS ACUPUNCTURE (HM06690) |●|●| | |●| | | |●| | | | |●|●| | | | | | | | | | | | |●| | | |●| | |●| | | | |●| | | | | | | |
| FAIRBOURNE CLINIC (HM07051) | | | | | | | | | | | | | | | | | | | | | | | | | | |●| | | | |●| | | | | | | |●| | | | | |●| |
| FEET TREAT (HM07186) | |●| | | | | | | | | | | | |●| | | | | | | | | | | | |●| | | |●| | |●| | | | | | | |●| | | |
| FERINGA, MARLIES (HM07233) |●|●| | |●| | | | | |●| | | |●| | |●| | | |●| | |●|●| |●| | | | | | | | | | | |●| |●| | | | | |
| HALL, BEVERLEY (HM08767) | |●| | |●| | | | | | | |●|●|●| | | |●| | | | |●|●| | |●|●| | | | | | | | | | | | |●| | | |●| |
| HALL, GRACE (HM08773) | |●| | |●| | | | | | | |●| |●| | | |●| | | | | | | | |●| | | | | | | | | | | | | | | | | |●| |
| HAZEL'S HOLISTIC HEALTH CARE (HM09294) |●| | | |●|●| | | | | | |●|●|●| | | |●| | | |●| | | | | |●|●| | |●| | |●| | |●| | | | | | | | | |
| HEWITT, ANDREW (HM09703) | |●| | |●| | | | | | | |●| |●| | | |●| | | | |●|●|●| |●|●| | | | | | | | | | | | | | | | | |●| |
| HILLSIDE OSTEOPATHIC PRACTICE (HM09806) | |●| | |●| | | | | | | | | | | | | | | | | | | |●| | | | | | | | | | | | | | | | | |●|●| |●| |

# I - S Conditions treated at Practices/Businesses

Business by County with Reference no.

| Business | Insomnia | Irritable Bowel Syndrome | Itching | Jet Lag | Joint Pain | Kidney Complaints | Lactose Intolerance | Laryngitis | Lethargy | Liver Disorders | Low Blood Pressure | Lung Problems | ME | Menopause | Migraine | Motion Sickness |
|---|---|---|---|---|---|---|---|---|---|---|---|---|---|---|---|---|
| KENT, JANET (HM11524) | ● | ● | | | | | | | ● | | ● | | ● | ● | ● | |
| KINGFISHERS COMP HEALTH CARE (HM11650) | ● | ● | | | ● | | | | ● | | ● | | | | ● | |
| LANGLEY CHIROPRACTORS CLINIC (HM11953) | | ● | | | ● | | | | | | | | ● | | ● | |
| LAVENDER, S (HM12029) | | | | | ● | | | | | | | | | | | |
| LIFE GUIDANCE (HM12344) | | ● | | | | | | | ● | | | | | | | |
| LISSADELL HOUSE PRACTICE (HM12457) | | ● | | | ● | ● | ● | | ● | ● | ● | | ● | ● | ● | |
| MAIDENHEAD CHIROPRACTIC (HM12933) | | ● | | | ● | | | | | | | | ● | | ● | |
| MAIDENHEAD PHYSIO & SPORTS (HM12934) | | | | | ● | | | | | | | | | | | |
| MCGREGOR, TONY (HM13504) | ● | | | | | | | | | | | | | | | |
| NASEBY ACUPUNCTURE CLINIC (HM14487) | ● | ● | ● | ● | ● | ● | ● | ● | ● | ● | ● | ● | ● | ● | ● | ● |
| NATURAL HEALTH CONSULTANCY (HM14591) | ● | ● | ● | ● | ● | ● | ● | ● | ● | ● | | ● | ● | ● | ● | ● |
| NATURAL THERAPY CLINIC (HM14656) | ● | ● | ● | ● | ● | ● | ● | ● | ● | ● | ● | ● | ● | ● | ● | ● |
| NATURAL THERAPY CLINIC (HM14655) | ● | ● | ● | ● | ● | ● | ● | ● | ● | ● | ● | ● | ● | ● | ● | ● |
| NEWBURY CHIROPRACTIC CENTRE (HM14851) | | ● | | | ● | | | | | | | | ● | | | |
| NEWBURY PHYSIOTHERAPY (HM14852) | | | | | ● | | | | | | | | | | | |
| NS3UK NUTRITION SERVICES (HM15099) | ● | ● | ● | ● | ● | | ● | | ● | | | | ● | ● | ● | |
| PETERS, JEAN (HM16086) | ● | ● | | | ● | ● | | | | | ● | | ● | ● | ● | |
| PIM HEALTH CLINIC (HM16301) | | ● | | | ● | | | | | | | | ● | | ● | |
| ROSEDALE CLINIC (HM17616) | | | | | ● | | | | | | | | | ● | ● | |
| SANDALL, S (HM17898) | | | | | ● | | | | | | | | | | | |
| SLOUGH SPORTS INJURIES CLINIC (HM18690) | | | | | ● | | | | | | | | | | | |
| SMETHURST, ALISON (HM18704) | | | | | | | | | | | | | ● | ● | | |
| SOUTH LODGE CONSULTING (HM18909) | | | | | | | | | | | | | | | | |
| STRINGER, FRANCES (HM19407) | | ● | | | ● | | | | | | | | ● | | ● | |
| THATCHAM CHIROPRACTIC CLINIC (HM19867) | | ● | | | ● | | | | | | | | ● | | ● | |
| TSENG, PATRICIA (HM20359) | ● | | | | ● | | | | ● | | ● | | ● | ● | ● | |
| WINNERSH HYPNOTHERAPY PRACTICE (HM21711) | ● | ● | | | | | | | ● | | | | | | | |
| WOOD, JEANIE M (HM21801) | | ● | | | ● | | | | | | | | ● | ● | ● | |
| WOODLEY HEALING CENTRE (HM21836) | ● | ● | ● | | ● | ● | ● | ● | ● | ● | ● | | ● | ● | ● | |
| **BRISTOL** | | | | | | | | | | | | | | | | |
| ANDERSON, KEITH (HM00830) | ● | | | | | | | | | | | | | | ● | |
| AQUARIUS HEALTH CENTRE (HM00959) | ● | ● | ● | ● | ● | ● | ● | ● | ● | ● | ● | ● | ● | ● | ● | ● |
| ARMSTRONG, ELIZABETH (HM01021) | | ● | | | ● | | | | | | | | | | | |
| ASS-DANCE MOVEMENT THERAPY (HM01268) | ● | | | | | | | | ● | | | | ● | ● | | |

| Business | Mouth Disorders | Mouth Ulcers | Multiple Sclerosis | Muscular Dystrophy | Musculo-skeletal | Nail Health | Nausea | Nerve Disorders | Nervous Disorders | Neuralgia | Obesity | Osteoporosis | Pain | Palpitations | Panic Attacks | Parkinson's Disease |
|---|---|---|---|---|---|---|---|---|---|---|---|---|---|---|---|---|
| KENT, JANET (HM11524) | | | | | | | ● | | ● | | ● | | | | | ● |
| KINGFISHERS COMP HEALTH CARE (HM11650) | | | | | | | | ● | ● | ● | | | ● | | | |
| LANGLEY CHIROPRACTORS CLINIC (HM11953) | | | ● | | | | | ● | ● | | | | ● | | | |
| LAVENDER, S (HM12029) | | | | | | | | | | | | | ● | ● | | |
| LIFE GUIDANCE (HM12344) | | | | | | | | | ● | | | | | | | |
| LISSADELL HOUSE PRACTICE (HM12457) | ● | ● | ● | | | ● | ● | ● | ● | ● | | ● | ● | | | |
| MAIDENHEAD CHIROPRACTIC (HM12933) | | | | | | | | ● | ● | | | | ● | | | |
| MAIDENHEAD PHYSIO & SPORTS (HM12934) | | | ● | | | | | | | | | | ● | | | |
| MCGREGOR, TONY (HM13504) | | | | | | | | | ● | | ● | | | | | |
| NASEBY ACUPUNCTURE CLINIC (HM14487) | ● | ● | ● | | | ● | ● | ● | ● | ● | | ● | ● | ● | ● | ● |
| NATURAL HEALTH CONSULTANCY (HM14591) | | | ● | | | | ● | ● | ● | ● | | | ● | ● | | ● |
| NATURAL THERAPY CLINIC (HM14656) | ● | ● | ● | ● | | ● | ● | ● | ● | ● | ● | ● | ● | ● | | ● |
| NATURAL THERAPY CLINIC (HM14655) | ● | ● | ● | | | ● | ● | ● | ● | ● | | ● | ● | ● | | |
| NEWBURY CHIROPRACTIC CENTRE (HM14851) | | | | | | | | ● | | ● | | ● | ● | | | |
| NEWBURY PHYSIOTHERAPY (HM14852) | | | ● | | | | | | | | | | ● | | | |
| NS3UK NUTRITION SERVICES (HM15099) | | ● | | | | | | | | | ● | ● | | ● | | |
| PETERS, JEAN (HM16086) | | | ● | | | ● | | | | | | | ● | ● | | |
| PIM HEALTH CLINIC (HM16301) | | | | | | | | ● | ● | ● | | ● | ● | | | |
| ROSEDALE CLINIC (HM17616) | | | | | | | ● | | | | | | ● | | | |
| SANDALL, S (HM17898) | | | | | | ● | | | | | | | | | | |
| SLOUGH SPORTS INJURIES CLINIC (HM18690) | | | ● | | | | | | | | | | | | | |
| SMETHURST, ALISON (HM18704) | | | ● | | | | | | | | | | ● | | | |
| SOUTH LODGE CONSULTING (HM18909) | | | | | | | | | | | | | ● | | | |
| STRINGER, FRANCES (HM19407) | | | | | | | | ● | ● | | | | ● | | | |
| THATCHAM CHIROPRACTIC CLINIC (HM19867) | | | | | | | | ● | | | | ● | ● | | | |
| TSENG, PATRICIA (HM20359) | | | ● | ● | | | | ● | ● | ● | | | ● | ● | | ● |
| WINNERSH HYPNOTHERAPY PRACTICE (HM21711) | | | | | | | | | | | ● | | | | | |
| WOOD, JEANIE M (HM21801) | | | | | | | | ● | ● | ● | | ● | ● | | | |
| WOODLEY HEALING CENTRE (HM21836) | | ● | ● | ● | | ● | ● | ● | ● | | ● | ● | ● | ● | | ● |
| **BRISTOL** | | | | | | | | | | | | | | | | |
| ANDERSON, KEITH (HM00830) | | | | | | | | | ● | | | | | | | |
| AQUARIUS HEALTH CENTRE (HM00959) | ● | ● | ● | ● | | ● | ● | ● | ● | ● | ● | ● | ● | ● | | ● |
| ARMSTRONG, ELIZABETH (HM01021) | | | | | | | | | | | ● | ● | ● | | | |
| ASS-DANCE MOVEMENT THERAPY (HM01268) | | | ● | ● | | | | | ● | | | | | | | ● |

| Business | Period Problems | Phobias | Piles | PMT | Pneumonia | Postural Problems | Pregnancy Help | Prostate Problems | Psoriasis | Raynaud's Disease | Recurrent Infections | Restless Legs | Rheumatoid Arthritis | Schizophrenia | Sciatica | Sexual Problems |
|---|---|---|---|---|---|---|---|---|---|---|---|---|---|---|---|---|
| KENT, JANET (HM11524) | | ● | | ● | | | ● | | | | | | | ● | | ● |
| KINGFISHERS COMP HEALTH CARE (HM11650) | ● | ● | ● | ● | | | | | ● | | | | | | ● | |
| LANGLEY CHIROPRACTORS CLINIC (HM11953) | | | | | | | | | | | | | | | ● | |
| LAVENDER, S (HM12029) | | | | ● | | | | | | | | | | | | |
| LIFE GUIDANCE (HM12344) | | ● | | | | | | | | | | | | | | |
| LISSADELL HOUSE PRACTICE (HM12457) | ● | | | ● | | | ● | | | ● | ● | ● | ● | | ● | |
| MAIDENHEAD CHIROPRACTIC (HM12933) | | | | | | | | | | | | | | | ● | |
| MAIDENHEAD PHYSIO & SPORTS (HM12934) | | | | | | | | | | | | | | | | |
| MCGREGOR, TONY (HM13504) | | ● | | | | | | | | | | | | | | ● |
| NASEBY ACUPUNCTURE CLINIC (HM14487) | ● | ● | ● | ● | | | ● | ● | ● | ● | | ● | ● | | ● | |
| NATURAL HEALTH CONSULTANCY (HM14591) | ● | ● | | ● | | | | | ● | ● | ● | ● | ● | | ● | |
| NATURAL THERAPY CLINIC (HM14656) | ● | ● | ● | ● | ● | | ● | ● | ● | ● | ● | ● | ● | ● | ● | ● |
| NATURAL THERAPY CLINIC (HM14655) | ● | ● | | ● | ● | | ● | ● | ● | ● | ● | ● | ● | | ● | ● |
| NEWBURY CHIROPRACTIC CENTRE (HM14851) | | | | | | | ● | | | | | | | | ● | |
| NEWBURY PHYSIOTHERAPY (HM14852) | | | | | | | | | | | | | | | | |
| NS3UK NUTRITION SERVICES (HM15099) | | | ● | ● | | | ● | | ● | ● | ● | | ● | ● | | |
| PETERS, JEAN (HM16086) | ● | | | ● | | | ● | | | | | ● | | | ● | |
| PIM HEALTH CLINIC (HM16301) | ● | | | ● | | | | | | ● | | | ● | | ● | |
| ROSEDALE CLINIC (HM17616) | | | | | | | | | | | | | | | ● | |
| SANDALL, S (HM17898) | | | | | | | | | | | | | | | | |
| SLOUGH SPORTS INJURIES CLINIC (HM18690) | | | | | | | | | | | | | | | | |
| SMETHURST, ALISON (HM18704) | | | | ● | | | ● | | | | | ● | | | | |
| SOUTH LODGE CONSULTING (HM18909) | | | | | | | | | | | | | ● | | ● | |
| STRINGER, FRANCES (HM19407) | | | | | | | | | | | | | | | ● | |
| THATCHAM CHIROPRACTIC CLINIC (HM19867) | | | | | | | | | | | | | | | ● | |
| TSENG, PATRICIA (HM20359) | ● | | | ● | | | ● | | | | | | ● | | ● | |
| WINNERSH HYPNOTHERAPY PRACTICE (HM21711) | | | | | | | | | | | | | | | | ● |
| WOOD, JEANIE M (HM21801) | | | | | | | | | | | | | ● | | ● | |
| WOODLEY HEALING CENTRE (HM21836) | ● | | | ● | | | ● | ● | ● | ● | ● | ● | ● | | ● | ● |
| **BRISTOL** | | | | | | | | | | | | | | | | |
| ANDERSON, KEITH (HM00830) | | | | | | | | | | | | | | | | |
| AQUARIUS HEALTH CENTRE (HM00959) | ● | ● | ● | ● | ● | | ● | ● | ● | ● | ● | ● | ● | ● | ● | ● |
| ARMSTRONG, ELIZABETH (HM01021) | | | | | | | | | | | | | | | ● | |
| ASS-DANCE MOVEMENT THERAPY (HM01268) | | ● | | | | | | | | | | | | ● | | |

# I - S Conditions treated at Practices/Businesses

| Business by County with Reference no. | Insomnia | Irritable Bowel Syndrome | Itching | Jet Lag | Joint Pain | Kidney Complaints | Lactose Intolerance | Laryngitis | Lethargy | Liver Disorders | Low Blood Pressure | Lung Problems | ME | Menopause | Migraine | Motion Sickness | Mouth Disorders | Mouth Ulcers | Multiple Sclerosis | Muscular Dystrophy | Musculo-skeletal | Nail Health | Nausea | Nerve Disorders | Nervous Disorders | Neuralgia | Obesity | Osteoporosis | Pain | Palpitations | Panic Attacks | Parkinson's Disease | Period Problems | Phobias | Piles | PMT | Pneumonia | Postural Problems | Pregnancy Help | Prostate Problems | Psoriasis | Raynaud's Disease | Recurrent Infections | Restless Legs | Rheumatoid Arthritis | Schizophrenia | Sciatica | Sexual Problems |
|---|---|---|---|---|---|---|---|---|---|---|---|---|---|---|---|---|---|---|---|---|---|---|---|---|---|---|---|---|---|---|---|---|---|---|---|---|---|---|---|---|---|---|---|---|---|---|---|---|
| AVON COMPLEMENTARY MEDICINE (HM01404) | | ● | | | ● | | ● | | ● | | | | ● | | | | | | | | | | | | | | | | | | | | | | | | | | | | | | | | | | | |
| BAGGLEY, J M (HM01536) | | | | | | | | | | | | | | | | | | | | | | ● | | | | | | | | | | | | | | | | | | | | | | | | | | |
| BEVAN, RUSS (HM02242) | ● | ● | ● | ● | ● | ● | ● | | ● | | ● | | ● | ● | ● | ● | ● | ● | ● | | | | ● | ● | ● | ● | ● | ● | ● | ● | | | ● | ● | | ● | | | | | ● | | ● | ● | | | ● | ● |
| BRISTOL HYPNOTHERAPY CLINIC (HM03063) | ● | ● | | | | | | | | | | | ● | | ● | | | | | | | | | | | | ● | | ● | ● | ● | | | ● | | | | | ● | | | | | | | | | ● |
| BRISTOL NATURAL HEALTH SERVICE (HM03064) | ● | ● | | | ● | ● | | | ● | ● | ● | ● | ● | ● | ● | ● | | | | | | | ● | | ● | ● | ● | | ● | ● | | ● | ● | ● | | ● | | | ● | ● | ● | | ● | ● | ● | | ● | ● |
| CASTLE CHIROPODY CLINIC (HM03828) | | | | | | | | | | | | | | | | | | | | | | ● | | | | | | | | | | | | | | | | | | | | | | | | | | |
| CHARLES CLINIC (HM04020) | | ● | | | ● | | | | | | | | ● | | | | | | | | | | | | | | | ● | ● | | | | | | | | | ● | | | | | | | | | ● | |
| CHERINGTON PRACTICE (HM04106) | | | | | ● | | | | | | | | | | | | | | | | | | | | | | | | | | | | | | | | | | | | | | | | | | | |
| CLARK, LYN (HM04566) | | ● | | | | | | | | | | | | | | | | | | | | ● | | | | | | | ● | | | | | | | ● | | | | | | | | | | | | |
| CLIFTON CHIROPRACTIC CLINIC (HM04666) | | ● | | | ● | ● | | | ● | ● | | | ● | | ● | | | | | | | | | ● | ● | | | ● | ● | | | | ● | | | | | | | | | ● | | | | | ● | |
| CLINIC OF NATURAL MEDICINE (HM04704) | ● | | | | ● | | | | | | | | ● | ● | ● | | | | | | | | ● | | | | | | ● | | | | | | | ● | | | ● | | | | | | | | | |
| CROSS HANDS CHIRO CLINIC (HM05478) | | ● | | | ● | | | | | | | | | ● | | | | | | | | | | ● | ● | | | ● | ● | | | | | | | | | | | | | | | | | | ● | |
| CTRE FOR KINESIOLOGY (HM05542) | ● | ● | ● | ● | ● | ● | ● | ● | ● | ● | ● | ● | ● | ● | ● | | | ● | | | | | ● | | | | ● | ● | ● | ● | | | ● | ● | ● | ● | | | | | ● | ● | ● | | ● | | | |
| DANCE VOICE THERAPY CENTRE (HM05709) | | | | | | | | | ● | | | | ● | | | | | | | ● | | | | ● | ● | | | | | | | ● | | ● | | | | | | | | | | | | ● | | |
| DOWRY CHIROPRACTIC CLINIC (HM06255) | | ● | | | ● | | | | | | | | | | | | | | | | | | | ● | | ● | | | ● | | | | | | | | | | | | | | | | | | ● | |
| FILE, CHRISTINE (HM07288) | ● | | | | ● | ● | | | | | ● | | ● | ● | ● | | | | | | | | ● | ● | | | | | ● | | | | | | | ● | | | | | | | | ● | ● | | | |
| FRANCIS, PATRICIA (HM07675) | | | | | | | | | | | | | | | | | | | | | | | | | | | | | ● | | | | | | | | | | | | | | | | | | | |
| FREEMAN, ANN (HM07719) | ● | ● | ● | ● | ● | | ● | ● | ● | ● | ● | ● | ● | ● | ● | ● | ● | ● | ● | | | | ● | | ● | ● | ● | ● | ● | ● | | ● | ● | ● | ● | ● | | | ● | ● | ● | ● | ● | ● | ● | | ● | |
| GARLAND, C (HM07889) | ● | ● | | | | | | | | | | | ● | ● | ● | | | | | | | | | | | | | | | | | | | | | | | | | | | | | | | | | |
| HARCOURT, A (HM08964) | | ● | | | ● | | | | | | | | ● | | ● | | | | | | | | | ● | | | | ● | ● | | | | | | | ● | | ● | ● | | | | | | | | | |
| HEALING WITH GABRIELLE TWINE (HM09360) | | ● | ● | | ● | ● | | ● | ● | ● | | ● | ● | ● | ● | | | | ● | ● | | | | ● | ● | ● | | ● | ● | ● | | ● | ● | | | ● | ● | | ● | | ● | | ● | | ● | | ● | |
| HEALTH & HEALING (HM09371) | ● | ● | ● | ● | ● | ● | ● | ● | ● | ● | ● | ● | ● | ● | ● | ● | ● | ● | ● | ● | | ● | ● | ● | ● | ● | ● | ● | ● | ● | | ● | ● | ● | ● | ● | ● | | ● | ● | ● | ● | ● | ● | ● | ● | ● | ● |
| HOPLEY, DENISE (HM10154) | | | | | ● | | | | | | | | | | | | | | | | | | | | | | | | ● | | | | | | | | | | | | | | | | | | ● | |
| HUDSON, JOHN (HM10313) | | | | | | | | | | | | | | | | | | | | | | | | | | | | | | | | | | ● | | | | | | | | | | | | | | |
| KEYNSHAM CHIROPRACTIC CLINÍC (HM11580) | | ● | | | ● | | | | | | | | ● | | ● | | | | | | | | | ● | ● | | | | ● | | | | | | | | | | | | | | | | | | ● | |
| KINGSWOOD CHIROPRACTIC CLINIC (HM11682) | | | | | ● | | | | | | | | ● | | ● | | | | | | | | | ● | ● | | | | ● | | | | | | | | | | | | | | | | | | ● | |
| KNIGHTSWOOD CLINIC (HM11762) | | | | | ● | | | | | | | | | | | | | | | | | | | | | | | | | | | | | | | | | | | | | | | | | | | |
| NAILSEA CHIROPRACTIC CLINIC (HM14460) | | | | | ● | | | | | | | | | | ● | | | | | | | | | ● | | ● | | ● | ● | | | | | | | | | | | | | | | ● | | | ● | |
| ORCHARD MEDICAL CENTRE (HM15364) | ● | ● | | | ● | ● | | ● | | | ● | | ● | ● | ● | | | | | | | ● | | ● | | | | | ● | ● | | | ● | | | ● | | | | | | | | | | | ● | |
| ORIENTAL MEDICINE PRACTICE (HM15387) | ● | ● | ● | ● | ● | ● | ● | ● | ● | ● | ● | ● | ● | ● | ● | ● | ● | ● | ● | ● | | | ● | ● | ● | ● | ● | ● | ● | ● | | | ● | | ● | ● | ● | | ● | ● | ● | ● | ● | ● | ● | | ● | ● |
| PARKER CLINIC (HM15683) | | | | | ● | | | | | | | | | | | | | | | | | | | ● | ● | | | ● | ● | | | | | | | | | | | | | | | | | | ● | |
| POCOCK, A (HM16391) | | | | | | | | | | | | | | | | | | | | | | ● | | | | | | | | | | | | | | | | | | | | | | | | | | |
| REDLANDS HOUSE CLINIC (HM17028) | | | | | ● | | | | | | | | | | | | | | | | | | | ● | ● | | | ● | ● | | | | | | | | | | | | | | | | | | ● | |
| REDMOND, CAROLINE (HM17031) | ● | ● | ● | ● | ● | ● | ● | ● | ● | ● | ● | ● | ● | ● | ● | ● | ● | ● | ● | ● | | ● | ● | ● | ● | ● | ● | ● | ● | ● | | ● | ● | ● | ● | ● | ● | | ● | ● | ● | ● | ● | ● | ● | ● | ● | ● |

# I - S Conditions treated at Practices/Businesses

| Business by County with Reference no. | Insomnia | Irritable Bowel Syndrome | Itching | Jet Lag | Joint Pain | Kidney Complaints | Lactose Intolerance | Laryngitis | Lethargy | Liver Disorders | Low Blood Pressure | Lung Problems | ME | Menopause | Migraine | Motion Sickness | Mouth Disorders | Mouth Ulcers | Multiple Sclerosis | Muscular Dystrophy | Musculo-skeletal | Nail Health | Nausea | Nerve Disorders | Nervous Disorders | Neuralgia | Obesity | Osteoporosis | Pain | Palpitations | Panic Attacks | Parkinson's Disease | Period Problems | Phobias | Piles | PMT | Pneumonia | Postural Problems | Pregnancy Help | Prostate Problems | Psoriasis | Raynaud's Disease | Recurrent Infections | Restless Legs | Rheumatoid Arthritis | Schizophrenia | Sciatica | Sexual Problems |
|---|---|---|---|---|---|---|---|---|---|---|---|---|---|---|---|---|---|---|---|---|---|---|---|---|---|---|---|---|---|---|---|---|---|---|---|---|---|---|---|---|---|---|---|---|---|---|---|---|
| RICHARD GIBBONS - ACUPUNCT (HM17244) | ● | ● |  |  | ● |  |  |  | ● |  |  | ● | ● | ● | ● |  |  |  |  |  |  |  | ● |  | ● | ● | ● |  | ● | ● |  |  | ● | ● |  | ● |  |  |  |  | ● |  |  |  | ● |  | ● | ● |
| STEVENS, BEN (HM19225) | ● |  |  |  | ● |  |  |  | ● |  |  |  |  | ● | ● |  |  |  |  |  |  |  | ● |  |  |  |  |  | ● |  |  |  |  |  |  | ● |  |  | ● |  |  |  |  |  |  |  |  |  |
| STIRLING, P (HM19302) | ● | ● | ● | ● | ● | ● | ● | ● | ● | ● | ● | ● | ● | ● | ● | ● | ● | ● | ● | ● |  | ● | ● | ● | ● | ● | ● | ● | ● | ● |  | ● | ● | ● | ● | ● | ● |  | ● | ● | ● | ● | ● | ● | ● | ● | ● | ● |
| STYLES, PATRICIA (HM19458) |  |  |  |  |  |  |  |  |  |  |  |  |  |  |  |  |  |  |  |  |  | ● |  |  |  |  |  |  |  |  |  |  |  |  |  |  |  |  |  |  |  |  |  |  |  |  |  |  |
| THOMAS, TRUDY (HM19958) |  |  |  |  |  |  |  |  |  |  |  |  |  |  |  |  |  |  |  |  |  | ● |  |  |  |  |  |  |  |  |  |  |  |  |  |  |  |  |  |  |  |  |  |  |  |  |  |  |
| TOLL HOUSE CLINIC (HM20120) |  | ● |  |  | ● |  |  |  |  |  |  |  |  |  |  | ● |  |  |  |  |  |  |  | ● |  | ● |  | ● | ● |  |  |  |  |  |  |  |  |  | ● |  |  |  |  |  | ● |  | ● |  |
| **BUCKINGHAMSHIRE** |  |  |  |  |  |  |  |  |  |  |  |  |  |  |  |  |  |  |  |  |  |  |  |  |  |  |  |  |  |  |  |  |  |  |  |  |  |  |  |  |  |  |  |  |  |  |  |  |
| ALTERNATE WAYS (HM00692) | ● | ● |  |  |  |  |  |  |  |  |  |  |  |  | ● |  |  |  |  |  |  |  |  |  |  |  |  |  |  |  |  |  |  |  |  |  |  |  |  |  |  |  |  |  |  |  |  |  |
| ALTERNATIVE THERAPIES TRAINING (HM00730) | ● | ● | ● | ● | ● | ● | ● | ● | ● | ● | ● | ● | ● | ● | ● | ● | ● | ● | ● | ● |  | ● | ● | ● | ● | ● | ● | ● | ● | ● |  | ● | ● | ● | ● | ● | ● |  | ● | ● | ● | ● | ● | ● | ● | ● | ● | ● |
| AMERSHAM CHIROPRACTIC CLINIC (HM00779) | ● | ● |  |  | ● |  |  |  |  |  |  |  |  |  |  |  |  |  |  |  |  |  |  | ● | ● | ● |  | ● | ● |  |  |  |  |  |  |  |  |  |  |  |  |  |  |  | ● |  | ● |  |
| AMERSHAM OSTEOPATHIC CLINIC (HM00780) | ● |  |  |  | ● |  |  |  | ● |  |  |  | ● |  | ● |  |  |  |  |  |  |  |  | ● |  | ● |  | ● | ● |  |  |  | ● |  |  | ● |  |  | ● |  |  |  |  |  |  |  | ● |  |
| ASHBERRY PHYSIOTHERAPY CLINIC (HM01188) |  |  |  |  | ● |  |  |  |  |  |  |  |  |  |  |  |  |  | ● |  |  |  |  |  |  |  |  |  |  |  |  |  |  |  |  |  |  |  |  |  |  |  |  |  |  |  |  |  |
| AYLESBURY CHIROPRACTIC CLINIC (HM01422) |  | ● |  |  | ● |  |  |  |  |  |  |  | ● |  |  |  |  |  |  |  |  |  |  | ● |  |  |  |  | ● |  |  |  |  |  |  |  |  |  |  |  |  |  |  |  |  |  | ● |  |
| AYLESBURY COMPLEMENTARY HEALTH (HM01423) | ● | ● |  | ● | ● |  |  |  | ● |  | ● |  | ● | ● | ● |  |  |  | ● |  |  |  |  | ● | ● |  | ● |  | ● | ● |  | ● | ● | ● |  | ● |  |  | ● | ● | ● | ● | ● |  | ● |  | ● |  |
| AYLESBURY VALE THERAPY (HM01425) | ● | ● | ● |  |  |  |  |  |  |  | ● |  | ● |  | ● |  |  |  |  |  |  | ● |  | ● | ● |  | ● |  | ● |  |  |  | ● | ● |  |  |  |  |  |  | ● |  |  | ● |  |  |  | ● |
| BANFIELD, KATIE (HM01657) | ● | ● |  |  | ● |  | ● |  |  |  |  |  | ● |  | ● |  |  |  |  |  |  |  |  |  |  | ● |  | ● | ● |  |  |  | ● |  |  | ● |  |  |  |  |  |  |  |  | ● |  | ● |  |
| BEACONSFIELD CHIRO CLINIC (HM01954) |  |  |  |  | ● |  |  |  |  |  |  |  | ● |  |  |  |  |  |  |  |  |  |  | ● |  |  |  | ● | ● |  |  |  |  |  |  |  |  |  |  |  |  |  |  |  |  |  | ● |  |
| BIGGS, SYLVIA (HM02294) |  | ● |  |  | ● |  |  |  |  |  | ● |  | ● | ● | ● |  |  |  | ● |  |  |  | ● |  |  |  |  |  | ● | ● |  |  | ● | ● |  | ● |  |  | ● |  |  |  |  |  |  |  | ● |  |
| BODY & SOUL (HM02565) | ● | ● |  |  |  |  |  |  |  |  |  |  |  | ● | ● |  |  |  |  |  |  |  |  |  |  |  |  |  | ● |  |  |  |  |  |  |  |  |  |  |  |  |  |  |  |  |  |  |  |
| BREEZE, T (HM02951) |  |  |  |  |  |  |  |  |  |  |  |  |  |  |  |  |  |  |  |  |  |  |  |  |  |  |  |  | ● |  |  |  |  |  |  |  |  |  |  |  |  |  |  |  |  |  | ● |  |
| BUCKINGHAM CHIROPRACTIC CLINIC (HM03310) |  | ● |  |  | ● |  |  |  |  |  |  |  | ● |  | ● |  |  |  | ● |  |  |  | ● | ● | ● | ● |  | ● | ● |  |  |  |  |  |  |  |  |  |  |  |  | ● |  |  |  |  | ● |  |
| CAMPBELL, LOUISE (HM03604) | ● |  |  |  |  | ● |  |  |  |  | ● |  | ● | ● | ● |  |  |  |  |  |  | ● | ● |  |  |  |  |  | ● |  |  |  | ● |  | ● | ● |  |  | ● |  |  |  |  |  |  |  |  |  |
| CAMPBELL, NIKKI (HM03605) | ● | ● |  |  | ● |  |  |  |  |  |  |  | ● | ● | ● |  |  |  | ● |  |  |  |  | ● | ● | ● |  |  | ● |  |  | ● |  |  |  | ● |  |  |  |  |  | ● |  |  | ● |  | ● |  |
| CASTLE STREET CLINIC (HM03837) | ● | ● |  |  | ● | ● | ● |  |  |  |  |  | ● | ● | ● | ● |  |  |  |  |  |  | ● |  |  | ● |  | ● | ● | ● |  |  | ● |  |  | ● |  |  | ● |  |  |  | ● | ● | ● |  | ● |  |
| CHILTERN AROMATHERAPY (HM04172) |  |  |  |  |  |  |  |  |  |  |  |  |  | ● | ● |  |  |  |  |  |  |  |  |  |  |  |  |  |  |  |  |  |  |  |  | ● |  |  |  |  |  |  |  |  |  |  |  |  |
| COACHING FOR SUCCESS (HM04750) | ● | ● |  |  |  |  |  |  |  |  |  |  |  |  |  |  |  |  |  |  |  |  |  |  | ● |  |  |  |  |  |  |  |  | ● |  |  |  |  |  |  | ● |  |  |  |  |  |  |  |
| COLDWELL, VERONICA (HM04810) | ● | ● | ● | ● | ● | ● | ● | ● | ● | ● | ● | ● | ● | ● | ● | ● | ● | ● | ● | ● |  | ● | ● | ● | ● | ● | ● | ● | ● | ● |  | ● | ● | ● | ● | ● | ● |  | ● | ● | ● | ● | ● | ● | ● | ● | ● | ● |
| COMPLEMENTARY HEALTH (HM04921) | ● | ● |  | ● | ● |  |  |  | ● |  | ● |  | ● | ● | ● |  |  |  |  |  |  |  |  | ● | ● |  | ● |  | ● | ● |  | ● | ● | ● |  | ● |  |  | ● | ● | ● | ● | ● |  | ● |  | ● |  |
| COMPLEMENTARY HEALTH CENTRE (HM04923) | ● | ● |  | ● | ● |  |  |  | ● |  | ● |  | ● | ● | ● |  |  |  |  |  |  |  |  | ● | ● |  | ● |  | ● | ● |  | ● | ● | ● |  | ● |  |  |  | ● | ● | ● | ● |  | ● |  | ● |  |
| DOIG, PAUL (HM06158) | ● | ● | ● |  |  | ● | ● | ● | ● | ● | ● | ● | ● | ● | ● |  | ● | ● |  |  |  |  | ● | ● | ● | ● |  |  |  | ● |  |  | ● | ● | ● | ● |  |  |  | ● |  |  | ● | ● | ● |  | ● | ● |
| DOWDELL, FIONA K (HM06234) |  |  |  |  | ● |  |  |  |  |  |  |  | ● |  | ● |  |  |  |  |  |  |  |  | ● |  |  |  |  | ● |  |  |  |  |  |  |  |  |  | ● |  |  |  |  |  |  |  | ● |  |
| EDWARDS, EMMA (HM06650) | ● | ● |  |  | ● |  |  |  |  |  | ● |  | ● | ● | ● |  |  |  |  |  |  |  | ● |  |  |  |  |  | ● |  |  |  |  |  |  | ● | ● |  | ● |  |  |  |  |  |  |  |  |  |
| ELAINE MCCARTHY REFLEXOLOGIST (HM06698) | ● | ● | ● | ● | ● | ● |  | ● | ● | ● | ● | ● | ● | ● | ● | ● | ● | ● | ● | ● |  |  | ● | ● | ● |  | ● | ● | ● | ● |  | ● | ● |  | ● | ● | ● |  | ● | ● | ● | ● | ● | ● | ● | ● | ● | ● |
| ENFIELD, CLAUDIA (HM06820) | ● | ● |  |  | ● | ● |  |  | ● | ● | ● |  | ● |  | ● |  |  |  |  |  |  |  |  |  |  |  |  |  |  |  |  |  |  |  |  |  |  |  |  |  |  |  |  |  |  |  |  |  |

# I - S Conditions treated at Practices/Businesses

| Business by County with Reference no. | Insomnia | Irritable Bowel Syndrome | Itching | Jet Lag | Joint Pain | Kidney Complaints | Lactose Intolerance | Laryngitis | Lethargy | Liver Disorders | Low Blood Pressure | Lung Problems | ME | Menopause | Migraine | Motion Sickness |
|---|---|---|---|---|---|---|---|---|---|---|---|---|---|---|---|---|
| FIRMAN, BARBARA (HM07332) | ● | ● | | ● | ● | ● | | | ● | | | ● | ● | ● | ● | |
| FLEET, BARBARA (HM07402) | ● | ● | | | | | | | | | | | | | | |
| GERRARDS CROSS SPORTS & BACK (HM08004) | | | | | | | | | | | | | | | | |
| HEATH, SUSAN (HM09454) | | | | | | | | | | | | | ● | ● | | |
| HOBBS, SALLY (HM09857) | ● | ● | ● | ● | ● | ● | ● | ● | ● | ● | ● | ● | ● | ● | ● | ● |
| HOLISTIC HEALING (HM09959) | ● | ● | | | ● | ● | | | | | | | ● | ● | ● | |
| HULCOTT END PRACTICE (HM10352) | | ● | | | ● | | | | | | | | ● | | | |
| J J COUNSELLING SERVICES (HM10798) | ● | | | | | | | | | | | | | ● | | |
| JOHNSON, HELEN (HM11074) | ● | ● | ● | ● | ● | ● | ● | ● | ● | ● | ● | ● | ● | ● | ● | ● |
| K BANFIELD NATUROPATHY/OSTEO (HM11288) | ● | ● | | | ● | | ● | | | | | | ● | | ● | |
| KENTISH, LORNE (HM11531) | ● | ● | | | ● | ● | | | | | ● | | ● | ● | ● | |
| LONG CRENDON OSTEOPATHS (HM12614) | | | | | ● | | | | | | | | | | | |
| MATTHEWS, FRANK (HM13306) | | | | | | | | | | | | | | | | |
| MIDDLE WAY RE-EDUCATION CTRE (HM13813) | | | | | ● | | | | ● | | | | ● | | | ● |
| MIND AND BODY (HM13959) | ● | | | | | | | | ● | | | | | | | |
| MIRZOEFF, PETER (HM13992) | ● | | | | | | | | | | | | | | | |
| O'NEIL, PAULA (HM15326) | ● | ● | | | ● | | | | ● | | | | | ● | ● | |
| OXFORDSHIRE BOWEN CLINIC (HM15545) | | | | | ● | | | | ● | | ● | ● | | | ● | |
| PATON, BARBARA (HM15823) | | ● | | | ● | | | | | | | | ● | | ● | |
| PHYSIO FIRST PRACTICE (HM16199) | | | | | ● | | | | | | | | | | | |
| PINEWOOD CHIROPODY PRACTICE (HM16312) | | | | | ● | | | | | | | | | | | |
| PRESTWOOD PHYSIOTHERAPY CLINIC (HM16562) | | | | | ● | | | | | | | | | | | |
| REIKI HEALTH CENTRE (HM17137) | ● | ● | | | | | | | | | | | | | ● | |
| RUNDLE, RICHARD (HM17752) | ● | ● | ● | ● | ● | ● | ● | ● | ● | ● | ● | ● | ● | ● | ● | |
| SHAW, FIONA (HM18335) | | | | | ● | | | | ● | ● | ● | | | | ● | |
| SHENLEY CHIROPRACTIC CLINIC (HM18399) | | ● | | | ● | | | | | | | | | | | |
| STEINBERG, PAMELA (HM19189) | ● | ● | ● | ● | ● | ● | ● | ● | ● | ● | ● | ● | ● | ● | ● | ● |
| TAYLOR, IAN E (HM19763) | | | | | | | | | | | | | | | | |
| TEACHERS OF ALEXNDR TECH (HM19806) | | ● | | | | | | | | | | | ● | | | |
| TODD, PAUL (HM20107) | | | | | | | | | | | | | | | | |
| TOMLIN, SUSAN M (HM20136) | ● | ● | | | ● | ● | | | | ● | ● | ● | ● | ● | ● | |
| TUDOR HOUSE CLINIC (HM20371) | | | | | ● | | | | | | | | | | | |
| WARDLAW, MICHAEL (HM20921) | | | | | | | | | | | | | | | | |
| WELLBURN (HM21154) | ● | ● | ● | ● | ● | ● | ● | ● | ● | ● | ● | ● | ● | ● | ● | ● |

| Business by County with Reference no. | Mouth Disorders | Mouth Ulcers | Multiple Sclerosis | Muscular Dystrophy | Musculo-skeletal | Nail Health | Nausea | Nerve Disorders | Nervous Disorders | Neuralgia | Obesity | Osteoporosis | Pain | Palpitations | Panic Attacks | Parkinson's Disease |
|---|---|---|---|---|---|---|---|---|---|---|---|---|---|---|---|---|
| FIRMAN, BARBARA (HM07332) | | | ● | ● | | ● | ● | | ● | | | | ● | ● | | ● |
| FLEET, BARBARA (HM07402) | | | | | | | | | | | | | | | | |
| GERRARDS CROSS SPORTS & BACK (HM08004) | | | | | | | | | | | | | ● | | | |
| HEATH, SUSAN (HM09454) | | | | | | | | | ● | | | | ● | | | |
| HOBBS, SALLY (HM09857) | ● | ● | ● | ● | | ● | ● | ● | ● | ● | ● | ● | ● | ● | | ● |
| HOLISTIC HEALING (HM09959) | | | ● | | | | ● | | | | | | ● | ● | | |
| HULCOTT END PRACTICE (HM10352) | | | | | | | | | | ● | | | ● | | | |
| J J COUNSELLING SERVICES (HM10798) | | | | | | | | | | | | | | | | |
| JOHNSON, HELEN (HM11074) | ● | ● | ● | ● | ● | ● | ● | ● | ● | ● | ● | ● | ● | ● | ● | ● |
| K BANFIELD NATUROPATHY/OSTEO (HM11288) | | | | | | | | | | ● | | ● | ● | | | |
| KENTISH, LORNE (HM11531) | | | | | | ● | ● | | | | | | ● | | | |
| LONG CRENDON OSTEOPATHS (HM12614) | | | | | | | | | | | | | ● | | | |
| MATTHEWS, FRANK (HM13306) | | | | | | | | | | | ● | | | | | |
| MIDDLE WAY RE-EDUCATION CTRE (HM13813) | | | | | | | | ● | ● | | | | | | | |
| MIND AND BODY (HM13959) | | | | | | | | | ● | | | | ● | ● | | |
| MIRZOEFF, PETER (HM13992) | | | | | | | | | ● | | ● | | ● | | | |
| O'NEIL, PAULA (HM15326) | | ● | | | | | | | | ● | | | ● | | | |
| OXFORDSHIRE BOWEN CLINIC (HM15545) | | | | | | | | ● | | ● | | | ● | | | |
| PATON, BARBARA (HM15823) | | | | | | | | ● | ● | | | ● | ● | | | ● |
| PHYSIO FIRST PRACTICE (HM16199) | | | | | | | | | | | | ● | ● | | | |
| PINEWOOD CHIROPODY PRACTICE (HM16312) | | | | | | ● | | | | | | | | | | |
| PRESTWOOD PHYSIOTHERAPY CLINIC (HM16562) | | | ● | | | | | | | | | | ● | | | |
| REIKI HEALTH CENTRE (HM17137) | | | | | | | | | | | | | | | | |
| RUNDLE, RICHARD (HM17752) | ● | ● | ● | ● | | | ● | ● | ● | ● | ● | ● | ● | ● | | ● |
| SHAW, FIONA (HM18335) | | | | | | | | | | | | | | | | |
| SHENLEY CHIROPRACTIC CLINIC (HM18399) | | | | | | | | ● | | | | | ● | | | |
| STEINBERG, PAMELA (HM19189) | ● | ● | ● | ● | | ● | ● | ● | ● | ● | ● | ● | ● | ● | | ● |
| TAYLOR, IAN E (HM19763) | | | | | | ● | | | | | | | | | | |
| TEACHERS OF ALEXNDR TECH (HM19806) | | | | | | | | | | | | ● | ● | | | |
| TODD, PAUL (HM20107) | | | | | | ● | | | | | | | | | | |
| TOMLIN, SUSAN M (HM20136) | | | ● | | | | | ● | | ● | | | ● | ● | | |
| TUDOR HOUSE CLINIC (HM20371) | | | | | | | | | | | | | ● | | | |
| WARDLAW, MICHAEL (HM20921) | | | | | | ● | | | | | | | | | | |
| WELLBURN (HM21154) | ● | ● | ● | | | ● | ● | ● | ● | ● | ● | ● | ● | ● | | ● |

| Business by County with Reference no. | Period Problems | Phobias | Piles | PMT | Pneumonia | Postural Problems | Pregnancy Help | Prostate Problems | Psoriasis | Raynaud's Disease | Recurrent Infections | Restless Legs | Rheumatoid Arthritis | Schizophrenia | Sciatica | Sexual Problems |
|---|---|---|---|---|---|---|---|---|---|---|---|---|---|---|---|---|
| FIRMAN, BARBARA (HM07332) | ● | ● | | ● | | | ● | ● | ● | ● | | ● | ● | | ● | ● |
| FLEET, BARBARA (HM07402) | | ● | | ● | | | | | | | | | | | | |
| GERRARDS CROSS SPORTS & BACK (HM08004) | | | | | | | | | | | | | ● | | ● | |
| HEATH, SUSAN (HM09454) | | | | | | | | | | | | | | | | ● |
| HOBBS, SALLY (HM09857) | ● | ● | ● | ● | ● | | ● | ● | ● | ● | ● | ● | ● | ● | ● | ● |
| HOLISTIC HEALING (HM09959) | ● | | | ● | | | | | | | | | | | ● | |
| HULCOTT END PRACTICE (HM10352) | | | | | | | | | | | | | ● | | | |
| J J COUNSELLING SERVICES (HM10798) | | ● | | ● | | | | | | | | | | | | ● |
| JOHNSON, HELEN (HM11074) | ● | ● | ● | ● | ● | ● | ● | ● | ● | ● | ● | ● | ● | ● | ● | ● |
| K BANFIELD NATUROPATHY/OSTEO (HM11288) | ● | | | ● | | | | | | | | | ● | | ● | |
| KENTISH, LORNE (HM11531) | ● | | | ● | | | ● | | | | | ● | | | | |
| LONG CRENDON OSTEOPATHS (HM12614) | | | | | | | | | | | | | | | ● | |
| MATTHEWS, FRANK (HM13306) | | ● | | | | | | | | | | | | | | |
| MIDDLE WAY RE-EDUCATION CTRE (HM13813) | | ● | | | | | | | | | | | | | ● | |
| MIND AND BODY (HM13959) | | ● | | | | | | | | | | | | | | |
| MIRZOEFF, PETER (HM13992) | | ● | | | | | | | | | | | | | | |
| O'NEIL, PAULA (HM15326) | ● | | | ● | | | ● | ● | ● | | ● | | | | ● | |
| OXFORDSHIRE BOWEN CLINIC (HM15545) | | | | | | | | | | | | | | | ● | |
| PATON, BARBARA (HM15823) | | | | | | | | | | | | | | | ● | |
| PHYSIO FIRST PRACTICE (HM16199) | | | | | | | | | | | | | | | ● | |
| PINEWOOD CHIROPODY PRACTICE (HM16312) | | | | | | | | | | | | | | | | |
| PRESTWOOD PHYSIOTHERAPY CLINIC (HM16562) | | | | | | | | | | | | | | | | |
| REIKI HEALTH CENTRE (HM17137) | | | | | | | | | | | | | | | | |
| RUNDLE, RICHARD (HM17752) | ● | ● | ● | ● | ● | | ● | ● | ● | ● | ● | ● | ● | ● | ● | ● |
| SHAW, FIONA (HM18335) | | | | ● | | | | | | | | | | | | |
| SHENLEY CHIROPRACTIC CLINIC (HM18399) | | | | | | | | | | | | | | | ● | |
| STEINBERG, PAMELA (HM19189) | ● | ● | ● | ● | ● | | ● | ● | ● | ● | ● | ● | ● | ● | ● | ● |
| TAYLOR, IAN E (HM19763) | | | | | | | | | | | | | | | | |
| TEACHERS OF ALEXNDR TECH (HM19806) | | | | | | | | | | | | | | | ● | |
| TODD, PAUL (HM20107) | | | | | | | | | | | | | | | | |
| TOMLIN, SUSAN M (HM20136) | ● | | | ● | | | | ● | | ● | | ● | ● | | ● | ● |
| TUDOR HOUSE CLINIC (HM20371) | | | | | | | | | | | | | | | | |
| WARDLAW, MICHAEL (HM20921) | | | | | | | | | | | | | | | | |
| WELLBURN (HM21154) | ● | ● | ● | ● | ● | | ● | ● | ● | ● | ● | ● | ● | ● | ● | ● |

# I - S Conditions treated at Practices/Businesses

| Business by County with Reference no. | Insomnia | Irritable Bowel Syndrome | Itching | Jet Lag | Joint Pain | Kidney Complaints | Lactose Intolerance | Laryngitis | Lethargy | Liver Disorders | Low Blood Pressure | Lung Problems | ME | Menopause | Migraine | Motion Sickness | Mouth Disorders | Mouth Ulcers | Multiple Sclerosis | Muscular Dystrophy | Musculo-skeletal | Nail Health | Nausea | Nerve Disorders | Nervous Disorders | Neuralgia | Obesity | Osteoporosis | Pain | Palpitations | Panic Attacks | Parkinson's Disease | Period Problems | Phobias | Piles | PMT | Pneumonia | Postural Problems | Pregnancy Help | Prostate Problems | Psoriasis | Raynaud's Disease | Recurrent Infections | Restless Legs | Rheumatoid Arthritis | Schizophrenia | Sciatica | Sexual Problems |
|---|---|---|---|---|---|---|---|---|---|---|---|---|---|---|---|---|---|---|---|---|---|---|---|---|---|---|---|---|---|---|---|---|---|---|---|---|---|---|---|---|---|---|---|---|---|---|---|---|
| WELLER, JACK (HM21156) | ● | ● |  |  |  |  |  |  |  |  |  |  | ● |  |  |  |  |  |  |  |  |  |  |  |  |  |  |  |  |  |  |  |  | ● |  |  |  |  |  |  |  |  |  |  |  |  |  |  |
| WEST WYCOMBE CHIRO CLINIC (HM21240) |  | ● |  |  | ● |  |  |  |  |  |  |  | ● |  |  |  |  |  |  |  |  |  |  | ● |  |  |  |  | ● |  |  |  |  |  |  |  |  |  |  |  |  |  |  |  |  |  | ● |  |
| WESTWOOD, TERRY (HM21287) |  |  |  |  |  |  |  |  |  |  |  |  |  |  |  |  |  |  |  |  |  |  |  |  |  |  | ● |  |  |  |  |  |  | ● |  |  |  |  |  |  |  |  |  |  |  |  |  |  |
| WOODWARD, MARGARET (HM21866) | ● | ● |  |  |  |  |  |  |  |  |  |  | ● |  | ● |  |  |  |  |  |  |  |  |  |  |  |  |  |  |  |  |  |  |  |  |  |  |  |  |  |  |  |  | ● |  |  |  |  |
| CAMBRIDGESHIRE |  |  |  |  |  |  |  |  |  |  |  |  |  |  |  |  |  |  |  |  |  |  |  |  |  |  |  |  |  |  |  |  |  |  |  |  |  |  |  |  |  |  |  |  |  |  |  |  |
| ACHILLES PHYSIOTHERAPY CLINIC (HM00161) |  |  |  |  | ● |  |  |  |  |  |  |  |  |  |  |  |  |  |  |  |  |  |  |  |  |  |  |  |  |  |  |  |  |  |  |  |  |  |  |  |  |  |  |  |  |  |  |  |
| ANDERSON, M (HM00834) |  | ● |  |  | ● |  |  |  |  |  |  |  |  |  |  |  |  |  |  |  |  |  |  | ● |  |  |  |  | ● |  |  |  |  |  |  |  |  |  |  |  |  |  |  |  |  |  | ● |  |
| ANDERSON, PAUL (HM00836) |  |  |  |  |  |  |  |  |  |  |  |  |  |  |  |  |  |  |  |  |  | ● |  |  |  |  |  |  |  |  |  |  |  |  |  |  |  |  |  |  |  |  |  |  |  |  |  |  |
| ARJUNA NATURAL HEALTH CENTRE (HM01000) | ● | ● | ● | ● | ● | ● | ● | ● | ● | ● | ● | ● | ● | ● | ● | ● | ● | ● | ● | ● |  | ● | ● | ● | ● | ● | ● | ● | ● | ● |  | ● | ● | ● | ● | ● | ● |  | ● | ● | ● | ● | ● | ● | ● | ● | ● | ● |
| BACK ON TRACK (HM01486) |  |  |  |  | ● |  |  |  |  |  |  |  |  |  |  |  |  |  |  |  |  |  |  |  |  |  |  |  | ● |  |  |  |  |  |  |  |  |  |  |  |  |  |  |  |  |  |  |  |
| BACK ON TRACK (HM01487) |  |  |  |  | ● |  |  |  |  |  |  |  |  |  |  |  |  |  |  |  |  |  |  |  |  |  |  |  | ● |  |  |  |  |  |  |  |  |  |  |  |  |  |  |  |  |  |  |  |
| BACK ON TRACK (HM01488) |  |  |  |  | ● |  |  |  |  |  |  |  |  |  |  |  |  |  |  |  |  |  |  |  |  |  |  |  |  |  |  |  |  |  |  |  |  |  |  |  |  |  |  |  |  |  |  |  |
| BENSON, HUGH (HM02168) | ● | ● | ● | ● | ● | ● | ● | ● | ● | ● | ● | ● | ● | ● | ● | ● | ● | ● | ● | ● |  | ● | ● | ● | ● | ● | ● | ● | ● | ● |  | ● | ● | ● | ● | ● | ● |  | ● | ● | ● | ● | ● | ● | ● | ● | ● | ● |
| BRAMPTON CHIROPRACTIC CLINIC (HM02906) | ● |  |  |  | ● |  |  |  | ● |  |  |  | ● |  | ● | ● |  |  |  |  |  |  |  | ● |  | ● |  |  | ● |  |  |  | ● |  |  |  |  |  |  |  |  |  | ● | ● |  |  | ● |  |
| CAMBRIDGE CHIROPRACTIC CENTRE (HM03572) |  | ● |  |  | ● |  |  |  |  |  |  |  |  |  |  |  |  |  |  |  |  |  |  | ● |  |  |  | ● | ● |  |  |  |  |  |  |  |  |  |  |  |  |  |  |  |  |  | ● |  |
| CAMBRIDGE TRAD ACUPUNC CENTRE (HM03578) | ● |  |  |  |  |  |  |  | ● |  |  |  |  | ● | ● |  |  |  |  |  |  |  |  |  |  |  |  |  | ● |  |  |  | ● |  |  | ● |  |  |  |  |  |  |  |  |  |  |  |  |
| CHIROPRATIC & HOM HEALTH CTRE (HM04408) | ● | ● |  | ● | ● | ● |  |  |  |  | ● |  | ● | ● | ● |  |  |  | ● | ● |  |  |  |  |  |  |  | ● | ● | ● |  |  | ● |  |  | ● |  |  | ● |  |  |  |  | ● | ● |  | ● |  |
| COMPLEMENTARY HEALTH CLINIC (HM04927) |  | ● |  |  | ● |  |  |  |  |  |  |  | ● | ● | ● |  |  |  | ● |  |  |  |  | ● |  | ● |  |  | ● |  |  |  | ● |  |  |  |  |  |  | ● |  |  |  | ● | ● |  | ● |  |
| COXELL REMEDIAL CLINIC (HM05324) |  | ● |  |  | ● |  |  |  |  |  |  |  |  |  |  |  |  |  |  |  | ● |  |  |  |  |  |  |  | ● |  |  |  |  |  |  |  |  |  |  |  |  |  |  | ● |  |  | ● |  |
| CUTTING, VALERIE (HM05648) | ● |  |  |  | ● | ● |  |  |  |  |  |  |  |  | ● |  |  |  |  |  |  |  | ● |  |  |  |  |  | ● |  |  |  | ● |  |  |  |  |  |  |  |  |  |  | ● |  |  | ● |  |
| FAULKNER, CINDY (HM07141) | ● | ● |  |  | ● | ● |  |  | ● |  | ● | ● | ● | ● | ● |  |  |  |  |  |  |  | ● |  | ● |  |  |  |  | ● |  |  | ● |  |  | ● |  |  | ● |  |  | ● |  |  |  |  | ● |  |
| GILBERT RD OSTEOPATHIC (HM08055) |  |  |  |  | ● |  |  |  |  |  |  |  |  |  |  |  |  |  |  |  |  |  |  | ● |  | ● |  |  | ● |  |  |  |  |  |  |  |  |  | ● |  |  |  |  |  |  |  | ● |  |
| HEALTH TEAM (HM09406) | ● | ● | ● | ● | ● | ● | ● | ● | ● | ● | ● | ● | ● | ● | ● | ● |  | ● |  |  |  | ● |  | ● | ● | ● | ● | ● | ● | ● |  |  | ● | ● | ● | ● |  |  | ● | ● | ● | ● | ● | ● | ● | ● | ● | ● |
| HYPNOSIS AND HEALTH (HM10495) | ● | ● |  | ● |  |  |  |  |  |  | ● |  | ● | ● | ● | ● |  |  | ● |  |  |  |  |  | ● |  | ● |  | ● |  |  |  | ● | ● |  | ● |  |  | ● |  | ● |  |  |  |  |  |  | ● |
| LIZ HALE HANDSON HEALTH (HM12495) | ● | ● | ● | ● | ● |  |  |  |  |  |  | ● | ● | ● | ● |  |  |  |  |  |  |  | ● |  | ● | ● |  |  | ● |  |  |  | ● |  |  | ● |  |  |  |  | ● |  |  | ● | ● |  | ● |  |
| LY, THI PHUNG (DR) (HM12754) | ● | ● | ● | ● | ● | ● |  | ● | ● | ● | ● | ● | ● | ● | ● | ● | ● | ● |  |  |  |  | ● |  | ● | ● | ● | ● | ● | ● |  |  | ● | ● | ● | ● | ● |  | ● | ● | ● | ● | ● | ● | ● |  | ● | ● |
| MAGUIRE, J () |  |  |  |  |  |  |  |  |  |  |  |  |  |  |  |  |  |  |  |  |  |  |  |  |  |  | ● |  |  |  |  |  |  |  |  |  |  |  |  |  |  |  |  |  |  |  |  |  |
| MATHIESON, M A (HM13290) |  |  |  |  |  |  |  |  |  |  |  |  |  |  |  |  |  |  |  |  |  | ● |  |  |  |  |  |  |  |  |  |  |  |  |  |  |  |  |  |  |  |  |  |  |  |  |  |  |
| MAYNARD, SUSANNE (HM13358) |  |  |  |  | ● |  |  |  |  |  |  |  |  |  |  |  |  |  |  |  |  |  |  |  |  |  |  |  |  |  |  |  |  |  |  |  |  |  |  |  |  |  |  |  |  |  |  |  |
| OUTSIDE IN (HM15507) |  |  |  | ● |  |  |  |  |  |  |  |  |  |  |  |  |  |  |  |  |  |  |  |  |  |  |  |  |  |  |  |  |  |  |  | ● |  |  |  |  |  |  |  |  |  |  |  |  |
| OXBOROUGH, JOY (HM15536) |  | ● | ● |  |  | ● | ● | ● | ● | ● | ● | ● | ● | ● | ● | ● | ● |  | ● | ● |  | ● | ● | ● | ● | ● | ● | ● | ● | ● |  |  |  | ● | ● | ● | ● |  |  | ● | ● | ● | ● | ● | ● | ● | ● |  |
| PHIL SEAL PSYCHOTHERAPY (HM16115) | ● | ● |  |  |  |  |  |  |  |  |  |  |  |  |  |  |  |  |  |  |  |  |  |  |  |  |  |  | ● |  | ● |  |  | ● |  |  |  |  |  |  |  |  |  |  |  |  |  |  |
| PRESTONS CHRTRD PHYSIOTHERAPY (HM16560) |  |  |  |  | ● |  |  |  |  |  |  |  |  |  |  |  |  |  |  |  | ● |  |  |  |  |  |  |  |  |  |  |  |  |  |  |  |  |  |  |  |  |  |  |  |  |  |  |  |
| REID, SUSAN (HM17121) |  | ● |  |  | ● |  |  |  | ● |  |  |  | ● | ● | ● |  |  |  | ● |  |  |  |  | ● | ● | ● |  | ● | ● |  |  |  | ● | ● |  | ● |  |  |  |  |  |  |  |  |  |  | ● |  |

# I - S Conditions treated at Practices/Businesses

| Business by County with Reference no. | Insomnia | Irritable Bowel Syndrome | Itching | Jet Lag | Joint Pain | Kidney Complaints | Lactose Intolerance | Laryngitis | Lethargy | Liver Disorders | Low Blood Pressure | Lung Problems | ME | Menopause | Migraine | Motion Sickness | Mouth Disorders | Mouth Ulcers | Multiple Sclerosis | Muscular Dystrophy | Musculo-skeletal | Nail Health | Nausea | Nerve Disorders |
|---|---|---|---|---|---|---|---|---|---|---|---|---|---|---|---|---|---|---|---|---|---|---|---|---|
| ROBINSON-ZEL, B (HM17508) | ● | | | | | | | | | | | | | | | | | | | | | | | |
| SMITH, JEANETTE (HM18752) | ● | | | | ● | ● | | | | | | ● | ● | ● | ● | | | | | | | | ● | ● |
| SPENCE, ALEX (HM18982) | | ● | | | ● | | | | | | | | | | | | | | | | | | | ● |
| TONG, JENNY (HM20154) | ● | | | | ● | ● | | | | | ● | ● | ● | ● | ● | | | | | | | ● | ● | ● |
| WASS, ANNETTE (HM20975) | ● | ● | ● | | ● | ● | ● | ● | ● | ● | ● | ● | ● | ● | ● | ● | ● | | | | | | ● | ● |
| WILKINSON, GLYNNIS (HM21506) | | | | | | | | | | | | | | | | | | | | | | ● | | |
| **CHANNEL ISLANDS** | | | | | | | | | | | | | | | | | | | | | | | | |
| ST SAMPSON'S MEDICAL CENTRE (HM19098) | | | | | ● | | | | | | | | | | ● | | | | | | | | | |
| **CHESHIRE** | | | | | | | | | | | | | | | | | | | | | | | | |
| A & H PAIN CLINIC (HM00016) | ● | ● | ● | | ● | | | | ● | | ● | | ● | ● | ● | | | | ● | | | | ● | ● |
| ADULT & CHILD FOOT CLINIC (HM00391) | | | | | ● | | | | | | | | | | | | | | | | | ● | | ● |
| AROMASPHERE (HM01083) | ● | ● | | | | | | | | | | | | ● | ● | | | | | | | | | |
| BACK PAIN CLINIC (HM01500) | | ● | | | ● | | | | | | | | ● | | ● | | | | ● | | | | | ● |
| BAXTER, GILLIAN (HM01927) | | | | | | | | | | | | | | | | | | | | | | ● | | |
| BERESFORD, KATHLEEN (HM02183) | ● | ● | | | | ● | | | | | ● | | ● | ● | ● | | | | | | | | ● | |
| BLOCH, PETER (HM02510) | | ● | | | ● | | | | | | | | ● | | ● | | | | | | | | | ● |
| BODY ESSENCES (HM02586) | ● | ● | | | | | | | | | | | | ● | ● | | | | | | | ● | | |
| BRAMHALL PARK PHYSIO CLINIC (HM02899) | | | | | ● | | | | | | | | | | | | | | ● | | | | | |
| CARMICHAEL CLINIC (HM03708) | ● | ● | | | ● | | | | ● | | | | | | ● | | | | | | | | ● | |
| CHEADLE HULME NATURAL HEALTH (HM04070) | ● | ● | | | ● | ● | | | | | | | ● | ● | ● | | | | | | | | ● | |
| CHESHIRE HEALTH CLINIC (HM04115) | | ● | | | ● | | | | | | | | ● | | ● | | | | ● | | | | | ● |
| CHESTER ALEXANDER TECH ST (HM04125) | | ● | | | ● | | | | | | | | ● | | | | | | | | | | | ● |
| CHESTER CHIROPODY (HM04126) | | | | | | | | | | | | | | | | | | | | | | ● | | |
| CHESTER CHIROPRACTIC CLINIC (HM04127) | | ● | | | ● | | | | | | | | | | | | | | | | | | | ● |
| CHESTER CLINIC (HM04128) | ● | ● | ● | | ● | ● | | ● | ● | ● | | ● | ● | ● | ● | ● | ● | ● | | | | | ● | ● |
| CHESTER HEALTH (HM04129) | ● | | | ● | ● | | | | ● | ● | | | ● | ● | ● | | | | | | | ● | ● | ● |
| CHESTER HEALTH & BEAUTY STUDIO (HM04130) | ● | | | ● | ● | | | | ● | ● | | | ● | ● | ● | | | | | | | ● | ● | ● |
| CHESTER HOMEOPATHIC CLINIC (HM04131) | ● | ● | ● | | ● | | ● | | ● | ● | ● | ● | ● | ● | ● | | | ● | ● | | | | | ● |
| CHESTER THERAPY CENTRE (HM04134) | | | | | | | | | | | | | | | | | | | | | | | | |
| CHINESE MEDICINE CENTRE (HM04257) | ● | ● | ● | ● | ● | ● | ● | ● | ● | ● | ● | ● | ● | ● | ● | ● | ● | ● | ● | ● | ● | ● | ● | ● |
| CHIROPODIST SURGERY (HM04295) | | | | | | | | | | | | | | | | | | | | | | | | |
| CLINIC OF ACUPUNCTURE (HM04684) | ● | ● | ● | | ● | ● | ● | | ● | ● | ● | ● | ● | ● | ● | ● | | ● | | | | | ● | ● |
| COLHOUN, PETER (HM04842) | | | | | | | | | | | | | | | | | | | | | | | | |
| CONGLETON COUNSELLING PRACTICE (HM04977) | ● | | | | | | | | | | | | ● | | | | | | | | | | | |

| Business by County with Reference no. | Nervous Disorders | Neuralgia | Obesity | Osteoporosis | Pain | Palpitations | Panic Attacks | Parkinson's Disease | Period Problems | Phobias | Piles | PMT | Pneumonia | Postural Problems | Pregnancy Help | Prostate Problems | Psoriasis | Raynaud's Disease | Recurrent Infections | Restless Legs | Rheumatoid Arthritis | Schizophrenia | Sciatica | Sexual Problems |
|---|---|---|---|---|---|---|---|---|---|---|---|---|---|---|---|---|---|---|---|---|---|---|---|---|
| ROBINSON-ZEL, B (HM17508) | | | | | | | | | | | | | | | | | | | | | | | | |
| SMITH, JEANETTE (HM18752) | | | | | ● | | | | ● | | | ● | | | ● | | | | | ● | | | ● | |
| SPENCE, ALEX (HM18982) | | | | ● | ● | | | | | | | | | ● | | | | | | | | | ● | |
| TONG, JENNY (HM20154) | | | | | ● | | | | ● | | | ● | | | ● | | | | | ● | | | ● | |
| WASS, ANNETTE (HM20975) | ● | ● | | | | ● | | | ● | | ● | ● | | | ● | ● | ● | ● | ● | ● | ● | | | |
| WILKINSON, GLYNNIS (HM21506) | | | | | | | | | | | | | | | | | | | | | | | | |
| **CHANNEL ISLANDS** | | | | | | | | | | | | | | | | | | | | | | | | |
| ST SAMPSON'S MEDICAL CENTRE (HM19098) | | | | | ● | | | | | | | | | | | | | | | | | | ● | |
| **CHESHIRE** | | | | | | | | | | | | | | | | | | | | | | | | |
| A & H PAIN CLINIC (HM00016) | | ● | ● | ● | ● | ● | | | ● | ● | ● | ● | | | | | ● | | | | | | ● | ● |
| ADULT & CHILD FOOT CLINIC (HM00391) | | | | ● | ● | | | | | | | | | | | | ● | ● | | ● | ● | | | |
| AROMASPHERE (HM01083) | | | | | | | | | | | | | | | | | | | | | | | | |
| BACK PAIN CLINIC (HM01500) | ● | | | | ● | | | | | | | | | | | | | | | | | | ● | |
| BAXTER, GILLIAN (HM01927) | | | | | | | | | | | | | | | | | | | | | | | | |
| BERESFORD, KATHLEEN (HM02183) | | | | | ● | | | | ● | | | ● | | | ● | | | | | ● | | | ● | |
| BLOCH, PETER (HM02510) | ● | | | | ● | | | | | | | | | | | | | | | | | | ● | |
| BODY ESSENCES (HM02586) | | | | | | | | | | | | | | | | | | | | | | | | |
| BRAMHALL PARK PHYSIO CLINIC (HM02899) | | | | | | | | | | | | | | | | | | | | | | | | |
| CARMICHAEL CLINIC (HM03708) | | ● | | | ● | ● | | | ● | | | ● | | | ● | | ● | | | | ● | | ● | |
| CHEADLE HULME NATURAL HEALTH (HM04070) | | | | | ● | | | | ● | | ● | ● | | | ● | | | | | ● | ● | | ● | |
| CHESHIRE HEALTH CLINIC (HM04115) | | | | ● | ● | | | | | | | | | ● | | | | | | | | | ● | |
| CHESTER ALEXANDER TECH ST (HM04125) | | | | ● | ● | | | | | | | | | | | | | | | | | | ● | |
| CHESTER CHIROPODY (HM04126) | | | | | | | | | | | | | | | | | | | | | | | | |
| CHESTER CHIROPRACTIC CLINIC (HM04127) | | | | | ● | | | | | | | | | | | | | | | | | | ● | |
| CHESTER CLINIC (HM04128) | ● | ● | ● | | ● | ● | | ● | ● | | ● | ● | | | ● | ● | ● | ● | ● | ● | ● | | ● | ● |
| CHESTER HEALTH (HM04129) | | | | | ● | | | | ● | | | ● | | | | | ● | ● | ● | | | | ● | |
| CHESTER HEALTH & BEAUTY STUDIO (HM04130) | | | | | ● | | | | ● | | | ● | | | | | ● | ● | ● | | | | ● | |
| CHESTER HOMEOPATHIC CLINIC (HM04131) | ● | | | ● | ● | ● | | | ● | ● | ● | ● | | | ● | ● | ● | ● | ● | | ● | ● | ● | ● |
| CHESTER THERAPY CENTRE (HM04134) | | | | | | | | | | ● | | | | | | | | | | | | | | |
| CHINESE MEDICINE CENTRE (HM04257) | ● | ● | ● | ● | ● | ● | ● | ● | ● | ● | ● | ● | ● | ● | ● | ● | ● | ● | ● | ● | ● | ● | ● | ● |
| CHIROPODIST SURGERY (HM04295) | | | | | | | | | | | | | | | | | | ● | ● | | | | | |
| CLINIC OF ACUPUNCTURE (HM04684) | ● | ● | | | ● | ● | | | ● | | ● | ● | | | ● | ● | ● | ● | ● | ● | ● | | ● | ● |
| COLHOUN, PETER (HM04842) | | ● | | ● | ● | | | | | | | | | | | | | | | ● | ● | | | |
| CONGLETON COUNSELLING PRACTICE (HM04977) | | | | | | | | | | | | | | | | | | | | | | | | |

# I - S Conditions treated at Practices/Businesses

Business by County with Reference no.

| | CONSTANTINE, J C (HM05012) | CREWE & NANT PHYSIO CLINIC (HM05431) | CROPPER, AGNES (HM05473) | DAVIES & ASSOCIATES (HM05791) | DEWHURST, PATRICA A (HM06049) | EDDIE, DAVID (HM06585) | EVANS, DI (HM06968) | FAGAN, B W (HM07042) | FIELD VIEW SURGERY (HM07259) | FINCH, WENDY (HM07302) | FIVE WAYS OSTEOPATHIC SURGERY (HM07381) | GRAHAM COOMBE - MCTIMONEY (HM08338) | HANDS ON PHYSIOTHERAPY (HM08913) | HAZELDENE, BARBARA (HM09292) | HEALD, M T (HM09316) | HIGHLEY, T J (HM09757) | HOWE, BARBARA (HM10261) | HYPNOS PRACTICE (HM10492) | IPHOFEN, RON (DR) (HM10712) | JANE HAMMOND THERAPY (HM10916) | JENKINSON, LEILA (HM10999) | JONES, J W (HM11155) | KNUTSFORD CHIROPRACTIC CLINIC (HM11775) | LEGGE, PAT (HM12176) | LOMAS, CLIFFORD (HM12574) | MACALLAN, STEPHEN (HM12815) | MARSH, F W (HM13147) | MEDICINE WHEEL (HM13670) | MEHTA HYPNOTHERAPY (HM13695) | MIDDLETON & ASSOCIATES (HM13817) | MISSION, CHAITANYA (HM13995) | MORTON, J V (HM14251) | NEEDHAM, ANGELA (HM14749) | NEW LIFE NATURAL HEALTH CARE (HM14821) |
|---|---|---|---|---|---|---|---|---|---|---|---|---|---|---|---|---|---|---|---|---|---|---|---|---|---|---|---|---|---|---|---|---|---|---|
| Sexual Problems | | | | | ● | | ● | | | | | | | | | | | ● | | | ● | | ● | | | ● | | | | | | | ● | ● |
| Sciatica | ● | | | ● | ● | ● | ● | ● | | ● | ● | ● | | ● | | | | | | | ● | | ● | | ● | ● | | | | ● | | | ● | ● |
| Schizophrenia | | | | | ● | | ● | | | | | | | | | | | | | | ● | | | | | | | | | | | | | ● |
| Rheumatoid Arthritis | ● | | | ● | ● | | | | | | ● | | | | | | | | | | ● | | ● | | | ● | | | | | | | ● | ● |
| Restless Legs | | | ● | | | | | | ● | | | ● | | ● | | | | | | | ● | | ● | | | ● | | | | | | ● | ● | ● |
| Recurrent Infections | | | | | ● | | | | | | | | | | | | | | | | ● | | ● | | | ● | | | | | | | ● | ● |
| Raynaud's Disease | | | | ● | ● | | | | | | | ● | | | | | | | | | ● | | | | | ● | | | | | | | | ● |
| Psoriasis | | | | | ● | | | | | | | | | | | | | ● | | | ● | | | | | ● | | | | | | | ● | ● |
| Prostate Problems | | | | | ● | | | | | | | | | | | | | | | | ● | | ● | | | ● | | | | | | | ● | ● |
| Pregnancy Help | | | ● | | ● | | ● | | | | | | | ● | | | | | | | ● | | ● | | | ● | | | | | | | ● | ● |
| Postural Problems | | | | | | | | | | | | | | | | ● | | | | | | | | | | | | | | | | | | |
| Pneumonia | | | | | | | | | | | | | | | | | | | | | ● | | | | | | | | | | | | ● | ● |
| PMT | | | ● | | ● | | ● | | | | | | | ● | | | ● | ● | | | ● | | ● | | | ● | | | | ● | | | ● | ● |
| Piles | | | | | ● | | | | | | | | | | | | | | | | ● | | | | | | | | | | | | ● | ● |
| Phobias | | | | | ● | | | | | | | | | | | | | ● | ● | ● | ● | | ● | | | | | | ● | ● | | | ● | ● |
| Period Problems | | | ● | | ● | | ● | | | | | ● | | | | | | | | | ● | ● | ● | | | ● | | | ● | ● | | | ● | ● |
| Parkinson's Disease | | | | | ● | | | | ● | | | | | | | | | | | | ● | ● | ● | | | ● | | | | | | ● | ● | ● |
| Panic Attacks | | | | | | | | | | | | | | | | | | ● | ● | | | | | | | | | | | | | | | |
| Palpitations | | | | | ● | | ● | | | | | | | ● | | | ● | | | | ● | | | | | ● | | | | | | | ● | ● |
| Pain | ● | | ● | ● | ● | ● | ● | ● | | | ● | ● | ● | ● | | | | ● | ● | | ● | ● | ● | | ● | ● | | | | ● | ● | ● | ● | ● |
| Osteoporosis | ● | | | ● | ● | | | | | | ● | | | | | | | | | | ● | | ● | | | | | | | ● | | ● | ● | ● |
| Obesity | | | | | ● | | | | | | | | | | | | | | ● | | ● | | | | | ● | | | | | | | ● | ● |
| Neuralgia | ● | | | ● | ● | | | | | | ● | ● | | | | | | ● | | | ● | | ● | | | ● | | | | ● | | | ● | ● |
| Nervous Disorders | | | | | ● | | | | | | | | | | | | | ● | ● | | ● | | ● | | | | | | | ● | | | ● | ● |
| Nerve Disorders | ● | | | ● | ● | | ● | ● | | | ● | ● | | | | | | | | | ● | ● | ● | | | ● | | | | ● | | | ● | ● |
| Nausea | | | ● | | ● | | ● | | | | | | | ● | | | | | ● | | ● | | ● | | | | | | | | | | ● | ● |
| Nail Health | | | | | ● | | ● | | ● | | | | | | ● | | | | | | ● | ● | | | | | ● | | | | | | | |
| Musculo-skeletal | | | | | | | | | | | | | | | | | | | | | | | | | | | | | | | | | | |
| Muscular Dystrophy | | | | | ● | | | | | | ● | | | | | | | | | | ● | | ● | | | | | | | | | | | ● |
| Multiple Sclerosis | | ● | | ● | ● | | | ● | | | ● | | ● | ● | | | | | | | ● | | ● | | | ● | | | | ● | | | ● | ● |
| Mouth Ulcers | | | | | ● | | | | | | | | | | | | | | | | ● | | | | | ● | | | | | | | ● | ● |
| Mouth Disorders | | | | | ● | | | | | | | | | | | | | | | | ● | | | | | ● | | | | | | | ● | ● |
| Motion Sickness | | | | | ● | | | | | | | | | | | | | | | | ● | | | | | | | | | | | | ● | ● |
| Migraine | ● | | ● | ● | ● | ● | ● | | | | ● | ● | | ● | | | ● | ● | | | ● | | ● | ● | ● | ● | | ● | | ● | ● | | ● | ● |
| Menopause | | | | | ● | | ● | | | | | | | ● | | | | | | | ● | | ● | ● | | ● | | | | ● | | | ● | ● |
| ME | ● | | ● | ● | ● | | ● | | | | ● | ● | | ● | | | ● | | | ● | ● | | ● | | ● | ● | | ● | | ● | | | ● | ● |
| Lung Problems | | | | | ● | | | | | | | | | | | | | | | | ● | | | | | ● | | | | | | | ● | ● |
| Low Blood Pressure | | | ● | | ● | | ● | | | | | | | | | | | | | | ● | | ● | | | ● | | | | ● | | | ● | ● |
| Liver Disorders | | | | | ● | | | | | | | | | | | | | | | | ● | | ● | | | ● | | | | | | | ● | ● |
| Lethargy | | | | | ● | | | | | | | | | | | | | | | | ● | | ● | | | ● | | | | ● | | | ● | ● |
| Laryngitis | | | | | ● | | | | | | | | | | | | | | | | ● | | | | | ● | | | | | | | ● | ● |
| Lactose Intolerance | | | | | ● | | | | | | | | | | | | | | | | ● | | | | | ● | | | | | | | ● | ● |
| Kidney Complaints | | | ● | | ● | | ● | | | | | | | ● | | | | | | | ● | | ● | | | ● | | | | | | | ● | ● |
| Joint Pain | ● | ● | ● | ● | ● | ● | ● | ● | ● | ● | ● | ● | ● | ● | | | | | | | ● | | ● | | | ● | | | ● | ● | ● | | ● | ● |
| Jet Lag | | | | | | | | | | | | | | | | | | | | | ● | | | | | | | | | | | | ● | ● |
| Itching | | | | | ● | | | | | | | | | | | | | | | | ● | ● | | | | ● | | | | | | | ● | ● |
| Irritable Bowel Syndrome | | | ● | | ● | ● | ● | | | | | ● | | ● | | | | ● | | | ● | | ● | ● | | ● | | ● | ● | ● | | | ● | ● |
| Insomnia | ● | | ● | | ● | ● | ● | | | | | | | ● | | | | ● | | | ● | | ● | ● | | ● | | | ● | | | | ● | ● |

www.healthmyself.com

Healthmyself Directory

England (by County)

CONDITIONS TREATED

I-S

# I - S Conditions treated at Practices/Businesses

Business by County with Reference no.

| Business by County with Reference no. | Insomnia | Irritable Bowel Syndrome | Itching | Jet Lag | Joint Pain | Kidney Complaints | Lactose Intolerance | Laryngitis | Lethargy | Liver Disorders | Low Blood Pressure | Lung Problems | ME | Menopause | Migraine | Motion Sickness | Mouth Disorders | Mouth Ulcers | Multiple Sclerosis | Muscular Dystrophy | Musculo-skeletal | Nail Health | Nausea | Nerve Disorders |
|---|---|---|---|---|---|---|---|---|---|---|---|---|---|---|---|---|---|---|---|---|---|---|---|---|
| NUTRITION AND ALLERGY CLINIC (HM15121) | ● | ● | ● | | ● | | ● | ● | ● | | ● | | ● | ● | ● | | | ● | ● | | | ● | ● | ● |
| OLD HALL CLINIC (HM15256) | ● | ● | ● | ● | ● | ● | | ● | ● | ● | | ● | ● | ● | ● | ● | ● | ● | | | | ● | ● | ● |
| PATON, W A (HM15825) | | | | | ● | | | | | | | | | | | | | | ● | | | | | |
| PENNYCOOK, AMANDA (HM15996) | | | | | | | | | | | | | | | | | | | | | | ● | | |
| PHOENIX CENTRE (HM16154) | | ● | | | | | | | | | | | | | ● | | | | | | | | | |
| PHYSIO & SPORTS INJURY CLINIC (HM16181) | | | | | ● | | | | | | | ● | | | | | | | | | | | | |
| PHYSIO PLUS (HM16203) | | | | | ● | | | | | | | | | | | | | | | | | | | |
| PHYSIO SPORTS INJURY CLINIC (HM16209) | | | | | ● | | | | | | | | | | | | | | ● | | | | | |
| POYNTON CHIROPRACTIC CLINIC (HM16519) | | | | | ● | | | | | | | | | | ● | | | | | | | | | ● |
| PRINCE, TANIA A (HM16622) | ● | ● | | | | | | | | | | | | | ● | | | | | | | | | |
| REDGRAVE, KENNETH (HM17025) | ● | ● | | | | | | | | | | | | | | | | | | | | | | |
| SANDBACH HYPNOSIS CLINIC (HM17899) | | | | | | | | | | | | | | | | | | | | | | | | |
| SAXELBY, M (HM17990) | | | | | | | | | | | | | | | | | | | | | | ● | | |
| SCENTED GARDENS (HM18011) | ● | ● | | | | | | | | | | | ● | ● | ● | | | | | | | | | |
| TEDSTONE, ALISON (HM19815) | | | | | | | | | | | | | | | | | | | | | | ● | | |
| THOMAS, BEVERLEY (HM19933) | | | | | | | | | | | | | | | | | | | | | | ● | | |
| THORNBER, A A (HM20016) | | | | | ● | | | | | | | | | | | | | | | | | | | |
| TIPLING, L (HM20087) | | | | | | | | | | | | | | | | | | | | | | ● | | |
| TRINITY HOUSE PRACTICE (HM20339) | | | | | ● | | | | | | | | | | | | | | | | | | | |
| TULLY, CHARLES (HM20388) | ● | | | | ● | | | | | | | ● | | | ● | | | | | | | | | ● |
| VALE ROYAL CHIROPRACTIC CLINIC (HM20552) | | ● | | | ● | | | | | | | | | | | | | | | | | | | ● |
| VALE ROYAL CHIROPRACTIC CLINIC (HM20553) | | ● | | | ● | | | | | | | | | | | | | | | | | | | ● |
| WARRINGTON CHIROPRACTIC CLINIC (HM20957) | | ● | | | ● | | | | | | | | | | ● | | | | | | | | | ● |
| WEAVER HOUSE CLINIC (HM21049) | | ● | ● | ● | ● | ● | ● | ● | ● | | | | ● | ● | ● | ● | ● | ● | ● | | | ● | ● | ● |
| WIDNES OSTEOPATHIC CLINIC (HM21459) | | | | | ● | | | | | | | | ● | ● | ● | | | | | | | | | |
| WILLIAMS OSTEOPATHIC CLINIC (HM21532) | | | | | ● | | | | | | | | ● | | | | | | | | | | | |
| **CLEVELAND** | | | | | | | | | | | | | | | | | | | | | | | | |
| ALEXANDER TECHNIQUE (HM00548) | ● | ● | | | ● | | | | ● | | ● | | ● | ● | ● | | | | ● | ● | | | ● | ● |
| BARNARD, SIMON (HM01732) | | | | | ● | | | | | | | | | | ● | | | | | | | | | ● |
| BODY BALANCE (HM02570) | | | | | ● | | | | | | | | | | | | | | | | | | | |
| ELLISON, TIM (HM06777) | | | | | ● | | | | | | | | | | | | | | | | | ● | | |
| HARTLEPOOL CHIROPRACTIC CLINIC (HM09138) | | | | | ● | | | | | | | | | | | | | | | | | | | ● |
| MERMAID CHIROPRACTIC PRACTICE (HM13749) | | ● | | | ● | | | | | | | | | | | | | | | | | | | ● |
| NATURAL THERAPY CENTRE (HM14637) | | | | | ● | | | | | | | | | ● | ● | | | | | | | | | |

| Business by County with Reference no. | Nervous Disorders | Neuralgia | Obesity | Osteoporosis | Pain | Palpitations | Panic Attacks | Parkinson's Disease | Period Problems | Phobias | Piles | PMT | Pneumonia | Postural Problems | Pregnancy Help | Prostate Problems | Psoriasis | Raynaud's Disease | Recurrent Infections | Restless Legs | Rheumatoid Arthritis | Schizophrenia | Sciatica | Sexual Problems |
|---|---|---|---|---|---|---|---|---|---|---|---|---|---|---|---|---|---|---|---|---|---|---|---|---|
| NUTRITION AND ALLERGY CLINIC (HM15121) | ● | | ● | ● | ● | ● | | ● | ● | | | ● | | | ● | ● | ● | ● | ● | ● | ● | ● | | ● |
| OLD HALL CLINIC (HM15256) | ● | ● | ● | | ● | ● | | | ● | ● | ● | ● | ● | | ● | ● | ● | ● | ● | ● | ● | | ● | |
| PATON, W A (HM15825) | | | | | ● | | | | | | | | | | | | | | | | | | | |
| PENNYCOOK, AMANDA (HM15996) | | | | | | | | | | | | | | | | | | | | | | | | |
| PHOENIX CENTRE (HM16154) | ● | | ● | | ● | | ● | | ● | ● | | ● | | | ● | | ● | | | | | | | ● |
| PHYSIO & SPORTS INJURY CLINIC (HM16181) | | | | | ● | | | ● | | | | | ● | | | | ● | ● | | | ● | | ● | |
| PHYSIO PLUS (HM16203) | | | | | | | | | | | | | | | | | | | | | | | | |
| PHYSIO SPORTS INJURY CLINIC (HM16209) | | | | | ● | | | | | | | | | | | | | | | | | | | |
| POYNTON CHIROPRACTIC CLINIC (HM16519) | | | | | ● | | | | | | | | | | ● | | | | | | | | ● | |
| PRINCE, TANIA A (HM16622) | | | ● | | ● | | | | | ● | | ● | | | ● | | ● | | | | | | | |
| REDGRAVE, KENNETH (HM17025) | | | | | | | | | | ● | | | | | | | | | | | | | | ● |
| SANDBACH HYPNOSIS CLINIC (HM17899) | | | | | | | | | | ● | | | | | | | | | | | | | | |
| SAXELBY, M (HM17990) | | | | | | | | | | | | | | | | | | | | | | | | |
| SCENTED GARDENS (HM18011) | | | | | | | | | | | | | | | | | | | | | | | | |
| TEDSTONE, ALISON (HM19815) | | | | | | | | | | | | | | | | | | | | | | | | |
| THOMAS, BEVERLEY (HM19933) | | | | | | | | | | | | | | | | | | | | | | | | |
| THORNBER, A A (HM20016) | | | | | | | | | | | | | | | | | | | | | | | | |
| TIPLING, L (HM20087) | | | | | | | | | | | | | | | | | | | | | | | | |
| TRINITY HOUSE PRACTICE (HM20339) | | | | | ● | | | | | | | | | | | | | | | | | | ● | |
| TULLY, CHARLES (HM20388) | ● | | | | ● | | | | | | | | | ● | | | | ● | | ● | ● | | ● | |
| VALE ROYAL CHIROPRACTIC CLINIC (HM20552) | | | | ● | ● | | | | | | | | | | | | | | | | | | ● | |
| VALE ROYAL CHIROPRACTIC CLINIC (HM20553) | | | | ● | ● | | | | | | | | | | | | | | | | | | ● | |
| WARRINGTON CHIROPRACTIC CLINIC (HM20957) | | | | | ● | | | | ● | | | | | | ● | | | | | | | | ● | |
| WEAVER HOUSE CLINIC (HM21049) | ● | ● | ● | ● | ● | ● | | | ● | | ● | ● | | | ● | ● | ● | ● | ● | ● | ● | | ● | ● |
| WIDNES OSTEOPATHIC CLINIC (HM21459) | | | | ● | ● | | | | | | | ● | | | | | | | | | | | ● | |
| WILLIAMS OSTEOPATHIC CLINIC (HM21532) | | | | | ● | | | | | | | | | | | | | | | | | | ● | |
| **CLEVELAND** | | | | | | | | | | | | | | | | | | | | | | | | |
| ALEXANDER TECHNIQUE (HM00548) | ● | ● | | ● | ● | ● | | ● | ● | ● | | ● | | | ● | | | | | ● | | | ● | |
| BARNARD, SIMON (HM01732) | | | | | ● | | | | | | | | | | | | | | | | | | ● | |
| BODY BALANCE (HM02570) | | | | | | | | | | | | | | | | | | | | | | | | |
| ELLISON, TIM (HM06777) | | | | | | | | | | | | | | | | | ● | ● | | | | | | |
| HARTLEPOOL CHIROPRACTIC CLINIC (HM09138) | | | | | ● | | | | | | | | | | | | | | | | | | ● | |
| MERMAID CHIROPRACTIC PRACTICE (HM13749) | | | | | ● | | | | | | | | | | | | | | | | | | ● | |
| NATURAL THERAPY CENTRE (HM14637) | | | | | ● | | | | ● | | | ● | | | | | | | | | | | ● | |

# I - S Conditions treated at Practices/Businesses

| Business by County with Reference no. | Insomnia | Irritable Bowel Syndrome | Itching | Jet Lag | Joint Pain | Kidney Complaints | Lactose Intolerance | Laryngitis | Lethargy | Liver Disorders | Low Blood Pressure | Lung Problems | ME | Menopause | Migraine | Motion Sickness | Mouth Disorders | Mouth Ulcers | Multiple Sclerosis | Muscular Dystrophy | Musculo-skeletal | Nail Health | Nausea | Nerve Disorders |
|---|---|---|---|---|---|---|---|---|---|---|---|---|---|---|---|---|---|---|---|---|---|---|---|---|
| NORTHERN GUILD-PSYCHOTHERAPY (HM15061) | | | | | | | | | | | | | | | | | | | | | | | | |
| RAINBOW BRIDGE SCHOOL (HM16875) |●|●|●|●|●|●|●|●|●|●|●|●|●|●|●|●|●|●|●|●| |●|●|●|
| REDCAR PHYSIO & SPORTS (HM17007) | | | | |●| | | | | | | | | | | | | |●| | | | | |
| RUSH, DENNIS (HM17754) |●|●| | | | | | |●| | | |●| | |●| | | | | | |●| |
| SKIPPINGS & ASSOCIATES (HM18657) | |●| | |●| | | | | | | | | | | | | | | | | | |●|
| STRESS COUNSELLING (HM19391) |●| | | | | | | | | | | | | | | | | | | | | | | |
| **CORNWALL** | | | | | | | | | | | | | | | | | | | | | | | | |
| AROMATICA (HM01135) |●|●| | | | | | | | | | |●|●|●| | |●| | | | | | |
| BANBURY, A E (HM01646) | |●| | |●| | | | | | | | | |●| | | | | | | | | |
| BARNNETT, ANN (HM01763) |●|●| | | |●| | | | |●| |●|●|●| | | |●|●| | | | |
| CARADON CHIROPRACTIC CLINIC (HM03656) | |●| | |●| | | | | | | |●|●|●| | | | | | | | |●|
| COMP HEALTH INITIATIVE (HM04912) |●|●|●|●|●|●|●|●|●|●|●|●|●|●|●|●|●|●|●|●| |●|●|●|
| DRAGE, STEPHEN (HM06279) | |●| | | | | | | | | | | | | | | | | | | |●| | |
| FEET FIRST (HM07180) |●|●| | |●| |●| | |●|●| |●|●|●|●| | |●| | | | |●|
| FORCE, GAYLE (HM07520) |●|●|●| |●|●| |●|●| |●|●|●|●|●| |●|●|●| | | | |●|
| HALL, PETER (HM08787) | | |●|●|●| | | | |●|●| |●|●|●| | | |●| | | | | |
| HAWKSLAND PHYSIOTHERAPY CENTRE (HM09233) | | | | |●| | | | | | | | | | | | | | | | | | |●|
| LIFE 'N' LIMB (HM12346) |●|●|●|●|●|●| |●|●| |●|●|●|●|●|●|●|●|●| | | |●|●|
| LIFE 'N' LIMB (HM12345) |●|●|●|●|●|●|●|●|●|●|●|●|●|●|●|●|●|●|●|●| |●|●|●|
| LIFE-WORK POTENTIAL (HM12368) |●|●|●| | | |●|●|●| | |●|●|●|●| |●|●| | | |●|●| |
| LISKEARD CHIROPRACTIC CLINIC (HM12453) | |●| | | | | | | | | | |●| |●| | | | | | | | |●|
| LISTER NATURAL HEALTH PRACTICE (HM12461) |●|●|●|●|●|●|●|●|●|●|●|●|●|●|●|●|●|●|●| | |●|●|●|
| MASTERS, B (HM13273) | |●| | |●| | | | | |●| |●| |●| | | |●| | | | |●|
| MORSE, EMMA (HM14239) |●|●| | | | | | | | | | | | | | | | | | | | | | |
| NEWQUAY CHIROPRACTIC CLINIC (HM14883) |●|●| | |●| |●| |●| |●| |●|●|●| | | | | | | | | |
| OSTEOPATHIC FAMILY CENTRE (HM15465) | |●| | |●| | | | | | |●|●|●|●|●| | | | | | |●|●|
| PENZANCE NATURAL HEALTH CENTRE (HM16006) | |●| | | | | | | | | | |●| |●| | | | | | | | | |
| ST AUSTELL CHIROPRACTIC CLINIC (HM19070) | |●| | |●| | | | | | | |●| |●| | | | | | | | |●|
| TRURO CHIROPRACTIC CLINIC (HM20354) | |●| | |●| | | | | | | |●| |●| | | | | | | | |●|
| TRURO OSTEOPATHIC PRACTICE (HM20356) | | | | |●| | | | | | | | | |●| | | | | | | | |●|
| VERA BOYES ACUPUNCTURE (HM20618) | |●| | |●| | | | | | | | | |●|●| | | | | | |●| |
| WEATHERHOGG, D J (HM21046) | | | | |●| | | | | | | | | |●| | | | | | | | | |
| WILLS, JONATHAN (HM21632) | | | | | | | | | | | | | | |●| | | | | | | | |●|
| WRIGHT, CYNTHIA (HM21929) |●| | | | | | | | | | | | | |●|●| | | | | | | | |

| Business by County with Reference no. | Nervous Disorders | Neuralgia | Obesity | Osteoporosis | Pain | Palpitations | Panic Attacks | Parkinson's Disease | Period Problems | Phobias | Piles | PMT | Pneumonia | Postural Problems | Pregnancy Help | Prostate Problems | Psoriasis | Raynaud's Disease | Recurrent Infections | Restless Legs | Rheumatoid Arthritis | Schizophrenia | Sciatica | Sexual Problems |
|---|---|---|---|---|---|---|---|---|---|---|---|---|---|---|---|---|---|---|---|---|---|---|---|---|
| NORTHERN GUILD-PSYCHOTHERAPY (HM15061) | | | | | | | | | |●| | | | | | | | | | | | | | |
| RAINBOW BRIDGE SCHOOL (HM16875) |●|●|●|●|●|●| |●|●|●|●|●|●| |●|●|●|●|●|●|●|●|●|●|
| REDCAR PHYSIO & SPORTS (HM17007) | | | | | | | | | | | | | | | | | | | | | | | | |
| RUSH, DENNIS (HM17754) |●| |●| |●| | | | |●| |●| | | | | | | |●| | | |●|
| SKIPPINGS & ASSOCIATES (HM18657) | | | | |●| | | | | | | | | | | | | | | | | |●| |
| STRESS COUNSELLING (HM19391) |●| | | | |●| | | |●| | | | | | | | | | | | | |●|
| **CORNWALL** | | | | | | | | | | | | | | | | | | | | | | | | |
| AROMATICA (HM01135) |●| | |●|●| | | |●| |●|●| | | | |●| | | |●| |●| |
| BANBURY, A E (HM01646) | |●| |●|●| | | | | | | | | | | | | | | | | |●| |
| BARNNETT, ANN (HM01763) | | | | |●|●| | |●| | |●| | |●| | | | | | | |●| |
| CARADON CHIROPRACTIC CLINIC (HM03656) |●| | | |●| | | | | | | | | | | | | | | | | |●| |
| COMP HEALTH INITIATIVE (HM04912) |●|●|●|●|●|●| |●|●|●|●|●|●| |●|●|●|●|●|●|●|●|●|●|
| DRAGE, STEPHEN (HM06279) | | |●| | | | | | |●| | | | | | | | | | | | | |●|
| FEET FIRST (HM07180) |●| |●| |●|●| |●|●| |●|●| | |●| | |●|●|●|●| |●| |
| FORCE, GAYLE (HM07520) |●|●|●| |●|●| | |●|●| |●| | |●|●|●|●|●|●|●|●|●|●|
| HALL, PETER (HM08787) |●|●| | |●| | | |●| | |●| | | | | |●|●| | | |●| |
| HAWKSLAND PHYSIOTHERAPY CENTRE (HM09233) | | | |●|●| | | | | | | | | | | | | | | | | |●| |
| LIFE 'N' LIMB (HM12346) |●|●|●| |●|●| | |●|●|●|●| | |●| |●|●|●|●|●| |●|●|
| LIFE 'N' LIMB (HM12345) |●|●|●|●|●|●| |●|●|●|●|●|●| |●|●|●|●|●|●|●|●|●|●|
| LIFE-WORK POTENTIAL (HM12368) |●| |●|●|●|●| | |●|●|●|●| | | |●|●| |●|●|●| | | |
| LISKEARD CHIROPRACTIC CLINIC (HM12453) | | | | |●| | | | | | | | | | | | | | | | | |●| |
| LISTER NATURAL HEALTH PRACTICE (HM12461) |●|●|●|●|●|●| | |●|●|●|●|●| |●|●|●|●|●|●|●| |●|●|
| MASTERS, B (HM13273) |●|●| |●|●| | | | | | | | | |●| | |●| |●|●| |●| |
| MORSE, EMMA (HM14239) | | | | |●| | | | | | | | | | | | | | | |●| | | |
| NEWQUAY CHIROPRACTIC CLINIC (HM14883) |●|●|●|●|●|●| | |●| | |●| | |●| |●| | | | |●|●| |
| OSTEOPATHIC FAMILY CENTRE (HM15465) |●|●| | |●| | | |●| |●|●|●| |●|●| | |●|●|●| |●| |
| PENZANCE NATURAL HEALTH CENTRE (HM16006) | | | | | | | | | | | | | | | | | | | | | | | | |
| ST AUSTELL CHIROPRACTIC CLINIC (HM19070) |●| | |●|●| | | | | | | | | | | | | | | | | |●| |
| TRURO CHIROPRACTIC CLINIC (HM20354) |●| | |●|●| | | | | | | | | | | | | | | | | |●| |
| TRURO OSTEOPATHIC PRACTICE (HM20356) | |●| | |●| | | | | | | | | |●| | | | | | | |●| |
| VERA BOYES ACUPUNCTURE (HM20618) | |●|●| |●| | | | | | | | | |●| | | | |●|●| |●| |
| WEATHERHOGG, D J (HM21046) | | | | | | | | | | | | | | | | | | | | | | |●| |
| WILLS, JONATHAN (HM21632) | |●| | |●| | | | | | | | | | | | | | | | | |●| |
| WRIGHT, CYNTHIA (HM21929) | | | | | | | | | |●| | | | | | | | | | | | | | |

# I - S Conditions treated at Practices/Businesses

| Business by County with Reference no. | Insomnia | Irritable Bowel Syndrome | Itching | Jet Lag | Joint Pain | Kidney Complaints | Lactose Intolerance | Laryngitis | Lethargy | Liver Disorders | Low Blood Pressure | Lung Problems | ME | Menopause | Migraine | Motion Sickness | Mouth Disorders | Mouth Ulcers | Multiple Sclerosis | Muscular Dystrophy | Musculo-skeletal | Nail Health | Nausea | Nerve Disorders | Nervous Disorders | Neuralgia | Obesity | Osteoporosis | Pain | Palpitations | Panic Attacks | Parkinson's Disease | Period Problems | Phobias | Piles | PMT | Pneumonia | Postural Problems | Pregnancy Help | Prostate Problems | Psoriasis | Raynaud's Disease | Recurrent Infections | Restless Legs | Rheumatoid Arthritis | Schizophrenia | Sciatica | Sexual Problems |
|---|---|---|---|---|---|---|---|---|---|---|---|---|---|---|---|---|---|---|---|---|---|---|---|---|---|---|---|---|---|---|---|---|---|---|---|---|---|---|---|---|---|---|---|---|---|---|---|---|
| **COUNTY DURHAM** |  |  |  |  |  |  |  |  |  |  |  |  |  |  |  |  |  |  |  |  |  |  |  |  |  |  |  |  |  |  |  |  |  |  |  |  |  |  |  |  |  |  |  |  |  |  |  |  |
| BALANCE HOLISTIC HEALTHCARE (HM01606) |  | ● | ● |  |  |  |  |  |  |  |  |  |  | ● | ● |  |  |  |  |  |  |  |  |  | ● |  |  |  | ● |  |  |  | ● | ● |  | ● |  |  |  |  |  |  |  |  |  |  |  |  |
| BODYWORK HEALTH CLUB & CLINIC (HM02639) | ● | ● |  |  |  |  |  |  |  |  |  |  |  |  |  |  |  |  |  |  |  |  |  |  |  |  |  |  |  |  |  |  |  |  |  |  |  |  |  |  |  |  |  |  |  |  |  |  |
| CALLAGHAN, M M (HM03548) |  |  |  |  |  |  |  |  |  |  |  |  |  |  |  |  |  |  |  |  |  | ● |  |  |  |  |  |  |  |  |  |  |  |  |  |  |  |  |  |  |  |  |  |  |  |  |  |  |
| EVANS, BRUCE (DR) (HM06958) |  |  |  |  | ● |  |  |  |  |  |  |  |  |  |  |  |  |  |  |  |  |  |  |  |  |  |  |  | ● |  |  |  |  |  |  |  |  |  |  |  |  |  |  |  |  |  | ● |  |
| FIONA OTTEWELL CHRTRD PHYSIO (HM07329) |  |  |  |  | ● |  |  |  |  |  |  |  |  |  |  |  |  |  |  |  |  |  |  |  |  |  |  | ● | ● |  |  |  |  |  |  |  |  |  |  |  |  |  |  |  |  |  |  |  |
| FOOTPRINTS (HM07507) |  |  |  |  |  |  |  |  |  |  |  |  |  |  |  |  |  |  |  |  |  | ● |  |  |  |  |  |  |  |  |  |  |  |  |  |  |  |  |  |  |  |  |  |  |  |  |  |  |
| HIND, CAROLE (HM09824) | ● | ● |  |  | ● |  |  |  |  |  |  |  | ● |  | ● |  |  |  | ● |  |  |  |  |  |  |  |  |  | ● |  |  |  | ● |  | ● | ● |  |  |  | ● |  |  |  |  |  |  | ● |  |
| HOBSON, I K (HM09864) |  |  |  |  | ● |  |  |  |  |  |  |  |  |  |  |  |  |  |  |  |  | ● |  |  |  |  |  |  |  |  |  |  |  |  |  |  |  |  |  |  |  |  |  |  |  |  |  |  |
| NEWCASTLE/NE TRANS MEDITA CTRE (HM14856) | ● | ● |  |  |  |  |  |  |  |  |  |  | ● |  | ● |  |  |  |  |  |  |  |  |  |  |  |  |  |  |  |  |  |  | ● |  |  |  |  |  |  |  |  |  |  |  |  |  |  |
| OLD PIT PRACTICE (HM15260) | ● |  |  |  | ● |  |  |  |  |  |  |  | ● |  |  |  |  |  |  |  |  |  |  |  |  |  |  |  | ● |  |  |  |  |  |  |  |  |  |  |  |  |  |  |  |  |  |  |  |
| SPOORS, L & D (HM19039) |  | ● |  |  | ● |  |  |  |  |  |  |  | ● |  |  |  |  |  |  |  |  |  |  |  |  |  |  |  | ● |  |  |  |  |  |  |  |  | ● | ● |  |  |  |  |  |  |  | ● |  |
| TEESDALE OSTEOPATHIC CLINIC (HM19817) |  | ● |  |  | ● |  |  |  |  |  |  |  | ● |  |  |  |  |  |  |  |  |  |  | ● | ● |  |  |  | ● |  |  |  |  |  |  |  |  | ● | ● |  |  |  |  |  |  |  | ● |  |
| TREATMENT ROOM (HM20302) |  |  |  |  | ● |  |  |  |  |  |  |  |  |  |  |  |  |  |  |  |  |  |  |  |  | ● |  |  | ● |  |  | ● |  |  |  |  |  |  |  |  |  | ● |  |  | ● |  | ● |  |
| WARWICK, ANDREA (HM20967) | ● | ● |  |  | ● |  |  |  | ● |  |  |  | ● | ● | ● |  |  |  | ● |  |  |  |  |  | ● |  |  |  | ● |  |  |  | ● | ● |  | ● |  |  |  |  |  |  |  |  | ● |  | ● |  |
| **CUMBRIA** |  |  |  |  |  |  |  |  |  |  |  |  |  |  |  |  |  |  |  |  |  |  |  |  |  |  |  |  |  |  |  |  |  |  |  |  |  |  |  |  |  |  |  |  |  |  |  |  |
| CUMBRIA PHYSIO & SPORTS CLINIC (HM05598) |  |  |  |  | ● |  |  |  |  |  |  |  |  |  |  |  |  |  | ● |  |  |  |  |  |  |  |  |  | ● |  |  |  |  |  |  |  |  |  |  |  |  |  |  |  |  |  |  |  |
| DEERING, CHRISTINE (HM05959) |  |  |  |  |  |  |  |  |  |  |  |  | ● |  |  |  |  |  |  |  |  |  |  |  | ● |  | ● |  |  |  |  |  |  | ● |  |  |  |  |  |  |  |  |  |  |  |  |  | ● |
| EDWARDS, D E (HM06648) |  |  |  |  |  |  |  |  |  |  |  |  |  |  |  |  |  |  |  |  |  |  |  |  |  |  |  |  |  |  |  |  |  | ● |  |  |  |  |  |  |  |  |  |  |  |  |  |  |
| FOOTWORKS (HM07515) |  |  |  |  |  |  |  |  |  |  |  |  |  |  |  |  |  |  |  |  |  | ● |  |  |  |  |  |  |  |  |  |  |  |  |  |  |  |  |  |  |  |  |  |  |  |  |  |  |
| GARNETT, JANE (HM07897) |  | ● |  |  |  |  |  |  |  |  |  |  |  |  |  |  |  |  |  |  |  |  |  |  |  |  |  |  | ● |  |  |  |  | ● |  |  |  |  |  |  |  |  |  |  |  |  |  |  |
| HERBS AND HELPERS (HM09668) | ● | ● | ● | ● | ● | ● |  |  | ● | ● |  | ● | ● | ● | ● |  |  | ● | ● |  |  |  | ● | ● | ● | ● |  | ● | ● | ● |  |  | ● |  |  | ● |  |  | ● | ● | ● | ● | ● | ● | ● |  | ● |  |
| HYPNOTHERAPY CENTRE (HM10525) |  |  |  |  |  |  |  |  |  |  |  |  |  |  | ● |  |  |  |  |  |  |  |  |  |  |  |  |  |  |  |  |  |  | ● |  |  |  |  |  |  |  |  |  |  |  |  |  |  |
| LIBRA THERAPY CENTRE (HM12328) |  |  |  |  |  |  |  |  |  |  |  |  | ● |  | ● |  |  |  |  |  |  |  |  |  |  |  |  |  |  |  |  |  |  |  |  |  |  |  |  |  |  |  |  |  |  |  |  |  |
| MCWATT, LIZ (HM13624) | ● | ● | ● |  | ● |  |  |  | ● | ● | ● |  |  | ● | ● |  |  | ● |  |  |  | ● | ● |  | ● |  |  |  |  | ● |  |  | ● |  | ● | ● |  |  |  |  |  |  | ● | ● | ● |  |  |  |
| RHAM, TRICIA (HM17217) | ● | ● |  |  | ● |  |  |  | ● |  | ● |  | ● | ● | ● |  |  |  | ● |  |  |  |  | ● | ● | ● |  | ● | ● |  |  | ● | ● | ● |  | ● |  |  | ● |  |  | ● |  | ● | ● |  | ● |  |
| RUBINSTEIN, ADAM (HM17724) |  |  |  |  | ● | ● |  |  |  | ● |  |  | ● |  | ● |  |  |  |  |  |  |  |  | ● | ● | ● |  |  | ● | ● |  |  | ● |  |  |  |  |  |  |  |  |  |  |  |  |  | ● | ● |
| RUBINSTEIN, ADAM (HM17725) |  |  |  |  | ● | ● |  |  |  | ● |  |  | ● |  | ● |  |  |  |  |  |  |  |  | ● | ● | ● |  |  | ● | ● |  |  | ● |  |  |  |  |  |  |  |  |  |  |  |  |  | ● | ● |
| SIMPLY PERFECT BY JAN (HM18581) |  |  |  |  |  |  |  |  |  |  |  |  |  |  |  |  |  |  |  | ● |  |  |  |  |  |  |  |  |  |  |  |  |  |  |  |  |  |  |  |  |  |  |  |  |  |  |  |  |
| SINGLETON, POLLY (HM18612) | ● | ● | ● | ● | ● | ● | ● | ● | ● | ● | ● | ● | ● | ● | ● | ● | ● | ● | ● | ● |  | ● | ● | ● | ● | ● | ● | ● | ● | ● |  | ● | ● | ● | ● | ● | ● |  | ● | ● | ● | ● | ● | ● | ● | ● | ● | ● |
| STRAWBERRY HOW CLINIC (HM19378) |  |  |  |  | ● |  |  |  |  |  |  |  |  |  | ● |  |  |  |  |  |  |  |  |  |  |  |  |  | ● |  |  |  | ● | ● |  |  | ● |  |  |  |  |  |  |  |  | ● | ● |  |
| THERAPY CENTRE (HM19898) | ● | ● | ● |  | ● | ● |  | ● | ● | ● | ● | ● | ● | ● | ● | ● | ● | ● | ● |  |  | ● | ● | ● | ● | ● |  | ● | ● | ● |  |  | ● | ● | ● | ● | ● |  | ● | ● | ● | ● | ● | ● | ● |  | ● |  |
| VULCANS LANE CHIROPODY (HM20720) |  |  |  |  |  |  |  |  |  |  |  |  |  |  |  |  |  |  |  |  |  | ● |  |  |  |  |  |  |  |  |  |  |  |  |  |  |  |  |  |  |  | ● |  |  |  |  |  |  |

# I - S Conditions treated at Practices/Businesses

| Business by County with Reference no. | Insomnia | Irritable Bowel Syndrome | Itching | Jet Lag | Joint Pain | Kidney Complaints | Lactose Intolerance | Laryngitis | Lethargy | Liver Disorders | Low Blood Pressure | Lung Problems | ME | Menopause | Migraine | Motion Sickness | Mouth Disorders | Mouth Ulcers | Multiple Sclerosis | Muscular Dystrophy | Musculo-skeletal | Nail Health | Nausea | Nerve Disorders | Nervous Disorders | Neuralgia | Obesity | Osteoporosis | Pain | Palpitations | Panic Attacks | Parkinson's Disease | Period Problems | Phobias | Piles | PMT | Pneumonia | Postural Problems | Pregnancy Help | Prostate Problems | Psoriasis | Raynaud's Disease | Recurrent Infections | Restless Legs | Rheumatoid Arthritis | Schizophrenia | Sciatica | Sexual Problems |
|---|---|---|---|---|---|---|---|---|---|---|---|---|---|---|---|---|---|---|---|---|---|---|---|---|---|---|---|---|---|---|---|---|---|---|---|---|---|---|---|---|---|---|---|---|---|---|---|---|
| **DERBYSHIRE** |||||||||||||||||||||||||||||||||||||||||||||||||
| ACUPUNCTURE CLINIC (HM00270) |●||||||||●||||●|●||||||||||||||||||||●|||●|||||||||||||●||
| ALTER-MED (HM00690) |●|●|●|●|●|●|●|●|●|●|●|●|●|●|●|●|●|●|●|●||●|●|●|●|●|●|●|●|●||●|●|●|●|●|●||●|●|●|●|●|●|●|●|●|●|
| AROMATHERAPY & REFLEX CTRE (HM01090) |●|●|●|●|●|●|●|●|●|●|●|●|●|●|●|●|●|●|●|●||●|●|●|●|●|●|●|●|●||●|●|●|●|●|●||●|●|●|●|●|●|●|●|●|●|
| BANKS, LINDA (HM01665) ||●|||||||||||●|●||||●|||||||●|||||●|||●|||●|||●|||||||●||
| BARROWCLIFFE, GRAHAM (DR) (HM01806) ||●||●|●|||●|||||||●|●|||||||||||||●|●|●|●||||●||●|●||||||||||●|●|
| BELPER BACKPAIN CLINIC (HM02110) ||||||||||||||||||||||||||||||●|||●||||||||||||||●||●|●||||
| BELPER HOMEOPATHY (HM02111) |●|●|●|●|●|●|●|●|●|●|●|●|●|●|●|●|●|●|●|●||●|●|●|●|●|●|●|●|●||●|●|●|●|●|●||●|●|●|●|●|●|●|●|●|●|
| BELPER NATURAL HEALTH CENTRE (HM02112) |●|●|●|●|●|●|●|●|●|●|●|●|●|●|●|●|●|●|●|●||●|●|●|●|●|●|●|●|●||●|●|●|●|●|●||●|●|●|●|●|●|●||●|●|
| BRADSHAW, P J (HM02878) |●|●|||||||||||||||||||||||●||●|||●|||||||||||||||●||||||
| CARRICK-SMITH, L (HM03744) ||||||||||||||||||||||||||||||||||●|||||||||||||||||||||||||
| CHIROPODY & PHYSIOTHERAPY (HM04303) |||||●|||||||||||||||||||||||||●|||||||||||||||||||●||||
| COVERLEY PHYSIOTHERAPY CLINIC (HM05284) |||||●||||||||||||||●||||||||||●|||||||||||||||||||||||||
| DARBY, ANN (HM05735) |●|●|||||||||||||●|||||||||||||||●||||||●|||||||||||●|||
| DERBYSHIRE SPORTS INJURIES (HM06014) |||||●|||||||||||||||||||||||||||||||||||||||||||||
| DRONFIELD PHYSIOTHERAPY CLINIC (HM06320) |||||●||||||||||||||●||||||||||●|||||||||||||||||||||||||
| ENJOY SPORT (HM06836) |||||●||||||||||●||||||||||||●|||●||||||||||||||||||||●||
| GARRISON-TODD, WENDY (HM07905) |●|●|●|●|●|●|●|●|●|●|●|●|●|●|●|●|●|●|●|●||●|●|●|●|●|●|●|●|●||●|●|●|●|●|●||●|●|●|●|●|●|●|●|●|●|
| HARDING, MANDY (HM08971) ||||||||||||||||||||||●||||||||||||||||||||||||||||
| HATHERSAGE HEALTH & THRPY CTRE (HM09198) |||||||||||||||||||||||||||||●|||||||||||||||||||||
| HIGGS, ANN (HM09734) ||●|||●|●|||●|●|●|●||●|●||||●||||●|●|●|●||●|●|●|||●|●|●|●|||●|●|●|●||●|●||●||
| HOUSE OF AROMATHERAPY (HM10216) |●|●||||||||||||●|●||||||||||||||||||||||●||||||||||||||
| ILKESTONE OSTEO & MED CTRE (HM10580) |●|●|||●||||||●||●|●|●||||●||||||●|||●|●|||●|●|||●||●|●||●||||●||●||
| JOHNSON, MELVYN (HM11086) |||||●||||||||●|||||||||||●||||●|●||||||||||●|●|||||||||●||
| KARDAHJI, F C (HM11319) |||||||||||||||||||||||||||||||||||||||||||||●||||
| KEMP, GILLIAN (HM11461) ||●|||||||||||●||||||●||||||||||●|||||●|||||||||||||||●||●||
| LANCASHIRE, A W (HM11915) |||||●||||||||●|||||||||||||||●|●|||||||||●|||||||||||||
| LIFESOLUTIONS (HM12359) |●|●|●||||||||||●|●|●|||||||●|●|●||||●|●|||●|●||●|||||||||||||●|
| MATLOCK PHYSIOTHERAPY CENTRE (HM13293) |●|●|●|●|●|●|●|●|●|●|●|●|●|●|●|●|●|●|●|●||●|●|●|●|●|●|●|●|●||●|●|●|●|●|●||●|●|●|●|●|●|●|●|●|●|
| MATTHEWS, A (HM13299) |●||●|●|●|●|●|●|●|●|●|●|●|●|●||||●|||●|●|●|●|●|●|●|●|●||●|●|●||●||||●|●|●|●|●|●||●|●|
| MATTHEWS, AMANDA (HM13301) |●||●|●|●|●|●|●|●|●|●|●|●|●|●||||●|||●|●|●|●|●|●|●|●|●||●|●|●||●|||●|●|●|●|●|●|●|●|●|●|
| NATURAL HEALTH CLINIC (HM14577) ||●|||●||||||||||||||||||||||||●|||||||||||||||||||●||||
| PHILIP STOCK - PHYSIOTHERAPIST (HM16120) |||||●|||||||||||||||●|||●||||●|●||||||||||●|||||||||●||
| PHYSIO ACTIVE (HM16193) |●|●|●|●|●|●||●|●||●|●|●|●|●|●|●|●|||||●|●|●|●|●||●|●||●|●|●|●|●|●||●|●|●|●|●|●|●||●||

www.healthmyself.com

Healthmyself Directory

# I - S Conditions treated at Practices/Businesses

Business by County with Reference no.

| Business by County with Reference no. | Insomnia | Irritable Bowel Syndrome | Itching | Jet Lag | Joint Pain | Kidney Complaints | Lactose Intolerance | Laryngitis | Lethargy | Liver Disorders | Low Blood Pressure | Lung Problems | ME | Menopause | Migraine | Motion Sickness | Mouth Disorders | Mouth Ulcers | Multiple Sclerosis | Muscular Dystrophy | Musculo-skeletal | Nail Health | Nausea | Nerve Disorders |
|---|---|---|---|---|---|---|---|---|---|---|---|---|---|---|---|---|---|---|---|---|---|---|---|---|
| SMITH, ALAN P (HM18711) |  | ● |  |  | ● |  |  |  |  |  |  |  | ● |  |  |  |  |  |  |  |  |  |  | ● |
| SPINK, BERNADETTE (HM19017) | ● | ● | ● | ● | ● |  |  |  | ● |  |  |  | ● | ● | ● |  | ● | ● |  |  |  |  | ● | ● |
| SPIRAC PHYSIOTHERAPY (HM19020) |  |  |  |  | ● |  |  |  |  |  |  |  |  |  |  |  |  |  | ● |  |  |  |  |  |
| STEVENSON, JACKIE (HM19249) | ● | ● | ● | ● | ● | ● | ● | ● | ● | ● | ● | ● | ● | ● | ● | ● | ● | ● | ● | ● |  | ● | ● | ● |
| TAYLOR, E F (HM19756) |  |  |  |  | ● |  |  |  |  |  |  |  |  |  | ● |  |  |  |  |  |  |  |  | ● |
| TAYLOR, E F (HM19757) |  |  |  |  | ● |  |  |  |  |  |  |  |  |  | ● |  |  |  |  |  |  |  |  | ● |
| TREEWICKS (HM20313) | ● |  |  |  |  |  |  |  |  |  |  |  |  |  |  |  |  |  |  |  |  |  |  |  |
| WHITTLE, S (HM21425) |  |  |  |  |  |  |  |  |  |  |  |  |  |  |  |  |  |  |  |  |  | ● |  |  |
| **DEVON** |  |  |  |  |  |  |  |  |  |  |  |  |  |  |  |  |  |  |  |  |  |  |  |  |
| ABBEYMEAD NATURAL HEALTH CTRE (HM00090) |  |  | ● |  |  |  |  |  | ● |  |  |  |  |  |  |  |  |  |  |  |  |  |  |  |
| ACUPUNCTURE CLINIC (HM00276) | ● | ● | ● | ● | ● | ● | ● | ● | ● | ● | ● | ● | ● | ● | ● | ● | ● | ● | ● | ● | ● | ● | ● | ● |
| ALISON MORTON PHYSIOTHERAPY (HM00579) |  |  | ● |  | ● |  |  |  |  |  |  |  |  | ● | ● |  |  |  | ● |  |  |  |  |  |
| ANNE RAWLINGS HYPNOTHERAPY (HM00901) | ● | ● | ● |  |  |  |  |  | ● |  |  |  | ● | ● |  |  |  |  |  |  |  |  |  |  |
| AWARENESS CENTRE (HM01415) | ● | ● | ● | ● | ● | ● | ● | ● | ● | ● | ● | ● | ● | ● | ● | ● | ● | ● | ● | ● |  | ● | ● | ● |
| BALL, ADRIAN (HM01624) |  |  |  |  | ● |  |  |  |  |  |  |  |  |  |  |  |  |  |  |  |  |  |  |  |
| BINMORE, F (HM02318) | ● | ● |  |  | ● | ● |  |  |  |  | ● |  | ● | ● | ● |  |  |  | ● |  |  |  | ● |  |
| BRIXHAM HEALING HANDS CENTRE (HM03105) |  | ● |  |  |  | ● |  |  |  |  |  |  | ● |  | ● |  |  |  | ● |  |  |  |  |  |
| CARPENTER, PAUL (HM03734) | ● | ● |  |  | ● | ● |  |  | ● |  | ● | ● | ● |  | ● |  |  |  |  |  |  | ● |  |  |
| CASTLE CHIROPRACTIC CLINIC (HM03829) |  |  |  |  | ● |  |  |  |  |  |  |  |  |  | ● |  |  |  |  |  |  |  |  | ● |
| CASTLEBRIDGE CHIRO & REFLEX (HM03844) |  |  |  |  |  |  |  |  |  |  |  |  |  |  |  |  |  |  |  |  |  | ● |  |  |
| CHELSTON CHIROPODY PRACTICE (HM04092) | ● |  |  |  |  | ● |  |  | ● |  | ● |  |  | ● | ● |  |  |  |  |  |  | ● |  |  |
| CHEMIN, CHRISTIAN (HM04098) |  |  |  |  | ● |  |  |  |  |  |  |  | ● |  | ● |  |  |  |  |  |  |  |  |  |
| CLINIC OF CHINESE MEDICINE (HM04687) |  |  |  |  | ● |  |  |  |  |  |  |  |  | ● | ● |  |  |  |  |  |  |  | ● |  |
| COLLEGE OF NATURAL NUTRITION (HM04851) |  | ● |  |  |  | ● | ● |  | ● | ● | ● | ● | ● | ● | ● |  |  |  | ● |  |  |  |  |  |
| COPE, ANNE (HM05134) |  |  |  |  | ● |  |  |  |  |  |  |  |  |  | ● |  |  |  |  |  |  |  |  |  |
| COX, MIRANDA (HM05316) |  |  |  |  |  |  |  |  |  |  |  |  | ● |  |  |  |  |  |  |  |  |  |  | ● |
| DEVONSHIRE HEALTH & RAQUET (HM06043) |  |  |  |  | ● |  |  |  |  |  |  |  |  |  |  |  |  |  |  |  |  |  |  |  |
| EAST DEVON CONSULTANCY (HM06512) | ● | ● | ● |  | ● |  | ● |  | ● |  |  |  | ● |  | ● |  | ● | ● | ● |  |  |  | ● |  |
| ELDON HEALTH CLINIC (HM06705) | ● | ● | ● |  | ● |  | ● | ● | ● | ● | ● |  | ● | ● | ● |  |  |  |  |  |  |  |  | ● |
| ELLIS, SUE (HM06773) |  |  |  |  | ● |  |  |  |  |  |  |  |  |  | ● |  |  |  |  |  |  |  | ● | ● |
| FOOT CLINIC & THERAPY ROOM (HM07474) |  |  |  |  |  |  |  |  |  |  |  |  |  |  |  |  |  |  |  |  |  | ● |  |  |
| FOOTEC MEDICAL (HM07500) |  |  |  |  |  |  |  |  |  |  |  |  |  |  |  |  |  |  |  |  |  |  |  |  |
| FUDGE, H (HM07777) |  |  |  |  | ● |  |  |  |  |  |  |  |  |  |  |  |  |  |  |  |  |  |  |  |
| GARRETTLEY, U (HM07902) | ● | ● |  |  | ● | ● |  |  |  |  | ● |  | ● | ● | ● |  |  |  |  |  |  |  | ● |  |

| Business by County with Reference no. | Nervous Disorders | Neuralgia | Obesity | Osteoporosis | Pain | Palpitations | Panic Attacks | Parkinson's Disease | Period Problems | Phobias | Piles | PMT | Pneumonia | Postural Problems | Pregnancy Help | Prostate Problems | Psoriasis | Raynaud's Disease | Recurrent Infections | Restless Legs | Rheumatoid Arthritis | Schizophrenia | Sciatica | Sexual Problems |
|---|---|---|---|---|---|---|---|---|---|---|---|---|---|---|---|---|---|---|---|---|---|---|---|---|
| SMITH, ALAN P (HM18711) |  |  |  | ● | ● |  |  |  |  |  |  |  |  | ● |  |  |  |  |  |  |  |  | ● |  |
| SPINK, BERNADETTE (HM19017) | ● | ● |  |  | ● |  |  |  | ● |  |  | ● |  |  |  | ● | ● | ● | ● |  | ● |  | ● |  |
| SPIRAC PHYSIOTHERAPY (HM19020) |  |  |  |  | ● |  |  |  |  |  |  |  |  |  |  |  |  |  |  |  |  |  |  |  |
| STEVENSON, JACKIE (HM19249) | ● | ● | ● | ● | ● | ● |  | ● | ● | ● | ● | ● | ● |  | ● | ● | ● | ● | ● | ● | ● | ● | ● | ● |
| TAYLOR, E F (HM19756) |  |  |  |  | ● |  |  |  |  |  |  |  |  | ● | ● |  |  |  |  |  |  |  | ● |  |
| TAYLOR, E F (HM19757) |  |  |  |  | ● |  |  |  |  |  |  |  |  | ● | ● |  |  |  |  |  |  |  | ● |  |
| TREEWICKS (HM20313) |  |  |  |  |  |  |  |  |  |  |  |  |  |  |  |  |  |  |  |  |  |  |  |  |
| WHITTLE, S (HM21425) |  |  |  |  |  |  |  |  |  |  |  |  |  |  |  |  |  |  |  |  |  |  |  |  |
| **DEVON** |  |  |  |  |  |  |  |  |  |  |  |  |  |  |  |  |  |  |  |  |  |  |  |  |
| ABBEYMEAD NATURAL HEALTH CTRE (HM00090) |  |  |  |  |  |  |  |  |  |  |  |  |  |  |  |  |  |  |  |  |  |  |  |  |
| ACUPUNCTURE CLINIC (HM00276) | ● | ● | ● | ● | ● | ● | ● | ● | ● | ● | ● | ● | ● |  | ● | ● | ● | ● | ● | ● | ● | ● | ● | ● |
| ALISON MORTON PHYSIOTHERAPY (HM00579) |  |  |  |  | ● |  |  |  | ● |  |  | ● |  |  |  |  |  |  |  |  |  |  |  |  |
| ANNE RAWLINGS HYPNOTHERAPY (HM00901) | ● |  |  |  |  | ● | ● |  | ● | ● |  | ● |  |  |  |  | ● |  | ● |  |  |  |  | ● |
| AWARENESS CENTRE (HM01415) | ● | ● | ● | ● | ● | ● |  | ● | ● | ● | ● | ● | ● |  | ● | ● | ● | ● | ● | ● | ● | ● | ● | ● |
| BALL, ADRIAN (HM01624) |  |  |  |  | ● |  |  |  |  |  |  |  |  |  |  |  |  |  |  |  |  |  | ● |  |
| BINMORE, F (HM02318) |  |  |  |  | ● | ● |  |  | ● |  |  | ● |  |  | ● |  |  |  |  | ● | ● |  | ● |  |
| BRIXHAM HEALING HANDS CENTRE (HM03105) |  |  |  |  | ● | ● |  |  |  |  |  | ● |  |  |  |  |  |  |  |  |  |  |  |  |
| CARPENTER, PAUL (HM03734) |  |  |  |  | ● |  |  |  |  |  |  |  |  |  |  |  |  |  |  |  |  |  |  |  |
| CASTLE CHIROPRACTIC CLINIC (HM03829) |  | ● |  |  | ● |  |  |  | ● |  |  |  |  |  |  |  |  |  |  | ● |  |  | ● |  |
| CASTLEBRIDGE CHIRO & REFLEX (HM03844) |  |  |  |  |  |  |  |  |  |  |  |  |  |  |  |  |  |  |  |  |  |  |  |  |
| CHELSTON CHIROPODY PRACTICE (HM04092) |  |  |  |  | ● |  |  |  |  |  |  |  |  |  |  |  |  |  |  |  |  |  |  |  |
| CHEMIN, CHRISTIAN (HM04098) |  | ● |  |  | ● | ● |  |  |  |  |  |  |  |  | ● |  |  |  | ● |  |  |  | ● |  |
| CLINIC OF CHINESE MEDICINE (HM04687) |  |  |  |  | ● |  |  |  | ● |  |  | ● |  |  |  |  |  |  |  |  |  |  |  |  |
| COLLEGE OF NATURAL NUTRITION (HM04851) |  |  | ● | ● |  | ● |  |  | ● |  |  | ● |  |  | ● | ● |  |  |  |  |  | ● |  |  |
| COPE, ANNE (HM05134) |  | ● |  |  | ● |  |  |  | ● |  |  | ● |  |  |  |  |  |  |  |  |  |  | ● |  |
| COX, MIRANDA (HM05316) | ● |  | ● |  | ● |  |  |  |  | ● |  |  |  |  |  |  |  |  |  |  |  |  |  |  |
| DEVONSHIRE HEALTH & RAQUET (HM06043) |  |  |  |  | ● |  |  |  |  |  |  |  |  |  |  |  |  |  |  |  |  |  |  |  |
| EAST DEVON CONSULTANCY (HM06512) |  | ● |  |  |  | ● |  | ● | ● |  |  | ● |  |  |  |  | ● | ● | ● | ● | ● | ● |  |  |
| ELDON HEALTH CLINIC (HM06705) |  | ● | ● | ● | ● |  |  |  | ● |  |  | ● |  |  |  |  | ● | ● | ● |  | ● |  | ● |  |
| ELLIS, SUE (HM06773) |  | ● |  | ● | ● |  |  |  |  |  |  |  |  |  |  |  |  |  |  | ● | ● |  | ● |  |
| FOOT CLINIC & THERAPY ROOM (HM07474) |  |  |  |  |  |  |  |  |  |  |  |  |  |  |  |  |  |  |  |  |  |  |  |  |
| FOOTEC MEDICAL (HM07500) |  |  |  |  |  |  |  |  |  |  |  |  |  |  |  |  |  |  |  |  | ● |  |  |  |
| FUDGE, H (HM07777) | ● |  |  |  | ● |  |  |  |  |  |  |  |  |  |  |  |  |  |  | ● |  |  | ● |  |
| GARRETTLEY, U (HM07902) |  |  |  |  | ● | ● |  |  | ● |  |  | ● |  |  | ● |  |  |  |  |  |  |  | ● |  |

# I - S Conditions treated at Practices/Businesses

Business by County with Reference no.

| Business | Insomnia | Irritable Bowel Syndrome | Itching | Jet Lag | Joint Pain | Kidney Complaints | Lactose Intolerance | Laryngitis | Lethargy | Liver Disorders | Low Blood Pressure | Lung Problems | ME | Menopause | Migraine | Motion Sickness |
|---|---|---|---|---|---|---|---|---|---|---|---|---|---|---|---|---|
| HEALTH CONSULTANCY (HM09382) | ● | ● | ● | ● | ● |  | ● | ● | ● | ● |  | ● | ● | ● | ● |  |
| HEALTH WAVES (HM09408) |  |  |  |  | ● |  |  |  | ● |  |  |  |  |  |  |  |
| IRIDOLOGY/NUTRITIONAL THER (HM10723) | ● | ● | ● | ● | ● | ● | ● | ● | ● | ● | ● | ● | ● | ● | ● | ● |
| J T SERVICES (HM10802) | ● |  |  |  | ● |  |  |  |  |  | ● | ● | ● |  |  | ● |
| JANE HYDE CHRTRD PHYSIO (HM10917) |  |  |  |  | ● |  |  |  |  |  |  |  |  |  |  |  |
| JEFFRIES, BARBARA (HM10972) |  |  |  |  |  |  |  |  |  |  |  |  | ● |  |  |  |
| JOHNSON, MICHAEL (HM11087) |  | ● |  |  | ● |  |  |  |  |  |  |  | ● | ● | ● |  |
| JULIE ADAMS REFLEXOLOGIST (HM11256) | ● | ● |  |  |  |  |  |  |  |  |  | ● |  |  | ● |  |
| KINGSBRIDGE COMP HLTH PRACTICE (HM11658) | ● | ● | ● | ● | ● | ● | ● | ● | ● | ● | ● | ● | ● | ● | ● | ● |
| KINGSBRIDGE PHYSICAL THERAPY (HM11659) |  |  |  |  | ● |  |  |  |  |  |  |  | ● |  |  |  |
| LIGHT TOUCH THERAPY TRAINING (HM12369) | ● | ● | ● | ● | ● | ● |  | ● | ● | ● |  | ● | ● | ● | ● | ● |
| LINDEMAN, A J (HM12415) | ● | ● | ● |  | ● | ● | ● | ● |  | ● | ● | ● | ● | ● | ● | ● |
| LION HOUSE SURGERY (HM12446) |  | ● |  |  | ● |  |  |  |  |  |  |  | ● |  | ● |  |
| MALLARDO, RENEE (HM12977) | ● | ● |  |  |  |  |  |  |  |  |  |  |  |  |  |  |
| MASON, MARCUS (HM13248) | ● | ● | ● | ● | ● | ● |  | ● | ● | ● | ● | ● | ● | ● | ● |  |
| MASSAGE RELAXING THERAPEUTIC (HM13262) | ● |  |  |  |  |  |  |  |  |  |  |  |  |  | ● |  |
| MONSHIN, DEBORAH J (HM14075) | ● | ● |  |  |  |  |  |  |  |  |  |  |  |  | ● |  |
| NELSON, PAUL (HM14781) | ● | ● | ● | ● | ● | ● |  | ● | ● | ● | ● | ● | ● | ● | ● | ● |
| NETHERWAY, JEAN (HM14789) | ● | ● |  |  | ● | ● |  |  |  |  |  |  |  | ● | ● |  |
| PAIGNTON PHYSIOTHERAPY (HM15576) |  |  |  |  | ● |  |  |  |  |  |  |  |  |  |  |  |
| PANNELL, R J (HM15636) |  |  |  |  | ● |  |  |  | ● |  | ● |  | ● |  | ● |  |
| PLAYERS, MEGAN (HM16365) | ● | ● | ● | ● | ● | ● | ● | ● | ● | ● | ● | ● | ● | ● | ● | ● |
| PLYMOUTH OSTEOPATHS (HM16388) |  |  |  |  | ● |  |  |  |  |  |  |  |  |  |  |  |
| REFLEXOLOGY CENTRE (HM17083) |  | ● |  |  |  |  |  |  |  |  |  |  | ● |  |  |  |
| RIVERSIDE CHIROPRACTIC CLINIC (HM17379) |  |  |  |  | ● |  |  |  |  |  |  |  |  |  | ● |  |
| ROSE & CROWN CLINIC (HM17598) | ● | ● | ● | ● | ● | ● | ● | ● | ● | ● | ● | ● | ● | ● | ● | ● |
| SANDERS, RACHEL (HM17916) |  |  |  |  |  |  |  |  |  |  |  |  |  |  |  |  |
| SCURR, PETER M (HM18160) |  |  |  |  | ● |  |  |  |  |  |  |  |  |  |  |  |
| SEELEY, JANICE (HM18194) | ● | ● | ● |  | ● | ● | ● | ● | ● | ● | ● | ● | ● | ● | ● | ● |
| SERENITY (HM18233) | ● | ● | ● | ● | ● | ● | ● | ● | ● | ● | ● | ● | ● | ● | ● | ● |
| STIMULUS FOR CHANGE (HM19296) | ● | ● |  |  |  |  |  |  | ● |  |  | ● | ● | ● | ● |  |
| TRANCE - FORMATIONS HEALING (HM20250) | ● | ● |  | ● |  |  |  |  |  |  | ● |  | ● | ● |  | ● |
| VITAL TOUCH (HM20703) | ● | ● |  |  |  |  |  |  |  |  |  |  |  |  |  |  |
| WALTERS, RICHARD (HM20882) | ● |  |  |  |  |  |  |  | ● |  |  |  |  | ● | ● |  |

| Business | Mouth Disorders | Mouth Ulcers | Multiple Sclerosis | Muscular Dystrophy | Musculo-skeletal | Nail Health | Nausea | Nerve Disorders | Nervous Disorders | Neuralgia | Obesity | Osteoporosis | Pain | Palpitations | Panic Attacks | Parkinson's Disease |
|---|---|---|---|---|---|---|---|---|---|---|---|---|---|---|---|---|
| HEALTH CONSULTANCY (HM09382) |  | ● | ● | ● |  |  | ● | ● | ● |  | ● | ● | ● | ● |  | ● |
| HEALTH WAVES (HM09408) |  |  |  |  |  |  |  |  |  |  |  |  |  |  |  |  |
| IRIDOLOGY/NUTRITIONAL THER (HM10723) | ● | ● | ● | ● | ● | ● | ● | ● | ● | ● | ● | ● | ● | ● | ● | ● |
| J T SERVICES (HM10802) |  |  |  |  |  |  |  |  |  |  |  |  | ● |  |  | ● |
| JANE HYDE CHRTRD PHYSIO (HM10917) |  |  |  |  |  |  |  |  |  |  |  |  |  |  |  |  |
| JEFFRIES, BARBARA (HM10972) |  |  |  |  |  |  |  |  | ● |  | ● |  |  |  |  |  |
| JOHNSON, MICHAEL (HM11087) |  |  |  |  |  |  |  |  | ● |  | ● |  | ● |  |  |  |
| JULIE ADAMS REFLEXOLOGIST (HM11256) |  |  |  |  |  |  |  | ● | ● |  |  |  | ● |  |  |  |
| KINGSBRIDGE COMP HLTH PRACTICE (HM11658) | ● | ● | ● | ● | ● | ● | ● | ● | ● | ● | ● | ● | ● | ● | ● | ● |
| KINGSBRIDGE PHYSICAL THERAPY (HM11659) |  |  |  |  |  |  |  |  |  |  |  | ● |  |  |  |  |
| LIGHT TOUCH THERAPY TRAINING (HM12369) | ● | ● | ● |  |  |  | ● | ● | ● | ● |  | ● | ● | ● |  |  |
| LINDEMAN, A J (HM12415) | ● | ● | ● | ● |  | ● |  | ● | ● | ● |  | ● | ● | ● |  | ● |
| LION HOUSE SURGERY (HM12446) |  |  |  |  |  |  |  | ● | ● |  |  |  | ● |  |  |  |
| MALLARDO, RENEE (HM12977) |  |  |  |  |  |  |  | ● | ● |  | ● |  | ● | ● |  |  |
| MASON, MARCUS (HM13248) |  | ● |  |  |  |  | ● | ● | ● | ● |  |  | ● | ● |  |  |
| MASSAGE RELAXING THERAPEUTIC (HM13262) |  |  |  |  |  |  |  |  |  |  | ● |  |  |  |  |  |
| MONSHIN, DEBORAH J (HM14075) |  |  |  |  |  |  |  | ● |  |  | ● |  |  |  |  |  |
| NELSON, PAUL (HM14781) | ● | ● |  |  |  | ● | ● | ● | ● | ● |  | ● | ● | ● |  |  |
| NETHERWAY, JEAN (HM14789) |  |  | ● |  |  |  |  |  |  |  |  |  | ● |  |  |  |
| PAIGNTON PHYSIOTHERAPY (HM15576) |  |  | ● |  |  |  |  |  |  |  |  |  | ● |  |  |  |
| PANNELL, R J (HM15636) |  |  |  | ● |  |  |  |  |  |  |  |  |  |  |  |  |
| PLAYERS, MEGAN (HM16365) | ● | ● | ● | ● |  | ● | ● | ● | ● | ● | ● | ● | ● | ● |  | ● |
| PLYMOUTH OSTEOPATHS (HM16388) |  |  |  |  |  |  |  |  |  | ● |  |  | ● |  |  |  |
| REFLEXOLOGY CENTRE (HM17083) |  |  |  |  |  |  |  |  |  |  |  |  |  |  |  |  |
| RIVERSIDE CHIROPRACTIC CLINIC (HM17379) |  |  |  |  |  |  |  | ● |  | ● |  | ● | ● |  |  |  |
| ROSE & CROWN CLINIC (HM17598) | ● | ● | ● | ● |  | ● | ● | ● | ● | ● | ● | ● | ● | ● |  | ● |
| SANDERS, RACHEL (HM17916) |  |  |  |  |  | ● |  |  |  |  |  |  |  |  |  |  |
| SCURR, PETER M (HM18160) |  |  |  |  |  | ● |  |  |  |  |  |  | ● |  |  |  |
| SEELEY, JANICE (HM18194) | ● | ● | ● | ● |  | ● |  | ● |  | ● |  | ● | ● | ● |  | ● |
| SERENITY (HM18233) | ● | ● | ● | ● |  | ● | ● | ● | ● | ● | ● | ● | ● | ● |  | ● |
| STIMULUS FOR CHANGE (HM19296) | ● | ● |  |  |  |  | ● |  | ● | ● |  |  | ● | ● |  |  |
| TRANCE - FORMATIONS HEALING (HM20250) |  |  |  |  |  |  |  |  | ● |  | ● |  | ● |  |  |  |
| VITAL TOUCH (HM20703) |  |  |  |  |  |  |  |  |  |  |  |  |  |  |  |  |
| WALTERS, RICHARD (HM20882) |  |  |  |  |  |  | ● |  |  |  |  |  | ● | ● |  |  |

| Business | Period Problems | Phobias | Piles | PMT | Pneumonia | Postural Problems | Pregnancy Help | Prostate Problems | Psoriasis | Raynaud's Disease | Recurrent Infections | Restless Legs | Rheumatoid Arthritis | Schizophrenia | Sciatica | Sexual Problems |
|---|---|---|---|---|---|---|---|---|---|---|---|---|---|---|---|---|
| HEALTH CONSULTANCY (HM09382) | ● | ● | ● | ● |  |  |  | ● | ● | ● | ● | ● | ● |  | ● | ● |
| HEALTH WAVES (HM09408) |  |  |  |  |  |  |  |  |  |  |  |  | ● |  |  |  |
| IRIDOLOGY/NUTRITIONAL THER (HM10723) | ● | ● | ● | ● | ● | ● | ● | ● | ● | ● | ● | ● | ● | ● | ● | ● |
| J T SERVICES (HM10802) |  |  |  | ● |  |  |  | ● | ● |  |  | ● | ● |  | ● |  |
| JANE HYDE CHRTRD PHYSIO (HM10917) |  |  |  |  |  |  |  |  |  |  |  |  |  |  | ● |  |
| JEFFRIES, BARBARA (HM10972) |  |  |  |  |  |  |  |  |  |  |  |  |  |  |  | ● |
| JOHNSON, MICHAEL (HM11087) |  | ● |  | ● |  |  |  | ● | ● |  |  |  |  |  | ● |  |
| JULIE ADAMS REFLEXOLOGIST (HM11256) |  |  |  |  |  |  |  |  |  |  |  |  |  |  | ● |  |
| KINGSBRIDGE COMP HLTH PRACTICE (HM11658) | ● | ● | ● | ● | ● | ● | ● | ● | ● | ● | ● | ● | ● | ● | ● | ● |
| KINGSBRIDGE PHYSICAL THERAPY (HM11659) |  |  |  |  |  |  |  |  |  |  |  | ● |  |  | ● |  |
| LIGHT TOUCH THERAPY TRAINING (HM12369) | ● | ● | ● | ● | ● |  | ● |  | ● | ● | ● | ● |  |  | ● |  |
| LINDEMAN, A J (HM12415) | ● |  | ● | ● | ● |  |  | ● | ● | ● | ● | ● | ● |  |  |  |
| LION HOUSE SURGERY (HM12446) |  |  |  |  |  |  |  |  |  |  |  |  |  |  | ● |  |
| MALLARDO, RENEE (HM12977) |  |  |  |  |  |  |  |  |  |  |  | ● |  |  |  | ● |
| MASON, MARCUS (HM13248) | ● | ● | ● | ● | ● |  | ● | ● | ● | ● | ● | ● | ● |  | ● | ● |
| MASSAGE RELAXING THERAPEUTIC (HM13262) |  |  |  |  |  |  |  |  |  |  |  |  |  |  |  |  |
| MONSHIN, DEBORAH J (HM14075) |  | ● |  | ● |  |  |  |  | ● |  |  |  |  |  |  | ● |
| NELSON, PAUL (HM14781) | ● | ● | ● | ● | ● |  | ● | ● | ● | ● | ● | ● | ● |  | ● | ● |
| NETHERWAY, JEAN (HM14789) | ● | ● |  | ● |  |  | ● |  |  |  |  |  | ● |  | ● |  |
| PAIGNTON PHYSIOTHERAPY (HM15576) |  |  |  |  |  |  |  |  |  |  |  |  |  |  |  |  |
| PANNELL, R J (HM15636) |  |  |  |  |  |  |  |  |  |  |  | ● |  |  |  |  |
| PLAYERS, MEGAN (HM16365) | ● | ● | ● | ● | ● |  | ● | ● |  | ● | ● | ● | ● | ● | ● | ● |
| PLYMOUTH OSTEOPATHS (HM16388) | ● |  |  |  |  |  | ● |  |  |  |  | ● |  |  | ● |  |
| REFLEXOLOGY CENTRE (HM17083) | ● |  |  | ● |  |  |  |  |  |  |  |  |  |  | ● |  |
| RIVERSIDE CHIROPRACTIC CLINIC (HM17379) |  |  |  |  |  |  |  |  |  |  |  | ● |  |  | ● |  |
| ROSE & CROWN CLINIC (HM17598) | ● | ● | ● | ● | ● |  | ● | ● | ● | ● | ● | ● | ● | ● | ● | ● |
| SANDERS, RACHEL (HM17916) |  |  |  |  |  |  |  |  |  |  |  |  |  |  |  |  |
| SCURR, PETER M (HM18160) |  |  |  |  |  |  |  |  |  |  |  |  | ● |  |  |  |
| SEELEY, JANICE (HM18194) | ● |  | ● | ● | ● |  |  | ● | ● | ● | ● | ● | ● |  | ● | ● |
| SERENITY (HM18233) | ● | ● | ● | ● | ● |  | ● | ● | ● | ● | ● | ● | ● | ● | ● | ● |
| STIMULUS FOR CHANGE (HM19296) | ● | ● |  | ● |  |  |  |  | ● |  | ● |  | ● |  |  | ● |
| TRANCE - FORMATIONS HEALING (HM20250) |  | ● |  | ● |  |  |  |  | ● |  |  | ● |  |  |  | ● |
| VITAL TOUCH (HM20703) |  |  |  | ● |  |  | ● |  |  |  |  |  |  |  |  |  |
| WALTERS, RICHARD (HM20882) |  |  |  | ● |  |  |  |  |  |  |  |  |  |  | ● |  |

www.healthmyself.com

# I - S Conditions treated at Practices/Businesses

| Business by County with Reference no. | Insomnia | Irritable Bowel Syndrome | Itching | Jet Lag | Joint Pain | Kidney Complaints | Lactose Intolerance | Laryngitis | Lethargy | Liver Disorders | Low Blood Pressure | Lung Problems | ME | Menopause | Migraine | Motion Sickness | Mouth Disorders | Mouth Ulcers | Multiple Sclerosis | Muscular Dystrophy | Musculo-skeletal | Nail Health | Nausea |
|---|---|---|---|---|---|---|---|---|---|---|---|---|---|---|---|---|---|---|---|---|---|---|---|
| WALTERS, RICHARD (HM20880) | ● | | | | | | | | ● | | | | | ● | ● | | | | | | | | ● |
| WILKINSON, MARY (HM21512) | | | | | | | | | | | | | | | ● | | | | ● | | | | |
| WILLIAMS CLINIC (HM21531) | ● | | | | ● | | | | | | | | | ● | ● | | | | | | | | ● |
| YOGA HEALTH STUDIO (HM22028) | ● | ● | | | | | | | | | | | ● | | ● | | | | ● | | | | |
| YORK HOUSE CHIROPRACTIC CLINIC (HM22045) | | | | | | | | | | | | | | | | | | | | | | | |
| DORSET | | | | | | | | | | | | | | | | | | | | | | | |
| ABBEY VIEW COMP CLINIC (HM00088) | ● | ● | ● | ● | ● | ● | ● | ● | ● | ● | ● | ● | ● | ● | ● | ● | ● | ● | ● | ● | | ● | ● |
| ALTERNATIVE APPROACH (HM00694) | | | | | ● | | | | | | | | | | | | | | | | | | |
| ARCHIBALD, LIZ (HM00980) | | | | | | | | | | | | | | | | | | | | | | | |
| ARNDALE CHIROPRACTIC (HM01031) | | | | | ● | | | | | | | | | | | | | | | | | | |
| AROMA TRANQUILITY (HM01064) | | | | | ● | | | | | | ● | | | | ● | | | | | | | | |
| ART OF REFLEXOLOGY (HM01154) | | | | | | | | | | | | | | | ● | | | | | | | | |
| AWDRY, ROBERT (HM01416) | ● | ● | ● | | ● | ● | ● | ● | ● | ● | ● | ● | ● | ● | ● | | ● | ● | | | | ● | ● |
| BACK IN BALANCE (HM01479) | | ● | | ● | ● | | | | | | | | ● | | ● | | | | | | | | |
| BACK IN FORM (HM01480) | | ● | | | ● | | | | | | | | | | | | | | | | | | |
| BELTAIN CENTRE (HM02116) | | ● | | | ● | | | | | | | | ● | | | | | | | | | | |
| BELTAIN CENTRE (HM02117) | ● | ● | | | | | | | ● | | | | | | ● | | | | | | | | |
| BOURNEMOUTH CTRE FOR COMP MED (HM02761) | ● | ● | ● | ● | ● | ● | ● | ● | ● | ● | ● | ● | ● | ● | ● | ● | ● | ● | | ● | | ● | ● |
| BOURNEMOUTH PHYSIO CLINIC (HM02762) | | | | | ● | | | | | | | | | | | | | | | | | | |
| BOWEN CLINIC (HM02771) | ● | ● | | | ● | ● | | | | | ● | ● | ● | ● | ● | | | | ● | | | | ● |
| BRANDON, DAVE (HM02912) | ● | ● | ● | ● | ● | ● | ● | ● | ● | ● | ● | ● | ● | ● | ● | ● | ● | ● | ● | ● | | ● | ● |
| BRIDPORT COMP MEDICINE CTRE (HM03019) | ● | ● | ● | ● | ● | ● | ● | ● | ● | ● | ● | ● | ● | ● | ● | ● | ● | ● | ● | ● | | ● | ● |
| BRIGHTER FUTURE (HM03040) | ● | ● | | | | | | | | | | | | | | | | | | | | | |
| BRIGHTER FUTURE (HM03039) | ● | ● | | | | | | | | | | | | | | | | | | | | | |
| BROADSTONE CENTRE COMP MED (HM03117) | ● | ● | ● | ● | ● | ● | | | ● | ● | ● | ● | ● | ● | ● | ● | | | ● | | | ● | ● |
| BROADSTONE CENTRE OF COMP MED (HM03118) | ● | ● | ● | ● | ● | ● | ● | ● | ● | ● | ● | ● | ● | ● | ● | ● | ● | ● | ● | ● | | ● | ● |
| BROWN, A D (HM03208) | | | | | | | | | | | | | | | | | | | | | | ● | |
| BURT, S (HM03429) | ● | ● | ● | | ● | ● | ● | ● | ● | ● | ● | ● | ● | ● | ● | ● | ● | ● | | | | ● | ● |
| BWT PODIATRY (HM03508) | | | | | ● | | | | | | | | | | | | | | | | | ● | |
| CARBERY PRACTICE (HM03657) | | | | | ● | | | | ● | | ● | | | | | | | | | | | | |
| CHARMINSTER CHIRO CLINIC (HM04036) | | ● | | | ● | | | | | | | | ● | | | | | | | | | | |
| CHINESE MEDICINE CENTRE (HM04254) | | | | | | | | | | | | | ● | | ● | | | | | | | | |
| CHINESE MEDICINE CLINIC (HM04258) | ● | ● | | | | | | | | | | | ● | | ● | | | | | | | | |
| CHIROPODY SERVICES (HM04338) | | | | | | | | | | | | | | | | | | | | | | ● | |

| Business by County with Reference no. | Nerve Disorders | Nervous Disorders | Neuralgia | Obesity | Osteoporosis | Pain | Palpitations | Panic Attacks | Parkinson's Disease | Period Problems | Phobias | Piles | PMT | Pneumonia | Postural Problems | Pregnancy Help | Prostate Problems | Psoriasis | Raynaud's Disease | Recurrent Infections | Restless Legs | Rheumatoid Arthritis | Schizophrenia | Sciatica | Sexual Problems |
|---|---|---|---|---|---|---|---|---|---|---|---|---|---|---|---|---|---|---|---|---|---|---|---|---|---|
| WALTERS, RICHARD (HM20880) | | | | | | ● | ● | | | ● | | | ● | | | | | | | | | | | ● | |
| WILKINSON, MARY (HM21512) | | | | | | ● | | | | | | | | | | ● | | | | | | | | ● | |
| WILLIAMS CLINIC (HM21531) | | | | | | ● | | | | ● | | | | | | | | ● | | | | | | | |
| YOGA HEALTH STUDIO (HM22028) | ● | | | ● | ● | | | | ● | | | | ● | | | | | | | | | ● | | | |
| YORK HOUSE CHIROPRACTIC CLINIC (HM22045) | | | | | | ● | | | | | | | | | | | | | | | | | | | |
| DORSET | | | | | | | | | | | | | | | | | | | | | | | | | |
| ABBEY VIEW COMP CLINIC (HM00088) | ● | ● | ● | ● | ● | ● | ● | | ● | ● | ● | ● | ● | ● | | ● | ● | ● | ● | ● | ● | ● | | ● | ● |
| ALTERNATIVE APPROACH (HM00694) | ● | | | | | ● | | | | | | | | | | | | | | | | | | ● | |
| ARCHIBALD, LIZ (HM00980) | | | | | | | | | | | ● | | | | | | | | | | | | | | |
| ARNDALE CHIROPRACTIC (HM01031) | | | | | | ● | | | | | | | | | | | | | | | | | | ● | |
| AROMA TRANQUILITY (HM01064) | | | | | | ● | | | | | | | | | | | | | ● | | | | | | |
| ART OF REFLEXOLOGY (HM01154) | | | | | | | | | | | | | | | | | | | | | | | | | |
| AWDRY, ROBERT (HM01416) | | ● | ● | ● | ● | ● | ● | | | ● | ● | ● | ● | ● | | ● | ● | ● | ● | ● | ● | ● | | ● | |
| BACK IN BALANCE (HM01479) | ● | ● | | | | | | | | | | | | | | | | | | | | | | ● | |
| BACK IN FORM (HM01480) | ● | | | | ● | ● | | | | | | | | | | | | | | | | | | ● | |
| BELTAIN CENTRE (HM02116) | | ● | | | | ● | | | | | ● | | | | | | | | | | ● | | | | ● |
| BELTAIN CENTRE (HM02117) | ● | ● | ● | ● | | | | | | | ● | | | | | ● | | ● | | | | | | | |
| BOURNEMOUTH CTRE FOR COMP MED (HM02761) | ● | ● | ● | ● | ● | ● | ● | | ● | ● | ● | ● | ● | | | ● | ● | ● | ● | ● | ● | ● | ● | ● | ● |
| BOURNEMOUTH PHYSIO CLINIC (HM02762) | | | | | | ● | | | | | | | | | | | | | | | | | | | |
| BOWEN CLINIC (HM02771) | | | | | | ● | | | ● | ● | | | ● | | | | | ● | | | | ● | | ● | |
| BRANDON, DAVE (HM02912) | ● | ● | ● | ● | ● | ● | ● | | ● | ● | ● | ● | ● | ● | | ● | ● | ● | ● | ● | ● | ● | ● | ● | ● |
| BRIDPORT COMP MEDICINE CTRE (HM03019) | ● | ● | ● | ● | ● | ● | ● | | ● | ● | ● | ● | ● | ● | | ● | ● | ● | ● | ● | ● | ● | ● | ● | ● |
| BRIGHTER FUTURE (HM03040) | | ● | | | | ● | | | | | ● | | | | | | | | | | | | | | ● |
| BRIGHTER FUTURE (HM03039) | | ● | | | | ● | | | | | ● | | | | | | | | | | | | | | ● |
| BROADSTONE CENTRE COMP MED (HM03117) | ● | ● | | ● | ● | ● | ● | | ● | ● | ● | | ● | | | ● | | ● | ● | ● | ● | ● | | ● | ● |
| BROADSTONE CENTRE OF COMP MED (HM03118) | ● | ● | ● | ● | ● | ● | ● | | ● | ● | ● | ● | ● | ● | | ● | ● | ● | ● | ● | ● | ● | ● | ● | ● |
| BROWN, A D (HM03208) | | | | | | | | | | | | | | | | | | | | | | | | | |
| BURT, S (HM03429) | ● | ● | | ● | ● | ● | ● | | | ● | | ● | ● | ● | | ● | ● | ● | ● | ● | ● | | | | |
| BWT PODIATRY (HM03508) | | | | | | | | | ● | | | | | | | | | | | | | | | | |
| CARBERY PRACTICE (HM03657) | ● | ● | | | ● | | | | | ● | | | | | | | ● | | | | | | | | ● |
| CHARMINSTER CHIRO CLINIC (HM04036) | ● | ● | | | | ● | | | | | | | | | | | | | | | | | | ● | |
| CHINESE MEDICINE CENTRE (HM04254) | | | | | | | | | | | | | | | | | | | | | | | | | |
| CHINESE MEDICINE CLINIC (HM04258) | | | | | | | | | | | | | | | | | | | | | | | | | |
| CHIROPODY SERVICES (HM04338) | | | | | | | | | | | | | | | | | | | | | | | | | |

# I - S Conditions treated at Practices/Businesses

| Business by County with Reference no. | Insomnia | Irritable Bowel Syndrome | Itching | Jet Lag | Joint Pain | Kidney Complaints | Lactose Intolerance | Laryngitis | Lethargy | Liver Disorders | Low Blood Pressure | Lung Problems | ME | Menopause | Migraine | Motion Sickness | Mouth Disorders | Mouth Ulcers | Multiple Sclerosis | Muscular Dystrophy | Musculo-skeletal | Nail Health | Nausea | Nerve Disorders | Nervous Disorders | Neuralgia | Obesity | Osteoporosis | Pain | Palpitations | Panic Attacks | Parkinson's Disease | Period Problems | Phobias | Piles | PMT | Pneumonia | Postural Problems | Pregnancy Help | Prostate Problems | Psoriasis | Raynaud's Disease | Recurrent Infections | Restless Legs | Rheumatoid Arthritis | Schizophrenia | Sciatica | Sexual Problems |
|---|---|---|---|---|---|---|---|---|---|---|---|---|---|---|---|---|---|---|---|---|---|---|---|---|---|---|---|---|---|---|---|---|---|---|---|---|---|---|---|---|---|---|---|---|---|---|---|---|
| CHIROPRACTIC TREATMENT CENTRE (HM04403) | | ● | | | ● | | | | | | | | ● | | | | | | | | | | | ● | ● | | | | ● | | | | | | | | | | | | | | | | | | ● | |
| CHRISTCHURCH CHIROPRACTIC CTRE (HM04435) | | ● | | | ● | | | | | | | | | | ● | | | | | | | | | ● | | | | ● | ● | | | | | | | ● | | | | | | | | | | | ● | |
| CHRISTCHURCH PHYSIO PRACTICE (HM04436) | | | | | ● | | | | | | | | | | | | | | | | | | | ● | | ● | | | ● | | | | | | | | | | | | | | | | | | ● | |
| CLARK, LYNN (HM04568) | | | | | | | | | | | | | | | | | | | | | | ● | | | | | | | | | | | | | | | | | | | | | | | | | | |
| COLLINWOOD, LOUIS (HM04884) | | ● | | | ● | | | | | | | | ● | | ● | | | | ● | ● | | | | ● | ● | | | | ● | | | | | | | | ● | | | | | | | | | | ● | |
| COMMUNITY CHIROPRACTIC CLINIC (HM04906) | | | | | ● | | | | | | | | | | | | | | | | | | | ● | | | | ● | ● | | | | | | | | | | | | | | | | | | ● | |
| DLP HYPNOTHERAPY CENTRE (HM06134) | ● | ● | | | | | | | | | | | ● | | | | | | | | | | | | ● | | ● | | | ● | | | | ● | | | | | | | | | | | | | | ● |
| EVANS, REBECCA MARY (HM06988) | | | | | ● | | | | | | | | | | | | | | | | | | | | | | | | ● | | | | | | | | | | | | | | | | | | | |
| FEET FIRST (HM07171) | | | | | | | | | | | | | | | | | | | | | | ● | | | | | | | | | | | | | | | | | | | | | | | | | | |
| FERNDOWN CHIROPRACTIC CLINIC (HM07239) | | ● | | | ● | | | | | | | | ● | | ● | | | | | | | | | ● | ● | | | | | | | | | | | | | | | | | | | | | | | |
| FREESPIRIT (HM07724) | ● | | ● | ● | ● | ● | | | | ● | ● | | ● | ● | ● | ● | ● | ● | ● | ● | | | ● | ● | ● | | | | ● | | | ● | ● | ● | | | | | | | | | | | ● | | | |
| FULL SPECTRUM THERAPY CENTRE (HM07786) | ● | ● | ● | ● | ● | ● | ● | ● | ● | ● | ● | ● | ● | ● | ● | ● | ● | ● | ● | ● | | ● | ● | ● | ● | ● | ● | ● | ● | ● | | ● | ● | ● | ● | ● | ● | | ● | ● | ● | ● | ● | ● | ● | ● | ● | ● |
| GLENCAIRE CLINIC (HM08145) | | ● | | | ● | | | | | | | | ● | | ● | | | | | | | | | ● | | | | ● | ● | | | | | | | | | ● | | | | | | | | | ● | |
| GODFREY, BRIAN (HM08184) | | ● | | | | | | | | | | | ● | ● | ● | | | | ● | | | | | | | | ● | ● | ● | | | | | | | ● | | | | | | | | | | | | ● |
| HAMPTON, ANNE (HM08886) | | | | | | | | | | | | | | | | | | | | | | ● | | | | | | | | | | | | | | | | | | | | | | | | | | |
| HARLING, MARIANNE (DR) (HM09010) | ● | ● | ● | ● | ● | ● | ● | ● | ● | ● | ● | ● | ● | ● | ● | ● | ● | ● | ● | | ● | ● | ● | ● | ● | ● | ● | ● | ● | ● | ● | ● | ● | ● | ● | ● | ● | ● | ● | ● | ● | ● | ● | ● | ● | ● | ● | ● |
| HIGHCLIFFE CHIROPRACTIC CLINIC (HM09749) | | | | | ● | | | | | | | | | | | | | | | | | | | | | ● | | | ● | | | | | | | | | | | | | | | | | | ● | |
| HIGHCLIFFE CHIROPRACTIC CLINIC (HM09748) | | ● | | | ● | | | | | | | | ● | | ● | | | | | | | | | ● | ● | | | | ● | | | | | | | | | | | | | | | | | | ● | |
| HOLISTIC HEALTH CENTRE (HM09973) | ● | ● | ● | ● | ● | ● | ● | ● | ● | ● | ● | ● | | ● | ● | ● | ● | ● | ● | ● | | | ● | | ● | | ● | ● | ● | ● | | ● | ● | ● | ● | ● | ● | | ● | ● | ● | ● | ● | ● | ● | | ● | ● |
| HOMEOPATHY HEALS (HM10081) | ● | ● | ● | ● | ● | ● | ● | | ● | | ● | | ● | ● | ● | ● | ● | ● | ● | ● | | ● | ● | ● | ● | ● | ● | ● | ● | ● | | ● | ● | ● | ● | ● | ● | | ● | ● | ● | ● | ● | ● | ● | ● | ● | ● |
| HOPKINS, H G (HM10149) | | ● | | | ● | | | | | | | | ● | | ● | | | | | | | | | ● | ● | | | | | | | | | | | | | | | | | | | | | | | |
| HORNE, SUE (HM10175) | ● | ● | ● | | ● | | | | | | | ● | ● | ● | ● | | | | | | | | | | | ● | | | ● | ● | | ● | ● | ● | | ● | | | | | | ● | | | ● | | ● | |
| JACKSON, A E (HM10817) | ● | ● | ● | ● | ● | ● | ● | ● | ● | ● | ● | ● | ● | ● | ● | ● | ● | ● | ● | ● | | ● | ● | ● | ● | ● | ● | ● | ● | ● | | ● | ● | ● | ● | ● | ● | | ● | ● | ● | ● | ● | ● | ● | ● | ● | ● |
| JELFS, MARTIN (HM10975) | | | | | | | | | | | | | | | | | | | | | | | | | ● | | | | | | | | | ● | | | | | | | | | | | | | | ● |
| KENNEDY, EDWARD (HM11491) | | | | | ● | | | | | | | | | | | | | | | | | | | | | | | | ● | | | | | | | | | ● | ● | | | | | | | | ● | |
| LEVER, I J (HM12261) | | | | | ● | | | | | | | | | | | | | | | | | | | ● | | | | | ● | | | | | | | | | ● | ● | | | | | | | | | |
| LOCK, ROBERT (HM12538) | ● | ● | ● | | ● | ● | | | | | ● | ● | ● | ● | ● | ● | | | | | | | ● | | ● | | ● | | ● | ● | | ● | ● | ● | | ● | | | | | ● | ● | | | ● | | ● | |
| MOTCOMBE PARK PHYSIOTHERAPY (HM14273) | | | | | ● | | | | | | | | | | | | | | ● | | | | | | | | | | | | | | | | | | | | | | | | | | | | | |
| NATURAL HEALTH CONSULTANCY (HM14592) | ● | ● | ● | ● | ● | ● | ● | ● | ● | ● | ● | ● | ● | ● | ● | ● | ● | ● | ● | ● | | ● | ● | ● | ● | ● | ● | ● | ● | ● | | ● | ● | ● | ● | ● | ● | | ● | ● | ● | ● | ● | ● | ● | ● | ● | ● |
| NEIJIA (HM14759) | ● | ● | ● | ● | ● | ● | | ● | ● | ● | ● | ● | ● | ● | ● | ● | ● | ● | ● | | | ● | ● | ● | ● | ● | ● | ● | ● | ● | | | ● | ● | ● | ● | ● | | ● | ● | ● | ● | ● | ● | ● | ● | ● | ● |
| PARTNERSHIP, BAKER (DR) (HM15764) | | | | | | | | | | | | | | | | | | | | | | | | | ● | | | | | | ● | | | ● | | | | | | | | | | | | | | |
| PHYSIO, MASSAGE & PR ACU (HM16210) | ● | ● | | | ● | | | | | | | | ● | | ● | | | | ● | | | | | ● | ● | ● | | ● | ● | | | | ● | ● | | ● | | | | | | ● | | ● | ● | | ● | |
| PRIDEAUX-BRUNE, COLETTE (HM16604) | ● | ● | ● | ● | ● | ● | ● | ● | ● | ● | ● | ● | ● | ● | ● | ● | ● | ● | ● | ● | | ● | ● | ● | ● | ● | ● | ● | ● | ● | | ● | ● | ● | ● | ● | ● | | ● | ● | ● | ● | ● | ● | ● | ● | ● | ● |
| PRIDMORE, JOSEPHINE (HM16605) | ● | ● | ● | ● | ● | ● | | | ● | ● | ● | ● | ● | ● | ● | ● | | | ● | | | ● | ● | ● | ● | | ● | ● | ● | ● | | ● | ● | ● | | ● | | | ● | | ● | ● | ● | ● | ● | | ● | ● |

# I - S Conditions treated at Practices/Businesses

| Business by County with Reference no. | Insomnia | Irritable Bowel Syndrome | Itching | Jet Lag | Joint Pain | Kidney Complaints | Lactose Intolerance | Laryngitis | Lethargy | Liver Disorders | Low Blood Pressure | Lung Problems | ME | Menopause | Migraine | Motion Sickness |
|---|---|---|---|---|---|---|---|---|---|---|---|---|---|---|---|---|
| PROSPECT HEALTH (HM16667) | | | | | ● | | | | | | | | | ● | | |
| ROLLS MILL COMP HEALTH CENTRE (HM17567) | | ● | ● | | ● | | | | | | | | ● | ● | ● | |
| ROWE, PENNY (HM17689) | ● | ● | ● | | ● | ● | ● | ● | ● | ● | ● | ● | ● | ● | ● | ● |
| ROY, COLLEEN (HM17710) | ● | ● | ● | ● | ● | ● | ● | ● | ● | ● | ● | ● | ● | ● | ● | ● |
| SHEBORNE CHIROPRACTIC CENTRE (HM18361) | | | | | ● | | | | | | | | | | ● | |
| SKELTON, JAN (HM18635) | | | | | | | | | | | | | | | | |
| SOUTHBOURNE HERBAL CLINIC (HM18924) | ● | ● | ● | ● | | ● | | | ● | ● | ● | ● | ● | ● | ● | ● |
| SOUTHBOURNE NATURAL HLTH CTRE (HM18925) | ● | ● | ● | ● | ● | ● | ● | ● | ● | ● | ● | ● | ● | ● | ● | ● |
| STANDISH-HAYES, QUENTIN (HM19125) | | ● | | | ● | | | | | | | | | | | |
| STEELE, T M (HM19183) | | ● | | | | | | | | | | | ● | | | |
| THORNTONS PHARMACY (HM20029) | ● | ● | ● | ● | ● | ● | ● | ● | ● | ● | ● | ● | ● | ● | ● | ● |
| TREAT FEET (HM20301) | | | | | | | | | | | | | | | | |
| TRUNDELL, C (HM20353) | | | | | | | | | | | | | | | | |
| WALTERS, RICHARD (HM20881) | ● | | | | | | | | ● | | | | | ● | ● | |
| WESSEX HEALTHY LIVING FOUND (HM21208) | ● | ● | | | ● | | | ● | ● | | ● | | ● | ● | ● | |
| WEST MOORS CHIROPRACTIC CLINIC (HM21230) | | ● | | | ● | | | | | | | | ● | | ● | |
| WIMBORNE CHIROPODY SURGERY (HM21687) | | | | | | | | | | | | | | | | |
| YELLOW HOUSE (HM22005) | ● | ● | ● | ● | ● | ● | ● | ● | ● | ● | ● | ● | ● | ● | ● | ● |
| ESSEX | | | | | | | | | | | | | | | | |
| ABBOT, LISA (HM00095) | | ● | | | ● | | | | | | | | | | ● | |
| ABBOTT, LISA (HM00099) | | ● | | | ● | | | | | | | | | | ● | |
| AEQUILIBRIUM (HM00407) | ● | ● | ● | | ● | ● | | ● | ● | ● | | ● | ● | ● | ● | |
| ARC HEALTHCARE (HM00968) | | ● | | | | | ● | | | ● | | | ● | | ● | |
| AROMATHERAPY CLINIC (HM01107) | ● | | | | ● | | | | | | | | | | ● | |
| ASHBY & ASSOCIATES (HM01194) | | | | | | | | | | | | | | | | |
| AVART, GILLIAN (HM01383) | ● | ● | | | ● | | | | | | | ● | ● | ● | ● | |
| BARKING PHYSICAL THERAPY CTRE (HM01715) | | | | | ● | | | | | | | | | | | |
| BAXTER, LISA (HM01929) | ● | ● | | | ● | ● | | | ● | | | | | ● | ● | |
| BENEDICTA (HM02125) | ● | | | ● | ● | | | | | | ● | | | ● | ● | |
| BE-WELL CLINIC (HM02251) | | | | ● | | | | | | | | | | ● | | |
| BODY BALANCE HEALTH SOLUTIONS (HM02571) | | | | | ● | | | | | | | | | | | |
| BRITISH INSTITUTE-HYPNOTHERAPY (HM03085) | | ● | | | | | | | | | | | | ● | | ● |
| BURNHAM PHYSIOTHERAPY CLINIC (HM03405) | | | | | ● | | | | | | | | | | | |
| CAIN, SHEILA (HM03538) | ● | ● | | | ● | | | | ● | | ● | | ● | ● | ● | |

| Business by County with Reference no. | Mouth Disorders | Mouth Ulcers | Multiple Sclerosis | Muscular Dystrophy | Musculo-skeletal | Nail Health | Nausea | Nerve Disorders | Nervous Disorders | Neuralgia | Obesity | Osteoporosis | Pain | Palpitations | Panic Attacks | Parkinson's Disease |
|---|---|---|---|---|---|---|---|---|---|---|---|---|---|---|---|---|
| PROSPECT HEALTH (HM16667) | ● | ● | | | | ● | | ● | ● | ● | | | ● | | | |
| ROLLS MILL COMP HEALTH CENTRE (HM17567) | | | ● | | | | | | | ● | | ● | | | | |
| ROWE, PENNY (HM17689) | ● | ● | ● | ● | | ● | ● | ● | ● | ● | ● | ● | ● | ● | | ● |
| ROY, COLLEEN (HM17710) | ● | ● | ● | ● | | ● | ● | ● | ● | ● | ● | ● | ● | ● | | ● |
| SHEBORNE CHIROPRACTIC CENTRE (HM18361) | | | | | | | | | | ● | | | ● | | | |
| SKELTON, JAN (HM18635) | | | | | | | | | | | | | | | | |
| SOUTHBOURNE HERBAL CLINIC (HM18924) | | ● | | | | | ● | | ● | ● | | | ● | ● | | ● |
| SOUTHBOURNE NATURAL HLTH CTRE (HM18925) | ● | ● | ● | ● | | ● | ● | ● | ● | ● | ● | ● | ● | ● | | ● |
| STANDISH-HAYES, QUENTIN (HM19125) | | | | | | | | ● | | | | | ● | | | |
| STEELE, T M (HM19183) | | | | | | | | ● | | | | | ● | | | |
| THORNTONS PHARMACY (HM20029) | ● | ● | ● | ● | | ● | ● | ● | ● | ● | ● | ● | ● | ● | | ● |
| TREAT FEET (HM20301) | | | | | | ● | | | | | | | | | | |
| TRUNDELL, C (HM20353) | | | | | | ● | | | | | | | | | | |
| WALTERS, RICHARD (HM20881) | | | | | | | ● | | | | | | ● | ● | | |
| WESSEX HEALTHY LIVING FOUND (HM21208) | | ● | | | | ● | ● | | | ● | ● | | ● | | | ● |
| WEST MOORS CHIROPRACTIC CLINIC (HM21230) | | | | | | | | ● | ● | | | | ● | | | |
| WIMBORNE CHIROPODY SURGERY (HM21687) | | | | | | ● | | | | | | | | | | |
| YELLOW HOUSE (HM22005) | ● | ● | ● | ● | | ● | ● | ● | ● | ● | ● | ● | ● | ● | | ● |
| ESSEX | | | | | | | | | | | | | | | | |
| ABBOT, LISA (HM00095) | | | | | | | | | | | | | | | | |
| ABBOTT, LISA (HM00099) | | | | | | | | | | | | | | | | |
| AEQUILIBRIUM (HM00407) | | | ● | | | | | ● | ● | ● | | ● | ● | ● | | ● |
| ARC HEALTHCARE (HM00968) | | | | | | | | | | | | | | | | |
| AROMATHERAPY CLINIC (HM01107) | | | | | | | ● | | | | | | ● | | | |
| ASHBY & ASSOCIATES (HM01194) | | | | | | ● | | | | | | | | | | |
| AVART, GILLIAN (HM01383) | | ● | ● | | | | | ● | ● | ● | ● | ● | ● | ● | | |
| BARKING PHYSICAL THERAPY CTRE (HM01715) | | | ● | | | | | | | | | | | | | |
| BAXTER, LISA (HM01929) | | | | | | | ● | ● | ● | | | ● | ● | | | |
| BENEDICTA (HM02125) | | | | | | | | | ● | | | | | ● | | |
| BE-WELL CLINIC (HM02251) | | | | | | | | | | | | | | | | |
| BODY BALANCE HEALTH SOLUTIONS (HM02571) | | | | | | | | | | | | | ● | | | |
| BRITISH INSTITUTE-HYPNOTHERAPY (HM03085) | | | | | | | | | ● | | ● | | | | | |
| BURNHAM PHYSIOTHERAPY CLINIC (HM03405) | | | ● | | | | | | | | | | | | | |
| CAIN, SHEILA (HM03538) | | | ● | | | | | | ● | | | | ● | ● | | |

| Business by County with Reference no. | Period Problems | Phobias | Piles | PMT | Pneumonia | Postural Problems | Pregnancy Help | Prostate Problems | Psoriasis | Raynaud's Disease | Recurrent Infections | Restless Legs | Rheumatoid Arthritis | Schizophrenia | Sciatica | Sexual Problems |
|---|---|---|---|---|---|---|---|---|---|---|---|---|---|---|---|---|
| PROSPECT HEALTH (HM16667) | | ● | | | | | | | | | | | | | | |
| ROLLS MILL COMP HEALTH CENTRE (HM17567) | | | | | | | | | | | | | ● | | ● | |
| ROWE, PENNY (HM17689) | ● | ● | ● | ● | ● | | ● | ● | ● | ● | ● | ● | ● | ● | ● | ● |
| ROY, COLLEEN (HM17710) | ● | ● | ● | ● | ● | | ● | ● | ● | ● | ● | ● | ● | ● | ● | ● |
| SHEBORNE CHIROPRACTIC CENTRE (HM18361) | ● | | | | | | | | | | | | | | ● | |
| SKELTON, JAN (HM18635) | | | | | | | | | | | | | | | ● | |
| SOUTHBOURNE HERBAL CLINIC (HM18924) | | ● | ● | ● | ● | | ● | ● | ● | ● | | ● | | ● | ● | |
| SOUTHBOURNE NATURAL HLTH CTRE (HM18925) | ● | ● | ● | ● | ● | | ● | ● | ● | ● | ● | ● | ● | ● | ● | ● |
| STANDISH-HAYES, QUENTIN (HM19125) | | | | | | | | | | | | | | | ● | |
| STEELE, T M (HM19183) | | | | | | ● | | | | | | | | | ● | |
| THORNTONS PHARMACY (HM20029) | ● | ● | ● | ● | ● | | ● | ● | ● | ● | ● | ● | ● | ● | ● | ● |
| TREAT FEET (HM20301) | | | | | | | | | | | | | | | | |
| TRUNDELL, C (HM20353) | | | | | | | | | | | | | | | | |
| WALTERS, RICHARD (HM20881) | ● | | | ● | | | | | | | | | | | ● | |
| WESSEX HEALTHY LIVING FOUND (HM21208) | ● | ● | | | ● | | ● | | ● | | ● | ● | | | ● | |
| WEST MOORS CHIROPRACTIC CLINIC (HM21230) | | | | | | | | | | | | | | | ● | |
| WIMBORNE CHIROPODY SURGERY (HM21687) | | | | | | | | | | | | | | | | |
| YELLOW HOUSE (HM22005) | ● | ● | ● | ● | ● | | ● | ● | ● | ● | ● | ● | ● | ● | ● | ● |
| ESSEX | | | | | | | | | | | | | | | | |
| ABBOT, LISA (HM00095) | ● | | | ● | | | ● | | | | ● | | | | ● | |
| ABBOTT, LISA (HM00099) | ● | | | ● | | | ● | | | | ● | | | | ● | |
| AEQUILIBRIUM (HM00407) | ● | | ● | ● | | | | | ● | | ● | | | | ● | |
| ARC HEALTHCARE (HM00968) | ● | | | ● | | | ● | | | | | | | | | |
| AROMATHERAPY CLINIC (HM01107) | | | | ● | | | | | ● | | | | | | | |
| ASHBY & ASSOCIATES (HM01194) | | | | | | | | | | | | | | | | |
| AVART, GILLIAN (HM01383) | ● | | | ● | | | ● | | ● | ● | ● | ● | ● | | ● | |
| BARKING PHYSICAL THERAPY CTRE (HM01715) | | | | | | | | | | | | | | | | |
| BAXTER, LISA (HM01929) | ● | | | ● | | | ● | | ● | | ● | | ● | | ● | |
| BENEDICTA (HM02125) | | | | ● | | | ● | | ● | ● | | | | | ● | |
| BE-WELL CLINIC (HM02251) | | | | ● | | | ● | | | | | | | | | |
| BODY BALANCE HEALTH SOLUTIONS (HM02571) | | | | | | | | | | | | | | | ● | |
| BRITISH INSTITUTE-HYPNOTHERAPY (HM03085) | | ● | | | | | ● | | | | | ● | | | | ● |
| BURNHAM PHYSIOTHERAPY CLINIC (HM03405) | | | | | | | | | | | | | | | | |
| CAIN, SHEILA (HM03538) | ● | | | ● | | | ● | ● | ● | ● | | ● | ● | | ● | |

# I - S Conditions treated at Practices/Businesses

Business by County with Reference no.

| Condition | CATON, PETER (HM03859) | CHAKRA ROSE (HM03942) | CHRIS MOSLIN HYPNOTHERAPIST (HM04433) | CLACTON CHIROPRACTIC CLINIC (HM04501) | CLARKE, M R (HM04593) | COKER, EILEEN (HM04800) | COMPLETE CHIROPRACTIC (HM04957) | COOK, JOE (HM05048) | COOPER, FELICITY (HM05104) | CROSS HANDS CHIRO CLINIC (HM05479) | CROWN CHIROPRACTIC CLINIC (HM05507) | CROWN CHIROPRACTIC CLINIC (HM05508) | DICKASON, J T (HM06067) | E A O C (HM06465) | EDWARDS, G E (HM06651) | ELECTROLYSIS CLINIC (HM06716) | ELMER CHIROPODY & PODIATRY SVS (HM06781) | EPPING OSTEOPATHY AND SPORTS (HM06854) | EPPING PHYSIOTHERAPY PRACTICE (HM06855) | ESSEX PHYSIO & SPORTS INJ CTRE (HM06938) | FARROW, VICKI (HM07135) | FLEUROMA (HM07418) | FOULKES, GEOFFREY LLOYD (HM07609) | FROST, JANICE (HM07761) | GENT, WENDY (HM07973) | GRAY, P A (HM08417) | HARLOW OSTEOPATHIC PRACTICE (HM09011) | HEALING ROOM (HM09349) | HYPNOTHERAPY & PSYCHO CONS (HM10508) | HYPNOTHERAPY CENTRE (HM10532) | HYPNOTHERAPY CENTRE (HM10530) | ISIS HOUSE THERAPY CENTRE (HM10768) | JACKSON, CYRIL (HM10832) | KELLY, GILLIAN (HM11431) |
|---|---|---|---|---|---|---|---|---|---|---|---|---|---|---|---|---|---|---|---|---|---|---|---|---|---|---|---|---|---|---|---|---|---|---|
| Sexual Problems | | | | | | ● | | ● | | | | | | | | | | | | | | | ● | ● | | | | | | ● | ● | | | |
| Sciatica | | | | ● | ● | ● | ● | ● | | | ● | ● | ● | ● | | | | ● | | | ● | | ● | ● | | | ● | ● | | | | | | |
| Schizophrenia | | ● | | | | | | | | | | | | | | | | | | | | | ● | ● | | | | | | | | | | |
| Rheumatoid Arthritis | | ● | | | | ● | | | ● | | | | | | | | ● | | | | | | ● | ● | ● | | | | | | | | | |
| Restless Legs | | | | | | ● | | ● | | | | | | | | | | | | | | ● | ● | ● | | | | | | | | | | |
| Recurrent Infections | | | | | | | | | | | | | | | | | | | | | | | ● | ● | | | | | | | | | | |
| Raynaud's Disease | | | | | | ● | | | | | | | | | | | | | | | | ● | ● | ● | | | | | | | | | | |
| Psoriasis | | | | | | ● | | ● | | | | | | | | | | | | | | ● | ● | ● | | | | ● | | | | | | |
| Prostate Problems | | ● | | | | ● | | | | | | | | | | | | | | | | | ● | ● | | | | | | | | | | |
| Pregnancy Help | | | | | | ● | | | | | | | | | | | | | | | | | ● | ● | | | | | | | | | | |
| Postural Problems | | | | | | | | | | | | | ● | | | | ● | | | | | | | | | | | | | | | | | |
| Pneumonia | | | | | | ● | | | | | | | | | | | | | | | | | ● | ● | | | | | | | | | | |
| PMT | | | | | | ● | | ● | | | | | | | | | | | | | | | ● | ● | | | | ● | | | | | | ● |
| Piles | | | | | | ● | | | | | | | | | | | | | | | | | ● | ● | | | | | | | | | | |
| Phobias | ● | ● | ● | | | | | ● | | | | | | | | | | | | | | | ● | ● | | | | | ● | ● | ● | | ● | |
| Period Problems | | | | | | ● | | | | | | | | | | | | | | | | | ● | ● | | | | ● | | | | | | ● |
| Parkinson's Disease | | ● | | | | | | | | | | | | | | | | | | | | | ● | | | | ● | | | | | | | |
| Panic Attacks | | | | | | | | | | | | | | | | | | | | | | | | | | | | | | ● | ● | | ● | |
| Palpitations | | | ● | | | | | | | | | | | | | | | | | | | | ● | ● | | | | | | | | | | |
| Pain | | ● | | ● | ● | ● | ● | ● | | | ● | ● | ● | | | | | ● | | | | ● | ● | ● | ● | | ● | ● | | | | | | |
| Osteoporosis | | | | ● | | ● | | | | | ● | ● | ● | | | | | | | | | | ● | ● | | | | | | | | | | |
| Obesity | ● | ● | ● | | | ● | | ● | | | | | | | | ● | | | | | | | ● | ● | | | | | | | | | | |
| Neuralgia | | | | | | ● | | | | | | | | | | | | ● | | | | | ● | ● | | | ● | ● | | | | | | |
| Nervous Disorders | ● | | | | | ● | | ● | | | | | | | | | | | | | | ● | ● | ● | | | | ● | | | | | | |
| Nerve Disorders | | | | ● | | ● | ● | | | | ● | ● | | | | | | | | | | | ● | ● | | | ● | | | | | | | |
| Nausea | | | | | | ● | | | | | | | | | | | | | | ● | | | ● | ● | | | | | | | | | | |
| Nail Health | | | | | | ● | | ● | | | | | | | ● | | | | | | | | ● | ● | | ● | | | | | | | | |
| Musculo-skeletal | | | | | | | | | | | | | | | | | | | | | | | | | | | | | | | | | | |
| Muscular Dystrophy | | | | | | ● | | | | | | | | | | | | | | | | | ● | ● | | | | | | | | | | |
| Multiple Sclerosis | | | | | | ● | | ● | | ● | | | | | | | | | | ● | | | ● | ● | | | | ● | | | | | | |
| Mouth Ulcers | | ● | | | | | | | | | | | | | | | | | | | | | ● | ● | | | | | | | | | | |
| Mouth Disorders | | | | | | | | | | | | | | | | | | | | | | | ● | ● | | | | | | | | | | |
| Motion Sickness | | | | | | | | | | | | | | | | | | | | | | ● | ● | ● | | | | | | | | | | |
| Migraine | | | | | ● | ● | | ● | | | | | | | | | | | ● | | | ● | ● | ● | | | | | | | | | | ● |
| Menopause | | | | | | ● | | | | | | | | | | | | | | | | | ● | ● | | | | ● | | | | | | ● |
| ME | ● | | | | | ● | | | | | ● | ● | | | | | | | | | | ● | ● | ● | | | ● | ● | | | | | | |
| Lung Problems | | | | | | | | | | | | | | | | | | | | | | | ● | ● | | | | | | | | | | |
| Low Blood Pressure | | | | | | ● | | | | | | | | | | | | | | | | ● | ● | ● | | | | ● | | | | | | |
| Liver Disorders | | ● | | | | | | | | | | | | | | | | | | | | | ● | ● | | | | | | | | | | |
| Lethargy | | | | | | ● | | | | | | | | | | | | | ● | | | | ● | ● | | | | ● | | | | | | ● |
| Laryngitis | | | | | | ● | | | | | | | | | | | | | | | | | ● | ● | | | | | | | | | | |
| Lactose Intolerance | | ● | | | | | | | | | | | | | | | | | | | | | ● | ● | | | | | | | | | | |
| Kidney Complaints | | | | | | | | | | | | | | | | | | | | | | | ● | ● | | | | | | | | | | |
| Joint Pain | | ● | | | ● | ● | ● | ● | | ● | ● | ● | ● | | | | | ● | ● | ● | | | ● | ● | ● | | ● | ● | | | | | | ● |
| Jet Lag | | | | | | ● | | | | | | | | | | | | | | | | | ● | ● | | | | | | | | | | |
| Itching | ● | | | | | ● | | ● | | | | | | | | | | | | | | | ● | ● | | | | | | | | | | |
| Irritable Bowel Syndrome | ● | ● | ● | ● | | ● | ● | ● | | | ● | ● | | | | | | | | | | | ● | ● | | | | ● | | | | ● | ● | |
| Insomnia | | | | | | ● | | ● | | | | | | | | | | | | ● | ● | | ● | ● | | | | | | | | ● | | ● |

England (by County)

CONDITIONS TREATED

I-S

www.healthmyself.com

# I - S Conditions treated at Practices/Businesses

| Business by County with Reference no. | Insomnia | Irritable Bowel Syndrome | Itching | Jet Lag | Joint Pain | Kidney Complaints | Lactose Intolerance | Laryngitis | Lethargy | Liver Disorders | Low Blood Pressure | Lung Problems | ME | Menopause | Migraine | Motion Sickness | Mouth Disorders | Mouth Ulcers | Multiple Sclerosis | Muscular Dystrophy | Musculo-skeletal | Nail Health | Nausea | Nerve Disorders | Nervous Disorders | Neuralgia |
|---|---|---|---|---|---|---|---|---|---|---|---|---|---|---|---|---|---|---|---|---|---|---|---|---|---|---|
| LAING, RICHARD (DR) (HM11866) | ● | ● | ● | ● | ● | ● |  | ● | ● |  | ● | ● | ● | ● | ● | ● | ● |  | ● |  |  |  | ● | ● | ● | ● |
| LA-SANTE AROMATHERAPY (HM11981) |  |  |  |  |  |  |  |  |  |  |  |  |  |  |  |  |  |  |  |  |  |  |  |  |  |  |
| LEIGH, MARTIN (HM12189) |  | ● |  |  | ● |  |  |  |  |  |  |  |  |  | ● |  |  |  |  |  |  |  |  |  |  | ● |
| LEVY, PAUL (HM12269) |  |  |  |  |  |  |  |  |  |  |  |  |  |  |  |  |  |  |  |  |  | ● |  |  |  |  |
| LINGWOOD CLINIC (HM12435) |  |  |  |  | ● |  |  |  |  |  |  |  |  |  | ● |  |  |  |  |  |  |  | ● |  |  |  |
| LONDON ROAD PHYSIO PRACTICE (HM12603) |  |  |  |  | ● |  |  |  |  |  |  |  |  |  |  |  |  |  | ● |  |  |  |  |  |  |  |
| MARTIN, LEIGH (HM13202) |  | ● |  |  | ● |  |  |  |  |  |  |  |  |  | ● |  |  |  |  |  |  |  |  |  |  | ● |
| MEDELY CLINIC (HM13647) | ● |  |  |  |  |  |  |  |  |  |  |  |  |  |  |  |  |  |  |  |  |  |  |  |  |  |
| MILES, C J (HM13855) |  |  |  |  |  |  |  |  |  |  |  |  |  |  |  |  |  |  |  |  |  | ● |  |  |  |  |
| MOONSTONE HEALING CENTRE (HM14111) | ● | ● |  |  | ● | ● |  |  | ● |  | ● | ● | ● | ● | ● |  |  |  |  |  |  |  | ● | ● | ● | ● |
| MOORE, SUSAN (HM14134) | ● | ● |  |  | ● |  |  |  |  |  | ● |  | ● |  | ● |  |  |  |  |  |  | ● | ● |  |  |  |
| MOUCHET, F (HM14282) |  |  |  |  |  |  |  |  |  |  |  |  |  |  |  |  |  |  |  |  |  |  |  |  |  |  |
| NATURAL REMEDY CENTRE (HM14620) | ● | ● | ● | ● | ● |  |  | ● | ● | ● | ● | ● | ● | ● | ● | ● | ● | ● |  |  |  | ● | ● |  | ● | ● |
| PALMER, DAVID J (HM15600) |  | ● |  |  | ● | ● |  |  | ● |  |  |  |  | ● | ● |  |  |  |  |  |  |  |  |  |  |  |
| PALMIST (HM15620) |  |  |  |  |  |  |  |  |  |  |  |  |  |  |  |  |  |  |  |  |  |  |  |  |  |  |
| PARVEZ, SHAUKAT (HM15771) | ● | ● | ● |  | ● |  |  |  |  |  |  |  | ● | ● | ● |  |  |  | ● | ● |  |  |  | ● | ● | ● |
| PEPPER, SUSAN (HM16010) |  |  |  |  | ● |  |  |  |  |  |  |  |  |  |  |  |  |  |  |  |  |  |  |  |  |  |
| PHARMACARE (HM16109) | ● | ● | ● | ● | ● |  | ● | ● | ● |  | ● | ● | ● | ● | ● | ● | ● | ● |  |  |  | ● | ● |  | ● | ● |
| PHYSIO & SPORTS INJURY CLINIC (HM16186) |  |  |  |  | ● |  |  |  |  |  |  |  |  |  |  |  |  |  |  |  |  |  |  | ● |  | ● |
| PINEWOOD PHYSIOTHERAPY CLINIC (HM16313) |  |  |  |  | ● |  |  |  |  |  |  |  | ● |  |  |  |  |  | ● | ● |  |  |  |  |  |  |
| PISCES NATURAL THERAPY CENTRE (HM16330) | ● | ● |  |  |  |  |  |  |  |  |  |  | ● |  |  |  |  |  |  |  |  |  |  |  |  |  |
| PRICE, G J (HM16572) | ● | ● |  | ● | ● |  |  |  |  |  | ● | ● |  | ● | ● |  |  |  |  |  |  |  | ● | ● |  | ● |
| PRIVATE HEALTH CENTRE CLINIC (HM16643) | ● | ● | ● | ● | ● | ● | ● | ● | ● | ● | ● | ● | ● | ● | ● | ● | ● | ● | ● | ● |  | ● | ● | ● | ● | ● |
| REFLEXOLOGY CLINIC (HM17088) | ● | ● |  |  | ● | ● |  |  | ● |  | ● | ● | ● | ● | ● |  |  |  | ● |  |  |  |  |  | ● |  |
| ROBINSON, DAVID (HM17466) |  |  |  |  |  |  |  |  |  |  |  |  |  |  |  |  |  |  |  |  |  |  |  |  |  |  |
| SCOTT, MARY (HM18124) | ● | ● | ● | ● | ● | ● | ● | ● | ● | ● | ● | ● | ● | ● | ● | ● | ● | ● | ● | ● |  | ● | ● | ● | ● | ● |
| SELF AWARENESS HEALING (HM18204) |  |  |  |  |  |  |  |  |  |  |  |  | ● |  |  |  |  |  |  |  |  |  |  |  | ● |  |
| SELVES, KATIE (HM18222) | ● | ● |  | ● | ● | ● | ● | ● | ● | ● | ● | ● | ● | ● | ● | ● |  |  |  |  |  |  | ● | ● | ● | ● |
| SEYMOUR, LOUISE (HM18259) |  |  |  |  |  |  |  |  |  |  |  |  |  |  |  |  |  |  |  |  |  | ● |  |  |  |  |
| SHELDON, PEGGY (HM18380) | ● | ● |  |  | ● | ● |  |  |  | ● |  |  | ● |  | ● |  |  |  |  |  |  |  |  |  |  |  |
| SOUTH, JO (HM18918) | ● | ● | ● | ● | ● | ● | ● | ● | ● | ● | ● | ● | ● | ● | ● | ● | ● | ● | ● | ● |  | ● | ● | ● | ● | ● |
| TRINITY CENTRE (HM20338) | ● | ● | ● | ● | ● | ● | ● | ● | ● | ● | ● | ● | ● | ● | ● | ● | ● | ● | ● | ● |  | ● | ● | ● | ● | ● |
| WAYNE-WRIGHT, M S (HM21043) |  |  |  |  |  |  |  |  |  |  |  |  |  |  |  |  |  |  |  |  |  | ● |  |  |  |  |
| WELLS HYPNOTHERAPY CLINIC (HM21167) |  | ● |  |  |  |  |  |  |  |  |  |  |  |  |  |  |  |  |  |  |  |  |  |  |  |  |

| Business by County with Reference no. | Obesity | Osteoporosis | Pain | Palpitations | Panic Attacks | Parkinson's Disease | Period Problems | Phobias | Piles | PMT | Pneumonia | Postural Problems | Pregnancy Help | Prostate Problems | Psoriasis | Raynaud's Disease | Recurrent Infections | Restless Legs | Rheumatoid Arthritis | Schizophrenia | Sciatica | Sexual Problems |
|---|---|---|---|---|---|---|---|---|---|---|---|---|---|---|---|---|---|---|---|---|---|---|
| LAING, RICHARD (DR) (HM11866) |  |  | ● | ● |  |  | ● | ● | ● | ● | ● |  |  |  | ● | ● | ● | ● | ● |  |  |  |
| LA-SANTE AROMATHERAPY (HM11981) |  |  | ● |  |  |  |  |  |  |  |  |  |  |  |  |  |  |  |  |  |  |  |
| LEIGH, MARTIN (HM12189) |  |  | ● |  |  |  |  |  |  |  |  |  |  |  |  |  |  |  |  |  | ● |  |
| LEVY, PAUL (HM12269) |  |  |  |  |  |  |  |  |  |  |  |  |  |  |  |  |  |  |  |  |  |  |
| LINGWOOD CLINIC (HM12435) |  |  | ● |  |  |  | ● | ● |  |  |  |  | ● |  |  |  |  |  |  |  | ● |  |
| LONDON ROAD PHYSIO PRACTICE (HM12603) |  |  | ● |  |  |  |  |  |  |  |  |  |  |  |  |  |  |  |  |  |  |  |
| MARTIN, LEIGH (HM13202) |  |  | ● |  |  |  |  |  |  |  |  |  |  |  |  |  |  |  |  |  | ● |  |
| MEDELY CLINIC (HM13647) |  |  | ● |  |  |  |  |  |  |  |  |  |  |  |  |  |  |  |  |  | ● |  |
| MILES, C J (HM13855) |  |  |  |  |  |  |  |  |  |  |  |  |  |  |  |  |  |  |  |  |  |  |
| MOONSTONE HEALING CENTRE (HM14111) | ● | ● | ● |  |  |  | ● | ● |  | ● |  |  |  |  |  |  |  |  | ● |  | ● | ● |
| MOORE, SUSAN (HM14134) |  |  | ● |  |  |  | ● |  |  | ● |  |  | ● |  |  |  |  | ● |  |  |  |  |
| MOUCHET, F (HM14282) |  |  |  |  |  |  |  |  |  |  |  |  |  |  |  |  |  |  |  |  |  | ● |
| NATURAL REMEDY CENTRE (HM14620) | ● | ● | ● | ● |  |  | ● | ● | ● | ● | ● |  | ● | ● | ● | ● | ● | ● | ● | ● | ● | ● |
| PALMER, DAVID J (HM15600) |  |  | ● |  |  |  |  |  |  | ● |  |  |  | ● |  |  |  |  |  |  | ● |  |
| PALMIST (HM15620) |  |  |  |  |  |  |  | ● |  |  |  |  |  |  |  |  |  |  |  |  |  |  |
| PARVEZ, SHAUKAT (HM15771) | ● | ● | ● | ● |  | ● | ● |  |  | ● |  |  | ● |  | ● | ● |  | ● | ● |  | ● | ● |
| PEPPER, SUSAN (HM16010) |  |  | ● |  |  |  |  |  |  |  |  |  | ● |  |  |  |  |  |  |  | ● |  |
| PHARMACARE (HM16109) | ● | ● | ● | ● |  | ● | ● | ● | ● | ● | ● |  | ● | ● | ● | ● | ● | ● | ● | ● | ● | ● |
| PHYSIO & SPORTS INJURY CLINIC (HM16186) |  | ● | ● |  |  | ● |  |  |  |  |  |  |  |  |  |  |  |  | ● |  | ● |  |
| PINEWOOD PHYSIOTHERAPY CLINIC (HM16313) |  | ● | ● |  |  |  |  |  |  |  |  |  |  |  |  | ● |  |  | ● |  | ● |  |
| PISCES NATURAL THERAPY CENTRE (HM16330) | ● |  |  |  |  |  |  | ● |  |  |  |  |  |  |  |  |  |  |  |  |  | ● |
| PRICE, G J (HM16572) | ● | ● | ● | ● |  |  | ● |  | ● | ● |  |  |  |  | ● |  |  | ● | ● |  | ● |  |
| PRIVATE HEALTH CENTRE CLINIC (HM16643) | ● | ● | ● | ● |  | ● | ● | ● | ● | ● | ● |  | ● | ● | ● | ● | ● | ● | ● | ● | ● | ● |
| REFLEXOLOGY CLINIC (HM17088) |  |  | ● | ● |  |  | ● | ● | ● |  |  |  | ● | ● |  | ● |  | ● |  |  | ● |  |
| ROBINSON, DAVID (HM17466) |  |  |  |  | ● |  |  | ● |  |  |  |  |  |  |  |  |  |  |  |  |  |  |
| SCOTT, MARY (HM18124) | ● | ● | ● | ● |  | ● | ● | ● | ● | ● | ● |  | ● | ● | ● | ● | ● | ● | ● | ● | ● | ● |
| SELF AWARENESS HEALING (HM18204) |  |  |  |  |  |  |  |  |  |  |  |  |  |  |  |  |  |  |  |  |  | ● |
| SELVES, KATIE (HM18222) |  | ● |  | ● |  |  | ● |  | ● | ● | ● |  |  | ● | ● | ● | ● |  | ● |  |  |  |
| SEYMOUR, LOUISE (HM18259) |  |  |  |  |  |  |  |  |  |  |  |  |  |  |  |  |  |  |  |  |  |  |
| SHELDON, PEGGY (HM18380) |  |  |  |  |  |  |  |  |  |  |  |  |  |  |  |  |  |  | ● |  |  |  |
| SOUTH, JO (HM18918) | ● | ● | ● | ● |  | ● | ● | ● | ● | ● | ● |  | ● | ● | ● | ● | ● | ● | ● | ● | ● | ● |
| TRINITY CENTRE (HM20338) | ● | ● | ● | ● |  | ● | ● | ● | ● | ● | ● |  | ● | ● | ● | ● | ● | ● | ● |  | ● | ● |
| WAYNE-WRIGHT, M S (HM21043) |  |  |  |  |  |  |  |  |  |  |  |  |  |  |  |  |  |  |  |  |  |  |
| WELLS HYPNOTHERAPY CLINIC (HM21167) |  |  |  |  | ● |  |  | ● |  |  |  |  |  |  |  |  |  |  |  |  |  |  |

# I - S Conditions treated at Practices/Businesses

| Business by County with Reference no. | Insomnia | Irritable Bowel Syndrome | Itching | Jet Lag | Joint Pain | Kidney Complaints | Lactose Intolerance | Laryngitis | Lethargy | Liver Disorders | Low Blood Pressure | Lung Problems | ME | Menopause | Migraine | Motion Sickness | Mouth Disorders | Mouth Ulcers | Multiple Sclerosis | Muscular Dystrophy | Musculo-skeletal | Nail Health | Nausea | Nerve Disorders | Nervous Disorders | Neuralgia | Obesity | Osteoporosis | Pain | Palpitations | Panic Attacks | Parkinson's Disease | Period Problems | Phobias | Piles | PMT | Pneumonia | Postural Problems | Pregnancy Help | Prostate Problems | Psoriasis | Raynaud's Disease | Recurrent Infections | Restless Legs | Rheumatoid Arthritis | Schizophrenia | Sciatica | Sexual Problems |
|---|---|---|---|---|---|---|---|---|---|---|---|---|---|---|---|---|---|---|---|---|---|---|---|---|---|---|---|---|---|---|---|---|---|---|---|---|---|---|---|---|---|---|---|---|---|---|---|---|
| WENTWORTH HEALTH CLINIC (HM21201) | | | | | | | | | | | ● | | | | ● | | | | | | | | | | | | | | ● | | | | | | | ● | | | | | ● | | | | | | | |
| WHEELER, M A (HM21316) | | | | | ● | | | | | | | | | | ● | | | | | | | | | | | | | | | | | | | | | | | | | | | | | | | | | |
| WHITE WATER HEALING CENTRE (HM21345) | ● | ● | | | ● | | | | ● | | | | ● | | ● | | | | | | | | | ● | ● | | | | ● | | | | | | | | | | | | | | | | ● | ● | ● | |
| WOODSIDE NATURAL HEALTH (HM21859) | ● | ● | ● | | ● | | | | | | | | | ● | ● | | | | ● | | | | | | ● | | | ● | ● | | | | ● | | | | | | | | | ● | | | ● | | ● | |
| **GLOUCESTERSHIRE** | | | | | | | | | | | | | | | | | | | | | | | | | | | | | | | | | | | | | | | | | | | | | | | | |
| ACUPUNCTURE CLINIC (HM00262) | ● | ● | ● | ● | ● | ● | | | | | ● | ● | ● | ● | ● | | | | ● | | | ● | ● | ● | ● | ● | | | ● | ● | | | ● | ● | ● | ● | ● | | ● | | ● | | ● | ● | ● | ● | ● | ● |
| ADAMS, PETER (HM00360) | ● | ● | ● | ● | ● | ● | ● | ● | ● | ● | ● | ● | ● | ● | ● | ● | ● | ● | ● | ● | | ● | ● | ● | ● | ● | | ● | ● | ● | | ● | ● | ● | ● | ● | ● | | ● | ● | ● | ● | ● | ● | ● | ● | ● | ● |
| ARTICHOKE NATURAL HEALTH (HM01168) | ● | ● | | | ● | | | | ● | | | | ● | ● | | | | | | | | | | | | | | | | | | | | | | | | | | | | | | | ● | | ● | |
| BISHOPS CLEEVE PHYSIO & SPORTS (HM02413) | | | | | ● | | | | | | | | | | | | | | | | | | | | | | | | ● | | | | | | | | | | | | | | | | | | | |
| BUNTON, LYNN (HM03354) | ● | ● | | | ● | | | | | | | | | ● | ● | | | | | | | | | | | | ● | | | | | | | | | ● | | | | | | | | ● | ● | | | |
| BURKE, JAYNE (HM03388) | ● | ● | | | ● | ● | | | | | ● | | ● | ● | ● | | | | ● | | | ● | ● | | | | | | ● | | | | ● | | ● | ● | | | ● | | | | | ● | | | ● | |
| CHELTENHAM HOLISTIC HLTH CTRE (HM04094) | ● | ● | ● | ● | ● | ● | ● | ● | ● | ● | ● | ● | ● | ● | ● | ● | ● | ● | ● | ● | | ● | ● | ● | ● | ● | ● | ● | ● | ● | | ● | ● | ● | ● | ● | ● | | ● | ● | ● | ● | ● | ● | ● | ● | ● | ● |
| CHELTENHAM HYPNOTHERAPY (HM04096) | ● | | | | | | | | | | | | | | | | | | | | | | | | ● | | | | | | | | | ● | | | | | | | | | | | | | | ● |
| CHELTENHAM PHYSIO/SPRTS CLNC (HM04097) | | | | | ● | | | | | | | | | | | | | | ● | | ● | | | | | | | | ● | | | | | | | | | | | | | | | | | | | |
| COMPLEMENTARY TOUCH (HM04950) | ● | | | | ● | | | | ● | | ● | | | | ● | | | | | | | | | | | | | | ● | | | | | | | | | | | | | | | ● | ● | | | |
| COOPER, ANGELA (HM05089) | | | | | | | | | | | | | | | | | | | | | | | | | | | | | | | ● | | | ● | | | | | | | | | | | | | | ● |
| COOPER, ANN (HM05090) | | ● | | | | ● | | | | | ● | | ● | ● | ● | | | | ● | | | | ● | | | | | | ● | | | | ● | | | ● | | | ● | | | ● | | | ● | | ● | |
| COTSWOLD PHYSIOTHERAPY CENTRE (HM05215) | | | | | ● | | | | | | | | ● | | | | | | ● | | | | | | | ● | | ● | ● | | | | | | | | | | | | | | | | ● | | ● | |
| ESSENTIAL BODYWORKS COMPANY (HM06899) | ● | ● | | | ● | | | | | | ● | | | | | | | | ● | ● | | | | ● | ● | | | | | | | | | | | | | | | | | | | | ● | | ● | |
| GREENWELL, DAVID (HM08498) | | ● | | | | | | | | | | | ● | | | | | | | | | | | | | | | | ● | | | | | ● | | ● | | | | | | | | | | | | |
| HYGEIA COLLEGE-COLOUR THERAPY (HM10476) | | | | | | | | | | | | | | | ● | | | | | | | | | | | | | | | | | | | | | | | | | | | | | | | | | |
| JOANNA SMITH AROMATHERAPY (HM11040) | ● | ● | | | ● | | | | | | | | | | ● | | | | | | ● | | | ● | | | | | | | | | ● | | | | | | | | | | | | | | | |
| LAWLER, R & G (HM12041) | ● | ● | | | | ● | | | | | ● | | ● | ● | ● | | | | | | | | ● | | | | | | ● | | | | | | ● | ● | | | ● | | | | | ● | | | | |
| LECKHAMPTON CHIROPRACTIC CLNC (HM12119) | | | | | ● | | | | | | | | | | ● | | | | | | | | | ● | | ● | | ● | ● | | | | | | | | | | | | | | | | | | ● | |
| MYERS, MERRILYN (HM14438) | | | | | | | | | | | | | | | | | | | | | | | | ● | | | | | | | | | | | | | | | | | | | | | | | | |
| NATURAL THERAPIES CLINIC (HM14633) | ● | ● | | | ● | ● | | | | | ● | ● | ● | | | | | | ● | | | | ● | | ● | | | | | ● | | | ● | ● | ● | ● | | | ● | | | | | | | | ● | |
| NATURAL THERAPY CENTRE (HM14649) | ● | | | | ● | | | | | | | | ● | | ● | | | | | | | | | ● | ● | ● | ● | | ● | | | | | ● | | ● | | | ● | | | | | | ● | | ● | |
| OLD CONVENT (HM15255) | | | | | | | | | | | | | | | ● | | | | | | | | | | | | | | | | | | | | | | | | | | | | | | | | ● | |
| OSTEOPATH (HM15445) | | | | | ● | | | | | | | | ● | | ● | | | | | | | | | | | | | ● | ● | | | | | | | | | | | | | | | | ● | | | |
| PENACHE (HM15960) | | ● | | | | | | | | | | | ● | ● | ● | | | | | | | | | | | | | | | | | | | | | | | | | | | | | | | | | |
| SHIATSU PRACTICE (HM18460) | ● | ● | | | ● | ● | | | | | | ● | | ● | ● | | | | ● | | | | ● | | ● | | | | ● | ● | | | ● | ● | ● | ● | | | ● | ● | | | | | | | ● | |
| SLATER, D C (HM18672) | | | | | | | | | | | | | | | | | | | | | | | | | | | | | | | ● | | | ● | | | | | | | | | | | | | | |
| SMYTH, DAVID (HM18830) | ● | ● | ● | ● | ● | ● | ● | ● | ● | ● | ● | ● | ● | ● | ● | ● | ● | ● | ● | ● | | ● | ● | ● | ● | ● | ● | ● | ● | ● | | ● | ● | ● | ● | ● | ● | | ● | ● | ● | ● | ● | ● | ● | ● | ● | ● |
| STOUT, HEATHER (HM19359) | ● | ● | ● | ● | ● | | ● | ● | ● | | | ● | ● | ● | ● | ● | | ● | ● | | | | ● | | ● | ● | | ● | ● | ● | | ● | ● | ● | ● | ● | | | ● | | ● | | ● | | | | ● | |

# I - S Conditions treated at Practices/Businesses

Business by County with Reference no.

| Business | Insomnia | Irritable Bowel Syndrome | Itching | Jet Lag | Joint Pain | Kidney Complaints | Lactose Intolerance | Laryngitis | Lethargy | Liver Disorders | Low Blood Pressure | Lung Problems | ME | Menopause | Migraine | Motion Sickness | Mouth Disorders | Mouth Ulcers | Multiple Sclerosis | Muscular Dystrophy | Musculo-skeletal | Nail Health | Nausea | Nerve Disorders |
|---|---|---|---|---|---|---|---|---|---|---|---|---|---|---|---|---|---|---|---|---|---|---|---|---|
| STROUD NATURAL HEALTH CLINIC (HM19422) | ● | ● | ● | ● | ● | ● | ● | ● | ● | ● | ● | ● | ● | ● | ● | ● | ● | ● | ● | ● | | ● | ● | ● |
| TREE OF LIFE CENTRE (HM20307) | ● | ● | | | ● | ● | | | | | ● | | ● | ● | ● | | | | ● | | | ● | ● | |
| VILLAGE CLINIC (HM20665) | | | | | ● | | | | | | | | | | | | | | ● | ● | | ● | | ● |
| VINEY HALL PHYSIOTHERAPY (HM20683) | | | | | ● | | | | | | | | | | | | | | | | | | | ● |
| WELLS, GEORGINA (HM21172) | | | | ● | ● | | | | | | ● | | | | | | | | | | | | ● | ● |
| YOGA DRUVAM JIVAN YOGA SOCIETY (HM22024) | ● | | | | | | | | | | ● | | | | | | | | | | | | | |
| **HAMPSHIRE** | | | | | | | | | | | | | | | | | | | | | | | | |
| ACUPUNCTURE & PHYSIO CLINIC (HM00245) | ● | ● | ● | ● | ● | ● | | ● | ● | ● | ● | ● | ● | ● | ● | ● | ● | ● | ● | ● | ● | | ● | ● |
| ALL - HEAL ACU & HERB CENTRE (HM00581) | ● | ● | ● | | ● | ● | | ● | ● | ● | ● | ● | ● | ● | ● | ● | | ● | ● | ● | | ● | ● | ● |
| ALLERGY THERAPY (HM00637) | ● | ● | ● | ● | ● | ● | ● | ● | ● | ● | ● | ● | ● | ● | ● | ● | ● | ● | ● | ● | | ● | ● | ● |
| ARTEMIS (HM01156) | ● | | | | | | | | | | | | | | | | | | | | | | | |
| AVENUE CLINIC (HM01389) | | ● | | | ● | | | | | | | | ● | | ● | | | | ● | ● | | | ● | ● |
| BOLDICK, KATHLEEN (HM02652) | ● | ● | | | ● | ● | | | | | ● | | ● | ● | ● | | | | | | | | ● | |
| BRADFORD HOUSE CHIRO CLINIC (HM02849) | | ● | | | ● | | | | | | | | ● | | ● | | | | | | | | | ● |
| BUCK, PETER (HM03306) | | | | | | | | | | | | | | | | | | | | | | ● | | |
| CARMICHAEL, GORDON (HM03709) | | | | | ● | | | | | | | | | | | | | | | | | | | |
| CASSELL, JOHN (HM03814) | ● | ● | ● | ● | ● | ● | ● | ● | ● | ● | ● | ● | ● | ● | ● | ● | ● | ● | ● | ● | | ● | ● | ● |
| CENTRE FOR COMP MEDICINE (HM03901) | ● | ● | ● | ● | ● | ● | ● | ● | ● | ● | ● | ● | ● | ● | ● | ● | ● | ● | ● | ● | ● | ● | ● | ● |
| CHILTERN COTTAGE CLINIC (HM04175) | ● | ● | ● | | ● | ● | | ● | ● | | | | ● | ● | ● | | ● | ● | ● | | | | ● | |
| CLEMENTS, CHRISTINE (HM04642) | | | | | ● | | | | | | | | | | | | | | | | | | | |
| COAST CLINIC (HM04752) | | | | | ● | | | | | | | | ● | | ● | | | | | | | | | |
| COLVILE, RICHARD (HM04895) | | ● | | | | | | | ● | | | | ● | | | | | | | | | | | |
| COMPLETE ANGEL HEALING CENTRE (HM04955) | ● | ● | | | ● | ● | | | | | ● | | ● | ● | ● | | | | ● | | | | | |
| CORELLO, LOUISE (HM05161) | ● | ● | ● | ● | ● | ● | | ● | ● | ● | ● | ● | ● | ● | ● | ● | | | | | | | ● | ● |
| CRAIG, PETER (HM05353) | | | | | | | | | | | | | | | | | | | | | | ● | | |
| CRANIOSACRAL THERAPY (HM05377) | ● | ● | | | ● | | | | ● | | ● | | ● | ● | ● | | | | ● | ● | | | | ● |
| CTRE FOR THE STUDY OF COMP MED (HM05543) | ● | ● | ● | ● | ● | ● | ● | ● | ● | ● | ● | ● | ● | ● | ● | ● | | ● | ● | | | | ● | |
| DOLPHIN STUDIOS (HM06165) | | ● | | | | | | | ● | | | | | | | | | | | | | | ● | |
| EASTLEIGH OSTEOPATHIC CLINIC (HM06544) | | ● | | | ● | | | | | | | | | | ● | | | | | | | | | |
| ENERGY EXCHANGE HOLISTIC CTRE (HM06816) | | | | | ● | | | | ● | | | | ● | | ● | | | | | | | | | |
| EVANS (HM06953) | | | | | | | | | | | | | | | | | | | | | | ● | | |
| FAIRFIELDS LANE WEST (HM07059) | ● | | | | ● | | | | | | | | ● | ● | ● | | | | ● | | | | | |
| FAMILY CHIRO & ALT MED CTRE (HM07081) | ● | ● | ● | ● | ● | ● | | ● | ● | ● | ● | ● | ● | ● | ● | | ● | ● | ● | | | ● | | ● |
| FIT FEET CHIROPODY (HM07361) | ● | ● | | | | | | | ● | ● | ● | | ● | | ● | | | | | | | ● | | |

| Business | Nervous Disorders | Neuralgia | Obesity | Osteoporosis | Pain | Palpitations | Panic Attacks | Parkinson's Disease | Period Problems | Phobias | Piles | PMT | Pneumonia | Postural Problems | Pregnancy Help | Prostate Problems | Psoriasis | Raynaud's Disease | Recurrent Infections | Restless Legs | Rheumatoid Arthritis | Schizophrenia | Sciatica | Sexual Problems |
|---|---|---|---|---|---|---|---|---|---|---|---|---|---|---|---|---|---|---|---|---|---|---|---|---|
| STROUD NATURAL HEALTH CLINIC (HM19422) | ● | ● | ● | ● | ● | ● | | ● | ● | ● | ● | ● | ● | | ● | ● | ● | ● | ● | ● | ● | ● | ● | ● |
| TREE OF LIFE CENTRE (HM20307) | | | | | ● | | | | ● | | ● | ● | | | ● | | | | | ● | | | ● | |
| VILLAGE CLINIC (HM20665) | | ● | | ● | ● | | | ● | | | | | | | | | | | | | ● | | ● | |
| VINEY HALL PHYSIOTHERAPY (HM20683) | | | | ● | ● | | | | | | | | | | | | | | | | ● | | ● | |
| WELLS, GEORGINA (HM21172) | ● | | | | ● | ● | | | | | | | | | ● | | | ● | | | ● | | ● | |
| YOGA DRUVAM JIVAN YOGA SOCIETY (HM22024) | | | | | | | | | | | | | | | | | | | | | | | | |
| **HAMPSHIRE** | | | | | | | | | | | | | | | | | | | | | | | | |
| ACUPUNCTURE & PHYSIO CLINIC (HM00245) | ● | ● | ● | ● | ● | ● | | ● | ● | | ● | ● | ● | | ● | | ● | ● | ● | ● | ● | | ● | |
| ALL - HEAL ACU & HERB CENTRE (HM00581) | ● | ● | ● | | ● | ● | | | ● | | ● | ● | | | ● | ● | ● | | | | | | ● | ● |
| ALLERGY THERAPY (HM00637) | ● | ● | ● | ● | ● | ● | | ● | ● | ● | ● | ● | ● | | ● | ● | ● | ● | ● | ● | ● | ● | ● | ● |
| ARTEMIS (HM01156) | ● | | | | | | | | | ● | | | | | | | | | | | | | | |
| AVENUE CLINIC (HM01389) | ● | ● | | ● | ● | | | ● | | | | | | | ● | | | ● | | ● | ● | | ● | |
| BOLDICK, KATHLEEN (HM02652) | | | | | ● | ● | | | ● | | | ● | ● | | ● | | | | | | | | ● | |
| BRADFORD HOUSE CHIRO CLINIC (HM02849) | ● | ● | | | ● | | | | | | | | | | | | | | | | | | ● | |
| BUCK, PETER (HM03306) | | | | | | | | | | | | | | | | | | | | | | | | |
| CARMICHAEL, GORDON (HM03709) | | | | | ● | | | | | | | | | | | | | | | ● | | | | |
| CASSELL, JOHN (HM03814) | ● | ● | ● | ● | ● | ● | | ● | ● | ● | ● | ● | ● | | ● | ● | ● | ● | ● | ● | ● | ● | ● | ● |
| CENTRE FOR COMP MEDICINE (HM03901) | ● | ● | ● | ● | ● | ● | ● | ● | ● | ● | ● | ● | ● | ● | ● | ● | ● | ● | ● | ● | ● | ● | ● | ● |
| CHILTERN COTTAGE CLINIC (HM04175) | ● | ● | | | ● | ● | | | ● | ● | | ● | | | | ● | ● | | ● | ● | | | | |
| CLEMENTS, CHRISTINE (HM04642) | | | | | ● | | | | | | | | | | | | | | | | | | ● | |
| COAST CLINIC (HM04752) | | | | | ● | | | | | | | ● | | | | | | | | | | | | |
| COLVILE, RICHARD (HM04895) | | | ● | ● | | | | | | | | ● | | | | | | | | | | | | ● |
| COMPLETE ANGEL HEALING CENTRE (HM04955) | | | | | ● | ● | | | ● | | | ● | | | ● | | | | | ● | ● | | ● | |
| CORELLO, LOUISE (HM05161) | ● | ● | | | ● | ● | | ● | ● | | ● | ● | ● | | ● | ● | ● | ● | ● | ● | | | ● | |
| CRAIG, PETER (HM05353) | | | | | | | | | | | | | | | | | | | | | | | | |
| CRANIOSACRAL THERAPY (HM05377) | ● | ● | | | | | | | ● | ● | | ● | | | ● | | ● | | | ● | | | | |
| CTRE FOR THE STUDY OF COMP MED (HM05543) | ● | ● | | | ● | ● | | | ● | ● | ● | ● | | | ● | ● | ● | ● | ● | ● | ● | ● | ● | ● |
| DOLPHIN STUDIOS (HM06165) | | | ● | | | ● | ● | | | ● | | | | | | | | | | | | | | |
| EASTLEIGH OSTEOPATHIC CLINIC (HM06544) | | ● | | | ● | | | | ● | | | ● | | | | | | | | | | | ● | |
| ENERGY EXCHANGE HOLISTIC CTRE (HM06816) | | | | | | | | | | ● | | | | | | | ● | | | | | ● | | |
| EVANS (HM06953) | | | | | | | | | | | | | | | | | | | | | | | | |
| FAIRFIELDS LANE WEST (HM07059) | | | | | ● | | | | | | | ● | | | | | | | | | | | ● | |
| FAMILY CHIRO & ALT MED CTRE (HM07081) | ● | ● | ● | ● | ● | ● | | ● | ● | ● | | ● | | | ● | ● | ● | ● | | ● | ● | | ● | |
| FIT FEET CHIROPODY (HM07361) | | | | | ● | | | ● | | | | | | | | | | | | ● | ● | | | |

# I - S Conditions treated at Practices/Businesses

| Business by County with Reference no. | Insomnia | Irritable Bowel Syndrome | Itching | Jet Lag | Joint Pain | Kidney Complaints | Lactose Intolerance | Laryngitis | Lethargy | Liver Disorders | Low Blood Pressure | Lung Problems | ME | Menopause | Migraine | Motion Sickness | Mouth Disorders | Mouth Ulcers | Multiple Sclerosis | Muscular Dystrophy | Musculo-skeletal | Nail Health | Nausea | Nerve Disorders | Nervous Disorders | Neuralgia | Obesity | Osteoporosis | Pain | Palpitations | Panic Attacks | Parkinson's Disease | Period Problems | Phobias | Piles | PMT | Pneumonia | Postural Problems | Pregnancy Help | Prostate Problems | Psoriasis | Raynaud's Disease | Recurrent Infections | Restless Legs | Rheumatoid Arthritis | Schizophrenia | Sciatica | Sexual Problems |
|---|---|---|---|---|---|---|---|---|---|---|---|---|---|---|---|---|---|---|---|---|---|---|---|---|---|---|---|---|---|---|---|---|---|---|---|---|---|---|---|---|---|---|---|---|---|---|---|---|
| FLEET & DISTRICT HYP CENTRE (HM07399) |●|●| | | | | | | | | | | | | | | | | | | | | | | | |●| |●| | | | |●| | | | | | | | | | | | | |●|
| FOOT SHOP (HM07486) | | | | | | | | | | | | | | | | | | | | | |●| | | | | | | | | | | | | | | | | | | | | | | | | | |
| FOREVER LIVING PRODUCTS (HM07555) | |●| | | | | | | | | | | | |●| | | | | | | | | | | | | | | |●| | |●| | | | | | | | | | | | | | |
| FOSSEY, LYNETTE (HM07585) |●|●| | |●| | | | | | | |●| |●| | | | | | | | | | | | | | | | | | | | | | | |●| | | | | | | | | |
| FOSTER, JAMES M ASSOCIATES (HM07593) | | | | | | | | | | | | | | | | | | | | | | | | | | | | | | | | | | | | | | | | | | | | |●| | | |
| FOX, ANTONY D (DR) (HM07631) |●|●|●|●|●|●|●|●|●|●|●|●|●|●|●|●|●|●|●|●| |●|●|●|●|●|●|●|●|●| |●|●|●|●|●| | | |●|●|●|●|●|●| |●| |
| GEE, L (HM07958) | | | | | | | | | | | | | | | | | | | | | | | | | | | | |●| | | | | | | | | | | | | | | | | | | |
| HANTSCARE (HM08947) | | | | |●| | | | | | | | | | | | | | | |●| | | | | | | |●| | | | | | | | | | | | | | | | | |●| |
| HAYLING ISLAND CHIRO CLINIC (HM09268) | | | | |●| | | | | | | | | |●| | | | | | | | |●| |●| | |●| | | | | | | | | | | | | | | |●| |●| |
| HEAL-ALL HERB AND ACU CTRE (HM09315) |●|●| |●|●| |●|●|●|●|●|●|●|●|●|●| |●|●|●| |●|●|●|●|●|●| |●|●| | |●| |●|●| | |●|●|●| | | | | | |●|●|
| HEARNE, BRIAN (HM09440) | | | | | | | | | | | | | | | | | | | | | |●| | | | | | | | | | | | | | | | | | | | | | | | | | |
| HERB MEDIC (HM09592) | |●| | | | | | | | | | | |●| | | | | | | | | | | | | | |●| | | |●| | |●| | | | | | | | | | | | |
| HIGH STREET CLINIC (HM09742) |●|●| | |●|●| | | | | | |●|●|●| | | |●| | |●| | | | | | |●|●| | |●| | |●| | | | | | | |●| | |●| |
| HOBBS, T J (HM09860) |●|●| | |●|●| |●| | |●| |●|●|●| | | |●| | | |●| | | | | |●|●| | |●| | | | | | | | | | | | | |●| |
| HOLISTIC ARTS STUDIOS (HM09948) |●|●| | | | | | | | | | | |●|●| | | | | | | | | | | | | | | | | |●| | |●| | | | | | | | | | | | |
| HOMOEOPATHIC CLINIC (HM10088) | |●| | |●| | | | | | | | | | | | | | | | | | |●| |●| | |●| | | | | | | | | | | | | | | | | |●| |
| HUTCHINGS, MARGARET (HM10448) |●| | | | | | | | | | | | | | | | | | | | | | | | | | | |●| | | | | | | | | | | | | | | | | | | |
| HYPNOSIS & STRESS COUNSELLING (HM10494) |●|●| | | | | | | | | | | | |●| | | | | | | | | | | |●| |●| | | | |●| | | | | | | | | | | | | | |
| HYPNOTHRPY FOR POSITIVE CHANGE (HM10542) |●|●|●| | | | | | | | | |●| |●|●| | | | | | | |●|●| |●| |●| |●| |●|●| |●| | |●| | | | |●| | | |●|
| INLPTA (HM10633) |●| | | | | | | |●| | | | | | | | | | | | | | | |●| |●| |●| | | | |●| | | | | | | | | | | | | | |
| INNER WHISPERS & THERAPY CTRE (HM10643) | | | | | | | | | | | | |●| |●| | | | | | | | | | | |●| | | | |●| | | | | | | | | | | | | | | | |
| JENKINS, RUSSELL (HM10994) |●|●|●|●|●|●|●|●|●|●|●|●|●|●|●|●|●|●|●|●| |●|●|●|●|●|●|●|●|●| |●|●|●|●|●|●| |●|●|●|●|●|●|●|●|●|●|
| JOYCE, HELEN G M (HM11236) | | | | |●| | | | | | | | | | | | | | | | | | | | | | |●| | | | | | | | | | | | | | | | | | |●| |
| KAY SILVER HYPNOTHERAPY (HM11349) |●|●| | | | | | |●| | | |●| | | | | | | | | | | | | | | |●| | | | |●| | | | | | | | | | | | | | |
| KD PHYSIOTHERAPY (HM11363) | | | | |●| | | | | | | | | | | | | |●| | | | | | | | | |●| | | | | | | | | | | | | | | | | | | |
| LEACH, TRICIA (HM12091) |●|●| | |●|●| | | | | | |●|●|●| | | | | | | | | | | | | |●|●| | |●| | |●| | |●| | | | | | | |●| |
| LEWIS, D J S (HM12288) |●|●|●|●|●|●| |●|●|●|●|●|●|●|●|●|●|●|●|●|●|●|●|●|●|●|●|●|●|●|●|●|●|●|●|●|●|●|●|●|●|●|●|●|●|●|●|●|
| LISLE, THOMAS (HM12455) | | | | | | | | | | | | | | | | | | | | | |●| | | | | | | | | | | | | | | | | | | | | | | | | | |
| LOCKHAMS THERAPY CENTRE (HM12545) | | | | | | | | |●| | | | | | | | | | | | | | | |●| | | |●| | | | | | | | | | | | | | | | | | | |
| LOWE, KENNETH (HM12699) | |●| | |●| | | | | | | | | |●| | | | | |●| | | | | | | |●| | | | | | | | | | | | | | |●|●| |●| |
| LYMINGTON CHIROPRACTIC CLINIC (HM12759) |●|●|●| |●| | | |●|●|●| | | |●|●| | | | | | | |●| |●| | |●| | | |●| | | | | | | | | |●| |●| |●| |
| MARLOR, J (HM13127) | | | | | | | | | | | | | | | | | | | | | |●| | | | | | | | | | | | | | | | | | | | | | | | | | |
| MELHUISH, J I (DR) (HM13705) | |●| | |●| | | | | | | |●| |●| | | | | | | | |●|●| | | |●| | | | | | | | | | | | | | | | | |●| |
| MINDWORKS HYPNOTHERAPY CLINIC (HM13969) |●|●| | | | | | | | | | |●| |●| | | | | | | | | | | | | |●|●| | | |●| | | | | | | | | | | | | |●|

# I - S Conditions treated at Practices/Businesses

| Business by County with Reference no. | Insomnia | Irritable Bowel Syndrome | Itching | Jet Lag | Joint Pain | Kidney Complaints | Lactose Intolerance | Laryngitis | Lethargy | Liver Disorders | Low Blood Pressure | Lung Problems | ME | Menopause | Migraine | Motion Sickness | Mouth Disorders | Mouth Ulcers | Multiple Sclerosis | Muscular Dystrophy | Musculo-skeletal | Nail Health | Nausea | Nerve Disorders | Nervous Disorders | Neuralgia | Obesity | Osteoporosis | Pain | Palpitations | Panic Attacks | Parkinson's Disease | Period Problems | Phobias | Piles | PMT | Pneumonia | Postural Problems | Pregnancy Help | Prostate Problems | Psoriasis | Raynaud's Disease | Recurrent Infections | Restless Legs | Rheumatoid Arthritis | Schizophrenia | Sciatica | Sexual Problems |
|---|---|---|---|---|---|---|---|---|---|---|---|---|---|---|---|---|---|---|---|---|---|---|---|---|---|---|---|---|---|---|---|---|---|---|---|---|---|---|---|---|---|---|---|---|---|---|---|---|
| NATURAL HEALTH SERVICE (HM14595) |●|●|●|●|●|●|●|●|●|●|●|●|●|●|●|●|●|●|●|●| |●|●|●|●|●|●|●|●|●| |●|●|●|●|●|●| |●|●|●|●|●|●|●|●|●|●|
| NATURES GATE (HM14688) | | | | | | | | | | | | | | | | | | | | | | | | | |●| | |●| | | | | | | | | |●| | | | | |●| |●| |
| NEW MILTON CHIROPRACTIC CLINIC (HM14825) | | | | |●| | | | | | | | | |●| | | | | | | | |●| |●| |●|●| | | | | | | | | | | | | | |●|●| |●| |
| NORMAN, J M (HM15004) | | | | | | | | | | | | | | | | | | | | | | | | | | | | |●| | | | | | |●| | | | | | | | | | | | |
| NORSWORTHY, CLAIRE (HM15017) | |●| | |●|●| | | | |●| |●|●|●| | | |●| | | |●| | | | | |●|●| | |●| | |●| | |●| | | | |●| | | | |
| PARCHMENT STREET CLINIC (HM15646) |●|●|●| |●|●| | |●|●|●| |●|●|●| | |●|●| | | |●|●|●|●|●| |●|●| | |●|●| |●| | |●|●|●|●| |●|●| |●|●|
| PHOENIX HOLISTIC CENTRE (HM16156) | |●| | | | | | | | | | | |●| | | | | | | | | | |●| | |●|●| | | | | | | | | | | | | | | | | | |●|
| PHYSIOTHERAPY CENTRE (HM16233) | | | | |●| | | | | | | | | | | | | |●| | | | | | | | | |●| | | | | | | | | | | | | | | | | | | |
| REIKI NATURAL HEALING CENTRE (HM17142) |●|●|●|●|●|●|●|●|●|●|●|●|●|●|●|●|●|●|●|●| |●|●|●|●|●|●|●|●|●| |●|●|●|●|●|●| |●|●|●|●|●|●|●|●|●|●|
| RICHARDS, CLAIRE (HM17249) |●| | | |●| | | | | | | | |●|●| | | | | | | | | |●| | | |●| | | |●| | |●| | | | | | | | | | | | |
| RINGWOOD CHIROPRACTIC CLINIC (HM17355) | |●| | |●| | | | | | | |●| |●| | | | | | | | |●|●| | | |●| | | | | | | | | | | | | | | | | |●| |
| RINGWOOD NATURAL HEALTH CLINIC (HM17357) |●|●|●| |●|●| | |●|●|●|●| |●|●| | | | | | | | | | | |●| |●|●| | |●| | |●| | | | |●| |●| | | |●| |
| RINGWOOD PHYSIOTHERAPY CENTRE (HM17358) | | | | |●| | | | | | | | | | | | | | | | | | | | | | | | | | | | | | | | | | | | | | | | | | | |
| S E E D INSTITUTE (HM17805) |●|●| | | | | | | | | | | |●|●| | | | | | | | | | | | | | | | | | | | | | | | | | | | | | | | | |
| SCANDINAVIAN CHIROPRACTIC CTRE (HM18002) | |●| | |●| | | | | | | |●| |●| | | | | | | | |●|●| | | |●| | | | | | | | | | | | | | | | | |●| |
| SIMCOE CLINIC (HM18549) |●|●| | |●|●| | | |●|●| |●|●|●| | | |●| | |●| |●| |●|●|●|●|●| | |●| |●|●| | |●|●|●|●|●|●|●| |●|●|
| SIMMONDS, J (HM18555) |●|●| | |●|●| |●|●|●|●|●|●|●|●| |●| |●| | | | |●|●|●| |●|●| | |●| | | |●| | | |●|●| |●| |●| | | |
| SOLENT CHIROPRACTIC CLINIC (HM18871) | |●| | |●| | | | | | | | | | | | | | | | | | | | | | |●|●| | | | | | | | | | | | | | | | | |●| |
| SOUTHGATE NAT THERAPY CLINIC (HM18937) |●|●| | |●|●| |●|●| |●|●|●|●|●|●| | |●| | | |●| | | | |●|●|●| |●|●|●|●|●|●| |●|●|●|●|●|●|●| |●| |
| SOUTHSEA CENTRE FOR COMP MED (HM18943) |●|●|●|●|●|●|●|●|●|●|●|●|●|●|●|●| |●|●| | | |●|●|●|●|●|●|●|●| |●|●|●|●|●|●| |●|●|●|●|●|●|●|●|●|●|
| THOMA, ANDREW (HM19923) | | | | |●| | | | | | | | | | | | | | | | | | | | | | | |●| | | | | | | | | | | | | | | | | |●| |
| TURNER, CATHY (HM20420) |●|●|●|●|●|●|●|●|●|●|●|●|●|●|●|●|●|●|●|●| |●|●|●|●|●|●|●|●|●| |●|●|●|●|●|●| |●|●|●|●|●|●|●|●|●|●|
| TWESLEDOWN PHYSIOTHERAPY (HM20449) | | | | |●| | | | | | | | | | | | | |●| | | | | | | | | | | | | | | | | | | | | | | | | | | | | |
| WELL HOUSE HOLISTIC HLTH CTRE (HM21138) |●|●|●|●|●|●|●|●|●|●|●|●|●|●|●|●|●|●|●|●| |●|●|●|●|●|●|●|●|●| |●|●|●|●|●|●| |●|●|●|●|●|●|●|●|●|●|
| WINCHESTER CHIROPRACTIC CLINIC (HM21691) | | | | |●| | | | | | | | | |●| | | | | |●| | | | |●| |●|●| | | | | | | | | | | |●| | | | | |●| |
| WINCHESTER HOM PRACTICE (HM21692) |●|●|●|●|●|●|●|●|●|●|●|●|●|●|●|●|●|●|●| | |●|●|●|●|●|●|●|●|●| |●|●|●|●|●|●| |●|●|●|●|●|●|●| |●|●|
| **HEREFORDSHIRE** | | | | | | | | | | | | | | | | | | | | | | | | | | | | | | | | | | | | | | | | | | | | | | | | |
| BEAUTY IS YOURS (HM01999) | |●| |●|●| | | | | |●| |●|●|●| | | |●| | | | | | | | | |●| | | | | | | | | | |●| | | |●|●| | | |
| BROADVIEW NATURAL HEALTH CTRE (HM03119) |●|●| | | | | | | | | | | | |●| | | | | |●| |●| | | | | |●| | | |●| | |●| | | | | | | | | | | | |
| HEREFORD CENTRE (HM09677) |●|●|●|●|●|●|●|●|●|●|●|●|●|●|●|●|●|●|●|●|●|●|●|●|●|●|●|●|●|●|●|●|●|●|●|●|●|●|●|●|●|●|●|●|●|●|●|●|
| HEREFORD CHIROPRACTIC CLINIC (HM09678) | | | | |●| | | | | | | |●| | | | | | | | | | |●| | | |●|●| | | | | | | | | | | | | | | | | |●| |
| JONES, KEVIN D G (HM11165) | | | | |●| | | | | | | | | | | | | |●| | | | |●| | | | |●| | | | | | | | | |●| | | | | | | |●| |
| LEDBURY NATURAL HEALTH CENTRE (HM12122) |●|●|●|●|●|●|●|●|●|●|●|●|●|●|●|●|●|●|●|●| |●|●|●|●|●|●|●|●|●| |●|●|●|●|●|●| |●|●|●|●|●|●|●|●|●|●|
| LEOMINSTER OSTEOPATHS (HM12221) |●|●| |●|●| | | |●| | | |●|●|●| | | |●| | | | | | |●| |●|●|●| |●|●| | |●| | |●|●| |●|●| |●| |●|●|

# I - S Conditions treated at Practices/Businesses

Business by County with Reference no.

| Business | Insomnia | Irritable Bowel Syndrome | Itching | Jet Lag | Joint Pain | Kidney Complaints | Lactose Intolerance | Laryngitis | Lethargy | Liver Disorders | Low Blood Pressure | Lung Problems | ME | Menopause | Migraine | Motion Sickness |
|---|---|---|---|---|---|---|---|---|---|---|---|---|---|---|---|---|
| TEDDER, CATHRINE (HM19814) | | | | | | | | | | | | | | | | |
| WILLCOCKS, T & S (HM21519) | | | | | ● | | | | | | | | ● | | ● | |
| **HERTFORDSHIRE** | | | | | | | | | | | | | | | | |
| ALLEN, JULIE & LEN (HM00613) | ● | ● | ● | | ● | ● | ● | ● | ● | ● | ● | ● | ● | ● | ● | ● |
| ALTERNATIVE CHOICES (HM00697) | ● | ● | ● | | | | | | | ● | | ● | ● | ● | ● | ● |
| ARNOLD, PETER & JACKIE (HM01036) | ● | ● | | | ● | | | | ● | | | | ● | ● | ● | |
| AROMA ROOM (HM01055) | | | | | | | | | | | | | | | | |
| AROMATHERAPY BY ANTONIO (HM01095) | ● | | | | | | | | | | | | | | | |
| ASHDOWN CLINIC (HM01205) | ● | ● | ● | | ● | | | | ● | | | | ● | ● | ● | |
| ASHWELL, MELBOURN & BALDOCK (HM01246) | | | | | ● | | | | | | | | ● | | | |
| ASSOCIATES HEAD & SHORT (HM01276) | | | | | | | | | | | | | | | | |
| ASSOCIATES HEAD & SHORT (HM01277) | | | | | | | | | | | | | | | | |
| ASSOCIATION OF STRESS MNGMT (HM01293) | | | | | ● | | | | ● | | | | | | ● | |
| AUTOGENIC TRAINING (HM01372) | ● | ● | ● | ● | ● | ● | | | | | ● | | ● | ● | ● | ● |
| BARNET CHIROPODY SURGERY (HM01757) | | | | | | | | | | | | | | | | |
| BASSETT CLINIC (HM01853) | | | | | ● | | | | | | | | | | ● | |
| BEAUCHAMP BAGENAL (HM01983) | ● | | | | ● | | | | | | | ● | | | ● | |
| BERKHAMSTED PHYSIO CLINIC (HM02193) | | | | | ● | | | | | | | | | | | |
| BETA HEALTH CLINIC (HM02229) | | | | | ● | | | | | | | | | ● | ● | |
| BIRTHWORKS (HM02399) | | | | | | | | | | | | | | | | |
| BISHOP'S STORTFORD HOMEOPATHIC (HM02416) | ● | | | ● | ● | | | | | | | | | ● | ● | |
| BODY MECHANICS THERAPY CLINIC (HM02598) | ● | | | | ● | | | | | | | | | | ● | |
| BOREHAMWOOD CHIRO CLINIC (HM02717) | | ● | | | ● | | | | | | | | ● | | | |
| BRIGGS-WILSON, A (HM03037) | | ● | | | | | | | | | | | ● | | | |
| BRIND, KEVIN (HM03053) | | | | | ● | | | | | | | | | | | |
| BURYHILL PHYSIOTHERAPY (HM03456) | | | | | ● | | | | | | | | | | | |
| BUTTERFIELD, ROBIN (HM03496) | | | | | ● | | | | | | | | ● | | ● | |
| CANNON, VALERIE (HM03635) | ● | ● | | | | ● | | | | | ● | | ● | ● | ● | |
| CHAUHAN, D K (HM04065) | ● | ● | ● | ● | ● | ● | ● | ● | ● | ● | ● | ● | ● | ● | ● | ● |
| CLARE JAMES HEALTH FOODS (HM04532) | | ● | | | | | | | | | | | | | | |
| CLNC OF ACU & CHINESE HRBL MED (HM04727) | | ● | | | ● | | | | ● | | | | ● | ● | ● | |
| CONISTON PHYSIOTHERAPY CLINIC (HM04980) | | | | | ● | | | | | | | | ● | | ● | ● |
| COOPER, FELICITY (HM05101) | | | | | | | | | | | | | | | | |
| DAVID HERBERT REFLEXOLOGY (HM05774) | ● | ● | | | ● | ● | | | | ● | ● | ● | ● | ● | ● | |

| Business | Mouth Disorders | Mouth Ulcers | Multiple Sclerosis | Muscular Dystrophy | Musculo-skeletal | Nail Health | Nausea | Nerve Disorders | Nervous Disorders | Neuralgia | Obesity | Osteoporosis | Pain | Palpitations | Panic Attacks | Parkinson's Disease |
|---|---|---|---|---|---|---|---|---|---|---|---|---|---|---|---|---|
| TEDDER, CATHRINE (HM19814) | | | | | | ● | | | | | | | | | | |
| WILLCOCKS, T & S (HM21519) | | | | | | | | | | | | | ● | | | |
| **HERTFORDSHIRE** | | | | | | | | | | | | | | | | |
| ALLEN, JULIE & LEN (HM00613) | ● | ● | | | | | ● | ● | ● | ● | ● | ● | ● | ● | | ● |
| ALTERNATIVE CHOICES (HM00697) | | | | | | | | | | | | | | | | |
| ARNOLD, PETER & JACKIE (HM01036) | | | | | | | | | | ● | | ● | ● | | | |
| AROMA ROOM (HM01055) | | | | ● | | | | | | | | | | | | |
| AROMATHERAPY BY ANTONIO (HM01095) | | | | | | | | | | | | | | | | |
| ASHDOWN CLINIC (HM01205) | | | | | | ● | | ● | | ● | ● | ● | ● | | | |
| ASHWELL, MELBOURN & BALDOCK (HM01246) | | | ● | | | | | ● | | ● | | ● | ● | | | |
| ASSOCIATES HEAD & SHORT (HM01276) | | | | | | ● | | | | | | | | | | |
| ASSOCIATES HEAD & SHORT (HM01277) | | | | | | ● | | | | | | | | | | |
| ASSOCIATION OF STRESS MNGMT (HM01293) | | | | | | | | | ● | | | | ● | ● | | |
| AUTOGENIC TRAINING (HM01372) | | | | | | | ● | | ● | | | | ● | ● | | |
| BARNET CHIROPODY SURGERY (HM01757) | | | | | | ● | | | | | | | | | | |
| BASSETT CLINIC (HM01853) | | | | | | | | | | ● | | | ● | | | |
| BEAUCHAMP BAGENAL (HM01983) | | | | | | | | ● | ● | | | | ● | | | |
| BERKHAMSTED PHYSIO CLINIC (HM02193) | | | ● | | | | | | | | | | ● | | | |
| BETA HEALTH CLINIC (HM02229) | | | | | | | ● | | | | | | ● | | | |
| BIRTHWORKS (HM02399) | | | | | | | | | | | | | | | | |
| BISHOP'S STORTFORD HOMEOPATHIC (HM02416) | | | | | | | | | | | ● | | | | | |
| BODY MECHANICS THERAPY CLINIC (HM02598) | | | | ● | | | | | | | | | | | | |
| BOREHAMWOOD CHIRO CLINIC (HM02717) | | | | | | | | ● | ● | ● | ● | ● | ● | | | |
| BRIGGS-WILSON, A (HM03037) | | | | | | | | | | | | | | | | |
| BRIND, KEVIN (HM03053) | | | | | ● | | | | | | | | | | | |
| BURYHILL PHYSIOTHERAPY (HM03456) | | | ● | | | | | | | | | | ● | | | |
| BUTTERFIELD, ROBIN (HM03496) | | | ● | ● | | | | | | | | ● | ● | | | |
| CANNON, VALERIE (HM03635) | | | ● | | | | | | | | | | ● | ● | | |
| CHAUHAN, D K (HM04065) | ● | ● | ● | ● | | ● | ● | ● | ● | ● | ● | ● | ● | ● | | ● |
| CLARE JAMES HEALTH FOODS (HM04532) | | | | | | | | | | | | | | | | |
| CLNC OF ACU & CHINESE HRBL MED (HM04727) | | | ● | | | | | | | | | ● | ● | ● | | |
| CONISTON PHYSIOTHERAPY CLINIC (HM04980) | | | | | | | | ● | | ● | | | ● | | | |
| COOPER, FELICITY (HM05101) | | | | | | | | | | | | | | | | |
| DAVID HERBERT REFLEXOLOGY (HM05774) | | | | | | | | ● | | | | | | | | ● |

| Business | Period Problems | Phobias | Piles | PMT | Pneumonia | Postural Problems | Pregnancy Help | Prostate Problems | Psoriasis | Raynaud's Disease | Recurrent Infections | Restless Legs | Rheumatoid Arthritis | Schizophrenia | Sciatica | Sexual Problems |
|---|---|---|---|---|---|---|---|---|---|---|---|---|---|---|---|---|
| TEDDER, CATHRINE (HM19814) | | | | | | | | | | | | | | | | |
| WILLCOCKS, T & S (HM21519) | | | | | | | | | | | | ● | | | ● | |
| **HERTFORDSHIRE** | | | | | | | | | | | | | | | | |
| ALLEN, JULIE & LEN (HM00613) | ● | ● | ● | ● | | | | ● | ● | ● | ● | ● | ● | | ● | ● |
| ALTERNATIVE CHOICES (HM00697) | | | | ● | | | ● | | | | | | | | | |
| ARNOLD, PETER & JACKIE (HM01036) | ● | | | ● | | | | | | | | | | | ● | |
| AROMA ROOM (HM01055) | | | | | | | | | | | | | | | | |
| AROMATHERAPY BY ANTONIO (HM01095) | | | | | | | | | | | | | | | | |
| ASHDOWN CLINIC (HM01205) | ● | ● | | ● | | | | | ● | ● | ● | ● | ● | | ● | |
| ASHWELL, MELBOURN & BALDOCK (HM01246) | | | | | | | | | | ● | | | ● | | ● | |
| ASSOCIATES HEAD & SHORT (HM01276) | | | | | | | | | | | | | ● | | | |
| ASSOCIATES HEAD & SHORT (HM01277) | | | | | | | | | | | | | ● | | | |
| ASSOCIATION OF STRESS MNGMT (HM01293) | ● | ● | | ● | | | | | ● | | | | ● | | | ● |
| AUTOGENIC TRAINING (HM01372) | ● | ● | ● | ● | | | ● | | ● | ● | ● | ● | | | | |
| BARNET CHIROPODY SURGERY (HM01757) | | | | | | | | | | | | | | | | |
| BASSETT CLINIC (HM01853) | | | | | | | | | | | | | | | ● | |
| BEAUCHAMP BAGENAL (HM01983) | | | | | | | | | | ● | | ● | ● | | ● | |
| BERKHAMSTED PHYSIO CLINIC (HM02193) | | | | | | | | | | | | | | | | |
| BETA HEALTH CLINIC (HM02229) | ● | | | ● | | | | | | | | | | | ● | |
| BIRTHWORKS (HM02399) | | | | | | | ● | | | | | | | | | |
| BISHOP'S STORTFORD HOMEOPATHIC (HM02416) | | ● | ● | ● | | | | | ● | | ● | | ● | | | |
| BODY MECHANICS THERAPY CLINIC (HM02598) | | | | | | | | | | | | | | | ● | |
| BOREHAMWOOD CHIRO CLINIC (HM02717) | ● | | | ● | | | ● | | | | | | | | ● | |
| BRIGGS-WILSON, A (HM03037) | | | | | | | | | | | | | | | | |
| BRIND, KEVIN (HM03053) | | | | | | | | | | | | | | | | |
| BURYHILL PHYSIOTHERAPY (HM03456) | | | | | | | | | | | | | | | | |
| BUTTERFIELD, ROBIN (HM03496) | | | | | | | | ● | ● | ● | | | | | | ● |
| CANNON, VALERIE (HM03635) | ● | | | ● | | | ● | | | | | | | | ● | |
| CHAUHAN, D K (HM04065) | ● | ● | ● | ● | ● | | ● | ● | ● | ● | ● | ● | ● | ● | ● | ● |
| CLARE JAMES HEALTH FOODS (HM04532) | | | | | | | | | | | | | | | | |
| CLNC OF ACU & CHINESE HRBL MED (HM04727) | | | ● | ● | | | | ● | ● | ● | | | ● | | ● | ● |
| CONISTON PHYSIOTHERAPY CLINIC (HM04980) | | | | | | | | | | ● | | ● | ● | | ● | |
| COOPER, FELICITY (HM05101) | | | | | | | | | | | | | ● | | | |
| DAVID HERBERT REFLEXOLOGY (HM05774) | ● | | | ● | | | | ● | ● | | | ● | | | ● | |

# I - S Conditions treated at Practices/Businesses

| Business by County with Reference no. | Insomnia | Irritable Bowel Syndrome | Itching | Jet Lag | Joint Pain | Kidney Complaints | Lactose Intolerance | Laryngitis | Lethargy | Liver Disorders | Low Blood Pressure | Lung Problems | ME | Menopause | Migraine | Motion Sickness |
|---|---|---|---|---|---|---|---|---|---|---|---|---|---|---|---|---|
| DEVINE, MARY (HM06036) | | | | | | | | | | | | | | | | |
| DOYLE, AUDREY (HM06257) | ● | ● | | ● | ● | ● | | ● | ● | ● | ● | ● | ● | ● | ● | |
| DUDGEON, DELIA (HM06353) | ● | ● | | | | | | | | | | | | | | |
| EVANS, HELEN (HM06975) | | | | | | | | | | | | | | | | |
| EVANS, HELEN (HM06976) | | | | | | | | | | | | | | | | |
| FEET RETREAT () | | | | | ● | | | | | | | | | | ● | |
| FREEMAN, FRANCES (HM07721) | ● | ● | ● | ● | ● | ● | ● | ● | ● | ● | ● | ● | ● | ● | ● | ● |
| GEMS (HM07969) | | | | | | | | | ● | | | | | | | |
| GENTLE FEET (HM07977) | ● | ● | | ● | ● | ● | | ● | ● | ● | ● | ● | ● | ● | ● | |
| GEOFF THIEL, COUNS & PSYCHO (HM07986) | | | | | | | | | | | | | | | | |
| GILLING, LINDA (HM08095) | ● | ● | ● | ● | ● | ● | | ● | ● | ● | ● | ● | ● | ● | ● | ● |
| GOODMAN, HENRY (HM08258) | ● | ● | | | | | | | | | | | | | | |
| GRAHAM & KERSTIN ELLIOTT (HM08336) | | ● | | | ● | | | | | | | | ● | | ● | |
| GROUNDS, L (HM08599) | ● | ● | | ● | ● | ● | | | ● | ● | ● | | | ● | | ● |
| HALAHAN, ELISABETH (HM08722) | ● | ● | ● | | ● | ● | ● | ● | ● | ● | ● | ● | ● | ● | ● | ● |
| HAMILTON-PETERS, R & J A (HM08849) | | ● | ● | | ● | | | | | | | | | | | |
| HARPENDEM OSTEOPATHIC PRACTICE (HM09035) | | | | | | | | | | | | | | | | |
| HARPENDEN CHIROPRACTIC CLINIC (HM09036) | | | | | ● | | | | | | | | | | | |
| HATHAWAY, ELIZABETH (HM09196) | | | | | | | | | | | | | ● | | | |
| HEALES CHIROPRACTIC CLINIC (HM09322) | | ● | | | ● | | | | | | | | | | | |
| HEALTHY AND WISE (HM09425) | ● | ● | ● | ● | ● | | | | | | | | ● | ● | ● | ● |
| HERTFORD NATURAL THERAPY CTRE (HM09690) | ● | | | | ● | | | | | | | | | ● | ● | |
| HODSDON, L M (HM09893) | | | | | | | | | | | | | | | | |
| HOLLENBERY, S (HM10019) | | | | | ● | | | | | | | | | | | |
| JACKSON, BARBARA (HM10830) | | | | | | | | | | | | | | | | |
| JENNIFER SAJIR PAED PHYSIO (HM11005) | | | | | | | | | | | | | | | | |
| JOE MILLER SPORTS INJURY (HM11045) | | | | | ● | | | | | | | | | | | |
| KEW, DEREK (HM11576) | ● | ● | | | | | | | | | | | ● | | | |
| KNEBWORTH PHYSIO CLINIC (HM11742) | | | | | ● | | | | | | | | | | | |
| LETCHWORTH-PHYSIOTHERAPY (HM12248) | | | | | ● | | | | | | | | | | | |
| LIFELINES (HM12355) | ● | ● | | | | | | | | | | | | ● | ● | |
| LINDY, D (HM12426) | | | | | ● | | | | | | | | | | | |
| MASON, L C (HM13247) | ● | ● | ● | | | | | | ● | | | | | | ● | ● |
| MAUREEN PRIDDLE (HM13328) | ● | ● | | | | | | | | | | | ● | ● | ● | |

| Business by County with Reference no. | Mouth Disorders | Mouth Ulcers | Multiple Sclerosis | Muscular Dystrophy | Musculo-skeletal | Nail Health | Nausea | Nerve Disorders | Nervous Disorders | Neuralgia | Obesity | Osteoporosis | Pain | Palpitations | Panic Attacks |
|---|---|---|---|---|---|---|---|---|---|---|---|---|---|---|---|
| DEVINE, MARY (HM06036) | | | | | | | | | | | | | ● | | |
| DOYLE, AUDREY (HM06257) | | | ● | ● | | ● | ● | ● | ● | ● | | ● | ● | ● | |
| DUDGEON, DELIA (HM06353) | | | | | | | | | | | | | | | |
| EVANS, HELEN (HM06975) | | | | | | ● | | | | | | | | | |
| EVANS, HELEN (HM06976) | | | | | | ● | | | | | | | | | |
| FEET RETREAT () | | | | | | | ● | | | | | | | | |
| FREEMAN, FRANCES (HM07721) | ● | ● | ● | ● | | ● | ● | ● | ● | ● | | ● | ● | ● | |
| GEMS (HM07969) | | | | | | | | ● | ● | | | | ● | | |
| GENTLE FEET (HM07977) | | | ● | ● | | | ● | ● | ● | ● | | ● | ● | ● | |
| GEOFF THIEL, COUNS & PSYCHO (HM07986) | | | | | | | | | ● | | | | | | |
| GILLING, LINDA (HM08095) | ● | ● | ● | ● | | ● | ● | ● | ● | ● | ● | ● | ● | ● | |
| GOODMAN, HENRY (HM08258) | | | | | | | | | ● | | | | | | |
| GRAHAM & KERSTIN ELLIOTT (HM08336) | | | | | | | | ● | ● | | | ● | ● | | |
| GROUNDS, L (HM08599) | ● | ● | ● | | | | ● | ● | ● | ● | | ● | | | |
| HALAHAN, ELISABETH (HM08722) | ● | ● | ● | | | ● | ● | ● | ● | ● | ● | ● | ● | ● | |
| HAMILTON-PETERS, R & J A (HM08849) | | | | | | | | | ● | | ● | | ● | | |
| HARPENDEM OSTEOPATHIC PRACTICE (HM09035) | | | | | | | | | | | | | ● | | |
| HARPENDEN CHIROPRACTIC CLINIC (HM09036) | | | | | | | | | | | | | ● | | |
| HATHAWAY, ELIZABETH (HM09196) | | | | | | | | ● | | | | ● | ● | | |
| HEALES CHIROPRACTIC CLINIC (HM09322) | | | | | | | | ● | | | | | ● | | |
| HEALTHY AND WISE (HM09425) | | | | | | | ● | ● | | | | | | | |
| HERTFORD NATURAL THERAPY CTRE (HM09690) | | | | | | | ● | | | | | | ● | | |
| HODSDON, L M (HM09893) | | | | | | ● | | | | | | | | | |
| HOLLENBERY, S (HM10019) | | | ● | | | | | | | | | | | | |
| JACKSON, BARBARA (HM10830) | | | | | | | | | | | | | | | |
| JENNIFER SAJIR PAED PHYSIO (HM11005) | | | | ● | | | | | | | | | | | |
| JOE MILLER SPORTS INJURY (HM11045) | | | | | | | | | | | | | ● | | |
| KEW, DEREK (HM11576) | | | | | | | ● | | ● | | ● | | ● | | |
| KNEBWORTH PHYSIO CLINIC (HM11742) | | | ● | | | | | ● | ● | | | ● | ● | | |
| LETCHWORTH-PHYSIOTHERAPY (HM12248) | | | ● | | | | | | | | | | ● | | |
| LIFELINES (HM12355) | | | | | | | | | | | | | ● | | |
| LINDY, D (HM12426) | | | | | | | | | | | | | ● | | |
| MASON, L C (HM13247) | | | | | | | ● | | ● | | ● | | | ● | |
| MAUREEN PRIDDLE (HM13328) | | | | | | | | | | | | | ● | | |

| Business by County with Reference no. | Parkinson's Disease | Period Problems | Phobias | Piles | PMT | Pneumonia | Postural Problems | Pregnancy Help | Prostate Problems | Psoriasis | Raynaud's Disease | Recurrent Infections | Restless Legs | Rheumatoid Arthritis | Schizophrenia | Sciatica | Sexual Problems |
|---|---|---|---|---|---|---|---|---|---|---|---|---|---|---|---|---|---|
| DEVINE, MARY (HM06036) | | | | | | | | | | | | | | | | | |
| DOYLE, AUDREY (HM06257) | ● | ● | ● | ● | ● | | | ● | ● | | | | ● | ● | | ● | |
| DUDGEON, DELIA (HM06353) | | ● | | | ● | | | | ● | | | | | | | ● | |
| EVANS, HELEN (HM06975) | | | | | | | | | | | | | | | | | |
| EVANS, HELEN (HM06976) | | | | | | | | | | | | | | | | | |
| FEET RETREAT () | | ● | | | | | | ● | | | | | | | | | |
| FREEMAN, FRANCES (HM07721) | ● | ● | ● | ● | ● | ● | | ● | ● | ● | ● | ● | ● | ● | ● | ● | ● |
| GEMS (HM07969) | | | ● | | | | | | | | | | | | | | |
| GENTLE FEET (HM07977) | ● | ● | ● | ● | ● | | | ● | ● | | | | ● | ● | | ● | |
| GEOFF THIEL, COUNS & PSYCHO (HM07986) | | | | | | | | | | | | | | | | | ● |
| GILLING, LINDA (HM08095) | ● | ● | | ● | ● | ● | | ● | ● | ● | ● | ● | ● | ● | | ● | |
| GOODMAN, HENRY (HM08258) | | | ● | | | | | | | | | | | | | | ● |
| GRAHAM & KERSTIN ELLIOTT (HM08336) | | | | | | | | | | | | | | | | ● | |
| GROUNDS, L (HM08599) | | | ● | | | | | | ● | | ● | | ● | ● | | | |
| HALAHAN, ELISABETH (HM08722) | | ● | ● | ● | ● | ● | | ● | ● | ● | ● | ● | ● | ● | | ● | ● |
| HAMILTON-PETERS, R & J A (HM08849) | | | ● | | ● | | | | | ● | | | | | | | ● |
| HARPENDEM OSTEOPATHIC PRACTICE (HM09035) | | | | | | | | | | | | | | | | ● | |
| HARPENDEN CHIROPRACTIC CLINIC (HM09036) | | | | | | | | | | | | | | | | | |
| HATHAWAY, ELIZABETH (HM09196) | | | | | | | | | | | | | | ● | | ● | |
| HEALES CHIROPRACTIC CLINIC (HM09322) | | | | | | | | | | | | | | | | ● | |
| HEALTHY AND WISE (HM09425) | | | ● | ● | ● | | | ● | ● | ● | | ● | | ● | | ● | |
| HERTFORD NATURAL THERAPY CTRE (HM09690) | | ● | ● | | ● | | | | | ● | | | | | | ● | |
| HODSDON, L M (HM09893) | | | | | | | | | | | | | | | | | |
| HOLLENBERY, S (HM10019) | | | | | | | | | | | | | | | | | |
| JACKSON, BARBARA (HM10830) | | | | | ● | | | | | | | | | | | | |
| JENNIFER SAJIR PAED PHYSIO (HM11005) | | | | | | | | | | | | | | | | | |
| JOE MILLER SPORTS INJURY (HM11045) | | | | | | | | | | | | | | | | ● | |
| KEW, DEREK (HM11576) | | | ● | | ● | | | | | ● | ● | | | | | | |
| KNEBWORTH PHYSIO CLINIC (HM11742) | ● | | | | | | | | | | | | | ● | | ● | |
| LETCHWORTH-PHYSIOTHERAPY (HM12248) | | | | | | | | | | | | | | | | | |
| LIFELINES (HM12355) | | ● | ● | | ● | | | | | | | | | | | | |
| LINDY, D (HM12426) | | | | | | | ● | | | | | | | | | | |
| MASON, L C (HM13247) | | ● | ● | | ● | | | | | ● | | | | | | | ● |
| MAUREEN PRIDDLE (HM13328) | | | | | ● | | | | | | | | | | | | |

# I - S Conditions treated at Practices/Businesses

| Business by County with Reference no. | Insomnia | Irritable Bowel Syndrome | Itching | Jet Lag | Joint Pain | Kidney Complaints | Lactose Intolerance | Laryngitis | Lethargy | Liver Disorders | Low Blood Pressure | Lung Problems | ME | Menopause | Migraine | Motion Sickness | Mouth Disorders | Mouth Ulcers | Multiple Sclerosis | Muscular Dystrophy | Musculo-skeletal | Nail Health | Nausea | Nerve Disorders | Nervous Disorders | Neuralgia | Obesity | Osteoporosis | Pain | Palpitations | Panic Attacks | Parkinson's Disease | Period Problems | Phobias | Piles | PMT | Pneumonia | Postural Problems | Pregnancy Help | Prostate Problems | Psoriasis | Raynaud's Disease | Recurrent Infections | Restless Legs | Rheumatoid Arthritis | Schizophrenia | Sciatica | Sexual Problems |
|---|---|---|---|---|---|---|---|---|---|---|---|---|---|---|---|---|---|---|---|---|---|---|---|---|---|---|---|---|---|---|---|---|---|---|---|---|---|---|---|---|---|---|---|---|---|---|---|---|
| MAYOR, DAVID F (HM13359) | ● | ● | ● |  | ● | ● |  |  | ● | ● | ● | ● | ● | ● | ● | ● |  |  |  |  |  |  | ● | ● | ● | ● |  |  | ● | ● |  |  | ● |  |  | ● |  |  | ● |  | ● | ● | ● | ● | ● | ● | ● |  |
| MCTIMONEY CHIROPRACTIC CLINIC (HM13612) |  |  |  |  |  |  |  |  |  |  |  |  |  |  |  |  |  |  |  |  |  |  |  |  |  |  |  |  | ● |  |  |  |  |  |  |  |  |  |  |  |  |  |  |  |  |  | ● |  |
| MELLERICK, N D (HM13708) |  |  |  |  | ● |  |  |  |  |  |  |  | ● |  |  |  |  |  |  |  |  |  |  | ● |  |  |  |  | ● |  |  |  |  |  |  |  |  | ● |  |  |  |  |  |  |  |  | ● |  |
| MIDAS TOUCH (HM13808) | ● | ● |  |  | ● |  |  |  | ● |  |  |  |  |  | ● |  |  |  | ● |  |  |  |  |  |  |  |  |  |  |  |  |  | ● |  |  | ● |  |  |  |  |  |  |  |  |  |  | ● |  |
| MID-HERTS ALEXANDER CENTRE (HM13827) | ● |  |  |  | ● |  |  |  |  |  |  | ● |  |  | ● |  |  |  |  |  |  |  |  | ● | ● |  |  |  | ● |  |  |  |  |  |  |  |  |  |  |  |  | ● |  | ● | ● |  | ● |  |
| NATURAL HEALTH CLINIC (HM14589) | ● |  |  |  | ● |  |  |  |  |  |  |  |  |  | ● |  |  |  |  |  |  |  |  |  |  |  |  |  | ● | ● |  |  | ● |  |  | ● |  |  |  |  |  |  |  |  |  |  | ● |  |
| NATURAL-BALANCE CO UK (HM14672) | ● | ● | ● |  |  |  |  |  |  | ● |  |  | ● | ● | ● | ● |  |  |  |  |  |  | ● | ● | ● | ● |  | ● |  |  |  |  | ● | ● | ● | ● |  |  | ● |  |  |  |  | ● |  |  | ● |  |
| O'HARA, JOHN (HM15246) |  |  |  |  | ● |  |  |  |  |  |  |  |  |  |  |  |  |  | ● |  |  |  |  | ● |  |  |  |  |  |  |  |  |  |  |  |  |  |  | ● |  |  |  |  |  | ● |  | ● |  |
| OPEN MINDS (HM15343) |  |  |  |  |  |  |  |  |  |  |  |  |  |  | ● |  |  |  |  |  |  |  |  |  |  |  |  |  |  |  |  |  |  |  |  |  |  |  |  |  |  |  |  |  |  |  |  |  |
| OSTEOPATHIC CLINIC (HM15459) | ● |  |  |  | ● |  |  |  |  |  |  |  |  |  | ● |  |  |  | ● |  |  |  |  |  |  | ● |  |  | ● |  |  |  |  |  |  | ● |  |  |  |  | ● | ● |  |  | ● |  | ● |  |
| OVERINGTON, KEL (HM15512) |  | ● |  |  |  | ● |  |  |  |  |  |  |  | ● |  |  |  |  | ● |  |  |  |  |  |  |  |  |  | ● | ● |  |  | ● | ● |  | ● |  |  |  |  |  |  |  |  |  |  | ● |  |
| PEEDLE, DAVID R (HM15938) |  |  |  |  |  |  |  |  |  |  |  |  |  |  |  |  |  |  |  |  |  | ● |  |  |  |  |  |  |  |  |  |  |  |  |  |  |  |  |  |  |  |  |  |  |  |  |  |  |
| PERRY, KAREN (HM16049) |  |  |  |  |  |  |  |  |  |  |  |  |  |  |  |  |  |  |  |  |  | ● |  |  |  |  |  |  |  |  |  |  |  |  |  |  |  |  |  |  |  |  |  |  |  |  |  |  |
| PERSONAL REFLECTIONS (HM16061) | ● | ● |  |  | ● | ● |  |  |  |  | ● |  | ● | ● | ● |  |  |  | ● | ● |  |  | ● |  |  |  |  |  | ● | ● |  |  | ● |  |  | ● |  |  | ● |  |  |  |  | ● |  |  | ● |  |
| PHYSIO & SPORTS INJURIES CLNC (HM16177) |  |  |  |  | ● |  |  |  |  |  |  |  |  |  | ● |  |  |  | ● | ● |  |  |  |  | ● |  |  |  | ● |  |  | ● |  |  |  |  |  |  |  |  |  |  |  | ● | ● |  | ● |  |
| PRIDDLE, PATRICK (HM16602) |  |  |  |  |  |  |  |  |  |  |  |  |  |  | ● |  |  |  |  |  |  |  |  |  |  |  |  |  |  |  |  |  |  | ● |  |  |  |  |  |  |  |  |  |  |  |  |  |  |
| PSYCHOTHERAPY (HM16726) | ● |  |  |  | ● |  |  |  |  |  |  |  | ● |  | ● |  |  |  |  |  |  |  |  | ● | ● |  | ● |  | ● |  |  |  |  |  |  |  |  |  |  |  |  |  |  |  |  |  |  |  |
| PURLYS (HM16769) |  | ● |  |  |  |  |  |  |  |  |  |  |  |  |  |  | ● | ● |  |  |  |  |  | ● |  |  |  |  | ● |  |  |  |  | ● |  |  |  |  |  |  |  |  |  |  |  |  |  |  |
| ROWLAND, JETHRO (HM17692) | ● | ● | ● | ● | ● | ● |  | ● |  | ● | ● | ● | ● | ● | ● | ● |  |  | ● |  |  |  | ● |  | ● | ● |  | ● | ● | ● |  | ● | ● | ● | ● | ● | ● |  | ● | ● | ● | ● | ● | ● | ● |  | ● | ● |
| S K REFLEXOLOGY (HM17811) |  | ● |  |  |  |  |  |  |  |  |  |  |  |  | ● |  |  |  |  |  |  |  |  |  |  |  |  |  |  |  |  |  |  | ● |  |  |  |  |  |  |  |  |  |  |  |  |  | ● |
| SHAW, CHRISTINE (HM18333) |  | ● |  |  | ● | ● |  |  | ● | ● | ● | ● | ● | ● | ● |  |  |  | ● |  |  |  |  | ● | ● | ● |  |  | ● |  |  |  | ● |  | ● | ● |  |  | ● | ● |  | ● |  | ● | ● |  | ● |  |
| SMITH, SUSAN (HM18813) | ● | ● |  |  |  |  |  |  |  |  |  |  | ● | ● | ● |  |  |  | ● |  |  |  |  |  |  |  |  |  | ● | ● |  |  | ● |  |  | ● |  |  | ● |  |  |  |  |  |  |  | ● |  |
| SOPWELL OSTEOPATHIC CLINIC (HM18894) |  | ● |  |  | ● |  |  |  |  |  |  |  |  |  | ● |  |  |  |  |  |  |  |  |  | ● |  |  |  | ● |  |  |  |  |  |  |  |  |  |  |  |  |  |  |  |  |  | ● |  |
| SOUTH, JO (HM18917) | ● | ● | ● | ● | ● | ● | ● | ● | ● | ● | ● | ● | ● | ● | ● | ● | ● | ● | ● | ● |  | ● | ● | ● | ● | ● | ● | ● | ● | ● |  | ● | ● | ● | ● | ● | ● |  | ● | ● | ● | ● | ● | ● | ● | ● | ● | ● |
| SPINOZA, DAVID (HM19019) |  |  |  |  | ● |  |  |  |  |  |  |  |  |  |  |  |  |  |  |  |  |  |  |  |  |  |  |  | ● |  |  |  |  |  |  |  |  |  |  |  |  |  |  |  |  |  |  |  |
| ST ALBANS CHIROPRACTIC CLINIC (HM19063) |  |  |  |  | ● |  |  |  |  |  |  |  | ● |  | ● |  |  |  |  |  |  |  |  | ● | ● | ● |  | ● | ● |  |  |  |  |  |  | ● |  |  |  |  |  |  |  |  |  |  | ● |  |
| STORT COUNS & PSYCHOTHERAPY (HM19351) |  | ● |  |  |  |  |  |  |  |  |  |  |  |  |  |  |  |  |  |  |  |  |  |  | ● |  |  |  |  |  |  |  |  | ● |  | ● |  |  |  |  |  |  |  |  |  |  |  |  |
| STORTFORD GRANGE PHYSIO CENTRE (HM19352) |  |  |  |  | ● |  |  |  |  |  |  |  |  |  |  |  |  |  | ● | ● |  |  |  |  |  |  |  |  | ● |  |  |  |  |  |  |  |  |  |  |  |  |  |  |  |  |  |  |  |
| SURVIVAL TRUST SURGERY (HM19526) | ● | ● | ● | ● | ● | ● | ● | ● | ● | ● | ● | ● | ● | ● | ● | ● | ● | ● | ● | ● |  | ● | ● | ● | ● | ● |  | ● | ● | ● |  | ● | ● | ● | ● | ● | ● |  | ● | ● | ● | ● | ● | ● | ● | ● | ● | ● |
| SWAN & SWAN (HM19572) |  |  |  |  |  |  |  |  |  |  |  |  |  |  |  |  |  |  |  |  |  | ● |  |  |  |  |  |  |  |  |  |  |  |  |  |  |  |  |  |  |  | ● |  | ● | ● |  | ● |  |
| THOMPSON, MARK () |  | ● |  |  | ● |  | ● |  | ● | ● | ● | ● | ● | ● | ● |  |  |  |  |  |  |  |  |  |  |  | ● | ● | ● | ● |  | ● |  |  |  | ● |  |  |  | ● |  |  |  | ● | ● |  | ● | ● |
| THOMPSON, MARK (HM19991) |  | ● |  |  | ● |  | ● |  | ● | ● | ● | ● | ● | ● | ● |  |  |  |  |  |  |  |  |  |  |  | ● | ● | ● | ● |  | ● |  |  |  | ● |  |  |  | ● |  |  |  | ● | ● |  | ● | ● |
| UNERMAN, EVE (HM20503) |  |  |  |  |  |  |  |  |  |  |  |  |  |  |  |  |  |  |  |  |  |  |  |  |  |  |  |  | ● |  |  |  | ● |  |  | ● |  |  | ● |  |  |  |  |  |  |  |  |  |
| WALKER, NEL (HM20791) |  |  |  |  |  |  |  |  |  |  |  |  |  |  |  |  |  |  |  |  |  |  |  |  |  |  |  |  | ● |  |  |  |  | ● |  |  |  |  |  |  |  |  |  |  |  |  |  | ● |

# I - S Conditions treated at Practices/Businesses

| Business by County with Reference no. | Insomnia | Irritable Bowel Syndrome | Itching | Jet Lag | Joint Pain | Kidney Complaints | Lactose Intolerance | Laryngitis | Lethargy | Liver Disorders | Low Blood Pressure | Lung Problems | ME | Menopause | Migraine | Motion Sickness | Mouth Disorders | Mouth Ulcers | Multiple Sclerosis | Muscular Dystrophy | Musculo-skeletal | Nail Health | Nausea | Nerve Disorders | Nervous Disorders | Neuralgia | Obesity | Osteoporosis | Pain | Palpitations | Panic Attacks | Parkinson's Disease | Period Problems | Phobias | Piles | PMT | Pneumonia | Postural Problems | Pregnancy Help | Prostate Problems | Psoriasis | Raynaud's Disease | Recurrent Infections | Restless Legs | Rheumatoid Arthritis | Schizophrenia | Sciatica | Sexual Problems |
|---|---|---|---|---|---|---|---|---|---|---|---|---|---|---|---|---|---|---|---|---|---|---|---|---|---|---|---|---|---|---|---|---|---|---|---|---|---|---|---|---|---|---|---|---|---|---|---|---|
| WALKER, RICHARD (HM20798) |●|●|●| |●| | | |●| | | | | |●| | | | | | | | | | | | | |●|●| | | |●| |●| | | | |●| | | |●| | |●|
| WATSON, KATHRYN (HM21015) |●|●|●|●|●|●| |●|●|●|●|●|●|●|●|●|●|●| | | | |●| |●| |●|●| |●| | |●| |●|●| | | |●|●|●|●|●|●| |●| |
| WELWYN CHIROPRACTIC CLINIC (HM21192) | |●| | |●| | | | | | | |●| |●| | | | | | | | |●|●| | | |●| | | | | | | | | | | | | | | | | |●| |
| WHITE, GRAHAM C (HM21355) |●|●|●|●|●|●|●|●|●|●|●|●|●|●|●|●|●|●|●|●| |●|●|●|●|●|●|●|●|●| |●|●|●|●|●|●| |●|●|●|●|●|●|●| |●|●|
| WOOD STREET CHIROPRACTIC CLNC (HM21780) | | | | |●| | | | | | | | | |●| | | | | | | | | | |●| | |●| | | | | | | | | | | | | | | | | |●| |
| WOOD STREET CLINIC (HM21781) | |●| | | | |●|●|●|●| |●|●|●|●| | | |●| | | |●| | | | | | | | | |●| | |●|●| | |●| | |●| | | | | |
| WORDSWORTH, LINDA (HM21890) |●|●| | |●| | | |●| |●| |●|●|●| | | |●| | | | | |●|●| | |●| | | |●| | |●| | |●| | | |●|●|●| |●| |
| WRIGHT, DOREEN (HM21931) |●|●|●|●|●|●|●|●|●|●|●|●|●|●|●|●|●|●|●|●| |●|●|●|●|●|●|●|●|●| |●|●|●|●|●|●| |●|●|●|●|●|●|●|●|●|●|
| WYE, DEBORAH (HM21969) | | | | | | | | | | | | | | | | | | | | | |●| | | | | | | | | | | | | | | | | | | | | | | | | | |
| WYNDHAM CLINIC (HM21977) | |●| | |●| |●| |●|●| | |●|●|●| | | |●| | | |●| | | | |●|●|●| | |●| |●|●| | | |●|●|●|●|●|●| |●| |
| **HUMBERSIDE** | | | | | | | | | | | | | | | | | | | | | | | | | | | | | | | | | | | | | | | | | | | | | | | | |
| BATH, ANN (HM01899) |●|●| | | | | | | | | | |●|●|●| | | | | | | | | | | | | |●| | | | | | |●| | | | | | | | | | | | |
| BRIGG CHIROPRACTIC CLINIC (HM03028) | |●| | |●| | | | | | | | | | | | | | | | | | |●| | | | |●| | | | | | | | | | | | | | | | | |●| |
| BRIGG SKIN SURGERY (HM03030) | | | | | | | | | | | | | | | | | | | | | | | | | | | | | | | | | | | | | | | | |●| | | | | | | |
| MESSINGHAM CHIROPODIST SURGERY (HM13761) | | | | | | | | | | | | | | | | | | | | | |●| | | | | | | | | | | | | | | | | | | | | | | | | | |
| PRIOSE COLES (HM16635) |●|●| | |●| |●| |●| | | |●|●|●| | | |●| | | | | |●|●| | | | | | |●| | |●| | | | |●|●| |●|●| | | |
| SCUNTHORPE CHIROPRACTIC CLINIC (HM18157) | | | | |●| | | | | | | | | | | | | | | | | | |●| |●| | |●| | | | | | | | | | | | | | | | | | |
| **HUMBERSIDE (NORTH)** | | | | | | | | | | | | | | | | | | | | | | | | | | | | | | | | | | | | | | | | | | | | | | | | |
| ACADEMY PHYSIOTHERAPY CLINIC (HM00149) | | | | |●| | | | | | | | | | | | | |●| | | | | | | | | | | | | | | | | | | | | | | | | | | | | |
| BEVERLEY CHIROPRACTIC CLINIC (HM02243) | | | | | | | | | | | | | | |●| | | | | | | | | | |●| | |●| | | |●| | | | | |●| | | | |●| | |●| |
| BRIDLINGTON CHIROPODY SURGERY (HM03018) | | | | | | | | | | | | | | | | | | | | | |●| | | | | | | | | | | | | | | | | | | | | | | | | | |
| DAMIAN P JOHNS (HM05704) | | | | | | | | | | | | | | | | | | | | | |●| | | | | | | | | | | | | | | | | | | | | | | | | | |
| GILBERDYKE SPORTS & INJURY (HM08054) | | | | |●| | | | | | | | | | | | | |●| | | | | | | | | | | | | | | | | | | | | | | | | | | | | |
| NATURAL THERAPIES (HM14629) |●|●|●|●|●|●| | |●|●| |●|●|●|●|●| | |●| | | |●|●| |●|●| |●| | | |●|●|●|●| | |●| |●|●| |●|●| |●| |
| NATURAL THERAPY CENTRE (HM14653) |●|●| | | | | | |●|●| | |●| |●| | | |●| | | | | |●|●|●| |●| | | | |●| |●| | |●| |●| | |●|●|●| |●|
| SAMANTHA WHITE AROMATICA (HM17877) |●|●| |●|●| | | | | | | | |●| | | |●| | | | | | |●| | | |●| | | |●| | |●| | |●| | | | |●| | | |●|
| **HUMBERSIDE (SOUTH)** | | | | | | | | | | | | | | | | | | | | | | | | | | | | | | | | | | | | | | | | | | | | | | | | |
| DAVIES, MICHAEL (HM05831) | | | | |●| | | | | | | | | | | | | | | | | | | | | | | |●| | | | | | | | | | | | | | | | | |●| |
| HARRISON-WILLIAMS (HM09113) | | | | | | | | | | | | | | | | | | | | | |●| | | | | | | | | | | | | | | | | | | | | | | | | | |
| HARRISON-WILLIAMS CHIROPODIST (HM09114) | | | | | | | | | | | | | | | | | | | | | |●| | | | | | | | | | | | | | | | | | | | | | | | | | |
| LOUISE HEALING CENTRE (HM12668) |●|●| | |●| | | |●| | | |●|●|●| | | |●| | | | |●|●| | | |●|●| |●| | | | | | | | | | | |●| | |●| |
| ROBINSON, KEITH (HM17488) | | | | | | | | | | | | | | | | | | | | | |●| | | | | | | | | | | | | | | | | | | | | | | | | | |
| SCARTHO OSTEOPATHIC PRACTICE (HM18007) | | | | |●| | | | | | | | | |●| | | | | | | | | | |●| | |●| | | | | | | | | | | | | | | |●| |●| |
| WALL, R A (HM20819) | | | | | | | | | | | | | | | | | | | | | |●| | | | | | |●| | | | | | | | | | | | | | | | | | | |

# I - S Conditions treated at Practices/Businesses

| Business by County with Reference no. | Insomnia | Irritable Bowel Syndrome | Itching | Jet Lag | Joint Pain | Kidney Complaints | Lactose Intolerance | Laryngitis | Lethargy | Liver Disorders | Low Blood Pressure | Lung Problems | ME | Menopause | Migraine | Motion Sickness | Mouth Disorders | Mouth Ulcers | Multiple Sclerosis | Muscular Dystrophy | Musculo-skeletal | Nail Health | Nausea | Nerve Disorders | Nervous Disorders | Neuralgia | Obesity | Osteoporosis | Pain | Palpitations | Panic Attacks | Parkinson's Disease | Period Problems | Phobias | Piles | PMT | Pneumonia | Postural Problems | Pregnancy Help | Prostate Problems | Psoriasis | Raynaud's Disease | Recurrent Infections | Restless Legs | Rheumatoid Arthritis | Schizophrenia | Sciatica | Sexual Problems |
|---|---|---|---|---|---|---|---|---|---|---|---|---|---|---|---|---|---|---|---|---|---|---|---|---|---|---|---|---|---|---|---|---|---|---|---|---|---|---|---|---|---|---|---|---|---|---|---|---|
| WEBB, C M (HM21057) | | | | | | | | | | | | | | | | | | | | | |●| | | | | | | | | | | | | | | | | | | | | | | | | | |
| ISLE OF WIGHT | | | | | | | | | | | | | | | | | | | | | | | | | | | | | | | | | | | | | | | | | | | | | | | | |
| CARISBROOKE HEALTH CENTRE (HM03687) | |●| | |●| | | | | | | | | | | | | | | | | | |●| | | | |●| | | | |●| | | | | |●| | | | | | | | | |
| GREENFIELD, BRIAN (HM08484) | | | | |●| | | | | |●| | | |●| | | | | | | | | | | | | |●| | | | | | | | | | | | | | | |●| | | |
| HOPE CLINIC (HM10134) |●|●|●|●|●|●|●|●|●|●|●|●|●|●|●|●|●|●|●|●| |●|●|●|●|●|●|●|●|●| |●|●|●|●|●|●| |●|●|●|●|●|●|●|●|●|●|
| HYPNOTHERAPY CONSULTANCY (HM10537) |●|●| | | | | | |●| | | |●| |●| | | | | | | | | |●| |●| |●| |●| |●|●| |●| | | | |●| | | | | | |●|
| SHEN CLINIC (HM18391) |●|●| | | | | | | | | | | | |●| | | | | | | | | | | |●| | | | | | |●| | | | | | | | | | | | | | |
| WRIGLEY, BARBARA (HM21956) |●|●| | | | | | | | | | | | |●| | | | | | | | | | | | | |●| | | | | | | | | | | | | | | | | | | |
| KENT | | | | | | | | | | | | | | | | | | | | | | | | | | | | | | | | | | | | | | | | | | | | | | | |
| ABBOTT, LISA (HM00098) | |●| | |●| | | | | | | | | |●| | | | | | | | | | | | | | | | | |●| | |●| | |●| | | |●| | | |●| |
| ABSOLUTE SOLUTIONS (HM00142) |●|●| |●| | | | |●| |●| |●| |●| | | | | | | | |●| | | | | | | | | |●| |●| | | | | | | | | | | | |
| ASHFORD CLINIC (HM01216) | | | | | | | | | | | | | | |●| | | | | | | | | | | | |●|●| | | |●| | |●| | |●| | | | | | | | | |
| ASHFORD OSTEOPATHIC CLINIC (HM01217) | | | | | | | | | | | | |●| |●| | | | |●| | | |●|●| | | |●| | | | | | | | | |●| | | | | |●| |●| |
| AYLESFORD MEDICAL CENTRE (HM01426) | | | | |●| | | | | | | | | |●| | | | | | | | | | | | | | | | | | | | | | | | | | | | | | |●| |
| AYLSHAM OSTEOPATHIC PRACTICE (HM01429) | | | | |●| | | | | | | |●| |●| | | | | | | | |●| |●| | |●| | | | | | | | | | | | |●| | | | |●| |
| BECKENHAM & BROMLEY (HM02017) | |●| | |●| | | | | | | |●| | | | | | | | | | |●| | | |●|●| | | | | | | | | | | | | | | | | |●| |
| BECKENHAM CHINESE MED CTRE (HM02019) | |●| | | | | | | | | | | | | | | | | | | | | | | | | | | | | | | | | | | | | | | | | | | | | |
| BENNETT, J P (HM02143) | | | | | | | | | | | | |●| | | | | | | | | | | | | | | | | | | | | | | | | | | | | | | | | | |
| BERGMANN, MARIA (DR) (HM02190) | | | | | | | | | | | | | | | | | | | | | | | | | | | | | | | | | | | | | | | |●| |●| | | |●| |
| BEXLEY OSTEOPATHIC CLINIC (HM02259) | |●| | | | | | | | | | |●| | | | | | | | | | |●| | | | |●| | | | | | | | |●| | | | | | | | |●| |
| BEXLEYHEATH NATURAL HEALTH (HM02262) |●|●|●|●|●|●|●|●|●|●|●|●|●|●|●|●|●|●|●|●| |●|●|●|●|●|●|●|●|●| |●|●|●|●|●|●| |●|●|●|●|●|●|●|●|●|●|
| BISHOP, SARAH (HM02411) | | | | |●| | | | | | | | | |●| | | | | | | | | | | | | |●| | | | | | | | | | | | | | | | | | | |
| BLACKFEN HYPNOTHERAPY (HM02442) |●|●| | | | | | | | |●| | |●| | | | | | | | | |●|●| |●| | | | | |●|●| |●| | | | |●| | | | | | |●|
| BLOSSOM AROMATHERAPY CENTRE (HM02521) |●|●| | | | | | | | | | | |●|●| | | | | | | | | | | | | | | | | | | |●| | | | | | | | | | | |
| BROMLEY CHIROPODY CENTRE (HM03142) | | | | | | | | | | | | | | | | | | | | | |●| | | | | | | | | | | | | | | | | | | | | | | | | |
| BROMLEY CHIROPRACTIC CLINIC (HM03143) | |●| | |●| | | | | | | |●| | | | | |●| | | | |●|●| |●|●|●| | | |●| | | | | | | | | | | | | |●| |
| BROMLEY OSTEOPATHIC CLINIC (HM03145) | |●| | |●| | | | | | | |●| | | | | | | | | | |●| | | |●|●| | | | | |●| |●| | | | | | | | |●| |
| CANTERBURY OSTEOPATHIC CLINIC (HM03641) |●|●| | |●| |●|●|●| |●| |●|●|●| | | |●| | | |●|●|●|●|●|●|●|●| | |●|●| |●|●| |●|●| | |●| |●| |●| |
| CARDWELL, MARTIN (HM03673) |●|●|●|●|●|●| |●|●|●|●|●|●|●|●|●| | |●|●| |●|●|●|●|●|●| |●|●| |●|●|●| |●|●| |●|●|●|●|●|●|●|●|●|●|
| CASTLE CLINIC (HM03830) |●|●|●|●|●|●|●|●|●|●|●|●|●|●|●|●|●|●|●|●| |●|●|●|●|●|●|●|●|●| |●|●|●|●|●|●| |●|●|●|●|●|●|●|●|●|●|
| CENTRE (HM03897) |●|●|●|●|●|●|●|●|●|●|●|●|●|●|●|●|●|●|●|●| |●|●|●|●|●|●|●|●|●| |●|●|●|●|●|●| |●|●|●|●|●|●|●|●|●|●|
| CHANDRA PDS (HM03982) |●| | | | | | | | | | | | | | | | | | | | | | | | | | | | | |●| | |●| | | | | | | | | | | | | | |
| CHANGE OF LIFE (HM03984) | | | | | | | | | | | | | | | | | | | | | | | | | | |●| | | | | | | | | | | | | |●| | | | | | | |
| CHINESE HERBAL MED & HLTH CARE (HM04200) | | | | | | | | | | | | | |●| | | | | | | | | | | | | | | | | | | | | | | | | | | | | | | | | | |

# I - S Conditions treated at Practices/Businesses

Business by County with Reference no.

| Business | Insomnia | Irritable Bowel Syndrome | Itching | Jet Lag | Joint Pain | Kidney Complaints | Lactose Intolerance | Laryngitis | Lethargy | Liver Disorders | Low Blood Pressure | Lung Problems | ME | Menopause | Migraine | Motion Sickness | Mouth Disorders | Mouth Ulcers | Multiple Sclerosis | Muscular Dystrophy | Musculo-skeletal | Nail Health | Nausea | Nerve Disorders | Nervous Disorders | Neuralgia | Obesity | Osteoporosis | Pain | Palpitations | Panic Attacks | Parkinson's Disease | Period Problems | Phobias | Piles | PMT | Pneumonia | Postural Problems | Pregnancy Help | Prostate Problems | Psoriasis | Raynaud's Disease | Recurrent Infections | Restless Legs | Rheumatoid Arthritis | Schizophrenia | Sciatica | Sexual Problems |
|---|---|---|---|---|---|---|---|---|---|---|---|---|---|---|---|---|---|---|---|---|---|---|---|---|---|---|---|---|---|---|---|---|---|---|---|---|---|---|---|---|---|---|---|---|---|---|---|---|
| CHINESE HERBAL MED ACU CTRE (HM04205) | ● | ● | | | | | | | | | | | ● | ● | | | | | ● | | | | | | | | | | | | | | | | | ● | | | | | | | | | | | | |
| CHIROPRACTIC PLUS (HM04402) | ● | ● | ● | ● | ● | ● | ● | ● | ● | ● | ● | ● | ● | ● | ● | ● | ● | ● | ● | ● | | ● | ● | ● | ● | ● | | ● | ● | ● | | | ● | ● | ● | ● | ● | | ● | ● | ● | ● | ● | ● | ● | | ● | ● |
| CHISLEHURST NATURAL HEALTH (HM04410) | ● | ● | ● | ● | ● | ● | ● | ● | ● | ● | ● | ● | ● | ● | ● | ● | ● | ● | ● | ● | | ● | ● | ● | ● | ● | ● | ● | ● | ● | | ● | ● | ● | ● | ● | ● | | ● | ● | ● | ● | ● | ● | ● | ● | ● | ● |
| CHISTLEHURST NATURAL HLTH CTRE (HM04411) | ● | ● | ● | ● | ● | ● | ● | ● | ● | ● | ● | ● | ● | ● | ● | ● | ● | ● | ● | ● | | ● | ● | ● | ● | ● | ● | ● | ● | ● | | ● | ● | ● | ● | ● | ● | | ● | ● | ● | ● | ● | ● | ● | ● | ● | ● |
| CHRISTINE CHINNERY COMP THER (HM04446) | ● | ● | ● | | ● | ● | | ● | ● | | ● | ● | ● | ● | ● | | | | | | | | ● | ● | ● | | ● | ● | ● | ● | | | ● | ● | ● | ● | ● | | ● | ● | ● | ● | ● | | ● | | ● | ● |
| CORRIGAN, PETER (HM05195) | | ● | | | | | | | | | | | | | | | | | | | | | | | | | | | | | | | | ● | | | | | | | | | | | | | | |
| COURT, SUSAN (HM05265) | | ● | | | ● | | | | | | | | | | ● | | | | ● | ● | | | | ● | | ● | | | ● | | | | ● | | | | | | ● | | | | | ● | ● | | ● | |
| COURT, SUSAN (HM05266) | | ● | | | ● | | | | | | | | | | ● | | | | ● | ● | | | | ● | | ● | | | ● | | | | ● | | | | | | ● | | | | | ● | ● | | ● | |
| COYSTEN & ASSOCIATES (HM05332) | ● | ● | | | ● | | | | | | | | ● | ● | ● | ● | | | | | | | ● | ● | ● | ● | | | ● | | | | ● | | | ● | | | ● | | | | | ● | | | ● | |
| CROIX, LINDA LA (HM05460) | | | | | | | | | | | | | | | ● | | | | | | | | | | | | | | | | | | | | | | | | | | | | | | | | | |
| DELTA MEDI CLINIC (HM05969) | | | | | ● | | | | | | | | | | | | | | | | | | | | | ● | | ● | | | | | | | | | | | | | | | | | ● | | | |
| DICKMAN, ANNIE (HM06080) | ● | ● | ● | ● | | ● | | | ● | | ● | ● | ● | ● | ● | | | | | | | | ● | | ● | ● | | | ● | | | ● | ● | | | ● | | | ● | | | | ● | ● | ● | | ● | |
| DILLON, MICHAEL (HM06100) | ● | ● | | | | | | | | | | | ● | | ● | ● | | | | | | | | ● | ● | | | | ● | | ● | | | ● | | ● | | | | | ● | | | | | | | ● |
| DIMENT, GORDON L (HM06105) | ● | ● | | | | | | | | | | | | | | | | | | | | | | | ● | | | | | | | | | ● | | | | | ● | | | | | | | | | ● |
| EARL, A (HM06496) | | | | | | | | | | | | | | | | | | | | | | | | | | | | | | | | | | ● | | | | | | | | | | | | | | |
| EDWARDS, R (HM06668) | | ● | | | ● | | | | | | | | | | | | | | | | | | | | | | | | ● | | | | | | | | | | | | | | | | | | ● | |
| EDWARDS, R, HERNE BAY (HM06670) | | ● | | | ● | | | | | | | | | | | | | | | | | | | ● | | | | | ● | | | | | | | | | | | | | | | | | | ● | |
| ELIZABETH ANNE (HM06736) | ● | | | | | | | | | | | | | | | | | | | | | | | | ● | | ● | | | | ● | | | ● | | | | | | | | | | | | | | |
| EUROPEAN AYUR-VEDA (HM06944) | ● | | | | ● | | | | | | | | | | | | | | | | | | | | | ● | ● | | ● | | | | | | | | | | | | | | | | ● | | | |
| EVEGATE CLINIC (HM06996) | ● | ● | ● | ● | ● | ● | ● | ● | ● | ● | ● | ● | ● | ● | ● | ● | ● | ● | ● | ● | | ● | ● | ● | ● | ● | ● | ● | ● | ● | | ● | ● | ● | ● | ● | ● | | ● | ● | ● | ● | ● | ● | ● | ● | ● | ● |
| EVOLUTION HEALTH (HM07014) | | | | ● | | | | | | | | | | | ● | | | | | | | | | | | ● | | | ● | | | | ● | | | | | | | | | | | | | | ● | |
| FALCONER, PATRICIA (HM07073) | | | | | | | | | | | | | | | ● | | | | | | | | | | | | | | | | | | | | | | | | | | | | | | | | | |
| FEET FIRST (HM07167) | | ● | | | ● | | | | | | | | | | ● | | | | ● | | | | | | | | | | ● | | | | | | | | | | | | | | | | | | | |
| FRANCIS-JONES, TREVOR (DR) (HM07679) | | | | | ● | | | | | | | | | | ● | | | | | ● | | | | | | | | | ● | | | | | | | | | ● | ● | | | | | | ● | | ● | |
| GIBSON, JAN (HM08040) | ● | ● | | | | | | | ● | | | | ● | | ● | | | | | | | | | | ● | | | | ● | ● | | | ● | ● | | | | | | | | | | | | | | ● |
| GILLINGHAM CLINIC OF COMP MED (HM08097) | ● | ● | ● | | ● | ● | | ● | ● | | ● | ● | ● | ● | ● | ● | | | | | | | ● | ● | | ● | ● | ● | ● | ● | | | ● | | ● | ● | ● | | ● | ● | ● | ● | ● | ● | ● | | ● | |
| GRAVESEND HOMOEOPATHY CLINIC (HM08404) | ● | ● | ● | ● | ● | ● | ● | ● | ● | ● | ● | ● | ● | ● | ● | ● | ● | ● | ● | | | ● | ● | ● | ● | ● | ● | ● | ● | ● | | | ● | ● | ● | ● | ● | | ● | ● | ● | ● | ● | ● | ● | | ● | ● |
| GUNN, JASON (HM08642) | | | | | ● | | | | | | | | | | | | | | | | | | | ● | | | | ● | ● | | | | | | | | | ● | | | | | | | | | | |
| HANNA, MARK (HM08931) | ● | ● | | | | | | | ● | | | | ● | | ● | | | | | | | | | ● | | | | | ● | ● | | | | ● | | | | | | | | | | | | ● | | ● |
| HAYES, JACQUELINE (HM09260) | ● | ● | | | ● | | | | ● | ● | ● | ● | ● | ● | ● | | | | ● | ● | | | ● | ● | | | | ● | ● | ● | | ● | ● | | ● | ● | ● | | ● | ● | | | | ● | ● | | ● | |
| HAZLEWOOD OSTEOPATHIC PRACTICE (HM09297) | | | | | ● | | | | | | | | | | ● | | | | | | | | | | | | | | | | | | | | | | | | | | | | | | | | | |
| HEAD TO TOE WELL-BEING (HM09300) | | ● | | | ● | | | | | | ● | | ● | | | | | | | | | | | | | | | | | | | | | | | ● | | | | | | | | | | | | |
| HEALING AND HERBS (HM09325) | ● | ● | | | ● | | | | | ● | | | ● | ● | | | | | ● | ● | | | | | | | | | ● | | | ● | ● | | | ● | | | | ● | ● | ● | | | ● | | | |
| HEATHSIDE CENTRE (HM09461) | ● | ● | ● | ● | ● | ● | ● | ● | ● | ● | ● | ● | ● | ● | ● | ● | ● | ● | ● | ● | | ● | ● | ● | ● | ● | ● | ● | ● | ● | | ● | ● | ● | ● | ● | ● | | ● | ● | ● | ● | ● | ● | ● | ● | ● | ● |

# I - S Conditions treated at Practices/Businesses

Business by County with Reference no.

| Business | Insomnia | Irritable Bowel Syndrome | Itching | Jet Lag | Joint Pain | Kidney Complaints | Lactose Intolerance | Laryngitis | Lethargy | Liver Disorders | Low Blood Pressure | Lung Problems | ME | Menopause | Migraine | Motion Sickness |
|---|---|---|---|---|---|---|---|---|---|---|---|---|---|---|---|---|
| HERTERICH, NIGEL (HM09688) | | | | | ● | | | | | | | | | | ● | |
| HOFFMAN, BRIAN ASSOCIATES (HM09900) | | | | | ● | | | | ● | | | | ● | | | |
| HOLMES, S A (HM10045) | ● | | | | | ● | | | ● | ● | ● | | | | ● | |
| HOPE CHIROPRACTIC (HM10133) | | ● | | | ● | | | | | | | | | | | |
| JACCQUELINE ELLISON PRACTICE (HM10811) | | | | | ● | | | | | | | | | | | |
| KARMERS CLINIQUE (HM11328) | ● | | | | ● | | | | | | | | | | ● | |
| KENT HOUSE CHIROPRACTIC CLINIC (HM11517) | | ● | | | ● | | | | | | | | | | | |
| KENT HOUSE CHIROPRACTIC CLINIC (HM11519) | | ● | | | ● | | | | | | | | ● | | ● | |
| KENT HOUSE CHIROPRACTIC CLINIC (HM11520) | | ● | | | ● | | | | | | | | | | | |
| KENT HOUSE CHIROPRACTIC CLINIC (HM11518) | | ● | | | ● | | | | | | | | | | | |
| KSC (HM11812) | ● | ● | ● | ● | ● | ● | ● | ● | ● | ● | ● | ● | ● | ● | ● | ● |
| LAMB, G BRIAN (HM11888) | | | ● | | ● | ● | | | | ● | ● | ● | ● | | ● | |
| LAVINGOTN, A (HM12034) | ● | ● | | | | | | | | | | | | ● | ● | |
| LEBOR, JILL (HM12115) | ● | ● | | ● | ● | ● | | ● | ● | ● | ● | ● | ● | ● | ● | ● |
| LIVING WELL CLINIC (HM12488) | | ● | | | ● | | | | | | | | | | | |
| LOBB, BRIAN W (HM12528) | | | | | | | | | | | | | | | ● | |
| LUGG, G (HM12732) | ● | ● | | | ● | | | | | | | | ● | ● | ● | |
| MABBERLEY, KATHIE (HM12812) | | ● | | ● | | | | | | | | | ● | ● | ● | |
| MAIDSTONE ACUPUNCTURE CLINIC (HM12935) | ● | ● | ● | ● | ● | ● | ● | ● | ● | ● | ● | ● | ● | ● | ● | ● |
| MARY CANNON - CLINICAL NUTRI (HM13221) | ● | ● | ● | | ● | | ● | ● | ● | ● | ● | | ● | ● | ● | ● |
| MASON & ASSOCIATES (HM13233) | | | | | ● | | | | | | | | ● | ● | ● | |
| MASON & ASSOCIATES (HM13232) | | ● | | | ● | | | | | | | | ● | ● | ● | |
| MATHER, SUE (HM13281) | ● | ● | ● | ● | ● | ● | ● | ● | ● | ● | ● | ● | ● | ● | ● | ● |
| MCDOWELL, S (HM13467) | | | | | ● | | | | | | | | | | | |
| MEADOWS (HM13630) | | | | | | | | | | | | | | | | |
| MEOPHAM CLINIC (HM13732) | | ● | | | | | | | | | | | ● | | | |
| MUIRHEAD, MARGARET (HM14323) | ● | ● | ● | ● | ● | ● | ● | ● | ● | ● | ● | ● | ● | ● | ● | ● |
| MULVANEY, ALISTAIR (HM14353) | | | ● | | ● | | | | | | | | | | | |
| NATURAL HEALTH CENTRE (HM14568) | ● | ● | ● | ● | ● | ● | ● | ● | ● | ● | ● | ● | ● | ● | ● | ● |
| NATURAL HEALTH CENTRE (HM14562) | | | | | | | | | | | | | | | ● | ● |
| NATURAL THERAPIST (HM14635) | ● | ● | ● | ● | ● | | ● | | ● | | ● | | ● | ● | ● | |
| NATURAL THERAPY CENTRE (HM14643) | | ● | | | | ● | | | | ● | | | | | | |
| OPTIVAVA (HM15352) | | | | | ● | | | | | | | | | | ● | |
| OSTEOPATHIC CLINIC (HM15461) | | ● | | | ● | | | | | | | | | | | |

| Business | Mouth Disorders | Mouth Ulcers | Multiple Sclerosis | Muscular Dystrophy | Musculo-skeletal | Nail Health | Nausea | Nerve Disorders | Nervous Disorders | Neuralgia | Obesity | Osteoporosis | Pain | Palpitations | Panic Attacks | Parkinson's Disease |
|---|---|---|---|---|---|---|---|---|---|---|---|---|---|---|---|---|
| HERTERICH, NIGEL (HM09688) | | | | | | | | | | | | | | | | |
| HOFFMAN, BRIAN ASSOCIATES (HM09900) | | | | | | | | | | | | | ● | | | |
| HOLMES, S A (HM10045) | | | | | | | | ● | ● | | | | | | | |
| HOPE CHIROPRACTIC (HM10133) | | | | | | | | ● | | | | | ● | | | |
| JACCQUELINE ELLISON PRACTICE (HM10811) | | | | | | | | | | | | | | | | |
| KARMERS CLINIQUE (HM11328) | | | ● | | | | | ● | | | | | ● | | | |
| KENT HOUSE CHIROPRACTIC CLINIC (HM11517) | | | | | | | | ● | | | | ● | ● | | | |
| KENT HOUSE CHIROPRACTIC CLINIC (HM11519) | | | | | | | | ● | ● | | | | ● | | | |
| KENT HOUSE CHIROPRACTIC CLINIC (HM11520) | | | | | | | | | | | | ● | ● | | | |
| KENT HOUSE CHIROPRACTIC CLINIC (HM11518) | | | | | | | | | ● | | | ● | ● | | | |
| KSC (HM11812) | ● | ● | ● | ● | | ● | ● | ● | ● | ● | ● | ● | ● | ● | | ● |
| LAMB, G BRIAN (HM11888) | ● | ● | ● | | | ● | ● | ● | ● | ● | ● | ● | ● | ● | | |
| LAVINGOTN, A (HM12034) | | | | | | | | | | | | | | | | |
| LEBOR, JILL (HM12115) | | ● | | | | | ● | | | | | | ● | ● | | ● |
| LIVING WELL CLINIC (HM12488) | | | | | | | | ● | ● | | | ● | ● | | | |
| LOBB, BRIAN W (HM12528) | | | | | | | | | ● | | | | ● | | | |
| LUGG, G (HM12732) | | | | | | ● | | | | | | | | | | |
| MABBERLEY, KATHIE (HM12812) | | | ● | | | | | | | | | | | | | ● |
| MAIDSTONE ACUPUNCTURE CLINIC (HM12935) | ● | | ● | | | | ● | ● | ● | ● | ● | ● | ● | ● | | ● |
| MARY CANNON - CLINICAL NUTRI (HM13221) | ● | ● | | | | ● | ● | | ● | ● | ● | ● | | ● | | |
| MASON & ASSOCIATES (HM13233) | | | | | | | | | | | | | ● | | | |
| MASON & ASSOCIATES (HM13232) | | | | | | | | | | | | | ● | | | |
| MATHER, SUE (HM13281) | ● | ● | ● | ● | | ● | ● | ● | ● | ● | ● | ● | ● | ● | | ● |
| MCDOWELL, S (HM13467) | | | | | | | | | | | | | | | | |
| MEADOWS (HM13630) | | | | | | | | | | | | | ● | | | |
| MEOPHAM CLINIC (HM13732) | | | | | | | | ● | | | | ● | ● | | | |
| MUIRHEAD, MARGARET (HM14323) | ● | ● | ● | ● | | ● | ● | ● | ● | ● | ● | ● | ● | ● | | |
| MULVANEY, ALISTAIR (HM14353) | | | | | | ● | | | | | | | ● | | | |
| NATURAL HEALTH CENTRE (HM14568) | ● | ● | ● | ● | | ● | ● | ● | ● | ● | ● | ● | ● | ● | | ● |
| NATURAL HEALTH CENTRE (HM14562) | | | | | | | | | | | ● | | ● | | | |
| NATURAL THERAPIST (HM14635) | | | ● | | | | | ● | ● | ● | ● | ● | ● | | | ● |
| NATURAL THERAPY CENTRE (HM14643) | | | | | | | | | | | | | | | | |
| OPTIVAVA (HM15352) | | | | | | | | | | | | | | | | |
| OSTEOPATHIC CLINIC (HM15461) | | | | | | | | ● | ● | | | | ● | | | |

| Business | Period Problems | Phobias | Piles | PMT | Pneumonia | Postural Problems | Pregnancy Help | Prostate Problems | Psoriasis | Raynaud's Disease | Recurrent Infections | Restless Legs | Rheumatoid Arthritis | Schizophrenia | Sciatica | Sexual Problems |
|---|---|---|---|---|---|---|---|---|---|---|---|---|---|---|---|---|
| HERTERICH, NIGEL (HM09688) | | | | | | | | | | | | | | | | |
| HOFFMAN, BRIAN ASSOCIATES (HM09900) | | | | | | | | | | ● | | | ● | | | |
| HOLMES, S A (HM10045) | | | | | | | | | | | | | | | ● | |
| HOPE CHIROPRACTIC (HM10133) | | | | | | | | | | | | | | | ● | |
| JACCQUELINE ELLISON PRACTICE (HM10811) | | | | | | | | | | | | | | | ● | |
| KARMERS CLINIQUE (HM11328) | ● | | | | | | | | | | | | | | ● | |
| KENT HOUSE CHIROPRACTIC CLINIC (HM11517) | | | | | | | | | | | | | | | ● | |
| KENT HOUSE CHIROPRACTIC CLINIC (HM11519) | | | | | | | | | | | | | | | ● | |
| KENT HOUSE CHIROPRACTIC CLINIC (HM11520) | | | | | | | | | | | | | | | ● | |
| KENT HOUSE CHIROPRACTIC CLINIC (HM11518) | | | | | | | | | | | | | | | ● | |
| KSC (HM11812) | ● | ● | ● | ● | ● | | ● | ● | ● | ● | ● | ● | ● | ● | ● | ● |
| LAMB, G BRIAN (HM11888) | ● | ● | ● | ● | | | | ● | ● | ● | ● | ● | ● | ● | ● | ● |
| LAVINGOTN, A (HM12034) | | | | ● | | | | | | | | | | | | |
| LEBOR, JILL (HM12115) | ● | ● | ● | ● | | | ● | ● | | ● | ● | ● | ● | | ● | |
| LIVING WELL CLINIC (HM12488) | | | | | | | | | | | | | | | ● | |
| LOBB, BRIAN W (HM12528) | | ● | | | | | | | | | | | | | | |
| LUGG, G (HM12732) | ● | | | ● | | | | | ● | ● | | ● | ● | | | |
| MABBERLEY, KATHIE (HM12812) | | | | ● | | | | | ● | | | | | | ● | |
| MAIDSTONE ACUPUNCTURE CLINIC (HM12935) | ● | ● | ● | ● | ● | | ● | ● | ● | ● | ● | ● | ● | ● | ● | ● |
| MARY CANNON - CLINICAL NUTRI (HM13221) | ● | | ● | ● | | | ● | | ● | ● | ● | ● | ● | | | |
| MASON & ASSOCIATES (HM13233) | | | | | | ● | ● | | | | | | | | ● | |
| MASON & ASSOCIATES (HM13232) | | | | | | ● | ● | | | | | | | | ● | |
| MATHER, SUE (HM13281) | ● | ● | ● | ● | ● | | ● | ● | ● | ● | ● | ● | ● | ● | ● | ● |
| MCDOWELL, S (HM13467) | | | | | | | | | | | | | | | | |
| MEADOWS (HM13630) | | | | | | | | | ● | | | | | | | |
| MEOPHAM CLINIC (HM13732) | | | | | | ● | | | | | | | | | ● | |
| MUIRHEAD, MARGARET (HM14323) | ● | ● | ● | ● | | | ● | ● | ● | ● | ● | ● | ● | ● | ● | ● |
| MULVANEY, ALISTAIR (HM14353) | | | | | | | | | ● | | | | ● | | | |
| NATURAL HEALTH CENTRE (HM14568) | ● | ● | ● | ● | ● | | ● | ● | ● | ● | ● | ● | ● | ● | ● | ● |
| NATURAL HEALTH CENTRE (HM14562) | | ● | | | | | | | | | | | | | | |
| NATURAL THERAPIST (HM14635) | ● | | ● | | ● | | | ● | ● | | | ● | ● | | ● | |
| NATURAL THERAPY CENTRE (HM14643) | | | | | | | | | | | | | | | | |
| OPTIVAVA (HM15352) | | | | | | | | | | | | | | | | |
| OSTEOPATHIC CLINIC (HM15461) | | | | | | ● | | | | | | | | | ● | |

www.healthmyself.com

# I - S Conditions treated at Practices/Businesses

| Business by County with Reference no. | Insomnia | Irritable Bowel Syndrome | Itching | Jet Lag | Joint Pain | Kidney Complaints | Lactose Intolerance | Laryngitis | Lethargy | Liver Disorders | Low Blood Pressure | Lung Problems | ME | Menopause | Migraine | Motion Sickness | Mouth Disorders | Mouth Ulcers | Multiple Sclerosis | Muscular Dystrophy | Musculo-skeletal | Nail Health | Nausea | Nerve Disorders |
|---|---|---|---|---|---|---|---|---|---|---|---|---|---|---|---|---|---|---|---|---|---|---|---|---|
| OSTEOPATHIC PRACTICE (HM15466) | | | | | | | | | | | | | | | ● | | | | | | | | | |
| PASSCHIER, MAREANNE SASSEN (HM15779) | ● | ● | ● | ● | ● | ● | ● | ● | ● | ● | ● | ● | ● | ● | ● | ● | ● | ● | ● | ● | | ● | ● | ● |
| PATERSON, MARGARET (HM15814) | ● | ● | | | ● | | | | ● | | ● | ● | ● | ● | ● | | | | | | | | | |
| PEARTON, GILL (HM15919) | ● | ● | ● | | ● | ● | ● | ● | ● | | ● | ● | ● | ● | ● | | | | | | | | ● | ● |
| PELE, ANDRI (HM15950) | | | | | | | | | | | | | | | ● | ● | | | | | | | | |
| PRINCES AVENUE OSTEOPATHIC (HM16623) | | ● | | | | | | | | | | | | | ● | | | | | | | | | ● |
| RALPH & EVANS (HM16906) | ● | ● | ● | | ● | ● | ● | ● | ● | ● | ● | ● | ● | ● | ● | | | ● | ● | | | | ● | ● |
| READ, CHARLES REG OSTEOPATH (HM16994) | | | | | | | | | | | | | | | | | | | | | | | | |
| REVEREND CAROL HADDERSLEY (HM17204) | ● | ● | ● | ● | ● | ● | ● | ● | ● | ● | ● | | ● | ● | ● | ● | ● | ● | ● | ● | | ● | ● | ● |
| RIDLEY, VICKY (HM17324) | ● | ● | ● | | ● | ● | ● | ● | ● | ● | ● | ● | ● | ● | ● | ● | ● | ● | ● | | | ● | ● | ● |
| ROCHESTER PHYSIO & SPORTS (HM17520) | | | | | ● | | | | | | | | | | | | | | ● | | | | | |
| ROMNEY MARSH OSTEOPATHS (HM17574) | ● | ● | ● | ● | ● | ● | | ● | ● | ● | | ● | ● | ● | ● | ● | | | ● | | | | ● | ● |
| ROSE, NAOMI (HM17612) | ● | ● | ● | | ● | | | | ● | | | | | ● | ● | | | | | | | | | |
| ROUND ROOM (HM17663) | ● | ● | | | ● | | | | | | ● | | ● | | ● | | | | ● | | | | | |
| SACKS, PATRICA (HM17828) | | | | | | | | | | | | | | | | | | | | | | ● | | |
| SANCTUM HOLISTIC THERAPY CTRE (HM17896) | | ● | | | | | | | | | | | | | ● | | | | | | | | | |
| SANDERS, PETER (HM17914) | | | | | ● | | | | | | | | | | ● | | | | | | ● | | | |
| SANDOWN CLINIC FOR COMP MED (HM17926) | ● | ● | ● | ● | ● | ● | ● | ● | ● | ● | ● | ● | ● | ● | ● | ● | ● | ● | ● | ● | | ● | ● | ● |
| SHEARER, GAYLE (HM18357) | | | | | ● | | | | | | | | | | ● | | | | | | | | | |
| SHIATSU (HM18451) | ● | | | | | | | | | | | | | | | | | | | | | | | |
| SOUTH LONDON HYPNOTHERAPY CTRE (HM18910) | ● | | ● | ● | | | | | ● | | ● | | ● | ● | ● | ● | | | ● | | | | ● | ● |
| SOUTHCOTE CHIROPRACTIC CLINIC (HM18927) | | | | | ● | | | | | | | | | | ● | | | | | | | | | |
| STARFIELDS HOLISTIC HLTH CTRE (HM19145) | ● | ● | ● | ● | ● | ● | ● | ● | ● | ● | ● | ● | ● | ● | ● | ● | ● | ● | ● | ● | ● | ● | ● | ● |
| STONE, CHARLES (HM19334) | | | | | | | | | | | | | | | | | | | | | | | | |
| STURGE, DEBBIE (HM19445) | | ● | | | | | | | | | | | | ● | | | | | | | | | | |
| SWAN, VIVA (HM19575) | ● | ● | ● | ● | ● | ● | ● | ● | ● | ● | ● | ● | ● | ● | ● | ● | ● | ● | ● | ● | | ● | ● | ● |
| SYCAMORE, TONI (HM19606) | | ● | | | | | | | | | | | | | | | | | | | | | | |
| TONBRIDGE CLINIC (HM20151) | | | | | ● | | | | | | | | | | ● | | | | | | | | | |
| TOWN, BERNICE (HM20199) | | | | | | | | | | | | | | | | | | | | | | ● | | |
| TURNER, ANDREA (HM20417) | | | | | | | | | | | | | ● | ● | ● | | | | | | | | | |
| VARNEY, MONICA (HM20591) | | ● | | ● | ● | | | | | | ● | | ● | ● | ● | | | | ● | | | | | ● |
| VILLAGE PHYSIOTHERAPY PRACTICE (HM20667) | | | | | ● | | | | | | | | | | | | | | | | | | | |
| VINCENT, EUNICE (HM20671) | ● | | | | | | | | | | | | | | | | | | | | | | | |
| VINES REIKI HEALING CENTRE (HM20680) | ● | ● | ● | ● | ● | ● | ● | ● | ● | ● | ● | ● | ● | ● | ● | ● | ● | ● | ● | ● | | ● | ● | ● |

| Business by County with Reference no. | Nervous Disorders | Neuralgia | Obesity | Osteoporosis | Pain | Palpitations | Panic Attacks | Parkinson's Disease | Period Problems | Phobias | Piles | PMT | Pneumonia | Postural Problems | Pregnancy Help | Prostate Problems | Psoriasis | Raynaud's Disease | Recurrent Infections | Restless Legs | Rheumatoid Arthritis | Schizophrenia | Sciatica | Sexual Problems |
|---|---|---|---|---|---|---|---|---|---|---|---|---|---|---|---|---|---|---|---|---|---|---|---|---|
| OSTEOPATHIC PRACTICE (HM15466) | | ● | | | ● | | | | | | | | | | ● | | | | | | | | ● | |
| PASSCHIER, MAREANNE SASSEN (HM15779) | ● | ● | ● | ● | ● | ● | | ● | ● | ● | ● | ● | ● | | ● | ● | ● | ● | ● | ● | ● | ● | ● | ● |
| PATERSON, MARGARET (HM15814) | | | | | ● | | | ● | ● | | | | | | ● | ● | | ● | | | ● | | ● | |
| PEARTON, GILL (HM15919) | | ● | | ● | ● | ● | | | ● | | ● | ● | | | ● | ● | ● | ● | ● | ● | | | ● | |
| PELE, ANDRI (HM15950) | | | ● | | ● | | | | | ● | | | | | | | | | | | | | | |
| PRINCES AVENUE OSTEOPATHIC (HM16623) | | ● | | | ● | | | | | | | | | | | | | | | | | | ● | |
| RALPH & EVANS (HM16906) | ● | ● | | ● | ● | ● | | | ● | ● | ● | ● | ● | | ● | ● | ● | ● | ● | ● | ● | | | |
| READ, CHARLES REG OSTEOPATH (HM16994) | | | | | ● | | | | | | | | | | | | | | | ● | | | ● | |
| REVEREND CAROL HADDERSLEY (HM17204) | ● | ● | ● | ● | ● | ● | | ● | ● | ● | ● | ● | ● | | ● | ● | ● | ● | ● | ● | ● | ● | ● | ● |
| RIDLEY, VICKY (HM17324) | ● | ● | ● | ● | ● | ● | | ● | ● | ● | ● | ● | ● | | ● | ● | ● | ● | ● | ● | ● | | ● | ● |
| ROCHESTER PHYSIO & SPORTS (HM17520) | | | | | ● | | | | | | | | | | | | | | | | | | | |
| ROMNEY MARSH OSTEOPATHS (HM17574) | ● | ● | | ● | ● | | | ● | ● | | | ● | | | | | | ● | ● | ● | ● | | ● | |
| ROSE, NAOMI (HM17612) | ● | | | | ● | | | | ● | | | ● | | | ● | | | | | | ● | ● | ● | |
| ROUND ROOM (HM17663) | | | | | ● | ● | | | ● | | | ● | | | ● | | ● | | | | | | | |
| SACKS, PATRICA (HM17828) | | | | | | | | | | | | | | | | | | | | | | | | |
| SANCTUM HOLISTIC THERAPY CTRE (HM17896) | | | | | | | | | | | | | | | | | | | | | | | | |
| SANDERS, PETER (HM17914) | | | | | | | | | | | | | | | | | | | | | | | | |
| SANDOWN CLINIC FOR COMP MED (HM17926) | ● | ● | ● | ● | ● | ● | | ● | ● | ● | ● | ● | ● | | ● | ● | ● | ● | ● | ● | ● | ● | ● | ● |
| SHEARER, GAYLE (HM18357) | | | | | ● | | | | | | | | | | ● | | | | | | | | ● | |
| SHIATSU (HM18451) | | | | | | | | | | | | | | | ● | | | | | | | | | |
| SOUTH LONDON HYPNOTHERAPY CTRE (HM18910) | ● | ● | ● | | ● | ● | | | ● | ● | | ● | | | | | ● | ● | | ● | | | | ● |
| SOUTHCOTE CHIROPRACTIC CLINIC (HM18927) | | ● | | | ● | | | | | | | | | | | | | | | ● | | | ● | |
| STARFIELDS HOLISTIC HLTH CTRE (HM19145) | ● | ● | ● | ● | ● | ● | ● | ● | ● | ● | ● | ● | ● | ● | ● | ● | ● | ● | ● | ● | ● | ● | ● | ● |
| STONE, CHARLES (HM19334) | | | | | | | ● | | | ● | | | | | | | | | | | | | | |
| STURGE, DEBBIE (HM19445) | | | | | | | | | | | | ● | | | | | | | | | | | | |
| SWAN, VIVA (HM19575) | ● | ● | ● | ● | ● | ● | | ● | ● | ● | ● | ● | ● | | ● | ● | ● | ● | ● | ● | ● | ● | ● | ● |
| SYCAMORE, TONI (HM19606) | ● | | | | | | | | | | | | | | | | | | | | | | | |
| TONBRIDGE CLINIC (HM20151) | | | ● | ● | | | | | | ● | | | | | | | | | | | ● | | | |
| TOWN, BERNICE (HM20199) | | | | | | | | | | | | | | | | | | | | | | | | |
| TURNER, ANDREA (HM20417) | | | | | ● | | | | ● | | | ● | | | ● | | ● | ● | | | ● | | | |
| VARNEY, MONICA (HM20591) | ● | | | | ● | | | ● | | | | ● | | | | | | | | | | | ● | |
| VILLAGE PHYSIOTHERAPY PRACTICE (HM20667) | | | | | | | | | | | | | | ● | | | | | | | | | | |
| VINCENT, EUNICE (HM20671) | | | | | | | | | | | | | | | | | | | | | | | | |
| VINES REIKI HEALING CENTRE (HM20680) | ● | ● | ● | ● | ● | ● | | ● | ● | ● | ● | ● | ● | | ● | ● | ● | ● | ● | ● | ● | ● | ● | ● |

# I - S Conditions treated at Practices/Businesses

| Business by County with Reference no. | Insomnia | Irritable Bowel Syndrome | Itching | Jet Lag | Joint Pain | Kidney Complaints | Lactose Intolerance | Laryngitis | Lethargy | Liver Disorders | Low Blood Pressure | Lung Problems | ME | Menopause | Migraine | Motion Sickness | Mouth Disorders | Mouth Ulcers | Multiple Sclerosis | Muscular Dystrophy | Musculo-skeletal | Nail Health | Nausea | Nerve Disorders | Nervous Disorders | Neuralgia | Obesity | Osteoporosis | Pain | Palpitations | Panic Attacks | Parkinson's Disease | Period Problems | Phobias | Piles | PMT | Pneumonia | Postural Problems | Pregnancy Help | Prostate Problems | Psoriasis | Raynaud's Disease | Recurrent Infections | Restless Legs | Rheumatoid Arthritis | Schizophrenia | Sciatica | Sexual Problems |
|---|---|---|---|---|---|---|---|---|---|---|---|---|---|---|---|---|---|---|---|---|---|---|---|---|---|---|---|---|---|---|---|---|---|---|---|---|---|---|---|---|---|---|---|---|---|---|---|---|
| WATLING STREET THERAPY CTRE (HM21001) | ● | ● | ● |  | ● | ● |  |  |  |  |  |  | ● | ● | ● |  |  | ● |  |  |  | ● | ● |  |  |  | ● | ● | ● | ● |  |  | ● |  |  | ● |  |  |  |  |  |  |  |  | ● |  |  |  |
| WEBB, JENNIFER (HM21067) |  |  |  |  |  |  |  |  |  |  |  |  | ● |  | ● |  |  |  |  |  |  |  |  |  |  |  |  |  | ● |  |  |  | ● |  |  |  |  |  |  |  |  |  |  |  | ● |  | ● |  |
| WELLS PHYSIO & SPORTS CLINIC (HM21168) |  |  |  |  | ● |  |  |  |  |  |  |  |  |  |  |  |  |  | ● |  | ● |  |  |  |  |  |  |  |  |  |  |  |  |  |  |  |  |  |  |  |  |  |  |  |  |  |  |  |
| WOOLF, JOY (HM21871) |  |  |  |  |  |  |  |  |  |  |  |  |  |  | ● |  |  |  |  |  |  |  |  |  |  |  |  |  | ● |  |  |  |  |  |  |  |  |  |  |  |  |  |  |  |  |  |  |  |
| LANCASHIRE |  |  |  |  |  |  |  |  |  |  |  |  |  |  |  |  |  |  |  |  |  |  |  |  |  |  |  |  |  |  |  |  |  |  |  |  |  |  |  |  |  |  |  |  |  |  |  |  |
| ABERNETHY, HILARY (HM00123) | ● | ● |  |  |  |  |  |  |  |  |  |  | ● |  |  |  |  |  | ● |  |  |  |  |  | ● |  | ● |  | ● | ● |  |  |  |  |  |  |  |  |  |  |  |  |  |  |  | ● |  |  |
| ACUPUNCTURE PRIVATE CLINIC (HM00317) | ● | ● |  |  |  |  |  |  |  |  |  |  |  |  | ● |  |  |  |  |  |  |  |  |  |  |  |  |  |  |  |  |  |  |  |  |  |  |  |  |  |  |  |  |  |  |  |  |  |
| ALPHAWAVE (HM00685) |  |  |  |  |  |  |  |  |  |  |  |  |  |  |  |  |  |  |  |  |  |  |  |  |  |  |  |  | ● |  |  |  |  | ● |  |  |  |  |  |  |  |  |  |  |  |  |  | ● |
| ALTERNATIVE MEDICINE (HM00715) | ● | ● | ● |  | ● | ● | ● | ● | ● |  | ● | ● | ● | ● | ● | ● | ● |  | ● |  |  |  | ● | ● | ● | ● | ● | ● | ● | ● |  | ● | ● | ● | ● | ● |  |  |  | ● | ● | ● | ● | ● | ● |  | ● |  |
| ALTERNATIVE MEDICINE PRACTICE (HM00721) | ● | ● | ● |  | ● | ● | ● | ● | ● |  | ● | ● | ● | ● | ● | ● |  | ● | ● |  |  |  | ● | ● | ● | ● | ● | ● | ● | ● |  |  | ● | ● | ● | ● |  |  |  | ● | ● | ● | ● | ● | ● |  | ● |  |
| BARRETT & LIPTROTT (HM01783) |  |  |  |  |  |  |  |  |  |  |  |  |  |  |  |  |  |  |  |  |  | ● |  |  |  |  |  |  |  |  |  |  |  |  |  |  |  |  |  |  |  |  |  |  |  |  |  |  |
| BEARLEY, CAROL (HM01969) | ● |  |  |  | ● | ● |  |  |  |  |  |  | ● |  | ● |  |  |  |  |  |  |  |  |  |  |  |  |  |  |  |  |  |  |  |  |  |  |  | ● |  |  |  |  |  |  |  |  |  |
| BEESTON, J (HM02061) |  |  |  |  | ● |  |  |  |  |  |  |  | ● |  | ● |  |  |  |  |  |  |  |  |  |  | ● |  | ● | ● |  |  |  |  |  |  |  |  |  |  |  |  |  |  | ● | ● |  | ● |  |
| BENTLEY AND ASSOCIATES (HM02172) |  |  |  |  | ● |  |  |  |  |  |  |  |  |  |  |  |  |  |  |  |  | ● |  |  | ● | ● |  |  | ● |  |  |  |  |  |  |  |  |  |  |  |  | ● |  |  | ● | ● | ● |  |
| BFMP (HM02265) |  | ● |  |  | ● | ● | ● | ● | ● | ● |  | ● | ● | ● |  |  |  |  |  |  |  |  |  | ● | ● | ● | ● | ● | ● | ● |  |  | ● |  |  | ● |  |  |  | ● | ● |  | ● | ● | ● |  | ● |  |
| BOLTON CHIROPRATIC CLINIC (HM02656) |  |  |  |  | ● |  |  |  |  |  |  |  |  |  | ● |  |  |  |  |  |  |  |  | ● | ● |  |  | ● | ● |  |  |  |  |  |  |  |  |  |  |  |  |  |  |  |  |  | ● |  |
| BOLTON CLINIC OF ACUPUNCTURE (HM02657) |  |  |  |  |  |  |  |  |  |  |  |  |  | ● | ● |  |  |  |  |  |  |  |  |  |  |  |  |  |  |  |  |  | ● |  |  | ● |  |  |  |  |  |  |  |  |  |  |  |  |
| BOLTON PHYSIOTHERAPY CLINIC (HM02658) |  |  |  |  | ● |  |  |  |  |  |  |  |  |  |  |  |  |  |  |  |  |  |  |  |  |  |  |  |  |  |  |  |  |  |  |  |  |  |  |  |  |  |  |  |  |  |  |  |
| BOLTON THERAPY CENTRE (HM02659) | ● | ● |  |  | ● |  |  |  | ● |  |  |  |  | ● | ● |  |  |  |  |  | ● |  | ● | ● | ● | ● |  | ● | ● |  |  |  | ● | ● |  | ● |  |  |  |  |  |  |  |  | ● |  | ● |  |
| BOLTON, VANESSA (HM02664) | ● | ● |  |  | ● | ● |  | ● | ● | ● | ● | ● | ● | ● | ● |  |  |  | ● |  |  |  | ● | ● | ● | ● |  |  | ● | ● |  |  | ● |  | ● | ● |  |  | ● | ● | ● |  | ● |  | ● |  | ● |  |
| BRIDGWATER, K A (HM03016) | ● | ● | ● | ● | ● | ● | ● | ● | ● | ● | ● | ● | ● | ● | ● | ● | ● | ● | ● | ● |  | ● | ● | ● | ● | ● | ● | ● | ● | ● |  | ● | ● | ● | ● | ● | ● |  | ● | ● | ● | ● | ● | ● | ● | ● | ● | ● |
| BROOKES, MICHAEL (HM03163) |  | ● |  | ● |  |  | ● |  | ● |  |  |  |  |  |  |  |  | ● |  |  |  |  |  |  |  |  |  |  |  |  |  |  |  |  |  | ● |  |  |  |  | ● |  |  |  |  |  |  |  |
| BURSCOUGH PHYSIOTHERAPY (HM03425) |  |  |  |  |  |  |  |  |  |  |  |  |  |  |  |  |  |  | ● |  |  |  |  | ● | ● |  |  |  |  |  |  | ● |  |  |  |  |  |  |  |  |  |  |  |  |  |  |  |  |
| CHARTERED PHYSIO & SPORTS (HM04041) |  |  |  |  | ● |  |  |  |  |  |  |  |  |  |  |  |  |  | ● |  |  |  |  |  |  |  |  |  |  |  |  |  |  |  |  |  |  |  |  |  |  |  |  |  |  |  |  |  |
| CLOUGHS - CHRTRD PHYSIO CLINIC (HM04735) |  |  |  |  | ● |  |  |  |  |  |  |  |  |  |  |  |  |  | ● |  |  |  |  |  |  |  |  |  | ● |  |  |  |  |  |  |  |  |  |  |  |  |  |  |  |  |  |  |  |
| COLES, RONNIE (HM04836) |  |  |  |  |  |  |  |  |  |  |  |  |  |  |  |  |  |  |  |  |  | ● |  |  |  |  |  |  |  |  |  |  |  |  |  |  |  |  |  |  |  |  |  |  |  |  |  |  |
| COMPLEMENTARY HEALTH SERVICES (HM04929) |  |  |  |  | ● |  |  |  |  |  |  |  |  |  |  |  |  |  |  |  |  |  |  |  |  |  |  |  |  |  |  |  |  |  |  |  |  |  |  |  |  |  |  |  |  |  |  |  |
| COTTAM, O N (HM05224) |  |  |  |  |  |  |  |  |  |  |  |  |  |  |  |  |  |  |  |  |  | ● |  |  |  |  |  |  |  |  |  |  |  |  |  |  |  |  |  |  |  |  |  |  |  |  |  |  |
| CRYSTAL & REIKI (HM05524) | ● | ● |  |  |  |  |  |  |  |  |  |  | ● |  | ● |  |  |  |  |  |  |  |  |  |  |  |  |  | ● |  |  |  |  |  |  |  |  |  |  |  |  |  |  |  |  |  |  |  |
| DAVIES, JOHNATHON (HM05819) |  |  |  |  |  |  |  |  |  |  |  |  |  |  |  |  |  |  |  |  |  | ● |  |  |  |  |  |  |  |  |  |  |  |  |  |  |  |  |  |  |  |  |  |  |  |  |  |  |
| DUCKWORTH, JEAN (HM06347) | ● | ● | ● | ● | ● | ● | ● | ● | ● | ● | ● | ● | ● | ● | ● | ● | ● | ● | ● |  |  | ● | ● | ● | ● | ● |  | ● | ● | ● |  | ● | ● | ● | ● | ● | ● |  | ● | ● | ● | ● | ● | ● | ● | ● | ● |  |
| GREENHALGH, A J T (HM08489) |  |  |  |  |  |  |  |  |  |  |  |  |  |  |  |  |  |  |  |  |  | ● |  |  |  |  |  |  |  |  |  |  |  |  |  |  |  |  |  |  |  |  |  |  |  |  |  |  |
| GROGAN, DIANA E (HM08592) | ● | ● |  |  | ● | ● |  |  |  |  |  |  | ● | ● | ● |  |  |  |  |  |  |  |  |  |  | ● |  |  | ● |  |  |  | ● |  |  | ● |  |  |  |  |  |  |  |  | ● |  | ● |  |
| HAMPSOM, JAMES (HM08878) |  |  |  |  | ● |  |  |  |  |  |  |  |  |  | ● |  |  |  |  |  |  |  | ● |  |  |  |  |  | ● |  |  |  | ● |  |  | ● |  |  |  |  |  |  |  |  |  |  |  |  |

# I - S Conditions treated at Practices/Businesses

| Business by County with Reference no. | Insomnia | Irritable Bowel Syndrome | Itching | Jet Lag | Joint Pain | Kidney Complaints | Lactose Intolerance | Laryngitis | Lethargy | Liver Disorders | Low Blood Pressure | Lung Problems | ME | Menopause | Migraine | Motion Sickness |
|---|---|---|---|---|---|---|---|---|---|---|---|---|---|---|---|---|
| HARDMAN, ALAN (HM08974) | | | | | | | | | | | | | | | | |
| HARMONIOUS HEALTHCARE (HM09015) | ● | ● | ● | | ● | ● | | | ● | | | | ● | ● | ● | |
| HEAVENS SCENT AROMATHERAPY (HM09478) | ● | | | | | | | | ● | | ● | | | | ● | |
| HEYWORTH, S (HM09716) | | | | | | | | | | | | | | | | |
| HOLDEN, JOHN H (HM09932) | | | | | | | | | | | | | | | | |
| JOHN HOLDEN ASSOCIATES (HM11051) | | | | | | | | | | | | | | | | |
| KELLY CHIROPODY (HM11424) | ● | | | | | | | | | | | | ● | | ● | |
| KENDEL HOUSE CLINIC (HM11479) | ● | ● | ● | | ● | | | | | | | | | ● | ● | |
| LAYNE, SUSAN G (HM12077) | ● | ● | | | ● | | | | ● | | | | ● | ● | ● | |
| LEYLAND PHYSIOTHERAPY CENTRE (HM12319) | | | | | ● | | | | | | | | | | | |
| MALKIN, DK, MANIP THERAPY (HM12975) | | | | | ● | | | | ● | | | | ● | | ● | |
| MOBILE CHIROPODIST (HM14027) | | | | | | | | | | | | | | | | |
| NATURAL HEALTH CENTRE (HM14566) | ● | ● | ● | | ● | | | | | | ● | | ● | ● | ● | |
| NELSON, S (HM14782) | ● | ● | | ● | ● | | | | | | ● | ● | ● | ● | ● | ● |
| ONE STOP HEALTH & BEAUTY (HM15323) | ● | ● | ● | ● | ● | ● | ● | ● | ● | ● | ● | ● | ● | ● | ● | ● |
| PEPPER, JOHN (HM16009) | ● | ● | | | | | | | ● | | | | ● | | ● | |
| PHYSIO AND SPORTS INJURIES (HM16195) | | | | | ● | | | | | | | | | | | |
| PURCELL, AMANDA (HM16762) | | | | | ● | | | | | | | | ● | | ● | |
| RAINBOW PREGNANCY ADVICE (HM16883) | | | | | | | | | | | | | | | | |
| RAMSBOTTOM PHYSIO CLINIC (HM16919) | | | | | ● | | | | | | | | | | | |
| RATCLIFFE, MARK (HM16949) | | | | | ● | | | | | | | | | | ● | |
| REMEDIAL MASSAGE/SPORTS (HM17175) | | | | | ● | | | | | | | | | | | |
| SMITH, CHRISTOPHER (DR) (HM18728) | | ● | | | | | | | | | | | | | | |
| ST GEORGES MULTI THERAPY CTRE (HM19075) | | ● | | | ● | | ● | | ● | | | | ● | | | |
| ST MARY'S CLINIC (HM19087) | | | | | ● | | | | ● | | | | | | ● | |
| TIP TOES (HM20086) | ● | ● | | | ● | | | | | | ● | | | | ● | |
| TRADITIONAL ACUPUNCTURE CLINIC (HM20220) | ● | ● | ● | | ● | ● | | | ● | ● | ● | ● | ● | ● | ● | ● |
| TRADITIONAL CHINESE MED CTRE (HM20223) | ● | ● | ● | | ● | ● | | | ● | | | | ● | ● | ● | |
| UPHAM, GILL (HM20522) | ● | ● | | | ● | | | | | | | ● | | ● | ● | |
| WATKINSON, BARBARA (HM20999) | ● | ● | | | ● | | | | ● | | | | ● | ● | ● | |
| WEST LANCS MCTIMONEY (HM21224) | | | | | ● | | | | | | | | ● | | ● | |
| WILSON, G (HM21656) | | ● | | | | | | | | | | | | | | |
| **LEICESTERSHIRE** | | | | | | | | | | | | | | | | |
| ACUPUNCTURE SERVICES (HM00320) | ● | ● | | | ● | | | | | | | | | | ● | |

| Business by County with Reference no. | Mouth Disorders | Mouth Ulcers | Multiple Sclerosis | Muscular Dystrophy | Musculo-skeletal | Nail Health | Nausea | Nerve Disorders | Nervous Disorders | Neuralgia | Obesity | Osteoporosis | Pain | Palpitations | Panic Attacks | Parkinson's Disease |
|---|---|---|---|---|---|---|---|---|---|---|---|---|---|---|---|---|
| HARDMAN, ALAN (HM08974) | | | | | | ● | | | | | | | | | | |
| HARMONIOUS HEALTHCARE (HM09015) | | | | | | ● | ● | ● | ● | ● | | | ● | ● | | |
| HEAVENS SCENT AROMATHERAPY (HM09478) | | | | | | | | | ● | | | | ● | | | |
| HEYWORTH, S (HM09716) | | | | | | ● | | | | | | | | | | |
| HOLDEN, JOHN H (HM09932) | | | | | | ● | | | | | | | | | | |
| JOHN HOLDEN ASSOCIATES (HM11051) | | | | | | ● | | | | | | | | | | |
| KELLY CHIROPODY (HM11424) | | | | | | | ● | | | | | | ● | | | |
| KENDEL HOUSE CLINIC (HM11479) | | | ● | | | | | | ● | | | ● | ● | | | ● |
| LAYNE, SUSAN G (HM12077) | | ● | ● | | | | ● | | ● | ● | | | ● | ● | | ● |
| LEYLAND PHYSIOTHERAPY CENTRE (HM12319) | | | ● | | ● | | | | | | | | ● | | | |
| MALKIN, DK, MANIP THERAPY (HM12975) | | | | ● | | | | | | ● | | ● | ● | | | |
| MOBILE CHIROPODIST (HM14027) | | | | | | ● | | | | | | | | | | |
| NATURAL HEALTH CENTRE (HM14566) | | | | | | | | ● | ● | | | | ● | | | |
| NELSON, S (HM14782) | | | ● | | | | | | | ● | | | ● | | | ● |
| ONE STOP HEALTH & BEAUTY (HM15323) | ● | ● | ● | ● | ● | ● | ● | ● | ● | ● | ● | ● | ● | ● | ● | ● |
| PEPPER, JOHN (HM16009) | | | | | | | | | ● | | | | ● | ● | | |
| PHYSIO AND SPORTS INJURIES (HM16195) | | | | | | | | | | ● | | ● | ● | | | |
| PURCELL, AMANDA (HM16762) | | | | | | | | | ● | | | | ● | | | |
| RAINBOW PREGNANCY ADVICE (HM16883) | | | | | | | | | | | | | | | | |
| RAMSBOTTOM PHYSIO CLINIC (HM16919) | | | ● | | | | | | | | | | | | | |
| RATCLIFFE, MARK (HM16949) | | | | | | | | | | ● | | | ● | | | |
| REMEDIAL MASSAGE/SPORTS (HM17175) | | | | | | | | | | | | | ● | | | |
| SMITH, CHRISTOPHER (DR) (HM18728) | | | | | | | | | | | | | ● | | | |
| ST GEORGES MULTI THERAPY CTRE (HM19075) | | | | | | | | | ● | | ● | | ● | | | |
| ST MARY'S CLINIC (HM19087) | | | | | | | | | | | | | ● | | | |
| TIP TOES (HM20086) | | | | | | | | | | | | | ● | | | |
| TRADITIONAL ACUPUNCTURE CLINIC (HM20220) | | | ● | | | | ● | | ● | ● | | | ● | ● | | |
| TRADITIONAL CHINESE MED CTRE (HM20223) | | ● | | | | | ● | | | | | | ● | | | |
| UPHAM, GILL (HM20522) | | | | | | | ● | | | | | | | | | |
| WATKINSON, BARBARA (HM20999) | | | | | | | | | | | | | ● | | | |
| WEST LANCS MCTIMONEY (HM21224) | | | ● | | | | | ● | | ● | | ● | ● | | | |
| WILSON, G (HM21656) | | | | | | | | | ● | | | | ● | | | |
| **LEICESTERSHIRE** | | | | | | | | | | | | | | | | |
| ACUPUNCTURE SERVICES (HM00320) | | | ● | | | | | ● | | | | | ● | | | ● |

| Business by County with Reference no. | Period Problems | Phobias | Piles | PMT | Pneumonia | Postural Problems | Pregnancy Help | Prostate Problems | Psoriasis | Raynaud's Disease | Recurrent Infections | Restless Legs | Rheumatoid Arthritis | Schizophrenia | Sciatica | Sexual Problems |
|---|---|---|---|---|---|---|---|---|---|---|---|---|---|---|---|---|
| HARDMAN, ALAN (HM08974) | | | | | | | | | | | | | | | | |
| HARMONIOUS HEALTHCARE (HM09015) | ● | | ● | ● | | | ● | ● | ● | ● | ● | ● | ● | | ● | |
| HEAVENS SCENT AROMATHERAPY (HM09478) | ● | | | ● | | | | | ● | | | | ● | | | |
| HEYWORTH, S (HM09716) | | | | | | | | | | | | | | | | |
| HOLDEN, JOHN H (HM09932) | | | | | | | | | | | | | | | | |
| JOHN HOLDEN ASSOCIATES (HM11051) | | | | | | | | | | | | | | | | |
| KELLY CHIROPODY (HM11424) | ● | | | | | | | | | | | | | | | |
| KENDEL HOUSE CLINIC (HM11479) | | ● | | ● | | ● | ● | | ● | ● | | ● | ● | | ● | |
| LAYNE, SUSAN G (HM12077) | | ● | | ● | | | | | ● | | ● | | ● | | ● | |
| LEYLAND PHYSIOTHERAPY CENTRE (HM12319) | | | | | | | | | | | | | | | | |
| MALKIN, DK, MANIP THERAPY (HM12975) | | | | | | | | | | | | ● | | | ● | |
| MOBILE CHIROPODIST (HM14027) | | | | | | | | | | | | | | | | |
| NATURAL HEALTH CENTRE (HM14566) | | | ● | ● | | | | | | | | | ● | | | |
| NELSON, S (HM14782) | ● | | ● | ● | | | ● | ● | ● | ● | ● | ● | ● | | ● | |
| ONE STOP HEALTH & BEAUTY (HM15323) | ● | ● | ● | ● | ● | ● | ● | ● | ● | ● | ● | ● | ● | ● | ● | ● |
| PEPPER, JOHN (HM16009) | ● | | | | | | | | | | ● | | | | | ● |
| PHYSIO AND SPORTS INJURIES (HM16195) | | | | | | | | | | | | | | | ● | |
| PURCELL, AMANDA (HM16762) | | | | | | ● | | | | | | | | | ● | |
| RAINBOW PREGNANCY ADVICE (HM16883) | | | | | | | ● | | | | | | | | | |
| RAMSBOTTOM PHYSIO CLINIC (HM16919) | | | | | | | | | | | | | | | | |
| RATCLIFFE, MARK (HM16949) | | | | | | | ● | ● | | | | | ● | | ● | |
| REMEDIAL MASSAGE/SPORTS (HM17175) | | | | | | | | | | | | | | | | |
| SMITH, CHRISTOPHER (DR) (HM18728) | | | | | | | | | | | | | | | ● | |
| ST GEORGES MULTI THERAPY CTRE (HM19075) | | ● | | ● | | | | | | | | | | | ● | |
| ST MARY'S CLINIC (HM19087) | | | | | | | | | | | | ● | | | ● | |
| TIP TOES (HM20086) | | | | | | | | | | | | ● | | | | |
| TRADITIONAL ACUPUNCTURE CLINIC (HM20220) | ● | | ● | ● | | | ● | | ● | ● | | ● | ● | | ● | |
| TRADITIONAL CHINESE MED CTRE (HM20223) | ● | | | ● | | | | ● | ● | | | | ● | | ● | ● |
| UPHAM, GILL (HM20522) | ● | ● | ● | ● | | | ● | | | | ● | | | | | |
| WATKINSON, BARBARA (HM20999) | ● | | | ● | | | ● | | | | ● | | | | ● | |
| WEST LANCS MCTIMONEY (HM21224) | ● | | | ● | | | | | | | | | ● | | ● | |
| WILSON, G (HM21656) | | | | | | | | | | | | | | | | ● |
| **LEICESTERSHIRE** | | | | | | | | | | | | | | | | |
| ACUPUNCTURE SERVICES (HM00320) | | ● | | | | | | | ● | | | | ● | | ● | ● |

# I - S Conditions treated at Practices/Businesses

Business by County with Reference no.

| Condition | ALBANY HOUSE (HM00479) | ANDREWS, SIMON C (HM00859) | ARCHWAY HSE NATURAL HLTH CTRE (HM00983) | AROMATHERAPY INTERNATIONAL (HM01115) | BROWN, RAY (HM03245) | CALM WATERS (HM03557) | CHIROPRACTIC CENTRE (HM04381) | CONLIFFE, LOUISE (HM04982) | DEADMAN, P J (HM05932) | GRAHAM SPOWAGE OSTEOPATHIC SVS (HM08340) | HASSETT, CHARLES (HM09187) | JACQUI BATES COUNSELLING (HM10866) | LEWIS, JACQUELINE (HM12296) | LOUGHBOROUGH OSTEOPATHIC (HM12660) | MELTON MOWBRAY PHYSIO CLINIC (HM13717) | NATURAL WAY HEALTH CENTRE (HM14669) | OADBY HOUSE (HM15140) | SCHOOL OF SPIRITUAL KNOWLEDGE (HM18085) | SHIRLEY FRANKLIN AROMATHERAPY (HM18485) | SUE CHARLES AROMATHERAPY (HM19466) | SUE RICKS COMP THERAPY (HM19467) | VICTORIA CLINIC (HM20650) | WENDY PRICE HOLISTIC RIDING (HM21198) | WILKINSON, GWEN (HM21507) | WOHL, M (DR) (HM21758) | LINCOLNSHIRE | ALEXANDER TECHNIQUE (HM00550) | BARN HOUSE PHYSIO CLINIC (HM01726) | BEVERLEYS (HM02246) | BOSTON CHIROPRACTIC CLINIC (HM02726) | CASTLEGATE OSTEO PRACTICE (HM03847) | CHIEN ACUPUNCTURE CLINIC (HM04161) | CLINIC OF NATURAL MEDICINE (HM04703) | COMPLEMENTARY THERAPY CENTRE (HM04946) |
|---|---|---|---|---|---|---|---|---|---|---|---|---|---|---|---|---|---|---|---|---|---|---|---|---|---|---|---|---|---|---|---|---|---|---|
| Sexual Problems | | ● | | | | ● | | | | | | | | | | | | | | | ● | | ● | | | | | | ● | | | | ● | |
| Sciatica | | ● | | | | ● | ● | ● | | ● | ● | | | | | | | ● | ● | ● | ● | ● | | | ● | | ● | | ● | ● | ● | ● | ● | ● |
| Schizophrenia | | ● | | | | ● | | | | | | | | | | | | | | | ● | | | | | | | | ● | | | | | |
| Rheumatoid Arthritis | | ● | | | | ● | | ● | | ● | | | | ● | | | | ● | | | ● | ● | | | | | | | ● | | ● | | ● | |
| Restless Legs | | ● | | | | ● | | | | ● | | | | | | | | ● | | | ● | ● | | | | | | | ● | | | | | ● |
| Recurrent Infections | | ● | | | | ● | | | | | | | | | | | | | | | ● | | | | | | | | ● | | | | ● | |
| Raynaud's Disease | | ● | | | | ● | | | | | | | | | | | | | | | ● | | | | ● | | | | ● | | ● | | ● | ● |
| Psoriasis | ● | ● | | | | ● | | | | | | | | | | | | | | ● | ● | | | | | | | | ● | | | ● | | |
| Prostate Problems | | ● | | | | ● | | | | | | | | | | | | ● | | | ● | | | | | | | | ● | | | | ● | |
| Pregnancy Help | | ● | | | | ● | | ● | | ● | | | | | | | | | | | ● | ● | | | ● | | | | ● | ● | ● | | ● | |
| Postural Problems | | | | | | | | | | | | | | | | | | | | | | | | | | | | | | | | | | |
| Pneumonia | | ● | | | | ● | | | | | | | | | | | | ● | | | ● | | | | | | | | ● | | | | ● | |
| PMT | | ● | | | | ● | | ● | | | | | | | | | | ● | ● | ● | ● | ● | ● | | | | | | ● | | | ● | ● | ● |
| Piles | | ● | | | | ● | | ● | | | | | | | | | | | | | ● | | | | | | | | ● | | | | ● | |
| Phobias | | ● | | | | ● | | ● | ● | | | ● | | | | | | | ● | | ● | ● | | | ● | | | | ● | | | | | |
| Period Problems | | ● | | | | ● | | ● | | | | | | | | | | ● | | | ● | ● | | | | | | | ● | | ● | ● | ● | |
| Parkinson's Disease | | ● | | | | ● | | | | | | | | | | | | ● | | ● | ● | | | | ● | | | | ● | | | | | |
| Panic Attacks | | | | | | | | | | | | | | | | | | | | | | | | | | | | | | | | | | |
| Palpitations | | ● | | | | ● | | ● | | | | | | | | | | ● | | | ● | ● | | | | | | | ● | | | | | |
| Pain | | ● | ● | ● | ● | ● | ● | ● | | ● | ● | | ● | ● | ● | ● | ● | ● | ● | | ● | ● | ● | | ● | | | ● | ● | ● | ● | ● | ● | ● |
| Osteoporosis | | ● | | | | ● | | | | | | | | | | | | ● | | | ● | ● | | | ● | | | | ● | ● | | | | ● |
| Obesity | | | | | | ● | | | | | | | | | | | | | | | ● | | ● | | ● | | | | ● | | | | | |
| Neuralgia | | ● | | | | ● | ● | | | ● | ● | | | | | | | ● | | | ● | ● | | | | | | | ● | ● | ● | | ● | ● |
| Nervous Disorders | | ● | | | | ● | | | | | | | | | | | | ● | ● | ● | ● | ● | | | ● | | | | ● | | ● | | | ● |
| Nerve Disorders | | ● | | | | ● | ● | | | ● | | | | | | | | ● | | | ● | | | | | | | | ● | ● | ● | | | |
| Nausea | | ● | | | | ● | | | | | | | | | | | | | | | ● | | | | | | | | ● | | | | | |
| Nail Health | | ● | | | | ● | | | | | | | | | | | | | | | ● | | | | | | | | ● | | | | | |
| Musculo-skeletal | | | | | | | | | | | | | | | | | | | | | | | | | | | | | | | | | | |
| Muscular Dystrophy | | ● | | | | ● | | | | | | | | | | | | ● | | | ● | | | | | | | | ● | | | | | |
| Multiple Sclerosis | | ● | | | | ● | | ● | | | | | ● | | | | ● | ● | | | ● | ● | | | ● | | | ● | ● | | | | | |
| Mouth Ulcers | | ● | | | | ● | | | | | | | | | | | | | | | ● | | | | | | | | ● | | | | ● | |
| Mouth Disorders | | ● | | | | ● | | | | | | | | | | | | | | | ● | | | | | | | | ● | | | | | |
| Motion Sickness | | ● | | | | ● | | | | | | | | | | | | | | | ● | | | | | | | | ● | | | | | |
| Migraine | ● | ● | ● | ● | | ● | ● | ● | | | | | ● | | | ● | | ● | | ● | ● | ● | ● | | ● | | | | ● | ● | ● | ● | ● | ● |
| Menopause | | ● | ● | ● | | ● | | ● | | | | | | | | | | ● | | ● | ● | ● | | | | | | | ● | | | ● | ● | |
| ME | | ● | | | ● | ● | | ● | | | | | | | | | | ● | | ● | ● | ● | ● | | ● | | ● | | ● | | | | ● | ● |
| Lung Problems | | ● | | | | ● | | | | | | | | | | | | ● | | | ● | ● | | | | | | | ● | | | | ● | |
| Low Blood Pressure | | ● | | | | ● | | | | | | | | | | | | | | | ● | ● | | | | | | | ● | | | | | |
| Liver Disorders | | ● | | | | ● | | | | | | | | | | | | | | | ● | | | | | | | | ● | | | | ● | |
| Lethargy | | ● | | | | ● | | | | | | | | | | | | ● | | | ● | ● | | | | | | | ● | | | ● | ● | |
| Laryngitis | | ● | | | | ● | | ● | | | | | | | | | | | | | ● | | | | ● | | | | ● | | | | | |
| Lactose Intolerance | | | | | | ● | | | | | | | | | | | | | | | ● | | | ● | | | | | ● | | | | ● | |
| Kidney Complaints | | ● | | | | ● | | | | | | | | | | | | ● | | | ● | | | | | | | | ● | | | | ● | ● |
| Joint Pain | ● | ● | ● | | | ● | ● | ● | | ● | ● | | ● | | ● | ● | ● | ● | | | ● | ● | | | ● | | | ● | ● | ● | ● | ● | ● | ● |
| Jet Lag | | | | | | ● | | ● | | | | | | | | | | ● | | | ● | | | | | | | | ● | | | | ● | |
| Itching | | ● | | | | ● | | ● | | | | | | | | | | | | | ● | | | | | | | | ● | | | | | |
| Irritable Bowel Syndrome | | ● | ● | ● | | ● | | ● | | | | | | | | | | ● | ● | ● | ● | ● | | | | | | | ● | ● | | | ● | |
| Insomnia | ● | ● | ● | ● | | ● | | | | | | | | | | | | | | ● | ● | | | | ● | | | | ● | | | ● | ● | |

www.healthmyself.com

# I - S Conditions treated at Practices/Businesses

| Business by County with Reference no. | Insomnia | Irritable Bowel Syndrome | Itching | Jet Lag | Joint Pain | Kidney Complaints | Lactose Intolerance | Laryngitis | Lethargy | Liver Disorders | Low Blood Pressure | Lung Problems | ME | Menopause | Migraine | Motion Sickness | Mouth Disorders | Mouth Ulcers | Multiple Sclerosis | Muscular Dystrophy | Musculo-skeletal | Nail Health | Nausea | Nerve Disorders |
|---|---|---|---|---|---|---|---|---|---|---|---|---|---|---|---|---|---|---|---|---|---|---|---|---|
| COXON CLINIC (HM05326) | | ● | | | ● | | | | | | | | | | | | | | ● | | | | | |
| EASTGATE HYPNOTHERAPY CENTRE (HM06541) | | ● | | | | | | | | | | | | | | | | | | | | | | |
| GOOD HEALTHKEEPING (HM08241) | ● | ● | ● | | ● | | ● | | ● | ● | ● | ● | ● | ● | ● | ● | | ● | ● | | | ● | ● | ● |
| GRANTHAM PHYSIO PRACTICE (HM08394) | | | | | ● | | | | | | | | | | | | | | | | | | | |
| HARRISON, FIONA (HM09098) | ● | ● | | | | | | | | | | | | ● | ● | | | | | | | | | |
| HORNCASTLE WAR MEMORIAL CENTRE (HM10172) | | ● | | | ● | | | | | | | | | | ● | | | | | | | | | ● |
| JUST JILLS (HM11282) | | ● | ● | ● | ● | | | | ● | | | | ● | ● | ● | ● | ● | | | | | ● | ● | ● |
| KESTEVEN NATURAL HEALTH CENTRE (HM11564) | ● | ● | ● | ● | ● | ● | ● | ● | ● | ● | ● | ● | ● | ● | ● | ● | ● | ● | ● | ● | | ● | ● | ● |
| LIFE (HM12335) | | | | | | | | | | | | | | | | | | | | | | | | |
| LINCOLN HERBAL TREATMENT CTRE (HM12407) | ● | ● | ● | ● | ● | ● | ● | ● | ● | ● | ● | ● | ● | ● | ● | ● | ● | ● | ● | | | ● | ● | ● |
| LIVING HEALTH (HM12485) | | | | | | | | | | | | | | | ● | | | | | | | | | ● |
| MARK RIDDLE HYPNOTHERAPY (HM13108) | ● | | | | | | | | | | | | | | | | | | | | | ● | | ● |
| MORLEY-KIRK, JOHN (HM14187) | ● | ● | | | | ● | | | ● | ● | ● | ● | ● | ● | ● | | | | ● | | | | | |
| NEWLAND CHIROPRACTIC CLINIC (HM14866) | | ● | | | ● | | | | | | | | | | ● | | | | ● | | | | | ● |
| REFLEXOLOGY CLINIC (HM17084) | ● | ● | | | ● | ● | | ● | ● | | | | ● | ● | ● | | | | ● | | | | | ● |
| REMEDIES (HM17176) | | | | | | | | | | | | | | | | | | | ● | ● | | | | |
| SALON, JANIES (HM17863) | | | | | | | | | | | | | | ● | ● | | | | | | | | | |
| SMITH, MICHAEL (HM18780) | ● | ● | | | | | | | | | | | | | ● | | | | | | | | | |
| WHITE, HEATHER (HM21357) | | ● | | | ● | | | | ● | | | | ● | ● | ● | ● | | | | | | | | |
| LONDON | | | | | | | | | | | | | | | | | | | | | | | | |
| FIRST PATH HYPNOTHERAPY (HM07338) | ● | ● | | | | | | | ● | | | | | ● | | | | | | | | | | |
| HARLEY STREET COMP MEDICINE (HM09001) | ● | ● | ● | ● | ● | ● | ● | ● | ● | ● | ● | ● | ● | ● | ● | ● | ● | ● | ● | ● | | ● | ● | ● |
| LONDON (GREATER) | | | | | | | | | | | | | | | | | | | | | | | | |
| 1ST ALTERNATIVE HEALTH CENTRE (HM00002) | | ● | | | ● | | | | | | | | ● | | ● | | | | | | | | | ● |
| ABBEY CENTRE (HM00071) | | | | | | | | | | | | | | | | | | | | | | | | |
| ABIGAIL'S (HM00126) | ● | ● | | | | | | | | | | | ● | ● | ● | | | | | | | | | |
| ABRAHAMS & BENNETT (HM00132) | | | | | | | | | | | | | | | | | | | | | | | | |
| ABRAHAMS & BENNETT (HM00133) | | | | | ● | | | | | | | | | | | | | | | | | | | |
| ACUMEDIC (HM00217) | ● | | | | ● | | | | | | ● | | | ● | ● | | | | | | | | ● | |
| ACUPUNCTURE & HERBAL CLINIC (HM00240) | | | | | ● | | | | | | | | | ● | ● | | | | | | | | | |
| ACUPUNCTURE CLINIC (HM00287) | ● | ● | ● | ● | ● | ● | ● | ● | ● | ● | ● | ● | ● | ● | ● | ● | ● | ● | ● | ● | | ● | ● | ● |
| ALEXANDER TECHNIQUE (HM00545) | | | | | | | | | | | | | | | | | | | | | | | | |
| ALEXANDER TECHNIQUE CENTRE (HM00555) | ● | | | | ● | ● | | | ● | | ● | ● | ● | | ● | ● | | | ● | | | | ● | ● |
| ALTERNATIVE HEALTH CENTRE (HM00705) | | ● | | | | | ● | | | | | | | | | | | | | | | | | |

| Business by County with Reference no. | Nervous Disorders | Neuralgia | Obesity | Osteoporosis | Pain | Palpitations | Panic Attacks | Parkinson's Disease | Period Problems | Phobias | Piles | PMT | Pneumonia | Postural Problems | Pregnancy Help | Prostate Problems | Psoriasis | Raynaud's Disease | Recurrent Infections | Restless Legs | Rheumatoid Arthritis | Schizophrenia | Sciatica | Sexual Problems |
|---|---|---|---|---|---|---|---|---|---|---|---|---|---|---|---|---|---|---|---|---|---|---|---|---|
| COXON CLINIC (HM05326) | | | | | ● | | | | | | | | | | | | | | | | | | ● | |
| EASTGATE HYPNOTHERAPY CENTRE (HM06541) | | | ● | | | | | | | ● | | | | | | | | | | | | | | |
| GOOD HEALTHKEEPING (HM08241) | | | ● | ● | | ● | | ● | ● | ● | ● | ● | ● | | ● | ● | ● | | ● | ● | ● | ● | | |
| GRANTHAM PHYSIO PRACTICE (HM08394) | | ● | | | ● | | | | | | | | | | | | | | | | ● | | | |
| HARRISON, FIONA (HM09098) | | | | | | | | | | | | | | | | | | | | | | | | |
| HORNCASTLE WAR MEMORIAL CENTRE (HM10172) | | ● | | ● | ● | | | | | | | | | | ● | | | | | | | | ● | |
| JUST JILLS (HM11282) | ● | ● | | | | ● | | | ● | | ● | | | | | | | | | | | | ● | |
| KESTEVEN NATURAL HEALTH CENTRE (HM11564) | ● | ● | ● | ● | ● | ● | | ● | ● | ● | ● | ● | ● | | ● | ● | ● | ● | ● | ● | ● | ● | ● | ● |
| LIFE (HM12335) | | | | | | | | | | | | | | | ● | | | | | | | | | |
| LINCOLN HERBAL TREATMENT CTRE (HM12407) | ● | ● | ● | ● | ● | ● | | | ● | ● | ● | ● | ● | | ● | ● | ● | ● | ● | ● | ● | ● | ● | ● |
| LIVING HEALTH (HM12485) | ● | ● | | ● | ● | ● | | | ● | | | | | | | | | | | | | | ● | |
| MARK RIDDLE HYPNOTHERAPY (HM13108) | ● | | | | | | | | | ● | | | | | | | | | | | | | | |
| MORLEY-KIRK, JOHN (HM14187) | | ● | | ● | ● | ● | | | | | | ● | | | ● | ● | ● | ● | | ● | ● | | ● | |
| NEWLAND CHIROPRACTIC CLINIC (HM14866) | ● | ● | | ● | ● | | | | | | | | | | ● | | | | | ● | ● | | ● | |
| REFLEXOLOGY CLINIC (HM17084) | ● | ● | | ● | ● | | | ● | ● | | | ● | | | | | | ● | | | ● | | ● | |
| REMEDIES (HM17176) | | | | | ● | | | | | | | | | | | | | | | | ● | | | |
| SALON, JANIES (HM17863) | | | | | ● | | | | | | | ● | | | | | | | | | | | | |
| SMITH, MICHAEL (HM18780) | | | ● | | | | | | | ● | | | | | | | | | | | | | | ● |
| WHITE, HEATHER (HM21357) | ● | | ● | | ● | | | | | ● | | | | | | | | | | | ● | | | |
| LONDON | | | | | | | | | | | | | | | | | | | | | | | | |
| FIRST PATH HYPNOTHERAPY (HM07338) | ● | | ● | | ● | | | | ● | ● | | ● | | | | | | | | | | | | ● |
| HARLEY STREET COMP MEDICINE (HM09001) | ● | ● | ● | ● | ● | ● | | ● | ● | ● | ● | ● | ● | | ● | ● | ● | ● | ● | ● | ● | ● | ● | ● |
| LONDON (GREATER) | | | | | | | | | | | | | | | | | | | | | | | | |
| 1ST ALTERNATIVE HEALTH CENTRE (HM00002) | | ● | | | ● | | | | ● | | | | | | ● | | | ● | | | ● | | ● | |
| ABBEY CENTRE (HM00071) | ● | | ● | | | | ● | | | ● | | | | | | | | | | | | | | ● |
| ABIGAIL'S (HM00126) | | | | | ● | | | | | | | ● | | | | | | | | | | | | |
| ABRAHAMS & BENNETT (HM00132) | | | | | ● | | | | | | | | | ● | ● | | | | | | | | ● | |
| ABRAHAMS & BENNETT (HM00133) | | | | | ● | | | | | | | | | ● | ● | | | | | | | | ● | |
| ACUMEDIC (HM00217) | ● | | ● | | ● | | | | ● | | | | | | | | ● | | | | | | ● | ● |
| ACUPUNCTURE & HERBAL CLINIC (HM00240) | | | | | ● | | | | ● | | | ● | | | | | ● | | | | | | | |
| ACUPUNCTURE CLINIC (HM00287) | ● | ● | ● | ● | ● | ● | | ● | ● | ● | ● | ● | ● | | ● | | ● | | ● | ● | ● | ● | ● | ● |
| ALEXANDER TECHNIQUE (HM00545) | | | | | | | | | | | | | | | | | | | | | | | ● | |
| ALEXANDER TECHNIQUE CENTRE (HM00555) | ● | ● | ● | ● | ● | ● | | | | ● | | | | | ● | | | | ● | | ● | | ● | |
| ALTERNATIVE HEALTH CENTRE (HM00705) | | | | | | | | | | | | | | | | | | | | | | | | |

# I - S Conditions treated at Practices/Businesses

| Business by County with Reference no. | ALTERNATIVE THERAPIES CENTRE (HM00728) | ALTERNATIVES COMP THERAPY CTRE (HM00743) | ANGEL HEART CENTRE (HM00867) | AUSTERBERRY, HELEN (HM01362) | AUSTERBERRY, HELEN (HM01363) | AVALON CHINESE MEDICINE CLINIC (HM01377) | AVATAR (HM01384) | AVENUE PSYCHOTHERAPY SERVICES (HM01391) | AYURVED HERBELI (HM01442) | BACK PAIN CENTRE (HM01498) | BACK PAIN CENTRE (HM01497) | BACK PAIN CENTRE (HM01499) | BACK PAIN CLINIC (HM01503) | BACK TO HEALTH - CHISWICK (HM01510) | BACK TO HEALTH - KINGSTON (HM01512) | BACK TO HEALTH - NORTH FINCHLEY (HM01513) | BACK TO HEALTH CHIRO CLINIC (HM01518) | BACK TO HEALTH-EALING (HM01519) | BARBICAN CENTRE (HM01693) | BARBICAN PODIATRY PRACTICE (HM01694) | BARNES CHIROPRACTIC HEALTHCARE (HM01740) | BARRIE, ALEXANDER (HM01798) | BAXTER, STEPHEN (HM01934) | BECKER, AMELY (HM02021) | BELMONT PHYSIOTHERAPY PRACTICE (HM02108) | BERNSTEIN, SAMUEL (HM02204) | BEST, JOHN G E (HM02224) | BLACKHEATH COMP THERAPIES CTRE (HM02450) | BLOOMSBURY ALEXANDER CENTRE (HM02516) | BLOOMSBURY THERAPY CENTRE (HM02518) | BOCOCK, RICHARD (HM02548) | BODYWISE (HM02637) | BOSTON CHIROPODY CLINIC (HM02725) | BRACKENBURY NTRL HEALTH CLNC (HM02837) |
|---|---|---|---|---|---|---|---|---|---|---|---|---|---|---|---|---|---|---|---|---|---|---|---|---|---|---|---|---|---|---|---|---|---|---|
| Sexual Problems | ● | | | | | ● | ● | ● | | | | | ● | | | | | | | | | | | ● | | | | | ● | ● | | | | |
| Sciatica | ● | ● | | | | ● | ● | | ● | ● | ● | ● | ● | ● | ● | ● | ● | ● | | | ● | ● | | | | | ● | | ● | ● | | ● | | ● |
| Schizophrenia | ● | | | | | | | ● | | | | | | | | | | | | | | | | | | | | | ● | ● | | | | |
| Rheumatoid Arthritis | ● | | | | | ● | | | | | | | ● | | | | | | ● | | ● | | | | | | | | ● | ● | | ● | ● | |
| Restless Legs | | | | | | ● | | | | | | | | | | | | | | | ● | ● | | | | | | | ● | ● | | ● | | |
| Recurrent Infections | ● | | | ● | ● | ● | | | | | | | ● | | | | | | | | | | | | | | | | ● | ● | ● | ● | ● | |
| Raynaud's Disease | | | | | | ● | | | | | | | | | | | | | | | | ● | | | | | | | ● | ● | ● | ● | ● | |
| Psoriasis | ● | ● | | | | ● | | | ● | | | | ● | | | | | | | | ● | | | | | | | | ● | ● | ● | ● | | |
| Prostate Problems | ● | | | | | ● | | | | | | | ● | | | | | | | | | ● | | | | | | | ● | ● | ● | ● | | |
| Pregnancy Help | ● | | | ● | ● | ● | ● | | | | ● | | | | | | | | | | | | | | | | | | ● | ● | ● | ● | | |
| Postural Problems | | | | | | | | | | ● | ● | ● | | | | | | | | | | | | | | | | | | | | | | |
| Pneumonia | ● | | | | | ● | | | | | | | | | | | | | | | | | | | | | | | ● | ● | | ● | | |
| PMT | ● | | | ● | ● | ● | | | ● | | | | ● | | | | | | | | | | | | | | | | ● | ● | ● | ● | | ● |
| Piles | ● | | | ● | ● | ● | | | ● | | | | ● | | | | | | | | | | | | | | | | ● | ● | ● | ● | | |
| Phobias | ● | | ● | | | ● | ● | ● | | | | | | | | | | | | | | | | ● | | ● | | | ● | ● | | | | |
| Period Problems | ● | ● | | ● | ● | ● | ● | | ● | | | | ● | | | | | | | | ● | | | | | | | | ● | ● | ● | ● | | ● |
| Parkinson's Disease | | | | | | ● | | | | | | | | | | | | | | | | ● | | | | | | | ● | ● | | ● | | |
| Panic Attacks | | | | | | | | ● | | | | | | | | | | | | | | | | | | | | | | | | | | |
| Palpitations | | ● | | ● | ● | ● | ● | | | | | | | | | | | | | | | ● | | | | | | | ● | ● | ● | ● | | |
| Pain | ● | ● | | ● | ● | ● | ● | | | ● | ● | ● | ● | ● | ● | ● | ● | ● | | | ● | ● | ● | | | | ● | ● | ● | ● | ● | ● | | ● |
| Osteoporosis | ● | ● | | | | ● | | | | | ● | ● | | | | | | | | | ● | | | | | | | | ● | ● | | ● | | |
| Obesity | | | ● | | | ● | ● | ● | | ● | | | | | | | | | | | | | | | | | | | ● | ● | | ● | | |
| Neuralgia | ● | | | | | ● | ● | | | | | | ● | | | | | | | | ● | ● | | | | | | | ● | ● | | ● | | |
| Nervous Disorders | ● | ● | ● | ● | ● | ● | | ● | | | | | ● | ● | ● | ● | ● | ● | | | | | | | | ● | | | ● | ● | ● | ● | | |
| Nerve Disorders | ● | | | | ● | ● | | ● | | | | ● | ● | ● | ● | ● | ● | ● | | | ● | ● | | | | | | | ● | ● | ● | ● | ● | |
| Nausea | ● | | | ● | ● | ● | | | | | | | | | | | | | | | | | | | | | | | ● | ● | | ● | | ● |
| Nail Health | ● | | | ● | ● | ● | | | ● | | | | | | | | | | | | | | | | | | | | ● | ● | | | | |
| Musculo-skeletal | | | | | | | | | | | | | | | | | | | | | | | | | | | | | | | | | | |
| Muscular Dystrophy | | | | | | ● | | | | | | | | | | | | | | | | | | | | | | | ● | ● | | | | |
| Multiple Sclerosis | | | | | | ● | | ● | | | | | | | | | | | | | ● | ● | | | ● | | | | ● | ● | | ● | | |
| Mouth Ulcers | ● | | | | | ● | | | ● | | | | ● | | | | | | | | | | | | | | | | ● | ● | | ● | | |
| Mouth Disorders | ● | | | | | ● | | | | | | | | | | | | | | | | | | | | | | | ● | ● | | ● | | |
| Motion Sickness | | | | | | ● | | | | | | | | | | | | | | | | | | | | | | | ● | ● | ● | ● | | |
| Migraine | ● | ● | | ● | ● | ● | ● | | ● | | ● | | ● | ● | ● | ● | ● | ● | | | ● | ● | | ● | | ● | | ● | ● | ● | ● | ● | | ● |
| Menopause | ● | ● | | ● | ● | ● | | | ● | | | | ● | | | | | | | | | | | | | | | | ● | ● | ● | ● | | ● |
| ME | ● | ● | | ● | ● | ● | | ● | ● | | | | | ● | ● | ● | ● | ● | | | | ● | ● | | | | | | ● | ● | ● | ● | | |
| Lung Problems | ● | | | | | ● | | | | | | | ● | | | | | | | | | ● | | | | | | | ● | ● | | ● | | |
| Low Blood Pressure | ● | | | | | ● | ● | | ● | | | | ● | | | | | | | | | ● | | | | | | | ● | ● | | ● | | |
| Liver Disorders | ● | | | | | ● | | | ● | | | | ● | | | | | | | | | ● | | | | | | | ● | ● | ● | ● | | |
| Lethargy | ● | ● | | ● | ● | ● | ● | ● | | | | | | | | | | | | | | ● | | | | | | | ● | ● | ● | ● | | |
| Laryngitis | ● | | | ● | ● | ● | | | | | | | ● | | | | | | | | | | | | | | | | ● | ● | ● | ● | | |
| Lactose Intolerance | | | | | | ● | | | ● | | | | | | | | | | | | | | | | | | | | ● | ● | | ● | | |
| Kidney Complaints | ● | | | | | ● | | | | | | | ● | | | | | | | | | ● | | | | | | | ● | ● | | ● | | |
| Joint Pain | ● | ● | | ● | ● | ● | ● | | ● | ● | ● | ● | ● | ● | ● | | ● | ● | | ● | ● | ● | | | ● | | ● | | ● | ● | | ● | | ● |
| Jet Lag | ● | | | ● | ● | ● | | | | | | | ● | | | | | | | | | | | | | | | | ● | ● | ● | | | |
| Itching | ● | ● | | ● | ● | ● | | | ● | | | | | | | | | | | | | | | | | | | | ● | ● | ● | ● | | |
| Irritable Bowel Syndrome | ● | ● | | ● | ● | ● | ● | | ● | ● | ● | ● | ● | ● | ● | ● | ● | ● | | | ● | ● | | | | ● | | | ● | ● | ● | ● | | |
| Insomnia | ● | ● | ● | ● | ● | ● | ● | ● | ● | | | | ● | | | | | | | | ● | | | | | ● | | | ● | ● | | ● | | |

# I - S Conditions treated at Practices/Businesses

| Business by County with Reference no. | Insomnia | Irritable Bowel Syndrome | Itching | Jet Lag | Joint Pain | Kidney Complaints | Lactose Intolerance | Laryngitis | Lethargy | Liver Disorders | Low Blood Pressure | Lung Problems | ME | Menopause | Migraine | Motion Sickness | Mouth Disorders | Mouth Ulcers | Multiple Sclerosis | Muscular Dystrophy | Musculo-skeletal | Nail Health | Nausea | Nerve Disorders |
|---|---|---|---|---|---|---|---|---|---|---|---|---|---|---|---|---|---|---|---|---|---|---|---|---|
| BRAHMA KUMARIS INNER SPACE (HM02886) | | | | | | | | | | | | | | | ● | | | | | | | | | |
| BRITISH AUTOGENIC SOCIETY (HM03076) | ● | ● | ● | ● | | | | | ● | | ● | | ● | ● | ● | | | | ● | | | | ● | |
| BRITISH HYPNOTHERAPY ASS (HM03084) | ● | ● | ● | | | | | | ● | | | | ● | ● | ● | | | | | | | | | |
| BRIXTON TAI CHI (HM03106) | | | | | | | | | | | | | | | | | | | | | | | | |
| BROOK GREEN OSTEOPATHY (HM03155) | | ● | | | ● | | | | | | | | | | ● | | | | | | | | | ● |
| BROOKS, CATHY (HM03175) | ● | ● | ● | ● | ● | ● | ● | ● | ● | | ● | | ● | ● | ● | ● | | ● | ● | | | | ● | ● |
| BROOKS, JANE (HM03177) | | | | | | | | | | | | | | | | | | | | | | | | |
| BROWN, ALISON R (HM03210) | | ● | | | | | | | | | | | ● | | ● | | | | | | | | | |
| BST FOUNDATION (HM03295) | | | | | | | | | | | | | | | | | | | | | | | | |
| BUCHANAN, ANGELA (HM03300) | | | | | ● | | | | | | | | | | | | | | ● | | | | | ● |
| BUCKLEY, BILLIE (HM03318) | | | | | | | | | | | | | | | | | | | | | | | | |
| BYRNE, JUDY (HM03516) | | ● | | | | | | | | | | | | | | | | | | | | | | |
| CASSIDY MEDICAL CENTRE (HM03815) | | | | | ● | | | | | | | | | | | | | | | | | | | ● |
| CENTRE FOR TRANSFORMATION (HM03920) | ● | ● | ● | ● | ● | ● | ● | | ● | ● | | | ● | ● | ● | ● | | | ● | | | ● | ● | |
| CHAPMAN, RUPERT (HM04009) | | | | | ● | | | | | | | | | | ● | | | | | | | | | ● |
| CHARTERHOUSE PHYSIOTHERAPY (HM04049) | | | | | ● | | | | | | | | | | | | | | | | | | | |
| CHARTERHOUSE PHYSIOTHERAPY (HM04048) | | | | | ● | | | | | | | | | | | | | | | | | | | |
| CHATSWORTH CLINIC (HM04063) | ● | ● | ● | ● | ● | ● | | ● | ● | ● | ● | ● | ● | ● | ● | ● | | ● | ● | | | | ● | ● |
| CHINESE MEDICAL CTRE OF LONDON (HM04245) | ● | ● | ● | ● | ● | ● | ● | ● | ● | ● | ● | ● | ● | ● | ● | ● | ● | ● | ● | ● | | ● | ● | ● |
| CHINESE SHOP (HM04269) | ● | ● | | | | | | | | | ● | | | ● | ● | | | | | | | | | |
| CHIROPRACTIC CLINIC (HM04393) | | ● | | | ● | | | | | | | | ● | | | | | | | | | | | ● |
| CHISWICK CHIROPRACTIC CLINIC (HM04412) | | ● | | | ● | | | | | | | | | | ● | | | | | | | | | ● |
| CITY HEALTH CENTRE (HM04496) | ● | ● | | | ● | | | ● | ● | | ● | ● | ● | ● | ● | ● | | | | | | | ● | ● |
| CLAIRE CHOUDHURY HERBAL PRAC (HM04507) | ● | ● | ● | | ● | | | ● | ● | | ● | ● | ● | ● | ● | | | ● | | | | | ● | |
| CLASSICAL OSTEOPATH (HM04610) | ● | ● | | | ● | ● | | ● | ● | ● | ● | ● | ● | | ● | | | | | | | | | ● |
| CLINIC FOR COUNSELLING (HM04681) | | | | | | | | | | | | | | | | | | | | | | | | |
| CLINIC FOR COUNSELLING (HM04680) | | | | | | | | | | | | | | | | | | | | | | | | |
| COLLEGE-PRACTICAL HOMEOPATHY (HM04855) | ● | | | | | | | | | | | | | | ● | | | | | | | | | |
| COMPLETE HEALTH CARE (HM04958) | ● | ● | ● | | ● | ● | ● | | ● | ● | ● | ● | ● | ● | ● | | | ● | ● | | | | ● | |
| CONNAUGHT SQUARE HYPNOTHERAPY (HM04986) | | | | | | | | | | | | | | | | | | | | | | | | |
| CONWAY, JONATHON (HM05029) | | | | | | | | | | | | | | | | | | | | | | | | |
| COUNSELLING & PSYCHOTHERAPY (HM05246) | | | | | | | | | | | | | ● | | ● | | | | | | | | | ● |
| COUNSELLING SERVICE (HM05252) | | | | | | | | | | | | | | | | | | | | | | | | |
| CRAVEN CLINIC (HM05385) | ● | | | | ● | | | | ● | | | | | ● | ● | | | | | | | | | |

| Business by County with Reference no. | Nervous Disorders | Neuralgia | Obesity | Osteoporosis | Pain | Palpitations | Panic Attacks | Parkinson's Disease | Period Problems | Phobias | Piles | PMT | Pneumonia | Postural Problems | Pregnancy Help | Prostate Problems | Psoriasis | Raynaud's Disease | Recurrent Infections | Restless Legs | Rheumatoid Arthritis | Schizophrenia | Sciatica | Sexual Problems |
|---|---|---|---|---|---|---|---|---|---|---|---|---|---|---|---|---|---|---|---|---|---|---|---|---|
| BRAHMA KUMARIS INNER SPACE (HM02886) | | | | | | | | | | | | | | | | | | | | | | | | |
| BRITISH AUTOGENIC SOCIETY (HM03076) | ● | ● | | | ● | ● | | | ● | ● | ● | ● | | | ● | | ● | ● | | ● | ● | | | |
| BRITISH HYPNOTHERAPY ASS (HM03084) | | | ● | | | ● | | | ● | ● | | ● | | | ● | | ● | | ● | | | | | ● |
| BRIXTON TAI CHI (HM03106) | | | | | | | | | | | | | | | ● | | | | | | | | | |
| BROOK GREEN OSTEOPATHY (HM03155) | | ● | | ● | ● | | | | ● | | | | | | ● | | | | | ● | ● | | ● | |
| BROOKS, CATHY (HM03175) | ● | ● | ● | | ● | ● | | | ● | ● | | ● | | | ● | ● | ● | ● | ● | ● | ● | | ● | |
| BROOKS, JANE (HM03177) | ● | | | | | | | | | ● | | | | | | | | | | | | | | |
| BROWN, ALISON R (HM03210) | | | | ● | ● | | | | | | | | | ● | ● | | | | | | | | ● | |
| BST FOUNDATION (HM03295) | | | | | | | | | | ● | | | | | | | | | | | | | | |
| BUCHANAN, ANGELA (HM03300) | | ● | | | ● | | | | | | | | | | | | | | | | ● | | ● | |
| BUCKLEY, BILLIE (HM03318) | | | | | | | | | | ● | | | | | | | | | | | | | | |
| BYRNE, JUDY (HM03516) | | | ● | | ● | | ● | | | ● | | | | | | | ● | | | | | | | |
| CASSIDY MEDICAL CENTRE (HM03815) | | ● | | | ● | | | | | | | | | | ● | | | | | | | | ● | |
| CENTRE FOR TRANSFORMATION (HM03920) | | ● | ● | | | ● | | | ● | ● | ● | ● | | | ● | ● | ● | | ● | ● | ● | | | ● |
| CHAPMAN, RUPERT (HM04009) | | ● | | | ● | | | | | | | | | | | | | | | | | | ● | |
| CHARTERHOUSE PHYSIOTHERAPY (HM04049) | | | | | | | | | | | | | | | | | | | | | | | | |
| CHARTERHOUSE PHYSIOTHERAPY (HM04048) | | | | | | | | | | | | | | | | | | | | | | | | |
| CHATSWORTH CLINIC (HM04063) | ● | ● | | ● | | ● | | | | ● | ● | ● | | | ● | ● | ● | ● | ● | ● | ● | | ● | ● |
| CHINESE MEDICAL CTRE OF LONDON (HM04245) | ● | ● | ● | ● | ● | ● | | ● | ● | ● | ● | ● | ● | | ● | ● | ● | ● | ● | | ● | ● | ● | ● |
| CHINESE SHOP (HM04269) | | ● | ● | ● | ● | ● | | | ● | | ● | ● | | | | | ● | | | | | | ● | |
| CHIROPRACTIC CLINIC (HM04393) | | | | | | | | | | | | | | | | | | | | | | | ● | |
| CHISWICK CHIROPRACTIC CLINIC (HM04412) | | ● | | | ● | | | | ● | | | | | ● | | | | | | ● | | | ● | |
| CITY HEALTH CENTRE (HM04496) | | ● | | ● | ● | ● | | | ● | | ● | ● | ● | | ● | ● | | ● | ● | ● | ● | | ● | ● |
| CLAIRE CHOUDHURY HERBAL PRAC (HM04507) | ● | ● | ● | | ● | ● | | | ● | | ● | ● | ● | | | ● | ● | ● | ● | | ● | | ● | |
| CLASSICAL OSTEOPATH (HM04610) | ● | ● | | ● | ● | ● | | | ● | | ● | ● | | | | | | ● | ● | ● | | | ● | |
| CLINIC FOR COUNSELLING (HM04681) | | | | | | | | | | ● | | | | | | | | | | | | | | |
| CLINIC FOR COUNSELLING (HM04680) | | | | | | | | | | ● | | | | | | | | | | | | | | |
| COLLEGE-PRACTICAL HOMEOPATHY (HM04855) | | | | | | | | | | | | | | | | | | | | | | | | |
| COMPLETE HEALTH CARE (HM04958) | ● | ● | ● | ● | ● | ● | | | ● | ● | ● | ● | | | ● | ● | ● | ● | ● | ● | ● | | ● | |
| CONNAUGHT SQUARE HYPNOTHERAPY (HM04986) | ● | | | | ● | | | | | | | | | | | | | | | | | | | |
| CONWAY, JONATHON (HM05029) | | | | | | | | | | ● | | | | | | | | | | | | | | |
| COUNSELLING & PSYCHOTHERAPY (HM05246) | | | | | ● | | | | | | | | | | | | | | | | | | | ● |
| COUNSELLING SERVICE (HM05252) | ● | | | | | | | | | | | | | | | | | | | | | | | |
| CRAVEN CLINIC (HM05385) | | | | | ● | | | | ● | ● | | ● | | | | | ● | | | | | | ● | |

# I - S Conditions treated at Practices/Businesses

Business by County with Reference no.

| Condition | CREATIVE INSIGHTS (HM05399) | CRISTA GALLI OSTEOPATHS (HM05446) | CTRE FOR CRANIO-SACRAL THERAPY (HM05540) | CTRE FOR THE STUDY OF COMP MED (HM05544) | DALTON, HELEN (HM05698) | DAVID WEISS HOMEOPATHY (HM05781) | DAVIS, JULIA (HM05854) | DAWSON, DAVID (DR) (HM05880) | DE BURGH, JULIE (HM05904) | DELROY, SANDRA (DR) (HM05968) | DENNIS MICHAEL PRACTICE (HM05990) | DENNISON, IAN (HM05996) | DISTANT HEALING (HM06123) | DOCKLANDS DENTAL/COMP HLTH (HM06141) | DREAM LINE (HM06296) | DREAMCATCHER (HM06298) | DULWICH PHYSIOTHERAPY (HM06383) | E.LONDON COMPLEMENTARY HEALTH (HM06479) | EALING COUNS & THERAPY CTRE (HM06488) | EAST WEST HERB SHOP (HM06527) | EAST WEST THERAPIES (HM06529) | EDGELL, MARJORY (HM06599) | EDGWARE NATURAL HEALTH CENTRE (HM06604) | ELLWOOD, CAROLINE (HM06780) | ELTHAM HYPNOTHERAPY ANALYSIS (HM06789) | ENFIELD CLINIC OF HERBAL MED (HM06818) | ENFIELD HYP & COUNSELLING (HM06819) | EQUILIBRIUM (HM06869) | EQUILIBRIUM COUNS/THRPY CTRE (HM06873) | FAIR, ANNETTE (HM07048) | FELDENKRAIS CENTRE (HM07190) | FLETCHER, CLARE (HM07410) | FLEXIBLE HOUR (HM07420) | FLOAT WORKS (HM07424) |
|---|---|---|---|---|---|---|---|---|---|---|---|---|---|---|---|---|---|---|---|---|---|---|---|---|---|---|---|---|---|---|---|---|---|---|
| Sexual Problems | | | | ● | | | ● | | | | | | | | ● | | | | ● | | | ● | | | ● | ● | ● | | | | | | | |
| Sciatica | | ● | ● | ● | ● | | ● | | | | ● | | ● | ● | | | | ● | | ● | ● | | | ● | | | | ● | | ● | | | | |
| Schizophrenia | | | | ● | | | ● | | | | | | ● | | | | | | | | | | | | ● | | | | | | | | | |
| Rheumatoid Arthritis | | ● | ● | ● | ● | ● | ● | | | | ● | | ● | | | | | ● | | ● | ● | | | | | | | ● | | | | | ● | |
| Restless Legs | | ● | ● | ● | ● | | ● | | | | ● | | | | | | | ● | | | ● | | | | | | | | | | | | | |
| Recurrent Infections | | ● | ● | ● | ● | ● | ● | | | | | | | | | | | ● | | ● | | | | | | ● | | | | | | | | |
| Raynaud's Disease | | ● | ● | ● | ● | | ● | | | | | | | | ● | | | ● | | ● | ● | | ● | | | ● | | | | | | | | |
| Psoriasis | | | | ● | ● | ● | ● | | | | | | ● | | | | | ● | | | ● | | ● | | ● | ● | | ● | | | | | | |
| Prostate Problems | | ● | ● | ● | ● | | ● | | | | | | ● | | | | | ● | | | | | | | | ● | | | | | | | | |
| Pregnancy Help | ● | ● | ● | ● | ● | | ● | | | | | | | | | | | ● | | | ● | ● | | ● | | ● | | ● | | | | | | ● |
| Postural Problems | | | | | | | | | | | | | | ● | | | | | | | | | | | | | | | | ● | | | | |
| Pneumonia | | ● | | | ● | | ● | | | | | | ● | | | | | ● | | | | | | | | | | | | | | | | |
| PMT | | ● | ● | ● | ● | ● | ● | | | | ● | | ● | | | | | ● | ● | ● | ● | ● | ● | ● | | ● | | ● | | | | | | |
| Piles | | ● | | ● | ● | | ● | | | | | | ● | | | | | ● | | | | | | | | | | | | | | | | |
| Phobias | ● | | | ● | ● | | ● | | ● | ● | | | ● | | | | | ● | | | ● | | ● | | ● | | ● | ● | ● | | | | | ● |
| Period Problems | | ● | ● | ● | ● | ● | ● | | | | | | ● | | | | | ● | | ● | ● | | | ● | | ● | | ● | | | | | | |
| Parkinson's Disease | | | ● | | | | ● | | | | | | | | | | | ● | | | | | | | | ● | | | | | | | | |
| Panic Attacks | | | | | | | | | | | | | | | | | | | | | | | | | ● | | | | | | | | | |
| Palpitations | ● | ● | | ● | ● | | ● | | | | | | ● | | | | | ● | | ● | | | ● | | ● | ● | | ● | ● | | | | | |
| Pain | ● | ● | ● | ● | ● | ● | ● | | | | | ● | ● | ● | | | ● | ● | | ● | | | ● | ● | ● | | ● | | ● | ● | ● | ● | | |
| Osteoporosis | | | | | ● | | ● | | | | | | ● | | ● | | | ● | | | | ● | | | | | | | | | | | | |
| Obesity | ● | | | | | | ● | | | | | | | | | | | ● | | | | ● | ● | | ● | | ● | ● | | | | | | |
| Neuralgia | | ● | ● | ● | ● | | ● | | | | | | ● | | | | | ● | ● | | | | | | ● | | | ● | | | | | | |
| Nervous Disorders | | | ● | ● | ● | | ● | | | | | | ● | | | | | ● | ● | ● | | | ● | | ● | ● | ● | ● | | | | | | |
| Nerve Disorders | | ● | ● | | ● | | ● | | | | | | ● | | | | | ● | ● | | | | | | | ● | | | | ● | | | | |
| Nausea | | ● | ● | ● | ● | | ● | | | | | | ● | | | | | ● | | ● | | | | | | ● | | ● | | | | | ● | |
| Nail Health | | | | | | | ● | | | | | | ● | | | | | | | | | | | | | | | | | | | | | |
| Musculo-skeletal | | | | | | | | | | | | | | | | | | | | | | | | | | | | | | | | | | |
| Muscular Dystrophy | | | | | | | ● | | | | | | ● | | | | | ● | | | | | | | | | | | | | | | | |
| Multiple Sclerosis | | | ● | ● | ● | | ● | | | ● | | | ● | | | | ● | ● | | | | | ● | | | | ● | ● | | | | | | |
| Mouth Ulcers | | | | ● | ● | | ● | | | | | | ● | | | | | ● | | | | | | | | ● | | | | | | | | |
| Mouth Disorders | | ● | ● | | | | ● | | | | | | ● | | | | | ● | | | | | | | | ● | | | | | | | | |
| Motion Sickness | | ● | ● | ● | ● | ● | ● | | | | | | | | | | | ● | | | | | | | | | | | | | | | ● | |
| Migraine | ● | ● | ● | ● | ● | ● | ● | | | | | | ● | | | | | ● | | ● | ● | | ● | | | ● | ● | ● | ● | ● | | ● | ● | |
| Menopause | | ● | ● | ● | ● | ● | ● | | | | | | | | | | | ● | | ● | ● | ● | ● | | | ● | | ● | | | | | | |
| ME | | ● | ● | ● | ● | ● | ● | ● | | | | | ● | | | | | ● | ● | ● | ● | ● | ● | | ● | ● | | ● | | | | | ● | |
| Lung Problems | | ● | ● | ● | ● | | ● | | | | | | ● | | | | | ● | | ● | | | | | | | | | | | | | | |
| Low Blood Pressure | | | ● | ● | ● | | ● | | | | | | | | | | | ● | | | ● | | | | | ● | | | | | | | | |
| Liver Disorders | | ● | ● | ● | ● | | ● | | | | | | ● | | | | | ● | | ● | ● | | | | | | | | | | | | | |
| Lethargy | | ● | ● | ● | ● | | ● | ● | | | | | | | ● | | | ● | ● | ● | ● | | | | | ● | | | | | | | ● | |
| Laryngitis | | ● | ● | ● | ● | ● | ● | | | | | | | | | | | ● | | | | | ● | | | ● | | | | | | | | |
| Lactose Intolerance | | | | ● | | | ● | ● | | | | | | | | | | | | | | | ● | | | ● | | ● | | | | | | |
| Kidney Complaints | | ● | | ● | ● | | ● | | | | | | ● | | | | | ● | | | | | | | | | | | | | | | | |
| Joint Pain | | ● | ● | ● | ● | ● | ● | ● | | | ● | ● | | ● | | | ● | ● | | ● | ● | | ● | | | | ● | ● | ● | ● | ● | ● | ● | |
| Jet Lag | | ● | | ● | ● | ● | ● | | | | | | | | | | | ● | | | | | | | | ● | | | | | | | ● | |
| Itching | | | | ● | ● | ● | ● | | | | | | ● | | | | | ● | | ● | | | | | | ● | | | | | | | | |
| Irritable Bowel Syndrome | ● | ● | ● | ● | ● | ● | ● | ● | | | | | ● | | | ● | | ● | | ● | ● | ● | ● | ● | ● | ● | ● | ● | | | | | ● | |
| Insomnia | ● | ● | ● | ● | ● | ● | ● | | ● | | | | ● | | | | | ● | | ● | ● | | ● | | ● | ● | ● | ● | | | | | ● | |

England (by County)

CONDITIONS TREATED

I-S

# I - S Conditions treated at Practices/Businesses

| Business by County with Reference no. | Insomnia | Irritable Bowel Syndrome | Itching | Jet Lag | Joint Pain | Kidney Complaints | Lactose Intolerance | Laryngitis | Lethargy | Liver Disorders | Low Blood Pressure | Lung Problems | ME | Menopause | Migraine | Motion Sickness | Mouth Disorders | Mouth Ulcers | Multiple Sclerosis | Muscular Dystrophy | Musculo-skeletal | Nail Health | Nausea | Nerve Disorders |
|---|---|---|---|---|---|---|---|---|---|---|---|---|---|---|---|---|---|---|---|---|---|---|---|---|
| FULHAM CLINIC (HM07781) | ● | ● | | | | ● | | | ● | | | ● | | ● | | | | | | | | | ● | |
| G T CONSULTANCY (HM07815) | ● | ● | | | | | | | | | | | | | | | | | | | | | | |
| GLASSMAN, DAVID (HM08128) | ● | | | | ● | ● | | | ● | | ● | ● | ● | | ● | ● | | | ● | ● | | | ● | ● |
| GODWIN, ROME (HM08194) | | | | | ● | | | | | | | | | | | | | | | | | | | |
| GREENWICH NATURAL HEALTH CTRE (HM08500) | | ● | | | ● | | | | | | | | ● | ● | ● | | | | | | | | | |
| GREIDINGER, CLIVE (HM08524) | ● | ● | | | | | | | | | | | | | | | | | | | | | | |
| HACKNEY HYPNOTHERAPY (HM08685) | ● | ● | | | | | | | | | | | | | | | | | | | | | | |
| HAIN, PATRICIA (HM08712) | ● | ● | | | ● | ● | ● | ● | ● | ● | ● | ● | ● | ● | ● | | | ● | ● | | | ● | ● | ● |
| HAMILTON, FIONA (HM08843) | | ● | | | ● | | | | | | | | | | | | | | | | | | | ● |
| HAMPSTEAD ACU/CHINESE HBL MED (HM08881) | | | | | ● | | | | | | | | | ● | ● | | | | | | | | | |
| HAREWOOD, MARCIA M (HM08991) | | ● | | | ● | | | | ● | ● | ● | | | | ● | | | | | | | | ● | |
| HARLEY ST STRESS MNGMT (HM08999) | ● | ● | ● | ● | | | | | ● | | | | ● | | ● | ● | | | | | | | ● | |
| HARLEY STREET TCM FERTILITY (HM09003) | | | | | | | | | | | | | ● | ● | | | | | | | | | | |
| HARLEY, KI (HM09006) | | | | | | | | | | | | | | | | | | | | | | | | |
| HARPER, SUZANNE G (HM09042) | ● | | | | ● | | | ● | | | ● | | | | ● | | | | | | | | ● | |
| HARPER, SUZANNE G (HM09041) | ● | ● | | | ● | | | ● | | | ● | | | | ● | | | | | | | | ● | |
| HARROW HEALTH CARE CENTRE (HM09121) | ● | ● | | | ● | | | | | | | | ● | ● | ● | ● | | | | | | | ● | |
| HAVELOCK-SEARLE, PAULINE (HM09206) | ● | ● | | | | | | | | | | | | | | | | | | | | | | |
| HAWKINS, JAN (HM09222) | ● | ● | | | | | | | | | | | ● | ● | | | | | ● | ● | | | | |
| HEALERS WORLD (HM09320) | ● | ● | ● | ● | ● | ● | ● | ● | ● | ● | ● | ● | ● | ● | ● | ● | ● | ● | ● | ● | | ● | ● | ● |
| HEALING ARTS UK (HM09326) | | | | | ● | | | | | | | | | | | | | | | | | | | |
| HEALTHY LIVING CENTRE (HM09429) | ● | ● | ● | ● | ● | ● | ● | ● | ● | ● | ● | ● | ● | ● | ● | ● | ● | ● | ● | ● | | ● | ● | ● |
| HERBAL CARE (HM09601) | ● | ● | ● | ● | ● | | | ● | ● | | ● | ● | ● | ● | ● | ● | ● | ● | ● | ● | | | ● | ● |
| HERBAL CARE (HM09600) | ● | ● | ● | ● | ● | | | ● | ● | | ● | ● | ● | ● | ● | ● | ● | ● | ● | ● | | | ● | ● |
| HERBMEDIC (HM09663) | ● | ● | ● | ● | ● | ● | ● | ● | ● | ● | ● | ● | ● | ● | ● | ● | ● | ● | ● | ● | | ● | ● | ● |
| HETHERTON, ANNE (HM09697) | ● | ● | ● | ● | ● | ● | ● | ● | ● | ● | ● | ● | ● | ● | ● | ● | ● | ● | ● | ● | | ● | ● | ● |
| HIGHBURY CENTRE (HM09746) | | | | | | | | | | | | | | | | | | | | | | | | |
| HILDRETH & COCKER (HM09767) | | | | | ● | | | | | | | | | | | | | | | | | | | |
| HOGARTH CLINIC (HM09907) | ● | ● | | ● | ● | ● | | | | ● | ● | ● | ● | ● | ● | ● | | | ● | ● | | | ● | ● |
| HOLMES, DAVID (HM10040) | | | | | | | | | | | | | | | | | | | | | | ● | | |
| HOME VISITING SERVICES (HM10069) | ● | ● | ● | ● | ● | ● | ● | ● | ● | ● | ● | ● | ● | ● | ● | ● | ● | ● | ● | | | | ● | |
| HONG TAD ACUPUNCTURE & HERBAL (HM10119) | ● | ● | ● | ● | ● | ● | ● | ● | ● | ● | ● | ● | ● | ● | ● | ● | ● | ● | ● | ● | | | ● | ● |
| HOPE, ANN (HM10137) | | | | | | | | | | | | | | | | | | | | | | ● | | |
| HOUSE OF MISTRY (HM10220) | ● | ● | ● | | ● | ● | | | | | ● | | | ● | ● | | ● | ● | | | | ● | ● | |

| Business by County with Reference no. | Nervous Disorders | Neuralgia | Obesity | Osteoporosis | Pain | Palpitations | Panic Attacks | Parkinson's Disease | Period Problems | Phobias | Piles | PMT | Pneumonia | Postural Problems | Pregnancy Help | Prostate Problems | Psoriasis | Raynaud's Disease | Recurrent Infections | Restless Legs | Rheumatoid Arthritis | Schizophrenia | Sciatica | Sexual Problems |
|---|---|---|---|---|---|---|---|---|---|---|---|---|---|---|---|---|---|---|---|---|---|---|---|---|
| FULHAM CLINIC (HM07781) | | | ● | | | | | | ● | | | ● | | | ● | ● | | | | | | | | ● |
| G T CONSULTANCY (HM07815) | | | ● | | ● | | | | | ● | | | | | | | ● | | | | | | | ● |
| GLASSMAN, DAVID (HM08128) | ● | ● | ● | ● | ● | ● | | | | ● | | | | | ● | | | | ● | | ● | | ● | |
| GODWIN, ROME (HM08194) | | | | | ● | | ● | | | | | | | | | | | | | | | | | |
| GREENWICH NATURAL HEALTH CTRE (HM08500) | | | | ● | ● | | | | ● | | | | | | ● | | | | | | | | ● | |
| GREIDINGER, CLIVE (HM08524) | | | | | | | | | | ● | | | | | | | | | | | | | | ● |
| HACKNEY HYPNOTHERAPY (HM08685) | | | ● | | ● | | | | | ● | | | | | | | | | | | | | | ● |
| HAIN, PATRICIA (HM08712) | | | ● | ● | ● | ● | | | ● | ● | ● | ● | | | ● | ● | ● | | ● | | ● | ● | ● | |
| HAMILTON, FIONA (HM08843) | | | | | ● | | | | | | | | | | ● | | | | | | | | ● | |
| HAMPSTEAD ACU/CHINESE HBL MED (HM08881) | | | | | ● | | | | ● | | | ● | | | | | | | | | | | ● | |
| HAREWOOD, MARCIA M (HM08991) | | ● | | | ● | ● | | | ● | | ● | ● | | | ● | ● | ● | | ● | ● | | | ● | |
| HARLEY ST STRESS MNGMT (HM08999) | ● | | ● | | ● | ● | | | ● | ● | | ● | | | ● | | | | | | | | | ● |
| HARLEY STREET TCM FERTILITY (HM09003) | | | | | | | | | ● | | | ● | | | | | | | | | | | | |
| HARLEY, KI (HM09006) | ● | | | | | | | | | ● | | | | | | | | | | | | | | |
| HARPER, SUZANNE G (HM09042) | ● | ● | | ● | ● | ● | | | ● | ● | | ● | | | ● | | | ● | ● | ● | ● | | ● | |
| HARPER, SUZANNE G (HM09041) | ● | ● | | ● | ● | ● | | | ● | ● | | ● | | | ● | | | ● | ● | ● | ● | | ● | |
| HARROW HEALTH CARE CENTRE (HM09121) | ● | ● | | ● | ● | | | | ● | | | ● | | | ● | | ● | ● | | ● | ● | | ● | |
| HAVELOCK-SEARLE, PAULINE (HM09206) | | | ● | | ● | | | | | ● | | | | | | | | | | | | | | ● |
| HAWKINS, JAN (HM09222) | ● | | ● | | | | | | | ● | | | | | | | | | | | | | | ● |
| HEALERS WORLD (HM09320) | ● | ● | ● | ● | ● | ● | | ● | ● | ● | ● | ● | ● | | ● | ● | ● | ● | ● | ● | ● | ● | ● | ● |
| HEALING ARTS UK (HM09326) | | | | | | | | | | | | | | | | | | ● | | | ● | | ● | |
| HEALTHY LIVING CENTRE (HM09429) | ● | ● | ● | ● | ● | ● | | ● | ● | ● | ● | ● | ● | | ● | ● | ● | ● | ● | ● | ● | ● | ● | ● |
| HERBAL CARE (HM09601) | ● | | ● | ● | ● | ● | | | ● | ● | ● | ● | ● | | ● | ● | ● | ● | ● | ● | ● | | ● | ● |
| HERBAL CARE (HM09600) | ● | | ● | ● | ● | ● | | | ● | ● | ● | ● | ● | | ● | ● | ● | ● | ● | ● | ● | | ● | ● |
| HERBMEDIC (HM09663) | ● | ● | ● | ● | ● | ● | | ● | ● | ● | ● | ● | ● | | | ● | ● | ● | ● | ● | ● | ● | ● | ● |
| HETHERTON, ANNE (HM09697) | ● | ● | ● | ● | ● | ● | | | ● | ● | ● | ● | ● | | ● | ● | ● | ● | ● | ● | ● | | ● | ● |
| HIGHBURY CENTRE (HM09746) | | | | | | | | | | | | | | | ● | | | | | | | | ● | |
| HILDRETH & COCKER (HM09767) | | | | ● | | | | | | | | | | | | | | | | | ● | | | |
| HOGARTH CLINIC (HM09907) | ● | ● | ● | ● | ● | ● | | | ● | | ● | ● | ● | | ● | | ● | ● | ● | ● | ● | ● | ● | |
| HOLMES, DAVID (HM10040) | | | | | | | | | | | | | | | | | | | | | | | | |
| HOME VISITING SERVICES (HM10069) | ● | ● | ● | ● | ● | ● | | | ● | | ● | ● | | | ● | ● | ● | ● | ● | | ● | | ● | ● |
| HONG TAD ACUPUNCTURE & HERBAL (HM10119) | ● | ● | ● | ● | ● | ● | | | ● | | | ● | ● | | ● | ● | ● | ● | ● | ● | ● | ● | ● | ● |
| HOPE, ANN (HM10137) | | | | | | | | | | | | | | | | | | | | | | | | |
| HOUSE OF MISTRY (HM10220) | ● | | | | ● | | | | ● | | ● | ● | | | ● | ● | | | | ● | ● | | ● | |

# I - S Conditions treated at Practices/Businesses

| Business by County with Reference no. | Insomnia | Irritable Bowel Syndrome | Itching | Jet Lag | Joint Pain | Kidney Complaints | Lactose Intolerance | Laryngitis | Lethargy | Liver Disorders | Low Blood Pressure | Lung Problems | ME | Menopause | Migraine | Motion Sickness | Mouth Disorders | Mouth Ulcers | Multiple Sclerosis | Muscular Dystrophy | Musculo-skeletal | Nail Health | Nausea | Nerve Disorders | Nervous Disorders | Neuralgia | Obesity | Osteoporosis | Pain | Palpitations | Panic Attacks | Parkinson's Disease | Period Problems | Phobias | Piles | PMT | Pneumonia | Postural Problems | Pregnancy Help | Prostate Problems | Psoriasis | Raynaud's Disease | Recurrent Infections | Restless Legs | Rheumatoid Arthritis | Schizophrenia | Sciatica | Sexual Problems |
|---|---|---|---|---|---|---|---|---|---|---|---|---|---|---|---|---|---|---|---|---|---|---|---|---|---|---|---|---|---|---|---|---|---|---|---|---|---|---|---|---|---|---|---|---|---|---|---|---|
| HOWARD, LYNNE (HM10240) | ● | ● | ● | ● | ● | ● | ● | ● | ● | ● | ● | ● | ● | ● | ● | ● | ● | ● | ● | ● | | ● | ● | ● | ● | ● | ● | ● | ● | ● | | ● | ● | ● | ● | ● | ● | | ● | ● | ● | ● | ● | ● | ● | ● | ● | ● |
| HUGHES, PAUL (HM10339) | ● | ● | ● | | | | | | | | ● | | | ● | | | | | | | | | | | ● | | | | | ● | | | ● | ● | ● | | ● | | | | ● | ● | ● | ● | ● | | ● | ● |
| HYDE BARKER & ASSOCIATES (HM10469) | | | | | | | | | | | | | | | | | | | | | | ● | | | | | | | | | | | | | | | | | | | | | | | | | | |
| INDEPENDENT PSYCHOLOGY SERVICE (HM10610) | | ● | | | | | | | | | | | ● | ● | | | | | | | | | | | ● | | ● | | ● | | | | | ● | | ● | | | | | | | | | | | | ● |
| INSIDE STORY (HM10650) | | ● | | | ● | | | | | | | | ● | | ● | | | ● | | | | | | | | | | | | ● | | | | | | | | | | | | | | | ● | | | |
| JACOBS, BRIAN M (HM10858) | ● | | | | | | | | | | | | | | | | | | | | | | | | | | ● | | | | | | | ● | | | | | | | | | | | | | | |
| JELFS, MARTIN (HM10976) | | | | | | | | | | | | | | | | | | | | | | | | | ● | | | | | | | | | ● | | | | | | | | | | | | | | ● |
| JELFS, MARTIN (HM10977) | | | | | | | | | | | | | | | | | | | | | | | | | ● | | | | | | | | | ● | | | | | | | | | | | | | | ● |
| JOSEPH CLINIC (HM11215) | | ● | | | ● | | | | | | | | | | | | | | | | | | | | | | | | ● | | | | | | | | | | | | | | | | | | | |
| KAGYU SAMYE DZONG LONDON (HM11294) | | | | | | | | | | | | | | | | | | | | | | | | | | | | | | | | | | | | ● | | | | | | | | | | | | |
| KALLAS, JEMIMA (HM11297) | ● | ● | ● | ● | | ● | | ● | ● | ● | ● | | ● | ● | ● | | ● | ● | | ● | | | ● | ● | ● | ● | ● | | ● | ● | | | ● | ● | ● | ● | | | | | ● | ● | ● | ● | | | | ● |
| KANE AND ROSS CLINICS (HM11309) | | ● | | | | | | | | | | | | | ● | | | | | | | | | | | | | | | | | | | | | | | | | | | | | | ● | | ● | |
| KEITH EGLETON HYPNOTHERAPY (HM11412) | ● | ● | ● | ● | | | | | | | | | ● | | ● | ● | | | ● | | | | | ● | ● | | ● | | ● | ● | ● | | ● | ● | | ● | | | | | ● | | | ● | | ● | | ● |
| KERN, MICHAEL (HM11544) | ● | ● | | ● | ● | ● | | | ● | ● | | | ● | | ● | | | | | | | | ● | ● | ● | ● | | | | ● | | | ● | | | ● | | | ● | | | ● | | | ● | | ● | |
| KIKAI SHIATSU CENTRE (HM11598) | ● | ● | | | ● | ● | | | | ● | | ● | ● | | ● | | | | | | | | ● | | | | | | ● | ● | | | ● | | | ● | | | | | | | | ● | ● | | ● | |
| KILBRIDE, PETER (HM11600) | ● | ● | | | | | | | | | | | | | | | | | | | | | | ● | | | | | ● | | | | | | | | | | | | ● | | | ● | | | | ● |
| KINGSBURY PSYCHOTHERAPY PRAC (HM11660) | | | | | | | | | | | | | | | | | | | | | | | | | ● | | | | | | | | | ● | | | | | | | | | | | | | | ● |
| KINGSGATE ACUPUNCTURE PRACTICE (HM11663) | ● | ● | ● | | ● | ● | | ● | ● | ● | ● | ● | ● | ● | ● | | | ● | ● | | | | ● | | ● | ● | | | | ● | | | ● | | ● | ● | | | ● | | | ● | | ● | | | ● | |
| LASSMAN, J (HM11986) | | | | | ● | | | | | | | | | ● | ● | | | | | | | | ● | | | | | | ● | | | | ● | | | ● | | | ● | | | | | | | | | |
| LEE COMPLEMENTARY HEALTH CTRE (HM12130) | | | | | | | | | | | | | | | | | | | | | | | | | | | | | | | ● | | | | | | | | | | | | | | | | | |
| LEVER CLINIC (HM12256) | | | | | ● | | | | ● | | | | | | ● | | | | | | | | | | | ● | | ● | ● | | | | | | | | | | | | | | | | ● | | ● | |
| LINDBERG FITNESS (HM12414) | | | | | | | | | | | | | | | | | | | | | | | | | | | | | | | | | | | | | | ● | | | | | | | | | | |
| LITTLE VENICE CHIROPODY (HM12469) | | | | | | | | | | | | | | | | | | | | | | ● | | | | | | | | | | | | | | | | | | | | | | | | | | |
| LIVING CENTRE CLINIC (HM12483) | ● | ● | ● | ● | ● | ● | | ● | ● | ● | ● | ● | ● | ● | ● | ● | | | | | | | ● | ● | ● | ● | | ● | ● | | | | ● | ● | | ● | | | ● | | ● | | | | ● | | ● | |
| LIZ DAWSON - PSYCHOTHERAPIST (HM12494) | | | | | | | | | ● | | | | | | | | | | | | | | | | | | | | | | | | | ● | | | | | | | | | | | | ● | | ● |
| LONDON INDIAN CHAMPISSAGE CTRE (HM12599) | ● | | | | | | | | | | | | | | | | | | | | | | | | | | | | | | | | | | | | | | | | | | | | | | ● | |
| LONDON SCHOOL OF OSTEOPATHY (HM12604) | | ● | | | ● | | | | | | | | | | | | | | | | ● | | | | | | | | ● | | | | | | | ● | | ● | | | | | | | ● | | | |
| LONDON SPINE AND JOINT CLINIC (HM12611) | | ● | | | ● | | | | | | | | | | ● | | | | | | | | | ● | ● | | | | ● | | | | | | | ● | | | ● | | | | | ● | ● | | ● | |
| LONGARETTI, ANTHONY (HM12623) | | | | | | | | | | | | | | | | | | | | | | | | | | | | | | | | | | | | | | | | | | | | | | | ● | |
| LOTUS CLINIC (HM12653) | ● | ● | ● | ● | ● | ● | | ● | ● | ● | | | ● | ● | ● | ● | ● | ● | | | | | ● | ● | ● | ● | ● | | ● | ● | | | ● | ● | ● | ● | | | ● | | ● | ● | ● | ● | | | ● | ● |
| LOW, JANET (DR) (HM12686) | ● | | | | | | | | | | | | | | | | | | | | | | | | ● | | | | | | | | | ● | | | | | | | | | | | | | | ● |
| LUXTON, PAULINE (HM12752) | | | | | ● | | | | | | | | | | | | | | | | | ● | | | | | | | | | | | | | | | | | | | | | | | | | | |
| MANLEY CLINIC (HM13016) | ● | ● | ● | ● | ● | ● | ● | ● | ● | ● | ● | ● | ● | ● | ● | ● | ● | ● | ● | ● | | ● | ● | ● | ● | ● | ● | ● | ● | ● | | | ● | ● | ● | ● | ● | | ● | ● | ● | ● | ● | ● | ● | | ● | ● |
| MARKS, DARREN HYPNOTHERAPY (HM13119) | | | | | | | | | | | | | | | | | | | | | | | | | | | | | ● | | | | | ● | | | | | | | | | | | | | | |

# I - S Conditions treated at Practices/Businesses

| Business by County with Reference no. | Insomnia | Irritable Bowel Syndrome | Itching | Jet Lag | Joint Pain | Kidney Complaints | Lactose Intolerance | Laryngitis | Lethargy | Liver Disorders | Low Blood Pressure | Lung Problems | ME | Menopause | Migraine | Motion Sickness | Mouth Disorders | Mouth Ulcers | Multiple Sclerosis | Muscular Dystrophy | Musculo-skeletal | Nail Health | Nausea | Nerve Disorders | Nervous Disorders | Neuralgia | Obesity | Osteoporosis | Pain | Palpitations | Panic Attacks | Parkinson's Disease | Period Problems | Phobias | Piles | PMT | Pneumonia | Postural Problems | Pregnancy Help | Prostate Problems | Psoriasis | Raynaud's Disease | Recurrent Infections | Restless Legs | Rheumatoid Arthritis | Schizophrenia | Sciatica | Sexual Problems |
|---|---|---|---|---|---|---|---|---|---|---|---|---|---|---|---|---|---|---|---|---|---|---|---|---|---|---|---|---|---|---|---|---|---|---|---|---|---|---|---|---|---|---|---|---|---|---|---|---|
| MARLBOROUGH THERAPY PRACTICE (HM13125) | ● | ● |  |  |  |  |  |  |  |  |  |  |  |  |  |  |  |  |  |  |  |  |  |  | ● |  | ● |  | ● |  |  |  |  |  |  |  |  |  |  |  |  |  |  |  |  |  |  |  |
| MATTHEWS, ROBERT (HM13312) | ● | ● |  | ● |  |  |  |  |  |  |  |  | ● |  | ● |  |  |  | ● |  |  |  |  |  | ● |  | ● |  | ● |  | ● | ● |  | ● |  |  |  |  |  |  |  |  |  |  |  |  |  | ● |
| MCCAFFREY, GERARDINE (HM13380) | ● | ● |  |  |  | ● |  |  |  | ● |  | ● | ● |  | ● |  |  |  |  |  |  | ● |  |  |  |  |  |  | ● |  |  |  | ● |  |  |  |  |  |  |  |  | ● |  |  |  |  | ● |  |
| MCCLOSKEY, P J (HM13409) |  |  |  |  | ● |  |  |  |  |  |  |  |  |  |  |  |  |  |  |  |  | ● |  | ● |  |  |  |  | ● |  |  |  |  |  |  |  |  |  |  |  | ● | ● | ● |  |  |  |  |  |
| MIDDLETON, IAN W (HM13821) | ● | ● |  |  |  | ● |  |  |  | ● |  |  | ● | ● | ● |  |  |  |  |  |  |  |  |  |  |  |  | ● |  |  |  |  | ● |  |  | ● |  |  | ● | ● | ● | ● | ● |  | ● |  |  |  |
| MILLS DE-WIN STUDIOS (HM13922) | ● | ● | ● | ● | ● | ● |  |  | ● | ● | ● | ● | ● | ● | ● |  |  |  | ● | ● |  | ● | ● | ● | ● | ● |  |  | ● |  |  | ● | ● |  | ● | ● |  |  |  |  |  |  |  | ● | ● |  | ● |  |
| MONTSERRAT CLINIC (HM14090) | ● | ● | ● | ● | ● | ● |  | ● | ● | ● | ● | ● | ● | ● | ● | ● | ● | ● |  |  |  |  | ● | ● | ● | ● | ● | ● | ● | ● |  | ● | ● | ● | ● | ● | ● |  | ● | ● | ● | ● | ● | ● | ● | ● | ● | ● |
| MOTHERSOLE, VINETA (HM20682) |  |  |  |  | ● |  |  |  |  |  |  |  |  |  |  |  |  |  |  |  |  |  |  |  |  | ● |  |  |  |  |  |  |  |  |  |  |  |  |  |  |  | ● |  |  |  |  |  |  |
| MOTTINGHAM HYPNOTHERAPY CTRE (HM14279) | ● | ● |  |  |  |  |  |  |  |  |  |  | ● |  | ● |  |  |  |  |  |  | ● | ● |  |  |  | ● |  | ● |  |  |  | ● | ● |  | ● |  |  |  |  |  |  |  |  |  | ● |  | ● |
| M-POWER (HM14308) | ● |  |  |  |  |  |  |  |  |  |  |  |  |  |  |  |  |  |  |  |  |  |  |  |  |  |  |  |  |  |  |  |  | ● |  |  |  |  |  |  |  |  |  |  |  |  |  |  |
| NEIL-ASHER, S (HM14761) |  |  |  |  | ● |  |  |  |  |  |  |  | ● |  |  |  |  |  |  |  |  |  |  | ● |  |  |  | ● | ● |  |  |  |  |  |  |  |  | ● |  |  |  |  |  |  |  |  | ● |  |
| NEILL, VICTORIA (HM14764) | ● |  |  |  | ● |  |  |  |  |  |  | ● | ● |  | ● |  |  |  |  |  |  |  | ● |  |  | ● |  | ● | ● |  |  | ● |  |  |  |  |  |  |  |  |  |  |  |  | ● |  | ● |  |
| NIEL-ASHER, S (HM14933) |  |  |  |  | ● |  |  |  |  |  |  |  | ● |  |  |  |  |  |  |  |  |  |  |  |  |  |  | ● | ● |  |  |  |  |  |  |  |  | ● |  |  |  |  |  |  |  |  | ● |  |
| NIELSEN, RITA C (HM14935) | ● | ● |  |  | ● | ● |  |  |  |  | ● | ● | ● | ● | ● |  |  |  | ● | ● |  |  | ● |  |  |  |  |  | ● | ● |  |  | ● |  |  | ● |  |  | ● |  |  |  |  |  |  |  | ● |  |
| NORTH POLE SCH OF T'AI-CHI (HM15094) | ● |  |  |  |  |  |  |  |  |  | ● |  |  |  |  |  |  |  |  |  |  |  |  |  |  |  |  |  |  |  |  |  |  |  |  |  |  |  |  |  |  |  |  |  |  |  |  |  |
| NORTHWOOD CLINIC (HM15067) |  |  |  |  | ● |  |  |  |  |  |  |  |  |  |  |  |  |  |  |  |  |  |  |  |  |  |  |  | ● |  |  |  |  |  |  |  |  |  |  |  |  |  |  | ● |  |  |  |  |
| NOTTING HILL TRAD ACU CTRE (HM15081) | ● |  |  |  | ● |  |  |  |  |  |  |  |  | ● | ● |  |  |  |  |  |  |  | ● |  |  |  |  |  | ● |  |  |  | ● |  |  | ● |  |  | ● |  | ● |  |  |  |  |  |  |  |
| NRTH LONDON ALEXANDER PRACTICE (HM15092) |  |  |  |  |  |  |  |  |  |  |  |  |  |  | ● |  |  |  |  |  |  |  |  |  |  |  |  | ● |  |  |  |  |  |  |  |  |  |  |  |  |  |  |  |  |  |  |  |  |
| NUTRITION FOR LIFE INT (HM15124) | ● | ● |  | ● | ● |  |  |  |  | ● |  |  | ● | ● | ● |  |  | ● | ● |  |  | ● | ● | ● | ● |  | ● | ● | ● |  |  |  | ● |  |  | ● |  |  |  | ● | ● |  |  |  | ● |  | ● |  |
| ORIENTAL MEDICINE (HM15386) | ● | ● | ● |  | ● | ● |  | ● | ● | ● | ● | ● | ● | ● | ● |  | ● | ● | ● | ● |  | ● | ● | ● | ● | ● | ● | ● | ● | ● |  | ● | ● |  | ● | ● | ● |  | ● | ● | ● | ● | ● | ● | ● | ● | ● | ● |
| OSTEOPATHIC ASSOCIATION CLINIC (HM15453) |  |  |  |  | ● |  |  |  |  |  |  |  |  |  |  |  |  |  |  |  |  |  |  |  |  |  |  |  | ● |  |  |  |  |  |  |  |  |  |  |  |  |  |  | ● |  |  | ● |  |
| OSTEOPATHIC PRACTICE (HM15471) |  | ● |  |  |  |  |  |  |  |  |  |  |  |  |  |  |  |  |  |  |  |  |  |  |  |  |  |  |  |  |  |  |  |  |  |  |  |  |  |  |  |  |  |  |  |  |  |  |
| OSTEOPATHIC PRACTICE (HM15470) | ● | ● |  | ● | ● | ● |  |  | ● |  |  | ● | ● |  | ● |  |  |  |  |  |  | ● |  |  |  | ● |  | ● | ● |  |  |  | ● |  | ● | ● | ● |  | ● |  |  | ● |  |  |  |  | ● | ● |
| OSTEOPATHIC PRACTICE (HM15467) |  |  |  |  | ● |  |  |  |  |  |  |  |  |  |  |  |  |  |  |  |  |  |  |  |  |  |  |  | ● |  |  |  |  |  |  |  |  |  |  |  |  |  |  |  |  |  | ● |  |
| OSTEOPATHIC PRACTICE (HM15473) |  |  |  |  | ● |  |  |  |  |  |  |  |  |  |  |  |  |  |  |  |  |  |  |  |  |  |  |  |  |  |  |  |  |  |  |  |  |  |  |  |  |  |  |  | ● |  |  |  |
| OTREMBA, KATHARINA (HM15496) | ● | ● | ● | ● | ● | ● | ● |  | ● | ● | ● |  | ● | ● | ● |  |  | ● |  |  |  | ● | ● |  | ● |  | ● |  | ● | ● |  |  | ● | ● |  | ● |  |  | ● |  | ● |  | ● | ● |  |  |  | ● |
| OUTCOMES (HM15502) | ● | ● |  | ● |  |  |  |  | ● |  |  |  | ● |  | ● |  |  |  |  |  |  |  | ● | ● | ● |  | ● |  | ● | ● |  |  | ● | ● |  | ● |  |  | ● |  | ● |  |  | ● | ● | ● |  | ● |
| PACIFIC WAVES PRODUCTIONS (HM15553) | ● | ● | ● |  |  |  |  |  | ● |  |  |  |  |  |  | ● |  |  |  |  |  |  |  |  | ● |  |  |  | ● | ● |  |  |  | ● |  | ● |  |  | ● |  |  |  |  | ● |  |  |  | ● |
| PALACE ROAD OSTEOPATHIC CLINIC (HM15590) |  |  |  |  | ● |  |  |  |  |  |  |  |  |  |  |  |  |  |  |  |  |  |  |  |  |  |  |  |  |  |  |  |  |  |  |  |  |  |  |  |  |  |  |  |  |  |  |  |
| PALFREYMAN, SUE (HM15592) |  | ● |  |  | ● |  |  |  |  |  |  |  | ● |  | ● |  |  |  |  |  |  |  |  |  |  | ● |  |  | ● |  |  |  |  |  |  |  |  |  | ● |  |  |  |  |  |  |  | ● |  |
| PAPOUTSIS, MARGARET (HM15642) |  |  |  |  |  |  |  |  |  |  |  |  |  |  |  |  |  |  |  |  |  |  |  |  |  |  |  |  |  |  |  |  |  |  |  |  |  |  |  |  |  |  |  |  |  |  | ● |  |
| PHYSIO ONE (HM16202) |  |  |  |  |  |  |  |  |  |  |  |  |  |  |  |  |  |  |  |  |  |  |  |  |  |  |  |  | ● |  |  |  |  |  |  |  |  | ● |  |  |  |  |  |  |  |  | ● |  |
| PHYSIO SOLUTIONS (HM16205) |  |  |  |  | ● |  |  |  |  |  |  |  | ● |  |  |  |  |  |  |  | ● |  |  |  |  |  |  | ● | ● |  |  |  |  |  |  |  |  |  |  |  |  |  |  |  |  |  | ● |  |
| PHYSIOTHERAPY PRACTICE (HM16253) |  |  |  |  |  |  |  |  |  |  |  |  |  |  |  |  |  |  |  |  |  |  |  |  |  |  |  | ● | ● |  |  | ● |  |  |  |  |  |  |  |  |  |  |  |  | ● |  | ● |  |

# I - S Conditions treated at Practices/Businesses

Business by County with Reference no.

| Business by County with Reference no. | Insomnia | Irritable Bowel Syndrome | Itching | Jet Lag | Joint Pain | Kidney Complaints | Lactose Intolerance | Laryngitis | Lethargy | Liver Disorders | Low Blood Pressure | Lung Problems | ME | Menopause | Migraine | Motion Sickness | Mouth Disorders | Mouth Ulcers | Multiple Sclerosis | Muscular Dystrophy | Musculo-skeletal | Nail Health | Nausea | Nerve Disorders |
|---|---|---|---|---|---|---|---|---|---|---|---|---|---|---|---|---|---|---|---|---|---|---|---|---|
| PINNER ROAD PHYSIOTHERAPY (HM16316) | | | | | ● | | | | | | | | | | | | | | ● | | | | | |
| PRICE, GILLIAN (HM16575) | ● | ● | ● | | ● | ● | | ● | ● | ● | ● | ● | ● | ● | ● | ● | ● | ● | ● | | | | ● | ● |
| PRICE, SANDRA (HM16594) | | | | | ● | | | | | | | | | | | | | | | | | | | |
| PRICE, SANDRA (HM16595) | | | | | ● | | | | | | | | | | | | | | | | | | | |
| PRIMROSE HEALING CENTRE (HM16616) | ● | ● | | | | | | | | | | | | ● | | | | | | | | | | ● |
| PRIVATE HEALTH CLINIC (HM16644) | ● | ● | ● | ● | ● | ● | ● | ● | ● | ● | ● | ● | ● | ● | ● | ● | ● | ● | ● | ● | | ● | ● | ● |
| PRIVATE PRACTICE (HM16649) | | | | | | | | | | | | | | | | | | | | | | | | |
| PSYCHOTHERAPY CENTRE (HM16734) | ● | ● | ● | | | | | | | | | | ● | | ● | | | | | | | | | |
| PSYCHOTHERAPY SERVICES (HM16737) | | | | | | | | | | | | | | | | | | | | | | | | |
| PUTNEY CHIROPRACTIC (HM16780) | | ● | | | ● | | | | | | | | | | ● | | | | | | | | | ● |
| RACHEL YOUNG - HYPNOTHERAPIST (HM16837) | ● | ● | ● | ● | ● | ● | | ● | ● | ● | ● | ● | ● | ● | ● | | | | | | | | | |
| RAEBURN, JO (HM16865) | ● | ● | ● | ● | ● | | | | | | ● | ● | ● | ● | ● | | | | | | | | ● | |
| RANDALL, CAROLINE (HM16926) | ● | ● | ● | ● | ● | ● | ● | ● | ● | ● | ● | ● | ● | ● | ● | ● | ● | ● | ● | ● | | ● | ● | ● |
| RAVENSCROFT CENTRE (HM16967) | ● | | | | | | | | ● | | | | ● | | | | | | | | | | | |
| READ, CHARLES (HM16993) | | | | | | | | | | | | | | | | | | | | | | | | |
| REEVE, MALCOLM (HM17060) | | | | | ● | | | | | | | | | | | | | | | | | | | |
| REFLEXOLOGY (HM17077) | ● | ● | | | ● | | ● | | ● | | ● | | ● | ● | ● | | | | | | | | | ● |
| REFLEXOLOGY CLINIC (HM17089) | | ● | | | | | | | | | | | | | ● | | | | | | | | | |
| RELAXATION PLACE (HM17166) | ● | ● | | | | | | | | | | | ● | ● | ● | | | | | | | | | |
| REPLINGHAM CLINIC (HM17195) | ● | ● | ● | | ● | ● | | | ● | ● | ● | | ● | ● | ● | | | | | | | | ● | |
| ROBERTS, MATT (HM17420) | ● | ● | | | | | | | | | | | | ● | | | | | | | | | | |
| ROBINSON, GABIE (HM17473) | | ● | | | | | | | | ● | | | | ● | ● | | | | | | | | | |
| ROEHAMPTON PHYSIO/SPORTS (HM17535) | | | | | ● | | | | | | | | | | | | | | ● | | | | | |
| ROSE, NICHOLAS (HM17613) | | | | | ● | | | | | | | | | | | | | | | | | | | ● |
| RUTHERFORD, BERWYN (HM17780) | | | | | ● | | | | | | | | | | | | | | | | | | | |
| SALTER, LIZ (HM17869) | ● | ● | ● | ● | ● | ● | ● | ● | ● | ● | | ● | ● | ● | ● | ● | ● | ● | ● | | | | ● | |
| SAYER CLINIC (HM17993) | | ● | | | ● | | | | | | | | | | ● | | | | | | | | | ● |
| SAYER CLINIC (HM17994) | | ● | | | ● | | | | | | | | | | | | | | | | | | | |
| SEARBY, JOE (HM18174) | ● | ● | | | ● | | | | ● | | | ● | | | ● | | | | | | | | | |
| SEEAR, MICHAEL (DR) (HM18189) | ● | ● | ● | ● | ● | ● | | | ● | ● | | ● | ● | ● | ● | | ● | ● | ● | | | | ● | ● |
| SEYMOUR PRACTICE (HM18257) | | | | | ● | | | | | | | | | | ● | | | | | | | | | |
| SHIATSU PLACE (HM18458) | ● | ● | | | ● | | | | | ● | ● | ● | ● | ● | ● | ● | | | | | | | ● | |
| SIMON, CAROLYN (HM18567) | | | | | ● | | | | | | | | | | | | | | | | | | | |
| SIMPLY HERBAL CLINIC (HM18577) | ● | ● | ● | ● | ● | ● | ● | ● | ● | ● | ● | ● | ● | ● | ● | ● | ● | ● | ● | ● | | ● | ● | ● |

| Business by County with Reference no. | Nervous Disorders | Neuralgia | Obesity | Osteoporosis | Pain | Palpitations | Panic Attacks | Parkinson's Disease | Period Problems | Phobias | Piles | PMT | Pneumonia | Postural Problems | Pregnancy Help | Prostate Problems | Psoriasis | Raynaud's Disease | Recurrent Infections | Restless Legs | Rheumatoid Arthritis | Schizophrenia | Sciatica | Sexual Problems |
|---|---|---|---|---|---|---|---|---|---|---|---|---|---|---|---|---|---|---|---|---|---|---|---|---|
| PINNER ROAD PHYSIOTHERAPY (HM16316) | | | | | ● | | | | | | | | | | | | | | | | | | | |
| PRICE, GILLIAN (HM16575) | ● | ● | ● | ● | ● | ● | | ● | ● | ● | ● | ● | | | ● | ● | ● | ● | ● | ● | ● | ● | ● | |
| PRICE, SANDRA (HM16594) | | | | | ● | | | | | | | | | ● | ● | | | | | | | | ● | |
| PRICE, SANDRA (HM16595) | | | | | ● | | | | | | | | | ● | ● | | | | | | | | ● | |
| PRIMROSE HEALING CENTRE (HM16616) | | | ● | | ● | | | | ● | ● | | ● | | | | | | | | | | | | ● |
| PRIVATE HEALTH CLINIC (HM16644) | ● | ● | ● | ● | ● | ● | | ● | ● | ● | ● | ● | ● | | ● | ● | ● | ● | ● | ● | ● | ● | ● | ● |
| PRIVATE PRACTICE (HM16649) | | | | | | | | | | ● | | | | | | | | | | | | | | |
| PSYCHOTHERAPY CENTRE (HM16734) | ● | | ● | | | | ● | | ● | ● | | ● | | | ● | | ● | | | | | | | ● |
| PSYCHOTHERAPY SERVICES (HM16737) | ● | | | | | | | | | ● | | | | | | | | | | | | | | |
| PUTNEY CHIROPRACTIC (HM16780) | | ● | | | ● | | | | | | | | | | | | | | | | | | ● | |
| RACHEL YOUNG - HYPNOTHERAPIST (HM16837) | | | ● | | ● | | | | | ● | | | ● | | ● | | ● | ● | ● | ● | | | ● | ● |
| RAEBURN, JO (HM16865) | | ● | | | ● | ● | | | ● | | ● | ● | ● | | ● | | ● | | | | ● | | | |
| RANDALL, CAROLINE (HM16926) | ● | ● | ● | ● | ● | ● | | ● | ● | ● | ● | ● | ● | | ● | ● | ● | ● | ● | ● | ● | ● | ● | ● |
| RAVENSCROFT CENTRE (HM16967) | ● | | | | ● | | | | | ● | | ● | | | | | | | | | | | | |
| READ, CHARLES (HM16993) | | | | | ● | | | | | | | | | | | | | | | ● | | | ● | |
| REEVE, MALCOLM (HM17060) | | | | | ● | | | | | | | | | | | | | | | | | | ● | |
| REFLEXOLOGY (HM17077) | ● | ● | | ● | ● | | | | ● | | ● | ● | | | ● | | | ● | | ● | ● | | | |
| REFLEXOLOGY CLINIC (HM17089) | | | | | | | | | | | | | | | | | | | | | | | | |
| RELAXATION PLACE (HM17166) | | | | | ● | | | | | | | ● | | | | | | | | | | | | |
| REPLINGHAM CLINIC (HM17195) | ● | | ● | ● | ● | | | | ● | ● | | ● | | | ● | | ● | | ● | | ● | | ● | |
| ROBERTS, MATT (HM17420) | | | ● | | ● | | | | ● | ● | | ● | | | | | | | | | | | | ● |
| ROBINSON, GABIE (HM17473) | | | | | | | | | | | | ● | | | | | ● | | | | ● | | | |
| ROEHAMPTON PHYSIO/SPORTS (HM17535) | | | | | | | | | | | | | | | | | | | | | | | | |
| ROSE, NICHOLAS (HM17613) | | ● | | | ● | | | | | | | | | | | | | | | ● | | | ● | |
| RUTHERFORD, BERWYN (HM17780) | | | | | | | | | | | | | | | | | | | | | | | ● | |
| SALTER, LIZ (HM17869) | ● | ● | ● | ● | ● | ● | | | ● | ● | ● | ● | ● | | ● | | ● | ● | ● | ● | ● | | | ● |
| SAYER CLINIC (HM17993) | ● | ● | | ● | ● | | | | ● | | | | | | | | | | | | | | ● | |
| SAYER CLINIC (HM17994) | | | | | ● | | | | | | | | | | | | | | | | | | ● | |
| SEARBY, JOE (HM18174) | ● | | | ● | | | | | | | | | | | | | | | | ● | ● | | ● | |
| SEEAR, MICHAEL (DR) (HM18189) | ● | ● | ● | ● | ● | | | | ● | ● | ● | ● | ● | | ● | ● | ● | ● | | ● | ● | | ● | ● |
| SEYMOUR PRACTICE (HM18257) | | | | | ● | | | | | | | | | | | | | | | | | | ● | |
| SHIATSU PLACE (HM18458) | ● | | | | ● | ● | | | ● | ● | | ● | | | ● | ● | | ● | ● | ● | ● | | ● | |
| SIMON, CAROLYN (HM18567) | | | | | ● | | | | | | | | | | | | | | | | | | | |
| SIMPLY HERBAL CLINIC (HM18577) | ● | ● | ● | ● | ● | ● | | ● | ● | ● | ● | ● | ● | | ● | ● | ● | ● | ● | ● | ● | ● | ● | ● |

# I - S Conditions treated at Practices/Businesses

| Business by County with Reference no. | Insomnia | Irritable Bowel Syndrome | Itching | Jet Lag | Joint Pain | Kidney Complaints | Lactose Intolerance | Laryngitis | Lethargy | Liver Disorders | Low Blood Pressure | Lung Problems | ME | Menopause | Migraine | Motion Sickness | Mouth Disorders | Mouth Ulcers | Multiple Sclerosis | Muscular Dystrophy | Musculo-skeletal | Nail Health | Nausea | Nerve Disorders |
|---|---|---|---|---|---|---|---|---|---|---|---|---|---|---|---|---|---|---|---|---|---|---|---|---|
| SIMPSON, STELLA (HM18599) | ● | ● | ● | | ● | ● | | | | ● | ● | ● | ● | ● | ● | | ● | ● | | | | | ● | ● |
| SLADE OSTEOPATHIC PRACTICE (HM18667) | | ● | | | ● | | | | | | | | | | ● | | | | | | | | | ● |
| SOUTH LONDON NATURAL HLTH CTRE (HM18911) | ● | ● | ● | ● | ● | ● | ● | ● | ● | ● | ● | ● | ● | ● | ● | ● | ● | ● | ● | ● | | ● | ● | ● |
| SOUTHFIELDS CLINIC (HM18935) | ● | | | | ● | | | | | | | | | ● | ● | | | | | | | | | |
| SPALL MEDICAL CENTRE (HM18957) | ● | | ● | | ● | ● | | | | ● | | | | ● | ● | | | ● | | | | ● | ● | ● |
| SPECIALIST HEALTH (HM18972) | | | | | ● | | | | | | | | | | | | | | | | | | | |
| SPENCER, PIERS (HM19001) | | | | | ● | | | | | | | | | | | | | | | | | | | |
| SPYROS MOUZOURIDES (HM19056) | ● | ● | ● | ● | ● | ● | ● | ● | ● | ● | ● | ● | ● | ● | ● | ● | ● | ● | ● | ● | | ● | ● | ● |
| STANMORE PHYSIO PRACTICE (HM19132) | | | | | ● | | | | | | | | | | | | | | | | | | | |
| STOBEZKI, YAEL (HM19307) | | | | | | | | | | | | | | | | | | | | | | | | |
| STRONG, STELLA (HM19419) | | | | | | | | | | | | | | | | | | | | | | | | |
| T C M HEALTHCARE (HM19640) | | ● | | | | | | | | | | | ● | ● | ● | | | | | | | | | ● |
| THOMPSON, MARK (HM19990) | | ● | | | ● | | ● | | ● | ● | ● | ● | ● | ● | ● | | | | | | | | | |
| THURGOOD, SIMON (HM20047) | | | | | ● | | | | | | | | | | | | | | | | | | | |
| TORRIDON COMP THERAPY CLINIC (HM20173) | | ● | | | ● | ● | | | | | ● | | ● | ● | ● | | | | ● | | | | | |
| TRADITIONAL ACUPUNCTURE CENTRE (HM20218) | ● | | | | ● | | | | ● | | | | | ● | ● | | | | | | | | ● | |
| TRANQUILITY (HM20255) | ● | ● | ● | ● | ● | ● | ● | ● | ● | | ● | ● | ● | ● | ● | ● | ● | ● | ● | ● | | ● | ● | ● |
| TROHEAR, PATRICIA (HM20345) | ● | ● | | | | | | | | | | | | | | | | | | | | | | |
| TURMAINE, VICKI (HM20410) | ● | ● | ● | ● | ● | ● | | ● | ● | ● | | | ● | ● | ● | ● | ● | ● | ● | | | | ● | ● |
| TURNBULL, JO (HM20413) | ● | ● | | ● | ● | ● | | | ● | ● | ● | | ● | ● | ● | | | | ● | | | | | ● |
| TURNER, TERI (HM20438) | | ● | | | ● | | | | | | | | | | ● | | | | | | | | | ● |
| TWICKENHAM PHYSIOFIRST CENTRE (HM20451) | | | | | ● | | | | | | | | | | | | | | ● | | | | | |
| UKCP (HM20490) | | | | | | | | | | | | | | | | | | | | | | | | |
| UNDERHILL, K (HM20496) | | | | | | | | | | | | | ● | | ● | | | | | | | | | |
| VALE PRACTICE (HM20551) | ● | ● | ● | ● | ● | ● | ● | ● | ● | ● | ● | ● | ● | ● | ● | ● | ● | ● | ● | ● | | ● | ● | ● |
| VANBRUGH PHYSIOTHERAPY CLINIC (HM20575) | ● | | | | ● | | | | | | | | ● | | | | | | ● | | | | | |
| WALK IN BACK RUB (HM20758) | | | | | | | | | | | | | | | | | | | | | | | | |
| WALK IN BACKRUB (HM20759) | | | | | | | | | | | | | | | ● | | | | | | | | | |
| WALK IN BACKRUB (HM20760) | | | | | | | | | | | | | | | ● | | | | | | | | | |
| WART, D (HM20959) | | | | | ● | | | | | | | | | | | | | | | | | | | |
| WARWICK ALTERNATIVE HEALTH (HM20961) | | | | | | ● | | | | | | | ● | ● | ● | | | | | | | ● | ● | |
| WEBER, MARALYN (HM21082) | ● | ● | ● | ● | ● | ● | ● | ● | ● | ● | ● | ● | ● | ● | ● | ● | ● | ● | ● | ● | | ● | ● | ● |
| WELL BEING (HM21131) | ● | ● | ● | ● | | | | | | | | | | ● | ● | ● | | | ● | | | | ● | |
| WEST LONDON HOLISTIC CENTRE (HM21226) | ● | ● | ● | | | | | | ● | | | | ● | ● | | | | | ● | | | | | ● |

| Business by County with Reference no. | Nervous Disorders | Neuralgia | Obesity | Osteoporosis | Pain | Palpitations | Panic Attacks | Parkinson's Disease | Period Problems | Phobias | Piles | PMT | Pneumonia | Postural Problems | Pregnancy Help | Prostate Problems | Psoriasis | Raynaud's Disease | Recurrent Infections | Restless Legs | Rheumatoid Arthritis | Schizophrenia | Sciatica | Sexual Problems |
|---|---|---|---|---|---|---|---|---|---|---|---|---|---|---|---|---|---|---|---|---|---|---|---|---|
| SIMPSON, STELLA (HM18599) | ● | ● | | | ● | ● | | | ● | ● | ● | ● | | | ● | | ● | ● | ● | ● | ● | | ● | ● |
| SLADE OSTEOPATHIC PRACTICE (HM18667) | | | | | ● | | | | | | | | | ● | | | | | | | | | ● | |
| SOUTH LONDON NATURAL HLTH CTRE (HM18911) | ● | ● | ● | ● | ● | ● | | ● | ● | ● | ● | ● | ● | | ● | ● | ● | ● | ● | ● | ● | ● | ● | ● |
| SOUTHFIELDS CLINIC (HM18935) | | | | | ● | | | | ● | | | ● | | | | | | | | | | | | |
| SPALL MEDICAL CENTRE (HM18957) | | | ● | | ● | ● | | | | | ● | | | | | ● | ● | | | | ● | | ● | ● |
| SPECIALIST HEALTH (HM18972) | | ● | | | ● | | | | | | | | | | | | | | | | | | ● | |
| SPENCER, PIERS (HM19001) | | | | | | | | | | | | | | | | | | | | | | | ● | |
| SPYROS MOUZOURIDES (HM19056) | ● | ● | ● | ● | ● | ● | | ● | ● | ● | ● | ● | ● | | ● | ● | ● | ● | ● | ● | ● | ● | ● | ● |
| STANMORE PHYSIO PRACTICE (HM19132) | | | | | ● | | | | | | | | | | | | | | | | | | | |
| STOBEZKI, YAEL (HM19307) | | | ● | | | | | | | ● | | | | | | | | | | | | | | |
| STRONG, STELLA (HM19419) | ● | ● | | | ● | | ● | | | | | | | | | | | | | | | | ● | |
| T C M HEALTHCARE (HM19640) | | | | | ● | | | | ● | | | ● | | | | | | | | | | | | |
| THOMPSON, MARK (HM19990) | | | ● | ● | ● | ● | | ● | | | | ● | | | | ● | | | | ● | ● | | ● | ● |
| THURGOOD, SIMON (HM20047) | | | | | | | | | | | | | | | | | | | | | | | | |
| TORRIDON COMP THERAPY CLINIC (HM20173) | | | | | ● | ● | | | | ● | | ● | | | | | | | | ● | | | ● | |
| TRADITIONAL ACUPUNCTURE CENTRE (HM20218) | | | | | ● | | | | ● | | | ● | | | | | ● | | | | | | | |
| TRANQUILITY (HM20255) | ● | | ● | ● | ● | ● | | | ● | ● | ● | ● | | | ● | | ● | ● | ● | ● | | | ● | |
| TROHEAR, PATRICIA (HM20345) | | | ● | | ● | ● | | | | ● | | | | | | | ● | | | | | | | |
| TURMAINE, VICKI (HM20410) | ● | ● | | | ● | ● | | | ● | ● | ● | ● | | | ● | ● | ● | ● | ● | ● | | | ● | ● |
| TURNBULL, JO (HM20413) | ● | | ● | | ● | ● | | | ● | | | ● | ● | | ● | ● | ● | ● | | | | | ● | |
| TURNER, TERI (HM20438) | | | | | ● | | | | | | | | | ● | | | | | | | | | ● | |
| TWICKENHAM PHYSIOFIRST CENTRE (HM20451) | | | | | | | | | | | | | | | | | | | | | | | | |
| UKCP (HM20490) | | | | | | | | | | ● | | | | | | | | | | | | ● | | ● |
| UNDERHILL, K (HM20496) | | | | | | | | | | | | | | | | | | | | | | | ● | |
| VALE PRACTICE (HM20551) | ● | ● | ● | ● | ● | ● | | ● | ● | ● | ● | ● | ● | | ● | ● | ● | ● | ● | ● | ● | ● | ● | ● |
| VANBRUGH PHYSIOTHERAPY CLINIC (HM20575) | | | | | ● | | | | | | | | | | | | | | | | | | | |
| WALK IN BACK RUB (HM20758) | | | | | ● | | | | | | | | | | | | | | | | | | | |
| WALK IN BACKRUB (HM20759) | | | | | ● | | | | | | | | | | | | | | | | | | | |
| WALK IN BACKRUB (HM20760) | | | | | ● | | | | | | | | | | | | | | | | | | | |
| WART, D (HM20959) | | | | | ● | | | | | | | | | | | | | | | | | | ● | |
| WARWICK ALTERNATIVE HEALTH (HM20961) | | | | | | | | | | ● | | ● | | | ● | | | | | | | | | ● |
| WEBER, MARALYN (HM21082) | ● | ● | ● | ● | ● | ● | | ● | ● | ● | ● | ● | ● | | ● | ● | ● | ● | ● | ● | ● | | ● | ● |
| WELL BEING (HM21131) | | | | | | ● | | | ● | ● | ● | ● | | | ● | ● | | | ● | ● | ● | | | |
| WEST LONDON HOLISTIC CENTRE (HM21226) | ● | | ● | | ● | ● | | | ● | ● | | ● | | | | | | | ● | | | | | ● |

# I - S Conditions treated at Practices/Businesses

| Business by County with Reference no. | Insomnia | Irritable Bowel Syndrome | Itching | Jet Lag | Joint Pain | Kidney Complaints | Lactose Intolerance | Laryngitis | Lethargy | Liver Disorders | Low Blood Pressure | Lung Problems | ME | Menopause | Migraine | Motion Sickness | Mouth Disorders | Mouth Ulcers | Multiple Sclerosis | Muscular Dystrophy | Musculo-skeletal | Nail Health | Nausea | Nerve Disorders | Nervous Disorders | Neuralgia | Obesity | Osteoporosis | Pain | Palpitations | Panic Attacks | Parkinson's Disease | Period Problems | Phobias | Piles | PMT | Pneumonia | Postural Problems | Pregnancy Help | Prostate Problems | Psoriasis | Raynaud's Disease | Recurrent Infections | Restless Legs | Rheumatoid Arthritis | Schizophrenia | Sciatica | Sexual Problems |
|---|---|---|---|---|---|---|---|---|---|---|---|---|---|---|---|---|---|---|---|---|---|---|---|---|---|---|---|---|---|---|---|---|---|---|---|---|---|---|---|---|---|---|---|---|---|---|---|---|
| WEST LONDON PSYCHOTHERAPY (HM21227) | ● | | | | | | | | | | | | ● | | | | | | | | | | | | ● | | ● | | | | | | | | | | | | | | | | | | | | | ● |
| WEST LONDON YOGA SHALA (HM21228) | | ● | | | | | | | | | ● | ● | | | | | | | | | | | | | ● | | | | | | | | ● | | ● | | | | | | | | | | | | | |
| WESTERN, G (HM21265) | | ● | | | | | | | | | | | ● | | | | | | | | | | | ● | | | | | ● | | | | | | | | | ● | | | | | | | | | ● | |
| WHITE HART LANE THERAPY CENTRE (HM21338) | | | | | ● | | | | | | | | | | ● | | | | ● | | | | | | | | | | | | | | | | | | | | | | | | | | | | ● | |
| WHOLE-BEING INTERACTIVE HYP (HM21435) | | | | | | | | | | | | | | | | | | | | | | | | | | | ● | | ● | | ● | | | ● | | | | | | | | | | | | | | |
| WIGHAM, A (HM21468) | | | | | | | | | | | | | ● | | | | | | | | | | | | | | | | | | | | | ● | | | | | | | | | | | | | | |
| WILKINSON, GILL (HM21505) | | | | | | | | | | | | | ● | | | | | | | | | | | | | | | | | | | | | ● | | | | | | | | | | | | | | |
| WILLIAMS, B A (HM21541) | ● | | | | ● | | | | | | | | | ● | ● | | | | | | | | | | | | | | ● | | | | | | | | | | | | ● | | | | | | | |
| WILLMOTT, SUSAN (HM21623) | ● | | ● | | | | | | ● | | | | | | | | | | | | | | | | | | ● | | ● | | | | | | | | | | | | | | | | | | | |
| WINCHMORE CLINIC OF OSTEOPATHY (HM21694) | | | | | | | | | | | | | ● | | ● | | | | | | | | | | | | | | ● | | | | | | | | | | | | | | | | | | ● | |
| WOODBERRY CLINIC (HM21815) | | | | | ● | | | | | | | | | | | | | | | | | | | ● | | | | | | | | | | | | | | | ● | | | | | | | | | |
| WOOLF, PERRY (HM21872) | | | | | ● | | | | | | | | | | | | | | | | | | | | | | | | ● | | | | | | | | | ● | | | | ● | | | | | ● | |
| WORLD OF LIGHT (HM21898) | ● | ● | ● | ● | ● | ● | ● | ● | ● | ● | ● | ● | ● | ● | ● | ● | ● | ● | ● | ● | | ● | ● | ● | ● | ● | ● | ● | ● | ● | | ● | ● | ● | ● | ● | ● | | ● | ● | ● | ● | ● | ● | ● | ● | ● | ● |
| WREN, ANTHONY (HM21920) | | | | | ● | | | | | | | | ● | | ● | | | | ● | | | | | | | ● | | | ● | | | | | | | | | ● | | | | | | | | | | |
| WRIGHT, JENNY (HM21936) | ● | ● | | | | | | | ● | | | | | ● | | | | | | | | ● | | | ● | | ● | | ● | | | | | | | | | | | | | | | | | | | |
| WYNNE-SIMMONS, A (DR) (HM21979) | ● | ● | ● | ● | ● | ● | ● | ● | ● | ● | ● | ● | ● | ● | ● | ● | ● | ● | ● | ● | | ● | ● | ● | | ● | | ● | ● | ● | | | ● | | ● | ● | ● | | ● | ● | ● | ● | ● | ● | ● | ● | ● | |
| YING, FRANK (HM22014) | | | | | ● | | | | | | | | ● | | | | | | | | | | | ● | | ● | | | ● | | | | | | | | | | | | | | | | | | ● | |
| YOGA THERAPY CENTRE (HM22033) | | | | | | | | | | | | | ● | | | | | | | | | | | | | | | | | | | | | | | ● | | | ● | | | | | | | | | |
| ZEN HEALTH CENTRE (HM22100) | ● | ● | ● | ● | ● | ● | ● | ● | ● | ● | ● | ● | ● | ● | ● | ● | ● | ● | ● | | | ● | ● | ● | ● | ● | ● | ● | ● | ● | | | ● | ● | ● | ● | ● | | ● | ● | ● | | ● | | ● | | ● | ● |
| ZEN SHIATSU & HEALING TAO (HM22101) | ● | ● | | | ● | ● | | | | | | | | ● | | | | | | | | | | | | | | ● | | | | | ● | | | ● | | | ● | ● | | | | | ● | | | ● |
| **MANCHESTER (GREATER)** | | | | | | | | | | | | | | | | | | | | | | | | | | | | | | | | | | | | | | | | | | | | | | | | |
| A SIR ROBERTS ALT PLACE (HM00045) | | ● | | | ● | | | | ● | | | | ● | ● | ● | | | | ● | ● | | | | | | | ● | | ● | ● | | | ● | ● | | ● | | | ● | ● | ● | | ● | ● | | | ● | ● |
| ACUMEDIC (HM00220) | ● | | | | ● | | | | | | ● | | | ● | ● | | | | | | | | ● | | ● | | ● | | ● | | | | ● | | | | | | | | ● | | | | | | ● | ● |
| ACUPUNCTURE CENTRE (HM00252) | ● | ● | | | ● | | | | | | | | | ● | ● | | | | | | | | ● | | | ● | | | ● | ● | | | ● | | | ● | | | | | | | | | ● | | ● | |
| ADVANCED PHYSIOTHERAPY CLINIC (HM00403) | | | | | ● | | | | | | | | | | | | | | | | | | | | | | | ● | ● | | | | | | | | | | | | | | | | ● | | ● | |
| ALL IN THE MIND (HM00582) | ● | ● | | | | | | | ● | | | | | | | | | | | | | ● | | | ● | | | | | ● | ● | | | ● | | | | | | | | | | | | | | |
| AROMATHERAPY BY SARA (HM01098) | | | | | | | | | | | | | | ● | ● | | | | | | | | | | | | | | | | | | | | | ● | | | | | | | | | | | | |
| AROMATHERAPY LADIES MASSAGE (HM01118) | ● | ● | ● | ● | ● | ● | ● | ● | ● | ● | ● | ● | ● | ● | ● | ● | ● | ● | ● | ● | | ● | ● | ● | ● | ● | ● | ● | ● | ● | | ● | ● | ● | ● | ● | ● | | ● | ● | ● | ● | ● | ● | ● | ● | ● | ● |
| ASTLEY COMPLEMENTARY CENTRE (HM01300) | ● | ● | | | | | ● | | | | | | ● | ● | ● | | | | | | | | | | ● | | | | ● | | | | | ● | | ● | | | | | | | | | | | | |
| BEAUTY THERAPY CENTRE (HM02006) | | | | | | | | | | | | | | | ● | | | | | | | | | | | | | | | | | | | | | | | | | | | | | | | | | |
| BRAMHALL CHIROPRACTIC CLINIC (HM02898) | | | | | ● | | | | | | | | ● | | | | | | | | | | | ● | | ● | | | ● | | | | ● | | | | | | ● | | | | | | | | ● | |
| BURGESS, KAREN (HM03377) | | | | | ● | | | | | | | ● | | | | | | | | | | ● | | | | ● | | ● | ● | | | | | | | | | | | | | ● | | | ● | | ● | |
| C CARTLEDGE REFLEXOLOGY (HM03521) | ● | ● | ● | ● | ● | ● | ● | ● | ● | ● | ● | ● | ● | ● | ● | ● | ● | ● | ● | ● | | ● | ● | ● | ● | ● | ● | ● | ● | ● | | ● | ● | ● | ● | ● | ● | | ● | ● | ● | ● | ● | ● | ● | ● | ● | ● |
| CHARTERED PHYSIOTHERAPY CLINIC (HM04046) | | | | | ● | | | | | | | | | | | | | | ● | | | | | ● | | ● | | | ● | | | ● | | | | | | | | | | | | | ● | | ● | |

# I - S Conditions treated at Practices/Businesses

Business by County with Reference no.

| Business by County with Reference no. | Insomnia | Irritable Bowel Syndrome | Itching | Jet Lag | Joint Pain | Kidney Complaints | Lactose Intolerance | Laryngitis | Lethargy | Liver Disorders | Low Blood Pressure | Lung Problems | ME | Menopause | Migraine | Motion Sickness |
|---|---|---|---|---|---|---|---|---|---|---|---|---|---|---|---|---|
| CHORLTON STRESS MANAGEMENT (HM04430) | ● | ● | | | | | | | | | | | | | | |
| CLARENDON CLINIC (HM04540) | | ● | | | ● | | | | ● | | | | | ● | | |
| COLLINGE, J C (HM04863) | | ● | | | ● | | | | | | | | | | | |
| COSGROVES PHYSIO-FIT CENTRE (HM05201) | | | | | | | | | | | | | | | | |
| CROSSWAY CLINIC (HM05491) | | | | | ● | | | | | | | | | | | |
| DAVEENA ASSOCIATES (HM05763) | | | | | | | | | | | | | | | | |
| DIDSBURY CHIROPRACTIC CLINIC (HM06090) | | | | | ● | | | | | | | | | | | |
| EVANS, DAVID (HM06967) | ● | ● | ● | | ● | | | ● | | | ● | | ● | ● | ● | |
| GOGIA, D R (DR) (HM08195) | | | | | | | | | | | | | | | | |
| GRAHAM COOMBE - MCTIMONEY (HM08337) | | ● | | | ● | | | | | | | | ● | | ● | |
| GUILD OF PRACTITIONERS (HM08627) | | | | | | | | | ● | | | | ● | | | |
| HOLMED CLINIC (HM10038) | | ● | | | ● | | | | | | | | ● | | ● | |
| HUMAN TOUCH CENTRE (HM10366) | | | | | ● | | | | | | | | ● | ● | ● | |
| IBBOTSON, GEOFF (DR) (HM10565) | | ● | | ● | | | | | | | | | ● | | ● | |
| M J HAYLETT - PHYSIOTHERAPIST (HM12802) | | | | ● | ● | | | | | | | | | | ● | |
| MOBILE COMPLEMENTARY THERAPIES (HM14029) | ● | | | | ● | | | | | | | | | | | |
| MOUNT STREET COMP THERAPIES (HM14291) | ● | ● | | | | | | | | | | | ● | ● | ● | |
| NICKI HAVES PHYSIO CLINIC (HM14923) | | | | | ● | | | | | | | | | | | |
| NIVERN, D (HM14954) | ● | | | | | | | | ● | | ● | | ● | ● | ● | |
| REJUVENATION (HM17154) | | | | | ● | | | | | | | | | | | |
| SCHOFIELD, G A (HM18018) | ● | | ● | | ● | ● | ● | | ● | ● | ● | ● | ● | ● | ● | |
| SHANGHAI ACUPUNCTURE CLINIC (HM18280) | ● | ● | ● | ● | ● | ● | ● | ● | ● | ● | ● | ● | ● | ● | ● | ● |
| ST JOHN STREET PHYSIO PRACTICE (HM19080) | | | | | ● | | | | | | | | | | | |
| STIRLING, DIANNE (HM19301) | ● | | | | | | | | ● | | | | | | ● | |
| SWINTON HEALTH FOODS (HM19600) | ● | ● | | | | ● | ● | | ● | ● | ● | | | | ● | |
| WAINWRIGHT, P (HM20739) | | | | | ● | | | | | | | | | | | |
| **MERSEYSIDE** | | | | | | | | | | | | | | | | |
| ABBEY FOOT CLINIC (HM00083) | | | | | | | | | | | | | | | | |
| ACUPUNCTURE CLINIC (HM00263) | ● | ● | | | ● | | | | | | ● | ● | ● | ● | ● | ● |
| AIGBURTH MCTIMONEY CLINIC (HM00427) | | ● | | | ● | | | | | | | | ● | | ● | |
| AINTREE OSTEOPATHIC (HM00439) | ● | ● | | | | | | | | | | | ● | | ● | |
| ALLERTON HEALTH CENTRE (HM00639) | | | | | ● | | | | ● | | | | | ● | ● | |
| BIMPSON, PETER (HM02311) | | | | | ● | | | | | | | | | | ● | |
| BOLTON, TOM (HM02663) | ● | | | | | | | | | | | | ● | | | |

| Business by County with Reference no. | Mouth Disorders | Mouth Ulcers | Multiple Sclerosis | Muscular Dystrophy | Musculo-skeletal | Nail Health | Nausea | Nerve Disorders | Nervous Disorders | Neuralgia | Obesity | Osteoporosis | Pain | Palpitations | Panic Attacks | Parkinson's Disease |
|---|---|---|---|---|---|---|---|---|---|---|---|---|---|---|---|---|
| CHORLTON STRESS MANAGEMENT (HM04430) | | | | | | | | ● | | | | | ● | | | |
| CLARENDON CLINIC (HM04540) | | | | | | | | | | ● | | | ● | | | |
| COLLINGE, J C (HM04863) | | | | | | | | | | | | ● | ● | | | |
| COSGROVES PHYSIO-FIT CENTRE (HM05201) | | | | | | | | | | ● | ● | ● | | | | |
| CROSSWAY CLINIC (HM05491) | | | | | | | | ● | | ● | | | ● | | | |
| DAVEENA ASSOCIATES (HM05763) | | | | | | | | | ● | | ● | | | ● | | |
| DIDSBURY CHIROPRACTIC CLINIC (HM06090) | | | | | | | | | | | | | | | | |
| EVANS, DAVID (HM06967) | | | ● | | | | | ● | ● | ● | ● | | ● | ● | | |
| GOGIA, D R (DR) (HM08195) | | | | | | | | | | | | | ● | | | |
| GRAHAM COOMBE - MCTIMONEY (HM08337) | | | | | | | | ● | | ● | | | ● | | | |
| GUILD OF PRACTITIONERS (HM08627) | | | | ● | | | | | | | | | ● | | | |
| HOLMED CLINIC (HM10038) | | | | | | | | ● | ● | | | | ● | | | |
| HUMAN TOUCH CENTRE (HM10366) | | | | | | | | | | | | | ● | | | |
| IBBOTSON, GEOFF (DR) (HM10565) | | | | | | | | | ● | | ● | | ● | | | |
| M J HAYLETT - PHYSIOTHERAPIST (HM12802) | | | | | | | | | | ● | | | ● | | | |
| MOBILE COMPLEMENTARY THERAPIES (HM14029) | | | | | | | | | | | | | ● | | | |
| MOUNT STREET COMP THERAPIES (HM14291) | | | | | | | | | | | | | | | | |
| NICKI HAVES PHYSIO CLINIC (HM14923) | | | ● | | | | | | | | | | | | | |
| NIVERN, D (HM14954) | | | ● | | | ● | ● | ● | ● | | | | ● | ● | | |
| REJUVENATION (HM17154) | | | | | | | | | | | | | ● | | | |
| SCHOFIELD, G A (HM18018) | | | ● | ● | | ● | ● | ● | ● | ● | ● | ● | ● | ● | | |
| SHANGHAI ACUPUNCTURE CLINIC (HM18280) | ● | ● | ● | ● | | ● | ● | ● | ● | ● | ● | ● | ● | ● | | ● |
| ST JOHN STREET PHYSIO PRACTICE (HM19080) | | | | | | | | | | | | | ● | | | ● |
| STIRLING, DIANNE (HM19301) | | | | | | | | ● | | | | | | | | |
| SWINTON HEALTH FOODS (HM19600) | | | | | | | | | | | | | | | | |
| WAINWRIGHT, P (HM20739) | | | | | | ● | | | | | | | | | | |
| **MERSEYSIDE** | | | | | | | | | | | | | | | | |
| ABBEY FOOT CLINIC (HM00083) | | | | | | ● | | | | | | | | | | |
| ACUPUNCTURE CLINIC (HM00263) | | | | | | | ● | ● | ● | ● | ● | ● | ● | | | ● |
| AIGBURTH MCTIMONEY CLINIC (HM00427) | | | ● | ● | | | | ● | ● | ● | | ● | ● | | | |
| AINTREE OSTEOPATHIC (HM00439) | | | | | | | | | ● | | | | ● | | | |
| ALLERTON HEALTH CENTRE (HM00639) | | | | | | | | | | | | | ● | | | |
| BIMPSON, PETER (HM02311) | | | | | | | | | | | | | ● | | | |
| BOLTON, TOM (HM02663) | | | | | | | | | | | | | | | ● | |

| Business by County with Reference no. | Period Problems | Phobias | Piles | PMT | Pneumonia | Postural Problems | Pregnancy Help | Prostate Problems | Psoriasis | Raynaud's Disease | Recurrent Infections | Restless Legs | Rheumatoid Arthritis | Schizophrenia | Sciatica | Sexual Problems |
|---|---|---|---|---|---|---|---|---|---|---|---|---|---|---|---|---|
| CHORLTON STRESS MANAGEMENT (HM04430) | | ● | | | | | | | ● | | | | | | | ● |
| CLARENDON CLINIC (HM04540) | ● | | | ● | | | | ● | | | ● | | | | ● | |
| COLLINGE, J C (HM04863) | | | | | | | | | | | | | ● | | ● | |
| COSGROVES PHYSIO-FIT CENTRE (HM05201) | | | | | | | | | | | | | ● | | ● | |
| CROSSWAY CLINIC (HM05491) | | ● | | | | ● | | | | | | | | | ● | |
| DAVEENA ASSOCIATES (HM05763) | | ● | | ● | | | | | | | | | | ● | | |
| DIDSBURY CHIROPRACTIC CLINIC (HM06090) | | | | | | | | | | | | | | | | |
| EVANS, DAVID (HM06967) | ● | ● | | ● | | | ● | | ● | ● | ● | | | | ● | ● |
| GOGIA, D R (DR) (HM08195) | | | | | | | | | | | | | | | | |
| GRAHAM COOMBE - MCTIMONEY (HM08337) | ● | | | | | | | | | ● | | ● | | | ● | |
| GUILD OF PRACTITIONERS (HM08627) | | | | | | | | | | | | | ● | | | |
| HOLMED CLINIC (HM10038) | | | | | | | | | | | | | | | ● | |
| HUMAN TOUCH CENTRE (HM10366) | | | | ● | | | ● | | ● | ● | | | ● | | | |
| IBBOTSON, GEOFF (DR) (HM10565) | | ● | | ● | | | | | ● | | | | | | | ● |
| M J HAYLETT - PHYSIOTHERAPIST (HM12802) | | | | | | | | | | | | | | | ● | |
| MOBILE COMPLEMENTARY THERAPIES (HM14029) | ● | | | | | | | | | | | ● | | | ● | |
| MOUNT STREET COMP THERAPIES (HM14291) | | | | | | | | | | | | | | | | |
| NICKI HAVES PHYSIO CLINIC (HM14923) | | | | | | | | | | | | | | | | |
| NIVERN, D (HM14954) | ● | | | ● | | | ● | | | ● | ● | ● | ● | | ● | ● |
| REJUVENATION (HM17154) | | | | | | | | | | | | | | | | |
| SCHOFIELD, G A (HM18018) | ● | ● | ● | ● | | | | | ● | ● | | | ● | ● | | ● |
| SHANGHAI ACUPUNCTURE CLINIC (HM18280) | ● | ● | ● | ● | ● | | ● | ● | ● | ● | ● | ● | ● | ● | ● | ● |
| ST JOHN STREET PHYSIO PRACTICE (HM19080) | | | | | | | | | | | | | ● | | | |
| STIRLING, DIANNE (HM19301) | | | | | | | | | | | | | | | | |
| SWINTON HEALTH FOODS (HM19600) | | | | | | | | | | | | | | | | |
| WAINWRIGHT, P (HM20739) | | | | | | | | | ● | | | | ● | | | |
| **MERSEYSIDE** | | | | | | | | | | | | | | | | |
| ABBEY FOOT CLINIC (HM00083) | | | | | | | | | | | | | | | | |
| ACUPUNCTURE CLINIC (HM00263) | ● | ● | ● | ● | | | | | ● | ● | | ● | ● | | ● | |
| AIGBURTH MCTIMONEY CLINIC (HM00427) | ● | | ● | | | | | | | ● | | ● | ● | | ● | |
| AINTREE OSTEOPATHIC (HM00439) | | | | ● | | | | | | ● | | | ● | | ● | |
| ALLERTON HEALTH CENTRE (HM00639) | | | | | | | | | | | | | | | ● | |
| BIMPSON, PETER (HM02311) | | | | | | | | | | | | | | | | |
| BOLTON, TOM (HM02663) | | ● | | ● | | | | | | | | | | | | |

# I - S Conditions treated at Practices/Businesses

| Business by County with Reference no. | Insomnia | Irritable Bowel Syndrome | Itching | Jet Lag | Joint Pain | Kidney Complaints | Lactose Intolerance | Laryngitis | Lethargy | Liver Disorders | Low Blood Pressure | Lung Problems | ME | Menopause | Migraine | Motion Sickness | Mouth Disorders | Mouth Ulcers | Multiple Sclerosis | Muscular Dystrophy | Musculo-skeletal | Nail Health | Nausea | Nerve Disorders | Nervous Disorders | Neuralgia | Obesity | Osteoporosis | Pain | Palpitations | Panic Attacks | Parkinson's Disease | Period Problems | Phobias | Piles | PMT | Pneumonia | Postural Problems | Pregnancy Help | Prostate Problems | Psoriasis | Raynaud's Disease | Recurrent Infections | Restless Legs | Rheumatoid Arthritis | Schizophrenia | Sciatica | Sexual Problems |
|---|---|---|---|---|---|---|---|---|---|---|---|---|---|---|---|---|---|---|---|---|---|---|---|---|---|---|---|---|---|---|---|---|---|---|---|---|---|---|---|---|---|---|---|---|---|---|---|---|
| BOYLE, ANDREW (HM02826) | ● | ● | | | ● | | | | ● | | | | ● | | ● | | | | | | | ● | | | | ● | | | ● | | | | ● | | | ● | | | | | ● | ● | ● | ● | ● | | ● | |
| BRENNAN, M A (HM02958) | | | | | | | | | | | | | | | | | | | | | | ● | | | | | | | | | | | | | | | | | | | | | | | | | | |
| CARTER, G R (HM03778) | | | | | | | | | | | | | | | | | | | | | | ● | | | | | | | | | | | | | | | | | | | | | | | | | | |
| CAWLEY, TONY (HM03871) | ● | ● | | | | | | | | | | | | | | | | | | | | | | | | | ● | | | | ● | | | ● | | | | | | | ● | | | | | | | |
| CONCANNON, DEIRDRE (HM04965) | | ● | | | ● | | | | | | | | ● | | | | | | | | | | | ● | | | | ● | ● | | | | | | | | | | | | | | | | | | ● | |
| D A F CLINIC (HM05655) | | ● | | | | | | | | | ● | | ● | | ● | | | | | | | ● | | | ● | | ● | | ● | ● | | | | | | | | | ● | ● | | | | | | | | |
| DARE TO CARE (HM05739) | | | | | | | | | | | | | | | ● | | | | | | | | | | | | | | ● | | | | ● | | | ● | | | | | | | | | | | | |
| FARMER, BARBARA (HM01681) | | | | | ● | | | | | | | | | | | | | | | | | | | | | ● | | ● | ● | | | | | | | | | | | | | | | | ● | | ● | |
| FRESHLEA PRIVATE CLINICS (HM07738) | | | | | ● | | | | | | | | | | | | | | | | | | | | | | | | ● | | | | | | | | | | | | | | | | | | ● | |
| GATEAUD, S (HM07924) | | ● | | | | | | | | | | | | | ● | | | | | | | | | | | | | ● | ● | | | | | | | | | ● | | | | | | | | | ● | |
| GROUNDS, L (HM08600) | | | | | | | | | | | | | | | | | | | | | | ● | | | | | | | | | | | | | | | | | | | | | | | | | | |
| HEAL TO TOE (HM09311) | ● | ● | ● | ● | ● | ● | ● | ● | ● | ● | ● | ● | ● | ● | ● | ● | ● | ● | ● | ● | | ● | ● | ● | ● | ● | ● | ● | ● | ● | | ● | ● | ● | ● | ● | | | ● | ● | ● | ● | ● | ● | ● | | ● | |
| HOLISTIC HEALTH CENTRE (HM09975) | ● | ● | ● | | ● | ● | | | | | | ● | ● | ● | ● | ● | | | | | | | | | | ● | | | ● | | | | ● | | ● | ● | | | | ● | ● | ● | ● | ● | ● | | ● | |
| HOPE STREET NATURAL HLTH CTRE (HM10136) | ● | | | | ● | | | | | | | | | ● | ● | | | | | | | | ● | | | | | | ● | | | | ● | | | ● | | | | | | | | | | | | |
| HYPNOCARE (HM10490) | | | | | | | | | | | | | | | | | | | | | | | | | | | ● | | | | | | | ● | | | | | | | | | | | | | | |
| JAMES, ANN (HM10880) | | | ● | | ● | | | | | | | | | | | | | | ● | ● | | ● | | ● | | | | ● | ● | | | ● | | | | | | | | | ● | ● | ● | ● | ● | | ● | |
| JARVIS, K R (HM10934) | | | | | | | | | | | | | | | | | | | | | | ● | | | | | | | | | | | | | | | | | | | | | | | | | | |
| MARKET STREET CHIROPODY CLINIC (HM13113) | | | | | | | | | | | | | | | | | | | | | | ● | | | | | | | | | | | | | | | | | | | | | | | | | | |
| MARSH, E C (HM13146) | | | | | | | | | | | | | | | | | | | | | | ● | | | | | | | | | | | | | | | | | | | | | | | | | | |
| MCLOUGHLIN, CLAIRE (HM13560) | | | | | | | | | | | | | | | | | | | | | | ● | | | | | | | | | | | | | | | | | | | | | | | | | | |
| NATURAL HEALTH CLINIC (HM14576) | ● | ● | ● | | ● | ● | | ● | ● | ● | | ● | ● | ● | ● | ● | ● | ● | ● | | | | ● | ● | ● | ● | | | ● | ● | | | ● | ● | ● | ● | ● | | ● | ● | ● | ● | ● | ● | ● | | ● | |
| PURE ESSENTIALS DIRECT (HM16764) | | | | | ● | | | | | | | | | | | | | | | | | | | | | | | | | | | | ● | | | ● | | | | | | | | | | | | |
| SANCTUARY NATURAL HEALTH (HM17893) | | | | | | | | | | | | | ● | | ● | | | | ● | | | | | | | | | | ● | | | | | | | | | | | | | ● | | | | | ● | |
| SCOTT, ANDREW (HM18107) | ● | ● | | | ● | | | | ● | | | ● | ● | ● | ● | ● | | | | | | | ● | | | | | | ● | ● | | | ● | | | ● | | | ● | ● | | | | | | | ● | |
| SEFTON PARK NATURAL THRPY CTRE (HM18198) | ● | | | | | | | | | | | | ● | | | | | | | | | | | | ● | | ● | | | | ● | | | | | | | | | | | | | | | | | ● |
| SIMPSON CLINIC (HM18584) | ● | ● | ● | ● | ● | ● | ● | ● | ● | ● | ● | ● | ● | ● | ● | ● | ● | ● | ● | ● | | ● | ● | ● | ● | ● | ● | ● | ● | ● | | ● | ● | ● | ● | ● | | | ● | ● | ● | ● | ● | ● | ● | | ● | |
| SOUTHPORT OSTEO & ACUPUNCTURE (HM18942) | | | | | | | | | | | | | | | | | | | | | | | | | | | | | ● | | | | | | | | | | | | | | | | | | ● | |
| STEINA SPORTS & PHYSIOTHERAPY (HM19188) | | | | | ● | | | | | | | | | | | | | | | | | | | | | | | | | | | | | | | | | | | | | | | | | | | |
| TARA SCHOOL OF HYPNOTHERAPY (HM19701) | | ● | | | | | | | | | | | | | | | | | | | | | | | ● | | ● | | ● | | | | | ● | | | | | | | ● | | | | | | | |
| THERAPY 21 (HM19890) | ● | | | | ● | | | | | | | | ● | | ● | | | | | | | | | | | | | | | | | | | | | | | | | | ● | | | | ● | | ● | |
| WILLIAMS CHIROPODY SERVICE (HM21530) | | | | | | | | | | | | | | | | | | | | | | ● | | | | | | | | | | | | | | | | | | | | | | | | | | |
| WILLIAMS, T H (HM21597) | | | | | | | | | | | | | | | | | | | | | | ● | | | | | | | | | | | | | | | | | | | | | | | | | | |
| WILLIAMS, TECWYN H (HM21598) | | | | | | | | | | | | | | | | | | | | | | ● | | | | | | | | | | | | | | | | | | | | | | | | | | |
| WIRRALL CLINIC (HM21730) | | | | | ● | | | | | | | | | | ● | | | | | | | | | | | | | | ● | | | | | | | | | | | | | | | | | | | |

www.healthmyself.com

# I - S Conditions treated at Practices/Businesses

| Business by County with Reference no. | Insomnia | Irritable Bowel Syndrome | Itching | Jet Lag | Joint Pain | Kidney Complaints | Lactose Intolerance | Laryngitis | Lethargy | Liver Disorders | Low Blood Pressure | Lung Problems | ME | Menopause | Migraine | Motion Sickness | Mouth Disorders | Mouth Ulcers | Multiple Sclerosis | Muscular Dystrophy | Musculo-skeletal |
|---|---|---|---|---|---|---|---|---|---|---|---|---|---|---|---|---|---|---|---|---|---|
| **MIDDLESEX** | | | | | | | | | | | | | | | | | | | | | |
| CLANRICARDE CLINIC (HM04526) | | ● | | | ● | ● | | ● | ● | ● | | | ● | | ● | ● | | | ● | | |
| **MIDLANDS (WEST)** | | | | | | | | | | | | | | | | | | | | | |
| 1ST CHIROPRACTIC UK (HM00006) | | ● | | | ● | | | | | | | | ● | | | | | | | | |
| 1ST CHIROPRACTIC UK (HM00005) | | ● | | | ● | | | | | | | | ● | | | | | | | | |
| A Q C H (HM00044) | ● | ● | ● | | ● | | ● | | ● | | ● | | ● | ● | ● | ● | | ● | ● | | |
| ABBEY CLINIC (HM00077) | | ● | | | ● | | | | | | | | | | | | | | ● | ● | |
| ABBIE HYPNOTHERAPY CENTRE (HM00093) | ● | ● | ● | ● | | | | | | | | | ● | | ● | ● | ● | | ● | | |
| ACUPUNCTURE HEALTH CLINIC (HM00312) | ● | | | | ● | | | | ● | | | | | ● | ● | | | | | | |
| ALCOCK, E C (HM00490) | | | | | | | | | | | | | | | | | | | | | |
| ALDA HOUSE NATURAL THERAPY (HM00492) | | ● | ● | | ● | ● | | | | ● | | ● | ● | ● | ● | | | ● | | | |
| ALDOUS, JOSIE (HM00503) | ● | ● | | | | | | | | | | | | | ● | | | | | | |
| ALLEN, ELAINE (HM00608) | ● | | ● | | | | | | | | | | | ● | ● | | | | | | |
| AROMA SANTE (HM01057) | ● | ● | ● | ● | ● | ● | ● | ● | ● | ● | ● | ● | ● | ● | ● | ● | ● | ● | ● | ● | |
| ARROW BANK CHIROPRACTIC CLINIC (HM01149) | | | | | ● | | | | | | | | | | | | | | | | |
| ASSOCIATION OF STRESS MNGMT (HM01288) | ● | ● | | ● | | | | | | | | | | | | | | | | | |
| BACKCARE & ACUPUNCTURE CLINIC (HM01526) | ● | ● | ● | ● | ● | ● | ● | | ● | ● | ● | ● | ● | ● | ● | ● | ● | ● | ● | | |
| BEAUTIFORM COLLEGE (HM01992) | | | | | ● | | | | | | | | | | | | | | | | |
| BILLINGHAM, S (HM02301) | ● | | | | | | | | | | | | | | ● | | | | ● | | |
| BIOENERGY PARTNERSHIP (HM02334) | | | | | ● | | | | | | | | ● | | ● | | | | | | |
| BIRMINGHAM ACU/CHIRO CLNC (HM02382) | ● | ● | ● | ● | ● | ● | ● | ● | ● | ● | ● | ● | ● | ● | ● | ● | ● | ● | ● | ● | |
| BIRMINGHAM PHYSIO CLINIC (HM02388) | | | | | ● | | | | | | | | | | | | | | | | |
| BIRMINGHAM TRAD ACU CENTRE (HM02390) | | | | | ● | | | | | | | | | | ● | | | | | | |
| BLAKE, D H (HM02479) | ● | ● | | | ● | | | | ● | | | | | ● | ● | ● | | ● | | | |
| BOLDMERE HYPNOTHERAPY (HM02653) | | ● | | | | | | | | | | | | | ● | | | | | | |
| BROWNHILL, D G (HM03257) | ● | ● | | | | | | | | | | | | | ● | | | | | | |
| BTAC (HM03296) | ● | ● | ● | | ● | | | | | | ● | ● | ● | ● | ● | | | | ● | | |
| BULLOCK, JULIE (HM03344) | | | | | | | | | | | | | | | | | | | | | |
| CARPENTER, DAVID (HM03727) | ● | ● | | | | ● | | | | | | | ● | | ● | ● | | | ● | | |
| CENTRE FOR NATURAL THERAPIES (HM03913) | ● | ● | ● | ● | ● | ● | ● | ● | ● | ● | ● | ● | ● | ● | ● | ● | ● | ● | ● | ● | |
| CHELMSLEY WOOD FOOT CLINIC (HM04086) | | | | | | | | | | | | | | | | | | | | | |
| CHEYLESMORE PHYSIO CLINIC (HM04147) | | | | | | | | | | | | | | | | | | | | | ● |
| CHIRO MED (HM04283) | ● | ● | ● | | | | | | ● | ● | ● | ● | ● | ● | ● | ● | | | ● | ● | |
| CHIROPRACTIC CLINIC (HM04388) | | ● | | | ● | | | | | | | | | | | | | | | | |

| Business by County with Reference no. | Nail Health | Nausea | Nerve Disorders | Nervous Disorders | Neuralgia | Obesity | Osteoporosis | Pain | Palpitations | Panic Attacks | Parkinson's Disease | Period Problems | Phobias | Piles | PMT | Pneumonia | Postural Problems | Pregnancy Help | Prostate Problems | Psoriasis | Raynaud's Disease | Recurrent Infections | Restless Legs | Rheumatoid Arthritis | Schizophrenia | Sciatica | Sexual Problems |
|---|---|---|---|---|---|---|---|---|---|---|---|---|---|---|---|---|---|---|---|---|---|---|---|---|---|---|---|
| **MIDDLESEX** | | | | | | | | | | | | | | | | | | | | | | | | | | | |
| CLANRICARDE CLINIC (HM04526) | ● | | ● | ● | ● | ● | ● | ● | | | ● | ● | | ● | ● | | | ● | ● | ● | ● | | | ● | | ● | ● |
| **MIDLANDS (WEST)** | | | | | | | | | | | | | | | | | | | | | | | | | | | |
| 1ST CHIROPRACTIC UK (HM00006) | | | ● | ● | | | | ● | | | | | | | | | | | | | | | | | | ● | |
| 1ST CHIROPRACTIC UK (HM00005) | | | | | | | | ● | | | | | | | | | | | | | | | | | | ● | |
| A Q C H (HM00044) | | ● | | ● | ● | ● | | ● | ● | | | ● | ● | | ● | | | ● | | ● | ● | ● | ● | | | | ● |
| ABBEY CLINIC (HM00077) | | | | | ● | | | ● | | | | | | | | | ● | | | | | | | ● | | ● | |
| ABBIE HYPNOTHERAPY CENTRE (HM00093) | | ● | ● | ● | | ● | | | | | | | ● | | | | | ● | | | | | | | | | |
| ACUPUNCTURE HEALTH CLINIC (HM00312) | | | | | | | | | | | | ● | | | ● | | | ● | | | | | | | | | |
| ALCOCK, E C (HM00490) | | | | | | | | | | | | | | | | | | | | | | | | ● | | | |
| ALDA HOUSE NATURAL THERAPY (HM00492) | ● | | ● | ● | ● | | | ● | ● | | | ● | ● | | ● | | | ● | ● | | | ● | | | | ● | |
| ALDOUS, JOSIE (HM00503) | | | | | | | | | | | | | | | | | | | | | | | | | | | |
| ALLEN, ELAINE (HM00608) | | | | | | | | | | | | | | | | | | | | | | | | | | | |
| AROMA SANTE (HM01057) | ● | ● | ● | ● | ● | ● | ● | ● | ● | | ● | ● | ● | ● | ● | ● | | ● | ● | ● | ● | ● | ● | ● | ● | ● | ● |
| ARROW BANK CHIROPRACTIC CLINIC (HM01149) | | | | | | | | ● | | | | | | | | | | | | | | | | | | | |
| ASSOCIATION OF STRESS MNGMT (HM01288) | | | | ● | | ● | | ● | | | | | ● | | ● | | | | | | | | | | | | |
| BACKCARE & ACUPUNCTURE CLINIC (HM01526) | | ● | ● | ● | ● | ● | ● | ● | ● | | ● | ● | ● | ● | ● | | | ● | ● | ● | ● | ● | ● | ● | | ● | |
| BEAUTIFORM COLLEGE (HM01992) | ● | | | | | | | ● | | | | | | | | | | | | | | | | ● | | | |
| BILLINGHAM, S (HM02301) | | | | | | | | | | | ● | ● | | | ● | | | | | | ● | | ● | | | | |
| BIOENERGY PARTNERSHIP (HM02334) | | | | | | | | ● | | | | | | | | | | | | | | | | | | | |
| BIRMINGHAM ACU/CHIRO CLNC (HM02382) | ● | ● | ● | ● | ● | ● | ● | ● | ● | | ● | ● | ● | ● | ● | ● | | ● | ● | ● | ● | ● | ● | ● | | ● | ● |
| BIRMINGHAM PHYSIO CLINIC (HM02388) | | | | | | | | | | | | | | | | | | | | | | | | | | | |
| BIRMINGHAM TRAD ACU CENTRE (HM02390) | | | ● | | | | | ● | | | | | | | | | ● | | | | | | | | | | |
| BLAKE, D H (HM02479) | | ● | ● | ● | | | ● | ● | | | | | | | | | | | | | | | | | | ● | |
| BOLDMERE HYPNOTHERAPY (HM02653) | | | | ● | | ● | | | | | | | ● | | | | | ● | | | | | | | | | |
| BROWNHILL, D G (HM03257) | | | ● | ● | | ● | | | ● | ● | | | ● | | | | | | | ● | | | | | | | ● |
| BTAC (HM03296) | | ● | | | | | | ● | ● | | | ● | | | ● | | | | | | ● | | ● | ● | | ● | ● |
| BULLOCK, JULIE (HM03344) | ● | | | | | | | | | | | | | | | | | | | | | | | | | | |
| CARPENTER, DAVID (HM03727) | | ● | ● | ● | | ● | | ● | ● | ● | | | ● | | ● | | | | | ● | | ● | ● | | | | ● |
| CENTRE FOR NATURAL THERAPIES (HM03913) | ● | ● | ● | ● | ● | ● | ● | ● | ● | | ● | ● | ● | ● | ● | ● | | ● | ● | ● | ● | ● | ● | ● | ● | ● | ● |
| CHELMSLEY WOOD FOOT CLINIC (HM04086) | ● | | | | | | | | | | | | | | | | | | | | | | | | | | |
| CHEYLESMORE PHYSIO CLINIC (HM04147) | | | | | | | | ● | | | | | | | | | | | | | | | | | | ● | |
| CHIRO MED (HM04283) | | ● | ● | | | | | | | | ● | ● | ● | | ● | | | ● | ● | ● | ● | ● | ● | ● | | ● | |
| CHIROPRACTIC CLINIC (HM04388) | | | ● | | | | ● | ● | | | | | | | | | | | | | | | | | | ● | |

# I - S Conditions treated at Practices/Businesses

Business by County with Reference no.

| Business | Insomnia | Irritable Bowel Syndrome | Itching | Jet Lag | Joint Pain | Kidney Complaints | Lactose Intolerance | Laryngitis | Lethargy | Liver Disorders | Low Blood Pressure | Lung Problems | ME | Menopause | Migraine | Motion Sickness | Mouth Disorders | Mouth Ulcers | Multiple Sclerosis | Muscular Dystrophy | Musculo-skeletal | Nail Health | Nausea | Nerve Disorders |
|---|---|---|---|---|---|---|---|---|---|---|---|---|---|---|---|---|---|---|---|---|---|---|---|---|
| CHIROPRACTORS OF WARWICK ROAD (HM04407) | | ● | | | | | | | | | | | | | | | | | | | | | | ● |
| CODSALL COMP THERAPIES (HM04778) | | | | | | | | | | | | | | | ● | | | | | | | | | |
| COMPLEMENTARY HEALING CENTRE (HM04919) | | | | | | | | | | | | | | | ● | | | | | | | | | |
| COMPLEMENTARY THERAPY CENTRE (HM04943) | | | | | | | | | | | | | | | | | | | | | | | | |
| COMPLEMENTARY THERAPY CENTRE (HM04947) | | | | | | | | | | | | | | | | | | | | | | | | |
| CREATIVE HEALTH CENTRE (HM05398) | ● | ● | | | | | | | | | | | ● | ● | ● | | | | | | | | | |
| CROFT, ANGELA (HM05453) | | ● | | | ● | | | | | | | | ● | | ● | | | | | | | | | |
| CRYSTAL CLEAR PRACTICE (HM05528) | ● | ● | ● | ● | ● | ● | ● | ● | ● | ● | ● | ● | ● | ● | ● | ● | ● | ● | ● | ● | | ● | ● | ● |
| CTIC (HM05535) | | | | | | | | | | | | | ● | | | | | | | | | | | |
| CTRE-REFLEX & AROMATHERAPY (HM05549) | ● | ● | | | ● | | | | | | | ● | ● | ● | ● | | | | ● | | | | | |
| DAVIS A STARKEY REM THERAP (HM05846) | ● | ● | | | ● | | | | | | ● | | | ● | ● | | | | ● | | | | | ● |
| DUDLEY PHYSIOTHERAPY CLINIC (HM06354) | | | | | ● | | | | | | | | | | | | | | | | | | | |
| ERDINGTHON NATURAL HEALTH CLNC (HM06880) | ● | ● | ● | ● | ● | ● | ● | ● | ● | ● | ● | ● | ● | ● | ● | ● | ● | ● | ● | ● | | ● | ● | |
| ESSENTIAL HEALTH (HM06909) | ● | | | | ● | | | | | | | | | | | | | | | | | | | |
| FAIRFAX PRIVATE THERAPY (HM07056) | ● | | | | ● | | | | ● | | ● | | | ● | ● | | | | | | | | ● | ● |
| FLETCHER, VICTOR JOHN (HM07416) | | | | | | | | | | | | | | | | | | | | | | ● | | |
| FORD, MARIA (HM07526) | | | | | | | | | | | | | | | | | | | | | | | | |
| FRESHWINDS CHARITABLE TRUST (HM07740) | ● | ● | ● | ● | ● | ● | ● | ● | ● | ● | ● | ● | ● | ● | ● | ● | ● | ● | ● | ● | | ● | ● | ● |
| GOLDEN PALMS (HM08207) | | | ● | | ● | | | | | | ● | ● | | | ● | | | | | | | | | |
| GREAT BARR OSTEO PRACTICE (HM08430) | | | | | | | | | | | | | | | | | | | | | | | | |
| GREEN VALLEY THERAPY CENTRE (HM08443) | ● | ● | ● | ● | ● | ● | ● | ● | ● | ● | ● | ● | ● | ● | ● | ● | ● | ● | ● | ● | | ● | ● | ● |
| GURPAL SINGH AROMA/REFLEX (HM08655) | ● | | | | | | | | | | | | ● | | ● | | | | | | | | | |
| HAGLEY CENTRE OF COMP MED (HM08701) | ● | ● | | | ● | | | | | | | | | | ● | | | | ● | | | | ● | ● |
| HALE ASSOCIATES (HM08727) | | ● | | | ● | | | | | | | | | | | | | | | | | | | ● |
| HALE, GEOFF (HM08732) | | ● | | | ● | | | | | | | | | | | | | | | | | | | ● |
| HALL GREEN ALTERN PRACTICE (HM08760) | ● | ● | ● | ● | ● | ● | ● | ● | ● | ● | ● | ● | ● | ● | ● | ● | ● | ● | ● | ● | | ● | ● | ● |
| HALL, SUSAN (HM08790) | ● | ● | | | ● | ● | | | ● | | ● | ● | ● | ● | ● | | | | ● | | | ● | ● | ● |
| HEALTH SHOP (HM09402) | ● | ● | ● | | ● | | | | | | | | ● | ● | ● | ● | ● | ● | | | | ● | ● | ● |
| HERBAL PHARMACY (HM09632) | ● | ● | ● | ● | ● | ● | ● | | ● | ● | ● | ● | ● | ● | ● | ● | ● | ● | | | | ● | ● | ● |
| HOGG, DEBBI (HM09913) | ● | ● | ● | ● | ● | ● | ● | ● | ● | ● | ● | ● | ● | ● | ● | ● | ● | ● | ● | ● | | ● | ● | ● |
| HOLISTIC HEALTH CENTRE (HM09972) | | | | | ● | | | | | | | | | | | | | | | | | | | |
| HOLLOWAY, P (HM10027) | ● | | | | | | | | ● | | | | | | ● | | | | | | | | | |
| HOLLY COTTAGE CHIRO CLINIC (HM10029) | | ● | | | ● | | | | | | | | ● | | ● | | | | | | | | | ● |
| HOMOEOPATHIC CLINIC/PHARMACY (HM10090) | ● | | ● | | | ● | | ● | ● | ● | | ● | ● | ● | ● | ● | ● | ● | ● | | | ● | | ● |

| Business | Nervous Disorders | Neuralgia | Obesity | Osteoporosis | Pain | Palpitations | Panic Attacks | Parkinson's Disease | Period Problems | Phobias | Piles | PMT | Pneumonia | Postural Problems | Pregnancy Help | Prostate Problems | Psoriasis | Raynaud's Disease | Recurrent Infections | Restless Legs | Rheumatoid Arthritis | Schizophrenia | Sciatica | Sexual Problems |
|---|---|---|---|---|---|---|---|---|---|---|---|---|---|---|---|---|---|---|---|---|---|---|---|---|
| CHIROPRACTORS OF WARWICK ROAD (HM04407) | | | | | ● | | | | | | | | | ● | | | | | | | | | ● | |
| CODSALL COMP THERAPIES (HM04778) | | | ● | | | | | | | | | | | | | | | | | | | | | |
| COMPLEMENTARY HEALING CENTRE (HM04919) | | | | | | | | | | | | | | | | | | | | | | | | |
| COMPLEMENTARY THERAPY CENTRE (HM04943) | | | | | | | | | | | | | | | | | | | | | ● | | | |
| COMPLEMENTARY THERAPY CENTRE (HM04947) | | | | | | | | | | | | | | | | | | | | | ● | | | |
| CREATIVE HEALTH CENTRE (HM05398) | | ● | | | ● | | | | ● | ● | | | | | | | ● | | | | ● | | ● | |
| CROFT, ANGELA (HM05453) | | | | ● | | | | | | | | | | | | | | | | | ● | | ● | |
| CRYSTAL CLEAR PRACTICE (HM05528) | ● | ● | ● | ● | ● | ● | | ● | ● | ● | ● | ● | ● | | ● | ● | ● | ● | ● | ● | ● | ● | ● | ● |
| CTIC (HM05535) | | | | | | | | | | | | | | | | | | | | | | | | |
| CTRE-REFLEX & AROMATHERAPY (HM05549) | | ● | | | | | | | ● | | | | | | | | | | | ● | | | ● | |
| DAVIS A STARKEY REM THERAP (HM05846) | | | | ● | ● | | | | ● | | | | | ● | ● | | | | | | | | ● | |
| DUDLEY PHYSIOTHERAPY CLINIC (HM06354) | | | | | | | | | | | | | | | | | | | | | | | | |
| ERDINGTHON NATURAL HEALTH CLNC (HM06880) | ● | ● | | ● | ● | ● | | ● | ● | ● | ● | ● | ● | | ● | ● | ● | ● | ● | ● | ● | ● | ● | ● |
| ESSENTIAL HEALTH (HM06909) | | | | | | | | | | | | | | | ● | | ● | | | | ● | | | |
| FAIRFAX PRIVATE THERAPY (HM07056) | ● | | | | | | | | | ● | | ● | | | | | | | | | ● | | ● | ● |
| FLETCHER, VICTOR JOHN (HM07416) | | | | | | | | | | | | | | | | | | | | | | | | |
| FORD, MARIA (HM07526) | | | | | ● | | | | ● | | | ● | | | | | | | | | | | | |
| FRESHWINDS CHARITABLE TRUST (HM07740) | ● | ● | ● | ● | ● | ● | | ● | ● | ● | ● | ● | ● | | ● | ● | ● | ● | ● | ● | ● | ● | ● | ● |
| GOLDEN PALMS (HM08207) | | | | | ● | | | | | | | | | | | | ● | | | | | | ● | |
| GREAT BARR OSTEO PRACTICE (HM08430) | | | | | ● | | | | | | | | | | ● | | | | | | | | | |
| GREEN VALLEY THERAPY CENTRE (HM08443) | ● | ● | ● | ● | ● | ● | | ● | ● | ● | ● | ● | ● | | ● | ● | ● | ● | ● | ● | ● | ● | ● | ● |
| GURPAL SINGH AROMA/REFLEX (HM08655) | | | | | | | | | | | | | | | | | | | | | | | | |
| HAGLEY CENTRE OF COMP MED (HM08701) | ● | | | | ● | | | | ● | ● | | ● | | | | | | | | | | | ● | |
| HALE ASSOCIATES (HM08727) | | | | | ● | | | | | | | | | ● | | | | | | | | | ● | |
| HALE, GEOFF (HM08732) | | | | | ● | | | | | | | | | ● | | | | | | | | | ● | |
| HALL GREEN ALTERN PRACTICE (HM08760) | ● | ● | ● | ● | ● | ● | | ● | ● | ● | ● | ● | ● | | ● | ● | ● | ● | ● | ● | ● | ● | ● | ● |
| HALL, SUSAN (HM08790) | ● | ● | | | ● | ● | | | ● | ● | ● | ● | ● | | ● | ● | ● | ● | | ● | ● | | ● | ● |
| HEALTH SHOP (HM09402) | | ● | ● | | ● | | | | ● | | ● | ● | | | | ● | | | | ● | ● | | ● | |
| HERBAL PHARMACY (HM09632) | ● | | ● | ● | ● | | | | ● | | ● | ● | | | ● | ● | ● | ● | ● | ● | ● | | ● | ● |
| HOGG, DEBBI (HM09913) | ● | ● | ● | ● | ● | ● | | ● | ● | ● | ● | ● | | | ● | ● | ● | ● | ● | ● | ● | | ● | ● |
| HOLISTIC HEALTH CENTRE (HM09972) | ● | | | | | | | | | ● | | | | | | | | | ● | | | | | |
| HOLLOWAY, P (HM10027) | | | | | | | | | | ● | | | | | | | | | | | | | | |
| HOLLY COTTAGE CHIRO CLINIC (HM10029) | ● | | | | ● | | | | | | | | | | | | | | | | | | ● | |
| HOMOEOPATHIC CLINIC/PHARMACY (HM10090) | ● | ● | ● | ● | ● | ● | | ● | ● | ● | ● | | ● | | ● | ● | ● | | ● | ● | ● | | ● | ● |

www.healthmyself.com

# I - S Conditions treated at Practices/Businesses

| Business by County with Reference no. | Insomnia | Irritable Bowel Syndrome | Itching | Jet Lag | Joint Pain | Kidney Complaints | Lactose Intolerance | Laryngitis | Lethargy | Liver Disorders | Low Blood Pressure | Lung Problems | ME | Menopause | Migraine | Motion Sickness | Mouth Disorders | Mouth Ulcers | Multiple Sclerosis | Muscular Dystrophy | Musculo-skeletal | Nail Health | Nausea | Nerve Disorders | Nervous Disorders | Neuralgia | Obesity | Osteoporosis | Pain | Palpitations | Panic Attacks | Parkinson's Disease | Period Problems | Phobias | Piles | PMT | Pneumonia | Postural Problems | Pregnancy Help | Prostate Problems | Psoriasis | Raynaud's Disease | Recurrent Infections | Restless Legs | Rheumatoid Arthritis | Schizophrenia | Sciatica | Sexual Problems |
|---|---|---|---|---|---|---|---|---|---|---|---|---|---|---|---|---|---|---|---|---|---|---|---|---|---|---|---|---|---|---|---|---|---|---|---|---|---|---|---|---|---|---|---|---|---|---|---|---|
| HOT-PAK (HM10206) | | | | | | | | | | | | | | | ● | | | | | | | | | | | | | | | | | | | | | | | | | | | | | | | | | |
| HUSBANDS, STEVE (HM10432) | ● | ● | ● | ● | ● | ● | ● | ● | ● | ● | ● | ● | ● | ● | ● | ● | ● | ● | ● | ● | | ● | ● | ● | ● | ● | ● | ● | ● | ● | | ● | ● | ● | ● | ● | ● | | ● | ● | ● | ● | ● | ● | ● | ● | ● | ● |
| INGRAM, CLARE (HM10624) | ● | ● | ● | | ● | ● | ● | ● | ● | ● | | ● | ● | ● | ● | ● | ● | ● | | | | | ● | ● | ● | ● | ● | | ● | ● | | | ● | | | ● | | | | ● | ● | | ● | ● | ● | | ● | ● |
| INNERSENSE (HM10647) | | ● | | | ● | | | | | | | | | | | | | | | | | | | | | | | | | | | | | | | | | | | | | | | | | | | |
| J BENSON CHIROPODIST (HM10793) | | | | | ● | | | | | | | | | | | | | | | | | ● | | | | | | | | | | | | | | | | | | | | | | | ● | | | |
| JOHNSON FOOTCARE (HM11061) | | | | | | | | | | | | | | | | | | | | | | ● | | | | | | | | | | | | | | | | | | | | | | | | | | |
| KEMPSON, STEVE (HM11468) | | | | | | | | | | | | | | | ● | | | | | | | | | | | | | | | | | | | ● | | | | | | | | | | | | | | |
| KEVIN FISHER CHIROPODY (HM11573) | | | | | | | | | | | | | | | | | | | | | | ● | | | | | | | | | | | | | | | | | | | | | | | | | | |
| LEWIS, MYRA (HM12305) | ● | ● | | | | | | | | | | | ● | ● | ● | | | | | | | | | | | | | | ● | | | | | | | ● | | | | | | | | | | | | |
| LIFE'S OPTION (HM12358) | | | | | | | | | | | | | | | ● | | | | | | | | | | | | | | | | | | | | | | | | | | | | | | | | | |
| LONGFORD PHYSIO & SPORTS (HM12627) | | | | | ● | | | | | | | | ● | | | | | | ● | ● | | | | ● | | ● | ● | ● | ● | | | ● | | | | | | | | | | | | | ● | | ● | |
| MCDERMOTT, J V (HM13447) | | | | | ● | | | | | | | | | | | | | | | | | | | | | | | ● | ● | | | | | | | | | ● | | | | | | | | | ● | |
| MIDLAND HYPNOTHERAPY CENTRE (HM13831) | ● | ● | ● | ● | ● | ● | ● | | ● | ● | ● | ● | ● | ● | ● | ● | ● | ● | ● | | | | ● | ● | ● | ● | ● | | ● | ● | | ● | ● | ● | | ● | | | ● | ● | ● | ● | ● | ● | ● | | ● | ● |
| MIDLAND HYPNOTHERAPY CENTRE (HM13830) | ● | ● | ● | ● | ● | ● | ● | | ● | ● | ● | ● | ● | ● | ● | ● | ● | ● | ● | | | | ● | ● | ● | | ● | | ● | ● | | ● | ● | ● | | ● | ● | | ● | ● | ● | ● | ● | ● | ● | | ● | ● |
| MIDLAND MEDICAL HOM PRACTICE (HM13833) | ● | ● | ● | ● | ● | ● | ● | ● | ● | ● | ● | ● | ● | ● | ● | ● | ● | ● | ● | ● | | ● | ● | ● | ● | ● | ● | ● | ● | ● | | ● | ● | ● | ● | ● | ● | | ● | ● | ● | ● | ● | ● | ● | ● | ● | ● |
| MIDLAND MEDICAL HOM PRACTICE (HM13832) | ● | ● | ● | ● | ● | ● | ● | ● | ● | ● | ● | ● | ● | ● | ● | ● | ● | ● | ● | ● | | ● | ● | ● | ● | ● | ● | ● | ● | ● | | ● | ● | ● | ● | ● | ● | | ● | ● | ● | ● | ● | ● | ● | ● | ● | ● |
| MIDLAND MEDICAL HOM PRACTICE (HM13834) | ● | ● | ● | ● | ● | ● | ● | ● | ● | ● | ● | ● | ● | ● | ● | ● | ● | ● | ● | ● | | ● | ● | ● | ● | ● | ● | ● | ● | ● | | ● | ● | ● | ● | ● | ● | | ● | ● | ● | ● | ● | ● | ● | ● | ● | ● |
| MIDLAND MEDICAL OSTEO PRACTICE (HM13835) | | | | | | | | | | | | | | | | | | | | | | | | | | | | | | | | | | | | | | | | | | | | | | | ● | |
| MIDLAND MEDICAL OSTEO PRACTICE (HM13836) | | | | | | | | | | | | | | | | | | | | | | | | | | | | | | | | | | | | | | | | | | | | | | | ● | |
| MIDLAND MEDICAL OSTEO PRACTICE (HM13837) | | | | | | | | | | | | | | | | | | | | | | | | | | | | | | | | | | | | | | | | | | | | | | | ● | |
| MORGAN, VALERIE (HM14177) | ● | ● | ● | ● | ● | ● | | ● | ● | | | ● | ● | ● | ● | ● | | | | | | | ● | | | | | | ● | | | | ● | | ● | ● | | | ● | | ● | | ● | | ● | | ● | |
| MORRIS, CLAIRE (HM14202) | | | | | | | | | | | | | | | | | | | | | | ● | | | | | | | | | | | | | | | | | | | | | | | | | | |
| MYATT, ANITA (HM14432) | ● | ● | ● | ● | ● | ● | ● | ● | ● | ● | ● | ● | ● | ● | ● | ● | ● | ● | ● | ● | | ● | ● | ● | ● | ● | ● | ● | ● | ● | | ● | ● | ● | ● | ● | ● | | ● | ● | ● | ● | ● | ● | ● | ● | ● | ● |
| NATURAL HEALTH CENTRE (HM14574) | ● | | | | ● | | | | | | | | | ● | ● | | | | | | | | ● | | | | | | ● | | | | ● | | | ● | | | | | | | | | | | | |
| NEWBRIDGE PHARMACY (HM14850) | ● | ● | ● | | ● | | | | ● | | | | ● | ● | ● | ● | | ● | | | | | | | ● | ● | | | ● | ● | | | ● | | | ● | | | ● | | | | | ● | ● | | ● | |
| OULTON FOOT CLINIC (HM15499) | | | | | | | | | | | | | | | | | | | | | | | ● | | | | | | | | | | | | | | | | | | | | | | | | | |
| PARK PRACTICE (HM15672) | ● | ● | ● | ● | ● | ● | ● | ● | ● | ● | ● | ● | ● | ● | ● | ● | ● | ● | ● | ● | | ● | ● | ● | ● | ● | ● | ● | ● | ● | | ● | ● | ● | ● | ● | ● | | ● | ● | ● | ● | ● | ● | ● | ● | ● | ● |
| PHYSIOTHERAPY CLINIC (HM16241) | | | | | ● | | | | | | | | | | | | | | | | | | | | | | | | ● | | | | | | | | | | | | | | | | | | | |
| PIKE, ELIZABETH G & J K (HM16286) | | | | | | | | | | | | | | | | | | | | | | ● | | | | | | | | | | | | | | | | | | | | | | | | | | |
| PILLATH, CHRISTINE (HM16297) | | ● | | | ● | | | | | | | | ● | | ● | | | | | | | | | ● | ● | | | | ● | | | | | | | | | ● | | | | | | | | | ● | |
| PLANT, ALISON () | ● | | | ● | | | | | ● | | | | | ● | ● | | | | | | | | | | | | | | ● | | | | ● | | | ● | | | | | | | | | | | ● | |
| PRISM THERAPIES (HM16636) | ● | ● | ● | | ● | | | | | | | | | | ● | | | | | | | ● | | | ● | | | | ● | | ● | | | ● | | | | | | | | | | | | | ● | |
| REMEDIAL MASSAGE THERAPY (HM17174) | | ● | | | ● | | | | | | | | | | ● | | | | ● | | | | | | | ● | | | ● | ● | | | | | | | | | | ● | | | | ● | ● | | ● | |
| ROMSLEY PHYSIOTHERAPY PRACTICE (HM17578) | ● | ● | | | ● | | | | | | | | | | ● | | | | | | | | | | | ● | | ● | ● | | | | | | | | | | | | | | | | ● | | | |

# I - S Conditions treated at Practices/Businesses

| Business by County with Reference no. | Insomnia | Irritable Bowel Syndrome | Itching | Jet Lag | Joint Pain | Kidney Complaints | Lactose Intolerance | Laryngitis | Lethargy | Liver Disorders | Low Blood Pressure | Lung Problems | ME | Menopause | Migraine | Motion Sickness | Mouth Disorders | Mouth Ulcers | Multiple Sclerosis | Muscular Dystrophy | Musculo-skeletal | Nail Health | Nausea | Nerve Disorders |
|---|---|---|---|---|---|---|---|---|---|---|---|---|---|---|---|---|---|---|---|---|---|---|---|---|
| SIDHOM, A (HM18529) | | | | | ● | | | | | | | | | | ● | | | | | | | | | |
| SOLIHULL CHIROPRACTIC CLINIC (HM18872) | | ● | | | ● | | | | | | | | ● | | | | | | | | | | | ● |
| SOMEWAY HERBAL CLINIC (HM18883) | ● | | | | ● | | | | | | | | | ● | ● | | | | | | | | | |
| ST PAULS OSTEOPATHY PRACTICE (HM19094) | | | | | ● | | | | | | | | ● | | ● | | | | | | | | | ● |
| STARKEY, DAVID (HM19147) | ● | ● | | | ● | | | | | | ● | | | ● | ● | | | | ● | | | | | ● |
| STOURBRIDGE ACU & OSTEO CTRE (HM19356) | | | | | ● | | | | | | | | | | | | | | | | | | | |
| SUCCESSWORKS (HM19461) | ● | | | | ● | | | | ● | | | | ● | | | | | | | | | | ● | |
| SUTTON COLDFIELD HEALTH CLINIC (HM19544) | | ● | ● | | ● | | | | | | | ● | ● | ● | ● | | | | ● | | | | | ● |
| TELLING, MELANIE (HM19823) | | | | | ● | ● | | | | | ● | | ● | ● | ● | | | | | | | | ● | ● |
| TELLING, MELANIE (HM19822) | ● | | | | ● | ● | | | | | | | ● | ● | ● | | | | | | | | ● | ● |
| THERAPY TRAINING COLLEGE (HM19911) | ● | ● | | | | | | | | | | | | | ● | | | | | | | | | |
| WALSALL PHYSIOTHERAPY CLINIC (HM20853) | | | | | ● | | | | | | | | | | | | | | ● | | | | | |
| WALSGRAVE CHIROPRACTIC CLINIC (HM20855) | | ● | | | ● | | | | | | | | | | | | | | | | | | | ● |
| WARD, JAQUELINE (HM20906) | ● | ● | | | | | | | | | | | | | | | | | | | | | | |
| WELL NATURAL HEALTH CENTRE (HM21139) | ● | ● | ● | ● | ● | ● | ● | ● | ● | ● | ● | ● | ● | ● | ● | ● | ● | ● | ● | ● | | ● | ● | ● |
| WELL NATURAL HEALTH CENTRE (HM21140) | ● | ● | ● | ● | ● | ● | ● | ● | ● | ● | ● | ● | ● | ● | ● | ● | ● | ● | ● | ● | | ● | ● | ● |
| WEST MIDLAND HYPNOTHERAPY (HM21229) | | | | | | | | | | | | | | | ● | ● | | | | | | | | |
| WESTON, JOHN (HM21278) | | | | | ● | | | | | | | | | | | | | | | | | | | |
| WESTWOOD, ANGELA (HM21285) | ● | | | | ● | ● | | | | | | | ● | | | | | | | | | | ● | |
| WHITE, SHELLEY (HM21378) | | ● | | | | | | | | | ● | | ● | ● | ● | | | | | | | | ● | |
| WHITEHALL, CAROL (HM21385) | | | | | | | | | | | | | | | | | | | | | | ● | | |
| WILLOWS CLNC COMP HEALTH CTRE (HM21630) | ● | ● | ● | | ● | ● | ● | ● | ● | ● | ● | ● | ● | ● | ● | ● | | ● | ● | | ● | | ● | ● |
| WITHYMOOR PHYSIOTHERAPY CLINIC (HM21749) | | | | | ● | | | | | | | | | | | | | | | | | | | |
| WOLVERHAMPTON CHINESE MED CTRE (HM21765) | ● | ● | ● | | ● | ● | | | ● | ● | | ● | ● | ● | ● | | | ● | ● | ● | | | ● | ● |
| ZEN HEALTH & BEAUTY (HM22099) | | | | | | | | | | | | | | | ● | | | | | | | | | |
| **NORFOLK** | | | | | | | | | | | | | | | | | | | | | | | | |
| ALTERNATIVE HEALTH CARE (HM00702) | | ● | | | ● | ● | | | | | ● | | ● | | ● | | | | ● | | | | ● | |
| AMALA CHIROPODY CENTRE (HM00760) | | | | | | | | | | | | | | | | | | | | | | | | |
| BODY BEAUTIFUL (HM02576) | ● | ● | | | | | | | | | ● | | ● | ● | ● | | | | | | | | ● | ● |
| BRUNSWICK PHYSIO (HM03280) | | | | | ● | | | | | | | | | | | | | | ● | | ● | | | |
| CHANDLER, ANN (HM03973) | | | | | ● | | | | | | | | | | | | | | ● | | | | | |
| CHASE PARK PRACTICE (HM04060) | | | | | | | | | ● | | | | | | | | | | | | | | | |
| CLASSICAL OSTEOPATH (HM04611) | ● | ● | | | ● | ● | | ● | ● | ● | ● | ● | ● | | ● | | | | | | | | | ● |
| COMER OSTEOPATHIC CLINIC (HM04897) | | ● | | | ● | | | | ● | | | | ● | | ● | | | | | | | | | |

| Business by County with Reference no. | Nervous Disorders | Neuralgia | Obesity | Osteoporosis | Pain | Palpitations | Panic Attacks | Parkinson's Disease | Period Problems | Phobias | Piles | PMT | Pneumonia | Postural Problems | Pregnancy Help | Prostate Problems | Psoriasis | Raynaud's Disease | Recurrent Infections | Restless Legs | Rheumatoid Arthritis | Schizophrenia | Sciatica | Sexual Problems |
|---|---|---|---|---|---|---|---|---|---|---|---|---|---|---|---|---|---|---|---|---|---|---|---|---|
| SIDHOM, A (HM18529) | | | | | ● | | | | | | | | | | | | | | | | | | ● | |
| SOLIHULL CHIROPRACTIC CLINIC (HM18872) | ● | | | | ● | | | | | | | | | | | | | | | | | | ● | |
| SOMEWAY HERBAL CLINIC (HM18883) | | | | | ● | | | | ● | | | | | | | | | | | | | | | |
| ST PAULS OSTEOPATHY PRACTICE (HM19094) | | ● | | ● | ● | ● | | | ● | | | ● | | | ● | | | ● | | ● | ● | | ● | |
| STARKEY, DAVID (HM19147) | | | | ● | ● | | | | ● | | | | | ● | ● | | | | | | | | ● | |
| STOURBRIDGE ACU & OSTEO CTRE (HM19356) | | | | | ● | | | | | | | | | | | | | | | | | | ● | |
| SUCCESSWORKS (HM19461) | ● | | | | | | | | | ● | | ● | | | | | | | | | | | | |
| SUTTON COLDFIELD HEALTH CLINIC (HM19544) | ● | ● | | ● | ● | | | | ● | | | ● | | | | | ● | | | | ● | | ● | |
| TELLING, MELANIE (HM19823) | | | | | ● | | | | ● | | | ● | | | ● | | | | | ● | ● | | | |
| TELLING, MELANIE (HM19822) | | | | | ● | | | | | | | ● | | | ● | | | | | ● | ● | | | |
| THERAPY TRAINING COLLEGE (HM19911) | | ● | ● | | ● | | | | ● | ● | | ● | | | ● | | | | | | | | | ● |
| WALSALL PHYSIOTHERAPY CLINIC (HM20853) | | | | | ● | | | | | | | | | | | | | | | | | | | |
| WALSGRAVE CHIROPRACTIC CLINIC (HM20855) | | | | | ● | | | | | | | | | | | | | | | | | | ● | |
| WARD, JAQUELINE (HM20906) | | | ● | | ● | ● | | | | ● | | | | | | | | | | | | | | |
| WELL NATURAL HEALTH CENTRE (HM21139) | ● | ● | ● | ● | ● | ● | | ● | ● | ● | ● | ● | ● | ● | ● | ● | ● | ● | ● | ● | ● | | ● | ● |
| WELL NATURAL HEALTH CENTRE (HM21140) | ● | ● | ● | ● | ● | ● | | ● | ● | ● | ● | ● | ● | | ● | ● | ● | ● | ● | ● | ● | ● | ● | ● |
| WEST MIDLAND HYPNOTHERAPY (HM21229) | ● | | | | | | | | | | | | | | | | | | | | | | | |
| WESTON, JOHN (HM21278) | | | | ● | ● | | | | | | | | | | | | | | | | ● | | ● | |
| WESTWOOD, ANGELA (HM21285) | | | | | | | | | ● | | | | | | | ● | | | | | | | | |
| WHITE, SHELLEY (HM21378) | | | | | | | | | ● | | | ● | | | ● | | | | | | | | | |
| WHITEHALL, CAROL (HM21385) | | | | | | | | | | | | | | | | | | | | | | | | |
| WILLOWS CLNC COMP HEALTH CTRE (HM21630) | ● | ● | ● | ● | ● | ● | ● | ● | ● | ● | ● | ● | | | ● | ● | ● | ● | ● | ● | ● | | ● | ● |
| WITHYMOOR PHYSIOTHERAPY CLINIC (HM21749) | | | | | | | | | | | | | | | | | | | | | | | | |
| WOLVERHAMPTON CHINESE MED CTRE (HM21765) | | | ● | | ● | ● | | | ● | | | ● | | | | ● | ● | | ● | | ● | | | ● |
| ZEN HEALTH & BEAUTY (HM22099) | | | | | | | | | | | | | | | | | | | | | | | | |
| **NORFOLK** | | | | | | | | | | | | | | | | | | | | | | | | |
| ALTERNATIVE HEALTH CARE (HM00702) | | | | ● | ● | ● | | | | ● | | ● | | | ● | | | | | | | | | |
| AMALA CHIROPODY CENTRE (HM00760) | | | | | | | | | | | | | | | | | | ● | | | | | | |
| BODY BEAUTIFUL (HM02576) | ● | | ● | | ● | | | ● | ● | | | | | | | | | | | | | | | |
| BRUNSWICK PHYSIO (HM03280) | | | | | | | | | | | | | | | | | | | | | | | | |
| CHANDLER, ANN (HM03973) | | | | | | | | | | | | | | | | | | | | | | | | |
| CHASE PARK PRACTICE (HM04060) | ● | | | | | | | | | ● | | | | | | | | | | | | | | ● |
| CLASSICAL OSTEOPATH (HM04611) | ● | ● | | ● | ● | ● | | | ● | | ● | ● | | | | | | ● | ● | ● | | | ● | |
| COMER OSTEOPATHIC CLINIC (HM04897) | | ● | | ● | ● | | | | | | | ● | | | ● | ● | ● | ● | ● | ● | ● | | ● | |

# I - S Conditions treated at Practices/Businesses

| Business by County with Reference no. | Insomnia | Irritable Bowel Syndrome | Itching | Jet Lag | Joint Pain | Kidney Complaints | Lactose Intolerance | Laryngitis | Lethargy | Liver Disorders | Low Blood Pressure | Lung Problems | ME | Menopause | Migraine | Motion Sickness | Mouth Disorders | Mouth Ulcers | Multiple Sclerosis | Muscular Dystrophy | Musculo-skeletal | Nail Health | Nausea | Nerve Disorders | Nervous Disorders | Neuralgia | Obesity | Osteoporosis | Pain | Palpitations | Panic Attacks | Parkinson's Disease | Period Problems | Phobias | Piles | PMT | Pneumonia | Postural Problems | Pregnancy Help | Prostate Problems | Psoriasis | Raynaud's Disease | Recurrent Infections | Restless Legs | Rheumatoid Arthritis | Schizophrenia | Sciatica | Sexual Problems |
|---|---|---|---|---|---|---|---|---|---|---|---|---|---|---|---|---|---|---|---|---|---|---|---|---|---|---|---|---|---|---|---|---|---|---|---|---|---|---|---|---|---|---|---|---|---|---|---|---|
| COMPLEMENTARY HEALTH CLINIC (HM04926) | | ● | | | ● | | | | | | | | ● | ● | ● | | | | ● | | | | | ● | | ● | | | ● | | | | ● | | | | | | | ● | | | | ● | ● | | ● | |
| COTTAGE CHIROPRACTIC CLINIC (HM05217) | | ● | | | ● | | | | | | | | ● | | | | | | | | | | | ● | ● | | | | ● | | | | | | | | | | | | | | | | | | ● | |
| COTTAGE CLINIC (HM05220) | ● | ● | ● | | | ● | | ● | ● | ● | ● | ● | | ● | ● | | ● | ● | ● | | | | ● | ● | ● | ● | ● | ● | ● | | | ● | ● | | ● | ● | | | ● | ● | ● | | ● | | ● | | ● | ● |
| COTTAGE NTRL HEALTH CLINIC (HM05222) | | | | | | | | | | | | | | | ● | | | | | | | | | | | | | | ● | | | | | | | | | | | | | | | | | | | |
| COUNTY HEALTH (HM05259) | ● | ● | ● | ● | ● | ● | | | ● | ● | | ● | ● | ● | ● | ● | | ● | | | | | ● | ● | ● | ● | | | | ● | | | ● | ● | ● | ● | ● | | ● | ● | ● | | ● | ● | ● | | | |
| DISS NATURAL HEALTH CLINIC (HM06121) | ● | ● | ● | | ● | | | | ● | ● | | ● | ● | | ● | ● | | | | | | | | | | | | | ● | ● | | | ● | | | ● | | | | | | | ● | ● | ● | | ● | |
| ELEMENTS OF HEALTH (HM06725) | ● | ● | ● | ● | ● | ● | ● | ● | ● | ● | ● | ● | ● | ● | ● | ● | ● | ● | | | | ● | ● | ● | ● | | ● | ● | ● | ● | | ● | ● | ● | ● | ● | | | ● | ● | ● | ● | ● | ● | ● | | ● | ● |
| ELLIS, STEPHEN (HM06772) | | ● | | | | | | | | | | | | | ● | | | | | | | | | ● | | | | | ● | | | | | | | ● | | | | | | | | | | | | |
| FISHER, JACK E (HM07355) | | | | | ● | | | | | | | | | | ● | | | | | | | | | | | | | | ● | | | | | | | | | | | | | | | | ● | | ● | |
| FORD OSTEOPATHIC CLINIC (HM07521) | | | | | ● | | | | | | | | | | | | | | | | | | | ● | ● | ● | | | ● | | | | | | | | | | ● | | | | | | | | ● | |
| GT YARMOUTH PHYSICAL THERAPY (HM08330) | | | | | ● | | | | | | | | | | | | | | | | | | | | | | | | ● | | | | | | | | | | | | | | | | | | ● | |
| HARGHAM HALL OSTEO PRACTICE (HM08992) | | | | | ● | | | | | | | | ● | | ● | | | | | | | | | ● | | ● | | | ● | | | | | | | | | | | | | ● | | | | | ● | |
| HOBSON, L A (HM09865) | | | | | | | | | | | | | | | | | | | | | | ● | | | | | | | | | | | | | | | | | | | | | | | | | | |
| HOMEOPATHIC CLINIC (HM10074) | ● | ● | ● | ● | ● | ● | ● | ● | ● | ● | ● | ● | ● | ● | ● | ● | ● | ● | ● | ● | | ● | ● | ● | ● | ● | ● | ● | ● | ● | | ● | ● | ● | ● | ● | ● | | ● | ● | ● | ● | ● | ● | ● | ● | ● | ● |
| JAMES, LINDA (HM10890) | ● | ● | | | | | | | | | | | ● | ● | ● | | | | | | | | | | | | | | ● | | | | | | | ● | | | | | | | | | | | | |
| JESSOP CLINIC (HM11021) | ● | | | | ● | | | | ● | | | | | ● | ● | | | | | | | | | | | ● | | | ● | | | | ● | | | ● | | | | | | ● | | ● | ● | | ● | |
| KING, SIMON (HM11644) | ● | ● | ● | ● | ● | ● | | ● | ● | ● | ● | ● | ● | ● | ● | ● | ● | ● | | | | | ● | ● | ● | ● | | | ● | ● | | | ● | ● | ● | ● | ● | | ● | ● | | ● | ● | ● | | | | ● |
| MONSON, J L B (HM14076) | | | | | | | | | | | | | | | | | | | | | | | | | | | | | | | | | | ● | | | | | | | | | | | | | | |
| NEW MARKET RD PHYSIO PRACTICE (HM14824) | | | | | ● | | | | | | | | | | | | | | ● | | | | | | | | | | | | | | | | | | | | | | | | | | | | | |
| NORFOLK CLINIC (HM14993) | ● | ● | ● | | | ● | ● | | | ● | ● | ● | ● | ● | ● | ● | ● | ● | | | | | ● | | | ● | | | ● | ● | | | ● | ● | ● | ● | ● | | | | ● | | ● | | | | ● | |
| NORFOLK NATURAL HEALTH SERVICE (HM14995) | | ● | | | ● | | ● | | ● | | ● | | ● | ● | ● | | | | | | | | | ● | ● | | | ● | ● | ● | | | ● | | | ● | | | | | | ● | | | | | ● | |
| NORMAN, A J (HM14999) | | ● | | | ● | | | | | | | | ● | | | | | | | | | | | ● | | | | | ● | | | | | | | | | | | | | | | | | | ● | |
| OLIVE GROVE BODY SCIENCE (HM15281) | | | | | | | | | | | | | | | | | | | | | | ● | | | | | | | | | | | | | | | | | | | ● | | | | | | | |
| PARK PHYSIOTHERAPY (HM15669) | | | | | ● | | | | | | | | | | ● | | | | | | | | | | | ● | | | ● | | | | | | | | | | | | | | | | | | ● | |
| QUEENS SQUARE SURGERY (HM16796) | ● | ● | ● | ● | ● | ● | ● | ● | ● | ● | ● | ● | ● | ● | ● | ● | ● | ● | ● | ● | | ● | ● | ● | ● | ● | ● | ● | ● | ● | | ● | ● | ● | ● | ● | ● | | ● | ● | ● | ● | ● | ● | ● | ● | ● | ● |
| RICHARDSON, ALAN (HM17268) | ● | ● | | | | | | | | | | | ● | | | | | | | | | | | | | | | | | | | | | ● | | | | | | | ● | | | | | | | |
| RIGBY COURT CLINIC (HM17331) | ● | ● | ● | | ● | | ● | ● | ● | ● | ● | ● | ● | ● | ● | ● | ● | ● | ● | | | | ● | ● | ● | ● | | ● | ● | ● | | ● | ● | ● | ● | ● | ● | | ● | ● | ● | ● | ● | ● | ● | | ● | ● |
| SHARP, DENISE (HM18307) | | ● | ● | | ● | ● | | | | | | | ● | ● | ● | | | | | | | | ● | | | | | | ● | ● | | | ● | | | ● | | | ● | | | | | ● | | | ● | |
| SHIATSU CENTRE (HM18453) | | | | | | | | | | | | | | | ● | | | | | | | | | | | | | | | | | | ● | | | | | | | | | | | | | | | |
| ST STEPHENS PRACTICE (HM19099) | | | | | ● | | | | ● | | | | | | ● | | | | | | | ● | | | | | | | ● | ● | | | | | | | | | | | | | | | | | ● | |
| WATTON PHYSIOTHERAPY CLINIC (HM21033) | | | | | ● | | | | | | | | | | | | | | ● | | | | | | | | | | | | | | | | | | | | | | | | | | | | | |
| WENDY JILLEY - MEDICAL HERB (HM21197) | ● | ● | ● | | ● | | | ● | ● | ● | ● | ● | ● | ● | ● | | ● | ● | ● | | | | ● | ● | ● | ● | | ● | | ● | | | ● | | | ● | | | ● | ● | ● | ● | ● | | ● | | | |
| WOBURN CLINIC (HM21755) | | ● | | | ● | | | | | | ● | | | ● | ● | | | | | | | | | | ● | | | | ● | ● | | | ● | ● | | ● | | | ● | | | | | | ● | | ● | ● |

# I - S Conditions treated at Practices/Businesses

| Business by County with Reference no. | Insomnia | Irritable Bowel Syndrome | Itching | Jet Lag | Joint Pain | Kidney Complaints | Lactose Intolerance | Laryngitis | Lethargy | Liver Disorders | Low Blood Pressure | Lung Problems | ME | Menopause | Migraine | Motion Sickness | Mouth Disorders | Mouth Ulcers | Multiple Sclerosis | Muscular Dystrophy | Musculo-skeletal | Nail Health | Nausea | Nerve Disorders | Nervous Disorders | Neuralgia | Obesity | Osteoporosis | Pain | Palpitations | Panic Attacks | Parkinson's Disease | Period Problems | Phobias | Piles | PMT | Pneumonia | Postural Problems | Pregnancy Help | Prostate Problems | Psoriasis | Raynaud's Disease | Recurrent Infections | Restless Legs | Rheumatoid Arthritis | Schizophrenia | Sciatica | Sexual Problems |
|---|---|---|---|---|---|---|---|---|---|---|---|---|---|---|---|---|---|---|---|---|---|---|---|---|---|---|---|---|---|---|---|---|---|---|---|---|---|---|---|---|---|---|---|---|---|---|---|---|
| **NORTHAMPTONSHIRE** | | | | | | | | | | | | | | | | | | | | | | | | | | | | | | | | | | | | | | | | | | | | | | | | |
| ACUPUNCTURE CLINIC (HM00275) | ● | | | | ● | | | | | | | | | ● | ● | | | | | | | | | | | | | | ● | | | | ● | | | ● | | | ● | | ● | | | | | | | |
| ALLEN HINDE - PHYSIOTHERAPIST (HM00598) | | | | | ● | | | | | | | ● | | | | | | | | | | | | ● | | ● | | | ● | | | | | | | | | | | | | | | | ● | | ● | |
| ANDREWS, S C (HM00857) | ● | ● | ● | | ● | ● | | ● | ● | ● | ● | ● | ● | ● | ● | ● | ● | ● | ● | ● | ● | ● | ● | ● | ● | ● | | ● | ● | ● | ● | ● | ● | ● | ● | ● | ● | ● | ● | ● | ● | ● | ● | ● | ● | ● | ● | ● |
| ANDREWS, SIMON C (HM00860) | ● | ● | ● | | ● | ● | | ● | ● | ● | ● | ● | ● | ● | ● | ● | ● | ● | ● | ● | | ● | ● | ● | ● | ● | | ● | ● | ● | | ● | ● | ● | ● | ● | ● | | ● | ● | ● | ● | ● | ● | ● | ● | ● | ● |
| ANNELISE (HM00906) | ● | ● | | | ● | | | | | | ● | | | | ● | | | | | | | | | | ● | | | | | | | | | | | ● | | | | | ● | | | | | | | |
| C F C M (HM03523) | ● | ● | ● | ● | ● | ● | | ● | ● | ● | | ● | ● | ● | ● | ● | ● | ● | | | | | ● | ● | ● | ● | | ● | ● | ● | | ● | ● | | ● | ● | | | | ● | ● | ● | ● | ● | ● | | ● | |
| CALLIS THERAPY FOUNDATION (HM03555) | ● | ● | ● | ● | ● | ● | ● | ● | ● | ● | ● | ● | ● | ● | ● | ● | ● | ● | ● | ● | | ● | ● | ● | ● | ● | ● | ● | ● | ● | | ● | ● | ● | ● | ● | ● | | ● | ● | ● | ● | ● | ● | ● | ● | ● | ● |
| DAVENTRY NATUREWORKS (HM05768) | | | | | ● | | | | | | | | | ● | ● | | | | | | | | ● | | | | | | ● | | | | ● | | | ● | | | | | | | | | | | ● | |
| DEVON PARADE CLINIC (HM06041) | ● | ● | ● | | ● | ● | | | | | | | ● | ● | ● | | | | ● | ● | | ● | ● | ● | ● | ● | ● | ● | ● | | | | ● | | | ● | | | ● | | ● | | | ● | ● | | ● | |
| ESSERY, TRICIA (HM06933) | | ● | | | ● | ● | | ● | | | ● | | ● | ● | ● | | | | ● | | | | ● | | | | | | ● | ● | | | ● | | | ● | | | ● | | | | | ● | ● | | ● | |
| GARVEY-WILLIAMS, RICHARD (HM07915) | ● | ● | | ● | ● | | | | ● | | | | ● | ● | ● | ● | | | | | | | | | | | | ● | ● | | | | ● | | | | | | | ● | | ● | | | ● | | ● | |
| GARVEY-WILLIAMS, RICHARD (HM07914) | | | | | ● | | | | ● | | | | ● | | ● | | | | | | | | | | | | | | ● | | | | | | | | | | | | | | | | ● | | ● | |
| GEDDES, PIPPA (HM07955) | ● | ● | ● | | ● | | | ● | ● | | ● | ● | ● | ● | ● | | ● | | | | | | | ● | ● | | | | ● | | | | ● | | | ● | | | | | | | ● | ● | ● | | ● | ● |
| JUST RELAX (HM11285) | ● | ● | ● | | ● | ● | | ● | ● | ● | ● | ● | ● | ● | ● | ● | ● | ● | ● | ● | | | ● | | | ● | | | ● | ● | | | ● | | | ● | | | ● | ● | | ● | ● | ● | ● | | ● | |
| LEE, STEPHEN (HM12146) | ● | ● | | | | | | | | | | | | ● | ● | | | ● | ● | | | | ● | | | | | | | ● | | | ● | | | ● | | | | | ● | | | | | | ● | |
| MAPLE TREE OSTEO PRACTICE (HM13061) | ● | ● | | | ● | | | ● | | | | | ● | ● | ● | ● | | | | | | | | | | ● | | | ● | | | | ● | ● | | | | | ● | | | | ● | | | | ● | |
| MOTLEY, MAUREEN (HM14277) | ● | ● | | | | | | | | | | | ● | ● | ● | | | | ● | | | | | | | | | | ● | | | | | | | ● | | | | | | | | | | | | |
| NENE VALLEY COMP THERAPIES (HM14785) | ● | ● | | | ● | | | ● | | | ● | | ● | ● | ● | | | | | | | | ● | | | | | | ● | | | | ● | | | ● | | | ● | | | | | | | | ● | |
| NORTHAMPTON CHIROPRACTIC (HM15051) | | ● | | | ● | | | | | | | | | | | | | | | | | | | | | | | | ● | | | | | | | | | | | | | | | | | | ● | |
| NORTHAMPTON CLINIC (HM15052) | ● | ● | | | | | | | | | | | ● | ● | ● | | | | | | | | | | | | | | | | | | | | | | | | | | | | | | | | | |
| REFLEXOLOGY CLINIC (HM17085) | ● | ● | ● | ● | ● | ● | ● | ● | ● | ● | ● | ● | ● | ● | ● | ● | | | ● | | | | ● | ● | ● | ● | | | ● | ● | | | ● | ● | ● | ● | ● | | ● | ● | ● | ● | ● | ● | | | ● | ● |
| TOWCESTER CHIROPRACTIC CLINIC (HM20194) | | | | | ● | | | | | | | | ● | | | | | | | | | | | | | ● | | ● | ● | | | | | | | | | | ● | | | | | | | | ● | |
| **NORTHUMBERLAND** | | | | | | | | | | | | | | | | | | | | | | | | | | | | | | | | | | | | | | | | | | | | | | | | |
| ACUCARE (HM00209) | | | | | ● | | | | | | | | | ● | ● | | | | | | | | | | | | | | ● | | | | ● | | | ● | | | | | | | | | | | | |
| AYRES, ELIZABETH (HM01433) | | | | | | | | | | | | | | | | | | | | | | ● | | | | | | | | | | | | | | | | | | | | | | | | | | |
| BOWEN TECHNIQUE STUDIO (HM02775) | | | | | ● | | | | | | | | | | | | | | | | | | | | | | | | ● | | | | | | | | | | | | | | | | | | | |
| EVISON, ALEX (HM07012) | ● | ● | | | | | | | ● | | | | ● | | ● | | | | | | | | | | ● | | ● | | | | | | | ● | | | | | | | | | | | | | | ● |
| FORSTER, LINDA (HM07570) | | ● | | | | | | | | | | | | | | | | | | | | | | | | | | | | | | | | | | | | | | | | | | | | | | |
| GREEN BATT PHYSIOTHERAPY (HM08434) | | | | | ● | | | | | | | | ● | | | | | | | | | | | ● | | ● | | | ● | | | | | | | | | | | | | | | | | | ● | |
| KI CLINIC (HM11591) | ● | ● | ● | ● | ● | ● | ● | ● | ● | ● | ● | ● | ● | ● | ● | ● | ● | | ● | ● | | ● | ● | ● | ● | | | | ● | | | | ● | ● | ● | ● | ● | | ● | ● | ● | | ● | ● | ● | | ● | |
| PHYSIOTHERAPY & SPORTS CLINIC (HM16223) | | | | | ● | | | | | | | | | | | | | | ● | | | | | | | | | | ● | | | | | | | | | | | | | | | | | | | |
| **NOTTINGHAMSHIRE** | | | | | | | | | | | | | | | | | | | | | | | | | | | | | | | | | | | | | | | | | | | | | | | | |
| ACUPUNCTURE CLINIC (HM00264) | | | | | ● | | | | | | | | | ● | ● | | | | | | | | | | | | | | ● | | | ● | ● | | | ● | | | | | ● | | | | | | | |

www.healthmyself.com

Healthmyself Directory

# I - S Conditions treated at Practices/Businesses

| Business by County with Reference no. | Insomnia | Irritable Bowel Syndrome | Itching | Jet Lag | Joint Pain | Kidney Complaints | Lactose Intolerance | Laryngitis | Lethargy | Liver Disorders | Low Blood Pressure | Lung Problems | ME | Menopause | Migraine | Motion Sickness | Mouth Disorders | Mouth Ulcers | Multiple Sclerosis | Muscular Dystrophy | Musculo-skeletal | Nail Health | Nausea | Nerve Disorders | Nervous Disorders | Neuralgia | Obesity | Osteoporosis | Pain | Palpitations | Panic Attacks | Parkinson's Disease | Period Problems | Phobias | Piles | PMT | Pneumonia | Postural Problems | Pregnancy Help | Prostate Problems | Psoriasis | Raynaud's Disease | Recurrent Infections | Restless Legs | Rheumatoid Arthritis | Schizophrenia | Sciatica | Sexual Problems |
|---|---|---|---|---|---|---|---|---|---|---|---|---|---|---|---|---|---|---|---|---|---|---|---|---|---|---|---|---|---|---|---|---|---|---|---|---|---|---|---|---|---|---|---|---|---|---|---|---|
| BEESTON PHYSIO & SPORTS CLNC (HM02060) | | | | | ● | | | | | | | | | | | | | | ● | | | | | | | | | | ● | | | | | | | | | | | | | | | | | | | |
| BOND, DIANORA (HM02669) | | | | | ● | | | | | | | | | | | | | | ● | ● | ● | | | ● | | ● | | ● | ● | | | ● | | | | | ● | ● | | | ● | | | | ● | | ● | |
| BULLEN-SPICER ASSOCIATES (HM03342) | ● | ● | | | | | | | ● | | | | ● | | | | | | | | | | | | ● | | ● | | | | | | | ● | | | | | | | | | | ● | | ● | | ● |
| CARITAS NATURAL HEALTH CLINIC (HM03688) | | ● | | | ● | | | | | | | | | | | | | | | | | | | | ● | | | | | | | | ● | | | | | | | | | | | | ● | | ● | |
| CENTRE FOR TRANSFORMATION (HM03921) | ● | ● | ● | ● | ● | ● | ● | | ● | ● | | | ● | ● | ● | ● | | | ● | | | ● | ● | | | ● | ● | | | ● | | | ● | ● | ● | ● | | | ● | ● | ● | | ● | ● | ● | | | ● |
| DEAN, MARTIN (HM05942) | ● | ● | | | ● | ● | | | ● | ● | ● | ● | ● | ● | ● | | | | | | | | | | | ● | | | ● | ● | | | ● | ● | ● | ● | | | ● | | ● | | ● | | | | ● | |
| EAST BRIDGEFORD PHYSIO NEEDS (HM06510) | | | | | ● | | | | | | | | | | | | | | ● | | | | | | | | | | ● | | | | | | | | | | | | | | | | | | | |
| GOTHAM VILLAGE PHSYO CLINIC (HM08308) | | | | | ● | | | | | | | | | | | | | | ● | | | | | | | | | | ● | | | | | | | | | | | | | | | | | | | |
| GREENWOOD, JULIA (HM08507) | | | | | | | | | | | | | | | | | | | | | | ● | | | | | | | | | | | | | | | | | | | | | | | | | | |
| HANDS ON HEALTH (HM08912) | | ● | | | ● | | | | | | | | | | | | | | | | | | | | ● | | | | | | | | ● | | | | | | | | | | | | ● | | ● | |
| IMPACT PHYSIO & SPORTS INJURIES (HM10590) | | | | | ● | | | | | | | | | | | | | | ● | | | | | | | | | | | | | | | | | | | | | | | | | | | | | |
| LIGHT UP YOUR LIFE (HM12370) | ● | ● | | | ● | ● | ● | | | ● | ● | | ● | ● | ● | | | | | | | | | | ● | | | ● | ● | | | | ● | ● | ● | | | | | | | | | | ● | | ● | |
| MORLEY-KIRK, JOHN (HM14188) | ● | ● | | | | ● | | | ● | ● | ● | ● | ● | ● | ● | | | | ● | | | | | | | ● | | ● | ● | ● | | | | | | ● | | | ● | ● | ● | ● | | ● | ● | | ● | |
| NATURAL HEALTH (HM14554) | ● | ● | ● | ● | ● | ● | | ● | ● | ● | ● | ● | ● | ● | ● | ● | ● | ● | ● | | | ● | ● | ● | ● | ● | ● | ● | ● | ● | | | ● | ● | ● | ● | ● | | ● | ● | ● | ● | ● | ● | ● | | ● | ● |
| NATURAL THERAPY CLINIC (HM14654) | ● | ● | ● | ● | ● | ● | ● | ● | ● | ● | ● | ● | ● | ● | ● | ● | ● | ● | ● | | | ● | ● | ● | ● | ● | ● | ● | ● | ● | | ● | ● | ● | ● | ● | ● | | ● | ● | ● | ● | ● | ● | ● | | ● | ● |
| NOTTINGHAM M S THERAPY CTRE (HM15083) | ● | ● | | | ● | ● | | | | | ● | | ● | ● | ● | | | | ● | | | | ● | | | | | | ● | ● | | | ● | | ● | ● | | | ● | | | | | ● | | | ● | |
| NOTTINGHAM NATURAL HEALTH CTRE (HM15084) | ● | ● | ● | ● | ● | ● | ● | ● | ● | ● | ● | ● | ● | ● | ● | ● | ● | ● | ● | ● | | ● | ● | ● | ● | ● | ● | ● | ● | ● | | ● | ● | ● | ● | ● | ● | | ● | ● | ● | ● | ● | ● | ● | ● | ● | ● |
| NOTTINGHAM SPORTS INJURY (HM15085) | | | | | ● | | | | | | | | | | | | | | ● | | | | | | | | | | ● | | | | | | | | | | | | | | | | | | | |
| OPTIMUM HEALTH (HM15348) | ● | ● | ● | ● | ● | ● | ● | ● | ● | ● | ● | ● | ● | ● | ● | ● | ● | ● | ● | ● | | ● | ● | ● | ● | ● | ● | ● | ● | ● | | ● | ● | ● | ● | ● | ● | | ● | ● | ● | ● | ● | ● | ● | ● | ● | ● |
| PARKSIDE STRESS MANAGEMENT (HM15722) | ● | ● | ● | ● | ● | ● | ● | ● | ● | ● | ● | ● | ● | ● | ● | ● | ● | ● | | | | ● | ● | ● | ● | ● | ● | ● | ● | ● | | | ● | ● | ● | ● | | | ● | | ● | | ● | ● | ● | | ● | |
| PHYSIO DIRECT (HM16197) | | | | | ● | | | | | | | | | | | | | | ● | | | | | | | | | | ● | | | | | | | | | | | | | | | | | | | |
| PHYSIODIRECT (HM16214) | | | | | ● | | | | | | | | | | | | | | ● | | | | | | | | | | ● | | | | | | | | | | | | | | | | | | | |
| PLAINS PHYSIO & BACK PAIN (HM16355) | | | | | ● | | | | | | | | | | | | | | ● | | | | | | | | | | ● | | | | | | | | | | | | | | | | | | | |
| RETFORD CHIROPRACTIC CLINIC (HM17200) | | ● | | | ● | | ● | | ● | | ● | | ● | | ● | | | | | | | | | ● | ● | ● | | ● | ● | ● | | | ● | | | ● | | | | | | | ● | | | | ● | |
| SEVENTHMOON NATURAL THRPY CTRE (HM18247) | ● | ● | ● | | ● | | | | ● | | | ● | ● | ● | ● | | | | ● | | | | | | | | | | ● | | ● | | ● | | | | | | ● | | | | | | | | ● | |
| SHEER TECHNIQUE (HM18368) | ● | ● | | ● | ● | ● | | ● | ● | ● | ● | ● | ● | ● | ● | ● | ● | ● | ● | ● | | ● | ● | ● | ● | ● | ● | ● | ● | ● | | | ● | ● | ● | ● | ● | | ● | ● | ● | | ● | ● | ● | | ● | ● |
| SHERWOOD PSYCHO TRAINING INS (HM18441) | ● | ● | | | | | | | | | | | | | | | | | | | | | | | ● | | | | | | | | | | | | | | | | | | | | | | | ● |
| SKELTON, CATHERINE () | ● | ● | ● | ● | ● | ● | ● | | ● | ● | | ● | ● | ● | ● | | | ● | ● | ● | | | ● | | | ● | ● | ● | ● | | | ● | ● | ● | ● | ● | | | ● | ● | ● | ● | ● | ● | ● | | ● | |
| SOUTHWELL ACUPUNCTURE CLINIC (HM18948) | ● | ● | ● | | ● | ● | ● | ● | ● | ● | ● | ● | ● | ● | ● | ● | | | | | | ● | ● | ● | ● | ● | | | ● | ● | | | | ● | | ● | ● | | ● | ● | ● | | | ● | ● | | | ● |
| TODD, S J (HM20108) | | | | | | | | | | | | | | | | | | | | | | | | | | | | ● | | | | | | | | | | | | | | | | | | | | |
| TOMLIN, NORMAN (HM20131) | | | | | ● | | | | | | | | ● | | ● | | | | | | | | | | | | | | ● | | | | | | | | | | | | | | | ● | | | ● | |
| TRADITIONAL ACUPUNCTURIST (HM20222) | ● | ● | ● | | ● | ● | | ● | ● | ● | | ● | ● | ● | ● | ● | | | | | | | ● | ● | ● | ● | | ● | ● | ● | | ● | ● | ● | | ● | | | ● | | | ● | ● | | ● | | ● | ● |
| VAUGHTON, NORMAN D (HM20601) | | | | | | | | | | | | | | | | | | | | | | | | | ● | | | | ● | | | | | ● | | | | | | | ● | | | | | | | |
| WELLBEING CENTRE (HM21149) | | | | | | | | | | | | | | | | | | | | | | | | | | | | | | | | | | ● | | | | | | | | | | | | | | |

# I - S Conditions treated at Practices/Businesses

Business by County with Reference no.

**OXFORDSHIRE**

| Business by County with Reference no. | Insomnia | Irritable Bowel Syndrome | Itching | Jet Lag | Joint Pain | Kidney Complaints | Lactose Intolerance | Laryngitis | Lethargy | Liver Disorders | Low Blood Pressure | Lung Problems | ME | Menopause | Migraine | Motion Sickness |
|---|---|---|---|---|---|---|---|---|---|---|---|---|---|---|---|---|
| ASHCROFT CLINIC (HM01198) | | ● | | | ● | | | | ● | | | | ● | | ● | |
| BACK IN LINE (HM01481) | | ● | | | ● | | | | | | | | ● | | ● | |
| BACK TO NORMAL CHIRO CLINIC (HM01522) | | | | | ● | | | | | | | | | | ● | |
| BLISS REMEDIES (HM02508) | ● | ● | | | ● | ● | | | | | ● | | ● | | ● | |
| COOPER, STEPHEN (HM05128) | | | | | | | | | | | | | | | | |
| COTTAGE CLINIC (HM05221) | ● | | | | | | | | | | | | ● | ● | ● | |
| EDULJEE, STELLA (HM06638) | ● | ● | | | ● | ● | | | | | | | ● | ● | ● | |
| FEET FIRST (HM07179) | ● | ● | | ● | ● | ● | | | | | | | | | | |
| FYSON, MELANIE (HM07806) | ● | ● | ● | | ● | | | ● | ● | | ● | | | ● | ● | ● |
| HANDS ON THERAPY (HM08915) | | | | | ● | | | | | | | | | | | |
| HELIX HOUSE (HM09522) | | | | | ● | | | | ● | | | | | | | |
| HUDSON, EMMA (HM10311) | | | | | ● | | | | | | | | | | ● | |
| HYPNOTHERAPY CENTRE (HM10516) | ● | | | | | | | | | | | | | | ● | |
| KIDLINGTON CHIROPRACTIC (HM11594) | | | | | ● | | | | | | | | ● | | | |
| KIDLINGTON HERBAL PRACTICE (HM11595) | ● | ● | ● | | ● | ● | | ● | ● | ● | ● | ● | ● | ● | ● | ● |
| KIDLINGTON OSTEO PRACTICE (HM11596) | | | | | ● | | | | | | | | | | | |
| MARRIOTT, HUGH (HM13138) | | | | | ● | | | | | | | | | | | |
| MIDSUMMER COTTAGE CLINIC (HM13845) | ● | ● | ● | | ● | | | ● | ● | ● | ● | ● | ● | ● | ● | ● |
| O'BRIEN, FRANCES (HM15179) | ● | | ● | | ● | | | | | | | | | ● | ● | |
| O'DONNELL, ELSPETH (HM15225) | | | | | | | | | | | | | | | | |
| OXFORD NUTRITION & ALLRGY CTRE (HM15541) | ● | ● | ● | ● | ● | | ● | ● | ● | ● | ● | | ● | ● | ● | |
| OXFORD TRANSCENDTL MEDITA CTRE (HM15544) | ● | ● | | | | | | | ● | | ● | | ● | | ● | |
| PARSONS STREET CLINIC (HM15747) | | ● | | | ● | | | | | ● | | | | | ● | |
| PLESTED, JOHN (HM16368) | | | | | ● | | | | | | | | | | | |
| POLLOCK, SUSAN (HM16418) | ● | | | | ● | | | | | | | | | | ● | |
| SIDEBOTTOM, MARGARET (HM18527) | | | | | ● | | | | | | | | | | | |
| SUMMERTON CLINIC (HM19498) | ● | ● | ● | ● | ● | ● | ● | ● | ● | ● | ● | ● | ● | ● | ● | ● |
| TOUCH OF NATURE (HM20188) | | ● | | | ● | | | | | | | | ● | | | |
| TWINE, I E (HM20453) | ● | ● | | ● | ● | | ● | | ● | | | | ● | ● | ● | ● |
| WANTAGE NATURAL HEALTH CENTRE (HM20891) | ● | ● | ● | ● | ● | ● | ● | ● | ● | ● | ● | ● | ● | ● | ● | ● |
| WANTAGE OSTEOPATHIC PRACTICE (HM20892) | | ● | | | ● | | | | | | | | | | ● | |
| WHEATLEY COMP THERAPY (HM21308) | | ● | | | | | | | | | ● | | | | | |
| WITNEY CHIROPRACTIC/CHIROPODY (HM21750) | | | | | ● | | | | | | | | | | ● | |

| Business by County with Reference no. | Mouth Disorders | Mouth Ulcers | Multiple Sclerosis | Muscular Dystrophy | Musculo-skeletal | Nail Health | Nausea | Nerve Disorders | Nervous Disorders | Neuralgia | Obesity | Osteoporosis | Pain | Palpitations | Panic Attacks | Parkinson's Disease |
|---|---|---|---|---|---|---|---|---|---|---|---|---|---|---|---|---|
| ASHCROFT CLINIC (HM01198) | | | | | | | | | | ● | | | ● | | | |
| BACK IN LINE (HM01481) | | | ● | | | | | ● | ● | ● | | ● | ● | | | |
| BACK TO NORMAL CHIRO CLINIC (HM01522) | | | | | | | | | | | | | ● | | | |
| BLISS REMEDIES (HM02508) | | | ● | | | ● | ● | ● | | | | | | ● | | |
| COOPER, STEPHEN (HM05128) | | | | | | | | | | | | | | | | |
| COTTAGE CLINIC (HM05221) | | | | | | | | | | | | | | | | |
| EDULJEE, STELLA (HM06638) | | | ● | ● | | | | | | | | | | | | |
| FEET FIRST (HM07179) | | | | | | ● | ● | | | | | | ● | | | |
| FYSON, MELANIE (HM07806) | | ● | | | | | ● | | | | | | | | | |
| HANDS ON THERAPY (HM08915) | | | | | | | | | | | | | ● | | | |
| HELIX HOUSE (HM09522) | | | | | | | ● | | | | | | ● | | | |
| HUDSON, EMMA (HM10311) | | | | | | | | ● | | ● | | | ● | | | |
| HYPNOTHERAPY CENTRE (HM10516) | | | | | | | | ● | ● | | ● | | ● | | | |
| KIDLINGTON CHIROPRACTIC (HM11594) | | | | | | | | ● | ● | ● | | | | | | |
| KIDLINGTON HERBAL PRACTICE (HM11595) | ● | ● | ● | | | | ● | | ● | ● | ● | ● | ● | ● | | |
| KIDLINGTON OSTEO PRACTICE (HM11596) | | | ● | ● | | | | | | | ● | ● | ● | ● | | |
| MARRIOTT, HUGH (HM13138) | | | | | | | | | | | | | ● | | | |
| MIDSUMMER COTTAGE CLINIC (HM13845) | | | ● | | | | ● | | | | | ● | ● | ● | | ● |
| O'BRIEN, FRANCES (HM15179) | | | | | | | | | | | | | ● | | | |
| O'DONNELL, ELSPETH (HM15225) | | | | | ● | | | | | | | | | | | |
| OXFORD NUTRITION & ALLRGY CTRE (HM15541) | ● | ● | ● | | | ● | ● | ● | ● | | ● | ● | ● | ● | | |
| OXFORD TRANSCENDTL MEDITA CTRE (HM15544) | | | ● | | | | | | | | | | | | | |
| PARSONS STREET CLINIC (HM15747) | | | | | | | ● | ● | ● | | | | ● | | | |
| PLESTED, JOHN (HM16368) | | | | | | | | | | | | | | | | |
| POLLOCK, SUSAN (HM16418) | | | | | | ● | | | | ● | | | ● | | | |
| SIDEBOTTOM, MARGARET (HM18527) | | | ● | | | | | | | | | | ● | | | |
| SUMMERTON CLINIC (HM19498) | ● | ● | ● | | | | ● | ● | ● | ● | | | ● | ● | | |
| TOUCH OF NATURE (HM20188) | | | | | | | | | | | | | | | | |
| TWINE, I E (HM20453) | | | | ● | | | | ● | ● | | ● | | ● | | | |
| WANTAGE NATURAL HEALTH CENTRE (HM20891) | ● | ● | ● | ● | | ● | ● | ● | ● | ● | ● | ● | ● | ● | | ● |
| WANTAGE OSTEOPATHIC PRACTICE (HM20892) | | | | | | | | | | | | ● | ● | | | |
| WHEATLEY COMP THERAPY (HM21308) | | | | | | | | | | | | | ● | | | |
| WITNEY CHIROPRACTIC/CHIROPODY (HM21750) | | | | | | | | ● | | ● | | | ● | | | |

| Business by County with Reference no. | Period Problems | Phobias | Piles | PMT | Pneumonia | Postural Problems | Pregnancy Help | Prostate Problems | Psoriasis | Raynaud's Disease | Recurrent Infections | Restless Legs | Rheumatoid Arthritis | Schizophrenia | Sciatica | Sexual Problems |
|---|---|---|---|---|---|---|---|---|---|---|---|---|---|---|---|---|
| ASHCROFT CLINIC (HM01198) | | | | | | | | | | ● | | ● | ● | | ● | |
| BACK IN LINE (HM01481) | | | | | | | | | | | | | | | ● | |
| BACK TO NORMAL CHIRO CLINIC (HM01522) | | | | | | | | | | | | ● | ● | | ● | |
| BLISS REMEDIES (HM02508) | | | | | | | | | | | | | | | | |
| COOPER, STEPHEN (HM05128) | | | | | | | | | | | | | | | ● | |
| COTTAGE CLINIC (HM05221) | | | | | | | | | | | | ● | | | | |
| EDULJEE, STELLA (HM06638) | | | | | | | | | | | | | | | | |
| FEET FIRST (HM07179) | ● | | | ● | | | ● | | | | | | | | ● | |
| FYSON, MELANIE (HM07806) | ● | ● | | ● | | | | | ● | | ● | | | | | |
| HANDS ON THERAPY (HM08915) | | | | | | | | | | | | | | | | |
| HELIX HOUSE (HM09522) | | | | | | | ● | | | | | | ● | | | |
| HUDSON, EMMA (HM10311) | | | | | | | | | | | | | | | | |
| HYPNOTHERAPY CENTRE (HM10516) | | ● | | | | | | | | | | | | | | ● |
| KIDLINGTON CHIROPRACTIC (HM11594) | | | | | | | | | | | | | | | ● | |
| KIDLINGTON HERBAL PRACTICE (HM11595) | ● | | ● | ● | ● | | | ● | ● | ● | ● | | ● | | ● | |
| KIDLINGTON OSTEO PRACTICE (HM11596) | | | | | | | | | | ● | | | | | ● | |
| MARRIOTT, HUGH (HM13138) | | | | | | | | | | | | | | | ● | |
| MIDSUMMER COTTAGE CLINIC (HM13845) | ● | | ● | ● | ● | | ● | ● | ● | ● | ● | ● | ● | ● | ● | ● |
| O'BRIEN, FRANCES (HM15179) | ● | | | ● | | | | | ● | | | | | | | |
| O'DONNELL, ELSPETH (HM15225) | | | | | | | | | | | | | ● | | ● | |
| OXFORD NUTRITION & ALLRGY CTRE (HM15541) | ● | | ● | ● | | | ● | ● | ● | ● | ● | ● | ● | ● | | |
| OXFORD TRANSCENDTL MEDITA CTRE (HM15544) | | ● | | ● | | | ● | | ● | | | | | | | |
| PARSONS STREET CLINIC (HM15747) | ● | | | | | | | | | | | | | | ● | |
| PLESTED, JOHN (HM16368) | | | | | | | | | | | | | | | | |
| POLLOCK, SUSAN (HM16418) | | | | | | | | | ● | ● | ● | ● | | | | |
| SIDEBOTTOM, MARGARET (HM18527) | | | | | | | | | | | | | | | | |
| SUMMERTON CLINIC (HM19498) | ● | | ● | ● | ● | | ● | ● | ● | ● | ● | ● | ● | | | |
| TOUCH OF NATURE (HM20188) | | | | | | | | | ● | | | | ● | | ● | |
| TWINE, I E (HM20453) | | ● | | ● | | | ● | | ● | ● | | ● | ● | | ● | |
| WANTAGE NATURAL HEALTH CENTRE (HM20891) | ● | ● | ● | ● | ● | | ● | ● | ● | ● | ● | ● | ● | ● | ● | ● |
| WANTAGE OSTEOPATHIC PRACTICE (HM20892) | | | | | | | | | | | | | ● | | ● | |
| WHEATLEY COMP THERAPY (HM21308) | | | | ● | | | | | | | | | | | | |
| WITNEY CHIROPRACTIC/CHIROPODY (HM21750) | | | | | | | | | | | | ● | | | ● | |

# I - S Conditions treated at Practices/Businesses

| Business by County with Reference no. | Insomnia | Irritable Bowel Syndrome | Itching | Jet Lag | Joint Pain | Kidney Complaints | Lactose Intolerance | Laryngitis | Lethargy | Liver Disorders | Low Blood Pressure | Lung Problems | ME | Menopause | Migraine | Motion Sickness | Mouth Disorders | Mouth Ulcers | Multiple Sclerosis | Muscular Dystrophy | Musculo-skeletal | Nail Health | Nausea | Nerve Disorders | Nervous Disorders | Neuralgia | Obesity | Osteoporosis | Pain | Palpitations | Panic Attacks | Parkinson's Disease | Period Problems | Phobias | Piles | PMT | Pneumonia | Postural Problems | Pregnancy Help | Prostate Problems | Psoriasis | Raynaud's Disease | Recurrent Infections | Restless Legs | Rheumatoid Arthritis | Schizophrenia | Sciatica | Sexual Problems |
|---|---|---|---|---|---|---|---|---|---|---|---|---|---|---|---|---|---|---|---|---|---|---|---|---|---|---|---|---|---|---|---|---|---|---|---|---|---|---|---|---|---|---|---|---|---|---|---|---|
| WITNEY NATURAL HEALTH CLINIC (HM21751) | ● | ● | ● | ● | ● | ● | ● | ● | ● | | ● | ● | ● | ● | ● | ● | ● | ● | ● | ● | | ● | ● | ● | ● | ● | ● | ● | ● | ● | | | ● | ● | ● | ● | ● | | ● | ● | ● | ● | ● | ● | ● | ● | ● | ● |
| **SHROPSHIRE** | | | | | | | | | | | | | | | | | | | | | | | | | | | | | | | | | | | | | | | | | | | | | | | | |
| ACUMEDIC (HM00218) | ● | | | | ● | | | | | | ● | | | ● | ● | | | | | | | | ● | | ● | | ● | | ● | | | | ● | | | | | | | | ● | | | | | | ● | ● |
| AYRES, JOHN (HM01434) | ● | ● | | | ● | | | | ● | | | | ● | | | | | | | | | | | | ● | | ● | | | | | | | ● | | | | | | | | | | | | | | ● |
| BODYLIFE CENTRE (HM02622) | ● | ● | | | | | | | | | | | ● | | | | | | ● | | | | | | | | ● | | | | | | | | | | | | | | | ● | | | | | | ● |
| BOOTH, ROBERT (HM02709) | | | | | ● | | | | | | | | | | | | | | ● | | | | | | | | | | ● | | | | | | | | | | | | | | | | | | | |
| COLERIDGE, JUDY (HM04831) | ● | ● | | | ● | | | | ● | | | | | ● | | | | | | | | | | | | | | | ● | | | | ● | | | ● | | | | | ● | | | ● | | | | |
| CORKE, A J (HM05167) | ● | | | | | | | | | | | | | | | | | | | | | | | | ● | | ● | | | | | | | ● | | | | | | | | | | | | | | |
| FULLERTON, N P (HM07792) | | | | | ● | | | | | | | | | | ● | | | | | | | | | ● | | ● | | | ● | | | | | | | | | | | | | | | | | | ● | |
| HALES OSTEOPATHIC PRACTICE (HM08743) | ● | ● | | | ● | ● | ● | | ● | ● | ● | ● | ● | ● | ● | ● | | ● | ● | | | | ● | | ● | ● | ● | ● | ● | ● | | | ● | | | ● | | | ● | ● | ● | ● | ● | ● | ● | | ● | |
| HEALING FOUNDATION (HM09334) | ● | ● | | | ● | ● | | | | | ● | | ● | ● | ● | | | | ● | | | | | | | | | | ● | | | | ● | ● | | | | | | | | | | | | | ● | |
| LUDLOW OSTEOPATHIC CLINIC (HM12727) | | | | | | | | | | | | | | | ● | | | | | | | | | | | | | | ● | | | | | | | | | | | | | | | | | | ● | |
| MEDAYD PHYSIOTHERAPY (HM13645) | | | | | ● | | | | | | | | | | | | | | ● | | | | | | | | | | ● | | | | | | | | | | | | | | | | | | | |
| MEDAYD PHYSIOTHERAPY (HM13644) | | | | | ● | | | | | | | | | | | | | | ● | | | | | | | | | | ● | | | | | | | | | | | | | | | | | | | |
| NEEDHAM, LYNDA M (HM14751) | | ● | | | ● | | | | | | | | | | ● | | | | | | | | | | | | ● | | | | | | ● | ● | | | | | | | | | | | ● | | ● | ● |
| OSTEOPATHIC (HM15449) | | ● | | | ● | | | | | | | | ● | ● | ● | | | ● | | | | | | ● | | ● | | | | | | | ● | | | | | | ● | | | | ● | | | | ● | |
| OSTLE, SAMANTHA (HM15480) | | ● | | | ● | | | | | | | | | | ● | | | | | | | | | | | ● | | | ● | | | | | | | | | | ● | | | | | | | | | |
| PEARSON, CHRISTINE (HM15911) | ● | ● | ● | ● | ● | ● | ● | ● | ● | ● | ● | ● | ● | ● | ● | ● | ● | ● | ● | ● | | ● | ● | ● | ● | ● | ● | ● | ● | ● | | ● | ● | ● | ● | ● | ● | | ● | ● | ● | ● | ● | ● | ● | ● | ● | ● |
| PHILLIPS, ANN (HM16124) | ● | ● | | | ● | | | | | | | | ● | ● | ● | | | | ● | | | | ● | | | | | | ● | ● | | | ● | | | ● | | | ● | | | | | ● | | | | |
| PREES COMPLEMENTARY THERAPIES (HM16533) | ● | | | | | | | | | | | | | | | | | | | ● | | | | | | | | | ● | | | | | ● | | | | | | | | | | | | | | |
| REYNOLDS, TESS (HM17216) | ● | ● | ● | | | ● | | | ● | ● | ● | ● | ● | ● | ● | | | ● | | | | | ● | | ● | ● | | | ● | ● | | | ● | ● | ● | ● | | | ● | | ● | ● | ● | ● | ● | | ● | |
| STONE, JANET (HM19336) | ● | ● | ● | ● | ● | ● | ● | ● | ● | ● | ● | ● | ● | ● | ● | ● | ● | ● | ● | ● | | ● | ● | ● | ● | ● | ● | ● | ● | ● | | ● | ● | ● | ● | ● | ● | | ● | ● | ● | ● | ● | ● | ● | ● | ● | ● |
| TAN & BEAUTY STUDIO (HM19676) | ● | ● | | | ● | ● | | | | | | | ● | ● | ● | | | | ● | | | | ● | | | | | | ● | ● | | | ● | | | ● | | | ● | | | | | ● | | | | |
| WALMSLEY, RUTH (HM20848) | ● | ● | | | ● | | | | ● | | | ● | ● | ● | | | | | ● | | | | | | ● | | | | ● | | | ● | | | | ● | | | ● | ● | | ● | ● | ● | ● | | ● | |
| WESTON, JOHN (HM21279) | | | | | | | | | | | | | | | | | | | | | | | | | | | | ● | ● | | | | | | | | | | | | | | | | ● | | ● | |
| WHITELEY, STEVEN (HM21400) | ● | ● | ● | ● | ● | ● | ● | ● | ● | ● | ● | ● | ● | ● | ● | ● | ● | ● | ● | ● | | ● | ● | ● | ● | ● | ● | ● | ● | ● | | ● | ● | ● | ● | ● | ● | | ● | ● | ● | ● | ● | ● | ● | ● | ● | ● |
| WILD ROSE (HM21488) | | ● | | | ● | | | | | | | | ● | ● | | | | | ● | | | | | ● | ● | | | ● | ● | | | | | | | | | | | | | | | | ● | | ● | |
| WILSON, AMANDA (HM21644) | | | | | | | | | | | | | | | | | | | | | | ● | | | | | | | | | | | | | | | | | | | | | | | | | | |
| **SOMERSET** | | | | | | | | | | | | | | | | | | | | | | | | | | | | | | | | | | | | | | | | | | | | | | | | |
| ABBEY CHIROPODY SERVICES (HM00074) | | | | | | | | | | | | | | | | | | | | | | ● | | | | | | | | | | | | | | | | | | | | | | | | | | |
| ALASKAN BACH FLOWER REMEDIES (HM00472) | | ● | | | | | | | | | | | | ● | ● | | | | | | | | | | | | | | | | | | | ● | | ● | | | | | | | | | | | | |
| ANDERSON, DAVID (HM00816) | | | | | | | | | | | | | | | | | | | | | | ● | | | | | | | | | | | | | | | | | | | | | | | | | | |
| ANSON, BARRIE (HM00916) | ● | ● | ● | ● | ● | ● | ● | ● | ● | ● | ● | ● | ● | ● | ● | ● | ● | ● | | | | ● | ● | ● | ● | ● | ● | ● | ● | ● | | | ● | ● | ● | ● | ● | | ● | ● | ● | ● | ● | ● | | | ● | ● |
| AUSSENS, MIEKE (HM01359) | | ● | | | ● | | | | | | | | ● | | ● | | | | ● | | | | | | | | | | ● | | | | | | | | | | | | | | | | | | | |

# I - S Conditions treated at Practices/Businesses

| Business by County with Reference no. | Insomnia | Irritable Bowel Syndrome | Itching | Jet Lag | Joint Pain | Kidney Complaints | Lactose Intolerance | Laryngitis | Lethargy | Liver Disorders | Low Blood Pressure | Lung Problems | ME | Menopause | Migraine | Motion Sickness | Mouth Disorders | Mouth Ulcers | Multiple Sclerosis | Muscular Dystrophy | Musculo-skeletal | Nail Health | Nausea | Nerve Disorders | Nervous Disorders | Neuralgia | Obesity | Osteoporosis | Pain | Palpitations | Panic Attacks | Parkinson's Disease | Period Problems | Phobias | Piles | PMT | Pneumonia | Postural Problems | Pregnancy Help | Prostate Problems | Psoriasis | Raynaud's Disease | Recurrent Infections | Restless Legs | Rheumatoid Arthritis | Schizophrenia | Sciatica | Sexual Problems |
|---|---|---|---|---|---|---|---|---|---|---|---|---|---|---|---|---|---|---|---|---|---|---|---|---|---|---|---|---|---|---|---|---|---|---|---|---|---|---|---|---|---|---|---|---|---|---|---|---|
| AVENUE CLINIC (HM01388) |●|●|●|●|●|●|●|●|●|●|●|●|●|●|●|●|●|●|●|●|●|●|●|●|●|●|●|●|●|●|●|●|●|●|●|●|●|●|●|●|●|●|●|●|●|●|●|●|
| BAILEY, LINDA R (HM01552) | |●| | | | |●| | | | | |●| | | | | | | | | | | | | |●|●| | | | |●| | |●| | | | | | | | | | | | |
| BATH ALEXANDER TECHNIQUE (HM01890) |●| | | |●| | | | | | | |●| |●| | | |●| | | | | | | | |●|●| | |●| | | | | |●| | | | | | |●| |●| |
| BATH NATURAL MEDICAL CENTRE (HM01893) |●| | | | | | | | | | | | | |●| | | | | | | | | | | | | | | | | | | | | | | | | | | | | | | | | |
| BATHPOOL CHIROPRACTIC CLINIC (HM01900) | |●| | |●| | | | | | | |●| | | | | |●| | |●| | |●| | |●|●| | | | | | |●| | | | | | | | | | |●| |
| BEECH HOUSE CLINIC (HM02046) | |●| | |●| | | | | | | |●| |●| | | | | | | | |●|●| | | |●| | | | | | | | | | | | | | | | | |●| |
| BOULEVARD PHARMACY (HM02739) |●|●|●|●|●| |●|●|●| | | |●|●|●|●|●|●| | | |●|●| |●|●|●|●|●|●| |●|●|●|●|●| | |●|●|●|●|●|●|●| |●|●|
| BRIDGET HEALING CENTRE (HM03008) |●|●|●|●|●|●|●|●|●|●|●|●|●|●|●|●|●|●|●|●| |●|●|●|●|●|●|●|●|●| |●|●|●|●|●|●| |●|●|●|●|●|●|●|●|●|●|
| CASTLE SURGERY (HM03840) | |●| | |●| | | | | | | |●| |●| | | | | | | | |●|●| | | |●| | | | | | | | | | | | | | | | | |●| |
| CHAMELEON OILS (HM03961) |●| |●| |●| | | | | | | | | | | | | | | | |●| | |●| | | |●| | | |●| | |●| | | | |●| | | | | | | |
| CHEDDAR COMP MEDICINE CTRE (HM04075) |●|●|●| |●| | | | | | | | |●|●| | | |●| | | | | | | | | |●| | | |●| | |●| | | | | | | | | | | | |
| CHINESE MEDICAL CENTRE (HM04238) |●| | | |●| | | | | |●| | |●|●| | | | | | | |●| |●| |●| |●| | | |●| | | | | | | |●| | | | | |●|●|
| CHIPPER, MARY (HM04278) | | | | |●| | | | | | | | |●| | | | | | | | | | | | | | | | | | | | | |●| | | | | | | | |●| | | |
| CLARKE GAIL & RAWLINSON MIKE (HM04581) | | | | |●| | | | | | | | | | | | | | | | | | | | | | | | | | | | | | | | |●| | | | | | | | |●| |
| CLINIC OF COMP MEDICINE (HM04689) |●|●|●| |●|●| |●|●| |●|●|●|●|●|●|●|●| | | | |●|●|●|●| | |●|●| | |●| |●|●|●| | |●|●|●|●|●|●| |●|●|
| CLISBY, JANE (HM04722) |●| | | | |●| | | | | | |●|●|●| | | | | | | |●| | | | | |●| | | | | | |●| | | | | | | | | | | |
| COMPLEMENTARY THERAPY (HM04942) | |●| | |●| |●| |●| | | |●| | | | | | | | | | | | | | | | | | | | | | | | | | | | | | | | | | |
| COOK, COLIN (HM05041) | | | | |●| | | | | | | | | |●| | | | | | | | |●| |●| |●|●| | | |●| | | | | | | | | | | | | |●| |
| COUNSULTING ROOMS (HM05253) |●|●| | | | | | | | | | | | | | | | | | | | | | |●| |●| |●|●| | | |●| | | | | | | | | | | | | |●|
| DAVIES, SALLY (HM05840) | | | | | | | | | | | | | |●|●| | | | | | | | | | | | | | | | | | | | | | | | | | | | | | | | |
| DEVONSHIRE SURGERY (HM06044) | |●| | |●| | | | | | | |●| |●| | | | | | | | | |●|●| | |●| | | | | | | | | | | | | | | | | |●| |
| EUROPEAN COLLEGE-BOWEN STUDIES (HM06946) |●|●|●| |●|●| | |●| | | |●| |●| | | |●| | | | | |●|●| | |●| | |●|●| |●|●| | |●| |●| | |●|●| |●| |
| FRANCES-WHITAKER, J A (HM07665) | | | | | | | | | | | | | | | | | | | | | | | | | | | | | | | | | | | | | | | | | | | |●| | | | |
| GLASTONBURY CHIROPRACTIC (HM08131) | |●| | |●| | | | | | | |●| |●| | | | | | | | |●|●| | |●|●| | | | | | |●| | | | | | | |●|●| |●| |
| GLASTONBURY EAST WEST CENTRE (HM08132) |●|●|●|●|●|●|●|●|●|●|●|●|●|●|●|●|●|●|●| | |●|●|●|●|●|●|●|●|●| |●|●|●|●|●|●| |●|●|●|●|●|●|●| |●|●|
| HELEN SMITH CHIROPODIST (HM09515) | | | | | | | | | | | | | | | | | | | | | |●| | | | | | | | | | | | | | | | | | | | | | | | | | |
| HOLISTIC HEALING CENTRE (HM09962) |●|●| | |●|●| | | | |●| |●|●|●| | | |●| | | | | | | | | |●|●| | | | | |●| | | | | | | | | | |●| |
| HUDSON, JOHN (HM10315) | | | | | | | | | | | | | | | | | | | | | | | | | | | | | | | | |●| | | | | | | | | | | | | | |
| HUXTABLE, ALISON (HM10461) | |●| | |●| | | | | | | | | | | | | | | | | | |●| | | |●|●| | | | | | | | |●| | | | | | | | |●| |
| JONES, BECKY (HM11125) |●|●| | | | | | |●| | | | | | |●| | | | | | | | | | |●| |●| | | | |●| | | | |●| | | | | |●| | | |
| JONES, RAYMOND (HM11190) | |●| | |●| | | | | | | | | | | | | | | | | | | | | | | |●| | | | | | | | | | | | | | | | | |●| |
| KIRKMEAD CENTRE (HM11718) |●|●| | | | | | | | | | |●|●|●| | | | | | | | | | | | | | | | | | | | | | | | | | | | | | | | | |
| LANSDOWN PHYSIOTHERAPY CLINIC (HM11964) | | | | |●| | | | | | | | | |●| | | | | | | | | | | | | |●| | | | | | | | | | | | | | | | | |●| |
| LEAVEY, J () | |●| | | | | | | | | | | | |●| | | | | | | | | | | | | | | | | | | | | | | | | | | | | | | | | |

# I - S Conditions treated at Practices/Businesses

| Business by County with Reference no. | Insomnia | Irritable Bowel Syndrome | Itching | Jet Lag | Joint Pain | Kidney Complaints | Lactose Intolerance | Laryngitis | Lethargy | Liver Disorders | Low Blood Pressure | Lung Problems | ME | Menopause | Migraine | Motion Sickness | Mouth Disorders | Mouth Ulcers | Multiple Sclerosis | Muscular Dystrophy | Musculo-skeletal | Nail Health |
|---|---|---|---|---|---|---|---|---|---|---|---|---|---|---|---|---|---|---|---|---|---|---|
| LOGAN, DAVID (HM12566) | | ● | | | | | | | | | | | | | | | | | | | | |
| MARY WILKINSON - MCTIMONEY (HM13225) | | | | | | | | | | | | | | | ● | | | | ● | | | |
| MARY WILKINSON - MCTIMONEY (HM13226) | | | | | | | | | | | | | | | ● | | | | ● | | | |
| MCLOUGHLIN, BRENDAN (HM13559) | | | | | | | | | | | | | | | | | | | | | | |
| MIDSOMER NORTON CHIROPRACTIC (HM13844) | | | | | ● | | | | | | | | | | | | | | | | | |
| MILSOM STREET CLINIC (HM13944) | | | | | ● | | | | | | | | | | | | | | | | | |
| NATURAL SPIRITUAL HEALING (HM14626) | ● | ● | | | ● | | | | | | | | ● | ● | ● | | | | ● | | | |
| NATURAL THERAPIES (HM14632) | ● | | | | | | | | | | | | | | ● | | | | | | | |
| NORSO BIOMAGNETICS UK (HM15016) | ● | ● | | ● | ● | | | | | | | | | | ● | | | | | | | |
| NUTRITION FOR LIFE (HM15123) | ● | ● | | ● | ● | ● | ● | | ● | ● | ● | | ● | | ● | | ● | ● | | ● | | ● |
| ORCHARD CLINIC (HM15360) | | ● | | | ● | | | | | | | | ● | | ● | | | | | | | |
| PARK HOUSE CLINIC (HM15666) | | | | | ● | | | | | | | | | | | | | | | | | |
| PARNELL, R H (HM15727) | | | | | | | | | | | | | | ● | ● | | | | | | | |
| PENNINGTON, PAM (HM15990) | | | | | | | | | | | | | | | | | | | | | | ● |
| PENNINGTON, PAM V (HM15991) | | | | | | | | | | | | | | | | | | | | | | ● |
| PITT, I T (HM16347) | | | | | | | | | | | | | | | | | | | | | | |
| PRESSURE WORKS (HM16544) | | | | | | | | | | | | | | | | | | | | | | |
| REED, W A (HM17046) | | | | | | | | | | | | | ● | ● | ● | | | | | | | |
| RICHARDS, M J (HM17261) | | | | | | | | | | | | | | | | | | | | | | ● |
| SHAMBHALA (HM18275) | | ● | | | | | ● | | ● | | | | ● | | | | | | | | | |
| SNOWDON, JANET (HM18843) | ● | ● | ● | ● | ● | ● | ● | ● | ● | ● | ● | ● | ● | ● | ● | ● | ● | ● | ● | ● | | ● |
| ST JAMES'S SURGERY (HM19079) | | | | | ● | | | | | | | | | | ● | | | | | | | |
| ST MICHAELS CHIROPRACTIC (HM19089) | | ● | | | ● | | | | | | | | | | | | | | | | | |
| ST MICHAEL'S HYPNOTHERAPY (HM19090) | ● | | | | | | | | | | | | | | | | | | | | | |
| STANLEY COURT SURGERY (HM19127) | | ● | | | ● | | | | | | | | ● | | | | | | | | | |
| STREET CHIROPRACTIC CLINIC (HM19383) | | | | | ● | | | | | | | | | | ● | | | | | | | |
| STREET CHIROPRACTIC CLINIC (HM19382) | | ● | | | ● | | | | | | | | ● | | | | | | | | | |
| STRESS CLINIC & NTRL HLTH CTRE (HM19389) | ● | ● | ● | ● | ● | ● | ● | | ● | ● | ● | ● | ● | ● | ● | ● | ● | ● | | | | |
| TARETH CENTRE (HM19704) | ● | ● | ● | ● | ● | ● | ● | ● | ● | ● | ● | ● | ● | ● | ● | ● | ● | ● | ● | ● | | ● |
| TAUNTON FOOT SURGERY (HM19722) | | | | | | | | | | | | | | | | | | | | | | ● |
| TAYLOR, GILLIAN (HM19760) | | | | | | | | | | | | | | | | | | | | | | ● |
| THOMPSON, G W (DR) (HM19978) | | | | | ● | | | | | | | | | | | | | | | | | |
| TURNPIKE SURGERY (HM20441) | | ● | | | ● | | | | | | | | ● | | | | | | | | | |
| WELLSPRING OSTEO/NTRL HEALTH (HM21181) | ● | ● | | | ● | ● | | | ● | | | ● | ● | ● | ● | | | | | | | |

| Business by County with Reference no. | Nausea | Nerve Disorders | Nervous Disorders | Neuralgia | Obesity | Osteoporosis | Pain | Palpitations | Panic Attacks | Parkinson's Disease | Period Problems | Phobias | Piles | PMT | Pneumonia | Postural Problems | Pregnancy Help | Prostate Problems | Psoriasis | Raynaud's Disease | Recurrent Infections | Restless Legs | Rheumatoid Arthritis | Schizophrenia | Sciatica | Sexual Problems |
|---|---|---|---|---|---|---|---|---|---|---|---|---|---|---|---|---|---|---|---|---|---|---|---|---|---|---|
| LOGAN, DAVID (HM12566) | | | | | | | | | ● | | | ● | | | | | | | | | | | | | | ● |
| MARY WILKINSON - MCTIMONEY (HM13225) | | | | | | | ● | | | | | | | | | | ● | | | | | | | | ● | |
| MARY WILKINSON - MCTIMONEY (HM13226) | | | | | | | ● | | | | | | | | | | ● | | | | | | | | ● | |
| MCLOUGHLIN, BRENDAN (HM13559) | | | | | | | | | | | | | | | | | | | | | | | | ● | | ● |
| MIDSOMER NORTON CHIROPRACTIC (HM13844) | | | | | | | ● | | | | | | | | | | | | | | | | | | ● | |
| MILSOM STREET CLINIC (HM13944) | | | | | | | ● | | | | | | | | | | | | | | | | | | ● | |
| NATURAL SPIRITUAL HEALING (HM14626) | | | | | | ● | ● | | | | | | | | | | ● | | | | | | | | | |
| NATURAL THERAPIES (HM14632) | | | ● | | | | ● | | | | | | | | | | | | | | | | | | | |
| NORSO BIOMAGNETICS UK (HM15016) | | | | | | ● | ● | | | | ● | | | | | | | | | | | ● | | | ● | |
| NUTRITION FOR LIFE (HM15123) | | | ● | | ● | | ● | | | | ● | | | ● | | | | | ● | ● | | | ● | | ● | |
| ORCHARD CLINIC (HM15360) | | ● | ● | | | | ● | | | | | | | | | | | | | | | | | | ● | |
| PARK HOUSE CLINIC (HM15666) | | | | | | | | | | | | | | | | | | | | | | | | | ● | |
| PARNELL, R H (HM15727) | | | | | | | ● | | | | ● | | | ● | | | | | | | | | | | | |
| PENNINGTON, PAM (HM15990) | | | | | | | | | | | | | | | | | | | | | | | | | | |
| PENNINGTON, PAM V (HM15991) | | | | | | | | | | | | | | | | | | | | | | | | | | |
| PITT, I T (HM16347) | | | | ● | | | | | | | | | | | | | | | | | | | | | ● | |
| PRESSURE WORKS (HM16544) | | | ● | | | | ● | | | | | | | | | | | | | | | | | | ● | |
| REED, W A (HM17046) | | | | | | | ● | | | | | | | ● | | | | | | | | | | | | |
| RICHARDS, M J (HM17261) | | | | | | | | | | | | | | | | | | | | | | | | | | |
| SHAMBHALA (HM18275) | | | ● | | ● | ● | ● | | | | ● | ● | | ● | | | | | | | | ● | | | ● | ● |
| SNOWDON, JANET (HM18843) | ● | ● | ● | ● | ● | ● | ● | ● | | ● | ● | ● | ● | ● | ● | | ● | ● | ● | ● | ● | ● | ● | ● | ● | ● |
| ST JAMES'S SURGERY (HM19079) | | | | ● | | ● | ● | | | | | | | | | | | | | | | | ● | | ● | |
| ST MICHAELS CHIROPRACTIC (HM19089) | | | | | | | ● | | | | | | | | | | | | | | | | | | | |
| ST MICHAEL'S HYPNOTHERAPY (HM19090) | | | | | | | | | | | | ● | | | | | | | | | | | | | | |
| STANLEY COURT SURGERY (HM19127) | | ● | ● | | | | ● | | | | | | | | | | | | | | | | | | ● | |
| STREET CHIROPRACTIC CLINIC (HM19383) | | ● | | ● | | ● | ● | | | | | | | | | | | | | | | ● | | | ● | |
| STREET CHIROPRACTIC CLINIC (HM19382) | | ● | ● | | | | ● | | | | | | | | | | | | | | | | | | ● | |
| STRESS CLINIC & NTRL HLTH CTRE (HM19389) | ● | ● | ● | ● | ● | ● | ● | ● | | | ● | ● | | ● | | | ● | ● | ● | ● | ● | ● | ● | | ● | ● |
| TARETH CENTRE (HM19704) | ● | ● | ● | ● | ● | ● | ● | ● | | ● | ● | ● | ● | ● | ● | | ● | ● | ● | ● | ● | ● | ● | ● | ● | ● |
| TAUNTON FOOT SURGERY (HM19722) | | | | | | | | | | | | | | | | | | | | | | | | | | |
| TAYLOR, GILLIAN (HM19760) | | | | | | | | | | | | | | | | | | | | | | | | | | |
| THOMPSON, G W (DR) (HM19978) | | ● | | | | | ● | | | | | | | | | | | | | | | | | | ● | |
| TURNPIKE SURGERY (HM20441) | | ● | ● | | | | ● | | | | | | | | | | | | | | | | | | ● | |
| WELLSPRING OSTEO/NTRL HEALTH (HM21181) | ● | ● | ● | ● | | | ● | | | | ● | ● | | ● | | | | | | | ● | ● | | | ● | |

# I - S Conditions treated at Practices/Businesses

| Business by County with Reference no. | Insomnia | Irritable Bowel Syndrome | Itching | Jet Lag | Joint Pain | Kidney Complaints | Lactose Intolerance | Laryngitis | Lethargy | Liver Disorders | Low Blood Pressure | Lung Problems | ME | Menopause | Migraine | Motion Sickness | Mouth Disorders | Mouth Ulcers | Multiple Sclerosis | Muscular Dystrophy | Musculo-skeletal | Nail Health | Nausea | Nerve Disorders | Nervous Disorders | Neuralgia | Obesity | Osteoporosis | Pain | Palpitations | Panic Attacks | Parkinson's Disease | Period Problems | Phobias | Piles | PMT | Pneumonia | Postural Problems | Pregnancy Help | Prostate Problems | Psoriasis | Raynaud's Disease | Recurrent Infections | Restless Legs | Rheumatoid Arthritis | Schizophrenia | Sciatica | Sexual Problems |
|---|---|---|---|---|---|---|---|---|---|---|---|---|---|---|---|---|---|---|---|---|---|---|---|---|---|---|---|---|---|---|---|---|---|---|---|---|---|---|---|---|---|---|---|---|---|---|---|---|
| WESTERN CHIROPRACTIC CLINIC (HM21263) | | ● | | ● | ● | | | | ● | | ● | | ● | | ● | ● | | | | | | | | ● | ● | ● | | ● | | ● | | | ● | | | ● | | | ● | | | | ● | ● | ● | | ● | |
| WILKINSON, MARY (HM21511) | | | | | | | | | | | | | | | ● | | | | ● | | | | | | | | | | ● | | | | | | | | | | ● | | | | | | | | ● | |
| WINCANTON CHIROPRACTIC CLINIC (HM21690) | | ● | | | ● | | | | | | | | ● | | ● | | | | | | | | | ● | ● | | | | ● | | | | | | | | | | | | | | | | | | ● | |
| YELLOW EMPEROR CORP (HM22004) | | ● | | | ● | | | | | | | | | ● | ● | | | | ● | | | | | | | | | | ● | | | | | | | ● | | | | | | | | | | | | |
| YEOVIL CHIROPRACTIC CLINIC (HM22008) | | ● | | | ● | | | | | | | | | | | | | | | | | | | | | | | | ● | | | | | | | | | | | | | | | | | | ● | |
| **STAFFORDSHIRE** | | | | | | | | | | | | | | | | | | | | | | | | | | | | | | | | | | | | | | | | | | | | | | | | |
| ALTERNATIVE THERAPY CENTRE (HM00735) | ● | ● | ● | | ● | ● | ● | ● | ● | ● | ● | ● | ● | ● | ● | | ● | ● | ● | | | ● | ● | ● | ● | ● | ● | | ● | ● | | ● | ● | ● | ● | ● | | | ● | ● | ● | ● | ● | ● | ● | | ● | ● |
| ALTERNATIVES (HM00741) | ● | ● | ● | ● | ● | ● | ● | ● | ● | ● | ● | ● | ● | ● | ● | ● | ● | ● | ● | ● | | ● | ● | ● | ● | ● | ● | ● | ● | ● | | ● | ● | ● | ● | ● | ● | | ● | ● | ● | ● | ● | ● | ● | ● | ● | ● |
| ANDERSON, G (HM00818) | | | | | | | | | | | | | | | ● | | | | | | | | | | | | | | | | | | | ● | | | | | | | | | | | | | | |
| BARCROFT, J M (HM01696) | | | | | ● | | | | | | | | | | ● | | | | | | | | | | | | | | | | | | | | | | | | | | | | | | | | | |
| BASFORD CHIROPRACTIC CLINIC (HM01842) | | ● | | | ● | | | | | | | | | | | | | | | | | | | ● | | | | | ● | | | | | | | | | ● | | | | | | | | | ● | |
| BLANK, CHRISTOPHER (HM02499) | | | | | | | | | | | | | | | | | | | | | | ● | | | | | | | | | | | | | | | | | | | | | | | | | | |
| BONNEBAIGT, ANDRE (HM02682) | | ● | | | | | | | | | | | | | ● | | | | | | | | | | | | | | | | | | | ● | | | | | | | | | | | | | | |
| BRADBURY, SHARON (HM02842) | | | | | ● | | | | | | | | | | | | | | | | | | | | | ● | | | ● | | | ● | | | | | | | ● | | | | | | | | ● | |
| BRAMPTON TREES CLINIC (HM02908) | | | | | ● | | | | | | | | | | | | | | ● | | | | | | | | | | ● | | | | | | | | | | | | | | | | | | | |
| BRIDGETT, A (HM03011) | | | | | ● | | | | | | | | | | ● | | | | ● | | | | | | | | | | ● | | | | | | | | | | | | | | | ● | ● | | ● | |
| BURKE, E (HM03385) | ● | | | | | | | | | | | | | | | | | | | | | | | ● | ● | | ● | | | | | | | ● | | | | | | | | | | | | | | |
| CASTLEFIELDS SURGERY (HM03846) | | | | | | | | | | | | | ● | | ● | | | | | | | | | | | | | | | | | | | | | | | | | | | | | | | | | |
| CHASE HEALTH FOODS (HM04055) | ● | ● | ● | ● | ● | ● | ● | ● | ● | ● | ● | ● | ● | ● | ● | ● | ● | ● | ● | ● | | ● | ● | ● | ● | ● | ● | ● | ● | ● | | ● | ● | ● | ● | ● | ● | | ● | ● | ● | ● | ● | ● | ● | ● | ● | ● |
| CHASE NATURAL THERAPY CENTRE (HM04059) | ● | ● | ● | ● | ● | ● | ● | ● | ● | ● | ● | ● | ● | ● | ● | ● | ● | ● | ● | ● | | ● | ● | ● | ● | ● | ● | ● | ● | ● | | ● | ● | ● | ● | ● | ● | | ● | ● | ● | ● | ● | ● | ● | ● | ● | ● |
| CITY CHIROPRACTIC CLINIC (HM04492) | | ● | | | ● | | | | | | | | ● | | ● | | | | | ● | | | | ● | ● | | | ● | ● | | | | | | | | | | | | | | | | | | ● | |
| CORNERSTONES PRACTICE (HM05182) | ● | ● | ● | ● | ● | ● | ● | ● | ● | ● | ● | ● | ● | ● | ● | ● | ● | ● | ● | ● | | ● | ● | ● | ● | ● | ● | ● | ● | ● | | ● | ● | ● | ● | ● | ● | | ● | ● | ● | ● | ● | ● | ● | ● | ● | ● |
| CRESCENT CLINIC (HM05417) | ● | ● | ● | ● | ● | ● | ● | ● | ● | ● | ● | ● | ● | ● | ● | ● | ● | ● | ● | ● | | ● | ● | ● | ● | ● | ● | ● | ● | ● | | ● | ● | ● | ● | ● | ● | | ● | ● | ● | ● | ● | ● | ● | ● | ● | ● |
| CRESCENT CLINIC FOR COMP MED (HM05418) | ● | | | | ● | | | | | | | | ● | | ● | | | | ● | | | | | | | | | | ● | | | | | | | | | | | | | | | | | | | |
| EDWARDS, ALLYN (HM06641) | ● | ● | | ● | ● | | | | ● | | ● | | ● | | ● | ● | | | ● | ● | | | | ● | ● | ● | | ● | | ● | | | | | ● | | | | | ● | | | | ● | ● | | ● | |
| EVANS, RICHARD (HM06989) | ● | ● | ● | ● | ● | ● | | | ● | ● | ● | ● | ● | ● | ● | | | | ● | | | ● | ● | ● | ● | ● | | | ● | ● | | ● | ● | ● | ● | ● | | | ● | ● | ● | ● | ● | ● | ● | | ● | |
| FOOT SOUL & BODYWORKS (HM07487) | ● | ● | ● | ● | ● | | | | | | | | ● | ● | | | | | | | | | ● | | | | | ● | ● | | | | ● | | | ● | | | | ● | ● | ● | | ● | ● | | ● | |
| FORTEY, C J (HM07579) | | | | | ● | | | | | | | | | | | | | | | | | | | | | | | | | | | | | | | | | | | | | | | | | | | |
| GASCOIGNE, DOROTHY (HM07917) | | | | | | | | | | | | | | | | | | | | | | | | | ● | | | | | | | | | | | | | | | | | | | | | | | |
| HALLARD, SHARON (HM08800) | | | | | | | | | | | | | | | ● | | | | | | | | | | | | | | | | | | | ● | | | | | | | | | | | | | | |
| ISHTA CENTRE (HM10761) | ● | ● | ● | ● | ● | ● | ● | ● | ● | ● | ● | ● | ● | ● | ● | ● | ● | ● | ● | ● | | ● | ● | ● | ● | ● | ● | ● | ● | ● | | ● | ● | ● | ● | ● | ● | | ● | ● | ● | ● | ● | ● | ● | ● | ● | ● |
| JOHNSON, JANICE (HM11079) | ● | ● | | | | | | | | | | | | | | | | | | | | | | | ● | | ● | | ● | ● | ● | | | ● | | | | | | | | | | | | | | |
| LOUISE BRITTLE (HM12667) | | | | | | | | | | | | | | | | | | | | | | | | | | | | | | | | | | | | | | | | | | | | | ● | | | |
| MILL BANK OSTEOPATHIC CLINIC (HM13865) | | ● | | | ● | | | | | | | | ● | | ● | | | | | | | | | ● | | | | | ● | | | | | | | | | | | | | | | | | | ● | |

# I - S Conditions treated at Practices/Businesses

Business by County with Reference no.

| Business | Insomnia | Irritable Bowel Syndrome | Itching | Jet Lag | Joint Pain | Kidney Complaints | Lactose Intolerance | Laryngitis | Lethargy | Liver Disorders | Low Blood Pressure | Lung Problems | ME | Menopause | Migraine | Motion Sickness |
|---|---|---|---|---|---|---|---|---|---|---|---|---|---|---|---|---|
| NARAYAN, MAMTA (HM14486) | | | | | | | | | | | | | | | | |
| NORBURY, SUSAN (HM14990) | ● | ● | ● | ● | ● | ● | ● | ● | ● | ● | ● | ● | ● | ● | ● | ● |
| O'CALLAGHAN, STEVE (HM15193) | ● | ● | | | ● | | | | ● | | | | ● | | ● | |
| PEACEHAVEN AROMATHERAPY (HM15877) | ● | ● | | | | | | | | | ● | | | ● | | |
| PRIORS PODIATRY PRACTICE (HM16629) | | | | | ● | | | | | | | | | | | |
| ROBERTS, KATE (HM17418) | | | | | | | | | | | | | | | | |
| STAFFORD CHIROPRACTIC CLINIC (HM19108) | | ● | | | ● | | | | | | | | | | ● | |
| STAFFORDSHIRE MCTIMONEY (HM19111) | | ● | | | ● | | | | ● | | | | | | ● | |
| SUSAN JAMES CONSULTANCY (HM19527) | | | | | | | | | | | | | | | | |
| TAMWORTH PHYSIOTHERAPY CLINIC (HM19675) | | | | | ● | | | | | | | | | | | |
| TE NOSCE (HM19803) | ● | ● | ● | ● | ● | ● | | ● | ● | | ● | | ● | ● | ● | |
| TUNSTALL HYPNOTHERAPY CENTRE (HM20401) | | ● | | | | | | | | | | | | | | |
| WHITBY, S E (HM21334) | | | | | ● | | | | | | | | | | | |
| YARNFIELD PARK- HEALTH/SPORTS (HM21989) | ● | ● | ● | ● | ● | ● | ● | ● | ● | ● | ● | ● | ● | ● | ● | ● |
| **SUFFOLK** | | | | | | | | | | | | | | | | |
| AJNA (HM00457) | | | | | | | | | | | | | | | ● | |
| BODY MECHANICS THERAPY CLINIC (HM02599) | | | | | ● | | | | | | | | | | | |
| CHARLTON CLINIC (HM04033) | | ● | | | ● | | | | | | | | | | | |
| CHURCHMAN & ASS REG OST (HM04475) | | | | | ● | | | | | | | | | | | |
| CHURCHMAN, BERYL (HM04478) | | | | | ● | | | | | | | | | | | |
| COLEBROOK, G (HM04820) | | | | | | | | | ● | | | | | | ● | |
| COOPER, A R (HM05088) | | | | | | | | | | | | | | | | |
| CT & IM LEITH (HM05534) | | ● | ● | | ● | ● | ● | | | | ● | | | | ● | |
| DENT, TRISH () | ● | ● | | | ● | | | | | | | | ● | ● | ● | |
| EVENKEEL (HM06997) | | | | | | | | | | | | | ● | ● | ● | |
| FELIXSTOWE PHYSIO PRACTICE (HM07203) | | | | | ● | | | | | | | | | | | |
| FRESHFIELDS OF ALDEBURGH (HM07737) | ● | ● | ● | ● | ● | ● | ● | ● | ● | ● | ● | ● | ● | ● | ● | ● |
| GREEN FARM CLINIC (HM08435) | | | | | ● | | | | | | | | | | | |
| GROSVENOR PHYSIOTHERAPY CLINIC (HM08597) | | | | | ● | | | | | | | | | | | |
| HARDY, MICHAEL (HM08984) | | | | | ● | | | | | | | | | | ● | |
| HEALING CONNECTIONS (HM09330) | ● | ● | ● | ● | ● | ● | | ● | ● | ● | ● | ● | ● | ● | ● | ● |
| HEALING HANDS (HM09336) | ● | ● | | | | | | | ● | | ● | | | ● | ● | |
| HITCHINS, ROSIE (HM09847) | ● | ● | | | | | | | | | | | | | ● | |
| HOPKINS, C J (HM10147) | ● | ● | | | | | | | | | | | ● | | ● | |

| Business | Mouth Disorders | Mouth Ulcers | Multiple Sclerosis | Muscular Dystrophy | Musculo-skeletal | Nail Health | Nausea | Nerve Disorders | Nervous Disorders | Neuralgia | Obesity | Osteoporosis | Pain | Palpitations | Panic Attacks | Parkinson's Disease |
|---|---|---|---|---|---|---|---|---|---|---|---|---|---|---|---|---|
| NARAYAN, MAMTA (HM14486) | | | | | | | | | | | | | ● | | | |
| NORBURY, SUSAN (HM14990) | ● | ● | ● | ● | | ● | ● | ● | ● | ● | ● | ● | ● | ● | | ● |
| O'CALLAGHAN, STEVE (HM15193) | | | ● | | | | | | | | | | | | | |
| PEACEHAVEN AROMATHERAPY (HM15877) | | | | | | | | | ● | | | | ● | | | |
| PRIORS PODIATRY PRACTICE (HM16629) | | | | | | | | | | | | | ● | | | |
| ROBERTS, KATE (HM17418) | | | | | | | | | ● | | | | | | | |
| STAFFORD CHIROPRACTIC CLINIC (HM19108) | | | | | | | | ● | | ● | | | ● | | | |
| STAFFORDSHIRE MCTIMONEY (HM19111) | | | ● | | | | | ● | | ● | | ● | ● | | | |
| SUSAN JAMES CONSULTANCY (HM19527) | | | | | | | | | | | | | ● | | | |
| TAMWORTH PHYSIOTHERAPY CLINIC (HM19675) | | | ● | | | | | | | | | | | | | |
| TE NOSCE (HM19803) | | ● | ● | | | ● | ● | ● | ● | ● | ● | ● | ● | ● | | |
| TUNSTALL HYPNOTHERAPY CENTRE (HM20401) | | | | | | | | | | | | | | | | |
| WHITBY, S E (HM21334) | | | ● | | | | | | | | | | ● | | | |
| YARNFIELD PARK- HEALTH/SPORTS (HM21989) | ● | ● | ● | ● | | ● | ● | ● | ● | ● | ● | ● | ● | ● | | ● |
| **SUFFOLK** | | | | | | | | | | | | | | | | |
| AJNA (HM00457) | | | | | | | | | | | | | | | | |
| BODY MECHANICS THERAPY CLINIC (HM02599) | | | | ● | | | | | | | | | ● | | | |
| CHARLTON CLINIC (HM04033) | | | | | | | | | | ● | ● | | ● | | | |
| CHURCHMAN & ASS REG OST (HM04475) | | | | | | | | | | ● | | | ● | | | |
| CHURCHMAN, BERYL (HM04478) | | | | | | | | | | ● | | | ● | | | |
| COLEBROOK, G (HM04820) | | | | | | | | | | | | | | | | |
| COOPER, A R (HM05088) | | | | | | ● | | | | | | | | | | |
| CT & IM LEITH (HM05534) | | | | | | | ● | ● | ● | ● | | ● | ● | | | |
| DENT, TRISH () | | | ● | | | | | | | | | | ● | | | |
| EVENKEEL (HM06997) | | | | | | ● | | | | | | | ● | | | |
| FELIXSTOWE PHYSIO PRACTICE (HM07203) | | | ● | | ● | | | | | | | | ● | | | |
| FRESHFIELDS OF ALDEBURGH (HM07737) | ● | ● | ● | ● | | ● | ● | ● | ● | ● | ● | ● | ● | ● | | |
| GREEN FARM CLINIC (HM08435) | | | ● | | | | | | | ● | | ● | ● | | | ● |
| GROSVENOR PHYSIOTHERAPY CLINIC (HM08597) | | | | | ● | | | | | | | | ● | | | |
| HARDY, MICHAEL (HM08984) | | | | | | | | | | | | | | | | |
| HEALING CONNECTIONS (HM09330) | ● | ● | ● | | | | ● | ● | ● | ● | ● | ● | ● | ● | | |
| HEALING HANDS (HM09336) | | | | | | | | | | ● | ● | | ● | | | |
| HITCHINS, ROSIE (HM09847) | | | | | | | | | | | | | | | | |
| HOPKINS, C J (HM10147) | | | | | | | | | | | ● | | | | | |

| Business | Period Problems | Phobias | Piles | PMT | Pneumonia | Postural Problems | Pregnancy Help | Prostate Problems | Psoriasis | Raynaud's Disease | Recurrent Infections | Restless Legs | Rheumatoid Arthritis | Schizophrenia | Sciatica | Sexual Problems |
|---|---|---|---|---|---|---|---|---|---|---|---|---|---|---|---|---|
| NARAYAN, MAMTA (HM14486) | | | | | | | | | | | | | | | | |
| NORBURY, SUSAN (HM14990) | ● | ● | ● | ● | ● | | ● | ● | ● | ● | ● | ● | ● | ● | ● | ● |
| O'CALLAGHAN, STEVE (HM15193) | | | | | | | | | | | | | ● | | ● | |
| PEACEHAVEN AROMATHERAPY (HM15877) | ● | | | ● | | | ● | | ● | | ● | | ● | | ● | |
| PRIORS PODIATRY PRACTICE (HM16629) | | | | | | | | | ● | ● | | ● | ● | | | |
| ROBERTS, KATE (HM17418) | | | | | | | | | | | | | | | | |
| STAFFORD CHIROPRACTIC CLINIC (HM19108) | | | | | | | | | | | | | ● | | ● | |
| STAFFORDSHIRE MCTIMONEY (HM19111) | ● | | | | | | ● | | | | | | ● | | ● | |
| SUSAN JAMES CONSULTANCY (HM19527) | ● | | | ● | | | | | | | | | | | | |
| TAMWORTH PHYSIOTHERAPY CLINIC (HM19675) | | | | | | | | | | | | | | | | |
| TE NOSCE (HM19803) | ● | | ● | ● | | | ● | ● | ● | ● | ● | ● | ● | | ● | |
| TUNSTALL HYPNOTHERAPY CENTRE (HM20401) | | | | | | | | | | | | | | | | ● |
| WHITBY, S E (HM21334) | | | | | | | | | | | | | | | | |
| YARNFIELD PARK- HEALTH/SPORTS (HM21989) | ● | ● | ● | ● | ● | | ● | ● | ● | ● | ● | ● | ● | ● | ● | ● |
| **SUFFOLK** | | | | | | | | | | | | | | | | |
| AJNA (HM00457) | | | | | | | | | | | | | | | | |
| BODY MECHANICS THERAPY CLINIC (HM02599) | | | | | | | | | | | | | | | | |
| CHARLTON CLINIC (HM04033) | | | | | | | | | | | | ● | ● | | ● | |
| CHURCHMAN & ASS REG OST (HM04475) | | | | | | | | | | | | | | | ● | |
| CHURCHMAN, BERYL (HM04478) | | | | | | | | | | | | | | | ● | |
| COLEBROOK, G (HM04820) | ● | | | | | | | | | | | | | | | |
| COOPER, A R (HM05088) | | | | | | | | | | | | | | | | |
| CT & IM LEITH (HM05534) | | | | | | | | ● | ● | | | ● | | | ● | |
| DENT, TRISH () | ● | | | ● | | | | | | | | | ● | | ● | |
| EVENKEEL (HM06997) | | | | | | | | | | | | | | | | |
| FELIXSTOWE PHYSIO PRACTICE (HM07203) | | | | | | | | | | | | | | | | |
| FRESHFIELDS OF ALDEBURGH (HM07737) | ● | ● | ● | ● | | | ● | ● | ● | | ● | ● | ● | | ● | |
| GREEN FARM CLINIC (HM08435) | | | | | | | | | | | | ● | ● | | ● | |
| GROSVENOR PHYSIOTHERAPY CLINIC (HM08597) | | | | | | | | | | | | | | | | |
| HARDY, MICHAEL (HM08984) | | | | ● | | | | | | | | | | | | |
| HEALING CONNECTIONS (HM09330) | ● | ● | ● | ● | ● | | ● | ● | ● | ● | ● | | ● | ● | ● | |
| HEALING HANDS (HM09336) | ● | ● | ● | ● | | | | ● | | | | | ● | | | ● |
| HITCHINS, ROSIE (HM09847) | | | | | | | | | | | | | | | | |
| HOPKINS, C J (HM10147) | | ● | | | | | ● | | | | | ● | | | | |

# I - S Conditions treated at Practices/Businesses

Business by County with Reference no.

| Business | Insomnia | Irritable Bowel Syndrome | Itching | Jet Lag | Joint Pain | Kidney Complaints | Lactose Intolerance | Laryngitis | Lethargy | Liver Disorders | Low Blood Pressure | Lung Problems | ME | Menopause | Migraine | Motion Sickness | Mouth Disorders | Mouth Ulcers | Multiple Sclerosis | Muscular Dystrophy | Musculo-skeletal | Nail Health | Nausea | Nerve Disorders | Nervous Disorders | Neuralgia |
|---|---|---|---|---|---|---|---|---|---|---|---|---|---|---|---|---|---|---|---|---|---|---|---|---|---|---|
| INNER SPACE SUFFOLK (HM10641) | ● | ● | ● | | ● | | | | | | | | | | ● | ● | | | | | | | | | | ● |
| IPSWICH CHIROPRACTIC CLINIC (HM10714) | | ● | | | ● | | ● | | | | | | | ● | ● | | | | | | | | ● | | ● | |
| IPSWICH PHYSIOTHERAPY PRACTICE (HM10715) | | | | | ● | | | | | | | | | | | | | | ● | | | | | | | |
| LAVENDER LODGE CLINIC (HM12023) | | ● | | | ● | | | | ● | | | | ● | | | | | | | | | | | | | ● |
| MALAROC (HM12961) | | | | | ● | | | | | | | | | | | | | | | | | | | | | |
| MANOR HOUSE (HM13039) | | | | | ● | | | | | | | | | | | | | | | | | | | | | |
| MARK CHURCH AROMATHERAPY (HM13106) | ● | ● | | | | | | | | | | | ● | ● | | | | | | | | | | | | |
| MASSAGE FOR HEALTH (HM13260) | | | | | ● | | | | | | | | ● | | ● | | | | | | | | | | | |
| MCTIMONEY CHIROPRACTIC CLINIC (HM13607) | | ● | ● | | ● | | | | | | | | | | ● | | | | | | | | | | ● | |
| MOHAN, TERRY (HM14046) | ● | ● | | | ● | | | | | | | | ● | | | | | | | | | | | | ● | ● |
| NATURECURES (HM14684) | ● | ● | | | ● | | | | ● | ● | | ● | ● | | ● | | | | | | | | ● | ● | ● | ● |
| NOAH'S ARK PSYCHOTHERAPY (HM14964) | ● | ● | | | | | | | ● | | | | ● | | ● | | | | | | | | ● | | | |
| PAGE, COLIN J (HM15570) | ● | ● | | | | | | | | | | | | | | | | | | | | | | | ● | |
| PAROLIN, PAUL (HM15728) | ● | ● | | | ● | | | | | | | | ● | | ● | | | | ● | | | | | | | |
| SHEROMA THERAPY (HM18435) | | | | | | | | | | | | | | | | | | | | | | | | | | |
| SPALDING, JULIE (HM18955) | ● | ● | | ● | ● | | | | ● | | | | ● | | ● | ● | | | ● | | | | ● | | ● | |
| SPRINGFIELD LODGE HEALTH CARE (HM19052) | ● | ● | ● | ● | ● | ● | ● | ● | ● | ● | ● | ● | ● | ● | ● | ● | ● | ● | ● | ● | | ● | ● | ● | ● | ● |
| ST MARYS PRACTICE (HM19088) | | | | | ● | | | | | | | | | | | | | | | | | | | | | |
| STEPHEN GORDON (HM19197) | | | | | | | | | | | | | | ● | ● | ● | ● | ● | ● | ● | | ● | ● | ● | ● | |
| STOWMARKET OSTEOPATHS (HM19363) | | | | | ● | | | | | | | | | | ● | | | | | | | | | ● | | ● |
| SUDBURY CHIROPRACTIC CLINIC (HM19462) | | | | | ● | | | | | | | | | | | | | | | | | | | ● | | ● |
| WEI CLINIC (HM21111) | ● | ● | ● | | ● | | | | ● | | ● | | ● | ● | ● | | | | ● | | | | ● | | ● | ● |
| WOOLPITPHYSIO (HM21881) | | | | | ● | | | | | | | | | | | | | | ● | | | | | | | |
| **SURREY** | | | | | | | | | | | | | | | | | | | | | | | | | | |
| ACE NUTRITION (HM00157) | ● | ● | ● | | ● | ● | ● | | | | ● | | ● | ● | ● | ● | | | ● | | | ● | ● | ● | ● | |
| ACORN HEALTH CLINIC (HM00177) | ● | | | | ● | | | | | | | | | ● | ● | | | | | | | | | | | |
| ACORN THERAPY CENTRE (HM00181) | ● | ● | | | | | | | ● | | | | | | ● | | | | | | | | | | ● | |
| ACUHERBAL CHINESE MEDICINE (HM00214) | | ● | | | | | | | | | | | | | ● | | | | | | | | | | | |
| ASCOT HOMEOPATHIC CLINIC (HM01177) | ● | ● | ● | ● | ● | ● | ● | ● | ● | ● | ● | ● | ● | ● | ● | ● | ● | ● | ● | | | | | | ● | |
| ASHTEAD CHARTERED PHYSIO SV (HM01230) | | | | | ● | | | | | | | | | | | | | | | | | | | | | |
| ASHTEAD CLINIC (HM01232) | | | | | ● | | | | | | | | | | ● | | | | | | | | | | | |
| ASTON CLINIC (HM01301) | | | | | ● | | | | | | | | | ● | ● | | | | | | | | ● | | | |
| ASW ALLERGY CONSULTANTS (HM01305) | ● | ● | ● | | ● | ● | ● | | ● | ● | ● | ● | ● | ● | ● | | | | | | | | ● | | ● | |
| AVENUE PHYSIO & SPORTS CLNC (HM01390) | | | | | ● | | | | | | | | | | | | | | ● | | | | | | | |

| Business | Obesity | Osteoporosis | Pain | Palpitations | Panic Attacks | Parkinson's Disease | Period Problems | Phobias | Piles | PMT | Pneumonia | Postural Problems | Pregnancy Help | Prostate Problems | Psoriasis | Raynaud's Disease | Recurrent Infections | Restless Legs | Rheumatoid Arthritis | Schizophrenia | Sciatica | Sexual Problems |
|---|---|---|---|---|---|---|---|---|---|---|---|---|---|---|---|---|---|---|---|---|---|---|
| INNER SPACE SUFFOLK (HM10641) | | | ● | | | | | | | | | | | | | | | ● | ● | | ● | |
| IPSWICH CHIROPRACTIC CLINIC (HM10714) | ● | | ● | | | | | | ● | ● | | | | | ● | | | ● | | | ● | |
| IPSWICH PHYSIOTHERAPY PRACTICE (HM10715) | | | ● | | | | | | | | | | | | | | | | | | | |
| LAVENDER LODGE CLINIC (HM12023) | | | ● | | | | | | | | | | | | | | | ● | | | ● | |
| MALAROC (HM12961) | | | | | | | | | | | | | | | | | | | ● | | ● | |
| MANOR HOUSE (HM13039) | | | ● | | | | | | | | | | | | | | | | | | ● | |
| MARK CHURCH AROMATHERAPY (HM13106) | | | ● | | | | ● | | | ● | | | ● | | ● | | | | | | | |
| MASSAGE FOR HEALTH (HM13260) | | | ● | | | | | | | | | | | | | | | | | | ● | |
| MCTIMONEY CHIROPRACTIC CLINIC (HM13607) | | | ● | | | | | | | | | | | | | | | | ● | | ● | |
| MOHAN, TERRY (HM14046) | | | ● | | | | | ● | | | | | | | | | | | | | ● | |
| NATURECURES (HM14684) | ● | ● | ● | | | | ● | ● | | ● | | | | | ● | | | ● | ● | | ● | ● |
| NOAH'S ARK PSYCHOTHERAPY (HM14964) | ● | | ● | | | | | ● | | | | | | | | | | | | | | ● |
| PAGE, COLIN J (HM15570) | | | | | | | | ● | | | | | | | | | | | | | | |
| PAROLIN, PAUL (HM15728) | | ● | ● | | | | | ● | | | | | | | | | | | ● | | ● | |
| SHEROMA THERAPY (HM18435) | | | ● | | | ● | | ● | | | | | | | | | | ● | | | ● | |
| SPALDING, JULIE (HM18955) | ● | ● | ● | ● | | | ● | ● | | ● | | | | | ● | | ● | ● | | | | ● |
| SPRINGFIELD LODGE HEALTH CARE (HM19052) | ● | ● | ● | ● | | ● | ● | ● | ● | ● | ● | | ● | ● | ● | ● | ● | ● | ● | ● | ● | ● |
| ST MARYS PRACTICE (HM19088) | | | ● | | | | | | | | | | | | | | | | | | ● | |
| STEPHEN GORDON (HM19197) | | | | | | | | | | | | | | | | | | | | | | |
| STOWMARKET OSTEOPATHS (HM19363) | | | ● | | | | | | | | | | | | | | ● | | | | ● | |
| SUDBURY CHIROPRACTIC CLINIC (HM19462) | | ● | | | | | | | | | | | | | | | | | | | | |
| WEI CLINIC (HM21111) | ● | ● | ● | ● | | | ● | | | ● | | | ● | | | ● | ● | ● | ● | | ● | |
| WOOLPITPHYSIO (HM21881) | | | | | | | | | | | | | | | | | | | | | | |
| **SURREY** | | | | | | | | | | | | | | | | | | | | | | |
| ACE NUTRITION (HM00157) | | | ● | ● | | | ● | | | ● | | | ● | ● | ● | ● | ● | ● | ● | | ● | |
| ACORN HEALTH CLINIC (HM00177) | | | ● | | | | | | | | | | | | | | | | | | | |
| ACORN THERAPY CENTRE (HM00181) | ● | | ● | | ● | | ● | ● | | ● | | | ● | | | | | | | | | ● |
| ACUHERBAL CHINESE MEDICINE (HM00214) | | | | | | | | | | | | | | | | | | | | | | |
| ASCOT HOMEOPATHIC CLINIC (HM01177) | ● | ● | ● | ● | | ● | ● | ● | ● | ● | | | ● | ● | ● | ● | ● | ● | | | ● | ● |
| ASHTEAD CHARTERED PHYSIO SV (HM01230) | | ● | ● | | | | | | | | | | ● | | | | | | ● | | ● | |
| ASHTEAD CLINIC (HM01232) | | | ● | | | | | | | | | | | | | | | | | | ● | |
| ASTON CLINIC (HM01301) | | | ● | | | | ● | | | ● | | | | | | | | | | | ● | |
| ASW ALLERGY CONSULTANTS (HM01305) | | ● | ● | ● | | | ● | | ● | ● | | | | ● | ● | ● | | | ● | | | |
| AVENUE PHYSIO & SPORTS CLNC (HM01390) | | | | | | | | | | | | | | | | | | | | | | |

# I - S Conditions treated at Practices/Businesses

| Business by County with Reference no. | Insomnia | Irritable Bowel Syndrome | Itching | Jet Lag | Joint Pain | Kidney Complaints | Lactose Intolerance | Laryngitis | Lethargy | Liver Disorders | Low Blood Pressure | Lung Problems | ME | Menopause | Migraine | Motion Sickness | Mouth Disorders | Mouth Ulcers | Multiple Sclerosis | Muscular Dystrophy | Musculo-skeletal | Nail Health | Nausea | Nerve Disorders | Nervous Disorders | Neuralgia | Obesity | Osteoporosis | Pain | Palpitations | Panic Attacks | Parkinson's Disease | Period Problems | Phobias | Piles | PMT | Pneumonia | Postural Problems | Pregnancy Help | Prostate Problems | Psoriasis | Raynaud's Disease | Recurrent Infections | Restless Legs | Rheumatoid Arthritis | Schizophrenia | Sciatica | Sexual Problems |
|---|---|---|---|---|---|---|---|---|---|---|---|---|---|---|---|---|---|---|---|---|---|---|---|---|---|---|---|---|---|---|---|---|---|---|---|---|---|---|---|---|---|---|---|---|---|---|---|---|
| BACK TO HEALTH (HM01508) | | ●| | | ●| | | | | | | | ●| | ●| | | | | | | | | ●| ●| | | | ●| | | | | | | | | | | | | | | | | | ●| |
| BACK TO HEALTH - GUILDFORD (HM01511) | | ●| | | ●| | | | | | | | ●| | ●| | | | | | | | | ●| ●| | | | ●| | | | | | | | | | | | | | | | | | ●| |
| BACK TO HEALTH - RICHMOND (HM01514) | | ●| | | ●| | | | | | | | ●| | ●| | | | | | | | | ●| ●| | | | ●| | | | | | | | | | | | | | | | | | ●| |
| BACK TO HEALTH - SUTTON (HM01515) | | ●| | | ●| | | | | | | | ●| | ●| | | | | | | | | ●| ●| | | | ●| | | | | | | | | | | | | | | | | | ●| |
| BACKCARE CLINIC (HM01527) | | | | | ●| | | | | | | | | | | | | | | | | | | | | ●| | ●| ●| | | | | | | | | | | | | | | | | | ●| |
| BAILEY, L J (HM01551) | | | | | ●| | | | | | | | | | ●| | | | | | | | | ●| | | | ●| ●| | | | | | | | | | | | | ●| | ●| ●| | ●| |
| BARNES, A K R (HM01743) | | | | | ●| | | | | | | | | | ●| | | | | | | | | | | ●| | | ●| | | | | | | | | | | | | | | | | | ●| |
| BARNSTEAD VILLAGE CLINIC (HM01769) | ●| | | | ●| | | | | | | | | | ●| | | | | | | | ●| | | | | | ●| | | | ●| | | | | | | | | | | | | | ●| |
| BATCHELOR, C (HM01863) | | | | | | | | | | | | | | | ●| | | | | | | | | | | | | | | | | | | | | | | | | | | | | | | | | |
| BAXTER, STEPHEN (HM01933) | | | | | | | | | | | | | ●| | | | | | | | | | | | | | | | ●| | | | | | | | | | | | | | | | | | | |
| BIGWOOD, SIMON (HM02295) | | | | | ●| | | | | | | | ●| ●| | | | | | | | | | | | | | | ●| | | | | | | | | | | | | | | | | | | |
| BIODYNAMICS (HM02332) | ●| ●| ●| ●| ●| ●| ●| ●| ●| ●| ●| ●| ●| ●| ●| ●| ●| ●| ●| ●| | ●| ●| ●| ●| ●| ●| ●| ●| ●| | ●| ●| ●| ●| ●| ●| | | ●| ●| ●| ●| ●| ●| ●| ●| ●|
| BOURNE HEALTH (HM02753) | | ●| | | | | | | | | ●| | ●| | ●| | | | | | | | | | | | | | ●| | | | | | | | | | ●| | | | | | ●| | | |
| BRABANT HOUSE CLINIC (HM02830) | ●| ●| ●| | ●| | ●| ●| ●| | | | ●| ●| ●| | | | | | | | ●| | | ●| ●| ●| ●| ●| | | ●| ●| | ●| | | | | ●| | ●| | ●| | ●| |
| BREWSTER, DAVID J (HM02980) | ●| ●| | | | | | | | | | | | | | | | | | | | | | | ●| | ●| | ●| ●| | | | ●| | | | | | | | | | | | | | ●|
| BST FOUNDATION (HM03294) | | | | | | | | | | | | | | | | | | | | | | | | | | | | | | | | | | ●| | | | | | | | | | | | | | |
| CAMBERLEY NATURAL THERAPY CTRE (HM03566) | ●| ●| | | | | | | ●| | | | ●| ●| ●| | | ●| | | | | | | | ●| | | | | | | ●| | ●| ●| | | | | | | | | ●| | ●| |
| CARLTON CLINIC (HM03700) | ●| ●| ●| ●| ●| ●| ●| ●| ●| ●| ●| ●| ●| ●| ●| ●| ●| ●| ●| ●| | ●| ●| ●| ●| ●| | ●| ●| ●| | ●| ●| ●| ●| ●| ●| | | ●| ●| ●| ●| ●| ●| ●| ●| |
| CATERHAM CHIROPRACTIC CLINIC (HM03853) | | ●| | | ●| | | | | | | | | | | | | | | | | | | ●| | | | | ●| | | | | | | | | | | | | | | | | | ●| |
| CHART LANE CLINIC (HM04039) | ●| ●| ●| ●| ●| ●| ●| ●| ●| ●| ●| ●| ●| ●| ●| ●| ●| ●| ●| ●| | ●| ●| ●| ●| ●| ●| ●| ●| ●| | ●| ●| ●| ●| ●| ●| | ●| ●| ●| ●| ●| ●| ●| ●| ●| ●|
| CHI CLINIC (HM04148) | ●| ●| ●| ●| ●| ●| ●| ●| ●| ●| ●| ●| ●| ●| ●| ●| ●| ●| ●| ●| | ●| ●| ●| ●| ●| ●| ●| ●| ●| | ●| ●| ●| ●| ●| ●| | ●| ●| ●| ●| ●| ●| ●| ●| ●| ●|
| CHIROPRACTIC CENTRE (HM04382) | | ●| | | ●| | | | | | | | ●| | | | | | | | | | | ●| | | | ●| ●| | | | | | | | | | | | | | | | | | | |
| CHRISTINE KEY HYPNOTHERAPIST (HM04447) | ●| ●| | | | | | | | | | | | | | | | | | | | | | | ●| | | | | | | | | ●| | | | | | | | | | | | | | ●|
| CITISPORT (HM04483) | | ●| | | ●| | ●| | | ●| | | ●| ●| ●| | | | | | | | | | | ●| ●| ●| ●| | | | ●| | | ●| | | | ●| | | ●| ●| ●| | ●| |
| CLEMENTS, J (HM04644) | ●| ●| | | ●| | | | ●| ●| ●| | | | ●| | | | ●| ●| | | | | | | | | ●| | | | | | | | | | | | | | | | | | | |
| COHEN, MICHAEL (HM04793) | ●| | | | | | | | | | | | | | | | | | | | | | | | ●| | ●| | | | | | | ●| | | | | | | | | | | | | | ●|
| CONFIDENTIAL COUNSELLING SVS (HM04975) | | | | | | | | | | | | | | | | | | | | | | | | | | | | | | | | | | ●| | | | | | | | | | | | | | |
| COX, JULIET (HM05307) | ●| | | | ●| | | | ●| | | | ●| | ●| | | | | | | | | ●| ●| | | ●| ●| | | | | | | | | | ●| | | | | ●| ●| | ●| |
| CROYDON HEALING CENTRE (HM05515) | ●| ●| ●| ●| ●| ●| ●| ●| ●| ●| ●| ●| ●| ●| ●| ●| ●| ●| ●| ●| | ●| ●| ●| ●| ●| ●| ●| ●| ●| | ●| ●| ●| ●| ●| ●| | ●| ●| ●| ●| ●| ●| ●| ●| ●| ●|
| CROYDON HYPNOTHERAPY (HM05516) | ●| ●| | | | | | | | | | | ●| | ●| | | | | | | ●| ●| | | | ●| | ●| | | | ●| ●| | ●| | | | | | | | | | ●| | ●|
| CUMMINS, ROZ (HM05617) | ●| ●| | | | ●| | | | | ●| | ●| ●| ●| | | | ●| | | | ●| | | | | | ●| ●| | | ●| | | ●| | | | | | | | ●| ●| | ●| |
| DORCHESTER HOUSE OSTEOPATHY (HM06195) | ●| ●| ●| ●| ●| ●| ●| ●| ●| ●| ●| ●| ●| ●| ●| ●| ●| ●| ●| ●| | ●| ●| ●| ●| ●| ●| ●| ●| ●| | ●| ●| ●| ●| ●| ●| | ●| ●| ●| ●| ●| ●| ●| ●| ●| ●|
| DORKING, PAUL (HM06200) | | | | | | | | | | | | | | | | | | | | | | | | | | | ●| | ●| | | | | ●| | ●| | | | | | | | | | | | ●|
| EDWARDS HEALTH CLINIC (HM06639) | ●| ●| ●| | | | | | ●| | | | | | ●| | | | | | | ●| ●| | ●| ●| ●| | ●| ●| | | ●| ●| | | | | | | | | | | | | | ●|

# I - S Conditions treated at Practices/Businesses

| Business by County with Reference no. | Insomnia | Irritable Bowel Syndrome | Itching | Jet Lag | Joint Pain | Kidney Complaints | Lactose Intolerance | Laryngitis | Lethargy | Liver Disorders | Low Blood Pressure | Lung Problems | ME | Menopause | Migraine | Motion Sickness | Mouth Disorders | Mouth Ulcers | Multiple Sclerosis | Muscular Dystrophy | Musculo-skeletal | Nail Health | Nausea | Nerve Disorders |
|---|---|---|---|---|---|---|---|---|---|---|---|---|---|---|---|---|---|---|---|---|---|---|---|---|
| ENOCK-SHORE, ANGELA (HM06845) | ● | ● | ● | | | | | | ● | | ● | | | | ● | | | | | | | ● | | |
| EPSOM CHIROPRACTIC CLINIC (HM06857) | | ● | | | ● | | | | | | | | | | | | | | | | | | | ● |
| EQUILIBRIUM OSTEOPATHIC (HM06876) | ● | ● | | | ● | | ● | | | | | | ● | ● | ● | | | | ● | | | | | ● |
| FARNBOROUGH CHIRO CLINIC (HM07111) | | | | | ● | | | | | | | | | | ● | | | | | | | | | |
| FEATHER, A J (HM07155) | | | | | ● | | | | | | | | | | | | | | | | | | | |
| GATEWAYS CENTRE (HM07928) | ● | | | | | | | | | | | | | ● | | | | | | | | | | |
| GAUVAIN, TONY (HM07934) | ● | | | | | | | | | | | | | | | | | | | | | ● | | ● |
| GLAISTER, BRIAN (DR) (HM08120) | | ● | | | | | | | | | | | | | | | | | | | | | | |
| GODDARD, TERRI (HM08180) | ● | | | ● | ● | | | | ● | | | | ● | | ● | | | | | | | | | |
| GOODLIFE NATURAL HEALTH CENTRE (HM08256) | | | | | ● | | | | | | | | | | | | | | | | | | | |
| GORDON, SARAH (HM08282) | ● | ● | | | | | | | | | | | ● | ● | ● | | | | | | | | | |
| GRAVELL, NICOLA (HM08401) | | | | | | | | | | | | | ● | | ● | | | | | | | | | |
| GUILDFORD PHYSIO & SPORTS (HM08632) | | | | | ● | | | | | | | | | | | | | | | | | | | |
| HAM CHIROPRACTIC CLINIC (HM08822) | | | | | ● | ● | | | | | | | | | ● | | | | | | | | ● | |
| HANDS ON HEALTH (HM08911) | | | | | ● | | | | | | | | | | ● | | | | | | | | | ● |
| HANFORD, S P (HM08925) | ● | | | | ● | | | | | | | | | | | | | | | | | | | |
| HARDY, JACK E (HM08981) | | | | | | | | | | | | | | | | | | | | | | | | |
| HARTLEY, GILL (HM09140) | | ● | | | ● | | | | | | | | | | ● | | | | | | | | | |
| HEAVEN MOUNTAIN TAIJI QUAN (HM09472) | | | | | ● | | | | | | | | | | | | | | | | | | | |
| HELIANTHUS PRACTICE (HM09518) | ● | ● | ● | ● | ● | ● | ● | ● | ● | ● | ● | ● | ● | ● | ● | ● | ● | ● | | | | ● | ● | ● |
| HERBAL KING (HM09628) | | | | | | | | | | | ● | | | | ● | | | | | | | | | |
| HERBALS (HM09647) | ● | ● | ● | ● | ● | ● | ● | ● | ● | ● | ● | ● | ● | ● | ● | ● | ● | ● | ● | | | ● | ● | ● |
| HILL, CHARLOTTE (HM09774) | | | | | ● | | | | | | | | ● | | | | | | | | | | | ● |
| HILLVIEW PHYSIO & SPORTS CLNC (HM09809) | | | | | ● | | | | | | | | | | | | | | ● | | | | | |
| HOLISTIC CENTRE (HM09949) | ● | ● | ● | ● | ● | ● | ● | ● | ● | ● | ● | ● | ● | ● | ● | ● | ● | ● | ● | ● | | ● | ● | ● |
| HOLISTIC HEALTH CENTRE (HM09971) | ● | | | | ● | | | | | | | | | ● | ● | | | | | | | | ● | |
| HOPPER, C A (HM10156) | | | | | | | | | | | | | | | | | | | | | | | | |
| HUMAN FOCUS RETURN TO WORK (HM10362) | | | | | ● | | | | | | | | ● | | | | | | | | | | | |
| INGLEDALE NATURAL HEALTH CTRE (HM10621) | | | | | ● | | | | | | | | | | | | | | | | | | | |
| INTEGRAL HEALTH (HM10690) | ● | ● | ● | ● | ● | ● | ● | ● | ● | ● | ● | ● | ● | ● | ● | ● | ● | ● | ● | ● | | ● | ● | ● |
| J V ASSOCIATES (HM10803) | ● | ● | | | | ● | ● | | ● | | ● | | ● | | ● | | | | ● | ● | | | ● | |
| KENT CLINIC OF NATURAL MED (HM11514) | ● | ● | ● | ● | ● | ● | ● | ● | ● | ● | ● | ● | ● | ● | ● | ● | ● | ● | ● | ● | | ● | ● | ● |
| KEW CHIROPRACTIC CLINIC (HM11575) | | | | | ● | | | | | | | | | | ● | | | | | | | | | |
| KINGSTON NATURAL HEALING CTRE (HM11677) | ● | ● | | ● | ● | | ● | | ● | | | ● | ● | ● | ● | | | | ● | | | | | |

| Business by County with Reference no. | Nervous Disorders | Neuralgia | Obesity | Osteoporosis | Pain | Palpitations | Panic Attacks | Parkinson's Disease | Period Problems | Phobias | Piles | PMT | Pneumonia | Postural Problems | Pregnancy Help | Prostate Problems | Psoriasis | Raynaud's Disease | Recurrent Infections | Restless Legs | Rheumatoid Arthritis | Schizophrenia | Sciatica | Sexual Problems |
|---|---|---|---|---|---|---|---|---|---|---|---|---|---|---|---|---|---|---|---|---|---|---|---|---|
| ENOCK-SHORE, ANGELA (HM06845) | ● | | | | | ● | | | ● | ● | | ● | | | | | ● | | | ● | | | | ● |
| EPSOM CHIROPRACTIC CLINIC (HM06857) | | | | | ● | | | | | | | | | | | | | | | | | | ● | |
| EQUILIBRIUM OSTEOPATHIC (HM06876) | | ● | ● | ● | ● | | | | ● | | ● | ● | | | ● | | | | | | ● | | ● | |
| FARNBOROUGH CHIRO CLINIC (HM07111) | | ● | | | ● | | | | ● | | | | | | | | | | | | | | ● | |
| FEATHER, A J (HM07155) | | | | | | | | | | | | | | | | | | | | | | | | |
| GATEWAYS CENTRE (HM07928) | ● | | | | | | | | | ● | | | | | | | | | | | | | | |
| GAUVAIN, TONY (HM07934) | | | | | | | | | | ● | | | | | | | | | | | | | | ● |
| GLAISTER, BRIAN (DR) (HM08120) | ● | | | | | | | | | ● | | | | | | | | | | | | | | |
| GODDARD, TERRI (HM08180) | | | | | ● | ● | | | ● | | | ● | | | | | | | | ● | | | ● | |
| GOODLIFE NATURAL HEALTH CENTRE (HM08256) | | | | | ● | | | | | | | | | | | | | | | | | | ● | |
| GORDON, SARAH (HM08282) | | | | | ● | | | | | | | ● | | | | | | | | | | | | |
| GRAVELL, NICOLA (HM08401) | ● | | ● | | ● | | | | ● | ● | | ● | | | ● | | ● | | | | | | | |
| GUILDFORD PHYSIO & SPORTS (HM08632) | | | | | | | | | | | | | | | | | | | | | | | | |
| HAM CHIROPRACTIC CLINIC (HM08822) | | | | | ● | | | | | | | | | | | | | | | | | | ● | |
| HANDS ON HEALTH (HM08911) | | | | | ● | | | | | | | | | | ● | | | | | | | | ● | |
| HANFORD, S P (HM08925) | | | | | | | | | | | | | | | | | | | | | | | ● | |
| HARDY, JACK E (HM08981) | | | ● | | | | ● | | | ● | | | | | | | | | | | | | | |
| HARTLEY, GILL (HM09140) | | | | | ● | | | | | | | | | | | | | | | | | | | |
| HEAVEN MOUNTAIN TAIJI QUAN (HM09472) | | | | ● | | | | | | | | | | | | | | | | | | | | |
| HELIANTHUS PRACTICE (HM09518) | ● | ● | ● | ● | ● | ● | | | ● | ● | ● | ● | ● | | ● | ● | ● | ● | ● | ● | ● | | ● | ● |
| HERBAL KING (HM09628) | | ● | | | | | | | | | | | | | ● | | ● | | | | ● | | | |
| HERBALS (HM09647) | ● | ● | ● | ● | ● | ● | | ● | ● | | ● | ● | ● | | ● | ● | ● | ● | ● | ● | ● | | ● | ● |
| HILL, CHARLOTTE (HM09774) | | | | ● | ● | | | | | | | | | ● | | | | | | | | | ● | |
| HILLVIEW PHYSIO & SPORTS CLNC (HM09809) | | | | | ● | | | | | | | | | | | | | | | | | | | |
| HOLISTIC CENTRE (HM09949) | ● | ● | ● | ● | ● | ● | | ● | ● | ● | ● | ● | ● | | ● | ● | ● | ● | ● | ● | ● | ● | ● | ● |
| HOLISTIC HEALTH CENTRE (HM09971) | | | | | ● | | | | | | | | | | | | | | | | | | | |
| HOPPER, C A (HM10156) | ● | | | | | | | | | | | | | | | | | | | | | | | |
| HUMAN FOCUS RETURN TO WORK (HM10362) | | | | | ● | | | | | | | | | | | | | | | | | | | |
| INGLEDALE NATURAL HEALTH CTRE (HM10621) | | | | | ● | | | | | | | | | | | | | | | | | | ● | |
| INTEGRAL HEALTH (HM10690) | ● | ● | ● | ● | ● | ● | | ● | ● | ● | ● | ● | ● | | ● | ● | ● | ● | ● | ● | ● | ● | ● | ● |
| J V ASSOCIATES (HM10803) | | | | | ● | | | ● | | | | | | | | | | | | | ● | | | |
| KENT CLINIC OF NATURAL MED (HM11514) | ● | ● | ● | ● | ● | ● | | | ● | | ● | | ● | | ● | ● | ● | ● | ● | ● | ● | ● | ● | ● |
| KEW CHIROPRACTIC CLINIC (HM11575) | | ● | | | ● | | | | | | | | | | | | ● | ● | | ● | ● | | ● | |
| KINGSTON NATURAL HEALING CTRE (HM11677) | ● | ● | ● | | ● | ● | | | | ● | | ● | | | ● | | ● | | ● | | ● | | ● | |

www.healthmyself.com

# I - S Conditions treated at Practices/Businesses

Business by County with Reference no.

| Business | Insomnia | Irritable Bowel Syndrome | Itching | Jet Lag | Joint Pain | Kidney Complaints | Lactose Intolerance | Laryngitis | Lethargy | Liver Disorders | Low Blood Pressure | Lung Problems | ME | Menopause | Migraine | Motion Sickness |
|---|---|---|---|---|---|---|---|---|---|---|---|---|---|---|---|---|
| KINGSTON OSTEOPATHS (HM11679) | | ● | | | ● | | | | | | | | ● | | ● | |
| KOLTHAMMER, JOHN (HM11780) | | | | | ● | | | | | | | | | | ● | |
| LEATHERHEAD CHIRO CLINIC (HM12114) | | | | | | | | | | | | | | | ● | |
| LONDON SPINE AND JOINT CLINIC (HM12610) | | | | | ● | | | | | | | | | | | |
| LOW, ROYSTON (HM12688) | ● | ● | | | ● | ● | | | | ● | | ● | | | ● | |
| MARKS, DARREN HYPNOTHERAPY (HM13120) | | | | | | | | | | | | | | | | |
| MARSON, JOY (HM13178) | | ● | | | | | ● | | ● | | | | ● | ● | ● | |
| MEEKS, FIONA (HM13683) | | | | | | ● | | | | | | | | | ● | |
| MEENEGHAN, TOM (HM13685) | ● | ● | ● | ● | ● | ● | | ● | ● | ● | ● | ● | ● | ● | ● | ● |
| MILFORD MASSAGE PRACTICE (HM13863) | | | | ● | | | | | | | | | | | ● | |
| MILLER CONSULTANCY (HM13880) | ● | | | ● | ● | | | ● | ● | | | | ● | ● | ● | ● |
| MIND AND BODY (HM13958) | ● | ● | | | ● | | | | ● | | ● | | ● | ● | ● | |
| MIST, CORINNE (HM13996) | ● | ● | | | | | | | | | ● | | | ● | ● | |
| NATURAL HEALING CENTRE (HM14541) | ● | ● | | | ● | ● | | | | | ● | | ● | ● | ● | |
| NATURAL HEALING CLINIC (HM14550) | | | | | ● | | | | | | | | | | | |
| NATURAL HEALTH PRACTICE (HM14594) | | ● | | | ● | | | | | | | | | | | |
| NATURAL SLEEP FOUNDATION (HM14624) | ● | | | | | | | | | | | | | | | |
| NICOLA FRY-HEALTH & BEAUTY (HM14927) | ● | ● | | ● | ● | | | | ● | | | | ● | ● | ● | |
| OLD WOKING GRANGE (HM15264) | ● | ● | | | ● | | ● | | ● | ● | ● | | ● | ● | ● | |
| OSTEOPATHY (HM15477) | | | | | ● | | | | | | | | ● | | ● | |
| PHILP, CHRISTINE (HM16147) | ● | ● | | | | | | | | | | | ● | ● | ● | |
| POWER, DAVID J (HM16503) | | | | | | | | | | | | | | | | |
| PRICE, SANDRA (HM16593) | | | | | ● | | | | | | | | | | | |
| RICHMOND PHYSIOTHERAPY (HM17301) | | | | | ● | | | | | | | | | | | |
| RIGAL, M (HM17330) | | | | | | | | | | | | | | | | |
| ROBYNA, ANNETTE (HM17516) | ● | ● | | ● | ● | | | | | | ● | | ● | ● | ● | |
| SARAH BOGUE HOMEOPATH (HM17944) | | ● | | | | | | | | | | ● | ● | ● | ● | |
| SAUMEEL PATEL ACU CLINIC (HM17950) | | | | | ● | | | | | | | | | ● | | |
| SAYER CLINIC (HM17992) | | ● | | | ● | | | | | | | | | | | |
| SCHONBERG, VERA (HM18078) | | ● | | | ● | | | | | | | | ● | | ● | |
| SCHOOL OF YOGA (HM18089) | | | | | ● | | | | | | | ● | | | ● | |
| SCORPIO PHYSIOTHERAPY (HM18103) | | | | | ● | | | | | | | | | | | |
| SELSDON COMP/RESP CLINIC (HM18220) | ● | ● | ● | ● | ● | ● | ● | ● | ● | ● | ● | ● | | ● | ● | ● |
| SEVEN SIGHS (HM18244) | | | | | ● | | | | | | | | | | | |

| Business | Mouth Disorders | Mouth Ulcers | Multiple Sclerosis | Muscular Dystrophy | Musculo-skeletal | Nail Health | Nausea | Nerve Disorders | Nervous Disorders | Neuralgia | Obesity | Osteoporosis | Pain | Palpitations | Panic Attacks | Parkinson's Disease |
|---|---|---|---|---|---|---|---|---|---|---|---|---|---|---|---|---|
| KINGSTON OSTEOPATHS (HM11679) | | | | | | | | ● | ● | ● | | ● | ● | | | |
| KOLTHAMMER, JOHN (HM11780) | | | | | | | | ● | | | | | ● | | | |
| LEATHERHEAD CHIRO CLINIC (HM12114) | | | | | | | | | | | | | | | | |
| LONDON SPINE AND JOINT CLINIC (HM12610) | | | | | | | | ● | | ● | | | ● | | | |
| LOW, ROYSTON (HM12688) | | | | | | | ● | ● | ● | ● | | | | ● | | |
| MARKS, DARREN HYPNOTHERAPY (HM13120) | | | | | | | | | | | | | ● | | | |
| MARSON, JOY (HM13178) | | | | | | | ● | | | | ● | ● | | | | |
| MEEKS, FIONA (HM13683) | | | ● | | | | | | | | | | | | | |
| MEENEGHAN, TOM (HM13685) | ● | ● | | | | ● | ● | ● | ● | ● | | ● | ● | ● | | |
| MILFORD MASSAGE PRACTICE (HM13863) | | | | | | | | | | | | | | | | |
| MILLER CONSULTANCY (HM13880) | | | ● | | | | | | ● | | ● | | ● | ● | ● | |
| MIND AND BODY (HM13958) | | | | | | | | | ● | ● | | ● | ● | ● | | |
| MIST, CORINNE (HM13996) | | | | | | | | | | | | | | | | |
| NATURAL HEALING CENTRE (HM14541) | | | ● | | | | | | | | | | ● | ● | | |
| NATURAL HEALING CLINIC (HM14550) | | | | | | | | | | | | | ● | | | |
| NATURAL HEALTH PRACTICE (HM14594) | | | | | | | | | | ● | | | | | | |
| NATURAL SLEEP FOUNDATION (HM14624) | | | | | | | | | | | | | | | | |
| NICOLA FRY-HEALTH & BEAUTY (HM14927) | | | | | | ● | | | ● | | ● | | | | | |
| OLD WOKING GRANGE (HM15264) | | | ● | ● | | | | | | | ● | | | | | |
| OSTEOPATHY (HM15477) | | | | | | | | | | ● | | | ● | | | |
| PHILP, CHRISTINE (HM16147) | | | | | | | | | | | | | | | | |
| POWER, DAVID J (HM16503) | | | | | | ● | | | | | | | | | | |
| PRICE, SANDRA (HM16593) | | | | | | | | | | | | | ● | | | |
| RICHMOND PHYSIOTHERAPY (HM17301) | | | ● | | | | | | | | | | | | | |
| RIGAL, M (HM17330) | | | | | | ● | | | | | | | | | | |
| ROBYNA, ANNETTE (HM17516) | | | | ● | | | | | | | | | ● | ● | | |
| SARAH BOGUE HOMEOPATH (HM17944) | | | | | | | | | | | | | | | | |
| SAUMEEL PATEL ACU CLINIC (HM17950) | | | | | | | | | | | | | ● | | | |
| SAYER CLINIC (HM17992) | | | | | | | | | | | | | ● | | | |
| SCHONBERG, VERA (HM18078) | | | | | | | | | | ● | ● | | ● | ● | | |
| SCHOOL OF YOGA (HM18089) | | | | | | | | | ● | | | | | | | |
| SCORPIO PHYSIOTHERAPY (HM18103) | | | | | | | | ● | | | | ● | ● | | | |
| SELSDON COMP/RESP CLINIC (HM18220) | ● | ● | ● | | | ● | ● | ● | ● | ● | ● | ● | ● | ● | | ● |
| SEVEN SIGHS (HM18244) | | | | | | | | | | | | | | | | |

| Business | Period Problems | Phobias | Piles | PMT | Pneumonia | Postural Problems | Pregnancy Help | Prostate Problems | Psoriasis | Raynaud's Disease | Recurrent Infections | Restless Legs | Rheumatoid Arthritis | Schizophrenia | Sciatica | Sexual Problems |
|---|---|---|---|---|---|---|---|---|---|---|---|---|---|---|---|---|
| KINGSTON OSTEOPATHS (HM11679) | ● | | | ● | ● | | ● | | | | | | ● | | ● | |
| KOLTHAMMER, JOHN (HM11780) | | | | | | | | | | | | | | | ● | |
| LEATHERHEAD CHIRO CLINIC (HM12114) | | | | | | | | | | | | | | | | |
| LONDON SPINE AND JOINT CLINIC (HM12610) | | | | | | | | | | | | | | | ● | |
| LOW, ROYSTON (HM12688) | | | ● | | | | | | | | | | ● | | ● | |
| MARKS, DARREN HYPNOTHERAPY (HM13120) | | ● | | | | | | | | | | | | | | |
| MARSON, JOY (HM13178) | ● | | | ● | | | ● | | ● | | | ● | ● | | | |
| MEEKS, FIONA (HM13683) | ● | | | ● | | | | | | | | | | | ● | |
| MEENEGHAN, TOM (HM13685) | ● | ● | ● | ● | | | | ● | ● | ● | ● | ● | ● | | ● | |
| MILFORD MASSAGE PRACTICE (HM13863) | | | | | | | | | | | | ● | ● | | ● | |
| MILLER CONSULTANCY (HM13880) | ● | ● | | | | | ● | ● | ● | ● | ● | ● | ● | ● | ● | ● |
| MIND AND BODY (HM13958) | ● | | | ● | | | | | ● | ● | | ● | ● | | ● | |
| MIST, CORINNE (HM13996) | | | | ● | | | ● | | | | | | | | | |
| NATURAL HEALING CENTRE (HM14541) | ● | ● | | ● | | | ● | | | | | ● | | | ● | |
| NATURAL HEALING CLINIC (HM14550) | | | | | | | | | | | | | | | ● | |
| NATURAL HEALTH PRACTICE (HM14594) | | | | | | | ● | | | | | | ● | | ● | |
| NATURAL SLEEP FOUNDATION (HM14624) | | | | | | | | | | | | | | | | |
| NICOLA FRY-HEALTH & BEAUTY (HM14927) | ● | | | ● | | | ● | | ● | | | | | | | |
| OLD WOKING GRANGE (HM15264) | | ● | | ● | | | | | ● | | | ● | ● | | | |
| OSTEOPATHY (HM15477) | | | | | | | ● | | | | | | | | ● | |
| PHILP, CHRISTINE (HM16147) | | | | | | | | | | | | | | | | |
| POWER, DAVID J (HM16503) | | | | | | | | | | | | | | | | |
| PRICE, SANDRA (HM16593) | | | | | | ● | ● | | | | | | | | ● | |
| RICHMOND PHYSIOTHERAPY (HM17301) | | | | | | | | | | | | | | | | |
| RIGAL, M (HM17330) | | | | | | | | | | | | | | | | |
| ROBYNA, ANNETTE (HM17516) | | | | ● | | | ● | | ● | ● | | ● | | | ● | |
| SARAH BOGUE HOMEOPATH (HM17944) | ● | | | ● | | | | | | | ● | | | | | |
| SAUMEEL PATEL ACU CLINIC (HM17950) | ● | | | ● | | | ● | | | | | | | | | |
| SAYER CLINIC (HM17992) | | | | | | | | | | | | | | | ● | |
| SCHONBERG, VERA (HM18078) | ● | ● | | | | | ● | | ● | ● | | | ● | | ● | |
| SCHOOL OF YOGA (HM18089) | | ● | | | | | ● | | | | | | | | ● | |
| SCORPIO PHYSIOTHERAPY (HM18103) | | | | | | | | | | | | | ● | | ● | |
| SELSDON COMP/RESP CLINIC (HM18220) | ● | ● | ● | ● | ● | | ● | ● | ● | | ● | ● | ● | | ● | ● |
| SEVEN SIGHS (HM18244) | | | | | | | | | | | | | | | | |

# I - S Conditions treated at Practices/Businesses

| Business by County with Reference no. | Insomnia | Irritable Bowel Syndrome | Itching | Jet Lag | Joint Pain | Kidney Complaints | Lactose Intolerance | Laryngitis | Lethargy | Liver Disorders | Low Blood Pressure | Lung Problems | ME | Menopause | Migraine | Motion Sickness | Mouth Disorders | Mouth Ulcers | Multiple Sclerosis | Muscular Dystrophy | Musculo-skeletal | Nail Health | Nausea | Nerve Disorders | Nervous Disorders | Neuralgia | Obesity | Osteoporosis | Pain | Palpitations | Panic Attacks | Parkinson's Disease | Period Problems | Phobias | Piles | PMT | Pneumonia | Postural Problems | Pregnancy Help | Prostate Problems | Psoriasis | Raynaud's Disease | Recurrent Infections | Restless Legs | Rheumatoid Arthritis | Schizophrenia | Sciatica | Sexual Problems |
|---|---|---|---|---|---|---|---|---|---|---|---|---|---|---|---|---|---|---|---|---|---|---|---|---|---|---|---|---|---|---|---|---|---|---|---|---|---|---|---|---|---|---|---|---|---|---|---|---|
| SHEPPERTON PHYSIOFIRST CENTRE (HM18425) | | | | |●| | | | | | | | | | | | | |●| | | | | | | | | | | | | | | | | | | | | | | | | | | | | |
| SIMMS, KATHERINE (HM18564) | | | | |●|●| | | | | | | | |●| | | | | | | | |●|●| | | |●| | |●| | | | | | | | | | | | |●| | | | |
| SURBITON NATURAL HEALTH CENTRE (HM19514) |●| | | |●| | | | | | | |●|●|●| | | | | | | | | | | | | |●| | | | | | | | | | | | |●| | | | | | | |
| SURREY HEALING SANCTUARY (HM19522) |●|●|●| |●|●| |●|●|●|●|●|●|●|●| | |●|●|●| |●|●|●|●| | |●|●|●| | |●| | |●| | | |●|●| |●| |●| |●| |
| SUTHERLAND, JENNY (HM19539) |●|●| | |●|●| | | | |●| |●|●|●| | | |●| | | | | | | | | |●|●| | |●| | |●| | |●| | | | |●| | |●| |
| SUTTON CHIROPRACTIC CLINIC (HM19543) | | | | |●| | | | | | | | | | | | | | | | | | | | | | | |●| | | | | | | | | | | | | | | | | |●| |
| TANSILL, LUCY (HM19689) | |●| | |●| | | | | | | | | |●| | | | | | | | | | | |●|●|●| | | | | | | | |●| | | | | | | | |●| |
| TELLING, PAUL (HM19824) | | | | |●| | | | | | | | | | | | | | | | | | | | | | | |●| | | | | | | | | | | | | | | | | | | |
| TOWNS, KATE (HM20202) | |●| | | | | | | | | | |●| |●| | | | | | | | | |●| | |●| | | | | |●| |●| | | |●|●| |●| | | | | |
| TRADITIONAL CHINESE MEDICINE (HM20225) | | | | |●|●| | | | | | |●| |●| | | |●| | | | | | | | | |●|●| | | | | | | | | | | | | | | | |●| |
| TRANSCENDENTAL MEDITATION (HM20266) |●|●| | | | | | | | | | |●| |●| | | | | | | | | |●| | | | | | | | | | | | | | | | | | | | |●| | |
| TURNER, R E (HM20435) | | | | |●| | | | | | | | | |●| | | | | | | | | | | | | | | | | | | | | | | | | | | | | | | | | |
| TWO STEPS REFLEXOLOGY (HM20458) | |●|●|●| | | |●| |●|●| |●|●|●|●| | | | | | |●|●|●|●| | |●|●| | |●| | |●| | | | | | | | |●| |●|●|
| WALKER, SARAH (HM20803) | |●| | | | | | | | |●| |●| |●| | | | | | | | | | | | | | | | |●| | | | | | |●| | | | | | | | | |
| WALLACE, SUE (HM20832) |●|●| | |●| | | | | | | |●| | | | | | | | | | | | | | | | | | | | | | | | | | | | | | | | | |●| |
| WHITWORTH, MICHAEL T (HM21431) | | | | | | | | | | | | | | | | | | | | | |●| | | | | | | | | | | | | | | | | | | | | | | | | | |
| WILKINSON, LESLEY (HM21510) | |●| |●|●| |●|●|●|●|●| |●|●|●|●|●|●|●|●| |●|●|●|●|●|●|●| | | | |●| |●|●| | | | | |●|●|●|●| |●|●|
| WILLIS, SALLY (HM21618) | | | | | | | | | | | | |●| | | | | | | | | | | | | |●| | | | | |●| | | | | | | | | | | | | | |
| WINTER, DAVID (HM21718) |●|●|●|●|●|●|●|●|●|●|●|●|●|●|●|●|●|●|●|●| |●|●|●|●|●|●|●|●|●| |●|●|●|●|●|●| |●|●|●|●|●|●|●|●|●|●|
| WOOD, VALERIE (HM21811) |●|●| | | | | | | | | | |●|●|●| | | | | | | | | | | | | | | | | | | | | | | | | | | | | | | | | |
| WOODLANDS NATURAL HLTH THERAPY (HM21832) |●|●| |●|●|●| | |●| |●|●|●|●|●|●| |●|●| | | | |●|●| | |●|●|●| |●|●|●|●|●| | | |●|●|●| |●| | |●| |
| **SUSSEX (EAST)** | | | | | | | | | | | | | | | | | | | | | | | | | | | | | | | | | | | | | | | | | | | | | | | | |
| ALBION CLINIC (HM00483) | |●| | |●| | | |●| |●| |●|●|●| | | |●| | | | |●|●|●| |●|●| | | | | | | | | | | | |●| |●|●| |●| |
| ALEXANDER TECHNIQUE (HM00549) | | | | |●| | | | | | | |●| |●| | | |●| | | | | | | | |●| | | |●| | | | | |●| | | | | | | | |●| |
| ALPHA HYPNOTHERAPY (HM00684) |●|●| | | | | | | | | | | | | | | | | | | | | | |●| | | | | | | | |●| | | | | | | | | | | | | | |
| ANGELA MATTHEWS HOMEOPATH (HM00873) |●|●| | | |●| | | |●| | | | |●| | | | | | | |●|●|●| | | | |●| | |●| | |●| | | | | | | | | | |●| |
| ARDERN FOOT & HEALTH CLINIC (HM00992) | | | | |●| | | | | | | |●|●|●| | | | | | |●|●| | | | | |●| | | |●|●| |●| | | | | | | |●| | | | |
| AROMA HAIR (HM01047) | | | | | | | | | | | | | |●|●| | | | | | | | | | | | | |●| | | | | | | | | |●| | | | | | | | | |
| ASHDOWN OSTEOPATHIC CENTRE (HM01206) | |●| | |●| | | | | | | |●| |●| | | |●| | | |●|●|●|●| |●|●| | |●|●|●| |●| | |●| |●| | | |●| |●| |
| BASSETT, N S (HM01857) | | | | |●| | | | | | | | | |●| | | | | | | | | | | | |●|●| | | | | | | | | |●| | | | |●|●| | | |
| BELVAIN, E (HM02118) | | | | | | | | | | | | | | |●| | | | | | | | | |●| | | | | | | | | | | | | | | | | | | | | | | |
| BEXHILL CHIROPRACTIC (HM02255) |●|●| | |●| | | | |●|●| | |●|●| | | |●| | | | |●| | | | |●| | |●| | | |●| |●| | | | | | |●| | | |
| BEXHILL OSTEOPATHIC PRACTICE (HM02257) |●|●| | |●| | | |●| | | | | |●| | | | | | | | | | |●| | |●| | | | | | | | | | | | | | |●| | | | |
| BRIGHTON & HOVE SPORTS CLINIC (HM03041) | | | | |●| | | | | | | | | | | | | |●| | | | | | | | | |●| | | | | | | | | | | | | | | | | | | |

www.healthmyself.com

Healthmyself Directory

# I - S Conditions treated at Practices/Businesses

| Business by County with Reference no. | Insomnia | Irritable Bowel Syndrome | Itching | Jet Lag | Joint Pain | Kidney Complaints | Lactose Intolerance | Laryngitis | Lethargy | Liver Disorders | Low Blood Pressure | Lung Problems | ME | Menopause | Migraine | Motion Sickness | Mouth Disorders | Mouth Ulcers | Multiple Sclerosis | Muscular Dystrophy | Musculo-skeletal | Nail Health | Nausea | Nerve Disorders |
|---|---|---|---|---|---|---|---|---|---|---|---|---|---|---|---|---|---|---|---|---|---|---|---|---|
| BRIGHTON ACUPUNCTURE CLINIC (HM03042) | ● | ● | | | ● | | | | ● | | | ● | ● | ● | ● | | | | | | | | ● | |
| BRIGHTON ALEXANDER TRAINING (HM03043) | | ● | | | ● | | | | | | | | | | ● | | | | | | | | | |
| BRIGHTON CHIROPRACTIC CLINIC (HM03044) | | ● | | | ● | | | | ● | | | | | ● | | | | | ● | | | | | ● |
| BRIGHTON HEALTH & RACQUET CLUB (HM03045) | | | | | ● | | | | | | | | | | | | | | | | | | | |
| BRIGHTON PHYSIOTHERAPY CLINIC (HM03048) | | | | | ● | | | | | | | | | | | | | | | | | | | |
| CANTERLA, MARGARET (HM03643) | ● | ● | ● | ● | ● | ● | ● | ● | ● | ● | ● | ● | ● | ● | ● | ● | ● | ● | ● | ● | | ● | ● | ● |
| CHARTERS PHYSIO & SPORTS (HM04050) | | | | | ● | | | | | | | | | | | | | | | | | | | |
| CLINCH, ADELE (HM04675) | | | | | | | | | | | | | | | | | | | | | | ● | | |
| CLINIC OF CHINESE MED & ACU (HM04685) | | | | | ● | | | | | | | | | | ● | | | | | | | | ● | |
| COMP THERAPY & TRAINING CENTRE (HM04915) | ● | ● | ● | ● | ● | ● | ● | ● | ● | ● | ● | ● | ● | ● | ● | ● | ● | ● | ● | ● | | ● | ● | ● |
| CONCEPTS PHYSIO & NUTRITION (HM04970) | ● | ● | ● | ● | ● | ● | ● | ● | ● | ● | ● | ● | ● | ● | ● | ● | ● | ● | ● | ● | | ● | ● | ● |
| COOK, ELAINE (HM05042) | ● | ● | ● | ● | ● | | | | ● | | ● | | ● | ● | ● | | | | | | | | | |
| COX, JULIET (HM05308) | ● | | | | ● | | | | ● | | | | ● | | ● | | | | | | | | | ● |
| CRESENT CLINIC (HM05422) | ● | ● | ● | ● | ● | ● | | | ● | ● | ● | ● | ● | ● | ● | ● | ● | ● | ● | | ● | ● | ● | ● |
| CROWBOROUGH CHIRO/COMP HLTH (HM05498) | | ● | ● | | | | | | | | | | | | ● | | | | ● | | | | | ● |
| CROWBOROUGH COMP THERAPISTS (HM05499) | ● | ● | | | ● | ● | | | | | ● | | ● | ● | ● | | | | ● | | | | | |
| CULL, BEN (HM05556) | | ● | | | | | | | ● | | | | ● | | ● | | | | | | | | | |
| CULLEN, MARGARET (HM05561) | | | | | | | | | | | | | | | | | | | | | | | | |
| DADSWELL, CLAIRE (HM05670) | ● | ● | ● | ● | ● | ● | ● | ● | ● | ● | ● | ● | ● | ● | ● | ● | ● | ● | | | | ● | ● | ● |
| DEEKS, STUART (HM05956) | ● | ● | ● | ● | ● | ● | | | ● | ● | ● | ● | ● | ● | ● | ● | ● | ● | ● | | | ● | ● | |
| DRIVE OSTEO AND SPORTS CLINIC (HM06314) | | ● | | | ● | | | | | | | | ● | | ● | | | | | | | | | |
| DRYDEN, B A (HM06332) | ● | | | | | | | | | | | | | | | | | | | | | | | |
| DYKE ROAD NATURAL HEALTH (HM06450) | ● | ● | ● | ● | ● | ● | ● | ● | ● | ● | ● | ● | ● | ● | ● | ● | ● | ● | ● | ● | | ● | ● | ● |
| EAST BOURNE CLINIC (HM06509) | | ● | | | ● | | | | | | | | ● | | | | | | | | | | | ● |
| EASTBOURNE CHIROPRACTIC CLINIC (HM06535) | | ● | | | ● | | | | | | | | | | | | | | | | | | | ● |
| FAIRCHILD, HAZEL (HM07052) | | ● | | | | | | | | | | | | | | | | | | | | | | |
| FAMILY FIRST (HM07087) | | | | | | | | | | | | | | | | | | | | | | | | |
| FIVEWAYS OSTEOPATHIC PRACTICE (HM07382) | | | | | | | | | | | | | | | ● | | | | | | | | | |
| FLOYD, MICHELLE (HM07438) | ● | ● | ● | ● | ● | ● | | ● | ● | ● | ● | ● | ● | ● | ● | ● | ● | ● | ● | | | ● | ● | ● |
| FOUNDATION, ANGELGATE (HM07615) | | ● | | | ● | ● | | | | ● | | | ● | ● | ● | | | | ● | | | | | |
| GEIGES, STEPHANIE (HM07967) | | | | | ● | | | | | | | | ● | | | | | | | | | | | ● |
| GOLDSTONE CLINIC (HM08230) | | | | | ● | | | | | | | | | | ● | | | | | | | | | |
| GOLDSTONE CLINIC (HM08229) | ● | ● | | | ● | | | | | | | | ● | ● | | | | | | | | | | ● |
| GONZALEZ, SOHANI (HM08237) | ● | ● | ● | ● | ● | ● | ● | ● | ● | ● | ● | ● | ● | ● | ● | ● | ● | ● | ● | ● | | ● | ● | ● |

| Business by County with Reference no. | Nervous Disorders | Neuralgia | Obesity | Osteoporosis | Pain | Palpitations | Panic Attacks | Parkinson's Disease | Period Problems | Phobias | Piles | PMT | Pneumonia | Postural Problems | Pregnancy Help | Prostate Problems | Psoriasis | Raynaud's Disease | Recurrent Infections | Restless Legs | Rheumatoid Arthritis | Schizophrenia | Sciatica | Sexual Problems |
|---|---|---|---|---|---|---|---|---|---|---|---|---|---|---|---|---|---|---|---|---|---|---|---|---|
| BRIGHTON ACUPUNCTURE CLINIC (HM03042) | | | | | | | | | ● | | | ● | | | ● | | | | | | | | ● | |
| BRIGHTON ALEXANDER TRAINING (HM03043) | | | | | | | | | | | | | | | | | | | | | | | | |
| BRIGHTON CHIROPRACTIC CLINIC (HM03044) | ● | | | ● | ● | | | | ● | | | | | | | | | | | ● | | | ● | |
| BRIGHTON HEALTH & RACQUET CLUB (HM03045) | | | | | ● | | | | | | | | | | | | | | | | | | | |
| BRIGHTON PHYSIOTHERAPY CLINIC (HM03048) | | | | | ● | | | | | | | | | | | | | | | | | | | |
| CANTERLA, MARGARET (HM03643) | ● | ● | ● | ● | ● | ● | | ● | ● | ● | ● | ● | ● | | ● | ● | ● | ● | ● | ● | ● | ● | ● | ● |
| CHARTERS PHYSIO & SPORTS (HM04050) | | | | | ● | | | | | | | | | | | | | | | | | | | |
| CLINCH, ADELE (HM04675) | | | | | | | | | | | | | | | | | | | | | | | | |
| CLINIC OF CHINESE MED & ACU (HM04685) | | | | | ● | | | | | | | | | | | | | | | | | | | |
| COMP THERAPY & TRAINING CENTRE (HM04915) | ● | ● | ● | ● | ● | ● | | ● | ● | ● | ● | ● | ● | | ● | ● | ● | ● | ● | ● | ● | ● | ● | ● |
| CONCEPTS PHYSIO & NUTRITION (HM04970) | ● | ● | ● | ● | ● | ● | | ● | ● | ● | ● | ● | ● | | ● | ● | ● | ● | | ● | ● | ● | ● | ● |
| COOK, ELAINE (HM05042) | ● | ● | | | ● | ● | | | ● | ● | ● | ● | | | ● | | | | | ● | ● | | ● | |
| COX, JULIET (HM05308) | ● | | | ● | ● | | | | | | | | | ● | ● | | | | | ● | ● | | ● | |
| CRESENT CLINIC (HM05422) | ● | ● | | ● | ● | ● | | ● | ● | ● | ● | ● | ● | | ● | ● | ● | | ● | | ● | | ● | ● |
| CROWBOROUGH CHIRO/COMP HLTH (HM05498) | ● | ● | ● | | ● | ● | | | ● | | | | | | ● | | | | | | | | ● | |
| CROWBOROUGH COMP THERAPISTS (HM05499) | | | | | ● | ● | | | ● | | | ● | | | ● | | | | | | ● | | ● | |
| CULL, BEN (HM05556) | ● | ● | | ● | ● | | | | | | | | | | | | | | | | | | ● | |
| CULLEN, MARGARET (HM05561) | | | | | | | | | | | | | | | | | | | | | | | | ● |
| DADSWELL, CLAIRE (HM05670) | ● | ● | ● | ● | ● | ● | | ● | ● | ● | ● | ● | ● | | ● | ● | ● | ● | ● | ● | ● | ● | ● | ● |
| DEEKS, STUART (HM05956) | ● | ● | | | ● | ● | | | ● | ● | ● | ● | ● | | ● | ● | ● | | ● | | ● | | | ● |
| DRIVE OSTEO AND SPORTS CLINIC (HM06314) | | | | | ● | | | | | | | | | | | | | | | ● | ● | | ● | |
| DRYDEN, B A (HM06332) | | | ● | | | | | | | ● | | | | | | | | | | | | | | |
| DYKE ROAD NATURAL HEALTH (HM06450) | ● | ● | ● | ● | ● | ● | | ● | ● | ● | ● | ● | ● | | ● | ● | ● | ● | ● | ● | ● | ● | ● | ● |
| EAST BOURNE CLINIC (HM06509) | ● | | | ● | ● | | | | | | | | | | | | | | | | | | ● | |
| EASTBOURNE CHIROPRACTIC CLINIC (HM06535) | ● | | | ● | ● | | | | | | | | | | | | | | | | | | ● | |
| FAIRCHILD, HAZEL (HM07052) | ● | | | | | | | | | | | | | | | | | | | | | | | |
| FAMILY FIRST (HM07087) | | | | | | | | | | ● | | | | | | | | | | | | | | ● |
| FIVEWAYS OSTEOPATHIC PRACTICE (HM07382) | | | | | ● | | | | | | | | | | | | | | | | ● | | ● | |
| FLOYD, MICHELLE (HM07438) | ● | ● | ● | ● | | ● | | ● | ● | ● | ● | ● | ● | | ● | ● | ● | ● | ● | ● | ● | ● | ● | ● |
| FOUNDATION, ANGELGATE (HM07615) | ● | | | ● | ● | ● | | ● | ● | | | ● | | | ● | ● | ● | | ● | | ● | | ● | |
| GEIGES, STEPHANIE (HM07967) | | | | ● | ● | | | | | | | | | ● | | | | | | | | | ● | |
| GOLDSTONE CLINIC (HM08230) | | | | | ● | | | | | | | | | | | | | | | | | | | |
| GOLDSTONE CLINIC (HM08229) | ● | | | ● | ● | | | | | | | | | | | | | | | | | | ● | |
| GONZALEZ, SOHANI (HM08237) | ● | ● | ● | ● | ● | ● | | ● | ● | ● | ● | ● | ● | | ● | ● | ● | ● | ● | ● | ● | ● | ● | ● |

# I - S Conditions treated at Practices/Businesses

| Business by County with Reference no. | Insomnia | Irritable Bowel Syndrome | Itching | Jet Lag | Joint Pain | Kidney Complaints | Lactose Intolerance | Laryngitis | Lethargy | Liver Disorders | Low Blood Pressure | Lung Problems | ME | Menopause | Migraine | Motion Sickness | Mouth Disorders | Mouth Ulcers | Multiple Sclerosis | Muscular Dystrophy | Musculo-skeletal | Nail Health | Nausea | Nerve Disorders | Nervous Disorders | Neuralgia | Obesity | Osteoporosis | Pain | Palpitations | Panic Attacks | Parkinson's Disease | Period Problems | Phobias | Piles | PMT | Pneumonia | Postural Problems | Pregnancy Help | Prostate Problems | Psoriasis | Raynaud's Disease | Recurrent Infections | Restless Legs | Rheumatoid Arthritis | Schizophrenia | Sciatica | Sexual Problems |
|---|---|---|---|---|---|---|---|---|---|---|---|---|---|---|---|---|---|---|---|---|---|---|---|---|---|---|---|---|---|---|---|---|---|---|---|---|---|---|---|---|---|---|---|---|---|---|---|---|
| GRIFFITHS, J (HM08567) | ● | ● | | | ● | | | | | | ● | | ● | | ● | | | | ● | | | | | | | | | | | | | | ● | | | ● | | | ● | | | | | ● | ● | | | |
| HART, RONALD (HM09131) | | | | | | | | | | | | | | | | | | | | | | ● | | | | | | | | | | | | | | | | | | | | | | | | | | |
| HART, RONALD (HM09130) | | | | | | | | | | | | | | | | | | | | | | ● | | | | | | | | | | | | | | | | | | | | | | | | | | |
| HAWKINS, LUKE (HM09224) | | | | | | | | | | | | | | | | | | | | | | ● | | | | | | | | | | | | | | | | | | | | | | | | | | |
| HEMMINGWAY CHIROPODIST (HM09537) | | | | | | | | | | | | | | | | | | | | | | ● | | | | | | | | | | | | | | | | | | | | | | | | | | |
| HERBAL HEALTH CLINIC (HM09617) | ● | ● | ● | | ● | ● | | ● | ● | ● | ● | ● | ● | ● | ● | ● | ● | ● | | | | | ● | | ● | ● | | | ● | ● | | | ● | ● | ● | ● | | | | ● | ● | ● | ● | ● | ● | | ● | |
| HOLDEN NATURAL HEALTH CLINIC (HM09927) | ● | ● | | | | ● | | | | | ● | | | | | | | | | | | | | | | | | | | | | | ● | | | ● | | | | | | | | | | | | |
| HOVE CHIROPRACTIC CLINIC (HM10227) | | ● | | | ● | | | | | | | | ● | | | | | | | | | | | ● | | | | | ● | | | | | | | | | | | | | | | | | | ● | |
| HOVE OSTEOPATHIC CLINIC (HM10228) | | | | | ● | | | | | | | | | | | | | | | | | | | | | | | | | ● | | | | | | | | | | | | | | | | | | |
| HUGHES, CLARE (HM10324) | | | | | ● | | | | | | | | ● | | | | | | | | | | | ● | ● | | | ● | ● | | | | | | | | | ● | | | | | | | | | ● | |
| HYSLOP, C P (HM10543) | ● | ● | ● | ● | ● | ● | ● | ● | ● | ● | ● | ● | ● | ● | ● | ● | ● | ● | ● | ● | | ● | ● | ● | ● | ● | ● | ● | ● | ● | | ● | ● | ● | ● | ● | ● | | ● | ● | ● | ● | ● | ● | ● | ● | ● | ● |
| JEMPSON, NICOLA (HM10978) | | | | | ● | | | | | | | | | | ● | | | | | | | | | | | | | | ● | | | | | | | | | | ● | | | | | | | | | |
| JOY, JANET (HM11231) | | ● | | | | | | | | | | | | | | | | | | | | | | | | | | | | | | | | ● | | | | | | | | | | | | | | |
| LEWES CHIROPRACTIC CLINIC (HM12271) | | ● | | | ● | | | | | | | | ● | | ● | | | | | | | | | ● | | ● | | ● | ● | | | | | | | | | | ● | | | | | | | | ● | |
| MCKEOWN, KAY (HM13532) | | ● | | | | | | | | | | | | | | | | | | | | | | | | | | | ● | | | | | | | | | | | | | | | | | | | |
| MEADOWSWEET (HM13634) | | | | ● | ● | | | | | | | | | ● | ● | | | | | | | | | | | | | | ● | | | ● | ● | | | | | ● | ● | | | | | | | | | |
| MURPHY, KEVIN (HM14387) | ● | | | | ● | | | | | | | | ● | | ● | | | | ● | | | | | ● | ● | ● | | ● | ● | | | | ● | | | ● | | | | | | | | ● | ● | | ● | |
| NEAT FEET (HM14742) | | | | | | | | | | | | | | | | | | | | | | ● | | | | | | | | | | | | | | | | | | | | | | | | | | |
| NEWICK PHYSIOTHERAPY CLINIC (HM14865) | | | | | ● | | | | | | | | | | | | | | ● | | ● | | | | | | | | ● | | | | | | | | | | | | | | | | | | | |
| OLD TOWN CHIROPRACTIC CLINIC (HM15263) | | | | | ● | | | | | | | | | | ● | | | | | | | | | | | | | | ● | | | | | | | | | | | | | | | | | | ● | |
| PRICE, JAMES (HM16583) | | | | | | | | | | | | | | | | | | | | | | ● | | | | | | | | | | | | | | | | | | | | | | | | | | |
| PRIORY HEIGHTS (HM16633) | | | | | ● | | | | | | | | | ● | ● | | | | | | | | | | | | | | ● | | | | ● | | | ● | | | | | | | | | | | | |
| REEVES, ALAN (HM17062) | | | | | | | | | | | | | | | | | | | | | | | | | | | | | | | | | | | | | | | | | | | | | | | | ● |
| REFLEXOLOGY FOR HEALTH (HM17095) | | ● | | | | ● | | | ● | | ● | | ● | ● | | | | | ● | | | | | ● | | | | | | | | | ● | | | ● | | | | | | | | | | | ● | |
| SANDERSON & ELEMENT (HM17919) | | | | | ● | | | | | | | | | | | | | | | | | | | ● | ● | | | ● | ● | | | | | | | | | | | | | | | | | | ● | |
| SANDERSON & ELEMENT (HM17920) | | | | | ● | | | | | | | | | | | | | | | | | | | ● | ● | | | ● | ● | | | | | | | | | | | | | | | | | | ● | |
| SANDERSON & ELEMENT (HM17922) | | | | | ● | | | | | | | | | | | | | | | | | | | ● | ● | | | ● | ● | | | | | | | | | | | | | | | | | | ● | |
| SCHOLL CENTRE (HM18032) | | | | | | | | | | | | | | | | | | | | | | ● | | | | | | | | | | | | | | | | | | | | | | | | | | |
| SUNDIAL HOUSE CHIROPRACTIC (HM19506) | | ● | | | ● | | | | | | | | | | | | | | | | | | | ● | ● | | | ● | ● | | | | | | | | | | | | | | | | | | ● | |
| TEALE, PAUL (HM19809) | | | | | ● | | | | | | | | | | ● | | | | | | | | | | | ● | | | | | | | | | | | | | | | | | | | | | ● | |
| TISSERAND (HM20095) | | | | | | | | | | | | | | | ● | | | | | | | | | | | | | | | | | | | | | | | | | | | | | | | | | |
| VALENCE ROAD OSTEOPATHS (HM20554) | | | | | | | | | | | | | | | | | | | | | | | | | | | | | | | | | | | | | | | | | | | | | | | ● | |
| WADHURST PHYSIO/SPORTS CLNC (HM20729) | | | | | ● | | | | | | | | | | | | | | ● | | ● | | | | | | | | | | | ● | | | | | | | | | | | | | | | | |
| WADHURST PHYSIO/SPORTS CLNC (HM20730) | | | | | ● | | | | | | | | | | | | | | ● | | ● | | | | | | | | | | | ● | | | | | | | | | | | | | | | | |

# I - S Conditions treated at Practices/Businesses

| Business by County with Reference no. | Insomnia | Irritable Bowel Syndrome | Itching | Jet Lag | Joint Pain | Kidney Complaints | Lactose Intolerance | Laryngitis | Lethargy | Liver Disorders | Low Blood Pressure | Lung Problems | ME | Menopause | Migraine | Motion Sickness |
|---|---|---|---|---|---|---|---|---|---|---|---|---|---|---|---|---|
| WALSH, M J (HM20865) | | | | | ● | | | | | | | | | | ● | |
| WEDLAKE-GRIFFITHS, J (HM21097) | | | | | ● | | | | | | | | | | | |
| WILBURY PHYSIOTHERAPY (HM21480) | | | | | ● | | | | | | | | | | | |
| WRIGHT, P A (HM21946) | | | | | | | | | | | | | | | | |
| **SUSSEX (WEST)** | | | | | | | | | | | | | | | | |
| ACORN CENTRE (HM00171) | | | | | | | | | ● | | | | ● | | ● | |
| ALAN SMITH CHIROPRACTOR (HM00470) | | | | | | | | | | | | | | | ● | |
| ANDREW BATHIE PRACTICE (HM00846) | ● | ● | | | | | | | | | | | ● | | ● | ● |
| ANGELA (HM00872) | | | | | ● | | | | | | | | | | | |
| AUROMA (HM01357) | | | | | | | | | | | | | | | ● | |
| AVALON HEALTH CENTRE (HM01380) | ● | ● | ● | ● | ● | ● | ● | ● | ● | ● | ● | ● | ● | ● | ● | ● |
| B O P (HM01452) | | | | | ● | | | | | | | | | | ● | |
| BACK 2 FITNESS CHIROPRACTIC (HM01476) | | ● | | | ● | | | | | | | | | | | |
| BALOOMBE OSTEOPATHIC & SPORTS (HM01641) | | | | | ● | | | | | | | | ● | | ● | |
| BARTHOLOMEW WAY CLINIC (HM01818) | | | | | ● | | | | | | | | | | | |
| BELLAMY PARTNERSHIP (HM02093) | | | | | ● | | | | | | | | | | ● | |
| BLACK, PAULINE (HM02425) | ● | ● | ● | ● | ● | ● | ● | ● | ● | ● | ● | ● | ● | ● | ● | ● |
| BODYGUIDE ALTERNATE (HM02619) | ● | ● | ● | ● | ● | ● | ● | ● | ● | ● | ● | ● | ● | ● | ● | ● |
| BOHNET, CAROLE (HM02648) | ● | ● | | | | | | | | | ● | | ● | ● | ● | |
| BRITCHIRO CLINIC (HM03068) | | ● | | | ● | | | | | | | | ● | | ● | |
| BURNS, L C (HM03417) | | | | | ● | | | | | | | | | | | |
| CARTLAND, ANN (HM03794) | | | | | | | | | | | | | | | | |
| CHANGES (HM03985) | ● | ● | ● | ● | ● | ● | | | ● | ● | | | | ● | ● | ● |
| CHICHESTER NATURAL HEALTH CTRE (HM04156) | ● | ● | ● | ● | ● | ● | ● | ● | ● | ● | ● | ● | ● | ● | ● | ● |
| CLAIRVOYANT - MEDIUM - HEALER (HM04514) | ● | | ● | ● | ● | ● | | ● | ● | ● | ● | ● | ● | ● | ● | |
| CLARKE, STEVEN (HM04604) | ● | | | | | | | | | | | | | | ● | |
| CORNERWEIGHS (HM05183) | | ● | | | | | ● | | | | | | | | ● | ● |
| DALLAS, PETER (HM05691) | ● | ● | | | ● | ● | | | | | ● | ● | ● | ● | ● | |
| DYER & ASSOCIATES (HM06444) | | ● | | | ● | | | | | | | | | | ● | |
| EMINATIONS ACUPUNCTURE CLINIC (HM06805) | ● | ● | ● | ● | ● | ● | | | ● | ● | ● | ● | ● | ● | ● | |
| FELPHAM NATURAL HEALTH CLINIC (HM07206) | | | | | ● | | | | | | | | ● | | | |
| FROST, CHARLES (HM07760) | ● | | | | | | | | | | | | | | ● | |
| FURNACE GREEN CHIRO CTRE (HM07800) | ● | ● | ● | ● | ● | ● | ● | ● | ● | ● | ● | ● | ● | ● | ● | ● |
| G & G FOOD SUPPLIES (HM07807) | | | | | | | | | | | | | | ● | | |

| Business by County with Reference no. | Mouth Disorders | Mouth Ulcers | Multiple Sclerosis | Muscular Dystrophy | Musculo-skeletal | Nail Health | Nausea | Nerve Disorders | Nervous Disorders | Neuralgia | Obesity | Osteoporosis | Pain | Palpitations | Panic Attacks | Parkinson's Disease |
|---|---|---|---|---|---|---|---|---|---|---|---|---|---|---|---|---|
| WALSH, M J (HM20865) | | | | | | | | ● | | | | | ● | | | |
| WEDLAKE-GRIFFITHS, J (HM21097) | | | | | | | | | | ● | | | | | | |
| WILBURY PHYSIOTHERAPY (HM21480) | | | ● | | | | | | | | | ● | ● | | | |
| WRIGHT, P A (HM21946) | | | | | | ● | | | | | | | | | | |
| **SUSSEX (WEST)** | | | | | | | | | | | | | | | | |
| ACORN CENTRE (HM00171) | | | | | | | | | ● | | | | | | | |
| ALAN SMITH CHIROPRACTOR (HM00470) | | | | | | | | | | ● | | | ● | ● | | |
| ANDREW BATHIE PRACTICE (HM00846) | ● | | | | | | ● | | ● | | ● | | ● | | | |
| ANGELA (HM00872) | | | | | | | | | | | | | | | | |
| AUROMA (HM01357) | | | | | | | | | | | | | | | | |
| AVALON HEALTH CENTRE (HM01380) | ● | ● | ● | ● | | ● | ● | ● | ● | ● | ● | ● | ● | ● | | ● |
| B O P (HM01452) | | | | | | | | | | ● | | ● | ● | | | |
| BACK 2 FITNESS CHIROPRACTIC (HM01476) | | | | | | | | ● | ● | | | ● | ● | | | |
| BALOOMBE OSTEOPATHIC & SPORTS (HM01641) | | | | | | | | | | | | ● | ● | | | |
| BARTHOLOMEW WAY CLINIC (HM01818) | | | | | | ● | | ● | | ● | | ● | ● | | | |
| BELLAMY PARTNERSHIP (HM02093) | | | | | | | | | | ● | | | | | | |
| BLACK, PAULINE (HM02425) | ● | ● | ● | | | ● | ● | ● | ● | ● | ● | ● | ● | ● | | |
| BODYGUIDE ALTERNATE (HM02619) | ● | ● | ● | ● | | ● | ● | ● | ● | ● | ● | ● | ● | ● | | ● |
| BOHNET, CAROLE (HM02648) | | | | | | | | | ● | | | | ● | | ● | |
| BRITCHIRO CLINIC (HM03068) | | | | | | | | ● | ● | | | | ● | | | |
| BURNS, L C (HM03417) | | | ● | | | | | | | | | | ● | | | |
| CARTLAND, ANN (HM03794) | | | | | | ● | | | | | | | | | | |
| CHANGES (HM03985) | | ● | ● | | | ● | ● | | ● | | | | | ● | | |
| CHICHESTER NATURAL HEALTH CTRE (HM04156) | ● | ● | ● | ● | | ● | ● | ● | ● | ● | ● | ● | ● | ● | | ● |
| CLAIRVOYANT - MEDIUM - HEALER (HM04514) | ● | ● | ● | | | ● | ● | ● | ● | ● | | | ● | ● | | ● |
| CLARKE, STEVEN (HM04604) | | | | | | ● | | | ● | | ● | | | | | |
| CORNERWEIGHS (HM05183) | | ● | | | | | | | | | | ● | | | | |
| DALLAS, PETER (HM05691) | | | | | | | | | ● | | | | ● | ● | | |
| DYER & ASSOCIATES (HM06444) | | | | | | | | ● | | | | ● | ● | | | |
| EMINATIONS ACUPUNCTURE CLINIC (HM06805) | | | | | | | ● | ● | ● | ● | ● | ● | ● | ● | | ● |
| FELPHAM NATURAL HEALTH CLINIC (HM07206) | | | | | | | | | | | | | | | | |
| FROST, CHARLES (HM07760) | | | | | | | | | ● | | | | | | | |
| FURNACE GREEN CHIRO CTRE (HM07800) | ● | ● | ● | ● | | ● | ● | ● | ● | ● | ● | ● | ● | ● | | ● |
| G & G FOOD SUPPLIES (HM07807) | | | | | | | | | | | | | | | | |

| Business by County with Reference no. | Period Problems | Phobias | Piles | PMT | Pneumonia | Postural Problems | Pregnancy Help | Prostate Problems | Psoriasis | Raynaud's Disease | Recurrent Infections | Restless Legs | Rheumatoid Arthritis | Schizophrenia | Sciatica | Sexual Problems |
|---|---|---|---|---|---|---|---|---|---|---|---|---|---|---|---|---|
| WALSH, M J (HM20865) | | | | | | | | | | | | | | | ● | |
| WEDLAKE-GRIFFITHS, J (HM21097) | | | | | | | | | | | | | ● | | ● | |
| WILBURY PHYSIOTHERAPY (HM21480) | | | | | | | | | | | | | | | | |
| WRIGHT, P A (HM21946) | | | | | | | | | | | | | | | | |
| **SUSSEX (WEST)** | | | | | | | | | | | | | | | | |
| ACORN CENTRE (HM00171) | | | | | ● | | | ● | ● | | | | ● | ● | ● | |
| ALAN SMITH CHIROPRACTOR (HM00470) | | | | | | | | | | | | ● | | | ● | |
| ANDREW BATHIE PRACTICE (HM00846) | | ● | | | | | | | ● | | | | | | | ● |
| ANGELA (HM00872) | | | | | | | | | | | | | | | | |
| AUROMA (HM01357) | | | | | | | | | | | | | | | | |
| AVALON HEALTH CENTRE (HM01380) | ● | ● | ● | ● | ● | | ● | ● | ● | ● | ● | ● | ● | ● | ● | ● |
| B O P (HM01452) | | | | | | | | | | | | | ● | | ● | |
| BACK 2 FITNESS CHIROPRACTIC (HM01476) | | | | | | | | | | | | | | | ● | |
| BALOOMBE OSTEOPATHIC & SPORTS (HM01641) | | | | | | | | | | | | | | | ● | |
| BARTHOLOMEW WAY CLINIC (HM01818) | | | | | | | | | | | | ● | ● | | ● | |
| BELLAMY PARTNERSHIP (HM02093) | | | | | | | | | | | | | | | ● | |
| BLACK, PAULINE (HM02425) | ● | ● | ● | ● | ● | | ● | ● | ● | ● | ● | ● | ● | | ● | ● |
| BODYGUIDE ALTERNATE (HM02619) | ● | ● | ● | ● | ● | | ● | ● | ● | ● | ● | ● | ● | ● | ● | ● |
| BOHNET, CAROLE (HM02648) | ● | | | ● | | | | | | | | | | | ● | |
| BRITCHIRO CLINIC (HM03068) | | | | | | | | | | | | | | | ● | |
| BURNS, L C (HM03417) | | | | | | | | | | | | | | | | |
| CARTLAND, ANN (HM03794) | | | | | | | | | | | | | | | | |
| CHANGES (HM03985) | ● | | | ● | | | ● | | ● | | ● | ● | | | ● | |
| CHICHESTER NATURAL HEALTH CTRE (HM04156) | ● | ● | ● | ● | ● | | ● | ● | ● | ● | ● | ● | ● | ● | ● | ● |
| CLAIRVOYANT - MEDIUM - HEALER (HM04514) | ● | ● | ● | ● | ● | | ● | ● | | | ● | ● | ● | | ● | ● |
| CLARKE, STEVEN (HM04604) | | ● | | | | | | | | | | | | ● | | |
| CORNERWEIGHS (HM05183) | | | | | | | | | | ● | | ● | | | | |
| DALLAS, PETER (HM05691) | ● | | | ● | | | ● | ● | ● | | | | | | ● | ● |
| DYER & ASSOCIATES (HM06444) | | | | | | ● | ● | | | | | | | | ● | |
| EMINATIONS ACUPUNCTURE CLINIC (HM06805) | ● | ● | ● | ● | ● | | ● | | ● | ● | ● | ● | ● | | ● | |
| FELPHAM NATURAL HEALTH CLINIC (HM07206) | | | | ● | | | | | ● | | | | | | ● | |
| FROST, CHARLES (HM07760) | | ● | | | | | | | | | | | | | | ● |
| FURNACE GREEN CHIRO CTRE (HM07800) | ● | ● | ● | ● | ● | | ● | ● | ● | ● | ● | ● | ● | ● | ● | ● |
| G & G FOOD SUPPLIES (HM07807) | | | | ● | | | | | | | | | | | | |

# I - S Conditions treated at Practices/Businesses

| Business by County with Reference no. | GARDINER, SAM (HM07876) | GRAVILLE, CHRIS (HM08405) | GREENFIELD, KAREN (HM08486) | HARRIS, PAUL A E (HM09084) | HEALTH IS HAPPINESS REFLEX (HM09390) | HEELER CENTRE (HM09498) | HORSHAM CHIROPRACTIC CENTRE (HM10191) | I C O M (HM10548) | JONES, NIGEL (HM11182) | JONES, WENDY (HM11203) | LITTLEHAMPTON NAT HLTH CTRE (HM12470) | MAYNARD, MARTIN A (HM13357) | MID SUSSEX CHIROPRACTIC CLINIC (HM13805) | MID SUSSEX HOMEOPATHIC CLINIC (HM13806) | MILLENNIUM HOMEOPATHY (HM13877) | MIND WORK SOLUTIONS (HM13967) | NUNN, SALLY (HM15108) | OSTEOPATHY AT ESQUIRE'S (HM15479) | PAIN & PARALYSIS SPECIALIST (HM15578) | PALMER, GAYLE (HM15606) | PALMER, GAYLE (HM15605) | PITT, KATHY (HM16349) | PORTLAND PHYSIOTHERAPY CLINIC (HM16451) | RICHARDSON, BRIAN J (HM17269) | ROOM FOR HEALING (HM17585) | SANDERSON & ELEMENT (HM17921) | SANDON, PATER H G (DR) (HM17925) | STEVENS, PAT (HM19238) | STOTT-DURHAM, ANDREW (HM19355) | SWAN, LAURIE C (HM19574) | TAYLOR, CHRISTIAN (HM19744) | TRANQUILLITY (HM20260) | WESTACOTT, EILEEN (HM21256) | WILSON, AVIS (HM21646) |
|---|---|---|---|---|---|---|---|---|---|---|---|---|---|---|---|---|---|---|---|---|---|---|---|---|---|---|---|---|---|---|---|---|---|---|
| Sexual Problems | ● | | | | | ● | | | | | ● | | | | ● | ● | ● | | | | | ● | | | | | ● | | | | ● | | | |
| Sciatica | | | | ● | ● | ● | ● | ● | ● | | ● | | ● | ● | ● | ● | ● | ● | ● | ● | ● | ● | | ● | ● | ● | ● | | | ● | ● | | | |
| Schizophrenia | | | | | | | | | | | ● | | | | ● | ● | ● | | | | | ● | | | | | ● | | | | ● | | | |
| Rheumatoid Arthritis | | | | | | | | ● | | | ● | | ● | ● | ● | ● | ● | ● | ● | ● | ● | ● | | ● | ● | | ● | | | | ● | ● | | |
| Restless Legs | ● | | | | ● | | | | | | ● | | | ● | ● | ● | ● | | ● | ● | ● | ● | | | ● | | ● | | | ● | ● | | | |
| Recurrent Infections | | | | | | | | ● | | | ● | | | ● | ● | ● | ● | | | ● | ● | ● | | | ● | | ● | | | ● | ● | | | |
| Raynaud's Disease | | | | | | ● | | ● | | | ● | | | ● | ● | ● | ● | | | ● | ● | ● | | | ● | | ● | | | | ● | | | |
| Psoriasis | | | | | | ● | | | | | ● | | ● | ● | ● | ● | ● | | | | | ● | | | ● | | ● | | | ● | ● | | | |
| Prostate Problems | | | | | | ● | | ● | | | ● | | ● | ● | ● | ● | ● | | | ● | ● | ● | | | ● | | ● | | | | ● | | | |
| Pregnancy Help | ● | | | | ● | | | ● | | | ● | | | ● | ● | ● | ● | ● | | ● | ● | ● | | | ● | | ● | | | | ● | | | |
| Postural Problems | | | | | | | | | | | | | | | | | | | | | | | | | | | | | | | | | | |
| Pneumonia | | | | | | | | | | | ● | | | | ● | ● | ● | | | ● | | ● | | | ● | | ● | | | | ● | | | |
| PMT | ● | ● | ● | | ● | ● | | ● | | | ● | | ● | ● | ● | ● | ● | | | ● | ● | ● | | | ● | | ● | | | | ● | | | |
| Piles | | | | | | | | | | | ● | | | ● | ● | ● | ● | | | ● | | ● | | | ● | | ● | | | | ● | | | |
| Phobias | ● | | | | | ● | | ● | | | ● | | | ● | ● | ● | ● | | | | | ● | | | ● | | ● | | | ● | ● | | | |
| Period Problems | ● | | ● | | ● | | | ● | | | ● | | ● | ● | ● | ● | ● | ● | | ● | ● | ● | | | ● | | ● | | | | ● | | ● | |
| Parkinson's Disease | | | | | | ● | | | | | ● | | | | ● | ● | ● | | | ● | ● | ● | | | ● | | ● | | | | ● | | | |
| Panic Attacks | | | | | | | | | | | | | | | | | | | | | | | | | | | | | | | | | | |
| Palpitations | | | | | ● | | | ● | | | ● | | ● | ● | ● | ● | ● | | | ● | ● | ● | | | ● | | ● | | | ● | ● | | | |
| Pain | ● | | | ● | ● | ● | ● | ● | | | ● | | ● | ● | ● | ● | ● | ● | ● | ● | ● | ● | ● | ● | ● | ● | ● | ● | | ● | ● | ● | ● | ● |
| Osteoporosis | | | | ● | | ● | | ● | | | ● | | ● | ● | ● | ● | ● | | | ● | ● | ● | | | ● | ● | ● | | | | ● | | | ● |
| Obesity | ● | | | | | | | ● | | | ● | | ● | | ● | ● | ● | | | | | ● | | | | | ● | | | ● | ● | ● | | |
| Neuralgia | | | | | | | | ● | | ● | ● | | ● | ● | ● | ● | ● | ● | ● | ● | ● | ● | | | ● | | ● | | | ● | ● | | | |
| Nervous Disorders | | | | ● | | ● | ● | ● | | | ● | | ● | ● | ● | ● | ● | | | ● | ● | ● | | | ● | ● | ● | ● | | ● | ● | ● | | |
| Nerve Disorders | ● | | | ● | | ● | ● | ● | | | ● | | ● | ● | ● | ● | ● | ● | ● | ● | ● | ● | | | ● | ● | ● | | | ● | ● | | | |
| Nausea | | | ● | | ● | | | ● | | | ● | | | ● | ● | ● | ● | | | ● | ● | ● | | | ● | | ● | | | | ● | | | |
| Nail Health | | | | | | | | | | | ● | ● | | | ● | ● | ● | | | | | ● | | ● | ● | | ● | | | | ● | | | |
| Musculo-skeletal | | | | | | | | | | | | | | | | | | | | | | | | | | | | | | | | | | |
| Muscular Dystrophy | | | | | | | | | | | ● | | | | ● | ● | ● | | | | | ● | | | | | ● | | | | ● | | | |
| Multiple Sclerosis | ● | | | | ● | ● | | ● | | | ● | | ● | | ● | ● | ● | | | | | ● | ● | | ● | | ● | | | | ● | | ● | |
| Mouth Ulcers | | | | | | | | | | | ● | | | ● | ● | ● | ● | | | | | ● | | | | | ● | | | | ● | | | |
| Mouth Disorders | | | | | | ● | | | | | ● | | | ● | ● | ● | ● | | | | | ● | | | ● | | ● | | | | ● | | | |
| Motion Sickness | ● | | | | | ● | | ● | | | ● | | | ● | ● | ● | ● | | | | | ● | | | | | ● | | | | ● | | | |
| Migraine | ● | ● | ● | | ● | ● | ● | ● | | | ● | | ● | ● | ● | ● | ● | ● | | ● | ● | ● | | | ● | | ● | | ● | | ● | | ● | ● |
| Menopause | ● | ● | | | ● | | | ● | | | ● | | | ● | ● | ● | ● | | | ● | ● | ● | | | ● | | ● | | | ● | ● | | | |
| ME | ● | | ● | | ● | ● | ● | ● | | | ● | | ● | ● | ● | ● | ● | ● | ● | ● | ● | ● | | | ● | | ● | | ● | ● | ● | ● | ● | |
| Lung Problems | | | | | | | | ● | | | ● | | | ● | ● | ● | ● | | | ● | ● | ● | | | ● | | ● | | | | ● | | | |
| Low Blood Pressure | ● | | | | ● | | | ● | | | ● | | | ● | ● | ● | ● | | | ● | | ● | | | ● | | ● | | | | ● | | | |
| Liver Disorders | | | | | | | | ● | | | ● | | | ● | ● | ● | ● | | | ● | ● | ● | | | ● | | ● | | | | ● | | | |
| Lethargy | | | | | | ● | | ● | | | ● | | | ● | ● | ● | ● | | | ● | ● | ● | | | ● | | ● | | | ● | ● | ● | | |
| Laryngitis | | | | | | | | | | | ● | | | ● | ● | ● | ● | | | ● | ● | ● | | | ● | | ● | | | | ● | | | |
| Lactose Intolerance | | | | | | ● | | | | | ● | | | | ● | ● | ● | | | ● | | ● | | | | | ● | | | | ● | | | |
| Kidney Complaints | | | ● | | ● | | | ● | | | ● | | ● | ● | ● | ● | ● | | | ● | ● | ● | | | ● | | ● | | | ● | ● | | | |
| Joint Pain | ● | | ● | ● | ● | ● | ● | ● | | ● | ● | | ● | ● | ● | ● | ● | ● | ● | ● | ● | ● | ● | ● | ● | ● | ● | ● | ● | | ● | ● | | ● |
| Jet Lag | | | | | | | | ● | | | ● | | | | ● | ● | ● | | | ● | | ● | | | ● | | ● | | | | ● | | | |
| Itching | | | | | | ● | | ● | | | ● | | | ● | ● | ● | ● | | | | | ● | | | ● | | ● | | | | ● | | | |
| Irritable Bowel Syndrome | ● | | | ● | ● | ● | ● | ● | ● | | ● | | ● | ● | ● | ● | ● | ● | ● | ● | ● | ● | | | ● | | ● | | | ● | ● | | | |
| Insomnia | ● | | ● | | ● | ● | | ● | | | ● | | ● | ● | ● | ● | ● | | | ● | | ● | | | ● | | ● | | | | ● | | ● | |

www.healthmyself.com

England (by County)

CONDITIONS TREATED

I-S

# I - S Conditions treated at Practices/Businesses

| Business by County with Reference no. | Insomnia | Irritable Bowel Syndrome | Itching | Jet Lag | Joint Pain | Kidney Complaints | Lactose Intolerance | Laryngitis | Lethargy | Liver Disorders | Low Blood Pressure | Lung Problems | ME | Menopause | Migraine | Motion Sickness |
|---|---|---|---|---|---|---|---|---|---|---|---|---|---|---|---|---|
| WOOD, J G (HM21798) | | | | | ● | | | | | | | ● | | | | |
| WORSFOLD, CHRISTINE (HM21903) | | | | | | | | | | | | | | | | |
| WORTHING CHIROPRACTIC CLINIC (HM21907) | | ● | | | ● | | | | | | | | ● | | | |
| WORTHING CLINIC OF ACUPUNCTURE (HM21908) | | | | | | | | | | | | | | ● | ● | |
| **TYNE AND WEAR** | | | | | | | | | | | | | | | | |
| ACUPUNCTURE & NAT MED CLINIC (HM00243) | ● | ● | ● | ● | ● | ● | ● | ● | ● | ● | ● | ● | ● | ● | ● | ● |
| AROMATHERAPY IN PRACTICE (HM01114) | | | | | | | | | | | | | ● | ● | | |
| B WIGRAM HEALING & REFLEXOLOGY (HM01455) | ● | | | | | | | | | | | | | | ● | |
| BALMORAL PHYSIOTHERAPY (HM01640) | | | | | ● | | | | | | | | | | | |
| BASS, MIKE (HM01850) | ● | ● | | ● | ● | ● | | | ● | ● | ● | | ● | ● | ● | ● |
| BODY BALANCE HOLISTIC THERAPY (HM02572) | ● | ● | | | | | | | | | | | | ● | ● | |
| CHIROPODY CLINIC (HM04324) | ● | ● | | | | ● | | | | | | | ● | ● | ● | |
| CONNECT PHYSICAL HEALTH CTRE (HM04989) | | ● | | | ● | | | | | | | | | | | |
| COOP, JOE (HM05082) | | | | | | | | | | | | | | | | |
| DENTON, A (HM05998) | ● | ● | | | ● | ● | | ● | | ● | ● | ● | ● | ● | ● | |
| DERWENT CENTRE (HM06020) | ● | ● | ● | ● | ● | ● | ● | ● | ● | ● | ● | ● | ● | ● | ● | ● |
| FAMILY CHIRO WELLNESS CENTRE (HM07083) | ● | ● | | | ● | ● | | | | ● | ● | ● | ● | | ● | |
| FEEL GOOD AROMATHERAPY (HM07164) | ● | ● | ● | | ● | ● | | ● | ● | ● | ● | ● | ● | ● | ● | |
| FOWLER, CHRISTINE (HM07628) | ● | ● | ● | ● | ● | ● | ● | ● | ● | ● | ● | ● | ● | ● | ● | ● |
| GATESHEAD COMPLEMENTARY HEALTH (HM07927) | | | | | | | | | | | | | | | | |
| HEALTH ALLIANCE CENTRE (HM09375) | | | | | ● | | | | | | | | | | ● | |
| HERBAL GARDEN AROMATHERAPY (HM09612) | ● | ● | ● | ● | ● | | | | | | | ● | ● | ● | ● | ● |
| HOLISTIC CHIROPRACTOR (HM09951) | | | | | ● | | | | | | | | | | | |
| HON, ARTHUR M R (HM10111) | | | | | ● | | | | | | | | | | | |
| HYPNOTHERAPY AND COUNSELLING (HM10514) | | | | | | | | | | | | | | | | |
| MCANELLY, J L (HM13368) | | | | | | | | | | | | | | | | |
| NATURAL SELECTION (HM14623) | ● | | | ● | | | | | | | | | | | | |
| NEW LIFE NATURAL HEALTH CARE (HM14820) | ● | ● | ● | ● | ● | ● | ● | ● | ● | ● | ● | ● | ● | ● | ● | ● |
| NEWCASTLE SPRTS INJ/THRPY CTRE (HM14855) | | | | | ● | | | | | | | | | ● | ● | |
| OSBORNE CLINIC (HM15420) | | ● | | | ● | | | | | | | | | | | |
| RAINBOW, RICHARD S (HM16887) | ● | | | | | | | | | | | | | | | |
| SCHOLL FOOTWEAR CENTRE (HM18077) | | | | | | | | | | | | | | | | |
| SHEN HOLISTIC THERAPIES (HM18392) | | ● | | | | | | | | | | | | | | |
| WESTOE PRACTICE (HM21277) | | | | | | | | | | | | | | | | |

| Business by County with Reference no. | Mouth Disorders | Mouth Ulcers | Multiple Sclerosis | Muscular Dystrophy | Musculo-skeletal | Nail Health | Nausea | Nerve Disorders | Nervous Disorders | Neuralgia | Obesity | Osteoporosis | Pain | Palpitations | Panic Attacks | Parkinson's Disease |
|---|---|---|---|---|---|---|---|---|---|---|---|---|---|---|---|---|
| WOOD, J G (HM21798) | | | ● | ● | | | | ● | | ● | | ● | ● | | | ● |
| WORSFOLD, CHRISTINE (HM21903) | | | | | | ● | | | | | | | | | | |
| WORTHING CHIROPRACTIC CLINIC (HM21907) | | | | | | | | ● | | | | ● | ● | | | |
| WORTHING CLINIC OF ACUPUNCTURE (HM21908) | | | | | | | | | | | | | ● | | | |
| **TYNE AND WEAR** | | | | | | | | | | | | | | | | |
| ACUPUNCTURE & NAT MED CLINIC (HM00243) | ● | ● | ● | ● | | ● | ● | ● | ● | ● | ● | ● | ● | ● | | ● |
| AROMATHERAPY IN PRACTICE (HM01114) | | | | | | | | | | | | | ● | | | |
| B WIGRAM HEALING & REFLEXOLOGY (HM01455) | | | ● | | | | ● | | ● | | | | | | | |
| BALMORAL PHYSIOTHERAPY (HM01640) | | | ● | | | | | | | | | | ● | | | |
| BASS, MIKE (HM01850) | | | | | | | ● | ● | ● | | | | ● | ● | | |
| BODY BALANCE HOLISTIC THERAPY (HM02572) | | | | | | | | | | | | | ● | | | |
| CHIROPODY CLINIC (HM04324) | | | | | | ● | | | | | | | | | | |
| CONNECT PHYSICAL HEALTH CTRE (HM04989) | | | | | | ● | | ● | | ● | | ● | ● | | | |
| COOP, JOE (HM05082) | | | | | | | | | | | | | | | | |
| DENTON, A (HM05998) | | | ● | | | | ● | | | | | | ● | ● | | |
| DERWENT CENTRE (HM06020) | ● | ● | ● | ● | ● | ● | ● | ● | ● | ● | ● | ● | ● | ● | ● | ● |
| FAMILY CHIRO WELLNESS CENTRE (HM07083) | | | ● | ● | | | ● | ● | ● | ● | | ● | ● | ● | | ● |
| FEEL GOOD AROMATHERAPY (HM07164) | ● | ● | ● | | | ● | ● | ● | ● | ● | ● | ● | ● | ● | | ● |
| FOWLER, CHRISTINE (HM07628) | ● | ● | ● | ● | | ● | ● | ● | ● | ● | ● | ● | ● | ● | | ● |
| GATESHEAD COMPLEMENTARY HEALTH (HM07927) | | | | ● | | | | | | | | | | | | |
| HEALTH ALLIANCE CENTRE (HM09375) | | | | | | | | | | ● | | | ● | | | |
| HERBAL GARDEN AROMATHERAPY (HM09612) | | ● | | | | | ● | ● | ● | ● | | | ● | | | |
| HOLISTIC CHIROPRACTOR (HM09951) | | | ● | | | | | ● | | | | | | | | |
| HON, ARTHUR M R (HM10111) | | | | | | | | | | | | | ● | | | |
| HYPNOTHERAPY AND COUNSELLING (HM10514) | | | | | | | | | ● | | | | | | | |
| MCANELLY, J L (HM13368) | | | | | | | | | | | | | | | | |
| NATURAL SELECTION (HM14623) | | | | | | | | | | | | | ● | | | |
| NEW LIFE NATURAL HEALTH CARE (HM14820) | ● | ● | ● | ● | | ● | ● | ● | ● | ● | ● | ● | ● | ● | | ● |
| NEWCASTLE SPRTS INJ/THRPY CTRE (HM14855) | | | ● | | | | | | | | | | ● | | | |
| OSBORNE CLINIC (HM15420) | | | ● | | | | | ● | | ● | ● | | ● | | | |
| RAINBOW, RICHARD S (HM16887) | | | | | | | | | ● | | ● | | ● | | | |
| SCHOLL FOOTWEAR CENTRE (HM18077) | | | | | | ● | | | | | | | | | | |
| SHEN HOLISTIC THERAPIES (HM18392) | | | | | | | | | | | | | | | | |
| WESTOE PRACTICE (HM21277) | | | | | | ● | | | | | | | | | | |

| Business by County with Reference no. | Period Problems | Phobias | Piles | PMT | Pneumonia | Postural Problems | Pregnancy Help | Prostate Problems | Psoriasis | Raynaud's Disease | Recurrent Infections | Restless Legs | Rheumatoid Arthritis | Schizophrenia | Sciatica | Sexual Problems |
|---|---|---|---|---|---|---|---|---|---|---|---|---|---|---|---|---|
| WOOD, J G (HM21798) | | | | | ● | | | | | | | | ● | | ● | |
| WORSFOLD, CHRISTINE (HM21903) | | | | | | | | | | | | | | | | |
| WORTHING CHIROPRACTIC CLINIC (HM21907) | | | | | | | | | | | | | | | ● | |
| WORTHING CLINIC OF ACUPUNCTURE (HM21908) | | | | ● | | | | | | | | | | | | |
| **TYNE AND WEAR** | | | | | | | | | | | | | | | | |
| ACUPUNCTURE & NAT MED CLINIC (HM00243) | ● | ● | ● | ● | ● | | ● | ● | ● | ● | ● | ● | ● | ● | ● | ● |
| AROMATHERAPY IN PRACTICE (HM01114) | | | | ● | | | | | | | | | | | | |
| B WIGRAM HEALING & REFLEXOLOGY (HM01455) | | | | | | | | | | | | | | | | |
| BALMORAL PHYSIOTHERAPY (HM01640) | | | | | | | | | | | | | | | | |
| BASS, MIKE (HM01850) | ● | | | ● | | | ● | ● | ● | | ● | ● | ● | | ● | |
| BODY BALANCE HOLISTIC THERAPY (HM02572) | | ● | | | | | | | | | | | ● | | | |
| CHIROPODY CLINIC (HM04324) | | | | | | | | | | | | | | | | |
| CONNECT PHYSICAL HEALTH CTRE (HM04989) | | | | | | | | | | | | | ● | | ● | |
| COOP, JOE (HM05082) | | ● | | | | | | | | | | | | | | |
| DENTON, A (HM05998) | ● | | ● | ● | | | ● | | | | | ● | ● | | ● | |
| DERWENT CENTRE (HM06020) | ● | ● | ● | ● | ● | ● | ● | ● | ● | ● | ● | ● | ● | ● | ● | ● |
| FAMILY CHIRO WELLNESS CENTRE (HM07083) | | | ● | ● | ● | | ● | ● | ● | ● | ● | ● | | | ● | ● |
| FEEL GOOD AROMATHERAPY (HM07164) | ● | ● | ● | ● | ● | | ● | ● | ● | ● | ● | ● | ● | | ● | |
| FOWLER, CHRISTINE (HM07628) | ● | ● | ● | ● | ● | | ● | ● | ● | ● | ● | ● | ● | ● | ● | ● |
| GATESHEAD COMPLEMENTARY HEALTH (HM07927) | | ● | | | | | | | | | | | | | | |
| HEALTH ALLIANCE CENTRE (HM09375) | | | | | | | | | | | | | | | ● | |
| HERBAL GARDEN AROMATHERAPY (HM09612) | ● | ● | | ● | | | ● | ● | ● | | ● | ● | ● | | ● | |
| HOLISTIC CHIROPRACTOR (HM09951) | | | | | | | | | | | | | | | ● | |
| HON, ARTHUR M R (HM10111) | | | | | | | | | | | | ● | | | ● | |
| HYPNOTHERAPY AND COUNSELLING (HM10514) | | ● | | | | | | | | | | | | | | |
| MCANELLY, J L (HM13368) | | ● | | | | | | | | | | | | | | |
| NATURAL SELECTION (HM14623) | | | | | | | | | | | | | | | | |
| NEW LIFE NATURAL HEALTH CARE (HM14820) | ● | ● | ● | ● | ● | | ● | ● | ● | ● | ● | ● | ● | ● | ● | ● |
| NEWCASTLE SPRTS INJ/THRPY CTRE (HM14855) | ● | | | ● | | | | | ● | | | | | | | |
| OSBORNE CLINIC (HM15420) | | | | ● | | | | | | | | | ● | | ● | |
| RAINBOW, RICHARD S (HM16887) | ● | ● | | ● | | | | | | | | | | | | ● |
| SCHOLL FOOTWEAR CENTRE (HM18077) | | | | | | | | | | | | | | | | |
| SHEN HOLISTIC THERAPIES (HM18392) | | | | | | | | | | | | | | | | |
| WESTOE PRACTICE (HM21277) | | | | | | | | | | | | | | | | |

# I - S Conditions treated at Practices/Businesses

| Business by County with Reference no. | Insomnia | Irritable Bowel Syndrome | Itching | Jet Lag | Joint Pain | Kidney Complaints | Lactose Intolerance | Laryngitis | Lethargy | Liver Disorders | Low Blood Pressure | Lung Problems | ME | Menopause | Migraine | Motion Sickness | Mouth Disorders | Mouth Ulcers | Multiple Sclerosis | Muscular Dystrophy | Musculo-skeletal | Nail Health | Nausea | Nerve Disorders | Nervous Disorders | Neuralgia | Obesity | Osteoporosis | Pain | Palpitations | Panic Attacks | Parkinson's Disease | Period Problems | Phobias | Piles | PMT | Pneumonia | Postural Problems | Pregnancy Help | Prostate Problems | Psoriasis | Raynaud's Disease | Recurrent Infections | Restless Legs | Rheumatoid Arthritis | Schizophrenia | Sciatica | Sexual Problems |
|---|---|---|---|---|---|---|---|---|---|---|---|---|---|---|---|---|---|---|---|---|---|---|---|---|---|---|---|---|---|---|---|---|---|---|---|---|---|---|---|---|---|---|---|---|---|---|---|---|
| WHITLEY BAY CHIROPRACTOR (HM21406) | | | | |●| | | | | | | | | | ●| | | | | | | | | | | | | |●| | | | | | | | | | | | | | | | | | | |
| WARWICKSHIRE | | | | | | | | | | | | | | | | | | | | | | | | | | | | | | | | | | | | | | | | | | | | | | | | |
| ACUPUNCTURE CLINIC (HM00279) |●| | | |●| | | |●| | | | |●|●| | | | | | | |●| | | | | |●| | | |●| | |●| | | | | | | | | | |●| |
| BARRATT'S HOMEOPATHY (HM01780) |●|●|●|●|●|●|●|●|●|●| |●|●|●|●|●|●|●| | | |●|●|●|●|●|●|●|●|●| |●|●|●|●|●|●| |●|●|●|●|●|●|●| |●|●|
| BIRTWELL, ANDREW (HM02400) | | | | | | | | | | | | | | | | | | | | | | | | |●| | | | | | | | | | | | | | | | | | | | | | |●|
| BRIEF COUNS & PSYCHOTHERAPY SV (HM03020) | | | | | | | | | | | | | | | | | | | | | | | | |●| | | | | | | | |●| | | | | | | | | | | | | |●|
| CHURCH LAWFORD CHIRO CLINIC (HM04463) | | | | |●| | | |●| | | |●| | | | | | | | | | | | |●| | |●| | | | | | | | | | | | | | | | | | | |
| CLIFTON OSTEOPATHIC PRACTICE (HM04669) | |●|●|●|●|●| | |●|●| |●|●|●|●| | |●|●| | | | | |●|●|●|●|●| | |●|●| |●|●| | |●|●|●|●|●|●|●| |●| |
| EDWARDS, IRENE & PETER (HM06656) | |●| | | | | | | | | | | | | | | | | | | | | | | | | | |●| |●| | |●| | | | | | | | | | | | | | |
| FIGHT (HM07282) | |●| | |●| | | | | | |●| | |●| | | | | | | | |●| | |●|●|●|●| | |●| | | | | | | | | | | |●|●| |●| |
| GREIG, E (HM08527) |●|●| | | | | | | | | | | | |●| | | | | | | | | | | | | |●| | | |●| | | | | | | | | | | | | |
| HEALTHPOINT (HM09414) |●| |●|●| | | |●| | | | | |●|●| | |●| | | | |●| | | | | |●| | |●| | |●| | | | | | | | | | |●| |
| HEART OF ENGLAND SHIATSU (HM09442) |●|●|●|●|●|●| | |●|●|●|●|●|●|●| | | |●| | | | |●|●|●| |●| |●| | |●|●| |●| | |●|●| | | |●|●| |●| |
| HEARTLANDS (HM09445) |●|●| | | | | | |●| |●| | | | |●| | | | | | | | |●| |●| |●|●| | | |●| | | | | | | | | | | | | |●|
| HERBAL ONE (HM09631) |●|●|●|●|●|●|●|●|●|●|●|●|●|●|●|●|●|●|●|●| |●|●|●|●|●|●|●|●|●| |●|●|●|●|●|●| |●|●|●|●|●|●|●|●|●|●|
| HOLYCOMBE (HM10060) | |●| | | | | | |●| | | | | |●| | | | | | | | | |●| | | | | | | | | | | | | | | | | | | | |●| |
| JAN LLOYD AROMATHERAPY (HM10913) |●|●| | | | | | |●| | | |●| |●| | | | | | | | | |●| | | |●| | | | |●| |●| | | | |●| | | |●| | | |
| LEAMINGTON SPA CHIRO CLINIC (HM12104) | |●| | |●| |●| | | | | |●| |●| | | | | | | |●|●| | | |●| | | | | | | | | | | | | | | | | |●| |
| LIFE-WAYS (HM12367) |●|●|●|●|●|●| |●|●|●|●|●|●|●|●|●|●|●|●| | |●|●|●|●|●|●|●|●|●| | |●|●|●|●|●| |●|●|●|●|●|●|●|●|●|●|
| NATURAL HEALTH CENTRE (HM14567) |●|●|●| |●|●|●| |●| |●|●|●|●|●|●| |●| | | | |●| |●|●|●|●|●|●| | |●|●| |●| | |●| |●| |●|●|●| |●| |
| NATURAL THERAPY CENTRE (HM14651) |●|●|●| |●|●| |●|●|●|●|●|●|●|●|●|●|●| | | | |●| |●|●| | |●|●| | |●|●|●|●| | |●|●| | |●| | | |●| |
| NEWEY, RACHEL (HM14862) |●|●| | |●| | | | | | | | | | | | | | | | | |●| | |●| | |●| | | |●| | | | | |●| | | | | | | |●| |
| NUNEATON CHIROPRACTIC CLINIC (HM15104) | |●| | |●| | | |●| | | | | | | | | | | | | | |●| | | |●|●| | | | | | | | | | | | | | | | |●| |
| PETERS, EVERARD (HM16085) |●| | | |●| | |●| | | | | | |●| | | | | | | | |●| |●| |●|●| | | | | | | | |●|●| |●| | | | | |●| |
| REFLEXOLOGY CLINIC (HM17091) | |●| | |●| | | | |●| |●| |●|●| | | | | | | | | | | | |●|●|●| | | | |●|●| | | |●|●|●| |●|●| |●| |
| REVITALIZE (HM17205) | |●| | | | | | | | | | | |●|●| | | | | | | | | | | | | | | | | | |●| |●| | | | | | | | | | | |
| RUSSELL, COLIN (HM17766) | | | | | | | | | | | | | | | | | | | | | |●| | | | | | | | | | | | | | | | | | | | | | | | | |
| SAVAGE, GERALD (HM17966) |●|●| |●| | | | |●| | | |●| |●| | | | | | | | |●|●| |●| |●|●| | | |●| | | | | | | | | |●| |●| |●|
| SHAWE AVENUE OSTEO PRACTICE (HM18351) | |●| | |●| | | | | | | | | | | | | |●| | | | | | |●| | |●| | | | | | | | |●| | | | | | |●| |●| |
| SHIATSU SOCIETY (HM18464) |●|●|●| |●|●| | | |●|●|●| |●|●| | | | | | | | | | | | |●|●|●| | |●|●| |●| | |●| | |●| |●|●|●|●|●|
| SMALLWOOD, P (HM18698) | | | | | | | | | | | | | | | | | | | | | |●| | | | | | | | | | | | | | | | | | | | | | | | | |
| STRATFORD PHYSIO CLINIC (HM19370) | | | | |●| | | | | | | | | | | | | |●| | | | | | | | | | | | | | | | | | | | | | | | | | | | |
| STUDLEY PHYSIOTHERAPY CENTRE (HM19442) | | | | |●| | | | | | | | | | | | | | | |●| | |●| |●| |●|●| | |●| | | | | | | | | | | | | | |●| |
| TOWERS, DIANA (HM20195) |●|●| |●| | | | | | | | | |●|●| | | | | | |●| |●|●| |●| |●| |●| | |●| | | | |●| | | | | | | | |●|

# I - S Conditions treated at Practices/Businesses

Business by County with Reference no.

| Business by County with Reference no. | Insomnia | Irritable Bowel Syndrome | Itching | Jet Lag | Joint Pain | Kidney Complaints | Lactose Intolerance | Laryngitis | Lethargy | Liver Disorders | Low Blood Pressure | Lung Problems | ME | Menopause | Migraine | Motion Sickness | Mouth Disorders | Mouth Ulcers | Multiple Sclerosis | Muscular Dystrophy | Musculo-skeletal | Nail Health | Nausea | Nerve Disorders |
|---|---|---|---|---|---|---|---|---|---|---|---|---|---|---|---|---|---|---|---|---|---|---|---|---|
| TRADITIONAL ACUPUNCTURE GROUP (HM20221) | ● | ● | | ● | ● | ● | | ● | ● | ● | ● | ● | ● | ● | ● | | | | ● | | | | ● | ● |
| WARWICK OSTEOPATHIC PRACTICE (HM20966) | | ● | ● | ● | ● | ● | | | ● | ● | | ● | ● | ● | ● | | | ● | ● | | | | | |
| WREN, PAULINE (HM21922) | ● | ● | | | | | | | ● | | | | ● | | | | | | | | | | | |
| WILTSHIRE | | | | | | | | | | | | | | | | | | | | | | | | |
| AMESBURY ABBEY CLINIC (HM00781) | | | | | ● | | | | | | | | | | | | | | ● | | | | | |
| ANDREWS, HAZEL (HM00852) | ● | ● | ● | | ● | | | | ● | | | | ● | ● | ● | ● | | ● | | | | | ● | |
| AVEBURY HYPNOTHERAPY PRACTICE (HM01386) | ● | ● | | | | | | | | | | | | | ● | | | ● | | | | | | ● |
| 'BACK IN LINE' (HM01482) | ● | | | ● | ● | | | | ● | | | | | | ● | | | | | | | | | |
| BLUNSDON ABBEY PHYSIOTHERAPY (HM02533) | | | | | ● | | | | | | | | | | | | | | ● | | | | | |
| CASTLE STREET CHIRO CLINIC (HM03836) | | | | | ● | | | | | | | | | | | | | | | | | | | |
| CRICKLADE ROAD PRACTICE (HM05439) | | ● | | | ● | | | | | | | | | | | | | | | | | | | |
| EASE MANAGEMENT CENTRE (HM06506) | ● | ● | | | | | | | ● | | | | ● | | | | | | | | | | | |
| ENGLISH, JOHN M (DR) (HM06834) | ● | ● | ● | | ● | ● | | ● | ● | ● | | ● | ● | ● | ● | ● | ● | ● | ● | | | | ● | |
| HEALTH HYDRO (HM09389) | ● | ● | ● | ● | ● | | | | ● | | | | ● | | ● | | | ● | | | | | ● | |
| HIGHWORTH PHYSIOTHERAPY CLINIC (HM09761) | | | | | ● | | | | | | | | | | | | | | ● | | | | | |
| HYPNOTHERAPY CENTRE (HM10529) | ● | ● | | | | | | | | | | | ● | ● | ● | ● | | | | | | | ● | ● |
| JENKINS, RUSSELL S (HM10996) | | | | | | | | | | | | | | | | | | | | | | | | |
| LEIGHTON REFLEXOLOGY CLINIC (HM12196) | ● | ● | | ● | | | | | ● | | ● | | ● | ● | ● | | | | | | | | | ● |
| LIFE-ENERGIES (HM12352) | ● | ● | ● | ● | ● | ● | | ● | ● | ● | ● | ● | ● | | ● | | ● | ● | ● | | | | | ● |
| LYON, P (HM12783) | | | | | ● | | | | | | | | | | | | | | | | | | | |
| MAGNO PULSE (HM12919) | ● | ● | | | ● | | | | | | ● | | ● | ● | ● | | | | ● | ● | | | | |
| MALMESBURY CHIROPRACTIC CLINIC (HM12982) | | ● | | | ● | | | | | | | | | | | | | | | | | | | |
| MARLBOROUGH CHIRO CLINIC (HM13122) | | | | | ● | | | | | | | | | | | | | | | | | | | ● |
| MARLBOROUGH NATURAL HLTH CTRE (HM13123) | ● | ● | ● | ● | ● | ● | ● | ● | ● | ● | ● | ● | ● | ● | ● | ● | ● | ● | ● | ● | | ● | ● | ● |
| MATHER, PAULINE (HM13280) | | ● | | ● | ● | | ● | | ● | ● | | | ● | ● | | | | | | | | | | |
| MOURANT, JENNIFER L (HM14298) | ● | ● | | | | | | | | | | | | | | | | | | | | | | |
| MULTI-THERAPY CENTRE (HM14352) | ● | ● | ● | | ● | | | ● | ● | ● | | | ● | ● | ● | | | ● | | | | | ● | |
| NATURAL THERAPY CENTRE (HM14639) | ● | ● | | | ● | | | | ● | | | | ● | ● | ● | | | | | | | | | ● |
| NATURALLY NUTRITION (HM14673) | ● | ● | | | ● | | ● | | ● | | ● | | ● | ● | ● | | | ● | ● | | | | | |
| OSTEOPATHS (HM15475) | | | | | ● | | | | | | | | | | | | | | | | | | | ● |
| PETER & CAROLINE (HM16071) | ● | | | | ● | | | | | | ● | | ● | | | | | | | | | | | |
| PETTIFER, JUSTINA (HM16095) | ● | ● | | | | | | | ● | | | | | | ● | | | | | | | ● | | ● |
| PHYSIOTHERAPY CLINIC (HM16247) | | | | | ● | | | | | | | | ● | | | | | | | | | | | ● |
| QUIRKE, G (HM16820) | | ● | | | | | | | | | | | | | | | | | | | | | | |

| Business by County with Reference no. | Nervous Disorders | Neuralgia | Obesity | Osteoporosis | Pain | Palpitations | Panic Attacks | Parkinson's Disease | Period Problems | Phobias | Piles | PMT | Pneumonia | Postural Problems | Pregnancy Help | Prostate Problems | Psoriasis | Raynaud's Disease | Recurrent Infections | Restless Legs | Rheumatoid Arthritis | Schizophrenia | Sciatica | Sexual Problems |
|---|---|---|---|---|---|---|---|---|---|---|---|---|---|---|---|---|---|---|---|---|---|---|---|---|
| TRADITIONAL ACUPUNCTURE GROUP (HM20221) | ● | ● | | ● | ● | ● | | ● | ● | ● | ● | ● | | | ● | ● | ● | ● | ● | ● | ● | | ● | |
| WARWICK OSTEOPATHIC PRACTICE (HM20966) | ● | ● | ● | ● | ● | | | ● | ● | | ● | ● | | | ● | ● | ● | ● | ● | ● | ● | | ● | |
| WREN, PAULINE (HM21922) | ● | | | | ● | | | | | ● | | | | | | | | | | | | | | |
| WILTSHIRE | | | | | | | | | | | | | | | | | | | | | | | | |
| AMESBURY ABBEY CLINIC (HM00781) | | | | | | | | | | | | | | | | | | | | | | | | |
| ANDREWS, HAZEL (HM00852) | ● | ● | | ● | ● | ● | | | ● | | ● | ● | | | ● | | ● | | | ● | ● | | ● | |
| AVEBURY HYPNOTHERAPY PRACTICE (HM01386) | ● | | ● | | | | | | | ● | | | | | | | | | | ● | | | | ● |
| 'BACK IN LINE' (HM01482) | | | | | ● | | | | | | | ● | | | | | | | | | | | ● | |
| BLUNSDON ABBEY PHYSIOTHERAPY (HM02533) | | | | | | | | | | | | | | | | | | | | | | | | |
| CASTLE STREET CHIRO CLINIC (HM03836) | | | | | ● | | | | | | | | | | | | | | | | | | | |
| CRICKLADE ROAD PRACTICE (HM05439) | | ● | | | ● | | | | ● | | | ● | | | ● | | ● | ● | | ● | ● | | ● | |
| EASE MANAGEMENT CENTRE (HM06506) | ● | | | | | | ● | | | ● | | | | | | | | | | | | ● | | |
| ENGLISH, JOHN M (DR) (HM06834) | ● | ● | | ● | ● | ● | | ● | ● | ● | ● | ● | ● | | ● | ● | ● | ● | ● | ● | ● | ● | ● | ● |
| HEALTH HYDRO (HM09389) | ● | ● | ● | | ● | | | | ● | ● | | ● | | | | | ● | ● | | ● | | ● | ● | |
| HIGHWORTH PHYSIOTHERAPY CLINIC (HM09761) | | | | | ● | | | | | | | | | | | | | | | | ● | | | |
| HYPNOTHERAPY CENTRE (HM10529) | ● | | ● | | ● | ● | | | | ● | | | | | | | | | | ● | | | | ● |
| JENKINS, RUSSELL S (HM10996) | | ● | | | ● | | | | | | | | | | | | | | | | | | ● | |
| LEIGHTON REFLEXOLOGY CLINIC (HM12196) | ● | ● | | | ● | | | | | | | ● | | | ● | | | | | ● | | | ● | |
| LIFE-ENERGIES (HM12352) | ● | ● | | ● | ● | | | ● | ● | | ● | ● | ● | | | ● | ● | ● | | | ● | | ● | ● |
| LYON, P (HM12783) | | | | | | | | | | | | | | ● | | | | | | | | | | |
| MAGNO PULSE (HM12919) | | | | | ● | | | | ● | | | ● | | | | | | ● | | ● | ● | | | |
| MALMESBURY CHIROPRACTIC CLINIC (HM12982) | ● | | | | ● | | | | | | | ● | | ● | ● | ● | | | | | | | ● | |
| MARLBOROUGH CHIRO CLINIC (HM13122) | | ● | | ● | ● | | | | | | | | | | | | | ● | | | ● | | ● | |
| MARLBOROUGH NATURAL HLTH CTRE (HM13123) | ● | ● | ● | ● | ● | ● | | ● | ● | ● | ● | ● | ● | | ● | ● | ● | ● | ● | ● | ● | ● | ● | ● |
| MATHER, PAULINE (HM13280) | | ● | | | ● | | | | ● | | | ● | | | | | | | | | | | ● | |
| MOURANT, JENNIFER L (HM14298) | | | | | | | | | | | | | | | | | | | | | | | | |
| MULTI-THERAPY CENTRE (HM14352) | | | ● | ● | | | ● | | ● | ● | ● | ● | ● | | ● | | ● | ● | ● | ● | ● | | ● | |
| NATURAL THERAPY CENTRE (HM14639) | ● | ● | | | ● | | | | ● | ● | ● | ● | | ● | | | | | ● | | ● | | ● | |
| NATURALLY NUTRITION (HM14673) | | | ● | ● | | | | ● | ● | | | ● | | | ● | ● | ● | | ● | ● | ● | ● | | |
| OSTEOPATHS (HM15475) | | ● | | | ● | | | | | | | | | | | | | ● | | | ● | | ● | |
| PETER & CAROLINE (HM16071) | | | | | | | | | | | | | | | | | | | | | ● | | | |
| PETTIFER, JUSTINA (HM16095) | ● | | | | ● | | | | | ● | | | | | ● | | | | | | | | | ● |
| PHYSIOTHERAPY CLINIC (HM16247) | | | | | ● | | | | | | | | | | | | | | | | | | ● | |
| QUIRKE, G (HM16820) | ● | | | | | | | | | ● | | | | | | | | | | | | | | |

# I - S Conditions treated at Practices/Businesses

| Business by County with Reference no. | Insomnia | Irritable Bowel Syndrome | Itching | Jet Lag | Joint Pain | Kidney Complaints | Lactose Intolerance | Laryngitis | Lethargy | Liver Disorders | Low Blood Pressure | Lung Problems | ME | Menopause | Migraine | Motion Sickness | Mouth Disorders | Mouth Ulcers | Multiple Sclerosis | Muscular Dystrophy | Musculo-skeletal | Nail Health | Nausea | Nerve Disorders | Nervous Disorders | Neuralgia | Obesity | Osteoporosis | Pain | Palpitations | Panic Attacks | Parkinson's Disease | Period Problems | Phobias | Piles | PMT | Pneumonia | Postural Problems | Pregnancy Help | Prostate Problems | Psoriasis | Raynaud's Disease | Recurrent Infections | Restless Legs | Rheumatoid Arthritis | Schizophrenia | Sciatica | Sexual Problems |
|---|---|---|---|---|---|---|---|---|---|---|---|---|---|---|---|---|---|---|---|---|---|---|---|---|---|---|---|---|---|---|---|---|---|---|---|---|---|---|---|---|---|---|---|---|---|---|---|---|
| RAINBOW NATURAL THERAPIES (HM16880) | | | | | | | | | | | | | | ● | ● | | | | | | | | | | | | | | ● | | | | | | | ● | | | ● | | | | | | | | | |
| SARUM PHYSIOTHERAPY CENTRE (HM17947) | | | | | ● | | | | | | | | | | | | | | ● | | | | | | | | | | | | | | | | | | | | | | | | | | | | | |
| SAWAYA, ALICIA (HM17982) | ● | ● | ● | ● | ● | ● | ● | ● | ● | ● | ● | ● | ● | ● | ● | ● | ● | ● | ● | ● | | ● | ● | ● | ● | ● | ● | ● | ● | ● | | ● | ● | ● | ● | ● | ● | | ● | ● | ● | ● | ● | ● | ● | ● | ● | ● |
| SHAFTSBURY PRACTICE (HM18266) | ● | ● | ● | ● | ● | ● | ● | ● | ● | ● | ● | ● | ● | ● | ● | ● | ● | ● | ● | ● | | ● | ● | ● | ● | ● | ● | ● | ● | ● | | ● | ● | ● | ● | ● | ● | | ● | ● | ● | ● | ● | ● | ● | ● | ● | ● |
| SHAVE, G M (HM18325) | | | | | | | | | | | | | | | | | | | | | | ● | | | | | | | | | | | | | | | | | | | | | | | | | | |
| SPIRITUAL HEALER (HM19026) | | | | | | | | | | | | | | | | | | | | | | | | | | | | | | | | | | | | ● | | | | | | | | | | | | |
| SWINDON CHIROPRACTIC CLINIC (HM19595) | | | | | ● | | | | | | | | | | ● | | | | | | | | | ● | | | | | ● | | | | | | | | | ● | ● | | | | | | | | ● | |
| TISBURY OSTEOPATHIC PRACTICE (HM20094) | | | | | ● | | | | | | | | ● | | | | | | | | | | | ● | | ● | | | ● | | | | ● | | | | | | ● | | | | | | | | ● | |
| WARMINSTER OSTEOPATHIC CLINIC (HM20929) | ● | ● | ● | | ● | | | | ● | ● | ● | | ● | ● | ● | ● | | | ● | | | | | | ● | ● | ● | | ● | ● | | | ● | ● | | ● | | | | ● | ● | | ● | ● | ● | | ● | ● |
| WATSON'S COURT CLINIC (HM21025) | | | | | ● | | | | | | | | | | | | | | | | | ● | | | | | | ● | | | | | | | | | | | | | | | | | | | | |
| WELLS, HENRIETTA (HM21175) | ● | ● | ● | ● | ● | ● | ● | ● | ● | ● | ● | ● | ● | ● | ● | ● | ● | ● | ● | ● | | ● | ● | ● | ● | ● | ● | ● | ● | ● | | ● | ● | ● | ● | ● | ● | | ● | ● | ● | ● | ● | ● | ● | ● | ● | ● |
| WESTBURY CHIROPRACTIC (HM21258) | | ● | | | ● | | | | | | | | ● | | | | | | | | | | | ● | ● | | | | ● | | | | | | | | | | | | | | | | | | ● | |
| WESTBURY REFLEXOLOGY CLINIC (HM21260) | ● | ● | | | ● | ● | | | | | | | ● | ● | ● | | | ● | | | | | ● | | | | | | ● | | | | ● | | | ● | | | ● | | | | | | ● | | | |
| WOOTTON BASSETT (HM21885) | | | | | ● | | | | | | | | | | | | | | | | | | | | | ● | | ● | ● | | | | | | | | | | | | | | | | ● | | ● | |
| **WORCESTERSHIRE** | | | | | | | | | | | | | | | | | | | | | | | | | | | | | | | | | | | | | | | | | | | | | | | | |
| 1ST CHIROPRACTIC UK (HM00007) | | ● | | | ● | | | | | | | | ● | | | | | | | | | | | ● | ● | | | | ● | | | | | | | | | | | | | | | | | | ● | |
| AINSLEY, S (HM00433) | | | | | ● | | | | | | | | | | | | | | | | | ● | | | | | | | | | | | | | | | | | | | | | | | | | ● | |
| BRETFORDTON CLINIC (HM02969) | | | | | ● | | | | | | ● | | ● | | ● | | | | | | | | | ● | ● | | | ● | ● | | | ● | | | | | | | | | | | | | ● | | ● | |
| BROMSGROVE CHIROPRACTIC CLINIC (HM03151) | | ● | | | ● | | | | | | | | ● | | ● | | | | | | | | | | | | | | ● | | | | | | | | | | | | | | | | | | ● | |
| CARYL, M D (HM03804) | | | | | | | | | | | | | | | | | | | | | | ● | | | | | | | | | | | | | | | | | | | | | | | | | | |
| DAVIES PODIATRY (HM05792) | | | | | | | | | | | | | | | | | | | | | | ● | | | | | | | | | | | | | | | | | | | | | | | | | | |
| EVESHAM NATURAL HEALTH CENTRE (HM07009) | ● | ● | ● | | ● | | | | ● | | ● | ● | ● | ● | ● | | | | ● | ● | | | ● | ● | ● | ● | | | ● | ● | | ● | ● | ● | | ● | | | ● | | ● | ● | ● | | ● | | ● | |
| FRONTIA (HM07757) | ● | ● | ● | ● | ● | | | | | | ● | | ● | ● | ● | ● | | ● | ● | | | | | ● | ● | ● | | ● | ● | ● | | | ● | ● | ● | ● | | | ● | ● | ● | ● | ● | ● | ● | | ● | |
| GIBBINS, JONATHAN (HM08022) | | ● | | | ● | | | | | | | | | | ● | | | | | | | | ● | ● | | ● | | ● | ● | | | | ● | | | | | | | | | | | ● | | | | |
| HINKS, MAXINE (HM09834) | | | | | | | | | | | | | | | ● | | | | | | | | | | | | | | | | | | | | | | | | | | | | | | | | | |
| HOLDEN, NINA (HM09933) | ● | | | | ● | ● | | | | | | | ● | ● | ● | | ● | ● | | | | | ● | ● | | | | | | | | | | | | | | | ● | ● | | | | | | | | |
| KITSON, P (HM11730) | | ● | | | ● | | | | | | | | | ● | | | | | | | | | | | | | | ● | ● | | | | | | | | | | | | | | | | | | ● | |
| KRISS, ADRIAN D (HM11803) | | | | | | | | | | | | | | | | | | | | | | ● | | | | | | | | | | | | | | | | | | | | | | | | | | |
| M THORLOW CHIROPODY (HM12810) | | | | | | | | | | | | | | | | | | | | | | ● | | | | | | | | | | | | | | | | | | | | | | | | | | |
| MALVERN NATURAL HEALTH CENTRE (HM12998) | ● | ● | ● | ● | ● | ● | ● | ● | ● | ● | ● | ● | ● | ● | ● | ● | ● | ● | ● | ● | | ● | ● | ● | ● | ● | ● | ● | ● | ● | | ● | ● | ● | ● | ● | ● | | ● | ● | ● | ● | ● | ● | ● | ● | ● | ● |
| MALVERN OSTEOPATHIC CLINIC (HM12999) | | | | | ● | | | | | | | | | | | | | | | | | | | | | | | | | | | | | | | | | | | | | | | | | | | |
| MARSTON, SUE (HM13179) | | | | | ● | | | | | | | | | ● | ● | | | | | | | | ● | | | | | | ● | | | | ● | | | ● | | | | | ● | | | | | | | |
| MEAKIN, D W (HM13637) | | | | | ● | | | | | | | | | | | | | | | | | | | | | | | | ● | | | | | | | | | | | | | | | | | | ● | |
| NATURAL HEALTH CENTRE (HM14564) | ● | | | | | | | | | | | | | ● | ● | | | | | | | | | | | ● | | | | | | | | | | | | | | | ● | | | | ● | | ● | |

www.healthmyself.com

# I - S Conditions treated at Practices/Businesses

| Business by County with Reference no. | Insomnia | Irritable Bowel Syndrome | Itching | Jet Lag | Joint Pain | Kidney Complaints | Lactose Intolerance | Laryngitis | Lethargy | Liver Disorders | Low Blood Pressure | Lung Problems | ME | Menopause | Migraine | Motion Sickness | Mouth Disorders | Mouth Ulcers | Multiple Sclerosis | Muscular Dystrophy | Musculo-skeletal |
|---|---|---|---|---|---|---|---|---|---|---|---|---|---|---|---|---|---|---|---|---|---|
| NOTTINGHAM, STUART (HM15086) | | | | | | | | | | | | | | | | | | | | | |
| OAKFIELD CLINIC (HM15150) | | | | | | | | | | | | ● | | | | | | | | | |
| PARDOE, DIANA T (HM15648) | ● | ● | | | | | | | | | | | | | | | | | | | |
| PERSHORE NAT THERAPY CLINIC (HM16057) | ● | ● | ● | ● | ● | ● | ● | ● | ● | ● | ● | ● | ● | ● | ● | ● | ● | ● | ● | ● | |
| R C C M (HM16829) | | | | | ● | | | | | | | | | | | | | | | | |
| REDDITCH CHIROPRACTIC CLINIC (HM17013) | | ● | | | ● | | | | | | | | ● | | | | | | | | |
| REDDITCH FOOTCARE SURGERY (HM17014) | | | | | | | | | | | | | | | | | | | | | |
| SOUTH WORCESTERSHIRE HYP (HM18915) | ● | ● | | | | | | | | | | | ● | | ● | | | | | | |
| STOKES, TERRY (HM19325) | ● | ● | ● | | ● | | | | ● | ● | | ● | ● | | ● | | | ● | | | |
| STONE, ANNE L (HM19329) | | | | | ● | | | | | | | ● | | | | | | | ● | | |
| WORCESTER NATURAL THERAPY CTRE (HM21886) | ● | ● | ● | ● | ● | ● | ● | ● | ● | ● | ● | ● | ● | ● | ● | ● | ● | ● | ● | ● | |
| YOUNG, JOANNA (HM22075) | ● | | | | ● | | | | | | | | ● | | ● | | | | | | |
| **YORKSHIRE (NORTH)** | | | | | | | | | | | | | | | | | | | | | |
| A TACTILE BUSINESS (HM00046) | ● | | | | | | | | | | | | | | | | | ● | ● | | |
| BAKER, LINDA (HM01587) | | | | | | | | | | | | | | | | | | | ● | | |
| BROADHEAD, J N & M (HM03114) | | | | | | | | | | | | | | | | | | | | | |
| BUSWELL, RONA (HM03471) | | | | | | | | | | ● | ● | | | | ● | | | | | | |
| CORDEL, MICHAEL (HM05160) | ● | ● | | | ● | | | | | | | ● | ● | | ● | | | | | | |
| CRAVEN CLINIC (HM05384) | ● | ● | ● | ● | ● | ● | ● | ● | ● | ● | ● | ● | ● | ● | ● | ● | ● | ● | ● | | |
| CROFT HOUSE CLINIC (HM05452) | | ● | | | ● | | | | | | | | | ● | ● | | | | | | |
| DOVE COURT CENTRE (HM06225) | ● | ● | ● | ● | ● | ● | ● | ● | ● | ● | ● | ● | ● | ● | ● | ● | ● | ● | ● | ● | |
| GRIFFIN, TRICIA (HM08555) | ● | ● | | | | | | | | | | | | ● | | | ● | | | | |
| HARROGATE HOLISTIC HEALTH CTRE (HM09116) | | ● | | | | | | | | | | | ● | ● | ● | | | | | | |
| HEALING CLINIC (HM09328) | ● | ● | ● | ● | ● | ● | ● | ● | ● | ● | ● | ● | ● | ● | ● | ● | ● | ● | ● | ● | |
| HIGHTHORN PHYSIOTHERAPY CLINIC (HM09759) | | | | | ● | | | | | | | | | | | | | | ● | | |
| HOBSON, I K (HM09863) | | | | | ● | | | | | | | | | | | | | | | | |
| LESZCZUK, PAULA (HM12245) | ● | ● | ● | ● | ● | ● | | ● | ● | ● | ● | ● | ● | ● | ● | ● | ● | ● | ● | ● | |
| LESZCZUK, PAULA (HM12246) | ● | ● | ● | ● | ● | ● | | ● | ● | ● | ● | ● | ● | ● | ● | ● | ● | ● | ● | ● | |
| LIFESUPPORT (HM12366) | ● | ● | ● | ● | ● | ● | | | ● | | | ● | ● | ● | ● | | | ● | | | |
| NANCY METCALFE MOBILE CONSULT (HM14468) | ● | | | | ● | | | | | | | | | | ● | | | | | | |
| NATURAL BALANCE (HM14515) | | | | | | | | | | | | | | | ● | | | | | | |
| PANACEA ACUPUNCTURE CLINIC (HM15628) | | | | | ● | | | | | | | | | | ● | | | | | | |
| PAULA LESZCZUK (HM15849) | ● | ● | ● | ● | ● | ● | | ● | ● | ● | ● | ● | ● | ● | ● | ● | ● | ● | ● | ● | |
| RATHBONE, DONNA (HM16955) | | | | | | | | | | | | | | | | | | | | | |

| Business by County with Reference no. | Nail Health | Nausea | Nerve Disorders | Nervous Disorders | Neuralgia | Obesity | Osteoporosis | Pain | Palpitations | Panic Attacks | Parkinson's Disease | Period Problems | Phobias | Piles | PMT | Pneumonia | Postural Problems | Pregnancy Help | Prostate Problems | Psoriasis | Raynaud's Disease | Recurrent Infections | Restless Legs | Rheumatoid Arthritis | Schizophrenia | Sciatica | Sexual Problems |
|---|---|---|---|---|---|---|---|---|---|---|---|---|---|---|---|---|---|---|---|---|---|---|---|---|---|---|---|
| NOTTINGHAM, STUART (HM15086) | | | | | ● | | | ● | | | | | | | | | | | | | | | | | | ● | |
| OAKFIELD CLINIC (HM15150) | | | | | | | | | | | | | | | | | | | | | ● | | | | | | |
| PARDOE, DIANA T (HM15648) | | | | | | | | | | | | | ● | | | | | | | ● | | | | | | | |
| PERSHORE NAT THERAPY CLINIC (HM16057) | ● | ● | ● | ● | ● | ● | ● | ● | ● | | ● | ● | ● | ● | ● | ● | | ● | ● | ● | ● | ● | ● | ● | ● | ● | ● |
| R C C M (HM16829) | | | | | | | | ● | | | | | | | | | | | | | | | | | | | |
| REDDITCH CHIROPRACTIC CLINIC (HM17013) | | | ● | ● | | | | ● | | | | | | | | | | | | | | | | | | ● | |
| REDDITCH FOOTCARE SURGERY (HM17014) | ● | | | | | | | | | | | | | | | | | | | | | | | | | | |
| SOUTH WORCESTERSHIRE HYP (HM18915) | | | | | | ● | | | | | | ● | ● | | ● | | | | | ● | | | | | | | |
| STOKES, TERRY (HM19325) | | | ● | | ● | | | ● | | | | | | | ● | | | | | ● | | | | | | ● | |
| STONE, ANNE L (HM19329) | | | | | | | | ● | | | ● | | | | | | | | | | | | | ● | | | |
| WORCESTER NATURAL THERAPY CTRE (HM21886) | ● | ● | ● | ● | ● | ● | ● | ● | ● | | ● | ● | ● | ● | ● | ● | | ● | ● | ● | ● | ● | ● | ● | ● | ● | ● |
| YOUNG, JOANNA (HM22075) | | | | | ● | | | ● | | | | ● | | | ● | | | | | | | ● | ● | | | ● | |
| **YORKSHIRE (NORTH)** | | | | | | | | | | | | | | | | | | | | | | | | | | | |
| A TACTILE BUSINESS (HM00046) | | | | | | | | | | | | | | | | | | | | | | | | | | | |
| BAKER, LINDA (HM01587) | | | | | | | | | | | | | | | | | | | | | | | | | | | |
| BROADHEAD, J N & M (HM03114) | ● | | | | | | | | | | | | | | | | | | | | | | | | | | |
| BUSWELL, RONA (HM03471) | | | | | | | | | | | | | | | | | | | | | | | | | | | |
| CORDEL, MICHAEL (HM05160) | | | | ● | ● | | | ● | ● | | | ● | | | | | | | ● | | | | ● | ● | | ● | ● |
| CRAVEN CLINIC (HM05384) | ● | ● | ● | ● | ● | ● | ● | ● | ● | | ● | ● | ● | ● | ● | ● | | ● | ● | ● | ● | ● | ● | ● | | ● | ● |
| CROFT HOUSE CLINIC (HM05452) | | | | | ● | | ● | ● | | | | ● | | | | | | ● | | | | | | | | ● | |
| DOVE COURT CENTRE (HM06225) | ● | ● | ● | ● | ● | ● | ● | ● | ● | | ● | ● | ● | ● | ● | ● | | ● | ● | ● | ● | ● | ● | ● | ● | ● | ● |
| GRIFFIN, TRICIA (HM08555) | | | | | | | | | | | | ● | | | ● | | | ● | | | | ● | | | | | |
| HARROGATE HOLISTIC HEALTH CTRE (HM09116) | | | | | | | | | | | | | | | | | | | | | | | | | | | |
| HEALING CLINIC (HM09328) | | ● | ● | ● | ● | ● | | ● | ● | | | ● | ● | ● | ● | ● | | ● | ● | ● | ● | ● | ● | ● | | ● | |
| HIGHTHORN PHYSIOTHERAPY CLINIC (HM09759) | | | | | | | | ● | | | | | | | | | | | | | | | | | | | |
| HOBSON, I K (HM09863) | ● | | | | | | | | | | | | | | | | | | | | | | | | | | |
| LESZCZUK, PAULA (HM12245) | ● | ● | ● | ● | ● | ● | ● | ● | ● | | ● | ● | ● | ● | ● | ● | | ● | ● | ● | ● | ● | ● | ● | | ● | ● |
| LESZCZUK, PAULA (HM12246) | ● | ● | ● | ● | ● | ● | ● | ● | ● | | ● | ● | ● | ● | ● | ● | | ● | ● | ● | ● | ● | ● | ● | | ● | ● |
| LIFESUPPORT (HM12366) | ● | ● | | ● | ● | | ● | ● | ● | | ● | ● | ● | | ● | | | ● | ● | ● | ● | | ● | ● | | ● | |
| NANCY METCALFE MOBILE CONSULT (HM14468) | | | | | | | | ● | | | | | | | | | | | | | | | | | | ● | |
| NATURAL BALANCE (HM14515) | | | | | | | | | | ● | | | | | | | | ● | | | | | | | | ● | |
| PANACEA ACUPUNCTURE CLINIC (HM15628) | | | | | | | | ● | | | | | | | | | | | | | | | | | | | |
| PAULA LESZCZUK (HM15849) | ● | ● | ● | ● | ● | ● | ● | ● | ● | | ● | ● | ● | ● | ● | ● | | ● | ● | ● | ● | ● | ● | ● | | ● | ● |
| RATHBONE, DONNA (HM16955) | ● | | | | | | | | | | | | | | | | | | | | | | | | | | |

# I - S Conditions treated at Practices/Businesses



Business by County with Reference no.

| | RIPON NATURAL HEALTH CENTRE (HM17365) | SHACKLETON, MAUREEN (HM18264) | SHAH, ATUL (HM18268) | SHEEHAN, NICHOLAS (HM18363) | SI SHEN CLINIC (HM18519) | SKIPTON CHIROPODY CENTRE (HM18658) | SMITH, C J (HM18723) | STATHER, M (HM19160) | STRATTON, FIONA (HM19372) | TERRY ANNE (HM19845) | YOGA FOR ALL (HM22026) | YORK CHIROPRACTIC CLINIC (HM22039) | YORK CLINIC (HM22040) | YORK COUNSELLING (HM22042) | YORKSHIRE (SOUTH) | ALTON & JAMES MED HERBAL (HM00748) | ANDERSON, A DUDLEY (HM00810) | BAWTRY PHYSIOTHERAPY PRACTICE (HM01918) | BONESETTER AND MANIPULATOR (HM02676) | BRAMLEY HALL CLINIC (HM02902) | BROOMHILL MEDICAL CENTRE (HM03193) | CARING CLINIC (HM03682) | COUNTRY PRACTICE (HM05256) | DORE PHYSIOTHERAPY PRACTICE (HM06196) | ESSENTIAL HARMONY (HM06907) | GORNEY, C (HM08296) | GRAPEVINE HEALTH (HM08399) | GRENOSIDE PHYSIOTHERAPY (HM08536) | HALLAMSHIRE NATURAL HLTH CTRE (HM08798) | HEALTHY FEET (HM09427) | HINCHLIFFE, JACKIE (HM09822) | HYPNOTHERAPY CENTRE (HM10515) | KIRBY, M (HM11702) | LLEWELLYN CONSULTANCY (HM12502) |
|---|---|---|---|---|---|---|---|---|---|---|---|---|---|---|---|---|---|---|---|---|---|---|---|---|---|---|---|---|---|---|---|---|---|---|
| Sexual Problems | ● | | ● | | | | | | | ● | | | ● | | | | ● | | | | | | | | | | ● | | | | | ● | | ● |
| Sciatica | ● | | ● | ● | | | ● | | ● | | | ● | ● | | | ● | | | ● | ● | | | | ● | | | ● | | ● | | ● | | ● | ● |
| Schizophrenia | | | | | | | | | | | | | ● | | | | | | | | | | | | | | | | | | | | | |
| Rheumatoid Arthritis | ● | | ● | | | | | | | | | | ● | | | ● | | | | ● | | ● | ● | | | | ● | | | ● | ● | | ● | ● |
| Restless Legs | ● | | ● | | | | | | | | ● | | ● | | | ● | | | | ● | | ● | | | | | ● | | | | | | ● | ● |
| Recurrent Infections | ● | | ● | | | | | | | | | | ● | | | ● | | | | ● | | ● | | | ● | | ● | | ● | | | ● | ● | ● |
| Raynaud's Disease | ● | | ● | | | | | | | ● | ● | | ● | | | ● | | | | ● | | ● | | | | | ● | | | ● | | | ● | ● |
| Psoriasis | ● | | ● | | | | | | ● | | | | ● | | | ● | | | | ● | | ● | | | | | ● | | ● | ● | ● | ● | ● | ● |
| Prostate Problems | | | ● | | | | | | | | | | ● | | | ● | | | | ● | | ● | | | | | ● | | ● | | | | ● | |
| Pregnancy Help | ● | | ● | | | | | | ● | | ● | | ● | | | | | | | ● | | | | | | | ● | | ● | | | ● | ● | ● |
| Postural Problems | | | | | | | | | | | | | | | | | | | | | | | | | | | | | | | | | | |
| Pneumonia | ● | | ● | | | | | | | | | | ● | | | | | | | ● | | | | | | | ● | | | | | | | |
| PMT | ● | | ● | | | | | | ● | ● | | | ● | ● | | ● | | | | ● | | ● | ● | | ● | | ● | | ● | | ● | ● | ● | ● |
| Piles | ● | | ● | | | | | | ● | | ● | | ● | | | ● | | | | ● | | ● | | | | | ● | | | | | | ● | ● |
| Phobias | ● | ● | | | | | | | | ● | | | ● | | | | ● | | | | | ● | | | | ● | ● | | | | | ● | ● | ● |
| Period Problems | ● | | ● | | | | | | ● | ● | ● | | ● | | | ● | | | | ● | | ● | ● | | ● | | ● | | ● | | ● | ● | ● | ● |
| Parkinson's Disease | ● | | ● | | | | | | | | | | ● | | | | | | | ● | | | | | | | ● | | | | ● | | | ● |
| Panic Attacks | | | | | | | | | | | | | | ● | | | | | | | | | | | | | | | | | | ● | | |
| Palpitations | ● | | ● | | | | | | ● | | | | ● | | | ● | | | | ● | | ● | | | | | ● | | | | | ● | ● | |
| Pain | ● | | ● | ● | | | ● | | ● | ● | | ● | ● | ● | | | ● | | | ● | | ● | | ● | ● | | ● | ● | ● | ● | ● | ● | ● | ● |
| Osteoporosis | ● | | ● | | | | | | | | | | ● | | | | | | | ● | | ● | | | | | ● | | | | | | ● | |
| Obesity | ● | | ● | | | | | | | ● | ● | | ● | | | | | | | ● | | | | | | | ● | | | | | ● | ● | ● |
| Neuralgia | ● | | ● | | | | | | | ● | | ● | ● | | | ● | | | | ● | | | | | | | ● | | | ● | | | ● | ● |
| Nervous Disorders | ● | | ● | | | | ● | | ● | ● | ● | | ● | ● | | ● | | | | | | ● | ● | | | | ● | | ● | | | ● | | ● |
| Nerve Disorders | | | ● | ● | | | ● | | | ● | | ● | ● | | | | | | | ● | | | | ● | | | ● | | | | | | ● | ● |
| Nausea | ● | | ● | | | | | | ● | ● | | | ● | | | | | | | ● | | ● | | | | | ● | | | | | ● | ● | ● |
| Nail Health | | | ● | | | ● | | ● | | | | | ● | | | | | | | | | ● | ● | | | | ● | | | ● | | ● | ● | ● |
| Musculo-skeletal | | | | | | | | | | | | | | | | | | | | | | | | | | | | | | | | | | |
| Muscular Dystrophy | ● | | | | | | | | | | | | ● | | | | | ● | | | | | | | | | ● | | | | | | | |
| Multiple Sclerosis | ● | | ● | | | | | | ● | | ● | | ● | | | | | | | ● | | ● | | | | | ● | ● | | | | | | ● |
| Mouth Ulcers | ● | | ● | | | | | | | | | | ● | | | ● | | | | ● | | ● | | | | | ● | | | | | | ● | ● |
| Mouth Disorders | ● | | ● | | | | | | | | | | ● | | | | | | | | | | | | | | ● | | | | | | ● | ● |
| Motion Sickness | ● | | ● | | | | | | ● | ● | | | ● | | | ● | | | | | | | | | | | ● | | | | | | ● | |
| Migraine | ● | | ● | ● | ● | | ● | | ● | | ● | ● | ● | ● | | ● | | | | | ● | ● | ● | | ● | | ● | | ● | | | ● | ● | ● |
| Menopause | ● | | ● | | | | | | ● | | | | ● | ● | | ● | | | | | | ● | ● | | ● | | ● | | ● | | | | ● | ● |
| ME | ● | | ● | | ● | | ● | | ● | ● | ● | | ● | ● | | ● | | | | ● | ● | ● | | | | | ● | | ● | | | ● | ● | ● |
| Lung Problems | ● | | ● | | | | | | ● | | | | ● | | | ● | | | | | | ● | | | | | ● | | | | | | ● | ● |
| Low Blood Pressure | ● | | ● | | | | | | | | ● | | ● | | | ● | | | | | | | | | ● | | ● | | ● | | | | ● | ● |
| Liver Disorders | ● | | ● | | | | | | | | | | ● | | | ● | | | | ● | | | | | | | ● | | | | | | ● | |
| Lethargy | ● | | ● | | | | | | ● | | ● | | ● | ● | | | | | | ● | | ● | | | ● | | ● | | ● | | | ● | ● | ● |
| Laryngitis | ● | | ● | | | | | | ● | | | | ● | | | | | | | | | ● | | | | | ● | | | | | | ● | |
| Lactose Intolerance | ● | | ● | | | | | | | | | | ● | | | ● | | | | | | ● | | | | | ● | | | | | | | |
| Kidney Complaints | ● | | ● | | | | | | | | | | ● | | | ● | | | | ● | | | | | | | ● | | | | | | ● | |
| Joint Pain | ● | | ● | ● | | | ● | | ● | ● | ● | ● | ● | | | ● | | ● | ● | ● | | ● | ● | ● | | | ● | ● | ● | ● | ● | ● | ● | ● |
| Jet Lag | ● | | ● | | | | | | | | ● | | ● | | | ● | | | | | | | | | | | ● | | | | | | | ● |
| Itching | ● | | ● | | | | | | ● | ● | | | ● | | | ● | | | | | | | | | | | ● | | | ● | | ● | ● | ● |
| Irritable Bowel Syndrome | ● | | ● | | | | ● | | ● | ● | ● | | ● | ● | | ● | | | | ● | ● | ● | | | ● | | ● | | ● | | | ● | ● | ● |
| Insomnia | ● | | ● | | | | | | ● | | ● | | ● | ● | | ● | | | | ● | | ● | ● | | ● | | ● | | | | ● | ● | ● | ● |

www.healthmyself.com

# I - S Conditions treated at Practices/Businesses

| Business by County with Reference no. | Insomnia | Irritable Bowel Syndrome | Itching | Jet Lag | Joint Pain | Kidney Complaints | Lactose Intolerance | Laryngitis | Lethargy | Liver Disorders | Low Blood Pressure | Lung Problems | ME | Menopause | Migraine | Motion Sickness | Mouth Disorders | Mouth Ulcers | Multiple Sclerosis | Muscular Dystrophy | Musculo-skeletal | Nail Health | Nausea | Nerve Disorders |
|---|---|---|---|---|---|---|---|---|---|---|---|---|---|---|---|---|---|---|---|---|---|---|---|---|
| M & B SERVICES (HM12794) | ● | ● | ● | ● | ● |  | ● | ● | ● |  | ● | ● | ● | ● | ● | ● |  |  | ● | ● |  | ● |  | ● |
| MEDICAL HERBALIST (HM13652) | ● | ● | ● | ● | ● | ● | ● | ● | ● | ● | ● | ● | ● | ● | ● | ● | ● | ● | ● | ● |  | ● | ● | ● |
| MILLINGTON, JANET (HM13917) | ● | ● | ● |  |  |  |  |  |  |  |  |  |  |  | ● |  |  |  |  |  |  |  |  |  |
| MOORGATE NATURAL HEALING CTRE (HM14138) | ● | ● | ● | ● | ● | ● | ● | ● | ● | ● | ● | ● | ● | ● | ● | ● | ● | ● | ● | ● |  | ● | ● | ● |
| NIGHTINGALE PHYSIO PRACTICE (HM14937) |  |  |  |  | ● |  |  |  |  |  |  |  |  |  |  |  |  |  |  |  |  |  |  |  |
| PAUL BOIZOT AROMATHERAPY (HM15839) | ● | ● |  |  |  |  |  |  |  |  |  |  |  |  | ● |  |  |  |  |  |  |  |  |  |
| SCHOLL CENTRE (HM18046) |  |  |  |  |  |  |  |  |  |  |  |  |  |  |  |  |  |  |  |  |  | ● |  |  |
| SEASONS BEAUTY CENTRE (HM18178) | ● | ● | ● | ● | ● | ● |  | ● | ● | ● | ● | ● | ● | ● | ● | ● | ● | ● | ● | ● |  | ● | ● | ● |
| SHEFFIELD NATURAL HEALTH CTRE (HM18372) | ● | ● | ● | ● | ● | ● | ● | ● | ● | ● | ● | ● | ● | ● | ● | ● | ● | ● | ● | ● |  | ● | ● | ● |
| SIMPSON, SARAH E (HM18598) |  |  |  |  |  |  |  |  |  |  |  |  |  |  |  |  |  |  |  |  |  | ● |  |  |
| STONES, KAREN (HM19343) | ● | ● | ● | ● | ● | ● | ● | ● | ● | ● | ● | ● | ● | ● | ● | ● | ● | ● | ● | ● |  | ● | ● | ● |
| TRIGG, REBECCA (HM20334) |  |  |  |  | ● |  |  |  |  |  |  |  |  |  | ● |  |  |  |  |  |  |  |  |  |
| WELLFOODS (HM21159) |  |  |  |  |  |  |  |  |  |  |  |  |  | ● |  |  |  |  |  |  |  |  |  |  |
| WELLFORCE (HM21160) | ● | ● | ● | ● | ● | ● | ● | ● | ● | ● | ● | ● | ● | ● | ● | ● | ● | ● | ● |  |  | ● | ● | ● |
| WELSH CHIROPRACTIC (HM21183) | ● | ● |  |  | ● | ● |  |  | ● |  |  |  | ● |  | ● |  |  |  |  |  |  |  |  | ● |
| WOMBWELL ACUPUNCTURE CLINIC (HM21770) |  |  |  |  | ● |  |  |  |  |  |  |  |  |  |  |  |  |  |  |  |  |  |  |  |
| **YORKSHIRE (WEST)** |  |  |  |  |  |  |  |  |  |  |  |  |  |  |  |  |  |  |  |  |  |  |  |  |
| A BARCHAM REFLEXOLOGY (HM00024) | ● | ● | ● | ● | ● | ● |  | ● | ● | ● | ● | ● | ● | ● | ● |  |  |  | ● |  |  |  | ● | ● |
| ACTIVE MINDS (HM00199) |  |  |  |  |  |  |  |  | ● |  |  |  |  |  |  |  |  |  |  |  |  |  |  |  |
| AIREDALE ALLERGY CENTRE (HM00441) |  | ● | ● |  | ● |  | ● |  | ● |  |  | ● | ● |  | ● |  |  |  |  |  |  |  | ● |  |
| ALEX TECH TEACHING CENTRE (HM00513) |  |  |  |  | ● |  |  |  |  |  |  |  |  |  | ● |  |  |  | ● |  |  |  |  |  |
| AMETHYST HEALING CENTRE (HM00783) |  | ● |  |  |  |  |  |  |  |  |  |  |  |  |  |  |  |  |  |  |  |  |  | ● |
| ARDENTE CHIROPODY SERVICE (HM00991) |  |  |  |  |  |  |  |  |  |  |  |  |  |  |  |  |  |  |  |  |  | ● |  |  |
| ASH, STACEY (HM01183) | ● |  |  |  |  |  |  |  |  |  |  |  |  | ● | ● |  |  |  |  |  |  |  |  |  |
| ASPEN CLINIC (HM01255) |  |  |  |  | ● |  |  |  |  |  |  |  |  |  |  |  |  |  | ● |  | ● |  |  |  |
| BENTLEY, J H (HM02173) |  |  |  |  | ● |  |  |  |  |  |  |  | ● |  | ● |  |  |  |  |  |  |  |  |  |
| BINGLEY HOMOEOPATHIC PRACTICE (HM02315) | ● | ● | ● | ● | ● | ● | ● | ● | ● | ● | ● | ● | ● | ● | ● | ● | ● | ● | ● | ● |  | ● | ● | ● |
| BODY ESSENCE (HM02585) | ● | ● |  |  |  |  |  |  |  |  |  |  | ● | ● | ● |  |  |  |  |  |  |  |  |  |
| BOYD HYPNOTHERAPY (HM02816) | ● | ● |  |  |  |  |  |  | ● |  |  |  | ● | ● | ● |  |  |  |  |  |  |  | ● |  |
| BRADFORD CHIROPODY & BIO CLNC (HM02846) |  |  |  |  |  |  |  |  |  |  |  |  |  |  |  |  |  |  |  |  |  | ● |  |  |
| BRADFORD CLINIC OF ALT MED (HM02848) | ● | ● | ● | ● | ● | ● | ● | ● | ● | ● | ● | ● | ● | ● | ● | ● | ● | ● | ● | ● |  | ● | ● | ● |
| BRAMIN CLINIC (HM02900) |  |  |  |  | ● |  |  |  |  |  |  |  |  |  |  |  |  |  |  |  |  |  |  | ● |
| BRAMLEY COMP THERAPY CLINIC (HM02901) | ● | ● | ● | ● | ● | ● | ● | ● | ● | ● | ● |  | ● | ● | ● | ● |  | ● | ● | ● |  |  | ● | ● |
| BRAY, D N (HM02928) |  |  |  |  | ● |  |  |  |  |  |  |  |  |  |  |  |  |  |  |  |  |  |  |  |

| Business by County with Reference no. | Nervous Disorders | Neuralgia | Obesity | Osteoporosis | Pain | Palpitations | Panic Attacks | Parkinson's Disease | Period Problems | Phobias | Piles | PMT | Pneumonia | Postural Problems | Pregnancy Help | Prostate Problems | Psoriasis | Raynaud's Disease | Recurrent Infections | Restless Legs | Rheumatoid Arthritis | Schizophrenia | Sciatica | Sexual Problems |
|---|---|---|---|---|---|---|---|---|---|---|---|---|---|---|---|---|---|---|---|---|---|---|---|---|
| M & B SERVICES (HM12794) | ● | ● |  | ● | ● | ● |  | ● | ● | ● |  | ● |  |  | ● |  |  |  | ● | ● | ● |  | ● | ● |
| MEDICAL HERBALIST (HM13652) | ● | ● | ● | ● | ● | ● |  | ● | ● | ● | ● | ● | ● |  | ● | ● | ● | ● | ● | ● | ● | ● | ● | ● |
| MILLINGTON, JANET (HM13917) | ● |  | ● |  |  |  |  |  |  | ● |  | ● |  |  |  |  | ● |  |  |  |  |  |  |  |
| MOORGATE NATURAL HEALING CTRE (HM14138) | ● | ● | ● | ● | ● | ● |  | ● | ● | ● | ● | ● | ● |  | ● | ● | ● | ● | ● | ● | ● | ● | ● | ● |
| NIGHTINGALE PHYSIO PRACTICE (HM14937) |  |  |  |  | ● |  |  |  |  |  |  |  |  |  |  |  |  |  |  |  |  |  |  |  |
| PAUL BOIZOT AROMATHERAPY (HM15839) |  | ● |  |  | ● |  |  |  |  |  |  | ● |  |  |  |  |  |  |  |  |  |  | ● |  |
| SCHOLL CENTRE (HM18046) |  |  |  |  |  |  |  |  |  |  |  |  |  |  |  |  |  |  |  |  |  |  |  |  |
| SEASONS BEAUTY CENTRE (HM18178) | ● | ● | ● | ● | ● | ● |  |  | ● | ● | ● | ● |  |  | ● | ● | ● | ● | ● | ● | ● |  | ● |  |
| SHEFFIELD NATURAL HEALTH CTRE (HM18372) | ● | ● | ● | ● | ● | ● |  | ● | ● | ● | ● | ● | ● |  | ● | ● | ● | ● | ● | ● | ● | ● | ● | ● |
| SIMPSON, SARAH E (HM18598) |  |  |  |  |  |  |  |  |  |  |  |  |  |  |  |  |  |  |  |  |  |  |  |  |
| STONES, KAREN (HM19343) |  | ● |  | ● | ● | ● |  |  | ● | ● | ● | ● | ● |  | ● | ● | ● | ● | ● | ● | ● |  | ● | ● |
| TRIGG, REBECCA (HM20334) |  |  |  |  | ● |  |  |  |  |  |  |  |  |  |  |  |  |  |  |  |  |  |  |  |
| WELLFOODS (HM21159) |  |  |  |  |  |  |  |  | ● |  |  | ● |  |  |  |  |  |  |  |  |  |  |  |  |
| WELLFORCE (HM21160) | ● | ● | ● | ● | ● | ● |  |  | ● | ● | ● | ● |  |  | ● | ● | ● | ● | ● | ● | ● |  | ● |  |
| WELSH CHIROPRACTIC (HM21183) |  | ● |  | ● | ● |  |  |  | ● |  |  | ● |  |  | ● |  |  |  |  | ● | ● |  | ● |  |
| WOMBWELL ACUPUNCTURE CLINIC (HM21770) |  |  |  |  | ● |  |  |  |  |  |  |  |  |  |  |  |  |  |  |  |  |  |  |  |
| **YORKSHIRE (WEST)** |  |  |  |  |  |  |  |  |  |  |  |  |  |  |  |  |  |  |  |  |  |  |  |  |
| A BARCHAM REFLEXOLOGY (HM00024) | ● |  |  |  | ● | ● |  |  | ● | ● |  | ● |  |  | ● | ● |  | ● | ● | ● | ● |  | ● |  |
| ACTIVE MINDS (HM00199) |  |  |  |  |  |  |  | ● |  |  |  |  |  |  |  |  |  |  |  |  |  |  |  |  |
| AIREDALE ALLERGY CENTRE (HM00441) |  | ● |  |  |  | ● |  |  |  |  |  |  |  |  |  |  |  |  |  | ● | ● |  |  |  |
| ALEX TECH TEACHING CENTRE (HM00513) |  |  |  |  | ● |  |  |  |  |  |  |  |  |  |  |  |  |  |  |  | ● |  | ● |  |
| AMETHYST HEALING CENTRE (HM00783) | ● |  |  |  |  |  |  |  |  |  |  |  |  |  |  |  | ● |  |  |  |  |  |  |  |
| ARDENTE CHIROPODY SERVICE (HM00991) |  |  |  |  |  |  |  |  |  |  |  |  |  |  |  |  |  |  |  |  |  |  |  |  |
| ASH, STACEY (HM01183) |  |  |  |  | ● |  |  |  | ● |  |  | ● |  |  | ● |  |  |  |  |  |  |  |  |  |
| ASPEN CLINIC (HM01255) |  |  |  |  | ● |  |  |  |  |  |  |  |  |  |  |  |  |  |  |  |  |  |  |  |
| BENTLEY, J H (HM02173) |  |  |  |  | ● |  |  |  |  |  |  |  |  |  |  |  |  |  |  |  |  |  |  |  |
| BINGLEY HOMOEOPATHIC PRACTICE (HM02315) | ● | ● | ● | ● | ● | ● |  | ● | ● | ● | ● | ● | ● |  | ● | ● | ● | ● | ● | ● | ● | ● | ● | ● |
| BODY ESSENCE (HM02585) |  |  |  |  | ● |  |  |  |  |  |  |  |  |  |  |  |  |  |  |  |  |  |  |  |
| BOYD HYPNOTHERAPY (HM02816) | ● |  | ● |  | ● |  |  |  | ● | ● |  | ● |  |  |  |  | ● |  |  |  | ● | ● | ● | ● |
| BRADFORD CHIROPODY & BIO CLNC (HM02846) |  |  |  |  |  |  |  |  |  |  |  |  |  |  |  |  |  |  |  |  |  |  |  |  |
| BRADFORD CLINIC OF ALT MED (HM02848) | ● | ● | ● | ● | ● | ● |  | ● | ● | ● | ● | ● | ● |  | ● | ● | ● | ● | ● | ● | ● | ● | ● | ● |
| BRAMIN CLINIC (HM02900) | ● |  |  | ● | ● |  |  |  |  |  |  |  |  |  |  |  |  |  |  |  |  |  | ● |  |
| BRAMLEY COMP THERAPY CLINIC (HM02901) | ● | ● | ● | ● | ● | ● | ● |  | ● | ● | ● | ● |  |  | ● |  | ● | ● | ● | ● | ● |  | ● | ● |
| BRAY, D N (HM02928) |  |  |  |  | ● |  |  |  |  |  |  |  |  |  |  |  |  |  |  |  |  |  |  |  |

# I - S Conditions treated at Practices/Businesses

Business by County with Reference no.

| Business | Insomnia | Irritable Bowel Syndrome | Itching | Jet Lag | Joint Pain | Kidney Complaints | Lactose Intolerance | Laryngitis | Lethargy | Liver Disorders | Low Blood Pressure | Lung Problems | ME | Menopause | Migraine | Motion Sickness | Mouth Disorders | Mouth Ulcers | Multiple Sclerosis | Muscular Dystrophy | Musculo-skeletal | Nail Health | Nausea | Nerve Disorders | Nervous Disorders | Neuralgia | Obesity | Osteoporosis | Pain | Palpitations | Panic Attacks | Parkinson's Disease | Period Problems | Phobias | Piles | PMT | Pneumonia | Postural Problems | Pregnancy Help | Prostate Problems | Psoriasis | Raynaud's Disease | Recurrent Infections | Restless Legs | Rheumatoid Arthritis | Schizophrenia | Sciatica | Sexual Problems |
|---|---|---|---|---|---|---|---|---|---|---|---|---|---|---|---|---|---|---|---|---|---|---|---|---|---|---|---|---|---|---|---|---|---|---|---|---|---|---|---|---|---|---|---|---|---|---|---|---|
| CALVERLEY ACUPUNCTURE CLINIC (HM03561) | ● | ● | | | | | | | | | | | ● | ● | ● | | | | ● | | | | ● | | ● | | ● | ● | | | | | ● | | | ● | | | ● | | | | | | ● | | | |
| CHAMPANERIA, S K (HM03963) | | ● | ● | | ● | | | | | | | | | | | | | | | | | | | | | | | | ● | | | | | | | ● | | | | | | | | | ● | | ● | |
| CHOICE AROMAS (HM04421) | ● | | | ● | ● | ● | | ● | ● | | | ● | ● | ● | ● | | | | | | | | | ● | ● | ● | | | | | | | ● | ● | | ● | | | | ● | ● | ● | | | ● | | ● | |
| CLARKE, DON (HM04586) | ● | | | | | | | | | | | | | ● | ● | | | | | | | | ● | | | | | | ● | | | | | | | | | | ● | | | | | | | | | |
| COOPER, SAFFRON (HM05126) | ● | ● | ● | ● | ● | ● | | ● | ● | ● | ● | ● | ● | ● | ● | ● | ● | ● | | | | ● | ● | ● | ● | ● | | | ● | ● | | | ● | ● | ● | ● | ● | | ● | | ● | ● | ● | ● | ● | | ● | ● |
| DESIGNING CHANGE (HM06022) | ● | | | | | | | | ● | | | | | | | | | | | | | | | | | | | | ● | | | | | ● | | | | | | | | | | | | | | ● |
| DRURY, WENDY (HM06331) | ● | ● | ● | | ● | ● | | ● | ● | ● | ● | ● | ● | ● | ● | | | | | | | | ● | ● | ● | ● | | | ● | | | | ● | | | ● | | | | | | | | | | | | |
| DUFFIELD (HM06360) | ● | ● | | | ● | ● | | | | | | | ● | | ● | | | | | | | | | | | | | | ● | | | | | | | | | | | | | | | | | | | |
| EQUA-LIBRA (HM06863) | ● | ● | | | | | | | ● | | | | | | | | | | | | | | | | ● | | | | | ● | | | | | | | | | | | | | | | ● | | | |
| FIGURA, CATHERINE MARIA (HM07283) | ● | ● | | | | | | | | | | | | ● | ● | | | | | | | | | | | | | | | | | | | | | | | | | | | | | | | | | |
| GILLETT, LIZ (HM08088) | | ● | | | | | | | | | | | ● | | ● | | | | | | | | | | | | | | | | | | | | | | | | | | | | | | | | | |
| HAMNETT, SHEILA (HM08870) | | ● | | | ● | | | | | | | | | | | | | | | | | | | | ● | | | | ● | | | | | | | | | | | | | | | | | | ● | |
| HANSON, S C (HM08944) | | | | | ● | | | | | | | | | | | | | | ● | ● | | ● | | ● | | ● | ● | ● | | | | ● | | | | | | | | | | ● | ● | ● | ● | | ● | |
| HEBDEN BRIDGE CENTRE (HM09487) | | | | | | | | | | | | | | | | | | | | | | | | | ● | | | | | | | | | ● | | | | | | | | | | | | | | |
| HERMITAGE OILS (HM09684) | | | | | ● | | | | | | | | | | | | | | | | | | | | | | | | | | | | | | | | | | | | ● | | | | | | | |
| HOBSON, ANNE (HM09862) | | | | | | | | | | | | | ● | ● | ● | | | | | | | | | | | | | | | | | | | | | | | | | | | | | | | | | |
| HOBSON, RICHARD (HM09867) | | | | | | | | | | | | | | | | | | | | | | | | | | | | | ● | | | | | ● | | | | | | | | | | | | | | |
| HOLME VALLEY SPORTS CLINIC (HM10036) | | | | | ● | | | | | | | | | | | | | | | | | | | | | | | | | | | | | | | | | | | | | | | | | | | |
| HOLMFIRTH PHYSIO/SPORTS INJURY (HM10048) | | | | | ● | | | | | | | | | ● | | | | | | | | | | | | | | | | | | | ● | | | ● | | | | | | | | | | | | |
| HOMEOPATHIC MEDICAL PRACTICE (HM10076) | | ● | | | ● | | | | | | | ● | ● | ● | ● | | | | ● | | | | | ● | ● | | | | | ● | | | ● | | | ● | | | ● | | ● | ● | ● | ● | ● | ● | | |
| HUNTER, REBECCA (HM10408) | ● | ● | ● | | ● | ● | | ● | ● | ● | ● | ● | ● | ● | ● | | | ● | ● | | | | ● | ● | ● | ● | ● | ● | ● | ● | | | ● | ● | ● | ● | ● | | ● | | | ● | ● | ● | | | ● | |
| J & J HARROP (HM10792) | | | | | | | | | | | | | | | | | | | | | | ● | | | | | | | | | | | | | | | | | | | | | | | | | | |
| JACKSON, ROGER D (HM10850) | | | | | ● | | | | | | | | | | | | | | | | | | | | | ● | | | | | | | | | | | | | | | | | | | | | ● | |
| KANG DA CLINIC (HM11313) | ● | ● | ● | ● | ● | ● | ● | ● | ● | ● | ● | ● | ● | ● | ● | ● | ● | ● | ● | ● | | ● | ● | ● | ● | ● | ● | ● | ● | ● | | ● | ● | | ● | ● | ● | | ● | ● | ● | ● | ● | ● | ● | | ● | ● |
| KINNAIRD, F M (HM11686) | ● | ● | | ● | | | | | ● | | | | | | | ● | | | | | | | ● | | ● | ● | ● | | ● | ● | | | | ● | | | | | | | | | | | | ● | | ● |
| LEEDS COUNSELLING & PSYCHO SVS (HM12158) | | | | | | | | | | | | | | | | | | | | | | | | | ● | | | | | | | | | | | | | | | | | | | | | | | ● |
| LPS TRAINING & CONSULTANCY (HM12713) | | | | | ● | | | | | | | | | | | | | | | | | | | | | | | | | | | | | | | | | | | | | | | | | | ● | |
| MOORFIELD FLOATATION (HM14137) | | | | | ● | | | | | | | | | | | | | | | | | | | | | | | | ● | | | | | | | | | | | | | | | | | | | |
| MORGAN, J D (DR) (HM14167) | ● | ● | | | | | | | | | | | | | ● | | | | | | | | | | ● | | ● | | | ● | | | | | | ● | | | | | | | | ● | | | | ● |
| MORLEY ACUPUNCTURE CLINIC (HM14180) | ● | ● | ● | ● | ● | ● | ● | ● | ● | ● | ● | ● | | ● | ● | ● | ● | ● | ● | ● | | ● | ● | ● | ● | ● | ● | ● | ● | ● | | ● | ● | ● | ● | ● | | | ● | ● | ● | ● | ● | ● | ● | ● | ● | ● |
| MORNINGTON PHYSIOTHERAPY (HM14193) | | | | | ● | | | | | | | | | | | | | | ● | | ● | | | ● | | ● | | ● | ● | | | ● | | | | | | | | | | | | | ● | | ● | |
| NATURES WORKROOM (HM14705) | ● | ● | ● | ● | ● | ● | ● | ● | ● | ● | ● | ● | ● | ● | ● | ● | ● | ● | ● | ● | | ● | ● | ● | ● | ● | ● | ● | ● | ● | | ● | ● | ● | ● | ● | ● | | ● | ● | ● | ● | ● | ● | ● | ● | ● | ● |
| NEILL-HIGGINS, CHRISTINA (HM14765) | | ● | ● | ● | ● | ● | | | | ● | ● | ● | ● | ● | ● | | | | | | | | | | ● | | | | ● | | ● | | ● | | ● | ● | | | ● | ● | ● | ● | | ● | ● | | ● | |
| NRTH LEEDS PHYSIO/SPRTS INJ (HM15091) | | | | | ● | | | | | | | | | | | | | | | | | | | ● | | | | ● | ● | | | | | | | | | | | | | | | | ● | | ● | |

www.healthmyself.com

# I - S Conditions treated at Practices/Businesses

| Business by County with Reference no. | Insomnia | Irritable Bowel Syndrome | Itching | Jet Lag | Joint Pain | Kidney Complaints | Lactose Intolerance | Laryngitis | Lethargy | Liver Disorders | Low Blood Pressure | Lung Problems |
|---|---|---|---|---|---|---|---|---|---|---|---|---|
| OWENS, PAULINE (HM15533) | ● | ● | | | ● | ● | | | | | ● | |
| PALLAS, ANDREW (HM15595) | | ● | ● | | ● | ● | | ● | ● | ● | | ● |
| PARKS, HILARY (HM15720) | ● | ● | | | ● | | | | | ● | ● | |
| PAYNE, AUDREY (HM15861) | | ● | | | ● | | | | ● | | | |
| POPPLEWELL, MARK (HM16437) | ● | ● | | | ● | | | | ● | | ● | ● |
| PRESTON, CATHY (HM16551) | | ● | | | | | | | ● | | | |
| RAINTREE HEALTH (HM16893) | | ● | ● | | ● | ● | ● | | ● | ● | ● | ● |
| RICHARDSON CLINIC (HM17266) | ● | ● | ● | ● | ● | ● | ● | ● | ● | ● | ● | ● |
| ROTHWELL SPORTS CENTRE (HM17658) | | | | | ● | | | | | | | |
| ROUNDHAY CHIROPRACTIC CLINIC (HM17667) | | | | | | | | | | | | |
| SALTAIRE COMP HEALTH STUDIO (HM17864) | ● | ● | ● | ● | ● | ● | ● | ● | ● | ● | ● | ● |
| SHACKLETON, JOHN A (HM18263) | | | | | ● | | | | | | | |
| SHERQIA, DARULSHAFA (HM18436) | ● | ● | ● | | ● | | | ● | ● | ● | ● | |
| SMITH, JANET (HM18751) | ● | ● | | | | | | | | | | |
| STEAD, JULIE ANN (HM19164) | ● | ● | | | | ● | | | | | | |
| SURGERY (HM19519) | ● | | | | ● | | | | | | | ● |
| SWAINE, PAULA (HM19565) | | | | | | | | | | | | |
| SYKES CLINIC (HM19610) | ● | ● | | | | | | | | | | |
| TORNTON, HOWARD (HM20172) | | | | | ● | | | | | | | |
| TRANSCENDENTAL MEDITATION (HM20285) | | | | | | | | | | | | |
| TUEL LANE PHYSIOTHERAPY CLINIC (HM20376) | | | | | ● | | | | | | | |
| WATKINS, JEAN (HM20996) | ● | ● | | | | | | | ● | | ● | |
| WEST YORKSHIRE CLINIC (HM21242) | ● | ● | ● | ● | ● | ● | | ● | ● | ● | ● | ● |
| WEST YORKSHIRE M S THRPY CTRE (HM21243) | | | | | | | | | | | | |
| WEST YORKSHIRE PHYSIO CENTRE (HM21244) | | | | | ● | | | | | | | |
| WETHERBY PHYSIO PRACTICE (HM21290) | | | | | ● | | | | | | | |
| WISE, CAROL (HM21732) | ● | ● | ● | ● | ● | ● | ● | ● | ● | ● | ● | ● |
| WOODHOUSE CLINIC (HM21826) | | ● | | | ● | | | | ● | | | |

| Business by County with Reference no. | ME | Menopause | Migraine | Motion Sickness | Mouth Disorders | Mouth Ulcers | Multiple Sclerosis | Muscular Dystrophy | Musculo-skeletal | Nail Health | Nausea | Nerve Disorders |
|---|---|---|---|---|---|---|---|---|---|---|---|---|
| OWENS, PAULINE (HM15533) | ● | ● | ● | | | | | | | ● | | ● |
| PALLAS, ANDREW (HM15595) | ● | ● | ● | | | | | | | | ● | ● |
| PARKS, HILARY (HM15720) | ● | ● | | | | | | | | | | |
| PAYNE, AUDREY (HM15861) | | | ● | | | | | | | | | |
| POPPLEWELL, MARK (HM16437) | ● | ● | ● | ● | | | | | | | ● | |
| PRESTON, CATHY (HM16551) | ● | | | | | | | | | | | |
| RAINTREE HEALTH (HM16893) | | ● | ● | | | | ● | | | | ● | ● |
| RICHARDSON CLINIC (HM17266) | ● | ● | ● | ● | ● | ● | ● | ● | | ● | ● | ● |
| ROTHWELL SPORTS CENTRE (HM17658) | | | | | | | | | | | | |
| ROUNDHAY CHIROPRACTIC CLINIC (HM17667) | | | | | | | | | | | | |
| SALTAIRE COMP HEALTH STUDIO (HM17864) | ● | ● | ● | ● | ● | ● | ● | ● | | ● | ● | ● |
| SHACKLETON, JOHN A (HM18263) | | | | | | | | | | ● | | |
| SHERQIA, DARULSHAFA (HM18436) | | | ● | | | | | | | | ● | ● |
| SMITH, JANET (HM18751) | ● | ● | ● | | | | | | | | | |
| STEAD, JULIE ANN (HM19164) | ● | ● | ● | | | | | | | ● | | |
| SURGERY (HM19519) | ● | | ● | ● | | | ● | | | | ● | ● |
| SWAINE, PAULA (HM19565) | | | | | | | | | | ● | | |
| SYKES CLINIC (HM19610) | ● | | ● | | | | | | | | | ● |
| TORNTON, HOWARD (HM20172) | | | ● | | | | | | | | | |
| TRANSCENDENTAL MEDITATION (HM20285) | | | ● | | | | | | | | | |
| TUEL LANE PHYSIOTHERAPY CLINIC (HM20376) | | | | | | | | | | | | |
| WATKINS, JEAN (HM20996) | | ● | ● | | | | ● | ● | | | | ● |
| WEST YORKSHIRE CLINIC (HM21242) | ● | ● | ● | ● | ● | ● | ● | ● | | ● | | ● |
| WEST YORKSHIRE M S THRPY CTRE (HM21243) | | | ● | | | | ● | | | | | |
| WEST YORKSHIRE PHYSIO CENTRE (HM21244) | | | | | | | | | | | | |
| WETHERBY PHYSIO PRACTICE (HM21290) | | | | | | | ● | | | | | |
| WISE, CAROL (HM21732) | ● | ● | ● | ● | ● | ● | ● | ● | | ● | ● | ● |
| WOODHOUSE CLINIC (HM21826) | ● | | ● | | | | | | | ● | | ● |

| Business by County with Reference no. | Nervous Disorders | Neuralgia | Obesity | Osteoporosis | Pain | Palpitations | Panic Attacks | Parkinson's Disease | Period Problems | Phobias | Piles | PMT |
|---|---|---|---|---|---|---|---|---|---|---|---|---|
| OWENS, PAULINE (HM15533) | | | | | ● | ● | | | ● | | ● | ● |
| PALLAS, ANDREW (HM15595) | ● | ● | ● | ● | ● | ● | | | ● | ● | ● | ● |
| PARKS, HILARY (HM15720) | | | | | | | | | | | | ● |
| PAYNE, AUDREY (HM15861) | | | | | ● | | | | ● | | | |
| POPPLEWELL, MARK (HM16437) | | ● | | | ● | ● | | | ● | | | ● |
| PRESTON, CATHY (HM16551) | ● | | ● | | ● | | | | | ● | | ● |
| RAINTREE HEALTH (HM16893) | ● | ● | ● | | ● | ● | | ● | ● | | ● | ● |
| RICHARDSON CLINIC (HM17266) | ● | ● | ● | ● | ● | ● | | ● | ● | ● | ● | ● |
| ROTHWELL SPORTS CENTRE (HM17658) | | | | | | | | | | | | |
| ROUNDHAY CHIROPRACTIC CLINIC (HM17667) | | | | | ● | | | | | | | |
| SALTAIRE COMP HEALTH STUDIO (HM17864) | ● | ● | ● | ● | ● | ● | | ● | ● | ● | ● | ● |
| SHACKLETON, JOHN A (HM18263) | | | | | | | | | | | | |
| SHERQIA, DARULSHAFA (HM18436) | ● | | | ● | ● | ● | | | ● | ● | ● | ● |
| SMITH, JANET (HM18751) | ● | ● | | | ● | | | | ● | | | ● |
| STEAD, JULIE ANN (HM19164) | | | | | ● | ● | | | ● | | | ● |
| SURGERY (HM19519) | | ● | | ● | ● | | | ● | | | | |
| SWAINE, PAULA (HM19565) | | | | | | | | | | | | |
| SYKES CLINIC (HM19610) | ● | ● | ● | | ● | | | | ● | ● | | ● |
| TORNTON, HOWARD (HM20172) | ● | | | | ● | | | | | | | |
| TRANSCENDENTAL MEDITATION (HM20285) | | | | | | | | | | | | |
| TUEL LANE PHYSIOTHERAPY CLINIC (HM20376) | | | | | | | | | | | | |
| WATKINS, JEAN (HM20996) | ● | | | | | | | | | | | ● |
| WEST YORKSHIRE CLINIC (HM21242) | ● | ● | ● | ● | ● | ● | | ● | ● | ● | ● | ● |
| WEST YORKSHIRE M S THRPY CTRE (HM21243) | | | | | | | | ● | | | | |
| WEST YORKSHIRE PHYSIO CENTRE (HM21244) | | | | | ● | | | | | | | |
| WETHERBY PHYSIO PRACTICE (HM21290) | | | | | ● | | | | | | | |
| WISE, CAROL (HM21732) | ● | ● | ● | ● | ● | ● | | ● | ● | ● | ● | ● |
| WOODHOUSE CLINIC (HM21826) | | ● | | | ● | ● | | | ● | | | ● |

| Business by County with Reference no. | Pneumonia | Postural Problems | Pregnancy Help | Prostate Problems | Psoriasis | Raynaud's Disease | Recurrent Infections | Restless Legs | Rheumatoid Arthritis | Schizophrenia | Sciatica | Sexual Problems |
|---|---|---|---|---|---|---|---|---|---|---|---|---|
| OWENS, PAULINE (HM15533) | | | ● | | | | | ● | | | ● | |
| PALLAS, ANDREW (HM15595) | | | ● | ● | ● | ● | ● | ● | ● | | ● | |
| PARKS, HILARY (HM15720) | | | | | | | | | | | | |
| PAYNE, AUDREY (HM15861) | | | | | | | | | ● | | ● | |
| POPPLEWELL, MARK (HM16437) | | | | | | ● | | ● | ● | | ● | |
| PRESTON, CATHY (HM16551) | | | | | | | | | | | | |
| RAINTREE HEALTH (HM16893) | ● | | | ● | ● | | | | ● | ● | ● | ● |
| RICHARDSON CLINIC (HM17266) | ● | | ● | ● | ● | ● | ● | ● | ● | ● | ● | ● |
| ROTHWELL SPORTS CENTRE (HM17658) | | | | | | | | | | | ● | |
| ROUNDHAY CHIROPRACTIC CLINIC (HM17667) | | | | | | | | | | | ● | |
| SALTAIRE COMP HEALTH STUDIO (HM17864) | ● | | ● | ● | ● | ● | ● | ● | ● | ● | ● | ● |
| SHACKLETON, JOHN A (HM18263) | | | | | | | | | | | | |
| SHERQIA, DARULSHAFA (HM18436) | | | | ● | ● | | ● | | ● | | ● | ● |
| SMITH, JANET (HM18751) | | | | | | | | | | | ● | |
| STEAD, JULIE ANN (HM19164) | | | | | | | | | | | ● | |
| SURGERY (HM19519) | | | | | | | | | ● | | ● | |
| SWAINE, PAULA (HM19565) | | | | | | | | | | | | |
| SYKES CLINIC (HM19610) | | | | | ● | | | | | | | ● |
| TORNTON, HOWARD (HM20172) | | ● | | | | | | | | | ● | |
| TRANSCENDENTAL MEDITATION (HM20285) | | | | | | | | | | | | |
| TUEL LANE PHYSIOTHERAPY CLINIC (HM20376) | | | | | | | | | | | | |
| WATKINS, JEAN (HM20996) | | | ● | | | | | | ● | | | |
| WEST YORKSHIRE CLINIC (HM21242) | ● | | ● | ● | ● | ● | ● | ● | ● | ● | ● | ● |
| WEST YORKSHIRE M S THRPY CTRE (HM21243) | | | | | | | | | | | ● | |
| WEST YORKSHIRE PHYSIO CENTRE (HM21244) | | | | | | | | | | | | |
| WETHERBY PHYSIO PRACTICE (HM21290) | | | | | | | | | | | | |
| WISE, CAROL (HM21732) | ● | | ● | ● | ● | ● | ● | ● | ● | ● | ● | ● |
| WOODHOUSE CLINIC (HM21826) | | | | | | | | | | | ● | |

# I - S Conditions treated at Practices/Businesses

Business by County with Reference no.

| Condition | BI-AURA THERAPY (HM02274) | ANNAPURNA NATURAL HEALTHCARE (HM00894) | BANDON CHIROPRACTIC CLINIC (HM01653) | BROOKFIELD PHYSIOTHERAPY (HM03167) | EAST CORK PHYSIOTHERAPY (HM06511) | HATTERSLEY, LAURENCE (HM09200) | HEALING THERAPIES (HM09354) | INS-CLINICAL HYP & PSYCHO (HM10661) | JONES, COLEEN (HM11131) | KEATING, MARY (HM11379) | MOORE-GROACKE, GILLIAN (DR) (HM14136) | PAUL DENNEHY - HYPNOTHERAPIST (HM15842) | RAVEN HILL CHIROPRACTIC CLINIC (HM16964) | SHIATSU (HM18452) | ABELIA COUNSELLING (HM00110) | ARDAGH ACUPUNCTURE CLINIC (HM00988) | ARDUNA COUNS & PSYCHOTHPY CTRE (HM00995) | BREE, JOHN (HM02947) | B-WELL HYPNOTHERAPY CLINIC (HM03506) | CHADHA, PRADEEP K (DR) (HM03933) | DUN LAOIRE HEALING ROOM (HM06389) | FAIRVIEW THERAPY CENTRE (HM07066) | FINISHING TOUCHES (HM07313) | FITZGERALD HYP-PSYCHOTHERAPY (HM07364) | HEALING PLACE (HM09347) | HEALING ROOM - DRUMCONDRA (HM09351) | HEALTH COUNSEL (HM09384) | HERBAL & ACUPUNCTURE (HM09595) | HOWTH COUNSELLING SERVICE (HM10294) |
|---|---|---|---|---|---|---|---|---|---|---|---|---|---|---|---|---|---|---|---|---|---|---|---|---|---|---|---|---|---|
| IRELAND | COUNTY CAVAN | COUNTY CORK | | | | | | | | | | | | | COUNTY DUBLIN | | | | | | | | | | | | | | |
| Sexual Problems | ● | | | | ● | ● | | ● | ● | | ● | ● | | | ● | | ● | ● | ● | ● | | ● | | | | | ● | ● | |
| Sciatica | ● | ● | ● | ● | ● | ● | ● | | | ● | | ● | | ● | | | | ● | ● | | | ● | | | ● | ● | | ● | |
| Schizophrenia | ● | | | | | | | | | | | | | | | | | ● | ● | | | | | | | | | | |
| Rheumatoid Arthritis | ● | | | ● | ● | ● | | | | | | | ● | | | ● | | ● | ● | | | | | | | | | ● | |
| Restless Legs | | | | | ● | | | | | ● | | ● | ● | ● | | | | | ● | | | | | | | | | ● | |
| Recurrent Infections | | | | | ● | | ● | | | | | ● | ● | | | | | ● | ● | | | | | | | ● | | ● | |
| Raynaud's Disease | | | | | ● | ● | | | | | | ● | ● | | | | | | ● | | | | | | | | | ● | |
| Psoriasis | ● | | | | ● | | | ● | | | | ● | | | | | | ● | ● | | | ● | | | | ● | | ● | |
| Prostate Problems | ● | | | | ● | | | | | | | ● | | | | | | ● | ● | | | | | | | | | ● | |
| Pregnancy Help | | | | | ● | | | | | | | | ● | ● | | | | ● | ● | | | ● | | | | | | | |
| Postural Problems | | | | | | | | | | | | | | | | | | | | | | | | | | | | | |
| Pneumonia | | | | | ● | | | | | | | | | | | | | ● | ● | | | | | | | | | | |
| PMT | ● | ● | | ● | ● | | ● | ● | | | ● | ● | ● | ● | | ● | | ● | ● | | | ● | | | | ● | | ● | |
| Piles | | | | | ● | | | | | | | | | | | | | ● | ● | | | | | | | | | | |
| Phobias | | | | | ● | | ● | ● | ● | | | ● | | ● | ● | | ● | ● | ● | ● | | ● | | | | | ● | | |
| Period Problems | ● | ● | | | ● | | ● | ● | | ● | | ● | ● | ● | | ● | | ● | ● | | | ● | | | | ● | | ● | |
| Parkinson's Disease | | | | ● | ● | | | | | | | ● | | | | | | ● | ● | | | | | | | | | | |
| Panic Attacks | | | | | | | | ● | | | | | | | ● | | | | | | | | | | | | | | |
| Palpitations | | | | ● | ● | | ● | ● | | ● | | ● | | ● | | | | ● | ● | | | ● | | | | ● | | ● | ● |
| Pain | ● | | ● | ● | ● | ● | ● | ● | | ● | ● | ● | ● | ● | ● | ● | | ● | ● | | | ● | | | ● | ● | | ● | |
| Osteoporosis | | | | ● | ● | | | | | | | | ● | | | | | ● | ● | | | | | | | ● | | ● | |
| Obesity | | | | ● | ● | | | ● | | | ● | ● | | | | | | | ● | ● | | | | | | | | ● | |
| Neuralgia | | | ● | | ● | | | ● | | | | ● | ● | ● | | ● | | ● | ● | | | ● | | | ● | | | ● | |
| Nervous Disorders | ● | | | ● | ● | ● | ● | ● | ● | | ● | ● | ● | ● | | | | ● | ● | ● | | ● | | | | ● | ● | | |
| Nerve Disorders | | | | ● | ● | ● | | ● | | | ● | ● | ● | ● | | | | ● | ● | ● | | | | | | ● | | | |
| Nausea | | | | ● | ● | | | | | ● | | ● | ● | ● | | | | ● | ● | | | ● | | | | ● | | ● | |
| Nail Health | | | | | | | | | | | | ● | ● | | | | | ● | ● | | | | ● | | | | | ● | |
| Musculo-skeletal | | | | | | | | | | | | | | | | | | | | | | | | | | | | | |
| Muscular Dystrophy | | | | ● | ● | | | | | | | | | | | | | ● | ● | | | | | | | | | | |
| Multiple Sclerosis | ● | | | ● | ● | | | ● | | | | | ● | | | ● | | ● | ● | | | | | | | | | | |
| Mouth Ulcers | ● | | | | | | | | | | | ● | ● | ● | | | | ● | ● | | | ● | | | | | | ● | |
| Mouth Disorders | | | | | ● | | | | | | | ● | ● | | | | | ● | ● | | | | | | | | | | |
| Motion Sickness | | | | | ● | | | ● | | | | ● | | | | | | ● | ● | | | | | | | | | | |
| Migraine | ● | | ● | | ● | | ● | ● | | | ● | ● | | ● | | ● | | ● | ● | | | ● | | | ● | ● | | ● | |
| Menopause | ● | ● | | | | | ● | ● | | | | ● | ● | ● | | | | ● | ● | | | ● | | | | ● | | ● | |
| ME | ● | | | ● | ● | | | ● | | | ● | | ● | ● | | ● | | ● | ● | ● | | ● | | ● | ● | ● | | ● | |
| Lung Problems | ● | | | | | | | | | | | | | ● | | ● | | ● | ● | | | ● | | | ● | ● | | | |
| Low Blood Pressure | ● | | | ● | | | ● | | | | | ● | ● | ● | | | | ● | ● | | | ● | | | | ● | | ● | |
| Liver Disorders | ● | | | | | | | | | | | ● | ● | ● | | | | ● | ● | | | ● | | | | | | ● | |
| Lethargy | ● | ● | | | | | ● | ● | | | | ● | ● | ● | | ● | | ● | ● | | | | | | | | | | ● |
| Laryngitis | ● | | | | | | | | | | | ● | | ● | | | | ● | ● | | | | | | | | | | |
| Lactose Intolerance | ● | | | | | | | | | | | | ● | | | | | ● | ● | | | | | | | ● | | | |
| Kidney Complaints | ● | | | | ● | | | | | | | ● | ● | ● | | | | ● | ● | | | ● | | | | ● | | | |
| Joint Pain | ● | | | ● | ● | ● | ● | | | | ● | ● | ● | | | ● | | ● | ● | | | ● | | | ● | ● | | | |
| Jet Lag | | ● | | | | | | ● | | | | ● | | ● | | | | ● | ● | | | | | | ● | | | | |
| Itching | | | | | ● | | | | | | | ● | | | | | | ● | ● | | | | | | | | | | |
| Irritable Bowel Syndrome | ● | | | ● | ● | | | ● | | ● | ● | ● | ● | ● | | | | ● | ● | ● | | ● | | | ● | ● | | ● | |
| Insomnia | ● | ● | | | ● | | ● | ● | | ● | | ● | | ● | ● | ● | | ● | ● | ● | ● | ● | ● | | ● | ● | | ● | |

www.healthmyself.com

Ireland (by County)

I-S CONDITIONS TREATED

# I - S Conditions treated at Practices/Businesses

Business by County with Reference no.

| Business by County with Reference no. | Insomnia | Irritable Bowel Syndrome | Itching | Jet Lag | Joint Pain | Kidney Complaints | Lactose Intolerance | Laryngitis | Lethargy | Liver Disorders | Low Blood Pressure | Lung Problems | ME | Menopause | Migraine | Motion Sickness |
|---|---|---|---|---|---|---|---|---|---|---|---|---|---|---|---|---|
| INNER CIRCLE HEALING CENTRE (HM10635) | | | | | | | | | | | | | | | | |
| INSTITUTE OF PSYCHOSOCIAL MED (HM10678) | | | | | | | | | | | | | | | | |
| KELLY, ANGELINA (HM11427) | ● | ● | | | ● | ● | | ● | ● | ● | | ● | ● | | ● | |
| LALLOO'S ACUPUNCTURE CLINIC (HM11881) | ● | ● | ● | ● | ● | ● | ● | ● | ● | ● | ● | ● | ● | ● | ● | ● |
| LITTLEJOHN CLINIC (HM12472) | | | | | ● | | | | | | | | | | ● | |
| MACLIAM, FIONNULA (HM12867) | ● | | | | | | | | | | | | | | | |
| MCHUGH HYPNOSIS & REFLEXOLOGY (HM13509) | ● | | | | ● | | | | | | | ● | | | ● | |
| MELT/TEMPLE BAR NATURAL (HM13716) | | | | | ● | ● | | | ● | ● | ● | ● | ● | ● | ● | ● |
| NATURAL SOLUTIONS (HM14625) | ● | | | ● | | | | | ● | | | | | | | |
| NUALA WOULFE BEAUTY SALON (HM15101) | | ● | | ● | | | | | | | | | | | | |
| RATHMINES CHIROPRACTIC CENTRE (HM16957) | | | | | ● | | | | | | | | | | | |
| T C M CENTRE (HM19639) | ● | ● | ● | | ● | ● | | ● | ● | ● | ● | ● | ● | ● | ● | |
| THERAPEUTICS (HM19888) | | | | | | | | | | | | | | | | |
| THEW, NIN (HM19916) | ● | ● | | | ● | ● | | ● | ● | ● | ● | ● | ● | ● | ● | |
| TOBIN, ROSALEEN (HM20105) | ● | | | | | | | | ● | | | | | | | |
| TRAD CHINESE MEDICINE/MASSAGE (HM20216) | ● | ● | | ● | ● | ● | | ● | | | | ● | | | ● | |
| TROY, ROSEMARY (HM20349) | | | | | | | | | | | | | | | | |
| COUNTY GALWAY | | | | | | | | | | | | | | | | |
| ALEXANDER TECHNIQUE CENTRE (HM00557) | | | | | | | | | ● | | | | | | ● | |
| BODYWATCH (HM02636) | | | | | | | | | | | | | | | | |
| O'COLMAIN, AIDAN (DR) (HM15203) | | | | | | | | | | | | | | | | |
| PRENDERGAST, KARL (HM16542) | | ● | | | ● | | | | | | | | | | ● | |
| COUNTY KERRY | | | | | | | | | | | | | | | | |
| ACUPUNCTURE CLINIC (HM00286) | ● | ● | ● | ● | ● | ● | | ● | ● | ● | ● | ● | ● | ● | ● | |
| WOODLAWN HOLISTIC THERAPY CTRE (HM21834) | | | | | | | | | | | | | | | ● | |
| COUNTY KILDARE | | | | | | | | | | | | | | | | |
| GREEN ROAD HEALING CENTRE (HM08441) | ● | ● | ● | ● | ● | | | ● | ● | | ● | ● | ● | ● | ● | ● |
| SHENANDOAH HEALING (HM18395) | ● | | | | | | | | ● | | | | | ● | ● | |
| COUNTY KILKENNY | | | | | | | | | | | | | | | | |
| BLUE ROOM (HM02528) | ● | ● | | | | | | | ● | | | | ● | | ● | |
| DULCAMARA (HM06375) | | ● | | | | ● | | | | ● | ● | | | ● | ● | |
| HOLISTIC HEALING CENTRE (HM09965) | ● | | | | ● | | | | ● | | | | ● | | ● | |
| COUNTY LIMERICK | | | | | | | | | | | | | | | | |
| HOLISTIC HEALING (HM09960) | ● | ● | | | ● | | | | | | ● | | | | | |

| Business by County with Reference no. | Mouth Disorders | Mouth Ulcers | Multiple Sclerosis | Muscular Dystrophy | Musculo-skeletal | Nail Health | Nausea | Nerve Disorders | Nervous Disorders | Neuralgia | Obesity | Osteoporosis | Pain | Palpitations | Panic Attacks | Parkinson's Disease |
|---|---|---|---|---|---|---|---|---|---|---|---|---|---|---|---|---|
| INNER CIRCLE HEALING CENTRE (HM10635) | | | | | | | | | | | | | | | | |
| INSTITUTE OF PSYCHOSOCIAL MED (HM10678) | | | | | | | | | ● | | | | | | | |
| KELLY, ANGELINA (HM11427) | | ● | | | | | | | ● | | | ● | ● | ● | | |
| LALLOO'S ACUPUNCTURE CLINIC (HM11881) | ● | ● | | ● | | | ● | ● | ● | ● | ● | ● | ● | ● | | |
| LITTLEJOHN CLINIC (HM12472) | | | | | | | | | | | | ● | | | | |
| MACLIAM, FIONNULA (HM12867) | | | | | | | | | ● | | | | | | | |
| MCHUGH HYPNOSIS & REFLEXOLOGY (HM13509) | | | ● | | | | | | ● | ● | ● | | | | | |
| MELT/TEMPLE BAR NATURAL (HM13716) | ● | ● | ● | | | | ● | ● | ● | | | ● | | | | ● |
| NATURAL SOLUTIONS (HM14625) | | | | | | | | | ● | | ● | | | | | |
| NUALA WOULFE BEAUTY SALON (HM15101) | | | | | | ● | | | ● | | | | | | | |
| RATHMINES CHIROPRACTIC CENTRE (HM16957) | | | | | | | | ● | | ● | | | ● | | | |
| T C M CENTRE (HM19639) | ● | ● | ● | | | | ● | | | ● | ● | ● | ● | ● | | ● |
| THERAPEUTICS (HM19888) | | | | | | | | ● | ● | | | | | | | |
| THEW, NIN (HM19916) | | ● | | | | | ● | | | | | | ● | ● | | |
| TOBIN, ROSALEEN (HM20105) | | | | | | | | | ● | | | | | | | |
| TRAD CHINESE MEDICINE/MASSAGE (HM20216) | | ● | | ● | | | ● | | | | | | ● | ● | | |
| TROY, ROSEMARY (HM20349) | | | | | | | | | | | | | | | | |
| COUNTY GALWAY | | | | | | | | | | | | | | | | |
| ALEXANDER TECHNIQUE CENTRE (HM00557) | | | | | | | | | | ● | | ● | ● | ● | | ● |
| BODYWATCH (HM02636) | | | | | | | | | | | ● | | | | | |
| O'COLMAIN, AIDAN (DR) (HM15203) | | | | | | | | | | | | | ● | | | |
| PRENDERGAST, KARL (HM16542) | | | | | | | | ● | | | | | ● | | | |
| COUNTY KERRY | | | | | | | | | | | | | | | | |
| ACUPUNCTURE CLINIC (HM00286) | | ● | | | | | ● | | ● | ● | | | ● | ● | | |
| WOODLAWN HOLISTIC THERAPY CTRE (HM21834) | | | ● | | | | | | | | | | ● | | | |
| COUNTY KILDARE | | | | | | | | | | | | | | | | |
| GREEN ROAD HEALING CENTRE (HM08441) | | | | | | | | ● | ● | ● | | | ● | ● | | |
| SHENANDOAH HEALING (HM18395) | | | | | | | | | ● | | | | ● | | | |
| COUNTY KILKENNY | | | | | | | | | | | | | | | | |
| BLUE ROOM (HM02528) | | | | | | | | | ● | | | | ● | | | |
| DULCAMARA (HM06375) | | | | | | | | | ● | | ● | | | | | |
| HOLISTIC HEALING CENTRE (HM09965) | | | | | | | | | ● | ● | | ● | ● | | | |
| COUNTY LIMERICK | | | | | | | | | | | | | | | | |
| HOLISTIC HEALING (HM09960) | | | ● | | | | ● | | | | | | ● | | | |

| Business by County with Reference no. | Period Problems | Phobias | Piles | PMT | Pneumonia | Postural Problems | Pregnancy Help | Prostate Problems | Psoriasis | Raynaud's Disease | Recurrent Infections | Restless Legs | Rheumatoid Arthritis | Schizophrenia | Sciatica | Sexual Problems |
|---|---|---|---|---|---|---|---|---|---|---|---|---|---|---|---|---|
| INNER CIRCLE HEALING CENTRE (HM10635) | | ● | | ● | | | | | | | | | | | | ● |
| INSTITUTE OF PSYCHOSOCIAL MED (HM10678) | | ● | | | | | | | | | | | | | | |
| KELLY, ANGELINA (HM11427) | ● | ● | ● | ● | | | ● | | ● | | ● | | ● | | ● | |
| LALLOO'S ACUPUNCTURE CLINIC (HM11881) | ● | ● | ● | ● | | | ● | ● | ● | ● | ● | ● | ● | ● | ● | ● |
| LITTLEJOHN CLINIC (HM12472) | | | | | ● | | ● | | | | | | | | | |
| MACLIAM, FIONNULA (HM12867) | | ● | | | | | | | | | | | | | | ● |
| MCHUGH HYPNOSIS & REFLEXOLOGY (HM13509) | | ● | | | | | | | ● | | | | ● | | ● | ● |
| MELT/TEMPLE BAR NATURAL (HM13716) | ● | | ● | ● | | | ● | | ● | | | | | ● | ● | |
| NATURAL SOLUTIONS (HM14625) | | ● | | | | | | | | | | | | | | ● |
| NUALA WOULFE BEAUTY SALON (HM15101) | ● | | | | | | | | | | | ● | | | ● | |
| RATHMINES CHIROPRACTIC CENTRE (HM16957) | | | | | | | | | | | | | | | ● | |
| T C M CENTRE (HM19639) | ● | | ● | ● | ● | | ● | ● | ● | ● | ● | ● | ● | | ● | ● |
| THERAPEUTICS (HM19888) | | | | | | | | | | | | | | | | |
| THEW, NIN (HM19916) | ● | | ● | ● | ● | | ● | ● | ● | ● | ● | ● | ● | | ● | ● |
| TOBIN, ROSALEEN (HM20105) | | | | | | | | | | | | | | | | |
| TRAD CHINESE MEDICINE/MASSAGE (HM20216) | ● | | | ● | | | | | | | | | | | ● | |
| TROY, ROSEMARY (HM20349) | | ● | | | | | | | | | | | | | | |
| COUNTY GALWAY | | | | | | | | | | | | | | | | |
| ALEXANDER TECHNIQUE CENTRE (HM00557) | | | | | | | | | | | | | ● | | ● | |
| BODYWATCH (HM02636) | | | | | | | | | | | | | | | | |
| O'COLMAIN, AIDAN (DR) (HM15203) | | | | | | | | | | | | | | | | |
| PRENDERGAST, KARL (HM16542) | ● | | | | | | | | | | | ● | | | ● | |
| COUNTY KERRY | | | | | | | | | | | | | | | | |
| ACUPUNCTURE CLINIC (HM00286) | ● | | ● | ● | ● | | | | | ● | ● | ● | ● | | | |
| WOODLAWN HOLISTIC THERAPY CTRE (HM21834) | | | | | | | | | | | | | | | ● | |
| COUNTY KILDARE | | | | | | | | | | | | | | | | |
| GREEN ROAD HEALING CENTRE (HM08441) | ● | | ● | ● | | | | | ● | ● | | ● | | | ● | |
| SHENANDOAH HEALING (HM18395) | | | ● | | | | | | | | | | | | ● | |
| COUNTY KILKENNY | | | | | | | | | | | | | | | | |
| BLUE ROOM (HM02528) | ● | ● | | | | | ● | | | | | | | | | ● |
| DULCAMARA (HM06375) | ● | | | ● | | | | | ● | ● | ● | | ● | | | |
| HOLISTIC HEALING CENTRE (HM09965) | | | | | | | | | | | | | ● | | ● | |
| COUNTY LIMERICK | | | | | | | | | | | | | | | | |
| HOLISTIC HEALING (HM09960) | | | | | | | | | | | | ● | | | | ● |

# I - S Conditions treated at Practices/Businesses

| Business by County with Reference no. | Insomnia | Irritable Bowel Syndrome | Itching | Jet Lag | Joint Pain | Kidney Complaints | Lactose Intolerance | Laryngitis | Lethargy | Liver Disorders | Low Blood Pressure | Lung Problems | ME | Menopause | Migraine | Motion Sickness | Mouth Disorders | Mouth Ulcers | Multiple Sclerosis | Muscular Dystrophy | Musculo-skeletal | Nail Health | Nausea | Nerve Disorders | Nervous Disorders | Neuralgia | Obesity | Osteoporosis | Pain | Palpitations | Panic Attacks | Parkinson's Disease | Period Problems | Phobias | Piles | PMT | Pneumonia | Postural Problems | Pregnancy Help | Prostate Problems | Psoriasis | Raynaud's Disease | Recurrent Infections | Restless Legs | Rheumatoid Arthritis | Schizophrenia | Sciatica | Sexual Problems |
|---|---|---|---|---|---|---|---|---|---|---|---|---|---|---|---|---|---|---|---|---|---|---|---|---|---|---|---|---|---|---|---|---|---|---|---|---|---|---|---|---|---|---|---|---|---|---|---|---|
| COUNTY LOUTH | | | | | | | | | | | | | | | | | | | | | | | | | | | | | | | | | | | | | | | | | | | | | | | | |
| HOLISTIC SOL NTRL HEALING CTRE (HM09989) | ● | | | | | | | | | | | | | | | | | | | | | ● | | | ● | | ● | | ● | | ● | | | ● | | | | | | | | | | | | | | |
| COUNTY MAYO | | | | | | | | | | | | | | | | | | | | | | | | | | | | | | | | | | | | | | | | | | | | | | | | |
| NATURAL HEALING CENTRE (HM14547) | ● | ● | ● | ● | ● | ● | | ● | ● | ● | ● | ● | ● | ● | ● | ● | ● | ● | ● | | | ● | ● | ● | ● | ● | ● | ● | ● | ● | | | ● | ● | ● | ● | ● | | ● | ● | ● | | ● | ● | ● | | ● | ● |
| TOBAR PHADRAIC (HM20102) | ● | ● | | | ● | | | | | | | | | ● | | | | | | | | | | | ● | | | | | | | | | | | | | | | | | | | | | | ● | |
| COUNTY MEATH | | | | | | | | | | | | | | | | | | | | | | | | | | | | | | | | | | | | | | | | | | | | | | | | |
| NATURAL MEDICINE CENTRE (HM14610) | ● | ● | ● | | ● | ● | ● | ● | ● | ● | ● | ● | ● | ● | ● | ● | ● | ● | | | | ● | ● | ● | ● | ● | ● | ● | ● | ● | | | ● | | ● | ● | ● | | ● | ● | ● | ● | ● | ● | ● | | ● | |
| COUNTY MONAGHAN | | | | | | | | | | | | | | | | | | | | | | | | | | | | | | | | | | | | | | | | | | | | | | | | |
| AROMA - ZONE (HM01043) | ● | | ● | | ● | | | | | | | | | | ● | | | | | | | | | | | | | | | | | | ● | | | | | | | | | | | | | | ● | |
| HEALTHY CHOICES (HM09426) | ● | ● | ● | | ● | ● | ● | | ● | | | | ● | ● | ● | | | ● | | | | | | | | | | | ● | | | | | | | | | | | | ● | | | | ● | | ● | |
| NORTHAMBER (HM15050) | ● | ● | ● | ● | ● | ● | ● | ● | ● | ● | ● | ● | ● | ● | ● | ● | ● | ● | ● | | | ● | ● | ● | ● | ● | ● | ● | ● | ● | | ● | ● | ● | ● | ● | ● | | ● | ● | ● | ● | ● | ● | ● | ● | ● | ● |
| COUNTY ROSCOMMON | | | | | | | | | | | | | | | | | | | | | | | | | | | | | | | | | | | | | | | | | | | | | | | | |
| HOLISTIC HEALTH FARM (HM09980) | ● | | | | ● | | | | | | | | | ● | | | | | | | | | | | ● | | | | | | | | ● | | | ● | | | | | | | | | ● | | | |
| COUNTY SLIGO | | | | | | | | | | | | | | | | | | | | | | | | | | | | | | | | | | | | | | | | | | | | | | | | |
| ANAM CHARA COUNSELLING (HM00802) | ● | | | | | | | | | | | | | | | | | | ● | | | | | | ● | | | | | ● | | | | ● | | | | | | | | | | | | | | ● |
| SLIGO CHIROPRACTIC (HM18686) | | | | | | ● | | | | ● | ● | ● | ● | ● | ● | | | | ● | | | | | ● | ● | ● | | ● | ● | | | | ● | | | | | | | | | | | | | | ● | |
| COUNTY TIPPERARY | | | | | | | | | | | | | | | | | | | | | | | | | | | | | | | | | | | | | | | | | | | | | | | | |
| KINSELLA, MARIE (HM11693) | | | | | | | | | | | | | | | | | | | | | | | | | ● | | | | | | | | | ● | | | | | | | | | | | | | | ● |
| COUNTY WESTMEATH | | | | | | | | | | | | | | | | | | | | | | | | | | | | | | | | | | | | | | | | | | | | | | | | |
| HOWE, JAN (HM10263) | ● | | | | ● | ● | | | | ● | | ● | ● | ● | | | | | | | | | | | | | | | ● | | | | | | | | | | | | | | | | | | ● | |
| COUNTY WEXFORD | | | | | | | | | | | | | | | | | | | | | | | | | | | | | | | | | | | | | | | | | | | | | | | | |
| FOURTH MOUNTAIN HOM AND ACU (HM07622) | ● | ● | ● | | ● | ● | ● | ● | ● | ● | | ● | ● | ● | ● | ● | ● | ● | ● | | | ● | ● | ● | ● | ● | ● | ● | ● | ● | | | ● | ● | ● | ● | ● | | ● | ● | ● | ● | ● | ● | ● | | ● | ● |
| JEFFARIES, PHILIP (HM10958) | | | | | ● | | | | | | | | | | ● | | | | | | | | | ● | | ● | | | ● | | | | ● | | | | | | | | | | | | | | | |
| JEFFARIES, PHILIP (HM10957) | | | | | ● | | | | | | | | | | ● | | | | | | | | | ● | | ● | | | ● | | | | ● | | | | | | | | | | | | | | | |
| MURPHY, MARY (HM14388) | ● | ● | | | | | | | ● | | | | | | | | | | | | | | | ● | ● | | | | ● | ● | | | | ● | | ● | | | | | | | | | | | | |
| OSTEOPATHIC PRACTICE (HM15474) | | ● | | | ● | | | | | | | ● | | | ● | | | | ● | | | | | ● | | ● | | | ● | | | | ● | | | | | | | | | | | ● | ● | | | |
| COUNTY WICKLOW | | | | | | | | | | | | | | | | | | | | | | | | | | | | | | | | | | | | | | | | | | | | | | | | |
| ARKLOW NATURAL HEALING CENTRE (HM01007) | ● | ● | ● | ● | ● | ● | | | | | | | ● | ● | ● | ● | | ● | ● | | | | ● | | | | | | ● | ● | | | ● | | ● | ● | | | ● | | ● | | ● | ● | ● | | | |
| HOLISTIC OPTIONS (HM09985) | ● | ● | | ● | ● | ● | | ● | ● | | ● | ● | ● | ● | ● | | | | | | | | ● | | ● | ● | ● | ● | ● | ● | | ● | ● | ● | ● | ● | ● | | | ● | ● | ● | | | ● | | ● | |
| JAMESON PERSONAL EXCELLENCE (HM10903) | ● | ● | | | | | | | ● | | | | | | ● | | | | | | | | | | ● | | ● | | ● | ● | | | ● | ● | | ● | | | | | ● | | | | | | | ● |
| MARK GOULDING - ACUPUNCTURIST (HM13107) | ● | ● | ● | | ● | ● | | ● | ● | ● | ● | ● | ● | ● | ● | ● | ● | ● | ● | ● | | | ● | ● | ● | ● | ● | ● | ● | ● | | ● | ● | ● | ● | ● | ● | | ● | ● | ● | ● | ● | ● | ● | | ● | ● |

# I - S Conditions treated at Practices/Businesses

|Business by County with Reference no.|Insomnia|Irritable Bowel Syndrome|Itching|Jet Lag|Joint Pain|Kidney Complaints|Lactose Intolerance|Laryngitis|Lethargy|Liver Disorders|Low Blood Pressure|Lung Problems|ME|Menopause|Migraine|Motion Sickness|Mouth Disorders|Mouth Ulcers|Multiple Sclerosis|Muscular Dystrophy|Musculo-skeletal|Nail Health|Nausea|Nerve Disorders|
|---|---|---|---|---|---|---|---|---|---|---|---|---|---|---|---|---|---|---|---|---|---|---|---|---|
|**NORTHERN IRELAND**| | | | | | | | | | | | | | | | | | | | | | | | |
|**COUNTY ANTRIM**| | | | | | | | | | | | | | | | | | | | | | | | |
|ACTIVE BALANCE CLINIC (HM00189)|●|●|●| |●| |●| |●|●|●|●|●|●|●| |●| | | | | | | |
|ALOE VERA (HM00669)|●|●|●|●| |●| |●| | | | |●|●|●| |●|●|●| | | | | |
|ANTRIM CHIROPRACTIC CLINIC (HM00923)| |●| | |●| | | | | | | | | | | | | | | | | | | |
|BALLYCLARE CHIROPRACTIC CLINIC (HM01636)| |●| | |●| | | | | | | |●| | | | | | | | | | |●|
|BALLYMONEY CHIROPRACTIC CLINIC (HM01639)| |●| | |●| | | | | | | | | | | | | | | | | | |●|
|BROWN, AVRIL (HM03215)| | | | | | | | | | | | | | | | | | | | | | | | |
|CREGAGH CHIROPRACTIC CLINIC (HM05412)| |●| | |●| | | | | | | |●| |●| | | | | | | | |●|
|EARLS, JAMES (HM06497)| | | | |●| | | | | | | |●| |●| | | | | | | | | |
|FINAGHY CHIROPRACTIC CLINIC (HM07295)| |●| | |●| | | | | | | | | | | | | | | | | | |●|
|FLORENCE SHARPE CHIROPODIST (HM07431)| | | | | | | | | | | | | | | | | | | | | |●| | |
|FRAMAR NATURAL HEALTH CLINIC (HM07654)|●|●|●|●|●|●|●|●|●|●|●| |●|●|●|●|●|●|●| | |●|●|●|
|GIVEN, CLIVE (HM08115)|●|●|●|●|●|●|●|●|●|●|●|●|●|●|●|●|●|●|●|●| |●|●|●|
|GLENGORMLEY CHIRO CLINIC (HM08151)| |●| | |●| | | | | | | | | | | | | | | | | | |●|
|HYPNOTHERAPY CENTRE (HM10521)| | | | | | | | | | | | | | | | | | | | | | | | |
|LAMBERT, RACHEL (HM11901)|●|●| | | | | | | | | | |●|●|●| | | | | | | | | |
|LISBURN CHIROPRACTIC CLINIC (HM12452)| | | | |●| | | | | | | | | | | | | | | | | | |●|
|MAXWELL, MARY (HM13337)|●| | | |●|●| | | | |●| |●| |●| | | | | | |●|●| |
|MCCARTNEY, W J (HM13401)| | | | | | | | | | | | | | | | | | | | | |●| | |
|MCCRYSTALS NATUROPATHIC CENTRE (HM13436)|●|●|●|●|●|●|●|●|●|●|●|●|●|●|●|●|●|●|●| | |●|●|●|
|MCCULLY, JOAN (HM13437)| | | | | | | | | | | | | | | | | | | | | |●| | |
|MYSTIC SCHEHERAZADE (HM14445)| | | | | | | | | | | | | | | | | | | | | | | | |
|REAY, H (HM17004)| | | | | | | | | | | | | | | | | | | | | |●| | |
|SCRABO HEALTH PRODUCTS (HM18143)|●|●|●|●|●|●|●|●|●|●|●|●|●|●|●|●|●|●|●| | |●|●|●|
|STEWART, S (HM19276)| | | | | | | | | | | | | | | | | | | | | |●| | |
|TODD, TREVOR (HM20109)| | | | | | | | | | | | | | | | | | | | | |●| | |
|W M RYAN AND SON (HM20722)| | | | |●| | | | | | | | | |●| | | | | | | |●| |
|YARO (HM21991)|●|●| | | | | | | | | | |●|●|●| | | | | | | | | |
|**COUNTY ARMAGH**| | | | | | | | | | | | | | | | | | | | | | | | |
|CRAIGAVON CHIROPRACTIC CLINIC (HM05355)| |●| | | | | | | | | | | | | | | | | | | | | |●|
|WILLIS, IAN (HM21614)| | | | | | | | | | | | | | | | | | | | | |●| | |

|Business by County with Reference no.|Nervous Disorders|Neuralgia|Obesity|Osteoporosis|Pain|Palpitations|Panic Attacks|Parkinson's Disease|Period Problems|Phobias|Piles|PMT|Pneumonia|Postural Problems|Pregnancy Help|Prostate Problems|Psoriasis|Raynaud's Disease|Recurrent Infections|Restless Legs|Rheumatoid Arthritis|Schizophrenia|Sciatica|Sexual Problems|
|---|---|---|---|---|---|---|---|---|---|---|---|---|---|---|---|---|---|---|---|---|---|---|---|---|
|**NORTHERN IRELAND**| | | | | | | | | | | | | | | | | | | | | | | | |
|**COUNTY ANTRIM**| | | | | | | | | | | | | | | | | | | | | | | | |
|ACTIVE BALANCE CLINIC (HM00189)| |●| |●|●|●| |●|●| |●|●| | | |●|●|●| | |●| |●| |
|ALOE VERA (HM00669)| | |●|●|●| | |●| | |●|●|●| | | |●|●| | |●| | | |
|ANTRIM CHIROPRACTIC CLINIC (HM00923)| | | |●|●| | | | | | | | | | | | | | | | | |●| |
|BALLYCLARE CHIROPRACTIC CLINIC (HM01636)|●| | |●|●| | | | | | | | | | | | | | | | | |●| |
|BALLYMONEY CHIROPRACTIC CLINIC (HM01639)| | | |●|●| | | | | | | | | | | | | | | | | |●| |
|BROWN, AVRIL (HM03215)| | | | | | |●| | | | | | | | | | | | | | | | |●|
|CREGAGH CHIROPRACTIC CLINIC (HM05412)|●| | | |●| | | | | | | | | | | | | | | | | |●| |
|EARLS, JAMES (HM06497)| | | | | | | | | | | | | | | | | | | | | | | | |
|FINAGHY CHIROPRACTIC CLINIC (HM07295)| | | |●|●| | | | | | | | | | | | | | | | | |●| |
|FLORENCE SHARPE CHIROPODIST (HM07431)| | | | | | | | | | | | | | | | | | | | | | | | |
|FRAMAR NATURAL HEALTH CLINIC (HM07654)|●|●|●|●|●| | | | | |●|●|●| | |●|●|●| |●|●| |●|●|
|GIVEN, CLIVE (HM08115)|●|●|●|●|●|●| |●|●|●|●|●|●| |●|●|●|●|●|●|●|●|●|●|
|GLENGORMLEY CHIRO CLINIC (HM08151)| | | | |●| | | | | | | | | | | | | | | | | |●| |
|HYPNOTHERAPY CENTRE (HM10521)| | | | | | |●| | |●| | | | | | | | | | | | | | |
|LAMBERT, RACHEL (HM11901)| | | | |●| | | | | | |●| | | | | | | | | | | | |
|LISBURN CHIROPRACTIC CLINIC (HM12452)| | | |●|●| | | | | | | | | | | | | | | | | |●| |
|MAXWELL, MARY (HM13337)| | | | |●| | | |●| | |●| | |●| | | | | | | | | |
|MCCARTNEY, W J (HM13401)| | | | | | | | | | | | | | | | | | | | | | | | |
|MCCRYSTALS NATUROPATHIC CENTRE (HM13436)|●|●|●|●|●|●| |●|●|●|●|●| | | |●|●|●|●|●|●| |●|●|
|MCCULLY, JOAN (HM13437)| | | | | | | | | | | | | | | | | | | | | | | | |
|MYSTIC SCHEHERAZADE (HM14445)| | | | |●| | | | | | | | | | | | | | | | | | | |
|REAY, H (HM17004)| | | | | | | | | | | | | | | | | | | | | | | | |
|SCRABO HEALTH PRODUCTS (HM18143)|●|●|●|●|●|●| |●|●|●|●|●|●| |●|●|●|●|●|●|●| |●| |
|STEWART, S (HM19276)| | | | | | | | | | | | | | | | | | | | | | | | |
|TODD, TREVOR (HM20109)| | | | | | | | | | | | | | | | | | | | | | | | |
|W M RYAN AND SON (HM20722)| |●| | |●| | | | | | | | | | | | | | | | | |●| |
|YARO (HM21991)| | | | | | | | | | | |●| | | | | | | | | | | | |
|**COUNTY ARMAGH**| | | | | | | | | | | | | | | | | | | | | | | | |
|CRAIGAVON CHIROPRACTIC CLINIC (HM05355)| | | |●|●| | | | | | | | | | | | | | | | | |●| |
|WILLIS, IAN (HM21614)| | | | | | | | | | | | | | | | | | | | | | | | |

# I - S Conditions treated at Practices/Businesses

Business by County with Reference no.

| Business | Insomnia | Irritable Bowel Syndrome | Itching | Jet Lag | Joint Pain | Kidney Complaints | Lactose Intolerance | Laryngitis | Lethargy | Liver Disorders | Low Blood Pressure | Lung Problems | ME | Menopause | Migraine | Motion Sickness |
|---|---|---|---|---|---|---|---|---|---|---|---|---|---|---|---|---|
| **COUNTY DOWN** | | | | | | | | | | | | | | | | |
| ARDS CHIROPRACTIC CLINIC (HM00993) | | ● | | | ● | | | | | | | | | | | |
| BANGOR CHIROPRACTIC CLINIC (HM01659) | | | | | | | | | | | | | | | | |
| BANGOR OSTEOPATHIC CLINIC (HM01660) | | | | | | | | | | | | | | | | |
| CHIROPRACTICE (HM04405) | | ● | | | ● | | | | | | | | | | | |
| COCHRANE, NIALL (HM04764) | | | | | | | | | | | | | | | | |
| HADDEN, MARLENE (HM08687) | ● | ● | | | | ● | | | | | | | ● | | ● | |
| LYCIUM CENTRE (HM12755) | ● | ● | ● | | ● | | | | ● | | ● | | ● | ● | ● | |
| MCCARTAN, DEBORAH (HM13392) | | | | | | | | | | | | | | | | |
| MCCLURG, T A (HM13412) | | | | | ● | | | | | | | | | | | |
| MCCUTCHEON, TINA (HM13441) | | ● | | | ● | | | | | | | | | | | |
| NEWRY CHIROPRACTIC CLINIC (HM14886) | | ● | | | ● | | | | | | | | | | | |
| NOBLE, ANDREW (DR) (HM14968) | | | | | ● | | | | | | | | | | | |
| NORTH DOWN CLINIC (HM15023) | | | | | | | | | | | | | ● | | ● | |
| PRINGLE CHIROPRACTIC (HM16626) | | ● | | | ● | | | | | | | | ● | | ● | |
| QUINN, BARBARA (HM16808) | | ● | | | ● | | | | | | | | ● | | | |
| REFLEXOLOGY CLINIC (HM17092) | ● | ● | | ● | | | | | | | | | | ● | ● | |
| YOGA CENTRE OF IRELAND (HM22023) | | | | | | | | | | | | | | | ● | |
| **COUNTY FERMANAGH** | | | | | | | | | | | | | | | | |
| ENNISKILLEN CHIRO CLINIC (HM06844) | | | | | ● | | | | | | | | ● | | ● | |
| **COUNTY LONDONDERRY** | | | | | | | | | | | | | | | | |
| CLARENDON CHIROPRACTIC CLINIC (HM04539) | | | | | ● | | | | | | | | | | | |
| CLAUDY CHIROPRACTIC CLINIC (HM04612) | | ● | | | ● | | | | | | | | | | | |
| CURRAN, MAUREEN (HM05630) | | | | | | | | | | | | | | | | |
| DISPENSERY (HM06117) | ● | ● | ● | ● | ● | ● | ● | ● | ● | ● | ● | ● | ● | ● | ● | ● |
| EQUILIBRIUM HOLISTIC CLINIC (HM06875) | ● | | | | | | | | | | | | | | ● | |
| FOYLE HYPNOTHERAPY CENTRE (HM07646) | ● | ● | | | | | | | ● | | | | ● | ● | ● | ● |
| LIFE TREE (HM12350) | | ● | | | | | ● | | ● | | | | | | | ● |
| MAGHERAFELT CHIRO CLINIC (HM12906) | | | | | ● | | | | | | | | | | | |
| **COUNTY TYRONE** | | | | | | | | | | | | | | | | |
| BRADLEY, R M (HM02871) | | | | | | | | | | | | | | | | |
| COOKSTOWN HERBAL CLINIC (HM05073) | ● | ● | ● | ● | ● | ● | ● | ● | ● | ● | ● | ● | ● | ● | ● | ● |
| DUNGANNON CHIROPRACTIC CLINIC (HM06405) | | ● | | | ● | | | | | | | | ● | | | |
| ROSEWOOD HEALTH CLINIC (HM17630) | ● | ● | ● | ● | ● | ● | ● | ● | ● | ● | ● | ● | ● | ● | ● | ● |

| Business | Mouth Disorders | Mouth Ulcers | Multiple Sclerosis | Muscular Dystrophy | Musculo-skeletal | Nail Health | Nausea | Nerve Disorders | Nervous Disorders | Neuralgia | Obesity | Osteoporosis | Pain | Palpitations | Panic Attacks | Parkinson's Disease |
|---|---|---|---|---|---|---|---|---|---|---|---|---|---|---|---|---|
| **COUNTY DOWN** | | | | | | | | | | | | | | | | |
| ARDS CHIROPRACTIC CLINIC (HM00993) | | | | | | | | ● | | | | | ● | | | |
| BANGOR CHIROPRACTIC CLINIC (HM01659) | | | | | | | | ● | | | | ● | ● | | | |
| BANGOR OSTEOPATHIC CLINIC (HM01660) | | | | | | | | ● | | ● | | | ● | | | |
| CHIROPRACTICE (HM04405) | | | | | | | | ● | ● | | | ● | ● | | | |
| COCHRANE, NIALL (HM04764) | | | | | | ● | | | | | | | | | | |
| HADDEN, MARLENE (HM08687) | | | ● | | | | ● | | | | | | ● | | | |
| LYCIUM CENTRE (HM12755) | | | ● | | | | | | | | | | ● | ● | | |
| MCCARTAN, DEBORAH (HM13392) | | | | | | ● | | | | | | | | | | |
| MCCLURG, T A (HM13412) | | | | | | ● | | | | | | | | | | |
| MCCUTCHEON, TINA (HM13441) | | | | | | | | | | | | | ● | | | |
| NEWRY CHIROPRACTIC CLINIC (HM14886) | | | | | | | | | | | | ● | ● | | | |
| NOBLE, ANDREW (DR) (HM14968) | | | | | | | | ● | | | | | ● | | | |
| NORTH DOWN CLINIC (HM15023) | | | | | | | | | | | | | | ● | | ● |
| PRINGLE CHIROPRACTIC (HM16626) | | | | | | | | ● | ● | ● | | | ● | | | |
| QUINN, BARBARA (HM16808) | | | | | | | | | | ● | | | ● | | | |
| REFLEXOLOGY CLINIC (HM17092) | | | | | | | | | | | | | | | | |
| YOGA CENTRE OF IRELAND (HM22023) | | | | | | | | | | | | | | | | |
| **COUNTY FERMANAGH** | | | | | | | | | | | | | | | | |
| ENNISKILLEN CHIRO CLINIC (HM06844) | | | | | | | | | | ● | | | ● | | | |
| **COUNTY LONDONDERRY** | | | | | | | | | | | | | | | | |
| CLARENDON CHIROPRACTIC CLINIC (HM04539) | | | | | | | | ● | | | | | ● | | | |
| CLAUDY CHIROPRACTIC CLINIC (HM04612) | | | | | | | | ● | ● | | | ● | ● | | | |
| CURRAN, MAUREEN (HM05630) | | | | | | | | | | | | | ● | | | |
| DISPENSERY (HM06117) | ● | ● | ● | ● | ● | ● | ● | ● | ● | ● | ● | ● | ● | ● | | ● |
| EQUILIBRIUM HOLISTIC CLINIC (HM06875) | | | | | | | | | | | | | | | | |
| FOYLE HYPNOTHERAPY CENTRE (HM07646) | | | | | | | | ● | ● | | ● | ● | ● | ● | | |
| LIFE TREE (HM12350) | | | | | | ● | | | | ● | | | | | | |
| MAGHERAFELT CHIRO CLINIC (HM12906) | | | | | | | | | | | | | ● | | | |
| **COUNTY TYRONE** | | | | | | | | | | | | | | | | |
| BRADLEY, R M (HM02871) | | | | | | ● | | | | | | | | | | |
| COOKSTOWN HERBAL CLINIC (HM05073) | ● | ● | ● | ● | | ● | ● | ● | ● | ● | ● | ● | ● | ● | | ● |
| DUNGANNON CHIROPRACTIC CLINIC (HM06405) | | | | | | | | ● | | | | ● | ● | | | |
| ROSEWOOD HEALTH CLINIC (HM17630) | ● | ● | ● | ● | | ● | ● | ● | ● | ● | ● | ● | ● | ● | | ● |

| Business | Period Problems | Phobias | Piles | PMT | Pneumonia | Postural Problems | Pregnancy Help | Prostate Problems | Psoriasis | Raynaud's Disease | Recurrent Infections | Restless Legs | Rheumatoid Arthritis | Schizophrenia | Sciatica | Sexual Problems |
|---|---|---|---|---|---|---|---|---|---|---|---|---|---|---|---|---|
| **COUNTY DOWN** | | | | | | | | | | | | | | | | |
| ARDS CHIROPRACTIC CLINIC (HM00993) | | | | | | | | | | | | | | | ● | |
| BANGOR CHIROPRACTIC CLINIC (HM01659) | | | | | | | | | | | | | | | ● | |
| BANGOR OSTEOPATHIC CLINIC (HM01660) | | | | | | | | | | | | | | | | |
| CHIROPRACTICE (HM04405) | | | | | | | | | | | | | | | ● | |
| COCHRANE, NIALL (HM04764) | | | | | | | | | | | | | | | | |
| HADDEN, MARLENE (HM08687) | ● | | | ● | | | ● | | | | | ● | | | ● | |
| LYCIUM CENTRE (HM12755) | ● | | | ● | | | | | ● | | | | ● | | ● | |
| MCCARTAN, DEBORAH (HM13392) | | | | | | | | | | | | | | | | |
| MCCLURG, T A (HM13412) | | | | | | | | | ● | ● | | ● | ● | | ● | |
| MCCUTCHEON, TINA (HM13441) | ● | | | ● | | | | | | | ● | | | | ● | |
| NEWRY CHIROPRACTIC CLINIC (HM14886) | | | | | | | | | | | | | | | ● | |
| NOBLE, ANDREW (DR) (HM14968) | | | | | | | | | | | | | | | ● | |
| NORTH DOWN CLINIC (HM15023) | | | | ● | | | | | ● | | | | | | ● | |
| PRINGLE CHIROPRACTIC (HM16626) | | | | | | | | | | | | | ● | | ● | |
| QUINN, BARBARA (HM16808) | | | | | | | | | | | | | | | ● | |
| REFLEXOLOGY CLINIC (HM17092) | | | | | | | ● | | | | | | | | | |
| YOGA CENTRE OF IRELAND (HM22023) | | | | | | | | | | | | | | | | |
| **COUNTY FERMANAGH** | | | | | | | | | | | | | | | | |
| ENNISKILLEN CHIRO CLINIC (HM06844) | | | | | | | | | | | | | | | ● | |
| **COUNTY LONDONDERRY** | | | | | | | | | | | | | | | | |
| CLARENDON CHIROPRACTIC CLINIC (HM04539) | | | | | | | | | | | | | | | ● | |
| CLAUDY CHIROPRACTIC CLINIC (HM04612) | | | | | | | | | | | | | | | ● | |
| CURRAN, MAUREEN (HM05630) | | | | | | | | | ● | ● | | | ● | | | |
| DISPENSERY (HM06117) | ● | ● | ● | ● | ● | ● | ● | ● | ● | ● | ● | ● | ● | ● | ● | ● |
| EQUILIBRIUM HOLISTIC CLINIC (HM06875) | | | | | | | | | | | | | | | | |
| FOYLE HYPNOTHERAPY CENTRE (HM07646) | ● | ● | | ● | | | | | ● | | | ● | | | ● | ● |
| LIFE TREE (HM12350) | | | | | | | | | | | ● | ● | | | ● | |
| MAGHERAFELT CHIRO CLINIC (HM12906) | | | | | | | | | | | | | | | ● | |
| **COUNTY TYRONE** | | | | | | | | | | | | | | | | |
| BRADLEY, R M (HM02871) | | | | | | | | | | | | | | | | |
| COOKSTOWN HERBAL CLINIC (HM05073) | ● | ● | ● | ● | ● | | ● | ● | ● | ● | ● | ● | ● | ● | ● | ● |
| DUNGANNON CHIROPRACTIC CLINIC (HM06405) | | | | | | | | | | | | | | | ● | |
| ROSEWOOD HEALTH CLINIC (HM17630) | ● | ● | ● | ● | ● | | ● | ● | ● | ● | ● | ● | ● | ● | ● | ● |

# I - S Conditions treated at Practices/Businesses

Business by County with Reference no.

| Business by County with Reference no. | Insomnia | Irritable Bowel Syndrome | Itching | Jet Lag | Joint Pain | Kidney Complaints | Lactose Intolerance | Laryngitis | Lethargy | Liver Disorders | Low Blood Pressure | Lung Problems | ME | Menopause | Migraine | Motion Sickness | Mouth Disorders | Mouth Ulcers | Multiple Sclerosis | Muscular Dystrophy | Musculo-skeletal | Nail Health |
|---|---|---|---|---|---|---|---|---|---|---|---|---|---|---|---|---|---|---|---|---|---|---|
| **SCOTLAND** | | | | | | | | | | | | | | | | | | | | | | |
| **ABERDEENSHIRE** | | | | | | | | | | | | | | | | | | | | | | |
| A WAY WITH THE FAERIES (HM00051) | | | | | | | | | | | | | | | ● | | | | | | | |
| ABERDEEN CHIROPRACTIC CLINIC (HM00114) | | ● | | | ● | | | | | | | | ● | | ● | | | | | | | |
| ALTERNATIVE PRACTICE (HM00723) | ● | ● | | | | | | | | | | | | | ● | | | | | | | |
| BANCHORY CHIROPODY PRACTICE (HM01649) | | | | | | | | | | | | | | | | | | | | | | ● |
| BEECHGROVE CLINIC (HM02050) | | | | | ● | | | | | | | | ● | | | | | | ● | | ● | |
| BON-ACCORD CHIROPODY (HM02667) | | | | | | | | | | | | | | | | | | | | | | ● |
| CHELSEA HOUSE CLINIC (HM04090) | ● | ● | | | | | | | | | | | | | ● | | | | | | | |
| CLAIRBAUX CLINIC (HM04506) | ● | | | | ● | | | | ● | | | | | ● | ● | | | | ● | | ● | |
| CLAIRBAUX CLINIC (HM04505) | ● | | | | ● | | | | ● | | | | | ● | ● | | | | ● | | | |
| DAB HANDS MASSAGE (HM05666) | ● | | | | | | | | | | | | | | | | | | | | | |
| DAVISON, FIONA (HM05865) | | | | | ● | | | | | | | | | | | | | | | | | |
| DEEVIEW AROMATHERAPY (HM05960) | ● | ● | | | ● | | | | ● | | | | ● | | | | | | | | | |
| GRAY, SHEILA (HM08419) | ● | ● | | | | | | | | | | | ● | ● | ● | | | | | | | |
| HUNTLY CHIROPRACTIC CLINIC (HM10412) | | ● | | | ● | | | | | | | | ● | | ● | | | | | | | |
| LEAL, DOUGLAS (HM12102) | | | | | | | | | | | | | | | | | | | | | | ● |
| MOSS PHARMACY (HM14262) | | | | | | | | | | | | | | | | | | | | | | ● |
| REIKI TRAINING CENTRE (HM17149) | | | | | | | | | | | | | | | | | | | | | | |
| RIVERSIDE CHIROPRACTIC CLINIC (HM17378) | | | | | ● | | | | | | | | | | ● | | | | | | | |
| ROSEMOUNT CENTRE (HM17623) | ● | ● | ● | | ● | ● | | ● | ● | ● | | ● | ● | ● | ● | ● | ● | | ● | | | |
| SAWYER, KEN (HM17985) | | | | | | | | | | | | | | | | | | | | | | |
| SERENDIPITY (HM18232) | | | | | | | | | | | | | | | ● | | | | | | | |
| STEPHENSON, L (HM19208) | | | | | | | | | | | | | | | | | | | | | | ● |
| TAGGART, RUTH (HM19652) | ● | | | | | | | | | | | | ● | ● | ● | | | | ● | | | |
| TOE TO HEEL - REFLEXOLOGY (HM20110) | ● | ● | | | ● | ● | | | | | ● | | ● | ● | ● | | | | ● | | | |
| TURRIFF CHIROPRACTIC CLINIC (HM20443) | | | | | ● | | | | | | | | | | | | | | | | | |
| WEST END PHYSIOTHERAPY (HM21219) | | | | | ● | | | | | | | | | | | | | | | | | |
| WILKEN, ANGEL (HM21492) | | | | | | | | | | | | | | | ● | | | | | ● | | |
| WOOD, A R (HM21783) | | | | | | | | | | | | | | | | | | | | | | ● |
| **ANGUS** | | | | | | | | | | | | | | | | | | | | | | |
| BAKER, P T (HM01593) | | ● | | | ● | | | | | | | | ● | | ● | | | | | | | |
| DRYDEN, PHILIP (HM06333) | | | | | | | | | | | | | | | | | | | | | | ● |

| Business by County with Reference no. | Nausea | Nerve Disorders | Nervous Disorders | Neuralgia | Obesity | Osteoporosis | Pain | Palpitations | Panic Attacks | Parkinson's Disease | Period Problems | Phobias | Piles | PMT | Pneumonia | Postural Problems | Pregnancy Help | Prostate Problems | Psoriasis | Raynaud's Disease | Recurrent Infections | Restless Legs | Rheumatoid Arthritis | Schizophrenia | Sciatica | Sexual Problems |
|---|---|---|---|---|---|---|---|---|---|---|---|---|---|---|---|---|---|---|---|---|---|---|---|---|---|---|
| **SCOTLAND** | | | | | | | | | | | | | | | | | | | | | | | | | | |
| **ABERDEENSHIRE** | | | | | | | | | | | | | | | | | | | | | | | | | | |
| A WAY WITH THE FAERIES (HM00051) | | | | | | | | | | | | | | | | | | | | | | | | | | |
| ABERDEEN CHIROPRACTIC CLINIC (HM00114) | | ● | ● | | | | ● | | | | | | | | | | | | | | | | | | ● | |
| ALTERNATIVE PRACTICE (HM00723) | | | | | | | | | | | | | | | | | | | | | | | | | | |
| BANCHORY CHIROPODY PRACTICE (HM01649) | | | | | | | | | | | | | | | | | | | | | | | | | | |
| BEECHGROVE CLINIC (HM02050) | | | | | | ● | ● | | | | | | | | | | | | | | | | ● | | ● | |
| BON-ACCORD CHIROPODY (HM02667) | | | | | | | | | | | | | | | | | | | | | | | | | | |
| CHELSEA HOUSE CLINIC (HM04090) | | | | | | | ● | | | | | | | | | | | | | | | | | | | |
| CLAIRBAUX CLINIC (HM04506) | | | | | | | ● | | | | ● | | | ● | | | | | | | | | | | | |
| CLAIRBAUX CLINIC (HM04505) | | | | | | | ● | | | | ● | | | ● | | | | | | | | | | | | |
| DAB HANDS MASSAGE (HM05666) | | | | | | | ● | | | | | | | | | | | | | | | | | | | |
| DAVISON, FIONA (HM05865) | | | | | | | ● | | | | | | | | | | | | | | | | | | ● | |
| DEEVIEW AROMATHERAPY (HM05960) | | | | | | | ● | | | | | | | | | | | | | | | ● | | | ● | |
| GRAY, SHEILA (HM08419) | | | ● | | | | ● | | | | ● | | | ● | | | | | ● | | | | | | ● | ● |
| HUNTLY CHIROPRACTIC CLINIC (HM10412) | | ● | ● | | | | ● | | | | | | | | | | | | | | | | | | ● | |
| LEAL, DOUGLAS (HM12102) | | | | | | | | | | | | | | | | | | | | | | | | | | |
| MOSS PHARMACY (HM14262) | | | | | | | | | | | | | | | | | | | | | | | | | | |
| REIKI TRAINING CENTRE (HM17149) | | | ● | | | | | | | | | | | | | | | | | | | | | | | |
| RIVERSIDE CHIROPRACTIC CLINIC (HM17378) | | ● | ● | | | | ● | | | | | | | | | | | | | | | | | | | |
| ROSEMOUNT CENTRE (HM17623) | | | ● | | ● | | ● | ● | | ● | | ● | ● | ● | ● | | ● | | ● | ● | ● | | ● | | ● | |
| SAWYER, KEN (HM17985) | | | | | | | | | | | | ● | | | | | | | | | | | | | | |
| SERENDIPITY (HM18232) | | | | | | | | | | | | | | | | | | | | | | | | | | |
| STEPHENSON, L (HM19208) | | | | | | | | | | | | | | | | | | | | | | | | | | |
| TAGGART, RUTH (HM19652) | | | | | | | | | | | | | | ● | | | | | | | | | | | | |
| TOE TO HEEL - REFLEXOLOGY (HM20110) | | | | | | | ● | ● | | | ● | | | ● | | | | ● | ● | ● | | ● | ● | | ● | |
| TURRIFF CHIROPRACTIC CLINIC (HM20443) | | | | | | | ● | | | | | | | | | | | | | | | | | | | |
| WEST END PHYSIOTHERAPY (HM21219) | | | | | | | ● | | | | | | | | | | | | | | | | | | | |
| WILKEN, ANGEL (HM21492) | | | | | | | | | | | | ● | | | | | | | | | | | | | | |
| WOOD, A R (HM21783) | | | | | | | | | | | | | | | | | | | | | | | | | | |
| **ANGUS** | | | | | | | | | | | | | | | | | | | | | | | | | | |
| BAKER, P T (HM01593) | | | | | | ● | ● | | | | | | | | | ● | ● | | | | | | | | ● | |
| DRYDEN, PHILIP (HM06333) | | | | | | | | | | | | | | | | | | | | | | | | | | |

# I - S Conditions treated at Practices/Businesses

| Business by County with Reference no. | Insomnia | Irritable Bowel Syndrome | Itching | Jet Lag | Joint Pain | Kidney Complaints | Lactose Intolerance | Laryngitis | Lethargy | Liver Disorders | Low Blood Pressure | Lung Problems | ME | Menopause | Migraine | Motion Sickness | Mouth Disorders | Mouth Ulcers | Multiple Sclerosis | Muscular Dystrophy | Musculo-skeletal | Nail Health |
|---|---|---|---|---|---|---|---|---|---|---|---|---|---|---|---|---|---|---|---|---|---|---|
| FOGGIE, MARGARET (HM07454) | | | | | | | | | | | | | | | | | | | | | | ● |
| HOLISTIC HEALING CENTRE (HM09964) | | ● | | | ● | | | | | | | | | | | | | | | | | |
| KIRRIEMUIR PHYSIO CLINIC (HM11723) | | | | | ● | | | | | | | | | | | | | | | | | |
| NICOLL, ELAINE (HM14929) | | | | | | | | | | | | | | | | | | | | | | ● |
| **ARGYLL AND BUTE** | | | | | | | | | | | | | | | | | | | | | | |
| ACTIVE CHIROPRACTIC (HM00195) | | | | | ● | | | | | | | | ● | | ● | | | | | | | |
| COMPLEMENTARY HEALTH CENTRE (HM04922) | | | | | ● | | | | | | | | | | | | | | | | | ● |
| GIBSON, RONALD J (HM08045) | ● | | | | ● | | | | ● | | ● | | | | ● | | | | | | | ● |
| HOMEOPATHIC PODIATRIST/REFLEX (HM10078) | | ● | | ● | | | | | | | ● | ● | ● | | | | | | ● | | | ● |
| NATURAL THERAPY CENTRE (HM14648) | ● | | | | | | | | | | | | ● | ● | ● | | | | ● | | | |
| REIKI LIGHT (HM17138) | | | | | | | | | | | | | ● | | ● | | | | | | | |
| **AYRSHIRE (EAST)** | | | | | | | | | | | | | | | | | | | | | | |
| CRUISE, M & M (HM05520) | | | | | | | | | | | | | | | | | | | | | | ● |
| LITTLEJOHN, S (HM12473) | | | | | | | | | | | | | | | | | | | | | | ● |
| LYNN BROWN CLINICAL AROM (HM12772) | ● | ● | ● | | ● | | | | ● | | ● | ● | ● | ● | ● | | | | ● | | | |
| **AYRSHIRE (NORTH)** | | | | | | | | | | | | | | | | | | | | | | |
| BODYSCENTS (HM02631) | ● | ● | | | | | | | | | | | ● | ● | ● | | | | | | | |
| BURNS, ALAN STEWART (HM03410) | | | | | | | | | | | | | | | | | | | | | | ● |
| CHIRO HEALTH CARE CLINIC (HM04282) | ● | ● | | | ● | ● | ● | | ● | | ● | | ● | ● | ● | | | | ● | | | |
| HANDS FOR FEET (HM08905) | | | | | | | | | | | | | | | | | | | | | | ● |
| PATON, MARY S (HM15824) | | | | | | | | | | | | | | | | | | | | | | ● |
| REID, E (HM17116) | ● | | | | ● | ● | | | | | ● | | ● | ● | ● | | | | | | | ● |
| **AYRSHIRE (SOUTH)** | | | | | | | | | | | | | | | | | | | | | | |
| BELL, W DOUGLAS (HM02091) | ● | ● | ● | ● | ● | ● | ● | ● | ● | ● | ● | ● | ● | ● | ● | ● | ● | ● | ● | ● | | ● |
| CARRICK CLINIC (HM03742) | | ● | | | ● | | | | ● | | ● | | | ● | ● | | | | | | | |
| CRUISE, M & M (HM05522) | | | | | | | | | | | | | | | | | | | | | | ● |
| ESSENCE OF HEALTH (HM06890) | ● | ● | ● | ● | ● | ● | ● | ● | ● | ● | ● | ● | ● | ● | ● | ● | ● | ● | ● | ● | | ● |
| HARDIE, ANNE (HM08966) | ● | ● | | | | | | | | | | | ● | ● | ● | | | | | | | |
| HEALTH STRESS & INJURIES (HM09404) | ● | ● | | | ● | | | | ● | | | | ● | ● | ● | | | | ● | | | |
| HEARTLAKE PHYSIOTHERAPY (HM09444) | | | | | ● | | | | | | | | | | | | | | ● | | | |
| HODGE, IAN (HM09874) | | ● | | | ● | | | | | | ● | | | | | | | | | | | |
| REID, A (HM17112) | | | | | | | | | | | | | | | | | | | | | | ● |
| SMITH, ALICIA (HM18712) | ● | ● | | | | | | | | | | | ● | | | | | | | | | |
| STEVENSON, SCOTT (HM19251) | | ● | | | | | | | | | | | ● | | ● | | | | | | | |

| Business by County with Reference no. | Nausea | Nerve Disorders | Nervous Disorders | Neuralgia | Obesity | Osteoporosis | Pain | Palpitations | Panic Attacks | Parkinson's Disease | Period Problems | Phobias | Piles | PMT | Pneumonia | Postural Problems | Pregnancy Help | Prostate Problems | Psoriasis | Raynaud's Disease | Recurrent Infections | Restless Legs | Rheumatoid Arthritis | Schizophrenia | Sciatica | Sexual Problems |
|---|---|---|---|---|---|---|---|---|---|---|---|---|---|---|---|---|---|---|---|---|---|---|---|---|---|---|
| FOGGIE, MARGARET (HM07454) | | | | | | | | | | | | | | | | | | | | | | | | | | |
| HOLISTIC HEALING CENTRE (HM09964) | | ● | | | | | | | | | | | | | | ● | | | | | | | | | ● | |
| KIRRIEMUIR PHYSIO CLINIC (HM11723) | | | | | | | ● | | | | | | | | | | | | | | | | | | | |
| NICOLL, ELAINE (HM14929) | | | | | | | | | | | | | | | | | | | | | | | | | | |
| **ARGYLL AND BUTE** | | | | | | | | | | | | | | | | | | | | | | | | | | |
| ACTIVE CHIROPRACTIC (HM00195) | | | | | ● | | ● | | | | | | | | | | | | | | | ● | | | ● | |
| COMPLEMENTARY HEALTH CENTRE (HM04922) | | | | | | | ● | | | | | | | | | | | | | | | | | | | |
| GIBSON, RONALD J (HM08045) | | | ● | | | | ● | | | | | | | | | | | | | ● | | | ● | | ● | |
| HOMEOPATHIC PODIATRIST/REFLEX (HM10078) | ● | ● | ● | | | | | | | ● | ● | | | ● | | | | | ● | ● | ● | ● | ● | | ● | |
| NATURAL THERAPY CENTRE (HM14648) | | | | | | | | | | | | | | ● | | | ● | | | | | ● | ● | | ● | |
| REIKI LIGHT (HM17138) | | | | | | | | | | | | | | | | | | | | | | | | | | |
| **AYRSHIRE (EAST)** | | | | | | | | | | | | | | | | | | | | | | | | | | |
| CRUISE, M & M (HM05520) | | | | | | | | | | | | | | | | | | | | | | | | | | |
| LITTLEJOHN, S (HM12473) | | | | | | | | | | | | | | | | | | | | | | | | | | |
| LYNN BROWN CLINICAL AROM (HM12772) | | ● | ● | ● | | | ● | ● | | ● | ● | ● | | ● | | | | | ● | | | ● | ● | | ● | |
| **AYRSHIRE (NORTH)** | | | | | | | | | | | | | | | | | | | | | | | | | | |
| BODYSCENTS (HM02631) | | | | | | | ● | | | | | | | ● | | | | | | | | | | | | |
| BURNS, ALAN STEWART (HM03410) | | | | | | | | | | | | | | | | | | | | | | | | | | |
| CHIRO HEALTH CARE CLINIC (HM04282) | | ● | ● | ● | | ● | ● | ● | | ● | ● | | | ● | | | | | ● | ● | ● | | ● | | ● | |
| HANDS FOR FEET (HM08905) | | | | | | | | | | | | | | | | | | | | | | | | | | |
| PATON, MARY S (HM15824) | | | | | | | | | | | | | | | | | | | | | | | | | | |
| REID, E (HM17116) | ● | | | | | | ● | ● | | | ● | | | ● | | | ● | | | | | ● | | | | |
| **AYRSHIRE (SOUTH)** | | | | | | | | | | | | | | | | | | | | | | | | | | |
| BELL, W DOUGLAS (HM02091) | ● | ● | ● | ● | ● | ● | ● | ● | | ● | ● | ● | ● | ● | ● | | ● | ● | ● | ● | ● | ● | ● | ● | ● | ● |
| CARRICK CLINIC (HM03742) | | | ● | ● | ● | | ● | ● | | | ● | | | ● | | | | ● | ● | | ● | | ● | | ● | |
| CRUISE, M & M (HM05522) | | | | | | | | | | | | | | | | | | | | | | | | | | |
| ESSENCE OF HEALTH (HM06890) | ● | ● | ● | ● | ● | ● | ● | ● | | ● | ● | ● | ● | ● | ● | | ● | ● | ● | ● | ● | ● | ● | ● | ● | ● |
| HARDIE, ANNE (HM08966) | | | | | | | ● | | | | | | | ● | | | | | | | | | | | | |
| HEALTH STRESS & INJURIES (HM09404) | | ● | ● | ● | ● | ● | ● | | | | ● | ● | | ● | | | ● | | | | | | | | ● | |
| HEARTLAKE PHYSIOTHERAPY (HM09444) | | | | | | | ● | | | | | | | | | | | | | | | | | | | |
| HODGE, IAN (HM09874) | | | ● | | ● | | ● | | | | | ● | | | | | | | | | | | | | | |
| REID, A (HM17112) | | | | | | | | | | | | | | | | | | | | | | | | | | |
| SMITH, ALICIA (HM18712) | | | ● | | | | ● | | ● | | | ● | | | | | | | ● | | | ● | | | | |
| STEVENSON, SCOTT (HM19251) | | | | | | | | | | | | ● | | | | | | | | | | | | | | |

# I - S Conditions treated at Practices/Businesses

Business by County with Reference no.

| Condition | CLACKMANNANSHIRE | DUMFRIES AND GALLOWAY | | | | | | | | EDINBURGH (CITY OF) | | | | | | | | | | | | | | | | | | | | | |
|---|---|---|---|---|---|---|---|---|---|---|---|---|---|---|---|---|---|---|---|---|---|---|---|---|---|---|---|---|---|---|---|
| | ALTERNATIVE MEDICAL CLINIC (HM00711) | BURTON, VICKY (HM03447) | CHLOE'S HERBS (HM04419) | DAVIDSON, MORAG (HM05788) | DUMFRIES HOLISTIC HEALTH CTRE (HM06386) | HEALTH STRESS & INJURIES CLNC (HM09405) | MCCLYMOUNT, JENNIFER (HM13416) | RANKINE, VANORA (HM16939) | SHARP, LINDA A (HM18314) | ACTIVE OSTEOPATHS (HM00200) | ALEXANDER TECHNIQUE (HM00517) | BABY HOLISTIC & MASSAGE (HM01464) | BIORADIANT HEALTH (HM02343) | BLACKHALL PHYSIOTHERAPY CLINIC (HM02445) | BLAIR, RICHARD (HM02475) | CHRISTIE, ADRIAN (HM04438) | E G H P (HM06468) | EDINBURGH ALEXANDER CENTRE (HM06606) | EDINBURGH HOMEOPATHIC CENTRE (HM06613) | EDINBURGH OSTEOPATHIC SURGERY (HM06615) | EDINBURGH PHYSIOTHERAPY CENTRE (HM06616) | EXCLUSIVE HYPNOTHERAPY (HM07019) | GARDINER, F (HM07872) | HAZEL, J M (HM09290) | HOLDEN, SHEENA (HM09934) | IN HARMONY AROMATHERAPY (HM10595) | J W PHYSIOTHERAPY & SPORTS (HM10804) | J W PHYSIOTHERAPY & SPORTS (HM10805) | JENAI (HM10980) | LIVING MIND (HM12487) | LOGAN, CAROL (HM12565) |
| Sexual Problems | | ● | | | ● | ● | | | | | | | | | | | ● | | | | | | | | | | | | | | ● |
| Sciatica | | | ● | | ● | ● | | | ● | ● | | | | | ● | | | ● | | ● | | | | | | | | | | | |
| Schizophrenia | | | | | ● | ● | | | | | | | | | | | | | | | | | | | | | | | | | |
| Rheumatoid Arthritis | ● | | | | ● | ● | | | ● | | | | | | | | | | | | | | ● | | | | ● | ● | | | |
| Restless Legs | ● | | ● | | ● | ● | | | ● | | | | | | | | | | | | | | | | | | | | | | |
| Recurrent Infections | | | ● | | ● | ● | | | | | | | | | | | | | | | | | | | | | | | | ● | |
| Raynaud's Disease | ● | | | | ● | ● | | | ● | | | | | | | | ● | | | | | | | | | | | | | | ● |
| Psoriasis | | | ● | | ● | ● | | | ● | | | | | | | | ● | | | | | | | | | | | | | | |
| Prostate Problems | | | ● | | ● | ● | | | ● | | | | | | | | | | | | | | | | | | | | | | |
| Pregnancy Help | ● | ● | ● | | ● | ● | | | ● | | | | | | ● | | | | | | | | | | | | | | | | |
| Postural Problems | | | | | | | | | | | | | | | | | | | | | | | | | | | | | | | |
| Pneumonia | | | ● | | ● | ● | | | | | | | | | | | | | | | | | | | | | | | | | |
| PMT | ● | | ● | | ● | ● | | | ● | | | | | | ● | | | | | | | | ● | | ● | | | | ● | | ● |
| Piles | | | ● | | ● | ● | | | ● | | | | | | | | | | | | | | | | | | | | | | |
| Phobias | ● | | | | ● | ● | | | ● | | | | | | | ● | ● | | | | | ● | | | | | | | | ● | ● |
| Period Problems | | ● | | | ● | ● | | | ● | | | | | | ● | | | | | | | | ● | | ● | | | | | | ● |
| Parkinson's Disease | | | | | ● | ● | | | | | | | | | | | | | | | | | | | | | ● | ● | | | |
| Panic Attacks | | | | | | | | | | | | | | | | ● | | | | | | | | | | | | | | | ● |
| Palpitations | | | ● | | ● | ● | | | ● | | | | | | ● | | | | | | | ● | | | | | | | | | |
| Pain | ● | ● | ● | | ● | ● | | | ● | ● | | ● | | | ● | | ● | | ● | ● | | | ● | | ● | | ● | ● | ● | ● | ● |
| Osteoporosis | | | ● | | ● | ● | | | ● | | | | | | | | | | | | | | | | | | ● | ● | | | |
| Obesity | | | | | ● | ● | | | | | | | | | | | | | | | | | | | | | | | | | |
| Neuralgia | | | ● | | ● | ● | | | ● | | | | | | ● | | ● | | | ● | | | | | | | ● | ● | | | |
| Nervous Disorders | ● | | ● | | ● | ● | | | | | | | | | | | ● | ● | | | | ● | ● | | | | | | | | ● |
| Nerve Disorders | ● | | ● | | ● | ● | | | | | | | | | | | | | | | | | ● | | | | ● | ● | | | |
| Nausea | | ● | ● | | ● | ● | | | ● | | | | | | ● | | | | | | | | | | | | | | | | |
| Nail Health | | | | ● | ● | ● | ● | ● | | | | | | | | | | | | | | | | ● | | | | | | | |
| Musculo-skeletal | | | | | | | | | | | | | | | | | | | | | | | | | | | ● | ● | | | |
| Muscular Dystrophy | | | | | ● | ● | | | | | | | | | | | | | | | | | ● | | | | | | | | |
| Multiple Sclerosis | | | | | ● | ● | | | | | | | | ● | | | | | | | | | ● | | | | ● | ● | | | |
| Mouth Ulcers | | | ● | | ● | ● | | | | | | | | | | | | | | | | | | | | | | | | | |
| Mouth Disorders | | | | | ● | ● | | | | | | | | | | | | | | | | | | | | | | | | | |
| Motion Sickness | | | | | ● | ● | | | ● | | | | | | | | | | | | | | | | | | | | | | |
| Migraine | ● | ● | ● | | ● | ● | | | ● | | ● | | ● | | ● | | ● | | ● | ● | | | ● | | ● | ● | ● | ● | ● | ● | ● |
| Menopause | | ● | ● | | ● | ● | | | ● | | | | | | | | | | | | | | ● | | | ● | | | ● | | |
| ME | | ● | ● | | ● | ● | | | ● | | | | | | ● | | ● | ● | | | | | | | | ● | ● | ● | ● | ● | |
| Lung Problems | | | ● | | ● | ● | | | ● | | | | | | ● | | | | | | | | | | | | | | | | |
| Low Blood Pressure | ● | ● | ● | | ● | ● | | | ● | | | | | | | | ● | | | | | | ● | | | | | | | | |
| Liver Disorders | | | ● | | ● | ● | | | | | | | | | ● | | | | | | | | ● | | | | | | | | |
| Lethargy | ● | | ● | | ● | ● | | | ● | | | | ● | | ● | | ● | | | | | | ● | | | | | | | ● | |
| Laryngitis | | | ● | | ● | ● | | | | | | | | | | | | | | | | | | | | | | | | | |
| Lactose Intolerance | | | ● | | ● | ● | | | | | | | | | | | ● | | | | | | | | | | | | | | |
| Kidney Complaints | | ● | | | ● | ● | | | ● | | | | | | ● | | | | | | | | | | | | | | | | |
| Joint Pain | ● | | ● | | ● | ● | | | ● | | | | ● | ● | ● | | ● | ● | ● | ● | ● | | ● | | | | ● | ● | | ● | |
| Jet Lag | | | | | ● | ● | | | | | | | | | | | | | | | | | | | | | | | | | ● |
| Itching | | | ● | | ● | ● | | | ● | | | | | | | | | | | | | | | | | | | | | | |
| Irritable Bowel Syndrome | ● | ● | ● | | ● | ● | | | ● | | | | | | | | ● | | | | | ● | ● | | ● | | | | ● | ● | ● |
| Insomnia | ● | ● | ● | | ● | ● | | | ● | | | | ● | | | | ● | | | | | | ● | | | | | | | ● | ● |

# I - S Conditions treated at Practices/Businesses

| Business by County with Reference no. | Insomnia | Irritable Bowel Syndrome | Itching | Jet Lag | Joint Pain | Kidney Complaints | Lactose Intolerance | Laryngitis | Lethargy | Liver Disorders | Low Blood Pressure | Lung Problems | ME | Menopause | Migraine | Motion Sickness | Mouth Disorders | Mouth Ulcers | Multiple Sclerosis | Muscular Dystrophy | Musculo-skeletal | Nail Health | Nausea | Nerve Disorders | Nervous Disorders | Neuralgia | Obesity | Osteoporosis | Pain | Palpitations | Panic Attacks | Parkinson's Disease | Period Problems | Phobias | Piles | PMT | Pneumonia | Postural Problems | Pregnancy Help | Prostate Problems | Psoriasis | Raynaud's Disease | Recurrent Infections | Restless Legs | Rheumatoid Arthritis | Schizophrenia | Sciatica | Sexual Problems |
|---|---|---|---|---|---|---|---|---|---|---|---|---|---|---|---|---|---|---|---|---|---|---|---|---|---|---|---|---|---|---|---|---|---|---|---|---|---|---|---|---|---|---|---|---|---|---|---|---|
| MACPHERSON, R G (HM12877) | | | | | | | | | | | | | | | | | | | | | | ● | | | | | | | | | | | | | | | | | | | | | | | | | | |
| MARCHMONT PHYSIOTHERAPY CLINIC (HM13073) | | | | | ● | | | | | | | | | | | | | | ● | | | | | | | | | | ● | | | | | | | | | | | | | | | | | | | |
| MARIPOSA AROMATHERAPY (HM13103) | ● | ● | | | | | | | | | | | ● | ● | ● | | | | | | | | | | | | | | ● | | | | | | | ● | | | | | | | | | | | | |
| MCVITTIE, D (HM13623) | | ● | | | ● | | | | ● | | ● | | ● | | ● | | | | | | | | | | | | | | | | | | ● | | | ● | | | ● | | | | | | | | | |
| MOBILE CHIROPODY SERVICES (HM14028) | | | | | | | | | | | | | | | | | | | | | | ● | | | | | | | | | | | | | | | | | | | | | | | | | | |
| MORNINGSIDE PODIATRY SERVICE (HM14192) | | | | | | | | | | | | | | | | | | | | | | ● | | | | | | | | | | | | | | | | | | | | | | | | | | |
| N H S (HM14449) | | | | | | | | | | | | | | | | | | | | | | ● | | | | | | | | | | | | | | | | | | | | | | | | | | |
| OLIVER & STODDARD (HM15285) | ● | ● | | | | ● | ● | | ● | ● | ● | | | | ● | | | | | | | | ● | | | | | | | | | | | | | | | | | | ● | | | | | | | |
| PATTERSON, YVONNE (HM15833) | | | | | | | | | | | | | ● | ● | ● | | | | | | | | | | | | | | ● | | | | | | | | | | | | | | | | | | | |
| PSYCHIC AND LIFE SOLUTIONS (HM16685) | | | | | | | | | | | | | | | | | | | | | | | | | ● | | | | | | | | | | | | | | | | | | | | | ● | | |
| ROBERT STONE THERAPEUTICS (HM17398) | | | | | | | | | ● | | | | | | | | | | | | | | | | | | | | | | | | | | | | | | | | | | | | | | | |
| RUMNEY, KATHLEEN (HM17748) | ● | ● | ● | ● | ● | ● | ● | ● | ● | ● | ● | ● | ● | ● | ● | ● | ● | ● | ● | ● | | ● | ● | ● | ● | ● | ● | ● | ● | ● | | ● | ● | ● | ● | ● | ● | | ● | ● | ● | ● | ● | ● | ● | ● | ● | ● |
| SHENTON, DIANNE (HM18402) | | | | | | | | | | | | | | | | | | | | | | ● | | | | | | | | | | | | | | | | | | | | | | | | | | |
| SKEDD, L A (HM18629) | | | | | | | | | | | | | | | | | | | | | | ● | | | | | | | | | | | | | | | | | | | | | | | | | | |
| TARA ROKPA ENDINBURGH (HM19699) | | ● | | | | | | | ● | ● | ● | | | | ● | | | | | | | | | | | | | | | | | | | | | | | | ● | | | | | | | | | |
| WARD, ELIZABETH (HM20900) | ● | | | | ● | | | | ● | | | | | | ● | | | | | | | | | | | | | | | | | | | | | | | | | | | | | | ● | | ● | |
| WELLBEING (HM21146) | | | | | | | | | | | | | | | ● | | | | | | | | | | | | | | | | | | | | | | | | | | | | | | | | | |
| **FALKIRK** | | | | | | | | | | | | | | | | | | | | | | | | | | | | | | | | | | | | | | | | | | | | | | | | |
| AESTHETICA TOTAL SKIN & BODY (HM00411) | ● | ● | | | | | | | | | | | ● | ● | ● | | | | | | | | | | | | | | | | | | | | | | | | | | | | | | | | | |
| FALKIRK CHIROPRACTIC CLINIC (HM07074) | | ● | | | ● | | | | | | | | | | | | | | | | | | | ● | | | | | ● | | | | | | | | | | | | | | | | | | ● | |
| GRANT, LESLIE & DAWN (HM08385) | | | | | | | | | | | | | | | | | | | | | | ● | | | | | | | | | | | | | | | | | | | | | | | | | | |
| GRANT, LESLIE AND DAWN (HM08386) | | | | | | | | | | | | | | | | | | | | | | ● | | | | | | | | | | | | | | | | | | | | | | | | | | |
| NATURAL HEALING CENTRE (HM14543) | ● | ● | | | ● | | | | | | ● | | ● | ● | ● | | | | | | | | ● | | | | | | | ● | | | ● | | | ● | | | | | | | | | ● | | ● | |
| **FIFE** | | | | | | | | | | | | | | | | | | | | | | | | | | | | | | | | | | | | | | | | | | | | | | | | |
| BODYNEEDS (HM02629) | ● | ● | ● | ● | ● | ● | ● | ● | ● | ● | ● | ● | ● | ● | ● | ● | ● | ● | ● | ● | | ● | ● | ● | ● | ● | ● | ● | ● | ● | | ● | ● | ● | ● | ● | ● | | ● | ● | ● | ● | ● | ● | ● | ● | ● | ● |
| CAMERON, WILLIAM (HM03588) | | | | | | | | | | | | | | | | | | | | | | ● | | | | | | | | | | | | | | | | | | | | | | | | | | |
| CAROLE'S MOBILE THERAPIST (HM03718) | ● | ● | | | | | | | | | | | | | ● | | | | | | | | | | | | | | | | | | | | | | | | | | | | | | | | | |
| COMPLEMENTARY THERAPY CLINIC (HM04949) | | ● | | | ● | | | | | | ● | | ● | ● | ● | | | ● | | | | | ● | | ● | | | | ● | | | | ● | ● | ● | ● | | | | | ● | | | | | | ● | |
| DAVIDSON, ANGELA (HM05785) | ● | ● | | | ● | ● | | | ● | ● | ● | ● | ● | ● | ● | | | | ● | | | ● | | ● | ● | ● | | ● | ● | | | | ● | | ● | ● | | | ● | ● | ● | ● | | ● | ● | | ● | |
| KEEP IN STEP (HM11394) | | | | | | | | | | | | | | | | | | | | | | ● | | | | | | | | | | | | | | | | | | | | | | | | | | |
| LEUTER, PAM () | ● | | | | ● | | | | | | | | | | ● | | | | | | | | | | | | | | | | | | | | | | | | | | | | | | | | | |
| NEAT FEET (HM14743) | ● | ● | | | ● | | | | | | ● | | ● | ● | ● | | | | | | | | ● | ● | ● | | | ● | ● | | | | ● | ● | | ● | ● | | ● | | | | | | ● | ● | ● | |
| O'BRIAN, D (HM15171) | | | | | | | | | | | | | | | | | | | | | | ● | | | | | | | | | | | | | | | | | | | | | | | | | | |
| SHEERINS, ROZ (HM18370) | | | | | | | | | | | | | | | | | | | | | | ● | | | | | | | | | | | | | | | | | | | | | | | | | | |

www.healthmyself.com

# I - S Conditions treated at Practices/Businesses

| Business by County with Reference no. | Insomnia | Irritable Bowel Syndrome | Itching | Jet Lag | Joint Pain | Kidney Complaints | Lactose Intolerance | Laryngitis | Lethargy | Liver Disorders | Low Blood Pressure | Lung Problems | ME | Menopause | Migraine | Motion Sickness | Mouth Disorders | Mouth Ulcers | Multiple Sclerosis | Muscular Dystrophy | Musculo-skeletal | Nail Health | Nausea | Nerve Disorders |
|---|---|---|---|---|---|---|---|---|---|---|---|---|---|---|---|---|---|---|---|---|---|---|---|---|
| ST ANDREWS OSTEOPATHS (HM19065) | | ● | | | ● | | | | | | | | ● | ● | ● | | | | | | | | | |
| TOLBOOTH HOUSE (HM20117) | | ● | ● | | | | | | | | | | | ● | | | | | | | | ● | | |
| TWA ACRES HYPNO TRAINING CTRE (HM20447) | ● | ● | | | | | | | | | | | ● | | ● | | | | ● | | | | | ● |
| **GLASGOW (CITY OF)** | | | | | | | | | | | | | | | | | | | | | | | | |
| ABOUT FACE (HM00131) | ● | | | | | | | | | | ● | | | | | | | | | | | | | |
| ACTIVE CHIROPRACTIC (HM00194) | | | | | ● | | | | | | | | ● | | ● | | | | | | | | | |
| ANDERSON DOE PODIATRY CLINIC (HM00809) | | | | | ● | | | | | | | | | | | | | | ● | | | | | |
| ANNE PENMAN THERAPY (HM00900) | ● | | | | | | | | | | | | | | ● | | | | | | | | | |
| BEHIND THE VEIL (HM02068) | ● | | | ● | | | | | ● | | ● | | ● | | ● | | | | | | | | ● | |
| BLACK, JIM (HM02424) | | | | | | | | | | | | | | | | | | | | | | ● | | |
| BOTHWELL PHYSIOTHERAPY (HM02733) | | | | | ● | | | | | | | | | | | | | | | | | | | ● |
| CARRICK STREET PHYSIO & SPORT (HM03743) | | | | | ● | | | | | | | | | | | | | | ● | | | | | |
| CLINIC AT CHARING CROSS (HM04679) | | | | | ● | | | | | | | | ● | | | | | | | | | | | |
| CONWAY, VALERIE (DR) (HM05034) | ● | ● | ● | | ● | ● | | ● | ● | ● | | ● | ● | ● | ● | ● | ● | ● | ● | | | | ● | ● |
| CONWAY, VALERIE A (DR) (HM05035) | ● | ● | ● | | ● | ● | | ● | ● | ● | | ● | ● | ● | ● | ● | ● | ● | ● | | | | ● | ● |
| FITZPATRICK, J H (HM07374) | | | | | | | | | | | | | | | | | | | | | | ● | | |
| HARVEST CLINIC (HM09152) | ● | ● | ● | | ● | ● | | | ● | | ● | | ● | ● | ● | | | | | | | ● | | |
| HOLISTIC HEALING & HYP (HM09961) | ● | | | | | | | | | | | | | | | | | | | | | | | |
| HUMAN PERFORMANCE CLINIC (HM10364) | ● | | | | | | | | | | | | | | | | | | | | | | | |
| LAMBERT, C W (HM11895) | | | | | | | | | | | | | | | | | | | | | | ● | | |
| LAURIE, A (HM12015) | | | | | | | | | | | | | | | | | | | | | | ● | | |
| LONG RIVER TAI CHI CIRCLE (HM12617) | | | | | | | | | | | ● | ● | | | ● | | | | | | | | | |
| MARY HERAGHTY AT HEALTHY FEET (HM13222) | | | | | | | | | | | | | ● | ● | ● | | | | ● | | | | | |
| MCLAREN, CATH RENA (HM13539) | ● | ● | | | ● | ● | | ● | ● | | ● | ● | ● | ● | ● | | | | | | | | ● | |
| MCLEAN, A M (HM13551) | | | ● | | ● | | | | | | | | | | | | | | ● | | | ● | | ● |
| MCTIMONEY CHIROPRACTIC CLINIC (HM13611) | | | | | | | | | | | | | | | | | | | | | | | | |
| NUTRITION WORLD (HM15126) | ● | ● | ● | ● | ● | ● | ● | ● | ● | ● | ● | ● | ● | ● | ● | ● | ● | ● | ● | ● | | ● | ● | ● |
| PLUIDGE, MARK (HM16379) | | | | | | | | | | | | | | | | | | | | | | ● | | |
| PSYCHIC & HEALING CENTRE (HM16684) | | | | | | | | | | | | | | | | | | | | | | | | |
| RHODIE, ANDREA (HM17231) | | | | | | | | | | | | | ● | ● | ● | | | | | | | | | |
| ROLLAND, C R (HM17563) | | | | | | | | | | | | | | | | | | | | | | ● | | |
| SCHOLL CENTRE (HM18039) | | | | | | | | | | | | | | | | | | | | | | ● | | |
| SHAWLANDS HYPNOTHERAPY CLINIC (HM18352) | | ● | | | | | | | | | | | ● | | ● | | | | | | | | | |
| SINO-HERBAL CLINIC (HM18615) | ● | | ● | | ● | ● | | | | ● | ● | ● | ● | ● | ● | | ● | ● | ● | ● | | | ● | ● |

| Business by County with Reference no. | Nervous Disorders | Neuralgia | Obesity | Osteoporosis | Pain | Palpitations | Panic Attacks | Parkinson's Disease | Period Problems | Phobias | Piles | PMT | Pneumonia | Postural Problems | Pregnancy Help | Prostate Problems | Psoriasis | Raynaud's Disease | Recurrent Infections | Restless Legs | Rheumatoid Arthritis | Schizophrenia | Sciatica | Sexual Problems |
|---|---|---|---|---|---|---|---|---|---|---|---|---|---|---|---|---|---|---|---|---|---|---|---|---|
| ST ANDREWS OSTEOPATHS (HM19065) | | | | ● | ● | | | | ● | | | | | | ● | | | ● | | ● | | | ● | |
| TOLBOOTH HOUSE (HM20117) | | | | ● | | | | | ● | ● | | | | | | | | | | | | | | |
| TWA ACRES HYPNO TRAINING CTRE (HM20447) | ● | ● | ● | | ● | | | | ● | ● | | ● | | | ● | | ● | | | | | | | ● |
| **GLASGOW (CITY OF)** | | | | | | | | | | | | | | | | | | | | | | | | |
| ABOUT FACE (HM00131) | ● | | | | | | | | | | | ● | | | | | | | | | | | | |
| ACTIVE CHIROPRACTIC (HM00194) | | | ● | | ● | | | | | | | | | | | | | | | ● | | | ● | |
| ANDERSON DOE PODIATRY CLINIC (HM00809) | | | | | | | | | | | | | | | | | | | | | | | | |
| ANNE PENMAN THERAPY (HM00900) | | | ● | | | | | | | ● | | ● | | | | | | | | | | | | |
| BEHIND THE VEIL (HM02068) | ● | | | | ● | | | | ● | | | ● | | | | | | | | ● | ● | | ● | |
| BLACK, JIM (HM02424) | | | | | | | | | | | | | | | | | | | | | | | | |
| BOTHWELL PHYSIOTHERAPY (HM02733) | ● | ● | | ● | ● | | | | | | | | | | | | | | | | | | ● | |
| CARRICK STREET PHYSIO & SPORT (HM03743) | | | | | ● | | | | | | | | | | | | | | | | | | | |
| CLINIC AT CHARING CROSS (HM04679) | | | | | | | | | ● | | | ● | | | | | | | | ● | | | | |
| CONWAY, VALERIE (DR) (HM05034) | ● | ● | | | ● | ● | | | ● | | | ● | ● | | ● | ● | ● | ● | ● | ● | ● | | ● | |
| CONWAY, VALERIE A (DR) (HM05035) | ● | ● | | | ● | ● | | | ● | | | ● | ● | | ● | ● | ● | ● | ● | ● | ● | | ● | |
| FITZPATRICK, J H (HM07374) | | | | | | | | | | | | | | | | | | | | | | | | |
| HARVEST CLINIC (HM09152) | ● | | ● | | ● | | | | ● | ● | ● | ● | | | ● | | ● | | | ● | ● | | ● | ● |
| HOLISTIC HEALING & HYP (HM09961) | | | ● | | | | | | | ● | | | | | | | | | | | | | | |
| HUMAN PERFORMANCE CLINIC (HM10364) | ● | | ● | | ● | ● | | | | ● | | | | | | | ● | | | | | | | ● |
| LAMBERT, C W (HM11895) | | | | | | | | | | | | | | | | | | | | | | | | |
| LAURIE, A (HM12015) | | | | | | | | | | | | | | | | | | | | | | | | |
| LONG RIVER TAI CHI CIRCLE (HM12617) | | | | | | | | | | | | | | | | | | | | | | | | |
| MARY HERAGHTY AT HEALTHY FEET (HM13222) | | | | | | | | | | | | ● | | | | | | | | | | | | |
| MCLAREN, CATH RENA (HM13539) | | ● | | | ● | ● | | | ● | | | ● | | | ● | | ● | ● | | ● | ● | | ● | |
| MCLEAN, A M (HM13551) | | ● | ● | ● | ● | | | ● | | | | | | | | | ● | ● | ● | ● | ● | | ● | |
| MCTIMONEY CHIROPRACTIC CLINIC (HM13611) | | | | | | | | | | | | | | | | | | | | | | | ● | |
| NUTRITION WORLD (HM15126) | ● | ● | ● | ● | ● | ● | | ● | ● | ● | ● | ● | ● | | ● | ● | ● | ● | ● | ● | ● | ● | ● | ● |
| PLUIDGE, MARK (HM16379) | | | | | | | | | | | | | | | | | | | | | | | | |
| PSYCHIC & HEALING CENTRE (HM16684) | | | | | ● | | | | | | | | | | | | | | | | | | | |
| RHODIE, ANDREA (HM17231) | | | | | | | | | | | | | | | | | | | | | | | | |
| ROLLAND, C R (HM17563) | | | | | | | | | | | | | | | | | | | | | | | | |
| SCHOLL CENTRE (HM18039) | | | | | | | | | | | | | | | | | | | | | | | | |
| SHAWLANDS HYPNOTHERAPY CLINIC (HM18352) | | | | | ● | | ● | | | ● | | | | | | | ● | | | | | | | |
| SINO-HERBAL CLINIC (HM18615) | ● | | ● | ● | ● | | | ● | ● | | ● | | | | | ● | ● | | | ● | ● | | | ● |

# I - S Conditions treated at Practices/Businesses

| Business by County with Reference no. | Insomnia | Irritable Bowel Syndrome | Itching | Jet Lag | Joint Pain | Kidney Complaints | Lactose Intolerance | Laryngitis | Lethargy | Liver Disorders | Low Blood Pressure | Lung Problems | ME | Menopause | Migraine | Motion Sickness | Mouth Disorders | Mouth Ulcers | Multiple Sclerosis | Muscular Dystrophy | Musculo-skeletal | Nail Health | Nausea | Nerve Disorders | Nervous Disorders | Neuralgia | Obesity | Osteoporosis | Pain | Palpitations | Panic Attacks | Parkinson's Disease | Period Problems | Phobias | Piles | PMT | Pneumonia | Postural Problems | Pregnancy Help | Prostate Problems | Psoriasis | Raynaud's Disease | Recurrent Infections | Restless Legs | Rheumatoid Arthritis | Schizophrenia | Sciatica | Sexual Problems |
|---|---|---|---|---|---|---|---|---|---|---|---|---|---|---|---|---|---|---|---|---|---|---|---|---|---|---|---|---|---|---|---|---|---|---|---|---|---|---|---|---|---|---|---|---|---|---|---|---|
| STEWART, JIM (DR) (HM19270) | ● | ● | | ● | | | | | | | | | ● | | ● | | | | | | | | | ● | ● | | ● | | | | | | | ● | | ● | | | | | | | | | | | | ● |
| THERAPY OF LIFE CLINIC (HM19905) | ● | ● | ● | ● | ● | ● | | | ● | ● | ● | ● | ● | ● | ● | ● | | ● | ● | ● | | | ● | ● | ● | ● | ● | ● | ● | ● | | | ● | ● | ● | ● | ● | | ● | | ● | | ● | ● | ● | ● | ● | |
| WEST END THERAPY CENTRE (HM21221) | ● | ● | ● | ● | ● | ● | ● | ● | ● | ● | ● | ● | ● | ● | ● | ● | ● | ● | ● | ● | | ● | ● | ● | ● | ● | ● | ● | ● | ● | | ● | ● | ● | ● | ● | ● | | ● | ● | ● | ● | ● | ● | ● | ● | ● | ● |
| **HIGHLAND** | | | | | | | | | | | | | | | | | | | | | | | | | | | | | | | | | | | | | | | | | | | | | | | | |
| BUMBLE - BEE'S PHYSIO (HM03347) | | | | | | | | | | | | | | ● | | | | | | | | | | | | | | ● | ● | | | | ● | | | | | | | | | | | | | | ● | |
| GENTLE WAYS (HM07980) | | ● | | | ● | | | | | | | | ● | | | | | | | | | | | | | | | ● | ● | | | | | | | | | | | | | | | | | | | |
| HARMONOLOGY CENTRE (HM09017) | ● | | | | | | | | | | | | | | | | | | ● | | | | | | | | | | ● | | | | | | | | | | | | | | | | | | | |
| HEALTH CORNER (HM09383) | | ● | | | ● | ● | | | ● | | | | | ● | ● | | | | | | | | | | | ● | | ● | ● | | | | ● | | | ● | | | ● | | | | ● | | | | ● | |
| PUFFIN HYDROTHERAPY POOL (HM16743) | | | | | ● | | | | | | | | | | | | | | ● | | | | | | | | | | ● | | | | | | | | | | | | | | | | | | | |
| TAYLOR, JUNE (HM19773) | ● | ● | | | ● | ● | | | | ● | ● | ● | ● | ● | ● | | | | | | | | ● | ● | ● | | | | ● | ● | | | ● | | | ● | | | ● | | | | ● | ● | | | ● | |
| WAH, G (HM20735) | ● | ● | | | ● | ● | | | | ● | ● | ● | ● | ● | ● | | | | | | | | ● | ● | ● | | | | ● | ● | | | ● | | | ● | | | ● | | | | ● | ● | | | ● | |
| **INVERCLYDE** | | | | | | | | | | | | | | | | | | | | | | | | | | | | | | | | | | | | | | | | | | | | | | | | |
| INVERCLYDE OSTEOPATHIC CLINIC (HM10704) | | ● | ● | ● | ● | | | ● | | | | | ● | ● | ● | | | | | | | | ● | ● | ● | ● | | | ● | ● | | | ● | ● | ● | ● | | | ● | ● | ● | ● | | | | | ● | |
| KELLERMANS (HM11418) | | | | | | | | | | | | | ● | ● | ● | | | | | | | | ● | | | | | | | | | | | | | | | | | | | | | | | | ● | |
| **LANARKSHIRE (NORTH)** | | | | | | | | | | | | | | | | | | | | | | | | | | | | | | | | | | | | | | | | | | | | | | | | |
| REGISTERED HOMEOPATH (HM17103) | ● | ● | ● | ● | ● | ● | ● | ● | ● | ● | ● | ● | ● | ● | ● | ● | ● | ● | ● | | | ● | ● | ● | ● | ● | | ● | ● | ● | | ● | ● | ● | ● | ● | ● | | | ● | | ● | ● | ● | ● | | ● | ● |
| SEMPRE LIBERA (HM18224) | ● | ● | | | | | | | | | | | | ● | ● | | | | | | | | | | | | | | | | | | | | | | | | | | | | | | | | | |
| STRATH NATURAL THERAPIES (HM19371) | ● | ● | | | | | | | | | | | | | ● | | | | | | | ● | | | ● | ● | ● | | ● | ● | | | | ● | | ● | | | | | | | | | | | | |
| **LANARKSHIRE (SOUTH)** | | | | | | | | | | | | | | | | | | | | | | | | | | | | | | | | | | | | | | | | | | | | | | | | |
| QUINN, JIM (HM16810) | ● | ● | ● | ● | ● | ● | ● | ● | ● | ● | ● | ● | ● | ● | ● | ● | ● | ● | ● | | ● | ● | ● | ● | ● | ● | ● | ● | ● | ● | ● | ● | ● | ● | ● | ● | ● | ● | ● | ● | ● | ● | ● | ● | ● | ● | ● | ● |
| ROBB, A (DR) (HM17387) | ● | ● | ● | ● | ● | ● | ● | ● | ● | ● | ● | ● | ● | ● | ● | ● | ● | ● | ● | ● | | ● | ● | ● | ● | ● | ● | ● | ● | ● | | ● | ● | ● | ● | ● | ● | | ● | ● | ● | ● | ● | ● | ● | ● | ● | ● |
| **LOTHIAN (EAST)** | | | | | | | | | | | | | | | | | | | | | | | | | | | | | | | | | | | | | | | | | | | | | | | | |
| AROMA (HM01042) | ● | ● | ● | ● | ● | ● | ● | ● | ● | ● | ● | ● | ● | ● | ● | ● | ● | ● | ● | ● | | ● | ● | ● | ● | ● | ● | ● | ● | ● | | ● | ● | ● | ● | ● | ● | | ● | ● | ● | ● | ● | ● | ● | ● | ● | ● |
| EAST LOTHIAN PHYSIO CENTRE (HM06518) | | | | | | | | | | | | | | | ● | | | | ● | | | | | ● | | ● | | ● | ● | | | ● | | | | | | | ● | | | | | | ● | | ● | |
| FRASER, GORDON (HM07696) | ● | ● | ● | ● | ● | ● | ● | ● | ● | ● | ● | ● | ● | ● | ● | ● | ● | ● | ● | ● | | ● | ● | ● | ● | ● | ● | ● | ● | ● | | ● | ● | ● | ● | ● | ● | | ● | ● | ● | ● | ● | ● | ● | ● | ● | ● |
| **LOTHIAN (MID)** | | | | | | | | | | | | | | | | | | | | | | | | | | | | | | | | | | | | | | | | | | | | | | | | |
| CRYSTAL SANCTUARY (HM05532) | ● | ● | | | | | | | ● | ● | ● | | | | ● | | | | | | | | | | | | | | ● | | | | | | | | | | | | | | | | | | | |
| HAMILTON, JAMES (HM08844) | ● | | | | ● | ● | | | | | ● | | ● | ● | ● | | | | | | | ● | ● | | | | | | ● | | | | ● | | | ● | | | | | | | | | | | | |
| NATURAL HEALTH CENTRE (HM14573) | ● | ● | ● | ● | ● | ● | ● | ● | ● | ● | ● | ● | ● | ● | ● | ● | ● | ● | ● | ● | | ● | ● | ● | ● | ● | ● | ● | ● | ● | | ● | ● | ● | ● | ● | ● | | ● | ● | ● | ● | ● | ● | ● | ● | ● | ● |
| NEW DUNDAS CLINIC (HM14817) | | | | | ● | | | | | | | | | | | | | | | | | | | | | ● | | | ● | | | | | | | | | | | | | | | | | | ● | |
| RADIANT COLOUR (HM16847) | ● | ● | | | | | | | | | | | ● | | ● | | | | | | | | | | | | | | | | | | | | | | | | | | | | | | | | | |
| SCOTTISH KINESIOLOGY CENTRE (HM18134) | ● | ● | ● | ● | ● | ● | ● | ● | ● | ● | ● | ● | ● | ● | ● | ● | ● | ● | ● | ● | | ● | ● | ● | ● | ● | ● | ● | ● | ● | | ● | ● | ● | ● | ● | ● | | ● | ● | ● | ● | ● | ● | ● | ● | ● | ● |
| **LOTHIAN (WEST)** | | | | | | | | | | | | | | | | | | | | | | | | | | | | | | | | | | | | | | | | | | | | | | | | |
| DUIGNAN, KAREN (HM06372) | | | | | | | | | | | | | | | | | | | | | | | | | | | | | | | | | | ● | | | | | | | | | | | | | | |

www.healthmyself.com

# I - S Conditions treated at Practices/Businesses

| Business by County with Reference no. | Insomnia | Irritable Bowel Syndrome | Itching | Jet Lag | Joint Pain | Kidney Complaints | Lactose Intolerance | Laryngitis | Lethargy | Liver Disorders | Low Blood Pressure | Lung Problems | ME | Menopause | Migraine | Motion Sickness | Mouth Disorders | Mouth Ulcers | Multiple Sclerosis | Muscular Dystrophy | Musculo-skeletal | Nail Health | Nausea | Nerve Disorders | Nervous Disorders | Neuralgia | Obesity | Osteoporosis | Pain | Palpitations | Panic Attacks | Parkinson's Disease | Period Problems | Phobias | Piles | PMT | Pneumonia | Postural Problems | Pregnancy Help | Prostate Problems | Psoriasis | Raynaud's Disease | Recurrent Infections | Restless Legs | Rheumatoid Arthritis | Schizophrenia | Sciatica | Sexual Problems |
|---|---|---|---|---|---|---|---|---|---|---|---|---|---|---|---|---|---|---|---|---|---|---|---|---|---|---|---|---|---|---|---|---|---|---|---|---|---|---|---|---|---|---|---|---|---|---|---|---|
| GILL, SHIRLEY (HM08080) | ● | ● | | | ● | | | | ● | ● | ● | | | ● | ● | | | | ● | ● | | | | ● | ● | | | | | | | | | | | ● | | | | | | | | | ● | | | |
| LINLITHGOW PHYSIO PRACTICE (HM12438) | | | | | ● | | | | | | | | | | | | | | ● | | | | | | | | | | | | | | | | | | | | | | | | | | | | | |
| VINCES, DENISE (HM20674) | ● | | | | ● | | | | ● | | ● | | ● | ● | ● | | | | | ● | | | | ● | ● | | | | ● | | | | ● | | | ● | | | | | ● | ● | | ● | ● | | | |
| **MORAY** | | | | | | | | | | | | | | | | | | | | | | | | | | | | | | | | | | | | | | | | | | | | | | | | |
| AROMANTIC (HM01080) | | | | | | | | | | | | | | | | | | | | | | | | | | | | | | | | | | | | | | | | | ● | | | | | | | |
| ELGIN CHIROPRACTIC CLINIC (HM06729) | | ● | | | ● | | | | | | | | ● | | ● | | | | | | | | | ● | ● | | | | ● | | | | | | | | | | | | | | | | | | ● | |
| FINDHORN FLOWER ESSENCES (HM07307) | | | | | | | | | | | | | | | ● | | | | | | | | | | | | | | | | | | | ● | | | | | | | | | | | | | | |
| HEALTHWORKS (HM09422) | ● | ● | ● | | ● | | | | ● | | ● | | ● | ● | ● | | | ● | | | | | ● | | ● | | | | ● | ● | | | ● | ● | | | | | ● | | ● | | | | | | ● | |
| **NORTHUMBERLAND** | | | | | | | | | | | | | | | | | | | | | | | | | | | | | | | | | | | | | | | | | | | | | | | | |
| SOLAR- PLEXUS (HM18864) | | ● | | | ● | | | | | | | | ● | ● | ● | | | | | | | | ● | | | | | | ● | ● | | | ● | | | ● | | | ● | | | | | ● | | | | |
| **ORKNEY ISLES** | | | | | | | | | | | | | | | | | | | | | | | | | | | | | | | | | | | | | | | | | | | | | | | | |
| A D S THOM (HM00030) | | | | | | | | | | | | | | | | | | | | | | ● | | | | | | | | | | | | | | | | | | | | | | | | | | |
| **PERTH AND KINROSS** | | | | | | | | | | | | | | | | | | | | | | | | | | | | | | | | | | | | | | | | | | | | | | | | |
| ACUPUNCTURE CLINIC (HM00288) | ● | ● | ● | ● | ● | ● | | ● | ● | ● | | ● | ● | ● | ● | ● | | | ● | | | | ● | ● | ● | ● | | ● | ● | ● | | ● | ● | | ● | ● | ● | | ● | ● | ● | ● | ● | ● | ● | | ● | |
| ACUPUNCTURE CLINIC DUNKELD (HM00289) | ● | ● | ● | ● | ● | ● | | ● | ● | | | ● | ● | ● | ● | ● | | | ● | | | | ● | ● | ● | ● | | ● | ● | ● | | ● | ● | | ● | ● | ● | | ● | ● | ● | ● | ● | ● | ● | | ● | |
| BACK PAIN & SPORTS CLINIC (HM01491) | | | | | ● | | | | | | | | | | ● | | | | | | ● | | | | | | | | | | | | | | | | | | | | | | | | ● | | ● | |
| LENDRICK LODGE (HM12210) | ● | | | | | | | | ● | | | | | | | | | | | | | | | ● | ● | | | | | | | | | | | | | | | | | | | | | | | |
| TAYLOR, D (HM19749) | ● | ● | | | | | | | | | | | ● | | | | | | ● | | | | | | | | ● | | ● | ● | | | | ● | | | | | | | | | | | | | | ● |
| **RENFREWSHIRE** | | | | | | | | | | | | | | | | | | | | | | | | | | | | | | | | | | | | | | | | | | | | | | | | |
| ALBA CENTRE (HM00473) | | | | | | | | | | | | | ● | ● | ● | | | | | | | | | | | | | | | | | | | ● | | ● | | | | | | | | | | | | |
| APT LASER THERAPY (HM00950) | | | | | | | | | | | | | | | | | | | | | | | | | | | ● | | | | | | | | | | | | | | | | | | | | | |
| BLACKHALL PARK CENTRE (HM02444) | ● | ● | | | ● | ● | | | | | ● | | ● | ● | ● | | | | ● | | | | | | | | | | ● | ● | | | ● | | | ● | | | ● | | | | | ● | | | ● | |
| DOUGLAS, ANNE S (HM06212) | | | | | ● | | | | | | | | | | | | | | ● | | | | | | | | | | ● | | | | | | | | | | | | | | | | | | | |
| FANNING, M W (HM07095) | ● | | | | ● | | | | | | ● | | ● | ● | ● | | | | ● | | | | | | | | | | ● | ● | | | | | | ● | | | | | | | | | | | | |
| PAISLEY CHIROPRACTIC CLINIC (HM15587) | | ● | | | ● | | | | ● | | | | ● | | ● | ● | | | | | | | | ● | ● | ● | | | ● | | | | ● | ● | | ● | | | ● | | | | | ● | | | ● | |
| PAISLEY NATURAL THERAPY CENTRE (HM15588) | ● | ● | ● | ● | ● | ● | ● | ● | ● | ● | ● | | ● | ● | ● | ● | ● | ● | ● | | | ● | ● | ● | | ● | ● | ● | ● | ● | | | ● | ● | | ● | | | ● | | ● | | | ● | ● | | ● | |
| PAISLEY PHYSIOTHERAPY CENTRE (HM15589) | | | | | ● | | | | | | | | | | | | | | | | | | | | | ● | | ● | ● | | | | | | | | | | ● | | | | | | ● | | ● | |
| RAINEY, MARTHA (HM16890) | ● | ● | | | ● | | | | ● | | ● | | | | | | | | ● | | | | | | | ● | ● | | ● | | | | | | | | | | | | | | | ● | | | | |
| ROSEWOOD AROMATHERAPY ROOM (HM17629) | | | | | | | | | | | | | | ● | ● | | | | | | | | | | | | | | ● | | | | | | | ● | | | | | | | | | | | | |
| **SCOTTISH BORDERS** | | | | | | | | | | | | | | | | | | | | | | | | | | | | | | | | | | | | | | | | | | | | | | | | |
| NATURES TOUCH (HM14698) | | | | | | | | | | | | | ● | ● | | | | | | | | | | | | | | | ● | | | | | | | | | | | | | | | | | | | |
| ST BOSWELLS CHIRO CLINIC (HM19072) | | | | | ● | | | | | | | | | | ● | | | | | | | | | | | ● | | | ● | | | | | | | | | | ● | | | | | | | | | |
| WATT, A S (HM21028) | | | | | | | | | | | | | | | | | | | | | | ● | | | | | | | | | | | | | | | | | | | | | | | | | | |
| WISHING WELL (HM21738) | ● | ● | ● | ● | ● | | ● | | ● | | | | ● | ● | ● | | ● | ● | ● | | | | | ● | ● | ● | ● | ● | ● | ● | | | ● | ● | ● | ● | ● | | ● | ● | ● | | ● | ● | ● | | ● | ● |

# I - S Conditions treated at Practices/Businesses

Business by County with Reference no.

| Condition | SHETLAND ISLANDS: LERWICK CHIROPRACTIC CLINIC (HM12231) |
|---|---|
| Sexual Problems | |
| Sciatica | |
| Schizophrenia | |
| Rheumatoid Arthritis | |
| Restless Legs | |
| Recurrent Infections | |
| Raynaud's Disease | |
| Psoriasis | |
| Prostate Problems | |
| Pregnancy Help | |
| Postural Problems | |
| Pneumonia | |
| PMT | |
| Piles | |
| Phobias | |
| Period Problems | |
| Parkinson's Disease | |
| Panic Attacks | |
| Palpitations | |
| Pain | ● |
| Osteoporosis | |
| Obesity | |
| Neuralgia | |
| Nervous Disorders | ● |
| Nerve Disorders | ● |
| Nausea | |
| Nail Health | |
| Musculo-skeletal | |
| Muscular Dystrophy | |
| Multiple Sclerosis | |
| Mouth Ulcers | |
| Mouth Disorders | |
| Motion Sickness | |
| Migraine | ● |
| Menopause | |
| ME | |
| Lung Problems | |
| Low Blood Pressure | |
| Liver Disorders | |
| Lethargy | |
| Laryngitis | |
| Lactose Intolerance | |
| Kidney Complaints | |
| Joint Pain | ● |
| Jet Lag | |
| Itching | |
| Irritable Bowel Syndrome | |
| Insomnia | |

# I - S Conditions treated at Practices/Businesses

| Business by County with Reference no. | Insomnia | Irritable Bowel Syndrome | Itching | Jet Lag | Joint Pain | Kidney Complaints | Lactose Intolerance | Laryngitis | Lethargy | Liver Disorders | Low Blood Pressure | Lung Problems | ME | Menopause | Migraine | Motion Sickness | Mouth Disorders | Mouth Ulcers | Multiple Sclerosis | Muscular Dystrophy | Musculo-skeletal | Nail Health | Nausea | Nerve Disorders |
|---|---|---|---|---|---|---|---|---|---|---|---|---|---|---|---|---|---|---|---|---|---|---|---|---|
| **WALES** | | | | | | | | | | | | | | | | | | | | | | | | |
| **BLAENAU GWENT** | | | | | | | | | | | | | | | | | | | | | | | | |
| ABERTILLERY PHYSIOTHERAPY (HM00125) | | | | | | | | | | | | | | | | | | | | | | | | |
| CLASSIC CLINIC (HM04606) | ● | ● | | | | | | | | | | | ● | ● | ● | | | | | | | | | |
| **BRIDGEND** | | | | | | | | | | | | | | | | | | | | | | | | |
| JENKINS, JOHN (HM10987) | ● | | | | | | | | | | | | | | | | | | | | | | | |
| PARKWOOD CHIROPRACTIC CLINIC (HM15725) | | | | | ● | | | | | | | | | | | | | | | | | | | ● |
| **CAERPHILLY** | | | | | | | | | | | | | | | | | | | | | | | | |
| OAKFIELD NATURAL HEALTH CENTRE (HM15151) | ● | ● | ● | ● | ● | ● | ● | ● | ● | ● | ● | ● | ● | ● | ● | ● | ● | ● | ● | ● | | ● | ● | ● |
| PARKWOOD CHIROPRACTIC CLINIC (HM15723) | | | | | ● | | | | | | | | | | ● | | | | | | | | | ● |
| **CARMARTHENSHIRE** | | | | | | | | | | | | | | | | | | | | | | | | |
| GREENWAY CONSULTANCY (HM08495) | ● | ● | | ● | | | | | | | ● | ● | ● | ● | ● | ● | | ● | | | | | | |
| HEALING HANDS (HM09339) | ● | ● | | | | | | | | | | | ● | | ● | | | | | | | | | |
| JABROO, C (HM10808) | ● | ● | ● | ● | ● | ● | ● | ● | ● | ● | ● | ● | ● | ● | ● | ● | ● | ● | ● | ● | | ● | ● | ● |
| SPENCER AROMATHERAPY (HM18990) | ● | ● | | | | | | | | | | | ● | | ● | | | | | | | | | |
| WAINWRIGHT, MARY (HM20738) | ● | ● | ● | ● | ● | ● | ● | ● | ● | ● | ● | ● | ● | ● | ● | ● | ● | ● | ● | ● | | ● | ● | ● |
| **CEREDIGION** | | | | | | | | | | | | | | | | | | | | | | | | |
| AMIES, SUSAN (HM00785) | | | | | | | | | | | | | | | | | | | | | | ● | | |
| CHERRY TREE CTRE FOR NTRL MED (HM04109) | ● | ● | ● | ● | ● | ● | ● | ● | ● | ● | ● | ● | ● | ● | ● | ● | ● | ● | ● | ● | | ● | ● | ● |
| COCKSEDGE, JOHN M (HM04774) | | | | | | | | | | | | | | | | | | | | | | ● | | |
| FFYNNONWEN NATURAL THRPY CTRE (HM07256) | | | | | | | | | | | | | ● | | ● | | | | | | | | | |
| **CONWY** | | | | | | | | | | | | | | | | | | | | | | | | |
| DREW, DAVID (HM06305) | | | | | ● | | | | | | ● | ● | ● | | ● | | | | | | | | | ● |
| HERBS FOR EVERYONE (HM09669) | ● | ● | ● | | ● | ● | | ● | ● | ● | ● | ● | ● | ● | ● | ● | ● | ● | ● | | | ● | ● | ● |
| MELA CENTRE OF OSTEOPATHY (HM13702) | | | | | ● | | | | | | | | | | | | | | | | | | | ● |
| MEWIS, R J (HM13782) | | | | | ● | | | | | | | | | | | | | | | | | | | |
| **DENBIGHSHIRE** | | | | | | | | | | | | | | | | | | | | | | | | |
| ALLIED PHYSIOTHERAPY (HM00646) | | | | | ● | | | | | | | | | | | | | | | | | | | |
| HEALING WAYS (HM09359) | ● | ● | ● | ● | ● | ● | ● | ● | ● | ● | ● | ● | ● | ● | ● | ● | ● | ● | ● | ● | | ● | ● | ● |
| MCGILL, L (HM13484) | | | | | | | | | | | | | | | | | | | | | | | | |
| ROY MORRIS CLINIC (HM17709) | ● | ● | | | ● | ● | | ● | ● | ● | ● | ● | ● | ● | ● | ● | ● | ● | ● | | | ● | ● | ● |
| **FLINTSHIRE** | | | | | | | | | | | | | | | | | | | | | | | | |
| A L J RILEY ASSOCIATES (HM00038) | ● | ● | | | ● | ● | ● | | | ● | ● | | | ● | ● | ● | | ● | | | | ● | ● | ● |

| Business by County with Reference no. | Nervous Disorders | Neuralgia | Obesity | Osteoporosis | Pain | Palpitations | Panic Attacks | Parkinson's Disease | Period Problems | Phobias | Piles | PMT | Pneumonia | Postural Problems | Pregnancy Help | Prostate Problems | Psoriasis | Raynaud's Disease | Recurrent Infections | Restless Legs | Rheumatoid Arthritis | Schizophrenia | Sciatica | Sexual Problems |
|---|---|---|---|---|---|---|---|---|---|---|---|---|---|---|---|---|---|---|---|---|---|---|---|---|
| **WALES** | | | | | | | | | | | | | | | | | | | | | | | | |
| **BLAENAU GWENT** | | | | | | | | | | | | | | | | | | | | | | | | |
| ABERTILLERY PHYSIOTHERAPY (HM00125) | | | | | ● | | | | | | | | | | | | | ● | | | ● | | ● | |
| CLASSIC CLINIC (HM04606) | | | | | ● | | | | | | | ● | | | | | | | | | | | | |
| **BRIDGEND** | | | | | | | | | | | | | | | | | | | | | | | | |
| JENKINS, JOHN (HM10987) | | | | | | | ● | | | ● | | | | | | | | | | | | | | |
| PARKWOOD CHIROPRACTIC CLINIC (HM15725) | | | | | ● | | | | | | | | | | | | | | | | | | ● | |
| **CAERPHILLY** | | | | | | | | | | | | | | | | | | | | | | | | |
| OAKFIELD NATURAL HEALTH CENTRE (HM15151) | ● | ● | ● | ● | ● | ● | | ● | ● | ● | ● | ● | ● | | ● | ● | ● | ● | ● | ● | ● | ● | ● | ● |
| PARKWOOD CHIROPRACTIC CLINIC (HM15723) | | ● | | ● | ● | | | | | | | | | | | | | | | ● | ● | | ● | |
| **CARMARTHENSHIRE** | | | | | | | | | | | | | | | | | | | | | | | | |
| GREENWAY CONSULTANCY (HM08495) | ● | | ● | | ● | ● | | | | ● | ● | ● | ● | | | | ● | ● | ● | | ● | | | ● |
| HEALING HANDS (HM09339) | | | | | | | | | | ● | | | | | | | | | | | | | | |
| JABROO, C (HM10808) | ● | ● | ● | ● | ● | ● | | ● | ● | ● | ● | ● | ● | | ● | ● | ● | ● | ● | ● | ● | ● | ● | ● |
| SPENCER AROMATHERAPY (HM18990) | | | | | | | | | | | | | | | | | | | | | | | | |
| WAINWRIGHT, MARY (HM20738) | ● | ● | ● | ● | ● | ● | | ● | ● | ● | ● | ● | ● | | ● | ● | ● | ● | ● | ● | ● | ● | ● | ● |
| **CEREDIGION** | | | | | | | | | | | | | | | | | | | | | | | | |
| AMIES, SUSAN (HM00785) | | | | | | | | | | | | | | | | | | | | | | | | |
| CHERRY TREE CTRE FOR NTRL MED (HM04109) | ● | ● | ● | ● | ● | ● | | ● | ● | ● | ● | ● | ● | | ● | ● | ● | ● | ● | ● | ● | ● | ● | ● |
| COCKSEDGE, JOHN M (HM04774) | | | | | | | | | | | | | | | | | | | | | | | | |
| FFYNNONWEN NATURAL THRPY CTRE (HM07256) | | | | | | ● | | | | | | | | | | | | | | | | | ● | |
| **CONWY** | | | | | | | | | | | | | | | | | | | | | | | | |
| DREW, DAVID (HM06305) | ● | | | | ● | ● | | | ● | ● | | ● | | | | | | | | | | ● | | ● |
| HERBS FOR EVERYONE (HM09669) | ● | ● | ● | ● | ● | ● | | ● | ● | ● | ● | ● | | | ● | ● | | ● | ● | ● | ● | | ● | ● |
| MELA CENTRE OF OSTEOPATHY (HM13702) | | ● | | ● | ● | | | | | | | | | | | | | | | | ● | | ● | |
| MEWIS, R J (HM13782) | | | | | ● | | | | | | | | | | | | | | | | | | ● | |
| **DENBIGHSHIRE** | | | | | | | | | | | | | | | | | | | | | | | | |
| ALLIED PHYSIOTHERAPY (HM00646) | | ● | | | ● | | | | | | | | | | | | | | | | | | ● | |
| HEALING WAYS (HM09359) | ● | ● | ● | ● | ● | ● | | ● | ● | ● | ● | ● | ● | | ● | ● | ● | ● | ● | ● | ● | ● | ● | ● |
| MCGILL, L (HM13484) | | | | | ● | | | | | ● | | ● | | | | | | | | | | | | ● |
| ROY MORRIS CLINIC (HM17709) | ● | ● | | ● | ● | ● | ● | | ● | ● | ● | ● | ● | | ● | ● | ● | | ● | ● | ● | | ● | |
| **FLINTSHIRE** | | | | | | | | | | | | | | | | | | | | | | | | |
| A L J RILEY ASSOCIATES (HM00038) | ● | ● | | | ● | | | | ● | | ● | ● | | | | ● | ● | | ● | ● | ● | | ● | ● |

# I - S Conditions treated at Practices/Businesses

| Business by County with Reference no. | Insomnia | Irritable Bowel Syndrome | Itching | Jet Lag | Joint Pain | Kidney Complaints | Lactose Intolerance | Laryngitis | Lethargy | Liver Disorders | Low Blood Pressure | Lung Problems | ME | Menopause | Migraine | Motion Sickness | Mouth Disorders | Mouth Ulcers | Multiple Sclerosis | Muscular Dystrophy | Musculo-skeletal | Nail Health | Nausea | Nerve Disorders | Nervous Disorders | Neuralgia | Obesity | Osteoporosis | Pain | Palpitations | Panic Attacks | Parkinson's Disease | Period Problems | Phobias | Piles | PMT | Pneumonia | Postural Problems | Pregnancy Help | Prostate Problems | Psoriasis | Raynaud's Disease | Recurrent Infections | Restless Legs | Rheumatoid Arthritis | Schizophrenia | Sciatica | Sexual Problems |
|---|---|---|---|---|---|---|---|---|---|---|---|---|---|---|---|---|---|---|---|---|---|---|---|---|---|---|---|---|---|---|---|---|---|---|---|---|---|---|---|---|---|---|---|---|---|---|---|---|
| BOOTS HEALTHCARE SERVICES (HM02711) | | | ● | | ● | | | | | | | | | | | | | | ● | ● | | ● | | | | | | ● | ● | | | ● | | | | | | | | | ● | ● | | | ● | | | |
| CHIROPODISTS SURGERY (HM04298) | | | | | | | | | | | | | | | | | | | | | | ● | | | | | | | | | | | | | | | | | | | | | | | | | | |
| GAFFNEY, ALMA (HM07827) | | | | | | | | | | | | | | | | | | | | | | ● | | | | | | | | | | | | | | | | | | | | | | | | | | |
| HYPNOTHERAPY CENTRE (HM10528) | ● | ● | | | | | | | | | | | ● | | | | | | ● | | | ● | | ● | | | ● | | | | | | | ● | | | | | | | ● | | | | | | | ● |
| **GLAMORGAN (VALE OF)** | | | | | | | | | | | | | | | | | | | | | | | | | | | | | | | | | | | | | | | | | | | | | | | | |
| ALEXANDER TECHNIQUE (HM00551) | | | | | ● | | | | | | | | | | | | | | | | | | | ● | | | | | ● | | | | | | | | | ● | | | | | | | | | ● | |
| ALEXANDER TECHNIQUE (HM00546) | | ● | | | ● | | | | | | | | | | | | | | | | | | | ● | | | | | ● | | | | | | | | | | | | | | | | | | ● | |
| AMETHYST HEALING CENTRE (HM00784) | ● | ● | | | | | | | | | | | ● | | ● | | | | | | | | | | | | | | | | | | | | | | | | | | | | | | | | | |
| AROMATHERAPY CLINIC (HM01105) | | | | ● | ● | | | | | | | | | ● | ● | | | | | | | | | | | | | | | | | | | | | ● | | | | | | | | ● | ● | | | |
| AYRE CENTRE OF HYPNOTHERAPY (HM01430) | | | | | | | | | | | | | | | | | | | | | | | | | | | ● | | | | | | | ● | | | | | | | | | | | | | | |
| BARRY OSTEOPATHIC CLINIC (HM01809) | | | | | ● | | | | | | | | | | | | | | | | | | | | | | | | ● | | | | | | | | | ● | | | | | | | | | ● | |
| BODY ESSENTIALS (HM02587) | | | | | | | | | | | | | | ● | ● | | | | | | | | | | | | | | | | | | | | | | | | | | | | | | | | | |
| BROWN, ANNE (HM03214) | | | | | ● | | | | | | | | | | | | | | | | | | | ● | | | | | ● | | | | | | | | | | | | | | | | ● | | ● | |
| CARDIFF CHIROPRACTIC CLINIC (HM03666) | | ● | | | ● | | | | | | | | ● | | | | | | | | | | | ● | | | | ● | ● | | | | | | | | | | | | | | | | | | ● | |
| CARDIFF HEALTH PRACTICE (HM03670) | | ● | | | | | | | | | | | | | | | | | | | | | | ● | | | | | ● | | | | | | | | | | | | | | | | | | ● | |
| CARDIFF HOMEOPATHIC CLINIC (HM03671) | ● | ● | ● | ● | ● | ● | ● | ● | ● | ● | ● | ● | ● | ● | ● | ● | ● | ● | ● | ● | | ● | ● | ● | ● | ● | ● | ● | ● | ● | | ● | ● | ● | ● | ● | ● | | ● | ● | ● | ● | ● | ● | ● | ● | ● | ● |
| CITY CENTRE CHIRO CLINIC (HM04488) | | ● | | | ● | | | | | | | | | | | | | | | | | | | | | | | ● | ● | | | | | | | | | | | | | | | | | | ● | |
| COWBRIDGE CHIRO/SPINAL REHAB (HM05289) | ● | ● | ● | ● | ● | ● | ● | ● | ● | ● | ● | ● | ● | ● | ● | ● | ● | ● | ● | ● | | ● | ● | ● | ● | ● | ● | ● | ● | ● | | ● | ● | ● | ● | ● | ● | | ● | ● | ● | ● | ● | ● | ● | | ● | ● |
| COWBRIDGE OSTEOPATH CLINIC (HM05290) | | | | | ● | | | | | | | | | | | | | | | | | | | | | | | | | | | | | | | | | ● | | | | | | | | | | |
| EVANS, STEVE (HM06990) | | | | | ● | | | | | | | | | | | | | | | | | | | | | | | | ● | | | | | | | | | | | | | | | | | | | |
| GLAMORGAN HEALTH & RACQUET (HM08122) | | | | | ● | | | | | | | | | | | | | | | | | | | | | | | | ● | | | | | | | | | | | | | | | | | | | |
| GRIMWADE, S (HM08586) | | | | | ● | | | | | | | | | | | | | | | | | | | | | ● | | | | | | | | | | | | | | | | | | | | | | |
| HENRIETTA CTRE FOR COMP THRPY (HM09565) | | | | | | | | | | | | | | | | | | | | | | | | | ● | | | | | | ● | | | ● | | | | | | | | | | | | | | ● |
| LLANISHEN PHYSIOTHERAPY CLINIC (HM12501) | | | | | ● | | | | | | | | | | | | | | ● | | | | | | | | | | | | | | | | | | | | | | | | | | | | | |
| MILES, ANDREW (HM13854) | | ● | | | | | | | | | | | | | ● | | | | | | | | | ● | | | | | ● | | | | | | | | | | | | | | | | | | ● | |
| MOBILE FOOTWORKS (HM14031) | | ● | | | ● | | | | | | | ● | ● | | ● | | | | ● | | | ● | | | | | | | ● | | | ● | | | | | | | | | | ● | | | ● | | | |
| MORGAN-AYRES, PAUL (PROF) (HM14178) | ● | ● | | | | | | | | | | | ● | | ● | | | | | | | | | | ● | ● | ● | | ● | | | | | ● | | ● | | | | | ● | | | | | ● | | ● |
| MULLINS, JOHN (HM14348) | | ● | | | | | | | | | | | ● | | ● | | | | | | | | | | | | | | | | | | ● | | | | | | | | | | | | | | ● | |
| NATURAL HEALTHCARE (HM14601) | ● | ● | ● | ● | ● | ● | | | | ● | ● | ● | ● | ● | ● | | | | | | | | | ● | ● | ● | ● | ● | ● | ● | | | ● | ● | ● | ● | | | | | | | | ● | ● | ● | ● | ● |
| PARKWOOD CHIROPRACTIC CLINIC (HM15726) | | | | | ● | | | | | | | | | | | | | | | | | | | ● | | | | | | | | | | | | | | | | | | | | | | | ● | |
| PARKWOOD CHIROPRACTIC CLINIC (HM15724) | | | | | ● | | | | | | | | | | | | | | | | | | | ● | | | | | ● | | | | | | | | | | | | | | | | | | ● | |
| PENARTH CHIROPRACTIC CLINIC (HM15961) | ● | | | | ● | | | | ● | | | | | ● | ● | | | | ● | | | | | | | | | ● | ● | | | | ● | | | | | | ● | | | | | | ● | | ● | |
| PENARTH HOMEOPATHY CLINIC (HM15962) | ● | ● | ● | ● | ● | ● | ● | ● | ● | ● | ● | ● | ● | ● | ● | ● | ● | ● | ● | ● | | ● | ● | ● | ● | ● | ● | ● | ● | ● | | ● | ● | ● | ● | ● | ● | | ● | ● | ● | ● | ● | ● | ● | ● | ● | ● |
| PENYLAN PODIATRIC CENTRE (HM16005) | | | | | | | | | | | | | | | | | | | | | | ● | | | | | | | | | | | | | | | | | | | | | | | | | | |

# I - S Conditions treated at Practices/Businesses

| Business by County with Reference no. | Insomnia | Irritable Bowel Syndrome | Itching | Jet Lag | Joint Pain | Kidney Complaints | Lactose Intolerance | Laryngitis | Lethargy | Liver Disorders | Low Blood Pressure | Lung Problems | ME | Menopause | Migraine | Motion Sickness | Mouth Disorders | Mouth Ulcers | Multiple Sclerosis | Muscular Dystrophy | Musculo-skeletal | Nail Health | Nausea | Nerve Disorders | Nervous Disorders | Neuralgia | Obesity | Osteoporosis | Pain | Palpitations | Panic Attacks | Parkinson's Disease | Period Problems | Phobias | Piles | PMT | Pneumonia | Postural Problems | Pregnancy Help | Prostate Problems | Psoriasis | Raynaud's Disease | Recurrent Infections | Restless Legs | Rheumatoid Arthritis | Schizophrenia | Sciatica | Sexual Problems |
|---|---|---|---|---|---|---|---|---|---|---|---|---|---|---|---|---|---|---|---|---|---|---|---|---|---|---|---|---|---|---|---|---|---|---|---|---|---|---|---|---|---|---|---|---|---|---|---|---|
| PHYSIO FIRST CENTRE (HM16198) | | | | ● | | | | | | | | | | | | | | ● | | | | | | | | | | | | | | | | | | | | | | | | | | | | | | |
| POLLEY, LYNDON (HM16413) | | | | | | | | | | | | | | | | | | | | | | ● | | | | | | | | | | | | | | | | | | | | | | | | | | |
| POLLEY, LYNDON (HM16414) | | | | | | | | | | | | | | | | | | | | | | ● | | | | | | | | | | | | | | | | | | | | | | | | | | |
| POLLEY, LYNDON (HM16415) | | | | | | | | | | | | | | | | | | | | | | ● | | | | | | | | | | | | | | | | | | | | | | | | | | |
| RENWICK, SARAH NADINE (HM17192) | ● | ● | | | | | | | | | | | | ● | ● | | | | | | | | | | | | | | | | | | ● | | | ● | | | | | ● | | | | | | | ● |
| RIDGE, D (HM17316) | | | | ● | | | | | | | | ● | | | | | | | | | | | | | | | | ● | ● | | | | | | | | | | | | | | | | | | ● | |
| RIDGE, D (HM17315) | | | | ● | | | | | | | | ● | | | | | | | | | | | | | | | | ● | ● | | | | | | | | | | | | | | | | | | ● | |
| SWANSEA VALLEY PHYSIO PRACTICE (HM19579) | | | | ● | | | | | | | | | | | | | | | | | | | | | ● | | | ● | | | | | | | | | | | | | | | | | | | ● | |
| GWYNEDD | | | | | | | | | | | | | | | | | | | | | | | | | | | | | | | | | | | | | | | | | | | | | | | | |
| CENTRE FOR WELL BEING (HM03922) | ● | ● | | | | | | | | | | | | | ● | | | | | | | | | | | | | | | | | | | | | | | | | | | | | | | | | |
| MOSSHILL HOLISTIC CENTRE (HM14270) | ● | ● | ● | ● | ● | ● | ● | ● | ● | ● | ● | ● | ● | ● | ● | ● | ● | ● | ● | ● | | ● | ● | ● | ● | ● | ● | ● | ● | ● | | ● | ● | ● | ● | ● | ● | | ● | ● | ● | ● | ● | ● | ● | ● | ● | ● |
| NATURAL THERAPY CLINIC (HM14660) | ● | ● | | ● | ● | | ● | | ● | | | | ● | ● | ● | | | | | | | | | | ● | | ● | | ● | | | | ● | | | ● | | | ● | | | | | | ● | | ● | |
| O'NEIL, L (HM15325) | ● | ● | | | | | | | ● | | | | | | ● | | | | | | | | | | | | | | | | | | | ● | | ● | | | ● | | | | | | | | | ● |
| ISLE OF ANGLESEY | | | | | | | | | | | | | | | | | | | | | | | | | | | | | | | | | | | | | | | | | | | | | | | | |
| CHALMERS, D G (HM03951) | | | | ● | | | | | | | | | | | | | | | | | | | | | | | | ● | | | | | | | | | | | | | | | | | | ● | |
| EPHRAIM, NONA (HM06851) | | | | | | | | | | | | | | | | | | | | | | | | | | | | | | | | | | | | | | | | | | | | | | | | ● |
| MONMOUTHSHIRE | | | | | | | | | | | | | | | | | | | | | | | | | | | | | | | | | | | | | | | | | | | | | | | | |
| ABERGAVENNY THERAPY CTRE (HM00121) | | ● | | | ● | ● | | | | | | | ● | ● | ● | | | | ● | | | | | | | | | | ● | ● | | | ● | | | ● | | | ● | | | | | ● | ● | | ● | |
| BROOKSIDE PHYSIO PRACTICE (HM03184) | | | | | ● | | | | | | | | | | ● | | | | | | | | | ● | | ● | | ● | ● | | | | ● | | | | | | | | | | | | | | ● | |
| ELECTROMAGNETIC PRODUCTS (HM06721) | | | | | ● | | | | | | | | | | ● | | | | | | ● | | | | | | | | ● | | | | | | | | | ● | | | | | | | ● | | | |
| HARMONY (HM09020) | ● | ● | ● | ● | ● | ● | ● | ● | ● | ● | ● | ● | ● | ● | ● | ● | ● | ● | ● | ● | | ● | ● | ● | ● | ● | ● | ● | ● | ● | | ● | ● | ● | ● | ● | ● | | ● | ● | ● | ● | ● | ● | ● | ● | ● | ● |
| NUTRITION CLINIC (HM15122) | ● | ● | | | ● | | ● | | ● | | ● | | ● | ● | ● | | | ● | ● | | | ● | ● | ● | ● | | ● | ● | ● | ● | | | ● | ● | ● | ● | | | ● | | ● | | ● | ● | ● | ● | ● | |
| TURFAEN CHIROPODY CLINIC (HM20407) | | | | | ● | | | | | | | | | | | | | | | | | ● | | | | | | | | | | | | | | | | | | | | | | | | | | |
| NEATH PORT TALBOT | | | | | | | | | | | | | | | | | | | | | | | | | | | | | | | | | | | | | | | | | | | | | | | | |
| ST JAMES MEDICAL CENTRE (HM19078) | ● | ● | ● | ● | ● | ● | ● | ● | ● | ● | ● | ● | ● | ● | ● | ● | ● | ● | ● | ● | | ● | ● | ● | ● | ● | ● | ● | ● | ● | | ● | ● | ● | ● | ● | ● | | ● | ● | ● | ● | ● | ● | ● | ● | ● | ● |
| NEWPORT | | | | | | | | | | | | | | | | | | | | | | | | | | | | | | | | | | | | | | | | | | | | | | | | |
| BAJJADA, JUNE (HM01572) | ● | ● | ● | | ● | | | | ● | | ● | | ● | | ● | | | | | | | | | | ● | ● | | | ● | ● | | | ● | | | | | | | | ● | ● | | ● | ● | | ● | |
| BEIGHTON, J W (HM02069) | ● | ● | ● | ● | ● | ● | | ● | ● | ● | ● | ● | ● | ● | ● | ● | ● | ● | ● | | | | ● | ● | ● | ● | | | ● | ● | | ● | ● | | ● | ● | ● | | ● | ● | ● | ● | ● | ● | ● | | ● | ● |
| BOWKETT, LYN (HM02792) | ● | ● | ● | ● | ● | ● | ● | ● | ● | ● | ● | ● | ● | ● | ● | ● | ● | ● | ● | ● | | ● | ● | ● | ● | ● | ● | ● | ● | ● | | ● | ● | ● | ● | ● | ● | | ● | ● | ● | ● | ● | ● | ● | ● | ● | ● |
| CLINIC OF HOLISTIC HEALTH (HM04693) | ● | ● | ● | ● | ● | ● | ● | ● | ● | ● | ● | ● | ● | ● | ● | ● | ● | ● | ● | ● | | ● | ● | ● | ● | ● | ● | ● | ● | ● | | ● | ● | ● | ● | ● | ● | | ● | ● | ● | ● | ● | ● | ● | ● | ● | ● |
| MOXLEY, SHIRLEY (HM14304) | | | | | ● | ● | | | ● | | | | | ● | ● | ● | | | ● | | | | ● | ● | ● | ● | | ● | ● | | | | ● | | | ● | | | ● | | ● | | | | ● | | ● | |
| OLIVER, MARION (HM15294) | ● | ● | | ● | ● | ● | | ● | ● | | ● | ● | ● | ● | ● | ● | ● | ● | ● | ● | | | ● | ● | ● | ● | ● | ● | ● | ● | | ● | ● | ● | | ● | | | ● | ● | ● | ● | | ● | ● | | ● | ● |
| PEMBROKESHIRE | | | | | | | | | | | | | | | | | | | | | | | | | | | | | | | | | | | | | | | | | | | | | | | | |
| CENTRE OF TRADITIONAL HEALING (HM03926) | | | | | | | | | | | | | | | ● | | | | | | | | | | | | | | | | | | | | | | | | | | | | | | | | | |

# I - S Conditions treated at Practices/Businesses

Business by County with Reference no.

| Business | Insomnia | Irritable Bowel Syndrome | Itching | Jet Lag | Joint Pain | Kidney Complaints | Lactose Intolerance | Laryngitis | Lethargy | Liver Disorders | Low Blood Pressure | Lung Problems |
|---|---|---|---|---|---|---|---|---|---|---|---|---|
| JABROO, C (HM10809) | ● | ● | ● | ● | ● | ● | ● | ● | ● | ● | ● | ● |
| **POWYS** | | | | | | | | | | | | |
| BRECON CLINIC (HM02944) | ● | ● | ● | | ● | ● | | ● | ● | ● | ● | ● |
| BRECON COMPLEMENTARY MED CTRE (HM02945) | ● | ● | ● | ● | ● | ● | ● | ● | ● | ● | ● | ● |
| CONROY, CHRISTINE (HM05007) | | | | ● | | | | | | | | |
| COVENT HOUSE NTRL HEALTH CTRE (HM05280) | ● | ● | ● | ● | ● | ● | ● | ● | ● | ● | ● | ● |
| GROVES, FRAN (HM08614) | | | | | ● | | | | | | | |
| HEALTH FOCUS (HM09386) | ● | ● | ● | | ● | ● | | | ● | ● | ● | |
| KILGOUR, KATHARINE () | | | | | ● | | | | | | | |
| LLANDRINDOD WELLS SPA TOWN (HM12499) | ● | ● | ● | ● | ● | ● | ● | ● | ● | ● | ● | ● |
| PEACE CLINIC (HM15876) | | ● | | | | | | | | | | |
| REFLEXOLOGY & ALLERGY THERAPY (HM17078) | ● | ● | | | | ● | | | ● | ● | ● | |
| SHEPPARD, HELEN (HM18421) | ● | ● | | | ● | | | | | | ● | ● |
| **RHONDDA CYNON TAFF** | | | | | | | | | | | | |
| LIFE CARING CENTRE (HM12338) | | | | | | | | | | | | |
| POLLEY, LYNDON (HM16416) | | | | | | | | | | | | |
| **SWANSEA** | | | | | | | | | | | | |
| ABERTAWE PHYSIOTHERAPY CLINIC (HM00124) | | | | | ● | | | | | | | |
| ACUPUNCTURE CENTRE (HM00254) | ● | | | | ● | | | | ● | | | |
| BURDEN, RICHARD (HM03370) | | ● | | | ● | | | | | ● | ● | |
| PEDORTHICS FOOT SGY PRACTICE (HM15935) | | | | | ● | | | | | | | |
| RODWAY & ASSOCIATES (HM17531) | | ● | | | ● | | | | | | | |
| **TORFAEN** | | | | | | | | | | | | |
| CLUB INDIGO (HM04741) | | | | | ● | | | | | | | |
| **WREXHAM** | | | | | | | | | | | | |
| HARMONY IN HEALTH (HM09028) | | ● | | | | | | | | | | |
| SENSORAMA (HM18229) | ● | ● | | | | | | | | | | |

| Business | ME | Menopause | Migraine | Motion Sickness | Mouth Disorders | Mouth Ulcers | Multiple Sclerosis | Muscular Dystrophy | Musculo-skeletal | Nail Health | Nausea | Nerve Disorders |
|---|---|---|---|---|---|---|---|---|---|---|---|---|
| JABROO, C (HM10809) | ● | ● | ● | ● | ● | ● | ● | ● | | ● | ● | ● |
| **POWYS** | | | | | | | | | | | | |
| BRECON CLINIC (HM02944) | ● | ● | ● | | ● | ● | ● | | | | ● | ● |
| BRECON COMPLEMENTARY MED CTRE (HM02945) | ● | ● | ● | ● | ● | ● | ● | ● | | ● | ● | ● |
| CONROY, CHRISTINE (HM05007) | | | | | | | | | | | | |
| COVENT HOUSE NTRL HEALTH CTRE (HM05280) | ● | ● | ● | ● | ● | ● | ● | | | | ● | ● |
| GROVES, FRAN (HM08614) | ● | | ● | | | | | | | | | |
| HEALTH FOCUS (HM09386) | ● | ● | ● | ● | | | ● | ● | | ● | | ● |
| KILGOUR, KATHARINE () | | | | | | | ● | | | | | |
| LLANDRINDOD WELLS SPA TOWN (HM12499) | ● | ● | ● | ● | ● | ● | ● | ● | | ● | ● | ● |
| PEACE CLINIC (HM15876) | ● | | ● | ● | | | | | | | | ● |
| REFLEXOLOGY & ALLERGY THERAPY (HM17078) | | ● | ● | | | | | | | | | |
| SHEPPARD, HELEN (HM18421) | ● | ● | ● | | | | ● | | | | | ● |
| **RHONDDA CYNON TAFF** | | | | | | | | | | | | |
| LIFE CARING CENTRE (HM12338) | | | | | | | | | | | | |
| POLLEY, LYNDON (HM16416) | | | | | | | | | | ● | | |
| **SWANSEA** | | | | | | | | | | | | |
| ABERTAWE PHYSIOTHERAPY CLINIC (HM00124) | | | ● | | | | | | | | | |
| ACUPUNCTURE CENTRE (HM00254) | | ● | ● | | | | | | | | ● | |
| BURDEN, RICHARD (HM03370) | ● | ● | | | | | | | | | | |
| PEDORTHICS FOOT SGY PRACTICE (HM15935) | | | | | | | | | | | | |
| RODWAY & ASSOCIATES (HM17531) | ● | | | | | | | | | | | |
| **TORFAEN** | | | | | | | | | | | | |
| CLUB INDIGO (HM04741) | | | | | | | | | | | | |
| **WREXHAM** | | | | | | | | | | | | |
| HARMONY IN HEALTH (HM09028) | ● | | | | | | | | | | | |
| SENSORAMA (HM18229) | | | ● | | | | | | | | | |

| Business | Nervous Disorders | Neuralgia | Obesity | Osteoporosis | Pain | Palpitations | Panic Attacks | Parkinson's Disease | Period Problems | Phobias | Piles | PMT |
|---|---|---|---|---|---|---|---|---|---|---|---|---|
| JABROO, C (HM10809) | ● | ● | ● | ● | ● | ● | | ● | ● | ● | ● | ● |
| **POWYS** | | | | | | | | | | | | |
| BRECON CLINIC (HM02944) | ● | ● | ● | ● | ● | ● | | ● | ● | ● | ● | ● |
| BRECON COMPLEMENTARY MED CTRE (HM02945) | ● | ● | ● | ● | ● | ● | | ● | ● | ● | ● | ● |
| CONROY, CHRISTINE (HM05007) | | | | | ● | | | | | | | |
| COVENT HOUSE NTRL HEALTH CTRE (HM05280) | ● | ● | ● | | ● | ● | | | ● | ● | ● | ● |
| GROVES, FRAN (HM08614) | | | | | ● | | | | | | | |
| HEALTH FOCUS (HM09386) | ● | ● | ● | ● | ● | | | | ● | ● | ● | ● |
| KILGOUR, KATHARINE () | | | | ● | ● | | | | | | | |
| LLANDRINDOD WELLS SPA TOWN (HM12499) | ● | ● | ● | ● | ● | ● | | ● | ● | ● | ● | ● |
| PEACE CLINIC (HM15876) | ● | | ● | | ● | | | | ● | ● | | ● |
| REFLEXOLOGY & ALLERGY THERAPY (HM17078) | | | | | | | | | | | | ● |
| SHEPPARD, HELEN (HM18421) | ● | ● | | | ● | ● | | | ● | | | ● |
| **RHONDDA CYNON TAFF** | | | | | | | | | | | | |
| LIFE CARING CENTRE (HM12338) | | | | | | | | | | | | |
| POLLEY, LYNDON (HM16416) | | | | | | | | | | | | |
| **SWANSEA** | | | | | | | | | | | | |
| ABERTAWE PHYSIOTHERAPY CLINIC (HM00124) | | ● | | ● | ● | | | | | | | |
| ACUPUNCTURE CENTRE (HM00254) | | | | | ● | | | | ● | | | ● |
| BURDEN, RICHARD (HM03370) | | | | ● | | | | | ● | | | ● |
| PEDORTHICS FOOT SGY PRACTICE (HM15935) | | | | | | | | | | | | |
| RODWAY & ASSOCIATES (HM17531) | | ● | | | ● | | | | | | | |
| **TORFAEN** | | | | | | | | | | | | |
| CLUB INDIGO (HM04741) | | | | | ● | | | | | | | |
| **WREXHAM** | | | | | | | | | | | | |
| HARMONY IN HEALTH (HM09028) | | | | | | | | | | | | ● |
| SENSORAMA (HM18229) | | | | | | | | | ● | | | ● |

| Business | Pneumonia | Postural Problems | Pregnancy Help | Prostate Problems | Psoriasis | Raynaud's Disease | Recurrent Infections | Restless Legs | Rheumatoid Arthritis | Schizophrenia | Sciatica | Sexual Problems |
|---|---|---|---|---|---|---|---|---|---|---|---|---|
| JABROO, C (HM10809) | ● | | ● | ● | ● | ● | ● | ● | ● | ● | ● | ● |
| **POWYS** | | | | | | | | | | | | |
| BRECON CLINIC (HM02944) | | | ● | ● | ● | ● | ● | ● | ● | | ● | ● |
| BRECON COMPLEMENTARY MED CTRE (HM02945) | ● | | ● | ● | ● | ● | ● | ● | ● | ● | ● | ● |
| CONROY, CHRISTINE (HM05007) | | | | | | ● | ● | | | | ● | |
| COVENT HOUSE NTRL HEALTH CTRE (HM05280) | | | ● | ● | ● | ● | ● | ● | ● | | ● | |
| GROVES, FRAN (HM08614) | | | | | | | | | | | | |
| HEALTH FOCUS (HM09386) | ● | | | ● | ● | | | ● | ● | | ● | |
| KILGOUR, KATHARINE () | | | | | | | | | | | ● | |
| LLANDRINDOD WELLS SPA TOWN (HM12499) | ● | | ● | ● | ● | ● | ● | ● | ● | ● | ● | ● |
| PEACE CLINIC (HM15876) | | | | | ● | | | | | | | ● |
| REFLEXOLOGY & ALLERGY THERAPY (HM17078) | | | | | | | | | | | | |
| SHEPPARD, HELEN (HM18421) | | | ● | ● | | | ● | ● | ● | | ● | |
| **RHONDDA CYNON TAFF** | | | | | | | | | | | | |
| LIFE CARING CENTRE (HM12338) | | | ● | | | | | | | | | |
| POLLEY, LYNDON (HM16416) | | | | | | | | | | | | |
| **SWANSEA** | | | | | | | | | | | | |
| ABERTAWE PHYSIOTHERAPY CLINIC (HM00124) | | | | | | | | | ● | | ● | |
| ACUPUNCTURE CENTRE (HM00254) | | | | | ● | | | | | | | |
| BURDEN, RICHARD (HM03370) | | | | | | | | | ● | | ● | |
| PEDORTHICS FOOT SGY PRACTICE (HM15935) | | | | | | | | | | | ● | |
| RODWAY & ASSOCIATES (HM17531) | | | | | | | | | | | ● | |
| **TORFAEN** | | | | | | | | | | | | |
| CLUB INDIGO (HM04741) | | | | | | | | | | | | |
| **WREXHAM** | | | | | | | | | | | | |
| HARMONY IN HEALTH (HM09028) | | | | | | | | | | | | |
| SENSORAMA (HM18229) | | | | | | | | | | | | |

# SECTION 4d

## S-W of Conditions treated at Practices

# S - W Conditions treated at Practices/Businesses and Specialist Treatment Categories

Specialist Treatment Categories: Children, Terminally Ill, Disabled, Horses, Dogs, CatS, Other Animals

| Business by County with Reference no. | Sexually Trans. Infections | Shingles | Sinus Problems | Skin Problems | Sleep Disorders | Slimming Help | Slipped Disk | Smoking Help | Sneezing | Snoring | Spinal Injuries | Sports Injuries | Sprains | Stammering | Stings | Stomach Problems | Stomach Ulcers | Stress | Sweating | Teeth Grinding | Tennis Elbow | Terminal Illness | Throat Problems | Thrush | Thyroid Problems | Tinnitis | Tiredness | Tonsilitis | Ulcers | Vaginal Problems | Varicose Veins | Verrucas | Vertigo | Viral Infections | Vomiting | Warts | Water Retention | Whiplash | Wind | Worms | Children | Terminally Ill | Disabled | Horses | Dogs | CatS | Other Animals |
|---|---|---|---|---|---|---|---|---|---|---|---|---|---|---|---|---|---|---|---|---|---|---|---|---|---|---|---|---|---|---|---|---|---|---|---|---|---|---|---|---|---|---|---|---|---|---|---|
| **ENGLAND** | | | | | | | | | | | | | | | | | | | | | | | | | | | | | | | | | | | | | | | | | | | | | | | |
| **BEDFORDSHIRE** | | | | | | | | | | | | | | | | | | | | | | | | | | | | | | | | | | | | | | | | | | | | | | | |
| ALOE VERA SPECIALISTS (HM00681) | | | ● | ● | ● | ● | | | ● | | | ● | | | ● | ● | ● | | | | ● | | ● | ● | | ● | ● | | | | | | | ● | | | | | ● | | ● | | ● | ● | ● | ● | ● |
| ALTERNATIVE THERAPY AT WORK (HM00732) | | | | | | | | | | | | | | | | | | | | | | | | | | | ● | | | | | | | | | | ● | | | | | | | | | | |
| AMPTHILL & FLITWICK CLINIC (HM00795) | | | | | | | ● | | | | | ● | ● | | | | | | | | ● | | | | | | | | | | | | | | | | | | | | ● | | ● | | | | |
| BEDFORD ACUPUNCTURE CLINIC (HM02032) | | | | ● | | | ● | ● | | | | ● | ● | | | | | | | | | | | | | | | | | | | | | | | | | | | | ● | | ● | | | | |
| BEDFORD CHIROPRACTIC SURGERY (HM02033) | | | | | | | ● | | | | ● | ● | ● | | | | | | | | ● | | | | | | | | | | | | | | | | | ● | | | ● | ● | ● | | | | |
| BEDFORD PHYSIOTHERAPY CENTRE (HM02035) | | | | | | | ● | | | | | ● | ● | | | | | | | | ● | | | | | | | | | | | | | | | | | | | | ● | | ● | | | | |
| BELLAMY, R D (HM02097) | | | | | | | ● | | | | | ● | ● | | | | | | | | ● | | | | | | ● | | | | ● | | | | | | | | | | ● | | ● | | | | |
| BOYCE, MICHAEL (HM02814) | | | | | ● | | | | | | | | | | | | | ● | | | | | | | | | | | | | | | | | | | | | | | ● | | ● | | | | |
| BURTON, MERILYNN (HM03444) | | | | | | | | | | | | | | | | | | | | | | | | | | | | | | | | ● | | | | ● | | | | | ● | ● | ● | | | | |
| CHARTERED PHYSIOTHERAPIST (HM04042) | | | | | | | ● | | | | | ● | ● | | | | | | | | ● | ● | | | | | | | | | | | | | | | | ● | | | ● | ● | ● | | | | |
| CLNC OF ACU & CHINESE HERB MED (HM04726) | | ● | ● | ● | ● | | ● | ● | | | | ● | ● | | | ● | | | | | ● | | | ● | ● | | ● | | | | | | ● | | | | ● | | | | | | | | | | |
| COULSTOCK, JUDY (HM05239) | | | ● | ● | ● | | | | | | | | | | | | | | ● | | | | | | | ● | ● | ● | | | | | | | ● | | | | | | | ● | | | | | |
| DA SILVA, CAROLE (HM05665) | | | | | | | | | | | | | | | | | | | | | | | | | | | ● | | | | | | | | | | | | | | | | | | | | |
| DISS, KATHRYN (HM06122) | | | | | | | ● | | | | ● | ● | ● | | | | | | | ● | ● | | | | | | ● | | | | | | | | | | | ● | | | ● | ● | ● | | | | |
| DUNTON CTRE-COUN/PSYCHOTHERAPY (HM06428) | | | | | | | | | | | | | | | | | | | | | | | | | | | | | | | | | | | | | | | | | ● | ● | ● | | | | |
| GOUGH, E & P T (HM08314) | | | | | | | | | | | | | | | | | | | | | | | | | | | | | | | | | | | | | | | | | ● | | ● | | | | |
| GROVE NATURAL THERAPY CLINIC (HM08610) | | | ● | ● | | | ● | | | | ● | ● | ● | | | | | | | | ● | | | | | | ● | | | | | | | | | | | ● | | | ● | ● | ● | | | | |
| HEALES CHIROPRACTIC CLINIC (HM09321) | | | | | | | ● | | | | ● | ● | ● | | | | | | | | ● | | | | | | | | | | | | | | | | | ● | | | | | | | | | |
| HOLISTIC HYPNOTHERAPY (HM09983) | | | | ● | ● | ● | ● | ● | | | | | ● | ● | | | | ● | | ● | | | | | | ● | ● | | | | | | | | | | | | | | ● | | | | | | |
| INWARD BOUND THERAPIES (HM10707) | | | | | ● | ● | | ● | | | | | | | | | | ● | | | | | | | | | | | | | | | | | | | | | | | | | ● | | | | |
| JENNIFER K HOUGH - PHYSIO (HM11004) | | ● | | | | | ● | | | | | ● | ● | | | | | | | | ● | | | | | | | | | | | | | | | | | | ● | | ● | ● | ● | | | | |
| JOHNSON, ANNE (HM11068) | | | | | | | ● | | | | | ● | ● | | | | | | | | ● | | | | | | | | | | | | | | | | | | | | ● | | | | | | |
| JOHNSTONS CHIROPODIST (HM11107) | | | | | | | | | | | | | | | | | | | | | | | | | | | | | | | | | | | | | | | | | ● | | ● | | | | |
| KEMPSTON CHIROPRACTIC CLINIC (HM11469) | | | | | | | ● | | | | ● | ● | ● | | | | | | | | ● | | | | | | | | | | | | | | | | | ● | | | ● | ● | ● | | | | |
| MAGNETS 4 HEALTH (HM12918) | | | | | ● | | ● | | | | | ● | ● | | | | | | | | ● | | | | | | | | | | | | | | | | | | | | | | | | | | |
| MULTIPLE SCLEROSIS THRPY CTRE (HM14351) | | | | ● | ● | | | | | | | | | | | | | | | | | | | | | | | | | | | | | | | | | | | | | | | | | | |
| OSBORN, HELEN (HM15418) | | | | | | | ● | | | | | ● | ● | | | | | ● | | | ● | | | | | | | | | | | | | | | | | | | | ● | ● | ● | | | | |
| PRICE, SARAH (HM16596) | | | | | | | | | | | | | | | | | | ● | | | | | | | | | ● | | | | | | | | | | ● | | | | ● | ● | | | | | |
| SCHOOL OF ICASA (HM18082) | ● | | | | | | | | | | | | | | | | | | | | | | | | | | | | | | | | | | | | | | | | | | ● | | | | |
| SHEER PERFECTION (HM18367) | | | ● | ● | ● | | | | | | | | | | | ● | | | | | | | | | ● | | ● | | | | | | | | | | ● | | ● | | | | | | | | |
| SPECTRUM HEALTH TRUST (HM18976) | | ● | ● | ● | ● | ● | ● | ● | ● | ● | | ● | ● | ● | ● | ● | ● | | ● | ● | ● | ● | ● | ● | ● | ● | ● | ● | ● | ● | ● | | ● | ● | ● | ● | ● | | ● | | ● | ● | ● | ● | ● | ● | ● |

# S - W Conditions treated at Practices/Businesses and Specialist Treatment Categories

Business by County with Reference no.

| Business by County with Reference no. | Sexually Trans. Infections | Shingles | Sinus Problems | Skin Problems | Sleep Disorders | Slimming Help | Slipped Disk | Smoking Help | Sneezing | Snoring | Spinal Injuries | Sports Injuries | Sprains | Stammering | Stings | Stomach Problems | Stomach Ulcers | Stress | Sweating | Teeth Grinding | Tennis Elbow | Terminal Illness | Throat Problems | Thrush |
|---|---|---|---|---|---|---|---|---|---|---|---|---|---|---|---|---|---|---|---|---|---|---|---|---|
| SPORT, ALEXANDER (HM19041) | | | | | ● | | ● | | | | | ● | ● | | | ● | | | | ● | | | | |
| SWEET BREEZE (HM19584) | ● | ● | ● | ● | ● | ● | ● | ● | ● | ● | | ● | ● | ● | ● | ● | ● | | ● | ● | ● | ● | ● | ● |
| THERAPY CENTRE (HM19894) | | | | | | | ● | | | | | ● | ● | | | | | | | | ● | | | |
| THOMPSON, MARTIN (HM19992) | | | | | | | | | | | | | ● | | | | | | | | | | | |
| WINTER, SALLY (HM21721) | | | | | | | | | | | | | | | | | | | | | | | | |
| WOODSIDE CLINIC (HM21857) | | | | ● | | | ● | | | | | ● | ● | | | ● | | ● | | | ● | | | |
| **BERKSHIRE** | | | | | | | | | | | | | | | | | | | | | | | | |
| 1ST CHIROPRACTIC CLINIC (HM00004) | | | | | | | ● | | | | ● | ● | ● | | | | | | | | ● | | | |
| ANABELLE'S THERAPEUTIC MASSAGE (HM00798) | | | | | | | | | | | | ● | ● | | | | | ● | | | | | | |
| ASCOT PHYSIOFIRST CENTRE (HM01178) | | | | | | | ● | | | | | ● | ● | | | | | | | | ● | | | |
| BACK TO HEALTH - WINDSOR (HM01516) | | | | | | | ● | | | | ● | ● | ● | | | | | | | | ● | | | |
| BERKSHIRE CHIROPRACTIC (HM02195) | | | | | | | ● | | | | ● | ● | ● | | | ● | | | | ● | ● | ● | | |
| BODY & SOUL (HM02561) | | | | | | | | | | | | | | | | | | ● | | | | | | |
| BRACKNELL CHIROPRACTIC CLINIC (HM02838) | | | | | | | ● | | | | ● | ● | ● | | | | | | | | ● | | | |
| BRUCE, ANN (HM03264) | | | | | | | | ● | | | | | | ● | | | | | | | | | | |
| BURNHAM CHIROPRACTIC CLINIC (HM03404) | | | | | | | ● | | | | ● | ● | ● | | | | | | | | ● | | | |
| CAMPBELL, ELSPETH (HM03597) | | | ● | ● | ● | ● | | ● | | | | | | ● | | ● | ● | ● | ● | ● | | ● | ● | ● |
| CASTLE HILL CLINIC (HM03833) | ● | ● | ● | ● | ● | ● | ● | ● | ● | ● | | ● | ● | | ● | ● | ● | | ● | ● | ● | | ● | ● |
| CAVERSHAM CHIROPRACTIC CLINC (HM03864) | | | | | | | ● | | | | ● | ● | ● | | | | | | | | | ● | | |
| CAVERSHAM FOOT CLINIC (HM03866) | | | | | | | | | | | | | | | | | | | | | | | | |
| CHEFLAND, GERTI (HM04084) | | | ● | | ● | | | | | ● | | ● | ● | | ● | ● | ● | | ● | ● | | | | |
| CHEUNG, JAMES T (DR) (HM04142) | | ● | ● | | ● | | | | | | | | | | | | | | | | | | | |
| COOKHAM CHIROPRACTIC CLINIC (HM05068) | | | ● | ● | ● | ● | ● | | | | ● | ● | ● | | | | | | ● | ● | ● | | | |
| COPPERTHWAITE, ERIC (HM05147) | | | | | | ● | | ● | | | | | | | | | | | | | | | | |
| DEAN RUSSELL & BRYDGES ROBERT (HM05936) | | | | | | | ● | | | | ● | ● | ● | | | | | | | | ● | | | |
| DEJODE, SONIA (HM05962) | | | | | | | ● | | | | ● | ● | ● | | | | | | | | ● | | | |
| EDNEY, C S (HM06625) | | | ● | ● | | | | | | | | | | | | | | | | | | | | |
| EDWARDS, JOHN (HM06659) | | | | | | ● | | ● | | | | | | | | | | | | | | | | |
| EIGHAN, PENELOPE (HM06689) | | | ● | ● | ● | | | | | | | ● | ● | ● | | ● | | | | ● | ● | | | |
| EIGHT WINDS ACUPUNCTURE (HM06690) | | ● | ● | ● | | | ● | | | | | ● | ● | | | | | | | | ● | | | |
| FAIRBOURNE CLINIC (HM07051) | | | | | | | ● | ● | | | | ● | | | | | | | | | | | | |
| FEET TREAT (HM07186) | | | | | | | | | | | | | | | ● | | | | | | | | | |
| FERINGA, MARLIES (HM07233) | | | ● | | ● | | | ● | | ● | | | | | | | | | ● | | | | ● | ● |
| HALL, BEVERLEY (HM08767) | | | | ● | | | ● | | | | ● | ● | ● | | | | | | | ● | ● | | | |

| Business by County with Reference no. | Thyroid Problems | Tinnitis | Tiredness | Tonsilitis | Ulcers | Vaginal Problems | Varicose Veins | Verrucas | Vertigo | Viral Infections | Vomiting | Warts | Water Retention | Whiplash | Wind | Worms | Specialist Treatment Categories: Children | Terminally Ill | Disabled | Horses | Dogs | CatS | Other Animals |
|---|---|---|---|---|---|---|---|---|---|---|---|---|---|---|---|---|---|---|---|---|---|---|---|
| SPORT, ALEXANDER (HM19041) | | | ● | | | | | | | | | | | | | | ● | ● | ● | | | | |
| SWEET BREEZE (HM19584) | ● | ● | ● | ● | ● | ● | ● | | ● | ● | ● | ● | ● | | ● | ● | ● | ● | ● | | | | |
| THERAPY CENTRE (HM19894) | | | | | | | | | | | | | | | | | ● | ● | ● | | | | |
| THOMPSON, MARTIN (HM19992) | | | | | | | | | | | | | | | | | ● | ● | ● | | | | |
| WINTER, SALLY (HM21721) | | | | | | | | | | | | | | | | | ● | ● | ● | | | | |
| WOODSIDE CLINIC (HM21857) | ● | | ● | | | | | | ● | ● | ● | | | | ● | | ● | | ● | | | | |
| **BERKSHIRE** | | | | | | | | | | | | | | | | | | | | | | | |
| 1ST CHIROPRACTIC CLINIC (HM00004) | | | | | | | | | | | | | | ● | | | ● | ● | ● | | | | |
| ANABELLE'S THERAPEUTIC MASSAGE (HM00798) | | | | | | | | | | | | | | | | | | | | | | | |
| ASCOT PHYSIOFIRST CENTRE (HM01178) | | | | | | | | | | | | | | | | | ● | ● | ● | | | | |
| BACK TO HEALTH - WINDSOR (HM01516) | | | | | | | | | | | | | | ● | | | ● | ● | ● | | | | |
| BERKSHIRE CHIROPRACTIC (HM02195) | | ● | | | | | | | | | | | | ● | | ● | ● | ● | ● | ● | ● | ● | ● |
| BODY & SOUL (HM02561) | | | | | | | | | | | | | | | | | ● | | ● | | | | |
| BRACKNELL CHIROPRACTIC CLINIC (HM02838) | | | | | | | | | | | | | | ● | | | ● | ● | ● | | | | |
| BRUCE, ANN (HM03264) | | | | | | | | | | | | | | | | | ● | ● | ● | | | | |
| BURNHAM CHIROPRACTIC CLINIC (HM03404) | | | | | | | | | | | | | | ● | | | ● | ● | ● | | | | |
| CAMPBELL, ELSPETH (HM03597) | ● | ● | ● | | ● | | | | ● | | | | | | ● | | ● | ● | ● | | | | |
| CASTLE HILL CLINIC (HM03833) | ● | ● | ● | ● | ● | ● | | | ● | ● | ● | ● | ● | | ● | ● | ● | | | | | | |
| CAVERSHAM CHIROPRACTIC CLINC (HM03864) | | | | | | | | | | | | | | ● | | | | | | | | | |
| CAVERSHAM FOOT CLINIC (HM03866) | | | | | ● | | | | | | | ● | | | | | ● | ● | ● | ● | ● | ● | ● |
| CHEFLAND, GERTI (HM04084) | ● | | ● | | | ● | ● | | ● | ● | ● | ● | ● | | ● | | ● | | ● | | | | |
| CHEUNG, JAMES T (DR) (HM04142) | | | ● | | | | | | | | ● | | | | | | ● | | ● | | | | |
| COOKHAM CHIROPRACTIC CLINIC (HM05068) | | ● | | | | | | | ● | | | | | ● | | | ● | ● | ● | | | | |
| COPPERTHWAITE, ERIC (HM05147) | | | | | | | | | | | | | | | | | ● | ● | ● | | | | |
| DEAN RUSSELL & BRYDGES ROBERT (HM05936) | | | | | | | | | | | | | | ● | | | ● | ● | ● | | | | |
| DEJODE, SONIA (HM05962) | | | | | | | | | | | | | | ● | | | ● | ● | ● | ● | | | |
| EDNEY, C S (HM06625) | | | | | | | | | | | | | | | | | ● | ● | ● | | | | |
| EDWARDS, JOHN (HM06659) | | | | | | | | | | | | | | | | | | | | | | | |
| EIGHAN, PENELOPE (HM06689) | | ● | ● | | | | ● | | ● | | | | ● | | ● | | ● | ● | ● | | | | |
| EIGHT WINDS ACUPUNCTURE (HM06690) | | | ● | | | | | | | | | | | | | | ● | ● | ● | | | | |
| FAIRBOURNE CLINIC (HM07051) | | | | | | | | | | | | | | | | | ● | ● | | | | | |
| FEET TREAT (HM07186) | ● | | | | | | | | | | | | ● | | ● | | ● | | | | | | |
| FERINGA, MARLIES (HM07233) | ● | | ● | | | | | | | | | ● | | | ● | | ● | | ● | | | | |
| HALL, BEVERLEY (HM08767) | | | ● | | | | | | | | | | | ● | | | ● | ● | ● | | | | |

# S - W Conditions treated at Practices/Businesses and Specialist Treatment Categories

Business by County with Reference no.

| Business by County with Reference no. | Sexually Trans. Infections | Shingles | Sinus Problems | Skin Problems | Sleep Disorders | Slimming Help | Slipped Disk | Smoking Help | Sneezing | Snoring | Spinal Injuries | Sports Injuries | Sprains | Stammering | Stings | Stomach Problems | Stomach Ulcers | Stress |
|---|---|---|---|---|---|---|---|---|---|---|---|---|---|---|---|---|---|---|
| HALL, GRACE (HM08773) | | | ● | ● | | | ● | | | | | ● | | | | | | |
| HAZEL'S HOLISTIC HEALTH CARE (HM09294) | | | ● | ● | | | | | | | | | | | | | | |
| HEWITT, ANDREW (HM09703) | | | | | | | ● | | | | | ● | ● | | | | | |
| HILLSIDE OSTEOPATHIC PRACTICE (HM09806) | | | | | | | ● | | | | | ● | ● | | | | | |
| KENT, JANET (HM11524) | | | | | ● | ● | | ● | | | | | | ● | | | | |
| KINGFISHERS COMP HEALTH CARE (HM11650) | | | | ● | ● | | | | | | | | ● | | | | | |
| LANE, CORINNE (HM11931) | | | | | | | | | | | | | | | | | | ● |
| LANGLEY CHIROPRACTORS CLINIC (HM11953) | | | | | | | ● | | | | ● | ● | ● | | | | | |
| LAVENDER, S (HM12029) | | | | | | | | | | | | | | | | | | ● |
| LIFE GUIDANCE (HM12344) | | | | | | ● | | ● | | | | | | ● | | ● | | ● |
| LISSADELL HOUSE PRACTICE (HM12457) | | ● | ● | ● | ● | ● | ● | ● | | | ● | ● | ● | | ● | ● | ● | |
| MAIDENHEAD CHIROPRACTIC (HM12933) | | | | | | | ● | | | | ● | ● | ● | | | | | |
| MAIDENHEAD PHYSIO & SPORTS (HM12934) | | | | | | | ● | | | | | ● | ● | | | | | |
| MCGREGOR, TONY (HM13504) | | | | | ● | ● | | ● | | | | | | ● | | | | |
| NASEBY ACUPUNCTURE CLINIC (HM14487) | | ● | ● | ● | ● | | | ● | ● | ● | | ● | ● | | | ● | ● | ● |
| NATURAL HEALTH CONSULTANCY (HM14591) | | ● | ● | ● | ● | | ● | ● | ● | | | | | ● | ● | ● | ● | |
| NATURAL THERAPY CLINIC (HM14655) | | ● | ● | ● | ● | ● | ● | ● | ● | ● | ● | ● | ● | ● | ● | ● | ● | |
| NATURAL THERAPY CLINIC (HM14656) | ● | ● | ● | ● | ● | ● | ● | ● | ● | | | ● | ● | ● | ● | ● | ● | |
| NEWBURY CHIROPRACTIC CENTRE (HM14851) | | | | | | | ● | | | | ● | ● | ● | | | | | |
| NEWBURY PHYSIOTHERAPY (HM14852) | | | | | | | ● | | | | | ● | ● | | | | | |
| NS3UK NUTRITION SERVICES (HM15099) | | | ● | | | | | | | | | | | | | | | |
| PETERS, JEAN (HM16086) | | | ● | ● | | | | | | | | ● | | | | | | ● |
| PIM HEALTH CLINIC (HM16301) | | | | | ● | ● | ● | | | | ● | ● | ● | | | | | |
| ROSEDALE CLINIC (HM17616) | | | ● | ● | | | ● | | | | | ● | ● | | | | | |
| SANDALL, S (HM17898) | | | | | | | ● | | | | | ● | ● | | | | | |
| SLOUGH SPORTS INJURIES CLINIC (HM18690) | | | | | | | ● | | | | | ● | ● | | | | | |
| SMETHURST, ALISON (HM18704) | | ● | ● | | ● | | | | | | | | ● | | | | | |
| SOUTH LODGE CONSULTING (HM18909) | | | | | | | ● | | | | | ● | ● | | | | | |
| STRINGER, FRANCES (HM19407) | | | | | | | ● | | | | ● | ● | ● | | | | | |
| THATCHAM CHIROPRACTIC CLINIC (HM19867) | | | | | | | ● | | | | ● | ● | ● | | | | | |
| TSENG, PATRICIA (HM20359) | | | ● | ● | ● | | ● | ● | | | | ● | ● | | | | | |
| WINNERSH HYPNOTHERAPY PRACTICE (HM21711) | | | | | | | | | | | | | | ● | | | | |
| WOOD, JEANIE M (HM21801) | | | | | | | ● | | | | ● | ● | ● | | | | | |
| WOODLEY HEALING CENTRE (HM21836) | | ● | ● | ● | | ● | | ● | ● | | | | | | | ● | ● | |

| Business by County with Reference no. | Sweating | Teeth Grinding | Tennis Elbow | Terminal Illness | Throat Problems | Thrush | Thyroid Problems | Tinnitis | Tiredness | Tonsilitis | Ulcers | Vaginal Problems | Varicose Veins | Verrucas |
|---|---|---|---|---|---|---|---|---|---|---|---|---|---|---|
| HALL, GRACE (HM08773) | | | | | | | | | | | | | | |
| HAZEL'S HOLISTIC HEALTH CARE (HM09294) | | | | | | | | | ● | | | | | |
| HEWITT, ANDREW (HM09703) | | | ● | | | | | | | | | | | |
| HILLSIDE OSTEOPATHIC PRACTICE (HM09806) | | | ● | | | | | ● | | | | | | |
| KENT, JANET (HM11524) | ● | ● | | | | | | | ● | | | | | |
| KINGFISHERS COMP HEALTH CARE (HM11650) | | | ● | | | | | | ● | | | | | |
| LANE, CORINNE (HM11931) | | | | | | | | | | | | | | |
| LANGLEY CHIROPRACTORS CLINIC (HM11953) | | | ● | | | | | | | | | | | |
| LAVENDER, S (HM12029) | | | | | | | | | | | | | | |
| LIFE GUIDANCE (HM12344) | | | | | | | | ● | | | | | | |
| LISSADELL HOUSE PRACTICE (HM12457) | ● | ● | ● | | | ● | | ● | ● | ● | ● | | | |
| MAIDENHEAD CHIROPRACTIC (HM12933) | | | ● | | | | | | | | | | | |
| MAIDENHEAD PHYSIO & SPORTS (HM12934) | | | ● | | | | | | | | | | | |
| MCGREGOR, TONY (HM13504) | | ● | | | | | | | | | | | | |
| NASEBY ACUPUNCTURE CLINIC (HM14487) | ● | ● | ● | | ● | ● | ● | | ● | ● | ● | | | |
| NATURAL HEALTH CONSULTANCY (HM14591) | ● | | ● | | ● | ● | ● | ● | ● | ● | | | | |
| NATURAL THERAPY CLINIC (HM14655) | ● | ● | ● | ● | ● | ● | ● | ● | ● | ● | ● | ● | ● | |
| NATURAL THERAPY CLINIC (HM14656) | ● | ● | ● | ● | ● | ● | ● | ● | ● | ● | ● | ● | ● | |
| NEWBURY CHIROPRACTIC CENTRE (HM14851) | | | ● | | | | | | | | | | | |
| NEWBURY PHYSIOTHERAPY (HM14852) | | | ● | | | | | | | | | | | |
| NS3UK NUTRITION SERVICES (HM15099) | | ● | | | | ● | ● | ● | ● | | | ● | ● | |
| PETERS, JEAN (HM16086) | | | | | | | | | ● | | | | | ● |
| PIM HEALTH CLINIC (HM16301) | | ● | ● | | | | | | | | | | | |
| ROSEDALE CLINIC (HM17616) | | | ● | | | | | | | | | | | |
| SANDALL, S (HM17898) | | | | | | | | | | | | | | ● |
| SLOUGH SPORTS INJURIES CLINIC (HM18690) | | | ● | | | | | | | | | | | |
| SMETHURST, ALISON (HM18704) | | | | | | | | | | | | | | |
| SOUTH LODGE CONSULTING (HM18909) | | | ● | ● | | | | | | | | | | |
| STRINGER, FRANCES (HM19407) | | | ● | | | | | | | | | | | |
| THATCHAM CHIROPRACTIC CLINIC (HM19867) | | | ● | | | | | | | | | | | |
| TSENG, PATRICIA (HM20359) | | | ● | ● | | | | | ● | | | | | |
| WINNERSH HYPNOTHERAPY PRACTICE (HM21711) | | | | | | | | | ● | | | | | |
| WOOD, JEANIE M (HM21801) | | | ● | | | | | | | | | | | |
| WOODLEY HEALING CENTRE (HM21836) | ● | | ● | | | | ● | | ● | | ● | ● | ● | |

| Business by County with Reference no. | Vertigo | Viral Infections | Vomiting | Warts | Water Retention | Whiplash | Wind | Worms | Specialist Treatment Categories: Children | Terminally Ill | Disabled | Horses | Dogs | CatS | Other Animals |
|---|---|---|---|---|---|---|---|---|---|---|---|---|---|---|---|
| HALL, GRACE (HM08773) | | | | | | | | | ● | ● | ● | | | | |
| HAZEL'S HOLISTIC HEALTH CARE (HM09294) | | | | | | | | | ● | ● | ● | | | | |
| HEWITT, ANDREW (HM09703) | | | | | | ● | | | ● | ● | ● | | | | |
| HILLSIDE OSTEOPATHIC PRACTICE (HM09806) | | | | | | | | | ● | ● | ● | | | | |
| KENT, JANET (HM11524) | ● | | | | | | | | ● | ● | ● | | | | |
| KINGFISHERS COMP HEALTH CARE (HM11650) | | | | | ● | | ● | | | | | | | | |
| LANE, CORINNE (HM11931) | | | | | | | | | | | | | | | |
| LANGLEY CHIROPRACTORS CLINIC (HM11953) | | | | | | ● | | | ● | ● | ● | | | | |
| LAVENDER, S (HM12029) | | | | | | | | | ● | ● | ● | | ● | ● | ● |
| LIFE GUIDANCE (HM12344) | | | | | | | | | | | | | | | |
| LISSADELL HOUSE PRACTICE (HM12457) | | | ● | ● | ● | ● | ● | ● | ● | ● | ● | | | | |
| MAIDENHEAD CHIROPRACTIC (HM12933) | | | | | | ● | | | ● | ● | ● | | ● | | |
| MAIDENHEAD PHYSIO & SPORTS (HM12934) | | | | | | | | | ● | ● | ● | | | | |
| MCGREGOR, TONY (HM13504) | | | | | | | | | | | | | | | |
| NASEBY ACUPUNCTURE CLINIC (HM14487) | ● | | ● | | ● | | ● | ● | ● | ● | ● | | | | |
| NATURAL HEALTH CONSULTANCY (HM14591) | ● | ● | ● | ● | ● | | ● | ● | ● | ● | ● | | | | |
| NATURAL THERAPY CLINIC (HM14655) | ● | ● | ● | ● | ● | ● | ● | ● | ● | ● | ● | | | | |
| NATURAL THERAPY CLINIC (HM14656) | ● | ● | ● | ● | ● | | ● | ● | ● | ● | | | | | |
| NEWBURY CHIROPRACTIC CENTRE (HM14851) | | | | | | ● | | | ● | ● | ● | | | | |
| NEWBURY PHYSIOTHERAPY (HM14852) | | | | | | | | | ● | ● | ● | | | | |
| NS3UK NUTRITION SERVICES (HM15099) | ● | | ● | ● | ● | | ● | ● | ● | ● | ● | | | | |
| PETERS, JEAN (HM16086) | | | | | | | | | ● | ● | ● | ● | ● | ● | |
| PIM HEALTH CLINIC (HM16301) | | | | | | ● | | | ● | ● | ● | | | | |
| ROSEDALE CLINIC (HM17616) | | | | | | | | | ● | ● | ● | | | | |
| SANDALL, S (HM17898) | | | | | | | | | ● | ● | ● | | | | |
| SLOUGH SPORTS INJURIES CLINIC (HM18690) | | | | | | | | | ● | ● | ● | | | | |
| SMETHURST, ALISON (HM18704) | | | | | ● | | | | ● | ● | | | | | |
| SOUTH LODGE CONSULTING (HM18909) | | | | | | | | | ● | ● | ● | | | | |
| STRINGER, FRANCES (HM19407) | | | | | | ● | | | ● | ● | ● | | | | |
| THATCHAM CHIROPRACTIC CLINIC (HM19867) | | | | | | ● | | | ● | ● | ● | | | | |
| TSENG, PATRICIA (HM20359) | ● | | | | ● | | | | ● | ● | ● | | | | |
| WINNERSH HYPNOTHERAPY PRACTICE (HM21711) | | | | | | | | | ● | | | | | | |
| WOOD, JEANIE M (HM21801) | | | | | | ● | | | ● | ● | ● | | | | |
| WOODLEY HEALING CENTRE (HM21836) | | ● | | ● | ● | | ● | ● | ● | ● | ● | | ● | ● | ● |

# S - W Conditions treated at Practices/Businesses and Specialist Treatment Categories

| Business by County with Reference no. | Sexually Trans. Infections | Shingles | Sinus Problems | Skin Problems | Sleep Disorders | Slimming Help | Slipped Disk | Smoking Help | Sneezing | Snoring | Spinal Injuries | Sports Injuries | Sprains | Stammering | Stings | Stomach Problems | Stomach Ulcers | Stress | Sweating | Teeth Grinding | Tennis Elbow | Terminal Illness | Throat Problems | Thrush | Thyroid Problems | Tinnitis | Tiredness | Tonsilitis | Ulcers | Vaginal Problems | Varicose Veins | Verrucas | Vertigo | Viral Infections | Vomiting | Warts | Water Retention | Whiplash | Wind | Worms | Specialist Treatment Categories: Children | Terminally Ill | Disabled | Horses | Dogs | CatS | Other Animals |
|---|---|---|---|---|---|---|---|---|---|---|---|---|---|---|---|---|---|---|---|---|---|---|---|---|---|---|---|---|---|---|---|---|---|---|---|---|---|---|---|---|---|---|---|---|---|---|---|
| **BRISTOL** | | | | | | | | | | | | | | | | | | | | | | | | | | | | | | | | | | | | | | | | | | | | | | | |
| ALEXANDER, KAREN (HM00565) | | | | | | | | | | | | | | | | | | | | | | | | | | | | | | | | | | | | | | | | | ● | ● | ● | | | | |
| ANDERSON, KEITH (HM00830) | | | | | | | | | | | | | | | | | | | | | | | | | | | | | | | | | | | | | | | | | ● | | | | ● | ● | |
| AQUARIUS HEALTH CENTRE (HM00959) | ● | ● | ● | ● | ● | ● | ● | ● | ● | ● | | ● | ● | ● | ● | ● | ● | | ● | ● | ● | ● | ● | ● | ● | ● | ● | ● | ● | ● | ● | | ● | ● | ● | ● | ● | | ● | ● | ● | ● | ● | | | | |
| ARMSTRONG, ELIZABETH (HM01021) | | | | | | | | | | | ● | ● | ● | | | | | | | | ● | | | | | | | | | | | | | | | | | ● | | | ● | ● | ● | | | | |
| AROMATHERAPY FOR LADIES (HM01110) | | | | | | | | | | | | | | | | | | | | | | | | | | | | | | | | | | | | | | | | | | | ● | | | | |
| ASS-DANCE MOVEMENT THERAPY (HM01268) | | | | | | | | | | | | | | | | | | | | | | | | | | | ● | | | | | | | | | | | | | | | | | | | | |
| AVON COMPLEMENTARY MEDICINE (HM01404) | | | | | | | | | | | | | | | | | | | | | | | | | | | ● | | | | | | | | | | | | | | ● | | | | | | |
| BAGGLEY, J M (HM01536) | | | | | | | | | | | | | | | | | | | | | | | | | | | | | | | | | | | | | | | | | ● | ● | ● | | | | |
| BEVAN, RUSS (HM02242) | | | ● | ● | ● | ● | | ● | ● | ● | | ● | ● | ● | | ● | | | ● | ● | | | ● | | ● | ● | ● | ● | | | ● | | ● | | ● | ● | ● | | ● | | ● | ● | ● | | | | |
| BRISTOL HYPNOTHERAPY CLINIC (HM03063) | | | | | ● | | | ● | | | | | | | | | | | | ● | | | | | | ● | ● | | | | | | | | ● | | | | | | | ● | | | | | |
| BRISTOL NATURAL HEALTH SERVICE (HM03064) | | | ● | ● | ● | ● | | ● | ● | ● | | | | | | ● | ● | | | | ● | | | ● | ● | ● | ● | ● | ● | | | | ● | | ● | | ● | | ● | ● | ● | ● | ● | | | | |
| CASTLE CHIROPODY CLINIC (HM03828) | | | | | | | | | | | | | | | | | | | | | | | | | | | | | | | | ● | | | | ● | | | | | ● | ● | ● | | | | |
| CHARLES CLINIC (HM04020) | | | | | | | ● | | | | ● | ● | ● | | | | | | | | ● | | | | | | | | | | | | | | | | | | | | ● | | ● | | | | |
| CHERINGTON PRACTICE (HM04106) | | | | | | | ● | | | | | ● | ● | | | | | | | | ● | | | | | | | | | | | | | | | | | | | | ● | ● | ● | | | | |
| CLARK, LYN (HM04566) | | | | | | | | | | | | | | | | | | ● | | | | | | | | | ● | | | | | | | | | | | | | | ● | ● | ● | | | | |
| CLIFTON CHIROPRACTIC CLINIC (HM04666) | | | | | | ● | ● | ● | | | | ● | ● | | | ● | | | | ● | ● | | | | | ● | | | | | | | ● | | | | | ● | | | ● | ● | ● | | | | |
| CLIFTON PRACTICE (HM04670) | | | | | | | | ● | | | | | | | | | | ● | | | | | | | | | | | | | | | | | | | | | | | ● | | ● | | | | |
| CLINIC OF NATURAL MEDICINE (HM04704) | | | ● | | ● | | | | | | | | | | | ● | | ● | | | | | | | | | | | | | ● | | | | | | | | | | | | | | | | |
| CROSS HANDS CHIRO CLINIC (HM05478) | | | | ● | | ● | | | | | ● | ● | ● | | | | | | | | ● | ● | | | | | | | | | | | | | | | | ● | | | ● | ● | ● | | | | |
| CTRE FOR KINESIOLOGY (HM05542) | | | ● | ● | ● | ● | | ● | ● | | | | | | | ● | | | | ● | | ● | ● | ● | ● | | ● | ● | ● | ● | | | ● | ● | | ● | ● | | ● | ● | ● | ● | | | | | |
| DANCE VOICE THERAPY CENTRE (HM05709) | | | | | ● | | | | | | | | | | | | | | | | | | | | | | ● | | | | | | | | | | | | | | ● | ● | ● | | | | |
| DOWRY CHIROPRACTIC CLINIC (HM06255) | | | | | | | ● | | | | ● | ● | ● | | | | | | | | ● | | | | | | | | | | | | | | | | | ● | | | ● | ● | ● | | | | |
| FILE, CHRISTINE (HM07288) | | | ● | | ● | | | | | | | | | | | ● | | ● | | | | | | | | | | | | | ● | | | | | | | | | | ● | ● | ● | | | | |
| FRANCIS, PATRICIA (HM07675) | | | | | | | | | | | | | | | | | | ● | | | | | | | | | | | | | | | | | | | | | | | ● | | | | | | |
| FREEMAN, ANN (HM07719) | | ● | ● | ● | ● | | | ● | ● | ● | | | | | ● | ● | ● | | ● | | ● | | ● | ● | ● | ● | ● | ● | ● | ● | ● | | ● | ● | ● | ● | ● | | ● | ● | ● | ● | ● | | | | |
| GARLAND, C (HM07889) | | | | | | | | | | | | | | | | | | ● | | | | | | | | | | | | | | | | | | | | | | | ● | ● | ● | | | | |
| HARCOURT, A (HM08964) | | | | | | | ● | | | | ● | ● | ● | | | | | | | | ● | | | | | | | | | | | | | | | | | ● | | | ● | | | | | | |
| HEALING WITH GABRIELLE TWINE (HM09360) | | ● | ● | ● | ● | | | | | | | ● | ● | | ● | ● | ● | | ● | | ● | ● | ● | | | | ● | | ● | ● | ● | | | | | ● | | | ● | | ● | ● | ● | ● | ● | ● | ● |
| HEALTH & HEALING (HM09371) | ● | ● | ● | ● | ● | ● | ● | ● | ● | ● | | ● | ● | ● | ● | ● | ● | | ● | ● | ● | ● | ● | ● | ● | ● | ● | ● | ● | ● | ● | | ● | ● | ● | ● | ● | | ● | ● | ● | ● | ● | | | | |
| HOPLEY, DENISE (HM10154) | | | | | | | | | | | | ● | ● | | | | | | | | | | | | | | | | | | | | | | | | | | | | ● | | | | | | |
| HUDSON, JOHN (HM10313) | | | | | | | | ● | | | | | | | | | | | | | | | | | | | | | | | | | | | | | | | | | ● | ● | ● | | | | |
| KEYNSHAM CHIROPRACTIC CLINÍC (HM11580) | | | | | | | ● | | | | ● | ● | ● | | | | | | | | ● | | | | | | | | | | | | | | | | | ● | | | ● | ● | ● | | | | |
| KINGSWOOD CHIROPRACTIC CLINIC (HM11682) | | | | | | | | | | | ● | ● | ● | | | | | | | | ● | | | | | | | | | | | | | | | | | ● | | | ● | ● | ● | | | | |

# S - W Conditions treated at Practices/Businesses and Specialist Treatment Categories

| Business by County with Reference no. | Sexually Trans. Infections | Shingles | Sinus Problems | Skin Problems | Sleep Disorders | Slimming Help | Slipped Disk | Smoking Help | Sneezing | Snoring | Spinal Injuries | Sports Injuries | Sprains | Stammering | Stings | Stomach Problems | Stomach Ulcers | Stress | Sweating | Teeth Grinding | Tennis Elbow | Terminal Illness | Throat Problems | Thrush | Thyroid Problems | Tinnitis | Tiredness | Tonsilitis | Ulcers | Vaginal Problems | Varicose Veins | Verrucas | Vertigo | Viral Infections | Vomiting | Warts | Water Retention | Whiplash | Wind | Worms | Specialist Treatment Categories: Children | Terminally Ill | Disabled | Horses | Dogs | CatS | Other Animals |
|---|---|---|---|---|---|---|---|---|---|---|---|---|---|---|---|---|---|---|---|---|---|---|---|---|---|---|---|---|---|---|---|---|---|---|---|---|---|---|---|---|---|---|---|---|---|---|---|
| KNIGHTSWOOD CLINIC (HM11762) | | | | | | |●| | | | |●|●| | | | | | | |●| | | | | | | | | | | | | | | | | | | |●|●|●| | | | |
| LAM RIM CTRE FOR WHOLE HEALTH (HM11883) | | | | | | | | | | | | | | | | | | | | | | | | | | | | | | | | | | | | | | | | |●| |●| | | | |
| NAILSEA CHIROPRACTIC CLINIC (HM14460) | | | | | | |●| | | | |●|●| | | | | | | |●| | | | |●| | | | | | |●| | | | | | | |●| | | | | | |
| NAYDLER, NICK (HM14711) | | | | | | | | | | | | | | | | | |●| | | | | | | | | | | | | | | | | | | | | | | | | | | | | |
| ORCHARD MEDICAL CENTRE (HM15364) | | |●| | | | | | | |●|●|●| | | | |●| | |●| | | | | | |●| | | |●| | |●| | |●| | |●|●|●| | | | |
| ORIENTAL MEDICINE PRACTICE (HM15387) | |●|●|●|●|●|●|●|●|●| |●|●|●| |●|●| |●|●|●| |●|●|●|●|●|●|●|●|●| |●| |●|●|●| |●|●|●| |●| | | | |
| PARKER CLINIC (HM15683) | | | | | | | | | | |●|●|●| | | | | | | |●| | | | | | | | | | | | | | | | |●| | |●|●|●| | | | |
| POCOCK, A (HM16391) | | | | | | | | | | | | | | | | | | | | | | | | | | | | | | | |●| | | | | | | | |●|●|●| | | | |
| REDLANDS HOUSE CLINIC (HM17028) | | | | | | |●| | | |●|●|●| | | | | | | |●| | | | | | | | | | | | | | | | |●| | |●|●|●| | | | |
| REDMOND, CAROLINE (HM17031) |●|●|●|●|●|●|●|●|●|●| |●|●|●|●|●|●| |●|●|●|●|●|●|●|●|●|●|●|●|●| |●|●|●|●|●| |●|●|●|●|●| | | | |
| RICHARD GIBBONS - ACUPUNCT (HM17244) | | |●| |●|●| |●|●| | | | | | |●| | | | |●|●| |●| |●|●| | | | | |●| |●| | | | | |●|●| | | | | |
| RISING DRAGON TAI CHI (HM17369) | | | | | | | | | | | | | | | | | |●| | | | | | | | | | | | | | | | | | | | | | | |●| | | | | |
| RISING DRAGON TAI CHI SCHOOL (HM17370) | | | | | | | | | | | | | | | | | |●| | | | | | | | | | | | | | | | | | | | | | | |●| | | | | |
| STEVENS, BEN (HM19225) | | |●|●|●| |●| | | | |●| | | | | | | | | | | | | | |●| | | | | | | |●| | | | | |●|●| | | | | |
| STIRLING, P (HM19302) |●|●|●|●|●|●|●|●|●|●| |●|●|●|●|●|●| |●|●|●|●|●|●|●|●|●|●|●|●|●| |●|●|●|●|●| |●|●|●|●|●| | | | |
| STYLES, PATRICIA (HM19458) | | | | | | | | | | | | | | | | | | | | | | | | | | | | | | | |●| | | | | | | | | | | | | | | |
| THOMAS, TRUDY (HM19958) | | | | | | | | | | | | | | | | | | | | | | | | | | | | | | | | | | | |●| | | | |●|●|●| | | | |
| TOLL HOUSE CLINIC (HM20120) | | | | | | |●| | | | |●|●| | | | | | | | | | | | | | | | | | | | | | | | |●| | |●| | | | | | |
| **BUCKINGHAMSHIRE** | | | | | | | | | | | | | | | | | | | | | | | | | | | | | | | | | | | | | | | | | | | | | | | |
| ALTERNATE WAYS (HM00692) | | | | | | | | | | | | | | | | | |●| | | | | | | | |●| | | | | | | | | | | | | |●|●|●| | | | |
| ALTERNATIVE THERAPIES TRAINING (HM00730) |●|●|●|●|●|●|●|●|●|●| |●|●|●|●|●|●| |●|●|●|●|●|●|●|●|●|●|●|●|●| |●|●|●|●|●| |●|●|●|●|●| | | | |
| AMERSHAM CHIROPRACTIC CLINIC (HM00779) | | | | | | |●| | | | |●|●| | | | | | |●|●| | | | |●| | | | | | | | | | | |●| | |●|●|●| | | | |
| AMERSHAM OSTEOPATHIC CLINIC (HM00780) | |●|●| |●| |●| | | | |●|●| | | | | | | |●| | |●| | |●| | | | | |●| | | | | | | |●| |●| | | | |
| ASHBERRY PHYSIOTHERAPY CLINIC (HM01188) | | | | | | |●| | | | |●|●| | | | | | | |●| | | | | | | | | | | | | | | | | | | |●|●|●| | | | |
| AYLESBURY CHIROPRACTIC CLINIC (HM01422) | | | | | | |●| | | |●|●|●| | | | | | | |●| | | | | | | | | | | | | | | | |●| | |●|●|●| | | | |
| AYLESBURY COMPLEMENTARY HEALTH (HM01423) | |●|●|●|●|●| |●|●|●| | | |●| | | |●| |●|●|●| |●| |●|●| | | | | | | | | | | | | |●|●|●|●|●|●|●|
| AYLESBURY VALE THERAPY (HM01425) | | | |●| |●| |●| |●| | | |●| | | | |●| | | | | | | | | | |●| | | | | |●| | | | |●|●|●| | | | |
| BANFIELD, KATIE (HM01657) | | |●|●| | |●| | | | |●|●| | |●| | | | |●| | |●|●| | | | | | | | | | | |●| |●| |●| |●| | | | |
| BEACONSFIELD CHIRO CLINIC (HM01954) | | | | | | |●| | | | |●|●| | | | | | | |●| | | | | | | | | | | | | | | | |●| | |●|●|●| | | | |
| BIGGS, SYLVIA (HM02294) | | |●| |●| | | | | | | | | | |●| | | | | | | | | |●| | | | | | | | | | |●| | |●|●|●| | | | |
| BODY & SOUL (HM02565) | | | |●|●| | | | | | | | | | | | |●| | | | | | | | | | | | | | | | | | | | | | | | | | | | | |
| BREEZE, T (HM02951) | | | | | | | | | | | | | | | | | | | | | | | | | | | | | | | | | | | | | | | | |●|●|●| | | | |
| BUCKINGHAM CHIROPRACTIC CLINIC (HM03310) | | | | | | |●| | | |●|●|●| | | | | | | |●| | | | | | | | | | | | | | | | |●| | |●|●|●|●|●|●|●|
| CAMPBELL, LOUISE (HM03604) | | |●| |●| | | | | | | | | | | | |●| | | | | | | | | | | | | | | | | | | | | | | |●|●| | | | |

# S - W Conditions treated at Practices/Businesses and Specialist Treatment Categories

Business by County with Reference no.

| Business | Sexually Trans. Infections | Shingles | Sinus Problems | Skin Problems | Sleep Disorders | Slimming Help | Slipped Disk | Smoking Help | Sneezing | Snoring | Spinal Injuries | Sports Injuries | Sprains | Stammering | Stings | Stomach Problems | Stomach Ulcers | Stress | Sweating |
|---|---|---|---|---|---|---|---|---|---|---|---|---|---|---|---|---|---|---|---|
| CAMPBELL, NIKKI (HM03605) | | | ● | | | | ● | | | | | ● | | | | | | | |
| CANDLEWELL CLINIC (HM03623) | | | | | | | | | | | | | | | | | | | |
| CASTLE STREET CLINIC (HM03837) | | | ● | ● | | | ● | ● | | | | ● | ● | | | ● | ● | | |
| CHILTERN AROMATHERAPY (HM04172) | | | | | | | | | | | | | | | | | | | |
| COACHING FOR SUCCESS (HM04750) | | | | ● | ● | | | ● | | | | ● | | | | | | | |
| COLDWELL, VERONICA (HM04810) | ● | ● | ● | ● | ● | ● | ● | ● | ● | ● | | ● | ● | ● | ● | ● | ● | | ● |
| COMPLEMENTARY HEALTH (HM04921) | | ● | ● | ● | ● | ● | | ● | ● | ● | | | | ● | | | | ● | |
| COMPLEMENTARY HEALTH CENTRE (HM04923) | | ● | | ● | ● | ● | | ● | ● | ● | | | | ● | | ● | | | ● |
| DOIG, PAUL (HM06158) | | ● | ● | ● | ● | | | | | | | | | ● | | ● | ● | | ● |
| DOWDELL, FIONA K (HM06234) | | | | | | | ● | | | | ● | ● | ● | | | | | | |
| EDWARDS, EMMA (HM06650) | | | ● | ● | ● | | | | | | | | | | | ● | | | |
| ELAINE MCCARTHY REFLEXOLOGIST (HM06698) | ● | | ● | ● | ● | ● | ● | | ● | ● | | ● | ● | | | ● | ● | | ● |
| ENFIELD, CLAUDIA (HM06820) | | | ● | ● | ● | | ● | | | | | ● | ● | | | ● | | | |
| FIRMAN, BARBARA (HM07332) | | | ● | ● | ● | | | | | ● | | | | ● | | | ● | ● | |
| FLEET, BARBARA (HM07402) | | | | | | | | | | | | | | | | | | ● | |
| GERRARDS CROSS SPORTS & BACK (HM08004) | | | | | | | ● | | | | | ● | ● | | | | | | |
| HEATH, SUSAN (HM09454) | | | | | | ● | | | | | | | | | | ● | | | |
| HOBBS, SALLY (HM09857) | ● | ● | ● | ● | ● | ● | ● | ● | ● | ● | | ● | ● | ● | ● | ● | ● | | ● |
| HOLISTIC HEALING (HM09959) | | | ● | ● | ● | | | | | | | | | | | | | ● | |
| HULCOTT END PRACTICE (HM10352) | | | | | | | ● | | | | | ● | ● | | | | | | |
| J J COUNSELLING SERVICES (HM10798) | | | | | ● | | | | | | | | | | | | | ● | |
| JOHNSON, HELEN (HM11074) | ● | ● | ● | ● | ● | ● | ● | ● | ● | ● | ● | ● | ● | ● | ● | ● | ● | ● | ● |
| K BANFIELD NATUROPATHY/OSTEO (HM11288) | | | ● | ● | | | ● | | | | | ● | ● | | | ● | | | |
| KENTISH, LORNE (HM11531) | | | ● | ● | ● | | | | | | | | | | | ● | | | |
| LONG CRENDON OSTEOPATHS (HM12614) | | | | | | | ● | | | | | ● | ● | | | | | | |
| MATTHEWS, FRANK (HM13306) | | | | | | ● | | ● | | | | | | | | | | ● | |
| MIDDLE WAY RE-EDUCATION CTRE (HM13813) | | | | | | | ● | | | | | | | ● | | | | | |
| MIND AND BODY (HM13959) | | | | | | | | | | | | | | | | | | | |
| MIRZOEFF, PETER (HM13992) | | | | | | | | ● | | | | | | | | | | ● | |
| MORRISSEY, BLANCHE (HM14236) | | | | | | | | | | | | | | | | | | | |
| O'NEIL, PAULA (HM15326) | | | ● | ● | ● | | | | | | | ● | ● | | | ● | ● | | |
| ORMSBY, NEIL (HM15399) | | | | | | | | | | | | | | | | | | | |
| OXFORDSHIRE BOWEN CLINIC (HM15545) | | | ● | | | | ● | | | | | ● | ● | | | ● | ● | | |
| PATON, BARBARA (HM15823) | | | | | | | ● | | | | ● | ● | ● | | | | | | |

| Business | Teeth Grinding | Tennis Elbow | Terminal Illness | Throat Problems | Thrush | Thyroid Problems | Tinnitis | Tiredness | Tonsilitis | Ulcers | Vaginal Problems | Varicose Veins | Verrucas | Vertigo | Viral Infections | Vomiting | Warts | Water Retention | Whiplash | Wind | Worms |
|---|---|---|---|---|---|---|---|---|---|---|---|---|---|---|---|---|---|---|---|---|---|
| CAMPBELL, NIKKI (HM03605) | ● | | ● | | | | ● | ● | | | | | | | | | | | | | |
| CANDLEWELL CLINIC (HM03623) | | | | | | | | | | | | | | | | | | | | | |
| CASTLE STREET CLINIC (HM03837) | | ● | | | ● | ● | | | | ● | | | | | | ● | | | | | |
| CHILTERN AROMATHERAPY (HM04172) | | | | | | | | ● | | | | | | | | | | | | | |
| COACHING FOR SUCCESS (HM04750) | | | | | | | | ● | | | | | | | | | | | | | |
| COLDWELL, VERONICA (HM04810) | ● | ● | ● | ● | ● | ● | ● | ● | ● | ● | ● | ● | | ● | ● | ● | ● | ● | | ● | ● |
| COMPLEMENTARY HEALTH (HM04921) | ● | ● | ● | | ● | | ● | ● | | | | | | | | | | | | | |
| COMPLEMENTARY HEALTH CENTRE (HM04923) | ● | ● | ● | | ● | | ● | ● | | | | | | | | | | | | ● | |
| DOIG, PAUL (HM06158) | ● | | | ● | ● | ● | ● | ● | ● | ● | ● | | | ● | | ● | ● | ● | | ● | |
| DOWDELL, FIONA K (HM06234) | | ● | | | | | | | | | | | | | | | | | ● | | |
| EDWARDS, EMMA (HM06650) | | | | | | | | ● | | | | | | | | | | | | | |
| ELAINE MCCARTHY REFLEXOLOGIST (HM06698) | ● | ● | ● | ● | ● | ● | ● | ● | ● | ● | ● | ● | | ● | ● | ● | | ● | | ● | |
| ENFIELD, CLAUDIA (HM06820) | | ● | | | | | | ● | | | | | | | | | | ● | ● | ● | |
| FIRMAN, BARBARA (HM07332) | | ● | ● | ● | ● | ● | ● | ● | | | | | | ● | | | | | | | |
| FLEET, BARBARA (HM07402) | | | | | | | | | | | | | | | | | | | | | |
| GERRARDS CROSS SPORTS & BACK (HM08004) | | ● | ● | | | | | | | | | | | | | | | | | | |
| HEATH, SUSAN (HM09454) | | | ● | ● | | | | ● | | | ● | | | | | | | | | | |
| HOBBS, SALLY (HM09857) | ● | ● | ● | ● | ● | ● | ● | ● | ● | ● | ● | ● | | ● | ● | ● | ● | ● | | ● | ● |
| HOLISTIC HEALING (HM09959) | | | | | | | | ● | | | | | | | | | | | | | |
| HULCOTT END PRACTICE (HM10352) | | ● | | | | | | ● | | | | | | | | | | | | | |
| J J COUNSELLING SERVICES (HM10798) | | | | | | | | ● | | | | | | | | | | | | | |
| JOHNSON, HELEN (HM11074) | ● | ● | ● | ● | ● | ● | ● | ● | ● | ● | ● | ● | ● | ● | ● | ● | ● | ● | ● | ● | ● |
| K BANFIELD NATUROPATHY/OSTEO (HM11288) | | ● | | | ● | ● | | | | | | | | | | | | ● | | ● | |
| KENTISH, LORNE (HM11531) | | | | | | | | ● | | | | | ● | | | | | | | | |
| LONG CRENDON OSTEOPATHS (HM12614) | | ● | | | | | | | | | | | | | | | | | | | |
| MATTHEWS, FRANK (HM13306) | | | | | | | | | | | | | | | | | | | | | |
| MIDDLE WAY RE-EDUCATION CTRE (HM13813) | | | | | | | ● | ● | | | | | | | | | | | | | |
| MIND AND BODY (HM13959) | | | ● | | | | | ● | | | | | | | | | | | | | |
| MIRZOEFF, PETER (HM13992) | | | | | | | | | | | | | | ● | | | | | | | |
| MORRISSEY, BLANCHE (HM14236) | | | | | | | | | | | | | ● | | | | ● | | | | |
| O'NEIL, PAULA (HM15326) | ● | ● | | | ● | ● | ● | ● | | ● | | | | | | | | | | ● | |
| ORMSBY, NEIL (HM15399) | | | | | | | | | | | | | | | | | | | | | |
| OXFORDSHIRE BOWEN CLINIC (HM15545) | | ● | | | | | ● | | | | | | | | | | | | | | |
| PATON, BARBARA (HM15823) | | ● | | | | | | ● | | | | | | | | | | | ● | | |

| Business | Specialist Treatment Categories: Children | Terminally Ill | Disabled | Horses | Dogs | CatS | Other Animals |
|---|---|---|---|---|---|---|---|
| CAMPBELL, NIKKI (HM03605) | ● | ● | ● | | | | |
| CANDLEWELL CLINIC (HM03623) | ● | ● | ● | ● | ● | ● | |
| CASTLE STREET CLINIC (HM03837) | ● | ● | ● | | | | |
| CHILTERN AROMATHERAPY (HM04172) | ● | ● | ● | | | | |
| COACHING FOR SUCCESS (HM04750) | ● | | | | | | |
| COLDWELL, VERONICA (HM04810) | ● | ● | ● | ● | ● | ● | ● |
| COMPLEMENTARY HEALTH (HM04921) | ● | ● | ● | | | | |
| COMPLEMENTARY HEALTH CENTRE (HM04923) | | | | | | | |
| DOIG, PAUL (HM06158) | ● | ● | | | | | |
| DOWDELL, FIONA K (HM06234) | ● | | | ● | ● | ● | ● |
| EDWARDS, EMMA (HM06650) | ● | ● | ● | | | | |
| ELAINE MCCARTHY REFLEXOLOGIST (HM06698) | ● | ● | ● | | | | |
| ENFIELD, CLAUDIA (HM06820) | ● | ● | ● | | | | |
| FIRMAN, BARBARA (HM07332) | ● | ● | ● | | ● | ● | |
| FLEET, BARBARA (HM07402) | ● | ● | ● | | | | |
| GERRARDS CROSS SPORTS & BACK (HM08004) | ● | ● | ● | | | | |
| HEATH, SUSAN (HM09454) | ● | ● | ● | | | | |
| HOBBS, SALLY (HM09857) | ● | ● | ● | | | | |
| HOLISTIC HEALING (HM09959) | ● | ● | ● | | | | |
| HULCOTT END PRACTICE (HM10352) | | | | | | | |
| J J COUNSELLING SERVICES (HM10798) | ● | ● | ● | | | | |
| JOHNSON, HELEN (HM11074) | ● | | ● | | | | |
| K BANFIELD NATUROPATHY/OSTEO (HM11288) | ● | | ● | | | | |
| KENTISH, LORNE (HM11531) | ● | ● | ● | | | | |
| LONG CRENDON OSTEOPATHS (HM12614) | ● | | ● | | | | |
| MATTHEWS, FRANK (HM13306) | | | ● | | | | |
| MIDDLE WAY RE-EDUCATION CTRE (HM13813) | ● | ● | ● | | | | |
| MIND AND BODY (HM13959) | | ● | ● | ● | ● | ● | ● |
| MIRZOEFF, PETER (HM13992) | | | | | | | |
| MORRISSEY, BLANCHE (HM14236) | ● | | | | | | |
| O'NEIL, PAULA (HM15326) | ● | | | | | | |
| ORMSBY, NEIL (HM15399) | | | ● | | | | |
| OXFORDSHIRE BOWEN CLINIC (HM15545) | ● | | | | | | |
| PATON, BARBARA (HM15823) | ● | | ● | | | | |

# S - W Conditions treated at Practices/Businesses and Specialist Treatment Categories

Business by County with Reference no.

| Business by County with Reference no. | Sexually Trans. Infections | Shingles | Sinus Problems | Skin Problems | Sleep Disorders | Slimming Help | Slipped Disk | Smoking Help | Sneezing | Snoring | Spinal Injuries | Sports Injuries | Sprains | Stammering | Stings | Stomach Problems | Stomach Ulcers | Stress | Sweating | Teeth Grinding | Tennis Elbow | Terminal Illness | Throat Problems | Thrush | Thyroid Problems | Tinnitis | Tiredness | Tonsilitis | Ulcers | Vaginal Problems | Varicose Veins | Verrucas | Vertigo | Viral Infections | Vomiting | Warts | Water Retention | Whiplash | Wind | Worms | Specialist Treatment Categories: Children | Terminally Ill | Disabled | Horses | Dogs | CatS | Other Animals |
|---|---|---|---|---|---|---|---|---|---|---|---|---|---|---|---|---|---|---|---|---|---|---|---|---|---|---|---|---|---|---|---|---|---|---|---|---|---|---|---|---|---|---|---|---|---|---|---|
| PHYSIO FIRST PRACTICE (HM16199) | | | | | | |●| | | | |●|●| | | | | | | |●| | | | | | | | | | | | | | | | | | | | | |●| | | | |
| PINEWOOD CHIROPODY PRACTICE (HM16312) | | | | | | | | | | | | | | | | | | | | | | | | | | | | | | | | | | | |●| | | | |●|●|●| | | | |
| PRESTWOOD PHYSIOTHERAPY CLINIC (HM16562) | | | | | | |●| | | | |●|●| | | | | | | |●| | | | | | | | | | | | | | | | | | | |●|●|●| | | | |
| PURTON HOUSE HOMEOPATHIC CTRE (HM16775) | | | | | | | | | | | | | | | | | | | | | | | | | | | | | | | | | | | | | | | | |●|●|●| | | | |
| REIKI HEALTH CENTRE (HM17137) | | | | | | | | | | | | | | | | | | | | | | | | | | | | | | | | | | | | | | | | |●|●|●| | | | |
| RUNDLE, RICHARD (HM17752) | |●|●|●|●|●|●|●|●|●| |●|●|●|●|●|●| |●|●|●|●|●|●|●|●|●|●|●|●|●| |●|●|●|●|●|●|●| |●|●|●|●|●|●| |
| SHAW, FIONA (HM18335) | | |●|●|●| | | | | | |●|●| | | | | | | |●| | | | | |●| | | | | | | | | | | | | |●|●|●| | | | |
| SHENLEY CHIROPRACTIC CLINIC (HM18399) | | | | | | |●| | | |●|●|●| | | | | | | |●| | | | | | | | | | | | | | | | |●| | |●|●|●| | | | |
| STEINBERG, PAMELA (HM19189) |●|●|●|●|●|●|●|●|●|●| |●|●|●|●|●|●| |●|●|●|●|●|●|●|●|●|●|●|●|●| |●|●|●|●|●| |●|●| |●|●| | | | |
| TAYLOR, IAN E (HM19763) | | | |●| | | | | | | |●| | | | | | | | | | | | | | | | | | | |●| | | | | | | | | | |●| | | | |
| TEACHERS OF ALEXNDR TECH (HM19806) | | | | | | |●| | | | |●|●| | | | |●| | |●| | | | | |●| | | | | | | | | | | | | |●|●|●| | | | |
| TODD, PAUL (HM20107) | | | | | | | | | | | | | | | | | | | | | | | | | | | | | | | | | | | | | | | | |●|●|●| | | | |
| TOMLIN, SUSAN M (HM20136) | | |●| |●| | | | | | | | | | |●| | | |●|●|●|●| | | |●| | | | | | |●|●| |●| | | |●|●|●| | | | |
| TUDOR HOUSE CLINIC (HM20371) | | | | | | |●| | | | |●|●| | | | | | | |●| | | | | | | | | | | | | | | | | | | |●|●|●| | | | |
| WARDLAW, MICHAEL (HM20921) | | | | | | | | | | | | | | | | | | | | | | | | | | | | | | | | | | | | | | | | |●|●|●| | | | |
| WELLBURN (HM21154) | |●|●|●|●|●|●|●|●|●| |●|●|●|●|●|●| |●|●|●|●|●|●|●|●|●| |●|●|●| |●|●|●|●|●| |●|●|●|●|●| | | | |
| WELLER, JACK (HM21156) | | | | |●|●| |●| | | | | |●| | | | | | | | | | | | | | | | | | | | | | | | | | | | | | | | |
| WEST WYCOMBE CHIRO CLINIC (HM21240) | | | | | | |●| | | |●|●|●| | | | | | | |●| | | | | | | | | | | | | | | | |●| | |●|●|●| | | | |
| WESTWOOD, TERRY (HM21287) | | | | | |●| |●| | | | | | | | | |●| | | | | | | | | | | | | | | | | | | | | | |●|●|●| | | | |
| WOODWARD, MARGARET (HM21866) | | |●|●|●| | | | | | | | | | |●| | | | | | | | | | | | | | | | | | | | |●| | | |●|●|●| | |●| |
| **CAMBRIDGESHIRE** | | | | | | | | | | | | | | | | | | | | | | | | | | | | | | | | | | | | | | | | | | | | | | | |
| ACHILLES PHYSIOTHERAPY CLINIC (HM00161) | | | | | | |●| | | | |●|●| | | | | | | |●| | | | | | | | | | | | | | | | | | | |●| | | | | | |
| ANDERSON, M (HM00834) | | | | | | |●| | | |●|●|●| | | | | | | |●| | | | | | | | | | | | | | | | |●| | |●|●|●| | | | |
| ANDERSON, PAUL (HM00836) | | | | | | | | | | | | | | | | | | | | | | | | | | | | | | | | | | | | | | | | |●|●|●| | | | |
| ARJUNA NATURAL HEALTH CENTRE (HM01000) |●|●|●|●|●|●|●|●|●|●| |●|●|●|●|●|●| |●|●|●|●|●|●|●|●|●|●|●|●|●| |●|●|●|●|●| |●|●|●|●|●| | | | |
| BACK ON TRACK (HM01486) | | | | | | |●| | | | |●|●| | | | | | | |●| | | | | | | | | | | | | | | | | | | |●|●|●| | | | |
| BACK ON TRACK (HM01487) | | | | | | |●| | | | |●|●| | | | | | | |●| | | | | | | | | | | | | | | | | | | |●|●|●| | | | |
| BACK ON TRACK (HM01488) | | | | | | |●| | | | |●|●| | | | | | | |●| | | | | | | | | | | | | | | | | | | |●|●|●| | | | |
| BENSON, HUGH (HM02168) | |●|●|●|●|●|●|●|●|●| |●|●|●|●|●|●| |●|●|●|●|●|●|●|●|●|●|●|●|●| |●|●|●|●|●| |●| |●| |●| | | | |
| BRAMPTON CHIROPRACTIC CLINIC (HM02906) | | |●| | | |●| | |●| |●| | | | | | | |●|●| | | | | |●| | | | | |●| | | | | | | |●| |●| | | | |
| CAMBRIDGE CHIROPRACTIC CENTRE (HM03572) | | | | | | | | | | |●|●|●| | | | | | | |●| | | | | | | | | | | | | | | | |●| | |●|●|●| | | | |
| CAMBRIDGE TRAD ACUPUNC CENTRE (HM03578) | |●|●|●| | |●| | | | |●|●| | | | | | | |●| | | | | |●| | | | | | | | | | | | | |●|●|●| | | | |
| CHIROPRATIC & HOM HEALTH CTRE (HM04408) | |●|●|●|●| |●|●| | | |●|●| | |●| |●| | |●| | | | | |●| | | |●| | | | | | | | | |●|●|●| |●| | |
| COMPLEMENTARY HEALTH CLINIC (HM04927) | |●|●| |●| | |●| | | |●|●| | | | | | | |●| | | | | |●| | | | | |●| | | |●| | | |●|●|●| | | | |

www.healthmyself.com

# S - W Conditions treated at Practices/Businesses and Specialist Treatment Categories

Business by County with Reference no.

| Business by County with Reference no. | Sexually Trans. Infections | Shingles | Sinus Problems | Skin Problems | Sleep Disorders | Slimming Help | Slipped Disk | Smoking Help | Sneezing | Snoring | Spinal Injuries | Sports Injuries | Sprains | Stammering | Stings | Stomach Problems |
|---|---|---|---|---|---|---|---|---|---|---|---|---|---|---|---|---|
| COXELL REMEDIAL CLINIC (HM05324) | | | | | | | ● | | | | | ● | ● | | | |
| CUTTING, VALERIE (HM05648) | | | ● | | | | | | | | | | | | | ● |
| FAULKNER, CINDY (HM07141) | | | ● | | ● | | | | | | | | | ● | | ● |
| GILBERT RD OSTEOPATHIC (HM08055) | | | | | | | | | | | | ● | ● | | | |
| HEAL, CHRISTIANNE (HM09313) | | | | | | | | | | | | | | | | |
| HEALTH TEAM (HM09406) | | | ● | ● | ● | ● | ● | ● | | | | ● | ● | ● | | ● |
| HYPNOSIS AND HEALTH (HM10495) | | | | ● | ● | ● | | ● | | | | | | ● | | ● |
| LIFELINE (HM12354) | | | | | | | | | | | | | | | | |
| LIZ HALE HANDSON HEALTH (HM12495) | | ● | ● | ● | ● | | ● | | | | | ● | ● | | | ● |
| LY, THI PHUNG (DR) (HM12754) | | ● | ● | ● | ● | ● | ● | ● | ● | ● | | ● | ● | | | ● |
| MAGUIRE, J () | | | | | | ● | | ● | | | | | | | | |
| MATHIESON, M A (HM13290) | | | | | | | | | | | | | | | | |
| MAYNARD, SUSANNE (HM13358) | | | | | | | ● | | | | | ● | ● | | | |
| OUTSIDE IN (HM15507) | | | | | ● | | | | | | | | | | | |
| OXBOROUGH, JOY (HM15536) | | ● | ● | ● | | ● | ● | ● | ● | ● | | ● | ● | | ● | ● |
| PHIL SEAL PSYCHOTHERAPY (HM16115) | | | | | | | | ● | | | | | | | | |
| PRESTONS CHRTRD PHYSIOTHERAPY (HM16560) | | | | | | | ● | | | | | ● | ● | | | |
| REID, SUSAN (HM17121) | | | | | ● | ● | ● | ● | ● | ● | ● | ● | ● | | | |
| REIKI (HM17126) | | | | | | | | | | | | | | | | |
| ROBINSON-ZEL, B (HM17508) | | | | | | | | | | | | | | ● | | |
| SMITH, JEANETTE (HM18752) | | | | | ● | | | | | | | | | | | ● |
| SPENCE, ALEX (HM18982) | | | | | | | ● | | | | ● | ● | ● | | | |
| TONG, JENNY (HM20154) | | | ● | | ● | | | | | | | | | | | ● |
| TRANSCENDENTAL MEDITATION (HM20286) | | | | | | | | | | | | | | | | |
| WASS, ANNETTE (HM20975) | | ● | ● | ● | ● | | | | | | | | | | | ● |
| WILKINSON, GLYNNIS (HM21506) | | | | | | | | | | | | | | | | |
| **CHANNEL ISLANDS** | | | | | | | | | | | | | | | | |
| ST SAMPSON'S MEDICAL CENTRE (HM19098) | | | | | | | ● | | | | | ● | | | | |
| **CHESHIRE** | | | | | | | | | | | | | | | | |
| A & H PAIN CLINIC (HM00016) | | ● | ● | ● | ● | ● | ● | ● | ● | | | ● | ● | | | ● |
| ADULT & CHILD FOOT CLINIC (HM00391) | | | | | | | | | | | | ● | ● | | | |
| ADVANCED SKIN THERAPY CLINIC (HM00404) | | | | ● | | | | | | | | | | | | |
| AMBLESIDE CLINIC (HM00773) | | | | | | | | | | | | | | | | |
| AROMASPHERE (HM01083) | | | | ● | ● | | | | | | | | | | | |

| Business by County with Reference no. | Stomach Ulcers | Stress | Sweating | Teeth Grinding | Tennis Elbow | Terminal Illness | Throat Problems | Thrush | Thyroid Problems | Tinnitis | Tiredness | Tonsilitis | Ulcers | Vaginal Problems | Varicose Veins | Verrucas |
|---|---|---|---|---|---|---|---|---|---|---|---|---|---|---|---|---|
| COXELL REMEDIAL CLINIC (HM05324) | | | | | ● | | | | | | ● | | | | | |
| CUTTING, VALERIE (HM05648) | | ● | | | | | ● | | | | ● | ● | | | | |
| FAULKNER, CINDY (HM07141) | ● | | ● | | | | | | ● | ● | ● | | | | | |
| GILBERT RD OSTEOPATHIC (HM08055) | | | | | ● | | | | | | | | | | | |
| HEAL, CHRISTIANNE (HM09313) | | ● | | | | | | | | | | | | | | |
| HEALTH TEAM (HM09406) | ● | | ● | ● | ● | ● | | ● | ● | ● | ● | | ● | ● | | |
| HYPNOSIS AND HEALTH (HM10495) | ● | | | ● | | ● | | | | | | | | | | |
| LIFELINE (HM12354) | | | | | | | | | | | | | | | | |
| LIZ HALE HANDSON HEALTH (HM12495) | | | ● | | ● | ● | ● | | | ● | ● | | | | | |
| LY, THI PHUNG (DR) (HM12754) | ● | | ● | ● | ● | ● | ● | ● | ● | ● | ● | ● | ● | ● | | |
| MAGUIRE, J () | | | | | | | | | | | | | | | | |
| MATHIESON, M A (HM13290) | | | | | | | | | | | | | | | | |
| MAYNARD, SUSANNE (HM13358) | | | | | ● | | | | | | | | | | | |
| OUTSIDE IN (HM15507) | | | | | | | | | | | | | | | | |
| OXBOROUGH, JOY (HM15536) | ● | | ● | | ● | | ● | ● | ● | ● | ● | ● | ● | ● | ● | |
| PHIL SEAL PSYCHOTHERAPY (HM16115) | | ● | | | | | | | | | | | | | | |
| PRESTONS CHRTRD PHYSIOTHERAPY (HM16560) | | | | | ● | | | | | | | | | | | |
| REID, SUSAN (HM17121) | | | | ● | ● | | | | | | ● | | | | | |
| REIKI (HM17126) | | | | | | | | | | | | | | | | |
| ROBINSON-ZEL, B (HM17508) | | | | | | | | | | | | | | | | |
| SMITH, JEANETTE (HM18752) | | | | | | | | | | | ● | | | | | |
| SPENCE, ALEX (HM18982) | | | | | ● | | | | | | | | | | | |
| TONG, JENNY (HM20154) | | | | | | | ● | | | | ● | ● | | | | |
| TRANSCENDENTAL MEDITATION (HM20286) | | ● | | | | | | | | | | | | | | |
| WASS, ANNETTE (HM20975) | ● | ● | ● | | | | ● | ● | ● | ● | ● | ● | ● | ● | ● | |
| WILKINSON, GLYNNIS (HM21506) | | | | | | | | | | | | | | | | |
| **CHANNEL ISLANDS** | | | | | | | | | | | | | | | | |
| ST SAMPSON'S MEDICAL CENTRE (HM19098) | | | | | ● | | | | | | | | | | | |
| **CHESHIRE** | | | | | | | | | | | | | | | | |
| A & H PAIN CLINIC (HM00016) | | | ● | | ● | | ● | | | ● | ● | ● | | | | |
| ADULT & CHILD FOOT CLINIC (HM00391) | | | | | | | | | | | | | | | ● | ● |
| ADVANCED SKIN THERAPY CLINIC (HM00404) | | | | | | | | | | | | | | | ● | |
| AMBLESIDE CLINIC (HM00773) | | | | | | | | | | | | | | | | |
| AROMASPHERE (HM01083) | | ● | | | | | | | | | | | | | | |

| Business by County with Reference no. | Vertigo | Viral Infections | Vomiting | Warts | Water Retention | Whiplash | Wind | Worms | Children | Terminally Ill | Disabled | Horses | Dogs | CatS | Other Animals |
|---|---|---|---|---|---|---|---|---|---|---|---|---|---|---|---|
| COXELL REMEDIAL CLINIC (HM05324) | | | | | | ● | | | | | | | | | |
| CUTTING, VALERIE (HM05648) | | | | | | | | | ● | ● | ● | | | | |
| FAULKNER, CINDY (HM07141) | | | ● | | ● | | | | ● | ● | | | | | |
| GILBERT RD OSTEOPATHIC (HM08055) | | | | | | | | | ● | | | | | | |
| HEAL, CHRISTIANNE (HM09313) | | | | | | | | | | ● | ● | | | | |
| HEALTH TEAM (HM09406) | ● | ● | | ● | ● | | ● | ● | ● | ● | ● | | | | |
| HYPNOSIS AND HEALTH (HM10495) | | | | | | | | | | ● | | | | | |
| LIFELINE (HM12354) | | | | | | | | | ● | | | | | | |
| LIZ HALE HANDSON HEALTH (HM12495) | | ● | | | ● | | ● | | ● | ● | ● | | | | |
| LY, THI PHUNG (DR) (HM12754) | ● | ● | ● | | ● | | ● | | ● | ● | | | | | |
| MAGUIRE, J () | | | | | | | | | ● | | | | | | |
| MATHIESON, M A (HM13290) | | | | ● | | | | | ● | ● | ● | | | | |
| MAYNARD, SUSANNE (HM13358) | | | | | | | | | ● | | ● | | | | |
| OUTSIDE IN (HM15507) | | | | | | | | | ● | | | | | | |
| OXBOROUGH, JOY (HM15536) | ● | ● | | | ● | | ● | ● | ● | ● | ● | | | | |
| PHIL SEAL PSYCHOTHERAPY (HM16115) | | | | | | | | | ● | ● | ● | | | | |
| PRESTONS CHRTRD PHYSIOTHERAPY (HM16560) | | | | | | | | | ● | ● | ● | | | | |
| REID, SUSAN (HM17121) | | | | | | ● | | | ● | ● | ● | | | | |
| REIKI (HM17126) | | | | | | | | | ● | ● | ● | | ● | ● | |
| ROBINSON-ZEL, B (HM17508) | | | | | | | | | | | | | | | |
| SMITH, JEANETTE (HM18752) | | | | | | | | | | | | | | | |
| SPENCE, ALEX (HM18982) | | | | | | ● | | | ● | | ● | | | | |
| TONG, JENNY (HM20154) | | | | | | | | | | | | | | | |
| TRANSCENDENTAL MEDITATION (HM20286) | | | | | | | | | ● | | | | | | |
| WASS, ANNETTE (HM20975) | | ● | ● | ● | ● | | ● | ● | ● | | | | | | |
| WILKINSON, GLYNNIS (HM21506) | | | | ● | | | | | ● | ● | | | | | |
| **CHANNEL ISLANDS** | | | | | | | | | | | | | | | |
| ST SAMPSON'S MEDICAL CENTRE (HM19098) | | | | | | | | | ● | | | | | | |
| **CHESHIRE** | | | | | | | | | | | | | | | |
| A & H PAIN CLINIC (HM00016) | ● | | ● | | ● | | ● | | ● | ● | ● | | | | |
| ADULT & CHILD FOOT CLINIC (HM00391) | | ● | | ● | ● | | | | ● | ● | ● | | | | |
| ADVANCED SKIN THERAPY CLINIC (HM00404) | | | | | | | | | ● | ● | ● | | | | |
| AMBLESIDE CLINIC (HM00773) | | | | | | | | | ● | ● | ● | | | | |
| AROMASPHERE (HM01083) | | | | | | | | | | | | | | | |

(Children, Terminally Ill, Disabled, Horses, Dogs, CatS, Other Animals: Specialist Treatment Categories)

# S - W Conditions treated at Practices/Businesses and Specialist Treatment Categories

Business by County with Reference no.

| Business | Sexually Trans. Infections | Shingles | Sinus Problems | Skin Problems | Sleep Disorders | Slimming Help | Slipped Disk | Smoking Help | Sneezing | Snoring | Spinal Injuries | Sports Injuries | Sprains | Stammering | Stings | Stomach Problems |
|---|---|---|---|---|---|---|---|---|---|---|---|---|---|---|---|---|
| BACHE CHIROPODY (HM01471) | | | | | | | | | | | | | | | | |
| BACK PAIN CLINIC (HM01500) | | | | | | | ● | | | | ● | ● | ● | | | |
| BAXTER, GILLIAN (HM01927) | | | | | | | | | | | | | | | | |
| BERESFORD, KATHLEEN (HM02183) | | | ● | ● | ● | | | | | | | | | | | |
| BLOCH, PETER (HM02510) | | | | | | | ● | | | | ● | ● | ● | | | |
| BODY ESSENCES (HM02586) | | | | ● | ● | | | | | | | | | | | |
| BRAMHALL PARK PHYSIO CLINIC (HM02899) | | | | | | | ● | | | | | ● | ● | | | |
| BURTON, J S (HM03436) | | | | | | | | | | | | | | | | |
| CARMICHAEL CLINIC (HM03708) | | ● | ● | ● | ● | | ● | ● | | | | ● | ● | | | |
| CHEADLE HULME NATURAL HEALTH (HM04070) | | | ● | ● | ● | | | | | | | | | | | ● |
| CHESHIRE HEALTH CLINIC (HM04115) | | | ● | | | | ● | ● | | | ● | ● | ● | | | |
| CHESTER ALEXANDER TECH ST (HM04125) | | | | | | | ● | | | | ● | ● | ● | | | |
| CHESTER CHIROPODY (HM04126) | | | | | | | | | | | | | | | | |
| CHESTER CHIROPRACTIC CLINIC (HM04127) | | | | | | | ● | | | | ● | ● | ● | | | |
| CHESTER CLINIC (HM04128) | | ● | ● | ● | ● | ● | ● | ● | | | | ● | ● | | | ● |
| CHESTER HEALTH (HM04129) | | | ● | ● | ● | | | | | | | | ● | | | ● |
| CHESTER HEALTH & BEAUTY STUDIO (HM04130) | | | ● | ● | ● | | | | | | | ● | ● | | | ● |
| CHESTER HOMEOPATHIC CLINIC (HM04131) | ● | | ● | ● | ● | | | | | | | ● | | | | ● |
| CHESTER THERAPY CENTRE (HM04134) | | | | | | | | | | | | | | | | |
| CHINESE MEDICINE CENTRE (HM04257) | ● | ● | ● | ● | ● | ● | ● | ● | ● | ● | ● | ● | ● | ● | ● | ● |
| CHIROPODIST SURGERY (HM04295) | | | | | | | | | | | | | | | | |
| CHIROPODY CORNER (HM04330) | | | | | | | | | | | | | | | | |
| CLINIC OF ACUPUNCTURE (HM04684) | | ● | ● | ● | ● | | ● | ● | | | | | | | | ● |
| COLHOUN, PETER (HM04842) | | | | | | | | | | | | ● | ● | | | |
| CONSTANTINE, J C (HM05012) | | | ● | | ● | | ● | | | | | ● | ● | | | |
| CREWE & NANT PHYSIO CLINIC (HM05431) | | | | | | | ● | | | | | ● | ● | | | |
| CROPPER, AGNES (HM05473) | | | ● | | ● | | | | | | | | | | | ● |
| DAVIES & ASSOCIATES (HM05791) | | | | | | | ● | | | | | ● | | | | |
| DEWHURST, PATRICA A (HM06049) | | ● | ● | ● | ● | ● | ● | | ● | ● | | | | ● | ● | ● |
| EDDIE, DAVID (HM06585) | | | ● | | ● | | | | | | | | | | | |
| EVANS, DI (HM06968) | ● | | ● | | ● | | | | | ● | | ● | ● | | | ● |
| FAGAN, B W (HM07042) | | ● | | | | | ● | | | | | ● | ● | | | |
| FEET FIRST MOBILE CHIROPODY SV (HM07183) | | | | | | | | | | | | | | | | |
| FIELD VIEW SURGERY (HM07259) | | | | ● | | | | | | | | ● | ● | | | |

| Business | Stomach Ulcers | Stress | Sweating | Teeth Grinding | Tennis Elbow | Terminal Illness | Throat Problems | Thrush | Thyroid Problems | Tinnitis | Tiredness | Tonsilitis | Ulcers | Vaginal Problems | Varicose Veins | Verrucas |
|---|---|---|---|---|---|---|---|---|---|---|---|---|---|---|---|---|
| BACHE CHIROPODY (HM01471) | | | | | | | | | | | | | | | | |
| BACK PAIN CLINIC (HM01500) | | | | | ● | | | | | | | | | | | |
| BAXTER, GILLIAN (HM01927) | | | | | | | | | | | | | | | | ● |
| BERESFORD, KATHLEEN (HM02183) | | | | | | | | | | | ● | | | | | |
| BLOCH, PETER (HM02510) | | | | | ● | | | | | | | | | | | |
| BODY ESSENCES (HM02586) | | ● | | | | | | | | | | | | | | |
| BRAMHALL PARK PHYSIO CLINIC (HM02899) | | | | | ● | | | | | | | | | | | |
| BURTON, J S (HM03436) | | | | | | | | | | | | | | | | |
| CARMICHAEL CLINIC (HM03708) | | | | | ● | | | | | | ● | | | | | |
| CHEADLE HULME NATURAL HEALTH (HM04070) | | | | | | | | | | | ● | | | | | |
| CHESHIRE HEALTH CLINIC (HM04115) | | ● | | | ● | | | | | | | | | | | |
| CHESTER ALEXANDER TECH ST (HM04125) | | | | | ● | | | | | | | | | | | |
| CHESTER CHIROPODY (HM04126) | | | | | | | | | | | | | | | | |
| CHESTER CHIROPRACTIC CLINIC (HM04127) | | | | | ● | | | | | | | | | | | |
| CHESTER CLINIC (HM04128) | ● | | ● | | ● | ● | ● | ● | ● | ● | ● | ● | ● | ● | | |
| CHESTER HEALTH (HM04129) | | | | | ● | ● | ● | ● | ● | ● | ● | ● | | | | |
| CHESTER HEALTH & BEAUTY STUDIO (HM04130) | | | | | ● | ● | ● | ● | ● | ● | ● | ● | | | | |
| CHESTER HOMEOPATHIC CLINIC (HM04131) | ● | | ● | ● | | | | ● | ● | ● | ● | ● | ● | ● | ● | |
| CHESTER THERAPY CENTRE (HM04134) | | | | | | | | | | | | | | | | |
| CHINESE MEDICINE CENTRE (HM04257) | ● | ● | ● | ● | ● | ● | ● | ● | ● | ● | ● | ● | ● | ● | ● | ● |
| CHIROPODIST SURGERY (HM04295) | | | | | | | | | | | | | | | | ● |
| CHIROPODY CORNER (HM04330) | | | | | | | | | | | | | | | | ● |
| CLINIC OF ACUPUNCTURE (HM04684) | | | ● | | ● | | ● | | ● | ● | ● | | | | | |
| COLHOUN, PETER (HM04842) | | | | | | | | | | | | | | | | |
| CONSTANTINE, J C (HM05012) | | | | | ● | | ● | | | | | | | | | |
| CREWE & NANT PHYSIO CLINIC (HM05431) | | | | | ● | | | | | | | | | | | |
| CROPPER, AGNES (HM05473) | | ● | | | | | | | | | | | | | | |
| DAVIES & ASSOCIATES (HM05791) | | | | | ● | ● | | | | | | | | | | |
| DEWHURST, PATRICA A (HM06049) | ● | | ● | | ● | ● | ● | ● | ● | ● | ● | ● | ● | ● | ● | |
| EDDIE, DAVID (HM06585) | | | | | | | | | | | ● | | | | | |
| EVANS, DI (HM06968) | ● | ● | | ● | ● | ● | ● | | ● | | ● | | | | ● | |
| FAGAN, B W (HM07042) | | | | | ● | | | | | | | | | | | |
| FEET FIRST MOBILE CHIROPODY SV (HM07183) | | | | | | | | | | | | | | | | ● |
| FIELD VIEW SURGERY (HM07259) | | | | | | | | | | | | | ● | | ● | |

| Business | Vertigo | Viral Infections | Vomiting | Warts | Water Retention | Whiplash | Wind | Worms | Children | Terminally Ill | Disabled | Horses | Dogs | CatS | Other Animals |
|---|---|---|---|---|---|---|---|---|---|---|---|---|---|---|---|
| BACHE CHIROPODY (HM01471) | | | | | | | | | ● | ● | ● | | | | |
| BACK PAIN CLINIC (HM01500) | | | | | | ● | | | ● | ● | ● | | | | |
| BAXTER, GILLIAN (HM01927) | | | | ● | | | | | | ● | ● | ● | | | |
| BERESFORD, KATHLEEN (HM02183) | | | | | | | | | ● | ● | ● | | | | |
| BLOCH, PETER (HM02510) | | | | | | ● | | | ● | ● | ● | | | | |
| BODY ESSENCES (HM02586) | | | | | | | | | ● | ● | ● | | | | |
| BRAMHALL PARK PHYSIO CLINIC (HM02899) | | | | | | | | | ● | ● | ● | | | | |
| BURTON, J S (HM03436) | | | | | | | | | ● | ● | ● | | | | |
| CARMICHAEL CLINIC (HM03708) | | | | | | | | | ● | ● | ● | | | | |
| CHEADLE HULME NATURAL HEALTH (HM04070) | | | | | | | | | ● | ● | ● | | | | |
| CHESHIRE HEALTH CLINIC (HM04115) | | | | | | ● | | | ● | | | | ● | ● | |
| CHESTER ALEXANDER TECH ST (HM04125) | | | | | | ● | | | ● | ● | ● | | | | |
| CHESTER CHIROPODY (HM04126) | | ● | | ● | | | | | ● | ● | ● | | | | |
| CHESTER CHIROPRACTIC CLINIC (HM04127) | | | | | | ● | | | ● | ● | ● | | | | |
| CHESTER CLINIC (HM04128) | ● | ● | ● | ● | ● | | | | ● | ● | ● | | | | |
| CHESTER HEALTH (HM04129) | | | | | ● | | | ● | ● | ● | ● | | | | |
| CHESTER HEALTH & BEAUTY STUDIO (HM04130) | | | | | ● | | | ● | ● | ● | ● | | | | |
| CHESTER HOMEOPATHIC CLINIC (HM04131) | | ● | | ● | | | ● | | ● | ● | ● | | | | |
| CHESTER THERAPY CENTRE (HM04134) | | | | | | | | | ● | ● | ● | | | | |
| CHINESE MEDICINE CENTRE (HM04257) | ● | ● | ● | ● | ● | ● | ● | ● | ● | ● | ● | | | | |
| CHIROPODIST SURGERY (HM04295) | | | | ● | | | | | ● | ● | ● | | | | |
| CHIROPODY CORNER (HM04330) | | | | | | | | | ● | ● | ● | | | | |
| CLINIC OF ACUPUNCTURE (HM04684) | ● | | ● | | ● | | ● | | ● | ● | ● | | | | |
| COLHOUN, PETER (HM04842) | | | | ● | ● | | | | ● | ● | ● | | | | |
| CONSTANTINE, J C (HM05012) | ● | | | | | | | | ● | ● | ● | | ● | ● | |
| CREWE & NANT PHYSIO CLINIC (HM05431) | | | | | | | | | ● | ● | ● | | | | |
| CROPPER, AGNES (HM05473) | | | | | | | | | ● | ● | ● | | | | |
| DAVIES & ASSOCIATES (HM05791) | ● | | | | | ● | | | ● | | ● | | | | |
| DEWHURST, PATRICA A (HM06049) | ● | ● | ● | ● | ● | | ● | | ● | ● | ● | | | | |
| EDDIE, DAVID (HM06585) | | | | | | ● | | | ● | ● | ● | | | | |
| EVANS, DI (HM06968) | | | | | | | | | ● | ● | ● | | | | |
| FAGAN, B W (HM07042) | | | | | | | | | ● | | ● | | | | |
| FEET FIRST MOBILE CHIROPODY SV (HM07183) | | | | ● | | | | | ● | ● | ● | | | | |
| FIELD VIEW SURGERY (HM07259) | | ● | | ● | | | | | ● | ● | ● | | | | |

www.healthmyself.com



# S - W Conditions treated at Practices/Businesses and Specialist Treatment Categories

| Business by County with Reference no. |  |  |  |  |  |  |  |  |  |  |  |  |  |  |  |  |  |  |  |  |  |  |  |  |  |  |  |  |  |  |  |  |  |  |  |  |  |  |  |  | Specialist Treatment Categories |  |  |  |  |  |  |
|---|---|---|---|---|---|---|---|---|---|---|---|---|---|---|---|---|---|---|---|---|---|---|---|---|---|---|---|---|---|---|---|---|---|---|---|---|---|---|---|---|---|---|---|---|---|---|---|
|  | Sexually Trans. Infections | Shingles | Sinus Problems | Skin Problems | Sleep Disorders | Slimming Help | Slipped Disk | Smoking Help | Sneezing | Snoring | Spinal Injuries | Sports Injuries | Sprains | Stammering | Stings | Stomach Problems | Stomach Ulcers | Stress | Sweating | Teeth Grinding | Tennis Elbow | Terminal Illness | Throat Problems | Thrush | Thyroid Problems | Tinnitis | Tiredness | Tonsilitis | Ulcers | Vaginal Problems | Varicose Veins | Verrucas | Vertigo | Viral Infections | Vomiting | Warts | Water Retention | Whiplash | Wind | Worms | Children | Terminally Ill | Disabled | Horses | Dogs | CatS | Other Animals |
| FINCH, WENDY (HM07302) |  |  |  |  |  |  | ● |  |  |  |  |  | ● |  |  |  |  | ● |  |  | ● |  |  |  |  |  |  |  |  |  |  |  |  |  |  |  |  |  |  |  | ● |  |  |  |  |  |  |
| FIVE WAYS OSTEOPATHIC SURGERY (HM07381) |  |  |  |  |  |  | ● |  |  |  |  | ● |  |  |  |  |  |  |  |  | ● |  |  |  |  |  |  |  |  |  |  |  | ● |  |  |  |  |  |  |  |  |  |  |  |  |  |  |
| GENTLE TOUCH (HM07979) |  |  |  | ● | ● | ● |  |  |  |  |  |  |  |  |  |  |  |  |  |  |  |  |  |  |  |  |  |  |  |  |  |  |  |  |  |  |  |  |  |  | ● | ● | ● |  |  |  |  |
| GRACE & ASSOCIATES (HM08331) |  |  |  |  |  |  |  |  |  |  |  |  |  |  |  |  |  |  |  |  |  |  |  |  |  |  |  |  |  |  |  | ● |  |  |  |  |  |  |  |  | ● | ● | ● |  |  |  |  |
| GRAHAM COOMBE - MCTIMONEY (HM08338) |  |  | ● |  |  |  | ● |  |  |  |  | ● |  |  |  |  |  |  |  |  | ● |  |  |  |  |  |  |  |  |  |  |  | ● |  |  |  |  |  |  |  | ● |  |  |  |  |  |  |
| HANDS ON PHYSIOTHERAPY (HM08913) |  |  |  |  |  |  | ● |  |  |  |  | ● | ● |  |  |  |  |  |  |  | ● |  |  |  |  |  |  |  |  |  |  |  |  |  |  |  |  |  |  |  | ● | ● |  |  |  |  |  |
| HAZELDENE, BARBARA (HM09292) |  |  | ● | ● | ● |  |  |  |  |  |  |  |  |  |  | ● |  | ● |  |  |  |  |  |  |  |  | ● |  |  |  |  |  |  |  |  |  |  |  |  |  | ● | ● | ● |  |  |  |  |
| HEALD, M T (HM09316) |  |  |  |  |  |  |  |  |  |  |  |  |  |  |  |  |  |  |  |  |  |  |  |  |  |  |  |  |  |  |  |  |  |  |  |  |  |  |  |  | ● | ● | ● |  |  |  |  |
| HIGHLEY, T J (HM09757) |  |  |  |  |  |  |  |  |  |  |  |  |  |  |  |  |  |  |  |  |  |  |  |  |  |  |  |  |  |  |  |  |  |  |  | ● |  |  |  |  |  |  |  |  |  |  |  |
| HOWE, BARBARA (HM10261) |  |  |  |  |  |  |  |  |  |  |  |  |  |  |  |  |  | ● |  |  |  |  |  |  |  |  | ● |  |  |  |  |  |  |  |  |  |  |  |  |  | ● | ● | ● |  |  |  |  |
| HUSKISSON, EILEEN (HM10434) |  |  |  |  |  |  |  |  |  |  |  |  |  |  |  |  |  |  |  |  |  |  |  |  |  |  |  |  |  |  |  | ● |  |  |  |  |  |  |  |  | ● | ● | ● |  |  |  |  |
| HYPNOS PRACTICE (HM10492) |  |  |  | ● |  | ● |  | ● |  |  |  |  |  | ● |  |  |  | ● |  | ● |  |  |  |  |  | ● |  |  |  |  |  |  |  |  |  | ● |  |  |  |  | ● |  |  |  |  |  |  |
| IPHOFEN, RON (DR) (HM10712) |  |  |  |  | ● |  |  | ● |  |  |  |  |  |  |  |  |  |  |  | ● |  |  |  |  |  |  |  |  |  |  |  |  |  |  |  |  |  |  |  |  | ● | ● | ● |  |  |  |  |
| JENKINSON, LEILA (HM10999) | ● | ● | ● | ● | ● | ● | ● | ● | ● | ● |  | ● | ● | ● | ● | ● | ● |  | ● | ● | ● | ● | ● | ● | ● | ● | ● | ● | ● | ● | ● |  | ● | ● | ● | ● | ● |  | ● | ● | ● | ● | ● |  |  |  |  |
| JONES, J W (HM11155) |  |  |  | ● |  |  |  |  |  |  |  |  |  |  |  |  |  |  | ● |  |  |  |  |  |  |  |  |  | ● |  |  |  |  | ● |  | ● |  |  |  |  | ● | ● | ● |  |  |  |  |
| KNUTSFORD CHIROPRACTIC CLINIC (HM11775) |  | ● | ● |  | ● |  | ● | ● | ● | ● | ● | ● | ● |  |  | ● |  |  | ● | ● | ● |  | ● |  |  | ● | ● | ● |  |  |  |  | ● |  |  |  |  | ● |  |  | ● | ● | ● |  |  |  |  |
| LEGGE, PAT (HM12176) |  |  |  |  | ● |  |  |  |  |  |  |  |  |  |  |  |  | ● |  |  |  |  |  |  |  |  |  |  |  |  |  |  |  |  |  |  |  |  |  |  |  |  |  |  |  |  |  |
| LOMAS, CLIFFORD (HM12574) |  |  | ● |  |  |  | ● |  |  |  |  |  |  |  |  |  |  |  |  |  | ● |  |  |  |  |  |  |  |  |  |  |  | ● |  |  |  |  |  |  |  | ● |  |  |  |  |  |  |
| MACALLAN, STEPHEN (HM12815) |  | ● | ● | ● | ● |  |  |  | ● |  |  |  |  |  |  | ● | ● |  | ● | ● | ● |  | ● | ● | ● |  | ● | ● | ● | ● |  |  | ● | ● | ● |  | ● |  | ● | ● | ● | ● | ● |  |  |  |  |
| MARSH, F W (HM13147) |  |  |  |  |  |  |  |  |  |  |  |  |  |  |  |  |  |  |  |  |  |  |  |  |  |  |  |  |  |  |  | ● |  |  |  |  |  |  |  |  | ● | ● | ● |  |  |  |  |
| MEDICINE WHEEL (HM13670) |  |  |  |  | ● |  |  |  |  |  |  |  |  |  |  |  |  | ● |  |  |  |  |  |  |  |  |  |  |  |  |  |  |  |  |  |  |  |  |  |  |  |  |  |  |  |  |  |
| MEHTA HYPNOTHERAPY (HM13695) |  |  |  | ● |  | ● |  | ● |  |  |  |  |  |  |  |  |  |  |  |  |  |  |  |  |  |  | ● |  |  |  |  |  |  |  |  |  |  |  |  |  | ● | ● | ● |  |  |  |  |
| MIDDLETON & ASSOCIATES (HM13817) |  |  | ● | ● |  |  | ● |  |  | ● |  | ● | ● |  |  |  |  |  |  |  | ● |  |  |  |  |  | ● |  |  |  |  |  |  |  |  |  |  | ● |  |  | ● | ● | ● |  |  |  |  |
| MISSION, CHAITANYA (HM13995) |  |  |  |  |  |  |  |  |  |  |  |  |  |  |  |  |  | ● |  |  |  |  |  |  |  |  | ● |  |  |  |  |  |  |  |  |  |  |  |  |  |  |  |  |  |  |  |  |
| MORTON, J V (HM14251) |  |  |  | ● |  |  |  |  |  |  |  |  | ● |  |  |  |  |  |  |  |  |  |  |  |  |  |  |  | ● |  |  | ● |  |  |  |  |  |  |  |  | ● | ● | ● |  |  |  |  |
| NEEDHAM, ANGELA (HM14749) |  | ● | ● | ● | ● | ● |  |  |  | ● |  | ● | ● | ● | ● | ● | ● |  | ● | ● | ● | ● | ● | ● | ● | ● | ● | ● | ● | ● | ● |  | ● | ● | ● | ● | ● |  | ● | ● | ● | ● | ● |  |  |  |  |
| NEW LIFE NATURAL HEALTH CARE (HM14821) |  | ● | ● | ● | ● | ● | ● |  | ● | ● |  | ● | ● |  | ● | ● | ● |  | ● | ● | ● | ● | ● | ● | ● | ● | ● | ● | ● | ● | ● |  | ● | ● | ● | ● | ● |  | ● | ● | ● | ● | ● |  |  |  |  |
| NEWTON, J C (HM14898) |  |  |  |  |  |  |  |  |  |  |  |  |  |  |  |  |  |  |  |  |  |  |  |  |  |  |  |  |  |  |  | ● |  |  |  |  |  |  |  |  | ● | ● | ● |  |  |  |  |
| NUTRITION AND ALLERGY CLINIC (HM15121) |  | ● | ● | ● | ● | ● |  | ● | ● | ● |  |  |  |  |  | ● | ● |  |  | ● | ● | ● | ● | ● | ● | ● | ● | ● | ● | ● | ● |  | ● | ● | ● |  | ● |  | ● |  | ● | ● | ● |  |  |  |  |
| OLD HALL CLINIC (HM15256) |  |  | ● | ● | ● |  |  |  | ● | ● |  | ● | ● | ● | ● | ● | ● |  | ● | ● |  |  | ● | ● | ● | ● | ● | ● | ● | ● | ● |  | ● | ● | ● | ● | ● |  | ● |  | ● | ● |  | ● | ● |  |  |
| PATON, W A (HM15825) |  |  |  |  |  |  | ● |  |  |  |  | ● | ● |  |  |  |  |  |  |  | ● |  |  |  |  |  |  |  |  |  |  |  |  |  |  |  |  |  |  |  | ● | ● | ● |  |  |  |  |
| PENNYCOOK, AMANDA (HM15996) |  |  |  |  |  |  |  |  |  |  |  |  |  |  |  |  |  |  |  |  |  |  |  |  |  |  |  |  |  |  |  | ● |  |  |  |  |  |  |  |  | ● | ● | ● |  |  |  |  |
| PHOENIX CENTRE (HM16154) |  |  |  | ● | ● | ● |  | ● |  |  |  |  |  | ● |  |  |  | ● |  | ● |  |  |  |  |  |  |  |  |  |  |  |  |  |  |  |  |  |  |  |  | ● | ● | ● |  |  |  |  |
| PHYSIO & SPORTS INJURY CLINIC (HM16181) |  |  |  | ● |  | ● | ● |  |  |  |  | ● | ● |  |  |  |  |  |  |  | ● |  |  |  |  |  |  |  |  |  |  |  |  |  |  |  |  |  |  |  | ● |  | ● | ● | ● | ● | ● |

# S - W Conditions treated at Practices/Businesses and Specialist Treatment Categories

| Business by County with Reference no. | Sexually Trans. Infections | Shingles | Sinus Problems | Skin Problems | Sleep Disorders | Slimming Help | Slipped Disk | Smoking Help | Sneezing | Snoring | Spinal Injuries | Sports Injuries | Sprains | Stammering | Stings | Stomach Problems | Stomach Ulcers | Stress | Sweating | Teeth Grinding | Tennis Elbow | Terminal Illness | Throat Problems | Thrush | Thyroid Problems | Tinnitis | Tiredness | Tonsilitis | Ulcers | Vaginal Problems | Varicose Veins | Verrucas | Vertigo | Viral Infections | Vomiting | Warts | Water Retention | Whiplash | Wind | Worms | Specialist Treatment Categories: Children | Terminally Ill | Disabled | Horses | Dogs | CatS | Other Animals |
|---|---|---|---|---|---|---|---|---|---|---|---|---|---|---|---|---|---|---|---|---|---|---|---|---|---|---|---|---|---|---|---|---|---|---|---|---|---|---|---|---|---|---|---|---|---|---|---|
| PHYSIO PLUS (HM16203) | | | | | | | ● | | | | | ● | ● | | | | | | | | ● | | | | | | | | | | | | | | | | | | | | ● | ● | ● | | | | |
| PHYSIO SPORTS INJURY CLINIC (HM16209) | | | | | | | ● | | | | | ● | ● | | | | | | | | ● | | | | | | | | | | | | | | | | | | | | ● | ● | ● | | | | |
| POYNTON CHIROPRACTIC CLINIC (HM16519) | | | | | | | ● | | | | | ● | | | | | | | | | ● | | | | | | | | | | | | | | | | | ● | | | ● | ● | ● | | | | |
| PREW, BEVERLEY (HM16566) | | | ● | | | | | | | | | | | | | | | | | | | | | | | | | | | | | | | | | | ● | | | | ● | ● | ● | | | | |
| PRINCE, TANIA A (HM16622) | | | | ● | | ● | | ● | | | | | | ● | | | | | | | | | | | | ● | | | | | | | | | | | | | | | | | | | | | |
| REDGRAVE, KENNETH (HM17025) | | | | | | | | | | | | | | | | ● | | | | | | | | | | | | | | | | | | | | | | | ● | | ● | | | | | | |
| RICHARDS, DAVID (HM17250) | | | | | | | | | | | | | | | | | | | | | | | | | | | | | | | | | | | | ● | | | | | ● | ● | ● | | | | |
| RICHARDS, KERRY L (HM17260) | | | | | | | | | | | | | | | | | | | | | | | | | | | | | | | | | | | | | | | | | ● | ● | ● | | | | |
| SANDBACH HYPNOSIS CLINIC (HM17899) | | | | | ● | ● | | ● | | | | | | | | | | | | | | | | | | | | | | | | | | | | | | | | | ● | ● | ● | | | | |
| SAXELBY, M (HM17990) | | | | | | | | | | | | | | | | | | | | | | | | | | | | | | | | ● | | | | | | | | | ● | ● | ● | | | | |
| SCENTED GARDENS (HM18011) | | | | ● | ● | | | | | | | | | | | | | ● | | | | | | | | | | | | | | | | | | | | | | | ● | ● | ● | | | | |
| TEDSTONE, ALISON (HM19815) | | | | | | | | | | | | | | | | | | | | | | | | | | | | | | | | ● | | | | | | | | | ● | | | | | | |
| THOMAS, BEVERLEY (HM19933) | | | | | | | | | | | | | | | | | | | | | | | | | | | | | | | | ● | | | | | | | | | ● | ● | ● | | | | |
| THORNBER, A A (HM20016) | | | | | | | ● | | | | | ● | ● | | | | | | | | | | | | | | | | | | | | | | | | | | | | ● | ● | ● | | | | |
| TIPLING, L (HM20087) | | | | | | | | | | | | | | | | | | | | | | | | | | | | | | | | ● | | | | | | | | | ● | ● | ● | | | | |
| TRINITY HOUSE PRACTICE (HM20339) | | | | | | | | | | | | ● | ● | | | | | | | | ● | | | | | | | | | | | | | | | | | | | | | | | | | | |
| TULLY, CHARLES (HM20388) | | | | | | ● | ● | | | | ● | ● | | ● | | | | ● | | ● | ● | | ● | | | | | | | | | | | | | | | ● | | | ● | ● | ● | | | | |
| TYRER, HELEN R (HM20473) | | | | | | | | | | | | | | | | | | | | | | | | | | | | | | | | ● | | | | | | | | | ● | ● | ● | | | | |
| VALE ROYAL CHIROPRACTIC CLINIC (HM20553) | | | | | | | | | | | | | | | | | | | | | ● | | | | | | | | | | | | | | | | | ● | | | | | | | | | |
| VALE ROYAL CHIROPRACTIC CLINIC (HM20552) | | | | | | | | | | | | ● | ● | | | | | | | | ● | | | | | | | | | | | | | | | | | ● | | | | | | | | | |
| WARRINGTON CHIROPRACTIC CLINIC (HM20957) | | | | | | | ● | | | | ● | ● | ● | | | ● | | | | ● | ● | | | | | ● | | | | | | | ● | | | | | ● | | | ● | | ● | | | | |
| WEAVER HOUSE CLINIC (HM21049) | | ● | ● | ● | ● | ● | | ● | ● | ● | | ● | ● | ● | ● | ● | | | ● | ● | ● | ● | ● | ● | ● | ● | ● | ● | ● | ● | ● | | ● | | ● | ● | ● | | ● | ● | ● | ● | ● | ● | ● | ● | |
| WIDNES OSTEOPATHIC CLINIC (HM21459) | | | | | | | ● | ● | | | | | | | | | | | | | | | | | | ● | | | | | | | | | | | | | | | ● | | ● | | | | |
| WILLIAMS OSTEOPATHIC CLINIC (HM21532) | | | ● | | ● | ● | | ● | | | | ● | ● | | | | | | | ● | ● | | | | | | | | | | | | | | | | | | | | ● | ● | ● | | | | |
| WOOLLEY, M E (HM21878) | | | | | | | | | | | | | | | | | | | | | | | | | | | | | | | | ● | | | | | | | | | ● | ● | ● | | | | |
| WYNNE-JONES, J (HM21978) | | | | | | | | | | | | | | | | | | | | | | | | | | | | | | | | | | | | | | | | | ● | ● | ● | | | | |
| **CLEVELAND** | | | | | | | | | | | | | | | | | | | | | | | | | | | | | | | | | | | | | | | | | | | | | | | |
| ALEXANDER TECHNIQUE (HM00548) | | | | | ● | | ● | | | | | ● | ● | ● | | | | | | ● | ● | | ● | | | ● | ● | | | | | | ● | | | | | | | | | | | | | | |
| BARNARD, SIMON (HM01732) | | | | | | | ● | | | | | ● | ● | | | | | | | | ● | | | | | | | | | | | | | | | | | | | | ● | | ● | | | | |
| BODY BALANCE (HM02570) | | | | | | | | | | | | ● | | | | | | ● | | | | | | | | | | | | | | | | | | | | | | | | | | | | | |
| ELLISON, TIM (HM06777) | | | | | | | | | | | | ● | | | | | | | | | | | | | | | | | | | | | | | | ● | | | | | | | | | | | |
| HARTLEPOOL CHIROPRACTIC CLINIC (HM09138) | | | | | | | ● | | | | ● | ● | ● | | | | | | | | ● | | | | | | | | | | | | | | | | | ● | | | ● | ● | ● | | | | |
| MERMAID CHIROPRACTIC PRACTICE (HM13749) | | | | | | | ● | | | | ● | ● | ● | | | | | | | | ● | | | | | | | | | | | | | | | | | ● | | | ● | ● | ● | | | | |
| NATURAL THERAPY CENTRE (HM14637) | | | ● | ● | | | ● | | | | | ● | ● | | | | | | | | | | | | | | ● | | | | | | | | | | | | | | ● | ● | ● | | | | |

# S - W Conditions treated at Practices/Businesses and Specialist Treatment Categories

Business by County with Reference no.

| Business | Sexually Trans. Infections | Shingles | Sinus Problems | Skin Problems | Sleep Disorders | Slimming Help | Slipped Disk | Smoking Help | Sneezing | Snoring | Spinal Injuries | Sports Injuries | Sprains | Stammering | Stings | Stomach Problems |
|---|---|---|---|---|---|---|---|---|---|---|---|---|---|---|---|---|
| NORTHERN GUILD-PSYCHOTHERAPY (HM15061) | | | | | | | | | | | | | | | | |
| RAINBOW BRIDGE SCHOOL (HM16875) | ● | ● | ● | ● | ● | ● | ● | ● | ● | ● | | ● | ● | ● | ● | ● |
| REDCAR PHYSIO & SPORTS (HM17007) | | | | | | | ● | | | | | ● | ● | | | |
| RUSH, DENNIS (HM17754) | | | | ● | ● | ● | | ● | | | | | | ● | | ● |
| SKIPPINGS & ASSOCIATES (HM18657) | | | | | | | ● | | | | ● | ● | ● | | | |
| STRESS COUNSELLING (HM19391) | | | | | | | | ● | | | | | | | | |
| CORNWALL | | | | | | | | | | | | | | | | |
| AROMATICA (HM01135) | | | ● | ● | ● | ● | | | | | | ● | ● | | ● | ● |
| BANBURY, A E (HM01646) | | | | | | | ● | | | | | ● | ● | | | ● |
| BARNNETT, ANN (HM01763) | | ● | ● | ● | ● | | | | | | | | | | | ● |
| BEARE, M E (HM01968) | | | | | | | | | | | | | | | | |
| CARADON CHIROPRACTIC CLINIC (HM03656) | | | | | | | ● | | | | ● | ● | ● | | | |
| CHIROPODIST/PODIATRIST (HM04296) | | | | | | | | | | | | | | | | |
| COMP HEALTH INITIATIVE (HM04912) | ● | ● | ● | ● | ● | ● | ● | ● | ● | ● | | ● | ● | ● | ● | ● |
| DRAGE, STEPHEN (HM06279) | | | | | | | | ● | | | | | | | | |
| FEET FIRST (HM07180) | | ● | ● | ● | ● | | ● | ● | | | | | | | | ● |
| FOOTCARE (HM07492) | | | | | | | | | | | | | | | | |
| FORCE, GAYLE (HM07520) | | ● | ● | ● | ● | | | ● | | | | ● | ● | ● | ● | ● |
| HALL, PETER (HM08787) | | | | ● | | | ● | | | | | ● | ● | | | |
| HAWKSLAND PHYSIOTHERAPY CENTRE (HM09233) | | | | | | | ● | | | | | ● | ● | | | |
| LIFE 'N' LIMB (HM12346) | | | ● | ● | ● | | | | | ● | | ● | ● | | ● | ● |
| LIFE 'N' LIMB (HM12345) | ● | ● | ● | ● | ● | ● | ● | ● | ● | ● | | ● | ● | ● | ● | ● |
| LIFE-WORK POTENTIAL (HM12368) | | ● | ● | ● | ● | | | ● | ● | | | ● | ● | | ● | ● |
| LISKEARD CHIROPRACTIC CLINIC (HM12453) | | | | | | | ● | | | | ● | ● | ● | | | |
| LISTER NATURAL HEALTH PRACTICE (HM12461) | ● | ● | ● | ● | ● | ● | ● | ● | ● | ● | | ● | ● | ● | ● | ● |
| MASTERS, B (HM13273) | | ● | | | | | ● | | | | ● | ● | ● | | | |
| MORSE, EMMA (HM14239) | | | | | | | | | | | | | | | | |
| NEWQUAY CHIROPRACTIC CLINIC (HM14883) | | | ● | | | ● | ● | ● | | | | ● | ● | | | ● |
| OSTEOPATHIC FAMILY CENTRE (HM15465) | | | ● | ● | ● | | ● | | | | | ● | ● | | | ● |
| PENZANCE NATURAL HEALTH CENTRE (HM16006) | | | | | | | | | | | | | | | | |
| REEVES, J (HM17066) | | | | | | | | | | | | | | | | |
| ST AUSTELL CHIROPRACTIC CLINIC (HM19070) | | | | | | | ● | | | | ● | ● | ● | | | |
| TRURO CHIROPRACTIC CLINIC (HM20354) | | | | | | | ● | | | | ● | ● | ● | | | |
| TRURO OSTEOPATHIC PRACTICE (HM20356) | | | | | | | ● | | | | | ● | ● | | | |

| Business | Stomach Ulcers | Stress | Sweating | Teeth Grinding | Tennis Elbow | Terminal Illness | Throat Problems | Thrush | Thyroid Problems | Tinnitis | Tiredness | Tonsilitis | Ulcers | Vaginal Problems | Varicose Veins |
|---|---|---|---|---|---|---|---|---|---|---|---|---|---|---|---|
| NORTHERN GUILD-PSYCHOTHERAPY (HM15061) | | ● | | | | | | | | | | | | | |
| RAINBOW BRIDGE SCHOOL (HM16875) | ● | | ● | ● | ● | ● | ● | ● | ● | ● | ● | ● | ● | ● | ● |
| REDCAR PHYSIO & SPORTS (HM17007) | | | | | ● | | | | | | | | | | |
| RUSH, DENNIS (HM17754) | | | ● | | | | | | | | ● | | | | |
| SKIPPINGS & ASSOCIATES (HM18657) | | | | | ● | | | | | | | | | | |
| STRESS COUNSELLING (HM19391) | | | | | | | | | | | ● | | | | |
| CORNWALL | | | | | | | | | | | | | | | |
| AROMATICA (HM01135) | | | | | ● | | ● | ● | | | ● | | | ● | |
| BANBURY, A E (HM01646) | | | | | ● | | | | | ● | | | | | |
| BARNNETT, ANN (HM01763) | | | | ● | | | | | | | ● | | | | |
| BEARE, M E (HM01968) | | | | | | | | | | | | | | | |
| CARADON CHIROPRACTIC CLINIC (HM03656) | | | | | ● | | | | | | | | | | |
| CHIROPODIST/PODIATRIST (HM04296) | | | | | | | | | | | | | | | |
| COMP HEALTH INITIATIVE (HM04912) | ● | | ● | ● | ● | ● | ● | ● | ● | ● | ● | ● | ● | ● | ● |
| DRAGE, STEPHEN (HM06279) | | ● | | | | | | | | | | | | | |
| FEET FIRST (HM07180) | ● | | | ● | | | ● | ● | ● | ● | | | | ● | ● |
| FOOTCARE (HM07492) | | | | | | | | | | | | | | | |
| FORCE, GAYLE (HM07520) | ● | | | ● | ● | ● | ● | | ● | ● | ● | ● | ● | ● | ● |
| HALL, PETER (HM08787) | ● | | ● | | ● | | | ● | | ● | ● | | ● | | |
| HAWKSLAND PHYSIOTHERAPY CENTRE (HM09233) | | | | | ● | | | | | | | | | | |
| LIFE 'N' LIMB (HM12346) | | | ● | ● | ● | ● | ● | ● | | | ● | | ● | | ● |
| LIFE 'N' LIMB (HM12345) | ● | ● | ● | ● | ● | ● | ● | ● | ● | ● | ● | ● | ● | ● | ● |
| LIFE-WORK POTENTIAL (HM12368) | ● | | ● | | | | ● | ● | | | ● | | | | |
| LISKEARD CHIROPRACTIC CLINIC (HM12453) | | | | | ● | | | | | | | | | | |
| LISTER NATURAL HEALTH PRACTICE (HM12461) | ● | | ● | ● | ● | ● | ● | ● | ● | ● | ● | ● | ● | ● | ● |
| MASTERS, B (HM13273) | | | | | ● | | | | | | | | | | |
| MORSE, EMMA (HM14239) | | | | | | | | | | | | | | | |
| NEWQUAY CHIROPRACTIC CLINIC (HM14883) | ● | | | ● | ● | | | | | ● | ● | | | | |
| OSTEOPATHIC FAMILY CENTRE (HM15465) | | | | ● | ● | | | | | ● | ● | ● | | | ● |
| PENZANCE NATURAL HEALTH CENTRE (HM16006) | | | | | | | | | | | | | | | |
| REEVES, J (HM17066) | | | | | | | | | | | | | | | |
| ST AUSTELL CHIROPRACTIC CLINIC (HM19070) | | | | | ● | | | | | | ● | | | | |
| TRURO CHIROPRACTIC CLINIC (HM20354) | | | | | ● | | | | | | ● | | | | |
| TRURO OSTEOPATHIC PRACTICE (HM20356) | | | | | ● | | | | | | | | | | |

| | | | | | | | | | | Specialist Treatment Categories | | | | | | |
|---|---|---|---|---|---|---|---|---|---|---|---|---|---|---|---|---|
| Business | Verrucas | Vertigo | Viral Infections | Vomiting | Warts | Water Retention | Whiplash | Wind | Worms | Children | Terminally Ill | Disabled | Horses | Dogs | CatS | Other Animals |
| NORTHERN GUILD-PSYCHOTHERAPY (HM15061) | | | | | | | | | | ● | ● | ● | | | | |
| RAINBOW BRIDGE SCHOOL (HM16875) | | ● | ● | ● | ● | ● | | ● | ● | | | | | | | |
| REDCAR PHYSIO & SPORTS (HM17007) | | | | | | | | | | ● | ● | ● | | | | |
| RUSH, DENNIS (HM17754) | | | | | ● | | | | | ● | | | | | | |
| SKIPPINGS & ASSOCIATES (HM18657) | | | | | | | ● | | | ● | ● | ● | | | | |
| STRESS COUNSELLING (HM19391) | | | | | | | | | | ● | | | | | | |
| CORNWALL | | | | | | | | | | | | | | | | |
| AROMATICA (HM01135) | | | | | ● | | | ● | | ● | | | | | | |
| BANBURY, A E (HM01646) | | ● | | | | | | | | | | | | | | |
| BARNNETT, ANN (HM01763) | | | | | | | | | | ● | ● | ● | | | | |
| BEARE, M E (HM01968) | ● | | | | | | | | | ● | ● | ● | | | | |
| CARADON CHIROPRACTIC CLINIC (HM03656) | | | | | | | ● | | | ● | ● | ● | | | | |
| CHIROPODIST/PODIATRIST (HM04296) | ● | | | | | | | | | ● | ● | ● | | | | |
| COMP HEALTH INITIATIVE (HM04912) | | ● | ● | ● | ● | ● | | ● | ● | ● | ● | ● | | | | |
| DRAGE, STEPHEN (HM06279) | | | | | | | | | | | | | | | | |
| FEET FIRST (HM07180) | | | | | | ● | | ● | | | | | | | | |
| FOOTCARE (HM07492) | ● | | | | | | | | | ● | ● | ● | | | | |
| FORCE, GAYLE (HM07520) | | | ● | | ● | ● | | ● | | ● | ● | ● | ● | ● | ● | ● |
| HALL, PETER (HM08787) | | | ● | | | ● | | ● | | | | | | | | |
| HAWKSLAND PHYSIOTHERAPY CENTRE (HM09233) | | | | | | | | | | ● | | ● | ● | ● | ● | ● |
| LIFE 'N' LIMB (HM12346) | | | ● | ● | ● | ● | | ● | | ● | ● | ● | | | | |
| LIFE 'N' LIMB (HM12345) | | ● | ● | ● | ● | ● | | ● | ● | ● | ● | ● | | | | |
| LIFE-WORK POTENTIAL (HM12368) | | ● | ● | | | ● | | ● | | ● | | ● | | | | |
| LISKEARD CHIROPRACTIC CLINIC (HM12453) | | | | | | | ● | | | ● | ● | ● | | | | |
| LISTER NATURAL HEALTH PRACTICE (HM12461) | | ● | | ● | ● | ● | | ● | | ● | ● | ● | | | | |
| MASTERS, B (HM13273) | | ● | | | | | ● | | | ● | ● | ● | | | | |
| MORSE, EMMA (HM14239) | | | | | | | | | | ● | | | | | | |
| NEWQUAY CHIROPRACTIC CLINIC (HM14883) | | ● | | | | | | ● | | ● | | | | | | |
| OSTEOPATHIC FAMILY CENTRE (HM15465) | | ● | | | | ● | ● | | | | | | | | | |
| PENZANCE NATURAL HEALTH CENTRE (HM16006) | | | | | | | | | | ● | ● | ● | | | | |
| REEVES, J (HM17066) | ● | | | | | | | | | ● | ● | ● | | | | |
| ST AUSTELL CHIROPRACTIC CLINIC (HM19070) | | | | | | | ● | | | | | | | | | |
| TRURO CHIROPRACTIC CLINIC (HM20354) | | | | | | | ● | | | | | | | | | |
| TRURO OSTEOPATHIC PRACTICE (HM20356) | | ● | | | | | | | | ● | | | | | | |

# S - W Conditions treated at Practices/Businesses and Specialist Treatment Categories

Business by County with Reference no.

| Business | Sexually Trans. Infections | Shingles | Sinus Problems | Skin Problems | Sleep Disorders | Slimming Help | Slipped Disk | Smoking Help | Sneezing | Snoring | Spinal Injuries | Sports Injuries | Sprains |
|---|---|---|---|---|---|---|---|---|---|---|---|---|---|
| VERA BOYES ACUPUNCTURE (HM20618) | | | ● | | | | | ● | | | | ● | |
| WEATHERHOGG, D J (HM21046) | | | | | | | ● | | | | | ● | ● |
| WILLS, JONATHAN (HM21632) | | | | | | | ● | | | | | ● | ● |
| WRIGHT, CYNTHIA (HM21929) | | | | | ● | ● | | ● | | | | | |
| **COUNTY DURHAM** | | | | | | | | | | | | | |
| BALANCE HOLISTIC HEALTHCARE (HM01606) | | | | | ● | | | | | | | | |
| BODYWORK HEALTH CLUB & CLINIC (HM02639) | | | | | ● | | | | | | | | |
| CALLAGHAN, M M (HM03548) | | | | | | | | | | | | | |
| EVANS, BRUCE (DR) (HM06958) | | | | | | | ● | | | | | ● | ● |
| FIONA OTTEWELL CHRTRD PHYSIO (HM07329) | | | | | | | | | | | | ● | ● |
| FOOTPRINTS (HM07507) | | | | | | | | | | | | | |
| HIND, CAROLE (HM09824) | | | ● | | | | | | | | | ● | ● |
| HOBSON, I K (HM09864) | | | | ● | | | | | | | | ● | ● |
| NATURAL HEALING CENTRE (HM14536) | | | | | | | | | | | | | |
| NEWCASTLE/NE TRANS MEDITA CTRE (HM14856) | | | | | ● | | | ● | | | | | |
| OLD PIT PRACTICE (HM15260) | | | | | | | ● | | | | | ● | ● |
| SPOORS, L & D (HM19039) | | | | | | | ● | | | | ● | ● | ● |
| TEESDALE OSTEOPATHIC CLINIC (HM19817) | | | | | | | ● | | | | ● | ● | ● |
| TREATMENT ROOM (HM20302) | | | | | | | ● | | | | | ● | ● |
| WARWICK, ANDREA (HM20967) | | | ● | ● | ● | | | ● | | | | ● | |
| **CUMBRIA** | | | | | | | | | | | | | |
| CUMBRIA PHYSIO & SPORTS CLINIC (HM05598) | | | | | | | ● | | | | | ● | ● |
| DEERING, CHRISTINE (HM05959) | | | | | | | | | | | | | |
| EDWARDS, D E (HM06648) | | | | | | ● | | ● | | | | | |
| FOOTWORKS (HM07515) | | | | | | | | | | | | ● | |
| GARNETT, JANE (HM07897) | | | | | ● | ● | | ● | | | | | |
| HARDWICKE, MICHAEL (HM08977) | | | | | | | | | | | | | |
| HERBS AND HELPERS (HM09668) | | ● | ● | ● | ● | | | | ● | | | | |
| HYPNOTHERAPY CENTRE (HM10525) | | | | | | ● | | ● | | | | | |
| LIBRA THERAPY CENTRE (HM12328) | | | | ● | ● | | | | | | | | |
| MCWATT, LIZ (HM13624) | | | ● | ● | | | | | ● | | | | |
| PETER STREET CLINIC (HM16075) | | | | | | | | | | | | | |
| RHAM, TRICIA (HM17217) | | | ● | | ● | | ● | | | ● | ● | ● | ● |
| RUBINSTEIN, ADAM (HM17724) | | | ● | | ● | | ● | | ● | ● | | | ● |

| Business | Stammering | Stings | Stomach Problems | Stomach Ulcers | Stress | Sweating | Teeth Grinding | Tennis Elbow | Terminal Illness | Throat Problems | Thrush | Thyroid Problems | Tinnitis | Tiredness |
|---|---|---|---|---|---|---|---|---|---|---|---|---|---|---|
| VERA BOYES ACUPUNCTURE (HM20618) | | | | | | | | ● | | | | | | ● |
| WEATHERHOGG, D J (HM21046) | | | | | | | | ● | | | | | | |
| WILLS, JONATHAN (HM21632) | | | | | | | | ● | | | | | | |
| WRIGHT, CYNTHIA (HM21929) | | | | | | | | | | | | | | |
| **COUNTY DURHAM** | | | | | | | | | | | | | | |
| BALANCE HOLISTIC HEALTHCARE (HM01606) | | | | | | | | | | | | | | |
| BODYWORK HEALTH CLUB & CLINIC (HM02639) | | | | | ● | | | | | | | | | |
| CALLAGHAN, M M (HM03548) | | | | | | | | | | | | | | |
| EVANS, BRUCE (DR) (HM06958) | | | | | | | | ● | | | | | | |
| FIONA OTTEWELL CHRTRD PHYSIO (HM07329) | | | | | | | | | | | | | | |
| FOOTPRINTS (HM07507) | | | | | | | | | | | | | | |
| HIND, CAROLE (HM09824) | | | ● | | | | | | | ● | | ● | ● | ● |
| HOBSON, I K (HM09864) | | | | | | | | | | | | | | |
| NATURAL HEALING CENTRE (HM14536) | | | | | | | | | | | | | | |
| NEWCASTLE/NE TRANS MEDITA CTRE (HM14856) | | | | | ● | | | | | | | | | |
| OLD PIT PRACTICE (HM15260) | | | | | | | | ● | | | | | | |
| SPOORS, L & D (HM19039) | | | | | | | | ● | | | | | | |
| TEESDALE OSTEOPATHIC CLINIC (HM19817) | | | | | | | | ● | | | | | | |
| TREATMENT ROOM (HM20302) | | | | | | | ● | ● | | | | | | |
| WARWICK, ANDREA (HM20967) | | | | | | | | ● | ● | | ● | | ● | ● |
| **CUMBRIA** | | | | | | | | | | | | | | |
| CUMBRIA PHYSIO & SPORTS CLINIC (HM05598) | | | | | | | | ● | | | | | | |
| DEERING, CHRISTINE (HM05959) | | | | | | | | | | | | | | ● |
| EDWARDS, D E (HM06648) | | | | | ● | | | | | | | | | |
| FOOTWORKS (HM07515) | | | | | | | | | | | | | | |
| GARNETT, JANE (HM07897) | | | | | ● | | | | | | | | | |
| HARDWICKE, MICHAEL (HM08977) | | | | | | | | | | | | | | |
| HERBS AND HELPERS (HM09668) | | | ● | ● | ● | ● | | | | ● | ● | ● | ● | ● |
| HYPNOTHERAPY CENTRE (HM10525) | | | | | | | | | | | | | | |
| LIBRA THERAPY CENTRE (HM12328) | | | | | | | | | | | | | | |
| MCWATT, LIZ (HM13624) | | | ● | | | | | | | | ● | ● | ● | ● |
| PETER STREET CLINIC (HM16075) | | | | | | | | | | | | | | |
| RHAM, TRICIA (HM17217) | | | ● | | | | ● | ● | | | | | ● | |
| RUBINSTEIN, ADAM (HM17724) | ● | | ● | | | | ● | ● | | | | | | ● |

| Business | Tonsilitis | Ulcers | Vaginal Problems | Varicose Veins | Verrucas | Vertigo | Viral Infections | Vomiting | Warts | Water Retention | Whiplash | Wind | Worms | Children | Terminally Ill | Disabled | Horses | Dogs | CatS | Other Animals |
|---|---|---|---|---|---|---|---|---|---|---|---|---|---|---|---|---|---|---|---|---|
| VERA BOYES ACUPUNCTURE (HM20618) | | | | | | ● | | | | | | | | ● | ● | ● | | | | |
| WEATHERHOGG, D J (HM21046) | | | | | | | | | | | | | | ● | | | | | | |
| WILLS, JONATHAN (HM21632) | | | | | | | | | | | | | | ● | | ● | | | | |
| WRIGHT, CYNTHIA (HM21929) | | | | | | | | | | | | | | ● | ● | ● | | | | |
| **COUNTY DURHAM** | | | | | | | | | | | | | | | | | | | | |
| BALANCE HOLISTIC HEALTHCARE (HM01606) | | | ● | | | | | | | | | | | ● | ● | ● | | | | |
| BODYWORK HEALTH CLUB & CLINIC (HM02639) | | | | | | | | | | | | | | ● | ● | ● | | | | |
| CALLAGHAN, M M (HM03548) | | | | | | | | | | | | | | ● | ● | ● | | | | |
| EVANS, BRUCE (DR) (HM06958) | | | | | | | | | | | | | | | | ● | | | | |
| FIONA OTTEWELL CHRTRD PHYSIO (HM07329) | | | | | | | | | | | | | | ● | | ● | | | | |
| FOOTPRINTS (HM07507) | | | | | ● | | | | | | | | | ● | ● | ● | | | | |
| HIND, CAROLE (HM09824) | | | | | | | | | | ● | | ● | | ● | ● | ● | | | | |
| HOBSON, I K (HM09864) | | | | | ● | | | | ● | | | | | ● | ● | ● | | | | |
| NATURAL HEALING CENTRE (HM14536) | | | | | | | | | | | | | | ● | ● | | | | | |
| NEWCASTLE/NE TRANS MEDITA CTRE (HM14856) | | | | | | | | | | | | | | ● | ● | ● | | | | |
| OLD PIT PRACTICE (HM15260) | | | | | | | | | | | | | | | | ● | | | | |
| SPOORS, L & D (HM19039) | | | | | | | | | | | ● | | | ● | | ● | | | | |
| TEESDALE OSTEOPATHIC CLINIC (HM19817) | | | | | | | | | | | ● | | | ● | ● | ● | | | | |
| TREATMENT ROOM (HM20302) | | | | | | | | | | | | ● | | ● | | ● | | | | |
| WARWICK, ANDREA (HM20967) | | | | | | | | | | | | ● | ● | ● | ● | ● | | | | |
| **CUMBRIA** | | | | | | | | | | | | | | | | | | | | |
| CUMBRIA PHYSIO & SPORTS CLINIC (HM05598) | | | | | | | | | | | | | | ● | ● | ● | | | | |
| DEERING, CHRISTINE (HM05959) | | | | | | | | | | | | | | ● | ● | | | | | |
| EDWARDS, D E (HM06648) | | | | | | | | | | | | | | ● | ● | ● | | | | |
| FOOTWORKS (HM07515) | | | | | | | | | ● | | | | | ● | ● | ● | | | | |
| GARNETT, JANE (HM07897) | | | | | | | | | | | | | | ● | ● | ● | | | | |
| HARDWICKE, MICHAEL (HM08977) | | | | | | | | | | | | | | ● | ● | ● | ● | | | |
| HERBS AND HELPERS (HM09668) | ● | ● | ● | ● | | ● | ● | ● | ● | ● | | ● | | ● | ● | | | | | |
| HYPNOTHERAPY CENTRE (HM10525) | | | | | | | | | | | | | | ● | ● | ● | | | | |
| LIBRA THERAPY CENTRE (HM12328) | | | | | | | | | | | | | | ● | ● | ● | | | | |
| MCWATT, LIZ (HM13624) | | | | | | | | | | ● | | ● | | ● | ● | ● | | | | |
| PETER STREET CLINIC (HM16075) | | | | | | | | | ● | | | | | ● | ● | ● | | | | |
| RHAM, TRICIA (HM17217) | | | | | | ● | | | | | | | | ● | ● | ● | | | | |
| RUBINSTEIN, ADAM (HM17724) | | | | | | | | | | | | | | ● | ● | ● | ● | ● | ● | |

(Children, Terminally Ill, Disabled, Horses, Dogs, CatS, Other Animals: Specialist Treatment Categories)

# S - W Conditions treated at Practices/Businesses and Specialist Treatment Categories

| Business by County with Reference no. | Sexually Trans. Infections | Shingles | Sinus Problems | Skin Problems | Sleep Disorders | Slimming Help | Slipped Disk | Smoking Help | Sneezing | Snoring | Spinal Injuries | Sports Injuries | Sprains | Stammering | Stings | Stomach Problems | Stomach Ulcers | Stress | Sweating | Teeth Grinding | Tennis Elbow | Terminal Illness | Throat Problems | Thrush | Thyroid Problems | Tinnitis | Tiredness | Tonsilitis | Ulcers | Vaginal Problems | Varicose Veins | Verrucas | Vertigo | Viral Infections | Vomiting | Warts | Water Retention | Whiplash | Wind | Worms | Specialist Treatment Categories: Children | Terminally Ill | Disabled | Horses | Dogs | CatS | Other Animals |
|---|---|---|---|---|---|---|---|---|---|---|---|---|---|---|---|---|---|---|---|---|---|---|---|---|---|---|---|---|---|---|---|---|---|---|---|---|---|---|---|---|---|---|---|---|---|---|
| RUBINSTEIN, ADAM (HM17725) | | | ● | | ● | | ● | | ● | ● | | | ● | ● | | ● | | | | ● | ● | | | | | | ● | | | | | | | | | | | | | | ● | ● | ● | ● | ● | ● | |
| SIMPLY PERFECT BY JAN (HM18581) | | | | | | | | | | | | | | | | | | | | | | | | | | | | | | | | | | | | | | | | | ● | | ● | | | | |
| SINGLETON, POLLY (HM18612) | ● | ● | ● | ● | ● | ● | ● | ● | ● | ● | | ● | ● | ● | ● | ● | ● | | ● | ● | ● | ● | ● | ● | ● | ● | ● | ● | ● | ● | ● | | ● | ● | ● | ● | ● | | ● | ● | ● | ● | ● | | | | |
| STRAWBERRY HOW CLINIC (HM19378) | | ● | ● | ● | ● | | ● | | | | | ● | ● | | | | ● | | | | | | | | | | ● | ● | | | ● | | ● | | ● | | | | | | ● | ● | ● | | | | |
| SWINDALE, TESSA (HM19594) | | | | | | | | | | | | | | | | | | | | | | | | | | | | | | | | ● | | | | ● | | | | | | | | | | | |
| THERAPY CENTRE (HM19898) | | ● | ● | ● | ● | ● | ● | ● | ● | | | ● | ● | | ● | ● | ● | | | | ● | ● | ● | ● | ● | ● | ● | ● | ● | ● | ● | | ● | ● | ● | ● | ● | | | | ● | ● | ● | | | | |
| VULCANS LANE CHIROPODY (HM20720) | | | | | ● | | | | | | | | ● | | | | | | | | | | | | | | | | | | | | | | | | ● | | | | | | ● | | | | |
| WILSON, P M (HM21664) | | | | | | | | | | | | | | | | | | | | | | | | | | | | | | | | ● | | | | ● | | | | | ● | ● | ● | | | | |
| **DERBYSHIRE** | | | | | | | | | | | | | | | | | | | | | | | | | | | | | | | | | | | | | | | | | | | | | | | |
| ACUPUNCTURE CLINIC (HM00270) | | ● | ● | ● | | | | | | | | ● | | | | | | | | | | | | | | | ● | | | | | | | | ● | | | | | | | ● | ● | | | | |
| ALTER-MED (HM00690) | ● | ● | ● | ● | ● | ● | ● | ● | ● | ● | | ● | ● | ● | ● | ● | ● | | ● | ● | ● | ● | ● | ● | ● | ● | ● | ● | ● | ● | ● | | ● | ● | ● | ● | ● | | ● | ● | | | | | | | |
| AROMATHERAPY & REFLEX CTRE (HM01090) | ● | ● | ● | ● | ● | ● | ● | ● | ● | ● | | ● | ● | ● | ● | ● | ● | | ● | ● | ● | ● | ● | ● | ● | ● | ● | ● | ● | ● | ● | | ● | ● | ● | ● | ● | | ● | ● | ● | ● | ● | | | | |
| BACH FLOWER REMEDIES (HM01469) | | | | | | | | | | | | | | | | | | ● | | | | | | | | | | | | | | | | | | | | | | | ● | ● | ● | | | | |
| BANKS, LINDA (HM01665) | | | ● | | ● | | | | | | | | | | | ● | | | | | | | | | | ● | ● | | | | | | | | | | | | | | ● | ● | ● | | | | |
| BARROWCLIFFE, GRAHAM (DR) (HM01806) | | ● | ● | | | ● | ● | ● | | | | | | | | | | | | ● | | | | | | | | | | | | | ● | | | | | | | | | | | | | | |
| BELPER BACKPAIN CLINIC (HM02110) | | | ● | | | | | | | | | ● | ● | | | | | | | ● | ● | | | | | ● | | ● | | | | | | | | | ● | | | | ● | | ● | | ● | | |
| BELPER HOMEOPATHY (HM02111) | ● | ● | ● | ● | ● | ● | ● | ● | ● | ● | | ● | ● | ● | ● | ● | ● | | ● | ● | ● | ● | ● | ● | ● | ● | ● | ● | ● | ● | ● | | ● | ● | ● | ● | ● | | ● | ● | ● | ● | ● | | | | |
| BELPER NATURAL HEALTH CENTRE (HM02112) | | ● | ● | ● | ● | ● | ● | ● | ● | ● | | ● | ● | ● | ● | ● | ● | | ● | ● | ● | ● | ● | ● | ● | ● | ● | ● | ● | ● | ● | | ● | ● | ● | ● | ● | | ● | ● | ● | ● | | | | | |
| BRADSHAW, P J (HM02878) | | | | ● | | | | ● | | | | | | ● | | | | | | ● | | ● | | | | ● | ● | | | | | | | | | | | | | | | ● | | | | | |
| CARRICK-SMITH, L (HM03744) | | | | | | | | | | | | | | | | | | | | | | ● | | | | | | | | | | | | | | | | | | | | | | | | | |
| CONTOUR DESIGNS (HM05021) | | | | | ● | ● | | ● | | | | | | | | | | ● | | | | | | | | | | | | | | | | | | | | | | | ● | ● | ● | | | | |
| COVERLEY PHYSIOTHERAPY CLINIC (HM05284) | | | | | | | ● | | | | | ● | ● | | | | | | | | ● | | | | | | | | | | | | | | | | | | | | ● | ● | ● | | | | |
| DARBY, ANN (HM05735) | | | | | | | | | | | | ● | | | | | | ● | | | | | | | | | | | | | | | | | | | | | | | ● | ● | ● | | | | |
| DERBYSHIRE SPORTS INJURIES (HM06014) | | | | | | | ● | | | | | ● | ● | | | | | | | | ● | | | | | | | | | | | | | | | | | | | | ● | ● | ● | | | | |
| DRONFIELD NAT HEALTH CLINIC (HM06319) | | | | | | | | | | | | | | | | | | | | | | | | | | | | | | | | | | | | | | | | | ● | ● | ● | | | | |
| DRONFIELD PHYSIOTHERAPY CLINIC (HM06320) | | | | | | | ● | | | | | ● | ● | | | | | | | | ● | | | | | | | | | | | | | | | | | | | | ● | ● | ● | | | | |
| ENJOY SPORT (HM06836) | | | | | | | ● | | | | | ● | ● | | | | | | | | ● | | | | | | | | | | | | | | | | | | | | ● | ● | ● | | | | |
| GARRISON-TODD, WENDY (HM07905) | ● | | ● | ● | ● | ● | ● | ● | ● | | | ● | ● | ● | ● | ● | ● | | ● | ● | ● | ● | ● | ● | ● | ● | ● | ● | ● | ● | ● | | ● | ● | ● | ● | ● | | ● | ● | ● | ● | ● | | | | |
| HARDING, MANDY (HM08971) | | | | | | | | | | | | | | | | | | | | | | | | | | | | | | | | | | | | | | | | | | ● | ● | | | | |
| HATHERSAGE HEALTH & THRPY CTRE (HM09198) | | | | | ● | | | | | | | | | | | | | ● | | | | | | | | | | | | | | | | | | | | | | | ● | ● | | | | | |
| HIGGS, ANN (HM09734) | | ● | ● | ● | ● | | | | | | | ● | ● | | | ● | | | | | ● | ● | | ● | | ● | | | | ● | | | ● | | | | | | | | ● | ● | ● | | | | |
| HOUSE OF AROMATHERAPY (HM10216) | | | | ● | ● | | | | | | | | | | | | | ● | | | | | | | | | | | | | | | | | | | | | | | ● | ● | ● | | | | |
| ILKESTONE OSTEO & MED CTRE (HM10580) | | | ● | ● | | | ● | | | | ● | ● | ● | | | | | | | | | | | | | | ● | | | | | | ● | | | | | ● | | | ● | | ● | | | | |
| JOHNSON, MELVYN (HM11086) | | | | | | | ● | | | | ● | ● | ● | | | | | | | | ● | | | | | | | | | | | | | | | | | ● | | | ● | | ● | | | | |

# S - W Conditions treated at Practices/Businesses and Specialist Treatment Categories

Specialist Treatment Categories: Children, Terminally Ill, Disabled, Horses, Dogs, CatS, Other Animals

| Business by County with Reference no. | Sexually Trans. Infections | Shingles | Sinus Problems | Skin Problems | Sleep Disorders | Slimming Help | Slipped Disk | Smoking Help | Sneezing | Snoring | Spinal Injuries | Sports Injuries | Sprains | Stammering | Stings | Stomach Problems | Stomach Ulcers | Stress | Sweating | Teeth Grinding | Tennis Elbow | Terminal Illness | Throat Problems | Thrush | Thyroid Problems | Tinnitis | Tiredness | Tonsilitis | Ulcers | Vaginal Problems | Varicose Veins | Verrucas | Vertigo | Viral Infections | Vomiting | Warts | Water Retention | Whiplash | Wind | Worms | Children | Terminally Ill | Disabled | Horses | Dogs | CatS | Other Animals |
|---|---|---|---|---|---|---|---|---|---|---|---|---|---|---|---|---|---|---|---|---|---|---|---|---|---|---|---|---|---|---|---|---|---|---|---|---|---|---|---|---|---|---|---|---|---|---|---|
| KARDAHJI, F C (HM11319) | | | | | | | | | | | |●| | | | | | | | | | | | | | | | | | | |●| | | | | | | | |●|●|●| | | | |
| KEMP, G D (HM11460) | | | | | | | | | | | | | | | | | | | | | | | | | | | | | | | |●| | | | | | | | | | | | | | | |
| KEMP, GILLIAN (HM11461) | | | | | |●|●|●| | | |●|●| | | | | | | |●| | | | | | | | | | | | | | | | | | | | | | | | | | |
| LANCASHIRE, A W (HM11915) | | | | | | |●| | | |●|●|●| | | | | | | |●| | | | | | | | | | | | | | | | |●| | |●|●|●| | | | |
| LIFESOLUTIONS (HM12359) | | | | |●|●| |●| | | | | |●| | | |●| |●| | | | | | | | | | | | | | | | | | | | |●|●| | | | | |
| MATLOCK PHYSIOTHERAPY CENTRE (HM13293) |●|●|●|●|●|●|●|●|●|●| |●|●|●|●|●|●| |●|●|●|●|●|●|●|●|●|●|●|●|●| |●|●|●|●|●| |●|●|●|●|●| | | | |
| MATTHEWS, A (HM13299) | |●|●|●|●|●|●|●|●|●| |●|●|●|●|●|●| |●| |●|●|●|●|●|●|●|●|●| |●| |●|●|●|●|●| |●| |●|●| | | | | |
| MATTHEWS, AMANDA (HM13301) | |●|●|●|●|●|●|●|●|●| |●|●|●|●|●|●| |●| |●|●|●|●|●|●|●|●|●| |●| |●|●|●|●|●| |●| |●|●|●| | | | |
| NATURAL HEALTH CLINIC (HM14577) | | | | | |●|●|●| | | |●|●| | | | | | | | | | | | | | | | | | | | | | | | | | | |●|●|●| | | | |
| PHILIP STOCK - PHYSIOTHERAPIST (HM16120) | |●| | | | | | | | | |●|●| | |●| | | | |●| | | | | | | | | | | |●| | | |●|●| | |●|●|●| | | | |
| PHYSIO ACTIVE (HM16193) |●|●|●|●|●| |●| |●| | |●|●| |●|●|●| |●|●|●|●|●|●|●|●|●|●|●|●|●| |●|●|●|●|●| |●|●|●| |●| | | | |
| SMITH, ALAN P (HM18711) | | | | | | |●| | | |●|●|●| | | | | | | |●| | | | | | | | | | | | | | | | |●| | |●| |●| | | | |
| SPINK, BERNADETTE (HM19017) | |●|●|●|●| |●| | | | |●|●| | | | |●| | |●| | |●| | |●|●|●|●|●| | |●| | | | | |●|●|●|●| | | | |
| SPIRAC PHYSIOTHERAPY (HM19020) | | | | | | |●| | | | |●|●| | | | | | | |●| | | | | | | | | | | | | | | | | | | |●|●|●| | | | |
| STEVENSON, JACKIE (HM19249) |●|●|●|●|●|●|●|●|●|●| |●|●|●|●|●|●| |●|●|●|●|●|●|●|●|●|●|●|●|●| |●|●|●|●|●| |●|●|●|●| | | | | |
| SYKES, PETER W (HM19617) | | | | | | | | | | | | | | | | | | | | | | | | | | | | | | | |●| | | | | | | | |●|●|●| | | | |
| TAYLOR, E F (HM19757) | | | | | | | | | | |●|●|●| | | | | | | |●| | | | | | | | | | | | | | | | |●| | |●|●|●| | | | |
| TAYLOR, E F (HM19756) | | | | | | | | | | |●|●|●| | | | | | | |●| | | | | | | | | | | | | | | | |●| | |●|●|●| | | | |
| TREEWICKS (HM20313) | | | | |●| | | | | | | | | | | | |●| | | | | | | | | | | | | | | | | | | | | | | |●|●| | | | |
| WHITEING CHIROPODISTS (HM21392) | | | | | | | | | | | | | | | | | | | | | | | | | | | | | | | | | | | | | | | | |●|●|●| | | | |
| WHITTLE, S (HM21425) | | | | | | | | | | | | | | | | | | | | | | | | | | | | | | | |●| | | | | | | | |●|●|●| | | | |
| **DEVON** | | | | | | | | | | | | | | | | | | | | | | | | | | | | | | | | | | | | | | | | | | | | | | | |
| ABBEYMEAD NATURAL HEALTH CTRE (HM00090) | | | | | | | | | | | | | | | | | | | | | | | | | | | | | | | | | | | | | | | | |●| | | | | | |
| ACUPUNCTURE CLINIC (HM00276) |●|●|●|●|●|●|●|●|●|●| |●|●|●|●|●|●|●|●|●|●|●|●|●|●|●|●|●|●|●|●| |●|●|●|●|●| |●|●| |●|●| | | | |
| ALISON MORTON PHYSIOTHERAPY (HM00579) | | |●|●| | |●| | | | |●|●| | | | | | | |●| | | | | |●| | | | | | | | | | | | | |●| |●| | | | |
| ANNE RAWLINGS HYPNOTHERAPY (HM00901) | | | |●|●|●| |●| | | | | |●| |●|●| | |●| | | | | | |●| | | | | | | | | | | | | |●|●| | | | | |
| ARCTURUES CLINIC (HM00987) | | | | | | | | | | | | | | | | | | | | | | | | | | | | | | | | | | | | | | | | |●|●|●| | | | |
| ASSOCIATED CHIROPODY SERVICES (HM01270) | | | | | | | | | | | | | | | | | | | | | | | | | | | | | | | |●| | | | | | | | |●|●|●| | | | |
| AWARENESS CENTRE (HM01415) |●|●|●|●|●|●|●|●|●|●| |●|●|●|●|●|●| |●|●|●|●|●|●|●|●|●|●|●|●|●| |●|●|●|●|●| |●|●|●|●|●|●|●|●|●|
| BALL, ADRIAN (HM01624) | | | | | | |●| | | | |●|●| | | | | | | |●| | | | | | | | | | | | | | | | | | | | | | | | | | |
| BARRETT, J (HM01790) | | | | | | | | | | | | | | | | | | | | | | | | | | | | | | | |●| | | | | | | | |●|●|●| | | | |
| BIDEFORD CHIROPRACTIC CLINIC (HM02283) | | | | | | | | | | | | | | | | | | | | | | | | | | | | | | | | | | | | | | | | |●| | |●|●|●|●|
| BINMORE, F (HM02318) | | |●|●|●| | | | | | | | | | | | | | | | | | | | | |●| | | | | | | | | | | | | |●| |●| | | | |
| BRIXHAM HEALING HANDS CENTRE (HM03105) | | |●| | | | | | | | | | | | |●| |●| | | | | | | | |●| | | | | | | | | | | | | |●|●|●| | | | |

www.healthmyself.com

Healthmyself Directory

# S - W Conditions treated at Practices/Businesses and Specialist Treatment Categories

| Business by County with Reference no. | Sexually Trans. Infections | Shingles | Sinus Problems | Skin Problems | Sleep Disorders | Slimming Help | Slipped Disk | Smoking Help | Sneezing | Snoring | Spinal Injuries | Sports Injuries | Sprains | Stammering | Stings | Stomach Problems | Stomach Ulcers | Stress | Sweating | Teeth Grinding | Tennis Elbow | Terminal Illness | Throat Problems | Thrush | Thyroid Problems | Tinnitis | Tiredness | Tonsilitis | Ulcers | Vaginal Problems | Varicose Veins | Verrucas | Vertigo | Viral Infections | Vomiting | Warts | Water Retention | Whiplash | Wind | Worms | Children (Specialist Treatment Categories) | Terminally Ill | Disabled | Horses | Dogs | CatS | Other Animals |
|---|---|---|---|---|---|---|---|---|---|---|---|---|---|---|---|---|---|---|---|---|---|---|---|---|---|---|---|---|---|---|---|---|---|---|---|---|---|---|---|---|---|---|---|---|---|---|---|
| CARPENTER, PAUL (HM03734) | | | ● | ● | ● | | | | | | | | | | | | | | | | | | | | | | ● | | | | | | | | | | ● | | ● | | | | | | | | |
| CASTLE CHIROPRACTIC CLINIC (HM03829) | | | | | | | ● | | | | | ● | ● | | | | | | | | ● | | | | | | | | | | | | | | | | | | | | ● | ● | ● | | | | |
| CASTLEBRIDGE CHIRO & REFLEX (HM03844) | | | | | | | | | | | | | | | | | | | | | | | | | | | | | | | | ● | | | | | | | | | | | | | | | |
| CHELSTON CHIROPODY PRACTICE (HM04092) | | | ● | ● | ● | | | | | | | | | | | ● | | | | | | | | | | | ● | | | | | | | | | | | | ● | | ● | ● | ● | | | | |
| CHEMIN, CHRISTIAN (HM04098) | | | ● | | | | ● | | | | | | ● | | | | | ● | | ● | ● | | | | | ● | | | | | | | ● | | | | | ● | | | ● | | ● | | | | |
| CLINIC OF CHINESE MEDICINE (HM04687) | | | ● | ● | | | | | | | | ● | | | | | | | | | | | | | | | ● | | | | | | | | | | | | | | ● | ● | ● | | | | |
| COLLEGE OF NATURAL NUTRITION (HM04851) | | | | ● | | ● | | | | | | | | | | ● | ● | | | | | ● | | ● | ● | ● | ● | | ● | | | | | | | | | | | | ● | ● | ● | | | | |
| COPE, ANNE (HM05134) | | | ● | | | ● | ● | | | | | ● | ● | | | ● | | | | | ● | | | | | | | | | | | | | | | | ● | | | | ● | | ● | | | | |
| COX, MIRANDA (HM05316) | | | | | ● | | | ● | | | | | | ● | | | | | | ● | | ● | | | | | ● | | | | | | | | | | | | | | ● | ● | ● | | | | |
| DEL MAR, ANTONIA (HM05963) | | | | | | | | | | | | | | | | | | | | | | | | | | | | | | | | | | | | | | | | | ● | | | | | | |
| DEVONSHIRE HEALTH & RAQUET (HM06043) | | | | | | | ● | | | | | ● | ● | | | | | | | | ● | | | | | | | | | | | | | | | | | | | | ● | ● | ● | | | | |
| EAST DEVON CONSULTANCY (HM06512) | | | ● | ● | ● | | | | ● | ● | | | | | | ● | ● | | ● | ● | | | ● | ● | | ● | ● | ● | ● | | | | | | ● | | | | ● | ● | ● | ● | | | | | |
| ELDON HEALTH CLINIC (HM06705) | | | ● | ● | ● | ● | ● | ● | ● | | | ● | ● | | | ● | ● | | ● | ● | ● | | | ● | ● | | ● | ● | | ● | ● | | ● | ● | ● | | | | ● | ● | | | | | | | |
| ELLIS, SUE (HM06773) | | | ● | | | | ● | | | | | ● | ● | | | ● | | | | | ● | | | | | ● | | | | | | | ● | | | | | | | | ● | | ● | ● | ● | ● | ● |
| FOOT CLINIC & THERAPY ROOM (HM07474) | | | | ● | | | | | | | | ● | ● | | | | | | | | | | | | | | | | | | | | | | | ● | | | | | ● | ● | ● | | | | |
| FOOTEC MEDICAL (HM07500) | | | | | | | | | | | | ● | | | | | | | | | | | | | | | | | | | | ● | | | | | | | | | ● | ● | ● | | | | |
| FUDGE, H (HM07777) | | | | | | | ● | | | | | ● | ● | | | | | | | | ● | | | | | | | | | | | | | | | | | | | | ● | | ● | | | | |
| GARRETTLEY, U (HM07902) | | | ● | ● | ● | | | | | | | | | | | ● | | | | | | | | | | | ● | | | | | | | | | | | | | | ● | ● | ● | | | | |
| HEALTH CONSULTANCY (HM09382) | | ● | ● | ● | ● | | ● | | | | | | ● | | ● | ● | ● | | ● | | ● | ● | ● | ● | ● | ● | ● | ● | ● | | | | ● | ● | ● | ● | ● | | ● | ● | | ● | ● | | | | |
| HEALTH WAVES (HM09408) | | | | | | | | | | | | | | ● | | | | | | | | | | | | | | | | | | | | | | | | | | | | | | | | | |
| HUME, PETER D (HM10370) | | | | | | | | | | | | | | | | | | | | | | | | | | | | | | | | ● | | | | | | | | | ● | ● | ● | | | | |
| IRIDOLOGY/NUTRITIONAL THER (HM10723) | ● | ● | ● | ● | ● | ● | ● | ● | ● | ● | ● | ● | ● | ● | ● | ● | ● | ● | ● | ● | ● | ● | ● | ● | ● | ● | ● | ● | ● | ● | ● | ● | ● | ● | ● | ● | ● | ● | ● | ● | ● | ● | ● | | | | |
| J T SERVICES (HM10802) | | | ● | ● | | | | | | | | ● | ● | | | | | | | | ● | | | | | | ● | | | | | | | | | | | | | | ● | | ● | ● | ● | ● | ● |
| JANE HYDE CHRTRD PHYSIO (HM10917) | | | | | | | | | | | | ● | ● | | | | | | | | | | | | | | | | | | | | | | | | | | | | ● | | | ● | ● | ● | ● |
| JEFFRIES, BARBARA (HM10972) | | | | | | | | | | | | | | | | | | | | | | ● | | | | | | | | | | | | | | | | | | | | ● | | | | | |
| JOHNSON, MICHAEL (HM11087) | | ● | ● | ● | ● | ● | | ● | | | | | ● | | ● | ● | | | ● | | | | | | | ● | ● | | | | | | ● | | | ● | | | | | ● | ● | ● | | | | |
| JULIE ADAMS REFLEXOLOGIST (HM11256) | | | ● | | ● | | | | | | | ● | ● | | | ● | | | | | ● | | | ● | ● | | ● | | | | | | | | | | ● | | ● | | ● | ● | ● | | | | |
| KINGSBRIDGE COMP HLTH PRACTICE (HM11658) | ● | ● | ● | ● | ● | ● | ● | ● | ● | ● | ● | ● | ● | ● | ● | ● | ● | ● | ● | ● | ● | ● | ● | ● | ● | ● | ● | ● | ● | ● | ● | ● | ● | ● | ● | ● | ● | ● | ● | ● | ● | ● | ● | | | | |
| KINGSBRIDGE PHYSICAL THERAPY (HM11659) | | | | | | | ● | | | | | ● | ● | | | | | | | | ● | | | | | | | | | | | | | | | | | | | | | | | | | | |
| LIGHT TOUCH THERAPY TRAINING (HM12369) | | ● | ● | ● | ● | | ● | ● | | | | ● | ● | ● | ● | | ● | ● | | | | | ● | ● | ● | ● | | ● | | ● | ● | | ● | ● | ● | ● | ● | | | | ● | ● | ● | | | | |
| LINDEMAN, A J (HM12415) | ● | ● | ● | ● | ● | | | | ● | | | | | | ● | ● | ● | | ● | ● | ● | | | ● | ● | ● | ● | ● | ● | ● | ● | | ● | ● | | ● | ● | | | ● | ● | ● | ● | | | | |
| LION HOUSE SURGERY (HM12446) | | | | | | | ● | | | | ● | ● | ● | | | | | | | | | | | | | | ● | | | | | | | | | | ● | ● | | | ● | ● | ● | | | | |
| MALLARDO, RENEE (HM12977) | | | | | | ● | | ● | | | | | | ● | | ● | | | ● | | | | | | | ● | ● | | | | | | | | | | | | | | ● | ● | ● | | ● | ● | |
| MASON, MARCUS (HM13248) | | ● | ● | ● | ● | | | | ● | | | | | | | ● | | | ● | ● | ● | | ● | | | ● | ● | ● | ● | ● | | | ● | | ● | | ● | | ● | | | | | | | | |

# S - W Conditions treated at Practices/Businesses and Specialist Treatment Categories

Business by County with Reference no.

| Business | Sexually Trans. Infections | Shingles | Sinus Problems | Skin Problems | Sleep Disorders | Slimming Help | Slipped Disk | Smoking Help | Sneezing | Snoring | Spinal Injuries | Sports Injuries | Sprains | Stammering | Stings | Stomach Problems | Stomach Ulcers | Stress | Sweating | Teeth Grinding | Tennis Elbow | Terminal Illness |
|---|---|---|---|---|---|---|---|---|---|---|---|---|---|---|---|---|---|---|---|---|---|---|
| MASSAGE RELAXING THERAPEUTIC (HM13262) | | | | | | ● | | | | | | ● | ● | | | | | ● | | | | |
| MONSHIN, DEBORAH J (HM14075) | | | | ● | | ● | | ● | | | | ● | | ● | | ● | ● | | ● | ● | | |
| NELSON, PAUL (HM14781) | ● | ● | ● | ● | ● | ● | | | ● | ● | | | ● | | ● | ● | ● | | | | ● | ● |
| NETHERWAY, JEAN (HM14789) | | | ● | | ● | | | | | | | ● | ● | | | ● | ● | ● | | | ● | |
| PAIGNTON PHYSIOTHERAPY (HM15576) | | | | | | | ● | | | | | ● | ● | | | | | | | | ● | |
| PANNELL, R J (HM15636) | | | | | | | ● | | | | | ● | ● | | | | | | | | | |
| PLAYERS, MEGAN (HM16365) | ● | | ● | ● | ● | ● | ● | ● | ● | ● | | ● | ● | ● | ● | ● | ● | | ● | ● | ● | |
| PLYMOUTH OSTEOPATHS (HM16388) | | | | | | | ● | | | | | ● | ● | | | | | | | | ● | |
| REFLEXOLOGY CENTRE (HM17083) | | | ● | | | | | | | | | | | | | | | | | | | |
| RENDLE, S (HM17182) | | | | | | | | | | | | | | | | | | | | | | |
| RIVERSIDE CHIROPRACTIC CLINIC (HM17379) | | | | | | | ● | | | | | ● | ● | | | | | | | | ● | |
| ROSE & CROWN CLINIC (HM17598) | ● | ● | ● | ● | ● | ● | ● | ● | ● | ● | | ● | ● | ● | ● | ● | ● | ● | ● | ● | ● | ● |
| SANDERS, RACHEL (HM17916) | | | | | | | | | | | | | | | | | | | | | | |
| SCURR, PETER M (HM18160) | | | | ● | | | | | | | | | | | | | | | | | | |
| SEELEY, JANICE (HM18194) | ● | ● | ● | ● | ● | | | ● | ● | | | | | | ● | ● | ● | | ● | ● | ● | |
| SERENITY (HM18233) | ● | ● | ● | ● | ● | ● | ● | ● | ● | ● | | ● | ● | ● | ● | ● | ● | | ● | ● | ● | ● |
| STIMULUS FOR CHANGE (HM19296) | | | | ● | ● | ● | | | ● | | | | | | ● | ● | ● | | ● | | | |
| TRANCE - FORMATIONS HEALING (HM20250) | | | | ● | ● | ● | | ● | | ● | | | | ● | | ● | | | | ● | | ● |
| VITAL TOUCH (HM20703) | | | ● | | | | | | | | | ● | | | | | | | | | ● | |
| WALTERS, RICHARD (HM20880) | | | ● | ● | | | | | | | | | | | | | | | | | | |
| WALTERS, RICHARD (HM20882) | | | ● | ● | | | ● | | | | | ● | ● | | | | | | | | ● | |
| WILKINSON, MARY (HM21512) | | | ● | | | | ● | | | | | ● | | | | | | | | | ● | |
| WILLIAMS CLINIC (HM21531) | | | ● | ● | ● | | ● | | | | | | | | | | | | | | | |
| WILLSHER, ERNEST R (HM21633) | | | | | | | | | | | | | | | | | | | | | | |
| YOGA HEALTH STUDIO (HM22028) | | | | | | | | | | | | | | | | | | ● | | | | |
| YORK HOUSE CHIROPODY (HM22044) | | | | | | | | | | | | | | | | | | | | | | |
| YORK HOUSE CHIROPRACTIC CLINIC (HM22045) | | | | | | | | | | | | ● | | | | | | | | | | |
| **DORSET** | | | | | | | | | | | | | | | | | | | | | | |
| ABBEY VIEW COMP CLINIC (HM00088) | ● | ● | ● | ● | ● | ● | ● | ● | ● | ● | ● | ● | ● | ● | ● | ● | ● | | ● | ● | ● | ● |
| ALTERNATIVE APPROACH (HM00694) | | | | | | | | | | | ● | ● | ● | | | | | | | | | |
| ARCHIBALD, LIZ (HM00980) | | | | | | ● | | ● | | | | | | | | | | | | | | |
| ARNDALE CHIROPRACTIC (HM01031) | | | | | | | ● | | | | ● | ● | ● | | | | | | | | | |
| AROMA TRANQUILITY (HM01064) | | | ● | ● | | | | | | | | | | | | | | ● | | | | |
| ART OF REFLEXOLOGY (HM01154) | | | ● | | | | | | | | | | | | | | | | | | | |

| Business | Throat Problems | Thrush | Thyroid Problems | Tinnitis | Tiredness | Tonsilitis | Ulcers | Vaginal Problems | Varicose Veins | Verrucas | Vertigo | Viral Infections | Vomiting | Warts | Water Retention | Whiplash | Wind | Worms | Children | Terminally Ill | Disabled | Horses | Dogs | CatS | Other Animals |
|---|---|---|---|---|---|---|---|---|---|---|---|---|---|---|---|---|---|---|---|---|---|---|---|---|---|
| MASSAGE RELAXING THERAPEUTIC (HM13262) | | | | | | | | | | | | | | | | | | | | | | | | | |
| MONSHIN, DEBORAH J (HM14075) | | | | | ● | | | | | | ● | | | | | | | | ● | ● | ● | | | | |
| NELSON, PAUL (HM14781) | ● | ● | ● | | ● | ● | ● | ● | ● | | ● | ● | ● | | | | ● | ● | ● | ● | ● | | | | |
| NETHERWAY, JEAN (HM14789) | | | | ● | ● | | | | | | | | | | | ● | | | ● | ● | ● | | | | |
| PAIGNTON PHYSIOTHERAPY (HM15576) | | | | | | | | | | | | | | | | | | | ● | ● | ● | | | | |
| PANNELL, R J (HM15636) | | | | | ● | | | | | | | | | | | | | | ● | ● | ● | | | | |
| PLAYERS, MEGAN (HM16365) | ● | ● | ● | ● | ● | ● | ● | ● | ● | | ● | ● | ● | ● | ● | | ● | ● | ● | ● | ● | | | | |
| PLYMOUTH OSTEOPATHS (HM16388) | | | | | | | | | | | | | | | | | | | | | | | | | |
| REFLEXOLOGY CENTRE (HM17083) | | | | | | | | | | | | | | | | | ● | | | | | | | | |
| RENDLE, S (HM17182) | | | | | | | | | | ● | | | | | | | | | ● | ● | ● | | | | |
| RIVERSIDE CHIROPRACTIC CLINIC (HM17379) | | | | ● | | | | | | | ● | | | | | | | | ● | ● | ● | | | | |
| ROSE & CROWN CLINIC (HM17598) | ● | ● | ● | ● | ● | ● | ● | ● | ● | | ● | ● | ● | ● | ● | | ● | ● | ● | ● | ● | | | | |
| SANDERS, RACHEL (HM17916) | | | | | | | | | | ● | | | | | | | | | ● | ● | ● | | | | |
| SCURR, PETER M (HM18160) | | | | | | | ● | | | ● | | | | ● | | | | | ● | ● | ● | | | | |
| SEELEY, JANICE (HM18194) | ● | ● | ● | ● | ● | ● | ● | ● | | | ● | ● | ● | ● | ● | | ● | ● | ● | | ● | | | | |
| SERENITY (HM18233) | ● | ● | ● | ● | ● | ● | ● | ● | ● | | ● | ● | ● | ● | ● | | ● | ● | ● | ● | ● | | | | |
| STIMULUS FOR CHANGE (HM19296) | ● | ● | | | ● | ● | | ● | | | | ● | ● | ● | | | ● | | ● | | | | | | |
| TRANCE - FORMATIONS HEALING (HM20250) | | | | ● | ● | | | ● | | | | | | | | | | | ● | ● | ● | ● | ● | ● | ● |
| VITAL TOUCH (HM20703) | | | | | | | | | ● | | | | | ● | | | | | ● | ● | ● | | | | |
| WALTERS, RICHARD (HM20880) | | | | | | | | | | | | | | | | | | | ● | ● | ● | | | | |
| WALTERS, RICHARD (HM20882) | | | | | ● | | | | | | | | | | | | | | | | | | | | |
| WILKINSON, MARY (HM21512) | | | | | | | | | | | | | | | | | | | ● | | ● | ● | ● | ● | ● |
| WILLIAMS CLINIC (HM21531) | | | | | ● | | | | | | | | ● | | | | | | | | | | | | |
| WILLSHER, ERNEST R (HM21633) | | | | | | | | | | ● | | | | | | | | | ● | ● | ● | | | | |
| YOGA HEALTH STUDIO (HM22028) | | | | | | | | | | | | | | | | | | | | ● | ● | | | | |
| YORK HOUSE CHIROPODY (HM22044) | | | | | | | | | | ● | | | | | | | | | ● | ● | ● | | | | |
| YORK HOUSE CHIROPRACTIC CLINIC (HM22045) | | | | | | | | | | | | | | | | | | | ● | ● | ● | | | | |
| **DORSET** | | | | | | | | | | | | | | | | | | | | | | | | | |
| ABBEY VIEW COMP CLINIC (HM00088) | ● | ● | ● | ● | ● | ● | ● | ● | ● | | ● | ● | ● | ● | ● | ● | ● | ● | ● | ● | ● | | | | |
| ALTERNATIVE APPROACH (HM00694) | | | | | | | | | | | | | | | | ● | | | ● | ● | ● | | | | |
| ARCHIBALD, LIZ (HM00980) | | | | | | | | | | | | | | | | | | | ● | | | | | | |
| ARNDALE CHIROPRACTIC (HM01031) | | | | | | | | | | | | | | | | ● | | | ● | ● | ● | | | | |
| AROMA TRANQUILITY (HM01064) | | | | | | | | | | | | | | | | | | | ● | ● | | | | | |
| ART OF REFLEXOLOGY (HM01154) | | | | | | | | | | | | | | | | | | | ● | ● | ● | | | | |

The last seven columns (Children to Other Animals) are headed "Specialist Treatment Categories".

# S - W Conditions treated at Practices/Businesses and Specialist Treatment Categories

| Business by County with Reference no. | | | | | | | | | | | | | | | | | | | | | | | | | | | | | | | | | | | | | | | | | Specialist Treatment Categories | | | | | | |
|---|---|---|---|---|---|---|---|---|---|---|---|---|---|---|---|---|---|---|---|---|---|---|---|---|---|---|---|---|---|---|---|---|---|---|---|---|---|---|---|---|---|---|---|---|---|---|
| | Sexually Trans. Infections | Shingles | Sinus Problems | Skin Problems | Sleep Disorders | Slimming Help | Slipped Disk | Smoking Help | Sneezing | Snoring | Spinal Injuries | Sports Injuries | Sprains | Stammering | Stings | Stomach Problems | Stomach Ulcers | Stress | Sweating | Teeth Grinding | Tennis Elbow | Terminal Illness | Throat Problems | Thrush | Thyroid Problems | Tinnitis | Tiredness | Tonsilitis | Ulcers | Vaginal Problems | Varicose Veins | Verrucas | Vertigo | Viral Infections | Vomiting | Warts | Water Retention | Whiplash | Wind | Worms | Children | Terminally Ill | Disabled | Horses | Dogs | CatS | Other Animals |
| AWDRY, ROBERT (HM01416) | | ● | ● | ● | ● | ● | | | ● | ● | | ● | ● | | ● | ● | ● | | | | ● | | ● | ● | ● | | ● | ● | ● | ● | ● | | ● | ● | ● | ● | | | ● | | ● | ● | ● | | | | |
| BACK IN BALANCE (HM01479) | | | | | | | ● | | | | ● | ● | ● | | | | | | | | ● | | | | | | | | | | | | | | | | | ● | | | ● | ● | ● | | | | |
| BACK IN FORM (HM01480) | | | | | | | | | | | ● | ● | ● | | | | | | | | ● | | | | | | | | | | | | | | | | | ● | | | ● | ● | ● | | | | |
| BELTAIN CENTRE (HM02117) | | | | ● | | ● | | ● | | | | | | | | | | | | | | | | | | | | | | | | | | | | | | | | | ● | ● | ● | | | | |
| BELTAIN CENTRE (HM02116) | | | | | | | | | | | | ● | | | | | | | | | | ● | | | | ● | ● | | | | | | | | | | | | | | ● | ● | ● | | | ● | ● |
| BOURNEMOUTH CTRE FOR COMP MED (HM02761) | | ● | ● | ● | ● | ● | ● | ● | ● | ● | | ● | ● | ● | ● | ● | ● | | ● | ● | ● | ● | ● | ● | ● | ● | ● | ● | ● | ● | ● | | ● | ● | ● | ● | ● | | ● | ● | ● | ● | ● | | | | |
| BOURNEMOUTH PHYSIO CLINIC (HM02762) | | | | | | | ● | | | | | ● | ● | | | | | | | | ● | | | | | | | | | | | | | | | | | | | | ● | ● | ● | | | | |
| BOWEN CLINIC (HM02771) | | | ● | ● | ● | | ● | | | | | ● | ● | | | ● | ● | | | | ● | | ● | | | ● | ● | | ● | | | | | | | | | | | | ● | ● | ● | | | | |
| BOWOOD HEALTH & BEAUTY CENTRE (HM02804) | | | | | | | | | | | | | | | | | | ● | | | | | | | | | | | | | | | | | | | | | | | | | | | | | |
| BRANDON, DAVE (HM02912) | ● | ● | ● | ● | ● | ● | ● | ● | ● | ● | | ● | ● | ● | ● | ● | ● | | ● | ● | ● | ● | ● | ● | ● | ● | ● | ● | ● | ● | ● | | ● | ● | ● | ● | ● | | ● | ● | ● | ● | ● | | | | |
| BRIDPORT COMP MEDICINE CTRE (HM03019) | ● | ● | ● | ● | ● | ● | ● | | | | ● | | | | | | | | | | | | | | | | | | | | | | | | | | | ● | | | ● | ● | ● | | | | |
| BRIGHTER FUTURE (HM03040) | | | | | | | | | | | | | | | | | | | | | | | | | | | | | | | | | | | | | | | | | ● | ● | ● | | | | |
| BRIGHTER FUTURE (HM03039) | | | | | | | | | | | | | | | | | | | | | | | | | | | | | | | | | | | | | | | | | ● | ● | ● | | | | |
| BROADSTONE CENTRE COMP MED (HM03117) | | ● | ● | ● | ● | ● | ● | ● | ● | ● | | ● | ● | ● | | ● | ● | | ● | ● | ● | ● | ● | ● | ● | ● | ● | | ● | ● | | | ● | ● | | | ● | | ● | | ● | ● | ● | | | | |
| BROADSTONE CENTRE OF COMP MED (HM03118) | ● | ● | ● | ● | ● | ● | ● | ● | ● | ● | ● | ● | ● | ● | ● | ● | ● | | ● | ● | ● | ● | ● | ● | ● | ● | ● | ● | ● | ● | ● | | ● | ● | ● | ● | ● | ● | ● | ● | ● | ● | ● | | | | |
| BROWN, A D (HM03208) | | | | | | | | | | | | | | | | | | | | | | | | | | | | | | | | | | | | ● | | | | | ● | ● | ● | | | | |
| BURT, S (HM03429) | ● | ● | ● | ● | ● | ● | | | ● | ● | | | | | | ● | ● | | | | | | ● | ● | ● | ● | ● | ● | ● | ● | ● | | ● | ● | ● | ● | ● | | ● | ● | ● | | | | | | |
| BWT PODIATRY (HM03508) | | | | | | | | | | | | | | | | | | | | | | | | | | | | | ● | | | | | | | | | | | | ● | | ● | | | | |
| CARBERY PRACTICE (HM03657) | | | | | | | ● | | | | | ● | ● | | | | | | | | ● | | | | | | ● | | | | | | | | | | | | | | ● | | ● | | | | |
| CHARMINSTER CHIRO CLINIC (HM04036) | | | | | | | ● | | | | ● | ● | ● | | | | | | | | ● | | | | | | | | | | | | | | | | | ● | | | | ● | ● | | | | |
| CHINESE MEDICINE CENTRE (HM04254) | | | | | ● | | | | | | | | | | | | | | | | | | | | | | | | | | | | | | | | | | | | ● | | ● | | | | |
| CHINESE MEDICINE CLINIC (HM04258) | | | | ● | ● | | | | | | | ● | | | | | | | | | | | | | | | | | | | | | | | | | | | | | | | | | | | |
| CHIROPODY SERVICES (HM04338) | | | | | | | | | | | | | | | | | | | | | | | | | | | | | | | | | | | | ● | | | | | ● | ● | ● | | | | |
| CHIROPRACTIC TREATMENT CENTRE (HM04403) | | | | | | | ● | | | | ● | ● | ● | | | | | | | | ● | | | | | | | | | | | | | | | | | ● | | | ● | ● | ● | | | | |
| CHRISTCHURCH CHIROPRACTIC CTRE (HM04435) | | | | | | | ● | | | | | ● | | | | ● | | | | ● | | | | | | | ● | | | | | | | | | | | | | | ● | | ● | | | | |
| CHRISTCHURCH PHYSIO PRACTICE (HM04436) | | | | | | | ● | | | | | ● | ● | | | | | | | | ● | | | | | | | | | | | | | | | | | | | | ● | | ● | | | | |
| CLARK, LYNN (HM04568) | | | | | | | | | | | | | | | | | | | | | | | | | | | | | | | | | | | | ● | | | | | ● | ● | ● | | | | |
| COLLINWOOD, LOUIS (HM04884) | | | ● | ● | ● | | ● | | | | ● | ● | ● | | | ● | | | | | ● | | | | ● | | | | | | | | ● | | ● | | | ● | | | ● | ● | ● | | | | |
| COMMUNITY CHIROPRACTIC CLINIC (HM04906) | | | | | | | | | | | | ● | ● | | | | | | | | | | | | | | | | | | | | | | | | | | | | ● | ● | ● | | | | |
| DLP HYPNOTHERAPY CENTRE (HM06134) | | | | | ● | ● | | ● | | | | | | ● | ● | | | ● | | ● | | | | | | | | | | | | | | | | | | | | | ● | ● | ● | | | | |
| DORSET RACQUETS & HEALTH CLUB (HM06205) | | | | | | | | | | | | | | | | | | ● | | | | | | | | | | | | | | | | | | | | | | | | | | | | | |
| EVANS, REBECCA MARY (HM06988) | | | | | | | | | | | | ● | ● | | | | | | | | ● | | | | | | | | | | | | | | | | | | | | | | | | | | |
| FEET FIRST (HM07171) | | | | | | | | | | | | | | | | | | | | | | | | | | | | | | | | | | | | ● | | | | | ● | ● | ● | | | | |
| FERNDOWN CHIROPRACTIC CLINIC (HM07239) | | | | | | | | | | | ● | | | | | | | | | | | | | | | | | | | | | | | | | | | ● | | | ● | ● | ● | | | | |

# S - W Conditions treated at Practices/Businesses and Specialist Treatment Categories

| Business by County with Reference no. | Sexually Trans. Infections | Shingles | Sinus Problems | Skin Problems | Sleep Disorders | Slimming Help | Slipped Disk | Smoking Help | Sneezing | Snoring | Spinal Injuries | Sports Injuries | Sprains | Stammering | Stings | Stomach Problems | Stomach Ulcers | Stress | Sweating | Teeth Grinding | Tennis Elbow | Terminal Illness | Throat Problems | Thrush |
|---|---|---|---|---|---|---|---|---|---|---|---|---|---|---|---|---|---|---|---|---|---|---|---|---|
| FREESPIRIT (HM07724) | | | | ● | | | | | | | | ● | ● | | ● | ● | ● | | | | | ● | | |
| FULL SPECTRUM THERAPY CENTRE (HM07786) | ● | ● | ● | ● | ● | ● | ● | ● | ● | ● | | ● | ● | ● | ● | ● | ● | | ● | ● | ● | ● | ● | ● |
| GLENCAIRE CLINIC (HM08145) | | | | | | | | | | | ● | ● | ● | | | | | | | | ● | | | |
| GODFREY, BRIAN (HM08184) | | | | | | | | ● | | ● | | | | | | | | | | ● | | ● | | |
| HAMPTON, ANNE (HM08886) | | | | | | | | | | | | | | | | | | | | | | | | |
| HARLING, MARIANNE (DR) (HM09010) | ● | ● | ● | ● | ● | ● | | ● | ● | ● | ● | ● | ● | ● | ● | ● | ● | ● | ● | ● | ● | ● | ● | ● |
| HIGHCLIFFE CHIROPRACTIC CLINIC (HM09749) | | | | | | | ● | | | | | ● | ● | | | | | | | ● | ● | | | |
| HIGHCLIFFE CHIROPRACTIC CLINIC (HM09748) | | | | | | | ● | | | | ● | ● | ● | | | | | | | | ● | | | |
| HOLISTIC HEALTH CENTRE (HM09973) | | ● | ● | ● | ● | ● | ● | ● | ● | ● | | ● | ● | ● | ● | ● | ● | | ● | | ● | | ● | ● |
| HOMEOPATHY HEALS (HM10081) | ● | ● | ● | ● | ● | ● | ● | ● | ● | ● | | ● | ● | ● | ● | ● | ● | | ● | ● | ● | ● | ● | ● |
| HOPKINS, H G (HM10149) | | | | | | | ● | | | | ● | ● | ● | | | | | | | | ● | | | |
| HORNE, SUE (HM10175) | | ● | | | | | | | | | | | | | | | | | | | ● | | | |
| JACKSON, A E (HM10817) | ● | ● | ● | ● | ● | ● | ● | ● | ● | ● | | ● | ● | ● | ● | ● | ● | | ● | ● | ● | ● | ● | ● |
| KENNEDY, EDWARD (HM11491) | | | | | | | ● | | | | ● | ● | ● | | | | | | | | ● | | | |
| LEVER, I J (HM12261) | | | | | | | ● | | | | ● | ● | ● | | | | | | | | ● | | | |
| LOCK, ROBERT (HM12538) | | ● | | ● | ● | ● | ● | ● | | | | | | ● | | ● | ● | | ● | | | | | |
| MOTCOMBE PARK PHYSIOTHERAPY (HM14273) | | | | | | | ● | | | | | ● | ● | | | | | | | | ● | | | |
| NATURAL HEALTH CONSULTANCY (HM14592) | ● | ● | ● | ● | ● | ● | ● | ● | ● | ● | | ● | ● | ● | ● | ● | ● | | ● | ● | ● | ● | ● | ● |
| NEIJIA (HM14759) | | ● | ● | ● | ● | ● | ● | ● | ● | ● | | ● | ● | ● | ● | ● | ● | | ● | ● | ● | ● | ● | |
| PARTNERSHIP, BAKER (DR) (HM15764) | | | | | | | | | | | | | | | | | | ● | | | | | | |
| PHYSIO, MASSAGE & PR ACU (HM16210) | | ● | ● | | | | ● | | | | | ● | ● | | | | | | | | ● | ● | | |
| PRIDEAUX-BRUNE, COLETTE (HM16604) | ● | ● | ● | ● | ● | ● | ● | ● | ● | ● | | ● | ● | ● | ● | ● | ● | | ● | ● | ● | ● | ● | ● |
| PRIDMORE, JOSEPHINE (HM16605) | | ● | ● | ● | ● | ● | ● | ● | ● | ● | | ● | ● | ● | | ● | ● | | ● | ● | ● | ● | ● | ● |
| PROSPECT HEALTH (HM16667) | | | | | ● | | | ● | | | | ● | ● | | | | | | | | | | | |
| ROBSON, VANESSA (HM17514) | | | | | | | | | | | | | | | | | | | | | | | | |
| ROLLS MILL COMP HEALTH CENTRE (HM17567) | | ● | | | | | ● | | | | | ● | ● | | | | | | | | ● | | | |
| ROWE, PENNY (HM17689) | ● | ● | ● | ● | ● | ● | ● | ● | ● | ● | | ● | ● | ● | ● | ● | ● | | ● | ● | ● | ● | ● | ● |
| ROY, COLLEEN (HM17710) | ● | ● | ● | ● | ● | ● | ● | ● | ● | ● | | ● | ● | ● | ● | ● | ● | | ● | ● | ● | ● | ● | ● |
| SHEBORNE CHIROPRACTIC CENTRE (HM18361) | | | | | | | ● | | | | | ● | ● | | | | | | | | ● | | | |
| SKELTON, JAN (HM18635) | | | ● | | | | | | | | | | | | | | | | | | | | | |
| SOUTHBOURNE HERBAL CLINIC (HM18924) | ● | ● | ● | ● | | | | | ● | | | ● | ● | | | ● | | | | ● | ● | | ● | ● |
| SOUTHBOURNE NATURAL HLTH CTRE (HM18925) | ● | ● | ● | ● | ● | ● | ● | ● | ● | ● | | ● | ● | ● | ● | ● | ● | | ● | ● | ● | ● | ● | ● |
| STANDISH-HAYES, QUENTIN (HM19125) | | | | | | | ● | | | | ● | ● | ● | | | | | | | | ● | | | |
| STEELE, T M (HM19183) | | | | | | | ● | | | | | ● | ● | | | | | | | | ● | | | |

| Business by County with Reference no. | Thyroid Problems | Tinnitis | Tiredness | Tonsilitis | Ulcers | Vaginal Problems | Varicose Veins | Verrucas | Vertigo | Viral Infections | Vomiting | Warts | Water Retention | Whiplash | Wind | Worms | Children (Specialist Treatment Categories) | Terminally Ill | Disabled | Horses | Dogs | CatS | Other Animals |
|---|---|---|---|---|---|---|---|---|---|---|---|---|---|---|---|---|---|---|---|---|---|---|---|
| FREESPIRIT (HM07724) | ● | ● | ● | | ● | | | | | | | | | | | | ● | ● | ● | | | | |
| FULL SPECTRUM THERAPY CENTRE (HM07786) | ● | ● | ● | ● | ● | ● | ● | | ● | ● | ● | ● | ● | | ● | ● | ● | ● | ● | | | | |
| GLENCAIRE CLINIC (HM08145) | | | | | | | | | | | | | | ● | | | ● | | ● | | | | |
| GODFREY, BRIAN (HM08184) | | ● | | | | | | | | | | | | | | | ● | ● | ● | | | | |
| HAMPTON, ANNE (HM08886) | | | | | | | | | | | | ● | | | | | ● | ● | ● | | | | |
| HARLING, MARIANNE (DR) (HM09010) | ● | ● | ● | ● | ● | ● | ● | ● | ● | ● | ● | ● | ● | ● | ● | ● | ● | | ● | | | | |
| HIGHCLIFFE CHIROPRACTIC CLINIC (HM09749) | | | | | | | | | | | | | | | | | ● | | ● | | | | |
| HIGHCLIFFE CHIROPRACTIC CLINIC (HM09748) | | | | | | | | | | | | | | ● | | | ● | ● | ● | | | | |
| HOLISTIC HEALTH CENTRE (HM09973) | ● | ● | ● | ● | ● | ● | ● | | ● | ● | ● | ● | ● | | ● | ● | ● | | ● | | ● | | |
| HOMEOPATHY HEALS (HM10081) | ● | ● | ● | ● | ● | ● | ● | | ● | ● | ● | ● | ● | | ● | ● | ● | ● | ● | | | | |
| HOPKINS, H G (HM10149) | | | | | | | | | | | | | | ● | | | ● | ● | ● | | | | |
| HORNE, SUE (HM10175) | | | ● | | | | | | | | | | | | | | | | | | | | |
| JACKSON, A E (HM10817) | ● | ● | ● | ● | ● | ● | ● | | ● | ● | ● | ● | ● | | ● | ● | ● | ● | ● | ● | ● | ● | ● |
| KENNEDY, EDWARD (HM11491) | | | | | | | | | | | | | | ● | | | | | ● | | | | |
| LEVER, I J (HM12261) | | | | | | | | | | | | | | ● | | | ● | | | | | | |
| LOCK, ROBERT (HM12538) | | | ● | | | | | | ● | | ● | | | | ● | | | ● | ● | | | | |
| MOTCOMBE PARK PHYSIOTHERAPY (HM14273) | | | | | | | | | | | | | | | | | ● | ● | ● | | | | |
| NATURAL HEALTH CONSULTANCY (HM14592) | ● | ● | ● | ● | ● | ● | ● | | ● | ● | ● | ● | ● | ● | ● | ● | ● | ● | ● | | | | |
| NEIJIA (HM14759) | ● | ● | ● | ● | ● | ● | ● | | ● | ● | ● | | ● | | ● | | ● | ● | ● | | | | |
| PARTNERSHIP, BAKER (DR) (HM15764) | | | | | | | | | | | | | | | | | | | | | | | |
| PHYSIO, MASSAGE & PR ACU (HM16210) | | ● | ● | | ● | | ● | | ● | | | | | | | | ● | | ● | | | | |
| PRIDEAUX-BRUNE, COLETTE (HM16604) | ● | ● | ● | ● | ● | ● | ● | | ● | ● | ● | ● | ● | | ● | ● | ● | ● | ● | | | | |
| PRIDMORE, JOSEPHINE (HM16605) | ● | ● | ● | | ● | ● | | | ● | ● | | | ● | | ● | | ● | ● | ● | | | | |
| PROSPECT HEALTH (HM16667) | | | ● | | | | | | | | | | | | | | ● | ● | ● | | | | |
| ROBSON, VANESSA (HM17514) | | | | | | | | ● | | | | ● | | | | | ● | ● | ● | | | | |
| ROLLS MILL COMP HEALTH CENTRE (HM17567) | | | | | | | | | | | | | | | | ● | ● | ● | ● | | | | |
| ROWE, PENNY (HM17689) | ● | ● | ● | ● | ● | ● | ● | | ● | ● | ● | ● | ● | | ● | ● | ● | ● | ● | | | | |
| ROY, COLLEEN (HM17710) | ● | ● | ● | ● | ● | ● | ● | | ● | ● | ● | ● | ● | | ● | ● | ● | ● | ● | | | | |
| SHEBORNE CHIROPRACTIC CENTRE (HM18361) | | ● | | | | | | | ● | | | | | | ● | | ● | ● | ● | | | | |
| SKELTON, JAN (HM18635) | | | | | | | | | | | | | | | | | ● | | ● | | | | |
| SOUTHBOURNE HERBAL CLINIC (HM18924) | ● | | ● | ● | ● | ● | ● | | ● | ● | ● | ● | ● | | ● | ● | ● | | | | | | |
| SOUTHBOURNE NATURAL HLTH CTRE (HM18925) | ● | ● | ● | ● | ● | ● | ● | | ● | ● | ● | ● | ● | | ● | ● | | | | | | | |
| STANDISH-HAYES, QUENTIN (HM19125) | | | | | | | | | | | | | | ● | | | ● | ● | ● | | | | |
| STEELE, T M (HM19183) | | | | | | | | | | | | | | ● | | | ● | | | | | | |

# S - W Conditions treated at Practices/Businesses and Specialist Treatment Categories

Business by County with Reference no.

| Business by County with Reference no. | Sexually Trans. Infections | Shingles | Sinus Problems | Skin Problems | Sleep Disorders | Slimming Help | Slipped Disk | Smoking Help | Sneezing | Snoring | Spinal Injuries | Sports Injuries | Sprains | Stammering | Stings | Stomach Problems | Stomach Ulcers | Stress | Sweating | Teeth Grinding | Tennis Elbow | Terminal Illness | Throat Problems | Thrush | Thyroid Problems | Tinnitis | Tiredness | Tonsilitis | Ulcers | Vaginal Problems | Varicose Veins | Verrucas | Vertigo | Viral Infections | Vomiting | Warts | Water Retention | Whiplash | Wind | Worms | Specialist Treatment Categories: Children | Terminally Ill | Disabled | Horses | Dogs | CatS | Other Animals |
|---|---|---|---|---|---|---|---|---|---|---|---|---|---|---|---|---|---|---|---|---|---|---|---|---|---|---|---|---|---|---|---|---|---|---|---|---|---|---|---|---|---|---|---|---|---|---|---|
| THORNTONS PHARMACY (HM20029) |●|●|●|●|●|●|●|●|●|●| |●|●|●|●|●|●| |●|●|●|●|●|●|●|●|●|●|●|●|●| |●|●|●|●|●| |●|●|●|●|●| | | | |
| TREAT FEET (HM20301) | | | | | | | | | | | |●| | | | | | | | | | | | | | | | | | | | | | | | | | | | |●|●|●| | | | |
| TRUNDELL, C (HM20353) | | | | | | | | | | | | | | | | | | | | | | | | | | | | | | | | | | | | | | | | |●|●|●| | | | |
| WALTERS, RICHARD (HM20881) | | |●|●| | |●| | | | |●|●| | | | | | | |●| | | | | | |●| | | | | | | | | | | | |●|●|●| | | | |
| WESSEX HEALTHY LIVING FOUND (HM21208) | |●|●|●|●|●| | |●| | | |●| | |●| |●| | |●| | |●| | |●| | | | | | | | |●|●| |●|●|●|●|●| | | | |
| WEST MOORS CHIROPRACTIC CLINIC (HM21230) | | | | | | |●| | | | |●|●| | | | | | | |●| | | | | | | | | | | | | | | | |●| | |●|●|●| | | | |
| WHITE FLOWER CENTRE (HM21337) | | | | | | | | | | | | | | | | | | | | | | | | | | | | | | | | | | | | | | | |●|●|●| | | | |
| WIMBORNE CHIROPODY SURGERY (HM21687) | | | | | | | | | | | | | | | | | | | | | | | | | | | | | | | | | | |●| | | | |●| |●| | | | |
| YELLOW HOUSE (HM22005) |●|●|●|●|●|●|●|●|●|●| |●|●|●|●|●|●| |●|●|●|●|●|●|●|●|●|●|●|●|●| |●|●|●|●|●| |●|●|●|●|●| | | | |
| **ESSEX** | | | | | | | | | | | | | | | | | | | | | | | | | | | | | | | | | | | | | | | | | | | | | | | |
| ABBOT, LISA (HM00095) | | |●| |●| | | | | | | | | | | | |●| | | | | | | | |●| | | | | | | | | | | |●| |●|●|●| | | | |
| ABBOTT, LISA (HM00099) | | |●| |●| | | | | | | | | | | | |●| | | | | | | | |●| | | | | | | | | | | |●| |●|●|●| | | | |
| AEQUILIBRIUM (HM00407) | | |●|●|●| |●| |●|●| |●|●| | |●|●| |●| |●| |●| |●|●|●|●| | |●| | | | | |●| |●| |●|●|●| | | | |
| ARC HEALTHCARE (HM00968) | | | | | | | | | | | | | | | | | | | | | | | |●| | | |●| | | | | | | | | | | | |●| | | | | | |
| AROMATHERAPY CLINIC (HM01107) | | | | | | |●| | | | | |●| | | | | | | | | | | | | |●| | | | | | | | | | | | | |●|●|●| | | | |
| ASHBY & ASSOCIATES (HM01194) | | | | | | | | | | | |●| | | | | | | | | | | | | | | | | | | |●| | | | | | | | |●|●|●| | | | |
| AVART, GILLIAN (HM01383) | |●| |●|●| | | | | | |●|●| |●|●|●| |●|●|●| | |●| |●|●| |●| | | | | | |●|●| | | |●| | | | | | |
| BARKING PHYSICAL THERAPY CTRE (HM01715) | | | | | | |●| | | | |●|●| | | | | | | |●| | | | | | | | | | | | | | | | | | | |●|●|●| | | | |
| BAXTER, LISA (HM01929) | | |●|●|●| |●| | | | | | | | |●| | | | |●| |●| | | |●| | | | | |●| | | |●| | | |●| | | | | | |
| BENEDICTA (HM02125) | | |●| |●| | | | | | | | | | | | |●| | | | | | | | |●| | | | | | | | | | | | | |●|●| | | | | |
| BE-WELL CLINIC (HM02251) | | | | | | | | | | | | | | | | | | | | | | | | | | | | | | | | | | | | | | | | |●|●| | | | | |
| BODY BALANCE HEALTH SOLUTIONS (HM02571) | | | | | | | | | | | |●| | | | | | | | | | | | | | | | | | | | | | | | | | | | | | | | | | | |
| BRENTWOOD CHIROPODY SURGERY (HM02963) | | | | | | | | | | | | | | | | | | | | | | | | | | | | | | | | | | | | | | | | |●|●|●| | | | |
| BRITISH INSTITUTE-HYPNOTHERAPY (HM03085) | | | | |●|●| |●| |●| | | | | | | | | | | | | | | | | | | | | | | | | | | | | | |●| | | | | | |
| BURNHAM PHYSIOTHERAPY CLINIC (HM03405) | | | | | | |●| | | | |●|●| | | | | | | |●| | | | | | | | | | | | | | | | | | | | |●|●| | | | |
| CAIN, SHEILA (HM03538) | |●|●|●|●| |●| | | | |●|●| | |●|●| | | |●|●| | |●|●|●|●| | | | | |●| | |●| |●|●|●|●|●|●|●|●|●|
| CATON, PETER (HM03859) | | | | |●| | |●| | | | | |●| | | | |●| | | | | | | |●| | | | | | | | | | | | | | | | | | | | |
| CHAKRA ROSE (HM03942) | | |●|●|●|●| |●| | | | | | | | | | | | | | | | |●| | | | | | | | | | | | | | | |●|●| | | | | |
| CHRIS MOSLIN HYPNOTHERAPIST (HM04433) | | | | |●|●| |●| | | | | | | | | | | | | | | | | | | | | | | | | | | | | | | | |●| | | | | | |
| CLACTON CHIROPRACTIC CLINIC (HM04501) | | | | | | |●| | | | |●|●| | | | | | | |●| | | | | | | | | | | | | | | | | | | | | | | | | |
| CLARKE, M R (HM04593) | | | | | | | | | | | |●|●| | | | | | | | | | | | | | | | | | | | | | | | | | | |●| | | | | | |
| COKER, EILEEN (HM04800) | |●|●|●|●|●| | | | | | | | |●|●| | |●|●|●| |●|●|●| |●|●| | | | | |●|●| |●| |●| |●|●|●| | | | |
| COMPLETE CHIROPRACTIC (HM04957) | | | | | | |●| | | | |●|●| | | | | | | |●| | | | | | | | | | | | | | | | |●| | |●|●|●| | | | |
| COOK, JOE (HM05048) | | | |●|●|●| |●| | | | | |●| | | | | |●| | | | | |●| | | | | |●| |●|●| | | | |●|●|●| | | | |

# S - W Conditions treated at Practices/Businesses and Specialist Treatment Categories

Business by County with Reference no.

| Business | Sexually Trans. Infections | Shingles | Sinus Problems | Skin Problems | Sleep Disorders | Slimming Help | Slipped Disk | Smoking Help | Sneezing | Snoring | Spinal Injuries | Sports Injuries | Sprains | Stammering | Stings | Stomach Problems |
|---|---|---|---|---|---|---|---|---|---|---|---|---|---|---|---|---|
| COOPER, FELICITY (HM05104) | | | | | | | | | | | | | | | | |
| CROFT, JOANNA (HM05455) | | | | | | | | | | | | | | | | |
| CROSS HANDS CHIRO CLINIC (HM05479) | | | | | | | ● | | | | | ● | ● | | | |
| CROWN CHIROPRACTIC CLINIC (HM05507) | | | | | | | ● | | | | ● | ● | ● | | | |
| CROWN CHIROPRACTIC CLINIC (HM05508) | | | | | | | ● | | | | | ● | ● | | | |
| DICKASON, J T (HM06067) | | | | | | | ● | | | | ● | ● | ● | | | |
| E A O C (HM06465) | | | | | | ● | ● | ● | | | | | ● | | | |
| EDWARDS, G E (HM06652) | | | | | | | | | | | | | | | | |
| EDWARDS, G E (HM06651) | | | | | | | | | | | | | | | | |
| ELECTROLYSIS CLINIC (HM06716) | | | | ● | | | | | | | | | | | | |
| ELMER CHIROPODY & PODIATRY SVS (HM06781) | | | | | | | | | | | | ● | | | | |
| EPPING OSTEOPATHY AND SPORTS (HM06854) | | | | | | | ● | | | | | ● | ● | | | |
| EPPING PHYSIOTHERAPY PRACTICE (HM06855) | | ● | ● | ● | | | ● | | | | | ● | ● | | | |
| ESSEX PHYSIO & SPORTS INJ CTRE (HM06938) | | | | | ● | | ● | | | | | ● | ● | | | |
| FARROW, VICKI (HM07135) | | | | | | | ● | | | | | | | | | |
| FLEUROMA (HM07418) | | | ● | ● | ● | ● | | | | | | | | | | |
| FOOT HEALTH CLINIC (HM07482) | | | | | | | | | | | | ● | ● | | | |
| FOULKES, GEOFFREY LLOYD (HM07609) | | ● | ● | ● | ● | ● | ● | ● | ● | ● | | ● | ● | ● | ● | ● |
| FROST, JANICE (HM07761) | | ● | ● | ● | ● | ● | ● | ● | ● | ● | | ● | ● | ● | ● | ● |
| FULTON, A J (HM07795) | | | | | | | | | | | | | | | | |
| FULTON, A J (HM07796) | | | | | | | | | | | | | | | | |
| GENT, WENDY (HM07973) | | | | ● | | | | | | | | ● | ● | | | |
| GRAY, P A (HM08417) | | | | | | | | | | | | | | | | |
| HADLEIGH PODIATRY CLINIC (HM08695) | | | | | | | | | | | | | | | | |
| HARLOW OSTEOPATHIC PRACTICE (HM09011) | | | | | | | ● | | | | | ● | ● | | | |
| HEALING ROOM (HM09349) | | | ● | ● | ● | | | | | | | ● | ● | | | ● |
| HOLISTIC HEALTH CLINIC (HM09978) | | | | | | | | | | | | | | | | |
| HYPNOTHERAPY & PSYCHO CONS (HM10508) | | | | | | ● | | ● | | | | | | | | |
| HYPNOTHERAPY CENTRE (HM10532) | | | | | | | ● | ● | | | | | | | | |
| HYPNOTHERAPY CENTRE (HM10530) | | | | | | ● | | ● | | | | | | | | |
| ISIS HOUSE THERAPY CENTRE (HM10768) | | | | | ● | ● | | | | | | | | | | |
| JACKSON, CYRIL (HM10832) | | | | | ● | ● | | ● | | | | | | | | |
| JOYNES, IAN (HM11239) | | | | | | | | | | | | | | | | |
| KELLY, GILLIAN (HM11431) | | ● | ● | ● | | | | | | | | ● | ● | | | |

| Business | Stomach Ulcers | Stress | Sweating | Teeth Grinding | Tennis Elbow | Terminal Illness | Throat Problems | Thrush | Thyroid Problems | Tinnitis | Tiredness | Tonsilitis | Ulcers | Vaginal Problems | Varicose Veins | Verrucas |
|---|---|---|---|---|---|---|---|---|---|---|---|---|---|---|---|---|
| COOPER, FELICITY (HM05104) | | | | | | | | | | | | | | | | |
| CROFT, JOANNA (HM05455) | | | | | | | | | | | | | | | | |
| CROSS HANDS CHIRO CLINIC (HM05479) | | | | | ● | | | | | | | | | | | |
| CROWN CHIROPRACTIC CLINIC (HM05507) | | | | | ● | | | | | | | | | | | |
| CROWN CHIROPRACTIC CLINIC (HM05508) | | | | | ● | | | | | | | | | | | |
| DICKASON, J T (HM06067) | | | | | ● | | | | | | | | | | | |
| E A O C (HM06465) | | | | | ● | | | | | | | | | | | |
| EDWARDS, G E (HM06652) | | | | | | | | | | | | | | | | ● |
| EDWARDS, G E (HM06651) | | | | | | | | | | | | | | | | ● |
| ELECTROLYSIS CLINIC (HM06716) | | | | | | | | | | | | | | | | |
| ELMER CHIROPODY & PODIATRY SVS (HM06781) | | | | | | | | | | | | | | | | ● |
| EPPING OSTEOPATHY AND SPORTS (HM06854) | | | | | ● | | | | | | | | | | | |
| EPPING PHYSIOTHERAPY PRACTICE (HM06855) | | | | | ● | | | | | | ● | | | | | |
| ESSEX PHYSIO & SPORTS INJ CTRE (HM06938) | | ● | | | ● | | | | | | ● | | | | | |
| FARROW, VICKI (HM07135) | | | | | | | | | | | ● | | | | | |
| FLEUROMA (HM07418) | | ● | | | | | | | | | ● | | | | | |
| FOOT HEALTH CLINIC (HM07482) | | | | | | | | | | | | | | | | |
| FOULKES, GEOFFREY LLOYD (HM07609) | ● | | ● | ● | ● | ● | ● | ● | ● | ● | ● | ● | ● | ● | ● | |
| FROST, JANICE (HM07761) | ● | | ● | ● | ● | ● | ● | ● | ● | ● | ● | ● | ● | ● | ● | |
| FULTON, A J (HM07795) | | | | | | | | | | | | | | | | ● |
| FULTON, A J (HM07796) | | | | | | | | | | | | | | | | ● |
| GENT, WENDY (HM07973) | | ● | | | | | | | | | | | | | | |
| GRAY, P A (HM08417) | | | | | | | | | | | | | | | | ● |
| HADLEIGH PODIATRY CLINIC (HM08695) | | | | | | | | | | | | | | | | ● |
| HARLOW OSTEOPATHIC PRACTICE (HM09011) | | | | | ● | | | | | | | | | | | |
| HEALING ROOM (HM09349) | | | | | ● | | | | | | ● | | | | | |
| HOLISTIC HEALTH CLINIC (HM09978) | | | | | | | | | | | | | | | | |
| HYPNOTHERAPY & PSYCHO CONS (HM10508) | | | | | | | | | | | | | | | | |
| HYPNOTHERAPY CENTRE (HM10532) | | ● | | | | | | | | | | | | | | |
| HYPNOTHERAPY CENTRE (HM10530) | | ● | | | | | | | | | | | | | | |
| ISIS HOUSE THERAPY CENTRE (HM10768) | | ● | | | | | | | | | ● | | | | | |
| JACKSON, CYRIL (HM10832) | | ● | | | | | | | | | | | | | | |
| JOYNES, IAN (HM11239) | | | | | | | | | | | | | | | | |
| KELLY, GILLIAN (HM11431) | | | | | | | | | | | ● | | | | | |

| Business | Vertigo | Viral Infections | Vomiting | Warts | Water Retention | Whiplash | Wind | Worms | Children | Terminally Ill | Disabled | Horses | Dogs | CatS | Other Animals |
|---|---|---|---|---|---|---|---|---|---|---|---|---|---|---|---|
| COOPER, FELICITY (HM05104) | | | | | | | | | ● | ● | ● | | | | |
| CROFT, JOANNA (HM05455) | | | | | | | | | | | | | ● | ● | ● |
| CROSS HANDS CHIRO CLINIC (HM05479) | | | | | | | | | | | | | | | |
| CROWN CHIROPRACTIC CLINIC (HM05507) | | | | | | ● | | | | | | | | | |
| CROWN CHIROPRACTIC CLINIC (HM05508) | | | | | | | | | | | | | | | |
| DICKASON, J T (HM06067) | | | | | | ● | | | ● | | ● | | | | |
| E A O C (HM06465) | | | | | | | | | | | | | | | |
| EDWARDS, G E (HM06652) | | | | | | | | | ● | ● | ● | | | | |
| EDWARDS, G E (HM06651) | | | | | | | | | ● | ● | ● | | | | |
| ELECTROLYSIS CLINIC (HM06716) | | | | | | | | | ● | ● | ● | | | | |
| ELMER CHIROPODY & PODIATRY SVS (HM06781) | | | | | | | | | ● | ● | ● | | | | |
| EPPING OSTEOPATHY AND SPORTS (HM06854) | | | | | | | | | ● | | ● | | | | |
| EPPING PHYSIOTHERAPY PRACTICE (HM06855) | | | | | | | | | ● | ● | ● | | | | |
| ESSEX PHYSIO & SPORTS INJ CTRE (HM06938) | | | | | | | | | ● | ● | ● | | | | |
| FARROW, VICKI (HM07135) | | | | | | | | | ● | ● | ● | | | | |
| FLEUROMA (HM07418) | | | | | | | | | ● | ● | ● | | | | |
| FOOT HEALTH CLINIC (HM07482) | | | | ● | | | | | ● | | ● | | | | |
| FOULKES, GEOFFREY LLOYD (HM07609) | ● | ● | ● | ● | ● | | ● | ● | ● | | ● | | | | |
| FROST, JANICE (HM07761) | ● | ● | ● | ● | ● | | ● | | ● | | ● | | | | |
| FULTON, A J (HM07795) | | | | | | | | | ● | ● | ● | | | | |
| FULTON, A J (HM07796) | | | | | | | | | | | | | | | |
| GENT, WENDY (HM07973) | | | | | | | | | ● | | | | | | |
| GRAY, P A (HM08417) | | | | | | | | | ● | ● | ● | | | | |
| HADLEIGH PODIATRY CLINIC (HM08695) | | | | | | | | | ● | ● | ● | | | | |
| HARLOW OSTEOPATHIC PRACTICE (HM09011) | | | | | | | | | ● | | ● | | | | |
| HEALING ROOM (HM09349) | | | | | ● | | | | ● | ● | ● | ● | ● | ● | ● |
| HOLISTIC HEALTH CLINIC (HM09978) | | | | | | | | | ● | ● | ● | | | | |
| HYPNOTHERAPY & PSYCHO CONS (HM10508) | | | | | | | | | ● | | ● | | | | |
| HYPNOTHERAPY CENTRE (HM10532) | | | | | | | | | | | ● | | | | |
| HYPNOTHERAPY CENTRE (HM10530) | | | | | | | | | ● | ● | ● | | | | |
| ISIS HOUSE THERAPY CENTRE (HM10768) | | | | | | | | | ● | ● | ● | | | | |
| JACKSON, CYRIL (HM10832) | | | | | | | | | ● | ● | ● | | | | |
| JOYNES, IAN (HM11239) | | | | | | | | | ● | ● | ● | | | | |
| KELLY, GILLIAN (HM11431) | | | | | | | | | | | | | | | |

(Children, Terminally Ill, Disabled, Horses, Dogs, CatS, Other Animals: Specialist Treatment Categories)

# S - W Conditions treated at Practices/Businesses and Specialist Treatment Categories

| Business by County with Reference no. | Sexually Trans. Infections | Shingles | Sinus Problems | Skin Problems | Sleep Disorders | Slimming Help | Slipped Disk | Smoking Help | Sneezing | Snoring | Spinal Injuries | Sports Injuries | Sprains | Stammering | Stings | Stomach Problems | Stomach Ulcers | Stress | Sweating | Teeth Grinding | Tennis Elbow | Terminal Illness | Throat Problems | Thrush | Thyroid Problems | Tinnitis | Tiredness | Tonsilitis | Ulcers | Vaginal Problems | Varicose Veins | Verrucas | Vertigo | Viral Infections | Vomiting | Warts | Water Retention | Whiplash | Wind | Worms | Specialist Treatment Categories: Children | Terminally Ill | Disabled | Horses | Dogs | CatS | Other Animals |
|---|---|---|---|---|---|---|---|---|---|---|---|---|---|---|---|---|---|---|---|---|---|---|---|---|---|---|---|---|---|---|---|---|---|---|---|---|---|---|---|---|---|---|---|---|---|---|---|
| LAING, RICHARD (DR) (HM11866) | | ● | ● | ● | ● | | | | ● | | | ● | ● | | ● | ● | ● | | ● | | ● | ● | ● | ● | ● | | ● | ● | ● | ● | ● | | ● | ● | ● | ● | ● | | ● | | ● | ● | ● | | | | |
| LA-SANTE AROMATHERAPY (HM11981) | | | | | ● | | | | | | | | | | | | | ● | | | | | | | | | | | | | | | | | | | | | | | ● | ● | ● | | | | |
| LEIGH, MARTIN (HM12189) | | | | | | | ● | | | | | ● | ● | | | ● | | | | | ● | | | | | ● | | | | | | | ● | | | | | | | | ● | | ● | | | | |
| LEVY, PAUL (HM12269) | | | | | | | | | | | | | | | | | | | | | | | | | | | | | | | | ● | | | | | | | | | ● | ● | ● | | | | |
| LINGWOOD CLINIC (HM12435) | | | ● | ● | ● | | ● | | | | | ● | ● | | | | | | | | ● | | | | | | | | | | | | | | | | | | | | ● | ● | ● | | | | |
| LONDON ROAD PHYSIO PRACTICE (HM12603) | | | | | | | ● | | | | | ● | ● | | | | | | | | ● | | | | | | | | | | | | | | | | | | | | ● | ● | ● | | | | |
| MARTIN, LEIGH (HM13202) | | | | | | | ● | | | | | ● | ● | | | ● | | | | | ● | | | | | ● | | | | | | | ● | | | | | | | | ● | | ● | | | | |
| MEDELY CLINIC (HM13647) | | | | | | | | | | ● | | ● | | | | | | | | | | | | | | | | | | | | | | | | | | | | | ● | | | | | | |
| MILES, C J (HM13855) | | | | | | | | | | | | | | | | | | | | | | | | | | | | | | | | ● | | | | | | | | | ● | ● | ● | | | | |
| MOONSTONE HEALING CENTRE (HM14111) | | | ● | | ● | ● | | ● | ● | | | | | | | | | | | | ● | | ● | | ● | ● | ● | ● | ● | | | | | | | | | | ● | | ● | ● | ● | | | | |
| MOORE, SUSAN (HM14134) | | | ● | | ● | | | | | | | | | | | | | ● | | | | | | | | | | | | | | ● | | | | | | | | | ● | ● | ● | | | | |
| MOSS, GRAEME (HM14264) | | | | | | | | | | | | | | | | | | | | | | | | | | | | | | | | | | | | | | | | | ● | ● | ● | | | | |
| MOUCHET, F (HM14282) | | | | | | | | | | | | | | | | | | | | | | | | | | | | | | | | | | | | | | | | | | ● | ● | | | | |
| NATURAL REMEDY CENTRE (HM14620) | ● | ● | ● | ● | ● | ● | ● | ● | ● | ● | | ● | ● | ● | ● | ● | ● | | ● | | ● | | ● | ● | ● | ● | ● | ● | ● | | ● | | ● | ● | ● | ● | | | ● | ● | ● | | ● | | ● | ● | |
| OSMAN, BRIAN (HM15435) | | | | | | | | | | | | | | | | | | | | | | | | | | | | | | | | | | | | | | | | | ● | ● | | | | | |
| PALMER, DAVID J (HM15600) | | | ● | | ● | | | | | | | ● | ● | | | | | | | | ● | | | | | ● | ● | | | | | | | | | | | | | | ● | ● | ● | | | | |
| PALMIST (HM15620) | | | | | ● | | | | | | | | | | | | | | | | | | | | | | | | | | | | | | | | | | | | ● | ● | ● | | | | |
| PARVEZ, SHAUKAT (HM15771) | | ● | ● | ● | ● | ● | ● | ● | ● | | | ● | ● | | | ● | ● | | | | ● | ● | | | | ● | ● | | | ● | | | | | | | ● | | ● | | ● | ● | ● | | | | |
| PEPPER, SUSAN (HM16010) | | | | | | | ● | | | | | | | | | | | | | | | | | | | | | | | | | | | | | | | | | | ● | | ● | | | | |
| PHARMACARE (HM16109) | | ● | ● | ● | ● | ● | | ● | ● | ● | | ● | ● | ● | ● | ● | ● | | ● | | ● | | ● | ● | ● | ● | ● | ● | ● | ● | ● | | ● | ● | ● | ● | ● | | ● | ● | ● | ● | ● | | | | |
| PHYSIO & SPORTS INJURY CLINIC (HM16186) | | | | | | | ● | | | | | ● | ● | | | | | | | | ● | | | | | | | | | | | | | | | | | | | | ● | | | | | | |
| PINEWOOD PHYSIOTHERAPY CLINIC (HM16313) | | | | | | | ● | | | | | ● | ● | | | | | | | | ● | | | | | | | | | | | | | | | | | | | | ● | | ● | | | | |
| PISCES NATURAL THERAPY CENTRE (HM16330) | | | | | ● | ● | | ● | | | | | | | | | | | | ● | | | | | | | ● | | | | | | | | | | | | | | ● | ● | | | | | |
| PRICE, G J (HM16572) | | | ● | ● | ● | ● | ● | | ● | | | ● | ● | | | ● | | | ● | | ● | | | | | | ● | | | | | | ● | | ● | | ● | | ● | | ● | | | | | | |
| PRIVATE HEALTH CENTRE CLINIC (HM16643) | ● | ● | ● | ● | ● | ● | ● | ● | ● | ● | | ● | ● | ● | ● | ● | ● | | ● | ● | ● | ● | ● | ● | ● | ● | ● | ● | ● | ● | ● | | ● | ● | ● | ● | ● | | ● | ● | ● | ● | ● | | | | |
| QUIT SMOKING CENTRE (HM16821) | | | | | | | | ● | | | | | | | | | | | | | | | | | | | | | | | | | | | | | | | | | | | | | | | |
| RAJA YOGA MEDITATION (HM16898) | | | | | | | | | | | | | | | | | | ● | | | | | | | | | | | | | | | | | | | | | | | | | | | | | |
| REFLEXOLOGY CLINIC (HM17088) | | | ● | | ● | ● | | | | | | | | | | ● | | | | | ● | | | | | ● | ● | | | | | | | | | | ● | | ● | | ● | ● | ● | | | | |
| ROBINSON, DAVID (HM17466) | | | | | ● | ● | | ● | | | | | | | | | | | | | | | | | | | | | | | | | | | | | | | | | ● | ● | | | | | |
| SANDERS, G (HM17909) | | | | | | | | | | | | | | | | | | | | | | | | | | | | | | | | ● | | | | | | | | | ● | ● | ● | | | | |
| SCOTT, MARY (HM18124) | ● | ● | ● | ● | ● | ● | ● | ● | ● | ● | | ● | ● | ● | ● | ● | ● | ● | ● | ● | ● | ● | ● | ● | ● | ● | ● | ● | ● | ● | ● | | ● | ● | ● | ● | ● | | ● | ● | ● | ● | ● | | | | |
| SELF AWARENESS HEALING (HM18204) | | | | | | | | | | | | | | | | | | | | | | ● | | | | | ● | | | | | | | | | | | | | | ● | ● | ● | | | | |
| SELVES, KATIE (HM18222) | | ● | ● | ● | ● | | | | | | | | | | | ● | ● | | ● | | | | ● | ● | | | ● | ● | ● | | ● | | | ● | | | ● | | ● | | ● | | | | | | |
| SEYMOUR, LOUISE (HM18259) | | | | | | | | | | | | | | | | | | | | | | | | | | | | | | | | | | | | ● | | | | | ● | ● | ● | | | | |

# S - W Conditions treated at Practices/Businesses and Specialist Treatment Categories

| Business by County with Reference no. | Sexually Trans. Infections | Shingles | Sinus Problems | Skin Problems | Sleep Disorders | Slimming Help | Slipped Disk | Smoking Help | Sneezing | Snoring | Spinal Injuries | Sports Injuries | Sprains | Stammering | Stings | Stomach Problems | Stomach Ulcers | Stress | Sweating | Teeth Grinding | Tennis Elbow | Terminal Illness | Throat Problems | Thrush | Thyroid Problems | Tinnitis | Tiredness | Tonsilitis | Ulcers | Vaginal Problems | Varicose Veins | Verrucas | Vertigo | Viral Infections | Vomiting | Warts | Water Retention | Whiplash | Wind | Worms | Specialist Treatment Categories: Children | Terminally Ill | Disabled | Horses | Dogs | CatS | Other Animals |
|---|---|---|---|---|---|---|---|---|---|---|---|---|---|---|---|---|---|---|---|---|---|---|---|---|---|---|---|---|---|---|---|---|---|---|---|---|---|---|---|---|---|---|---|---|---|---|---|
| SHELDON, PEGGY (HM18380) | | | ● | | | | ● | | | | | ● | ● | | | | | | | | ● | | | | | | ● | | | | | | | | | | | ● | | | ● | ● | ● | | | | |
| SOUTH, JO (HM18918) | ● | ● | ● | ● | ● | ● | ● | ● | ● | ● | | ● | ● | ● | ● | ● | ● | | ● | ● | ● | ● | ● | ● | ● | ● | ● | ● | ● | ● | ● | | ● | ● | ● | ● | ● | | ● | ● | ● | ● | ● | | | | |
| TRINITY CENTRE (HM20338) | ● | ● | ● | ● | ● | ● | ● | ● | ● | ● | | ● | ● | ● | ● | ● | ● | | ● | ● | ● | ● | ● | ● | ● | ● | ● | ● | ● | ● | ● | | ● | ● | ● | ● | ● | | ● | ● | ● | ● | ● | | | | |
| WADDINGTON, R M (HM20726) | | | | | | | | | | | | | | | | | | | | | | | | | | | | | | | | ● | | | | | | | | | ● | ● | ● | | | | |
| WALK CHIROPODIST (HM20757) | | | | | | | | | | | | | | | | | | | | | | | | | | | | | | | | ● | | | | | | | | | ● | ● | ● | | | | |
| WAYNE-WRIGHT, M S (HM21043) | | | | | | | | | | | | | | | | | | | | | | | | | | | | | | | | | | | | | | | | | ● | ● | ● | | | | |
| WELLS HYPNOTHERAPY CLINIC (HM21167) | | | | | ● | ● | | ● | | | | | | | | | | ● | | | | | | | | | | | | | | | | | | | | | | | ● | ● | ● | | | | |
| WENTWORTH HEALTH CLINIC (HM21201) | | | | ● | | | | | | | | ● | | | | | | ● | | | | | | | | | | | | | | | | | | | | | | | ● | ● | ● | | | | |
| WETHERALL, STUART (HM21289) | | | | | | | | | | | | | | | | | | | | | | | | | | | | | | | | | | | | | | | | | ● | ● | ● | | | | |
| WHEELER, M A (HM21317) | | | | | | | | | | | | | | | | | | | | | | | | | | | | | | | | | | | | | | | | | ● | ● | ● | | | | |
| WHEELER, M A (HM21316) | | | | | | | ● | | | | | ● | ● | | | | | | | | | | | | | | | | | | | | | | | | | | | | ● | ● | ● | | | | |
| WHITE WATER HEALING CENTRE (HM21345) | | | | | | | ● | | | | | | | | | | | | | | | | | | | | ● | | | | | | | | | | | | | | ● | ● | | | | | |
| WOODSIDE NATURAL HEALTH (HM21859) | | | ● | ● | ● | | ● | | | | | ● | ● | | | ● | | | | ● | ● | | | | | ● | ● | | | | | | | | | | ● | | ● | | ● | | ● | | | | |
| **GLOUCESTERSHIRE** | | | | | | | | | | | | | | | | | | | | | | | | | | | | | | | | | | | | | | | | | | | | | | | |
| ACUPUNCTURE CLINIC (HM00262) | | ● | ● | ● | ● | | ● | | ● | | | | ● | ● | ● | ● | ● | | ● | ● | ● | ● | ● | | ● | ● | ● | | ● | | ● | | ● | | ● | | ● | | ● | | ● | ● | ● | | | | |
| ADAMS, PETER (HM00360) | ● | ● | ● | ● | ● | | ● | | ● | ● | | ● | ● | ● | ● | ● | ● | | ● | ● | ● | ● | ● | ● | ● | ● | ● | ● | ● | ● | ● | | ● | ● | ● | ● | ● | | ● | ● | ● | ● | ● | | | | |
| AGASCAR, ROBIN (HM00416) | | | | | | ● | | ● | | | | | | | | | | ● | | | | | | | | | | | | | | | | | | | | | | | ● | ● | ● | | | | |
| ARTICHOKE NATURAL HEALTH (HM01168) | | | | ● | | ● | | | | | | ● | | | | | | | | | ● | | | | | | ● | | | | | | | | | | | | | | ● | | ● | | | | |
| BISHOPS CLEEVE PHYSIO & SPORTS (HM02413) | | | | | | | ● | | | | | ● | ● | | | | | | | | ● | | | | | | | | | | | | | | | | | | | | ● | ● | ● | | | | |
| BUNTON, LYNN (HM03354) | | | ● | ● | ● | | | | | | | | | | | ● | ● | | | | | | | | | | ● | | | | | | | | | ● | ● | | | | ● | ● | ● | | | | |
| BURKE, JAYNE (HM03388) | | | ● | ● | ● | | | | | | | ● | | ● | | | | | | | | | ● | | | | ● | | | | | | | | | | | | | | ● | ● | ● | | | | |
| CHELTENHAM CLINIC & TRAD ACU (HM04093) | | | | | | | | | | | | | | | | | | | | | | | | | | | | | | | | | | | | | | | | | ● | | | | | | |
| CHELTENHAM HOLISTIC HLTH CTRE (HM04094) | ● | ● | ● | ● | ● | ● | ● | ● | ● | ● | | ● | ● | ● | ● | ● | ● | ● | ● | ● | ● | ● | ● | ● | ● | ● | ● | ● | ● | ● | ● | | ● | ● | ● | ● | ● | | ● | ● | ● | ● | ● | | | | |
| CHELTENHAM HYPNOTHERAPY (HM04096) | | | | | | ● | | ● | | | | | | | | | | | | | | | | | | | | | | | | | | | | | | | | | | | | | | | |
| CHELTENHAM PHYSIO/SPRTS CLNC (HM04097) | | | | | | | ● | | | | | ● | ● | | | | | | | | ● | | | | | | | | | | | | | | | | | | | | ● | | ● | | | | |
| COMPLEMENTARY TOUCH (HM04950) | | | ● | ● | ● | | | | | | | ● | ● | | | | | | | | | | | | | | ● | | | | | | | | | | ● | | ● | | ● | ● | ● | | | | |
| COOPER, ANGELA (HM05089) | | | | | | ● | | ● | | | | | | | | | | ● | | | | | | | | | ● | | | | | | | | | | | | | | ● | ● | ● | | | | |
| COOPER, ANN (HM05090) | | | ● | ● | | | | | | | | | | | | | | ● | | | | | | | ● | | | | ● | | | | | | ● | | ● | | | | ● | ● | ● | | | | |
| COTSWOLD PHYSIOTHERAPY CENTRE (HM05215) | | ● | ● | | | | ● | | | | | ● | ● | | | | | | | | ● | | | | | | | | ● | | | | ● | | | | | | | | ● | ● | ● | | | | |
| ESSENTIAL BODYWORKS COMPANY (HM06899) | | | ● | | | | | | | | | ● | ● | | | | | | | | ● | ● | | | | | ● | | | | | | | | | | ● | | | | ● | ● | ● | | | | |
| GREENWELL, DAVID (HM08498) | | ● | | | ● | ● | | ● | | | | | | | | | | | | ● | | | | | | ● | | | | | | | | | | ● | | | | | ● | ● | | | | | |
| HYGEIA COLLEGE-COLOUR THERAPY (HM10476) | | | | | ● | | | | | | | | | | | | | ● | | | | | | | | | | | | | | | | | | | | | | | ● | ● | ● | | | | |
| JOANNA SMITH AROMATHERAPY (HM11040) | | | ● | | | | | | | | ● | ● | | | | | | ● | | | ● | | | | | | | | | | | | | | | | | | | | | | | | | | |
| LAWLER, R & G (HM12041) | | | ● | ● | ● | | | | | | | | | | | | | ● | ● | | | | ● | | | | ● | | | | | | | | | | | | | | ● | ● | ● | | | | |

www.healthmyself.com

# S - W Conditions treated at Practices/Businesses and Specialist Treatment Categories

| Business by County with Reference no. | Sexually Trans. Infections | Shingles | Sinus Problems | Skin Problems | Sleep Disorders | Slimming Help | Slipped Disk | Smoking Help | Sneezing | Snoring | Spinal Injuries | Sports Injuries | Sprains | Stammering | Stings | Stomach Problems | Stomach Ulcers | Stress | Sweating | Teeth Grinding | Tennis Elbow | Terminal Illness | Throat Problems | Thrush | Thyroid Problems | Tinnitis | Tiredness | Tonsilitis | Ulcers | Vaginal Problems | Varicose Veins | Verrucas | Vertigo | Viral Infections | Vomiting | Warts | Water Retention | Whiplash | Wind | Worms | Specialist Treatment Categories: Children | Terminally Ill | Disabled | Horses | Dogs | CatS | Other Animals |
|---|---|---|---|---|---|---|---|---|---|---|---|---|---|---|---|---|---|---|---|---|---|---|---|---|---|---|---|---|---|---|---|---|---|---|---|---|---|---|---|---|---|---|---|---|---|---|---|
| LECKHAMPTON CHIROPRACTIC CLNC (HM12119) | | | | | | | ● | | | | | ● | ● | | | | | | | | | | | | | | | | | | | | | | | | | | | | ● | ● | ● | | | | |
| MYERS, MERRILYN (HM14438) | | | | | ● | | | | | | | | | | | | | | | | | | | | | | | | | | | | | | | | | | | | ● | ● | | | | | |
| NATURAL THERAPIES CLINIC (HM14633) | | | ● | ● | ● | | ● | | | | | ● | ● | ● | | ● | ● | | ● | ● | | | ● | | ● | | ● | ● | | | | | | | | | | | | | ● | ● | ● | | | | |
| NATURAL THERAPY CENTRE (HM14649) | | | ● | ● | ● | ● | | ● | | | | ● | ● | ● | | | | | | | | | | | | ● | ● | | | | | | | | | | ● | | ● | | ● | ● | ● | | | | |
| OLD CONVENT (HM15255) | | | | | | | | | | | | ● | | | | | | | | | | | | | | | | | | | | | | | | | | | | | ● | ● | ● | | | | |
| OSTEOPATH (HM15445) | | | | | | | | | | | | ● | ● | | | | | | | | ● | | | | | | | | | | | | | | | | | | | | ● | | ● | | | | |
| PENACHE (HM15960) | | | | ● | ● | | | | | | | | | | | | | ● | | | | | | | | | | | | | | | | | | | | | | | ● | ● | ● | | | | |
| SHIATSU PRACTICE (HM18460) | | | ● | | ● | | | | | | | ● | ● | | | ● | ● | | | ● | ● | | ● | | | | ● | | ● | | | | ● | | | | | | ● | | ● | ● | ● | | | | |
| SLATER, D C (HM18672) | | | | | | | | ● | | | | | | | | | | | | | | | | | | | | | | | | | | | | | | | | | ● | ● | ● | | | | |
| SMYTH, DAVID (HM18830) | | ● | ● | ● | ● | ● | ● | ● | ● | ● | | ● | ● | ● | ● | ● | ● | | ● | ● | ● | ● | ● | ● | ● | ● | ● | ● | ● | ● | ● | | ● | ● | ● | ● | ● | | ● | ● | ● | ● | ● | ● | ● | ● | ● |
| STOUT, HEATHER (HM19359) | | ● | ● | ● | ● | | ● | | | | | ● | ● | | ● | ● | ● | | ● | | ● | | ● | | | | ● | ● | ● | ● | ● | | ● | ● | ● | ● | ● | | ● | | ● | ● | ● | | | | |
| STROUD NATURAL HEALTH CLINIC (HM19422) | ● | ● | ● | ● | ● | ● | ● | ● | ● | ● | | ● | ● | ● | ● | ● | ● | | ● | ● | ● | ● | ● | ● | ● | ● | ● | ● | ● | ● | ● | | ● | ● | ● | ● | ● | | ● | ● | ● | ● | ● | | | | |
| TREE OF LIFE CENTRE (HM20307) | | | ● | ● | ● | | | | | | | ● | | ● | | | | | | | | | ● | | | | ● | | | | | | | | | | | | | | ● | ● | ● | ● | | | |
| VILLAGE CLINIC (HM20665) | | | | | | | ● | | | | | ● | ● | | | | | | | | ● | | | | | | | | | | | ● | | | | | | | | | ● | | | | | | |
| VINEY HALL PHYSIOTHERAPY (HM20683) | | | | | | | ● | | | | | ● | ● | | | | | | | | ● | | | | | | | | | | | | | | | | | | | | ● | ● | ● | | | | |
| WELLS, GEORGINA (HM21172) | | ● | | ● | ● | | | ● | | | | | ● | | ● | | | | ● | | | | ● | ● | | | ● | | ● | ● | | | | ● | | | | | ● | | ● | ● | ● | | | | |
| YOGA DRUVAM JIVAN YOGA SOCIETY (HM22024) | | | | | | | | | | | | | | | | | | | | | | | | | | | | | | | | | | | | | | | | | ● | ● | ● | | | | |
| **HAMPSHIRE** | | | | | | | | | | | | | | | | | | | | | | | | | | | | | | | | | | | | | | | | | | | | | | | |
| ACUPUNCTURE & PHYSIO CLINIC (HM00245) | | ● | ● | ● | ● | ● | ● | ● | ● | | | ● | ● | | | ● | | | ● | | ● | ● | ● | | | ● | ● | | | | ● | | ● | | ● | | ● | | ● | | ● | ● | ● | | | | |
| ALL - HEAL ACU & HERB CENTRE (HM00581) | | ● | ● | ● | ● | ● | ● | ● | ● | | | ● | | | | ● | ● | | ● | | ● | | ● | ● | ● | ● | ● | ● | ● | ● | ● | | ● | | ● | | ● | | ● | ● | ● | | ● | | | | |
| ALLERGY THERAPY (HM00637) | ● | ● | ● | ● | ● | ● | ● | ● | ● | ● | | ● | ● | ● | ● | ● | ● | | ● | ● | ● | ● | ● | ● | ● | ● | ● | ● | ● | ● | ● | | ● | ● | ● | ● | ● | | ● | ● | | | | | | | |
| ARMSTRONG, ANNA (HM01018) | | | | | | | | | | | | | | | | | | | | | | | | | | | | | | | | | | | | | | | | | ● | ● | ● | | | | |
| ARMSTRONG, ANNA (HM01017) | | | | | | | | | | | | | | | | | | | | | | | | | | | | | | | | | | | | | | | | | ● | ● | ● | | | | |
| ARTEMIS (HM01156) | | | | | ● | | | ● | | | | | | | | | | | | | | | | | | | | | | | | | | | | | | | | | | | | | | | |
| AVENUE CLINIC (HM01389) | | | | | | | | | | | | ● | ● | | | | | | ● | | ● | | | | | ● | | | | | | | ● | | | | | | | | ● | | ● | | | | |
| BOLDICK, KATHLEEN (HM02652) | | | ● | | ● | | | | | | | | | | | | | | | | | | | | | | ● | | | | | | | | | | | | | | ● | ● | ● | | | | |
| BOTHWICK, JOHN (HM02734) | | | | | | | | | | | | ● | | | | | | | | | | | | | | | | | | | | | | | | | | | | | | | | | | | |
| BRADFORD HOUSE CHIRO CLINIC (HM02849) | | | | | | | ● | | | | ● | ● | ● | | | | | | | | ● | | | | | | | | | | | | | | | | | ● | | | ● | ● | ● | | | | |
| BUCK, PETER (HM03306) | | | | | | | | | | | | | | | | | | | | | | | | | | | | | | | | | | | | | | | | | ● | ● | ● | | | | |
| CARMICHAEL, GORDON (HM03709) | | | | | | | | | | | | ● | ● | | | | | | | | | | | | | | | | | | | | | | | | | | | | ● | ● | | | | | |
| CASSELL, JOHN (HM03814) | ● | ● | ● | ● | ● | ● | ● | ● | ● | ● | ● | ● | ● | ● | ● | ● | ● | | ● | ● | ● | ● | ● | ● | ● | ● | ● | ● | ● | ● | ● | | ● | ● | ● | ● | ● | ● | ● | ● | ● | ● | ● | | | | |
| CENTRE FOR COMP MEDICINE (HM03901) | ● | ● | ● | ● | ● | ● | ● | ● | ● | ● | ● | ● | ● | ● | ● | ● | ● | ● | ● | ● | ● | ● | ● | ● | ● | ● | ● | ● | ● | ● | ● | ● | ● | ● | ● | ● | ● | ● | ● | ● | ● | ● | ● | | | | |
| CHILTERN COTTAGE CLINIC (HM04175) | | | ● | ● | ● | | | | ● | | | | | ● | ● | ● | | ● | ● | | | | ● | ● | | | ● | ● | ● | ● | | | | ● | ● | ● | ● | | | ● | ● | | | | | | |
| CLEMENTS, CHRISTINE (HM04642) | | | ● | | | | ● | | | | | ● | ● | | | | | | | | ● | | | | | ● | | | | | | | | | | | | | | | ● | ● | ● | | | | |

# S - W Conditions treated at Practices/Businesses and Specialist Treatment Categories

| Business by County with Reference no. | Sexually Trans. Infections | Shingles | Sinus Problems | Skin Problems | Sleep Disorders | Slimming Help | Slipped Disk | Smoking Help | Sneezing | Snoring | Spinal Injuries | Sports Injuries | Sprains | Stammering | Stings | Stomach Problems | Stomach Ulcers | Stress |
|---|---|---|---|---|---|---|---|---|---|---|---|---|---|---|---|---|---|---|
| COAST CLINIC (HM04752) | | | | | | | | | | | | ● | ● | | | | | ● |
| COLVILE, RICHARD (HM04895) | | | | ● | | ● | | | | | | | | | | | ● | |
| COMPLETE ANGEL HEALING CENTRE (HM04955) | | | ● | ● | ● | | | | | | | | | | | ● | ● | |
| CORELLO, LOUISE (HM05161) | | ● | ● | ● | ● | | | ● | | | | ● | | | | ● | ● | |
| CRAIG, PETER (HM05353) | | | | | | | | | | | | | | | | | | |
| CRANIOSACRAL THERAPY (HM05377) | | | ● | ● | ● | | | | | | | | | | | ● | | |
| CTRE FOR THE STUDY OF COMP MED (HM05543) | | ● | ● | ● | | | ● | | ● | | | | | ● | ● | ● | ● | |
| DOLPHIN STUDIOS (HM06165) | | | | | ● | ● | | ● | | | | | | | | | | |
| EASTLEIGH OSTEOPATHIC CLINIC (HM06544) | | | | | | | ● | | | | | ● | ● | | | ● | | |
| EDGAR, A (HM06596) | | | | | | | | | | | | | | | | | | |
| ENERGY EXCHANGE HOLISTIC CTRE (HM06816) | | | | | | | | | | | | | | | | | | |
| EVANS (HM06953) | | | | | | | | | | | | | | | | | | |
| FAIRFIELDS LANE WEST (HM07059) | | | ● | | ● | | | | | ● | | ● | | | | | | |
| FAMILY CHIRO & ALT MED CTRE (HM07081) | ● | ● | ● | ● | ● | ● | ● | ● | | ● | | ● | ● | | ● | ● | | ● |
| FIT FEET CHIROPODY (HM07361) | | | ● | ● | ● | | | | | | | | | | | ● | | |
| FLEET & DISTRICT HYP CENTRE (HM07399) | | | | | ● | ● | | ● | | | | | | ● | | | | |
| FOOT SHOP (HM07486) | | | | | | | | | | | | | | | | | | |
| FOREVER LIVING PRODUCTS (HM07555) | | | | ● | | | | ● | | | | | | | | | | ● |
| FOSSEY, LYNETTE (HM07585) | | | | | | | | | | | | | | | | | | ● |
| FOSTER, JAMES M ASSOCIATES (HM07593) | | | | | | | | | | | | ● | | | | | | |
| FOX, ANTONY D (DR) (HM07631) | ● | ● | ● | ● | ● | ● | ● | | | ● | | ● | ● | ● | ● | ● | ● | |
| GEE, L (HM07958) | | | | | | | | | | | | ● | ● | | | | | ● |
| HANTSCARE (HM08947) | | | | | | | | | | | | ● | ● | | | | | |
| HAYLING ISLAND CHIRO CLINIC (HM09268) | | | | | | | ● | | | | | ● | ● | | | | | |
| HEAL-ALL HERB AND ACU CTRE (HM09315) | | ● | ● | ● | ● | ● | ● | ● | ● | | | ● | | | | ● | ● | |
| HEARNE, BRIAN (HM09440) | | | | | | | | | | | | | | | | | | |
| HERB MEDIC (HM09592) | | | | ● | | | | | | | | | | | | | | ● |
| HIGH STREET CLINIC (HM09742) | | | ● | ● | ● | | | | | | | ● | ● | | | | | |
| HOBBS, T J (HM09860) | | | ● | ● | ● | | | | | | | | | | | ● | | |
| HOLISTIC ARTS STUDIOS (HM09948) | | | ● | | ● | | | | | | | ● | | | | ● | | |
| HOMOEOPATHIC CLINIC (HM10088) | | | | | | | ● | | | | | ● | ● | | | | | |
| HYPNOSIS & STRESS COUNSELLING (HM10494) | | | | | | ● | | ● | | | | | | | | | | |
| HYPNOTHRPY FOR POSITIVE CHANGE (HM10542) | | | | ● | ● | ● | | ● | | | | | | ● | | ● | | ● |
| INLPTA (HM10633) | | | | | ● | | | ● | | | | | | ● | | | | |

| Business by County with Reference no. | Sweating | Teeth Grinding | Tennis Elbow | Terminal Illness | Throat Problems | Thrush | Thyroid Problems | Tinnitis | Tiredness | Tonsilitis | Ulcers | Vaginal Problems | Varicose Veins | Verrucas | Vertigo | Viral Infections | Vomiting | Warts | Water Retention | Whiplash | Wind | Worms |
|---|---|---|---|---|---|---|---|---|---|---|---|---|---|---|---|---|---|---|---|---|---|---|
| COAST CLINIC (HM04752) | | | | | | | | | | | | | | | | | | | | | | |
| COLVILE, RICHARD (HM04895) | | | | | | ● | | | ● | | | | | | | | | | ● | | | |
| COMPLETE ANGEL HEALING CENTRE (HM04955) | | | | | ● | | | | ● | | | | | | | | | | | | | |
| CORELLO, LOUISE (HM05161) | | | ● | ● | ● | | ● | ● | ● | ● | ● | | | | | ● | ● | | | | | |
| CRAIG, PETER (HM05353) | | | | | | | | | | | | | | | | | | ● | | | | |
| CRANIOSACRAL THERAPY (HM05377) | | ● | ● | ● | | | | ● | ● | | | | | | ● | | | | | | | |
| CTRE FOR THE STUDY OF COMP MED (HM05543) | ● | | ● | ● | ● | ● | ● | ● | ● | ● | ● | ● | | | ● | ● | ● | ● | | | ● | |
| DOLPHIN STUDIOS (HM06165) | | | | | | ● | | | ● | | | | | | | | | | | | | |
| EASTLEIGH OSTEOPATHIC CLINIC (HM06544) | | | ● | | | | | | | | | | | | | | | | | | | |
| EDGAR, A (HM06596) | | | | | | | | | | | | | | ● | | | | | | | | |
| ENERGY EXCHANGE HOLISTIC CTRE (HM06816) | | | | | | | | | | | | | | | | | | | | | | |
| EVANS (HM06953) | | | | | | | | | | | | | | ● | | | | | | | | |
| FAIRFIELDS LANE WEST (HM07059) | | | ● | | | ● | | ● | | | | ● | | | | | | | | | | |
| FAMILY CHIRO & ALT MED CTRE (HM07081) | ● | ● | ● | | | ● | ● | ● | ● | | | | ● | | ● | ● | | | ● | | ● | |
| FIT FEET CHIROPODY (HM07361) | | | | | | | | | ● | | | ● | | | | | | | ● | | ● | |
| FLEET & DISTRICT HYP CENTRE (HM07399) | | | | | | | | | | | | | | | | | | | | | | |
| FOOT SHOP (HM07486) | | | | | | | | | | | | | | | | | | | | | | |
| FOREVER LIVING PRODUCTS (HM07555) | | | | | | | | | | | | | | | | | | | | | | |
| FOSSEY, LYNETTE (HM07585) | | | | | | | | | | | | | | | | | | | | | | |
| FOSTER, JAMES M ASSOCIATES (HM07593) | | | | | | | | | | | | | | | | | | | | | | |
| FOX, ANTONY D (DR) (HM07631) | ● | ● | ● | ● | ● | ● | ● | ● | ● | ● | ● | ● | ● | | ● | ● | ● | ● | ● | | ● | ● |
| GEE, L (HM07958) | | | ● | | | | | | | | | | | | | | | | | | | |
| HANTSCARE (HM08947) | | | ● | | | | | | | | | | | | | | | | | | | |
| HAYLING ISLAND CHIRO CLINIC (HM09268) | | | ● | | | | | ● | | | | | | | | | | | | | | |
| HEAL-ALL HERB AND ACU CTRE (HM09315) | ● | | ● | | ● | ● | ● | ● | ● | ● | ● | ● | ● | | ● | | ● | | ● | | ● | ● |
| HEARNE, BRIAN (HM09440) | | | | | | | | | | | | | | | | | | | | | | |
| HERB MEDIC (HM09592) | | | | | | | | | | | | | | | | | | | | | | |
| HIGH STREET CLINIC (HM09742) | | | ● | | | | | | ● | | | | | | | | | | | | | |
| HOBBS, T J (HM09860) | | | | | | | | | ● | | | | | | | | | | | | | |
| HOLISTIC ARTS STUDIOS (HM09948) | | | | | | | | | ● | | | | | | | | | | ● | | | |
| HOMOEOPATHIC CLINIC (HM10088) | | ● | ● | | | | | ● | | | | | | | | | | | | | | |
| HYPNOSIS & STRESS COUNSELLING (HM10494) | | | | | | | | | | | | | | | | | | | | | | |
| HYPNOTHRPY FOR POSITIVE CHANGE (HM10542) | ● | ● | | | | | | ● | ● | | | | | | | | | | | | | |
| INLPTA (HM10633) | | | | | | | | | ● | | | | | | | | | | | | | |

| Business by County with Reference no. | Specialist Treatment Categories: Children | Terminally Ill | Disabled | Horses | Dogs | CatS | Other Animals |
|---|---|---|---|---|---|---|---|
| COAST CLINIC (HM04752) | ● | ● | ● | | | | |
| COLVILE, RICHARD (HM04895) | ● | | ● | | | | |
| COMPLETE ANGEL HEALING CENTRE (HM04955) | ● | ● | | ● | ● | ● | ● |
| CORELLO, LOUISE (HM05161) | ● | ● | ● | | | | |
| CRAIG, PETER (HM05353) | ● | ● | ● | | | | |
| CRANIOSACRAL THERAPY (HM05377) | ● | ● | ● | | | | |
| CTRE FOR THE STUDY OF COMP MED (HM05543) | ● | ● | ● | | | | |
| DOLPHIN STUDIOS (HM06165) | ● | ● | ● | | | | |
| EASTLEIGH OSTEOPATHIC CLINIC (HM06544) | | | | | | | |
| EDGAR, A (HM06596) | ● | ● | ● | | | | |
| ENERGY EXCHANGE HOLISTIC CTRE (HM06816) | ● | ● | ● | | | | |
| EVANS (HM06953) | ● | ● | ● | | | | |
| FAIRFIELDS LANE WEST (HM07059) | ● | | ● | | | | |
| FAMILY CHIRO & ALT MED CTRE (HM07081) | ● | ● | ● | ● | ● | ● | ● |
| FIT FEET CHIROPODY (HM07361) | ● | ● | ● | | | | |
| FLEET & DISTRICT HYP CENTRE (HM07399) | ● | | | | | | |
| FOOT SHOP (HM07486) | ● | | ● | | | | |
| FOREVER LIVING PRODUCTS (HM07555) | | | | | | | |
| FOSSEY, LYNETTE (HM07585) | ● | ● | ● | | | | |
| FOSTER, JAMES M ASSOCIATES (HM07593) | ● | ● | ● | | | | |
| FOX, ANTONY D (DR) (HM07631) | ● | ● | | | | | |
| GEE, L (HM07958) | ● | ● | ● | | | | |
| HANTSCARE (HM08947) | ● | | | | | | |
| HAYLING ISLAND CHIRO CLINIC (HM09268) | | | | | | | |
| HEAL-ALL HERB AND ACU CTRE (HM09315) | ● | | ● | | | | |
| HEARNE, BRIAN (HM09440) | ● | ● | ● | | | | |
| HERB MEDIC (HM09592) | | | | | | | |
| HIGH STREET CLINIC (HM09742) | ● | ● | ● | | | | |
| HOBBS, T J (HM09860) | ● | ● | ● | | | | |
| HOLISTIC ARTS STUDIOS (HM09948) | ● | ● | ● | | | | |
| HOMOEOPATHIC CLINIC (HM10088) | | | | | | | |
| HYPNOSIS & STRESS COUNSELLING (HM10494) | ● | ● | ● | | | | |
| HYPNOTHRPY FOR POSITIVE CHANGE (HM10542) | ● | ● | ● | | | | |
| INLPTA (HM10633) | | | | | | | |

# S - W Conditions treated at Practices/Businesses and Specialist Treatment Categories

Business by County with Reference no.

| Business by County with Reference no. | Sexually Trans. Infections | Shingles | Sinus Problems | Skin Problems | Sleep Disorders | Slimming Help | Slipped Disk | Smoking Help | Sneezing | Snoring | Spinal Injuries | Sports Injuries | Sprains | Stammering | Stings | Stomach Problems |
|---|---|---|---|---|---|---|---|---|---|---|---|---|---|---|---|---|
| INNER WHISPERS & THERAPY CTRE (HM10643) | | | | | | | | | | | | | | | | |
| JENKINS, RUSSELL (HM10994) | ● | ● | ● | ● | ● | ● | ● | ● | ● | ● | | ● | ● | ● | ● | ● |
| JOYCE, HELEN G M (HM11236) | | | | | | | ● | | | | | | ● | | | |
| KAY SILVER HYPNOTHERAPY (HM11349) | | | | | ● | ● | | ● | | | | | | | | ● |
| KD PHYSIOTHERAPY (HM11363) | | | | | | | ● | | | | | ● | ● | | | |
| LEACH, TRICIA (HM12091) | | | ● | | ● | | | | | | | | | | | ● |
| LEWIS, D J S (HM12288) | ● | ● | ● | ● | ● | | | ● | ● | ● | ● | ● | ● | ● | ● | ● |
| LISLE, THOMAS (HM12455) | | | | | | | | | | | | | | | | |
| LOCKHAMS THERAPY CENTRE (HM12545) | | | | | | | | | | | | ● | | | | |
| LOWE, KENNETH (HM12699) | | | | | | | ● | | | | | ● | ● | | | |
| LYMINGTON CHIROPRACTIC CLINIC (HM12759) | | | | ● | | | ● | | | | | ● | ● | | | ● |
| MARLOR, J (HM13127) | | | | | | | | | | | | | | | | |
| MELHUISH, J I (DR) (HM13705) | | | | | | | ● | | | | ● | ● | ● | | | |
| MINDWORKS HYPNOTHERAPY CLINIC (HM13969) | | | | | ● | | | ● | | | | | | | | |
| NATURAL HEALTH SERVICE (HM14595) | ● | ● | ● | ● | ● | ● | ● | ● | ● | ● | | ● | ● | ● | ● | ● |
| NATURES GATE (HM14688) | | | | | | | ● | | | | | | | | | |
| NEW MILTON CHIROPRACTIC CLINIC (HM14825) | | | | | | | ● | | | | ● | ● | ● | | | |
| NORMAN, J M (HM15004) | | | | | ● | | | | | | | | | | | |
| NORSWORTHY, CLAIRE (HM15017) | | | ● | ● | ● | | | | | | | | | | | ● |
| PARCHMENT STREET CLINIC (HM15646) | | ● | ● | ● | ● | | | ● | ● | ● | | ● | ● | ● | | ● |
| PHOENIX HOLISTIC CENTRE (HM16156) | | | | ● | | | | ● | | | | ● | | | | |
| PHYSIOTHERAPY CENTRE (HM16233) | | | | | | | ● | | | | | ● | ● | | | |
| REIKI NATURAL HEALING CENTRE (HM17142) | ● | ● | ● | ● | ● | ● | ● | ● | ● | ● | | ● | ● | ● | ● | ● |
| RICHARDS, CLAIRE (HM17249) | | | ● | | | | | | | | | | | | | |
| RINGWOOD CHIROPRACTIC CLINIC (HM17355) | | | | | | | ● | | | | ● | ● | ● | | | |
| RINGWOOD NATURAL HEALTH CLINIC (HM17357) | | | ● | ● | | | | ● | | | | ● | | | | ● |
| RINGWOOD PHYSIOTHERAPY CENTRE (HM17358) | | | | | | | ● | | | | | ● | ● | | | |
| S E E D INSTITUTE (HM17805) | | | | | | | | | | | | | | | | |
| SCANDINAVIAN CHIROPRACTIC CTRE (HM18002) | | | | | | | ● | | | | ● | ● | ● | | | |
| SIMCOE CLINIC (HM18549) | | | ● | ● | | | ● | | | | | ● | | | | ● |
| SIMMONDS, J (HM18555) | | | ● | ● | ● | | ● | | | | | ● | ● | | | ● |
| SOLENT CHIROPRACTIC CLINIC (HM18871) | | | | | | | | | | | | ● | ● | | | |
| SOUTHGATE NAT THERAPY CLINIC (HM18937) | | ● | ● | ● | ● | | ● | | | | | ● | ● | | | ● |
| SOUTHSEA CENTRE FOR COMP MED (HM18943) | ● | ● | ● | ● | ● | ● | ● | ● | ● | ● | | ● | ● | ● | | ● |

| Business by County with Reference no. | Stomach Ulcers | Stress | Sweating | Teeth Grinding | Tennis Elbow | Terminal Illness | Throat Problems | Thrush | Thyroid Problems | Tinnitis | Tiredness | Tonsilitis | Ulcers | Vaginal Problems | Varicose Veins | Verrucas |
|---|---|---|---|---|---|---|---|---|---|---|---|---|---|---|---|---|
| INNER WHISPERS & THERAPY CTRE (HM10643) | | ● | | | | | | | | | | | | | | |
| JENKINS, RUSSELL (HM10994) | ● | | ● | ● | ● | ● | ● | ● | ● | ● | ● | ● | ● | ● | ● | |
| JOYCE, HELEN G M (HM11236) | | | | | ● | | | | | | | | | | | |
| KAY SILVER HYPNOTHERAPY (HM11349) | | | | | | | | ● | | | ● | | | | | |
| KD PHYSIOTHERAPY (HM11363) | | | | | ● | | | | | | | | | | | |
| LEACH, TRICIA (HM12091) | | | | | | | | | | | ● | | | | | |
| LEWIS, D J S (HM12288) | ● | ● | ● | ● | ● | ● | ● | ● | ● | ● | ● | ● | ● | ● | ● | ● |
| LISLE, THOMAS (HM12455) | | | | | | | | | | | | | | | | ● |
| LOCKHAMS THERAPY CENTRE (HM12545) | | | | | | | | | | | ● | | | | | |
| LOWE, KENNETH (HM12699) | | | | | ● | | | | | | | | | | | |
| LYMINGTON CHIROPRACTIC CLINIC (HM12759) | | | | | | | | ● | | | ● | | ● | | | |
| MARLOR, J (HM13127) | | | | | | | | | | | | | | | | |
| MELHUISH, J I (DR) (HM13705) | | | | | ● | | | | | | | | | | | |
| MINDWORKS HYPNOTHERAPY CLINIC (HM13969) | | ● | | | | | | | | | ● | | | | | |
| NATURAL HEALTH SERVICE (HM14595) | ● | | ● | ● | ● | ● | ● | ● | ● | ● | ● | ● | ● | ● | ● | |
| NATURES GATE (HM14688) | | | | | | ● | | | | | | | | | | |
| NEW MILTON CHIROPRACTIC CLINIC (HM14825) | | | | | ● | | | | | ● | | | | | | |
| NORMAN, J M (HM15004) | | ● | | | | | | | | | | | | | | |
| NORSWORTHY, CLAIRE (HM15017) | | | | | | | | | | | ● | | | | | |
| PARCHMENT STREET CLINIC (HM15646) | ● | | ● | | ● | | ● | | ● | ● | ● | | ● | ● | | |
| PHOENIX HOLISTIC CENTRE (HM16156) | | | | | | ● | | | | | ● | | | | | |
| PHYSIOTHERAPY CENTRE (HM16233) | | | | | ● | | | | | | | | | | | |
| REIKI NATURAL HEALING CENTRE (HM17142) | ● | | ● | ● | ● | ● | ● | ● | ● | ● | ● | ● | ● | ● | ● | |
| RICHARDS, CLAIRE (HM17249) | | | | | | | | | ● | | ● | | | | | |
| RINGWOOD CHIROPRACTIC CLINIC (HM17355) | | | | | ● | | | | | | | | | | | |
| RINGWOOD NATURAL HEALTH CLINIC (HM17357) | ● | | | ● | ● | | ● | ● | ● | ● | ● | | ● | ● | | |
| RINGWOOD PHYSIOTHERAPY CENTRE (HM17358) | | | | | ● | | | | | | | | | | | |
| S E E D INSTITUTE (HM17805) | | ● | | | | | | | | | | | | | | |
| SCANDINAVIAN CHIROPRACTIC CTRE (HM18002) | | | | | ● | | | | | | | | | | | |
| SIMCOE CLINIC (HM18549) | ● | | | | ● | | | ● | ● | ● | ● | | | | ● | |
| SIMMONDS, J (HM18555) | ● | | ● | | ● | ● | ● | | ● | ● | ● | ● | | ● | | |
| SOLENT CHIROPRACTIC CLINIC (HM18871) | | | | | ● | | | | | | | | | | | |
| SOUTHGATE NAT THERAPY CLINIC (HM18937) | ● | | | | ● | ● | ● | ● | ● | | ● | ● | | | | |
| SOUTHSEA CENTRE FOR COMP MED (HM18943) | ● | | ● | ● | ● | | ● | ● | ● | ● | ● | ● | ● | ● | ● | |

| Business by County with Reference no. | Vertigo | Viral Infections | Vomiting | Warts | Water Retention | Whiplash | Wind | Worms | Specialist Treatment Categories: Children | Terminally Ill | Disabled | Horses | Dogs | CatS | Other Animals |
|---|---|---|---|---|---|---|---|---|---|---|---|---|---|---|---|
| INNER WHISPERS & THERAPY CTRE (HM10643) | | | | | | | | | ● | ● | ● | | | | |
| JENKINS, RUSSELL (HM10994) | ● | ● | ● | ● | ● | | ● | ● | ● | ● | ● | | | | |
| JOYCE, HELEN G M (HM11236) | | | | | | | | | | | | | | | |
| KAY SILVER HYPNOTHERAPY (HM11349) | ● | | | | | | ● | | ● | ● | ● | | | | |
| KD PHYSIOTHERAPY (HM11363) | | | | | | | | | ● | ● | ● | | | | |
| LEACH, TRICIA (HM12091) | | | | | | | | | ● | ● | ● | | | | |
| LEWIS, D J S (HM12288) | ● | ● | ● | ● | ● | ● | ● | ● | ● | ● | ● | ● | ● | ● | ● |
| LISLE, THOMAS (HM12455) | | | | | | | | | ● | ● | ● | | | | |
| LOCKHAMS THERAPY CENTRE (HM12545) | | | | | | | | | ● | ● | ● | ● | ● | ● | ● |
| LOWE, KENNETH (HM12699) | | | | | | | | | ● | | | | | | |
| LYMINGTON CHIROPRACTIC CLINIC (HM12759) | | | | | ● | | | | ● | ● | ● | | | | |
| MARLOR, J (HM13127) | | | | | | | | | ● | ● | ● | | | | |
| MELHUISH, J I (DR) (HM13705) | | | | | | ● | | | ● | ● | ● | | | | |
| MINDWORKS HYPNOTHERAPY CLINIC (HM13969) | | | | | | | | | ● | ● | ● | | | | |
| NATURAL HEALTH SERVICE (HM14595) | ● | ● | ● | ● | ● | | ● | ● | ● | ● | ● | | | | |
| NATURES GATE (HM14688) | | | | | | | | | | ● | ● | | | | |
| NEW MILTON CHIROPRACTIC CLINIC (HM14825) | ● | | | | | | | | ● | ● | ● | | | | |
| NORMAN, J M (HM15004) | | | | | | | | | ● | ● | ● | | | | |
| NORSWORTHY, CLAIRE (HM15017) | | | | | | | | | ● | ● | ● | | | | |
| PARCHMENT STREET CLINIC (HM15646) | ● | ● | ● | | ● | | ● | | | | | | | | |
| PHOENIX HOLISTIC CENTRE (HM16156) | | | | | | | | | ● | ● | ● | | | | |
| PHYSIOTHERAPY CENTRE (HM16233) | | | | | | | | | ● | | ● | | | | |
| REIKI NATURAL HEALING CENTRE (HM17142) | ● | ● | ● | ● | ● | | ● | ● | ● | ● | ● | ● | ● | ● | ● |
| RICHARDS, CLAIRE (HM17249) | | | | | | | | | ● | ● | ● | | | | |
| RINGWOOD CHIROPRACTIC CLINIC (HM17355) | | | | | | ● | | | ● | ● | ● | | | | |
| RINGWOOD NATURAL HEALTH CLINIC (HM17357) | | | | ● | | | ● | | ● | | | | | | |
| RINGWOOD PHYSIOTHERAPY CENTRE (HM17358) | | | | | | | | | ● | ● | ● | | | | |
| S E E D INSTITUTE (HM17805) | | | | | | | | | ● | | | | | | |
| SCANDINAVIAN CHIROPRACTIC CTRE (HM18002) | | | | | | ● | | | ● | ● | ● | | | | |
| SIMCOE CLINIC (HM18549) | ● | | | | ● | | ● | | ● | ● | ● | ● | | | |
| SIMMONDS, J (HM18555) | ● | ● | | | ● | | ● | | ● | ● | ● | | | | |
| SOLENT CHIROPRACTIC CLINIC (HM18871) | | | | | | | | | ● | ● | ● | | | | |
| SOUTHGATE NAT THERAPY CLINIC (HM18937) | | ● | ● | | | | | | ● | ● | ● | | | | |
| SOUTHSEA CENTRE FOR COMP MED (HM18943) | ● | ● | ● | | ● | | | | ● | ● | ● | | | | |

# S - W Conditions treated at Practices/Businesses and Specialist Treatment Categories

| Business by County with Reference no. | Sexually Trans. Infections | Shingles | Sinus Problems | Skin Problems | Sleep Disorders | Slimming Help | Slipped Disk | Smoking Help | Sneezing | Snoring | Spinal Injuries | Sports Injuries | Sprains | Stammering | Stings | Stomach Problems | Stomach Ulcers | Stress | Sweating | Teeth Grinding | Tennis Elbow | Terminal Illness | Throat Problems | Thrush | Thyroid Problems | Tinnitis | Tiredness | Tonsilitis | Ulcers | Vaginal Problems | Varicose Veins | Verrucas | Vertigo | Viral Infections | Vomiting | Warts | Water Retention | Whiplash | Wind | Worms | Specialist Treatment Categories: Children | Terminally Ill | Disabled | Horses | Dogs | CatS | Other Animals |
|---|---|---|---|---|---|---|---|---|---|---|---|---|---|---|---|---|---|---|---|---|---|---|---|---|---|---|---|---|---|---|---|---|---|---|---|---|---|---|---|---|---|---|---|---|---|---|---|
| THOMA, ANDREW (HM19923) | | | | | | | ● | | | | | ● | | | | | | | | | ● | | | | | | | | | | | | | | | | | | | | | | | | | | |
| TURNER, CATHY (HM20420) | ● | ● | ● | ● | ● | ● | ● | ● | ● | ● | | ● | ● | ● | ● | ● | ● | | ● | ● | ● | ● | ● | ● | ● | ● | ● | ● | ● | ● | ● | | ● | ● | ● | ● | ● | | ● | ● | ● | ● | ● | | | | |
| TWESLEDOWN PHYSIOTHERAPY (HM20449) | | | | | | | ● | | | | | ● | ● | | | | | | | | ● | | | | | | | | | | | | | | | | | | | | ● | | | | | | |
| VINCE, LINDA (HM20668) | | | | | | | | | | | | | | | | | | | | | | | | | | | | | | | | | | | | | | | | | ● | ● | ● | | | | |
| WELL HOUSE HOLISTIC HLTH CTRE (HM21138) | ● | ● | ● | ● | ● | ● | ● | ● | ● | ● | | ● | ● | ● | ● | ● | ● | | ● | ● | ● | ● | ● | ● | ● | ● | ● | ● | ● | ● | ● | | ● | ● | ● | ● | ● | | ● | ● | ● | ● | ● | | | | |
| WINCHESTER CHIROPRACTIC CLINIC (HM21691) | | | | | | | ● | | | | | ● | ● | ● | | | | | | | ● | | | | | ● | | | | | | | ● | | | | | | | | | | | | | | |
| WINCHESTER HOM PRACTICE (HM21692) | ● | ● | ● | ● | ● | ● | ● | ● | ● | ● | | ● | ● | ● | ● | ● | ● | | ● | ● | ● | ● | ● | ● | ● | ● | ● | ● | ● | ● | ● | | ● | ● | ● | ● | ● | | ● | ● | ● | ● | ● | | | | |
| **HEREFORDSHIRE** | | | | | | | | | | | | | | | | | | | | | | | | | | | | | | | | | | | | | | | | | | | | | | | |
| BEAUTY IS YOURS (HM01999) | | | ● | ● | | ● | | | | | | | ● | | | ● | | | | | ● | | | | | | ● | | | | | | | | | | | | | | ● | | | | | | |
| BROADVIEW NATURAL HEALTH CTRE (HM03119) | | | | | | | | | | | | | | | | | | | | | | | | | | | | | | | | | | | | | | | | | ● | ● | ● | | | | |
| HEREFORD CENTRE (HM09677) | ● | ● | ● | ● | ● | ● | ● | ● | ● | ● | ● | ● | ● | ● | ● | ● | ● | ● | ● | ● | ● | ● | ● | ● | ● | ● | ● | ● | ● | ● | ● | ● | ● | ● | ● | ● | ● | ● | ● | ● | ● | ● | ● | | | | |
| HEREFORD CHIROPRACTIC CLINIC (HM09678) | | | | | | | ● | | | | | ● | ● | | | | | | | | ● | | | | | | | | | | | | | | | | | ● | | | | | | | | | |
| JONES, KEVIN D G (HM11165) | | | | | | | ● | | | | | ● | ● | | | | | | | | | | | | | | | | | | | | | | | | | | | | ● | | ● | | | | |
| LEDBURY NATURAL HEALTH CENTRE (HM12122) | ● | ● | ● | ● | ● | ● | ● | ● | ● | ● | | ● | ● | ● | ● | ● | ● | | ● | ● | ● | ● | ● | ● | ● | ● | ● | ● | ● | ● | ● | | ● | ● | ● | ● | ● | | ● | ● | ● | ● | ● | | | | |
| LEOMINSTER OSTEOPATHS (HM12221) | | ● | ● | | ● | ● | ● | | | | | ● | | | | | | | | ● | | | | ● | ● | ● | ● | | | | ● | | ● | | | | | | | | ● | ● | ● | | | | |
| TEDDER, CATHRINE (HM19814) | | | | | | | | | | | | | | | | | | | | | | | | | | | | | | | | | | | | | | | | | ● | ● | ● | | | | |
| WILLCOCKS, T & S (HM21519) | | | | | | | | | | | | ● | | | | | | | | | ● | | | | | | | | | | | | | | | | | | | | ● | ● | ● | ● | ● | ● | ● |
| **HERTFORDSHIRE** | | | | | | | | | | | | | | | | | | | | | | | | | | | | | | | | | | | | | | | | | | | | | | | |
| ALDER, DENNIS (HM00497) | | | | | | | | | | | | | | | | | | | | | | | | | | | | | | | | ● | | | | | | | | | ● | ● | ● | | | | |
| ALLEN, JULIE & LEN (HM00613) | | ● | ● | ● | ● | ● | ● | ● | ● | ● | | | ● | ● | ● | ● | ● | | ● | ● | ● | | ● | ● | ● | ● | ● | ● | ● | ● | ● | | ● | ● | ● | ● | ● | | ● | ● | ● | ● | | | | | |
| ALTERNATIVE CHOICES (HM00697) | | | | | ● | | | | | | | ● | | | | | | | | | | | | | | | | | | | | | | | | | | | | | ● | ● | ● | | | | |
| ARNOLD, PETER & JACKIE (HM01036) | | ● | ● | ● | | | | | ● | | | ● | ● | | | | | | | | | | ● | ● | | ● | ● | | | | | | | | | | | | | | ● | | ● | ● | ● | | |
| AROMA ROOM (HM01055) | | | | | ● | | | | | | | | | | | | | ● | | | | | | | | | | | | | | | | | | | | | | | ● | ● | ● | | | | |
| AROMATHERAPY BY ANTONIO (HM01095) | | | | | ● | | | | | | | | | | | | | | | | | | | | | | | | | | | | | | | | | | | | | | ● | | | | |
| ASHDOWN CLINIC (HM01205) | | ● | ● | ● | ● | ● | ● | ● | | ● | | ● | ● | | | ● | ● | | ● | ● | ● | | | | | ● | ● | ● | ● | | | | | | | ● | | | ● | | | | | | | | |
| ASHWELL, MELBOURN & BALDOCK (HM01246) | | | | | | | ● | | | | | ● | ● | | | | | | | | ● | | | | | | | | | | | | | | | | | | | | ● | | ● | | | | |
| ASSOCIATES HEAD & SHORT (HM01277) | | | | | | | | | | | | ● | | | | | | | | | | | | | | | | | | | | | | | | | | | | | ● | ● | ● | | | | |
| ASSOCIATES HEAD & SHORT (HM01276) | | | | | | | | | | | | ● | | | | | | | | | | | | | | | | | | | | | | | | | | | | | ● | ● | ● | | | | |
| ASSOCIATION OF STRESS MNGMT (HM01293) | | | | | | | | ● | | | | | | | | | | | | | | | | | | | ● | | | | | | | | | | | | | | | | | | | | |
| AUTOGENIC TRAINING (HM01372) | | | ● | ● | ● | ● | ● | ● | | ● | | ● | ● | ● | | ● | ● | ● | ● | ● | | ● | ● | | | ● | ● | | | | | | ● | | ● | | | | ● | | ● | ● | ● | | | | |
| BARNET CHIROPODY SURGERY (HM01757) | | | | | | | | | | | | ● | | | | | | | | | | | | | | | | | | | | ● | | | | ● | | | | | | ● | ● | ● | | | |
| BASSETT CLINIC (HM01853) | | | | | | | ● | | | | | ● | ● | | | | | | | | ● | | | | | | | | | | | | | | | | | | | | ● | | | | | | |
| BEAUCHAMP BAGENAL (HM01983) | | | | | | ● | ● | | | | | ● | ● | | | ● | | ● | | ● | ● | | ● | | | | | | | | | | | | | | | ● | | | ● | ● | ● | | | | |
| BERKHAMSTED PHYSIO CLINIC (HM02193) | | | | | | | ● | | | | | ● | ● | | | | | | | | ● | | | | | | | | | | | | | | | | | | | | ● | ● | ● | | | | |

www.healthmyself.com

# S - W Conditions treated at Practices/Businesses and Specialist Treatment Categories

Business by County with Reference no.

| Business by County with Reference no. | Sexually Trans. Infections | Shingles | Sinus Problems | Skin Problems | Sleep Disorders | Slimming Help | Slipped Disk | Smoking Help | Sneezing | Snoring | Spinal Injuries | Sports Injuries | Sprains | Stammering | Stings | Stomach Problems | Stomach Ulcers | Stress | Sweating | Teeth Grinding | Tennis Elbow | Terminal Illness | Throat Problems | Thrush |
|---|---|---|---|---|---|---|---|---|---|---|---|---|---|---|---|---|---|---|---|---|---|---|---|---|
| BETA HEALTH CLINIC (HM02229) | | | ● | ● | | | ● | | | | | ● | ● | | | | | | | | ● | | | |
| BISHOP'S STORTFORD HOMEOPATHIC (HM02416) | | ● | ● | | ● | | | | | | | | ● | | | ● | ● | | | ● | | | | |
| BODY MECHANICS THERAPY CLINIC (HM02598) | | | | | | | | | | ● | | ● | ● | | | | | ● | | | ● | | | |
| BOREHAMWOOD CHIRO CLINIC (HM02717) | | | ● | | | ● | ● | | | | | ● | ● | | | ● | | ● | | | ● | | | |
| BRIGGS-WILSON, A (HM03037) | | | | | | | | | | | | | | | | | | | | | | | | |
| BRIND, KEVIN (HM03053) | | | | | | | ● | | | | | ● | ● | | | | | | | | ● | | | |
| BURYHILL PHYSIOTHERAPY (HM03456) | | | | | | | ● | | | | | ● | ● | | | | | | | | ● | | | |
| BUTTERFIELD, ROBIN (HM03496) | | | | | | | ● | | | | | ● | | | | | | | | | ● | | | |
| CANNON, VALERIE (HM03635) | | | ● | ● | ● | | | | | | | | | | | ● | | | | | | | | |
| CHAUHAN, D K (HM04065) | ● | ● | ● | ● | ● | ● | ● | ● | ● | ● | | ● | ● | ● | ● | ● | ● | | ● | ● | ● | ● | ● | ● |
| CHOPRA, S (HM04427) | | | | | | | | | | | | | | | | | | | | | | | | |
| CHOPRA, S (HM04426) | | | | | | | | | | | | | | | | | | | | | | | | |
| CLARE JAMES HEALTH FOODS (HM04532) | | | | | ● | | | | | | | | | | | | | | | | | | | |
| CLNC OF ACU & CHINESE HRBL MED (HM04727) | | ● | ● | ● | ● | | ● | ● | | | | ● | ● | | | ● | | | | | ● | | | ● |
| CONISTON PHYSIOTHERAPY CLINIC (HM04980) | | | ● | | | | ● | | | | | ● | ● | | | | | | | | | | | |
| COOPER, FELICITY (HM05101) | | | | | | | | | | | | | | | | | | | | | | | | |
| DAVID HERBERT REFLEXOLOGY (HM05774) | | | ● | ● | ● | | | | | | | | | | | ● | ● | | | | ● | | | |
| DEVINE, MARY (HM06036) | | | | | | | | | | | | | | | | | | | | | | | | |
| DOYLE, AUDREY (HM06257) | | | ● | ● | ● | | | | | | | | | | | ● | ● | | | ● | | ● | ● | |
| DUDGEON, DELIA (HM06353) | | | | | | | | | | | | | | | | | | | | | | | | |
| EVANS, HELEN (HM06975) | | | | ● | | | | | | | | | | | | | | | | | | | | |
| EVANS, HELEN (HM06976) | | | | ● | | | | | | | | | | | | | | | | | | | | |
| FEET RETREAT () | | ● | ● | ● | ● | | | | | | | | | | | | | | | ● | | | | |
| FREEMAN, FRANCES (HM07721) | ● | ● | ● | ● | ● | ● | ● | | ● | ● | | ● | ● | ● | ● | ● | ● | | ● | ● | ● | ● | ● | ● |
| GEMS (HM07969) | | | | | | | | | | | | | | | | | | ● | | | | | | |
| GENTLE FEET (HM07977) | | | ● | ● | ● | | | | | | | | | | | ● | ● | | | ● | | ● | ● | |
| GEOFF THIEL, COUNS & PSYCHO (HM07986) | | | | | | | | | | | | | | | | | | ● | | | | | | |
| GILLING, LINDA (HM08095) | | ● | ● | | ● | | ● | | ● | ● | | ● | ● | | ● | ● | ● | | ● | | ● | ● | ● | ● |
| GOODMAN, HENRY (HM08258) | | | | | ● | ● | | ● | | | | | | ● | | | | | | | | | | |
| GRAHAM & KERSTIN ELLIOTT (HM08336) | | | | | | | ● | ● | | | ● | ● | ● | | | | | | | | ● | | | |
| GROUNDS, L (HM08599) | | | ● | ● | ● | ● | | ● | | | | | | | ● | ● | ● | | | | | | | |
| HALAHAN, ELISABETH (HM08722) | | ● | ● | | ● | ● | ● | | ● | ● | | | ● | ● | ● | ● | ● | | ● | ● | ● | ● | ● | ● |
| HAMILTON-PETERS, R & J A (HM08849) | | | | ● | ● | ● | | ● | | | | | | ● | | | | | | ● | | | ● | |
| HARPENDEM OSTEOPATHIC PRACTICE (HM09035) | | | ● | | | | | | | | | ● | ● | | | | | | | | ● | | | |

| Business by County with Reference no. | Thyroid Problems | Tinnitis | Tiredness | Tonsilitis | Ulcers | Vaginal Problems | Varicose Veins | Verrucas | Vertigo | Viral Infections | Vomiting | Warts | Water Retention | Whiplash | Wind | Worms | Children | Terminally Ill | Disabled | Horses | Dogs | CatS | Other Animals |
|---|---|---|---|---|---|---|---|---|---|---|---|---|---|---|---|---|---|---|---|---|---|---|---|
| BETA HEALTH CLINIC (HM02229) | | | ● | | | | | | | | | | | ● | | | ● | ● | ● | | | | |
| BISHOP'S STORTFORD HOMEOPATHIC (HM02416) | | ● | | ● | ● | ● | | | | ● | ● | | | | ● | ● | | | | ● | | ● | |
| BODY MECHANICS THERAPY CLINIC (HM02598) | | ● | | | | | | | | | | | | | | | ● | ● | ● | | | | |
| BOREHAMWOOD CHIRO CLINIC (HM02717) | | | ● | | | | | | ● | | | | | ● | | | ● | | ● | | | | |
| BRIGGS-WILSON, A (HM03037) | | | | | | | | | | | | | | | | | ● | | | ● | ● | ● | ● |
| BRIND, KEVIN (HM03053) | | | | | | | | | | | | | | | | | ● | | ● | | | | |
| BURYHILL PHYSIOTHERAPY (HM03456) | | | | | | | | | | | | | | | | | | | | | | | |
| BUTTERFIELD, ROBIN (HM03496) | | | | | | | ● | | | | | | | | | | ● | ● | ● | | | | |
| CANNON, VALERIE (HM03635) | | ● | ● | | | | | | | | | | | | | | ● | ● | ● | | | | |
| CHAUHAN, D K (HM04065) | ● | ● | ● | ● | ● | ● | ● | | ● | ● | ● | ● | ● | | ● | ● | | | | | | | |
| CHOPRA, S (HM04427) | | | | | | | | ● | | | | | | | | | ● | ● | ● | | | | |
| CHOPRA, S (HM04426) | | | | | | | | ● | | | | | | | | | ● | ● | ● | | | | |
| CLARE JAMES HEALTH FOODS (HM04532) | | | | | | | | | | | | ● | | | | | | | | | | | |
| CLNC OF ACU & CHINESE HRBL MED (HM04727) | ● | | ● | | | | | | ● | | | | ● | | | | | | | | | | |
| CONISTON PHYSIOTHERAPY CLINIC (HM04980) | | ● | ● | | ● | | | | ● | | | | | | | | ● | ● | ● | | | | |
| COOPER, FELICITY (HM05101) | | | | | | | | | | | | | | | | | ● | ● | ● | | | | |
| DAVID HERBERT REFLEXOLOGY (HM05774) | ● | | ● | | | | | | | | | | | | | | ● | ● | | | | | |
| DEVINE, MARY (HM06036) | | | | | | | | | | | | | | | | | ● | ● | ● | | | | |
| DOYLE, AUDREY (HM06257) | ● | | ● | | ● | ● | ● | ● | | | ● | | ● | | ● | | ● | ● | ● | | | | |
| DUDGEON, DELIA (HM06353) | | | | | | | | | | | | | | | | | ● | | | | | | |
| EVANS, HELEN (HM06975) | | | | | ● | | | | | | | ● | | | | | | | | | | | |
| EVANS, HELEN (HM06976) | | | | | ● | | | | | | | ● | | | | | ● | ● | ● | | | | |
| FEET RETREAT () | | | | ● | | | ● | | | | | | | | | | ● | ● | ● | | | | |
| FREEMAN, FRANCES (HM07721) | ● | ● | ● | ● | ● | ● | ● | | ● | ● | ● | ● | ● | | ● | ● | ● | ● | ● | | | | |
| GEMS (HM07969) | | | | | | | | | | | | | | | | | ● | | ● | | | | |
| GENTLE FEET (HM07977) | ● | | ● | | ● | ● | ● | | | | ● | | ● | | ● | | ● | ● | ● | | | | |
| GEOFF THIEL, COUNS & PSYCHO (HM07986) | | | | | | | | | | | | | | | | | | | | | | | |
| GILLING, LINDA (HM08095) | ● | ● | ● | ● | ● | ● | ● | | ● | ● | ● | ● | ● | | ● | | ● | ● | ● | | | | |
| GOODMAN, HENRY (HM08258) | | | ● | | | | | | | | | | | | | | ● | ● | | | | | |
| GRAHAM & KERSTIN ELLIOTT (HM08336) | | | | | | | | | | | | | | ● | | | ● | ● | ● | | | | |
| GROUNDS, L (HM08599) | ● | ● | ● | | | | | | ● | | | | ● | | ● | | ● | ● | ● | | | | |
| HALAHAN, ELISABETH (HM08722) | ● | ● | ● | ● | ● | ● | ● | | ● | ● | ● | ● | ● | | ● | ● | ● | | ● | | | | |
| HAMILTON-PETERS, R & J A (HM08849) | | | ● | | | | | | | | | ● | | | | | ● | | ● | | | | |
| HARPENDEM OSTEOPATHIC PRACTICE (HM09035) | | ● | | | | | | | | | | | | | | | ● | | ● | | | | |

# S - W Conditions treated at Practices/Businesses and Specialist Treatment Categories

Business by County with Reference no.

| Business | Sexually Trans. Infections | Shingles | Sinus Problems | Skin Problems | Sleep Disorders | Slimming Help | Slipped Disk | Smoking Help | Sneezing | Snoring | Spinal Injuries | Sports Injuries | Sprains | Stammering |
|---|---|---|---|---|---|---|---|---|---|---|---|---|---|---|
| HARPENDEN CHIROPRACTIC CLINIC (HM09036) | | | | | | | | | | | | ● | ● | |
| HATHAWAY, ELIZABETH (HM09196) | | | | | | | ● | | | | | ● | ● | |
| HEALES CHIROPRACTIC CLINIC (HM09322) | | | | | | | ● | | | | ● | ● | ● | |
| HEALTHY AND WISE (HM09425) | | | ● | ● | ● | | | | ● | | | | ● | |
| HERTFORD NATURAL THERAPY CTRE (HM09690) | | | ● | ● | | | | | | | | ● | ● | |
| HODSDON, L M (HM09893) | | | | | | | | | | | | | | |
| HOLLENBERY, S (HM10019) | | | | | | | ● | | | | | ● | ● | |
| JACKSON, BARBARA (HM10830) | | | | | | | | | | | | | | |
| JENNIFER SAJIR PAED PHYSIO (HM11005) | | | | | | | | | | | | | | |
| JOE MILLER SPORTS INJURY (HM11045) | | | | | | | ● | | | | | ● | ● | |
| JONES, ALAN (HM11115) | | | | | | | | | | | | | | |
| KEW, DEREK (HM11576) | | | | ● | ● | ● | | ● | | | | | | |
| KNEBWORTH PHYSIO CLINIC (HM11742) | | ● | | | | | ● | | | | | ● | ● | |
| LETCHWORTH-PHYSIOTHERAPY (HM12248) | | | | | | | ● | | | | | ● | ● | |
| LEWIN, ROCHELLE (HM12273) | | | | | | | | | | | | | | |
| LIFELINES (HM12355) | | | | | ● | | | | | | | | | |
| LINDY, D (HM12426) | | | | | | | | | | | | ● | ● | |
| MASON, L C (HM13247) | | | | | ● | ● | | ● | | | | | | ● |
| MAUREEN PRIDDLE (HM13328) | | | | | ● | ● | | | | | | | | |
| MAYOR, DAVID F (HM13359) | | ● | ● | ● | ● | | ● | ● | ● | | | ● | ● | |
| MCTIMONEY CHIROPRACTIC CLINIC (HM13612) | | | | | | | | | | | | | | |
| MELLERICK, N D (HM13708) | | | | | | | ● | | | | ● | ● | ● | |
| MIDAS TOUCH (HM13808) | | | ● | | | | | | | | | | | |
| MID-HERTS ALEXANDER CENTRE (HM13827) | | | | | | ● | ● | | | | ● | ● | ● | |
| NATURAL HEALTH CLINIC (HM14589) | | | | | | | | | | | | ● | ● | |
| NATURAL-BALANCE CO UK (HM14672) | | | ● | ● | ● | | | | | | | | ● | |
| O'HARA, JOHN (HM15246) | | | ● | | | | | | | | | | | |
| OPEN MINDS (HM15343) | | | | | ● | | | | | | | ● | | |
| OSTEOPATHIC CLINIC (HM15459) | | | ● | ● | ● | | ● | ● | | | | ● | ● | |
| OVERINGTON, KEL (HM15512) | | | ● | | ● | | | | | | | ● | | |
| PEEDLE, DAVID R (HM15938) | | | | | | | | | | | | | | |
| PERRY, KAREN (HM16049) | | | | | | | | | | | | | | |
| PERSONAL REFLECTIONS (HM16061) | | | ● | | ● | | | | | | | | | |
| PHYSIO & SPORTS INJURIES CLNC (HM16177) | | ● | | | | | ● | | | | | ● | ● | |

| Business | Stings | Stomach Problems | Stomach Ulcers | Stress | Sweating | Teeth Grinding | Tennis Elbow | Terminal Illness | Throat Problems | Thrush | Thyroid Problems | Tinnitis | Tiredness | Tonsilitis | Ulcers | Vaginal Problems |
|---|---|---|---|---|---|---|---|---|---|---|---|---|---|---|---|---|
| HARPENDEN CHIROPRACTIC CLINIC (HM09036) | | | | | | | ● | | | | | | | | | |
| HATHAWAY, ELIZABETH (HM09196) | | | | | | | ● | | | | | | | | | |
| HEALES CHIROPRACTIC CLINIC (HM09322) | | | | | | | ● | | | | | | | | | |
| HEALTHY AND WISE (HM09425) | | ● | | | | | | | ● | | | | | ● | | |
| HERTFORD NATURAL THERAPY CTRE (HM09690) | | | | | | | ● | | | | | | ● | | | |
| HODSDON, L M (HM09893) | | | | | | | | | | | | | | | | |
| HOLLENBERY, S (HM10019) | | | | | | | ● | | | | | | | | | |
| JACKSON, BARBARA (HM10830) | | | | ● | | | | | | | | | | | | |
| JENNIFER SAJIR PAED PHYSIO (HM11005) | | | | | | | | | | | | | | | | |
| JOE MILLER SPORTS INJURY (HM11045) | | | | | | | ● | | | | | | | | | |
| JONES, ALAN (HM11115) | | | | | | | | | | | | | | | | |
| KEW, DEREK (HM11576) | | | | | | ● | | | | | | ● | | | | |
| KNEBWORTH PHYSIO CLINIC (HM11742) | | | | | | | ● | | | | | | | | | |
| LETCHWORTH-PHYSIOTHERAPY (HM12248) | | | | | | | ● | | | | | | | | | |
| LEWIN, ROCHELLE (HM12273) | | | | ● | | | | | | | | | | | | |
| LIFELINES (HM12355) | | | | ● | | | | | | | | | ● | | | |
| LINDY, D (HM12426) | | | | | | | ● | | | | | | | | | |
| MASON, L C (HM13247) | | ● | | | ● | ● | | | | | | | | | | |
| MAUREEN PRIDDLE (HM13328) | | | | ● | | | | | | | | | | | | |
| MAYOR, DAVID F (HM13359) | | ● | ● | | | | ● | | ● | ● | | | ● | | ● | |
| MCTIMONEY CHIROPRACTIC CLINIC (HM13612) | | | | | | | | | | | | | | | | |
| MELLERICK, N D (HM13708) | | | | | | | ● | | | | | | | | | |
| MIDAS TOUCH (HM13808) | | | | | | | | | | ● | | | | ● | | |
| MID-HERTS ALEXANDER CENTRE (HM13827) | | ● | | ● | | ● | ● | | ● | | | | | | | |
| NATURAL HEALTH CLINIC (HM14589) | | | | ● | | | | | | | | | | | | |
| NATURAL-BALANCE CO UK (HM14672) | ● | | | | ● | | | | | ● | ● | | ● | ● | | |
| O'HARA, JOHN (HM15246) | | | | | | | | | | | | ● | | | | |
| OPEN MINDS (HM15343) | | | | | | | | | | | | | | | | |
| OSTEOPATHIC CLINIC (HM15459) | | | | | | | ● | | | | | | ● | | | |
| OVERINGTON, KEL (HM15512) | | ● | | ● | | | ● | | | | | | | | | |
| PEEDLE, DAVID R (HM15938) | | | | | | | | | | | | | | | | |
| PERRY, KAREN (HM16049) | | | | | | | | | | | | | | | | |
| PERSONAL REFLECTIONS (HM16061) | | ● | | | | | | | | | | | ● | | | |
| PHYSIO & SPORTS INJURIES CLNC (HM16177) | | | | | | | ● | | | | | | | | | ● |

| Business | Varicose Veins | Verrucas | Vertigo | Viral Infections | Vomiting | Warts | Water Retention | Whiplash | Wind | Worms | Children | Terminally Ill | Disabled | Horses | Dogs | CatS | Other Animals |
|---|---|---|---|---|---|---|---|---|---|---|---|---|---|---|---|---|---|
| HARPENDEN CHIROPRACTIC CLINIC (HM09036) | | | | | | | | | | | ● | ● | ● | | | | |
| HATHAWAY, ELIZABETH (HM09196) | | | | | | | | | | | ● | ● | ● | | | | |
| HEALES CHIROPRACTIC CLINIC (HM09322) | | | | | | | | ● | | | ● | ● | ● | | | | |
| HEALTHY AND WISE (HM09425) | | | | | | ● | | | ● | ● | ● | | | | | | |
| HERTFORD NATURAL THERAPY CTRE (HM09690) | | | | | ● | | | | | | ● | ● | ● | | | | |
| HODSDON, L M (HM09893) | | | | | | | | | | | ● | ● | ● | | | | |
| HOLLENBERY, S (HM10019) | | | | | | | | | | | ● | | | | | | |
| JACKSON, BARBARA (HM10830) | | | | | | | | | | | | ● | ● | | | | |
| JENNIFER SAJIR PAED PHYSIO (HM11005) | | | | | | | | | | | ● | | ● | | | | |
| JOE MILLER SPORTS INJURY (HM11045) | | | | | | | | | | | ● | | ● | | | | |
| JONES, ALAN (HM11115) | | ● | | | | | | | | | ● | ● | ● | | | | |
| KEW, DEREK (HM11576) | | | | | | | | | | | | | | | | | |
| KNEBWORTH PHYSIO CLINIC (HM11742) | | | | | | | | | | | ● | ● | ● | | | | |
| LETCHWORTH-PHYSIOTHERAPY (HM12248) | | | | | | | | | | | ● | | | | | | |
| LEWIN, ROCHELLE (HM12273) | | | | | | | | | | | ● | ● | ● | | | | |
| LIFELINES (HM12355) | | | | | | | | | | | ● | ● | ● | | | | |
| LINDY, D (HM12426) | | | | | | | | ● | | | ● | | ● | | | | |
| MASON, L C (HM13247) | | | | | | | ● | | | | ● | | | | | | |
| MAUREEN PRIDDLE (HM13328) | | | | | | | | | | | ● | ● | ● | | | | |
| MAYOR, DAVID F (HM13359) | ● | | ● | ● | | | | | ● | | ● | ● | ● | | | | |
| MCTIMONEY CHIROPRACTIC CLINIC (HM13612) | | | | | | | | | | | ● | | ● | | | | |
| MELLERICK, N D (HM13708) | | | | | | | | ● | | | ● | | ● | | | | |
| MIDAS TOUCH (HM13808) | | | | | | | | | | | | ● | ● | | | | |
| MID-HERTS ALEXANDER CENTRE (HM13827) | | | | | | | | ● | | | ● | | ● | | | | |
| NATURAL HEALTH CLINIC (HM14589) | | | | | | | | ● | | | ● | ● | ● | | | | |
| NATURAL-BALANCE CO UK (HM14672) | | | ● | | | | ● | | | | ● | ● | ● | | | | |
| O'HARA, JOHN (HM15246) | | | | | | | | | | | ● | ● | | | | | |
| OPEN MINDS (HM15343) | | | | | | | | | | | | ● | ● | | | | |
| OSTEOPATHIC CLINIC (HM15459) | | | | | | | | | | | ● | ● | ● | | | | |
| OVERINGTON, KEL (HM15512) | | | | | | | | | | | ● | ● | ● | | | | |
| PEEDLE, DAVID R (HM15938) | | | | | | | | | | | ● | ● | ● | | | | |
| PERRY, KAREN (HM16049) | | ● | | | | | | | | | ● | ● | ● | | | | |
| PERSONAL REFLECTIONS (HM16061) | | | | | | | | | | | ● | ● | ● | | | | |
| PHYSIO & SPORTS INJURIES CLNC (HM16177) | | | | | | | | | | | ● | | ● | | | | |

Specialist Treatment Categories: Children, Terminally Ill, Disabled, Horses, Dogs, CatS, Other Animals

www.healthmyself.com

# S - W Conditions treated at Practices/Businesses and Specialist Treatment Categories

Business by County with Reference no.

| Business | Sexually Trans. Infections | Shingles | Sinus Problems | Skin Problems | Sleep Disorders | Slimming Help | Slipped Disk | Smoking Help | Sneezing | Snoring | Spinal Injuries | Sports Injuries | Sprains | Stammering | Stings | Stomach Problems | Stomach Ulcers | Stress |
|---|---|---|---|---|---|---|---|---|---|---|---|---|---|---|---|---|---|---|
| PRIDDLE, PATRICK (HM16602) |  |  |  |  |  |  |  |  |  |  |  |  |  |  |  |  |  | ● |
| PSYCHOTHERAPY (HM16726) |  |  |  | ● | ● | ● |  | ● |  |  |  |  |  |  |  | ● |  | ● |
| PURLYS (HM16769) |  |  |  |  |  | ● |  | ● |  |  |  |  |  |  |  |  |  | ● |
| ROWLAND, JETHRO (HM17692) |  | ● | ● | ● | ● |  |  | ● | ● |  |  |  |  |  |  | ● | ● | ● |
| S K REFLEXOLOGY (HM17811) |  |  |  |  | ● |  |  |  |  |  |  | ● |  |  |  | ● |  |  |
| SHAW, CHRISTINE (HM18333) |  | ● | ● |  |  |  |  |  |  |  |  |  |  |  |  |  |  |  |
| SMITH, SUSAN (HM18813) |  |  | ● |  |  |  |  |  |  |  |  |  |  |  |  | ● |  |  |
| SOPWELL OSTEOPATHIC CLINIC (HM18894) |  |  |  |  |  |  | ● |  |  |  |  | ● |  |  |  | ● |  |  |
| SOUTH, JO (HM18917) | ● | ● | ● | ● | ● | ● | ● | ● | ● | ● |  | ● | ● | ● | ● | ● | ● |  |
| SOUTHDOWN CHIROPODY PRACTICE (HM18929) |  |  |  |  |  |  |  |  |  |  |  |  |  |  |  |  |  |  |
| SPINOZA, DAVID (HM19019) |  |  |  |  |  |  | ● | ● |  |  |  |  |  |  |  |  |  |  |
| ST ALBANS CHIROPRACTIC CLINIC (HM19063) |  |  |  |  |  | ● | ● | ● | ● | ● |  | ● | ● |  |  |  |  |  |
| STORT COUNS & PSYCHOTHERAPY (HM19351) |  |  |  |  |  |  |  | ● |  |  |  |  |  |  |  |  |  |  |
| STORTFORD GRANGE PHYSIO CENTRE (HM19352) |  |  |  |  |  |  | ● |  |  |  |  |  |  |  |  |  |  |  |
| SURVIVAL TRUST SURGERY (HM19526) | ● | ● | ● | ● | ● | ● | ● | ● | ● | ● |  | ● | ● | ● | ● | ● | ● |  |
| SWAN & SWAN (HM19572) |  |  |  | ● |  |  |  |  |  |  |  | ● | ● |  |  |  |  |  |
| THOMPSON, MARK (HM19991) |  |  | ● | ● |  |  | ● |  |  |  |  | ● | ● |  |  | ● | ● |  |
| THOMPSON, MARK () |  |  | ● | ● |  |  | ● |  |  |  |  | ● | ● |  |  | ● | ● |  |
| UNERMAN, EVE (HM20503) |  |  |  |  |  |  |  |  |  |  |  |  |  |  |  |  |  | ● |
| WALKER, NEL (HM20791) |  |  |  |  | ● |  |  |  |  |  |  |  |  |  |  |  |  |  |
| WALKER, RICHARD (HM20798) |  |  |  | ● | ● | ● |  | ● |  |  |  |  |  | ● |  |  |  |  |
| WATSON, KATHRYN (HM21015) |  | ● | ● | ● | ● |  |  | ● |  |  |  |  |  |  | ● | ● | ● |  |
| WELWYN CHIROPRACTIC CLINIC (HM21192) |  |  |  |  |  |  | ● |  |  |  | ● | ● | ● |  |  |  |  |  |
| WHITE, GRAHAM C (HM21355) |  | ● | ● | ● | ● | ● | ● | ● | ● | ● |  | ● | ● | ● | ● | ● | ● |  |
| WOOD STREET CHIROPRACTIC CLNC (HM21780) |  |  |  |  |  |  | ● |  |  |  |  | ● | ● |  |  |  |  |  |
| WOOD STREET CLINIC (HM21781) |  | ● | ● | ● |  |  |  | ● |  |  |  |  |  |  |  | ● | ● |  |
| WORDSWORTH, LINDA (HM21890) |  |  | ● | ● | ● |  |  |  |  |  |  | ● |  |  |  |  |  |  |
| WRIGHT, DOREEN (HM21931) | ● | ● | ● | ● | ● | ● | ● | ● | ● | ● |  | ● | ● | ● | ● | ● | ● |  |
| WRIGHT, KAREN (HM21940) |  |  |  |  |  |  |  |  |  |  |  | ● |  |  |  |  |  |  |
| WYE, DEBORAH (HM21969) |  |  |  |  |  |  |  |  |  |  |  |  |  |  |  |  |  |  |
| WYNDHAM CLINIC (HM21977) |  | ● | ● | ● |  |  | ● |  | ● |  |  | ● | ● |  |  | ● | ● |  |
| **HUMBERSIDE** |  |  |  |  |  |  |  |  |  |  |  |  |  |  |  |  |  |  |
| BATH, ANN (HM01899) |  |  |  | ● |  |  |  |  |  |  |  |  |  |  |  |  |  | ● |
| BRIGG CHIROPRACTIC CLINIC (HM03028) |  |  |  |  |  |  | ● |  |  |  | ● | ● | ● |  |  |  |  |  |

| Business | Sweating | Teeth Grinding | Tennis Elbow | Terminal Illness | Throat Problems | Thrush | Thyroid Problems | Tinnitis | Tiredness | Tonsilitis | Ulcers | Vaginal Problems | Varicose Veins | Verrucas | Vertigo | Viral Infections | Vomiting | Warts | Water Retention | Whiplash | Wind | Worms |
|---|---|---|---|---|---|---|---|---|---|---|---|---|---|---|---|---|---|---|---|---|---|---|
| PRIDDLE, PATRICK (HM16602) |  |  |  |  |  |  |  |  |  |  |  |  |  |  |  |  |  |  |  |  |  |  |
| PSYCHOTHERAPY (HM16726) |  |  |  |  | ● |  |  |  | ● |  |  |  |  |  |  |  |  |  |  |  |  |  |
| PURLYS (HM16769) |  | ● |  |  |  |  |  |  |  |  |  |  |  |  |  |  |  |  |  |  |  |  |
| ROWLAND, JETHRO (HM17692) | ● | ● | ● |  | ● | ● | ● |  |  | ● | ● | ● |  |  |  |  | ● |  | ● |  | ● |  |
| S K REFLEXOLOGY (HM17811) |  |  |  |  |  |  |  |  |  |  |  |  |  |  |  |  |  |  |  |  |  |  |
| SHAW, CHRISTINE (HM18333) |  |  |  |  |  |  | ● | ● | ● |  |  |  | ● |  |  |  |  |  | ● |  |  |  |
| SMITH, SUSAN (HM18813) |  |  |  |  |  |  |  |  |  |  |  |  |  |  |  |  |  |  |  |  |  |  |
| SOPWELL OSTEOPATHIC CLINIC (HM18894) |  |  | ● |  |  |  |  | ● | ● |  |  |  |  |  |  |  |  |  |  |  |  |  |
| SOUTH, JO (HM18917) | ● | ● | ● | ● | ● | ● | ● | ● | ● | ● | ● | ● | ● |  | ● | ● | ● | ● | ● |  | ● | ● |
| SOUTHDOWN CHIROPODY PRACTICE (HM18929) |  |  |  |  |  |  |  |  |  |  |  |  |  |  |  |  |  | ● |  |  |  |  |
| SPINOZA, DAVID (HM19019) |  |  | ● |  |  |  |  |  |  |  |  |  |  |  |  |  |  |  |  |  |  |  |
| ST ALBANS CHIROPRACTIC CLINIC (HM19063) |  | ● | ● |  |  |  |  |  |  |  |  |  |  |  |  |  |  |  |  |  |  |  |
| STORT COUNS & PSYCHOTHERAPY (HM19351) |  |  |  | ● |  |  |  |  | ● |  |  |  |  |  |  |  |  |  |  |  |  |  |
| STORTFORD GRANGE PHYSIO CENTRE (HM19352) |  |  |  |  |  |  |  |  |  |  |  |  |  |  |  |  |  |  |  |  |  |  |
| SURVIVAL TRUST SURGERY (HM19526) | ● | ● | ● | ● | ● | ● | ● | ● | ● | ● | ● | ● | ● |  | ● | ● | ● | ● | ● |  | ● | ● |
| SWAN & SWAN (HM19572) |  |  |  |  |  |  |  |  |  |  | ● |  |  | ● |  |  |  |  |  |  |  |  |
| THOMPSON, MARK (HM19991) |  | ● | ● |  |  | ● | ● |  | ● |  |  |  | ● |  |  |  |  |  |  |  | ● |  |
| THOMPSON, MARK () |  | ● | ● |  |  | ● | ● |  | ● |  |  |  | ● |  |  |  |  |  |  |  | ● |  |
| UNERMAN, EVE (HM20503) |  |  |  |  |  |  |  |  |  |  |  |  |  |  |  |  |  |  |  |  |  |  |
| WALKER, NEL (HM20791) |  |  |  |  |  |  |  |  |  |  |  |  |  |  |  |  |  |  |  |  |  |  |
| WALKER, RICHARD (HM20798) |  | ● |  | ● |  |  |  | ● | ● |  |  |  |  |  |  |  |  | ● |  |  |  |  |
| WATSON, KATHRYN (HM21015) | ● |  |  |  | ● | ● |  |  | ● | ● | ● | ● | ● |  |  | ● | ● |  | ● |  | ● | ● |
| WELWYN CHIROPRACTIC CLINIC (HM21192) |  |  | ● |  |  |  |  |  |  |  |  |  |  |  |  |  |  |  |  | ● |  |  |
| WHITE, GRAHAM C (HM21355) | ● | ● | ● | ● | ● | ● | ● | ● | ● | ● | ● | ● | ● |  | ● | ● | ● | ● | ● |  | ● | ● |
| WOOD STREET CHIROPRACTIC CLNC (HM21780) |  |  | ● |  |  |  |  |  |  |  |  |  |  |  |  |  |  |  |  |  |  |  |
| WOOD STREET CLINIC (HM21781) |  |  |  |  | ● | ● | ● |  | ● | ● | ● | ● |  |  |  | ● |  | ● | ● |  | ● | ● |
| WORDSWORTH, LINDA (HM21890) | ● |  |  | ● | ● |  | ● | ● | ● |  |  |  |  |  | ● |  |  |  |  |  | ● |  |
| WRIGHT, DOREEN (HM21931) | ● | ● | ● | ● | ● | ● | ● | ● | ● | ● |  | ● | ● |  | ● | ● | ● | ● | ● |  | ● | ● |
| WRIGHT, KAREN (HM21940) |  |  |  |  |  |  |  |  |  |  |  |  |  | ● |  |  |  |  |  |  |  |  |
| WYE, DEBORAH (HM21969) |  |  |  |  |  |  |  |  |  |  |  |  |  | ● |  |  |  |  |  |  |  |  |
| WYNDHAM CLINIC (HM21977) |  |  | ● | ● |  | ● |  |  | ● | ● |  |  |  |  |  | ● | ● |  | ● |  | ● |  |
| **HUMBERSIDE** |  |  |  |  |  |  |  |  |  |  |  |  |  |  |  |  |  |  |  |  |  |  |
| BATH, ANN (HM01899) |  |  |  |  |  |  |  |  |  |  |  |  |  |  |  |  |  |  |  |  |  |  |
| BRIGG CHIROPRACTIC CLINIC (HM03028) |  |  | ● |  |  |  |  |  |  |  |  |  |  |  |  |  |  |  |  | ● |  |  |

| Business | Specialist Treatment Categories: Children | Terminally Ill | Disabled | Horses | Dogs | CatS | Other Animals |
|---|---|---|---|---|---|---|---|
| PRIDDLE, PATRICK (HM16602) | ● | ● | ● |  |  |  |  |
| PSYCHOTHERAPY (HM16726) |  |  |  |  |  |  |  |
| PURLYS (HM16769) | ● |  | ● |  |  |  |  |
| ROWLAND, JETHRO (HM17692) | ● |  |  |  |  |  |  |
| S K REFLEXOLOGY (HM17811) | ● | ● |  |  | ● |  |  |
| SHAW, CHRISTINE (HM18333) | ● | ● |  |  |  |  |  |
| SMITH, SUSAN (HM18813) | ● | ● | ● |  |  |  |  |
| SOPWELL OSTEOPATHIC CLINIC (HM18894) | ● |  |  |  |  |  |  |
| SOUTH, JO (HM18917) | ● | ● | ● |  |  |  |  |
| SOUTHDOWN CHIROPODY PRACTICE (HM18929) | ● | ● | ● |  |  |  |  |
| SPINOZA, DAVID (HM19019) | ● |  | ● |  |  |  |  |
| ST ALBANS CHIROPRACTIC CLINIC (HM19063) | ● | ● | ● |  |  |  |  |
| STORT COUNS & PSYCHOTHERAPY (HM19351) |  | ● |  |  |  |  |  |
| STORTFORD GRANGE PHYSIO CENTRE (HM19352) | ● | ● | ● |  |  |  |  |
| SURVIVAL TRUST SURGERY (HM19526) | ● | ● | ● |  |  |  |  |
| SWAN & SWAN (HM19572) | ● | ● | ● |  |  |  |  |
| THOMPSON, MARK (HM19991) | ● |  |  |  |  |  |  |
| THOMPSON, MARK () | ● |  |  |  |  |  |  |
| UNERMAN, EVE (HM20503) | ● | ● | ● |  |  |  |  |
| WALKER, NEL (HM20791) |  |  |  |  |  |  |  |
| WALKER, RICHARD (HM20798) | ● | ● | ● |  |  |  |  |
| WATSON, KATHRYN (HM21015) | ● | ● | ● |  |  |  |  |
| WELWYN CHIROPRACTIC CLINIC (HM21192) | ● |  | ● |  |  |  |  |
| WHITE, GRAHAM C (HM21355) | ● | ● | ● |  |  |  |  |
| WOOD STREET CHIROPRACTIC CLNC (HM21780) |  |  |  |  |  |  |  |
| WOOD STREET CLINIC (HM21781) | ● |  | ● |  |  |  |  |
| WORDSWORTH, LINDA (HM21890) | ● | ● | ● |  |  |  |  |
| WRIGHT, DOREEN (HM21931) | ● | ● | ● |  |  |  |  |
| WRIGHT, KAREN (HM21940) | ● | ● | ● |  |  |  |  |
| WYE, DEBORAH (HM21969) | ● | ● | ● |  |  |  |  |
| WYNDHAM CLINIC (HM21977) | ● | ● |  |  |  |  |  |
| **HUMBERSIDE** |  |  |  |  |  |  |  |
| BATH, ANN (HM01899) |  |  |  |  |  |  |  |
| BRIGG CHIROPRACTIC CLINIC (HM03028) | ● | ● | ● |  |  |  |  |

# S - W Conditions treated at Practices/Businesses and Specialist Treatment Categories

| |||||||||||||||||||||||||||||||||||||||||Specialist Treatment Categories|||||||
|---|---|---|---|---|---|---|---|---|---|---|---|---|---|---|---|---|---|---|---|---|---|---|---|---|---|---|---|---|---|---|---|---|---|---|---|---|---|---|---|---|---|---|---|---|---|---|---|
| Business by County with Reference no. | Sexually Trans. Infections | Shingles | Sinus Problems | Skin Problems | Sleep Disorders | Slimming Help | Slipped Disk | Smoking Help | Sneezing | Snoring | Spinal Injuries | Sports Injuries | Sprains | Stammering | Stings | Stomach Problems | Stomach Ulcers | Stress | Sweating | Teeth Grinding | Tennis Elbow | Terminal Illness | Throat Problems | Thrush | Thyroid Problems | Tinnitis | Tiredness | Tonsilitis | Ulcers | Vaginal Problems | Varicose Veins | Verrucas | Vertigo | Viral Infections | Vomiting | Warts | Water Retention | Whiplash | Wind | Worms | Children | Terminally Ill | Disabled | Horses | Dogs | CatS | Other Animals |
| BRIGG SKIN SURGERY (HM03030) ||||●|||||||||||||||||||||||||||||||||||||||||||||
| PRIOSE COLES (HM16635) ||●|●|●|●||||||●|●|||●|●|||||||●|●|●|●|●|●||||||||||||●||●|||||||
| SCUNTHORPE CHIROPRACTIC CLINIC (HM18157) |||||||●||||||●|●||||||||●||||||||||||||||||||●|||||||
| HUMBERSIDE (NORTH) ||||||||||||||||||||||||||||||||||||||||||||||||
| ACADEMY PHYSIOTHERAPY CLINIC (HM00149) |||||||●||||||●|●||||||||●||||||||||||||||||||●|||||||
| BEVERLEY CHIROPRACTIC CLINIC (HM02243) |||||||●||||||●|●|||||||●|●|||||●||||||||||||||||●|||||||
| BRIDLINGTON CHIROPODY SURGERY (HM03018) ||||||||||||||||||||||||||||||||●||||●|||||●|●|●|||||
| DAMIAN P JOHNS (HM05704) ||||||||||||||||||||||||||||||||●||||||||●|●|●|||||
| GILBERDYKE SPORTS & INJURY (HM08054) |||||||●||||||●|●||||||||●||||||||||||||||||||●|||||||
| NATURAL THERAPIES (HM14629) ||●|●|●|●|●|●|●||||●|●|||●|●||●|●|●|●|●|●|●|●|●||||●||●|||●|●||●||●|●|●|||||
| NATURAL THERAPY CENTRE (HM14653) |||||●|●||●|||||||●||||||●||●||||●|●|||||||||||||||●|●||||||
| SAMANTHA WHITE AROMATICA (HM17877) ||●|●||||||||||●|●||||||||||●||||●|●|||||||||●|||||||●|||||
| HUMBERSIDE (SOUTH) ||||||||||||||||||||||||||||||||||||||||||||||||
| DAVIES, MICHAEL (HM05831) |||||||||||||●||||||||●||||||||||||||||||●|||●||●|||||
| HARRISON-WILLIAMS (HM09113) |||||||||||||||||||||||||||||||||||||||||●|●|●|||||
| HARRISON-WILLIAMS CHIROPODIST (HM09114) |||||||||||||||||||||||||||||||||||||||||●|●|●|||||
| LOUISE HEALING CENTRE (HM12668) |||●||●|●||●||||●|●|||●|||||●|●|||●||●|||●|●||●||||●||||●|●|●||●|●||
| ROBINSON, KEITH (HM17488) |||||||||||||||||||||||||||||||||||||||||●|●|●|||||
| SCARTHO OSTEOPATHIC PRACTICE (HM18007) |||||||●||||||●|●|||||||||||||||||||||||||||||●|●|●|||||
| WALL, R A (HM20819) |||||||||||||●|●||||||||●||||||||||||||||||||●|●|●|||||
| WEBB, C M (HM21057) |||||||||||||||||||||||||||||||||||||||||●|●|●|||||
| ISLE OF WIGHT ||||||||||||||||||||||||||||||||||||||||||||||||
| BURROWS, MARY (HM03424) ||||||||||||||||||||||||||||||||●||||||||●|●|●|||||
| CARISBROOKE HEALTH CENTRE (HM03687) |||||||●||||||●|||||||||●||●||||●|||||●||||||||●|●|●|||||
| FLANDERS, H (HM07391) ||||||||||||||||||||||||||||||||●||||||||●|●|●|||||
| FOOTSTEPS (HM07510) ||||||||||||||||||||||||||||||||●||||||||●|●|●|||||
| FOOTSTEPS THERAPY CENTRE (HM07513) ||||||||||||||||||||||||||||||||●|||||||||||||||
| GREENFIELD, BRIAN (HM08484) |||●|||||||||●|●||||||||●|●||||●|●||||||●||||||||●|●||||||
| HOPE CLINIC (HM10134) |●|●|●|●|●|●|●|●|●|●||●|●|●|●|●|●||●|●|●|●|●|●|●|●|●|●|●|●|●||●|●|●|●|●||●|●|●|●|●|||||
| HYPNOTHERAPY CONSULTANCY (HM10537) ||||●|●|●||●|||||||●|||||●|●||||||●|●||||||||||||||●|||||||
| SHEN CLINIC (HM18391) ||||●|●|||||||●|●|||||●|||||||||||||||||||||||||●||●|||||
| TAYLOR, S A (HM19791) |||||||||||||||||||||||||||||||||||||||||●|●|●|||||
| TOUCH FOR HEALTH (HM20186) |||||||||||||●|●||||||||||||||||||||||||||||||||||
| WRIGLEY, BARBARA (HM21956) ||||||||||||||||||●|||||||||||||||||||||||●|●|●|||||

www.healthmyself.com

# S - W Conditions treated at Practices/Businesses and Specialist Treatment Categories

| Business by County with Reference no. | Sexually Trans. Infections | Shingles | Sinus Problems | Skin Problems | Sleep Disorders | Slimming Help | Slipped Disk | Smoking Help | Sneezing | Snoring | Spinal Injuries | Sports Injuries | Sprains | Stammering | Stings | Stomach Problems | Stomach Ulcers | Stress | Sweating | Teeth Grinding | Tennis Elbow | Terminal Illness | Throat Problems | Thrush | Thyroid Problems | Tinnitis | Tiredness | Tonsilitis | Ulcers | Vaginal Problems | Varicose Veins | Verrucas | Vertigo | Viral Infections | Vomiting | Warts | Water Retention | Whiplash | Wind | Worms | Specialist Treatment Categories: Children | Terminally Ill | Disabled | Horses | Dogs | CatS | Other Animals |
|---|---|---|---|---|---|---|---|---|---|---|---|---|---|---|---|---|---|---|---|---|---|---|---|---|---|---|---|---|---|---|---|---|---|---|---|---|---|---|---|---|---|---|---|---|---|---|---|
| KENT | | | | | | | | | | | | | | | | | | | | | | | | | | | | | | | | | | | | | | | | | | | | | | | |
| ABBOTT, LISA (HM00098) | | |●| |●| | | | | | | | | | | | | | | | | | | | | |●| | | | | | | | | | | |●| |●|●|●| | | | |
| ABSOLUTE SOLUTIONS (HM00142) | | | | |●|●| |●| | | | | |●| | | | | |●| | | | | | |●| | | | | | | | | | | | | |●|●|●| | | | |
| ALEXANDER TECHNIQUE (HM00553) | | | | | | | | | | | | |●| | | | | | | | | | | | | | | | | | | | | | | | | | | |●|●|●| | | | |
| ASHFORD CLINIC (HM01216) | | | | | | | | | | | | | | | | | |●| | | | | | | | | | | | | | | | | | | | | | |●|●|●| | | | |
| ASHFORD OSTEOPATHIC CLINIC (HM01217) | | |●| | | |●| | | | |●|●| | | | | | | |●| | | | |●| | | | | | |●| | | | | | | |●| |●| |●| | |
| AYLESFORD MEDICAL CENTRE (HM01426) | | | | | | | | | | | | | | | | | | | | |●| | | | | | | | | | | | | | | | | | | |●| | | | | | |
| AYLSHAM OSTEOPATHIC PRACTICE (HM01429) | | |●| | | |●| | | | |●|●| | | | | | | |●| | | | | | | | | | | | | | | | | | | |●|●|●| |●| | |
| BECKENHAM & BROMLEY (HM02017) | | | | | | |●| | | |●|●|●| | | | | | | |●| | | | | | | | | | | | | | | | |●| | |●|●|●| | | | |
| BECKENHAM CHINESE MED CTRE (HM02019) | | | |●| | | | | | | | | | | | | | | | | | | | | | | | | | | | | | | | | | | | |●|●|●| | | | |
| BENNETT, J P (HM02143) | | | | |●| | |●| | | | | |●| | | | | | | | | | | | | | | | | | | | | | | | | | | | |●| | | | |
| BERGMANN, MARIA (DR) (HM02190) | | | |●| | | | | | | | | | | | | |●| | | | | | | | | | | | | | | | | | | | | | | |●| | | | | |
| BEXLEY OSTEOPATHIC CLINIC (HM02259) | | | | | | |●| | | |●|●|●| | | | | | | |●| | | | | | | | | | | | | | | | |●| | |●| |●| | | | |
| BEXLEYHEATH NATURAL HEALTH (HM02262) |●|●|●|●|●|●|●|●|●|●| |●|●|●|●|●|●| |●|●|●|●|●|●|●|●|●|●|●|●|●| |●|●|●|●|●| |●|●|●|●|●| | | | |
| BISHOP, SARAH (HM02411) | | |●| | | |●| | | | | | | | | | | | | |●| | | | | | | | | | | | | | | | | | | |●|●|●| | | | |
| BLACKFEN HYPNOTHERAPY (HM02442) | |●| | |●|●| | | | | | | |●| | | | | |●| | | | | |●| | | |●| | | | | | | | | | |●| | | | | | |
| BLOSSOM AROMATHERAPY CENTRE (HM02521) | | | |●|●| | | | | | | | | | | | |●| | | | | | | | | | | | | | | | | | | | | | | | | | | | | |
| BROMLEY CHIROPODY CENTRE (HM03142) | | | | | | | | | | | |●| | | | | | | | | | | | | | | | | | | |●| | | | | | | | |●|●|●| | | | |
| BROMLEY CHIROPRACTIC CLINIC (HM03143) | | | |●|●|●|●|●| | |●|●|●|●| | | | |●| |●| | | | | |●| | | | | | | | | | |●| | |●|●|●| | | | |
| BROMLEY OSTEOPATHIC CLINIC (HM03145) | | | | | | |●| | | |●|●|●| | | | | | | |●| | | | | | | | | | | | | | | | |●| | |●| |●| | | | |
| CANTERBURY OSTEOPATHIC CLINIC (HM03641) | | |●|●|●|●|●|●| | | |●|●| | |●|●| | |●|●|●|●|●|●|●|●|●|●| | | |●| | | |●| | | |●|●|●| | | | |
| CARDWELL, MARTIN (HM03673) | |●|●|●|●|●|●|●|●|●| |●|●|●|●|●|●| |●|●|●|●|●| |●|●|●|●|●|●|●| |●|●| |●|●| |●|●|●|●|●|●|●|●|●|
| CASTLE CLINIC (HM03830) |●|●|●|●|●|●|●|●|●|●| |●|●|●|●|●|●| |●|●|●|●|●|●|●|●|●|●|●|●|●| |●|●|●|●|●| |●|●|●|●|●|●| | | |
| CENTRE (HM03897) |●|●|●|●|●|●|●|●|●|●| |●|●|●|●|●|●|●|●|●|●|●|●|●|●|●|●|●|●|●|●| |●|●|●|●|●| |●|●| | | | | | | |
| CHANDRA PDS (HM03982) | | | | |●| | |●| | | | | | | | | | | | | | | | | | | | | | | | | | | | | | | | |●|●|●| | | | |
| CHANGE OF LIFE (HM03984) | | | | | |●| | | | | | | | | | |●| | | | | | | | | | | | | | | | | | | | | | |●|●|●| | | | |
| CHINESE HERBAL MED & HLTH CARE (HM04200) | | | |●| | | | | | | | | | | | | | | | | | | | | | | | | | | | | | | | | | | |●| |●| | | | |
| CHINESE HERBAL MED ACU CTRE (HM04205) | | | |●| | | | | | | | | | | | | |●| | | | | | | | | | | | | | | | | | | | | | |●|●|●| | | | |
| CHIROPRACTIC PLUS (HM04402) |●|●|●|●|●|●|●|●|●|●| |●|●|●|●|●|●| |●|●|●|●|●|●|●|●|●|●|●|●|●| |●|●|●|●|●| |●|●|●|●|●| | | | |
| CHISLEHURST NATURAL HEALTH (HM04410) |●|●|●|●|●|●|●|●|●|●| |●|●|●|●|●|●| |●|●|●|●|●|●|●|●|●|●|●|●|●| |●|●|●|●|●| |●|●|●|●|●| | | | |
| CHISTLEHURST NATURAL HLTH CTRE (HM04411) |●|●|●|●|●|●|●|●|●|●| |●|●|●|●|●|●| |●|●|●|●|●|●|●|●|●|●|●|●|●| |●|●|●|●|●| |●|●|●|●|●| | | | |
| CHRISTINE CHINNERY COMP THER (HM04446) | |●|●|●|●|●|●| |●|●| |●|●| |●|●|●| |●| |●|●|●|●|●|●|●|●|●|●|●| | |●|●|●|●| |●| |●|●|●| | | | |
| CORRIGAN, PETER (HM05195) | | | | |●|●| |●| | | | | | | | | |●| | | | | | | | | | | | | | | | | | | | | | | |●| | | | | |
| COURT, SUSAN (HM05265) | |●|●| |●| |●| | | | |●|●| | | | | | | |●| | | | |●|●| | | | | | | | | | | | | |●|●|●| | | | |

# S - W Conditions treated at Practices/Businesses and Specialist Treatment Categories

Business by County with Reference no.

| Business by County with Reference no. | Sexually Trans. Infections | Shingles | Sinus Problems | Skin Problems | Sleep Disorders | Slimming Help | Slipped Disk | Smoking Help | Sneezing | Snoring | Spinal Injuries | Sports Injuries | Sprains | Stammering | Stings | Stomach Problems | Stomach Ulcers | Stress |
|---|---|---|---|---|---|---|---|---|---|---|---|---|---|---|---|---|---|---|
| COURT, SUSAN (HM05266) | | ● | ● | | ● | | ● | | | | | ● | ● | | | | | |
| COYSTEN & ASSOCIATES (HM05332) | | | ● | | | | ● | | | | | ● | ● | | | ● | | |
| CROIX, LINDA LA (HM05460) | | | | | | | | | | | | | | | | | | ● |
| DELTA MEDI CLINIC (HM05969) | | | | | | | ● | | | | | ● | ● | | | | | |
| DICKMAN, ANNIE (HM06080) | | | ● | ● | ● | | | | | | | ● | ● | | ● | ● | | ● |
| DILLON, MICHAEL (HM06100) | | | | | ● | ● | | ● | | | | | | ● | | | | ● |
| DIMENT, GORDON L (HM06105) | | | | | ● | ● | | ● | | | | | | ● | | | | |
| EARL, A (HM06496) | | | | | ● | ● | | ● | | | | | | | | | | ● |
| EDWARDS, R (HM06668) | | | | | | | ● | | | | ● | ● | ● | | | | | |
| EDWARDS, R, HERNE BAY (HM06670) | | | | | | | ● | | | | ● | ● | ● | | | | | |
| ELIZABETH ANNE (HM06736) | | | | | | ● | | ● | | | | | | | | | | |
| EUROPEAN AYUR-VEDA (HM06944) | | | ● | ● | ● | | | | | | | | | | | | | |
| EVEGATE CLINIC (HM06996) | ● | ● | ● | ● | ● | ● | ● | ● | ● | ● | | ● | ● | ● | ● | ● | ● | |
| EVOLUTION HEALTH (HM07014) | | | ● | | | | ● | | | | | ● | ● | | | | | |
| FALCONER, PATRICIA (HM07073) | | | | | | | | | | | | | | | | | | ● |
| FEET FIRST (HM07167) | | | | | | | | | | | | | | | | | | |
| FRANCIS-JONES, TREVOR (DR) (HM07679) | | | | | | | ● | | | | ● | ● | ● | | | | | ● |
| GIBSON, JAN (HM08040) | | | | | ● | ● | | ● | | | | | | ● | | | | |
| GILLINGHAM CLINIC OF COMP MED (HM08097) | ● | ● | ● | ● | ● | | ● | | | ● | | ● | ● | | ● | ● | | |
| GRAVESEND HOMOEOPATHY CLINIC (HM08404) | | ● | ● | ● | ● | ● | ● | ● | ● | ● | | ● | ● | ● | ● | ● | ● | ● |
| GUNN, JASON (HM08642) | | | | | | | ● | | | | ● | ● | ● | | | | | |
| HANNA, MARK (HM08931) | | | | | ● | | | ● | | ● | | | | ● | | | | |
| HAWKHURST NATURAL THERAPIES (HM09216) | | | | | | | | | | | | | | | | | | |
| HAYES, JACQUELINE (HM09260) | | ● | ● | | ● | | ● | | ● | ● | | ● | ● | ● | | ● | ● | |
| HAZLEWOOD OSTEOPATHIC PRACTICE (HM09297) | | | | | | | | | | | | | | | | | | |
| HEAD TO TOE WELL-BEING (HM09300) | | | ● | | | | | | | | | | | | | | | |
| HEALING AND HERBS (HM09325) | | | ● | ● | ● | | ● | | | | | ● | ● | | | ● | ● | |
| HEATHSIDE CENTRE (HM09461) | ● | ● | ● | ● | ● | ● | ● | ● | ● | ● | | ● | ● | ● | ● | ● | ● | |
| HERTERICH, NIGEL (HM09688) | | | | | | | | | | | | ● | ● | | | | | |
| HOFFMAN, BRIAN ASSOCIATES (HM09900) | | | | | | | | | | | | ● | ● | | | | | |
| HOLMES, S A (HM10045) | | | ● | ● | ● | | | | | | | | | | | | | |
| HOPE CHIROPRACTIC (HM10133) | | | | | | | | | | | ● | ● | ● | | | | | |
| ISIS (HM10763) | | | | | | | | | | | | | | | | | | |
| JACCQUELINE ELLISON PRACTICE (HM10811) | | | | | | | | | | | | ● | | | | | | |

| Business by County with Reference no. | Sweating | Teeth Grinding | Tennis Elbow | Terminal Illness | Throat Problems | Thrush | Thyroid Problems | Tinnitis | Tiredness | Tonsilitis | Ulcers | Vaginal Problems | Varicose Veins | Verrucas | Vertigo | Viral Infections | Vomiting | Warts | Water Retention | Whiplash | Wind | Worms |
|---|---|---|---|---|---|---|---|---|---|---|---|---|---|---|---|---|---|---|---|---|---|---|
| COURT, SUSAN (HM05266) | | | ● | | | | | ● | ● | | | | | | | | | | | | | |
| COYSTEN & ASSOCIATES (HM05332) | | ● | ● | | | | | ● | | | | | | | ● | | | | | | | |
| CROIX, LINDA LA (HM05460) | | | | | | | | | | | | | | | | | | | | | | |
| DELTA MEDI CLINIC (HM05969) | | | | | | | | | | | | | | | | | | | | | | |
| DICKMAN, ANNIE (HM06080) | | | ● | | ● | ● | ● | ● | ● | ● | | | ● | | | | | | | | | |
| DILLON, MICHAEL (HM06100) | | | | ● | | | | ● | | | | | | | | | | | | | | |
| DIMENT, GORDON L (HM06105) | | | | | | | | | | | | | | | | | | | | | | |
| EARL, A (HM06496) | | | | | | | | | | | | | | | | | | | | | | |
| EDWARDS, R (HM06668) | | | ● | | | | | | | | | | | | | | | | | ● | | |
| EDWARDS, R, HERNE BAY (HM06670) | | | | | | | | | | | | | | | | | | | | ● | | |
| ELIZABETH ANNE (HM06736) | | | | | | | | | | | | | | | | | | | | | | |
| EUROPEAN AYUR-VEDA (HM06944) | | | | | | | | | | | | | ● | | | | | | | | | |
| EVEGATE CLINIC (HM06996) | ● | ● | ● | ● | ● | ● | ● | ● | ● | ● | ● | ● | ● | | ● | ● | ● | ● | ● | | ● | ● |
| EVOLUTION HEALTH (HM07014) | | ● | ● | | | | | | | | | | | | | | | | | | | |
| FALCONER, PATRICIA (HM07073) | | | | | | | | | | | | | | | | | | | | | | |
| FEET FIRST (HM07167) | | | | | | | | | | | | | | | | | | | | | | |
| FRANCIS-JONES, TREVOR (DR) (HM07679) | | | ● | | | | | | | | | | | | | | | | | ● | | |
| GIBSON, JAN (HM08040) | | ● | | ● | | | | | | | | | | | | | ● | | | | | |
| GILLINGHAM CLINIC OF COMP MED (HM08097) | | ● | | ● | ● | ● | ● | ● | ● | ● | | ● | ● | | ● | | ● | ● | | | | |
| GRAVESEND HOMOEOPATHY CLINIC (HM08404) | ● | ● | ● | ● | ● | ● | ● | ● | ● | ● | ● | ● | ● | | ● | ● | ● | ● | ● | | ● | ● |
| GUNN, JASON (HM08642) | | | | | | | | | | | | | | | | | | | | ● | | |
| HANNA, MARK (HM08931) | | ● | | | | | | ● | | | | | | | | | | | | | | |
| HAWKHURST NATURAL THERAPIES (HM09216) | | | | | | | | | | | | | | | | | | | | | | |
| HAYES, JACQUELINE (HM09260) | ● | ● | ● | ● | | | | | ● | ● | | | ● | | ● | | ● | | ● | | ● | |
| HAZLEWOOD OSTEOPATHIC PRACTICE (HM09297) | | | ● | | | | | | | | | | | | | | | | | | | |
| HEAD TO TOE WELL-BEING (HM09300) | | | | | | | | | | | | | | | | | | | ● | | | |
| HEALING AND HERBS (HM09325) | | | ● | ● | | ● | | | ● | ● | ● | ● | | | | ● | | ● | ● | | | |
| HEATHSIDE CENTRE (HM09461) | ● | ● | ● | ● | ● | ● | ● | ● | ● | ● | ● | ● | ● | | ● | ● | ● | ● | ● | | ● | ● |
| HERTERICH, NIGEL (HM09688) | | | ● | | | | | | | | | | | | | | | | | | | |
| HOFFMAN, BRIAN ASSOCIATES (HM09900) | | | ● | | | | | | | | | | ● | | | | | | | | | |
| HOLMES, S A (HM10045) | | | | | | | | | ● | | | | | | | | | | ● | | ● | |
| HOPE CHIROPRACTIC (HM10133) | | | ● | | | | | | | | | | | | | | | | | ● | | |
| ISIS (HM10763) | | | | | | | | | | | | | | | | | | | | | | |
| JACCQUELINE ELLISON PRACTICE (HM10811) | | | ● | | | | | | | | | | | | | | | | | | | |

**Specialist Treatment Categories**

| Business by County with Reference no. | Children | Terminally Ill | Disabled | Horses | Dogs | CatS | Other Animals |
|---|---|---|---|---|---|---|---|
| COURT, SUSAN (HM05266) | ● | ● | ● | | | | |
| COYSTEN & ASSOCIATES (HM05332) | ● | ● | | | | | |
| CROIX, LINDA LA (HM05460) | ● | | | | | | |
| DELTA MEDI CLINIC (HM05969) | ● | | ● | | | | |
| DICKMAN, ANNIE (HM06080) | ● | | | | ● | | |
| DILLON, MICHAEL (HM06100) | ● | ● | ● | | | | |
| DIMENT, GORDON L (HM06105) | ● | | | | | | |
| EARL, A (HM06496) | ● | ● | | | | | |
| EDWARDS, R (HM06668) | ● | ● | ● | | | | |
| EDWARDS, R, HERNE BAY (HM06670) | ● | ● | ● | | | | |
| ELIZABETH ANNE (HM06736) | ● | | | | | | |
| EUROPEAN AYUR-VEDA (HM06944) | | | | | | | |
| EVEGATE CLINIC (HM06996) | | | | | | | |
| EVOLUTION HEALTH (HM07014) | ● | | ● | | | | |
| FALCONER, PATRICIA (HM07073) | ● | ● | ● | | | | |
| FEET FIRST (HM07167) | ● | ● | ● | | | | |
| FRANCIS-JONES, TREVOR (DR) (HM07679) | ● | ● | ● | | | | |
| GIBSON, JAN (HM08040) | ● | ● | ● | | ● | ● | |
| GILLINGHAM CLINIC OF COMP MED (HM08097) | ● | ● | ● | | | | |
| GRAVESEND HOMOEOPATHY CLINIC (HM08404) | ● | ● | ● | | | | |
| GUNN, JASON (HM08642) | ● | | ● | | | | |
| HANNA, MARK (HM08931) | ● | | | | | | |
| HAWKHURST NATURAL THERAPIES (HM09216) | ● | ● | ● | | | | |
| HAYES, JACQUELINE (HM09260) | ● | ● | ● | ● | ● | ● | ● |
| HAZLEWOOD OSTEOPATHIC PRACTICE (HM09297) | ● | ● | ● | | | | |
| HEAD TO TOE WELL-BEING (HM09300) | | | | | | | |
| HEALING AND HERBS (HM09325) | ● | ● | | | | | |
| HEATHSIDE CENTRE (HM09461) | ● | ● | ● | | | | |
| HERTERICH, NIGEL (HM09688) | ● | | | | | | |
| HOFFMAN, BRIAN ASSOCIATES (HM09900) | ● | ● | ● | ● | ● | ● | ● |
| HOLMES, S A (HM10045) | | ● | ● | | | | |
| HOPE CHIROPRACTIC (HM10133) | ● | ● | ● | | | | |
| ISIS (HM10763) | ● | ● | ● | ● | ● | ● | ● |
| JACCQUELINE ELLISON PRACTICE (HM10811) | | | | | | | |

# S - W Conditions treated at Practices/Businesses and Specialist Treatment Categories

| Business by County with Reference no. | | | | | | | | | | | | | | | | | | | | | | | | | | | | | | | | | | | | | | | | | Specialist Treatment Categories | | | | | | |
|---|---|---|---|---|---|---|---|---|---|---|---|---|---|---|---|---|---|---|---|---|---|---|---|---|---|---|---|---|---|---|---|---|---|---|---|---|---|---|---|---|---|---|---|---|---|---|
| | Sexually Trans. Infections | Shingles | Sinus Problems | Skin Problems | Sleep Disorders | Slimming Help | Slipped Disk | Smoking Help | Sneezing | Snoring | Spinal Injuries | Sports Injuries | Sprains | Stammering | Stings | Stomach Problems | Stomach Ulcers | Stress | Sweating | Teeth Grinding | Tennis Elbow | Terminal Illness | Throat Problems | Thrush | Thyroid Problems | Tinnitis | Tiredness | Tonsilitis | Ulcers | Vaginal Problems | Varicose Veins | Verrucas | Vertigo | Viral Infections | Vomiting | Warts | Water Retention | Whiplash | Wind | Worms | Children | Terminally Ill | Disabled | Horses | Dogs | CatS | Other Animals |
| KARMERS CLINIQUE (HM11328) | | | ● | ● | | | | | | | | ● | | | | | | | | | | | | | | ● | ● | | | | | | ● | | | | | | | | ● | ● | ● | | | | |
| KENT HOUSE CHIROPRACTIC CLINIC (HM11519) | | | | | | | ● | | | | ● | ● | ● | | | | | | | | ● | | | | | | | | | | | | | | | | | ● | | | ● | ● | ● | | | | |
| KENT HOUSE CHIROPRACTIC CLINIC (HM11517) | | | | | | | ● | | | | ● | ● | ● | | | | | | | | ● | | | | | | | | | | | | | | | | | ● | | | ● | ● | ● | | | | |
| KENT HOUSE CHIROPRACTIC CLINIC (HM11518) | | | | | | | ● | | | | ● | ● | ● | ● | | | | | | | ● | | | | | | | | | | | | | | | | | ● | | | ● | ● | ● | | | | |
| KENT HOUSE CHIROPRACTIC CLINIC (HM11520) | | | | | | | ● | | | | ● | ● | ● | | | | | | | | ● | | | | | | | | | | | | | | | | | ● | | | ● | ● | ● | | | | |
| KSC (HM11812) | ● | ● | ● | ● | ● | ● | ● | ● | ● | ● | | ● | ● | ● | ● | ● | ● | | ● | ● | ● | ● | ● | ● | ● | ● | ● | ● | ● | ● | ● | | ● | ● | ● | ● | ● | | ● | ● | ● | ● | ● | | | | |
| LAMB, G BRIAN (HM11888) | | ● | ● | ● | ● | ● | ● | | ● | ● | | ● | ● | ● | ● | ● | ● | | ● | ● | ● | | ● | | ● | ● | ● | ● | ● | | ● | | ● | ● | ● | | ● | | ● | ● | ● | ● | ● | | | | |
| LAVINGOTN, A (HM12034) | | | | ● | ● | | | | | | | | | | | | | ● | | | | | | | | | | | | | | | | | | | | | | | ● | ● | ● | | | | |
| LEBOR, JILL (HM12115) | | | ● | ● | ● | | ● | | ● | | | ● | ● | | | ● | | | | ● | ● | | ● | | ● | ● | ● | | | | | | | | | | ● | | ● | | ● | ● | ● | | | | |
| LEBRET, A F (HM12117) | | | | | | | | | | | | | | | | | | | | | | | | | | | | | | | | | | | | | | | | | ● | ● | ● | | | | |
| LIVING WELL CLINIC (HM12488) | | | | | | | | | | | ● | ● | ● | | | | | | | | ● | | | | | | | | | | | | | | | | | ● | | | ● | ● | ● | | | | |
| LOBB, BRIAN W (HM12528) | | | | | | | | ● | | | | | | | | | | | | | | | | | | | | | | | | | | | | | | | | | | | | | | | |
| LUGG, G (HM12732) | | | ● | ● | ● | | | | | | | ● | | | | | | | | | | | | | | | | | | | | | | | | | | | | | ● | ● | ● | | | | |
| MABBERLEY, KATHIE (HM12812) | | | ● | | | | | | | | | ● | ● | | | | | | | | ● | | | | | ● | | | | | | | | | | | | | | | ● | ● | ● | | | | |
| MAIDSTONE ACUPUNCTURE CLINIC (HM12935) | ● | ● | ● | ● | ● | ● | ● | ● | ● | ● | | ● | ● | ● | | ● | ● | | ● | ● | ● | | ● | ● | ● | ● | ● | ● | ● | ● | ● | | ● | | | | ● | | | | | | | | | | |
| MARY CANNON - CLINICAL NUTRI (HM13221) | | | ● | ● | ● | ● | | | | | | | | | | ● | ● | | ● | | | | ● | ● | ● | ● | ● | ● | ● | ● | ● | | | ● | ● | | ● | | ● | ● | ● | | ● | | | | |
| MASON & ASSOCIATES (HM13232) | | | | | | | ● | | | | ● | ● | ● | | | | | | | | ● | | | | | | | | | | | | | | | | | ● | | | ● | ● | ● | | | | |
| MASON & ASSOCIATES (HM13233) | | | | | | | ● | | | | ● | ● | ● | | | | | | | | ● | | | | | | | | | | | | | | | | | ● | | | ● | | ● | | | | |
| MATHER, SUE (HM13281) | ● | ● | ● | ● | ● | ● | ● | ● | ● | ● | | ● | ● | ● | ● | ● | ● | | ● | ● | ● | ● | ● | ● | ● | ● | ● | ● | ● | ● | ● | | ● | ● | ● | ● | ● | | ● | ● | ● | ● | ● | | | | |
| MCDOWELL, S (HM13467) | | | | | | | | | | | | | | | | | | | | | | | | | | | | | | | | | | | | | | | | | ● | | ● | | | | |
| MEADOWS (HM13630) | | | | ● | ● | | | | | | | | | | | | | | | | | | | | | | | | | | | | | | | | | | | | ● | ● | ● | ● | ● | ● | ● |
| MEOPHAM CLINIC (HM13732) | | | | | | | ● | | | | ● | ● | ● | | | | | | | | ● | | | | | | | | | | | | | | | | | ● | | | ● | ● | ● | | | | |
| MUIRHEAD, MARGARET (HM14323) | ● | ● | ● | ● | ● | ● | | ● | ● | ● | | | | | ● | ● | | | | | ● | ● | ● | ● | ● | ● | ● | ● | ● | ● | ● | | ● | ● | ● | ● | ● | | ● | ● | ● | ● | ● | | | | |
| MULVANEY, ALISTAIR (HM14353) | | | | ● | | | | | | | | | ● | | | | | | | | | | | | | | | | | | | | | | | ● | | | | | ● | | ● | | | | |
| NATURAL HEALTH CENTRE (HM14568) | ● | ● | ● | ● | ● | ● | ● | ● | ● | ● | | ● | ● | ● | ● | ● | ● | | ● | ● | ● | ● | ● | ● | ● | ● | ● | ● | ● | ● | ● | | ● | ● | ● | ● | ● | | ● | ● | ● | ● | ● | | | | |
| NATURAL HEALTH CENTRE (HM14562) | | | | ● | | | | ● | | | | | | ● | | | | ● | ● | ● | | | | | | | ● | | | | | | ● | | | | | | | | ● | ● | ● | | | | |
| NATURAL THERAPIST (HM14635) | | | ● | ● | ● | | ● | | | | | ● | ● | | | ● | ● | | | | | | | | | ● | ● | | | | ● | | ● | | | | ● | | | | ● | | ● | | | | |
| NATURAL THERAPY CENTRE (HM14643) | | | | | | | | | | | | | | | | | | | | | | | | | | | | | | | | | | | | | | | | | ● | ● | ● | | | | |
| OPTIVAVA (HM15352) | | | | | | | | | | | | | | | | | | | | | | | | | | | | | | | | | | | | | | | | | ● | ● | ● | | | | |
| OSTEOPATHIC CLINIC (HM15461) | | | | | | | ● | | | | ● | ● | ● | | | | | | | | ● | | | | | | | | | | | | | | | | | ● | | | ● | ● | ● | | | | |
| OSTEOPATHIC PRACTICE (HM15466) | | | | | | | ● | | | | | ● | ● | | | | | | | | | | | | | | | | | | | | | | | | | | | | ● | | | | | | |
| PASSCHIER, MAREANNE SASSEN (HM15779) | ● | ● | ● | ● | ● | ● | ● | ● | ● | ● | | ● | ● | ● | ● | ● | ● | | ● | ● | ● | ● | ● | ● | ● | ● | ● | ● | ● | ● | ● | | ● | ● | ● | ● | ● | | ● | ● | ● | ● | ● | | | | |
| PATERSON, MARGARET (HM15814) | | | ● | | ● | | ● | | | | | ● | ● | | | | | | | ● | ● | ● | ● | | ● | ● | ● | | | | | | | ● | | | | | | | ● | ● | ● | | | | |
| PEARTON, GILL (HM15919) | | | ● | ● | ● | | ● | | | ● | | ● | ● | | | ● | ● | | | ● | ● | | ● | | ● | ● | ● | | ● | | | | | ● | | ● | | | ● | | ● | ● | | | | | |

# S - W Conditions treated at Practices/Businesses and Specialist Treatment Categories

| | | | | | | | | | | | | | | | | | | | | | | | | | | | | | | | | | | | | | | | | | Specialist Treatment Categories | | | | | | |
|---|---|---|---|---|---|---|---|---|---|---|---|---|---|---|---|---|---|---|---|---|---|---|---|---|---|---|---|---|---|---|---|---|---|---|---|---|---|---|---|---|---|---|---|---|---|---|
| Business by County with Reference no. | Sexually Trans. Infections | Shingles | Sinus Problems | Skin Problems | Sleep Disorders | Slimming Help | Slipped Disk | Smoking Help | Sneezing | Snoring | Spinal Injuries | Sports Injuries | Sprains | Stammering | Stings | Stomach Problems | Stomach Ulcers | Stress | Sweating | Teeth Grinding | Tennis Elbow | Terminal Illness | Throat Problems | Thrush | Thyroid Problems | Tinnitis | Tiredness | Tonsilitis | Ulcers | Vaginal Problems | Varicose Veins | Verrucas | Vertigo | Viral Infections | Vomiting | Warts | Water Retention | Whiplash | Wind | Worms | Children | Terminally Ill | Disabled | Horses | Dogs | CatS | Other Animals |
| PELE, ANDRI (HM15950) |||●||||●||||||●||||●|●|●|||||||●||||||●||||||||●|●|●|||||
| PHYSIOTHERAPY CENTRE (HM16230) |||||||||||●|||||||||||||||||||||||||||||||||●|●|●|||||
| PRINCES AVENUE OSTEOPATHIC (HM16623) |||||||●|||||●|●|||||||||||||||||||||||||||||||||●|||||||
| RALPH & EVANS (HM16906) ||●|●|●|●||||●|||||||●|●||●||||●|●|●|●|●|●|●|●|●||●|●|●|●|●||●||●|||||||
| READ, CHARLES REG OSTEOPATH (HM16994) |||||||●|||||●|●||||||||●|||||●|||||||||||||||●|●|●|||||
| REVEREND CAROL HADDERSLEY (HM17204) |●|●|●|●|●|●|●|●|●|●||●|●|●|●|●|●||●|●|●|●|●|●|●|●|●|●|●|●|●||●|●|●|●|●||●|●|●|●|●||●|●||
| RIDLEY, VICKY (HM17324) |●|●|●|●|●|||●|●|●||●|●|●|●|●|●||●||●|●|●|●|●|●|●|●|●|●|●||●|●||●|●||●|●|●|●|●||●|●|●|
| ROCHESTER PHYSIO & SPORTS (HM17520) |||||||●|||||●|●||||||||●|||||||||||||||||||||●||●|||||
| ROMNEY MARSH OSTEOPATHS (HM17574) |||●||||●|||||●|●|||●|●||||●||●||●|●|●|||||||●||||||||●|●|●|||||
| ROSE, NAOMI (HM17612) |||●|●|●||||||||●||||||●|||●|●|||||●||||●||||||●||||●|●|●|||||
| ROUND ROOM (HM17663) ||||●|●|||||||||||||●|||||||||●||||||||||||||||●|||||
| SACKS, PATRICA (HM17828) |||||||||||||||||||||||||||||||||●||||●|||||●|●|●||●|●||
| SANCTUM HOLISTIC THERAPY CTRE (HM17896) ||||●|●|||||||||||||●||||||||||||||||||||||||||||||
| SANDERS, PETER (HM17914) |||||||●|||||●|●||||||||●|||||||||||||||||||||●|●|●|||||
| SANDOWN CLINIC FOR COMP MED (HM17926) |●|●|●|●|●|●|●|●|●|●||●|●|●|●|●|●||●|●|●|●|●|●|●|●|●|●|●|●|●||●|●|●|●|●||●|●||||||||
| SHEARER, GAYLE (HM18357) |||||||●|||||●|●||||||||●|||||||||||||||||||||●||●|||||
| SHIATSU (HM18451) |||||●||||||●||||●||||||||||||●||||||||||||||●|●||||||
| SOUTH LONDON HYPNOTHERAPY CTRE (HM18910) ||●|●|●|●|●||●|●|●||||●||●|●||●|●|||●|||●|●|||●||||●|●|●|||●||●|●|●|||||
| SOUTHCOTE CHIROPRACTIC CLINIC (HM18927) |||||||●|||||●|●||||||||●|||||||||||||||||||||●||●|||||
| STARFIELDS HOLISTIC HLTH CTRE (HM19145) |●|●|●|●|●||●||●|●|●|●|●|●||●|●|●|●|●|●|●|●|●|●|●|●|●|●|●|●|●|●|●|●|●|●|●|●|●||●|●|●|●|●|●|●|
| STONE, CHARLES (HM19334) ||||||●||●|||||||||||●|||||||||||||||||||||||●||●|||||
| STURGE, DEBBIE (HM19445) ||||●||●||||||||||||||||||●|●||●|||||||||||||●||●|●|●|||||
| SWAN, VIVA (HM19575) |●|●|●|●|●|●|●|●|●|●||●|●|●|●|●|●||●|●|●|●|●|●|●|●|●|●|●|●|●||●|●|●|●|●||●|●||||||||
| SYCAMORE, TONI (HM19606) ||||●|●|||||||||||||||||||||||||||||||||||||||||||||
| TONBRIDGE CLINIC (HM20151) |||●|●|●|●|●|●|●|●||●|●||||||||●||||||●||||||●||||||||●|●|●|||||
| TOWN, BERNICE (HM20199) |||||||||||||||||||||||||||||||||●||||●|||||●|●|●|||||
| TURNER, ANDREA (HM20417) |||●||||||||||||||||●|||||||||●||||||||||||||||●|●||||||
| TURNER, PENNY (HM20434) |||||||||||||||||||●||||||||||||||||||||||||||||||
| USEFUL THERAPIES (HM20534) |||||||||||||||||||||||||||||||||||||||||●|●|●|||||
| VARNEY, MONICA (HM20591) |||●||●|●|||||●||||●|||||||●|||||●|||||||||||||●||●|●||||||
| VILLAGE PHYSIOTHERAPY PRACTICE (HM20667) |||||||●|||||●|●||||||||●||||||||||||||||●||||||||||
| VINCENT, EUNICE (HM20671) |||||||||||||||||||●||||||||||||||||||||||||●|●|||||
| VINES REIKI HEALING CENTRE (HM20680) |●|●|●|●|●|●|●|●|●|●||●|●|●|●|●|●||●|●|●|●|●|●|●|●|●|●|●|●|●||●|●|●|●|●||●|●|●|●|●|||||
| WATLING STREET THERAPY CTRE (HM21001) ||●|●|●|●|●||●||||●|●|||||||●|●||||||●|●||||||||●|●||●||●|●|●|||||

www.healthmyself.com

Healthmyself Directory

# S - W Conditions treated at Practices/Businesses and Specialist Treatment Categories

| Business by County with Reference no. | Sexually Trans. Infections | Shingles | Sinus Problems | Skin Problems | Sleep Disorders | Slimming Help | Slipped Disk | Smoking Help | Sneezing | Snoring | Spinal Injuries | Sports Injuries | Sprains | Stammering | Stings | Stomach Problems | Stomach Ulcers | Stress | Sweating | Teeth Grinding | Tennis Elbow | Terminal Illness | Throat Problems | Thrush | Thyroid Problems | Tinnitis | Tiredness | Tonsilitis | Ulcers | Vaginal Problems | Varicose Veins | Verrucas | Vertigo | Viral Infections | Vomiting | Warts | Water Retention | Whiplash | Wind | Worms | Specialist Treatment Categories: Children | Terminally Ill | Disabled | Horses | Dogs | CatS | Other Animals |
|---|---|---|---|---|---|---|---|---|---|---|---|---|---|---|---|---|---|---|---|---|---|---|---|---|---|---|---|---|---|---|---|---|---|---|---|---|---|---|---|---|---|---|---|---|---|---|---|
| WEBB, JENNIFER (HM21067) | | | ● | | | | | | | | | | | | | | | | | | | | | | | | | | | | | | | | | | | | | | ● | | | | | | |
| WELLS PHYSIO & SPORTS CLINIC (HM21168) | | | | | | | ● | | | | | ● | ● | | | | | | | | ● | | | | | | | | | | | | | | | | | | | | ● | | | | | | |
| WOLFE, ROBERT (HM21762) | | | | | | | | | | | | ● | | | | | | | | | | | | | | | | | | | | ● | | | | ● | | | | | ● | ● | ● | | | | |
| WOOLF, JOY (HM21871) | | | | | | | | | | | | | | | | | | ● | | | | | | | | | | | | | | | | | | | | | | | | | | | | | |
| **LANCASHIRE** | | | | | | | | | | | | | | | | | | | | | | | | | | | | | | | | | | | | | | | | | | | | | | | |
| ABERNETHY, HILARY (HM00123) | | | | | ● | ● | | | | | | | | | | | | | | | | | | | | | ● | | | | | | | | | | | | | | ● | ● | ● | | | | |
| ACUPUNCTURE PRIVATE CLINIC (HM00317) | | | | | | | | ● | | | | | | | | | | | | | | | | | | | | | | | | | | | | | | | | | | | | | | | |
| ALPHAWAVE (HM00685) | | | | | | | | ● | | | | | | | | | | ● | | | | | | | | | | | | | | | | | | | | | | | ● | ● | ● | | | | |
| ALTERNATIVE MEDICINE (HM00715) | | ● | ● | ● | ● | ● | ● | ● | ● | ● | | ● | ● | ● | | ● | ● | | ● | | ● | | | ● | | ● | ● | ● | ● | | ● | | ● | | | ● | ● | ● | ● | ● | ● | ● | ● | | | | |
| ALTERNATIVE MEDICINE PRACTICE (HM00721) | | ● | ● | ● | ● | ● | ● | ● | ● | ● | | ● | ● | ● | | ● | ● | | ● | | ● | | ● | ● | | ● | ● | ● | ● | | ● | | ● | | ● | ● | ● | | ● | ● | ● | ● | ● | | | | |
| BACUP HOLISTIC THERAPIES (HM01532) | | | | | | | | | | | | | | | | | | ● | | | | | | | | | | | | | | | | | | | | | | | ● | ● | ● | ● | ● | ● | ● |
| BARRETT & LIPTROTT (HM01783) | | | | | | | | | | | | | | | | | | | | | | | | | | | | | | | | ● | | | | ● | | | | | | ● | ● | ● | | | |
| BEARLEY, CAROL (HM01969) | | | ● | | ● | | | | | | | | | | | | | ● | | | | | | | | | | | | | ● | | | | | | | | | | ● | ● | ● | | | | |
| BEESTON, J (HM02061) | | ● | | | | | ● | | | | | ● | ● | | | | | | | | ● | | | | | | | | | | | | ● | | | | | | | | | | ● | | | | |
| BENTLEY AND ASSOCIATES (HM02172) | | | | | | | ● | | | | | ● | ● | | | | | | | | ● | | | | | | | | | | | | | | | ● | | | | | ● | ● | ● | | | | |
| BFMP (HM02265) | | ● | ● | ● | ● | ● | ● | ● | | | | | ● | | | ● | ● | | | | ● | | ● | ● | ● | ● | ● | ● | ● | | | | ● | ● | ● | ● | ● | | ● | ● | ● | | | | | | |
| BIOS NATURE CLINIC (HM02344) | | | | | | | | | | | | | | | | | | | | | | | | | | | | | | | | | | | | | | | | | ● | ● | ● | ● | | | |
| BOLTON CHIROPRATIC CLINIC (HM02656) | | | | | | | | | | | ● | ● | ● | | | | | | | | ● | | | | | | | | | | | | | | | | | ● | | | ● | ● | ● | | | | |
| BOLTON CLINIC OF ACUPUNCTURE (HM02657) | | | ● | ● | | | | | | | | ● | | | | | | | | | | | | | | | ● | | | | | | | | | | | | | | ● | ● | ● | | | | |
| BOLTON PHYSIOTHERAPY CLINIC (HM02658) | | | | | | | ● | | | | | ● | ● | | | | | | | | ● | | | | | | | | | | | | | | | | | | | | ● | ● | ● | | | | |
| BOLTON THERAPY CENTRE (HM02659) | | ● | ● | | ● | | ● | ● | | | | ● | ● | | | | | ● | | ● | ● | | | | | ● | ● | | | | | | ● | | ● | | | ● | ● | | ● | | ● | | | | |
| BOLTON, VANESSA (HM02664) | | ● | ● | ● | ● | | | | | | | | | | | ● | | | | | ● | | ● | | ● | | ● | | | ● | ● | | ● | | | | ● | | ● | | ● | | | | | | |
| BRIDGWATER, K A (HM03016) | ● | ● | ● | ● | ● | ● | ● | ● | ● | ● | | ● | ● | ● | ● | ● | ● | ● | ● | ● | ● | ● | ● | ● | ● | ● | ● | ● | ● | ● | ● | | ● | ● | ● | ● | ● | | ● | ● | ● | ● | ● | | | | |
| BROOKES, MICHAEL (HM03163) | | | | ● | | | | | | | | | | | | ● | | | | | | | | ● | | | | | | | | | | | | | | | | | ● | ● | ● | | | | |
| BURSCOUGH PHYSIOTHERAPY (HM03425) | | | | | | | | | | | ● | | | | | | | | | | | | | | | | | | | | | | | | | | | | | | | | ● | | | | |
| CHARTERED PHYSIO & SPORTS (HM04041) | | | | | | | ● | | | | | ● | ● | | | | | | | | ● | | | | | | | | | | | | | | | | | | | | ● | ● | ● | | | | |
| CLOUGHS - CHRTRD PHYSIO CLINIC (HM04735) | | | | | | | ● | | | | | ● | ● | | | | | | | | ● | | | | | | | | | | | | | | | | | | | | ● | | ● | | | | |
| COLES, RONNIE (HM04836) | | | | | | | | | | | | | | | | | | | | | | | | | | | | | | | | ● | | | | | | | | | | | | | | | |
| COMPLEMENTARY HEALTH SERVICES (HM04929) | | | | | | | ● | | | | | | ● | | | | | | | ● | | | | | | | | | | | | | | | | | | | | | ● | | ● | | | | |
| COTTAM, O N (HM05224) | | | | | | | | | | | | | | | | | | | | | | | | | | | | | | | | | | | | | | | | | ● | ● | ● | | | | |
| CRYSTAL & REIKI (HM05524) | | | | ● | ● | | | | | | | | | | | | | ● | | | | | | | | | | | | | | | | | | | | | | | ● | ● | ● | | | | |
| DAVIES, JOHNATHON (HM05819) | | | | | | | | | | | | | | | | | | | | | | | | | | | | | | | | ● | | | | | | | | | ● | ● | ● | | | | |
| DOUGLAS, CAROLINE (HM06213) | | | | | | | | | | | | | | | | | | | | | | | | | | | | | | | | ● | | | | | | | | | ● | ● | ● | | | | |
| DUCKWORTH, JEAN (HM06347) | | ● | ● | ● | ● | | | ● | ● | ● | | ● | ● | ● | ● | ● | ● | | ● | ● | ● | ● | ● | ● | ● | ● | ● | ● | ● | ● | ● | | ● | ● | ● | ● | ● | | ● | ● | ● | ● | ● | | | | |

# S - W Conditions treated at Practices/Businesses and Specialist Treatment Categories

Business by County with Reference no.

| Business by County with Reference no. | Sexually Trans. Infections | Shingles | Sinus Problems | Skin Problems | Sleep Disorders | Slimming Help | Slipped Disk | Smoking Help | Sneezing | Snoring | Spinal Injuries | Sports Injuries | Sprains | Stammering | Stings | Stomach Problems | Stomach Ulcers | Stress | Sweating | Teeth Grinding |
|---|---|---|---|---|---|---|---|---|---|---|---|---|---|---|---|---|---|---|---|---|
| GEE, D (HM07957) | | | | | | | | | | | | | | | | | | | | |
| GINSBERG, ANNE (HM08111) | | | | | | | | | | | | | | | | | | | | |
| GREENHALGH, A J T (HM08489) | | | | | | | | | | | | | | | | | | | | |
| GROGAN, DIANA E (HM08592) | | | ● | ● | | | ● | ● | | | | ● | | | | ● | | | | |
| HAMPSOM, JAMES (HM08878) | | | ● | ● | ● | | | | | | | ● | | | | | | | | |
| HARDMAN, ALAN (HM08974) | | | | | | | | | | | | | | | | | | | | |
| HARMONIOUS HEALTHCARE (HM09015) | | ● | ● | ● | ● | | ● | | ● | | | ● | ● | | ● | ● | | | ● | |
| HAYDOCK, CLAIRE (HM09254) | | | | | | | | | | | | | | | | | | | | |
| HEAVENS SCENT AROMATHERAPY (HM09478) | | | ● | ● | | | | | | | | | ● | | | | | ● | | |
| HEYWORTH, S (HM09716) | | | | | | | | | | | | | | | | | | | | |
| HOLDEN, JOHN H (HM09932) | | | | | | | | | | | | | | | | | | | | |
| JOHN HOLDEN ASSOCIATES (HM11051) | | | | | | | | | | | | ● | | | | | | | | |
| KELLY CHIROPODY (HM11424) | | | | | ● | | | | | | | ● | ● | | | ● | | ● | | |
| KENDEL HOUSE CLINIC (HM11479) | | | ● | ● | ● | | ● | ● | | | ● | ● | ● | | | | | | | |
| LAYNE, SUSAN G (HM12077) | | | ● | ● | | | | ● | | | | | | ● | | | | | ● | ● |
| LEYLAND PHYSIOTHERAPY CENTRE (HM12319) | | | | | | | ● | | | | | ● | ● | | | | | | | |
| MALKIN, DK, MANIP THERAPY (HM12975) | | | | | | | ● | | | | | ● | ● | | | | | | | |
| MOBILE CHIROPODIST (HM14027) | | | | | | | | | | | | | | | | | | | | |
| NATURAL HEALTH CENTRE (HM14566) | | ● | ● | ● | | | | ● | | | | ● | ● | | | | | | | |
| NELSON, S (HM14782) | | | ● | ● | ● | | ● | | | | | | | ● | | ● | ● | | | ● |
| ONE STOP HEALTH & BEAUTY (HM15323) | ● | ● | ● | ● | ● | ● | ● | ● | ● | ● | ● | ● | ● | ● | ● | ● | ● | ● | ● | ● |
| PEPPER, JOHN (HM16009) | | | | ● | ● | | | | | | | | | | | ● | | | | |
| PHYSIO AND SPORTS INJURIES (HM16195) | | | | | | | ● | | | | | ● | ● | | | | | | | |
| PURCELL, AMANDA (HM16762) | | | | | | | ● | | | | ● | ● | ● | | | | | | | |
| RAMSBOTTOM PHYSIO CLINIC (HM16919) | | | | | | | ● | | | | | ● | ● | | | | | | | |
| RATCLIFFE, MARK (HM16949) | | | ● | | | | ● | | | | | ● | ● | | | | | | | |
| REMEDIAL MASSAGE/SPORTS (HM17175) | | | | | | | ● | | | | | ● | ● | | | | | | | |
| SMITH, CHRISTOPHER (DR) (HM18728) | | | | | | | | | | | | ● | ● | | | | | | | |
| SPIRITUAL THERAPIST (HM19029) | | | | | | | | | | | | | | | | ● | | | | |
| ST GEORGES MULTI THERAPY CTRE (HM19075) | | | ● | ● | | ● | | ● | | | | | | ● | ● | | | | | ● |
| ST MARY'S CLINIC (HM19087) | | | | | | | ● | | | | | ● | ● | | | | | | | |
| TATTERSALL, KAREN (HM19719) | | | | | | | | | | | | | | | | | | | | |
| TINKER, D C (HM20083) | | | | | | | | | | | | | | | | | | | | |
| TIP TOES (HM20086) | | | ● | ● | ● | | | | ● | ● | | | | | | | | | | |

| Business by County with Reference no. | Tennis Elbow | Terminal Illness | Throat Problems | Thrush | Thyroid Problems | Tinnitis | Tiredness | Tonsilitis | Ulcers | Vaginal Problems | Varicose Veins | Verrucas | Vertigo | Viral Infections | Vomiting | Warts | Water Retention | Whiplash | Wind | Worms |
|---|---|---|---|---|---|---|---|---|---|---|---|---|---|---|---|---|---|---|---|---|
| GEE, D (HM07957) | | | | | | | | | | | | ● | | | | ● | | | | |
| GINSBERG, ANNE (HM08111) | | | | | | | | | | | | | | | | | | | | |
| GREENHALGH, A J T (HM08489) | | | | | | | | | | | | | | | | ● | | | | |
| GROGAN, DIANA E (HM08592) | ● | | | | | ● | | | | | | | ● | | | | | | | |
| HAMPSOM, JAMES (HM08878) | | | | | | | ● | | | | | | | | | | | | | |
| HARDMAN, ALAN (HM08974) | | | | | | | | | | | | | | | | | | | | |
| HARMONIOUS HEALTHCARE (HM09015) | ● | | | ● | ● | | ● | | | | ● | | ● | ● | ● | | ● | | ● | |
| HAYDOCK, CLAIRE (HM09254) | | | | | | | | | | | | | | | | ● | | | | |
| HEAVENS SCENT AROMATHERAPY (HM09478) | | | | ● | | | ● | | | | | | | | | | ● | | | |
| HEYWORTH, S (HM09716) | | | | | | | | | | | | | | | | | | | | |
| HOLDEN, JOHN H (HM09932) | | | | | | | | | | | | | | | | ● | | | | |
| JOHN HOLDEN ASSOCIATES (HM11051) | | | | | | | | | | | | | | | | | | | | |
| KELLY CHIROPODY (HM11424) | | | | | ● | | ● | ● | | | | | | | | ● | | | | |
| KENDEL HOUSE CLINIC (HM11479) | ● | ● | | ● | | ● | ● | | ● | | ● | | ● | ● | ● | ● | ● | ● | ● | |
| LAYNE, SUSAN G (HM12077) | ● | ● | ● | | | ● | ● | | | | ● | | ● | | | | ● | | | |
| LEYLAND PHYSIOTHERAPY CENTRE (HM12319) | ● | | | | | | | | | | | | | | | | | | | |
| MALKIN, DK, MANIP THERAPY (HM12975) | ● | | | | | | ● | | | | | | | | | | | | | |
| MOBILE CHIROPODIST (HM14027) | | | | | | | | | | | | | | | | | | | | |
| NATURAL HEALTH CENTRE (HM14566) | ● | | | ● | ● | | ● | | | | ● | | | | ● | ● | ● | | ● | |
| NELSON, S (HM14782) | ● | | ● | ● | ● | | | ● | | ● | | | | | | | ● | | ● | |
| ONE STOP HEALTH & BEAUTY (HM15323) | ● | ● | ● | ● | ● | ● | ● | ● | ● | ● | ● | ● | ● | ● | ● | ● | ● | ● | ● | ● |
| PEPPER, JOHN (HM16009) | | ● | | | | ● | ● | | | ● | | | | | | | | | ● | |
| PHYSIO AND SPORTS INJURIES (HM16195) | ● | | | | | | | | | | | | | | | | | ● | | |
| PURCELL, AMANDA (HM16762) | ● | | | | | | | | | | | | | | | | | ● | | |
| RAMSBOTTOM PHYSIO CLINIC (HM16919) | ● | | | | | | | | | | | | | | | | | | | |
| RATCLIFFE, MARK (HM16949) | ● | | | | | | | | | | | | | | | | | | | |
| REMEDIAL MASSAGE/SPORTS (HM17175) | ● | | | | | | | | | | | | | | | | | | | |
| SMITH, CHRISTOPHER (DR) (HM18728) | | | | | | | | | | | | | | | | | | | | |
| SPIRITUAL THERAPIST (HM19029) | | | | | | | | | | | | | | | | | | | | |
| ST GEORGES MULTI THERAPY CTRE (HM19075) | | | | | | | | | | | | | | | | | | | | |
| ST MARY'S CLINIC (HM19087) | ● | | | | | | | | | | | | | | | | | | | |
| TATTERSALL, KAREN (HM19719) | | | | | | | | | | | | ● | | | | | | | | |
| TINKER, D C (HM20083) | | | | | | | | | | | | | | | | ● | | | | |
| TIP TOES (HM20086) | | | | | | ● | ● | | | | | | | | | | ● | | ● | |

Specialist Treatment Categories

| Business by County with Reference no. | Children | Terminally Ill | Disabled | Horses | Dogs | CatS | Other Animals |
|---|---|---|---|---|---|---|---|
| GEE, D (HM07957) | ● | | ● | | | | |
| GINSBERG, ANNE (HM08111) | ● | ● | ● | ● | ● | ● | ● |
| GREENHALGH, A J T (HM08489) | ● | ● | ● | | | | |
| GROGAN, DIANA E (HM08592) | | | ● | | | | |
| HAMPSOM, JAMES (HM08878) | ● | ● | ● | | | | |
| HARDMAN, ALAN (HM08974) | ● | ● | ● | | | | |
| HARMONIOUS HEALTHCARE (HM09015) | ● | ● | ● | | | | |
| HAYDOCK, CLAIRE (HM09254) | ● | ● | ● | | | | |
| HEAVENS SCENT AROMATHERAPY (HM09478) | | | | | | | |
| HEYWORTH, S (HM09716) | ● | ● | ● | | | | |
| HOLDEN, JOHN H (HM09932) | ● | ● | ● | | | | |
| JOHN HOLDEN ASSOCIATES (HM11051) | ● | ● | ● | | | | |
| KELLY CHIROPODY (HM11424) | ● | ● | ● | | | | |
| KENDEL HOUSE CLINIC (HM11479) | ● | ● | ● | | | | |
| LAYNE, SUSAN G (HM12077) | ● | ● | ● | | | | |
| LEYLAND PHYSIOTHERAPY CENTRE (HM12319) | ● | ● | ● | | | | |
| MALKIN, DK, MANIP THERAPY (HM12975) | ● | | | | | | |
| MOBILE CHIROPODIST (HM14027) | ● | ● | ● | | | | |
| NATURAL HEALTH CENTRE (HM14566) | ● | | ● | | ● | ● | |
| NELSON, S (HM14782) | ● | | | | | | |
| ONE STOP HEALTH & BEAUTY (HM15323) | ● | ● | ● | | | | |
| PEPPER, JOHN (HM16009) | | ● | ● | ● | ● | ● | ● |
| PHYSIO AND SPORTS INJURIES (HM16195) | ● | | ● | | | | |
| PURCELL, AMANDA (HM16762) | ● | | ● | | | | |
| RAMSBOTTOM PHYSIO CLINIC (HM16919) | ● | | ● | | | | |
| RATCLIFFE, MARK (HM16949) | ● | | ● | | | | |
| REMEDIAL MASSAGE/SPORTS (HM17175) | ● | | | | | | |
| SMITH, CHRISTOPHER (DR) (HM18728) | ● | ● | ● | | | | |
| SPIRITUAL THERAPIST (HM19029) | ● | ● | ● | ● | ● | ● | ● |
| ST GEORGES MULTI THERAPY CTRE (HM19075) | ● | ● | ● | | | | |
| ST MARY'S CLINIC (HM19087) | ● | ● | ● | | | | |
| TATTERSALL, KAREN (HM19719) | ● | ● | ● | | | | |
| TINKER, D C (HM20083) | ● | ● | ● | | | | |
| TIP TOES (HM20086) | ● | ● | ● | | | | |

# S - W Conditions treated at Practices/Businesses and Specialist Treatment Categories

Business by County with Reference no.

| Business by County with Reference no. | Sexually Trans. Infections | Shingles | Sinus Problems | Skin Problems | Sleep Disorders | Slimming Help | Slipped Disk | Smoking Help | Sneezing | Snoring | Spinal Injuries | Sports Injuries | Sprains | Stammering | Stings | Stomach Problems | Stomach Ulcers | Stress | Sweating | Teeth Grinding | Tennis Elbow | Terminal Illness | Throat Problems | Thrush | Thyroid Problems | Tinnitis | Tiredness | Tonsilitis | Ulcers | Vaginal Problems | Varicose Veins | Verrucas | Vertigo | Viral Infections | Vomiting | Warts | Water Retention | Whiplash | Wind | Worms | Specialist Treatment Categories: Children | Terminally Ill | Disabled | Horses | Dogs | CatS | Other Animals |
|---|---|---|---|---|---|---|---|---|---|---|---|---|---|---|---|---|---|---|---|---|---|---|---|---|---|---|---|---|---|---|---|---|---|---|---|---|---|---|---|---|---|---|---|---|---|---|---|
| TOMLINSON, ELIZABETH (HM20141) | | | | ● | | | | | | | | | | | | | | | | | | | | | | | | | | | | ● | | | | ● | | | | | | | | | | | |
| TRADITIONAL ACUPUNCTURE CLINIC (HM20220) | | ● | ● | ● | ● | | | ● | | | | | | | | ● | | | ● | | ● | | ● | ● | | ● | ● | | | | | | | | ● | | ● | | ● | | | | | | | | |
| TRADITIONAL CHINESE MED CTRE (HM20223) | | ● | ● | ● | ● | | | | | | | ● | ● | | | ● | ● | | | | ● | | | | | | ● | | | | | | ● | | ● | ● | ● | | ● | | ● | ● | ● | | | | |
| UPHAM, GILL (HM20522) | | | ● | ● | ● | | | | | | | | ● | | ● | ● | | | ● | | | | ● | | | ● | ● | ● | | ● | | | | | | | | | | | ● | ● | ● | | | | |
| WATKINSON, BARBARA (HM20999) | | | ● | | ● | | | | | | | | | | | ● | | | | | ● | ● | | | | ● | ● | | | | | | | | | | | | | | ● | ● | ● | | | | |
| WEST LANCS MCTIMONEY (HM21224) | | | ● | | | | ● | | | | | ● | | | | | | | | ● | ● | | | | | ● | ● | | | | | | | | | | | | | | ● | ● | ● | | | | |
| WILSON, G (HM21656) | | | | | | | | ● | | | | | | ● | | | | ● | | | | | | | | | | | | | | | | | | | | | | | ● | ● | ● | | | | |
| YEAMAN, DAVID (HM21996) | | | | | | | | | | | | | | | | | | | | | | | | | | | | | | | | ● | | | | | | | | | ● | ● | ● | | | | |
| **LEICESTERSHIRE** | | | | | | | | | | | | | | | | | | | | | | | | | | | | | | | | | | | | | | | | | | | | | | | |
| ACUPUNCTURE SERVICES (HM00320) | | | ● | | | | ● | ● | | | | ● | ● | | | ● | | | ● | | ● | | | | | | ● | | | | | | ● | | | | | | | | | ● | ● | | | | |
| ALBANY HOUSE (HM00479) | | | | ● | | | | | | | | | | | | | | | | | | | | | | | | | | | | | | | | | | | | | ● | | | | | | |
| ANDREWS, SIMON C (HM00859) | ● | ● | ● | ● | ● | | | ● | ● | ● | | ● | ● | ● | ● | ● | ● | | ● | ● | ● | ● | ● | ● | ● | ● | ● | ● | ● | ● | ● | | ● | ● | ● | ● | ● | | ● | ● | ● | ● | ● | | | | |
| ARCHWAY HSE NATURAL HLTH CTRE (HM00983) | | | | ● | ● | | | | | | | ● | | | | | | ● | | | | | | | | | | | | | | | | | | | | | | | ● | ● | ● | | | | |
| AROMATHERAPY INTERNATIONAL (HM01115) | | | | ● | ● | | | | | | | | | | | | | ● | | | | | | | | | | | | | | | | | | | | | | | ● | ● | ● | | | | |
| AYURVEDIC HERBAL CLINIC (HM01444) | | | | | | | | | | | | | | | | | | | | | | | | | | | | | | | | | | | | | | | | | ● | ● | ● | | | | |
| BROWN, RAY (HM03245) | | | ● | | | | | | | | | | | | | | | | | | | | | | | | | | | | | | | | | | | | | | ● | ● | ● | | | | |
| CALM WATERS (HM03557) | ● | ● | ● | ● | ● | ● | ● | ● | ● | ● | | ● | ● | ● | ● | ● | ● | | ● | ● | ● | ● | ● | ● | ● | ● | ● | ● | ● | ● | ● | | ● | ● | ● | ● | ● | | ● | ● | ● | ● | ● | | | | |
| CHIROPRACTIC CENTRE (HM04381) | | | ● | | | | ● | | | | | ● | ● | | | | | | | | ● | | | | | | | | | | | | | | | | | | | | ● | ● | ● | | | | |
| CONLIFFE, LOUISE (HM04982) | | ● | ● | ● | ● | | | | ● | | | | ● | | ● | ● | | | ● | | ● | | ● | ● | ● | ● | ● | ● | | ● | ● | | ● | | ● | ● | ● | | ● | | ● | | | ● | ● | ● | ● |
| DEADMAN, P J (HM05932) | | | | | | | | | | | | | | | | | | | | | | | | | | | | | | | | | | | | | | | | | ● | ● | ● | | | | |
| FAIRWEATHER, S & E (HM07068) | | | | | | | | | | | | ● | | | | | | ● | | | | | | | | | | | | | | | | | | | | | | | | ● | ● | | | | |
| GLENFIELD PRACTICE (HM08150) | | | | | | | | | | | | | | | | | | | | | | | | | | | | | | | | | | | | | | | | | ● | | ● | | | | |
| GRAHAM SPOWAGE OSTEOPATHIC SVS (HM08340) | | | | | | | ● | | | | | ● | ● | | | | | | | | ● | | | | | | | | | | | | ● | | | | | | | | ● | | ● | | | | |
| HASSETT, CHARLES (HM09187) | | | | | | | ● | | | | | ● | ● | | | | | | | | ● | | | | | | | | | | | | | | | | | | | | | | | | | | |
| JACQUI BATES COUNSELLING (HM10866) | | | | | | ● | | ● | | | | | | | | | | | | | | | | | | | | | | | | | | | | | | | | | | | | | | | |
| LEWIS, JACQUELINE (HM12296) | | | | | | | | | | | | | ● | | | | | | | | | | | | | | | | | | | | | | | | | | | | ● | ● | ● | | | | |
| LOUGHBOROUGH OSTEOPATHIC (HM12660) | | | | | | | ● | | | | | ● | ● | | | | | | | | ● | | | | | | | | | | | | | | | | | | | | ● | | ● | | | | |
| MELTON MOWBRAY PHYSIO CLINIC (HM13717) | | | | | | | ● | | | | | ● | ● | | | | | | | | ● | | | | | | | | | | | | | | | | | | | | ● | | | | | | |
| NATURAL WAY HEALTH CENTRE (HM14669) | | | ● | ● | | | | | | | | | ● | | | | | | | | | | | | | | ● | | | | | | | | | | | | | | ● | ● | ● | | | | |
| OADBY HOUSE (HM15140) | | | | | | | ● | | | | | ● | ● | | | | | | | | ● | | | | | | | | | | | | | | | | | | | | ● | | ● | | | | |
| SCHOOL OF SPIRITUAL KNOWLEDGE (HM18085) | ● | ● | ● | ● | ● | | ● | | | | | | | | | ● | ● | | | | ● | ● | ● | | ● | ● | ● | ● | | ● | | | | | | | | | | | ● | ● | ● | | | | ● |
| SHIRLEY FRANKLIN AROMATHERAPY (HM18485) | | | | | | | | | | | | ● | | | | | | | | | | ● | | | | | | | | | | | | | | | | | | | | ● | | | | | |
| STERN, J (HM19217) | | | | | | | | | | | | | | | | | | | | | | | | | | | | | | | | | | | | | | | | | ● | ● | ● | | | | |
| SUE CHARLES AROMATHERAPY (HM19466) | | | | ● | ● | | | | | | | | | | | | | | | | | | | | | | | | | | | | | ● | | | ● | | | | ● | ● | | | | | |

# S - W Conditions treated at Practices/Businesses and Specialist Treatment Categories

| Business by County with Reference no. | Sexually Trans. Infections | Shingles | Sinus Problems | Skin Problems | Sleep Disorders | Slimming Help | Slipped Disk | Smoking Help | Sneezing | Snoring | Spinal Injuries | Sports Injuries | Sprains | Stammering | Stings | Stomach Problems | Stomach Ulcers | Stress | Sweating | Teeth Grinding | Tennis Elbow | Terminal Illness | Throat Problems | Thrush | Thyroid Problems | Tinnitis | Tiredness | Tonsilitis | Ulcers | Vaginal Problems | Varicose Veins | Verrucas | Vertigo | Viral Infections | Vomiting | Warts | Water Retention | Whiplash | Wind | Worms | Specialist Treatment Categories: Children | Terminally Ill | Disabled | Horses | Dogs | CatS | Other Animals |
|---|---|---|---|---|---|---|---|---|---|---|---|---|---|---|---|---|---|---|---|---|---|---|---|---|---|---|---|---|---|---|---|---|---|---|---|---|---|---|---|---|---|---|---|---|---|---|---|
| SUE RICKS COMP THERAPY (HM19467) | ● | ● | ● | ● | ● | ● | ● | ● | ● | ● | | ● | ● | ● | ● | ● | ● | ● | ● | ● | ● | ● | ● | ● | ● | ● | ● | ● | ● | ● | ● | | ● | ● | ● | ● | ● | | ● | ● | ● | ● | ● | | | | |
| VICTORIA CLINIC (HM20650) | | | ● | | ● | | ● | | | ● | | ● | ● | | | | | | | | ● | | | | | | ● | | | | | | ● | | | | ● | | | | ● | ● | ● | | | | |
| WENDY PRICE HOLISTIC RIDING (HM21198) | | | | | | ● | | ● | | | | | | | | | | ● | | | | | | | | | ● | | | | | | | | | | | | | | ● | | | ● | ● | ● | ● |
| WILKINSON, GWEN (HM21507) | | | | | | | | | | | | | | | | | | | | | | | | | | ● | | | | | | | | | | | | | | | ● | ● | ● | | | | |
| WOHL, M (DR) (HM21758) | | | | | | ● | ● | ● | | ● | | ● | | | | | | ● | | | | | ● | | | | ● | | | | | | | | | | | | | | ● | | ● | ● | ● | ● | ● |
| LINCOLNSHIRE | | | | | | | | | | | | | | | | | | | | | | | | | | | | | | | | | | | | | | | | | | | | | | | |
| ALEXANDER TECHNIQUE (HM00550) | | | | | | | ● | | | | | | | | | | | | | | | | | | | | | | | | | | | | | | | | | | | | ● | | | | |
| BARN HOUSE PHYSIO CLINIC (HM01726) | | | | | | | ● | | | | | ● | ● | | | | | | | | ● | | | | | | | | | | | | | | | | | | | | | ● | | ● | | | |
| BEVERLEYS (HM02246) | ● | ● | ● | ● | ● | ● | ● | ● | ● | ● | | ● | ● | ● | ● | ● | ● | | ● | ● | ● | ● | ● | ● | ● | ● | ● | ● | ● | ● | ● | | ● | ● | ● | ● | ● | | ● | ● | ● | ● | ● | | | | |
| BOSTON CHIROPRACTIC CLINIC (HM02726) | | | | | | | ● | | | | ● | ● | ● | | | | | | | | ● | | | | | | | | | | | | | | | | | ● | | | ● | ● | ● | | | | |
| CASTLEGATE OSTEO PRACTICE (HM03847) | | ● | | | | | ● | | | | | ● | ● | | | ● | | | | | ● | | | | | | | | | | | | ● | | | | | | | | ● | ● | ● | | | | |
| CHIEN ACUPUNCTURE CLINIC (HM04161) | | | ● | ● | ● | | ● | | | | | ● | ● | | | | | | | | ● | | | | | | ● | | | | | | | | ● | | | | | | ● | ● | ● | | | | |
| CLINIC OF NATURAL MEDICINE (HM04703) | | | | | ● | ● | ● | | | | | ● | ● | | ● | ● | ● | | | | ● | | ● | ● | ● | | ● | ● | ● | ● | | | | ● | | | | | | ● | ● | | ● | | | | |
| COMPLEMENTARY THERAPY CENTRE (HM04946) | | | | | ● | | | ● | | | | | | ● | | | | | | | | | | | | | | | | | | | | | | | | | | | ● | ● | ● | | | | |
| COXON CLINIC (HM05326) | | | | | | | ● | ● | | | | ● | ● | | | ● | | | | | ● | | | | | | | | | | | | | | | | | | | | ● | ● | ● | | | | |
| DORMAN, KARL (HM06201) | | | | | | | ● | | | | | | | | | | | | | | ● | | | | | | | | | | | | | | | | | ● | | | ● | ● | ● | | | | |
| EASTGATE HYPNOTHERAPY CENTRE (HM06541) | | | | | | ● | | ● | | | | | | ● | | | | | | | | | | | | | | | | | | | | | | | | | | | | | | | | | |
| GOOD HEALTHKEEPING (HM08241) | | ● | ● | ● | ● | ● | | | ● | | | | ● | | ● | ● | ● | | ● | ● | | | ● | ● | ● | ● | ● | ● | ● | ● | ● | | ● | ● | ● | ● | ● | | ● | ● | ● | ● | | | | | |
| GRANTHAM PHYSIO PRACTICE (HM08394) | | | | | | | ● | | | | | ● | | | | | | | | | ● | | | | | | | | | | | | | | | | | | | | ● | | ● | | | | |
| HARRISON, FIONA (HM09098) | | | ● | ● | | | | | | | | | | | | | | ● | | | | | | | | | | | | | | | | | | | | | | | ● | ● | ● | | | | |
| HEART TO HEART (HM09443) | | | | | | | | | | | | | | | | | | | | | | | | | | | | | | | | | | | | | | | | | | ● | | | | | |
| HORNCASTLE WAR MEMORIAL CENTRE (HM10172) | | | | | | ● | ● | | | | ● | ● | ● | | | | | | | | ● | | | | | | | | | | | | | | | | | | | | ● | ● | ● | | | | |
| JUST JILLS (HM11282) | | ● | ● | | | | | | | | | | ● | | ● | | | | | ● | | | | ● | | ● | ● | | | | | | ● | | | ● | ● | | ● | ● | ● | ● | | | ● | ● | |
| KESTEVEN NATURAL HEALTH CENTRE (HM11564) | ● | ● | ● | ● | ● | ● | ● | ● | ● | ● | | ● | ● | ● | ● | ● | ● | | ● | ● | ● | ● | ● | ● | ● | ● | ● | ● | ● | ● | ● | | ● | ● | ● | ● | ● | | ● | ● | ● | ● | ● | | | | |
| LINCOLN HERBAL TREATMENT CTRE (HM12407) | | ● | ● | ● | ● | ● | | | ● | ● | | | | | ● | ● | ● | | ● | ● | ● | ● | ● | ● | ● | ● | ● | ● | ● | ● | ● | | ● | ● | ● | ● | ● | | ● | ● | ● | ● | ● | | | | |
| LIVING HEALTH (HM12485) | | | ● | ● | | | ● | | | | ● | ● | ● | | | | | | | ● | ● | | | | | | ● | | | | | | | | | | | ● | | | ● | ● | ● | | | | |
| MARK RIDDLE HYPNOTHERAPY (HM13108) | | | | | ● | ● | | ● | | | | | | | | | | | | | | | | | | | | | | | | | | | | | | | | | | | | | | | |
| MORLEY-KIRK, JOHN (HM14187) | | ● | ● | ● | ● | | | | | | | | | | | ● | ● | | | | ● | ● | | ● | ● | ● | ● | | | | ● | | | ● | | | ● | | ● | ● | ● | ● | ● | | ● | | |
| NEWLAND CHIROPRACTIC CLINIC (HM14866) | | | ● | | | | | | | | | ● | ● | | | ● | | | | ● | ● | | | | | ● | | | | | | | ● | | | | | ● | | | ● | ● | ● | | | | |
| REFLEXOLOGY CLINIC (HM17084) | | | ● | ● | ● | | ● | | | | | ● | | | | ● | | ● | ● | | ● | ● | ● | | ● | | ● | | | | | | | | | | | | | | ● | ● | ● | | | | |
| REMEDIES (HM17176) | | | | | | | | | | | | ● | ● | | | | | | | ● | | | | | | | | | | | | | | | | | | | | | ● | ● | ● | | | | |
| SALON, JANIES (HM17863) | | | | ● | ● | | | | | | | | | | | | | ● | | | | | | | | | | | | | | | | | | | | | | | | | | | | | |
| SMITH, MICHAEL (HM18780) | | | | | ● | ● | | ● | | | | | | | | | | | | | | | | | | | | | | | | | | | | | | | | | ● | | ● | | | | |
| WHITE, HEATHER (HM21357) | | | ● | | ● | ● | | ● | | ● | | | | | | ● | | | | | | ● | | | | | ● | | | | | | | | | | | | | | ● | ● | ● | | | | |

# S - W Conditions treated at Practices/Businesses and Specialist Treatment Categories

Business by County with Reference no.

| Business by County with Reference no. | Sexually Trans. Infections | Shingles | Sinus Problems | Skin Problems | Sleep Disorders | Slimming Help | Slipped Disk | Smoking Help | Sneezing | Snoring | Spinal Injuries | Sports Injuries | Sprains | Stammering | Stings | Stomach Problems | Stomach Ulcers | Stress | Sweating | Teeth Grinding | Tennis Elbow | Terminal Illness | Throat Problems | Thrush | Thyroid Problems | Tinnitis | Tiredness | Tonsilitis | Ulcers | Vaginal Problems | Varicose Veins | Verrucas | Vertigo | Viral Infections | Vomiting | Warts | Water Retention | Whiplash | Wind | Worms | Specialist Treatment Categories: Children | Terminally Ill | Disabled | Horses | Dogs | CatS | Other Animals |
|---|---|---|---|---|---|---|---|---|---|---|---|---|---|---|---|---|---|---|---|---|---|---|---|---|---|---|---|---|---|---|---|---|---|---|---|---|---|---|---|---|---|---|---|---|---|---|---|
| WINTERTON, SUZANNE (HM21725) | | | | | | | | | | | | | | | | | | | | | | | | | | | | | | | | | | | | | | | | | ● | ● | ● | ● | ● | ● | ● |
| **LONDON** | | | | | | | | | | | | | | | | | | | | | | | | | | | | | | | | | | | | | | | | | | | | | | | |
| FIRST PATH HYPNOTHERAPY (HM07338) | | | | | ● | ● | | | | | | | | ● | | | | | ● | ● | | | | | | | ● | | | | | | ● | | | | | | | | ● | ● | ● | | | | |
| HARLEY STREET COMP MEDICINE (HM09001) | ● | ● | ● | ● | ● | ● | ● | ● | ● | ● | | ● | ● | ● | ● | ● | ● | | ● | ● | ● | ● | ● | ● | ● | ● | ● | ● | ● | ● | ● | | ● | ● | ● | ● | ● | | ● | ● | ● | ● | ● | | | | |
| **LONDON (GREATER)** | | | | | | | | | | | | | | | | | | | | | | | | | | | | | | | | | | | | | | | | | | | | | | | |
| 1ST ALTERNATIVE HEALTH CENTRE (HM00002) | | | ● | ● | | | ● | | | ● | | ● | ● | | | | | | | | ● | | ● | | | ● | | | | | | | | | | | | | | | ● | ● | ● | | | | |
| ABBEY CENTRE (HM00071) | | | | | ● | | | ● | | | | | | ● | | ● | | | | | | | | | | | | | | | | | | | | | | | | | ● | ● | ● | | | | |
| ABBEYWOOD CHIROPODY CLINIC (HM00091) | | | | | | | | | | | | | | | | | | | | | | | | | | | | | | | | ● | | | | | | | | | ● | ● | ● | | | | |
| ABIGAIL'S (HM00126) | | | | ● | ● | | | | | | | | | | | | | ● | | | | | | | | | | | | | | | | | | | | | | | ● | ● | ● | | | | |
| ABRAHAMS & BENNETT (HM00133) | | | | | | | ● | | | | | ● | | | | | | | | | ● | | | | | | | | | | | | | | | | | ● | | | ● | | ● | | | | |
| ABRAHAMS & BENNETT (HM00132) | | | | | | | ● | | | | | ● | | | | | | | | | ● | | | | | | | | | | | | | | | | | ● | | | ● | | ● | | | | |
| ACORN THERAPY CENTRE (HM00182) | | | | | | ● | | ● | | | | | | | | | | ● | | | | | | | | | | | | | | | | | | | | | | | ● | ● | ● | | | | |
| ACUMEDIC (HM00217) | | | | ● | ● | ● | | ● | ● | | | ● | | | | ● | | | | | | | | | | | | | | | | | | | | | ● | | | | ● | ● | ● | | | | |
| ACUPUNCTURE & HERBAL CLINIC (HM00240) | | | ● | ● | | | ● | | | | | ● | | | | | | | | | ● | | | | | | ● | | | | | | | | | | | | | | ● | | ● | | | | |
| ACUPUNCTURE CLINIC (HM00287) | ● | ● | ● | ● | ● | ● | ● | ● | ● | ● | | ● | ● | ● | ● | ● | ● | | ● | ● | ● | ● | ● | ● | ● | ● | ● | ● | ● | ● | ● | | ● | ● | ● | ● | ● | | ● | | ● | ● | ● | | | | |
| ALEXANDER TECHNIQUE (HM00552) | | | | | | | | | | | | | | | | | | | | | | | | | | | | | | | | | | | | | | | | | ● | ● | ● | ● | ● | ● | |
| ALEXANDER TECHNIQUE (HM00547) | | | | | | | ● | | | | | ● | | | | | | | | | | | | | | | | | | | | | | | | | | | | | ● | | | | | | |
| ALEXANDER TECHNIQUE (HM00545) | | | | | | | ● | | | | | ● | | | | | | | | ● | ● | | | | | | | | | | | | | | | | | | | | ● | | ● | | | | |
| ALEXANDER TECHNIQUE CENTRE (HM00555) | | | | | | ● | ● | ● | | ● | | ● | ● | ● | | ● | ● | | | ● | ● | | ● | | | ● | ● | | ● | | ● | | ● | | | | | | | | | | | | | | |
| ALLEN, CAROL (HM00603) | | | | | | | | | | | | | | | | | | | | | | | | | | | | | | | | | | | | | | | | | ● | ● | ● | | | | |
| ALTERNATIVE THERAPIES CENTRE (HM00728) | | ● | ● | ● | ● | ● | ● | ● | ● | ● | | ● | ● | ● | ● | ● | ● | | ● | ● | ● | ● | ● | ● | ● | | ● | ● | ● | ● | ● | | ● | ● | ● | ● | ● | | ● | ● | ● | ● | ● | | | | |
| ALTERNATIVES COMP THERAPY CTRE (HM00743) | | | ● | ● | ● | | | ● | ● | ● | | ● | ● | | | | | | | ● | ● | | | ● | | ● | ● | | | | | | | | | | | | | | ● | | | | | | |
| ANGEL HEART CENTRE (HM00867) | | | | | ● | ● | | ● | | | | | | | | | | ● | | | | | | | | | ● | | | | | | | | | | | | | | ● | ● | | | | | |
| AUSTERBERRY, HELEN (HM01363) | | ● | ● | ● | ● | | | | ● | | | | ● | | ● | ● | | | | | | | ● | ● | | | ● | ● | | ● | | | | ● | ● | ● | | | ● | | ● | ● | ● | | | | |
| AUSTERBERRY, HELEN (HM01362) | | ● | ● | ● | ● | | | | ● | | | | ● | | ● | ● | | | | | | | ● | ● | | | ● | ● | | ● | | | | ● | ● | ● | | | ● | | ● | ● | ● | | | | |
| AVALON CHINESE MEDICINE CLINIC (HM01377) | ● | ● | ● | ● | ● | ● | ● | ● | ● | ● | | ● | ● | | ● | ● | ● | | ● | | ● | ● | ● | ● | ● | ● | ● | ● | ● | ● | ● | | ● | ● | ● | ● | ● | | ● | ● | ● | ● | ● | | | | |
| AVATAR (HM01384) | | | ● | | ● | ● | | ● | | ● | | | | | | | | | | ● | | | | | | ● | ● | | | | | | | | | | ● | | | | ● | ● | ● | | | | |
| AVENUE PSYCHOTHERAPY SERVICES (HM01391) | | | | | ● | | | | | | | | | | | | | | | | | | | | | | | | | | | | ● | | | | | | | | | | | | | | |
| AYURVED HERBELI (HM01442) | | | ● | ● | | | | ● | | | | | | | | ● | ● | | | | | | | | | | ● | | | ● | | | | | ● | | | | ● | | ● | | ● | | ● | ● | |
| BACK PAIN CENTRE (HM01498) | | | | | | | ● | | | | ● | ● | ● | | | | | | | | ● | | | | | | | | | | | | | | | | | ● | | | ● | | ● | | | | |
| BACK PAIN CENTRE (HM01497) | | | | | | | ● | | | | ● | ● | ● | | | | | | | | ● | | | | | | | | | | | | | | | | | ● | | | ● | | ● | | | | |
| BACK PAIN CENTRE (HM01499) | | | | | | | ● | | | | ● | ● | ● | | | | | | | | ● | | | | | | | | | | | | | | | | | ● | | | ● | | ● | | | | |
| BACK PAIN CLINIC (HM01503) | | ● | ● | | ● | ● | ● | | | | ● | ● | ● | | | ● | ● | | ● | ● | ● | | ● | ● | ● | | ● | | ● | | ● | | ● | ● | ● | ● | ● | | ● | | ● | | | | | | |
| BACK TO HEALTH - CHISWICK (HM01510) | | | | | | | ● | | | | | | | | | | | | | | ● | | | | | | | | | | | | | | | | | ● | | | ● | ● | ● | | | | |

# S - W Conditions treated at Practices/Businesses and Specialist Treatment Categories

Business by County with Reference no.

| Business by County with Reference no. | Sexually Trans. Infections | Shingles | Sinus Problems | Skin Problems | Sleep Disorders | Slimming Help | Slipped Disk | Smoking Help | Sneezing | Snoring | Spinal Injuries | Sports Injuries | Sprains | Stammering | Stings | Stomach Problems | Stomach Ulcers | Stress | Sweating |
|---|---|---|---|---|---|---|---|---|---|---|---|---|---|---|---|---|---|---|---|
| BACK TO HEALTH - KINGSTON (HM01512) | | | | | | | ● | | | | ● | ● | ● | | | | | | |
| BACK TO HEALTH - NORTH FINCHLEY (HM01513) | | | | | | | ● | | | | | ● | ● | | | | | | |
| BACK TO HEALTH CHIRO CLINIC (HM01518) | | | | | | | ● | | | | ● | ● | ● | | | | | | |
| BACK TO HEALTH-EALING (HM01519) | | | | | | | ● | | | | | | | | | | | | |
| BARBICAN CENTRE (HM01693) | | | | | | | | | | | | | | | | | | | |
| BARBICAN PODIATRY PRACTICE (HM01694) | | | | | | | | | | | | ● | | | | | | | |
| BARNES CHIROPRACTIC HEALTHCARE (HM01740) | | | | | ● | | ● | | | | | ● | ● | | | ● | | | |
| BARRIE, ALEXANDER (HM01798) | | | ● | | | | ● | | | | | ● | ● | | | ● | ● | | |
| BECKER, AMELY (HM02021) | | | | | ● | | | | | | | | | | | | | | |
| BELMONT PHYSIOTHERAPY PRACTICE (HM02108) | | | | | | | ● | | | | | ● | ● | | | | | | |
| BERNSTEIN, SAMUEL (HM02204) | | | | | ● | ● | | ● | | | | | | ● | | | | | |
| BEST, JOHN G E (HM02224) | | | | | | | ● | | | | | ● | ● | | | | | | |
| BEVERLEY CLINIC (HM02244) | | | | | | | | | | | | | | | | | | | |
| BLACKHEATH COMP THERAPIES CTRE (HM02450) | | | | | | | | | | | | ● | | | | | | | |
| BLOOMSBURY ALEXANDER CENTRE (HM02516) | ● | ● | ● | ● | ● | ● | ● | ● | ● | ● | | ● | ● | ● | ● | ● | ● | | ● |
| BLOOMSBURY THERAPY CENTRE (HM02518) | ● | ● | ● | ● | ● | ● | ● | ● | ● | ● | | ● | ● | ● | ● | ● | ● | | ● |
| BOCOCK, RICHARD (HM02548) | | | | ● | ● | | | | | | | | | | ● | ● | | | |
| BODYWISE (HM02637) | | ● | ● | ● | ● | | ● | ● | ● | ● | | ● | ● | | ● | ● | ● | | ● |
| BOSTON CHIROPODY CLINIC (HM02725) | | | | ● | | | | | | | | ● | | | | | | | |
| BRACKENBURY NTRL HEALTH CLNC (HM02837) | | | ● | ● | | | ● | | | | | ● | ● | | | | | | |
| BRAHMA KUMARIS INNER SPACE (HM02886) | | | | | | | | | | | | | | | | | | ● | |
| BRANDON, NICHOLAS (HM02914) | | | | | | | | | | | | | | | | | | | |
| BRITISH AUTOGENIC SOCIETY (HM03076) | | | ● | | ● | ● | | ● | ● | | | | | | | | ● | | |
| BRITISH HYPNOTHERAPY ASS (HM03084) | | | | ● | ● | ● | | | | | | | | ● | | | | | ● |
| BRIXTON TAI CHI (HM03106) | | | | | | | | | | | | | | | | | | ● | |
| BROOK GREEN OSTEOPATHY (HM03155) | | | ● | | | | ● | | | | | ● | ● | | | ● | | | |
| BROOKS, CATHY (HM03175) | | ● | ● | ● | ● | | | ● | ● | | | ● | ● | ● | ● | ● | ● | | |
| BROOKS, JANE (HM03177) | | | | | | | | | | | | | | | | | | | |
| BROWN, ALISON R (HM03210) | | | | | | | ● | | | | ● | ● | ● | | | | | | |
| BST FOUNDATION (HM03295) | | | | | | | | ● | | | | | | | | | | ● | |
| BUCHANAN, ANGELA (HM03300) | | | | | | | ● | | | | | ● | ● | | | | | | |
| BUREN, VAN (HM03371) | | | | | | | | | | | | | | | | | | ● | |
| BYRNE, JUDY (HM03516) | | | | ● | ● | ● | | ● | | ● | | | | | | | | | |
| CASSIDY MEDICAL CENTRE (HM03815) | | | | | | | | | | | | ● | ● | | | | | | |

| Business by County with Reference no. | Teeth Grinding | Tennis Elbow | Terminal Illness | Throat Problems | Thrush | Thyroid Problems | Tinnitis | Tiredness | Tonsilitis | Ulcers | Vaginal Problems | Varicose Veins | Verrucas | Vertigo | Viral Infections | Vomiting | Warts | Water Retention | Whiplash | Wind | Worms |
|---|---|---|---|---|---|---|---|---|---|---|---|---|---|---|---|---|---|---|---|---|---|
| BACK TO HEALTH - KINGSTON (HM01512) | | ● | | | | | | | | | | | | | | | | | ● | | |
| BACK TO HEALTH - NORTH FINCHLEY (HM01513) | | ● | | | | | | | | | | | | | | | | | | | |
| BACK TO HEALTH CHIRO CLINIC (HM01518) | | ● | | | | | | | | | | | | | | | | | ● | | |
| BACK TO HEALTH-EALING (HM01519) | | | | | | | | | | | | | | | | | | | ● | | |
| BARBICAN CENTRE (HM01693) | | | | | | | | | | | | | | | | | | | | | |
| BARBICAN PODIATRY PRACTICE (HM01694) | | | | | | | | | | | | | | | | | ● | | | | |
| BARNES CHIROPRACTIC HEALTHCARE (HM01740) | ● | ● | | | | | ● | ● | | | | | | ● | | | | | | ● | |
| BARRIE, ALEXANDER (HM01798) | | ● | | | | | ● | ● | | | | | | ● | | | | | | ● | ● |
| BECKER, AMELY (HM02021) | | | | | | | | ● | | | | | | | | | | | | | |
| BELMONT PHYSIOTHERAPY PRACTICE (HM02108) | | ● | | | | | | | | | | | | | | | | | | | |
| BERNSTEIN, SAMUEL (HM02204) | ● | | | | | | | | | | | | | | | | | | | | |
| BEST, JOHN G E (HM02224) | | ● | | | | | | | | | | | | | | | | | | | |
| BEVERLEY CLINIC (HM02244) | | | | | | | | | | | | | | | | | | | | | |
| BLACKHEATH COMP THERAPIES CTRE (HM02450) | | | | | | | | | | | | | | | | | | | | | |
| BLOOMSBURY ALEXANDER CENTRE (HM02516) | ● | ● | ● | ● | ● | ● | ● | ● | ● | ● | ● | ● | | ● | ● | ● | | ● | | ● | |
| BLOOMSBURY THERAPY CENTRE (HM02518) | ● | ● | ● | ● | ● | ● | ● | ● | ● | ● | ● | ● | | ● | ● | ● | ● | ● | | ● | |
| BOCOCK, RICHARD (HM02548) | | | | | ● | | | ● | ● | | | | | | ● | ● | ● | | | | |
| BODYWISE (HM02637) | | ● | ● | ● | ● | ● | ● | ● | ● | ● | ● | ● | | ● | ● | ● | ● | ● | | ● | ● |
| BOSTON CHIROPODY CLINIC (HM02725) | | | | | | | | | | ● | | | | | | | | | | | |
| BRACKENBURY NTRL HEALTH CLNC (HM02837) | | ● | | | | | | ● | | | | | | | | | | | | | |
| BRAHMA KUMARIS INNER SPACE (HM02886) | | | | | | | | | | | | | | | | | | | | | |
| BRANDON, NICHOLAS (HM02914) | | | | | | | | | | | | | | | | | | | | | |
| BRITISH AUTOGENIC SOCIETY (HM03076) | ● | ● | ● | | | ● | ● | ● | | | | | | | | | | | | | |
| BRITISH HYPNOTHERAPY ASS (HM03084) | | | | | | | | ● | | | ● | | | ● | | | | | | | |
| BRIXTON TAI CHI (HM03106) | | | | | | | | | | | | | | | | | | | | | |
| BROOK GREEN OSTEOPATHY (HM03155) | ● | ● | | | | | | | | | | | | | | | | | | ● | |
| BROOKS, CATHY (HM03175) | ● | ● | ● | | ● | ● | ● | ● | ● | | ● | ● | | | ● | ● | ● | ● | | ● | ● |
| BROOKS, JANE (HM03177) | | | | | | | | | | | | | | | | | | | | | |
| BROWN, ALISON R (HM03210) | | ● | | | | | | | | | | | | | | | | | ● | | |
| BST FOUNDATION (HM03295) | | | | | | | | | | | | | | | | | | | | | |
| BUCHANAN, ANGELA (HM03300) | | ● | | | | | | | | | | | | | | | | | | | |
| BUREN, VAN (HM03371) | | | | | | | | | | | | | | | | | | | | | |
| BYRNE, JUDY (HM03516) | | | | | | | | | | | | | | | | | | | | | |
| CASSIDY MEDICAL CENTRE (HM03815) | | ● | | | | | | | | | | | | | | | | | | | |

| Business by County with Reference no. | Specialist Treatment Categories: Children | Terminally Ill | Disabled | Horses | Dogs | CatS | Other Animals |
|---|---|---|---|---|---|---|---|
| BACK TO HEALTH - KINGSTON (HM01512) | ● | ● | ● | | | | |
| BACK TO HEALTH - NORTH FINCHLEY (HM01513) | ● | ● | ● | | | | |
| BACK TO HEALTH CHIRO CLINIC (HM01518) | ● | ● | ● | | | | |
| BACK TO HEALTH-EALING (HM01519) | ● | ● | ● | | | | |
| BARBICAN CENTRE (HM01693) | ● | ● | ● | | | | |
| BARBICAN PODIATRY PRACTICE (HM01694) | ● | | ● | | | | |
| BARNES CHIROPRACTIC HEALTHCARE (HM01740) | ● | ● | ● | | | | |
| BARRIE, ALEXANDER (HM01798) | ● | | ● | | | | |
| BECKER, AMELY (HM02021) | | | | | | | |
| BELMONT PHYSIOTHERAPY PRACTICE (HM02108) | | | | | | | |
| BERNSTEIN, SAMUEL (HM02204) | ● | | | | | | |
| BEST, JOHN G E (HM02224) | ● | | ● | | | | |
| BEVERLEY CLINIC (HM02244) | ● | | | | | | |
| BLACKHEATH COMP THERAPIES CTRE (HM02450) | | | | | | | |
| BLOOMSBURY ALEXANDER CENTRE (HM02516) | ● | ● | ● | | | | |
| BLOOMSBURY THERAPY CENTRE (HM02518) | ● | ● | ● | | | | |
| BOCOCK, RICHARD (HM02548) | ● | ● | ● | | | | |
| BODYWISE (HM02637) | ● | ● | ● | | | | |
| BOSTON CHIROPODY CLINIC (HM02725) | ● | ● | ● | | | | |
| BRACKENBURY NTRL HEALTH CLNC (HM02837) | ● | ● | | | | | |
| BRAHMA KUMARIS INNER SPACE (HM02886) | ● | ● | ● | | | | |
| BRANDON, NICHOLAS (HM02914) | ● | ● | ● | ● | ● | ● | ● |
| BRITISH AUTOGENIC SOCIETY (HM03076) | ● | ● | | | | | |
| BRITISH HYPNOTHERAPY ASS (HM03084) | ● | | | | | | |
| BRIXTON TAI CHI (HM03106) | | | ● | | | | |
| BROOK GREEN OSTEOPATHY (HM03155) | ● | ● | ● | | | | |
| BROOKS, CATHY (HM03175) | ● | ● | ● | | | | |
| BROOKS, JANE (HM03177) | ● | | | | | | |
| BROWN, ALISON R (HM03210) | ● | | ● | | | | |
| BST FOUNDATION (HM03295) | ● | ● | ● | | | | |
| BUCHANAN, ANGELA (HM03300) | ● | | ● | | | | |
| BUREN, VAN (HM03371) | | | | | | | |
| BYRNE, JUDY (HM03516) | ● | ● | ● | | | | |
| CASSIDY MEDICAL CENTRE (HM03815) | | | | | | | |

# S - W Conditions treated at Practices/Businesses and Specialist Treatment Categories

| Business by County with Reference no. | Sexually Trans. Infections | Shingles | Sinus Problems | Skin Problems | Sleep Disorders | Slimming Help | Slipped Disk | Smoking Help | Sneezing | Snoring | Spinal Injuries | Sports Injuries | Sprains | Stammering | Stings | Stomach Problems | Stomach Ulcers | Stress | Sweating | Teeth Grinding | Tennis Elbow | Terminal Illness | Throat Problems | Thrush | Thyroid Problems | Tinnitis | Tiredness | Tonsilitis | Ulcers | Vaginal Problems | Varicose Veins | Verrucas | Vertigo | Viral Infections | Vomiting | Warts | Water Retention | Whiplash | Wind | Worms | Specialist Treatment Categories: Children | Terminally Ill | Disabled | Horses | Dogs | CatS | Other Animals |
|---|---|---|---|---|---|---|---|---|---|---|---|---|---|---|---|---|---|---|---|---|---|---|---|---|---|---|---|---|---|---|---|---|---|---|---|---|---|---|---|---|---|---|---|---|---|---|---|
| CENTRE FOR TRANSFORMATION (HM03920) | | ● | ● | ● | ● | | | | | | | | ● | | ● | ● | ● | | ● | ● | ● | | ● | ● | ● | ● | | | | ● | ● | | ● | | | ● | ● | | ● | | ● | ● | | | | | |
| CHAPMAN, RUPERT (HM04009) | | | ● | | | | | | | | | ● | | | | | | | | | ● | | | | | | | | | | | | | | | | | | | | ● | | ● | | | | |
| CHARTERHOUSE PHYSIOTHERAPY (HM04049) | | | | | | | ● | | | | | ● | ● | | | | | | | | ● | | | | | | | | | | | | | | | | | ● | | | ● | | ● | | | | |
| CHARTERHOUSE PHYSIOTHERAPY (HM04048) | | | | | | | ● | | | | | ● | ● | | | | | | | | ● | | | | | | | | | | | | | | | | | | | | ● | | ● | | | | |
| CHATSWORTH CLINIC (HM04063) | | ● | ● | ● | ● | | ● | | ● | | | | ● | | ● | ● | ● | | | | ● | | ● | ● | ● | | ● | ● | ● | ● | ● | | ● | ● | ● | ● | ● | | ● | ● | ● | ● | ● | | | | |
| CHINESE MEDICAL CTRE OF LONDON (HM04245) | ● | ● | ● | ● | ● | ● | ● | ● | ● | ● | | ● | ● | | | ● | ● | | ● | ● | ● | | ● | ● | ● | ● | ● | ● | ● | ● | ● | | ● | ● | ● | ● | ● | | ● | ● | ● | ● | ● | | | | |
| CHINESE SHOP (HM04269) | | ● | ● | ● | ● | | | | | | | ● | ● | | ● | | | | | | ● | | | | | ● | ● | | | | | | ● | | | | ● | | | | ● | | ● | | | | |
| CHIRON CTRE-BODY PSYCHOTHERAPY (HM04288) | | | | | | | | | | | | | | | | | | | | | | | | | | | | | | | | | | | | | | | | | | ● | ● | | | | |
| CHIROPRACTIC CLINIC (HM04393) | | | | | | | ● | | | | ● | ● | ● | | | | | | | | ● | | | | | | | | | | | | | | | | | ● | | | ● | ● | ● | | | | |
| CHISWICK CHIROPRACTIC CLINIC (HM04412) | | | | | | | | | | | | ● | ● | | | | ● | | | | ● | | | | | | | | | | | | ● | | | | | ● | | | ● | ● | ● | | | | |
| CITY HEALTH CENTRE (HM04496) | | ● | ● | | ● | | ● | | ● | ● | | ● | ● | ● | | ● | ● | | | ● | ● | ● | ● | | ● | ● | ● | ● | | ● | ● | | ● | ● | ● | | ● | | | | ● | ● | | | | | |
| CLAIRE CHOUDHURY HERBAL PRAC (HM04507) | | ● | ● | ● | ● | ● | | ● | ● | | | | | | | ● | ● | | ● | | | | | ● | | ● | ● | ● | ● | | ● | | | ● | ● | ● | ● | | ● | | ● | ● | ● | | | | |
| CLASSICAL OSTEOPATH (HM04610) | | | ● | | | | ● | | | | | ● | ● | | | ● | ● | | ● | ● | ● | ● | ● | | ● | ● | ● | ● | ● | | | | | | | | | ● | ● | | ● | ● | | | | | |
| COLLEGE-PRACTICAL HOMEOPATHY (HM04855) | | | | ● | ● | ● | | | | | | | | | | | | ● | | | | | | | | | | | | | | | | | | | | | | | ● | ● | ● | | | | |
| COMPLETE HEALTH CARE (HM04958) | | ● | ● | ● | ● | ● | ● | ● | ● | ● | | ● | ● | | | ● | ● | | ● | ● | ● | | ● | ● | ● | ● | ● | ● | ● | ● | ● | | ● | ● | ● | | ● | | ● | | | | | | | | |
| CONNAUGHT SQUARE HYPNOTHERAPY (HM04986) | | | | | ● | ● | ● | ● | | | | | | | | | | | | ● | | | | | | | | | | | | | ● | | | | | | | | | | | | | | |
| CONWAY, JONATHAN (HM05028) | | | | | ● | ● | | ● | | | | | | | | | | | | | | | | | | | | | | | | | | | | | | | | | ● | ● | ● | | | | |
| CONWAY, JONATHON (HM05029) | | | | | ● | ● | | ● | | | | | | | | | | ● | | | | | | | | | | | | | | | | | | | | | | | ● | ● | ● | | | | |
| COUNSELLING & PSYCHOTHERAPY (HM05246) | | | | | | | | | | | | | | | | | | | | | | | | | | | | | | | | | | | | | | | | | ● | ● | ● | | | | |
| COUNSELLING SERVICE (HM05252) | | | | | | ● | | ● | | | | | | | | | | ● | | | | | | | | | | | | | | | | | | | | | | | | | | | | | |
| CRAVEN CLINIC (HM05385) | | ● | ● | ● | | | ● | | | | | ● | ● | | | | | | | | ● | | | | | | ● | | | | | | | | ● | | | | | | | | | | | | |
| CREATIVE INSIGHTS (HM05399) | | | | ● | ● | ● | | ● | ● | ● | | | | | | | | | | ● | | ● | | | | ● | | | | | | | | | | | | | | | | ● | | | | | |
| CRISTA GALLI OSTEOPATHS (HM05446) | | | ● | | ● | | ● | | ● | ● | | ● | ● | | | ● | ● | | ● | ● | ● | ● | ● | | ● | ● | ● | ● | | ● | ● | | ● | ● | | | ● | | ● | | ● | ● | ● | | | | |
| CTRE FOR CRANIO-SACRAL THERAPY (HM05540) | | | ● | ● | ● | | | | | | | ● | ● | ● | | ● | ● | | ● | ● | ● | | ● | | ● | ● | ● | ● | ● | | | | ● | | | | | | | | ● | ● | ● | | | | |
| CTRE FOR THE STUDY OF COMP MED (HM05544) | | ● | ● | ● | | | ● | | ● | | | | | ● | ● | ● | ● | | ● | | ● | ● | ● | ● | ● | ● | ● | ● | ● | ● | | | ● | ● | ● | ● | | | ● | | ● | ● | ● | | | | |
| DALTON, HELEN (HM05698) | ● | ● | ● | ● | ● | | | | ● | ● | | | ● | ● | ● | ● | ● | | ● | ● | ● | | ● | ● | ● | | ● | ● | ● | ● | ● | | ● | ● | ● | ● | | | ● | ● | ● | ● | ● | | | | |
| DAVID WEISS HOMEOPATHY (HM05781) | | | ● | ● | ● | | | | ● | | | | | | | ● | | | | | | | | ● | | | ● | ● | | | | | | | | | | | ● | | ● | ● | | | | | |
| DAVIS, JULIA (HM05854) | ● | ● | ● | ● | ● | ● | ● | ● | ● | ● | | ● | ● | ● | ● | ● | ● | | ● | ● | ● | ● | ● | ● | ● | ● | ● | ● | ● | ● | ● | | ● | ● | ● | ● | ● | | ● | ● | ● | ● | ● | | | | |
| DAWSON, DAVID (DR) (HM05880) | | | | | | | | | | | | | | | | | | | | | | | | | | | ● | | | | | | | | | | | | | | ● | | | | | | |
| DE BURGH, JULIE (HM05904) | | | | | | ● | | ● | | | | | | | | | | ● | | | | | | | | | | | | | | | | | | | | | | | ● | | | | | | |
| DELROY, SANDRA (DR) (HM05968) | | | | | | | | | | | | | | | | | | ● | | | | ● | | | | | | | | | | | | | | | | | | | ● | ● | ● | | | | |
| DENNIS MICHAEL PRACTICE (HM05990) | | | | | | | ● | | | | | ● | | | | | | | | | ● | | | | | ● | | | | | | | | | | | | | | | ● | | ● | | | | |
| DENNISON, IAN (HM05996) | | | | | | | | | | | | ● | ● | | | | | ● | | | | | | | | | | | | | | | | | | | | | | | ● | ● | ● | | | | |
| DISTANT HEALING (HM06123) | | ● | ● | ● | ● | | ● | ● | | | | ● | ● | | ● | ● | | | | | | ● | ● | | ● | ● | ● | | | | ● | | | ● | | ● | ● | | ● | ● | ● | ● | ● | ● | ● | ● | |

# S - W Conditions treated at Practices/Businesses and Specialist Treatment Categories

Business by County with Reference no.







Specialist Treatment Categories: Other Animals, CatS, Dogs, Horses, Disabled, Terminally Ill, Children

| Condition | DOCKLANDS DENTAL/COMP HLTH (HM06141) | DREAMCATCHER (HM06298) | DULWICH PHYSIOTHERAPY (HM06383) | E.LONDON COMPLEMENTARY HEALTH (HM06479) | EALING COUNS & THERAPY CTRE (HM06488) | EAST WEST HERB SHOP (HM06527) | EAST WEST THERAPIES (HM06529) | EDGELL, MARJORY (HM06599) | EDGWARE NATURAL HEALTH CENTRE (HM06604) | ELLWOOD, CAROLINE (HM06780) | ELTHAM HYPNOTHERAPY ANALYSIS (HM06789) | ENFIELD CLINIC OF HERBAL MED (HM06818) | ENFIELD HYP & COUNSELLING (HM06819) | EQUILIBRIUM (HM06869) | EQUILIBRIUM COUNS/THRPY CTRE (HM06873) | FAIR, ANNETTE (HM07048) | FELDENKRAIS CENTRE (HM07190) |
|---|---|---|---|---|---|---|---|---|---|---|---|---|---|---|---|---|---|
| Other Animals | | | | | | | ● | | | | | | | | | | |
| CatS | | | | | | | ● | | | | | | | | | | |
| Dogs | | | | | | | | | | | | | | | | | |
| Horses | | | | | | | | | | | | | | | | | |
| Disabled | ● | ● | | ● | | | ● | | ● | ● | ● | | ● | | | ● | ● |
| Terminally Ill | ● | ● | | ● | | | ● | ● | ● | ● | | | ● | | | ● | |
| Children | ● | ● | ● | ● | | ● | ● | | ● | | ● | | ● | ● | | ● | ● |
| Worms | | | | ● | | | | | | | | ● | | | | | |
| Wind | | | | ● | ● | ● | ● | | ● | ● | | ● | | | | | |
| Whiplash | ● | | | | | | | | | | | | | | | ● | |
| Water Retention | | | | ● | | | ● | | | | | ● | | ● | | | |
| Warts | | | | ● | | | | | | | | ● | | | | | |
| Vomiting | | | | ● | | ● | | | | | | ● | | | | | |
| Viral Infections | | | | ● | | | | | ● | | | ● | | ● | | | |
| Vertigo | | | | ● | | ● | | | | | | ● | | ● | | | |
| Verrucas | | | | | | | | | | | | | | | | | |
| Varicose Veins | | | | ● | | | | | | | | ● | | | | | |
| Vaginal Problems | | | | ● | | ● | | | | | | ● | | | | | |
| Ulcers | | | | ● | | | | | | | | ● | | | | | |
| Tonsilitis | | | | ● | | | | | | | | ● | | | | | |
| Tiredness | | | | ● | ● | ● | | | ● | ● | | ● | ● | ● | | | |
| Tinnitis | | | | ● | | | | | | | | ● | | | | | |
| Thyroid Problems | | | | ● | ● | ● | | | | | ● | ● | | ● | | | |
| Thrush | | | | ● | ● | ● | | | ● | ● | | ● | | | | | |
| Throat Problems | | | | ● | | ● | | | | | | ● | | | | | |
| Terminal Illness | | | | ● | | | | ● | | | | | | | | | |
| Tennis Elbow | ● | | ● | ● | | ● | ● | | ● | | | | | | | ● | |
| Teeth Grinding | | | | ● | | | | ● | | | | | | | | | |
| Sweating | | | | ● | | | | | | | ● | ● | | | | | |
| Stress | | | | ● | | | | | | | | | | | | | |
| Stomach Ulcers | | | | ● | ● | | | | ● | | | ● | | | | | |
| Stomach Problems | | | | ● | ● | ● | ● | | ● | | ● | ● | | | | | |
| Stings | | | | ● | | | | | | | | ● | | | | | |
| Stammering | | | | ● | | | | ● | | | | | | | | | |
| Sprains | ● | | ● | ● | | | | | | ● | | | | | | ● | |
| Sports Injuries | ● | | ● | ● | | | | | ● | | | | | ● | | ● | |
| Spinal Injuries | ● | | | | | | | | | | | | | | | ● | |
| Snoring | | | | ● | | | | | | | | ● | | | | | |
| Sneezing | | | | ● | | | | | | | | ● | | | | | |
| Smoking Help | | | | ● | ● | | | ● | ● | | ● | ● | ● | ● | ● | | |
| Slipped Disk | ● | | ● | ● | | | | | | ● | | | | ● | | | |
| Slimming Help | | | | ● | | | | | | | ● | ● | ● | ● | | | |
| Sleep Disorders | | ● | | ● | | ● | | ● | ● | | ● | ● | ● | ● | | | |
| Skin Problems | | ● | | ● | ● | ● | | | ● | | | ● | | ● | | | |
| Sinus Problems | | ● | | ● | ● | ● | ● | | ● | | | ● | | ● | | | |
| Shingles | | | | ● | | | | | | | | | | | | | |
| Sexually Trans. Infections | | | | | | | | | | | | ● | | | | | |

| Condition | FERGUSON, WILMA (HM07232) | FLETCHER, CLARE (HM07410) | FLEXIBLE HOUR (HM07420) | FLOAT WORKS (HM07424) | FRY, HOWARD (HM07772) | FULHAM CLINIC (HM07781) | G T CONSULTANCY (HM07815) | GEORGE (HM07987) | GLASSMAN, DAVID (HM08128) | GODWIN, ROME (HM08194) | GREENWICH NATURAL HEALTH CTRE (HM08500) | GREIDINGER, CLIVE (HM08524) | GROUP ANALYTIC PRACTICE (HM08605) | HACKNEY HYPNOTHERAPY (HM08685) | HAIN, PATRICIA (HM08712) | HAMILTON, FIONA (HM08843) | HAMPSTEAD ACU/CHINESE HBL MED (HM08881) |
|---|---|---|---|---|---|---|---|---|---|---|---|---|---|---|---|---|---|
| Other Animals | | | | | | | | | | | | | | | | | |
| CatS | | | | | | | | | | | | | | | | | |
| Dogs | | | | | | | | | | | | | | | | | |
| Horses | | | | | | | | | | | | | | | | | |
| Disabled | ● | | | | | | | ● | ● | ● | | ● | ● | | ● | ● | ● |
| Terminally Ill | ● | | | | | | | ● | ● | | ● | | ● | | ● | | ● |
| Children | ● | | | | | ● | ● | ● | ● | | ● | ● | ● | ● | ● | ● | ● |
| Worms | | | | | | | | | | | | | | | ● | | |
| Wind | | | ● | | | ● | | | | | | | | | ● | | |
| Whiplash | | | | | | | | | | | | | | | | | |
| Water Retention | | | | | | ● | | | | | | | | | ● | | |
| Warts | | | | | ● | | | | | | | | | | | | |
| Vomiting | | | | | | | | | | | | | | | | | |
| Viral Infections | | | | | | ● | | | | | | | | | | | |
| Vertigo | | | | | | | | | ● | | | | | | | | |
| Verrucas | | | | | | | | ● | | | | | | | | | |
| Varicose Veins | | | | | | ● | | | ● | | | | | | | | |
| Vaginal Problems | | | | | | ● | | | | | | | | | | | |
| Ulcers | | | | | | | | | ● | | | | | | ● | | |
| Tonsilitis | | | | | | ● | | | | | | | | | ● | | ● |
| Tiredness | | ● | ● | | | ● | ● | | ● | | | | | | ● | | ● |
| Tinnitis | | | ● | | | ● | | | ● | | | | | | ● | | |
| Thyroid Problems | | | | | | | | | | | | | | | ● | | |
| Thrush | | | | | | | | | | | | | | | ● | | |
| Throat Problems | | | | | | ● | | | ● | | | | | | ● | | |
| Terminal Illness | | | | | | | | | ● | | | | | | ● | | |
| Tennis Elbow | | | ● | | | ● | | | ● | | ● | | | | ● | ● | ● |
| Teeth Grinding | | | | | | ● | ● | | ● | | | | | ● | | | |
| Sweating | | | ● | | | ● | | | | | | | | ● | | | |
| Stress | | | | ● | | | ● | | | | | | ● | ● | | | |
| Stomach Ulcers | | | | | | ● | | | ● | | | | | | ● | | |
| Stomach Problems | | | ● | | | ● | | | ● | | | | | | ● | | |
| Stings | | | | | | | | | | | | | | | | | |
| Stammering | | | | | | | ● | | ● | | | ● | | ● | | | |
| Sprains | | | | | | ● | | | ● | | | | | | ● | ● | ● |
| Sports Injuries | | | ● | ● | | ● | | | ● | | ● | | | | ● | ● | ● |
| Spinal Injuries | | | | | | | | | | | | | | | | | |
| Snoring | | | | | | ● | | | ● | | | | | ● | | | |
| Sneezing | | | | | | | | | | | | | | | | | |
| Smoking Help | | | | | | | ● | | ● | | ● | ● | | ● | | | |
| Slipped Disk | | | | | | | | | ● | | ● | | | | | ● | ● |
| Slimming Help | | | | | | | ● | | ● | | ● | | | ● | ● | | |
| Sleep Disorders | | | ● | | | ● | ● | | | | | | | ● | ● | | |
| Skin Problems | | ● | | | | ● | | | | | | | | | ● | | ● |
| Sinus Problems | | ● | | | | ● | | | | | | | | | ● | | ● |
| Shingles | | | | | | ● | | | | | | | | | | | |
| Sexually Trans. Infections | | | | | | | | | | | | | | | | | |

# S - W Conditions treated at Practices/Businesses and Specialist Treatment Categories

Business by County with Reference no.

| Business by County with Reference no. | Sexually Trans. Infections | Shingles | Sinus Problems | Skin Problems | Sleep Disorders | Slimming Help | Slipped Disk | Smoking Help | Sneezing | Snoring | Spinal Injuries | Sports Injuries | Sprains | Stammering | Stings | Stomach Problems | Stomach Ulcers | Stress |
|---|---|---|---|---|---|---|---|---|---|---|---|---|---|---|---|---|---|---|
| HAREWOOD, MARCIA M (HM08991) | | ● | ● | ● | | ● | ● | | | | | ● | ● | | | ● | | |
| HARLEY ST STRESS MNGMT (HM08999) | | | | ● | ● | ● | | ● | | | | | | ● | | | | ● |
| HARLEY STREET TCM FERTILITY (HM09003) | | | | ● | | | | | | | | | | | | | | |
| HARPER, SUZANNE G (HM09042) | | | ● | ● | ● | ● | ● | ● | | | | ● | ● | | | ● | | |
| HARPER, SUZANNE G (HM09041) | | | ● | | ● | ● | ● | ● | | | | ● | ● | | | ● | | |
| HARROW HEALTH CARE CENTRE (HM09121) | | ● | ● | ● | ● | | ● | ● | | | | ● | ● | | | | | |
| HATHA YOGA/COUNSELLING (HM09195) | | | | | | | | | | | | | | | | | | |
| HAVELOCK-SEARLE, PAULINE (HM09206) | | | | | ● | ● | | ● | | | | | | ● | | | | |
| HAWKINS, JAN (HM09222) | | | | | | | | | | | | | | | | | | |
| HEAL, CHRISTIANNE (HM09314) | | | | | | | | | | | | | | | | | | |
| HEALERS WORLD (HM09320) | ● | ● | ● | ● | ● | ● | ● | ● | ● | ● | | ● | ● | ● | ● | ● | ● | |
| HEALING ARTS UK (HM09326) | | | | | | | ● | | | | | ● | ● | | | | | |
| HEALTHY LIVING CENTRE (HM09429) | ● | ● | ● | ● | ● | ● | ● | ● | ● | ● | | ● | ● | ● | ● | ● | ● | |
| HELEN BERNAT - FITNESS TRAINER (HM09511) | | | | | | ● | | | | | | | | | | | | |
| HERBAL CARE (HM09600) | ● | ● | ● | ● | ● | ● | ● | ● | ● | | | ● | ● | | ● | ● | ● | |
| HERBAL CARE (HM09601) | ● | ● | ● | ● | ● | ● | ● | ● | ● | | | ● | ● | | ● | ● | ● | |
| HERBMEDIC (HM09663) | ● | ● | ● | ● | ● | ● | ● | ● | ● | ● | | ● | ● | | ● | ● | ● | |
| HETHERTON, ANNE (HM09697) | | ● | ● | ● | ● | ● | ● | ● | ● | ● | | ● | ● | ● | ● | ● | ● | |
| HIGHBURY CENTRE (HM09746) | | | | | | | | | | | | | | | | | | |
| HILDRETH & COCKER (HM09767) | | | | | | | | | | | | | | | | | | |
| HOBBS, SALLY (HM09858) | | | | | | | | | | | | | | | | | | |
| HOGARTH CLINIC (HM09907) | | ● | ● | ● | ● | | ● | ● | | | | ● | ● | | | ● | ● | |
| HOLMES, DAVID (HM10040) | | | | | | | | | | | | | | | | | | |
| HOME VISITING SERVICES (HM10069) | | ● | ● | ● | ● | | | ● | ● | | | ● | ● | | | ● | ● | |
| HOMOEOPATHIC HEALTH CENTRE (HM10095) | | | | | | | | | | | | | | | | | | |
| HONG TAD ACUPUNCTURE & HERBAL (HM10119) | | ● | ● | ● | ● | ● | ● | ● | ● | | | ● | ● | | | ● | ● | |
| HOPE, ANN (HM10137) | | | | | | | | | | | | | | | | | | |
| HOUSE OF MISTRY (HM10220) | | | | ● | | ● | | ● | ● | ● | | ● | ● | | ● | ● | ● | |
| HOWARD, LYNNE (HM10240) | ● | ● | ● | ● | ● | ● | ● | ● | ● | ● | | ● | ● | ● | ● | ● | ● | |
| HUGHES, PAUL (HM10339) | | ● | ● | ● | ● | | | ● | ● | | | ● | ● | ● | ● | ● | ● | |
| HYDE BARKER & ASSOCIATES (HM10469) | | | | | | | | | | | | | | | | | | |
| INDEPENDENT PSYCHOLOGY SERVICE (HM10610) | | | | | ● | | | | | | | | | | | | | |
| INSIDE STORY (HM10650) | | | ● | ● | ● | | | | | | | | | | | ● | | |
| JACOBS, BRIAN M (HM10858) | | | | | ● | | | ● | | | | | | | | | | |

| Business by County with Reference no. | Sweating | Teeth Grinding | Tennis Elbow | Terminal Illness | Throat Problems | Thrush | Thyroid Problems | Tinnitis | Tiredness | Tonsilitis | Ulcers | Vaginal Problems | Varicose Veins | Verrucas | Vertigo | Viral Infections | Vomiting | Warts | Water Retention | Whiplash | Wind | Worms |
|---|---|---|---|---|---|---|---|---|---|---|---|---|---|---|---|---|---|---|---|---|---|---|
| HAREWOOD, MARCIA M (HM08991) | ● | ● | ● | | ● | ● | | ● | ● | ● | | ● | | | | ● | ● | ● | ● | | ● | ● |
| HARLEY ST STRESS MNGMT (HM08999) | | ● | | ● | | | | | ● | | | | | | ● | | | | | | | |
| HARLEY STREET TCM FERTILITY (HM09003) | | | | | | | | | | | | | | | | | | | | | | |
| HARPER, SUZANNE G (HM09042) | ● | ● | ● | | ● | ● | ● | ● | ● | | | | | | ● | ● | ● | | | ● | | |
| HARPER, SUZANNE G (HM09041) | ● | ● | ● | | ● | ● | | ● | ● | | | | | | ● | ● | ● | | | ● | | |
| HARROW HEALTH CARE CENTRE (HM09121) | | | ● | | | ● | ● | ● | | | | | | | | | | | | | | |
| HATHA YOGA/COUNSELLING (HM09195) | | | | | | | | | | | | | | | | | | | | | | |
| HAVELOCK-SEARLE, PAULINE (HM09206) | | | | | | | | | | | | | | | | | | | | | | |
| HAWKINS, JAN (HM09222) | | | | ● | | | | | | | | | | | | | | | | | | |
| HEAL, CHRISTIANNE (HM09314) | | | | ● | | | | | | | | | | | | | | | | | | |
| HEALERS WORLD (HM09320) | ● | ● | ● | ● | ● | ● | ● | ● | ● | ● | ● | ● | ● | | ● | ● | ● | ● | ● | | ● | ● |
| HEALING ARTS UK (HM09326) | | | ● | | | | | | | | | | | | | | | | | | | |
| HEALTHY LIVING CENTRE (HM09429) | ● | ● | ● | ● | ● | ● | ● | ● | ● | ● | ● | ● | ● | | ● | ● | ● | ● | ● | | ● | ● |
| HELEN BERNAT - FITNESS TRAINER (HM09511) | | | | | | | | | | | | | | | | | | | | | | |
| HERBAL CARE (HM09600) | ● | | ● | | ● | ● | ● | ● | ● | ● | ● | ● | | | ● | ● | ● | ● | ● | | ● | ● |
| HERBAL CARE (HM09601) | ● | | ● | | ● | ● | ● | ● | ● | ● | ● | ● | | | ● | ● | ● | ● | ● | | ● | ● |
| HERBMEDIC (HM09663) | ● | ● | ● | ● | ● | ● | ● | ● | ● | ● | ● | ● | ● | | ● | ● | ● | ● | ● | | ● | ● |
| HETHERTON, ANNE (HM09697) | ● | ● | ● | | ● | ● | ● | ● | ● | ● | ● | ● | ● | | ● | ● | ● | ● | ● | | ● | ● |
| HIGHBURY CENTRE (HM09746) | | | ● | | | | | | | | | | | | | | | | | | | |
| HILDRETH & COCKER (HM09767) | | | | | | | | | | | | | | | | | | | | | | |
| HOBBS, SALLY (HM09858) | | | | | | | | | | | | | | | | | | | | | | |
| HOGARTH CLINIC (HM09907) | ● | | ● | ● | | | | ● | ● | | ● | | | | ● | ● | ● | | ● | | | |
| HOLMES, DAVID (HM10040) | | | | | | | | | | | | | | ● | | | | | | | | |
| HOME VISITING SERVICES (HM10069) | ● | | ● | ● | ● | ● | ● | ● | ● | ● | ● | ● | ● | | | ● | ● | ● | ● | | ● | ● |
| HOMOEOPATHIC HEALTH CENTRE (HM10095) | | | | | | | | | | | | | | | | | | | | | | |
| HONG TAD ACUPUNCTURE & HERBAL (HM10119) | ● | ● | ● | ● | ● | ● | ● | ● | ● | ● | ● | ● | ● | | ● | ● | ● | ● | ● | | ● | |
| HOPE, ANN (HM10137) | | | | | | | | | | | | | | | | | | ● | | | | |
| HOUSE OF MISTRY (HM10220) | | | ● | | ● | ● | ● | ● | ● | ● | ● | ● | ● | | | | | ● | ● | | ● | ● |
| HOWARD, LYNNE (HM10240) | ● | ● | ● | ● | ● | ● | ● | ● | ● | ● | ● | ● | ● | | ● | ● | ● | ● | ● | | ● | ● |
| HUGHES, PAUL (HM10339) | ● | ● | | ● | ● | ● | ● | ● | ● | ● | ● | ● | ● | | ● | ● | ● | ● | ● | | ● | ● |
| HYDE BARKER & ASSOCIATES (HM10469) | | | | | | | | | | | | | | | | | | | | | | |
| INDEPENDENT PSYCHOLOGY SERVICE (HM10610) | | | | | | | | | | | | | | | | | | | | | | |
| INSIDE STORY (HM10650) | | | | | | ● | | | ● | | | | | | | | | | | | | |
| JACOBS, BRIAN M (HM10858) | | | | | | | | | | | | | | | | | | | | | | |

| Business by County with Reference no. | Specialist Treatment Categories: Children | Terminally Ill | Disabled | Horses | Dogs | CatS | Other Animals |
|---|---|---|---|---|---|---|---|
| HAREWOOD, MARCIA M (HM08991) | | | | | | | |
| HARLEY ST STRESS MNGMT (HM08999) | ● | | | | | | |
| HARLEY STREET TCM FERTILITY (HM09003) | | | | | | | |
| HARPER, SUZANNE G (HM09042) | | | | | | | |
| HARPER, SUZANNE G (HM09041) | ● | | | | | | |
| HARROW HEALTH CARE CENTRE (HM09121) | ● | ● | ● | | | | |
| HATHA YOGA/COUNSELLING (HM09195) | ● | | | | | | |
| HAVELOCK-SEARLE, PAULINE (HM09206) | ● | ● | ● | | | | |
| HAWKINS, JAN (HM09222) | | ● | ● | | | | |
| HEAL, CHRISTIANNE (HM09314) | | ● | | | | | |
| HEALERS WORLD (HM09320) | ● | ● | ● | | | | |
| HEALING ARTS UK (HM09326) | ● | ● | ● | ● | ● | ● | ● |
| HEALTHY LIVING CENTRE (HM09429) | ● | ● | ● | | | | |
| HELEN BERNAT - FITNESS TRAINER (HM09511) | | | | | | | |
| HERBAL CARE (HM09600) | ● | | ● | | | | |
| HERBAL CARE (HM09601) | ● | | ● | | | | |
| HERBMEDIC (HM09663) | ● | ● | ● | | | | |
| HETHERTON, ANNE (HM09697) | ● | | | | | | |
| HIGHBURY CENTRE (HM09746) | ● | ● | ● | | | | |
| HILDRETH & COCKER (HM09767) | | | | ● | ● | ● | |
| HOBBS, SALLY (HM09858) | ● | ● | ● | | | | |
| HOGARTH CLINIC (HM09907) | ● | ● | ● | | | | |
| HOLMES, DAVID (HM10040) | ● | ● | ● | | | | |
| HOME VISITING SERVICES (HM10069) | ● | ● | ● | | | | |
| HOMOEOPATHIC HEALTH CENTRE (HM10095) | ● | | | | | | |
| HONG TAD ACUPUNCTURE & HERBAL (HM10119) | ● | | ● | | | | |
| HOPE, ANN (HM10137) | ● | | ● | | | | |
| HOUSE OF MISTRY (HM10220) | | | | | | | |
| HOWARD, LYNNE (HM10240) | ● | ● | ● | | | | |
| HUGHES, PAUL (HM10339) | ● | ● | ● | ● | ● | ● | ● |
| HYDE BARKER & ASSOCIATES (HM10469) | ● | ● | ● | | | | |
| INDEPENDENT PSYCHOLOGY SERVICE (HM10610) | | | | | | | |
| INSIDE STORY (HM10650) | ● | | ● | | | | |
| JACOBS, BRIAN M (HM10858) | | | | | | | |

# S - W Conditions treated at Practices/Businesses and Specialist Treatment Categories

Business by County with Reference no.

| Business by County with Reference no. | Sexually Trans. Infections | Shingles | Sinus Problems | Skin Problems | Sleep Disorders | Slimming Help | Slipped Disk | Smoking Help | Sneezing | Snoring | Spinal Injuries | Sports Injuries | Sprains | Stammering | Stings | Stomach Problems | Stomach Ulcers | Stress | Sweating | Teeth Grinding |
|---|---|---|---|---|---|---|---|---|---|---|---|---|---|---|---|---|---|---|---|---|
| JEWERS, M S (HM11025) | | | | | | | | | | | | | | | | | | | | |
| JOSEPH CLINIC (HM11215) | | | | | | | ● | | | | | ● | | | | | | | | |
| KAGYU SAMYE DZONG LONDON (HM11294) | | | | | | | | | | | | | | | | | | | | |
| KALLAS, JEMIMA (HM11297) | | ● | ● | ● | ● | | | ● | ● | ● | | | | ● | | ● | ● | | ● | ● |
| KANE AND ROSS CLINICS (HM11309) | | | | | | | | | | | | | | | | | | | | |
| KEITH EGLETON HYPNOTHERAPY (HM11412) | | | | ● | ● | ● | | ● | | ● | | | | ● | | ● | ● | ● | ● | ● |
| KERN, MICHAEL (HM11544) | | | | | ● | | ● | | | | | | | ● | | ● | | | | ● |
| KIKAI SHIATSU CENTRE (HM11598) | | | | | | | | | | | | ● | | | | ● | | | | |
| KILBRIDE, PETER (HM11600) | | | | | ● | ● | | ● | | ● | | | | | | | | | ● | ● |
| KINGSGATE ACUPUNCTURE PRACTICE (HM11663) | | ● | ● | ● | ● | | ● | ● | | | | ● | ● | | | ● | ● | | ● | |
| KINGSLEY, NOEL (HM11667) | | | | | | | | | | | | | | | | | | | | |
| KIRSH, MALCOLM (DR) (HM11725) | | | | | | | | | | | | | | | | | | ● | | |
| KIRSH, MALCOLM (DR) (HM11724) | | | | | | | | | | | | | | | | | | ● | | |
| KLEIN, JEMMA (HM11737) | | | | | | | | | | | | | | | | | | | | |
| LASSMAN, J (HM11986) | | | ● | ● | ● | | | | | | | | | | | | | | | |
| LEE COMPLEMENTARY HEALTH CTRE (HM12130) | | | | | | | ● | | | | | | | | | | | | | |
| LEVER CLINIC (HM12256) | | | | | | | ● | | | | | ● | ● | | | | | | | |
| LITTLE VENICE CHIROPODY (HM12469) | | | | ● | | | | | | | | ● | | | | | | | | |
| LIVING CENTRE CLINIC (HM12483) | | ● | ● | ● | ● | ● | ● | ● | ● | ● | | ● | ● | | | ● | | | | |
| LIZ DAWSON - PSYCHOTHERAPIST (HM12494) | | | | | ● | | | ● | | | | | | | | | | | | |
| LONDON ASS OF PRIMAL PSYCHO (HM12583) | | | | | | | | | | | | | | | | | | | | |
| LONDON INDIAN CHAMPISSAGE CTRE (HM12599) | | | | | | | ● | | | | | | | | | | | ● | | |
| LONDON SCHOOL OF OSTEOPATHY (HM12604) | | | | | | | | | | | | | | | | | | | | |
| LONDON SPINE AND JOINT CLINIC (HM12611) | | | | | | | ● | | | | | ● | ● | | | | | | | |
| LONGARETTI, ANTHONY (HM12623) | | | | | | | | | | | | ● | | | | | | | | |
| LOTUS CLINIC (HM12653) | | ● | ● | ● | ● | ● | | ● | ● | ● | | | ● | ● | ● | ● | ● | | ● | ● |
| LOW, JANET (DR) (HM12686) | | | | | | | | | | | | | | | | | | | | |
| LUXTON, PAULINE (HM12752) | | | | | | | | | | | | | | | | | | ● | | |
| MANLEY CLINIC (HM13016) | | ● | ● | ● | ● | ● | ● | ● | ● | ● | | ● | ● | ● | ● | ● | ● | | ● | ● |
| MARIE, SOUTA (HM13099) | | | | | | | | | | | | | | | | | | ● | | |
| MARKS, DARREN HYPNOTHERAPY (HM13119) | | | | | ● | ● | | ● | | | | | | | | | | ● | | |
| MARLBOROUGH THERAPY PRACTICE (HM13125) | | | | | ● | | | ● | | | | | | | | | | | | ● |
| MATTHEWS, ROBERT (HM13312) | | | | | ● | ● | | ● | | ● | | | | ● | | | | ● | | ● |
| MCCAFFREY, GERARDINE (HM13380) | | | ● | | ● | | | | | | | | | | | ● | | | | |

| Business by County with Reference no. | Tennis Elbow | Terminal Illness | Throat Problems | Thrush | Thyroid Problems | Tinnitis | Tiredness | Tonsilitis | Ulcers | Vaginal Problems | Varicose Veins | Verrucas | Vertigo | Viral Infections | Vomiting | Warts | Water Retention | Whiplash | Wind | Worms |
|---|---|---|---|---|---|---|---|---|---|---|---|---|---|---|---|---|---|---|---|---|
| JEWERS, M S (HM11025) | | | | | | | | | | | | ● | | | | | | | | |
| JOSEPH CLINIC (HM11215) | ● | | | | | | | | | | | | ● | | | | | | | |
| KAGYU SAMYE DZONG LONDON (HM11294) | | | | | | | | | | | | | | | | | | | | |
| KALLAS, JEMIMA (HM11297) | | | ● | ● | ● | ● | ● | ● | ● | ● | ● | | ● | | ● | ● | | | ● | |
| KANE AND ROSS CLINICS (HM11309) | | | | | | | | | | | | | | | | | | | | |
| KEITH EGLETON HYPNOTHERAPY (HM11412) | | | | | | ● | ● | | | | | | | | | | | | | |
| KERN, MICHAEL (HM11544) | | | ● | | | ● | ● | | | | | | ● | | | | | | | |
| KIKAI SHIATSU CENTRE (HM11598) | | | | | | | ● | | | | | | | | | | | | | |
| KILBRIDE, PETER (HM11600) | | | | | | ● | | | | | | | | | | | | | | |
| KINGSGATE ACUPUNCTURE PRACTICE (HM11663) | ● | | ● | | ● | ● | ● | ● | | | | | | | ● | | ● | | ● | |
| KINGSLEY, NOEL (HM11667) | | | | | | | | | | | | | | | | | | | | |
| KIRSH, MALCOLM (DR) (HM11725) | | | | | | | | | | | | | | | | | | | | |
| KIRSH, MALCOLM (DR) (HM11724) | | | | | | | | | | | | | | | | | | | | |
| KLEIN, JEMMA (HM11737) | | | | | | | | | | | | ● | | | | | | | | |
| LASSMAN, J (HM11986) | | | | | | | ● | | | | | | | | | | | | | |
| LEE COMPLEMENTARY HEALTH CTRE (HM12130) | ● | | | | | | | | | | | | | | | | | | | |
| LEVER CLINIC (HM12256) | ● | | | | | | ● | | ● | | | | | | | | | | | ● |
| LITTLE VENICE CHIROPODY (HM12469) | | | | | | | | | | | | ● | | ● | | ● | | | | |
| LIVING CENTRE CLINIC (HM12483) | ● | | | ● | | | ● | | | | | | | | | | ● | | | |
| LIZ DAWSON - PSYCHOTHERAPIST (HM12494) | | | | | | | ● | | | | | | | | | | | | | |
| LONDON ASS OF PRIMAL PSYCHO (HM12583) | | ● | | | | | | | | | | | | | | | | | | |
| LONDON INDIAN CHAMPISSAGE CTRE (HM12599) | | | | | | | ● | | | | | | | | | | | | | |
| LONDON SCHOOL OF OSTEOPATHY (HM12604) | | | | | | | | | | | | | | | | | | ● | | |
| LONDON SPINE AND JOINT CLINIC (HM12611) | ● | | | | | | | | | | | | | | | | | | | |
| LONGARETTI, ANTHONY (HM12623) | ● | | | | | | | | | | | | | | | | | | | |
| LOTUS CLINIC (HM12653) | | | ● | ● | ● | ● | ● | ● | ● | ● | ● | | ● | ● | ● | ● | ● | | ● | ● |
| LOW, JANET (DR) (HM12686) | | | | | | | | | | | | | | | | | | | | |
| LUXTON, PAULINE (HM12752) | | | | | | | | | | | | | | | | ● | | | | |
| MANLEY CLINIC (HM13016) | ● | | ● | ● | ● | ● | ● | ● | ● | ● | ● | | ● | ● | ● | ● | ● | | ● | ● |
| MARIE, SOUTA (HM13099) | | | | | | | | | | | | | | | | | | | | |
| MARKS, DARREN HYPNOTHERAPY (HM13119) | | | | | | | | | | | | | | | | | | | | |
| MARLBOROUGH THERAPY PRACTICE (HM13125) | | ● | | | | | | | | | | | | | | | | | | |
| MATTHEWS, ROBERT (HM13312) | | | | | | ● | | | | | | | | | | | | | | |
| MCCAFFREY, GERARDINE (HM13380) | | | ● | | ● | | ● | | | | | ● | | | | | ● | | | |

Specialist Treatment Categories

| Business by County with Reference no. | Children | Terminally Ill | Disabled | Horses | Dogs | CatS | Other Animals |
|---|---|---|---|---|---|---|---|
| JEWERS, M S (HM11025) | ● | ● | ● | | | | |
| JOSEPH CLINIC (HM11215) | ● | | | | | | |
| KAGYU SAMYE DZONG LONDON (HM11294) | ● | ● | ● | | | | |
| KALLAS, JEMIMA (HM11297) | | ● | | | | | |
| KANE AND ROSS CLINICS (HM11309) | ● | | | | | | |
| KEITH EGLETON HYPNOTHERAPY (HM11412) | | | | | | | |
| KERN, MICHAEL (HM11544) | ● | ● | ● | | | | |
| KIKAI SHIATSU CENTRE (HM11598) | | | | | | | |
| KILBRIDE, PETER (HM11600) | | ● | ● | | | | |
| KINGSGATE ACUPUNCTURE PRACTICE (HM11663) | ● | | | | | | |
| KINGSLEY, NOEL (HM11667) | ● | | ● | | | | |
| KIRSH, MALCOLM (DR) (HM11725) | ● | ● | ● | | | | |
| KIRSH, MALCOLM (DR) (HM11724) | | ● | ● | | | | |
| KLEIN, JEMMA (HM11737) | ● | ● | ● | | | | |
| LASSMAN, J (HM11986) | ● | | | | | | |
| LEE COMPLEMENTARY HEALTH CTRE (HM12130) | ● | ● | ● | | | | |
| LEVER CLINIC (HM12256) | ● | ● | ● | | | | |
| LITTLE VENICE CHIROPODY (HM12469) | ● | ● | ● | | | | |
| LIVING CENTRE CLINIC (HM12483) | ● | ● | ● | | | | |
| LIZ DAWSON - PSYCHOTHERAPIST (HM12494) | | ● | | | | | |
| LONDON ASS OF PRIMAL PSYCHO (HM12583) | | | | | | | |
| LONDON INDIAN CHAMPISSAGE CTRE (HM12599) | | | | | | | |
| LONDON SCHOOL OF OSTEOPATHY (HM12604) | ● | ● | ● | | | | |
| LONDON SPINE AND JOINT CLINIC (HM12611) | | | | | | | |
| LONGARETTI, ANTHONY (HM12623) | | | | | | | |
| LOTUS CLINIC (HM12653) | ● | ● | ● | | | | |
| LOW, JANET (DR) (HM12686) | ● | ● | ● | | | | |
| LUXTON, PAULINE (HM12752) | ● | ● | ● | | ● | | |
| MANLEY CLINIC (HM13016) | ● | | | | | | |
| MARIE, SOUTA (HM13099) | | | | | | | |
| MARKS, DARREN HYPNOTHERAPY (HM13119) | | ● | ● | | | | |
| MARLBOROUGH THERAPY PRACTICE (HM13125) | ● | ● | ● | | | | |
| MATTHEWS, ROBERT (HM13312) | ● | ● | ● | | | | |
| MCCAFFREY, GERARDINE (HM13380) | ● | ● | ● | | | | |

# S - W Conditions treated at Practices/Businesses and Specialist Treatment Categories

| | | | | | | | | | | | | | | | | | | | | | | | | | | | | | | | | | | | | | | | | | Specialist Treatment Categories | | | | | | |
|---|---|---|---|---|---|---|---|---|---|---|---|---|---|---|---|---|---|---|---|---|---|---|---|---|---|---|---|---|---|---|---|---|---|---|---|---|---|---|---|---|---|---|---|---|---|---|---|
| Business by County with Reference no. | Sexually Trans. Infections | Shingles | Sinus Problems | Skin Problems | Sleep Disorders | Slimming Help | Slipped Disk | Smoking Help | Sneezing | Snoring | Spinal Injuries | Sports Injuries | Sprains | Stammering | Stings | Stomach Problems | Stomach Ulcers | Stress | Sweating | Teeth Grinding | Tennis Elbow | Terminal Illness | Throat Problems | Thrush | Thyroid Problems | Tinnitis | Tiredness | Tonsilitis | Ulcers | Vaginal Problems | Varicose Veins | Verrucas | Vertigo | Viral Infections | Vomiting | Warts | Water Retention | Whiplash | Wind | Worms | Children | Terminally Ill | Disabled | Horses | Dogs | CatS | Other Animals |
| MCCLOSKEY, P J (HM13409) | | | | ● | | | | | | | | ● | ● | | | | | | ● | | | | | | | | | | ● | | | ● | | ● | | ● | | | | | ● | ● | ● | | | | |
| MEYERSON, SIMON (HM13789) | | | | | | | | | | | | | | | | | | ● | | | | | | | | | | | | | | | | | | | | | | | ● | ● | ● | | | | |
| MIDDLETON, IAN W (HM13821) | | | ● | ● | | | | | | | | | | | | ● | ● | | ● | | | | ● | ● | ● | ● | | ● | ● | | ● | | | ● | | | ● | | | | ● | ● | ● | | | | |
| MILLS DE-WIN STUDIOS (HM13922) | | | ● | ● | ● | | ● | | | | | ● | ● | | | ● | | | | ● | ● | ● | | | ● | ● | ● | | | | ● | | | | | | ● | | ● | | ● | ● | ● | | | | |
| MONTSERRAT CLINIC (HM14090) | ● | ● | ● | ● | ● | ● | ● | ● | ● | ● | | ● | ● | ● | ● | ● | ● | ● | ● | ● | ● | ● | ● | ● | ● | ● | ● | ● | ● | ● | ● | | ● | ● | ● | ● | ● | | ● | ● | ● | | ● | | | | |
| MOTHERSOLE, VINETA (HM20682) | | | | ● | | | | | | | | ● | ● | | | | | | | | | | | | | | | | | | | | | | | ● | | | | | | ● | ● | | | | |
| MOTTINGHAM HYPNOTHERAPY CTRE (HM14279) | | | ● | ● | ● | ● | | ● | | | | | | ● | | | | | | ● | | | ● | | | | | | | | | | | | | | | | | | | | | | | | |
| M-POWER (HM14308) | | | | | | ● | | ● | | | | | | | | | | | | | | | | | | | | | | | | | | | | | | | | | | | | | | | |
| NATURAL HEALTH CLINIC (HM14575) | | | | | | | | | | | | | | | | | | | | | | | | | | | | | | | | | | | | | | | | | ● | | ● | | | | |
| NEIL-ASHER, S (HM14761) | | | | | | | ● | | | | | ● | ● | | | | | | | | ● | | | | | | | | | | | | | | | | | ● | | | ● | | ● | | | | |
| NEILL, VICTORIA (HM14764) | | ● | ● | | | | ● | | | | | ● | ● | | | | | | | | ● | | | | | ● | | | | | | | ● | | | | | | | | ● | ● | ● | | | | |
| NEW CROSS NATURAL THRPY CTRE (HM14814) | | | | | | | | | | | | | | | | | | | | | | | | | | | | | | | | | | | | | | | | | ● | | | | | | |
| NIEL-ASHER, S (HM14933) | | | | | | | ● | | | | | ● | ● | | | | | | | | ● | | | | | | | | | | | | | | | | | ● | | | ● | | ● | | | | |
| NIELSEN, RITA C (HM14935) | | ● | ● | ● | ● | | | | | | | | | | | ● | | | | | | | | | | ● | ● | ● | | | | | | | | | | | | | ● | ● | ● | | | | |
| NORTH POLE SCH OF T'AI-CHI (HM15094) | | | | | | | | | | | | | | | | | | | | | | | | | | | ● | | | | | | | | | | | | | | | | | | | | |
| NORTHWOOD CLINIC (HM15067) | | | | | | | | | | | | ● | ● | | | | | | | | | | | | | | | | | | | | | | | | | | | | ● | ● | ● | | | | |
| NOTTING HILL TRAD ACU CTRE (HM15081) | | | ● | ● | ● | | | | | | | ● | ● | | | | | | | | ● | | | | | | ● | | | | | | | | ● | | | | | | ● | ● | ● | | | | |
| NUTRITION FOR LIFE INT (HM15124) | | | ● | | ● | ● | | ● | | ● | | ● | ● | | | ● | ● | | | | | ● | ● | ● | | | ● | | | | ● | | | | ● | | | | ● | ● | ● | ● | ● | | | | |
| O'CONNOR, PENNY (HM15214) | | | | | | | | | | | | | | | | | | | | | | | | | | | | | | | | | | | | | | | | | ● | ● | | | | | |
| ORIENTAL MEDICINE (HM15386) | ● | ● | ● | ● | ● | ● | ● | ● | ● | ● | | ● | ● | | ● | ● | ● | | ● | ● | ● | ● | ● | ● | ● | ● | ● | ● | ● | ● | ● | | ● | ● | ● | ● | ● | | ● | | ● | ● | ● | | | | |
| OSTEOPATHIC ASSOCIATION CLINIC (HM15453) | | | | | | | ● | | | | | ● | ● | | | | | | | | ● | | | | | | | | | | | | | | | | | | | | | | ● | | | | |
| OSTEOPATHIC PRACTICE (HM15470) | | | ● | ● | ● | | ● | | | ● | | ● | ● | | ● | | | | | ● | ● | | | | | ● | | | | | | | ● | | | | | | ● | | ● | ● | ● | | | | |
| OSTEOPATHIC PRACTICE (HM15467) | | | | | | | ● | | | | | ● | | | | | | | | | ● | | | | | | | | | | | | | | | | | | | | ● | | | | | | |
| OSTEOPATHIC PRACTICE (HM15473) | | | | | | | ● | | | | | ● | | | | | | | | | ● | | | | | ● | | | | | | | | | | | | | | | ● | | | | | | |
| OTREMBA, KATHARINA (HM15496) | | | ● | ● | ● | ● | | ● | ● | | | | | ● | ● | ● | ● | | ● | ● | | | | ● | ● | ● | ● | ● | ● | ● | | | | | ● | ● | ● | | ● | | ● | ● | ● | | | | |
| OUTCOMES (HM15502) | | | ● | ● | ● | ● | | ● | | | | | | ● | | ● | ● | | ● | ● | | | | ● | | ● | ● | | | | | | ● | | ● | ● | | | | | | | | | | | |
| PACIFIC WAVES PRODUCTIONS (HM15553) | | | | ● | ● | ● | | ● | | ● | | | | ● | | | | | ● | ● | | | | | | | ● | | | | | | ● | | | | | | ● | | ● | | | | | | |
| PALACE ROAD OSTEOPATHIC CLINIC (HM15590) | | | | | | | | | | | | | | | | | | | | | ● | | | | | | | | | | | | | | | | | | | | | | | | | | |
| PALFREYMAN, SUE (HM15592) | | | | | | | ● | | | | | ● | ● | | | | | | | | ● | | | | | | | | | | | | | | | | | | | | ● | | | | | | |
| PAPOUTSIS, MARGARET (HM15642) | | | | | | | ● | | | | | ● | ● | | | | | | | | ● | | | | | | | | | | | | | | | | | | | | | | | | | | |
| PATEL, J C (HM15788) | | | | | | | | | | | | ● | | | | | | | | | | | | | | | | | | | | ● | | | | | | | | | ● | ● | ● | | | | |
| PHYSIO ONE (HM16202) | | ● | | | | | | | | | | ● | ● | | | | | | | | | | | | | | | | | | | | ● | | | | | ● | | | ● | | | | | | |
| PHYSIO SOLUTIONS (HM16205) | | | | | | | ● | | | | | ● | ● | | | | | | | | ● | | | | | | | | | | | | | | | | | | | | ● | | ● | | | | |
| PHYSIOTHERAPY PRACTICE (HM16253) | | | | | | | | | | | | ● | | | | | | ● | | | ● | | | | | | | | | | | | | | | | | | | | ● | ● | ● | | | | |

# S - W Conditions treated at Practices/Businesses and Specialist Treatment Categories

Business by County with Reference no.

| Business | Sexually Trans. Infections | Shingles | Sinus Problems | Skin Problems | Sleep Disorders | Slimming Help | Slipped Disk | Smoking Help | Sneezing | Snoring | Spinal Injuries | Sports Injuries | Sprains | Stammering | Stings | Stomach Problems | Stomach Ulcers | Stress |
|---|---|---|---|---|---|---|---|---|---|---|---|---|---|---|---|---|---|---|
| PINNER ROAD PHYSIOTHERAPY (HM16316) | | | | | | | ● | | | | | ● | ● | | | | | |
| PODIATRY CLINIC (HM16393) | | | | | | | | | | | | ● | | | | | | |
| PRICE, GILLIAN (HM16575) | | ● | ● | ● | ● | ● | ● | ● | ● | ● | | ● | ● | | | ● | ● | |
| PRICE, SANDRA (HM16595) | | | | | | | ● | | | | ● | ● | ● | | | | | |
| PRICE, SANDRA (HM16594) | | | | | | | ● | | | | ● | ● | ● | | | | | |
| PRIMROSE HEALING CENTRE (HM16616) | | | | | ● | ● | | ● | | | | | | ● | | | | |
| PRIVATE HEALTH CLINIC (HM16644) | ● | ● | ● | ● | ● | ● | ● | ● | ● | ● | | ● | ● | ● | ● | ● | ● | |
| PRIVATE PRACTICE (HM16649) | | | | | | | | | | | | | | | | | | |
| PROPERT, DAVID (HM16666) | | | | | | | | | | | | | | | | | | |
| PSYCHOTHERAPY CENTRE (HM16734) | | | | ● | ● | | | | | | | | | ● | | | | |
| PUTNEY CHIROPRACTIC (HM16780) | | | | | | | ● | | | | | ● | | | | | | |
| RACHEL YOUNG - HYPNOTHERAPIST (HM16837) | | | ● | ● | ● | ● | | ● | | | | ● | ● | ● | | ● | ● | |
| RAEBURN, JO (HM16865) | | ● | ● | ● | ● | | | | | | | ● | ● | | | ● | | |
| RANDALL, CAROLINE (HM16926) | ● | ● | ● | ● | ● | ● | ● | ● | ● | ● | | ● | ● | ● | ● | ● | ● | |
| RAVENSCROFT CENTRE (HM16967) | | | | | ● | | | ● | | | | | | | | | | |
| READ, CHARLES (HM16993) | | | | | | | ● | | | | | ● | ● | | | | | |
| REEVE, MALCOLM (HM17060) | | | | | | | ● | | | | | | ● | | | | | |
| REFLEXOLOGY (HM17077) | | | ● | ● | ● | | | | | | | | | | | | | |
| REFLEXOLOGY CLINIC (HM17089) | | | | | | | | | | | | | | | | | | |
| RELAXATION PLACE (HM17166) | | | | ● | | | | | | | | | | | | | | ● |
| REPLINGHAM CLINIC (HM17195) | | | ● | ● | ● | ● | ● | ● | | | | ● | ● | | | ● | | |
| ROBERTS, MATT (HM17420) | | | | | ● | | | ● | | | | | | ● | | | | |
| ROBINSON, GABIE (HM17473) | | | ● | ● | ● | | | | | | | | | | | ● | | |
| ROEHAMPTON PHYSIO/SPORTS (HM17535) | | | | | | | ● | | | | | ● | ● | | | | | |
| ROSE, NICHOLAS (HM17613) | | | | | | | | | | | | ● | ● | | | | | |
| RUTHERFORD, BERWYN (HM17780) | | | ● | | | | ● | | | | | ● | ● | | | | | |
| SALTER, LIZ (HM17869) | ● | ● | ● | ● | ● | | | ● | ● | | | | | ● | ● | ● | ● | |
| SAYER CLINIC (HM17994) | | | | | | | | | | | ● | ● | ● | | | | | |
| SAYER CLINIC (HM17993) | | | | | | | ● | | | | ● | ● | ● | | | | | |
| SEARBY, JOE (HM18174) | | | ● | | ● | | ● | | | ● | | ● | ● | ● | | ● | | |
| SEEAR, MICHAEL (DR) (HM18189) | | | ● | ● | ● | ● | | ● | ● | | | | | ● | | ● | ● | ● |
| SEYMOUR PRACTICE (HM18257) | | | | | | | ● | | | | | ● | ● | | | | | |
| SHIATSU PLACE (HM18458) | | | ● | ● | ● | | ● | | | | | ● | | | | ● | ● | |
| SHIATSU STUDIO (HM18465) | | | | | | | | | | | | | | | | | | ● |

| Business | Sweating | Teeth Grinding | Tennis Elbow | Terminal Illness | Throat Problems | Thrush | Thyroid Problems | Tinnitis | Tiredness | Tonsilitis | Ulcers | Vaginal Problems | Varicose Veins | Verrucas | Vertigo | Viral Infections | Vomiting | Warts | Water Retention | Whiplash | Wind | Worms |
|---|---|---|---|---|---|---|---|---|---|---|---|---|---|---|---|---|---|---|---|---|---|---|
| PINNER ROAD PHYSIOTHERAPY (HM16316) | | | ● | | | | | | | | | | | | | | | | | | | |
| PODIATRY CLINIC (HM16393) | | | | | | | | | | | | | | | | | | ● | | | | |
| PRICE, GILLIAN (HM16575) | ● | ● | ● | | ● | ● | ● | ● | ● | ● | ● | ● | ● | | ● | ● | ● | | ● | | ● | |
| PRICE, SANDRA (HM16595) | | | ● | | | | | | | | | | | | | | | | | ● | | |
| PRICE, SANDRA (HM16594) | | | ● | | | | | | | | | | | | | | | | | ● | | |
| PRIMROSE HEALING CENTRE (HM16616) | ● | ● | | | | | | | ● | | | | | | ● | | | | | | | |
| PRIVATE HEALTH CLINIC (HM16644) | ● | ● | ● | ● | ● | ● | ● | ● | ● | ● | ● | ● | ● | | ● | ● | ● | ● | ● | | ● | ● |
| PRIVATE PRACTICE (HM16649) | | | | | | | | | ● | | | | | | | | | | | | | |
| PROPERT, DAVID (HM16666) | | | | | | | | | | | | | | | | | | | | | | |
| PSYCHOTHERAPY CENTRE (HM16734) | | | | | | | | | | | | ● | | | ● | | | | | | | |
| PUTNEY CHIROPRACTIC (HM16780) | | ● | | | | | | | | | | | | | | | | | | | | |
| RACHEL YOUNG - HYPNOTHERAPIST (HM16837) | ● | ● | ● | ● | ● | | ● | ● | ● | | ● | | | | | | | | | | ● | |
| RAEBURN, JO (HM16865) | | ● | | ● | ● | ● | | ● | ● | | | | ● | | | | | ● | ● | | | |
| RANDALL, CAROLINE (HM16926) | ● | ● | ● | ● | ● | ● | ● | ● | ● | ● | ● | ● | ● | | ● | ● | ● | ● | ● | | ● | ● |
| RAVENSCROFT CENTRE (HM16967) | | | | | | | | | ● | | | | | | | | | | | | | |
| READ, CHARLES (HM16993) | | | ● | | | | | ● | | | | | | | | | | | | | | |
| REEVE, MALCOLM (HM17060) | | | ● | | | | | | | | | | | | | | | | | | | |
| REFLEXOLOGY (HM17077) | | | | | | | ● | | ● | | | | ● | | | | | | ● | | ● | |
| REFLEXOLOGY CLINIC (HM17089) | | | | | | | | | | | | | | | | | | | | | | |
| RELAXATION PLACE (HM17166) | | | | | | | | | | | | | | | | | | | | | | |
| REPLINGHAM CLINIC (HM17195) | | ● | ● | ● | | | | ● | ● | | ● | | | | ● | | | | | | | |
| ROBERTS, MATT (HM17420) | | | | | | | | | ● | | | | | | ● | | | | | | | |
| ROBINSON, GABIE (HM17473) | | | | | | | | | ● | | | | | | | | | ● | ● | | | |
| ROEHAMPTON PHYSIO/SPORTS (HM17535) | | | ● | | | | | | | | | | | | | | | | | | | |
| ROSE, NICHOLAS (HM17613) | | | ● | | | | | | | | | | | | | | | | | | | |
| RUTHERFORD, BERWYN (HM17780) | | | ● | | | | | | | | | | | | | | | | | | | |
| SALTER, LIZ (HM17869) | ● | ● | | | ● | ● | ● | | ● | ● | ● | ● | | | ● | ● | ● | ● | | | ● | ● |
| SAYER CLINIC (HM17994) | | | ● | | | | | | | | | | | | | | | | | ● | | |
| SAYER CLINIC (HM17993) | | | ● | | | | | ● | | | | | | | ● | | | | | ● | | |
| SEARBY, JOE (HM18174) | | ● | ● | | ● | | | | ● | | | | | | | | | | | | | |
| SEEAR, MICHAEL (DR) (HM18189) | | ● | ● | | | | ● | ● | ● | ● | | | | | | | | | | | | |
| SEYMOUR PRACTICE (HM18257) | | | ● | | | | | | | | | | | | | | | | | | | |
| SHIATSU PLACE (HM18458) | ● | ● | ● | ● | ● | | | ● | ● | | ● | | ● | | | | ● | | ● | | ● | |
| SHIATSU STUDIO (HM18465) | | | | | | | | | | | | | | | | | | | | | | |

| Business | Specialist Treatment Categories: Children | Terminally Ill | Disabled | Horses | Dogs | CatS | Other Animals |
|---|---|---|---|---|---|---|---|
| PINNER ROAD PHYSIOTHERAPY (HM16316) | ● | ● | ● | | | | |
| PODIATRY CLINIC (HM16393) | ● | | ● | | | | |
| PRICE, GILLIAN (HM16575) | | ● | ● | | | | |
| PRICE, SANDRA (HM16595) | ● | | ● | | | | |
| PRICE, SANDRA (HM16594) | ● | ● | ● | | | | |
| PRIMROSE HEALING CENTRE (HM16616) | | | | | | | |
| PRIVATE HEALTH CLINIC (HM16644) | ● | ● | ● | | | | |
| PRIVATE PRACTICE (HM16649) | ● | | ● | | | | |
| PROPERT, DAVID (HM16666) | ● | ● | ● | | | | |
| PSYCHOTHERAPY CENTRE (HM16734) | | | | | | | |
| PUTNEY CHIROPRACTIC (HM16780) | ● | ● | ● | | | | |
| RACHEL YOUNG - HYPNOTHERAPIST (HM16837) | ● | ● | ● | | | | |
| RAEBURN, JO (HM16865) | ● | ● | ● | | | | |
| RANDALL, CAROLINE (HM16926) | | ● | ● | | | | |
| RAVENSCROFT CENTRE (HM16967) | ● | ● | | | | | |
| READ, CHARLES (HM16993) | ● | ● | ● | | | | |
| REEVE, MALCOLM (HM17060) | ● | | ● | | | | |
| REFLEXOLOGY (HM17077) | ● | ● | ● | | | | |
| REFLEXOLOGY CLINIC (HM17089) | ● | | | | | | |
| RELAXATION PLACE (HM17166) | ● | ● | ● | | | | |
| REPLINGHAM CLINIC (HM17195) | ● | ● | | | | | |
| ROBERTS, MATT (HM17420) | | | | | | | |
| ROBINSON, GABIE (HM17473) | ● | ● | ● | | | | |
| ROEHAMPTON PHYSIO/SPORTS (HM17535) | | | ● | | | | |
| ROSE, NICHOLAS (HM17613) | | | | | | | |
| RUTHERFORD, BERWYN (HM17780) | ● | | ● | | | | |
| SALTER, LIZ (HM17869) | ● | ● | | | | | |
| SAYER CLINIC (HM17994) | | | | | | | |
| SAYER CLINIC (HM17993) | ● | ● | ● | | | | |
| SEARBY, JOE (HM18174) | ● | | | | | | |
| SEEAR, MICHAEL (DR) (HM18189) | | | | | | | |
| SEYMOUR PRACTICE (HM18257) | ● | | | | | | |
| SHIATSU PLACE (HM18458) | ● | ● | ● | | | | |
| SHIATSU STUDIO (HM18465) | ● | ● | | | | | |

# S - W Conditions treated at Practices/Businesses and Specialist Treatment Categories

| Business by County with Reference no. | Sexually Trans. Infections | Shingles | Sinus Problems | Skin Problems | Sleep Disorders | Slimming Help | Slipped Disk | Smoking Help | Sneezing | Snoring | Spinal Injuries | Sports Injuries | Sprains | Stammering | Stings | Stomach Problems | Stomach Ulcers | Stress | Sweating | Teeth Grinding | Tennis Elbow |
|---|---|---|---|---|---|---|---|---|---|---|---|---|---|---|---|---|---|---|---|---|---|
| SIMON, CAROLYN (HM18567) | | | | | | | ● | | | | | | | | | | | | | | |
| SIMPLY HERBAL CLINIC (HM18577) | | ● | ● | ● | ● | ● | | ● | ● | ● | | ● | ● | | ● | ● | ● | | ● | ● | ● |
| SIMPSON, STELLA (HM18599) | ● | ● | ● | ● | ● | | ● | ● | ● | ● | | ● | ● | | | ● | ● | | ● | | ● |
| SLADE OSTEOPATHIC PRACTICE (HM18667) | | | | | | | ● | | | | ● | ● | ● | | | | | | | | ● |
| SOUTH LONDON NATURAL HLTH CTRE (HM18911) | ● | ● | ● | ● | ● | ● | ● | ● | ● | ● | | ● | ● | ● | ● | ● | ● | | ● | ● | ● |
| SOUTHFIELDS CLINIC (HM18935) | | | ● | ● | | | ● | | | | | ● | | | | | | | | | ● |
| SPALL MEDICAL CENTRE (HM18957) | ● | | | ● | ● | ● | | ● | ● | ● | | ● | ● | | | ● | ● | | ● | ● | ● |
| SPECIALIST HEALTH (HM18972) | | | | | | | ● | | | | | ● | ● | | | | | ● | | | ● |
| SPENCER, PIERS (HM19001) | | | | | | | ● | | | | | ● | ● | | | | | | | | ● |
| SPYROS MOUZOURIDES (HM19056) | ● | ● | ● | ● | ● | ● | ● | ● | ● | | | | | | ● | ● | ● | | ● | | ● |
| STANMORE PHYSIO PRACTICE (HM19132) | | | | | | | ● | | | | | ● | | | | | | | | | ● |
| STOBEZKI, YAEL (HM19307) | | | | | | | | | | | | | | | | | | ● | | | |
| STRONG, STELLA (HM19419) | | | | | | | ● | | | | | | | | | | | | | | |
| T C M HEALTHCARE (HM19640) | | ● | ● | ● | | | | | | | | | | | | | | | | | |
| THOMPSON, MARK (HM19990) | | | ● | ● | | | ● | | | | | ● | ● | | | ● | ● | | | ● | ● |
| THURGOOD, SIMON (HM20047) | | | | | | | ● | | | | | ● | | | | | | | | | |
| TORRIDON COMP THERAPY CLINIC (HM20173) | | | ● | ● | ● | | | ● | | | | | | | | ● | | | | | |
| TRADITIONAL ACUPUNCTURE CENTRE (HM20218) | | ● | ● | ● | | | ● | | | | | ● | | | | | | | | | |
| TRANQUILITY (HM20255) | | | ● | ● | ● | ● | ● | ● | ● | ● | | ● | ● | ● | ● | ● | ● | | ● | ● | ● |
| TROHEAR, PATRICIA (HM20345) | | | | | ● | ● | | ● | | | | | | | | | ● | | | | |
| TURMAINE, VICKI (HM20410) | | ● | ● | ● | ● | | | | ● | | | | ● | ● | ● | ● | | | ● | ● | ● |
| TURNBULL, JO (HM20413) | | ● | ● | | ● | | | ● | | | | ● | | | | ● | | | ● | | |
| TURNER, TERI (HM20438) | | | | | | | ● | | | | ● | ● | ● | | | | | | | | ● |
| TWICKENHAM PHYSIOFIRST CENTRE (HM20451) | | | | | | | ● | | | | | ● | ● | | | | | | | | ● |
| UKCP (HM20490) | | | | | ● | | | ● | | | | | | | | | | | | | |
| UNDERHILL, K (HM20496) | | | ● | | | | ● | | | | | ● | ● | | | | | | | ● | ● |
| VALE PRACTICE (HM20551) | ● | ● | ● | ● | ● | ● | ● | ● | ● | ● | | ● | ● | ● | ● | ● | ● | | ● | ● | ● |
| VANBRUGH PHYSIOTHERAPY CLINIC (HM20575) | | | | | | | ● | | | | | ● | ● | | | | | | | | ● |
| WALK IN BACK RUB (HM20758) | | | | | | | | | | | | | | | | | | ● | | | |
| WALK IN BACKRUB (HM20759) | | | | | | | | | | | | | | | | | | ● | | | |
| WALK IN BACKRUB (HM20760) | | | | | | | | | | | | | | | | | | ● | | | |
| WART, D (HM20959) | | | | | | | ● | | | | | ● | ● | | | | | | | | ● |
| WARWICK ALTERNATIVE HEALTH (HM20961) | | | ● | | ● | | | | | | | | | | | ● | | ● | | | |
| WEBER, MARALYN (HM21082) | | | ● | ● | ● | ● | | | ● | ● | | ● | ● | ● | | ● | ● | | ● | | ● |

| Business by County with Reference no. | Terminal Illness | Throat Problems | Thrush | Thyroid Problems | Tinnitis | Tiredness | Tonsilitis | Ulcers | Vaginal Problems | Varicose Veins | Verrucas | Vertigo | Viral Infections | Vomiting | Warts | Water Retention | Whiplash | Wind | Worms | Specialist Treatment Categories: Children | Terminally Ill | Disabled | Horses | Dogs | CatS | Other Animals |
|---|---|---|---|---|---|---|---|---|---|---|---|---|---|---|---|---|---|---|---|---|---|---|---|---|---|---|
| SIMON, CAROLYN (HM18567) | | | | | | | | | | | | | | | | | | | | | | | | | | |
| SIMPLY HERBAL CLINIC (HM18577) | | ● | ● | ● | ● | ● | ● | ● | ● | ● | | ● | ● | ● | ● | ● | | ● | ● | ● | ● | ● | | | | |
| SIMPSON, STELLA (HM18599) | ● | ● | ● | ● | ● | ● | ● | ● | ● | ● | | ● | ● | ● | | ● | | ● | | | ● | ● | | | | |
| SLADE OSTEOPATHIC PRACTICE (HM18667) | | | | | | | | | | | | | | | | | ● | | | ● | | ● | | | | |
| SOUTH LONDON NATURAL HLTH CTRE (HM18911) | ● | ● | ● | ● | ● | ● | ● | ● | ● | ● | | ● | ● | ● | ● | ● | | ● | ● | ● | ● | ● | | | | |
| SOUTHFIELDS CLINIC (HM18935) | | | | | | ● | | | | | | | | | | | | | | | | | | | | |
| SPALL MEDICAL CENTRE (HM18957) | | ● | ● | ● | | | ● | ● | ● | ● | | | | | ● | | | | | ● | ● | ● | | | | |
| SPECIALIST HEALTH (HM18972) | | | | | | | | | | | | | | | | | | | | ● | | ● | | | | |
| SPENCER, PIERS (HM19001) | | | | | | | | | | | | | | | | | | | | | | | | | | |
| SPYROS MOUZOURIDES (HM19056) | ● | ● | ● | ● | ● | ● | ● | ● | ● | ● | | ● | ● | ● | ● | ● | | ● | ● | ● | ● | ● | | | | |
| STANMORE PHYSIO PRACTICE (HM19132) | | | | | | | | | | | | | | | | | | | | | | | | | | |
| STOBEZKI, YAEL (HM19307) | | | | | | ● | | | | | | | | | | | | | | | ● | | | | | |
| STRONG, STELLA (HM19419) | | | | | | | | | | | | | | | | | | | | ● | | | | | | |
| T C M HEALTHCARE (HM19640) | | | | ● | | ● | | | ● | | | | | | | | | | | | | | | | | |
| THOMPSON, MARK (HM19990) | | | ● | ● | | ● | | | | ● | | | | | | | | ● | | ● | | | | | | |
| THURGOOD, SIMON (HM20047) | | | | | | | | | | | | | | | | | | | | ● | | ● | | | | |
| TORRIDON COMP THERAPY CLINIC (HM20173) | | | | | | ● | | | | | | | | | | | | | | ● | ● | ● | | | | |
| TRADITIONAL ACUPUNCTURE CENTRE (HM20218) | | | | | | ● | | | | | | | | | | | | | | ● | ● | ● | | | | |
| TRANQUILITY (HM20255) | | ● | ● | ● | ● | ● | ● | ● | ● | ● | | ● | ● | ● | ● | ● | | ● | | ● | ● | ● | | | | |
| TROHEAR, PATRICIA (HM20345) | | | | | | | | | | | | | | | | | | | | ● | | | | | | |
| TURMAINE, VICKI (HM20410) | | | ● | ● | ● | ● | ● | ● | ● | ● | | ● | ● | ● | ● | ● | | ● | ● | ● | | ● | | | | |
| TURNBULL, JO (HM20413) | ● | ● | | ● | ● | ● | | | | ● | | | | | | ● | | | ● | ● | ● | ● | | | | |
| TURNER, TERI (HM20438) | | | | | | | | | | | | | | | | | ● | | | ● | | ● | | | | |
| TWICKENHAM PHYSIOFIRST CENTRE (HM20451) | | | | | | | | | | | | | | | | | | | | ● | ● | ● | | | | |
| UKCP (HM20490) | | | | | | | | | | | | ● | | | | | | | | | | | | | | |
| UNDERHILL, K (HM20496) | | | | | ● | | | | | | | ● | | | | | | | | ● | | | | | | |
| VALE PRACTICE (HM20551) | ● | ● | ● | ● | ● | ● | ● | ● | ● | ● | | ● | ● | ● | ● | ● | | ● | ● | ● | | | | | | |
| VANBRUGH PHYSIOTHERAPY CLINIC (HM20575) | | | | | | | | | | | | | | | | | | | | ● | | ● | | | | |
| WALK IN BACK RUB (HM20758) | | | | | | | | | | | | | | | | | | | | | | | | | | |
| WALK IN BACKRUB (HM20759) | | | | | | | | | | | | | | | | | | | | | | | | | | |
| WALK IN BACKRUB (HM20760) | | | | | | | | | | | | | | | | | | | | | | | | | | |
| WART, D (HM20959) | | | | | | | | | | | | | | | | | ● | | | ● | | ● | | | | |
| WARWICK ALTERNATIVE HEALTH (HM20961) | | ● | | | | ● | | | ● | | | | | | | | | | | ● | ● | ● | | | | |
| WEBER, MARALYN (HM21082) | ● | ● | ● | ● | ● | ● | ● | ● | ● | ● | | ● | ● | ● | ● | ● | | ● | | ● | ● | | | | | |

# S - W Conditions treated at Practices/Businesses and Specialist Treatment Categories

| Business by County with Reference no. | | | | | | | | | | | | | | | | | | | | | | | | | | | | | | | | | | | | | | | | | Specialist Treatment Categories | | | | | | |
|---|---|---|---|---|---|---|---|---|---|---|---|---|---|---|---|---|---|---|---|---|---|---|---|---|---|---|---|---|---|---|---|---|---|---|---|---|---|---|---|---|---|---|---|---|---|---|
| | Sexually Trans. Infections | Shingles | Sinus Problems | Skin Problems | Sleep Disorders | Slimming Help | Slipped Disk | Smoking Help | Sneezing | Snoring | Spinal Injuries | Sports Injuries | Sprains | Stammering | Stings | Stomach Problems | Stomach Ulcers | Stress | Sweating | Teeth Grinding | Tennis Elbow | Terminal Illness | Throat Problems | Thrush | Thyroid Problems | Tinnitis | Tiredness | Tonsilitis | Ulcers | Vaginal Problems | Varicose Veins | Verrucas | Vertigo | Viral Infections | Vomiting | Warts | Water Retention | Whiplash | Wind | Worms | Children | Terminally Ill | Disabled | Horses | Dogs | CatS | Other Animals |
| WELL BEING (HM21131) | | | ● | ● | ● | | | | | ● | | | | | | | ● | | | ● | ● | | | ● | ● | ● | | ● | | ● | | | | | ● | ● | | | ● | | ● | ● | ● | | | | |
| WEST LONDON HOLISTIC CENTRE (HM21226) | | | | ● | ● | ● | | ● | | | | | | ● | | ● | | | | | | | | | | | ● | | | | | | | | | | | | | | | | | | | | |
| WEST LONDON PSYCHOTHERAPY (HM21227) | | | | | ● | | | | | | | | | | | | | | | | | | | | | | | | | | | | | | | | | | | | ● | ● | ● | | | | |
| WEST LONDON YOGA SHALA (HM21228) | | | | | | | ● | | | | | ● | ● | | | | | | | | | | | | | | | | | | | | | | | | | | | | ● | ● | ● | | | | |
| WESTERN, G (HM21265) | | | | | | | ● | | | | ● | ● | ● | | | | | | | | ● | | | | | | | | | | | | | | | | | ● | | | ● | | ● | | | | |
| WHITE HART LANE THERAPY CENTRE (HM21338) | | | | | | | ● | | | | | ● | ● | | | | | | | | ● | | | | | | | | | | | | | | | | | ● | | | | | | | | | |
| WHOLE-BEING INTERACTIVE HYP (HM21435) | | | | | | ● | | ● | | | | | | | | | | ● | | | | | | | | | | | | | | | | | | | | | | | ● | ● | ● | | | | |
| WIGHAM, A (HM21468) | | | | | | | | | | | | | | | | | | ● | | | | | | | | | | | | | | | | | | | | | | | | ● | | | | | |
| WILLIAMS, B A (HM21541) | | | ● | ● | | | ● | | | | | ● | | | | | | | | | | | | | | | ● | | | | | | | | | | | | | | ● | ● | ● | | | | |
| WILLIAMS, IAN (HM21565) | | | | | | | | | | | | | | | | | | | | | | | | | | | | | | | | ● | | | | | | | | | ● | ● | ● | | | | |
| WILLMOTT, SUSAN (HM21623) | | | | | ● | ● | | ● | | | | | | | | | | | | | | | | | | | ● | | | | | | | | | | | | | | | ● | | | | | |
| WILSON, CHRISTOPHER (HM21651) | | | | | | | | | | | | | | | | | | | | | | | | | | | | | | | | | | | | | | | | | ● | ● | ● | | | | |
| WINCHMORE CLINIC OF OSTEOPATHY (HM21694) | | | | | | | ● | | | | | ● | ● | | | | | | | | ● | | | | | | | | | | | | | | | | | | | | ● | ● | ● | | | | |
| WOODBERRY CLINIC (HM21815) | | | | | | | | | | | | ● | ● | | | | | | | | ● | | | | | | | | | | | | | | | | | | | | ● | | | | | | |
| WOOLF, PERRY (HM21872) | | | | ● | | | | | | | | ● | ● | | | | | | | | | | | | | | | | | | ● | ● | | | | ● | | | | | | | | | | | |
| WORLD OF LIGHT (HM21898) | ● | ● | ● | ● | ● | ● | ● | ● | ● | ● | | ● | ● | ● | ● | ● | ● | | ● | ● | ● | ● | ● | ● | ● | ● | ● | ● | ● | ● | ● | | ● | ● | ● | ● | ● | | ● | ● | ● | ● | ● | | | | |
| WREN, ANTHONY (HM21920) | | | ● | | ● | | | | | | | | | | | | | | | | | | | | | ● | | | | | | | | | | | | | | | ● | ● | ● | | | | |
| WRIGHT, JENNY (HM21936) | | | | | ● | ● | | ● | | | | | | ● | | | | | | ● | | | | | | | | | | | | | | | | | | | | | ● | ● | | | | | |
| WYNNE-SIMMONS, A (DR) (HM21979) | | ● | ● | ● | ● | | | | ● | | | ● | ● | ● | ● | ● | ● | | | | | | ● | ● | ● | | ● | ● | ● | ● | ● | | ● | ● | ● | | ● | | ● | ● | | | | | | | |
| YING, FRANK (HM22014) | | | | | | | ● | | | | | ● | ● | | | | | | | | ● | | | | | | | | | | | | | | | | | | | | ● | | | | | | |
| YOGA THERAPY CENTRE (HM22033) | | | | | | | | | | | | | | | | | | | | | | | | | | | | | | | | | | | | | | | | | | ● | ● | | | | |
| ZEN HEALTH CENTRE (HM22100) | ● | ● | ● | ● | ● | ● | ● | ● | ● | ● | | ● | ● | | ● | ● | ● | | ● | | ● | ● | ● | ● | ● | ● | ● | ● | ● | ● | ● | | ● | ● | ● | ● | ● | | ● | ● | ● | ● | ● | | | | |
| ZEN SHIATSU & HEALING TAO (HM22101) | | | | | | | | | | | | | | | | | | | ● | ● | | ● | | | | | | | | | | | | | | | | | ● | | | | | | | | |
| MANCHESTER (GREATER) | | | | | | | | | | | | | | | | | | | | | | | | | | | | | | | | | | | | | | | | | | | | | | | |
| A SIR ROBERTS ALT PLACE (HM00045) | | ● | ● | ● | ● | ● | ● | ● | | ● | | ● | ● | ● | | | | | | | ● | ● | | ● | | ● | ● | | | | ● | | | | | ● | | | | | ● | ● | ● | | | | |
| A6 CHIROPODY PRACTICE (HM00055) | | | | | | | | | | | | | | | | | | | | | | | | | | | | | | | | | | | | | | | | | ● | ● | ● | | | | |
| ACUMEDIC (HM00220) | | | | ● | ● | ● | | ● | ● | | | ● | | | | ● | | | | | | | | | | | | | | | | | | | | | ● | | | | ● | ● | ● | | | | |
| ACUPUNCTURE CENTRE (HM00252) | | ● | | | ● | | | ● | ● | | | | | | | | ● | | | | ● | | | | | ● | ● | | | ● | | | ● | | | | | | | | ● | ● | | | | | |
| ADVANCED CHIROPODY SURGERY (HM00394) | | | | | | | | | | | | | | | | | | | | | | | | | | | | | | | | | | | | ● | | | | | ● | ● | ● | | | | |
| ADVANCED PHYSIOTHERAPY CLINIC (HM00403) | | | | | | | ● | | | | | ● | ● | | | | | | | | ● | | | | | | | | | | | | | | | | | ● | | | ● | | ● | | | | |
| ALL IN THE MIND (HM00582) | | | | | | ● | | | | | | | | ● | | | | | | ● | | | | | | | ● | | | | | | | | | | | | | | | | | | | | |
| AROMATHERAPY BY SARA (HM01098) | | | | ● | ● | | | | | | | | | | | | | ● | | | | | | | | | | | | | | | | | | | | | | | | | | | | | |
| AROMATHERAPY LADIES MASSAGE (HM01118) | ● | ● | ● | ● | ● | ● | ● | ● | ● | ● | | ● | ● | ● | ● | ● | ● | | ● | ● | ● | ● | ● | ● | ● | ● | ● | ● | ● | ● | ● | | ● | ● | ● | ● | ● | | ● | ● | ● | ● | ● | | | | |
| ASTLEY COMPLEMENTARY CENTRE (HM01300) | | | | | ● | | | ● | | | | ● | | | | | | | | | ● | | | | | | | | | | | ● | | | | ● | | | | | ● | ● | ● | | | | |

# S - W Conditions treated at Practices/Businesses and Specialist Treatment Categories

Business by County with Reference no.

| Business by County with Reference no. | Sexually Trans. Infections | Shingles | Sinus Problems | Skin Problems | Sleep Disorders | Slimming Help | Slipped Disk | Smoking Help | Sneezing | Snoring | Spinal Injuries | Sports Injuries | Sprains | Stammering | Stings | Stomach Problems |
|---|---|---|---|---|---|---|---|---|---|---|---|---|---|---|---|---|
| BEAUTY THERAPY CENTRE (HM02006) | | | | | | | | | | | | | | | | |
| BRAMHALL CHIROPRACTIC CLINIC (HM02898) | | | | ● | | | | | | | | ● | | | | |
| BURGESS, KAREN (HM03377) | | | | | | | ● | | | | | ● | ● | | | |
| C CARTLEDGE REFLEXOLOGY (HM03521) | ● | ● | ● | ● | ● | ● | ● | ● | ● | ● | | ● | ● | ● | ● | ● |
| CHARTERED PHYSIOTHERAPY CLINIC (HM04046) | | | | | | | ● | | | | | ● | ● | | | |
| CHORLTON STRESS MANAGEMENT (HM04430) | | | | | | ● | | ● | | | | | | ● | | |
| CLARENDON CLINIC (HM04540) | | | ● | | | | ● | | | | | ● | ● | | | |
| COHEN, D (DR) (HM04789) | | | | | | | | | | | | | | | | |
| COLLINGE, J C (HM04863) | | | | | | | | | | | | | ● | | | |
| COSGROVES PHYSIO-FIT CENTRE (HM05201) | | | | | | ● | ● | | | | | ● | ● | | | |
| CROSSWAY CLINIC (HM05491) | | | | | ● | | ● | | | | | ● | ● | | | |
| DAVEENA ASSOCIATES (HM05763) | | | | | ● | | | | | | | | | | | |
| DIDSBURY CHIROPRACTIC CLINIC (HM06090) | | | | | | | | | | | | | | | | |
| EVANS, DAVID (HM06967) | | | | ● | ● | ● | | ● | | | | | | ● | | ● |
| GRAHAM COOMBE - MCTIMONEY (HM08337) | | | ● | | | | ● | | | | | ● | | | | |
| GUILD OF PRACTITIONERS (HM08627) | | | | | | | ● | | | | | | | | | |
| HIGH PEAK HOLISTIC CENTRE (HM09738) | | | | | | | | | | | | | | | | |
| HOLMED CLINIC (HM10038) | | | | | | | ● | | | | ● | ● | ● | | | |
| HORRIDGE, S P (HM10182) | | | | | | | | | | | | | | | | |
| HUMAN TOUCH CENTRE (HM10366) | | | | | ● | ● | | | | | | ● | | | | |
| IBBOTSON, GEOFF (DR) (HM10565) | | | | | ● | ● | | ● | | | | | | | | |
| M J HAYLETT - PHYSIOTHERAPIST (HM12802) | | | | | | | ● | | | | | ● | ● | | | |
| MOBILE COMPLEMENTARY THERAPIES (HM14029) | | | ● | | ● | | ● | | | | | ● | ● | | | |
| MOUNT STREET COMP THERAPIES (HM14291) | | | | ● | ● | | | | | | | | | | | |
| NICKI HAVES PHYSIO CLINIC (HM14923) | | | | | | | ● | | | | | ● | ● | | | |
| NIVERN, D (HM14954) | | | ● | ● | ● | ● | | | | | | ● | ● | | | |
| REFLEXOLOGY & CHIROPODY (HM17079) | | | | | | | | | | | | | | | | |
| REJUVENATION (HM17154) | | | | | | | | | | | | ● | ● | | | |
| SCHOFIELD, G A (HM18018) | | ● | ● | ● | ● | | | ● | | ● | | ● | ● | ● | | ● |
| SHANGHAI ACUPUNCTURE CLINIC (HM18280) | ● | ● | ● | ● | ● | ● | ● | ● | ● | ● | | ● | ● | ● | ● | ● |
| ST JOHN STREET PHYSIO PRACTICE (HM19080) | | | | | | | | | | | | ● | ● | | | |
| STIRLING, DIANNE (HM19301) | | | | | | | | | | | | | | | | |
| SWINTON HEALTH FOODS (HM19600) | | | ● | ● | ● | | | | | | | | | | | |
| WAINWRIGHT, P (HM20739) | | | | | | | | | | | | | | | | |

| Business by County with Reference no. | Stomach Ulcers | Stress | Sweating | Teeth Grinding | Tennis Elbow | Terminal Illness | Throat Problems | Thrush | Thyroid Problems | Tinnitis | Tiredness | Tonsilitis | Ulcers | Vaginal Problems | Varicose Veins | Verrucas | Vertigo |
|---|---|---|---|---|---|---|---|---|---|---|---|---|---|---|---|---|---|
| BEAUTY THERAPY CENTRE (HM02006) | | ● | | | | | | | | | | | | | | | |
| BRAMHALL CHIROPRACTIC CLINIC (HM02898) | | | | ● | ● | | | | | ● | ● | | | | | | ● |
| BURGESS, KAREN (HM03377) | | | | | ● | | | | | | | | | | | | ● |
| C CARTLEDGE REFLEXOLOGY (HM03521) | ● | | ● | ● | ● | ● | ● | ● | ● | ● | ● | ● | ● | ● | ● | | ● |
| CHARTERED PHYSIOTHERAPY CLINIC (HM04046) | | | | | ● | | | | | | | | | | | | |
| CHORLTON STRESS MANAGEMENT (HM04430) | | | | | | | | | | | | | | | | | |
| CLARENDON CLINIC (HM04540) | | | ● | | ● | | | | | | ● | | | ● | | | ● |
| COHEN, D (DR) (HM04789) | | | | ● | | | | | | | | | | | | | |
| COLLINGE, J C (HM04863) | | | | | ● | | | | | | | | | | | | |
| COSGROVES PHYSIO-FIT CENTRE (HM05201) | | | | | ● | | | | | | | | | | | | |
| CROSSWAY CLINIC (HM05491) | | | | | ● | | | | | | ● | | | | | | |
| DAVEENA ASSOCIATES (HM05763) | | | | | | | | | | | | | | | | | |
| DIDSBURY CHIROPRACTIC CLINIC (HM06090) | | | | | ● | | | | | | | | | | | | ● |
| EVANS, DAVID (HM06967) | ● | | | ● | | | ● | | | ● | ● | | ● | ● | | | ● |
| GRAHAM COOMBE - MCTIMONEY (HM08337) | | | | | ● | | | | | | | | | | | | ● |
| GUILD OF PRACTITIONERS (HM08627) | | | | | ● | | | | | | | | | | | | |
| HIGH PEAK HOLISTIC CENTRE (HM09738) | | ● | | | | | | | | | | | | | | | |
| HOLMED CLINIC (HM10038) | | | | | ● | | | | | | | | | | | | |
| HORRIDGE, S P (HM10182) | | | | | | | | | | | | | | | | | |
| HUMAN TOUCH CENTRE (HM10366) | | ● | | | | | | | | | | | | | | | |
| IBBOTSON, GEOFF (DR) (HM10565) | | | | | | ● | | | | | | | | | | | |
| M J HAYLETT - PHYSIOTHERAPIST (HM12802) | | | | | | | | | | | | | | | | | |
| MOBILE COMPLEMENTARY THERAPIES (HM14029) | | | | | ● | | | | | | | | | | | | |
| MOUNT STREET COMP THERAPIES (HM14291) | | ● | | | | | | | | | | | | | | | |
| NICKI HAVES PHYSIO CLINIC (HM14923) | | | | | ● | | | | | | | | | | | | |
| NIVERN, D (HM14954) | | | | | ● | ● | ● | | | | ● | ● | | | | | |
| REFLEXOLOGY & CHIROPODY (HM17079) | | | | | | | | | | | | | | | | | |
| REJUVENATION (HM17154) | | | | | | | | | | | | | | | | | |
| SCHOFIELD, G A (HM18018) | ● | | | | | ● | ● | | ● | ● | ● | ● | | | | ● | |
| SHANGHAI ACUPUNCTURE CLINIC (HM18280) | ● | | ● | ● | ● | ● | ● | ● | ● | ● | ● | ● | ● | ● | ● | | ● |
| ST JOHN STREET PHYSIO PRACTICE (HM19080) | | | | | ● | | | | | | | | | | | | |
| STIRLING, DIANNE (HM19301) | | ● | | | | | | | | | | | | | | | |
| SWINTON HEALTH FOODS (HM19600) | | ● | | | | | | | | | ● | | | | | | |
| WAINWRIGHT, P (HM20739) | | | | | | | | | | | | | ● | | | | |

| | | | | | | | | Specialist Treatment Categories | | | | | | |
|---|---|---|---|---|---|---|---|---|---|---|---|---|---|---|
| Business by County with Reference no. | Viral Infections | Vomiting | Warts | Water Retention | Whiplash | Wind | Worms | Children | Terminally Ill | Disabled | Horses | Dogs | CatS | Other Animals |
| BEAUTY THERAPY CENTRE (HM02006) | | | | | | | | | | | | | | |
| BRAMHALL CHIROPRACTIC CLINIC (HM02898) | | | | | | | | | | | | | | |
| BURGESS, KAREN (HM03377) | | | ● | | ● | | | ● | | ● | | | | |
| C CARTLEDGE REFLEXOLOGY (HM03521) | ● | ● | ● | ● | | ● | ● | ● | ● | ● | | | | |
| CHARTERED PHYSIOTHERAPY CLINIC (HM04046) | | | | | | | | ● | | ● | | | | |
| CHORLTON STRESS MANAGEMENT (HM04430) | | | | | | | | ● | ● | ● | | | | |
| CLARENDON CLINIC (HM04540) | | | | | | | | | | | | | | |
| COHEN, D (DR) (HM04789) | | ● | | | | | ● | ● | | | | | | |
| COLLINGE, J C (HM04863) | | | | | | | | | | ● | | | | |
| COSGROVES PHYSIO-FIT CENTRE (HM05201) | | | | | ● | | | ● | | ● | | | | |
| CROSSWAY CLINIC (HM05491) | | | | | | | | ● | | ● | | | | |
| DAVEENA ASSOCIATES (HM05763) | | | | | | | | | | | | | | |
| DIDSBURY CHIROPRACTIC CLINIC (HM06090) | | | | | | | | ● | | ● | | | | |
| EVANS, DAVID (HM06967) | | | ● | | | | | ● | | | | | | |
| GRAHAM COOMBE - MCTIMONEY (HM08337) | | | | | | | | ● | | | | | | |
| GUILD OF PRACTITIONERS (HM08627) | | | | | | | | ● | ● | ● | | | | |
| HIGH PEAK HOLISTIC CENTRE (HM09738) | | | | | | | | | | | | | | |
| HOLMED CLINIC (HM10038) | | | | | ● | | | ● | ● | ● | | | | |
| HORRIDGE, S P (HM10182) | | | | | | | | ● | ● | ● | | | | |
| HUMAN TOUCH CENTRE (HM10366) | | | | | | | | | | | | | | |
| IBBOTSON, GEOFF (DR) (HM10565) | | | | | | | | | ● | ● | | | | |
| M J HAYLETT - PHYSIOTHERAPIST (HM12802) | | | | | | | | ● | | ● | | | | |
| MOBILE COMPLEMENTARY THERAPIES (HM14029) | | | | ● | | | | | | | | | | |
| MOUNT STREET COMP THERAPIES (HM14291) | | | | | | | | ● | ● | ● | | | | |
| NICKI HAVES PHYSIO CLINIC (HM14923) | | | | | | | | ● | | ● | | | | |
| NIVERN, D (HM14954) | ● | | ● | ● | | ● | | ● | ● | | ● | ● | ● | |
| REFLEXOLOGY & CHIROPODY (HM17079) | | | | | | | | ● | ● | ● | | | | |
| REJUVENATION (HM17154) | | | | | | | | ● | ● | ● | | | | |
| SCHOFIELD, G A (HM18018) | | | ● | ● | | ● | | ● | ● | ● | | | | |
| SHANGHAI ACUPUNCTURE CLINIC (HM18280) | ● | ● | ● | ● | | ● | ● | | | | | | | |
| ST JOHN STREET PHYSIO PRACTICE (HM19080) | | | | | | | | ● | | ● | | | | |
| STIRLING, DIANNE (HM19301) | | | | | | | | ● | | ● | | | | |
| SWINTON HEALTH FOODS (HM19600) | | | | | | | | | | | | | | |
| WAINWRIGHT, P (HM20739) | | | ● | | | | | ● | ● | ● | | | | |

# S - W Conditions treated at Practices/Businesses and Specialist Treatment Categories

Business by County with Reference no.

Specialist Treatment Categories: Children, Terminally Ill, Disabled, Horses, Dogs, CatS, Other Animals

| Business by County with Reference no. | Sexually Trans. Infections | Shingles | Sinus Problems | Skin Problems | Sleep Disorders | Slimming Help | Slipped Disk | Smoking Help | Sneezing | Snoring | Spinal Injuries | Sports Injuries | Sprains | Stammering | Stings | Stomach Problems | Stomach Ulcers | Stress | Sweating | Teeth Grinding | Tennis Elbow | Terminal Illness | Throat Problems | Thrush | Thyroid Problems | Tinnitis | Tiredness | Tonsilitis | Ulcers | Vaginal Problems | Varicose Veins | Verrucas | Vertigo | Viral Infections | Vomiting | Warts | Water Retention | Whiplash | Wind | Worms | Children | Terminally Ill | Disabled | Horses | Dogs | CatS | Other Animals |
|---|---|---|---|---|---|---|---|---|---|---|---|---|---|---|---|---|---|---|---|---|---|---|---|---|---|---|---|---|---|---|---|---|---|---|---|---|---|---|---|---|---|---|---|---|---|---|---|
| MERSEYSIDE | | | | | | | | | | | | | | | | | | | | | | | | | | | | | | | | | | | | | | | | | | | | | | | |
| ABBEY FOOT CLINIC (HM00083) | | | | | | | | | | | | | | | | | | | | | | | | | | | | | | | | | | | | | | | | | ● | ● | ● | | | | |
| ACUPUNCTURE CLINIC (HM00263) | | ● | ● | ● | ● | ● | ● | ● | ● | | | ● | ● | | | ● | ● | | ● | | ● | | | | | ● | ● | | | | | | ● | | | | | | | | ● | | ● | | ● | | |
| AIGBURTH MCTIMONEY CLINIC (HM00427) | | | ● | | ● | | ● | | | ● | | ● | ● | | | | | | | | ● | | | | | ● | ● | | | | ● | | ● | | | | ● | | ● | | ● | ● | ● | | | | |
| AINTREE OSTEOPATHIC (HM00439) | | ● | ● | ● | ● | | ● | ● | | | | ● | ● | | | ● | | | | | ● | | | | | ● | ● | | | | | | ● | | | | | | | | ● | | ● | | | | |
| ALLERTON HEALTH CENTRE (HM00639) | | | ● | ● | ● | | | | | | | ● | | | | | | | | | | | | | | | ● | | | | | | | | | | | ● | | | ● | ● | ● | | | | |
| BIMPSON, PETER (HM02311) | | | | | | | | | | | | | | | | | | ● | | | | | | | | | | | | | | | | | | | | | | | ● | ● | ● | | | | |
| BOLTON, TOM (HM02663) | | | | | | ● | | ● | | | | | | | | | | ● | | | | | | | | | | | | | | | | | | | | | | | | ● | ● | | | | |
| BOYLE, ANDREW (HM02826) | | ● | ● | ● | | | ● | | | | | ● | ● | | | | | | | ● | ● | | | | | | | | | | | ● | | ● | | ● | | | | | ● | ● | ● | | | | |
| BRENNAN, M A (HM02958) | | | | | | | | | | | | ● | | | | | | | | | | | | | | | | | | | | ● | | | | | | | | | ● | ● | ● | | | | |
| CARTER, G R (HM03778) | | | | | | | | | | | | ● | | | | | | | | | | | | | | | | | | | | ● | | | | ● | | | | | ● | ● | ● | | | | |
| CAWLEY, TONY (HM03871) | | | | | | ● | | ● | | | | | | ● | | | | ● | | | | | | | | | | | | | | | | | | | | | | | | | | | | | |
| CONCANNON, DEIRDRE (HM04965) | | | | | | | | | | | ● | ● | ● | | | | | | | | ● | | | | | | | | | | | | | | | | | ● | | | | | | | | | |
| D A F CLINIC (HM05655) | | | | | ● | | | | | | | ● | | | | | | | ● | | | | | | ● | | ● | | | | | | ● | | | ● | | | | | | | | | | | |
| DARE TO CARE (HM05739) | | | | | | | ● | | | | | ● | ● | | | | | | | | ● | | | | | | ● | | | | | | | | | | | | | | ● | ● | ● | | | | |
| FARMER, BARBARA (HM01681) | | ● | | | | | ● | | | | | ● | ● | | | | | | | | ● | | | | | | | | | | | | ● | | | | | | | | | | ● | | | | |
| FRESHLEA PRIVATE CLINICS (HM07738) | | | | | | | ● | | | | | ● | ● | | | | | | | | ● | | | | | | | | | | | | | | | | | | | | ● | | ● | | | | |
| GATEAUD, S (HM07924) | | | | | | | ● | | | | ● | ● | ● | | | | | | | | | | | | | | | | | | | | | | | | | ● | | | ● | | ● | ● | ● | ● | |
| GROUNDS, L (HM08600) | | | | | | | | | | | | | | | | | | | | | | | | | | | | | | | | | | | | | | | | | ● | ● | ● | | | | |
| HEAL TO TOE (HM09311) | | ● | ● | ● | ● | ● | ● | ● | ● | ● | | ● | ● | ● | ● | ● | ● | | ● | | ● | ● | ● | ● | ● | ● | ● | ● | ● | ● | ● | | ● | ● | ● | ● | ● | | ● | | ● | ● | ● | | | | |
| HOLISTIC HEALTH CENTRE (HM09975) | | ● | ● | ● | ● | | ● | ● | | | | ● | ● | | | ● | | | | | | | | ● | | ● | ● | | ● | ● | ● | | ● | ● | ● | ● | | | ● | ● | ● | | ● | | | | |
| HOPE STREET NATURAL HLTH CTRE (HM10136) | | | ● | ● | | | | | | | | | | | | | | | | | | | | | | | ● | | | | | | | | | | | | | | ● | ● | ● | | | | |
| HYPNOCARE (HM10490) | | | | | | ● | | | | | | | | | | | | ● | | | | | | | | | | | | | | | | | | | | | | | | ● | ● | ● | | | |
| JACKSONS (HM10854) | | | | | | | | ● | | | | | | | | | | | | | | | | | | | | | | | | | | | | | | | | | ● | | ● | | | | |
| JAMES, ANN (HM10880) | | | | ● | | | ● | | | | | ● | ● | | ● | | | | | | | | | | ● | | ● | | | | ● | ● | | ● | | ● | | | | | ● | ● | ● | | | | |
| JARVIS, K R (HM10934) | | | | | | | | | | | | | | | | | | | | | | | | | | | | | | | | ● | | | | | | | | | ● | ● | ● | | | | |
| KNOWLES, JANICE (HM11771) | | | | | | | | | | | | | | | | | | | | | | | | | | | | | | | | ● | | | | | | | | | ● | ● | ● | | | | |
| MARKET STREET CHIROPODY CLINIC (HM13113) | | | | | | | | | | | | | | | | | | | | | | | | | | | | | | | | ● | | | | ● | | | | | ● | ● | ● | | | | |
| MARSH, E C (HM13146) | | | | | | | | | | | | | | | | | | | | | | | | | | | | | | | | ● | | | | | | | | | ● | | ● | | | | |
| MCLOUGHLIN, CLAIRE (HM13560) | | | | | | | | | | | | | | | | | | | | | | | | | | | | | | | | ● | | | | ● | | | | | ● | ● | ● | | | | |
| NATURAL HEALTH CLINIC (HM14576) | | | ● | ● | ● | | ● | | ● | | | ● | ● | | ● | ● | ● | | ● | | ● | ● | ● | ● | ● | ● | ● | ● | ● | ● | ● | | ● | ● | ● | ● | ● | | ● | ● | ● | ● | ● | | | | |
| NATUROPATHIC HEALTH CENTRE (HM14709) | | | | | | | | | | | | | | | | | | | | | | | | | | | | | | | | | | | | | | | | | ● | | ● | | | | |
| NELSON, PATRICIA (HM14780) | | | | | | | | | | | | | | | | | | | | | | | | | | | | | | | | ● | | | | | | | | | ● | ● | ● | | | | |
| PURE ESSENTIALS DIRECT (HM16764) | | | | ● | | | | | | | | | | | | | | ● | | | | | | | | | | | | | | | | | | | | | | | | | | | | | |

# S - W Conditions treated at Practices/Businesses and Specialist Treatment Categories

Business by County with Reference no.

| Business by County with Reference no. | Sexually Trans. Infections | Shingles | Sinus Problems | Skin Problems | Sleep Disorders | Slimming Help | Slipped Disk | Smoking Help | Sneezing | Snoring | Spinal Injuries | Sports Injuries | Sprains | Stammering | Stings | Stomach Problems | Stomach Ulcers | Stress | Sweating | Teeth Grinding | Tennis Elbow | Terminal Illness | Throat Problems | Thrush |
|---|---|---|---|---|---|---|---|---|---|---|---|---|---|---|---|---|---|---|---|---|---|---|---|---|
| SANCTUARY NATURAL HEALTH (HM17893) | | | | | | | | | | | | ● | ● | | | | | ● | | | | | | |
| SCOTT, ANDREW (HM18107) | | | ● | ● | ● | | ● | | | | | ● | ● | | | ● | | | ● | ● | ● | | ● | |
| SEFTON PARK NATURAL THRPY CTRE (HM18198) | | | | | ● | ● | ● | | | | | ● | ● | | | ● | | | | | ● | | | |
| SIMPSON CLINIC (HM18584) | ● | ● | ● | ● | ● | ● | ● | ● | ● | ● | | ● | ● | ● | ● | ● | ● | | | ● | ● | | ● | ● |
| SOUTHPORT OSTEO & ACUPUNCTURE (HM18942) | | | | | | | ● | | | | | ● | ● | | | | | | | | ● | | | |
| STEINA SPORTS & PHYSIOTHERAPY (HM19188) | | | | | | | ● | | | | | ● | ● | | | | | | | | ● | | | |
| SUMMERS, ALFRED A (HM19487) | | | | | | | | | | | | | | | | | | | | | | | | |
| TARA SCHOOL OF HYPNOTHERAPY (HM19701) | | | | | ● | ● | | ● | | | | | | ● | | | | | | | | | | |
| THERAPY 21 (HM19890) | | | | ● | | | | | | | | | | | | | | ● | | | ● | | | |
| WEST WIRRAL CHIROPRACTIC (HM21239) | | | | | | | | | | | ● | | | | | | | | | | | | | |
| WILLIAMS, CATHERINE (HM21546) | | | | | | | | | | | | | | | | | | | | | | | | |
| WIRRALL CLINIC (HM21730) | | | ● | ● | | | ● | | | | | ● | ● | | | | | | | | ● | | | |
| **MIDDLESEX** | | | | | | | | | | | | | | | | | | | | | | | | |
| CLANRICARDE CLINIC (HM04526) | | ● | ● | | | | ● | | | | | ● | ● | | | | | | | | ● | | ● | ● |
| **MIDLANDS (WEST)** | | | | | | | | | | | | | | | | | | | | | | | | |
| 1ST CHIROPRACTIC UK (HM00005) | | | | | | | ● | | | | | ● | ● | | | | | | | | ● | | | |
| 1ST CHIROPRACTIC UK (HM00006) | | | | | | | ● | | | | ● | ● | ● | | | | | | | | ● | | | |
| A Q C H (HM00044) | | ● | ● | ● | ● | ● | | ● | | ● | | | | ● | | ● | ● | | ● | ● | | ● | ● | ● |
| ABBEY CLINIC (HM00077) | | | | | | | ● | | | | | ● | ● | | | | | | | | ● | | | |
| ABBIE HYPNOTHERAPY CENTRE (HM00093) | | | | | ● | | | ● | | | | | | | | ● | | | | | | | | |
| ACUPUNCTURE HEALTH CLINIC (HM00312) | | ● | ● | ● | ● | | | | | | | ● | ● | | | | | | | | | | | |
| ALCOCK, E C (HM00490) | | | | | | | | | | | | | | | | | | | | | | | | |
| ALDA HOUSE NATURAL THERAPY (HM00492) | | ● | ● | ● | ● | | ● | | ● | | | ● | ● | | ● | ● | ● | | | | ● | | ● | ● |
| ALDOUS, JOSIE (HM00503) | | | | | | | | | | | | | | | | | | ● | | | | | | |
| ALLEN, ELAINE (HM00608) | | | | ● | ● | | | | | | | | | | | | | ● | | | | | | |
| AROMA SANTE (HM01057) | ● | ● | ● | ● | ● | ● | ● | ● | ● | ● | | ● | ● | ● | ● | ● | ● | | ● | ● | ● | ● | ● | ● |
| ARROW BANK CHIROPRACTIC CLINIC (HM01149) | | | | | | | | | | | | ● | ● | | | | | | | | | | | |
| ASSOCIATION OF STRESS MNGMT (HM01288) | | | | | | ● | | ● | | | | | | | | | | | | ● | | | | |
| BACKCARE & ACUPUNCTURE CLINIC (HM01526) | | ● | ● | ● | ● | ● | ● | ● | ● | ● | | ● | ● | | | ● | ● | ● | ● | ● | ● | ● | ● | ● |
| BEAUTIFORM COLLEGE (HM01992) | | | | ● | | ● | | | | | | | | | | | | | | | | | | |
| BILLINGHAM, S (HM02301) | | | ● | ● | ● | | | | | | | | | | | | | | | | | ● | | |
| BIRMINGHAM ACU/CHIRO CLNC (HM02382) | | ● | ● | ● | ● | ● | ● | ● | ● | ● | ● | ● | ● | ● | ● | ● | ● | | ● | ● | ● | ● | ● | ● |
| BIRMINGHAM PHYSIO CLINIC (HM02388) | | | | | | | ● | | | | | ● | ● | | | | | | | | ● | | | |
| BIRMINGHAM TRAD ACU CENTRE (HM02390) | | | | | | | | | | | | ● | | | | | | ● | | | | | | |

| Business by County with Reference no. | Thyroid Problems | Tinnitis | Tiredness | Tonsilitis | Ulcers | Vaginal Problems | Varicose Veins | Verrucas | Vertigo | Viral Infections | Vomiting | Warts | Water Retention | Whiplash | Wind | Worms | Children | Terminally Ill | Disabled | Horses | Dogs | CatS | Other Animals |
|---|---|---|---|---|---|---|---|---|---|---|---|---|---|---|---|---|---|---|---|---|---|---|---|
| SANCTUARY NATURAL HEALTH (HM17893) | | | | | | | | | | | | | | | | | ● | ● | ● | | | | |
| SCOTT, ANDREW (HM18107) | | | ● | | | | | | | | | | ● | | | | ● | | ● | | | | |
| SEFTON PARK NATURAL THRPY CTRE (HM18198) | | | ● | | | | | | | | | | | | | | ● | ● | ● | | | | |
| SIMPSON CLINIC (HM18584) | ● | ● | ● | ● | ● | ● | ● | | ● | | ● | ● | ● | | ● | ● | ● | ● | ● | ● | ● | ● | ● |
| SOUTHPORT OSTEO & ACUPUNCTURE (HM18942) | | | | | | | | | | | | | | | | | ● | | ● | | | | |
| STEINA SPORTS & PHYSIOTHERAPY (HM19188) | | | | | | | | | | | | | | | | | ● | ● | ● | | | | |
| SUMMERS, ALFRED A (HM19487) | | | | | | | | | | | | | | | | | ● | ● | ● | | | | |
| TARA SCHOOL OF HYPNOTHERAPY (HM19701) | | | | | | | | | | | | | | | | | | | | | | | |
| THERAPY 21 (HM19890) | | | | | | | | | | | | | | | | | | ● | ● | | ● | | |
| WEST WIRRAL CHIROPRACTIC (HM21239) | | | | | | | | | | | | | | ● | | | ● | ● | ● | | | | |
| WILLIAMS, CATHERINE (HM21546) | | | | | | | | | | | | | | | | | ● | ● | ● | | | | |
| WIRRALL CLINIC (HM21730) | | | | | | | | | | | | | | | | | | ● | ● | | | | |
| **MIDDLESEX** | | | | | | | | | | | | | | | | | | | | | | | |
| CLANRICARDE CLINIC (HM04526) | ● | ● | | | | | ● | | | ● | | ● | | | | ● | ● | ● | ● | | | | |
| **MIDLANDS (WEST)** | | | | | | | | | | | | | | | | | | | | | | | |
| 1ST CHIROPRACTIC UK (HM00005) | | | | | | | | | | | | | | ● | | | ● | ● | ● | | | | |
| 1ST CHIROPRACTIC UK (HM00006) | | | | | | | | | | | | | | ● | | | | | | | | | |
| A Q C H (HM00044) | ● | ● | ● | | ● | | | | ● | | ● | ● | ● | | ● | | ● | ● | ● | | | | |
| ABBEY CLINIC (HM00077) | | | | | | | | | | | | | | ● | | | | | | | | | |
| ABBIE HYPNOTHERAPY CENTRE (HM00093) | | | ● | | | | | | | | | | | | | | ● | ● | ● | | | | |
| ACUPUNCTURE HEALTH CLINIC (HM00312) | | | ● | | | | | | | | ● | | | | | | ● | ● | | | | | |
| ALCOCK, E C (HM00490) | | | | | | | | | | | | | | | | | ● | ● | ● | | | | |
| ALDA HOUSE NATURAL THERAPY (HM00492) | ● | | ● | ● | | ● | | | ● | ● | | ● | ● | | ● | ● | ● | ● | ● | | | | |
| ALDOUS, JOSIE (HM00503) | | | | | | | | | | | | | | | | | ● | ● | ● | | | | |
| ALLEN, ELAINE (HM00608) | | | | | | | | | | | | | | | | | ● | ● | ● | | | | |
| AROMA SANTE (HM01057) | ● | ● | ● | ● | ● | ● | ● | | ● | ● | ● | ● | ● | | ● | ● | ● | ● | ● | | | | |
| ARROW BANK CHIROPRACTIC CLINIC (HM01149) | | | | | | | | | | | | | | | | | ● | ● | ● | | | | |
| ASSOCIATION OF STRESS MNGMT (HM01288) | | | | | | | | | | | | | | | | | | | | | | | |
| BACKCARE & ACUPUNCTURE CLINIC (HM01526) | ● | ● | ● | ● | ● | ● | ● | | ● | ● | ● | ● | ● | | ● | ● | ● | ● | ● | ● | ● | | |
| BEAUTIFORM COLLEGE (HM01992) | | | | | | | | | | | | | | | | | | | | | | | |
| BILLINGHAM, S (HM02301) | ● | | | ● | | | | | | | | | | | | | | | | | | | |
| BIRMINGHAM ACU/CHIRO CLNC (HM02382) | ● | ● | ● | ● | ● | | ● | | ● | ● | ● | ● | ● | ● | ● | | ● | ● | ● | | | | |
| BIRMINGHAM PHYSIO CLINIC (HM02388) | | | | | | | | | | | | | | | | | ● | | | | | | |
| BIRMINGHAM TRAD ACU CENTRE (HM02390) | | | ● | | | | | | | | | | | | | | | | | | | | |

# S - W Conditions treated at Practices/Businesses and Specialist Treatment Categories

| Business by County with Reference no. | Sexually Trans. Infections | Shingles | Sinus Problems | Skin Problems | Sleep Disorders | Slimming Help | Slipped Disk | Smoking Help | Sneezing | Snoring | Spinal Injuries | Sports Injuries | Sprains | Stammering | Stings | Stomach Problems | Stomach Ulcers | Stress | Sweating | Teeth Grinding | Tennis Elbow | Terminal Illness | Throat Problems | Thrush | Thyroid Problems | Tinnitis |
|---|---|---|---|---|---|---|---|---|---|---|---|---|---|---|---|---|---|---|---|---|---|---|---|---|---|---|
| BLAKE, D H (HM02479) | | | | | | | ● | | | | ● | ● | ● | | | | | | | | ● | | | | | ● |
| BOLDMERE HYPNOTHERAPY (HM02653) | | | | ● | ● | ● | | ● | | | | | | ● | | | | | | ● | | | | | | ● |
| BROWNHILL, D G (HM03257) | | | | | ● | ● | | ● | | | | | | ● | | | | ● | | | | | | | | |
| BTAC (HM03296) | | ● | ● | ● | ● | | ● | | | | | | | | | ● | ● | | ● | ● | ● | | ● | | ● | ● |
| BULLOCK, JULIE (HM03344) | | | | | | | | | | | | | | | | | | | | | | | | | | |
| CALLAGHAN, R M & J (HM03549) | | | | | | | | | | | | | | | | | | | | | | | | | | |
| CARPENTER, DAVID (HM03727) | | | | ● | ● | ● | | | | | | ● | | | | ● | ● | | ● | ● | | | | | | |
| CENTRAL CHIROPODY CLINIC (HM03888) | | | | | | | | | | | | | | | | | | | | | | | | | | |
| CENTRE FOR NATURAL THERAPIES (HM03913) | ● | ● | ● | ● | ● | ● | ● | ● | ● | ● | | ● | ● | ● | ● | ● | ● | | ● | ● | ● | ● | ● | ● | ● | ● |
| CHEER, MARIE (HM04082) | | | | | | | | | | | | | | | | | | ● | | | | | | | | |
| CHELMSLEY WOOD FOOT CLINIC (HM04086) | | | | | | | | | | | | | | | | | | | | | | | | | | |
| CHEYLESMORE PHYSIO CLINIC (HM04147) | | | | | | | ● | | | | | ● | ● | | | | | | | | ● | | | | | |
| CHIRO MED (HM04283) | | | ● | ● | ● | ● | ● | ● | ● | | | ● | ● | | | ● | | | ● | ● | | ● | | | | ● |
| CHIROPRACTIC CLINIC (HM04388) | | | | | | | | | | | | ● | ● | | | | | | | | ● | | | | | |
| CHIROPRACTORS OF WARWICK ROAD (HM04407) | | | | | | | | | | | | ● | ● | | | | | | | | | | | | | |
| CODSALL COMP THERAPIES (HM04778) | | | | | | ● | | | | | | | | | | | | ● | | | | | | | | |
| COMPLEMENTARY HEALING CENTRE (HM04919) | | | | ● | ● | | | | | | | ● | | | | | | | | | | | | | | |
| COMPLEMENTARY THERAPY CENTRE (HM04947) | | | | | | | | | | | | ● | | | | | | | | | | | | | | |
| COMPLEMENTARY THERAPY CENTRE (HM04943) | | | | | | | | | | | | ● | | | | | | | | | | | | | | |
| CREATIVE HEALTH CENTRE (HM05398) | | | | | ● | ● | | ● | | ● | | ● | ● | | | ● | | | | ● | ● | | | | | |
| CROFT, ANGELA (HM05453) | | | | ● | | | | | | | | | | | | | | ● | | | | | | | | |
| CRYSTAL CLEAR PRACTICE (HM05528) | ● | ● | ● | ● | ● | ● | ● | ● | ● | ● | | ● | ● | ● | ● | ● | ● | | ● | ● | ● | ● | ● | ● | ● | ● |
| CTIC (HM05535) | | | | | | ● | | | | | | | | | | | | | | | | | | | | |
| CTRE-REFLEX & AROMATHERAPY (HM05549) | | ● | ● | | ● | | | | | | | | | | | | | | | | | | | | | |
| DAVIS A STARKEY REM THERAP (HM05846) | | | | | | | ● | | | | ● | ● | ● | | | | | | | | | | | | ● | |
| DHANA, P N (HM06053) | | | | | | | | | | | | | | | | | | | | | | | | | | |
| DUDLEY PHYSIOTHERAPY CLINIC (HM06354) | | | | | | | ● | | | | | ● | ● | | | | | | | | ● | | | | | |
| ERDINGTHON NATURAL HEALTH CLNC (HM06880) | ● | ● | ● | ● | ● | ● | ● | ● | ● | ● | | ● | ● | ● | ● | ● | ● | | ● | ● | ● | ● | ● | ● | ● | ● |
| ESSENTIAL HEALTH (HM06909) | | | ● | ● | | | | | | | | | | | | | | | | | | | | | | ● |
| EVE GRAYWOLF LUNG PSYC CONS (HM06995) | | | | | | | | | | | | | | | | | | | | | | | | | | |
| FAIRFAX PRIVATE THERAPY (HM07056) | | | ● | ● | ● | ● | | | | | | | | | ● | ● | | | | | | | | | | |
| FORD, MARIA (HM07526) | | | | | | | | | | | | | | | | | | ● | | | | | | | | |
| FRESHWINDS CHARITABLE TRUST (HM07740) | ● | ● | ● | ● | ● | ● | ● | ● | ● | ● | | ● | ● | ● | ● | ● | ● | | ● | ● | ● | ● | ● | ● | ● | ● |
| GOLDEN PALMS (HM08207) | | | ● | | | | | | | | | ● | | | | | | | | | | | | ● | | |

| Business by County with Reference no. | Tiredness | Tonsilitis | Ulcers | Vaginal Problems | Varicose Veins | Verrucas | Vertigo | Viral Infections | Vomiting | Warts | Water Retention | Whiplash | Wind | Worms | Specialist Treatment Categories: Children | Terminally Ill | Disabled | Horses | Dogs | CatS | Other Animals |
|---|---|---|---|---|---|---|---|---|---|---|---|---|---|---|---|---|---|---|---|---|---|
| BLAKE, D H (HM02479) | ● | | | | | | ● | | | | | ● | | | ● | | | | | | |
| BOLDMERE HYPNOTHERAPY (HM02653) | | | | | | | | | | | | | | | ● | ● | | | | | |
| BROWNHILL, D G (HM03257) | | | | | | | | | | | | | | | ● | ● | | | | | |
| BTAC (HM03296) | ● | ● | ● | | | | ● | | | | | | | | ● | | | | | | |
| BULLOCK, JULIE (HM03344) | | | | | | ● | | | | | | | | | ● | ● | ● | | | | |
| CALLAGHAN, R M & J (HM03549) | | | | | | | | | | ● | | | | | ● | ● | ● | | | | |
| CARPENTER, DAVID (HM03727) | ● | | | | | | ● | | ● | | | | | | ● | ● | ● | | | | |
| CENTRAL CHIROPODY CLINIC (HM03888) | | | | | | | | | | ● | | | | | ● | ● | ● | | | | |
| CENTRE FOR NATURAL THERAPIES (HM03913) | ● | ● | ● | ● | ● | | ● | ● | ● | ● | ● | | ● | ● | ● | | ● | | ● | ● | ● |
| CHEER, MARIE (HM04082) | | | | | | | | | | | | | | | | | | | | | |
| CHELMSLEY WOOD FOOT CLINIC (HM04086) | | | | | | | | | | | | | | | ● | ● | ● | | | | |
| CHEYLESMORE PHYSIO CLINIC (HM04147) | | | | | | | | | | | | | | | | | | | | | |
| CHIRO MED (HM04283) | ● | | | | | | ● | ● | | | ● | | ● | | ● | ● | ● | | | | |
| CHIROPRACTIC CLINIC (HM04388) | | | | | | | | | | | | | | | ● | ● | ● | | | | |
| CHIROPRACTORS OF WARWICK ROAD (HM04407) | | | | | | | | | | | | ● | | | ● | ● | ● | | | | |
| CODSALL COMP THERAPIES (HM04778) | | | | | | | | | | | | | | | ● | | | | | | |
| COMPLEMENTARY HEALING CENTRE (HM04919) | | | | | | | | | | | | | | | | | | | | | |
| COMPLEMENTARY THERAPY CENTRE (HM04947) | | | | | | | | | | | | ● | | | ● | ● | ● | | | | |
| COMPLEMENTARY THERAPY CENTRE (HM04943) | | | | | | | | | | | | ● | | | ● | ● | ● | | | | |
| CREATIVE HEALTH CENTRE (HM05398) | | | | ● | | | | | | | | | | | | | | | | | |
| CROFT, ANGELA (HM05453) | | | | | | | | | | | | | | | ● | ● | ● | | | | |
| CRYSTAL CLEAR PRACTICE (HM05528) | ● | ● | ● | ● | ● | | ● | ● | ● | ● | ● | | ● | ● | ● | ● | ● | | ● | ● | ● |
| CTIC (HM05535) | | | | | | | | | | | | | | | | ● | ● | | | | |
| CTRE-REFLEX & AROMATHERAPY (HM05549) | | | | | ● | | | | | | | | | | ● | ● | ● | | | | |
| DAVIS A STARKEY REM THERAP (HM05846) | ● | | | | | | | | | | | ● | | | ● | | ● | | | | |
| DHANA, P N (HM06053) | | | | | | | | | | | | | | | ● | ● | ● | | | | |
| DUDLEY PHYSIOTHERAPY CLINIC (HM06354) | | | | | | | | | | | | | | | | | ● | | | | |
| ERDINGTHON NATURAL HEALTH CLNC (HM06880) | ● | ● | ● | ● | ● | | ● | ● | ● | ● | ● | | ● | ● | ● | ● | ● | | | | |
| ESSENTIAL HEALTH (HM06909) | | | | | | | | | | | | | | | ● | ● | ● | | | | |
| EVE GRAYWOLF LUNG PSYC CONS (HM06995) | | | | | | | | | | | | | | | ● | ● | | | | | |
| FAIRFAX PRIVATE THERAPY (HM07056) | ● | | | | | | | | | | ● | | | | ● | | | | | | |
| FORD, MARIA (HM07526) | | | | | | | | | | | | | | | ● | ● | ● | | | | |
| FRESHWINDS CHARITABLE TRUST (HM07740) | ● | ● | ● | ● | ● | | ● | ● | ● | ● | ● | | ● | ● | ● | ● | | | | | |
| GOLDEN PALMS (HM08207) | ● | | | | | | | | | | | | | | ● | ● | ● | | | | |

# S - W Conditions treated at Practices/Businesses and Specialist Treatment Categories

| Business by County with Reference no. | Sexually Trans. Infections | Shingles | Sinus Problems | Skin Problems | Sleep Disorders | Slimming Help | Slipped Disk | Smoking Help | Sneezing | Snoring | Spinal Injuries | Sports Injuries | Sprains | Stammering | Stings | Stomach Problems | Stomach Ulcers | Stress | Sweating | Teeth Grinding | Tennis Elbow | Terminal Illness | Throat Problems | Thrush | Thyroid Problems | Tinnitis | Tiredness | Tonsilitis | Ulcers | Vaginal Problems | Varicose Veins | Verrucas | Vertigo | Viral Infections | Vomiting | Warts | Water Retention | Whiplash | Wind | Worms | Specialist Treatment Categories: Children | Terminally Ill | Disabled | Horses | Dogs | CatS | Other Animals |
|---|---|---|---|---|---|---|---|---|---|---|---|---|---|---|---|---|---|---|---|---|---|---|---|---|---|---|---|---|---|---|---|---|---|---|---|---|---|---|---|---|---|---|---|---|---|---|---|
| GREAT BARR OSTEO PRACTICE (HM08430) | | | | | | |●| | | | |●|●| | | | | | | |●| | | | | | | | | | | | | | | | | | | |●| | | | | | |
| GREEN VALLEY THERAPY CENTRE (HM08443) |●|●|●|●|●|●|●|●|●|●| |●|●|●|●|●|●| |●|●|●|●|●|●|●|●|●|●|●|●|●| |●|●|●|●|●| |●|●|●|●|●| | | | |
| HAGLEY CENTRE OF COMP MED (HM08701) | |●| | | | | |●| | | |●|●| | | | | | | | | | | | | | | | | | | | | | | | | |●| |●|●|●| | | | |
| HALE ASSOCIATES (HM08727) | | | | | | |●| | | |●|●|●| | | | | | | |●| | | | | | | | | | | | | | | | |●| | | | | | | | | |
| HALE, GEOFF (HM08732) | | | | | | |●| | | |●|●|●| | | | | | | |●| | | | | | | | | | | | | | | | |●| | |●| |●| | | | |
| HALL GREEN ALTERN PRACTICE (HM08760) |●|●|●|●|●|●|●|●|●|●| |●|●|●|●|●|●| |●|●|●|●|●|●|●|●|●|●|●|●|●| |●|●|●|●|●| |●|●|●|●|●| | | | |
| HALL, SUSAN (HM08790) | | |●|●|●|●| | |●|●| | | | | |●|●| | | |●| | |●| |●| |●| | | | |●|●| | |●| |●| |●|●|●| | | | |
| HARTNESS, R (HM09149) | | | | | | | | | | | | | | | | | | | | | | | | | | | | | | | |●| | | | | | | | |●|●|●| | | | |
| HEALTH SHOP (HM09402) | | |●|●|●|●| | |●|●| |●|●| |●|●| | | | | | | |●|●|●|●| | |●|●| |●| | |●|●| |●|●|●| |●|●|●|●|●|
| HERBAL PHARMACY (HM09632) |●|●|●|●|●|●| |●|●|●| | | | |●|●|●| |●| | | |●|●|●|●|●|●|●|●|●| | |●|●|●|●| |●|●|●| |●| | | | |
| HIGGS, R W (HM09737) | | | | | | | | | | | | | | | | | | | | | | | | | | | | | | | | | | | | | | | | |●| | | | | | |
| HOGG, DEBBI (HM09913) | |●|●|●|●|●|●|●|●|●| |●|●|●| |●|●|●|●|●|●|●|●|●|●|●|●|●|●|●| | |●|●|●|●|●| |●| |●|●|●| | | | |
| HOLISTIC HEALTH CENTRE (HM09972) | | | | | | | | | | | | | | | |●| | | | | | | | | | |●| | | | | | | | | | | | | |●|●|●| | | | |
| HOLLOWAY, P (HM10027) | | | | | |●| |●| | | | | |●| | | |●| | | | | | | | |●| | | | | | | | | | | | | |●|●|●| | | | |
| HOLLY COTTAGE CHIRO CLINIC (HM10029) | | | | | | |●| | | |●|●|●| | | | | | | |●| | | | | | | | | | | | | | | | |●| | |●|●|●| | | | |
| HOMOEOPATHIC CLINIC/PHARMACY (HM10090) |●|●|●|●|●|●|●|●|●|●| |●|●|●| |●|●| |●| | | | | | | | |●|●|●|●| |●|●|●|●|●| |●|●|●| |●| |●|●| |
| HOT-PAK (HM10206) | | | | | | | | | | | |●|●| | | | |●| | | | | | | | | | | | | | | | | | | | | | |●|●|●|●|●|●|●|
| HUSBANDS, STEVE (HM10432) |●|●|●|●|●|●|●|●|●|●| |●|●|●|●|●|●| |●|●|●|●|●|●|●|●|●|●|●|●|●| |●|●|●|●|●| |●|●|●|●|●| | | | |
| INGRAM, CLARE (HM10624) | |●|●|●|●| | | |●| | | | | | |●| | |●|●|●| |●|●|●|●|●|●|●|●| | | |●| |●|●| |●| |●| | | | | | |
| INNERSENSE (HM10647) | | | | | | | | | | | | | | | | | |●| | | | | | | | | | | | | | | | | | | | | | |●|●|●| | | | |
| JOHNSON FOOTCARE (HM11061) | | | | | | | | | | | | | | | | | | | | | | | | | | | | | | | | | | | |●| | | | |●|●|●| | | | |
| KEMPSON, STEVE (HM11468) | | | | |●|●| | | | | | | | | | | |●| | | | | | | | | | | | | | | | | | | | | | |●| |●| | | | |
| KEVIN FISHER CHIROPODY (HM11573) | | | | | | | | | | | | | | | | | | | | | | | | | | | | | | | |●| | | | | | | | |●|●|●| | | | |
| LEWIS, MYRA (HM12305) | | | |●|●| | | | | | | | | | | | |●| | | | | | | | | | | | | | | | | | | | | | | | | | | | |
| LIFE'S OPTION (HM12358) | | | | | | | | | | | | | | | | | |●| | | | | | | | | | | | | | | | | | | | | | | | | | | | |
| LONGFORD PHYSIO & SPORTS (HM12627) | |●| | | | |●| | | | |●|●| | | | | | | |●| | | | | | | | | | | | | | | | |●| | | |●| | | | |
| MAPES, JANET (HM13059) | | | | | | | | | | | | | | | | | | | | | | | | | | | | | | | | | | | | | | | | |●|●|●| | | | |
| MCDERMOTT, J V (HM13447) | | | | | | |●| | | |●|●|●| | | | | | | |●| | | | | | | | | | | | | | | | |●| | |●|●|●| | | | |
| MIDLAND HYPNOTHERAPY CENTRE (HM13830) | |●|●|●|●|●| |●|●|●| |●| |●|●|●|●| |●|●|●| |●|●|●|●|●| |●|●| | |●| |●|●|●| |●| |●|●|●| | | | |
| MIDLAND HYPNOTHERAPY CENTRE (HM13831) | |●|●|●|●|●| |●|●|●| |●| |●| |●|●| |●|●|●| |●|●|●|●|●| |●|●| | |●| |●|●|●| |●| |●|●|●| | | | |
| MIDLAND MEDICAL HOM PRACTICE (HM13833) |●|●|●|●|●|●|●|●|●|●| |●|●|●|●|●|●| |●|●|●|●|●|●|●|●|●|●|●|●|●| |●|●|●|●|●| |●|●|●| |●| | | | |
| MIDLAND MEDICAL HOM PRACTICE (HM13832) |●|●|●|●|●|●|●|●|●|●| |●|●|●|●|●|●| |●|●|●|●|●|●|●|●|●|●|●|●|●| |●|●|●|●|●| |●|●|●| |●| | | | |
| MIDLAND MEDICAL HOM PRACTICE (HM13834) |●|●|●|●|●|●|●|●|●|●| |●|●|●|●|●|●| |●|●|●|●|●|●|●|●|●|●|●|●|●| |●|●|●|●|●| |●|●|●| |●| | | | |
| MIDLAND MEDICAL OSTEO PRACTICE (HM13837) | | | | | | |●| | | | | | | | | | | | | |●| | | | | | | | | | | | | | | | | | | | | | | | | | |

# S - W Conditions treated at Practices/Businesses and Specialist Treatment Categories

Business by County with Reference no.

| Business | Sexually Trans. Infections | Shingles | Sinus Problems | Skin Problems | Sleep Disorders | Slimming Help | Slipped Disk | Smoking Help | Sneezing | Snoring | Spinal Injuries | Sports Injuries |
|---|---|---|---|---|---|---|---|---|---|---|---|---|
| MIDLAND MEDICAL OSTEO PRACTICE (HM13836) | | | | | | | ● | | | | | |
| MIDLAND MEDICAL OSTEO PRACTICE (HM13835) | | | | | | | ● | | | | | |
| MORGAN, VALERIE (HM14177) | | ● | ● | ● | ● | | ● | | | | | ● |
| MORRIS, CLAIRE (HM14202) | | | | ● | | | | | | | | ● |
| MYATT, ANITA (HM14432) | ● | ● | ● | ● | ● | ● | ● | ● | ● | ● | | ● |
| NATURAL HEALTH CENTRE (HM14574) | | | ● | ● | | | | | | | | ● |
| NEWBRIDGE PHARMACY (HM14850) | | | ● | ● | ● | | ● | | | | | ● |
| OULTON FOOT CLINIC (HM15499) | | | | | | | | | | | | |
| PARK PRACTICE (HM15672) | ● | ● | ● | ● | ● | ● | ● | ● | ● | ● | | ● |
| PAUL MAWER PSYCHOLGICAL SVS (HM15843) | | | | | | | | | | | | |
| PHYSIOTHERAPY CLINIC (HM16241) | | | | | | | ● | | | | | ● |
| PIKE, ELIZABETH G & J K (HM16286) | | | | | | | | | | | | |
| PILLATH, CHRISTINE (HM16297) | | | | | | | ● | | | | ● | ● |
| PLANT, ALISON () | | | ● | | | | | | | | | |
| PRISM THERAPIES (HM16636) | | | | ● | | ● | | ● | | ● | | ● |
| REMEDIAL MASSAGE THERAPY (HM17174) | | | ● | | | | ● | | | | | ● |
| RICHARDSON, CYRIL (HM17273) | | | | | | | | | | | | |
| ROBINSON, JOHN (HM17484) | | | | | | | | | | | | |
| ROMSLEY PHYSIOTHERAPY PRACTICE (HM17578) | | | ● | | | | | | | | | ● |
| SEITAI/SHIATSU & MANIPULATION (HM18202) | | | | | | | | | | | | ● |
| SIDHOM, A (HM18529) | | | | | | | ● | | | | | ● |
| SOLIHULL CHIROPRACTIC CLINIC (HM18872) | | | | | | | ● | | | | ● | ● |
| SOMEWAY HERBAL CLINIC (HM18883) | | | ● | ● | ● | | | | | | | ● |
| ST PAULS OSTEOPATHY PRACTICE (HM19094) | | | ● | ● | ● | | ● | | | | | ● |
| STARKEY, DAVID (HM19147) | | | | | | | ● | | | | ● | ● |
| STOURBRIDGE ACU & OSTEO CTRE (HM19356) | | | | | | | | | | | | ● |
| SUCCESSWORKS (HM19461) | | | | | | | | | | | | |
| SUTTON COLDFIELD HEALTH CLINIC (HM19544) | | ● | | | | | ● | ● | | | | ● |
| TELLING, MELANIE (HM19822) | | | ● | ● | ● | | ● | | | | | ● |
| TELLING, MELANIE (HM19823) | | | ● | ● | ● | | ● | | | | | |
| THERAPY TRAINING COLLEGE (HM19911) | | | | | ● | ● | | ● | | | | |
| WALSALL PHYSIOTHERAPY CLINIC (HM20853) | | | | | | | ● | | | | | ● |
| WALSGRAVE CHIROPRACTIC CLINIC (HM20855) | | | | | | | ● | | | | ● | ● |
| WARD, JAQUELINE (HM20906) | | | | ● | | ● | | ● | | ● | | |

| Business | Sprains | Stammering | Stings | Stomach Problems | Stomach Ulcers | Stress | Sweating | Teeth Grinding | Tennis Elbow | Terminal Illness | Throat Problems | Thrush |
|---|---|---|---|---|---|---|---|---|---|---|---|---|
| MIDLAND MEDICAL OSTEO PRACTICE (HM13836) | | | | | | | | | ● | | | |
| MIDLAND MEDICAL OSTEO PRACTICE (HM13835) | | | | | | | | | ● | | | |
| MORGAN, VALERIE (HM14177) | ● | | | ● | ● | | ● | | | | | ● |
| MORRIS, CLAIRE (HM14202) | ● | | | | | | | | | | | |
| MYATT, ANITA (HM14432) | ● | ● | ● | ● | ● | | ● | ● | ● | ● | ● | ● |
| NATURAL HEALTH CENTRE (HM14574) | | | | | | | | | ● | | | |
| NEWBRIDGE PHARMACY (HM14850) | ● | | ● | | | | | | ● | | | |
| OULTON FOOT CLINIC (HM15499) | | | | | | | | | | | | |
| PARK PRACTICE (HM15672) | ● | ● | ● | ● | ● | ● | ● | ● | ● | ● | ● | ● |
| PAUL MAWER PSYCHOLGICAL SVS (HM15843) | | | | | | | | | | | | |
| PHYSIOTHERAPY CLINIC (HM16241) | ● | | | | | | | | ● | | | |
| PIKE, ELIZABETH G & J K (HM16286) | | | | | | | | | | | | |
| PILLATH, CHRISTINE (HM16297) | ● | | | | | | | | ● | | | |
| PLANT, ALISON () | | | | | | ● | | | | | | |
| PRISM THERAPIES (HM16636) | | ● | | | | | | ● | ● | | | |
| REMEDIAL MASSAGE THERAPY (HM17174) | ● | | | ● | ● | | | | ● | | ● | |
| RICHARDSON, CYRIL (HM17273) | | | | | | | | | | | | |
| ROBINSON, JOHN (HM17484) | | | | | | | | | | | | |
| ROMSLEY PHYSIOTHERAPY PRACTICE (HM17578) | ● | | | | | | | | ● | | | |
| SEITAI/SHIATSU & MANIPULATION (HM18202) | | | | | | ● | | | | | | |
| SIDHOM, A (HM18529) | ● | | | | | | | | ● | | | |
| SOLIHULL CHIROPRACTIC CLINIC (HM18872) | ● | | | | | | | | ● | | | |
| SOMEWAY HERBAL CLINIC (HM18883) | ● | | | | | | | | ● | | | |
| ST PAULS OSTEOPATHY PRACTICE (HM19094) | ● | | | | | | | ● | ● | | | |
| STARKEY, DAVID (HM19147) | ● | | | | | | | | | | | |
| STOURBRIDGE ACU & OSTEO CTRE (HM19356) | ● | | | | | | | | ● | | | |
| SUCCESSWORKS (HM19461) | | | | | | | | | | | | |
| SUTTON COLDFIELD HEALTH CLINIC (HM19544) | | | | | ● | | ● | | ● | | | |
| TELLING, MELANIE (HM19822) | | ● | | ● | | ● | | | | | ● | |
| TELLING, MELANIE (HM19823) | | | | ● | | ● | | | | | ● | |
| THERAPY TRAINING COLLEGE (HM19911) | | ● | | | | | | ● | | | | |
| WALSALL PHYSIOTHERAPY CLINIC (HM20853) | ● | | | | | | | | ● | | | |
| WALSGRAVE CHIROPRACTIC CLINIC (HM20855) | ● | | | | | | | | ● | | | |
| WARD, JAQUELINE (HM20906) | | ● | | | | ● | | ● | | | | |

| Business | Thyroid Problems | Tinnitis | Tiredness | Tonsilitis | Ulcers | Vaginal Problems | Varicose Veins | Verrucas | Vertigo | Viral Infections | Vomiting | Warts |
|---|---|---|---|---|---|---|---|---|---|---|---|---|
| MIDLAND MEDICAL OSTEO PRACTICE (HM13836) | | | | | | | | | | | | |
| MIDLAND MEDICAL OSTEO PRACTICE (HM13835) | | | | | | | | | | | | |
| MORGAN, VALERIE (HM14177) | | | ● | ● | | | | | | | ● | |
| MORRIS, CLAIRE (HM14202) | | | | | | | | | | | | ● |
| MYATT, ANITA (HM14432) | ● | ● | ● | ● | ● | ● | ● | | ● | ● | ● | ● |
| NATURAL HEALTH CENTRE (HM14574) | | | ● | | | | | | | | ● | |
| NEWBRIDGE PHARMACY (HM14850) | ● | | ● | ● | | | | | | | | |
| OULTON FOOT CLINIC (HM15499) | | | | | | | | | | | | ● |
| PARK PRACTICE (HM15672) | ● | ● | ● | ● | ● | ● | ● | | ● | ● | ● | ● |
| PAUL MAWER PSYCHOLGICAL SVS (HM15843) | | | | | | | | | | | | |
| PHYSIOTHERAPY CLINIC (HM16241) | | | | | | | | | | | | |
| PIKE, ELIZABETH G & J K (HM16286) | | | | | | | | | | | | ● |
| PILLATH, CHRISTINE (HM16297) | | | | | | | | | | | | |
| PLANT, ALISON () | | | ● | | | | | | | | | ● |
| PRISM THERAPIES (HM16636) | | ● | | | | | | | | | | |
| REMEDIAL MASSAGE THERAPY (HM17174) | | ● | | | ● | | | | | | | |
| RICHARDSON, CYRIL (HM17273) | | | | | | | | | | | | ● |
| ROBINSON, JOHN (HM17484) | | | | | | | | | | | | |
| ROMSLEY PHYSIOTHERAPY PRACTICE (HM17578) | | | | | | | | | | | | |
| SEITAI/SHIATSU & MANIPULATION (HM18202) | | | | | | | | | | | | |
| SIDHOM, A (HM18529) | | | | | | | | | | | | |
| SOLIHULL CHIROPRACTIC CLINIC (HM18872) | | | | | | | | | | | | |
| SOMEWAY HERBAL CLINIC (HM18883) | | | ● | | | | | | | | | |
| ST PAULS OSTEOPATHY PRACTICE (HM19094) | | ● | ● | | | | | | ● | | | |
| STARKEY, DAVID (HM19147) | ● | | ● | | | | | | | | | |
| STOURBRIDGE ACU & OSTEO CTRE (HM19356) | | | | | | | | | | | | |
| SUCCESSWORKS (HM19461) | | | | | | | | | ● | | | |
| SUTTON COLDFIELD HEALTH CLINIC (HM19544) | | | ● | | | | | | | | | |
| TELLING, MELANIE (HM19822) | ● | | | ● | | ● | ● | | | | | |
| TELLING, MELANIE (HM19823) | | | | ● | | ● | ● | | | | | |
| THERAPY TRAINING COLLEGE (HM19911) | | ● | ● | | | | | | | | | |
| WALSALL PHYSIOTHERAPY CLINIC (HM20853) | | | | | | | | | | | | |
| WALSGRAVE CHIROPRACTIC CLINIC (HM20855) | | | | | | | | | | | | |
| WARD, JAQUELINE (HM20906) | | | | | | | | | | | | |

| Business | Water Retention | Whiplash | Wind | Worms | Children | Terminally Ill | Disabled | Horses | Dogs | CatS | Other Animals |
|---|---|---|---|---|---|---|---|---|---|---|---|
| MIDLAND MEDICAL OSTEO PRACTICE (HM13836) | | | | | | | | | | | |
| MIDLAND MEDICAL OSTEO PRACTICE (HM13835) | | | | | | | | | | | |
| MORGAN, VALERIE (HM14177) | ● | | | | ● | ● | | | | | |
| MORRIS, CLAIRE (HM14202) | | | | | ● | ● | ● | | | | |
| MYATT, ANITA (HM14432) | ● | | ● | ● | ● | ● | ● | ● | ● | ● | |
| NATURAL HEALTH CENTRE (HM14574) | | | | | | | | | | | |
| NEWBRIDGE PHARMACY (HM14850) | | | | | | | | | | | |
| OULTON FOOT CLINIC (HM15499) | | | | | ● | ● | | | | | |
| PARK PRACTICE (HM15672) | ● | | ● | ● | ● | ● | ● | | | | |
| PAUL MAWER PSYCHOLGICAL SVS (HM15843) | | | | | ● | | | | | | |
| PHYSIOTHERAPY CLINIC (HM16241) | | | | | ● | ● | ● | | | | |
| PIKE, ELIZABETH G & J K (HM16286) | | | | | ● | ● | ● | | | | |
| PILLATH, CHRISTINE (HM16297) | | ● | | | ● | ● | ● | | | | |
| PLANT, ALISON () | | | | | | | | | | | |
| PRISM THERAPIES (HM16636) | | | | | ● | | | | | | |
| REMEDIAL MASSAGE THERAPY (HM17174) | | | | | ● | ● | ● | | | | |
| RICHARDSON, CYRIL (HM17273) | | | | | ● | | ● | | | | |
| ROBINSON, JOHN (HM17484) | | | | | ● | ● | ● | | | | |
| ROMSLEY PHYSIOTHERAPY PRACTICE (HM17578) | | | | | ● | ● | ● | | | | |
| SEITAI/SHIATSU & MANIPULATION (HM18202) | | | | | | | | | | | |
| SIDHOM, A (HM18529) | | | | | ● | ● | ● | | | | |
| SOLIHULL CHIROPRACTIC CLINIC (HM18872) | | ● | | | ● | ● | ● | | | | |
| SOMEWAY HERBAL CLINIC (HM18883) | | | | | ● | ● | ● | | | | |
| ST PAULS OSTEOPATHY PRACTICE (HM19094) | | | | | ● | ● | ● | | | | |
| STARKEY, DAVID (HM19147) | | ● | | | ● | | ● | | | | |
| STOURBRIDGE ACU & OSTEO CTRE (HM19356) | | | | | | | | | | | |
| SUCCESSWORKS (HM19461) | | | | | ● | ● | ● | ● | ● | ● | ● |
| SUTTON COLDFIELD HEALTH CLINIC (HM19544) | ● | | | | ● | ● | ● | | | | |
| TELLING, MELANIE (HM19822) | | | | | ● | ● | ● | | | | |
| TELLING, MELANIE (HM19823) | | | | | ● | ● | ● | | | | |
| THERAPY TRAINING COLLEGE (HM19911) | ● | | | | ● | | ● | | | | |
| WALSALL PHYSIOTHERAPY CLINIC (HM20853) | | | | | ● | ● | ● | | | | |
| WALSGRAVE CHIROPRACTIC CLINIC (HM20855) | | ● | | | ● | ● | ● | | | | |
| WARD, JAQUELINE (HM20906) | | | | | | | | | | | |

(Children, Terminally Ill, Disabled, Horses, Dogs, CatS, Other Animals: Specialist Treatment Categories)

# S - W Conditions treated at Practices/Businesses and Specialist Treatment Categories

Business by County with Reference no.

| Business | Sexually Trans. Infections | Shingles | Sinus Problems | Skin Problems | Sleep Disorders | Slimming Help | Slipped Disk | Smoking Help | Sneezing | Snoring | Spinal Injuries | Sports Injuries | Sprains | Stammering | Stings | Stomach Problems |
|---|---|---|---|---|---|---|---|---|---|---|---|---|---|---|---|---|
| WELL NATURAL HEALTH CENTRE (HM21140) | ● | ● | ● | ● | ● | ● | ● | ● | ● | ● | | ● | ● | ● | ● | ● |
| WELL NATURAL HEALTH CENTRE (HM21139) | ● | ● | ● | ● | ● | ● | ● | ● | ● | ● | ● | ● | ● | ● | ● | ● |
| WEST MIDLAND HYPNOTHERAPY (HM21229) | | | | | | | | | | | | | | | | |
| WESTON, JOHN (HM21278) | | | | | | | ● | | | | | ● | ● | | | |
| WESTWOOD, ANGELA (HM21285) | | | ● | ● | ● | | | | | | | | | | | |
| WHITE, SHELLEY (HM21378) | | | | | ● | | | | | | | | | | | |
| WHITEHALL, CAROL (HM21385) | | | | | | | | | | | | | | | | |
| WILLOWS CLNC COMP HEALTH CTRE (HM21630) | | | ● | ● | ● | ● | ● | ● | ● | ● | ● | ● | ● | ● | | ● |
| WITHYMOOR PHYSIOTHERAPY CLINIC (HM21749) | | | | | | | ● | | | | | ● | ● | | | |
| WOLVERHAMPTON CHINESE MED CTRE (HM21765) | | ● | ● | ● | ● | ● | | ● | | ● | | ● | ● | | | ● |
| ZEN HEALTH & BEAUTY (HM22099) | | | | | ● | | | | | | | | | | | |
| **NORFOLK** | | | | | | | | | | | | | | | | |
| ALTERNATIVE HEALTH CARE (HM00702) | | | ● | ● | ● | | | | | | | | | | | ● |
| AMALA CHIROPODY CENTRE (HM00760) | | | | | | | | | | | | | | | | |
| BODY BEAUTIFUL (HM02576) | | | | | ● | ● | | | | | | | | | | |
| BRUNSWICK PHYSIO (HM03280) | | | | | | | ● | | | | | ● | ● | | | |
| CARSON, KAREN (HM03770) | | | | | | | | | | | | | | | | |
| CHANDLER, ANN (HM03973) | | | | | | | ● | | | | | ● | ● | | | |
| CHASE PARK PRACTICE (HM04060) | | | | | | | | | | | | | | | | |
| CHIROPODIST (HM04291) | | | | | | | | | | | | | | | | |
| CHIROPODISTS (HM04297) | | | | | | | | | | | | | | | | |
| CLASSICAL OSTEOPATH (HM04611) | | | ● | | | | ● | | | | | ● | ● | | | ● |
| COMER OSTEOPATHIC CLINIC (HM04897) | | | ● | | | | ● | | | | | ● | ● | | | ● |
| COMPLEMENTARY HEALTH CLINIC (HM04926) | | ● | ● | | ● | | | ● | | | | ● | ● | | | |
| COTTAGE CHIROPRACTIC CLINIC (HM05217) | | | | | | | ● | | | | ● | ● | ● | | | |
| COTTAGE CLINIC (HM05220) | | ● | ● | ● | ● | | | | | | | | | | | ● |
| COUNTY HEALTH (HM05259) | | ● | ● | ● | ● | | | ● | ● | ● | | ● | ● | | ● | ● |
| DISS NATURAL HEALTH CLINIC (HM06121) | | | ● | ● | ● | | ● | ● | | | | | ● | | | |
| ELEMENTS OF HEALTH (HM06725) | | | ● | ● | ● | ● | ● | ● | ● | ● | | ● | ● | ● | ● | ● |
| ELLIS, STEPHEN (HM06772) | | | | ● | | | | ● | | | | ● | ● | | | |
| FIRST STEP FOOTCARE (HM07340) | | | | | | | | | | | | | | | | |
| FISHER, JACK E (HM07355) | | | | | | | ● | | | | | | | | | |
| FORD OSTEOPATHIC CLINIC (HM07521) | | | | | | | ● | | | | | ● | ● | | | |
| GEARY, A G (HM07951) | | | | | | | | | | | | | | | | |

| Business | Stomach Ulcers | Stress | Sweating | Teeth Grinding | Tennis Elbow | Terminal Illness | Throat Problems | Thrush | Thyroid Problems | Tinnitis | Tiredness | Tonsilitis | Ulcers | Vaginal Problems | Varicose Veins | Verrucas |
|---|---|---|---|---|---|---|---|---|---|---|---|---|---|---|---|---|
| WELL NATURAL HEALTH CENTRE (HM21140) | ● | | ● | ● | ● | ● | ● | ● | ● | ● | ● | ● | ● | ● | ● | |
| WELL NATURAL HEALTH CENTRE (HM21139) | ● | | ● | ● | ● | ● | ● | ● | ● | ● | ● | ● | ● | ● | ● | |
| WEST MIDLAND HYPNOTHERAPY (HM21229) | | | | | | | | | | | | | | | | |
| WESTON, JOHN (HM21278) | | | | | ● | | | | | | | | | | | |
| WESTWOOD, ANGELA (HM21285) | | | | ● | | | | | | | | ● | | | ● | |
| WHITE, SHELLEY (HM21378) | | | | | ● | | | ● | ● | | | ● | | | | |
| WHITEHALL, CAROL (HM21385) | | | | | | | | | | | | | | | | ● |
| WILLOWS CLNC COMP HEALTH CTRE (HM21630) | | | ● | | ● | ● | ● | ● | ● | ● | ● | | | ● | ● | ● |
| WITHYMOOR PHYSIOTHERAPY CLINIC (HM21749) | | | | | ● | | | | | | | | | | | |
| WOLVERHAMPTON CHINESE MED CTRE (HM21765) | ● | | ● | | ● | | ● | | | ● | ● | | ● | ● | | |
| ZEN HEALTH & BEAUTY (HM22099) | | | | | | | | | | | | | | | | |
| **NORFOLK** | | | | | | | | | | | | | | | | |
| ALTERNATIVE HEALTH CARE (HM00702) | ● | ● | | | | | | | | | ● | | | | | |
| AMALA CHIROPODY CENTRE (HM00760) | | | | | | | | | | | | | | | | ● |
| BODY BEAUTIFUL (HM02576) | | | | | | | | ● | | | ● | | | | | |
| BRUNSWICK PHYSIO (HM03280) | | | | | ● | | | | | | | | | | | |
| CARSON, KAREN (HM03770) | | | | | | | | | | | | | | | | ● |
| CHANDLER, ANN (HM03973) | | | | | ● | | | | | | | | | | | |
| CHASE PARK PRACTICE (HM04060) | | | | | | | | | | | ● | | | | | |
| CHIROPODIST (HM04291) | | | | | | | | | | | | | | | | |
| CHIROPODISTS (HM04297) | | | | | | | | | | | | | | | | |
| CLASSICAL OSTEOPATH (HM04611) | ● | | ● | ● | ● | ● | ● | | ● | ● | ● | ● | ● | | | |
| COMER OSTEOPATHIC CLINIC (HM04897) | ● | | | | | | | ● | | ● | ● | | | | | |
| COMPLEMENTARY HEALTH CLINIC (HM04926) | | | | | ● | | | | | | ● | | | | | |
| COTTAGE CHIROPRACTIC CLINIC (HM05217) | | | | | ● | | | | | | | | | | | |
| COTTAGE CLINIC (HM05220) | | | ● | | | | | ● | | ● | ● | | ● | ● | ● | |
| COUNTY HEALTH (HM05259) | ● | | ● | ● | ● | | ● | ● | ● | ● | ● | ● | ● | ● | ● | |
| DISS NATURAL HEALTH CLINIC (HM06121) | | | ● | | ● | | ● | ● | | ● | ● | | | | | |
| ELEMENTS OF HEALTH (HM06725) | ● | | ● | ● | ● | ● | ● | ● | ● | ● | ● | ● | ● | ● | ● | |
| ELLIS, STEPHEN (HM06772) | | ● | | | | | | | | | | | | | | |
| FIRST STEP FOOTCARE (HM07340) | | | | | | | | | | | | | | | | ● |
| FISHER, JACK E (HM07355) | | | | | ● | | | | | | | | | | | |
| FORD OSTEOPATHIC CLINIC (HM07521) | | | | | | | | | | | | | | | | |
| GEARY, A G (HM07951) | | | | | | | | | | | | | | | | |

| Business | Vertigo | Viral Infections | Vomiting | Warts | Water Retention | Whiplash | Wind | Worms | Children (Specialist Treatment Categories) | Terminally Ill | Disabled | Horses | Dogs | CatS | Other Animals |
|---|---|---|---|---|---|---|---|---|---|---|---|---|---|---|---|
| WELL NATURAL HEALTH CENTRE (HM21140) | ● | ● | ● | ● | ● | | ● | ● | ● | ● | ● | | | | |
| WELL NATURAL HEALTH CENTRE (HM21139) | ● | ● | ● | ● | ● | ● | ● | ● | ● | ● | ● | | | | |
| WEST MIDLAND HYPNOTHERAPY (HM21229) | | | | | | | | | ● | ● | ● | | | | |
| WESTON, JOHN (HM21278) | | | | | | | | | ● | | ● | | | | |
| WESTWOOD, ANGELA (HM21285) | | | | | | | | | | | | | | | |
| WHITE, SHELLEY (HM21378) | | | | | | | | | ● | ● | ● | | | | |
| WHITEHALL, CAROL (HM21385) | | | | | | | | | ● | ● | ● | | | | |
| WILLOWS CLNC COMP HEALTH CTRE (HM21630) | ● | ● | ● | ● | ● | ● | ● | | ● | ● | ● | | | | |
| WITHYMOOR PHYSIOTHERAPY CLINIC (HM21749) | | | | | | | | | ● | | ● | | | | |
| WOLVERHAMPTON CHINESE MED CTRE (HM21765) | | | ● | | ● | | ● | | ● | | ● | | ● | ● | |
| ZEN HEALTH & BEAUTY (HM22099) | | | | | | | | | ● | ● | ● | | | | |
| **NORFOLK** | | | | | | | | | | | | | | | |
| ALTERNATIVE HEALTH CARE (HM00702) | | | | | | | | | ● | ● | ● | | | | |
| AMALA CHIROPODY CENTRE (HM00760) | | | | | | | | | ● | ● | ● | | | | |
| BODY BEAUTIFUL (HM02576) | | | | | ● | | | | | | | | | | |
| BRUNSWICK PHYSIO (HM03280) | | | | | | | | | ● | ● | ● | | | | |
| CARSON, KAREN (HM03770) | | | | | | | | | | | | | | | |
| CHANDLER, ANN (HM03973) | | | | | | | | | ● | ● | ● | | | | |
| CHASE PARK PRACTICE (HM04060) | | | | | | | | | | ● | | | | | |
| CHIROPODIST (HM04291) | | | | | | | | | ● | ● | ● | | | | |
| CHIROPODISTS (HM04297) | | | | | | | | | ● | ● | ● | | | | |
| CLASSICAL OSTEOPATH (HM04611) | ● | | | | | ● | ● | | ● | ● | | | | | |
| COMER OSTEOPATHIC CLINIC (HM04897) | ● | | | | | | | | ● | ● | ● | | | | |
| COMPLEMENTARY HEALTH CLINIC (HM04926) | ● | | | | ● | | | | ● | ● | ● | | | | |
| COTTAGE CHIROPRACTIC CLINIC (HM05217) | | | | | | ● | | | | ● | ● | ● | | | |
| COTTAGE CLINIC (HM05220) | | ● | | | ● | | | ● | ● | | | | | | |
| COUNTY HEALTH (HM05259) | ● | ● | ● | ● | ● | | ● | ● | ● | | ● | | | | |
| DISS NATURAL HEALTH CLINIC (HM06121) | ● | ● | | | | | ● | | ● | ● | ● | ● | ● | ● | ● |
| ELEMENTS OF HEALTH (HM06725) | ● | ● | ● | ● | ● | | ● | ● | ● | | | | | | |
| ELLIS, STEPHEN (HM06772) | | | | | | | | | | ● | ● | | | | |
| FIRST STEP FOOTCARE (HM07340) | | | | ● | | | | | ● | ● | ● | | | | |
| FISHER, JACK E (HM07355) | | | | | | | | | ● | | ● | | | | |
| FORD OSTEOPATHIC CLINIC (HM07521) | | | | | | | | | ● | | ● | | | | |
| GEARY, A G (HM07951) | | | | | | | | | ● | ● | ● | | | | |

# S - W Conditions treated at Practices/Businesses and Specialist Treatment Categories

| Business by County with Reference no. | Sexually Trans. Infections | Shingles | Sinus Problems | Skin Problems | Sleep Disorders | Slimming Help | Slipped Disk | Smoking Help | Sneezing | Snoring | Spinal Injuries | Sports Injuries | Sprains | Stammering | Stings | Stomach Problems | Stomach Ulcers | Stress | Sweating | Teeth Grinding | Tennis Elbow | Terminal Illness | Throat Problems | Thrush | Thyroid Problems | Tinnitis | Tiredness | Tonsilitis | Ulcers | Vaginal Problems | Varicose Veins | Verrucas | Vertigo | Viral Infections | Vomiting | Warts | Water Retention | Whiplash | Wind | Worms | Specialist Treatment Categories: Children | Terminally Ill | Disabled | Horses | Dogs | CatS | Other Animals |
|---|---|---|---|---|---|---|---|---|---|---|---|---|---|---|---|---|---|---|---|---|---|---|---|---|---|---|---|---|---|---|---|---|---|---|---|---|---|---|---|---|---|---|---|---|---|---|---|
| GT YARMOUTH PHYSICAL THERAPY (HM08330) | | | | | | | ● | | | | | ● | ● | | | | | | | | ● | | | | | | ● | | | | | | | | | | | | | | ● | | ● | | | | |
| HARGHAM HALL OSTEO PRACTICE (HM08992) | | | ● | | | | ● | | | | | ● | ● | | | | | | | | ● | | | | | | | | | | | | | | | | | | | | ● | ● | ● | | ● | | |
| HOBSON, L A (HM09865) | | | | | | | | | | | | | | | | | | | | | | | | | | | | | | | | | | | | | | | | | ● | ● | ● | | | | |
| HOMEOPATHIC CLINIC (HM10074) | ● | ● | ● | ● | ● | ● | ● | ● | ● | ● | | ● | ● | ● | ● | ● | ● | | ● | ● | ● | ● | ● | ● | ● | ● | ● | ● | ● | ● | ● | | ● | ● | ● | ● | ● | | ● | ● | ● | ● | ● | ● | ● | ● | ● |
| JAMES, LINDA (HM10890) | | | | ● | ● | | | | | | | | | | | | | ● | | | | | | | | | | | | | | | | | | | | | | | ● | ● | ● | | | | |
| JESSOP CLINIC (HM11021) | | | ● | | ● | | ● | | | | | ● | ● | | | | | | | | ● | | | | ● | | ● | | | | | | | | | | | | | | | | | | | | |
| KING, SIMON (HM11644) | | ● | ● | ● | ● | ● | | ● | ● | ● | | ● | ● | ● | ● | ● | ● | | ● | ● | ● | | ● | ● | ● | ● | ● | ● | ● | ● | ● | | ● | ● | ● | ● | ● | | ● | | ● | ● | ● | | | | |
| MONSON, J L B (HM14076) | | | | | | | | | | | | | | | | | | ● | | | | | | | | | | | | | | | | | | | | | | | | | | | | | |
| NEW MARKET RD PHYSIO PRACTICE (HM14824) | | | | | | | | | | | | | | | | | | | | | ● | | | | | | | | | | | | | | | | | | | | ● | | ● | | | | |
| NORFOLK CLINIC (HM14993) | | | ● | ● | | | | ● | ● | ● | | ● | ● | | | ● | ● | | ● | ● | ● | | | ● | ● | ● | ● | ● | ● | ● | | | ● | ● | ● | ● | ● | | ● | ● | ● | | | | | | |
| NORFOLK NATURAL HEALTH SERVICE (HM14995) | | | ● | ● | ● | ● | | ● | | | | | | | | ● | | | | | | | | | | | | | | | | | | ● | | | ● | | ● | | ● | ● | ● | | | | |
| NORMAN, A J (HM14999) | | | | | ● | ● | ● | | | | ● | ● | ● | | | | | | | | ● | | | | | | | | | | | | | | | | | ● | | | ● | ● | ● | | | | |
| OLIVE GROVE BODY SCIENCE (HM15281) | | | | ● | | | | | | | | | | | | | | | | | | | | | | | | | | | | | | | | | | | | | ● | ● | ● | | | | |
| PARK PHYSIOTHERAPY (HM15669) | | | | | | | ● | | | | | ● | ● | | | | | | | | ● | | | | | | | | | | | | | | | | | | | | ● | | ● | | | | |
| QUEENS SQUARE SURGERY (HM16796) | ● | ● | ● | ● | ● | ● | ● | ● | ● | ● | | ● | ● | ● | ● | ● | ● | | ● | ● | ● | ● | ● | ● | ● | ● | ● | ● | ● | ● | ● | | ● | ● | ● | ● | ● | | ● | ● | ● | ● | ● | | | | |
| RICHARDSON, ALAN (HM17268) | | ● | | | | | | ● | | | | | | | | | | | | | | | ● | ● | | | | | | | | | | ● | | | | | | | ● | | | | | | |
| RIGBY COURT CLINIC (HM17331) | | ● | ● | ● | ● | | | ● | ● | ● | | ● | ● | ● | ● | ● | ● | | ● | ● | ● | ● | ● | ● | ● | ● | ● | ● | ● | ● | ● | | ● | ● | ● | ● | ● | | ● | ● | ● | ● | ● | | | | |
| SHARP, DENISE (HM18307) | | ● | ● | ● | ● | | | | | | | | | | | ● | | | | | | | | | | | ● | | | | | | | | | | | | | | ● | ● | ● | | | | |
| SHIATSU CENTRE (HM18453) | | | | | | | | | | | | ● | | | | | | | | | ● | | | | | | ● | | | | | | | | | | | ● | | | ● | ● | ● | | | | |
| ST STEPHENS PRACTICE (HM19099) | | ● | ● | | ● | | | | | | | ● | ● | | | | | | | | | | | | | | | | | | | | | | ● | | | ● | | | ● | ● | ● | | | | |
| WATTON PHYSIOTHERAPY CLINIC (HM21033) | | | | | | | ● | | | | | ● | ● | | | | | | | | ● | | | | | | | | | | | | | | | | | | | | ● | ● | ● | | | | |
| WELLBEING NATURALLY (HM21152) | | | | | | | | | | | | | | | | | | | | | | | | | | | | | | | | | | | | | | | | | ● | ● | ● | | | | |
| WENDY JILLEY - MEDICAL HERB (HM21197) | | ● | ● | ● | ● | | | | ● | ● | | | | | ● | ● | ● | | ● | | | | ● | ● | | ● | ● | ● | ● | ● | ● | | | ● | ● | ● | ● | | ● | | ● | ● | ● | | | | |
| WOBURN CLINIC (HM21755) | | | | | | ● | ● | ● | | | | | | | | ● | | | | ● | | | | | | | ● | | | | | | | ● | | | ● | | | | ● | ● | ● | | | | |
| NORTHAMPTONSHIRE | | | | | | | | | | | | | | | | | | | | | | | | | | | | | | | | | | | | | | | | | | | | | | | |
| ACUPUNCTURE CLINIC (HM00275) | | | ● | ● | | | ● | | | | | ● | ● | | | | | | | | ● | | | | | | ● | | | | | | | | | | | | | | ● | ● | ● | | | | |
| ALLEN HINDE - PHYSIOTHERAPIST (HM00598) | | | | | | | ● | | | | | ● | ● | | | | | | | | ● | | | | | | | | | | | | | | | | | | | | ● | | ● | | | | |
| ANDREWS, S C (HM00857) | ● | ● | ● | ● | ● | | | ● | ● | ● | ● | ● | ● | ● | ● | ● | ● | ● | ● | ● | ● | ● | ● | ● | ● | ● | ● | ● | ● | ● | ● | ● | ● | ● | ● | ● | ● | ● | ● | ● | ● | ● | ● | | | | |
| ANDREWS, SIMON C (HM00860) | ● | ● | ● | ● | ● | | | ● | ● | ● | | ● | ● | ● | ● | ● | ● | | ● | ● | ● | ● | ● | ● | ● | ● | ● | ● | ● | ● | ● | | ● | ● | ● | ● | ● | | ● | ● | ● | ● | ● | | | | |
| ANNELISE (HM00906) | | | ● | ● | | | | | | | | | | | | | | | | | | | | | | ● | | | | | | | | | | | | | | | ● | | ● | | | | |
| ARBOURS (HM00965) | | | | | | | | | | | | | | | | | | | | | | | | | | | | | | | | | | | | | | | | | ● | ● | ● | | | | |
| C F C M (HM03523) | | ● | ● | ● | | | ● | | | | | ● | ● | ● | ● | ● | ● | | ● | ● | ● | | ● | ● | | ● | ● | ● | ● | ● | ● | | ● | ● | ● | ● | ● | | ● | ● | ● | ● | ● | | | | |
| CALLIS THERAPY FOUNDATION (HM03555) | ● | ● | ● | ● | ● | ● | ● | ● | ● | ● | | ● | ● | ● | ● | ● | ● | | ● | ● | ● | ● | ● | ● | ● | ● | ● | ● | ● | ● | ● | | ● | ● | ● | ● | ● | | ● | ● | ● | ● | ● | | | | |
| CLINTON HOUSE CHIROPODY (HM04719) | | | | | | | | | | | | ● | | | | | | | | | | | | | | | | | | | | | | | | | | | | | ● | | ● | | | | |

# S - W Conditions treated at Practices/Businesses and Specialist Treatment Categories

Business by County with Reference no.

Columns Children to Other Animals: Specialist Treatment Categories

| Business by County with Reference no. | Sexually Trans. Infections | Shingles | Sinus Problems | Skin Problems | Sleep Disorders | Slimming Help | Slipped Disk | Smoking Help | Sneezing | Snoring | Spinal Injuries | Sports Injuries | Sprains | Stammering | Stings | Stomach Problems | Stomach Ulcers | Stress | Sweating | Teeth Grinding | Tennis Elbow | Terminal Illness | Throat Problems | Thrush | Thyroid Problems | Tinnitis | Tiredness | Tonsilitis | Ulcers | Vaginal Problems | Varicose Veins | Verrucas | Vertigo | Viral Infections | Vomiting | Warts | Water Retention | Whiplash | Wind | Worms | Children | Terminally Ill | Disabled | Horses | Dogs | CatS | Other Animals |
|---|---|---|---|---|---|---|---|---|---|---|---|---|---|---|---|---|---|---|---|---|---|---|---|---|---|---|---|---|---|---|---|---|---|---|---|---|---|---|---|---|---|---|---|---|---|---|---|
| DAVENTRY NATUREWORKS (HM05768) | | | | | | |●| | | | |●|●| | | | | | | |●| | | | | |●| | | | | | | |●| | | | | | | | | | | | |
| DEVON PARADE CLINIC (HM06041) | |●|●|●|●| |●|●| | | |●|●| | | | |●| | |●| | | | | |●| | | | |●| | | | | | | | |●| |●| | | | |
| ESSERY, TRICIA (HM06933) | | |●|●|●| | | | | | | | | | | | | | | | | | | | | |●| | | | | | | | | | | | | |●|●|●| | | | |
| GARVEY-WILLIAMS, RICHARD (HM07915) | | | |●| | |●| | | | |●|●| | |●|●| |●| |●| | | |●|●|●| |●| | | |●| | | | | | | |●|●|●| | | | |
| GARVEY-WILLIAMS, RICHARD (HM07914) | | | | | | |●| | | | |●|●| | | | | | | |●| | | | | | | | | | | | | | | | | | | |●|●|●| | | | |
| GEDDES, PIPPA (HM07955) | | |●|●|●| | | | | | | | | | | |●| |●| |●| |●|●|●| |●|●| |●| | | | | | |●| |●| |●|●|●| | | | |
| JUST RELAX (HM11285) | |●|●|●|●| |●|●| |●| |●|●| | |●| | | | |●| |●| |●|●|●| | | |●| |●| | | |●| |●| |●|●|●| | | | |
| LEE, STEPHEN (HM12146) | |●|●|●| | | | | | | |●|●| | |●| |●| | |●| | | | | |●|●| | | | | | | | | | | | | | | | | | | |
| MAPLE TREE OSTEO PRACTICE (HM13061) | | |●| |●| | | | |●| |●|●| | |●|●| | | |●| |●| | | |●| | | | | |●| | | | | | | |●| |●| | | | |
| MOTLEY, MAUREEN (HM14277) | | | |●|●| | | | | | | | | | | | |●| | | | | | | | | | | | | | | | | | | | | | | | |●| | | | |
| NENE VALLEY COMP THERAPIES (HM14785) | | | |●|●| | | | | | | | | | |●| |●| | | | | | | | |●| | | | | | | | | | | | | |●|●|●| | | | |
| NORTHAMPTON CHIROPRACTIC (HM15051) | | | | | | |●| | | | |●|●| | | | | | | |●| | | | | | | | | | | | | | | | |●| | |●|●|●| | | | |
| NORTHAMPTON CLINIC (HM15052) | | | |●|●| | | | | | | | | | | | |●| | | | | | | | | | | | | | | | | | | | | | |●|●|●| | | | |
| REFLEXOLOGY CLINIC (HM17085) | |●|●|●|●|●|●|●|●|●| |●|●|●| |●|●| |●|●|●|●|●|●|●|●|●|●|●|●| | |●| | | |●| |●| |●|●|●| | | | |
| TOWCESTER CHIROPRACTIC CLINIC (HM20194) | | | | | | |●| | | | |●|●| | | | | | | | | | | | | |●| | | | | | | | | | | | | |●|●|●|●|●|●|●|
| **NORTHUMBERLAND** | | | | | | | | | | | | | | | | | | | | | | | | | | | | | | | | | | | | | | | | | | | | | | | |
| ACUCARE (HM00209) | | |●|●| | |●| | | | |●|●| | | | | | | |●| | | | | |●| | | | | | | | | | | | | |●|●|●| | | | |
| AYRES, ELIZABETH (HM01433) | | | | | | | | | | | | | | | | | | | | | | | | | | | | | | | | | | | | | | | |●|●|●| | | | |
| BOWEN TECHNIQUE STUDIO (HM02775) | | | | | | |●| | | | |●|●| | | | | | | |●| | | | | | | | | | | | | | | | | | | |●| |●| | | | |
| EVISON, ALEX (HM07012) | | | |●|●|●| |●| | | | | | | | | |●|●|●| | | | | | |●| | | | | | | | | | | | | | | | | | | | |
| FORSTER, LINDA (HM07570) | | | | | |●| | | | | | | | | | | | | | | | | | | | | | | | | | | | | | | | | | |●| | | | | | |
| GREEN BATT PHYSIOTHERAPY (HM08434) | | | | | | |●| | | | |●| | | | | | | | |●| | | | | | | | | | | | | | | | | | | |●| |●| | | | |
| KI CLINIC (HM11591) | |●|●|●|●|●| |●|●|●| |●|●|●|●|●|●| |●|●|●|●|●|●|●|●|●|●| |●|●| |●|●|●| |●| |●| |●|●|●| | | | |
| MEAD, BRUCE (HM13626) | | | | | | | | | | | | | | | | | | | | | | | | | | | | | | | |●| | | | | | | | |●|●|●| | | | |
| PHYSIOTHERAPY & SPORTS CLINIC (HM16223) | | | | | | |●| | | | |●|●| | | | | | | |●| | | | | | | | | | | | | | | | | | | |●|●|●| | | | |
| **NOTTINGHAMSHIRE** | | | | | | | | | | | | | | | | | | | | | | | | | | | | | | | | | | | | | | | | | | | | | | | |
| ACUPUNCTURE CLINIC (HM00264) | | |●|●| | |●| | | | |●|●| | | | | | | |●| | | | | | | | | | | | | | | | | | | |●| |●| | | | |
| BEESTON PHYSIO & SPORTS CLNC (HM02060) | | | | | | |●| | | | |●|●| | | | | | | |●| | | | | | | | | | | | | | | | | | | |●| |●| | | | |
| BOND, DIANORA (HM02669) | |●|●| | | |●| | | | |●|●| | | | | | | |●| | | | | | | | | | | | | | | | | | | |●|●|●|●|●|●|●|
| BRAHMA KUMARIS WORLD (HM02891) | | | | | | | | | | | | | | | | | |●| | | | | | | | | | | | | | | | | | | | | | | | | | | | | |
| BROADLEY, RICHARD (HM03116) | | | | | | | | | | | | | | | | | | | | | | | | | | | | | | | | | | | | | | | | | |●|●| | | | |
| BULLEN-SPICER ASSOCIATES (HM03342) | | | | |●|●| |●| | | | | |●| |●| | |●|●| | | | | | |●| | | | | | | | | | | | | |●|●|●| | | | |
| CARITAS NATURAL HEALTH CLINIC (HM03688) | | |●| | | | | | | | |●| | | | | | | | | | | | | | |●| | | | | | | | | | | | | | | | | | | | |
| CENTRE FOR TRANSFORMATION (HM03921) | |●|●|●|●| | | | | | | |●| |●|●|●| |●|●|●| |●|●|●|●| | | |●|●| |●| | |●|●| |●| |●|●| | | | | |

# S - W Conditions treated at Practices/Businesses and Specialist Treatment Categories

| Business by County with Reference no. | Sexually Trans. Infections | Shingles | Sinus Problems | Skin Problems | Sleep Disorders | Slimming Help | Slipped Disk | Smoking Help | Sneezing | Snoring | Spinal Injuries | Sports Injuries | Sprains | Stammering | Stings | Stomach Problems | Stomach Ulcers | Stress | Sweating | Teeth Grinding | Tennis Elbow | Terminal Illness | Throat Problems | Thrush | Thyroid Problems |
|---|---|---|---|---|---|---|---|---|---|---|---|---|---|---|---|---|---|---|---|---|---|---|---|---|---|
| DEAN, MARTIN (HM05942) |  |  | ● | ● | ● |  | ● | ● | ● |  |  | ● | ● |  | ● | ● | ● |  | ● |  | ● |  | ● | ● | ● |
| EAST BRIDGEFORD PHYSIO NEEDS (HM06510) |  |  |  |  |  |  | ● |  |  |  |  | ● | ● |  |  |  |  |  |  |  | ● |  |  |  |  |
| GOTHAM VILLAGE PHSYO CLINIC (HM08308) |  |  |  |  |  |  | ● |  |  |  |  | ● | ● |  |  |  |  |  |  |  | ● |  |  |  |  |
| GREENWOOD, JULIA (HM08507) |  |  |  |  |  |  |  |  |  |  |  |  |  |  |  |  |  |  |  |  |  |  |  |  |  |
| HANDS ON HEALTH (HM08912) |  |  | ● |  |  |  |  |  |  |  |  | ● |  |  |  |  |  |  |  |  |  |  |  |  |  |
| IMPACT PHYSIO & SPORTS INJURIES (HM10590) |  |  |  |  |  |  | ● |  |  |  |  | ● | ● |  |  |  |  |  |  |  | ● |  |  |  |  |
| KENNETH C HUGGINS HYPNOTHERAPY (HM11501) |  |  |  |  |  |  |  |  |  |  |  |  |  |  |  |  |  |  |  |  |  |  |  |  |  |
| LIGHT UP YOUR LIFE (HM12370) |  |  | ● |  | ● |  | ● |  |  |  |  |  | ● |  |  | ● | ● |  |  |  |  |  | ● |  |  |
| MANSFIELD CHIROPODY (HM13046) |  |  |  |  |  |  |  |  |  |  |  |  |  |  |  |  |  |  |  |  |  |  |  |  |  |
| MORLEY-KIRK, JOHN (HM14188) |  | ● | ● | ● | ● |  |  |  |  |  |  |  |  |  |  | ● | ● |  |  |  | ● | ● |  | ● | ● |
| NATURAL HEALTH (HM14554) |  | ● | ● | ● | ● | ● | ● | ● | ● | ● |  | ● | ● |  | ● | ● | ● |  | ● | ● | ● |  | ● | ● | ● |
| NATURAL THERAPY CLINIC (HM14654) |  | ● | ● | ● | ● | ● | ● | ● | ● | ● |  | ● | ● |  | ● | ● | ● |  | ● | ● | ● |  | ● | ● | ● |
| NOTTINGHAM M S THERAPY CTRE (HM15083) |  |  | ● | ● | ● |  |  |  |  |  |  | ● |  |  |  | ● | ● |  |  |  |  |  |  |  |  |
| NOTTINGHAM NATURAL HEALTH CTRE (HM15084) | ● | ● | ● | ● | ● | ● | ● | ● | ● | ● |  | ● | ● | ● | ● | ● | ● | ● | ● | ● | ● | ● | ● | ● | ● |
| NOTTINGHAM SPORTS INJURY (HM15085) |  |  |  |  |  |  | ● |  |  |  |  | ● | ● |  |  |  |  |  |  |  | ● |  |  |  |  |
| OPTIMUM HEALTH (HM15348) | ● | ● | ● | ● | ● | ● | ● | ● | ● | ● |  | ● | ● | ● | ● | ● | ● | ● | ● | ● | ● | ● | ● | ● | ● |
| PARKSIDE STRESS MANAGEMENT (HM15722) |  |  | ● | ● | ● | ● |  |  | ● |  |  |  |  |  | ● | ● | ● |  | ● | ● | ● |  | ● | ● |  |
| PHYSIO DIRECT (HM16197) |  |  |  |  |  |  | ● |  |  |  |  | ● | ● |  |  |  |  |  |  |  | ● |  |  |  |  |
| PHYSIODIRECT (HM16214) |  |  |  |  |  |  | ● |  |  |  |  | ● | ● |  |  |  |  |  |  |  | ● |  |  |  |  |
| PLAINS PHYSIO & BACK PAIN (HM16355) |  |  |  |  |  |  | ● |  |  |  |  | ● | ● |  |  |  |  |  |  |  | ● |  |  |  |  |
| RETFORD CHIROPRACTIC CLINIC (HM17200) |  |  | ● | ● |  |  | ● |  |  |  | ● | ● | ● |  |  | ● |  |  |  | ● | ● |  |  |  |  |
| SEVENTHMOON NATURAL THRPY CTRE (HM18247) |  |  | ● | ● |  |  |  | ● |  |  |  |  |  |  |  | ● |  |  |  |  |  |  |  |  | ● |
| SHEER TECHNIQUE (HM18368) |  | ● | ● | ● | ● | ● | ● | ● | ● | ● |  | ● | ● | ● | ● | ● |  |  | ● | ● | ● | ● | ● | ● | ● |
| SHERWOOD PSYCHO TRAINING INS (HM18441) |  |  |  |  | ● |  |  |  |  |  |  |  |  |  |  |  |  |  |  |  |  |  |  |  |  |
| SKELTON, CATHERINE () |  | ● | ● | ● |  | ● | ● | ● |  |  |  |  |  |  |  | ● |  |  |  | ● | ● |  | ● | ● | ● |
| SOUTHWELL ACUPUNCTURE CLINIC (HM18948) |  | ● | ● | ● | ● |  |  |  | ● | ● |  | ● | ● |  | ● | ● | ● |  | ● | ● | ● | ● | ● | ● | ● |
| TOMLIN, NORMAN (HM20131) |  |  |  |  |  |  | ● |  |  |  |  | ● | ● |  |  |  |  |  |  |  | ● |  |  |  |  |
| TRADITIONAL ACUPUNCTURIST (HM20222) |  |  | ● | ● | ● | ● | ● | ● | ● |  |  | ● | ● |  |  | ● | ● |  | ● |  | ● | ● | ● | ● |  |
| VAUGHTON, NORMAN D (HM20601) |  |  |  |  |  | ● |  | ● |  |  |  |  |  |  |  |  |  | ● |  | ● |  |  |  |  |  |
| WELLBEING CENTRE (HM21149) |  |  |  |  |  |  |  |  |  |  |  |  |  |  |  |  |  | ● |  |  |  |  |  |  |  |
| OXFORDSHIRE |  |  |  |  |  |  |  |  |  |  |  |  |  |  |  |  |  |  |  |  |  |  |  |  |  |
| ASHCROFT CLINIC (HM01198) |  | ● |  |  |  | ● | ● |  |  |  |  | ● | ● |  |  |  |  |  |  |  | ● |  |  | ● |  |
| BACK IN LINE (HM01481) |  |  |  |  |  |  | ● |  |  |  | ● | ● | ● |  |  |  |  |  |  |  | ● |  |  |  |  |
| BACK TO NORMAL CHIRO CLINIC (HM01522) |  |  |  |  |  |  | ● |  |  |  |  | ● | ● |  |  |  |  |  |  |  | ● |  |  |  |  |

| Business by County with Reference no. | Tinnitis | Tiredness | Tonsilitis | Ulcers | Vaginal Problems | Varicose Veins | Verrucas | Vertigo | Viral Infections | Vomiting | Warts | Water Retention | Whiplash | Wind | Worms | Specialist Treatment Categories: Children | Terminally Ill | Disabled | Horses | Dogs | CatS | Other Animals |
|---|---|---|---|---|---|---|---|---|---|---|---|---|---|---|---|---|---|---|---|---|---|---|
| DEAN, MARTIN (HM05942) | ● | ● |  |  |  |  |  |  |  | ● |  | ● |  |  |  | ● | ● |  |  |  |  |  |
| EAST BRIDGEFORD PHYSIO NEEDS (HM06510) |  |  |  |  |  |  |  |  |  |  |  |  |  |  |  | ● |  | ● |  |  |  |  |
| GOTHAM VILLAGE PHSYO CLINIC (HM08308) |  |  |  |  |  |  |  |  |  |  |  |  |  |  |  | ● | ● | ● |  |  |  |  |
| GREENWOOD, JULIA (HM08507) |  |  |  |  |  |  | ● |  |  |  |  |  |  |  |  | ● | ● | ● |  |  |  |  |
| HANDS ON HEALTH (HM08912) |  | ● |  |  |  |  |  |  |  |  |  |  |  |  |  |  |  |  |  |  |  |  |
| IMPACT PHYSIO & SPORTS INJURIES (HM10590) |  |  |  |  |  |  |  |  |  |  |  |  |  |  |  | ● |  | ● |  |  |  |  |
| KENNETH C HUGGINS HYPNOTHERAPY (HM11501) |  |  |  |  |  |  |  |  |  |  |  |  |  |  |  | ● | ● | ● |  |  |  |  |
| LIGHT UP YOUR LIFE (HM12370) | ● | ● |  |  |  |  |  |  |  |  |  |  |  |  |  | ● | ● | ● |  |  |  |  |
| MANSFIELD CHIROPODY (HM13046) |  |  |  |  |  |  | ● |  |  |  |  |  |  |  |  | ● | ● | ● |  |  |  |  |
| MORLEY-KIRK, JOHN (HM14188) | ● | ● |  |  |  | ● |  |  | ● |  |  | ● |  | ● | ● | ● | ● | ● |  | ● |  |  |
| NATURAL HEALTH (HM14554) | ● | ● | ● | ● | ● | ● |  | ● | ● | ● | ● | ● |  | ● |  | ● |  | ● |  |  |  |  |
| NATURAL THERAPY CLINIC (HM14654) | ● | ● | ● | ● | ● | ● |  | ● | ● | ● | ● | ● |  | ● | ● | ● |  | ● |  |  |  |  |
| NOTTINGHAM M S THERAPY CTRE (HM15083) |  | ● |  |  |  |  |  |  |  |  |  |  |  |  |  | ● | ● | ● |  |  |  |  |
| NOTTINGHAM NATURAL HEALTH CTRE (HM15084) | ● | ● | ● | ● | ● | ● |  | ● | ● | ● | ● | ● |  | ● | ● | ● | ● | ● |  |  |  |  |
| NOTTINGHAM SPORTS INJURY (HM15085) |  |  |  |  |  |  |  |  |  |  |  |  |  |  |  | ● |  | ● |  |  |  |  |
| OPTIMUM HEALTH (HM15348) | ● | ● | ● | ● | ● | ● |  | ● | ● | ● | ● | ● |  | ● | ● | ● | ● | ● | ● | ● | ● | ● |
| PARKSIDE STRESS MANAGEMENT (HM15722) |  | ● | ● | ● | ● | ● |  | ● | ● | ● | ● | ● |  | ● | ● | ● | ● | ● |  |  |  |  |
| PHYSIO DIRECT (HM16197) |  |  |  |  |  |  |  |  |  |  |  |  |  |  |  | ● | ● | ● |  |  |  |  |
| PHYSIODIRECT (HM16214) |  |  |  |  |  |  |  |  |  |  |  |  |  |  |  | ● | ● | ● |  |  |  |  |
| PLAINS PHYSIO & BACK PAIN (HM16355) |  |  |  |  |  |  |  |  |  |  |  |  |  |  |  | ● |  | ● |  |  |  |  |
| RETFORD CHIROPRACTIC CLINIC (HM17200) |  | ● |  |  |  |  |  | ● |  |  |  | ● | ● |  |  | ● |  | ● |  |  |  |  |
| SEVENTHMOON NATURAL THRPY CTRE (HM18247) |  | ● |  |  |  |  |  |  |  |  |  |  |  |  |  | ● | ● | ● |  |  |  |  |
| SHEER TECHNIQUE (HM18368) | ● | ● | ● | ● | ● | ● |  | ● | ● | ● | ● | ● |  | ● | ● | ● | ● | ● | ● | ● | ● | ● |
| SHERWOOD PSYCHO TRAINING INS (HM18441) |  |  |  |  |  |  |  |  |  |  |  |  |  |  |  |  |  |  |  |  |  |  |
| SKELTON, CATHERINE () |  |  |  |  |  |  |  |  | ● |  | ● |  |  | ● | ● | ● | ● | ● |  |  |  |  |
| SOUTHWELL ACUPUNCTURE CLINIC (HM18948) | ● | ● | ● | ● | ● | ● |  | ● | ● | ● |  | ● |  | ● |  | ● | ● |  |  |  |  |  |
| TOMLIN, NORMAN (HM20131) |  |  |  |  |  |  |  |  |  |  |  |  |  |  |  | ● |  | ● |  |  |  |  |
| TRADITIONAL ACUPUNCTURIST (HM20222) |  | ● | ● |  |  |  |  | ● |  | ● |  | ● |  | ● |  | ● | ● | ● |  |  |  |  |
| VAUGHTON, NORMAN D (HM20601) |  |  |  |  |  |  |  |  |  |  |  |  |  |  |  | ● |  | ● |  |  |  |  |
| WELLBEING CENTRE (HM21149) |  |  |  |  |  |  |  |  |  |  |  |  |  |  |  | ● |  | ● |  |  |  |  |
| OXFORDSHIRE |  |  |  |  |  |  |  |  |  |  |  |  |  |  |  |  |  |  |  |  |  |  |
| ASHCROFT CLINIC (HM01198) |  | ● |  |  |  |  |  |  |  |  |  |  |  |  |  |  |  |  |  |  |  |  |
| BACK IN LINE (HM01481) |  |  |  |  |  |  |  |  |  |  |  |  | ● |  |  |  |  |  |  |  |  |  |
| BACK TO NORMAL CHIRO CLINIC (HM01522) |  |  |  |  |  |  |  |  |  |  |  |  |  |  |  | ● | ● | ● | ● | ● |  |  |

# S - W Conditions treated at Practices/Businesses and Specialist Treatment Categories

Business by County with Reference no.

| Business by County with Reference no. | Sexually Trans. Infections | Shingles | Sinus Problems | Skin Problems | Sleep Disorders | Slimming Help | Slipped Disk | Smoking Help | Sneezing | Snoring | Spinal Injuries | Sports Injuries | Sprains | Stammering | Stings | Stomach Problems | Stomach Ulcers | Stress | Sweating | Teeth Grinding | Tennis Elbow | Terminal Illness | Throat Problems | Thrush |
|---|---|---|---|---|---|---|---|---|---|---|---|---|---|---|---|---|---|---|---|---|---|---|---|---|
| BLISS REMEDIES (HM02508) | | ● | ● | | ● | | | | | | | | ● | | | | | | | | | | | |
| COOPER, STEPHEN (HM05128) | | | | | | | | | | | | | | ● | | | | | | | | | | |
| CORRIE REIKI HEALING (HM05192) | | | | | | | | | | | | | | | | | | | | | | | | |
| COTTAGE CLINIC (HM05221) | | | | | | | | | | | | | | | | | | | | | | | | |
| EDULJEE, STELLA (HM06638) | | | | | | | ● | | | | | ● | ● | | | ● | | | | | | | | |
| FEET FIRST (HM07179) | | | ● | | ● | | | | | | | | | | | | | | | | ● | | | |
| FYSON, MELANIE (HM07806) | | ● | ● | ● | ● | | | | | | | | ● | | ● | ● | | | ● | | | | ● | ● |
| HANDS ON THERAPY (HM08915) | | | | | | | | | | | | ● | ● | | | | | | | | | | | |
| HELIX HOUSE (HM09522) | | | ● | | | | ● | | | | | | ● | ● | | | | | | | ● | | | |
| HUDSON, EMMA (HM10311) | | | | | | | ● | | | | | | ● | | | | | | | | ● | | | |
| HYPNOTHERAPY CENTRE (HM10516) | | | | | ● | ● | | ● | | ● | | | | ● | | | | | | ● | | | | |
| KIDLINGTON CHIROPRACTIC (HM11594) | | | | | | | ● | | | | | | | | | | | | | | ● | | | |
| KIDLINGTON HERBAL PRACTICE (HM11595) | | ● | ● | ● | ● | ● | | ● | | ● | | | | | | ● | ● | | ● | | | | ● | ● |
| KIDLINGTON OSTEO PRACTICE (HM11596) | | | | | | | ● | | | | | ● | ● | | | | | | | | ● | | | |
| MARRIOTT, HUGH (HM13138) | | | ● | | | | ● | | | | | ● | ● | | | | | | | | | | | |
| MIDSUMMER COTTAGE CLINIC (HM13845) | | ● | ● | ● | ● | ● | ● | | | | | ● | ● | | ● | ● | ● | | ● | | ● | ● | ● | ● |
| O'BRIEN, FRANCES (HM15179) | | | ● | ● | ● | | ● | | | | | ● | ● | | | | | | | | | | | |
| O'DONNELL, ELSPETH (HM15225) | | | | | | | | | | | | ● | ● | | | | | | | | ● | | | |
| OXFORD NUTRITION & ALLRGY CTRE (HM15541) | | | ● | ● | ● | ● | | ● | ● | ● | | ● | | | | ● | ● | ● | ● | ● | | | | ● |
| OXFORD TRANSCENDTL MEDITA CTRE (HM15544) | | | | ● | ● | | | ● | | | | | | ● | | | ● | | | | | ● | | |
| PARSONS STREET CLINIC (HM15747) | | | | | | | ● | | | | | ● | ● | | | | | | | | ● | | | |
| PLESTED, JOHN (HM16368) | | | | | | | | | | | | ● | ● | | | | | | | | | | | |
| POLLOCK, SUSAN (HM16418) | | | | ● | ● | | | | | | | ● | ● | | | | | | | | ● | | | |
| SIDEBOTTOM, MARGARET (HM18527) | | | | | | | ● | | | | | ● | ● | | | | | | | | ● | | | |
| SUMMERTON CLINIC (HM19498) | | ● | ● | ● | ● | | | | ● | | | | | | ● | ● | ● | | | | | | ● | ● |
| TOUCH OF NATURE (HM20188) | | | ● | | | ● | | | | | | | | | | | | ● | | | | | | |
| TWINE, I E (HM20453) | | | ● | ● | ● | ● | ● | ● | ● | ● | | ● | ● | | | | | | ● | | ● | ● | | |
| WANTAGE NATURAL HEALTH CENTRE (HM20891) | ● | ● | ● | ● | ● | ● | ● | ● | ● | ● | | ● | ● | ● | ● | ● | ● | | ● | ● | ● | ● | ● | ● |
| WANTAGE OSTEOPATHIC PRACTICE (HM20892) | | | | | | | ● | | | | | ● | ● | | | | | | | | ● | | | |
| WHEATLEY COMP THERAPY (HM21308) | | | | | | | | | | | | ● | | | | | | | | | | | | |
| WITNEY CHIROPRACTIC/CHIROPODY (HM21750) | | | | | | | ● | | | | | ● | ● | | | | | | | ● | ● | | | |
| WITNEY NATURAL HEALTH CLINIC (HM21751) | ● | ● | ● | ● | ● | ● | ● | ● | ● | ● | | ● | ● | ● | ● | ● | ● | | ● | | ● | | ● | ● |
| SHROPSHIRE | | | | | | | | | | | | | | | | | | | | | | | | |
| ACUMEDIC (HM00218) | | | | ● | ● | ● | | ● | ● | | | ● | | | | ● | | | | | | | | |

| Business by County with Reference no. | Thyroid Problems | Tinnitis | Tiredness | Tonsilitis | Ulcers | Vaginal Problems | Varicose Veins | Verrucas | Vertigo | Viral Infections | Vomiting | Warts | Water Retention | Whiplash | Wind | Worms | Children (Specialist Treatment Categories) | Terminally Ill | Disabled | Horses | Dogs | CatS | Other Animals |
|---|---|---|---|---|---|---|---|---|---|---|---|---|---|---|---|---|---|---|---|---|---|---|---|
| BLISS REMEDIES (HM02508) | | | ● | | | | | | | | ● | | | | | | ● | ● | ● | | | | |
| COOPER, STEPHEN (HM05128) | | | ● | | | | | | | | | | | | | | ● | | ● | | | | |
| CORRIE REIKI HEALING (HM05192) | | | | | | | | | | | | | | | | | ● | ● | ● | ● | ● | ● | ● |
| COTTAGE CLINIC (HM05221) | | | ● | | | | | | | | | | | | | | | ● | | | | | |
| EDULJEE, STELLA (HM06638) | | | ● | | | | | | | | | | | | | | ● | ● | ● | | | | |
| FEET FIRST (HM07179) | ● | | ● | | ● | | | | | | | ● | | | | | ● | ● | ● | | | | |
| FYSON, MELANIE (HM07806) | | | ● | ● | | | | | | ● | ● | | ● | | ● | | ● | | | | | | |
| HANDS ON THERAPY (HM08915) | | | | | | | | | | | | | | | | | ● | ● | ● | | | | |
| HELIX HOUSE (HM09522) | | ● | ● | | | | | | | | | | | | | | ● | | | | | | |
| HUDSON, EMMA (HM10311) | | | | | | | | | | | | | | | | | | | | | | | |
| HYPNOTHERAPY CENTRE (HM10516) | | | | | | | | | | | | | | | | | ● | ● | ● | | ● | ● | ● |
| KIDLINGTON CHIROPRACTIC (HM11594) | | ● | | | | | | | | | | | | | | | ● | ● | | | | | |
| KIDLINGTON HERBAL PRACTICE (HM11595) | ● | ● | ● | ● | ● | | ● | | ● | | ● | ● | ● | | ● | ● | ● | | | | | | |
| KIDLINGTON OSTEO PRACTICE (HM11596) | | ● | | | | | | | | | | | | | | | ● | | | | | | |
| MARRIOTT, HUGH (HM13138) | | | | | | | | | | | | | | | | | ● | ● | ● | | | | |
| MIDSUMMER COTTAGE CLINIC (HM13845) | ● | ● | ● | ● | ● | ● | ● | | ● | ● | ● | ● | ● | | ● | ● | ● | ● | ● | | | | |
| O'BRIEN, FRANCES (HM15179) | | | ● | | | | | | | | | | | | | | ● | ● | ● | | | | |
| O'DONNELL, ELSPETH (HM15225) | | | | | | | | | | | | | | | | | ● | | ● | | | | |
| OXFORD NUTRITION & ALLRGY CTRE (HM15541) | ● | ● | ● | ● | ● | ● | ● | | ● | ● | ● | | ● | | ● | | ● | | ● | | | | |
| OXFORD TRANSCENDTL MEDITA CTRE (HM15544) | | | ● | | | | | | | | | | | | | | ● | ● | ● | | | | |
| PARSONS STREET CLINIC (HM15747) | ● | ● | ● | | | | | | | | | | | | | | | | | | | | |
| PLESTED, JOHN (HM16368) | | | | | | | | | | | | | | | | | ● | ● | ● | | | | |
| POLLOCK, SUSAN (HM16418) | | | | | | | ● | ● | | ● | | ● | ● | | | | ● | ● | ● | | | | |
| SIDEBOTTOM, MARGARET (HM18527) | | | | | | | | | | | | | | | | | ● | ● | ● | | | | |
| SUMMERTON CLINIC (HM19498) | | ● | ● | ● | ● | ● | ● | | | ● | ● | ● | ● | | ● | ● | ● | ● | ● | | | | |
| TOUCH OF NATURE (HM20188) | | | ● | | | | | | | | | | ● | | | | ● | ● | ● | | | | |
| TWINE, I E (HM20453) | | | ● | | ● | | | | | | | ● | ● | | ● | | ● | ● | ● | | | | |
| WANTAGE NATURAL HEALTH CENTRE (HM20891) | ● | ● | ● | ● | ● | ● | ● | | ● | ● | ● | ● | ● | | ● | ● | ● | ● | ● | | | | |
| WANTAGE OSTEOPATHIC PRACTICE (HM20892) | | | | | | | | | | | | | | | | | ● | ● | ● | | | | |
| WHEATLEY COMP THERAPY (HM21308) | | | | | | | | | | | | | ● | | | | ● | ● | ● | | | | |
| WITNEY CHIROPRACTIC/CHIROPODY (HM21750) | | | | | | | | | ● | | | | | | | | ● | ● | ● | | | | |
| WITNEY NATURAL HEALTH CLINIC (HM21751) | ● | ● | ● | ● | ● | ● | ● | | ● | ● | ● | ● | ● | | ● | ● | ● | ● | ● | | | | |
| SHROPSHIRE | | | | | | | | | | | | | | | | | | | | | | | |
| ACUMEDIC (HM00218) | | | | | | | | | | | | | ● | | | | ● | ● | ● | | | | |

# S - W Conditions treated at Practices/Businesses and Specialist Treatment Categories

| Business by County with Reference no. | Sexually Trans. Infections | Shingles | Sinus Problems | Skin Problems | Sleep Disorders | Slimming Help | Slipped Disk | Smoking Help | Sneezing | Snoring | Spinal Injuries | Sports Injuries | Sprains | Stammering | Stings | Stomach Problems | Stomach Ulcers | Stress | Sweating | Teeth Grinding |
|---|---|---|---|---|---|---|---|---|---|---|---|---|---|---|---|---|---|---|---|---|
| AYRES, JOHN (HM01434) | | | | | ● | | | ● | | | | | | | | | | | | |
| BEATTIE, R G (HM01979) | | | | | | | | | | | | | | | | | | | | |
| BODYLIFE CENTRE (HM02622) | | | | | | | | | | | | ● | | | | | | | | |
| BOOTH, ROBERT (HM02709) | | | | | | | ● | | | | | ● | ● | | | | | | | |
| COLERIDGE, JUDY (HM04831) | | | | | ● | | | | | | | ● | ● | | | | | | | ● |
| CORKE, A J (HM05167) | | | | | | ● | | ● | | | | | | | | | | ● | | |
| FULLERTON, N P (HM07792) | | | ● | | | | ● | | | | | ● | ● | | | | | | | |
| HALES OSTEOPATHIC PRACTICE (HM08743) | | | ● | ● | | ● | ● | ● | | ● | | ● | ● | | | ● | ● | | ● | |
| HEALING FOUNDATION (HM09334) | | | ● | | ● | | | | | | | | | | | ● | | | | |
| LUDLOW OSTEOPATHIC CLINIC (HM12727) | | | | | | | ● | | | | | | | | | | | | | |
| MADDOCKS CLINIC (HM12898) | | | | | | | | | | | | | | | | | | | | |
| MEDAYD PHYSIOTHERAPY (HM13644) | | | | | | | ● | | | | | ● | ● | | | | | | | |
| MEDAYD PHYSIOTHERAPY (HM13645) | | | | | | | ● | | | | | ● | ● | | | | | | | |
| NEEDHAM, LYNDA M (HM14751) | | | | | ● | ● | | ● | | | | ● | | ● | | | | | | |
| OSTEOPATHIC (HM15449) | | | ● | | ● | | ● | | | | | ● | ● | | | ● | ● | | | |
| OSTLE, SAMANTHA (HM15480) | | | | | | | | | | | | ● | | | | | | | | |
| PEARSON, CHRISTINE (HM15911) | ● | ● | ● | ● | ● | ● | ● | ● | ● | ● | | ● | ● | ● | ● | ● | ● | | ● | ● |
| PHILLIPS, ANN (HM16124) | | | ● | ● | ● | | | | | | | ● | | | | | | ● | | |
| PREES COMPLEMENTARY THERAPIES (HM16533) | | | | | ● | ● | | ● | | | | | | | | | | ● | | |
| REYNOLDS, TESS (HM17216) | | ● | ● | | ● | | | | | | | | | | | ● | ● | | ● | |
| SHREWSBURY SOLE CARE (HM18507) | | | | | | | | | | | | | | | | | | ● | | |
| STONE, JANET (HM19336) | ● | ● | ● | ● | ● | ● | ● | ● | ● | ● | | ● | ● | ● | ● | ● | ● | | ● | ● |
| TAN & BEAUTY STUDIO (HM19676) | | | ● | ● | ● | | | | | | | | | | | ● | | | | |
| WALMSLEY, RUTH (HM20848) | | | ● | | ● | | | | | | | | ● | | | ● | | ● | ● | ● |
| WESTON, JOHN (HM21279) | | | | | | | ● | | | | | ● | ● | | | | | | | |
| WHITELEY, STEVEN (HM21400) | ● | ● | ● | ● | ● | ● | ● | ● | ● | ● | | ● | ● | ● | ● | ● | ● | ● | ● | ● |
| WILD ROSE (HM21488) | | | | | ● | | ● | ● | ● | ● | | ● | ● | | | ● | | | | |
| WILSON, AMANDA (HM21644) | | | | | | | | | | | | ● | | | | | | | | |
| SOMERSET | | | | | | | | | | | | | | | | | | | | |
| ABBEY CHIROPODY SERVICES (HM00074) | | | | | | | | | | | | | | | | | | | | |
| ALASKAN BACH FLOWER REMEDIES (HM00472) | | | | ● | ● | | | | | | | ● | ● | | | | | | | |
| ANDERSON, DAVID (HM00816) | | | | | | | | | | | | | | | | | | | | |
| ANSON, BARRIE (HM00916) | | ● | ● | ● | ● | ● | | ● | ● | | | | ● | ● | ● | ● | ● | | ● | ● |
| AUSSENS, MIEKE (HM01359) | | | | | | | | | | | | ● | | | | | | ● | | |

| Business by County with Reference no. | Tennis Elbow | Terminal Illness | Throat Problems | Thrush | Thyroid Problems | Tinnitis | Tiredness | Tonsilitis | Ulcers | Vaginal Problems | Varicose Veins | Verrucas | Vertigo | Viral Infections | Vomiting | Warts | Water Retention | Whiplash | Wind | Worms |
|---|---|---|---|---|---|---|---|---|---|---|---|---|---|---|---|---|---|---|---|---|
| AYRES, JOHN (HM01434) | | ● | | | | | | | | | | | | | | | | | | |
| BEATTIE, R G (HM01979) | | | | | | | | | | | | ● | | | | | | | | |
| BODYLIFE CENTRE (HM02622) | | | | | | | ● | | | | | | | | | | | | | |
| BOOTH, ROBERT (HM02709) | ● | | | | | | | | | | | | | | | | | | | |
| COLERIDGE, JUDY (HM04831) | | | | | | | ● | | | | | | | | | | ● | | | |
| CORKE, A J (HM05167) | | | | | | | | | | | | | | | | | | | | |
| FULLERTON, N P (HM07792) | ● | | | | | | | | | | | | | | | | | | | |
| HALES OSTEOPATHIC PRACTICE (HM08743) | ● | | ● | ● | ● | ● | ● | | ● | | | | ● | | ● | | ● | | ● | ● |
| HEALING FOUNDATION (HM09334) | | | | | | | ● | | | | | | | | | | | | | |
| LUDLOW OSTEOPATHIC CLINIC (HM12727) | ● | | | | | | | | | | | | ● | | | | | | | |
| MADDOCKS CLINIC (HM12898) | | | | | | | | | | | | | | | | | | | | |
| MEDAYD PHYSIOTHERAPY (HM13644) | ● | | | | | | | | | | | | | | | | | | | |
| MEDAYD PHYSIOTHERAPY (HM13645) | ● | | | | | | | | | | | | | | | | | | | |
| NEEDHAM, LYNDA M (HM14751) | ● | | | | | ● | ● | | | | | | | | | | | | | |
| OSTEOPATHIC (HM15449) | ● | | | | | ● | ● | | | | ● | | ● | | | | | | | |
| OSTLE, SAMANTHA (HM15480) | | | | | | | ● | | | | | | | | | | | | | |
| PEARSON, CHRISTINE (HM15911) | ● | ● | ● | ● | ● | ● | ● | ● | ● | ● | ● | | ● | ● | ● | ● | ● | | ● | ● |
| PHILLIPS, ANN (HM16124) | | | | | | | ● | | | | | | | | | | | | | |
| PREES COMPLEMENTARY THERAPIES (HM16533) | | | | | | | | | | | | | | | | | | | | |
| REYNOLDS, TESS (HM17216) | ● | | ● | | | ● | ● | | | | | | ● | | ● | | | | | |
| SHREWSBURY SOLE CARE (HM18507) | | | | | | | | | | | | | | | | | | | | |
| STONE, JANET (HM19336) | ● | ● | ● | ● | ● | ● | ● | ● | ● | ● | ● | | ● | ● | ● | ● | ● | | ● | ● |
| TAN & BEAUTY STUDIO (HM19676) | | | | | | | ● | | | | | | | | | | | | | |
| WALMSLEY, RUTH (HM20848) | ● | ● | | | | | ● | | | | ● | | | | | | ● | | | |
| WESTON, JOHN (HM21279) | ● | | | | | | | | | | | | | | | | | | | |
| WHITELEY, STEVEN (HM21400) | ● | ● | ● | ● | ● | ● | ● | ● | ● | ● | ● | | ● | ● | ● | ● | ● | | ● | ● |
| WILD ROSE (HM21488) | ● | | | | | | ● | | | | | | | | | | | | | |
| WILSON, AMANDA (HM21644) | | | | | | | | | | | | ● | | | | | | | | |
| SOMERSET | | | | | | | | | | | | | | | | | | | | |
| ABBEY CHIROPODY SERVICES (HM00074) | | | | | | | | | | | | | | | | ● | | | | |
| ALASKAN BACH FLOWER REMEDIES (HM00472) | | | | | | | | | | | | | | | | | | | | |
| ANDERSON, DAVID (HM00816) | | | | | | | | | | | | ● | | | | ● | | | | |
| ANSON, BARRIE (HM00916) | ● | ● | ● | ● | ● | ● | ● | ● | ● | ● | ● | | ● | ● | ● | ● | ● | | ● | |
| AUSSENS, MIEKE (HM01359) | ● | | | | | | ● | | | | | | | | | | | ● | | |

| Business by County with Reference no. | Specialist Treatment Categories: Children | Terminally Ill | Disabled | Horses | Dogs | CatS | Other Animals |
|---|---|---|---|---|---|---|---|
| AYRES, JOHN (HM01434) | ● | ● | | | | | |
| BEATTIE, R G (HM01979) | ● | ● | ● | | | | |
| BODYLIFE CENTRE (HM02622) | | | | | | | |
| BOOTH, ROBERT (HM02709) | ● | ● | ● | | | | |
| COLERIDGE, JUDY (HM04831) | | ● | ● | | | | |
| CORKE, A J (HM05167) | | | | | | | |
| FULLERTON, N P (HM07792) | ● | ● | ● | | | | |
| HALES OSTEOPATHIC PRACTICE (HM08743) | ● | | ● | | | | |
| HEALING FOUNDATION (HM09334) | ● | ● | ● | | | | |
| LUDLOW OSTEOPATHIC CLINIC (HM12727) | ● | | | | | | |
| MADDOCKS CLINIC (HM12898) | ● | ● | ● | | | | |
| MEDAYD PHYSIOTHERAPY (HM13644) | ● | ● | ● | | | | |
| MEDAYD PHYSIOTHERAPY (HM13645) | ● | ● | ● | | | | |
| NEEDHAM, LYNDA M (HM14751) | | ● | ● | | | | |
| OSTEOPATHIC (HM15449) | ● | | | | ● | ● | |
| OSTLE, SAMANTHA (HM15480) | ● | | | ● | ● | ● | |
| PEARSON, CHRISTINE (HM15911) | ● | ● | ● | | | | |
| PHILLIPS, ANN (HM16124) | ● | ● | ● | | | | |
| PREES COMPLEMENTARY THERAPIES (HM16533) | ● | ● | ● | | | | |
| REYNOLDS, TESS (HM17216) | ● | ● | ● | | | | |
| SHREWSBURY SOLE CARE (HM18507) | ● | ● | ● | | | | |
| STONE, JANET (HM19336) | ● | ● | ● | | | | |
| TAN & BEAUTY STUDIO (HM19676) | | ● | ● | | | | |
| WALMSLEY, RUTH (HM20848) | | ● | | | | | |
| WESTON, JOHN (HM21279) | ● | | ● | | | | |
| WHITELEY, STEVEN (HM21400) | ● | ● | ● | | | | |
| WILD ROSE (HM21488) | ● | ● | ● | | | | |
| WILSON, AMANDA (HM21644) | ● | ● | ● | | | | |
| SOMERSET | | | | | | | |
| ABBEY CHIROPODY SERVICES (HM00074) | ● | ● | ● | | | | |
| ALASKAN BACH FLOWER REMEDIES (HM00472) | ● | | ● | | | | |
| ANDERSON, DAVID (HM00816) | ● | ● | ● | | | | |
| ANSON, BARRIE (HM00916) | ● | ● | ● | | | | |
| AUSSENS, MIEKE (HM01359) | ● | ● | ● | | | | |

# S - W Conditions treated at Practices/Businesses and Specialist Treatment Categories

| Business by County with Reference no. | Sexually Trans. Infections | Shingles | Sinus Problems | Skin Problems | Sleep Disorders | Slimming Help | Slipped Disk | Smoking Help | Sneezing | Snoring | Spinal Injuries | Sports Injuries | Sprains | Stammering | Stings | Stomach Problems | Stomach Ulcers | Stress | Sweating | Teeth Grinding | Tennis Elbow | Terminal Illness | Throat Problems | Thrush | Thyroid Problems | Tinnitis | Tiredness | Tonsilitis | Ulcers | Vaginal Problems | Varicose Veins | Verrucas | Vertigo | Viral Infections | Vomiting | Warts | Water Retention | Whiplash | Wind | Worms | Specialist Treatment Categories: Children | Terminally Ill | Disabled | Horses | Dogs | CatS | Other Animals |
|---|---|---|---|---|---|---|---|---|---|---|---|---|---|---|---|---|---|---|---|---|---|---|---|---|---|---|---|---|---|---|---|---|---|---|---|---|---|---|---|---|---|---|---|---|---|---|---|
| AVENUE CLINIC (HM01388) | ● | ● | ● | ● | ● | ● | ● | ● | ● | ● | ● | ● | ● | ● | ● | ● | ● | ● | ● | ● | ● | ● | ● | ● | ● | ● | ● | ● | ● | ● | ● | ● | ● | ● | ● | ● | ● | ● | ● | ● | ● | ● | ● | | | | |
| BAILEY, LINDA R (HM01552) | | | ● | | | ● | | | ● | ● | | | | | | | | | | | | | | ● | | | | | | ● | | | | | | | ● | | | | ● | ● | ● | | | | |
| BATH ALEXANDER TECHNIQUE (HM01890) | | | | | ● | | | | | | | ● | | | | | | | | | | | | | | | | | | | | | ● | | | | | ● | | | | | ● | | | | |
| BATH NATURAL MEDICAL CENTRE (HM01893) | | | | ● | | | | | | | | | | | | | | ● | | | | | | | | | | | | | | | | | | | | | | | ● | ● | ● | | | | |
| BATHPOOL CHIROPRACTIC CLINIC (HM01900) | | | | | | | | | | | | ● | | | | | | | | | ● | | | | | | ● | | | | | | | | | | | | | | ● | | ● | | | | |
| BEECH HOUSE CLINIC (HM02046) | | | | | | | ● | | | | ● | ● | ● | | | | | | | | ● | | | | | | | | | | | | | | | | | ● | | | ● | ● | ● | | | | |
| BOULEVARD PHARMACY (HM02739) | | ● | ● | ● | ● | ● | ● | ● | ● | ● | | ● | ● | | ● | ● | ● | | ● | ● | ● | ● | ● | ● | ● | ● | ● | ● | ● | | ● | | ● | ● | ● | ● | ● | | ● | ● | ● | ● | ● | ● | ● | ● | ● |
| BRIDGET HEALING CENTRE (HM03008) | ● | ● | ● | ● | ● | ● | ● | ● | ● | ● | | ● | ● | ● | ● | ● | ● | | ● | ● | ● | ● | ● | ● | ● | ● | ● | ● | ● | ● | ● | | ● | ● | ● | ● | ● | | ● | ● | | | | | | | |
| CANDY, TIM (HM03624) | | | | | | | | | | | | | | | | | | | | | | | | | | | | | | | | | | | | | | | | | | | | ● | ● | ● | ● |
| CASTLE SURGERY (HM03840) | | | | | | | ● | | | | ● | ● | ● | | | | | | | | ● | | | | | | | | | | | | | | | | | ● | | | ● | ● | ● | | | | |
| CHAMELEON OILS (HM03961) | | | | ● | ● | | | | | | | | | | | | | | | | | | | | | | | | | | | | | ● | | | | | | | ● | ● | ● | | | | |
| CHEDDAR COMP MEDICINE CTRE (HM04075) | | | ● | ● | ● | | ● | | | | | ● | ● | | | | | ● | | | ● | | | | | | ● | | | | | | | | | | | | | | | | | | | | |
| CHINESE MEDICAL CENTRE (HM04238) | | | | ● | ● | ● | | ● | ● | | | ● | | | | ● | | | | | | | | | | | | | | | | | | | | | ● | | | | ● | ● | ● | | | | |
| CHIPPER, MARY (HM04278) | | | ● | | | | | | | | | | | | | | | ● | | | | | | | | | | | | | | | | | | | ● | | | | ● | ● | ● | | | | |
| CHIROPODY SURGERY (HM04344) | | | | | | | | | | | | | | | | | | | | | | | | | | | | | | | | ● | | | | | | | | | ● | ● | ● | | | | |
| CLARKE GAIL & RAWLINSON MIKE (HM04581) | | | | | | | | | | | | | | | | | | | | | | | | | | | | | | | | | | | | | | | | | ● | | | | | | |
| CLINIC OF COMP MEDICINE (HM04689) | | ● | ● | ● | ● | | ● | | ● | | | ● | ● | | ● | ● | ● | | ● | ● | ● | | ● | ● | ● | | ● | ● | ● | ● | ● | | ● | ● | ● | ● | ● | | ● | ● | ● | | ● | | | | |
| CLISBY, JANE (HM04722) | | | ● | | | | | | | | | | | | | ● | | | | | | | ● | | | | | ● | | | | | | | ● | | | | | | ● | ● | ● | | | | |
| COMPLEMENTARY THERAPY (HM04942) | | | | | | | | | | | | | | | | | | | | | | | | | | | ● | | | | | | | | | | | | | | ● | | | | | | |
| COOK, COLIN (HM05041) | | ● | ● | | | | ● | | | | | ● | ● | | | | | | | | ● | | | | | ● | | | | | | | | | | | | | | | ● | | ● | | | | |
| COUNSULTING ROOMS (HM05253) | | | | ● | ● | | | ● | | | | | | ● | | | | | | ● | | | | | | ● | | | | | | | | | | | | | | | | ● | ● | | | | |
| DAVIES, SALLY (HM05840) | | | | | | | | | | | | | | | | | | ● | | | | | | | | | | | | | | | | | | | | | | | | | | | | | |
| DEVONSHIRE SURGERY (HM06044) | | | | | | | ● | | | | ● | ● | ● | | | | | | | | ● | | | | | | | | | | | | | | | | | ● | | | ● | ● | ● | | | | |
| EUROPEAN COLLEGE-BOWEN STUDIES (HM06946) | | ● | ● | | ● | | ● | | | | | ● | ● | | | | | | ● | | ● | | | | | ● | | | | | | | ● | | | | ● | | | | ● | ● | ● | ● | | | |
| FRANCES-WHITAKER, J A (HM07665) | | | | | | | | | | | | ● | ● | | | | | | | | | | | | | | | | | | | | | | | ● | | | | | ● | ● | ● | | | | |
| GLASTONBURY CHIROPRACTIC (HM08131) | | | | | | | ● | | | | ● | ● | ● | | | | | | | | ● | | | | | | | | | | | | | | | | | ● | | | ● | ● | ● | | | | |
| GLASTONBURY EAST WEST CENTRE (HM08132) | ● | ● | ● | ● | ● | ● | ● | ● | ● | ● | | ● | ● | ● | ● | ● | ● | | ● | ● | ● | | ● | ● | ● | ● | ● | ● | ● | ● | ● | | ● | ● | ● | ● | ● | | ● | ● | ● | | | | | | |
| HELEN SMITH CHIROPODIST (HM09515) | | | | | | | | | | | | | | | | | | | | | | | | | | | | | | | | | | | | | | | | | ● | ● | ● | | | | |
| HOLISTIC HEALING CENTRE (HM09962) | | | ● | ● | ● | | | | | | | | | | | ● | | | | | | | | | | | ● | | | | | | | | | | | | | | ● | ● | ● | | | | |
| HUDSON, JOHN (HM10315) | | | | | | | | ● | | | | | | | | | | | | | | | | | | | | | | | | | | | | | | | | | ● | ● | ● | | | | |
| HUXTABLE, ALISON (HM10461) | | | | | | | ● | | | | | ● | ● | | | | | | | | ● | | | | | | | | | | | | | | | | | ● | | | ● | | ● | | | | |
| HYPNOTHERAPY IN HUTTON (HM10540) | | | | | | | | | | | | | | | | | | | | | | | | | | | | | | | | | | | | | | | | | ● | ● | | | | | |
| JONES, BECKY (HM11125) | | | | ● | ● | ● | | ● | ● | ● | | | | ● | | | | | | ● | | ● | | | | | ● | | | | | | | | | | | | | | ● | ● | ● | | | | |
| JONES, RAYMOND (HM11190) | | | | | | | | | | | | ● | ● | | | | | | | | | | | | | | | | | | | | | | | | | | | | ● | ● | ● | | | | |

# S - W Conditions treated at Practices/Businesses and Specialist Treatment Categories

| Business by County with Reference no. | Sexually Trans. Infections | Shingles | Sinus Problems | Skin Problems | Sleep Disorders | Slimming Help | Slipped Disk | Smoking Help | Sneezing | Snoring | Spinal Injuries | Sports Injuries | Sprains | Stammering | Stings | Stomach Problems | Stomach Ulcers | Stress | Sweating | Teeth Grinding | Tennis Elbow | Terminal Illness | Throat Problems | Thrush | Thyroid Problems | Tinnitis | Tiredness | Tonsilitis | Ulcers | Vaginal Problems | Varicose Veins | Verrucas | Vertigo | Viral Infections | Vomiting | Warts | Water Retention | Whiplash | Wind | Worms | Specialist Treatment Categories: Children | Terminally Ill | Disabled | Horses | Dogs | CatS | Other Animals |
|---|---|---|---|---|---|---|---|---|---|---|---|---|---|---|---|---|---|---|---|---|---|---|---|---|---|---|---|---|---|---|---|---|---|---|---|---|---|---|---|---|---|---|---|---|---|---|---|
| KIRKMEAD CENTRE (HM11718) | | | | | | | | | | | | | | | | | |●| | | | | | | | | | | | | | | | | | | | | | |●|●|●| | | | |
| LANSDOWN PHYSIOTHERAPY CLINIC (HM11964) | | | | | | |●| | | | |●|●| | | | | | | |●| | | | | | | | | | | |●| | | | | | | | | | | | | | |
| LEAVEY, J () | | | | | | | | | | | | | | | | | |●| | | | | | | | | | | | | | | | | | | | | | |●|●|●| | | | |
| LOGAN, DAVID (HM12566) | | | | | |●| |●| | | | | | | | | |●| | | | | | | | | | | | | | | | | | | | | | |●|●| | | | | |
| MARY WILKINSON - MCTIMONEY (HM13226) | | |●| | | |●| | | | |●| | | | | | | | |●| | | | | | | | | | | | | | | | | | | |●| |●|●|●|●|●|
| MARY WILKINSON - MCTIMONEY (HM13225) | | |●| | | |●| | | | |●| | | | | | | | |●| | | | | | | | | | | | | | | | | | | | | | | | | | |
| MIDSOMER NORTON CHIROPRACTIC (HM13844) | | | | | | | | | | | | | | | |●|●| | | | | | | | | | | | | | | | | | | | | | | |●|●|●| | | | |
| MILSOM STREET CLINIC (HM13944) | | | | | | |●| | | |●|●|●| | | | | | | |●| | | | | | | | | | | | | | | | |●| | |●|●|●| | | | |
| NATURAL SPIRITUAL HEALING (HM14626) | | | | |●| | | | | | | | | | | | | | | | |●| | | | | | | | | | | | | | | | | | |●|●|●|●|●|●|●|
| NATURAL THERAPIES (HM14632) | | |●| |●| | | | | | | | | | | | | | | | | | | | | |●| | | | | | | | | | | | | |●|●| | | | | |
| NORSO BIOMAGNETICS UK (HM15016) | | | | |●| | | | | | | |●| | | | | | | |●| | | | | |●| | | | | | | | | | | | | |●|●|●|●|●|●|●|
| NUTRITION FOR LIFE (HM15123) | | |●|●|●|●| | | |●| | |●| | |●| | |●| | | |●| | |●|●| |●| | | |●|●|●| |●| |●| |●|●|●|●|●|●| |
| ORCHARD CLINIC (HM15360) | | | | | | |●| | | |●|●|●| | | | | | | | | | | | | |●| | | | | | | | | |●|●| | |●|●|●| | | | |
| PARK HOUSE CLINIC (HM15666) | | | | | | |●| | | | |●|●| | | | | | | |●| | | | | | | | | | | | | | | | | | | |●|●|●| | | | |
| PARNELL, R H (HM15727) | | |●| | | | | | | | | | | | | | | | | | | | | | | |●| | | | | | | | | | | | | |●|●|●| | | | |
| PARRY, J M (HM15738) | | | | | | | | | | | | | | | | | | | | | | | | | | | | | | | |●| | | | | | | | |●|●|●| | | | |
| PENNINGTON, PAM (HM15990) | | | | | | | | | | | | | | | | | | | | | | | | | | | | | | | | | | | |●| | | | |●|●|●| | | | |
| PERKINS, L (HM16026) | | | | | | | | | | | | | | | | | | | | | | | | | | | | | | | |●| | | | | | | | |●|●|●| | | | |
| PITT, I T (HM16347) | | |●| | | | | | | | |●|●| | | | | | | |●| | | | | | | | | | | | | | | | | | | |●| |●| | | | |
| PRESSURE WORKS (HM16544) | | | | | | | | | | | |●|●| | | | | | | |●| | | | | | | | | | | | | | | | | | | |●|●|●| | | | |
| REED, W A (HM17046) | | | | | | | | | | | |●| | | | | |●| | | | | | | | | | | | | | | | | | | | | | |●|●|●| | | | |
| RICHARDS, M J (HM17261) | | | | | | | | | | | | | | | | | | | | | | | | | | | | | | | | | | | |●| | | | |●|●|●| | | | |
| SHAMBHALA (HM18275) | | | | |●| |●|●| | | |●|●| | |●| | | | |●| | | | | |●| | | | | | |●| | |●| | |●| | | | | | | |
| SNOWDON, JANET (HM18843) |●|●|●|●|●|●|●|●|●|●| |●|●|●|●|●|●| |●|●|●|●|●|●|●|●|●|●|●|●|●| |●|●|●|●|●| |●|●|●|●|●| | | | |
| ST JAMES'S SURGERY (HM19079) | | | | | | |●| | | | |●|●| | | | | | | |●| | | | | | | | | | | | | | | | | | | |●| | | | | | |
| ST MICHAELS CHIROPRACTIC (HM19089) | | | | | | | | | | | |●|●| | | | | | | | | | | | | | | | | | | | | | | | | | | |●|●|●| | | | |
| ST MICHAEL'S HYPNOTHERAPY (HM19090) | | | | |●|●| |●| | | | | | | | | |●| | | |●| | | | |●| | | | | | | | | | | | | |●|●| | | | | |
| STANLEY COURT SURGERY (HM19127) | | | | | | |●| | | |●|●|●| | | | | | | |●| | | | | | | | | | | | | | | | |●| | | | | | | | | |
| STREET CHIROPRACTIC CLINIC (HM19383) | | | | | | |●| | | | |●|●| | | | | | | |●| | | | |●| | | | | | |●| | | | | | | |●| | | | | | |
| STREET CHIROPRACTIC CLINIC (HM19382) | | | | | | |●| | | |●|●|●| | | | | | | |●| | | | | | | | | | | | | | |●| |●| | | | | | | | | |
| STRESS CLINIC & NTRL HLTH CTRE (HM19389) | | |●|●|●|●|●|●|●|●| |●|●|●| |●|●| |●|●|●|●|●|●|●|●|●| |●|●|●| |●| |●| |●| |●|●|●|●|●| | | | |
| TARETH CENTRE (HM19704) |●|●|●|●|●|●|●|●|●|●| |●|●|●|●|●|●| |●|●|●|●|●|●|●|●|●|●|●|●|●| |●|●|●|●|●| |●|●|●|●|●| | | | |
| TAUNTON FOOT SURGERY (HM19722) | | | | | | | | | | | | | | | | | | | | | | | | | | | | | | | | | | | | | | | | |●|●|●| | | | |
| TAYLOR, GILLIAN (HM19760) | | | | | | | | | | | | | | | | | | | | | | | | | | | | | | | | | | | |●| | | | |●|●|●| | | | |

# S - W Conditions treated at Practices/Businesses and Specialist Treatment Categories

| Business by County with Reference no. | Sexually Trans. Infections | Shingles | Sinus Problems | Skin Problems | Sleep Disorders | Slimming Help | Slipped Disk | Smoking Help | Sneezing | Snoring | Spinal Injuries | Sports Injuries | Sprains | Stammering | Stings | Stomach Problems | Stomach Ulcers | Stress | Sweating | Teeth Grinding | Tennis Elbow | Terminal Illness | Throat Problems | Thrush | Thyroid Problems | Tinnitis | Tiredness | Tonsilitis | Ulcers | Vaginal Problems | Varicose Veins | Verrucas | Vertigo | Viral Infections | Vomiting | Warts | Water Retention | Whiplash | Wind | Worms | Specialist Treatment Categories: Children | Terminally Ill | Disabled | Horses | Dogs | CatS | Other Animals |
|---|---|---|---|---|---|---|---|---|---|---|---|---|---|---|---|---|---|---|---|---|---|---|---|---|---|---|---|---|---|---|---|---|---|---|---|---|---|---|---|---|---|---|---|---|---|---|
| TERRACE THRPY PSYCHO/NTRL HLTH (HM19843) | | | | | | | | | | | | | | | | | | | | | | | | | | | | | | | | | | | | | | | | | ● | ● | ● | | | | |
| THOMPSON, G W (DR) (HM19978) | | | | | | | ● | | | | ● | ● | ● | | | | | | | | | | | | | | | | | | | | | | | | | ● | | | ● | | ● | | | | |
| TURNPIKE SURGERY (HM20441) | | | | | | | ● | | | | ● | ● | ● | | | | | | | | ● | | | | | | | | | | | | | | | | | ● | | | ● | ● | ● | | | | |
| WELLSPRING OSTEO/NTRL HEALTH (HM21181) | | | ● | ● | ● | | ● | ● | | | | ● | ● | | | ● | | | ● | ● | ● | ● | ● | | ● | | ● | | | | | | ● | | | | | | | | ● | ● | ● | | | | |
| WESTERN CHIROPRACTIC CLINIC (HM21263) | | ● | ● | | | | ● | | | ● | ● | ● | ● | | | ● | | | | ● | ● | | | | | ● | ● | ● | | | | | ● | | | | | ● | | | ● | ● | ● | | | | |
| WILKINSON, MARY (HM21511) | | | ● | | | | ● | | | | | ● | | | | | | | | | ● | | | | | | | | | | | | | | | | | | | | | | | | | | |
| WINCANTON CHIROPRACTIC CLINIC (HM21690) | | | | | | | ● | | | | ● | ● | ● | | | | | | | | ● | | | | | | | | | | | | | | | | | ● | | | ● | | ● | | | | |
| YELLOW EMPEROR CORP (HM22004) | | | | | | | | ● | | | | ● | | | | ● | | | | | | | | | | | ● | | | | | | | | | | | | | | ● | | ● | | | | |
| YEOVIL CHIROPRACTIC CLINIC (HM22008) | | | | | | | | | | | | ● | ● | | | | | | | | | | | | | | | | | | | | | | | | | | | | ● | ● | ● | | | | |
| **STAFFORDSHIRE** | | | | | | | | | | | | | | | | | | | | | | | | | | | | | | | | | | | | | | | | | | | | | | | |
| ALTERNATIVE THERAPY CENTRE (HM00735) | | ● | ● | ● | ● | ● | ● | ● | ● | ● | | ● | ● | ● | ● | ● | ● | | ● | ● | ● | ● | ● | ● | ● | ● | ● | ● | ● | | ● | | ● | | ● | | ● | | ● | | ● | ● | ● | | | | |
| ALTERNATIVES (HM00741) | ● | ● | ● | ● | ● | ● | ● | ● | ● | ● | | ● | ● | ● | ● | ● | ● | | ● | ● | ● | ● | ● | ● | ● | ● | ● | ● | ● | ● | ● | | ● | ● | ● | ● | ● | | ● | ● | ● | ● | ● | | | | |
| ANDERSON, G (HM00818) | | | | | | ● | | ● | | | | | | | | | | | | | | | | | | | | | | | | | | | | | | | | | ● | ● | ● | | | | |
| BARCROFT, J M (HM01696) | | | | | | | | | | | | ● | ● | | | | | | | | | | | | | | | | | | | ● | | | | | | | | | ● | ● | ● | | | | |
| BASFORD CHIROPRACTIC CLINIC (HM01842) | | | | | | | ● | | | | ● | ● | ● | | | | | | | | ● | | | | | | | | | | | | | | | | | ● | | | ● | ● | ● | | | | |
| BLANK, CHRISTOPHER (HM02499) | | | | | | | | | | | | | | | | | | | | | | | | | | | | | | | | ● | | | | | | | | | ● | ● | ● | | | | |
| BONNEBAIGT, ANDRE (HM02682) | | | | | | ● | | ● | | | | | | | | | | | | | | | | | | | | | | | | | | | | | | | | | ● | ● | ● | | | | |
| BORE ST POD & CHIROP PRACTICE (HM02716) | | | | | | | | | | | | ● | | | | | | | | | | | | | | | | | | | | | | | | ● | | | | | ● | | ● | | | | |
| BRADBURY, SHARON (HM02842) | | | | | | | ● | | | | | ● | ● | | | | | | | | ● | | | | | | | | | | | | | | | | | | | | | | | | | | |
| BRAMPTON TREES CLINIC (HM02908) | | | | | | | ● | | | | | ● | ● | | | | | | | | ● | | | | | | | | | | | | | | | | | | | | ● | ● | ● | | | | |
| BRIDGETT, A (HM03011) | | | | | | | ● | | | | | ● | ● | | | | | | | | ● | | | | | | | | | | | | | | | | | | | | ● | ● | | | | | |
| BURKE, E (HM03385) | | | | | ● | ● | | ● | | | | | | | | | | | | | | | | | | | ● | | | | | | | | | | | | | | | | | | | | |
| CASTLEFIELDS SURGERY (HM03846) | | | | | | | | | | | | ● | | | | | | | | | ● | | | | | | | | | | | | | | | | | | | | ● | ● | ● | | | | |
| CHASE HEALTH FOODS (HM04055) | ● | ● | ● | ● | ● | ● | ● | ● | ● | ● | | ● | ● | ● | ● | ● | ● | | ● | ● | ● | ● | ● | ● | ● | ● | ● | ● | ● | ● | ● | | ● | ● | ● | ● | ● | | ● | | | | | | | | |
| CHASE NATURAL THERAPY CENTRE (HM04059) | ● | ● | ● | ● | ● | ● | ● | ● | ● | ● | | ● | ● | ● | ● | ● | ● | ● | ● | ● | ● | ● | ● | ● | ● | ● | ● | ● | ● | ● | ● | | ● | ● | ● | ● | ● | | ● | ● | ● | ● | ● | | | | |
| CITY CHIROPRACTIC CLINIC (HM04492) | | | | | | | ● | | | | ● | ● | ● | | | | | | | | ● | | | | | | ● | | | | | | | | | | | ● | | | ● | ● | ● | | | | |
| CORNERSTONES PRACTICE (HM05182) | ● | ● | ● | ● | ● | ● | ● | ● | ● | ● | | ● | ● | ● | ● | ● | ● | | ● | ● | ● | ● | ● | ● | ● | ● | ● | ● | ● | ● | ● | | ● | ● | ● | ● | ● | | ● | ● | | | | | | | |
| CRESCENT CLINIC (HM05417) | ● | ● | ● | ● | ● | ● | ● | ● | ● | ● | | ● | ● | ● | ● | ● | ● | | ● | ● | ● | ● | ● | ● | ● | ● | ● | ● | ● | ● | ● | | ● | ● | ● | ● | ● | | ● | ● | ● | ● | ● | | | | |
| CRESCENT CLINIC FOR COMP MED (HM05418) | | | ● | ● | | | ● | | | | | ● | ● | | | | | | | | ● | | | | | | ● | | | | | | | | | | | | | | ● | ● | ● | | | | |
| EDWARDS, ALLYN (HM06641) | | | ● | | ● | | ● | | | | | ● | ● | | | | | | ● | | ● | | | | | ● | ● | | | | | | ● | | | | | | ● | | ● | | ● | | | | |
| ESSENTIAL HEALTH (HM06911) | | | | | | | | | | | | | | | | | | | | | | | | | | | | | | | | | | | | | | | | | ● | ● | ● | | | | |
| EVANS, RICHARD (HM06989) | | ● | ● | ● | ● | | | | | | | ● | ● | | | ● | ● | | ● | ● | ● | ● | ● | ● | ● | ● | ● | | | | ● | | ● | ● | ● | | ● | | ● | | ● | ● | ● | | | | |
| FEET FIRST (HM07176) | | | | | | | | | | | | | | | | | | | | | | | | | | | | | | | | ● | | | | | | | | | ● | ● | ● | | | | |
| FOOT SOUL & BODYWORKS (HM07487) | | | ● | | ● | | | | | | | | | | | ● | | | | | ● | | | | | | ● | | | | | | | | | | | | ● | | ● | ● | ● | | ● | ● | ● |

# S - W Conditions treated at Practices/Businesses and Specialist Treatment Categories

| Business by County with Reference no. | Sexually Trans. Infections | Shingles | Sinus Problems | Skin Problems | Sleep Disorders | Slimming Help | Slipped Disk | Smoking Help | Sneezing | Snoring | Spinal Injuries | Sports Injuries | Sprains | Stammering | Stings | Stomach Problems | Stomach Ulcers | Stress | Sweating | Teeth Grinding | Tennis Elbow | Terminal Illness | Throat Problems | Thrush | Thyroid Problems | Tinnitis | Tiredness | Tonsilitis | Ulcers | Vaginal Problems | Varicose Veins | Verrucas | Vertigo | Viral Infections | Vomiting | Warts | Water Retention | Whiplash | Wind | Worms | Specialist Treatment Categories: Children | Terminally Ill | Disabled | Horses | Dogs | CatS | Other Animals |
|---|---|---|---|---|---|---|---|---|---|---|---|---|---|---|---|---|---|---|---|---|---|---|---|---|---|---|---|---|---|---|---|---|---|---|---|---|---|---|---|---|---|---|---|---|---|---|
| FORTEY, C J (HM07579) | | | | | | | | | | | | ● | | | | | | | | | | | | | | | | | | | | | | | | | | | | | ● | | | | | | |
| GASCOIGNE, DOROTHY (HM07917) | | | | | | | | | | | | | | | | | | | | | | | | | | | | | | | | | | | | | | | | | ● | ● | ● | | | | |
| GASCOYNE, P (HM07920) | | | | | | | ● | | | | | ● | ● | | | | | | | | | | | | | | | | | | | ● | | | | | | | | | ● | ● | ● | | | | |
| HALLARD, SHARON (HM08800) | | | | | ● | ● | | ● | | | | | | | | | | | | | | | | | | | | | | | | | | | | | | | | | | | | | | | |
| IBBS, ROGER (HM10566) | | | | | | | | | | | | | | | | | | | | | | | | | | | | | | | | ● | | | | | | | | | ● | ● | ● | | | | |
| ISHTA CENTRE (HM10761) | ● | ● | ● | ● | ● | ● | ● | ● | ● | ● | | ● | ● | ● | ● | ● | ● | | ● | ● | ● | ● | ● | ● | ● | ● | ● | ● | ● | ● | ● | | ● | ● | ● | ● | ● | | ● | | ● | ● | ● | | | | |
| JOHNSON, JANICE (HM11079) | | | | | ● | ● | | ● | | | | | | | | | | ● | | | | | | | | | | | | | | | | | | | | | | | ● | ● | | | | | |
| LOUISE BRITTLE (HM12667) | | | | | | | | | | | | ● | | | | | | | | | | | | | | | | | | | | | | | | | | | | | ● | ● | ● | | | | |
| MARCONI, L R (HM13076) | | | | | | | | | | | | | | | | | | | | | | | | | | | | | | | | ● | | | | | | | | | ● | ● | ● | | | | |
| MELLOR, J SIMON (HM13709) | | | | | | | | | | | | | | | | | | | | | | | | | | | | | | | | | | | | | | | | | ● | ● | ● | | | | |
| MILL BANK OSTEOPATHIC CLINIC (HM13865) | | | ● | | | | ● | | | | | ● | ● | | | | | | | | ● | | | | | | | | | | | | ● | | | | | | | | ● | | ● | | | | |
| NARAYAN, MAMTA (HM14486) | | | | | | | | | | | | ● | ● | | | | | | | | | | | | | | | | | | | | | | | | | | | | ● | | | | | | |
| NORBURY, SUSAN (HM14990) | ● | ● | ● | ● | ● | ● | ● | ● | ● | ● | | ● | ● | ● | ● | ● | ● | | ● | ● | ● | ● | ● | ● | ● | ● | ● | ● | ● | ● | ● | | ● | ● | ● | ● | ● | | ● | ● | ● | ● | ● | | | | |
| O'CALLAGHAN, STEVE (HM15193) | | | | | | | | | | | | ● | | | | | | | | | ● | | | | | | ● | | | | ● | | | | | | | | | | ● | ● | ● | | | | |
| PAYTON, ANTHONY (HM15875) | | | | | | | | | | | | | | | | | | | | | | | | | | | | | | | | ● | | | | | | | | | ● | ● | ● | | | | |
| PEACEHAVEN AROMATHERAPY (HM15877) | | | ● | ● | ● | | | | | | | | | | | | | ● | | | | | | | | | ● | | | | | | | ● | | ● | ● | | | | ● | ● | ● | | | | |
| PEACH, F J (HM15879) | | | | | | | | | | | | | | | | | | | | | | | | | | | | | | | | ● | | | | | | | | | ● | ● | ● | | | | |
| PLANT, R M (HM16359) | | | | | | | | | | | | | | | | | | | | | | | | | | | | | | | | ● | | | | | | | | | ● | ● | ● | | | | |
| PRIORS PODIATRY PRACTICE (HM16629) | | | | ● | | | | | | | | ● | ● | | | | | | | | | | | | | | | | | | | | | | | | | | | | ● | | ● | | | | |
| REECE, P & BRADSHAW, J (HM17039) | | | | | | | | | | | | | | | | | | | | | | | | | | | | | | | | ● | | | | | | | | | ● | ● | ● | | | | |
| ROBERTS, KATE (HM17418) | | | | | | | | | | | | | | | | | | ● | | | | | | | | | | | | | | | | | | | | | | | ● | ● | ● | | | | |
| SAGGU, S (HM17838) | | | | | | | | | | | | | | | | | | | | | | | | | | | | | | | | | | | | | | | | | ● | ● | ● | | | | |
| STAFFORD CHIROPRACTIC CLINIC (HM19108) | | | | | | | ● | | | | ● | ● | ● | | | | | | | | ● | | | | | | | | | | | | ● | | | | | ● | | | ● | ● | ● | | | | |
| STAFFORDSHIRE MCTIMONEY (HM19111) | | | ● | | | | ● | | | | | ● | ● | | | | | | | ● | ● | | | | | ● | | | | | | | ● | | | | | | | | ● | ● | ● | | | | |
| SUSAN JAMES CONSULTANCY (HM19527) | | | | | | | | | | | | | | | | | | | | | | | | | ● | | ● | | | | | | | | | | | | | | | | | | | | |
| TAMWORTH PHYSIOTHERAPY CLINIC (HM19675) | | | | | | | ● | | | | | ● | ● | | | | | | | | ● | | | | | | | | | | | | | | | | | | | | ● | ● | ● | | | | |
| TE NOSCE (HM19803) | | ● | ● | ● | ● | ● | | ● | ● | ● | | ● | ● | | ● | ● | ● | | ● | | ● | | ● | ● | ● | ● | ● | ● | ● | | ● | | | ● | | | | | ● | ● | ● | | ● | | | | |
| VALERIE BETTANY CLINIC (HM20558) | | | | | | | | | | | | | | | | | | | | | | | | | | | | | | | ● | | | | | ● | | | | | | | | | | | |
| WATSON, G T (HM21008) | | | | | | | | | | | | | | | | | | | | | | | | | | | | | | | | ● | | | | ● | | | | | ● | ● | ● | | | | |
| WHITBY, S E (HM21334) | | | | | | | ● | | | | | ● | ● | | | | | | | | ● | | | | | | | | | | | | | | | | | | | | ● | ● | ● | | | | |
| YARNFIELD PARK- HEALTH/SPORTS (HM21989) | ● | ● | ● | ● | ● | ● | ● | ● | ● | ● | | ● | ● | ● | ● | ● | ● | | ● | ● | ● | ● | ● | ● | ● | ● | ● | ● | ● | ● | ● | | ● | ● | ● | ● | ● | | ● | ● | | | | | | | |
| **SUFFOLK** | | | | | | | | | | | | | | | | | | | | | | | | | | | | | | | | | | | | | | | | | | | | | | | |
| AJNA (HM00457) | | | | | | | | | | | | | | | | | | ● | | | | | | | | | | | | | | | | | | | | | | | | | | | | | |
| BODY MECHANICS THERAPY CLINIC (HM02599) | | | | | | | | | | | | ● | ● | | | | | | | | ● | | | | | | | | | | | | | | | | | | | | ● | ● | ● | | | | |

www.healthmyself.com

# S - W Conditions treated at Practices/Businesses and Specialist Treatment Categories

Business by County with Reference no.

| Business by County with Reference no. | Sexually Trans. Infections | Shingles | Sinus Problems | Skin Problems | Sleep Disorders | Slimming Help | Slipped Disk | Smoking Help | Sneezing | Snoring | Spinal Injuries | Sports Injuries | Sprains | Stammering | Stings | Stomach Problems | Stomach Ulcers | Stress | Sweating |
|---|---|---|---|---|---|---|---|---|---|---|---|---|---|---|---|---|---|---|---|
| CHARLTON CLINIC (HM04033) | | | | | | ● | ● | | | | | ● | ● | | | | | | |
| CHURCHMAN & ASS REG OST (HM04475) | | | | | | | ● | | | | | ● | ● | | | | | | |
| CHURCHMAN, BERYL (HM04478) | | | | | | | ● | | | | | ● | ● | | | | | | |
| CLAIRVOYANT SERVICES (HM04518) | | | | | | | | | | | | | | | | | | | |
| COLEBROOK, G (HM04820) | | | ● | | ● | | | | | | | | | | | | | | |
| COOPER, A R (HM05088) | | | | | | | | | | | | | | | | | | | |
| CT & IM LEITH (HM05534) | | ● | ● | ● | | | ● | ● | | | | ● | ● | | ● | ● | ● | | |
| DENT, TRISH () | | | | | | | | | | | | | | | | | | ● | |
| EVENKEEL (HM06997) | | | | | ● | ● | | | | | | | | | | | | | |
| FELIXSTOWE PHYSIO PRACTICE (HM07203) | | | | | | | ● | | | | | ● | ● | | | | | | |
| FRESHFIELDS OF ALDEBURGH (HM07737) | | ● | ● | ● | ● | ● | ● | ● | ● | ● | | ● | ● | ● | ● | ● | ● | | ● |
| GREEN FARM CLINIC (HM08435) | | | | | | | | | | | | ● | ● | | | | | | |
| GROSVENOR PHYSIOTHERAPY CLINIC (HM08597) | | | | | | | ● | | | | | ● | ● | | | | | | |
| HARDY, MICHAEL (HM08984) | | | | | | | | | | | | | | | | | | | |
| HEALING CONNECTIONS (HM09330) | ● | ● | ● | ● | ● | | | ● | ● | ● | | ● | ● | | ● | ● | ● | | ● |
| HEALING HANDS (HM09336) | | | ● | | | ● | | ● | | | | | | | | | | | |
| HITCHINS, ROSIE (HM09847) | | | | | ● | | | | | | | | | | | | | ● | |
| HOPKINS, C J (HM10147) | | | | | | | | ● | | | | | | | | | | ● | |
| INNER SPACE SUFFOLK (HM10641) | | | ● | | ● | | ● | | | | | ● | ● | | | | | | |
| IPSWICH CHIROPRACTIC CLINIC (HM10714) | | ● | ● | | ● | ● | | ● | | | | ● | ● | | | | | | |
| IPSWICH PHYSIOTHERAPY PRACTICE (HM10715) | | | | | | | ● | | | | | ● | ● | | | | | | |
| LAVENDER LODGE CLINIC (HM12023) | | | | | | | ● | | | | | ● | ● | | | | | | |
| MALAROC (HM12961) | | | | | | | ● | | | | | ● | ● | | | | | | |
| MANOR HOUSE (HM13039) | | | | | | | ● | | | | | ● | ● | | | | | | |
| MARK CHURCH AROMATHERAPY (HM13106) | | | ● | ● | | | | | | | | | | | | | | | |
| MASSAGE FOR HEALTH (HM13260) | | | ● | | | | | | | | | ● | | | | | | | |
| MCTIMONEY CHIROPRACTIC CLINIC (HM13607) | | | ● | ● | ● | | ● | | | | | ● | ● | | | | | | |
| MOHAN, TERRY (HM14046) | | | | | ● | | | | | | | | | | | | | | |
| NATURECURES (HM14684) | | | ● | ● | ● | ● | ● | ● | | | | ● | ● | | | ● | ● | | |
| NOAH'S ARK PSYCHOTHERAPY (HM14964) | | | | | ● | ● | | ● | | | | | | ● | | | | | |
| PAGE, COLIN J (HM15570) | | | | | | ● | | ● | | | | | | | | | | ● | |
| PAROLIN, PAUL (HM15728) | | | ● | | ● | | ● | | | | | ● | ● | | | | | | |
| SHEROMA THERAPY (HM18435) | | | | | | | | ● | | | | | | | | | | | |
| SPALDING, JULIE (HM18955) | | | | ● | ● | ● | | ● | | | | | | ● | | | | ● | |

| Business by County with Reference no. | Teeth Grinding | Tennis Elbow | Terminal Illness | Throat Problems | Thrush | Thyroid Problems | Tinnitis | Tiredness | Tonsilitis | Ulcers | Vaginal Problems | Varicose Veins | Verrucas | Vertigo | Viral Infections | Vomiting | Warts | Water Retention | Whiplash | Wind | Worms |
|---|---|---|---|---|---|---|---|---|---|---|---|---|---|---|---|---|---|---|---|---|---|
| CHARLTON CLINIC (HM04033) | | ● | | | | | | | | | | | | | | | | | | | |
| CHURCHMAN & ASS REG OST (HM04475) | | ● | | | | | | | | | | | | | | | | | | | |
| CHURCHMAN, BERYL (HM04478) | | ● | | | | | | | | | | | | | | | | | | | |
| CLAIRVOYANT SERVICES (HM04518) | | | | | | | | | | | | | | | | | | | | | |
| COLEBROOK, G (HM04820) | | | | | | | | ● | | | | | | | | | | | | ● | |
| COOPER, A R (HM05088) | | | | | | | | | | | | | | | | | ● | | | | |
| CT & IM LEITH (HM05534) | | ● | | | | | | | | | | ● | | | | | | ● | | ● | |
| DENT, TRISH () | | | | | | | | ● | | | | | | | | | | | | | |
| EVENKEEL (HM06997) | | | | | | | | | | | | | | | | | | | | ● | |
| FELIXSTOWE PHYSIO PRACTICE (HM07203) | | ● | | | | | | | | | | | | | | | | | | | |
| FRESHFIELDS OF ALDEBURGH (HM07737) | ● | ● | | ● | ● | ● | ● | ● | ● | ● | ● | | | ● | ● | ● | ● | ● | | ● | ● |
| GREEN FARM CLINIC (HM08435) | | ● | | | | | | | | | | | | | | | | | | | |
| GROSVENOR PHYSIOTHERAPY CLINIC (HM08597) | | | | | | | | | | | | | | | | | | | | | |
| HARDY, MICHAEL (HM08984) | | | | | | | | | | | | | | | | | | | ● | | |
| HEALING CONNECTIONS (HM09330) | ● | ● | ● | ● | ● | ● | ● | ● | ● | ● | | ● | | ● | ● | ● | ● | ● | | ● | |
| HEALING HANDS (HM09336) | | | | | | | | ● | | | | | | | | | | | | | |
| HITCHINS, ROSIE (HM09847) | | | | | | | | | | | | | | | | | | | | | |
| HOPKINS, C J (HM10147) | ● | ● | ● | | | | ● | | | | | | | | | | | | | | |
| INNER SPACE SUFFOLK (HM10641) | | ● | | | | | | | | | | | | | | | | | | | |
| IPSWICH CHIROPRACTIC CLINIC (HM10714) | | ● | | | | ● | ● | | | | | | | | | | | ● | | ● | ● |
| IPSWICH PHYSIOTHERAPY PRACTICE (HM10715) | | ● | | | | | | | | | | | | | | | | | | | |
| LAVENDER LODGE CLINIC (HM12023) | | ● | | | | | | ● | | | | | | | | | | ● | | | |
| MALAROC (HM12961) | | ● | | | | | | | | | | | | | | | | | | | |
| MANOR HOUSE (HM13039) | | ● | | | | | | | | | | | | | | | | | | | |
| MARK CHURCH AROMATHERAPY (HM13106) | | | | | | | | | | | | ● | | | | | | | | | |
| MASSAGE FOR HEALTH (HM13260) | ● | | | | | | | | | | | | | | | | | | | | |
| MCTIMONEY CHIROPRACTIC CLINIC (HM13607) | ● | ● | | | | | | ● | | | | | | | | | | | | ● | |
| MOHAN, TERRY (HM14046) | ● | | | | | | | | | | | | | | | | | | | | |
| NATURECURES (HM14684) | | ● | | | | | ● | ● | | | | | | | | | | | | | |
| NOAH'S ARK PSYCHOTHERAPY (HM14964) | | | | | | | | ● | | | | | | | | ● | | | | | |
| PAGE, COLIN J (HM15570) | | | | | | | | | | | | | | | | | | | | | |
| PAROLIN, PAUL (HM15728) | ● | ● | | | | | ● | ● | | | | | | | | | | | | | |
| SHEROMA THERAPY (HM18435) | | | ● | | | | | ● | | | | | | | | | | | | | |
| SPALDING, JULIE (HM18955) | ● | | ● | | | | ● | ● | | | | | | | ● | ● | | | | | |

Specialist Treatment Categories

| Business by County with Reference no. | Children | Terminally Ill | Disabled | Horses | Dogs | CatS | Other Animals |
|---|---|---|---|---|---|---|---|
| CHARLTON CLINIC (HM04033) | ● | | ● | | | | |
| CHURCHMAN & ASS REG OST (HM04475) | ● | | | ● | ● | | |
| CHURCHMAN, BERYL (HM04478) | ● | | | ● | ● | | |
| CLAIRVOYANT SERVICES (HM04518) | | | ● | | | | |
| COLEBROOK, G (HM04820) | | | ● | | | | |
| COOPER, A R (HM05088) | ● | ● | ● | | | | |
| CT & IM LEITH (HM05534) | ● | | | | | | |
| DENT, TRISH () | ● | | ● | | | | |
| EVENKEEL (HM06997) | ● | ● | ● | ● | ● | ● | |
| FELIXSTOWE PHYSIO PRACTICE (HM07203) | ● | ● | ● | | | | |
| FRESHFIELDS OF ALDEBURGH (HM07737) | ● | ● | | | | | |
| GREEN FARM CLINIC (HM08435) | ● | | ● | | | | |
| GROSVENOR PHYSIOTHERAPY CLINIC (HM08597) | ● | ● | ● | | | | |
| HARDY, MICHAEL (HM08984) | ● | ● | ● | | | | |
| HEALING CONNECTIONS (HM09330) | ● | ● | ● | | | | |
| HEALING HANDS (HM09336) | ● | ● | ● | | | | |
| HITCHINS, ROSIE (HM09847) | | | | | | | |
| HOPKINS, C J (HM10147) | ● | ● | ● | | | | |
| INNER SPACE SUFFOLK (HM10641) | ● | | ● | | | | |
| IPSWICH CHIROPRACTIC CLINIC (HM10714) | ● | | ● | | | | |
| IPSWICH PHYSIOTHERAPY PRACTICE (HM10715) | ● | | ● | | | | |
| LAVENDER LODGE CLINIC (HM12023) | ● | ● | ● | | | | |
| MALAROC (HM12961) | ● | | ● | | | | |
| MANOR HOUSE (HM13039) | ● | ● | ● | | | | |
| MARK CHURCH AROMATHERAPY (HM13106) | ● | ● | ● | | | | |
| MASSAGE FOR HEALTH (HM13260) | ● | ● | ● | | | | |
| MCTIMONEY CHIROPRACTIC CLINIC (HM13607) | ● | | ● | | | | |
| MOHAN, TERRY (HM14046) | ● | ● | ● | | | | |
| NATURECURES (HM14684) | ● | ● | ● | | | | |
| NOAH'S ARK PSYCHOTHERAPY (HM14964) | ● | | | | | | |
| PAGE, COLIN J (HM15570) | ● | | | | | | |
| PAROLIN, PAUL (HM15728) | ● | ● | ● | | | | |
| SHEROMA THERAPY (HM18435) | | ● | ● | | | | |
| SPALDING, JULIE (HM18955) | ● | ● | | | | | |

# S - W Conditions treated at Practices/Businesses and Specialist Treatment Categories

Specialist Treatment Categories: Children, Terminally Ill, Disabled, Horses, Dogs, CatS, Other Animals

| Business by County with Reference no. | Sexually Trans. Infections | Shingles | Sinus Problems | Skin Problems | Sleep Disorders | Slimming Help | Slipped Disk | Smoking Help | Sneezing | Snoring | Spinal Injuries | Sports Injuries | Sprains | Stammering | Stings | Stomach Problems | Stomach Ulcers | Stress | Sweating | Teeth Grinding | Tennis Elbow | Terminal Illness | Throat Problems | Thrush | Thyroid Problems | Tinnitis | Tiredness | Tonsilitis | Ulcers | Vaginal Problems | Varicose Veins | Verrucas | Vertigo | Viral Infections | Vomiting | Warts | Water Retention | Whiplash | Wind | Worms | Children | Terminally Ill | Disabled | Horses | Dogs | CatS | Other Animals |
|---|---|---|---|---|---|---|---|---|---|---|---|---|---|---|---|---|---|---|---|---|---|---|---|---|---|---|---|---|---|---|---|---|---|---|---|---|---|---|---|---|---|---|---|---|---|---|---|
| SPRINGFIELD LODGE HEALTH CARE (HM19052) | ● | ● | ● | ● | ● | ● | ● | ● | ● | ● |  | ● | ● | ● | ● | ● | ● |  | ● | ● | ● | ● | ● | ● | ● | ● | ● | ● | ● | ● | ● |  | ● | ● | ● | ● | ● |  | ● | ● | ● | ● | ● |  |  |  |  |
| ST MARYS PRACTICE (HM19088) |  |  |  |  |  |  | ● |  |  |  |  | ● | ● |  |  |  |  |  |  |  | ● |  |  |  |  |  |  |  |  |  |  |  |  |  |  |  |  |  |  |  | ● | ● | ● |  |  |  |  |
| STEPHEN GORDON (HM19197) |  |  |  |  |  |  |  |  |  |  |  |  |  |  |  |  |  |  |  |  |  |  |  |  |  |  |  |  |  |  |  |  |  |  |  |  |  |  |  |  | ● | ● | ● |  |  |  |  |
| STOWMARKET OSTEOPATHS (HM19363) |  |  | ● |  |  |  | ● |  |  |  |  | ● | ● | ● |  |  |  |  |  | ● | ● |  |  |  |  | ● |  |  |  |  |  |  | ● |  |  |  |  |  |  |  | ● |  | ● |  |  |  |  |
| SUDBURY CHIROPRACTIC CLINIC (HM19462) |  |  |  |  |  |  | ● |  |  |  |  |  |  |  |  |  |  |  |  |  |  |  |  |  |  |  |  |  |  |  |  |  |  |  |  |  |  |  |  |  |  |  |  |  |  |  |  |
| WEI CLINIC (HM21111) |  |  | ● | ● | ● | ● |  | ● |  |  |  |  |  |  |  | ● |  |  | ● |  | ● |  | ● | ● | ● | ● | ● |  |  | ● |  |  |  |  |  |  |  |  |  |  |  |  |  |  | ● | ● |  |
| WOOLPITPHYSIO (HM21881) |  |  |  |  |  |  | ● |  |  |  |  | ● | ● |  |  |  |  |  |  |  | ● |  |  |  |  |  |  |  |  |  |  |  |  |  |  |  |  |  |  |  |  |  |  |  |  |  |  |
| **SURREY** |  |  |  |  |  |  |  |  |  |  |  |  |  |  |  |  |  |  |  |  |  |  |  |  |  |  |  |  |  |  |  |  |  |  |  |  |  |  |  |  |  |  |  |  |  |  |  |
| ACE NUTRITION (HM00157) |  |  | ● | ● | ● | ● |  |  |  |  |  |  |  |  |  | ● | ● |  | ● |  | ● |  |  | ● | ● |  | ● |  | ● | ● | ● |  |  | ● |  | ● |  |  | ● | ● | ● |  |  |  |  |  |  |
| ACORN HEALTH CLINIC (HM00177) |  |  | ● | ● | ● |  |  |  |  |  |  | ● |  |  |  |  |  |  |  |  |  |  |  |  |  |  | ● |  |  |  |  |  |  |  |  |  |  |  |  |  | ● |  | ● |  |  |  |  |
| ACORN THERAPY CENTRE (HM00181) |  |  |  |  | ● | ● |  | ● |  |  |  |  |  | ● |  |  |  |  |  | ● |  | ● |  |  |  |  | ● |  |  |  |  |  |  |  |  |  |  |  |  |  | ● | ● | ● |  |  |  |  |
| ACUHERBAL CHINESE MEDICINE (HM00214) |  |  | ● |  |  |  |  |  |  |  |  |  |  |  |  |  |  | ● |  |  |  |  |  |  |  |  |  |  |  |  |  |  |  |  |  |  |  |  |  |  | ● | ● | ● |  |  |  |  |
| ASCOT HOMEOPATHIC CLINIC (HM01177) |  | ● | ● | ● | ● |  |  |  | ● | ● |  | ● | ● |  | ● | ● | ● |  | ● | ● | ● |  | ● | ● | ● |  | ● | ● | ● | ● | ● |  | ● | ● | ● | ● | ● |  | ● | ● | ● |  |  |  |  |  |  |
| ASHTEAD CHARTERED PHYSIO SV (HM01230) |  |  |  |  |  |  | ● |  |  |  |  | ● | ● |  |  |  |  |  |  |  | ● |  |  |  |  |  |  |  |  |  |  |  |  |  |  |  |  |  |  |  |  |  | ● |  |  |  |  |
| ASHTEAD CLINIC (HM01232) |  |  |  |  |  |  |  |  |  |  |  | ● |  |  |  |  |  |  |  |  |  |  |  |  |  |  |  |  |  |  |  |  |  |  |  |  |  |  |  |  | ● | ● | ● |  |  |  |  |
| ASTON CLINIC (HM01301) |  |  | ● | ● |  |  | ● | ● |  |  |  | ● | ● |  |  |  |  |  |  |  | ● |  |  |  |  |  | ● |  |  |  |  |  |  |  | ● |  |  |  |  |  | ● | ● | ● |  |  |  |  |
| ASW ALLERGY CONSULTANTS (HM01305) |  |  | ● | ● | ● |  |  |  |  |  |  |  |  |  | ● | ● | ● |  |  |  |  |  | ● | ● | ● | ● | ● |  |  | ● | ● |  |  | ● | ● |  |  |  | ● |  | ● |  | ● |  |  |  |  |
| AVENUE PHYSIO & SPORTS CLNC (HM01390) |  |  |  |  |  |  | ● |  |  |  |  | ● | ● |  |  |  |  |  |  |  | ● |  |  |  |  |  |  |  |  |  |  |  |  |  |  |  |  |  |  |  | ● | ● | ● |  |  |  |  |
| BACK TO HEALTH (HM01508) |  |  |  |  |  |  | ● |  |  |  |  | ● | ● |  |  |  |  |  |  |  | ● |  |  |  |  |  |  |  |  |  |  |  |  |  |  |  |  | ● |  |  | ● | ● | ● |  |  |  |  |
| BACK TO HEALTH - GUILDFORD (HM01511) |  |  |  |  |  |  | ● |  |  |  |  | ● | ● |  |  |  |  |  |  |  | ● |  |  |  |  |  |  |  |  |  |  |  |  |  |  |  |  |  |  |  | ● | ● | ● |  |  |  |  |
| BACK TO HEALTH - RICHMOND (HM01514) |  |  |  |  |  |  | ● |  |  |  | ● | ● | ● |  |  |  |  |  |  |  | ● |  |  |  |  |  |  |  |  |  |  |  |  |  |  |  |  | ● |  |  | ● | ● | ● |  |  |  |  |
| BACK TO HEALTH - SUTTON (HM01515) |  |  |  |  |  |  | ● |  |  |  | ● | ● | ● |  |  |  |  |  |  |  | ● |  |  |  |  |  |  |  |  |  |  |  |  |  |  |  |  | ● |  |  | ● | ● | ● |  |  |  |  |
| BACKCARE CLINIC (HM01527) |  |  |  |  |  |  |  |  |  |  |  | ● |  |  |  |  |  |  |  |  | ● |  |  |  |  |  |  |  |  |  |  |  |  |  |  |  |  | ● |  |  | ● |  | ● |  |  |  |  |
| BAILEY, L J (HM01551) |  |  | ● |  |  |  | ● |  |  |  |  | ● | ● |  |  |  |  |  |  |  | ● |  |  |  |  |  |  |  |  |  |  |  |  |  |  |  |  |  |  |  |  |  | ● |  |  |  |  |
| BARNES, A K R (HM01743) |  |  |  |  |  |  | ● |  |  |  |  | ● | ● |  |  |  |  |  |  |  | ● |  |  |  |  |  |  |  |  |  |  |  |  |  |  |  |  | ● |  |  | ● |  | ● |  |  |  |  |
| BARNSTEAD VILLAGE CLINIC (HM01769) |  |  | ● | ● |  |  |  |  |  |  |  | ● | ● |  |  |  |  |  |  |  | ● |  |  |  |  |  | ● |  |  |  |  |  |  |  |  |  |  |  |  |  | ● | ● | ● |  |  |  |  |
| BATCHELOR, C (HM01863) |  |  |  |  |  |  |  |  |  |  |  |  |  |  |  |  |  |  |  |  |  |  |  |  |  |  |  |  |  |  |  |  |  |  |  |  |  |  |  |  |  | ● | ● |  |  |  |  |
| BIGWOOD, SIMON (HM02295) |  |  | ● | ● |  |  | ● |  |  |  |  | ● |  |  |  |  |  |  |  |  |  |  |  |  |  |  | ● |  |  |  |  |  |  |  |  |  |  |  |  |  |  |  |  |  |  |  |  |
| BIODYNAMICS (HM02332) | ● | ● | ● | ● |  |  |  | ● |  |  |  | ● | ● |  |  | ● | ● |  |  |  | ● | ● | ● | ● | ● | ● | ● | ● | ● | ● | ● |  | ● | ● | ● | ● | ● |  | ● | ● | ● | ● | ● | ● | ● | ● | ● |
| BOURNE HEALTH (HM02753) |  |  |  | ● |  |  |  |  |  |  |  | ● |  |  |  |  |  |  |  |  |  |  |  |  |  |  |  |  |  |  |  |  |  |  |  |  |  |  |  |  | ● | ● | ● |  |  |  |  |
| BRABANT HOUSE CLINIC (HM02830) |  | ● | ● | ● | ● | ● | ● | ● | ● | ● |  | ● | ● |  |  | ● |  |  | ● | ● | ● |  | ● | ● |  | ● | ● | ● |  |  |  |  | ● |  |  | ● |  |  |  |  | ● |  |  |  |  |  |  |
| BREWSTER, DAVID J (HM02980) |  |  |  | ● | ● | ● |  | ● |  | ● |  |  |  | ● |  |  |  |  | ● | ● |  | ● |  |  |  | ● | ● |  |  |  |  |  |  |  | ● |  |  |  |  |  |  |  |  |  |  |  |  |
| BST FOUNDATION (HM03294) |  |  |  |  |  |  |  | ● |  |  |  |  |  |  |  |  |  | ● |  |  |  |  |  |  |  |  |  |  |  |  |  |  |  |  |  |  |  |  |  |  | ● | ● | ● |  |  |  |  |
| CAMBERLEY NATURAL THERAPY CTRE (HM03566) |  | ● | ● | ● |  |  |  | ● |  |  |  |  |  |  |  |  |  |  |  |  | ● |  |  |  |  |  | ● |  |  |  |  |  |  |  |  |  |  |  |  |  | ● |  | ● |  |  |  |  |

www.healthmyself.com

Healthmyself Directory

# S - W Conditions treated at Practices/Businesses and Specialist Treatment Categories

| Business by County with Reference no. | | | | | | | | | | | | | | | | | | | | | | | | | | | | | | | | | | | | | | | | Specialist Treatment Categories | | | | | | |
|---|---|---|---|---|---|---|---|---|---|---|---|---|---|---|---|---|---|---|---|---|---|---|---|---|---|---|---|---|---|---|---|---|---|---|---|---|---|---|---|---|---|---|---|---|---|---|
| | Sexually Trans. Infections | Shingles | Sinus Problems | Skin Problems | Sleep Disorders | Slimming Help | Slipped Disk | Smoking Help | Sneezing | Snoring | Spinal Injuries | Sports Injuries | Sprains | Stammering | Stings | Stomach Problems | Stomach Ulcers | Stress | Sweating | Teeth Grinding | Tennis Elbow | Terminal Illness | Throat Problems | Thrush | Thyroid Problems | Tinnitis | Tiredness | Tonsilitis | Ulcers | Vaginal Problems | Varicose Veins | Verrucas | Vertigo | Viral Infections | Vomiting | Warts | Water Retention | Whiplash | Wind | Worms | Children | Terminally Ill | Disabled | Horses | Dogs | CatS | Other Animals |
| CARLTON CLINIC (HM03700) | ● | ● | ● | ● | ● | ● | ● | ● | ● | ● | | ● | ● | | ● | ● | ● | | ● | ● | ● | | ● | ● | ● | ● | ● | ● | ● | | ● | | ● | ● | ● | | ● | | ● | | ● | ● | ● | ● | ● | | |
| CATERHAM CHIROPRACTIC CLINIC (HM03853) | | | | | | | ● | | | | | ● | ● | | | | | | | | ● | | | | | | | | | | | | | | | | | ● | | | ● | ● | ● | | | | |
| CHART LANE CLINIC (HM04039) | ● | ● | ● | ● | ● | | | ● | ● | ● | | ● | ● | ● | ● | ● | ● | | | ● | ● | | ● | ● | ● | ● | ● | ● | ● | ● | ● | | ● | ● | ● | ● | ● | | ● | ● | ● | | ● | | | | |
| CHI CLINIC (HM04148) | ● | ● | ● | ● | ● | ● | ● | ● | ● | ● | | ● | ● | ● | ● | ● | ● | | ● | ● | ● | ● | ● | ● | ● | ● | ● | ● | ● | ● | ● | | ● | ● | ● | ● | ● | | ● | ● | ● | ● | ● | | | | |
| CHIROPRACTIC CENTRE (HM04382) | | | | | | | ● | | | | ● | | ● | | | | | | | | ● | | | | | | | | | | | | | | | | | ● | | | | | | | | | |
| CHRISTINE KEY HYPNOTHERAPIST (HM04447) | | | | | ● | ● | | ● | | | | | | ● | | | | | | | | | | | | | | | | | | | | | | | | | | | | | | | | | |
| CITISPORT (HM04483) | | | | | | ● | ● | | | | | ● | ● | | | ● | ● | | | | | ● | | | ● | | ● | | | | | | | | | | | ● | | ● | ● | ● | ● | | | | |
| CLEMENTS, J (HM04644) | | | ● | ● | ● | | | | | | | | | | | | | | | | | | | | | | ● | | | | | | | | | | ● | | ● | | ● | ● | ● | | | | |
| COHEN, MICHAEL (HM04793) | | | | | ● | ● | | ● | | | | | | | | | | | | | | | | | | | ● | | | | | | | | | | | | | | | ● | | | | | |
| CONFIDENTIAL COUNSELLING SVS (HM04975) | | | | | | | | | | | | | | | | | | | | | | | | | | | | | | | | | ● | | | | | | | | | ● | ● | | | | |
| COX, JULIET (HM05307) | | | | | | | ● | | | | | ● | | ● | | | | | | ● | ● | | ● | | | | ● | | | | | | | | | | | ● | | | ● | ● | ● | | | | |
| CRANLEIGH CHIROPRACTIC CLINIC (HM05381) | | | | | | | | | | | | | | | | | | | | | | | | | | | | | | | | | | | | | | | | | ● | | ● | ● | ● | | |
| CROYDON HEALING CENTRE (HM05515) | ● | ● | ● | ● | ● | ● | ● | ● | ● | ● | | ● | ● | ● | ● | ● | ● | | ● | ● | ● | ● | ● | ● | ● | ● | ● | ● | ● | ● | ● | | ● | ● | ● | ● | ● | | ● | ● | ● | ● | ● | ● | ● | ● | ● |
| CROYDON HYPNOTHERAPY (HM05516) | | | ● | ● | ● | ● | | ● | | | | | | ● | | | | | | ● | | | ● | | | | | | | | | | | | | | | | | | | | | | | | |
| CUMMINS, ROZ (HM05617) | | | ● | ● | ● | | | | | | | | | | | ● | | | | | | | | | | | ● | | | | | | | | | | | | | | ● | ● | ● | ● | ● | ● | ● |
| DORCHESTER HOUSE OSTEOPATHY (HM06195) | ● | ● | ● | ● | ● | ● | ● | ● | ● | ● | | ● | ● | ● | ● | ● | ● | | ● | ● | ● | ● | ● | ● | ● | ● | ● | ● | ● | ● | ● | | ● | ● | ● | ● | ● | | ● | ● | ● | ● | ● | | | | |
| DORKING, PAUL (HM06200) | | | | | ● | ● | | ● | | | | | | | | | | ● | | | | | | | | | | | | | | | | | | | | | | | ● | ● | ● | | | | |
| EDWARDS HEALTH CLINIC (HM06639) | | | | ● | ● | ● | | ● | | | | | | ● | | ● | | | | ● | | ● | ● | | | ● | ● | | ● | ● | | | ● | | ● | ● | | | ● | | | ● | ● | | | | |
| ENOCK-SHORE, ANGELA (HM06845) | | | ● | ● | ● | ● | | ● | | | | | | | | | | | | | | | | | | ● | ● | | | | | | | | | | | | | | ● | ● | ● | | | | |
| EPSOM CHIROPRACTIC CLINIC (HM06857) | | | | | | | ● | | | | ● | ● | ● | | | | | | | | ● | | | | | | | | | | | | | | | | | ● | | | ● | ● | ● | | | | |
| EQUILIBRIUM OSTEOPATHIC (HM06876) | | | ● | | | | ● | | | | | ● | ● | | | ● | ● | | | ● | ● | | | | | | ● | | | | ● | | ● | | | | | | | | ● | ● | ● | | | | |
| FARNBOROUGH CHIRO CLINIC (HM07111) | | | | | | | ● | | | | | ● | ● | | | | | | | | ● | | | | | | | | | | | | | | | | | | | | ● | | | | | | |
| FEATHER, A J (HM07155) | | | | | | | | | | | | | ● | | | | | | | | | | | | | | | | | | | | | | | | | | | | ● | ● | ● | | | | |
| FOOT CARE CENTRE (HM07466) | | | | | | | | | | | | | | | | | | | | | | | | | | | | | | | | | | | | ● | | | | | ● | ● | ● | | | | |
| GATEWAYS CENTRE (HM07928) | | | | | | | | | | | | | | | | | | | | | | | | | | | | | | | | | | | | | | | | | ● | ● | ● | | | | |
| GAUVAIN, TONY (HM07934) | | | | | | ● | | ● | | | | | | | | | | | | ● | | | | | | | ● | | | | | | | | | | | | | | ● | | | | | | |
| GODDARD, TERRI (HM08180) | | | ● | | | | | | | | | ● | | | | | | ● | | | ● | | | | | ● | ● | | | | | | ● | | | | | | | | ● | | | | | | |
| GOODLIFE NATURAL HEALTH CENTRE (HM08256) | | | | | | | ● | | | | | ● | ● | | | | | | | | ● | | | | | | | | | | | | | | | | | | | | | | | | | | |
| GORDON, SARAH (HM08282) | | | | ● | ● | | | | | | | ● | | | | | | ● | | | | | | | | | | | | | | | | | | | | | | | | | | | | | |
| GRAVELL, NICOLA (HM08401) | | | | ● | ● | ● | | ● | | | | | | ● | | | | | ● | ● | | ● | | | | ● | ● | | | | | | | | | | | | | | | ● | | | | | |
| GUILDFORD PHYSIO & SPORTS (HM08632) | | | | | | | ● | | | | | ● | ● | | | | | | | | | | | | | | | | | | | | | | | | | | | | ● | ● | ● | | | | |
| HAM CHIROPRACTIC CLINIC (HM08822) | | | | | | | ● | | | | | ● | ● | | | | | | | | ● | | | | | | | | | | | | ● | | | | | | | | ● | | | | | | |
| HANDS ON HEALTH (HM08911) | | | | | | | ● | | | | | ● | ● | | | | | | | ● | ● | | | | | | | | | | | | | | | | | | | | ● | ● | ● | | | | |
| HANFORD, S P (HM08925) | | | | | | | | | | | | | | | | | | | | | | | | | | | ● | | | | | | | | | | ● | | | | ● | | | | | | |

# S - W Conditions treated at Practices/Businesses and Specialist Treatment Categories

Business by County with Reference no.

| Business by County with Reference no. | Sexually Trans. Infections | Shingles | Sinus Problems | Skin Problems | Sleep Disorders | Slimming Help | Slipped Disk | Smoking Help | Sneezing | Snoring | Spinal Injuries | Sports Injuries | Sprains | Stammering | Stings | Stomach Problems | Stomach Ulcers | Stress |
|---|---|---|---|---|---|---|---|---|---|---|---|---|---|---|---|---|---|---|
| HARDY, JACK E (HM08981) | | | | | ● | ● | | ● | | | | | | ● | | | | |
| HARTLEY, GILL (HM09140) | | | ● | | ● | | | | | | | | ● | | | | | |
| HEAVEN MOUNTAIN TAIJI QUAN (HM09472) | | | | | | | ● | | | | | | | | | | | |
| HELIANTHUS PRACTICE (HM09518) | | ● | ● | ● | ● | ● | ● | ● | ● | ● | | ● | ● | | ● | ● | ● | |
| HERBAL KING (HM09628) | ● | | | ● | | ● | | | | | | | | | | ● | ● | ● |
| HERBALS (HM09647) | | ● | ● | ● | ● | ● | ● | ● | ● | ● | | ● | ● | | ● | ● | ● | |
| HILL, CHARLOTTE (HM09774) | | | | | | | ● | | | | ● | ● | ● | | | | | |
| HILLVIEW PHYSIO & SPORTS CLNC (HM09809) | | | | | | | ● | | | | | ● | ● | | | | | |
| HOLISTIC CENTRE (HM09949) | ● | ● | ● | ● | ● | ● | ● | ● | ● | ● | | ● | ● | ● | ● | ● | ● | |
| HOLISTIC HEALTH CENTRE (HM09971) | | | ● | ● | ● | | | | | | | ● | | | | | | |
| HOPPER, C A (HM10156) | | | | | | | | | | | | | | | | | | |
| HUMAN FOCUS RETURN TO WORK (HM10362) | | | | | | | | | | | | ● | ● | | | | | |
| INGLEDALE NATURAL HEALTH CTRE (HM10621) | | | | | | | ● | | | | | ● | ● | | | | | |
| INTEGRAL HEALTH (HM10690) | ● | ● | ● | ● | ● | ● | ● | ● | ● | ● | | ● | ● | ● | ● | ● | ● | |
| J V ASSOCIATES (HM10803) | | | ● | ● | ● | | | | | | | | | | | | | |
| KENT CLINIC OF NATURAL MED (HM11514) | ● | ● | ● | ● | ● | ● | ● | ● | ● | ● | | ● | ● | ● | ● | ● | ● | |
| KEW CHIROPRACTIC CLINIC (HM11575) | | | | | | | ● | | | | | ● | ● | | | | | |
| KINGSTON NATURAL HEALING CTRE (HM11677) | | ● | ● | ● | | | | ● | | | | ● | ● | ● | | ● | | |
| KINGSTON OSTEOPATHS (HM11679) | | | | | | | ● | | | | | ● | ● | | | ● | | |
| KOLTHAMMER, JOHN (HM11780) | | | | | | | | | | | | ● | | | | | | |
| LEATHERHEAD CHIRO CLINIC (HM12114) | | | | ● | ● | | | | | | | | | | | | | |
| LONDON SPINE AND JOINT CLINIC (HM12610) | | | | | | | ● | | | | | ● | ● | | | | | |
| LOW, ROYSTON (HM12688) | | | ● | ● | | | ● | ● | | | | ● | ● | | | ● | ● | |
| MARKS, DARREN HYPNOTHERAPY (HM13120) | | | | | ● | ● | | ● | | | | | | | | | | ● |
| MARSON, JOY (HM13178) | | | | ● | | ● | | ● | | | | | | | | ● | ● | |
| MEDICAL HYPNOTHERAPY CLINIC (HM13653) | | | | | | ● | | ● | | | | | | | | | | |
| MEEKS, FIONA (HM13683) | | | ● | | | | | | | | | | | | | | | ● |
| MEENEGHAN, TOM (HM13685) | | ● | ● | ● | ● | | | ● | ● | ● | | ● | ● | | ● | ● | ● | |
| MILFORD MASSAGE PRACTICE (HM13863) | | | | | | | ● | | | | | ● | ● | | | | | ● |
| MILLER CONSULTANCY (HM13880) | | ● | ● | ● | ● | ● | | ● | ● | ● | | | | ● | | ● | ● | ● |
| MIND AND BODY (HM13958) | | | ● | ● | ● | | | ● | | | | ● | | | | ● | | |
| MIST, CORINNE (HM13996) | | | ● | ● | ● | | | | | | | | | | | | | |
| MOSS PHARMACY PODIATRY (HM14263) | | | | | | | | | | | | | | | | | | |
| NATURAL HEALING CENTRE (HM14541) | | | ● | ● | ● | | | | | | | | | | | ● | | ● |

| Business by County with Reference no. | Sweating | Teeth Grinding | Tennis Elbow | Terminal Illness | Throat Problems | Thrush | Thyroid Problems | Tinnitis | Tiredness | Tonsilitis | Ulcers | Vaginal Problems | Varicose Veins | Verrucas | Vertigo | Viral Infections | Vomiting | Warts | Water Retention | Whiplash | Wind | Worms |
|---|---|---|---|---|---|---|---|---|---|---|---|---|---|---|---|---|---|---|---|---|---|---|
| HARDY, JACK E (HM08981) | | | | ● | | | | | | | | | | | | | | | | | | |
| HARTLEY, GILL (HM09140) | | ● | | | | | | | | | | | | | | | | | | | | |
| HEAVEN MOUNTAIN TAIJI QUAN (HM09472) | | | | | | | | | | | | | | | | | | | | | | |
| HELIANTHUS PRACTICE (HM09518) | ● | ● | ● | | ● | ● | ● | ● | ● | ● | ● | ● | ● | | ● | ● | ● | ● | ● | | ● | ● |
| HERBAL KING (HM09628) | | | | | ● | | | ● | | | | | | | | ● | | | | | | ● |
| HERBALS (HM09647) | ● | ● | ● | | ● | ● | ● | ● | ● | ● | ● | ● | ● | | ● | ● | ● | ● | ● | | ● | ● |
| HILL, CHARLOTTE (HM09774) | | | ● | | | | | | | | | | | | | | | | | ● | | |
| HILLVIEW PHYSIO & SPORTS CLNC (HM09809) | | | ● | | | | | | | | | | | | | | | | | | | |
| HOLISTIC CENTRE (HM09949) | ● | ● | ● | ● | ● | ● | ● | ● | ● | ● | ● | ● | ● | | ● | ● | ● | ● | ● | | ● | ● |
| HOLISTIC HEALTH CENTRE (HM09971) | | | | | | | | | ● | | | | | | | | | | | | | |
| HOPPER, C A (HM10156) | | | | | | | | | | | | | | | | | | | | | | |
| HUMAN FOCUS RETURN TO WORK (HM10362) | | | ● | | | | | | | | | | | | | | | | | ● | | |
| INGLEDALE NATURAL HEALTH CTRE (HM10621) | | | ● | | | | | | | | | | | | | | | | | | | |
| INTEGRAL HEALTH (HM10690) | ● | ● | ● | ● | ● | ● | ● | ● | ● | ● | ● | ● | ● | | ● | ● | ● | ● | ● | | ● | ● |
| J V ASSOCIATES (HM10803) | | | | | | | | | ● | | | | | | | | | | | | | |
| KENT CLINIC OF NATURAL MED (HM11514) | ● | ● | ● | | ● | ● | ● | ● | ● | ● | ● | ● | ● | | ● | ● | ● | ● | ● | | ● | ● |
| KEW CHIROPRACTIC CLINIC (HM11575) | | | ● | | | | | ● | | | | | | | ● | | | | | | | |
| KINGSTON NATURAL HEALING CTRE (HM11677) | | ● | ● | ● | | | | | ● | | | | ● | | ● | | | | | | ● | |
| KINGSTON OSTEOPATHS (HM11679) | | | ● | | | | | ● | | | | | | | ● | | | | | | | |
| KOLTHAMMER, JOHN (HM11780) | | | ● | | | | | | | | | | | | | | | | | ● | | |
| LEATHERHEAD CHIRO CLINIC (HM12114) | | | | | | | | | | | | | | | | | | | | | | |
| LONDON SPINE AND JOINT CLINIC (HM12610) | | | ● | | | | | | | | | | | | | | | | | | | |
| LOW, ROYSTON (HM12688) | | | ● | | | | | ● | | | | | | | ● | | | | ● | | ● | |
| MARKS, DARREN HYPNOTHERAPY (HM13120) | | | | | | | | | | | | | | | | | | | | | | |
| MARSON, JOY (HM13178) | | | | | | ● | ● | | ● | | ● | | | | | | | | ● | | ● | |
| MEDICAL HYPNOTHERAPY CLINIC (HM13653) | | | | | | | | | | | | | | | | | | | | | | |
| MEEKS, FIONA (HM13683) | | ● | | | | | | | | | | | | | | | | | | | | |
| MEENEGHAN, TOM (HM13685) | ● | ● | ● | ● | ● | ● | ● | | ● | ● | ● | | | | ● | ● | ● | ● | ● | | ● | ● |
| MILFORD MASSAGE PRACTICE (HM13863) | | | | | | | | | | | | | | | | | | | | | | |
| MILLER CONSULTANCY (HM13880) | ● | ● | ● | ● | ● | | | ● | ● | | ● | | | | ● | | ● | ● | | | | |
| MIND AND BODY (HM13958) | | | ● | | | | ● | | ● | | | | | | | | | | ● | | ● | |
| MIST, CORINNE (HM13996) | | | | | | | | | ● | | | | | | | | | | ● | | ● | |
| MOSS PHARMACY PODIATRY (HM14263) | | | | | | | | | | | | | | ● | | | | | | | | |
| NATURAL HEALING CENTRE (HM14541) | | | | | | | | | ● | | | | | | | | | | | | | |

| Business by County with Reference no. | Specialist Treatment Categories: Children | Terminally Ill | Disabled | Horses | Dogs | CatS | Other Animals |
|---|---|---|---|---|---|---|---|
| HARDY, JACK E (HM08981) | ● | ● | ● | | | | |
| HARTLEY, GILL (HM09140) | ● | ● | ● | | | | |
| HEAVEN MOUNTAIN TAIJI QUAN (HM09472) | ● | ● | ● | ● | ● | ● | |
| HELIANTHUS PRACTICE (HM09518) | ● | | ● | | | | |
| HERBAL KING (HM09628) | ● | ● | ● | | | | |
| HERBALS (HM09647) | ● | | ● | | | | |
| HILL, CHARLOTTE (HM09774) | ● | | ● | | | | |
| HILLVIEW PHYSIO & SPORTS CLNC (HM09809) | ● | | ● | | | | |
| HOLISTIC CENTRE (HM09949) | ● | ● | ● | | | | |
| HOLISTIC HEALTH CENTRE (HM09971) | ● | ● | ● | | | | |
| HOPPER, C A (HM10156) | | ● | | | | | |
| HUMAN FOCUS RETURN TO WORK (HM10362) | | | ● | | | | |
| INGLEDALE NATURAL HEALTH CTRE (HM10621) | | | | | | | |
| INTEGRAL HEALTH (HM10690) | ● | ● | ● | ● | ● | ● | ● |
| J V ASSOCIATES (HM10803) | ● | | ● | ● | ● | ● | |
| KENT CLINIC OF NATURAL MED (HM11514) | ● | ● | ● | | | | |
| KEW CHIROPRACTIC CLINIC (HM11575) | ● | | ● | | | | |
| KINGSTON NATURAL HEALING CTRE (HM11677) | ● | ● | ● | | | | |
| KINGSTON OSTEOPATHS (HM11679) | ● | ● | | | | | |
| KOLTHAMMER, JOHN (HM11780) | ● | | ● | | | | |
| LEATHERHEAD CHIRO CLINIC (HM12114) | ● | ● | ● | | | | |
| LONDON SPINE AND JOINT CLINIC (HM12610) | ● | ● | ● | | | | |
| LOW, ROYSTON (HM12688) | ● | | | | | | |
| MARKS, DARREN HYPNOTHERAPY (HM13120) | | ● | ● | | | | |
| MARSON, JOY (HM13178) | ● | | | | | | |
| MEDICAL HYPNOTHERAPY CLINIC (HM13653) | ● | ● | ● | | | | |
| MEEKS, FIONA (HM13683) | ● | ● | ● | | | | |
| MEENEGHAN, TOM (HM13685) | ● | ● | ● | | | | |
| MILFORD MASSAGE PRACTICE (HM13863) | ● | | | | | | |
| MILLER CONSULTANCY (HM13880) | ● | ● | ● | | | | |
| MIND AND BODY (HM13958) | ● | ● | | | | | |
| MIST, CORINNE (HM13996) | ● | ● | ● | | | | |
| MOSS PHARMACY PODIATRY (HM14263) | ● | ● | ● | | | | |
| NATURAL HEALING CENTRE (HM14541) | ● | ● | ● | ● | ● | ● | ● |

# S - W Conditions treated at Practices/Businesses and Specialist Treatment Categories

Business by County with Reference no.

| Specialist Treatment Categories / Conditions | NATURAL HEALING CLINIC (HM14550) | NATURAL HEALTH PRACTICE (HM14594) | NATURAL SLEEP FOUNDATION (HM14624) | NICHOLLS, VERITY (HM14915) | NICOLA FRY-HEALTH & BEAUTY (HM14927) | OLD WOKING GRANGE (HM15264) | OSTEOPATHY (HM15477) | PHILP, CHRISTINE (HM16147) | PHOENIX (HM16152) | POWER, DAVID J (HM16503) | PRICE, SANDRA (HM16593) | RICHMOND PHYSIOTHERAPY (HM17301) | RIGAL, M (HM17330) | ROBYNA, ANNETTE (HM17516) | ROSE, CYNTHIA J (HM17605) | SARAH BOGUE HOMEOPATH (HM17944) | SAUMEEL PATEL ACU CLINIC (HM17950) | SAYER CLINIC (HM17992) | SCHONBERG, VERA (HM18078) | SCHOOL OF YOGA (HM18089) | SCORPIO PHYSIOTHERAPY (HM18103) | SELSDON COMP/RESP CLINIC (HM18220) | SEVEN SIGHS (HM18244) | SHEPPERTON PHYSIOFIRST CENTRE (HM18425) | SIMMS, KATHERINE (HM18564) | STEWART, I (HM19267) | SURBITON NATURAL HEALTH CENTRE (HM19514) | SURREY HEALING SANCTUARY (HM19522) | SUTHERLAND, JENNY (HM19539) | SUTTON CHIROPRACTIC CLINIC (HM19543) | TANSILL, LUCY (HM19689) | TELLING, PAUL (HM19824) | TOWNS, KATE (HM20202) | TRADITIONAL CHINESE MEDICINE (HM20225) |
|---|---|---|---|---|---|---|---|---|---|---|---|---|---|---|---|---|---|---|---|---|---|---|---|---|---|---|---|---|---|---|---|---|---|---|
| Other Animals | | | | | | | | | | | | | | | | | | | | | | | | | | | | | | | | | | |
| CatS | | | | | | | | | | | | | | | | | | | | | | | | | | | | | | | | | | |
| Dogs | | | | | | | | | | | | | | | | | | | | | | | | | | | | | | | | | | |
| Horses | | | | | | | | | | | | | | | | | | | | | | | | | | | | | | | | | | |
| Disabled | ● | ● | ● | ● | ● | | | ● | ● | ● | ● | ● | ● | | | | ● | | | | | ● | ● | ● | | ● | ● | ● | ● | ● | | | | ● |
| Terminally Ill | ● | | | ● | | | | ● | | ● | ● | ● | | | ● | | ● | | | | | ● | ● | ● | ● | ● | ● | ● | ● | ● | | | | ● |
| Children | ● | ● | ● | ● | ● | | ● | ● | | ● | ● | ● | ● | ● | | | ● | | ● | | ● | ● | ● | ● | ● | ● | ● | ● | ● | ● | ● | | | ● |
| Worms | | | | | | ● | | | | | | | | | | | | | | | | ● | | | | | | | | | | | | |
| Wind | | ● | | | | ● | | | | | | | | | | | | | | | | ● | | | | | | | | | | | | |
| Whiplash | | | | | | | | | | | ● | | | | | | | ● | | | | | | | | | | | | | ● | | | |
| Water Retention | | ● | | | ● | | | | | | | | | | | | | | | | | ● | | | | | | | | | | | | |
| Warts | | | | | | | | | | | | | ● | | | ● | | | | | | ● | | | | ● | | ● | | | | | | |
| Vomiting | | | | | | | | | | | | | | | | | | | | | | ● | | | | | | ● | | | | | | ● |
| Viral Infections | | | | | | | | | | | | | | | | | | | | | | ● | | | | | | ● | | | | | | |
| Vertigo | | | | | | | ● | | | | | | | | | | | | | | | ● | | | | | | | | | | | | |
| Verrucas | | | | | | | | | | ● | | | | | | | | | | | | | | | | ● | | | | | | | | |
| Varicose Veins | | | | | ● | | | | | | | | | | | | | | | | | ● | | | | | | | | | | | | |
| Vaginal Problems | | | | | | | | | | | | | | | | | | | | | | ● | | | | | | | | | | | | |
| Ulcers | | | | | | | | | | | | | | | | | | | | | | ● | | | | | | ● | | | | | | |
| Tonsilitis | | | | | | | | | | | | | | | | | | | | | | ● | | | | | | ● | | | | | | |
| Tiredness | | ● | | | ● | ● | | | | | | | | ● | | ● | ● | | | ● | | ● | | | | | ● | ● | ● | | | | ● | |
| Tinnitis | | | | | | ● | ● | | | | | | | | | | | | | | | ● | | | | | | ● | | | | | | |
| Thyroid Problems | | | | | | ● | | | | | | | | | | | | | | | | ● | | | | | | ● | | | | | | |
| Thrush | | | | | | ● | | | | | | | | | | | | | | | | ● | | | | | | | | | | | | |
| Throat Problems | | | | | | | | | | | | | | | | | | | | | | ● | | | | | | ● | | | | | | |
| Terminal Illness | | | | | | | | | | | | | | | | | | | | | | ● | | | | | | ● | | | | | | |
| Tennis Elbow | ● | ● | | | | | ● | | | | ● | ● | | | | | ● | ● | | | ● | ● | | ● | | | | | | | ● | | | |
| Teeth Grinding | | | | | | | | | | | | | | | | | | | | | | ● | | | | | | | | | | | | |
| Sweating | | | | | | ● | | | | | | | | | | | | | | | | ● | | | | | | | | | | | | |
| Stress | | | | | | | | ● | | | | | | | | | | | | | | | | | | | | | | | | ● | | |
| Stomach Ulcers | | | | | | ● | | | | | | | | | | | | | | | | ● | | | | | | ● | | | | | | |
| Stomach Problems | | | | | | ● | | | | | | | | | | ● | | | | | | ● | | | | | | ● | ● | | | | | ● |
| Stings | | | | | | | | | | | | | | | | | | | | | | ● | | | | | | ● | | | | | | |
| Stammering | | | | | | | | | | | | | | | | | | | | | | ● | | | | | | | | | | | | |
| Sprains | | ● | | | | | ● | | | | ● | ● | | ● | | | ● | ● | | | ● | ● | | ● | | | | ● | | ● | ● | ● | | ● |
| Sports Injuries | ● | ● | | | | | ● | | | | ● | ● | ● | ● | | | ● | ● | | | ● | ● | | ● | | | | ● | | ● | ● | ● | | ● |
| Spinal Injuries | | | | | | | | | | | ● | | | | | | | ● | | | | | | | | | | | | | ● | | | |
| Snoring | | | | | | | | | | | | | | | | | | | | | | ● | | | | | | | | | ● | | | |
| Sneezing | | | | | | | | | | | | | | | | | | | | | | ● | | | | | | | | | ● | | | |
| Smoking Help | | | | | | ● | | | | | | | | | | | | | ● | | | ● | | | | | | | | | ● | | | |
| Slipped Disk | | | | | | | ● | | | | ● | ● | | | | | ● | | | | ● | ● | | ● | | | | ● | | ● | ● | | | |
| Slimming Help | | | | | ● | ● | | | | | | | | | | | | | ● | | | ● | | | | | | | | | | | | |
| Sleep Disorders | | | ● | | | ● | | ● | | | | | | ● | | ● | | | ● | ● | | ● | | | ● | | | ● | ● | | | | | ● |
| Skin Problems | | | | | ● | ● | | | | | | | ● | | | ● | ● | | | | | ● | | | | | ● | ● | ● | | | | ● | |
| Sinus Problems | | | | | ● | | | | | | | | | | | ● | ● | | | | | ● | | | | | ● | ● | ● | | | | | ● |
| Shingles | | | | | | | | | | | | | | | | | | | | | | ● | | | | | | ● | | | | | | ● |
| Sexually Trans. Infections | | | | | | | | | | | | | | | | | | | | | | | | | | | | | | | | | | |

# S - W Conditions treated at Practices/Businesses and Specialist Treatment Categories

Business by County with Reference no.

| Business | Sexually Trans. Infections | Shingles | Sinus Problems | Skin Problems | Sleep Disorders | Slimming Help | Slipped Disk | Smoking Help | Sneezing | Snoring | Spinal Injuries | Sports Injuries | Sprains | Stammering | Stings | Stomach Problems |
|---|---|---|---|---|---|---|---|---|---|---|---|---|---|---|---|---|
| TRANSCENDENTAL MEDITATION (HM20266) | | | | | | | | ● | | | | | | | | |
| TURNER, R E (HM20435) | | | | | | | ● | | | | | | | | | |
| TWO STEPS REFLEXOLOGY (HM20458) | | ● | ● | ● | ● | | | | ● | | | | ● | ● | | ● |
| WALKER, SARAH (HM20803) | | | | | | | | | | | | | | | | |
| WALLACE, SUE (HM20832) | | | | | | | | | | | | ● | | | | |
| WEYBRIDGE CHIROPRACTIC CLINIC (HM21293) | | | | | | | | | | | | ● | | | | |
| WILKINSON, LESLEY (HM21510) | ● | ● | ● | ● | ● | ● | | ● | ● | ● | | ● | | ● | | ● |
| WILLIS, SALLY (HM21618) | | | | | | | | | | | | | | | | |
| WINTER, DAVID (HM21718) | ● | ● | ● | ● | ● | ● | ● | ● | ● | ● | | ● | ● | ● | ● | ● |
| WOOD, VALERIE (HM21811) | | | | ● | ● | | | | | | | | | | | |
| WOODLANDS NATURAL HLTH THERAPY (HM21832) | | ● | ● | ● | ● | | | | | ● | | | | | | ● |
| **SUSSEX (EAST)** | | | | | | | | | | | | | | | | |
| ALBION CLINIC (HM00483) | | | | | | | ● | | | | ● | ● | ● | | | |
| ALEXANDER TECHNIQUE (HM00549) | | | | | | | ● | | | | | | | | | |
| ALPHA HYPNOTHERAPY (HM00684) | | | | | ● | ● | | ● | | | | | | | | |
| ANGELA MATTHEWS HOMEOPATH (HM00873) | | | ● | ● | ● | | | ● | | | | | | | | |
| ARDERN FOOT & HEALTH CLINIC (HM00992) | | | ● | | ● | | | | | | | | | | | |
| AROMA HAIR (HM01047) | | | | | | | | ● | | | | | | | | |
| ASHDOWN OSTEOPATHIC CENTRE (HM01206) | | | ● | | | | ● | | | | | ● | ● | | | |
| BASSETT, N S (HM01857) | | | ● | | | | ● | | | | | ● | ● | | | |
| BELVAIN, E (HM02118) | | | | ● | ● | | | | | | | | | | | |
| BEXHILL CHIROPRACTIC (HM02255) | | | ● | | ● | | | | | | | ● | ● | | | |
| BEXHILL OSTEOPATHIC PRACTICE (HM02257) | | | | | | | ● | ● | | | | ● | ● | | | |
| BLACKER, JOHN (HM02441) | | | | | | | | | | | | | | | | |
| BRIGHTON & HOVE SPORTS CLINIC (HM03041) | | | | | | | ● | | | | | ● | ● | | | |
| BRIGHTON ACUPUNCTURE CLINIC (HM03042) | | ● | | ● | ● | | | ● | ● | | | | | | | ● |
| BRIGHTON ALEXANDER TRAINING (HM03043) | | | | | | | | | | | | | | | | |
| BRIGHTON CHIROPRACTIC CLINIC (HM03044) | | | | | | | | ● | | | | ● | ● | | | |
| BRIGHTON HEALTH & RACQUET CLUB (HM03045) | | | | | | | ● | | | | | ● | ● | | | |
| BRIGHTON PHYSIOTHERAPY CLINIC (HM03048) | | | | | | | ● | | | | | ● | ● | | | |
| CANTERLA, MARGARET (HM03643) | ● | ● | ● | ● | ● | ● | ● | ● | ● | ● | | ● | ● | ● | ● | ● |
| CHARTERS PHYSIO & SPORTS (HM04050) | | | | | | | ● | | | | | ● | ● | | | |
| CLINCH, ADELE (HM04675) | | | | | | | | | | | | | | | | |
| CLINIC OF CHINESE MED & ACU (HM04685) | | | ● | ● | | | | | | | | | | | | |

| Business | Stomach Ulcers | Stress | Sweating | Teeth Grinding | Tennis Elbow | Terminal Illness | Throat Problems | Thrush | Thyroid Problems | Tinnitis | Tiredness | Tonsilitis | Ulcers | Vaginal Problems | Varicose Veins | Verrucas |
|---|---|---|---|---|---|---|---|---|---|---|---|---|---|---|---|---|
| TRANSCENDENTAL MEDITATION (HM20266) | | ● | | | | | | | | | ● | | | | | |
| TURNER, R E (HM20435) | | | | | | | | | | | | | | | | |
| TWO STEPS REFLEXOLOGY (HM20458) | | | ● | | | | ● | | ● | | ● | ● | | | | |
| WALKER, SARAH (HM20803) | | | | | | | | | | | | | | | | |
| WALLACE, SUE (HM20832) | | | | | | | | | | | ● | | | | | |
| WEYBRIDGE CHIROPRACTIC CLINIC (HM21293) | | | | | | | | | | | | | | | | |
| WILKINSON, LESLEY (HM21510) | | | ● | ● | ● | | ● | ● | ● | | ● | ● | | ● | ● | |
| WILLIS, SALLY (HM21618) | | ● | | | | | | | | | | | | | | |
| WINTER, DAVID (HM21718) | ● | | ● | ● | ● | ● | ● | ● | ● | ● | ● | ● | ● | ● | ● | |
| WOOD, VALERIE (HM21811) | | ● | | | | | | | | | | | | | | |
| WOODLANDS NATURAL HLTH THERAPY (HM21832) | | | | | ● | | | ● | ● | | ● | | | | | |
| **SUSSEX (EAST)** | | | | | | | | | | | | | | | | |
| ALBION CLINIC (HM00483) | | | | | ● | | | | | | ● | | | | | |
| ALEXANDER TECHNIQUE (HM00549) | | | | | ● | | | | | | ● | | | | | |
| ALPHA HYPNOTHERAPY (HM00684) | | ● | | | | | | | | | | | | | | |
| ANGELA MATTHEWS HOMEOPATH (HM00873) | | | ● | | | | ● | ● | | | ● | | | | | |
| ARDERN FOOT & HEALTH CLINIC (HM00992) | | | | | | | ● | | | | ● | | | | ● | |
| AROMA HAIR (HM01047) | | ● | | | | | | | | | | | | | | |
| ASHDOWN OSTEOPATHIC CENTRE (HM01206) | | | | | ● | | | | | ● | | | | | | |
| BASSETT, N S (HM01857) | | | | | ● | | | | | ● | | | | | | |
| BELVAIN, E (HM02118) | | | | | | | | | | | | | | | | |
| BEXHILL CHIROPRACTIC (HM02255) | | ● | | | ● | | | | | | ● | | | | | |
| BEXHILL OSTEOPATHIC PRACTICE (HM02257) | | | | ● | ● | | | | | ● | | | | | | |
| BLACKER, JOHN (HM02441) | | | | | | | | | | | | | | | | |
| BRIGHTON & HOVE SPORTS CLINIC (HM03041) | | | | | ● | | | | | | | | | | | |
| BRIGHTON ACUPUNCTURE CLINIC (HM03042) | ● | | ● | | ● | | ● | | | | ● | | ● | | | |
| BRIGHTON ALEXANDER TRAINING (HM03043) | | | | | | | | | | | | | | | | |
| BRIGHTON CHIROPRACTIC CLINIC (HM03044) | | | | | | | | | | | ● | | | | | |
| BRIGHTON HEALTH & RACQUET CLUB (HM03045) | | | | | ● | | | | | | | | | | | |
| BRIGHTON PHYSIOTHERAPY CLINIC (HM03048) | | | | | ● | | | | | | | | | | | |
| CANTERLA, MARGARET (HM03643) | ● | | ● | ● | ● | ● | ● | ● | ● | ● | ● | ● | ● | ● | ● | |
| CHARTERS PHYSIO & SPORTS (HM04050) | | | | | ● | | | | | | | | | | | |
| CLINCH, ADELE (HM04675) | | | | | | | | | | | | | | | | |
| CLINIC OF CHINESE MED & ACU (HM04685) | | | | | | | | | | | ● | | | | | |

| Business | Vertigo | Viral Infections | Vomiting | Warts | Water Retention | Whiplash | Wind | Worms | Children | Terminally Ill | Disabled | Horses | Dogs | CatS | Other Animals |
|---|---|---|---|---|---|---|---|---|---|---|---|---|---|---|---|
| TRANSCENDENTAL MEDITATION (HM20266) | | | | | | | | | ● | | | | | | |
| TURNER, R E (HM20435) | | | | | | | | | ● | | ● | | ● | | |
| TWO STEPS REFLEXOLOGY (HM20458) | ● | | | | ● | | | | ● | ● | ● | | | | |
| WALKER, SARAH (HM20803) | | | | | ● | | ● | | ● | ● | ● | | | | |
| WALLACE, SUE (HM20832) | | | | | | | | | | | | | | | |
| WEYBRIDGE CHIROPRACTIC CLINIC (HM21293) | | | | | | | | | ● | | | | | | |
| WILKINSON, LESLEY (HM21510) | | ● | ● | ● | ● | | ● | ● | ● | ● | ● | ● | ● | ● | ● |
| WILLIS, SALLY (HM21618) | | | | | | | | | | | | | | | |
| WINTER, DAVID (HM21718) | ● | ● | ● | ● | ● | | ● | ● | ● | ● | | | | | |
| WOOD, VALERIE (HM21811) | | | | | | | | | | | | | | | |
| WOODLANDS NATURAL HLTH THERAPY (HM21832) | | | | | ● | | | | ● | | | | | | |
| **SUSSEX (EAST)** | | | | | | | | | | | | | | | |
| ALBION CLINIC (HM00483) | | | | | | ● | | | ● | ● | ● | | | | |
| ALEXANDER TECHNIQUE (HM00549) | | | | | | | | | | | | | | | |
| ALPHA HYPNOTHERAPY (HM00684) | | | | | | | | | ● | ● | ● | | | | |
| ANGELA MATTHEWS HOMEOPATH (HM00873) | | ● | | ● | | | | | ● | ● | ● | | | | |
| ARDERN FOOT & HEALTH CLINIC (HM00992) | | | | | | | | | ● | | ● | | | | |
| AROMA HAIR (HM01047) | | | | | | | | | | | | | | | |
| ASHDOWN OSTEOPATHIC CENTRE (HM01206) | | | | | | | | | ● | ● | ● | ● | ● | | |
| BASSETT, N S (HM01857) | ● | | | | | | | | | | | | | | |
| BELVAIN, E (HM02118) | | | | | | | | | | | | | | | |
| BEXHILL CHIROPRACTIC (HM02255) | | | | | | ● | | | ● | ● | ● | | | | |
| BEXHILL OSTEOPATHIC PRACTICE (HM02257) | ● | | | | | | | | ● | ● | ● | | | | |
| BLACKER, JOHN (HM02441) | | | | | | | | | ● | ● | ● | | | | |
| BRIGHTON & HOVE SPORTS CLINIC (HM03041) | | | | | | | | | ● | ● | ● | | | | |
| BRIGHTON ACUPUNCTURE CLINIC (HM03042) | | | | | | | | | ● | | | | | | |
| BRIGHTON ALEXANDER TRAINING (HM03043) | | | | | | | | | ● | ● | ● | | | | |
| BRIGHTON CHIROPRACTIC CLINIC (HM03044) | | | | | ● | | | | ● | ● | ● | | | | |
| BRIGHTON HEALTH & RACQUET CLUB (HM03045) | | | | | | | | | ● | ● | ● | | | | |
| BRIGHTON PHYSIOTHERAPY CLINIC (HM03048) | | | | | | | | | ● | ● | ● | | | | |
| CANTERLA, MARGARET (HM03643) | ● | ● | ● | ● | ● | | ● | ● | ● | ● | ● | | | | |
| CHARTERS PHYSIO & SPORTS (HM04050) | | | | | | | | | ● | ● | ● | | | | |
| CLINCH, ADELE (HM04675) | | | | ● | | | | | | ● | ● | | | | |
| CLINIC OF CHINESE MED & ACU (HM04685) | | | ● | | | | | | ● | ● | ● | | | | |

(Children, Terminally Ill, Disabled, Horses, Dogs, CatS, Other Animals: Specialist Treatment Categories)

# S - W Conditions treated at Practices/Businesses and Specialist Treatment Categories

| Business by County with Reference no. | Sexually Trans. Infections | Shingles | Sinus Problems | Skin Problems | Sleep Disorders | Slimming Help | Slipped Disk | Smoking Help | Sneezing | Snoring | Spinal Injuries | Sports Injuries | Sprains | Stammering | Stings | Stomach Problems | Stomach Ulcers | Stress | Sweating | Teeth Grinding | Tennis Elbow | Terminal Illness | Throat Problems | Thrush | Thyroid Problems | Tinnitis | Tiredness | Tonsilitis | Ulcers | Vaginal Problems | Varicose Veins | Verrucas | Vertigo | Viral Infections | Vomiting | Warts | Water Retention | Whiplash | Wind | Worms | Specialist Treatment Categories: Children | Terminally Ill | Disabled | Horses | Dogs | CatS | Other Animals |
|---|---|---|---|---|---|---|---|---|---|---|---|---|---|---|---|---|---|---|---|---|---|---|---|---|---|---|---|---|---|---|---|---|---|---|---|---|---|---|---|---|---|---|---|---|---|---|---|
| COMP THERAPY & TRAINING CENTRE (HM04915) | ● | ● | ● | ● | ● | ● | ● | ● | ● | ● | | ● | ● | ● | ● | ● | ● | | ● | ● | ● | ● | ● | ● | ● | ● | ● | ● | ● | ● | ● | | ● | ● | ● | ● | ● | | ● | ● | ● | ● | ● | | | | |
| CONCEPTS PHYSIO & NUTRITION (HM04970) | ● | ● | ● | ● | ● | ● | ● | ● | ● | ● | | ● | ● | ● | ● | ● | ● | | ● | ● | ● | ● | ● | ● | ● | ● | ● | ● | ● | ● | ● | | ● | ● | ● | ● | ● | | ● | | ● | ● | ● | ● | ● | ● | ● |
| COOK, ELAINE (HM05042) | | | | | ● | | | | | | | ● | | | | | | | | | ● | | | | | ● | ● | | | | | | | | | | | | ● | | ● | | | | | | |
| COX, JULIET (HM05308) | | | | | | | ● | | | | | ● | | ● | | | | | | ● | ● | | ● | | | | ● | | | | | | | | | | | ● | | | | | | | | | |
| CRESENT CLINIC (HM05422) | | ● | ● | ● | ● | | ● | ● | ● | ● | | ● | ● | | ● | ● | ● | | ● | ● | ● | | ● | ● | ● | ● | ● | ● | ● | ● | ● | | ● | ● | ● | ● | ● | | ● | ● | ● | ● | ● | | | | |
| CROWBOROUGH CHIRO/COMP HLTH (HM05498) | | | ● | ● | | | | | | | | | | | | ● | ● | | | ● | ● | | | | | | | | | | | | ● | | ● | | | | ● | | ● | ● | ● | | | | |
| CROWBOROUGH COMP THERAPISTS (HM05499) | | | ● | ● | ● | | | | | | | | | | | | | ● | | | | | | | | | ● | | | | | | | | | | | | | | ● | ● | ● | | | | |
| CULL, BEN (HM05556) | | | | | | ● | ● | ● | | | | ● | ● | | | | | | | ● | ● | | | | | | ● | | | | | | | | | | | | | | ● | ● | ● | | | | |
| DADSWELL, CLAIRE (HM05670) | ● | ● | ● | ● | ● | ● | | ● | ● | ● | | ● | ● | ● | ● | ● | ● | | ● | ● | ● | ● | ● | ● | ● | ● | ● | ● | ● | ● | ● | | ● | ● | ● | ● | ● | | ● | ● | | | | | | | |
| DEEKS, STUART (HM05956) | | ● | ● | ● | ● | | | ● | ● | | | | ● | | ● | ● | ● | | ● | ● | ● | | ● | ● | ● | ● | ● | ● | ● | ● | ● | | ● | ● | ● | ● | ● | | ● | ● | ● | ● | ● | | | | |
| DRIVE OSTEO AND SPORTS CLINIC (HM06314) | | | | | | | ● | | | | | ● | ● | | | | | | | ● | ● | | | | | | | | | | | | | | | | | | | | ● | | ● | | | | |
| DRYDEN, B A (HM06332) | | | | | | | | ● | | | | | | | | | | | | | | | | | | ● | | | | | | | | | | | | | | | | | ● | | | | |
| DYKE ROAD NATURAL HEALTH (HM06450) | ● | ● | ● | ● | ● | ● | ● | ● | ● | ● | | ● | ● | ● | ● | ● | ● | | ● | ● | ● | ● | ● | ● | ● | ● | ● | ● | ● | ● | ● | | ● | ● | ● | ● | ● | | ● | ● | ● | ● | ● | | | | |
| EAST BOURNE CLINIC (HM06509) | | | | | | | ● | | | | | ● | ● | | | | | | | | ● | | | | | | | | | | | | | | | | | | | | ● | | ● | | | | |
| EAST, MARY EDGINTON (HM06531) | | | | | | | | | | | | | | | | | | | | | | | | | | | | | | | | | | | | | | | | | ● | ● | ● | | | | |
| EASTBOURNE CHIROPRACTIC CLINIC (HM06535) | | | | | ● | | ● | | | | ● | ● | ● | | | | | | | | ● | | | | | | | | | | | | | | | | | ● | | | ● | ● | ● | | | | |
| EATON, MARION (HM06563) | | | | | | | | | | | | | | | | | | | | | | | | | | | | | | | | | | | | | | | | | ● | ● | ● | | | | |
| FAIRCHILD, HAZEL (HM07052) | | | | | | | | | | | | | | | | | | | | | | | | | | | | | | | | | | | | | | | | | | | ● | | | | |
| FAMILY FIRST (HM07087) | | | | | ● | ● | | ● | | | | ● | ● | | | | | | | | ● | | | | | | | | | | | | | | | | | | | | ● | ● | ● | | | | |
| FIVEWAYS OSTEOPATHIC PRACTICE (HM07382) | | | | | | | ● | | | | | ● | ● | | | | | | | | ● | | | | | | | | | | | | | | | | | | | | ● | | ● | | | | |
| FLOYD, MICHELLE (HM07438) | | ● | ● | ● | ● | | | | ● | ● | | ● | ● | ● | ● | ● | ● | | ● | ● | ● | ● | ● | ● | ● | ● | ● | ● | ● | ● | ● | | ● | ● | ● | ● | ● | | ● | ● | ● | ● | ● | | | | |
| FOUNDATION, ANGELGATE (HM07615) | | | ● | ● | | ● | | | | | | | ● | | | ● | ● | | | | ● | ● | | | ● | ● | ● | | | | | | | | | | ● | | ● | | ● | ● | ● | | | | |
| GATEHOUSE THERAPY CENTRE (HM07925) | | | | | | | | | | | | | | | | | | | | | | | | | | | | | | | | | | | | | | | | | ● | ● | ● | | | | |
| GEIGES, STEPHANIE (HM07967) | | | | | | | ● | | | | ● | ● | ● | | | | | | | | ● | | | | | | | | | | | | | | | | | | | | ● | ● | ● | | | | |
| GOLDSTONE CLINIC (HM08230) | | | | | | | | | | | | | | | | | | | | | | | | | | | | | | | | | | | | | | | | | ● | ● | ● | | | | |
| GOLDSTONE CLINIC (HM08229) | | | | | ● | ● | | | | | ● | ● | ● | | | | | | | | ● | | | | | | ● | | | | | | ● | | | | | ● | | | ● | ● | ● | | | | |
| GONZALEZ, SOHANI (HM08237) | ● | ● | ● | ● | ● | | | ● | ● | | | ● | ● | ● | ● | ● | ● | | ● | ● | ● | ● | ● | ● | ● | ● | ● | ● | ● | ● | ● | | ● | ● | ● | ● | ● | | ● | ● | ● | ● | | | | | |
| GRIFFITHS, J (HM08567) | | | | | | | | | | | | ● | ● | | | | | | | | ● | | | | | | ● | | | | | | | | | | | | | | ● | ● | ● | | | | |
| HART, RONALD (HM09131) | | | | | | | | | | | | | | | | | | | | | | | | | | | | | | | | | | | | | ● | | | | ● | ● | ● | | | | |
| HART, RONALD (HM09130) | | | | | | | | | | | | | | | | | | | | | | | | | | | | | | | | | | | | | | | | | ● | ● | ● | | | | |
| HAWKINS, LUKE (HM09224) | | | | | | | | | | | | ● | ● | | | | | | | | | | | | | | | | | | | | | | | ● | | | | | ● | ● | ● | | | | |
| HEMMINGWAY CHIROPODIST (HM09537) | | | | | | | | | | | | | | | | | | | | | | | | | | | | | | | | ● | | | | ● | | | | | ● | ● | ● | | | | |
| HERBAL HEALTH CLINIC (HM09617) | | ● | ● | ● | ● | | | | ● | | | ● | ● | | ● | ● | ● | | ● | ● | ● | | ● | ● | ● | ● | ● | ● | ● | | ● | | ● | ● | | ● | ● | | ● | | ● | | | | | | |
| HOLDEN NATURAL HEALTH CLINIC (HM09927) | | | | | | | | ● | | | | | | | ● | | | | | | | | | | | | | | | | | | | ● | | ● | | | | | ● | ● | ● | | | | |

# S - W Conditions treated at Practices/Businesses and Specialist Treatment Categories

Business by County with Reference no.

**SUSSEX (WEST)**

| Business | Sexually Trans. Infections | Shingles | Sinus Problems | Skin Problems | Sleep Disorders | Slimming Help | Slipped Disk | Smoking Help | Sneezing | Snoring | Spinal Injuries | Sports Injuries | Sprains | Stammering | Stings | Stomach Problems |
|---|---|---|---|---|---|---|---|---|---|---|---|---|---|---|---|---|
| HOVE CHIROPRACTIC CLINIC (HM10227) | | | | | | | ● | | | | ● | ● | ● | | | |
| HOVE OSTEOPATHIC CLINIC (HM10228) | | | | | | | ● | | | | | ● | ● | | | |
| HUGHES, CLARE (HM10324) | | | | | | | ● | | | | ● | ● | ● | | | |
| HYSLOP, C P (HM10543) | ● | ● | ● | ● | ● | ● | ● | ● | ● | ● | | ● | ● | ● | ● | ● |
| JEMPSON, NICOLA (HM10978) | | | | | | | | | | | | | | | | |
| JOY, JANET (HM11231) | | | | | ● | | | ● | | | | | | | | |
| LEWES CHIROPRACTIC CLINIC (HM12271) | | | | | | | ● | | | | ● | ● | ● | | | |
| MCKEOWN, KAY (HM13532) | | | | | | | ● | | | | | | | | | |
| MEADOWSWEET (HM13634) | | | | | | | | | | | | ● | ● | | | |
| MURPHY, KEVIN (HM14387) | | | | | ● | | ● | | | ● | | ● | ● | | | |
| NEAT FEET (HM14742) | | | | | | | | | | | | | | | | |
| NEWICK PHYSIOTHERAPY CLINIC (HM14865) | | | | | | | ● | | | | | ● | ● | | | |
| OLD TOWN CHIROPRACTIC CLINIC (HM15263) | | | | | | | ● | | | | | ● | | | | |
| PRICE, JAMES (HM16583) | | | | | | | | | | | | | | | | |
| PRIORY HEIGHTS (HM16633) | | | ● | ● | | | | ● | | | | ● | | | | |
| REEVES, ALAN (HM17062) | | | | | | | | | | | | | | | | |
| REFLEXOLOGY FOR HEALTH (HM17095) | | | ● | | ● | | | | | | | | | | | ● |
| SANDERSON & ELEMENT (HM17919) | | | | | | | | | | | | | ● | ● | | |
| SANDERSON & ELEMENT (HM17920) | | | | | | | | | | | | ● | ● | | | |
| SANDERSON & ELEMENT (HM17922) | | | | | | | | | | | | | ● | ● | | |
| SCHOLL CENTRE (HM18032) | | | | | | | | | | | | | | | | |
| SIMPSON, HEATHER (HM18588) | | | | | | | | | | | | | | | | |
| SUNDIAL HOUSE CHIROPRACTIC (HM19506) | | | | | | | | | | | | ● | ● | | | |
| TEALE, PAUL (HM19809) | | | | | | | ● | | | | | ● | ● | | | |
| TISSERAND (HM20095) | | | | | | | | | | | | | | | | |
| TRENCHARD, ABIGAIL (HM20319) | | | | | | | | | | | | | | | | |
| VALENCE ROAD OSTEOPATHS (HM20554) | | | | | | | ● | | | | | ● | ● | | | |
| WADHURST PHYSIO/SPORTS CLNC (HM20730) | | | | | | | ● | | | | | ● | ● | | | |
| WADHURST PHYSIO/SPORTS CLNC (HM20729) | | | | | | | ● | | | | | ● | ● | | | |
| WALSH, M J (HM20865) | | | | | | | ● | | | | | ● | ● | | | |
| WEDLAKE-GRIFFITHS, J (HM21097) | | | | | | | ● | | | | | ● | ● | | | |
| WILBURY PHYSIOTHERAPY (HM21480) | | | | | | | ● | | | | | ● | ● | | | |
| WRIGHT, P A (HM21946) | | | | | | | | | | | | ● | | | | |

| Business | Stomach Ulcers | Stress | Sweating | Teeth Grinding | Tennis Elbow | Terminal Illness | Throat Problems | Thrush | Thyroid Problems | Tinnitis | Tiredness | Tonsilitis | Ulcers | Vaginal Problems | Varicose Veins | Verrucas |
|---|---|---|---|---|---|---|---|---|---|---|---|---|---|---|---|---|
| HOVE CHIROPRACTIC CLINIC (HM10227) | | | | | ● | | | | | | | | | | | |
| HOVE OSTEOPATHIC CLINIC (HM10228) | | | | | ● | | | | | | | | | | | |
| HUGHES, CLARE (HM10324) | | | | | ● | | | | | | | | | | | |
| HYSLOP, C P (HM10543) | ● | | ● | ● | ● | ● | ● | ● | ● | ● | ● | ● | ● | ● | ● | |
| JEMPSON, NICOLA (HM10978) | | ● | | | | | | | | | | | | | | |
| JOY, JANET (HM11231) | | | | | | | | | | | | | | | | |
| LEWES CHIROPRACTIC CLINIC (HM12271) | | | | | ● | | | | | | | | | | | |
| MCKEOWN, KAY (HM13532) | | | | | | | | | | | | | | | | |
| MEADOWSWEET (HM13634) | | | | | ● | | | | | | | | | | | |
| MURPHY, KEVIN (HM14387) | | | | | ● | | | | | ● | | | | | | |
| NEAT FEET (HM14742) | | | | | | | | | | | | | | | | |
| NEWICK PHYSIOTHERAPY CLINIC (HM14865) | | | | | ● | | | | | | | | | | | |
| OLD TOWN CHIROPRACTIC CLINIC (HM15263) | | | | | ● | | | | | | | | | | | |
| PRICE, JAMES (HM16583) | | | | | | | | | | | | | | | | ● |
| PRIORY HEIGHTS (HM16633) | | | | | | | | | | | ● | | | | | |
| REEVES, ALAN (HM17062) | | | | | | | | | | | | | | | | |
| REFLEXOLOGY FOR HEALTH (HM17095) | | | | ● | | | ● | | ● | | ● | | | | | |
| SANDERSON & ELEMENT (HM17919) | | | | | | | | | | | | | | | | |
| SANDERSON & ELEMENT (HM17920) | | | | | | | | | | | | | | | | |
| SANDERSON & ELEMENT (HM17922) | | | | | | | | | | | | | | | | |
| SCHOLL CENTRE (HM18032) | | | | | | | | | | | | | | | | |
| SIMPSON, HEATHER (HM18588) | | | | | | | | | | | | | | | | |
| SUNDIAL HOUSE CHIROPRACTIC (HM19506) | | | | | ● | | | | | | | | | | | |
| TEALE, PAUL (HM19809) | | | | | | | | | | | | | | | | |
| TISSERAND (HM20095) | | ● | | | | | | | | | | | | | | |
| TRENCHARD, ABIGAIL (HM20319) | | ● | | | | | | | | | | | | | | |
| VALENCE ROAD OSTEOPATHS (HM20554) | | | | | ● | | | | | | | | | | | |
| WADHURST PHYSIO/SPORTS CLNC (HM20730) | | | | | ● | | | | | | | | | | | |
| WADHURST PHYSIO/SPORTS CLNC (HM20729) | | | | | ● | | | | | | | | | | | |
| WALSH, M J (HM20865) | | | | | ● | | | | | | | | | | | |
| WEDLAKE-GRIFFITHS, J (HM21097) | | | | | ● | | | | | | | | | | | |
| WILBURY PHYSIOTHERAPY (HM21480) | | | | | ● | | | | | | | | | | | |
| WRIGHT, P A (HM21946) | | | | | | | | | | | | | | | | |

| Business | Vertigo | Viral Infections | Vomiting | Warts | Water Retention | Whiplash | Wind | Worms | Children | Terminally Ill | Disabled | Horses | Dogs | CatS | Other Animals |
|---|---|---|---|---|---|---|---|---|---|---|---|---|---|---|---|
| HOVE CHIROPRACTIC CLINIC (HM10227) | | | | | | ● | | | ● | ● | ● | | | | |
| HOVE OSTEOPATHIC CLINIC (HM10228) | | | | | | | | | ● | ● | ● | | | | |
| HUGHES, CLARE (HM10324) | | | | | | | | | ● | ● | ● | | | | |
| HYSLOP, C P (HM10543) | ● | ● | ● | ● | ● | | ● | ● | ● | ● | ● | | | | |
| JEMPSON, NICOLA (HM10978) | | | | | | | | | ● | ● | ● | | | | |
| JOY, JANET (HM11231) | | | | | | | | | | | | | | | |
| LEWES CHIROPRACTIC CLINIC (HM12271) | ● | | | | | ● | | | ● | ● | ● | | | | |
| MCKEOWN, KAY (HM13532) | | | | | | | | | | | | | | | |
| MEADOWSWEET (HM13634) | | | | | | | | | ● | ● | ● | | | | |
| MURPHY, KEVIN (HM14387) | ● | | | | | | | | ● | ● | ● | ● | ● | ● | ● |
| NEAT FEET (HM14742) | | | | ● | | | | | ● | ● | ● | | | | |
| NEWICK PHYSIOTHERAPY CLINIC (HM14865) | | | | | | | | | | | ● | | | | |
| OLD TOWN CHIROPRACTIC CLINIC (HM15263) | | | | | | | | | ● | | | | | | |
| PRICE, JAMES (HM16583) | | | | ● | | | | | ● | ● | ● | | | | |
| PRIORY HEIGHTS (HM16633) | | | | | | | | | | | ● | | | | |
| REEVES, ALAN (HM17062) | | | | | | | | | | ● | | | | | |
| REFLEXOLOGY FOR HEALTH (HM17095) | ● | | | | ● | | ● | | ● | ● | ● | | | | |
| SANDERSON & ELEMENT (HM17919) | | | | | | | | | ● | ● | ● | | | | |
| SANDERSON & ELEMENT (HM17920) | | | | | | | | | ● | ● | ● | | | | |
| SANDERSON & ELEMENT (HM17922) | | | | | | | | | ● | ● | ● | | | | |
| SCHOLL CENTRE (HM18032) | | | | ● | | | | | ● | ● | ● | | | | |
| SIMPSON, HEATHER (HM18588) | | | | | | | | | | | | | ● | ● | ● |
| SUNDIAL HOUSE CHIROPRACTIC (HM19506) | | | | | | | | | ● | | | | | | |
| TEALE, PAUL (HM19809) | | | | | | | | | ● | | ● | | | | |
| TISSERAND (HM20095) | | | | | | | | | | | | | | | |
| TRENCHARD, ABIGAIL (HM20319) | | | | | | | | | | | | | | | |
| VALENCE ROAD OSTEOPATHS (HM20554) | | | | | | ● | | | ● | | ● | | | | |
| WADHURST PHYSIO/SPORTS CLNC (HM20730) | | | | | | | | | ● | ● | ● | | | | |
| WADHURST PHYSIO/SPORTS CLNC (HM20729) | | | | | | | | | ● | ● | ● | | | | |
| WALSH, M J (HM20865) | | | | | | | | | ● | ● | ● | | | | |
| WEDLAKE-GRIFFITHS, J (HM21097) | | | | | | | | | ● | | ● | | | | |
| WILBURY PHYSIOTHERAPY (HM21480) | | | | | | | | | ● | ● | ● | | | | |
| WRIGHT, P A (HM21946) | | | | ● | | | | | ● | ● | ● | | | | |

(Children, Terminally Ill, Disabled, Horses, Dogs, CatS and Other Animals: Specialist Treatment Categories)

# S - W Conditions treated at Practices/Businesses and Specialist Treatment Categories

| Business by County with Reference no. | Sexually Trans. Infections | Shingles | Sinus Problems | Skin Problems | Sleep Disorders | Slimming Help | Slipped Disk | Smoking Help | Sneezing | Snoring | Spinal Injuries | Sports Injuries | Sprains | Stammering | Stings | Stomach Problems | Stomach Ulcers | Stress | Sweating | Teeth Grinding | Tennis Elbow | Terminal Illness | Throat Problems | Thrush | Thyroid Problems | Tinnitis | Tiredness | Tonsilitis | Ulcers | Vaginal Problems | Varicose Veins | Verrucas | Vertigo | Viral Infections | Vomiting | Warts | Water Retention | Whiplash | Wind | Worms | Specialist Treatment Categories: Children | Terminally Ill | Disabled | Horses | Dogs | CatS | Other Animals |
|---|---|---|---|---|---|---|---|---|---|---|---|---|---|---|---|---|---|---|---|---|---|---|---|---|---|---|---|---|---|---|---|---|---|---|---|---|---|---|---|---|---|---|---|---|---|---|---|
| ACORN CENTRE (HM00171) | | | | | | | | | | | | | | | | | ● | | | | ● | | | ● | | ● | ● | | | | | | | | | | | | | | ● | ● | ● | ● | ● | ● | ● |
| ACUPUNCTURE CLINIC (HM00277) | | | | | | | | | | | | | | | | | | | | | | | | | | | | | | | | | | | | | | | | | ● | ● | ● | | ● | | |
| ALAN SMITH CHIROPRACTOR (HM00470) | | | ● | | | | | | | | | ● | ● | | | | | | | ● | ● | | | | | | | | | | | | ● | | | | | | | | ● | | | | | | |
| ANDREW BATHIE PRACTICE (HM00846) | | | | | ● | ● | | ● | | ● | | ● | | ● | | | | | | ● | | | | | | ● | ● | | | | | | ● | | | | | | | | ● | | | | | | |
| ANGELA (HM00872) | | | | | | | | | | | | | | | | | | ● | | | | | | | | | | | | | | | | | | | | | | | ● | ● | ● | ● | ● | ● | |
| AUROMA (HM01357) | | | | | | | | | | | | | | | | | | ● | | | | | | | | | | | | | | | | | | | | | | | | | | | | | |
| AVALON HEALTH CENTRE (HM01380) | ● | ● | ● | ● | ● | ● | ● | ● | ● | ● | | ● | ● | ● | ● | ● | ● | | ● | ● | ● | ● | ● | ● | ● | ● | ● | ● | ● | ● | ● | | ● | ● | ● | ● | ● | | ● | ● | ● | ● | ● | | | | |
| B O P (HM01452) | | | ● | | | | ● | | | | | ● | ● | | | | | | | | ● | | | | | ● | | | | | | | ● | | | | | | | | | | | | | | |
| BACK 2 FITNESS CHIROPRACTIC (HM01476) | | | | | | | | | | | | ● | ● | | | | | | | | ● | | | | | | | | | | | | | | | | | | | | ● | ● | ● | | | | |
| BALOOMBE OSTEOPATHIC & SPORTS (HM01641) | | | | | | | | | | | | | | | | | | | | | | | | | | | | | | | | | | | | | | | | | ● | ● | ● | | | | |
| BARTHOLOMEW WAY CLINIC (HM01818) | | | | ● | | | | | | | | ● | ● | | | | | | ● | | | | | | | | | | | | ● | | | ● | | ● | ● | | | | ● | ● | ● | | | | |
| BELLAMY PARTNERSHIP (HM02093) | | | | | | | ● | | | | | ● | ● | | | | | | | | | | | | | | | | | | | | | | | | | | | | ● | | | | | | |
| BLACK, PAULINE (HM02425) | | ● | ● | ● | ● | | | | ● | | | ● | ● | ● | ● | ● | ● | | ● | ● | ● | ● | ● | ● | ● | ● | ● | ● | ● | ● | ● | | ● | ● | ● | ● | ● | | ● | ● | ● | ● | ● | | | | |
| BODYGUIDE ALTERNATE (HM02619) | ● | ● | ● | ● | ● | ● | ● | ● | ● | ● | | ● | ● | ● | ● | ● | ● | | ● | ● | ● | ● | ● | ● | ● | ● | ● | ● | ● | ● | ● | | ● | ● | ● | ● | ● | | ● | ● | ● | ● | ● | | | | |
| BOHNET, CAROLE (HM02648) | | | ● | | ● | | | | | | | ● | | | | | | ● | | | ● | | | | | | | | | | | | | | | | | | | | | | | | | | |
| BRITCHIRO CLINIC (HM03068) | | | | | | | ● | | | | ● | ● | ● | | | | | | | | ● | | | | | | | | | | | | | | | | | ● | | | ● | ● | ● | | | | |
| BURNS, L C (HM03417) | | | | | | | ● | | | | | ● | ● | | | | | | | | ● | | | | | | | | | | | | | | | | | | | | ● | ● | ● | | | | |
| CARTLAND, ANN (HM03794) | | | | | | | | | | | | | | | | | | | | | | | | | | | | | | | | | | | | | | | | | ● | ● | ● | | | | |
| CASH, G G (HM03811) | | | | | | | | | | | | | | | | | | | | | | | | | | | | | | | | ● | | | | ● | | | | | ● | ● | ● | | | | |
| CHANGES (HM03985) | | ● | ● | ● | ● | | | | | | | | ● | | | ● | | | ● | | | | | ● | ● | | ● | | | | | | ● | | | ● | ● | | | | ● | ● | | | ● | ● | ● |
| CHASE, PETER (HM04061) | | | | | | | | | | | | | | | | | | | | | | | | | | | | | | | | ● | | | | | | | | | | ● | ● | | | | |
| CHICHESTER NATURAL HEALTH CTRE (HM04156) | ● | ● | ● | ● | ● | ● | ● | ● | ● | ● | | ● | ● | ● | ● | ● | ● | | ● | ● | ● | ● | ● | ● | ● | ● | ● | ● | ● | ● | ● | | ● | ● | ● | ● | ● | | ● | ● | ● | ● | ● | | | | |
| CHIROPODIST () | | | | | | | | | | | | | | | | | | | | | | | | | | | | | | | | ● | | | | | | | | | ● | ● | ● | | | | |
| CLAIRVOYANT - MEDIUM - HEALER (HM04514) | | ● | ● | ● | ● | ● | ● | ● | | | | ● | | ● | ● | ● | ● | | ● | ● | ● | ● | ● | ● | ● | ● | ● | ● | ● | ● | ● | | ● | ● | ● | ● | | | | | ● | ● | ● | ● | ● | ● | ● |
| CLARKE, STEVEN (HM04604) | | | | | ● | ● | | | | | | | | | | | | | ● | | | | | | | | | | | | | | | | | | | | | | ● | ● | ● | | | | |
| CORNERWEIGHS (HM05183) | | | | | | | | | | | | | | | | | | | | | | | | ● | | | | | | | | | | | | | | | | | | | | | | | |
| DALLAS, PETER (HM05691) | | | ● | ● | ● | | | | | | | ● | | | | | | | ● | | | | | | | | ● | | | | | | | | | | ● | | | | ● | | | | | | |
| DYER & ASSOCIATES (HM06444) | | | | | | | ● | | | | ● | ● | ● | | | | | | | | ● | | | | | | | | | | | | | | | | | ● | | | ● | | ● | | | | |
| EMINATIONS ACUPUNCTURE CLINIC (HM06805) | ● | ● | ● | ● | ● | | | ● | | | | ● | ● | | | ● | ● | | ● | ● | ● | ● | ● | ● | ● | ● | ● | ● | ● | ● | ● | | ● | ● | ● | ● | ● | | ● | ● | ● | ● | ● | | | | |
| FELPHAM NATURAL HEALTH CLINIC (HM07206) | | | | | | | | | | | | ● | ● | | | | | | | | ● | | | | | | | | | | | | | | | | | | | | ● | ● | | | | | |
| FROST, CHARLES (HM07760) | | | | | ● | ● | | ● | | | | | | | | | | | | | | | | | | | | | | | | | | | | ● | | | | | ● | | ● | | | | |
| FURNACE GREEN CHIRO CTRE (HM07800) | ● | ● | ● | ● | ● | ● | ● | ● | ● | ● | | ● | ● | ● | ● | ● | ● | | ● | ● | ● | ● | ● | ● | ● | ● | ● | ● | ● | ● | ● | | ● | ● | ● | ● | ● | | ● | ● | ● | | ● | | | | |
| G & G FOOD SUPPLIES (HM07807) | | | | | | | | | | | | | | | | | | | | | | | | ● | | | | | | | | | | | | | | | | | | | | | | | |
| GARDINER, SAM (HM07876) | | | | | ● | ● | | ● | | ● | | | | | | | | ● | | ● | | | | | | | ● | | | | | | | | | | | | | | ● | ● | ● | | | | |

# S - W Conditions treated at Practices/Businesses and Specialist Treatment Categories

| | | | | | | | | | | | | | | | | | | | | | | | | | | | | | | | | | | | | | | | | | Specialist Treatment Categories | | | | | | |
|---|---|---|---|---|---|---|---|---|---|---|---|---|---|---|---|---|---|---|---|---|---|---|---|---|---|---|---|---|---|---|---|---|---|---|---|---|---|---|---|---|---|---|---|---|---|---|
| Business by County with Reference no. | Sexually Trans. Infections | Shingles | Sinus Problems | Skin Problems | Sleep Disorders | Slimming Help | Slipped Disk | Smoking Help | Sneezing | Snoring | Spinal Injuries | Sports Injuries | Sprains | Stammering | Stings | Stomach Problems | Stomach Ulcers | Stress | Sweating | Teeth Grinding | Tennis Elbow | Terminal Illness | Throat Problems | Thrush | Thyroid Problems | Tinnitis | Tiredness | Tonsilitis | Ulcers | Vaginal Problems | Varicose Veins | Verrucas | Vertigo | Viral Infections | Vomiting | Warts | Water Retention | Whiplash | Wind | Worms | Children | Terminally Ill | Disabled | Horses | Dogs | CatS | Other Animals |
| GRAVILLE, CHRIS (HM08405) | | | | | | | | | | | | | | | | | | ● | | | | | | | | | | | | | | | | | | | | | | | | | | | | | |
| GREENFIELD, KAREN (HM08486) | | | | | ● | | | | | | | | | | | ● | | ● | | | | | | | | | | | | | | | | | | | | | | | ● | ● | ● | | | | |
| HARRIS, PAUL A E (HM09084) | | | | | | | | | | | | ● | ● | | | | | | | | ● | | | | | | | | | | | | | | | | | | | | ● | ● | ● | | | | |
| HEALTH IS HAPPINESS REFLEX (HM09390) | | | ● | ● | ● | | | | | | | | | | | ● | | | | | | | | | | | ● | | | | | | | | | | | | | | ● | ● | ● | | | | |
| HEELER CENTRE (HM09498) | | ● | ● | ● | ● | | | ● | | | | ● | ● | | | | | | | | ● | | | | ● | | ● | | | | | | | | | | ● | | | | ● | | ● | | | | |
| HORSHAM CHIROPRACTIC CENTRE (HM10191) | | | | | | | ● | | | | ● | ● | ● | | | | | | | | ● | | | | | | | | | | | | | | | | | ● | | | ● | ● | ● | | | | |
| I C O M (HM10548) | | | ● | ● | ● | | ● | ● | | | | ● | ● | | | ● | | ● | ● | ● | ● | | ● | | ● | ● | ● | | | | | | ● | | ● | | ● | | ● | | ● | ● | ● | | | | |
| JONES, NIGEL (HM11182) | | | | | | | ● | | | | | ● | ● | | | | | | | | ● | | | | | | | | | | | | | | | | | ● | | | ● | ● | ● | | | | |
| JONES, WENDY (HM11203) | | | | | | | | | | | | ● | ● | | | | | | | | ● | | | | | | | | | | | | | | | | | | | | | | | | | | |
| LITTLEHAMPTON NAT HLTH CTRE (HM12470) | ● | ● | ● | ● | ● | ● | ● | ● | ● | ● | | ● | ● | ● | ● | ● | ● | | ● | ● | ● | ● | ● | ● | ● | ● | ● | ● | ● | ● | ● | | ● | ● | ● | ● | ● | | ● | ● | ● | ● | ● | | ● | ● | ● |
| MAYNARD, MARTIN A (HM13357) | | | | | | | | | | | | | | | | | | | | | | | | | | | | | | | | ● | | | | ● | | | | | ● | ● | ● | | | | |
| MID SUSSEX CHIROPRACTIC CLINIC (HM13805) | | ● | ● | ● | ● | ● | ● | ● | ● | ● | | ● | ● | | | ● | ● | | ● | | ● | | ● | ● | ● | ● | ● | ● | ● | | | | ● | | | | | | ● | | ● | ● | ● | | | | |
| MID SUSSEX HOMEOPATHIC CLINIC (HM13806) | | ● | ● | ● | ● | | | | ● | | | ● | ● | | ● | ● | ● | | ● | | ● | | ● | ● | | ● | ● | ● | ● | ● | ● | | ● | ● | ● | ● | ● | | ● | ● | ● | ● | | | | | |
| MILLENNIUM HOMEOPATHY (HM13877) | ● | ● | ● | ● | ● | ● | ● | ● | ● | ● | | ● | ● | ● | ● | ● | ● | | ● | ● | ● | ● | ● | ● | ● | ● | ● | ● | ● | ● | ● | | ● | ● | ● | ● | ● | | ● | ● | ● | ● | ● | | | | |
| MIND WORK SOLUTIONS (HM13967) | ● | ● | ● | ● | ● | ● | ● | ● | ● | ● | | ● | ● | ● | ● | ● | ● | | ● | ● | ● | ● | ● | ● | ● | ● | ● | ● | ● | ● | ● | | ● | ● | ● | ● | ● | | ● | ● | ● | ● | ● | | | | |
| NUNN, SALLY (HM15108) | ● | ● | ● | ● | ● | ● | ● | ● | ● | ● | | ● | ● | ● | ● | ● | ● | | ● | ● | ● | ● | ● | ● | ● | ● | ● | ● | ● | ● | ● | | ● | ● | ● | ● | ● | | ● | ● | ● | ● | ● | | | | |
| OSTEOPATHY AT ESQUIRE'S (HM15479) | | | ● | | | | ● | | | | | | ● | | | | | | | | ● | | | | | | | | | | | | | | | | | | | | ● | ● | ● | | | | |
| PAIN & PARALYSIS SPECIALIST (HM15578) | | | | | | | ● | | | | | ● | ● | | | | | ● | | | ● | | | | | | ● | | | | | | | | | | | ● | | | ● | ● | ● | ● | ● | ● | ● |
| PALMER, GAYLE (HM15605) | | | ● | | ● | | ● | | ● | ● | | ● | ● | ● | | ● | | | | ● | ● | ● | | | ● | ● | ● | ● | ● | ● | | | ● | | | | | | ● | | ● | ● | ● | | | | |
| PALMER, GAYLE (HM15606) | | ● | ● | ● | ● | | ● | | | ● | | ● | ● | | | ● | ● | | ● | ● | ● | ● | ● | | ● | ● | ● | ● | ● | ● | ● | | ● | ● | ● | | ● | | ● | | ● | ● | ● | | ● | | |
| PITT, KATHY (HM16349) | ● | ● | ● | ● | ● | ● | ● | ● | ● | ● | | ● | ● | ● | ● | ● | ● | | ● | ● | ● | ● | ● | ● | ● | ● | ● | ● | ● | ● | ● | | ● | ● | ● | ● | ● | | ● | ● | ● | ● | ● | | | | |
| PORTLAND PHYSIOTHERAPY CLINIC (HM16451) | | | | | | | ● | | | | | ● | ● | | | ● | | | | | ● | | | | | | | | | | | | | | | | | | | | ● | | ● | | | | |
| RICHARDSON, BRIAN J (HM17269) | | | | | | | | | | | | ● | ● | | | | | | ● | | | | | | | | | | | | | | | | | | | | | | ● | | ● | | | | |
| RICHARDSON, JANET (HM17282) | | | | | | | | | | | | | | | | | | | | | | | | | | | | | | | | ● | | | | | | | | | ● | ● | ● | | | | |
| ROOM FOR HEALING (HM17585) | | ● | ● | ● | ● | | ● | | | | | ● | ● | | | ● | ● | | ● | | ● | ● | ● | ● | ● | ● | ● | ● | ● | ● | | | ● | ● | | | ● | | ● | ● | ● | ● | ● | | | | |
| SANDERSON & ELEMENT (HM17921) | | | | | | | | | | | | | ● | ● | | | | | | | | | | | | | | | | | | | | | | | | | | | ● | ● | ● | | | | |
| SANDON, PATER H G (DR) (HM17925) | ● | ● | ● | ● | ● | ● | ● | ● | ● | ● | | ● | ● | ● | ● | ● | ● | | ● | ● | ● | ● | ● | ● | ● | ● | ● | ● | ● | ● | ● | | ● | ● | ● | ● | ● | | ● | ● | ● | ● | ● | | | | |
| SMITH, BARBARA (HM18720) | | | | | | | | | | | | | | | | | | | | | | | | | | | | | | | | ● | | | | | | | | | ● | ● | ● | | | | |
| STEVENS, PAT (HM19238) | | | | ● | | | | | | | | ● | ● | | | | | | | | | | | | | | | | | | | | | | | | | | | | ● | ● | ● | | | | |
| STOTT-DURHAM, ANDREW (HM19355) | | | | | | | | | | | | ● | ● | | | | | | | | | | | | | | | | | | | | | | | | | | | | ● | ● | ● | ● | ● | ● | ● |
| SWAN, LAURIE C (HM19574) | | | ● | ● | ● | | | | | | | | | | | ● | | | ● | | | | ● | ● | | | | | | | | | | | | | | | | | ● | | | | | | |
| TAYLOR, CHRISTIAN (HM19744) | ● | ● | ● | ● | ● | ● | ● | ● | ● | ● | | ● | ● | ● | ● | ● | ● | | ● | ● | ● | ● | ● | ● | ● | ● | ● | ● | ● | ● | ● | | ● | ● | ● | ● | ● | | ● | ● | ● | ● | ● | | | | |
| TAYLOR, JAMES M (HM19767) | | | | | | | | | | | ● | | | | | | | | | | | | | | | | | | | | | | | | | | | | | | ● | ● | ● | | | | |
| TRANQUILLITY (HM20260) | | | | ● | | ● | | ● | | | | | | | | | | | | | | | | | | | ● | | | | | | | | | | | | | | ● | ● | ● | | ● | ● | ● |

www.healthmyself.com

Healthmyself Directory

# S - W Conditions treated at Practices/Businesses and Specialist Treatment Categories

| | | | | | | | | | | | | | | | | | | | | | | | | | | | | | | | | | | | | | | | | | Specialist Treatment Categories | | | | | | |
|---|---|---|---|---|---|---|---|---|---|---|---|---|---|---|---|---|---|---|---|---|---|---|---|---|---|---|---|---|---|---|---|---|---|---|---|---|---|---|---|---|---|---|---|---|---|---|
| Business by County with Reference no. | Sexually Trans. Infections | Shingles | Sinus Problems | Skin Problems | Sleep Disorders | Slimming Help | Slipped Disk | Smoking Help | Sneezing | Snoring | Spinal Injuries | Sports Injuries | Sprains | Stammering | Stings | Stomach Problems | Stomach Ulcers | Stress | Sweating | Teeth Grinding | Tennis Elbow | Terminal Illness | Throat Problems | Thrush | Thyroid Problems | Tinnitis | Tiredness | Tonsilitis | Ulcers | Vaginal Problems | Varicose Veins | Verrucas | Vertigo | Viral Infections | Vomiting | Warts | Water Retention | Whiplash | Wind | Worms | Children | Terminally Ill | Disabled | Horses | Dogs | CatS | Other Animals |
| WESTACOTT, EILEEN (HM21256) | | | | | | | | | | | | | | | | | | ● | | | | | | | | | | | | | | | | | | | | | | | ● | ● | ● | | | | |
| WILSON, AVIS (HM21646) | | | | ● | | | | | | | | | | | | | | | | | | | | | | | ● | | | | ● | | | | | ● | | | | | | | | | | | |
| WOOD, J G (HM21798) | | ● | | ● | | | ● | | | | | ● | ● | | | | | | | | ● | | | | | | | | | | | | ● | | | | | | | | ● | | ● | | | | |
| WORSFOLD, CHRISTINE (HM21903) | | | | | | | | | | | | | | | | | | | | | | | | | | | | | | | | | | | | ● | | | | | ● | ● | ● | | | | |
| WORTHING CHIROPRACTIC CLINIC (HM21907) | | | | | | | ● | | | | ● | ● | ● | | | | | | | | ● | | | | | | | | | | | | | | | | | ● | | | ● | ● | ● | | | | |
| WORTHING CLINIC OF ACUPUNCTURE (HM21908) | | | ● | ● | | | | | | | | ● | | | | | | | | | | | | | | | | | | | | | | | | | | | | | | | | | | | |
| YORK, TIM (HM22054) | | | | | | | | | | | | ● | | | | | | ● | | | ● | | | | | | | | | | | | | | | | | | | | ● | | ● | | | | |
| TYNE AND WEAR | | | | | | | | | | | | | | | | | | | | | | | | | | | | | | | | | | | | | | | | | | | | | | | |
| ACUPUNCTURE & NAT MED CLINIC (HM00243) | ● | ● | ● | ● | ● | ● | ● | ● | ● | ● | | ● | ● | ● | ● | ● | ● | | ● | ● | ● | ● | ● | ● | ● | ● | ● | ● | ● | ● | ● | | ● | ● | ● | ● | ● | | ● | ● | ● | ● | ● | | | | |
| AROMATHERAPY IN PRACTICE (HM01114) | | | | ● | ● | | | | | | | | | | | | | ● | | | | | | | | | | | | | | | | | | | | | | | ● | ● | ● | | | | |
| B WIGRAM HEALING & REFLEXOLOGY (HM01455) | | ● | | | | | | | | | | | | | | | | | | ● | | ● | | | | ● | | | | | | | | | | | | | | | ● | ● | ● | ● | ● | ● | ● |
| BALMORAL PHYSIOTHERAPY (HM01640) | | | | | | | ● | | | | | ● | ● | | | | | | | | ● | | | | | | | | | | | | | | | | | | | | ● | ● | ● | | | | |
| BASS, MIKE (HM01850) | | ● | ● | | ● | | | | ● | | | ● | ● | | | ● | | | | ● | ● | ● | | | ● | | ● | | | | | | ● | ● | ● | | ● | | ● | | | ● | ● | | | | |
| BODY BALANCE HOLISTIC THERAPY (HM02572) | | | | | | | | | | | | | | | | | | ● | | | | | | | | | | | | | | | | | | | | | | | ● | ● | ● | | | | |
| BRAHMA KUMARIS WORLD (HM02890) | | | | | | | | | | | | | | | | | | | | | | | | | | | | | | | | | | | | | | | | | ● | ● | ● | | | | |
| CHIROPODY CLINIC (HM04324) | | | | | | | | | | | | | | | | ● | | ● | | | | | ● | | | | ● | | | | | ● | | | | | | | | | | | | | | | |
| CONNECT PHYSICAL HEALTH CTRE (HM04989) | | | | | | ● | ● | | | | | ● | ● | | | | | | | | ● | | | | | | | | | | | | ● | | | | | | | | ● | | | | | | |
| COOP, JOE (HM05082) | | | | | | | | | | | | | | | | | | | | | | | | | | | | | | | | | | | | | | | | | ● | ● | ● | | | | |
| DENTON, A (HM05998) | | | ● | ● | ● | | | | ● | | | ● | ● | | | ● | | | ● | | | | ● | | | | ● | ● | | | | | ● | | | | | | | | ● | ● | ● | | | | |
| DERWENT CENTRE (HM06020) | ● | ● | ● | ● | ● | ● | ● | ● | ● | ● | ● | ● | ● | ● | ● | ● | ● | ● | ● | ● | ● | ● | ● | ● | ● | ● | ● | ● | ● | ● | ● | ● | ● | ● | ● | ● | ● | ● | ● | ● | ● | ● | ● | | ● | ● | ● |
| EARDLEY, D & J (HM06492) | | | | | | | | | | | | | | | | | | | | | | | | | | | | | | | | | | | | | | | | | ● | ● | ● | | | | |
| EQUILIBRIUM (HM06867) | | | | | | | | | | | | | | | | | | | | | | | | | | | | | | | | | | | | | | | | | ● | | | | | | |
| FAMILY CHIRO WELLNESS CENTRE (HM07083) | | | ● | ● | ● | ● | ● | | | ● | | ● | ● | | | ● | ● | | ● | ● | ● | | | | | ● | ● | | | | | | ● | | | | | | | | ● | | | | | | |
| FEEL GOOD AROMATHERAPY (HM07164) | | ● | ● | ● | ● | | ● | | ● | ● | | ● | ● | | ● | ● | ● | | ● | | ● | ● | ● | ● | ● | ● | ● | ● | ● | ● | ● | | | ● | | ● | ● | | ● | ● | ● | ● | ● | ● | ● | ● | ● |
| FOWLER, CHRISTINE (HM07628) | ● | ● | ● | ● | ● | ● | ● | ● | ● | ● | | ● | ● | ● | ● | ● | ● | | ● | ● | ● | ● | ● | ● | ● | ● | ● | ● | ● | ● | ● | | ● | ● | ● | ● | ● | | ● | ● | ● | ● | ● | | | | |
| GATESHEAD COMPLEMENTARY HEALTH (HM07927) | | | | | | ● | | ● | | | | | | | | | | ● | | | | | | | | | | | | | | | | | | | | | | | ● | ● | ● | | | | |
| HEALTH ALLIANCE CENTRE (HM09375) | | | | | | | ● | | | | | ● | ● | | | | | | | | | | | | | | | | | | | | | | | | | | | | | | | | | | |
| HERBAL GARDEN AROMATHERAPY (HM09612) | | ● | ● | ● | ● | ● | | ● | ● | ● | | ● | ● | | ● | ● | ● | | | | ● | ● | ● | ● | | ● | ● | ● | | ● | ● | | ● | ● | | ● | ● | | ● | ● | ● | ● | ● | ● | ● | ● | ● |
| HOLISTIC CHIROPRACTOR (HM09951) | | | | | | | ● | | | | | | | | | | | | | | | | | | | | | | | | | | | | | | | | | | ● | ● | ● | ● | ● | ● | ● |
| HON, ARTHUR M R (HM10111) | | | | | | | ● | | | | | ● | ● | | | | | | | | ● | | | | | | | | | | | | | | | | | | | | ● | | ● | ● | ● | ● | ● |
| HYPNOTHERAPY AND COUNSELLING (HM10514) | | | | ● | ● | ● | | ● | | | | | | | | | | | | ● | | | | | | ● | | | | | | | | | | | | | | | ● | | | | | | |
| MCANELLY, J L (HM13368) | | | | | | ● | | ● | | | | | | | | | | ● | | | | | | | | | | | | | | | | | | | | | | | ● | ● | ● | | | | |
| NATURAL SELECTION (HM14623) | | | | | | | | | ● | | | | | | | | | | | | | | | | | | ● | | | | | | | | | | ● | | ● | | ● | | ● | | | | |
| NEW LIFE NATURAL HEALTH CARE (HM14820) | ● | ● | ● | ● | ● | ● | ● | ● | ● | ● | | ● | ● | ● | ● | ● | ● | | ● | ● | ● | ● | ● | ● | ● | ● | ● | ● | ● | ● | ● | | ● | ● | ● | ● | ● | | ● | ● | ● | ● | ● | | | | |

# S - W Conditions treated at Practices/Businesses and Specialist Treatment Categories

| Business by County with Reference no. | | | | | | | | | | | | | | | | | | | | | | | | | | | | | | | | | | | | | | | | | Specialist Treatment Categories | | | | | | |
|---|---|---|---|---|---|---|---|---|---|---|---|---|---|---|---|---|---|---|---|---|---|---|---|---|---|---|---|---|---|---|---|---|---|---|---|---|---|---|---|---|---|---|---|---|---|---|---|
| | Sexually Trans. Infections | Shingles | Sinus Problems | Skin Problems | Sleep Disorders | Slimming Help | Slipped Disk | Smoking Help | Sneezing | Snoring | Spinal Injuries | Sports Injuries | Sprains | Stammering | Stings | Stomach Problems | Stomach Ulcers | Stress | Sweating | Teeth Grinding | Tennis Elbow | Terminal Illness | Throat Problems | Thrush | Thyroid Problems | Tinnitis | Tiredness | Tonsilitis | Ulcers | Vaginal Problems | Varicose Veins | Verrucas | Vertigo | Viral Infections | Vomiting | Warts | Water Retention | Whiplash | Wind | Worms | Children | Terminally Ill | Disabled | Horses | Dogs | CatS | Other Animals |
| NEWCASTLE SPRTS INJ/THRPY CTRE (HM14855) | | |●|●| | |●| | | | |●|●| | | | | | | |●| | | | | |●| | | | | | | | | | | | | |●|●|●| | | | |
| OSBORNE CLINIC (HM15420) | | |●| | | |●|●| | | |●|●| | | | | | |●|●| | | | |●| | | |●| | | | | | | | |●| |●|●|●| | | | |
| RAINBOW, RICHARD S (HM16887) | | | | | | | |●| | | | | | | | | | | |●| | | | | | | | | | | | | | | |●| | | | |●| |●| | | | |
| RICHARDSON, DEBORAH (HM17276) | | | | | | | | | | | | | | | | | | | | | | | | | | | | | | | | | | | | | | | | |●|●|●| | | | |
| SCHOLL FOOTWEAR CENTRE (HM18077) | | | | | | | | | | | | | | | | | | | | | | | | | | | | | | | | | | | | | | | | |●|●|●| | | | |
| SHEN HOLISTIC THERAPIES (HM18392) | | | |●|●| | | | | | | | | | | | | | | | | | | | | | | | | | | | | | | | | | | | | | | | | | |
| WESTOE PRACTICE (HM21277) | | | | | | | | | | | | | | | | | | | | | | | | | | | | | | | | | | | | | | | | |●|●|●| | | | |
| WHITLEY BAY CHIROPRACTOR (HM21406) | | | | | | | | | | |●|●|●| | | | | | | | | | | | | | | | | | | | | | | | | | | |●|●|●| | | | |
| **WARWICKSHIRE** | | | | | | | | | | | | | | | | | | | | | | | | | | | | | | | | | | | | | | | | | | | | | | | |
| ACUPUNCTURE CLINIC (HM00279) | | |●|●| | |●| | | | |●|●| | | | | | | | | | | | | |●| | | | | | | |●| | | | | |●|●|●| | | | |
| BARRATT'S HOMEOPATHY (HM01780) | |●|●|●|●| |●|●|●|●| |●|●| |●|●|●| |●|●|●|●|●|●|●|●|●|●|●|●|●| |●|●|●|●|●| |●|●|●|●|●| | | | |
| BIRTWELL, ANDREW (HM02400) | | | | | | | | | | | | | | | | | | | | | | | | | | | | | | | | | | | | | | | | |●|●|●| | | | |
| BRIEF COUNS & PSYCHOTHERAPY SV (HM03020) | | | | |●| | | | | | | | | | | | | | |●| | | | | | | | | | | | | | | | | | | | | | | | | | | |
| CHURCH LAWFORD CHIRO CLINIC (HM04463) | | | | | | |●| | | | |●|●| | | | | | |●|●| | | | | | | | | | | | | | | | | | | |●|●|●| | | | |
| CLIFTON OSTEOPATHIC PRACTICE (HM04669) | |●|●|●|●|●|●| | |●| |●|●| | |●|●| | |●|●|●|●|●|●|●|●| |●|●|●| |●| | |●|●| |●| |●|●|●| | |●| |
| EDWARDS, IRENE & PETER (HM06656) | | | | |●|●| |●| | | | | | | | | | | | | | | | | | | | | | | | | | | | | | | | |●|●|●| | | | |
| FIGHT (HM07282) | | | |●| |●|●| | | | |●|●| | | | | | |●|●| | | | | | | | | |●| |●| | | | | | | |●|●|●| | | | |
| GREIG, E (HM08527) | | | | | |●| |●| | | | | | | | | | | | | | | | | | | | | | | | | | | | | | | | | |●| | | | | |
| HEALTHPOINT (HM09414) | |●| | | | | |●| | | |●|●| | | | | |●| |●| | | | |●| |●| | | | |●| | | | | | | | | | | | | | |
| HEART OF ENGLAND SHIATSU (HM09442) | | | |●|●| |●| | | | | | |●| | | | | | |●| | | | |●|●| | | |●| | | | | |●| | | | | | | | | | |
| HEARTLANDS (HM09445) | | | | |●|●| |●| | | |●| | | |●|●| | |●| | | | | | |●| | | | | | | | | | | | | |●| | | | | | |
| HERBAL ONE (HM09631) |●|●|●|●|●|●|●|●|●|●| |●|●|●|●|●|●| |●|●|●|●|●|●|●|●|●|●|●|●|●| |●|●|●|●|●| |●|●|●|●|●| | | | |
| HOLYCOMBE (HM10060) | | | | | | | | | | | | | | | | | | | | | | | | | | |●| | | | | | | | | | | | | |●|●|●| | | | |
| JAN LLOYD AROMATHERAPY (HM10913) | | |●|●|●| | | | | | |●|●| | | | | | | |●|●| | | | |●| | | | | | | | | | | | | |●|●|●| | | | |
| LEAMINGTON SPA CHIRO CLINIC (HM12104) | | | |●| | |●| | | |●|●|●| | | | | | | |●| | | | | | | | | | | | | | | | |●| | |●|●|●| | | | |
| LIFE-WAYS (HM12367) | |●|●|●|●|●| |●|●|●| |●|●|●|●|●|●| |●|●|●| |●|●|●|●|●|●|●|●|●| |●|●|●|●|●| |●|●|●|●|●| | | | |
| MYERS, MARION (HM14437) | | | | | | | | | | | | | | | | | | | | | | | | | | | | | | | | | | | | | | | | | |●| | | | | |
| NATURAL HEALTH CENTRE (HM14567) | |●|●|●|●| |●|●| | | |●|●| | |●|●| | | |●| | |●| |●|●|●|●|●| | | |●| | |●| |●| |●|●|●| | | | |
| NATURAL THERAPY CENTRE (HM14651) | |●|●|●|●| | | |●|●| |●|●| |●|●|●| |●| |●| |●|●|●|●|●|●|●|●| | |●|●|●|●|●| |●| |●| | | | | | |
| NEWEY, RACHEL (HM14862) | | |●| | | |●| | | | |●|●| | | | | | |●|●| | | | | |●| | | | | | | | | | | |●| |●|●| | | | | |
| NUNEATON CHIROPRACTIC CLINIC (HM15104) | | | | |●|●|●|●| |●| |●|●| | | | | | | |●| | | | | | | | | | | | | | | | |●| | |●|●|●| | | | |
| PETERS, EVERARD (HM16085) | | |●| |●| |●| | | | |●|●|●| | | | | |●|●|●|●| | |●|●|●| | | | |●| | | | | | | |●|●|●| | | | |
| REFLEXOLOGY CLINIC (HM17091) | | |●| | | |●| | | | | | | | |●| | | | | | |●| |●|●| | | |●|●| | | | | |●| | | |●|●| | | | | |
| REVITALIZE (HM17205) | | | | | | | | | | | | | | | | | |●| | | | | | | | | | | | | | | | | | | | | | |●|●|●| | | | |

# S - W Conditions treated at Practices/Businesses and Specialist Treatment Categories

Business by County with Reference no.

Specialist Treatment Categories: Children, Terminally Ill, Disabled, Horses, Dogs, CatS, Other Animals

| Business by County with Reference no. | Sexually Trans. Infections | Shingles | Sinus Problems | Skin Problems | Sleep Disorders | Slimming Help | Slipped Disk | Smoking Help | Sneezing | Snoring | Spinal Injuries | Sports Injuries | Sprains | Stammering | Stings | Stomach Problems | Stomach Ulcers | Stress | Sweating | Teeth Grinding | Tennis Elbow | Terminal Illness | Throat Problems | Thrush | Thyroid Problems | Tinnitis | Tiredness | Tonsilitis | Ulcers | Vaginal Problems | Varicose Veins | Verrucas | Vertigo | Viral Infections | Vomiting | Warts | Water Retention | Whiplash | Wind | Worms | Children | Terminally Ill | Disabled | Horses | Dogs | CatS | Other Animals |
|---|---|---|---|---|---|---|---|---|---|---|---|---|---|---|---|---|---|---|---|---|---|---|---|---|---|---|---|---|---|---|---|---|---|---|---|---|---|---|---|---|---|---|---|---|---|---|---|
| RUSSELL, COLIN (HM17766) | | | | | | | | | | | | ● | | | | | | | | | | | | | | | | | | | | | | | | | | | | | ● | ● | ● | | | | |
| SAVAGE, GERALD (HM17966) | | | | | ● | ● | | ● | | ● | | | | ● | | | | ● | ● | ● | | ● | | | | | ● | | | | | | ● | | | | | | | | ● | ● | ● | | | | |
| SHAND, GRAHAM (HM18278) | | | | | | | | | | | | ● | ● | | | | | | | | ● | | | | | | | | | | | | | | | | | | | | ● | | ● | | | | |
| SHAWE AVENUE OSTEO PRACTICE (HM18351) | | | | | | | | | | | | ● | ● | | | | | | | | ● | | | | | | | | | | | | | | | | | ● | | | | | | | | | |
| SHIATSU SOCIETY (HM18464) | | | ● | ● | | | ● | ● | | | | ● | ● | | | ● | ● | | ● | ● | ● | | ● | | | ● | ● | ● | | ● | | | | | ● | | ● | | ● | | | | | | | | |
| SMALLWOOD, P (HM18698) | | | | | | | | | | | | ● | | | | | | | | | | | | | | | | | | | | ● | | | | | | | | | ● | ● | ● | | | | |
| STRATFORD ACU & HOLISTIC HLTH (HM19369) | | | | | | | | | | | | | | | | | | | | | | | | | | | | | | | | | | | | | | | | | ● | ● | | | | | |
| STRATFORD PHYSIO CLINIC (HM19370) | | | | | | | ● | | | | | ● | ● | | | | | | | | ● | | | | | | | | | | | | | | | | | | | | ● | ● | ● | | | | |
| STUDLEY PHYSIOTHERAPY CENTRE (HM19442) | | | | | | | ● | | | | | ● | ● | | | | | | | | ● | | | | | | | | | | | | | | | | | | | | | | ● | | | | |
| TOWERS, DIANA (HM20195) | | | | | ● | ● | | ● | | | | | | ● | | | | | | | | ● | | | | | ● | | | | | | | | | | | | | | ● | ● | ● | | | | |
| TRADITIONAL ACUPUNCTURE GROUP (HM20221) | | ● | ● | ● | ● | ● | | ● | | | | ● | ● | ● | | ● | ● | | ● | ● | ● | ● | ● | ● | ● | ● | ● | | ● | | ● | | ● | ● | ● | | ● | | ● | | ● | ● | ● | | | | |
| WARWICK OSTEOPATHIC PRACTICE (HM20966) | | ● | ● | ● | ● | ● | ● | | | ● | | ● | ● | | | ● | ● | | | ● | ● | ● | | ● | ● | ● | ● | | ● | ● | ● | | ● | | | ● | ● | | ● | | ● | ● | ● | | | ● | |
| WREN, PAULINE (HM21922) | | | | | | | | ● | | | | | | | | | | | | | | | | | | | ● | | | | | | | | | | | | | | ● | ● | | ● | ● | ● | ● |
| **WILTSHIRE** | | | | | | | | | | | | | | | | | | | | | | | | | | | | | | | | | | | | | | | | | | | | | | | |
| AMESBURY ABBEY CLINIC (HM00781) | | | | | | | ● | | | | | ● | ● | | | | | | | | ● | | | | | | | | | | | | | | | | | | | | ● | ● | ● | | | | |
| ANDREWS, HAZEL (HM00852) | | | ● | ● | ● | | | ● | ● | | | ● | ● | | | ● | ● | | ● | ● | ● | | | | | ● | ● | | | ● | | | ● | | ● | | ● | | ● | | | ● | ● | | | | |
| AVEBURY HYPNOTHERAPY PRACTICE (HM01386) | | | | | ● | ● | | ● | | | | | | | | ● | | | | | | | | | | | | | | | | | | | | | | | | | ● | ● | | | | | |
| 'BACK IN LINE' (HM01482) | | | | ● | | | | | | | | | | | | | | ● | | | | | | | | | ● | | | | | | | | | | | | | | ● | ● | | | | | |
| BLUNSDON ABBEY PHYSIOTHERAPY (HM02533) | | | | | | | ● | | | | | ● | ● | | | | | | | | ● | | | | | | | | | | | | | | | | | | | | ● | ● | ● | | | | |
| CASTLE STREET CHIRO CLINIC (HM03836) | | | | | | | | | | | | ● | ● | | | | | | | | | | | | | | | | | | | | | | | | | | | | ● | ● | ● | | | | |
| CRICKLADE ROAD PRACTICE (HM05439) | | | ● | ● | ● | ● | ● | ● | | | | ● | ● | | | | | | | | ● | | | ● | | | ● | | | | | | | | | | | | | | ● | | ● | | | | |
| EASE MANAGEMENT CENTRE (HM06506) | | | | | ● | | | | | | | | | | | | | ● | | ● | | | | | | | ● | | | | | | | | | | | | | | | | | | | | |
| ENGLISH, JOHN M (DR) (HM06834) | ● | ● | ● | ● | ● | | ● | ● | ● | | | | ● | ● | ● | ● | ● | | ● | ● | ● | | ● | ● | ● | ● | ● | ● | ● | ● | ● | | ● | ● | ● | ● | ● | | ● | ● | ● | | | | | | |
| HEALTH HYDRO (HM09389) | | ● | ● | ● | ● | ● | ● | ● | ● | ● | | ● | ● | | | | | | ● | | ● | | | ● | | | ● | | | ● | | | | | | | | | ● | | ● | ● | ● | | | | |
| HIGHWORTH PHYSIOTHERAPY CLINIC (HM09761) | | | | | | | | | | | | ● | ● | | | | | | | | ● | | | | | | | | | | | | | | | | | | | | ● | | ● | ● | ● | ● | ● |
| HYPNOTHERAPY CENTRE (HM10529) | | | ● | ● | ● | ● | | ● | ● | | | | | ● | | ● | | | | | | | | | | ● | ● | | | | | | | | | | | | ● | | | | | | | | |
| JENKINS, RUSSELL S (HM10996) | | | | | | | ● | | | | | ● | ● | | | | | | | | ● | | | | | | | | | | | | | | | | | | | | ● | ● | ● | | | | |
| LEIGHTON REFLEXOLOGY CLINIC (HM12196) | | | ● | | ● | | | | | | | | | | | | | | | | | | | | ● | | ● | ● | | | | | | | | | | | | | ● | | ● | | | | |
| LIFE-ENERGIES (HM12352) | | | ● | ● | | | ● | | ● | ● | | ● | ● | | ● | ● | ● | | | | ● | | | | | ● | | ● | | | | | | ● | | ● | | | | | ● | ● | ● | ● | ● | ● | ● |
| LYON, P (HM12783) | | | | | | | | | | | | | | | | | | ● | | | | | | | | | | | | | | | | | | | | | | | ● | ● | ● | | | | |
| MAGNO PULSE (HM12919) | | | | ● | ● | | | | | | | ● | ● | | | | | | | | ● | | | | ● | ● | ● | | | | ● | | | | | | | | | | | | ● | ● | ● | ● | ● |
| MALMESBURY CHIROPRACTIC CLINIC (HM12982) | | | | | | | ● | | | | | ● | ● | | | | | | | | ● | | | | | | | | | | | | | | | | | ● | | | ● | ● | ● | | | | |
| MARLBOROUGH CHIRO CLINIC (HM13122) | | | | | | | ● | | | | | ● | ● | | | | | | | | ● | | | | | | | | | | | | | | | | | | | | ● | ● | ● | | | | |
| MARLBOROUGH NATURAL HLTH CTRE (HM13123) | ● | ● | ● | ● | ● | ● | ● | ● | ● | ● | | ● | ● | ● | ● | ● | ● | | ● | ● | ● | ● | ● | ● | ● | ● | ● | ● | ● | ● | ● | | ● | ● | ● | ● | ● | | ● | ● | ● | ● | ● | | | | |

# S - W Conditions treated at Practices/Businesses and Specialist Treatment Categories

| Business by County with Reference no. | Sexually Trans. Infections | Shingles | Sinus Problems | Skin Problems | Sleep Disorders | Slimming Help | Slipped Disk | Smoking Help | Sneezing | Snoring | Spinal Injuries | Sports Injuries | Sprains | Stammering | Stings | Stomach Problems | Stomach Ulcers | Stress | Sweating | Teeth Grinding | Tennis Elbow | Terminal Illness | Throat Problems |
|---|---|---|---|---|---|---|---|---|---|---|---|---|---|---|---|---|---|---|---|---|---|---|---|
| MATHER, PAULINE (HM13280) | | | | | | | ● | | | | | ● | ● | | | | | | | ● | ● | | |
| MCTIMONEY CHIROPRACTIC CLINIC (HM13604) | | | | | | | | | | | | | | | | | | | | | | | |
| MOURANT, JENNIFER L (HM14298) | | | | | | | | | | | | | | | | | | | | | | | |
| MULTI-THERAPY CENTRE (HM14352) | ● | ● | ● | ● | ● | | | | ● | | | | | | | ● | ● | ● | | | | | ● |
| NATURAL THERAPY CENTRE (HM14639) | | | ● | | ● | ● | ● | ● | | ● | | ● | ● | ● | | ● | | ● | | ● | ● | | |
| NATURALLY NUTRITION (HM14673) | | ● | ● | ● | | ● | | ● | | | | ● | | | | ● | ● | | | | | | ● |
| OSTEOPATHS (HM15475) | | | ● | | | | ● | | | | | ● | ● | | | | | | | | ● | | |
| PETER & CAROLINE (HM16071) | | | ● | | ● | | | | | | | | | | | | | | | | | | |
| PETTIFER, JUSTINA (HM16095) | | | | | ● | ● | | ● | | | | | | ● | | | | | | ● | | | |
| PHYSIOTHERAPY CLINIC (HM16247) | | | | | | ● | ● | | | | | ● | ● | | | | | | | | ● | | |
| QUIRKE, G (HM16820) | | | | | ● | | | ● | | | | | | | | | | | | | | | |
| RAINBOW NATURAL THERAPIES (HM16880) | | | | | | | | | | | | | | | | | | ● | | | | | |
| SARUM PHYSIOTHERAPY CENTRE (HM17947) | | | | | | | ● | | | | | ● | ● | | | | | | | | ● | | |
| SAWAYA, ALICIA (HM17982) | ● | ● | ● | ● | ● | ● | ● | ● | ● | ● | | ● | ● | ● | ● | ● | ● | | ● | ● | ● | ● | ● |
| SHAFTSBURY PRACTICE (HM18266) | ● | ● | ● | ● | ● | ● | ● | ● | ● | ● | | ● | ● | ● | ● | ● | ● | | ● | ● | ● | ● | ● |
| SHAVE, G M (HM18325) | | | | | | | | | | | | | | | | | | | | | | | |
| SPIRITUAL HEALER (HM19026) | | | | | | | | | | | | | | | | | | ● | | | | | |
| SWINDON CHIROPRACTIC CLINIC (HM19595) | | | | | | | | | | | ● | ● | ● | | | | | ● | | | ● | | |
| TISBURY OSTEOPATHIC PRACTICE (HM20094) | | | ● | | | | | | | | | | ● | | | | | | | ● | ● | | |
| WARMINSTER OSTEOPATHIC CLINIC (HM20929) | | ● | ● | | ● | ● | ● | ● | | | | ● | ● | | | ● | | | | ● | ● | | |
| WATSON'S COURT CLINIC (HM21025) | | | | ● | | | | | | | | ● | | | | | | | | | | | |
| WELLS, HENRIETTA (HM21175) | ● | ● | ● | ● | ● | ● | ● | ● | ● | ● | | ● | ● | ● | ● | ● | ● | | ● | ● | ● | ● | ● |
| WESTBURY CHIROPRACTIC (HM21258) | | | | | | | ● | | | | ● | ● | ● | | | | | | | | ● | | |
| WESTBURY REFLEXOLOGY CLINIC (HM21260) | | | | | ● | | | | | | | | | | | | | ● | | | | | ● |
| WOOTTON BASSETT (HM21885) | | | | | | | ● | | | | | ● | ● | | | | | | | | ● | | |
| **WORCESTERSHIRE** | | | | | | | | | | | | | | | | | | | | | | | |
| 1ST CHIROPRACTIC UK (HM00007) | | | | | | | ● | | | | ● | | ● | ● | | | | | | | ● | | |
| AINSLEY, S (HM00433) | | | | | | | ● | | | | | ● | ● | | | | | | | | | | |
| BRETFORDTON CLINIC (HM02969) | | | | | | | ● | | | | | ● | ● | | | | | | | | ● | | |
| BROMSGROVE CHIROPRACTIC CLINIC (HM03151) | | | | | | | ● | | | | ● | ● | ● | | | | | | | | ● | | |
| CARYL, M D (HM03804) | | | | | | | | | | | | | | | | | | | | | | | |
| DAVIES PODIATRY (HM05792) | | | | | | | | | | | | | | | | | | | | | | | |
| EVESHAM NATURAL HEALTH CENTRE (HM07009) | | | ● | ● | ● | | ● | ● | | | | ● | ● | ● | ● | ● | ● | | | | ● | ● | ● |
| FRONTIA (HM07757) | | ● | ● | ● | ● | | ● | ● | ● | ● | | ● | ● | | | ● | ● | | ● | | ● | | ● |

| Business by County with Reference no. | Thrush | Thyroid Problems | Tinnitis | Tiredness | Tonsilitis | Ulcers | Vaginal Problems | Varicose Veins | Verrucas | Vertigo | Viral Infections | Vomiting | Warts | Water Retention | Whiplash | Wind | Worms | Specialist Treatment Categories: Children | Terminally Ill | Disabled | Horses | Dogs | CatS | Other Animals |
|---|---|---|---|---|---|---|---|---|---|---|---|---|---|---|---|---|---|---|---|---|---|---|---|---|
| MATHER, PAULINE (HM13280) | | ● | | ● | | | | | | | | | | | | | | | ● | ● | ● | ● | ● | |
| MCTIMONEY CHIROPRACTIC CLINIC (HM13604) | | | | | | | | | | | | | | | | | | ● | ● | ● | ● | ● | ● | ● |
| MOURANT, JENNIFER L (HM14298) | | | | ● | | | | | | | | | | | | | | ● | | ● | | | | |
| MULTI-THERAPY CENTRE (HM14352) | ● | ● | | ● | ● | ● | ● | | | | ● | ● | ● | | | ● | ● | ● | ● | ● | | | | |
| NATURAL THERAPY CENTRE (HM14639) | | ● | ● | ● | | ● | | | | | | | ● | | | | | ● | ● | ● | ● | ● | ● | ● |
| NATURALLY NUTRITION (HM14673) | ● | ● | ● | ● | | ● | | ● | | | ● | | | ● | | ● | ● | ● | ● | ● | | | | |
| OSTEOPATHS (HM15475) | | | ● | | | | | | | ● | | | | | | | | | | | | | | |
| PETER & CAROLINE (HM16071) | | | | ● | | | | | | | | | | | | | | | | | | | | |
| PETTIFER, JUSTINA (HM16095) | | | ● | ● | | | | | | ● | | | | | | | | ● | | ● | | | | |
| PHYSIOTHERAPY CLINIC (HM16247) | | | | | | | | | | | | | | | | | | ● | ● | ● | | | | |
| QUIRKE, G (HM16820) | | | | | | | | | | | | | | | | | | ● | | | | | | |
| RAINBOW NATURAL THERAPIES (HM16880) | | | | | | | | | | | | | | | | | | | ● | ● | | | | |
| SARUM PHYSIOTHERAPY CENTRE (HM17947) | | | | | | | | | | | | | | | | | | ● | ● | ● | | | | |
| SAWAYA, ALICIA (HM17982) | ● | ● | ● | ● | ● | ● | ● | ● | | ● | ● | ● | ● | ● | | ● | ● | ● | ● | ● | | | | |
| SHAFTSBURY PRACTICE (HM18266) | ● | ● | ● | ● | ● | ● | ● | ● | | ● | ● | ● | ● | ● | | ● | ● | ● | ● | ● | | | | |
| SHAVE, G M (HM18325) | | | | | | | | | ● | | | | ● | | | | | ● | ● | ● | | | | |
| SPIRITUAL HEALER (HM19026) | | | | | | | | | | | | | | | | | | ● | ● | ● | ● | ● | ● | ● |
| SWINDON CHIROPRACTIC CLINIC (HM19595) | | | | | | | | | | | | | | | ● | | | ● | ● | ● | | | | |
| TISBURY OSTEOPATHIC PRACTICE (HM20094) | | | | | | | | | | | | | | | | | | ● | ● | ● | | | | |
| WARMINSTER OSTEOPATHIC CLINIC (HM20929) | ● | | | ● | | | ● | | | ● | | ● | | ● | ● | ● | | ● | ● | ● | ● | ● | ● | ● |
| WATSON'S COURT CLINIC (HM21025) | | | | | | | | | ● | | | | ● | | | | | ● | ● | ● | | | | |
| WELLS, HENRIETTA (HM21175) | ● | ● | ● | ● | ● | ● | ● | ● | | ● | ● | ● | ● | ● | | ● | ● | ● | ● | ● | | | | |
| WESTBURY CHIROPRACTIC (HM21258) | | | | | | | | | | | | | | | ● | | | | | | | | | |
| WESTBURY REFLEXOLOGY CLINIC (HM21260) | | | | | | | | | | | | | | | | | | ● | ● | ● | | | | |
| WOOTTON BASSETT (HM21885) | | | | | | | | | | | | | | | | | | | | | | | | |
| **WORCESTERSHIRE** | | | | | | | | | | | | | | | | | | | | | | | | |
| 1ST CHIROPRACTIC UK (HM00007) | | | | | | | | | | | | | | | ● | | | ● | ● | ● | | | | |
| AINSLEY, S (HM00433) | | | | | | | | | | | | | | | | | | ● | | ● | | | | |
| BRETFORDTON CLINIC (HM02969) | | | | | | | | | | | | | | | | | | ● | | ● | | | | |
| BROMSGROVE CHIROPRACTIC CLINIC (HM03151) | | | | | | | | | | | | | | | ● | | | ● | ● | ● | | | | |
| CARYL, M D (HM03804) | | | | | | | | | ● | | | | | | | | | ● | ● | ● | | | | |
| DAVIES PODIATRY (HM05792) | | | | | | | | | ● | | | | | | | | | ● | ● | ● | | | | |
| EVESHAM NATURAL HEALTH CENTRE (HM07009) | | ● | | ● | | | ● | | | ● | | | | ● | | ● | ● | ● | | ● | | | | |
| FRONTIA (HM07757) | ● | | ● | ● | ● | ● | ● | ● | | ● | ● | ● | ● | ● | | ● | | ● | ● | ● | | ● | | |

# S - W Conditions treated at Practices/Businesses and Specialist Treatment Categories

| | | | | | | | | | | | | | | | | | | | | | | | | | | | | | | | | | | | | | | | | | Specialist Treatment Categories | | | | | | |
|---|---|---|---|---|---|---|---|---|---|---|---|---|---|---|---|---|---|---|---|---|---|---|---|---|---|---|---|---|---|---|---|---|---|---|---|---|---|---|---|---|---|---|---|---|---|---|---|
| Business by County with Reference no. | Sexually Trans. Infections | Shingles | Sinus Problems | Skin Problems | Sleep Disorders | Slimming Help | Slipped Disk | Smoking Help | Sneezing | Snoring | Spinal Injuries | Sports Injuries | Sprains | Stammering | Stings | Stomach Problems | Stomach Ulcers | Stress | Sweating | Teeth Grinding | Tennis Elbow | Terminal Illness | Throat Problems | Thrush | Thyroid Problems | Tinnitis | Tiredness | Tonsilitis | Ulcers | Vaginal Problems | Varicose Veins | Verrucas | Vertigo | Viral Infections | Vomiting | Warts | Water Retention | Whiplash | Wind | Worms | Children | Terminally Ill | Disabled | Horses | Dogs | CatS | Other Animals |
| GIBBINS, JONATHAN (HM08022) | | |●| | | |●| | | | |●|●| | | | | | | |●| | | | | | | | | | | | | | | | | | | |●| |●|●|●|●|●|
| HINKS, MAXINE (HM09834) | | | |●|●| | | | | | | | | | | | |●| | | | | | | | | | | | | | | | | | | | | | |●|●|●| | | | |
| HOLDEN, NINA (HM09933) | | | | |●| | | | | | | | | | | | |●| | | | |●| |●| | | | | | | | | | | | | | | |●| |●| | | | |
| JONES, VAL (HM11200) | | | | | | | | | | | | | | | | | | | | | | | | | | | | | | | | | | | | | | | | |●|●|●| | | | |
| KITSON, P (HM11730) | | | | | | |●| | | |●|●|●| | | | | | | |●| | | | | | | | | | | | | | | | |●| | |●|●|●| |●| | |
| KRISS, ADRIAN D (HM11803) | | | | | | | | | | | | | | | | | | | | | | | | | | | | | | | | | | | |●| | | | |●|●| | | | | |
| M THORLOW CHIROPODY (HM12810) | | | | | | | | | | | | | | | | | | | | | | | | | | | | | | | |●| | | | | | | | |●|●|●| | | | |
| MALVERN NATURAL HEALTH CENTRE (HM12998) |●|●|●|●|●|●|●|●|●|●| |●|●|●|●|●|●| |●|●|●|●|●|●|●|●|●|●|●|●|●| |●|●|●|●|●| |●|●| | | | | | | |
| MALVERN OSTEOPATHIC CLINIC (HM12999) | | | | | | | | | | | |●|●| | | | | | | |●| | | | | | | | | | | | | | | | | | | |●|●|●| | | | |
| MARSTON, SUE (HM13179) | | |●|●|●| | | | | | | | | | | | | | | | | | | | | |●| | | | | | | | | | | | | |●| | | | | | |
| MEAKIN, D W (HM13637) | | | | | | |●| | | | |●|●| | | | | | | |●| | | | | | | | | | | | | | | | |●| | |●| |●| | | | |
| NATURAL HEALTH CENTRE (HM14564) | | | | | |●| |●| | | |●|●| | |●| | | | |●| | | | | | | | | | | | | | | | | | | |●|●|●| | | | |
| NOTTINGHAM, STUART (HM15086) | | | | | | |●| | | | |●|●| | | | | | | |●| | | | | | | | | | | | | | | | | | | |●| | | | | | |
| NURCHIR (HM15110) | | | |●| | | | | | | |●|●| | | | | | | | | | | | | | | | | | |●| | | |●| | | | |●|●|●| | | | |
| OAKFIELD CLINIC (HM15150) | | | | | | | | | |●| | | | | | | | | | | | | | | | | | | | | | | | | | | | | | |●| | | | | | |
| PARDOE, DIANA T (HM15648) | | |●|●|●|●| |●| | | | | | | | | | | | | | | | | | | | | | | | | | | | | | | | | | | | | | | |
| PERSHORE NAT THERAPY CLINIC (HM16057) |●|●|●|●|●|●|●|●|●|●| |●|●|●|●|●|●| |●|●|●|●|●|●|●|●|●|●|●|●|●| |●|●|●|●|●| |●|●|●|●|●| | | | |
| R C C M (HM16829) | | | | | | |●| | | | |●|●| | | | | | | |●| | | | | | | | | | | | | | | | | | | |●|●|●| | | | |
| REDDITCH CHIROPRACTIC CLINIC (HM17013) | | | | | | |●| | | |●|●|●| | | | | | | |●| | | | | | | | | | | | | | | | |●| | |●|●|●| | | | |
| REDDITCH FOOTCARE SURGERY (HM17014) | | | | | | | | | | | | | | | | | | | | | | | | | | | | | | | | | | | |●| | | | |●|●|●| | | | |
| SOUTH WORCESTERSHIRE HYP (HM18915) | | | |●|●|●| |●| | | | | |●| |●| | | |●| | | | | |●|●| | | | | | | | | | | | | |●| | | | | | |
| STOKES, TERRY (HM19325) | |●| |●| | |●| | | | |●| | | |●| | | |●|●| | | |●| |●|●|●| | | | | | |●| | |●|●|●|●|●| | | | |
| STONE, ANNE L (HM19329) | | | | | | | | | | | |●|●| | | | | | | |●| | | | | | | | | | | | | | | | | | | |●| |●| | | | |
| VINE HERBAL PRODUCTS (HM20677) | | | | | | | | | | | | | | | | | | | | | | | | | | | | | | | | | | | | | | | | | | | |●|●| | |
| WORCESTER NATURAL THERAPY CTRE (HM21886) |●|●|●|●|●|●|●|●|●|●| |●|●|●|●|●|●|●|●|●|●|●|●|●|●|●|●|●|●|●|●| |●|●|●|●|●| |●|●|●|●|●| | | | |
| YOUNG, JOANNA (HM22075) | | |●| | | |●| | | | |●|●| | | | | | | |●| |●| | | | | | | | | |●|●| | | | | | |●|●|●| | | | |
| **YORKSHIRE (NORTH)** | | | | | | | | | | | | | | | | | | | | | | | | | | | | | | | | | | | | | | | | | | | | | | | |
| BAKER, LINDA (HM01587) | | | | | | | | | | | | | | | | | | | | | | | | | | | | | | | | | | | | | | | | | |●|●|●|●|●|●|
| BARRASS, K I (HM01778) | | | | | | | | | | | | | | | | | | | | | | | | | | | | | | | |●| | | | | | | | |●|●|●| | | | |
| BLACK, SAUL (HM02428) | | | | | | | | | | | | | | | | | | | | | | | | | | | | | | | |●| | | | | | | | |●|●|●| | | | |
| BROADHEAD, J N & M (HM03114) | | | | | | | | | | | |●| | | | | | | | | | | | | | | | | | | |●| | | | | | | | |●|●|●| | | | |
| BUSWELL, RONA (HM03471) | | |●|●|●| | | | | | | | | | |●|●| | | | | | | | | |●| |●| | | | | | | |●| |●| |●|●|●| | | | |
| CHIROPODIST (HM04292) | | | | | | | | | | | | | | | | | | | | | | | | | | | | | | | |●| | | | | | | | |●|●|●| | | | |
| CORDEL, MICHAEL (HM05160) | |●|●| |●| |●|●|●|●| |●|●| | |●|●| | | |●| | | |●|●|●|●| | | | | | |●| |●| | | |●| |●| | | | |

# S - W Conditions treated at Practices/Businesses and Specialist Treatment Categories

| Business by County with Reference no. | | | | | | | | | | | | | | | | | | | | | | | | | | | | | | | | | | | | | | | | | Specialist Treatment Categories | | | | | | |
|---|---|---|---|---|---|---|---|---|---|---|---|---|---|---|---|---|---|---|---|---|---|---|---|---|---|---|---|---|---|---|---|---|---|---|---|---|---|---|---|---|---|---|---|---|---|---|
| | Sexually Trans. Infections | Shingles | Sinus Problems | Skin Problems | Sleep Disorders | Slimming Help | Slipped Disk | Smoking Help | Sneezing | Snoring | Spinal Injuries | Sports Injuries | Sprains | Stammering | Stings | Stomach Problems | Stomach Ulcers | Stress | Sweating | Teeth Grinding | Tennis Elbow | Terminal Illness | Throat Problems | Thrush | Thyroid Problems | Tinnitis | Tiredness | Tonsilitis | Ulcers | Vaginal Problems | Varicose Veins | Verrucas | Vertigo | Viral Infections | Vomiting | Warts | Water Retention | Whiplash | Wind | Worms | Children | Terminally Ill | Disabled | Horses | Dogs | CatS | Other Animals |
| CRAVEN CLINIC (HM05384) | | ● | ● | ● | ● | ● | ● | ● | ● | | | ● | ● | | ● | ● | ● | | ● | ● | ● | ● | ● | ● | ● | ● | ● | ● | ● | ● | ● | | ● | ● | ● | ● | ● | | ● | ● | ● | ● | ● | | | | |
| CROFT HOUSE CLINIC (HM05452) | | | ● | | | | ● | | | | | ● | ● | | | | | | | | ● | | | | | | | | | | | | | | | | | | | | ● | | ● | | | | |
| DOVE COURT CENTRE (HM06225) | ● | ● | ● | ● | ● | ● | ● | ● | ● | ● | | ● | ● | ● | ● | ● | ● | | ● | ● | ● | ● | ● | ● | ● | ● | ● | ● | ● | ● | ● | | ● | ● | ● | ● | ● | | ● | ● | ● | ● | ● | | | | |
| EASY WAY YORKSHIRE (HM06557) | | | | | | | | ● | | | | | | | | | | | | | | | | | | | | | | | | | | | | | | | | | | | | | | | |
| GRIFFIN, TRICIA (HM08555) | | ● | | | ● | | | | | | | | | | | ● | | | | | | | | ● | | | ● | | | ● | | | | | | ● | ● | | ● | | ● | ● | ● | | | | |
| HARROGATE HOLISTIC HEALTH CTRE (HM09116) | | | | | | | | ● | | | | | | | | ● | | ● | | | | | | ● | | | | | | | | | | | | | | | | | | | ● | | | | |
| HEALING CLINIC (HM09328) | | ● | ● | ● | ● | ● | ● | ● | ● | ● | | ● | ● | ● | | ● | ● | | ● | ● | ● | ● | ● | ● | ● | ● | ● | ● | ● | ● | ● | | ● | ● | ● | ● | ● | | ● | ● | ● | ● | ● | | | | |
| HESCOTT, J D (HM09692) | | | | | | | | | | | | | | | | | | | | | | | | | | | | | | | | | | | | | | | | | ● | ● | ● | | | | |
| HIGHTHORN PHYSIOTHERAPY CLINIC (HM09759) | | | | | | | ● | | | | | ● | ● | | | | | | | | ● | | | | | | | | | | | | | | | | | | | | ● | ● | ● | | | | |
| HOBSON, I K (HM09863) | | | | ● | | | | | | | | ● | ● | | | | | | | | | | | | | | | | | | | ● | | | | ● | | | | | ● | ● | ● | | | | |
| KNOWLES, J (HM11770) | | | | | | | | | | | | | | | | | | | | | | | | | | | | | | | | ● | | | | | | | | | ● | ● | ● | | | | |
| LESZCZUK, PAULA (HM12245) | | ● | | ● | ● | | ● | ● | ● | ● | | | ● | | ● | ● | ● | | ● | ● | ● | ● | ● | ● | ● | ● | ● | ● | ● | ● | ● | | ● | ● | ● | ● | ● | | ● | ● | ● | ● | ● | ● | ● | ● | ● |
| LESZCZUK, PAULA (HM12246) | | ● | ● | ● | ● | | ● | ● | ● | ● | | | ● | | ● | ● | ● | | ● | ● | ● | ● | ● | ● | ● | ● | ● | ● | ● | ● | ● | | ● | ● | ● | ● | ● | | ● | ● | ● | ● | ● | ● | ● | ● | ● |
| LIFESUPPORT (HM12366) | | | ● | ● | ● | | | ● | ● | | | ● | ● | | | ● | | ● | ● | ● | ● | ● | ● | ● | ● | ● | ● | | ● | ● | ● | | ● | ● | | ● | ● | | ● | | ● | ● | ● | ● | ● | ● | |
| NANCY METCALFE MOBILE CONSULT (HM14468) | | | | | | | | | | | | | | | | | | | | | ● | | | | | | | | | | | | | | | | | | | | ● | | ● | | | | |
| NATURAL BALANCE (HM14515) | | | | | | | | | | | | | | | | | | | | | | | | | | | | | | | | | | | | | | ● | | | ● | ● | ● | | | | |
| PANACEA ACUPUNCTURE CLINIC (HM15628) | | | ● | ● | | | | | | | | | | | | | | | | | | | | | | | | | | | | | | | | | | | | | | | | | | | |
| PAULA LESZCZUK (HM15849) | | ● | ● | ● | ● | | ● | ● | ● | ● | | | ● | | ● | ● | ● | | ● | ● | ● | ● | ● | ● | ● | ● | ● | ● | ● | ● | ● | | ● | ● | ● | ● | ● | | ● | ● | ● | ● | ● | ● | ● | ● | ● |
| RATHBONE, DONNA (HM16955) | | | | | | | | | | | | | | | | | | | | | | | | | | | | | | | | | | | | | | | | | ● | ● | | | | | |
| RIPON NATURAL HEALTH CENTRE (HM17365) | ● | ● | ● | ● | ● | | ● | | | ● | | ● | ● | | ● | ● | ● | | ● | | ● | ● | ● | ● | ● | ● | ● | ● | ● | | ● | | ● | ● | ● | ● | ● | | | ● | ● | ● | ● | | | | |
| RYEDALE CLINIC (HM17803) | | | | | | | | | | | | | | | | | | | | | | | | | | | | | | | | | | | | | | | | | ● | | | | | | |
| SHACKLETON, MAUREEN (HM18264) | | | | | | ● | | ● | | | | | | | | | | ● | | | | | | | | | | | | | | | | | | | | | | | ● | ● | ● | | | | |
| SHAH, ATUL (HM18268) | ● | ● | ● | ● | ● | ● | ● | ● | ● | ● | | ● | ● | | ● | ● | ● | | ● | ● | ● | ● | ● | ● | ● | ● | ● | ● | ● | ● | ● | | ● | ● | ● | ● | ● | | ● | ● | ● | ● | ● | | | | |
| SHEEHAN, NICHOLAS (HM18363) | | | | | | | ● | | | | | ● | ● | | | | | | | | ● | | | | | | | | | | | | | | | | | | | | | | | | | | |
| SI SHEN CLINIC (HM18519) | | | | | | | | | | | | | | | | | | ● | | | | | | | | | | | | | | | | | | | | | | | ● | ● | ● | | | | |
| SKIPTON CHIROPODY CENTRE (HM18658) | | | | | | | | | | | | | | | | | | | | | | | | | | | | | | | | | | | | ● | | | | | ● | ● | ● | | | | |
| SMITH, C J (HM18723) | | | | | | | ● | | | | ● | ● | ● | | | | | | | | ● | | | | | | | | | | | | | | | | | ● | | | | | | | | | |
| STATHER, M (HM19160) | | | | | | | | | | | | | | | | | | | | | | | | | | | | | | | | ● | | | | | | | | | ● | ● | ● | | | | |
| STRATTON, FIONA (HM19372) | | | ● | | ● | | | | ● | | | ● | | | | ● | | | | | ● | ● | ● | ● | ● | | ● | | | | | | | ● | ● | | | | | | | ● | ● | | | | |
| TERRY ANNE (HM19845) | | | | | | | | ● | | ● | | ● | ● | ● | | ● | ● | | | | | | ● | | | ● | ● | ● | | | | | | | | | | | | | ● | ● | | | | | |
| YOGA FOR ALL (HM22026) | | | ● | | ● | ● | | ● | | | | | | | | | | | | | | | | | | ● | ● | | | | ● | | | | | | | | ● | | ● | | ● | | | | |
| YORK CHIROPRACTIC CLINIC (HM22039) | | | | | | | ● | | | | | ● | ● | | | | | | | | ● | | | | | | | | | | | | ● | | | | | | | | ● | | | | | | |
| YORK CLINIC (HM22040) | ● | ● | ● | ● | ● | ● | ● | ● | ● | ● | | ● | ● | ● | ● | ● | ● | | ● | ● | ● | ● | ● | ● | ● | ● | ● | ● | ● | ● | ● | | ● | ● | ● | ● | ● | | ● | ● | ● | ● | ● | | | | |
| YORK COUNSELLING (HM22042) | | | | | ● | ● | | ● | | | | | | | | | | ● | | ● | | | | | | | | | | | | | | | | | | | | | | ● | | | | | |

# S - W Conditions treated at Practices/Businesses and Specialist Treatment Categories

| | | | | | | | | | | | | | | | | | | | | | | | | | | | | | | | | | | | | | | | | | Specialist Treatment Categories | | | | | | |
|---|---|---|---|---|---|---|---|---|---|---|---|---|---|---|---|---|---|---|---|---|---|---|---|---|---|---|---|---|---|---|---|---|---|---|---|---|---|---|---|---|---|---|---|---|---|---|
| Business by County with Reference no. | Sexually Trans. Infections | Shingles | Sinus Problems | Skin Problems | Sleep Disorders | Slimming Help | Slipped Disk | Smoking Help | Sneezing | Snoring | Spinal Injuries | Sports Injuries | Sprains | Stammering | Stings | Stomach Problems | Stomach Ulcers | Stress | Sweating | Teeth Grinding | Tennis Elbow | Terminal Illness | Throat Problems | Thrush | Thyroid Problems | Tinnitis | Tiredness | Tonsilitis | Ulcers | Vaginal Problems | Varicose Veins | Verrucas | Vertigo | Viral Infections | Vomiting | Warts | Water Retention | Whiplash | Wind | Worms | Children | Terminally Ill | Disabled | Horses | Dogs | CatS | Other Animals |
| YORKSHIRE (SOUTH) | | | | | | | | | | | | | | | | | | | | | | | | | | | | | | | | | | | | | | | | | | | | | | |
| ALTON & JAMES MED HERBAL (HM00748) | | ● | ● | ● | ● | | | ● | ● | ● | | | | | | ● | ● | | ● | | | | ● | ● | ● | ● | ● | ● | ● | ● | ● | | | ● | ● | ● | ● | | ● | ● | ● | ● | ● | | | | |
| ANDERSON, A DUDLEY (HM00810) | | | | | ● | ● | | ● | | | | | | ● | | | | ● | | | | | | | | | | | | | | | | | | | | | | | ● | ● | ● | | | | |
| BAWTRY PHYSIOTHERAPY PRACTICE (HM01918) | | | | | | | ● | | | | | ● | ● | | | | | | | | | ● | | | | | | | | | | | | | | | | | | | ● | | ● | | | | |
| BLUFF, ANN (HM02529) | | | | | | | | | | | | | | | | | | | | | | | | | | | | | | | | | | | | | | | | | ● | ● | ● | | | | |
| BONESETTER AND MANIPULATOR (HM02676) | | | | | | | ● | | | | | | | | | | | | | | | | | | | | | | | | | | | | | | | | | | ● | | | | | | |
| BOON, G M (HM02690) | | | | | | | | | | | | ● | | | | | | | | | | | | | | | | | | | | ● | | | | | | | | | ● | ● | ● | | | | |
| BRAMLEY HALL CLINIC (HM02902) | | ● | ● | ● | ● | ● | ● | | ● | ● | | ● | ● | | | ● | ● | | ● | | ● | | | ● | ● | ● | ● | ● | | ● | | | ● | ● | ● | | ● | | ● | ● | ● | ● | ● | | | | |
| BRANKIN, M & K (HM02917) | | | | | | | | | | | | | | | | | | | | | | | | | | | | | | | | | | | | | | | | | ● | ● | ● | | | | |
| BRANKLIN, M & K (HM02918) | | | | | | | | | | | | | | | | | | | | | | | | | | | | | | | | | | | | | | | | | ● | ● | ● | | | | |
| BROOMHILL MEDICAL CENTRE (HM03193) | | | | ● | ● | | | | | | | | | | | | | ● | | | | | | | | | | | | | | | | | | | | | | | ● | ● | ● | | | | |
| CARING CLINIC (HM03682) | | ● | ● | ● | | | | | | ● | | | | | | ● | ● | | ● | ● | ● | | ● | ● | | | ● | ● | ● | ● | ● | | | ● | ● | ● | ● | | ● | | ● | | | | | | |
| CHIROPODY SURGERY (HM04342) | | | | | | | | | | | | | | | | | | | | | | | | | | | | | | | | | | | | | | | | | ● | ● | ● | | | | |
| CLAIRE LOUISE (HM04510) | | | | | | | | | | | | | | | | | | | | | | | | | | | | | | | | | | | | ● | | | | | ● | ● | ● | | | | |
| COUNTRY PRACTICE (HM05256) | | | ● | ● | | | | | | | | ● | | | | | | | ● | | | | | | | | | | | | | | | | | ● | | | | | ● | ● | | | | | |
| DORE PHYSIOTHERAPY PRACTICE (HM06196) | | | | | | | ● | | | | | ● | ● | | | | | | | | | | | | | | | | | | | | | | | | | | | | | | | ● | | | |
| EATON, T C (HM06565) | | | | | | | | | | | | | | | | | | | | | | | | | | | | | | | | ● | | | | | | | | | ● | ● | ● | | | | |
| ESSENTIAL HARMONY (HM06907) | | | ● | ● | ● | | | | | | | | ● | | ● | | | | | | | | | | | | ● | | | | | | | | | | ● | | | | | | | | | | |
| FISHER, CHRISTINE A (HM07349) | | | | | | | | | | | | | | | | | | | | | | | | | | | | | | | | | | | | | | | | | ● | ● | ● | | | | |
| GORNEY, C (HM08296) | | | | | | | | | | | | | | | | | | ● | | | | | | | | | | | | | | | | | | | | | | | ● | ● | ● | | | | |
| GRAPEVINE HEALTH (HM08399) | ● | ● | ● | ● | ● | ● | | ● | ● | ● | | ● | ● | ● | ● | ● | ● | | ● | ● | ● | ● | ● | ● | ● | ● | ● | ● | ● | | ● | | ● | ● | ● | ● | ● | | ● | ● | ● | ● | ● | | | | |
| GRENOSIDE PHYSIOTHERAPY (HM08536) | | | | | | | ● | | | | | ● | ● | | | | | | | | ● | | | | | | | | | | | | | | | | | | | | ● | | | | | | |
| HALLAMSHIRE NATURAL HLTH CTRE (HM08798) | | | ● | ● | | | ● | | | | | ● | ● | ● | | ● | ● | | | ● | ● | | | ● | ● | | ● | | | ● | | | | ● | | | ● | | ● | | ● | ● | ● | | | | |
| HEALTHY FEET (HM09427) | | | | ● | | | | | | | | ● | ● | | | | | | ● | | | | | | | | | | | | | ● | | ● | | ● | | | | | ● | ● | ● | | | | |
| HINCHLIFFE, JACKIE (HM09822) | | ● | ● | ● | ● | | | | | ● | | | | | | | | ● | | | | | | ● | | | ● | ● | | | | | | ● | | ● | | | | | ● | | ● | | | | |
| HYPNOTHERAPY CENTRE (HM10515) | | | | ● | ● | ● | | ● | | ● | | | | ● | | ● | | | | ● | | | | | | ● | ● | | | | | | | | ● | ● | | | | | ● | ● | ● | | | | |
| KIRBY, M (HM11702) | | | ● | ● | ● | ● | | ● | | | | ● | ● | | ● | ● | ● | | ● | ● | ● | ● | ● | ● | ● | ● | ● | ● | ● | ● | ● | | ● | ● | ● | ● | ● | | ● | ● | ● | ● | ● | | | | |
| LAISTER, MARTIN (HM11868) | | | | | | | | | | | | | | | | | | | | | | | | | | | | | | | | | | | | | | | | | ● | ● | ● | | | | |
| LLEWELLYN CONSULTANCY (HM12502) | | ● | ● | ● | ● | ● | | ● | ● | ● | | ● | ● | ● | ● | ● | ● | | ● | ● | ● | ● | ● | ● | | ● | ● | ● | | | | | ● | ● | ● | ● | ● | | ● | | ● | ● | ● | ● | ● | ● | ● |
| M & B SERVICES (HM12794) | | | ● | ● | ● | ● | | ● | | | | | | | | ● | ● | | | ● | ● | ● | ● | | | ● | ● | | | | | | | ● | | | ● | | ● | | ● | ● | ● | | | | |
| MEDICAL HERBALIST (HM13652) | ● | ● | ● | ● | ● | ● | ● | ● | ● | ● | | ● | ● | ● | ● | ● | ● | | ● | ● | ● | ● | ● | ● | ● | ● | ● | ● | ● | ● | ● | | ● | ● | ● | ● | ● | | ● | ● | ● | ● | | | | | |
| MILLINGTON, JANET (HM13917) | | | | | ● | ● | | ● | | | | | | ● | | ● | | | | | | | | | | | | | | | | | | | | | | | | | | | | | | | |
| MOORGATE NATURAL HEALING CTRE (HM14138) | ● | ● | ● | ● | ● | ● | ● | ● | ● | ● | | ● | ● | ● | ● | ● | ● | | ● | ● | ● | ● | ● | ● | ● | ● | ● | ● | ● | ● | ● | | ● | ● | ● | ● | ● | | ● | ● | ● | ● | ● | | | | |
| NIGHTINGALE PHYSIO PRACTICE (HM14937) | | | | | | | | | | | | ● | ● | | | | | | | | ● | | | | | | | | | | | | | | | | | | | | ● | ● | ● | | | | |

# S - W Conditions treated at Practices/Businesses and Specialist Treatment Categories

Business by County with Reference no.

| Business by County with Reference no. | Sexually Trans. Infections | Shingles | Sinus Problems | Skin Problems | Sleep Disorders | Slimming Help | Slipped Disk | Smoking Help | Sneezing | Snoring | Spinal Injuries | Sports Injuries | Sprains | Stammering | Stings | Stomach Problems | Stomach Ulcers | Stress | Sweating | Teeth Grinding | Tennis Elbow | Terminal Illness | Throat Problems | Thrush | Thyroid Problems | Tinnitis | Tiredness | Tonsilitis | Ulcers | Vaginal Problems | Varicose Veins | Verrucas | Vertigo | Viral Infections | Vomiting | Warts | Water Retention | Whiplash | Wind | Worms | Specialist Treatment Categories: Children | Terminally Ill | Disabled | Horses | Dogs | CatS | Other Animals |
|---|---|---|---|---|---|---|---|---|---|---|---|---|---|---|---|---|---|---|---|---|---|---|---|---|---|---|---|---|---|---|---|---|---|---|---|---|---|---|---|---|---|---|---|---|---|---|---|
| PAUL BOIZOT AROMATHERAPY (HM15839) |  |  | ● |  |  |  |  |  |  |  |  |  |  |  |  | ● |  |  |  |  |  |  |  |  |  |  |  |  |  |  |  |  |  |  |  |  |  |  |  |  | ● | ● | ● |  |  |  |  |
| SCHOLL CENTRE (HM18046) |  |  |  |  |  |  |  |  |  |  |  |  |  |  |  |  |  |  |  |  |  |  |  |  |  |  |  |  |  |  |  | ● |  |  |  |  |  |  |  |  |  |  |  |  |  |  |  |
| SEASONS BEAUTY CENTRE (HM18178) |  |  | ● | ● | ● | ● | ● | ● | ● | ● |  | ● | ● |  | ● | ● | ● |  | ● | ● | ● | ● | ● | ● | ● | ● | ● | ● | ● | ● | ● |  | ● | ● | ● | ● | ● |  | ● |  | ● | ● | ● |  |  |  |  |
| SHARRON CHIROPODY CLINIC (HM18324) |  |  |  |  |  |  |  |  |  |  |  |  |  |  |  |  |  |  |  |  |  |  |  |  |  |  |  |  |  |  |  | ● |  |  |  |  |  |  |  |  | ● | ● | ● |  |  |  |  |
| SHEFFIELD NATURAL HEALTH CTRE (HM18372) | ● | ● | ● | ● | ● | ● | ● | ● | ● | ● |  | ● | ● | ● | ● | ● | ● |  | ● | ● | ● | ● | ● | ● | ● | ● | ● | ● | ● | ● | ● |  | ● | ● | ● | ● | ● |  | ● | ● | ● | ● | ● |  |  |  |  |
| STONES, KAREN (HM19343) |  | ● | ● | ● | ● |  | ● | ● | ● | ● |  | ● | ● | ● | ● | ● | ● |  | ● |  | ● |  | ● | ● | ● | ● | ● | ● | ● | ● | ● |  | ● | ● | ● | ● | ● |  | ● |  | ● | ● | ● |  |  |  |  |
| TRIGG, REBECCA (HM20334) |  |  | ● | ● |  |  |  |  |  |  |  | ● |  |  |  |  |  |  |  |  |  |  |  |  |  |  | ● |  |  |  |  |  |  |  |  |  |  |  |  |  | ● |  |  |  |  |  |  |
| VINSON, CAROL (HM20686) |  |  |  |  |  |  |  |  |  |  |  |  |  |  |  |  |  |  |  |  |  |  |  |  |  |  |  |  |  |  |  |  |  |  |  |  |  |  |  |  | ● | ● | ● |  |  |  |  |
| WELLFORCE (HM21160) |  | ● | ● | ● | ● |  |  | ● | ● | ● |  | ● | ● | ● | ● | ● | ● |  | ● | ● | ● | ● | ● | ● | ● | ● | ● | ● | ● | ● | ● |  | ● | ● | ● | ● | ● |  | ● | ● |  |  |  |  |  |  |  |
| WELSH CHIROPRACTIC (HM21183) |  |  | ● | ● | ● |  | ● | ● |  |  |  | ● | ● |  |  | ● |  |  |  | ● | ● |  |  |  |  | ● | ● |  |  |  |  |  | ● |  |  |  |  |  |  |  | ● | ● | ● |  |  |  |  |
| WHITE HOUSE PHYSIOTHERAPY (HM21340) |  |  |  |  |  |  |  |  |  |  |  |  |  |  |  |  |  |  |  |  |  |  |  |  |  |  |  |  |  |  |  |  |  |  |  |  |  |  |  |  | ● | ● | ● |  |  |  |  |
| WHITEING, J P (HM21393) |  |  |  |  |  |  |  |  |  |  |  | ● |  |  |  |  |  |  |  |  |  |  |  |  |  |  |  |  |  |  |  |  |  |  |  |  |  |  |  |  | ● | ● | ● |  |  |  |  |
| WILSON, JOHN PAUL (HM21658) |  |  |  |  |  |  |  |  |  |  |  |  |  |  |  |  |  |  |  |  |  |  |  |  |  |  |  |  |  |  |  | ● |  |  |  |  |  |  |  |  |  |  |  |  |  |  |  |
| WOMBWELL ACUPUNCTURE CLINIC (HM21770) |  |  |  |  |  | ● | ● |  |  |  |  | ● | ● |  |  |  |  |  |  |  | ● |  |  |  |  |  |  |  |  |  |  |  |  |  |  |  |  |  |  |  | ● |  |  |  |  |  |  |
| **YORKSHIRE (WEST)** |  |  |  |  |  |  |  |  |  |  |  |  |  |  |  |  |  |  |  |  |  |  |  |  |  |  |  |  |  |  |  |  |  |  |  |  |  |  |  |  |  |  |  |  |  |  |  |
| A BARCHAM REFLEXOLOGY (HM00024) |  |  | ● |  | ● |  | ● |  |  |  |  | ● |  |  |  | ● |  |  |  |  | ● |  |  | ● | ● |  | ● |  |  | ● |  |  | ● |  |  |  | ● |  | ● |  | ● | ● | ● |  |  |  |  |
| ACTIVE MINDS (HM00199) |  |  |  |  |  |  |  |  |  |  |  |  |  |  |  |  |  | ● |  |  |  |  |  |  |  |  | ● |  |  |  |  |  |  |  |  |  |  |  |  |  |  |  |  |  |  |  |  |
| AIREDALE ALLERGY CENTRE (HM00441) |  |  | ● | ● | ● |  |  |  |  |  |  |  |  |  |  | ● |  |  | ● |  |  |  | ● | ● |  |  | ● |  |  |  |  |  |  |  |  |  |  |  | ● |  | ● |  |  |  |  |  |  |
| ALEX TECH TEACHING CENTRE (HM00513) |  |  |  |  |  |  | ● |  |  |  |  | ● | ● | ● |  |  |  |  |  | ● | ● |  | ● |  |  |  | ● |  |  |  |  |  |  |  |  |  |  |  |  |  | ● | ● | ● |  |  |  |  |
| AMETHYST HEALING CENTRE (HM00783) |  |  |  |  |  |  |  |  |  |  |  |  |  |  |  |  |  | ● |  | ● |  |  |  |  |  |  |  |  |  |  |  |  |  |  |  |  |  |  |  |  | ● | ● | ● |  |  |  |  |
| ARDENTE CHIROPODY SERVICE (HM00991) |  |  |  |  |  |  |  |  |  |  |  |  |  |  |  |  |  |  |  |  |  |  |  |  |  |  |  |  |  |  |  |  |  |  |  | ● |  |  |  |  | ● | ● | ● |  |  |  |  |
| ASH, STACEY (HM01183) |  |  | ● | ● |  |  | ● |  |  |  |  | ● | ● |  |  |  |  |  |  |  | ● |  |  |  |  |  | ● |  |  |  |  |  |  |  |  |  |  |  |  |  |  | ● | ● |  |  |  |  |
| ASPEN CLINIC (HM01255) |  |  |  |  |  |  | ● |  |  |  |  | ● | ● |  |  |  |  |  |  |  | ● |  |  |  |  |  |  |  |  |  |  |  |  |  |  |  |  |  |  |  | ● | ● | ● |  |  |  |  |
| BENTLEY, J H (HM02173) |  |  |  |  |  |  |  |  |  |  |  |  |  |  |  |  |  | ● |  |  |  | ● |  |  |  |  |  |  |  |  |  |  |  |  |  |  |  |  |  |  | ● | ● |  |  |  |  |  |
| BINGLEY HOMOEOPATHIC PRACTICE (HM02315) | ● | ● | ● | ● | ● | ● | ● | ● | ● | ● |  | ● | ● | ● | ● | ● | ● |  | ● | ● | ● | ● | ● | ● | ● | ● | ● | ● | ● | ● | ● |  | ● | ● | ● | ● | ● |  | ● | ● | ● | ● | ● |  |  |  |  |
| BODY ESSENCE (HM02585) |  |  |  | ● | ● |  |  |  |  |  |  |  |  |  |  |  |  | ● |  |  |  |  |  |  |  |  |  |  |  |  |  |  |  |  |  |  |  |  |  |  | ● | ● | ● |  |  |  |  |
| BOYD HYPNOTHERAPY (HM02816) |  |  |  | ● | ● | ● |  | ● |  | ● |  | ● | ● | ● |  | ● |  |  |  | ● |  |  |  |  |  |  | ● |  |  |  |  |  |  |  |  | ● |  |  |  |  |  |  | ● |  |  |  |  |
| BRADFORD CHIROPODY & BIO CLNC (HM02846) |  |  |  |  |  |  |  |  |  |  |  | ● |  |  |  |  |  |  |  |  |  |  |  |  |  |  |  |  |  |  |  |  |  |  |  | ● |  |  |  |  |  |  |  |  |  |  |  |
| BRADFORD CLINIC OF ALT MED (HM02848) | ● | ● | ● | ● | ● | ● | ● | ● | ● | ● |  | ● | ● | ● | ● | ● | ● |  | ● | ● | ● | ● | ● | ● | ● | ● | ● | ● | ● | ● | ● |  | ● | ● | ● | ● | ● |  | ● | ● | ● | ● | ● |  |  |  |  |
| BRAMIN CLINIC (HM02900) |  |  |  |  |  |  |  |  |  |  | ● | ● | ● |  |  |  |  |  |  |  | ● |  |  |  |  |  |  |  |  |  |  |  |  |  |  |  |  | ● |  |  | ● | ● | ● |  |  |  |  |
| BRAMLEY COMP THERAPY CLINIC (HM02901) |  | ● | ● | ● | ● | ● | ● | ● | ● | ● |  | ● | ● | ● | ● | ● | ● | ● | ● | ● | ● |  | ● | ● | ● | ● | ● |  | ● | ● | ● |  | ● | ● | ● | ● | ● |  | ● | ● | ● | ● | ● |  |  |  |  |
| BRAY, D N (HM02928) |  |  |  |  |  |  |  |  |  |  |  |  |  |  |  |  |  | ● |  |  |  |  |  |  |  |  |  |  |  |  |  |  |  |  |  |  |  |  |  |  | ● |  | ● |  |  |  |  |
| BROWN, PAT (HM03243) |  |  |  |  |  |  |  |  |  |  |  |  |  |  |  |  |  | ● |  |  |  |  |  |  |  |  |  |  |  |  |  |  |  |  |  |  |  |  |  |  | ● | ● | ● |  |  |  |  |
| CALVERLEY ACUPUNCTURE CLINIC (HM03561) |  |  | ● |  | ● | ● |  | ● |  |  |  | ● | ● |  |  | ● | ● |  | ● | ● | ● |  |  |  |  | ● | ● |  |  |  |  |  |  |  |  |  |  |  |  |  |  |  |  |  |  |  |  |

# S - W Conditions treated at Practices/Businesses and Specialist Treatment Categories

| Business by County with Reference no. | Sexually Trans. Infections | Shingles | Sinus Problems | Skin Problems | Sleep Disorders | Slimming Help | Slipped Disk | Smoking Help | Sneezing | Snoring | Spinal Injuries | Sports Injuries | Sprains | Stammering | Stings | Stomach Problems |
|---|---|---|---|---|---|---|---|---|---|---|---|---|---|---|---|---|
| CHAMPANERIA, S K (HM03963) | | ● | | ● | | | | ● | ● | | | | | | | ● |
| CHOICE AROMAS (HM04421) | | | | | | | | | | | | | | | | |
| CLARKE, DON (HM04586) | | | ● | ● | | | | | | | | ● | | | | |
| COOPER, SAFFRON (HM05126) | ● | ● | ● | ● | ● | | | | ● | ● | | ● | ● | ● | ● | ● |
| DESIGNING CHANGE (HM06022) | | | | | | | | ● | | | | | | | | |
| DIATHERMY CLINIC (HM06064) | | | | | | | | | | | | | | | | |
| DRURY, WENDY (HM06331) | | | ● | ● | ● | | | | | | | | | | | ● |
| DUFFIELD (HM06360) | | | ● | | | | | | | | | ● | ● | | | |
| EQUA-LIBRA (HM06863) | | | ● | ● | | ● | | ● | | | | | | | | |
| FIGURA, CATHERINE MARIA (HM07283) | | | | ● | ● | | | | | | | | | | | |
| GILLETT, LIZ (HM08088) | | | | | | | | | | | | | | | | |
| HAMER-BLOOM, S (HM08832) | | | | | | | | | | | | | | | | |
| HAMNETT, SHEILA (HM08870) | | | | | | | | | | | | ● | ● | | | |
| HANSON, S C (HM08944) | | | | | | | ● | | | | | ● | ● | | | |
| HEBDEN BRIDGE CENTRE (HM09487) | | | | | | | | | | | | | | | | |
| HERMITAGE OILS (HM09684) | | ● | | ● | | | | | | | | | | | | |
| HOBSON, ANNE (HM09862) | | | | | | | | | | | | | | | | |
| HOBSON, RICHARD (HM09867) | | | | | | | | ● | | | | | | | | |
| HOLME VALLEY SPORTS CLINIC (HM10036) | | | | | | | ● | | | | | ● | ● | | | |
| HOLMFIRTH PHYSIO/SPORTS INJURY (HM10048) | | | | | ● | | ● | | | | | ● | ● | | | |
| HOMEOPATHIC MEDICAL PRACTICE (HM10076) | | ● | ● | ● | ● | | | | | | | | | | | ● |
| HOMEOPATHY FOR CHILDREN (HM10080) | | | | | | | | | | | | | | | | |
| HUNTER, REBECCA (HM10408) | | ● | ● | ● | ● | | | ● | ● | | | ● | ● | | | ● |
| J & J HARROP (HM10792) | | | | | | | | | | | | | | | | |
| JACKSON, ROGER D (HM10850) | | | | | | | ● | | | | | ● | ● | | | |
| KANG DA CLINIC (HM11313) | ● | ● | ● | ● | ● | ● | ● | | | | | ● | ● | | | ● |
| KINGSMITH, ANNE-MARIE (HM11673) | | | | | | | | | | | | | | | | |
| KINNAIRD, F M (HM11686) | | | | ● | ● | ● | | ● | | | | ● | | ● | | ● |
| LEEDS COUNSELLING & PSYCHO SVS (HM12158) | | | | | | | | | | | | | | | | |
| LPS TRAINING & CONSULTANCY (HM12713) | | | | | | | ● | | | | | ● | ● | | | |
| MOORFIELD FLOATATION (HM14137) | | | | | | | | | | | | | | | | |
| MORGAN, J D (DR) (HM14167) | | | | | ● | ● | | ● | | ● | | | | ● | | |
| MORLEY ACUPUNCTURE CLINIC (HM14180) | | ● | ● | ● | ● | ● | ● | ● | ● | ● | | ● | ● | ● | | ● |
| MORNINGTON PHYSIOTHERAPY (HM14193) | | ● | | | | | ● | | | | | ● | ● | | | |

| Business by County with Reference no. | Stomach Ulcers | Stress | Sweating | Teeth Grinding | Tennis Elbow | Terminal Illness | Throat Problems | Thrush | Thyroid Problems | Tinnitis | Tiredness | Tonsilitis | Ulcers | Vaginal Problems | Varicose Veins | Verrucas |
|---|---|---|---|---|---|---|---|---|---|---|---|---|---|---|---|---|
| CHAMPANERIA, S K (HM03963) | ● | | | | | | | ● | | | | | | | | |
| CHOICE AROMAS (HM04421) | | ● | | | | | | | | | ● | | | | | |
| CLARKE, DON (HM04586) | | | | | | | | | | | ● | | | | | |
| COOPER, SAFFRON (HM05126) | ● | | ● | ● | ● | ● | ● | ● | | ● | ● | ● | ● | ● | ● | |
| DESIGNING CHANGE (HM06022) | | ● | | | | | | | | | ● | | | | | |
| DIATHERMY CLINIC (HM06064) | | | | | | | | | | | | | | | | |
| DRURY, WENDY (HM06331) | ● | | | | | | ● | | ● | ● | ● | | | | | |
| DUFFIELD (HM06360) | | | | | | | | | | | | | | | | |
| EQUA-LIBRA (HM06863) | | | | | | | | | | | ● | | | | | |
| FIGURA, CATHERINE MARIA (HM07283) | | ● | | | | | | | | | | | | | | |
| GILLETT, LIZ (HM08088) | | | | | | | | | | | | | | | | |
| HAMER-BLOOM, S (HM08832) | | | | | | | | | | | | | | | | |
| HAMNETT, SHEILA (HM08870) | | ● | | | | | | | | | | | | | | |
| HANSON, S C (HM08944) | | | | | | | | | ● | | | | | | | ● |
| HEBDEN BRIDGE CENTRE (HM09487) | | | | | | | | | | | | | | | | |
| HERMITAGE OILS (HM09684) | | | | | | | | | | | | | | | | |
| HOBSON, ANNE (HM09862) | | ● | | | | | | | | | | | | | | |
| HOBSON, RICHARD (HM09867) | | ● | | | | | | | | | | | | | | |
| HOLME VALLEY SPORTS CLINIC (HM10036) | | | | | ● | | | | | | | | | | | |
| HOLMFIRTH PHYSIO/SPORTS INJURY (HM10048) | | | | | ● | | | | | | | | | | | |
| HOMEOPATHIC MEDICAL PRACTICE (HM10076) | ● | | | | | | ● | ● | ● | ● | ● | ● | ● | ● | | |
| HOMEOPATHY FOR CHILDREN (HM10080) | | | | | | | | | | | | | | | | |
| HUNTER, REBECCA (HM10408) | ● | ● | ● | ● | ● | ● | ● | | ● | ● | ● | | | ● | ● | |
| J & J HARROP (HM10792) | | | | | | | | | | | | | | | | |
| JACKSON, ROGER D (HM10850) | | | | | ● | | | | | | | | | | | |
| KANG DA CLINIC (HM11313) | ● | | ● | | ● | | ● | ● | ● | ● | ● | ● | ● | ● | ● | |
| KINGSMITH, ANNE-MARIE (HM11673) | | | | | | | | | | | | | | | | |
| KINNAIRD, F M (HM11686) | | | ● | ● | | | | | | ● | ● | | | | | |
| LEEDS COUNSELLING & PSYCHO SVS (HM12158) | | ● | | | | | | | | | | | | | | |
| LPS TRAINING & CONSULTANCY (HM12713) | | | | | ● | | | | | | | | | | | |
| MOORFIELD FLOATATION (HM14137) | | ● | | | | | | | | | | | | | | |
| MORGAN, J D (DR) (HM14167) | | | | ● | | | | | | | | | | | | |
| MORLEY ACUPUNCTURE CLINIC (HM14180) | ● | | ● | | ● | ● | ● | ● | ● | ● | ● | ● | ● | ● | ● | |
| MORNINGTON PHYSIOTHERAPY (HM14193) | | | | | ● | | | | | | | | | | | |

| Business by County with Reference no. | Vertigo | Viral Infections | Vomiting | Warts | Water Retention | Whiplash | Wind | Worms | Specialist Treatment Categories: Children | Terminally Ill | Disabled | Horses | Dogs | CatS | Other Animals |
|---|---|---|---|---|---|---|---|---|---|---|---|---|---|---|---|
| CHAMPANERIA, S K (HM03963) | | | | ● | | | | | ● | ● | ● | | | | |
| CHOICE AROMAS (HM04421) | | | | | | | | | | | | | | | |
| CLARKE, DON (HM04586) | | | ● | | | | | | ● | ● | ● | | | | |
| COOPER, SAFFRON (HM05126) | ● | ● | ● | ● | ● | | ● | ● | ● | ● | ● | | | | |
| DESIGNING CHANGE (HM06022) | ● | | | | | | | | ● | | ● | | | | |
| DIATHERMY CLINIC (HM06064) | | | | ● | | | | | ● | | ● | | | | |
| DRURY, WENDY (HM06331) | | | | | ● | | | | ● | | | | | | |
| DUFFIELD (HM06360) | | | | | | | | | ● | ● | ● | | | | |
| EQUA-LIBRA (HM06863) | | | | | | | | | ● | | ● | | | | |
| FIGURA, CATHERINE MARIA (HM07283) | | | | | | | | | | | | | | | |
| GILLETT, LIZ (HM08088) | | | | | | | | | ● | ● | ● | | | | |
| HAMER-BLOOM, S (HM08832) | | | | ● | | | | | ● | ● | ● | | | | |
| HAMNETT, SHEILA (HM08870) | | | | | | | | | ● | ● | ● | | | | |
| HANSON, S C (HM08944) | | | | ● | | | | | ● | ● | | | | | |
| HEBDEN BRIDGE CENTRE (HM09487) | | | | | | | | | | | ● | | | | |
| HERMITAGE OILS (HM09684) | | | | | | | | | ● | | ● | | | | |
| HOBSON, ANNE (HM09862) | | | | | | | | | | | ● | | | | |
| HOBSON, RICHARD (HM09867) | | | | | | | | | ● | ● | ● | | | | |
| HOLME VALLEY SPORTS CLINIC (HM10036) | | | | | | | | | ● | ● | ● | | | | |
| HOLMFIRTH PHYSIO/SPORTS INJURY (HM10048) | | | | | | | | | ● | | ● | | | | |
| HOMEOPATHIC MEDICAL PRACTICE (HM10076) | ● | | | | | | | | | ● | ● | ● | | | |
| HOMEOPATHY FOR CHILDREN (HM10080) | | | | | | | | | ● | | | | | | |
| HUNTER, REBECCA (HM10408) | ● | ● | ● | | ● | | ● | | ● | ● | | | | | |
| J & J HARROP (HM10792) | | | | ● | | | | | ● | ● | ● | | | | |
| JACKSON, ROGER D (HM10850) | | | | | | | | | | | | | | | |
| KANG DA CLINIC (HM11313) | ● | ● | ● | ● | ● | | ● | ● | ● | ● | ● | | | | |
| KINGSMITH, ANNE-MARIE (HM11673) | | | | | | | | | ● | ● | ● | | | | |
| KINNAIRD, F M (HM11686) | ● | | ● | | | | ● | | | ● | ● | | | | |
| LEEDS COUNSELLING & PSYCHO SVS (HM12158) | | | | | | | | | ● | | | | | | |
| LPS TRAINING & CONSULTANCY (HM12713) | | | | | | | | | ● | ● | ● | | | | |
| MOORFIELD FLOATATION (HM14137) | | | | | | | | | | | | | | | |
| MORGAN, J D (DR) (HM14167) | | | | ● | | | | | ● | | | | | | |
| MORLEY ACUPUNCTURE CLINIC (HM14180) | ● | ● | ● | ● | ● | | ● | | ● | ● | ● | | | | |
| MORNINGTON PHYSIOTHERAPY (HM14193) | ● | | | | | | | | ● | ● | ● | | ● | ● | |

# S - W Conditions treated at Practices/Businesses and Specialist Treatment Categories

| Business by County with Reference no. | Sexually Trans. Infections | Shingles | Sinus Problems | Skin Problems | Sleep Disorders | Slimming Help | Slipped Disk | Smoking Help | Sneezing | Snoring | Spinal Injuries | Sports Injuries | Sprains | Stammering | Stings | Stomach Problems | Stomach Ulcers | Stress | Sweating | Teeth Grinding | Tennis Elbow | Terminal Illness | Throat Problems | Thrush | Thyroid Problems | Tinnitis | Tiredness | Tonsilitis | Ulcers | Vaginal Problems | Varicose Veins | Verrucas | Vertigo | Viral Infections | Vomiting | Warts | Water Retention | Whiplash | Wind | Worms | Children | Terminally Ill | Disabled | Horses | Dogs | CatS | Other Animals |
|---|---|---|---|---|---|---|---|---|---|---|---|---|---|---|---|---|---|---|---|---|---|---|---|---|---|---|---|---|---|---|---|---|---|---|---|---|---|---|---|---|---|---|---|---|---|---|---|
| NATURES WORKROOM (HM14705) | ● | ● | ● | ● | ● | ● | ● | ● | ● | ● | | ● | ● | ● | ● | ● | ● | | ● | ● | ● | ● | ● | ● | ● | ● | ● | ● | ● | ● | ● | | ● | ● | ● | ● | ● | | ● | ● | ● | ● | ● | | | | |
| NEILL-HIGGINS, CHRISTINA (HM14765) | | | ● | ● | | | | | | | | | | | | ● | ● | | | | | ● | | ● | ● | ● | | | | | | | | ● | | | | | ● | | ● | ● | ● | | | | |
| NRTH LEEDS PHYSIO/SPRTS INJ (HM15091) | | | | | | | ● | | | | | ● | ● | | | | | | | | ● | | | | | | | | | | | | | | | | | | | | ● | | | | | | |
| OWENS, PAULINE (HM15533) | | | ● | ● | ● | | | | | | | | | ● | | ● | | | | | | | ● | | | | ● | ● | | | | | | | | | | | | | | | | | | | |
| PALLAS, ANDREW (HM15595) | | | ● | ● | | ● | ● | | ● | | | ● | ● | | | ● | | | | ● | ● | | ● | ● | | ● | ● | ● | | | ● | | ● | ● | | | ● | | ● | | ● | ● | ● | | | | |
| PARKS, HILARY (HM15720) | | | ● | ● | ● | | | | | | | | | | | ● | | ● | | | | | | | | | ● | | | | | | | | | ● | ● | ● | | | ● | | | | | | |
| PAYNE, AUDREY (HM15861) | | | ● | | | | | | | | | | | | | | | ● | | | | | | | | | | | | | | | | | | | | | | | ● | | ● | | | | |
| POPPLEWELL, MARK (HM16437) | | ● | ● | | ● | | | | | | | ● | ● | | | ● | ● | | ● | | ● | | | | | | ● | | | | | | | | ● | | ● | | ● | | | | | | | | |
| PRESTON, CATHY (HM16551) | | | | | ● | | | ● | | | | | | | | | | | | | | ● | | | | | ● | | | | | | | | | | | | | | ● | ● | | | | | |
| RAINTREE HEALTH (HM16893) | ● | | | ● | | ● | | | | | | ● | | | ● | ● | ● | | | | | | ● | ● | | | ● | ● | ● | ● | | | ● | ● | | ● | | | ● | ● | | | | | | | |
| RICHARDSON CLINIC (HM17266) | ● | ● | ● | ● | ● | ● | ● | ● | ● | ● | | ● | ● | ● | ● | ● | ● | | ● | ● | ● | ● | ● | ● | ● | ● | ● | ● | ● | ● | ● | | ● | ● | ● | ● | ● | | ● | ● | ● | ● | ● | | | | |
| ROTHWELL SPORTS CENTRE (HM17658) | | | | | | | ● | | | | | ● | ● | | | | | | | | ● | | | | | | | | | | | | | | | | | | | | ● | ● | ● | | | | |
| ROUNDHAY CHIROPRACTIC CLINIC (HM17667) | | | | | | | | | | | | ● | ● | | | | | | | | | | | | | | | | | | | | | | | | | | | | ● | | | | | | |
| SALTAIRE COMP HEALTH STUDIO (HM17864) | ● | ● | ● | ● | ● | ● | ● | ● | ● | ● | | ● | ● | ● | ● | ● | ● | | ● | ● | ● | ● | ● | ● | ● | ● | ● | ● | ● | ● | ● | | ● | ● | ● | ● | ● | | ● | ● | | ● | ● | | | | |
| SHACKLETON, JOHN A (HM18263) | | | | | | | | | | | | ● | ● | | | | | | | | | | | | | | | | | | | | | | | | | | | | ● | ● | ● | | | | |
| SHERQIA, DARULSHAFA (HM18436) | | ● | | ● | ● | | | | ● | | | | | | | ● | ● | | | | | | | | | | ● | | ● | | ● | | ● | ● | | | ● | | | | ● | | | | | | |
| SMITH, JANET (HM18751) | | | ● | | | | | | | | | ● | ● | | | | | | | | ● | | ● | | | | | | | | | | | | | | | | | | ● | | | | | | |
| STEAD, JULIE ANN (HM19164) | | | | | ● | | | | | | | | | | | ● | | | | | | | | | | | ● | | | | | ● | | | | | | | | | ● | ● | ● | | | | |
| SURGERY (HM19519) | | ● | ● | | | | ● | ● | | | | ● | ● | | | | | | | | ● | | | | | ● | | | | | | | | | | ● | | | | | ● | | | | | | |
| SYKES CLINIC (HM19610) | | | | ● | ● | ● | | ● | | | | | | | | | | ● | | | | | | | | ● | | | | | | | | | | | | | | | ● | ● | ● | | | | |
| TORNTON, HOWARD (HM20172) | | | | | | | ● | | | | ● | ● | | | | | | | | | ● | | | | | | | | | | | | | | | | | ● | | | ● | | | | | | |
| TRANSCENDENTAL MEDITATION (HM20285) | | | | | | | | | | | | | | | | | | ● | | | | | | | | | ● | | | | | | | | | | | | | | | | | | | | |
| TUEL LANE PHYSIOTHERAPY CLINIC (HM20376) | | | | | | | ● | | | | | ● | ● | | | | | | | | ● | | | | | | | | | | | | | | | | | | | | ● | ● | ● | | | | |
| WATKINS, JEAN (HM20996) | | | ● | ● | ● | | | | | | | | | | | ● | ● | | | | | | | | | | ● | | | ● | | | | | | | ● | | ● | | ● | ● | ● | | | | |
| WEST YORKSHIRE CLINIC (HM21242) | ● | ● | ● | ● | ● | ● | ● | ● | ● | ● | | ● | ● | ● | ● | ● | ● | | ● | ● | ● | ● | ● | ● | ● | ● | ● | ● | ● | ● | ● | | ● | ● | ● | | ● | | ● | | ● | ● | ● | | | | |
| WEST YORKSHIRE M S THRPY CTRE (HM21243) | | | ● | | | | | | | | | | | | | | | | | | | | | | | | | | | | | | | | | | | | | | ● | ● | ● | | | | |
| WEST YORKSHIRE PHYSIO CENTRE (HM21244) | | | | | | | ● | | | | | ● | ● | | | | | | | | ● | | | | | | | | | | | | | | | | | | | | ● | ● | ● | | | | |
| WETHERBY PHYSIO PRACTICE (HM21290) | | | | | | | ● | | | | | ● | ● | | | | | | | | ● | | | | | | | | | | | | | | | | | | | | ● | | | | | | |
| WIDDOPP, BRIAN (HM21455) | | | | | | | | | | | | | | | | | | | | | | | | | | | | | | | | | | | | | | | | | ● | ● | ● | | | | |
| WISE, CAROL (HM21732) | ● | ● | ● | ● | ● | ● | ● | ● | ● | ● | | ● | ● | ● | ● | ● | ● | | ● | ● | ● | ● | ● | ● | ● | ● | ● | ● | ● | ● | ● | | ● | ● | ● | ● | ● | | ● | ● | ● | ● | ● | | | | |
| WOODHOUSE CLINIC (HM21826) | | | | ● | | | ● | | | | | ● | ● | | | | | | | ● | ● | | | | | ● | | | | ● | | | ● | | | ● | | | | | ● | | | | | | |

(Children, Terminally Ill, Disabled, Horses, Dogs, CatS, Other Animals: Specialist Treatment Categories)

# S - W Conditions treated at Practices/Businesses and Specialist Treatment Categories

Business by County with Reference no.

| Business | Sexually Trans. Infections | Shingles | Sinus Problems | Skin Problems | Sleep Disorders | Slimming Help | Slipped Disk | Smoking Help | Sneezing | Snoring | Spinal Injuries | Sports Injuries | Sprains | Stammering | Stings | Stomach Problems | Stomach Ulcers | Stress | Sweating | Teeth Grinding | Tennis Elbow | Terminal Illness | Throat Problems | Thrush |
|---|---|---|---|---|---|---|---|---|---|---|---|---|---|---|---|---|---|---|---|---|---|---|---|---|
| **IRELAND** | | | | | | | | | | | | | | | | | | | | | | | | |
| **COUNTY CAVAN** | | | | | | | | | | | | | | | | | | | | | | | | |
| BI-AURA THERAPY (HM02274) | | | ● | ● | ● | | ● | | | | | | ● | ● | | ● | ● | ● | | | ● | ● | ● | |
| **COUNTY CORK** | | | | | | | | | | | | | | | | | | | | | | | | |
| ANNAPURNA NATURAL HEALTHCARE (HM00894) | | | ● | | ● | | | ● | | | | | | | | | | | | ● | | | | |
| BANDON CHIROPRACTIC CLINIC (HM01653) | | | | | | | | | | | | | | | | | | | | | ● | | | |
| BROOKFIELD PHYSIOTHERAPY (HM03167) | | | | ● | | | | | | | | ● | ● | | | | | | | ● | | | | ● |
| EAST CORK PHYSIOTHERAPY (HM06511) | | ● | ● | ● | ● | ● | ● | ● | ● | ● | | ● | ● | | | ● | ● | | ● | ● | ● | ● | ● | ● |
| HATTERSLEY, LAURENCE (HM09200) | | | ● | | | | ● | | | | | ● | ● | | | | | | | ● | ● | | | |
| HEALING THERAPIES (HM09354) | | | | | | | | | | | | | | | | | | | | | | | | |
| HERBAL DISPENSARY (HM09610) | | | | | | | | | | | | | | | | | | | | | | | | |
| INS-CLINICAL HYP & PSYCHO (HM10661) | | | | ● | ● | ● | | ● | | ● | | | | ● | | ● | | | ● | ● | | ● | | |
| KEATING, MARY (HM11379) | | | ● | | ● | | | ● | | | | | ● | | | ● | ● | | | | ● | | | ● |
| MOORE-GROACKE, GILLIAN (DR) (HM14136) | | | | | ● | ● | | | | | | | | ● | | | | ● | | | | | | |
| PAUL DENNEHY - HYPNOTHERAPIST (HM15842) | | | | | ● | ● | | ● | ● | ● | | ● | | ● | ● | ● | ● | | ● | ● | ● | ● | ● | |
| RAVEN HILL CHIROPRACTIC CLINIC (HM16964) | | ● | ● | ● | ● | ● | ● | ● | | | ● | ● | ● | | ● | ● | ● | | ● | ● | | | | ● |
| SHIATSU (HM18452) | | | ● | | ● | | ● | | | | | ● | | | | ● | | | | | | | | ● |
| **COUNTY DUBLIN** | | | | | | | | | | | | | | | | | | | | | | | | |
| ABELIA COUNSELLING (HM00110) | | | | | | ● | | ● | | | | | | ● | | | | | | ● | | | | |
| ARDAGH ACUPUNCTURE CLINIC (HM00988) | | ● | ● | ● | ● | | ● | ● | | | | ● | | | | ● | ● | | | | ● | | | |
| ARDUNA COUNS & PSYCHOTHPY CTRE (HM00995) | | | | | | | | | | | | | | | | | | | | | | | | |
| BREE, JOHN (HM02947) | ● | ● | ● | ● | ● | | | | | ● | | ● | ● | | | ● | ● | | | | | ● | ● | |
| B-WELL HYPNOTHERAPY CLINIC (HM03506) | ● | ● | ● | ● | ● | ● | ● | ● | ● | ● | | ● | ● | ● | ● | ● | ● | ● | ● | ● | ● | ● | ● | ● |
| CHADHA, PRADEEP K (DR) (HM03933) | | | | | ● | | | ● | | | | | | | | | | | | | | | | |
| DUN LAOIRE HEALING ROOM (HM06389) | | | | | | | | | | | | | | | | | | ● | | | | | | |
| FAIRVIEW THERAPY CENTRE (HM07066) | | | ● | ● | ● | | ● | ● | | | | ● | | | | ● | | | | | ● | ● | | ● |
| FITZGERALD HYP-PSYCHOTHERAPY (HM07364) | | | | | ● | | | ● | | | | | | | | | | | | | | | | |
| HEALING PLACE (HM09347) | | | ● | | | | ● | | | | | ● | ● | | | ● | | | | ● | ● | | | |
| HEALING ROOM - DRUMCONDRA (HM09351) | | | ● | ● | ● | | | | | | | | | | | ● | | | | ● | | ● | | |
| HEALTH COUNSEL (HM09384) | | | | | | | | ● | | | | | | | | | | | | | | | | |
| HERBAL & ACUPUNCTURE (HM09595) | | ● | ● | ● | ● | | | ● | | ● | | ● | ● | | | ● | ● | | ● | | ● | | ● | ● |
| HERBAL HEALTH SERVICES (HM09618) | | | | | | | | | | | | | | | | | | | | | | | | |
| HOWTH COUNSELLING SERVICE (HM10294) | | | | | ● | | | | | | | | | | | | | | | | | | | |

Specialist Treatment Categories: Children, Terminally Ill, Disabled, Horses, Dogs, CatS, Other Animals

| Business | Thyroid Problems | Tinnitis | Tiredness | Tonsilitis | Ulcers | Vaginal Problems | Varicose Veins | Verrucas | Vertigo | Viral Infections | Vomiting | Warts | Water Retention | Whiplash | Wind | Worms | Children | Terminally Ill | Disabled | Horses | Dogs | CatS | Other Animals |
|---|---|---|---|---|---|---|---|---|---|---|---|---|---|---|---|---|---|---|---|---|---|---|---|
| **IRELAND** | | | | | | | | | | | | | | | | | | | | | | | |
| **COUNTY CAVAN** | | | | | | | | | | | | | | | | | | | | | | | |
| BI-AURA THERAPY (HM02274) | ● | ● | ● | ● | ● | | ● | | | | | | ● | | | | ● | ● | ● | ● | | | |
| **COUNTY CORK** | | | | | | | | | | | | | | | | | | | | | | | |
| ANNAPURNA NATURAL HEALTHCARE (HM00894) | | ● | ● | | | | | | | | | | | | | | ● | ● | ● | | | | |
| BANDON CHIROPRACTIC CLINIC (HM01653) | | | | | | | | | | | | | | | | | ● | ● | ● | | | | |
| BROOKFIELD PHYSIOTHERAPY (HM03167) | | | ● | | | | | | | | | | | | | | ● | ● | ● | | | | |
| EAST CORK PHYSIOTHERAPY (HM06511) | ● | ● | ● | ● | ● | | | | ● | | ● | | ● | | ● | | | | | | | | |
| HATTERSLEY, LAURENCE (HM09200) | | ● | ● | | ● | | | | | | | | | | | | ● | | ● | | | | |
| HEALING THERAPIES (HM09354) | | | ● | | | | | | | | | | | | | | ● | ● | ● | ● | ● | ● | ● |
| HERBAL DISPENSARY (HM09610) | | | | | | | | | | | | | | | | | ● | ● | ● | | | | |
| INS-CLINICAL HYP & PSYCHO (HM10661) | | ● | | | | | | | ● | | ● | ● | | | | | ● | | | | | | |
| KEATING, MARY (HM11379) | | | ● | | | | | | | | | | ● | | | | | | | | | | |
| MOORE-GROACKE, GILLIAN (DR) (HM14136) | | | | | | | | | | | | | | | | | ● | ● | ● | | | | |
| PAUL DENNEHY - HYPNOTHERAPIST (HM15842) | ● | ● | ● | | ● | ● | | | ● | | ● | ● | ● | | ● | ● | ● | ● | ● | | | | |
| RAVEN HILL CHIROPRACTIC CLINIC (HM16964) | | ● | ● | ● | ● | | | | | | ● | ● | ● | ● | ● | ● | | | | | | | |
| SHIATSU (HM18452) | | | ● | | | | | | | | | | ● | ● | ● | | ● | ● | ● | | | | |
| **COUNTY DUBLIN** | | | | | | | | | | | | | | | | | | | | | | | |
| ABELIA COUNSELLING (HM00110) | | | | | | | | | | | | | | | | | | | | | | | |
| ARDAGH ACUPUNCTURE CLINIC (HM00988) | | ● | ● | | ● | | | | | | | | | | ● | | | | | | | | |
| ARDUNA COUNS & PSYCHOTHPY CTRE (HM00995) | | | | | | | | | | | | | | | | | ● | ● | | | | | |
| BREE, JOHN (HM02947) | ● | ● | ● | ● | ● | ● | ● | | ● | ● | | | | | | | ● | ● | ● | ● | ● | ● | |
| B-WELL HYPNOTHERAPY CLINIC (HM03506) | ● | ● | ● | ● | ● | ● | ● | | ● | ● | ● | ● | ● | | ● | ● | ● | ● | | | | | |
| CHADHA, PRADEEP K (DR) (HM03933) | | | | | | | | | | | | | | | | | | | ● | | | | |
| DUN LAOIRE HEALING ROOM (HM06389) | | | | | | | | | | | | | | | | | ● | ● | ● | ● | ● | ● | ● |
| FAIRVIEW THERAPY CENTRE (HM07066) | | | ● | | ● | ● | ● | | | | | | | | | | ● | ● | ● | | | | |
| FITZGERALD HYP-PSYCHOTHERAPY (HM07364) | | | | | | | | | | | | | | | | | ● | | | | | | |
| HEALING PLACE (HM09347) | | ● | ● | | | | | | | | ● | | | | ● | | ● | ● | | | | | |
| HEALING ROOM - DRUMCONDRA (HM09351) | | ● | ● | | | | | | | | | | | | ● | | ● | ● | ● | | | | |
| HEALTH COUNSEL (HM09384) | | | | | | | | | | | | | | | | | | ● | | | | | |
| HERBAL & ACUPUNCTURE (HM09595) | ● | | ● | | ● | ● | | | | ● | | | | | | | ● | | | | | | |
| HERBAL HEALTH SERVICES (HM09618) | | | | | | | | | | | | | | | | | ● | ● | ● | | | | |
| HOWTH COUNSELLING SERVICE (HM10294) | | | | | | | | | | | | | | | | | ● | | | | | | |

# S - W Conditions treated at Practices/Businesses and Specialist Treatment Categories

Business by County with Reference no.

| Business by County with Reference no. | Sexually Trans. Infections | Shingles | Sinus Problems | Skin Problems | Sleep Disorders | Slimming Help | Slipped Disk | Smoking Help | Sneezing | Snoring | Spinal Injuries | Sports Injuries | Sprains | Stammering | Stings | Stomach Problems | Stomach Ulcers | Stress |
|---|---|---|---|---|---|---|---|---|---|---|---|---|---|---|---|---|---|---|
| INNER CIRCLE HEALING CENTRE (HM10635) | | | | | | | | ● | | | | ● | ● | ● | | | | |
| KELLY, ANGELINA (HM11427) | | | ● | ● | ● | | | | | | | | | | | ● | | |
| LALLOO'S ACUPUNCTURE CLINIC (HM11881) | | ● | ● | ● | ● | ● | ● | ● | ● | ● | | ● | ● | ● | ● | ● | ● | |
| LITTLEJOHN CLINIC (HM12472) | | | ● | | | | | | | | | ● | ● | | | ● | ● | |
| MACLIAM, FIONNULA (HM12867) | | | | | ● | | | | | | | | | | | | | ● |
| MCHUGH HYPNOSIS & REFLEXOLOGY (HM13509) | | | | | ● | ● | | ● | | | | | | | | | | |
| MELT/TEMPLE BAR NATURAL (HM13716) | | ● | ● | ● | ● | ● | | ● | ● | ● | | ● | ● | | | | | |
| NATURAL SOLUTIONS (HM14625) | | | | | ● | ● | | ● | | ● | | | | ● | | | | |
| NUALA WOULFE BEAUTY SALON (HM15101) | | | ● | ● | | ● | | | | | | | | | | ● | | |
| RATHMINES CHIROPRACTIC CENTRE (HM16957) | | | | | | | ● | | | | | ● | ● | | | | | |
| T C M CENTRE (HM19639) | | ● | ● | ● | ● | ● | ● | ● | ● | | | ● | ● | | ● | ● | ● | |
| THERAPEUTICS (HM19888) | | | | ● | | ● | | | | | | | | | | | | |
| THEW, NIN (HM19916) | | | ● | ● | ● | | | | ● | | | | | | | ● | ● | ● |
| TOBIN, ROSALEEN (HM20105) | | | | | ● | | | | | | | | | | | | | |
| TRAD CHINESE MEDICINE/MASSAGE (HM20216) | | | ● | | ● | | | | | ● | | ● | ● | | | | ● | |
| **COUNTY GALWAY** | | | | | | | | | | | | | | | | | | |
| ALEXANDER TECHNIQUE CENTRE (HM00557) | | | | | ● | | ● | | | | | ● | | ● | | | | |
| O'COLMAIN, AIDAN (DR) (HM15203) | | | | | ● | | | | | | | | | | | | | |
| PRENDERGAST, KARL (HM16542) | | | ● | | | | ● | | | | | ● | ● | | | | | |
| **COUNTY KERRY** | | | | | | | | | | | | | | | | | | |
| ACUPUNCTURE CLINIC (HM00286) | | ● | ● | ● | ● | | | ● | ● | | | | ● | | | ● | ● | |
| DALY, CHARLES (HM05699) | | | | | | | | | | | | ● | | | | | | |
| WOODLAWN HOLISTIC THERAPY CTRE (HM21834) | | | | ● | | | | | | | | | | | | | | |
| **COUNTY KILDARE** | | | | | | | | | | | | | | | | | | |
| GREEN ROAD HEALING CENTRE (HM08441) | | ● | ● | | ● | | | | | | | | | ● | | ● | | |
| SHENANDOAH HEALING (HM18395) | | | | ● | ● | | | | | | | ● | ● | | | | | |
| **COUNTY KILKENNY** | | | | | | | | | | | | | | | | | | |
| BLUE ROOM (HM02528) | | | | | ● | | | | | | | | | | | | | |
| DULCAMARA (HM06375) | | | ● | | | | | | | | | | | | | ● | ● | |
| HOLISTIC HEALING CENTRE (HM09965) | | | ● | | | | ● | | | | | ● | ● | | | | | |
| MOLLEREAU, ANNE MARIE (HM14052) | | | | | | | | | | | | | | | | | | |
| **COUNTY LIMERICK** | | | | | | | | | | | | | | | | | | |
| HOLISTIC HEALING (HM09960) | | | ● | ● | ● | | | ● | | ● | | | | | | ● | | |
| **COUNTY LONGFORD** | | | | | | | | | | | | | | | | | | |

| Business by County with Reference no. | Sweating | Teeth Grinding | Tennis Elbow | Terminal Illness | Throat Problems | Thrush | Thyroid Problems | Tinnitis | Tiredness | Tonsilitis | Ulcers | Vaginal Problems | Varicose Veins | Verrucas | Vertigo | Viral Infections | Vomiting | Warts | Water Retention | Whiplash | Wind | Worms |
|---|---|---|---|---|---|---|---|---|---|---|---|---|---|---|---|---|---|---|---|---|---|---|
| INNER CIRCLE HEALING CENTRE (HM10635) | | | | | | | | | | | | | | | | | | | | | | |
| KELLY, ANGELINA (HM11427) | | | ● | | ● | ● | ● | ● | ● | ● | | ● | | | ● | ● | ● | ● | | | | |
| LALLOO'S ACUPUNCTURE CLINIC (HM11881) | ● | ● | ● | ● | ● | ● | ● | ● | ● | ● | ● | ● | ● | | ● | ● | ● | ● | ● | | ● | ● |
| LITTLEJOHN CLINIC (HM12472) | | | | | ● | | | | | | | | | | | | | | | | | |
| MACLIAM, FIONNULA (HM12867) | | | | | | | | | | | | | | | | | | | | | | |
| MCHUGH HYPNOSIS & REFLEXOLOGY (HM13509) | ● | ● | | | | | | | | | | | | | | | | | | | | |
| MELT/TEMPLE BAR NATURAL (HM13716) | | | | | | ● | | ● | ● | | | ● | | | | ● | ● | | | | ● | |
| NATURAL SOLUTIONS (HM14625) | | ● | | | | ● | | ● | ● | | | | | | ● | | | | | | | |
| NUALA WOULFE BEAUTY SALON (HM15101) | | | | | | | ● | | | | | | | | | | | | | | | |
| RATHMINES CHIROPRACTIC CENTRE (HM16957) | | | ● | | | | | ● | | | | | | | | ● | | | | | | |
| T C M CENTRE (HM19639) | ● | | ● | ● | ● | ● | ● | ● | ● | ● | ● | ● | | | ● | ● | ● | ● | ● | | ● | ● |
| THERAPEUTICS (HM19888) | | | | | | | | | ● | | | | ● | | | | | | ● | | | |
| THEW, NIN (HM19916) | ● | ● | ● | | | ● | ● | | ● | ● | | ● | | | | ● | ● | | ● | | ● | |
| TOBIN, ROSALEEN (HM20105) | | | | | | | | | ● | | | | | | | | | | | | | |
| TRAD CHINESE MEDICINE/MASSAGE (HM20216) | ● | ● | ● | | ● | ● | | ● | ● | | ● | | | | | | ● | | ● | | | |
| **COUNTY GALWAY** | | | | | | | | | | | | | | | | | | | | | | |
| ALEXANDER TECHNIQUE CENTRE (HM00557) | | ● | ● | | ● | | | | | | | | | | | | | | | | | |
| O'COLMAIN, AIDAN (DR) (HM15203) | | | | | | | | | | | | | | | | | | | | | | |
| PRENDERGAST, KARL (HM16542) | | | ● | | | | | | | | | | | | | | | | | | | |
| **COUNTY KERRY** | | | | | | | | | | | | | | | | | | | | | | |
| ACUPUNCTURE CLINIC (HM00286) | ● | ● | ● | | ● | ● | ● | ● | ● | ● | ● | ● | ● | | ● | | ● | | ● | | ● | ● |
| DALY, CHARLES (HM05699) | | | | | | | | | | | | | | | | | | | | | | |
| WOODLAWN HOLISTIC THERAPY CTRE (HM21834) | | | | | | | | | | ● | | | | | | | | | | | | ● |
| **COUNTY KILDARE** | | | | | | | | | | | | | | | | | | | | | | |
| GREEN ROAD HEALING CENTRE (HM08441) | | | ● | | | ● | ● | ● | ● | ● | | ● | | | | | ● | ● | ● | | ● | |
| SHENANDOAH HEALING (HM18395) | | | | | | | | | ● | | | | | | ● | | | | | | | |
| **COUNTY KILKENNY** | | | | | | | | | | | | | | | | | | | | | | |
| BLUE ROOM (HM02528) | | | | ● | | | ● | | ● | | | | | | | | | | | | | |
| DULCAMARA (HM06375) | | | | | | ● | ● | | ● | ● | ● | | ● | | | ● | | ● | ● | | | ● |
| HOLISTIC HEALING CENTRE (HM09965) | | | ● | | | | | | ● | | | | | | | | | | | | | |
| MOLLEREAU, ANNE MARIE (HM14052) | | | | | | | | | | | | | | | | | | | | | | |
| **COUNTY LIMERICK** | | | | | | | | | | | | | | | | | | | | | | |
| HOLISTIC HEALING (HM09960) | | | ● | | | | | ● | ● | | | | | | ● | | | | | | ● | |
| **COUNTY LONGFORD** | | | | | | | | | | | | | | | | | | | | | | |

| Business by County with Reference no. | Specialist Treatment Categories: Children | Terminally Ill | Disabled | Horses | Dogs | CatS | Other Animals |
|---|---|---|---|---|---|---|---|
| INNER CIRCLE HEALING CENTRE (HM10635) | ● | ● | | | | | |
| KELLY, ANGELINA (HM11427) | ● | | ● | | | | |
| LALLOO'S ACUPUNCTURE CLINIC (HM11881) | ● | ● | ● | | | | |
| LITTLEJOHN CLINIC (HM12472) | ● | ● | ● | | ● | | |
| MACLIAM, FIONNULA (HM12867) | | | | | | | |
| MCHUGH HYPNOSIS & REFLEXOLOGY (HM13509) | ● | ● | ● | | | | |
| MELT/TEMPLE BAR NATURAL (HM13716) | ● | ● | | ● | | | |
| NATURAL SOLUTIONS (HM14625) | ● | ● | ● | | ● | | |
| NUALA WOULFE BEAUTY SALON (HM15101) | | | | | | | |
| RATHMINES CHIROPRACTIC CENTRE (HM16957) | ● | | | | | | |
| T C M CENTRE (HM19639) | ● | ● | ● | | | | |
| THERAPEUTICS (HM19888) | | | | | | | |
| THEW, NIN (HM19916) | | | | | | | |
| TOBIN, ROSALEEN (HM20105) | ● | ● | ● | | | | |
| TRAD CHINESE MEDICINE/MASSAGE (HM20216) | | | | | | | |
| **COUNTY GALWAY** | | | | | | | |
| ALEXANDER TECHNIQUE CENTRE (HM00557) | ● | ● | ● | | | | |
| O'COLMAIN, AIDAN (DR) (HM15203) | ● | ● | ● | | | | |
| PRENDERGAST, KARL (HM16542) | ● | ● | | | | | |
| **COUNTY KERRY** | | | | | | | |
| ACUPUNCTURE CLINIC (HM00286) | ● | | | | | | |
| DALY, CHARLES (HM05699) | | | | | | | |
| WOODLAWN HOLISTIC THERAPY CTRE (HM21834) | | ● | ● | | | | |
| **COUNTY KILDARE** | | | | | | | |
| GREEN ROAD HEALING CENTRE (HM08441) | | | | | | | |
| SHENANDOAH HEALING (HM18395) | ● | ● | ● | | | | |
| **COUNTY KILKENNY** | | | | | | | |
| BLUE ROOM (HM02528) | | | | | | | |
| DULCAMARA (HM06375) | ● | ● | ● | | | | |
| HOLISTIC HEALING CENTRE (HM09965) | ● | ● | ● | | | | |
| MOLLEREAU, ANNE MARIE (HM14052) | | | | ● | | | |
| **COUNTY LIMERICK** | | | | | | | |
| HOLISTIC HEALING (HM09960) | ● | | ● | | | | |
| **COUNTY LONGFORD** | | | | | | | |

# S - W Conditions treated at Practices/Businesses and Specialist Treatment Categories

| Business by County with Reference no. | Sexually Trans. Infections | Shingles | Sinus Problems | Skin Problems | Sleep Disorders | Slimming Help | Slipped Disk | Smoking Help | Sneezing | Snoring | Spinal Injuries | Sports Injuries | Sprains | Stammering | Stings | Stomach Problems | Stomach Ulcers | Stress | Sweating | Teeth Grinding | Tennis Elbow | Terminal Illness | Throat Problems | Thrush | Thyroid Problems | Tinnitis | Tiredness | Tonsilitis | Ulcers | Vaginal Problems | Varicose Veins | Verrucas | Vertigo | Viral Infections | Vomiting | Warts | Water Retention | Whiplash | Wind | Worms | Specialist Treatment Categories: Children | Terminally Ill | Disabled | Horses | Dogs | CatS | Other Animals |
|---|---|---|---|---|---|---|---|---|---|---|---|---|---|---|---|---|---|---|---|---|---|---|---|---|---|---|---|---|---|---|---|---|---|---|---|---|---|---|---|---|---|---|---|---|---|---|---|
| LONGFORD BEAUTY CLINIC (HM12626) |  |  |  | ● |  | ● |  |  |  |  |  |  |  |  |  |  |  |  |  |  |  |  |  |  |  |  |  |  |  |  |  |  |  |  |  |  |  |  |  |  |  |  | ● |  |  |  |  |
| COUNTY LOUTH |  |  |  |  |  |  |  |  |  |  |  |  |  |  |  |  |  |  |  |  |  |  |  |  |  |  |  |  |  |  |  |  |  |  |  |  |  |  |  |  |  |  |  |  |  |  |  |
| HOLISTIC SOL NTRL HEALING CTRE (HM09989) |  |  |  |  |  | ● |  | ● |  |  |  |  |  | ● |  |  |  |  |  |  |  |  |  |  |  |  | ● |  |  |  |  |  |  |  |  |  |  |  |  |  | ● | ● | ● |  |  |  |  |
| COUNTY MAYO |  |  |  |  |  |  |  |  |  |  |  |  |  |  |  |  |  |  |  |  |  |  |  |  |  |  |  |  |  |  |  |  |  |  |  |  |  |  |  |  |  |  |  |  |  |  |  |
| NATURAL HEALING CENTRE (HM14547) |  | ● | ● | ● | ● | ● | ● | ● | ● | ● |  |  | ● |  | ● | ● | ● |  | ● | ● | ● | ● | ● | ● | ● |  | ● | ● | ● | ● | ● |  | ● | ● | ● | ● | ● |  | ● | ● | ● | ● | ● | ● | ● | ● | ● |
| TOBAR PHADRAIC (HM20102) |  |  |  |  | ● | ● |  |  |  |  |  |  |  |  |  |  |  |  |  |  |  | ● |  |  |  |  |  |  |  |  |  |  |  |  |  |  |  |  |  |  | ● | ● | ● |  |  |  |  |
| COUNTY MEATH |  |  |  |  |  |  |  |  |  |  |  |  |  |  |  |  |  |  |  |  |  |  |  |  |  |  |  |  |  |  |  |  |  |  |  |  |  |  |  |  |  |  |  |  |  |  |  |
| NATURAL MEDICINE CENTRE (HM14610) | ● | ● | ● | ● | ● | ● |  | ● | ● | ● |  | ● | ● | ● | ● | ● | ● |  | ● | ● | ● | ● | ● | ● |  | ● | ● | ● | ● | ● | ● |  | ● | ● | ● | ● | ● |  | ● | ● |  |  |  |  |  |  |  |
| COUNTY MONAGHAN |  |  |  |  |  |  |  |  |  |  |  |  |  |  |  |  |  |  |  |  |  |  |  |  |  |  |  |  |  |  |  |  |  |  |  |  |  |  |  |  |  |  |  |  |  |  |  |
| AROMA - ZONE (HM01043) |  |  |  |  |  |  |  |  |  |  |  |  | ● |  |  |  |  |  |  |  |  |  |  |  |  |  |  |  |  |  |  |  |  |  |  | ● |  |  |  |  | ● | ● | ● |  |  |  |  |
| HEALTHY CHOICES (HM09426) |  |  | ● | ● | ● |  | ● | ● |  |  |  | ● | ● |  |  | ● | ● |  |  |  | ● |  |  |  |  |  |  |  |  |  |  |  |  |  |  |  |  |  |  |  | ● |  | ● |  |  |  |  |
| NORTHAMBER (HM15050) |  | ● | ● | ● | ● | ● | ● | ● | ● | ● |  | ● | ● | ● | ● | ● | ● |  | ● | ● | ● | ● | ● | ● | ● | ● | ● | ● | ● | ● | ● |  | ● | ● | ● | ● | ● |  | ● | ● | ● | ● | ● |  |  |  |  |
| COUNTY ROSCOMMON |  |  |  |  |  |  |  |  |  |  |  |  |  |  |  |  |  |  |  |  |  |  |  |  |  |  |  |  |  |  |  |  |  |  |  |  |  |  |  |  |  |  |  |  |  |  |  |
| HOLISTIC HEALTH FARM (HM09980) |  |  | ● |  | ● |  |  |  |  |  |  |  |  |  |  |  |  |  |  |  |  |  |  |  |  | ● |  |  |  |  |  |  |  |  |  |  |  |  |  |  | ● | ● | ● |  | ● |  |  |
| COUNTY SLIGO |  |  |  |  |  |  |  |  |  |  |  |  |  |  |  |  |  |  |  |  |  |  |  |  |  |  |  |  |  |  |  |  |  |  |  |  |  |  |  |  |  |  |  |  |  |  |  |
| ANAM CHARA COUNSELLING (HM00802) |  |  |  |  |  |  |  |  |  |  |  |  |  |  |  |  |  | ● |  |  |  | ● |  |  |  |  |  |  |  |  |  |  |  |  |  |  |  |  |  |  |  | ● | ● |  |  |  |  |
| SLIGO CHIROPRACTIC (HM18686) |  |  |  |  |  |  | ● | ● |  |  |  |  | ● |  |  | ● | ● |  |  |  | ● |  |  | ● | ● | ● | ● | ● |  |  |  |  |  |  |  |  |  |  |  |  | ● | ● | ● |  |  |  |  |
| COUNTY TIPPERARY |  |  |  |  |  |  |  |  |  |  |  |  |  |  |  |  |  |  |  |  |  |  |  |  |  |  |  |  |  |  |  |  |  |  |  |  |  |  |  |  |  |  |  |  |  |  |  |
| KINSELLA, MARIE (HM11693) |  |  |  |  |  |  |  |  |  |  |  |  |  |  |  |  |  |  |  |  |  |  |  |  |  |  |  |  |  |  |  |  |  |  |  |  |  |  |  |  |  | ● |  |  |  |  |  |
| COUNTY WESTMEATH |  |  |  |  |  |  |  |  |  |  |  |  |  |  |  |  |  |  |  |  |  |  |  |  |  |  |  |  |  |  |  |  |  |  |  |  |  |  |  |  |  |  |  |  |  |  |  |
| HOWE, JAN (HM10263) |  |  | ● | ● |  |  |  |  |  |  |  |  |  |  |  | ● |  | ● |  |  |  |  |  |  | ● |  |  |  |  |  |  |  |  |  |  |  |  |  |  |  | ● | ● | ● |  |  |  |  |
| COUNTY WEXFORD |  |  |  |  |  |  |  |  |  |  |  |  |  |  |  |  |  |  |  |  |  |  |  |  |  |  |  |  |  |  |  |  |  |  |  |  |  |  |  |  |  |  |  |  |  |  |  |
| FOURTH MOUNTAIN HOM AND ACU (HM07622) | ● | ● | ● | ● | ● | ● | ● | ● | ● | ● |  | ● | ● |  | ● | ● | ● |  | ● | ● | ● |  | ● | ● | ● |  | ● | ● | ● | ● |  |  | ● | ● | ● | ● |  |  |  | ● | ● |  | ● |  |  |  |  |
| JEFFARIES, PHILIP (HM10958) |  |  |  |  |  |  | ● |  |  |  |  | ● | ● |  |  |  |  |  |  |  | ● |  |  |  |  |  |  |  |  |  |  |  | ● |  |  |  |  |  |  |  |  |  |  |  |  |  |  |
| JEFFARIES, PHILIP (HM10957) |  |  |  |  |  |  | ● |  |  |  |  | ● | ● |  |  |  |  |  |  |  | ● |  |  |  |  |  |  |  |  |  |  |  | ● |  |  |  |  |  |  |  |  |  |  |  |  |  |  |
| MURPHY, MARY (HM14388) |  |  |  |  | ● | ● |  |  |  |  |  |  |  |  |  |  |  |  |  | ● |  |  |  |  |  |  | ● |  |  |  |  |  |  |  |  |  |  |  |  |  |  |  |  |  |  |  |  |
| OSTEOPATHIC PRACTICE (HM15474) |  |  |  |  |  |  | ● |  |  |  |  | ● | ● |  |  |  |  |  |  |  | ● |  |  |  |  |  |  |  |  |  |  |  |  |  |  |  |  |  |  |  | ● | ● |  |  |  |  |  |
| COUNTY WICKLOW |  |  |  |  |  |  |  |  |  |  |  |  |  |  |  |  |  |  |  |  |  |  |  |  |  |  |  |  |  |  |  |  |  |  |  |  |  |  |  |  |  |  |  |  |  |  |  |
| ARKLOW NATURAL HEALING CENTRE (HM01007) |  |  | ● | ● | ● |  |  | ● | ● |  |  | ● | ● |  | ● | ● | ● |  | ● | ● | ● |  | ● |  | ● | ● | ● | ● | ● | ● | ● |  | ● | ● | ● | ● |  |  | ● | ● | ● | ● | ● |  |  |  |  |
| HOLISTIC OPTIONS (HM09985) |  | ● | ● | ● | ● | ● |  | ● |  |  |  | ● | ● |  | ● | ● | ● |  |  |  | ● |  | ● | ● | ● | ● | ● | ● | ● |  | ● |  | ● | ● | ● |  | ● |  | ● |  | ● | ● | ● |  |  |  |  |
| JAMESON PERSONAL EXCELLENCE (HM10903) |  |  |  |  | ● | ● |  | ● |  | ● |  |  |  | ● |  | ● | ● |  |  | ● |  |  |  |  |  | ● |  |  | ● | ● |  |  |  |  | ● |  |  |  |  |  | ● | ● | ● |  |  |  |  |
| MARK GOULDING - ACUPUNCTURIST (HM13107) |  | ● | ● | ● | ● | ● | ● | ● | ● | ● |  | ● | ● | ● |  | ● | ● |  | ● | ● | ● | ● | ● | ● | ● | ● | ● | ● | ● | ● | ● |  | ● | ● | ● | ● | ● |  | ● | ● | ● | ● | ● |  |  |  |  |

# S - W Conditions treated at Practices/Businesses and Specialist Treatment Categories

Business by County with Reference no.

## NORTHERN IRELAND

### COUNTY ANTRIM

| Business | Sexually Trans. Infections | Shingles | Sinus Problems | Skin Problems | Sleep Disorders | Slimming Help | Slipped Disk | Smoking Help | Sneezing | Snoring | Spinal Injuries | Sports Injuries | Sprains | Stammering | Stings | Stomach Problems | Stomach Ulcers | Stress |
|---|---|---|---|---|---|---|---|---|---|---|---|---|---|---|---|---|---|---|
| ACTIVE BALANCE CLINIC (HM00189) | | | | ● | ● | ● | | ● | | | | | ● | ● | | | ● | ● |
| ALOE VERA (HM00669) | | ● | ● | ● | ● | ● | | | | | | ● | ● | | ● | ● | ● | |
| ANTRIM CHIROPRACTIC CLINIC (HM00923) | | | | | | | ● | | | | | ● | ● | | | | | |
| BALLYCLARE CHIROPRACTIC CLINIC (HM01636) | | | | | | | ● | | | | ● | ● | ● | | | | | |
| BALLYMONEY CHIROPRACTIC CLINIC (HM01639) | | | | | | | ● | | | | ● | ● | ● | | | | | |
| BROWN, AVRIL (HM03215) | | | | | | | | | | | | | | | | | | ● |
| CHIROPODIST (HM04290) | | | | | | | | | | | | | | | | | | |
| CRAWFORD, J G (HM05392) | | | | | | | | | | | | | | | | | | |
| CREGAGH CHIROPRACTIC CLINIC (HM05412) | | | | | | | ● | | | | ● | ● | ● | | | | | |
| EARLS, JAMES (HM06497) | | | | | | | | | | | | | | | | | | |
| FAMILY CHIRO CLINIC BALLYMENA (HM07082) | | | | | | | | | | | | | | | | | | |
| FINAGHY CHIROPRACTIC CLINIC (HM07295) | | | | | | | ● | | | | ● | ● | ● | | | | | |
| FLORENCE SHARPE CHIROPODIST (HM07431) | | | | | | | | | | | | | | | | | | |
| FRAMAR NATURAL HEALTH CLINIC (HM07654) | | ● | ● | ● | ● | ● | ● | ● | ● | ● | | ● | ● | | ● | ● | ● | |
| GIVEN, CLIVE (HM08115) | ● | ● | ● | ● | ● | ● | ● | ● | ● | ● | | ● | ● | ● | ● | ● | ● | ● |
| GLENGORMLEY CHIRO CLINIC (HM08151) | | | | | | | ● | | | | ● | ● | ● | | | | | |
| HYPNOTHERAPY CENTRE (HM10521) | | | | | | ● | | ● | | | | | | | | | | |
| LAMBERT, RACHEL (HM11901) | | | | ● | | | | | | | | | | | | | | ● |
| LISBURN CHIROPRACTIC CLINIC (HM12452) | | | | | | | ● | | | | ● | ● | ● | | | | | |
| MAXWELL, MARY (HM13337) | | | ● | | | | | | | | | | | | | ● | | |
| MCCARTNEY, W J (HM13401) | | | | | | | | | | | | | | | | | | |
| MCCRYSTALS NATUROPATHIC CENTRE (HM13436) | ● | ● | ● | ● | ● | ● | ● | ● | ● | ● | | ● | ● | ● | ● | ● | ● | |
| MYSTIC SCHEHERAZADE (HM14445) | | | | | ● | ● | | | | | | | | | | | | |
| NTH IRELAND MUSIC THER TRUST (HM15100) | | | | | | | | | | | | | | | | | | |
| REAY, H (HM17004) | | | | | | | | | | | | | | | | | | |
| SCRABO HEALTH PRODUCTS (HM18143) | | ● | ● | ● | ● | ● | | ● | ● | ● | | | ● | | ● | ● | ● | |
| STEWART, S (HM19276) | | | | | | | | | | | | | | | | | | |
| TODD, TREVOR (HM20109) | | | | | | | | | | | | | | | | | | |
| W M RYAN AND SON (HM20722) | | | | | | | ● | | | | | ● | ● | | | | | |
| YARO (HM21991) | | | | | ● | | | | | | | | | | | | | ● |

| Business | Sweating | Teeth Grinding | Tennis Elbow | Terminal Illness | Throat Problems | Thrush | Thyroid Problems | Tinnitis | Tiredness | Tonsilitis | Ulcers | Vaginal Problems | Varicose Veins | Verrucas | Vertigo | Viral Infections | Vomiting | Warts | Water Retention | Whiplash | Wind | Worms |
|---|---|---|---|---|---|---|---|---|---|---|---|---|---|---|---|---|---|---|---|---|---|---|
| ACTIVE BALANCE CLINIC (HM00189) | ● | ● | | | | ● | | ● | | | | | ● | | | | | | ● | | ● | |
| ALOE VERA (HM00669) | | | ● | | ● | ● | ● | | ● | ● | ● | | ● | | | | ● | ● | ● | | ● | ● |
| ANTRIM CHIROPRACTIC CLINIC (HM00923) | | | ● | | | | | | | | | | | | | | | | | | | |
| BALLYCLARE CHIROPRACTIC CLINIC (HM01636) | | | ● | | | | | | | | | | | | | | | | | ● | | |
| BALLYMONEY CHIROPRACTIC CLINIC (HM01639) | | | ● | | | | | | | | | | | | | | | | | ● | | |
| BROWN, AVRIL (HM03215) | | | | | | | | | | | | | | | | | | | | | | |
| CHIROPODIST (HM04290) | | | | | | | | | | | | | | | | | | ● | | | | |
| CRAWFORD, J G (HM05392) | | | | | | | | | | | | | | | | | | | | | | |
| CREGAGH CHIROPRACTIC CLINIC (HM05412) | | | ● | | | | | | | | | | | | | | | | | ● | | |
| EARLS, JAMES (HM06497) | | | ● | | | | | | | | | | | | | | | | | | | |
| FAMILY CHIRO CLINIC BALLYMENA (HM07082) | | | | | | | | | | | | | | | | | | | | | | |
| FINAGHY CHIROPRACTIC CLINIC (HM07295) | | | ● | | | | | | | | | | | | | | | | | ● | | |
| FLORENCE SHARPE CHIROPODIST (HM07431) | | | | | | | | | | | | | | ● | | | | | | | | |
| FRAMAR NATURAL HEALTH CLINIC (HM07654) | ● | | ● | | ● | ● | ● | ● | ● | ● | ● | | ● | | ● | | ● | ● | | | ● | ● |
| GIVEN, CLIVE (HM08115) | ● | ● | ● | ● | ● | ● | ● | ● | ● | ● | ● | ● | ● | | ● | ● | ● | ● | ● | | ● | ● |
| GLENGORMLEY CHIRO CLINIC (HM08151) | | | ● | | | | | | | | | | | | | | | | | ● | | |
| HYPNOTHERAPY CENTRE (HM10521) | | | | | | | | | | | | | | | | | | | | | | |
| LAMBERT, RACHEL (HM11901) | | | | | | | | | | | | | | | | | | | | | | |
| LISBURN CHIROPRACTIC CLINIC (HM12452) | | | ● | | | | | | | | | | | | | | | | | ● | | |
| MAXWELL, MARY (HM13337) | | | | | | | | | ● | ● | | | ● | | | | | ● | | | | |
| MCCARTNEY, W J (HM13401) | | | | | | | | | | | | | | ● | | | | ● | | | | |
| MCCRYSTALS NATUROPATHIC CENTRE (HM13436) | ● | ● | ● | ● | ● | ● | ● | ● | ● | ● | ● | ● | ● | | ● | ● | ● | ● | ● | | ● | ● |
| MYSTIC SCHEHERAZADE (HM14445) | | | | | | | | | | | | | | | | | | | | | | |
| NTH IRELAND MUSIC THER TRUST (HM15100) | | | | | | | | | | | | | | | | | | | | | | |
| REAY, H (HM17004) | | | | | | | | | | | | | | ● | | | | ● | | | | |
| SCRABO HEALTH PRODUCTS (HM18143) | ● | ● | ● | | ● | ● | ● | ● | ● | ● | ● | ● | ● | | ● | ● | ● | ● | ● | | ● | ● |
| STEWART, S (HM19276) | | | | | | | | | | | | | | | | | | | | | | |
| TODD, TREVOR (HM20109) | | | | | | | | | | | | | | | | | | | | | | |
| W M RYAN AND SON (HM20722) | | | ● | | | | | ● | | | | | | | | | | | | | | |
| YARO (HM21991) | | | | | | | | | | | | | | | | | | | | | | |

**Specialist Treatment Categories**

| Business | Children | Terminally Ill | Disabled | Horses | Dogs | CatS | Other Animals |
|---|---|---|---|---|---|---|---|
| ACTIVE BALANCE CLINIC (HM00189) | ● | ● | ● | | | | |
| ALOE VERA (HM00669) | ● | ● | ● | ● | ● | ● | ● |
| ANTRIM CHIROPRACTIC CLINIC (HM00923) | ● | ● | ● | | | | |
| BALLYCLARE CHIROPRACTIC CLINIC (HM01636) | ● | ● | ● | | | | |
| BALLYMONEY CHIROPRACTIC CLINIC (HM01639) | ● | ● | ● | | | | |
| BROWN, AVRIL (HM03215) | | | ● | | | | |
| CHIROPODIST (HM04290) | ● | ● | ● | | | | |
| CRAWFORD, J G (HM05392) | ● | ● | ● | | | | |
| CREGAGH CHIROPRACTIC CLINIC (HM05412) | | | | | | | |
| EARLS, JAMES (HM06497) | | | | | | | |
| FAMILY CHIRO CLINIC BALLYMENA (HM07082) | ● | ● | ● | | | | |
| FINAGHY CHIROPRACTIC CLINIC (HM07295) | ● | ● | ● | | | | |
| FLORENCE SHARPE CHIROPODIST (HM07431) | ● | ● | ● | | | | |
| FRAMAR NATURAL HEALTH CLINIC (HM07654) | ● | | ● | | | | |
| GIVEN, CLIVE (HM08115) | ● | ● | ● | | | | |
| GLENGORMLEY CHIRO CLINIC (HM08151) | ● | ● | ● | | | | |
| HYPNOTHERAPY CENTRE (HM10521) | ● | ● | ● | | | | |
| LAMBERT, RACHEL (HM11901) | ● | ● | ● | | | | |
| LISBURN CHIROPRACTIC CLINIC (HM12452) | ● | ● | ● | | | | |
| MAXWELL, MARY (HM13337) | | | | | | | |
| MCCARTNEY, W J (HM13401) | ● | ● | ● | | | | |
| MCCRYSTALS NATUROPATHIC CENTRE (HM13436) | ● | ● | ● | ● | ● | | |
| MYSTIC SCHEHERAZADE (HM14445) | | ● | ● | | | | |
| NTH IRELAND MUSIC THER TRUST (HM15100) | ● | ● | ● | | | | |
| REAY, H (HM17004) | ● | ● | ● | | | | |
| SCRABO HEALTH PRODUCTS (HM18143) | ● | | ● | | ● | | |
| STEWART, S (HM19276) | ● | ● | ● | | | | |
| TODD, TREVOR (HM20109) | ● | ● | ● | | | | |
| W M RYAN AND SON (HM20722) | ● | ● | ● | | | | |
| YARO (HM21991) | ● | ● | | | | | |

### COUNTY ARMAGH

# S - W Conditions treated at Practices/Businesses and Specialist Treatment Categories

Business by County with Reference no.

| Business | Sexually Trans. Infections | Shingles | Sinus Problems | Skin Problems | Sleep Disorders | Slimming Help | Slipped Disk | Smoking Help | Sneezing | Snoring | Spinal Injuries | Sports Injuries | Sprains | Stammering | Stings | Stomach Problems | Stomach Ulcers | Stress | Sweating | Teeth Grinding | Tennis Elbow |
|---|---|---|---|---|---|---|---|---|---|---|---|---|---|---|---|---|---|---|---|---|---|
| CAMPBELL, FIONA (HM03598) | | | | | | | | | | | | | | | | | | | | | |
| CRAIGAVON CHIROPRACTIC CLINIC (HM05355) | | | | | | | ● | | | | | | ● | | | | | | | | ● |
| LYON, HARRIETTE (HM12780) | | | | | | | | | | | | | | | | | | | | | |
| WILLIS, IAN (HM21614) | | | | | | | | | | | | | | | | | | | | | |
| **COUNTY DOWN** | | | | | | | | | | | | | | | | | | | | | |
| ARDS CHIROPRACTIC CLINIC (HM00993) | | | | | | | ● | | | | ● | ● | ● | | | | | | | | ● |
| BANGOR CHIROPRACTIC CLINIC (HM01659) | | | | | | | | | | | ● | ● | ● | | | | | | | | |
| BANGOR OSTEOPATHIC CLINIC (HM01660) | | | | | | | ● | | | | | ● | ● | | | | | | | | |
| CHIROPRACTICE (HM04405) | | | | | | | ● | | | | | ● | ● | | | | | | | | ● |
| COCHRANE, NIALL (HM04764) | | | | | | | | | | | | | | | | | | | | | |
| FAMILY CHIROPRACTIC CLINIC (HM07085) | | | | | | | | | | | | | | | | | | | | | |
| HADDEN, MARLENE (HM08687) | | ● | ● | ● | ● | | | ● | | ● | | | | | | ● | | | | | ● |
| LYCIUM CENTRE (HM12755) | | | ● | ● | ● | | | | | | | ● | ● | | | ● | | | ● | | ● |
| MCCARTAN, DEBORAH (HM13392) | | | | | | | | | | | | | | | | | | | | | |
| MCCLURG, T A (HM13412) | | | | | | | | | | | | ● | ● | | | | | | | | |
| MCCUTCHEON, TINA (HM13441) | | | | ● | | | ● | ● | | | | ● | | | | ● | | | | | ● |
| NEWRY CHIROPRACTIC CLINIC (HM14886) | | | | | | | | | | | ● | ● | ● | | | | | | | | ● |
| NOBLE, ANDREW (DR) (HM14968) | | | | | | | ● | | | | ● | ● | ● | | | | | | | | ● |
| NORTH DOWN CLINIC (HM15023) | | | | | | | ● | | | | | ● | | | | | | | | | ● |
| PRINGLE CHIROPRACTIC (HM16626) | | | ● | | | | ● | ● | | | ● | ● | ● | | | ● | ● | | | | ● |
| QUINN, BARBARA (HM16808) | | | | | | | ● | | | | | ● | | | | | | | | | ● |
| REFLEXOLOGY CLINIC (HM17092) | | | ● | | | | | | | | | | | | | | | | | | |
| YOGA CENTRE OF IRELAND (HM22023) | | | | | | | | | | | | | | | | | | ● | | | |
| **COUNTY FERMANAGH** | | | | | | | | | | | | | | | | | | | | | |
| ENNISKILLEN CHIRO CLINIC (HM06844) | | | | | | | ● | | | | | ● | ● | | | | | | | | ● |
| **COUNTY LONDONDERRY** | | | | | | | | | | | | | | | | | | | | | |
| CLARENDON CHIROPRACTIC CLINIC (HM04539) | | | | | | | ● | | | | ● | ● | ● | | | | | | | | ● |
| CLAUDY CHIROPRACTIC CLINIC (HM04612) | | | | | | | | | | | | ● | ● | | | | | | | | ● |
| CURRAN, MAUREEN (HM05630) | | | ● | ● | | | | | | | | | | | | | | ● | | | |
| DISPENSERY (HM06117) | | ● | ● | ● | ● | ● | ● | ● | ● | ● | ● | ● | ● | ● | ● | ● | ● | ● | ● | ● | ● |
| EQUILIBRIUM HOLISTIC CLINIC (HM06875) | | | | | | | | | | | | ● | | | | | | | | | |
| FEET FIRST (HM07174) | | | | | | | | | | | | | | | | | | | | | |
| FOYLE HYPNOTHERAPY CENTRE (HM07646) | | | | | ● | ● | | ● | | | | | | ● | | | | ● | ● | ● | |
| LIFE TREE (HM12350) | | ● | ● | ● | | | | | | | | | | | | | | | ● | | ● |

| Business | Terminal Illness | Throat Problems | Thrush | Thyroid Problems | Tinnitis | Tiredness | Tonsilitis | Ulcers | Vaginal Problems | Varicose Veins | Verrucas | Vertigo | Viral Infections | Vomiting | Warts | Water Retention | Whiplash | Wind | Worms | Specialist Treatment Categories: Children | Terminally Ill | Disabled | Horses | Dogs | CatS | Other Animals |
|---|---|---|---|---|---|---|---|---|---|---|---|---|---|---|---|---|---|---|---|---|---|---|---|---|---|---|
| CAMPBELL, FIONA (HM03598) | | | | | | | | | | | ● | | | | | | | | | | | | | | | |
| CRAIGAVON CHIROPRACTIC CLINIC (HM05355) | | | | | | | | | | | | | | | | | | | | ● | ● | ● | | | | |
| LYON, HARRIETTE (HM12780) | | | | | | | | | | | ● | | | | ● | | | | | | | | | | | |
| WILLIS, IAN (HM21614) | | | | | | | | | | | ● | | | | ● | | | | | ● | ● | ● | | | | |
| **COUNTY DOWN** | | | | | | | | | | | | | | | | | | | | | | | | | | |
| ARDS CHIROPRACTIC CLINIC (HM00993) | | | | | | | | | | | | | | | | | ● | | | ● | ● | ● | | | | |
| BANGOR CHIROPRACTIC CLINIC (HM01659) | ● | | | | | | | | | | | | | | | | | | | ● | ● | ● | | | | |
| BANGOR OSTEOPATHIC CLINIC (HM01660) | | | | | | | | | | | | | | | | | | | | | | | | | | |
| CHIROPRACTICE (HM04405) | | | | | | | | | | | | | | | ● | | ● | | | ● | ● | ● | | | | |
| COCHRANE, NIALL (HM04764) | | | | | | | | | | | ● | | | | | | | | | ● | ● | ● | | | | |
| FAMILY CHIROPRACTIC CLINIC (HM07085) | | | | | | | | | | | | | | | | | | | | ● | ● | ● | | | | |
| HADDEN, MARLENE (HM08687) | | ● | | | | ● | | | | ● | | | | | | ● | | | | ● | ● | ● | ● | | | |
| LYCIUM CENTRE (HM12755) | | | | | | ● | | | | | | | | | | ● | | ● | | ● | | | | | | |
| MCCARTAN, DEBORAH (HM13392) | | | | | | | | | | | ● | | | | ● | | | | | | | | | | | |
| MCCLURG, T A (HM13412) | | | | | | | | | | ● | | | | | ● | | | | | ● | ● | ● | | | | |
| MCCUTCHEON, TINA (HM13441) | | | ● | | | ● | ● | | | | | | | | | | | ● | | ● | | | | | | |
| NEWRY CHIROPRACTIC CLINIC (HM14886) | | | | | | | | | | | | | | | | | ● | | | ● | ● | | | | | |
| NOBLE, ANDREW (DR) (HM14968) | | | | | | | | | | | | | | | | | ● | | | ● | ● | ● | ● | ● | | ● |
| NORTH DOWN CLINIC (HM15023) | | | | | ● | | | | | | | ● | | | | | | | | ● | | ● | | | | |
| PRINGLE CHIROPRACTIC (HM16626) | | | | | ● | | | | | | | ● | | | | | ● | | | ● | ● | ● | ● | ● | ● | ● |
| QUINN, BARBARA (HM16808) | | | | | | | | | | | | | | | | | | | | ● | | ● | | | | |
| REFLEXOLOGY CLINIC (HM17092) | ● | | | | ● | | | | | | | ● | | | | ● | | | | ● | ● | | | | | |
| YOGA CENTRE OF IRELAND (HM22023) | | | | | | | | | | | | | | | | | | | | | | ● | | | | |
| **COUNTY FERMANAGH** | | | | | | | | | | | | | | | | | | | | | | | | | | |
| ENNISKILLEN CHIRO CLINIC (HM06844) | | | | | | | | | | | | | | | | | | | | ● | | ● | | | | |
| **COUNTY LONDONDERRY** | | | | | | | | | | | | | | | | | | | | | | | | | | |
| CLARENDON CHIROPRACTIC CLINIC (HM04539) | | | | | | | | | | | | | | | | | ● | | | ● | ● | ● | | | | |
| CLAUDY CHIROPRACTIC CLINIC (HM04612) | | | | | | | | | | | | | | | | | ● | | | ● | ● | ● | | | | |
| CURRAN, MAUREEN (HM05630) | | | | | | | | | | | | | | | | | | | | ● | ● | ● | | | | |
| DISPENSERY (HM06117) | ● | ● | ● | ● | ● | ● | ● | ● | ● | ● | | ● | ● | ● | ● | ● | ● | ● | ● | ● | ● | ● | | | | |
| EQUILIBRIUM HOLISTIC CLINIC (HM06875) | | | | | | | | | | | | | | | | | | | | ● | ● | ● | | | | |
| FEET FIRST (HM07174) | | | | | | | | | | | ● | | | | ● | | | | | ● | ● | ● | | | | |
| FOYLE HYPNOTHERAPY CENTRE (HM07646) | ● | | | | ● | ● | | | ● | | | ● | | | | ● | | | | ● | ● | ● | | | | |
| LIFE TREE (HM12350) | | ● | ● | | ● | ● | | ● | ● | | | ● | ● | | ● | | | | | ● | | ● | | | | |

# S - W Conditions treated at Practices/Businesses and Specialist Treatment Categories

Business by County with Reference no.

| Condition | MAGHERAFELT CHIRO CLINIC (HM12906) | COUNTY TYRONE | COOKSTOWN HERBAL CLINIC (HM05073) | DUNGANNON CHIROPRACTIC CLINIC (HM06405) | ROSEWOOD HEALTH CLINIC (HM17630) |
|---|---|---|---|---|---|
| **Specialist Treatment Categories** | | | | | |
| Other Animals | | | | | |
| CatS | | | | | |
| Dogs | | | | | |
| Horses | | | | | |
| Disabled | ● | | ● | ● | ● |
| Terminally Ill | ● | | | ● | ● |
| Children | ● | | ● | ● | ● |
| Worms | | | ● | | ● |
| Wind | | | ● | | ● |
| Whiplash | | | | ● | |
| Water Retention | | | ● | | ● |
| Warts | | | ● | | ● |
| Vomiting | | | ● | | ● |
| Viral Infections | | | ● | | ● |
| Vertigo | | | ● | | ● |
| Verrucas | | | | | |
| Varicose Veins | | | ● | | ● |
| Vaginal Problems | | | ● | | ● |
| Ulcers | | | ● | | ● |
| Tonsilitis | | | ● | | ● |
| Tiredness | | | ● | | ● |
| Tinnitis | ● | | ● | | ● |
| Thyroid Problems | | | ● | | ● |
| Thrush | | | ● | | ● |
| Throat Problems | | | ● | | ● |
| Terminal Illness | | | ● | | ● |
| Tennis Elbow | ● | | ● | ● | ● |
| Teeth Grinding | | | ● | | ● |
| Sweating | | | ● | | ● |
| Stress | | | | | |
| Stomach Ulcers | | | ● | | ● |
| Stomach Problems | | | ● | | ● |
| Stings | | | ● | | ● |
| Stammering | | | ● | | ● |
| Sprains | ● | | ● | ● | ● |
| Sports Injuries | ● | | ● | ● | ● |
| Spinal Injuries | | | | ● | |
| Snoring | | | ● | | ● |
| Sneezing | | | ● | | ● |
| Smoking Help | | | ● | | ● |
| Slipped Disk | ● | | ● | ● | ● |
| Slimming Help | | | ● | | ● |
| Sleep Disorders | | | ● | | ● |
| Skin Problems | | | ● | | ● |
| Sinus Problems | ● | | ● | | ● |
| Shingles | | | ● | | ● |
| Sexually Trans. Infections | | | ● | | ● |

# S - W Conditions treated at Practices/Businesses and Specialist Treatment Categories

Business by County with Reference no.

| Business | Sexually Trans. Infections | Shingles | Sinus Problems | Skin Problems | Sleep Disorders | Slimming Help | Slipped Disk | Smoking Help | Sneezing | Snoring | Spinal Injuries | Sports Injuries | Sprains | Stammering | Stings | Stomach Problems | Stomach Ulcers | Stress | Sweating | Teeth Grinding |
|---|---|---|---|---|---|---|---|---|---|---|---|---|---|---|---|---|---|---|---|---|
| **SCOTLAND** | | | | | | | | | | | | | | | | | | | | |
| **ABERDEENSHIRE** | | | | | | | | | | | | | | | | | | | | |
| A WAY WITH THE FAERIES (HM00051) | | | | | | | | | | | | | | | | | | | | |
| ABERDEEN CHIROPRACTIC CLINIC (HM00114) | | | | | | | | | | | ● | ● | ● | | | | | | | |
| ALTERNATIVE PRACTICE (HM00723) | | | | | | | | | | | | ● | | | | | | | | |
| BANCHORY CHIROPODY PRACTICE (HM01649) | | | | ● | | | | | | | | | | | | | | | | |
| BEECHGROVE CLINIC (HM02050) | | | ● | | | ● | ● | | | | | ● | ● | | | | | | | |
| BON-ACCORD CHIROPODY (HM02667) | | | | | | | | | | | | | | | | | | | | |
| CHELSEA HOUSE CLINIC (HM04090) | | | | | | | | | | | | | | | | | | ● | | |
| CITY BEACH (HM04486) | | | | ● | | ● | | | | | | | | | | | | | | |
| CLAIRBAUX CLINIC (HM04506) | | ● | ● | ● | | | ● | | | | | ● | ● | | | | | | | |
| CLAIRBAUX CLINIC (HM04505) | | ● | ● | ● | | | ● | | | | | ● | ● | | | | | | | |
| DAVISON, FIONA (HM05865) | | | | | | | ● | | | | | ● | ● | | | | | | | |
| DEEVIEW AROMATHERAPY (HM05960) | | | | | | | | | | | | | | | | | | | | |
| GRAY, SHEILA (HM08419) | | | ● | | ● | | | | | | | ● | | | | ● | | | | |
| HANDS ACROSS THE VOID (HM08904) | | | | | | | | | | | | | | | | | | | | |
| HUNTLY CHIROPRACTIC CLINIC (HM10412) | | | | | | | ● | | | | | ● | ● | | | | | | | |
| LEAL, DOUGLAS (HM12102) | | | | | | | | | | | | | | | | | | | | |
| MOSS PHARMACY (HM14262) | | | | | | | | | | | | | | | | | | | | |
| REIKI TRAINING CENTRE (HM17149) | | | | | ● | | | | | | | | | | | | | | | |
| RIVERSIDE CHIROPRACTIC CLINIC (HM17378) | | | | | | | | | | | | ● | ● | | | | | | | |
| ROSEMOUNT CENTRE (HM17623) | | | | ● | ● | ● | | ● | ● | ● | | ● | ● | ● | | ● | ● | ● | | |
| SAWYER, KEN (HM17985) | | | | | | ● | | ● | | | | | | | | | | | | |
| SERENDIPITY (HM18232) | | | | ● | ● | ● | | | | | | | | | | | | | | |
| TAGGART, RUTH (HM19652) | | | | ● | | | | | | | | ● | | | | | | ● | | |
| TOE TO HEEL - REFLEXOLOGY (HM20110) | | | ● | | | | | | | | | | ● | | | ● | | | | ● |
| TURRIFF CHIROPRACTIC CLINIC (HM20443) | | | | | | | | | | | | ● | ● | | | | | | | |
| WEST END PHYSIOTHERAPY (HM21219) | | | | | | | ● | | | | | ● | ● | | | | | | | |
| WILKEN, ANGEL (HM21492) | | | ● | ● | | | | | | | | | | | | | | | | |
| WOOD, A R (HM21783) | | | | | | | | | | | | | | | | | | | | |
| **ANGUS** | | | | | | | | | | | | | | | | | | | | |
| BAKER, P T (HM01593) | | | | | | | ● | | | | | ● | ● | | | | | | | |
| DRYDEN, PHILIP (HM06333) | | | | | | | | | | | | | | | | | | | | |

| Business | Tennis Elbow | Terminal Illness | Throat Problems | Thrush | Thyroid Problems | Tinnitis | Tiredness | Tonsilitis | Ulcers | Vaginal Problems | Varicose Veins | Verrucas | Vertigo | Viral Infections | Vomiting | Warts | Water Retention | Whiplash | Wind | Worms |
|---|---|---|---|---|---|---|---|---|---|---|---|---|---|---|---|---|---|---|---|---|
| **SCOTLAND** | | | | | | | | | | | | | | | | | | | | |
| **ABERDEENSHIRE** | | | | | | | | | | | | | | | | | | | | |
| A WAY WITH THE FAERIES (HM00051) | | | | | | | | | | | | | | | | | | | | |
| ABERDEEN CHIROPRACTIC CLINIC (HM00114) | ● | | | | | | | | | | | | | | | | | ● | | |
| ALTERNATIVE PRACTICE (HM00723) | | | | | | ● | | | | | | | | | | | | | | |
| BANCHORY CHIROPODY PRACTICE (HM01649) | | | | | | | | | | | | | | | | ● | | | | |
| BEECHGROVE CLINIC (HM02050) | ● | | | | | | | | | | | | | | | | | | | |
| BON-ACCORD CHIROPODY (HM02667) | | | | | | | | | | | | | | | | ● | | | | |
| CHELSEA HOUSE CLINIC (HM04090) | | | | | | | | | | | | | | | | | | | | |
| CITY BEACH (HM04486) | | | | | | | | | | | | | | | | | | | | |
| CLAIRBAUX CLINIC (HM04506) | ● | | | | | | ● | | | | | | | | | | | | | |
| CLAIRBAUX CLINIC (HM04505) | ● | | | | | | ● | | | | | | | | | | | | | |
| DAVISON, FIONA (HM05865) | | | | | | | | | | | | | | | | | | | | |
| DEEVIEW AROMATHERAPY (HM05960) | | | | | | | ● | | | | | | | | | | | | | |
| GRAY, SHEILA (HM08419) | ● | | | | | | | | | | | | | | | | ● | | | |
| HANDS ACROSS THE VOID (HM08904) | | | | | | | | | | | | | | | | | | | | |
| HUNTLY CHIROPRACTIC CLINIC (HM10412) | ● | | | | | | | | | | | | | | | | | ● | | |
| LEAL, DOUGLAS (HM12102) | | | | | | | | | | | | | | | | | | | | |
| MOSS PHARMACY (HM14262) | | | | | | | | | | | | | | | | | | | | |
| REIKI TRAINING CENTRE (HM17149) | | | | | | | | | | | | | | | | | | | | |
| RIVERSIDE CHIROPRACTIC CLINIC (HM17378) | | | | | | | | | | | | | | | | | | | | |
| ROSEMOUNT CENTRE (HM17623) | ● | ● | ● | | | ● | ● | | ● | | ● | | ● | | ● | ● | | | | ● |
| SAWYER, KEN (HM17985) | | | | | | | | | | | | | | | | | | | | |
| SERENDIPITY (HM18232) | | | | | | ● | | | | | | | | | | | | | | |
| TAGGART, RUTH (HM19652) | | | | | | ● | | | | | | | | | | | | ● | | |
| TOE TO HEEL - REFLEXOLOGY (HM20110) | ● | ● | | ● | ● | ● | ● | | | | | | ● | | | | ● | | | |
| TURRIFF CHIROPRACTIC CLINIC (HM20443) | | | | | | | | | | | | | | | | | | | | |
| WEST END PHYSIOTHERAPY (HM21219) | ● | | | | | | | | | | | | | | | | | | | |
| WILKEN, ANGEL (HM21492) | | | | | | | | | | | | | | | | | | | | |
| WOOD, A R (HM21783) | | | | | | | | | | | | | | | | | | | | |
| **ANGUS** | | | | | | | | | | | | | | | | | | | | |
| BAKER, P T (HM01593) | ● | | | | | | | | | | | | | | | | | ● | | |
| DRYDEN, PHILIP (HM06333) | | | | | | | | | | | | ● | | | | ● | | | | |

| Business | Children | Terminally Ill | Disabled | Horses | Dogs | CatS | Other Animals |
|---|---|---|---|---|---|---|---|
| | **Specialist Treatment Categories** | | | | | | |
| **SCOTLAND** | | | | | | | |
| **ABERDEENSHIRE** | | | | | | | |
| A WAY WITH THE FAERIES (HM00051) | ● | | ● | ● | ● | ● | ● |
| ABERDEEN CHIROPRACTIC CLINIC (HM00114) | ● | ● | ● | | | | |
| ALTERNATIVE PRACTICE (HM00723) | ● | ● | ● | ● | ● | ● | |
| BANCHORY CHIROPODY PRACTICE (HM01649) | ● | ● | ● | | | | |
| BEECHGROVE CLINIC (HM02050) | ● | ● | ● | | | | |
| BON-ACCORD CHIROPODY (HM02667) | ● | ● | ● | | | | |
| CHELSEA HOUSE CLINIC (HM04090) | ● | ● | ● | | | | |
| CITY BEACH (HM04486) | | ● | | | | | |
| CLAIRBAUX CLINIC (HM04506) | ● | ● | ● | | | | |
| CLAIRBAUX CLINIC (HM04505) | ● | ● | ● | | | | |
| DAVISON, FIONA (HM05865) | ● | | ● | | | | |
| DEEVIEW AROMATHERAPY (HM05960) | | | | | | | |
| GRAY, SHEILA (HM08419) | ● | ● | ● | | | | |
| HANDS ACROSS THE VOID (HM08904) | | ● | ● | | | | |
| HUNTLY CHIROPRACTIC CLINIC (HM10412) | ● | ● | ● | | | | |
| LEAL, DOUGLAS (HM12102) | ● | ● | ● | | | | |
| MOSS PHARMACY (HM14262) | ● | | ● | | | | |
| REIKI TRAINING CENTRE (HM17149) | ● | | | | | | |
| RIVERSIDE CHIROPRACTIC CLINIC (HM17378) | ● | ● | ● | | | | |
| ROSEMOUNT CENTRE (HM17623) | ● | ● | ● | | | | |
| SAWYER, KEN (HM17985) | ● | ● | ● | | | | |
| SERENDIPITY (HM18232) | ● | | ● | | | | |
| TAGGART, RUTH (HM19652) | ● | ● | ● | | | | |
| TOE TO HEEL - REFLEXOLOGY (HM20110) | ● | ● | ● | | | | |
| TURRIFF CHIROPRACTIC CLINIC (HM20443) | ● | ● | ● | | | | |
| WEST END PHYSIOTHERAPY (HM21219) | | | | | | | |
| WILKEN, ANGEL (HM21492) | ● | ● | | | | | |
| WOOD, A R (HM21783) | ● | ● | ● | | | | |
| **ANGUS** | | | | | | | |
| BAKER, P T (HM01593) | ● | | | | | | |
| DRYDEN, PHILIP (HM06333) | ● | ● | ● | | | | |

# S - W Conditions treated at Practices/Businesses and Specialist Treatment Categories

Specialist Treatment Categories: Children, Terminally Ill, Disabled, Horses, Dogs, CatS, Other Animals

| Business by County with Reference no. | Sexually Trans. Infections | Shingles | Sinus Problems | Skin Problems | Sleep Disorders | Slimming Help | Slipped Disk | Smoking Help | Sneezing | Snoring | Spinal Injuries | Sports Injuries | Sprains | Stammering | Stings | Stomach Problems | Stomach Ulcers | Stress | Sweating | Teeth Grinding | Tennis Elbow | Terminal Illness | Throat Problems | Thrush | Thyroid Problems | Tinnitis | Tiredness | Tonsilitis | Ulcers | Vaginal Problems | Varicose Veins | Verrucas | Vertigo | Viral Infections | Vomiting | Warts | Water Retention | Whiplash | Wind | Worms | Children | Terminally Ill | Disabled | Horses | Dogs | CatS | Other Animals |
|---|---|---|---|---|---|---|---|---|---|---|---|---|---|---|---|---|---|---|---|---|---|---|---|---|---|---|---|---|---|---|---|---|---|---|---|---|---|---|---|---|---|---|---|---|---|---|---|
| FOGGIE, MARGARET (HM07454) | | | | | | | | | | | | | | | | | | | | | | | | | | | | | | | | | | | | ● | | | | | | | | | | | |
| HOLISTIC HEALING CENTRE (HM09964) | | | | | | | | | | | ● | ● | ● | | | | | | | | ● | | | | | | | | | | | | | | | | | ● | | | ● | | ● | | | | |
| KIRRIEMUIR PHYSIO CLINIC (HM11723) | | | | | | | ● | | | | | ● | ● | | | | | | | | ● | | | | | | | | | | | | | | | | | | | | ● | ● | ● | | | | |
| NATURAL HEALTH & CHIROPODY (HM14558) | | | | | | | | | | | | | | | | | | | | | | | | | | | | | | | | | | | | | | | | | ● | | | | | | |
| NICOLL, ELAINE (HM14929) | | | | | | | | | | | | | | | | | | | | | | | | | | | | | | | | ● | | | | ● | | | | | | | | | | | |
| ARGYLL AND BUTE | | | | | | | | | | | | | | | | | | | | | | | | | | | | | | | | | | | | | | | | | | | | | | | |
| ACTIVE CHIROPRACTIC (HM00195) | | | | | | ● | | | | | | ● | ● | | | | | | | | ● | | | | | | ● | | | | | | | | | | | | | | ● | | | | | | |
| COMPLEMENTARY HEALTH CENTRE (HM04922) | | | | | | | ● | | | | | ● | ● | | | | | | | | | | | | | | | | | | | | | | | | | | | | ● | ● | ● | | | | |
| GIBSON, RONALD J (HM08045) | | | | | ● | | ● | | | | | | ● | | | | | | | | | | | | | | ● | | | | | | | | | ● | | | | | ● | | ● | | | | |
| GRAPEVINE (HM08398) | | | | | | | | | | | | | | | | | | | | | | | | | | | | | | | | | | | | | | | | | ● | ● | ● | | | | |
| HOMEOPATHIC PODIATRIST/REFLEX (HM10078) | | | | ● | | ● | | ● | | | | ● | ● | ● | | | | | | | | ● | | | | | ● | | | | | | | | | ● | ● | | ● | | ● | ● | ● | | | | |
| NATURAL THERAPY CENTRE (HM14648) | | | | | | | ● | ● | | | | ● | | | | ● | | | | | ● | | | ● | | | | | | | ● | | ● | ● | | | | | | | ● | | ● | | | | |
| REIKI LIGHT (HM17138) | | | | | ● | | | | | | | | | | | | | ● | | | | | | | | | | | | | | | | | | | | | | | ● | ● | ● | | | | |
| AYRSHIRE (EAST) | | | | | | | | | | | | | | | | | | | | | | | | | | | | | | | | | | | | | | | | | | | | | | | |
| CRUISE, M & M (HM05520) | | | | | | | | | | | | | | | | | | | | | | | | | | | | | | | | ● | | | | ● | | | | | ● | ● | ● | | | | |
| LITTLEJOHN, S (HM12473) | | | | | | | | | | | | | | | | | | | | | | | | | | | | | | | | ● | | | | | | | | | ● | ● | ● | | | | |
| LYNN BROWN CLINICAL AROM (HM12772) | | | ● | ● | ● | | | ● | | | | ● | ● | | | ● | | | | | ● | ● | ● | ● | ● | | ● | | | | ● | | | ● | | | ● | | ● | | ● | ● | ● | | | | |
| MCCABE, P J (HM13376) | | | | | | | | | | | | | | | | | | | | | | | | | | | | | | | | ● | | | | | | | | | | | | | | | |
| REID, ELIZABETH (HM17117) | | | | | | | | | | | | | | | | | | | | | | | | | | | | | | | | | | | | | | | | | ● | ● | ● | | ● | ● | |
| AYRSHIRE (NORTH) | | | | | | | | | | | | | | | | | | | | | | | | | | | | | | | | | | | | | | | | | | | | | | | |
| BODYSCENTS (HM02631) | | | | | ● | ● | | | | | | | | | | | | ● | | | | | | | | | | | | | | | | | | | | | | | ● | ● | ● | | | | |
| BURNS, ALAN STEWART (HM03410) | | | | | | | | | | | | | | | | | | | | | | | | | | | | | | | | ● | | | | ● | | | | | ● | ● | ● | | | | |
| CHIRO HEALTH CARE CLINIC (HM04282) | | | ● | | ● | ● | ● | | | | | ● | ● | | | ● | | | | ● | ● | | | | | | ● | | | | | | | | | | ● | ● | | | ● | ● | ● | | | | |
| HANDS FOR FEET (HM08905) | | | | | | | | | | | | | | | | | | | | | | | | | | | | | | | | | | | | ● | | | | | ● | ● | ● | | | | |
| PATON, MARY S (HM15824) | | | | | | | | | | | | ● | | | | | | | | | | | | | | | | | | | | | | | | ● | | | | | ● | ● | ● | | | | |
| REID, E (HM17116) | | | ● | | ● | | | | | | | | | | | ● | | | | | | | ● | | | | ● | ● | | | | ● | | | | ● | | | | | ● | ● | ● | | | | |
| AYRSHIRE (SOUTH) | | | | | | | | | | | | | | | | | | | | | | | | | | | | | | | | | | | | | | | | | | | | | | | |
| BELL, W DOUGLAS (HM02091) | ● | ● | ● | ● | ● | ● | ● | ● | ● | ● | | ● | ● | ● | ● | ● | ● | | ● | ● | ● | ● | ● | ● | ● | ● | ● | ● | ● | ● | ● | | ● | ● | ● | ● | ● | | ● | ● | ● | ● | ● | ● | ● | ● | |
| CARRICK CLINIC (HM03742) | | | ● | ● | | | ● | ● | | | | ● | ● | | | ● | | | ● | | ● | | | ● | | | ● | | | ● | | | | | | | | | | | | | | | | | |
| CRUISE, M & M (HM05522) | | | | | | | | | | | | | | | | | | | | | | | | | | | | | | | | ● | | | | | | | | | ● | ● | ● | | | | |
| ESSENCE OF HEALTH (HM06890) | ● | ● | ● | ● | ● | ● | ● | ● | ● | ● | | ● | ● | ● | ● | ● | ● | | ● | ● | ● | ● | ● | ● | ● | ● | ● | ● | ● | ● | ● | | ● | ● | ● | ● | ● | | ● | ● | ● | ● | ● | | | | |
| HARDIE, ANNE (HM08966) | | | | ● | ● | | | | | | | ● | | | | | | ● | | | | | | | | | | | | | | | | | | | | | | | ● | ● | ● | | | | |
| HEALTH STRESS & INJURIES (HM09404) | | ● | ● | ● | ● | ● | ● | ● | ● | ● | | ● | ● | | | ● | | ● | ● | ● | ● | | | | | | ● | | | | | | | | | | ● | | | | ● | ● | ● | | | | |
| HEARTLAKE PHYSIOTHERAPY (HM09444) | | | | | | | ● | | | | | ● | ● | | | | | | | | ● | | | | | | | | | | | | | | | | | | | | ● | | ● | | | | |

# S - W Conditions treated at Practices/Businesses and Specialist Treatment Categories

| Business by County with Reference no. | Sexually Trans. Infections | Shingles | Sinus Problems | Skin Problems | Sleep Disorders | Slimming Help | Slipped Disk | Smoking Help | Sneezing | Snoring | Spinal Injuries | Sports Injuries | Sprains | Stammering | Stings | Stomach Problems | Stomach Ulcers | Stress | Sweating | Teeth Grinding |
|---|---|---|---|---|---|---|---|---|---|---|---|---|---|---|---|---|---|---|---|---|
| HODGE, IAN (HM09874) | | | | | ● | ● | | ● | | | | | | | | | | | | ● |
| ORIENTAL HEALTH CENTRE (HM15381) | | | | | | | | ● | | | | ● | | | | | | | | |
| REID, A (HM17112) | | | | | | | | | | | | | | | | | | | | |
| SMITH, ALICIA (HM18712) | | | | ● | ● | ● | | ● | | | | | | | | | | ● | | ● |
| STEVENSON, SCOTT (HM19251) | | | | | ● | | | | | | | | | | | | | ● | | |
| CLACKMANNANSHIRE | | | | | | | | | | | | | | | | | | | | |
| ALTERNATIVE MEDICAL CLINIC (HM00711) | | | ● | ● | ● | | ● | | | ● | | ● | ● | | | | | | | |
| DUMFRIES AND GALLOWAY | | | | | | | | | | | | | | | | | | | | |
| BURTON, VICKY (HM03447) | | | | ● | | | | | | | | | | | | ● | | | | |
| CHLOE'S HERBS (HM04419) | | | ● | ● | | | | | | | | ● | ● | | ● | ● | ● | | | |
| DAVIDSON, MORAG (HM05788) | | | | | | | | | | | | | | | | | | | | |
| DUMFRIES HOLISTIC HEALTH CTRE (HM06386) | ● | ● | ● | ● | ● | ● | ● | ● | ● | ● | | ● | ● | ● | ● | ● | ● | | ● | ● |
| HEALTH STRESS & INJURIES CLNC (HM09405) | ● | ● | ● | ● | ● | ● | ● | ● | ● | ● | | ● | ● | ● | ● | ● | ● | | ● | ● |
| MCCLUNE, LORNA (HM13410) | | | | | | | | | | | | | | | | | | | | |
| MCCLYMOUNT, JENNIFER (HM13416) | | | | | | | | | | | | | | | | | | | | |
| RANKINE, VANORA (HM16939) | | | | | | | | | | | | | | | | | | | | |
| SHARP, LINDA A (HM18314) | | ● | ● | ● | ● | | ● | ● | ● | | | ● | ● | | | ● | ● | | ● | ● |
| EDINBURGH (CITY OF) | | | | | | | | | | | | | | | | | | | | |
| ACTIVE OSTEOPATHS (HM00200) | | | | | | | | | | | | | | | | | | | | |
| ALEXANDER TECHNIQUE (HM00517) | | | | | | | | | | | | | | | | | | ● | | |
| BABY HOLISTIC & MASSAGE (HM01464) | | | | | ● | | | | | | | | | | | | | | | |
| BIORADIANT HEALTH (HM02343) | | | | | ● | | | | | | | | | | | | | ● | | |
| BLACKHALL PHYSIOTHERAPY CLINIC (HM02445) | | | | | | | ● | | | | | ● | ● | | | | | | | |
| BLAIR, RICHARD (HM02475) | | | ● | | ● | | | | | | | ● | ● | | | ● | | | | ● |
| CARRS, ALLEN (HM03762) | | | | | | | | ● | | | | | | | | | | | | |
| CHRISTIE, ADRIAN (HM04438) | | | | | | | | ● | | | | | | | | | | ● | | |
| DRUMMOND, IAN (HM06326) | | | | | | ● | | ● | | | | | | | | | | | | |
| E G H P (HM06468) | | | | | ● | ● | | ● | | | | | | ● | | ● | | | | ● |
| EDINBURGH ALEXANDER CENTRE (HM06606) | | | ● | | | | | | | | | | | ● | | | | | | |
| EDINBURGH FLOATARIUM (HM06611) | | | | | | | | | | | | | | | | | | ● | | |
| EDINBURGH HOMEOPATHIC CENTRE (HM06613) | | | | | | | ● | | | | | ● | ● | | | | | | | |
| EDINBURGH OSTEOPATHIC SURGERY (HM06615) | | | | | | | ● | | | | | ● | | | | | | | | |
| EDINBURGH PHYSIOTHERAPY CENTRE (HM06616) | | | | | | | ● | | | | | ● | ● | | | | | | | |
| EXCLUSIVE HYPNOTHERAPY (HM07019) | | | | | ● | ● | | ● | | | | | | ● | | | | | | |

| Business by County with Reference no. | Tennis Elbow | Terminal Illness | Throat Problems | Thrush | Thyroid Problems | Tinnitis | Tiredness | Tonsilitis | Ulcers | Vaginal Problems | Varicose Veins | Verrucas | Vertigo | Viral Infections | Vomiting | Warts | Water Retention | Whiplash | Wind | Worms | Specialist Treatment Categories: Children | Terminally Ill | Disabled | Horses | Dogs | CatS | Other Animals |
|---|---|---|---|---|---|---|---|---|---|---|---|---|---|---|---|---|---|---|---|---|---|---|---|---|---|---|---|
| HODGE, IAN (HM09874) | | | | | | ● | | | | | | | ● | | | | | | | | | | | | | | |
| ORIENTAL HEALTH CENTRE (HM15381) | | | | | | | | | | | | | | | | | | | | | ● | ● | ● | | | | |
| REID, A (HM17112) | | | | | | | | | | | | ● | | | | | | | | | ● | ● | ● | | | | |
| SMITH, ALICIA (HM18712) | | | | | | ● | | | | | | | | | | | | | | | ● | ● | | | | | |
| STEVENSON, SCOTT (HM19251) | | | | | | | | | | | | | | | | | | | | | ● | ● | ● | | | | |
| CLACKMANNANSHIRE | | | | | | | | | | | | | | | | | | | | | | | | | | | |
| ALTERNATIVE MEDICAL CLINIC (HM00711) | | | | | | ● | ● | | | | | | ● | | | | | | | | ● | ● | ● | | | | |
| DUMFRIES AND GALLOWAY | | | | | | | | | | | | | | | | | | | | | | | | | | | |
| BURTON, VICKY (HM03447) | | | ● | | | | ● | | | ● | | | | | | | | | | | ● | ● | ● | | | | |
| CHLOE'S HERBS (HM04419) | | ● | ● | ● | | | ● | ● | ● | ● | | | | ● | | | | | ● | ● | ● | ● | | | ● | ● | |
| DAVIDSON, MORAG (HM05788) | | | | | | | | | | | | | | | | | | | | | ● | ● | ● | | | | |
| DUMFRIES HOLISTIC HEALTH CTRE (HM06386) | ● | ● | ● | ● | ● | ● | ● | ● | ● | ● | ● | | ● | ● | ● | ● | ● | | ● | ● | ● | ● | ● | | | | |
| HEALTH STRESS & INJURIES CLNC (HM09405) | ● | ● | ● | ● | ● | ● | ● | ● | ● | ● | ● | | ● | ● | ● | ● | ● | | ● | ● | ● | ● | ● | | | | |
| MCCLUNE, LORNA (HM13410) | | | | | | | | | | | | ● | | | | | | | | | ● | ● | ● | | | | |
| MCCLYMOUNT, JENNIFER (HM13416) | | | | | | | | | | | | ● | | | | | | | | | | | | | | | |
| RANKINE, VANORA (HM16939) | | | | | | | | | | | | | | | | | | | | | ● | ● | ● | | | | |
| SHARP, LINDA A (HM18314) | ● | | ● | ● | ● | ● | ● | | | ● | ● | | ● | ● | ● | | ● | | ● | | | | | ● | ● | | |
| EDINBURGH (CITY OF) | | | | | | | | | | | | | | | | | | | | | | | | | | | |
| ACTIVE OSTEOPATHS (HM00200) | | | | | | | | | | | | | | | | | | | | | ● | | ● | | | | |
| ALEXANDER TECHNIQUE (HM00517) | | | | | | | | | | | | | | | | | | | | | ● | | ● | | | | |
| BABY HOLISTIC & MASSAGE (HM01464) | | | | | | | | | | | | | | | | | | | | | | | | | | | |
| BIORADIANT HEALTH (HM02343) | | | | | | | ● | | | | | | | | | | | | | | ● | ● | ● | | | | |
| BLACKHALL PHYSIOTHERAPY CLINIC (HM02445) | ● | | | | | | | | | | | | | | | | | | | | ● | ● | ● | | | | |
| BLAIR, RICHARD (HM02475) | ● | | | | | | | | | | | | | | | | ● | | | | ● | ● | ● | | | | |
| CARRS, ALLEN (HM03762) | | | | | | | | | | | | | | | | | | | | | | ● | ● | | | | |
| CHRISTIE, ADRIAN (HM04438) | | | | | | | | | | | | | | | | | | | | | ● | ● | ● | | | | |
| DRUMMOND, IAN (HM06326) | | | | | | | | | | | | | | | | | | | | | ● | ● | ● | | | | |
| E G H P (HM06468) | | | | | | ● | ● | | | ● | | | ● | | | | | | | | ● | | | | | | |
| EDINBURGH ALEXANDER CENTRE (HM06606) | | | | | | | | | | | | | | | | | | | | | | | | | | | |
| EDINBURGH FLOATARIUM (HM06611) | | | | | | | | | | | | | | | | | | | | | | | | | | | |
| EDINBURGH HOMEOPATHIC CENTRE (HM06613) | ● | | | | | | ● | | | | | | | | | | | | | | ● | ● | ● | | | | |
| EDINBURGH OSTEOPATHIC SURGERY (HM06615) | ● | | | | | | | | | | | | | | | | | | | | ● | | | | | | |
| EDINBURGH PHYSIOTHERAPY CENTRE (HM06616) | ● | | | | | | | | | | | | | | | | | | | | ● | ● | ● | | | | |
| EXCLUSIVE HYPNOTHERAPY (HM07019) | | | | | | | | | | | | | | | | | | | | | ● | ● | ● | | | | |

# S - W Conditions treated at Practices/Businesses and Specialist Treatment Categories

Specialist Treatment Categories: Children, Terminally Ill, Disabled, Horses, Dogs, CatS, Other Animals

| Business by County with Reference no. | Sexually Trans. Infections | Shingles | Sinus Problems | Skin Problems | Sleep Disorders | Slimming Help | Slipped Disk | Smoking Help | Sneezing | Snoring | Spinal Injuries | Sports Injuries | Sprains | Stammering | Stings | Stomach Problems | Stomach Ulcers | Stress | Sweating | Teeth Grinding | Tennis Elbow | Terminal Illness | Throat Problems | Thrush | Thyroid Problems | Tinnitis | Tiredness | Tonsilitis | Ulcers | Vaginal Problems | Varicose Veins | Verrucas | Vertigo | Viral Infections | Vomiting | Warts | Water Retention | Whiplash | Wind | Worms | Children | Terminally Ill | Disabled | Horses | Dogs | CatS | Other Animals |
|---|---|---|---|---|---|---|---|---|---|---|---|---|---|---|---|---|---|---|---|---|---|---|---|---|---|---|---|---|---|---|---|---|---|---|---|---|---|---|---|---|---|---|---|---|---|---|---|
| GARDINER, F (HM07872) | | | ● | ● | ● | | | | ● | ● | | | | | | ● | | | | | | | | | | | ● | | | | | | | | | | ● | | ● | | ● | ● | ● | | | | |
| HAZEL, J M (HM09290) | | | | | | | | | | | | | | | | | | | | | | | | | | | | | | | | ● | | | | ● | | | | | ● | ● | ● | | | | |
| HOLDEN, SHEENA (HM09934) | | | ● | | | | | | | | | | | | | | | ● | | | | | | | | | ● | | | | | | | | | | | | | | ● | ● | ● | | | | |
| IN HARMONY AROMATHERAPY (HM10595) | | | | ● | ● | ● | | | | | | | | | | | | ● | | | | | | | | | | | | | | | | | | | | | | | | | | | | | |
| J W PHYSIOTHERAPY & SPORTS (HM10805) | | ● | | | | | ● | | | | | ● | ● | | | | | | | | ● | | | | | ● | | | | | | | | | | | | | | | ● | ● | ● | | | | |
| J W PHYSIOTHERAPY & SPORTS (HM10804) | | ● | | | | | ● | | | | | ● | ● | | | | | | | | ● | | | | | ● | | | | | | | | | | | | | | | ● | ● | ● | | | | |
| JENAI (HM10980) | | | | ● | ● | | | | | | | | | | | | | ● | | | | | | | | | | | | | | | | | | | | | | | ● | ● | ● | | | | |
| KELLY, T G (HM11446) | | | | | | | | | | | | | | | | | | | | | | | | | | | | | | | | ● | | | | | | | | | ● | ● | ● | | | | |
| KELLY, T G (HM11447) | | | | | | | | | | | | | | | | | | | | | | | | | | | | | | | | ● | | | | ● | | | | | ● | ● | ● | | | | |
| LIVING MIND (HM12487) | | | ● | | ● | | | ● | | | | | | | | ● | ● | ● | | ● | | | | | | ● | ● | | | | | | | | | | | | | | ● | ● | ● | | | | |
| LOGAN, CAROL (HM12565) | | | | | ● | | | | | | | ● | | | | ● | | | | ● | | | ● | | | | ● | | | | | | | | | | | | | | ● | ● | ● | | | | |
| MACPHERSON, R G (HM12877) | | | | | | | | | | | | | | | | | | | | | | | | | | | | | | | | ● | | | | ● | | | | | ● | ● | ● | | | | |
| MARCHMONT PHYSIOTHERAPY CLINIC (HM13073) | | | | | | | ● | | | | | ● | ● | | | | | | | | ● | | | | | | | | | | | | | | | | | | | | | | | | | | |
| MARIPOSA AROMATHERAPY (HM13103) | | | | ● | ● | | | | | | | | | | | | | ● | | | | | | | | | | | | | | | | | | | | | | | ● | ● | ● | | | | |
| MARSHALL, S C (HM13171) | | | | | | | | | | | | | | | | | | | | | | | | | | | | | | | | ● | | | | | | | | | ● | ● | ● | | | | |
| MCDONALD, DAVID S (HM13456) | | | | | | | | | | | | | | | | | | | | | | | | | | | | | | | | | | | | | | | | | ● | ● | ● | | | | |
| MCVITTIE, D (HM13623) | | | | | | | | | | | | | | | | ● | | | | | | | | | ● | ● | ● | | | | | | | | | | | | | | ● | | | | | | |
| MOBILE CHIROPODY SERVICES (HM14028) | | | | | | | | | | | | | | | | | | | | | | | | | | | | | | | | ● | | | | ● | | | | | ● | ● | ● | | | | |
| MORNINGSIDE PODIATRY SERVICE (HM14192) | | | | | | | | | | | | | | | | | | | | | | | | | | | | | | | | ● | | | | ● | | | | | ● | ● | ● | | | | |
| N H S (HM14449) | | | | | | | | | | | | | | | | | | | | | | | | | | | | | | | | | | | | | | | | | ● | ● | ● | | | | |
| OLIVER & STODDARD (HM15285) | | | ● | ● | ● | | | | | | | | | | | ● | | | | | | | | | | | ● | | | | | | | | | | | | | | | | | | | | |
| PATTERSON, YVONNE (HM15833) | | | | ● | ● | | | | | | | | | | | | | ● | | | | | | | | | | | | | | | | | | | | | | | ● | | ● | | | | |
| PSYCHIC AND LIFE SOLUTIONS (HM16685) | | | | | | | | | | | | | | | | | | ● | | | | | | | | | | | | | | | | | | | | | | | | | | | | | |
| RUMNEY, KATHLEEN (HM17748) | ● | ● | ● | ● | ● | ● | ● | ● | ● | ● | | ● | ● | ● | ● | ● | ● | | ● | ● | ● | ● | ● | ● | ● | ● | ● | ● | ● | ● | ● | | ● | ● | ● | ● | ● | | ● | ● | ● | ● | ● | | | | |
| SHENTON, DIANNE (HM18402) | | | | | | | | | | | | | | | | | | | | | | | | | | | | | | | | | | | | | | | | | ● | ● | ● | | | | |
| SKEDD, L A (HM18629) | | | | | | | | | | | | | | | | | | | | | | | | | | | | | | | | | | | | ● | | | | | ● | ● | ● | | | | |
| TARA ROKPA ENDINBURGH (HM19699) | | | ● | ● | ● | | | | | | | | | | | | | | | | | | | | | | ● | | | | | | | | | | | | | | ● | ● | ● | | | | |
| WARD, ELIZABETH (HM20900) | | | | | ● | | | | | | | | ● | | | | | | | | | | | | | | ● | | | | | | | | | | | | | | ● | ● | ● | | | | |
| WELLBEING (HM21146) | | | | | ● | | | | | | | | | | | | | ● | | | | | | | | | | | | | | | | | | | | | | | ● | ● | ● | | ● | ● | |
| **FALKIRK** | | | | | | | | | | | | | | | | | | | | | | | | | | | | | | | | | | | | | | | | | | | | | | | |
| AESTHETICA TOTAL SKIN & BODY (HM00411) | | | | ● | ● | | | | | | | | | | | | | ● | | | | | | | | | | | | | | | | | | | | | | | | | | | | | |
| ANGUS WILLIAMSON CLINIC (HM00885) | | | | | ● | | | | | | | ● | | | | | | ● | | | | | | | | | | | | | | | | | | | | | | | ● | ● | ● | | | | |
| FALKIRK CHIROPRACTIC CLINIC (HM07074) | | | | | | | ● | | | | | ● | ● | | | | | | | | ● | | | | | | | | | | | | | | | | | ● | | | ● | ● | ● | | | | |
| GRANT, LESLIE & DAWN (HM08385) | | | | | | | | | | | | | | | | | | | | | | | | | | | | | | | | ● | | | | | | | | | ● | ● | ● | | | | |

www.healthmyself.com

# S - W Conditions treated at Practices/Businesses and Specialist Treatment Categories

| Business by County with Reference no. | Sexually Trans. Infections | Shingles | Sinus Problems | Skin Problems | Sleep Disorders | Slimming Help | Slipped Disk | Smoking Help | Sneezing | Snoring | Spinal Injuries | Sports Injuries | Sprains | Stammering | Stings | Stomach Problems | Stomach Ulcers | Stress | Sweating | Teeth Grinding | Tennis Elbow | Terminal Illness | Throat Problems | Thrush | Thyroid Problems | Tinnitis | Tiredness | Tonsilitis | Ulcers | Vaginal Problems | Varicose Veins | Verrucas | Vertigo | Viral Infections | Vomiting | Warts | Water Retention | Whiplash | Wind | Worms | Specialist Treatment Categories: Children | Terminally Ill | Disabled | Horses | Dogs | CatS | Other Animals |
|---|---|---|---|---|---|---|---|---|---|---|---|---|---|---|---|---|---|---|---|---|---|---|---|---|---|---|---|---|---|---|---|---|---|---|---|---|---|---|---|---|---|---|---|---|---|---|---|
| GRANT, LESLIE AND DAWN (HM08386) | | | | | | | | | | | | | | | | | | | | | | | | | | | | | | | | ● | | | | ● | | | | | ● | ● | ● | | | | |
| KELIMAR CLINIC (HM11416) | | | | | | | | | | | | ● | ● | | | | | ● | | | | | | | | | | | | | | | | | | | | | | | ● | ● | ● | | | | |
| NATURAL HEALING CENTRE (HM14543) | | | | | | | ● | | | | | | | | | | | | | | | | | | | | | | | | | | | | | | ● | | | | ● | ● | | | | | |
| **FIFE** | | | | | | | | | | | | | | | | | | | | | | | | | | | | | | | | | | | | | | | | | | | | | | | |
| BODYNEEDS (HM02629) | ● | ● | ● | ● | ● | ● | ● | ● | ● | ● | | ● | ● | ● | ● | ● | ● | | ● | ● | ● | ● | ● | ● | ● | ● | ● | ● | ● | ● | ● | | ● | ● | ● | ● | ● | | ● | ● | ● | ● | ● | | | | |
| CAMERON, WILLIAM (HM03588) | | | | | | | | | | | | | | | | | | | | | | | | | | | | | | | | | | | | | | | | | ● | ● | ● | | | | |
| CAROLE'S MOBILE THERAPIST (HM03718) | | | | | ● | | | | | | | | | | | | | | | | | | | | | | | | | | | | | | | | | | | | ● | ● | ● | | | | |
| COMPLEMENTARY THERAPY CLINIC (HM04949) | | | ● | | ● | ● | | | | | | ● | ● | | ● | ● | ● | | | | ● | | | | | ● | ● | | ● | | | | | | | ● | | | | | ● | | ● | | | | |
| DAVIDSON, ANGELA (HM05785) | | ● | ● | ● | ● | | | | | | | | | | | ● | ● | ● | ● | | | ● | | | ● | ● | ● | ● | | | | | | ● | | | | | | | ● | ● | ● | | | | |
| KEEP IN STEP (HM11394) | | | | | | | | | | | | | | | | | | | | | | | | | | | | | | | | | | | | | | | | | ● | ● | ● | | | | |
| LEUTER, PAM () | | | | | ● | | | | | | | | | | | | | ● | | | | | | | | | | | | | | | | | | | | | | | ● | ● | ● | ● | ● | ● | ● |
| NATURAL REMEDY CLINIC (HM14621) | | | | | | | | | | | | | | | | | | | | | | | | | | | | | | | | | | | | | | | | | ● | | | | | | |
| NEAT FEET (HM14743) | | | ● | ● | ● | | | | | | | ● | ● | | | | | | | | | ● | | | ● | | ● | ● | | | ● | | | | | | ● | | | | ● | ● | ● | | | | |
| O'BRIAN, D (HM15171) | | | | | | | | | | | | | | | | | | | | | | | | | | | | | | | | | | | | | | | | | ● | ● | ● | | | | |
| SHEERINS, ROZ (HM18370) | | | | | | | | | | | | | | | | | | | | | | | | | | | | | | | | | | | | | | | | | ● | ● | ● | | | | |
| ST ANDREWS OSTEOPATHS (HM19065) | | ● | ● | | | | ● | | | | | ● | ● | | | | | | | | ● | | | | | | ● | | | | ● | | | | | | | | | | ● | | | | ● | | |
| TOLBOOTH HOUSE (HM20117) | | | | ● | | ● | ● | ● | | | | ● | | | | | | | | | | | | | | | | | | | | ● | | | | ● | | | | | ● | | ● | | | | |
| TWA ACRES HYPNO TRAINING CTRE (HM20447) | | | | | ● | | | ● | | | | | | ● | | ● | ● | | | ● | | ● | | | | | ● | | | | | | ● | | | | | | | | ● | ● | ● | | | | |
| **GLASGOW (CITY OF)** | | | | | | | | | | | | | | | | | | | | | | | | | | | | | | | | | | | | | | | | | | | | | | | |
| ABOUT FACE (HM00131) | | | ● | ● | ● | | | | | | | | | | | | | | | | | | | | | | | | | | | | | | | ● | ● | | | | | | | | | | |
| ACTIVE CHIROPRACTIC (HM00194) | | | | | | ● | | | | | | ● | ● | | | | | | | | ● | | | | | | ● | | | | | | | | | | | | | | ● | | | | | | |
| ANDERSON DOE PODIATRY CLINIC (HM00809) | | | | | | | | | | | | ● | ● | | | | | | | | ● | | | | | | | | | | | ● | | | | | | | | | ● | ● | ● | | | | |
| ANNE PENMAN THERAPY (HM00900) | | | | | ● | ● | | ● | | | | | | | | | | | | | | | | | | | ● | | | | | | | | | | | | | | ● | ● | ● | | | | |
| BEARSDEN CHIROPRACTIC CLINIC (HM01971) | | | | | | | | | | | | | | | | | | | | | | | | | | | | | | | | | | | | | | | | | ● | | ● | | | | |
| BEHIND THE VEIL (HM02068) | | | | | | | | | | | | | ● | ● | | ● | | | ● | | | | | | | | | | | | | | | | | | | | | | ● | ● | ● | | | | |
| BLACK, JIM (HM02424) | | | | | | | | | | | | | | | | | | | | | | | | | | | | | | | | ● | | | | | | | | | ● | ● | ● | | | | |
| BOTHWELL PHYSIOTHERAPY (HM02733) | | | | | | | ● | | | | ● | ● | ● | | | | | | | | ● | | | | | | | | | | | | | | | | | ● | | | ● | ● | ● | | | | |
| CARRICK STREET PHYSIO & SPORT (HM03743) | | | | | | | ● | | | | | ● | ● | | | | | | | | ● | | | | | | | | | | | | | | | | | | | | | | | | | | |
| CLINIC AT CHARING CROSS (HM04679) | | | | | ● | ● | | ● | | | | ● | | ● | | | | | | ● | ● | | | | | ● | | | | | | | | | | ● | | | | | ● | | | | | | |
| CONWAY, VALERIE (DR) (HM05034) | | ● | ● | ● | ● | | | | ● | | | | ● | | | ● | ● | | ● | | ● | | ● | ● | | | ● | ● | ● | ● | | | | ● | ● | ● | ● | | ● | | ● | ● | ● | | | | |
| CONWAY, VALERIE A (DR) (HM05035) | | ● | ● | ● | ● | | | | ● | | | | ● | | | ● | ● | | ● | | ● | | ● | ● | | | ● | ● | ● | ● | | | | ● | ● | ● | ● | | ● | | ● | ● | ● | | | | |
| FITZPATRICK, J H (HM07374) | | | | | | | | | | | | | | | | | | | | | | | | | | | | | | | | ● | | | | ● | | | | | | | | | | | |
| FOOTSURE (HM07514) | | | | | | | | | | | | | | | | | | | | | | | | | | | | | | | | | | | | | | | | | ● | ● | ● | | | | |
| HARVEST CLINIC (HM09152) | | | ● | ● | ● | ● | ● | ● | | ● | | ● | ● | ● | ● | ● | ● | | ● | ● | ● | ● | | | | | ● | | ● | | ● | | | | | ● | ● | | ● | | ● | ● | ● | | | | |

# S - W Conditions treated at Practices/Businesses and Specialist Treatment Categories

| Business by County with Reference no. | Sexually Trans. Infections | Shingles | Sinus Problems | Skin Problems | Sleep Disorders | Slimming Help | Slipped Disk | Smoking Help | Sneezing | Snoring | Spinal Injuries | Sports Injuries | Sprains | Stammering | Stings | Stomach Problems | Stomach Ulcers | Stress | Sweating | Teeth Grinding | Tennis Elbow | Terminal Illness | Throat Problems | Thrush | Thyroid Problems | Tinnitis | Tiredness | Tonsilitis | Ulcers | Vaginal Problems | Varicose Veins | Verrucas | Vertigo | Viral Infections | Vomiting | Warts | Water Retention | Whiplash | Wind | Worms | Specialist Treatment Categories: Children | Terminally Ill | Disabled | Horses | Dogs | CatS | Other Animals |
|---|---|---|---|---|---|---|---|---|---|---|---|---|---|---|---|---|---|---|---|---|---|---|---|---|---|---|---|---|---|---|---|---|---|---|---|---|---|---|---|---|---|---|---|---|---|---|---|
| HOLISTIC HEALING & HYP (HM09961) | | | | | ● | | | ● | | | | | | ● | | | | | | ● | | | | | | | | | | | | | | | | | | | | | ● | ● | ● | | | | |
| HUMAN PERFORMANCE CLINIC (HM10364) | | | | ● | ● | ● | | ● | | | | | | ● | | | | | | ● | | | | | | | | | | | | | | | | | | | | | ● | ● | ● | | | | |
| LAMBERT, C W (HM11895) | | | | | | | | | | | | | | | | | | | | | | | | | | | | | | | | ● | | | | | | | | | ● | ● | ● | | | | |
| LASER THERAPY CENTRE (HM11984) | | | | | | ● | | ● | | | | | | | | | | ● | | | | | | | | | | | | | | | | | | | | | | | | | | | | | |
| LAURIE, A (HM12015) | | | | | | | | | | | | | | | | | | | | | | | | | | | | | | | | | | | | | | | | | ● | ● | ● | | | | |
| LONG RIVER TAI CHI CIRCLE (HM12617) | | | ● | | ● | | | | | | | | | | | | | | | | | | | | | | ● | | | | | | | | | | | | | | ● | | | | | | |
| MARY HERAGHTY AT HEALTHY FEET (HM13222) | | | | | | | | | | | | | | | | | | | | | | | | | | | | | | | | | | | | ● | | | | | ● | | ● | | | | |
| MCLAREN, CATH RENA (HM13539) | | | ● | ● | ● | | | | | | | | | | | ● | | | ● | | ● | | ● | | ● | ● | ● | ● | | ● | | | | | | | ● | | ● | | ● | | ● | | | | |
| MCLEAN, A M (HM13551) | | | | ● | | | | | | | | ● | ● | | | | | | ● | | | | | | | | | | ● | | ● | | | | | ● | ● | | | | ● | ● | ● | | | | |
| MCTIMONEY CHIROPRACTIC CLINIC (HM13611) | | | | | | | ● | | | | | ● | | | | | | | | | | | | | | | | | | | | | | | | | | | | | ● | | ● | | | | |
| NUTRITION WORLD (HM15126) | ● | ● | ● | ● | ● | ● | ● | ● | ● | ● | | ● | ● | | ● | ● | ● | | ● | ● | ● | ● | ● | ● | ● | ● | ● | ● | ● | ● | ● | | ● | ● | ● | ● | ● | | ● | ● | ● | ● | ● | | | | |
| PLUIDGE, MARK (HM16379) | | | | | | | | | | | | | | | | | | | | | | | | | | | | | | | | | | | | | | | | | ● | ● | | | | | |
| PSYCHIC & HEALING CENTRE (HM16684) | | | | | | | | | | | | | | | | | | | | | | | | | | | | | | | | | | | | | | | | | | ● | ● | | | | |
| RHODIE, ANDREA (HM17231) | | | | ● | ● | | | | | | | | | | | | | ● | | | | | | | | | | | | | | | | | | | | | | | | | | | | | |
| ROLLAND, C R (HM17563) | | | | | | | | | | | | | | | | | | | | | | | | | | | | | | | | ● | | | | | | | | | ● | ● | ● | | | | |
| SCHOLL CENTRE (HM18039) | | | | | | | | | | | | | | | | | | | | | | | | | | | | | | | | ● | | | | | | | | | ● | ● | ● | | | | |
| SHAWLANDS HYPNOTHERAPY CLINIC (HM18352) | | | | | | ● | | ● | | | | | | ● | | | | | | | | | | | | ● | | | | ● | | | | | | | | | | | ● | ● | ● | | | | |
| SINO-HERBAL CLINIC (HM18615) | ● | ● | ● | ● | ● | ● | | ● | ● | ● | | ● | | | | ● | ● | | ● | | ● | | ● | ● | ● | | ● | ● | ● | | ● | | ● | | ● | ● | ● | | | | | | | | | | |
| STEWART, JIM (DR) (HM19270) | | | | | ● | ● | | ● | | | | | | ● | | | | | | ● | | ● | | | | ● | | | | ● | | | | | | | | | | | | | | | | | |
| THERAPY OF LIFE CLINIC (HM19905) | | ● | ● | ● | ● | ● | ● | ● | | | | ● | ● | | ● | ● | ● | | ● | | ● | ● | ● | ● | ● | | ● | | ● | | ● | | | ● | ● | ● | ● | | | | ● | ● | ● | ● | ● | ● | |
| WEST END THERAPY CENTRE (HM21221) | ● | ● | ● | ● | ● | ● | ● | ● | ● | ● | | ● | ● | ● | ● | ● | ● | | ● | ● | ● | ● | ● | ● | ● | ● | ● | ● | ● | ● | ● | | ● | ● | ● | ● | ● | | ● | ● | ● | ● | ● | | | | |
| **HIGHLAND** | | | | | | | | | | | | | | | | | | | | | | | | | | | | | | | | | | | | | | | | | | | | | | | |
| BUMBLE - BEE'S PHYSIO (HM03347) | | | ● | | | | ● | | | | | ● | ● | | | | | | | | ● | | | | | | | | | | | | | | | | | | | | ● | ● | ● | | | | |
| GENTLE WAYS (HM07980) | | | | | ● | | | | | | | | ● | ● | | | | ● | | ● | | ● | | ● | | ● | ● | | | | | | | | | | ● | | | | ● | ● | ● | | | ● | ● |
| HARMONOLOGY CENTRE (HM09017) | | | | | ● | | | | | | | | | | | | | ● | | | | | | | | | | | | | | | | | | | | | | | | | | | | | |
| HEALTH CORNER (HM09383) | | | | | ● | | ● | | | | | ● | | | | | | | | ● | ● | | | | | | | | | | | | | | | | ● | | | | ● | ● | ● | | | | |
| PUFFIN HYDROTHERAPY POOL (HM16743) | | | | | | | ● | | | | | ● | ● | | | | | | | | ● | | | | | | | | | | | | | | | | | | | | ● | ● | ● | | | | |
| TAYLOR, JUNE (HM19773) | | | ● | ● | ● | | | | | ● | | | | | | | | ● | | ● | | | | | | | ● | ● | ● | | | | | | | | ● | | ● | | ● | ● | ● | | | | |
| WAH, G (HM20735) | | ● | ● | ● | ● | | | | | ● | | | | | | | | ● | | ● | | | | | | ● | ● | ● | ● | ● | ● | | ● | | | | ● | | ● | | ● | ● | ● | | | | |
| **INVERCLYDE** | | | | | | | | | | | | | | | | | | | | | | | | | | | | | | | | | | | | | | | | | | | | | | | |
| INVERCLYDE OSTEOPATHIC CLINIC (HM10704) | | | | ● | | | ● | | | | | ● | ● | | | | | | ● | | ● | ● | | ● | | ● | ● | ● | ● | ● | ● | | ● | ● | ● | ● | ● | | ● | | | | | | | | |
| KELLERMANS (HM11418) | | | | ● | | | | | | | | ● | | | | | | ● | | | ● | | | | | | | | | | | | | | | | | | | | ● | ● | ● | | | | |
| **LANARKSHIRE (NORTH)** | | | | | | | | | | | | | | | | | | | | | | | | | | | | | | | | | | | | | | | | | | | | | | | |
| REGISTERED HOMEOPATH (HM17103) | ● | ● | ● | ● | ● | | | | ● | ● | | ● | ● | ● | ● | ● | ● | | ● | ● | ● | ● | ● | ● | ● | ● | ● | ● | ● | ● | ● | | ● | ● | ● | ● | ● | | ● | | ● | ● | ● | | | | |

www.healthmyself.com

Healthmyself Directory

# S - W Conditions treated at Practices/Businesses and Specialist Treatment Categories

| Business by County with Reference no. | Sexually Trans. Infections | Shingles | Sinus Problems | Skin Problems | Sleep Disorders | Slimming Help | Slipped Disk | Smoking Help | Sneezing | Snoring | Spinal Injuries | Sports Injuries | Sprains | Stammering | Stings | Stomach Problems | Stomach Ulcers | Stress | Sweating | Teeth Grinding |
|---|---|---|---|---|---|---|---|---|---|---|---|---|---|---|---|---|---|---|---|---|
| SEMPRE LIBERA (HM18224) | | | | | | | | | | | | | | | | | | ● | | |
| SMITH, IRENE B (HM18748) | | | | | | | | | | | | | | | | | | | | |
| STRATH NATURAL THERAPIES (HM19371) | | | | | ● | ● | | ● | | | | | | ● | | | | ● | | ● |
| LANARKSHIRE (SOUTH) | | | | | | | | | | | | | | | | | | | | |
| QUINN, JIM (HM16810) | ● | ● | ● | ● | ● | ● | ● | ● | ● | ● | ● | ● | ● | ● | ● | ● | ● | ● | ● | ● |
| ROBB, A (DR) (HM17387) | ● | ● | ● | ● | ● | ● | ● | ● | ● | ● | | ● | ● | ● | ● | ● | ● | | ● | ● |
| LOTHIAN (EAST) | | | | | | | | | | | | | | | | | | | | |
| AROMA (HM01042) | ● | ● | ● | ● | ● | ● | ● | ● | ● | ● | | ● | ● | ● | ● | ● | ● | | ● | ● |
| EAST LOTHIAN PHYSIO CENTRE (HM06518) | | ● | | | | | | | | | | ● | ● | | | | | | | |
| FRASER, GORDON (HM07696) | ● | ● | ● | ● | ● | ● | ● | ● | ● | ● | | ● | ● | ● | ● | ● | ● | | ● | ● |
| LOTHIAN (MID) | | | | | | | | | | | | | | | | | | | | |
| CRYSTAL SANCTUARY (HM05532) | | | ● | ● | ● | | | | | | | | | | | | | | | |
| HAMILTON, JAMES (HM08844) | | | ● | | | | | | | | | | | | | ● | | | | |
| NATURAL HEALTH CENTRE (HM14573) | ● | ● | ● | ● | ● | ● | ● | ● | ● | ● | | ● | ● | ● | ● | ● | ● | | ● | ● |
| NEW DUNDAS CLINIC (HM14817) | | | | | | | ● | | | | | ● | ● | | | | | | | |
| RADIANT COLOUR (HM16847) | | | | | ● | | | | | | | | | | | | | ● | | |
| SCOTTISH KINESIOLOGY CENTRE (HM18134) | ● | ● | ● | ● | ● | ● | ● | ● | ● | ● | | ● | ● | ● | ● | ● | ● | | ● | ● |
| LOTHIAN (WEST) | | | | | | | | | | | | | | | | | | | | |
| DUIGNAN, KAREN (HM06372) | | | | | | | | ● | | | | | | | | | | ● | | |
| GILL, SHIRLEY (HM08080) | | | ● | ● | ● | | | | | | | | | | | | | ● | | |
| LINLITHGOW PHYSIO PRACTICE (HM12438) | | | | | | | ● | | | | | ● | ● | | | | | | | |
| VINCES, DENISE (HM20674) | | | ● | ● | ● | | | | | | | | | | | ● | ● | | | |
| MORAY | | | | | | | | | | | | | | | | | | | | |
| AROMANTIC (HM01080) | | | ● | ● | | | | | | | | | ● | | | | | | | |
| ELGIN CHIROPRACTIC CLINIC (HM06729) | | | | | | | ● | | | | ● | ● | ● | | | | | | | |
| FINDHORN FLOWER ESSENCES (HM07307) | | | | | ● | | | | | | | | | | | | | ● | | |
| HEALTHWORKS (HM09422) | | | | ● | ● | | ● | ● | | | | ● | ● | | | ● | ● | | ● | |
| NORTHUMBERLAND | | | | | | | | | | | | | | | | | | | | |
| SOLAR- PLEXUS (HM18864) | | | | | | | | | | | | | | | | | | ● | | |
| ORKNEY ISLES | | | | | | | | | | | | | | | | | | | | |
| A D S THOM (HM00030) | | | | | | | | | | | | | | | | | | | | |
| PERTH AND KINROSS | | | | | | | | | | | | | | | | | | | | |
| ACUPUNCTURE CLINIC (HM00288) | | ● | ● | ● | ● | | ● | ● | ● | ● | | ● | ● | | | ● | ● | | ● | |
| ACUPUNCTURE CLINIC DUNKELD (HM00289) | | ● | ● | ● | ● | | ● | ● | ● | ● | | ● | ● | | | ● | ● | | ● | |

| Business by County with Reference no. | Tennis Elbow | Terminal Illness | Throat Problems | Thrush | Thyroid Problems | Tinnitis | Tiredness | Tonsilitis | Ulcers | Vaginal Problems | Varicose Veins | Verrucas | Vertigo | Viral Infections | Vomiting | Warts | Water Retention | Whiplash | Wind | Worms | Specialist Treatment Categories: Children | Terminally Ill | Disabled | Horses | Dogs | CatS | Other Animals |
|---|---|---|---|---|---|---|---|---|---|---|---|---|---|---|---|---|---|---|---|---|---|---|---|---|---|---|---|
| SEMPRE LIBERA (HM18224) | | | | | | | | | | | | | | | | | | | | | ● | ● | ● | | | | |
| SMITH, IRENE B (HM18748) | | | | | | | | | | | | | | | | | | | | | ● | | ● | | | | |
| STRATH NATURAL THERAPIES (HM19371) | | | ● | | | ● | | | | | | | | | | | | | | | ● | ● | ● | | | | |
| LANARKSHIRE (SOUTH) | | | | | | | | | | | | | | | | | | | | | | | | | | | |
| QUINN, JIM (HM16810) | ● | ● | ● | ● | ● | ● | ● | ● | ● | ● | ● | ● | ● | ● | ● | ● | ● | ● | ● | ● | ● | ● | ● | | | | |
| ROBB, A (DR) (HM17387) | ● | ● | ● | ● | ● | ● | ● | ● | ● | ● | ● | | ● | ● | ● | ● | ● | | ● | ● | ● | ● | ● | | | | |
| LOTHIAN (EAST) | | | | | | | | | | | | | | | | | | | | | | | | | | | |
| AROMA (HM01042) | ● | ● | ● | ● | ● | ● | ● | ● | ● | ● | ● | | ● | ● | ● | ● | ● | | ● | ● | ● | ● | ● | | | | |
| EAST LOTHIAN PHYSIO CENTRE (HM06518) | ● | | | | | ● | | | | | | | ● | | | | | | | | | | | | | | |
| FRASER, GORDON (HM07696) | ● | ● | ● | ● | ● | ● | ● | ● | ● | ● | ● | | ● | ● | ● | ● | ● | | ● | ● | ● | ● | ● | | | | |
| LOTHIAN (MID) | | | | | | | | | | | | | | | | | | | | | | | | | | | |
| CRYSTAL SANCTUARY (HM05532) | | | | | | | ● | | | | | | | | | | ● | | ● | | ● | ● | ● | | | | |
| HAMILTON, JAMES (HM08844) | | | ● | | | | ● | ● | | | | | | | | | | | | | ● | ● | ● | | | | |
| NATURAL HEALTH CENTRE (HM14573) | ● | ● | ● | ● | ● | ● | ● | ● | ● | ● | ● | | ● | ● | ● | ● | ● | | ● | ● | | | | | | | |
| NEW DUNDAS CLINIC (HM14817) | ● | | | | | | | | | | | | | | | | | ● | | | ● | | ● | | | | |
| RADIANT COLOUR (HM16847) | | | | | | | ● | | | | | | | | | | | | | | ● | | | ● | ● | ● | ● |
| SCOTTISH KINESIOLOGY CENTRE (HM18134) | ● | ● | ● | ● | ● | ● | ● | ● | ● | ● | ● | | ● | ● | ● | ● | ● | | ● | ● | ● | ● | ● | | | | |
| LOTHIAN (WEST) | | | | | | | | | | | | | | | | | | | | | | | | | | | |
| DUIGNAN, KAREN (HM06372) | | | | | | | | | | | | | | | | | | | | | ● | ● | ● | | | | |
| GILL, SHIRLEY (HM08080) | | | | | | | ● | | | | | | | | | | ● | | ● | | ● | ● | ● | | | | |
| LINLITHGOW PHYSIO PRACTICE (HM12438) | ● | | | | | | | | | | | | | | | | | | | | ● | | | | | | |
| VINCES, DENISE (HM20674) | ● | | | | | ● | ● | | | | | | | | | | ● | | ● | | | | ● | | | | |
| MORAY | | | | | | | | | | | | | | | | | | | | | | | | | | | |
| AROMANTIC (HM01080) | | | | | | | | | | | ● | | | | | ● | | | | | ● | | | ● | ● | ● | ● |
| ELGIN CHIROPRACTIC CLINIC (HM06729) | ● | | | | | | | | | | | | | | | | | ● | | | ● | ● | ● | | | | |
| FINDHORN FLOWER ESSENCES (HM07307) | | | | | | | | | | | | | | | | | | | | | | | | | | | |
| HEALTHWORKS (HM09422) | ● | | ● | ● | ● | | ● | ● | ● | ● | | | ● | ● | ● | ● | ● | | ● | ● | ● | | | | | | |
| NORTHUMBERLAND | | | | | | | | | | | | | | | | | | | | | | | | | | | |
| SOLAR- PLEXUS (HM18864) | | | | | | | | | | | | | | | | | | | | | ● | ● | ● | | | | |
| ORKNEY ISLES | | | | | | | | | | | | | | | | | | | | | | | | | | | |
| A D S THOM (HM00030) | | | | | | | | | | | | ● | | | | | | | | | ● | ● | ● | | | | |
| PERTH AND KINROSS | | | | | | | | | | | | | | | | | | | | | | | | | | | |
| ACUPUNCTURE CLINIC (HM00288) | ● | | ● | ● | ● | | ● | ● | | ● | | | ● | ● | ● | | ● | | ● | | | | | | | | |
| ACUPUNCTURE CLINIC DUNKELD (HM00289) | ● | | ● | ● | ● | | ● | ● | | ● | | | ● | ● | ● | | ● | | ● | | | | | | | | |

# S - W Conditions treated at Practices/Businesses and Specialist Treatment Categories

Business by County with Reference no.

| Business by County with Reference no. | Sexually Trans. Infections | Shingles | Sinus Problems | Skin Problems | Sleep Disorders | Slimming Help | Slipped Disk | Smoking Help | Sneezing | Snoring | Spinal Injuries | Sports Injuries | Sprains | Stammering | Stings | Stomach Problems | Stomach Ulcers | Stress | Sweating | Teeth Grinding | Tennis Elbow | Terminal Illness | Throat Problems | Thrush | Thyroid Problems | Tinnitis | Tiredness | Tonsilitis | Ulcers | Vaginal Problems | Varicose Veins | Verrucas | Vertigo | Viral Infections | Vomiting | Warts | Water Retention | Whiplash | Wind | Worms | Children (Specialist Treatment Categories) | Terminally Ill | Disabled | Horses | Dogs | CatS | Other Animals |
|---|---|---|---|---|---|---|---|---|---|---|---|---|---|---|---|---|---|---|---|---|---|---|---|---|---|---|---|---|---|---|---|---|---|---|---|---|---|---|---|---|---|---|---|---|---|---|---|
| AUCHTERARDER CHIROPODY (HM01343) | | | | | | | | | | | | | | | | | | | | | | | | | | | | | | | | ● | | | | | | | | | ● | ● | ● | | | | |
| BACK PAIN & SPORTS CLINIC (HM01491) | | | | | | | ● | | | | | ● | ● | | | | | | | | ● | | | | | | | | | | | | | | | | | | | | ● | | ● | | | | |
| HOWIE, TOM R (HM10283) | | | | | | | | | | | | | | | | | | | | | | | | | | | | | | | | ● | | | | | | | | | ● | ● | ● | | | | |
| HOWIE, TOM R (HM10284) | | | | | | | | | | | | | | | | | | | | | | | | | | | | | | | | ● | | | | | | | | | ● | ● | ● | | | | |
| LENDRICK LODGE (HM12210) | | | | | ● | | | | | | | | | | | | | | | | | | | | | | ● | | | | | | | | | | | | | | ● | ● | ● | | | | |
| STEVENSON, IAN W (HM19246) | | | | | | | | | | | | | | | | | | | | | | | | | | | | | | | | ● | | | | | | | | | ● | ● | ● | | | | |
| TAYLOR, D (HM19749) | | | | | | ● | | ● | | | | | | ● | | | | | | ● | | ● | | | | ● | ● | | | | | | | | | ● | | | | | ● | ● | ● | | | | |
| **RENFREWSHIRE** | | | | | | | | | | | | | | | | | | | | | | | | | | | | | | | | | | | | | | | | | | | | | | | |
| ALBA CENTRE (HM00473) | | | | | | | | | | | | | | | | | | | | | | | | | | | | | | | | | | | | | | | | | ● | ● | ● | | | | |
| APT LASER THERAPY (HM00950) | | | | | | | | ● | | | | | | | | | | ● | | | | | | | | | | | | | | | | | | | | | | | | ● | | | | | |
| BLACKHALL PARK CENTRE (HM02444) | | | ● | ● | ● | | ● | | | | | ● | ● | | | ● | | | | | | | | | | | ● | | | | | | | | | | | | | | ● | ● | ● | | | | |
| DOUGLAS, ANNE S (HM06212) | | | | | | | ● | | | | | ● | ● | | | | | | | | ● | | | | | | | | | | | | | | | | | | | | | | | | | | |
| FANNING, M W (HM07095) | | | | | | | | | | | | | | | | | | ● | | | | | | | | | | | | | | | | | | | | | | | ● | ● | ● | | | | |
| LINTON, UNNA (HM12444) | | | | | | | | | | | | | | | | | | | | | | | | | | | | | | | | ● | | | | | | | | | ● | ● | ● | | | | |
| PAISLEY CHIROPRACTIC CLINIC (HM15587) | | | | | ● | | ● | | | | | ● | ● | | | ● | | | | | ● | | | | | ● | | | | | | | ● | | | | | | | | ● | ● | ● | | | | |
| PAISLEY NATURAL THERAPY CENTRE (HM15588) | | ● | ● | ● | ● | ● | ● | ● | ● | | | ● | ● | ● | ● | ● | ● | | ● | | ● | | ● | ● | ● | ● | ● | ● | ● | | | | ● | | ● | | ● | | ● | | ● | | | ● | ● | | ● |
| PAISLEY PHYSIOTHERAPY CENTRE (HM15589) | | | | | | | ● | | | | | ● | ● | | | | | | | | ● | | | | | | | | | | | | | | | | | | | | | | | | | | |
| RAINEY, MARTHA (HM16890) | | | ● | ● | ● | | | | | | | | | | | | | | | | | | | | | | ● | | | | | | | | | | | | | | | | ● | | | | |
| ROSEWOOD AROMATHERAPY ROOM (HM17629) | | | | ● | ● | | | | | | | ● | | | | | | ● | | | ● | | | | | | | | | | | | | | | | | | | | | | | | | | |
| **SCOTTISH BORDERS** | | | | | | | | | | | | | | | | | | | | | | | | | | | | | | | | | | | | | | | | | | | | | | | |
| HOGARTH, JAMES (HM09908) | | | | | | | | | | | | | | | | | | | | | | | | | | | | | | | | ● | | | | | | | | | ● | ● | ● | | | | |
| L W FOOTCARE (HM11844) | | | | | | | | | | | | | | | | | | | | | | | | | | | | | | | | ● | | | | | | | | | ● | ● | ● | | | | |
| NATURES TOUCH (HM14698) | | | | | ● | | | | | | | | | | | | | ● | | | | | | | | | | | | | | | | | | | | | | | ● | ● | ● | | | | |
| ST BOSWELLS CHIRO CLINIC (HM19072) | | | | | | | | | | | | ● | ● | | | | | | | | ● | | | | | ● | | | | | | | | ● | | | | | | | ● | | ● | | | | |
| WATT, A S (HM21028) | | | | | | | | | | | | | | | | | | | | | | | | | | | | | | | | | | | | | | | | | ● | ● | ● | | | | |
| WISHING WELL (HM21738) | | ● | ● | ● | ● | ● | | ● | | | | ● | ● | | | ● | | | ● | | ● | | | ● | ● | ● | ● | | ● | ● | ● | | | ● | | ● | ● | | ● | ● | ● | ● | ● | ● | ● | ● | ● |
| **SHETLAND ISLANDS** | | | | | | | | | | | | | | | | | | | | | | | | | | | | | | | | | | | | | | | | | | | | | | | |
| LERWICK CHIROPRACTIC CLINIC (HM12231) | | | | | | | | | | | | ● | ● | | | | | | | | | | | | | | | | | | | | | | | | | | | | | | | | | | |

# S - W Conditions treated at Practices/Businesses and Specialist Treatment Categories

| Business by County with Reference no. | Sexually Trans. Infections | Shingles | Sinus Problems | Skin Problems | Sleep Disorders | Slimming Help | Slipped Disk | Smoking Help | Sneezing | Snoring | Spinal Injuries | Sports Injuries | Sprains | Stammering | Stings | Stomach Problems | Stomach Ulcers | Stress | Sweating | Teeth Grinding | Tennis Elbow | Terminal Illness | Throat Problems | Thrush | Thyroid Problems | Tinnitis | Tiredness | Tonsilitis | Ulcers | Vaginal Problems | Varicose Veins | Verrucas | Vertigo | Viral Infections | Vomiting | Warts | Water Retention | Whiplash | Wind | Worms | Specialist Treatment Categories: Children | Terminally Ill | Disabled | Horses | Dogs | CatS | Other Animals |
|---|---|---|---|---|---|---|---|---|---|---|---|---|---|---|---|---|---|---|---|---|---|---|---|---|---|---|---|---|---|---|---|---|---|---|---|---|---|---|---|---|---|---|---|---|---|---|---|
| **WALES** | | | | | | | | | | | | | | | | | | | | | | | | | | | | | | | | | | | | | | | | | | | | | | | |
| **BLAENAU GWENT** | | | | | | | | | | | | | | | | | | | | | | | | | | | | | | | | | | | | | | | | | | | | | | | |
| ABERTILLERY PHYSIOTHERAPY (HM00125) | | | | | | | ● | | | | | ● | ● | | | | | | | | ● | | | | | | | | | | | | | | | | | | | | ● | | | | | | |
| CLASSIC CLINIC (HM04606) | | | | ● | ● | | | | | | | ● | | | | | | ● | | | | | | | | | | | | | | | | | | | | | | | ● | ● | ● | | | | |
| **BRIDGEND** | | | | | | | | | | | | | | | | | | | | | | | | | | | | | | | | | | | | | | | | | | | | | | | |
| ALTERNATIVE HEALING CENTRE (HM00698) | | | | | | | | | | | | | | | | | | | | | | | | | | | | | | | | | | | | | | | | | ● | ● | ● | | | | |
| JENKINS, JOHN (HM10987) | | | | | ● | ● | | ● | | | | | | | | | | ● | | | | | | | | | | | | | | | | | | | | | | | ● | ● | ● | | | | |
| PARKWOOD CHIROPRACTIC CLINIC (HM15725) | | | | | | | ● | | | | ● | ● | ● | | | | | | | | | | | | | | | | | | | | | | | | | ● | | | | | | | | | |
| **CAERPHILLY** | | | | | | | | | | | | | | | | | | | | | | | | | | | | | | | | | | | | | | | | | | | | | | | |
| OAKFIELD NATURAL HEALTH CENTRE (HM15151) | ● | ● | ● | ● | ● | ● | ● | ● | ● | ● | | ● | ● | ● | ● | ● | ● | | ● | ● | ● | ● | ● | ● | ● | ● | ● | ● | ● | ● | ● | | ● | ● | ● | ● | ● | | ● | ● | | | | | | | |
| PARKWOOD CHIROPRACTIC CLINIC (HM15723) | | | | | | | ● | | | | | ● | ● | | | | | | | | ● | | | | | | | | | | | | | | | | | | | | ● | | ● | | | | |
| **CARMARTHENSHIRE** | | | | | | | | | | | | | | | | | | | | | | | | | | | | | | | | | | | | | | | | | | | | | | | |
| GREENWAY CONSULTANCY (HM08495) | | ● | ● | ● | ● | ● | | ● | ● | ● | | ● | | ● | ● | ● | ● | | ● | | ● | | ● | ● | | | ● | | ● | | | | ● | ● | | ● | | | ● | | ● | | ● | | ● | ● | ● |
| HEALING HANDS (HM09339) | | | | | | | | | | | | | | | | | | | | | | | | | | | | | | | | | | | | | | | | | ● | ● | ● | ● | | | |
| JABROO, C (HM10808) | ● | ● | ● | ● | ● | ● | ● | ● | ● | ● | | ● | ● | ● | ● | ● | ● | | ● | ● | ● | ● | ● | ● | ● | ● | ● | ● | ● | ● | ● | | ● | ● | ● | ● | ● | | ● | ● | | | | | | | |
| SPENCER AROMATHERAPY (HM18990) | | | | | | | | | | | | ● | | | | | | ● | | | | | | | | | | | | | | | | | | | | | | | ● | ● | ● | | | | |
| WAINWRIGHT, MARY (HM20738) | ● | ● | ● | ● | ● | ● | ● | ● | ● | ● | | ● | ● | ● | ● | ● | ● | | ● | ● | ● | ● | ● | ● | ● | ● | ● | ● | ● | ● | ● | | ● | ● | ● | ● | ● | | ● | ● | ● | ● | ● | | | | |
| **CEREDIGION** | | | | | | | | | | | | | | | | | | | | | | | | | | | | | | | | | | | | | | | | | | | | | | | |
| AMIES, SUSAN (HM00785) | | | | | | | | | | | | | | | | | | | | | | | | | | | | | | | | | | | | ● | | | | | ● | ● | ● | | | | |
| CHERRY TREE CTRE FOR NTRL MED (HM04109) | ● | ● | ● | ● | ● | ● | ● | ● | ● | ● | | ● | ● | ● | ● | ● | ● | | ● | ● | ● | ● | ● | ● | ● | ● | ● | ● | ● | ● | ● | | ● | ● | ● | ● | ● | | ● | ● | ● | ● | ● | | | | |
| COCKSEDGE, JOHN M (HM04774) | | | | | | | | | | | | | | | | | | | | | | | | | | | | | | | | ● | | | | | | | | | ● | ● | ● | | | | |
| FFYNNONWEN NATURAL THRPY CTRE (HM07256) | | | | | | | | | | | | | | | | | | | | | | | | | | | | | | | | | | | | | | | | | ● | ● | | | | | |
| JONES, B E (HM11122) | | | | | | | | | | | | | | | | | | | | | | | | | | | | | | | | ● | | | | | | | | | ● | ● | ● | | | | |
| LEWIS, D MICHAEL (HM12289) | | | | | | | | | | | | | | | | | | | | | | | | | | | | | | | | ● | | | | | | | | | ● | ● | ● | | | | |
| **CONWY** | | | | | | | | | | | | | | | | | | | | | | | | | | | | | | | | | | | | | | | | | | | | | | | |
| DREW, DAVID (HM06305) | ● | | | ● | | | | | | | | | | | | ● | ● | | | | | ● | ● | | | | ● | | | ● | | | | ● | | | | | | | ● | ● | ● | ● | ● | ● | ● |
| HERBS FOR EVERYONE (HM09669) | | ● | ● | ● | ● | ● | | | ● | ● | | ● | ● | | ● | ● | ● | | | | ● | ● | ● | ● | ● | ● | ● | ● | ● | ● | ● | | ● | ● | ● | ● | ● | | ● | ● | ● | ● | ● | ● | ● | ● | ● |
| MELA CENTRE OF OSTEOPATHY (HM13702) | | | | | | | ● | | | | | ● | ● | | | | | | | | ● | | | | | | | | | | | | | | | | | | | | ● | | ● | | | | |
| MEWIS, R J (HM13782) | | | | | | | | | | | ● | ● | ● | | | | | | | | | | | | | | | | | | | | | | | | | ● | | | ● | ● | ● | | | | |
| **DENBIGHSHIRE** | | | | | | | | | | | | | | | | | | | | | | | | | | | | | | | | | | | | | | | | | | | | | | | |
| ALLIED PHYSIOTHERAPY (HM00646) | | | | | | | ● | | | | | ● | ● | | | | | | | | | | | | | | | | | | | | | | | ● | | | | | ● | | ● | | | | |
| HEALING WAYS (HM09359) | ● | ● | ● | ● | ● | ● | ● | ● | ● | ● | | ● | ● | ● | ● | ● | ● | | ● | ● | ● | ● | ● | ● | ● | ● | ● | ● | ● | ● | ● | | ● | ● | ● | ● | ● | | ● | ● | | | | | | | |
| MCGILL, L (HM13484) | | | | | | | | | | | | | | | | | | ● | | | | | | | | | | | | | | | | | | | | | | | ● | ● | ● | | | | |

# S - W Conditions treated at Practices/Businesses and Specialist Treatment Categories

| | | | | | | | | | | | | | | | | | | | | | | | | | | | | | | | | | | | | | | | | | Specialist Treatment Categories | | | | | | |
|---|---|---|---|---|---|---|---|---|---|---|---|---|---|---|---|---|---|---|---|---|---|---|---|---|---|---|---|---|---|---|---|---|---|---|---|---|---|---|---|---|---|---|---|---|---|---|---|
| Business by County with Reference no. | Sexually Trans. Infections | Shingles | Sinus Problems | Skin Problems | Sleep Disorders | Slimming Help | Slipped Disk | Smoking Help | Sneezing | Snoring | Spinal Injuries | Sports Injuries | Sprains | Stammering | Stings | Stomach Problems | Stomach Ulcers | Stress | Sweating | Teeth Grinding | Tennis Elbow | Terminal Illness | Throat Problems | Thrush | Thyroid Problems | Tinnitis | Tiredness | Tonsilitis | Ulcers | Vaginal Problems | Varicose Veins | Verrucas | Vertigo | Viral Infections | Vomiting | Warts | Water Retention | Whiplash | Wind | Worms | Children | Terminally Ill | Disabled | Horses | Dogs | CatS | Other Animals |
| ROY MORRIS CLINIC (HM17709) | | ● | ● | ● | ● | | ● | ● | | ● | | ● | ● | | ● | ● | ● | | | ● | ● | | ● | ● | ● | ● | ● | ● | ● | ● | ● | | ● | ● | ● | ● | ● | | ● | ● | | | | | | | |
| FLINTSHIRE | | | | | | | | | | | | | | | | | | | | | | | | | | | | | | | | | | | | | | | | | | | | | | | |
| A L J RILEY ASSOCIATES (HM00038) | | ● | ● | ● | ● | | | | | | | ● | ● | | ● | ● | ● | | ● | | ● | | | ● | | | ● | | ● | | | | | | | | ● | | ● | | ● | ● | ● | ● | ● | ● | ● |
| BOOTS HEALTHCARE SERVICES (HM02711) | | | | ● | | | | | | | | ● | ● | | | | | | | | | | | | | | | | ● | | ● | | | | | ● | | | | | ● | ● | ● | | | | |
| CHIROPODISTS SURGERY (HM04298) | | | | | | | | | | | | | | | | | | | | | | | | | | | | | | | | | | | | ● | | | | | ● | ● | | | | | |
| GAFFNEY, ALMA (HM07827) | | | | | | | | | | | | | | | | | | | | | | | | | | | | | | | | ● | | | | | | | | | ● | ● | ● | | | | |
| HYPNOTHERAPY CENTRE (HM10528) | | | | | | ● | | ● | | | | | | | | | | | | ● | | | | | | ● | | | ● | | | | | | | | | | | | ● | | ● | | | | |
| REECE, JULIE (HM17038) | | | | | | | | | | | | | | | | | | | | | | | | | | | | | | | | | | | | | | | | | ● | ● | ● | | | | |
| GLAMORGAN (VALE OF) | | | | | | | | | | | | | | | | | | | | | | | | | | | | | | | | | | | | | | | | | | | | | | | |
| ALEXANDER TECHNIQUE (HM00546) | | | | | | | ● | | | | | ● | ● | | | | | | | | | | | | | | | | | | | | | | | | | | | | ● | ● | ● | | | | |
| ALEXANDER TECHNIQUE (HM00551) | | | | | | | ● | | | | ● | ● | ● | | | | | | | | ● | | | | | | | | | | | | | | | | | ● | | | ● | ● | ● | | | | |
| AMETHYST HEALING CENTRE (HM00784) | | | | ● | ● | | | | | | | | | | | | | ● | | | | | | | | | | | | | | | | | | | | | | | ● | | | | | | |
| AROMATHERAPY CLINIC (HM01105) | | | ● | ● | | | | | | | | | | | | | | | | | | | | | | | | | | | | | | | | | | | | | | | | | | | |
| AYRE CENTRE OF HYPNOTHERAPY (HM01430) | | | | | ● | ● | | ● | | | | | | | | | | ● | | | | | | | | | | | | | | | | | | | | | | | ● | ● | | | | | |
| BARRY OSTEOPATHIC CLINIC (HM01809) | | | | | | | ● | | | | ● | ● | ● | | | | | | | | ● | | | | | | | | | | | | | | | | | ● | | | | | ● | | | | |
| BODY ESSENTIALS (HM02587) | | | | | | | | | | | | | | | | | | ● | | | | | | | | | | | | | | | | | | | | | | | | | | | | | |
| BROWN, ANNE (HM03214) | | | | | | | ● | | | | | ● | ● | | | | | | | | ● | | | | | | | | | | | | | | | | | | | | | | | | | | |
| CARDIFF CHIROPRACTIC CLINIC (HM03666) | | | | | | | ● | | | | ● | ● | ● | | | | | | | | ● | | | | | | | | | | | | | | | | | ● | | | ● | ● | ● | | | | |
| CARDIFF HEALTH PRACTICE (HM03670) | | | | | | | ● | | | | ● | ● | ● | | | | | | | | ● | | | | | | | | | | | | | | | | | ● | | | | | | | | | |
| CARDIFF HOMEOPATHIC CLINIC (HM03671) | ● | ● | ● | ● | ● | ● | ● | ● | ● | ● | | ● | ● | ● | ● | ● | ● | | ● | ● | ● | ● | ● | ● | ● | ● | ● | ● | ● | ● | ● | | ● | ● | ● | ● | ● | | ● | ● | ● | ● | ● | | | | |
| CITY CENTRE CHIRO CLINIC (HM04488) | | | | | | | ● | | | | ● | ● | ● | | | | | | | | ● | | | | | | | | | | | | | | | | | ● | | | ● | ● | ● | | | | |
| COWBRIDGE CHIRO/SPINAL REHAB (HM05289) | ● | ● | ● | ● | ● | ● | ● | ● | ● | ● | ● | ● | ● | ● | | ● | ● | | ● | ● | ● | ● | ● | ● | ● | ● | ● | ● | ● | ● | ● | | ● | ● | ● | ● | ● | ● | ● | ● | ● | ● | ● | | | | |
| COWBRIDGE OSTEOPATH CLINIC (HM05290) | | | | | | | ● | | | | | ● | ● | | | | | | | | ● | | | | | | | | | | | | | | | | | | | | ● | ● | ● | | | | |
| EVANS, STEVE (HM06990) | | | | | | | ● | | | | | ● | ● | | | | | | | | ● | | | | | | | | | | | | | | | | | | | | ● | | | | | | |
| GLAMORGAN HEALTH & RACQUET (HM08122) | | | | | | | ● | | | | | ● | ● | | | | | | | | ● | | | | | | | | | | | | | | | | | | | | ● | ● | ● | | | | |
| GRIMWADE, S (HM08586) | | | ● | | | | | | | | | ● | ● | | | | | | | | ● | | | | | | ● | | | | | | | | | | | | ● | | ● | | | | | | |
| HENRIETTA CTRE FOR COMP THRPY (HM09565) | | | | | ● | | | | | | | | | | | | | ● | | | | | | | | | | | | | | | | | | | | | | | ● | ● | ● | | | | |
| JUDY COURIE - REFLEX & AROMA (HM11250) | | | | | | | | | | | | ● | | | | | | | | | | | | | | | | | | | | | | | | | | | | | ● | ● | ● | | | | |
| LLANISHEN PHYSIOTHERAPY CLINIC (HM12501) | | | | | | | ● | | | | | ● | ● | | | | | | | | ● | | | | | | | | | | | | | | | | | | | | ● | ● | ● | | | | |
| MILES, ANDREW (HM13854) | | | | | | | | | | | ● | ● | ● | | | | | | | | ● | | | | | | | | | | | | | | | | | ● | | | ● | ● | ● | | | | |
| MOBILE FOOTWORKS (HM14031) | | | ● | | ● | | | | | | | ● | | | | | | | | | ● | ● | | | ● | ● | ● | | | | | | | | | ● | ● | | | | ● | ● | ● | | | | |
| MORGAN-AYRES, PAUL (PROF) (HM14178) | | ● | | | ● | ● | | ● | | | | | | ● | | ● | ● | | ● | ● | | ● | | | | ● | ● | | ● | | | | | | | | | | | | ● | ● | ● | | | | |
| MULLINS, JOHN (HM14348) | | | ● | | | | ● | | | | | | ● | | | ● | ● | | | | ● | | | | | | | | | | | | | | | | | | ● | | ● | | | | | | |
| NATURAL HEALTHCARE (HM14601) | | | | ● | ● | ● | | ● | ● | | | | | | | | | ● | | | ● | | | | | ● | ● | | | | | | | | | | ● | | ● | | ● | | ● | | | | |

# S - W Conditions treated at Practices/Businesses and Specialist Treatment Categories

Business by County with Reference no.

| Business by County with Reference no. | Sexually Trans. Infections | Shingles | Sinus Problems | Skin Problems | Sleep Disorders | Slimming Help | Slipped Disk | Smoking Help | Sneezing | Snoring | Spinal Injuries | Sports Injuries | Sprains | Stammering | Stings | Stomach Problems | Stomach Ulcers | Stress | Sweating | Teeth Grinding | Tennis Elbow | Terminal Illness | Throat Problems | Thrush | Thyroid Problems | Tinnitis | Tiredness | Tonsilitis | Ulcers | Vaginal Problems | Varicose Veins | Verrucas | Vertigo | Viral Infections | Vomiting | Warts | Water Retention | Whiplash | Wind | Worms | Specialist Treatment Categories: Children | Terminally Ill | Disabled | Horses | Dogs | CatS | Other Animals |
|---|---|---|---|---|---|---|---|---|---|---|---|---|---|---|---|---|---|---|---|---|---|---|---|---|---|---|---|---|---|---|---|---|---|---|---|---|---|---|---|---|---|---|---|---|---|---|---|
| PARKWOOD CHIROPRACTIC CLINIC (HM15726) | | | | | | | ● | | | | ● | ● | ● | | | | | | | | | | | | | | | | | | | | | | | | | ● | | | ● | ● | ● | | | | |
| PARKWOOD CHIROPRACTIC CLINIC (HM15724) | | | | | | | ● | | | | ● | ● | ● | | | | | | | | ● | | | | | | | | | | | | | | | | | ● | | | ● | ● | ● | | | | |
| PENARTH CHIROPRACTIC CLINIC (HM15961) | | | ● | ● | ● | | ● | | | | | ● | ● | | | | | | | ● | ● | | | | | ● | ● | | | | | | ● | | | | | ● | | | | | | | | | |
| PENARTH HOMEOPATHY CLINIC (HM15962) | | ● | ● | ● | ● | ● | ● | ● | ● | ● | | ● | ● | ● | ● | ● | ● | | ● | ● | ● | ● | ● | ● | ● | ● | ● | ● | ● | ● | ● | | ● | ● | ● | ● | ● | | ● | ● | | ● | ● | | | | |
| PENYLAN PODIATRIC CENTRE (HM16005) | | | | | | | | | | | | | | | | | | | | | | | | | | | | | | | | | | | | ● | | | | | ● | ● | ● | | | | |
| PHYSIO FIRST CENTRE (HM16198) | | | | | | | ● | | | | | ● | ● | | | | | | | | ● | | | | | | | | | | | | | | | | | | | | ● | ● | ● | | | | |
| POLLEY, LYNDON (HM16414) | | | | | | | | | | | | | | | | | | | | | | | | | | | | | | | | | | | | ● | | | | | ● | ● | ● | | | | |
| POLLEY, LYNDON (HM16413) | | | | | | | | | | | | | | | | | | | | | | | | | | | | | | | | ● | | | | | | | | | ● | ● | ● | | | | |
| POLLEY, LYNDON (HM16415) | | | | | | | | | | | | | | | | | | | | | | | | | | | | | | | | ● | | | | ● | | | | | ● | ● | ● | | | | |
| RENWICK, SARAH NADINE (HM17192) | | | ● | ● | ● | | | | | | | ● | | | | | | | | | | | | ● | | | | | | | ● | | | | | | ● | | ● | | ● | ● | ● | | ● | ● | |
| RIDGE, D (HM17315) | | | | | | | ● | | | | | ● | ● | | | | | | | | ● | | | | | | | | | | | | | | | | | ● | | | | | ● | | | | |
| RIDGE, D (HM17316) | | | | | | | ● | | | | | ● | ● | | | | | | | | ● | | | | | | | | | | | | | | | | | ● | | | ● | | ● | | | | |
| SIMS, TRACEY (HM18602) | | | | | | | | | | | | | | | | | | | | | | | | | | | | | | | | ● | | | | ● | | | | | | | | | | | |
| SWANSEA VALLEY PHYSIO PRACTICE (HM19579) | | | | | | | ● | | | | | ● | ● | | | | | | | | ● | | | | | | | | | | | | | | | | | | | | ● | | | | | | |
| WALSH, J A (HM20859) | | | | | | | | | | | | | | | | | | | | | | | | | | | | | | | | | | | | ● | | | | | ● | ● | ● | | | | |
| GWYNEDD | | | | | | | | | | | | | | | | | | | | | | | | | | | | | | | | | | | | | | | | | | | | | | | |
| CENTRE FOR WELL BEING (HM03922) | | | | | | | | | | | | | | | | | | ● | | | | | | | | | | | | | | | | | | | | | | | ● | ● | ● | | | | |
| MOSSHILL HOLISTIC CENTRE (HM14270) | ● | ● | ● | ● | ● | ● | ● | ● | ● | ● | | ● | ● | ● | ● | ● | ● | ● | ● | ● | ● | ● | ● | ● | ● | ● | ● | ● | ● | ● | ● | | ● | ● | ● | ● | ● | | ● | ● | ● | ● | ● | | | | |
| NATURAL THERAPY CLINIC (HM14660) | | ● | ● | ● | ● | ● | | ● | ● | ● | | ● | ● | ● | | ● | ● | | ● | | ● | | | ● | | ● | ● | | | | | | ● | | | | ● | | ● | | ● | ● | ● | | | | |
| O'NEIL, L (HM15325) | | | | ● | ● | | | ● | | | | | | | | | | | | | | | | | | | | | | | | | ● | | | | | | | | ● | ● | ● | | | | |
| ISLE OF ANGLESEY | | | | | | | | | | | | | | | | | | | | | | | | | | | | | | | | | | | | | | | | | | | | | | | |
| CHALMERS, D G (HM03951) | | | | | | | | | | | | ● | ● | | | | | | | | ● | | | | | | | | | | | | | | | | | | | | | | ● | | | | |
| MONMOUTHSHIRE | | | | | | | | | | | | | | | | | | | | | | | | | | | | | | | | | | | | | | | | | | | | | | | |
| ABERGAVENNY THERAPY CTRE (HM00121) | | | ● | ● | | | | | | | | ● | | | | ● | | | | | | | ● | | | | ● | | | | | | | | | | | | | | ● | ● | ● | | | | |
| BROOKSIDE PHYSIO PRACTICE (HM03184) | | ● | ● | | | | ● | | | | | ● | ● | | | | | | | | ● | | | | | ● | | | | | | | | | | | | | | | ● | | ● | | | | |
| ELECTROMAGNETIC PRODUCTS (HM06721) | | | | | | | | | | | | ● | ● | | | | | ● | | | ● | | | | | | | | ● | | | | | | | | | ● | | | | | | ● | ● | ● | ● |
| HARMONY (HM09020) | ● | ● | ● | ● | ● | ● | ● | ● | ● | ● | | ● | ● | | ● | ● | ● | | ● | ● | ● | ● | ● | ● | ● | ● | ● | ● | ● | ● | ● | | ● | ● | ● | ● | ● | | ● | | ● | ● | ● | | | | |
| NUTRITION CLINIC (HM15122) | | | ● | ● | ● | ● | | | | | | ● | ● | | ● | ● | ● | ● | | | ● | | ● | ● | ● | ● | ● | ● | ● | ● | | | ● | ● | ● | | ● | | ● | | ● | | | | | | |
| TURFAEN CHIROPODY CLINIC (HM20407) | | | | | | | | | | | | ● | ● | | | | | | | | | | | | | | | | ● | | | | | | | ● | | | | | ● | | ● | | | | |
| NEATH PORT TALBOT | | | | | | | | | | | | | | | | | | | | | | | | | | | | | | | | | | | | | | | | | | | | | | | |
| ST JAMES MEDICAL CENTRE (HM19078) | ● | ● | ● | ● | ● | ● | ● | ● | ● | ● | | ● | ● | ● | ● | ● | ● | | ● | ● | ● | ● | ● | ● | ● | ● | ● | ● | ● | ● | ● | | ● | ● | ● | ● | ● | | ● | ● | ● | ● | ● | | | | |
| NEWPORT | | | | | | | | | | | | | | | | | | | | | | | | | | | | | | | | | | | | | | | | | | | | | | | |
| BAJJADA, JUNE (HM01572) | | ● | ● | | ● | ● | ● | ● | | | | ● | ● | | | | | | | ● | ● | | ● | ● | ● | ● | ● | | | | | | ● | | | | | | ● | | ● | ● | ● | | | ● | |
| BEIGHTON, J W (HM02069) | ● | ● | ● | ● | ● | | ● | | ● | ● | | | | | ● | ● | ● | | ● | ● | ● | ● | ● | ● | ● | ● | ● | ● | ● | ● | ● | | ● | ● | ● | ● | ● | | ● | ● | ● | ● | | ● | ● | ● | ● |

# S - W Conditions treated at Practices/Businesses and Specialist Treatment Categories

| Business by County with Reference no. | Sexually Trans. Infections | Shingles | Sinus Problems | Skin Problems | Sleep Disorders | Slimming Help | Slipped Disk | Smoking Help | Sneezing | Snoring | Spinal Injuries | Sports Injuries | Sprains | Stammering | Stings | Stomach Problems | Stomach Ulcers | Stress |
|---|---|---|---|---|---|---|---|---|---|---|---|---|---|---|---|---|---|---|
| BOWKETT, LYN (HM02792) | ● | ● | ● | ● | ● | ● | ● | ● | ● | ● |  | ● | ● | ● | ● | ● | ● |  |
| CLINIC OF HOLISTIC HEALTH (HM04693) | ● | ● | ● | ● | ● | ● | ● | ● | ● | ● |  | ● | ● | ● | ● | ● | ● |  |
| MOXLEY, SHIRLEY (HM14304) |  |  | ● | ● | ● |  | ● | ● | ● |  |  | ● | ● |  |  | ● |  |  |
| OLIVER, MARION (HM15294) |  | ● | ● | ● | ● |  |  |  |  |  |  |  |  |  |  | ● | ● |  |
| **PEMBROKESHIRE** |  |  |  |  |  |  |  |  |  |  |  |  |  |  |  |  |  |  |
| CENTRE OF TRADITIONAL HEALING (HM03926) |  |  |  |  |  |  |  |  |  |  |  |  |  |  |  |  |  | ● |
| JABROO, C (HM10809) | ● | ● | ● | ● | ● | ● | ● | ● | ● | ● |  | ● | ● | ● | ● | ● | ● |  |
| **POWYS** |  |  |  |  |  |  |  |  |  |  |  |  |  |  |  |  |  |  |
| BRECON CLINIC (HM02944) |  | ● | ● | ● | ● | ● | ● | ● | ● | ● |  | ● | ● | ● |  | ● | ● |  |
| BRECON COMPLEMENTARY MED CTRE (HM02945) | ● | ● | ● | ● | ● | ● | ● | ● | ● | ● |  | ● | ● | ● | ● | ● | ● |  |
| CONROY, CHRISTINE (HM05007) |  |  | ● |  |  |  |  |  |  |  |  |  |  |  |  |  |  |  |
| COVENT HOUSE NTRL HEALTH CTRE (HM05280) |  | ● | ● | ● | ● | ● |  | ● | ● | ● |  |  | ● | ● | ● | ● | ● |  |
| GROVES, FRAN (HM08614) |  |  |  |  |  |  |  |  |  |  |  | ● | ● |  |  |  |  |  |
| HEALTH FOCUS (HM09386) |  | ● | ● | ● | ● | ● | ● | ● | ● |  |  | ● | ● | ● | ● | ● | ● |  |
| HERBAL HELPLINE (HM09619) |  |  |  |  |  |  |  |  |  |  |  |  |  |  |  |  |  |  |
| KILGOUR, KATHARINE () |  | ● |  |  |  |  |  |  |  |  |  | ● | ● |  |  |  |  |  |
| LLANDRINDOD WELLS SPA TOWN (HM12499) | ● | ● | ● | ● | ● | ● | ● | ● | ● | ● |  | ● | ● | ● | ● | ● | ● |  |
| PEACE CLINIC (HM15876) |  |  |  |  | ● | ● |  | ● |  |  |  |  |  | ● |  |  |  |  |
| REFLEXOLOGY & ALLERGY THERAPY (HM17078) |  |  | ● | ● | ● |  |  |  |  |  |  |  |  |  |  |  |  |  |
| SHEPPARD, HELEN (HM18421) |  |  | ● | ● | ● |  |  |  |  |  |  | ● | ● |  |  | ● |  |  |
| **RHONDDA CYNON TAFF** |  |  |  |  |  |  |  |  |  |  |  |  |  |  |  |  |  |  |
| POLLEY, LYNDON (HM16416) |  |  |  |  |  |  |  |  |  |  |  |  |  |  |  |  |  |  |
| **SWANSEA** |  |  |  |  |  |  |  |  |  |  |  |  |  |  |  |  |  |  |
| ABERTAWE PHYSIOTHERAPY CLINIC (HM00124) |  | ● |  |  |  |  | ● |  |  |  |  | ● | ● |  |  |  |  |  |
| ACUPUNCTURE CENTRE (HM00254) |  | ● | ● | ● | ● |  | ● |  |  |  |  | ● | ● |  |  |  |  |  |
| BURDEN, RICHARD (HM03370) |  |  |  |  |  |  |  |  |  |  |  |  | ● |  |  | ● | ● |  |
| I R C H (HM10554) |  |  |  |  |  |  |  |  |  |  |  |  |  |  |  |  |  |  |
| PEDORTHICS FOOT SGY PRACTICE (HM15935) |  |  |  |  |  |  |  |  |  |  |  | ● |  |  |  |  |  |  |
| RODWAY & ASSOCIATES (HM17531) |  |  |  |  |  |  | ● |  |  |  |  | ● | ● |  |  |  |  |  |
| WATKINS, PHILIPPA (HM20997) |  |  |  |  |  |  |  |  |  |  |  |  |  |  |  |  |  |  |
| **TORFAEN** |  |  |  |  |  |  |  |  |  |  |  |  |  |  |  |  |  |  |
| CLUB INDIGO (HM04741) |  |  |  |  |  |  | ● |  |  |  |  | ● | ● |  |  |  |  |  |
| **WREXHAM** |  |  |  |  |  |  |  |  |  |  |  |  |  |  |  |  |  |  |
| HARMONY IN HEALTH (HM09028) |  |  | ● | ● |  |  |  |  |  |  |  |  |  |  |  |  |  | ● |

| Business by County with Reference no. | Sweating | Teeth Grinding | Tennis Elbow | Terminal Illness | Throat Problems | Thrush | Thyroid Problems | Tinnitis | Tiredness | Tonsilitis | Ulcers | Vaginal Problems | Varicose Veins | Verrucas | Vertigo | Viral Infections | Vomiting | Warts | Water Retention | Whiplash | Wind | Worms |
|---|---|---|---|---|---|---|---|---|---|---|---|---|---|---|---|---|---|---|---|---|---|---|
| BOWKETT, LYN (HM02792) | ● | ● | ● | ● | ● | ● | ● | ● | ● | ● | ● | ● | ● |  | ● | ● | ● | ● | ● |  | ● | ● |
| CLINIC OF HOLISTIC HEALTH (HM04693) | ● | ● | ● | ● | ● | ● | ● | ● | ● | ● | ● | ● | ● |  | ● | ● | ● | ● | ● |  | ● | ● |
| MOXLEY, SHIRLEY (HM14304) |  |  |  | ● |  |  | ● |  | ● |  |  |  |  |  |  |  |  |  |  |  |  |  |
| OLIVER, MARION (HM15294) | ● |  | ● | ● | ● | ● | ● | ● | ● | ● |  | ● |  |  | ● |  |  |  | ● |  | ● |  |
| **PEMBROKESHIRE** |  |  |  |  |  |  |  |  |  |  |  |  |  |  |  |  |  |  |  |  |  |  |
| CENTRE OF TRADITIONAL HEALING (HM03926) |  |  |  |  |  |  |  |  |  |  |  |  |  |  |  |  |  |  |  |  |  |  |
| JABROO, C (HM10809) | ● | ● | ● | ● | ● | ● | ● | ● | ● | ● | ● | ● | ● |  | ● | ● | ● | ● | ● |  | ● | ● |
| **POWYS** |  |  |  |  |  |  |  |  |  |  |  |  |  |  |  |  |  |  |  |  |  |  |
| BRECON CLINIC (HM02944) | ● | ● | ● | ● | ● | ● | ● | ● | ● |  | ● | ● | ● |  | ● |  | ● |  | ● |  | ● |  |
| BRECON COMPLEMENTARY MED CTRE (HM02945) | ● | ● | ● | ● | ● | ● | ● | ● | ● | ● | ● | ● | ● |  | ● | ● | ● | ● | ● |  | ● | ● |
| CONROY, CHRISTINE (HM05007) |  |  | ● |  |  |  |  | ● |  |  |  |  |  |  |  |  |  |  |  |  |  |  |
| COVENT HOUSE NTRL HEALTH CTRE (HM05280) | ● | ● | ● | ● | ● | ● | ● | ● | ● | ● | ● | ● | ● |  | ● | ● | ● | ● | ● |  | ● | ● |
| GROVES, FRAN (HM08614) |  |  | ● |  |  |  |  |  |  |  |  |  |  |  |  |  |  |  |  | ● |  |  |
| HEALTH FOCUS (HM09386) | ● |  | ● |  | ● | ● | ● | ● | ● |  |  | ● |  |  | ● |  |  | ● | ● |  | ● |  |
| HERBAL HELPLINE (HM09619) |  |  |  |  |  |  |  |  |  |  |  |  |  |  |  |  |  |  |  |  |  |  |
| KILGOUR, KATHARINE () |  |  |  |  |  |  |  |  |  |  |  |  |  |  |  |  |  |  |  |  |  |  |
| LLANDRINDOD WELLS SPA TOWN (HM12499) | ● | ● | ● | ● | ● | ● | ● | ● | ● | ● | ● | ● | ● |  | ● | ● | ● | ● | ● |  | ● | ● |
| PEACE CLINIC (HM15876) |  |  |  |  |  |  |  |  |  |  |  |  |  |  |  |  |  | ● |  |  |  |  |
| REFLEXOLOGY & ALLERGY THERAPY (HM17078) |  |  |  |  |  | ● |  |  | ● |  |  | ● |  |  |  |  |  |  | ● |  | ● |  |
| SHEPPARD, HELEN (HM18421) |  |  | ● |  | ● |  | ● | ● | ● | ● |  |  |  |  | ● |  |  |  | ● |  | ● |  |
| **RHONDDA CYNON TAFF** |  |  |  |  |  |  |  |  |  |  |  |  |  |  |  |  |  |  |  |  |  |  |
| POLLEY, LYNDON (HM16416) |  |  |  |  |  |  |  |  |  |  |  |  |  | ● |  |  |  | ● |  |  |  |  |
| **SWANSEA** |  |  |  |  |  |  |  |  |  |  |  |  |  |  |  |  |  |  |  |  |  |  |
| ABERTAWE PHYSIOTHERAPY CLINIC (HM00124) |  |  | ● |  |  |  |  |  |  |  |  |  |  |  |  |  |  |  |  |  |  |  |
| ACUPUNCTURE CENTRE (HM00254) |  |  | ● |  |  |  |  |  | ● |  |  |  |  |  |  |  |  |  |  |  |  |  |
| BURDEN, RICHARD (HM03370) |  |  |  |  |  | ● | ● |  | ● | ● |  | ● |  |  |  | ● |  |  |  |  | ● | ● |
| I R C H (HM10554) |  |  |  |  |  |  |  |  |  |  |  |  |  |  |  |  |  |  |  |  |  |  |
| PEDORTHICS FOOT SGY PRACTICE (HM15935) |  |  |  |  |  |  |  |  |  |  |  |  |  |  |  |  |  | ● |  |  |  |  |
| RODWAY & ASSOCIATES (HM17531) |  |  | ● |  |  |  |  |  |  |  |  |  |  |  |  |  |  |  |  | ● |  |  |
| WATKINS, PHILIPPA (HM20997) |  |  |  |  |  |  |  |  |  |  |  |  |  |  |  |  |  |  |  |  |  |  |
| **TORFAEN** |  |  |  |  |  |  |  |  |  |  |  |  |  |  |  |  |  |  |  |  |  |  |
| CLUB INDIGO (HM04741) |  |  | ● |  |  |  |  |  |  |  |  |  |  |  |  |  |  |  |  |  |  |  |
| **WREXHAM** |  |  |  |  |  |  |  |  |  |  |  |  |  |  |  |  |  |  |  |  |  |  |
| HARMONY IN HEALTH (HM09028) |  |  |  |  |  |  |  |  |  |  |  |  |  |  |  |  |  |  |  |  |  |  |

| Business by County with Reference no. | Specialist Treatment Categories: Children | Terminally Ill | Disabled | Horses | Dogs | CatS | Other Animals |
|---|---|---|---|---|---|---|---|
| BOWKETT, LYN (HM02792) | ● | ● | ● |  |  |  |  |
| CLINIC OF HOLISTIC HEALTH (HM04693) | ● | ● | ● |  |  |  |  |
| MOXLEY, SHIRLEY (HM14304) | ● | ● | ● |  |  |  |  |
| OLIVER, MARION (HM15294) | ● | ● | ● |  |  |  |  |
| **PEMBROKESHIRE** |  |  |  |  |  |  |  |
| CENTRE OF TRADITIONAL HEALING (HM03926) | ● | ● | ● |  |  |  |  |
| JABROO, C (HM10809) |  |  |  |  |  |  |  |
| **POWYS** |  |  |  |  |  |  |  |
| BRECON CLINIC (HM02944) | ● | ● | ● |  |  |  |  |
| BRECON COMPLEMENTARY MED CTRE (HM02945) | ● | ● | ● |  |  |  |  |
| CONROY, CHRISTINE (HM05007) | ● | ● | ● | ● | ● | ● | ● |
| COVENT HOUSE NTRL HEALTH CTRE (HM05280) | ● | ● | ● |  |  |  |  |
| GROVES, FRAN (HM08614) | ● | ● | ● | ● | ● |  |  |
| HEALTH FOCUS (HM09386) | ● | ● | ● |  |  |  |  |
| HERBAL HELPLINE (HM09619) | ● | ● |  | ● | ● |  | ● |
| KILGOUR, KATHARINE () |  |  | ● |  |  |  |  |
| LLANDRINDOD WELLS SPA TOWN (HM12499) |  |  |  |  |  |  |  |
| PEACE CLINIC (HM15876) |  | ● | ● |  |  |  |  |
| REFLEXOLOGY & ALLERGY THERAPY (HM17078) | ● | ● | ● |  |  |  |  |
| SHEPPARD, HELEN (HM18421) | ● | ● | ● |  |  |  |  |
| **RHONDDA CYNON TAFF** |  |  |  |  |  |  |  |
| POLLEY, LYNDON (HM16416) | ● | ● | ● |  |  |  |  |
| **SWANSEA** |  |  |  |  |  |  |  |
| ABERTAWE PHYSIOTHERAPY CLINIC (HM00124) | ● |  | ● |  |  |  |  |
| ACUPUNCTURE CENTRE (HM00254) | ● | ● | ● |  |  |  |  |
| BURDEN, RICHARD (HM03370) | ● |  |  |  |  |  |  |
| I R C H (HM10554) | ● | ● | ● |  |  |  |  |
| PEDORTHICS FOOT SGY PRACTICE (HM15935) | ● |  | ● |  |  |  |  |
| RODWAY & ASSOCIATES (HM17531) | ● |  | ● |  |  |  |  |
| WATKINS, PHILIPPA (HM20997) | ● | ● | ● |  |  |  |  |
| **TORFAEN** |  |  |  |  |  |  |  |
| CLUB INDIGO (HM04741) | ● | ● | ● |  |  |  |  |
| **WREXHAM** |  |  |  |  |  |  |  |
| HARMONY IN HEALTH (HM09028) | ● | ● | ● | ● | ● | ● |  |

HEALTH MYSELF

# SECTION 5

## Useful Addresses of Health Food Shops

# ENGLAND

## BEDFORDSHIRE

- **FIRST HEALTH FOR VITAMINS**, 87-88 Market Hall, The Luton Arndale Centre, **LUTON**, LU1 2TB
(T) 01582 451170
- **HERBALIFE INDEPENDENT DISTRIBUTOR**, 9 Willenhall Close, **LUTON**, LU3 3XX
(T) 01582 591906
- **HOLLAND & BARRETT**, 10 Horn Lane, Harpur Centre, **BEDFORD**, MK40 1TP
(T) 01234 352866
- **HOLLAND & BARRETT**, 158 The Luton Arndale Centre, **LUTON**, LU1 2TJ
(T) 01582 482574
- **HUGE SUPPLEMENTS**, 43 Clevedon Road, **LUTON**, LU2 9EB
(T) 08003 892071
- **NATURAL HEALTH SERVICE (THE)**, 18 West Street, **DUNSTABLE**, LU6 1SX
(T) 01582 668899
- **NATURE'S HARVEST**, 19 North Street, **LEIGHTON BUZZARD**, LU7 7EF
(T) 01525 371378
- **NIGHTINGALES WHOLEFOODS**, 18 West Street, **DUNSTABLE**, LU6 1SX
(T) 01582 670461
- **PUMPERNICKEL**, 7 The Arcade, **BEDFORD**, MK40 1NS
(T) 01234 348179
- **SHERRY'S HEALTH FOODS**, 58 High Street, **BIGGLESWADE**, SG18 0LJ
(T) 01767 220020
- **SKYBIO LTD**, Tythe Farm, Staploe Road, Wyboston, **BEDFORD**, MK44 3AT
(T) 01480 477733
- **WHOLE FOODS BEDFORD**, 1 Thurlow Street, **BEDFORD**, MK40 1LR
(T) 01234 219618
- **WOODS SUPPLEMENTS**, Maxet House, Liverpool Road, **LUTON**, LU1 1RS
(T) 01582 650011

## BERKSHIRE

- **ABBOTS**, 231 High Street, **CROWTHORNE**, RG45 7AQ
(T) 01344 772491
- **ACE NUTRITION LTD**, 4 Ruscombe Gdns, Datchet, **SLOUGH**, SL3 9BG
(T) 01753 544002
- **ACTIVE HEALTH LTD**, Unit 12/Lakeside Business Pk, Swan Lane, **SANDHURST**, GU47 9DN
(T) 01252 861666
- **ALDRAH HEALTH & LEISURE (EUROPE) LTD**, Ascot House, 29a High Street, **ASCOT**, SL5 7HG
(T) 01344 872774
- **BLUE GREEN PLANET LTD**, PO Box 1454, **SLOUGH**, SL3 9YS
(T) 01753 544002
- **BRIGHT IDEAS**, Ascot House, 29a High Street, **ASCOT**, SL5 7HG
(T) 01344 872826
- **CITADEL SERVICES**, 5 Weycrofts, **BRACKNELL**, RG42 1TD
(T) 01344 644555
- **G N C**, 79 Nicholsons Walk, **MAIDENHEAD**, SL6 1LB
(T) 01628 783594
- **G N C LTD**, 96 Peascod Street, **WINDSOR**, SL4 1DH
(T) 01753 860618
- **GARLANDS ORGANIC SHOP**, 6 Reading Road, Pangbourne, **READING**, RG8 7LY
(T) 01189 844770
- **HEALTH & DIET CENTRES LTD**, 2/Brook House, Northbrook Street, **NEWBURY**, RG14 1AH
(T) 01635 528165
- **HEALTH & DIET CENTRES LTD**, 65 Princess Square, **BRACKNELL**, RG12 1LS
(T) 01344 411870
- **HEALTH OF THE NATION**, P O Box 4833, Henley Road, Wargrave, **READING**, RG10 8XY
(T) 01189 401794
- **HEALTH PERCEPTION (UK) LTD**, 12 Lakeside Business Pk, Swan Lane, **SANDHURST**, GU47 9DN
(T) 01252 861454
- **HEALTH PERCEPTION UK LTD**, Chavey Down Road, Winkfield Row, **BRACKNELL**, RG42 7NY
(T) 01344 893499
- **HERBALIFE**, 6 Perth Trading Estate, Perth Avenue, **SLOUGH**, SL1 4DW
(T) 01753 898600
- **HERBALIFE INDEPENDENT DISTRIBUTER**, 1 Leverkusen Road, **BRACKNELL**, RG12 7SQ
(T) 01344 307477
- **HERBALIFE INDEPENDENT DISTRIBUTOR**, 19 Kingstable Street, Eton, **WINDSOR**, SL4 6AB
(T) 01753 622177
- **HIPP NUTRITION**, 165 Main Street, New Greenham Park, Greenham, **THATCHAM**, RG19 6HN
(T) 01635 528250
- **HOLLAND & BARRETT**, 105a Northbrook Street, **NEWBURY**, RG14 1AA
(T) 01635 552218
- **HOLLAND & BARRETT**, 2 Union Street, **READING**, RG1 1EU
(T) 01189 507825
- **HOLLAND & BARRETT**, 22 High Street, **BRACKNELL**, RG12 1LL
(T) 01344 455313
- **HOLLAND & BARRETT**, 58 Broad Street Mall, **READING**, RG1 7QE
(T) 01189 572787
- **HOLLAND & BARRETT**, 69 High Street, **MAIDENHEAD**, SL6 1JX
(T) 01628 789622
- **HOLLAND & BARRETT**, Unit 14 The Queensmere Centre, **MAIDENHEAD**, SL6 1DB
(T) 01753 694355
- **JULIAN GRAVES LTD**, 5 The Observatory, High Street, **SLOUGH**, SL1 1LE
(T) 01753 530582
- **JULIAN GRAVES LTD**, 90 Queensmere, **SLOUGH**, SL1 1DG
(T) 01753 823794
- **KIWIS BEES KNEES LTD**, 89A Grove Road, **WINDSOR**, SL4 1HT
(T) 01753 840559
- **SMITHKLINE BEECHAM**, 11 Stoke Poges Lane, **SLOUGH**, SL1 3NW
(T) 01753 533433
- **SMITHKLINE BEECHAM**, Norreys Drive, **MAIDENHEAD**, SL6 4BL
(T) 01628 426400
- **SQUIRREL'S**, 65 High Street, Burnham, **SLOUGH**, SL1 7JX
(T) 01628 666122
- **SUTHERLAND HEALTH LTD**, Unit 1 Rivermead, Pipers Way, **THATCHAM**, RG19 4EP
(T) 01635 874488
- **THAMES VALLEY HOMOEPATHIC NETWORK**, 41a Hanover Way, **WINDSOR**, SL4 5NN
(T) 01753 830945
- **VITALITY FOODS**, 20 Peach Street, **WOKINGHAM**, RG40 1XG
(T) 01189 775797

## BRISTOL

- **BAY TREE (THE)**, 176 Henleaze Road, BS9 4NE
(T) 01179 621115
- **BEE HEALTHY**, 130 Stoke Lane, Westbury-on-Trym, BS9 3RJ
(T) 01179 622848
- **BODYWISE (UK) LTD**, Unit 23 Marsh La Industrial Estate, Marsh Lane, Easton-in-Gordano, **EASTON-IN-GORDANO**, BS20 0NH
(T) 01275 371764
- **C M INTERNATIONAL**, 78 Wordsworth Road, BS7 0DZ
(T) 01179 075164
- **CAULDRON FOODS LTD**, Unit 1/2, Portishead Business Pk, Portishead, **PORTISHEAD**, BS20 7BF
(T) 01275 818448
- **CLIFTON HEALTH FOODS & DELICATESSEN**, 67-69 Queens Road, Clifton, BS8 1QL
(T) 01179 291600
- **E & H HEALTH SHOP**, 94 Mina Road, BS2 9XW
(T) 01179 830250
- **EARTH FORCE**, 1 Upper Belmont Road, BS7 9DG
(T) 01179 049930
- **ESSENTIAL TRADING CO-OPERATIVE**, Unit 3 Lodge Causeway, BS16 3JB
(T) 01179 583550
- **HEALTH SCENTS**, 14 Broad Street, Staple Hill, BS16 5NX
(T) 01179 701582
- **HEALTH WISE**, 27 North Walk, Yate, BS37 4AP
(T) 01454 322168
- **HEALTHCARE INTERNATIONAL**, 5 Ninth Avenue, BS7 0QW
(T) 01179 312888
- **HOLLAND & BARRETT**, 14 St Marys Way, Thornbury, BS35 2BH
(T) 01454 417201
- **HOLLAND & BARRETT**, 21 Clifton Down Shopping Centre, Whiteladies Road, BS8 2NN
(T) 01179 738188
- **HOLLAND & BARRETT**, 83 The Horsefair, BS1 3JP
(T) 01179 293170
- **HOLLAND & BARRETT**, 87-89 High Street, Nailsea, BS48 1AW
(T) 01275 810106
- **HOLLAND & BARRETT**, Lower Level/The Mall, 36 Cribbs Causeway Regional Shopping Ce, Patchway, **PATCHWAY**, BS34 5GG
(T) 01179 592270
- **HOLLAND & BARRETT**, Unit 2 Odeon Development, Broadmead, BS1 3DN
(T) 01179 260557
- **JULIAN GRAVES LTD**, Broadmead Gallery, Broadmead, BS1 3XB
(T) 01179 220664
- **LA RUCA**, 89 Gloucester Road, Bishopston, BS7 8AS
(T) 01179 446810
- **MOTHER NATURE**, 100 High Street, Portishead, BS20 6AJ
(T) 01275 817178
- **NATURAL HEALTH CO (THE)**, Saville Ct Business Centre, 10 Saville Place, BS8 4EJ
(T) 01275 394944
- **NATURAL WOMAN**, 21 Wellington Park, BS8 2UW
(T) 01179 466649
- **PIPPIN HARRIS**, 8 The Precinct, Portishead, BS20 6AH
(T) 01275 846263
- **POWER SPORTS**, 6 The Old Malthouse, Little Ann Street, BS2 9EB
(T) 01179 551379
- **PROLAB NURTRITION EUROPE**, Collins Street, BS11 9JJ
(T) 01179 380800
- **SCOOPAWAY**, 113 Gloucester Road, Bishopston, BS7 8AT
(T) 01179 872199
- **STAPLES WHOLEFOODS**, 10 St. Catherines Place, BS3 4HG
(T) 01179 537102
- **STEVENS L**, 20 St. Edyths Road, BS9 2ES
(T) 01179 877115
- **STONEGROUND HEALTH FOODS**, 5 The Mall, BS8 4DP
(T) 01179 741260
- **SUNFLOWER WHOLEFOODS**, 359 Gloucester Road, Horfield, BS7 8TG
(T) 01179 240833
- **TOTAL HEALTH CARE**, 57 Elmdale Road, Bedminster, BS3 3JD
(T) 01179 664625
- **WILD OATS WHOLEFOODS**, 9-11 Lower Redland Road, BS6 6TB
(T) 01179 731967

## BUCKINGHAMSHIRE

- **BACK TO NATURE**, 14 Cornwalls Centre, High Street, **BUCKINGHAM**, MK18 1SB
(T) 01280 812694
- **C F S RESOURCES**, Pine Tree Lodge, Green End Road, Radnage, **HIGH WYCOMBE**, HP14 4BY
(T) 01494 483222

- **COUNTRY FINE FOODS**, Unit 11 Park Street Industrial Estate, Osier Way, **AYLESBURY**, HP20 1EB (T) 01296 394153
- **EVERFRESH NATURAL FOODS**, Gatehouse Cl, Gatehouse Industrial Area, **AYLESBURY**, HP19 8DE (T) 01296 425333
- **GARY RODRIGUES**, 64 Hithercroft Road, **HIGH WYCOMBE**, HP13 5RH (T) 01494 439634
- **HALDANE FOODS LTD**, Howard Way, Interchange Park, **NEWPORT PAGNELL**, MK16 9PY (T) 01908 211311
- **HEALTH & DIET CENTRES LTD**, 2d Station Road, **GERRARDS CROSS**, SL9 8EL (T) 01753 889040
- **HEALTH SHOP LTD (THE)**, 12 The Highway, **BEACONSFIELD**, HP9 1QQ (T) 01494 678787
- **HEALTHRIGHT**, 27 High Street, **CHESHAM**, HP5 1BG (T) 01494 771267
- **HEALTHRIGHT**, 48c Friars Square, **AYLESBURY**, HP20 2SP (T) 01296 397022
- **HERBALIFE DISTRIBUTOR**, 8 Kendal Cl, **SLOUGH**, SL2 5HX (T) 01753 532089
- **HOLLAND & BARRETT**, 100 Sycamore Road, **AMERSHAM**, HP6 5EN (T) 01494 727273
- **HOLLAND & BARRETT**, 6 The Arcade, Octagon Centre, **HIGH WYCOMBE**, HP11 2HR (T) 01494 526605
- **HOLLAND & BARRETT**, Unit 16 Brunel Centre, The Concourse, Bletchley, **MILTON KEYNES**, MK2 2BH (T) 01908 642437
- **HOLLAND & BARRETT**, Unit 17 The Food Centre, **MILTON KEYNES**, MK9 3NT (T) 01908 690721
- **JULIAN GRAVES LTD**, 4-5 Octagon Parade, **HIGH WYCOMBE**, HP11 2HU (T) 01494 535533
- **LIBRAVITA TECHNOLOGY**, 53 The Parade, **BOURNE END**, SL8 5SB (T) 07000 818818
- **LICHTWER PHARMA UK**, Regency House, Dedmere Road, **MARLOW**, SL7 1FJ (T) 01628 487780
- **NEWSTART**, 20 Stafford Grove, Shenley Church End, **MILTON KEYNES**, MK5 6AY (T) 01908 501876
- **NIKKEN UK LTD**, Matrix House, 2 North Fourth Street, **MILTON KEYNES**, MK9 1NJ (T) 01908 202400
- **NUTRITIONAL HEALTHCARE INTERNATIONAL**, PO Box 346, **MARLOW**, SL7 1WH (T) 01628 477538
- **ONLY NATURAL**, 41 St Peters Court, High Street, Chalfont St. Peter, **GERRARDS CROSS**, SL9 9QQ (T) 01753 889441
- **RELIV UK LTD**, The Gatehouse/Fryers Works, Abercromby Avenue, **HIGH WYCOMBE**, HP12 3BW (T) 01494 539733
- **SELF-CARE PRODUCTS LTD**, 30 Sycamore Road, **AMERSHAM**, HP6 5DR (T) 01494 722741
- **SUNRIDER EUROPE**, Unit 14 Plover Close, Interchange Park, **NEWPORT PAGNELL**, MK16 9PS (T) 01908 616006
- **UNI-VITE EXPORT LTD**, 50 Aylesbury Road, Aston Clinton, **AYLESBURY**, HP22 5AH (T) 01296 630900
- **VEGEWORLD CO LTD**, 36 Benbow Court, Shenley Church End, **MILTON KEYNES**, MK5 6JG (T) 01908 506613
- **YVES PONROY (UK) LTD**, Unit 1 Fairview Industrial Estate, Raans Road, **AMERSHAM**, HP6 6JY (T) 01494 729970

## CAMBRIDGESHIRE

- **ARJUNA WHOLEFOODS**, 12 Mill Road, **CAMBRIDGE**, CB1 2AD (T) 01223 364845
- **BE-WELL NUTRITIONAL PRODUCTS LTD**, 20 Kings Street Industrial Estate, Langtoft, **PETERBOROUGH**, PE6 9NF (T) 01778 560868
- **CAMBRIDGE COMMODITY LTD**, 83a Lynn Road, **ELY**, CB6 1DD (T) 01353 667258
- **CAMBRIDGE HEALTH FOOD**, 5 Bridge Street, **CAMBRIDGE**, CB2 1UA (T) 01223 350433
- **DAILY BREAD CO-OPERATIVE (CAMBRIDGE) LTD**, Unit 3 Kilmaine Close, **CAMBRIDGE**, CB4 2PH (T) 01223 423177
- **FRESH ROYAL JELLY CO**, Coven Wood Cottage, Mill Hill, Weston Colville, **CAMBRIDGE**, CB1 5NY (T) 01223 290282
- **GRANTA PROCESSORS**, Mill Lane, Whittlesford, **CAMBRIDGE**, CB2 4XL (T) 01223 834100
- **HEALTH PARTNERSHIP**, 47 Pound Cl, Burwell, **CAMBRIDGE**, CB5 0EP (T) 01638 618120
- **HOLLAND & BARRETT**, 1 Coronation Parade, High Street, **ELY**, CB7 4LB (T) 01353 662330
- **HOLLAND & BARRETT**, 33 Long Causeway, **PETERBOROUGH**, PE1 1YJ (T) 01733 311268
- **HOLLAND & BARRETT**, 4-6 Bradwells Court, **CAMBRIDGE**, CB1 1NH (T) 01223 368914
- **HOLLAND & BARRETT**, 58 Eden Hall, Grafton Centre, **CAMBRIDGE**, CB1 1PS (T) 01223 314544
- **HOLLAND & BARRETT**, Unit 6 St Benedicts Court, **HUNTINGDON**, PE18 6PN (T) 01480 417203
- **HUMET HEALTHCARE LTD**, Unit 2, Forge Cl, Eaton Socon/St. Neots, **HUNTINGDON**, PE19 3TP (T) 01480 403769
- **LANDAUER HONEY LTD**, Top Barn, Fowlmere Road, Newton, **CAMBRIDGE**, CB2 5PG (T) 01223 872444
- **LIFEPLUS EUROPE LTD**, Howard Road, Eaton Socon, **ST. NEOTS**, PE19 8GB (T) 01480 477230
- **NATURAL CHOICE**, Merryland, **ST. IVES**, PE27 5ED (T) 01480 467320
- **OUTSIDE IN (CAMBRIDGE) LTD**, Unit 21 Scotland Road Estate, Dry Drayton, **CAMBRIDGE**, CB3 8AT (T) 01954 211955
- **PETERBOROUGH HEALTH FOOD CENTRE**, 25 Westgate, **PETERBOROUGH**, PE1 1PZ (T) 01733 566807
- **ST NEOTS HEALTH FOOD CENTRE**, 2 Church Walk, **ST. NEOTS**, PE19 1JH (T) 01480 218106
- **WISBECH WHOLEFOODS**, 8 North Street, **WISBECH**, PE13 1NP (T) 01945 464468

## CHESHIRE

- **ALPHA HEALTH & BEAUTY**, 30a The Precinct, Cheadle Hulme, **CHEADLE**, SK8 5BB (T) 01614 828153
- **BIO OIL RESEARCH LTD**, 64 Welsh Row, **NANTWICH**, CW5 5EU (T) 01270 629323
- **CEDAR HEALTH LTD**, Pepper Road, Hazel Grove, **STOCKPORT**, SK7 5BW (T) 01614 831235
- **CHESHIRE WHOLEFOODS LTD**, Stendall Road, Stadium Industrial Estate, **CHESTER**, CH1 4LU (T) 01244 375205
- **CONGLETON HEALTH STORE (THE)**, 8 Bridge Street, **CONGLETON**, CW12 1AY (T) 01260 299795
- **COUNTRY BUMPKIN (THE)**, 4a Cross Street, **ALTRINCHAM**, WA14 1EQ (T) 01619 414663
- **COUNTRY LIVING HEALTH STORE**, 94-98 Park Lane, Poynton, **STOCKPORT**, SK12 1RE (T) 01625 876115
- **COUNTRYWORLD LTD**, Common Lane, Culcheth, **WARRINGTON**, WA3 4EH (T) 01925 765448
- **DEMETER WHOLEFOODS**, 12 Welles Street, **SANDBACH**, CW11 1GT (T) 01270 760445
- **DUTTONS HEALTH FOODS**, 8 Godstall Lane, **CHESTER**, CH1 1LN (T) 01244 316255
- **FIT AS A FIDDLE**, 108 Mill Street, **MACCLESFIELD**, SK11 6NR (T) 01625 612555
- **FIT AS A FIDDLE**, 41-43 Albert Road, **WIDNES**, WA8 6JA (T) 01514 202866
- **FULL OF BEANS**, 93 Witton Street, **NORTHWICH**, CW9 5DR (T) 01606 41778
- **GOOD FOOD SHOP**, 2 Melbourne Street, **STALYBRIDGE**, SK15 2JE (T) 01613 049225
- **GOOD HEALTH**, 13 Armentieres Square, **STALYBRIDGE**, SK15 2BR (T) 01613 388385
- **GRANARY (THE)**, 108 Northgate Street, **CHESTER**, CH1 2HT (T) 01244 318553
- **GRANARY (THE)**, 20b The Market, Princess Street, **CHESTER**, CH1 2HH (T) 01244 349892
- **HAZELNUT HEALTH FOODS**, 307 London Road, Hazel Grove, **STOCKPORT**, SK7 4PS (T) 01614 831576
- **HEALTH FOOD CENTRE**, 41 Oxford Road, **ALTRINCHAM**, WA14 2ED (T) 01619 284399
- **HEALTH RACK**, The Forum Shopping Centre, Northgate Street, **CHESTER**, CH1 2BY (T) 01244 401245
- **HEALTH REACTION**, PO Box 241, **STOCKPORT**, SK1 1EG (T) 01614 464887
- **HEALTH SHOP (THE)**, Moss Lane Surgery, Moss Lane, Madeley, **CREWE**, CW3 9PR (T) 01782 751275
- **HEALTHCARE**, 55 Albert Road, **WIDNES**, WA8 6JS (T) 01514 229244
- **HEALTHCARE INTERNATIONAL**, 3 Armitstead Road, **SANDBACH**, CW11 3LP (T) 01270 763841
- **HEALTHY HERBS**, Tatton Street, **KNUTSFORD**, WA16 6AB (T) 01565 755022
- **HERBALIFE**, 21 Caesars Cl, Castlefields, **RUNCORN**, WA7 2JU (T) 01928 775095
- **HERBALIFE**, 54 Acton Avenue, Appleton, **WARRINGTON**, WA4 5PT (T) 01925 268897
- **HERBALIFE DISTRIBUTOR**, Ruskin Room, Drury Lane, **KNUTSFORD**, WA16 6HA (T) 01565 621006
- **HERES HEALTH**, Market Hall, The Mall, **HYDE**, SK14 2QT (T) 01613 666909
- **HOLLAND & BARRETT**, 39 High Street, **NANTWICH**, CW5 5DB (T) 01270 610041
- **HOLLAND & BARRETT**, 4 The Mall, **SALE**, M33 7XZ (T) 01619 051894
- **HOLLAND & BARRETT**, 52 The Mall, **WARRINGTON**, WA1 1QE (T) 01925 418424
- **HOLLAND & BARRETT**, 7 Paddock Row, Grosvenor Precinct, **CHESTER**, CH1 1ED (T) 01244 348153
- **HOLLAND & BARRETT**, 70 George Street, **ALTRINCHAM**, WA14 1RF (T) 01619 296716

- **HOLLAND & BARRETT**, 72 High Street, **NORTHWICH**, CW9 5AU
(T) 01606 42073
- **HOLLAND & BARRETT**, 77 Town Square, Halton Lea, **RUNCORN**, WA7 2EU
(T) 01928 791188
- **HOLLAND & BARRETT**, 97 Princes Street, **STOCKPORT**, SK1 1RW
(T) 01614 802314
- **HOLLAND & BARRETT**, Unit 4 Mill Street Mall, Grosvenor Centre, **MACCLESFIELD**, SK11 6AJ
(T) 01625 424256
- **HONEYSUCKLE HEALTH FOODS**, 4 Hawthorn Lane, **WILMSLOW**, SK9 1AA
(T) 01625 526144
- **JULIAN GRAVES LTD**, 6 Northgate Street, **CHESTER**, CH1 2HQ
(T) 01244 313017
- **LIFE STYLE FITNESS DIRECT**, 3 Silk Street, **CONGLETON**, CW12 4DH
(T) 01260 297905
- **M & R HEALTH FOODS**, 1 The Mallards, Off Field Bank Road, **MACCLESFIELD**, SK11 8PT
(T) 01625 572673
- **MARPLE HEALTH FOODS**, 72a Stockport Road, Marple, **STOCKPORT**, SK6 6AB
(T) 01614 275662
- **MILLMARK FOODS**, 101 Main Street, **FRODSHAM**, WA6 7AB
(T) 01928 735151
- **NATURES REMEDIES**, 10 Time Square, **WARRINGTON**, WA1 2AR
(T) 01925 444885
- **NEW LIFE PRODUCTS LTD**, 20 Green Lane, Poynton, **STOCKPORT**, SK12 1TJ
(T) 01625 850994
- **NUTRITION FOR LIFE**, 78 Halton Road, **RUNCORN**, WA7 5SB
(T) 01928 576233
- **NUTRITION FOR LIFE (UK) LTD**, 1 Easter Court, Europa Boulevard, Westbrook, **WARRINGTON**, WA5 5ZZ
(T) 01925 496600
- **NUTRITION POINT LTD**, 13 Taurus Pk, Europa Boulevard, Westbrook, **WARRINGTON**, WA5 5ZT
(T) 07041 544044
- **NUTTERS UK LTD**, 13-15 Brierley Business Centre, Mirion Street, **CREWE**, CW1 2AZ
(T) 01270 500217
- **PADMA UK**, Bramhall Moor Technology Park, Pepper Road, Hazel Grove, **STOCKPORT**, SK7 5BW
(T) 01614 834662
- **PANTRY (THE)**, 3 Lindow Parade, Chapel Lane, **WILMSLOW**, SK9 5JL
(T) 01625 524822
- **PEAK HEALTH LTD**, 12 Britannia Road, **SALE**, M33 2AA
(T) 01619 621210
- **PRIMA HEALTH PRODUCTS LTD**, Brook House, 6 Penryn Avenue, **SALE**, M33 3PG
(T) 01619 698948
- **SALUS (UK) LTD**, 17 Grosvenor Grange, Woolston, **WARRINGTON**, WA1 4SF
(T) 01925 815841
- **SPARKLES**, 13 Wilmslow Road, **CHEADLE**, SK8 1DW
(T) 01614 285756
- **USANA**, 44 School Lane, Hartford, **NORTHWICH**, CW8 1PE
(T) 01606 782154
- **WILSONS WHOLEFOOD**, 7 Compstall Road, Romiley, **STOCKPORT**, SK6 4BT
(T) 01614 946446

## CLEVELAND

- **ALOE VERA ADVICE CENTRE (THE)**, 10 High Street, **YARM**, TS15 9AE
(T) 01642 898560
- **BLACKS HEALTH FOOD CENTRE**, 7 Regency West Mall, **STOCKTON-ON-TEES**, TS18 1EF
(T) 01642 679087
- **FARMACE HEALTH STORES**, 4 West Dyke Road, **REDCAR**, TS10 1DZ
(T) 01642 490102
- **FOR GOODNESS SAKE**, 11 Gilkes Street, **MIDDLESBROUGH**, TS1 5ET
(T) 01642 219249
- **FOR GOODNESS SAKE**, 28 Westgate, **GUISBOROUGH**, TS14 6BA
(T) 01287 637074
- **FOR GOODNESS SAKE**, Parkway Shopping Centre, Coulby Newham, **MIDDLESBROUGH**, TS8 0TJ
(T) 01642 599075
- **HEALTH RACK**, Cleveland Centre, **MIDDLESBROUGH**, TS1 2NW
(T) 01642 219881
- **HOLLAND & BARRETT**, 14 Oberhausen Mall, Hill Street Shopping Centre, **MIDDLESBROUGH**, TS1 1TB
(T) 01642 220179
- **HOLLAND & BARRETT**, 16 Castle Way, **STOCKTON-ON-TEES**, TS18 1AL
(T) 01642 671127
- **HOLLAND & BARRETT**, 184 Middleton Grange Shopping Centre, **HARTLEPOOL**, TS24 7RR
(T) 01429 860810
- **NATURES STORE**, 107 High Street, Great Ayton, **MIDDLESBROUGH**, TS9 6BW
(T) 01642 723351
- **SALTBURN HEALTH FOODS**, Unit 5 Station Buildings, Station Square, **SALTBURN-BY-THE-SEA**, TS12 1AQ
(T) 01287 624622
- **SELECTIONS**, 2 High Street, Sedgefield, **STOCKTON-ON-TEES**, TS21 2AU
(T) 01740 620456

## CORNWALL

- **A & N HEALTH FOODS**, 62 Fore Street, **SALTASH**, PL12 6JW
(T) 01752 844926
- **BRAN TUB (THE)**, 7/Market House Arcade, Fore Street, **BODMIN**, PL31 2JA
(T) 01208 76625
- **BUDE HEALTH STORE**, 8 Lansdown Road, **BUDE**, EX23 8BH
(T) 01288 352425
- **COUNTRY FAYRE**, Higher Penquite Farm, St. Breward, **BODMIN**, PL30 4NX
(T) 01208 850897
- **COUNTRY FAYRE**, Polmorla Road, **WADEBRIDGE**, PL27 7ND
(T) 01208 814141
- **COUNTRY STORE (THE)**, 3 Bond Street, **REDRUTH**, TR15 2QA
(T) 01209 215012
- **GOOD HEALTH**, Tregenna Place, **ST. IVES**, TR26 1SB
(T) 01736 794726
- **GRANARY (THE)**, 15d Causewayhead, **PENZANCE**, TR18 2SN
(T) 01736 361869
- **GRANARY (THE)**, Higher Newham Lane, Newham, **TRURO**, TR1 2ST
(T) 01872 274343
- **HEALTH SHOP (THE)**, Market House Arcade, **LAUNCESTON**, PL15 8EP
(T) 01566 774300
- **HENDRAS**, 8 Lemon Street, **TRURO**, TR1 2LQ
(T) 01872 223799
- **HOLLAND & BARRETT**, 1 Frances Street, **TRURO**, TR1 3DN
(T) 01872 272991
- **HOLLAND & BARRETT**, 13-14 Aylmer Square, **ST. AUSTELL**, PL25 5LL
(T) 01726 73548
- **HOLLAND & BARRETT**, 3 Market Place, **PENZANCE**, TR18 2JA
(T) 01736 331855
- **HOLLAND & BARRETT**, 42 Market Street, **FALMOUTH**, TR11 3AJ
(T) 01326 319327
- **JILLY ORGANIC WHOLEFOODS**, Biscombes Lane, **CALLINGTON**, PL17 7LB
(T) 01579 384356
- **MUSTARD SEED (THE)**, Boscawen Road, **PERRANPORTH**, TR6 0EW
(T) 01872 571421
- **N P S NATRADERM**, P O Box 9, **HELSTON**, TR13 8HJ
(T) 01326 564565
- **NATURAL STORE**, 16 High Street, **FALMOUTH**, TR11 2AB
(T) 01326 311507
- **NATURAL STORE**, 3 The Parade, **HELSTON**, TR13 8RT
(T) 01326 564226
- **PURE THING (THE)**, 4 East Street, **NEWQUAY**, TR7 1BH
(T) 01637 876772
- **RICHARDS HEALTH FOODS**, Bread Street, **PENZANCE**, TR18 2EQ
(T) 01736 362828
- **SHARCARE LTD**, Unit 2 Parade House, The Parade, **LISKEARD**, PL14 6AF
(T) 01579 342828
- **SPICE OF LIFE (THE)**, The Market House, Higher Market Street, **LOOE**, PL13 1BW
(T) 01503 265092
- **SUNFLOWER WHOLEFOODS**, 16a Cross Street, **CAMBORNE**, TR14 8EX
(T) 01209 715970

## COUNTY DURHAM

- **B K S MARKETING**, Unit 12 Dudley Road, **DARLINGTON**, DL1 4GG
(T) 01325 484646
- **BLACKS HEALTH FOOD CENTRE**, 91 Claypath, **DURHAM**, DH1 1RG
(T) 01913 843197
- **FOOD WEIGHHOUSE (THE)**, 14 Bondgate, **DARLINGTON**, DL3 7JE
(T) 01325 483119
- **HBM**, Ashleigh, Stockton Road, **SEAHAM**, SR7 0NS
(T) 01915 813183
- **HEALTH WAREHOUSE (THE)**, 15 Post House Wynd, **DARLINGTON**, DL3 7LU
(T) 01325 468570
- **HOLLAND & BARRETT**, 13 Millburngate, **DURHAM**, DH1 4SL
(T) 01913 842374
- **HOLLAND & BARRETT**, 5 Queen Street, **DARLINGTON**, DL3 6SH
(T) 01325 365656
- **MOLLY'S WHOLEFOOD STORE**, 11 Front Street, Framwellgate Moor, **DURHAM**, DH1 5EJ
(T) 01913 862216
- **SEASONS WHOLEFOODS**, Bridge End, **CHESTER LE STREET**, DH3 3RE
(T) 01913 880050
- **VERD MARKETING**, 9 Cherry Tree Drive, Sunnybrow, **CROOK**, DL15 0XG
(T) 01388 747836
- **VITACOLL LTD**, 109 Stanhope Rd South, **DARLINGTON**, DL3 7SF
(T) 01325 240122
- **VITAL SPARK NUTRITION**, 17 Van Mildert Close, **PETERLEE**, SR8 2NJ
(T) 01915 862634

## CUMBRIA

- **APPLESEEDS**, 59 Market Street, **ULVERSTON**, LA12 7LT
(T) 01229 583394
- **BRAMBLES WHOLE FOODS**, 5 Bridge Street, **APPLEBY-IN-WESTMORLAND**, CA16 6QH
(T) 01768 353588
- **CHRYSALIS WHOLEFOODS**, 33c High Street, **WIGTON**, CA7 9NJ
(T) 01697 349559
- **EDEN VALLEY WHOLEFOODS**, 34 The Market, Scotch Street, **CARLISLE**, CA3 8QX
(T) 01228 546853
- **F & V FOODS**, 53 Market Street, **DALTON-IN-FURNESS**, LA15 8AW
(T) 01229 465544
- **FELLSIDE WHOLEFOODS**, 11 Allhallows Lane, **KENDAL**, LA9 4JH
(T) 01539 722344
- **GOLDEN HARVEST HEALTH FOODS**, 22 Harrington Road, **WORKINGTON**, CA14 3ED
(T) 01900 66132
- **GRANARY (THE)**, 24 Market Place, **COCKERMOUTH**, CA13 9NQ
(T) 01900 822633
- **HALF MOON WHOLEFOODS**, 14 Front Street, **BRAMPTON**, CA8 1NG
(T) 01697 73775

- **HARLEY FOODS LTD**, Blindcrake Hall, Blindcrake, **COCKERMOUTH**, CA13 0QP (T) 01900 823037
- **HEALTH BONUS**, Wall Nook, Beckside, Cartmel, **GRANGE-OVER-SANDS**, LA11 7SP (T) 01539 536043
- **HEALTH RACK**, Crag Brow, Bowness-on-Windermere, **WINDERMERE**, LA23 3BX (T) 01539 488368
- **HOLLAND & BARRETT**, 2 Globe Lane, Lanes Shopping Centre, **CARLISLE**, CA3 8NX (T) 01228 530827
- **HOLLAND & BARRETT**, 54 Stricklandgate, **KENDAL**, LA9 4ND (T) 01539 733828
- **JULIAN GRAVES LTD**, 34 Devonshire Arcade, **PENRITH**, CA11 7SS (T) 01768 895221
- **JULIAN GRAVES LTD**, 55 Quarry Rigg, Bowness-on-Windermere, **WINDERMERE**, LA23 3DU (T) 01539 443372
- **KAN FOODS WHOLEFOOD SHOP (THE)**, 9 New Shambles, **KENDAL**, LA9 4TS (T) 01539 721190
- **KERSHAW'S HEALTH FOODS**, 127 Queen Street, **WHITEHAVEN**, CA28 7QF (T) 01946 66627
- **LIVING WELL**, 26 The Square, **MILNTHORPE**, LA7 7QJ (T) 01539 563870
- **NATURES HEALTH STORE**, 1 King Street, **PENRITH**, CA11 7AR (T) 01768 899262
- **NICHOLSON HOUSE COFFEE SHOP**, 14 St Georges Terrace, **MILLOM**, LA18 4DB (T) 01229 774534
- **PASTURES NEW**, 64 Scott Street, **BARROW-IN-FURNESS**, LA14 1QE (T) 01229 833043
- **SALAD SPROUTS**, Friars Croft, Allithwaite Road, Cartmel, **GRANGE-OVER-SANDS**, LA11 7SB (T) 01539 536592
- **SUNDANCE WHOLEFOODS**, 33 Main Street, **KESWICK**, CA12 5BL (T) 01768 774712

## DERBYSHIRE

- **ACADIA PRODUCTS**, PO Box 5210, Newton, **ALFRETON**, DE55 5ZQ (T) 01773 875555
- **ATOPIC QUEST LTD**, 243 Ashbourne Road, Turnditch, **BELPER**, DE56 2LL (T) 01773 550180
- **BEANO'S WHOLEFOOD**, Holme Road, Matlock Bath, **MATLOCK**, DE4 3NU (T) 01629 57130
- **BEE WELL PRODUCTS LTD**, Laurel Cottage Apiaries, Hockley Lane, Wingerworth, **CHESTERFIELD**, S42 6QQ (T) 01246 220130
- **BLACK PETER HEALTH CARE LTD**, William Nadin Way, **SWADLINCOTE**, DE11 0BB (T) 01283 228300
- **CRUSTY COB (THE)**, 1b Market Street, **HEANOR**, DE75 7NR (T) 01773 769260
- **FRUIT & NUTS**, 10 Station Road, Mickleover, **DERBY**, DE3 5GH (T) 01332 515637
- **GLOSSOP WHOLE FOOD**, 8 Henry Street, **GLOSSOP**, SK13 8BW (T) 01457 865678
- **GOOD HEALTH FOODS**, Unit 4/Corn Exchange, Albert Street, **DERBY**, DE1 2DS (T) 01332 383997
- **GOOD HEALTH FOODS LTD**, 2 Soresby Street, **CHESTERFIELD**, S40 1JN (T) 01246 272530
- **HARVEST MOON**, Unit 15 Peak Village, Chatsworth Road, Rowsley, **MATLOCK**, DE4 2JE (T) 01629 733877
- **HEALTH & DIET FOOD CO LTD**, Stubley Lane, **DRONFIELD**, S18 1PF (T) 01246 413294
- **HERBATICUS**, 76 Snape Hill Lane, **DRONFIELD**, S18 2GP (T) 01246 411949
- **HIGH FIVE LTD**, Derwent Business Centre, Clarke Street, **DERBY**, DE1 2BU (T) 01332 724747
- **HOLLAND & BARRETT**, 1 Crown Square, **MATLOCK**, DE4 3AT (T) 01629 57737
- **HOLLAND & BARRETT**, 17 Spring Gardens Centre, **BUXTON**, SK17 6DF (T) 01298 71021
- **HOLLAND & BARRETT**, 18 Crown Walk, **DERBY**, DE1 2NP (T) 01332 360664
- **HOLLAND & BARRETT**, 29a Bath Street, **ILKESTON**, DE7 8AH (T) 01159 447626
- **HOLLAND & BARRETT**, 8 St Peters Way, **DERBY**, DE1 2NR (T) 01332 381062
- **HOLLAND & BARRETT RETAIL LTD**, 59 Low Pavement, **CHESTERFIELD**, S40 1PB (T) 01246 232536
- **M P BIO SCIENCE INTERNATIONAL LTD**, Edgemoor Estate, Bishops Lane, **BUXTON**, SK17 6UP (T) 01298 27777
- **MARKET WHOLEFOODS**, The Shambles, Mellor Road, New Mills, **HIGH PEAK**, SK22 4DW (T) 01663 747550
- **MCNEIL CONSUMER NUTRITIONALS**, 1 Millenium Way, Dunston Technology Park, **CHESTERFIELD**, S41 8ND (T) 01246 451400
- **NATURAL CHOICE**, 24 St John Street, **ASHBOURNE**, DE6 1GH (T) 01335 346096
- **NATURAL CHOICE**, 44 Oxford Street, **RIPLEY**, DE5 3AP (T) 01773 570239
- **NATURAL CHOICE**, 5 The Shambles, **CHESTERFIELD**, S40 1PX (T) 01246 558550
- **NATURAL CHOICE**, 96 High Street, **ALFRETON**, DE55 7BE (T) 01773 833226
- **NATURAL HEALTH**, 13 High Street, Long Eaton, **NOTTINGHAM**, NG10 1HY (T) 01159 731628
- **NATURES WAY**, 11 Park Farm Centre, Allestree, **DERBY**, DE22 2QN (T) 01332 552055
- **NUTRI (IMPORTS & EXPORTS) LTD**, Buxton Road, New Mills, **HIGH PEAK**, SK22 3JU (T) 01663 746559
- **ORCHARD HEALTH FOODS**, 29 Castlefields Main Centre, **DERBY**, DE1 2PE (T) 01332 360829
- **SUNFLOWER HEALTH STORE**, 20 Market Place, **ILKESTON**, DE7 5QA (T) 01159 304750
- **TOTAL HEALTH**, 19 King Street, Duffield, **BELPER**, DE56 4EU (T) 01773 824641
- **WILD CARROTVEGETARIAN CAFE**, 5 Bridge Street, **BUXTON**, SK17 6BS (T) 01298 22843

## DEVON

- **ALOE DISTRIBUTION CO**, 5 Bindon Road, **EXETER**, EX4 9HN (T) 01392 466000
- **ALOE VERA BUSINESS CENTRE**, Pounds Mead, Hillsview, **BRAUNTON**, EX33 2LA (T) 01271 817020
- **ALOE VERA EXMOUTH**, 2 Brookhayes Cl, **EXMOUTH**, EX8 3AD (T) 01395 271496
- **AQUASOURCE (UK) LTD**, 12 Oaktree Place/Matford Business Park, Marsh Barton Trading Estate, **EXETER**, EX2 8WA (T) 01392 822155
- **ARK (THE)**, 38 East Street, Ashburton, **NEWTON ABBOT**, TQ13 7AX (T) 01364 653020
- **ATRI DRIED FRUIT LTD**, Unit B1-B6 Dunkeswell Business Park, Dunkeswell Industrial Estate, **HONITON**, EX14 4RA (T) 01404 891989
- **B NATURAL**, 14 The Strand, **EXMOUTH**, EX8 1AD (T) 01395 279144
- **BEANFEAST WHOLEFOODS**, 2 The Arcade, Fore Street, **OKEHAMPTON**, EX20 1EX (T) 01837 52387
- **BIDEFORD HEALTH FOODS**, 14 Mill Street, **BIDEFORD**, EX39 2JT (T) 01237 472715
- **BODZ**, 50 Exeter Road, **EXMOUTH**, EX8 1PY (T) 01395 225066
- **CITY WHOLEFOODS**, 14 South Street, **EXETER**, EX1 1DZ (T) 01392 250925
- **CITY WHOLEFOODS**, 67 Magdalen Road, **EXETER**, EX2 4TA (T) 01392 252295
- **COUNTRY FAYRE HEALTH FOODS**, 5 Duke Street, **DARTMOUTH**, TQ6 9PY (T) 01803 834576
- **CROSSWAYS STORES**, 68 Victory Street, **PLYMOUTH**, PL2 2DA (T) 01752 563205
- **EXMOUTH HEALTH FOOD STORES**, 19 High Street, **EXMOUTH**, EX8 1NP (T) 01395 265741
- **GALEN HEALTH**, 4/Lockyer Mews, Paddons Row, **TAVISTOCK**, PL19 0HF (T) 01822 618488
- **GANESHA**, 1 Dolphin Co, High Street, **HONITON**, EX14 1LS (T) 01404 43225
- **GANESHA WHOLE FOODS**, Sidmouth Shopping Centre, High Street, **SIDMOUTH**, EX10 8LE (T) 01395 578526
- **GANESHA WHOLE FOODS**, Simpson House, South Street, **AXMINSTER**, EX13 5AD (T) 01297 33957
- **GOLDEN HAMPER (THE)**, 19 Queen Street, **SEATON**, EX12 2NY (T) 01297 21076
- **GREENLIFE SHOP (THE)**, 11-13 Fore Street, **TOTNES**, TQ9 5DA (T) 01803 866738
- **GRIFFIN WHOLEFOODS**, 120 East Street, **SOUTH MOLTON**, EX36 3BU (T) 01769 572372
- **GUYS WHOLE FOODS & FRUITERERS**, 5 Blackboy Road, **EXETER**, EX4 6SG (T) 01392 259338
- **HEALTH FOOD STORE**, Unit F Gammon Walk, **BARNSTAPLE**, EX31 1DJ (T) 01271 345624
- **HEALTHFOODS UNLIMITED**, 181 Cowick Street, **EXETER**, EX4 1AA (T) 01392 495258
- **HEALTHWISE**, 81 Fore Street, **KINGSBRIDGE**, TQ7 1AB (T) 01548 857707
- **HEALTHY PULSES**, 174 Sidwell Street, **EXETER**, EX4 6RH (T) 01392 250552
- **HEALTHY PULSES**, 49 Eastlake Street, **PLYMOUTH**, PL1 1BU (T) 01752 261669
- **HEALTHY WAY (THE)**, 30 High Street, **ILFRACOMBE**, EX34 9DA (T) 01271 865883
- **HERBALIFE**, 10 Barton Villas, **DAWLISH**, EX7 9QJ (T) 01626 865665
- **HERBS & HONEY**, 77 Fore Street, St. Marychurch, **TORQUAY**, TQ1 4PU (T) 01803 314901
- **HOLLAND & BARRETT**, 15 The Crossways Shopping Centre, **PAIGNTON**, TQ4 5BL (T) 01803 559193
- **HOLLAND & BARRETT**, 16 Waterbeer Street, **EXETER**, EX4 3EH (T) 01392 277494
- **HOLLAND & BARRETT**, 16-18 Princesshay, **EXETER**, EX1 1LY (T) 01392 251590

- **HOLLAND & BARRETT**, 22 Courtenay Street, **NEWTON ABBOT**, TQ12 2DT
(T) 01626 353141
- **HOLLAND & BARRETT**, 28 Union Street, **TORQUAY**, TQ2 5PW
(T) 01803 212215
- **HOLLAND & BARRETT**, 35 Fore Street, **TIVERTON**, EX16 6LZ
(T) 01884 256690
- **HOLLAND & BARRETT**, 58 Cornwall Street, **PLYMOUTH**, PL1 1LR
(T) 01752 661822
- **HOLLAND & BARRETT**, 92 High Street, **BARNSTAPLE**, EX31 1HR
(T) 01271 328295
- **HOLLAND & BARRETT**, Fore Street, **SIDMOUTH**, EX10 8AF
(T) 01395 512535
- **HOLLAND & BARRETT**, Unit 2 36 Royal Parade, **PLYMOUTH**, PL1 1DU
(T) 01752 661076
- **JULIAN GRAVES LTD**, 33 Fleet Street, **TORQUAY**, TQ2 5DJ
(T) 01803 201502
- **JULIAN GRAVES LTD**, 37 Green Lanes Shopping Centre, **BARNSTAPLE**, EX31 1UL
(T) 01271 321518
- **KILWORTHY KAPERS**, 11 King Street, **TAVISTOCK**, PL19 0DS
(T) 01822 615039
- **MARKET HEALTH FOODS**, Market Hall, Market Street, **NEWTON ABBOT**, TQ12 2RJ
(T) 01626 202076
- **NATURES WAY**, 1 North Road, **HOLSWORTHY**, EX22 6EJ
(T) 01409 254305
- **NICHOLSONS WHOLEFOOD & HEALTH SHOP**, 12 Fore Street, **KINGSBRIDGE**, TQ7 1NY
(T) 01548 854347
- **NUTTERS**, 14 Bank Street, **TEIGNMOUTH**, TQ14 8AW
(T) 01626 776246
- **ORCHARD WHOLE FOODS**, 16 High Street, **BUDLEIGH SALTERTON**, EX9 6LQ
(T) 01395 442508
- **ORCHARD WHOLEFOODS**, 5a Mill Street, **OTTERY ST. MARY**, EX11 1AB
(T) 01404 812109
- **P S B PARTNERSHIP**, 73 Dartmouth Road, **PAIGNTON**, TQ4 5AF
(T) 01803 528022
- **PINE PANTRY**, 7 Bolton Street, **BRIXHAM**, TQ5 9BZ
(T) 01803 856140
- **POPPADUMS**, 2 Waterloo Street, **TEIGNMOUTH**, TQ14 8AS
(T) 01626 772510
- **POPPADUMS**, 39a The Strand, **DAWLISH**, EX7 9PT
(T) 01626 863128
- **PRESTON HEALTH STORES**, 300 Torquay Road, **PAIGNTON**, TQ3 2ER
(T) 01803 522233
- **REAPERS HEALTHFOODS**, 18 Bampton Street, **TIVERTON**, EX16 6AA
(T) 01884 255310
- **RICKARD-LANES**, 47 Mayflower Street, **PLYMOUTH**, PL1 1QL
(T) 01752 665175
- **SACKS**, 80 High Street, **TOTNES**, TQ9 5SN
(T) 01803 863263
- **SEASONS**, 8 Well Street, **EXETER**, EX4 6QR
(T) 01392 201282
- **SEEDS BAKERY**, 11-12 Burke Road, **TOTNES**, TQ9 5XL
(T) 01803 864249
- **SEEDS HEALTH STORE**, 22 Duke Street, **DARTMOUTH**, TQ6 9PZ
(T) 01803 833200
- **SOUTHERN HEALTH FOODS**, Church Street, **SIDMOUTH**, EX10 8LZ
(T) 01395 514777
- **SUMMERBEE PRODUCTS**, Windsor House, Lime Avenue, **TORQUAY**, TQ2 5JL
(T) 01803 212965
- **TORBAY HEALTH STORE**, 28 Hyde Road, **PAIGNTON**, TQ4 5BY
(T) 01803 527251
- **TOTNES HEALTH SHOP (THE)**, 35 High Street, **TOTNES**, TQ9 5NP
(T) 01803 862526

## DORSET

- **AUTOHEALTH LTD**, 356 Lymington Road, Highcliffe, **CHRISTCHURCH**, BH23 5EY
(T) 01425 280990
- **BAY TREE (THE)**, 15 Pennys Walk, **FERNDOWN**, BH22 9TH
(T) 01202 896096
- **BAY TREE (THE)**, 24 Saxon Square, **CHRISTCHURCH**, BH23 1QB
(T) 01202 481817
- **BOSCOMBE HEALTH FOODS**, 8 Royal Arcade, **BOURNEMOUTH**, BH1 4BT
(T) 01202 301947
- **COUNTRY FOODS**, 19 Station Road, **SWANAGE**, BH19 1AB
(T) 01929 427057
- **DISCOUNT HEALTH STORE**, 96 Dolphin Centre, **POOLE**, BH15 1SS
(T) 01202 674193
- **DISCOUNT HEALTH STORE (THE)**, 18 Westbourne Arcade, **BOURNEMOUTH**, BH4 9AY
(T) 01202 764064
- **DOWN TO EARTH NATURAL FOODS**, E, 18 Princes Street, **DORCHESTER**, DT1 1TW
(T) 01305 268325
- **EARTH FOODS**, 75 Southbourne Grove, **BOURNEMOUTH**, BH6 3QU
(T) 01202 422465
- **ESSENTIALLY YOURS**, 24 Hillbrow Road, **BOURNEMOUTH**, BH6 5NT
(T) 01202 430878
- **FOOD FOR THOUGHT**, 64 Cheap Street, **SHERBORNE**, DT9 3BJ
(T) 01935 814262
- **FOREVER LIVING PRODUCTS (UK) LTD**, 11 Melford Court, St. Peters Road, **BOURNEMOUTH**, BH1 2LS
(T) 01202 293300
- **FRUITS OF THE EARTH**, 2a Victoria Grove, **BRIDPORT**, DT6 3AA
(T) 01308 425827
- **HARVEST FOODS**, 29 St Catherines Road, **BOURNEMOUTH**, BH6 4AE
(T) 01202 420998
- **HEALTH & DIET CENTRES LTD**, Unit 31/Sovereign Centre, Christchurch Road, **BOURNEMOUTH**, BH1 4SX
(T) 01202 300059
- **HEALTH FOOD CENTRE (THE)**, 23/Hampshire Centre, Castle La West, **BOURNEMOUTH**, BH8 9UW
(T) 01202 522778
- **HEALTH FOODS**, 60 West Street, **BRIDPORT**, DT6 3QP
(T) 01308 423236
- **HEALTH MINISTRY (THE)**, 16 High Street, **CHRISTCHURCH**, BH23 1AY
(T) 01202 471152
- **HEALTHCARE**, 227 Ashley Road, **POOLE**, BH14 9DS
(T) 01202 730555
- **HELEN'S WHOLEFOOD STORE**, 61 St Mary Street, **WEYMOUTH**, DT4 8PP
(T) 01305 777261
- **HELIANTHE HEALTH FOODS**, 14 Bell Street, **SHAFTESBURY**, SP7 8AE
(T) 01747 853555
- **HOLLAND & BARRETT**, 14 Market Place, **BLANDFORD FORUM**, DT11 7EB
(T) 01258 450661
- **HOLLAND & BARRETT**, 23 The Arcade, **BOURNEMOUTH**, BH1 2AF
(T) 01202 297713
- **HOLLAND & BARRETT**, 33 St Mary Street, **WEYMOUTH**, DT4 8PN
(T) 01305 766485
- **HOLLAND & BARRETT**, 54 South Street, **DORCHESTER**, DT1 1DQ
(T) 01305 251857
- **JULIAN GRAVES LTD**, 213 High Street, **POOLE**, BH15 1BY
(T) 01202 678802
- **JULIAN GRAVES LTD**, Tudor Arcade, South Street, **DORCHESTER**, DT1 1BN
(T) 01305 257934
- **JULIAN GRAVES LTD**, Unit 22/Sovereign Centre, Christchurch Road, **BOURNEMOUTH**, BH1 4SX
(T) 01202 395729
- **LYME GREEN WHOLEFOODS**, 57-58 Broad Street, **LYME REGIS**, DT7 3QF
(T) 01297 444936
- **MASONS**, 12 Dunyeats Road, **BROADSTONE**, BH18 8AG
(T) 01202 693935
- **MASONS HEALTH FOODS**, 1585 Wimborne Road, **BOURNEMOUTH**, BH10 7BB
(T) 01202 594700
- **MOORDOWN ALOE VERA PRODUCTS**, 48 King Edward Avenue, **BOURNEMOUTH**, BH9 1TZ
(T) 01202 522983
- **NATURALIFE**, 18 Antelope Walk, **DORCHESTER**, DT1 1BE
(T) 01305 250110
- **NATURALIFE WHOLEFOODS**, 22 South Street, **BRIDPORT**, DT6 3NQ
(T) 01308 459690
- **PERFORMANCE FOODS**, 228 Holdenhurst Road, **BOURNEMOUTH**, BH8 8AX
(T) 01202 391275
- **PURBECK WHOLEFOODS**, 37 North Street, **WAREHAM**, BH20 4AD
(T) 01929 552332
- **RAINBOW BRIDGE CENTRE (THE)**, 19 Trinity Road, **WEYMOUTH**, DT4 8TJ
(T) 01305 775552
- **REAL MEAT CO (THE)**, 14 Bournemouth Road, **POOLE**, BH14 0ES
(T) 01202 747972
- **SPILL THE BEANS**, 6a West Street, **WIMBORNE**, BH21 1JN
(T) 01202 888989
- **SUN COTTAGE**, Unit 7 Hybris Business Park, Crossways, **DORCHESTER**, DT2 8BF
(T) 01305 854540
- **SUNFRUIT INTERNATIONAL**, 147 Rosemary Road, **POOLE**, BH12 3HE
(T) 01202 730234
- **WINTON HEALTH FOODS**, 33 Withermoor Road, **BOURNEMOUTH**, BH9 2NU
(T) 01202 527871

## ESSEX

- **ABBEY HEALTH FOODS**, 3 Sun Street, **WALTHAM ABBEY**, EN9 1ER
(T) 01992 650014
- **ALL NATURAL**, 27 Pier Avenue, **CLACTON-ON-SEA**, CO15 1QE
(T) 01255 435629
- **BVS CORAL CARLO LTD**, 17 Burlescoombe Road, **SOUTHEND-ON-SEA**, SS1 3QG
(T) 01702 589855
- **CAPITAL CLIFF LTD**, P O Box 4444, **EPPING**, CM16 7BY
(T) 01279 414787
- **CHIGWELL HEALTH FOODS**, 5 Brook Parade, High Road, **CHIGWELL**, IG7 6PB
(T) 020 8501 0222
- **CHINESE HERB HEALTH CENTRE**, 105 Cranbrook Road, **ILFORD**, IG1 4PU
(T) 020 8478 8808
- **CORNFLOWER WHOLEFOODS**, 49 High Street, Brightlingsea, **COLCHESTER**, CO7 0AQ
(T) 01206 306679
- **D & A HEALTH & PET FOODS**, 94 Connaught Avenue, **FRINTON-ON-SEA**, CO13 9PT
(T) 01255 679603
- **DOUBLE DRAGON**, 4 Tring Cl, **ILFORD**, IG2 7LQ
(T) 020 8554 3848
- **FOOD BOX (THE)**, 72 Station Parade, **BARKING**, IG11 8EA
(T) 020 8594 8354
- **FOOD FOR THOUGHT**, 4 Cameron Road, **ILFORD**, IG3 8LA
(T) 020 8597 4388
- **GLENS HEALTH FOODS**, 20 New London Road, **CHELMSFORD**, CM2 0SW
(T) 01245 350881

- **GREENS**, 37 Rectory Grove, **LEIGH-ON-SEA**, SS9 2HA
(T) 01702 475338
- **GRIFFINS WEIGH**, 18 Short Wyre Street, **COLCHESTER**, CO1 1LN
(T) 01206 545386
- **HEALTH LINE**, 32 Corbets Tey Road, **UPMINSTER**, RM14 2AD
(T) 01708 220495
- **HEALTHY LIVING**, 31 Newland Street, **WITHAM**, CM8 2AF
(T) 01376 520374
- **HERBAL INN**, 35a The Meadows, **CHELMSFORD**, CM2 6FD
(T) 01245 266128
- **HERBALIFE INDEPENDENT DISTRIBUTOR**, 21 Natal Road, **ILFORD**, IG1 2HA
(T) 020 8514 4350
- **HOLLAND & BARRETT**, 1 Broad Walk, **HARLOW**, CM20 1HX
(T) 01279 437166
- **HOLLAND & BARRETT**, 11 Station Road, **CLACTON-ON-SEA**, CO15 1TD
(T) 01255 435551
- **HOLLAND & BARRETT**, 25 King Street, **SAFFRON WALDEN**, CB10 1EU
(T) 01799 516736
- **HOLLAND & BARRETT**, 250 Thurrock Lakeside Shopping Centre, West Thurrock, **GRAYS**, RM20 2ZG
(T) 01708 869226
- **HOLLAND & BARRETT**, 285 High Road, **LOUGHTON**, IG10 1AH
(T) 020 8508 4009
- **HOLLAND & BARRETT**, 42 Eastgate Centre, **BASILDON**, SS14 1AE
(T) 01268 282084
- **HOLLAND & BARRETT**, 4-5 Exchange Way, **CHELMSFORD**, CM1 1XB
(T) 01245 258748
- **HOLLAND & BARRETT**, 5 Priory Walk, **COLCHESTER**, CO1 1LG
(T) 01206 369129
- **HOLLAND & BARRETT**, 52 Cranbrook Road, **ILFORD**, IG1 4NF
(T) 020 8553 2808
- **HOLLAND & BARRETT**, 55a High Street, **RAYLEIGH**, SS6 7EW
(T) 01268 779249
- **HOLLAND & BARRETT**, 6 The Mall, **GRAYS**, RM17 6QE
(T) 01375 387357
- **HOLLAND & BARRETT**, 7 Pelhams Lane, **COLCHESTER**, CO1 1JT
(T) 01206 546009
- **HOLLAND & BARRETT**, 9 Chapel High, **BRENTWOOD**, CM14 4BX
(T) 01277 210478
- **HOLLAND & BARRETT**, 9 Southchurch Road, **SOUTHEND-ON-SEA**, SS1 2NE
(T) 01702 615415
- **HOLLAND & BARRETT**, Unit 17 Laurie Walk, **ROMFORD**, RM1 3RT
(T) 01708 722349
- **JULIAN GRAVES LTD**, Unit 38 Harvey Centre, **HARLOW**, CM20 1XP
(T) 01279 451000
- **KEY ELEMENTS INTERNATIONAL LTD**, Unit 24, Buckingham Square, **WICKFORD**, SS11 8YQ
(T) 01268 761902
- **LIFESTYLES EURO**, 1 Sable Court, Sylvan Way, Laindon, **BASILDON**, SS15 6TU
(T) 01268 548969
- **MAGKEN (SERVICES) LTD**, 278-280 London Road, **WESTCLIFF-ON-SEA**, SS0 7JG
(T) 01702 351341
- **MAN SHUEN HONG LONDON**, 4 Tring Close, **ILFORD**, IG2 7LQ
(T) 020 8554 3838
- **NATURAL FOODS**, 27 Sir Isaacs Walk, **COLCHESTER**, CO1 1JJ
(T) 01206 542844
- **NATURAL WAY (THE)**, 14 New Street, **BRAINTREE**, CM7 1ES
(T) 01376 329009
- **NATURES TABLE**, 8 The Walk, 128a High Street, **BILLERICAY**, CM12 9YB
(T) 01277 655444
- **ORCHID NUTRICARE LTD**, Haven Quay, Haven Road, **COLCHESTER**, CO2 8JE
(T) 01206 798845
- **ORCHID NUTRICARE LTD**, Haven Quay, Haven Road, **COLCHESTER**, CO2 8XX
(T) 01206 798844
- **PILGRIMS NATURAL**, 4 King Georges Place, **MALDON**, CM9 5BZ
(T) 01621 858605
- **RAW NUTRITION**, 16 Hepburn Cl, Chafford Hundred, **GRAYS**, RM16 6LZ
(T) 01375 483767
- **SHENFIELD HEALTH**, 27 Hutton Road, Shenfield, **BRENTWOOD**, CM15 8JU
(T) 01277 260739
- **SUNRISE HEALTH FOODS**, 31 Spa Road, **HOCKLEY**, SS5 4PH
(T) 01702 207017
- **SUNSHINE WHOLE FOODS**, 3 Hernshaw, Herongate, **BRENTWOOD**, CM13 3PE
(T) 01277 812161
- **SYNERGY SALES GROUP**, Rivendell House, Queens Road, West Bergholt, **COLCHESTER**, CO6 3HE
(T) 01206 240000
- **T M HEALTH SHOP**, 348 London Road, **WESTCLIFF-ON-SEA**, SS0 7JJ
(T) 01702 335327
- **UK HEALTH PRODUCTS**, 6 Sussex Road, **COLCHESTER**, CO3 3QH
(T) 01206 710851
- **VITAMIN FACTORY (THE)**, P O Box 5880, **BASILDON**, SS14 3GH
(T) 07071 780079
- **VIVENDI HEALTH CARE DIRECT**, Logan House, 110 Church Road, Tiptree, **COLCHESTER**, CO5 0AB
(T) 01621 810995
- **WAYLAND HEALTHCARE PRODUCTS**, 266 Harwich Road, Little Clacton, **CLACTON-ON-SEA**, CO16 9PX
(T) 01255 862090
- **WICKFORD HEALTH STORE**, 15 The Broadway, **WICKFORD**, SS11 7AD
(T) 01268 733710

## GLOUCESTERSHIRE

- **BROADBENT GRANARY WHOLEFOODS**, Market Square, **NEWENT**, GL18 1PS
(T) 01531 821922
- **CHELTENHAM NUTRITION CENTRE**, 133 Bath Road, **CHELTENHAM**, GL53 7LT
(T) 01242 514150
- **CHELTENHAM NUTRITION CENTRE**, 28 Winchcombe Street, **CHELTENHAM**, GL52 2LX
(T) 01242 529934
- **COTSWOLD NATURAL FOOD STORE**, 30 Long Street, **WOTTON-UNDER-EDGE**, GL12 7BT
(T) 01453 844424
- **FOREST HEALTH FOODS**, Bridge House, Newerne Street, **LYDNEY**, GL15 5RF
(T) 01594 843498
- **G R LANE**, Sisson Road, **GLOUCESTER**, GL1 3QB
(T) 01452 524012
- **GREEN SHOP (THE)**, Bisley, **STROUD**, GL6 7BX
(T) 01452 770629
- **HARVEST HOME**, Fountain Street, Nailsworth, **STROUD**, GL6 0BL
(T) 01453 832986
- **HOLEHEARTED**, 48 High Street, **STONEHOUSE**, GL10 2NA
(T) 01453 826521
- **HOLLAND & BARRETT**, 20 Regent Arcade, Regent Street, **CHELTENHAM**, GL50 1JZ
(T) 01242 528749
- **HOLLAND & BARRETT**, 24 Cricklade Street, **CIRENCESTER**, GL7 1JH
(T) 01285 641068
- **HOLLAND & BARRETT**, 3 St Michaels Buildings, Eastgate Street, **GLOUCESTER**, GL1 1PD
(T) 01452 311281
- **INTRA DISTRIBUTOR**, Frocester Farm, Peter Street, Frocester, **STONEHOUSE**, GL10 3TQ
(T) 01453 821508
- **JULIAN GRAVES LTD**, Beechwood Place Shopping Centre, High Street, **CHELTENHAM**, GL50 1DQ
(T) 01242 254849
- **JUST WHOLEFOODS**, Unit 16 Cirencester Business Estate, Love Lane, **CIRENCESTER**, GL7 1YG
(T) 01285 651910
- **MOTHER NATURE**, 2 Bedford Street, **STROUD**, GL5 1AY
(T) 01453 758202
- **NATURES WAY**, 69 Cricklade Street, **CIRENCESTER**, GL7 1HY
(T) 01285 651360
- **ORIGINAL CANDY CO (THE)**, Units 14-15 Horcott Industrial Estate, Horcott Road, **FAIRFORD**, GL7 4BX
(T) 01285 711227
- **PROTEC HEALTH INTERNATIONAL LTD**, P O Box 137, **CIRENCESTER**, GL7 5YW
(T) 01285 715120
- **SPRING FINE FOODS (WESTERN) LTD**, Spring Fine Foods, Nash Lane, Abbeymead, **GLOUCESTER**, GL4 4SD
(T) 01452 720175
- **SUNSHINE HEALTH SHOP**, 25 Church Street, **STROUD**, GL5 1JL
(T) 01453 763923
- **TEWKESBURY NUTRITION CENTRE**, 98 High Street, **TEWKESBURY**, GL20 5JZ
(T) 01684 299620
- **W E ANDERTON**, 4 College Court, **GLOUCESTER**, GL1 2NJ
(T) 01452 414808
- **WHOLEFOOD SHOP (THE)**, The Square, Stow on the Wold, **CHELTENHAM**, GL54 1AF
(T) 01451 832194
- **WYEDEAN WHOLEFOODS**, 13 Market Street, **CINDERFORD**, GL14 2SD
(T) 01594 825455
- **WYEDEAN WHOLEFOODS**, 15 Market Place, **COLEFORD**, GL16 8AW
(T) 01594 810303
- **WYEDEAN WHOLEFOODS**, 18 Newerne Street, **LYDNEY**, GL15 5RF
(T) 01594 841907
- **ZEBRA WHOLEFOODS**, 306 High Street, **CHELTENHAM**, GL50 3JF
(T) 01242 241070

## HAMPSHIRE

- **AIRCOM HEALTH & NUTRITION**, Clarendon Court, Over Wallop, **STOCKBRIDGE**, SO20 8HU
(T) 01264 782174
- **ALOE VERA CENTRE**, 1 Cortina Way, Hedge End, **SOUTHAMPTON**, SO30 0JJ
(T) 01489 691266
- **ARROWMED LTD**, Alderney House, 58 Normandy Street, **ALTON**, GU34 1DE
(T) 01420 544424
- **AVON WINES & WHOLEFOODS**, 10 High Street, **FORDINGBRIDGE**, SP6 1AX
(T) 01425 652258
- **BARNYARD FOODS**, 49-51A West Street, **ALRESFORD**, SO24 9AU
(T) 01962 733187
- **BEANIE'S**, 77B High Street, **FAREHAM**, PO16 7AW
(T) 01329 822916
- **BENNETT GROUP (THE)**, Churchill House, Jubilee Road, **WATERLOOVILLE**, PO7 7RF
(T) 023 9225 3424
- **BRAN TUB (THE)**, 20 Lavant Street, **PETERSFIELD**, GU32 3EW
(T) 01730 267043
- **G N C LIVEWELL**, 48a Kingswell Path, Cascades Centre, **PORTSMOUTH**, PO1 4RR
(T) 023 9285 1552
- **HAVANT HEALTH FOOD STORE**, 7 North Street Arcade, **HAVANT**, PO9 1PX
(T) 023 9247 5736
- **HAYLING HEALTH FOODS**, 20 Mengham Road, **HAYLING ISLAND**, PO11 9BL
(T) 023 9246 0047

- **HEALTH & DIET CENTRE**, 419 Shirley Road, **SOUTHAMPTON**, SO15 3JF (T) 023 8077 6279
- **HEALTH & DIET CENTRES LTD**, 14 East Street, **SOUTHAMPTON**, SO14 3HE (T) 023 8063 4680
- **HEALTH & DIET CENTRES LTD**, 7 Wellington Way, **WATERLOOVILLE**, PO7 7ED (T) 023 9226 6822
- **HEALTH GARDEN (THE)**, 38 Mengham Road, **HAYLING ISLAND**, PO11 9BL (T) 023 9264 8390
- **HEALTH SHOP (THE)**, 113a Stoke Road, **GOSPORT**, PO12 1LR (T) 023 9258 3201
- **HELANBECK PROVISIONS**, 6a High Street, Hythe, **SOUTHAMPTON**, SO45 6AH (T) 023 8084 7987
- **HERBAL LIFE DISTRIBUTION**, 33 Carmarthen Avenue, **PORTSMOUTH**, PO6 2AG (T) 023 9237 0559
- **HERBALIFE**, 58 Dover Street, **SOUTHAMPTON**, SO14 6GL (T) 023 8033 3054
- **HERBALIFE DISTRIBUTOR**, 55 Woodlands Road, Baughurst, **TADLEY**, RG26 5NS (T) 01189 811775
- **HERBALIFE INDEPENDENT DISTRIBUTOR**, Green Acre, Hatchet Green, Hale, **FORDINGBRIDGE**, SP6 2NB (T) 01725 513452
- **HOLLAND & BARRETT**, 10 Kingsmead, **FARNBOROUGH**, GU14 7SL (T) 01252 543638
- **HOLLAND & BARRETT**, 118 High Street, **GOSPORT**, PO12 1DU (T) 023 9258 9948
- **HOLLAND & BARRETT**, 17 Mayfair House, Town Centre, **BASINGSTOKE**, RG21 7JT (T) 01256 346170
- **HOLLAND & BARRETT**, 18 East Street, **SOUTHAMPTON**, SO14 3HG (T) 023 8021 1859
- **HOLLAND & BARRETT**, 19 The Swan Centre, **EASTLEIGH**, SO50 5SG (T) 023 8061 4789
- **HOLLAND & BARRETT**, 233 Fleet Road, **FLEET**, GU13 8BN (T) 01252 625671
- **HOLLAND & BARRETT**, 240 Commercial Road, **PORTSMOUTH**, PO1 1HG (T) 023 9282 5416
- **HOLLAND & BARRETT**, 33 High Street, **WINCHESTER**, SO23 9BL (T) 01962 843194
- **HOLLAND & BARRETT**, 34 Union Street, **ALDERSHOT**, GU11 1EW (T) 01252 336684
- **HOLLAND & BARRETT**, 41 Chantry Centre, Service Yard, **ANDOVER**, SP10 1RL (T) 01264 335075
- **HOLLAND & BARRETT**, 55 Osborn Mall, **FAREHAM**, PO16 0PW (T) 01329 239641
- **HOLLAND & BARRETT**, 63 Osborne Road, **SOUTHSEA**, PO5 3LS (T) 023 9282 2662
- **HOLLAND & BARRETT**, 9 Westbrook Walk, **ALTON**, GU34 1HZ (T) 01420 82260
- **HONEYSUCKLE SNACKS LTD**, The Croft, Foreman Road, Ash Green, **ALDERSHOT**, GU12 6HD (T) 01252 315639
- **INTERHEALTH**, 21 Sandhurst Lane, Blackwater, **CAMBERLEY**, GU17 0DQ (T) 01252 890083
- **JULIAN GRAVES LTD**, 18 Rams Walk, **PETERSFIELD**, GU32 3JA (T) 01730 264056
- **JULIAN GRAVES LTD**, 28 Wellington Centre, **ALDERSHOT**, GU11 1DB (T) 01252 329946
- **JULIAN GRAVES LTD**, 55 Cascades, **PORTSMOUTH**, PO1 4RJ (T) 023 9287 4719
- **JULIAN GRAVES LTD**, Chantry Centre, Service Yard, **ANDOVER**, SP10 1RL (T) 01264 337891
- **LABHUC HEALTH SERVICES**, 95 Barton Court Avenue, Barton-on-sea, **NEW MILTON**, BH25 7E (T) 01425 899176
- **MANNATECH LTD**, Pinewood, Chineham, **BASINGSTOKE**, RG24 8AL (T) 01256 698001
- **NATURAL HEALTH CO (THE)**, 7 Albion Place, Hartley Wintney, **HOOK**, RG27 8RL (T) 01252 844943
- **NATURALLY HEALTH FOODS**, 5 Waterloo Court, **ANDOVER**, SP10 1QJ (T) 01264 332375
- **NEW FOREST ORGANICS**, 31 Carrington Lane, Milford on Sea, **LYMINGTON**, SO41 0RA (T) 01590 641395
- **ORD RIVER TEA TREE OIL PTY LTD**, Cedar Suite, Winchester Road, **ALRESFORD**, SO24 9EZ (T) 01962 734080
- **PEPPERCORN NATURAL FOODS**, 11 Latimer Street, **ROMSEY**, SO51 8DF (T) 01794 513499
- **PITTMANS HEALTHY OPTIONS**, 63 High Street, **LYNDHURST**, SO43 7BE (T) 023 8028 4174
- **SCOLTOCKS NATURAL FOODS**, 1a Market Place, **RINGWOOD**, BH24 1AN (T) 01425 473787
- **SCOLTOCKS NATURAL FOODS**, 35 Station Road, **NEW MILTON**, BH25 6HR (T) 01425 619090
- **SESAME HEALTH STORE**, 26 The Square, **LIPHOOK**, GU30 7AH (T) 01428 722188
- **SOUTHSEA HEALTH SHOP**, 241 Albert Road, **SOUTHSEA**, PO4 0JR (T) 023 9275 3458
- **SPICE OF LIFE**, 3 Bemisters Lane, **GOSPORT**, PO12 1HB (T) 023 9250 1912
- **SUNRIDER INDEPENDANT DISTRIBUTOR**, 242 Avondale, Ash Vale, **ALDERSHOT**, GU12 5NQ (T) 01252 524516
- **SWEET JOE PYE**, 31 St Thomas Street, **LYMINGTON**, SO41 9NE (T) 01590 672931
- **TIME FOR CHANGE**, 167 Fawcett Road, **SOUTHSEA**, PO4 0DH (T) 023 9281 8786
- **V I P DIRECT NUTRITION LTD**, 22 Whitefield Road, **NEW MILTON**, BH25 6DF (T) 01425 611000
- **VITAL INGREDIENTS (THE)**, 67 Bedford Place, **SOUTHAMPTON**, SO15 2DS (T) 023 8033 7139
- **VITALITY HEALTH FOODS**, 29 Wote Street, **BASINGSTOKE**, RG21 7NE (T) 01256 364904
- **WINCHESTER HEALTH FOOD CENTRE**, 41 Jewry Street, **WINCHESTER**, SO23 8RY (T) 01962 851113

## HEREFORDSHIRE

- **ESKLEY SHEEP MILK SUPPLIES**, Llanbaddon, Michaelchurch Escley, **HEREFORD**, HR2 0PR (T) 01981 510294
- **FODDER WHOLEFOODS**, 26-27 Church Street, **HEREFORD**, HR1 2LR (T) 01432 358171
- **GEORGE'S**, 25 High Street, **KINGTON**, HR5 3AX (T) 01544 231400
- **GRAVES JULIAN LTD**, Flat 1/Maylord Orchards, Gomond Street, **HEREFORD**, HR1 2DA (T) 01432 275599
- **HARVESTORE HEALTH FOODS**, 47 Eign Gate, **HEREFORD**, HR4 0AB (T) 01432 268209
- **HERBAL LIFE**, Unit 6 Hatton Gardens Industrial Estate, **KINGTON**, HR5 3RB (T) 01544 230699
- **HERBALIFE INDEPENDENT DISTRIBUTOR**, The Cottage, Sunset Yard, Sunset, **KINGTON**, HR5 3RF (T) 01544 231425
- **HOLLAND & BARRETT**, 8 High Street, **LEOMINSTER**, HR6 8LZ (T) 01568 615455
- **LEDBURY WHOLEFOODS**, 82 The Homend, **LEDBURY**, HR8 1BX (T) 01531 632889
- **NITTY GRITTY WHOLEFOODS**, 24 West Street, **LEOMINSTER**, HR6 8ES (T) 01568 611600
- **RODETTE INTERNATIONAL LTD**, The Rhos, Hillhampton Lane, Shobdon, **LEOMINSTER**, HR6 9NE (T) 01568 708731
- **SALAD BOWL (THE)**, 30 Union Street, **HEREFORD**, HR1 2BT (T) 01432 355712
- **SURVIVAL FOODS**, Units 1-2 Cobnash Industrial Estate, Kingsland, **LEOMINSTER**, HR6 9RW (T) 01568 708344

## HERTFORDSHIRE

- **A C M TRADING**, 73B High Street, Stotfold, **HITCHIN**, SG5 4LD (T) 01462 733405
- **A W ENTERPRISES**, 2/Horwood Cottages, Back Lane, Letchmore Heath, **WATFORD**, WD2 8EH (T) 01923 853431
- **CLARE JAMES**, 13a Hempstead Road, **KINGS LANGLEY**, WD4 8BJ (T) 01923 263195
- **CROFT NATURAL HEALTH**, 16a High Street, **HITCHIN**, SG5 1AT (T) 01462 436881
- **DOWN TO EARTH WHOLEFOODS**, 7 Amwell End, **WARE**, SG12 9HP (T) 01920 463358
- **EXTREME MUSCLE & FITNESS**, 13a London Road, **ST. ALBANS**, AL1 1LA (T) 01727 854485
- **FAIRHAVEN WHOLEFOODS LTD**, 27 Jubilee Trade Centre, Jubilee Road, **LETCHWORTH**, SG6 1SP (T) 01462 675300
- **FOREVER LIVING PRODUCTS**, Little Hyde Hall, Hatfield Heath Road, **SAWBRIDGEWORTH**, CM21 9HX (T) 01279 725845
- **FULL OF BEANS**, 2 Church Street, **SAWBRIDGEWORTH**, CM21 9AB (T) 01279 726002
- **GARNELL CORPORATION**, 13a London Road, **ST. ALBANS**, AL1 1LA (T) 01727 842222
- **GLUTEN FREE FOODS**, Unit 270/Centennial Pk, Centennial Avenue, Elstree, **BOREHAMWOOD**, WD6 3SS (T) 020 8952 0052
- **GOOD FOOD SHOP**, 4 Old Cross, **HERTFORD**, SG14 1RB (T) 01992 550101
- **GOOD LIVING**, 8 Pinnocks Lane, **BALDOCK**, SG7 6DS (T) 01462 896421
- **GRAINS HEALTH FOOD SHOP**, 25 Market Place, **HATFIELD**, AL10 0LJ (T) 01707 274912
- **HARMONY**, 53 High Street, **TRING**, HP23 5AG (T) 01442 822311
- **HEALTHY & WISE ORGANIC CENTRE**, 84 High Street, **HARPENDEN**, AL5 2SP (T) 01582 761435
- **HERBALFE DISTRIBUTOR**, 62 Westerdale, **HEMEL HEMPSTEAD**, HP2 5TJ (T) 01442 402292
- **HERBALIFE**, 42 Furlong Way, Great Amwell, **WARE**, SG12 9TE (T) 01920 468387
- **HERBALIFE**, 6a Hermitage Road, **HITCHIN**, SG5 1BS (T) 01462 456111

- **HERBALIFE**, Watford Road, **ST. ALBANS**, AL2 3JZ
(T) 01727 768321
- **HERBALIFE DISTRIBUTOR**, 6 Scrubbitts Park Road, **RADLETT**, WD7 8JP
(T) 01923 853476
- **HERBALIFE DISTRIBUTOR**, 95 River Meads, Stanstead Abbotts, **WARE**, SG12 8EL
(T) 01920 877667
- **HOLLAND & BARRETT**, 11 Leys Avenue, **LETCHWORTH**, SG6 3EA
(T) 01462 678289
- **HOLLAND & BARRETT**, 12a South Street, **BISHOP'S STORTFORD**, CM23 3AT
(T) 01279 651637
- **HOLLAND & BARRETT**, 13 French Row, **ST. ALBANS**, AL3 5DU
(T) 01727 866562
- **HOLLAND & BARRETT**, 187 Marlowes, **HEMEL HEMPSTEAD**, HP1 1BB
(T) 01442 211356
- **HOLLAND & BARRETT**, 19a Town Square, **STEVENAGE**, SG1 1BP
(T) 01438 351417
- **HOLLAND & BARRETT**, 25-27 Bircherley Green, **HERTFORD**, SG14 1BN
(T) 01992 504751
- **HOLLAND & BARRETT**, 54 Howardsgate, **WELWYN GARDEN CITY**, AL8 6BP
(T) 01707 376285
- **HOLLAND & BARRETT**, 6 Angel Pavement, **ROYSTON**, SG8 9AS
(T) 01763 249468
- **HOLLAND & BARRETT**, 65 The Parade, High Street, **WATFORD**, WD1 1LJ
(T) 01923 221602
- **HOLLAND & BARRETT**, 94 Hermitage Road, **HITCHIN**, SG5 1DG
(T) 01462 451643
- **HOLLAND & BARRETT**, Unit 44 Queensway, **STEVENAGE**, SG1 1BA
(T) 01438 727749
- **HYGIENE & PROTECTION CO LTD**, 1 Danesbury Pk Danesbury Pk Road, **WELWYN**, AL6 9SA
(T) 01438 840542
- **JULIAN GRAVES LTD**, The Galleria, Comet Way, **HATFIELD**, AL10 0XR
(T) 01707 276386
- **METRO HEALTH STORE & CLINIC**, 13 Leeming Road, **BOREHAMWOOD**, WD6 4EB
(T) 020 8386 6696
- **MOCWUR ASSOCIATES**, 4 Pages Croft, **BERKHAMSTED**, HP4 1BX
(T) 01494 896701
- **NATURAL CONNECTION LTD**, 21 Sleapcross Gardens, Smallford, **ST. ALBANS**, AL4 0RX
(T) 01727 821721
- **NATURAL HEALTH CO (INTERNATIONAL) LTD (THE)**, The Maltings, Bridge Street, **HITCHIN**, SG5 2DE
(T) 01462 436777
- **NATURAL HEALTH PRODUCTS**, Unit 11 Wedgwood Court, Wedgwood Way, **STEVENAGE**, SG1 4QR
(T) 01438 222244
- **NATURAL WAY (THE)**, 15 Florence Walk, North Street, **BISHOP'S STORTFORD**, CM23 2NZ
(T) 01279 465850
- **NEW OUTLOOK**, The Maltings, Roydon Road, Stanstead Abbotts, **WARE**, SG12 8HG
(T) 01920 877877
- **OASIS WHOLEFOODS**, 112 High Street, **RICKMANSWORTH**, WD3 1AQ
(T) 01923 896600
- **PERFORMANCE BEVERAGES LTD**, Conbar House, Mead Lane, **HERTFORD**, SG13 7AP
(T) 01992 535077
- **POTTERS BAR HEALTH FOODS**, 21 The Broadway, Darkes Lane, **POTTERS BAR**, EN6 2HX
(T) 01707 652255
- **SOJO PRODUCTS LTD**, Audley House, North Bridge Road, **BERKHAMSTED**, HP4 1EH
(T) 01442 255569
- **SOLGAR VITAMINS & HERBS**, Aldbury, **TRING**, HP23 5PT
(T) 01442 890355
- **SYCAMORE WHOLEFOODS**, 214C Hatfield Road, **ST. ALBANS**, AL1 4LW
(T) 01727 855401
- **TAYLOR JACKSON HEALTH PRODUCTS**, Orchard Villa, Porters Park Drive, Shenley, **RADLETT**, WD7 9DS
(T) 01923 853111
- **TONTUP & CO**, 4 Pages Croft, **BERKHAMSTED**, HP4 1BX
(T) 01494 896701
- **VICTORIA HEALTHFOODS**, 137 The Harlequin, **WATFORD**, WD1 2TL
(T) 01923 227297
- **WHOLISTIC RESEARCH CO LTD**, The Old Forge, Mill Green, **HATFIELD**, AL9 5NZ
(T) 01707 262686

## HUMBERSIDE (NORTH)

- **BRIDLINGTON HEALTH FOOD STORE**, 10a Manor Street, **BRIDLINGTON**, YO15 2SA
(T) 01262 601867
- **FOOD FOR THOUGHT**, 550 Holderness Road, **HULL**, HU9 3ES
(T) 01482 711192
- **HERON JOHN H LTD**, 145 Boothferry Road, **GOOLE**, DN14 6NB
(T) 01405 764271
- **HOLLAND & BARRETT**, 47 King Street, **BRIDLINGTON**, YO15 2DB
(T) 01262 676006
- **JULIAN GRAVES LTD**, Unit 18 The Promenades Shopping Centre, **BRIDLINGTON**, YO15 2DX
(T) 01262 608058
- **PEPPERCORN**, 89 Pasture Road, **GOOLE**, DN14 6BP
(T) 01405 769875
- **PEPPERCORN 84**, 11 Railway Street, Pocklington, **YORK**, YO42 2QR
(T) 01759 303275
- **POWER HEALTH PRODUCTS LTD**, Airfield Industrial Estate, Pocklington, **YORK**, YO42 1NR
(T) 01759 302595
- **SEVEN SEAS LTD**, Hedon Road, **HULL**, HU9 5NJ
(T) 01482 375234

## HUMBERSIDE (SOUTH)

- **HEALTH RACK**, Friargate, Freshney Place, **GRIMSBY**, DN31 1ED
(T) 01472 340938
- **HOLLAND & BARRETT**, 61 Friargate, Freshney Place, **GRIMSBY**, DN31 1QQ
(T) 01472 344115
- **HOLTON HEALTH PRODUCTS**, Unit 2 Louth Road, Holton-le-Clay, **GRIMSBY**, DN36 5YN
(T) 01472 824444
- **JULIAN GRAVES LTD**, 2-4 Flottergate Mall, **GRIMSBY**, DN31 1QX
(T) 01472 353327
- **LEMVEJ HERBAL**, 17 Station Avenue, New Waltham, **GRIMSBY**, DN36 4Q
(T) 01472 309176
- **ORIENTAL SPICES**, 189 Freeman Street, **GRIMSBY**, DN32 7AS
(T) 01472 241130

## ISLE OF MAN

- **BIO-MONDE PREPARATIONS LTD**, Unit C1-C2 Balthane Industrial Estate, Balthane, **BALLASALLA**, IM9 2AG
(T) 01624 827580
- **CASTLETOWN HEALTH STORE**, 21 Malew Street, **CASTLETOWN**, IM9 1AD
(T) 01624 825812
- **HOLLAND & BARRETT LTD**, Unit 2, 26-30 Strand Street, **DOUGLAS**, IM1 2EG
(T) 01624 676527
- **ISLE OF MAN HEALTH FOOD CENTRE**, 90 Bucks Road, **DOUGLAS**, IM1 3AG
(T) 01624 675647
- **MAYLIN B**, Bay View Road, **PORT ST. MARY**, IM9 5AL
(T) 01624 836966
- **MOTHER NATURE**, 42 Parliament Street, **RAMSEY**, IM8 1AN
(T) 01624 815118

## ISLE OF WIGHT

- **COWES HEALTH FOODS**, 8 High Street, **COWES**, PO31 7RZ
(T) 01983 282070
- **HEALTHY OPTIONS**, Tacloban, Main Road, Arreton, **NEWPORT**, PO30 3AD
(T) 01983 530230
- **HOLLAND & BARRETT**, 1 High Street, **RYDE**, PO33 2PN
(T) 01983 565257
- **HOLLAND & BARRETT**, 52 St James Street, **NEWPORT**, PO30 1LQ
(T) 01983 522121
- **RALPHS HEALTH FOODS**, 64-65 St James Street, **NEWPORT**, PO30 1LQ
(T) 01983 522353
- **SHANKLIN HEALTH STORE**, 25 High Street, **SHANKLIN**, PO37 6JW
(T) 01983 863063
- **WEST WIGHT WHOLE FOODS**, Clarence Buildings, Avenue Road, **FRESHWATER**, PO40 9UU
(T) 01983 754891

## KENT

- **ADVANCE NUTRITION**, 14 Mount Pleasant Road, **TUNBRIDGE WELLS**, TN1 1QU
(T) 01892 515927
- **ADVANCE NUTRITION LTD**, 14 Mount Pleasant Road, **TUNBRIDGE WELLS**, TN1 1QU
(T) 01892 515927
- **ALL THE BEST HEALTH FOOD**, 16 The Broadway, **BROADSTAIRS**, CT10 2AD
(T) 01843 604408
- **ALLIED HEALTH**, Medway House, Medway Street, **MAIDSTONE**, ME14 1JS
(T) 01622 750770
- **ALOE VERA**, 4, Coppings Brook Cottages, Leigh, **TONBRIDGE**, TN11 8PP
(T) 01732 741454
- **ALOE VERA & BEE PRODUCTS**, 22 Evans Road, Willesborough, **ASHFORD**, TN24 0UA
(T) 01233 643034
- **BEDROCK SUPPLIES**, 68 West Street, **SITTINGBOURNE**, ME10 1AR
(T) 01795 422465
- **BEE NATURAL PRODUCTS (UK) LTD**, 26 Beacon Road, **BROADSTAIRS**, CT10 3DF
(T) 01227 720881
- **CANTERBURY NUTRITION CENTRE**, 2-3 Iron Bar Lane, **CANTERBURY**, CT1 2HN
(T) 01227 788277
- **CANTERBURY WHOLEFOODS**, 10 The Borough, **CANTERBURY**, CT1 2DR
(T) 01227 464623
- **CORNUCOPIA**, 4 High Street, **WHITSTABLE**, CT5 1BQ
(T) 01227 770075
- **DOUG REES**, 4 Coppings Brook Cottages, Leigh, **TONBRIDGE**, TN11 8PP
(T) 07071 283684
- **DOVER HEALTH FOOD CENTRE**, Unit 16 Charlton Centre, High Street, **DOVER**, CT16 1TS
(T) 01304 210970
- **ECOFLOW INDEPENDENT DISTRIBUTOR**, Idleigh Cottage, Idleigh Ct Road, Meopham, **GRAVESEND**, DA13 0JR
(T) 01474 872942
- **ESPECIALLY HEALTH**, 119 High Street, **SEVENOAKS**, TN13 1UP
(T) 01732 741181
- **FLYNNS BEE FARMS LTD**, Elmley Road, Minster on Sea, **SHEERNESS**, ME12 3SS
(T) 01795 874935
- **FOOD FOR LIVING**, 1 Market Place, **DARTFORD**, DA1 1EX
(T) 01322 278790
- **FOOD FOR LIVING**, 8 Wellington Parade, Blackfen Road, **SIDCUP**, DA15 9NB
(T) 020 8304 3874
- **FOREVER LIVING PRODUCTS**, 25 Southlands Road, **BROMLEY**, BR2 9QR
(T) 020 8313 3506
- **FOREVER LIVING PRODUCTS**, Unit B5 Hillborough Business Park, Sweechbridge Road, **HERNE BAY**, CT6 6TE
(T) 01227 749926

- **FOREVER LIVING PRODUCTS GOUDHURST KENT**, Unit 2/Crown Yard, Bedgebury Road, Goudhurst, **CRANBROOK**, TN17 2QZ
(T) 01580 212322
- **G N C**, 254 The Glades Shopping Centre, High Street, **BROMLEY**, BR1 1DN
(T) 020 8290 5938
- **HARVEST HEALTH FOODS**, 31 Queen Street, **RAMSGATE**, CT11 9DZ
(T) 01843 583135
- **HEALTH HOUSE (THE)**, 116 High Street, **CHATHAM**, ME4 4BY
(T) 01634 409291
- **HEALTH MATTERS**, 34 Chatsworth Parade, **ORPINGTON**, BR5 1DE
(T) 01689 824953
- **HEALTH MATTERS**, 8 Widmore Road, **BROMLEY**, BR1 1SE
(T) 020 8460 3894
- **HEALTH OPTIONS**, 5 Belmont Road, **WHITSTABLE**, CT5 1QJ
(T) 01227 772242
- **HERB & SPICE SHOP**, The Priory Shopping Centre, Westgate Road, **DARTFORD**, DA1 2AR
(T) 01322 228737
- **HERBAL HEALTH LTD**, 39 Earl Street, **MAIDSTONE**, ME14 1PF
(T) 01622 663443
- **HERBAL RESEARCH INTERNATIONAL LTD**, PO Box 60, **TUNBRIDGE WELLS**, TN2 3ZA
(T) 01892 528628
- **HERBALIFE**, Idleigh Cottage, Idleigh Court Road, Meopham, **GRAVESEND**, DA13 0JR
(T) 01474 872363
- **HERBALIFE DISTRIBUTOR**, 72 Sandford Road, **SITTINGBOURNE**, ME10 1PX
(T) 01795 427002
- **HERBALIFE INDEPENDENT DISTRIBUTOR**, 2 Hill Farm Close, High Halstow, **ROCHESTER**, ME3 8SS
(T) 01634 251181
- **HOLLAND & BARRETT**, 10 The Centre, **MARGATE**, CT9 1JG
(T) 01843 228131
- **HOLLAND & BARRETT**, 11 Swanley Centre, **SWANLEY**, BR8 7TG
(T) 01322 666910
- **HOLLAND & BARRETT**, 15 High Street, **RAMSGATE**, CT11 9AB
(T) 01843 852568
- **HOLLAND & BARRETT**, 17 Hempstead Valley Shopping Centre, Hempstead, **GILLINGHAM**, ME7 3PB
(T) 01634 375796
- **HOLLAND & BARRETT**, 19 Calverley Road, **TUNBRIDGE WELLS**, TN1 2TH
(T) 01892 539287
- **HOLLAND & BARRETT**, 203 High Street, **CHATHAM**, ME4 4BG
(T) 01634 830735
- **HOLLAND & BARRETT**, 216 High Street, **BECKENHAM**, BR3 1EN
(T) 020 8650 3562
- **HOLLAND & BARRETT**, 219 High Street, **ORPINGTON**, BR6 0NZ
(T) 01689 874773
- **HOLLAND & BARRETT**, 23 Mount Pleasant Road, **TUNBRIDGE WELLS**, TN1 1NT
(T) 01892 533077
- **HOLLAND & BARRETT**, 27 The Mall, **BEXLEYHEATH**, DA6 7JJ
(T) 020 8298 7930
- **HOLLAND & BARRETT**, 345 Dukes Walk, Chequers Centre, **MAIDSTONE**, ME15 6AS
(T) 01622 765277
- **HOLLAND & BARRETT**, 35 Biggin Street, **DOVER**, CT16 1BU
(T) 01304 241426
- **HOLLAND & BARRETT**, 38 High Street, **DEAL**, CT14 6HE
(T) 01304 371664
- **HOLLAND & BARRETT**, 41 High Street, **CANTERBURY**, CT1 2RY
(T) 01227 787861
- **HOLLAND & BARRETT**, 49 Bellegrove Road, **WELLING**, DA16 3PB
(T) 020 8301 1887
- **HOLLAND & BARRETT**, 56 High Street, **BROMLEY**, BR1 1EG
(T) 020 8460 3883
- **HOLLAND & BARRETT**, 76 High Street, **SHEERNESS**, ME12 1NL
(T) 01795 581097
- **HOLLAND & BARRETT**, 8 Kempthorne Street, St Georges Centre, **GRAVESEND**, DA11 0TA
(T) 01474 321838
- **HOLLAND & BARRETT**, 80 Sandgate Road, **FOLKESTONE**, CT20 2AA
(T) 01303 243646
- **HOLLAND & BARRETT**, 87 High Street, Charing, **ASHFORD**, TN27 0LS
(T) 01233 620392
- **HOLLAND & BARRETT**, 96 High Street, **SITTINGBOURNE**, ME10 4PH
(T) 01795 476664
- **J & B HEALTH FOODS & AROMATICS**, 9 Beckenham Road, **WEST WICKHAM**, BR4 0QR
(T) 020 8777 8721
- **JUST HEALTH**, 49 High Street, **GILLINGHAM**, ME7 1BQ
(T) 01634 851145
- **LAMBERTS HEALTHCARE LTD**, P O Box 1, **TUNBRIDGE WELLS**, TN2 3EQ
(T) 01892 552121
- **LIFESTYLES HEALTHCARE (EUROPE) LTD**, Nevill Estate, Danegate, Eridge Green, **TUNBRIDGE WELLS**, TN3 9JA
(T) 01892 750511
- **LYRICAL HEALTH & BODY CARE**, 60 Pilgrims Way East, Otford, **SEVENOAKS**, TN14 5QW
(T) 01959 522411
- **MICHAEL'S**, Northdown Road, Northdown Industrial Park, St. Peters, **BROADSTAIRS**, CT10 3JP
(T) 01843 604602
- **NATURAL CHOICE**, 106 Mortimer Street, **HERNE BAY**, CT6 5EB
(T) 01227 741887
- **NATURAL DISTRIBUTION**, 11-12 Willesborough Ind Pk, Willesborough, **ASHFORD**, TN24 0TD
(T) 01233 636761
- **NATURAL LIFE**, 66 Grosvenor Road, **TUNBRIDGE WELLS**, TN1 2AS
(T) 01892 543834
- **NATURAL PRODUCT CO (THE)**, 16 Horsley Road, **ROCHESTER**, ME1 1UW
(T) 01634 408491
- **NATURES BEST HEALTH PRODUCTS LTD**, Unit 1, Lamberts Road, **TUNBRIDGE WELLS**, TN2 3EH
(T) 01892 552117
- **NEW DAWN ENTERPRISE**, 118 Gipsy Road, **WELLING**, DA16 1JE
(T) 020 8303 4514
- **NUT STOP**, Castle House, Castle Hill Avenue, **FOLKESTONE**, CT20 2TQ
(T) 01303 246885
- **NUTRALIFE UK LTD**, Omicron House, Fircroft Way, **EDENBRIDGE**, TN8 6EL
(T) 01732 866686
- **ORGANIC HEALTH (CANTERBURY)**, Unit 22 Maynard Road, Wincheap Industrial Estate, **CANTERBURY**, CT1 3RH
(T) 01227 472774
- **PEPPERS**, 115 High Street, **DEAL**, CT14 6BB
(T) 01304 375349
- **PEPPERS HEALTH FOOD**, 115 High Street, **HYTHE**, CT21 5JH
(T) 01303 267573
- **PLAMIL FOODS LTD**, Bowles Well Gardens, **FOLKESTONE**, CT19 6PQ
(T) 01303 850588
- **RAINHAM HEALTH FOOD CENTRE**, 28 Rainham Shopping Centre, Rainham, **GILLINGHAM**, ME8 7HW
(T) 01634 362267
- **SCOTTS**, 8 High Street, **DOVER**, CT16 1DR
(T) 01304 214790
- **SHEPTONHURST LTD**, 105 Dover Road, **FOLKESTONE**, CT20 1NL
(T) 01303 242196
- **SUPPLEMENT WAREHOUSE**, 3 Mid Kent Shopping Centre, Castle Road, **MAIDSTONE**, ME16 0PU
(T) 01622 752131
- **TEKNO FUEL SPORTS DRINKS**, P O Box 603, **GILLINGHAM**, ME8 0AE
(T) 01634 233272
- **TUDOR HEALTH LTD**, 2 Bramble Close, Hildenborough, **TONBRIDGE**, TN11 9HG
(T) 01732 833115
- **VEGETARE OF CRANBROOK**, 43 High Street, **CRANBROOK**, TN17 3EE
(T) 01580 712263
- **WINDMILL HEALTH STORE**, 20 Windmill Street, **GRAVESEND**, DA12 1AS
(T) 01474 534394

## LANCASHIRE

- **ALBION HOUSE ENTERPRISES**, 85 Albion Street, **BURNLEY**, BB11 4JG
(T) 01282 416202
- **APHRODITE**, 1a Priory Lane, Penwortham, **PRESTON**, PR1 0AR
(T) 01772 746555
- **APPLE HEALTH CARE**, Stall 67 Market Hall, Market Square, **BURNLEY**, BB11 1AZ
(T) 01282 412111
- **ARTHRO VITE LTD**, 5 Dicconson Ter, Lytham, **LYTHAM ST. ANNES**, FY8 5JY
(T) 01253 735736
- **BARE HEALTH FOOD STORE**, 19 Princes Cresent, **MORECAMBE**, LA4 6BY
(T) 01524 420894
- **BENNETTS NATURAL PRODUCTS**, 209 Blackburn Road, Wheelton, **CHORLEY**, PR6 8EY
(T) 01254 831520
- **BLACKPOOL NUTRITION CENTRE**, 22 Deansgate, **BLACKPOOL**, FY1 1BN
(T) 01253 749077
- **BODY CARE**, 23 Church Street, **BARNOLDSWICK**, BB18 5UR
(T) 01282 816008
- **BODY HEALTH**, Market Hall, Bow Street, **ASHTON-UNDER-LYNE**, OL6 6BZ
(T) 01613 433287
- **BOWLAND & HARRET HEALTH FOOD CENTRE**, 24 Topping Street, **BLACKPOOL**, FY1 3AQ
(T) 01253 752563
- **BURY NUTRITION CENTRE**, 6 The Mall, **BURY**, BL9 0QQ
(T) 01617 616445
- **CHORLEY HEALTH FOOD STORES**, 18 New Market Street, **CHORLEY**, PR7 1DB
(T) 01257 276146
- **CLEVELEYS HEALTH FOOD STORE**, 44 Victoria Road West, **THORNTON-CLEVELEYS**, FY5 1BU
(T) 01253 864030
- **D & H PERSONAL HEALTH CARE**, 14 Princess Street, Haslingden, **ROSSENDALE**, BB4 6NN
(T) 01706 211041
- **DANDELION HEALTH & HEALING**, 59 Woodlands Road, **LYTHAM ST. ANNES**, FY8 1DA
(T) 01253 738779
- **DERMALIFE**, Unit 304/Kingfisher Business Centre, Burnley Road, Rawtenstall, **ROSSENDALE**, BB4 8ES
(T) 01706 220522
- **E M C HEALTH FOODS**, 19 Union Street, **ACCRINGTON**, BB5 1PL
(T) 01254 399577
- **E M C HEALTH FOODS**, 20 Market Square, **BURNLEY**, BB11 1AZ
(T) 01282 427555
- **FARNWORTH HEALTH FOODS**, 112 Market Street, Farnworth, **BOLTON**, BL4 9AE
(T) 01204 862531
- **FOOD WEIGH HOUSE LTD (THE)**, 13 Guildhall Arcade, Lancaster Road, **PRESTON**, PR1 1HR
(T) 01772 200609
- **GARSTANG HEALTH FOOD STORES**, High Street, Garstang, **PRESTON**, PR3 1FA
(T) 01995 602833

- **GENERAL NUTRITION CENTRE**, 155 Market Hall, Arndale Centre, **MANCHESTER**, M4 2EB (T) 01618 192201
- **GOOD HEALTH FOODS LTD**, 1A Princess Parade, **BURY**, BL9 0QL (T) 01617 637573
- **GOOD HEALTH FOODS LTD**, Arndale Centre, **MANCHESTER**, M4 2HU (T) 01618 319881
- **GOOD HEALTHFOODS LTD**, 8 Albion Street, **OLDHAM**, OL1 3BB (T) 01616 260699
- **GOOD LIFE PRODUCTS**, PO Box 86, Royton, **OLDHAM**, OL2 5DA (T) 01616 271069
- **GOODHEALTH PRODUCTS**, Saddleworth Business Centre, Huddersfield Road, Delph, **OLDHAM**, OL3 5DF (T) 01457 829220
- **HABANA FOODS**, Pechell Street, Ashton-on-Ribble, **PRESTON**, PR2 2RN (T) 01772 715244
- **HEALTH & PURE FOODS**, 36-37 Market Hall, Market Street, **PRESTON**, PR1 2JD (T) 01772 254015
- **HEALTH & VEGETARIAN STORE**, 2 Worsley Avenue, **MANCHESTER**, M40 9NA (T) 01616 834456
- **HEALTH FOOD CENTRE**, 113 Yorkshire Street, **ROCHDALE**, OL16 1DR (T) 01706 648141
- **HEALTH FOOD CENTRE BOLTON**, Deansgate Chambers, 152 Deansgate, **BOLTON**, BL1 1BB (T) 01204 525084
- **HEALTH RACK**, 1 Orchard Street, **PRESTON**, PR1 2EN (T) 01772 561936
- **HEALTH RACK**, 18 Makinson Arcade, **WIGAN**, WN1 1PL (T) 01942 323858
- **HEALTH RACK**, 22 Bank Hey Street, **BLACKPOOL**, FY1 4RS (T) 01253 295925
- **HEALTH RACK LTD**, 25 Ainsworth Street, **BLACKBURN**, BB1 6AS (T) 01254 690490
- **HEALTH RACK LTD**, Clitheroe Road, Dutton, **PRESTON**, PR3 2YT (T) 01254 779200
- **HEALTHCARE INTERNATIONAL**, 5 Chestnut Drive, **LEIGH**, WN7 3JW (T) 01942 672542
- **HEALTHIER EATING.COM**, Lion Mill, Fitton Street, Royton, **OLDHAM**, OL2 5JX (T) 01616 337001
- **HEALTH-N-BREW**, M41 Market Hall, Common Garden Street, **LANCASTER**, LA1 1XD (T) 01524 388555
- **HEALTHY OPTION (THE)**, Food Hall, Market Way, **SALFORD**, M6 5HG (T) 01617 369663
- **HELLONS HEALTH FOOD STORE**, 84 Highfield Road, **BLACKPOOL**, FY4 2JF (T) 01253 343427
- **HERB STALL (THE)**, 1 King Street, **LANCASTER**, LA1 1JN (T) 01524 32916
- **HERBALIFE INDEPENDANT DISTRIBUTOR**, 12 Grizedale Avenue, Garstang, **PRESTON**, PR3 1WD (T) 01995 605823
- **HERES HEALTH**, 107 Market Hall, Market Street, **ASHTON-UNDER-LYNE**, OL6 6BZ (T) 01613 304447
- **HERE'S HEALTH**, 39-41, Indoor Market Hall, **OLDHAM**, OL1 3BG (T) 01616 243045
- **HOLLAND & BARRETT**, 122 Arndale Centre, **MANCHESTER**, M4 2EA (T) 01618 345975
- **HOLLAND & BARRETT**, 24 Euston Road, **MORECAMBE**, LA4 5DD (T) 01524 401383
- **HOLLAND & BARRETT**, 26 Newport Street, **BOLTON**, BL1 1NB (T) 01204 385954
- **HOLLAND & BARRETT**, 26 Penny Street, **LANCASTER**, LA1 1UA (T) 01524 848633
- **HOLLAND & BARRETT**, 3 Cobden Court, **BLACKBURN**, BB1 7JG (T) 01254 693010
- **HOLLAND & BARRETT**, 33 Corporation Street, **BLACKPOOL**, FY1 1EJ (T) 01253 299393
- **HOLLAND & BARRETT**, 33 The Mall, **BURNLEY**, BB11 1BA (T) 01282 459833
- **HOLLAND & BARRETT**, 37 Spindles Shopping Centre, **OLDHAM**, OL1 1HD (T) 01616 220180
- **HOLLAND & BARRETT**, 39 Raven Way, **SALFORD**, M6 5LD (T) 01617 366524
- **HOLLAND & BARRETT**, 51 St Annes Road West, **LYTHAM ST. ANNES**, FY8 1SB (T) 01253 712022
- **HOLLAND & BARRETT**, 97 Friargate Walk, St Georges Shopping Centre, **PRESTON**, PR1 2NQ (T) 01772 253152
- **HOLLAND & BARRETT**, Moor Street, **ORMSKIRK**, L39 2AA (T) 01695 578686
- **HOLLAND & BARRETT**, Unit 12 Arndale Centre, Cornhill, **ACCRINGTON**, BB5 1EX (T) 01254 235114
- **HOLLAND & BARRETT**, Unit 22 Ladysmith Centre, Staveleigh Walk, **ASHTON-UNDER-LYNE**, OL6 7JJ (T) 01613 396552
- **HOLLAND & BARRETT**, Unit 34, New Market Hall, **WIGAN**, WN1 1PX (T) 01942 826425
- **HOUSTON HEALTH SHOP**, 34 Yorkshire Street, **MORECAMBE**, LA3 1QE (T) 01524 419407
- **JEANS HEALTH FOODS**, Market Hall, Market Parade, **BURY**, BL9 0BD (T) 01617 612145
- **JEANS HEALTH FOODS LTD**, Unit 2 Bolton Market, Ashburner Street, **BOLTON**, BL1 1TJ (T) 01204 366287
- **JOHN HOOL**, 10b Market Hall, Knowsley Street, **BOLTON**, BL1 2AR (T) 01204 391663
- **JULIAN GRAVES LTD**, 21 Hounds Hill Centre, Victoria Street, **BLACKPOOL**, FY1 4HU (T) 01253 294344
- **LIBRA LANCASHIRE LTD**, 98 Church Road, Tarleton, **PRESTON**, PR4 6UP (T) 01772 816100
- **LONSDALE HEALTH PRODUCTS LTD**, Unit 4 Ingleton Industrial Estate, Ingleton, **CARNFORTH**, LA6 3NU (T) 01524 241007
- **LYTHAM HEALTH FOOD STORE**, 12a Park Street, **LYTHAM ST. ANNES**, FY8 5LU (T) 01253 739551
- **MAHARISHI AYUR-VEDA PRODUCTS**, Beacon House, Willow Walk, **SKELMERSDALE**, WN8 6UR (T) 01695 51015
- **MAWSONS**, 57 George Street, **OLDHAM**, OL1 1LT (T) 01616 248182
- **MAWSON'S HEALTHFOODS**, 16 Rochdale Road, Royton, **OLDHAM**, OL2 6QJ (T) 01616 260341
- **MEDICAL INNOVATIONS**, Newlands Medical Centre, 315 Chorley New Road, **BOLTON**, BL1 5BP (T) 01204 842830
- **MOOREY'S HEALTH STORE**, Mini Shop F, Five Day Market, **BLACKBURN**, BB1 6AS (T) 01254 53245
- **MORECAMBE HEALTH FOOD CENTRE**, 9 Pedder Street, **MORECAMBE**, LA4 5DY (T) 01524 413733
- **MOSSLEY WHOLEFOODS**, 11-13 Arundel Street, Mossley, **ASHTON-UNDER-LYNE**, OL5 0NY (T) 01457 837743
- **NATIONAL MSM HELPLINE**, 3 Victoria Road, **LYTHAM ST. ANNES**, FY8 1LE (T) 01253 721001
- **NATURAL CHOICE**, 13 Bridge Street, **DARWEN**, BB3 2AA (T) 01254 773311
- **NATURAL CHOICE**, 4-6 Market Place, **POULTON-LE-FYLDE**, FY6 7AY (T) 01253 893952
- **NATURAL HEALTH PRODUCTS**, 29 St Annes Road West, **LYTHAM ST. ANNES**, FY8 1SB (T) 01253 789090
- **NATURAL OPTIONSHEALTH PRODUCTS LTD**, Kingcraig Court, Kingcraig Road, **BLACKPOOL**, FY2 0FY (T) 01253 479111
- **NATURE FARE**, 5 Towngate, Leyland, **PRESTON**, PR5 1EN (T) 01772 434693
- **NATURE STORE**, 4a Lord Street, **LEIGH**, WN7 1DP (T) 01942 671068
- **NATURES AID LTD**, St. Georges Park, Kirkham, **PRESTON**, PR4 2DQ (T) 01772 686231
- **NATURE'S BEST**, 74a Bryn Street, Ashton-in-Makerfield, **WIGAN**, WN4 9AU (T) 01942 204038
- **NELSON NUTRITION**, 24 Marsden Mall, Arndale Centre, **NELSON**, BB9 9SL (T) 01282 618066
- **NORFORD HEALTH FOODS**, Unit 1 Indoor Market, **ROCHDALE**, OL16 1EA (T) 01706 355387
- **NUT CENTRE (THE)**, 112 Manchester Retail Market, Arndale Centre, **MANCHESTER**, M4 2EA (T) 01618 323294
- **NUT CENTRE (THE)**, Stall 55-56 Market Hall, Market Street, **PRESTON**, PR1 2JD (T) 01772 823382
- **NUTRATECH**, 5 Hall Street, **BURNLEY**, BB11 1QJ (T) 01282 456902
- **NUTRISPORT**, Great George Street, **WIGAN**, WN3 4DL (T) 01942 519111
- **ONLY NATURAL**, 64 Standishgate, **WIGAN**, WN1 1DG (T) 01942 236239
- **PAUL'S AROMATHERAPY & NATURAL WELL BEING CENTRE**, 36a Clifton Street, **LYTHAM ST. ANNES**, FY8 5EW (T) 01253 794179
- **PAY & SAVE**, Unit 6 Market Place, **ROCHDALE**, OL16 1EB (T) 01706 523439
- **POWERBECK SPORTS**, Unit 17/18/Victoria Industrial Estate, Victoria Street, **LEIGH**, WN7 5SE (T) 01942 269677
- **PRESTON HEALTH FOOD STORES**, 26 Guildhall Street, **PRESTON**, PR1 3NU (T) 01772 257617
- **RESEARCH PROJECTS LTD**, Unit 5-6/Waterfront Marine Business Pk B, Dock Road, **LYTHAM ST. ANNES**, FY8 5AQ (T) 01253 731330
- **SCIENCE IN SPORT LTD**, Ashwood, Brockhall Village, Old Langho, **BLACKBURN**, BB6 8BB (T) 01254 246060
- **SCI-FIT UK**, Unit 11/Locke Industrial Estate, Emmett Street, Horwich, **BOLTON**, BL6 7PN (T) 01204 698988
- **SIMPLY NATURAL**, 14 Poulton Street, Kirkham, **PRESTON**, PR4 2AB (T) 01772 671489
- **SINGLE STEP COOPERATIVE LTD**, 78a Penny Street, **LANCASTER**, LA1 1XN (T) 01524 63021
- **ULTIMATE NUTRITION**, 3-4 Maritime Street, **FLEETWOOD**, FY7 7PB (T) 01253 774000
- **WELLSPRING HEALTH ASSOCIATES**, 1 Swan Courtyard, Castle Street, **CLITHEROE**, BB7 2DQ (T) 01200 429777

**WHEATSHEAF HEALTH FOODS**, 23 Burscough Street, **ORMSKIRK**, L39 2EG (T) 01695 579833

**WHEELTON HEALTHCARE CENTRE**, 209 Blackburn Road, Heapey, **CHORLEY**, PR6 8EP (T) 01254 830122

**WIGNA WHOLEFOODS**, Unit 1 Bradley Hall Trading Estate, Bradley Lane, Standish, **WIGAN**, WN6 0XQ (T) 01257 424632

**WILD OATS**, 48 Mount Street, **FLEETWOOD**, FY7 6LD (T) 01253 779125

## LEICESTERSHIRE

**AU NATURAL**, 9 Cross Street, Blaby, **LEICESTER**, LE8 4FD (T) 01162 789888

**CLAYBROOK MILL LTD**, Hall House, Hall Lane, Ullesthorpe, **LUTTERWORTH**, LE17 5DD (T) 01455 202443

**CURRENT AFFAIRS**, 9a Loseby Lane, **LEICESTER**, LE1 5DR (T) 01162 510887

**ELF FOODS**, 38 Market Street, **LOUGHBOROUGH**, LE11 3ER (T) 01509 212424

**ESSENTIAL CONSUMER PRODUCTS LTD**, 7A Church Walks, **HINCKLEY**, LE10 1DW (T) 01455 233733

**FARM GATE PRODUCTS**, Chestnut Avenue, Oadby, **LEICESTER**, LE2 5JH (T) 01162 713086

**GOOD HEALTH FOODS LTD**, Unit 3 Market Centre, Market Place, **LEICESTER**, LE1 5HQ (T) 01162 532783

**GOOD HEALTH FOODS MR W BAILE**, 46b Market Place, **LEICESTER**, LE1 5GF (T) 01162 623565

**GOODNESS FOODS**, 18 Silver Street, **LEICESTER**, LE1 5ET (T) 01162 624859

**HALDANE FOODS LTD**, Unit 25 Hayhill, Barrow upon Soar, **LOUGHBOROUGH**, LE12 8LD (T) 01509 816611

**HEALTH & WHOLE FOODS**, 13 Sibson Road, Birstall, **LEICESTER**, LE4 4DX (T) 01162 671677

**HEALTHY HERITAGE**, 11 Manor Walk, **MARKET HARBOROUGH**, LE16 9BP (T) 01858 431250

**HEALTHY LIVING**, 3 Odeon Arcade, **LEICESTER**, LE1 5HJ (T) 01162 539097

**HOLLAND & BARRETT**, 33 Horsefair Street, **LEICESTER**, LE1 5BP (T) 01162 621547

**HOLLAND & BARRETT**, 5 Humberstone Mall, **LEICESTER**, LE1 3YB (T) 01162 516270

**JULIAN GRAVES LTD**, 3 Clocktower Mall, Haymarket Shopping Centre, **LEICESTER**, LE1 3YA (T) 01162 531115

**LEICESTER WHOLEFOOD CO-OPERATIVE LTD**, Unit 3 Freehold Street, **LEICESTER**, LE1 2LX (T) 01162 512525

**LIFEPLAN PRODUCTS LTD**, Unit 1 Elizabethan Way, **LUTTERWORTH**, LE17 4ND (T) 01455 556281

**NATURAL CHOICE**, 51 Belvoir Road, **COALVILLE**, LE67 3PD (T) 01530 811125

**NATURAL CHOICE**, 7 Edwards Centre, Regent Street, **HINCKLEY**, LE10 0BB (T) 01455 635254

**NATURES DISPENSARY**, 7 Mill Street, **OAKHAM**, LE15 6EA (T) 01572 771231

**NAWNAL HEALTH PRODUCTS**, 43 Howards Close, Loughborough, **LEICESTER**, LE11 4T (T) 01420 409176

**PAUL'S TOFU**, Unit 9 66 Snow Hill, **MELTON MOWBRAY**, LE13 1PD (T) 01664 560572

**PEPPERS WHOLE FOODS**, 59a Queens Road, **LEICESTER**, LE2 1TT (T) 01162 702974

**QUALITY KITCHEN**, 11 Bradgate Drive, Ratby, **LEICESTER**, LE6 0LB (T) 01162 883735

**SHEPHERDBOY LTD**, Cross Street, Syston, **LEICESTER**, LE7 2JG (T) 01162 602992

**THORPES HEALTH FOODS**, 25 Burton Street, **MELTON MOWBRAY**, LE13 1AE (T) 01664 562727

**WIGSTON HEALTH FOOD & DIET**, 17 Leicester Road, **WIGSTON**, LE18 1NR (T) 01162 889424

## LINCOLNSHIRE

**BEST OF HEALTH (THE)**, Tillbridge Farm, Tillbridge Road, Sturton by Stow, **LINCOLN**, LN1 2DS (T) 01427 787282

**BOSTON HEALTH FOODS**, 12 Church Street, **BOSTON**, PE21 6NW (T) 01205 367709

**BRIAN HARDY LTD**, 19 Wide Bargate, **BOSTON**, PE21 6SR (T) 01205 362121

**COUNTRY FAYRE**, 25 Watergate, **GRANTHAM**, NG31 6NS (T) 01476 578581

**GOOD FOR YOU**, 23 Silver Street, **GAINSBOROUGH**, DN21 2DT (T) 01427 616617

**GRANTHAM HEALTH STORE**, 6 Kings Walk, **GRANTHAM**, NG31 6NL (T) 01476 573720

**GREEN PARK HEALTH & NUTRUTION**, Central Park Farm, Station Road, Knaith, **GAINSBOROUGH**, DN21 5HD (T) 01427 613259

**GREENS HEALTH FOODS**, 175 High Street, **LINCOLN**, LN5 7AF (T) 01522 524874

**HOLBEACH WHOLEFOODS**, 32 High Street, Holbeach, **SPALDING**, PE12 7DY (T) 01406 422149

**HOLLAND & BARRETT**, 319 High Street, **LINCOLN**, LN5 7DW (T) 01522 567615

**HOLLAND & BARRETT**, 35 Hall Place, **SPALDING**, PE11 1SG (T) 01775 724220

**HOLLAND & BARRETT**, 37 Lumley Road, **SKEGNESS**, PE25 3LL (T) 01754 764412

**HOLLAND & BARRETT**, 47 Market Place, **BOSTON**, PE21 6NF (T) 01205 359712

**HOLLAND & BARRETT**, 57 High Street, **STAMFORD**, PE9 2AW (T) 01780 480387

**HONEYPOT HEALTH FOODS**, 96 Lumley Road, **SKEGNESS**, PE25 3ND (T) 01754 767387

**JULIAN GRAVES LTD**, Waterside Shopping Centre, High Street, **LINCOLN**, LN2 1AP (T) 01522 576747

**KEMISTORE**, 46 High Street, **MABLETHORPE**, LN12 1AD (T) 01507 473686

**MOTHER NATURE**, Bristol Arcade, **SLEAFORD**, NG34 7ST (T) 01529 303875

**NATURAL REMEDY WAREHOUSE**, 4 Broadgate House, Westlode Street, **SPALDING**, PE11 2AF (T) 01775 724994

**PIONEER TRADING CO**, 5a High Street, Tattershall, **LINCOLN**, LN4 4LE (T) 01526 345613

**SILVER LANE WHOLE FOODS**, 2 Silver Lane, **STAMFORD**, PE9 2BT (T) 01780 755710

**SPICE OF LIFE**, 4 The Burghley Centre, Hereward Street, **BOURNE**, PE10 9EG (T) 01778 394735

## LINCOLNSHIRE (NORTH)

**COUNTRY COTTAGE (THE)**, 10 College Yard, **BRIGG**, DN20 8JL (T) 01652 657486

**HOLLAND & BARRETT**, 37 High Street, **SCUNTHORPE**, DN15 6SB (T) 01724 278157

**KEEP YOURSELF RIGHT 2**, 4 Ravendale Street North, **SCUNTHORPE**, DN15 6NE (T) 01724 854236

## LONDON (GREATER)

**2 FIGS**, 101 Newington Green Road, **LONDON**, N1 4QY (T) 020 7690 6811

**21ST CENTURY HEALTH LTD**, 2 Fitzhardinge Street, **LONDON**, W1H 9PN (T) 020 7935 5440

**A NAGEENA LTD**, Block D St Anns Row, Limehouse, **LONDON**, E14 7HN (T) 020 7538 5713

**ACETA LTD**, 214 Old Brompton Road, **LONDON**, SW5 0BX (T) 020 7373 9818

**ALARA**, 58-60 Marchmont Street, **LONDON**, WC1N 1AB (T) 020 7837 1172

**ALARA WHOLEFOODS LTD**, 110-112 Camley Street, **LONDON**, NW1 0PF (T) 020 7387 9303

**ALOE VERA**, 163 Brent Street, **LONDON**, NW4 4DH (T) 020 8203 8255

**ALOE VERA**, London House, 100 New Kings Road, **LONDON**, SW6 4LX (T) 020 7731 8855

**ALOE VERA CONSULTANT**, 47 Canadian Avenue, **LONDON**, SE6 3AU (T) 020 8690 3988

**ALOE VERA HEALTH PRODUCTS & INFORMATION SERVICE**, 55 Amity Grove, **LONDON**, SW20 0LQ (T) 020 8241 1463

**ALTERNATIVE HEALTH CENTRE**, 1369 High Road, **LONDON**, N20 9LN (T) 020 8445 2675

**AMERIFIT EUROPE LTD**, 38 Ferme Park Road, **LONDON**, N4 4ED (T) 020 8374 5869

**APPLEJACKS**, Unit 28 The Mall, The Stratford Centre, **LONDON**, E15 1XD (T) 020 8519 5809

**ARMSTRONG ENTERPRISES**, 33 Mawbey House, Old Kent Road, **LONDON**, SE1 5PG (T) 020 7232 2370

**AZIZA NATURAL SOAPS**, Unit 30d Camden Lock Place, Chalk Farm Road, **LONDON**, NW1 8AL (T) 020 7482 4242

**AZURE**, Unit 4 Old Garden House/The Lanterns, Bridge Lane, **LONDON**, SW11 3AD (T) 020 7223 8787

**B GREEN**, 104 Ballards Lane, **LONDON**, N3 2DN (T) 020 8343 1002

**BACK TO EDEN**, 120A Lower Clapton Road, **LONDON**, E5 0QR (T) 020 8510 9777

**BALDWINS WHOLE FOODS**, 171-173 Walworth Road, **LONDON**, SE17 1RW (T) 020 7701 4892

**BALHAM WHOLEFOODS & HEALTH STORE**, 8 Bedford Hill, **LONDON**, SW12 9RG (T) 020 8673 4842

**BARNSBURY HEALTH FOODS**, 285 Caledonian Road, **LONDON**, N1 1EF (T) 020 7607 7344

**BEIJING TONG REN TANE (UK) LTD**, 124 Shaftesbury Avenue, **LONDON**, W1V 7DJ (T) 020 7287 0098

**BELLEDONNA HEALTH FOOD**, 5 Westbury Parade, **LONDON**, SW12 9DZ (T) 020 8673 3121

**BIOCEUTICALS LTD**, 26 Zennor Road, **LONDON**, SW12 0PS (T) 020 8675 5664

- **BIONAL (UK) LTD**, 7 Ingate Place, **LONDON**, SW8 3NS
(T) 020 7720 8820
- **BIO-SYNERGY LTD**, 55 Paddington Street, **LONDON**, W1M 3RQ
(T) 020 8444 4405
- **BODY ACTIVE**, Charing Cross Underground Shopping Concourse, 5 Adelaide Street, **LONDON**, WC2N 4HZ
(T) 020 7240 1363
- **BODY DESIGN COMPANY LTD**, 41 Brook Meadow, **LONDON**, N12 7DB
(T) 020 8446 7029
- **BODYWATCH HOME TESTING KITS**, 60 Wimpole Street, **LONDON**, W1M 7DE
(T) 020 7486 7278
- **BRAES GROUP LTD**, Masters House, 107 Hammersmith Road, **LONDON**, W14 0QH
(T) 020 7602 4455
- **BUDDHIST CO-OPERATIVE**, 5 Hindmans Road, **LONDON**, SE22 9NF
(T) 020 8693 9951
- **BUMBLEBEE NATURAL FOODS**, 30 Brecknock Road, **LONDON**, N7 0DD
(T) 020 7607 1935
- **BUSHWACKER WHOLEFOODS**, 132 King Street, **LONDON**, W6 0QU
(T) 020 8748 2061
- **C K F HEALTH CARE**, 260 Upper Street, **LONDON**, N1 2UQ
(T) 020 7359 1126
- **CAPITAL HEALTH LTD**, P O Box 27207, **LONDON**, N11 3WL
(T) 020 8361 8466
- **CERES HEALTH FOODS**, 427a Upper Richmond Road West, **LONDON**, SW14 7PJ
(T) 020 8878 7403
- **CHANGES INTERNATIONAL INDEPENDENT DISTRIBUTORS**, 19 Pennyford Court, Henderson Drive, **LONDON**, NW8 8UF
(T) 020 7289 6670
- **CHATFIELD LABORATORIES**, Kramer Mews, **LONDON**, SW5 9JG
(T) 020 7370 4664
- **CHELSEA HEALTH FOOD**, 402 Kings Road, **LONDON**, SW10 0LJ
(T) 020 7352 4663
- **COLTSFOOT & KELP**, 106 Northfield Avenue, **LONDON**, W13 9RT
(T) 020 8566 0830
- **COLTSFOOT KELP**, 106 Northfield Avenue, **LONDON**, W13 9RT
(T) 020 8567 3548
- **COMMUNITY FOODS LTD**, Unit 2 M1 Cross, Brent Terrace, **LONDON**, NW2 1LT
(T) 020 8208 2966
- **COOPERS NATURAL FOODS**, 17 Lower Marsh, **LONDON**, SE1 7RJ
(T) 020 7261 9314
- **CORNUCOPIA**, 51 Chelsea Manor Street, **LONDON**, SW3 5RZ
(T) 020 7352 7403
- **CORNUCOPIA HEALTH FOODS**, 64 St Marys Road, **LONDON**, W5 5EX
(T) 020 8579 9431
- **COUNTRY LIFE NATURAL FOOD SHOP LTD**, 3-4 Warwick Street, **LONDON**, W1R 5WA
(T) 020 7434 2838
- **COUNTRYSIDE WHOLEFOODS**, 19 Forty Hill, **ENFIELD**, EN2 9HT
(T) 020 8363 2933
- **CRYSTAL**, 17 Westow Street, **LONDON**, SE19 3RY
(T) 020 8771 1503
- **DANDELION NATURAL FOODS**, 120 Northcote Road, **LONDON**, SW11 6QU
(T) 020 7350 0902
- **DAY PLUS ONE**, Unit 11b Crusader Industrial Estate, 167 Hermitage Road, **LONDON**, N4 1LZ
(T) 020 8802 1088
- **DIET & HEALTH**, 28 Watling Avenue, **EDGWARE**, HA8 0LR
(T) 020 8952 9629
- **DIRECT ASSECT**, 3 St Stephens Mews, **LONDON**, W2 5QZ
(T) 020 7243 1238
- **ECOLABS LTD**, 3 Adam & Eve Mews, **LONDON**, W8 6UG
(T) 020 7460 8101
- **EDGWARE NATURAL HEALTH FOODS & CLINIC & MAIL ORDER**, 128 High Street, **EDGWARE**, HA8 7EL
(T) 020 8952 9566
- **EDMONTON HEALTH FOOD CENTRE**, 36 North Square, **LONDON**, N9 0HW
(T) 020 8807 8787
- **EKUNBAYO MAJESTY**, 56 Church Road, **LONDON**, SE19 2EZ
(T) 020 8771 6973
- **ERDIC LTD**, 12 Harley Street, **LONDON**, W1N 1AA
(T) 08456 0770274
- **EURODOT LTD**, 2a Windermere Road, **LONDON**, N19 5SG
(T) 020 7263 2113
- **FIELDWAY**, 43a Deptford Bridge, **LONDON**, SE8 4HH
(T) 020 8469 0604
- **FINCHLEY HEALTH FOOD CENTRE**, 745 High Road, **LONDON**, N12 0BP
(T) 020 8445 8743
- **FINEMIX FOODS**, 7-11 Minerva Road, **LONDON**, NW10 6HJ
(T) 020 8838 5078
- **FINSTEAD LTD**, 242 North End Road, **LONDON**, SW6 1NL
(T) 020 7385 4440
- **FOOD & FITNESS**, 43 Old Church Road, **LONDON**, E4 6SJ
(T) 020 8524 0722
- **FOOD FOR ALL**, 3 Cazenove Road, **LONDON**, N16 6PA
(T) 020 8806 4138
- **FOOD FOR THOUGHT**, 154 High Street, **HOUNSLOW**, TW3 1LR
(T) 020 8572 0310
- **FOREVER LIVING**, 166 Bramley Road, **LONDON**, N14 4HX
(T) 020 8449 4806
- **FOREVER LIVING PRODUCTS**, Area 210 Office/Trident Business Centre, 89 Bickersteth Road, **LONDON**, SW17 9SH
(T) 020 8516 7761
- **FOREVER YOUNG INTERNATIONAL LTD**, St Martins Way, **LONDON**, SW17 0JH
(T) 020 8944 7442
- **FRIENDS HEALTH FOODS**, 83 Roman Road, **LONDON**, E2 0QN
(T) 020 8980 1843
- **FRUIT GARDEN (THE)**, 21 Melcombe Street, **LONDON**, NW1 6AG
(T) 020 7935 5161
- **G M C**, 212 Upper Street, **LONDON**, N1 1RL
(T) 020 7226 3422
- **GAIA**, 123 St Margarets Road, **TWICKENHAM**, TW1 2LH
(T) 020 8892 2262
- **GENERAL NUTRITION CENTRE**, 104 Marylebone High Street, **LONDON**, W1M 3DB
(T) 020 7935 8412
- **GENERAL NUTRITION CENTRES**, 7 Chequers Square, **UXBRIDGE**, UB8 1LN
(T) 01895 254538
- **GHIR HEALTH FOODS LTD**, 426 Barking Road, **LONDON**, E6 2SA
(T) 020 8471 7576
- **GINNI ENTERPRISES**, 4 Gladstone Road, **SOUTHALL**, UB2 5BB
(T) 020 8843 1970
- **GOLDEN ORIENT LTD**, 17 Earlham Street, **LONDON**, WC2H 9LL
(T) 020 7836 5545
- **GOOD HEALTH SHOP (THE)**, 47 High Street, Whitton, **TWICKENHAM**, TW2 7LB
(T) 020 8894 9487
- **GOOD LIFE HEALTH FOOD**, 7 Broadway Parade, **LONDON**, N8 9DE
(T) 020 8340 0601
- **GRANARY (THE)**, 165 High Street North, **LONDON**, E6 1JB
(T) 020 8552 5988
- **GREEN EARTH**, 260 West End Lane, **LONDON**, NW6 1LJ
(T) 020 7433 1664
- **GREEN EARTH WHOLEFOODS**, 49 Stoke Newington Church Street, **LONDON**, N16 0AR
(T) 020 7923 1477
- **GREEN HOUSE (THE)**, Unit 65-67 Markethall/Wood Green Shopping City, High Road, **LONDON**, N22 6YE
(T) 020 8881 1471
- **GREENLANDS HEALTH FOOD SHOP**, Greenwich Market, **LONDON**, SE10 9HZ
(T) 020 8293 9176
- **GREENS**, 11-13 Strutton Ground, **LONDON**, SW1P 2HY
(T) 020 7222 4588
- **HAELAN CENTRE (THE)**, 41 The Broadway, **LONDON**, N8 8DT
(T) 020 8340 4258
- **HAMPSTEAD HEALTH SHOP LTD**, 57 Hampstead High Street, **LONDON**, NW3 1QH
(T) 020 7435 6418
- **HARRINGTON P**, Flat E 15 Kingwood Road, **LONDON**, SW6 6SP
(T) 020 7386 0627
- **HAYES HEALTH FOODS**, 814c Uxbridge Road, **HAYES**, UB4 0RS
(T) 020 8561 1624
- **HEALTH & DIET CENTRES LTD**, 151 Putney High Street, **LONDON**, SW15 1SU
(T) 020 8788 0944
- **HEALTH & DIET CENTRES LTD**, 201 Centre Court Shopping Centre, 4 Queens Road, **LONDON**, SW19 8YE
(T) 020 8947 3583
- **HEALTH & DIET CENTRES LTD**, 243 Muswell Hill Broadway, **LONDON**, N10 1DE
(T) 020 8444 7717
- **HEALTH & DIET CENTRES LTD**, 31 Tranquil Vale, **LONDON**, SE3 0BU
(T) 020 8318 0448
- **HEALTH & DIET CENTRES LTD**, 5 Jerdan Place, **LONDON**, SW6 1BE
(T) 020 7385 0015
- **HEALTH 2000**, 145 Talgarth Road, **LONDON**, W14 9DA
(T) 07967 030161
- **HEALTH CARE**, 41A Hurlstone Road, **LONDON**, SE25 6JD
(T) 020 8240 9157
- **HEALTH CRAZE**, 115 Earls Court Road, **LONDON**, SW5 9RL
(T) 020 7244 7784
- **HEALTH CRAZE**, 24 Old Brompton Road, **LONDON**, SW7 3DL
(T) 020 7589 5870
- **HEALTH FARM SHOP**, 6 Camberwell Church Street, **LONDON**, SE5 8QU
(T) 020 7703 7130
- **HEALTH FIRST**, 644 Kingsbury Road, **LONDON**, NW9 9HN
(T) 020 8238 9336
- **HEALTH FOOD CENTRE**, 156 Balham High Road, **LONDON**, SW12 9BN
(T) 020 8265 7532
- **HEALTH FOODS**, 767 Fulham Road, **LONDON**, SW6 5HA
(T) 020 7736 8848
- **HEALTH ZONE**, 30 Wimbledon Hill Road, **LONDON**, SW19 7PA
(T) 020 8944 1133
- **HEALTHFOOD CENTRE**, 11 Warren Street, **LONDON**, W1P 5DA
(T) 020 7387 9289
- **HEALTHPOINT EUROPE**, 42 High Street, **HARROW**, HA1 3LL
(T) 020 8423 3475
- **HEALTHQUEST LTD**, 7 Brampton Road, **LONDON**, NW9 9BX
(T) 020 8206 2066
- **HEALTHWISE**, 5 Manor House, The Green, **SOUTHALL**, UB2 4BJ
(T) 020 8893 5126
- **HEALTHY HARVEST FOOD STORE (THE)**, Squires Garden Centre, Sixth Cross Road, **TWICKENHAM**, TW2 5PA
(T) 020 8943 0692
- **HENDON HEALTH FOOD CENTRE**, 125 Brent Street, **LONDON**, NW4 2DX
(T) 020 8202 9165

- **HERBALIFE**, 13 Cope Place, **LONDON**, W8 6AA (T) 020 7937 2000
- **HERBALIFE**, 2 Clarence Place, **LONDON**, E5 8HN (T) 020 8986 3963
- **HERBALIFE**, 86 Wanlip Road, **LONDON**, E13 8QP (T) 020 7474 4594
- **HERBALIFE**, P O Box 27738, **LONDON**, E5 9FN (T) 020 8806 1166
- **HERBALIFE DISTRIBUTOR**, 33 Thornsett Road, **LONDON**, SE20 7XB (T) 020 8778 8719
- **HERBALIFE DISTRIBUTOR**, 51 Welbeck Street, **LONDON**, W1A 4UA (T) 020 7935 0506
- **HERBALIFE DISTRIBUTOR**, 85 Forburg Road, **LONDON**, N16 6HR (T) 020 8806 7948
- **HERBALIFE INDEPENDENT DISTRIBUTOR**, 125 Windmill Lane, **GREENFORD**, UB6 9DZ (T) 020 8813 0967
- **HERBALIFE INDEPENDENT DISTRIBUTOR**, 157 Highbury Quadrant, **LONDON**, N5 2TG (T) 020 7226 8351
- **HERBALIFE INDEPENDENT DISTRIBUTOR**, 25 Aylestone Avenue, **LONDON**, NW6 7AE (T) 08001 63946
- **HERBALIFE INDEPENDENT DISTRIBUTOR**, 341 Lea Bridge Road, **LONDON**, E10 7LA (T) 020 8923 1113
- **HERBALIFE WEIGHT LOSS GAIN SUPERVISOR**, 106 North End House, Fitzjames Ave, **LONDON**, W14 0RY (T) 020 7603 1467
- **HIBBS G M INDEPENDENT HERBALISED DISTRIBUTOR**, 465 Twickenham Road, **ISLEWORTH**, TW7 7DZ (T) 020 8892 1933
- **HIGHBURY HEALTH FOODS**, 25-27 Highbury Corner, **LONDON**, N5 1RA (T) 020 7609 9471
- **HILDRETH & COCKER LTD**, Freepost, **LONDON**, SW12 0ZT (T) 020 7274 0006
- **HOLLAND & BARRETT**, 10 Warwick Way, **LONDON**, SW1V 1RU (T) 020 7834 4796
- **HOLLAND & BARRETT**, 112 Shepherds Bush Centre, Shepherds Bush Green, **LONDON**, W12 8PP (T) 020 8743 1045
- **HOLLAND & BARRETT**, 121 Muswell Hill Road, **LONDON**, N10 3HS (T) 020 8883 1154
- **HOLLAND & BARRETT**, 123 Oxford Street, **LONDON**, W1R 1TF (T) 020 7287 3624
- **HOLLAND & BARRETT**, 129-131 High Road, **LONDON**, N22 6BB (T) 020 8889 4759
- **HOLLAND & BARRETT**, 13 King Street, **TWICKENHAM**, TW1 3SD (T) 020 8891 6696
- **HOLLAND & BARRETT**, 133a High Street North, **LONDON**, E6 1HZ (T) 020 8552 6090
- **HOLLAND & BARRETT**, 137 Putney High Street, **LONDON**, SW15 1SU (T) 020 8785 7018
- **HOLLAND & BARRETT**, 139 Kensington Church Street, **LONDON**, W8 7LP (T) 020 7727 9011
- **HOLLAND & BARRETT**, 14 Northways Parade, **LONDON**, NW3 5EN (T) 020 7722 5920
- **HOLLAND & BARRETT**, 16 Embankment Place, **LONDON**, WC2N 6NN (T) 020 7839 4988
- **HOLLAND & BARRETT**, 17-19 Pantile Walk, **UXBRIDGE**, UB8 1LT (T) 01895 237841
- **HOLLAND & BARRETT**, 185 High Street, **HOUNSLOW**, TW3 1BL (T) 020 8572 6066
- **HOLLAND & BARRETT**, 191-200 Camden High Street, **LONDON**, NW1 7BT (T) 020 7485 9477
- **HOLLAND & BARRETT**, 192 Earls Court Road, **LONDON**, SW5 9QF (T) 020 7370 6868
- **HOLLAND & BARRETT**, 198 Eltham High Street, **LONDON**, SE9 1BJ (T) 020 8859 7075
- **HOLLAND & BARRETT**, 21 Central Square, **WEMBLEY**, HA9 7AJ (T) 020 8902 6959
- **HOLLAND & BARRETT**, 21-23 Shorts Gardens, **LONDON**, WC2H 9AS (T) 020 7836 5151
- **HOLLAND & BARRETT**, 220 Fulham Road, **LONDON**, SW10 9NB (T) 020 7352 9939
- **HOLLAND & BARRETT**, 22-24 College Road, **HARROW**, HA1 1BE (T) 020 8427 4794
- **HOLLAND & BARRETT**, 260 Kensington High Street, **LONDON**, W8 6NA (T) 020 7603 2751
- **HOLLAND & BARRETT**, 29 The Arndale Centre, **LONDON**, SW18 4TE (T) 020 8871 3706
- **HOLLAND & BARRETT**, 3 Mitcham Road, **LONDON**, SW17 9PA (T) 020 8767 8552
- **HOLLAND & BARRETT**, 3 Selborne Walk, **LONDON**, E17 7JR (T) 020 8520 5459
- **HOLLAND & BARRETT**, 31 Upper Street, **LONDON**, N1 0PN (T) 020 7359 9117
- **HOLLAND & BARRETT**, 319 High Holborn, **LONDON**, WC1V 7PB (T) 020 7242 0459
- **HOLLAND & BARRETT**, 32 Queensway, **LONDON**, W2 4QW (T) 020 7727 6449
- **HOLLAND & BARRETT**, 332 Green Lanes, **LONDON**, N13 5TW (T) 020 8886 6769
- **HOLLAND & BARRETT**, 36 Brunswick Centre, **LONDON**, WC1N 1AE (T) 020 7278 4640
- **HOLLAND & BARRETT**, 38 Church Street, **ENFIELD**, EN2 6BA (T) 020 8367 3944
- **HOLLAND & BARRETT**, 416 Chiswick High Road, **LONDON**, W4 5TF (T) 020 8994 1683
- **HOLLAND & BARRETT**, 42 Kilburn High Road, **LONDON**, NW6 4HJ (T) 020 7624 9297
- **HOLLAND & BARRETT**, 452 Holloway Road, **LONDON**, N7 6QA (T) 020 7607 3933
- **HOLLAND & BARRETT**, 5 Kings Mall, King Street, **LONDON**, W6 0PZ (T) 020 8748 9792
- **HOLLAND & BARRETT**, 51 Johns Road, **LONDON**, SW11 1QP (T) 020 7228 6071
- **HOLLAND & BARRETT**, 55 St Johns Wood High Street, **LONDON**, NW8 7NL (T) 020 7586 5494
- **HOLLAND & BARRETT**, 6 New Broadway, **LONDON**, W5 2XA (T) 020 8840 1070
- **HOLLAND & BARRETT**, 61 Broadway, **LONDON**, W13 9BP (T) 020 8840 7558
- **HOLLAND & BARRETT**, 67 Riverdale, **LONDON**, SE13 7ER (T) 020 8297 9559
- **HOLLAND & BARRETT**, 68 The Broadway, **LONDON**, SW19 1RQ (T) 020 8542 7486
- **HOLLAND & BARRETT**, 7 North Mall, **LONDON**, N9 0EQ (T) 020 8807 6711
- **HOLLAND & BARRETT**, 71-73 Kings Road, **LONDON**, SW3 4NX (T) 020 7352 4130
- **HOLLAND & BARRETT**, 78 Baker Street, **LONDON**, W1M 1DL (T) 020 7935 3544
- **HOLLAND & BARRETT**, 81 Golders Green Road, **LONDON**, NW11 8EN (T) 020 8455 5811
- **HOLLAND & BARRETT**, 81 Powis Street, **LONDON**, SE18 6JB (T) 020 8316 5490
- **HOLLAND & BARRETT**, 90 The Mall, The Stratford Centre, **LONDON**, E15 1XQ (T) 020 8536 0467
- **HOLLAND & BARRETT**, Aldgate Bars Shopping Centre, 1 Whitechapel High Street, **LONDON**, E1 1DU (T) 020 7481 3791
- **HOLLAND & BARRETT**, Catford Centre, 33 Winslade Way, **LONDON**, SE6 4JU (T) 020 8690 3903
- **HOLLAND & BARRETT**, The High, Streatham High Road, **LONDON**, SW16 1HA (T) 020 8769 1418
- **HOLLAND & BARRETT**, Unit 2b Dalston Cross Shopping Centre, **LONDON**, E8 2LX (T) 020 7923 9113
- **HOLLAND & BARRETT**, Unit 9 Aylesham Centre, Rye Lane, **LONDON**, SE15 5EW (T) 020 7639 3354
- **HOLLAND & BARRETT**, Unit W16 Shopping Centre, Brent Cross, **LONDON**, NW4 3FG (T) 020 8202 8669
- **HOLLAND & BARRETT**, Victoria Station, Unit 15 Victoria Place, **LONDON**, SW1W 9SJ (T) 020 7828 5480
- **HOLLAND & BARRETT**, West One Shopping Centre, 381 Oxford Street, **LONDON**, W1R 1FE (T) 020 7493 7988
- **HOLLAND & BARRETT LTD**, 25 Surrey Quays Shopping Centre, Redriff Road, **LONDON**, SE16 7LL (T) 020 7231 1043
- **HONEY HEALTH**, 83 High Road, **LONDON**, E18 2QP (T) 020 8530 6136
- **HONEY TREE (THE)**, 340 Norwood Road, **LONDON**, SE27 9AF (T) 020 8670 0288
- **HOUSE OF MISTRY**, 15-17 South End Road, **LONDON**, NW3 2PT (T) 020 7794 0848
- **HUMAN NATURE**, 13 Malvern Road, **LONDON**, NW6 5PS (T) 020 7328 5452
- **IDRISS NATURAL FOODS LTD**, Units 9-10 Brember Road, **HARROW**, HA2 8AX (T) 020 8864 9827
- **IRENE STEIN LTD**, 1a Nichol Close, **LONDON**, N14 6JP (T) 020 8886 6000
- **IRENE STIN LTD**, 1a Nichol Close, **LONDON**, N14 6JP (T) 08001 46441
- **JAYSONS WHOLESALE**, Unit 28 Stadium Business Centre, North End Road, **WEMBLEY**, HA9 0AT (T) 020 8795 4850
- **JUICEMOOSE UK LTD**, 28 James Street, **LONDON**, W1M 5HS (T) 020 7487 2882
- **KENKKO GROUP LTD**, Kenkko House, 8 Heriot Road, **LONDON**, NW4 2DG (T) 020 8202 6600
- **KOREAN RED GINSENG CO LTD (THE)**, P O Box 16018, **LONDON**, SW11 3WH (T) 020 7585 0312
- **KUDOS**, 256 Edgware Road, **LONDON**, W2 1DS (T) 020 7724 3904
- **KUDOS VITAMINS & HERBALS LTD**, 2nd Floor Parkway House, Sheen Lane, **LONDON**, SW14 8LS (T) 020 8392 6524
- **L SPENCER**, 120A Lower Clapton Road, **LONDON**, E5 0QR (T) 020 8510 9524
- **LIFE ESSENCE LTD**, Unit 15 Chiltonian Industrial Estate, Manor Lane, **LONDON**, SE12 0TX (T) 020 8297 7888
- **LIFE PLUS INDEPENDENT MEMBER**, 22 Westbourne Gdns, **LONDON**, W2 5PU (T) 020 7221 3668

- **LONDON DISTRIBUTORS**, 47 Farringdon Road, **LONDON**, EC1M 3JB (T) 020 7916 9773
- **LPU HEALTH CLUB**, 122 Kilburn High Road, **LONDON**, NW6 4HY (T) 020 7328 1515
- **MAGNA JEWELLERY LTD**, Po Box 338, **EDGWARE**, HA8 8HZ (T) 020 8958 9719
- **MANOR HEALTH FOODS**, 93 Victoria Road, **RUISLIP**, HA4 9BH (T) 01895 672386
- **MARIGOLD HEALTH FOODS LTD**, 102 Camley Street, **LONDON**, NW1 0PF (T) 020 7388 4515
- **MARKET PLACE HEALTH FOODS**, 8 Market Place, **LONDON**, W3 6QS (T) 020 8993 3848
- **MARKHAM PRODUCTS LTD**, 2-5 Old Bond Street, **LONDON**, W1X 3TB (T) 020 7491 7993
- **MARTIN WELLS**, 55 Mount Pleasant Road, **LONDON**, NW10 3EH (T) 020 8357 9557
- **MEERAS HEALTH FOOD CENTRE**, 2 High Street, **LONDON**, NW10 4LX (T) 020 8965 7610
- **MILLENNIUM HEALTH FOODS**, Unit 50B/Ealing Broadway Centre, The Broadway, **LONDON**, W5 5JY (T) 020 8840 6949
- **MISTRYS CHEMIST**, 16-18 Station Parade, **LONDON**, NW2 4NH (T) 020 8450 7002
- **MISTRY'S HEALTH FOOD STORE**, 18 Station Parade, **LONDON**, NW2 4NH (T) 020 8450 0025
- **MONTIGNAC BOUTIQUE**, 160 Old Brompton Road, **LONDON**, SW5 0BA (T) 020 7370 2010
- **MRS R LEE**, Golders Green Road, **LONDON**, NW11 9AT (T) 07930 356435
- **MULTILINKS LTD**, 12 The Broadway, **SOUTHALL**, UB1 1PS (T) 020 8867 9660
- **NATALIE HEALTH FOOD**, 245 Imperial Drive, **HARROW**, HA2 7HE (T) 020 8868 0695
- **NATURAL HEALTHCARE**, 89 Lonsdale Avenue, **WEMBLEY**, HA9 7EW (T) 020 8903 1931
- **NATURAL RISE FOODS**, 21 Bernard Road, **LONDON**, N15 4NE (T) 020 8808 2007
- **NATURAL WAY (THE)**, 1b The Avenue, **LONDON**, E4 9LB (T) 020 8523 5123
- **NATURE CHOICE LTD**, 7 Falcons Court, St Martins Way, **LONDON**, SW17 0JH (T) 020 8944 5584
- **NATURE'S CHOICE**, 47 Church Lane, **LONDON**, E11 1HE (T) 020 8539 4196
- **NATURE'S GOLD**, 783a Fulham Road, **LONDON**, SW6 5HD (T) 020 7736 1600
- **NATURE'S WAY HEALTH SHOP**, 252 Streatham High Road, **LONDON**, SW16 1HS (T) 020 8769 0065
- **NATUROSAN HEALTH PRODUCTS**, 32 Sylvester Road, **LONDON**, N2 8HN (T) 020 8343 3403
- **NIKKEN INDEPENDENT DISTRIBUTOR**, 3 Haldan Road, **LONDON**, E4 9JJ (T) 020 8531 4175
- **NUT HOUSE LTD**, 341 Mare Street, **LONDON**, E8 1HY (T) 020 8525 0090
- **NUT HOUSE LTD (THE)**, 448 Bethnal Green Road, **LONDON**, E1 6LA (T) 020 7739 5456
- **NUTMAN (THE)**, Park Royal Business Centre, 9-17 Park Royal Road, **LONDON**, NW10 7LQ (T) 020 8965 1112
- **NUTRITION & BEAUTY CENTRE**, 246 Upper Tooting Road, **LONDON**, SW17 7EX (T) 020 8672 5417
- **NUTRITION WORKS**, 18 Dollis Hill Estate, Brook Road, **LONDON**, NW2 7BZ (T) 020 8450 2522
- **NUTSTOP**, Platford 1 Metropolitan Line, Baker Street, **LONDON**, W1M 1DA (T) 020 7224 4064
- **OLIVE TREE**, 84 Willesden Lane, **LONDON**, NW6 7TA (T) 020 7328 9078
- **OPTIMUM NUTRITION CO (THE)**, 13 Blades Court, **LONDON**, W6 9DJ (T) 020 8870 9490
- **PANACEA (HEALTH) LTD**, Hallmark Trading Estate, Fourth Way, **WEMBLEY**, HA9 0LB (T) 020 8795 3730
- **PARADISE FOODS**, 164 Kentish Town Road, **LONDON**, NW5 2JS (T) 020 7284 3402
- **PEACHES HEALTH**, 143 High Street, Wanstead, **LONDON**, E11 2RL (T) 020 8530 3617
- **PEPPERCORNS NATURAL HEALTH FOODS**, 193-195 West End Lane, **LONDON**, NW6 2LJ (T) 020 7328 6874
- **PHARMADASS LTD**, 16 Aintree Road, **GREENFORD**, UB6 7LA (T) 020 8991 0035
- **PIKME DRY FRUITS & NUTS**, 2 Ashcombe Gardens, **EDGWARE**, HA8 8HS (T) 020 8958 3018
- **PLANET ORGANIC**, 42 Westbourne Grove, **LONDON**, W2 5SH (T) 020 7221 7171
- **PORTOBELLO WHOLEFOODS**, 266 Portobello Road, **LONDON**, W10 5TY (T) 020 8968 9133
- **POSITIVE ENERGY**, 14a Lime Gr, **LONDON**, W12 8EA (T) 020 8477 5766
- **PREMIER FRUIT & NUT LTD**, Premier House, 325 Streatham High Road, **LONDON**, SW16 3NT (T) 020 8679 8226
- **PROCELL LTD**, 440 West Green Road, **LONDON**, N15 3PT (T) 020 8889 5050
- **PROVENDER**, 103 Dartmouth Road, **LONDON**, SE23 3HT (T) 020 8699 4046
- **PUREALOE**, 341 Lea Bridge Road, **LONDON**, E10 7LA (T) 020 8521 1166
- **QUEENS HEALTH SHOP**, 64 Gloucester Road, **LONDON**, SW7 4QT (T) 020 7584 4815
- **QUITELYNN LTD**, 682 Holloway Road, **LONDON**, N19 3NP (T) 020 7263 6570
- **REAL FARE NUTRITION CENTRE**, 296 Chiswick High Road, **LONDON**, W4 1PA (T) 020 8995 2293
- **REGINA HEALTH LTD**, Alexandra Grove, **LONDON**, N12 8NU (T) 020 8446 6644
- **RESPECT FOR LIFE**, Warwick House/Angell Town Estate, Overton Road, **LONDON**, SW9 7JP (T) 020 7501 9800
- **REVITAL HEALTH PLACE**, 3a The Colonnade, 123-151 Buckingham Palace Road, **LONDON**, SW1W 9TB (T) 020 7976 6615
- **REVITAL HEALTH SHOP**, 35 High Road, **LONDON**, NW10 2TE (T) 020 8459 3382
- **REVITAL LTD**, 78 High Street, **RUISLIP**, HA4 7AA (T) 01895 629950
- **RHEMA UK LTD**, Coach House, 72 Rowfant Road, **LONDON**, SW17 7AS (T) 020 8488 8111
- **ROAD TO GOOD HEALTH**, 388 Norwood Road, **LONDON**, SE27 9AA (T) 020 8333 1858
- **RUISLIP HEALTH FOODS**, 22 High Street, **RUISLIP**, HA4 7AN (T) 01895 638187
- **RYE WHOLEFOODS**, 35 Myddelton Street, **LONDON**, EC1R 1UA (T) 020 7278 5878
- **S HENDRICKSON**, 2 Scholefield Road, **LONDON**, N19 3EX (T) 020 7272 9484
- **SABONA RHEUMATIC RELIEF CO LTD**, 4 Blythe Mews, Blythe Road, **LONDON**, W14 0HW (T) 020 7603 0656
- **SCITEC EUROPE**, Brisbane Avenue, **LONDON**, SW19 3AF (T) 020 8543 5999
- **SECOND NATURE WHOLEFOODS**, 78 Wood Street, **LONDON**, E17 3HX (T) 020 8520 7995
- **SESAME WHOLEFOODS**, 128 Regents Park Road, **LONDON**, NW1 8XL (T) 020 7586 3779
- **SHEEL HEALTH & HERBAL**, 312-314 Lewisham Road, **LONDON**, SE13 7PA (T) 020 8244 0809
- **SILVERSTONE FOODS**, 71a Wentworth Street, **LONDON**, E1 7TD (T) 020 8881 7262
- **SLOANE HEALTH SHOP**, 27 King's Road, **LONDON**, SW3 4RP (T) 020 7730 7046
- **SOVEREIGN HEALTH**, 14 Eastbourne Avenue, **LONDON**, W3 6JN (T) 020 8896 3706
- **SPIRALHAVEN LTD**, Unit 28 Cumberland Business Park, Cumberland Avenue, **LONDON**, NW10 7AX (T) 020 8965 7810
- **STAY HEALTHY NATURALLY**, 111 Wembley Park Drive, **WEMBLEY**, HA9 8HG (T) 020 8903 8683
- **SUN FOODS LTD**, 17 Marshgate Lane Business Centre, **LONDON**, E15 2NH (T) 020 8519 8080
- **SUN FOREST WHOLEFOODS**, 21 Broad Street, **TEDDINGTON**, TW11 8QZ (T) 020 8977 1151
- **SUNRIDER EUROPE**, 4th Floor, 14-20 Shand Street, **LONDON**, SE1 2ES (T) 020 7940 8000
- **SUNRIDER INDEPENDANT DISTRIBUTOR**, 158 Shirland Road, **LONDON**, W9 2BT (T) 020 7266 0173
- **SUPPLEMENT WAREHOUSE**, 160 Hermon Hill, **LONDON**, E18 1QH (T) 020 8989 6665
- **SWISSHEALTH**, 11 St Mary Abbots Terrace, **LONDON**, W14 8NX (T) 020 7602 5344
- **TANGERINE DREAM**, 3 Ravenscourt Close, **RUISLIP**, HA4 7PP (T) 01895 624001
- **TEMPLE HEALTH FOODS**, 17 Temple Fortune Parade, **LONDON**, NW11 0QS (T) 020 8458 6087
- **TENS HEALTH LTD**, 108 George Lane, South Woodford, **LONDON**, E18 1AD (T) 020 8532 2310
- **TODAYS LIVING**, 92 Clapham High Street, **LONDON**, SW4 7UL (T) 020 7622 1772
- **TONY'S NATURAL FOODS**, 10 Caledonian Road, **LONDON**, N1 9DU (T) 020 7837 5223
- **TOP QUALITY NATURAL FOOD & NUTS**, PO Box 2465, **LONDON**, NW7 3QJ (T) 020 8906 3080
- **TOTAL BODY CARE**, Unit 26 4 Silicon Centre, 26-28 Wadsworth Road, **GREENFORD**, UB6 7JD (T) 020 8997 8319
- **TRANS-GLOBE DISTRIBUTING & MARKETING LTD**, 31 Bedford Square, **LONDON**, WC1B 3EG (T) 020 7314 1567
- **TRIOLET INTERNATIONAL LTD**, 5 Lawn Road, **LONDON**, NW3 2XS (T) 020 7722 2866
- **TROPICAL WHOLEFOODS**, Unit 9 Industrial Estate, Hamilton Road, **LONDON**, SE27 9SF (T) 020 8670 1114

- **ULTIMATE HEALTH**, 51 Welbeck Street, **LONDON**, W1M 7HE
(T) 020 7935 0506
- **V R C**, 12b Bittacy Hill, Mill Hill, **LONDON**, NW7 1LB
(T) 020 8343 0222
- **VAL & SONS**, 37 Iberia House, Hornsey Rise, **LONDON**, N19 3ND
(T) 020 7686 1108
- **VEGAN DIRECT LTD**, 74 Bidwell Gardens, **LONDON**, N11 2AU
(T) 020 8374 8001
- **VEGETARIA**, 25 Half Moon Lane, **LONDON**, SE24 9JU
(T) 020 7274 5759
- **VEGETARIAN FOODS UK LTD**, Security House, 2 Romford Road, **LONDON**, E15 4BZ
(T) 020 8521 6227
- **VENUS HEALTH FOOD STORE**, 141c High Street, **LONDON**, E17 7DB
(T) 020 8520 3085
- **VICTORIA HEALTH FOODS**, 99 Muswell Hill Broadway, **LONDON**, N10 3RS
(T) 020 8444 2355
- **VICTORIA HEALTH FOODS**, Unit 23/Broadwalk Shopping Centre, Station Road, **EDGWARE**, HA8 7BD
(T) 020 8905 6931
- **VITA HEALTH FOODS**, 565 Lea Bridge Road, **LONDON**, E10 7EQ
(T) 020 8539 3245
- **VITACARE LTD**, Unit 1/Utopia Village, 7 Chalcot Road, **LONDON**, NW1 8LH
(T) 020 7722 4300
- **VITAFOOD KNUFINKE**, 37-38 Long Acre, **LONDON**, WC2E 9JT
(T) 020 7836 0666
- **VITAL NUTRITION LTD**, 4 Quex Road, **LONDON**, NW6 4PJ
(T) 020 7624 8557
- **VITALITY HEALTH SHOP**, 1 Merton High Street, **LONDON**, SW19 1DD
(T) 020 8544 9433
- **VITAMEX (UK) LTD**, 338 Euston Road, **LONDON**, NW1 3BT
(T) 020 7544 8635
- **WELL BEAN**, 9 Old Dover Road, **LONDON**, SE3 7BT
(T) 020 8858 6854
- **WELL BEING FOODS**, 19 Sydenham Road, **LONDON**, SE26 5EX
(T) 020 8659 2003
- **WEMBLEY HEALTH FOOD CENTRE (THE)**, 536 High Road, **WEMBLEY**, HA9 7BS
(T) 020 8900 2684
- **WHOLE EARTH FOODS LTD**, 2 Valentine Place, **LONDON**, SE1 8QH
(T) 020 7633 5900
- **WHOLEFOOD**, 24 Paddington Street, **LONDON**, W1M 4DR
(T) 020 7935 3924
- **WHOLEMEAL SHOP (THE)**, 190 Well Street, **LONDON**, E9 6QT
(T) 020 8985 1822
- **WILKINS NATURAL FOODS**, 53 Marsham Street, **LONDON**, SW1P 3DP
(T) 020 7222 4038
- **ZEST**, 38 Upper Street, **LONDON**, N1 0PN
(T) 020 7704 6680
- **ZINAXIN**, Palladium House, 1-4 Argyll Street, **LONDON**, W1V 2LD
(T) 020 7328 9797

## MANCHESTER (GREATER)

- **BG SPORTS & HEALTH SUPPLIES**, Unit 6/Old Co-Op Buildings, High Street, Worsley, **MANCHESTER**, M28 3JH
(T) 01617 903983
- **CHEMICAL NUTRITIONAL PRODUCTS LTD**, Unit 10 Alpha Court, Windmill Lane Industrial Estate, Denton, **MANCHESTER**, M34 3RB
(T) 01613 201212
- **CHORLTON WHOLE FOODS**, 64 Beech Road, **MANCHESTER**, M21 9EG
(T) 01618 816399
- **CLARE'S HEALTH FOOD SHOP**, 22 Queens Walk, Droylsden, **MANCHESTER**, M43 7AD
(T) 01613 015287
- **FOREVER LIVING PRODUCTS**, 15 Marham Close, **MANCHESTER**, M21 7GD
(T) 01618 606313
- **GOOD LIFE VICTORIA (THE)**, 6 Victoria Station Approach, **MANCHESTER**, M3 1NY
(T) 01618 345224
- **HEALTH & DIET FOOD CO LTD**, Units B1-B2 & C1-C2/Europa Trading Estate, Stoneclough Road, Radcliffe, **MANCHESTER**, M26 1GG
(T) 01204 707420
- **HOLLAND & BARRETT**, 607 Wilbraham Road, **MANCHESTER**, M21 9AN
(T) 01618 811539
- **HOLLAND & BARRETT**, 87 Deansgate, **MANCHESTER**, M3 2BW
(T) 01618 345923
- **HOLLAND & BARRETT**, F10 Arndale Shopping Centre, Middleton, **MANCHESTER**, M24 4EL
(T) 01616 433180
- **HOLLAND & BARRETT**, Unit66 Arndale Centre, Stretford, **MANCHESTER**, M32 9BD
(T) 01618 655229
- **HOLLAND & BARRETT LTD**, 8 Peel Avenue, The Trafford Centre, **MANCHESTER**, M17 8BL
(T) 01617 472699
- **JEAN'S HEALTH FOODS LTD**, 17 Festival Village, The Trafford Centre, **MANCHESTER**, M17 8FS
(T) 01617 471117
- **LAUGHING LENTAL (THE)**, 10 King Edwards Buildings, Bury Old Road, **SALFORD**, M7 4QJ
(T) 01617 405766
- **NATURE'S GRACE**, 37 Barlow Moor Road, **MANCHESTER**, M20 6TW
(T) 01614 346784
- **OASIS FOOD & DRINK CO LTD**, Ennis Cl, Roundthorn Industrial Estate, **MANCHESTER**, M23 9LE
(T) 01612 838888
- **ORGANIX WHOLEFOODS LTD**, Sevendale House, 7 Dale Street, **MANCHESTER**, M1 1JA
(T) 01612 280220
- **SOYA HEALTH FOODS LTD**, Unit 4 Guinness Road, Trafford Park, **MANCHESTER**, M17 1SD
(T) 01618 720549
- **SWINTON HEALTH FOODS**, 177 Moorside Road, Swinton, **MANCHESTER**, M27 9LD
(T) 01617 930091
- **UNICORN GROCERY LTD**, 89 Albany Road, **MANCHESTER**, M21 0BN
(T) 01618 610010
- **VILLAGE HEALTH FOOD STORE (THE)**, 47 Church Street, Eccles, **MANCHESTER**, M30 0BJ
(T) 01617 889745
- **WITHINGTON HEALTH FOODS**, 486 Wilmslow Road, **MANCHESTER**, M20 3BG
(T) 01614 456696

## MERSEYSIDE

- **ABACA**, 255 Woolton Road, Childwall, **LIVERPOOL**, L16 8NA
(T) 01517 226669
- **ALLERGY AID SHOP (THE)**, 83 Pensby Road, Heswall, **WIRRAL**, CH60 7RB
(T) 01513 484488
- **ALOE TO YOU**, 11 Halcyon Road, **BIRKENHEAD**, CH41 2UG
(T) 01516 533958
- **ALOE VERA**, 5 Solar Road, **LIVERPOOL**, L9 9AS
(T) 01515 257137
- **ALOE VERA UK**, 72 Oldfield Drive, Heswall, **WIRRAL**, CH60 9HF
(T) 01513 424160
- **ATHENA INTERNATIONAL**, Laurel Business Centre, 15 Laurel Road, **LIVERPOOL**, L7 0LJ
(T) 01512 808384
- **BIRKDALE HEALTH STORE**, 35b Liverpool Road, **SOUTHPORT**, PR8 4AG
(T) 01704 564353
- **BODYCARE HEALTH SHOP**, 27 Bridge Street, **NEWTON-LE-WILLOWS**, WA12 9BE
(T) 01925 220313
- **EUROPAD LTD**, 4 Kelvin Park, Dock Road, **BIRKENHEAD**, CH41 1LT
(T) 01516 502280
- **FOODS OF THE WORLD**, 18 Ormskirk Street, **ST. HELENS**, WA10 1BJ
(T) 01744 29491
- **GRANARY (THE)**, 17 Pensby Road, Heswall, **WIRRAL**, CH60 7RA
(T) 01513 427428
- **GRANARY (THE)**, 2 Parkgate Road, **NESTON**, CH64 9XE
(T) 01513 531331
- **GRANARY (THE)**, Care Of Kwik Save, 374 Woodchurch Road, **BIRKENHEAD**, CH42 8PG
(T) 01516 080411
- **HEALTH RACK**, 185 Lord Street, **SOUTHPORT**, PR8 1PF
(T) 01704 510580
- **HEALTH RACK**, 7 Church Square, **ST. HELENS**, WA10 1AF
(T) 01744 29899
- **HEALTH RACK**, Parkside, Strand Shopping Centre, **BOOTLE**, L20 4ST
(T) 01519 335606
- **HEALTH RACK**, Unit 44 Tontine Market, Lagrange Arcade, **ST. HELENS**, WA10 1BL
(T) 01744 22907
- **HEALTHY BITE**, 35 Crosby Road North, **LIVERPOOL**, L22 4QB
(T) 01519 288188
- **HERBALIFE**, 13 Fulwood Road, **LIVERPOOL**, L17 9PX
(T) 01517 288725
- **HOLLAND & BARRETT**, 10 The Palatine, Strand Shopping Centre, **BOOTLE**, L20 4SN
(T) 01519 229157
- **HOLLAND & BARRETT**, 12 Station Arcade, Chapel Street, **SOUTHPORT**, PR8 1BH
(T) 01704 530734
- **HOLLAND & BARRETT**, 17 Whitechapel, **LIVERPOOL**, L1 6DS
(T) 01512 368911
- **HOLLAND & BARRETT**, 28 Marina Walk, **ELLESMERE PORT**, CH65 0BN
(T) 01513 559228
- **HOLLAND & BARRETT**, 3a Bold Street, **LIVERPOOL**, L1 4DJ
(T) 01517 089343
- **HOLLAND & BARRETT**, 4 Cherry Square, **WALLASEY**, CH44 5XU
(T) 01516 397707
- **HOLLAND & BARRETT**, 6 Borough Pavement, Grange Precinct, **BIRKENHEAD**, CH41 2XX
(T) 01516 477327
- **HOLLAND & BARRETT**, 8 Hardshaw Centre, **ST. HELENS**, WA10 1EB
(T) 01744 20821
- **KOMBUCHA HEALTH LTD**, Unit A3B/Small Business Centre, Brunswick Way, Brunswick Business Park, **LIVERPOOL**, L3 4BD
(T) 01517 090008
- **LIFESTYLES**, 230 Guildford Road, **SOUTHPORT**, PR8 4NQ
(T) 01772 489157
- **MARKET HEALTH FOOD STORE**, 39-52 King Street, **SOUTHPORT**, PR8 1LG
(T) 01704 535795
- **MILLENNIA HEALTH**, 144 Seabank Road, **WALLASEY**, CH45 1HG
(T) 01516 395982
- **NATURAL WAYS**, 6 Market Street, **SOUTHPORT**, PR8 1HH
(T) 01704 545210
- **NATURES GATE**, 248 Smithdown Road, **LIVERPOOL**, L15 5AH
(T) 01517 342425
- **ONLY NATURAL**, 48 Westfield Street, **ST. HELENS**, WA10 1QF
(T) 01744 759797
- **PRESCOT HEALTH SHOP**, 13 Eccleston Street, **PRESCOT**, L34 5QA
(T) 01512 925062
- **SEFTON PARK HEALTH FOODS**, 8 Lawrence Road, **LIVERPOOL**, L15 0EG
(T) 01517 337545
- **SOUTHPORT HEALTH FOOD SHOP**, 25 Market Street, **SOUTHPORT**, PR8 1HJ
(T) 01704 531448
- **TAITS**, 83-85 Dale Street, **LIVERPOOL**, L2 2HT
(T) 01512 362338

- **THORNBY HEALTH STORE**, 66 Brows Lane, **LIVERPOOL**, L37 4ED (T) 01704 877330
- **TOTAL HEALTH CARE**, 34 Grange Road, **SOUTHPORT**, PR9 9AD (T) 01704 530646
- **TUCKERBINS KIRKBY**, 8 Telegraph Way, **LIVERPOOL**, L32 8US (T) 01515 485155
- **WENDY LLOYD AUDIO PRODUCTIONS LTD**, 1A Grosvenor Road, **WIRRAL**, CH47 3BS (T) 01516 321206
- **WOOLTON VILLAGE HEALTH FOODS**, 5 Allerton Road, Woolton, **LIVERPOOL**, L25 7RA (T) 01514 282386
- **ZANZA HEALTH CARE**, A1 Kingfisher Business Pk, Hawthorne Road, **BOOTLE**, L20 6PF (T) 01519 224640

## MIDDLESEX

- **NORTHWOOD HEALTH FOODS**, 3 Rowland Place, Green Lane, **NORTHWOOD**, HA6 1AB (T) 01923 824882

## MIDLANDS (WEST)

- **ALOE VERA ADVISORY CENTRE**, 123a Birmingham Road, **COVENTRY**, CV5 9GR (T) 024 7640 2837
- **ALPHA THE NATURAL WAY**, 44 Market Street, **KINGSWINFORD**, DY6 9LB (T) 01384 277257
- **BEST OF HEALTH (THE)**, Safeguard House, Intown, **WALSALL**, WS1 1SQ (T) 01922 610890
- **BIOCARE LTD**, Lakeside Centre, 180 Lifford Lane, **BIRMINGHAM**, B30 3NU (T) 01214 333727
- **CAMBRIDGE DIET CENTRE**, 27 Glebe Drive, **SUTTON COLDFIELD**, B73 5SZ (T) 01216 057499
- **COUNTRY CUPBOARD (THE)**, 94 The Green, Kings Norton, **BIRMINGHAM**, B38 8RS (T) 01214 584411
- **DROP IN THE OCEAN**, 17 City Arcade, **COVENTRY**, CV1 3HX (T) 024 7622 5273
- **GENERAL NUTRITION CENTRE**, 58 Broadgate, **COVENTRY**, CV1 1NF (T) 024 7622 1336
- **GENERAL NUTRITION CENTRE**, 63 The Pallasades, **BIRMINGHAM**, B2 4XJ (T) 01216 338216
- **GNC LTD**, Unit 99 The Merry Hill Centre, **BRIERLEY HILL**, DY5 1SY (T) 01384 480908
- **GNC-GENERAL NUTRITION CENTRE**, 30 Bradford Mall, Saddlers Centre, **WALSALL**, WS1 1YT (T) 01922 720671
- **GOOD HEALTH FOODS**, 19 Old Square, **WALSALL**, WS1 1QA (T) 01922 638989
- **GOOD HEALTHFOODS LTD**, 15 Shelton Square, **COVENTRY**, CV1 1DG (T) 024 7663 2774
- **GREEN VALLEY TRADING CO**, 135 Stratford Road, Shirley, **SOLIHULL**, B90 3AY (T) 01217 440690
- **HARVEST HEALTH FOODS**, 34 The Square, Aldridge, **WALSALL**, WS9 8QS (T) 01922 745245
- **HEALTH & BEAUTY**, Stalls 28 & 29 Market Hall, Market Street, **BILSTON**, WV14 0DN (T) 01902 498284
- **HEALTH & HERBS**, 39 Lower High Street, **WEDNESBURY**, WS10 7AQ (T) 01215 053019
- **HEALTH FOOD CENTRE**, 146-148 High Street, **SOLIHULL**, B91 3SY (T) 01217 050134
- **HEALTH HARMONY**, 347 Kenilworth Road, Balsall Common, **COVENTRY**, CV7 7DL (T) 01676 530288
- **HEALTH SHOP (THE)**, 19 Silvercourt, **WALSALL**, WS8 6HA (T) 01543 372742
- **HEALTH SHOP (THE)**, 22 Market Centre, High Street, Bloxwich, **WALSALL**, WS3 2JE (T) 01922 710004
- **HEALTH SHOP (WILLENHALL) (THE)**, 3 Cross Street, **WILLENHALL**, WV13 1PG (T) 01902 601035
- **HEALTH STORE (THE)**, 10a Burnett Road, **SUTTON COLDFIELD**, B74 3EJ (T) 01213 534169
- **HEALTH WORLD**, Care Of Spencers Instore Shops, The Merry Hill Centre, **BRIERLEY HILL**, DY5 1SY (T) 01384 482363
- **HOLLAND & BARRETT**, 11 Churchill Shopping Centre, **DUDLEY**, DY1 1PJ (T) 01384 230610
- **HOLLAND & BARRETT**, 11-13 Queens Arcade, **WOLVERHAMPTON**, WV1 3NL (T) 01902 420937
- **HOLLAND & BARRETT**, 1-3 Priory Square, **BIRMINGHAM**, B4 7LG (T) 01212 367869
- **HOLLAND & BARRETT**, 132 High Street, Erdington, **BIRMINGHAM**, B23 6RS (T) 01213 829897
- **HOLLAND & BARRETT**, 215 Stratford Road, Shirley, **SOLIHULL**, B90 3AH (T) 01217 336880
- **HOLLAND & BARRETT**, 2160 Coventry Road, Sheldon, **BIRMINGHAM**, B26 3JB (T) 01217 420313
- **HOLLAND & BARRETT**, 22 Grosvenor Shopping Centre, Northfield, **BIRMINGHAM**, B31 2JU (T) 01214 754932
- **HOLLAND & BARRETT**, 32 Ryemarket, **STOURBRIDGE**, DY8 1HJ (T) 01384 374112
- **HOLLAND & BARRETT**, 33 Alcester Road South, **BIRMINGHAM**, B14 7JQ (T) 01214 447000
- **HOLLAND & BARRETT**, 33 Cornbow Centre, Hagley Mall, **HALESOWEN**, B63 4AJ (T) 01215 850496
- **HOLLAND & BARRETT**, 34-36 Park Street, **WALSALL**, WS1 1NG (T) 01922 611348
- **HOLLAND & BARRETT**, 43 Queens Square, Sandwell Centre, **WEST BROMWICH**, B70 7NJ (T) 01215 535523
- **HOLLAND & BARRETT**, 54-55 The Pallasades, **BIRMINGHAM**, B2 4XH (T) 01216 330104
- **HOLLAND & BARRETT**, 6 City Arcade, **COVENTRY**, CV1 3HX (T) 024 7622 2752
- **HOLLAND & BARRETT**, 84 High Street, **SOLIHULL**, B91 3TA (T) 01217 092153
- **HOLLAND & BARRETT**, 98 Church Street, **BILSTON**, WV14 0AX (T) 01902 496489
- **HOLLAND & BARRETT**, 99a High Street, Harborne, **BIRMINGHAM**, B17 9NR (T) 01214 276494
- **HOLLAND & BARRETT**, One Stop Shopping Centre, Walsall Road, Perry Barr, **BIRMINGHAM**, B42 1AA (T) 01213 311599
- **HOLLAND & BARRETT**, Sainsbury Centre, 31-57 Lower Parade, **SUTTON COLDFIELD**, B72 1XX (T) 01213 212439
- **HOLLAND & BARRETT**, West Orchard Shopping Centre, Smithford Way, **COVENTRY**, CV1 1QL (T) 024 7623 0107
- **HOUSE OF HEALTH (THE)**, 6/Carlton House, 18 Mere Green Road, **SUTTON COLDFIELD**, B75 5BS (T) 01213 087020
- **JULIAN GRAVES LTD**, 210 The Parade, **SUTTON COLDFIELD**, B72 1PA (T) 01213 212713
- **JULIAN GRAVES LTD**, Unit 95, Off Second Avenue, **KINGSWINFORD**, DY6 7JU (T) 01384 282700
- **JUST HEALTH**, Arcadian Shopping Centre, Ladywell Walk, **BIRMINGHAM**, B5 4TD (T) 01216 225923
- **LEPPIN HEALTH PRODUCTS LTD**, Unit 10 Tile Cross Trading Estate, Tile Cross Road, **BIRMINGHAM**, B33 0NW (T) 01217 796619
- **LIFESTYLE**, 139 Daventry Road, **COVENTRY**, CV3 5HD (T) 024 7650 2147
- **MOTHER NATURE BABYFOOD'S LTD**, Arena Studios, 126 Morville Street, **BIRMINGHAM**, B16 8DG (T) 01214 558011
- **NATURAL WORLD FOODS LTD**, 23 Central Square, High Street, Erdington, **BIRMINGHAM**, B23 6RY (T) 01216 813838
- **NATURAL WORLD FOODS LTD**, 596 Bearwood Road, **SMETHWICK**, B66 4BW (T) 01214 202145
- **NATURES HEALTH SHOP**, Unit 52 Swan Shopping Centre, Coventry Road, Yardley, **BIRMINGHAM**, B26 1AD (T) 01216 930688
- **NATURE'S HEALTH SHOP**, Unit 52 Swan Centre, Coventry Road, Yardley, **BIRMINGHAM**, B25 8AD (T) 01217 082888
- **NUT CENTRE (THE)**, 15-20 Retail Market Stalls, Bull Ring Centre, **BIRMINGHAM**, B5 4PJ (T) 01216 431278
- **NUT CENTRE (THE)**, Edgbaston Street, **BIRMINGHAM**, B5 4RB (T) 01216 667131
- **NUTMEG**, 1 Maypole Street, Wombourne, **WOLVERHAMPTON**, WV5 9JB (T) 01902 324952
- **NUTRITION FOR LIFE**, 28 Hazelhurst Road, Kings Heath, **BIRMINGHAM**, B14 7PJ (T) 01214 411707
- **OFFICE SECURITY**, 33 York Street, **WOLVERHAMPTON**, WV1 3RN (T) 01902 454491
- **P G INTERNATIONAL**, 11 Mirfield Road, **BIRMINGHAM**, B33 0AA (T) 01216 040788
- **PENN**, 58 Warstones Road, **WOLVERHAMPTON**, WV4 4LP (T) 01902 345055
- **PREMIER HEALTH**, 2 Wolfe Road, **COVENTRY**, CV4 9UP (T) 024 7642 2050
- **QUEST VITAMINS LTD**, 8 Venture Way, Aston Science Park, **BIRMINGHAM**, B7 4AP (T) 01213 590056
- **ROSEMARY'S**, 2-3 Mander Square, Mander Centre, **WOLVERHAMPTON**, WV1 3NN (T) 01902 427520
- **ROSEMARY'S HEALTH-FOOD SHOP**, 3 Lower Hall Lane, **WALSALL**, WS1 1RH (T) 01922 636640
- **SUPERSAVE LOOSE FOODS**, 46 Bull Ring, **BIRMINGHAM**, B5 5DB (T) 01216 430011
- **TROPICANA HEALTH & FITNESS**, 53 Lichfield Road, **BIRMINGHAM**, B6 5RW (T) 01213 281270
- **TUBBS WHOLEFOODS**, Unit 13 Victoria Passage, **STOURBRIDGE**, DY8 1DP (T) 01384 440311
- **WEIGH & SAVE**, 8 Birmingham Street, Churchill Shopping Centre, **DUDLEY**, DY2 7BL (T) 01384 243808
- **WISE WEIGH**, 33-34 Retail Market, **COVENTRY**, CV1 3HT (T) 024 7652 5034
- **YOURS NATURALLY**, 204 High Street, **DUDLEY**, DY1 1PB (T) 01384 455210

## NORFOLK

- **ARTHURS WHOLEFOODS & CRAFTS**, 3a Wellington Road, **DEREHAM**, NR19 2BP (T) 01362 697750
- **BARLEY SACK HEALTH FOODS**, 15 Norwich Street, **DEREHAM**, NR19 1BX (T) 01362 694486
- **CAMBRIDGE HEALTH PLAN**, Deben House, Magdalen Street, **NORWICH**, NR3 1JE (T) 01603 760777

- **CROMER KITCHEN (THE)**, 3 Church Street, **CROMER**, NR27 9ER
(T) 01263 512383
- **DIANE'S PANTRY**, 8 Market Place, Reepham, **NORWICH**, NR10 4JJ
(T) 01603 871075
- **DIRECT MERCANTILE CO (THE)**, Sackville Place, 44-48 Magdalen Street, **NORWICH**, NR3 1JU
(T) 07020 951088
- **EAGLESFIELD WHOLEFOODS**, 132 Magdalen Street, **NORWICH**, NR3 1JD
(T) 01603 620931
- **FRAGRANT AIR (PRODUCTS) LTD**, Washingford House, Cookes Road, Bergh Apton, **NORWICH**, NR15 1AA
(T) 01508 550924
- **GREEN PARROT WHOLEFOODS**, 89 Market Place, **SWAFFHAM**, PE37 7AQ
(T) 01760 724704
- **GUY'S HEALTH FOODS**, 35 Norwich Street, **DEREHAM**, NR19 1AD
(T) 01362 693402
- **HEALTH FOOD CENTRE**, 91 High Street, Gorleston, **GREAT YARMOUTH**, NR31 6RQ
(T) 01493 662162
- **HEALTH FOOD CENTRE (THE)**, 27 Market Place, **NORTH WALSHAM**, NR28 9BS
(T) 01692 403219
- **HOLLAND & BARRETT**, 15-16 Norfolk Street, **KING'S LYNN**, PE30 1AN
(T) 01553 765969
- **HOLLAND & BARRETT**, 19-21 White Lion Street, **NORWICH**, NR2 1PX
(T) 01603 762955
- **HOLLAND & BARRETT**, 9-10 Victoria Arcade, **GREAT YARMOUTH**, NR30 2NU
(T) 01493 855316
- **KIKI LTD**, 3 Windsor Avenue, **GREAT YARMOUTH**, NR30 4EA
(T) 01493 857878
- **LYDIAS HEALTH FOOD SHOP**, Melbourne House, Church Street, **ATTLEBOROUGH**, NR17 2AH
(T) 01953 456228
- **NATURAL FOOD STORE**, 4 Exchange Street, **NORWICH**, NR2 1AT
(T) 01603 613228
- **NATURAL FOOD STORE**, 84-85 Provision Market, **NORWICH**, NR2 1ND
(T) 01603 766723
- **NATURAL FOODSTORE**, Norfolk House Yard, St Nicholas Street, **DISS**, IP22 4LB
(T) 01379 651832
- **NUTMEG (THE)**, 30b High Street, **SHERINGHAM**, NR26 8JR
(T) 01263 825881
- **RAINBOW WHOLEFOODS**, 16 Dove Street, **NORWICH**, NR2 1DE
(T) 01603 625560
- **RAINBOW WHOLEFOODS**, 21 Whitelodge Business Estate, Hall Road, **NORWICH**, NR4 6DG
(T) 01603 630484
- **RAY UNDRILL WHOLEFOODS**, 1 St Nicholas Court, **NORTH WALSHAM**, NR28 9BY
(T) 01692 402559
- **RAY UNDRILL WHOLEFOODS**, Grove Corner Cottage, Knapton Grove, Knapton, **NORTH WALSHAM**, NR28 0RS
(T) 01692 404340
- **WHOLEFOOD WAREHOUSE**, 1b Trafalgar Industrial Estate, Sovereign Way, **DOWNHAM MARKET**, PE38 9SW
(T) 01366 382260
- **WYMONDHAM HEALTH FOODS**, 17 Market Street, **WYMONDHAM**, NR18 0AJ
(T) 01953 603738

## NORTHAMPTONSHIRE

- **CAMBRIDGE MANUFACTURING CO LTD**, Stafford House, Brakey Road, Weldon North Industrial Estate, **CORBY**, NN17 5LU
(T) 01536 403678
- **CORTAFLEX**, Willow Farm Cottage, Clay Coton, **NORTHAMPTON**, NN6 6JU
(T) 01788 869000
- **DAILY BREAD CO-OPERATIVE LTD**, The Old Laundry, Bedford Road, **NORTHAMPTON**, NN4 7AD
(T) 01604 621531
- **GOOD EARTH CATALOGUE CO LTD**, 25 High Street, Silverstone, **TOWCESTER**, NN12 8US
(T) 08702 411770
- **GOOD HEALTH FOODS**, 21 Gold Street, **NORTHAMPTON**, NN1 1RA
(T) 01604 233860
- **GOOD LIFE (THE)**, 5 The Ridings Arcade, The Ridings, **NORTHAMPTON**, NN1 1EZ
(T) 01604 621280
- **GOODNESS FOODS WHOLESALE**, South March, Long March Industrial Estate, **DAVENTRY**, NN11 4PH
(T) 01327 706611
- **GRANOVITA UK LTD**, 4-5 Stanton Cl, Finedon Road Industrial Estate, **WELLINGBOROUGH**, NN8 4HN
(T) 01933 273717
- **HEALTH QUEST**, 8 Wood Street, **NORTHAMPTON**, NN1 2ED
(T) 01604 630125
- **HOLLAND & BARRETT**, 34 High Street, **KETTERING**, NN16 8SU
(T) 01536 417209
- **HOLLAND & BARRETT**, 43 Queens Square, **CORBY**, NN17 1PD
(T) 01536 408914
- **HOLLAND & BARRETT**, 8 Mercers Row, **NORTHAMPTON**, NN1 2QL
(T) 01604 639603
- **HONEY POT (THE)**, 4 Bishops Court, **DAVENTRY**, NN11 4NP
(T) 01327 312595
- **HOUSE OF GOODNESS LTD**, South March, Long March Industrial Estate, **DAVENTRY**, NN11 4PH
(T) 01327 704474
- **KEG 9**, 22 Silver Street, **WELLINGBOROUGH**, NN8 1AY
(T) 01933 222499
- **KETTERING HEALTH FOODS**, 103 Montagu Street, **KETTERING**, NN16 8PA
(T) 01536 410208
- **MARTLET NATURAL FOODS**, 10-14 Ise Valley Industrial Estate, Meadow Close, **WELLINGBOROUGH**, NN8 4BH
(T) 01933 442022
- **PILMORES OF DURHAM**, 78 High Street, **RUSHDEN**, NN10 0PQ
(T) 01933 316469
- **SELECT HEALTH CARE (UK) LTD**, 112-114 Mill Road, **KETTERING**, NN16 0RJ
(T) 01536 417714
- **VELVET ENERGY UK LTD**, Westlands, Long Buckby Road, **DAVENTRY**, NN11 5LT
(T) 01327 704223
- **VUJPIM VITAL LIFE**, 1 Kite's Close, East Hunsbury, **NORTHAMPTON**, NN4 0QR
(T) 01472 309176

## NOTTINGHAMSHIRE

- **BLOSSOMS NOTTINGHAM LTD**, 32 Front Street, Arnold, **NOTTINGHAM**, NG5 7EL
(T) 01159 676564
- **CERES**, 31 Nottingham Road, Eastwood, **NOTTINGHAM**, NG16 3AN
(T) 01773 769540
- **CORSONS**, 29-31 Central Avenue, West Bridgford, **NOTTINGHAM**, NG2 5GQ
(T) 01159 814080
- **DIFFCHAMB LTD**, Block 3 Unit 12 Old Mill La Industrial Estate, Mansfield Woodhouse, **MANSFIELD**, NG19 9BG
(T) 01623 626220
- **DOWN TO EARTH**, 6a Market Place, **SOUTHWELL**, NG25 0HE
(T) 01636 812012
- **FITZPATRICKS**, 1 Carlton Square, Carlton, **NOTTINGHAM**, NG4 3BP
(T) 01159 563000
- **FLORIDA HEALTH**, 4 Castle Boulevard, **NOTTINGHAM**, NG7 1FB
(T) 01159 413112
- **FRUIT BASKET (THE)**, 4 Gordon Road, West Bridgford, **NOTTINGHAM**, NG2 5LN
(T) 01159 817014
- **GNC**, Unit 70 215 Upper Level, Victoria Centre, **NOTTINGHAM**, NG1 3QN
(T) 01159 584810
- **GOOD HEALTH**, 73 Carolgate, **RETFORD**, DN22 6EB
(T) 01777 706384
- **GOOD HEALTH FOODS**, 12 Stockwell Gate, **MANSFIELD**, NG18 1LE
(T) 01623 633455
- **HEALTH FOOD STORE (THE)**, 19 Leeming Street, **MANSFIELD**, NG18 1NA
(T) 01623 652224
- **HEALTH FOODS PLUS**, Unit 11 The Idlewells, **SUTTON-IN-ASHFIELD**, NG17 1BL
(T) 01623 558467
- **HEALTH STORES PARTNERSHIP**, Queens Road, **NOTTINGHAM**, NG2 3AS
(T) 01159 555255
- **HEALTHWISE**, 11 Plains Road, **NOTTINGHAM**, NG3 5JH
(T) 01159 625487
- **HIZIKI WHOLEFOOD COLLECTIVE LTD**, 15 Goose Gate, **NOTTINGHAM**, NG1 1FE
(T) 01159 505523
- **HOLLAND & BARRETT**, 1 St Marks Lane, **NEWARK**, NG24 1XS
(T) 01636 605025
- **HOLLAND & BARRETT**, 13 The Broadwalk, The Broad Marsh Centre, **NOTTINGHAM**, NG1 7LE
(T) 01159 799409
- **HOLLAND & BARRETT**, 36 High Street, Hucknall, **NOTTINGHAM**, NG15 7HG
(T) 01159 638683
- **HOLLAND & BARRETT**, 55 Four Seasons Centre, **MANSFIELD**, NG18 1SX
(T) 01623 634543
- **HOLLAND & BARRETT**, 617 Mansfield Road, **NOTTINGHAM**, NG5 2BY
(T) 01159 624527
- **HOLLAND & BARRETT**, 7 Carolgate, **RETFORD**, DN22 6BZ
(T) 01777 711963
- **HOLLAND & BARRETT**, 95 Victoria Centre, **NOTTINGHAM**, NG1 3QE
(T) 01159 580753
- **HOLLAND & BARRETT**, Unit 2 C-Operative Development, High Road, Beeston, **NOTTINGHAM**, NG9 2LF
(T) 01159 224302
- **KIRKGATE HEALTHFOODS**, 42 Kirkgate, **NEWARK**, NG24 1AB
(T) 01636 612230
- **NATURAL FOOD CO**, 37a Mansfield Road, **NOTTINGHAM**, NG1 3FB
(T) 01159 559914
- **NUTRITION FOR LIFE**, 17 Ascot Drive, **MANSFIELD**, NG18 3BX
(T) 01623 409988
- **NUTRITIONAL ANALYSIS**, 12 Hillsway Cresent, **MANSFIELD**, NG18 5DS
(T) 01623 620218
- **OPTIMUM HEALTH PRODUCTS LTD**, 3/Chapel Mews Court, Chapel Street, Beeston, **NOTTINGHAM**, NG9 3HB
(T) 01159 677000
- **PLANET HEALTH**, 4 Castle Boulevard, **NOTTINGHAM**, NG7 1FB
(T) 01159 419007
- **ROOTS NATURAL FOODS**, 526 Mansfield Road, **NOTTINGHAM**, NG5 2FR
(T) 01159 609014
- **ROSEMARYS HEALTH FOODS**, 6 Lincoln Street, **NOTTINGHAM**, NG1 3DJ
(T) 01159 505072
- **TWIN LABORATORIES INCORPORATED**, 3-5 High Pavement, **NOTTINGHAM**, NG1 1HF
(T) 01159 897323
- **USANA**, 163 Toton Lane, Stapleford, **NOTTINGHAM**, NG9 7JD
(T) 01159 176126
- **WHITE'S HERBAL & HEALTH FOODS**, 1a Potter Street, **WORKSOP**, S80 2AD
(T) 01909 473349

- **WORKSOP HEALTH SHOP**, 19 Ryton Street, **WORKSOP**, S80 2AY (T) 01909 531660

## OXFORDSHIRE

- **ALLERGYFREE DIRECT LTD**, Unit 5/Centre Mead, Osney Mead, **OXFORD**, OX2 0ES (T) 01865 722003
- **BEAN BAG NATURAL HEALTH**, 2 Wesley Walk, High Street, **WITNEY**, OX8 6ZJ (T) 01993 773922
- **E M S**, 21 Elizabeth Rise, **BANBURY**, OX16 9LZ (T) 01295 264093
- **GNC GENERAL NUTRITION CENTRE**, 17 Westgate, **OXFORD**, OX1 1NU (T) 01865 249219
- **GOOD FOOD SHOP CHARLBURY LTD**, 39 Sheep Street, Charlbury, **CHIPPING NORTON**, OX7 3RR (T) 01608 811157
- **HADDDENHAM HEALTHCARE**, 27 Croft Road, **THAME**, OX9 3JF (T) 01844 218330
- **HERBALIFE DISTRIBUTOR**, 21 Isis Avenue, **BICESTER**, OX6 8GR (T) 01869 324102
- **HIGH HEALTH FOODS LTD**, 41 Market Place, **HENLEY-ON-THAMES**, RG9 2AA (T) 01491 573764
- **HOLLAND & BARRETT**, 100 London Road, Headington, **OXFORD**, OX3 9AJ (T) 01865 764578
- **HOLLAND & BARRETT**, 3 King Edward Street, **OXFORD**, OX1 4HS (T) 01865 243407
- **HOLLAND & BARRETT**, 6 Castle Centre, **BANBURY**, OX16 5UH (T) 01295 277909
- **HOLLAND & BARRETT**, 6 Golden Cross, **OXFORD**, OX1 3EU (T) 01865 792102
- **HOLLAND & BARRETT**, 6/Suffolk House, 263 Banbury Road, **OXFORD**, OX2 7HN (T) 01865 552523
- **HOLLAND & BARRETT RETAIL LTD**, 47 Market Place, **WANTAGE**, OX12 8AW (T) 01235 768965
- **LIFESTYLE HEALTHCARE LTD**, Centenary Business Park, Station Road, **HENLEY-ON-THAMES**, RG9 1DS (T) 01491 411767
- **NATURES HARVEST**, 4a Church Lane, **BANBURY**, OX16 5LR (T) 01295 253208
- **OXFORD NUTRITION LTD**, P O Box 110, **WITNEY**, OX8 7FJ (T) 01993 709752
- **OXFORD WHOLEFOODS LTD**, Unit 5 Centremead, Osney Mead, **OXFORD**, OX2 0ES (T) 01865 244122
- **PAM SAVINS**, 3 Wesley Lane, **BICESTER**, OX6 7JU (T) 01869 241405
- **PANTRY (THE)**, 31 Acre End Street, Eynsham, **WITNEY**, OX8 1PF (T) 01865 882271
- **PERUVIAN IMPORTS**, 12 Halifax Road, **BICESTER**, OX6 7TG (T) 01869 369839
- **UHURU WHOLEFOODS**, 58 Cowley Road, **OXFORD**, OX4 1HZ (T) 01865 248249
- **ULTRAPHARM LTD**, Unit 2-3 Centenary Business Park, Station Road, **HENLEY-ON-THAMES**, RG9 1DS (T) 01491 578016
- **WANTAGE HEALTH FOOD STORE**, 16 Wallingford Street, **WANTAGE**, OX12 8AX (T) 01235 768199

## SHROPSHIRE

- **ACORN**, 2 St Marys Street, **BRIDGNORTH**, WV16 4DW (T) 01746 761896
- **DUTTONS HEALTH FOODS**, 15 Albion Hill, **OSWESTRY**, SY11 1QA (T) 01691 656934
- **ENTERTAINING ELEPHANTS**, 43b High Street, **CHURCH STRETTON**, SY6 6BX (T) 01694 723922
- **FUTURE PHYSIQUE**, Chatbrook Cottage, Hunger Hill, Condover, **SHREWSBURY**, SY5 7BJ (T) 01743 874290
- **HARVEST WHOLEFOODS**, Glebe Farm, Lydham, **BISHOPS CASTLE**, SY9 5HB (T) 01588 638990
- **HEALTHCARE INTERNATIONAL**, Inglenook Cottage, Heath Road, Prees Heath, **WHITCHURCH**, SY13 2AE (T) 01948 664483
- **HEALTHY THYME**, 2 Bradford Street, **SHIFNAL**, TF11 8AT (T) 01952 462009
- **HOLLAND & BARRETT**, 13 New Street, Wellington, **TELFORD**, TF1 1LU (T) 01952 243720
- **HOLLAND & BARRETT**, 3 The Square, **SHREWSBURY**, SY1 1LA (T) 01743 357611
- **HOLLAND & BARRETT**, 34 Sherwood Street, Telford Shopping Centre, Town Centre, **TELFORD**, TF3 4BW (T) 01952 291356
- **HOLLAND & BARRETT**, 4 Butcher Row, **SHREWSBURY**, SY1 1UW (T) 01743 272016
- **HONEYSUCKLE WHOLEFOODS**, 53 Church Street, **OSWESTRY**, SY11 2SZ (T) 01691 653125
- **MICHAEL & BRENDA YORK**, Mallards Close, Alveley, **BRIDGNORTH**, WV15 6JL (T) 01746 780144
- **NATURES SUNSHINE PRODUCTS**, Unit 5 Hortonwood 32, **TELFORD**, TF1 4EU (T) 01952 671600
- **NEWPORT HEALTH FOOD CENTRE**, 6a St. Mary Street, **NEWPORT**, TF10 7AB (T) 01952 814000
- **SHERWOOD WHOLEFOODS**, 1 Wilkinson Walk, **MARKET DRAYTON**, TF9 1PW (T) 01630 655155
- **VICKS HEALTHIWAYS**, 13 Market Street, Wellington, **TELFORD**, TF1 1DT (T) 01952 242526
- **WILD THYME WHOLEFOOD WORKERS CO-OPERATIVE**, 1-2 Castle Gates, **SHREWSBURY**, SY1 2AQ (T) 01743 364559

## SOMERSET

- **BURNHAM HEALTH FOOD CENTRE**, 4 Victoria Street, **BURNHAM-ON-SEA**, TA8 1AL (T) 01278 783866
- **CERES NATURAL FOODS**, 42 Princes Street, **YEOVIL**, BA20 1EQ (T) 01935 428791
- **COBBS**, Unit 7 Brunel Shopping Centre, **SOMERTON**, TA11 7PY (T) 01458 274066
- **COUNTRY HARVEST**, 8 The Courtyard, St James Street, **TAUNTON**, TA1 1JR (T) 01823 252843
- **EVERGREEN**, 61 Station Road, **TAUNTON**, TA1 1PA (T) 01823 322414
- **FROME WHOLEFOODS**, 8 Cheap Street, **FROME**, BA11 1BN (T) 01373 473334
- **G N C**, 5 Southgate, **BATH**, BA1 1TD (T) 01225 471093
- **GREEN SHOP (THE)**, High Street, Midsomer Norton, **BATH**, BA3 2DA (T) 01761 418857
- **H S L HEALTH SCREENING LTD**, 1 Church Square, **TAUNTON**, TA1 1SA (T) 01823 325023
- **HARVEST NATURAL FOODS**, 37 Walcot Street, **BATH**, BA1 5BN (T) 01225 465519
- **HEALTH BOX (THE)**, 5 St Johns House, Church Street, **YEOVIL**, BA20 1HE (T) 01935 411156
- **HOLLAND & BARRETT**, 13 Glovers Walk, **YEOVIL**, BA20 1LH (T) 01935 421785
- **HOLLAND & BARRETT**, 19 Meadow Street, **WESTON-SUPER-MARE**, BS23 1QG (T) 01934 620020
- **HOLLAND & BARRETT**, 2 Fore Street, **CHARD**, TA20 1PH (T) 01460 63435
- **HOLLAND & BARRETT**, 20 Angel Place, Shopping Centre, **BRIDGWATER**, TA6 3TQ (T) 01278 452567
- **HOLLAND & BARRETT**, 22 High Street, **WELLS**, BA5 2SG (T) 01749 677665
- **HOLLAND & BARRETT**, 29 Old Market Centre, **TAUNTON**, TA1 3TP (T) 01823 275300
- **HOLLAND & BARRETT**, 6 Cheap Street, **BATH**, BA1 1NE (T) 01225 330091
- **HOLLAND & BARRETT**, 6 Station Road, **CLEVEDON**, BS21 6NH (T) 01275 342049
- **JULIAN GRAVES LTD**, 1 The Podium, Northgate Street, **BATH**, BA1 5AL (T) 01225 448404
- **JULIAN GRAVES LTD**, Unit 9 The Sovereign Centre, High Street, **WESTON-SUPER-MARE**, BS23 1HL (T) 01934 643144
- **KOMBUCHA SUPPLIES UK**, The Hollies, Mill Hill, Wellow, **BATH**, BA2 8QJ (T) 01225 833150
- **MALTHOUSE (THE)**, 208 High Street, Worle, **WESTON-SUPER-MARE**, BS22 6JE (T) 01934 513867
- **NATURALIFE**, Unit 7 The George Shopping Centre, **CREWKERNE**, TA18 7LU (T) 01460 76568
- **NATURES WAY**, 4 Cornhill, **WELLINGTON**, TA21 8LU (T) 01823 667666
- **NEW WORLD PRODUCTS**, 6 Curlew Close, **MINEHEAD**, TA24 6UW (T) 01643 707121
- **PROBIOTICS INTERNATIONAL LTD**, Matts Lane, **STOKE-SUB-HAMDON**, TA14 6QE (T) 01935 822921
- **QUALITY FOODS**, Unit 3 Broadway Court, Miles Street, **BATH**, BA2 4HX (T) 01225 336800
- **QUEENSWOOD NATURAL FOODS**, 2 Robins Drive, **BRIDGWATER**, TA6 4DL (T) 01278 423440
- **RIVERSIDE JUICE BAR**, 18 The Podium, Northgate Street, **BATH**, BA1 5AL (T) 01225 444457
- **SEASONS WHOLEFOOD**, 10 George Street, **BATH**, BA1 2EH (T) 01225 469730
- **SUE'S PANTRY**, Bow Street, **LANGPORT**, TA10 9PR (T) 01458 252853
- **SUNSEED**, 12 South Street, **WELLINGTON**, TA21 8NS (T) 01823 662313
- **SUSTAINABLE LIFE**, Lower Rocks, Compton Street, Butleigh, **GLASTONBURY**, BA6 8SF (T) 01458 850998
- **TOPFIT HEALTH PRODUCTS LTD**, 156 Old Church Road, **CLEVEDON**, BS21 7TU (T) 01275 340042
- **TOUCAN WHOLEFOODS**, 7 Floyds Corner, **MINEHEAD**, TA24 5UW (T) 01643 706101
- **WHOLEFOOD STORE (THE)**, 29 High Street, **GLASTONBURY**, BA6 9DR (T) 01458 831004

## STAFFORDSHIRE

- **BEECHWOOD HEALTH & NUTRITION**, Croxall Road, Edingale, **TAMWORTH**, B79 9JH (T) 01827 383016
- **BOOTS HEALTH & HERBAL STORES**, 39-41 Merrial Street, **NEWCASTLE**, ST5 2AE (T) 01782 617463

- **BRECKLES WHOLEFOODS**, 14 Stanley Street, **LEEK**, ST13 5HG
(T) 01538 387660
- **CHADWICKS HEALTH SHOP**, 35 Paradise Street, **STOKE-ON-TRENT**, ST6 5AG
(T) 01782 819707
- **CHASE HEALTH FOODS**, 4 Mill Street, **STAFFORD**, ST16 2AJ
(T) 01785 608181
- **FINE HEALTH LTD**, Unit 10/Chasewood Pk Business Centre, Hednesford Road, Heath Hayes, **CANNOCK**, WS12 5XR
(T) 01543 274783
- **FOOD FOR THOUGHT**, 57 Tamworth Street, **LICHFIELD**, WS13 6JW
(T) 01543 253726
- **FOOD FOR THOUGHT**, 6 Wolverhampton Road, Codsall, **WOLVERHAMPTON**, WV8 1PE
(T) 01902 842646
- **FOOD FOR THOUGHT**, Unit 6 The Market Hall, Market Place, **BURTON-ON-TRENT**, DE14 1HE
(T) 01283 510423
- **GOOD HEALTH FOODS**, Ladysmith Farm, Hoar Cross, **BURTON-ON-TRENT**, DE13 8QS
(T) 01283 575648
- **GOOD HEALTH FOODS LTD**, 5 Middle Entry, **TAMWORTH**, B79 7NJ
(T) 01827 310894
- **GOOD HEALTH FOODS LTD**, Unit 3 The Levels Industrial Estate, The Levels, **RUGELEY**, WS15 1RD
(T) 01889 577767
- **GRAPE & GRAIN**, 25 Lower Gungate, **TAMWORTH**, B79 7AT
(T) 01827 62133
- **HEALTH MATTERS**, 21-23 The Strand, **STOKE-ON-TRENT**, ST3 2JF
(T) 01782 319333
- **HEALTH RACK**, Parkway/Potteries Shopping Centre, Market Square, **STOKE-ON-TRENT**, ST1 1PS
(T) 01782 272228
- **HERBIES**, 22 High Street, Cheadle, **STOKE-ON-TRENT**, ST10 1AF
(T) 01538 754488
- **HERBIES**, 72 High Street, Biddulph, **STOKE-ON-TRENT**, ST8 6AS
(T) 01782 522133
- **HERBIES**, High Street, **STONE**, ST15 8AJ
(T) 01785 817745
- **HOLLAND & BARRETT**, 1 Gaolgate Street, **STAFFORD**, ST16 2BG
(T) 01785 252758
- **HOLLAND & BARRETT**, 14a George Street, **TAMWORTH**, B79 7LN
(T) 01827 65891
- **HOLLAND & BARRETT**, 29 High Street, **NEWCASTLE**, ST5 1QZ
(T) 01782 713059
- **HOLLAND & BARRETT**, 3 St Modwens Walk, The Precinct, **BURTON-ON-TRENT**, DE14 1HL
(T) 01283 533747
- **HOLLAND & BARRETT**, 41 Market Street, **LICHFIELD**, WS13 6LA
(T) 01543 256782
- **HOLLAND & BARRETT**, 8 Underhill Walk, **BURTON-ON-TRENT**, DE14 1DE
(T) 01283 740078
- **HOLLAND & BARRETT**, 8 Upper Market Square, **STOKE-ON-TRENT**, ST1 1NS
(T) 01782 266126
- **HOLLAND & BARRETT**, Unit 21, Cannock Shopping Centre, **CANNOCK**, WS11 1WS
(T) 01543 500046
- **JULIAN GRAVES LTD**, Watling Street, Gailey, **STAFFORD**, ST19 5PP
(T) 01902 798402
- **MENSCARE (UK) LTD**, 101 Smithfield Road, **UTTOXETER**, ST14 7LD
(T) 01889 569467
- **MUSCLEMANIA**, 1 Mitchells Court, **TAMWORTH**, B79 7AF
(T) 01827 66341
- **NATURE'S STORE LTD**, Unit 2 Jamage Road Industrial Estate, Talke Pits, **STOKE-ON-TRENT**, ST7 1XN
(T) 01782 794300
- **PEAK PLUS LTD**, Woodside Lodge, Ramshorn Road, Oakamoor, **STOKE-ON-TRENT**, ST10 3BZ
(T) 01538 703704
- **REAL FOOD CO (THE)**, 50 Sandbach Road South, Alsager, **STOKE-ON-TRENT**, ST7 2LP
(T) 01270 873322
- **SUREPHARM SERVICES LTD**, Unit 2 H Bretby Business Park, Bretby, **BURTON-ON-TRENT**, DE15 0YZ
(T) 01283 224337
- **WARRENS HEALTH PRODUCTS**, Unit C Richmond Park/Levels Industrial Estate, The Levels, **RUGELEY**, WS15 1RD
(T) 01889 578878

## SUFFOLK

- **ANGLIAN SPORTS NUTRITION**, Tayfen Road, **BURY ST. EDMUNDS**, IP32 6BH
(T) 01284 717166
- **ANIMAL HEALTH SUPPLIES**, Station Road, Framlingham, **WOODBRIDGE**, IP13 9EE
(T) 01728 621070
- **B HEALTHY SOLUTIONS**, Brookside, Pinmill Road, Chelmondiston, **IPSWICH**, IP9 1JF
(T) 01473 780155
- **COMB-A-WAY**, PO Box 18, Benhall, **SAXMUNDHAM**, IP17 1NB
(T) 01728 604480
- **FOOD FOR THOUGHT**, 189 London Rd South, **LOWESTOFT**, NR33 0DR
(T) 01502 581040
- **FRUITS OF THE EARTH CO-OP**, 67 Upper Orwell Street, **IPSWICH**, IP4 1HP
(T) 01473 211282
- **GOBBLIN WHOLEFOODS LTD**, Station Road Industrial Estate, Station Road, Elmswell, **BURY ST. EDMUNDS**, IP30 9HR
(T) 01359 241841
- **GOLDEN HARVEST**, 96 North Street, **SUDBURY**, CO10 1RF
(T) 01787 376214
- **HEALTH FOOD & HERBS**, 9 The Traverse, **BURY ST. EDMUNDS**, IP33 1BJ
(T) 01284 754986
- **HERBALIFE**, Middleton Road, **SUDBURY**, CO10 7NT
(T) 01787 319071
- **HOLLAND & BARRETT**, 17 The Britten Centre, **LOWESTOFT**, NR32 1LR
(T) 01502 500832
- **HOLLAND & BARRETT**, 27 Westgate Street, **IPSWICH**, IP1 3DR
(T) 01473 233477
- **HOLLAND & BARRETT**, 6 Brentgovel Street, **BURY ST. EDMUNDS**, IP33 1EB
(T) 01284 706677
- **HOLLAND & BARRETT**, 7 Butter Market, **IPSWICH**, IP1 1BE
(T) 01473 219153
- **HOLLAND & BARRETT**, 7 The Rookery, **NEWMARKET**, CB8 8EQ
(T) 01638 561511
- **HOLLAND & BARRETT**, 8-10 Market Place, **STOWMARKET**, IP14 1DP
(T) 01449 676046
- **HOLLAND & BARRETT**, 91 Hamilton Road, **FELIXSTOWE**, IP11 7AS
(T) 01394 671796
- **HONEYROSE PRODUCTS LTD**, Tomo Business Park, Creeting Road, **STOWMARKET**, IP14 5AY
(T) 01449 612137
- **HUNGATE HEALTH STORE**, 4 Hungate, **BECCLES**, NR34 9TL
(T) 01502 715009
- **LOAVES & FISHES**, 52 The Thoroughfare, **WOODBRIDGE**, IP12 1AL
(T) 01394 385650
- **MANNATECH**, Pond Cottage, The Street, Lidgate, **NEWMARKET**, CB8 9PW
(T) 01638 500391
- **OREGANO HEALTH FOODS**, 169-171 London Road North, **LOWESTOFT**, NR32 1HG
(T) 01502 582907
- **PERFECT PERFORMANCE PRODUCTS**, 13-15 Victoria Way, **NEWMARKET**, CB8 7SH
(T) 01638 662589
- **SIMPLY DELICIOUS**, 70 High Street, **LEISTON**, IP16 4BZ
(T) 01728 833078
- **SUNFLOWER**, 101 High Street, Hadleigh, **IPSWICH**, IP7 5EJ
(T) 01473 823219
- **YOXFORD NATURAL FOOD STORE**, High Street, Yoxford, **SAXMUNDHAM**, IP17 3EP
(T) 01728 668520

## SURREY

- **ABSOLUTE HEALTHCARE LTD**, 191 Banstead Road South, **SUTTON**, SM2 5LW
(T) 020 8770 1997
- **ALOE VERA HEALTH & BEAUTY PRODUCTS**, Cornerways, Pyrford Road, **WEST BYFLEET**, KT14 6RH
(T) 01932 341257
- **ALOE VERA PRODUCT CENTRE**, 13 Scott Close, **EPSOM**, KT19 9NY
(T) 020 8397 7300
- **ALOE VERA PRODUCTS**, 42 Raleigh Road, **RICHMOND**, TW9 2DX
(T) 020 8940 2402
- **ARKOPHARMA (UK) LTD**, Unit 7 Redlands Centre, Redlands, **COULSDON**, CR5 2HT
(T) 020 8763 1414
- **AROMANTICA**, 16 St Martins Walk, **DORKING**, RH4 1UT
(T) 01306 742005
- **ASHFORD HEALTH STORES**, 10 Station Road, **ASHFORD**, TW15 2UP
(T) 01784 244975
- **AUSTRALIAN EMU OIL DIRECT**, 49 Portland Road, **ASHFORD**, TW15 3BU
(T) 01784 255400
- **BEAUTY PRODUCTS INTERNATIONAL LTD**, Copsem House, 44 Copsem Lane, **ESHER**, KT10 9HJ
(T) 01372 842211
- **BREWHURST HEALTH FOOD SUPPLIES LTD**, Abbot Cl, Byfleet, **WEST BYFLEET**, KT14 7JP
(T) 01932 354211
- **BRITANNIA HEALTH PRODUCTS**, Forum House, 41-51 Brighton Road, **REDHILL**, RH1 6YS
(T) 01737 773741
- **CROOK KEVIN**, 20 Woodland Way, **MORDEN**, SM4 4DS
(T) 020 8542 3710
- **EDEN PRODUCTS**, The Hatches, Frimley Green, **CAMBERLEY**, GU16 6HG
(T) 01252 408371
- **FERROSAN HEALTH CARE LTD**, Beaver House, York Close, Byfleet, **WEST BYFLEET**, KT14 7HN
(T) 01932 336366
- **FOOD FOR THOUGHT**, 2-6 Haydon Place, **GUILDFORD**, GU1 4LL
(T) 01483 533841
- **FOOD FOR THOUGHT**, 30-32 Frimley High Street, Frimley, **CAMBERLEY**, GU16 5JD
(T) 01276 691996
- **FOOD FOR THOUGHT**, 38 Market Place, **KINGSTON UPON THAMES**, KT1 1JQ
(T) 020 8546 7806
- **FOR GOODNESS SAKE**, 15 Stoneleigh Broadway, **EPSOM**, KT17 2JA
(T) 020 8393 4701
- **G N C**, 35 Oakdene Parade, **COBHAM**, KT11 2LR
(T) 01932 864553
- **GENERAL DIETARY LTD**, P O Box 38, **KINGSTON UPON THAMES**, KT2 7YP
(T) 020 8336 2323
- **GENERAL NUTRITION CENTRE**, 28 The Friary, **GUILDFORD**, GU1 4YN
(T) 01483 452607
- **GNC-GENERAL NUTRITION CENTRE**, 85 North End, **CROYDON**, CR0 1TJ
(T) 020 8688 3147
- **GOOD LIFE HEALTH FOODS**, 1 Waterloo Road, **EPSOM**, KT19 8AY
(T) 01372 742095
- **GRAYSHOTT HEALTH STORE**, Grove House, Headley Road, Grayshott, **HINDHEAD**, GU26 6LE
(T) 01428 604046

- **HARPERS GROUP**, Parallel House, 32 London Road, **GUILDFORD**, GU1 2AB (T) 08705 275139
- **HASLEMERE HEALTHFOODS**, 71 Weyhill, **HASLEMERE**, GU27 1HN (T) 01428 658294
- **HEALTH & DIET CENTRES LTD**, 35 The Precinct, High Street, **EGHAM**, TW20 9HN (T) 01784 436402
- **HEALTH & DIET CENTRES LTD**, 81 High Street, **GODALMING**, GU7 1AW (T) 01483 424353
- **HEALTH & DIET CENTRES LTD**, Seymour House, Lower South Street, **GODALMING**, GU7 1BZ (T) 01483 410600
- **HEALTH FOOD CENTRE (THE)**, 62 The Broadway, **SURBITON**, KT6 7HR (T) 020 8399 3932
- **HEALTH FOODS CHEAM VILLAGE**, 60 The Broadway, Cheam, **SUTTON**, SM3 8BD (T) 020 8643 5132
- **HEALTH MATTERS**, 90 Edenfield Gardens, **WORCESTER PARK**, KT4 7DY (T) 020 8873 0942
- **HEALTH WEALTH & BEAUTY**, 11 Willowhayne Gdns, **WORCESTER PARK**, KT4 8TH (T) 020 8241 6193
- **HEALTHWISE**, 146 Molesey Road, **WALTON-ON-THAMES**, KT12 4RD (T) 01932 252143
- **HERBALIFE**, 14 Norfolk House/Courtlands, Sheen Road, **RICHMOND**, TW10 5AT (T) 020 8332 7057
- **HERBALIFE DISTRIBUTER**, 111 Lavender Avenue, **MITCHAM**, CR4 3RS (T) 020 8687 1043
- **HERBALIFE DISTRIBUTOR**, 14a Thrupps Lane, **WALTON-ON-THAMES**, KT12 4LY (T) 01932 253717
- **HERBALIFE INDEPENDENT DISTRIBUTOR**, 66 Rymer Road, **CROYDON**, CR0 6EE (T) 020 8654 2294
- **HOLLAND & BARRETT**, 1 Kings Shade Walk, High Street, **EPSOM**, KT19 8EB (T) 01372 741928
- **HOLLAND & BARRETT**, 1098-1099 Whitgift Centre, **CROYDON**, CR0 1UU (T) 020 8681 5174
- **HOLLAND & BARRETT**, 12-13 Apple Market, **KINGSTON UPON THAMES**, KT1 1JE (T) 020 8541 1378
- **HOLLAND & BARRETT**, 14 Wolsey Walk, **WOKING**, GU21 1XU (T) 01483 726019
- **HOLLAND & BARRETT**, 185 High Street, **DORKING**, RH4 1RU (T) 01306 889654
- **HOLLAND & BARRETT**, 19 Church Walk, **CATERHAM**, CR3 6RT (T) 01883 330125
- **HOLLAND & BARRETT**, 19 Grace Reynolds Walk, **CAMBERLEY**, GU15 3SN (T) 01276 64043
- **HOLLAND & BARRETT**, 19 High Street, **WEYBRIDGE**, KT13 8AX (T) 01932 847649
- **HOLLAND & BARRETT**, 19 The Belfry, Station Road, **REDHILL**, RH1 1SE (T) 01737 778809
- **HOLLAND & BARRETT**, 20 Swan Court, High Street, **LEATHERHEAD**, KT22 8AH (T) 01372 378682
- **HOLLAND & BARRETT**, 23 The Centre, **WALTON-ON-THAMES**, KT12 1QJ (T) 01932 220774
- **HOLLAND & BARRETT**, 29 The Elmsleigh Centre, **STAINES**, TW18 4QB (T) 01784 459218
- **HOLLAND & BARRETT**, 3 The Friary, **GUILDFORD**, GU1 4YL (T) 01483 537207
- **HOLLAND & BARRETT**, 50 London Road, **MORDEN**, SM4 5BE (T) 020 8685 0375
- **HOLLAND & BARRETT**, 50a George Street, **RICHMOND**, TW9 1HJ (T) 020 8940 1007
- **HOLLAND & BARRETT**, 5a West Street, **FARNHAM**, GU9 7DN (T) 01252 714876
- **HOLLAND & BARRETT**, 68 High Street, **REIGATE**, RH2 9AP (T) 01737 248260
- **HOLLAND & BARRETT**, 95 High Street, **NEW MALDEN**, KT3 4BP (T) 020 8942 6694
- **JAGULANA LTD**, Hamilton House, 39 Kings Road, **HASLEMERE**, GU27 2QA (T) 01428 656725
- **JESSUP MARKETING**, White Robins, St Georges Road, **WEYBRIDGE**, KT13 0EP (T) 01932 854825
- **JULIAN GRAVES LTD**, 1034 Whitgift Centre, **CROYDON**, CR0 1UU (T) 020 8686 4313
- **JULIAN GRAVES LTD**, The Friary Centre, The Friary, **GUILDFORD**, GU1 4YU (T) 01483 450110
- **L C A GROUP**, 16-18 Pampisford Road, **PURLEY**, CR8 2NE (T) 020 8645 9863
- **L D MALLET MORGAN**, Clock Barn Lodge, Hambledon Road, Busbridge, **GODALMING**, GU8 4AY (T) 01483 429374
- **LIFE STYLE NATURAL HEALTH CENTRE**, The Hersham Centre, Hersham, **WALTON-ON-THAMES**, KT12 4HL (T) 01932 254624
- **LIFEPULSE**, 2 Anderson Drive, **ASHFORD**, TW15 1BE (T) 01784 258282
- **MILLENNIUM HEALTH FOODS**, Unit G29/Bentalls Shopping Centre, Wood Street, **KINGSTON UPON THAMES**, KT1 1TR (T) 020 8549 8341
- **MULTIPOWER FITNESS & NUTRITION**, 41-51 Brighton Road, **REDHILL**, RH1 6YS (T) 01737 773030
- **NATURES SUNSHINE PRODUCTS DISTRIBUTOR**, 23 Chestnut Avenue, **ESHER**, KT10 8JF (T) 07000 782927
- **NEWTON CONSUMER PRODUCTS**, 2 Mansfield Road, **SOUTH CROYDON**, CR2 6HN (T) 020 8688 1018
- **NOAH'S HEALTH FOOD STORES**, 4 South Parade, Stafford Road, **WALLINGTON**, SM6 9AJ (T) 020 8647 1724
- **OAKWOOD HEALTH**, Ad Mail 353, **GUILDFORD**, GU1 1BZ (T) 08003 18887
- **OLIVERS WHOLEFOOD STORE**, 5 Station Approach, Kew Gardens, **RICHMOND**, TW9 3QB (T) 020 8948 3990
- **ORCHARD CLINIC**, Little Orchard, Brentmoor Road, West End, **WOKING**, GU24 9QG (T) 01276 855529
- **ORTIS**, 63 Hampton Court Way, **THAMES DITTON**, KT7 0LT (T) 020 8398 9888
- **OXTED HEALTH FOODS**, 75 Station Road East, **OXTED**, RH8 0AX (T) 01883 730060
- **PANACEA HEALTHCARE LTD**, The Clockhouse, Pasture Wood, Holmbury St. Mary, **DORKING**, RH5 6LQ (T) 01306 731133
- **PUMPKIN PATCH (THE)**, 10 High Street, **BANSTEAD**, SM7 2LJ (T) 01737 371007
- **PURLEY WHOLE FOODS**, 48 High Street, **PURLEY**, CR8 2AA (T) 020 8668 1293
- **R B ENTERPRISES**, 54 Beresford Avenue, **SURBITON**, KT5 9LJ (T) 020 8241 9275
- **SLOANE HEALTH SHOP ROOTCARE LTD**, 50 High Street, **ESHER**, KT10 9QY (T) 01372 465864
- **SOMA HEALTH**, Little Mead Industrial Estate, Little Mead, **CRANLEIGH**, GU6 8ND (T) 01483 277533
- **SURBITON WHOLEFOODS**, 14 Claremont Road, **SURBITON**, KT6 4QU (T) 020 8399 2772
- **VEGA NUTRITIONAL LTD**, 20 Hersham Centre, Hersham Green, Hersham, **WALTON-ON-THAMES**, KT12 4HL (T) 01932 267337
- **VILLAGE HEALTH FOODS**, 5b High Street, **CATERHAM**, CR3 5UE (T) 01883 345633
- **VITAMEDIPHARM**, Unit 22 Addington Business Centre, Vulcan Way, New Addington, **CROYDON**, CR0 9UG (T) 01689 843733
- **WASSEN INTERNATIONAL LTD**, Unit 14 Mole Business Park, Randalls Road, **LEATHERHEAD**, KT22 7BA (T) 01372 379828
- **WHOLEFOOD SHOP (THE)**, 96 High Street, **CROYDON**, CR0 1ND (T) 020 8686 6167
- **WORKOUT WORLD**, 19-21 Keeley Road, **CROYDON**, CR0 1TE (T) 020 8686 4309
- **XYROFIN (UK) LTD**, 41-51 Brighton Road, **REDHILL**, RH1 6YS (T) 01737 773732

## SUSSEX (EAST)

- **21ST CENTURY HEALTH**, Brookstone, Innhams Wood, **CROWBOROUGH**, TN6 1TE (T) 01892 669404
- **A M P (WHOLESALE) LTD**, 7 Swift Close, Ridgewood, **UCKFIELD**, TN22 5PY (T) 01825 765678
- **ACTIVE INTERNATIONAL**, Gate House Farm, Northiam Road, Staplecross, **ROBERTSBRIDGE**, TN32 5RP (T) 01580 830505
- **AU NATUREL INC**, Pavilion Buildings, Old Steine, **BRIGHTON**, BN1 1EL (T) 01273 693010
- **AUSTRIAN MOOR PRODUCTS LTD**, White Ladies, Maresfield, **UCKFIELD**, TN22 2HH (T) 01825 762658
- **BATTLE WHOLEFOOD**, 83 High Street, **BATTLE**, TN33 0AQ (T) 01424 772435
- **BIO NUTRITION**, PO Box 2611, **EASTBOURNE**, BN21 4LQ (T) 01323 731531
- **FAMILY FIRST**, 41 Terminus Road, **EASTBOURNE**, BN21 3QL (T) 01323 734505
- **FINBARR'S WHOLE FOODS & ORGANIC WINES**, 57 George Street, **HASTINGS**, TN34 3EE (T) 01424 443025
- **FOREVER LIVING PRODUCTS**, 94 Church Street, Willingdon, **EASTBOURNE**, BN22 0HU (T) 01323 501774
- **FUEL4BODIES**, 17 Marine Court, **ST. LEONARDS-ON-SEA**, TN38 0DX (T) 01424 422011
- **FULL OF BEANS**, 96-97 High Street, **LEWES**, BN7 1XH (T) 01273 472627
- **G N C**, Unit 43, Churchill Square, **BRIGHTON**, BN1 2TD (T) 01273 710150
- **HAILSHAM HEALTH FOODS**, 2 St. Marys Walk, **HAILSHAM**, BN27 1AF (T) 01323 441126
- **HEALTH FOOD STORES**, 11 London Road, **BEXHILL-ON-SEA**, TN39 3JR (T) 01424 212203
- **HEALTH PLUS**, Dolphin House, 30 Lushington Road, **EASTBOURNE**, BN21 4LL (T) 01323 737374
- **HEALTH STORE**, 26 Church Street, **SEAFORD**, BN25 1LD (T) 01323 893473
- **HEALTHIBODY**, 52 High Street, **NEWHAVEN**, BN9 9PA (T) 01273 512957
- **HEALTHLINK**, 21f Station Road, Portslade, **BRIGHTON**, BN41 1GX (T) 01273 420120



 

- **HEALTHWISE**, 44b Cooden Sea Road, **BEXHILL-ON-SEA**, TN39 4SL (T) 01424 844075
- **HERBALIFE**, 121 Lansdowne Place, **HOVE**, BN3 1FP (T) 01273 723884
- **HIGHER NATURE LTD**, Nutrition Centre, Burwash Common, **ETCHINGHAM**, TN19 7LX (T) 01435 883484
- **HILLS MARKETING (HERBS & VITAMINS)**, Hill Farm, Magrees Lane, Broad Oak, **HEATHFIELD**, TN21 8TR (T) 01435 868682
- **HOLLAND & BARRETT**, 10 Devonshire Road, **BEXHILL-ON-SEA**, TN40 1AS (T) 01424 216860
- **HOLLAND & BARRETT**, 105 London Road, **BRIGHTON**, BN1 4JG (T) 01273 696209
- **HOLLAND & BARRETT**, 21 Queens Road, **HASTINGS**, TN34 1QY (T) 01424 427253
- **HOLLAND & BARRETT**, 62 Arndale Centre, **EASTBOURNE**, BN21 3NW (T) 01323 646790
- **HOLLAND & BARRETT**, 66-68 North Street, **BRIGHTON**, BN1 1RE (T) 01273 746343
- **HOLLAND & BARRETT**, 68 George Street, **HOVE**, BN3 3YD (T) 01273 321873
- **INFINITY FOODS CO-OPERATIVE LTD**, 67b Norway Street, Portslade, **BRIGHTON**, BN41 1AE (T) 01273 424060
- **ITS ONLY NATURAL**, 90 High Street, **UCKFIELD**, TN22 1PU (T) 01825 761270
- **JULIAN GRAVES LTD**, 39 Arndale Centre, **EASTBOURNE**, BN21 3NW (T) 01323 410890
- **JULIAN GRAVES LTD**, Priory Meadow Shopping Centre, Queens Square, **HASTINGS**, TN34 1PH (T) 01424 717919
- **LANSDOWN HEALTH FOODS**, 44 Cliffe High Street, **LEWES**, BN7 2AN (T) 01273 474681
- **MOTHERHEMP SHOP**, 22 Gardner Street, **BRIGHTON**, BN1 1UP (T) 01273 818047
- **NEW ZEAL HEALTH PRODUCTS**, 20 Old Steine, **BRIGHTON**, BN1 1EL (T) 01273 600005
- **NUTRIMAX**, The Old Cottage, Sparks, Northiam, **RYE**, TN31 6JP (T) 01580 831830
- **POSTLETHWAITE HERBAL PRODUCTS**, Marley Lane, Sedlescombe, **BATTLE**, TN33 0QP (T) 01424 774498
- **REFLEX NUTRITION LTD**, 77a Rutland Road, **HOVE**, BN3 5FE (T) 01273 297295
- **RIO TRADING CO (HEALTH) LTD**, 2 Centenary Industrial Estate, Hughes Road, **BRIGHTON**, BN2 4AW (T) 01273 570987
- **RYE WHOLEFOODS**, 90 High Street, **RYE**, TN31 7JN (T) 01797 223495
- **SEAFORD HEALTH STORE**, 26 Church Street, **SEAFORD**, BN25 1LD (T) 01323 893473
- **SEAFORD LABORATORIES LTD**, Cradle Hill Industrial Estate, **SEAFORD**, BN25 3JE (T) 01323 896779
- **SPORTS NUTRITION CO LTD (THE)**, 5 Frederick Terrace, Frederick Place, **BRIGHTON**, BN1 1AX (T) 01273 202322
- **STEWART DISTRIBUTION**, 44 Park Cr Ter, **BRIGHTON**, BN2 3HE (T) 01273 625988
- **SUNNY FOODS**, 76 Beaconsfield Road, **BRIGHTON**, BN1 6DD (T) 01273 507879
- **TENDRING HEALTH STORE**, 26a High Street, **HAILSHAM**, BN27 1BJ (T) 01323 840170
- **TRACE MINERALS (UK) LTD**, Lower Road, **FOREST ROW**, RH18 5HE (T) 01342 824684
- **TRINITY WHOLEFOODS**, 3 Trinity Street, **HASTINGS**, TN34 1HG (T) 01424 430473
- **USANA DISTRIBUTORS**, 49 Hartfield Road, **FOREST ROW**, RH18 5BY (T) 01342 824222
- **VITAL SOURCE**, 34 Adelaide Cresent, **HOVE**, BN3 2JJ (T) 01273 747704
- **WEALDON WHOLEFOODS CO-OPERATIVE LTD**, High Street, **WADHURST**, TN5 6AA (T) 01892 783065
- **WHOLE FOODS GALORE**, 2 Oxford Ter, Hailsham Road, **HEATHFIELD**, TN21 8AA (T) 01435 866532

## SUSSEX (WEST)

- **BEST CARE PRODUCTS**, 73 Garden Wood Road, **EAST GRINSTEAD**, RH19 1RX (T) 01342 410303
- **CERES HEALTH FOOD**, 29 Goring Road, Goring-by-Sea, **WORTHING**, BN12 4AR (T) 01903 242023
- **CORNERWEIGHS**, Elm Lodge, 1 Caudle Street, **HENFIELD**, BN5 9DQ (T) 01273 492794
- **G & G FOOD SUPPLIES LTD**, Vitality House, 2-3 Imberhorne Way, **EAST GRINSTEAD**, RH19 1RL (T) 01342 312811
- **GREEN PEOPLE CO LTD (THE)**, Brighton Road, Handcross, **HAYWARDS HEATH**, RH17 6BZ (T) 01444 401444
- **H B L HEALTH PRODUCTS**, 63 Birkdale Drive, Ifield, **CRAWLEY**, RH11 0TU (T) 01293 402437
- **H L R INTERNATIONAL**, Tara Hill, Henfield Road, Upper Beeding, **STEYNING**, BN44 3TF (T) 01903 813813
- **HEALING LIGHT HEALTH FOODS**, 5 Buckingham Road, **SHOREHAM-BY-SEA**, BN43 5UA (T) 01273 453705
- **HEALTH FLAIR**, 130 Montague Street, **WORTHING**, BN11 3HG (T) 01903 209470
- **HERB CO (THE)**, 2 Bramley Nursery, School Lane, Ashurst Wood, **EAST GRINSTEAD**, RH19 3QW (T) 01342 823650
- **HERBAL & HEALTH**, 2 Elm Cottages, Worthing Road, Southwater, **HORSHAM**, RH13 7DT (T) 01403 731796
- **HERBALIFE**, South Gables, Birchwood Grove Road, **BURGESS HILL**, RH15 0DN (T) 01444 236003
- **HOLLAND & BARRETT**, 11 Warwick Street, **WORTHING**, BN11 3DF (T) 01903 231274
- **HOLLAND & BARRETT**, 123 The Street, Rustington, **LITTLEHAMPTON**, BN16 3DN (T) 01903 784101
- **HOLLAND & BARRETT**, 17 London Road, **BOGNOR REGIS**, PO21 1PQ (T) 01243 830354
- **HOLLAND & BARRETT**, 19 North Street, **CHICHESTER**, PO19 1LB (T) 01243 778898
- **HOLLAND & BARRETT**, 22 The Orchards, **HAYWARDS HEATH**, RH16 3TH (T) 01444 453991
- **HOLLAND & BARRETT**, 25 London Road, **EAST GRINSTEAD**, RH19 1AL (T) 01342 325089
- **HOLLAND & BARRETT**, 6 County Mall, **CRAWLEY**, RH10 1FF (T) 01293 565913
- **HOLLAND & BARRETT**, 71 Church Walk, **BURGESS HILL**, RH15 9BQ (T) 01444 242724
- **HOLLAND & BARRETT**, Unit 6 Swan Walk, **HORSHAM**, RH12 1HQ (T) 01403 274353
- **JULIAN GRAVES LTD**, Unit 46, Swan Walk, **HORSHAM**, RH12 1PT (T) 01403 754918
- **LIFESTYLES**, 24 Homefield Avenue, **BOGNOR REGIS**, PO22 6AN (T) 01243 587314
- **MEDEX SCIENTIFIC UK LTD**, 4 Denne Road, **HORSHAM**, RH12 1JE (T) 01403 218999
- **MIDHURST HEALTH STORE**, Rumbolds Hill, **MIDHURST**, GU29 9BY (T) 01730 810820
- **NATURAL HEALTH & BEAUTY**, PO Box 35, **CRAWLEY**, RH11 8YU (T) 01293 419914
- **NATURAL WAY**, 33a Carfax, **HORSHAM**, RH12 1EE (T) 01403 262228
- **NATURE'S WAY FOODS LTD**, Walnut Tree Farm, Vinnetrow Road, Runcton, **CHICHESTER**, PO20 6QB (T) 01243 790099
- **NUTRI HEALTH (UK) LTD**, Downlands Farm, Drayton Lane, Merston, **CHICHESTER**, PO20 6EL (T) 01243 775992
- **SELF HEALTH ENTERPRISES LTD**, Bulrushes Farm, Coombe Hill Road, **EAST GRINSTEAD**, RH19 4LZ (T) 01342 300023
- **SPENCO HEALTHCARE INTERNATIONAL LTD**, 45 London Road, **HORSHAM**, RH12 1AN (T) 01403 321900
- **STEYNING HEALTH FOODS**, 108 High Street, **STEYNING**, BN44 3RD (T) 01903 815953
- **SYNPHARMA INTERNATIONAL LTD**, 9 Kings Court, Kings Road, **HORSHAM**, RH13 5PP (T) 01403 217772
- **TOP TABLE**, 4 West Street, Storrington, **PULBOROUGH**, RH20 4EE (T) 01903 745900
- **TOWN & COUNTRY WEIGH**, 7 East Street, **HORSHAM**, RH12 1HH (T) 01403 210090
- **TWINLAB**, P O Box 150, **ARUNDEL**, BN18 9SW (T) 01903 885800
- **VITAMINERAL**, 14 Estcots Drive, **EAST GRINSTEAD**, RH19 3DA (T) 01342 314440
- **VITA-RITE.COM LTD**, 12 Ring Road, **LANCING**, BN15 0QF (T) 01903 752657
- **WHOLESALE NUTRITION LTD**, Wyman House, Shopwhyke Road, **CHICHESTER**, PO20 6AA (T) 01243 771700
- **XYNERGY HEALTH PRODUCTS**, Unit 5b Old Station Yard, Elsted, **MIDHURST**, GU29 0JT (T) 01730 813642

## TYNE AND WEAR

- **ALMONDS & RAISINS HEALTH FOODS LTD**, 6 Princess Square, **NEWCASTLE UPON TYNE**, NE1 8ER (T) 01912 615959
- **CAMBRIDGE DIET**, 56 Stuart Gardens, **NEWCASTLE UPON TYNE**, NE15 9LT (T) 01912 677128
- **FARAH HEALTH**, Unit 1/The Adelaide Centre, Adelaide Ter, **NEWCASTLE UPON TYNE**, NE4 8BE (T) 01912 737001
- **FOOD FOR THOUGHT**, 28 Astley Road, Seaton Delaval, **WHITLEY BAY**, NE25 0DG (T) 01912 375935
- **HEALTH AND BEAUTY CLINIC (THE)**, 11-13 Crossley Ter, Arthurs Hill, **NEWCASTLE UPON TYNE**, NE4 5NY (T) 01912 735100
- **HEALTH FAYRE**, Grand Hotel Buildings, Percy Street, **NEWCASTLE UPON TYNE**, NE1 7RY (T) 01912 323172
- **HEALTH INTERNATIONAL**, 23 Windsor Gardens, **WHITLEY BAY**, NE26 3BG (T) 01912 517772

- **HERVALIFE DISTRIBUTOR**, 2 Pontdyke, **GATESHEAD**, NE10 8LP (T) 01914 421383
- **HOLLAND & BARRETT**, 11 Bigg Market, **NEWCASTLE UPON TYNE**, NE1 1UN (T) 01912 327540
- **HOLLAND & BARRETT**, 21 Blandford Street, **SUNDERLAND**, SR1 3JP (T) 01915 656249
- **HOLLAND & BARRETT**, 287-289 Whitley Road, **WHITLEY BAY**, NE26 2TA (T) 01912 516107
- **HOLLAND & BARRETT**, 5 Cameron Walk, Metrocentre, **GATESHEAD**, NE11 9YR (T) 01914 602546
- **HOLLAND & BARRETT**, 8 Denmark Centre, **SOUTH SHIELDS**, NE33 2LR (T) 01914 559724
- **HONEY TREE (THE)**, 68 Heaton Road, **NEWCASTLE UPON TYNE**, NE6 5HL (T) 01912 402589
- **LOW FELL HEALTH STORE**, 558 Durham Road, **GATESHEAD**, NE9 6HX (T) 01914 822882
- **MANDALA WHOLE FOODS**, 43 Manor House Road, **NEWCASTLE UPON TYNE**, NE2 2LY (T) 01912 810045
- **MILBURNS**, Unit 29 Newgate Shopping Centre, **NEWCASTLE UPON TYNE**, NE1 5RS (T) 01912 329091
- **MILBURNS HEALTH FOODS**, 13 Mistletoe Road, **NEWCASTLE UPON TYNE**, NE2 2DX (T) 01912 813533
- **MOTHER NATURE**, 8 Railway Street, **NORTH SHIELDS**, NE29 6QD (T) 01912 963853
- **MOTHER NATURE**, Gateshead Indoor Market, Trinity Square, **GATESHEAD**, NE8 1AG (T) 01914 782598
- **NUTMEG WHOLEFOODS**, 34 Station Road, Gosforth, **NEWCASTLE UPON TYNE**, NE3 1QD (T) 01912 130496
- **PEAK BODY NUTRITION**, 5 Biddick Lane, **WASHINGTON**, NE38 8AB (T) 01914 154603
- **WELLBEING HEALTH SHOP**, Unit 92 Wessington Square, The Galleries, **WASHINGTON**, NE38 7RT (T) 01914 165012
- **WILD OATS**, Unit 2b Ryles Buildings, Park View, **WHITLEY BAY**, NE26 3ND (T) 01912 515987

## WARWICKSHIRE

- **A MATTHEWMAN**, The Grange, Welford Road, Long Marston, **STRATFORD-UPON-AVON**, CV37 8RH (T) 01789 721830
- **AROVITE LTD**, The Precinct, School Road, Wellesbourne, **WARWICK**, CV35 9NL (T) 01789 841538
- **GOOD HEALTH FOODS LTD**, 5a Stratford Street, **NUNEATON**, CV11 5BS (T) 024 7637 0833
- **GRAINSTORE (THE)**, 5 Market Street, **ATHERSTONE**, CV9 1ET (T) 01827 720072
- **HEALTH EMPORIUM (THE)**, 44 The Square, **KENILWORTH**, CV8 1EB (T) 01926 850115
- **HEALTH FOOD STORE**, 59 Mill Street, **BEDWORTH**, CV12 8JX (T) 024 7631 5627
- **HEALTH SHOP (THE)**, 6 Coventry Street, **NUNEATON**, CV11 5SZ (T) 024 7634 6200
- **HOLLAND & BARRETT**, 2 Market Place, **NUNEATON**, CV11 4EA (T) 024 7635 2649
- **HOLLAND & BARRETT**, 20-22 High Street, **WARWICK**, CV34 4AP (T) 01926 409305
- **HOLLAND & BARRETT**, 36a High Street, **RUGBY**, CV21 3BW (T) 01788 570280
- **HOLLAND & BARRETT**, 55 Warwick Street, **LEAMINGTON SPA**, CV32 5JR (T) 01926 421775
- **HOLLAND & BARRETT**, Samuel Ryder House, Townsend Drive, Attleborough Fields Ind Estate, **NUNEATON**, CV11 6XW (T) 01455 251900
- **KAIRE EUROPE LTD**, Wharf Street, **WARWICK**, CV34 5LB (T) 01926 411113
- **MARGARET HILLS**, Unit 7 Millar Court, 43 Station Road, **KENILWORTH**, CV8 1JD (T) 01926 850019
- **MATTHEWMAN A**, Longbridge Manor, Longbridge, **WARWICK**, CV34 6RB (T) 01926 497007
- **NATURAL CHOICE**, 2 Chestnut House, North Street, **RUGBY**, CV21 2AG (T) 01788 562148
- **RHODES DYNAMIX**, 4 Chapel Court, Holly Walk, **LEAMINGTON SPA**, CV32 4YS (T) 01926 424000
- **RUGBY HEALTH FOODS**, 15 Albert Street, **RUGBY**, CV21 2SD (T) 01788 579222
- **RUPERTS HEATH FOOD**, 36 Sheep Street, **SHIPSTON-ON-STOUR**, CV36 4AF (T) 01608 664116
- **STRATFORD HEALTH FOODS**, Unit 1 Greenhill Street, **STRATFORD-UPON-AVON**, CV37 6LF (T) 01789 292353
- **VITALL INTERNATIONAL INDEPENDENT DISTRIBUTORS**, 21 Fairway, **NUNEATON**, CV11 6NP (T) 024 7635 1356
- **WARWICK HEALTH FOOD CENTRE**, 40a Brook Street, **WARWICK**, CV34 4BL (T) 01926 494311
- **YOUR GOOD HEALTH**, Leamington Road, Princethorpe, **RUGBY**, CV23 9PU (T) 01926 632827

## WILTSHIRE

- **ALOE VERA**, Burbage Wharf, Burbage, **MARLBOROUGH**, SN8 3BJ (T) 01672 810920
- **ALOE VERA STORE**, 55 Castle Road, **SALISBURY**, SP1 3RH (T) 01722 415105
- **ASHTANGA**, 13 Fairwood Road, Dilton Marsh, **WESTBURY**, BA13 3SN (T) 01373 859313
- **BIO HAZARD DIRECT LTD**, Moonleaze Farm, Braydon, **SWINDON**, SN5 0AQ (T) 01666 860849
- **CAUSEWAY HEALTH FOODS & HOMEBREW**, 4 The Causeway, **CHIPPENHAM**, SN15 3BT (T) 01249 659431
- **CHLORELLA PRODUCTS LTD**, Draycott Foliat, **SWINDON**, SN4 0HX (T) 01793 741122
- **FOREVER LIVING PRODUCTS**, Old Sarum Park, Old Sarum, **SALISBURY**, SP4 6EB (T) 01722 341116
- **GENERAL NUTRITION CENTRE**, 14-16 Brunel Plaza, **SWINDON**, SN1 1LF (T) 01793 520385
- **GRAVES JULIAN LTD**, Unit 11/The Wilton Shopping Village, King Street, Wilton, **SALISBURY**, SP2 0RS (T) 01722 741346
- **HEALTHY LIFE (THE)**, 4 Little Brittox, **DEVIZES**, SN10 1AR (T) 01380 725558
- **HOLLAND & BARRETT**, 1 Market Place, **WARMINSTER**, BA12 9AY (T) 01985 847965
- **HOLLAND & BARRETT**, 15 The Shires, **TROWBRIDGE**, BA14 8AT (T) 01225 776056
- **HOLLAND & BARRETT**, 17 Brunnel Shopping Centre, Brunel Plaza, **SWINDON**, SN1 1LF (T) 01793 521235
- **HOLLAND & BARRETT**, 59 Silver Street, **SALISBURY**, SP1 2NG (T) 01722 324064
- **JULIAN GRAVES LTD**, 28 Butcher Row, **SALISBURY**, SP1 1EP (T) 01722 421141
- **LARKHALL NATURAL HEALTH LTD**, Newmarket Avenue, White Horse Business Park, **TROWBRIDGE**, BA14 0XQ (T) 01225 711677
- **MALMESBURY WHOLEFOODS**, 29 Abbey Row, **MALMESBURY**, SN16 0AG (T) 01666 823030
- **NATURE'S ENERGY**, 7 Standings Close, Nine Elms, **SWINDON**, SN5 9UG (T) 01793 887574
- **NATURES LARDER**, 96 Victoria Road, **SWINDON**, SN1 3BD (T) 01793 521831
- **PANCEUTICS LTD**, P O Box 1358, **SWINDON**, SN3 4GP (T) 01793 822275
- **REAPERS WHOLEFOODS**, 22a Silver Street, **TROWBRIDGE**, BA14 8AE (T) 01225 777024
- **SALISBURY HEALTH FOODS**, 15 Queen Street, **SALISBURY**, SP1 1EY (T) 01722 335965
- **SAUNDERS ORGANICS**, 8b High Street, **MARLBOROUGH**, SN8 1LT (T) 01672 513838
- **SEGLAN & CO**, Norris Hill Farm House, Norris Hill, Brokerswood, **WESTBURY**, BA13 4E (T) 01323 459176
- **SPICE OF LIFE (THE)**, 33 Silver Street, **BRADFORD-ON-AVON**, BA15 1JX (T) 01225 864351
- **SWINDON PULSE WHOLEFOODS CO-OPERATIVE**, 27 Curtis Street, **SWINDON**, SN1 5JU (T) 01793 692016
- **WILD THYMES**, Unit 2/Hughenden Yard, High Street, **MARLBOROUGH**, SN8 1LT (T) 01672 516373
- **WILTON WHOLEFOODS**, Unit 5 The Business Centre, Morgans Vale Road, Redlynch, **SALISBURY**, SP5 2HA (T) 01725 513122
- **WISE SAGE WHOLEFOODS**, 8 High Street, **CALNE**, SN11 0BS (T) 01249 812675

## WORCESTERSHIRE

- **ALOE VERA FOREVER LIVING PRODUCTS**, Ridgeway Cross, Cradley, **MALVERN**, WR13 5JS (T) 01886 880088
- **BEEWELL**, 4 Royal Arcade, Bridge Street, **PERSHORE**, WR10 1AG (T) 01386 556577
- **BODYCARE**, 17 Josiah Mason Mall, Rowland Hill Centre, **KIDDERMINSTER**, DY10 1EJ (T) 01562 750007
- **BRAN TUB WHOLEFOODS (THE)**, Belle Vue Ter, **MALVERN**, WR14 4AU (T) 01684 891191
- **CYTOPLAN LTD**, Unit 8 Hanley Workshops, Hanley Swan, **WORCESTER**, WR8 0DX (T) 01684 310099
- **FOREVER LIVING PRODUCTS**, Poachers Barn, Sandlin, Leigh Sinton, **MALVERN**, WR13 5DN (T) 01886 833661
- **GENERAL NUTRITION CENTRE**, C7 Chapel Walk, **WORCESTER**, WR1 3LD (T) 01905 612639
- **HEALTH FOOD CENTRE**, 69a St. Johns, **WORCESTER**, WR2 5AG (T) 01905 425888
- **HOLE IN THE WALL**, 20 Market Street, **TENBURY WELLS**, WR15 8BQ (T) 01584 811429
- **HOLLAND & BARRETT**, 10 King Charles Square, Swan Centre, **KIDDERMINSTER**, DY10 2BA (T) 01562 748822
- **HOLLAND & BARRETT**, 13 Royal Square, Kingfisher Shopping Centre, **REDDITCH**, B97 4HU (T) 01527 64384
- **HOLLAND & BARRETT**, 15 High Street, **BROMSGROVE**, B61 8AJ (T) 01527 836949



 

- **HOLLAND & BARRETT**, 22 Mealcheapen Street, **WORCESTER**, WR1 2DQ (T) 01905 28153
- **HOLLAND & BARRETT**, 23 Abbey Gate, **EVESHAM**, WR11 4BG (T) 01386 40854
- **HOLLAND & BARRETT**, 38 High Street, **PERSHORE**, WR10 1DP (T) 01386 556495
- **HOLLAND & BARRETT**, 45 High Street, **STOURPORT-ON-SEVERN**, DY13 8BU (T) 01299 822463
- **JULIAN GRAVES LTD**, 41 Friary Walk, **WORCESTER**, WR1 3LE (T) 01905 611129
- **JULIAN GRAVES LTD**, Unit 6, Evesham Country Pk, Twyford, **EVESHAM**, WR11 4TP (T) 01386 45168
- **MYPLAN LTD**, Old Colwall, **MALVERN**, WR13 6HF (T) 01684 540441
- **NATURAL FARE**, 9 Talbot Square, Cleobury Mortimer, **KIDDERMINSTER**, DY14 8BQ (T) 01299 270103
- **NATURES OWN LTD**, Unit 8 Hanley Workshops, Hanley Road, Hanley Swan, **WORCESTER**, WR8 0DX (T) 01684 310022
- **R & E A BUCKINGHAM**, The Smallholding, Chadbury Road, Chadbury, **EVESHAM**, WR11 4TD (T) 01386 765538
- **ROSEMARYS HEALTH FOODS**, 10 The Shambles, **WORCESTER**, WR1 2RF (T) 01905 612190
- **SUNSHINE HEALTH SHOP**, 3 Vine Street, **EVESHAM**, WR11 4RE (T) 01386 443757

## YORKSHIRE (NORTH)

- **ALTERNATIVES**, Chapel Street, Easingwold, **YORK**, YO61 3AF (T) 01347 822215
- **BEE HEALTH**, Sneatondale Honey Farm, Racecourse Road, East Ayton, **SCARBOROUGH**, YO13 9HT (T) 01723 864001
- **BEECHAM HEALTH FOODS**, 16 Yorkersgate, **MALTON**, YO17 7AB (T) 01653 695145
- **COUNTRY PRODUCTS**, 11a Centre Park, Rudgate, Tockwith, **YORK**, YO26 7QF (T) 01423 358858
- **FIRST SEASON**, 1 St Anns Lane, **WHITBY**, YO21 3PF (T) 01947 601608
- **FOOD FOR THOUGHT**, 2 Ryedale Court, The Village, Haxby, **YORK**, YO32 3SA (T) 01904 765878
- **FOUNTAINS HEALTH STORES**, 7 North Street, **RIPON**, HG4 1JY (T) 01765 604726
- **GOLDEN HARVEST HEALTH SHOP (THE)**, 24a Aberdeen Walk, **SCARBOROUGH**, YO11 1XW (T) 01723 365660
- **GRANARY (THE)**, 13 Church Lane, **SELBY**, YO8 4PQ (T) 01757 708516
- **GREEN HOUSE (THE)**, 5 Station Parade, **HARROGATE**, HG1 1UF (T) 01423 502580
- **HEALTH DIRECT**, Brereton Lodge, Goathland, **WHITBY**, YO22 5JR (T) 01947 896037
- **HEALTH RACK**, 16 Stonegate, **YORK**, YO1 8AS (T) 01904 624467
- **HEALTHY LIFE NATURAL FOOD CENTRE**, 10 High Street, **SKIPTON**, BD23 1JZ (T) 01756 790619
- **HELLENIA**, Dallamires Lane, **RIPON**, HG4 1TT (T) 01765 603816
- **HERB OF GRACE**, 11 Castlegate, **KNARESBOROUGH**, HG5 8AR (T) 01423 862351
- **HERBALIFE DISTRIBUTION**, 6 Lawson Avenue, Boroughbridge, **YORK**, YO51 9UU (T) 01423 325554
- **HOLLAND & BARRETT**, 1a James Street, **HARROGATE**, HG1 1QS (T) 01423 503469
- **HOLLAND & BARRETT**, 28 Coney Street, **YORK**, YO1 1ND (T) 01904 627257
- **HOLLAND & BARRETT**, 30 Market Place, **THIRSK**, YO7 1LB (T) 01845 526868
- **HOLLAND & BARRETT**, Unit 18 Brunswick Pavilion, Somerset Terrace, **SCARBOROUGH**, YO11 2PA (T) 01723 501369
- **HUPWUS HEALTH PRODUCTS**, Chandlers, Town Hill, Hebden, **SKIPTON**, BD23 5D (T) 01733 286176
- **JULIAN GRAVES LTD**, Craven Court, High Street, **SKIPTON**, BD23 1DG (T) 01756 790270
- **LIFEPLAN PRODUCTS LTD**, 4 Franklins Yard, Fossgate, **YORK**, YO1 9TN (T) 01904 620809
- **MARK CHADBOURNE & NICOLA LESTER**, 69 Crowberry Drive, **HARROGATE**, HG3 2UF (T) 01423 564237
- **NATURAL CHOICE**, 11 Silver Street, **KNARESBOROUGH**, HG5 8AJ (T) 01423 867705
- **QUALITY HEALTH FOODS**, 3 Westminster Arcade, Parliament Street, **HARROGATE**, HG1 2RN (T) 01423 541154
- **SCOOP VALUE**, 18 Finkle Street, **SELBY**, YO8 4DS (T) 01757 213475
- **SHEPHERDS PURSE**, 95 Church Street, **WHITBY**, YO22 4BH (T) 01947 820228
- **TULLIVERS**, 1-2 Colliergate, **YORK**, YO1 8BP (T) 01904 636437
- **VICTORIA HEALTH FOOD CENTRE**, 91 Victoria Road, **SCARBOROUGH**, YO11 1SL (T) 01723 369895
- **WIVES KITCHEN**, 11 Finkle Street, **RICHMOND**, DL10 4QA (T) 01748 822210
- **YORK NUT CENTRE (THE)**, 21 Market Street, **YORK**, YO1 8SL (T) 01904 641205

## YORKSHIRE (SOUTH)

- **A J SERVICES**, 12/Walton Court, Bocking Lane, **SHEFFIELD**, S8 7BH (T) 01142 495033
- **A1 ALOE VERA NATURAL HEALTH PRODUCTS**, The Barn, Beverleys Road, **SHEFFIELD**, S8 9BR (T) 01142 589187
- **ALLSPORTS INTERNATIONAL LTD**, Wheatley Hall Road, **DONCASTER**, DN2 4LP (T) 01302 325163
- **ALOE VERA & BEE PRODUCTS**, 37 Folds Cresent, **SHEFFIELD**, S8 0EP (T) 01142 811348
- **BEAN BEANIE WHOLEFOOD**, 205-207 Crookes Valley Road, **SHEFFIELD**, S10 1BA (T) 01142 681662
- **CORNCROFT CONCEPTS LTD**, Millennium House, 30 Junction Road, **SHEFFIELD**, S11 8XB (T) 01142 631990
- **DOWN TO EARTH**, 406 Sharrow Vale Road, **SHEFFIELD**, S11 8ZP (T) 01142 685220
- **FREEWALKER HEALTH CO (THE)**, Springfield House, Rands Lane, Armthorpe, **DONCASTER**, DN3 3DY (T) 01302 302362
- **HARVEST TYME**, 43 Middlewood Road, **SHEFFIELD**, S6 4GW (T) 01142 347803
- **HEALTH RACK**, 15 May Day Green, **BARNSLEY**, S70 1RH (T) 01226 779950
- **HEALTH RACK**, 22 St. Sepulchre Gate, **DONCASTER**, DN1 1SW (T) 01302 343109
- **HEALTHCARE PRODUCTS (UK) LTD**, 111 Halifax Road, **SHEFFIELD**, S6 1LB (T) 01142 349994
- **HERBAFAYRE**, 2a Ecclesfield Road, Chapeltown, **SHEFFIELD**, S35 1TD (T) 01142 455026
- **HERBAFAYRE**, 9 Eastwood Lane, **ROTHERHAM**, S65 1EQ (T) 01709 376401
- **HERBAL DELIGHTS**, 15 Hoyland Road, Hoyland, **BARNSLEY**, S74 0LT (T) 01226 350091
- **HERBALIFE**, 10 Queen Victoria Road, **SHEFFIELD**, S17 4HT (T) 01142 363992
- **HOLLAND & BARRETT**, 10 Barkers Pool, **SHEFFIELD**, S1 2HB (T) 01142 755438
- **HOLLAND & BARRETT**, 19 Cheapside, **BARNSLEY**, S70 1RQ (T) 01226 770069
- **HOLLAND & BARRETT**, 23 Frenchgate, **DONCASTER**, DN1 1PZ (T) 01302 360082
- **HOLLAND & BARRETT**, Unit 47 Crystal Peaks, Eckington Way, Crystal Peaks, **SHEFFIELD**, S20 7PP (T) 01142 510369
- **IN A NUTSHELL**, 31 Chesterfield Road, **SHEFFIELD**, S8 0RL (T) 01142 508555
- **JOHNSON ASSOCIATES**, 6 Hoober Court, Rawmarsh, **ROTHERHAM**, S62 7LH (T) 01709 710316
- **LEMBAS LTD**, Unit 7 Meersbrook Works, Valley Road, **SHEFFIELD**, S8 9FT (T) 01142 586056
- **LOMPAK FOOD PACKING**, Unit 14/Swinton Meadows Industrial Estate, Meadow Way, Swinton, **MEXBOROUGH**, S64 8AB (T) 01709 570176
- **MARKET HEALTH STORE (THE)**, Market Place, **DONCASTER**, DN1 1NG (T) 01302 369139
- **NATURES TRAIL**, 665 Ecclesall Road, **SHEFFIELD**, S11 8PT (T) 01142 665984
- **NEW ROOTS**, 347 Glossop Road, **SHEFFIELD**, S10 2HP (T) 01142 721971
- **NUTRITION FOR LIFE INTERNATIONAL**, 10 Laverack Street, **SHEFFIELD**, S13 8TR (T) 01142 697841
- **S P N (UK) LTD**, 24 Sandringham Road, **DONCASTER**, DN2 5HU (T) 01302 761755
- **SHEFFIELD WHOLEFOOD STORE**, 174 Norfolk Street, **SHEFFIELD**, S1 2JH (T) 01142 721608
- **WELLFOODS LTD**, Units 6/Mapplewell Business Pk, Blacker Road, Mapplewell, **BARNSLEY**, S75 6BP (T) 01226 381712
- **WICKER HERBAL STORE**, 195 Castle Market, **SHEFFIELD**, S1 2AF (T) 01142 723632
- **WOMBWELL HEALTH STORE**, 51a High Street, Wombwell, **BARNSLEY**, S73 8HS (T) 01226 341300
- **ZED WHOLEFOODS**, 3 Nether Edge Road, **SHEFFIELD**, S7 1RU (T) 01142 552153

## YORKSHIRE (WEST)

- **ARCON (UK) LTD**, 48 Station Road, Holywell Green, **HALIFAX**, HX4 9AW (T) 01422 377115
- **B R PHARMACEUTICALS**, Unit 51/Broom Mills, Coal Hill Lane, Farsley, **PUDSEY**, LS28 5NA (T) 01132 565836
- **BACTACOTE LTD**, Stanley Road, **BRADFORD**, BD2 1AS (T) 01274 720505
- **BEANO WHOLEFOODS**, 36 New Briggate, **LEEDS**, LS1 6NU (T) 01132 435737

- **BEAR WHOLEFOODS (THE)**, 29 Rochdale Road, **TODMORDEN**, OL14 7LA
(T) 01706 813737
- **BIG APPLE (THE)**, Unit 1 Morley Market, Queen Street, Morley, **LEEDS**, LS27 8EG
(T) 01132 534525
- **BRAN TUB (THE)**, 33b High Street, Yeadon, **LEEDS**, LS19 7SP
(T) 01132 502524
- **CHEVIN HEALTH & WHOLEFOOD STORE**, 44 Boroughgate, **OTLEY**, LS21 1AE
(T) 01943 850323
- **DE RIT (UK) LTD**, Tenterfields Business Park, Burnley Road, Luddendenfoot, **HALIFAX**, HX2 6EQ
(T) 01422 885523
- **ENGLISH HERBAL**, 20 Eastgate, **LEEDS**, LS2 7JL
(T) 01132 451095
- **FINE FOOD HEALTH STORES**, 123 Queensgate Market, Birkby, **HUDDERSFIELD**, HD2 2UJ
(T) 01484 530211
- **FOOD THERAPY**, 11 Northgate, **HALIFAX**, HX1 1UR
(T) 01422 350826
- **FOOD WEIGHOUSE LTD**, 66 Carlton Street, **CASTLEFORD**, WF10 1DB
(T) 01977 603140
- **FUNNY FOODS**, 42 Station Road, **OSSETT**, WF5 8AY
(T) 01924 273255
- **GOOD FOOD STORE (THE)**, 4b Main Street, Garforth, **LEEDS**, LS25 1EZ
(T) 01132 868965
- **GOOD LIFE (THE)**, 32 Market Place, **WETHERBY**, LS22 6NE
(T) 01937 587564
- **GOODHEALTH**, 7 Queen Street, Horbury, **WAKEFIELD**, WF4 6LP
(T) 01924 266669
- **GREEN HEALTH SHOP (THE)**, 27 Northgate, **CLECKHEATON**, BD19 3HH
(T) 01274 871488
- **GREEN HEALTH SHOP (THE)**, 9 The Moors Shopping Centre, South Hawksworth Street, **ILKLEY**, LS29 9LB
(T) 01943 816435
- **HALFMOON HEALTH FOODS**, 6 Half Moon Street, **HUDDERSFIELD**, HD1 2HE
(T) 01484 456392
- **HALFMOON HEALTH FOODS**, 6 Half Moon Street, **HUDDERSFIELD**, HD1 2JJ
(T) 01484 310161
- **HEALTH FOOD STORES**, 20-22 Market Arcade, **HALIFAX**, HX1 1NX
(T) 01422 353991
- **HEALTH IMPORTS LTD**, Young Street, **BRADFORD**, BD8 9RE
(T) 01274 487662
- **HEALTH PUBLICATIONS LTD**, 48 Station Road, Holywell Green, **HALIFAX**, HX4 9AW
(T) 01422 376434
- **HEALTH RACK**, Arndale Mall, Kirkgate Centre, **BRADFORD**, BD1 1TQ
(T) 01274 732110
- **HEALTH RACK (THE)**, Pack Horse Walk, **HUDDERSFIELD**, HD1 2RT
(T) 01484 540405
- **HEALTH SHOP (THE)**, 19-20 Market Hall, Kirkgate, **SHIPLEY**, BD18 3QU
(T) 01274 582635
- **HEALTH WISE**, 29 Westgate Market, **HALIFAX**, HX1 1PF
(T) 01422 340313
- **HEALTHILIFE LTD**, Charlestown House, Otley Road, Baildon, **SHIPLEY**, BD17 7JS
(T) 01274 595021
- **HEALTHLIFE DIRECT**, Charlestown House, Otley Road, Baildon, **SHIPLEY**, BD17 7JS
(T) 01274 589026
- **HEALTHY LIFESTYLE**, 127b Main Street, Garforth, **LEEDS**, LS25 1AF
(T) 01132 860202
- **HELIOS WHOLE FOODS**, 225 King Cross Road, **HALIFAX**, HX1 3JL
(T) 01422 330445
- **HEMINGWAYS**, 24 Corporation Street, **DEWSBURY**, WF13 1QG
(T) 01924 465634
- **HERBS & HEALTH FOODS**, 517 Great Horton Road, **BRADFORD**, BD7 4EG
(T) 01274 573369
- **HOLLAND & BARRETT**, 11 All Saints Walk, The Ridings Centre, **WAKEFIELD**, WF1 1US
(T) 01924 367195
- **HOLLAND & BARRETT**, 11 Arndale Centre, **LEEDS**, LS15 8ET
(T) 01132 648326
- **HOLLAND & BARRETT**, 11 The Princess Of Wales Precinct, **DEWSBURY**, WF13 1NH
(T) 01924 462625
- **HOLLAND & BARRETT**, 19 Brook Street, **ILKLEY**, LS29 8AA
(T) 01943 817162
- **HOLLAND & BARRETT**, 37 Merrion Centre, **LEEDS**, LS2 8NG
(T) 01132 342828
- **HOLLAND & BARRETT**, 4 Crown Street, **HALIFAX**, HX1 1TT
(T) 01422 365794
- **HOLLAND & BARRETT**, 58 Kirkgate, **BRADFORD**, BD1 1QT
(T) 01274 723289
- **HOLLAND & BARRETT**, 64 Towngate, **KEIGHLEY**, BD21 3QE
(T) 01535 663338
- **HOLLAND & BARRETT**, 95 New Street, **HUDDERSFIELD**, HD1 2TW
(T) 01484 548963
- **HOLLAND & BARRETT**, Bond Street, Centre Plaza, **LEEDS**, LS1 5ER
(T) 01132 467011
- **HOLLAND & BARRETT**, Unit 14 Carlton Lane Shopping Centre, Carlton Street, **CASTLEFORD**, WF10 1BA
(T) 01977 603858
- **J & S ENTERPRISES**, Chapel House, Timble, **OTLEY**, LS21 2NN
(T) 01943 880288
- **J DODD & CO LTD (EST 1882)**, 6 Byram Street, **HUDDERSFIELD**, HD1 1BX
(T) 01484 420028
- **MARVELS HEALTH SHOP**, 60 High Street, **NORMANTON**, WF6 2AL
(T) 01924 891333
- **MRS BEE'S HEALTH FOODS**, Sefton Mews, 134a High Street, Boston Spa, **WETHERBY**, LS23 6BW
(T) 01937 842827
- **NATURAL CHOICE**, 72 Westbourne Road, **HUDDERSFIELD**, HD1 4LE
(T) 01484 513162
- **NATURAL FOOD STORE**, 23 North Lane, Headingley, **LEEDS**, LS6 3HW
(T) 01132 784944
- **NATURES STORE**, 6 Marygate, **WAKEFIELD**, WF1 1NX
(T) 01924 368430
- **NATURES STORE**, 7 Market Hall Kiosks, Carlton Street, **CASTLEFORD**, WF10 1BG
(T) 01977 515949
- **NATUREWAY**, 122 Harrogate Road, **LEEDS**, LS7 4NY
(T) 01132 696801
- **NUT SHOP (THE)**, Row A & B, Kirkgate Market, **LEEDS**, LS2 7HW
(T) 01132 455267
- **OAKWOOD**, 458 Roundhay Road, **LEEDS**, LS8 2HU
(T) 01132 179977
- **OFFSHOOT**, 20 Cavendish Street, **KEIGHLEY**, BD21 3RG
(T) 01535 606589
- **PURELY NATURAL**, 94a Town Street, Horsforth, **LEEDS**, LS18 4AP
(T) 01132 580283
- **RAINTREE HEALTH (UK) LTD**, PO Box 12, Thornton, **BRADFORD**, BD13 3YD
(T) 01274 832880
- **REDDIHOUGH J E**, 410 Skipton Road, **KEIGHLEY**, BD20 6HP
(T) 01535 605369
- **RYECORN WHOLEFOODS**, 112 Commercial Street, **BRIGHOUSE**, HD6 1AQ
(T) 01484 711835
- **SAVANT DISTRIBUTION LTD**, 15 Iveson Approach, **LEEDS**, LS16 6LJ
(T) 01132 301993
- **TUJKIG HEALTHILIFE**, 38 Lowergate, Paddock, **HUDDERSFIELD**, HD3 4ER
(T) 01472 309176
- **VITRITION (UK) LTD**, Unit 7/Victoria Spring Business Pk, Wormald Street, **LIVERSEDGE**, WF15 6RA
(T) 01924 410400
- **WAKEFIELD HEALTH FOODS (HERBALIST)**, 11 Market Way, **WAKEFIELD**, WF1 1QJ
(T) 01924 367132
- **WESLEY & GELDARD**, 46 Market Street, **HEBDEN BRIDGE**, HX7 6AA
(T) 01422 845217
- **YOUR NUTS**, 14a Towngate, Holmfirth, **HUDDERSFIELD**, HD7 1HA
(T) 01484 680126
- **YOUR NUTS**, Unit 10 Springfield Mills, Norman Road, Denby Dale, **HUDDERSFIELD**, HD8 8TH
(T) 01484 864902

## NORTHERN IRELAND

### COUNTY ANTRIM

- **ALOE HEALTH PRODUCTS**, 17 Larkfield Road, **BELFAST**, BT4 1QE
(T) 028 9067 1428
- **ALOE VERA CENTRE**, 338 Ballyclare Road, **NEWTOWNABBEY**, BT36 4TQ
(T) 08000 351151
- **ALOE VERA PRODUCT CENTRE**, 338 Ballyclare Road, **NEWTOWNABBEY**, BT36 4TQ
(T) 028 9034 2695
- **BALSAN HYDRO THERAPY**, Unit 12 North City Business Centre, 2 Duncairn Gardens, **BELFAST**, BT15 2GG
(T) 028 9074 5512
- **BEST OF HEALTH NORTHERN IRELAND**, 73 Largy Road, **CRUMLIN**, BT29 4RS
(T) 028 9445 4955
- **EATWELL FOODS**, 413 Lisburn Road, **BELFAST**, BT9 7EW
(T) 028 9066 4362
- **EDEN HEALTH**, Smithfield, **LISBURN**, BT28 1TH
(T) 028 9260 3641
- **FOREVER LIVING PRODUCTS**, Carrickfergus Ind Centre, Belfast Road, **CARRICKFERGUS**, BT38 8PH
(T) 028 9336 5649
- **FRAMAR HEALTH**, 595 Lisburn Road, **BELFAST**, BT9 7GS
(T) 028 9068 1018
- **FRAMAR HEALTH PRODUCTS**, 391 Ormeau Road, **BELFAST**, BT7 3GP
(T) 028 9069 4210
- **HEALTH CARE INTERNATIONAL**, 46 Kennedy Drive, **LISBURN**, BT27 4HZ
(T) 028 9260 1550
- **NATURAL HEALTH PRODUCTS**, 11 Railway Street, **LISBURN**, BT28 1XG
(T) 028 9266 2551
- **NATURE CARE**, Unit 3 Shopping Precinct, High Street, **ANTRIM**, BT41 4BN
(T) 028 9442 8651
- **NATURE NOOK (THE)**, 4 Victoria Street, **BALLYMONEY**, BT53 6DW
(T) 028 2766 4178
- **NATURES WAY**, 305 Upper Newtownards Road, **BELFAST**, BT4 3JH
(T) 028 9047 1333
- **NATURE'S WAY**, 305 Upper Newtownards Road, **BELFAST**, BT4 3JH
(T) 028 9065 6694
- **NUT-MEG (THE)**, 9a Lombard Street, **BELFAST**, BT1 1RB
(T) 028 9024 9984
- **QUINTESSENCE HEALTH SHOP**, 327 Antrim Road, **BELFAST**, BT15 2HF
(T) 028 9035 1590
- **RICHWELL MARKETING LTD**, 18 Old Saintfield Road, Carryduff, **BELFAST**, BT8 8EY
(T) 028 9081 2323



 

**ROYAL DYNASTY**, 23 Irish Quarter West, **CARRICKFERGUS**, BT38 8AS
(T) 028 9335 5700

**SCOOP & HEALTH**, 15 Bloomfield Avenue, **BELFAST**, BT5 5AA
(T) 028 9045 2586

**SCOOP-A-MARKET**, 8 Castle Street, **BELFAST**, BT1 1BL
(T) 028 9024 1072

**TRAMWAYS**, Unit 9 Tramways Shopping Centre, Farmley Road, **NEWTOWNABBEY**, BT36 7TS
(T) 028 9083 0574

**WATAIR ENTERPRISES**, 4 Mount Aboo Park, **BELFAST**, BT10 0DJ
(T) 028 9020 2224

## COUNTY ARMAGH

**CYBERFLEX PERFORMANCE FITNESS UK LTD**, 2 Village Walk, Portadown, **CRAIGAVON**, BT63 5TL
(T) 028 3833 6955

**HEALTH BIN (THE)**, 17 Union Street, Lurgan, **CRAIGAVON**, BT66 8DY
(T) 028 3832 8458

**HEALTH BIN (THE)**, 5 Church Street, Portadown, **CRAIGAVON**, BT62 3LG
(T) 028 3833 2882

**NATURES ESSENCE**, 6 William Street, Lurgan, **CRAIGAVON**, BT66 6JA
(T) 028 3831 6469

**ZEST HEALTH CENTRE**, 18 Thomas Street, **ARMAGH**, BT61 7PX
(T) 028 3751 1651

## COUNTY DOWN

**ASHDENE HEALTH**, 42 Banbridge Road, Rathfriland, **NEWRY**, BT34 5PQ
(T) 028 4063 0842

**CASTLE HEALTH STORE**, 8b Castle Street, Comber, **NEWTOWNARDS**, BT23 5DZ
(T) 028 9187 8227

**EDEN HEALTH PRODUCTS**, 10 Newry Street, **BANBRIDGE**, BT32 3HA
(T) 028 4066 2841

**FRED STOREY (BELFAST) LTD**, 5a High Street, Comber, **NEWTOWNARDS**, BT23 5HJ
(T) 028 9187 0033

**HARVEST HEALTH FOODS & HOME BREW**, Unit 6 Kingsway, 5 Monaghan Street, **NEWRY**, BT35 6BB
(T) 028 3026 7967

**HARVEST NATURAL FOOD STORE**, 2c-2d King Street, **BANGOR**, BT20 3AH
(T) 028 9145 1979

**IONA SHOP**, 27 Church Road, **HOLYWOOD**, BT18 9BU
(T) 028 9042 8597

**LIFESPRING INTERNATIONAL**, Ards Business Centre, Jubilee Road, **NEWTOWNARDS**, BT23 4YH
(T) 028 9181 9787

**MERVIN ROULSTON ALOE VERA PRODUCTS**, 12 Castle Street, Comber, **NEWTOWNARDS**, BT23 5DZ
(T) 028 9187 1048

**NATURAL HEALTH CENTRE (THE)**, 20 Margaret Street, **NEWRY**, BT34 1DF
(T) 028 3025 2940

**NATURAL TOUCH (THE)**, 1 Main Street, Saintfield, **BALLYNAHINCH**, BT24 7AA
(T) 028 9751 1414

## COUNTY FERMANAGH

**HEALTHY LIFE**, 12 Paget Lane, **ENNISKILLEN**, BT74 7HT
(T) 028 6632 2862

**NATURES CHOICE**, 30 East Bridge Street, **ENNISKILLEN**, BT74 7BT
(T) 028 6632 8993

## COUNTY LONDONDERRY

**BOOTS STORES LTD**, Unit 11-12 Meadow Lane Shopping Centre, Moneymore Road, **MAGHERAFELT**, BT45 6PR
(T) 028 7963 4365

**HEALTH FOOD STORE (THE)**, 62 The Promenade, **PORTSTEWART**, BT55 7AF
(T) 028 7083 2660

**HEALTH MINISTRY (THE)**, 4 Tullyheran Road, **MAGHERA**, BT46 5JQ
(T) 028 7964 4444

**HERB GARDEN (THE)**, 8a Stone Row, **COLERAINE**, BT52 1EP
(T) 028 7032 9277

**LIFE TREE**, 37 Spencer Road, **LONDONDERRY**, BT47 6AA
(T) 028 7134 2865

**NATURAL REMEDIES**, 3 The Mall, **LIMAVADY**, BT49 0AD
(T) 028 7776 4794

**SANTE**, 5 Union Hall Place, **LONDONDERRY**, BT48 6LU
(T) 028 7126 3020

**TNHM LTD**, 4 Tullyheran Road, **MAGHERA**, BT46 5JQ
(T) 028 7964 4999

**TONIQ**, 12 Bridge Street, **LONDONDERRY**, BT48 6JZ
(T) 028 7130 8606

## COUNTY TYRONE

**FARM HEALTH PRODUCTS LTD**, 59 Market Street, **OMAGH**, BT79 0AA
(T) 028 8224 5361

**NATURE TRAIL**, 20 Bridge Street, **OMAGH**, BT78 1BX
(T) 028 8224 0388

**NATURE TRAIL**, 39 Castle Street, **OMAGH**, BT78 1DD
(T) 028 8224 0365

# SCOTLAND

## ABERDEENSHIRE

**ALOE VERA (SCOTLAND)**, Aldersyde House, New Byth, **TURRIFF**, AB53 5XD
(T) 01888 544496

**COUNTRY WAYS**, 11 Hanover Street, **FRASERBURGH**, AB43 9HQ
(T) 01346 510350

**GRAMPIAN HEALTH FOOD**, 5 Crown Street, **ABERDEEN**, AB11 6HA
(T) 01224 590886

**HOLLAND & BARRETT**, 49 Netherkirkgate, **ABERDEEN**, AB10 1AU
(T) 01224 648810

**HOLLAND & BARRETT**, Unit 2 Trinity Centre, Union Street, **ABERDEEN**, AB11 6BE
(T) 01224 581737

**NATURE'S LARDER**, 60 Holburn Street, **ABERDEEN**, AB10 6BX
(T) 01224 588120

## ANGUS

**CORNKIST (THE)**, 13 West High Street, **FORFAR**, DD8 1BE
(T) 01307 468497

**GOODNESS ME**, 106 Gray Street, Broughty Ferry, **DUNDEE**, DD5 2DN
(T) 01382 736344

**HEALTH HAVEN (THE)**, 95 High Street, **CARNOUSTIE**, DD7 7EA
(T) 01241 857700

**HOLLAND & BARRETT**, 20 The Wellgate, **DUNDEE**, DD1 2DB
(T) 01382 205726

**HOLLAND & BARRETT**, 229 High Street, **ARBROATH**, DD11 1DZ
(T) 01241 434565

**NATURELLE**, 59 Castle Street, **FORFAR**, DD8 3AG
(T) 01307 468738

**STOBSWELL MEAL STORE**, 156 Albert Street, **DUNDEE**, DD4 6QW
(T) 01382 462099

**TAYSIDE HEALTH FOODS**, 42 Commercial Street, **DUNDEE**, DD1 3EJ
(T) 01382 201660

**WEIGH & SAVE**, Care Kwik Save Pitkerro Road, **DUNDEE**, DD4 8ES
(T) 01382 510765

## ARGYLL

**MILLSTONE WHOLEFOODS**, 15 High Street, **OBAN**, PA34 4BG
(T) 01631 562704

## ARGYLL AND BUTE

**ECO HEALTH & GRAINSTORE**, 50 Hillfoot Street, **DUNOON**, PA23 7DT
(T) 01369 705106

**GRAPEVINE (THE)**, 49 Victoria Street, **ROTHESAY**, PA20 0AP
(T) 01700 504414

**HEALTHCRAFT**, 62 West Princes Street, **HELENSBURGH**, G84 8UG
(T) 01436 674993

**HOLLAND & BARRETT**, 45 Sylvania Way, **CLYDEBANK**, G81 2RR
(T) 01419 528644

**HOLLAND & BARRETT**, 61 High Street, **DUMBARTON**, G82 1LS
(T) 01389 730754

**PULSE (THE)**, Mafeking Place, Burnbank Street, **CAMPBELTOWN**, PA28 6JD
(T) 01586 552411

**WHOLEFOOD CENTRE**, 83 Argyll Street, **DUNOON**, PA23 7DH
(T) 01369 703892

## AYRSHIRE (EAST)

**HOLLAND & BARRETT**, 6 The Cross, **KILMARNOCK**, KA1 1LR
(T) 01563 574304

**SERIOUSLY HEALTHY LTD**, 81 Main Road, Crookedholm, **KILMARNOCK**, KA3 6JU
(T) 01563 555850

**YVONNE'S HEALTH FOODS & CRAFTS**, 1 Avenue Square, Stewarton, **KILMARNOCK**, KA3 5AB
(T) 01560 486890

## AYRSHIRE (NORTH)

**A3 HEALTH FOOD SHOP**, 20A Ritchie Street, **WEST KILBRIDE**, KA23 9AL
(T) 01294 829656

**BIOFORCE (UK) LTD**, 2 Breuster Place, Riverside Business Park, **IRVINE**, KA11 5DD
(T) 01294 277344

**HOLLAND & BARRETT**, 11 Rivergate, **IRVINE**, KA12 8EH
(T) 01294 278815

**HOLLAND & BARRETT**, 29 Nelson Street, **LARGS**, KA30 8LN
(T) 01475 686167

**VALLEY HEALTH PRODUCTS**, 7 Bellard Walk, **WEST KILBRIDE**, KA23 9JL
(T) 01294 829997

**VILLAGE SHOP**, Shore Road, Lamlash, **BRODICK**, KA27 8LA
(T) 01770 700349

## AYRSHIRE (SOUTH)

**HOLLAND & BARRETT**, 13 Academy Street, **TROON**, KA10 6HR
(T) 01292 311833

**HOLLAND & BARRETT**, 17 Carrick Street, **AYR**, KA7 1NS
(T) 01292 261099

**NATURAL INSTINCTS**, 20 Hope Street, **AYR**, KA7 1LT
(T) 01292 282661

**SWISS HEALTH PRODUCTS LTD**, Auchenkyle, Southwood Road, **TROON**, KA10 7EL
(T) 01292 317785

## DUMFRIES AND GALLOWAY

**DUMFRIES HEALTH & WHOLEFOODS**, 29-31 English Street, **DUMFRIES**, DG1 2BU
(T) 01387 261065

**JAN DE VRIES HEALTHCARE LTD**, 52 Hanover Street, **STRANRAER**, DG9 7RP
(T) 01776 704702

**NEWTON STEWART HEALTH FOOD SHOP**, 18-20 Queen Street, **NEWTON STEWART**, DG8 6JL
(T) 01671 402023

**SUNRISE WHOLEFOODS**, 49 King Street, **CASTLE DOUGLAS**, DG7 1AE
(T) 01556 504455

## EDINBURGH (CITY OF)

**GREENLINE PRODUCTS**, Redford Road, **EDINBURGH**, EH13 0AS
(T) 08006 16282

**HANOVER HEALTH FOODS**, 40 Hanover Street, **EDINBURGH**, EH2 2DR
(T) 01312 254291

- **HENDERSON'S OF HANOVER STREET**, 92 Hanover Street, **EDINBURGH**, EH2 1DR
(T) 01312 256694
- **HOLLAND & BARRETT**, 18 Nicolson Street, **EDINBURGH**, EH8 9HL
(T) 01316 676002
- **I S O (EDINBURGH)**, 57-59 South Clerk Street, **EDINBURGH**, EH8 9PP
(T) 01316 225101
- **JORDAN VALLEY WHOLEFOODS**, 8 Nicolson Street, **EDINBURGH**, EH8 9DH
(T) 01315 566928
- **MULBERRY HOUSE**, Inverleith Row, **EDINBURGH**, EH3 5LS
(T) 01315 583303
- **NATURES GATE**, 83 Clerk Street, **EDINBURGH**, EH8 9JG
(T) 01316 682067
- **NUT CO (THE)**, Waverley Shopping Centre, Princes Street, **EDINBURGH**, EH1 1BQ
(T) 01315 574959
- **PRIVATE LINES**, 60 Elm Row, **EDINBURGH**, EH7 4AQ
(T) 01315 576842
- **REAL FOODS LTD**, 37 Broughton Street, **EDINBURGH**, EH1 3JU
(T) 01315 571911
- **REAL FOODS LTD**, 8 Brougham Street, **EDINBURGH**, EH3 9JH
(T) 01312 281201
- **ROOTS WHOLEFOODS**, 60 Newington Road, **EDINBURGH**, EH9 1QN
(T) 01316 682888
- **RYAN'S WHOLEFOODS**, Hailes Park Industrial Estate, Dumbryden Drive, **EDINBURGH**, EH14 2QR
(T) 01314 777055
- **SCOOP-A-MARKET**, 29 Newkirkgate, **EDINBURGH**, EH6 6AB
(T) 01315 550186

## FALKIRK

- **COUNTRY FAYRE**, 13 South Street, **BO'NESS**, EH51 0EA
(T) 01506 826382
- **HOLLAND & BARRETT**, 45 High Street, FK1 1ES
(T) 01324 633397
- **WUHFOS BROS**, 27 Adam Crescent, Stenhousemuir, **LARBERT**, FK5 4DG
(T) 01323 459176

## FIFE

- **ALOE INTERNATIONAL (EUROPE) LTD**, 8/Edison House, Fullerton Road, **GLENROTHES**, KY7 5QR
(T) 01592 612000
- **ARCHTURUS HEALTH CARE LTD**, Strathenry House, Strathenry, **GLENROTHES**, KY6 3HY
(T) 01592 620865
- **HEALTH FOOD & MORE**, 9 Albany Gate, **GLENROTHES**, KY7 5NP
(T) 01592 769333
- **HEALTH FOODSTORE**, 2 Whytehouse Avenue, **KIRKCALDY**, KY1 1UW
(T) 01592 266651
- **HOLLAND & BARRETT**, 132 High Street, Dysart, **KIRKCALDY**, KY1 2YU
(T) 01592 205349
- **HOLLAND & BARRETT**, 31 Kingsgate Centre, **DUNFERMLINE**, KY12 7QU
(T) 01383 624915
- **NATURES WAY**, 27 High Street East, **ANSTRUTHER**, KY10 3DQ
(T) 01333 311077
- **PREMIER HEALTH FOODS**, 15 Bridge Street, **DUNFERMLINE**, KY12 8AQ
(T) 01383 730365
- **ST ANDREWS HEALTH FOODS**, 123 Market Street, **ST. ANDREWS**, KY16 9PE
(T) 01334 478887
- **TEMPLETONS**, 93 Market Street, **ST. ANDREWS**, KY16 9NX
(T) 01334 473950

## GLASGOW (CITY OF)

- **EVERGREEN WHOLEFOODS**, 18 Nithsdale Road, **GLASGOW**, G41 2AN
(T) 01414 221303
- **FORREST & NIVEN LTD**, 54 Dundas Street, **GLASGOW**, G1 2AQ
(T) 01414 006070
- **GOODHEALTH GRAIN & PET STORE**, 3 Mugdock Road, Milngavie, **GLASGOW**, G62 8PD
(T) 01419 566352
- **GRANARY (THE)**, 34 Busby Road, Clarkston, **GLASGOW**, G76 7XJ
(T) 01416 380001
- **GRASSROOTS**, 20 Woodlands Road, **GLASGOW**, G3 6UR
(T) 01413 533278
- **HEALTH FOOD SHOP**, 10 Dixon Avenue, **GLASGOW**, G42 8ED
(T) 01414 238675
- **HERBALIFE**, 195 Maxwell Avenue, Bearsden, **GLASGOW**, G61 1HS
(T) 01419 424106
- **HOLLAND & BARRETT**, 9 Queen Street, **GLASGOW**, G1 3ED
(T) 01412 213425
- **HOLLAND & BARRETT**, 94 Sauchiehall Street, **GLASGOW**, G2 3DE
(T) 01413 311188
- **HOLLAND & BARRETT**, The Forge, **GLASGOW**, G31 4EB
(T) 01415 518420
- **LA TEA DOH**, 136 Nithsdale Road, **GLASGOW**, G41 5RB
(T) 01414 243224
- **MASSIMO'S**, 243 Newlands Road, **GLASGOW**, G44 4EJ
(T) 01416 370575
- **NATRUAL BALANCE**, 633 Great Western Road, **GLASGOW**, G12 8RE
(T) 01415 795596
- **NATURAL BALANCE**, 633 Great Western Road, **GLASGOW**, G12 8RE
(T) 01415 795550
- **QUALITY DELI & HEALTH FOODS**, 123 Douglas Street, **GLASGOW**, G2 4HF
(T) 01413 312984
- **VITALITY DIRECT**, P O Box 5126, Clarkston, **GLASGOW**, G76 8YN
(T) 01413 030074

## HIGHLAND

- **BOREALIS PRODUCTS**, Old Pier Road, **ISLE OF SKYE**, IV49 8AE
(T) 01471 822669
- **HEALTH FOOD CENTRE**, 5 Princes Street, **THURSO**, KW14 7BQ
(T) 01847 893561
- **HEALTH FOOD SHOP (THE)**, 45 High Street, **ALNESS**, IV17 0PT
(T) 01349 883088
- **HEALTH SHOP (THE)**, 1 Falconers Lane, **NAIRN**, IV12 4DS
(T) 01667 453997
- **HEALTH SHOP (THE)**, 20 Baron Taylors Street, **INVERNESS**, IV1 1QG
(T) 01463 233104
- **HEALTHY DELI (THE)**, 19 High Street, **DINGWALL**, IV15 9RU
(T) 01349 866177
- **HIGHLAND WHOLEFOODS LTD**, Unit 6 13 Harbour Road, **INVERNESS**, IV1 1SY
(T) 01463 712393
- **HOLLAND & BARRETT**, 34 Eastgate, **INVERNESS**, IV2 3NA
(T) 01463 234267
- **JACKSON'S WHOLEFOODS**, Park Road, **PORTREE**, IV51 9EP
(T) 01478 613326
- **WEIGH IN SHOP (THE)**, 40b Baron Taylors Street, **INVERNESS**, IV1 1QG
(T) 01463 237414

## LANARKSHIRE (NORTH)

- **AIRDRIE GRAIN & HEALTH FOODS**, 37 Hallcraig Street, **AIRDRIE**, ML6 6AH
(T) 01236 754291
- **BEST OF HEALTH (THE)**, Unit 7 Mallard Way, Strathclyde Business Park, **BELLSHILL**, ML4 3BF
(T) 01698 740777
- **ESSENTIALLY YOURS**, Unit A9, Block14 Coltness Lane, **GLASGOW**, G33 4DR
(T) 01417 663400
- **FOREVER LIVING PRODUCTS PRODUCT CENTRE**, 10 Mollins Court, Cumbernauld, **GLASGOW**, G68 9HP
(T) 01236 782054
- **HOLLAND & BARRETT**, 34 Brandon Parade South, **MOTHERWELL**, ML1 1RB
(T) 01698 230929
- **HOLLAND & BARRETT**, 66 Graham Street, **AIRDRIE**, ML6 6DB
(T) 01236 751551
- **JULIAN GRAVES LTD**, Dunottar Avenue, **COATBRIDGE**, ML5 4LS
(T) 01236 437881

## LANARKSHIRE (SOUTH)

- **ALIVE HEALTH FOOD**, The Plaza Shopping Centre, East Kilbride, **GLASGOW**, G74 4LH
(T) 07710 454953
- **BODY NATURAL (THE)**, 44 Wellgate, **LANARK**, ML11 9DT
(T) 01555 661400
- **HOLLAND & BARRETT**, Unit 23 The Olympia, East Kilbride, **GLASGOW**, G74 1PG
(T) 01355 232627
- **NUTRITIONAL WORLD**, The Plaza, East Kilbride, **GLASGOW**, G74 1LW
(T) 01355 574869
- **WHOLEFOOD HARVEST**, 8 Main Street, **STRATHAVEN**, ML10 6AJ
(T) 01357 522605

## LOTHIAN (EAST)

- **FOOD FOR THOUGHT**, 13 Hardgate, **HADDINGTON**, EH41 3JW
(T) 01620 823196
- **GENESIS NETWORK UK**, 10, Eweford, **DUNBAR**, EH42 1RF
(T) 01368 864834

## LOTHIAN (MID)

- **ENGINE SHED SHOP (THE)**, 123 Bruntsfield Place, **EDINBURGH**, EH10 4EQ
(T) 01312 296494
- **GOOD FOOD**, 255 Morningside Road, **EDINBURGH**, EH10 4RD
(T) 01314 529020
- **MILLARS OF MORNINGSIDE**, 414 Morningside Road, **EDINBURGH**, EH10 5HY
(T) 01314 472468

## LOTHIAN (WEST)

- **A T SUPPLEMENTAL**, 17 Waverley Ind Units, Waverley Street, **BATHGATE**, EH48 4HY
(T) 01506 650777
- **BRAMIK FOODS WHOLESALE**, East Mains Industrial Estate, East Mains Industrial Estate, **BROXBURN**, EH52 5AU
(T) 01506 856661
- **EXTREME NUTRITION**, 9b Young Street, **WEST CALDER**, EH55 8EG
(T) 01506 870222
- **HERBALIFE**, The Hayloft, 3 Barns Court, East Whitburn, **BATHGATE**, EH47 8ET
(T) 01501 744959
- **HOLLAND & BARRETT**, 67 Almondvale Centre, Almondvale South, **LIVINGSTON**, EH54 6NB
(T) 01506 430021
- **LINPHARMA LTD**, P O Box 13511, **LINLITHGOW**, EH49 7YH
(T) 01506 848649
- **MILLSTONE (THE)**, 131-133 High Street, **LINLITHGOW**, EH49 7EJ
(T) 01506 847270
- **PROSOYA EUROPE LTD**, Unit 2/3, Kingsthorne Pk, Houstoun Industrial Estate, **LIVINGSTON**, EH54 5DB
(T) 01506 433777

## MORAY

- **BALANCE**, 59 High Street, **FOCHABERS**, IV32 7DU
(T) 01343 821443
- **HEALTH CORNER (THE)**, 41b High Street, **GRANTOWN-ON-SPEY**, PH26 3EG
(T) 01479 870400

- **KINBRO HEALTH FOODS**, 40 South Street, **ELGIN**, IV30 1JX
(T) 01343 549318
- **PHOENIX APOTHECARY (THE)**, The Park, Findhorn, **FORRES**, IV36 3TZ
(T) 01309 691044

## NORTHUMBERLAND

- **ALOE VERA CENTRE (UK) LTD**, 3 Drivers Lane, **BERWICK-UPON-TWEED**, TD15 1ER
(T) 01289 302893
- **GOOD LIFE SHOP (THE)**, 50 High Street, **WOOLER**, NE71 6BG
(T) 01668 281700
- **HANNY'S HEALTH FOODS**, 41a Bondgate Within, **ALNWICK**, NE66 1SX
(T) 01665 604401
- **HEALTHI CHOICE BLYTH**, 32 Bowes Street, **BLYTH**, NE24 1BE
(T) 01670 365426
- **HERITAGE HEALTH**, 6 Bellway House, Woodhorn Road, **ASHINGTON**, NE63 0AE
(T) 01670 816729
- **HOLLAND & BARRETT**, 23 Station Road, **ASHINGTON**, NE63 9UZ
(T) 01670 853883
- **HOLLAND & BARRETT**, 31-33 Fore Street, **HEXHAM**, NE46 1LU
(T) 01434 609067
- **MARKET SHOP (THE)**, 48 Bridge Street, **BERWICK-UPON-TWEED**, TD15 1AQ
(T) 01289 307749
- **PHARMA NORD (UK) LTD**, Telford Court, **MORPETH**, NE61 2DB
(T) 01670 519989

## PERTH AND KINROSS

- **GLENRIE FITNESS FOODS**, Wester Tillyrie House, Milnathort, **KINROSS**, KY13 0RW
(T) 01577 865535
- **HIGHLAND HEALTH STORE**, 7-16 St. John Street, **PERTH**, PH1 5SP
(T) 01738 628102
- **NATURE'S CORNER**, Cross Street, **CALLANDER**, FK17 8EA
(T) 01877 330200
- **NATUREWORKS**, 10 Linden Park Terrace, Milnathort, **KINROSS**, KY13 9XY
(T) 01577 861861
- **R CARRUTHERS**, 3 Atholl Road, **PITLOCHRY**, PH16 5BX
(T) 01796 472735
- **TREASURE ISLAND**, Unit 1, Mill Lane, **PITLOCHRY**, PH16 5BH
(T) 01796 473074
- **WUVHOS ASSOCIATES**, 5 Cottage, Scone Of Lethenby, **PERTH**, PH2 6AB
(T) 01924 850176

## RENFREWSHIRE

- **FOXBAR RESOURCE CENTRE**, 59 Amochrie Road, **PAISLEY**, PA2 0LB
(T) 01505 816600
- **GRAIN STORE (THE)**, 16 John Wood Street, **PORT GLASGOW**, PA14 5HU
(T) 01475 742721
- **HEALTH & HERBS**, The Paisley Centre, 23 High Street, **PAISLEY**, PA1 2AF
(T) 01418 485312
- **HEALTH WELL (THE)**, 5 High Street, **JOHNSTONE**, PA5 8JZ
(T) 01505 325642
- **HOLLAND & BARRETT**, 23 Hamilton Way, **GREENOCK**, PA15 1JJ
(T) 01475 552553
- **HOLLAND & BARRETT**, Unit 2 The Cross, Gilmour Street, **PAISLEY**, PA1 1EE
(T) 01418 485989
- **NEWLOOK HEALTH**, 254 Abbey Mill Business Centre, **PAISLEY**, PA1 1TJ
(T) 01418 490440

## SCOTTISH BORDERS

- **HEALTH FOOD SHOP (THE)**, 31 Bank Street, **GALASHIELS**, TD1 1EN
(T) 01896 758085
- **KELSO WHOLEFOODS**, 52 Woodmarket, **KELSO**, TD5 7AX
(T) 01573 225664

## SHETLAND ISLANDS

- **HEALTH CRAFT**, 12 Commercial Road, **LERWICK**, ZE1 0LX
(T) 01595 692924
- **SCOOP WHOLEFOODS**, Toll Clock Shopping Centre, North Road, **LERWICK**, ZE1 0PE
(T) 01595 695888

## STIRLING

- **STIRLING HEALTH FOOD STORE**, 29 Dumbarton Road, FK8 2LQ
(T) 01786 464903

## WESTERN ISLES

- **GRAIN & HEALTH FOOD STORE**, 5 Cromwell Street, **STORNOWAY**, HS1 2DB
(T) 01851 702255

# WALES

## BLAENAU GWENT

- **GOOD HEALTH SHOP (THE)**, 17 Beaufort Street, Brynmawr, **EBBW VALE**, NP23 4AG
(T) 01495 313896
- **JULIAN GRAVES LTD**, Victoria Road, **EBBW VALE**, NP23 6UN
(T) 01495 304600
- **NATURAL WONDERS**, 101 Bailey Street, Brynmawr, **EBBW VALE**, NP23 4DN
(T) 01495 315300

## BRIDGEND

- **HOLLAND & BARRETT**, Wyndham House, Wyndham Street, CF31 1ED
(T) 01656 653748
- **TROFF ANIMAL HEALTH (THE)**, 36 Nolton Street, CF31 3BN
(T) 01656 668744

## CAERPHILLY

- **EVENING PRIMROSE OIL CO LTD**, New Road, Tir-y-Berth, **HENGOED**, CF82 8SJ
(T) 01443 812183
- **HEALTH WITH HERBS**, Unit 19, The Market Place, **BLACKWOOD**, NP12 1AU
(T) 01495 228851

## CARMARTHENSHIRE

- **AARDVARK WHOLEFOODS**, 2 Mansel Street, **CARMARTHEN**, SA31 1QX
(T) 01267 232497
- **ELIZABETH BENNETT**, 19 The Market Precinct, **LLANELLI**, SA15 1YF
(T) 01554 757246
- **GO MANGO WHOLEFOODS**, 4/Black Lion Mews, High Street, **CARDIGAN**, SA43 1HJ
(T) 01239 614727
- **HEALTH LEADS UK LTD**, Crown Buildings, High Street, Bancyfelin, **CARMARTHEN**, SA33 5ND
(T) 01267 211800
- **HOLLAND & BARRETT**, 16 Stepney Street, **LLANELLI**, SA15 3UP
(T) 01554 744131
- **HOLLAND & BARRETT**, Blue Street, **CARMARTHEN**, SA31 3LE
(T) 01267 237198
- **ICECRYSTAL LTD**, Swiss Valley Farm, Felinfoel, **LLANELLI**, SA14 8LZ
(T) 01554 771203
- **IECHYD DA**, 11 Broad Street, **LLANDOVERY**, SA20 0AR
(T) 01550 720703
- **JELFS HEALTH & HERBAL STORES**, 8 Wind Street, **AMMANFORD**, SA18 3DN
(T) 01269 595703
- **M J HALL**, Mill House, Mill Street, St. Dogmaels, **CARDIGAN**, SA43 3DY
(T) 01239 613999
- **NATURES BOUNTY**, Dinarth Hall, Bridge Street, **LLANDYSUL**, SA44 4BA
(T) 01559 363360
- **OWL'S WISDOM (THE)**, Sycamore Street, **NEWCASTLE EMLYN**, SA38 9AJ
(T) 01239 711729
- **RIVERSIDE HEALTH**, Adpar, **NEWCASTLE EMLYN**, SA38 9EH
(T) 01239 711440
- **T & H ANDREWS**, 55 Pendre, **CARDIGAN**, SA43 1JR
(T) 01239 612187
- **TOTAL HEALTHCARE**, Tenby Road, St. Clears, **CARMARTHEN**, SA33 4JN
(T) 01994 231660
- **WAVELEY STORES**, 23 Lammas Street, **CARMARTHEN**, SA31 3AL
(T) 01267 236521
- **WHOLEFOOD STORE**, 2 Bridge Street, **LAMPETER**, SA48 7HG
(T) 01570 423317

## CEREDIGION

- **MAETH Y MEYSYDD**, 16 Chalybeate Street, **ABERYSTWYTH**, SY23 1HS
(T) 01970 612946
- **TROPICAL FOREST PRODUCTS**, P O Box 92, Blaenplwyf, **ABERYSTWYTH**, SY23 4DJ
(T) 01970 832511
- **WINDSOR HEALTH CENTRE**, 42 Terrace Road, **ABERYSTWYTH**, SY23 2AE
(T) 01970 612915

## CONWY

- **COUNTRY KITCHEN**, 10 Sea View Road, **COLWYN BAY**, LL29 8DG
(T) 01492 533329
- **HOLLAND & BARRETT**, 51 Mostyn Street, **LLANDUDNO**, LL30 2NN
(T) 01492 870814
- **HOLLAND & BARRETT**, Unit 9 Colwyn Centre, Sea View Road, **COLWYN BAY**, LL29 8DG
(T) 01492 534336
- **INCREASED PERFORMANCE**, 64 Abergele Road, **COLWYN BAY**, LL29 7PP
(T) 01492 535758
- **LOVELLS**, 8 Gloddaeth Street, **LLANDUDNO**, LL30 2DS
(T) 01492 877091
- **NATURAL CHOICE (THE)**, 14 Colwyn Avenue, Rhos on Sea, **COLWYN BAY**, LL28 4RB
(T) 01492 549520
- **NATURE'S WAY**, 4a Market Street, **ABERGELE**, LL22 7AA
(T) 01745 826444

## DENBIGHSHIRE

- **FRESH'N HEALTHY**, 177-179 High Street, **PRESTATYN**, LL19 9AY
(T) 01745 886648
- **HOLLAND & BARRETT**, 30 High Street, **DENBIGH**, LL16 3RY
(T) 01745 816965
- **HOLLAND & BARRETT**, 58 High Street, **RHYL**, LL18 1TW
(T) 01745 355044
- **RUTHIN WHOLE FOODS**, Chester House, Well Street, **RUTHIN**, LL15 1AH
(T) 01824 702778
- **WHOLEBAKE**, Ty'n Llidiart Industrial Estate, **CORWEN**, LL21 9RR
(T) 01490 412297

## FLINTSHIRE

- **A L J RILEY**, Surgery House, Halkyn, **HOLYWELL**, CH8 8DL
(T) 01352 781138
- **HOLYWELL WHOLEFOODS**, 2 Victoria Square, High Street, **HOLYWELL**, CH8 7TF
(T) 01352 714032
- **MOLD HEALTH STORES**, 1 Earl Road, **MOLD**, CH7 1AX
(T) 01352 757172
- **PARRISH'S FLOR & HEALTH FOODS**, Unit 11-12 Central Precinct, Brunswick Road, **BUCKLEY**, CH7 2EF
(T) 01244 543239
- **SHOTTON HEALTH FOODS**, 62a Chester Road West, Shotton, **DEESIDE**, CH5 1BY
(T) 01244 830702

## GLAMORGAN (VALE OF)

- **ALLIED HEALTH LTD**, 68a Cowbridge Road East, **CARDIFF**, CF11 9DU
(T) 029 2030 0848
- **BEANFREAKS LTD**, 3 St Mary Street, **CARDIFF**, CF10 1AT
(T) 029 2025 1671
- **BLUE LAKE HEALTH & NUTRITION**, Tara, Llanmaes, **LLANTWIT MAJOR**, CF61 2XR
(T) 01446 795333

- **CABBAGE PATCH**, 94 Barry Road, **BARRY**, CF63 1BB (T) 01446 722754
- **CANTON HEALTH FOODS**, 218 Cowbridge Road East, **CARDIFF**, CF5 1GX (T) 029 2039 7983
- **COUNTRY FAYRE**, 4 James Street, Pontarddulais, **SWANSEA**, SA4 1HY (T) 01792 830224
- **EXCEL NUTRITION**, 8 Mount Stuart Square, **CARDIFF**, CF10 5EE (T) 029 2040 1745
- **G N C GENERAL NUTRITION CENTRE**, 40 Town Wall, St. Davids Centre, **CARDIFF**, CF10 2DQ (T) 029 2034 2094
- **HEALTH WITH HERBS**, 127 Holton Road, **BARRY**, CF63 4HP (T) 01446 741602
- **HEALTH WITH HERBS**, Unit 6 Cwrt-Y-Castell, **CAERPHILLY**, CF83 1NU (T) 029 2086 7706
- **HEALTHCARE SHOP**, 832 Newport Road, Rumney, **CARDIFF**, CF3 4LH (T) 029 2036 1427
- **HEALTHWISE**, 89 Beulah Road, **CARDIFF**, CF14 6LW (T) 029 2076 5733
- **HOLLAND & BARRETT**, 4 Queen Street, **NEATH**, SA11 1DL (T) 01639 645745
- **HOLLAND & BARRETT**, 41 Commercial Street, **ABERDARE**, CF44 7RW (T) 01685 871051
- **JAHRAM HEALTH FOODS**, 1 Price Street, Cefn Coed, **MERTHYR TYDFIL**, CF48 2L (T) 029 2050 1176
- **M I MARKETING**, Priory Fields, Corntown, **BRIDGEND**, CF35 5BG (T) 01656 649955
- **MARKETING DIRECT**, P O Box 164, **CARDIFF**, CF5 4YT (T) 029 2057 7973
- **NATURAL SELECTION HEALTH FOODS**, 27 Whitcombe Street, **ABERDARE**, CF44 7AU (T) 01685 877066
- **NATURE'S TABLE LTD**, Unit 1 Tyndall Industrial Estate, Tyndall Street, **CARDIFF**, CF10 4BP (T) 029 2049 0683
- **NEATH HEALTH STORE**, C51 General Market, Green Street, **NEATH**, SA11 1DP (T) 01639 642665
- **PULSE WHOLEFOODS**, 171 Kings Road, **CARDIFF**, CF11 9DE (T) 029 2022 5873
- **RICHARDSON'S HEALTH FOODS**, Victoria Road, **PENARTH**, CF64 3EG (T) 029 2071 1044
- **ROATH HEALTH FOODS**, 39 Wellfield Road, **CARDIFF**, CF24 3PA (T) 029 2048 6023
- **VYDEX ANIMAL HEALTH LTD**, PO Box 164, **CARDIFF**, CF5 4YT (T) 029 2057 8578
- **WHITCHURCH HEALTH FOODS**, 53c Merthyr Road, Whitchurch, **CARDIFF**, CF14 1DD (T) 029 2061 8716
- **WORLD OF HEALTH & HERBS (THE)**, 24 Royal Arcade, **CARDIFF**, CF10 1AE (T) 029 2022 9048

## GWENT

- **EUROCAPS LTD**, Crown Business Pk, Dukestown, **TREDEGAR**, NP22 4EF (T) 01495 308900
- **HEALTH WITH HERBS**, 39 Commercial Street, **TREDEGAR**, NP22 3DJ (T) 01495 725668

## GWYNEDD

- **DIMENSIONS**, 15 Holyhead Road, **BANGOR**, LL57 2EG (T) 01248 351562
- **ELADON LTD**, 63 High Street, **BANGOR**, LL57 1NR (T) 01248 370059
- **FLAME LILY HEALTH STORE**, Trefellyn High Street, **TYWYN**, LL36 9AD (T) 01654 711570
- **HALO FOODS LTD**, 11-12 Pendre Industrial Estate, **TYWYN**, LL36 9LW (T) 01654 711171
- **HOLLAND & BARRETT**, 253 High Street, **BANGOR**, LL57 1PB (T) 01248 355934
- **JUST NATURAL**, 4 Pool Hill, **CAERNARFON**, LL55 1NP (T) 01286 674748
- **TAST FOOD SHOP (THE)**, Harbour Road, Abersoch, **PWLLHELI**, LL53 7AU (T) 01758 713456
- **VEGONIA WHOLEFOODS**, 49 High Street, **PORTHMADOG**, LL49 9LR (T) 01766 515195

## ISLE OF ANGLESEY

- **WHOLE THING (THE)**, 5 Field Street, **LLANGEFNI**, LL77 7EH (T) 01248 724832

## MERTHYR TYDFIL

- **HOLLAND & BARRETT**, 13 Graham Way, CF47 8EG (T) 01685 382086

## MONMOUTHSHIRE

- **AQUARIUS HEALTHCARE LTD**, Symondscliffe Way, Portskewett, **CALDICOT**, NP26 5PW (T) 01291 437000
- **CHEPSTOW HEALTH FOODS**, 23A Moor Street, **CHEPSTOW**, NP16 5DB (T) 01291 625997
- **COGHILL RESEARCH LABS**, Ker Menez, Lower Race, **PONTYPOOL**, NP4 5UH (T) 01495 767755
- **CORNUCOPIA**, Market Street, **ABERGAVENNY**, NP7 5SD (T) 01873 855346
- **HOLLAND & BARRETT**, 4b High Street, **ABERGAVENNY**, NP7 5RY (T) 01873 850429
- **HOLLAND & BARRETT**, 73 Monnow Street, **MONMOUTH**, NP25 3EW (T) 01600 772153
- **WARRENS**, The Market, **PONTYPOOL**, NP4 6JW (T) 01495 763225

## NEATH PORT TALBOT

- **HEALTH WITH HERBS**, 7 Riverside, **PORT TALBOT**, SA13 1EJ (T) 01639 884391
- **HOLLAND & BARRETT**, 17 Aberafan Centre, **PORT TALBOT**, SA13 1PB (T) 01639 871971
- **PEAK PERFORMANCE**, 8A Parry Road, **PORT TALBOT**, SA12 7TR (T) 01639 886850
- **TOTAL HEALTHCARE**, 2 Brombil Gdns, **PORT TALBOT**, SA13 2AX (T) 01639 884988

## NEWPORT

- **BEANFREAKS LTD**, 5 Chartist Towers, Upper Dock Street, NP20 1DW (T) 01633 666150
- **HOLLAND & BARRETT**, 42A Commercial Street, NP20 1LP (T) 01633 264596

## PEMBROKESHIRE

- **HARVEST STORES**, 2a St James Street, **NARBERTH**, SA67 7DB (T) 01834 861022
- **HEALTHWISE**, 25 High Street, **HAVERFORDWEST**, SA61 2BW (T) 01437 767017
- **HOLLAND & BARRETT**, 16 Riverside Quay, **HAVERFORDWEST**, SA61 2LJ (T) 01437 762723
- **NATURAL GROCER & HOME BREW SHOP (THE)**, 15-17 Quay Street, **HAVERFORDWEST**, SA61 1BG (T) 01437 767499
- **WHOLEFOODS OF NEWPORT**, East Street, **NEWPORT**, SA42 0SY (T) 01239 820773

## POWYS

- **CHEESE 'N' CHIVES**, Cavendish House, 21 High Street, **BUILTH WELLS**, LD2 3DL (T) 01982 551171
- **GOOD FOOD DISTRIBUTORS**, Unit 35 Ddole Road Industrial Estate, **LLANDRINDOD WELLS**, LD1 6DF (T) 01597 824720
- **HOLLAND & BARRETT**, Bethel Square, **BRECON**, LD3 7JP (T) 01874 610329
- **MACBEAN WHOLEFOODS**, 13 High Street, **NEWTOWN**, SY16 2NX (T) 01686 627002
- **NATURAL FOODS**, 17 Great Oak Street, **LLANIDLOES**, SY18 6BU (T) 01686 412306
- **QUARRY CAFE (THE)**, Glasgow House, 13 Heol Maengwyn, **MACHYNLLETH**, SY20 8EB (T) 01654 702624
- **QUARRY SHOP (THE)**, 27 Heol Maengwyn, **MACHYNLLETH**, SY20 8EB (T) 01654 702339
- **SUPER SCOOP**, Unit 2 26-27 Short Bridge Street, **NEWTOWN**, SY16 1AA (T) 01686 625754
- **VANS GOOD FOOD SHOPS**, Middleton Street, **LLANDRINDOD WELLS**, LD1 5ET (T) 01597 823074

## RHONDDA CYNON TAFF

- **BARBARA'S KITCHEN**, PO Box 54, **PONTYCLUN**, CF72 8WD (T) 01443 229304
- **BODYWISE HEALTH SHOP**, 208 High Street, **TREORCHY**, CF42 6AS (T) 01443 777064
- **HEALTH WITH HERBS**, 6c Taff Street, **PONTYPRIDD**, CF37 4UL (T) 01443 405091
- **HEALTHCARE**, 87a Dunraven Street, **TONYPANDY**, CF40 1AP (T) 01443 441292
- **J LOBB & SONS LTD**, 43 Talbot Road, Talbot Green, **PONTYCLUN**, CF72 8AD (T) 01443 224254
- **ORGANIC WHOLEFOODS & HOMEBREW**, 8 Mill Street, **PONTYPRIDD**, CF37 2SN (T) 01443 406583
- **PACIFIC NUTRITION**, Business Development Centre, Main Avenue, Treforest Industrial Estate, **PONTYPRIDD**, CF37 5UR (T) 01443 844030

## SWANSEA

- **GRANARY (THE)**, Castleton Walk, Newton Road, Mumbles, **MUMBLES**, SA3 4AX (T) 01792 367791
- **HEALTH & HERBS**, 5-7 Picton Arcade, SA1 3BH (T) 01792 654053
- **HEALTH WORLD**, 16d Swansea Market, SA1 3PE (T) 01792 646364
- **HOLLAND & BARRETT**, 10 Union Street, SA1 3EF (T) 01792 644011
- **KILLAY HEALTH SHOP**, 2 Goetre Fawr Road, Killay, SA2 7QS (T) 01792 206816

## TORFAEN

- **BEANFREAKS**, 7 Caradoc Road, **CWMBRAN**, NP44 1PP (T) 01633 482507
- **HOLLAND & BARRETT**, 16 South Walk, **CWMBRAN**, NP44 1PU (T) 01633 865040

## WREXHAM

- **BEANSTALK NATURAL FOODS**, 14 Central Arcade, LL11 1AG (T) 01978 364447

# *Complementary Treatments Explained*

## Absent Healing

Projecting healing powers over a distance. By "Spiritual Healing" it is meant the healing of the sick in body, mind or spirit by means of prayer or meditation (whether or not in the presence of the patient) and laying on of hands. Spiritual Healing is the art and science of assisting the restoration of health at all levels of being irrespective of where ill health has manifested. Distinctions of race, class, sex or religion are irrelevant. No affirmation of religious faith is required of the patient. By the laying on of hands, by atonement through meditation and prayer, whether or not in the presence of the patient, a healer seeks to induce a beneficial effect upon a patient's life force at all levels of existence. Spiritual healing may be given for any illness, stress or injury as a therapy, which has no side effects and is complementary to any other therapy. The medically diagnosed nature of severity of the illness is unimportant with regard to outcome. Those who feel that they lack harmony of body, mind and Spirit may seek Spiritual Healing. This lack of balance or harmony manifests, as illness of some sort and therefore equilibrium needs to be restored. Spiritual Healing ensures that the Spirit gets the healing it needs to distribute to the mind or body it occupies.

## Acupressure

An ancient massage skill. A mixture of Massage and Acupuncture. Used in conjunction with Naturopathy. Instead of the use of needles, it is the use of firm thumb and hand pressure at key "pressure points" but at the same energy points used in Acupuncture. Acupressure is an ancient Chinese total body treatment, given through clothing on pressure points, to stimulate the flow and improve circulation of energy throughout the body. Like its Japanese equivalent Shiatsu, Acupressure requires no needles relying instead on the thumbs, palms, heels of the hands and elbows, (sometimes knees and feet) to apply held pressure on vital points on the body. Along with pressure point treatment, gentle stretching and corrective exercises are also used. Acupressure is the pressing of acupoints, but Tui Na (or Tuina, pronounced "twee-nah") makes use of many different strokes that are applied to acupoints, channels and muscle groups. Most importantly, Tui Na is a physical expression of the flow of Qi energy from one human being to another. When done with correct intent, the strokes and techniques stimulate an exchange of Qi energy between the practitioner and the patient, and this is the secret healing power of Tui Na. Point Holding, developed by Karen Peterson and John Walsh, is a particular form of Acupressure that balances the body's energy by applying pressure to specific acupoints to remove blockage and stimulate energy flow within the meridians (energy pathways). What distinguishes Point Holding from other form of Acupressure is that requires multiple practitioners to hold Acupressure points up to two hours.

## Acupuncture

The use of needles to treat diseases and ailments. Certain areas of the body are said to be along energy pathways and the needles effectively unblock, increase or decrease the flow of energy along these pathways. Diseases or certain indications affect the balance of the energy pathways also. Minor electrical voltages can enhance Acupuncture needles and their positive effects as well. Acupuncture can also be used in conjunction with heat produced by burning specific herbs, this is called Moxibustion. In addition, a non-invasive method of massage therapy, called Acupressure can also be effective.

## Alexander Technique

Improving general health and even specific indications through better posture. The use of gentle manipulation and the direction of better posture is said to be of use in reducing stress and mental awareness. The Alexander Technique is a way of learning how to get rid of harmful tension in the body and is a method that works to change (movement) habits in our everyday activities. It is a simple and practical method for improving ease and freedom of movement, balance, support and coordination. The technique teaches the use of the appropriate amount of effort for a particular activity, giving more energy for all your activities. It is not a series of treatments or exercises, but rather a re-education of the mind and body. The Alexander Technique is a method, which helps a person discover a new balance in the body by releasing unnecessary tension. It can be applied to sitting, lying down, standing, walking, lifting, and other daily activities. "The Alexander Technique is an intelligent way to solve body problems!"

## Allergy Testing

Any of several tests used to determine the substance(s) to which a person is allergic. There are many methods of Allergy Testing. Among the more common are the skin tests, elimination-type tests, and the radioallergosorbent test (RAST). Specific methods vary. The scratch test (one of the most common methods) involves placement of a small amount of suspected allergy-causing substances (allergens) on the skin (usually the forearm, upper arm, or the back), and then scratching or pricking the skin so that the allergen is introduced under the skin surface. The skin is observed closely for signs of a reaction, usually swelling and redness of the site. Results are usually obtained within about 20 minutes, and several suspected allergens can be tested at the same time. A similar method involves injection of a small amount of allergen under the surface of the skin (intradermal) and watching for a reaction at the site. Skin tests are most useful for respiratory allergies (in which the allergen is inhaled), a penicillin allergy, and insect bite allergies. Food allergies are usually tested by using various "elimination" diets (in which the suspected food(s) are eliminated from the diet for several weeks and then gradually re-introduced one at a time while the person is observed for signs of an allergic reaction). Because food allergies are often affected by what the person thinks they might be allergic to, a double-blind test may be advised. In this test, suspected foods and placebos (inert substances) are given in a disguised form. The person being tested and the health care provider are both unaware of whether the particular substance being tested in that session is a placebo or a food substance (a 3rd party knows the identity of the substances and identifies them with some sort of code). This test requires several sessions if more than one substance is under investigation. The RAST is a laboratory test performed on blood. It tests for the amount of specific IgE antibodies in the blood (which are present if there is a "true" allergic reaction).

## Anthroposohical Medicine

An extension of medical practice on the basis of the comprehensive view of the human being provided by spiritual science. A mix of conventional medicine, Naturopathy, and Homeopathy. Diagnosis is based on allopathic medicine. Treatment includes dietary changes, homeopathic medicines, art and movement therapies, spiritual and psychological counselling. An all-encompassing approach to better health.

## Aromatherapy

Aromatherapy is the art and science of helping living things toward wholeness and balance using the essential oils, which can be extracted from plants. Essential oils seem to work in three ways. If used in baths, compresses, or cosmetics, the very small molecules involved will be absorbed through the skin and into the capillaries that underlie it. Or if used in vaporisers or diffusers, they will be breathed in and absorbed through the respiratory mucosa. Then they are carried by the blood through the body to the different organs they target to exert their physical effects. They are also absorbed in the nasal mucosa and taken up by scent receptors, which send signals through the nerves to the limbic system. This is the area of the brain where memories associated with strong emotions are stored. It also links directly to the parts of the brain that control many of the automatic functions of the body, such as blood pressure, heart rate, respirations, and gut movements. Thus the essential oils can have a strong effect on the emotions, both through the body functions associated with them and through memory. Essential oils can have an effect on one's spiritual energy outlets...clearing, stimulating, slowing, or opening according to their own very conviction. Thus their association with churches, meditation, and spiritual work for centuries.

## Art Therapy

Art Therapy is a process where one combines mind and body, and internal and external experiences and then relates them into chosen formalities of art: line, shape, colour, form, size, texture, content, etc. It is a non-verbal form of communication and expression, and both the art process and the art product contribute to the conversation, which may transpire both within the creator himself as well as with others. An issue, feeling, or thought may be relayed more easily or with more truthfulness through the means of creating 2-D and 3-D art rather than through the art of conversation alone. Freud expressed the potential difficulties in verbal communication in terms of translating dream imagery into words: "I could draw it," a dreamer often says, "but I don't know how to say it" (Lewis, 1996). There are two ways art may be used therapeutically. Art as therapy is concerned with the expression of art for academic, aesthetic, or cultural aims. It is believed that one may reconcile emotional conflicts and foster self-awareness and personal growth through the creative process. It is a product-oriented approach. Professionals who can provide this service are art therapists, therapeutic art educators, or therapeutic artists.

## Aura Therapy

How would you like to dramatically reduce your stress and anxiety, feel more peaceful and relaxed, gain perceptual clarity, feel greater joy and confidence, increase your energy, improve your physical health, and awaken you to your holiness? You can do all this by removing imbalances in your human energy field and aura. These energy blocks manifest themselves as stress and anxiety. Removing the blocks restores the natural energy flow resulting in feelings of peace and harmony. When aligned and balanced, the aura is radiant energy, a living light. The aura serves the transformational agendas of the soul, it is constructed such that imbalance can be incorporated into the ego structure. Part of our life is to create blocks, which we use as stepping-stones. Our issues and concerns appear as blocks and distortions in the energy field. Physical and emotional trauma, self-judgment and limiting beliefs, or external psychic pressures from individuals, groups or institutional belief systems cause these blocks and distortions. Psychological and spiritual wounds condense, even into physical disease, to assist us to complete the soul's imperative to fulfil our nature. Although these patterns in the aura represent energy limitations, each one also holds a key to greater spiritual realisation and strengthening. They are adversaries that become allies as we work to transform them. Each dilemma is linked internally to a solution that awakens our holiness. Our beliefs, judgments, attitudes, and trauma affect the containment and movement of energy within our consciousness. Blocks are an attempt to protect. As such, they become integrated into the sustaining structure of our personality. As we create meaning in response to trauma, we adapt to the meaning as if it were normal. Thus, the trauma and the meaning we constructed in response become normalised into our psyche. We adapt to the level of our injury. While the ego adapts to trauma, the soul continues to pursue transformation. In the deepest sense, our aura is out of balance as one phase in a process caused by our drive to awaken spiritually and transform the quality of our lives and our experience. In a more conventional sense, any concern, trauma, or issue that brings one to counselling or requires therapy reflects in the Aura as an imbalance. Blocks and imbalances help us answer the age-old questions: Who am I? What am I? What do I want? The more energised and integrated the aura, the faster the process. Transformation and realisation can be instantaneous. The Aura wants to be in balance. As we grow wiser, we are more attentive to the care and maintenance of ourselves as energy. It is in our nature to seek new experience and then transform that experience into understanding, strength, and awareness. Blocks are a natural increment of human destiny. To have a perfectly balanced Aura, one's development and attitudes on all three of these levels (physical, emotional, and mental-spiritual) must be in perfect atonement with the Infinite. For example, should a man become involved in an intense argument with another person leading to an exchange of physical blows, the disharmonies will show in both the mental and physical auras and the auric fields will be disrupted. The Aura carries scars just as the physical body carries its scars. Emotionally and spiritually as the affected person strives for a better balance, the wounds become laced just as a physician will sew up a cut on the physical body. Consequently, as we live, grow, decide what is right and what is wrong, rationalize and compromise, our aura is in a constant state of flux. How the aura is transformed depends upon our ideas, attitudes, endeavours, and the state of consciousness in which we live. There is no doubt that our personality; soul condition, hidden self, and physical condition are revealed clearly through the vibrations and formation of the Aura. A trained Noetic Field Therapist can tell the emotional and spiritual development of a person by the scars and lacings in the Aura.

## Auricular Therapy

The insertion of needles into acupuncture points in the ear that relate to specific parts of the body. Used frequently for quit smoking and weight loss therapy. Also Known as ear acupuncture.

## Auto Suggestion

Through Hypnotism it is the production of a psychical condition in which the faculty of receiving impressions by suggestion and where the power to act upon and carry out the suggestions is greatly increased.

## Autogenic Training

Autogenic, which means "self-regulation or -generation," refers to the way in which your mind can influence your body to balance the self-regulative systems that control circulation, breathing, heart rate, and so on. Autogenic training allows you to control stress by training your autonornic nervous system to become relaxed. It is suggested that you learn progressive relaxation first. Autogenic Training will then teach you to respond, in a passive manner, to verbal and visual cues that reduce tension. By focusing on relaxing phrases and images, the training conditions positive, relaxing responses, such as rhythmic breathing and heart rate and a warm, relaxed, heavy feeling throughout the body. Autogenic training is based on the notion of passive concentration: that is, you try to achieve your goal of relaxation by not working actively to do so (as in progressive relaxation).

Practice Autogenic Training twice each day in order to maximize the benefits. Choose times and places that are feasible for an uninterrupted session. Wear comfortable clothes. Sit or be in a position that allows total support for your entire body. When you begin autogenic training, first work on reducing your heart rate and calming your breathing; then you can move on to trying to evoke warm, heavy, relaxed sensations in your limbs and body.

## Aversion Therapy

A type of Psychotherapy, designed to cause a patient to reduce or avoid an undesirable behaviour pattern by conditioning him to associate the behaviour with an undesirable stimulus. The chief stimuli used in the therapy are electrical and chemical. In the electrical therapy, the patient is given a lightly painful shock whenever the undesirable behaviour is aroused; this method has been used in the treatment of sexual deviations. In the chemical therapy, the patient is given a drug that produces unpleasant effects, such as nausea, when combined with the undesirable behaviour; this method has been common in the treatment of alcoholism, the therapeutic drug and the alcohol together causing the nausea.

## Ayurvedic Medicine

Ayurveda is a holistic system of healing which evolved among the Brahmin sages of ancient India some 3000-5000 years ago. There are several aspects of this system of medicine which distinguish it from other approaches to health care: It focuses on establishing and maintaining balance of the life energies within us, rather than focusing on individual symptoms. It recognises the unique constitutional differences of all individuals and therefore recommends different regimens for different types of people. Although two people may appear to have the same outward symptoms, their energetic constitutions may be very different and therefore call for very different remedies. Ayurveda is a complete medical system, which recognises that ultimately all intelligence and wisdom, flows from one Absolute source (Paramatman). Health manifests by the grace of the Absolute acting through the laws of Nature (Prakriti). Ayurveda assists Nature by promoting harmony between the individual and Nature by living a life of balance according to her laws. Ayurveda describes three fundamental universal energies which regulate all natural processes on both the macrocosmic and microcosmic levels. That is, the same energies which produce effects in the various galaxies and star systems are operating at the level of the human physiology—in your own physiology. These three universal energies are known as the Tridosha. Finally, the ancient Ayurvedic physicians realised the need for preserving the alliance of the mind and body and offers mankind tools for remembering and nurturing the subtler aspects of our humanity. Ayurveda seeks to heal the fragmentation and disorder of the mind-body complex and restore wholeness and harmony to all people.

## Baby Massage

"Touch is a primary need which must be met if the infant is to develop as a healthy human being, able to love, to play, to think critically and unprejudicially." The skin is the largest sensory organ in the body and touch is one of the most powerful of all the human senses. The sense of touch has been detected in embryos less than 8 weeks old and massage is one of the best ways for both a carer and their baby to benefit from the advantages of touch. The bonding process between a baby and his/her carer plays a vital role in helping the child to grow up feeling secure and having a positive self image. A number of researchers have found that positive touch plays a greater role in this process than food and eating. Massage can play an important role in the bonding process between parent and child, by allowing time and space for the parent and child to get to know each other and communicate in an intimate and positive way. Massage can help a baby to feel more secure if it is done regularly because this is a time when s/he has your undivided attention, which can be hard for new (and second or more time round) mums. Massage can increase a child's self-awareness as they develop and help them to become less body conscious. "Parenthood" is not automatic and parents do not always know what to do and this makes some people very anxious. Massage therefore provides time to relax and get to know each other when there are few other demands pressed upon you, so helping to build up the level of confidence in both parent and child. Massage helps to relax and calm both giver and receiver. This can be of particular benefit if you have a fretful baby, as a baby's distress affects the carer who often becomes increasingly agitated which further upsets the baby. A massage can help both baby and carer to relax and calm down. In the USA, researchers have found that the skin has an immunological function. The epidermis produces a substance similar to the hormone produced by the thymus gland, which is active in producing T-cell differentiation, and positive touch increases the production of this substance. Thus a baby's immune system can be strengthened through regular massage, which in turn can help improve a baby's resistance to disease. In certain situations massage can act as an alternative to drugs, for example with colic. There is some debate about what colic actually is, but whatever the true definition many people find that their baby cries regularly in the early evening. Some find that gentle

abdominal massage helps, while others have found that the early evening is a stressful time for all the family and by dedicating time to massage the baby, the time and attention given has helped reduce the baby's apparent distress. Similarly a gentle abdominal massage can help with wind and constipation and a gentle head massage can help relieve the pain experienced when teething. If a baby is having difficulty in weaning, a massage followed by a bottle may help as the baby is still receiving a close tactile encounter with their mother. Baby massage helps to provide a child with strong foundations to grow into
a physically and emotionally healthy adult."

## Bach Remedies

Each of the 38 remedies discovered by Dr Bach is directed at a particular characteristic or emotional state. To select the remedies you need you only need to think about the sort of person you are and the way you are feeling. Then you take the remedies you need. Here is a list of the 38 remedies and their indications. , Agrimony - mental torture behind a cheerful face, Aspen - fear of unknown things, Beech – intolerance, Centaury - the inability to say 'no', Cerato - lack of trust in one's own decisions, Cherry Plum - fear of the mind giving way, Chestnut Bud - failure to learn from mistakes, Chicory - selfish, possessive love, Clematis - dreaming of the future without working in the present, Crab Apple - the cleansing remedy, also for self-hatred, Elm - overwhelmed by responsibility, Gentian - discouragement after a setback, Gorse - hopelessness and despair, Heather - self-centeredness and self-concern, Holly - hatred, envy and jealousy, Honeysuckle - living in the past, Hornbeam - procrastination, tiredness at the thought of doing something, Impatiens - impatience , Larch - lack of confidence, Mimulus - fear of known things, Mustard - deep gloom for no reason, Oak - the plodder who keeps going past the point of exhaustion, Olive - exhaustion following mental or physical effort, Pine - guilt, Red Chestnut - over-concern for the welfare of loved ones, Rock Rose - terror and fright, Rock Water - self-denial, rigidity and self-repression, Scleranthus - inability to choose between alternatives, Star of Bethlehem - shock, Sweet Chestnut - Extreme mental anguish, when everything has been tried and there is no right left, Vervain - over-enthusiasm, Vine - dominance and inflexibility, Walnut - protection from change and unwanted influences, Water Violet - pride and aloofness, White Chestnut - unwanted thoughts and mental arguments, Wild Oat - uncertainty over one's direction in life, Wild Rose - drifting, resignation, apathy, Willow - self-pity and resentment, There is also a combination remedy called Rescue Remedy.

## Bates Method

Dr W H Bates was a respected American Ophthalmologist who practised mainly in New York. He noticed that the vision of many of his patients was extremely variable and realised that this meant it could be improved. He later gave up his orthodox practice in order to devote his life to discovering, then showing others, how long sight, short sight and astigmatism could be prevented and improved in children and adults without the use of glasses. What does the method entail? Learning to keep the eyes and mind relaxed while becoming ever more interested in the world around. Special techniques are used to give extra stimulus where this is needed, but the emphasis is on improving the use of the eyes in everyday life. Is there any guarantee that it will work? No! It is an educational method and everything depends on the pupil's ability and willingness to learn. However, most of those who take it up seriously do experience substantial benefit.

## Beauty Therapy

A plethora of techniques used to improve personal perception and outward view towards self esteem, confidence and attractiveness. Ranging from Manicure to Skin exfoliation.

## Bio-Energetics

Gentle Bio-Energetics is an educational and therapeutic model designed to integrate verbal and body therapies for healing and growth. The 'gentle' aspect refers to the role of the therapist/helper as being non-invasive and nurturing, in both the touch and verbal interventions used. 'Bio-Energetics' refers to the individual's life energy, how it flows freely or is blocked by emotional armour resulting from traumatic life experiences. Bio-Energetic Analysis is a form of analytic Psychotherapy which combines work with the body and with the mind to promote health and enhance one's pleasure in living. With the help of a psycho-developmental lens, the Bio-Energetic therapist assists the client to see how early childhood experiences have affected the client's adult perception of self and behaviour towards others. The client is guided to an understanding of how early life experiences, for example, unmet needs, have affected the client's ability to be fully alive in the world. Early life traumas are understood to impact the client as an adult on both the level of the personality (psyche) and on the level of the body (soma). The Bio-Energetic therapist thus views the client as a psycho-somatic unity. Mind and body, to the bioenergetic therapist, are dynamically intertwined. The psychological defences a client uses to manage emotional pain - rationalisation, denial and suppression - are also anchored in the body where they appear as unique muscular patterns which inhibit self-awareness. A client's psychological defences combined with muscular holding patterns create a unique character logical defensive structure. The Bio-Energetic therapist studies each aspect of this defensive structure. Physical exercises are designed that are uniquely suited to challenge the client's muscular defences. The therapist carefully explores with each client what it would feel like to begin to release tightened muscles through movement and deeper breathing. As the body work progresses, the client normally uncovers beliefs and experiences emotions which have been repressed since childhood. With the help of the Bio-Energetic therapist, the client begins to understand that habitual defences combined with chronic muscular tensions and self limiting cognitive beliefs were once a recipe for survival in an early environment that was not supportive of the client's being. In current life as an adult, however, these same defences, physical tensions, and mental beliefs inhibit the client's capacity for joy, happiness, love, sadness, sensuality, and healthy anger. Physical exercises and the emotions they release form an important part of Bio-Energetic Psychotherapy; equally important is the analytic work. The client's expressions, defences, and ways of relating to the Bio-Energetic therapist provide the raw material from which the therapist assists the client to uncover personal meaning, integrate newly expressed feelings into an authentic identity, and relate to self and others in more satisfying ways. Bio-Energetic Analysis engages with each client's physical, emotional, and cognitive being in the world. The bioenergetic therapist uses knowledge of developmental psychology to understand the aetiology of each client's difficulties. Bio-Energetic Analysis is, however, a present-focused Psychotherapy, in that the therapist begins with each client's presenting problems and with an assessment of the client's here-and-now vitality in the context of present relationships. Gradually, through body work, analysis, and the experience of a safe, healthy, supportive connection with the therapist, the client discovers greater capacity for joy, for integrity and for creative self-expression in life.

## Biofeedback

Biofeedback is a therapeutic technique that helps clients develop the ability to control certain physiological processes. The means to do this include monitoring the physiological response in the client and displaying the signals generated by the monitoring technique to the therapist and client. The client uses this biological feedback to learn about and gain control of his/her responses. Biofeedback is, therefore, an educational process in which the client is helped to learn to control certain physiological processes, but it is the client who assumes the responsibility for and becomes an active participant in his/her own improvement. The therapist utilizes different techniques to facilitate the acquisition of such control (none of the techniques used in the Counselling Centre include surgical or pharmacological adjuncts). An additional benefit of this program is that the client increases his/her feelings of self-control and personal mastery because it is him/her who produces the desired changes by following the therapist's instructions and practicing regularly.

## Biomagnetic Therapy

Magnetic energy is a structuring force of the universe. As such, it is a reflection of the order that causes the infinite stars and planets throughout the galaxies to revolve and spin at incredible velocities while remaining in their respective orbits. As one of the four fundamental forces of nature along with gravity, nuclear energy and radioactivity, electromagnetism is equivalent in definition to the Traditional Chinese Medicine (TCM) concept of 'Qi', or the East Indian Ayurvedic definition of 'Prana'. These concepts are what many in the West, regard as the 'life force'.

## Biomechanics

See Kinesiology. Fundamentally the relationship between physiological structure and the biochemical influences on biological structure.

## Bonesetting

See Chiropractics

## Bowen Therapy

Simply stated, the Bowen Technique allows the body to reset and heal itself. A Bowen treatment consists of a series of gentle moves on skin (or through light clothing), with the client usually lying on a bed or comfortable treatment couch. A treatment session usually lasts from half an hour to an hour and frequently results in a deep sense of overall relaxation, allowing the body to recharge and balance itself. Recent studies have shown the beneficial effects of deep levels of relaxation on our immune and hormonal systems. However, the Bowen Technique can also be extremely effective for musculo-skeletal problems such as back pain, sports injuries and many other ailments and discomforts. There are many theories as to how the Bowen Technique works, but none that completely explain its holistic effect and often outstanding results. The body is a highly complex unit dependent upon the balance of all its aspects. Whilst the orthodox medical profession still tend to take a symptomatic view of disease, Bowen is truly holistic in its approach. One Bowen move may address the entire system producing maximum results with minimal intervention. Unlike some other hands-on disciplines, the Bowen Technique does not impose a particular approach on the client. Instead, it encourages a gentle response which empowers the body's own resources to heal itself. Bowen moves are, in themselves, a study in delicacy, being light, gentle and very precise. Frequent pauses between moves give the body time to respond and benefit. This treatment involves a gentle, dynamic system of muscle and connective tissue moves which balance the body and stimulate energy flows. Bowen Therapy is used to treat a wide range of chronic musculo-skeletal problems. This unique physical/vibrational approach to healing sends a gentle signal to the body that allows the neuromuscular system to reset all tension levels thus promoting natural healing. The relaxation and relief one feels is profound and lasting, affecting the muscular, skeletal, digestive, respiratory and energetic systems. Bowen Therapy is a way of giving the body the gentle hint that it needs to find its own way back to health and balance

## Chinese Herbal Medicine

Chinese herbs are selected and combined in formulas based on principles that have no relation whatsoever to Bio-Chemistry. Before looking at the principles that comprise Chinese Herbal Medicine Theory take note of these words of caution. Please don't prescribe or recommend Chinese herbs for yourself or others. Especially if you are pregnant, it's imperative that you consult a professional before taking any herbs. 1)Without training and experience you will most probably not get the relief you seek. 2)You may make yourself more uncomfortable. 3)There are a handful of Chinese herbs that are dangerous when not used according to classical principles. Dang Gui - Angelica Root is a good example. It's being advertised as "The Woman's Herb". "Used for centuries in China for women's health problems". That's true but it certainly isn't the whole story. Which "women's health problem" do you have? If you're having irregular or no periods Dang Gui - Angelica will probably be helpful because it nourishes and moves blood. If you're spotting blood during pregnancy don't take Dang Gui - Angelica because it can cause miscarriage by its action of moving blood. Increasing the risk is the fact that there are three other forms of Angelica and all have different herbal actions.

## Chiropody

Chiropody deals with a wide range of foot disorders and problems, such as corns, calluses, blisters, various nail problems, as well as skin, joint and bone conditions. What is less well appreciated is that it may also help with a number of other problems which may be associated with poor foot functioning - for example low back pain, hip problems, knee pains, neck stiffness, and ankle weakness. We tend to underestimate the importance of well maintained feet to our general well-being. Chiropody takes on a new significance when one becomes aware that the average person takes 18,000 steps per day and shifts the equivalent of one hundred tonnes of bodyweight for every mile walked. The 26 bones and 23 muscles of the foot are therefore crucial to a well-balanced existence in several senses! For this reason it is a therapy worth considering not just for crisis management or simple maintenance; regular check-ups can be an excellent way of preventing problems developing through early diagnosis. The more common name for this approach in most countries is Podiatry. Chiropody, Podiatric medicine and Podology are largely synonymous terms. In the NHS the community Podiatry service aims to provide assessment, diagnosis and treatment of lower limb pathologies enabling patients to attain mobility. The service aims to be need led with care based on patient centred treatment plans which include foot health education. Where appropriate, this will be in conjunction with relatives, carers and other health professionals. The range of services provided covers routine, maintenance and palliative care, Bio-Mechanics (many clinics are run jointly with the Physiotherapy service) and Nail Surgery.

## Chiropractics

Chiropractics is a branch of the healing arts concerned with human health and disease processes. Doctors of Chiropractics are physicians who consider man as an integrated being, but give special attention to spinal mechanics, musculo-skeletal, neurological, vascular, nutritional, and environmental relationships. In simple language, Chiropractics is preventative health care. Doctors of Chiropractics were early pioneers of holistic health care offering an alternative to medicine through management and treatment of health disorders by employing proper lifestyles, diet, nutritional therapies, exercise, and care of the spine and nervous system. Chiropractics is: the largest, drugless health profession in the world, the second largest health profession overall, and one of the fastest growing health care professions in the western world. What's the difference between a Chiropractor and an Osteopath? This should be a really good joke, along the lines of, "Well, a Chiropractor makes your joints go 'pop' while an Osteopath ....." The trouble is, an Osteopath does exactly the same thing. But demanding that your practitioner 'pops' your joints is like insisting that a doctor writes a prescription every time you see him/her. There are many other, often more appropriate, interventions at her disposal. , The Public's misunderstandings of these traditions are a direct result of both professions' lack of communication. Both train for a minimum of four to five years. Chiropractors use short-lever techniques (focusing manipulation on one vertebrae at a time) with some long-lever techniques, whilst osteopaths more commonly use long-lever techniques (affecting the spine through rotation at the shoulders and hips) with some short-lever techniques. Osteopaths maybe associated with the gentle Cranial-Sacral Technique, but Chiropractors too use Sacral-Occipital Technique (the difference is in name only.) Even their history runs parallel, unsurprising when you consider that the two eager and impressionable young men who founded Osteopathy, Andrew Taylor Still, and Daniel David Palmer, founder of Chiropractics, spent their early manhood in the mid-America of the mid-1800's and were exposed a plethora of folk medicines. Among them Irish immigrant bone-setters; Chinese Tui Na practitioners (similar to physiotherapists); and native Americans bone men. One could say that manipulation, in all probability, was the first medical intervention to be invented. It may not have been subtle, but even cave-men must have had a few dislocated shoulders or stiff backs put to rest, one way or another. Neil Austin, a chiropractor working in London, explained that whatever subtle differences that existed between the two professions have virtually been eliminated through an expanded education and training programme. "The range of techniques being taught to both groups have converged in recent years, so that now it's the quality of the practitioner that counts." The theoretical differences are historical, and play little role in present day management of back problems. Considering that our own Western traditional medical curriculum was only developed in the mid-1800s, it is surprising that allopathic doctors got the upper hand at all, especially in the treatment of painful and restrictive back conditions. Yet just this year Western medics admitted that their traditional recommendation of bed rest for back pain only prolongs the discomfort. Restricting corsets and braces for conditions such as ankyolosing spondylitis (an inflammatory condition which often leads to fusing of the vertebrae, leading to complete immobility at that joint) have not yet been thrown out as a treatment by many older doctors, even though this treatment does more harm than good. As Osteopaths and Chiropractors have maintained all along, mobility at the joints is essential. These professionals are trained well enough (infinitely better than your doctor when it comes to musculo-skeletal disease) to recognise when to manipulate and when not to. They do not rotate a herniated disc, nor do they treat an osteoporotic woman in the same manner as they would a burly footballer who has put his back out while training. They also read x-rays and use them when there is a suspicion of structural change or tumour. Chiropractors use x-rays a little more often than Osteopaths, (Chiropractors are trained to take x-rays as well as to read them) but both are aware of the associated health hazards and are reluctant to use them without some justification. This is in direct contrast to Western practitioners. Radiation from x-rays has an accumulative effect especially in bone. Doctors should know, as they are twice as likely and Radiologists ten times as likely to die from leukaemia as the general public, and some scientists have linked the substantial increase in the general incidence of Leukaemia to the routine use of x-rays, especially when coupled with exposure from other sources! In any case, as Sean Durkan, an osteopath working in London, explained, x-rays tell little about what is happening in common conditions such as herniated (slipped) disc. To see this in detail one would need to look at an MRI scan, although as Durkan further explained, the palpatory skills and clinical judgment of the practitioner will count for more than any high tech equipment in the majority of cases. The moral of the story is, a well trained Osteopath or Chiropractor is able to judge when a back needs some conventional medical intervention, better than a conventional doctor can judge when to recommend manipulative therapies. As Austin explained, "we spend five years studying the musculo-skeletal system and everything that can impact on it in detail. This is as much time as doctors spend going over the whole body. They are trained generalists, we are the specialists in this area." And the future for the two professions? Austin conceded, "I think basically the historical differences will be forgotten and I think that very soon the two professions, in the United Kingdom at least, will unite."

## Clinical Ecology

It is a medical orientation which looks upon disease as an individual's specific reaction to environmental insults in terms of adaptation. Since individual susceptibility is a major component in this reaction, successful stabilisation or reversal of this reaction depends upon the person learning its nature and becoming able to identify the environmental excitants. Only in this way can they become master of their destiny. It is not so much the physician as the individual's understanding and attitude that can modify the individual susceptibility factor. Clinical ecologists are approaching a wide range of physical and mental disorders of obscure origin and unfavourable prognosis using this concept. The concept is not new, but currently, because of the drug orientation of medical practice, it is not widely appreciated. The clinical ecology orientation for successful application is dependent upon the individual's willingness to alter his way of living, eating and even thinking in order to cope with environmental reaction.

## Cognitive Therapy

Cognitive Therapy and Research is a broadly conceived interdisciplinary journal whose main function is to stimulate and communicate research and theory on the role of cognitive processes in human adaptation and adjustment. It attempts to integrate such diverse areas of Psychology as clinical, cognitive, counselling developmental, experimental, learning, personality, and social. Cognitive Therapy is the most heavily researched form of Psychotherapy and has proven effectiveness in the treatment of several psychiatric illnesses, including depression and anxiety. It is based on the idea that people with psychiatric disorders have maladaptive patterns of thinking. By understanding and changing these patterns, a patient may bring about positive changes in his or her mental functioning. Cognitive Therapy is a widely used form of Psychotherapy that focuses on changing dysfunctional cognitions (thoughts), emotions, and behaviour. A computerised learning program emphasises the form of Cognitive Therapy developed over the last thirty years by Aaron T. Beck and co-workers. Cognitive Therapy is based on the theory that individuals with depression, anxiety, and other emotional disorders have maladaptive patterns of information processing and related behavioural difficulties. One of the primary targets of Cognitive Therapy is the identification of negative or distorted automatic thoughts. These cognitions are the relatively autonomous thoughts that occur rapidly while an individual is in the midst of a particular situation or is recalling significant events from the past. Patients with depression and anxiety have many more negative or fearful automatic thoughts than control subjects, and these distorted cognitions stimulate painful emotional reactions. In addition, negative automatic thoughts can be associated with behaviours (e.g., helplessness, withdrawal, or avoidance) that make the problem worse. In depression or anxiety disorders, there is often a "vicious cycle" of dysfunctional cognitions, emotions, and behaviours. Automatic thoughts are frequently based on faulty logic or errors in reasoning. Cognitive Therapy is directed, in part, at helping patients recognise and change these cognitive errors (sometimes called cognitive distortions). Some of the commonly described cognitive errors include: all or nothing thinking, personalisation, ignoring the evidence, and overgeneralisation. In cognitive therapy, patients are usually taught how to detect cognitive errors and to use this skill in developing a more rational style of thinking. Another focus of cognitive therapy is on underlying schemas. These cognitive structures are thought to be the templates, or basic rules, for interpreting information from the environment. Schemas (sometimes termed core beliefs) can be either adaptive or maladaptive. Cognitive therapists assist patients in modifying problematic schemas. Generally, cognitive therapy for dysfunctional schemas is more complex and demanding than therapeutic work with automatic thoughts. Cognitive Therapy also includes a number of behavioural interventions such as activity scheduling and graded task assignments. These procedures are used to reverse behavioural pathology and to influence cognitive functioning. The relationship between cognition and behaviour is considered to be a "two way street." If behaviour improves, there is usually a salutatory effect on cognition. In a similar manner, cognitive changes can lead to behavioural gains. Thus, Cognitive therapists often combine cognitive and behavioural techniques in clinical practice.

## Colonic Hydrotherapy

Colonic Hydrotherapy is an internal bath that helps cleanse the colon of poisons, gas, accumulated faecal matter and mucous deposits. Such techniques were first recorded in 1500BC, and have been used in traditional and naturopathic medicine since that time. Using sterilised equipment, filtered water is gently introduced into the rectum which progressively softens and expels faecal matter and compacted deposits. Essentially for anyone with a condition aggravated or caused totally or in part by auto toxicity, and where the resulting improved elimination aids healing. Most diets include mucous forming foods like dairy products - eggs, sugar, flour etc and even those people on relatively good diets and who have regular bowel movements have old hardened accumulations of mucoid deposits which hinder proper elimination and need periodic cleansing. Colon Hydrotherapy is beneficial to people suffering from: Constipation, Diarrhoea, Mucous Colitis, Colitis, Spastic Colon, Diverticulitis, Liver Sluggishness, Halitosis, Headaches, Flatulence, Haemorrhoids, Skin problems (acne, eczema, psoriasis), Abdominal Bloating, Asthma, Allergies, Fatigue, Lethargy. It is also beneficial prior to and following barium enemas and during therapeutic fasting. Some complex conditions such as Crohn's Disease, Myalgic Encephalomyelitis (ME) and Intestinal Candida are also helped by the resultant detoxifying effect of Colonic Hydrotherapy.

## Colour Therapy

The use of colour through out time has proven to be a very powerful tool to help us configure our minds, body and soul to a more stable, peaceful and unity of being. This process goes back to ancient times and is still being used in institutions for mentally disabled to normal everyday use. All types of religion have used this method of power to enable themselves for the better. Of course this is not a permanent cure so, please advice your physician if a problem is serious. Do not forget there are more than pharmaceutical ways to receive medicine i.e. holistic. Do what you feel not what you are told; we know our bodies better than anyone. Red: A powerful colour that has always been associated with vitality and ambition. It can help overcome negative thoughts. However, it is also associated with anger; if we have too much red in our system, or around us, we may feel irritable, impatient and uncomfortable. Pink: emotionally soothing and calming and gives a feeling of gentle warmth and nurturing. It lessens feelings of irritation and aggression, surrounding us with a sense of love and protection. It also alleviates loneliness, despondency, over sensitivity and vulnerability. While red relates more to sexuality, pink is associated with unselfish love. Orange: Orange is a joyous colour. It frees and releases emotions and alleviates feelings of self-pity, lack of self worth and unwillingness to forgive. It stimulates the mind, renewing interest in life; it is a wonderful antidepressant and lifts the spirits. Apricot/Peach is good for nervous exhaustion. Yellow: Yellow is also a happy, bright and uplifting colour, a celebration of sunny days. It is associated with the intellectual side of the mind and the expression of thoughts. It therefore aids the powers of discernment and discrimination, memory and clear thinking, decision-making and good judgment. It also helps good organization, assimilation of new ideas and the ability to see different points of view. It builds self-confidence and encourages an optimistic attitude. Conversely, dull yellow can be the colour of fear. Green: Green has a strong affinity with nature, helping us connect with empathy to others and the natural world. We instinctively seek it out when under stress or experiencing emotional trauma. It creates a feeling of comfort, laziness and relaxation, calmness and space, lessening stress, balancing and soothing the emotions. Dark green represents the onset of death and is nondescript, unassertive, a negation of life and joy. Lime and olive green can have a detrimental effect on both physical and emotional health since sickly yellow and green are associated with the emotions of envy, resentment and possessiveness. Turquoise: We associate blue greens with the refreshing and cool ocean. It is therefore invigorating, cooling and calming. Like green, turquoise is good for mental strain and tiredness or feeling washed out. It is an elevating colour that encourages us to make a sparkling fresh start. Turquoise is also helpful for feelings of loneliness, since it heightens communication, sensitivity and creativity. Blue: A cool, calming colour and is associated with a higher part of the mind than yellow. It represents the night, so it makes us feel calm and relaxed as if we are being soothed by the deep blue of the night sky. Light and soft blue, make us feel quiet and protected from all the bustle and activity of the day and alleviate insomnia. Blue inspires mental control, clarity and creativity. Midnight blue has a strong sedative effect on the mind, allowing us to connect to our intuitive and feminine side. Too much dark blue can be depressing, however, Indigo, Violet and Purple have a deep affect on the psyche and have been used in psychiatric care to help calm and pacify patients suffering from a number of mental and nervous disorders. These colours balance the mind and help transform obsessions and fears. Indigo is a powerful, psychic colour associated with the ride of the brain and stimulates intuition and imagination. It is also a strong sedative. Violet and purple are colours of transformation at a very deep level, bringing peace and combating shock or fear. They have a cleansing effect in emotional disturbances. They are also connected with artistic and musical impulses, mystery and sensitivity to beauty and high ideals, stimulating creativity, inspiration, sensitivity, spirituality and compassion. Violet can exert strong psychic influences, however a person attracted by it has to guard against living in a fantasy world. Purple is associated with psychic protection. Magenta: When we are feeling despondent and worried about our condition, or are feeling angry and frustrated, magenta draws us out of this attitude and lets our spirits soar. It is a spiritual colour but also with practical overtones, associated with a compassion, support and kindness. From a negative perceptive, magenta, like violet, makes us desire to be lifted out of the demanding world and avoid challenges. It can also be too relaxing. So avoid magenta if you are chronically depressed or introverted. White: The colour of ultimate purity is white. It is an all-round colour of protection, bringing peace and comfort, alleviating emotional shock and despair and helping inner cleansing of emotions, thoughts and spirit. If you need time and space to reflect on you life, white can give you a feeling of freedom and uncluttered openness. Too much white, however, can be cold and isolating because white separates us from other people. Black: This colour is comforting, protective and mysterious. It is associated with silence, the infinite and the feminine life force-passive, uncharted and mysterious. Black can also prevent us from growing and changing. We often cloak ourselves in black to hide from the world. Grey: Associated with independence, self-reliance, self-control, grey acts as a shield from outside influence. However, grey generally has a negative feeling- thick grey clouds, fog and smoke. Grey is the colour of evasion and non-commitment since it is neither black nor white. It relates to walling everything off, remaining separate, uncommitted and uninvolved, inevitably leading to loneliness. It also denotes self-criticism. Silver: The colour of the moon, which is ever changing. It relates to the feminine principle and the emotional, sensitive aspect of the mind. It balances, harmonizes and is mentally cleansing. Gold: Like yellow, gold is associated with the sun and is therefore related to abundance and power, higher ideals, wisdom and understanding. It is mentally revitalising, energising and inspiring and helpful for fear, uncertainty and lack of interest. Pale gold is excellent for depression and sharpens the mind. Brown: The colour of Mother Earth, brown brings a sense of stability, alleviating insecurity. However, it also relates to bottling up of emotion, a retreat from and a fear of the outside world and also narrow-mindedness. This often results from a lack of self-worth. From a website specialising in Colour Healing: "This system of Colour Healing is a new paradigm for the sick, especially for those who are doomed at present while being treated with orthodox medicine. Colour Therapy treatment works by matching the frequency wavelength of a colour to that of a disease, virus or infection. Patients can spend days connected with a bracelet and wire to a coloured tabulation, which in time will neutralise the disease. It's basically works like a radio, you have to match the radio signal frequency with the tuner to work and it's the same with Colour Therapy, you must match the colour frequency with the disease. This system of Colour Healing is seen by practitioners to kill bacterial and virus infections provided you complete the treatments. Colour Therapy destroys microbes but cannot supply bodily needs that are deficient nor can it repair any physical damage or physical ailments. On your own accord you may take vitamins, minerals or need to fulfil a complete diet which is abundant in natural and raw foods. Also very important to restoring health is a daily intake of good water. You may need a physician to prescribe additional medication which is necessary to your well being, our system does not supply medical services. During Colour Treatments, the colour which matches the frequency of the microbe you are infected with is fed back to our system by means of a radio carrier wave. You are directly connected to the colour and oscillator machine. We do not absent healing because it is a form of faith healing. Our way does its work by machine alone and so any number of people can be treated at the same time. Bloodstream infections are the easiest to kill because all the microbes circulate under the connection of the machine. Infections in organs and flesh take longer. It all depends on your circulation, your age, your vitality, your size and the nature of the disease. Overdose is impossible with this treatment machine because as soon as a particular microbe is killed there is nothing left that its particular colour can work on. Wrong colours also have no effect in this machine. In both the above cases nothing happens. A simple coil however produces a harmful radiation of the "iridium" frequency but Liley's machine does not. It is completely free of all harmful effects. This means that there is no side effects either, so the treatment is 100% safe, because the only thing that happens is a reduction of infection. Often you can feel this. Colour treatments are by one colour tabulation at a time and not by the whole lot mixed up together. Colours are applied separately and alternately so each gives its maximum effect and is not slowed down by the presence of the other colours. The latest electronic colour machine often kills off infections faster than your body can take advantage of. This means that recuperation continues on after the treatment ceases.

## Complementary Therapy (Alternative)

Alternative medicine is coming out of the closet: once dismissed as wholesale quackery, this increasingly accepted field has been changing health-care systems the world over. All specialties have been affected by the adoption of complementary therapies, including oncology. However, most oncologists are not familiar with the alternative therapies used by many of their patients. Unconventional therapies are called "complementary" because they are often used to supplement mainstream medicine or to calm the symptoms of terminal illness with non-invasive treatments that carry minimal or no side effects. Complementary therapies are used in conjunction with, rather than instead of, conventional treatment; relaxation therapy is an example. Today, most alternative medicine is used as an integral part of a wellness-oriented lifestyle. There is no simple definition, because alternative medicine is many things to many people, there is no one-line answer that would define the term simply and clearly and satisfy everyone. This reason alone is why it can be so difficult for some people to get a clear sense of just what alternative medicine is - and what it is not. The truth is, one simple definition can't possibly describe all that professionals now consider "alternative medicine." Alternative medicine is made up of a rich array of techniques, modalities and medical systems that, for the most part, are unfamiliar to the majority of the public. They are, therefore, an "alternative" to what most people are using when they need health care. Almost all alternative medical techniques are founded on a holistic perspective of health. In other words, when diagnosing and treating a person, consideration is given to the whole person including the physical, emotional, mental and spiritual aspects of who he or she is. Much of what we call alternative medicine comes to us from other cultures or from ancient healing traditions. For example, the use of herbs is found all over the world in many cultures including Native Americans. Acupuncture comes specifically from ancient China and has been documented as being in use as early as 2697 B.C. Contrary to popular belief, many alternative medical techniques are used everyday by people from all walks of life. Alternative medicine is also defined by what it is not. Alternative medicines are medical interventions not taught widely at medical schools or generally available at hospitals. Complementary and alternative medicine is defined through a social process as those practices that do not form part of the dominant system for managing health and disease.

## Counselling

To provide Counselling is to provide a supportive relationship for the counselee as the counsellor seeks to listen, understand and enable the counselee to think through problems and issues, and to take action that will help him to function more effectively. The role of counselling is constantly changing as more and more people of all ages, from children to pensioners, male and female struggle as they come face to face with dilemmas in their lives. Stress - at work or at home, lack of self confidence, relationship problems with friends and families, and internal conflict, fear and guilt can all add to the confusion, sadness and feelings of depression and tiredness. Counselling methods will help you to take control of your life again. By encouraging you to look at the possibilities in conjunction with the problems, you will start to see how to improve your life, using ways which will help you again and again.

## Cranial Osteopathy

The Cranial approach is an extremely gentle form of Osteopathy invaluable for the treatment of babies and children although adults may also benefit. Disturbances and limitations both within the bones of the skull and throughout the body are identified and corrected. Gentle pressure or sensations of warmth and relaxation can be felt as releases occur. Nine out of ten children suffer trauma in the birth process. It is advisable for every infant to be checked at birth particularly after a lengthy delivery or if forceps or ventouse have been used. The new mother will also benefit from treatment . Problems in babies and children which may be alleviated include disturbed sleep patterns, excessive crying, colic, glue ear, recurrent coughs and colds, developmental delay and behavioural problems. Cranial Osteopathy (or as it is sometimes called " Cranio-sacral Osteopathy") is a very gentle, yet extremely powerful, system of osteopathic medicine which uses the patient's " Cranial Rhythm" (also known as the " Primary Respiratory or Involuntary Mechanism") for evaluation and treatment. What is the Cranial Rhythm? It is a cyclical expansion and contraction of all the tissues of the body, which occurs 8-18 times a minute, is distinct from all other known body rhythms (i.e. heartbeat, breathing rate) and can be felt in all parts of the body. The movement is of very small amplitude, therefore it takes practitioners with a very finely developed sense of touch to feel it. This rhythm was first described in the early 1900's by Dr. William G. Sutherland and its existence was confirmed in a series of laboratory tests in the1960's and '70's. There is much debate as to what causes the rhythm and why it is there; it has often been observed to continue for a few minutes after the heart and breathing stops when someone dies, leading us to presume it is a movement of a very primitive or basic level of body function; some have compared it to the inherent movement of singled celled organisms (e.g. amoebas), suggesting that the cells of the body still behave, individually, in this way even though they are part of a far more complicated and organised system. How do you feel it? Using very gentle, light touch practitioners will examine the cranial rhythm in various areas of your body; this doesn't hurt and feels very pleasant and relaxing. What can you tell by feeling it? Practitioners compare what your rhythm is doing to what they consider normal; this gives them an insight into what stresses and strains your body is under at present and as a result of its past; it also shows them what state your body is in, if it's healthy, stressed, tired etc. Above all they are assessing the function of your body and how it is working, with a view to helping it to restore itself to health. What things can it help? It can help wide variety of conditions, and is particularly useful in, but not limited to, the treatment of the following: Infants and children; Colic and other digestive problems; sleeplessness; crying/upset/whinging babies; learning difficulties; persistent coughs and colds; glue ear; hyperactivity etc. adults; back, neck and head aches; most common digestive problems; sinusitis; stress; sleeping difficulties; etc.

## Cranio-Sacral Therapy

Cranio-Sacral Therapy is an exceptionally gentle yet extremely powerful form of treatment which can be helpful to most people and in most conditions - from minor aches and pains to severe and persistent chronic health problems. It is a profound healing process which can influence the deeply held patterns of disease - both physical and psychological - which accumulate throughout life as a result of injury and illness and become held into the body tissues, leading to ill-health and dysfunction. It has the potential to transform these patterns of restriction and resistance in our lives at a very fundamental level, thereby eliminating disease and restoring health. How does it work? Cranio-Sacral Therapy involves a very gentle touch of the practitioners' hands, both for diagnosis and for treatment. This light contact may be taken up on the cranium, the sacrum or any other part of the body as appropriate. Through this light touch the practitioner is able to pick up subtle patterns of motion within the body - rhythms, pulls, pulsations - emanating from deep within the core structures of the body. These movements are a reflection of Cranio-Sacral motion which is expressed in all tissues throughout the body. Every condition affecting a person influences this movement, creating asymmetries or restrictions to Cranio-Sacral motion. The Cranio-Sacral Therapist can therefore diagnose every condition through the corresponding patterns of resistance within the Cranio-Sacral system. By responding appropriately to these patterns - in other words by gently allowing the subtle movements deep within the body to unwind themselves - the Cranio-Sacral Therapist can enable and facilitate the release of Cranio-Sacral restrictions. Release at these profound regulatory levels in turn enables the release of disease conditions throughout the body. What does it involve? Cranio-Sacral Therapy is most often carried out with the client lying down, fully clothed in a quiet and peaceful environment. Treatment is usually experienced as a very profound relaxation which may pervade the whole person, physically, mentally and emotionally, often accompanied by a feeling of lightness and ease. The gentle approach of Cranio-Sacral Therapy is entirely non-invasive. The subtle interaction of two systems - brought together by this light contact - stimulates and enhances self-healing mechanisms within the body to respond, release and open up to a more balanced healthy state. What can it treat? Cranio-Sacral Therapy is primarily concerned with creating and maintaining a healthy, balanced state on all levels. This underlying state of well-being enables the body's own healing mechanisms to operate at optimum level, and therefore enables the body to eliminate disease and restore health. Cranio-Sacral Therapy works on many different levels and influences many different structures within the body. It influences the musculo-skeletal system, the nervous system, the cardiovascular-vascular system, the immune system, the organs, the connective tissues, the fluids and the energy systems of the body. It therefore has widespread and profound effects on conditions affecting all of these systems. Because it treats the whole person it can influence all conditions affecting the whole person or any part of the person. Cranio-Sacral Therapy therefore has a very wide range of applications. It is suitable for all ages from newborn babies to the elderly, including all ages and stages in between. It is particularly valuable in babies and children since the establishment of healthy patterns at an early age sets patterns for the whole future of that individual, both in their health and in their abilities. It is also particularly renowned for its profound influence on the effects of Birth Trauma - the effects of which may range from learning difficulties, hyperactivity and ear-infections to epilepsy and cerebral palsy. Cranio-Sacral Therapy is also particularly valuable in solving and resolving difficult and persistent conditions. The following are just a few examples of the many conditions that might benefit from Cranio-Sacral treatment: Headaches, Migraines, Period Pains, Asthma, Sinusitis, Bronchitis, Cystitis, Frozen Shoulder, Arthritis, Sciatica, Sprained Ankle, Joint Disorders, RSI, Digestive Problems, Whiplash Injuries, Spinal Curvatures, Back Pain, Neck Pain, Persistent pain anywhere in the body, Tension, Anxiety, Insomnia, Visual Disturbances, Lack of Energy, Problems during and after Pregnancy, Depression, Post-Operative Effects, Adhesions, Baby Care, Colic, Pyloric Stenosis, Feeding Difficulties, Ear Infections, Glue Ear, Tonsillitis, ENT Problems, Compression of the skull due to a difficult birth, with its many after effects, Learning Difficulties, Dyslexia, Squint, Lazy Eye, Hyperactivity, Autism, Epilepsy, Cerebral Palsy, Behavioural Disorders, Tantrums, Obsessional Behaviour, Dental and TMJ Problems, Head Injuries, and their subtle influence on personality and mental state, Meningitis and its chronic, consequences, Post Viral Syndrome, ME, Glandular Fever, Fatigue, The after effects of any chronic illness or debilitating disease.

## Cryo Surgery

Surgical techniques using temperatures at or below freezing. The use of freezing as a special surgical technique to destroy or excise tissue.

## Crystal Healing

We all have a sixth sense - intuition that most of us very rarely listen to. Intuition is the sense that something is going to happen before it does. The degree of your ability depends on how much you believe and how often you practice. Crystals can help you to use your natural abilities. Crystal healing is using the energy from the crystal channelled through the healer so that any imbalance in the body may be put back to get your energy flowing around the body again. These days many shops sell crystals so go and have a browse around. It is your choice which one to buy. You choose - no one else, after all it will be your crystal for you to work with. When you find some crystals the next step is to choose one for yourself - but how. Relax, take a good look at them and consider which one draws you to it. Let your intuition work for you. When you have chosen your crystal, bought it and taken it home, the next step is to cleanse it. There are various ways to do this and one of the easiest is probably water cleansing. Visualise cleansing the crystal while rinsing it in the water - picture all that negative energy washing away. The next stage is to charge the crystal, to do this you could place them on a windowsill in the light of the sun or moon for a short period of time. Having chosen cleansed and charged your crystals you then need to care for them. Use them for the purpose for which they were intended, feel them, handle them and talk to them. You need to tune into your crystal, communicate with it. This may not happen at first but persevere and remain calm, it may help to play relaxing music quietly in the background. You need to keep your crystals in a bag, this should be made from natural fibre. You need to practice with your crystals. Feel the energy from it and feel the energy between your hands.

Eventually you should be able to use this to remove a persons energy blocks and renew their Chakra's. There are different crystals for different areas of the body for example; amethyst for the crown, sodalite for the brow, blue lace agate for the throat and so it goes on down the body covering all eight chakras. Alternatively you could try a session with a crystal healer and see what you experience. I have done this and found the flow of energy from her hands to be amazing, but that is something you will have to discover for yourself. Here are ways crystals can be used to augment energy healing, also known as therapeutic touch or healing touch. In all energy healing work, the healing can be instantaneous if the healer is connected to truth and the recipient is receptive. It's important to remember that the healer is simply a channel for pure positive energy. The patient is the one who is responsible for accepting the healing. As a healer, it's wise to remember that when we spiritually ask for aid in helping another in any way, we immediately summon great help from Spirit. When we forget who we are and begin to focus on the negative or that which is unwanted, we create imbalances in our energy fields that can lead to disease. The key to rebalancing the energy field is to focus not at all on what is not wanted (the ailment), but to visualize only what is wanted (perfect health) with positive expectancy. Finally, there are no hard rules for energy healing. It's an intuitive and inspired process. Trust that if you set a high intention, all you have to do is allow magic to happen! A simple crystal healing is to place crystals of the appropriate colour and energy at corresponding chakra points. This will cleanse and energize the chakras. Here is a list of the chakras with stones that may prove beneficial: Root chakra: Jasper (bloodstone), garnet, onyx, rubies. Second chakra(womb): hematite, moonstone. Third chakra (solar plexus): citrine, amber, topaz. Fourth chakra (heart): rose quartz, Chinese Fluorite. Fifth chakra (throat): aquamarine, turquoise. Sixth chakra (third eye): sapphire, turquoise, and amethyst. Seventh chakra (crown): clear quartz or amethyst. It's a good idea to "stroke down" and cleanse the aura energetically before applying the energies of the stones, one by one, to the chakras. Begin with the root chakra, and imagine energy rising from the base of the spine up through the crown of the head as you move upward. Visualize each chakra being energized and expanding in turn. Clear quartz can be used to simply magnify all healing efforts. Try holding a point in your hand as you scan the aura (point facing out), and then face the point in as you send healing and harmonizing energy. Another powerful healing technique involves the use of two clear quarts points. Sit at the feet of the patient with the point of the crystal in your right hand facing in at the bottom of the patient's left foot, and the point of the crystal in your left hand pointing out at the bottom of the patient's right foot. Send energy up through your right hand (patient's left foot) and visualize it channelling all through the body, all up the left side, and through and down the right side and out the right foot. Imagine a continue circle of energy going in and flowing out. The key is to visualise ease of flow and balance. Visualise all stagnant energies breaking up and melting down, and new clarity and flow being established. All unwanted energies will be washed through, and new vitality and well-being will fill the energy field.

## Cupping

Cupping is a technique that involves applying suction to the body surface. The suction is traditionally created using a small glass or bamboo cup and a flame. A cotton ball soaked in alcohol is ignited to produce a very hot flame. This flame is briefly placed within the jar to instantly heat the air inside. The flame is quickly withdrawn and the open face of the cup is placed against the skin. The air cools as quickly as it was heated creating a vacuum. As a result, the tissue beneath the cup is lifted. Cupping may either be fixed or running. Fixed cupping is simply applying the cup to the skin and leaving it stationary. With running cupping, the skin is lubricated allowing the cup to be moved across the skin in a massaging motion to cover a larger area. Sensation- Cupping is described as a sucking sensation. It is not at all uncomfortable, but can feel a little strange. Sometimes cupping will leave a very superficial discoloration of the skin. This discoloration may range from red to purple in colour and is the result of blood congestion in the local area. It is not accompanied with any discomfort and usually resolves in a couple of days. Indications - In Chinese medicine, cupping is used to bring pathogens and stagnation to the surface in order for it to be released from the body. Cupping is usually applied to the back and is commonly used for upper respiratory infections and back pain. The suction created by cupping is very good for releasing muscle spasms in the upper and lower back. Traditionally, this technique was frequently used to draw pus out of skin abscesses.

## Cymatics

Cymatics was developed in the 1960s by British medical doctor and Osteopath, Dr. Peter Manners. The therapy grew out of early research into electromagnetic energy and the concept that every living thing - person, animal, plant or organism is surrounded by an energy field that resonates at its own particular frequency. Professor Gaveau of the Sorbonne in Paris, Dr. Brunner from Germany, Dr. Harold S Burr from Yale University and Swiss scientist Dr. Hans Jenny, were all individually involved in research into the phenomenon in the 1950s. The results of their work was collated by Dr. Manners and developed into the therapy of Cymatics. Unlike many other types of complementary therapy, Cymatics exploits the scientific possibilities of 20th century medicine and according to Dr. Peter Manners, "is founded on a true knowledge of man". Consequently, the medical profession is mostly appreciative of what it has to offer. In fact, the treatment has proved to be so successful, painless and easy to perform, that it is rapidly growing in popularity. There are now Cymatic clinics in Britain, Europe, Japan, Australia and others are soon to open in Brazil and Mexico. Cymatics comes from the Greek word "kyma" meaning "a great wave". Cymatic Therapy is a form of sound therapy, based in the principal that every cell in the body, of which there are believed to be millions, is controlled by and electromagnetic field which resonates at its own particular sound frequency. When we are well this frequency is steady and constant, but any dysfunction or disease upsets the harmony of the body and the area affected then generates an increased resonance. The practitioner uses the Cymatic machinery to generate a frequency identical to that of healthy cells. His aim is to support what the cells are trying to do naturally, therefore aiding the healing process and restoring the body to good health and harmony. How does it work? Cymatic practitioners use special equipment to generate the required frequencies of harmonics to stimulate the affected cells in all areas of the body. Originally, the equipment was very large, cumbersome and expensive, but today it is much smaller, in fact about the size of a small brief case. Treatment is applied by means of a large hand-held applicator, or via Cymatic probes which are small pencil-like applicators used to treat small areas. The practitioner chooses the treatment from around 850 frequencies, all of which have been calculated over a period of years. The treatment is then directed at the area of the body causing the problem. This may be the point of pain but often is not. Treatment works in the same way for all problems. If you have muscular pain, for example, the energy of that muscle and the frequency of its field will have been changed by the injury or condition affecting it. Transmitting a corrective frequency into the muscle can re-balance its energy and almost immediately relieve the pain experienced. In an asthmatic condition, for example, the asthmatic tension is released so that the patient is able to breathe more easily. Viral conditions on the other hand, can be cured. The sound waves set up a condition in the body which make it intolerable for the virus to remain. What happens in a consultation ? The first treatment lasts for an hour or more and begins with a normal check-up. If necessary the practitioner will take your pulse, blood pressure, listen to your chest and carry out any other relevant conventional medical diagnostic tests. But in the case of injury where the nature of the condition is obvious this is not usually required. The practitioner will go on to ask you for details about; Your general health and any condition that you might be suffering from What sort of food you eat in your normal diet . He will also require details of your occupation and will want to know any aspects of your life style that may also contribute to your condition. Practitioner's trained in other forms of complimentary therapies such as acupuncture or osteopathy may also use elements of those systems in the diagnosis. When he has arrived at his diagnosis the practitioner will take you into a treatment room. Depending upon the treatment required you might be asked to lie on a couch or sit on a specially designed structure in which you can rest your head, neck and shoulders so that you are relaxed and ready for treatment. Treatment can sometimes take the form of "Aqua Sonics" in which case it takes place in a heated pool in an air-conditioned building. The molecular structure of water can be heated altered by certain sound frequencies, making it an easier medium in which people with mobility problems can move. People with arthritis, rheumatoid problems and physical disability are often treated in this way. Even patients with paralysis can experience some sense of movement because of their own dilation in the water. The nature and length of treatment depends on your condition. For example, a difficult viral condition may need to be treated with several different frequencies for 45 to 60 minutes, but something as straightforward as arthritis could benefit from just 30 minutes of treatment. Treatment in the pool may last as little as 20 minutes because it can be so relaxing that you may want to fall asleep. In all cases the sensation is pleasant, relaxing and slightly stimulating as sound frequencies are transmitted through you body. How many sessions do I need ? It is impossible to say. It depends on the nature of you condition, how long you had it and your body's individual healing ability. Treatment is believed to speed up a person's healing rate by 50 per cent. You are recommended to have treatment twice a week to begin with and then once a week until the problem is cleared. You should start to see some positive benefits by about the third treatment. Which problems can it help ? The therapy reduces pain and inflammation and helps improve mobility. It has been noted as a successful treatment for conditions such as arthritis, rheumatism, back pain, post-operative healing, sport injuries, bone fractures and muscular injury. But Dr. Manners states that every condition, illness or psychological state can be treated or improved by the technique because it releases tension in the system and allows the mind and body to return to a normal level. Is it safe ? Cymatic therapy, administered by a qualified therapy is perfectly safe for everyone , irrespective of age or level of fitness. Pregnant women, very young babies and the very frail and elderly can all be treated with Cymatics. In over 30 years of practice there have been no recorded side effects arising from the treatment.

## Dance Movement Therapy

Dance is the most fundamental of the arts, involving direct expression through the body. It is an intimate and powerful medium for therapy. Based on the assumption that body and mind are interrelated, dance/movement therapy is defined by the American Dance Therapy Association as "the Psychotherapeutic use of movement as a process which furthers the emotional, cognitive and physical integration of the individual." Dance/movement therapy effects changes in feelings, cognition, physical functioning, and behaviour. Dance as therapy came into existence in the 1940s, especially through the pioneering efforts of Marian Chace. Psychiatrists in Washington, D.C., found that their patients were deriving benefits from attending Chace's unique dance classes. As a result, Chace was asked to work on the back wards of St. Elizabeth's Hospital with patients who had been considered too disturbed to participate in regular group activities. A non-verbal group approach was needed and dance/movement therapy met that need. The American Dance Therapy Association (ADTA) was founded in 1966 by 73 charter members in 15 states. Now, the Association has grown to nearly 1200 members in 46 states and 20 foreign countries. ADTA maintains a registry of dance/movement therapists who meet specific educational and clinical practice standards. The title "Dance Therapist Registered" (DTR) is granted to entry-level dance/movement therapists who have a master's degree which includes 700 hours of supervised clinical internship. The advanced level of registry, Academy of Dance Therapists Registered (ADTR), is awarded only after DTRs have completed 3,640 hours of supervised clinical work in an agency, institution, or special school, with additional supervision from an ADTR. In addition, as part of their written application for review by the credentials committee, applicants for ADTR must document their understanding of theory and practice. The association has a code of ethics and has established standards for professional practice, education and training. Dance/movement therapy academic programs stress coursework in dance/movement therapy theory and practice, movement observation and analysis, human development, psychopathology, cultural diversity, research skills, and group work. In 1979, ADTA established an approval process for the purpose of evaluating these programs. Research and scholarly writings are published in the American Journal of Dance Therapy and in publications funded by the Marian Chace Memorial Fund of the ADTA. Today, in addition to those with severe emotional disorders, people of all ages and varying conditions receive dance/movement therapy. Examples of these are individuals with eating disorders, adult survivors of violence, sexually and physically abused children, dysfunctional families, the homeless, autistic children, the frail elderly, and substance abusers. An evolving area of specialization is using dance/movement therapy in disease prevention and health promotion programs and with those who have chronic medical conditions. Many innovative programs provide dance/movement therapy for people with cardiovascular disease, hypertension, chronic pain, or breast cancer. Research has been undertaken on the effects of dance/movement therapy in special settings (such as prisons and centres for the homeless) and with specific populations including the learning disabled, frail elderly, emotionally disturbed, depressed and suicidal, mentally retarded, substance abusers, visually and hearing impaired, psychotic, and autistic. Those with physical problems (such as amputations, traumatic brain injury, stroke, and chronic pain) and with chronic illnesses (such as anorexia and bulimia, cancer, Alzheimer's disease, cystic fibrosis, heart disease, diabetes, asthma, AIDS, and arthritis) have also been studied. In institutions, dance/movement therapists may work as administrators as well as clinicians. Dance/movement therapists who are ADTRs in good standing are also qualified to teach, provide supervision, and engage in private practice.

## Dietician

An expert in formulating a diet plan based on need and results. Not just for weight loss but also for indications where diet coordination may help in treating intolerances, allergies and certain diseases.

## Do-In

The ancient form of Chinese self massage pronounced dough-in aims to prevent disease, rather than cure it. Closely related to Shiatsu Massage techniques. Shiatsu is a (relatively) modern Japanese development of the ancient Chinese healing art doin-ankyo. It is massage incorporating oriental Ki and meridian knowledge. "Do" also means way or path and "Ki" is the Energy/movement - usually used in the sense of life energy and very important in Acupuncture.

## Douching

A form of hydrotherapy in which a jet or jets of water are hosed onto parts of the body. Believed to many benefits including muscle stimulation, circulation improvements, sedative effects and easing of muscular tension and other pain. Used too clean areas of orifices that are accessible externally. Not recommended as vaginal contraceptive.

## Dowsing

Diagnosis by the use of a divining rod or pendulum suspended by a thread, of the client and/or the client's environment. It is claimed that a dowser can locate areas of disease within the body and also areas of geopathic stress within buildings which could be causing the disease. To dowse is to search, with the aid of simple hand held tools or instruments, for that which is otherwise hidden from view or knowledge. It can be applied to searches for a great number of artefacts and entities. It is most commonly known by most people in association with searching for underground water; not surprising considering the absolute need for water by man and his animals and cultivated plants which sustain him. What is less readily known is that dowsing can be also used for searching for other underground features such as archaeological remains, cavities and tunnels, oil, veins of mineral ore, underground building services, missing items and occasionally missing persons. Although no thorough scientific explanations for dowsing has yet been found it is frequently acknowledged that there is some correlation between the dowsing reaction and changes in magnetic flux when dowsing on site. What is more difficult for the newcomer to accept is that dowsing can be carried out at a distance and, moreover, the distance itself has no bearing on the results; dowsing can be carried out for something in the next room or the next continent. This is of immense practical use for site dowsers who save themselves and their clients valuable time by initially, at least, dowsing at a distance to seek the direction of the nearest source, for example, or actually dowsing over a map of an area to determine more precisely the target of the search. This particular faculty is frequently used by those practitioners using dowsing in the area of health when they are able to dowse for causative factors and suitable remedies at a distance from the patient, employing a sample or witness of the person, for example, on which to focus their attention.

## Drama Therapy

Drama Therapy is the systematic and intentional use of drama/theatre processes and products to achieve the therapeutic goals of symptom relief, emotional and physical integration, and personal growth. Drama Therapy is an active, experiential approach that facilitates the client's ability to tell his/her story, solve problems, set goals, express feelings appropriately, achieve catharsis, extend the depth and breadth of inner experience, improve interpersonal skills and relationships, and strengthen the ability to perform personal life roles while increasing flexibility between roles. Drama therapists are trained in theatre arts, Psychology, Psychotherapy and Drama Therapy. Areas of study include improvisation, puppetry, role-playing, mask work, pantomime, theatrical production, psychodrama, developmental psychology, theories of personality, and group process.

## Electrolypolysis

Finally, a way to get rid of unwanted fat from specific areas of your body without painful surgery. Electrolypolysis and Lymph Drainage are proven methods of removing fat, activating inactive fat cells to provide you with a new a slimmer you. Discovered about 20 years ago by Doctors, the procedure has now become affordable and non-invasive. Electrolypolysis can reduce your figure by inches, possibly even one whole size even after the first session using low voltage currents through non-invasive skin electrodes. How does it work? Cellulite is the fat that accumulates in specific areas of our bodies. Electrolypolysis targets these problem areas, such as, your waist, hips and thighs. It breaks down the fat in your cells into a substance your body can easily get rid of. This substance travels out of the fat cells into the lymphatic system and is then excreted by the kidneys as urine. What does it feel like? There is no pain involved in this process. It will produce a tingling feeling, much like a tickle or an itch. There is no muscle contraction or discomfort. How long will it last? Providing you eat a healthy diet, exercise regularly and do not gain a substantial amount of weight, these results will be permanent.

## Electrotherapy

The human body is a web, a complex and intertwined mass of neurons and synapses that crackle with electricity and send messages across millions of nerve pathways. Everything that you think, feel, smell, touch — even if you aren't aware of it — has a corresponding and intricate neurological reaction. Pleasure, pain, happiness, fear, heat, cold, etc, come from tiny sparks of electricity that jump between nerves and eventually get translated by your brain into sensations and feelings that you recognise. Sometimes the messages that your body sends are undesirable — pain, for example. Or, you don't have the ability to send certain messages altogether — such as those that might help heal an injured limb or low back. Electrotherapy, on the other hand, can change these signals for therapeutic benefit. By interrupting, altering or inducing certain electrical impulses, electrotherapy devices — such as the TENS (transcutaneous electrical nerve stimulation) and neuromuscular stimulation products can help control pain, promote muscle rehabilitation and facilitate fluid movement. That's why health care professionals prescribe their use for a variety of circumstances including lower back pain, joint stiffness, muscle spasm, sports-related injury and post-operative treatments.

## Faith Healing

The use of prayer in healing began in human prehistory and continues to this day. Contemporary surveys reveal that most people pray and that they pray frequently, and almost always when their loved ones are ill. What do mental healing and spiritual healing mean? The terms 'mental healing' and 'spiritual healing' are frequently used interchangeably. What does 'spiritual' mean in this context? For many healers, spiritual healing is an integral part of their personal religion. Yet this cannot be the whole story because spiritual and prayer-based healing is universal. It cannot be attributed to any particular religious point of view. It occurs in monotheistic traditions such as Buddhism just as it does in the theistic traditions of the West and in animistic societies as well. What is the unifying principle in mental-spiritual healing that seemingly transcends personal religious views? Is mental-spiritual healing a direct effect of mind or consciousness? Are personal religious interpretations irrelevant? What is the most fundamental, basic requirement for mental-spiritual healing, without which it cannot occur? , One of the most thorough and innovative studies of this field is by psychologist Lawrence LeShan. LeShan found that mental-spiritual healing methods are of two main types. In type 1 healing, which he considered the most important and prevalent, the healer enters a prayerful, altered state of consciousness in which he views himself and the patient as a single entity. There need be no physical contact and there is no attempt to "do anything" or "give something" to the person in need. Type 1 healers uniformly emphasize the importance of empathy, love, and caring in this process. These healers state that this type of healing is a natural process that does not violate the laws of innate bodily function but rather speeds up ordinary healing — a very rapid self-repair or self-recuperation. Type 2 healers, on the other hand, do touch the patient and describe some "flow of energy" through their hands to the patient's area of pathology. Feelings of heat are common in both the patient and the healer. In this mode, the healer tries to heal. How does this type of healing occur? How does this type of healing occur? There is no explanation within contemporary medical science. The lack of an explanation for these events causes many people to dismiss them without investigating the evidence: Since they cannot occur, they do not occur. Proponents of this foregone conclusion regard any "evidence" for mental healing as illusory, nothing more than artefacts of poor experimentation or data processing, or chance results of complex random processes.

## Family Therapy

It deals with such problems as divorce, bereavement, school troubles and "other life-changes that cause pain". Family therapists work with whole families and family members. It is something of a myth that they only work with the whole family, often they work with individuals, couples and other involved people such as doctors, teachers and family friends. Family therapists believe it is important to consider individuals within their personal and family relationships. These people add meaning and support to life. The types of problems family therapists work with vary but include relationship difficulties, divorce and separation, illness in parents or children, bereavement, school and college difficulties and other life-changes that cause upset and pain. Family therapists help individuals who feel they have been damaged by their family experiences. They work with specific conditions (in association with other professionals) such as anorexia, bulimia, ADHD, depression, encopresis, enuresis and other conditions affecting family life.

## Feldenkrais Methodology

Feldenkrais methodology utilises "awareness through movement" whereby a therapist verbally guides a patient through (precise) movements in an effort to undo habitual postures and movement patterns that may have had a deleterious effect on, for instance, the cervical or lumbar spine.6,7 Feldenkrais practitioners also utilize a concept called "functional integration," an extension of awareness through movement, whereby a therapist will use tactile clues to guide a patient through better movement patterns. By design, the Feldenkrais method is individualised, and therefore difficult to objectify. Nevertheless, studies have been performed to assess its value in the treatment of musculo-skeletal injury. In part, it relies on the practitioner being aware not only of the patient's body and movements, but those of his or her own. Although there is clear intent to be objective, by definition, Feldenkrais technique moulds treatment to match the individual, and must include non-specific nuances including those brought into treatment by the therapist. In addition, there is a strong aspect of psychosocial awareness as a part of the treatment regimen, further making objective evaluation complicated. As a methodology it is perhaps best known as a form of physical therapy. This is in fact a great shame, as it tends to hide the real sophistication of the art, which is more as a learning methodology. A Feldenkrais Practitioner would not think in terms of fixing someone's sore shoulder for example. Rather they would think more in terms of helping that person learn more about the way they are organising themselves in such ways that the symptom ceases to exist. If all that happens is the alleviating of the symptom without an educative process then it will reappear.

Common results for those who practise this method can be greater sensitivity in all areas of life, graceful movement, improved performance - not just physically - and an ability to work with change more easily and with greater sophistication.

## Feng Shui

Feng Shui is the practice of living harmoniously with the energy of the surrounding environment which naturally leads to the art of placement, not only of buildings, but also of everything within them. Traditionally taught and practised in the Far East it was originally used as a way of divining where to site graves. It was also drawn upon to decide when and where to build a home, a community or an entire city. These same principles were then applied to the arrangement of the home, the use of various rooms and so on. This wisdom was not only understood and practised in the Far East, as all parts of the world have drawn on traditional ideas for the design and position of homes and places of worship. In Europe, there are pre-historic, medieval and more modern structures that have been built in a certain fashion and on certain sites for a specific purpose. This collective practice of the art of placement can include: traditional Feng Shui, modern interpretation of feng shui, geomancy, dowsing, space clearing and astrology. Feng Shui, literally means wind and water. It is an ancient Chinese study of the natural environment. Feng Shui can determine the best or most favourable location for anyone and assist that person to avoid his or her worst or least desirable location in any environment. This environment can be at the office, home, or any place that they are at. Feng Shui makes the determination based on the year the individual is born, the environment surrounding them and through the movements of the solar system. Throughout ancient China, classical Feng Shui was a closely guarded discipline used as a tool to ensure the good health, wealth and power of the imperial dynasties. The keepers of this secret knowledge were the Feng Shui masters, the highly respected scientists and astronomers who were charged with sustaining the good fortune and prosperity of the royal court. These masters of Chinese geomancy were very selective of their protégées and extremely wary of sharing their Feng Shui knowledge with any outsider. As a result, few who claimed to be Feng Shui masters even knew the basic theories, which meant even fewer could practice with proficiency. To this day, Feng Shui charlatans continue to shroud their ignorance in cloaks of mystery and ritual. They take a "shotgun" approach to prescribing wind Chimes and mirrors, embellishing their charade with some incense and prayer. Actually, a classical Feng Shui reading involves no guesswork. Every building has unique energy characteristics that need to be individually addressed, so be wary of practitioners who offer fixed or occult "cures". Their prescribed remedies may actually do more harm than good.

## Floral Essence Therapy (Bach's)

Some call them "Nature's Prozac," but depression is only one of many emotional imbalances they are used for. To some, the idea seems just too good to be true: Take a few drops a day of a harmless, pleasant-tasting liquid, and your anxiety or depression or other negative emotions will just melt away. Yet for many people, including many PWAs, that appears to be just what happens. They are flower remedies developed in the 1930s by noted British bacteriologist and homeopathic physician Edward Bach. These and other more recently developed flower essences - and there are now hundreds of other lines of essences in addition to the original ones developed by Dr. Bach, made from flowers worldwide - are still one of the best-kept secrets among natural therapies. These gentle healers are non-toxic, non habit-forming essences of flowering plants that help to rebalance negative emotional states such as fear, anxiety, depression, and poor self-image. Flower essences have no floral scent or taste, and are not related to aromatherapy, which is closer to herbology. Rather, like homeopathy, they are classified as "vibrational" or "subtle energy" medicine. Like many other natural therapies, flower essences act on the level of the individual's innate healing capacity, or healing intelligence. Taking them is rather like rebooting one's inner computer, restoring order to a system that has gone off course. There is as yet no clear scientific explanation for how or why these essences work. Author Mechtild Scheffer, in her book Bach Flower Therapy: Theory and Practice, describes the action of the Bach remedies as "healing by restoring harmony in awareness." In one of a very few double-blind, controlled studies done thus far, a study conducted in California in 1979 by Michael S. Weinglas found that use of the Bach remedies enhanced creativity, deepened self-understanding and self-acceptance, and increased humour. Los Angeles practitioner Yolanda Lacombe believes that the essences help the immune system by strengthening a person's sense of protective boundaries, reinforcing the distinction between self and non-self - which is, when you think about it, just what the immune system does. Flower essences may be used in conjunction with any other therapy, and they can be especially effective when used along with psychotherapy. Each flower essence deals with a particular emotional state. In the Bach flower remedies, the original essences developed in England by Edward Bach, there are 38 different individual remedies. There is also one combination - called "Rescue Remedy," "Calming Essence," or "Five Flower Formula," depending on the manufacturer - that is particularly useful for coping with high-stress or emergency situations, such as accidents, exams, dentists' appointments, or temper tantrums. Rescue Remedy also comes in a cream form that is wonderfully soothing for burns, stings, cuts, and other skin afflictions. Flower essences can be used equally effectively with adults, children, animals, and plants. There are two basic ways to use the essences. On an occasional basis, such as for temporary stress or anxiety, they may be administered by putting two drops (four in the case of Rescue Remedy) directly under the tongue or adding them to any beverage. For long-term treatment of more chronic problems, such as fears or trauma, a formula can be made up containing one or more remedies (up to a combination of six) in a one-ounce dropper bottle. The formula is then taken several times a day for a month or more. This method achieves much deeper, longer-lasting results.

## Flotation Therapy

Flotation Therapy was developed from the early work of Dr. John Lilly who was a neurophysiologist and psychoanalyst. In 1954 he conducted research into how the brain would react when it was denied external stimulation. He devised flotation tanks which were originally called sensory deprivation chambers. When the therapeutic benefits of these chambers were realized the name was changed to Flotation Therapy. Flotation Therapy is a way of isolating the mind and body from any external stimuli. This in turn helps produce deep relaxation. , The treatment involves the patient lying in a sound proof tank of water. The water has salts and minerals dissolved into it which enables the body to float. These days most flotation tanks are installed in health clubs. The tanks measure around 8ft long by 4ft wide. Generally most people prefer to float naked. You will be given ear plugs to use. The flotation takes place in complete darkness. Some flotation tanks may play relaxation tapes or there may be a two way microphone so you may talk to a practitioner.

## Gait Analysis

Quantitative Gait Analysis is useful in objective documentation of walking ability as well as identifying the underlying causes for walking abnormalities in patients with cerebral palsy, stroke, head injury and other neuromuscular problems. The results of Gait Analysis have been shown to be useful in determining the best course of treatment in these patients.

## Gem Essence Therapy

Gem essences like homeopathic remedies and flower essences are becoming very popular in the alternative healing field. These three modalities form the foundation of "Vibrational Medicine", each created with the intent of working with the more subtle (or vibrational) aspects of our beings. These subtle aspects include the mind and thought patterns, the heart and the entire spectrum of human emotion and the spirit essence which is the highest frequency of all. As we all learn more about the effects that our thoughts and feelings have upon our physical state of well-being we can with the help of vibrational medicine, be better able to heal the very causes of many imbalances that can and do manifest in the denser physical body. These subtle mental, emotional and spiritual energies form the very blueprint of a person's being and can be successfully comforted, healed and balanced with the correct remedy.

## Gestalt Therapy

Phenomenology is a discipline that helps people stand aside from their usual way of thinking so that they can tell the difference between what is actually being perceived and felt in the current situation and what is residue from the past. A Gestalt exploration respects, uses and clarifies immediate, "naive" perception "undebauched by learning". Gestalt Therapy treats what is "subjectively" felt in the present, as well as what is "objectively" observed, as real and important data. This contrasts with approaches that treat what the patient experiences as "mere appearances" and uses interpretation to find "real meaning." The goal of Gestalt phenomenological exploration is awareness, or insight. "Insight is a patterning of the perceptual field in such a way that the significant realities are apparent; it is the formation of a gestalt in which the relevant factors fall into place with respect to the whole". In Gestalt Therapy insight is clear understanding of the structure of the situation being studied. Awareness without systematic exploration is not ordinarily sufficient to develop insight. Therefore, Gestalt Therapy uses focused awareness and experimentation to achieve insight. How one becomes aware is crucial to any phenomenological investigation. The phenomenologist studies not only personal awareness but also the awareness process itself. The patient is to learn how to become aware of awareness. How the therapist and the patient experience their relationship is of special concern in Gestalt Therapy .

## Hellerwork

Hellerwork began in 1978 when Joseph Heller (1940) left his position as the first President of the Rolf Institute to start training his first class of students at Sky High ranch in the California desert. As well as Dr. Rolf, whom Joseph Heller acknowledges with the utmost respect, Heller also incorporated Judith

Aston's movement work and the metaphysics of Dr. Brugh Joy in the foundations of Hellerwork. Further influences on the development of Hellerwork have included Hal Stone's Voice Dialogue work, and his inclusive approach has allowed many contributions that Heller's more than 750 students have brought to the work. Heller's work is an education of the body, through the body. In the process and it is a process that takes about 10 hours, usually done in weekly hours, all sorts of aches and pains and problems begin to clear up. Clients are empowered to continue the process for themselves and maintain and improve the initial results of the programme The essence of Hellerwork incorporates (and I use the word consciously) the concept of Integration, a word rooted in the Latin verb tegere, to touch. So by one definition Integration could be defined as being in touch with yourself through your body. Another key concept in Hellerwork is Synergy, a (now much abused) term first popularised by Buckminster Fuller in the 60's. In the context of Hellerwork, synergy is the unexpected and valuable impact of the mind, body and spirit working together better and the improved internal satisfaction and external effectiveness and ease that this generates. Tthe rate at which learning can occur is truly staggering" Joseph Heller Hellerwork is a multi-layered experience which reaches the parts massage does not. It includes a deep and systematic massage of the connective tissues which restores freedom of movement and more choice to the body in question. The system works from the outside in and from the bottom up, bringing increased order and symmetry to the physical structure, and a feeling of lightness and ease. The deep. slow movements used in the bodywork bring more consciousness into the body and allow the client to feel into previously inaccessible areas. Together with this uniquely powerful bodywork method, sometimes described as myo-fascial treatment, are added movement education and a conversation to relate mind and body. Movement education seeks to improve habitual use of the body in the ordinary everyday activities of sitting, standing and walking. By adding choice to the client's repertoire of movement the client is empowered to change habitual patterns that may be holding tension related problems in place. The conversation explores the mind/body relationship. If thoughts, feelings, attitudes, beliefs and opinions are interfering with the person's ability to release the build-up of chronic tension that we all tend to suffer from, then those issues can also be brought to consciousness in a gentle and respectful way. Becoming aware of these mind/body connections, the client takes the first steps towards a level of release in the body that is more significant than that afforded by a mechanical massage. The major results reported by clients of Hellerwork are increased vitality and energy, improved posture, flexibility, breathing and the ability to be comfortable in one's body. There is an experience often described as being "10 years younger". As an educational process you don't have to have a problem to benefit from Hellerwork. On the other hand it is also a very therapeutic experience, and just in the process of going through the series, all sorts of problems tend to clear up. My own personal experience was that it was a severe backache that brought me to Hellerwork. I learned through this that my worst problems are also my greatest opportunities, and I welcome and honour the "problems" that my clients bring to me, because generally they are what gets us into action in life. Hellerwork is about making whole - putting the disparate parts back together into a more coherent system. Wholeness is healing. As an experience of wholeness, Hellerwork can help you get in touch more with your true purpose in life, it can align your body with your brilliant mind and it can help expand and focus your energy on what's really important for you The kind of culture that most of us live in is characterised by an increasing pace of life, increasing stress from electromagnetic, noise and light pollution and a dissonance between mind, body and spirit. We tend to do sedentary jobs, commute long distances to work and spend a lot of time in front of televisions and computers. When we do exercise it is often in basement gyms with harsh lighting, in air conditioned rooms using linear movements and steel machinery. Now more than ever we need ways of getting in touch with ourselves, literally. New ways which do not perpetuate the harder, faster, superficial, material, mechanical values of industrial society. The new ways include slower, more conscious, organic, integrated, softer more intelligent approaches which are more individually tailored to people's needs. Witness the explosion of interest in Yoga, Pilates, Meditation, Tai Chi, and Homoeopathy. Hellerwork is a cutting-edge soft technology for facilitating a more flexible future capable of helping you assimilate the rapid rate of change in today's world. Hellerwork - fitness for lazy intelligent people.

## Herbal Medicine

Treatment of indications, diseases and disorders using herbal extracts and medicines. Herbal therapy is the most ancient form of health care known to humankind. Herbs have been used in all cultures throughout history. Extensive scientific documentation now exists concerning their use for health conditions, including premenstrual syndrome, indigestion, insomnia, heart disease, cancer and HIV.

## Holistic Healing

Whole body treatment that includes virtually all complementary medical treatments and expertise.

## Homeopathy

The fundamental criteria for Homeopathy is the law of similar, described by Hippocrates and developed by Hahnemann as : "SIMILIA SIMILIBUS CURENTUR". It means that a medication that can provoke symptoms during experimentation, can also heal the spontaneous same symptoms. Homeopathy is "a system of medical practice that treats a disease especially by the administration of minute doses of a remedy that would in healthy persons produce symptoms similar to those of the disease", "The Similum or Law of Similars: This basic law of homeopathy is similia similibus currentur: 'let likes be cured with like'. Based on this premise, the first Homeopathic principle states that any substance that can make you ill can also cure you - anything that is capable of producing symptoms of disease in a healthy person can cure those symptoms in a sick person. By 'symptom' the Homeopath means those changes that are felt by the patient (subjective) or observed (objective), which may be associated with a particular disease, or state of disease, and which are the outward expression of that state" . Homeopathy is a 200-year-old medical system you can use at home to help treat family members with a wide spectrum of acute health problems. It offers a way to gently stimulate your inner healing resources through recognising and reinforcing the adaptive reaction of the body's natural defences. By choosing the correct, individually suited homeopathic medicine from the plant, mineral, animal, or chemical kingdom, you can successfully stimulate the body's own defences, you can complement your family's efforts toward good health with these safe, natural medicines that provide an effective, inexpensive alternative to conventional medicine ". Homeopathy was begun in Germany by Samuel Hahnemann (1755-1845) and established as a major natural health-care force in the 1800s in America. It is a natural pharmaceutical science that utilizes substances from the plant, mineral and animal kingdoms and is based on the premise that these naturally occurring substances can cure disease symptoms similar to those they produce if taken in overdose. Each medicine is individually prescribed according to how it stimulates the immune and defence systems of the sick person. Sometimes it is called the "royal medicine."

## Hopi Ear Candles

Glands in the ear canal secrete a substance called Cerumen, which helps to cleanse the ear of debris. This collects as wax and tiny hairs in the ear remove it without our help or without us noticing. Earwax is important as it protects the ear from infection. Problems arise when there is a build-up of too much ear wax. Many people attempt to poke objects such as cotton buds into their ears in an attempt to clean them. This usually pushes the wax further down into the auditory canal where it can become compacted. In this hardened form it is unlikely to escape naturally & if left for a long period it may harden, causing blocked ears, earache, reduced/dull hearing, itching, ear & head noises. Often, pain from the pressure of wax on the sensitive lining of the ear canal, which becomes swollen, makes the blocking sensation worse. Many older people assume their hearing difficulties are age-related when, in fact, it is more commonly due to years of inadequate cleansing. Soap can enter the auditory canal and actually harden earwax. Having ones ears syringed is an unpleasant experience, which can lead to perforated eardrums. Hopi Ear Candles are named after the native American tribe who first introduced this gentle therapy to the West. The Hopi nation (translated Hopi means "peaceful ones") are renowned for their extensive knowledge of healing and their spiritual lifestyle. The Hopi candle is not a candle as such but a hollow tube made out of cotton flax. To stiffen the flax they are impregnated with herb oils whose healing properties have been known to the Hopi Tribe for hundreds of years. The treatment is very gentle and relaxing and takes 30-60 minutes depending on the condition being treated. The candle is placed over the ear orifice and ignited, it is only allowed to burn to within 4" of the end of the candle. As it burns it produces a gentle local heat. The warm air combined with the oil and herbs soften the wax and draws it into the base of the candle, the candle is then removed and the ear and surrounding area is then massaged, the treatment is repeated on the other side.

## Humanistic Psychology

Humanistic Psychology is a value orientation that holds a hopeful, constructive view of human beings and of their substantial capacity to be self-determining. It is guided by a conviction that intentionality and ethical values are strong psychological forces, among the basic determinants of human behaviour. This conviction leads to an effort to enhance such distinctly human qualities as choice, creativity, the interaction of the body, mind and spirit, the capacity to become more aware, free, responsible, life-affirming and trustworthy. Humanistic Psychology acknowledges that the mind is strongly influenced by determining forces in society and in the unconscious, and that some of these are negative and destructive. Humanistic Psychology nevertheless emphasizes the independent dignity and worth of human beings and their conscious capacity to develop personal competence and self respect. This value orientation has led to the development of therapies to facilitate personal and interpersonal skills and to enhance the quality of life. Since there is much difficulty involved in inner growth, humanistic psychologists often stress the importance of courageously learning to take responsibility for oneself as one confronts personal transitions. The difficulty of encouraging personal growth is matched by the difficulty of developing appropriate institutional and organizational environments in which human beings can flourish. Clearly, societies both help and hinder human growth. Because nourishing environments can make an important contribution to the development of healthy personalities, human needs should be given priority when fashioning social policies. This becomes increasingly critical in a rapidly changing world threatened by such dangers as nuclear war, overpopulation and the breakdown of traditional social structures. Many humanistic psychologists stress the importance of social change, the challenge of modifying old institutions and inventing new ones able to sustain both human development and organisational efficacy. Thus the humanistic emphasis on individual freedom should be matched by recognition of our interdependence and our responsibilities to one another, to society and culture, and to the future. All of these special concerns point toward the need for a more complete knowledge of the quality of human experience. Humanistic Psychology is best known as a body of theory and systems of Psychotherapy, but it is also an approach to scholarship and research, to inquiry informed by a strong sense of purpose. The purpose is to provide a level of understanding that can promote the power of personal choice and the care and effectiveness of social groups. Humanistic Psychology recognizes that human existence consists of multiple layers of reality: the physical, the organic and the symbolic. In considering these components it advocates the use of a variety of research approaches to study their characteristics and intentions. It contests the idea - traditionally held by the behavioural sciences - that the only legitimate research method is an experimental test using quantified data. It argues for the use of additional methods specifically designed to study the organic and symbolic realms. Humanistic psychology is strongly supportive of phenomenological and clinical approaches to the study of the human position in the order of life. It also encourages the discovery of new research approaches which seek to further understand the richness in the depth of human being. The symbolic dimension of consciousness is of special interest . It is in this realm of our lives - a uniquely human realm - that meaning value, culture, personal decision and responsibility are expressed and manifested. The humanities are thus important resources in humanistic psychology research. Another thing the humanistic approach brings into account is the fact that society's ideas about what counts as legitimate knowledge constitutes a certain kind of power over our lives. The assumption that knowledge is confined to what can be directly perceived and publicly measured leads easily to the conclusion that personal values, meaning and decision lack a larger significance or interpretation. The value-based position taken by Humanistic Psychology implies a commitment to the use of research approaches that provide access to all characteristics of human existence.

## Hydrotherapy

Hydrotherapy is the use of water, ice, steam and hot and cold temperatures to maintain and restore health. Treatments include full body immersion, stream baths, saunas, sitz baths, colonic irrigation and the application of hot, and/or cold compresses. Hydrotherapy is effective for treating a wide range of conditions and can easily be used in the home as part of a self-care program.

## Hypnosis

History has dutifully locked Hypnosis in a box whose label reads, "Danger - unlock hidden powers at your own risk; may contain mystical ideas and open your mind to the unknown; evil thoughts may try and possess you." Hidden powers - mystical and unknown, potentially evil (or socially unacceptable) thoughts - Hypnosis lets them out. Are you scared? Are you scared of your own thoughts, your own powers, and your own hidden inner potential? Hypnosis frees your mind and psyche from the inner critic, that part of you that mimics the people in your past who told you what to do and what you can and can't do. Actually, no one knows what the mind is truly capable of, other than it's a lot more than what has ever been proven. The mind resists being made to prove itself, but then miraculously demonstrates talents you didn't even know you had in unexpected ways and unsupervised moments - such as, knowing something before it happens or providing superhuman strength in emergencies. The trick is to set your mind free to do its stuff. That's what hypnosis, good Hypnosis, does. Hypnosis relaxes and/or distracts your conscious, critical mind, (the socially programmed mind), and allows your inner child out to play and experiment, or, if you'd rather, you can say, allows the inner psyche, with your personal psychic powers, to perform what it is capable of without that internal critic nagging away and draining your psychic juices. These wonderful Hypnosis meditations can let you begin a process of internal awareness, of self-realisation and discovery that can truly transform your world. This doesn't mean that you don't have to do anything. These hypnosis experiences do not take away your personal power, they give you power and strengthen the powers you already possess. You have to want to realize your dreams and be wiling to put forth active effort. You must learn to allow your inner psyche to produce the changes that will, sometimes, even seem to threaten the order of your pre-existing systems, the socially programmed ones with their fear and limitations written into your script.

Now, through the use of these recordings, positive things are about to happen within the scope of your own real-time limitations.

## Hypnotherapy

A therapy technique that uses hypnosis and self hypnosis to benefit patients

## Indian Head Massage

Indian Head Massage has been practised in India for over 1000 years and was originally used as a technique to keep long, thick hair in healthy condition. It only involved massage of the head and hair. However, the modern Indian Head Massage includes the upper back, shoulders, neck, upper arms, scalp and face. The neck and shoulders are where tension is particularly prone to accumulate and Indian Head Massage helps to eliminate muscle tension in these areas. Indian Head Massage works with a firm and gentle rhythm to help un-knot blockages and relieve the uncomfortable build-up of muscular tension. It relaxes the scalp and helps tone up the subcutaneous muscles, helping to relieve headaches and eyestrain. It also stimulates scalp circulation, which helps to strengthen and improve the texture of the hair. The massage to the face has a very soothing effect and increases lymphatic drainage, removing toxins from the facial area. Indian Head Massage can also help with sinus problems. Some allergies and hay fever can be considerably assisted and it has the added benefit of calming the emotions too, promoting relaxation and relieving stress. After a medical form has been completed and the creams and/or oils to be used have been chosen, you will be asked to remove your shirt or blouse and any jewellery. You will be given a towel to wrap around yourself, so that your upper back and shoulders are exposed. Then you will sit on a chair, and either lean forward into a pillow or stay sitting up, according to your choice. Your back, upper arms, neck and scalp are then massaged. Your therapist may ask you to lie on a couch for the facial part of the massage. The skin is massaged with either cream or oil depending upon the client's skin type and the scalp can be massaged using the skin's natural ability to produce it's own secretions, or, if desired, oil can be used. This can be beneficial to improve the texture of the hair and scalp and is nice to have done if the massage is being done towards the end of the day. Then the client can sleep overnight with the oil in the hair allowing it to seep in gently to maximise the conditioning effect. What are the contraindications or conditions that must not use this type of massage? Some types of Cancer, Epilepsy, Migraines, Thrombosis/Embolism, Advanced Heart Condition, Diabetes, Skin Disorders in some circumstances. There are other more minor conditions that may contraindicate. What we would do for most health conditions is send a letter to your doctor explaining that you would like an Indian Head Massage and ask his permission to proceed. An Indian Head Massage takes about 45 minutes.

## Inhalation Therapy

When steam rooms are scented with aromatic substances, it's called Inhalation Therapy. The most common is eucalyptus, but lemongrass and lavender are becoming popular choices. Sea air is simulated by using sea salts for thalassotherapy. Thalassotherapy is hydrotherapy using seawater-based products. At spas that specialise in this, you may find yourself immersed in actual filtered seawater in a tub or shower. Others offer seawater mineral salts dissolved in a whirlpool bath. "Inhalation Therapy" defined as an allied health specialty with medical direction in the treatment, management, control, diagnostic evaluation and care of patients with deficiencies and abnormalities with the cardiopulmonary system. Oxygen Therapy is a common Inhalation Technique.

## Iridology

Iridology (sometimes referred to as iris diagnosis) is based on the bizarre belief that each area of the body is represented by a corresponding area in the iris of the eye (the coloured area around the pupil). According to this viewpoint, a person's state of health and disease can be diagnosed from the colour, texture and location of various pigment flecks in the eye. Iridology practitioners claim to diagnose "imbalances" that can be treated with vitamins, minerals, herbs and similar products. Some also claim that the eye markings can reveal a complete history of past illnesses as well as previous treatment. One textbook, for example, states that a white triangle in the appropriate area indicates appendicitis, but a black speck indicates that the appendix had been removed by surgery. Iridology charts - dozens of which exist - vary somewhat in the location and interpretation of their iris signs. Sclerology is similar to iridology but interprets the shape and condition of blood vessels on the white portion (sclera) of the eyeball. Some iridologists use computers to help them analyse eye photographs and select the products they recommend

## Kinesiology

Kinesiology is a multidisciplinary science encompassing three primary areas of study. These areas are Biomechanics, Exercise Physiology, and Psychomotor Behaviour. Kinesiologists use these three primary sciences to study human movement. There are many different fields that Kinesiologists are employed in. Kinesiologists working in the rehabilitative field are concerned about (with) maximizing motor and perceptual abilities as well as the individual's total well-being. There are three different rehabilitative fields that Kinesiologists could be involved in. Kinesiologists working with individuals with cardiac problems would complete assessments on the efficiency of the cardiorespiratory system. Following their assessment they would develop a rehabilitation plan that would involve modifying lifestyle behaviours. Kinesiologists use various assessment techniques to allow detailed diagnoses of movement problems. The information derived from the assessment can then be used to develop appropriate rehabilitation programs. Kinesiologists working with special populations would assess and may re-educate or set up rehabilitative programs. The different populations that they may work with include: the developmentally delayed, physically disabled, brain damaged, elderly, emotionally disturbed or any other special problem. In the workplace there are many complex interactions between the worker, machine, and environment. In this setting, Kinesiologists are concerned with the assessment and the prescription of solutions to problems. Kinesiologists deal with such issues as man and machine interactions, matching skill level with job demands, employee fitness, fatigue, design of equipment, and health and safety. Kinesiology Ergonomists assess suitability of ergonomic design of workstations. They provide suggestions for modifications and assistive devices.

## Kirlian Photography

Named after Semyon Kirlian, an inventor and electrician from Krasnodar, Russia. This is a controversial technique for photographing objects in the presence of a high-frequency, high-voltage, low-amperage electrical field, the photographs of which show glowing, multicoloured emanations said to be auras or biofields. There is no evidence that Kirlian photography is a paranormal phenomenon. Some researchers say it reveals a physical form of psychic energy. Others believe that it reveals the etheric body, one of the layers of the aura believed to permeate all living things and that an understanding of this energy will lead to greater insights into medicine, psychology, psychic healing, PSI, and dowsing. Critics say the technique shows nothing more than a discharge of electricity, which can be produced under certain conditions. Kirlian used his own hand for his first experiment, and photographed a strange glow radiating from the fingertips. He and his wife, Valentina, a biologist, experimented with photographing both live and inanimate subjects. Their work was brought to the attention of the West in the 1960s and response in the scientific community was mixed. Kirlian photos are said to reveal health and emotion by changes in the brightness, colours, and patterns of the light. Experiments in the 1970s at the University of California showed changes in a plant's glow when approached by a human hand and pricked. When part of a leaf was cut off, a glowing outline of the amputated portion still appeared on film. Subsequent research found that the glow around humans similarly reflected changes in emotional state. Psychic healers and Uri Geller were photographed with hares of light streaming from their fingertips when engaged in their respective activities. Some Kirlian enthusiasts consider the phantom leaf phenomenon as evidence for the existence of an etheric body. However, critics say the phenomenon disproves Kirlian Photography altogether — if there really was a biofield, then the aura should disappear when an organism dies. Supporters nonetheless foresee applications of Kirlian Photography in diagnostic medicine.

## Laser Treatment

Laser (very focused and high intensity light waves) treatment is used in treating poor eyesight, removing hair and also repairing scars.

## Light Therapy

Light Therapy techniques range from the most simple and traditional ("Get outside and get some sunshine and fresh air", your grandmother told you) to the most high-tech and sophisticated forms of light-assisted psychotherapy (which was developed in California, of course). These therapies may be categorised by the form of light used, from simple to sophisticated: Bright Light, Coloured Light, flickering Light, Coloured Flickering Light, Polarised Light. Bright Light Therapy: The importance of light for health and vitality was perhaps more obvious in ancient times than it is today. People living close to nature have an immediate appreciation of the sun, perhaps even worship it religiously, in a way that is lost when one is insulated from nature by many layers of technology. Even a hundred years ago the medical value of sunlight was still well appreciated. Wounds were known to heal more quickly and with less scarring when sunlight was used as a disinfectant. Tuberculosis clinics flourished in the high mountains of Switzerland. Rickets responded to sunlight. But sitting around in the sunlight takes time and seems boring in today's busy world, so the discovery of antibiotics in the middle of this century pushed aside most of these slow but natural cures. Taking a pill is sometimes cheaper and more convenient than staying at a sanatorium. The modern rediscovery of Light Therapy occurred in a more psychological context. Season Affective Disorder (SAD), also known as winter depression, was identified as a light deficiency problem which could be corrected with exposure to bright light, especially on awakening in the morning. Of all the forms of Light Therapy, bright light treatment for SAD is by far the most thoroughly researched and the most accepted by mainstream medicine. Scientific journal articles on SAD number in the hundreds by now . Several companies on both sides of the Atlantic manufacture "light boxes", sources of bright artificial light for SAD sufferers to sit by during breakfast. There is even a battery-operated light "visor", worn on the head, to shine light directly into the eyes while allowing the wearer to move about. The ultimate high-tech natural treatment is a light "alarm clock", a dawn simulator, which turns on a gradually brightening light source, starting an hour or two before rising time and reaching its maximum when the (indoor) sun rises and it's time to get up! Once the day is started, there is still the problem of inadequate and artificial indoor lighting in the workplace or schoolroom. Conventional fluorescent lamps emit light which is deficient in many of the colours and wavelengths of natural sunlight. Numerous studies have shown the benefits of replacing these lamps with full-spectrum fluorescents, more closely imitating sunlight. Workplace health statistics improve, school performance improves, even dental caries in school children was shown to decrease under full-spectrum lights. These were large studies with large control groups for comparisons. These results are not really too surprising. Humans evolved outdoors, in sunlight. When light enters the eyes and strikes the retina, the resultant nerve signals pass not only to the visual cortex of the brain, so we can see objects, but also, over separate nerve pathways, to other brain structures including the hypothalamus, the pineal and pituitary systems, and the limbic system, causing hormonal and emotional effects. Visual perception is not the only function of the eyes; they are also the openings through which light, almost like a nutrient, reaches the brain. Coloured Light Therapy: This "nutrient" view of light naturally leads one to consider the effects of different colours of light, selections from the rainbow spectrum of white light. At one sales table at the LIGHT'98 conference visitors could try wearing spectacles of different colours (not just rose coloured specs) and experience the depressive calm of blue-violet specs and the stimulation of yellow ones. A large study in schools in Alberta, Canada, conducted over a whole school year, compared pupils in classrooms with conventional fluorescent lights and dull coloured walls against pupils in classrooms with full-spectrum lighting and walls painted with warm colours. Both changes separately showed significant improvements in academic performance and discipline and decreases in absenteeism due to illness, and the combination of changes was even more effective. There is also an entire school of optometrists who use coloured light to treat patients. In the 1920's and 1930's Dr. Harry Spitler developed a system known as Syntonic Optometry which uses coloured light, shone into the patients eyes, to treat a variety of physiological and emotional disorders, far beyond the traditional bounds of optometry. The light is shone into the patients' eyes from a special light source equipped with a variety of coloured filters. The underlying principle of this therapy is to balance the activities of the sympathetic and parasympathetic nervous systems using colours that are either stimulating or calming. Practitioners can be found in many countries, though the treatment is most widespread in the US. Flickering Light Therapy: If bright light and coloured light can have such an effect on the brain, mind, and body, it is to be expected that flickering light would have even more effect. Flickering light certainly grabs one's attention; neurologically speaking, neurons tend to report only changing stimuli, quickly tiring of anything steady. So flickering light might be considered to be a more aggressive form of Light Therapy, for more severe conditions. A small but growing body of research studies documents the benefits of this form of Light Therapy, technically known as photic stimulation. Flickering light is shone into the eyes either from a mask or goggles worn by the patient or by having the patient sit in front of a larger flickering light source one or two feet away. Typically the treatment is applied for 15 or 20 minutes per day. In a hospital trial in London, flickering light therapy proved more effective than any previously published treatment for premenstrual syndrome (PMS), and two separate published studies in the US have shown significant improvement in children with learning disorders such as attention deficit disorder. Several other studies have shown good results in the reduction of chronic pain, including the pain of TMJ, and a photic stimulation device is currently being marketed to dentists' offices for this purpose. The neurological basis for this form of light therapy is suggested by studies by Dr. Norman Shealy in Missouri, who found increases in the levels of various hormones and neurochemicals after patients had been treated for 20 minutes with flickering light . Coloured Flickering Light Therapy: Some of the most impressive and moving reports at the LIGHT'98 conference involved the use of coloured flickering light as a catalyst in the process of psychotherapy. Here the more subtle emotional effect of different colours is combined with the penetrating effect of flickering light to accelerate the therapeutic process of uncovering and bringing out deeply buried emotional material for processing and relief. Clearly this procedure is highly dependent on the skill of the therapist; the selection of light colour and flash frequency is an interactive process, involving a high level of awareness and even intuition on the part of the therapist . A live demonstration of this technique with a volunteer subject was one of the more astounding moments of the conference. Light Therapy not involving the Eyes: Some forms of Light Therapy involve shining light on parts of the body other than the eyes. The use of blue light as a treatment for neo-natal jaundice is a well-established medical procedure. A recent study reported that merely shining light on the backs of subjects' knees was sufficient to alter the timing of the internal circadian body clock; this suggests that the effects of bright light on SAD, described above, may not be entirely mediated through the eyes. At the LIGHT'98 conference several practitioners reported on body work with laser light or coloured light applied to acupuncture points in a modern-day version of traditional Chinese medicine. Another particularly impressive presentation reported on work done in Russia, over many years with thousands of patients, using a technique known as blood photo-modification in which blood is drawn from the patient, circulated though a glass tube where it is irradiated with laser light, and then returned directly to the patient; astounding results were reported with a wide range of diseases. Although it is a dramatic example of the use of light, the photodynamic therapy treatment for cancer is not discussed in this article, since it is really an improved form of chemotherapy, rather than actual Light Therapy.

## Macrobiotics

Macrobiotics is the art and science of health and longevity through the study and understanding of the relation and interactions between ourselves, the foods we eat, the lifestyles we choose to lead, and the environments in which we live. The Macrobiotic approach is based on the view that we are the result of and are continually influenced by our total environment, which ranges from the foods we eat and our daily social interactions to the climate and geography in which we live. In considering all factors that influence our lives, the Macrobiotic approach to health and healing views sickness as the natural attempt of the body to return to a more harmonious and dynamic state with the natural environment. As what we choose to eat and drink and how we live our lives are primary environmental factors that influence our health and create who we are, the macrobiotic approach emphasizes the importance of proper dietary and lifestyle habits. The macrobiotic approach is based on principles, theories and practices that have been known to philosophers, scholars and physicians throughout history. The term "Macrobiotics" comes from Greek ("macro" meaning "large" or "long", and "bios" meaning "life") and was first coined by Hippocrates, the father of western medicine. Its most recent development stems from Michio Kushi who was inspired by philosopher-writer Georges Ohsawa. George Ohsawa published numerous works in Japanese, English and French, which combined the western traditions of Macrobiotics with 5,000 years of traditional oriental medicine. By using macrobiotic principles to address and adjust environmental, dietary and lifestyle influences, thousands of individuals have been able to prolong their lives by recovering from a wide range of illnesses including heart disease, cancer, diabetes and many others (view some of these recovery testimonials on our library pages). The macrobiotic approach to health recovery can be used along with conventional and alternative medical treatment and intervention and is compatible with and adaptable to all forms of religious and traditional cultural practices. Some traditional and basic macrobiotic practices include eating more whole grains, beans and fresh vegetables, increasing variety in food selections and traditional cooking methods, eating regularly and less in quantity, chewing more and maintaining an active and positive life and mental outlook. General dietary and lifestyle guidelines for persons living in a temperate, four seasons climate have been established by Michio Kushi. These guidelines outline basic dietary proportions along with healthier lifestyle habits and are not intended to define a specific regimen that one must follow, as additional adjustments are required for individual application which will vary according to personal situations. If you are seeking specific advice we recommend that you visit the Kushi Institute and meet with a Macrobiotic Counsellor. The Kushi Institute's week-long training program "The Way to Health" is also recommended, as it gives you the skills and knowledge to put your counsellor's advice into practice correctly.

## Magnetic Therapy

The use of magnets as therapeutic devices is not new. Magnetic Therapy has been practiced for thousands of years and was mentioned in ancient writings from many cultures. It has become an alternative treatment method for many medical conditions. Magnetic Therapy is well advanced in Japan, China, India, Australia and Germany. There is growing interest from other countries including Great Britain, Holland, Canada and the United States. The World Health Organization published a study in 1987 that essentially laid to rest the notion that magnets in the strengths commonly used for therapeutic uses have any detrimental effect on the human body. Magnetic Therapy is based on the biological effects of magnetic fields on the living organism. When magnetic fields are properly applied (polarity, intensity and frequency) there is a reaction that is utilized in the treatment of illness, the alleviation of pain and the general promotion of well being. A magnetic field penetrates every single cell being exposed to the field. This in turn influences the ions within the cell to enhance ion exchange that will improve the oxygen utilization of the cell. This is important for the healing and regeneration process.

## Manual Lymph Drainage

Manual Lymph Drainage (MLD): a very light and gentle manual treatment technique to improve the activity of intact lymph vessels, to assist in moving fluid around areas of obstruction, and stimulate the immune system. MLD was specifically developed to help the body transport water substances from loose connective tissue via the lymph system. The technique is highly specialized and requires extensive training: it does not resemble "massage" beyond the placing of the therapist's hands on the client's body. Manual Lymph Drainage or Complex Decongestive therapy is the treatment of choice for oedema problems. Therapists who perform this technique require over many many hours of training to learn special light stroking and pumping techniques that encourage reabsorption or removal of fluids from the swollen tissues. A complete understanding of the physiology of the lymphatic vessels enables the therapist to assist the body in forming new lymph pathways to replace damaged or absent ones. The treatment includes a combination of Manual Lymph Drainage, complex bandaging, exercise and skin care, and encourages the patient to manage care at home. The results of treatment with Manual Lymph Drainage is a decrease in swelling, reduction of pain, reduction of scar tissue and a calming effect on the autonomic nervous system. There are many other pathologies that respond to this specialised form of massage. Among them are acne, various forms of arthritis, pelvic disorders such as endometriosis, arterial and venous ulcerations, stroke, spinal and various other orthopaedic injuries as well as post surgical oedemas.

## Massage

Massage stimulates the lymphatic system facilitating the removal of stored toxins, which contribute to aching muscles. Therapists offer a variety of expert techniques, from which is designed the ideal combination to give the best type of massage: Therapeutic and Remedial Massage can give relief to tension, spasm and to ease aching backs etc after exertion. It can also alleviate the pain of muscle injuries and accelerate their healing. Relaxing Massage can reduce tension & relieve negative effects of everyday stress giving a totally relaxed feeling of well being. Stimulating Massage can restore the body's natural energy levels.

## Massage (Therapeutic)

Therapeutic Massage is one of the oldest treatments used by mankind. Records show the ancient Chinese, Hindus, Egyptians, Greeks and Romans used this hands-on therapy to soothe aches and pains. Today, people of all ages are enjoying the health benefits of massage. New research is linking the human touch to improved immune functioning. Healing through touch, or the laying on of hands which has its origins in ancient times. It is mentioned in the Bible. Therapeutic Healing Massage: - is a combination of therapeutic massage, hands-on healing and positional release. Positional release is a technique of working with sore muscles by passively applying a stretch to relieve the strain. It helps find relief from neck, shoulder, back pain and chronic ailments. Increases feelings of well-being. Relaxes tight, sore muscles. Helps in circulation of blood and lymph. Reduces stress and anxiety. Relieves muscular back pain. Helps in general relaxation. Helps improve immune system functioning. In addition, restores energy flow, resulting in increased energy and vitality.

## McTimoney Chiropractic

Daniel D. Palmer introduced the term 'chiropractic' to mean adjustments of the bones made by the hands alone, from the Greek words 'kheir' meaning 'hand' and 'praktikos' meaning 'done by'. He founded the first school of chiropractic, Palmer College in Iowa, and was succeeded by his son B. J. Palmer. It was one of his early students, Dr. Mary Walker DC, who taught chiropractic to John McTimoney in the 1950s. McTimoney was to further develop the techniques he was taught and extended their use to animals. The swiftness of the adjustments he devised requires great sensitivity and skill, and once mastered the McTimoney method has proved to be extremely effective. Chiropractic is a drugless and non-surgical form of therapy, and with the McTimoney gentle approach and reliance on the hand, it has not deviated from the original ideals of chiropractic. Because of these unique qualities, the 'John McTimoney method' is distinguished from other manipulative methods. McTimoney chiropractic is holistic - concerned with the welfare of the whole body. This emphasis on causes rather than symptoms has growing public appeal. At the same time the medical profession increasingly recognises chiropractic as an effective therapeutic technique. Such widespread acceptance is marked by the Chiropractors Act 1994 with a view to regulating professional standards and educational institutions for all chiropractors in the UK. Currently McTimoney practitioners represent over a third of the entire UK chiropractic profession. The nervous system is responsible for all body functions. The correct alignment of vertebrae in the spinal column is vital to maintain nerve pathways. Misalignments, in the body can occur at any time. They may be related to accidents, sporting activities, household tasks, emotional and physical stress, even a bad mattress. Some causes are so subtle that changes can occur without the patient's knowledge as symptoms can take years to arise.

Chiropractors believe that much ill health in adult life may be related to accidents in childhood. When subluxations occur, a person can experience pain - of any description, of any duration, anywhere down the course of the nerve. This may lead to malfunction in either the muscles or internal organs. For example, tingling fingers can often be caused by subluxation of the neck vertebrae. The McTimoney chiropractor will examine by hand (palpate) the bones and joints of the body to check for imbalance, however slight. Any problems found are corrected with various adjustments which are effective and safe. The bones are never forced into place, but by adjusting with a very rapid thrust and immediate release, the bone 'toggles' towards its correct position. By easing muscle tension and using the natural elasticity of tendons attached to the bone, the treatment is relatively gentle and comfortable to receive. Anyone from babies to the elderly can benefit. If areas of the body are out of balance, they can affect the whole; therefore the entire body is assessed at each treatment. McTimoney chiropractic aims to restore nerve function in order to promote natural health. This involves re-educating the patient's muscles and bones into a better alignment. It is also a preventive therapy and can greatly improve overall health and well-being. Regular check ups are recommended to ensure that the body maintains a healthy balance. Special care after falls etc. can prevent disease from arising. John McTimoney was a pioneer in developing his method for the treatment of animals. This was a major breakthrough, bringing understanding of the causes of animal 'disease', difficult behaviour and poor performance. Those practitioners who treat animals have undergone a thorough training to qualify for this specialised branch of the profession. For more than 30 years, McTimoney animal chiropractors have been helping horses, dogs, cats and farm animals - the range of animals treated has even widened to include some 'exotic' species. Again, the whole body is assessed and treated to eliminate the cause, not just to deal with the symptoms. Treatment requires the approval of the owner's veterinary surgeon and a growing number of vets now refer cases to a McTimoney animal chiropractor.

## Meditation

The word "meditation" conjures up the picture of a bearded man sitting cross-legged in front of an entrance to a cave or high on a mountain top. Climbing the mountain and reaching him is part of the arduous journey toward self-fulfilment, self-improvement. Once we find him we ask, "What is the meaning of life?" or "How do we achieve peace in ourselves and our lives?" This all-knowing man tells us the answers are "inside ourselves" and tells us to go and contemplate. It would be best to call meditation relaxation – conscious relaxation, chosen relaxation. These are words that are more universally understood, more comfortable. Meditating is actually easier than you might imagine. Most of us have dabbled in meditation by participating in conscious relaxation. Maybe during an exercise class or to manage pain at the dentist or anxiety before a test. We start by paying attention to our breathing. The practical effort to focus completely on our breathing takes our minds away from the "mind clutter" that constantly tries to invade our mind and eliminate feelings that will lead to a time of calm. With repeated effort the goal of clearing your mind – to think of nothing, does occur and the process of meditation takes on its own energy. The result is peace, serenity, calmness, eventually opening yourself to new insights. "Too much stress, stress reduction, chill out, let it go, detach" – familiar phrases to all of us. Our world is fast, fun and exciting. It is also challenging, trying, demanding and frightening. These two sides of our lives produce stress, emotional reactions, anxiety, worry and anticipation. Our bodies and minds can tolerate only so much of any of these. After a while, each of us reaches a saturation point and the results become uncomfortable at best; for some it may be unbearable, even unendurable. No magic pill is available to eliminate these feelings. The reality is, as the wise old man said, the answer is inside all of us. To manage these universal concerns we must go inside ourselves. Among the steps we can take is the learning and practicing of meditation. With time and faith in the commitment to practice frequently, (daily meditating is ideal), during your meditation time you may "leave the moment." A feeling of separation exists where the mind is clear, clean and blank. You will still hear sounds around you, but they will not interfere with your meditation. Sometimes you may weep — you may not even be aware of what is making you weep. It is your own emotions having a voice of their own. Sometimes you may feel a smile across your face :-) that is contentment showing itself. Sometimes you may fall asleep and awaken truly refreshed. There is no right or wrong behaviour during your meditation. It is your time for you. Everyone deserves this kind of personal attention. This is a self-care activity; loving oneself! Teach it to your children instead of a time-out in their room or corner. Teach it to your friends, family, anyone who will listen. We can share this gift and get back as we give. We are all better because of each person who meditates. The peace and joy felt by those who meditate enters the world for all of us as positive energy. From it the world is a better place. Imagine if we all practiced meditation! Chi Kung is an ancient Chinese exercise system of energy work using breath, movement, and meditation for building health and vitality. Chi or Qi means vital energy; Gong or Kung means to work with or to train. Thus Qi Gong means to work with one's Qi. Qi Gong is used as a therapy for the treatment of chronic diseases, to produce anaesthesia and may help to cure cancer alone or in conjunction with chemotherapy. Qi Gong is performed everyday by millions of Chinese who want to stay healthy and prevent illness or simply because they enjoy it. Qi Gong is used in martial arts and other sports to strengthen muscles, increase endurance and to heighten one's awareness.

## Metamorphic Therapy

The Metamorphic Technique is a simple approach to self healing and creativity within the individual. The practitioner uses a light touch to focus attention on the spinal reflex in the feet, hands and head, which was found to correspond to the time before birth. It was during that period that we established the basis of the characteristics on which we live our life now. The word "technique" is defined as a way of approaching a task that perfects itself in the doing. As a catalyst the practitioner must remain detached from achieving particular results. In this context it is up to the life force of the people receiving sessions to release their creative potential, transforming their inner patterns under the guidance of their innate intelligence. The Technique is easily learned and is ideal for use within the family or in institutions, since no specific environment is needed. After sessions people often notice immediate physical or emotional change, or changes in their situation, reflecting perhaps the inner transformation of some life patterns. This can take place at a subtle level so that it is hardly noticed by the conscious mind but those around them will pick up the differences. No special healing skill is needed to perform the Metamorphic Technique other than an attitude of detachment and of allowing complete freedom to the person to transform in whatever way is right for them. The Metamorphic Technique does not involve the treatment of symptoms but provides an environment in which a movement out of old patterns occurs, at both the physical and psychological levels. As people get a deeper insight into themselves, so the need for the symptoms can disappear. Consequently the Technique may be received by itself, or in conjunction with other approaches such as orthodox or complementary medicine, although it is not part of them. The Metamorphic Technique is easy for people to use regularly, being simple to apply and pleasant to experience.

## Miasm Therapy

Homeopaths regard the patient's symptom profile as a systemic manifestation of an underlying chronic disorder called a miasm. Miasms are serious disturbances of what homeopaths call the patient's vital force that are inherited from parents at the time of conception. German doctor Samuel Hahnemann, who developed homeopathy in the late 18th century, believed that the parents' basic lifestyle, their emotional condition and habitual diet, and even the atmospheric conditions at the time of conception would affect the number and severity of Miasms passed on to the child. Hahnemann himself distinguished three miasms: the psoric, which he considered the most universal source of chronic disease in humans; the syphilitic; and the sycotic, which he attributed to gonorrhoea . Later homeopaths identified two additional Miasms, the cancernic and the tuberculinic. The remaining major source of miasms is allopathic medicine. It is thought that specific allopathic treatments? particularly smallpox vaccinations , cortisone preparations, major tranquillisers, and antibiotics? can produce additional layers of miasms in the patient's constitution. Constitutional prescribing evaluates the person's current state or miasmic picture, and selects a remedy intended to correct or balance that state. The homeopath may prescribe a different remedy for each Miasmic layer over time, but gives only one remedy at a time directed at the person's current state. The basic principle governing the prescription of each successive remedy is the law of similars, or "like cures like".

## Moxibustion

Counter irritation produced by placing on the skin and igniting a cone or cylinder of moxa, a tuft of soft combustible substance popularly used in the Orient as a cautery and counterirritant. Moxibustion treats and prevents diseases by applying heat to points or certain locations of the human body. The material used is mainly " moxa - wool " in the form of a cone or stick. For centuries, moxibustion and acupuncture have been used in clinical practice, thus they are usually termed together in Chinese. Moxibustion is generally applied to the yang portion first, then the yin portion; clinically it is applied to the upper part first and then the lower part. Treat the back first, the abdominal region second; the head and body first and the four extremities second. But the sequence should be given according to the pathological conditions. The volume for moxibustion, including the size of moxa cone or duration of the moxa stick application should be in parallel to the patients' pathological conditions, general constitution, age and the site where moxibustion is to be applied. Generally, three to seven moxa cones are used for each point, and ten to fifteen minutes for the application of moxa stick.

## Mud Therapy

Next time you see a child lolling in the mud, think twice before chastising the infant, iInstead, join in the fun. Mud, claim naturopaths, has the potential to improve blood circulation and removes unwanted heat from the body. Mud, when applied properly on the body, has a soothning effect, say the naturopaths while claiming that "mud therapy" is even beneficial in the treatment of a number of skin diseases including eczema. Mud is defined as "hyper thermal" or "hypothermalised mud", deriving from mixing of a solid component (organic and/or inorganic clay) with mineral water (salso-bromo-iodic). Mud consists of 53% clay, 36% minerals, 7% organic substances and 4% water. Mineral water as well as temperature & chemical components influence the development of the maturing process of typical micro flora. Depending upon the local effects it has wide range in alternative medicine. Depending on the case it can be applied as partial body wrapping, partial bath and full bath. The Local effects of Mud Therapy are: 1). Increase pulse rate, 2). Increase body temperature, 3). Improve vascularisation, 4). Stimulate metabolic exchange in cartilage, 5). Local anti-inflammatory, 6). Resolvent, 7). Analgesic, 8). Muscle relaxing and smoothing, 9). Revitalising action, 10). Stimulate bone cell activity in the joints, 11). Cell trophism, 12). Production of synovial fluid, 13). Improve reactivity of body itself against disease-causing agents. Mud treatments bring relieve to arthrosis, spondylitis, psoriatic arthritis, dysmetabolic rheumatism, periarthritis, tendonitis, tendonitis, bursitis, fibrositis, some post-traumatic muscular hypotonia, hypo trophy and muscular rigidity. Mineral-enriched mud helps people who are suffering from psoriasis, eczema, acne and variety of other skin ailments.

## Music Therapy

Music therapy is the prescribed use of music by a qualified person to effect positive changes in the psychological, physical, cognitive, or social functioning of individuals with health or educational problems. Music therapists assess emotional well-being, physical health, social functioning, communication abilities, and cognitive skills through musical responses; design music sessions for individuals and groups based on client needs using music improvisation, receptive music listening, song writing, lyric discussion, music and imagery, music performance, and learning through music; participate in interdisciplinary treatment planning, ongoing evaluation, and follow up. Those who benefit include:- children, adolescents, adults, and the elderly with mental health needs, developmental and learning disabilities, Alzheimer's disease and other aging related conditions, substance abuse problems, brain injuries, physical disabilities, and acute and chronic pain, including mothers in labour. Music therapists working psychiatric hospitals, rehabilitative facilities, medical hospitals, outpatient clinics, day care treatment centres, agencies serving developmentally disabled persons, community mental health centres, drug and alcohol programs, senior centres, nursing homes, hospice programs, correctional facilities, halfway houses, schools, and private practice. Music therapy allows persons with mental health needs to: explore personal feelings, make positive changes in mood and emotional states, have a sense of control over life through successful experiences, practice problem solving, and resolve conflicts leading to stronger family and peer relationships

## Naturopathy

Naturopathic medicine is an alternative to conventional medicine based on the idea that with the help of special diets, herbs, and other natural supplements the body will heal itself. Overall, it is a less intrusive approach to healing than conventional medicine, which relies largely on drugs that treat symptoms, but not root causes. Naturopathy is very popular all over the world, including Europe, where herbal medicine is the medicine of first choice for close to half of German physicians and close to 25% of the prescriptions written in France are homeopathic. There is also the safety factor to consider. There isn't a single documented case of anyone dying of an herb, vitamin, or homeopathic product in the last ten years. Naturopathic Medicine is the field of health care which works with the body's own efforts to allow optimum expression of physiological, mental/emotional, and physical health, given the individual's genetic make up and environment. Naturopathy is an approach to health care that promotes and maintains health. It recognises that there are laws governing human function and our natural environment; Every living thing has vitality, this is known as the principle of vitalism. There is a healing power in nature. The body heals itself because of its innate vitality. A medicine given to a dead body will produce no effects; thus medicines act only to stimulate the innate healing power of the body. There is an invariable connection between the structural, biochemical and mental/emotional elements of all living beings. This is known as the triad of health. There is an interaction of the whole person; dysfunction in one part of the body inevitably leads to dysfunction elsewhere, just as dysfunction in one part of the Naturopathic triad means all parts of the triad will be affected. People are genetically, bio chemically, structurally and emotionally different from one another: they are individuals. We interact with our environment; health is a reflection of a harmonious interaction. There is an important difference between acute and chronic disease. Acute diseases are the result of the expression of the body's homoeostatic mechanisms attempting to re-establish balance. For example a high fever is produced to combat infection in order to aid the immunological defence mechanisms. All disease starts with a disruption to the body's homoeostatic mechanisms; health is a return to balance of these mechanisms. Health is more than the absence of disease; health is when all aspects of an individual's biochemical, mental/emotional and physical being are in balance.

The human body has adapted to its environment over millions of years, it has come to expect certain foods for its fuel, clean water, a certain amount of fresh air and sunlight, and a certain amount of exercise and rest/relaxation. Naturopathic medicine is the application of these laws in a clinical setting to maintain, improve or establish health in patients. It is therefore not a technique but an approach to health care. The defining elements of Naturopathy are: That it always seeks to work with the body's own self-correcting mechanisms, or efforts to maintain homoeostasis. That it always attempts to address all three aspects of the naturopathic triad. That it regards education of the patient as highly as treatment of the patient. That it always seeks to address lifestyle factors that are contributing to the problem and re-educate the patient into a lifestyle more conducive to health.

## Neuro-Linguistic Program

Neuro-linguistic programming (NLP) is the study of how people think and experience life. The goal of NLP is to aid in problem solving. NLP tries to help people solve problems by looking at how the person defines a problem. NLP takes into account a person's beliefs, attitudes, and strategies used in decision making. It also looks at how a person will respond to situations and problems. By looking at these aspects of human behaviour, practitioners of NLP can help a person figure out new ways to approach problems, in order to solve them. An NLP practitioner works with people to study the structure of their personal experience. NLP makes these basic assumptions: The mind and the body are part of the same system. Every behaviour has a positive intention. All behaviour is useful in some context. All the resources we need are available in our own psychology. Human interaction is always systematic. The meaning of one person's communication to another is reflected in the response of the other person. There is no failure, only feedback. "If it is possible for someone, it is possible for me." "I am responsible for creating my own experience, and I am responsible for what happens to me.NLP has studied people who do things well and developed concepts by looking at: the structure and processes they used to achieve a given task their beliefs and attitudes, their use of resources and how they handled difficulties. NLP then built a model to help people think through the way they do things. The model also helps people apply new solutions to problems they may have. NLP assumes that if one person can do something well, then others can also be taught to do something well. NLP seems to work well for people who suffer from phobias or fears. By studying people who do not have a certain fear, the person with a phobia can learn from them. The person's responses, beliefs, and values can be changed to reduce or remove the impact of the phobia. A variety of models are used to help people adjust to situations. These models help people examine what they do now and what they might do differently. The following 5 senses are closely examined visual, or sight , auditory, which processes sound kinesthetic, responsible for touch and feelings, gustatory, or taste, olfactory, or smell. NLP considers the whole sensory experience to help the person make changes. The more real the memory or the representation, the greater the person's ability to understand and change. Practitioners use a variety of models that help them assist others in making changes. These models help the practitioner ask the right questions. They also help practitioners gauge physical feedback to a stimulus or experience. People are guided through experiences without interfering with their memory or process. A number of different models can be used. Some use talking or hypnotherapy, and some are assisted with computer programs. NLP techniques have been used as therapy, as a self-help program, as a method to improve learning, athletics, or sales techniques, as a way of questioning to recognize and improve communication and problem solving. NLP continues to be developed and aligned with other fields. In NLP, the workings of the brain are studied in order to see what can be learned. The goal of NLP is to imitate human excellence in order to improve behaviour.

## Neurotherapy

Neurotherapy, also called EEG biofeedback or neurofeedback, is a form of alternative medicine that can help to cure a wide range of psychological disorders, but also help a person improve their quality of life regardless of whether they have a psychological problem or not. It can also be used as a starting point to treat many other physiological problems. The theory of neurotherapy works on the premise that the brain has four main frequencies, delta, theta, alpha and beta. If a brain is emitting the delta frequency this signifies a state of deep sleep. Theta frequency brain waves suggest that a person is highly relaxed, perhaps daydreaming. Alpha waves show that an individual is generally relaxed, whilst beta waves mean that the patient is in a state of over arousal. High-tech perceptive equipment is used to monitor patients' brainwaves, and the good thing concerning this analysis is that it is comprehensively non-intrusive – one hardly knows it is taking place. If the equipment shows that the brainwaves tend to be lower than normal, it suggests that the patient may be depressed, or lethargic. If the reading is higher than normal, the patient may be anxious and unable to unwind. Once the brain patterns of the individual have been established, it is up to the therapist to make the patient more aware of when a particular brain wave is occurring, and also train the person to regulate brain frequency themselves.

By doing this, the affected person eventually doesn't need the help of the therapist, having gained the ability to assess and self-mediate. One ingenious system has been developed to help the patient learn this practice. They learn how to play a video game, in which the character can only be moved by the correct brain frequency (the patient is wired up in such a way so the video game can detect a change in their brain frequency). After several sessions with the video game, the patient will have developed the ability to recognise and alter particular brain waves. The analysis in neurotherapy also extends further than monitoring merely brainwaves. Many therapists test for such things as enzymes, hormones and nerve reflexes. Once this biofeedback has been analysed, action can be taken, usually in the form of pressure on the nerve channels of an affected part of the body. This in turn causes the body to react by producing the necessary biochemical to fight the affliction. It is seen as a far better way of solving the problem than a prescription drug, which would ease the symptoms, but not necessarily get to the cause of the problem. Neurotherapy is an excellent form of alternative medicine. Although mainly used to treat patients with such problems as epilepsy, depression and post-traumatic stress disorder, it can be used by healthy people to better understand the psycho-physiological workings of the brain. The technique of biofeedback can also be used to monitor other parts of the body and then take appropriate action to remedy a wide range of physiological complaints

## Nutritional Therapy

Nutritional therapy is a system of healing based on the belief that food, as nature intended, provides the medicine we need to obtain and maintain a state of health: our food is our medicine and our medicine is our food. Although some health problems require specific medication, many conditions can be relieved effectively with nutritional therapy. These include disorders ranging from chronic fatigue, energy loss, insomnia and depression, to backache, skin complaints, asthma, and headaches. Nutritional therapy will also benefit you if you have no specific illness, but want to maintain a state of optimum health. It is safe for babies and children as well as adults, and the change of eating patterns that is typically prescribed usually has far fewer side effects than synthetic medicines. Nutritional therapy is a holistic discipline; nutrition as the key to good health is the all-embracing fundamental principle used since the time of the famous Greek doctor and founder of western medicine, Hippocrates, to help people of all ages to stay at their personal peak of energy and vitality. Today, new insights of food scientists play a significant role in the practice of nutritional therapy as preventative medicine. During the last fifty years, many wonderful breakthroughs have improved our understanding of the role of food in our lives. But at the same time, many of us are realizing that food is the cornerstone which, in our modern lifestyle, has been rejected by the builder. The speed at which we live and work — the pressure of the deadline — pushes us into a fast-eating culture, where quality of food becomes secondary. Eating on the job, on the run, under pressure, denies us the experience, the purpose, and the role of food. Eventually it denies us our very lifestyle. Modern supermarkets are stocked with many instant meals, but more often than not, these meals are far lower in nutritional value than those prepared at home with fresh organically grown ingredients. For all the benefits agribusiness has brought the people of the Western world, the disadvantages of the modern food industry include extensive use of chemicals in food production. There is also a loss of the vitality intrinsic in newly harvested food because many products are transported vast distances before they reach their destination. Of course, this is the case with many of the so-called "fresh" foods on our supermarket shelves, as well as with those dishes that have been pre-cooked and packaged before reaching the supermarkets. Lifestyle and nutrition are intimately linked, and our lifestyle defines itself partly from the tradition of the country we live in, and partly from our attitudes. How do you really want to live? Given the choice, would you prefer to eat well every day, to exercise, to breathe clean air as often as possible, to drink a reasonable amount of water in order to keep your bloodstream clean and able to wash out toxins? This choice is available to all of us, but to exercise it we need to understand the impact on our well-being of different foods and learn from direct experience what kind of eating pattern best suits our lifestyle.

## Orgone Therapy (Reichian Therapy)

Medical Orgone therapy is a unique approach to treating emotional and physical illness by reducing or eliminating those barriers that block the natural expressions of emotion and healthy sexual feeling. This method of treatment was developed by Austrian psychiatrist and scientist Wilhelm Reich, M.D. (1897-1957). After years of clinical and experimental laboratory research, Reich concluded that emotions, sexual feelings, and all life processes are expressions of a biological energy in the body. He further concluded that this life energy is related to bioelectricity but is fundamentally different. He called this energy "Orgone energy". Reich theorized that Orgone energy fills the universe and pulsates in all living things. He believed that deep, genuine love and the ability to experience a gratifying orgasm mutually with one's partner are the fullest and deepest expressions of our being and are central to maintaining optimal health. Reich contended that in almost all individuals, the flow and release of Orgone energy are blocked by chronic muscle contractions in various areas of the body and by emotional attitudes adopted early in life. The "nice little girl" who never gets angry, and the "strong, brave boy" who never shows fear and sadness are but two examples of such attitudes that prevent the full and rational expressions of natural emotions. Blocked emotions interfere with pleasure in the life and cause sexual feelings to become disconnected from tender emotions of love. Without emotional release, anxiety develops, which further increases physical and emotional contraction. This cycle results in a range of problems such as feelings of emptiness, depression, irrational fears, and self-destructive behaviour. Medical Orgone therapy employs direct work on the body, especially on spastic muscles, with verbal therapy to bring about a healthy state accompanied by satisfaction in one's work and love life. Medical Orgone therapy is based on Wilhelm Reich's theory of armouring. The method of treatment developed from observations on the movement and blockage of energy in the body. Infants and children naturally feel pleasure and reach out to the world. If these impulses are frustrated, the child contracts and develops methods to adapt to the stress. If frustrations continue, these defensive reactions become chronic and extend into adult life even when they are no longer needed. For example, a child may develop a submissive manner to deal with an angry parent and then as an adult react submissively to all authority figures, even when it would be better to be assertive. Other common examples of "character armour" are found in individuals who present themselves as aloof, superior, "cool," sophisticated, cute, or special. Medical Orgonomists consider these character attitudes to be manifested in actual muscular rigidities (muscular armour), which hold back intolerable or unacceptable emotions such as anger, fear, or sadness. Individuals are usually unaware of their muscular armour or that their physical problems, such as headaches, stiff neck, or back pain, are often rooted in repressed emotions. Armouring forms in infancy, and early childhood as defence against painful feelings, but it is not a satisfactory solution because it later interferes with healthy emotional life and energy discharge. Medical Orgone therapy strives to eliminate chronic armour to restore the individual to more natural functioning in all aspects of his or her life. The medical Orgonomist is trained to understand the patient in all respects and diagnose the patterns of character and physical armour. Because all medical Orgone therapists are physicians who also have specialized training in psychiatry, they are equipped to diagnose physical conditions and work directly on their patients. Treatment includes character analysis and the release of buried emotions facilitated by breathing and direct work on spastic muscles. The therapy does not focus much on psychological causes or delve deeply into past relationships with parents. Therapy is also used to treat infants and children. The removal of early armouring allows the child to develop with a natural energy flow, emotional aliveness, and a sense of well-being. Treatment helps to prevent the development in adult life. It is important to note that the techniques used in this therapy are not the same as those in some other methods used to address physical tension such as acupressure, massage, and deep breathing. Character analysis also has its own specific techniques, which should not be confused with positive affirmations, guided self-examination, and similar therapeutic approaches. Medical Orgone therapy is a unique approach to the prevention and treatment of a wide range of mental and physical conditions. Medical Orgonomists report successful treatment of the full range of emotional symptoms and relationship problems. Serious conditions such as depression, schizophrenia, panic disorder, and ADHD can often be treated without resorting to medications. Reich concluded, and present-day physicians who practice medical Orgone therapy concur, that the elimination of armouring, in and of itself, restores natural, healthy functioning. Patients regain their natural capacities to enjoy satisfaction in love, work, and the pursuit of knowledge.

## Oriental Diagnosis

Every organ in your body is mirrored on the periphery. For example, your face will show the state of all your organs. For those who know how to read the signs, it means that you can start healing a weak organ BEFORE it becomes a problem (this is called preventative medicine). Other parts of the body can be used for Oriental Diagnosis : The hands, feet, tongue, eyes, voice, smell etc. Oriental medicine has evolved over several thousand years and is now widely practised as either acupuncture or herbal medicine throughout the world. The underlying principles have remained unchanged over the centuries and the real aim of oriental healing is to encourage the prevention of disease rather than dealing with first aid situations. A vital part of this fascinating system is the diagnostic methods that are used. If you have ever visited an acupuncturist or a Chinese herbal medicine practitioner, they will always examine the pulses on your wrist, look at your tongue, listen to your voice, perhaps palpate the abdomen, and ask you many questions about your diet, lifestyle, sleeping patterns, etc. Part of the visual diagnosis that they all use is to look at discolorations, spots, blemishes, puffiness or dryness of the skin on the face. Each area of the face reveals the current health of the major internal organs and forms part of - not all - the diagnostic procedure. In this feature you will be able to ascertain from the symptoms whether there are any underlying imbalances that may be occurring. They may not necessarily reveal themselves as acute or chronic problems at this stage, but in the spirit of prevention, they are worth noting and considering what changes you could make to your diet or lifestyle to strengthen the organ concerned. If you have always been looking for symptomatic or superficial ways to remedy dry skin or rashes on your face and had little success, then it may well be worth your while considering looking much further beneath the surface to the underlying cause from an oriental medicine perspective. This is the key to success with the oriental approach to healing.

## Orthomolecular Medicine

Orthomolecular medicine describes the practice of preventing and treating disease by providing the body with optimal amounts of substances which are natural to the body. Now more commonly known as Megavitamin Therapy. The term "orthomolecular" was first used by Linus Pauling in a paper he wrote in the journal Science in 1968. This paper first described the theoretical foundations for what was later to become a specialty within complementary medicine. The key idea in orthomolecular medicine is that genetic factors are central not only to the physical characteristics of individuals, but also to their biochemical milieu. Biochemical pathways of the body have significant genetic variability in terms of transcriptional potential and individual enzyme concentrations, receptor-ligand affinities and protein transporter efficiency. Diseases such as atherosclerosis, cancer, schizophrenia or depression are associated with specific biochemical abnormalities which are either causal or aggravating factors of the illness. In the orthomolecular view, it is possible that the provision of vitamins, amino acids, trace elements, electrolytes or fatty acids in amounts sufficient to correct biochemical abnormalities will be therapeutic in preventing or treating such diseases.

## Orthotics

People have been wearing shoes since the dawn of time to make life's hard road more bearable. Early shoe designs dating back thousands of years suggest that appearance has always been as important as comfort, if not more important. The shoe was a status symbol. As shoes became more accessible to the general population, people demanded better comfort. At this time shoes were made the same. There was no such thing as a left or right shoe (a concept that would not catch on until the 1800s.) Early innkeepers recognized that most weary travellers complained of foot pain. The first insoles were made by innkeepers from matted animal hair retrieved from the local barn (later called felt). Over time, shoe makers, or cobblers, modified the innkeepers' foot pads and began to add leather materials to the insides of shoes to create a better, more comfortable fit, the first arch supports were born. Early arch supports were made by laminating layers of leather strips together and then shaping the arch support by hand for wearing inside shoes. These new arch supports helped create a new level of comfort for people wearing shoes. The only problem was that arch supports were often bulky and heavy. By the early 1900's electricity and bench grinders made cutting down leather laminated devices much faster and therefore more affordable for the general population. In addition, lighter and softer materials were combined with leather blanks to create an additional level of comfort. The next major enhancement came in the 1960s when a new generation of thermoplastics was introduced to the marketplace. Thermoplastics mould to a form, such as a replica of your foot, when hot. Once cooled, the material retains the moulded shape of the form. Thermoplastics, such as polypropylene, are lightweight especially in comparison to leather and foam materials. More importantly, thermoplastics provide a strong, durable, and thin orthotic that can support the foot and body while fitting into modern style shoes. As a further plus, polypropylene is recyclable. The introduction of thermoplastic materials led to new theories about how to make arch supports. Instead of using a shoe last to make the device, medical professionals began using a mould or cast of a person's foot, thereby creating a true orthotic. The medical definition of an orthotic is a brace that supports a specific body structure. More importantly, scientific principles were (and continue to be) applied to the foot's structure and to foot orthotics to develop foot supports that can actually control the function of feet, legs, hips, back, and neck. Since the 1960's, the art of custom orthotic making has been continually enhanced so that today it is possible to build an orthotic that can help correct the foot deformities (such as bunions, flat feet, etc.) that cause typical aches and pains in the feet, legs, hips, back, and neck—the types of aches and pains people in all cultures and all parts of world experience. The custom orthotic is typically prescribed by a licensed Foot Care Professional who is Medically trained. Orthotics are fabricated by Professional Orthotic Laboratories. Medically Prescribed Custom Orthotics can be compared to eye glasses: Foot Orthotics (or eye glasses) do not change your body, but instead assist you in performing to a higher level. If you don't wear them, they are not helping you. If you need glasses and wear them, seeing and reading become much easier. The same applies to Custom Orthotics. If you need them, they can greatly enhance your general comfort and well-being. If you depend on your feet to work or play, you will find it hard to live without foot orthotics once you have a pair. Foot Care Professionals and Foot Orthotic Laboratories provide a full range of products for the consumer, from inexpensive insoles to totally custom foot orthotics made to perform under very specific conditions, such as snow skiing or for hard-to-fit women's dress shoes. The future promises a continuing stream of enhancements.

## Osteomyology

Osteomyology is a system of physical treatment which combines joint manipulation with soft tissue massage, corrective exercises, electrotherapy and other natural healing methods. The treatment of chronic pain is one of the central aspects of the professional work of an Osteomyologist. This ranges from the long term results of untreated sports and work-related injuries to the arthritis of the elderly. Osteomyologists work to alleviate pain, to improve mobility and to make patients' lives more comfortable. Much long-term, chronic pain is caused by degenerative changes to the body's framework. Nobody can reverse the changes which have taken place. However, treatment using gentle, manual techniques on joints, muscles and ligaments may often ease pain, reduce swelling and improve the mobility and range of joint movement. Age is no barrier to this treatment as treatment is tailored to the needs of each individual. Consideration of a patient's life style is relevant to treatment as habitual incorrect use of the body leads to strain of muscles and joints. Exercises to do at home may also be advised to reduce muscle spasm and to improve the way joints work, even though they may be worn. Osteomyologists are trained in diagnosis. They use their hands to discover the underlying causes of pain, through sensitive touch and mobility testing. They may also ask for diagnostic imaging to assess the seriousness of your condition. A visit to your GP may be suggested when an underlying medical condition is considered to be a possible cause of the discomfort you are experiencing. There are times when it is wise for you to take medication as well as receiving physical treatments. Sometimes, too, surgery may be necessary, such as for hip replacements, and in these instances, it is important to see the appropriate specialist.

## Osteopathy

Osteopathy is a distinctive and complete system of health care, based on broad principles that "offer a way of thinking and acting in relation to questions of health and disease" (Dr. I. M. Korr). The procedures it uses in diagnosis and treatment promote healthy functioning in a person by correcting mechanical imbalances within and between the structures of the body. By structures we mean the muscles, bones, ligaments, organs, and fascia. The fascia is a very thin layer of tissue that is found under the skin. Correcting the mechanical imbalances in the structures is done by restoring, maintaining, and improving the harmonious working of the nervous and musculo-skeletal systems. The name osteopathy (given to the therapy by Dr. Still) comes from the Greek osteon (bone) and pathos (to suffer), so it literally means suffering of the bone. The name has created some confusion, leading people to think that an osteopath treats only conditions of the bones. However, Dr. Still chose the name because he recognized the importance of a properly functioning musculo-skeletal system for the total well-being of the individual. Osteopathy and orthodox medicine have many things in common: they both use the scientific knowledge of anatomy and physiology, as well as clinical methods of investigation. In this respect, they have a similar language. The greatest differences, however, lie in the way patients are evaluated and in the approach to treatment. As a general rule, the orthodox medical approach focuses on the end product of the problem — that is, on the illness. Treatment aims to redress the balance by giving drugs or carrying out surgery. Osteopaths focus on tracing the changes in function that have occurred over a period of time. This is in order to try to understand the chain of events that have altered the relationship between structure and function, resulting in the present complaint. A typical example might be a six-year-old boy who, while playing, falls very hard on his bottom. He cries bitterly and complains of pain over his sacrum for a week or so. A kiss and "rub it better" console him. During a sudden growth spurt as a teenager, the same boy complains of low back ache. By the age of eighteen, he has his first attack of sciatica, which is helped by anti-inflammatory and muscle relaxant medicine. He gives up his favourite sport, rowing, because it seems to aggravate the problem. In his late twenties, married with a young child and a stressful job, he begins to have an irritable colon and attacks of cystitis. He takes antibiotics and changes his diet. At the age of forty, he has a major attack of low back pain and sciatica and is in bed for two weeks. At this point, hoping to avoid surgery, he visits an osteopath.

## Paranormal Therapies

Phenomena that are characterised as Paranormal is a form of alternative therapy, and is exercised by people that allegedly give order to paranormal powers, that are not (yet) scientifically proven but with these powers claim they can carry out medical actions. Includes Faith Healing, Charismatic Healing and to some extent ESP, Extrasensory Perception.

## Pattern Therapies

The belief that patterns profoundly affect state of well being, health and the environment can be used in a number of complementary medical treatments.

## Physiotherapy

Physiotherapy centres itself in the analysis and evaluation of the movement and posture, based in the structure and function of the body, using specific educational and therapeutic approaches, based essentially in movements, manipulative therapies and physical and natural means, with the aim of health promotion and prevention of the disease, to prepare or to rehabilitate, individuals with dysfunctions of physical, mental, growth nature, or others such as pain, with the objective of helping them to achieve the best functionality and life quality. Usually given on the NHS after surgical treatment as rehabilitation.

## Phytotherapy

Phytotherapy or Herbal Medicine as it is also known is the oldest system of medicine and is used extensively throughout the world. It is supported by the World Health organisation and involves the use of plant and plant products for their healing properties to promote better health. Phytotherapy aims to treat each person as an individual with their own set of unique requirements for optimal health. This means that most people suffering from both short and long term illnesses can be helped by Phytotherapy. Herbal medicines are 100% natural; and are prepared from domestically grown plants or collected from the wild. They are prescribed to improve the functioning of the body's systems resulting in the restoration of a balanced state of health

## Pilates

Imagine an exercise program that you look forward to, that engages you, and that leaves you refreshed and alert with a feeling of physical and mental well-being. The Pilates Method (pronounced puh-LAH-teez) of body conditioning will do all this...and more. Developed in the 1920s by the legendary physical trainer and founder of the Pilates Studio®, Joseph H. Pilates, The Method is an exercise system focused on improving flexibility and strength for the total body without building bulk. Not surprisingly, some of the first people to use the Pilates Method were dancers such as Martha Graham and George Balanchine. The Pilates Method is not just exercise, however. It is a series of controlled movements engaging your body and mind, performed on specifically designed exercise apparatus and supervised by extensively trained teachers.

## Podiatry

Podiatry is the management of foot disorders and the problems associated with general health conditions, which manifest themselves in the feet and the lower limb. The foot is a highly complex structure which can develop problems that can affect a patients overall health and well-being. Some foot problems result in serious and devastating consequences if appropriate podiatry treatment is not provided. Podiatrists provide a fully comprehensive foot care service to patients and are trained to work with other health care professionals and medical teams. Podiatrists are specialists who are trained to diagnose and devise treatment plans and carry out treatment to all age groups. Management ranges from simple nail care to nail surgery, from the mechanical correction of gait and posture to more complex surgical techniques. Effective practice requires a strong combination of practical skills and academic ability. Podiatrists have an interest in people, a caring and considerate attitude and excellent communication skills.

## Polarity Therapy

Polarity Therapy is a multidimensional system of healing that combines Ayurvedic principles, bodywork, counselling, awareness skills, diet and polarity stretching exercises to balance the flow of energy within the body. This Holistic therapy developed by Dr. Randolph Stone, a naturopath, chiropractor and osteopath works on body, mind and spirit to help the client to heal himself naturally and take responsibility for his own health and wellness. Polarity Therapy is a comprehensive health system involving energy-based bodywork, diet, exercise and self- awareness. It works with the Human Energy Field, electro- magnetic patterns expressed in mental, emotional and physical experience. In Polarity Therapy, health is viewed as a reflection of the condition of the energy field, and therapeutic methods are designed to balance the field for health benefit. Polarity Therapy as stated was developed by Randolph Stone (1890-1981), who conducted a thorough investigation of energy in the healing arts over the course of his 60 year medical career. Drawing information from a wide range of sources, he found that the Human Energy Field is affected by touch, diet, movement, sound, attitudes, relationships, life experience, trauma and environmental factors. Since Polarity Therapy lends an energy-based perspective to all these subjects, the scope of Polarity practice is often very broad, with implications for health professionals in many therapeutic disciplines. As a result, Polarity has strong, mutually supportive connections to many other holistic health systems. Basic characteristics of the Human Energy Field are described in many sources, both ancient and modern. For example, the term "Polarity" refers to the universal pulsation of expansion/contraction or repulsion/attraction known as

Yang and Yin in Oriental therapies. Similarly, Polarity integrates the "Three Principles and Five Chakras" of Aryuvedic tradition, and has been called the modern manifestation of ancient Hermetic Philosophy. At the same time Polarity Therapy also enjoys rich ties to modern science, which has confirmed its essential theme of energetic relationship as the basis of all phenomena. The Application of Polarity Therapy, In the Polarity model, health is experienced when energy systems function in their natural state; energy flows smoothly without significant blockage or fixation. When energy is unbalanced, blocked or fixed due to stress or other factors, pain and disease arise. Blockages generally manifest in sequence from the subtle to the dense levels of the field. Polarity Therapy seeks to find the blockages and release energy to normal flow patterns, and to maintain the Energy Field in an open, flexible condition. In a typical Polarity Therapy session, the practitioner assesses energetic attributes using palpation, observation and interview methods. Sessions usually take 60-90 minutes, do not require disrobing, and involve both touch and verbal interaction. Touch contact may be light, medium or firm.

n the session, the practitioner supports the client in increasing self-awareness of subtle energetic sensations, which are often experienced as tingling, warmth, expansion or wavelike movement. The results of Polarity Therapy sessions vary, and may include profound relaxation, new insight into energetic patterns and their implications, and relief from numerous specific problematic situations.

## Postural Integration

A body-centred therapy that uses touch, deep tissue massage, energy work, awareness skills and a particular client-practitioner relationship. Developed by Jack Painter in the late 1960's it is based on his personal development and experience in Rolfing, Bioenergetics, acupuncture, yoga, breath therapy, neo-Reichian bodywork, Gestalt and Meditation. Postural Integration doesn't claim to be a psychotherapy or a therapy for all ailments although the benefits affect the whole person in his psychophysical totality. It is above all a method for Transformation and Personal Growth.

## Primal Therapy

A method of psychotherapy that treats neurosis by teaching patients to relive traumatic experiences and to express feelings through Angry Screaming and other verbal or physical acts of aggression. Primal Therapy is a natural therapy pioneered by Dr. Arthur Janov in the late 1960's. It is based on his hypothesis that neurosis is a disorder of feeling. Janov postulated that we are born beings of need: we need to be fed, kept warm, allowed to develop and grow, and nurtured in many differing but specific ways. If we are denied any of these needs for any length of time then we hurt. If the denial is strong enough then we switch off that need, that is we bury the hurt feelings that ensue. In this way we erode our capacity to feel, not only the bad but also the good feelings. The process involves the original creation of the unconscious mind and marks the dawning of symbolic behaviour and the creation of neurosis. In Primal Therapy clients are helped and guided to feel these original trauma for the first time. What was a life threatening hurt for a three year old can be felt and integrated as a twenty three year old. In a safe and controlled environment (darkened lights, padded, safe room) and usually talking about events that disturb the client in the present, she or he is guided back to the primal event and all it's attendant pain. The process is necessarily gradual and can take from nine months to two years to make major inroads to effect the recovery and create an "ex-neurotic". Dr. Janov has also pioneered the comprehension of these processes (the creation of neurosis and it's healing during Primal Therapy) by the development of Primal Theory. Primal Therapy drew worldwide attention after the publication of Janov's book "The Primal Scream". This somewhat sensational title has led to many misconceptions about the therapy. Traditionally, formal therapy takes the form of a three week intensive with a follow up group and sessions. Dr. Janov claimed it was the cure for neurosis, and reading "The Primal Scream" one expects some kind of miracle to happen, if not in the first three weeks then soon after. Time has proved that neurosis takes a lot of hard work and dedication to unravel on the part of the client and a lot of experience and skill on the part of the therapist. Post-Primal people are not superhuman, miraculously cured by an intensive course of "screaming". The cure exists in finding a way of living a feeling life in a world that often makes it hard to do just that. Therapy gives one the means to drain off the levels of tension that the neurotic has grown up making and then gives him a dynamic means of handling tensions that life itself might create. Importantly one gets a true insight into one's behaviour and the ability to change the way one acts and reacts. Therapy only works and continues to maintain health on the twin footing of feeling and resolving painful situations and making changes in one's life appropriate to any revealed insight.

## Psionic Therapy

Psionics/Radionics is based on the understanding that every person's energy patterns or rhythms are as unique to them as their fingerprints, and that every part of their body, down to the cell level, reflects these 'vibrations'. When illness, injury, infection, stress, pollution, malnutrition, or poor hygiene cause these patterns to become imbalanced or interrupted the energy is altered. This altered energy pattern can be read from any part of the body and treated by sending messages, with an instrument, to the body in order that the body may heal itself through the restored flow of energy. A 'witness', which is something such as a lock of hair, a blood spot, or a fingernail clipping from the patient, is placed into the machine which will pick up its energy rhythm. Using this rhythm, coded messages are sent from the instrument back to the patient to correct imbalances discovered through the initial analysis. There is no need for the patient to be anywhere near the machine to take place. It is said that effects have been felt by patients' long distances from the machine. Psionics/Radionics can treat any type of illness, although medical emergencies and life-threatening illnesses or injuries should always be treated by a medical doctor. Radionics has also been used to treat animals and plants. Cerebrex Radionic/Psionic devices are not meant to usurp traditional medical procedure. This technology is offered in the spirit of exploration and experimentation only and thus is in no way in misalignment with mainstream medical and psychological procedure.

## Psychotherapy

Psychotherapy is the provision by qualified practitioners of a formal and professional relationship within which patient(s)/client(s) can profitably explore difficult, and often painful, emotions and experiences. These may include feelings of anxiety, depression, trauma, or perhaps the loss of meaning in one's life. It is a process which seeks to help the person gain an increased capacity for choice, through which the individual becomes more autonomous and self determined. Psychotherapy may be provided for individuals or children, couples, families and groups

## Pyramid Power

There is a great mystical knowledge hidden within the inner depths of the Great Pyramid. The square base means that the Pyramid is solidly founded on nature and its immutable laws; the angles represent Silence, Profundity, Intelligence and Truth. The south side of the pyramid signifies Cold, the north side represents Heat, the west side symbolises Darkness and the east side, Light. The triangular sides typify the three-fold spiritual power. Many believe in the mystic spiritual powers of the Pyramids.

## Pyschosynthesis

Pyschosynthesis is an approach to human development fostered by Roberto Assagioli (1888 -1974) beginning around 1910 and continuing to the present day. It is both a theory and practice where the focus is to achieve a synthesis, a coming together, of the various parts of an individual's personality into a more cohesive self. That person can then function in a way that is more life-affirming and authentic. Another major aspect of psychosynthesis is its affirmation of the spiritual dimension of the person, i.e. the "higher" or "transpersonal" self. The higher self is seen as a source of wisdom, inspiration, unconditional love, and the will to meaning in our lives. Psychosynthesis is founded on the basic premise that human life has purpose and meaning and that we participate in an orderly universe structured to facilitate the evolution of consciousness. A corollary is that each person's life has purpose and meaning within this broader context and that it is possible for the individual to discover this. Psychosynthesis has had a profound impact on the human potential movement. For example, the use of guided imagery and the concept of sub personalities originate in Psychosynthesis. Psychosynthesis therapy provides a safe and supportive atmosphere for the exploration of personal issues and concerns. It honours the client's developmental level and unique ways of working. The process begins with what is foreground in the person's life and moves the client in the direction of the fullest expression of his or her own potential. The concerns and issues dealt with include: personal, interpersonal, or family conflict and alienation, death, dying, or unresolved grief over the loss of a loved one, professional burnout and/or exploring a change of career, recognition of addictive/co-dependent behaviour patterns, abuse, abandonment, or incest in childhood or adolescence, somatic concerns - physical illness, chronic pain, or health care difficulty in making choices or in achieving certain goals. unfulfilled spiritual longing or a sense of duality between the psychological and spiritual aspects of life, a need to find deeper meaning in one's life, or a sense that "something is missing." Since the process of psychosynthesis is unique to each individual, the work may involve one in a variety of different activities. These could include development and use of the will, integration of the physical, mental, emotional, spiritual, and social aspects of life, learning to dis-identify from self- limiting identifications, concepts, and roles, exploration of values, meaning, and purpose, and unblocking obstacles to creative expression. The work itself draws from a diverse range of techniques and methods, depending on what is natural and most appropriate for each person. Within the psychosynthesis framework, practitioners utilize guided imagery, hypnotherapy, gestalt, movement, assertive training, family systems work, breath-work, art therapy, journal writing, and meditation, among other techniques.

During the psychosynthesis process, each person is encouraged to seek guidance increasingly from within him or herself, and taught how to proceed independently, safely, and effectively without the assistance of the psychosynthesis guide.

## Qigong

Qigong combines movement, meditation, and breath regulation to enhance the flow of vital energy in the body, improve blood circulation, and enhance immune functions. Because Qigong can be used by the healthy as well as the severely ill, it is one of the most broadly applicable systems of self-care in the world. In China, it is estimated that 200 million people practice Qigong everyday.

## Reflexology

The ancient healing art of reflexology has been known to man for many thousands of years. It was first practiced by the early Indian, Chinese and Egyptian peoples. In 1913 Dr. William Fitzgerald, an American ear, nose and throat surgeon, introduced this therapy to the West. He noted that pressure on specific parts of the body could have an anaesthetising effect on a related area. Developing this theory, he divided the body into ten equal and vertical zones, ending in the fingers and toes. He concluded that pressure on one part of a zone could affect everything else within that zone. Thus, reflex areas on the feet and hands are linked to other areas and organs of the body within the same zone. In the 1930's, Eunice Ingham, a therapist, further developed and refined the zone therapy into what is now known as foot reflexology. She observed that congestion or tension in any part of the foot mirrors congestion or tension in a corresponding part of the body. Thus, when you treat the big toes there is a related effect in the head, and treating the whole foot can have a relaxing and healing effect on the whole body. On your first visit there is a preliminary talk with the practitioner. The reflexologist then begins to work on your feet, or hands if necessary, noting problem areas. There may be discomfort in some places, but it is fleeting, and is an indication of congestion or imbalance in a corresponding part of the body. For the most part, the sensation is pleasant and soothing. Reflexology will relax you while stimulating the body's own healing mechanisms. Usually a treatment session lasts for about one hour. A course of treatment varies in length depending on your body's needs. Your reflexologist will discuss this with you at the first session. After the first treatment or two your body may respond in a very definite way: you may have a feeling of well-being and relaxation; or you may feel lethargic, nauseous or tearful, but this is transitory. It is, however, vital information for reflexologists, as it shows how your body is responding to treatment. Since reflexology treats the whole person, not the symptoms of disease, most people benefit from treatment. The therapy brings relief to a wide range of acute and chronic conditions, and is suitable for all ages. Once your body is in-tune, it is wise to have regular treatments in order to help maintain health and well-being. An increasing number of people are using this safe, natural therapy as a way of relaxing, balancing and harmonising the body.

## Reichian Therapy (Orgone Therapy)

Orgone therapy (also known as Reichian therapy) is a holistic body-mind psychotherapy which addresses the bioenergetic underpinnings of psycho/emotional distress. It was developed by Wilhelm Reich, M.D. a pioneer in the study of bioenergy and emotional processes, who proposed that one's psychological and emotional distress results from the blocking of his or her experience and expression of life affirming emotions (sadness, joy, anger, grief, longing, and fear). Reich termed this blocking "armouring". Armouring develops during the course of one's lifetime in response to hurtful or non-nurturing environments and the need to defend oneself from painful emotions. Armouring is expressed in one's beliefs, attitudes, and interpersonal behaviour; and in one's posture, breathing style, and pattern of muscular tensions. Armouring restricts the movement of energy and gives rise to painful emotions such as shame, anxiety, guilt, defensive anger and unresolved grief. Armouring diminishes one's capacity to experience healthy aggression, intimacy, and sexual excitation and pleasure. Through the use of dialogue, breathing, and bodily movement Orgone therapy works to help one first recognize and then lessen chronic patterns of armouring. As one's armouring diminishes, previously bound energy flows more naturally, allowing for more natural and healthy functioning.

WHO MAY BENEFIT FROM ORGONE THERAPY? Individuals with emotional or interpersonal difficulties. This includes depression, anxiety, low self- esteem, and relationship problems at home or at work. These difficulties may be long term or as a result of a current crisis or trauma. Individuals who have been raised in families marked by abusive parent-child relationships and/or alcohol or drug abuse. Such family systems often leave family members with painful emotions and feelings of low self-esteem and emotional distress. Individuals suffering from stress related muscular tensions or psychosomatic disorders, which are often a result of unexpressed emotions. Individuals who feel emotionally inhibited or blocked in their daily life.

## Reiki

Reiki (pronounced Ray-Key) is a method of natural healing based on the application of what the name literally means, Universal Life Force Energy. In its simplest form using Reiki is simply the practitioner placing their hands on the recipient with the intent of bringing healing, and willing for Reiki energy to flow. There is a set of hand positions traditionally taught which give good coverage over the recipient's entire body. It is not necessary to follow those positions, they are merely taught as a starting position from which the practitioner can learn. If there is a specific area of concern the practitioner can keep his/her hands right there for as long as necessary.

## Remedial Massage

The benefits of massage are becoming increasingly recognised in recent years. However, public perception can often have massage directly related to stress relief and muscle aches and pains, when, in fact, the benefits of massage are so much more. A qualified remedial massage therapist can be of help to you in many ways: Tissue manipulation to relieve muscle spasm and tension, Lymphatic circulation, Facilitating movement by prevent formation of adhesions, Increasing blood flow, Stimulation of skin, nerves, glands, the immune system and tissue metabolism, Improving muscle tone - excellent for pre and post competition for active sports people, Alleviates pain - helps lessen inflammation and oedema and always gives stress relief.

## Rogerian Therapy

Rogerian therapy involves the therapist's entry into the client's unique phenomenological world. In mirroring this world, the therapist does not disagree or point out contradictions (Shaffer, 1978). Neither does he/she attempt to delve into the unconscious. The focus is on immediate conscious experience. Rogers (1977) describes therapy as a process of freeing a person and removing obstacles so that normal growth and development can proceed and the client can become independent and self-directed. During the course of therapy the client moves from rigidly of self-perception to fluidity. Certain conditions are necessary for this process. A "growth promoting climate" requires the therapist to be congruent, have unconditional positive regard for the client as well as show empathic understanding. Congruence on the part of the therapist refers to her/his ability to be completely genuine whatever the self of the moment. While it is necessary during therapy h/she is not expected to be a completely congruent person all the time, as such perfection is impossible. Empathy refers to understanding the client's feelings and personal meanings as they are experienced and communicating this back to the person. While unconditional positive regard involves relating from therapist to client not as a scientist to an object of study, but as a person to a person. He feels this client to be a person of self-worth, of value no matter what his condition, his behaviour or his feelings. He respects him for what he is, and accepts him as he is, with his potentialities Rogers' strong belief in the positive nature of human beings is based on his many years of clinical experience, working with a wide variety of individuals. The theory of person-centred therapy suggests any client, no matter what the problem, can improve without being taught anything specific by the therapist, once he/she accepts and respects themselves. The resources all lie within the client. While this may be so, this type of therapy many not be effective for severe psychopathologies such as schizophrenia (which today is considered to have strong biological component) or other disorders such as phobias, obsessive-compulsive disorder or even depression (currently effectively treated with drugs and cognitive therapy). Rogers himself noted that every theory, including his own, contains "an unknown (and perhaps at that time unknowable) amount of error and mistaken inference. His belief was that a theory should serve as a stimulus to further creative thinking. I believe he has succeeded in this intention. This theory has very strong heuristic value and continues to generate debate and interest. The theory further focuses on the whole individual as he/she experiences the world. Agency and free will are not undermined in this model. It gives considerable attention to the concept of self and the suggestion that we can all overcome damages inflicted in childhood is very appealing. Full functioning is no the exclusive domain of a very lucky few. It is, at least theoretically, attainable for many. Rogers does not assume women are inferior to men and his "sexist" language was corrected in his later writings. It also recognises persons as the most important focus in the study of personality.

## Rolfing

Rolfers see structure as a series of inter-connected and inter-related bony segments. Our bodies are designed to provide internal support for all these segments. Large sections provide support for sections that are above them as well as rest upon sections that are below them. An example of this is the relationship between the pelvis and the legs: Some people have developed a habit of storing tremendous amounts of tension through their hips, buttocks, and legs. This prevents their hip girdle from easily resting upon their leg bones in a way that provides maximum energy, range of motion, stability and stamina. The more we overload our musculature to compensate for our inability to move with grace and fluidity in our bodies, the more we tire ourselves unnecessarily. The more we allow for this system of internal support to operate in the way it was designed to operate, the more our bodies become a vehicle for our full physical expression. Through Rolfing we let go into ideal posture rather than hold to achieve it. Rolfers and teachers of Rolf Movement Integration address these disruptions in structural balance in the bodies of our students and clients. We teach through hands-on manipulation and provide cues and prompts that help people regain structural integrity. We are interested in the ways our feet contact the ground as well as the ways our heads float effortlessly on top. Through the use of metaphor, we teach elongation without effort. One of the hallmarks of Rolfing is the attainment of improved posture as a function of surrendering tension and strain, as opposed to learning new ways of working hard. Clients often hear that they are not coming to learn to work harder in their bodies; they are coming to work less hard. Dr. Ida Rolf, who founded this system, often clarified the difference between posture and balance. The Latin word, ponere, has the same root as posture and means "to put" or "to place". As a result of interpreting posture in such a manner, people often acquire the habit of holding a static, "correct" position. Through Rolfing, however, we continuously seek out a dynamic, creative balance in our bodies that is quite different than putting or placing body parts in one place and then keeping them in that place. Posture, as is taught through Rolfing, is a creative, fluid process. We move with correct posture, we do not hold. We learn the inherent balance of a properly aligned structure and let gravity do the work of providing support.

## Seichem (See also Reiki)

Reiki is a natural healing method that was developed in the early 20th century in Japan. The word Reiki is a combination of two Japanese words: Rei and Ki. Rei means spiritual intelligence or supernatural force; Ki means life energy. In the Western world Reiki is mostly described as Universal life force energy, or Spiritually guided life force energy. The energy is channelled by a Reiki practitioner and goes to the places in the body where healing is most needed. Tera Mai Reiki was developed by Kathleen Milner and is based on the Usui System of Natural Healing, which is the original Reiki system founded by Mikao Usui. The Tera Mai system includes three other healing energies, together with the Reiki energy these are named Seichem. Tera Mai is a registered trade mark; this ensures that everybody who decides to learn Tera Mai Reiki receives the same initiations, no matter who the teacher is. Page 44 of 50

## Shiatsu

The Japanese word Shiatsu is composed of a character meaning finger (shi) and another character meaning pressure (atsu). Shiatsu is the proper application of carefully placed pressure on specific points on the surface of the human body. Pressure is applied with the fingers and hands to eliminate pain and fatigue to stimulate the body's natural self-curative abilities. Shiatsu is primarily a way to prevent the development of sickness and a therapy ideally suited to human body. Shiatsu tries to always keep the body in top condition so that symptoms requiring medical attention do not develop. Characteristics of Shiatsu Therapy are:- 1. Immediate assessment 2. No medicine or mechanical devices needed 3. Some experience discomfort if they are unusually stiff 4. Suitable to all age groups 5. Resistance to sickness 6. Sense of mutual trust and reliance 7. Total treatment . Shiatsu strives to help eliminate ailments and prevent their recurrence and the development of other ailments. Pressure applied by the hands on certain points of the skin stimulates the body's natural recuperative powers and removes fatigue by causing the diffusion of the lactic acid and carbon dioxide that accumulate among the tissues to cause muscular stiffness and stagnation of the blood. These accumulations of fatigue-causing materials apply abnormal pressure on the nerves, blood, and lymph vessels. This causes irregular internal secretions and peculiarities in the skeletal system and internal organs. By diffusing fatigue-causing accumulations, shiatsu pressure restores flexibility to the muscle tissues and relieves pain-producing systems. Shiatsu treatment is concerned mainly with the 660 pressure ponits (tsubo) where blood vessels, lymph vessels, nerves, and the ductless glands of the endocrine system tend to concentrate or to branch. Namikoshi Shiatsu therapy has organized the tsubo in a system that is based on physiology and pathology.

## Silva Method

In 1969 a man named Jose Silva formally introduced a self-evolvement course he had been developing for over 20 years. By combining a metronome with meditation and self-hypnosis techniques, users quickly learn how to control states of consciousness normally associated with long term meditation. A variety of tools can be taught which enable people to manage their lives and to access information normally associated with intuition and ESP. Here is a general description: to function at the Alpha brain wave level (normally associated with the dream state) and to use both brain hemispheres in harmony, develop and maintain a positive mental attitude no matter what the circumstances around you, how to relax mentally and physically, go to sleep without drug, wake up without an alarm clock, stay awake and alert longer when needed without drugs, remember and generate dreams for problem solving, relieve and stop having headaches and migraines, visualisation skills for changing self image , develop memory skills pain and bleeding control to accelerate healing , quickly and easily eliminate or develop habits , develop ESP abilities , The Silva Method is currently being taught in 103 countries and 29 languages.

## Sound Therapy

Effectively used in many hospitals as part of the treatment for Alzheimer's disease, the monks of Tibet discovered the healing power of overtone chanting thousands of years ago. The basic tenet behind sound therapy is that everything in the universe is in a constant state of vibration. If true, the cells of the human body constantly vibrate, meaning that sound can either relax or agitate, heal or harm. Most commonly employs the direct application of the voice, music and other sounds. It is used effectively to reduce pain and inflammation, especially in conditions such as arthritis, back pain and soft-tissue damage

## Spiritual Healing

Spiritual Healing is Essential Healing. Its pathway works through the Essential, or Vital Energy flow of the body. Spiritual healing is not what Jesus did. He performed miracles and gave out miracles. Miracles work through the virtual energy flow to the body, not through the vital energy flow of the body. The Essenes were masters at spiritual healing. When we talk about Spiritual Healing, we talk of 'transfer energy healing' that is, transfer of 'power' to cause the body to heal itself because it is low on its 'power' to do so. Spiritual Healing is not Applied healing, although it may use parts of Applied Healing techniques from time to time in order to assist the healing process. Applied healing works on treating the "effect", the "result" or the "symptom". Spiritual Healing re-tunes and re-balances the bodies 'energies' allowing it to function more fully on what it has. It works on treating the "cause", often a deep emotional imbalance. One of many, which we as biological humans bury rather than get rid of ourselves, because the human body can usually handle our stressful situations by suppressing them inwardly. Spiritual Healing is not natural healing, it is supernatural healing. It may cause natural healing to occur naturally as a result of treatment, because the supernatural causes the body to do so.

## Sports Massage

Sports Massage is used primarily for the serious athlete who trains continuously. It focuses on the muscles relevant to the client's particular athletic activity. It also includes pre-event, post-event and maintenance techniques that promote greater athletic endurance and performance, and also lessens the chance of injury and reduces recovery time.

## Stress Therapy

Stress Management Practitioners teach patients how to lessen the impact of stress on their well-being. Exact techniques vary depending on the practitioner's training and interests.

## Swedish Body Massage

A wonderful way to treat yourself to the experience of deep relaxation while at the same time benefiting from increased circulation, tension reduction and muscle rejuvenation. It is a great way to get rid of achy muscles or stored up tension and stresses in our busy everyday life. If you feel good this massage will make you feel even better. Encourages body to release endorphins bringing a stressed out body back to normal functioning. Chronic stress causes chronic tension, trigger points and poor circulation. Swedish massage relieves these problems allowing the body normal rest. Massage can be thought of as a one-hour vacation from stress. Research has confirmed that massage reduces anxiety and increases feelings of well being. Because massage is a sensory experience, therapeutic massage contributes to a healthy immune system.

## T'ai-Chi Ch'uan

The ability to centre the mind is really that of keeping the mind interested and involved in the experience of the present moment. This is understood to be the foundation of T'ai Chi because from this state of attention comes the possibility to change, correct, and heal. To facilitate this process T'ai Chi uses a physical location, the lower abdomen/pelvis, which is called the Tan T'ien in Chinese. This represents the true body centre in the sense that it's the natural movement and feeling centre. With this specific body awareness we can begin the process of distributing the attention more evenly and equally throughout the body. The ability to spread attention throughout the body is understood in Chinese medicine to be one of the most important elements of good health because it's indicative of the relationship between the mind and the body. Unlike the prevailing Western view that one must work hard for the experience we call being healthy. In T'ai Chi health is understood to be natural (and therefore effortless) to that individual who has achieved balance and harmony between body and mind. The essence of T'ai Chi practice is not to learn a set of movements, nor to become talented in a system of self-defence, although these abilities may occur during the course of practice. The intention of T'ai Chi is to allow one the opportunity to become more aware of the natural laws which govern change; not just change in the body as affects physical, structural movement, but rather principles of change and movement that govern every aspect of our lives and the world around us. The exercises of the practice simply provide us with an opportunity to explore that process of discovery.

## Tantra Therapy

Tantra is a system for expanding consciousness, and Mantras are holistic, mystic words, which are chanted repeatedly to awaken internal insight, spiritual and psychic awareness. Tantra is an ancient Indian system propounded by Lord Shiva for the uplifting of human secret power during the Kaliyuga (iron age). The root of human spiritual growth lies in the Muladhara Chakra at the base of the sacral in a dormant state. Tantra-mantra is a fundamental tool used to activate the universal source of vast living energy in the human body (kundalini), for enlightenment and to achieve a state of super consciousness. These ancient techniques also assist in the healing of psychosomatic disorders and sexual dysfunction, and are used for increasing willpower, spiritual, psychic and sexual enhancement. Linked to Ayurveda, the traditional holistic medical system of India, using a constitution based model for determining your state of health. Rather than treating the symptoms of disease directly, Ayurvedic treatment aims to rebalance your doshas according to your constitution, resulting in a body and mind that is healthy and sound. By becoming familiar with your own unique dosha pattern you can lead a life that is more in harmony with your individual nature. Ayurveda describes a complete system for restoring, maintaining and enhancing health, advocating the use of natural healing methods tailored to the individual - such as life style changes, Himalayan Herbal/Mineral remedies, Detoxification treatments, Rejuvenation preparations and Yogic and Tantric practices.

## Tera-Mai (See Reiki)

Everybody can learn to work with the Terra-Mai Reiki energy. No special abilities or skills are required to be able to channel the healing energies. During a Reiki course the body is attuned to the Reiki energies. The ability to channel the energy always remains. Reiki is taught in three levels in which information about the history and the use of Reiki is given. For each level there are initiations, also called attunements, in which the body is prepared for channelling the Reiki energy.

## Thought Field Therapy

Discovered and developed by Dr. Roger Callahan PhD, a Californian clinical psychologist with over 40 years of experience, Thought Field Therapy (TFT) is a totally unique form of meridian therapy. It is best described as a natural, drug-free, non-invasive system to eliminate the cause of negative emotions. Quite simply the addressing of specific energy meridian points on the body in a precise and defined sequence, TFT has been shown to have an unprecedented success rate of up to 98%. Now in its twentieth year of development, TFT is probably the only therapy currently available for the treatment of psychological problems and emotional challenges that can genuinely claim to offer a cure. Most individuals experience significant, usually complete, relief from their problem within a few minutes. No other treatment presently available, conventional, complementary or alternative can claim the same success, speed and completeness. The key to this extraordinary success has been Dr. Callahan's discovery of the natural code that governs psychological problems, and an effective treatment for the phenomenon of Psychological Reversal - the tendency for some individuals to unconsciously self-sabotage their own recovery despite outwardly seeking to rid themselves of their problem. Thought Field Therapy... is extraordinarily powerful, in that individuals receive nearly immediate relief from their suffering, has no adverse side effects. Does not require the individual to talk about their problem, something that often causes considerable distress or embarrassment and which discourages many for seeking treatment in the first place. Are extremely efficient, treatment times of 10 minutes or less not uncommon.

## Touch Therapy

Healing through touch is one of the oldest therapies in the world. Touch has always been a most effective method of healing. The energy that flows through the hands can refresh, regenerate, revitalize. The laying on of hands can create great physical-mental changes in the hands of a person who understands that touch sometimes can be as effective as drugs or surgery. The mobilisation of the soft tissue, which may include skin, fascia, tendons, ligaments, and muscles, for the purpose of establishing good physical condition. The term shall include effleurage, petrissage, tapotement, compression, vibration, stretching, heliotherapy, superficial hot and cold applications, topical applications, or other therapy, which involves movement either by hand, forearm, elbow, or foot, for the purpose of therapeutic massage. Massage therapy may include the external application and use of herbal or chemical preparations and lubricants such as salts, powders, liquids, non-prescription creams, mechanical devises such as T-bars, thumpers, body support systems, heat lamps, hot and cold packs, salt glow, steam cabinet baths or hydrotherapy. The term includes any massage, movement therapy, massage technology, myotherapy, massotherapy, oriental massage techniques, structural integration, or polarity therapy. The term shall not include laser therapy, microwave, injection therapy, manipulation of the joints, or any diagnosis or treatment of an illness that normally involves the practice of medicine, chiropractic, physical therapy, podiatry, nursing, occupational therapy, veterinary, acupuncture, osteopathy, orthopaedics, hypnosis, or naturopathies.

## Transactional Analysis

Transactional Analysis (TA) is a theory of personality and social psychology within the humanistic tradition. Eric Berne, the founder of TA, re-examined the basic assumptions held by psychiatry and, from his pioneering work as a radical scientist, developed the theory of Transactional Analysis. As an educational approach, Transactional Analysis offers a framework for understanding personality, human development, communications and personal life patterns. TA provides ways to describe and explain both internal experience and interpersonal behaviour in an innovative and accessible manner. Because of its emphasis on the interactional aspects of communication, it is invaluable in all branches of education, as well as other areas where the understanding of people is of central importance to professional effectiveness. Three philosophical concepts underpin Transactional Analysis in education. Respect for the dignity of all human beings and empathic acceptance of them, as people are essential qualities for effective educators. These qualities are at the heart of successful relationships between teachers and learners. People at all ages and stages of development are capable of learning to take responsibility for their decisions and actions. Educational difficulties can be addressed effectively with co-operative goodwill and a coherent theoretical framework, which makes sense of the human dynamics involved. The process of educational Transactional Analysis is contractual, so that all parties know where they stand, and what agreements have been made for what purposes. Throughout the process, the ideas and methods of TA are used openly to promote informed co-operation and the sharing of power between all parties.

## Tui-na

A system of medical massage that uses the theories of Traditional Chinese Medicine (TCM) to treat many different diseases. Practiced continually in China and throughout the Orient for more than 2,500 years. In Japan, Korea, Vietnam, Tibet and Cambodia (among others) the medicine has been adapted and changed slightly to fit their specific cultures.

## Vibrational Therapy

All is energy, all energy vibrates and has a frequency of vibration. Some fall into the "range" of hearing, some into the "range" of physical sight. Some vibrate at a rate that make them "feel solid" by other objects (such as our fingertips), which are also vibrating at this rate of "solid". When a body is "out of its vibrational rate", it is out of balance, and is perceived as in disease by the "sense" that resonates to this frequency of vibration, our sight, our hearing, our touch, etc. There are also frequencies we "perceive" that although "out of range" of our "normal" means of perception (the five senses), are being perceived by our "sixth" sense. These would be the auric/etheric/spiritual bodies, etc. And they, too, when out of their right frequency rate, are perceived to be out of balance. Bringing things back into their right rate of frequency, re-establishing balance is the correct definition of the art of healing. Therefore, understanding and developing perception of frequencies and then creating means to re-balance irregular frequencies are the necessary steps for a Light Worker to become a true "healer".

## Visualisation Therapy

This technique, also called guided imagery, is used to promote physical, mental and emotional health by imagining positive images and desired outcomes to specific situations. It is used in traditional societies and in religious communities such as Tibetan Buddhists who focus on the image of a deity when asking for healing. Visualisation therapy is believed to encourage activity in the right hemisphere of the brain, related to creativity and emotions. Many athletes claim to have had competitive success by using visualisation. Visualisation therapy is often used as an adjunct to conventional cancer treatment.

## Vitamin Therapy

The treatment of indications related to low levels of vitamins. Providing the body with the essentials of life.

## Voice Therapy

Hoarseness is the term often used by patients to describe changes in their voice quality. The causes of hoarseness are determined after obtaining a detailed medical history of the circumstances preceding the onset of hoarseness and performing a thorough physical examination. The latter may include visualisation of the vocal cords, possibly using indirect laryngoscopes, flexible nasolaryngoscopy or strobovideolaryngoscopy. In the absence of an upper respiratory tract infection, any patient with hoarseness persisting for more than two weeks requires a complete evaluation. When the patient has a history of tobacco use, cancer of the head and neck must be considered and ruled out. Voice abuse is one of the most common causes of hoarseness and can lead to other vocal pathologies such as vocal nodules. Good vocal hygiene can prevent and treat some pathology, and voice therapy is a cornerstone of management in some cases of hoarseness. Auditory Verbal Therapy is a process of developing language, which gives hearing-impaired children the tools to develop speech and auditory skills. The therapy operates on the principle that usable hearing is common to 95% of all hearing impaired children. With powerful hearing aids or cochlear implants and continual stimulation of sounds, these children can learn to listen. Babies with normal hearing learn to communicate by becoming aware of sound, mimicking the sounds they hear and, through interacting with family members, learn that sounds have meaning. Hearing impaired babies can learn language in the same way but they need to be taught how to become aware of sound. This is what Auditory Verbal Therapy does - it teaches them how to listen. The approach is parent-centred and the auditory-verbal therapist's main tasks are to assess the hearing and language capabilities of the child and to teach the parent / caregiver to encourage the child's emerging skills in listening, speech and language. Hearing-impaired children who learn to listen and speak have the opportunity of being integrated into regular classes in their neighbourhood schools, learning alongside their hearing peers.

## Ying & Yang

The concepts of Yin and Yang and the Five Agents provided the intellectual framework of much of Chinese scientific thinking especially in fields like biology and medicine The organs of the body were seen to be interrelated in the same sorts of ways as other natural phenomena, and best understood by looking for correlations and correspondences. Illness was seen as a disturbance in the balance of Yin and Yang or the Five Agents caused by emotions, heat or cold, or other influences. Therapy thus depended on accurate diagnosis of the source of the imbalance. The earliest surviving medical texts are fragments of manuscript from early Han tombs. Besides general theory, these texts cover drugs, gymnastics, minor surgery, and magic spells. The text which was to become the main source of medical theory also apparently dates from the Han. It is the Yellow Emperor's Classic of Medicine, supposed to have been written during the third millennium BCE by the mythical Yellow Emperor. The Yellow Emperor said "The principle of Yin and Yang is the foundation of the entire universe. It underlies everything in creation. It brings about the development of parenthood; it is the root and source of life and death it is found with the temples of the gods In order to treat and cure diseases one must search for their origins. "Heaven was created by the concentration of Yang, the force of light, earth was created by the concentration of Yin, the forces of darkness. Yang stands for peace and serenity; Yin stands for confusion and turmoil. Yang stands for destruction; Yin stands for conservation. Yang brings about disintegration; Yin gives shape to things.... The pure and lucid element of light is manifested in the upper artifices and the turbid element of darkness is manifested in the lower orifices. Yang, the element of light, originates in the pores. Yin, the element of darkness, moves within the five viscera. Yang the lucid force of light truly is represented by the four extremities- and Yin the turbid force of darkness stores the power of the six treasures of nature. Water is an embodiment of Yin as fire is an embodiment of Yang. Yang creates the air, while Yin creates the senses, which belong to the physical body When the physical body dies; the spirit is restored to the air, its natural environment. The spirit receives its nourishment through the air, and the body receives its nourishment through the senses. "If Yang is overly powerful, then Yin may be too weak. If Yin is particularly strong, then Yang is apt to be defective If the male force is overwhelming, then there will be excessive heat. If the female force is overwhelming, then there will be excessive cold. Exposure to repeated and severe heat will induce chills. Cold injures the body while heat injures the spirit When the spirit is hurt, severe pain will ensue. When the body is hurt, there will be swelling. Thus, when severe pain occurs first and swelling comes on later, one may infer that a disharmony in the spirit has done harm to the body. Likewise, when swelling appears first and severe pain is felt later on, one can say that a dysfunction in the body has injured the spirit.... "Nature has four seasons and five elements. To grant long life, these seasons and elements must store up the power of creation in cold, heat, dryness, moisture, and wind. Man has five viscera in which these five climates are transformed into joy, anger, sympathy, and grief. And fear. The emotions of joy and anger are injurious to the spirit just as cold and heat are injurious to the body. Violent anger depletes Yin; violent joy depletes Yang. When rebellious emotions rise to Heaven the pulse expires and leaves the body When joy and anger are without moderation, then cold and heat exceed all measure, and life is no longer secure. Yin and Yang should be respected to an equal extent. The Yellow Emperor asked, "Is there any alternative to the law of Yin and Yang?" Qi Bo answered: "When Yang is the stronger, the body is hot, the pores are closed, and people begin to pant; they become boisterous and coarse and do not perspire. They become feverish, their mouths are dry and sore, their stomachs feel tight, and they die of constipation. When Yang is the stronger, people can endure winter but not summer. When Yin is the stronger, the body is cold and covered with perspiration. People realize they are ill; they tremble and feel chilly. When they feel chilled, their spirits become rebellious. Their stomachs can no long digest food and they die. When Yin is stronger, people can endure summer but not winter. Thus Yin and Yang alternate. Their ebbs and surges vary, and so does the character of the diseases." The Yellow Emperor asked, "Can anything be done to harmonize and adjust these two principles of nature?" Qi Bo answered: "If one has the ability to know the seven injuries and the eight advantages, one can bring the two principles into harmony. If one does not know how to use this knowledge, his life will be doomed to early decay. By the age of forty the Yin force in the body has been reduced to one-half of its natural vigour and an individual's youthful prowess has deteriorated. By the age of fifty the body has grown heavy. The ears no longer hear well. The eyes no longer see clearly By the age of sixty the life producing power of Yin has declined to a very low level. Impotence sets in The nine orifices no longer benefit each other.... Those who seek wisdom beyond the natural limits will retain good hearing and clear vision. Their bodies will remain light and strong. Although they grow old in years, they will stay able-bodied and vigorous and be capable of governing to great advantage. For this reason the ancient sages did not rush into the affairs of the world. In their pleasures and joys they were dignified and tranquil. They did what they thought best and did not bend their will or ambition to the achievement of empty ends Thus their allotted span of life was without limit, like that of Heaven and earth. This is the way the ancient sages controlled and conducted themselves. "By observing myself I learn about others, and their diseases become apparent to me. By observing the external symptoms, I gather knowledge about the internal diseases One should watch for things out of the ordinary One should observe minute and trifling things and treat them as if the were big and important. When they are treated the danger they pose will be dissipated. Experts in examining patients judge their general appearance; they feel their pulse and determine whether it is Yin or Yang that causes the disease.... To determine whether Yin or Yang predominates, one must be able to distinguish a light pulse of low tension from a hard pounding one. With a disease of Yang, Yin predominates With a disease of Yin, Yang predominates When one is filled with vigour and strength, Yin and Yang are in proper harmony

## Yoga

Yoga instruction is a general term for a range of body-mind exercise practices used to access consciousness and encourage physical and mental well being. Some forms concentrate on achieving perfection in posture and alignment of the body; others aim at mental control to access higher consciousness. Between these two forms are yoga's that focus on the interrelationship of body, mind, and energy. In Yoga Therapy, some yoga teachers emphasise yoga exercises that relieve stress, improve circulation or boost the immune system. This gentle form of low impact exercise can often be tailored to help people with limited mobility due to stroke, arthritis or other chronic diseases. See also Ayurveda.

## Zen Therapy

A branch of Mahayana Buddhism which developed in China during the sixth and seventh centuries. Zen stresses the importance of the enlightenment experience and the futility of rational thought, intellectual study and religious ritual in attaining this; a central element of Zen is zazen, a meditative practice which seeks to free the mind of all thought and conceptualisation. "Zen Buddhism", commonly called "Zen," developed from Buddhism, which originated in India around 600 BC. As Buddhism gained popularity and moved eastward through China and to Japan, local philosophies and religions, notably Taoism (pronounced "Daoism"), were mingled together with Buddhism. New schools were formed in China, such as "Chan", which became "Zen" in Japan. Retaining the original message of the Buddha, stress was put on meditative practice, downplaying rational thought and the study of scripture and ritual. The keystone of Buddhism is the "Four Noble Truths:" Existence is suffering., Our typical road in life is to maximize pleasure and minimize unpleasantries, but we often find that eliminating all pain and discomfort is not possible. Around 600 B.C., a prince in India named Siddhartha Guatama lived a sheltered life in a palace. As the story goes, Prince Siddhartha saw sickness, pain, and death one day as he stole a peek at the world outside the palace. The Prince decided to search for the cause of such suffering in the world, as well as a cure. Suffering is caused by desires and attachments. We all start forming attachments to things before the day we are born. The moment we are separated from these things, we feel loss, anxiety, and sadness. We develop cravings for things: wealth, prestige, and cars. Cravings and desires create suffering if not met. Even when we possess the items, we covet them and protect them (jealously) for fear of losing them (and these don't have to be tangible things-pride, status, even happiness itself are included). The world is an ever-changing, impermanent place- the more things we cling to, the more we lose when they change or go away. There is a way to end worldly suffering. Siddhartha wandered around for many years, alone or with the sadhus (Hindu holy men) who also lead meagre lives. Through meditation, he was finally able to rid himself of all attachments to the world, in the experience called "satori" (awakening or enlightenment). The way to end all worldly suffering is to follow the "Eightfold Path" to satori. The "Eightfold Path" is the code of moral conduct for Buddhists to follow. Following the Path helps to clear the mind and body of the "dust" of the world, being the attachments and desires that keep us suffering and away from satori. As we gain insight, the path becomes easier and more natural to follow. Zen emphasizes the 8th part of the path, "right concentration," or on the meditative aspect of the Path, but all parts are intertwined together.

## Zero Balancing

This technique developed by Fritz Smith MD integrates a Western anatomical view of structure with Eastern concepts of body energy. In a session, the therapist moves through a set protocol designed to enhance energy flow and a sense of physical well-being. The Zero Balancing Association was founded in 1991 to promote and support the teaching and practice of Zero-Balancing, a hands on body/mind system designed by Dr Fritz Smith in 1973 to align body energy with the body's physical structure. It represents the integration of Eastern views of energy with Western views of science, and teaches how to use energy as a working tool in relation to body structure. The hallmarks of ZB are the integration of the client's body energy with their body structure; creating clearer, stronger fields of energy in the body/mind; and balancing energy in the densest tissues of the body, the bone and skeletal system. The desired outcome of a Zero Balancing session is to help relieve physical and mental symptoms; to improve the ability to deal with life stresses; to organise vibratory fields thereby promoting the sense of wholeness and well being.

HEALTH MYSELF

# Practitioner Entry Request Form

If you would like the opportunity to enter your Complementary Medicine Practice **FREE OF CHARGE** into this unique directory then follow any of the easy steps below:

- Fill in the request form below and send it to: **FREEPOST HCC PUBLISHING LTD**
- Fax: **08707 541667**
- Tel: **08707 541676**
- Email: **information@healthmyself.com**
- Visit: **www.healthmyself.com**

Please send a more detailed questionnaire to this Practice, to ensure our details are entered correctly in the Healthmyself Directory.

| | |
|---|---|
| **Your Name** | |
| **Business Name** | |
| **Address** | |
| **County /Postcode** | |
| **Contact Name** | |
| **Job Title** | |
| **Telephone / Fax** | T: F: |
| **Web Address** | www |
| **Email** | |

**Business Type** *(please tick)*

- Complementary Medicine ☐
- Manipulative Structural Therapy ☐
- Mind Body Medicine ☐
- Touch Therapy ☐
- Self Help Treatment ☐
- Medicinal Therapy ☐
- Oriental Medicine ☐
- Postural Therapy ☐

Tear here

HEALTH MYSELF

# How to use the Directory

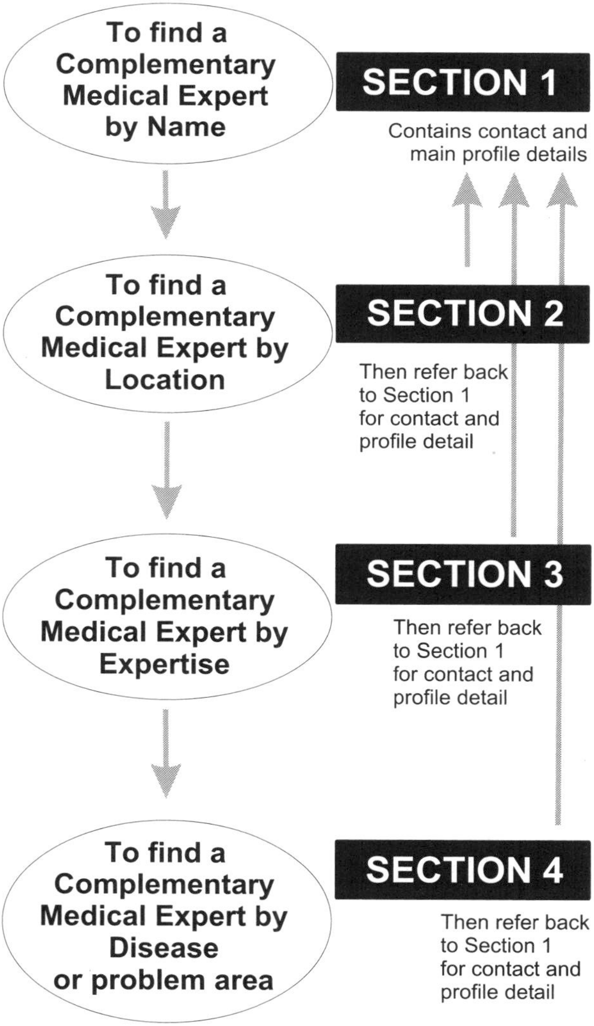

# SECTION 1 Overview

## A-Z of all 22,000 Complementary Medicine Practices

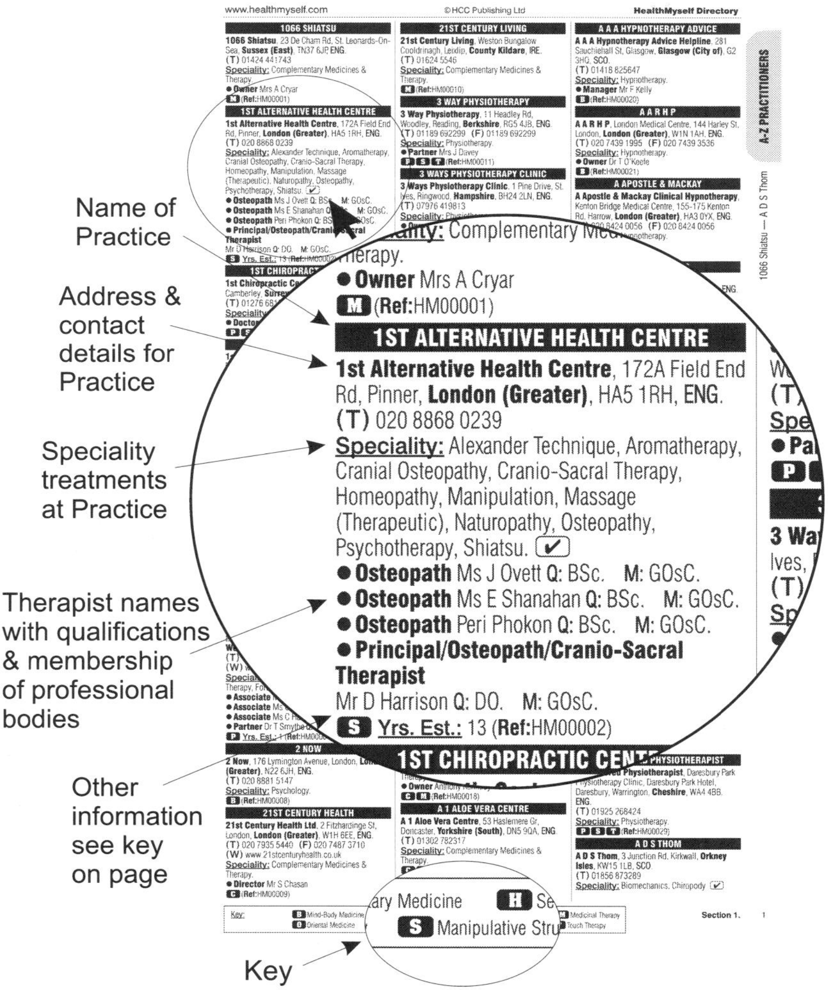


**All other sections following refer back to this section 1**

# SECTION 2 Overview

## A-Z of all Complementary Medicine Practices by County by Town within Country

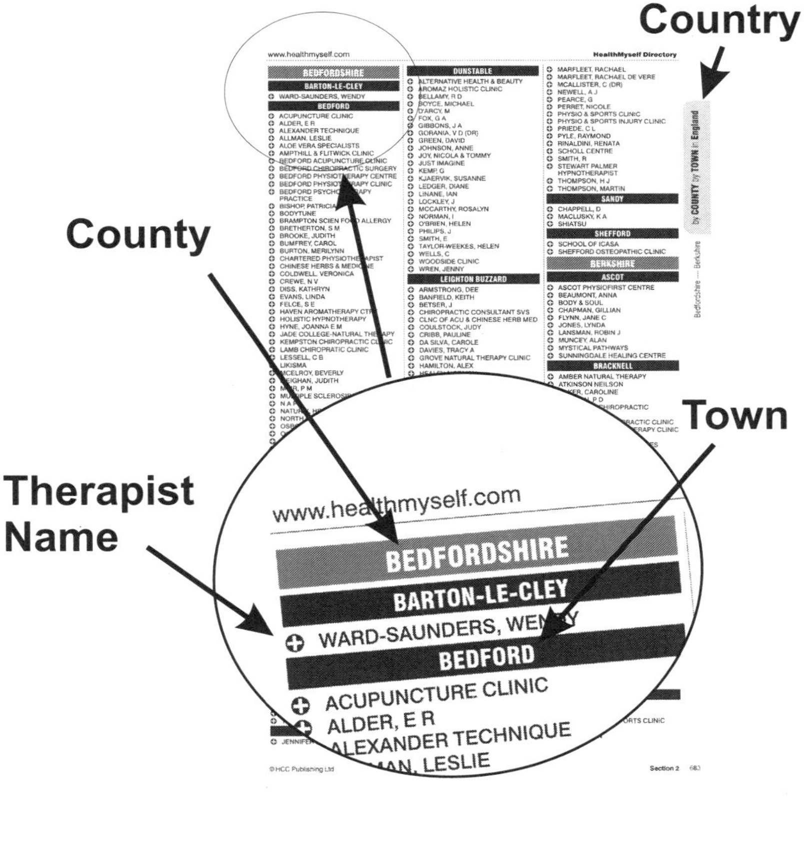


Once you have located a practice simply refer back to Section 1 for contact details or go to another section and expand on your search further.

# SECTION 3 Overview

## A-Z of Complementary Medicine Practices by County identified by types of Therapy Expertise

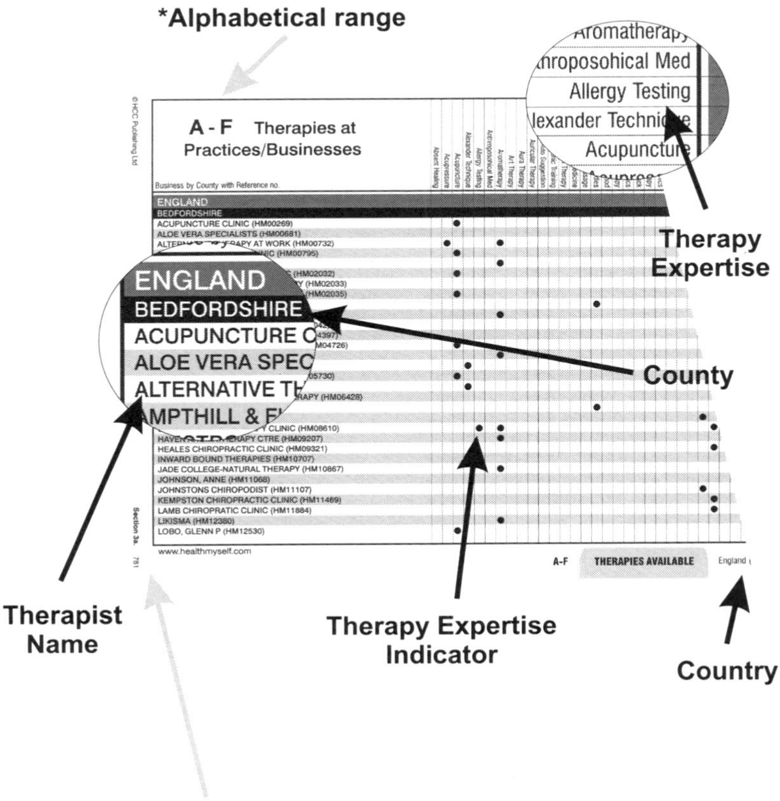


* Section 3 is split into 3 parts, (a, b, c) to cover the alphabetical range.

Once you have located a practice simply refer back to Section 1 for contact details or go to another section and expand on your search further.

# SECTION 4 Overview

## A-Z of Complementary Medicine Practices by County identified by problems, indications or diseases treated

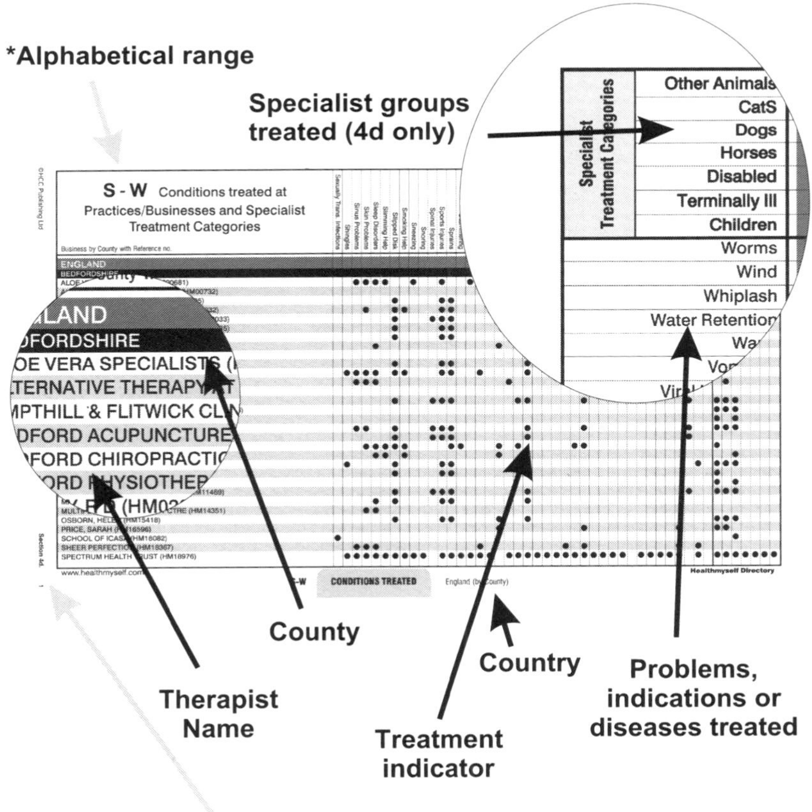


* Section 4 is split into 4 parts, (a, b, c, d) to cover the alphabetical range.

Once you have located a practice simply refer back to Section 1 for contact details or go to another section and expand on your search